W9-CNC-484

25 Dec 06

Mr. Schinnerer –

You have helped me tremendously the past few months in finding my first home. During this time, your passion for architecture has been on full display, and I hope this book will compliment it. I appreciate all your help.

Happy Holidays.

– Josh

Home

NEW DIRECTIONS IN
WORLD ARCHITECTURE
AND DESIGN

Home

NEW DIRECTIONS IN WORLD ARCHITECTURE AND DESIGN

MILLENNIUM HOUSE

First published in 2006 by
Millennium House Pty Ltd
52 Bolwarra Rd, Elanora Heights
NSW, 2101, Australia

ISBN 10: 1-921209-01-1
ISBN 13: 978-1-921209-01-7

SALES
For all sales, please contact:
Millennium House Pty Ltd
52 Bolwarra Rd, Elanora Heights
NSW, 2101, Australia
Phone: (612) 9970 6850   Fax: (612) 9970 8136
Email: rightsmanager@millenniumhouse.com.au

PHOTOGRAPHERS
Millennium House would like to hear from photographers interested in supplying photographs

Printed in China
Color separation by Pica Digital Pte Ltd, Singapore

Publisher Gordon Cheers

Associate publisher Margaret Olds

Project manager Tracy Tucker

Art director Stan Lamond

Chief text editor Loretta Barnard

Editors Monica Berton, Helen Cooney, Heather Jackson, Susan Page, Janet Parker

Coordinator, Parts 1 & 3 Monica Berton

Picture research Monica Berton, Helen Cooney, Tracy Tucker

Cover design Stan Lamond, Anthony Wyld

Designers Stan Lamond, Lena Lowe, Ingo Voss

Initial design concept Anthony Wyld

Digital image control Andrew Davies

Index Di Harriman

Production Bernard Roberts

Publishing assistants Elissa Coxon, Julie Tucker

Photographers are acknowledged on page 574

Photographs on preliminary pages:

Pages 2–3: Crescent House, Wallace E Cunningham
Page 4: Slat House, David Hertz Architects
Pages 6–7: Chesa Futura, Foster and Partners; Küchel Architects
Pages 8–9: Quito House, Carlos Zapata Studio
Page 11: Mataja Residence, Belzberg/Wittman Collaborative
Page 13: Skybox, Melling:Morse Architects
Page 14: Casa Cusenza, Van Tilburg, Banvard & Soderbergh

Consultants

Michael Webb lives and works in Los Angeles, USA, and is the author of more than twenty books on architecture and design including *Art/Invention/House*, *Adventurous Wine Architecture*, and *Brave New Houses*. He is also a regular contributor to *Architectural Digest*, *The Architectural Review*, and *Frame and Mark*.

Chris Abel is an architecture writer and lecturer of international renown, based in Sydney, Australia. He has taught at major universities in many parts of the world and is the author of more than 100 publications of theory and criticism.

Professor Alexander Cuthbert, University of New South Wales, Australia, has had more than 30 years academic and professional experience, living and working in Europe, North America, Asia, and Australasia, in the fields of architecture, urban design, and urban planning.

Professor Philip Goad, Melbourne University, Australia, is internationally known for his research in a variety of areas, including architectural theory and design. He is an authority on modern Australian architecture and has worked extensively as an architect, conservation consultant, and curator.

Douglas Lloyd Jenkins is one of New Zealand's best known and most respected design, art, and architecture writers. In 2005 he was awarded the Montana Medal for Non-Fiction, New Zealand's top literary prize, for his book *At Home: A Century of New Zealand Design*.

Professor 'Ora Joubert, University of Pretoria, South Africa, is an acclaimed architect, with work featuring in more than fifty national and international publications. As well as academic commitments, she is the editor of a forthcoming book on contemporary South African architecture.

CONTRIBUTING WRITERS

Part 1 Alexander Cuthbert, Ayu Suartika

Part 2 Nigel Bartlett, Philip Goad, Linda Hunt, Marlowe Richards, Barry Stone, Russell Walden, and the architects

Part 3 Michael Chapman, Samantha Levy, Miles Lewis, Jamie Inglis, Raju Mazumdar, Barry Stone, Russell Walden, Nadia Watson, and Tracey Woods

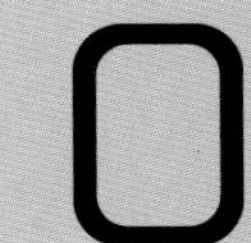

ntents

Chapter 10

Outer City 178

Chapter 11

Future City 266

contents (continued)

Part 2
Home Today (continued)

FREEMASONS BUILDING
CANDLES

Preface

Home is an enlightening tribute to architecture, containing rich illustrative photos, technical drawings, and descriptive text. The pages depict the cultural traditions of housing throughout history, featuring a broad range of innovative homes of the present day, and a guide to architects who are leaders in their field.

In the Introduction, architectural writer Michael Webb looks at the evolution of home in the Americas, from the dwellings of early settlers to the Modernist creations of Frank Lloyd Wright and Irving Gill, and the South American push inspired by Le Corbusier. Michael Webb puts the American homes featured in this book into context.

In Part 1, Professor Alexander Cuthbert considers the home as the universal physical medium of expression for humans. Drawing examples from across the globe and across time, he considers the cultural, symbolic, religious, and spiritual dimensions of home.

Part 2 of the book is devoted to exploring an international array of homes, designed by some of the most significant architects of the modern era. A wide selection of images provides a spatial context to plans, elevations, and section drawings. The home descriptions are written by the architects themselves, or a nominated writer, and these provide invaluable insights into the architects' design intents and their creative solutions to logistic, heritage, and environmental problems. The descriptions also provide an appreciation of the architects' design philosophy. The homes have been ordered alphabetically by name within broad categories, including In the City, Outer City, Future City, In the Country, By the Water, and In Your Dreams. Readers can seek out their favorite architects in the book's index.

Part 3 of the book is set out in an easy-to-use A–Z format and includes profiles of significant architects and designers who have shaped architectural trends in the past century.

Enjoy viewing some of today's most significant, architecturally designed homes from around the world created by the artists of modern-day architecture.

Introduction

Houses of the Americas

SETTLERS' HOMES

The Americas span the entire range of the world's geography, from polar ice caps to tropical rainforests by way of arid deserts, lofty mountains, vast plains, and the longest coastline of any continent. Culturally, the range is much narrower. The British took over from Dutch and French rulers in North America; the Spanish settled Central and South America, and the Portuguese seized control of Brazil. That established distinct legacies of building that initially overrode local conditions, just as the colonialists ignored or suppressed whatever native traditions they encountered.

The Spanish were even more determined than the British to impose their will on their new domains and the Laws of the Indies provided a blueprint for every new town and city from the sixteenth century on. And yet, the remoteness of these settlements and the scarcity of sophisticated materials encouraged local builders to create a simpler architecture of adobe blocks, clay tiles, and rough-hewn wooden beams, reserving dressed stone and rich ornament for cathedrals and centers of administration. The hacienda was a model that provided security and enclosure for families and livestock.

In North America, early settlers adapted the same models of wood-frame and brick construction they had practiced at home, and utilized the same pattern books for ornament and the treatment of facades. The cottages and mansions of New England played subtle variations on English styles until well after the original 13 states declared independence. As settlers moved westward through the nineteenth century, they developed new models, and absorbed the Spanish traditions of Texas and California. The false fronts of Main Street in every western town, the Victorian exuberance of the merchant class, and the Arts and Crafts bungalows are now cherished as historic relics.

THE AMERICAN HOME

As the United States became richer, more populous and diversified, architectural eclecticism flourished. The new rich sought an instant pedigree, as they still do, by building extravagant copies of European castles and palaces, and the middle classes sought status with decorative overlays on humbler structures. Regional styles spread across the country, starting with the wood-frame houses that were shipped as kits around Cape Horn to San Francisco following the Gold Rush of 1849. Today's tract builders offer a menu of styles, from Mediterranean to Cape Cod, in suburban developments that have a cookie-cutter sameness in every state. The house became the "home," a stand-alone symbol of personal status and the American way of life, with deep emotional and economic associations. Huge resources are poured into the construction, furnishing, and landscaping of homes. Although American-style suburbs now encircle the globe, no country has such a fixation on size and surface style as the USA.

In contrast, poverty and corruption has held back development in most Latin American countries. Tradition still rules, and the opulent estates and luxury apartments of the affluent are a shocking contrast to the teeming shanty towns that surround most cities. Houses that would excite no attention in the USA are protected by high walls, surveillance cameras, and armed guards. Bodyguards drive owners to work or to shop in armored cars. The open plans and clean lines of contemporary architecture are compromised by the pervasive feeling of insecurity.

Modernism was a late arrival and has shallow roots in the Americas, except for office towers where the USA led the world. In southern California, Irving Gill used thin planes of concrete to create a pared-down version of the Spanish Missions, and Frank Lloyd Wright employed textured concrete blocks to build houses that were inspired by Mexican temples. In the 1920s, R.M. Schindler and Richard Neutra moved to Los Angeles from their native Vienna, transplanting progressive European ideas to this far shore. Philip Johnson popularized the concept of the International Modern style in an exhibition that was inaugurated in 1932 at the fledgling Museum of Modern Art in New York. It provoked a lively debate, but few Americans wanted to live that way until postwar euphoria and an emphasis on the practical over the pure made it seem less threatening. Even then, the Case Study House program yielded only 24 realized designs in the years 1945–63, and few developers embraced those ideas.

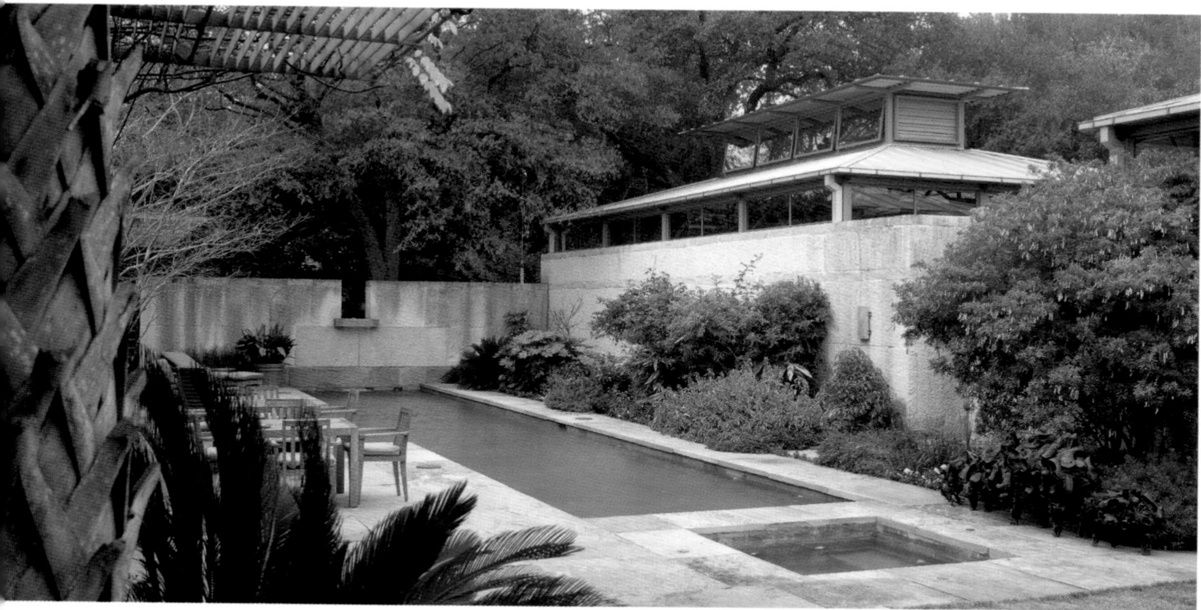

LEFT
The House of Courts in Texas, features three internal courtyards. Architects Lake | Flato were inspired by the Spanish missions, warehouses, and early stone houses common in the Texan landscape.

ABOVE
The "Miesian box" visible at the front of Studio Pali Fekete's House on Blue Jay Way creates an arresting facade for the home. The glass-walled sitting room doubles as a protective eave for the home's entry.

ABOVE
In almost impossible contrast with the teeming and strife-ridden streets of São Paulo, Brazil, Isay Weinfeld's Casa Marrom stands in serene splendor, a haven of beauty in a blighted metropolis. For the clients, the home expresses their relaxed way of living.

ABOVE
At the entry to Kanner Architect's Malibu House, the varied roof lines preview the "ladder of space and volume" that awaits. This Californian home by the sea was inspired by the work of Mexican Pritzker-winning architect Luis Barrigan, who was famed for the way he worked with space and light. The Cubist work of Irving Gill was another important influence.

RIGHT
In House C, TEN Arquitectos have achieved a vivid sense of space on a relatively small building site by incorporating large voids into a three-level residence. The Modernist design of the home is representative of a range of cosmopolitan homes found in Mexico City today.

In South America, Le Corbusier spread the Modernist gospel on lecture tours and through his writings, but local architects had to wait to realize their dreams – in Uruguay from 1930 on, and later in Mexico, Brazil, and Cuba, but rarely elsewhere. The forces of reaction were deeply entrenched, especially in Argentina and the Andean republics, and the visionary capital of Brasilia was completed just as a military coup overthrew the elected government and drove Oscar Niemeyer, the godfather of Brazilian Modernism, into exile. The Modernist honeymoon in Cuba ended soon after Castro seized power and took the geriatric Soviet Union as his model. Architects and their clients emigrated en masse.

Whatever a country's politics or wealth, innovative residences are always rare. With few exceptions, builders and their customers prefer the tried and true — the house that doesn't stand out from the crowd. A family may crave larger rooms and the badges of wealth (from lofty porticoes to fancy cars), but they also want to fit in with their neighbors. Homeowners typically reject every departure from the norm, as spontaneously as small children refuse to eat the unfamiliar. Community design codes mandate shapes and color palettes, seeking a respectable uniformity. The challenge for the few enlightened clients and talented architects is to maneuver around these whimsical constraints or find a site that's unregulated, while responding to the topography and climate, as well as to the scale and character of the surroundings.

ABOVE
Outside of his usual landscape of the desert, architect Will Bruder created the almost futuristic Sky Arc Residence on a wooded hillside overlooking San Francisco Bay. The home is sheathed in a skin of dulled pewter-gray zinc and green-tinted glass with curved sun canopies fabricated from aqueous fiberglass.

LEFT
Reminiscent of a bird's outstretched wings, Carlos Zapata's daring Quito House hovers on its dramatic clifftop location on the edge of Cumbaya Valley looking toward Cotopaxi, Ecuador's highest active volcano.

Things used to be a lot simpler. In 1946, Palm Springs was a scattered community of second homes, a two-hour drive across the desert from Los Angeles. Frank Sinatra had just made his first million and strolled through the open door of an architect's office on Palm Drive. E. Stewart Williams had taken over the practice from his father, but he was out, and the entertainer spoke to his brother. He wanted a house with a pool, to be finished in three months so that he could spend Christmas there with his family. And it should be Colonial style. Williams met the deadline, but built a modern, flat-roofed residence. "Sinatra had heard of Colonial but he'd probably never seen one, and he was entirely satisfied with what I gave him," Williams later recalled. The nearest neighbor was probably a mile away, and many of the free spirits who wintered in Palm Springs in those early years were willing to try something new. Edgar Kaufmann Sr, a department store mogul, had commissioned Frank Lloyd Wright to build Fallingwater as his summer house in Pennsylvania, outraging his peers, but he encountered no opposition to his 1947 Neutra desert house.

Today, every move may be contested. A German art-collector bought a waterfront lot on the Gulf Coast of Florida, and commissioned a purist white house from Richard Meier. When the architect heard it was in a gated community he feared the worst and tried to back out, but the client insisted, and he built a model with a dramatic V-profile roof and submitted it for approval. The review board had heard of Meier and treated him with respect, but were deeply disturbed when they saw that the pitched roof they had mandated was apparently upside down. Meier calmly responded that nothing in their exhaustive code said it had to be done in the conventional way and, to their fury, he prevailed. The constraints inspired him to do one of his finest, most original designs.

Ever since Ayn Rand's lurid novel, *The Fountainhead,* and the real-life example of Wright tyrannizing his clients, architects have enjoyed an unjustified reputation for arrogance and imposing their own ideas on reluctant clients. A few have tried, but it's not good strategy; the choice is too wide and most people call on former clients to ask if they are well satisfied. In contrast to the off-the-shelf models builders offer, architects can tailor a house to your personal needs and desires. It will take much longer and cost more, but it's a life-long investment that will bring untold rewards. The houses included in this book may be rooted in place and the local vernacular, but they make daring leaps into the unknown, carrying their lucky owners to places they never dreamed of.

For sheer exuberance, it's hard to surpass the house that Carlos Zapata designed for a young art-loving couple high in the Andes, just outside Quito, the historic capital of Ecuador. The Venezuela-born architect lived in the area as a child, although he now practices in New York, and the clients are friends. They asked him for a house that would make them feel as though they were levitating, and Zapata sketched a plan that resembles a bird in flight, with an extended terrace and main bedroom oriented toward one lofty peak and a partially covered pool branching off toward another.

The hillside house that John Patkau designed on the Vancouver waterfront is tightly confined by its neighbors, and its exuberance is contained within a narrow slot of space. The client, a Chinese businessman, wanted a house that would maximize views of the natural harbor and pull light into every room, and the architect has achieved this by raising the lap pool and allowing the light to filter though the water and splash down from skylights, turning the simple linear volume into a luminous, multi-leveled belvedere.

Builders prefer flat sites that speed construction, but architects are inspired by steep gradients, and some of the best houses are perched on precipices. Will Bruder is a man of the desert who has built several expressive houses around his home base of Phoenix. In contrast, Sky Arc, a recent residence for a software inventor who sold his company at an early age to enjoy his family and music, hugs a wooded hillside looking out to San Francisco Bay. Poured concrete anchors the house to the slope, curved canopies of aqueous fiberglass modulate the light, and the woodsy, colorful interior makes a connection with the pines and madrona trees to either side. It's a house that embraces and frames the landscape; and it is both free-flowing and snug within.

Sharon Johnston and Mark Lee, a husband–wife partnership in Los Angeles, were commissioned to build a spec house on the edge of Santa Monica Canyon. To maximize the volume while minimizing the number of caissons required for the foundations, they designed a flared concrete base and a steel frame that tapers in at the top, and is covered with a spray-on polymer skin that unifies roof and walls. The owner parks her car and enters at the middle level, where glass sliders open two sides of the lofty living room to a panoramic view over the canyon.

Some houses take their character from one or two materials that are employed in a boldly expressive way. A house by Brigitte Shim and Howard Sutcliffe in the suburbs of Toronto is named the Weathering Steel House for its rusted steel (Cor-Ten) cladding, which requires no maintenance and withstands the rigors of the Canadian climate. Within this hard carapace is a house that contrasts exposed poured concrete with the rich tones of fir, mahogany, and cherrywood.

David Chun was commissioned to build an expansive family house for his Korean-born parents in a leafy neighborhood of West Los Angeles. As a Modernist, he had no compunction in creating a base of poured concrete, but he overcame the reservations of his clients by treating the lofty living room as a giant cabinet with maple floors, cherry paneling, redwood soffits, and straight-grain Douglas fir doors and windows. He demonstrated that wood is the magic button, convincing skeptics that modern does not need to feel cold and alien.

ABOVE LEFT
Architect John Patkau describes Shaw House, on the Vancouver waterfront, as an "essay in light, water, and concrete." The entrance to the home is located directly under the lap pool, so the whole area is illuminated by the pattern of light that passes through the pool's glass bottom.

TOP
With Weathering Steel House, Brigitte Shim and Howard Sutcliffe set out to create a home that would make an emphatic statement in its suburban Toronto neighborhood. The "no maintenance" steel cladding was chosen because of the way it interacts with nature, darkening slowly as it weathers.

ABOVE
From the exterior, Hill House, by architects Johnston Marklee & Associates, looks like a white geometric sculpture built into the hillside. The interior, created by the dynamic form of the home, makes the most of the views across Rustic and Sullivan canyons to Santa Monica Bay.

Many of the best architect-designed houses are studies in minimalism, eliminating everything that's inessential to focus attention on the landscape and the life within.

The planned community of Sea Ranch on the northern California coastline began, 40 years ago, with woodsy houses and a condo block that drew inspiration from the past and from the rugged landscape. Buzz Yudell, who was a partner of the late Charles Moore, and his wife Tina Beebe, who was employed by Charles and Ray Eames, worked in the spirit of those original buildings in designing their own stripped-down summer house. They built a Cubist compound of redwood siding with shallow-pitched corrugated metal roofs that seem to disappear as you approach.

Another bucolic hideaway is located at the bottom of a canyon in Big Sur, an area of stunning natural beauty to the south of San Francisco. French-born architect Anne Fougeron employed cedar battens to screen the street facade, copper that will weather to a soft brown, and glass clerestories to pull in natural light when the sun dips below the walls of the canyon. Thanks to the earthy tones of the natural materials and the refinement of the detailing, this house sits lightly on the land.

Many of the best architect-designed houses are studies in minimalism, eliminating everything that's inessential to focus attention on the landscape and the life within.

A patron of contemporary art invited Jim Jennings to design a guest house for visiting artists on a ranch in the Alexander Valley of northern California. Jennings made a cut through a grassy knoll, and treated the poured concrete retaining walls as a container for two identical suites that open up to precisely framed views at either end and also share a central courtyard. The walls are slightly angled to each other to force the perspective, and are incised by New York artist David Rabinowitch.

The houses of the two Iranian-born sisters, Gisue and Mojgan Hariri, are celebrated for their elegant simplicity, and both qualities are evident in their Belmont House residence, near San Francisco, in which they deftly combined the dominant types of "architecture" in the region: Mexican pueblo style and the mobile-trailer home. A paradoxical mix that inspires.

ABOVE
Yudell-Beebe House at Sea Ranch was designed by and for its inhabitants, architect Buzz Yudell and design colorist Tina Beebe. The house was developed in response to the rhythms and elements of the rugged coast of northern California.

TOP RIGHT
Acknowledging the ecologically fragile nature of the site in Big Sur, northern California, Jackson Family Retreat, by Fougeron Architecture, is a Modernist structure that sits lightly on the land. Steel columns lift the structure 3 ft (1 m) off the ground, to reduce its impact and to protect it from flooding.

ABOVE RIGHT
The two dominant architectural styles of the San Francisco suburb of Belmont (the mobile-trailer home and the pueblo style of housing) have been captured by Hariri & Hariri – Architecture in the design of Belmont House. The Mexican-influenced heavy stuccoed walls are visible at the lower level of the house; the metal-clad volume sits atop its solid base.

RIGHT
The starkly minimalist walls of Jim Jennings' Visiting Artists House mark the entry to one of two self-contained suites in which visiting artists might stay. The long walls integrate with the curve of the land by literally cutting through the hill on which the home sits.

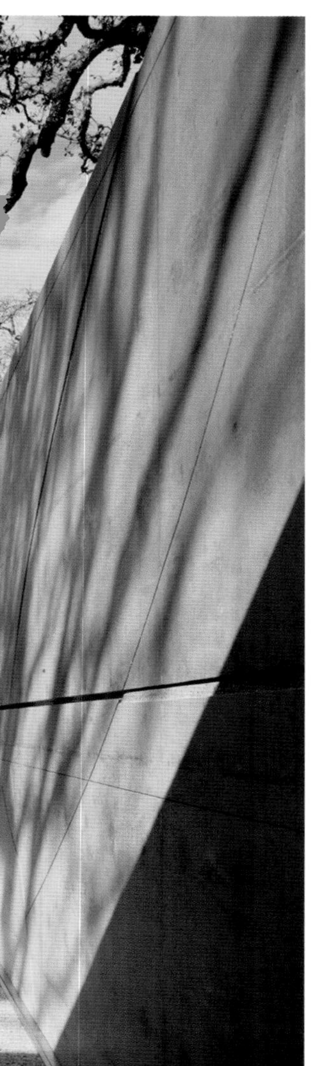

ABOVE
With Desert House, Marmol Radziner + Associates developed an exciting prototype for an eco-friendly prefabricated custom house. The home consists of four prefabricated house modules and six deck modules, all built off-site and transported to the client's chosen location.

ABOVE RIGHT
Pugh + Scarpa's Solar Umbrella is situated in an area populated mostly with single-story bungalows. The home, inspired by Paul Rudolph's Umbrella House of 1953, incorporates both passive and active solar design techniques and is a bold precedent for the Venice area of California.

From the birth of the modern movement 80 years ago, architects have dreamed of making good design available to a broad public, employing prefabrication to simplify construction and achieve cost savings through standardization. Few designs have progressed beyond the prototype stage. The design-build firm of Leo Marmol and Ron Radziner has established its own factory in an effort to control quality and offer a variety of customized models. Marmol created the first house for himself and his wife, shipping steel-framed modular units and assembling them on a desert site outside Los Angeles. The product of this initial venture has the solidity and refinement of the firm's site-built houses, but the cost was lower, and the time required for site preparation and final assembly was substantially less.

The late Franklin Israel was a master of subtle inflections, imparting a dynamic sense of movement to every space he designed. Before his death, in 1996, he sketched a house for a cliff-side site in West Los Angeles, and this was fleshed out by his partners, Barbara Callas and Steven Shortridge, who now have their own firm. A steel-troweled gray stucco facade shuts out traffic noise, and its sharp angles herald the interlocking volumes of the interior, which step down the precipitous slope and open up to decks overlooking the ocean. There's a harmonious balance of solid and void, and axes that tie the varied spaces together.

Energy conservation has become an increasingly high priority as public awareness of global warming becomes more widespread and the cost of power escalates. Green architecture is the hallmark of buildings designed by Gwynne Pugh and Lawrence Scarpa, a partnership in West Los Angeles, and Scarpa named his own house the Solar Umbrella. A steel-framed addition to a modest bungalow contains a new living area that opens to a walled yard and a master suite that is cantilevered over the old structure. The entire house is naturally ventilated, and an array of photovoltaic panels generates more energy than the house consumes, doubling as a sun shade. Recycled materials are used throughout, thus reducing costs.

INNOVATION AND COLLABORATION

Most of the houses featured here are one-offs, but they display a wealth of ideas that other architects and clients can adapt to their own projects. Creativity and practicality, elegance and economy, adventure and a sense of rootedness are carefully balanced. They represent a collaboration between audacious clients and innovative designers who shed all preconceptions in the search for a fresh approach. These are houses that point the way forward, in contrast to most of their neighbors, which vainly attempt to recreate the past.

Michael Webb

Los Angeles writer Michael Webb is the author of more than twenty books on architecture and design.

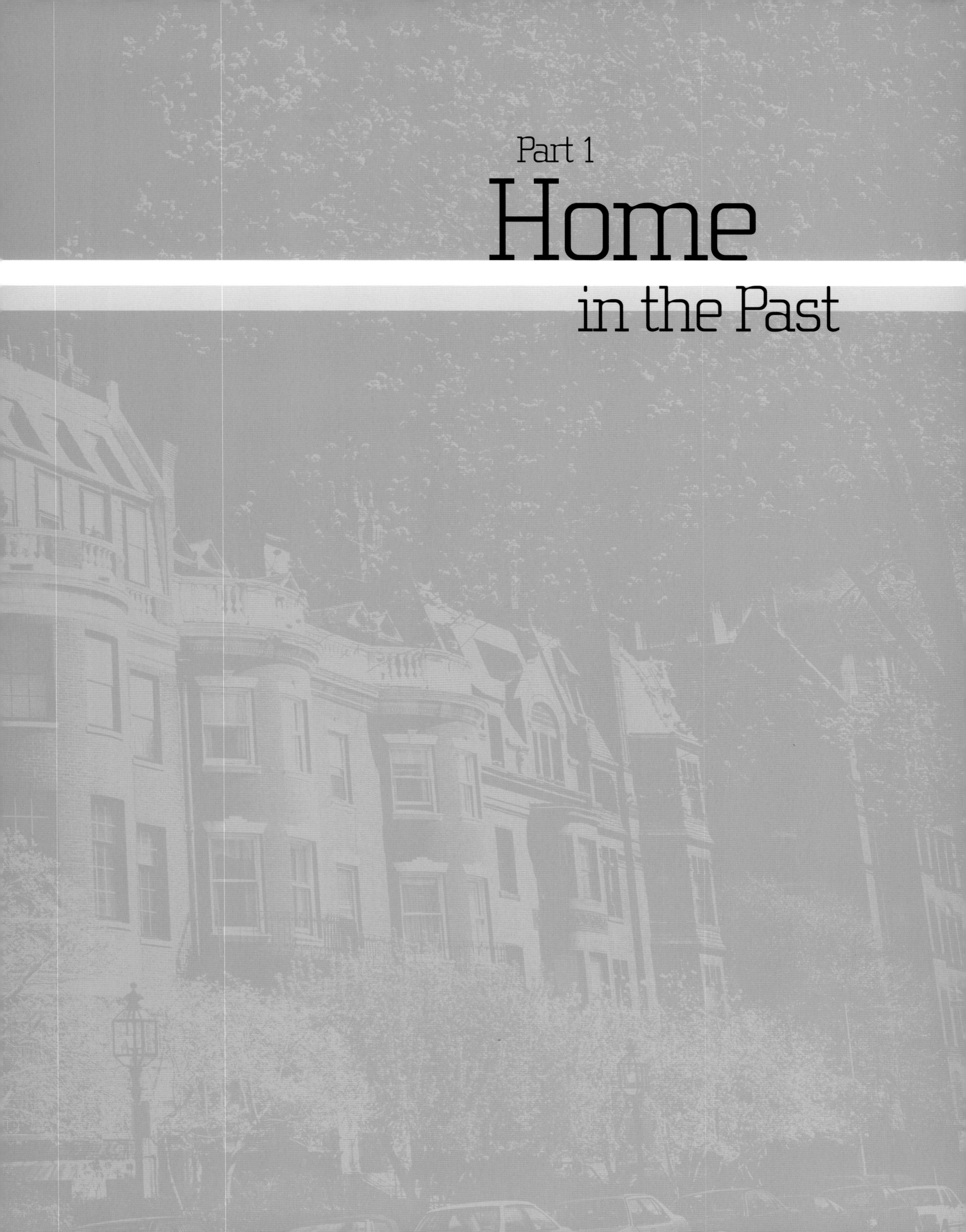

Part 1

Home in the Past

Introduction

Home is the ultimate paradox: It can be a building, a destination, or a concept. Home at its most elementary is merely a house – a place where we perform functional tasks for ourselves such as washing, cooking and eating, personal hygiene, storing material possessions, investing money, and other activities. But home has purposes beyond the material; it has an historical and spiritual purpose. We say: "Home is where the heart is" – a thought which opens up a universe of emotion. Here we use the idea of home to signify the place where journeys end; a place we somehow arrive back to, though not necessarily from where we departed. Despite this, home also connotes the idea of a return – a homecoming of some kind to the same people, whether it is to where a partner resides, to one's children or friends, or to a familiar landscape. Here the connection in our minds moves beyond the functional into the realm of feelings.

In this section we integrate function and emotion with concept, as we set out to illustrate the complexity of home and its historic, symbolic, religious, and spiritual dimensions. In essence, home reflects an archeology of qualities that are integrated in highly complex ways. In exploring the idea of home over historical time, it is fair to say that while homes range from primitive grass huts to immense palaces, they all perform the same tasks in different ways and in different proportions. Neither can we draw any conclusions about the symbolic richness of people's lives from the physical quality of their houses. The Aboriginal people of Australia had the most elementary shelters, yet lived in a world without parallel in our modern societies. Their concept of home stretched out to encompass the entire symbolic universe of the Dreamtime. Conversely, the physical dimensions and apparent wealth of grand castles and palaces were no indication of a similar richness in the lives of kings and queens, or of dictators and other tyrants.

Homes in the past have also had a significant impact on the homes of today in form, design, and appearance to the extent that it is impossible to isolate ourselves from the effects of history. At whatever time, homes have had to adapt to similar climates, geographies, systems of beliefs, and the adoption of the family unit as a universal norm. However grand, most homes have used certain basic features such as pitched roofs for insulation and drainage, windows for daylight, and doors for access. In this manner our homes are a direct reflection of our physiology and in most cases mirror the human condition. In many areas, building materials are limited and homes, however large or important, have a similar appearance dictated by nature.

The effects of history are also revealed in the work of famous architects, each one being significantly affected by their own learning, and also by each other. Hence today we see stylistic and design influences continuing over thousands of years, from ancient Greece and Rome and the Italian Renaissance, to the Georgian architecture in Britain and into contemporary design today. Much of this has been directly copied as a vocabulary or "language" of architecture. Architects have also adopted the spirit of home as personal influences, and we find examples such as traditional Japanese architecture, the Greek villages in the Cyclades, Italian hill towns and Scottish castles personally affecting many of the great contemporary architects.

TOP
Trulli houses from Puglia, Italy. These houses display the timeless qualities of utility and beauty. They also combine together into one continuous facade, hence helping to form a town as well as a series of homes.

LEFT
Homes in the Cyclades, Greece. The islands of the Cyclades form part of the mythology of ancient Greece and are steeped in history and legend. The villages of Mykonos, Ios, and Santorini have inspired architects for generations. Absolute simplicity of color and a complex integration of individual architectural elements have created unique and beautiful homes for the islanders.

TOP RIGHT
Fishing boats in a canal, Venice, Italy. This view shows another side to the usual grandeur of Venice. An ordinary street in an ordinary neighborhood displays a rich tapestry of color alongside the canal, demonstrating how even the most elementary of buildings can contribute vibrancy to urban life.

FAR RIGHT
Courtyard of a building, Jaipur, India. This building, with its elegant and spacious courtyard, is well adapted to the heat of the Indian climate. The richly decorated facades with crafted balconies, doors, windows, and entry way, show how a simple courtyard and a single tree can provide a beautiful living environment.

But we must also remember that the concept of home cannot be isolated from that of community. As home is a reflection of the self and family, it is also a reflection of a larger social world, varying from a small tribe to today's mega-urban regions. Lifestyles, customs, and traditions practiced at home are seldom unique and are connected to society by systems of communication such as language, mail, boats, roads, air transport and today's mass media and electronic communication. Even the actual form of home is in many cases sacrificed to the greater social good. At the village level, homes are frequently organized in some collective configuration for defense, against some form of adversity in nature, or from other people. Homes may be designed to symbolize a god or gods, so that the ritual display of a particular deity will grant protection from evil forces. Similarly, in larger settlements and cities, high-rise apartments (that even existed 2000 years ago in the *insulae* of ancient Rome) represent a singular loss of identity in the interests of collective life.

In the following pages we illustrate the wonder that is home in many examples drawn from across the world – from the polar icecaps and the tropics, to outer space. These all attest to the sheer vastness of creativity and imagination that characterizes the human condition in its responses to nature and function, to family, spirituality, aesthetics, and social life. In all of this, home is the universal medium where these qualities become distilled and refined in physical space, a testament to the singularity of our collective universe.

Chapter 1

Home as Nature

The terms "refuge" or "sanctuary" are ways of expressing the meaning of home in relation to the natural world. Refuge implies a passive attitude and experience: Some place to which one can escape, or flee from enemies; a place of security or asylum; a sanctuary or a place where people go for safekeeping. There we can avoid the fear associated with natural forces such as earthquakes, tsunamis or other extreme climatic changes. In this context home reflects attitudes to nature, and as a refuge, is designed to mitigate its worst effects. There is also a significant overlap between humanity's relationship to other peoples and animals, and its attitude to the natural world. While both are extremely material considerations, relationships to nature are also philosophical, religious, and spiritual (as discussed in Home as Spirit).

AN ENEMY TO BE TAMED?

Western civilization has for centuries followed the dictum "multiply and subdue the Earth:" A philosophy which might just see the extinction of the human species. India's renowned political and social reformer, Mohandas Gandhi, when asked about his views on western life, replied that he thought it would be a good idea. Western attitudes accepted humanity as the predominant force in the world. Attitudes to nature as a world to be conquered, and imperialism as a political philosophy, were not wholly unrelated. In contrast, there have been countless examples of the huge respect that early nomadic and hunter-gatherer people had for nature, as it provided refuge, food, and overall prosperity. From the Inuit people in the Arctic Circle and the Plains Indians of North America (the Sioux, Blackfoot, Cheyenne, Crow, Kiowa, and Comanche), to the Dayak people of Borneo and the Maori in New Zealand, nature was God and their survival was ensured by this belief. However, nature within western civilization has been viewed as an enemy to be tamed, its resources exploited, and all assistance denied in time of need. This is seen in humanity's struggle to preserve rainforests, agree on carbon dioxide emissions, reduce the use of fossil fuels, and the destruction of animal and marine species. Today, these same attitudes are slowly bringing us to the point where our beliefs may not survive because they will have destroyed the material basis upon which they were constructed. Nature will no longer be capable of providing the refuge that it has so generously allowed in the past, since it has been suffocated by its own inhabitants.

The first of our species survived by hunting animals and gathering food from their environment. Hence, they were known as "hunter-gatherers." Few such people remain, most having become extinct as civilization gradually evolved into the globalized world of today. The ones that do exist in minute numbers are found in such places as Papua New Guinea (the Dani and Tambanum), the Amazon Basin (the Yanoamo, Tampiri, Bororo and Guarani), and up until relatively recently, in Australia (the Australian Aborigines). Their lives remain threatened by development that is not only destroying their culture, but also the plant and animal species that they depend on for their survival. For many of these peoples, and others like them, scattered across the planet, home has no material existence – the actual creation of permanent structures is unknown. Most use temporary dwellings for protection from the elements, from wild animals if such creatures exist, and even from the spirit and other worlds that structure their cosmology. Home is built, if it is built at all, from basic natural materials, in most cases from vegetation in the form of tree bark, branches, strong grasses such as papyrus, bamboo, leaves, and other substances. In other situations, cave and cliff dwellings abound, either underground or cut into rock.

In nomadic hunter-gatherer societies, people saw themselves as part of nature, somehow balancing off advantages against disadvantages, but without the idea that nature was somehow an enemy. Dependence on nature was respected and worshiped in a multitude of ways, where animistic beliefs allocated god-like powers to inanimate and animate objects and creatures. Forests, lakes and streams, plants and animals were alive with spirit, and integration with nature was absolute. Nonetheless, home still had to be located and designed in such a manner as to fend off wild animals, vermin, and insects, and to provide insulation from heat and cold. Torrential rain, typhoons, dust and snow storms also had to be resisted, as well as earthquakes, volcanic eruptions, and serious flooding. Therefore, the evolution of home gave rise to infinite and progressive forms of refuge, as well as a unique use of natural materials depending on which force of nature happened to predominate in any region. Examples include the use of steeply pitched roofs to resist torrential rain or mud-brick for insulation.

LEFT
A local village hut, Sepik River, Papua New Guinea. In contrast to the various types of natural disasters that mother Earth may bring us, it also provides an immense range of basic natural materials. This house is almost entirely built from grass and leaves collected from its surroundings. Being built on stilts, the structure protects its occupants from flooding as well as providing cooling ventilation.

TOP
An illuminated igloo, Hudson Bay, Manitoba, Canada. The word "igloo" is derived from the Inuktitut word *iglu* which means "house." Nowadays, the igloo is commonly associated with the snow house – a form of shelter protecting its occupants from the freezing harsh climate of the Arctic. Its construction requires blocks of hard field snow which are structurally sufficient to condense and interlock ice crystals that hold the dome.

OPPOSITE
Rock-hewn dwellings, Uchisar, Turkey. This is an example of home situated in the Cappadocia region. These homes represent an amazing adaptation of people to the hilly and rocky living environment. Earthquakes and volcanic eruptions are believed to be the major reasons for the formation of such strange terrain then, for hundreds of years, the people of this region dug into the soft but firm rock to create these unusual dwellings.

MUD-BRICK AND STRAW

The geographic distribution of similarly built forms and spaces are referred to as "typologies," and while the range of individual types of building are infinite, certain generic or commonly held features in mass construction of structure and form can usually be identified. The simple reason for this resides in the properties and qualities of materials, which are derived from nature. While the contemporary use of brick, for example, is widespread, buildings are restricted by the fact that brick cannot be used in tension, limiting brick to specific dimensions that utilize its compressive stress to best advantage. Combined with the type of kiln and the heat of the firing process, the use of different types of clay also decides strength, what color bricks or tiles eventually adopt, and therefore the height of walls that can be constructed. Similar considerations apply to all other materials, limiting and influencing how home materializes from nature, and deciding how efficiently home can be adapted to its environment.

Heat and cold have been tamed for millennia by the use of mud-brick structures, which are simultaneously extremely cheap, widely available, and incredibly effective. In many cases, the only difference between mud-brick and brick is that the former is only fired by the heat of the sun, and therefore has a much weaker crushing strength. Mud-brick remains the predominant building resource for the majority of the Earth's population, as is thatch as a roofing material. Mud-brick has a multitude of local names, one of the most common being the word "adobe," which is used in North and Central America. Adobe bricks are without doubt one of the most superior building materials ever invented, being readily available for free, and an efficient insulator against heat and cold. Frequently made from a mixture of mud and straw, adobe has been used to build whole cities; the largest pyramid ever built was constructed at Chan Chan in Peru from mud-bricks. Entire towns such as Gao and Timbuktu in Mali, or the desert cities in the Yemen are built from adobe. San'a, the Yemeni capital, is largely constructed from mud-brick, and buildings can reach ten stories in height. Taos Pueblo in New Mexico, built by the Tiwi Indians, is also a wonderful example of the combined use of mud-brick with a defensive structure. The building complex is up to five stories high in places, and houses cannot be distinguished from each other or from the settlement as a whole. Even the traditional ovens, which were used for baking, were built from adobe. The Tiwi created an extremely efficient defensive system by only allowing access to homes through the roof of the structure, and in historic photographs there are only a few doors visible. Photographs that are more recent show an increase in doorways. Given the transition to modern society, this suggests that the need for floor level access has been increased. While Taos Pueblo is relatively "modern" in the ancient world, Catal Huyuk in Anatolia in Turkey has a similar form. So in this context the confluence between nature, refuge, home, and settlement becomes absolute.

After mud-brick for building walls, strong grasses in the form of straw have traditionally been used as a walling and roofing material, either independently or in combination with mud, although adobe could also be adapted to roofing over small areas. Straw was frequently used as an additive to mud-bricks for increased strength, resilience or insulation, depending on the use to which it was put. The addition of straw increased the tensile quality of the brick, which only had strength in compression and cracked easily under differential loading. The essential property of any insulating material is that it does not allow the efficient passage of heat across its width. Adobe did this due to its high insulating properties, and straw had similar abilities since it contained a sealed air space between each joint in the material. When straw was used for roofing, and laid at a reasonable pitch, rotting was prevented through the efficient drainage of rainwater. It could then last many years without replacement, and has been used across the world, from the romantic thatched cottages of rural England to the Batak houses in Sumatra and the kainga and pataka houses built by the Maori in New Zealand.

Thatch has therefore been used in a plethora of forms as defense against nature and as a refuge for local people. Probably the best example of its use has been by the Marsh Arabs (Ma'dan) of Iraq. Reed boats were used for transport, and on top of reed islands, entire houses were built from the same material, which could last up to 20 years – even longer on dry land. The Marsh Arabs nearly became extinct under Saddam Hussein's rule, when the supply of water to the marshes was cut off. Fortunately, this situation has now been corrected and the Ma'dan is returning to their traditional way of life.

In many early societies, stored crops also required a refuge in the form of granaries, which had the same thatched roof as home. The granaries of early people became an art form in themselves, as in the Gurunsi of Upper Volta or the Tata in Chad. Even today, grain silos are one of the most dominant architectural features of the American mid-west, and have provided inspiration for many modern architects.

LIVING WITH THE ELEMENTS

Torrential rains and tropical storms usually have been resisted in several different ways. The best forms were those that had steeply pitching roofs, as we can see from many indigenous homes, such as those of the Batak in Sumatra, the Jolong people of South Vietnam and the various peoples from the islands of Micronesia. In addition, flooding was frequently dealt with either by having floating structures or through the use of stilts, which raised the building above the water level, such as those in Papua New Guinea or the Solomon Islands.

Even today, grain silos are one of the most dominant architectural features of the American mid-west, and have provided inspiration for many modern architects.

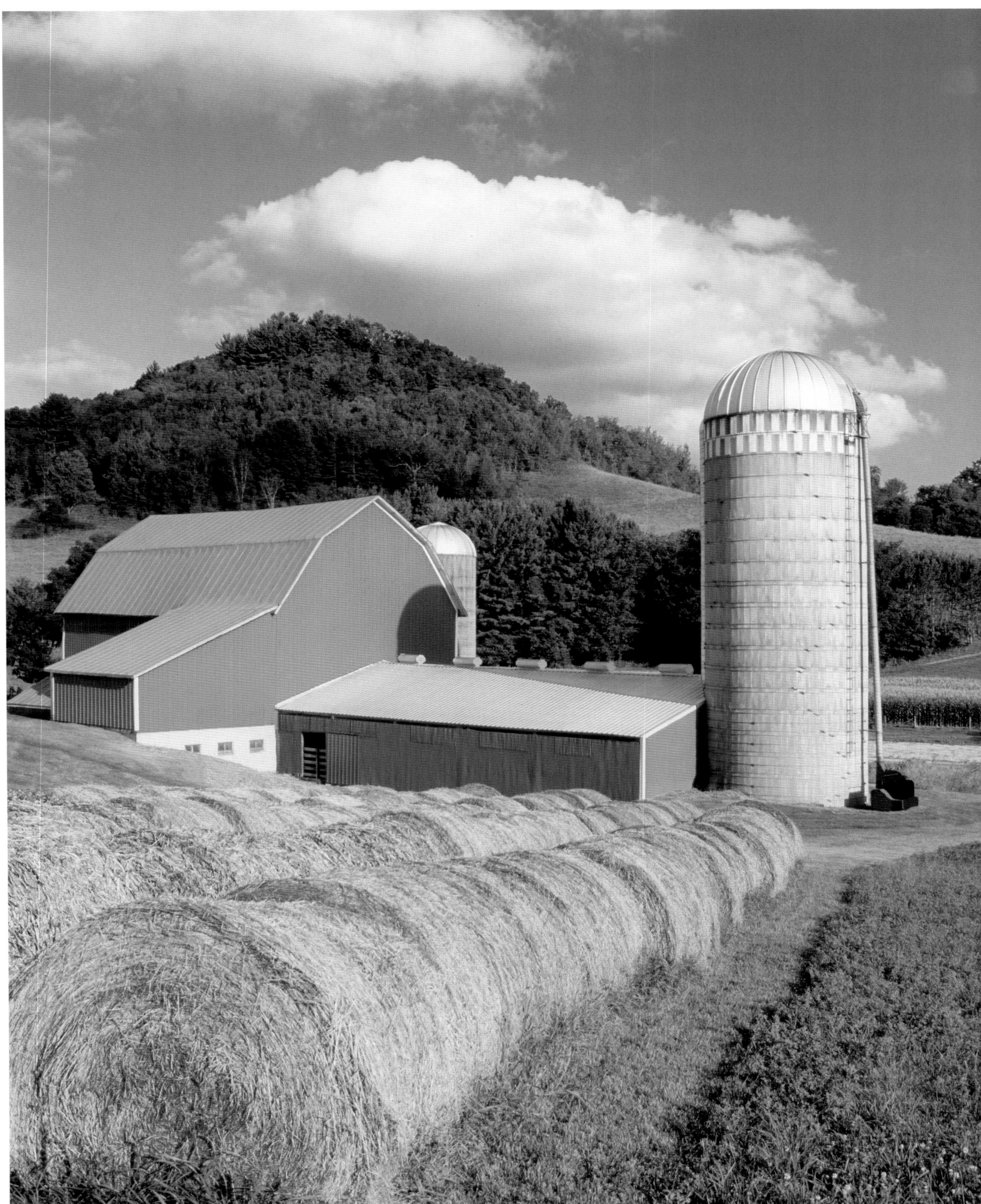

TOP LEFT
A traditional thatched cottage in Great Tew, Oxfordshire, England. In thatched houses the main structure is built from stone, brick or wood, and the roof from straw or other dried grasses. Organic materials such as straw, water reed, sedge, rushes, and heather have been long-crafted for roofing purposes. In most European countries, for example, wheat stems have been widely used.

TOP FAR LEFT
Taos Pueblo village, near Taos, New Mexico, USA. This is one of the ancient settlements of the Pueblo people, a native American community who have continuously maintained their original form of habitation up to the present time. Its uniqueness is inextricably linked to the existence of multi-storied residential dwellings whose strength relies in the use of adobe or mud-bricks.

RIGHT
A farmhouse with a grain silo in the American mid-west. While this type of dwelling fulfills its residential purpose, it is designed to accommodate farming activity. The grain silo is usually used for storing wheat. They are a feature of home in many American mid-west states, and their cylindrical forms signify their relationship to nature and food storage.

FOLLOWING PAGES
A traditional guesthouse of the Marsh people between the Euphrates and Tigris rivers in southern Iraq. This form of dwelling has its entire structure made out of bundles of reeds, and can be easily rebuilt when the structure becomes weak from flooding, age, or accident.

Earthquakes were quite another story, and there was little or no defense against volcanic eruptions, mud slides and tsunamis, except not building in areas prone to these natural disasters. Nonetheless, the design of home remained ingenious. Wooden structures were frequently designed with flexible joints, which allowed for settlement and lateral movement, since rigid structures were most at risk from earthquakes. In Bali, for example, the actual structure of the traditional Balinese house was also partially isolated from the dividing walls, offering an additional level of protection from the shifting of tectonic plates under the earth, by partially separating form from structure. In other areas, such as Japan, which is seriously earthquake prone, nature provided bamboo, allowing traditional buildings to be lightweight and sliding panels for walls (*shoji*) to be largely made out of paper. Without doubt, traditional Japanese architecture represents the pinnacle of technology when it comes to carpentry in wooden buildings. Joints between wooden members were arguably the most complex ever created, with hundreds of different types to suit all known circumstances. In many cases, joints were manufactured without even the use of wooden dowels, let alone the steel nails popularly used in the west. While buildings frequently burned down, they were relatively safe during earthquakes because of their flexibility and absence of mass. Lightweight homes using traditional materials were also less prone to damage during a storm, and in cases where houses collapsed, allowed the salvaging of materials for reuse. While firestorms were also threatening, it was a singularly easier task to rebuild such homes than those made from heavier and more enduring materials.

In South America, the Inca people also invented polygonal walling to resist earthquakes. This method of construction used stone as a material, which settled and became stronger when it was vibrated, although this method of construction was probably not used to house the poor. Nonetheless, excellent examples of polygonal walling remain visible in Cuzco, Peru, where Spanish colonists used structures as the foundations for their own homes. The colonists, however, proved to be a worse disaster than that of any natural force, decimating the population through war and pestilence, particularly smallpox. Therefore, the Incas used the power of nature as a refuge when they fled the advance of the Spanish conquistadors, escaping to the inaccessible regions of the Andes, and to fortresses such as those at Machu Picchu, Pisac, and Ollantaytambo.

So the landscape itself can provide refuge in a variety of different ways. Fortresses were built on hilltops, the very vastness and heat of the desert offered protection, islands created isolation, and even marshes allowed for sanctuary. Indeed the city of Venice was first established by a group of refugees fleeing from Padua around about the sixth century. (The great historian Lewis Mumford notes that the marshes and shallow waters of the Adriatic replaced the defensive properties of stone walls, while observing that other forms of refuge can be as effective without the construction of massive defensive systems.) The marshes were slowly turned into islands through dredging, and over one and a half millennia later, Venice developed into the city it is today. Italy is also home to another form of refuge – the hill town. These were not the same kind of hill town as the Incas had built, which relied on the secrecy of remoteness as well as mountainous terrain. Towns such as San Gimignano, Todi, Montepulciano, Montefalco, Montecastello and a host of others were permanent settlements where the hilltop and town had the same identity. The people of San Gimignano even enhanced this situation by building tower homes that can still be seen today. Combined with a maze of streets, the town became an even more impenetrable refuge.

While early habitation was undoubtedly crude and unsophisticated, this held no implication for the sensibilities of early peoples. The Aboriginal population of Australia possessed a highly advanced consciousness in relation to a unified cosmology of matter, energy and spirit. Arguably, their awareness went well beyond that of contemporary modern life by several levels. The world was not measured by possessions or defined by omnipotent and fearful gods. Not only was their relationship to their environment unsurpassed, it was inextricably linked with their concept of existence

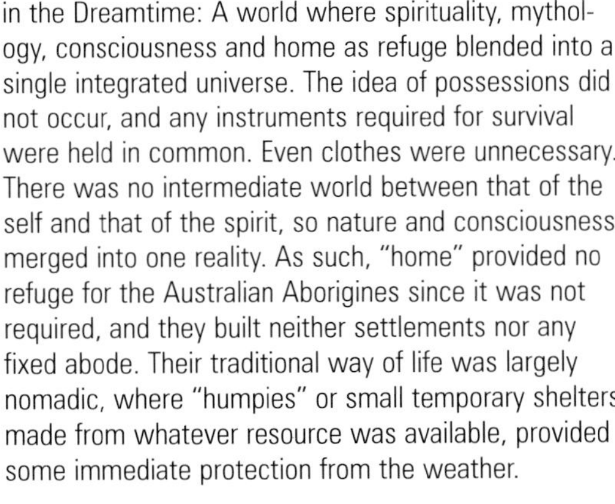

in the Dreamtime: A world where spirituality, mythology, consciousness and home as refuge blended into a single integrated universe. The idea of possessions did not occur, and any instruments required for survival were held in common. Even clothes were unnecessary. There was no intermediate world between that of the self and that of the spirit, so nature and consciousness merged into one reality. As such, "home" provided no refuge for the Australian Aborigines since it was not required, and they built neither settlements nor any fixed abode. Their traditional way of life was largely nomadic, where "humpies" or small temporary shelters made from whatever resource was available, provided some immediate protection from the weather.

Nature as refuge has therefore had a massive effect on home, as well as settlement. Nature has provided an infinite variety of climates, geographies, and materials that have supported habitation for countless millennia. There is no doubt, however, that we have not chosen to learn from our ancestors. Nature can no longer provide unconditional refuge from its own power, nor can it survive without our active participation. Since we have now achieved the Biblical mandate of dominion over nature, it is now time to question whether another strategy based on worship and respect for nature might be a more effective way to guarantee our refuge and hence our survival for the foreseeable future.

TOP FAR LEFT
Interior of a traditional Japanese house. Traditional Japanese house design is a consummate example of relating interior and exterior elements to create a balanced living environment. Natural building materials are used. Wide sliding doors and mobile internal partitions create an unsurpassed sense of space.

FAR LEFT
Polygonal walling in Cuzco in the Peruvian Andes. The city is believed to have been the center of the Inca Empire from the fourteenth to the fifteenth century. Such walls had defensive purposes, as well as protection from earthquakes due to their extreme stability and size. As structures, they are also a high art form.

TOP CENTRE
An Italian hill town forming the background to the San Biagio Church, Montepulciano, Tuscany, Italy. The hilly contours of the region inspired the Italians to form tower homes at the summit. Hilltops have always been considered a safe living environment against attack from enemies.

ABOVE
Gamble House, Pasadena, California, USA. Commissioned by David and Mary Gamble, this outstanding house was designed by architects Charles Sumner Greene and Henry Mather Greene in 1908. The use of timber, wide terraces, cross ventilation, and an indoor-outdoor living environment are carefully designed and crafted to create a harmonious home.

TOP
Fallingwater, Bear Run, Pennsylvania, USA. Built by the legendary architect Frank Lloyd Wright for Edgar Kaufmann in 1935, Fallingwater is perhaps one of the most famous homes in America. In this design, Wright creates an organic relationship with nature, mimicking the natural rock ledges that are created by a rushing mountain stream.

Chapter 2

Home as Defense

The concept of home as defense looks at home as protection from living creatures, including other human beings. This concept is primal and remains with us today. Home as defense is also dictated by climate, geography, and nature. This view is discussed in Home as Nature.

ACTIVE DEFENSE

As society has evolved from its primitive origins, it has become clear that the idea of defense has intensified and is of greater concern. There is a well-known saying in Britain that "an Englishman's home is his castle:" An unambiguous reference to the defensive structures that castles represent. The phrase "an Englishman's home is his palace" would have an altogether different significance; palaces being a place for display and entertainment, where any external threat has already been accommodated. These days, people define their lives by the ownership of commodities – cars, jewelry, computers, plasma televisions – so there is much more to be protected than just our physical bodies, as was the only requirement in ancient times. While modern life has unquestioned benefits over prior standards of living, it is also permeated by criminal activity from the state and corporate level, down to individuals. This generates the need not only for extensive security systems in homes, but also for complex surveillance systems throughout most cities in the developed world.

Active defense has from time immemorial been concerned with building walls, usually against warring neighbors, and the concept of "wall" is also used as a metaphor for a variety of defensive conditions – in technology, in psychology, and physically. Walls have adopted many forms and in the past have been physically built from every possible material available, including wood, stone and water (moats), often in combination. Israel is in the process of building a wall 800 miles long (650 km) along the West Bank, and the United States of America is considering a similar wall along its entire border with Mexico. At one level, the history of civilization is the history of progressive warfare between individuals, tribes, fiefdoms, states, and nations. The Great Wall of China is probably the greatest of these, built to keep out nomadic Mongolian and Manchurian tribes from the 3rd century BCE onwards. From Biblical times, the walls of Jericho remain an archetype for all defensive structures, and even the Romans had to build Hadrian's Wall across the whole of Britain to keep the blue woad-painted savages from Scotland on their own territory. Even animals have been used as defensive elements during warfare – Hannibal is well remembered for using elephants to fight the Romans – and movies of the Wild West are replete with images of cowboys using their horses as a protective wall against the original inhabitants. At the other end of the scale, animals also represented a need for serious defense, and many early forms of settlement constructed defensive walls against predators. Africa and India were home to the most dangerous species of animals – lions, tigers, cheetahs, and rogue elephants – and protection from these marauding carnivores was ubiquitous. Mass settlements from the Cameroon exhibit a huge range of huts constructed in a circle that were simultaneously defensive fortifications from animals, storage places for grain, and rooms for various sizes of family where more than one wife was the norm. The same is true of the Zulu Kraal in South Africa. Therefore, from our beginning as a species, humanity has viewed home both as a place to be defended and as a refuge for protection and solace.

TOP
A medicine man in front of his beehive hut, Natal, South Africa. This kind of house is decorated with various types of animal heads which are believed to have the power to defend against unwanted forces such as evil spirits. Evil spirits are considered to harm human health, bring bad luck, and affect relationships with others.

LEFT
Buckingham Palace, London, England. This is the official residence of the British head of state. To a great extent the palace is a symbolic representation of British sovereignty and the strength of its defenses that were part of the historic success of the British Empire. Buckingham Palace is a venue for numerous official state occasions and celebrations.

OPPOSITE
The Great Wall of China. Built from the 3rd century BCE onwards, the wall was intended to form a defensive structure, and coincidentally isolated China from the rest of the world. Attacks by the Mongols, however, demonstrated that the wall was ineffective and could be easily breached. It has been recognized as a UNESCO World Heritage Site since 1987.

Home then became the second "wall," since most cities were forced to construct defensive systems in the form of immense battlements and moats, or to locate on unscaleable hilltops.

POWER AND PROTECTION

As society developed and nomadic peoples everywhere became organized into communities of fixed settlements based on agriculture, surplus energy became stored not only in agricultural products, but also in materials mined from the earth, such as precious stones, gold, silver, and copper. A materialized concept of history proposes that communities are only representative of human labor – the labor it took to make them. An extended division of labor was created when social production reached a point where manufacture exceeded consumption and a quantum of labor could be freed to perform work not related to survival. This is how priests, artists and other professions arose. Progression from one historical period to another depended on how much labor had been stored in specific material forms. In turn new forms of power came into being, which were built on sectarian knowledge (priests), collective energy (armies), or organized social life (governments). The first forms of social organization that superseded hunter-gatherers, tribes and nomadic peoples are traditionally referred to as slave states, slavery representing the next level of social development. Not only did home remain a defensive environment, it now became located in towns and cities where slavery was a defining form of wealth, with slaves being variously used for physical labor, their intellectual abilities (not all slaves were uneducated and many were used as scribes, doctors or for whatever skill they owned), a form of currency, and even substitute foot soldiers. Slave states abounded over historical time. The worlds of the ancient Sumerians, Egyptians, Olmecs, Toltecs and Aztecs were all built on slavery. Slaves were one-third of the population of ancient Greece, the birthplace of democracy. More recently, the Incas of South America also based their culture on slavery, as indeed did the United States of America up until the civil war. Hence, another layer of defense was added to the idea of home, since it was not merely individual, house, or family that had to be protected, but states that had acquired enemies. Defense fell into the hands of professional armies conscripted by the state, whose job it was to protect its citizens from becoming slaves themselves. Home then became the second "wall," since most cities were forced to construct defensive systems in the form of immense battlements and moats, or to locate on unscaleable hilltops.

TOP LEFT
Thatched huts, Machu Picchu, Peru. An example of the 150 houses discovered in Machu Picchu, a sacred site to the Inca people located in the Peruvian Andes, 9060 ft (2800 m) above sea level. It was the main center to which the Incas fled in order to escape the invasion of the Spanish in 1532.

ABOVE
The hill town of San Gimignano, Tuscany, Italy. The selection of a hilltop as the site for this town provided a prime defensive opportunity as well as a unique urban form. The town built a series of towers to exaggerate the height of the village, which offered a more threatening image to any potential enemy.

Not only did "home" become secondary to "wall," and "citizen" to "soldier," the concept now acquired a whole new meaning since different classes of people had come into being. While hunter-gatherers existed in a state of shared wealth and power, slave states had allowed social stratification, and hence an unequal distribution of wealth to come about. On this basis, new forms of home evolved across the medieval period into the Renaissance that had never previously been contemplated. The beginning of conspicuous consumption was born, where excess wealth was not merely possessed; it was also exhibited, albeit for the specific function of protection. Where defense was concerned, this meant citadels, castles and fortresses, usually at the center of a settlement or town. There are few places in the world where defensive homes for those in power were not constructed. The home of the king, prince, dictator, or demi-god needed protection both from other powers, and frequently from their own people. Even today, there are few governments that do not possess special silos for the powerful, such as bunkers for the defense of the privileged in the event of a nuclear war.

In medieval times, warring states or fiefdoms built fortresses all over Europe. Scotland is a first-class example of this, where the country is littered with castles of all kinds. Edinburgh Castle is a perfect model of home as defense, as are the castles at Craigievar, Fyvie and Huntly. Similarly the Bastide towns of France such as Carcassonne, Villereal, and Monpazier are outstanding showpieces of walled towns of the medieval period. Italian hill towns such as San Gimignano, Assisi and Todi, also made effective use of the landscape, where hilltops provided near perfect defense against attack.

From the late Renaissance onwards, castles were no longer built (despite the naming of Hearst Castle in California in 1947, designed by Julia Morgan for Sir William Randolph Hearst, the newspaper magnate). Wars now took place between nations, and the homes of the rich took the form of grand palaces. Opulence was now exhibited on an unprecedented scale, as we can see from castles all over Europe. However, increased diversification in social classes combined with a transition from feudal society into the modern world meant that defense once again returned to the basic features required by personal security. Opulence continued and the castle gave way to the palace, as in the splendor of Chateau de Fontainebleau near Paris in France, Villa Aldobrandini near Frascati in Italy, Zwinger Palace in Dresden, and Buckingham Palace in London. While this still meant keeping out unwanted individuals, the number of typologies of home increased dramatically as urban life started to accelerate in its diversity of income classes and forms of labor.

Since home has always been caught up in human conflict in one form or another, it has had to provide its own defense, or to take part in some type of collective system, where social energy could be harnessed to provide what individuals could not. For example, the construction of defensive walls, moats and even houses was a collective effort from people in a society. Human belief systems and psychology also contribute to our understanding of home. For example, in Islamic cultures where women are not allowed out of the home unless accompanied by a male relative, balconies are designed so they can see out to the world of men, but they cannot be seen themselves. This is evident in Mughal or Rajput architecture in India, or in most cities in the Middle East. Home then becomes a defensive wall in terms of social and religious practices, where the entire form of the building, and indeed whole cities, are constructed to encompass religious dogma. There are, of course, many degrees of variation depending on the specific needs of the belief system.

In a much less extreme form, home everywhere is influenced by the cultural worldview of its occupants, in particular their protection from real or perceived threats, such as evil spirits and threatening gods. In many rural communities today, residents still do not feel the need to lock doors and windows when they leave the house. But in most modern urban areas, sophisticated electronics replace the friendly surveillance of community. Electrical devices provide internal surveillance, with direct connections to private security firms, and complex locking mechanisms on all the doors and windows, or even specially trained and selected dogs. At the biological level, the idea of defense is even built into our neurological systems, one-half dealing with fight and flight, or attack and escape, the other dealing with relaxation and rest. Therefore, the concept of defense is a primal part of our psychosomatic make-up, which has evolved along with the actual changes to our physical body over millions of years of evolution.

MODERN SURVEILLANCE

Defense applies not only to the simple physical act of keeping out unwanted people, it is also relevant to the virtual world, where electronic communication has become an invasive part of our home. Clearly, the idea of home as somewhere to be defended is increasing rather than decreasing in both its significance and cost. The burgeoning use of electronic communication for shopping, banking, education, and a plethora of other uses, also demands defensive networks and systems. The Internet is itself mutating into new and unexpected forms that require complex networks and strategies to protect its function. Previously unknown forms of defense such as "firewalls," "virus protection," "spam filters," "spyware" and so on, are now commonplace. Defense in the third millennium now requires highly sophisticated protection to ensure both personal and physical security at home, while at the same time it limits physical movement, replacing it with electronic communication. To use an extreme case, it is obvious that anyone who can work entirely from home – an increasing percentage of the population – need never leave unless they become sick, since other basic services such as banking, shopping, and entertainment can all be provided for electronically in a virtual world. Even money becomes irrelevant in this context. An evolving idea of home is therefore intimately linked to parallel defensive networks and systems.

So today's post-modern society also belongs to a parallel and virtual world of electronic communication and being. Here, a new and insidious process in the form of surveillance systems is now in place, which can be used for both defense, as well as encroachment into the home. There is no clear boundary between these two processes. Their use contains one of the great ethical problems of our times – the degree to which human rights should be sacrificed to individual and collective security.

TOP LEFT
Zwinger Palace, Dresden, Germany. Designed by the famous eighteenth-century architect, Matthaus Daniel Poppelmann, Zwinger Palace is one of Germany's most prominent landmarks. It was built on a site formerly used as a castle, whose inner and outer walls functioned as massive barriers from invasions.

FAR LEFT
Cliff dwellings of the Mesa Verde National Park, Colorado, USA. This is one of the most remarkable sites on Earth for any series of homes ever built. It is located near the top of a canyon wall under a huge overhang, offering supreme defensive qualities as well as protection from the elements.

ABOVE
A traditional home in Bahrain. This is an example of home in an Islamic society where women's activities must be invisible to the outside world. Balconies and terraces of these houses are designed to allow women to have views on events taking place outside the dwelling without anyone being able to see them.

RIGHT
Hill House, Helensburgh, Scotland. This house is the finest domestic building ever designed by the master architect, Charles Rennie Mackintosh. He borrowed its design features from Scottish baronial castles, and was a formative influence in the Art Nouveau movement. Simple, clean lines and natural colors characterize the house.

Chapter 3

Home as Cloister

The concept of home as cloister opens up the question of typologies once again. The word "cloister" has a variety of possible interpretations: It immediately conjures up the idea of courtyard and the geometry of the square; something hidden, secretive, protected, internal, and private. In formal terms, the cloister or courtyard represents the square at the domestic level, but there is also a direct analogy with the square at the city level. Two great typologies have ruled the development of urban life: The street and the square. Roads are about points and lines and the movement between them. The street has been for centuries the key to transportation, and the words "shopping" and "street" have long been synonymous. Streets are conduits for commerce and communication, services and transport. Roads and streets have been important to civilized life from ancient times, and Roman roads are famous for setting in place many of the major trajectories of contemporary European transportation. Overall, the Romans built around 50,000 miles (80,500 km) of roads. The Fosse Way in England and the Appian Way in Italy are classic examples, and the construction method used lasted over 2,000 years before it was surpassed by modern technology.

THE SQUARE

The square on the other hand, even as a geometric concept, is not about movement but about rest and other associated activities, such as contemplation, reflection and discussion. At least since Hellenic times, over 2,500 years ago, the square has structured cities through the medium of a gridiron plan, and ancient Greek colonial towns in Asia Minor, such as Miletus, Priene and Pergamon, are famous as the predecessors of contemporary gridiron planning. However, gridiron planning was also a part of Asian urbanization. Japanese cities such as Kyoto and Nara, as well as the Chinese cities of Chang'an, Luoyang and Yangzhou, are all famous as early examples of gridiron planning. Today this is also evident in the United States of America where the entire country is based on cadastral gridiron planning; that is, the division of land into square or rectilinear sections, New York being a prime example. Therefore, the use of the grid as a fundamental geometric structure has been formative to urban development. But at that level, the grid remains a two-dimensional concept. Cities also demand the third dimension of height, as well as transformation in the fourth dimension – the space of time and history. This is the realm of urban design, where adapted spaces are generated for human use.

Squares have various uses when it comes to human interaction. The Greek square or agora was the archetypal urban form that encapsulated the concepts of discourse and philosophy, as well as that of commerce and the exchange of goods. The Greek home was built around the idea of a square or cloister, and was also the chosen form of the Romans who came after them. The agora – the central urban space of Greek cities – was the ultimate statement of urban life, where conversation was as important as commodities. Citizens gathered to exchange ideas, to gossip, or perhaps to listen to famous philosophers such as Socrates, Plato, Euripides, or Epicurus. The agora was usually constructed with generous colonnades, which encouraged dialog, debate, and conversation in all of its forms by providing a space which sequestered individuals from the often searing heat of summer. The reconstructed Stoa of Attalos is a perfect example of this and can be seen today in Athens. The agora gradually developed over history as the space around which western cities were built, and a space upon which the future development of democracy was predicated. It was the locus of military drills, festivals, elections, and spectacles, and was the place where the entire administration of the city was located. The great squares of the world owe their existence to the agora, and many European cities have a dominant "square" where the identity of the city and its social life circulates. We can name, for example, Trafalgar Square in London, St Mark's Square in Venice, Times Square in New York, and Place des Vosges in Paris. While Asian cities owe no allegiance to the Greeks, they are not immune from having their own important urban squares, such as Tiananmen Square in Beijing, Tugu Monas (Monas Square) in Jakarta and Sanam Luang in Bangkok. Each of these squares have also been associated with civil unrest, and it is clear that one of the functions of the square in urban life has been as a place where civil society has expressed its grievances against tyrannical states and governments of all kinds, in both eastern and western cultures.

How then does this translate at the level of domestic life? The idea of cloister is not limited to home, but is a form of home. In architecture, the term "cloister" applies to any square form that is centered on a colonnaded courtyard and which has a variety of spaces on the periphery. The use of that particular type of space in Europe evolved from monastic life to which it was eminently suited. In medieval times, the Guilds, which were the basis of organized labor, generated their own collective system to regulate working conditions and educate their members. This unified system was given the Latin name *universitas*, the original form of the university in western culture. From cloister and *universitas*, the modern university was born as form and function. University quadrangles became the adopted symbol of higher learning. However, this was also repeated over time in government and other institutions, such as hospitals, prisons, and asylums. So when we look at the idea of home as cloister throughout history, we also see that its adopted form was not arbitrary. It was tailored to a variety of human needs such as safety, security, privacy, the isolation of domestic functions, and the capacity to adapt to a variety of different climatic conditions and materials. Examples include the wonderful Spanish colonial courtyard houses in Mexico with their cool interiors and large hammocks for siesta, to the Arab cities in the deserts of Yemen, and the delicately framed simplicity of traditional Japanese houses with enclosed Zen gardens. Even the British system of new towns adopted the courtyard house as part of their architectural vocabulary for public housing.

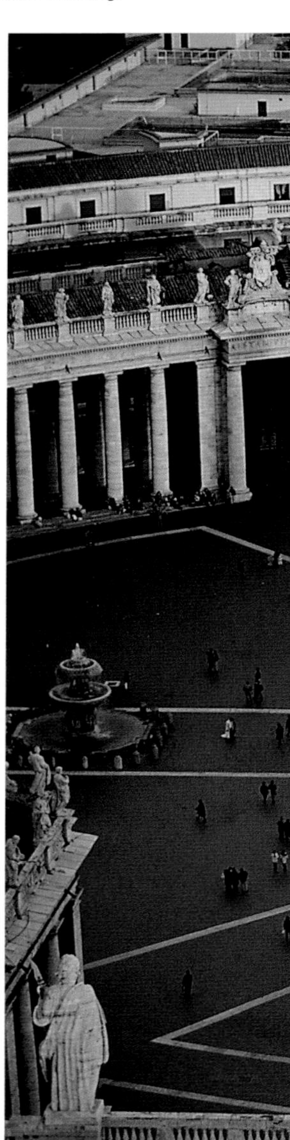

TOP
The Appian Way, Rome, Italy. The Romans depended on roads being built to link all parts of its empire. Roads and streets have been the key to commerce and transport for centuries and the words "shopping" and "street" have long been synonymous. The street is the most elementary urban form.

RIGHT
St Peter's Square, Vatican City, Italy. This is probably the most significant square in the Christian world as well as being an architectural and urban masterpiece. It is here that the Pope gives his annual blessing to Catholics all around the world.

TOP LEFT
Stoa of Attalos, Athens, Greece. This restored cloister was originally a two-story commercial building and a precursor for many contemporary architectural and urban forms. The presence of colonnades on both floors promoted interaction, dialog, and debate among visitors. There were rooms on both floors for commercial purposes.

TOP RIGHT
The Lion Court, Alhambra Palace, Granada, Spain. The court is the central feature of the Harem – one section of the Alhambra Palace that ties three rooms together: The Hall of the Two Sisters; the Hall of the Abencerrajes; and the Hall of the Kings. The basin of the magnificent Lion Fountain is supported by 12 marble lions.

FOLLOWING PAGES
Former hospital courtyard, Mexico City, Mexico. The courtyard is a basic domestic and urban form that appears all over the world. The central fountain is a cooling device, and the garden offers every room a view of greenery and flowers.

THE COURTYARD HOUSE

The courtyard house as cloister has therefore had a huge range of applications throughout the world, and across the entire historical spectrum. In addition, certain cultures, such as that of Islam, have traditionally favored the courtyard form. The position of women in this society and the need for extreme privacy within the blank walls that the courtyard offers means that the cloister is tailor-made for people of the Muslim faith. The traditional Islamic courtyard house, particularly that of the wealthy, can frequently reach a height exceeding three or four stories, and can be found in cities such as Cairo, Fez, Aleppo, Damascus or Baghdad. For Islam, this type of housing contains at least three important features. First, the building height means that on the upper floors, balconies can be constructed that permit views out without anyone looking in, such as the mushrabiya shutters used in Egypt or the carved and ornate balconies of Mughal architecture. This also suggests social segregation of women to the upper floors, and men and the more public functions of storage and entertainment to the ground floor. Second, the courtyard house offers both an outside and an inside to its occupants. In those Islamic states where women cannot freely move about, the courtyard becomes a place that doubles for the public space of the city. It is an area where relatives and friends can meet in relative privacy and comfort within the acceptable norms of their culture. In addition, it offers a semi-public space whereby people may enter from the street, without directly intruding into the domestic space of the home. Third, the higher form of the courtyard house also allows a "chimney" effect to take place. With the careful integration of a fountain at ground level, the courtyard allows air to be cooled as it passes through the fountain or pond, also cooling the rooms at higher levels as the air rises up. In fact, this device serves the same function as a flue in a fire, except it is used for cooling rather than heating.

Courtyard design is favored in Muslim countries because it offers both closure and exposure – closure from the outside world and exposure within the family.

The courtyard is not limited to Islamic architecture in the Middle East, India, Africa and a few other locations. Its generic benefits have been widely adopted in many other regions. In China, at the urban level, the idea of cloister was also implicit, and it remained the dominant form for hundreds of years. Wealth was measured not by the height or grandeur of a building, but by the extent of its walls. The same form was used with great effect in the Heavenly City in Beijing, which is structured around two ceremonial squares. The traditional Chinese house in Beijing was bounded by lanes called *hutongs* with their internal courtyards called *si he yuan*. However, its existence has been widely threatened since the low-rise nature of the courtyard house represents a huge barrier to development. It is already being replaced by high-rise apartments and a process of importing western domestic typologies that the American scholar Tony King refers to as "villafication." China's extraordinary growth over the last 20 years and its expectations for the future suggest that the traditional courtyard house may soon be consigned to museum environments in designated conservation areas, and vast tracts of these beautiful old houses have already been extinguished from Chinese cities.

The traditional Balinese courtyard house is yet another application of the widespread use of the cloister as architectural form. Because of the prevalence of Balinese Hinduism, the courtyard has a somewhat different function from other locations. For example, in contrast to the Islamic courtyard which can be built over as many floors as construction methods and wealth will allow, in Bali, religious practices forbid construction that is higher than the average height of coconut trees (49 ft/15 m). In addition, the external wall does not denote the actual structure of the house, since the space it encloses is subdivided into nine squares called Sanga Mandala. Each square has a different function and may be occupied by a different building form. The family shrine occupies the northeast corner and the central space is usually an open courtyard. This space is usually quite large and is the common area used by the family on a daily basis, as well as the location for rituals and celebrations. Traditional Balinese society and cosmology also revolves around the principle that the prime function of home is that of a shrine for the ancestors. Family members are therefore custodians of home in perpetuity, but do not "own" it. For that reason, in contrast to materialistic societies elsewhere, Balinese homes have no value as commodities, and only have value in use. They are in a very real sense, religious cloisters.

The courtyard and the archetype of the cloister have had universal application across a wide range of climatic conditions, although the form has predominated in hot or warm temperate zones. Psychologically, this architectural structure is introspective, segregated, of limited horizon, self-centered, and concentrated on family life. These qualities are necessary to society and will continue to serve the world's inhabitants for centuries to come.

OPPOSITE
Interior of an Islamic school, Morocco. Courtyard design is favored in Muslim countries because it offers both closure and exposure – closure from the outside world and exposure within the family. The design also protects its occupants from hot, dry climatic conditions.

ABOVE
Casa de Montego, Mexico. A classic Mexican home for the wealthy. This courtyard house has a wide veranda that borders the courtyard. A large hammock and outside furniture demonstrate the use of the veranda as an extension of the living space, allowing residents to enjoy the interior landscape of the courtyard.

TOP
Summer Palace, Yiheyuan, China. In today's China, courtyard houses represent a huge barrier to development. Due to the rapid growth in both population and development over the last 20 years, these houses have been replaced by high-rise apartments.

Chapter 4

Home as Spirit

Home as spirit concerns the relationship between humanity and the unseen world in its many guises. The function of home under this ideology encompasses everything from organized religion and animistic beliefs, to the worlds of black magic or voodoo. Home as spirit focuses on safeguarding occupants from all manner of unseen forces, the representation of gods, and ceremonies in their worship or offerings to appease them. Overall, these practices seek to maintain equilibrium within the home, where health, wealth and happiness are commonly held aspirations. Also important is the position of home as a place where family beliefs are nourished. This notion incorporates believing in some kind of god in the form of organized religion, existence after death, particular ideologies and practices in life, as well as the power accorded to individuals within society such as those of seer, jro taksu, shaman, witchdoctor, medicine man or priest.

A PLACE OF PRAYER AND REMEMBRANCE

These meanings of home as spirit suggest two main concepts: Home as a place of worship, and home as a memoir. The notion of worship imbeds a devotion to natural spirits, deities, the idea of God and its manifestations. The spirit world is not homogeneous. Some spirits are good, some bad, and some relatively benign. Some protect health, some the environment, some food supplies, and some are harnessed in the interest of harming others. Such religious observance may ask for blessings in the manner of a good harvest, protection from accidents, physical strength, good weather, family success, abundant crops, forgiveness from wrongdoing, or healing for illnesses. Vernacular societies frequently have specific homes dedicated to their gods and healers in the form of spirit or medicine houses. Worship may also be directed to evil spirits not to bring any misfortune or disturbance to the household's living environment. People from the Ivory Coast, for example, implant a huge masked dancer doll on stilts in front of their homes for protection. Countless examples exist of this kind of practice.

The notion of home as a memoir first embraces the idea of remembrance where home remains a repository for the soul. The soul of every family member is to be perpetuated and respected, even though the person may no longer be in the physical world. Second, home also represents the locus for a commemoration of legendary figures, values, or memorable deeds embraced by communities and societies at a larger scale.

LEFT
Taj Mahal, Agra, India. The Taj Mahal, a symbol of eternal love, was built in 1631 by Shah Jahan, the fifth Mughal emperor, in reminiscence of his second wife, Mumtaz Mahal, a Muslim princess from Persia. The building was designed by the Iranian architect, Ustad Isa.

TOP
A house in Ivory Coast, Africa. A large-scale, masked dancer doll on stilts is installed in front of this dwelling to dispatch all invisible evil spirits. They are unwanted and deemed to possess powers that inflict hazards and harm to the home's residents.

Therefore, devotion to higher, invisible forces has been part of daily life, maintained from generation to generation in various societies across history and within every type of human group be it hunter-gatherer, nomadic, slave state, medieval, or modern. The Greeks believed that their ancient gods had been overthrown by the Titans: A group of 12 new gods (Zeus, Poseidon, Hades, Hestia, Hera, Ares, Athena, Apollo, Aphrodite, Hermes, Artemis, and Hephaestus), whose sacred home was Mount Olympus. In every home in ancient Greece, there was a shrine or shrines to these gods. The same was true of the Romans, who also worshiped a group of 12 different gods. Even at that time the great sages of China, Lao Tse and Confucius, had established Taoism (based on Buddhism) and Confucianism respectively, and shrines to these ideologies have been an integral part of home across the whole of Asia for over 2,500 years. To accommodate these practices and other forms of observance of spirit, home offers the most immediate space for private contemplation and prayer. In most places, this takes the shape of a family altar or shrine where, for example, a statue of Siddhartha Gautama, Lao Tan, or Kung-fu-tse sits, surrounded with incense, flowers, and other offerings. Similar practices are also common in Japanese families. Shinto, the indigenous faith of Japanese people has no founder, scriptures or sutras. Shinto gods are called Kami and are represented in the forces of nature. Amaterasu, the sun god, was the most important deity. Japan's other religion, Zen Buddhism, had similar forms of worship, but since it had no personified gods, objects were usually used for meditation in the form of a flower, a painting or even a hand-drawn circle representing the cosmos. In addition, a family altar may also be present in the home, which is specifically devoted to paying respect to a family's ancestors.

In communities of early peoples who still function today, life still takes place within the governing compass of the spirit world. For instance, The Abelam village situated between the Sepik River and the Prince Alexander Mountains in northern Papua New Guinea has a ceremonial spirit house referred as Haus Tambaran. This is an "all-roof" house. The whole structure slopes to the ground at the back and the frame is constructed by bamboo poles forming a high-peaked ridge at the front. The prominent role of ritual and spirit is demonstrated from the scale of the Haus Tambaran which can reach 82 ft (25 m) in height. This is five to six times higher than the height of houses built next to and opposite it. While ordinary dwellings do not have decorative elements, the Haus Tambaran has its upper front wall decorated with blue and red oval-shaped ornaments, symbolic faces, cassowaries, and flying foxes. Abelam people secure the lower part of the front facade of this ceremonial house with plaited mats with two entrances, whereas living houses have none of these securities.

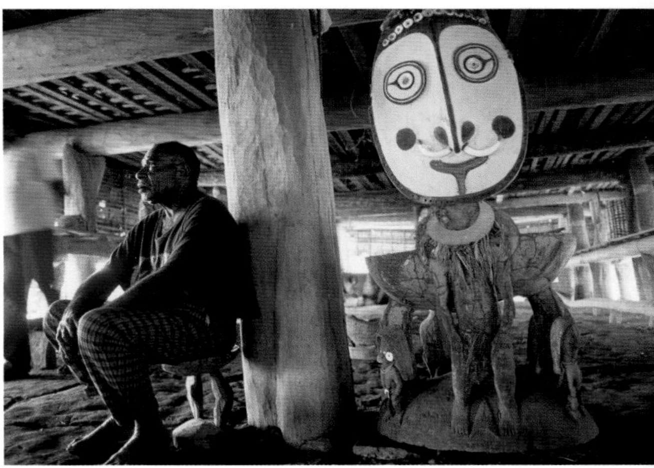

RIGHT
Interior of a Haus Tambaran, Palambei Village, Papua New Guinea. These lively symbols in the forms of carvings or masks, used in a Haus Tambaran, are imbued with the religious beliefs of the people. Based on the principles of totenism and animism, these creations are made to drive out bad spirits.

TOP
Statues of Buddha, Bangkok, Thailand. In Thailand, where Buddhism is widely practiced, it is common to find an altar located at a prominent part of the house. A statue of Buddha is usually accompanied by offerings such as flowers.

ABOVE RIGHT
Graceland, Memphis, Tennessee, USA. The former home of rock legend Elvis Presley from the late 1950s until his death in 1973. It is now a museum showcasing his remarkable career and the site of his grave.

The significance of home as a medium for the spirit world, a space of transaction, meditation and prayer, is evident within the vernacular house of the Balinese in Indonesia. It exhibits singular generic qualities and demonstrates in great detail the extent to which home as spirit is defined by, and embedded within, family life. It is the locus where the macrocosmic forces of gods and nature determine the daily life of the people. The traditional Balinese courtyard house or compound is divided into nine zones, called Sanga Mandala. The family shrine is called Merajan or Sanggah and is located in the most sacred zone Utama-Utama – usually at the northeast corner of Tanah Sikut Satak (the site where the house is). Other domestic functions are located in relation to the family shrine and are not negotiable. Bathrooms, WCs, washing areas, kitchens etc. are already determined before anyone decides to build a traditional house. The Merajan has several smaller shrines each of which is devoted to a deva or deity, the god's manifestations, and the family's ancestors, whose souls have received further ceremonies following a cremation rite. In order to safeguard the house from "bad" spirits, there are also small shrines located at every corner of the house. For similar purposes, there is another shrine built just in front of the main entrance, as one enters the compound. While some shrines are built with stone foundations, timber structures, grass straw, or palm sugar husk roofing, most are wholly constructed from soft natural volcanic stone quarried close by or collected from adjacent rivers. Even the placing of floors has ritual significance, with the kitchen at the lowest level and the shrine having the highest elevation.

Thus spirit worship in the Balinese home infuses both behavior and architecture. A woman who is menstruating is not allowed to enter or even stand near the shrine. In this circumstance, she is also exempted from involvement in the preparation of offerings, ceremonies, and prayer. Family members and non-family members who are in mourning are also restricted from entering. All equipment used for ritual, including other matters relating to these shrines, is not usually mixed with those utilized for other purposes, despite the fact that their functions overlap. Some families even have an additional building and kitchen to support the operation of the family shrines. Offerings are made to the ancestors on a daily basis. Apart from a daily offering, each family holds a bigger ceremony to celebrate the day when the shrines were completed. It comes every 210 days (six Balinese months) – the day when family members and relatives coming from the same ancestral line meet, pray, and gather for meals. In a traditional family compound, a significant portion of the family's annual income can be spent on offerings and ceremonies.

Therefore, the observation of ritual complexity carried by home goes beyond mere physical experience. In Bali and other Indonesian societies, every stage of constructing a home involves a series of observances that may come in various forms of ceremony, offerings, and sacrifices. In order to invite "good" spirits and calm down "bad" forces, such rituals may have to take place on a specific day according to a particular calendar. Types of building materials used, the selection of site, and distinctive choices of symbolic and decorative forms are all part of the effort to deploy spiritual significance to home. Failing to fulfill any of these procedures may be regarded as a direct cause for insecurity, illness, bad luck, or psychological discomfort experienced by members of the household.

Measuring the Tanah Sikut Satak, site clearing, putting in foundations, fitting columns and beams, roofing, etc., are all commenced on a particular day. Each involves offerings and ceremony. Building materials used for shrines should be the finest available in terms of quality and durability. In circumstances where these practices cannot be performed, negligence may be excused by performing other special ritual ceremonies. Such ceremonies are also applied when the sacred value of a family shrine is disturbed or compromised by any means. At another level, even the spirit of the owner is incorporated into the home by constructing a special scale based on his actual physical being. Such measuring sticks form the basis for all elements in the construction process.

TOP LEFT
Animism-Hinduism practices in Balinese society. Balinese daily life is closely linked to this belief system. No day passes without offerings to the gods. The Balinese calendar dictates hundreds of special ceremonies and events every year.

HERO WORSHIP

In today's society, home as spirit is also represented in the process of conservation where homes of society's greatest representatives, good or bad, have been protected for posterity. These rise above the importance of individuals and are emblematic of entire histories – the rule of presidents, victory in war, the development of art and literature, and other accomplishments. In this context, houses are consciously preserved in order to commemorate and memorialize a past that is not only significant to a particular family but also to a wider audience, community, or country. In the United States of America, for example, the house of Thomas Jefferson at Monticello near Charlottesville, Virginia, is a wonderful piece of architecture that celebrates this famous president. Alternatively, the simple birthplace of Elvis Presley in Tupelo, Mississippi is also a form of shrine for millions of Americans, as is his house, Graceland, in Memphis.

Paradoxically, it would appear that as society has progressed, the relationship between home as spirit and its reflection in dwelling form has decreased with an overall increase in the complexity of social development. Expressions of home as spirit have been gradually simplified or even eliminated over time. In fact, societies wrongly labeled "primitive" are much closer to home as spirit than most homes today, which are largely bereft of spiritual content and expression. In the developed world, new gods such as Nike, Sony, and Chanel, have arisen to reflect today's Mount Olympus of consumer society and commodity fetishism.

TOP CENTRE
North lawn of the White House, Washington DC, USA. The official residence of the President of the United States of America, the White House was conceived by George Washington, who selected its actual location. Its development began in 1792 and it was completed in 1800 in the Classical style of architecture.

TOP RIGHT
10 Downing Street, London, England. The historic home and office of the Prime Minister of the United Kingdom, this building is of modest appearance and does not reflect the important activities held inside it. It symbolizes that the government remains close to the ordinary life of the people.

ABOVE
Home interior of a Shaker community. The spartan nature of Shaker religious beliefs is reflected in their whole environment. The design of artefacts is simple yet beautiful. The minimal use of furniture also reflects this philosophy. Simplicity is a widely acknowledged value of Shaker communities.

Chapter 5

Home as Journey

Home as journey has had a long history, from the trading caravans of the Great Silk Route to the space capsules that NASA has sent to the moon. While the nomad is central to our idea of home as an experience of movement, the concept also has many variations.

NOMADISM

In the strict sense of the word, "nomadism" only has two interpretations. Pastoral nomadic life was a symbiosis between humans and animals, where movement was demanded because animals of whatever kind had depleted the landscape of food. One theory of pastoral nomadism is that it grew out of the activities of hunter-gatherer people; another is that it evolved much later after mixed farming had developed. In any event, pastoral nomads were dependent on animal husbandry, and their lifestyle allowed them to exploit a variety of different landforms so, technically, it is a form of farming, replacing plants with animals. The domestication of goats, horses, sheep, cattle, and other creatures allowed this form of nomadism to evolve. The Mongols, Magyars and Moors were typical examples of this. Pastoral nomadism was also dictated by the seasons, where migration was imposed by the passage from one season to another.

True nomadism, however, required no justification for movement – it was just natural behavior, rather than staying in one place. Historic nomadic peoples populated all forms of landscape: the Bedouin and Tuareg of the desert, the Pygmies of the central African jungle, the Innu people of Quebec and Labrador, or the Moken sea gypsies of the Surin Islands in southern Thailand. Therefore, nomadism even included movement over water, and the nomadic Hakka boat people of southern China can be seen in anchorages in Hong Kong today.

TOP
Example of an Aboriginal wurley, Australia. This hut exemplifies the journeys of the largely nomadic lifestyle of the Australian Aborigines. Home is an endless journey following the myths and legends of the Dreamtime – their spiritual world. All forms of home were crude, temporary, and disposable.

LEFT
A hut of the Bambendjelle tribe, Makao, Democratic Republic of the Congo. The construction of this temporary hut coincides with the tribe's constant movement in search of food. This migration is also necessary to avoid disastrous damage potentially caused by bad weather conditions.

MOBILE "HOMES"

The development of home in these contexts also bred a variety of physical dwellings. Both true nomadism and pastoral nomadism led to the construction of an immense variety of structures that were sometimes fixed (to be revisited at the same time the following year), or that were transported by camel, horse or other animals such as the llama and guanaco of Peru. Many true nomads, such as the pygmy tribes of the Ituri Forest in the Democratic Republic of the Congo or the Australian Aborigines, only had the most minimal of temporary and disposable structures. Since nomadism took place in all kinds of climatic conditions, home had to be adapted accordingly. The Inuit built temporary ice huts called "igloos" whenever they needed refuge. The Mongols developed circular buildings called "yurts," which were suited to the high winds of the Steppe, which were also used by the Kirghiz people in the Gobi desert. In America the Plains Indians developed the "tepee," which was a superb adaptation to climatic conditions. It also satisfied the need for a demountable structure. The tepee could be transported as the tribe moved, being used predominantly during periods of hunting buffalo. It used a framework of long poles in a conical form, covered with animal skins as a protective membrane. Ventilation through the apex of the tepee allowed a central fire to be lit for heating and cooking. The outside was usually decorated with symbolic images. Today animal skins have been replaced by high quality canvas, and tepees built according to the original design are still in vogue and can now be purchased by mail order. The other structure used by the Plains Indians was the wigwam, which is often confused with the tepee. It was, however, an entirely different form, built in the shape of a dome from flexible tree branches covered with rush matting, and was usually used to store grain.

The Bedouin Arabs developed an altogether different form of tent home; a structure that could easily cover a large area and accommodate many people. The Bedouin account for 10 percent of the population of the central Middle East. Their nomadic lifestyle is based in the desert environments of Saudi Arabia, Yemen, Israel, Syria, as well as Egypt, Tunisia, and Libya in North Africa. It is estimated that in Saudi Arabia alone there are around 700,000 Bedouin people. Most are Sunni Muslims, but there are also a small number of Christians because any Bedouin who believed in Jesus Christ was put to death. The Bedouin tent was usually black in color and extremely lightweight, being made from wool strips and lightweight timbers in compression. Its shape is very like the advanced tent forms used today by contemporary architects, where steel and powerful synthetic materials parallel the Bedouin use of rope and canvas. The tent was nonetheless a simple affair, based on a series of vertical poles with a horizontal membrane stretched over them and fixed with ropes into the ground. Like most nomadic people, the concept of furniture was alien, and people sat, conversed, and slept on the floor.

The idea of nomad is by no means confined to early forms of social organization, and it has had many equivalents as society has evolved. The Romany people are one such example and are found throughout Europe and Asia. Originating from northwest India, they migrated through Persia and Turkey, and hence into Western Europe. The Romany have been given many names by local people, including the English "gypsy" and the French *tzigane*, and they have suffered serious persecution over their entire history, which originated 800 to 1000 years ago. This has continued right into the modern period, when they were declared "sub-human" by the Nazis and sent to concentration camps. One traditional form of Romany home recognized throughout Europe has been the highly decorated horse-drawn caravan or cart. These carts have been used for centuries and in many cases, have been superseded today by motor homes, often with air-conditioning, a bathroom and the usual amenities of modern homes. While many Romany remain nomadic, significant numbers have decided to live in fixed settlements, with some 70 percent of today's Romany population residing in small towns such as Hameau Tzigane in Grasse, France, or Shuto Orizari in Skopje, Macedonia.

ABOVE
A typical caravan used by the Romany people. A precursor of the mobile home, the caravan is one of the original features of gypsy life. Originally pulled by horses, most gypsies now use some kind of mechanical transport, such as cars or vans. Caravans were also moving art forms, using complex decorative features and bright colors.

TOP
Native American dwelling, Great Plains, USA. The tepee as a nomadic dwelling has two distinct features: It has a hole at the top that allows an open fire and cooking activities to take place inside; and it uses 10 poles as a basic frame, covered with animal skins, which is easily transportable on horseback.

FOLLOWING PAGES
Bedouin tents, the Sahara, Morocco. In Arabic, *bedouin* means "inhabitant of the desert." The bedouin build their tents to accommodate family members and to serve their guests. In the 1950s and 60s, however, the bedouin started to change their nomadic lifestyle to settle and work in cities across the Middle East.

Technology has also extended the concept of home into space, with space flights and space stations now transporting home out into the universe.

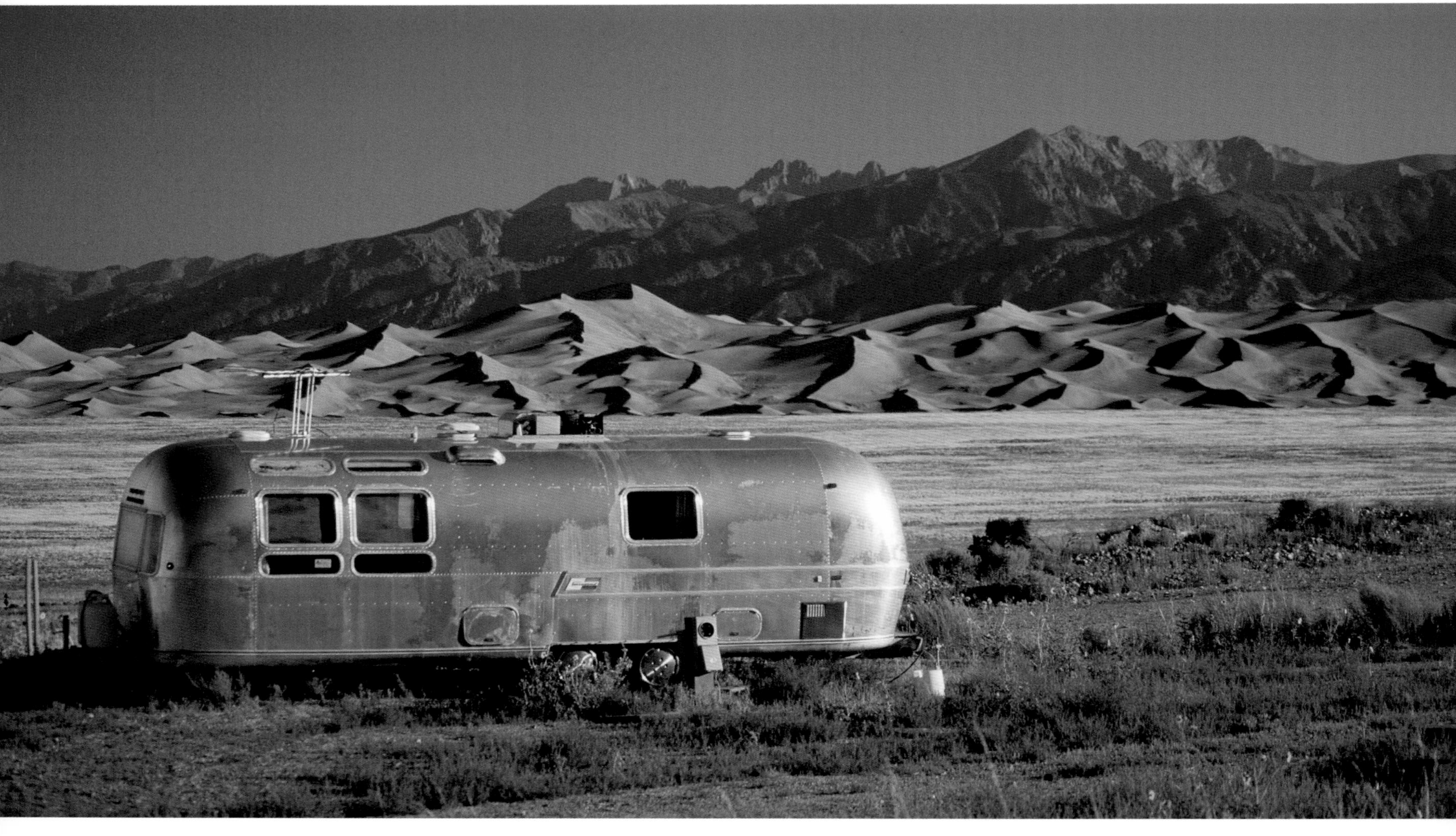

MODERN MIGRATION

In today's globalized world, home as journey has taken on new meanings as modern forms of conflict, disease, economic opportunity and lifestyle have taken place. The greatest of these is probably migration due to famine, persecution and unemployment. Legal migration to the United States of America is now approaching one million per annum. Since the system of registration as a resident of a particular village was abolished in China, 200 million people have left rural areas for cities, with 40 million on the move at any one time. The United Nations (UNHCR) currently estimates a total of approximately 175 million migrants worldwide. In addition to this, there are approximately 12 million refugees, which suggests about 200 million persons are moving home in some form or another at any one time. Today, for those who have suffered from political persecution, war, disease or natural disasters, home has taken on the forms of temporary tent settlements and other places of detention across the globe. This is most prevalent in Africa. Here, home as journey has become suspended until people can return to their original settlement, or be welcomed by some other country. Unfortunately, refugee camps have a habit of turning into semi-permanent forms of home as the world's capacity to absorb these populations is resisted.

Home as journey in the modern world is not, however, limited to migrants and refugees. Wealth and technology also manufacture their own forms of home as journey, as seen in the mobile home. Greater retirement incomes combined with advanced health care has allowed people in developed countries to chose mobility rather than belonging to a fixed settlement. In addition, it is a much cheaper form of home. Rather than having a huge percentage of one's savings locked up in fixed capital, home as journey can be bought for a tenth of the price. This form of home is on the increase. The mobile home is now ubiquitous, with many new models developing since the original and iconic Airstream Trailer of the United States, or the Volkswagen Microbus of Europe, both popular in the 1950s. Having worked for 40 or 50 years, many retirees enjoying good health now buy some form of mobile home that is self-contained or requires towing. Sometimes both are used together, where a self-powered mobile home also tows a car, offering a more flexible system of transportation. Mobile homes assemble into temporary settlements at designated sites for specified periods, and then move to the next destination. These are altogether different from what is called a trailer park, where homes are indeed mobile, but hardly ever move from an initial fixed location.

The mobile home phenomenon is predominantly limited to wealthy countries and/or those with large land masses, such as the United States of America or Australia. Since the formation of the European Economic Community (EEC), movement across national boundaries and the transfer of certain benefits has also opened up increased possibilities across the whole of Europe.

ABOVE
The Airstream Trailer. For decades, the Airstream Trailer has been an icon of American life. It also represented the ultimate in quality mobile homes with a sleek aluminum outer shell and a highly finished interior. The smooth, cigar-shaped exterior gave it its name "airstream," which symbolized the design.

Technology has also extended the concept of home into space, with space flights and space stations now transporting home out into the universe. Oil rigs also represent home as journey, at least temporarily, for those who must work on location throughout the world. The same is true of ocean liners, and huge, floating settlements such as *The World*: a ship comprised of luxury private apartments, which travels to the four corners of the globe. As the world's population increases, it is expected that mobility for whatever reason is also likely to increase. An evolving trend is to combine home as journey with electronic communication, where people become what author Steven Roberts has called "technomads," with online nomadic living and support wherever home happens to be. The possible combination of electronic communication, flexible transport, and accommodation with the virtual world promises that new and unheralded forms of home as journey are on their way.

TOP LEFT
Trailers or caravans have been widely used as temporary homes for people who are traveling. This is especially true of many western countries where large distances are best covered by taking one's home along. Recreational vehicles provide people with the comfort of a moving home – a space to sleep, cook, dine in, wash, and relax.

ABOVE
An emergency shelter at Cape Hallett, Antarctica. Cape Hallett was the site for New Zealand and the United States of America's joint research base in Antarctica (1957–73). This type of shelter was commonly used to protect researchers who worked on the project from the constant cold weather conditions of Antarctica.

TOP RIGHT
Gemini Space Capsule docking in orbit. The ultimate mobile home traveling at thousands of miles per hour and providing every basic service necessary for survival. However, in contrast to other mobile forms of home, space capsules have highly limited performance specifications, with little room for errors of judgment.

Chapter 6
Home as Art

Throughout history, home for people in every single topography and climate has always had a symbolic function. The reason for this is obvious: People live not only in the material world of their own physical requirements, but also in environments where societies express their collective history, beliefs, aspirations, emotions, the exhibition of power and authority, and even fears and tribulations. From the time humanity first came into consciousness, the imagination has been harnessed as the mechanism by which representation of other worlds could be realized. Today, we call this "art" and it is a concept of modernity to the extent that a small painting by the French impressionist Vincent Van Gogh can sell for upwards of US$50 million dollars. To this degree, art has simply become part of contemporary investment strategies for the wealthy, in the process changing art from any practical function into collector's items for state-controlled art galleries and private entrepreneurs.

AN IDEA OF BEAUTY

Although the word "art" is useful in describing certain functions of home, it can also be misleading. Art as a concept has little validity over history unless we consider both its context and practice. In ancient times, art did not exist as we know it today. As modernism was the first epoch to conceive of itself as a separate "bit" of history – a period apart, independent, and definable from the rest – so it was the first to reappropriate the function of art from the symbolic to the material, from the sacred to the profane, and from the world of the spirit to that of money, wealth, and power.

When examining home as art, it is important to consider the relationship between "art" and "aesthetics." While these terms are commonly tied together, there is no necessary relationship between them. In ancient Greek *aestheta* means "perceptible things" and it was not until the eighteenth century that aesthetics became related to the idea of beauty, first in German and then in English. Therefore, our concepts of beauty, art, and aesthetics are a direct product of our time and have little to do with how history has dealt with systems for representing consciousness. There is a famous Balinese saying: "We have no art, we simply do everything as well as we can." This indicates a condition that had existed for millennia, where the function of art was to support the daily life of people and where it had no exchange value. Art was simply the best anyone could do in whatever activity they were undertaking. Without doubt, home was organized around material processes and was structured around these activities: Fire for cooking, animal skins and blankets for sleeping, space to tell stories and transmit the oral history of the people. However, the symbolic world was at least equal to the material, and was often more important. While there has always been a collective dimension to home where communities celebrated their relation to family life, home has always played its own important part in rituals and ceremonies, such as those associated with the birth of children, rites of passage, marriage, and the journey beyond life into the worlds of gods and spirits. In each case, home as art was fully integrated. It did not occupy a separate space of objectivity and contemplation, and the world of "otherness" was expressed both through the human body in trance, dance, or meditation, or through fetishes, painting, objects carved from wood, metal and stone, and even in the layout of space, both within the dwelling and its relationship to other buildings in the community. The ancient caves of Lascaux in France have highly decorated interiors, as do the Tassilli frescoes in cave dwellings of the Sahara desert. In contrast to the idea that art was dependent on a complex division of labor required to release labor from toil, in Lascaux we find that art celebrated life and was necessary to its success.

TOP
A prominent mural of the Gyantse Kumbum Monastery, Gyantse, Tibet. Being the largest stupa in Tibet, this monastery has four floors with chapels of different sizes and is filled with statues and murals. *Kumbum* in Tibetan means 100,000 images. This is one of the few monasteries surviving after the destruction caused by Chinese occupation.

LEFT
Lascaux cave painting, Lascaux, France. Some of the earliest forms of home – caves – were decorated with highly stylized and symbolic paintings. In contrast to the idea that art is dependant on a complex division of labor required to release labor from toil, the Lascaux painting in France demonstrates that the celebration of life was necessary to its success.

RIGHT
An example of Maori carving, New Zealand. Traditional Maori homes are works of art with carved and painted beams and lintels, highly woven tapestries made from reeds as well as elaborately sculpted and ornate panels and supporting columns.

TOP FAR RIGHT
Aboriginal hand painting, Australia. The Australian Aborigines had all manner of art totems, sculptures, fetishes, implements etc., which were frequently a representation of natural phenomena such as lightning, storms, animals, and vegetation of all kinds. This example demonstrates its use in cave painting.

FAR RIGHT
Tokyo Bay, Japan. This bathroom is built based on feng shui principles. It is designed to overlook the bay, which is considered to bring positive "chi" or energy not only to the house, but also to its occupants.

ART IS CULTURE

Home as art has many dimensions. One of the most basic is the relationship to the cosmos, where the positioning of home frequently reflected religious or spiritual dimensions. Positioning was often directly related to compass points, or the rising and setting of the sun. In the ancient Chinese practice of feng shui, particular geographic features and relationships are important, and elements called dragon lines help "chi" (the circulating life energy found in all things) flow naturally in the landscape. For example, having mountains behind and water in front of an abode was always desirable. The Cheyenne Indians always adopted a circular camp form with the entrance to the east, which was also the orientation for the doorway in all the tepees. Groupings of tents symbolized clan structures, human life cycles, and relationships to the Earth such as hunting and the production of crops.

The relationship between mythology and art was absolute in the life of Australia's Aborigines to the extent that the life of every individual was the perfect expression of a unity with every living creature and feature of the physical landscape. A film called *Where the Green Ants Dream* (1984) by the famous German director Wim Wenders personified the ongoing conflict between corporations and indigenous communities. In his film, the local Australian Aboriginal community refused to allow any disruption to the Earth, because that was the place "where the green ants dream." While the Aborigines had no dwellings, they had all manner of "art" totems, sculptures, fetishes, implements etc., which were frequently a representation of natural phenomena such as lightning, storms, animals, and vegetation of all kinds.

Home as art even has zoomorphic qualities where the actual form of the house or settlement mimics some kind of animal, as in the tortoise of the Lunda Kingdom of Angola or the village of Boum Massenia in Chad, which takes the form of a rhinoceros. The human body has also been used as art, as in the anthropomorphic plans of the Fali people in Cameroon. While early people frequently based the form of home on the representation of living creatures, all materials used to construct home also lent themselves to some manner of adornment, and the use of natural dyes and paints was widespread. No part of any building was immune to decoration or carving. Traditional Maori homes, for example, have carved and painted beams and lintels, highly woven tapestries made from reeds as wall panels, and elaborately sculpted and ornate supporting columns. The Haida Indians of British Columbia also erected huge carved totem poles as part of home, which had huge symbolic significance.

Even as long ago as the ancient Egyptians, architecture was still influenced by religion and ritual, as seen in the pyramids and mastabas constructed for the dead.

ABOVE
The Marble Court, Palace of Versailles, France. Commissioned by Louis XIV, development of the Palace of Versailles began in 1669 and was built over the next 25 years by architects Louis Le Vau and Jules Hardouin-Mansart, with the world-famous André Le Nôtre designing the landscape. After its construction, Versailles had a tremendous influence on French architecture and the arts.

TOP
The Great Temple of Ramses II, Abu Simbel, Egypt. This is one of the cut-rock temples located in the ancient Wawat in Nubia. The temple's giant facade is about 125 ft (38 m) long and 102 ft (31 m) high and is dedicated to the New Kingdom's most prominent gods: Ptah (god of creation), Amun-Re (god of greatness), Re-Harakhte (god of the sun), and Ramses II himself.

ALL IN THE DETAIL

It is clear that art as we know it today became increasingly detached from daily life as civilization evolved. Part of this was due to the progress of architecture as a discrete art form. Art was applied to home by experts rather than being created based on traditional rituals, conventions, and beliefs. Even as long ago as the ancient Egyptians, architecture was still influenced by religion and ritual, as seen in the pyramids and mastabas constructed for the dead, and the temples and other ritual places as homes for the gods. In ancient Greece and Rome, the courtyard house had been established as the standard art form. Apart from the building itself, experts were then used, as they have been until today, to create art in the form of murals, paintings, sculptures and landscape features using both plants and objects such as fountains to generate home as art. In many ways, this process reached its pinnacle during the Renaissance and Baroque periods, where the concentration of wealth into private hands combined with the ability to express this wealth through material means is unsurpassed even today. The homes of the world's greatest

billionaires such as Bill Gates, Warren Buffet, and Karl Albrecht fade into obscurity when compared to those of the last 500 years. For example, the Palace of Versailles near Paris, commissioned by Louis XIV, was started in 1669, and was built over the next 25 years by architects Louis Le Vau and Jules Hardouin-Mansart with the world-famous André Le Nôtre designing the landscape. Approximately 36,000 workers were employed in its construction. Later, Buckingham Palace in London was initiated by King George IV around 1820, and was designed and supervised by the architect John Nash. But such extravagant homes were by no means unique, and the whole of Europe and Asia are replete with the most incredible examples of home as art: The Chateau of Chambord in the Loire Valley (1519–47) designed by Domenico da Cortona, Belvedere Palace in Vienna (1714–22) by Johann Lucas von Hildebrandt, Blenheim Palace in England (1705–22) by Sir John Vanbrugh, and the Winter Palace in St Petersburg (1762) by Bartolomeo Rastrelli. All these palaces are consummate examples of home as art because they incorporate painting, sculpture, wood carving, landscaping, and architectural detailing.

Home as the art of architecture really came into being with the creation of modern professions and institutions: The Royal Institute of British Architects being the first such establishment to take concrete form in 1834. Since then, the development of home as the art of architecture has been influenced by recent history, social development, and technological advances. Many architects also continued the tradition of designing everything in the building including furniture and fittings, so they created an easily identifiable style. Prime examples were Frank Lloyd Wright (Fallingwater, Bear Run, Pennsylvania, 1935), Charles Rennie Mackintosh (Hill House, Helensburgh, Scotland, 1902–03), Antonio Gaudi (the Casa Mila, 1905–10, and Casa Batllo, 1905–07 in Barcelona), Ludwig Mies van der Rohe (The Farnsworth House, Plano, Illinois, 1951), and the Greene Brothers (Gamble House, Pasadena, California, 1908). Home as art is not, however, limited to individual buildings, and some remarkable housing complexes have also had a huge influence, such as Auguste Perret's apartment building on the Rue Franklin in Paris (1903), Le Corbusier's Unite d'Habitation in Marseilles (1947–52), Ralph Erskine's Byker Redevelopment in Newcastle-upon-Tyne, England (1973–78), and the Palace of Abraxas by Ricardo Bofill in Marne-La-Vallée, France (1978–83). Overall, history has provided us with all the evidence we need to consider home as art in a multiplicity of dimensions, providing for material needs and raising the spirit in countless ways.

ABOVE
Casa Batllo, Barcelona, Spain. Translated as the "House of Bones," Casa Batllo is one of Antonio Gaudi's masterpieces. Gaudi pioneered the Art Nouveau movement and built this apartment building between 1905–07. His style has an organic, skeletal quality which clearly distinguishes his buildings from others in the city.

Chapter 7

Home as Facade

The word "facade" is a French word meaning "front," but it also has another meaning of "false" or "illusory." When we say that a person is "putting on a facade," we mean that they are pretending to be something that they are not; they are hiding their true feelings or personality. However, "facade" is also used to describe the front of a building, usually facing the street. The idea of something "false" also applies to buildings, since a facade usually does not tell you much about what is going on inside. For all practical purposes a building usually has five surfaces. The facade seen from the street therefore only allows one of these surfaces to be seen. This also raises an interesting conundrum for architects, namely whether or not facades come into the realm of what we call "architecture" since only one surface is usually designed, and it is normally part of a continuous frontage stretching the entire length of a street.

AT FACE VALUE

Without doubt, the concepts "street" and "facade" are inseparably linked. Furthermore, facades are usually composed of many buildings, usually houses, and they all look the same. Facades are usually made up of a single repeated module. There may, however, be subtle variations either in each single unit or indeed over the entire surface where central or terminal features may act to unify the overall design, as in the famous terraces of John Nash in London. Facades also imply the idea of "front" and "back," a practice from which modern architecture has tried to escape, since buildings are supposed to be unified sculptural objects that do not place a premium on any single aspect. In this paradigm, there can be no fronts or backs, only buildings. Overall, this implies that the terrace is an urban form rather than an architectural one.

While it is possible to design a street without having it bounded by facades, it is not possible to design a continuous facade without making a street in the process. Similarly, it is highly unusual to use a continuous facade for homes without designing the basic unit from which the facade is composed. As a broad generalization, we can therefore say that the evolution of the contemporary city has been in many cases dependent on the application of the idea of facade to domestic purposes. In the process, this created streets that were the very foundation of urbanization. This fact can be evidenced in some of the great cities of the world, particularly in Europe. Paris is famous for its boulevards that are bounded by continuous facades around six stories high. In Britain, both Bath and Edinburgh are famous for their Georgian terraces usually around four to six stories high, and London is also well-known for its extensive Edwardian terraces.

Barcelona has magnificent *avenidas* bordered by extensive facades fringed with rows of street trees, and the Gran Via de les Corts Catalanes – truly one of the great streets of the world. New York is renowned for its "brownstone" terraces, which were the very basis for the development of Manhattan, extending north over the entire length of the island, from Battery Park to West 220th Street near the Cloisters Museum. Other examples abound, from Buenos Aires in Argentina to the medieval facades of Florence and Venice, or the magnificent terraces of the Ringstrasse in Vienna. In every case, facadism was the device that generally married middle class respectability to the public space of the street in the central city. Working class people in industrial areas usually occupied significantly poorer quality terraced housing close to their source of work.

Home as facade was used extensively in Europe, the Americas, and Russia, having singularly less application in the East. At least part of this had to do with how social class was defined, what construction materials and skills were available, and how the political economy of a country determined what constituted wealth. In addition, tradition and custom played a huge part. In China, for example, the conspicuous display of wealth was not socially acceptable, and the homes of the wealthy almost never rose above a single story in height. The preferred use of the courtyard form for domestic use meant that the homes of the wealthy were defined by the size of the compound, not how tall or elaborately decorated the building was. In essence, the traditional Chinese *hutong* or alley was in fact another type of facade, usually one that had no qualities at all other than a few gates, which allowed entry from the alley into the domestic space of home.

LEFT
Workers' houses, Fushun, China. Fushun is an industrialized city with almost 63 percent of its 2 million residents working in various industrial companies, mainly coal mining. Housing quality and environment in this city remains a serious concern.

TOP
Cumberland Terrace, Regent's Park, London, England. Completed in 1827, this residential unit was designed in the Neoclassical style by one of Britain's most famous architects, John Nash.

OPPOSITE
Brownstone houses, Brooklyn, New York City, USA. New York's "brownstones" typify the city's urban development. These elegant homes in the form of a continuous facade epitomize the cosmopolitan charm of the districts from 225th Street to lower Manhattan.

FOLLOWING PAGES
Hundertwasser House, Vienna, Austria. This apartment complex was designed by the Austrian artist, Friedensreich Hundertwasser. He tried to humanize the tendency to standardize units and is known for his riotous colors and unorthodox facades.

BIRTH OF THE TERRACE

One fine example of the use of the terrace in urbanization comes from Edinburgh in Scotland, referred to as "the Athens of the North." The clarity of Edinburgh's historical growth is a classic example of urban development due to the precision and visibility of its architecture, and seldom is history displayed so precisely in built form. The ancient city is prominent in a castle built on top of a volcanic plug, glaciation having determined the form of the medieval city that falls away from the ridgeline on both sides. The center of the medieval town runs down the ridge called "the Royal Mile" to the Palace of Holyroodhouse at the bottom, a spectacular and seldom used home for the British Royal Family. At the beginning of the eighteenth century, conditions in the medieval town (itself a series of facades or "closes") had become so bad and offensive to the rich that they decided to build another environment to escape what they termed "the smoky beehives of the unwashed." This has since been referred to as the "New Town," a bastion of middle class gentility, which it has maintained to the present time. The New Town was located roughly a kilometre away from the castle, on the other side of a small lake, and the competition for the master plan was won by James Craig in 1766, when he was only 22 years old. The New Town was laid out on a gridiron plan, using the device of the facade on every street to construct homes for the professional classes. Each part of the gridiron had a central garden held in common by adjacent properties. Although these gardens remain inaccessible to the public, they provided Edinburgh with significant open spaces in the very center of the city. Home as facade was therefore laid down over the last 250 years as the adopted form for the entire city center, through Georgian, and Victorian times, and into the modern period. Along with Bath, Edinburgh is one of the best examples of Georgian architecture and planning in Britain.

ABOVE
Victoria Street, Edinburgh, Scotland. This view of Victoria Street down towards West Bow and the Grassmarket – the oldest part of Edinburgh – showcases a continuous facade. The buildings contain both shops and apartments, and the street has been formed over centuries of development and redevelopment as the city grew.

While it is possible to design a street without having it bounded by facades, it is not possible to design a continuous facade without making a street in the process.

At the time they originated around 1750, similar terraces formed the heart of the bourgeois city throughout Europe. Homes such as these had never been seen before. They were bright, airy, and full of light; built from stone that would seldom age; secure from criminals; and maintained neighborliness and conversation through proximity and common front and back gardens. They had wide streets and sidewalks, street trees and clarity of purpose. Depending on the topography, at least one basement was built below ground, sometimes two. Behind the common facade, however, two basic forms of housing were deployed. The first was the division of the facade into a specified number of vertically organized homes over four to six stories, limited by height given that elevators had not yet been invented. Here, class structure was apparent with the servants occupying the basement and the attic, with family reception and dining rooms on the ground floor and bedrooms on the first and second floors. The other form of housing, sometimes referred to as the "tenement," used an entirely different structure with a common door to the street. Each separate unit of the facade was segregated horizontally into apartments that usually occupied opposite sides of the common stair. This form was much more prevalent in France than in Britain. Few of the immense facades created by Napoleon III and his architect Baron Hausmann hide homes over four or five stories. They feature direct access to the street and are singularly limited to apartment dwelling. Perhaps the collective memory of the French Revolution of 1789 inhibited the obvious demonstration of wealth represented in the vertical division of facade into home. In addition, since most terraces were built by speculative builders, as indeed are most homes today, there were significant variations within houses and apartments across all aspects of planning and construction. Homes seldom had fewer than three to four bedrooms, and the internal spaces had immense variation in layout. Homes built in the eighteenth century demonstrated magnificent work by all trades, with complex plaster cornices and ceiling roses, huge skirting boards at floor level, beautifully carved doors and window details, and a widespread use of etched glass, handmade tiles, and other decorative elements. Even the stone and wrought iron work were art forms in themselves.

The use of the facade was not solely the purview of the middle classes. About the time that James Craig designed Edinburgh's New Town, one of the greatest events in human history was taking shape in the form of the Industrial Revolution. Not only did this generate the wealth that allowed a burgeoning middle class and its adopted form of housing, it also dramatically increased land values. With the need to house workers close to mines and factories, the row house – the working class equivalent of the bourgeois terrace – came into existence. All the great centers of production from Glasgow and Manchester to Pittsburgh, Lyons and Frankfurt had to accommodate workers in the smallest possible space in close proximity to work. The row house became a ubiquitous form of home, with standard housing units crushed together in narrow streets, with minimal facilities and little amenity. The heartland of the Industrial Revolution, the English Midlands, is still using row housing built at the end of the nineteenth century, many of which, like the mines and equipment used in production, are now conservation items for visiting tourists. These types of home as facade were also featured by the famous pop group the Beatles in a scene from the film *Yellow Submarine*. Here, a small external door on the outside (signifying poverty and hence identification with the community), has been converted into a single huge home by knocking out the internal partitions. Therefore, the facade is indeed an adaptable urban form that has served its purpose well under a diversity of circumstances. Nonetheless, while retaining its capacity for privacy and illusion at an individual level, it advertises, in no uncertain manner, the social purpose for which it was constructed.

ABOVE
Row houses, Back Bay, Boston, Massachusetts, USA. These apartments from Boston are the equivalent of the New York "brownstones" and give the area much of its character. Back Bay has always been an up-market area for wealthy professionals.

TOP LEFT
Homes built in the eighteenth century demonstrated a magnificent attention to detail with complex ceiling roses, plaster cornices, beautifully carved doors and windows, and a widespread use of etched glass, handmade tiles, and other decorative elements.

Chapter 8

Home as Function

As we have seen, home has a diversity of functions. In different places and at different times, home has protected humans from nature, other people, gods, and evil spirits. It is a place for celebration and decoration, and a sanctuary for religious observance. At another level, home provides a place to work; make love; sleep or rest; to cook; to provide privacy, warmth or coolness; and perhaps somewhere to take care of washing and personal hygiene. In all of these cases, however, there are a plethora of ways in which these functions can be both performed and expressed. If we look at the astonishing variety of homes, we cannot even make general assumptions about how these various functions are incorporated, except perhaps in the developed world of today. Even there, huge cultural differences predominate.

DOMESTIC RITES AND RULES

We have already noted that some nomadic people, such as the Australian Aborigines or the Ituri pygmies of the Democratic Republic of the Congo, do not even possess a physical structure to call home. In these cultures, the overall functions of home exist as part of nature. Food does not come standardized, processed, canned, or frozen. Food is living nature, and is usually alive until just before it is eaten. The rain or river provides for washing, and even the spirits exist in plants and animals. In more settled times, many ancient cultures also provided for certain traditional domestic functions to take place in commonality, such as bathing, with the bath being a collective concept in both ancient Greece and Rome. The Romans, in particular, built baths wherever they had colonies, which at that time was most of the known western world. Bath in England, named after its Roman baths, can still be seen today. Many Roman baths were also fed by huge aqueducts that transported water as far as 62 miles (100 km). Probably the greatest examples of these were the Baths of Diocletian and the Baths of Caracalla, remnants of which can also be seen today in modern Rome. (The Baths of Diocletian were the largest ever built, being completed in 305 CE, they functioned for 230 years until the Goths cut off the supply of water to the city.) One can also find collective parallels in all other domestic functions, such as eating, sleeping, and making love. All these functions have taken place collectively in one form or another, for example, in primitive rituals, ancient bacchanalian rites, Roman orgies, and various rites of solstice and celebrations during the Medieval period, while others related to witchcraft and Satanism.

Even these normally accepted functions of home have a huge variety of expression. Sleeping, for instance, can be practiced simply by lying down anywhere and going to sleep with no support for either head or body, to the use of immense and complicated structures either on, or raised above the ground, such as Victorian four-poster beds. In between we find beds made from a variety of materials, from straw and horsehair to solid cotton pads, as in the Japanese futon, or woven as in the Mexican hammock, which comes in all sizes up to the "matrimonio" that can hold an entire family. Even head supports have huge variation, from the solid wooden or reed pillows of the Chinese to luxurious pillows made from the wool of animals, breast feathers of geese, or today's synthetic fibers. After sleeping, home probably has the universal function of preparing and eating food. Anthropologists have for centuries studied the significance of both in the symbolic sense as well as the functional, although these usually overlap in complex ways.

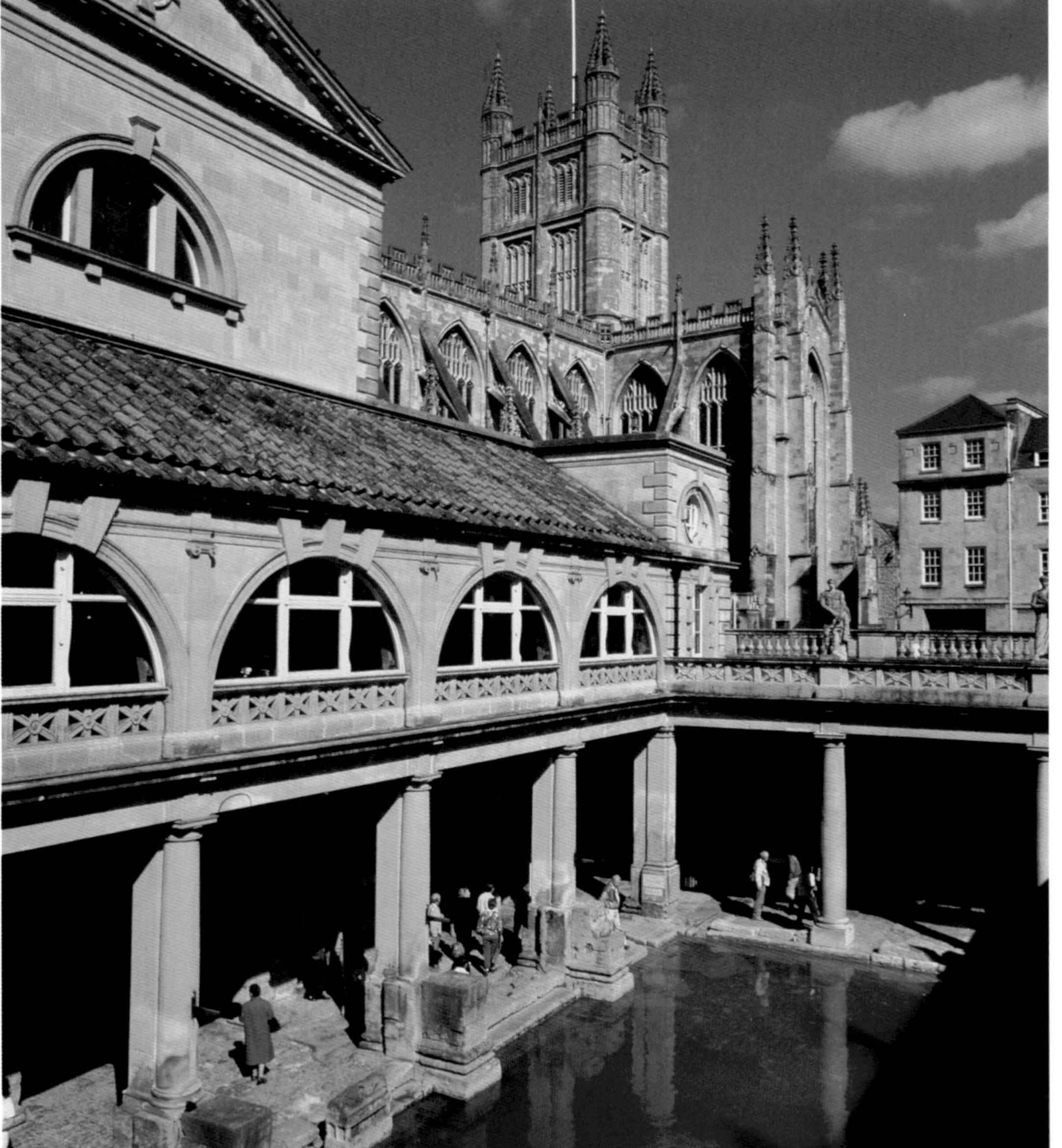

LEFT
Roman Public Baths, Bath, England. Bath is one of the greatest Georgian cities in England. It is the site of historic Roman baths from which derives its name. Bathing was one of the most important leisure activities of the ancient Romans and was practiced as a communal activity.

TOP
One of the prime functions of home is the preparation of food, and each culture has its own very different customs. Traditional Japanese homes like this one do not use furniture in the western sense. Family meals are served on a table and enjoyed sitting on tatami-covered floors.

Cathedrals were adorned with all types of art. While the stonework in many cases was elaborately sculpted and carved, the expression of structure dominated.

The famous French anthropologist Claude Levi-Strauss wrote two books entitled *The Raw and the Cooked* and *The Origin of Table Manners* which dealt with this subject – how and where food was prepared, for what purposes and locations, and the manners associated with time and place. Levi-Strauss and others have described in great detail the symbolic and ritual functions involved in eating and the entire panoply of associations that food has had over the centuries. More recently, Margaret Visser has written about *The Rituals of Dinner*, where table manners, eating rituals and food taboos are covered in detail. Visser explains that every human society has eating rules and from these rules, manners in deportment, behavior and speech have followed. Conforming to these rules creates harmony, orderliness and class distinctions and, in excess, snobbery. Even the technology of eating has evolved from simply eating with fingers to the use of wooden chopsticks and metal instruments. Where eating has risen to a high art, a dozen different implements, including glasses and plates, may be used for the same meal. Cutlery can also be used differently. For example, the spoon replaces the knife in certain Asian countries such as the Philippines or Indonesia, and is used for cutting as well as drinking. In some cultures, the knife is used to cut the food after it is placed between the teeth, rather than on the plate. Every object, function, and process dealing with food is culturally designated.

While all of the above considerations relate to the *functions* of home, we are also concerned here with home itself as *function*. Most early cultures have built extremely functional homes as far as their structure is concerned, such as the igloo, tepee, yurt, or mud-brick house. One can also argue that even the stark simplicity of Classical Greek architecture was still very functional, despite the fact that temples were painted in bright colors with all kinds of added decoration. The same can be said about the great cathedrals of the Medieval and Gothic periods; that the functions of the buildings were totally expressed in their form. Cathedrals were adorned with all types of art. While the stonework in many cases was elaborately sculpted and carved, the expression of structure dominated. Ross King's book *Brunelleschi's Dome* is a masterly account of the immense functional considerations that went into the erection of the great dome of Santa Maria del Fiore in Florence.

RIGHT
Basilica Santa Maria del Fiore, Florence, Italy. As shown, this cathedral has a distinctive 148 ft-wide (45 m-wide) dome resembling a lily flower – the symbol of Florence. It was designed by the famous architect, Arnolfo de Cambio in 1296, but took decades to complete due to the fact that the dome had to be invented as it was being built.

THE RISE OF ARCHITECTURE

By the twentieth century, however, architecture had become well established both as an art form and as a professional activity, and architectural history has classified particular styles in accordance with the periods which they occupied. Hence, students learn about the Assyrian, Babylonian, Greek, Roman, Medieval, Gothic, and Modern periods. If they are lucky, they will also learn about the immense complexity of Asian art and architecture in the Americas, China, India and other places. These periods are further subdivided into a huge diversity of other typologies. But by the end of the nineteenth century in Europe, a new movement in architecture had evolved which was called the Art Nouveau (or New Art), which in turn progressed into another period called Art Deco. All of this transpired over a period of around 40 years from 1890 to 1930. Both styles relied on using decorative features in building design and all associated elements such as furniture and furnishings. The Art Nouveau used extremely fluid organic forms, and architects Charles Plumet, Baron Victor Horta, Charles Rennie Mackintosh, Hector Guimard, and Antonio Gaudi are prime examples of this style of art. In Vienna at the *Fin De Siècle* (end of the nineteenth century), the Viennese Secession created its own adaptation in the work of architects Otto Wagner and Adolf Loos, and in the paintings of Gustav Klimt and Egon Schiele.

The Art Nouveau morphed into the Art Deco, where decorative arts were still of high priority, although by that time, around 1910, the fluid biotic forms of the Art Nouveau were giving way to the more geometric yet still stylized forms of the Art Deco. In contrast to earlier historical periods, both of these art forms were of relatively short duration, even when they are considered together. In many ways it is easier to think of them as facets of the same style, rather than two separate styles. Both in a very real sense heralded the advent of Functionalism that followed shortly after World War I. In many ways, both styles could be considered diversions to the central function of architecture. Functionalism became the architecture of Modernism and existed in its heyday for half a century (from approximately 1925 to 1975), although its principles have many adherents, even today.

LEFT
The main bedroom in Hill House, Helensburgh, Scotland. Designed by Scotland's most famous architect, Charles Rennie Mackintosh, Hill House contrasts a highly functional exterior with a more decorative yet spartan interior.

FUNCTIONALISM

Functionalism in architecture refers to home as well as other buildings in a particular way. In marked contrast to the decorative periods that preceded it, Functionalism believed that pursuing beauty by adding more and more decoration was both futile as well as false. It maintained that beauty in architecture could only be achieved if exactly the opposite position was adopted – the elimination of all decorative features throughout the entire building. The idea expressed by the famous architect Ludwig Mies van der Rohe that "less is more" became the aesthetic agenda for half of the twentieth century. This position has probably never had a more profound manifestation than his Barcelona Pavilion of 1929, a building which had no purpose at all other than expressing a new architectural philosophy. The domestic scale of the Pavilion resembles an up-market, contemporary home of today, even though it was built more than 75 years ago. The Pavilion's internal walls were independent to its structure and could be moved at will. Being a master of Functionalism, Mies van der Rohe still believed that "God is in the details." Clarity of function, beginning with structure, became the prime purpose of modern architecture. For the Functionalist, the idea that "beauty is truth, truth beauty," correlated truth to the surgical exposure of the inner workings of architecture, stripping away every unnecessary element until the "truth" of the building was revealed.

The constellation of ideas which surrounded Functionalism became crystallized in one of the most famous design institutions that the world has ever seen – the Bauhaus. Opened in Weimar, Germany, in 1919, under the direction of master architect Walter Gropius, the Bauhaus employed world-famous artists such as Paul Klee, Wassilly Kandinsky, and Laszlo Moholy-Nagy. Weimar was considered the ground of genius, with Johann Wolfgang von Goethe, Friedrich Christoph von Schiller and Franz Liszt also once calling it home. The Bauhaus moved to Dessau in 1930 under the tutelage of Mies van der Rohe at approximately the same time as the Barcelona Pavilion was being built. The Bauhaus philosophy undoubtedly had the most profound influence over the art of architecture in the twentieth century. While its basic design philosophy centered on function as beauty, the deeper meaning behind Functionalism was the concept that in harnessing mass production to Functionalist design, objects of beauty which until that time had only been afforded by the wealthy, could now be brought within the reach of ordinary citizens. Unfortunately, Functionalism in design was also pursued as functional social science and eugenics, a philosophy which we refer to as Fascism or National Socialism. The Third Reich closed down the Bauhaus in 1933, and the Diaspora of many Bauhaus staff spread Functionalism to many other countries, particularly the United States of America.

ABOVE
Rue Franklin Apartments, Paris, France. This wonderful block of apartments in the Art Deco style illustrates how even high-rises can provide beautiful homes. The detailing of the building is quite exceptional, having been designed by Auguste Perret, a famous French architect who pioneered the use of concrete in some of his other buildings.

TOP LEFT
Barcelona Pavilion, Barcelona, Spain. This house was designed by the world-famous architect, Ludwig Mies van der Rohe and was built for the 1929 World's Fair in Barcelona. Like many architects, he derived inspiration from traditional Japanese architecture. While this is not a "home" as such, it is an archetype of the homes he designed and a perfect model of his architectural philosophy.

ABOVE
Farnsworth House, Plano, Illinois, USA. This transparent glass house is the perfect embodiment of Mies van der Rohe's great passion for minimalism and Functionalism. Though it was claimed unliveable by its owner, Dr Farnsworth, this house has long been regarded as a symbol and true representation of modern architecture in the twentieth century.

TOP
Interior of the Glass House, New Canaan, Connecticut, USA. Designed by the famous American architect, Philip Johnson, this steel-framed glass house is a classic example of the International Style seen in America in the late 1940s. Johnson was clearly inspired by Mies van der Rohe's design of Farnsworth House.

Home played a central role in the expression of Functionalism, and for many of the Bauhaus architects and those who came after them, the domestic scale of home represented the smallest spatial unit where an entire philosophy or its variants could be rendered manifest. Indeed, many of the Modernists are as famous for their residences as they are for much larger projects. In 1929, Pierre Chareau built an apartment in Paris called La Maison de Verre (The Glass House) which remains today an archetype in the development of Functionalism. In exactly the same year, Mies van der Rohe was completing The Tugendhat home in Brno in the Czech Republic. Along with the Farnsworth House in the United States of America (1951), Mies van der Rohe built two icons in the domestic sphere of home, both masterpieces of contemporary architecture. Mies van der Rohe's concept in both houses took his basic philosophy to its ultimate conclusion, whereby every single element in the building was expressed in its uttermost simplicity, creating one continuous and endless flow of space out of minimal architectural elements. Indeed, the Farnsworth House actually constituted a single space subdivided by partitions. The great American architect, Philip Johnson, followed Mies van der Rohe's example by building a similar home in New Canaan, Connecticut, which was also called The Glass House (1949) because it had no external solid walls and for all practical purposes was very transparent.

Examples of Functionalism are therefore ubiquitous, and have adopted many differing forms of expression throughout the world. Other classics are Le Corbusier's Villa Savoye (1928–29) at Poissy in France (as well as his "domino" housing), and the Rietveld-Schroder House (1924–25) in Utrecht by Gerrit Rietveld. The latter example was part of The Netherlands' own unique contribution to Modernism. This came in the form of a movement called De Stijl (the Style) – one which was also seriously influenced by the artists Piet Mondrian and Theo van Doesburg. More recent examples are Richard Meier's Douglas House (1973) in Harbor Springs, Michigan, and Rem Koolhaas' house, the Villa Dall'Ava (1991) in Saint Cloud, France. Tragically, Functionalism, like many movements in art, made inflated claims for its own accomplishments. Many so-called Functionalist buildings were so dysfunctional in human terms that their owners refused to occupy them, as in Mies van der Rohe's Farnsworth House. People simply did not want to live in environments that were functional to the point of sterility. One might even argue that the Functionalists did not build homes, they built houses – and to what extent can one belong to a glass box? In addition, many such houses were unsustainable in today's terms, where huge expanses of glass turned them into refrigerators in the winter and ovens in the summer. In a book entitled *With Man in Mind*, Constance Perrin neatly sums up the core problem of Functionalism by quoting Mies van der

The idea that home is not a physical space but a space of meaning, association, history, and inheritance, became a central concern in Post-modernism.

Rohe: "If anyone will tell us architects what people need, we'll tell them how to build it." Perrin's reprise was that since no one apparently ever told him what they needed, he continued to build for himself. Functionalism's greatest error therefore was in assuming that the truth of home lay in the perfect use of materials in delineating space, rather than in the perfect satisfaction of needs – the emotional and psychological requirements of individuals; a problem that began to be addressed in the advent of Post-modernism around 1975.

TOP LEFT
Rietveld-Schroder House, Utrecht, The Netherlands. Commissioned by Mrs Schroder-Schrader, the house was designed by Gerrit Rietveld. It is a monument to The Netherlands' own movement in modern architecture called De Stijl. Rietveld's style differed substantially from others, yet he followed the same laws of Functionalism.

TOP RIGHT
A home in Seaside, Florida, USA. The town of Seaside in Florida is one of the formative projects in a new architectural style called New Urbanism. It is characterized by a desire to recreate the qualities of small town USA. It resorts to many images borrowed from the past, such as clapboard exteriors, front gardens, picket fences, town squares etc., and overall exhibits a nostalgia for the past.

THE HOME OF THE FUTURE

Post-modern architecture evolved out of the defects of Modernism. In concentrating on minimalism and the elimination of any extraneous detail, the Modernists also deprived culture of a vast range of meanings that had previously been expressed in architectural features. In a very real sense, the Modernists got as far away from the individual's needs for meaning in their environment as was possible. Over the last 40 years, Post-modernism has set about correcting this error by deliberately creating buildings that are rich in historical and cultural referents. The idea that home is not a physical space but a space of meaning, association, history, and inheritance, became of central concern. Post-modernism is also eclectic, in that it does not apply the same formula to every problem, as is the case in Functionalism. The result is a variety in design, rich in symbolic meaning, and expressive of human sentiment and emotion. Many of the most famous Post-modern architects have built "homes," including Frank Gehry, Coop Himmelblau, Bernard Tschumi, and Robert Venturi. The latter architect built a home called the Vanna Venturi House (1962) that is a prime example of the genre and contains a huge array of references to classical architecture in its construction.

While Post-modern architecture is not formulaic, a movement has evolved within it called New Urbanism, or alternatively, Traditional New Design (TND), Neo Traditionalism or Neo Eclecticism. This style heavily relies on certain common traditional features, such as doors, windows, picket fences, verandas, and wood shingles. New Urbanism is burdened by nostalgia for the lifestyles of the 1950s, along with images of Cape Cod villages and Prairie homes. Of prime concern is reinstating the traditional values and images of the past, characterized by small town USA, with walkable environments, front gardens, picket fences, town squares, village centers and the rest. The town of Seaside, Florida is a classic example, but literally hundreds of local authorities have now adopted New Urbanism as the chosen development model. It has also mutated into adaptations for sub-cultures, with cities like Santa Ana in California advertising Latino New Urbanism where houses have balconies and are painted bright yellows, blues and pinks, adapted to the Latino personality and culture. Like it or not, New Urbanism has precipitated a landslide of conservative values in urban design and it remains to be seen where its future lies.

Part 2

Home Today

Chapter 9

In the City

Living in compact spaces in close proximity to others requires a home that enhances social interaction – while also providing places for solitude and privacy.

Whether it is a dwelling in the depths of a metropolis, or a house on a sunny suburban block, city homes are characteristically governed by the constraints of urban density.

The city is a great place to live – vibrant with its diverse cultures, its history reflected in the architecture, and its network of road and rail a constant hum. But larger populations can create over-crowding, and more buildings and infrastructure result in less available space and limited access to the natural environment.

It is this dense urban context that informs our modern home design in the city.

PERSONAL RETREAT

The antidote to the complexity of the outside world is the simplicity of the interior environment. Clean lines in an ordered environment with simple, accessible forms are pleasing to the eye and relieve the mind.

Increasing population requires interaction with many people on a daily basis. As a result, people are becoming more inward focused to maintain a sense of personal space and their homes are a reflection of this. A high fence encloses the property, a drive-in garage eliminates chance interaction with neighbors and the front veranda, a place to sit and watch the world go by, has all but vanished.

Homes are now designed to meet the needs of the occupants: spaces to live, work, and play. There really is little need to leave.

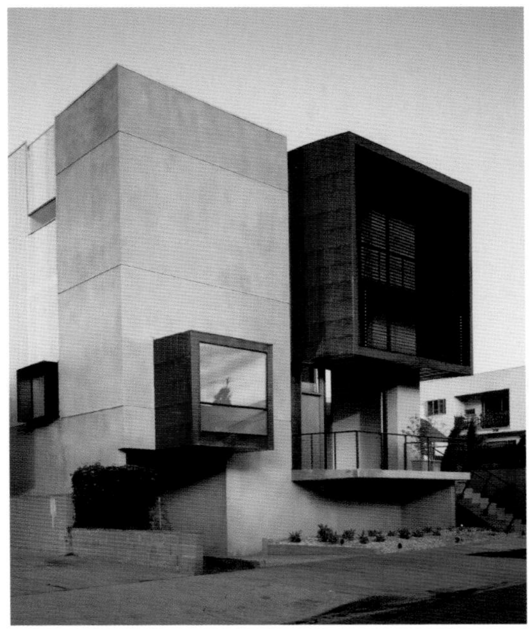

COMPACT FOOTPRINT

Buildings have sprung up on much of the available land in the city, and construction space is at a premium. To avoid urban sprawl, homes are now constrained to a compact footprint. Designing a multi-level dwelling is a simple solution to getting the most out of a reduced spatial allotment.

A multi-functional room is also an efficient use of space. The kitchen and dining room is combined with the living room in an "open plan" concept, thus reducing the size of each area, but giving a feeling of increased overall space. Architecturally, there are several tricks to give the illusion of space. For example, the exterior environment becomes an extension of the interior space when full height windows are used.

CONTRIVED NATURE

As increased infrastructure erodes the natural environment, immediate access to nature has become limited. In response, design for the city dwelling has created purposeful touchstones to nature.

The built form of a dwelling can capitalize on the external environment. A strategically placed window frames the view to a garden, tree, or water feature, like a precious piece of artwork. A balcony steps out onto a lofty view overlooking the city below. A small courtyard becomes a private oasis.

ABOVE
Orange Grove,
Pugh + Scarpa Architects

TOP RIGHT
Legal / Illegal House,
Manuel Herz Architecture & Urbanism

OPPOSITE
1532 House,
Fougeron Architecture

THE CITY HOME

Living in the city has some very challenging design constraints. Space is limited in a densely built urban setting, which increases proximity to neighbors and often offers limited access to nature. As a result, a home within the city is characterized by a compact footprint, homes that optimize a sense of privacy and have revitalizing references to nature.

11th Street House CALIFORNIA, USA

Koning Eizenberg Architecture

Constructed	2001
Home type	Two-story family home
Structure	Standard wood-framing

ABOVE
The house has a quiet but evocative presence from the street with layers of tall grasses concealing a small outdoor patio that is reached by an oversized sliding door. The front door is located on the side.

OPPOSITE
A view from the outdoor room looking back toward the house where glazing sets up a strong indoor–outdoor connection. The stucco wall is detailed to appear to float above and provides a backdrop to the overscaled pop-out window to the main bedroom.

"The 11th Street house is very straightforward. A few simple overscaled moves are used to transcend expectations of the potential of cost-conscious conventional construction. The house is light-filled and organized around a big outdoor room."

Julie Eizenberg

ECONOMICAL CONTEMPORARY DESIGN

In 1998 the Shines bought a very small teardown single-family house in Santa Monica, California. After about a year they were ready to improve their living situation. Having happily lived in a speculative condominium designed by Koning Eizenberg Architects for another client, the Shines trusted them to build an economical contemporary design.

Money was always a key issue for the owners, who were nervous about over-extending their resources. The architects first looked at a remodel/addition, but as the economy continued to improve, the Shines felt more comfortable building a new home. By then the design was established.

The architects have always seen practical parameters as opportunities to reassess conventional outcomes, rather than as limitations. So, although they briefly flirted with a redesign, the original approach did not seem to them to be at all compromised. In fact, the limitations of accepting conventional layouts (the existing conditions) and construction approaches (cost), had pushed them to look at how to infuse ordinary construction with a contemporary sensibility.

OPEN PLAN, OPEN LIVING

The design was developed not so much as a custom house but more as a speculative contemporary house for design-savvy, middle-class families – something you could buy from a catalog with a few variations. The house has three bedrooms upstairs and a study/guestroom as well as a home-office downstairs supplementing the usual living, dining, and family rooms.

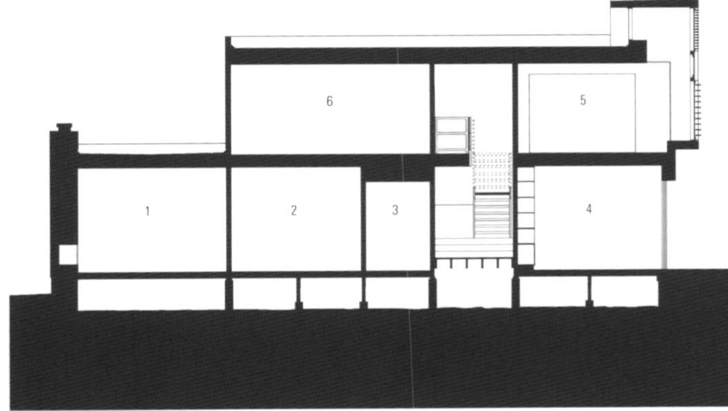

1 living
2 bedroom 1
3 laundry
4 bedroom 2
5 bedroom 3
6 main bedroom

EAST–WEST SECTION

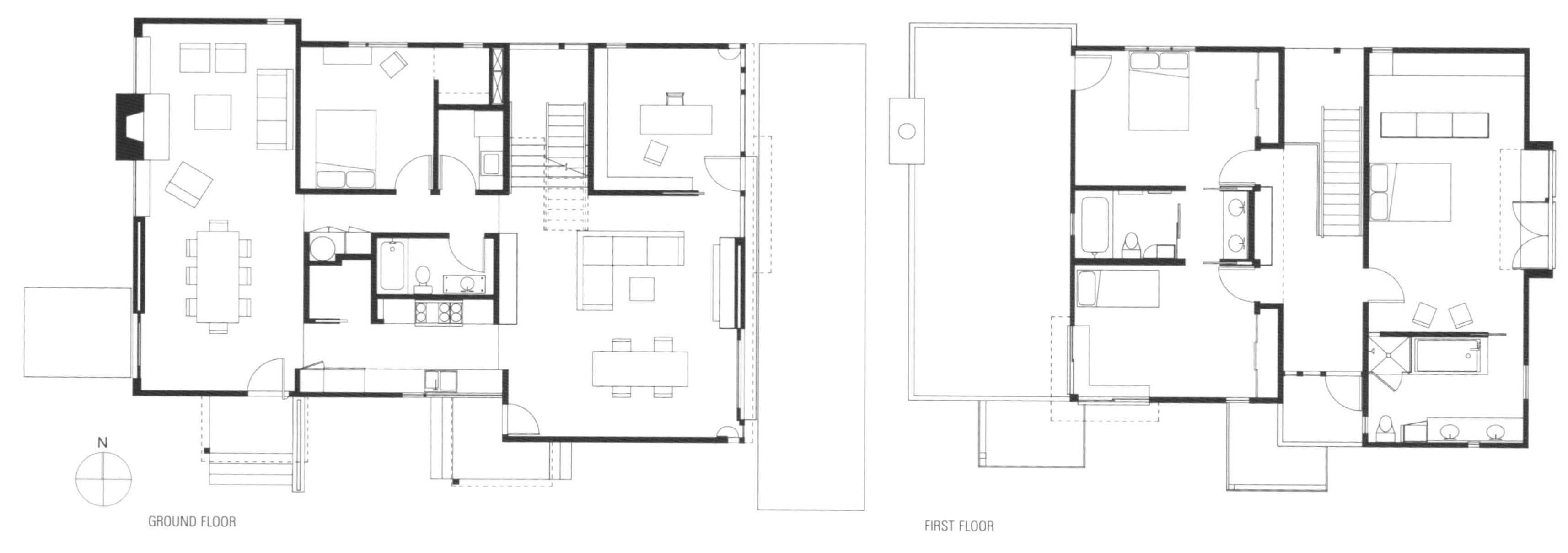
N
GROUND FLOOR
FIRST FLOOR

The downstairs spaces spiral around the kitchen with a simple open plan that establishes strong connections to the outside. The building(s) are used to enhance the creation of a strong social outside space – an outdoor living room. Even the detached garage – the standard throwaway – is upgraded just a little (and painted a sky blue) as it forms the fourth wall to the outside space flanked by the house to the west and hedges to the north and south.

GIVING THE HOUSE AN IDENTITY

Koning Eizenberg Architecture also consciously included the oversized picture-frame doors that have become somewhat of a signature for their residential projects as a way of providing a "feature" trademark for the design. Houses, they believe, need identity and status-merchandising strategies, just like other design products such as cars or clothes. Otherwise, they tried to keep demanding detailing to a minimum, focusing on the large, dramatic pop-out window to the main bedroom and the glazing in the living areas that make the house feel so open.

The house, including the garage, at approximately 3,500 sq ft (325 sq m) was completed for about US$570,000 in 2001. On the west side of Los Angeles, this was "as cheap as you could get" using the conventional architect/general contractor approach. There was no "sweat-equity" or "nifty delivery" method involved here, just a tweaking of the system with a good contractor and a trusting client.

FAR LEFT
The living/dining areas face the street. Neither client nor architect liked shades, so tall grasses were used to screen the interior. The planting is supplemented by translucent rolldown shades to control the effects of the sun. It is a serene space that includes an oversized wood-framed sliding door, maple flooring, and a painted medium-density fiberboard (MDF) ceiling and feature wall.

TOP LEFT
The kitchen is a concentration of color and texture within the quiet colors and finishes that characterize the rest of the house. Kitchens are always energetic places and the green glass tile and orange painted cabinets heighten this characteristic. Glimpses of the kitchen contribute fragments of color to the adjacent living spaces.

ABOVE
The main bedroom has a small area of space with a high ceiling that draws light from glazing on two sides. The unexpected and exaggerated change of scale and texture (Douglas fir plywood) provides a dramatic effect for minimum expenditure. The bedroom windows have exterior wood slats to provide added pattern, as well as shade from the morning sun.

1532 House SAN FRANCISCO, USA

Fougeron Architecture

Constructed	2005
Home type	Three-level family home
Structure	Glass, steel, stucco, and wood

"This design expresses my commitment to true contextualism: relating the house to the natural forces of the steep site; integrating its spaces with land, light, and view; placing it firmly within its San Francisco slope rather than perched on stilts. The result is a contemporary restatement of the city's bold spirit in the artistic vocabulary of its owners."

Anne Fougeron

ABOVE
The demure facade playfully and respectfully reinterprets a familiar San Francisco building form with traditional materials, translating the bay window of the front-facing artist's studio into a monocle design. The house is integrated fully into the extra-deep lot, using the steep site's various levels of grade to interlock its complex spaces.

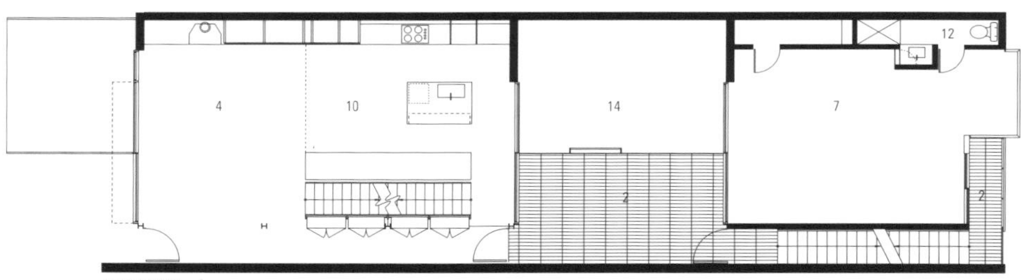

LEVEL THREE

LEVEL TWO

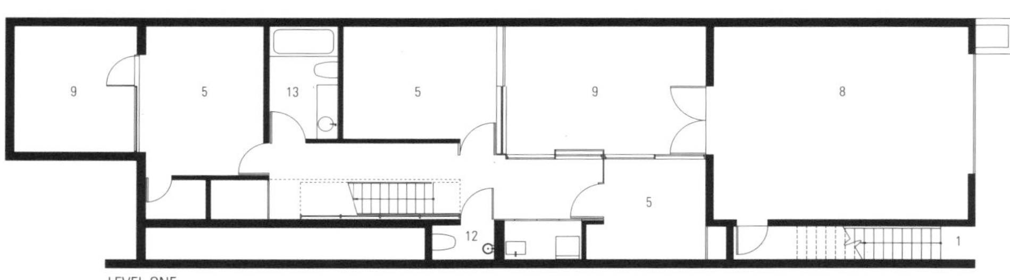

LEVEL ONE

1 entry
2 deck
3 bridge
4 living
5 bedroom
6 main bedroom
7 artist's studio
8 garage
9 courtyard
10 kitchen/dining
11 study
12 WC
13 bathroom
14 open to below

ABOVE AND LEFT
The living area's placement at the rear of the house, level with the backyard, creates the fluid beauty and privacy of indoor/outdoor California living. Flooding the center of the house with light. The middle courtyard (left) transforms every inner space, giving all rooms a gleaming double aspect.

COURTYARDS AND LIGHT

This new house, in-filled on an existing 25-ft (7.5-m) wide lot in San Francisco, includes two distinct volumes that are separated by an interior courtyard. The structure at the front has a garage at street level with a painting studio above it. The back volume is the main house, with the bedrooms on the lower level, the living spaces in the middle, and an intimate main bedroom suite situated on the top floor, facing southwest onto the backyard garden.

The design of this project uses two sectional moves: horizontal and vertical. The horizontal move creates two courtyards – one in the middle and one at the back of the house – while the vertical move digs the lower bedrooms down to the garage and street level. The combination of these two moves serves to interlock the house to the site as well as the surrounding urban fabric, thus interweaving the inside and outside spaces with a play of light and dark. The inspiration for this weave of complex spatial relationships came directly from the artist/owner's paintings, which are abstractions based on fabrics and their many contextual relationships.

CONTROLLING NATURAL LIGHT

Throughout this sectional interplay, the floor-to-ceiling windows, glass floors, and skylights manipulate the natural light and allow it to penetrate deep into all rooms. The house is transparent from the street to the backyard, offering a rare glimpse into an intimate world that is usually closed behind the doors and facades of San Francisco homes.

The main floor of the house – an open floor plan with kitchen, dining, and living spaces – is punctuated by a two-story space for the staircase, and is on ground level with the rear yard. A setback of the building on the third floor opens the house to spectacular views of the bay and the Golden Gate Bridge.

OUTDOOR SPACES GALORE

The house has seven outdoor spaces, all with distinctive qualities and views: the front deck off the studio, the deck on top of the studio, the lower level courtyard, the entry level deck off the court-yard, the back courtyard, the glass and wood walkway, and the backyard. These seven decks and spaces unfurl right around the living areas of the house, thereby unlocking the visual complexity of the structure and its site. Sensitive landscaping by Ron Lutsko integrates the plan.

This house boldly introduces a new building typology to San Francisco. It is a house of courtyards and light that brings new life to the world of the city's residential architecture, and allows for new modes of indoor/outdoor living.

ABOVE
At the top of the house, in a garden-view glass bay, sits the quaint main bedroom suite. Scaled for intimacy, with a lowered ceiling, this floating retreat feels a world away from the city street at the opposite end of the site.

RIGHT
In a reference to the owner's engagement with fabric in her artworks, the glass railings on the custom steel staircase incorporate a pattern of woven strands. The design concept echoes throughout the house: two light courts interwoven with two distinct volumes in an innovative, complex rhythm.

The viewer's eye in this artist's home is kept in constant motion, exposing from a multitude of angles what and who is on display. This visual enticement, and the size and scale of the interior spaces, lend beautifully to the flow of life within and throughout the house.

LEFT
From all vantage points of the open-plan main floor, the sectional interplay of the house offers visual surprises. The glass and wood walkway (above right) yields yet another charm when accessed at rooftop level: breathtaking views of the San Francisco skyline and the Golden Gate Bridge.

Alamo Street Loft TEXAS, USA

Lake | Flato Architects

Constructed 2001
Home type Urban loft/studio
Structure Exposed steel framing inserted into existing brick shell building

"We took the burned-out shell of a building and transformed it into an 'industrial hacienda.' The open plan is filled with natural light from the saw-toothed roof, and with views of interior courtyards. The result is a home that screens out the urban environment and expresses the building's industrial past through the creative use of steel and concrete."

Lake | Flato Architects

OUT OF THE ASHES

A 1920s industrial building in inner city San Antonio, which was damaged in a devastating fire, was the palette upon which the architects worked to transform the remaining building into a comfortable living and studio space. The owner and architect had already begun working on creating a loft space to accommodate work and living when the fire gutted the inside of the building. Essentially, only the shell remained.

The "shell" set the scene for an open plan, airy new dwelling. The original wooden roof structure was replaced with a saw-toothed, steel-framed roof that secured the free-standing brick walls. This roof style, with its alternating clear glass and dark plywood, reflects the old factories in the San Antonio area and is a feature of the building. It also allows plenty of light into the interior and, even on the most overcast days, no other lighting is necessary. Ironically, if it hadn't been for the fire, the ceiling would have been much lower than its current 20 ft (6 m).

The fire also warped some steel walls in one of the factory's old rooms. The architect took advantage of this to create the dining area, giving it an artistic edginess. The walls, floor, and ceiling are covered with sheets of steel. The overall result is one of elegant minimalism.

TWO BUILDINGS, ONE UNIT

There are two buildings on the site that were once adjoining warehouses – one is now used for living and one for work. The main building offers wide volumes of space and contains the generous central living area, dining room, kitchen, and bedrooms. Barn-style doors separate the bedroom from the living area. The whole home has an open airy feel, not surprising, given the ceiling height. The other building contains studio space, living space, guest rooms, service areas, and a garage. The layout is reminiscent of a Spanish hacienda.

There is a narrow alley that runs between the two buildings and leads into a large central courtyard with a pool, which provides a tranquil interlude in an industrialized setting. The alley itself was transformed into the entry area.

MATERIALS MEANT TO LAST

The materials were chosen for their sturdy qualities – steel was used for the framing and railings, the brick walls were retained, and steel and translucent glass cladding was used for the facades. Concrete fiberboard (a mixture of cement, concrete, and recycled paper) was set into the exterior walls of the original brick structure. This not only preserves the historic character of the exterior of the building, it also offers privacy for the owner.

The cement floors were rubbed with old crank-case oil and finished with wax, an environmentally friendly alternative to chemical-based concrete stains.

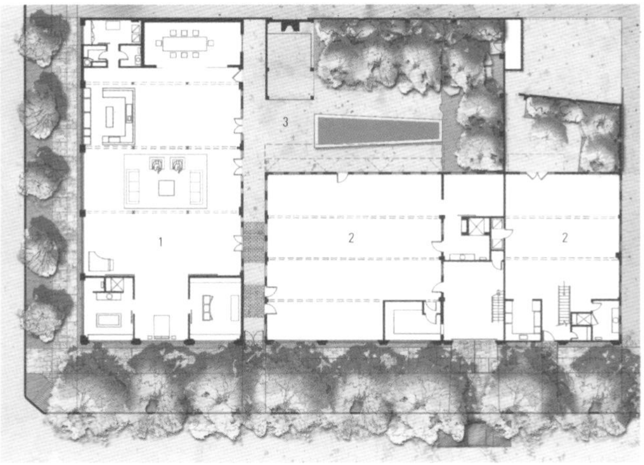

1 living loft
2 studio
3 pool and courtyard

ABOVE LEFT
A lap pool is the focal point of the courtyard. This water element helps to soften the hard edges of the industrial materials – concrete, steel, and brick.

TOP LEFT
Stained concrete fiberboard panels and high windows infill between brick piers, providing separation and privacy from the street.

TOP
A structural steel frame was inserted into the existing masonry structure. Clerestory windows allow light to fill the living space, even on cloudy days.

ABOVE
Stained concrete floors and smooth plywood paneling on the walls and ceiling provide warmth to the industrial aesthetic.

Bellevue Hill House SYDNEY, AUSTRALIA

buzacottwebber

Constructed 2005
Home type Single-story family home
Structure Steel frame, concrete floor slab, timber framing, plasterboard, and corrugated steel roofing

"This house is all about allowing for a relaxed family lifestyle in Sydney's great climate, while taking advantage of its position high on a hillside with great city views. This is a house I would be happy to live in myself."
Stephen Buzacott

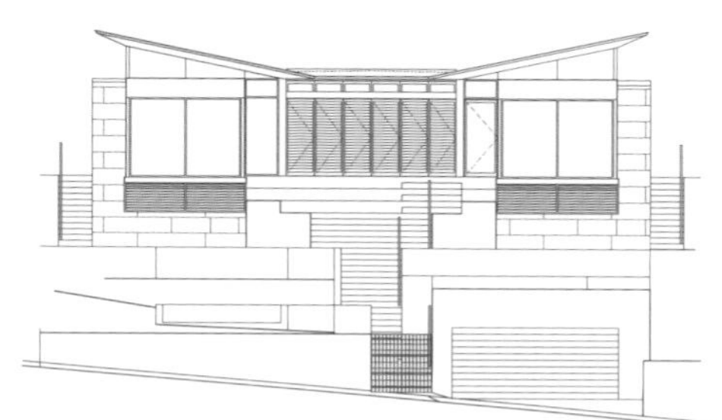

ABOVE RIGHT
Perched high above street level, entry to the house is via terraced gardens, paved patios, and grassed areas. Placed between the two wings, the western courtyard affords spectacular views of the city skyline and the Sydney Harbour Bridge. The western elevation is screened both for privacy and solar control with adjustable and retractable aluminum venetian blinds.

OPPOSITE
The burnished concrete paving of the rear eastern courtyard extends into the light and sunny kitchen/family room, giving flow and continuity between outdoor and indoor areas. The kitchen, with its uncluttered profle, is designed to integrate with the overall space. A walk-through pantry and laundry area is accessed via a joinery door beside the refrigerator.

DESIGNS ON OUTDOOR LIFESTYLE

This relatively large 3,000-sq-ft (280-sq-m) site is located in the rugged coastal landscape typical of much of eastern Sydney and its inland waterways. The site is steeply graded, exposed, elevated, and east–west in aspect on the western slope of Bellevue Hill. Reflecting Sydney's benign climate, this house is designed for an outdoor lifestyle, and is focused on the full enjoyment of the surrounding landscape and views.

The simple plan grew out of the brief for a single-level house and a request to retain the original 1920s cottage, by locating a new wing along the southern side of the site to form two outdoor spaces. The cost of retaining the cottage, however, far outweighed the benefit to the overall project. The H-shaped plan evolved from the original design – flipping the proposed bed-room wing to the overshadowed northern edge of the site and arranging the living spaces along the sunnier southern edge became the intelligent solution.

A VIEW TO PRIVACY

The H-shaped plan forms two courtyard spaces, which directly relate to the surrounding internal spaces. The larger eastern courtyard is shielded from cold winter and hot summer westerly winds, allowing a protected and private outdoor living space with a small lap pool extending into the garden. The smaller western courtyard opens to the western city skyline view and flows out to a small stepped terrace that connects to the terraced front garden. The dining room forms the link between the two side pavilions and opens up on both sides, allowing the courtyard spaces and view to flow through the entire house.

The entry is via long stairs which rise past the secluded side patios and the terraced gardens. This leads to a small stepped terrace; here, visitors can rest and take in the western view over the city skyline and Sydney Harbour Bridge. Entry to the house is through the western atrium, which then leads through to the rear

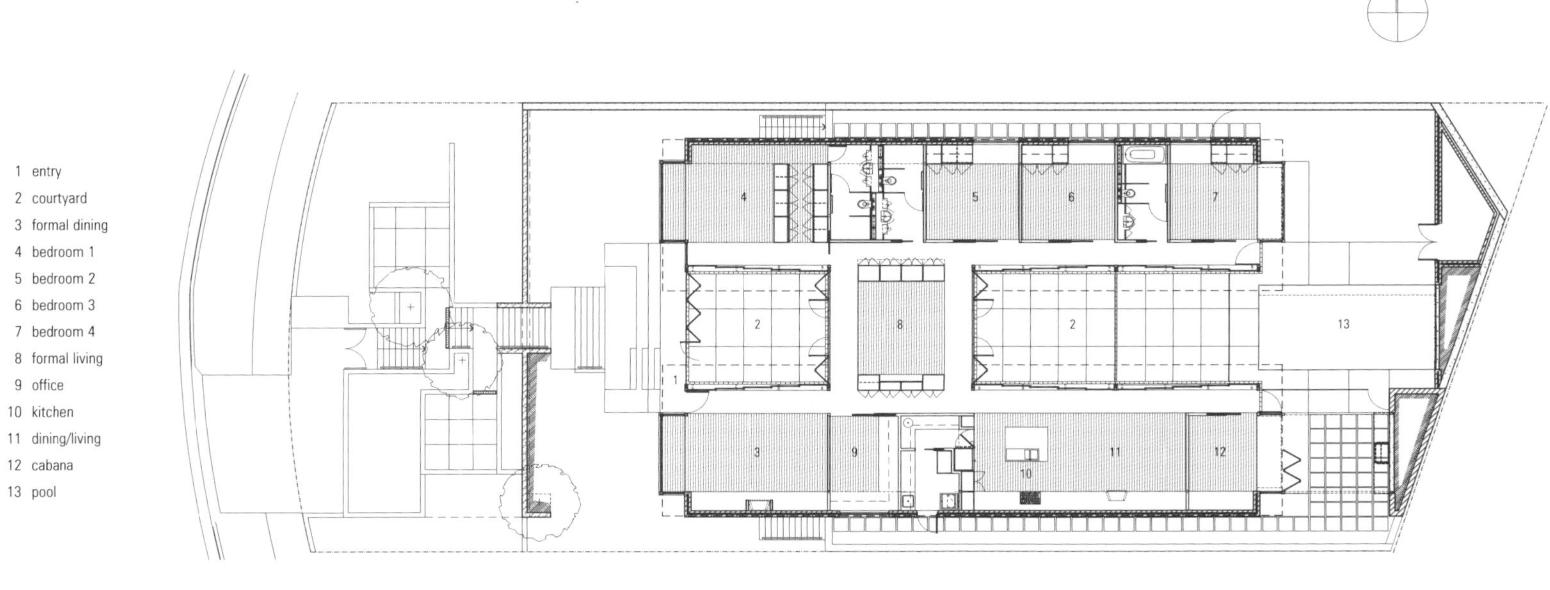
N
1 entry
2 courtyard
3 formal dining
4 bedroom 1
5 bedroom 2
6 bedroom 3
7 bedroom 4
8 formal living
9 office
10 kitchen
11 dining/living
12 cabana
13 pool

ABOVE
The 10 ft (3 m) doors can be fully retracted, allowing the interior and exterior spaces to combine, effectively doubling the size of the living areas.

of the house along the edges of the atria. The extension of the exterior floor finish into the interior blurs the delineation between inside and outside.

LIGHT AND SPACE

The open design complements a close family lifestyle. The family entertains constantly and this house allows for a range of both formal and informal gatherings. Sliding and folding glass walls around the courtyards open up the interiors to the outside, making what is a modestly sized house feel larger and more spacious. In contrast, the side walls facing the boundary are masonry, acting as a container for the house and giving privacy to the interior. Highlight windows are located along both the northern and southern sides of the home, maximizing flow-through ventilation and light, and giving a view of the sky from the interior. The resulting mono-pitched roof form gives the interior a heightened sense of airiness and space while focusing the eye on the atria.

MAXIMIZING LOW KEY MATERIALS

Materials are low key – off-white concrete, steel, timber floors, white-painted plasterboard walls and ceilings, blackbutt-veneered joinery with insets and highlights of Calacatta marble. The windows are 10 ft (3 m) high, clear anodized aluminum and solar glass with rendered masonry walls to the boundary walls and terraced gardens. The roof is finished in corrugated steel.

This house is designed for an outdoor lifestyle, and is focused on the full enjoyment of the surrounding landscape and views.

ABOVE
The dining room is a calming, timber-paneled space that is regularly used for family meals, quiet contemplation, and newspaper-reading. It also connects the two courtyards, linking the main areas and consolidating the spatial flow throughout the entire house.

RIGHT
All bedrooms have built-in wardrobes and desks. This light-filled child's room has a bay window facing the rear garden and swimming pool. The large cavity sliding doors give a direct connection to the central courtyard beyond.

Casa D'Água SÃO PAULO, BRAZIL

Isay Weinfeld

Construction 2002–2003
Home type Four-level family dwelling
Structure Poured concrete

"Our clients are people with a great regard for nature and a deep appreciation of outdoor living. With this in mind, we designed a house where they could feel closer to nature, and forget they live in São Paulo, an 18 million-strong metropolis. It seems that after moving into this house they don't go to their getaway spot in the countryside as often as they once did."
Isay Weinfeld

TOP RIGHT
The office on level four is surrounded by glass, so the owner can enjoy the view while working. The treetops in the foreground give way to the city skyline in the distance.

RIGHT
The entry hallway is actually a narrow pool – in the first half, it is a stone path leading to the central patio; in the second half, it is a lap pool extending to the back of the block.

WATER FEATURE

A narrow pool runs alongside the house, from the entry to the back of the block. In the first section of the pool, large granite stones, which are anchored to the bottom slab, seem to skip across the water surface, forming a pathway to the central patio. A little further on, this pool becomes a lap pool that stretches to the back wall of the block.

LONG AND NARROW

The block's long and narrow shape inspired the architects to create a central patio that divides the building into two blocks. This allows for good insulation in all the rooms – they all face either north, east, or west. Outdoors, thick natural-twine ropes make a natural curtain that shades the patio and filters the sunlight, creating dappled patterns of light and shade.

The house is spread over four levels, and all the spaces are arranged according to their primary functions. For example, the garage and utility rooms are on level one, while the dining and living rooms, kitchen, and laundry areas are located on level two. Level three contains a family room and the bedrooms; and finally, level four comprises a small office and a terrace.

As they have three adult children, the owners wanted their bedroom to be private and set apart from the others. So on level three the three bedrooms with ensuites and a private living room are located in one wing, while the main bedroom is located in the other.

MERGING NEW AND OLD

It was the clients' wish that the house would not look, or feel, "new." So the architects proposed that it be built with some elements from the clients' farm. For instance, rough stones cover the boundary walls, and recycled timber was used for flooring in the bedrooms. The rust stains on the wood were retained, providing a link with times long past. These older elements are a reference to the family's lifestyle and history as well as their special relationship with nature.

GARDEN OF DELIGHTS

The landscaping around the house includes orchids, ferns, and bromeliads, many of which grow in the small crevices of the external wall. The back garden contains various types of underbrush, as well as flowering plants such as daisies and lilies, and a jabuticaba tree, a member of the myrtle family, with white flowers and blue-black berries. On the terrace on level four, there are several potted fruit trees, including pomegranate, tangerine, pitanga, and lemon trees.

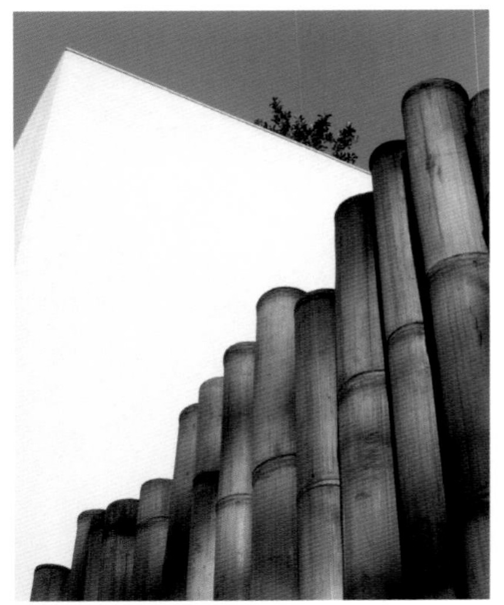

1 entry
2 ramp
3 dining
4 living
5 lap pool
6 kitchen
7 bedroom
8 main bedroom
9 family
10 office
11 roof terrace

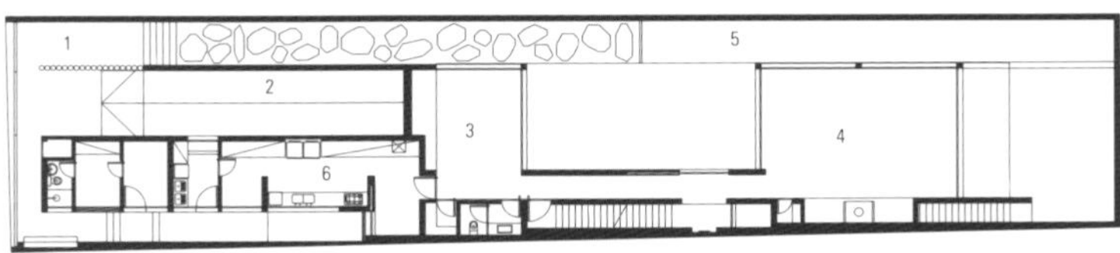

LEVEL TWO

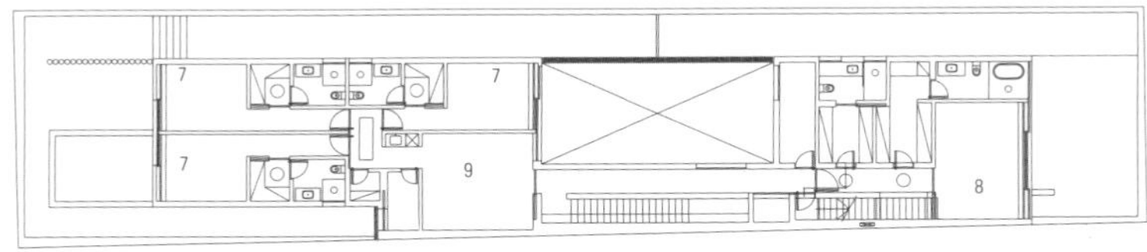

LEVEL THREE

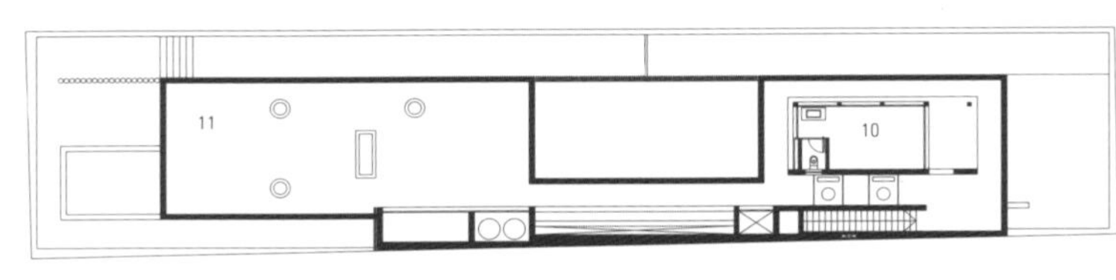

LEVEL FOUR

TOP LEFT
This detail of the front facade shows the partition of bamboo canes separating the pedestrian entrance from the garage ramp.

LEFT
The stairway leading to level one is made of stone. A recess built into the ceiling allows daylight to illuminate the space. A bas relief sculpture set into the wall lends a historic note.

The older elements of the home are a reference to the family's lifestyle and history as well as their special relationship with nature.

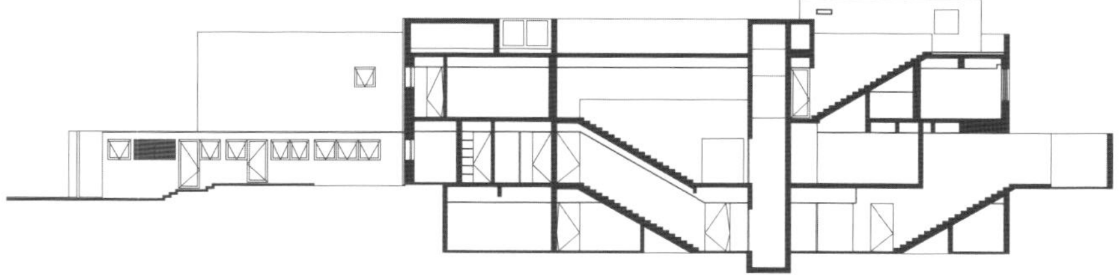

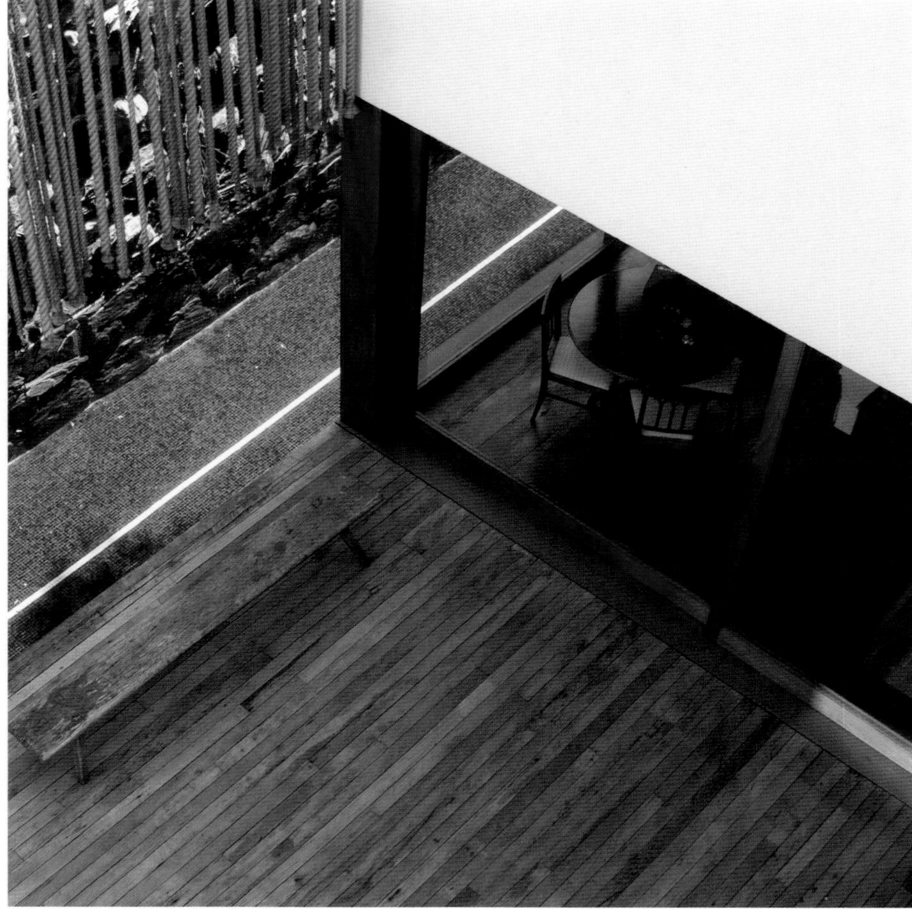

ABOVE
The open wooden deck is integrated into the dining and living rooms via large sliding glass doors. A curtain of natural twine hangs down from a beam on level four, screening the patio from the sun.

LEFT
The entry path leads from the street to the central patio of wooden decking. Rough stones from the owners' country estate cover the side wall, where native orchids grow in small crevices.

Casa Perellos ZEJTUN, MALTA

Architecture Project

Construction	2001–2005
Home type	Two-story, single-family terraced palazzo
Structure	Traditional masonry, steel frame

"Here was a special and uniquely noble property, despite its size, which had regrettably lost much of its luster and, through generations of neglect, fallen into disrepair. Seeing the palazzo reborn was a joy. Restoring it to its former elegance and infusing it with its righteous status in the village was extremely satisfying."
Architecture Project

A LONG AND NOBLE HISTORY

During the late seventeenth and early eighteenth centuries, the eastern half of the island of Malta flourished. Having fortified the southern harbors against invasions by Mediterranean corsairs, the Knights of Malta ushered in a period of peace and prosperity.

Sitting on a strategic vantage point overlooking the harbors, the town of Zejtun was much sought after by the nobles and Knights of the island. Many built palaces and also contributed financially to the establishment of new churches, including the church of Saint Catherine of Alexandria, the town's patron.

Built during this period, Casa Perellos was the country residence of the Grand Master at the time, a Spaniard, Ramon Perellos y Rocafull (1697–1720). Perellos was a great lover of the arts and a benevolent administrator.

RESTORATION TO GLORY

Casa Perellos is located within the historic core of the village. It is an intimate retreat – not large, yet stately and noble. Together with much of the town, the property suffered damage during World War II, when it was converted to different uses. During the early phases of the refurbishment works, an air-raid shelter, cut from the rock, was uncovered adjacent to the cellar. Political turbulence during the latter half of the twentieth century resulted in the residence suffering severe neglect and abandonment.

LEFT
As with many Mediterranean buildings, the pool helps to cool the air within the shady walled garden of Casa Perellos. During the day, citrus trees provide shelter from the midday sun; on warm summer evenings, their fragrance wafts across the courtyard and throughout the palazzo.

ABOVE
This glass and steel extension houses the kitchen on the ground floor, a guest room above, and a main bedroom suite on top.

ABOVE LEFT
The original courtyard structures, including the arched screen and the well head, have been painstakingly restored to their former splendor.

The recent meticulous refurbishment of the property restores to the house its serene dignity and nobility, as well as its princely standing in the architectural and social fabric of the town. The works involved the complete restoration of the fabric and the redecoration of the interiors. With minimum intervention, the original spaces and volumes were recreated. In the interiors, contemporary interventions are grafted onto the simple volumes of the eighteenth-century spaces, the original details being retained and restored wherever possible.

DELICATE, DECORATIVE, DURABLE

To the rear of the building, two lateral wings of glass and steel emphasize the delicacy of the original decoration. These extend from the main volume, reaching out to the garden, parallel to the house's main axis. These extensions house the kitchen (set in the heart of the garden), a guest bedroom, bathrooms for the two bedroom wings on the first floor, and additional service spaces. Faced in folding hardwood louvered shutters, the filtered daylight casts a gentle glow on the surfaces within, while the rooms become extensions of the garden beyond.

Between the wings, the courtyard and its attached garden becomes the central living room of the "palazzo," a tranquil and sheltered space for relaxation, overlooked by the balcony to the centrally placed family room at first-floor level.

Leading away from the courtyard, the original garden path had led to a small fountain and water bowl, set within a niche surmounted by the Grand Master's coat of arms. The remaining stretch of this path has been replaced by a linear pool of water set among a small number of preserved leafy citrus trees, which shade it from the harsh summer light and excessive heat.

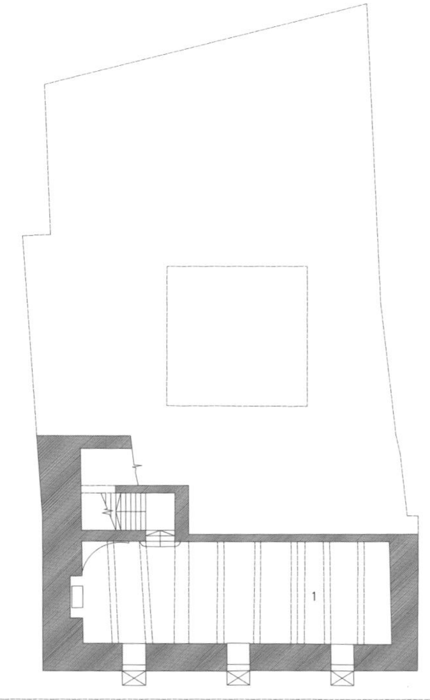

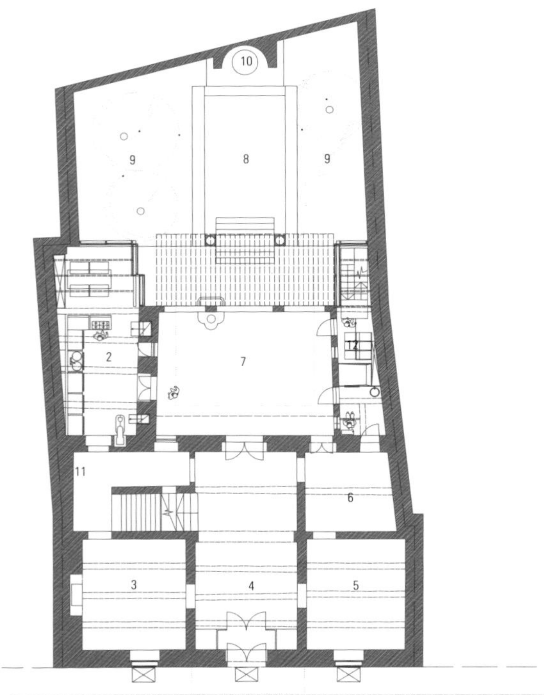

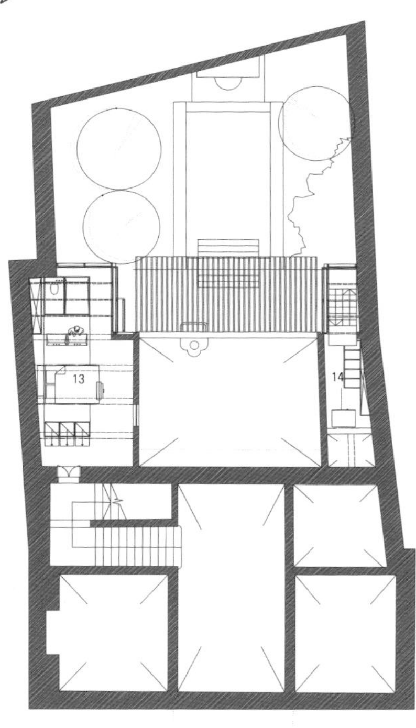

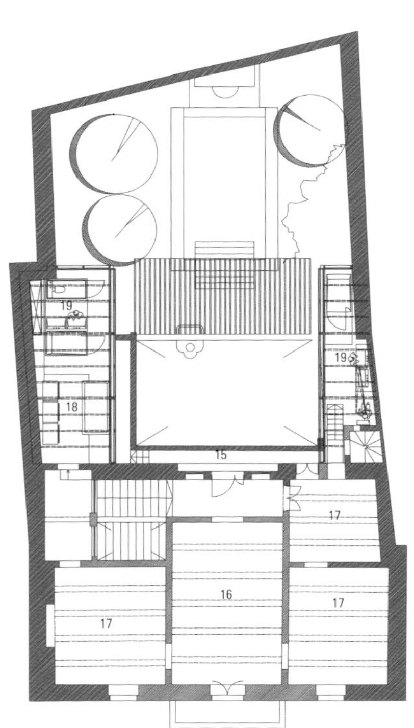

1 family
2 kitchen
3 dining
4 hall
5 study
6 playroom
7 courtyard
8 pool
9 orange grove
10 fountain
11 pantry
12 storage
13 guest bedroom
14 laundry
15 terrace
16 family
17 bedroom
18 dressing
19 bathroom

The recent meticulous refurbishment of the property restores to the house its serene nobility and dignity.

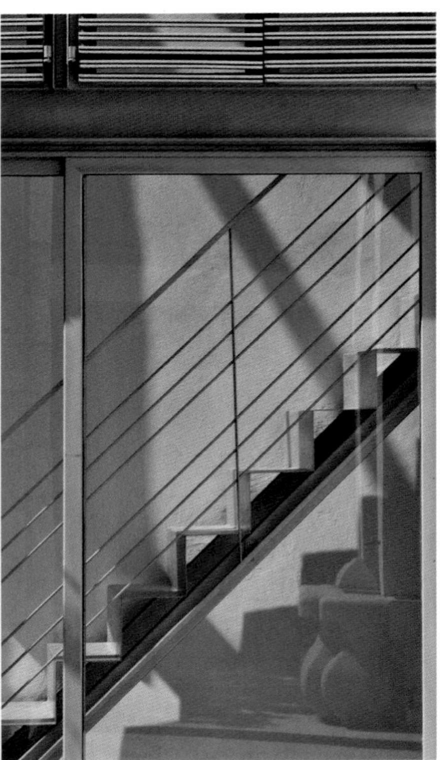

ABOVE
The elegant main bathroom is located in one of the wings of the new extension. It receives abundant filtered light through the wooden shutters.

FAR LEFT
Original details have been retained and restored wherever possible. The calming ambience of the entrance hall opens to the tranquil courtyard and garden.

LEFT
A glimpse through sliding glass doors reveals the sleek steel staircase that gives access to the laundry. The understated details of the new additions help form this impressive restoration project into a complementary and coherent whole.

Charter House Apartments MELBOURNE, AUSTRALIA

Jackson Clements Burrows Architects

Constructed	2002
Home type	Office block and inner city apartments
Structure	Timber and steel frame, with zinc cladding placed on original brick building

"This project attempts to demonstrate an appropriate contemporary response to architectural and cultural heritage considerations. The result is a distinct and identifiable contemporary extension, which complements the existing building through its conscious connections in form, reinforcing the verticality of the impressive Federation Warehouse style."

Jackson Clements Burrows Architects

A NOBLE HERITAGE

The original Charter House was constructed in Melbourne during the commercial resurgence that followed the depression of the early 1890s. The house was commissioned in 1905 by a large Melbourne printing company, Charles Troedel & Co, to accommodate their burgeoning printing works and offices. Architect Nahum Barnet was engaged to design the premises, which have been described as an example of the Federation Warehouse style.

The printing company occupied the building until 1932 before moving to larger premises in South Melbourne. A well-known Melbourne architectural company, A & K Henderson, then bought the site and a year later made some major alterations, which included re-positioning the entry, building a large ground floor lobby and installing a passenger lift. All offices in the building were completely refurbished.

Today, Charter House is regarded as an important heritage building. It is located in Bank Place opposite the Mitre Tavern, which is the central business district's oldest building. There are a number of other significant heritage sites in the vicinity.

REDEVELOPING HISTORY

One of the major requests in the redevelopment brief was for a rooftop extension that incorporated residential apartments. Given the historical significance of the building, a sensitive approach was required. The architect considered the recommendations made by the planning department of the city council and their heritage advisers. This resulted in an evolutionary design process that allowed for the testing of opportunities for a more contemporary architecture that would not compromise the original building.

VERTICAL EXTENSION AND SEPARATION

The architectural styles in the rooftop extension have been separated, and the extension itself is a "wrapped extrusion." The lower level of the new work is limited to the space within the external walls of the original structure. The upper levels are not confined to this limitation and merge well with the outer limits of the original facade and the accompanying detail.

SWEEPING FORM

The sweep of the new built form has the effect of diminishing the visual volume from street level. It also connects in a formal way with the mansard roof of an adjacent rooftop extension (a favored solution in the city council's planning guidelines). Two balconies extrude through the new form, which further emphasizes the distortion. The zinc facade sweeps across the extension – the architect likens the effect to a piece of curling paper, an image that sits nicely with the history of the building and its early use as a printing works.

A MARRIAGE BETWEEN OLD AND NEW

Deep windows are like punctuation marks in the facade, and the standing seams have been strategically positioned in order to more closely reflect the heritage aspect and detail of the building. This also results in a strong visual connection between the two architectural styles, and ensures that the contrasting ideas sit well together and complement one another. The outcome is that the extension, while contemporary and distinctive, also balances the existing building through the use of connecting forms. The Federation Warehouse style is retained but given a modern flavor.

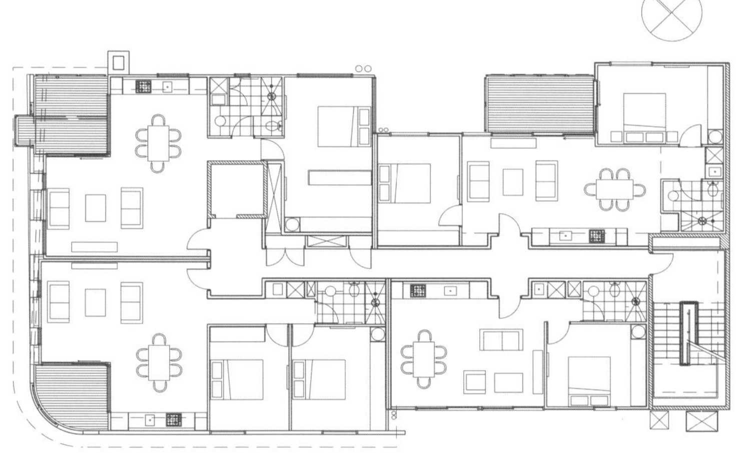

LEFT
The architecture of the new extension echoes the detailing and fenestration of the existing building. The form sweeps backwards from the corner to engage with the mansard roof beyond, while the changing geometry is subtly accentuated by the protruding balconies.

FAR LEFT
The apartment living spaces have generously proportioned decks, an abundance of natural light, and expansive views of the city.

ABOVE
Balconies provide much-needed private outdoor space for the apartments, which are nestled among the city towers of the central business district.

FOLLOWING PAGES
The modern rooftop extension complements the heritage fabric of Melbourne's Bank Place and provides a strong architectural identity for Charter House with the surrounding context.

Cremorne Street House AUCKLAND, NEW ZEALAND

Stevens Lawson Architects

Constructed 2004
Home type Two-story family home
Structure Concrete blocks, GRC, timber, and zinc

"Shapes and textures are contrasted and repeated throughout the house and landscape creating a sense of harmony, complexity, and visual delight. The triangular geometries repeated throughout establish an integrated theme that engenders a personal character to the house."

Gary Lawson and Nicholas Stevens

PUBLIC FACE, PRIVATE MASK

This family house is situated on a quiet street in the inner Auckland suburb of Herne Bay. Honed concrete blocks, dark stained timber, and white pre-cast concrete have been combined in an intensive sculptural composition. The cast concrete facade acts simultaneously as a public sculpture, and as a protective mask for the private spaces behind.

The living spaces are laid out in a linear progression along the length of the site, connecting the front courtyard to the rear courtyard. This continuous space steps down several levels, following the land's natural slope, defining distinct living and dining areas. The three bedrooms are on the upper floor along with the "sky lounge." The sky lounge functions as a private living space with separate stair access, or as an extension to the main bedroom suite.

The southern side houses garaging, service court, laundry, bathroom, and study. One unusual feature is the double staircase, one leading to the sky lounge and the other to the bedrooms. While it may not appear to make sense at first, it resolves a circulation dilemma and provides one of the most engaging moments in the house.

JOURNEY THROUGH THE HOUSE

The visitor enters through a slatted gate, alongside a block wall, passes by the front courtyard, slips under the sculpted facade, through the heavy crafted timber pivot door, into a dark gallery with a red velvet curtain, turns right to pass through a gap in the wall, and descends into an elongated living space, which steps down toward the rear courtyard, and has a sculpted ceiling and irregular spaced vertical slot windows down one side. From there ascend to the sky lounge.

FORMS AND MOTIFS

The sculpted front facade has a dual function – to provide privacy and protection, but also to give something back to the street. The architects see it as a mask, its form reminiscent of Pacific tapa patterns, origami, and Modernist design. It is made of glass reinforced concrete (GRC) and formed in one large mold.

Thematic motifs recur throughout the house. One is of triangulated forms, a Pacific reference, which can be seen in the front facade, the front door, the living room ceilings, the kitchen bar, the Noguchi paper ceiling light, and the garden plan. The other is of irregular spacing and random patterns, which can be seen in the slot windows, driveway paving, the sliding timber

ABOVE
View from the front courtyard looking through to the rear lawn and lap pool. The main entry is positioned within the series of honed block walls, which slice through into the interior creating a strong interplay with the folded ceiling of the living, dining, and kitchen beyond.

RIGHT
Looking along the lap pool reveals the open-ended plan of the house, with living and kitchen contained between the parallel honed block walls. The sky lounge sits atop, within the end of the upper level, capturing great views of the harbor and the setting sun.

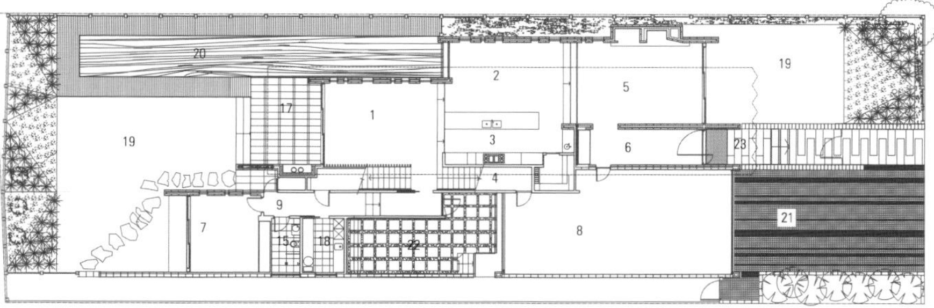

GROUND FLOOR

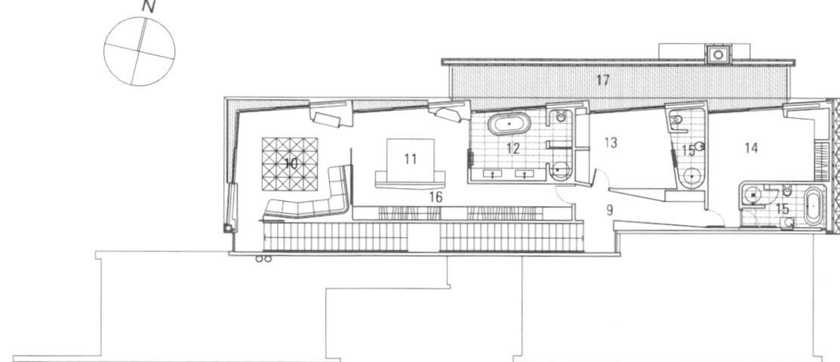

FIRST FLOOR

1 living	6 entry	11 bedroom 1	16 dressing	21 motorcourt
2 dining	7 study/guest	12 ensuite	17 terrace	22 service court
3 kitchen	8 garage	13 bedroom 2	18 laundry	23 entry court
4 store	9 hallway	14 bedroom 3	19 lawn	
5 lounge	10 sky lounge	15 bathroom	20 pool	

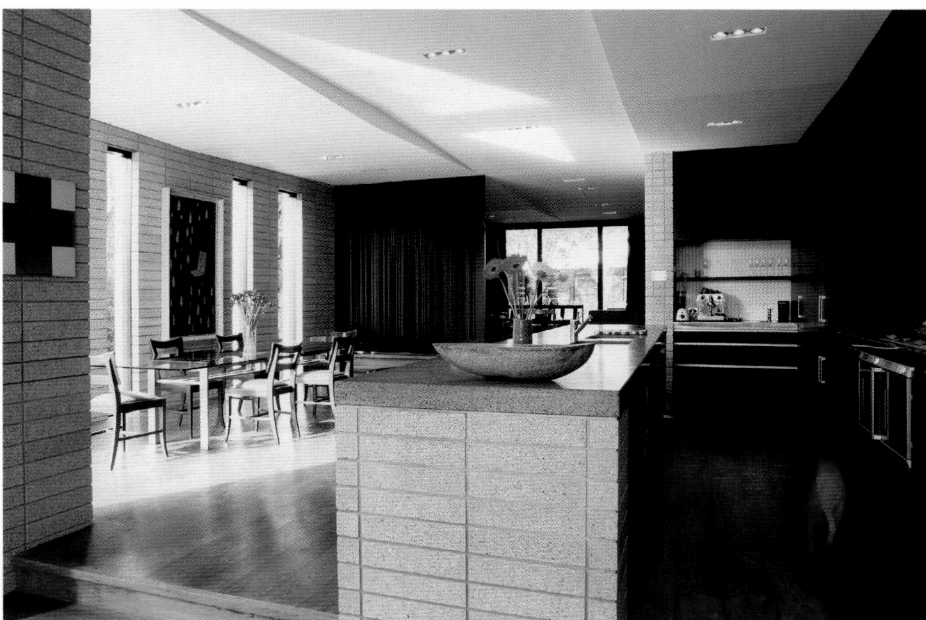

ABOVE
The concrete terrazzo-topped island bench with honed block sides, provides another linear element to the kitchen and dining area. The pleated ceiling and the textured timber sliding door to the living space, combined with art and classic furniture, add a further layer of interest to the rich material palette used throughout the house.

doors, the stairway screen, and the bathroom floor tiles. These variations on a theme give the house a particular resonance.

CRAFT AND QUALITY MATERIALS

Materials with texture and richness have been used: elongated honed concrete blocks, dark timber floors and joinery, velour carpets, velvet curtains, leather upholstery. There is a stark contrast between the earthiness of concrete and the plushness of velvet.

Although austere in one way, it is also a tactile and sensuous house, with a restrained sense of luxury.

The architects are practitioners of contemporary architecture, with its Modernist underpinnings, but are also interested in historic architecture, traditional Japanese architecture with its dark timber, sliding screens, asymmetry, level changes, and flowing spaces, and the New Zealand regionalism of John Scott. The aim is to create multiple readings.

Fabric Wall Residence FUKUOKA, JAPAN

Kazuhiko Oishi Architecture Atelier

Constructed	2004
Home type	Single dwelling
Structure	Polycarbonate slabs and polyester fabric walls on cement slabs

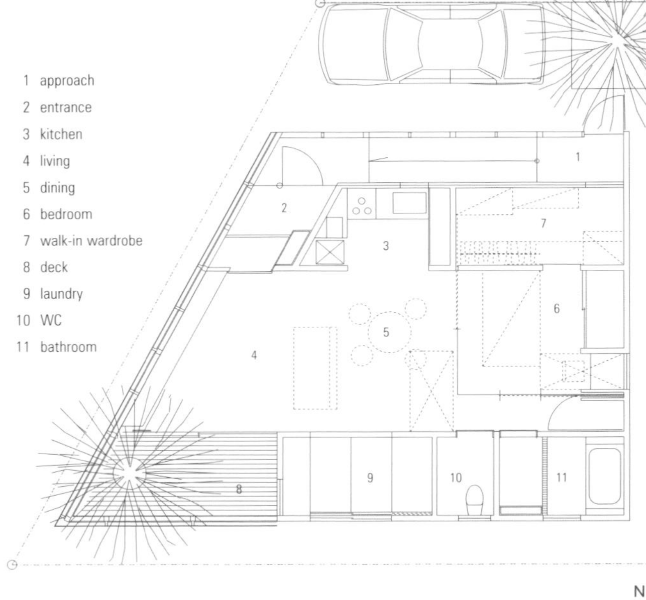

ABOVE
The architect's use of polycarbonate cellular slabs provides the client with complete privacy; the fabric sheath adds warmth and mutes the exterior scenery and lights. In consideration of the client's stage in life, ramps for wheelchair access lead to the entry at the far right.

RIGHT
A narrow hallway leads to the entry of the home. The distinctive "fabric" walls acknowledge the client's association with dress design in her youth.

"This is a compact dwelling designed to accommodate the very basic needs of its ageing client for maintenance, security, and functionality."

Kazuhiko Oishi

MODERNIST ENCLAVE

The city of Fukuoka on Japan's southernmost island of Kyushu is developing a deserved reputation as a wellspring of Modernism. Isolated from the mainland, and also from the mainland's history and traditional approach to architecture, in recent years Fukuoka has attracted a wealth of creative artists who are catering to a new demographic of discerning, wealthy, and informed clients.

POLYCARBONATE SKIN

This renaissance is typified in Kazuhiko Oishi's Fabric Wall Residence. Located on a small 1,410-sq-ft-(131-sq-m-) corner site in a busy residential street, this compact dwelling is set on a series of concrete slabs, giving the house a raised appearance.

In response to the client's need for high-level security, coupled with the restrictions of the site, the home's exterior is composed of a double-skin of polycarbonate hollow cellular slabs with a blue and green polyester fiber cloth sheath. The "fabric," and the way it wraps around the home like a sash belt are an acknowledgment of the client's association with dress design in her youth.

The materials allows for thermal flow, and constantly changes appearance, depending upon the weather, lighting conditions, and the observer's perspective.

LIGHT FILTER

The light from the surrounding buildings becomes muted as it passes through the opaque polycarbonate skin. Providing privacy from the street, the thin walls are both a characteristic of traditional Japanese architecture and a response to the region's reasonably mild climate.

The interior of the house is a one-room space, set between a flat wooden ceiling and a timber floor, which is raised above the ground. The house is naturally ventilated – air enters the home through floor vents and exits via two elevated windows.

TRADITIONAL IDEA

The home has an open plan living, dining, sleeping, and tatami quarters but the single space can be divided and areas made private by mobile internal partitions that run in two directions. A private guest sleeping area can be created in this way.

Set within the external polycarbonate wall, an exterior deck is open to the sky and provides the interior's only view of a naturally lit environment.

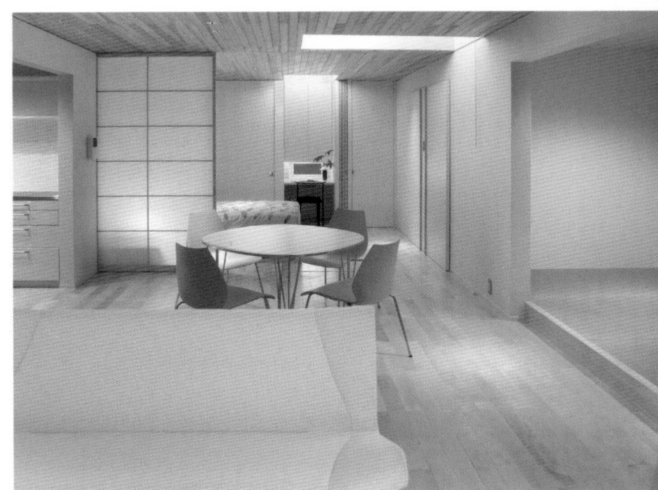

ABOVE
The arrangement of space in this compact ultra-modern home recalls traditional Japanese design. The effect is accentated by the use of pale timbers and sliding screens.

TOP
The importance of the private terrace is seen in the amount of unfiltered light it admits to the interior and also in the way it frames the tree, giving the home an important reference to nature.

Horizon Apartments SYDNEY, AUSTRALIA

Harry Seidler & Associates

Construction	1996–1999
Home type	Forty-three story apartment building
Structure	Reinforced concrete columns and structural facade, toughened cantilevered glass balustrades, and pre-stressed concrete floors

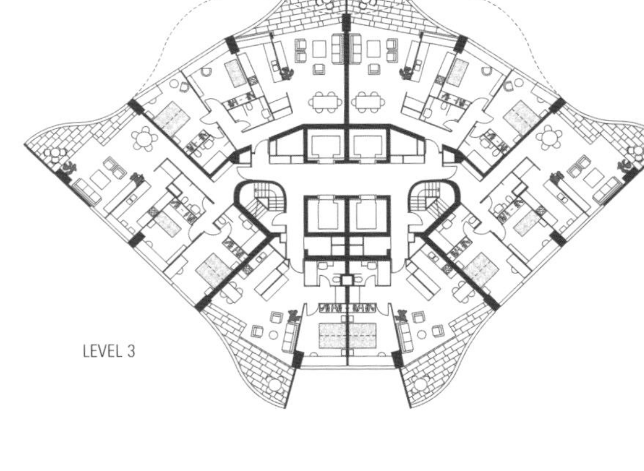

LEVEL 3

"From a distance, the curved balconies provide a scintillating, animated pattern, terminating with a cap of continuous balconies to the penthouse. The deliberate restricted palette of external materials reinforces the tower's sculptural, monolithic appearance."

Harry Seidler & Associates

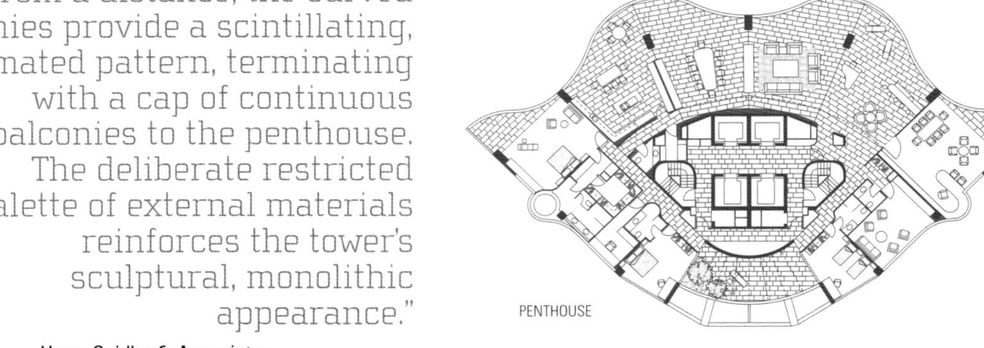

PENTHOUSE

ABOVE
A quirk in local planning rules meant the site for the Horizon Apartments was exempt from height restrictions. In order to relate to the streetscape of the surrounding inner-city terrace houses, the height was lowered, and three, four-story terraces were built along street frontages.

Planning authorities in Sydney are not generally favorable to high-rise developments in designated suburban areas, so plans had to be considered carefully before submission and subsequent permission to build was granted. Horizon Apartments was designed so that visual obstructions to views were kept to a minimum. In addition, the slimness of the building meant that it would cast fewer shadows than larger, taller buildings.

This 43-level tower was designed to obtain the widest possible outlook over Sydney Harbour and across to the Opera House and the Sydney Harbour Bridge. To achieve this, the tower was shaped to expose the sweep of the view from north to west.

FANTASTIC FLEXIBILITY

The apartment tower consists of two penthouses, 18 three-bedroom apartments, 157 two-bedroom apartments and 45 one-bedroom apartments. In the townhouses, there is one three-bedroom apartment, eight two-bedroom apartments, and 22 one-bedroom/studio apartments.

Floor space in the apartment tower is divided evenly between living and bedroom areas, giving each apartment a high degree of flexibility of function.

The units on the first six floors have their living area in the center, so that the lower garden apartment building does not obstruct their views. There is a range of outlook choices on the next 24 levels depending on the position of living areas and terraces on successive levels. This gives residents a choice of views – either the city skyline or beautiful Sydney Harbour.

The views are even more expansive in the higher apartments, extending out to the Pacific Ocean. The orientation of the balconies also alters in the larger apartments, which are situated in the top quarter of the tower, permitting even more dramatic views.

SEEING WHAT'S OUTSIDE

The living areas and main bedrooms have full glass walls to capture views. Narrower horizontal windows are installed in the kitchens and other bedrooms. Terrace overhangs or exterior awnings provide effective protection from the heat of the sun, and also remove the need for venetian blinds, which would detract from the views.

All balconies have a distinct shape and are large enough to accommodate outdoor furniture and cooking facilities. Each apartment is also individually air-conditioned. The entire top floor of the tower is crowned with a lavish penthouse.

REST AND RECREATION

The site was excavated to accommodate a five-level, 500-car basement garage, with a centrally placed elevator providing access to the entrance lobby. There are extensive recreational facilities for the apartment-dwellers, with a barbecue area, swimming pool, and tennis court, which are visible from the terraces of the surrounding low-rise apartments. The remainder of the site has been extensively landscaped.

The split-level lower studio/garden units each have either a ground-floor private patio, or an upper-floor, or roof-level terrace.

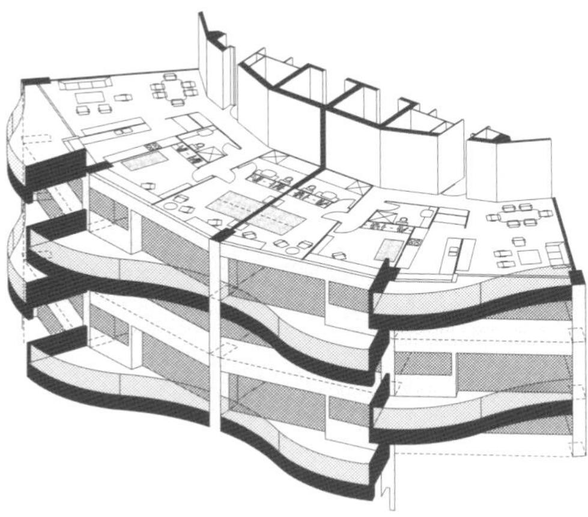

LEFT
The combined living and dining areas have full glass walls to exploit the dramatic views of the city and harbor.

ABOVE
The higher the apartment, the more expansive the view. The spacious curved balconies can accommodate outdoor furniture and cooking facilities. The terrace overhangs provide protection from the weather and also eliminate the need for venetian blinds.

House C MEXICO CITY, MEXICO

TEN Arquitectos

Constructed	2004
Home type	Three-level residence
Structure	Reinforced concrete frames and concrete slabs

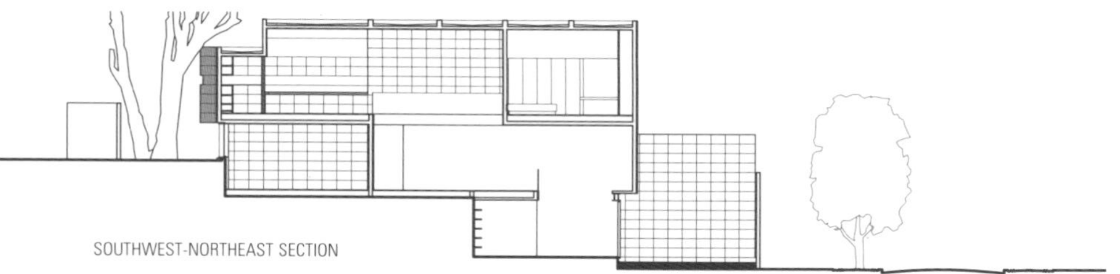
SOUTHWEST-NORTHEAST SECTION

ABOVE
This view of the exterior of House C illustrates the high degree of privacy required by the clients because of the building's exposed corner location. The brutalist nature of the exterior eastern wall is softened by the presence of the skylight alongside a soaring "keep," and also by the overtly Modernist, angular form of the wall itself.

TOP RIGHT
Functionalism can be seen in the second-level family room – an expansive living area where every articulation between spaces has been erased. House C's L-shaped design provides a sense of inter-connectedness as one looks out out the window across the central courtyard to the kitchen and guest bedrooms beyond.

FAR RIGHT
Here the courtyard is showcased as the central focus of House C. A sense of privacy, if not intimacy, is achieved by the high wrap-around facades. The extensive use of glass helps to fuse the interior and exterior spaces.

"The clients' brief was for a multistory family home on a narrow, exposed site that would incorporate views, while at the same time providing security and privacy. The owners wanted an open-plan design with lots of light and a sense of space throughout the house, as well as privacy and quiet for the bedrooms on the upper level."

TEN Arquitectos

The design of TEN Arquitectos' House C is representative of the range of cosmopolitan residential architecture that can be found throughout twenty-first century Mexico City today.

PRIVACY AND SECURITY

House C is a single-family residence situated on a difficult, sloping site of approximately 4,305 sq ft (400 sq m) in one of the most expensive and exclusive neighborhoods in the city – Lomas de Chapultepec, the Beverly Hills of Mexico City.

A hallmark of TEN Arquitectos' work is their insistence on an intimate dialogue with the client at every stage of development. The project team of Enrique Norten, Bernardo Gomez-Pimienta and Jorge Luis Perez devised the L-shaped plan, with the living areas oriented in a northerly aspect to maximize privacy from the busy streetscape to the building's south. Highly exposed due to its corner-site locale, the home's massive southern wall also provides a level of security highly sought after in a suburb where private security firms, and walls 10 ft (3 m) high or more, are not uncommon.

The L-shaped plan, coupled with House C's high parting wall enclosure, reinforce the interior/exterior spaces as the central focus of the home.

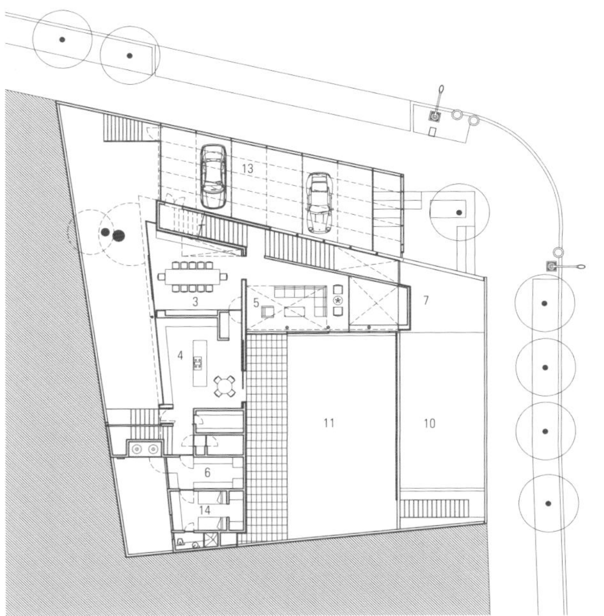

LEVEL TWO

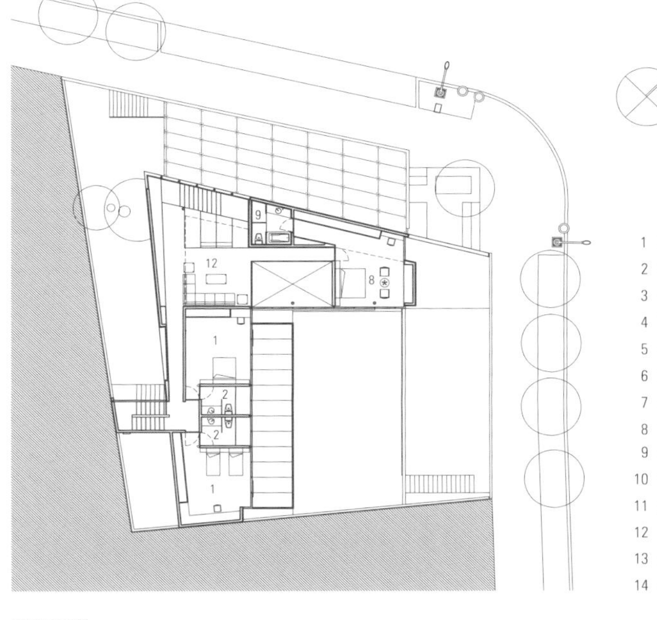

LEVEL THREE

1 bedroom
2 bathroom
3 dining
4 kitchen
5 living
6 laundry
7 reflective pool
8 main bedroom
9 main bathroom
10 terrace
11 garden
12 family
13 garage
14 service area

The L-shaped plan, coupled with House C's high parting wall enclosure, reinforce the interior/exterior spaces as the central focus of the house.

OPPOSITE
The horizontal limitations imposed by the relatively small size of the building site did not prevent the architects from achieving a vivid sense of space. This openness was achieved by incorporating large voids into the design and building "up." An external wall appears to disappear into the interior, enhancing the building's sense of balance, while at the same time providing continuity between the interior and exterior.

ABOVE
The hallway connects the three bedrooms and the family room on the second floor. Despite its narrowness, the hallway has a sense of openness, provided by diffused light from an elongated window in the building's western wall, as well as by downlights and a high ceiling.

TOP RIGHT
This view of the family room demonstrates the architects' minimalist approach and keen sense of the practical – the generously proportioned central built-in serves as a work bench and storage area.

LINKING THE LEVELS

The main entrance's double height strongly emphasizes the horizontality of the courtyard reflecting pool, seen beyond a window to the left of the entry, as well as the verticality of the two flights of stairs on the right. These stairs link the primary living spaces below, to the main bedroom on the upper level, which is isolated from noisy living areas by a hallway. The hallway is lit from above by a vertical skylight on the building's western wall.

Each of the two guest bedrooms, also on the upper level, has its own bathroom and affords expansive views over the central courtyard and beyond.

The primary living, dining, and outdoor/interior spaces are located on the middle floor and linked by stairs on the eastern side of the house to the bedrooms and family room above, as well as to the library and stone-paved courtyard below. The ground floor also contains the home's six-car garage and a small storage area.

EXTERNAL AND INTERNAL VIEWS

Throughout the home there is an artful interplay of space and view, enhanced by the continuity of external and internal materials, which fuses interior and exterior spaces.

Large, uncluttered living spaces allow a wide variety of functions. The interplay effect reaches its peak in the top-floor family room, which has extensive views of the interior. From this vantage point, the double height of the ground-floor library and living room weaves these rooms into the panoramic skyline, lending the distant city views a certain immediacy.

House for Art Collectors SYDNEY, AUSTRALIA

Marsh Cashman Koolloos Architects

Construction	2000–2001
Home type	Single dwelling, contemporary terrace house
Structure	Three level, concrete slab floor with load-bearing brickwork

"The terrace house type is identified and expressed with close reference to its predecessors, but is also re-evaluated and transformed into a more open, flowing and dynamic form and spatial experience...the spatial experience was most important to us in this project, with elements of surprise and drama, containment and modesty, serenity and enigma."

Mark Cashman

ABOVE
This view from the first floor bridge down into the central void looks like a series of "boxes," but each has a purpose. The suspended zinc clad box contains the main bedroom walk-in wardrobe. It drops down to become the ceiling over the kitchen area. The large concrete slab at ground level is the kitchen's island bench; the black box along the kitchen wall encloses cupboards; the pink strip is a cupboard light.

ABOVE RIGHT
The shelves housing the library are a space-saving dividing wall, separating the studio at the eastern end of the house from the dining and kitchen areas.

The House for Art Collectors is a residence to house art and books, the two great passions of its occupants. The house had to be spacious, with a central void space and a Modernist style. Both owners required a working space.

The project was part of a new subdivision and, coincidentally, a redevelopment of a former art gallery in an urban part of Sydney. The subdivision created a row of long, narrow allotments. The client purchased one of the middle lots and although the home is freestanding, it is sandwiched between two other houses of similar scale and size. The surrounding context is predominantly residential with a mixture of house types and styles ranging from historic to contemporary.

EXPRESSIVE AND ENIGMATIC

The simple rectangular building form and structural system of concrete floors, with load-bearing brickwork and lightweight roof, combine harmoniously with generally simple finishes, such as cement-rendered walls and steel-troweled, tinted concrete floors.

The use of "floating rectangular boxes" both internally and externally are designed to break down any sense of division between the inside and outside. The design invites visitors to enter and journey through the sequence of spaces – areas that express elements of the occupants' personalities, while not giving too much away.

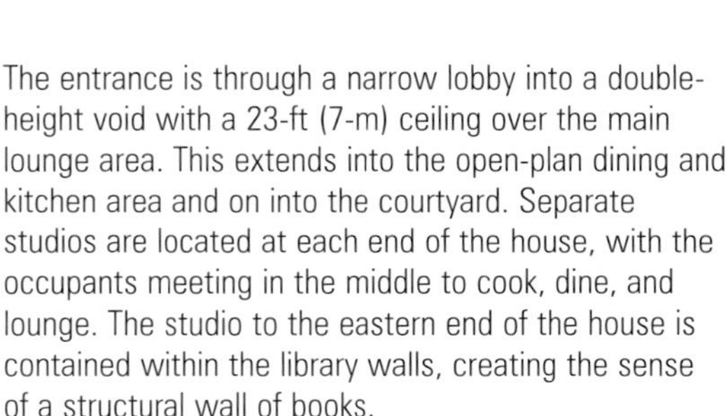

The entrance is through a narrow lobby into a double-height void with a 23-ft (7-m) ceiling over the main lounge area. This extends into the open-plan dining and kitchen area and on into the courtyard. Separate studios are located at each end of the house, with the occupants meeting in the middle to cook, dine, and lounge. The studio to the eastern end of the house is contained within the library walls, creating the sense of a structural wall of books.

The central outdoor area provides a private living space with a lap pool and garden. The upper level contains bedrooms for owners and guests and the basement level, to the rear, houses a garage and storage area.

THE CHALLENGES OF LIGHT AND HEAT

With the site's east–west orientation along a narrow site, moderating heat in the west-facing living area while maximizing light was a challenge. The central courtyard allows plenty of daylight and sunlight to penetrate the interior, while motorized blinds on the glazed walls screen the hot afternoon sun when necessary. A central roof light, equipped with motorized opening windows, lets in northern sunlight and southern daylight to the central interior on both levels, while also creating good air movement through stack-effect ventilation.

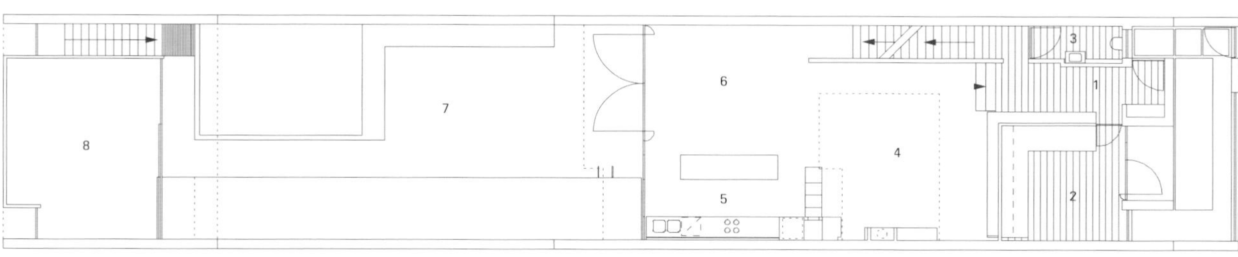

GROUND FLOOR

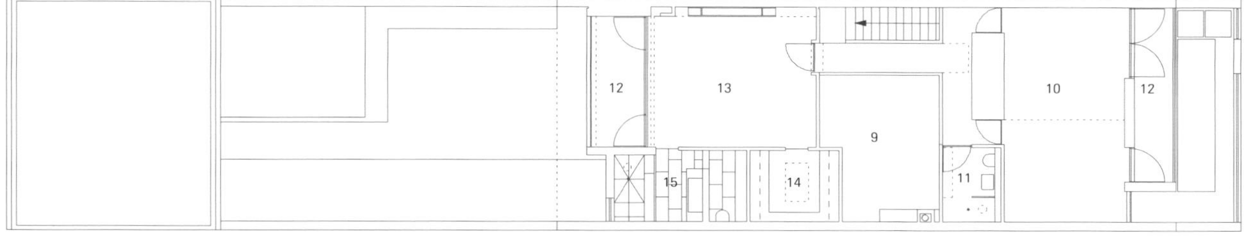

FIRST FLOOR

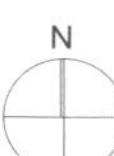

1 entry
2 study 1
3 wc
4 living
5 kitchen
6 dining
7 courtyard/pool
8 study 2
9 open to below
10 guests
11 bathroom
12 balcony
13 main bedroom
14 walk-in wardrobe
15 ensuite

LEFT
The simple hot-dip galvanized finish on the steel-framed windows creates a "barely there" separation between inside and out. Local views are possible at the upper level and can be enjoyed from a balcony off the main bedroom.

ABOVE
A lap pool and courtyard lie between one of the studies and the main living area. With the site's east–west orientation, the central courtyard maximizes penetration of the northern sun to the center of the living areas. The courtyard tree, which will grow large, provides both visual privacy to a neighboring apartment block and shading in summer. The high courtyard wall extends and encompasses the rear studio and the courtyard.

House Mongolia JOHANNESBURG, SOUTH AFRICA

Hugh Fraser

Constructed 2003
Home type Free-standing, single-family residence
Structure Single story with load-bearing brickwork; timber and corrugated iron roofing

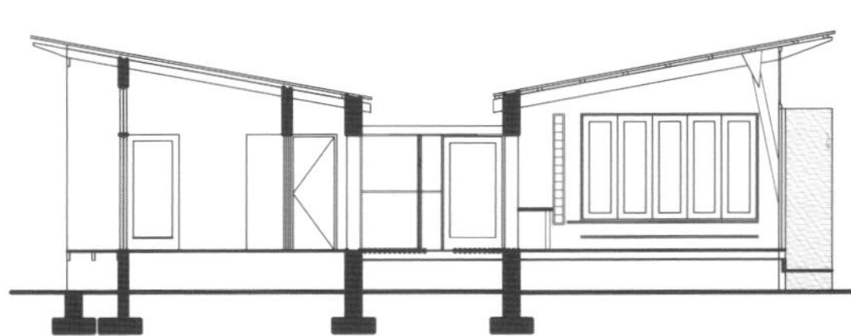

"Johannesburg is not universally perceived as one of the world's beautiful cities. However, it probably has more trees than any other city on the planet. This house was positioned in a particularly sylvan setting and I sought to exploit the nature of the site."

Hugh Fraser

ABOVE
The north orientation of House Mongolia helps maximize sunlight penetration, which in mid-winter lasts only a short time. In summer, light and heat are intense. Lush vegetation to the side of the main living area shields the house from the hot afternoon sun, offering cool respite when temperatures soar.

SPACE FOR LIFE AND WORK

Architect Hugh Fraser wanted to build a comfortable and practical home that blended in with the leafy surroundings of his urban Johannesburg home site. As a single practicing architect, he also wanted a separate office on the same property. As to the significance of the quirky appellation, the property had been registered under the name "Mongolian Properties." Fraser liked the name – and so it stayed.

The large, gently sloping site was already heavily landscaped with exotic and indigenous trees. Rather than remove them, Fraser decided to position the house among them.

CHOOSING MATERIALS

In some rooms, the floors are suspended timber (eucalypt) on concrete foundations, and in others, they are suspended concrete. This choice was made because the soil on the property is largely clay and prone to instability. Concrete serves to stabilize the foundations. Doors and windows are framed in meranti timber. South African pine was chosen for the roof, which is also covered with corrugated iron sheeting.

GREEN INTEGRATION

The abundance of trees on the site inspired Fraser to integrate them into the overall design. His prime consideration was to take advantage of what the site had to offer – in particular to make the most of the leafy views.

The house consists of two pavilions, with the living areas in the front, facing north, the sleeping areas at the back, and the entrance sitting in the middle. Because the house faces north, the strong summer sun may have posed a problem, therefore positioning the pavilions correctly on the site was an important consideration. However, the number of trees and their proximity to the house offers adequate protection, helping maintain a pleasant temperature year round.

A NATURAL ENTRANCE

The house is located deep within its forest setting, approximately 100 ft (30 m) away from car access and parking. Visitors make the journey to the house down a winding, tree-studded path. Once reached, the entrance area features a native tree growing up through the space, boxed in behind glass panels.

All rooms – living, dining and kitchen area, bedrooms and two bathrooms – are enveloped by the surrounding vegetation, helping to blur the boundaries between inside and out. Doors open out onto the garden, effectively increasing the size of the living areas.

FORM AND FUNCTION

Furniture and fittings form part of the architecture of House Mongolia. The kitchen is designed as a unit on wheels with open shelves. The shutters in the main bedroom open independently of the glass doors, and the shower is placed outside in the garden.

ABOVE
Much of the house opens out onto the garden. The outdoor environment essentially becomes part of the interior, adding to the available living space.

RIGHT
As winter approaches, the deciduous trees discard their protective canopy, exposing the exterior of the house to more intense light. As a result, the house becomes more sculptural, the starkness of the outside color blending well with the surrounding hues.

Jalan Tempinis KUALA LUMPUR, MALAYSIA

Seksan Design

Construction	1995–2000
Home type	Two-story family home
Structure	Overburnt bricks, steel, and exposed concrete

"The objective is a process designed to capture and imbed the passage of time into the fabric of the building, not unlike the natural changes that happen in a temporal landscape."

Seksan

A GARDEN HOUSE

Tucked away in a quaint neighborhood of Kuala Lumpur, this is a house undergoing the natural weathering and disintegration process of any organic structure, subtly incorporating this entropy into the additions and modifications made on the existing 1970s semi-detached building.

Conceptualized primarily as a "garden house" into which the visitor must first untangle themselves through the structured curtain of red-rooted *Cissus* creepers at the entrance, the house splits into a series of almost "accidental" living and garden spaces that begin to define the vocabulary of the dwelling.

LOCAL MATERIALS

The house, with a land area of 4,000 sq ft (370 sq m) was converted to a studio and home office in 1995, when most of the trees in the garden were planted. The brief was to both transform and convert it back into a home of 3,000 sq ft (280 sq m) to accommodate an expanding family with children and dogs. Further remodeling was carried out in 2001 and 2005.

It was important for the house to reflect and adapt to the fluctuating changes and needs of the family. The design had to reflect a personal reinterpretation of the working-class aesthetic, glorifying the use of local and cheap building materials and leaving things unfinished to let time, children, and dogs have their turn to make their mark on the surroundings.

LEFT
The cool, neutral palette, the display of traditional and contemporary artifacts, and the use of everyday materials helps tie the interior of the earthy and laid-back living area into its all-important surroundings.

ABOVE
A hammock takes pride of place in the living area, blurring the boundaries between inside and out. The vertical lines created by the palm trunks heightens the sense of a treetop retreat in the middle of the city.

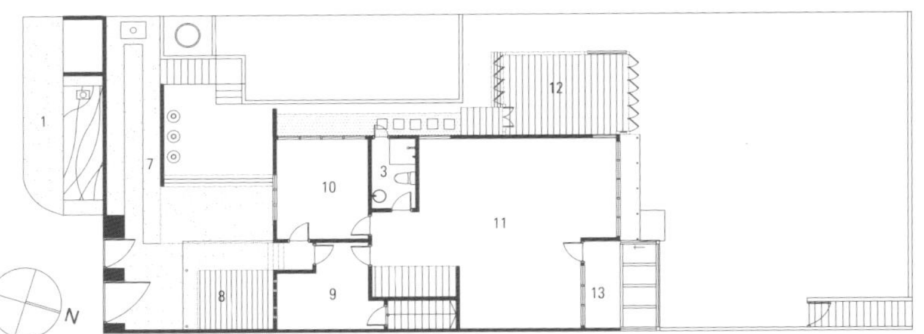

FIRST FLOOR

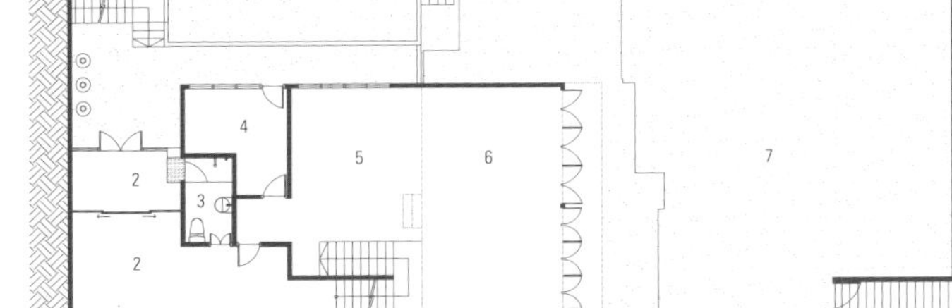

GROUND FLOOR

1 street
2 bedroom
3 bathroom
4 kitchen
5 dining
6 living
7 garden
8 meeting platform
9 study
10 reception
11 studio
12 tree-house
13 glasshouse

CAPTURING THE PASSAGE OF TIME

The layering of materials such as overburnt bricks, steel, and exposed concrete provide the perfect canvas for the garden to permeate the perforations of the architectural envelope. The aging of materials, and the patina of wear and tear is reflected back into the living spaces, diffusing the boundaries of interior and exterior, light and shadow, porous and solid.

WALK THROUGH THE HOUSE

Once through the lush entrance, a flight of stairs delivers the visitor into the wide living area that spills into a palm-shaded garden cooled by an adjacent water feature. The trees provide a canopy, filtering the sky and the external surroundings, creating dappled patches of light and shadow, which skim the surface of the brick-paved courtyard. The living space divides into the open kitchen and dining area and merges into the courtyard, which is accessible from the entrance level.

The sleeping space on the first level slips into a small tree-house extension that overlooks the paved courtyard below. The light-filled bathroom, overlooking the kitchen courtyard, opens out toward the sky.

An impressive collection of paintings, sculptures, and bric-a-brac adorn every corner of the house. Overlooking the spaces below is a roof garden that spills color, texture, and form to the surprised visitor climbing the ladder that accesses it.

Like a favorite chair, which through years of use and abuse has the indelible imprint of the owner, this house comes to root in a symbiotic relationship of family, plants, trees, and the land.

TOP LEFT
Large fold-back doors open onto the paved courtyard with its grove of palms and fountain.

OPPOSITE
A small tree-house extension overlooks the courtyard and provides a pleasant outdoor dining area.

TOP RIGHT
The small, multi-purpose courtyard is both a children's play area and an adult's retreat. Custom-built wire-mesh outdoor furniture is a testament to the resourcefulness encouraged by the architect. By using local and cheap building materials, the house is imbued with a sense of continual change, without forgoing concepts of style, longevity, and comfort.

ABOVE
"Reclining" on a purpose-built platform, this stainless steel sculpture makes a bold statement in the courtyard.

Legal / Illegal House COLOGNE, GERMANY

Manuel Herz Architecture & Urbanism

Constructed	2003
Home type	Mixed-use (two apartments, one office), five-level building
Structure	Concrete and glass

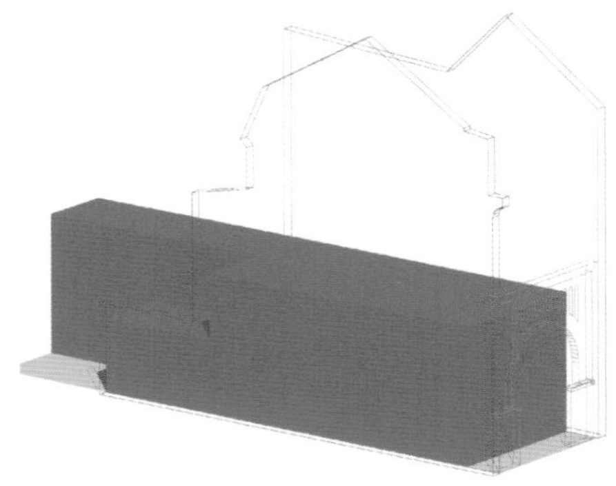

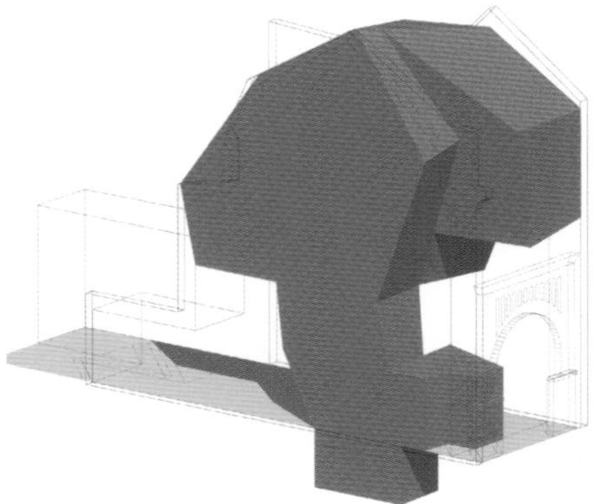

RIGHT
The building's "legal" volume (green) complies with the rules of the local building code, including that it be set back 3 ft (1 m) from the historic facade. The "illegal" volume (red) exceeds the maximum permitted floor area. It spans from street level upwards, through the legal volume, the upper levels curving back down to complete a partial loop around the historic front gate. There is no differentiation between walls, floors, and roof.

LEFT
The free-form, "goggle-eyed" illegal structure seems to jut out defiantly against the rules and regulations imposed by local planning authorities.

"To diagnose the psychosis of a suburb means working on the symptoms. These symptoms become apparent via both the built and non-built environments. They are made visible in the scale of the urban fabric as well as on the scale of a building. They are written into the local code and rules governing the development of that suburb."

Manuel Herz

ABOVE
The windows and skylights of the illegal section of the building look toward the sky and onto the neighboring terraces. Every faceted surface throws a shadow across one of the adjoining sites, something forbidden by German planning law.

FOLLOWING PAGES
Illegal/Legal jauntily celebrates its individuality among the nineteeth-century facades of the landmark buildings, while still paying homage to their prestige and position in the streetscape. As foreign as the structure might seem in the area, it acts upon the history, the state of the urban fabric, and attempts to enrich the immediate context.

A SUBURB IN DISCONTENT

Located south of the medieval border of Cologne, Bayenthal was founded in the middle of the nineteenth century and was incorporated into the district of Cologne in the 1880s in the wake of a large municipal reform. The founding of Bayenthal and its primary source of development goes back to its first discontent – "industrial discontent."

In other parts of the world, in the first half of the nineteenth century, industrial wheels were turning, but in Prussia things were slow. Germany had little of the new technology. Gustav Mevissen, a developer and financial speculator from Cologne, changed this when he founded Kölner Maschinenbau AG (the Cologne Machine Construction Company Ltd) in 1856, which soon grew to be a major player in Germany's steel market, gaining contracts to build bridges, cathedral roofs, and other buildings of cultural significance. The factory shaped Bayenthal's urban fabric enormously.

CITIZENS IN DISCONTENT

The gap between rich and poor was starkly evident in the housing of the time, with workers living in very congested and overcrowded conditions. Only meters away from these homes was a wasteland, originally intended to be used as an extension of the factory. The extension did not eventuate and the site remained an artificial wasteland. Adequate housing was lacking in the neighborhood and higher rent could be demanded of the tenants, most of whom were factory workers. The owners of the company discovered, as a secondary means of income, that the market value of the sites they owned increased once development plans had been set up for those sites. It was never intended that the "planned" developments be carried out, rather, the intention was to raise the market value. This combination of factors contributed to the general quality of the neighborhood, which is one of missing identity, or missing character.

POOR PLANNING

A large development was constructed in the 1960s with over 1,000 apartments on the site. In the 1970s an urban master plan was proposed for Bayenthal, to stem the flow of families moving to rural areas – the population had decreased by 25 percent at this time. The plan removed the tram line in the main street, the street width was doubled, and the density of construction was to be halved by building mainly fully detached buildings. Suburbia was to move in.

This development plan, which remains the binding by-law since that time, has never been applied, for two reasons. First, most houses on the main road were classed as historical landmarks so they could not be demolished, and as a consequence the road could not be widened. Second, the maximum density construction was so low that making a profit was impossible, so investors decided to stay away.

Not a single exterior wall is standing upright and the differentiation between wall, roof, and floor is dissolved.

COOL AND CALCULATING

The prerequisite of the project is based purely on a cost-benefit calculation. A developer decided that the only way to utilize what was considered a commercially unviable site in the main street was to invest in "architecture." That way, marketability would be increased and thus, also, profit on the investment.

LEGAL VOLUME

The 18-ft (5.5-m) wide and 82-ft (25-m) deep site, in combination with all rules, fire regulations, building laws, the municipal development plan, and the rules of "construction near landmark buildings" resulted in a clearly defined and non-ambiguous volume. Form follows the law. A transparent and orthogonal volume was devised, which steps back from the building's historic facade by 3 ft (1 m), and thereby complies with the municipal building line set out in the development plan. According to the plan, a construction is not allowed to cover the whole site, so a stepping down of the volume is created by making terraces on each level in the back part of the site. This volume of the building is formulated according to all laws and binds itself to the rules. This is the "legal" volume.

ILLEGAL VOLUME

The second volume is formed through different measures. It is the defiant volume. How many rules can be disregarded in a place dominated and strangled by rules? As a whole, this volume is not allowed to exist at all, because its complete floor area exceeds the maximum permitted. Hence, the volume in itself is illegal. Being a non-orthogonal, free-formed body, it is mainly opaque and traces a path from street level through the gate, moving up the floors, piercing through them, and facing with its main mass at the upper levels back down upon the street, thereby completing a loop around the historic gate.

Fire regulations are disregarded and the main mass encroaches the street again, crossing the municipal building line. Not a single exterior wall is standing upright and the differentiation between wall, roof, and floor – the main categories of building elements in architecture – is dissolved. It is covered with a bright-red polyurethane coating which allows for a "construction without details" and forms a continuous skin over all surfaces of the building. This is the "illegal" volume, being disrespectful as it is of the German building code and the laws and regulations of that site in particular.

VIEWING THE CONTEXT AS THE CAPITAL

The building is a reaction to the urbanization of this part of Cologne. It introduces a foreign body into the urban fabric, and moves right up to the limits of the site, or rather, exceeds them, in its ratio of mass, its measurement, its complexity, and its materials. It ruthlessly overloads the site. It may be an architectural intervention that is not in the best interest of the suburb, but on the other hand, maybe it has a self-sufficiency. It expresses the economic situation, the constellation of laws and rules to form, and the socio-cultural condition of the suburb in a built form.

LEFT AND ABOVE
The stairwell follows the angular, non-orthogonal structure of the exterior. It also functions as a light well, allowing shafts of sunlight from the numerous skylights above to penetrate the lower levels of the building.

TOP
The cantilevered staircase appears to float within the stairwell without dominating the space. The gaps between the stair treads enable light to flow throughout the space and also permit views through to the glass doors beyond.

The Lowe Apartment LONDON, ENGLAND

Brookes Stacey Randall Architects

Completed 1995
Home type Apartment
Structure Steel frame, concrete floor, steel and timber mezzanine level, steel and glass stair

"The project has been described as 'redefining high-tech,' which I think is because it is a very warm environment; it is comfortable to spend time in. The technology helps achieve this, keeping it calm, rather than dominating. The client trained as an architect so was able to quickly grasp our ideas and give clear feedback, which helped enormously."

Nik Randall (now of Space Craft Architects)

ABOVE
The existing curved ceiling of the apartment has been combined with two curved walls to accentuate the center of the main space. Three large pull-out "pods" transform the main space into a functional and flexible area – either a dressing room, recording room, or dining/kitchen space. The rooflight opens hydraulically, so that on warm nights the owner can lie in bed and gaze at the stars.

FLEXIBILITY OF USE

Chris Lowe of the UK band Pet Shop Boys requested a flexible living space to fit within the top floor of a converted warehouse. The challenge was to maximize the sense of space, while generating flexible accommodation choices. The main volume is designed as a single room, the function of which can change depending on the facilities brought into use.

The storage area is equipped with three large pull-out "pods," each providing a different facility for the main space. By pulling out a particular pod, the space changes from kitchen/dining room to dressing room to music and recording room. The pods were designed to be flexible – all storage boxes, shelves, clothes rails, and work surfaces are fully interchangeable. Their configuration can change as the owner's needs change. When concealed, there is no evidence of the pods' tracks or wheels. The development of the pods demonstrated a successful collaboration between architect, engineer, and contractor – an optimal mix of expertise for the realization of an innovative design.

SPACE, LIGHT, AND PRIVACY

Although diversity of use was a major consideration, the architect also aimed to maintain and enhance the sense of space. The stair, with its glass treads and risers, provides minimal visual interruption to the overall volume. This is achieved by using the glass structurally, forming a folded plate in one direction and a truss in the other. No other structure is then required to hold the treads in space.

The roof area is brought into everyday use by doubling as a terrace, accessed via a folded plate-glass stair and a hydraulically opening rooflight. In summer the owner can lie in bed beneath the stars with the rooflight open and enjoy views of London's skyline.

The glass in the kitchen and dining areas is held from behind by a stainless steel support. The frame of each pane pivots to maintain privacy and allows control over the view. Although the apartment is relatively small, the repeated connections to the external environment increase the generous sense of the space.

THE LIGHT SIDE OF LIVING

The lighting concept enhances the architecture rather than simply lighting the space. Window screens are lit from behind to allow a gentle transition from day to night. Downlights can be dimmed to provide soft light to the kitchen/dining area, and the birch-faced screens contain fluorescent tubes for an even light.

The main wall runs the entire length of the apartment, disappearing around the curve to the entrance. It is lit by flush rectangular ceiling downlights.

LEFT
Recessed ceiling downlights in the bathroom are directed onto the rear of the folding screens. The sleek fittings include a heated towel rack, stainless steel bath, and a shower head with a pressure switch linked to an integrated fiber-optic light.

ABOVE LEFT
The circulation of the apartment has been designed to maximize a sense of scale, concealing views and revealing them as the user moves through the space. Privacy in the main living area is provided by pivoting glass screens covered with a birch veneer; these also generate a warm, gentle radiance.

ABOVE
The glass treads and risers of the stairs provides minimal visual interruption, allowing light to flow throughout the entire volume. Daylight is modified through a combination of translucent screens, opaque blinds, and louvers, allowing total control over the degree of privacy and light.

McAssey House SYDNEY, AUSTRALIA

Ian Moore Architects

Constructed 2005
Home type Four-level, four-bedroom family home
Structure Steel frame, concrete floor slabs, and reinforced concrete block retaining walls

"The difficulties imposed by the steeply sloping site, height limits, and four large gum trees have driven the design to produce the stepped, two-pavilion form that breaks down the scale of this large house. The small, stone-cladding tiles, with their texture and minor color variations, further reduce the scale, and complement and contrast with the trunks of the large trees retained on the site."

Ian Moore

ABOVE
The home is split into two pavilions of differing heights, each orientated differently from the other, following the irregular boundaries of the site. The placement of the pavilions has allowed the four large gum trees that graced the original site to remain. The color and texture of the trees are reflected in the exterior surfaces of basalt stone cladding and bronze aluminum.

LEFT
From the street, the house reads as a modest two story structure, although it is actually four stories high. A steel and timber entry bridge slips between the two pavilions and through a frameless glass sliding entry door.

TOP RIGHT
The main living area, visible here, is linked by the exterior timber deck to the family living area. These two areas are the only spaces on the same level across the two pavilions.

APPEARANCES CAN BE DECEIVING

An irregular-shaped block of land on a slope above Sydney's Balmoral Beach is the site of this four-bedroom home. Topography and local council height restrictions were used to create the stepped, two-pavilion form. From the street, the house appears to be two stories, rather than its actual four stories.

An entry bridge slips into the wedge of space between the two pavilions, and tumbles down a long staircase to the deck and plunge pool below. Basalt cladding and hardwood decking flow through the frameless, sliding-glass door into this space, emphasizing its treatment as an exterior, rather than an interior space.

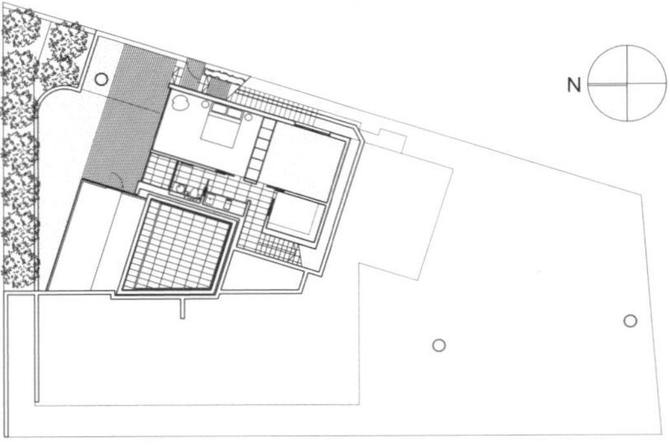

LOWEST LEVEL

A SENSUAL SKIN FOR THE HOME

Local council requirements that the house have a predominantly stone facade led to the choice of stone cladding. That the stonework is non-structural, is evident in the street facade of the two cantilevered pavilions – in the lack of grouting between the tiles and in the thickness of the tiles, visible at the corners and in the reveals. Also, thin sections of steel beam and column have been clad in bronze aluminum. Structural logic was not the driver here – rather, perfecting the shifting scales, textures, and colors of the skin.

PERFECT PAVILIONS

The main bedroom and ensuite are on the upper level of the western pavilion, and there is a roof terrace above the entry space. Immediately below are the music room/study, which overlook the double height dining area and from which there are stunning views of Sydney Harbour. Kitchen, dining, and living areas are located on the lower level, with the guest bathroom and utility room both within the kitchen "pod."

The children's bedrooms and bathrooms are on the upper level of the eastern pavilion, and a second living area and garage are on the level beneath. The lowest level of the home contains a wine cellar, gym, and self-contained guest accommodation.

The two living areas are the only spaces on the same level across the two pavilions. They are linked by a northeast facing timber deck. The plunge pool is set between these two areas.

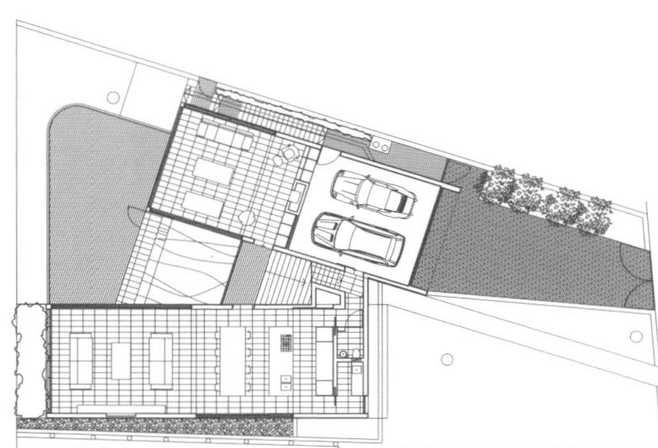
LEVEL TWO

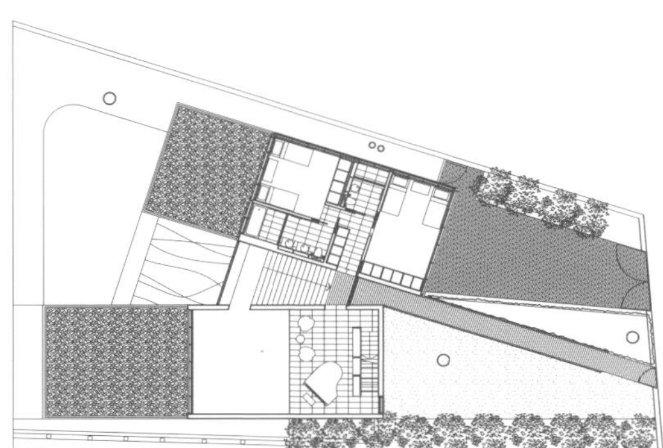
LEVEL THREE

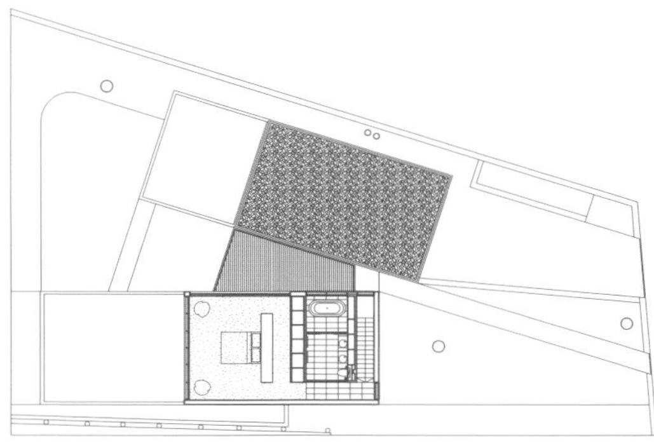
TOP LEVEL

TOP LEFT
After entering from street level, the wedge-shaped main staircase, between the two pavilions, descends dramatically to a landing that looks over the plunge pool. The stone-clad walls of the stairwell continue the theme set by the exterior, also maintaining the separation between pavilions.

TOP RIGHT
The transition from exterior to interior occurs at the stone-clad portals at the base of the main staircase – visible here, the opening into the main living area. The glass louvers effectively moderate natural ventilation.

ABOVE
Stainless steel and American oak create the kitchen's pleasing clean lines. Behind the American oak-clad storage pod lies a bathroom and utility room.

MARVELLOUS MATERIALS

The house frame is lightweight steel, which serves two purposes: first, to allow the creation of large, clear spans to help sliding doors integrate inside and outside spaces; second, to keep excavation and construction of retaining walls on the slope to a minimum. The steel beams and columns that are not part of the continuous wall plane are clad in bronze-anodized aluminum, which matches the door, window frames, and louvers. Basalt slabs are used on the floors of all living areas and bathrooms. As well, basalt wall tiles are used in the bathroom.

American oak is used for air-conditioning grilles, and joinery units – in the kitchen the oak is complemented by stainless steel benchtops. The concrete roofs are covered in large, dark gray rock ballast, providing continuity with the texture and color of the basalt cladding.

ENERGY EFFICIENCY

To reduce energy consumption, numerous passive environmental principles were integrated into the design. All living areas and bedrooms enjoy a north-easterly aspect, with cross-ventilation provided through glass sliding doors and louvers. Floor to ceiling glass lets in plenty of natural light; outside aluminum louvers provide shade.

The stone-tiled concrete floor and the 12-in- (300-mm-) thick insulated external walls and roof have a high thermal mass, thus protecting the home from extremes of temperature. A water tank beneath the rear deck collects rainwater from the roof, which is then used in the garden.

An entry bridge slips into the wedge of space between the two pavilions, and tumbles down a long staircase to the deck and plunge pool below.

LEFT
The plunge pool, viewed from the roof terrace above the main staircase. The pool is lined with the same basalt stone as the exterior walls. This image clearly shows the divergent angles of the two pavilions.

ABOVE
The main living room is glazed on three sides with views to Sydney Harbour and Balmoral Beach, and to the plunge pool, visible at right. The fourth wall contains built-in storage and a fireplace. The simple material palette of American oak, basalt stone, and bronze aluminum throughout the home ties the various areas together.

Metro Hollywood Transit Village CALIFORNIA, USA

Kanner Architects

Completed	2003
Home type	Multi-level apartment block
Structure	Heavy steel moment frames for support over the subway station; and plaster, glass, and paint

"The project is more about social impact than its design aesthetic. The design was approached with the idea that high-density, transit-oriented development can be achieved within reasonable budgets and with architecturally interesting design and materials. The increasing need for multi-family housing in a city with so little open space means developers and architects have to be more creative and thoughtful to avoid creating uninteresting, unlivable, and unsafe structures that simply serve to warehouse people."
Kanner Architects

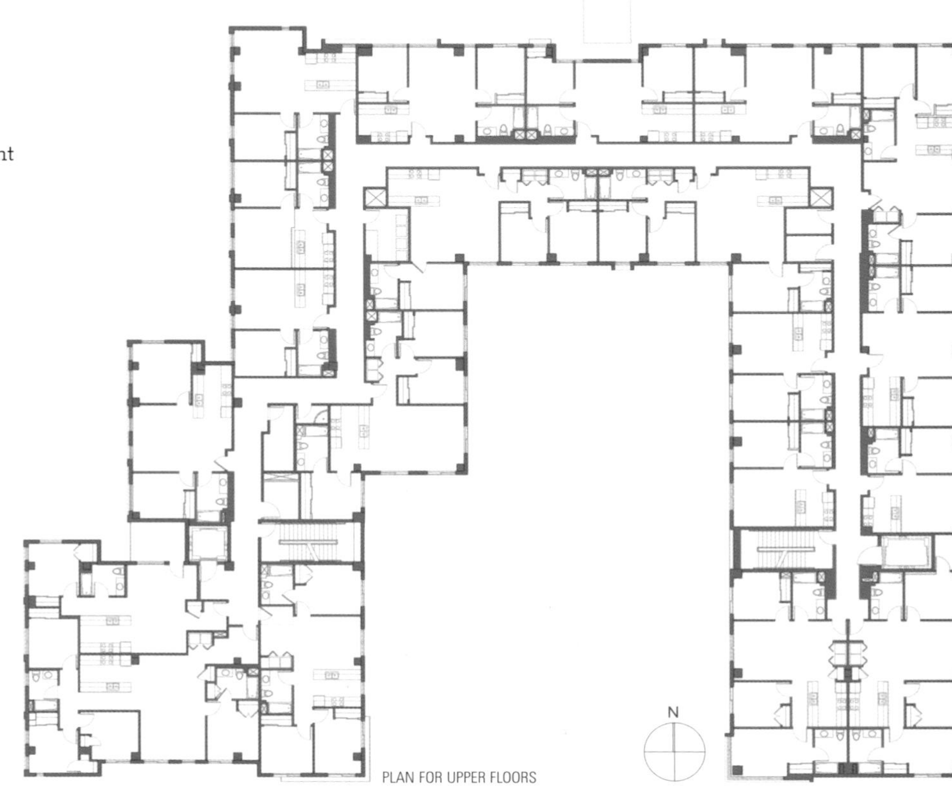

PLAN FOR UPPER FLOORS

STYLISH YET COMPLETELY AFFORDABLE

The corner of Hollywood Boulevard and Western Avenue in Hollywood is the site for this mixed-used development. Consisting of 60 mostly two- or three-bedroom home units, it sits above 10,000 sq ft (930 sq m) of retail space and a child care center. The development, designed for low-income families, is built above a subway station, so the challenge was to design a structurally sound building that came in on budget. Its central location means that the residents are easily able to commute into and around the city by subway and other public transport.

The interiors of the units are simple and spacious. The fixtures and appliances maintain the project's theme of being interesting without breaking the budget.

ABOVE
At a busy intersection in the heart of a revitalized Hollywood, Metro Hollywood Transit Village was designed with rooftop photovoltaic panels to reduce energy bills for residents.

OPPOSITE
Considering that the project sits on top of a subway station, the main design challenge was creating an inexpensive, yet structurally sound and interesting building, on a typically tight budget for "affordable" housing.

ENERGIZING BENEFITS

The architects designed Metro Hollywood as a model that exhibited social and environmental benefits for its residents, as well as being aesthetically pleasing. One area that was of particular concern for the architect was energy efficiency. Photovoltaic panels – the wing-like pieces on the roof – were placed there to lower energy usage. As a result this building performs at least 20 percent more efficiently than state codes require.

To maintain a sense of unity with the neighborhood, Metro Hollywood's large courtyard has been lined up with the existing courtyard of a nearby housing project. The effect of this is to create a large open space between the two developments. The colorful design with its modern features complements the design of the subway station that sits beneath the development.

SCHEDULING AND BUDGETARY CHALLENGES

A number of challenges confronted the architect on this project. The construction schedule was extremely tight, and had to be fast-tracked through approvals, in part because of deadlines to secure state funding for "affordable" housing.

The heavy steel frames needed to support the building above the subway station were expensive, which meant the architect had to devise cost-effective design elements elsewhere in the structure. One creative response was to reduce the number and size of the windows in the development, and to position them cleverly in both a vertical and horizontal configuration. This had the effect of limiting the noise from the street as well as the underground trains. The windows were also soundproofed.

Another strategy to stay within the constraints of the budget was to use painted plaster instead of more costly materials to replicate the colorful design of the Metro station.

Metro Hollywood Transit Village, built at the front-end of a focused revitalization of the east Hollywood community, puts people in affordable residences that they can be proud to call home and that are near to jobs and/or transportation to jobs and amenities.

TOP LEFT
In this typical top-floor corner unit, butt-glazed corner windows and simple bright interior colors effectively receive and spread light. Rooms feel spacious and bright as a result, and provide wide-angle views of the city.

FAR LEFT
Painted plaster panels on the building's exterior refer to the color scheme of the tiles in the existing subway station construction. Kanner Architects expanded on the original colors, which were basic primary hues, to develop a more dynamic and rich color scheme for the facade and finishes.

ABOVE
Strategic window orientations and protruding window details break up an otherwise simple and smooth north elevation. Touches of color and unexpected placement of routine items such as windows help bring the building to life without the need to spend money on extravagant materials or structural tricks.

RIGHT
The western elevation illustrates the raised deck upon which the project was designed. Stairs lead up to the main approach on Western Avenue and a ramp descends into the subterranean parking. The top floor isn't a floor at all, but a screen to hide the building's mechanical equipment. Strategically arranged venting grills perform a function similar to that of the windows on lower levels.

WESTERN ELEVATION

Mica House LONDON, ENGLAND

Stanton Williams Architects

Constructed 1997
Home type Penthouse apartment
Structure Steel frame top floor placed on existing warehouse building

"We tracked the path of the sun throughout the day and from season to season to make maximum use of light flowing into the apartment. The effect is a living space constantly changed by nature...the plan was to view the inside and outside as one space. We did this by careful use of glass, stainless steel, overlapping levels, screens, and sliding panels inside, with cedar decking outside."

Stanton Williams

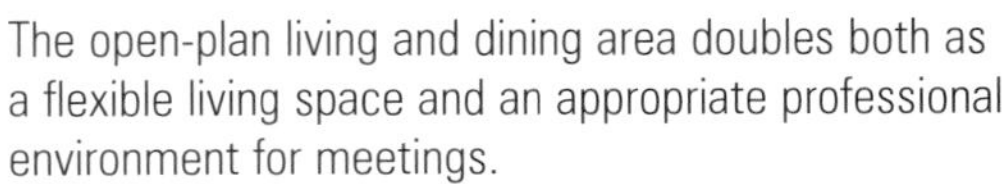

ABOVE
The living and dining area, the studio, and the main bedroom all open onto the cedar-decked terrace. The minimal glazing structure and the continuity of timber allow the interior and exterior spaces to dissolve seamlessly into one another.

ABOVE RIGHT
The careful balance of structural form with the optimum amount of glass has enabled spectacular natural illumination and reflection within the penthouse. The spatial arrangement affords a large degree of multi-use – spaces feel united by using only a limited palette of materials.

FLEXIBILITY AND FREEDOM

This flexible, light-filled apartment on the top of a refurbished factory in north London's Islington district offers multi-purpose interiors that adapt to the living and working needs of the owner.

Rather than adhering to formally defined home and office environments, the space accommodates whatever is required at the time. To avoid the "working from home" elements, the client wanted a pared-back gallery ambience – a space that is open, light, white, and furnished sparingly. The L-shaped penthouse apartment opens along its entire length onto a spacious terrace with a full-height sliding glazed wall that makes it a natural extension of the interior.

FINDING THE PERFECT PLACE

The client discovered an existing warehouse boasting 360° views. This warehouse block had been granted a change of use from light industrial to residential. Architect Paul Williams then developed an open-plan design that would afford not only comfort for the owner, but also a stimulating and appropriate backdrop for meetings and creative work.

LOOKING AT LIGHT

Driven by the orchestration of light entering the building from morning to night, the concept focused upon the color shifts of daylight throughout the day. Hence, no color is used inside; abundant light and its changing hues constantly redefines the space.

The open-plan living and dining area doubles both as a flexible living space and an appropriate professional environment for meetings.

A private elevator delivers visitors directly to the lobby of the apartment. Here the eye is drawn to the full height glass doors with views over London. The living space opens to a large, roof terrace decked in cedar.

MOVEMENT THROUGH SPACE

Three sycamore timber planes define the sleeping spaces – one pivots and folds flush into the wall, another is a door cut within a panel, and the third slides straight out of a wall.

Sycamore flooring is used throughout the apartment, and within the main living space the floor is folded up to conceal the kitchen units.

DEFINING INTERIOR SPACES

By maintaining a limited palette of materials, the plaster walls define the internal volume and reflect light around the space. Design was meticulous, with flat radiators flushed into walls, underfloor heating below the engineered sycamore boards, and sun-shading blinds concealed within the ceiling.

Other than the custom-built furniture, all elements were designed by Stanton Williams as integral sculptural entities in the project. The fixed kitchen and sliding doors allow other internal elements to become individual items in their own right.

1 back terrace
2 shower
3 bedroom 2
4 main bedroom
5 living
6 terrace
7 bathroom
8 lobby
9 elevator
10 studio
11 landing
12 kitchen
13 bedroom 3

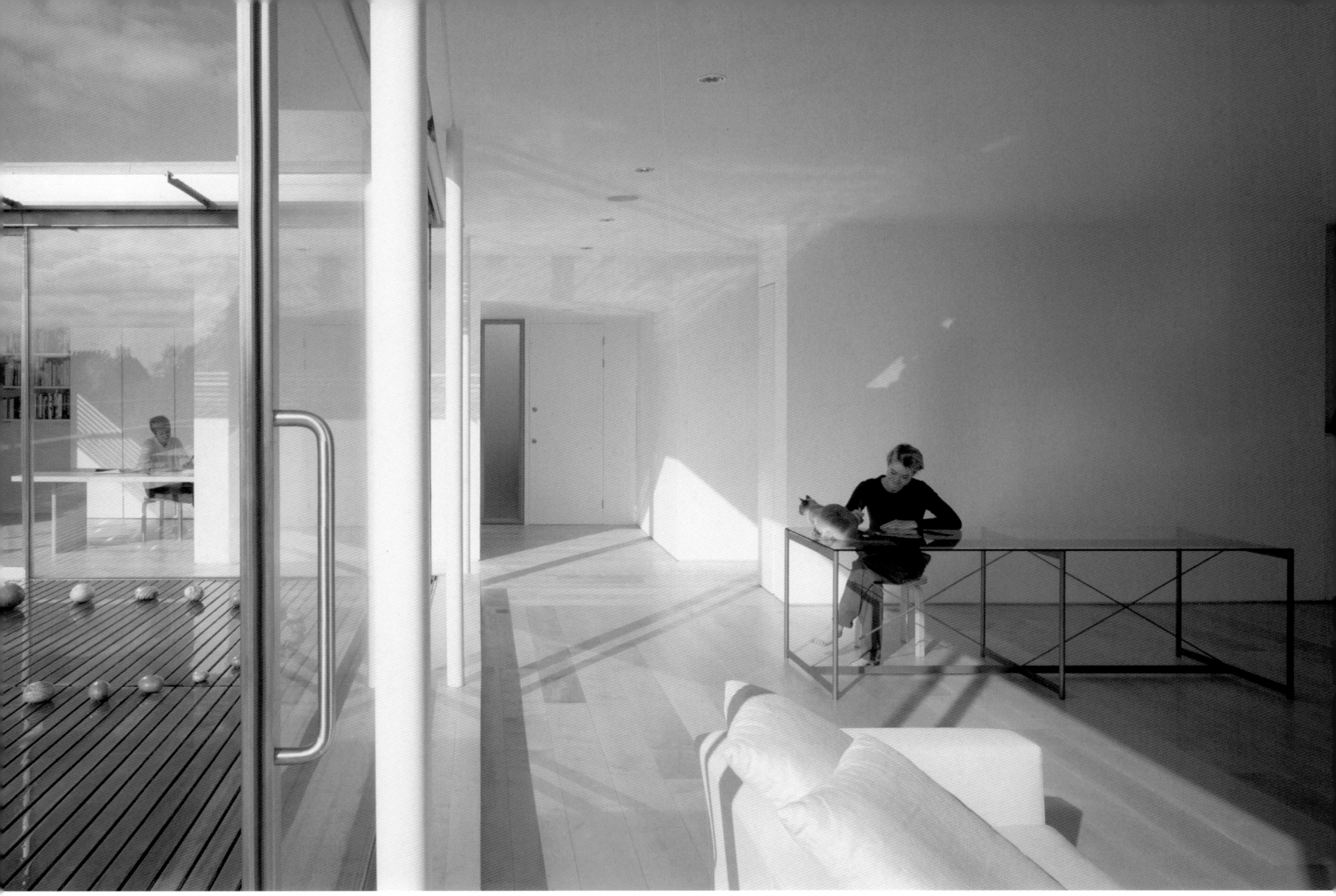

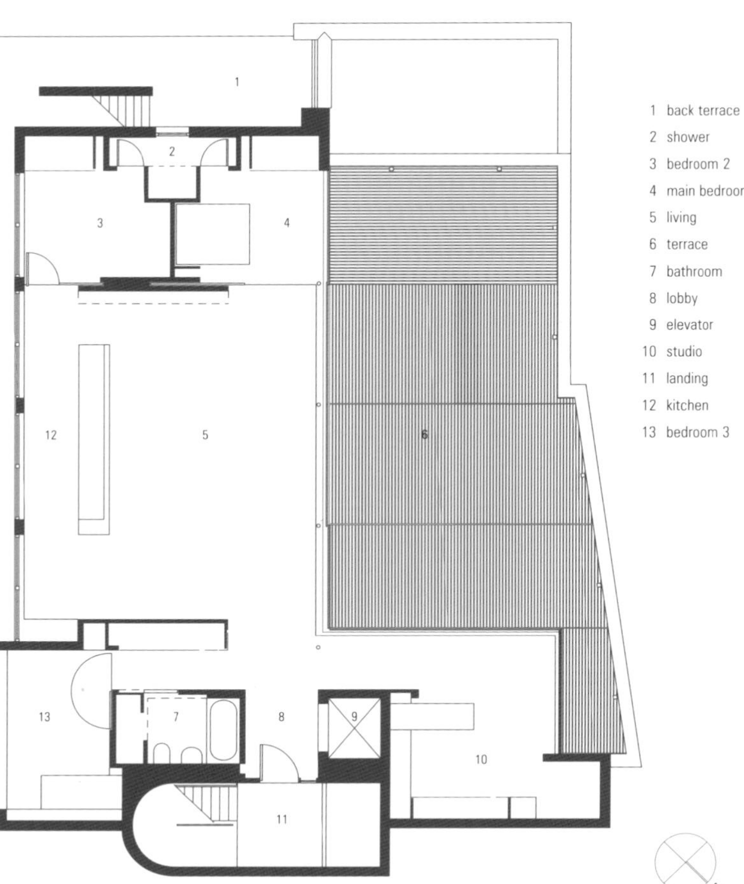

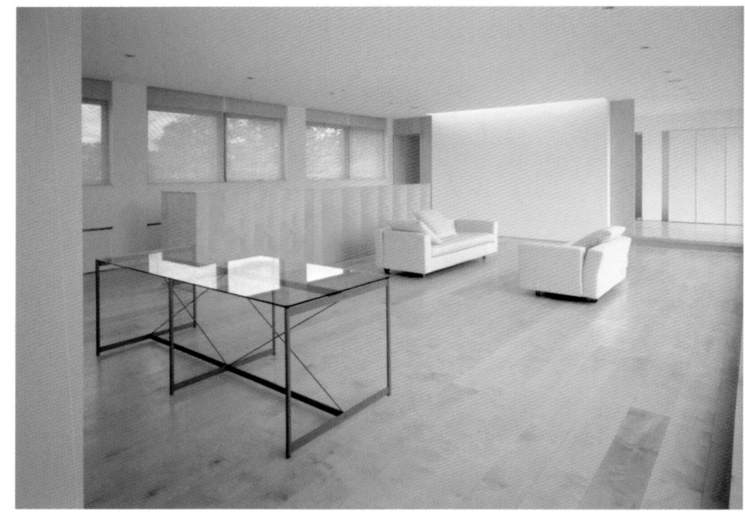

ABOVE
The simple, open-plan living and dining area doubles as both a meeting room for work and as after-hours space for the family. The kitchen is hidden by a timber screen, and a row of small windows provides a backdrop to the full-height glazing of the terrace-facing wall. The end wall is animated by natural light from the carefully carved roof light. A sycamore screen slides out of the wall creating privacy for the main bedroom.

Mitchinson Residence SYDNEY, AUSTRALIA

Stephen Varady Architecture

Construction	2003–2004
Home type	Two-story house, behind single-story historic terrace facade
Structure	Extensive alterations and additions

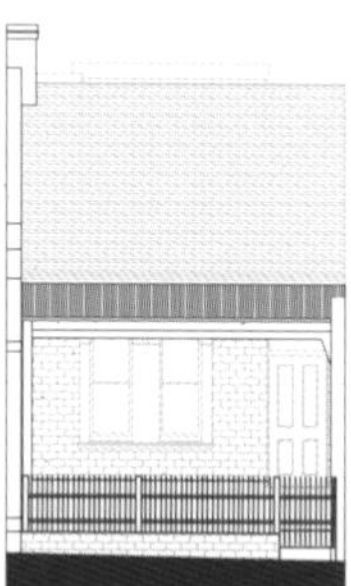

"For this project, the owner made a brave decision. She had already commissioned someone else for a design, with plans ready for council approval. She saw one of our projects and decided to start the design process again. The completed house is the outcome of a successful client/architect relationship"

Stephen Varady

ABOVE
The client desired parking but no garage and a garden, so the garage door motor is part of a mechanical sculpture that hangs over this open courtyard. To complete this ensemble, a concrete planter box hovers above. This screens views from the residential and office towers in the distance.

RIGHT
Stairway to Heaven. The stair has been used as a dramatic transition zone between the more open living areas downstairs and the private bedrooms upstairs, by focusing the view on the northern sky at the top. The transition has been further heightened through the use of red on the walls, ceiling, and floor.

WHITE AND LIGHT

This new design subverts the conventional terrace-house configuration by creating a spiral circulation path though the new house. With north to the front of the house, a courtyard was inserted into the center of the plan to draw natural light into the previously dark spaces at the rear. The staircase faces north so that it doubles as a lightshaft, bringing the low winter sunshine into the rear kitchen and dining spaces.

The client wanted a white house, as a backdrop for artworks and special personal items, but the staircase was to be a strong feature using a bright color. Red was chosen, creating a beautiful red tube, charging the senses each time one travels up or down the staircase. At different times of the day and during the different seasons, the quality of light passing through the stairwell shifts from subtle to dramatic, bathing the lower spaces in strong sunshine or soft light. The living, dining, and kitchen areas are all in one, reducing their overall size while maintaining a feeling of space, a feeling that is further heightened by "borrowing" space from the adjacent central courtyard and rear garden.

SLEEPING IN STYLE

The landing at the top of the staircase leads to the bedrooms. It has a glass floor – another method of drawing more light into the living spaces below. The bedrooms are large and private, and each has its own bathroom. To achieve a greater feeling of space, the main bedroom and ensuite "borrow" space and light

from each other through the use of a clear glass wall, allowing two modest-sized spaces to feel much bigger than they really are. The highlight windows around all four sides of the ensuite create a light-filled space that is totally private in a very constrained inner-city setting.

INTERSECTING ELEMENTS

The overall design is a sculptural composition of intersecting forms, and this is followed through with a composition of sculptural ceiling elements in the living/dining/kitchen space.

Finally, this project is the latest in an ongoing exploration of sculptural form. The architect is constantly searching for poetic sculptural forms that do not compromise the use of the spaces within. The composition of this project is a series of intersecting rectilinear elements – from the large scale to the small scale – from the overall form to the smaller sculptured ceiling of the living/dining/kitchen space.

SCREENING FROM THE OUTSIDE

The site has two street frontages. A sensitive facade was designed for the rear, which incorporates a garage door and gate. Local council insisted that some visibility be maintained from the street into the rear garden, so the garage door has a series of angled blades that give a greater sense of openness between the garden and the street, while totally blocking any view into the rear of the house.

TOP FAR LEFT
The clear glass floor landing at the top of the staircase allows for more natural light and sunshine to reach the ground floor, and also provides a dramatic transition from the staircase to the bedrooms.

LEFT
A view of the kitchen, dining, living area, and courtyard showing the composition of spaces with sculptured elements on the ceiling. The stairwell also doubles as a lightshaft, with the low winter northern sun shining right down onto the floor of the southern end of the house.

Mt Eden House AUCKLAND, NEW ZEALAND

South Pacific Architecture

Constructed	2006
Home type	Suburban, single dwelling
Structure	Two-and-a-half story concrete house

"I was very keen to work with the solidness of rock, which aside from its many attractive qualities, helped influence a decision toward a more affordable concrete construction."

Megan Rule

ABOVE
A single, cedar-paneled sliding door against a raw, prefabricated concrete panel exterior offers a simple gesture to the inner suburban street, while also disguising a third level of living space within the home.

TOP RIGHT
Glazed cedar-sliding doors open off the main living area onto a north-facing deck and a secluded back garden. A series of strip timber louvers, across the north-facing perimeter wall, offers secure cross-ventilation, while subtly connecting the two concrete panel structures.

PROBLEMS WITH THE SITE

Making maximum use of a small Auckland in-fill site, Mt Eden House is located on the rocky Mt Eden lava flow, with dry wall scoria boundaries. The surrounding housing is quite varied. In this part of Auckland, town planning regulations stipulated that new homes had to resemble villas, and this, along with a limited budget and a restrictive space of only 4,300 sq ft (400 sq m), posed something of a challenge for the architect.

The architect looked at the two-story buildings in the area, in particular the Martha Mine pumphouse in near-by Waihi, and applied its utilitarian qualities to her design, while keeping at the back of her mind some of the elements of thirteenth century monastic buildings – such as proportion, use of light, and solidity.

The size and location of the site made crane access and maneuverability difficult. The site also contained a sewer line junction and a stormwater soakpit (a chamber in the rock for natural drainage). Rock cutting was also required – rock and fertile soil were stock-piled for later landscaping of the site.

READY-MADE REMEDIES

The architect used prefabricated panel technology borrowed from commercial warehousing. This allowed for rapid construction and the bulk of the house went up over several days.

Another aspect of the design is that it offers a degree of adaptability, providing the potential for two independently operating or self-contained parts within a single residence, or perhaps, in the future, two separate residences.

Precast concrete panels were used in a further effort to economize. The panels were limited to two modular lengths of 10½ ft (3.2 m) and 4 ft (1.2 m). From these, there is a natural evolution into two major, equally sized "concrete containers," from which four minor, equally sized skylit bay windows protrude. These bay windows have wooden frames, which fit in well with older houses in the area. They provide visual relief to the exterior and interior edges of the house, while also disguising the concrete panel joints within mitered corners. In addition, they allow filtered light into both the north and south ends of the house.

LEVELS AND LIGHT

In between the two concrete containers, there is a central circulation staircase and entry space. The main living level sits above a basement entry and garage level. A deck opens off the first floor kitchen and living areas, giving a view of the rear north-facing garden.

CHARACTERISTIC FITTINGS

The double-hung windows in the bays are situated just above floor level, and when they are fully open are at handrail height. Setting them back into the rooms, as one would hang a picture frame, gives the striking effect of light and shade.

The finishing of Mt Eden House is notable for its simple use of raw materials, and the effective juxtaposition of timber and concrete. The fittings are generally inexpensive, with the joinery and interior cladding done in pine and plywood.

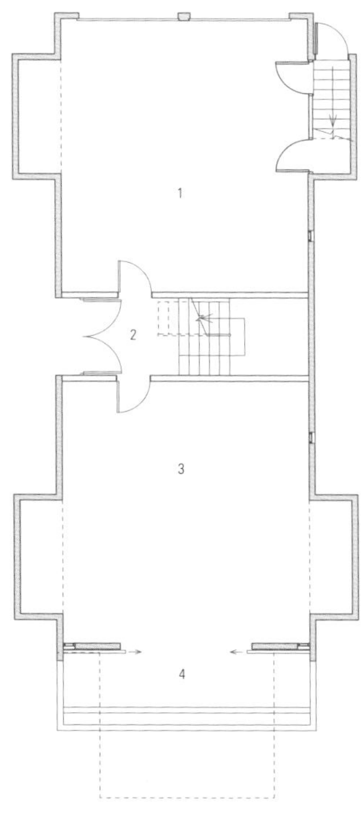

GARDEN LEVEL

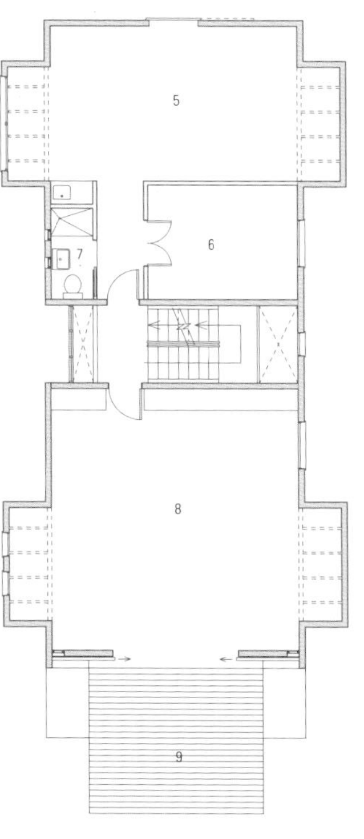

GROUND FLOOR

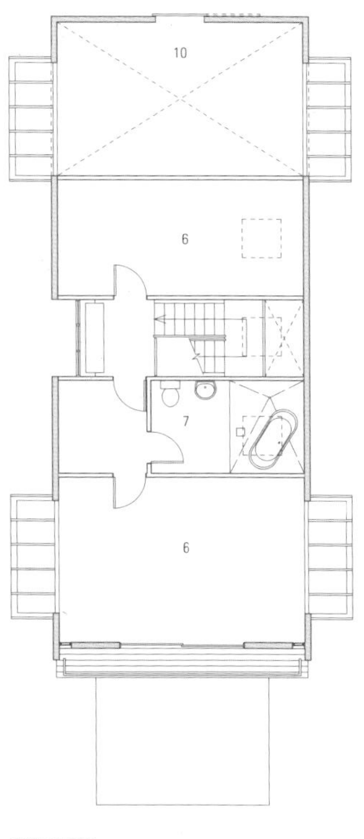

FIRST FLOOR

1 garage
2 entry
3 workshop
4 courtyard
5 studio
6 bedroom
7 bathroom
8 living/kitchen
9 deck
10 open to below

LEFT
Two "concrete living containers" are divided by a central circulation staircase – constructed almost entirely of pine and plywood. Translucent sheet cladding filters light onto a raw interior of timber against concrete.

ABOVE
Viewed from the bedroom loft above, the skylit bay – and the distinct alcove of light-filled space it creates – modulates the exterior and interior edges of the home. At the same time, it provides a means to disguise concrete panel joints within mitered corners.

Orange Grove CALIFORNIA, USA

Pugh + Scarpa Architects

Constructed 2006
Home type Multi-family loft condominiums
Structure Cast-in-place concrete on the first floor; conventional wood framing above the concrete

"Charles Eames once said that ideas are not subject to ownership but exist in the world and are waiting to be snatched up and worked upon. In selecting an idea to develop or work upon, Eames described the responsibility that came with this. He said that a designer must treat the ideas with the utmost of care and invention, otherwise, the ideas would be ruined forever for all others."

Pugh + Scarpa Architects

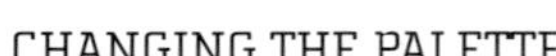

CHANGING THE PALETTE

Orange Grove makes a bold new architectural statement in the City of West Hollywood. It is a sensitively designed building that blends in well with the neighborhood, which is characterized by traditional bungalow-style, single-family dwellings. What makes Orange Grove special, however, is the manner in which it diverges from the overwhelming mood of the area, and yet remains compatible with it. The material palette and scale is different – rather than use traditional pitched roof forms, Orange Grove has been designed using Modernist principles. So it is eclectic and unconventional, but still sits consistently in its surroundings.

The large balcony in the front facade gives the building a strong relationship to the streetscape, yet Orange Grove is certainly distinct from nearby houses and other buildings.

A SENSE OF SCULPTURE

The large-scale elements of the building instill it with drama, but it is also broken down into manageable human-scale parts, and then further divided into two different buildings. Because of its flaunting of convention, Orange Grove can, in a sense, be likened to the Schindler House, which is an icon of Californian Modernism located only a short distance away. As with the Schindler House, the windows, balcony and

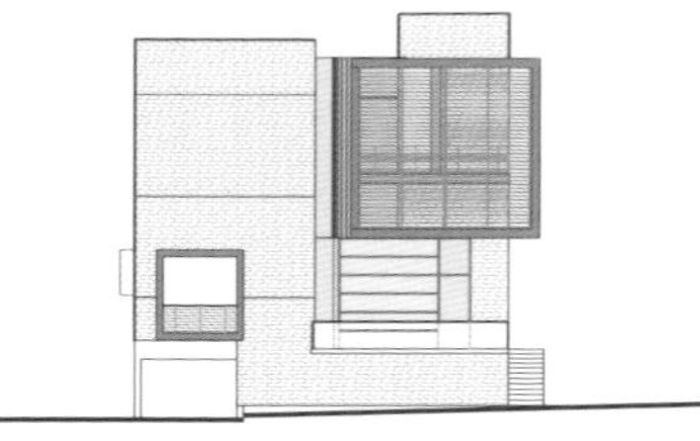

East elevation

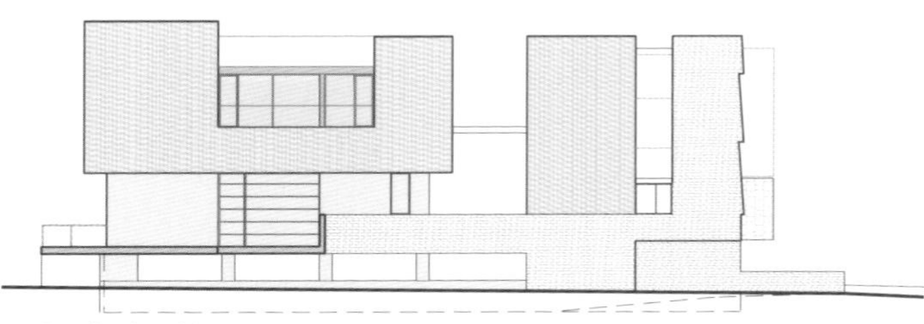

South elevation

ABOVE
The bedroom flows out to the terrace, which opens both spaces onto the street, connecting the whole structure to the neighborhood.

RIGHT
The building mass is broken into smaller elements that fit into the scale of the street and the neighboring structures of mainly bungalow-style homes.

NO
PARKING
8AM TO 10AM
FRIDAYS
NO
PARKING

ABOVE
Unit number five features a sky-lit, 20-ft (6-m) high mezzanine and 18-ft (5.5-m) ceilings in the living space. The effect successfully demonstrates the architects' vision of simple interior volumes of space.

TOP
Detail of the private area upstairs, with its distinctive horizontal opening that frames the city view to the south. The design creates a cosy atmosphere as well as inviting the outside world inside.

OPPOSITE
The light filled volume of the small living space opens out to the street when the garage door is open.

other typical architectural elements of Orange Grove have a sculptural essence to them. The windows have been inserted into the spaces between different sections of the building.

BALANCING TENSIONS

One way to describe the design of Orange Grove is as a subtle balance of tensions. A three-dimensional composition is created by the strategic placement of windows, doors, balconies, and building volumes. This generates a feeling of fluidity to the building. Each part of the structure has a clearly defined shape – for example, the corrugated metal surround enclosing the second floor balcony in the north and east facades.

Another example of this demarcation can be seen in the two square-profile balcony surrounds in the front facade. One of them is small and open at the front, while the other is large and veiled with stainless steel slats. Yet in spite of these contrasts, each balcony maintains a sense of overall balance and is closely related to other elements of the building.

LIGHT, SPACE, AND ART

The architects wanted all the elements of the building to be interpreted as abstract, so even though a window is a window, it also can be seen as a slit, or as a framed box.

Orange Grove encapsulates the notion – and reality – of large, simple interior volumes of space. It is a model whose foundations are space, light, and the industrial materials of the loft, which is the antithesis of the bungalow. In this regard, the building responds to the wishes of a burgeoning niche market of clients who want something distinctive and open, and which caters to their lifestyle choices.

Parnell House AUCKLAND, NEW ZEALAND

Crosson Clarke Carnachan Architects

Constructed 2002
Home type Single dwelling
Structure Concrete slab lower floor, timber upper floor and wall framing

"This is an exploration of the dichotomy between the architectural style of an 1870s Victorian cottage and a modern, minimalist design. The project was about combining and modifying a nineteenth-century building to fit a twenty-first century lifestyle."

Simon Carnachan

ABOVE
The facade of the house had to be retained due to local planning restrictions, which listed the home as a heritage building.

RADICAL REFORM

The original cottage on this site was built in the 1870s for a sea captain, and because of its history, the local planning authorities stipulated that the facade be retained in order to comply with the area's heritage zoning. The original cottage interior, however, has been completely replaced.

The brief for Parnell House was to remove the existing, badly constructed, sub-standard "lean-to" and replace it with a new double height addition. One of the most effective ways of reducing the bulk of the building was to locate the new kitchen, bathroom, and service areas underneath the existing house.

The architect decided to leave the existing cottage and its front veranda and to completely refurbish the rest of the exterior of the building, so that it was in the same style as other houses in the area, thus maintaining the character, scale, and appearance of the street.

The original chimney conceals a skylight to the guest bedroom, and a loft has been added in the roof space, which has views across to the adjacent reserve and the city beyond.

Another decision was to provide a negative detail/recess to isolate the new addition from the cottage. This meant that the simple cottage shape with its pyramidal roof was not only maintained, but accentuated.

VANISHING ACTS

The walls were removed from the original cottage layout, although the original hallway was kept. The main bedroom now opens to natural light and pleasing views. The sandblasted glass sliders can close off the bedroom for privacy. The ensuite and wardrobe are extensions of the main bedroom, rather than separate rooms, giving the feeling of openness.

MORE THAN JUST PARKING

Another consideration for the site was car parking. This was provided on site by disguising the front of the garages and then recessing them so that they resembled walls coming from the side of the house. As well, louvers were added to clad the garage doors – this kept the horizontal weatherboard look at the front of the house.

EAST ELEVATION

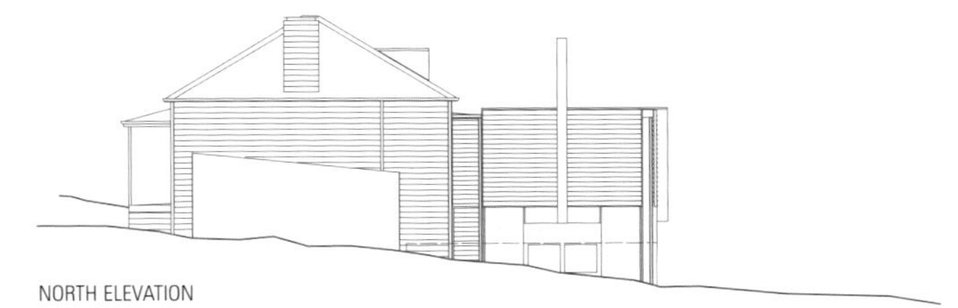

NORTH ELEVATION

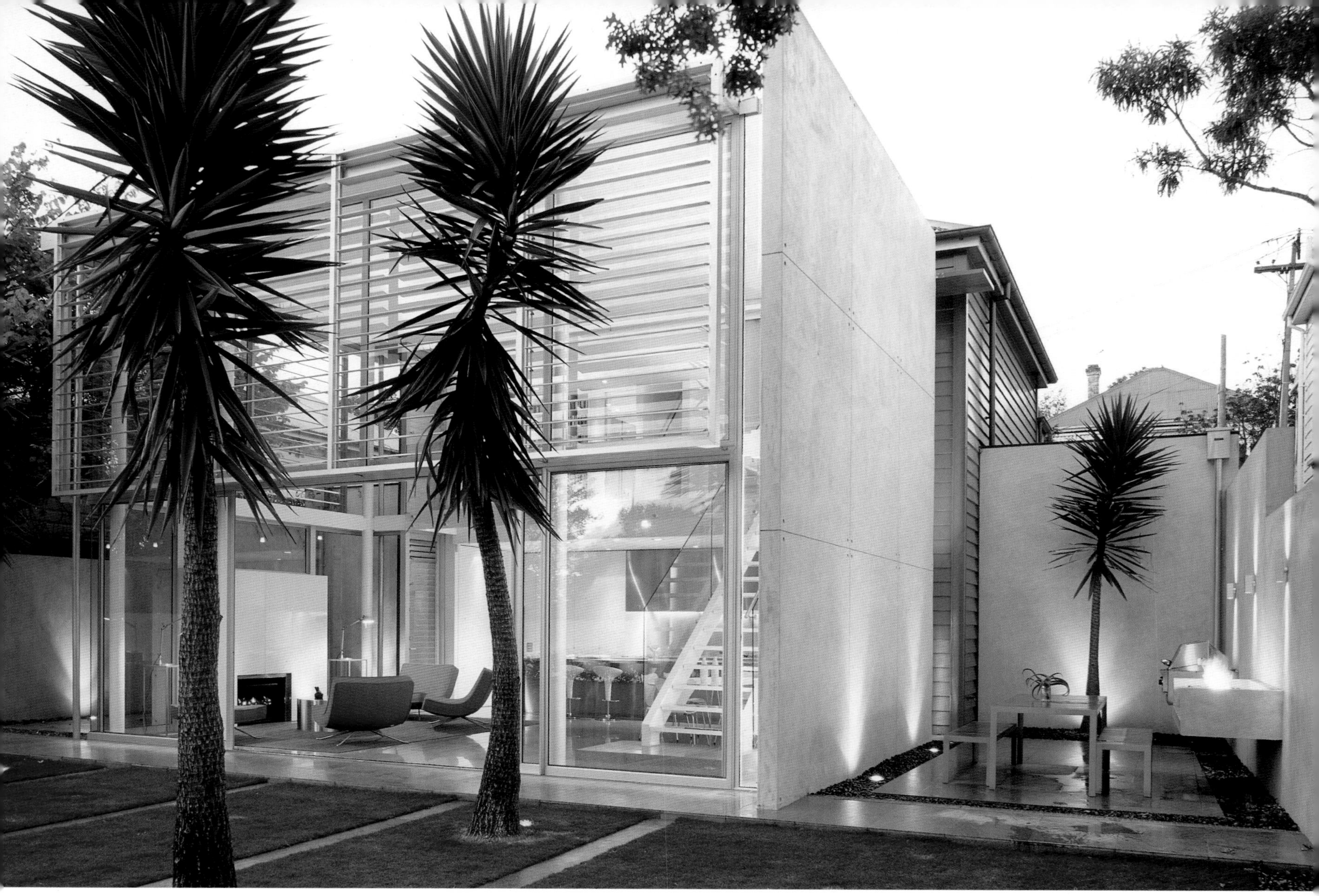

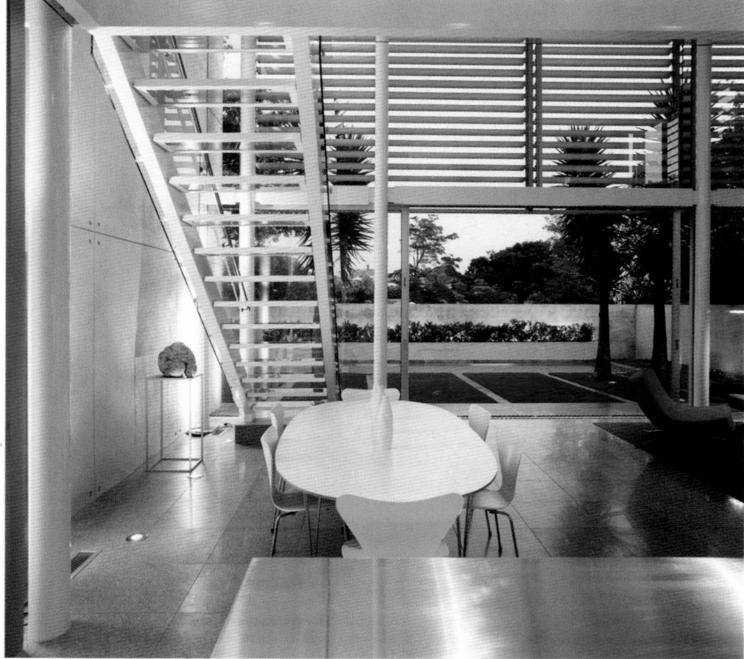

1 garage
2 main bedroom and bathroom
3 bedroom
4 bathroom
5 open to below
6 kitchen
7 dining/living
8 library
9 veranda

GROUND FLOOR

FIRST FLOOR

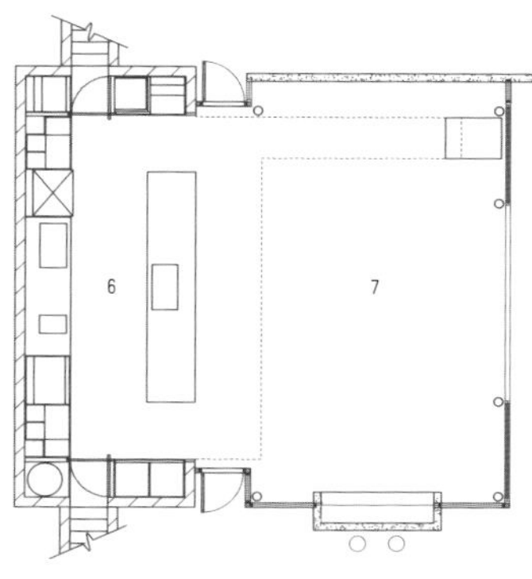

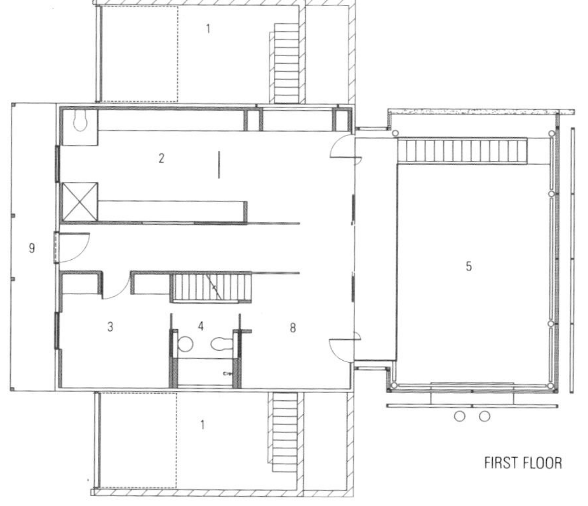

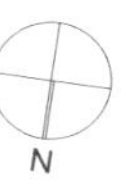

TOP
The rear courtyard features grass with inlaid tile lines, and yuccas, selected for their dramatic foliage. The gas flares and table are perfect for evening outdoor dining.

ABOVE
The glass and steel stairs, and the exterior louvers over the glass box at the rear of the house are functional, while also adding a sleek charm to the structure.

Louvers were also used over glazed areas to continue the horizontal weatherboard appearance. In fact, the garage performed another function – it disguised the building in the backyard and minimized the view from the street.

SMALL, SIMPLE, SUPER

The level of the new addition was constructed under the gutter line of the existing house, and the whole essence of the idea was to keep the addition simple and small.

Materials are also simple and minimalist. The timber floor is oiled tawa, a native New Zealand timber, and the appliances are stainless steel. The glass walkway and stairs are stylish and elegant, and the exterior louvers are aluminum. Colored halogen lights are recessed into the floor in the entry hall, providing a warm welcome.

The courtyard is the essence of simplicity. The lawn is inlaid with honed basalt tiles, which add warmth and texture, and four yuccas were planted to add a striking foliage feature to the area. The lap pool and jacuzzi are separated by glass.

ABOVE
Pivot doors are designed to look like part of the kitchen and also to provide access to the garages, which are located on either side of the house.

TOP LEFT
The kitchen is white and stainless steel, with a stainless-steel island bench. The glass walkway allows "borrowed" light from above into the kitchen below.

OPPOSITE
The exterior view looking from the rear courtyard. The exterior louvers are aluminum with aerofoil-shaped blades. They are adjustable in order to offer protection from the afternoon sun.

Skybox WELLINGTON, NEW ZEALAND

Melling:Morse Architects

Construction	2001–2002
Home type	City house, single dwelling
Structure	Three-level timber box bolted to steel frame

"The visible separation of the Skybox from my office building beneath is far more than an architectural conceit. The concept really works – aided by the wind slapping against its underbelly, there is no awareness inside the box of the sometimes stressful world it seeks to escape."

Gerald Melling

ABOVE
The underbelly of the Skybox is deliberately exposed to both the eye and the elements. An electric hoist is a valuable conveyance for furniture, appliances, boxes of groceries, as well as bicycles.

RIGHT
Egmont Street is a narrow mid-city alleyway of early twentieth-century warehouses, most of which have been re-engineered and adapted for apartments over the past decade. On its lofty steel frame, the Skybox is inserted into a gap above the continuous wall of brickwork that lines the west side of the street.

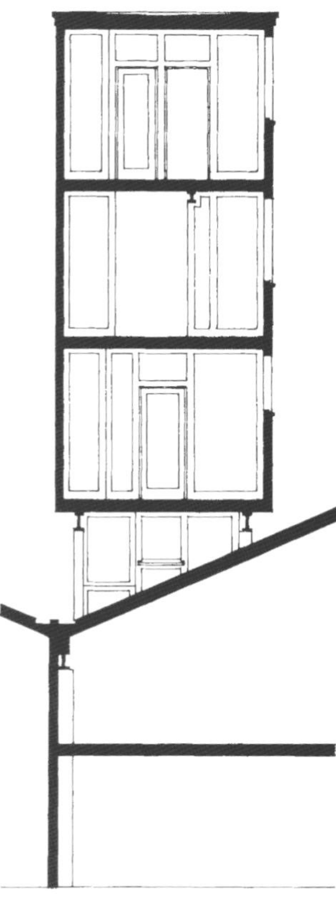

LEFT

Heavily glazed on three of its four sides (east, north, and west), the Skybox is an effective solar heater. Its system of fenestration is a gentle satire on the archetypal Modernist curtain-wall of the commercial building, here constructed in natural timber with infill panels of fixed glazing, louvers, and flat colorsteel sheet glued to plywood. The vertical orange neon "Skybox" sign is a participatory gesture to the 24-hour life of the city.

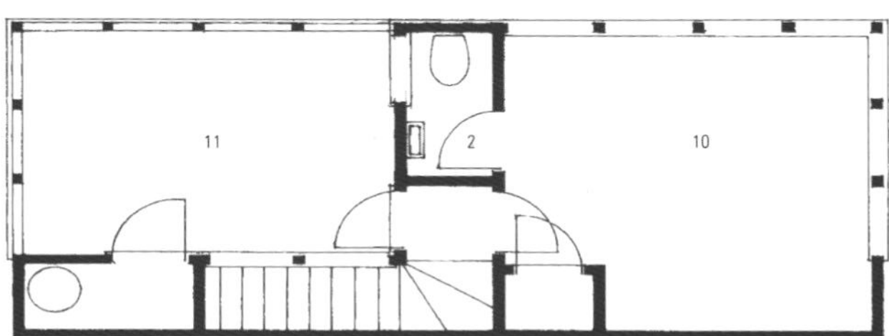

LEVEL THREE

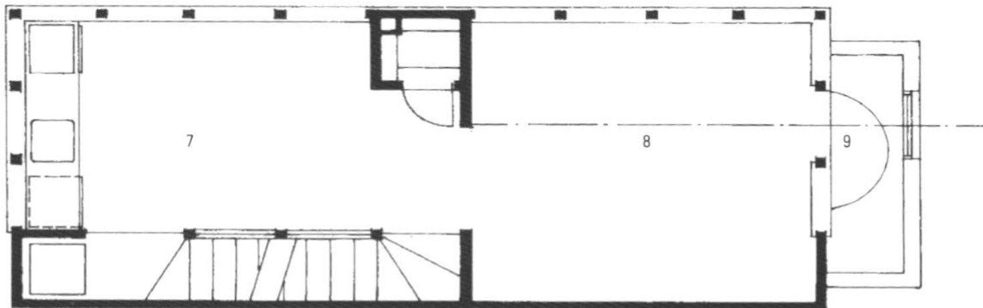

LEVEL TWO

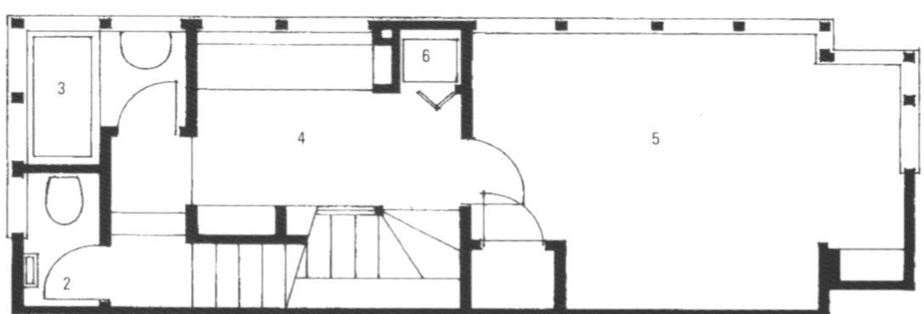

LEVEL ONE

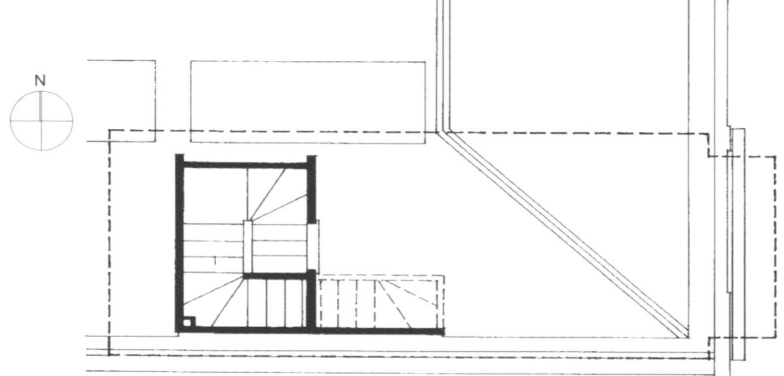

STAIRCASE SHAFT

1 staircase
2 WC
3 bathroom
4 study
5 main bedroom
6 laundry
7 kitchen/dining
8 living/sitting area
9 balcony
10 guest bedroom
11 loggia

TOP RIGHT
The east-facing nose of the sitting area (level 2) becomes a morning balcony, cantilevered over the street. The glazed gate in the balustrade wall opens to allow access for items lifted from the street on the electric hoist. All the internal timbers are environmentally-friendly macrocarpa, which does not require chemical treatment.

RIGHT
The staircase arrives at the study (level 1), running between a wall of bookshelves (the "library") and a wall of opal glass, which "borrows" and enhances sunlight into the staircase shaft. Wall and ceiling linings are predominantly colorsteel sheet on plywood or plasterboard.

ABOVE
A macrocarpa and stainless-steel kitchen bench abuts the western end of level 2, overlooking an urban village of assorted apartments in adjacent buildings, both old and new. Window glass is direct-glazed into exposed structural framework (macrocarpa posts and lintels); the louvers are assembled kit-sets.

REINVENTING WELLINGTON

Melling:Morse Architects are known for their small timber houses, which have been enlivening the hinterlands of Wellington (the capital city of New Zealand) for more than a decade. This pursuit of domestic architectural opportunity has now continued into the heart of the city, down a narrow lane lined with colonial brickwork and the ghosts of an early twentieth-century red-light district. Gerald Melling's Skybox, his own living accommodation above his office warehouse, suggests an architecture of limitless urban possibility.

In recent years, Wellington has been relentlessly reinventing itself through the inhabitation of its core. Along with new apartment blocks, domestically converted commercial and historic buildings have brought new life to the nation's cultural and administrative hub. Like most cities, however, the center of Wellington tends towards architectural chaos. Melling's response has been to bring order to his air space.

LIVING AND WORKING IN THE SAME – YET DIFFERENT – SPACE

The notion of live/work/play in the same location is the new urban paradigm. While endorsing this, Melling recognizes the sanity in an appropriate degree of segregation – hence the Skybox displays a physical, visual, and conceptual independence from the office building beneath it, connected only by the concealed umbilical cord of its staircase shaft. A lofty steel frame slung high over the roof of the existing building provides a platform for the box's apparent autonomy.

NARROW FOOTPRINT, WIDE VISION

The narrow footprint (11½ ft x 26 ft [3.5 m x 8 m]) of the Skybox is defined by its supporting steel frame. The box itself is made up of three layers of plywood-braced timber frame, using a 36 in (900 mm) planning grid and 9 ft (2.7 m) ceiling heights. The lowest level – with main bedroom, study, and bathroom – is deliberately reclusive, reflected in higher window-sill heights than those of the upper two layers. The intermediate level is an open space for kitchen, dining, and living, with a small, east-facing balcony cantilevered over the street. The top floor provides a guest room and a covered loggia.

Clad in vertical corrugated steel, the cold south face of the Skybox is completely closed. All other facades open to the warmth of the sun, the views, and the adjacent cityscape.

SUMPTUOUS SKIN

The Skybox's skin is a consistent, low-maintenance grid framed in macrocarpa and filled with direct glazing, glass louvers, colorsteel sheet, and plywood. While the external rough-sawn timber is allowed to weather to a natural silver-gray, internal timbers are dressed smooth and sealed against steel-clad linings – a sophisticated counterpoint of soft versus hard, warm versus cool, human versus slick.

Straddling an industrial warehouse of humble origin, the Skybox moves – quite literally, layer by layer – from the ordinary to the extraordinary. Planning approvals were only reluctantly granted by city fathers who imagined the Skybox as tilting at windmills. Certainly, it rocks in a gust of wind, but rarely has a New Zealand architect been so well-cradled under Pacific moons.

Solar Umbrella CALIFORNIA, USA

Pugh + Scarpa Architects

Constructed	2005
Home type	Single-family home renovation and addition
Structure	Tilt-up concrete, steel, and wood framing

"Kiesler once wrote, 'Our Western world has been overrun by masses of art objects. What we really need are not more and more objects, but an objective.'"

Pugh + Scarpa Architects

ABOVE
It was important to the clients to integrate principles of sustainability into the design, so the architects looked at the whole site and took advantage of as many opportunities as possible in order to create a sustainable living environment. This included reorienting the house 180° for better solar orientation.

RIGHT
The old backyard has been transformed into a new entry court. Instead of using concrete or stone when remodeling the home, the architects used decomposed granite and gravel hardscape, including a storm-water retention basin, which allows the ground to absorb water as well as alleviate urban run-off to the ocean – a vast improvement on less environmentally friendly alternatives. The landscaping is purposely low maintenance and is complemented by the use of drought-tolerant xeriscaping, which also sits well with the texture and colors of the house.

SUSTAINABLE LIVING

Venice, California is populated with mostly single-story bungalows, and the Solar Umbrella is a bold precedent for the area, its double-story, environmentally sensitive form setting a standard for a new generation of Modernist architecture. The site is 41 ft (12.5 m) wide and 100 ft (30 m) long. The existing 650-sq-ft (60.5-sq-m) bungalow was transformed into a 1,900-sq-ft (176.5-sq-m) residence that proclaims itself ready for the challenges of the twenty-first century.

Inspired by Paul Rudolph's "Umbrella House" of 1953, the Solar Umbrella is a modern reinvention of the solar canopy, which provides thermal resistance to hot summers and protection against cold winters. Sustainability was important, so the architects looked at the whole site and took advantage of as many opportunities as possible to create a sustainable living environment.

CAPTURING THE SUN'S ENERGY

Using both active and passive solar design techniques, energy consumption is neutral. In addition, the majority of the materials used in the interior are made from recycled or renewable products. All materials used for the building itself and the landscaping around it were chosen because of their aesthetic and actual impact on the site. The result is an artistic sensory experience.

Another consideration the architects took into account was aspect – they rotated the residence 180° from its original orientation, so what used to be the front and main entry at the north became the back facing south. As well as allowing optimal exposure to the southern sunlight, this gave the architects more space, and a chance to create a more welcoming introduction to the building.

Solar panels are wrapped around the south elevation. They protect the building from the intensity of the sun, and also absorb and transform the captured sunlight into usable energy – in fact, all the electricity in the home is provided by this strategy. The solar canopy is functional, performing the role of energy collector, but also aesthetically pleasing, with an interesting experimental effect.

EXPANDING SPACES

One wall at the south was removed, and the primary layout of the existing dwelling retained. The original bungalow was quite compact, and now there is a large addition to the south – it includes a new entry, living area, main bedroom, and laundry and storage areas.

The kitchen, formerly at the back of the house, now opens up into a large living area, which in its turn, opens out to a generously sized front yard. A glass

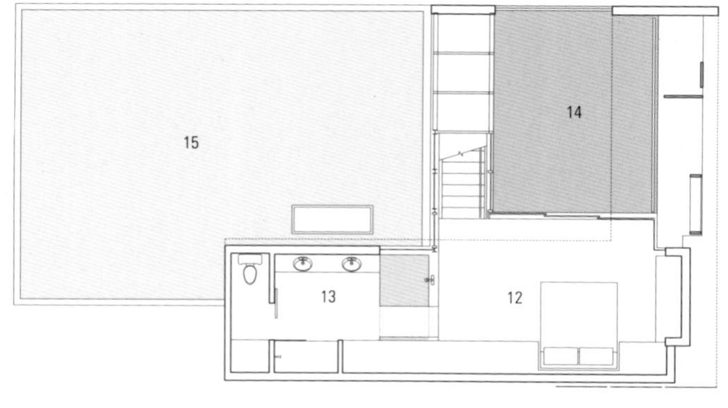

FIRST FLOOR

1 study
2 closet
3 bedroom
4 bathroom
5 dining room
6 kitchen
7 living room
8 utility closet
9 laundry
10 fish pond
11 jacuzzi
12 main bedroom
13 main bathroom
14 terrace
15 roof below

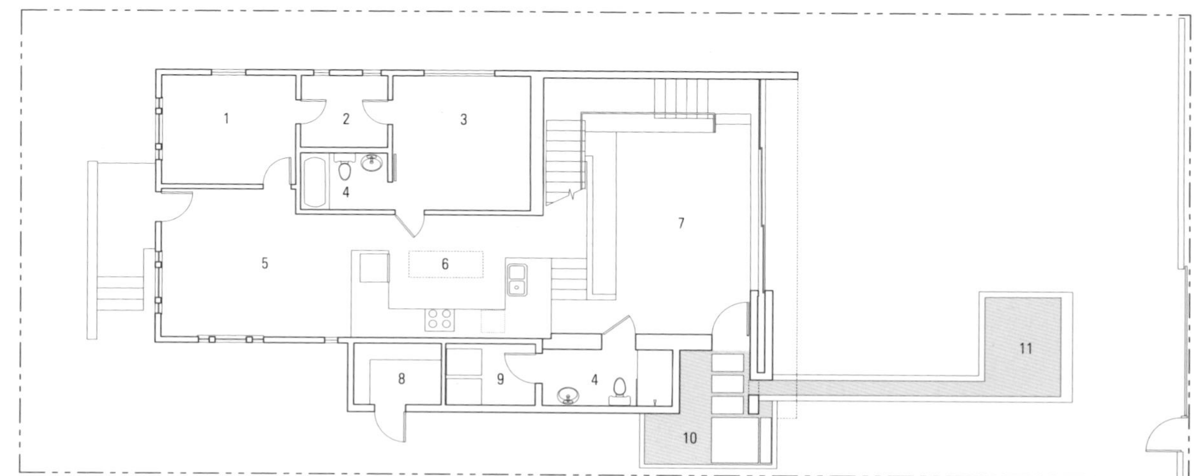

GROUND FLOOR

wall in the living area marks the boundary between inside and outside, and creates a visual walkway from one end of the site to the other.

EXTERIOR SPACES, INTERIOR FEEL

Exterior spaces are thought of as "outdoor rooms" and the architects have achieved this by creating strong visual and physical links between the interior and exterior, resulting in a more energetic relationship between the two.

This blurring of boundaries is further accentuated by the entry area along the western edge of the site. A concrete pool – a convincing landscape element in its own right – marks the route to the front door. At the entry, the pool cascades into a lower level of water. A variation on the concept of the welcome mat is provided by the stepping stones. They are immersed in water and create an exciting invitation to the inside of the home. Once again, the outside and the inside come together.

The main bedroom is on the second level and demonstrates the strategy of interlocking space. It is situated above the living area and accessed by a set of floating, folded-plate steel stairs. The room opens onto a covered terrace overlooking the garden, extending the bedroom space outside. The overall impression is of a loft exposed to the outside. The bedroom terrace not only brings the outside in, it also provides the front elevation with a view of the garden.

This deep terrace carves out an exterior space within the visual bounds of the building envelope and provides the front elevation with a unique character. The second level is not enclosed at all, but rather, it is protected by the planes that wrap around it.

LIGHT AND TRANSPARENCY

The design is given depth and richness through the composition of interlocking solid and open spaces. Views are visible from the front to the back, giving the house a transparent quality. These "visual corridors" contain the formal elements of the home, such as stairs, guardrails, bearing walls, structural columns, built-in furniture, and cabinetwork, but they vary in density, texture, and color.

Natural light is plentiful and the stepped roofs and clerestory windows emphasize the light and generate light and shadow at various times of the day, which serves to enliven the more permanent fixtures of the design. The outcome is a layered composition with plenty of interest, both formal and informal.

MATERIALS FOR BEAUTY AND PERFORMANCE

The materials used in the residence have been artfully used as design features, for example, an acoustic panel, made from recycled newspaper, was palm-sanded and employed as the finish material for the custom-made cabinets. Oriented strand board, a structural grade building material, became the main flooring material besides concrete.

FAR LEFT
The new living space flows unbroken into the entry court. Privacy screens made from steel and industrial brooms shield the main bedroom, on the second floor, from direct view.

ABOVE
In the kitchen/dining area the natural cherry dining table is complemented by the cabinets and flooring. Both of these are made from oriented strand board, which is both cost effective and meets with the owner's wishes of using long-lasting and environmentally responsible materials.

TOP RIGHT
An airy, light filled space is created by having the main bedroom opening out onto a covered terrace that overlooks the garden. The feeling of space is further accentuated as the bedroom flows seamlessly into the light filled main bathroom.

RIGHT
Detail of the floating, perforated steel staircase leading to the main bedroom. The medium and design of the staircase, off the main living area, continues with the theme of flooding the house in light, and is an architectural feature in its own right.

SOMA House SAN FRANCISCO, USA

Jim Jennings Architecture

Completed 1998
Home type Two-story, single-family residence
Structure Steel, translucent glass, concrete, and wood

"Every client desires some degree of invention from their architect. With this house, invention occurred not only in the design and physical making of the place, but in the infusion of a type and standard of living into a part of town where it hadn't previously existed."
Jim Jennings

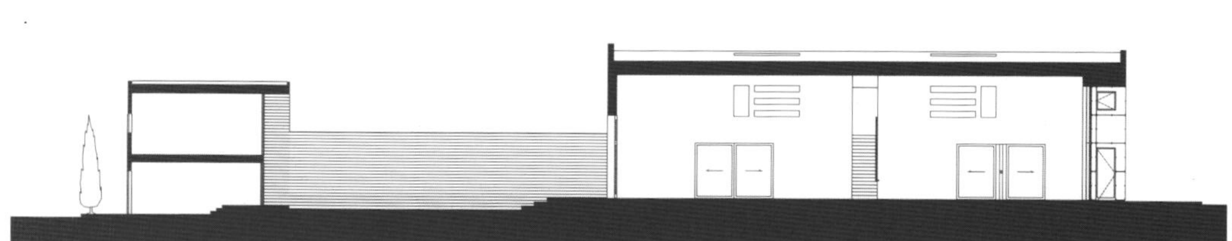

ABOVE
SOMA's street elevation is a modern graphic presence in a transitional urban neighborhood. Steel panels make up the bulk of the facade; a two-story, four-part grid of translucent glass, a smooth counterpoint to the hard metal, allows diffused light into the main interior.

TOP RIGHT
An interior courtyard is situated between the main house and the studio/guesthouse. The limestone-paved terrace is flanked by rows of black-trunk bamboo in pebbles. A wood screen wraps the courtyard and forms a contrasting element with the home's concrete rear wall.

ELUSIVE EDGE

Located in San Francisco's south of Market district (SOMA) – an industrial precinct with few single-family residences – SOMA House retains the foundations and concrete walls of its former function as an old commercial building, and presents a modern yet enigmatic face to the denizens of this gritty urban neighborhood.

ABSTRACTED FORMS

The house, courtyard, and separate studio/guesthouse span from the busy street frontage to the rear alley. The building's inscrutable facade features translucent glass and perforated steel. The steel is spaced away from the building wall so that small holes in each panel focus light inside. In a "camera obscura" effect, multiple images are projected onto the translucent glass interior walls, which when viewed from the inside display the abstracted motion of the exterior. Apart from this element of visual complexity, the spacious interiors are light-filled, minimally detailed, and serene.

The heart of the two-story house is a long and high living/dining area that runs along half the building and opens to the courtyard. This airy space, capped by a barrel-vaulted ceiling, features white walls, swaths of wood and steel, and a light-colored travertine floor. The other half contains a kitchen, pantry and study/office on the ground level and two bedrooms overhead, reached via a poured-concrete stairway.

The living area is mostly maintained as one open-plan space. However, sliding partitions of translucent glass, framed in mahogany and blued steel, are sometimes used to seal off the front area as an office conference room. The partitions can also divide the study and kitchen from the main area.

TRANSLUCENT ILLUMINATIONS

Natural light signifies the house. An abundance of diffused northern light, ushered through the translucent glass at the front, is balanced by bright sunlight from the south, streaming through the glass wall to the courtyard. Skylights are scattered above both floors.

Translucent glass bands, set in rectangular reliefs, bring copious light into the massive bedrooms and ensuite bathrooms. Although each bedroom has a lower, more intimate ceiling than the living area below, they are not identical; the southern bedroom has roof access, while the northern bedroom has a walk-in wardrobe and part of the "camera obscura" effect on its bathroom wall. Both bathrooms are sheathed in limestone.

The rectangular courtyard is lined in Alaskan yellow cedar planks, echoing the siding of the adjacent building. The minimalist look of the rest of the house continues with the use of limestone pavers, pebbles, and black-trunk bamboo for landscaping. With no transparent windows on the perimeter, the courtyard is the building's sole link to the natural environment.

ABOVE RIGHT
The glazed front door, largely hidden from the street, is tucked into a recess in the steel facade. The perforated steel transmits light to the interior through a translucent glass wall for a "camera obscura" effect.

RIGHT
The studio/guesthouse also incorporates an alley garage. Alaskan yellow cedar planks and floor-to-ceiling glass are the predominant materials of this secondary structure, whose upper level looks out over the private outdoor area.

1 living
2 office
3 bathroom
4 kitchen
5 pantry
6 courtyard
7 garage
8 bedroom
9 walk-in wardrobe

ABOVE
Sliding panels of mahogany, blued steel, and glass allow the main space to be subdivided for flexibility of use. Here, the panels close off the main living space to create a temporary meeting area. The front door is at center left; next to it is the translucent glass interior wall that is at the back of the exterior steel facade.

RIGHT
The vaulted ceiling of the main living area incorporates motorized skylights that ventilate the two-story volume. Multiple sources of natural light illuminate the space. Blued-steel panels define the fireplace wall and subtly contrast with the wood. Steel also surrounds the opening to the kitchen, at left.

OPPOSITE
Concrete sheer walls are left exposed in the stairway off the living area, the plugholes complementing the perforations of the exterior steel. A light sculpture by John Wigmore is predominant in the living area beyond. The mahogany stairs lead to the main bedrooms.

Urale Arapai House AUCKLAND, NEW ZEALAND

Malcolm Walker Architects

Constructed 2004
Home type Two-story family house
Structure Masonry, concrete slab floors, and absorbent acoustic ceilings

"My clients commented that up to 30 people have stayed for a week and there still seemed plenty of room. They said it had been designed for hard 'coconuts' and wild Samoan kids. The hallway takes a 'thrashing.' This is music to an architect, whose job it is to provide a place that complements and enhances their clients' way of living."
Malcolm Walker Architects

ABOVE
In a heritage area occupied mainly by Victorian villas, the street elevation gives a nod to this predominant neighborhood form, and includes a backward salute to the traditional veranda. The entrance wall is clad in translucent fiberglass, giving a generous and unexpected sunlit introduction to the house.

TOP RIGHT
Within the simple plan of the house there remains a spatial complexity. The stairs and main circulation point pivots around the "big step." The translucent nature of the hall gives a sense of being connected with the outdoors. Large pivot and sliding doors facilitate the indoor/outdoor feel to the rooms.

PACIFIC ISLAND LIFESTYLE

Located on a tiny inner-city site, the Urale Arapai House needed to be a dwelling for a robust and social family of eight with an extended Pacific island family of playwrights, television producers, musicians, film-makers, and sportspeople. With six children, a steady stream of visitors, and short- and long-term guests, the design had to provide space as well as privacy.

The owners have lived in the area for many years, in a suburb once home to many Pacific island families. These days, few remain. Real estate prices and lack of adequate space have forced them to relocate. Urale Arapai House is the owners' declaration that they intend to remain in the area and to bring their family up there.

ROBUST MATERIALS

The family's lifestyle includes a broad range of activities, from rugby in the hallway to the care of infants, from quiet homework assignments to band practice – many occurring at the same time. Careful planning was required in order to accommodate these pursuits.

A busy house requires resilient materials. The architect chose a strapped and lined concrete block with pre-stressed concrete floors. Absorbent acoustic ceilings were installed in the main living area.

FINDING FORM

Local planning authorities have strict regulations regarding special character requirements, so the architect drew on neighboring Victorian villas as a reference for form and context. Another reference – this time to the practicalities of Pacific living – inspired the deep veranda and the shaded outdoor areas.

The form is essentially that of a split villa. The traditional central hallway of the villa plan has now been set at one side. Instead of being used as merely a circulation device, the upper and lower hallways have been expanded and fenestrated as social spaces. These feed into simple rooms that provide a retreat from the energy of the household – essential in a house that is, by the owner's admission, the loudest in the street.

The rooms themselves are not fixed territory in the conventional sense; usage and occupation is fluid. Consistent with this, the upper bathroom is planned to be both ensuite to the parents' room and a general household bathroom. Large pivot and sliding doors are used between the circulation spaces and social rooms, to further include and manage the hallways as social areas and as integral areas of the house.

As owner Arnette Arapai comments, "Europeans have a sense of *this is my space*; Island families do not."

The downstairs living room has spaces adjoining it – the kitchen, hallway, window seat, auxiliary family room, and outdoor room all operate independently of each other. Dining is informal and usually happens outside or at the kitchen servery. The family room, adjacent to the living room, serves as a formal dining room, entertainment space, or adult refuge.

NATIVE LANDSCAPES

Landscaping is underway, using a mix of native New Zealand and Pacific island plants such as frangipanis, nikau palms, flaxes, and black bamboo, with black taros for ground cover. It is a clear reference to the Pacific origins of the residents, but the plants are also selected for hardiness and visual interest against the raw concrete of the walls.

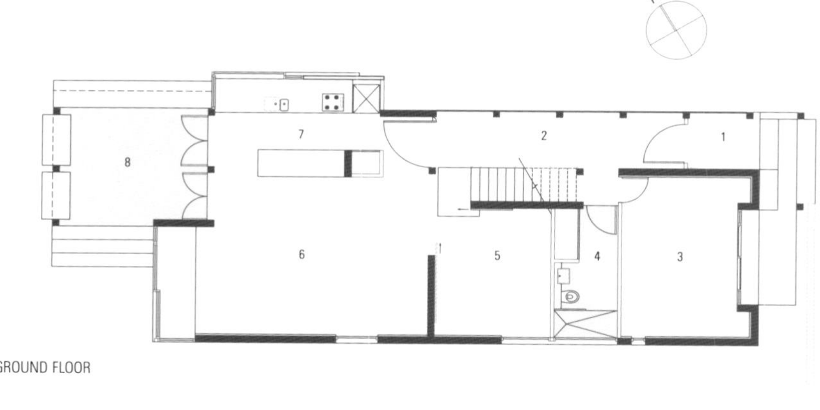

GROUND FLOOR

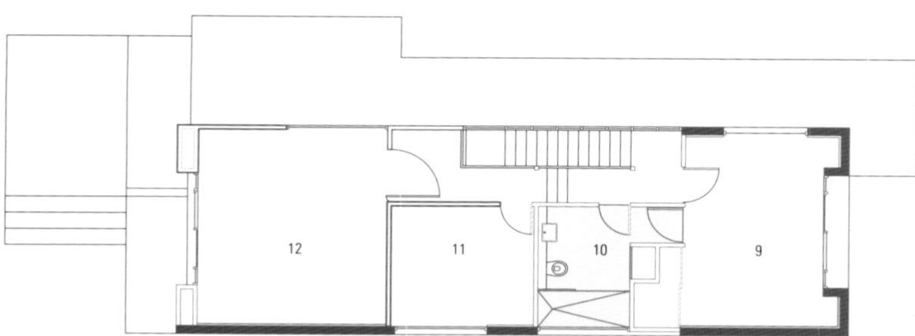

FIRST FLOOR

1 entry
2 hallway
3 bedroom
4 bathroom
5 bedroom/family
6 living
7 kitchen
8 deck
9 bedroom
10 bathroom
11 bedroom
12 living/bedroom

ABOVE
A hall runs down one side of the house and includes the kitchen on its journey from the front door to the backyard. The main living area is to the right.

LEFT
To the rear of the house, the outdoor room (on left) is perfectly suited to the maritime climate and Pacific lifestyle, and is an important and fully utilized space.

Weathering Steel House TORONTO, CANADA

Shim-Sutcliffe Architects

Constructed	2001
Home type	Single dwelling, residential house
Structure	Wood frame, steel columns, and beams clad with weathering steel on a plywood backing

"The design of this project is an emphatic critique of the material and spatial banality of the surrounding suburban neighborhood. We hope that the Weathering Steel House offers the possibility of a much richer physical experience – one that engages all the senses."

Brigitte Shim and Howard Sutcliffe

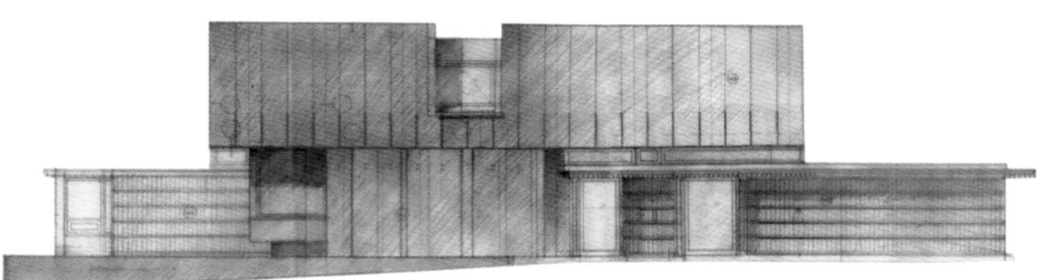

NORTH ELEVATION

TOP RIGHT
Winter view of the street elevation (facing north) showing the home's weathering steel cladding and the retaining wall in the foreground, also in weathering steel.

FAR RIGHT
View of the ravine-side of the house, showing the reflecting pool and adjoining swimming pool extending from the center of the structure into the wintry garden. The many windows facing south draw in the maximum amount of warmth from the sun, while also capturing views of the ravine and city skyline beyond.

CREATING A CONTRAST WITH THE EXISTING HOUSING

In the Toronto garden suburb of Don Mills, 1960s ranch bungalows and their surrounding landscaping are being levelled to be replaced by substantial, clumsy, historically referential monster houses. Constructed of beige brick, taupe-colored stucco and reconstituted stone, these new houses form the new ideal suburban dream house. Complemented by decorative and ornamental landscaping, they are the antithesis of their Modernist predecessors.

Weathering Steel House sits in direct contrast to this context. Materially rich, dark, and abstract, it creates a clear threshold to the world within, to the site it creates, and to the ravine edge over which it looks. The L-shaped house frames a reconfigured landscape created around shaped, tree-covered mounds and a sweeping meadow. Imbedding itself into the center of the house, the reflecting pool and swimming pool beyond form the intermediary between building and landscape, weaving reflected light, motion, and sound into the heart of the project.

LIGHT AND MOVEMENT

From the street this house is seemingly much more opaque than adjacent buildings; meanwhile, sculptural cut-outs in the elevation offer precise transparent glimpses of the ravine beyond. Upon entering the home, a circulation space parallel to the front elevation connects the garage entry, front entry, basement courtyard, and second level in one continuous slice of vertical and horizontal space. From the entry, one catches a glimpse of the ravine treetops beyond, before rising up a few steps to the main living level. From here the landscape and the house unfold, with the linear watercourse weaving internal and external space together.

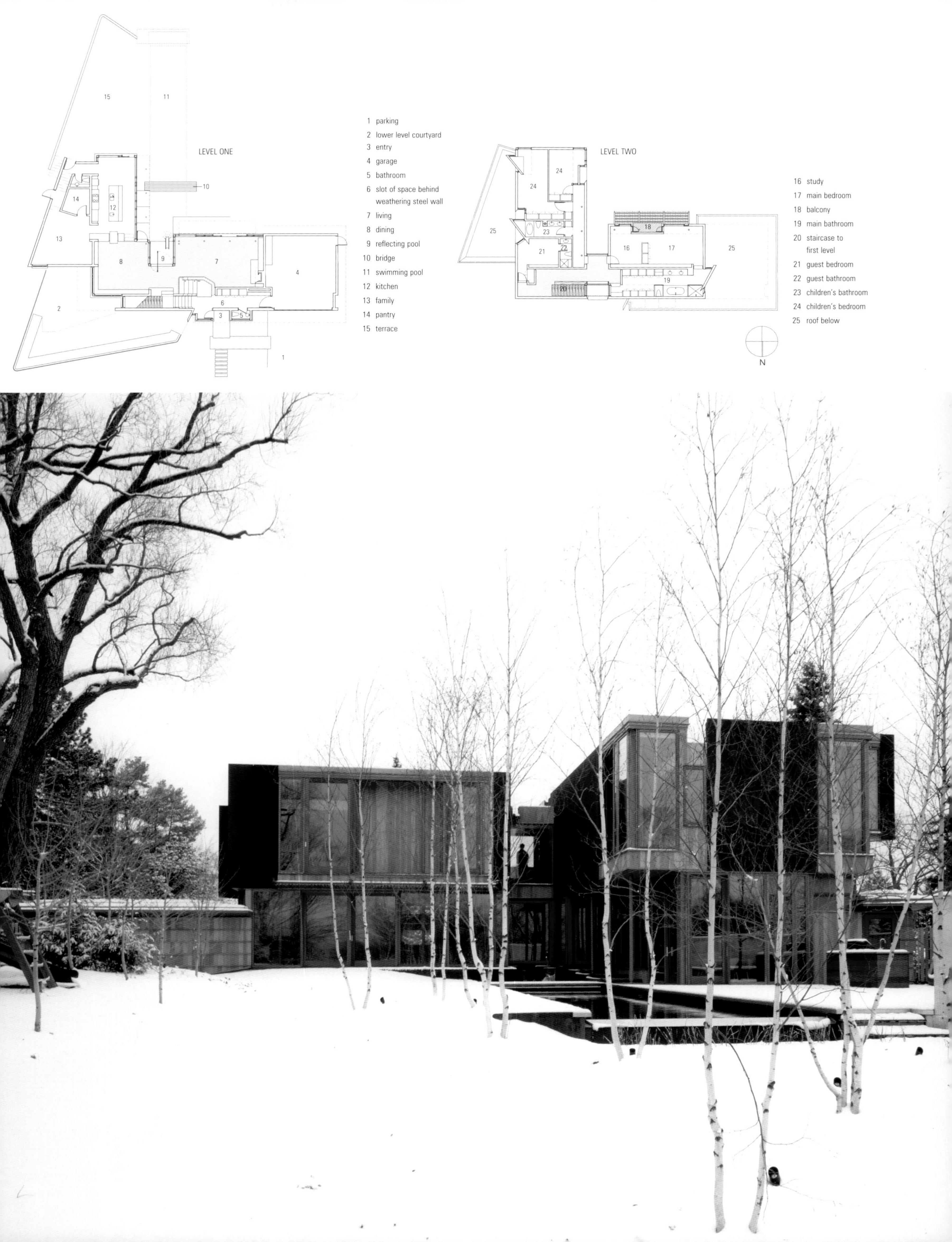
LEVEL ONE
1 parking
2 lower level courtyard
3 entry
4 garage
5 bathroom
6 slot of space behind weathering steel wall
7 living
8 dining
9 reflecting pool
10 bridge
11 swimming pool
12 kitchen
13 family
14 pantry
15 terrace
LEVEL TWO
16 study
17 main bedroom
18 balcony
19 main bathroom
20 staircase to first level
21 guest bedroom
22 guest bathroom
23 children's bathroom
24 children's bedroom
25 roof below
N

TOP LEFT
Imbedding itself into the center of the house, the reflecting pool connects the building with the exterior landscape, while also bringing reflected light, motion, and sound into the heart of the home.

LEFT
View of the entry with the staircase to the second level and the staircase to the lower level visible. The lower level courtyard is beyond the door. The main living level is a few steps up from the entry.

ABOVE
A skylight and inverted bay window drops a pool of light on the landing of the staircase to the second level, terminating at the end of the reflecting pool axis. The rich chocolate walls tie together the natural finishes of timber and concrete.

A skylight and inverted bay window drops a pool of light on the landing of the staircase to the second level, terminating at the end of the reflecting pool axis. On the second level, this inverted bay window and large window on the south side of the house help to form a "bridge" between the main bedroom and the children's wing.

THE CHALLENGE OF CLIMATE

Toronto is situated on the northern shore of Lake Ontario, and is part of a large freshwater system known as the Great Lakes. The site's adjacency to this body of water creates a technically challenging climatic condition ranging from –40ºF to 104ºF (–40ºC to 40ºC). The passive solar design of the project responds directly to this challenge – with few windows and much of the service and circulation on the north side and the public rooms on the south side, where there is maximum solar gain, as well as views of the verdant ravine and city skyline beyond.

CREATING TEXTURES

The building cladding is weathering steel, which was selected because of its direct interaction with nature, allowing, as it does, the richly textured skin to darken slowly. Because weathering steel is usually fabricated in large sections for bridges and other civil engineering works, the channels and all the fixed components of this cladding system were break-formed from weathering steel plate.

ABOVE
View of the light-filled living area with floating cabinet, fireplace, and wood storage cavity beyond. The spare furnishings and neutral color palette afford the room a natural warmth.

Westcliff Estate JOHANNESBURG, SOUTH AFRICA

studioMAS architects + urban designers

Construction	2001–2002
Home type	Three-story family home
Structure	Off-shutter concrete carcass with stone and aluminum cladding

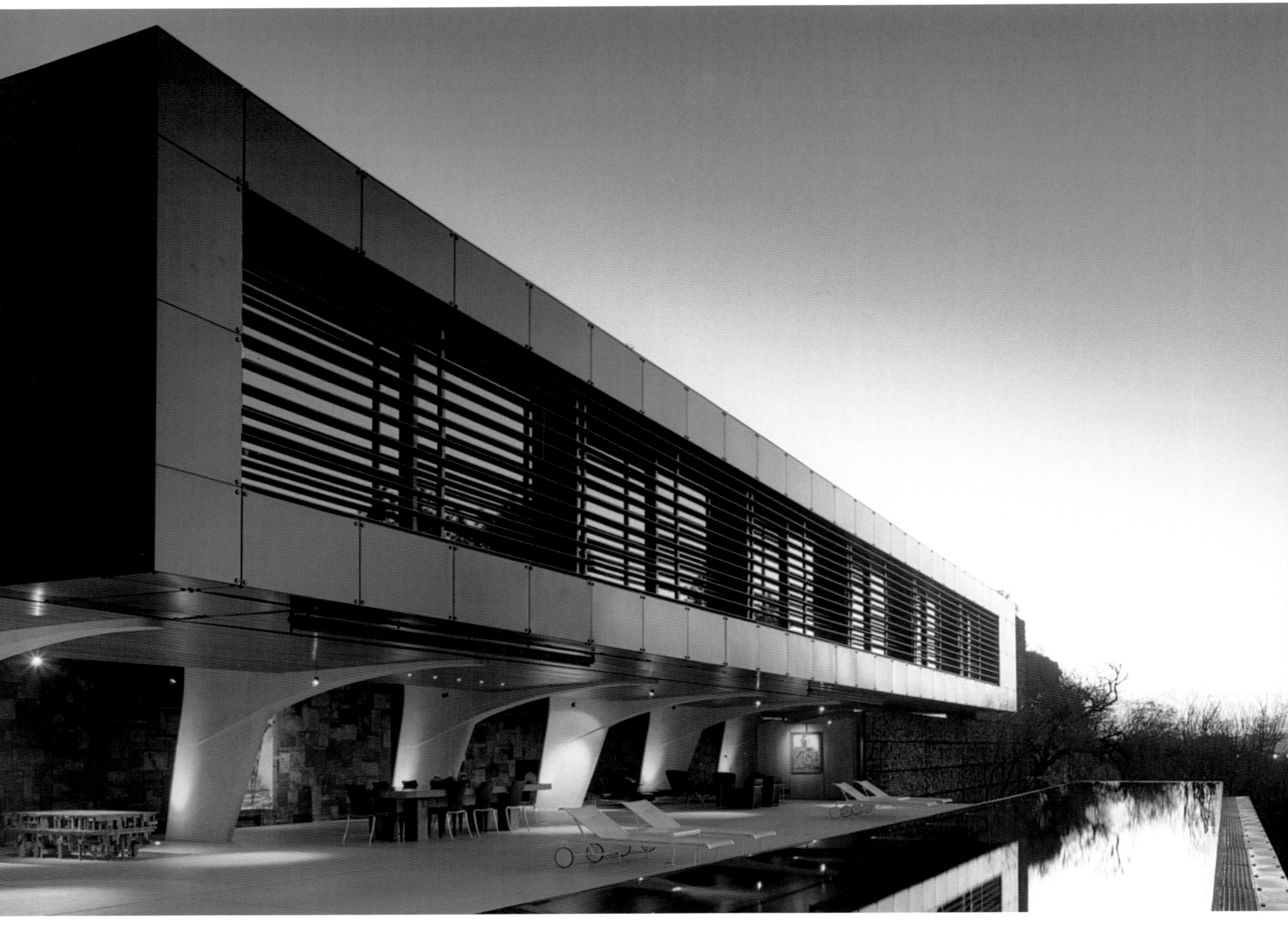

ABOVE
As the afternoon light fades, owners enjoy views from the entertainment/living area looking across the swimming pool. Two glass sliding doors open from the internal living space to the patio.

"Our goal was to design a twenty-first century African house that embodies the 'new values' of modern South Africa – respect for the land, for its setting, and for the people."

Pierre Swanepoel

MODERNISM IN AN AFRICAN CONTEXT

Considered by some to be a seminal work of Johannesburg Modernism, Westcliff Estate was designed to sit on a steep site, partially submerged into the slope at the back. The site was originally subdivided from the 100-year-old Rand Lord property, now a school for disabled children. The school could not use this part of the site owing to the extreme slope, and the home's location is in an area where much of the natural vegetation had been destroyed.

The expansive views, the breathtaking landscape, and the tempered Highveld weather demanded a building that was open to its surroundings; one that invites the landscape inside. The raised pool and wide patio obscure views of neighboring houses at the front of the property, while the structural columns frame the more distant vistas.

TREE MOTIFS

The tree-like columns hold the bedrooms high in the "treetops," while the open-plan living area is under the tree-trunks next to the "river" – the pool. This narrative reflects very literally how many South Africans choose to live their lives – close to nature. The roof opens to invite in the winter sun, its rays also warming the dark slate wall in the windless colder months. To further support the tree analogy, the structures that guide the automated roof resemble the long, dramatic leaves of the bird of paradise plant (*Strelitzia*).

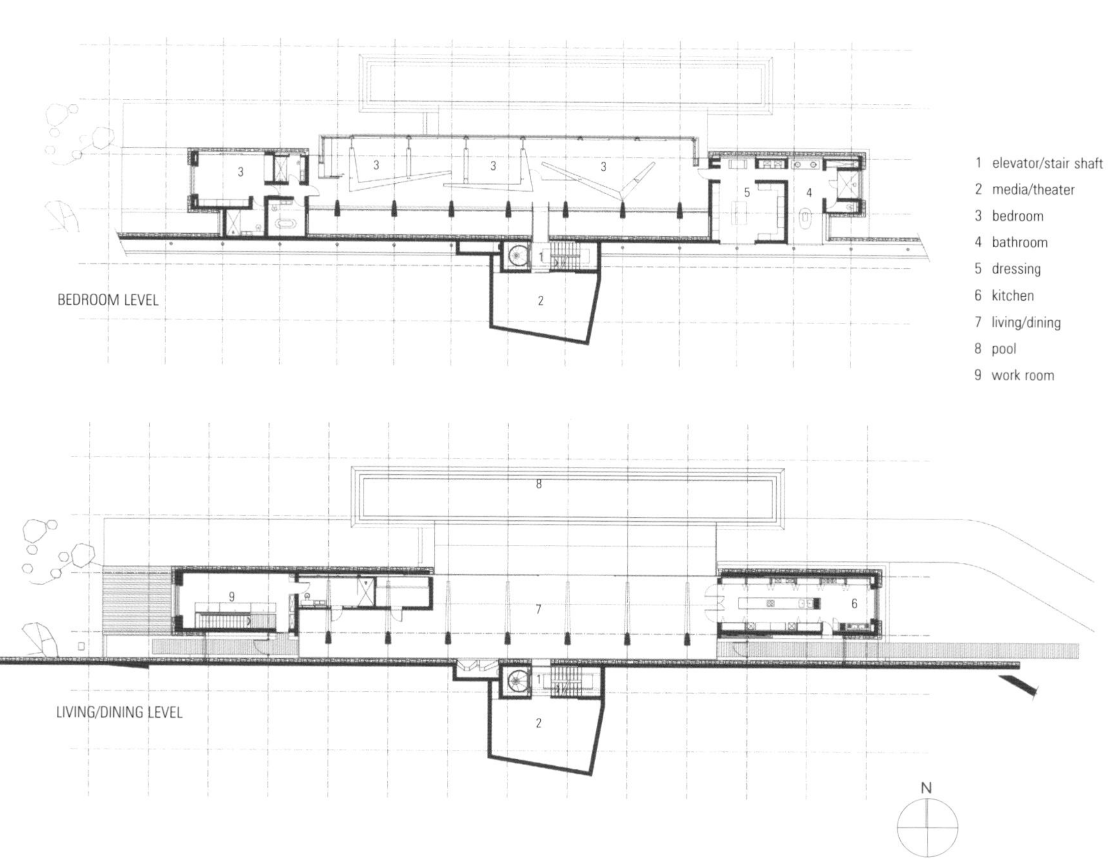

TOP LEFT
An aerial view of Westcliff Estate showing the roof, pool, and patio area. Most of the landscape in front of the building was rehabilitated using only indigenous trees and grasses.

ABOVE
Looking east from the garden, across the deck toward the study. The shutters and glass fold and slide down respectively to expose the inside to the surrounding gardens.

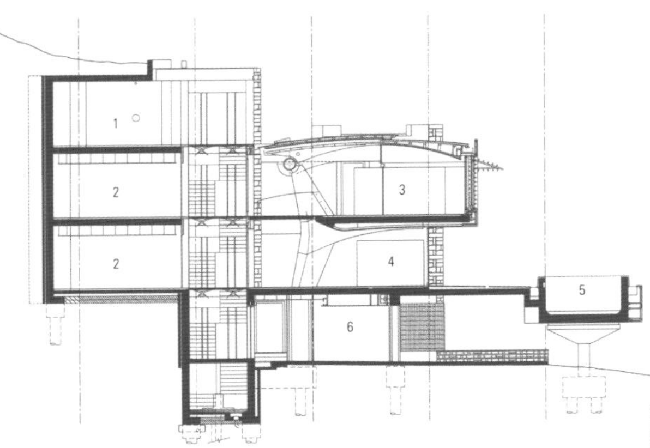

1 study
2 theater/media
3 bedroom
4 living/dining
5 pool
6 parking

LETTING IN THE LANDSCAPE

Visitors to this impressive home park in front of the retaining wall under the trees. They then approach from the east via a narrow, boarded ramp that is complete with an electrically operated, vertically sliding steel gate. Entry to the house is bordered by a retaining wall and two rubble dry stone walls contained by wire cages. Views to the northern landscape are hidden until the living space is entered, when the spectacular scene is revealed. Large glass doors slide away into the two flanking structures to integrate the patio, swimming pool, and the living space.

Seven tree-like columns support the bedrooms above and create a spacious living area underneath, with no obstruction between the pool, terrace, and magnificent panorama beyond. The impression is of sitting under a tree with one's back leaning against the trunk. The interplay between the organic and the rectilinear forms is a reflection of a desire to be part of nature, but also to be protected from it.

Furnishings are sparse; there is a deliberate feeling of emptiness, which allows the surrounding landscape to become the protagonist.

The main bedroom is the farthest east of the home's four bedrooms; it has an ensuite bathroom and a dressing room in the flanking structure. Thorn-shaped, removable cupboards delineate the other bedrooms, ensuring privacy and flexible storage for each space.

Stone from the site, in conjunction with concrete, was used in the construction of the house, affirming the building's connection with its surroundings.

The house is fully automated, allowing the family to change the internal environment in response to the climate outside. The notion of door, window, and roof is questioned in the design – the roof opens, the doors and windows disappear to give access to the outside landscape, inviting it in to become part of the interior. Some believe Westcliff Estate heralds the emergence of the new African house, or at least offers an alternative to the typical Eurocentric notion of building.

ABOVE
The imposing glass-floored elevator delivers occupants and visitors speedily to their desired level within the house.

LEFT
A view from the living room looking north across the entertainment area, pool, and beyond to leafy Johannesburg, a city considered to be part of the biggest urban forest in the world.

RIGHT
The automated roof opens over the living space, allowing the family to control the internal environment in response to the conditions outside.

Wind House SINGAPORE

WOHA

Construction	2004–2006
Home type	Two-story detached dwelling
Structure	Reinforced concrete with steelwork, and pad footings

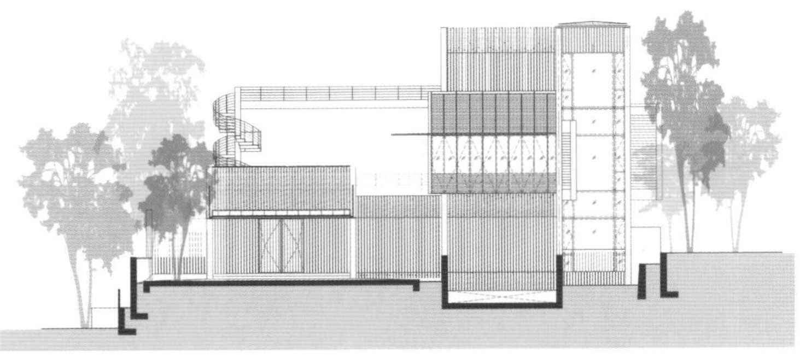

NORTH ELEVATION

"This private family residence was designed as a 'machine' to capture Singapore's light breezes ... in order to avoid the need for air-conditioning as much as possible."

Richard Hassell

LEFT
A steel bridge links the pool on level one to a roof terrace and roof garden, complete with overflow bathtub, on level two. Passive cooling methods figure prominently in the house design – breezes are directed over the swimming pool and water features to produce evaporatively cooled air, which then enters the house through open windows and doors.

LIFE IS A BREEZE

The clients requested a home that not only took advantage of Singapore's breezes and the extensive views of the nearby Botanic Gardens, but one that also delivered privacy and seclusion. The design process involved in-depth research into local wind patterns. Although Singapore has an equatorial climate with light breezes, comfort in the sometimes oppressive heat can be increased substantially by small increases in wind velocity and, in turn, by directing wind to activity locations in and around the home.

HARVESTING THE WIND

A series of devices was selected to act as wind "harvesters." Walls are extended beyond the building envelope to capture wind and thus increase the air pressure on openings. Selected blocks in the wall are omitted to form openings, light recesses, or service penetrations. Deflectors direct passing air into the home to increase air volume, and large overhangs deflect wind traveling up the hill slopes and direct it down into rooms and terraces.

Wind "towers" create air movement throughout the house. At each end of the circulation void, the two highest points of the house have electrically operated louvers. These can be opened on the leeward side of the prevailing wind to create a negative pressure, drawing warm air up and out of the home.

Inside the home, sliding doors stack to reduce the barrier to air movement; pocket doors slide out of the way when in use; bathroom walls move out from the main walls to create cross-ventilated louvered slots; and bedroom doors incorporate sliding joinery, which can be opened for ventilation while still maintaining privacy.

MINIMAL BARRIERS AND WIND-COOLING

The architectural envelope is minimized where possible to create a secure perimeter without blocking the wind. Vertical aluminum screens, constructed using angles that repeat the deflection strategy at a much smaller scale, present a minimal barrier to breezes. Internal openings allow breezes to permeate the house from end to end and back to front. The classically traditional device of "enfilade" – a series of aligned doors or openings – facilitates air flow throughout the house from one room to another.

Other environmental measures employed included both passive and active devices: wind is directed over water as it enters the house from different directions to create evaporative cooling; large overhangs keep out direct light; roof gardens shade the structure, and absorb both light energy and carbon; and water is heated by pumps on the roof for use in the home.

PATTERN AND TEXTURE

Extensive layering of diverse architectural "surfaces" – water, metal mesh, grass, concrete, plaster and paint, timber, fabric, aluminum, screens, walls – make a textural statement in the landscape. These are visually weightless, suspended in three dimensions throughout the site.

LIFESTYLE AND ART

The house is designed around the lifestyle of the owner. Gardens and water elements are everywhere, from the basement to the roof, and the main bedroom features an overflow bathtub adjoining a water garden. Entertaining is of great importance – the house has a Western and a Chinese dining room, an outdoor Asian kitchen, a barbecue, pool, and pavilion.

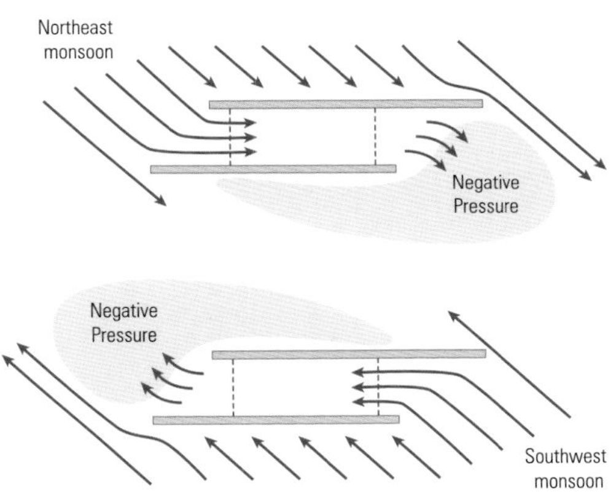

ABOVE
This diagram shows how the walls of the house extend beyond the building envelope to capture the air movement created by the southeast and northwest monsoons. This generates areas of negative pressure that then draw cool breezes through the house.

TOP
In order to keep the wind "harvesting" potential at a premium, the house is enclosed with aluminum screen walls, creating a secure perimeter and a visually pleasing facade without blocking the breezes.

ABOVE RIGHT
Walls, overflow spout, and roof eaves protrude from the main walls to form a striking graphic pattern on the house exterior. The window overhangs are important in providing much-needed summer shade and a cooler internal temperature.

FOLLOWING PAGES
Entertainment areas are given prominence in the design, reflecting their importance in the owners' lifestyle. Careful placement of the house on the site allows all rooms to engage with the outdoor areas, the pool, and the tropical vegetation.

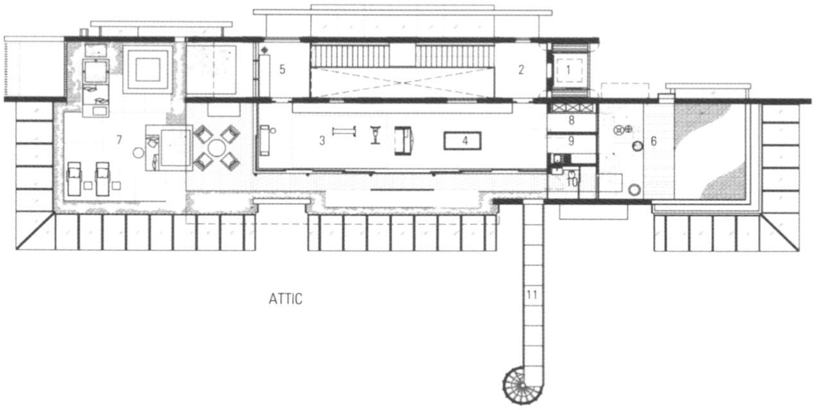

1 elevator
2 elevator lobby
3 gym
4 billiard room
5 gallery
6 roof
7 roof terrace
8 store
9 pantry
10 bathroom
11 bridge

ATTIC

1 roof terrace
2 bridge
3 bedroom
4 family
5 elevator lobby
6 elevator
7 gallery
8 pantry
9 main study
10 main bedroom
11 dressing
12 main bathroom
13 bathroom
14 water garden
15 roof garden
16 planter box

LEVEL TWO

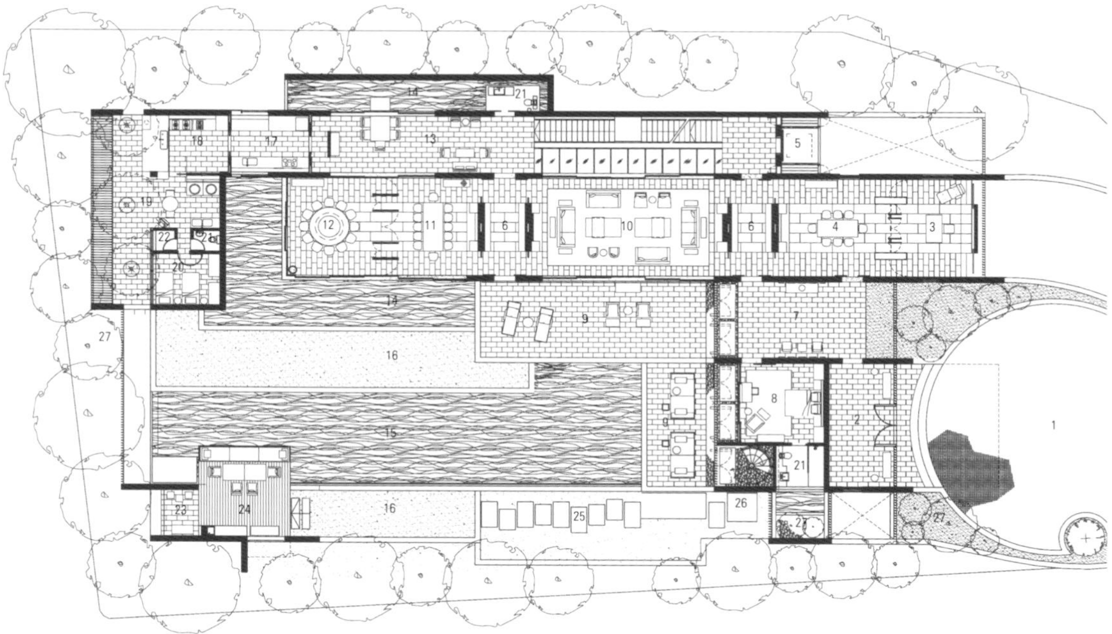

1 port-cochere
2 entry
3 study
4 meeting
5 elevator
6 passage
7 foyer
8 guest room
9 terrace
10 living
11 Western dining
12 Chinese dining
13 gallery
14 water gallery
15 swimming pool
16 lawn
17 dry kitchen
18 wet kitchen
19 utility
20 maid
21 bath
22 shower
23 barbecue
24 pavilion
25 stepping stones
26 outdoor shower
27 garden

LEVEL ONE

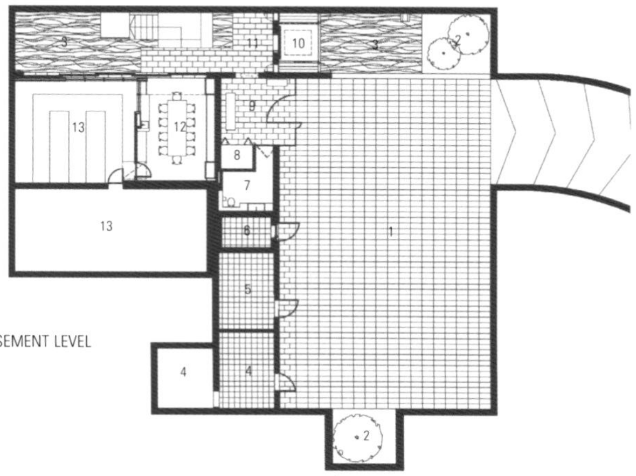

1 garage
2 garden
3 reflection pool
4 pool pump
5 store
6 household shelter
7 powder room
8 shoe rack
9 entry
10 elevator
11 elevator lobby
12 wine dining
13 wine cellar

BASEMENT LEVEL

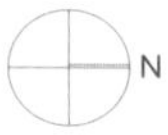

N

ABOVE
Looking across the water gallery from the Chinese dining area toward the pavilion and swimming pool. A "layering" of spaces creates an understated opulence, and emphasizes the connection between the interior and the surrounding gardens.

RIGHT
A wall of windows maximizes the views. They open out fully, providing minimal barrier to the light breezes. Translucent fine aluminum mesh affords privacy without impeding the dappled light that filters through from the tropical gardens.

LEFT
The entrance screen was created using angled, vertical aluminum panes, which repeats the wind deflection strategy integrated into the house design but on a micro scale. Behind the screen, the entrance features a sky-lit cast-concrete mural by Australian artist, Bruce Reynolds. The mural weaves together Chinese symbolic icons, family memories, and local elements.

ABOVE
The interior openings link the areas between the deflector walls. A series of aligned doors allows the breeze to flow through the house from one room to another – spaces are connected by staircases and a glass-floored bridge.

Chapter 10

Outer City

Despite the commute and the influence of neighboring properties, a home on the city fringe has both rural serenity and access to urban amenity.

A short drive past the city limits, turn off the highway onto a quiet road and approach a house partially concealed from view by tall trees. This is the perfect setting for a home on the city fringe, and it has the best of both worlds – an urban lifestyle within a rural setting.

The city fringe is an area of transition between the city and the country, with many of the homes built on large blocks of remnant farmland, or virgin land. Homes here generally have a relatively large footprint and are more aesthetically diverse compared with their generic cousins in the sprawling subdivisions nearby. While the city is close, it is not immediately accessible, and this semi-rural setting still requires home design to loosely fit within the existing context.

ACCESSIBILITY

Appealing to a variety of lifestyles, the outer city home's location takes advantage of both rural and urban environments, although neither area is instantly available. As a result, there is a lot of time spent away from the home, both for work and play.

Reliance on the car is a key feature in the design of houses in the outer city. Arrival at the home is rarely on foot. The once proud and welcoming front door is often consigned to an inferior location, tucked behind a large garage that dominates the front of the house. And the garage houses more than a vehicle, it is frequently a storehouse of props for an array of outdoor activities.

SPACIOUS FOOTPRINT

A home on a subtsantial area of land has the luxury of a spacious footprint. However, the outer city location does not have the actual seclusion found in the rural setting, and the sense of space is limited by distinct property boundaries, and the possibility of being overlooked by neighbors.

Large interior spaces that are clearly defined are a design feature for this type of home. Specialist areas create a sense of privacy within the home – a playroom for children, or a parents' retreat.

A sizeable backyard is a feature of the outer city home's environment, and access to it is an essential element for the lifestyle of the homeowners. A private open area, the backyard may be an extension of the home's interior space, or simply the transition between internal and external space.

CONTEXTUAL INFLUENCE

The aesthetic diversity of the city fringe is not without limitations, and a home designed for this location is influenced by its context, and must complement the neighborhood.

A free-standing, detached dwelling is typical of the outer city location. The scale of the home and the type of building materials used, will ideally fit in with the proximate buildings. The aesthetic must also be sensitive to the surroundings – the home integrating with the texture of the landscape in which it is sited.

THE OUTER CITY HOME

This location gives the best of both worlds – a serene, semi-rural environment, but also one that is close enough to the city to take advantage of all that it has to offer.

ABOVE
Oshry Residence,
Studio Pali Fekete Architects (SPF:a)

TOP RIGHT
Floating House,
Ngiom Partnership

OPPOSITE
Hill House,
Johnston Marklee & Associates

Amy Loh House SUNGEI BOLAH, MALAYSIA

Jimmy Lim (CSL Associates)

Constructed 2002
Home type Multi-level home
Structure Concrete frame with brick infill

"In architecture, nothing is more important than listening to the client and creating an environment for them that effortlessly caters to their needs and maximizes their happiness."

Jimmy Lim

ABOVE
The swimming pool is seen here extending from double doors. The area provides the occupants with an outdoor lounging and swimming area, with the gazebo (in partial view to the right) providing shade from the harsh tropical sun.

THE LOCATION

Amy Loh House is situated in a gated golf course community in the western suburbs of Kuala Lumpur.

Located along a narrow 8,000-sq-ft (750-sq-m) block on a steep incline that slopes away from the street, the home has been constructed diagonally across the site on a 45° axis due to the peculiarities of the site's topography. This axis increases the home's sense of space, resulting in a multi-level structure partially raised on stilts to minimize environmental impact and eliminate the need for the "cut and fill" approach so common in developments of this type.

OPEN SPACES

For this design the architect was interested in pursuing a theory of openness made possible by an absence of internal walls, thus creating vast, separate areas visually connected to one another. Large spaces such as the living room, the central focus of the house, are spanned by a network of beams, with massive columns that support the roof structure in the absence of internal walls.

The home's roof is a blend of traditionally spreading eaves and pitched terracotta tiles. Metal sheeting was also required to provide the curvature necessary to follow the unorthodox parabolic double axis that takes the Amy Loh house in two different directions.

NATURAL AIR-CONDITIONING

The home has no air-conditioning, instead relying upon air wells and cross-ventilation to encourage wind movement. The home's interior is lavishly decorated with carved doorways and high windows that permit rising warm air to escape, thus creating a natural flow and movement of air.

Decorative windows in the living areas use recycled stained glass from Indonesia and are framed in local Chengal hardwood, one of the densest species of timber and highly resistant to white ants.

The main bedroom is situated near to an outdoor swimming pool on the upper level that is accessed through sliding doors. Water from the pool cascades through a void to the ground floor between the downstairs living and dining rooms and into a reflecting pool.

TOP LEFT
Pitched roofs with spreading eaves and white plaster-rendered exteriors are a Jimmy Lim signature, both effective means of temperature control in the harsh tropical climate.

TOP RIGHT
Recycled stained glass from Indonesia provides an ornamental touch to this side panel in the home's lobby. Timber is a practical building element in the tropics due to its ability to absorb and dissipate heat without transferring it to the interior.

ABOVE
The rich color of the Chengal hardwood combined with the intricate patterning of the window design create an ever-changing interplay of light and shade in the living area.

Beau Constance CAPE TOWN, SOUTH AFRICA

Metropolis

Construction	2003–2004
Home type	Two level, free-standing residence
Structure	Steel and concrete

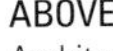

"...the house is essentially a loose arrangement of planes defining a set of relationships for dwelling as an integral part of the landscape..."

Jon Jacobson

ABOVE
Architecturally speaking, Beau Constance is a collection of cubic forms made up of individual planes, which are nestled into a wild and mountainous landscape.

ABOVE RIGHT
Walls of glass in the living room connect the main home to a variety of outside entertainment areas for different seasonal use. Wrap-around timber slats provide sun-control and a sense of enclosure.

Beau Constance is located in a rural strip between leafy suburban Constantia and the rugged slopes of the Vlakkenberg mountains. A newly developed wine farm, it enjoys an unspoilt natural setting, with spectacular views of the Cape Peninsula below, and pristine forested mountain slopes all around.

The design of Beau Constance was developed so as not to compromise the unique site, while at the same time departing from the solid white walls and pitched roofs of traditional Cape wineland architecture. In its place, the architects pursued an architecture of generous voids, floating horizontal planes, and natural materials that would completely merge with its surroundings.

THE RESIDENCE

The residence and its associated spa pavilion are sited on an elongated platform tucked into a fold in the steep mountainside, completely isolated from surrounding neighbors. The house does not have a specific orientation. It was conceived as a filter through which the landscape could enter from all directions.

The accommodation is therefore organized around a system of outdoor courtyards, simultaneously shaping and being shaped by the building. The courtyards allow shelter from strong southeasterly winds in summer, allow views from all parts of the building, and create an unimpeded flow of space from inside to outside.

SEPARATE SCULPTURAL ELEMENTS

The house touches lightly on the landscape. It is arranged into two "boxes," formed by floating concrete flat roofs and turned-down timber screen walls. All the elements of the house – suspended floors, stairs, and external and internal walls, are expressed as separate sculptural elements, floating in a loose composition, under the "sheltering sky" of the overarching forms.

The accommodation is organized into three interlocking volumes, with services in one single-story block, the double-volume kitchen/dining/family room in another, and the living room, study, and bedrooms in a third slightly higher block, with an underground wine cellar and entertainment area beneath.

The farm folds itself around a natural gully, incorporating rolling vineyards on its lower slopes, and a steep craggy mountainside higher up.

ABOVE
The house hovers above the ground plane, flowing through to the landscape beyond.

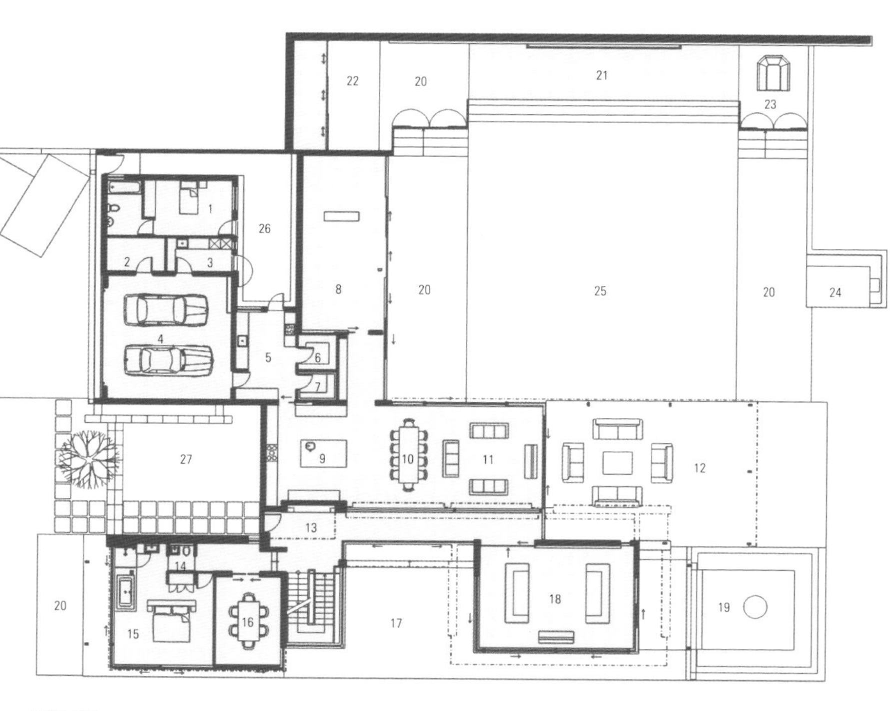

LEVEL ONE

25

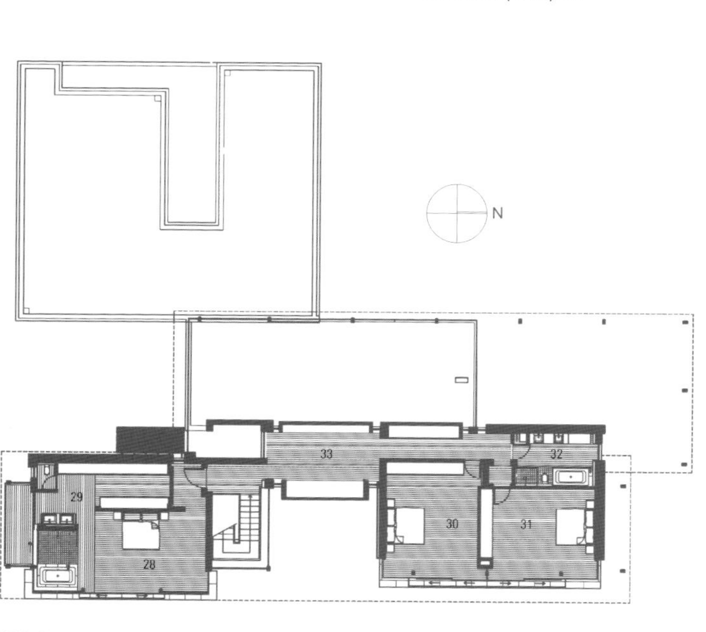

LEVEL TWO

1 staff quarters
2 office
3 utility
4 garage
5 scullery
6 pantry
7 cold room
8 playroom
9 kitchen
10 dining
11 family
12 north terrace
13 entry
14 guest WC
15 guest suite
16 study
17 east terrace
18 living
19 outside seating
20 deck
21 pool
22 pool seating
23 jacuzzi
24 barbecue
25 lawn
26 courtyard
27 entrance court
28 main bedroom
29 main bathroom
30 bedroom
31 bedroom
32 bathroom
33 TV room

ABOVE
Transparency and volume allow an easy flow of inside-outside space in all directions.

OPPOSITE
A continuous membrane of glass under a concrete canopy emphasizes the experience of the sweeping views beyond.

Entry is from the south into a formal courtyard. An axial movement spine from the front door to the north patio defines circulation on both levels, and structures a progressive series of views of the landscape. The living level is designed for regular entertainment and an extroverted outdoor lifestyle.

By contrast, the bedrooms are entirely private. They float over the living level in a self-contained "capsule" linked to the central volume by narrow slot windows. They are less "bed rooms" and more shelves in the landscape. The ensuite has been recast as a sculptural object within the space of the main bedroom, which responds to the necessities and pleasures of bathing.

UNION OF ARCHITECTURE AND NATURE

Structurally, the house is essentially a series of thin concrete slabs, supported on slim steel columns, and stabilized by a number of free-standing concrete walls and columns. The lightness and delicacy of the structure contributes to the lack of materiality required by the architectural concept.

Materials themselves are chosen for their resonance with the colors of the site: stone, raw concrete, and sun-bleached balau.

At Beau Constance, shelter and enclosure have been reduced to an essence, to create a union between architecture and nature. It is simultaneously about making place and about finding a place in the landscape.

RIGHT
Stone, timber, and off-shutter concrete are the primary materials, integrating the home with the color tones and textures of the surrounding landscape. A separate recreational building, containing the spa, shown here, demonstrates the beauty and functionality of these materials.

FOLLOWING PAGES
The physical and conceptual center of the house is the double-volume kitchen/dining/family room, from which courtyards and living spaces radiate in all directions. It is at once the farm kitchen, the center of family life, and the "center of the landscape" – a vantage point from which the entire farm and its surrounding context can be experienced and appreciated. The focus of the kitchen is the framed view of the summit of the Vlakkenberg.

Belmont House CALIFORNIA, USA

Hariri & Hariri - Architecture

Construction	1999–2002
Home type	Single family residence
Structure	Concrete and lightweight steel frame

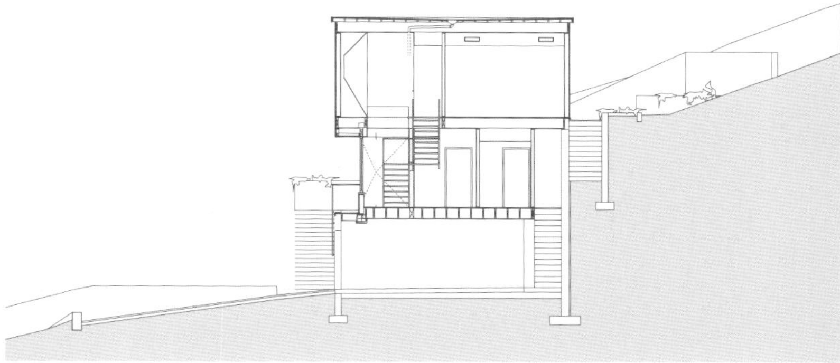

"What is expressed here is this paradoxical human desire to be part of the new and the old, the heavy and the light, the earth and the sky, the rooted and the mobile simultaneously."

Gisue Hariri

CREATING A HYBRID

This deceptively simple house is built straight into a hill in Belmont, near San Francisco. The New York architects wanted to explore the synthesis between the two dominant types of architecture in the region, namely the mobile-trailer home and the Mexican pueblo style of housing. The owners, who work in Silicon Valley, are a young couple with a child, and are representative of the new demographic that is emerging in the area.

To gain access to the house, the visitor follows a curved concrete retaining wall that edges the long driveway up to the entry. Concrete steps lead to the mid-entry level, where a long veranda with a blue stucco wall leads to the extra-large rusted steel front door – a dramatic statement in the overall design. This takes the visitor into the entrance hall, where a sculptural staircase invites one to the upper main floor.

PUEBLO INFLUENCES

The Mexican pueblo influence is evident in the lower level of the house, the heavy, stuccoed concrete walls providing texture, color, and warmth. The east side of the house contains the entry and gallery area, while the generously sized children's area sits on the west side.

The upper level of the home contains the main bedroom and ensuite at one end, with open loft living at the other. This part of the house contains the open-plan living room, dining area, and kitchen, a library in the center, and a home office at the other end. All these spaces open to a terrace and hillside at the back of the house.

TOP RIGHT
The rectangular volume of the upper floors floats over its solid concrete base, as if ready to "move on." A series of concrete steps takes one from the driveway to the mid-entry level.

RIGHT
Reminiscent of Mexican pueblo architecture, the heavy blue stucco walls ground the structure, anchoring the seemingly lightweight metal-wrapped upper floors.

OPPOSITE
Inspired equally by the iconic mobile-trailer home and Mexican pueblo architecture, the home is an expression of the old and the new, the heavy and the light. A curved concrete retaining wall directs the way uphill into the driveway.

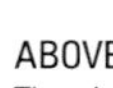

MOBILE-HOME INFLUENCES

The influence of the mobile-trailer home can be seen in the upper level of the house, which is a large rectangular volume wrapped in metal sitting atop a solid base. It appears to hover over the lower level. Natural light and cross-ventilation come from the large openings in this rectangle, which also allow sweeping views of both the hill and valley.

SUCCESSFUL MERGING OF STYLES

The architects saw the marriage of the two styles as an expression of the human desire to be part of the new and the old, the heavy and the light – it is something of a paradox to be rooted to the ground and yet presenting a "mobile" vision.

One of the considerations the architects took into account was a comment by the editor of the *New York Times*, Blaine Harden, who said, "The American house has been swelling for decades. It has swollen even though a smaller family lives in it. Even the hulking and ostentatious suburban McMansion is bulking up, as mega-houses pop up across the United States."

Belmont House attempts to reverse this trend and show that "less is more." What is important to these architects is to connect to the culture and landscape that one builds on. In their opinion, to be original one has to understand and interpret the architecture of both the old and the new.

TOP LEFT
The interplay of old and new, evident in Belmont House's exterior, enters the interior of the home, with the aged steel door giving way to a stark and sculptural staircase.

CENTER
The oversized rusted steel door creates a dramatic entrance door, pivoting into the entrance hall. Its obvious weight and strength are in sharp contrast to the sparse decoration and lightweight fixtures beyond.

ABOVE
The airy main upper level contains the living, dining, and kitchen areas, as well as a library at the center, and the main bedroom and home-office at either end. All open onto a terrace and hillside views.

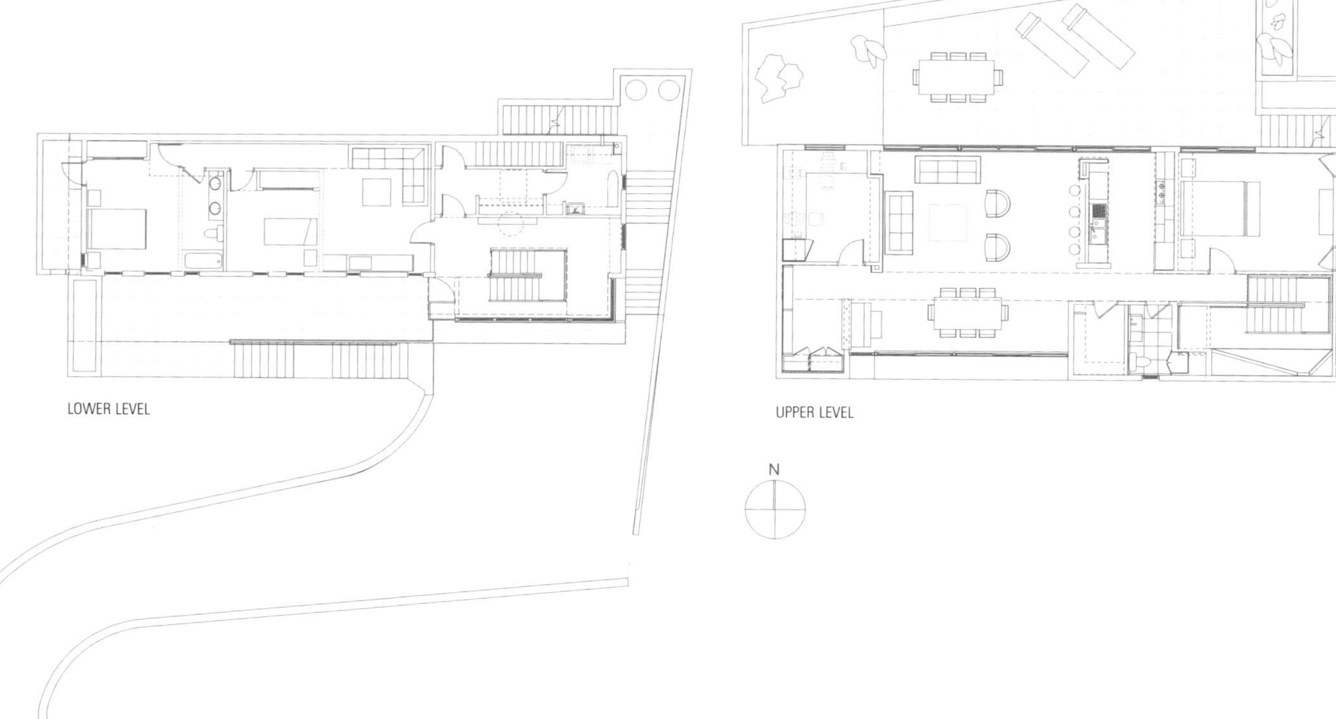
LOWER LEVEL
UPPER LEVEL
N

Benedict Canyon Residence CALIFORNIA, USA

Griffin Enright Architects

Constructed 2005
Home type Single-dwelling contemporary house
Structure Single-level concrete slab floor, wood, and steel frame

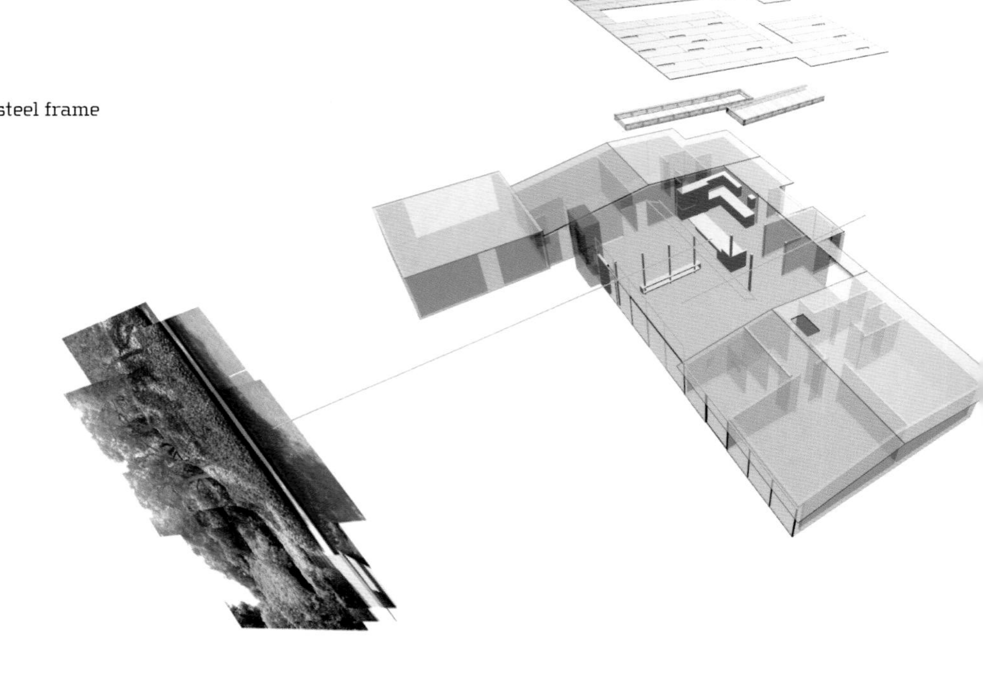

"The orchestration of both natural and artificial light creates ever-changing lighting conditions throughout the day, while the reflective quality of the floor and ceiling creates a dynamic spatial condition, blurring inside and out and up and down."

Griffin Enright Architects

TOP RIGHT
The exploded view of the home shows the interrelationship between the light boxes, the skylight, and the interior areas and view beyond.

ABOVE
The family room and living room, both with expansive views of the garden, are separated by a floating shelf. Steel columns hold and support the birch veneer timber divider that functions as an attractive book or display case.

A MODERNIST RENOVATION

For the extensive renovation of this 2,600-sq-ft (240-sq-m) mid-century house on a hillside site in Los Angeles, the client desired a transformation to make the house more true to the spirit of its Modernist origins, including bringing more natural light inside and exploiting and extending the dazzling views of the canyon setting and its indigenous wildlife.

A portion of the original gabled roof was replaced with an extended plane of the same angle, yielding a continuous upwardly sweeping surface. This new roof element was folded up and after replacing a stucco wall with a 50-ft (15-m) wide wall of glass, the rear facade became a large glazed surface that opened up the house. From the inside, there are now unobstructed views of the landscape and pool, and from the outside, the house is completely transparent in daylight and transforms into a glowing box in the dark.

INFUSING SPACES WITH LIGHT

In the interior, nearly all of the existing finishes were demolished and four interior walls were eliminated to create open, airy, light-infused public spaces. Within the new loft-like space, discrete functional areas are defined through changes in the ceiling, placement of furniture, custom-designed built-ins, and lighting. For example, a custom piece was designed – made of wood and supported by steel columns – that appears to float between the living area and den, and functions as both a bookcase and room divider. Similarly, a custom-made, cherry-veneered and stainless steel island defines the kitchen.

A FOCUS ON THE CEILING

The ceiling became a significant component of the overall design. It was designed to slope with a plywood panel system housing seemingly randomly placed track light fixtures. This system is punctuated by the intersection of two light boxes and a skylight. The light boxes are composed of resin panels with imbedded sea grass, creating a soft, glowing, filtered lighting effect. The light boxes are oriented to provide visual connections to the entry and the backyard. In an analogous fashion, the long, narrow skylight is positioned to mirror the main circulation of the house, casting striking patterns of shadows.

FINE FINISHING

To give visual interest to the floor, the concrete was stained and finished with an epoxy resin that has an almost liquid quality. The sloping ceiling, reflective surfaces, and the play of light and shadow make the space dynamic and full of energy, blurring distinctions between floor and ceiling and interior and exterior.

TOP RIGHT
The view from the rear of the house creates a somewhat voyeuristic feeling about the glazed wall, sitting, as it does, against the clear pool reflection. The nearly transparent rear wall is visually extended by its mirror image in the water; a design feature recognized by Venetian architects for hundreds of years.

RIGHT
A view from the centrally located living area looking up to the intersecting skylight and light boxes. The uplifting effect is achieved by literally raising the roof. This juxtaposition of the natural environment (the sky) with materials that incorporate nature underscores the desire to blend exterior and interior.

N
1 entry
2 dining
3 living
4 family
5 kitchen
6 bathroom
7 bedroom
8 bedroom
9 garage
10 bedroom
11 WC
12 main bedroom
13 main bathroom

CH House BARCELONA, SPAIN

BAAS Jordi Badia/Mercé Sangenís

Constructed	2000
Home type	Two-story family home
Structure	Concrete walls, metallic pillars

"The house was conceived as a small matchbox gently dropped on the grass, closed on the southern side because of the close proximity of the neighbors, and open on the northern side where the garden is wider."

BAAS Jordi Badia/Mercé Sangenís

ABOVE
The kitchen protrudes from the northern side, providing a "window" to this part of the garden. This side of the house is relatively closed as it is overlooked by a neighboring property. The use of white concrete and wood inside and outside creates a unified theme.

TOP RIGHT
The living areas of the house are one large space connected on a diagonal section. The interior of the house is organized around an internal patio that separates the living spaces from the children's and guest bedrooms, illuminating the interior and controlling the temperature.

INDIVIDUAL STYLE AND FORM

La Garriga is a popular holiday destination, located close to Barcelona, between the plain of the Vallès and the foothills of Montseny Mountain.

CH House is situated on a trapezoid-shaped block of land and can be accessed from two streets, each on a different level. The main entry is on the upper level while the other sits on the lower level, along with the garage and swimming pool. The inside of the house is arranged around two major spaces that are clearly delineated, according to their function.

The exterior of the house makes a strong individual statement, which is somewhat out of context with the neighborhood. Constructed in white concrete and wood, CH House resembles a rectangular box neatly placed on the site. This provides privacy without compromising the volume of the interior.

THE CENTRAL NUCLEUS

With its small courtyard, the entry is the focal point of the interior. Leading off from this area are the children's and guest bedrooms, positioned along the eastern facade. The rest of the house has been designed as a single space, with strategically placed furniture creating three separate spaces, all of which open out to the western facade.

The living room is part of the central space and close to the entry, while the dining room adjoins the living room and the kitchen. The stairs lead to the top floor of the house, their layout strengthening the axis that crosses the dwelling over much of its length.

PRIVATE SPACES

The bedrooms are hidden behind a slatted wall. An interior courtyard flows through an anteroom to the children's bedrooms, and the guest room is quite separate from the private family areas.

The main bedroom opens out to the house's western facade and the dressing room leads to the interior courtyard. The ensuite is primarily timber, with natural light provided by a skylight in the shower area. The walls of the ensuite blend with the garden and have been placed at an angle to both provide privacy and admit filtered light to the entry.

EXCITING EXTERIORS

The back street entrance functions as an outdoor foyer or porch. From this point, visitors enter the house by walking along an interior cobbled path to the interior courtyard, which is paved to complement the rest of the streetscape. The intoxicating perfumes of a lemon tree and lavender permeate the interior of the house.

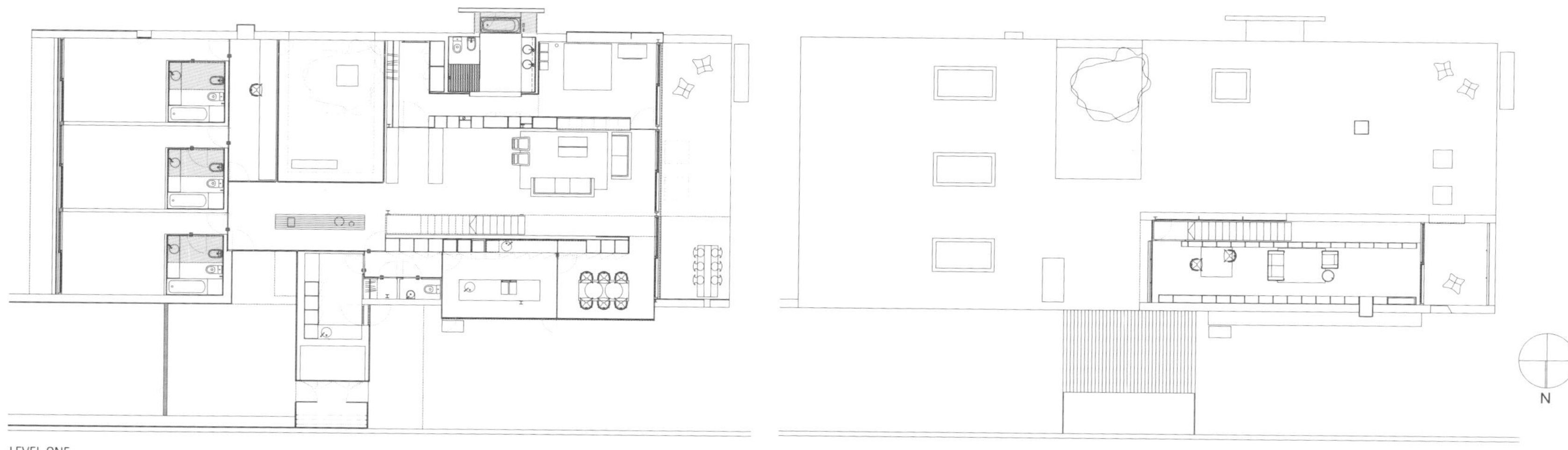

LEFT
Both the children's and guest bedrooms are behind a wooden slatted wall, which protects this part of the house from noise while lending it some privacy.

FAR LEFT
The open stairway acts as an axis running east–west, allowing views of the whole house. Open shelving on the upper level to the right of the stairway doubles as a low wall or partition.

ABOVE
The house was conceived as a small matchbox that has been gently dropped on the grass. It is closed on the lateral side to provide privacy from the neighboring property but open where the garden is deeper.

Cliff House CAPE TOWN, SOUTH AFRICA

Van der Merwe Miszewski Architects

Construction	1999–2001
Home type	Three-level family home
Structure	Concrete frame with glass infill panels; timber and lightweight steel frame decks and timber shutters

"The site is heavily wooded with poplars and pines that are common to the area, and it has spectacular views toward Table Mountain, the city, and the sea."

Van der Merwe Miszewski Architects

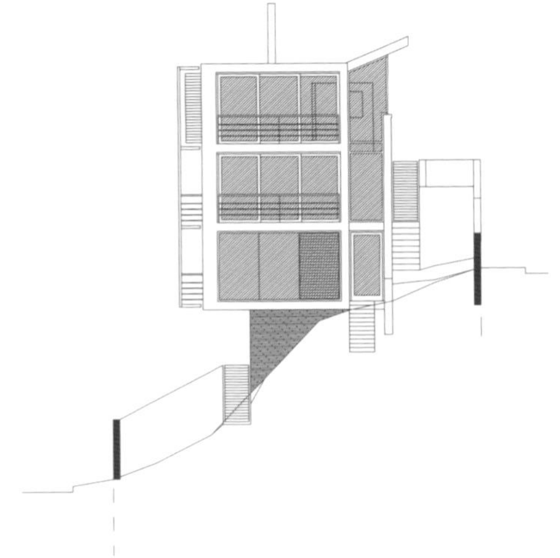

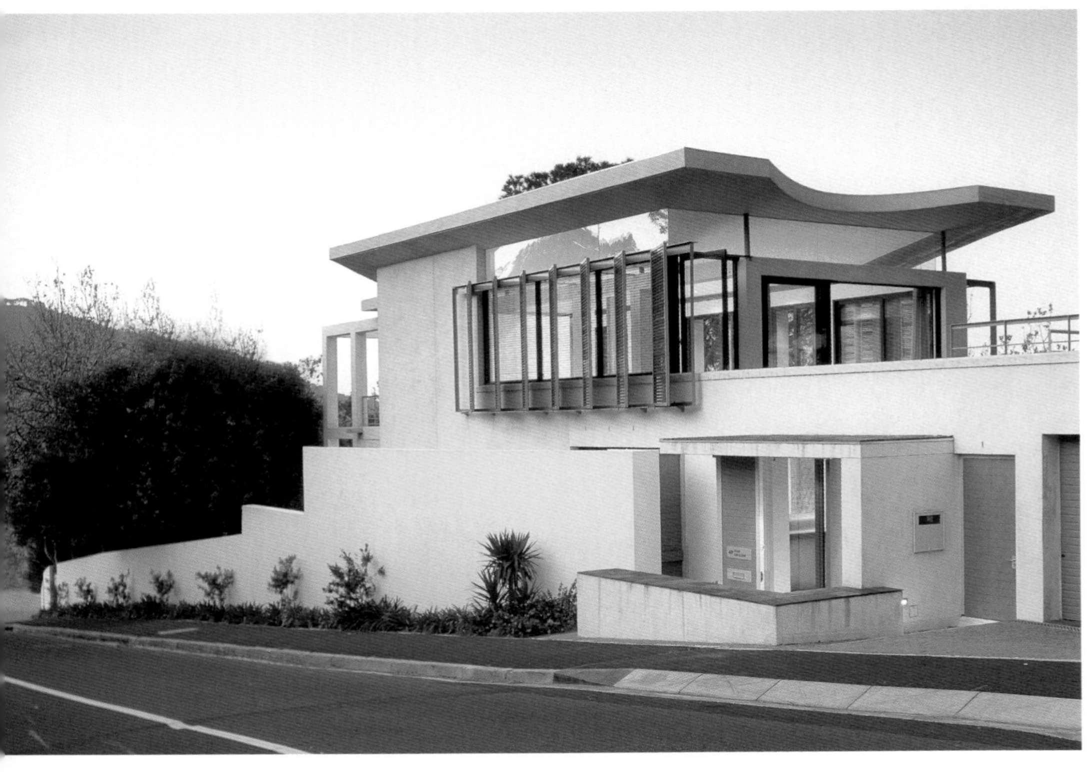

RESPECTING THE LAND

Cliff House is built on a long narrow site that is 45 ft (14 m) wide by 228 ft (70 m) long. Located in a heavily wooded area in a suburb of Cape Town, it has panoramic views toward Table Mountain, the cityscape, and the ocean. Two considerations early in the design process were to maximize access to the views and to retain as many of the trees on the site as possible in order to provide privacy, noise reduction, and protection from the sun.

The architects were asked to come up with a design that accommodated the usual living spaces – living room, dining room, kitchen, three bedrooms, bathrooms, and a study area – as well as a self-contained flat that could be used for visitors or staff, plenty of storage space, and a double garage.

The site configuration influenced the form of the house, a rectangular building sitting parallel to the natural contours of the land. This approach reduced the need for extensive excavation. There is a strong reference to nature in the design, as the modular arrangement admits plenty of light and ventilation, even to the lower parts of the house.

CLIFFTOP VIEWS TO THE SEA

In the middle of the three levels, the main entrance to the house leads directly into the living and dining areas. These are bound by a terrace that extends the living area to the outside and immediately draws the

eye to the ocean views. A fireplace in the center of this area warms the house. This level also contains the garage as well as private access to the flat and laundry below.

A suspended staircase connects this level to the bedrooms and bathrooms on the one below, and to the upper level, which contains the study, the study terrace, and the rooftop terrace, all of which boast fine views of the mountains and the sea. The location of the stair allows uninterrupted views through the "view-facing" facades.

LAYERED AND SURPRISING

The northwestern facade is a solid wall with strategically placed openings that afford particular views, such as to the mountains. There are also doors leading to the garage and main entry. The northeastern facade is primarily a gallery structure, and timber decks provide protection from the sun in the hottest part of the day. The timber and supporting lightweight steel frame structure were chosen to contrast with the concrete finish on the rest of the house, and to give it a warm, textured ambience. The window shutters are also timber.

A central entry court, planted with native and exotic plants, is set in the middle of the rectangle of the house. The overall impression is that the home has a number of layers that provide the visitor with a variety of experiences.

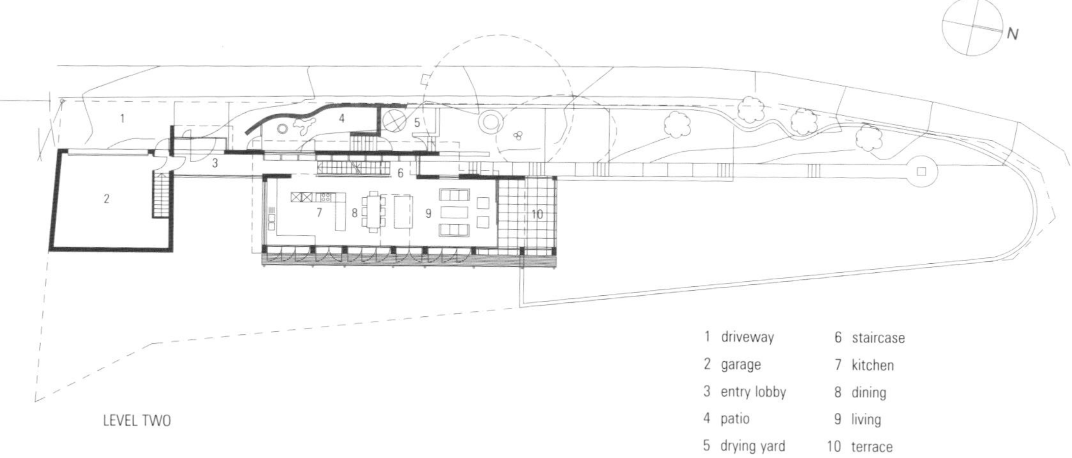

FAR LEFT
The western facade shows the main entrance on the middle level. Pivoting timber screens control the amount of sunlight to the study on the upper level, while the roof slab tilts up along its western and southern edges to allow extensive views toward Table Mountain.

TOP LEFT
In contrast to the western facade, the eastern facade comprises an elevated and modulated concrete grid structure. Timber shutters screen the in-fill glazing, and a lightweight steel and timber balcony echoes the primary structural grid.

ABOVE
On the middle level, the kitchen can be seen beyond the living room. Sliding doors to the left open onto the east-facing balconies with their views toward the city and the sea. The stairs to the right link this level with the study above and the bedrooms below.

Exploded House BODRUM, TURKEY

GAD-Gokhan Avcioglu NEW YORK, USA

Constructed	2005
Home type	Three-story family house
Structure	Glass, steel, concrete, and local natural stone

"The house successfully reflects GAD Architecture's working principles, which are sustainability, eco-friendliness, and micro-climate. This project is also very successful in terms of combining geographical and local conditions with today's contemporary technology."

GAD Architecture

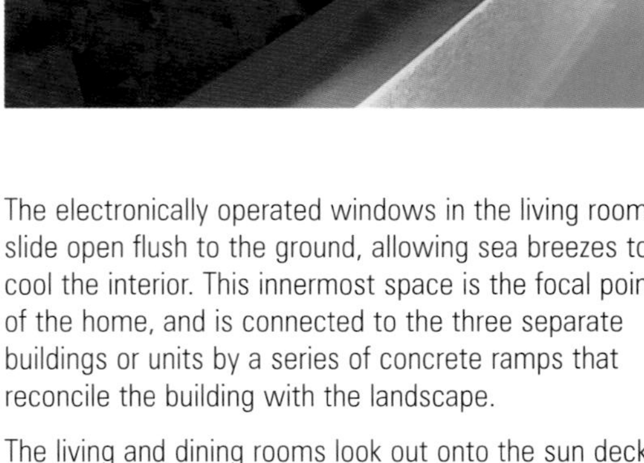

TOP
The natural cooling system for the house consists of a pool on the roof of the main building. Rainwater collects here, then cascades onto the next roof before being recirculated.

ABOVE
On the southeastern side of the house are the study, the unit on the left, and the main bedroom, on the right. A glass atrium connects these two separate buildings.

HISTORIC SETTING

Bodrum is a Mediterranean port and trade settlement in the southwest of Turkey. The area boasts a rich 3,000-year history, which includes the Hellenistic, Roman, and Ottoman periods. The venerated scientist Heredot was born here, and sculptures by renowned artists such as Leochares, Bryaxis, and Timotheos were once exhibited here. These works are now held in museum collections around the world.

METAPHOR FOR A SINGLE BUILDING

The owners have a vast antique collection reflecting the rich history of the area. They wanted a home that would complement and display their collection without making them feel as if they were living in a museum.

The local outdated building codes restricted new forms of architecture being introduced. To overcome this and to create a more flexible building type, the architects created a house with three separate buildings linked by a glass atrium – a metaphor for a single building that has been "exploded" into many parts.

Each unit, which complies with the regulation size of 800 sq ft (75 sq m), has a separate function. There is a main bedroom and ensuite; a kitchen and dining room; and a guesthouse with an adjacent study.

The central glass atrium has a dual function – it is the entry to the building as well as the main living area. Floor to ceiling windows allow 180° vistas of the stunning landscape and bay.

The electronically operated windows in the living room slide open flush to the ground, allowing sea breezes to cool the interior. This innermost space is the focal point of the home, and is connected to the three separate buildings or units by a series of concrete ramps that reconcile the building with the landscape.

The living and dining rooms look out onto the sun deck and swimming pool. From here, the ramp leads down the hillside to a guest unit (an additional self-contained apartment), which is nestled in the landscape and hidden from the house above.

PART OF THE LANDSCAPE

The open plan of the main house ensures that it is light and airy, a must in summer. As a secondary precaution, the roof of the building is covered with pools that collect rainwater. The water cascades from one roof to another and then recirculates, thus creating a natural cooling system for a hot climate.

The "Exploded House" harmonizes with the natural environment. When observed from above, the pools mirror the surrounding landscape and the panoramic views of the bay, helping to mask the presence of the building on the hill.

1 living
2 dining
3 study
4 main bedroom
5 pool
6 sun deck
7 guest unit

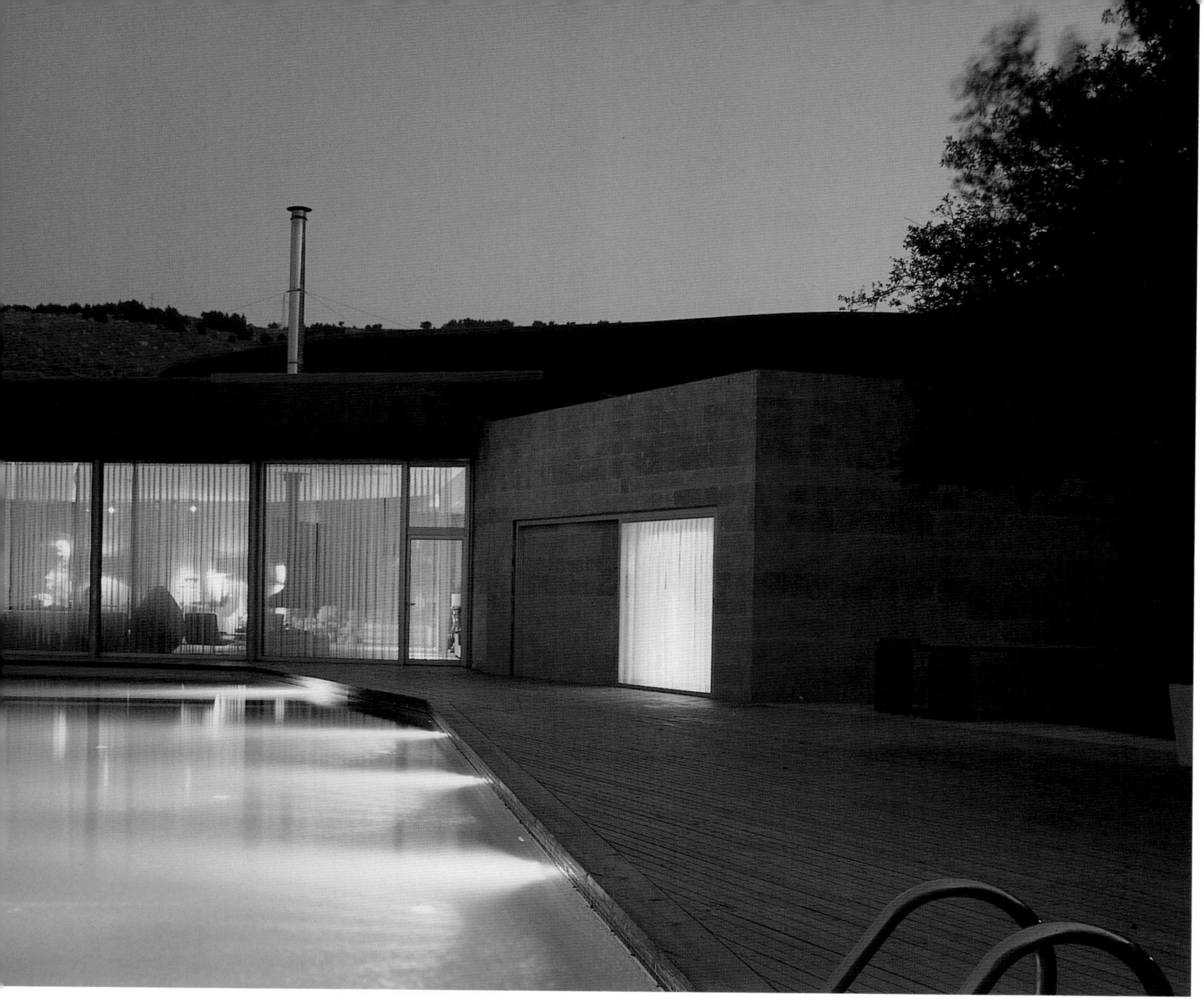

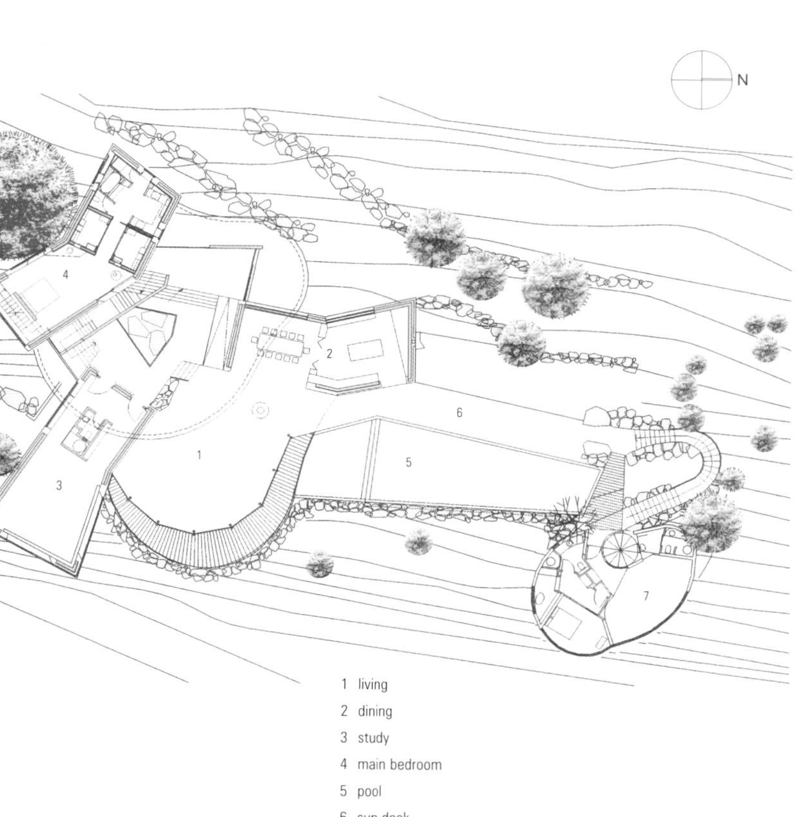

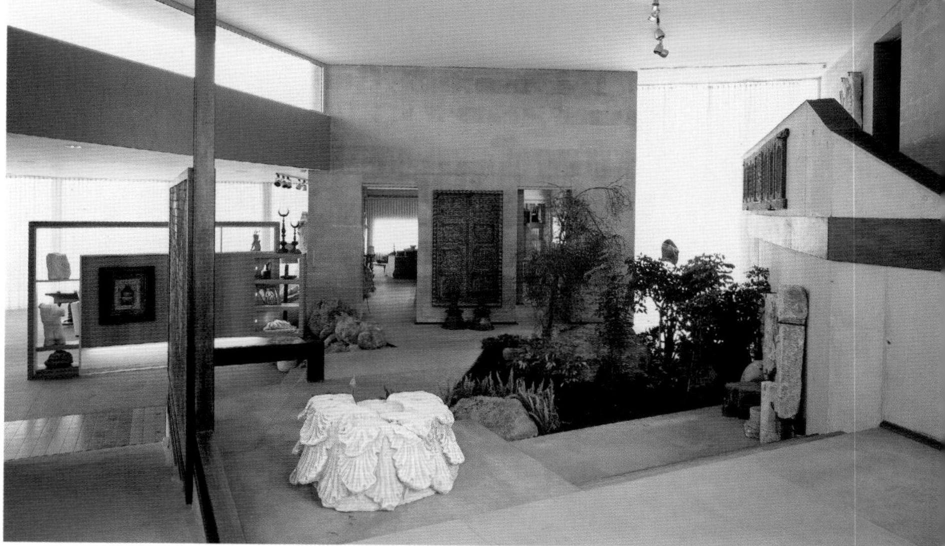

TOP
The home comprises three separate buildings, each with a separate function. The kitchen and dining room unit, seen here, look out over the swimming pool and sun deck. The structure itself forms a low-profile against the rising rocky terrain behind.

ABOVE
The neutral color palette of the living room, together with the indoor garden, and rough-texture, natural finishes, connect the interior with the sun-bleached terrain outside, at the same time providing the perfect backdrop for the owners' art collection.

Floating House SUNGAI BULOH, MALAYSIA

Ngiom Partnership

Constructed 2005
Home type Two-level family home
Structure Concrete, glass, and aluminum

FRONT

"Water – and the floating qualities it possesses – was the inspiration for this dramatic home. The ambience of Floating House is completely determined by the overriding motif of water."

Teng-Ngiom Lim

A "FLOATING" HOUSE

Sierramas, a gated community in Sungai Buloh, about 12 miles (20 km) from Kuala Lumpur, is the site for this dramatic house. Situated on the edge of a cliff, the house appears to float on water. It is this dazzling point of reference that dominates the overall impression of the structure.

MELDING OUTSIDE AND INSIDE

The formal responses to the setting are complemented by both lyrical and metaphysical responses, and the surrounding environment is integrated into the design of the house. The walls have been purposefully designed with a transparent quality, to make the boundaries between the inside and the outside appear somewhat ephemeral. The architect sees this as a desirable facet of the home. As the trees and other plants reach maturity, the distinction between exterior and interior spaces will be reduced further, uniting the built environment with the natural surroundings.

This blurring of boundaries between outside and inside is again accentuated when the glass louvers are opened. As the outside world enters the house, the sound of water quite naturally becomes integral to the inside spaces. Water is an important element of the design – it unites the house with the landscape.

ABOVE
The understated front of the house is expressed only by a carport and a water tower. Light streams through glass panels in the carport roof, separating it from the main house, and flooding the back wall in light. The water tower anchors the carport to the main house.

TOP RIGHT
The pathways along the side of the house leading to the main entrance mirror each other in form and structure; the one on the right, steps over water, and launches the "floating house".

OPPOSITE
The house floats over a pool of water and over the edge of the cliff, pointing toward the horizon. While the rest of the house is open and accessible, the balcony is private, and can be reached only from the bedrooms, ensuring that it remains a secluded retreat.

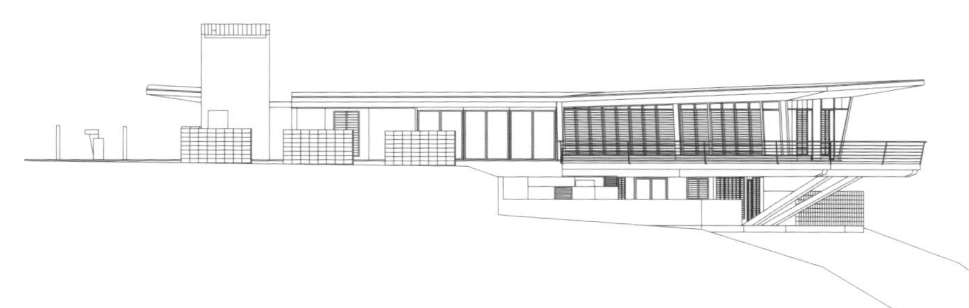

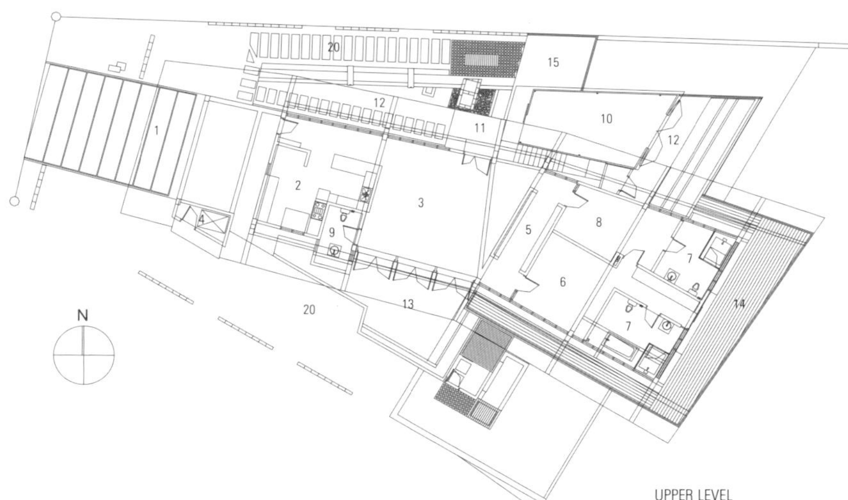

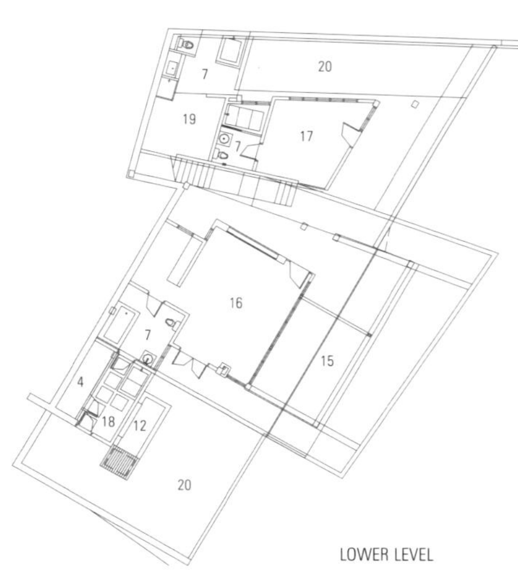

1 carport
2 kitchen
3 main hall
4 services
5 library
6 main bedroom
7 bathroom
8 bedroom
9 WC
10 dining
11 entry
12 water feature
13 pool
14 balcony
15 terrace
16 guest bedroom
17 maid's room
18 outdoor shower
19 laundry
20 garden

WATER IS THE KEY

The owner's love for water is expressed in the style of the bathrooms. On the ground floor, they are located in areas with the highest ceilings, and the walls are glazed almost from floor to ceiling, washing the rooms with natural light during the day. To accentuate the invitation of light, the main bathroom has an additional skylight. Part of the bathroom is extended over the main pool, so that glass, light, and water come together through their fluidity, lightness, and visual permeability.

Each of the larger bedrooms is visibly connected to a distinct water body – the main bedroom flows out to the main pool, and the second bedroom on the ground floor is linked to a water feature. The ground floor main bedroom is connected to both a garden and water feature. The various pools create a tranquil environment throughout the home, bringing the external environment inside.

The kitchen, too, looks out on water. The room has its own skylight, connecting the blue of the water with the blue of the sky, creating a serene indoor/outdoor flow.

The terrace on the ground floor faces the back of the slope and is accessible only from the bedrooms, connecting this part of the house to the environment.

The roof of the carport is joined to the main building by a row of glass panels that allow natural light to wash the back wall. The carport itself is a single thin concrete slab anchored by the water tower.

FAR TOP LEFT
The principal part of the house and deck floats over the lower garden. The edge of the main pool is visible in the foreground.

TOP RIGHT
The home's tapering walls result in a large roof overhang, which effectively shades the interior – a decided asset in a tropical climate. The deck looks back toward the main pool.

TOP LEFT
The main bathroom is spacious and well lit. A combination of light, glass, glazed tiles, and water makes the bathroom a liquid and sensual place.

RIGHT
The walls have a transparent quality, blurring the boundary between inside and outside, The interplay between glass, light, and water creates an ambience of cool serenity.

Heise House SYDNEY, AUSTRALIA

Peter Downes Designs

Completed	2002
Home type	Single family dwelling
Structure	Steel and timber

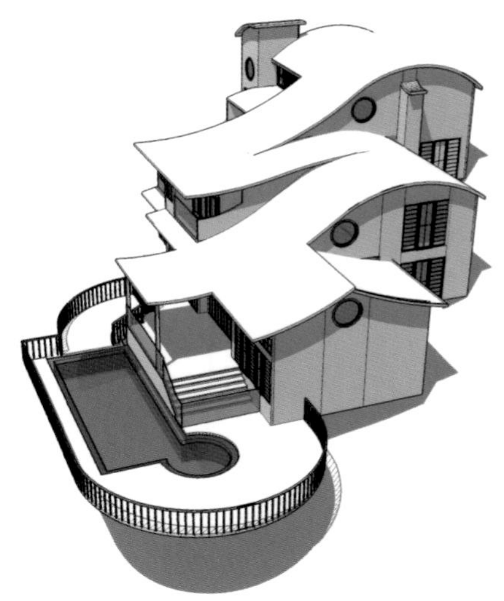

"I have a deep and lifelong love of the Australian landscape, and one of the ways I express this emotion is by designing houses on unspoilt bush sites. And the challenge becomes even more interesting when the site is steep, as the design inevitably becomes a three-dimensional exercise. So this project for me is close to being perfect."

Peter Downes

ABOVE
This computer image shows the swooping and diving roof lines of the house as it cascades down the steep site. The articulated plan shape meant that many of the significant trees on the original site were retained.

LEFT
The convoluted roof lines produced many geometrically interesting ceiling shapes, highlighted by the use of bold, contrasting colors throughout the home. Australian hardwoods were used extensively to capture the bush spirit.

TOP RIGHT
Exposed steel was used as a design element to emphasize the curved roof lines, and to visually link the indoors and outdoors. Multifold doors connect the family room to the covered outdoor entertaining area, which leads to the lower level deck and pool via wide timber stairs.

FAR RIGHT
Nestled amongst the gum trees, and perched on the edge of the precipitous slope, the modest entry gives little hint of the size of the structure below.

BUSH RETREAT

The owners needed a large family home to accommodate their three daughters and one son, with sufficient living spaces to help preserve a sense of order. The family includes several musicians, so space was needed in the living area for a grand piano. The house was also to take maximum advantage of the uninterrupted bush views from as many of the rooms as possible, to provide a respite from the owners' busy professional lives.

Because the house is located on a steep block with no usable outdoor areas, the owners wanted a pool surrounded by large decks, all connected to the living areas. And they also wanted something unique.

DESIGN SOLUTIONS

Twenty minutes drive from the Sydney CBD, the site was 360 sq ft (4,000 sq m) of indigenous forest in Beecroft, with a fall of 52 ft (16 m) – the equivalent of five stories – over the building area. The clients had already had a previous unsympathetic design rejected by the local council and were anxious to get it right the second time around.

The first step in the design process was to identify all the significant trees, and then to try to fit a house between them. A zigzag outline was sketched up that saved all but one tree, and at the same time produced

a sunny northeast aspect for the house, as well as uninterrupted bush views from all the living areas and the main bedroom.

Three main floor levels were needed to compensate for the slope and to provide sufficient floor space (some 4,000 sq ft [360 sq m] in total), with the lowest (living) level further split by a 3-ft (1-m) drop, and then another 3-ft (1-m) drop to the pool and associated decks.

The top level contains the garage, a large utility room, and the entry. The middle level contains all the bedrooms while all three separate living areas are on the lowest level.

The main living areas open via multifold doors onto a covered entertaining deck, with wide steps leading to the pool decks.

CURVES AND SWOOPS

The swooping, curved rooflines ensured compliance with the overall height limit, while disguising the bulk and scale of the building as it steps down the site. An additional benefit of the curved rooflines was varied and interesting ceiling geometry, artfully highlighted by bold color selections.

Lightweight construction with minimum excavation was chosen as the most cost effective and environmentally friendly building methodology.

Further interest was added to the design by mixing painted weatherboards and corrugated steel cladding, both with vertical shadow lines to complement the design.

LIGHT AND PRIVACY

The use of obscure glass and glass bricks solved potential privacy issues for some of the secondary rooms that look out on adjoining dwellings. Skylights and carefully positioned highlight windows bathe the interior with natural light and provide views of the tree canopy and sky.

Hill House CALIFORNIA, USA

Johnston Marklee and Associates

Constructed 2004
Home type Three-level, single-family home
Structure Concrete, steel, and timber

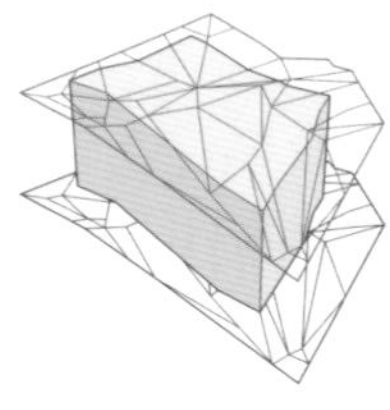

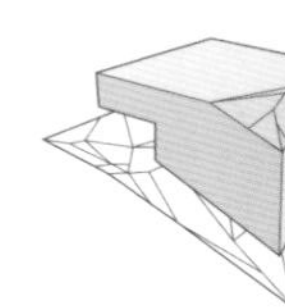

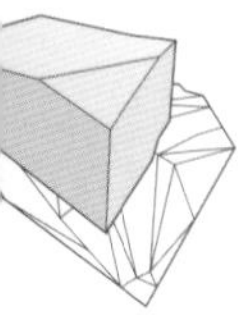

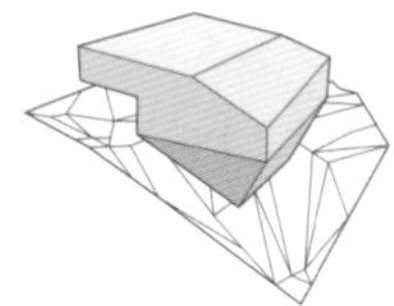

"The Hill House was designed under conditions generated by modern problems of hillside building. Sited on a steep uneven, downhill slope, the design of the house utilizes the restrictions of hillside and zoning ordinances to create a spatial and structural opportunity – adopting the zoning envelope as a building form. The dynamic form minimizes the distinction between roof and wall planes while maximizing the distinction between interior and exterior."

Johnston Marklee & Associates

The site is an irregular-shaped block of land on a sloping hillside that has sweeping views across Rustic and Sullivan canyons to Santa Monica Bay. Local planning authorities have placed stringent restrictions on hillside construction so that the natural terrain is not compromised. The architects of Hill House used these restrictions to advantage, by incorporating them into the design and blending the house into the hillside.

PUSHING THE ENVELOPE

The fixed zoning envelope was the basis for the design, and the architect compressed the home's individual components into specific patterns. Non-structural walls and partitions were kept to a minimum. The upper level contains a semi-private loft space; the lower level contains the main bedroom, and between these two levels sits the central living and dining spaces. The levels are connected by a steel and glass staircase. The walls and ceiling of the interior have been shaped to emphasize the geometric feel of the house. They also double as storage spaces.

WONDERFUL WINDOWS

The windows have been strategically installed to get the most from views, and to allow plenty of light and air circulation. The lie of the land, with its impressive views of the canyon and ocean in three directions, means that the rear of the house actually appears as if it were the front. Sliding glass doors merge the inside with the outside. The windows to the bedrooms are recessed, permitting views to the outside, but preventing outsiders from looking in. Skylights have been placed both in the flat and sloped roofs, and create a three-dimensional ambience.

PICTURE PERFECT MATERIALS

The elastomeric cement exterior coating gives the house a continuity with its surroundings, as the roof and walls appear as a unified expression. The lavender color was inspired by the color of the bark of local eucalyptus trees and serves to merge the house with the landscape. As the day lengthens, the light changes and creates an interplay with the colors of the spectrum. Inside the house, polished Carrara marble and glossy countertops contribute to a seamless feeling. Coupled with the enameled steel and lacquered wood finishes, and the dark walnut flooring and cabinetry, the effect is complete.

Native California grasses have been planted in the garden, softening the slope. These are counterbalanced with dramatic succulent plants, well suited to the temperate climate of California.

STURDINESS AND STRENGTH

The home's challenging location demanded a strong assembly and the architects chose concrete, steel, and timber as their major construction materials. Nine 35 ft (10.5 m) deep, reinforced concrete piles form the foundation for the house; these are held together by a system of grade beams. From the foundation, the concrete walls are set at a slope, rather than vertically. A steel frame comes out of the concrete base to create the central core of the house and the cantilevered overhang at the home's entrance.

TOP LEFT AND ABOVE
Three-dimensional models illustrate the different requirements of the Hillside Zoning Ordinance as applied to the site to generate the maximum allowable building volume.

LEFT
The geometric shape of the house, as seen from across Santa Monica Canyon, is the zoning ordinance made visible on the hillside, with each inflection of the mass registering the topographic nuances of the site. The resulting sculptural design seamlessly engages with the surrounding site.

TOP
To express the continuity of the building skin and to minimize the conventional distinctions between roof and wall planes, an elastomeric cement exterior coating material was used. Oversized openings, which are oriented away from the street in favor of canyon and ocean views, puncture through the seamless skin.

ABOVE
The inclined walls rise perpendicularly from the grade instead of vertically, giving the house the figure of a "prevented fall" against the landscape.

TOP LEFT
Clerestory windows above the bookshelves draw light into the study from a skylight above, which brings direct light into the mezzanine-level bathroom and closet.

TOP RIGHT
The placement of a skylight window on the sloped roof further blurs the conventional differentiation between roof and wall. Indirect light sources and unanticipated views from these openings further enhance the three-dimensional quality of the space.

ABOVE
An open floor plan, high ceilings, and lofted upper level allow for dramatic views and natural light to be experienced throughout the house. With few interior partitions, the living spaces are flexible and able to accommodate contemporary lifestyles.

Public and private living areas are arranged within the fixed building envelope; thus the setbacks of the irregularly formed lot result in "shaped" living spaces.

ABOVE
Light from the upper levels of the home cascades down the folded steel staircase into the sitting room of the more secluded main bedroom. The sculptural open staircase stitches together the three levels of the house.

Hofbauer House VIENNA, AUSTRIA

Pichler & Traupmann Architects

Construction	2000–2001
Home type	Three-story family home
Structure	Concrete slab floor and walls with steel columns

SECOND FLOOR

FIRST FLOOR

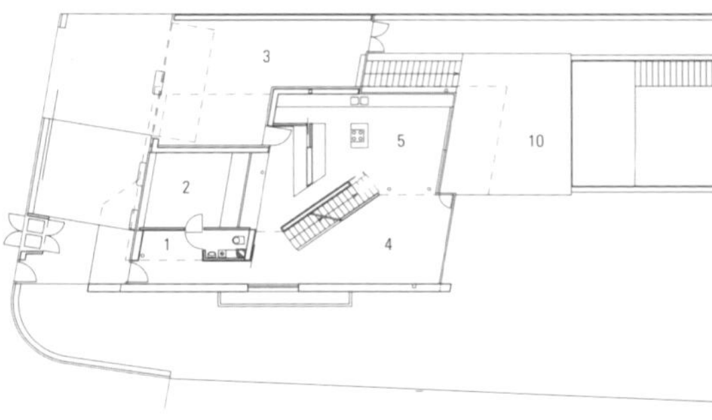

GROUND FLOOR

1 hall
2 office
3 garage
4 living
5 dining
6 library/study
7 main bedroom
8 bedroom
9 open to below
10 terrace

"Not only should space be capable of flowing from the inside out and the outside in, the spatial shell should also awaken from its autonomous state and architecturally merge inside and out in an analogous, flowing gesture. In addition, we go beyond classical Modernisms, 'Platonic solids,' and structural homogeneity in the direction of dynamic duality."

Pichler & Traupmann

A CITY SUBURB

In the northern part of Vienna-Floridsdorf, between the Old Danube (an old, cut-off branch of the river used as a recreational area) and the "New" Danube (a popular bathing place built as flood protection), there has been a dramatic increase in the price of building sites over recent years. This is one of the few remaining urban areas with loosely scattered single-family housing developments that lies close to the city center. Two nearby underground railway lines connect it to the rest of the city and surrounding urban areas.

Building only started in this area in the 1920s. It had once been a gravel bank, also serving for a time as a garbage tip. As no large-scale housing complexes had been built here, a plot size of about 10,800 sq ft (1,000 sq m) – the standard elsewhere – developed, and the permitted built area was set at 1,600 sq ft (150 sq m). This is the most common house size, and it is much in demand.

FLOWING SPACES

The clients' brief for a family home required the architects to maximize the area of the house, so a multilevel design utilizing various volumes was the solution.

An indoor pool and garage are at basement and ground floor level, automatically raising the living and private spaces. Typical of Pichler & Traupmann's design strategy is the diagonal axis at the center of the house, formed by staircases that open up broad views of the city. For example, the nearby Donauturm (Danube Tower), the symbol of the district, can be clearly seen from the upper levels.

The two-story living hall is linked with the upper levels by a library/study on the landing. That work area also functions as a kind of punctuation mark, leading to the bedrooms on the upper floors.

On several sides of the house, exterior platforms have been built, so as to link the internal spaces with the outdoor environment.

"FOLDED" SURFACES

Viennese building regulations allow for a certain leeway. For instance, the permitted height of eaves can be exceeded in some parts of the building as long as other parts are below the permitted height. The architects exploited this regulation by creating a complex composition.

The signature of the architects is the interlocking of various volumes. Within the house, it can be seen in the continuous surface that is "folded" back and forth a number of times – from wall to ceiling and back – creating a sense of continuity inside and out.

The architects have consistently used white render, metal sheeting, slate, and wood to give the house a harmonious but defined look.

FAR LEFT
The diagonal flight of wooden stairs links the two-story living hall with the double-height library/study above. The stairs also bridge the gap between the white plastered structural walls and the wooden lining.

ABOVE
This night view shows the spatial concept of the design: two intertwined double-story volumes are wrapped by a continuously "folded" surface. The furnishings and fittings lend the house a sleek, minimalist look.

TOP
The spaces are layered so that the floor of the library/study hovers above the dining area. White plaster has been used for the main surfaces, wood for the secondary elements, and gray paint for the structural elements.

ABOVE
The pool area was devised as a Modernist interpretation of a wellspring in a cave. Slate has been used on the walls and floor to connect the pool to the earth. Light shines only from the pool and floors, creating a warm and seductive ambience.

House and Atelier Lang-Kröll BAVARIA, GERMANY

Florian Nagler Architekten

Construction	2000–2002
Home type	Family residence with atelier
Structure	Two-story, timber construction on a basement of fairfaced concrete cladding; polycarbonate elements

TOP
The view from the northern side of the house shows the town of Gleissenberg in the distance. The house nestles into the hillside so that the entrance to the upper level is at ground level.

ABOVE
The southern side shows the home's traditional shape, which helps it to harmonize with the neighborhood. The large studio window on the upper level provides scenic views.

"Our philosophy is to concentrate our attention on the project's local conditions – topography, urban structure, and social environment – and to unite function, construction, and design. Moreover, on this project the very small budget was an important criterion, which influenced our design."
Florian Nagler

HOME AND STUDIO IN ONE

Gabriele Lang-Kröll and Peter Lang wanted to build a house for themselves and their four children near Cham, a small town in Bavaria, in a transition area between the Bavarian and the Bohemian forests. An artist who mainly works with large-sized woodcuts, Lang required a studio that could accommodate both a painting area and some machines for printing. On the one hand the project was determined by the small budget, on the other by both the clients and the public authority's open-minded attitude toward architecture.

PREFABRICATED UNITS

The house was built in a more or less marginal development area on the outskirts of Gleissenberg. Such is the form of the roof and the position of the house that it fits in with the neighboring buildings.

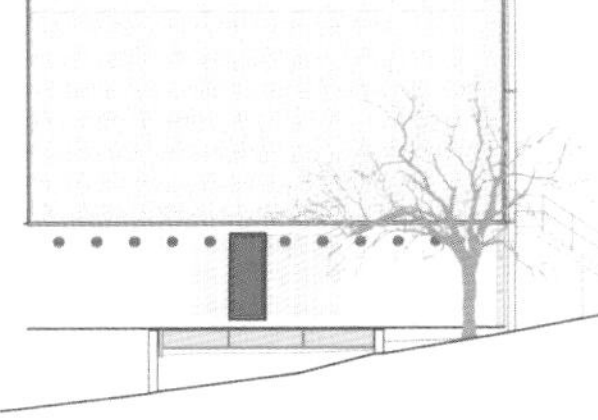

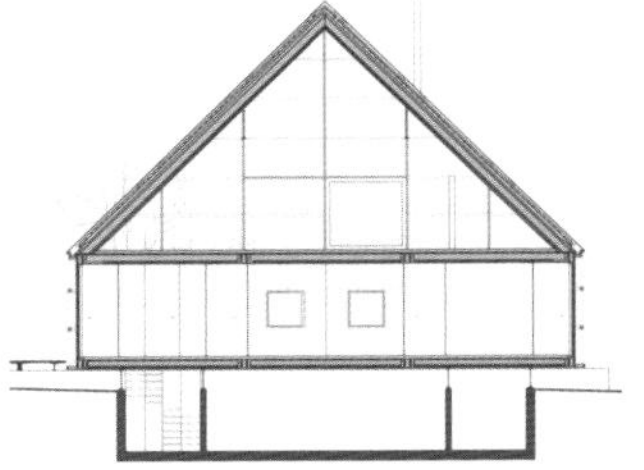

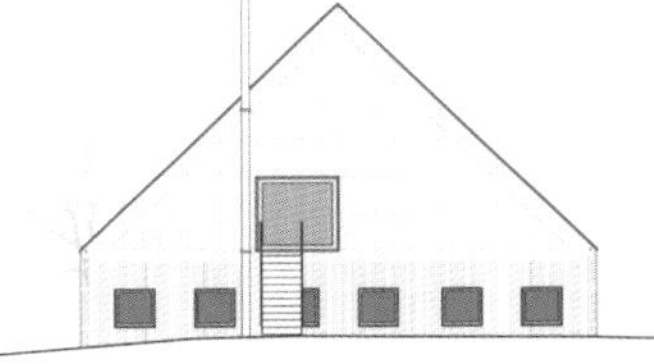

LEFT
Here the house is shown from the southwestern side. The sheltered entrance is nestled under a deep overhang and flanked by stacks of firewood, which is used to heat the house in winter.

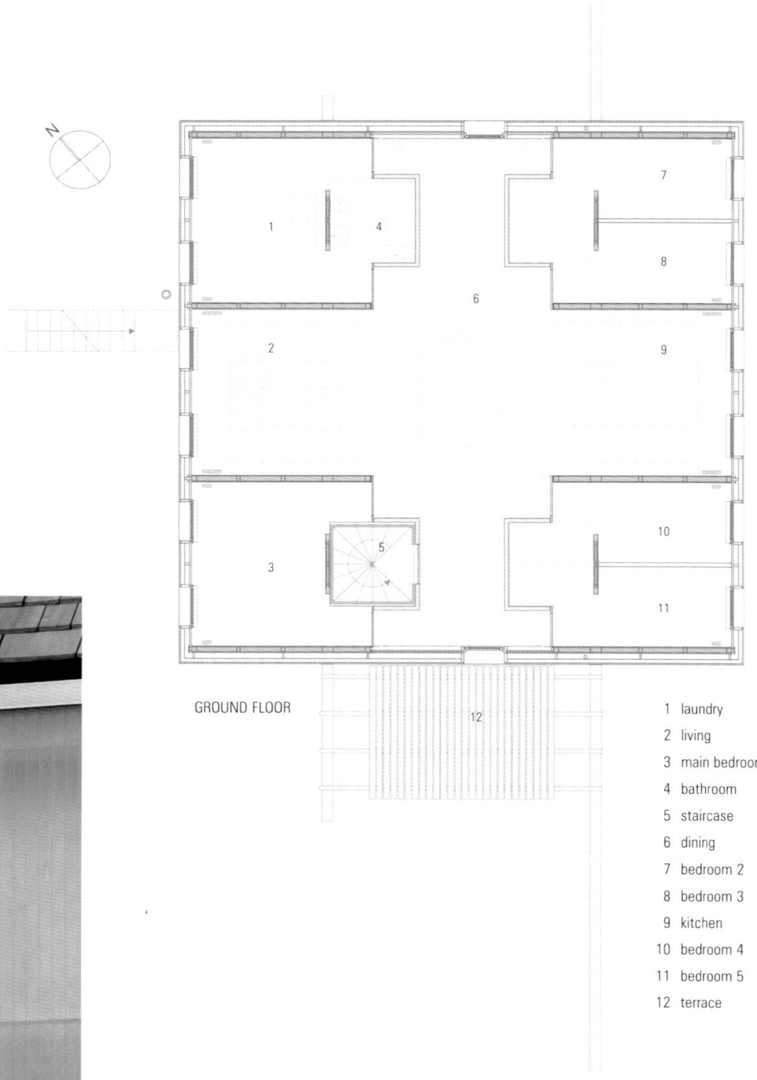

GROUND FLOOR

1 laundry
2 living
3 main bedroom
4 bathroom
5 staircase
6 dining
7 bedroom 2
8 bedroom 3
9 kitchen
10 bedroom 4
11 bedroom 5
12 terrace

ABOVE
A detail of the transparent double-wall facade, featuring the polycarbonate cladding and one of the ventilation holes, which are left open in the warmer months and closed during winter.

The timber construction stands on a basement, formed by two walls of fairfaced concrete that run parallel to the contour lines. Assembled from 14 prefabricated floor and wall units of different sizes, the house is a maximum size of 13½ x 41 feet (4.1 x 12.48 m). The overhang is created by beams that form walls in the ground floor. The floor units bear on these walls and are bolted together. Some short walls above the concrete walls in the basement take over the cross-bracing.

MAXIMIZING SPACES

The entrance, heating installation, and a workshop are located in the basement. The area is used as a roofed access, a carport, and storage area for firewood. The ground floor contains all the living areas. The studio is located in the first floor under the self-supporting roof.

The house has a neutral floor plan, so the young family can be flexible with their living space. One big room for the family is surrounded by several small rooms.

NATURAL LIGHT AND VENTILATION

A transparent double-wall facade creates a bright atmosphere both in the living area and in the light-flooded studio, so there is no need for artificial light in the daytime. The space between the inner and outer facade can be turned from summer to winter mode by simply covering the ventilation holes.

SIMPLE MATERIALS, STYLISH RESULT

The ceiling is made of rough fir wood, and all the cladding is made of polycarbonate, so there is no timber left exposed to the weather.

The clapboard roof and the simple connector system for the polycarbonate elements allowed the owners to participate in the building process. With the help of friends, the couple mounted the roof covering and the cladding. Moreover, Gabriele Lang-Kröll, who is a carpenter, built the wooden spiral staircase according to the architect's plans.

LEFT
The family's living space is a flexible area that can be changed over time to suit the growing family's needs. One of the ventilation holes can be seen in the transparent wall behind the dining area.

ABOVE
The top floor of the house contains Peter Lang's studio, which faces north and overlooks a picturesque view. Filled with natural light, it has its own entrance through a sliding glass door.

House of Courts TEXAS, USA

Lake | Flato Architects

Constructed 1997
Home type Suburban villa
Structure One-story steel frame with limestone walls and metal roofs

"The goal was to create a private haven that was friendly to the owner's art collection. We pushed the buildings to the outer edges of the lot, creating three internal courtyards. The stone walls are the defining element. They are about creating space internally rather than making a connection to the site."

Lake | Flato Architects

ABOVE
The house turns its back to the street and focuses inward toward the courtyards. The front door is reached by following a path that zigzags between large rough-cut boulders.

LEFT
A steel and glass gallery wraps around the perimeter of the primary courtyard, creating the transition from indoors to outdoors. White oak floors are banded with Colorado sandstone. The ceilings are exposed, acoustic-metal decking.

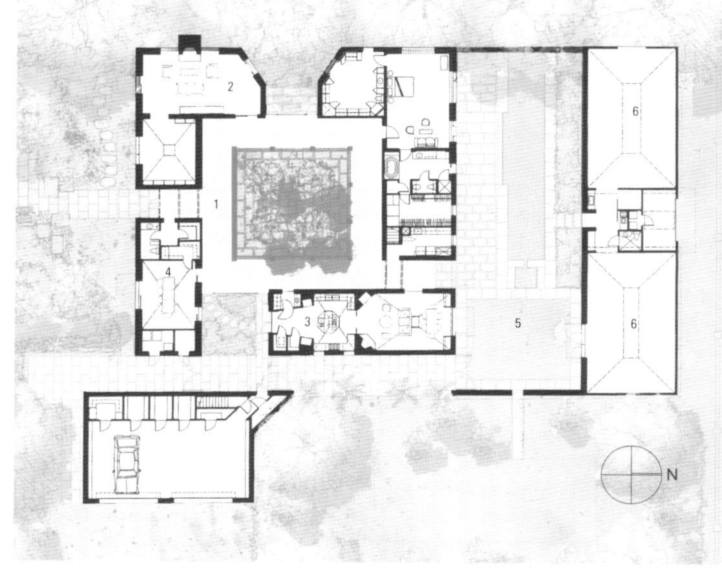

1 gallery
2 living
3 kitchen
4 dining
5 pool courtyard
6 studio

ART FOR ART'S SAKE

The architects were asked to design a house that would accommodate the impressive art collection of the owner. They took some inspiration from the essential simplicity of Texan architecture, seen in the warehouses, missions, and early stone houses that are part of the Texan landscape. The house is located in a "well-to-do suburb" populated with spacious homes, and the idea was to create an unassuming haven in the midst of the surrounding affluence.

The house is 12,580 sq ft (1,169 sq m) and has three internal courtyards, one of which has a pool. The center of the house – a large hall with high clerestory windows – contains the bulk of the owner's art collection. In the middle of this is a sculpture courtyard measuring 30 sq ft (2.8 sq m). Metal-and-glass windows and doors create a spacious gallery feeling.

PODS FOR PRIVACY

At the corners of the house sit the private and functional spaces – the bedrooms, living and dining areas, a study, and a kitchen. There is a careful delineation between the public and private areas. The private areas, called "pods" by the architect, resemble small pavilions. The wide doorways lead directly to the courtyards and garden, almost bringing nature inside the house. A row of oak trees provides shade in the courtyard garden.

PROTECTION FROM THE SUN

The roofs are metal, and those on the "pods" are topped with shaded glass lanterns that reduce the effects of the sun. This was an intentional move in order to protect the works of art from the sun, while simultaneously showing them to advantage. In the gallery area, the windows are tinted glass, filtering the potentially damaging ultraviolet rays from works by artists as varied as Picasso and de Kooning.

Another consideration in the design was ventilation. All the doors and windows open fully and breezeways are created by the positioning of the courtyards. This is critical in the hot climate of San Antonio.

STONE FOR SOLIDITY

The facade of the house is constructed of large slabs of local limestone, called "Old Yella," cut by local masons into 3 ft (90 cm) blocks and interwoven with Texan gray stone. Entry is through a recessed door built into a low wall at the front of the home. Internal walls are clad with limestone, and the floors are white oak banded in Colorado sandstone, which offers a warm contrast to the preponderance of stone in the house.

DECORATING WITH FLAIR

The high ceilings gave the owner more freedom in choosing the interior design and furnishings. Installation art sits comfortably with tall dressers and large antique candlesticks. The house, both inside and outside, is a statement of individuality in a suburban locale.

TOP LEFT
A pool courtyard separates the main house from the studio, grounded by its heavy limestone walls but lightened by the steel, lantern-like roofs that float above.

ABOVE
This rooftop view illustrates the concept of separate pods for separate functions, such as living, dining, and sleeping.

House on Blue Jay Way LOS ANGELES, USA

Studio Pali Fekete architects (SPF:a)

Construction	2002–2004
Home type	Single dwelling
Structure	Four-level steel and glass structure with teak plywood skin on top level

"This house is very special to me. You feel as if you are floating in space...a great sensation. You also get to feel the connection with all levels of the home at one time. It was quite a task to get it just right – building on a 45° angle isn't that simple, but the end result made it all worthwhile."

Zoltan E. Pali

NORTHEAST PERSPECTIVE

TOP FAR LEFT
Initial elevation drawings put the "Miesian box" on the canyon side of the home, but building requirements and future design revisions moved the glass-walled sitting room to the opposite side of the home, where it doubles as a canopy for the home's entry door.

ABOVE
Sun sets over the home's private pool area. The pool is equipped with extra features, such as color LED lighting and special fountain elements to enhance the ambience.

RENOVATING WITH VISION

Although technically a renovation project, only the foundation of the original Blue Jay Way house remains standing in this West Hollywood architectural icon. Although he is known for his spectacular historic preservation work, architect Zoltan Pali found nothing in the home's original design worth preserving. However, in order to maintain city entitlements on the land from the 1980s, the new design had to maintain some of the existing structure or it would lose up to half its height and size. The solution, which maintains the exact footprint of the original house for legal reasons, actually increased the square footage by almost 20 percent. As is often the case, constraints provided a catalyst for a uniquely beautiful architectural solution.

EXPANDING HORIZONS

The existing structure was inefficient and unsuccessful architecturally, minimizing rather than maximizing the home's greatest asset – its extravagant 180° views. New building and safety requirements enforced after the 1994 Northridge earthquake made it easier to maintain the appearance of remodeling, under the pretext of shoring up the foundation. In actuality, however, the architect replaced the original design with an entirely new structure.

"INSERTING" SPACE AND CREATING LEVELS

Perched on a steep, nearly 45° grade, the house appears to be a three-level structure from the street. Were it possible to approach from the rear, however, one would see four distinct levels, jutting vertically from the slope. Without increasing the building envelope, a lower floor was created in the unique 20-ft (6-m) tall "crawlspace," which had existed underneath the floor of the original home due to the steep hillside. The architect dug underneath the house to "insert" the extra level of living space, in much the same way that architects in New York insert pocket theaters into historic building envelopes.

The homeowner enters a three-car garage on the second level, and once inside is greeted by a narrow, 22-ft (6.7-m) long window at car's eye level. Guests enter through the outer gate, serenaded by a water

LEVEL ONE

LEVEL TWO

LEVEL THREE

1 gym
2 laundry
3 media/theater
4 office
5 game room/wine cellar
6 garage
7 window into pool from level one
8 family
9 kitchen
10 dining
11 living
12 balcony
13 pool
14 deck
15 guest bathroom
16 guest bedroom
17 walk-in wardrobe
18 main bathroom
19 main bedroom
20 sitting
21 basement below with bar, dance floor, and DJ booth

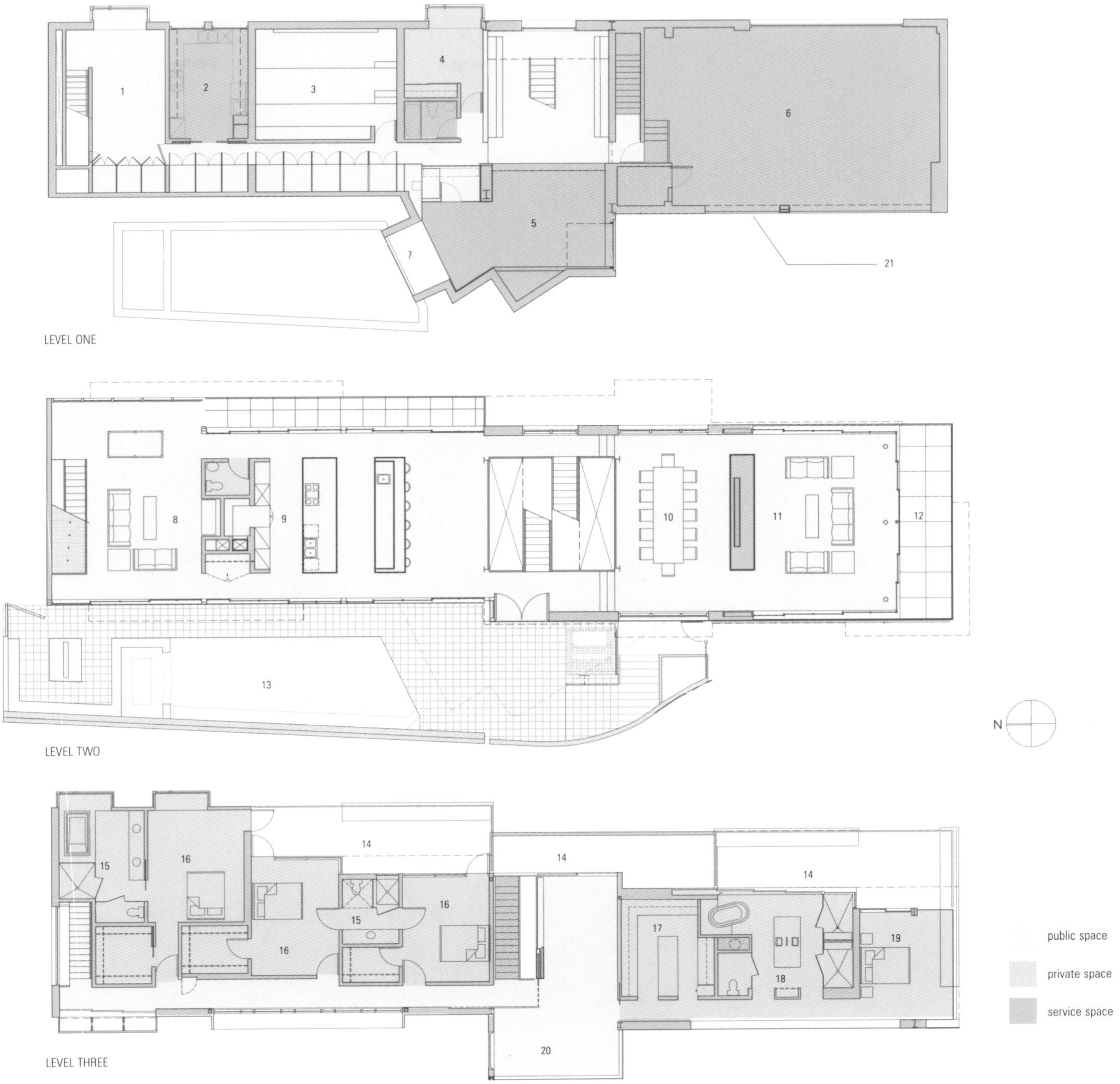

public space
private space
service space

feature that doubles as a privacy screen to the game room on the second floor. Guests ascend an outer stair past the 42-ft (12.8-m) fountain/swimming pool and enter the home on a clean, transparent level surrounded by glass. The long glass plinth cuts horizontally through the building's mass at the center, offering the home's public areas – living, dining, and kitchen – the most open view and floor plan. The main elements are located centrally and low to the walnut floor so that the views to the outside are not impeded.

A PLACE FOR WORK AND PLAY

The main floor's circulation plan flows around the perimeter, promoting changing vistas and connection with the outdoors as one moves freely between living room, dining room, and kitchen. A limestone water feature doubles as a bench and provides low separation between living and dining areas. Below, two concrete levels house entertainment and work spaces, including a media/home theater room with

LEFT
The kitchen has two island benches, helping to provide unbroken visual contact between the dining and living areas.

FAR LEFT
An imposing main stairwell connects all levels of the house and assists in creating the illusion of higher ceilings.

All four bedrooms open to an east-facing terrace to enjoy the radiant Los Angeles sunshine, predictable for most of the year.

stadium seating, glass-ceiling wine cellar (visible through the floor of the kitchen), pool table lounge, exercise room with windows overlooking the canyon, laundry room, and home office. The entire structure revolves around a generously cut 16-ft (4.8-m) main stairwell, making the home's standard ceiling heights feel higher and lighter.

THE HEIGHT OF HOME ENTERTAINMENT

Descending lower into the hillside, along a wood-paneled interior stair, one is transported to another place and time. A seductive 800-sq-ft (74-sq-m) night club with full bar offers guests all the pleasures of the Sunset Strip without the cover charge or drive down the hill. The lounge is equipped with a dual turntable DJ mix station and top-of-the-line sound system. Clad in teak wall panels of varying size and grain orientation, the lounge's rounded mirrors and white leather sofas efficiently transport the visitor to Soho in the 1970s. A mirrored ball, colored lights, and fog machine complete the mood, and a smoking terrace showcases breathtaking views of the Los Angeles basin at night.

MAXIMIZING VISTAS

The home's living quarters sit on the highest level, offering respite from ambient sound and vistas that seem to touch the sky above. The architect clad the upper residential level of the home in warm teak plywood panels. A main suite sits directly above the living room, sharing equally magnificent 180° vistas through 4-ft (1.2-m) high windows visible from the bed. Only steps from the bedside, a sitting lounge eases the journey to wakefulness with Barcelona chairs and a window-side view for morning coffee and a glance at the morning paper. A flat screen television inconspicuously awaits those who prefer "broadcast" news, mounted flush with the western wall and invisible to those who enter the room.

TRANSPARENT DESIGN, SUBTLE RESULT

Behind the master bed, a transparent shower "partitions" the bedroom from its luxurious bathroom, featuring limestone floors, an "overflow" bath, two pedestal sinks and an oversized walk-in wardrobe with two separate entry doors. A toilet and bidet are tucked away behind blue translucent glass.

A PLACE IN THE SUN

Three other bedrooms occupy the home's teak level, one with its own bathroom, the other two sharing a Jack-and-Jill style bathroom. All four bedrooms open to a shared east-facing terrace to enjoy the radiant Los Angeles sunshine, predictable for most of the year. The terrace is minimally landscaped with native plants and lined with a comfortable, cushioned bench for lounging. West of the bedrooms, a long and narrow eye-level window spans the entire entry corridor.

Perforating the smooth, marine-grade teak on the upper level, a Miesian steel-and-glass reading room juts out over the front entry, paying tribute to the legendary Modernist, while also offering western sun to the main suite, and conveniently providing shelter over the home's front entry.

ABOVE
Upon entry into the home, visitors are immediately greeted by expansive views across the Los Angeles basin.

LEFT
A long, low limestone water feature creates an elegant and understated separation between the dining area and living room.

FAR LEFT
The bed in the main suite faces the home's most spectacular views. A glass shower behind the bed separates the sleeping area from the main bathroom.

House X1 SUNGAI BULOH, MALAYSIA

Ngiom Partnership

Constructed	2003
Home type	Five-level, single-family residence
Structure	Steel, concrete, and glass

"Site terrains often have poetic values and provide limits within which the architect must work. Other constraints include budgets and planning authorities. The architect naturally must always have a design agenda, and in the case of House X1, this is related to both spatial and formal qualities, as well as a certain lyricism, all the while mindful of the restrictions imposed by site conditions and climate."

Teng-Ngiom Lim

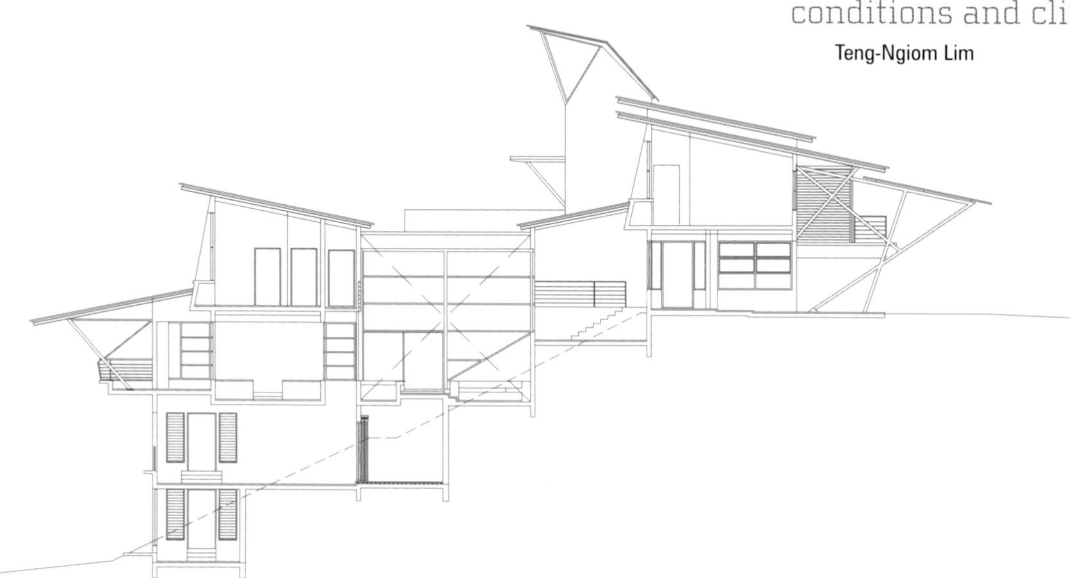

STEEP SITE CHALLENGES

Sungai Buloh is located about 12 miles (20 km) from Kuala Lumpur. The steep site, with an incline of 29°, was densely vegetated and had a small brook running across it. The house was purposely orientated toward the back of the site because it afforded the best views over the vegetation and beyond. This posed some difficulties, however, particularly as the site was quite narrow and flared at the back.

The architect wanted to keep the house as close to the slope as possible. To achieve this, a central courtyard breaks the house into two distinct parts. The courtyard space, conceived as a cubic void, is the link with all parts of the house. There is a visual link between the top and bottom of the slope, and a spatial link, which allows the passage of air to travel from the bottom to the top of the house. This breezeway is emphasized by the formation of a wind shaft, which terminates at the rooftop.

MAXIMIZING TERRAIN

The line of slope of the site dictated the planes of the house, which slowly open and flare out toward the back. The lower part of the house is set into the incline, and so it maintains an even temperature. The upper part of the house sits on top, giving the effect of a minimal barrier between the interior and exterior. Prominent roof overhangs help to moderate temperatures.

TOP
The turret at the top of the house holds the water tank, which is warmed by the sun's rays. The turret also functions as a wind funnel, discharging rising warm air from the main house. Access to the observation deck is underneath the turret.

ABOVE
The street elevation is on the cliff's edge and possesses an austere simplicity. The main spaces of the house open toward the woods at the back. The slender struts supporting the roof echo the tall bamboos flourishing along the sides of the house.

LEFT
The slope of the site dictates the various planes of the house, which closely follow the same orientation. The spaces that are sandwiched between the line of the roof and the line of the land flare open toward the back.

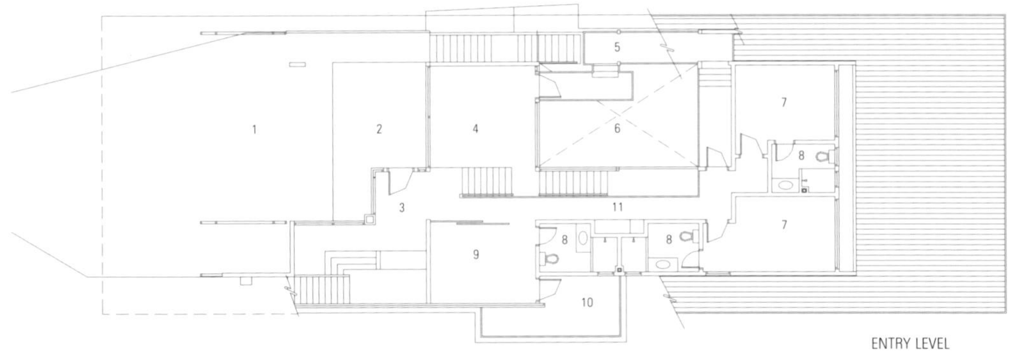

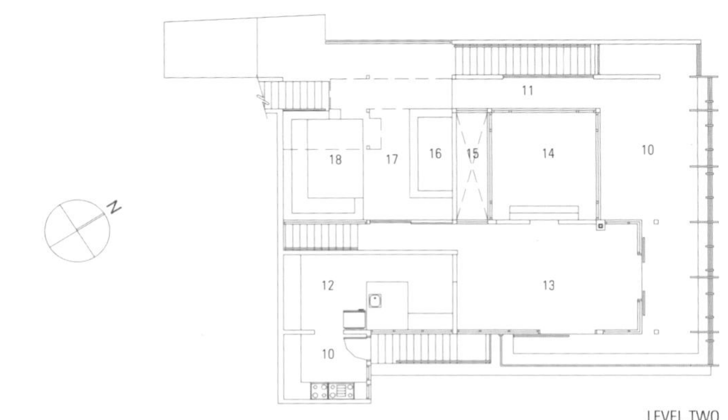

1 carport
2 entrance
3 foyer
4 family
5 bridge
6 void over courtyard
7 bedroom
8 bathroom
9 study
10 terrace
11 gallery
12 kitchen
13 dining
14 living
15 open to below
16 water feature
17 courtyard
18 sunken sitting area

USING LYRICISM

The architect considered the notion of lyricism in his design – something that is achieved when space, form, and materials react favorably with the light. He believes that architecture is successful when the climatic conditions are also taken into account. The natural landscape plays an important role – in fact, it should be considered as integral to the project. In House X1, the interior and the landscape blend, the walls becoming a transparent skin, blurring the visual barrier between the outside and inside spaces.

THE HOUSE AS ART

The architect believes that architecture should be a work of art. The canvas consists of the materials used; the backdrop is the surrounding landscape. The quality of light is a major criterion upon which art is judged – and so it is with architecture. Light also accentuates the natural qualities of solids, voids, and other textural spaces. Where light is soft and gentle, then space takes over; where light is weak, space takes on a dreamlike ambience. There is no internal decoration – the house is considered a work of art in itself. It also interacts with the natural environment – the wind, the rain, the sunlight. The sculptural poetry of the dwelling depends on the quality of light, so the house is kept white – a badge of purity and sincerity.

SIGNIFICANT FORM AND FUNCTION

Form is a critical element of the design, with the abstract preferred to the ordinary. Any deviation comes from the requirements of function, once again, emanating from the essence of natural light.

FAR LEFT
The house is visually connected throughout, with minimal barriers between the internal and external spaces. The courtyard, with its lush garden, is located in the middle of the house – this central location allows shafts of light to penetrate and illuminate all internal areas.

LEFT
Bathed in light throughout the day, the staircase leads to the bedrooms. The act of moving up and down through the light has a lyrical quality to it. The bench at the foot of the stairs is crafted from black-pigmented concrete and is yet another area to sit and contemplate the changing patterns of light during the day.

ABOVE
Viewed from the upper entrance, the house has an obvious synergy, with no distinguishable barrier between the various internal spaces and the external environment. The bridge integrates the inside with the outside; the courtyard brings the outside to the inside.

Jayasundere House COLOMBO, SRI LANKA

Varuna de Silva

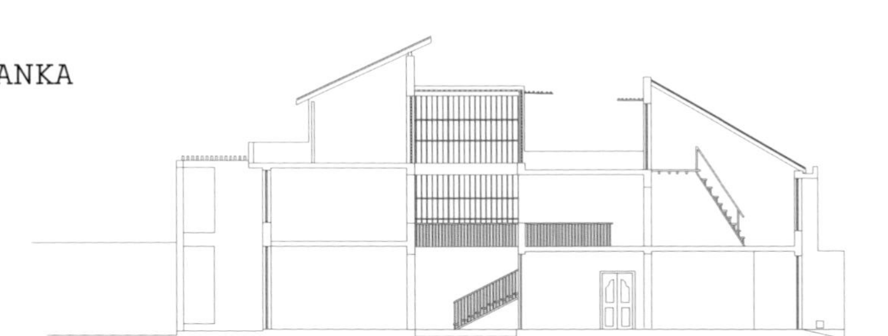

Constructed 2001
Home type Three-level family home
Structure Brick, concrete, steel, glass, and timber

"The house is located just outside Colombo's inner city limits, in a densely populated urban setting, sandwiched between two houses. The challenge was to maximize the available space yet provide comfort and functionality."
Varuna de Silva

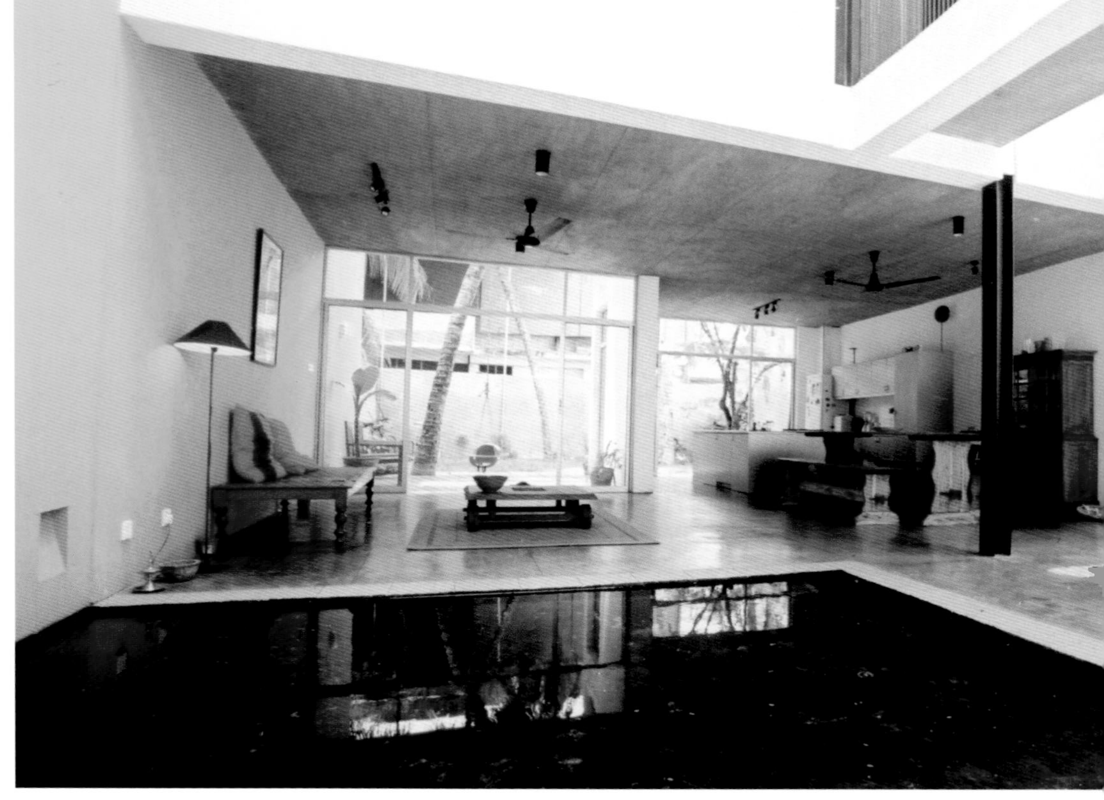

WHEN SIZE MATTERS

Small plot sizes are common in Colombo, so house design must always take this into account. Measuring 25 x 94 ft (7.5 x 28.5 m) and facing a busy street, Jayasundere House is located in a narrow side garden belonging to the client's parents' home. The house is built to the boundaries in front and on either side, but local regulations insist that a rear space be left open to the sky: This space has become the garden.

TRADITIONAL BUT CONTEMPORARY

The clients wanted a comfortable but unconventional three-bedroom home with separate work areas.

Because of the narrowness of the site, the architect was inspired by the traditional Sri Lankan courtyard house, so the middle of this house was opened to the sky in the traditional manner to admit plenty of natural light and ventilation. This design has the added benefit of keeping the house cool, a critical factor in this hot tropical location.

By keeping partition walls to a minimum, the house seems larger than it is, and the interior spaces flow into one another. Light materials were used in the design of the stairs to maintain this fluid ambience.

On the ground level, the office, storeroom, and powder room have walls. All the other spaces flow into one another and also open out into the garden, thus blurring the division between outside and inside.

LIGHT AND MOVEMENT

The husband's home office is connected to the carport, which is part of the house. The central triple-height void, which opens to the sky, provides light and air. A reflecting pool between the office and the living areas provides a quiet serenity in the middle of the house.

The owners love to entertain, so the kitchen area was placed in the center of the living and dining rooms. The reflecting pool is on one side, the veranda on the other, and the garden sits beyond.

UP ON THE ROOF

On level two, there is a family area and main bedroom with walk-in dressing room and ensuite. The two other bedrooms share a bathroom. The main bedroom and bathroom look over the garden; the other rooms, each with a timber mezzanine deck, look over the street.

Cantilevered concrete steps provide access to the roof terrace of the house. The wife's home office is also on the third level, with access to the roof terraces – an entertainment and play space.

SIMPLICITY AND STYLE

A cut and polished cement floor is just one of the basic finishes in the house. Aluminium French windows open to the garden and the roof terrace. The interior doors have been recycled from an old building. An orange-colored feature wall runs along the length of the house, providing a fascinating interplay of light and shadow as the day grows longer.

TOP LEFT
The shallow reflecting pool in the middle of the house acts as a buffer between the office and the living area, which includes the kitchen, and living and dining rooms. It also brings much needed light and ventilation into the long narrow plot. The glass walls to the garden beyond create a feeling of spaciousness.

ABOVE
The rear of the house becomes the "front," as it opens out to the mandatory rear space – the garden. The orange wall, which runs along the length of the house, ends with the double-height veranda outside the living room, complementing the "greenness" of the garden.

TOP
A steep steel checker plate and C purlin (roof beam) "ladder" provides access to the mezzanine deck.

TOP RIGHT
The middle of the house becomes its "heart," where the whole structure opens out vertically. The top is protected from the weather by a steel and glass roof, and the thin steel grilles and handrails make the building seem lighter.

1 study
2 main bedroom
3 family lounge
4 bedroom 2
5 bedroom 3
6 kitchen
7 living & dining
8 office
9 garage
10 veranda
11 open to below
12 garden
13 reflecting pool
14 open-air terrace

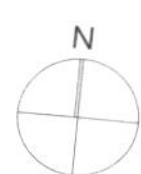

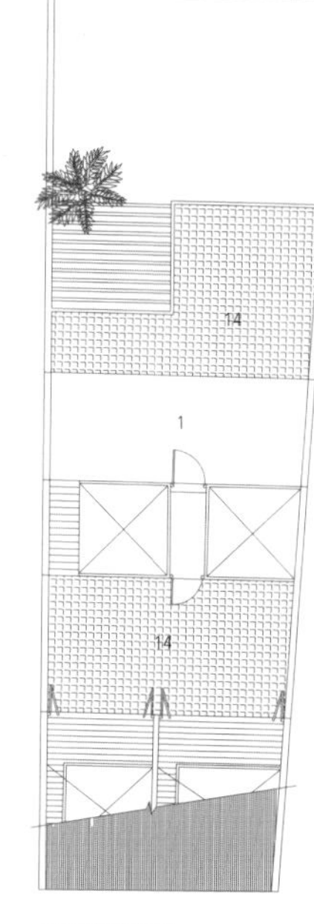

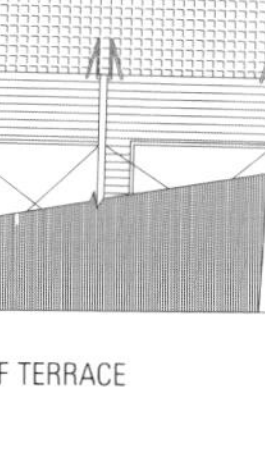

ROOF TERRACE

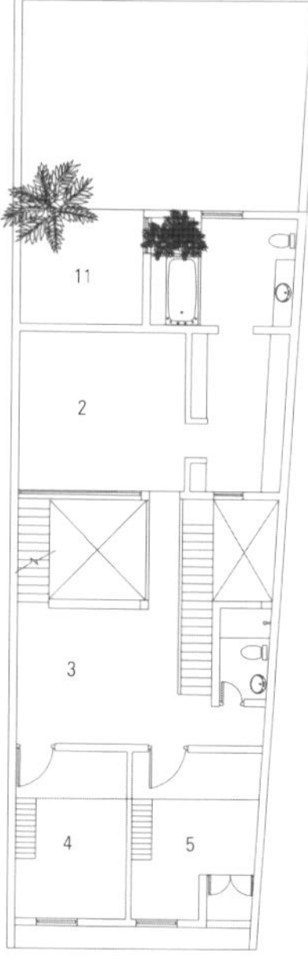

LEVEL TWO

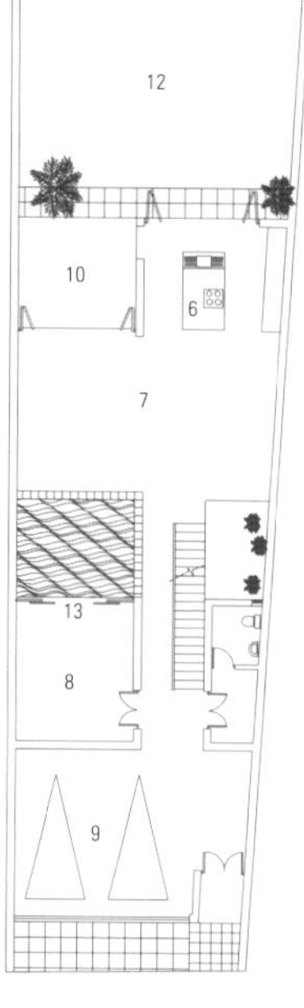

LEVEL ONE

The Mews VALLETTA, MALTA

Architecture Project

Construction	1994–1998
Home type	Four single-family residences
Structure	Stone-clad concrete frame base with load-bearing masonry above

"The project sought to fuse the current Maltese preference for the detached villa and garden with the vernacular, cubic, Mediterranean-village farmhouse structure to create an updated idiom for the suburban residence. The villas were arranged to promote opportunities for social interaction through an array of private, semi-private, and public spaces; these external spaces becoming the fulcrum of the complex."

Architecture Project

A CLUSTER OF UNITS

"The Mews" in Kappara, a charming suburb of Malta's capital city Valletta, is a condominium consisting of four homes located on a corner suburban site. The units are clustered around a spacious, central courtyard. This shared courtyard area is elevated above street level in order to accommodate a lower level of private parking – a cool, well-ventilated undercroft.

COMBINING TRADITIONAL FORMS WITH MODERN IDEAS

The project takes its cue from the Mediterranean *ortus clauses*, meaning "closed garden," and the local vernacular dwelling type – the two-story, Maltese-village farmhouse, with its solid external facades and central courtyard. The built fabric has been organized to create a balance between solid and void, and light and shade. The result is a natural equilibrium, where outside and inside merge without ever losing their definition. While the cubic massing echoes the local style, the solid podium walls are suggestive of Malta's historic fortifications.

The raised ground floor is dedicated to landscaping, with the central courtyard acting as the first in a series of threshold spaces that mediate between the street and the interiors of the homes. The main living spaces, in turn, lead out onto the surrounding private gardens. Each home has been designed as an extension of the central courtyard and the garden spaces creating a complex spatial and social environment – comprising private, semi-private, and public domains in a friendly, village-like setting.

The kitchen area, located in a corner of each unit, has been glazed in order to eliminate any feelings of enclosure and solidity – also providing a pleasant view from the kitchen out over the garden, which separates the homes from the perimeter wall.

WARM AND COOL AIR

Through the careful juxtaposition of open and closed spaces, the reservoir of cool air that accumulates in the sheltered court is evenly distributed throughout the four homes. Airflow occurs through slatted wooden openings, which were inspired by the traditional multi-layered Maltese windows with their practical louvered shutters. Warmer air, which rises unobstructed through the vertical voids within the homes themselves, is then extracted at the roof level.

PRIVATE SPACES

Each apartment has three bedrooms, the main with an ensuite. The homes extend from the lower parking level within the podium through to the family room and roof terraces. These are elevated above the surrounding suburbs to catch glimpses of Valletta and its beautiful harbors.

LEFT
The transition from the central courtyard to the staircase in each apartment is through a multi-layered door and screen. The white exterior walls with panels of blue mosaic tiles give The Mews a Mediterranean feel.

TOP RIGHT
Clean lines and simple interior finishes complement the light-filled homes. The timber finishes provide sophistication and warmth.

1 entry
2 living
3 kitchen
4 courtyard
5 garden
6 pantry
7 roof
8 common courtyard
9 staircase to garages
10 pond

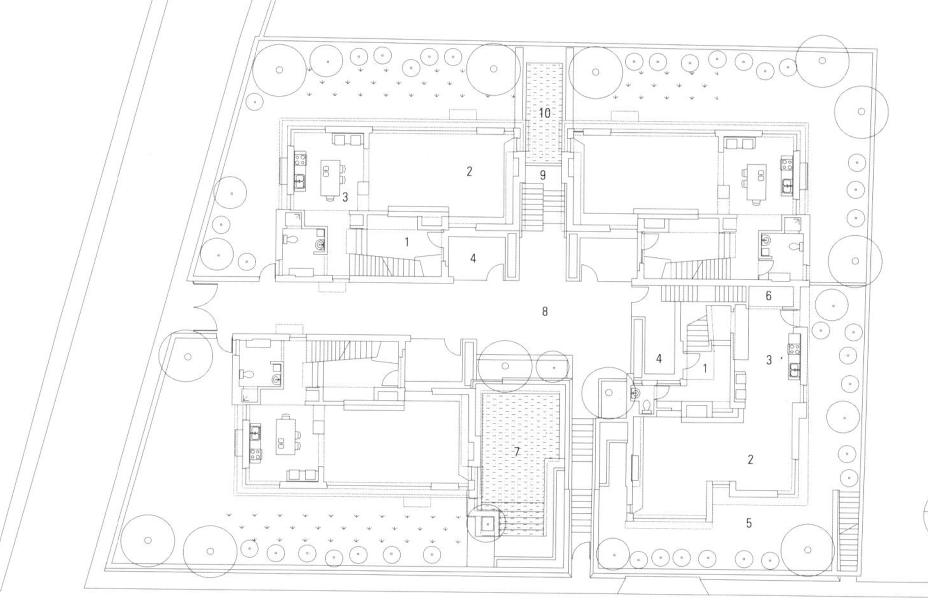

ABOVE
The Mews apartments sit above street level, on top of a private parking area. The elevated dwellings enjoy glimpses of Valletta city and its surrounding harbors.

Mosewich House BRITISH COLUMBIA, CANADA

D'Arcy Jones Design

Construction	2003–2004
Home type	Single-family dwelling
Structure	Wood-frame construction, finished in stucco

"This design expands on themes of asymmetry, continuity of form, and subtraction; the house's proportions were exaggerated and carved, transforming conventional wood frame construction into something substantial and dense. My preoccupation with section as a key determiner of how spaces feel is articulated through a range of interior and exterior spaces that are both simple and complex."

D'Arcy Jones

ABOVE
Glowing like a lantern in the trees, the house appears to be extruded from its rocky site. A muted stucco "brow" provides visual compression: a blunt form that exaggerates the fine linear detailing of the glass openings and scales down the height of the three-level house.

LEFT
Set back from the street, the house is nestled in a desert landscape. Shadowy window recesses protect the interior from the hot summer sun. A south-facing private courtyard is hinted at through five narrow slots in the wall.

VALLEY VIEWS, DEEP ROOTS

Perched on the edge of a steep slope in a natural setting, this pragmatic suburban home is surrounded by a variety of house types. Although formally different from the neighboring houses, the house is sensitive to the neighborhood's scale and materiality, while deferring to its immediate site and the desert landscape of the Thompson River valley.

Native vegetation was retained to provide a landscape buffer between the house and road – the front exterior is dotted with existing Ponderosa pines, sagebrush, and bunch-grass, in-filled with new indigenous plantings. To merge interior spaces with the landscape, a private courtyard unites the kitchen and dining areas. Intimate views of rock outcroppings contrast with long views to the river valley below.

STRONG MATERIALS

To meet budgetary constraints, no structural steel was used in the construction of the house. Rather, the house was built using conventional North American wood-frame construction, finished with conventional stucco. The structural capabilities of engineered lumber create the airy feel of the house, with its open spaces and generous overhangs.

1 hallway
2 rock garden
3 garden
4 dining
5 terrace
6 media room
7 jacuzzi/terrace

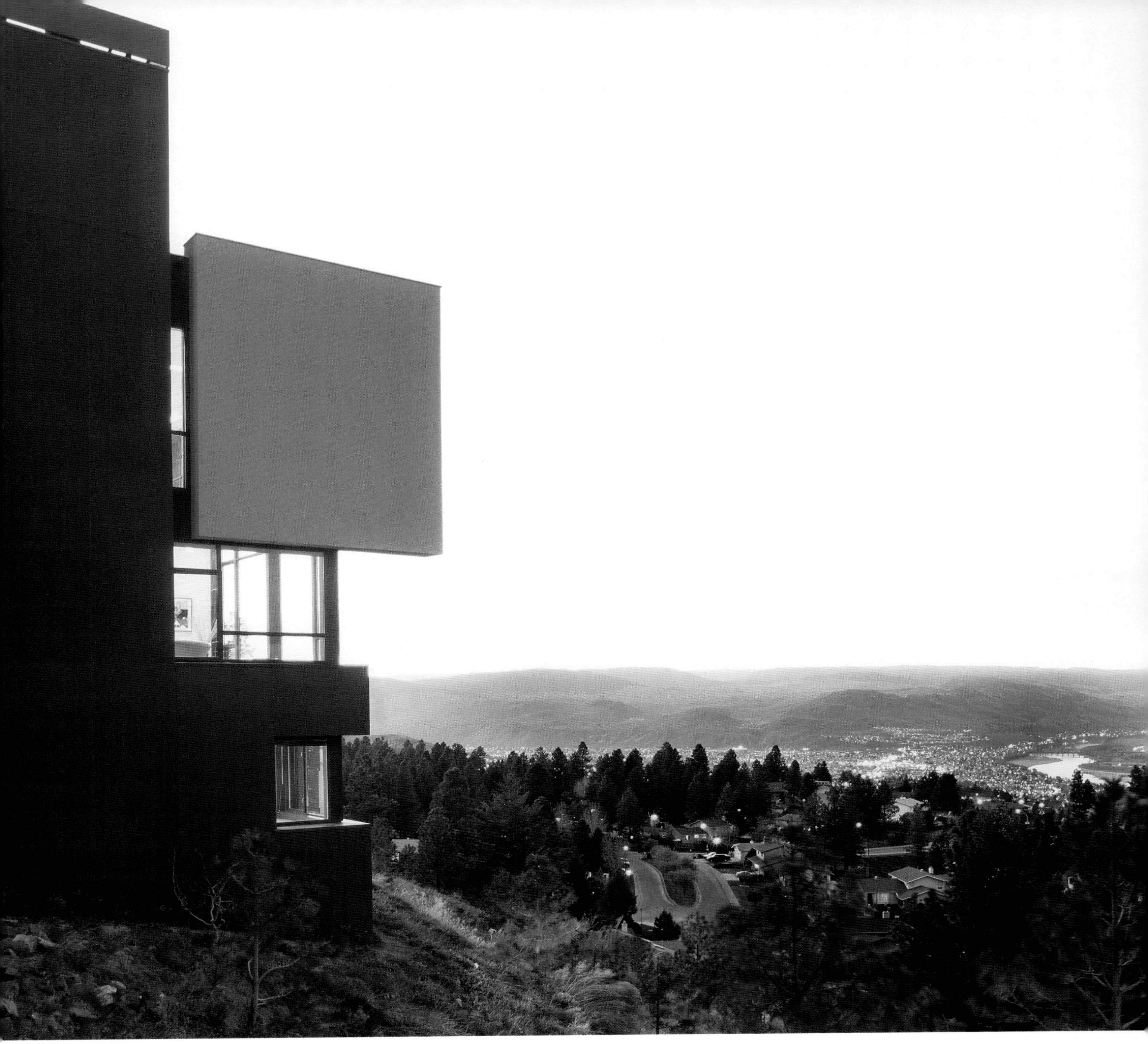

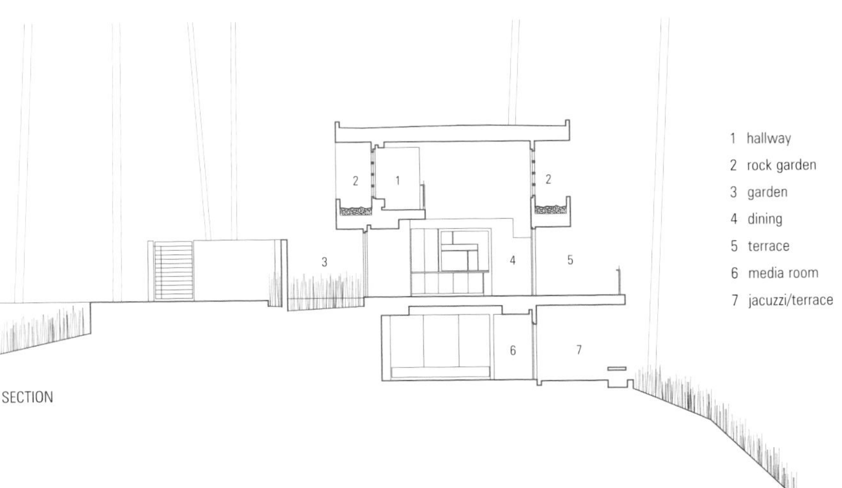

ABOVE
Overlooking the Thompson River valley at sunset, the muted stucco mass folds down to become an abstract floating plane. Separated from the dark mass of the chimney by transparent glass openings, it frames 270° views from the living area's corner windows.

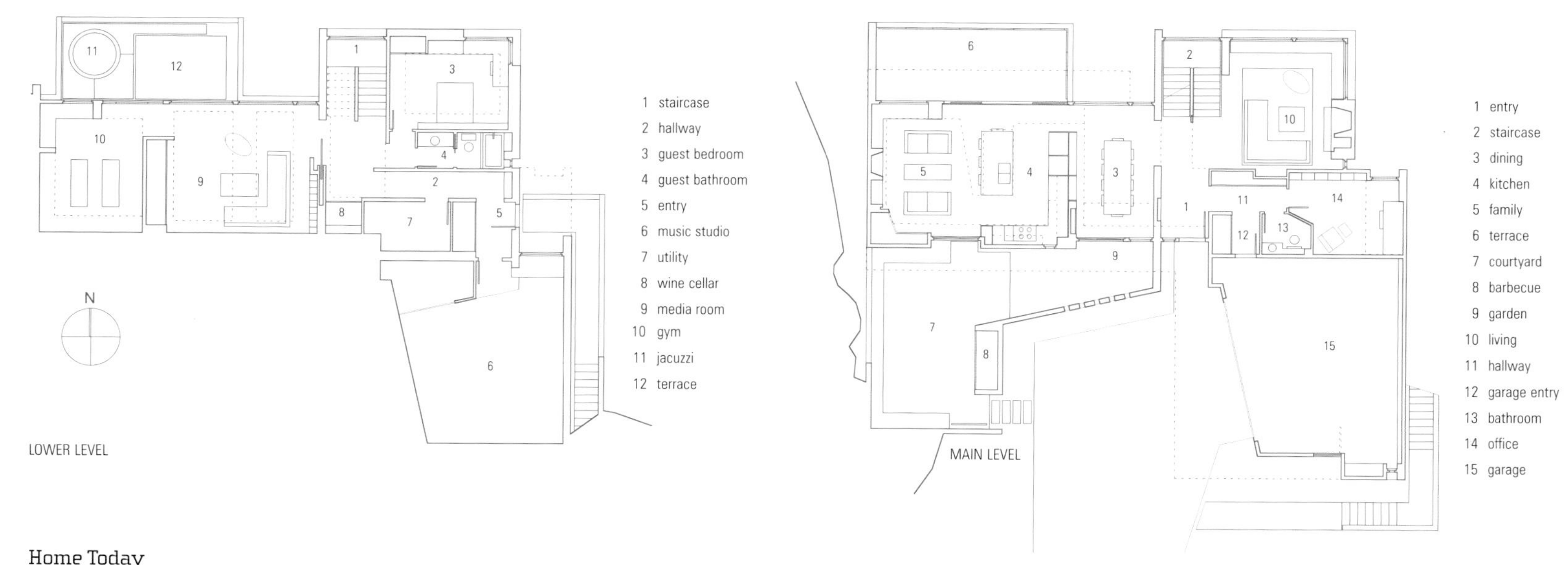
1 staircase
2 hallway
3 guest bedroom
4 guest bathroom
5 entry
6 music studio
7 utility
8 wine cellar
9 media room
10 gym
11 jacuzzi
12 terrace
N
LOWER LEVEL
1 entry
2 staircase
3 dining
4 kitchen
5 family
6 terrace
7 courtyard
8 barbecue
9 garden
10 living
11 hallway
12 garage entry
13 bathroom
14 office
15 garage
MAIN LEVEL

FAR LEFT
The double-height living area is dominated by a large chimney and open fireplace. The recessed stone panels mirror the rock outcroppings in the courtyard, while the chunky cherry mantle repeats the L-shaped asymmetry that occurs throughout the house.

TOP LEFT
A steel and maple staircase plunges through the core of the house, linking all three levels. The stairs' steel enclosure frames cropped internal views through the house, from the living area to the kitchen. A skylight over the stairs acts like a sundial through the day, constantly changing the steel mesh's level of transparency.

LEFT
The living area's mullions and floating stucco planes give human scale to a double-height space. The cherry storage ledge provides a sense of containment and security, to counter any feelings of vertigo.

INTERIOR VOIDS

The design and form of the house was primarily considered from the interior. A dark-tinted stucco mass grounds the house, visually linking courtyard walls, terraces, chimneys, and shear walls, thereby giving the impression of one continuous solid. In contrast is a muted stucco mass that wraps asymmetrically to frame panoramic views. Interior spaces are defined by modulating the voids between these two contrasting stucco masses. When the stucco masses extend inside the house, the threshold is defined with floor-to-ceiling glass, translucent in some locations for light and privacy. Windows were not considered as punched openings, but rather as voids between the two contrasting stucco masses.

SEEING AND HEARING

The clients are a young couple with two children. Upper level bedroom areas are separated for privacy with double-height dining and living areas, creating a voluminous central space naturally lit from the north and south. In the middle of this open space, a sculptural maple and steel staircase connects the home's three levels.

One of the clients is a drummer. A hidden feature of the lower level is a sound-proof recording studio tucked under the garage.

The client's comprehensive collection of Canadian art is strategically displayed throughout the home's circulation routes.

SHADE AND CONTRAST

Shade is provided by deep cantilevered overhangs. Cross-ventilation comes from carefully located operable windows, reducing reliance on air-conditioning. The largest glass openings in the house take advantage of north and east light, with the south-facing openings shaded from the strong summer sun. To keep the interior shaded during the hottest part of the day, the southwest walls of the house are blank.

The balance of dark and light, an abstraction of the immediate landscape, was realized by providing a small area of dark stucco in all the main living spaces, to reduce interior glare during hot summer days and foggy winters. This theme of contrast is carried to all the interior finishes; floors are maple and slate, with dark cherry built-in ledges functioning as storage chests and extra seating.

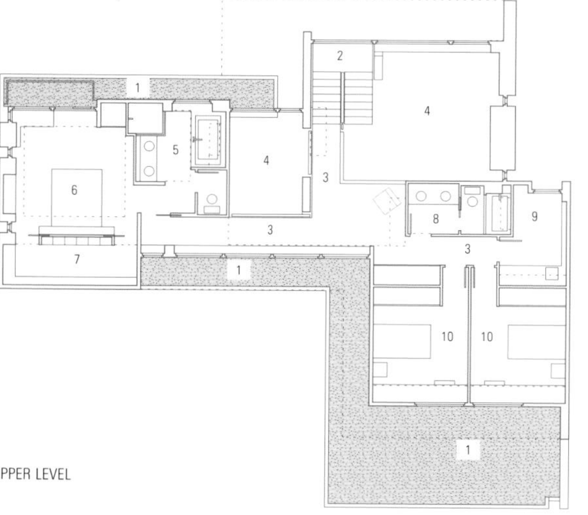

UPPER LEVEL

1 rock garden
2 staircase
3 hallway
4 open to below
5 main bathroom
6 main bedroom
7 wardrobe
8 bathroom
9 utility
10 bedroom

Oshry Residence CALIFORNIA, USA

Studio Pali Fekete architects (SPF:a)

Construction	2002–2004
Home type	Single-family dwelling
Structure	Concrete friction pile foundation, steel frame superstructure, plaster, glass, and limestone

"The glass bridge is more than a hallway – it is one of many places in the home that bid one a momentary pause, overlooking the profound beauty of the canyon."

Zoltan E. Pali

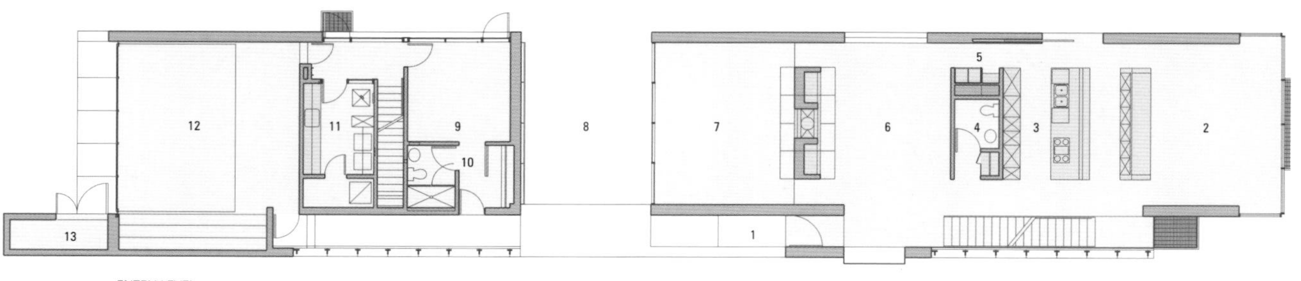

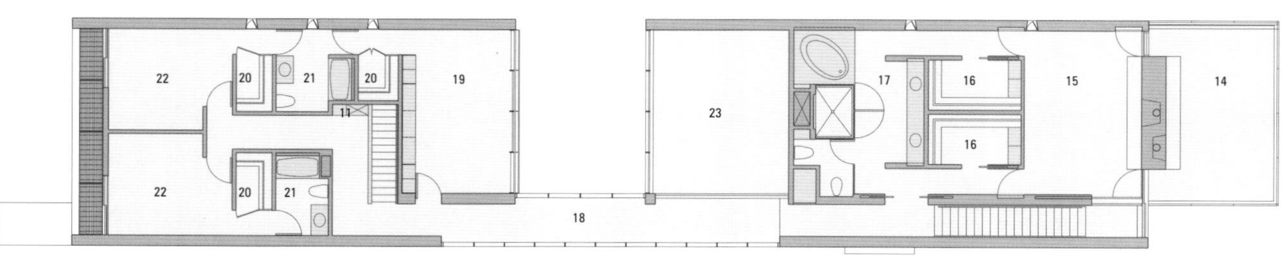

1 entry
2 family
3 kitchen
4 WC
5 pantry
6 dining
7 living
8 courtyard
9 maid
10 bathroom
11 utility
12 garage
13 storage
14 deck
15 main bedroom
16 walk-in wardrobe
17 main bathroom
18 bridge
19 study
20 closet
21 bathroom
22 bedroom
23 open to below

LEFT
On the outward side of the home, the two volumes are connected by a glass bridge which overlooks a courtyard. The eastern elevation is shielded from direct sunlight on the ground floor by a series of limestone louvers.

ABOVE
A steep canyon below the home's eastern elevation provides a dramatic vista to the entry corridor. The facade is straightforwardly minimalist.

BEAUTIFUL, WHITE, MINIMALIST

The client's request was for a "white house" with minimalist beauty to be set on a narrow pad of land in the upmarket Stone Canyon region of Bel Air, blessed with spectacular views. The client, a designer by trade, wanted the freedom to work from home periodically without his workspace interfering with his home life. Overall, the structure is designed to minimize the geological impact (and hence the cost) of construction on the precipitous site, while maximizing the variety of views offered as one moves through the home.

A CHALLENGING SITE

Not only was the land a steep grade, the soil was not suitable for residential development with a standard foundation, so the structure needed to be rooted with concrete friction piles dug 90 ft (27 m) below the surface. The cost of this, and the challenge of staging construction on a 45° grade, was a fundamental aspect of the project's design. Strict zoning guidelines for hillside lots, as well as the client's requirements, created a tapestry of challenges that invigorated Zoltan E. Pali, who sees architecture as the "art" of solving such problems poetically.

BRIDGING CONNECTION

Organizing the home along a narrow floor plan and incorporating an outdoor courtyard as livable space minimized the number of foundation piles needed for a sound structure; it also provided an answer to the client's request for indoor/outdoor connection. The design explores new expressions of transparency and connectivity; two distinct volumes are connected by an iconic glass bridge on the upper level with a central courtyard on the ground floor. The layout juxtaposes notions of private and public separation against this

indoor/outdoor connection. Traveling across the bridge from private to public living areas, floor-to-ceiling glass reveals exceptional views. The impact of direct sun is mitigated through a series of limestone louvers. These fixed white planes, spaced at intervals along the first floor, provide shading without obstructing views; they also cast shadow patterns throughout the day.

FINE-TUNING FOR COMFORT

Pali fine-tuned a plan to maximize both comfort and connection to the outdoors. Kitchen, dining, and sitting rooms face southeast, each space flowing into the next. Perched discreetly atop the kitchen and family room, the main suite and private terrace share a similar southeastern orientation. The kitchen's single rear wall is centrally placed and circulation around its perimeter leads to formal dining and living rooms.

The dining room is punctuated at its northwestern end by a long, narrow window, which frames the lush greenery of the backyard. The western edge of the living room backs up to a glass wall looking out to the central courtyard. The western volume contains a garage, two guest bedrooms, and the office. Canyon views can be enjoyed through the transparent bridge.

ABOVE
The minimalist wood-burning fireplace offers glowing evening warmth during winter and a clean, space-saving solution to fuel storage in the living room.

RIGHT
The striking glass bridge provides a dreamlike meeting space between the private and public areas. Windows across the bridge slide open to allow warmer air to escape during hot days.

ABOVE
A light-filled formal living room features double-height ceilings and a connection with the paved courtyard via sliding glass doors.

LEFT
The spacious main bathroom displays clean lines, minimal fuss-free finishes, and plenty of practical storage.

Pacaembu House SÃO PAULO, BRAZIL

Marcio Kogan Arquiteto

Construction	2003-2005
Home type	Two-level family home
Structure	Concrete and wood

"With Pacaembu House, we aimed for the sort of architectural synthesis spoken of by the abstract painter Vassily Kandinsky in his studies on the relationship between movement and tension that exists in design. Each element in Pacaembu House adds to the clarity of the visual composition."

Marcio Kogan & Gabriel Kogan

MODEL OF MODERNITY

Pacaembu House, named in honor of São Paulo's monument to football, Pacaembu Stadium, is the product of one of Brazil's leading lights of Modernism, Marcio Kogan.

Located in one of the city's most affluent neighborhoods, the home is an unashamed model of Modernity – its elongated box-like shape achieves visual synthesis through the architect's boldly sparing use of architectural elements.

The orderly instincts of the designer are expressed in his use of vast longitudinal concrete walls, which purposefully define the home's perimeters, provide security, and give form to its open living spaces.

The home's northern elevation is dominated by its double-fronted, white concrete facade, which ties the structure together, supporting the upper level and forming a false balcony for the bedrooms.

Although two-story, the exterior presents three horizontal layers. Concrete dominates the outer two layers with a middle recessed layer alternately glazed and lined with dark timber slats.

INTERPLAY OF MATERIALS

The living area extends onto a wooden deck in seamless transition.

Here, the dynamic between exterior and interior is that of a single space. From inside looking out, the color, texture, and design proportion of the perimeter wall form part of the interior decoration, playing in perfect harmony with the interior furnishings.

Similarly, the carefully positioned trees relate to the wall behind, as do sketchlines on a canvas, while at the same time their sketchy forms are in sharp contrast with two richly colored, sculpted chairs in the living room. The effect as a whole is that of looking at an abstract painting.

A pool lies between the wall and wooden deck and a pebbled garden extends from the eastern end of the deck, where more mature trees grow.

THE INTERIOR

The heart of Pacaembu House is its massive living room, decorated in the style of the 1950s with low-slung modular furniture and an elongated console along its southern wall.

A dining room, galley-style kitchen, and employee quarters complete the downstairs area, while upstairs the main bedroom and children's bedrooms, all with ensuites, face north with views into the courtyard.

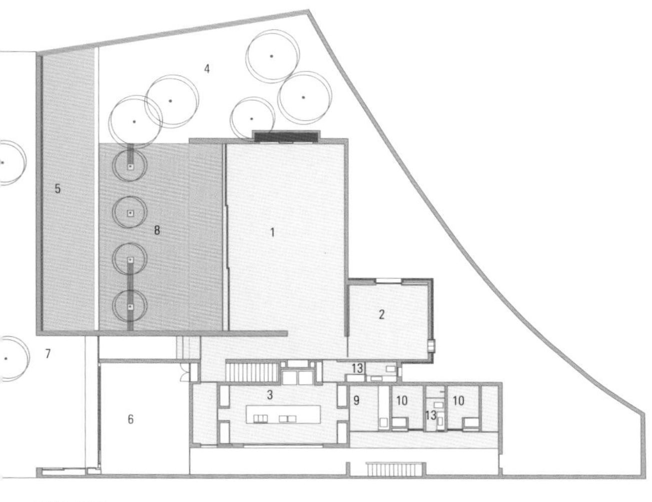

LEVEL ONE

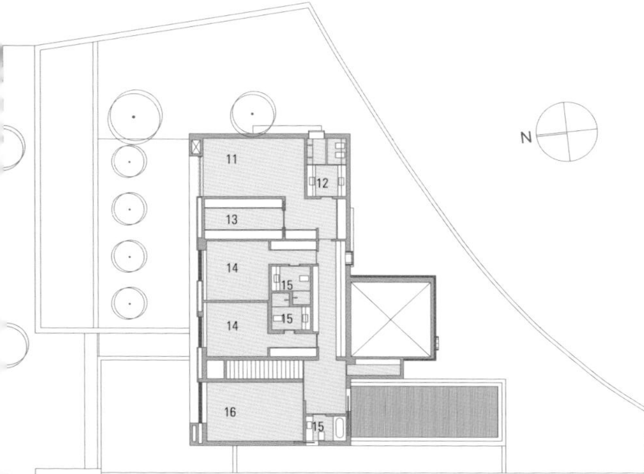

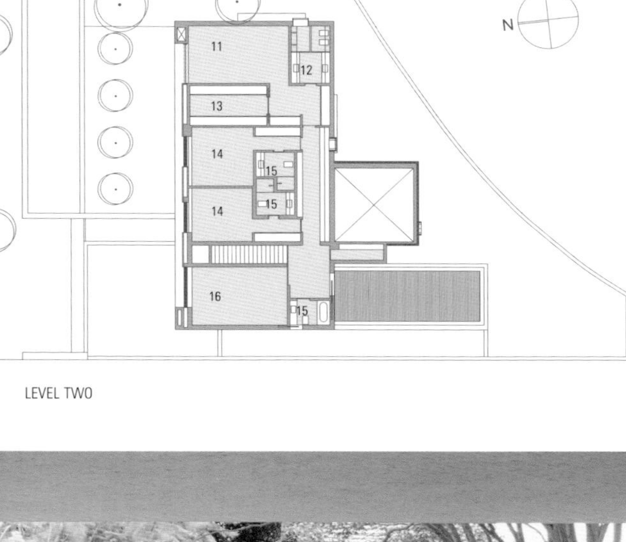

LEVEL TWO

1 living
2 dining
3 kitchen
4 garden
5 pool
6 garage
7 entry
8 deck
9 laundry
10 employee quarters
11 main bedroom
12 ensuite
13 dressing
14 bedroom
15 bathroom
16 TV room

TOP LEFT
The minimalist simplicity of the living room, with its low-slung console and modular furniture, is reinforced by the absence of internal partitions. The owners are able to indulge completely in the large expanse.

LEFT
An understated interplay of colors and textures. The deck and pool are nicely framed by the broad concrete overhang, which softens the transition between the indoor and outdoor spaces while also filtering light into the living room.

ABOVE
Nightfall brings a sense of intimacy and warmth. On the deck, the restrained, sensitive lighting illuminates the trees and draws the eye upward through the foliage.

FOLLOWING PAGES
Here the exterior deck and living room are seen as one complete whole – a clean, seamless union of indoor and outdoor spaces unencumbered by frames or columns. Despite the enormity of the space, it is completely private.

Rokko Housing I, II, and III KOBE, JAPAN

Tadao Ando Architect and Associates

Construction	1981–2002
Home type	Nine-story low-rise apartment housing
Structure	Reinforced concrete

ABOVE
Neatly manicured greenery adorns the rooftop of Rokko II. The indoor swimming pool is an important communal facility for residents. It can also be easily accessed by residents of the neighboring Rokko I.

"The planning of Rokko Housing I began with a struggle over terrain and a dialogue with nature. In Rokko II this evolved into communicating more actively with nature, bringing nature inside the architecture. In Rokko III special attention was placed on the public spaces, which are the source of ventilation and lighting, and serve as devices to promote dialogues among people, and with nature. Through them I wished to express the wonderful richness and joy of living together."

Tadao Ando

OPPOSITE
Nestled in the existing landscape and following the steeply sloping terrain, the building heights of Rokko I, II, and III were kept low so that the structures would blend into the verdant setting.

ROKKO I – A VIEW TO COLLECTIVE HOUSING

Set on the edge of the Rokko Mountains in Kobe, the plan of this new collective housing concept takes advantage of the 60° slope of the land and the lush natural surroundings. Rokko Housing is located in the residential area of Hyogo, the south-facing site offering a panoramic view from Osaka Bay to Kobe. The architect's intention was to create a new style of communal living – one which reinforced a relationship between nature, and public and private space. An integral factor in achieving this goal was to employ a grid system to control the overall structure.

NATURAL INCLINATIONS

The architect wanted to plan this development keeping nature firmly in mind, noting that building projects in Japan have not always been developed in an environmentally sound manner. There was no plan to make radical changes to the topography, but rather to make use of the natural inclinations of the land. The building is, in fact, built right into the landscape, stepping down as the slope descends. To amalgamate the building into its surroundings the structure was sunk into the ground to keep the height down.

The building consists of a group of units that measure 17½ x 15¾ ft (5.3 x 4.8 m). Each unit has a terrace, and there is a range of views available depending on the unit's location within the development. The symmetrical plan allows for intentional gaps, which function as plaza areas and have the effect of uniting the building. Ventilation and insulation is promoted by the dry areas at the edges of the building.

Because the topography is irregular, there is a naturally occurring asymmetry in the structure of the development. One of the results of this is that the outdoor walkway has become the center of the project. The landscaping is designed to interact directly with the building. The geometric shapes accentuate the architecture's artificiality, with the consequence that the beauty of the natural surroundings is heightened.

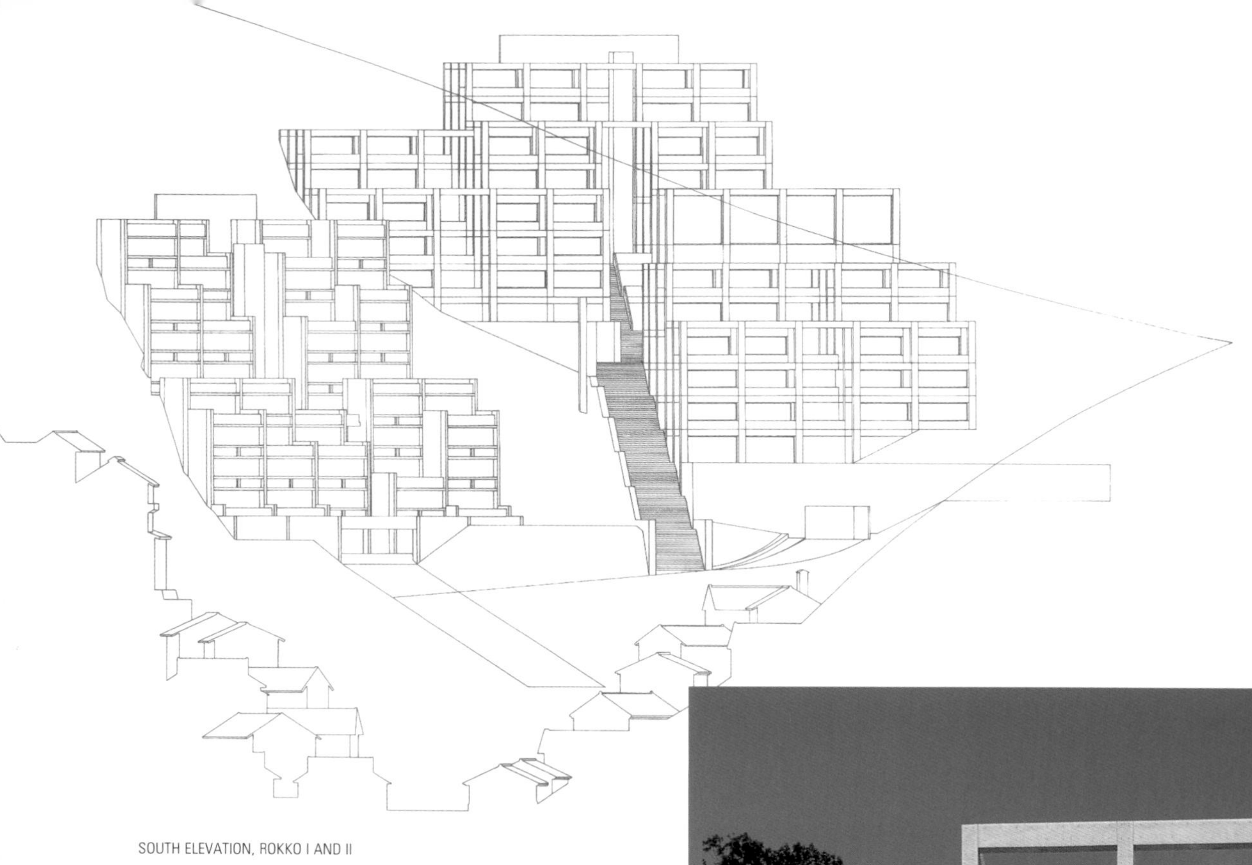

SOUTH ELEVATION, ROKKO I AND II

ROKKO II – AMALGAMATE WITH NATURE

The site for Rokko Housing II is four times bigger than that of Rokko Housing I. It also sits on a 60° slope, the steep incline leading the architect to further explore his desire to integrate the structure with the natural landscape. There was an interesting advantage in this regard – the site is located in a ravine, making it easier to merge the building with its surroundings.

A uniform grid of 17 x 17 ft (5.2 x 5.2 m) was adopted for this building, which consists of three complexes. Although all three are connected, they are quite individual in form. An asymmetric plan was generated when the grid was applied to the complexes, creating an authentic architectural order overall.

FACILITIES FOR EVERYONE

The architect strongly believes that a new building should contribute a level of meaning to its surroundings and its occupants, so an indoor pool was included, a facility that could be accessed by both Rokko Housing I and II residents. Another benefit was the addition of a peaceful rooftop plaza on the intermediate level, which allows magnificent views of the ocean and provides a pleasant communal space for social interaction among the residents.

Further expanding on his plan, the architect envisaged a third project for another nearby site, combining not only residences for older people, but also a kindergarten. There is a particular harmony between children and senior citizens, and their proximity in the plan further demonstrates the importance of communal space and social connection in the Rokko Housing II concept.

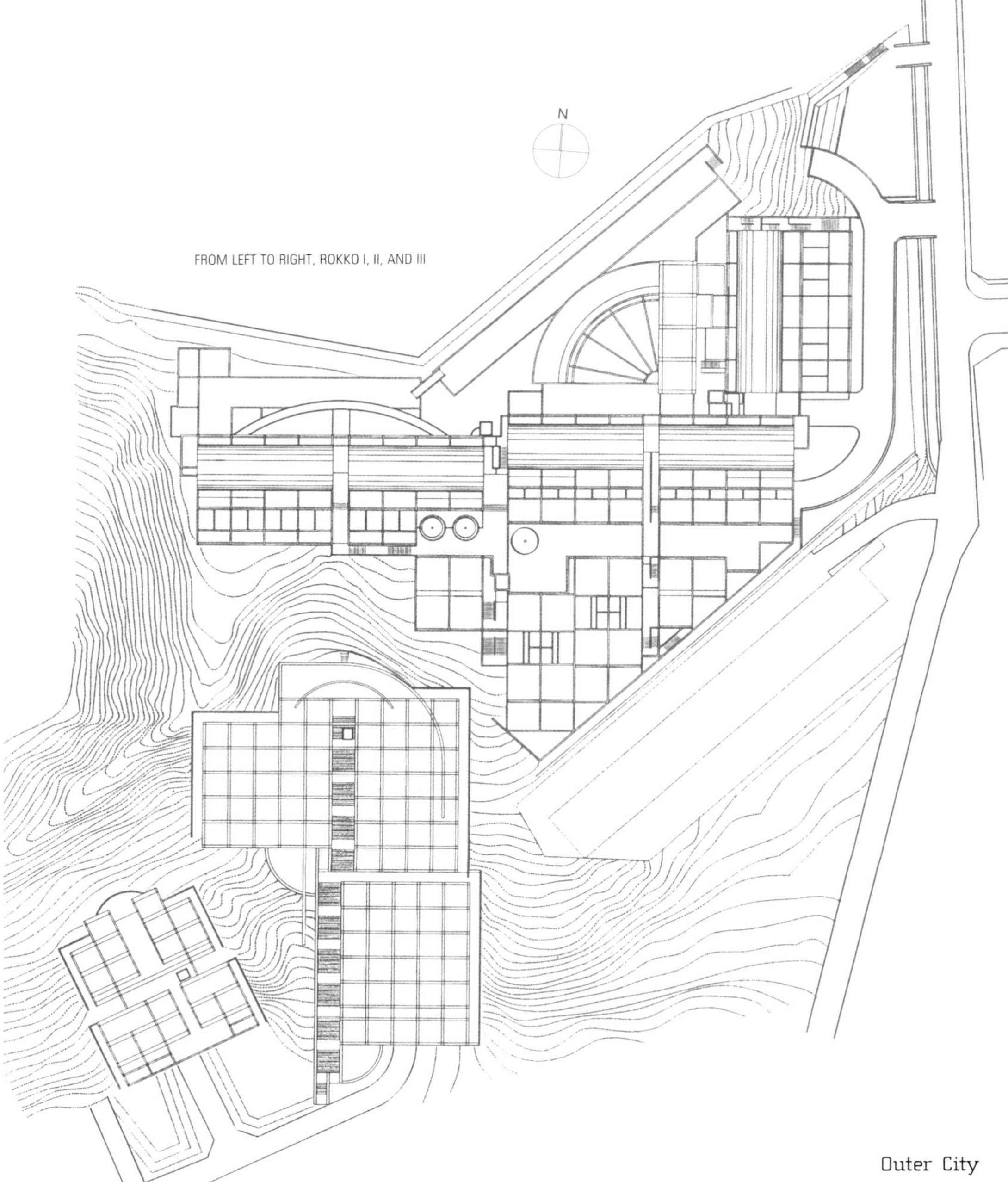

FROM LEFT TO RIGHT, ROKKO I, II, AND III

LEFT
The central stairway of Rokko II provides an axis point for the architecture as a whole. Although a rigid grid system was applied to the project, it did not sacrifice flexibility of layout or choice of vistas in the modular design.

ABOVE
The three-dimensional alley space of Rokko II links the public and private areas of the housing.

TOP
Spectacular views toward Kobe city are available from the high-rise units, looking across the rooftop greenery of Rokko III.

ROKKO III – A LIFESTYLE CHOICE

With the construction of the third housing complex in this development, the architect wanted to offer a lifestyle that closely reflected the location. He began thinking about the project before completing Rokko Housing II and had already put ideas on paper before he was asked to realize the concept as part of the recovery housing implemented for people whose homes had been destroyed in the Great Hanshin earthquake of 1995. In keeping with the ambience of the first two developments, the new site also offered beautiful views across the sea and the port of Kobe.

The structure of Rokko Housing III is once again arranged on a grid, this time measuring 22½ x 24½ ft (6.9 x 7.5 m), stepped over an elevation of 50 ft (15 m). Two of the blocks face south, right into the central axis of Rokko Housing II. One block faces east into the main walkway, and on the south side of the site there is a group of courtyard dwellings. The northern section of the site faces onto a garden. The parking area is hidden at a lower point.

LOOKING OUT AND IN

Each unit in Rokko Housing III has its own individual vista, affording residents a sense of individuality sometimes lacking in larger communal developments of this type.

One of the important community facilities open to all residents in Rokko Housing III is a swimming pool, which also has a view across the extensive gardens. There are other significant community considerations – one block of homes is specifically designed for the needs of senior citizens and also caters for residents with disabilities.

REAL INTERACTION

Walkways link the landscaped garden areas in the lower-level courtyard homes. This was an intentional exercise, the idea being that the path functions as communal space, as it did in the earlier projects. The hillside, which rises around the garden spaces, expands the communal areas by association.

The expanded communal areas, coupled with the housing complex, makes it easy for a real interaction between people and the natural environment. It also makes it easy for people to meet and enjoy one another's company, thus reinforcing and promoting the perception of living together in harmony.

The architect has been planning a fourth development in the Rokko Housing project, where he hopes to elaborate on the notion of close communal living intermingled with the pleasures of inhabiting the natural world.

The architect's intention was to create a new style of communal living – one which reinforced a relationship between nature, and public and private space.

ABOVE
The amphitheater-like quality of the central plaza in Rokko II creates a stately gathering place for residents.

LEFT
The individual dwellings within Rokko II complex retain a close relationship with nature and possess wonderful views toward Kobe city. Abundant natural light and a high degree of privacy add to the relaxed and inviting ambience of the homes.

TOP LEFT
The design of each apartment in Rokko II took into consideration the spatial qualities that best suited the stepped composition of the project.

Santa Monica House CALIFORNIA, USA

Chun Studio

Construction 2000–2002
Home type Single dwelling, contemporary courtyard house
Structure Two-level, concrete slab and raised floor construction with poured-in-place concrete walls and wood siding

"The genesis of the house was sub-dividing a standard rectangular lot into a series of exterior gardens and interior rooms by overlaying a grid. The house is an aggregation of these separate spaces – the design priority was establishing interesting spatial relationships to each part. The matrix of these relationships establishes a rich texture of stimulating adjacencies between interior rooms, and between interior rooms and exterior gardens."

David Chun

TOP RIGHT
Wooden screens surround the courtyard side of the family room. This sitting area faces the open courtyard toward the living room and the rock garden beyond. Views from this perspective capture the porosity and transparency of being in between the private and public rooms of the house.

PRIORITY: PRIVACY

The house was designed for the architect's parents, who requested a garden retreat away from the public realm, so privacy was a high priority. The context is a suburban neighborhood with an eclectic style of homes, all subdivided in rows of standard rectangular lots. The expansive openness of the interior spaces is modern in quality, and the finished materials are left to express their natural beauty, providing a sense of warmth and permanence to the house.

LAYERING THE EFFECT

Santa Monica House is H-shaped and is structured by three principal layers of space as one moves from the street to the rear garden. The first is the opaque layer (front of the building or street facade); the second is a transparent layer (central courtyard); and the third is the semi-transparent layer (rear of building).

The opaque layer is the two-story bar facing the street. It establishes a clear division between what is "in" and what is "out." In a sense, this buffer sets up the house to be able to invent its own separate private environment. The symmetrical street facade draws the visitor to its center by a two-story void that serves as an entry vestibule. This void space is a moment of transition from the opacity of the exterior wall to the transparency of its interior spaces. The 21-ft (6.4-m) wall is a statement of privacy that overwhelms the passerby, but dematerializes for the entering visitor.

EVEN WHEN OUTSIDE, YOU'RE INSIDE

The home is entered via 9-ft (2.7-m), pivoting, stainless steel doors – the home is exposed (transparent layer). The central courtyard and outdoor gardens can be viewed simultaneously through large floor to ceiling windows. The living room is flanked by two outdoor gardens: the central courtyard and the rock garden.

LEFT
The opaque layer is the two-story bar facing the street. It establishes a clear division between what is "in" and what is "out." In a sense, this buffer sets up the home to be able to invent its own separate private environment. The symmetrical street facade draws the visitor to its center by a two-story void that serves as an entry vestibule.

ABOVE
The living room is flanked by two outdoor gardens: the central courtyard and the rock garden. The room opens out onto the central courtyard via large accordion doors, When the doors are open the interior and exterior spaces are seamless.

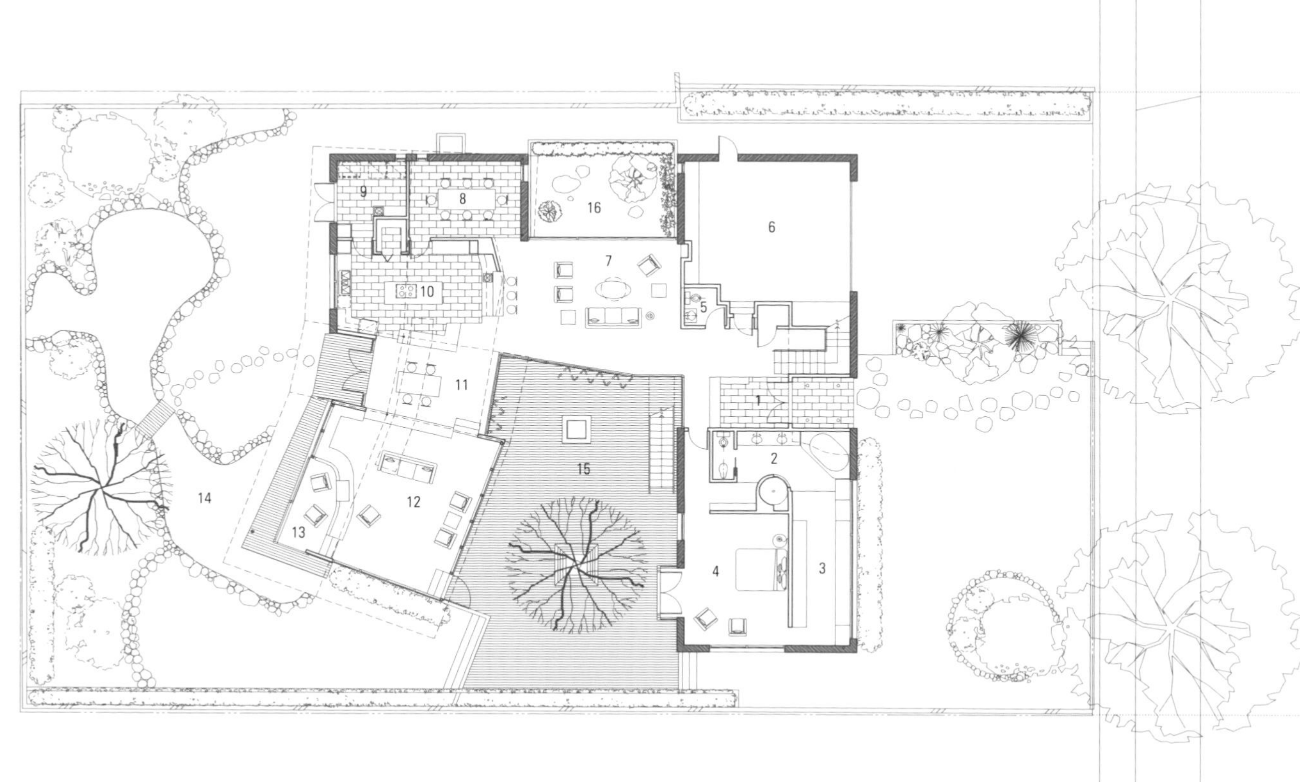

The living room opens onto the central courtyard by large accordion doors where the interior and the exterior can be made seamless. The sense of inside and outside is further challenged not just by the physical openings, but by the relationship to the outer opaque layer. Independent of the living room, the exterior courtyard space still feels very much inside the domestic compound.

The last semi-transparent layer is the rear one-story bar facing the back garden. It is composed of all the everyday domestic spaces (family room, kitchen, breakfast, and dining). This bar bends toward the rear and engages the garden with a covered viewing deck that hovers over the garden pond. In the family room, wooden screens direct the focus toward the rear garden by subtly veiling the central courtyard. The kitchen has direct access to all adjacent spaces. Its floor level is at the highest elevation, from which one steps down to the breakfast room, and from there down again into the family room. The relationship of these three rooms together creates a theater-like atmosphere.

CREATING LAYERS OF MEANING

The playful relationships of adjacent and overlapping spaces creates a constantly changing perception when moving through different layers of the home. The openness of the plan, and the large sheets of glass that dominate the perimeter walls of the home, create space that rhythmically expand and contract; first within the home, then out to the gardens and beyond.

The openness of the plan, and the large sheets of glass...create space that rhythmically expands and contracts...

LEFT
Looking out toward the courtyard from the kitchen, the foreground shows a fire pit (for warmth and barbecues) that is a focal point at the center of the property. It is a social gathering place for casual outdoor dining and conversation, and a place of interaction as all the rooms of the home have visual access to this central location.

ABOVE
The family room is a sunken, glass pavilion surrounded by lush gardens. The sunken floor and its dark color palette create intimacy and ground the room, while the surrounding glass walls allow commanding views to the perimeter of the property. Inside the room, the focal point is an open fireplace with a stainless-steel-clad flue suspended from the ceiling. Just beyond the fireplace is a small study area that opens out to the rear garden through floor to ceiling sliding glass doors.

TOP RIGHT
The living room is flanked by two outdoor gardens: the central courtyard and the rock garden. The rock garden is a "viewing garden," seen here from the living room. It is a careful and deliberately composed garden of rocks and small plantings that mimic larger gardens by way of proportion.

RIGHT
The semi-transparent layer is the rear, one-story bar facing the rear garden. It comprises the family room, kitchen, breakfast, and dining – the everyday domestic spaces. This bar bends toward the rear and engages the garden with a covered viewing deck that hovers over the koi pond.

The School House LONDON, ENGLAND

Brookes Stacey Randall Architects

Constructed	1996
Home type	Apartment within refurbished school
Structure	Load-bearing brickwork, structural steel mezzanine level, steel and glass stair and mezzanine

"The design approach was to make a distinction between the old and the new, allowing the original building to read clearly, with the new insertions touching the original fabric as lightly as possible. The design is not fixed but has the inherent flexibility to change, on both a daily and long-term basis. We love living there; especially Louis, who plays cricket in the main space."

Nik Randall (now of Space Craft Architects)

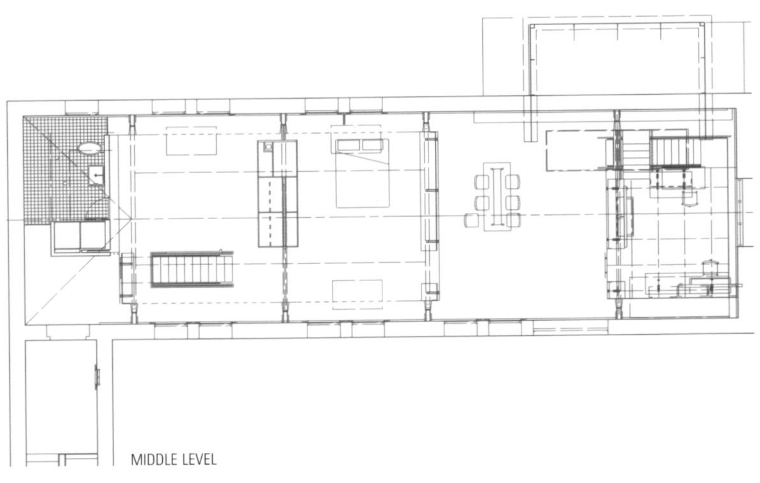

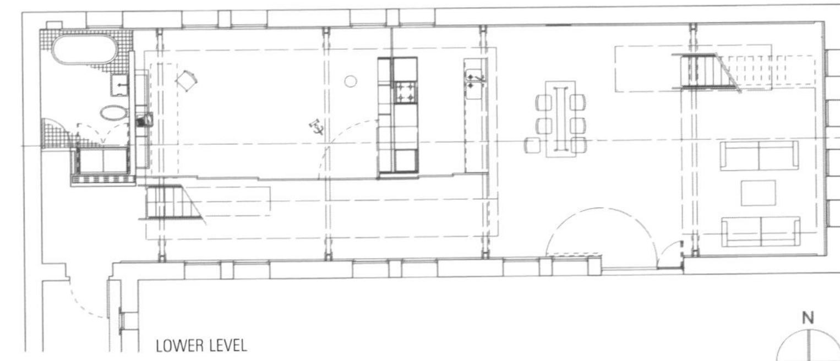

ABOVE
Clever use of sliding screens and custom-built storage units transform the main area into kitchen, dining, living, office, and play spaces. The glass-floored studio houses textile designer Suzsi Corio's materials.

ABOVE
The kitchen is generally open to the living area but can also be closed off with retractable screens. The apartment's middle level is defined by large platforms – this one above the kitchen is covered in birch plywood and coir matting – which tie in with the original timber trusses and help sustain a sense of vertical space. Efficient heating for the apartment is provided by a pressurized hot water system. Radiators are recessed into the wall linings and a strong fan pushes the warm air into the volume of the house.

BACK TO SCHOOL

Architect Nik Randall converted a Victorian school, built in 1871, into a private apartment for himself and his family. The large space, which originally housed two classrooms, perfectly suited Randall's desire for adaptability – where areas changed their function depending on the needs of the moment. An innovative approach to space and cleverly designed storage units made these transformations possible.

A LESSON IN SPACE

The height of the interior (some 24½ ft [7.5 m]) allowed plenty of space for three levels. The main family area is located on the lower level, as are the kitchen, living, dining, and office areas. There are no walls, and hence no defined rooms, with all spaces merging into one another. Where necessary, sliding screens are used to delineate areas within the volume. Randall's young son, Louis, has a large free area to play in; this same area can be used as an office, or it converts easily into a comfortable sleeping space for guests. This flexibility is achieved by using custom-built storage units, which can accommodate a range of functions, including a roll-out futon mattress.

The middle level of the apartment contains the bedrooms and dressing areas, and a studio for Randall's partner, textile designer Suzsi Corio. Large platforms are the focal point here, creating a sense of space, while still retaining the ambience of the original building. These platforms, which sit above the main living space beneath, define this level.

The floor of the larger platform is birch-faced plywood and coir matting. The floor of the studio is glass, which dramatically opens the area to the spaces below. A skylight lets in plenty of natural light. There are only two spaces on the top level, serving as sleeping areas, play space, or storage space, as required.

LIGHT AND COLOR

Lighting has been designed to suit the apartment's flexible floor plan. It is possible to evenly light the entire home. The architect also wanted the lighting to complement the style of the building, and to be discreet – the light fittings are flush, thus emphasizing the light, not the light fitting.

The color scheme also enhances the architectural purpose. A lime-yellow wall separates the main sitting area from the rest of the lower space. Kitchen and storage units are in soft shades of gray-green, and side walls and ceilings are off-white. The overall effect is subdued, yet it permits distinction between the home's different spaces. Creative use of color and light have resulted in a warm, flexible, modern home that manages to preserve its link with the past.

Casa Serrano SANTIAGO, CHILE

Felipe Assadi and Christophe Rousselle

Constructed	2006
Home type	Three-level residence
Structure	Concrete and steel frame on concrete slab

"The objective was to create a house that maximized the 180° views of Santiago and the surrounding mountains. The living areas are transparent spaces enclosed in glass, regulating light into the interior and set alongside a framework of concrete that is supported by steel columns."
Felipe Assadi

A DOMINANT PRESENCE

An imposing design dominating its surroundings, Casa Serrano comprises three living areas contained within a cocoon of reinforced concrete over a steel frame.

The living areas on the lower levels are organized around a central tower, which tie the building together while facilitating the movement of cooling breezes. Internal steel columns support the northern and southern facades and make a strong visual statement. A central fireplace acts as a partition between the dining and living areas, which lead to a ground-level, north-facing courtyard, where the koi pond points like a finger toward the panoramic views.

The middle level contains the main bedroom and a second bedroom, which open onto a common west-facing balcony. Two other bedrooms open onto a walled, north-facing, inner courtyard accessed by a series of sliding glass doors. A large glazed exterior affords views into the adjacent living room below. There are two more bedrooms, both of which open onto balconies. All four bedrooms have ensuites.

EXOTIC SKIN

Almendrillo, an exotic hardwood from the Amazon rainforest, is used for the west-facing decking on the middle level. The upper level houses the study, where the north-facing, reinforced-concrete exterior is sheathed in a second skin of almendrillo. This lends the concrete exterior warmth, texture, and human scale. Light filters through a series of tiny, randomly placed windows.

CELEBRATION OF CUBISM

Casa Serrano deliberately confronts its surroundings rather than seamlessly blending with them. The result is a bold, formal statement that brings an international voice to the city of Santiago.

ABOVE
The void above the hallway neatly sets off the otherwise elongated floor plan. Downlights and hardwood floors bring a softness and intimacy to a living area that is flooded with views of Santiago city.

TOP RIGHT
The elegant almendrillo skin on the north-facing wall provides both continuity and contrast with the west-facing deck and inner courtyard below. Randomly placed windows in the wall introduce an intricate interplay of light into the upper level study.

RIGHT
The streetscape view of the house is an unashamedly Modernist statement. The home's domineering mass is accentuated by enclosing the two west-facing bedrooms in timber-clad, reinforced concrete.

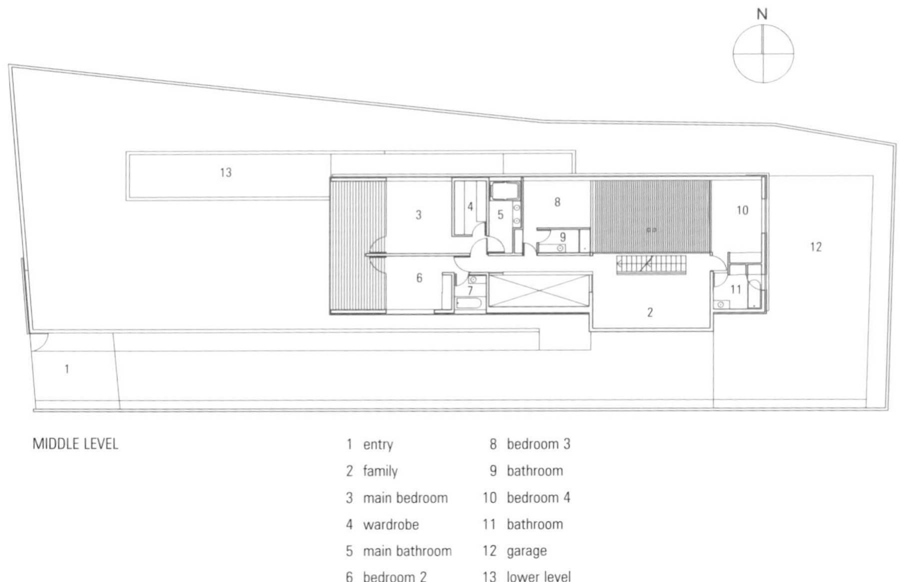

MIDDLE LEVEL

1 entry
2 family
3 main bedroom
4 wardrobe
5 main bathroom
6 bedroom 2
7 bathroom
8 bedroom 3
9 bathroom
10 bedroom 4
11 bathroom
12 garage
13 lower level koi pond

ABOVE
A centrally placed fireplace in the living space on the lower level provides the room's focal point, its flue soaring through the ceiling into the courtyard above. Glass exterior walls on three sides flood the room with light.

Studio and Apartment House Huber LUCERNE, SWITZERLAND

Graser Architekten

Construction	2002–2003
Home type	Two apartments and two studios with an open staircase between
Structure	Wooden frame for the inner structure, cloth for the outer cover

"Our design work focuses on flexibility and the capacity to alter things along the way – and we apply our technical knowledge to the use of prefabricated materials. There are no right or wrong materials or forms for us, and to a certain extent we renounce ostentation. Under no circumstances must the 'form' of the project arise from our personal preferences – rather from the personal preferences of the client."

Jürg Graser

ABOVE
Viewed from the northeastern side of the building, House Huber sits lightly on the landscape, tucking into a curve of the road. The parking area is under the box-like front of the house.

RIGHT
A transitional space housing the lightweight staircase links the three levels as well as the two buildings. This connecting space acts as both a balcony and a terrace.

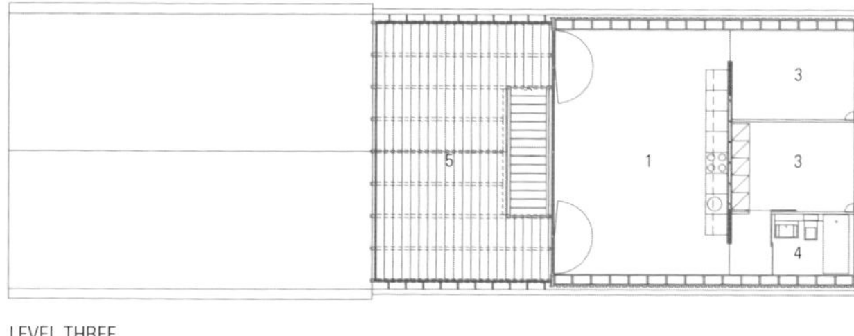

LEVEL THREE

1 living
2 studio
3 bedroom
4 bathroom
5 staircase
6 patio

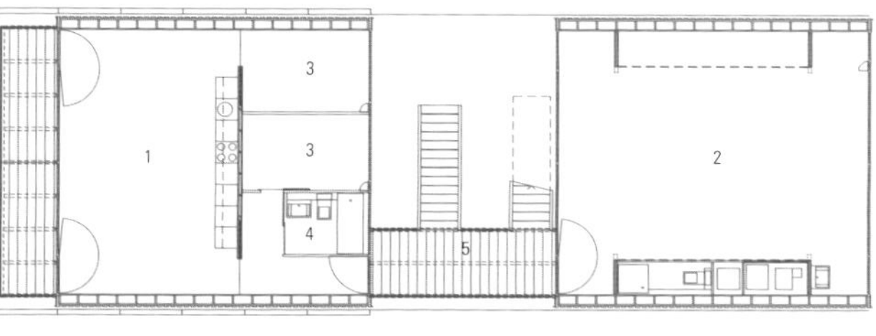

LEVEL TWO

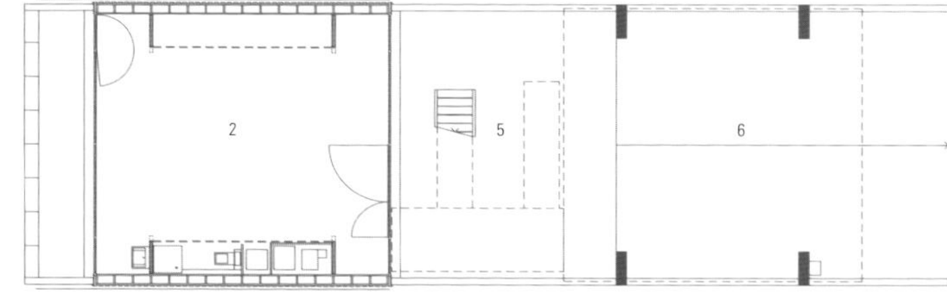

LEVEL ONE

MODERN INTERPRETATION

House Huber is situated in one of the oldest areas of Emmenbrücke in Lucerne, Switzerland. The house lies between a southern slope in the east, dotted with villas dating from the end of the nineteenth century, and a plain in the west, which contains single-family houses dating from the post-World War II period. The building site was once part of an old farm that extended over the whole area. The last farm building was torn down in 2002.

The new building reacts to the uniqueness of its location in two ways. First, it assumes the geometry of the old house, hinting at the original building complex. It also allows for the curve in the adjacent road, so the house sits comfortably in its surroundings. Second, the height and the number of stories in the new building are a kind of reinterpretation of a typical farmhouse – traditionally both a working and a living space – but with a modern twist.

MULTIFUNCTIONAL SPACE

Like all forms of design, architecture is subject to various trends, and these days, a minimalist formal expression – where architecture can be reduced to a two-dimensional plane – seems to be the fashion. Yet in spite of the move away from the structurally "self-contained" buildings of the recent past, there is no doubt that we are still fascinated by the relationship between structure and space.

In House Huber, there are two completely closed supporting longitudinal walls, which serve to frame the dual functions of working and living areas. Large transverse windows allow the free flow of light into these rooms. There is also a double height void situated between the two building apartments, which is used by both of them. This spatial element is a transitional space between the homes. Combined with the entry and the parking area under the second apartment, the area becomes a larger L-shaped multifunctional space.

ADDING VALUE

For the architects designing this project, budgetary constraints gave rise to creative solutions, encouraging the production of a structure with a style all its own. The architects were interested in looking at the basic space and then "adding value" to it. This meant that extra funds were allocated to a few specific elements that architecturally enhanced the project.

HIGH-TECH MATERIALS

The outer cover of the building is made of cloth – an efficient, high-tech material that adds an aesthetic dimension to the project, setting the building apart from its conventional setting. The durable cloth is multifunctional, serving as a sunshade, weather barrier, and air cushion. All these factors add to the passive energy balance of the project.

TOP LEFT
The cloth roof covering admits lots of natural light to the triple-height space between the two modules, while the large surface windows allow discreet views between the interiors of the two living areas.

ABOVE
The transparent effect of the cloth outer cover, which protects the interior from sun and glare, is echoed in the perforated metal plates on the stair treads. The whole building has a light, and light-filled, feel.

Ward Residence CALIFORNIA, USA

Marmol Radziner + Associates

Construction	2000–2003
Home type	Two-level house, single-family residence
Structure	Concrete block, steel, and glass

"The Ward Residence introduces a series of contrasts into the site: the solid volumes and the light glass pavilions, the rough structural nature of the concrete block with the burnished finish of the blocks, the light colored walls and the dark stained oak floors. These contrasts create a simple yet sensitive solution to the steep site."

Marmol Radziner + Associates

ABOVE
The Ward Residence is set in a steep hillside peppered with numerous large trees. During construction, much effort was spent protecting the original trees on the land, since the indoor/outdoor interaction is so important to the concept of the home.

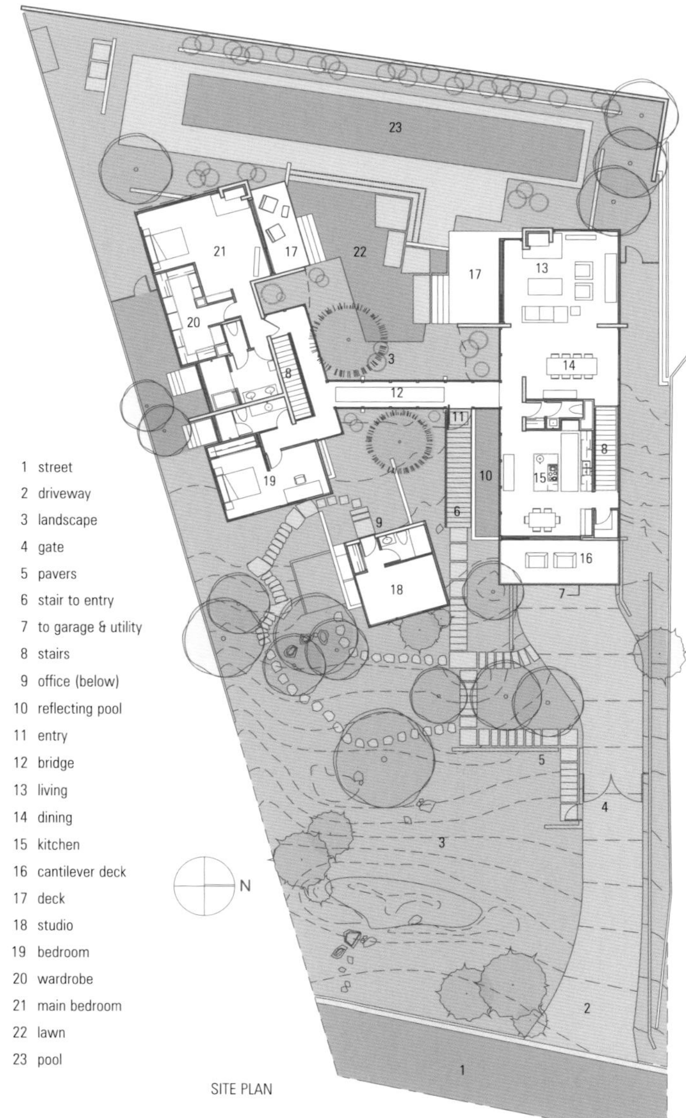

SEPARATE YET INTEGRATED

Situated in Rustic Canyon, one of the most serene areas in Los Angeles, this new residence offers views of the canyon and gently sloping hillsides to the east. The neighborhood has a rich architectural history, including residences by Ray Kappe, Pierre Koenig, and A. Quincy Jones, and provides local precedents for the ideals of Modernism. The Ward Residence takes lessons from these Modern neighbors, including the natural material palette and resolve for indoor/outdoor living, while making new design and material innovations.

Keeping with the notion of establishing a serene garden-like environment, the home's 4,000-sq-ft (370-sq-m) mass appears smaller because of the organization of the living and working spaces within three seemingly separate pavilions. Arranged according to the requirements of public use, private domains, and functional work areas, the separate volumes perch delicately atop solid masses of burnished concrete blocks imbedded in the hillside. A glass-enclosed walkway bridges the two masses, taking optimal advantage of the location and surrounding landscape. The landscape flows below and past the glazed entry hall as it bridges the public and private volumes of the home.

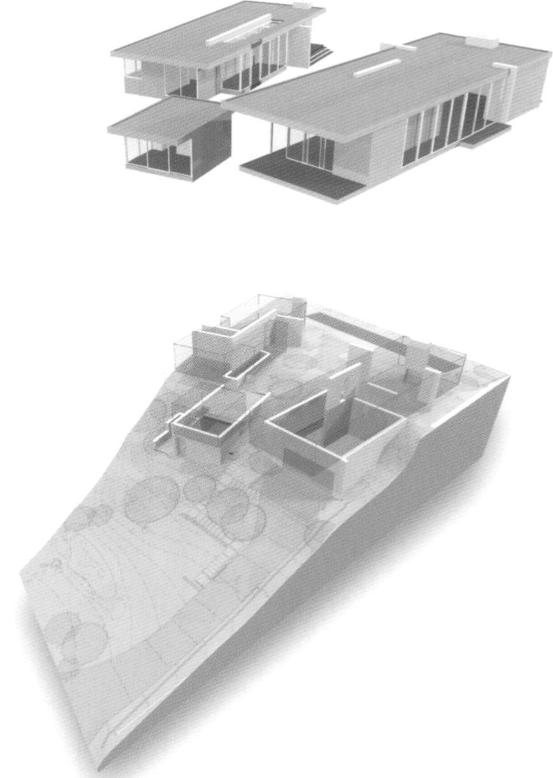

EXPLOITING TOPOGRAPHY

Materials of burnished concrete block, galvanized steel paneling, and glass complement the openness of the design and the careful integration of the object-like forms on the site. Filtering in the landscape, the site introduces a skewed procession upon entry that leads up to the pavilions and provides glimpses of additional structures beyond.

A double cantilevered guest house rests on top of the studio, accentuating the breezeway and creating an intimate arrival area. Working with the landscape into one pictorial image, the simple lap pool lines the back of the property.

The design utilizes the opportunities of the site's natural topography and foliage to provide privacy and separation from neighboring lots. By shifting the home forward and away from the neighboring yards, the design exploits the steep site and builds within the hillside, allowing for additional stories. By keeping the structures below tree level, the home's focus becomes more introverted – a retreat within a lush hillside garden. During construction, a great deal of effort was spent ensuring the safety of the trees native to the site.

ABOVE
The house reveals itself as a progression from the solid masonry walls imbedded in the hillside, up into the lighter steel and glass pavilions above. The main approach to the house flows between the skewed positioning of the double cantilevered guest pavilion, on the left, and the cantilevered deck off the kitchen, on the right.

TOP RIGHT
"Volumes," made from stacked concrete masonry, sit within the steep hillside and provide the base for the steel and glass pavilions to float above. The three glass pavilions divide the house into public, private, and functional work areas. The contrast between the visual weight of the masonry volumes and the lightness of the upper pavilions create different experiences throughout the site.

ABOVE
Looking back at the home from the cantilevered deck off the kitchen, the view reveals the close interaction of indoor and outdoor spaces. The steel structure provides the support necessary to create the large expanses of glass.

RIGHT
The water feature outside the kitchen directly connects natural elements to the interior of the home.

BLURRING BOUNDARIES

The home consistently blurs the distinction between interior and exterior spaces through the use of exposed natural materials, large expanses of glass, and significant outdoor living spaces. The living room and main bedroom each have direct access to the backyard, while a separate cantilevered balcony opens up the kitchen to surrounding treetops. A large window in the main bathroom provides protected views that can be enjoyed from the Japanese cedar hot tub.

A SOLID MOTIF

The concrete block is a defining motif in the home, for the masonry flows between the inside and outside of the home, acting both as a structural material and an exposed finished surface. All textures, from the craggy "split-faced" to sandblasted precision, and colors, from pale white to warm gray, were considered during the material selection process. The final choice, a custom fabricated block of white concrete with burnished faces was selected for its unique beauty and its ability to play off the rustic nature of the site.

ABOVE
The burnished concrete block is a central motif in both the interior and exterior of the home – seen here, in the fireplace surround and engaged column.

LEFT
The master bathroom combines a material palette of cedar casework, burnished concrete block, and stainless steel to create an intimate feel in this private space. The cedar hot tub reveals the Japanese influence on the design.

FOLLOWING PAGES
A lap pool runs the length of the backyard, emphasizing the horizontality of the steel and glass pavilions. Running almost parallel to the pool, a glass-enclosed walkway bridges the public and private areas of the home.

Chapter 11

Future City

A new era of home design is unfolding. Homes of the future will maximize our limited resources, and use new techniques and materials that will be more sensitive to the environment.

Consider living in a home made of glass, where a voice-activated electric current turns the walls opaque on command. Or perhaps your home will be made of cardboard, plastic, or even rubber. Whatever your vision of the future might be, one thing is certain – home design in the city of the future will be motivated by the limited availability of resources.

With natural resources dwindling, homes will be designed for more efficient use of space, using innovative new materials that reduce the impact of humans on the environment. Technology will revolutionize conventional design, and traditional building methods will be replaced as home design becomes more complex.

INGENUITY OF FORM

Complex design and more efficient use of space will result in ingenious forms. Computer-3D modelling, one of the new technologies, allows architects to study their designs dynamically, examining them from every angle to resolve problems. This results in much more creative freedom, and organic forms are beginning to emerge as possible design solutions.

One innovation is to manipulate space: Rooms can now expand or contract as walls are moved along a track in the ceiling. These wall panels can be hidden away in a wall cavity, giving the illusion of more space, or turned at different angles to totally reconfigure the space.

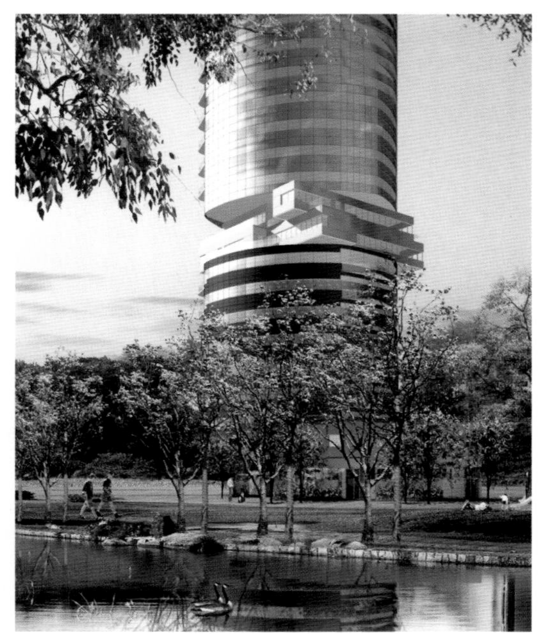

ABOVE
Shanghai Star Mei Hwa Estate, Ben Wood Studio Shanghai

TOP RIGHT
Moriyama House, Ryue Nishizawa

OPPOSITE
Living Tomorrow Pavilion, UN Studio

CONSTRUCTION TECHNOLOGY

The burden on our natural resources is being reduced by both innovative design and the development of new building materials, such as composite materials and those that can be dismantled and reused. Such materials demand the development of compatible building techniques.

Modular home design is a novel construction technology. The prefabricated modular components are designed once and then manufactured with computer assistance, with services included, and reconfigured for each site. This process reduces product waste and makes construction on site more efficient.

SUSTAINABILITY

Limited access to resources and an increasing awareness of the environment has created an ethos of conservation that has unleashed a flood of invention in the areas of renewable energy and recycled materials.

We can power our homes by harnessing wind energy, and we can also use the sun to heat water simply and effectively. We are already recycling paper and plastics to make items such as carpet, insulation, and structural elements for the home. Floors need not be made of hardwood. Instead, a photograph of real wood can be laminated onto recycled plastic sheets.

INNOVATIVE DESIGN

The city of the future will see the emergence of a new, innovative design movement that will embrace new materials and building techniques, resulting in new shapes and organic forms. This shift will require us to re-examine our understanding of what home is and will make us redefine ourselves, our lifestyles, and our relationships in response to our new surroundings.

Gardner 1050 LOS ANGELES, USA

Lorcan O'Herlihy Architects

Constructed	2006
Home type	Three-story apartment building
Structure	Steel and wood frame with cement-board cladding, timber, and glass

"Density is a critical issue in Los Angeles. This project represents an inventive way of dealing with housing for the masses. By creating a central light well and wrapping the building around this space, the central void becomes the heart of the project, providing circulation, light, and a place for social interaction."

Lorcan O'Herlihy

A NEW ARCHITECTURAL LANDSCAPE

West Hollywood has become increasingly urbanized over recent years, and the Gardner 1050 project of 10 housing units, south of the famous Santa Monica Boulevard, has made a significant contribution to the architectural landscape of the district. The architects used various approaches, such as incorporating courtyards into the design of the building, to give the units a distinctive appearance, thus distinguishing them from more commonplace styles in the area.

A CENTRAL COURTYARD

A major design consideration was to connect the indoor and outdoor spaces to maximize flexibility for the residents. Individual units are essentially wrapped around a courtyard in the center of the project, which measures 15,000 sq ft (about 4,600 sq m). The architects' strategic use of a simple form and refined materials has allowed variations in how the scale and facade of the building are perceived.

On the western facade, cedar slats placed around the cut-away box have been used to create a translucent exterior "skin." The courtyard sits inside this area. A glass-clad staircase makes a dramatic statement, immediately drawing the eye to this stark vertical exclamation mark. The staircase also marks the entry to the building and provides a subdued light in the evenings, enhancing the exterior.

MASTERFUL MATERIALS

For appearance and durability, the architects chose a painted cement-board cladding system as one of the main materials. The other primary materials used are transparent glass panels, horizontal cedar slats, and painted aluminum window frames.

The cedar slats cover the whole second level and also double as a screen for the entry to the garage and the third level's outside community area. Wood has also been used on the first and third levels to extend the wood theme.

EXCITING EXTERIOR, INTIMATE INTERIOR

The courtyard and interior of the project truly define it. Simultaneously spacious and intimate, the courtyard features drought-tolerant native shrubs, perfectly offset by the integral seating. A fountain close to the entry provides a tranquil ambience, and also contributes to the open feeling of the space.

Stainless steel cables run up to the level three walkways, providing the foundations for a hanging garden from that level. The steel gratings here also create a pattern of light and shadow on the courtyard below. The paving is a green-tinted concrete that complements the glass at the front entry.

SETTING A HIGH QUALITY BENCHMARK

One of the project's most successful attributes is its provision of medium-density housing within an esthetically pleasing structure.

LEFT
Wood is used as a feature on the fireplace wall, extending the exterior "skin" into the interior. The expansive windows and glass door fill the room with light and create an esthetic rarely evident in medium-density housing.

ABOVE
Cedar slats frame an exterior deck, providing both shade and privacy. The slats on the exterior walls not only unify the whole structure but also help break up the different elements.

1 bedroom
2 main bedroom
3 dressing
4 bath 1
5 hallway
6 ensuite
7 living
8 kitchen

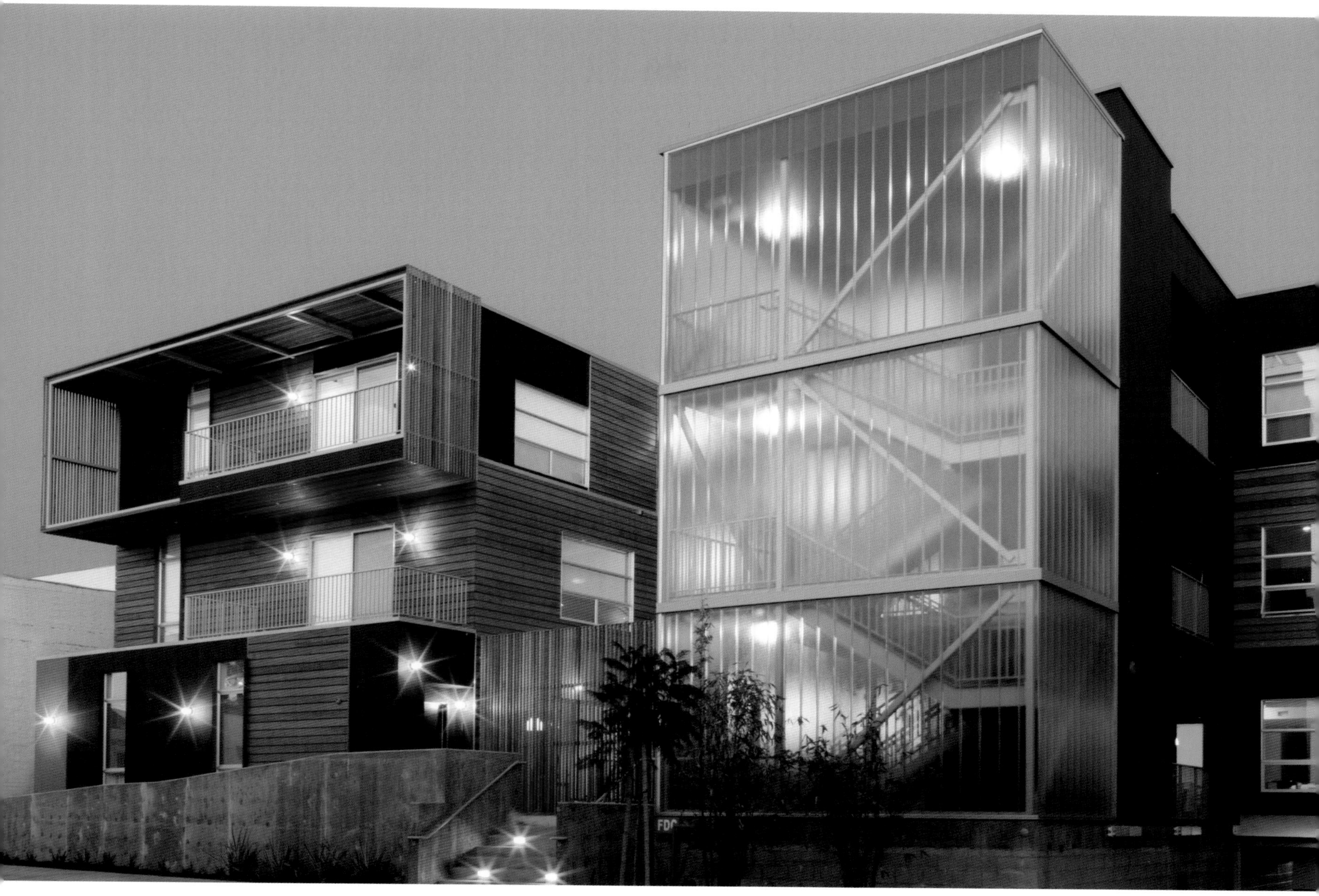

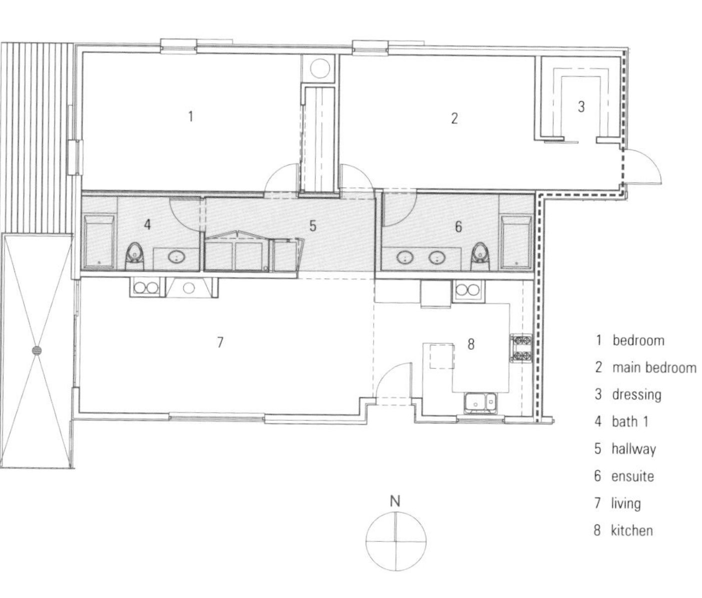

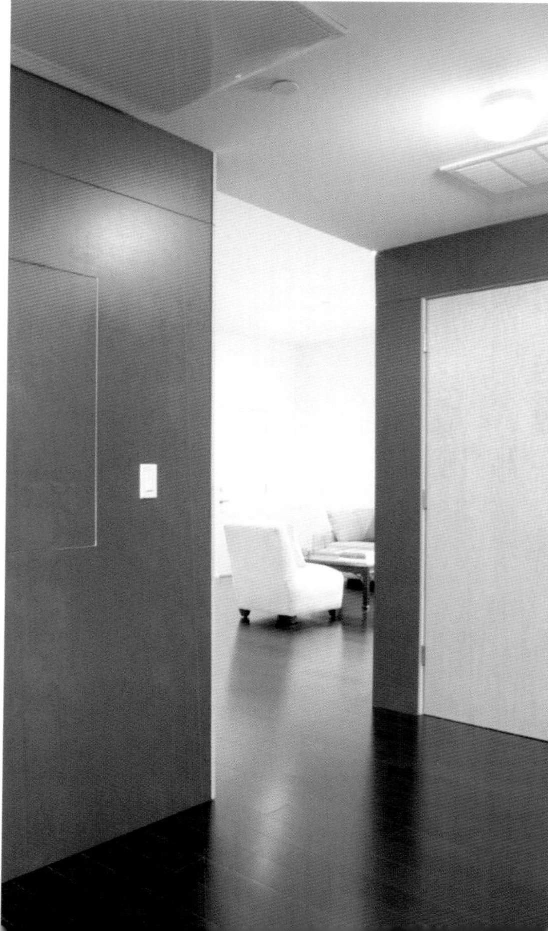

ABOVE
The architects see the Gardner 1050 project as establishing an innovative precedent for this part of West Hollywood's architectural environment. The translucent glass stairwell is a feature of the eye-catching facade. It also provides a strong vertical element in an otherwise horizontal composition.

LEFT
Bold color in the hallway provides a dynamic contrast with the pale-themed living room beyond.

Living Tomorrow AMSTERDAM, THE NETHERLANDS

UNStudio

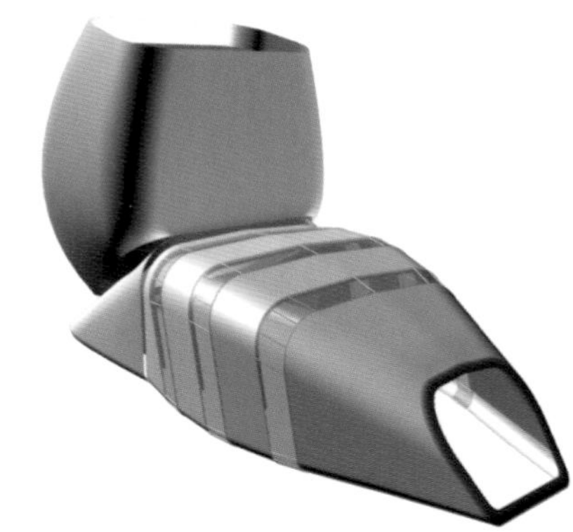

Constructed 2002
Home type Future-oriented living and working prototype, temporary building (5 years) – showroom
Structure Stucco and corrugated iron over concrete

"Living Tomorrow is a temporary building designed to raise people's awareness of future trends in housing and business. We needed to demonstrate that cutting-edge technology need not be too complex and can still be made to serve people's needs."
UNStudio

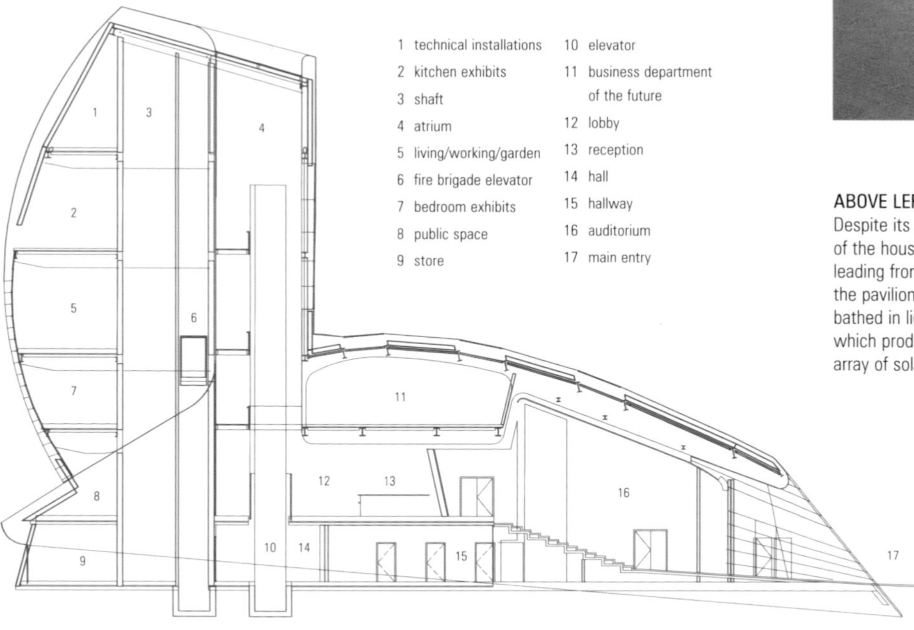

ABOVE LEFT
Despite its location in the middle of the house, this staircase – leading from the auditorium to the pavilion's reception area – is bathed in light from a glass roof, which produces electricity via an array of solar energy panels.

TOP
UNStudio's vision of what the future may hold – a curvaceously shaped combined office and living space.

ABOVE
Multi-tasked, wall-mounted LCD screens adjust lights, operate blinds, fill rooms with soft music, and even ignite the living area's gas fireplace.

TOP RIGHT
This view of the exterior is an assault on the senses, with its stucco over concrete blocks, load-bearing concrete panels, corrugated metal, and enormous expanses of 40-ft- (12-m-) high glass. Air voids in the concrete blocks beneath the stucco provide ample insulation and require minimal maintenance.

SHOWCASE FOR THE FUTURE

The Living Tomorrow Pavilion, on Arena Boulevard in Amsterdam, is a futuristic building designed by UNStudio, a network of architects, graphic designers, builders, and quantity surveyors headed by architect Ben van Berkel and art historian Caroline Bos. The building and its contents have an exhibition life of five years. After that, another Living Tomorrow Pavilion featuring new technologies will be constructed.

The building is designed to raise awareness of future trends in housing and in the workplace, and to nurture a spirit of innovation among professionals and the general public. It showcases cutting-edge technology while researchers develop and demonstrate concepts that may be integrated into the homes of the future.

CORPORATE SUPPORT

The project is supported by companies such as Bose, Microsoft, and Unilever, who provide prototypes of their products. In this way it serves as a platform for some of the world's most innovative corporations, who can discuss their products with the consumer.

A LIGHT FOOTPRINT

UNStudio's radical design gives a glimpse of what the future may hold. Fluid and curvaceous exterior walls achieve continuity between the horizontal and vertical planes as well as the internal and external spaces. The design triumphantly mimics the helicoidal system of DNA – its two spiral circuits intersect with each other over all levels.

All the materials used in the pavilion's construction are either recyclable or have a low impact on the environment. The building's own footprint is minimal, with less than half the lot assigned to it being used for the building. The remainder is used for staging various bi-annual open-air events.

BOOT SHAPE

Although the layout varies, the pavilion consists of two spaces – one horizontal, and the other vertical, much like a boot. The "foot" usually contains the office of the future, a meeting room, an auditorium and event hall, while the "leg" usually houses the kitchen exhibits and living quarters. Some spaces are reserved for the public.

The building is heated and cooled using solar energy and extensive natural ventilation systems. As an alternative to designated bedrooms, occupants may choose to sleep in "cocoons" within the living area. These circle-shaped beds can close up, and each has its own integrated multimedia system.

Communications and connectivity are paramount. The websites have speech technology, and electricity is supplied via transparent solar cells. A computer in the kitchen even provides recipes to help you lose weight, while ambient lighting in soft, muted shades of blue, green, and gray adjust to your mood.

In the pavilion, ideas are shelved if they fail to meet expectations. For example, the refrigerator that reordered food was discarded for being too clumsy and complicated to operate.

Longlands Mill CHESHIRE, ENGLAND

Space Craft Architects

Construction	2007–2008
Home type	Apartments, offices, studios, and shops
Structure	Steel frame with pre-cast concrete floors

"We are very excited by the ideas we have developed for this project, especially the spaces to be opened up alongside the Canal and the River Tame. Our design will allow views through the site from the river to the canal, and beyond. It will also generate new routes to link the area together and help revitalize the town center."

Nik Randall

AN EYE ON HISTORY

Between the River Tame and the Huddersfield Narrow Canal in the center of Stalybridge, Cheshire, sits the 4.5 acre (1.8 ha) Longlands Mill site. Space Craft Architects won a recent competition to decide who would design a mixed-use scheme for the site. Space Craft was selected because they were seen to epitomize a design-led approach and also because of their inspired body of work to date. The company's ideas for the mixed-use development, incorporating the old with the new, were the most sympathetic to the site's history – there are some surviving mill buildings from centuries gone by.

A THREE-PRONGED FOCUS

Space Craft put forward three primary objectives for the development. First, they wanted to guarantee the future of the surviving mill buildings by performing appropriate alterations, giving them practical new uses, and constructing new buildings that were complementary to the existing ones. Second, they wanted to revitalize Stalybridge by amalgamating the original site with the surrounding semi-urban environment. Third, Space Craft wanted to design and build a broad range of both commercial and residential accommodation.

LOOKING TO THE FUTURE

The Space Craft proposal looks to the future, beyond the requirements of the site itself. They have the big picture in mind, and have identified possible retail prospects and the creation of more public space and transport infrastructure. Architect Nik Randall, a director of the company, sees their proposal as a way of rejuvenating the town center.

The proposal includes more than 250 new homes, offices, cafés, and restaurants, as well as a range of retail and other commercial spaces. As the town of Stalybridge sits at the foot of the Pennines, there is also a proposal for a hotel in the master plan.

Space Craft are spending time at the site with Urban Splash, the developer for the project, to finalize the design ideas, and also to restore those parts of the Mill complex that have been heritage-listed. This will set the scene for the proposed refurbishment of the site into residential apartments and commercial space.

The conversion of the Longlands Mill building has been designed to express the original cast-iron columns and timber roof trusses in such a way that they harmonize with the character of the apartments and shared spaces. The new buildings will comprise spacious, interlocking double-height apartments, maximizing the sense of space while keeping them affordable.

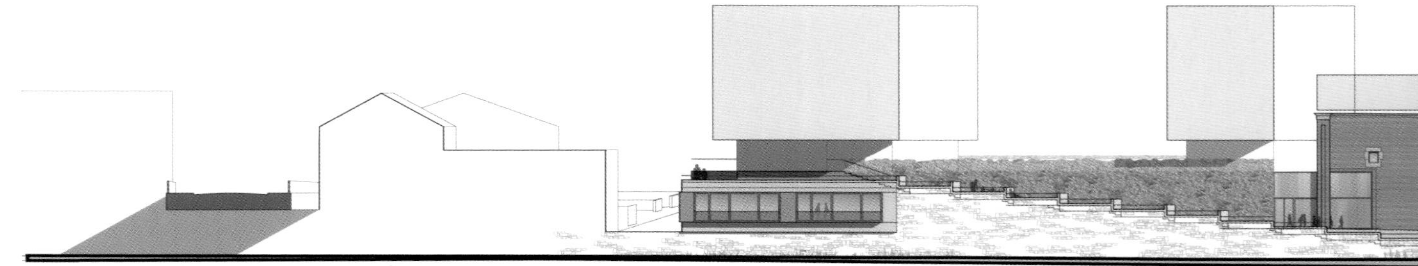

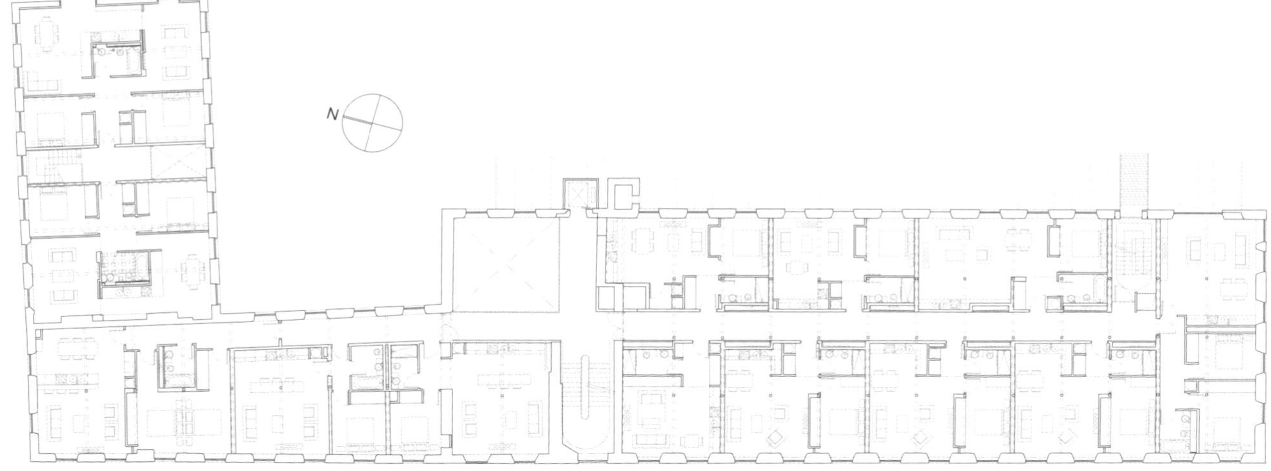

SECOND LEVEL

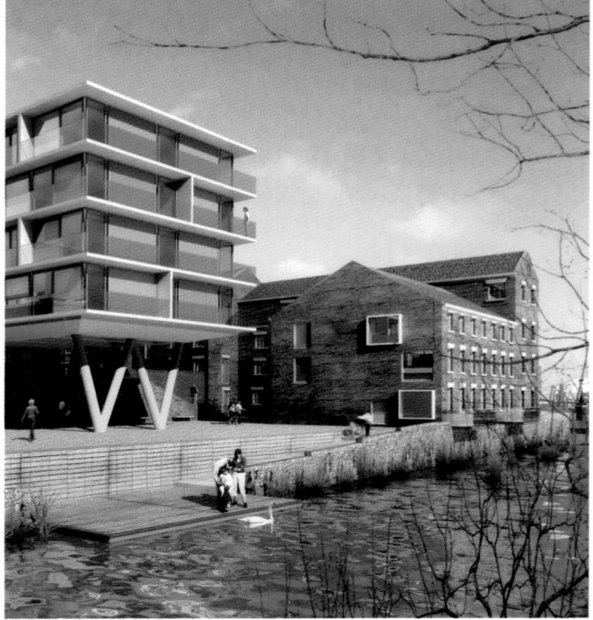

TOP LEFT
An aerial view of the proposed development, which is designed to enhance the commercial and economic life of Stalybridge, shows how the entire site is flanked by the canal and the river.

LEFT
The town's history is bound up with the heritage-listed mill buildings, so Space Craft wanted to restore these as well as incorporate modern architectural ideas.

ABOVE
The development will provide public access to the River Tame and the Huddersfield Narrow Canal, creating new parklands along these waterways and rejuvenating the entire site.

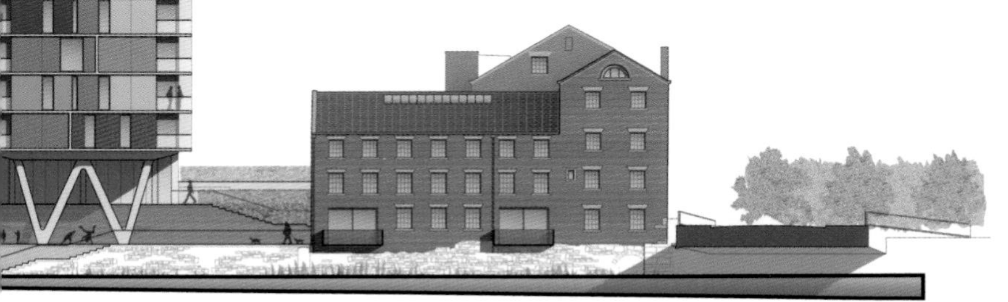

Moriyama House TOKYO, JAPAN

Ryue Nishizawa

Constructed 2005
Home type Single dwelling [owner's house] and five apartments
Structure Three levels and basement, concrete, plated steel, and glass

ABOVE
Variations in the footprint, floor plan, and height of each of the Moriyama buildings convey the impression of a town in miniature, full of harmoniously contrasting forms and pleasantly differing perspectives for its inhabitants. Common structural elements and styles provide a sense of community and shared values.

"Moriyama House is a community in miniature, composed of individually proportioned buildings on a small parcel of land in a typically urban setting. Its ten separate volumes cater to the varying needs of its occupants, as well as creating a series of connected individual gardens all open to the surroundings."
Ryue Nishizawa

In a densely populated area of Tokyo, the architect Ryue Nishizawa, and his associates, Ippei Takahashi and Kimihiko Okada, took a modest 3,000-sq-ft (290-sq-m) site and constructed a cluster of subterranean and aboveground two- and three-story towers. These fit in perfectly with their surrounding urban environment, while at the same time providing an innovative solution to the specific needs of the client.

ALTERNATIVE MODEL OF HABITATION

Although technically a single dwelling for its owner, Moriyama House is in fact a collection of ten separate self-contained buildings – exploring the theory of fragmenting a structure into its constituent parts. The result is an alternative model of habitation, which gives the owner the flexibility of living in any one of the spaces or moving between them as his mood or needs dictate.

The interior of each of the ten buildings contains varying combinations of kitchens, living rooms, and bedrooms, so the owner also has the option to rent any of the spaces for an additional income source.

SHARED GARDENS

Tiny landscaped areas weave in and out of the structures, designed by the architect to create a series of "Schreber Gardens," (a German tradition of leasing people small, allotted public spaces in which to grow vegetables, fruit, and flowers). In addition these spaces function as common areas where people can interact.

The walls of Moriyama House have been prefabricated out of plated steel so as to be as thin as possible – and to maximize the living and outdoor areas, on what is a typically small parcel of Tokyo real estate.

TURNING PRIVACY ON ITS HEAD

The buildings reflect an unorthodox approach to the issue of privacy: One bathroom is located outside, and cannot be accessed from within; another home includes an uncurtained glass wall, which faces the public courtyard. The architect hopes to cultivate openness among the occupants.

COMMUNITY AND HARMONY

Flung across the site in perfect proportion and harmony, Moriyama House's collection of towers, landscaped areas, and intricate network of pathways and alleyways follows the Japanese tradition of small residential dwellings, creating a community unto itself.

Moriyama House's many white concrete facades create a minimalist maze of Cubism, reminiscent of the paintings of Piet Mondrian and of the purity of Modernism in the 1920s.

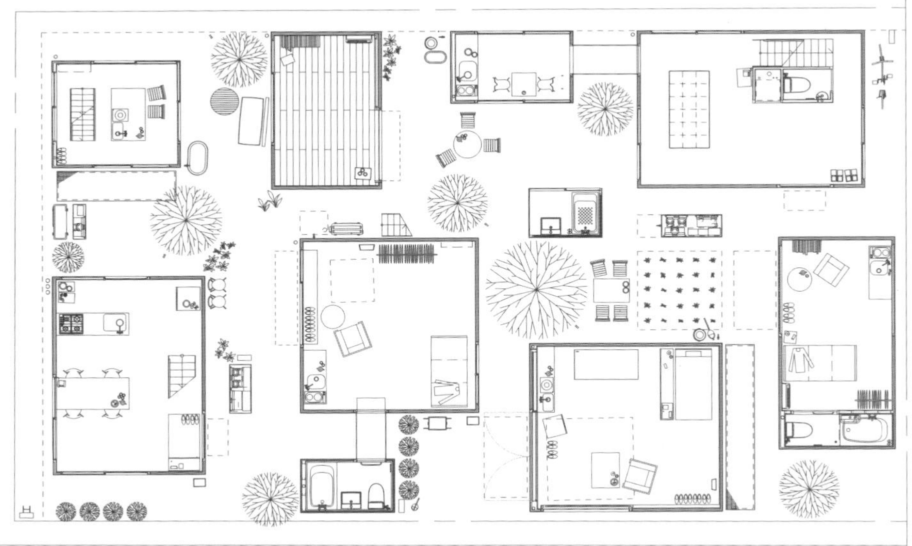

ABOVE LEFT
Large picture windows give a sense of openness and warmth to the small rooms, while also embracing expansive city views. Minimal ornamentation, characteristic of the project, is accentuated by the almost "invisible" window frames.

ABOVE
A myriad of open spaces is created from the location of Moriyama House's buildings – ranging from long, narrow alleyways to broader landscaped spaces such as the one pictured here. Ornamental trees and shrubs provide texture to spaces where the focus of the inhabitants is directed inwards through glass areas that face each other.

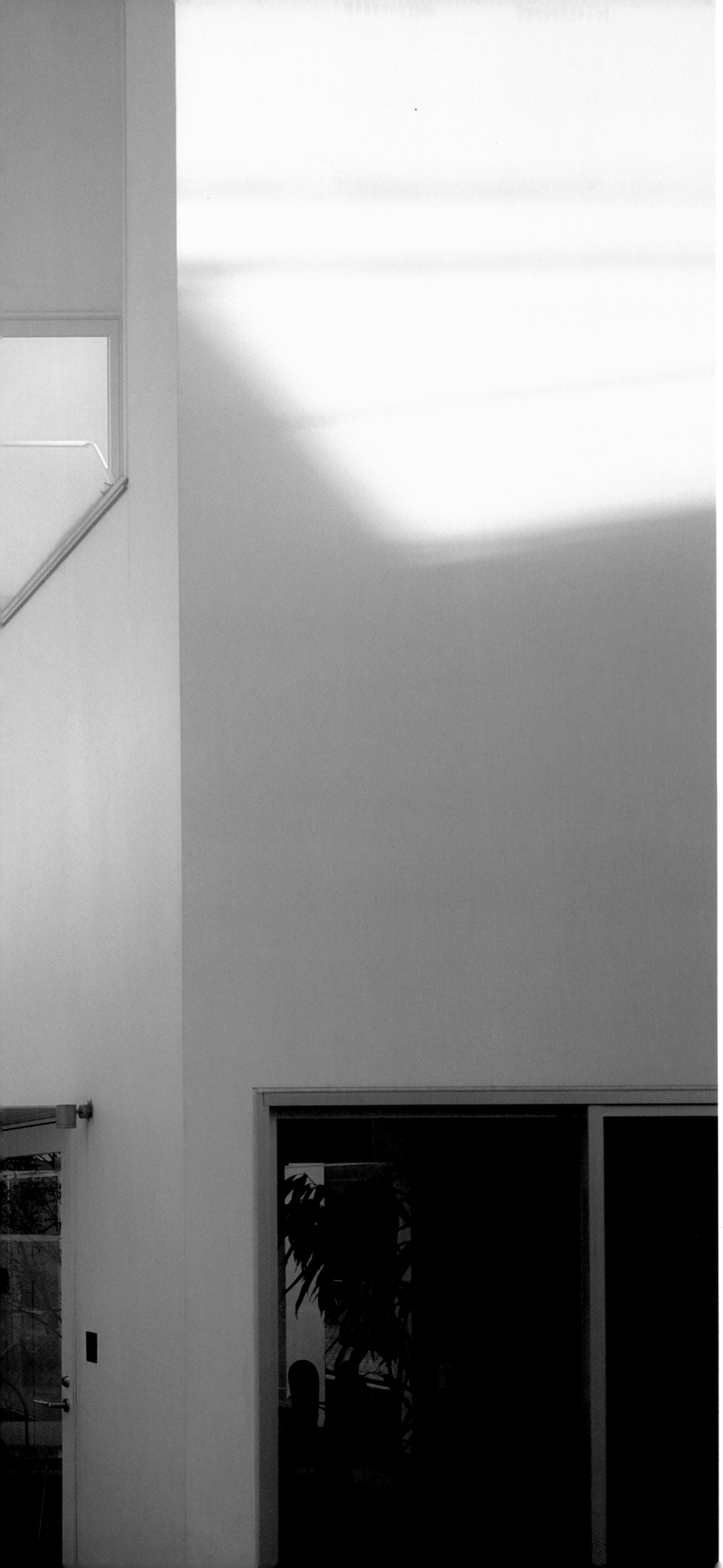

LEFT
Despite the close proximity of the separate buildings, there is no sense of clutter or density. Rather, the Moriyama buildings together have a sense of wholeness, each element part of a beautifully crafted entity. Narrow alleyways provide access points to entryways and connect the outdoor spaces.

ABOVE
In such compact living space, staircases are necessarily functional – narrow with minimal balustrading, shallow treads, and high angles. Their design typifies the architect's approach of maximizing internal spaces without compromising functionality.

One Room, Three Ways

John Aspinall C3D INTERACTIVE

"To have imagined, 20 years ago, that an architect would have the opportunity to observe a digital representation of a design proposal in context would have pushed the limits of credibility. However, the current reality is exactly that, and more."

John Aspinall

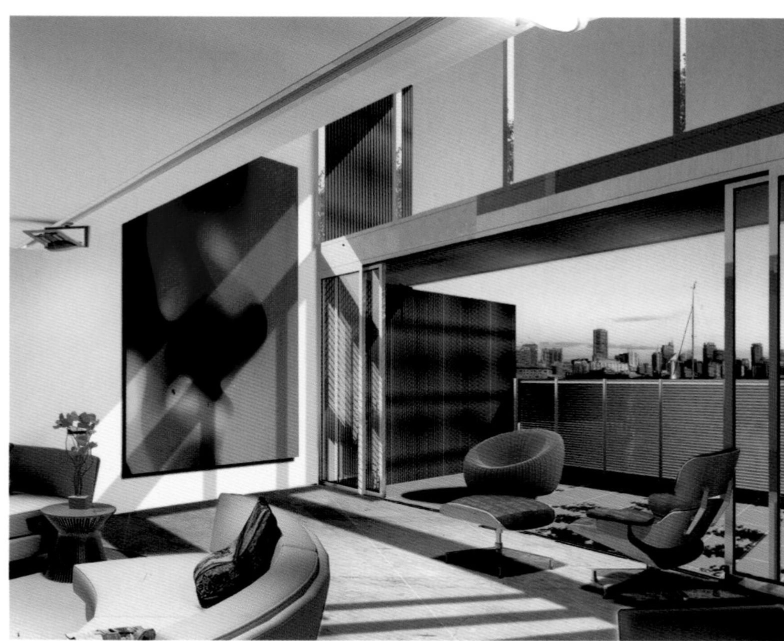

ABOVE AND RIGHT
The same basic shell can take on a series of quite different characters reflecting the owner's tastes. CAD technology permits a visual assessment of the impact of various furniture styles, even down to the choice of artwork.

TOP RIGHT
By utilizing computer visualization programs, with their extensive libraries of "modeled" furniture, clients can consider a vast range of design options.

COMPUTER AIDED DESIGN

It is now within the technical capabilities of most architectural practices to generate photo realistic images and even animations of design proposals. For architects, the arrival of Computer Aided Design (CAD) promised a radical alternative to existing design solutions. However, for the majority of architectural practices, CAD represents little more than computer-aided drafting, reducing documentation production times dramatically. At the other extreme, stand the pioneers of CAD, who recognize the huge potential at their fingertips.

STATE OF THE ART COMPUTER TECHNOLOGY

Frank Gehry's current work represents the "state of the art" in terms of pushing computer technology to its limits within the field of architecture. By searching for ways to help contractors better understand highly complex geometrical forms, Gehry's office began to develop its own specific software. This was based upon an existing package, CATIA, a purely three-

dimensional modeling program, originally created in France to design jet fighters and adapted by Boeing for commercial aircraft. This has now evolved to a point where physical models, still Gehry's preferred methods of schematic design, can be digitally scanned into the computer. From here, the design is further refined and developed to a point where exact quantities and geometries can be fed directly to the building contractor from the CAD model.

A further benefit of this approach is an increased dialogue between the architect and sub-contractor at the design development stage, which will lead to considerable cost and time saving and, perhaps, an even greater involvement from, and respect for, the architect beyond the production of documentation.

INTERACTIVE DESIGN PROCESSES

At a more practical level, many architectural practices are beginning to see the advantages of a more interactive design process, using currently available CAD technology.

Architecturally, the interactive model's greatest strength still remains within the design development stage and its ability to evolve and respond with the speed and accuracy necessary to produce an optimal design solution.

Specialized visualization studios now utilize software originally developed within the film industry, where speed is essential, to encourage all members of building design teams to assess the impact of new developments in context – internally and externally – from the earliest stages of concept design.

EFFECTIVE RESOLUTION

The progression of the three-dimensional model follows several defined stages that reflect the iterative process of design, from geometric considerations into compositional concerns involving material, surface texture, colors, and lighting. The visual portrayal of any potentially contentious areas of the design facilitates rapid and effective resolution of any issues.

It is the intention of interactive visualization studios to continue developing and enhancing these ideas, permitting a far more streamlined and effective design process.

This will lead to considerable time and cost savings for all members of the design team. More importantly, in creating an environment in which architectural design can be more critically and objectively assessed, standards of design, both in terms of resolution and quality, will inevitably improve.

ABOVE
The same room takes on a completely different identity in this rendering. The starkness of the 1990s apartment is softened by the inclusion of rich textures and materials.

Parque Espana MEXICO CITY, MEXICO

TEN Arquitectos

Constructed 2001
Home type Multilevel residence with underground garage
Structure Concrete frames and waffled slabs

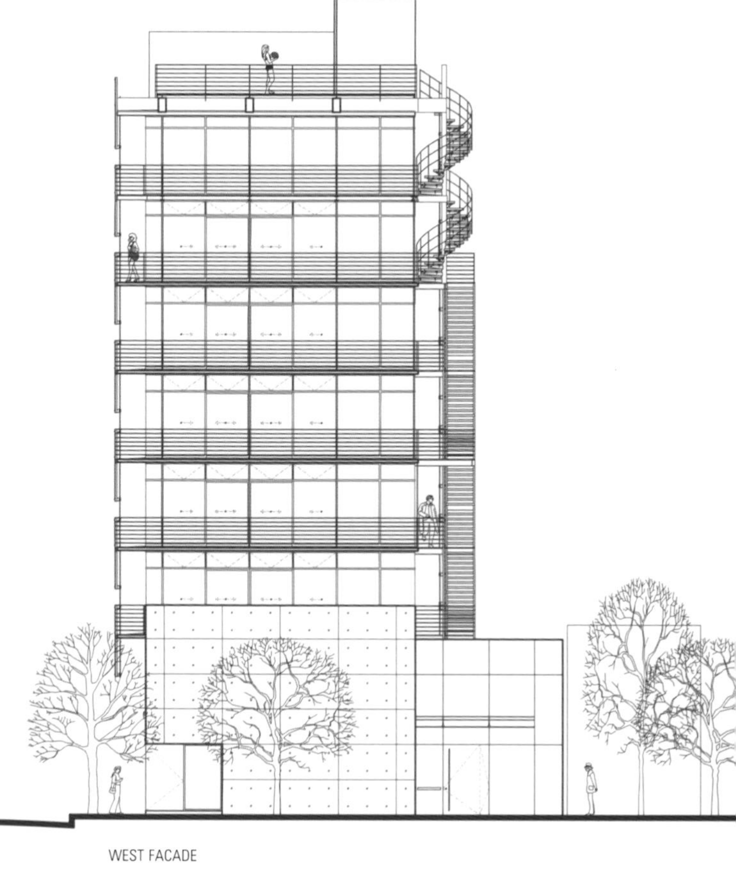

WEST FACADE

"Our clients wanted a modern building that would house family apartments and a penthouse above an art gallery and garage. The site is very exposed, so we wanted to give each apartment privacy without sacrificing either light or the views to the Parque Espana across the street."

TEN Arquitectos

With its innovative, grid-like exterior of aluminum and glass, TEN Arquitectos' multilevel residential building on a tight corner site is ideally located in one of Mexico City's densest urban environments.

A MODERN OUTLOOK

Situated in the Colonia Condesa district opposite the Parque Espana, a lovely city park built in 1921 to celebrate Mexico's victory in the War of Independence, the building consists of six single-family apartments and one two-story rooftop penthouse, all set above a contemporary art gallery on the ground floor. There is also an adjacent residents' garage with parking for 14 cars.

The clean modern lines of the building's facade of aluminum and glass reflect the changing face of Mexico City's most modern district, which blends traditional colonial architecture with splendid examples of Modernity, all set among tree-lined streets with alfresco restaurants.

The building's design is characterized by immaculate proportions and a considered layering of elements and materials. The external stairs and balconies provide a lively composition for streetscape views of the building.

ROOFTOP GARDEN

Each apartment contains two bedrooms that are centrally located along a narrow floor plan, with living areas on either side and services such as laundry, pantry, and storage placed along the eastern side.

ABOVE
This exterior view of the building from the Parque Espana across the street reveals the Modernist simplicity and angular form of the ground-floor concrete facade, as well as the cavernous entrance to the art gallery. Its straight lines and classical form typify TEN Arquitectos' approach to design – buildings that derive their character less from their shape than from the way they were built.

ABOVE
The building's western facade shows an extensive use of glass, which seems to welcome the passerby into the project. Sliding, transparent fabric screens reinvent expansive, framed views of the surrounding neighborhood from the building's interior. Generous balconies provide ample space for entertaining.

TOP RIGHT
This ground level view illustrates the building's exquisite sense of proportion and how neatly it fits into the surrounding streetscape. Ornamentation is non-existent in a building where functionality and the pursuit of Modernism – as seen in the repetitious nature of the partitioning – is regarded as paramount.

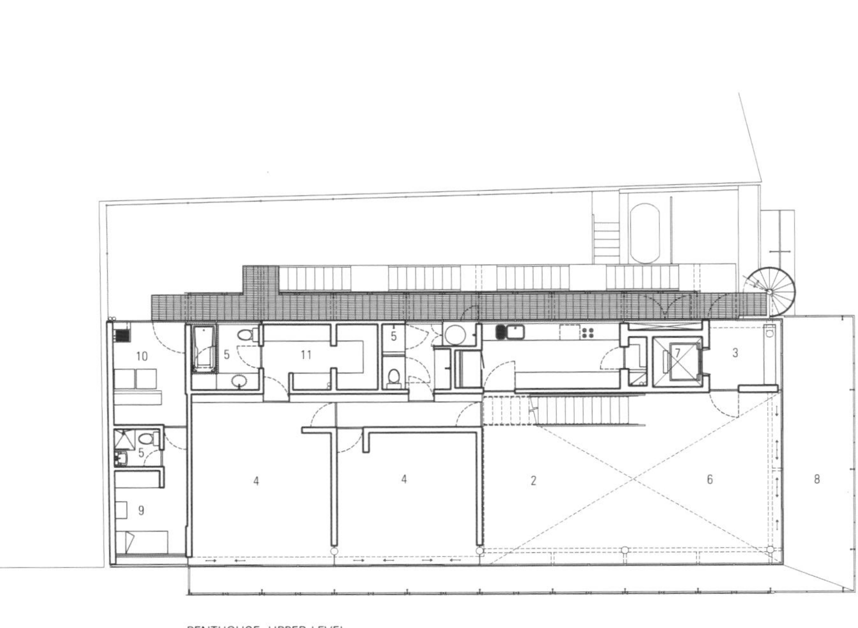

PENTHOUSE, UPPER LEVEL

1 kitchen
2 dining
3 hallway
4 bedroom
5 bathroom
6 living
7 elevator
8 terrace
9 service area
10 utility
11 dressing room

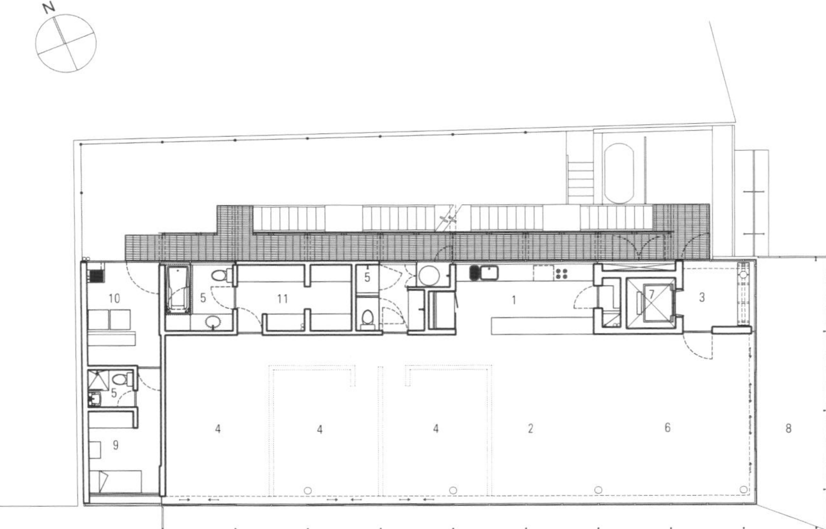

TYPICAL FLOOR PLAN

ABOVE
This interior view of the penthouse demonstrates how a generous room height can give a sense of space even to a narrow living area. The amount of light is controlled by the use of fabric filters on the windows.

The building's southern elevation provides views to Parque Espana by means of a cantilevered terrace. The bedrooms above the street on the western side are sheltered by an elegant, slim balcony set in the foreground of elaborate, continuously sliding partitions of translucent fabric, all contained within an intricate framework of aluminum. In addition to filtering out ultraviolet rays and harsh sunlight, they provide privacy and a random order that is constantly changing.

All residents share a roof garden, complete with lap pool and wood-decking surround. These elements assist in the "rediscovery of the rooftop" in a city where rooftops are normally occupied by nothing more than building machinery and clotheslines.

Service stairs connect every level, allowing access to each apartment via bridges. An external spiral staircase leading to the roof garden is recessed into the building's eastern corner. The two-story penthouse consists of an upper level loft containing a main bedroom, a guest suite, two bathrooms, and a family room. Its lower level is a massive, functional open space, flooded with light from the 15-ft- (5-m-) high windows on its western facade. The kitchen, laundry, and a downstairs bathroom are located behind a large partition that anchors the stairs leading to the rooms above.

DESIGN AWARD

In Parque Espana, the principal designer, Enrique Norten, has demonstrated his ability to produce a building that is both technically innovative, in its use of complex industrial materials, and sensitive to the surrounding streetscape.

The Parque Espana development received the Design Excellence in Housing Award from the Boston Society of Architects in 2004.

The clean modern lines of the building's facade of aluminum and glass reflect the changing face of Mexico City's most modern district...

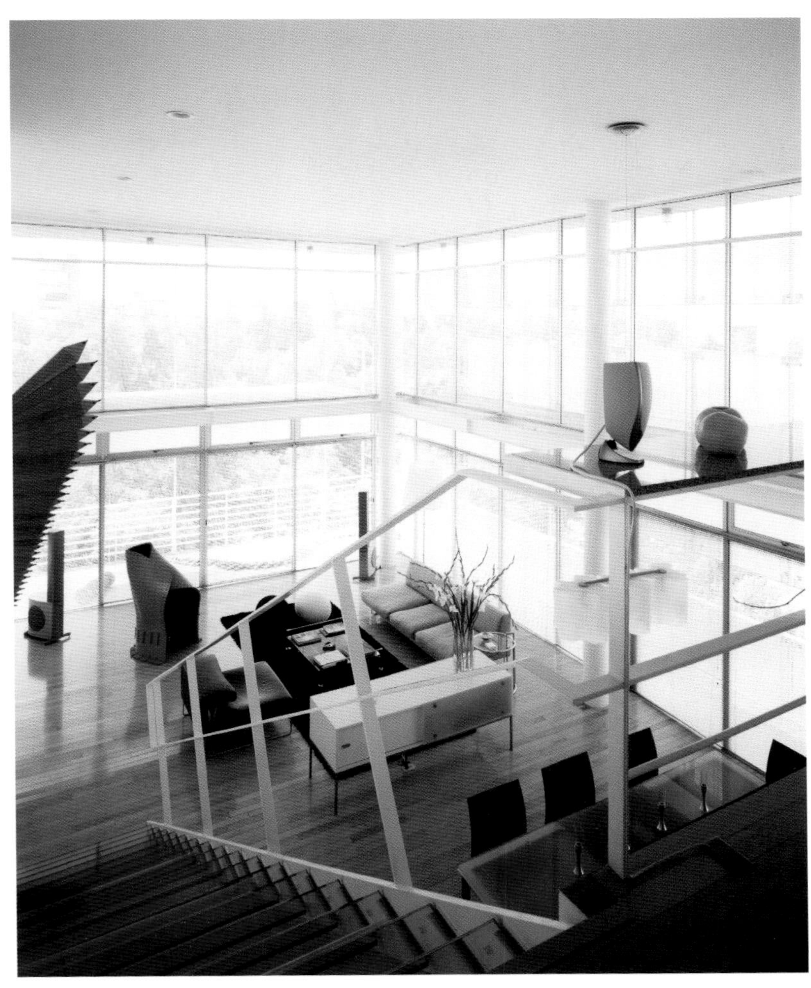

ABOVE
This interior view of the living area is taken from the second level of the penthouse. The importance of the "void" in architecture is seen in the designer's refusal to extend the loft further into the living area simply in order to gain more space.

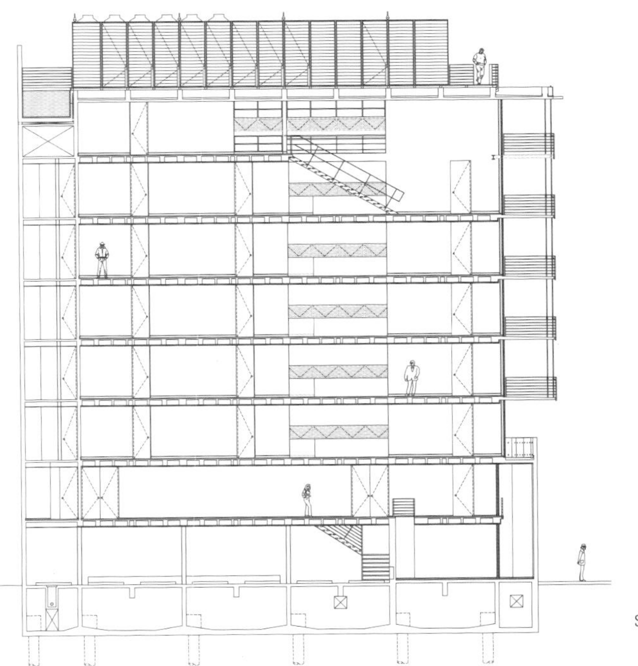

SECTION VIEW

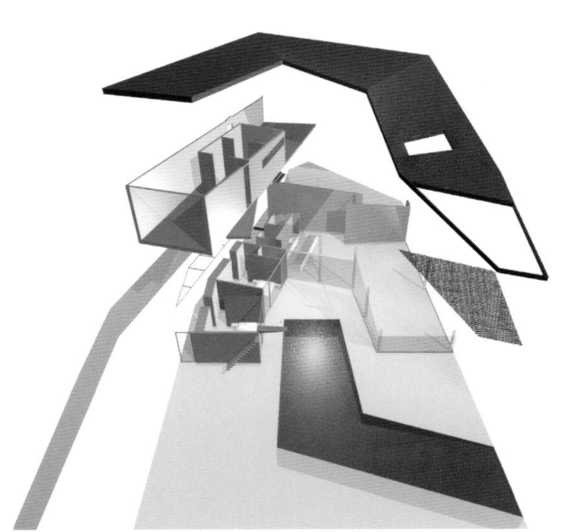

Ramp House BODRUM, TURKEY

GAD-Gokhan Avcioglu NEW YORK, USA

Construction	Yet to be completed
Home type	Multi-level family home
Structure	Steel core and fibrous concrete

"The 'Ramp House' reinterprets traditional dwellings in the area, yet its angular structure...fits into the clefts in the hillside and remains in keeping with the natural environment..."

GAD Architecture

BUILDING REGULATIONS

Bodrum is a seaside resort in southwestern Turkey, overlooking the blue Aegean Sea. The area has a long history, going back some 3,000 years, and as a result local planning authorities impose strict regulations on new building developments. In order to gain approval to build here, the architects had to either devise an innovative interpretation of the traditional villa-style home that predominates in the area or relate the design in some way to the town's ancient roots.

ANCIENT INSPIRATION

And so they did. The design of Ramp House was inspired by the Mausoleum of Halicarnassus, one of the Seven Wonders of the Ancient World. Built in about 350 BCE and renowned for its unique design, the Mausoleum had four steep staircases, one on each side. The distinctive "ramps" in Ramp House are a modern interpretation of this design.

Still at the planning stage, the home is 4000 sq ft (370 sq m) and will be built from a steel core and covered in fibrous concrete. The design blends with the undulating landscape and incorporates a multi-functional rooftop terrace. Conveniently, the ramp access to the roof provides a neat solution to accommodating the owner's collection of motor cycles – the parking area is on top of the house. This way too, the first level, with its courtyard and pool area, will be kept clear of vehicles, allowing unimpeded views of the water and the valley.

There is also a roof terrace at the top of the house, which serves as an observation deck and entertaining area. In the hotter months, this will also be an inviting space, where one can sleep under the stars.

OPEN LIVING

Overlapping floor planes in the house adapt to the shape of the land. A ramp leading to a roof terrace can be accessed by both foot and bike, and expansive views of the valley and the bay can be enjoyed from all areas of the house.

The design of the house is very open, and the living spaces are generously proportioned. Because the climate in this part of Turkey is very hot, it is vital to create a flexible connection between the interior and exterior spaces. Floor to ceiling glass windows help to create this connection, allowing plenty of fresh air to circulate around the house. Their other function is to give sweeping views from every room.

TOP
An exploded view of the "Ramp House" showing how the rooms relate to each other.

LEFT
Defying the traditional style of the area, yet remaining in harmony with it, the architects found inspiration for the angles and "ramps" in the ancient Mausoleum of Halicarnassus.

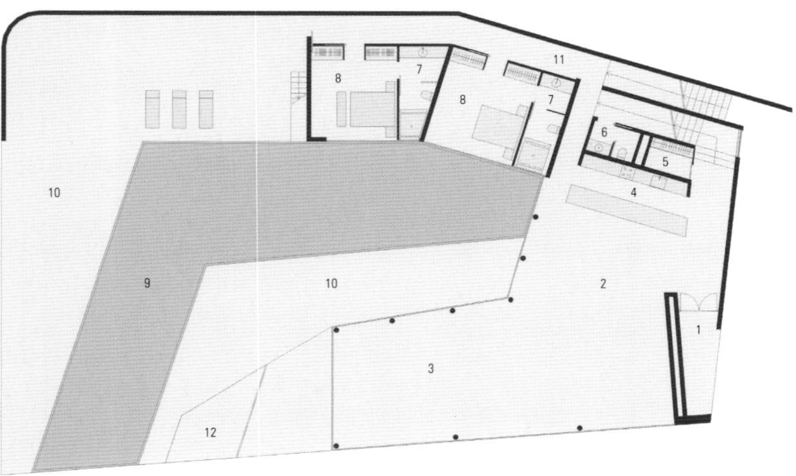

LEVEL ONE

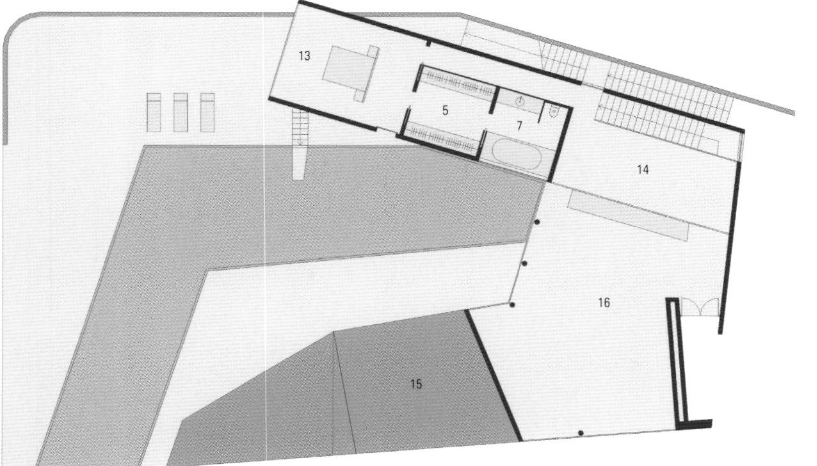

LEVEL TWO

1 entry
2 dining
3 living
4 kitchen
5 dressing
6 toilet
7 ensuite
8 bedroom
9 pool
10 courtyard
11 rooftop terrace entry
12 ramp to roof
13 main bedroom
14 mezzanine
15 roof
16 roof terrace

TOP
Defined by angles, the living room and the pool beyond become part of the landscape, tucked into the cleft of the hillside. One of the architects' signatures is the use of a neutral palette for interior finishes – easy on the eye and reflective of the natural landscape outside,

ABOVE
The roof ramp of the elongated living and dining room section almost collapses into the pool, which like everything else is both streamlined and angular.

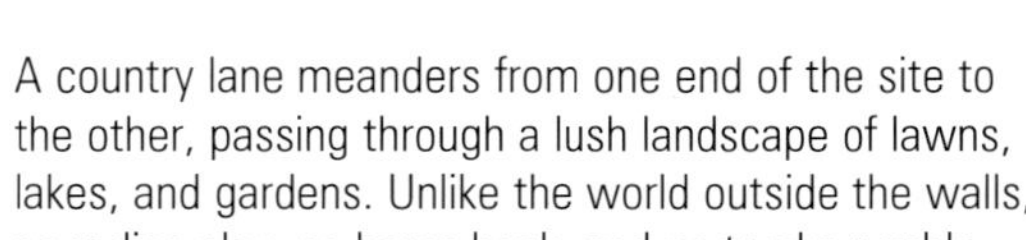

Shanghai Star Mei Hwa Estate SHANGHAI, CHINA

Ben Wood Studio Shanghai

Construction	In progress
Home type	Restored historic villas and contemporary villas; high-rise apartments with panoramic views
Structure	Villas: brickwork. Apartments: beam-free, flat plate tubular structural system

"The goal of this project is to create the most unique and prestigious residential address in Shanghai, and, indeed, in China. The generous amount of land in the Mei Hwa Estate allows the creation of many amenities usually not found in densely populated Shanghai. Here people live, entertain, and enjoy the things that mean the most to them."

Ben Wood

LIVING AN EXCLUSIVE LIFESTYLE

The villas, apartments, and gardens of Mei Hwa Estate form a secluded and tranquil living space for the residents, protected from the outside by a bamboo screen wall and dense shrubbery. In Shanghai, no other residential complex so close to the city enjoys such a large expanse of landscaped gardens.

There are 20 existing villas within the site, of English, French, and German styles. Of these, seven will be retained, and nine new villas constructed in a contemporary style, compatible in scale and size with the historic villas. Each villa will have a private garden featuring a south-facing lawn and a water feature. Both old and new villas will be located on existing landscaped roads – the old and new, side by side in a country landscape.

There are four high-rise towers within the complex, each positioned artfully on the site so as to create a particular relationship with the surrounding landscape.

PRIVATE GARDENS, HIDDEN DELIGHTS

The gardens of the estate are designed to be seen and enjoyed only from inside the estate. At the entrance to the estate, a low stone and copper gatehouse greets visitors, and overhead a trellis connects this building to the screen wall surrounding the complex.

A country lane meanders from one end of the site to the other, passing through a lush landscape of lawns, lakes, and gardens. Unlike the world outside the walls, no radios play, no horns honk, and no trucks rumble.

The recreational facilities in the complex are situated at the southern end of the site, so the north gardens, with small curved lake and undulating beds of ornamental grasses and fragrant flowers, remain the more tranquil space. The southern gardens are the setting for the South Lake Towers. Also in the area are small pavilions, covered arbors, rose gardens, playgrounds, tennis courts, and a band shell for live concerts.

LEFT
Lakeside villas are to be constructed in a contemporary style compatible in scale and size with the existing historic villas. Each villa will have a private garden with a unique water feature. Large outdoor terraces provide areas for entertainment and relaxation.

PANORAMIC PLEASURES

Outlook is important for all the residences. The northern garden apartments look out on the north lake and gardens, framed by the foliage of mature trees, many more than 75 years old. Each villa by the south lake comprises two duplex apartments, both of which enjoy ground level views of the lake and common gardens from their living and dining areas.

Panoramic views of the district can be enjoyed from the living and dining areas of the tower apartments. Like the large trees that surround the towers, the cladding of the building is predominantly green – green stone panels alternate with bands of glass, which reflect the surroundings.

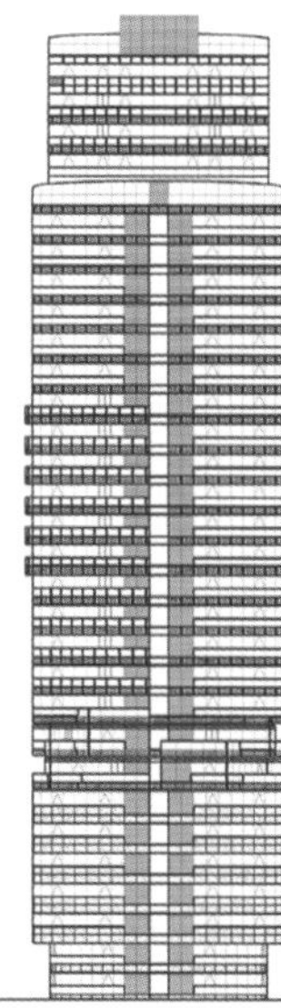

MASTERFUL MATERIALS

The tower structure is tubular, comprising a reinforced concrete core that forms shear walls, with reinforced concrete columns providing the outer ring at the building edge. To minimize the thickness of flat plate, inner columns are incorporated between the core and outer-ring columns. The outer-ring columns are set back from the building edge so that the curtain wall is supported by the cantilever flat plate.

THE ORGANIZATION OF SPACES

There are two apartments per level in the towers – half are three bedroom, and the remainder are either four bedroom or two bedroom.

All units have a small maid's room, bath, and balcony adjacent the kitchen. A separate elevator connecting to a service lobby at the ground floor provides direct access to each kitchen and maid's area.

Two garden or sky penthouses share an entire floor of each tower. There is a great deal of flexibility in the size and configuration of these luxury homes. The penthouses have an area of approximately 4,140 sq ft (385 sq m), but can be made smaller or larger depending on the arrangement and size of the balconies and roof terraces.

ABOVE
Apartments in the towers have floor areas ranging from 1,980 sq ft (184 sq m) to 4,150 sq ft (385 sq m): Floors two to eight are garden apartments; floors nine to 10, garden penthouses, boasting extensive balconies and outdoor terraces; floors 11 to 30, sky apartments; and floors 31 to 32 sky penthouses.

RIGHT
A contemporary lifestyle is accommodated in residences that range in character from a restored mid-twentieth century villa to a modern penthouse apartment atop one of the 32-story South Lake Towers.

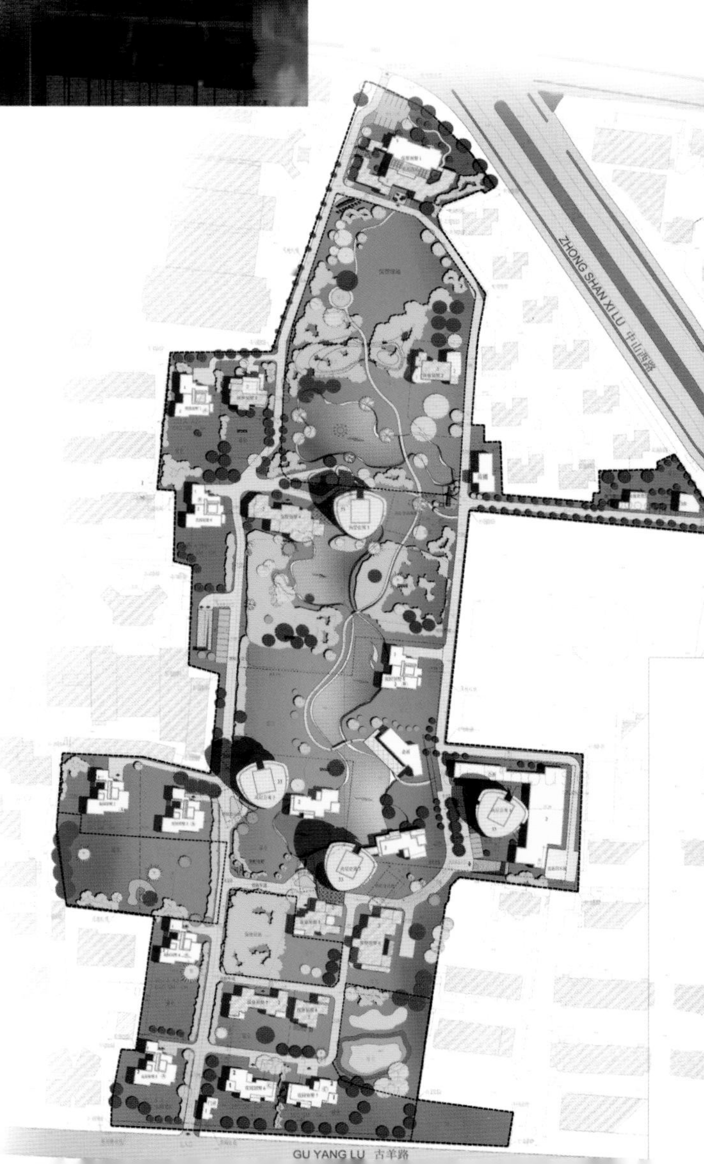

Skyhouse, London LONDON, ENGLAND

Marks Barfield Architects

Home type Apartment tower block, 30–50 stories high

Structure 180 homes per 2.5 acres (1 hectare); concrete, steel, and glass

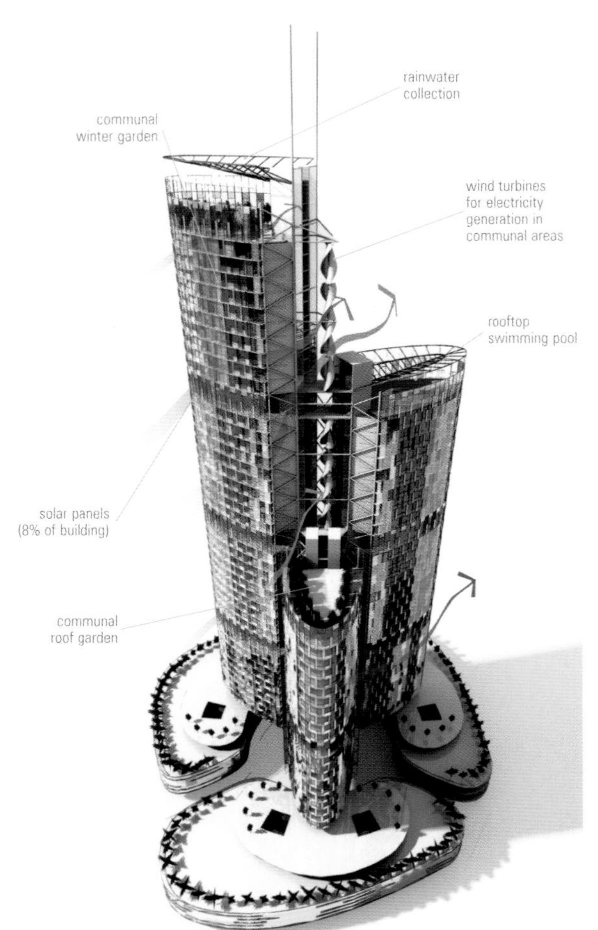

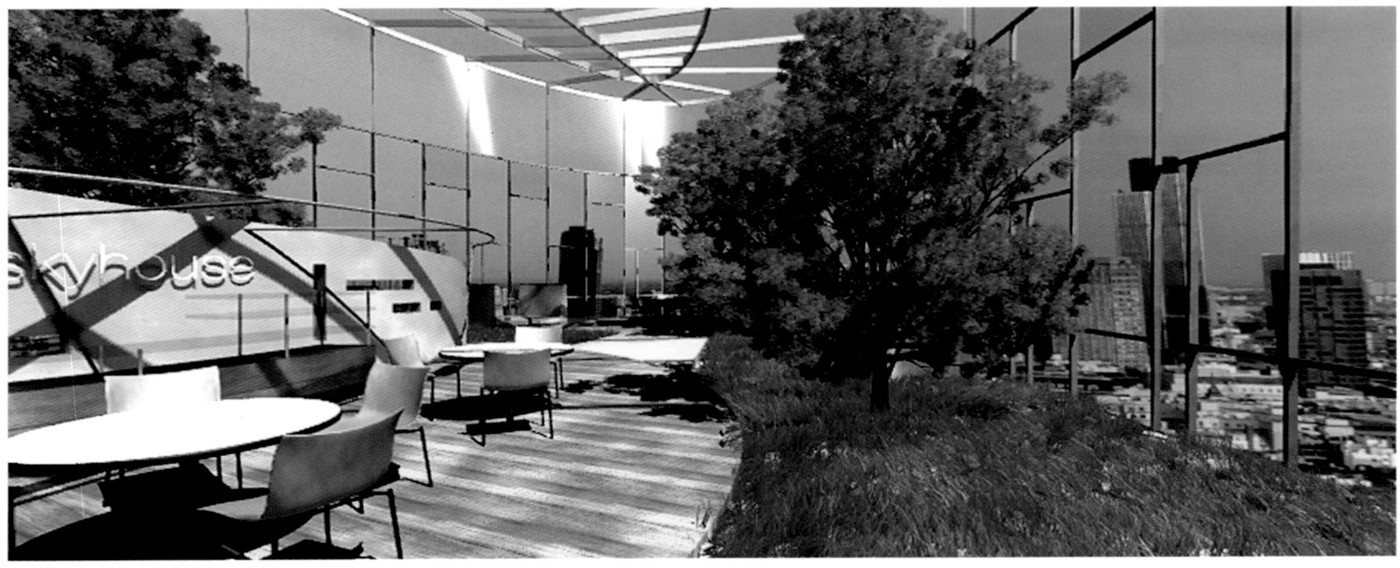

"These aren't the old tower blocks that everyone loathes. Skyhouse has learnt from the past. We have designed buildings that look beautiful, set them in wonderful landscapes, focused heavily on quality of life and sought to meet commercial, environmental, political, and social housing requirements. In short, we think we have created a future way to live – a symbol of modern Britain."

Julia Barfield and David Marks

Architects David Marks and Julia Barfield set themselves a challenge – to redress a paucity of housing options for key sector workers in London by creating high-density, affordable, and aesthetically pleasing apartments that make clever use of light and space, and also offer fantastic views. The emphasis is on building an environment where people want to live, rather than a place where they have to live.

The project integrates within its tall exterior a wide range of housing choices and sizes, including shops, health clubs, and gardens. It uses green technology, including the renewable energy sources of solar and wind, as well as the latest insulation and recycling systems.

PRACTICALLY UNCONVENTIONAL

The aim of Skyhouse is to offer affordable apartment living to teachers, nurses, and police – key sector workers that sometimes have difficulty purchasing a home in an expensive city. Clusters of Skyhouses can be built within the setting of a new urban parkland, without disturbing London's historic sightlines – close to places of employment yet a world away from city hustle and bustle.

HIGH-RISE WITH HEART

Skyhouse takes a fresh look at the concept of residential tower blocks, making them places where people actually want to live. This is reflected in the provision of communal amenities: a rooftop swimming pool and double-height "skygardens" and "skylobbies," all with spectacular city views. The ground level is set in a pleasing, landscaped, or mixed-use urban context. Security is maintained via secure underground parking and a 24-hour concierge. Proximity to shopping and transport are other community positives.

THE GREEN SCENE

Integral to the project is the use of sustainable green technologies, which are cost-saving: Eight percent of the building is covered in solar panels; floor to ceiling glazing affords not only panoramic views but passive solar heating; high insulation and a resultant low demand for heating; wind turbines generate electricity for communal areas; and rainwater is collected from the rooftop and stored for use in skygarden areas.

LEFT
Enormous glass panels and a louvered glass roof envelop the teardrop rooftop pool. The pool is an important inclusion in the Skyhouse design concept – it helps create a focal point and meeting place for residents.

TOP
Double-height communal skygardens are a key feature of the project. The architects believe these areas, with their expansive city views and relaxed "green" environments, are a crucial part of creating places where people actually want to live. There is also an emphasis on security, convenience, and sustainability. "Green" initiatives, such as rainwater collection systems, recycling, wind-generated electricity, and solar panels are integrated into the structure.

ABOVE
A range of homes, from affordable one- or two-bedroom apartments to more expensive three- or four-bedroom duplexes can be accommodated within the structure. Extensive use of glass and high quality contemporary finishes add to the relaxed, urban appeal.

Tyson Street House MELBOURNE, AUSTRALIA

Jackson Clements Burrows Architects

Constructed	2005
Home type	Two-story family home
Structure	Timber frame, glass, steel, and polycarbonate cladding

"This project involved the replacement of a weatherboard cottage that was covered by a heritage overlay with a new two-story home. On the basis that the local council recommends retaining such buildings, the project called for an innovative response. The house is concealed behind a photographic image of the original cottage, which has been applied as a graphic overlay to a three-dimensional facade. Could this ironic gesture be an example of the streetscape ultimately preserved by the problem itself?"

Jackson Clements Burrows Architects

CONTEXT, DECAY, AND HERITAGE

Located in a narrow back street in inner-city Melbourne, the original single-fronted weatherboard cottage on the site was in a state of decay. The client's brief to the architects was to replace the existing house with a new two-story family residence. In the architects' opinion, the decrepit dwelling had little or no heritage significance – the council heritage adviser disagreed, however, suggesting that the house made a significant contribution to the character of streetscape. A compromise had to be reached.

The client was keen to avoid the time and cost implications of possible planning tribunal hearings. Predictably, they were told that the council's heritage advice would be to replace the existing structure with a building similar in form, scale, and detail to that of the surrounding buildings.

IDEAS AND EXPLORATION

The architects accepted the notion of appropriate form and scale for a property bound by heritage constraints, but questioned the validity of designing yet another "polite" contextual building as a means of commemorating the existing streetscape. They took a lateral approach to the vexing problem, formulating an innovative and workable solution. They explored the idea of context and memory by making it "virtual" – in essence, they attempted to immerse the new house into an image of the old house.

VIRTUALITY OR REALITY?

The architects worked on creating a new form – one that was of a scale and proportion appropriate to the small site (just 3,000 sq ft [280 sq m]) and to the neighboring buildings. The new facade was then clad in glazed panels and superimposed with a photographic image of the original single-story house at 1:1 scale. The image was printed on adhesive film and applied to the inside face of the glass panels, where it would be protected from sun and rain exposure. The image wraps itself around the panels, complementing the roof forms of the neighboring houses and reflecting the sky above. This configuration also helped to diminish the scale of the upper story. In this way, the single-story streetscape could be preserved by concealing the larger and higher form of the new house.

RIGHT
Employing inventive "smoke and mirror" tactics to satisfy the council's heritage requirements, the modern facade of the new house preserves the history and appearance of the single-story streetscape by concealing it behind an photo-realistic image of the original dwelling.

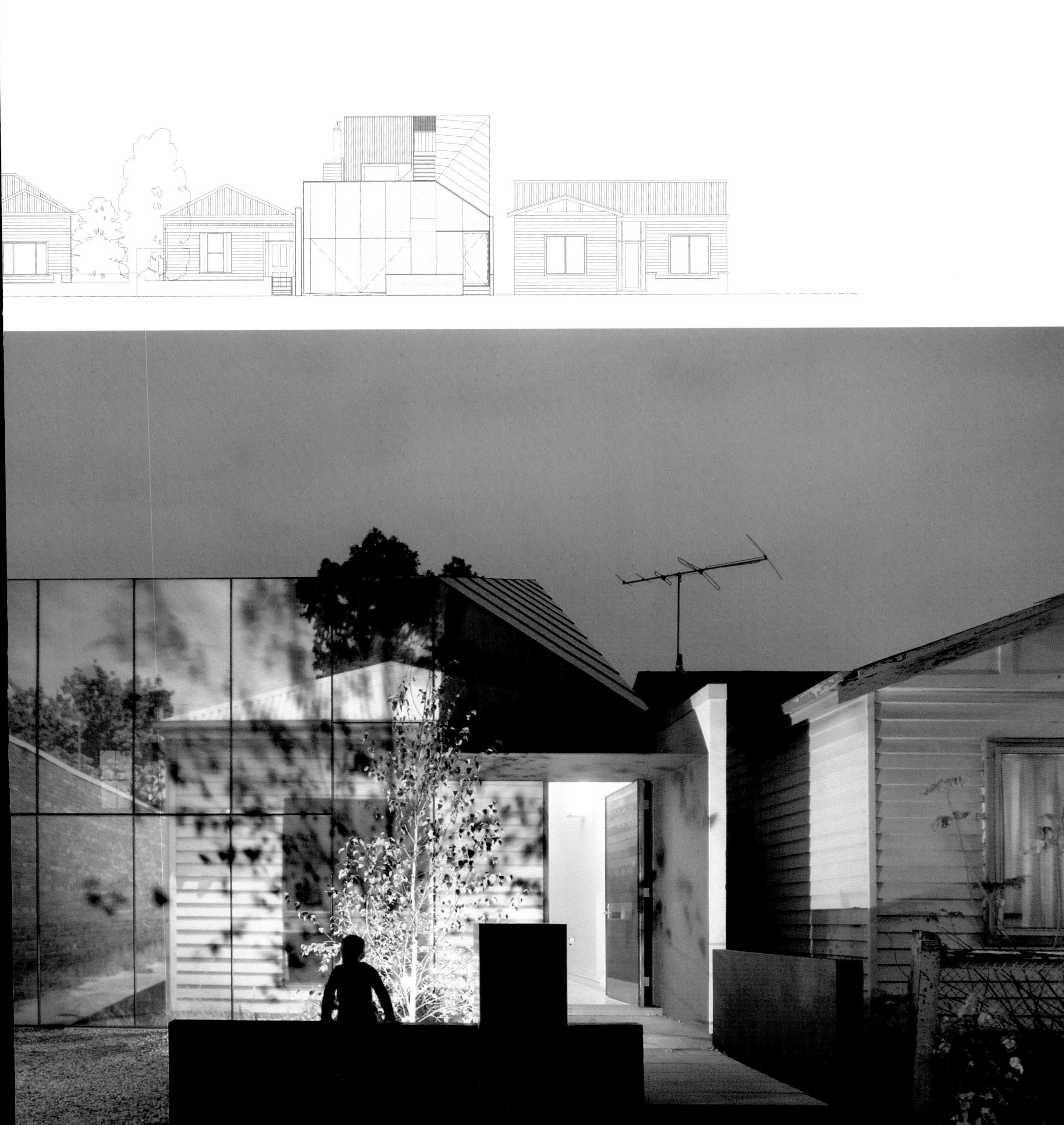

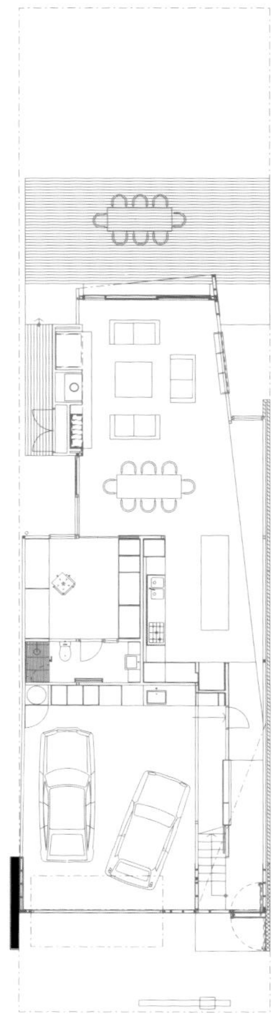

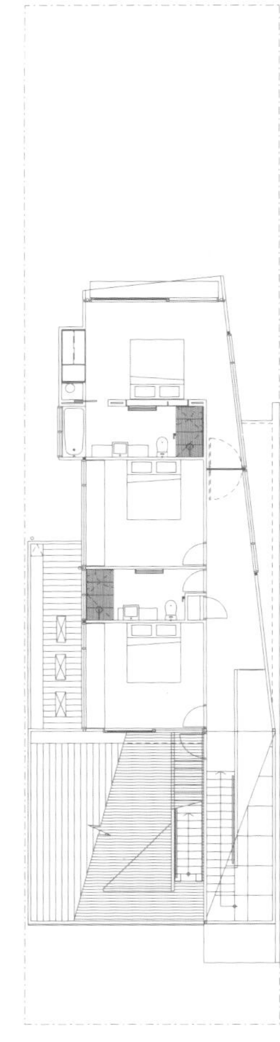

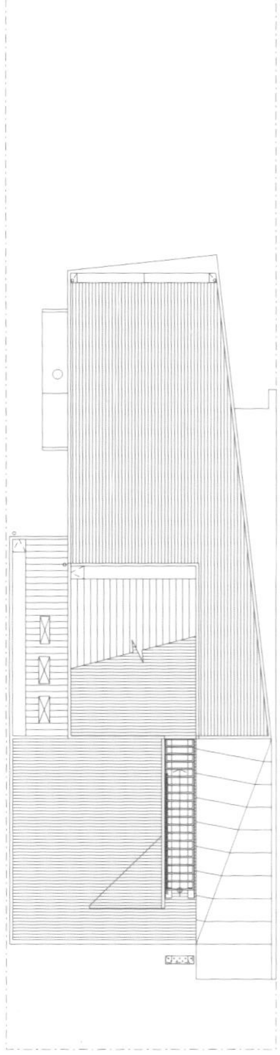

GROUND FLOOR

FIRST FLOOR

ROOF

INTERIOR RELATIONSHIPS

The living area, kitchen, bathrooms, bedrooms, roof decks, and double lock-up garage are concealed behind the photographic facade of the original dwelling. The house unfolds as a series of protected private spaces, opening out to interact with the garden and city views at the rear. A large lemon-scented gum tree is the only physical remnant of the original site. It was retained as a focal point for the garden, and its importance is recognized throughout the house interior by the use of colored laminate panels, sampled from the tones of the tree's seasonal bark and leaves.

COMMENTARY THROUGH ARCHITECTURE

This project is a response to the difficulties that may be encountered when required to create architectural solutions within heritage zones. It attempts to give rise to further debate about the sometimes conflicting aims of preservation and innovation within an architectural framework. In this sense, it is both a critique of the process and a surreal architectural solution.

PREVIOUS PAGES
The first floor roof deck provides a sculptural outdoor space to enjoy the expansive city views. Environmentally responsible principles were adopted during construction of the house, including the use of sustainable regrowth timber throughout.

RIGHT
Cost and energy efficiencies were integral to the project – external cladding materials are low maintenance, and glazing areas are limited and appropriately orientated to utilize their passive heating and cooling properties.

TOP
The multicolored laminate panels used in the kitchen echo the changing hues of the garden's lemon-scented gum tree. Two layers of polycarbonate cladding provide filtered natural daylight from the roof deck into the main entry area of the house.

ABOVE
An elegant choice of interior finishes imbues the light-filled and relaxed living/dining area with warmth and sophistication. The adjoining brick side fence, visible through the large window, pays homage to the cottage that originally stood on the site.

Voler House SAN DIEGO, USA

Wallace E Cunningham

Construction	2006–2008
Home type	"Two-level" residence
Structure	Post-tensioned concrete floor slabs, steel frame superstructure, and structural glazing system

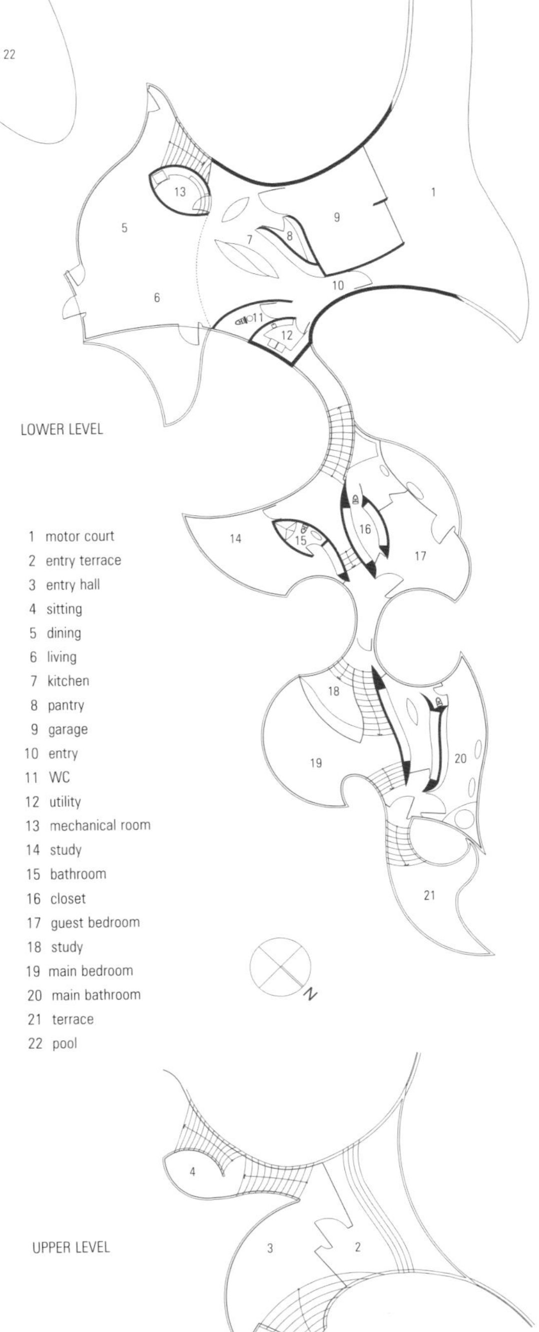

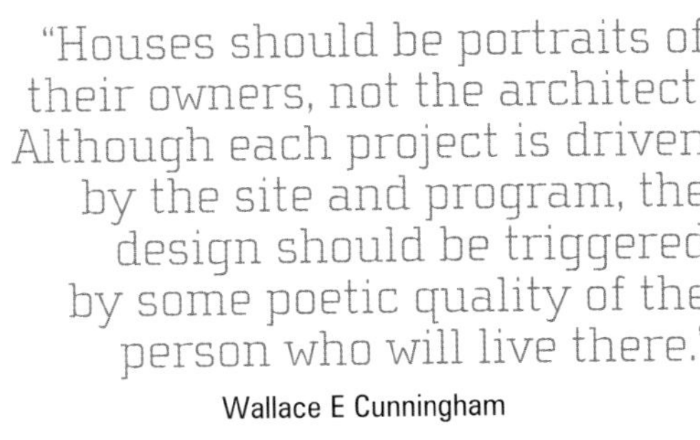

"Houses should be portraits of their owners, not the architect. Although each project is driven by the site and program, the design should be triggered by some poetic quality of the person who will live there."

Wallace E Cunningham

ABOVE
The building has a sense of "movement" – the inert structure seemingly trying to free itself from its earthly restraints. Slender structural supports provide minimal distraction, allowing one to enjoy the sheer audacity of it all.

RIGHT
The scale and complexity of the roof is apparent here, with each section corresponding to a living area below and designed to maximize views to the north, east, and west. The driveway and motor court can be seen in the upper right of the picture.

Descending along a rocky escarpment overlooking beautiful Lake Hodges, 31 miles (50 km) north of San Diego on the San Dieguito River, is the site for Voler House.

The home's dynamic roofline resembles the pattern generated by the blades of a helicopter slowly coming to a halt – already it is an emblematic icon of organic architecture.

VERSATILE MATERIALS

Designed in titanium, which is 30 percent lighter than steel and 50 percent stronger, the roof has a bronze patina (a thin greenish layer of copper sulfate with anti-corrosive properties), adding durability and virtually eliminating maintenance.

The home's curvaceous design permits light to enter it at varying angles throughout the day creating an intricate interplay of angles and shapes. Walls become palettes for abstract patterns of shadow and reflection that constantly alter the mood of the home, giving inanimate, inert surfaces a sense of movement.

The scarf-like roof triumphantly demonstrates the philosophy of its designer – that buildings are not merely visual objects, but that they also need to radiate emotion. The titanium-clad covering is seemingly suspended above the site with its structural elements situated outside the bounds of the building envelope.

The versatility of concrete is evident in the many sculptured internal spaces, resulting in an expression of character that is difficult to obtain with more traditional materials, such as stone or steel.

The practicality of architectural grade cast-in-place concrete is reflected in its ability to withstand earthquakes, in its energy gain that reduces heating and cooling costs, and its ability to resist pest and water damage.

HARMONIZING WITH THE ENVIRONMENT

A sculptural reflection of the clients, the home's design is governed by the need to maintain a constant physical and visual connection to the landscape. It tumbles and cascades down a rocky escarpment always in harmony with the environment, its directions determined by pre-existing granite outcrops and the site's topography.

Internal and external spaces are obliquely defined due to large expanses of frameless glass that permit the penetration of light throughout. Undulating ceilings climb skyward to maximize the vistas beyond.

Transitional stairways spiral their way through the interior following the contours of the ground below. Kitchen benchtops, bathroom vanities, and closets are designed to mimic the curved contours of the house.

Access to the home is via an upper level terrace that descends into the living/dining area. A central hallway curls its way through the interior providing a sense of discovery, with fresh spaces constantly revealing themselves. Beyond the guest bedroom with attached bathroom and study lie the main bedroom with its study and main bathroom. Next to this sleeping area, a private north-facing terrace provides views over Lake Hodges and beyond.

ABOVE
The combination of Voler House's titanium and cast-in-place concrete perfectly complements the home's granite surrounds. Terraced living areas make full use of the site's natural topography in a design that harmonizes with, rather than dominates, the environment.

Wall House AUROVILLE, INDIA

Anupama Kundoo BERLIN, GERMANY

Constructed 2000
Home type Three-level family home
Structure Brick masonry, RCC frame structure, timber, terracotta

"I believe that given the environmental crises facing us today, architects need to find appropriate technologies to build permanent buildings with the least possible impact. I don't think we need to keep inventing new materials, but rather to find innovative ways of using the same old healthy materials from the local area to suit our modern needs. This has been my quest."
Anupama Kundoo

ECOLOGICAL EMPATHY

This residence is remarkable in a number of ways: First, it uses environmentally friendly building materials and alternative technologies; second, it is energy efficient; and third, it suits both its climate and its surroundings. The architects and owners explored ways to maximize these qualities, so the house is eco-friendly in the way it handles water and waste.

In order to optimize the amount of air circulation, the house is oriented to the southeast. The plan is linear, and the house contains a long rectangular space within the brick masonry shell. The areas of the house are organized into a long row, with a hallway separating the various indoor spaces. Each area has been strategically positioned so that there is a fluidity between the alcoves and projections, which sit on the northeastern side of the house, and the large 14-ft (4.3-m) overhang of the main vaulted roof on the southwestern side.

TRANSPARENCY AND PRIVACY

The large living areas are open, while the more private spaces of the bedrooms are isolated from the rest of the house without being apart from it. The house essentially follows a simple design: There are clear delineations between the interior spaces, but the volume is designed so that the divisions between the inside and the outside are somewhat blurred.

These spaces flow out into the garden, reached by a long flight of steps. Timber is one of the main elements of the southwestern facade, and the use of mesh gives an impression of transparency. This allows views to the outside but also offers shade from the sun, protecting the interior from heat and glare.

DERIVING NEW FROM OLD

The facades of the house are exposed brick, and have been scaled back to the smaller proportions of traditional bricks. They have been set in a lime mortar with 10 percent cement added for strength. The walls are either 4, 8, or 12 in (10, 20, or 30 cm) thick, and as they deviate from the normal 1:2 proportion, bonds were specifically designed for them. These "achakal" bricks also play a structural role in the ground floor.

The house is double height, which boosts the cross-ventilation in the interior. Catenary vaults with hollow clay tubes provide insulation and have the added bonus of reducing the use of steel in the building. The guest bedroom features a flat terraced roof, which comprises extruded clay modules over partly pre-cast beams. These are quite common in the neighborhood, as they offer effective insulation for houses with flat roofs.

EARTHY RESPONSES

On the middle level, terracotta pots were used as fillers. This strategy increased the depth of the concrete while simultaneously reducing the amount of concrete and steel required. It is interesting to note that this area did not require insulation. Overall, this has led to lower energy demands. In addition, solar photovoltaics supply electricity. Solar energy also powers a water heater and a water pump.

1 entry
2 terrace
3 outdoor living
4 kitchen
5 store
6 studio
7 guest bedroom
8 bathroom
9 lotus pond

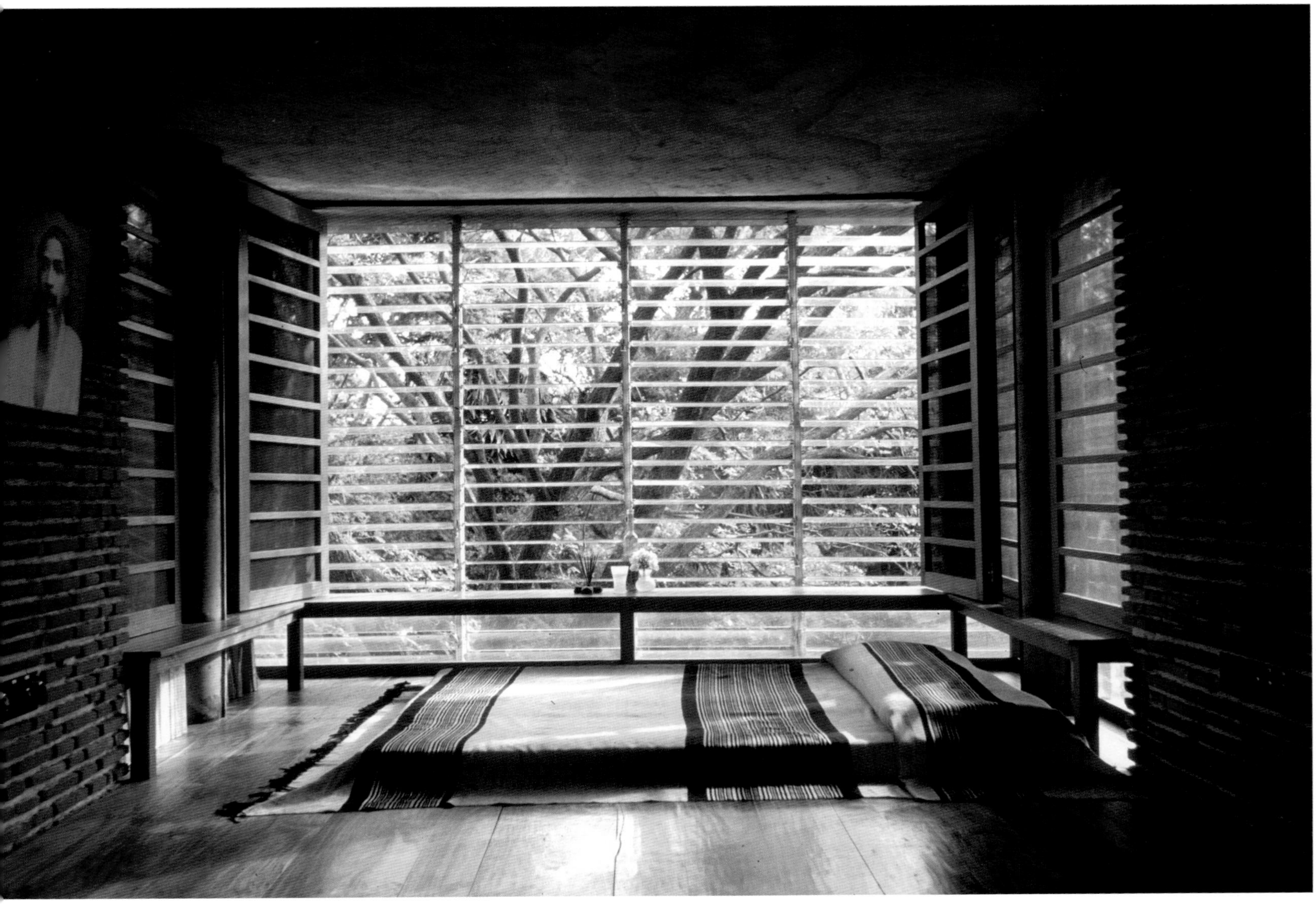

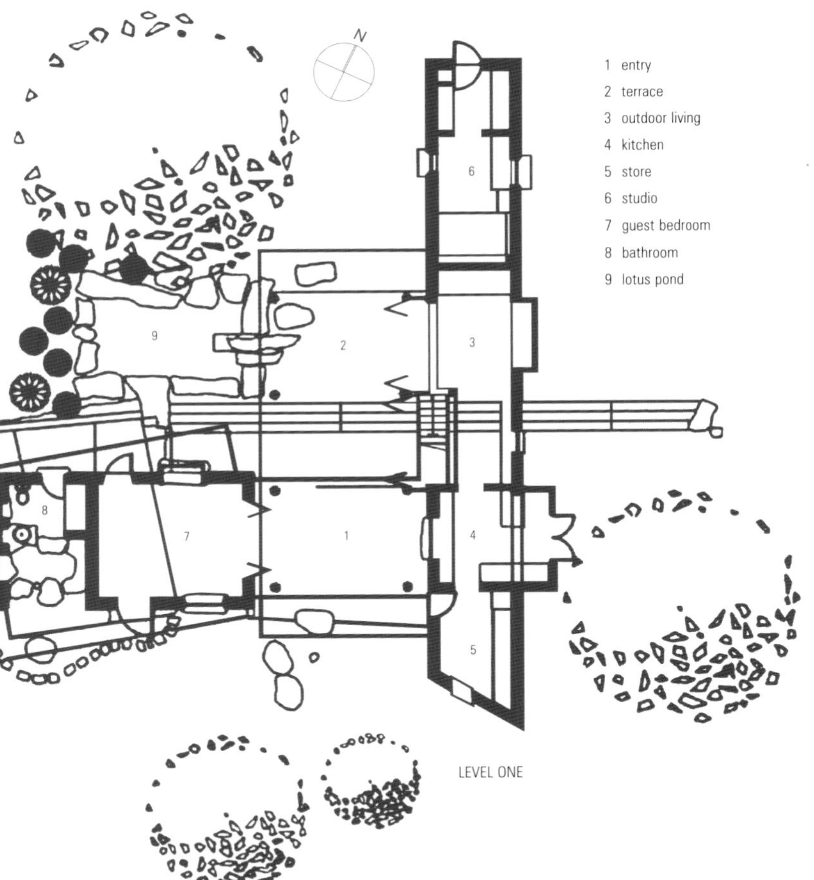

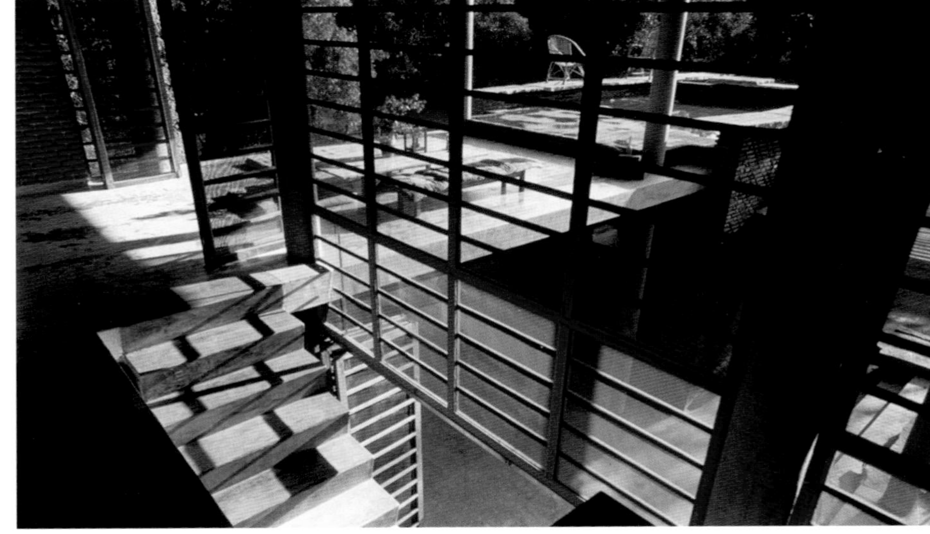

FAR LEFT
Supported by concrete columns, the vault shelters the house from the southwestern sun while also creating a transition space for various activities, such as outdoor living and dining – a must in a hot, humid climate.

TOP
The bedroom alcove projects out of the "wall" beneath the rain tree. Mesh screens keep mosquitoes at bay while also controlling the amount of glare from the southwestern sun during the late afternoon.

ABOVE
The lotus pond on the upper level lends an atmosphere of quiet contemplation to the terrace, which projects from the southwestern side of the building. The stairs lead down to the garden.

Zhujiajiao Cambridge Water Town SHANGHAI, CHINA

Ben Wood Studio

Constructed	2005
Home type	Contemporary style villas, townhouses, combining the traditional Chinese courtyard house style
Structure	Two–four level, load-bearing brickwork

"In modern China, we want both the old and the new. Using the age-old principles of water town planning, this master plan connects us with our history. At the same time a community of new homes with contemporary amenities provides us with a modern lifestyle."

Ben Wood

THE BEAUTY OF WATER

The beauty of a water town comes from an organic relationship between mankind and nature, and this relationship gives form to the built environment: The architect sees it as DNA expressed in the art of architecture.

The layout for this modern-day water town was derived from historic patterns of settlement. The physical relationship between buildings and water and public access to both water and buildings were the key organizing principles. Water is within walking distance of every home. Following a more than one-thousand-year-old tradition, the village center is located in the middle of the site, at the intersection of several canals.

TRADITION MEETS MODERNITY

As well as tradition, the project had to embrace a modern lifestyle, so the architect's challenge was to effectively blend new and old, innovation and tradition, change and continuity.

RIGHT
Inspired by the adjacent Zhujiajiao Old Water Town, the architect created new canals and built the villas around them. The architect's vision was to create a complex for families with a modern lifestyle, who also wished to be connected to nature and tradition.

TOP RIGHT
The vertical composition of the three-story villas is a reinterpation of the traditional Chinese architectural style. It retains the quality of intimacy of the older style, but unlike its predecessors it has plenty of light and natural air circulation.

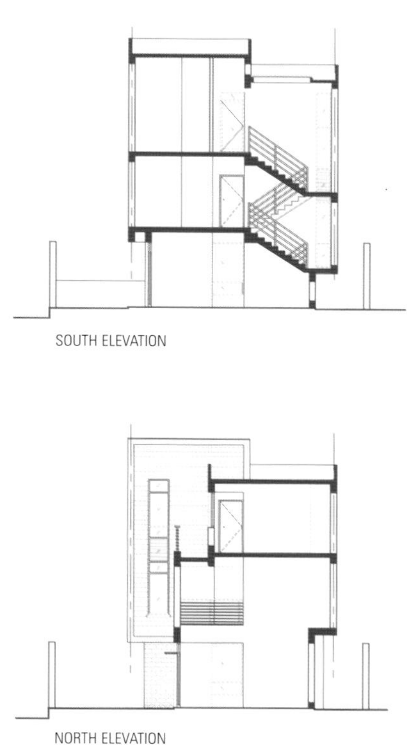

SOUTH ELEVATION

NORTH ELEVATION

THREE-STORY VILLA

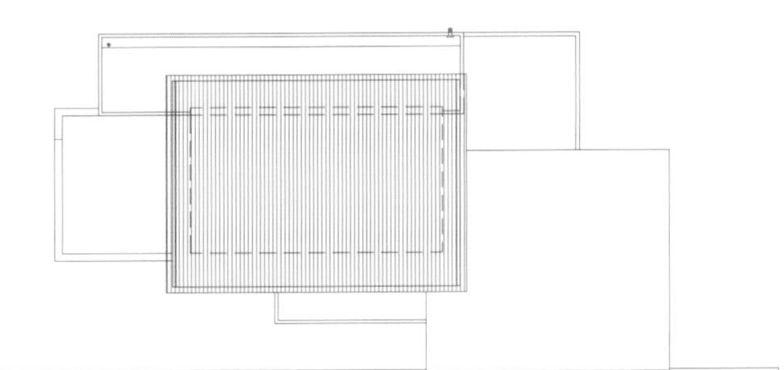

ROOF LEVEL

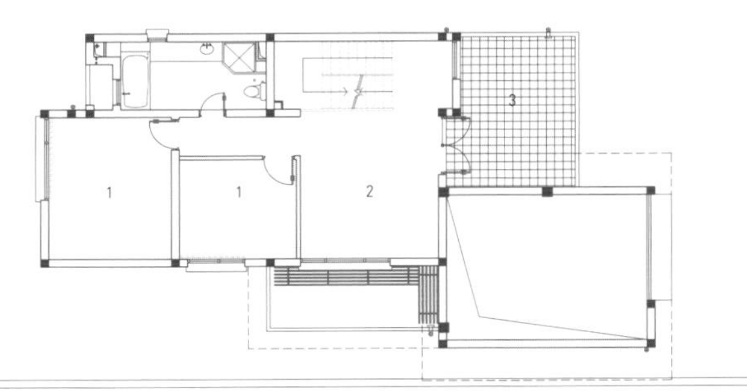

LEVEL TWO

1 guest
2 family
3 terrace
4 employee quarters
5 breakfast
6 kitchen
7 dining
8 living
9 main bedroom

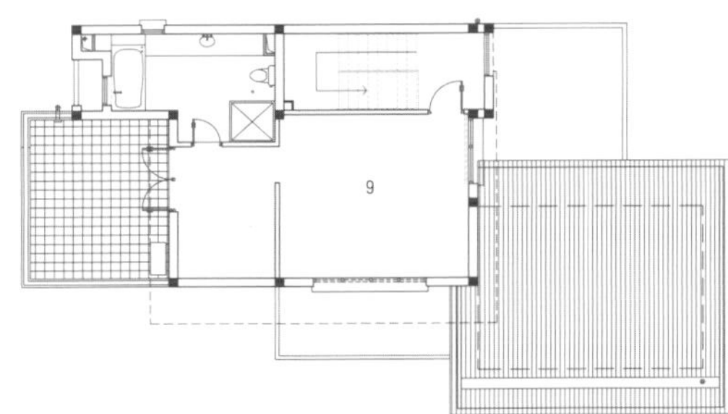

LEVEL THREE

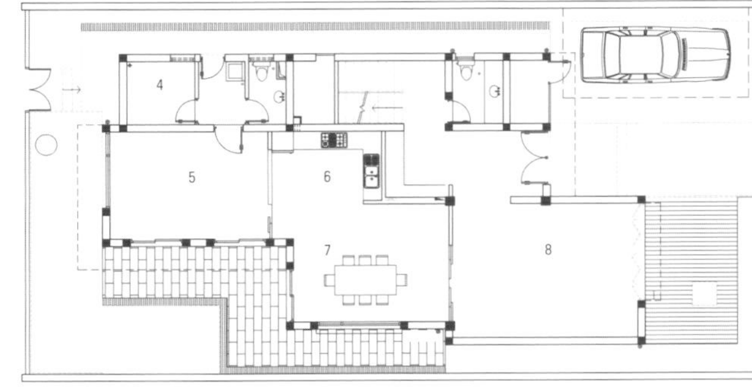

LEVEL ONE

ABOVE
Glass doors in the dining room open out to the home's courtyard, making it an extension of the living area.

RIGHT
Each three-story villa contains a spacious double-height sitting room with a glazed wall on one side and a folding glass door on the other, ensuring ample light and cross ventilation.

HISTORIC TIES

The historic Zhujiajiao Old Water Town is adjacent to the current site. Known as the "Venice of Shanghai," the old town is one of four famous old "cultural towns" in Shanghai. The new site works with the old.

Three sides of the current site are surrounded by water, and a river goes through it from the northwest corner. To emphasize the town's character, new canals were built around old ones. This also meant that the village center and townhouses could be situated around the water.

"Water alleys" and "street alleys" are the fabric of a traditional water town, both with specific functions. Water alleys were the main channels for traffic, commodity transportation, and connections to neighboring villages; street alleys were filled with necessary supply stores, side-by-side for ease of shopping and communication.

COURTYARD STYLE

The vertical composition of the courtyard houses is a new interpretation of a traditional Chinese architectural style. It achieves the essence of intimacy of traditional courtyard houses, while at the same time resolving the disadvantages of poor air circulation and lack of natural light.

The courtyard extends the living area from the dining room via glass doors.

SOMETHING FOR EVERYONE

About 55 percent of the town's homes are villas with two to three floors. The main bedroom of the three-story house is on the third floor with private bathroom and balcony. The first floor, with a fixed glass wall on one side and a folding glass door on the other, functions as the main sitting room. Large glass windows allow a connection to the outdoor yards. Each house has its own parking and an employee's room adjacent to the breakfast room and kitchen.

About 45 percent of the homes are townhouses with three to four floors. Two townhouses are linked by bridges on the second and third floors. They share an inner courtyard with a public staircase, which creates the feeling of being in a garden before entering the home. The upper unit entrance is on the third floor.

Gray bricks and roof tiles are the main materials for traditional houses in southeast China and these were the inspiration for Zhujiajiao Cambridge Water Town. Large glass walls on the first floors let in plenty of natural light, and connect the interiors visually and spatially with the exterior.

ABOVE
Surronded by a lotus lake, the community center is the focal point of the water town. The large terrace on the top floor overlooks the whole of Zhujiajiao Cambridge Water Town.

Chapter 12

In the Country

A home in the country embraces the natural environment, inviting designs that capture views of the landscape while at the same time harmonizing with it.

The main design intent of a home beyond the city limits – perhaps a farmhouse surrounded by pasture or a cottage tucked among the trees – is to exploit the intimate relationship it has with the natural landscape.

Living in a rural setting has the advantage of being in a vast private space with nature right at the doorstep. This can foster a desire to protect the existing vegetation, so homes are often built with a greater sensitivity to the landscape.

But the remote location may mean there are no existing infrastructure and utilities. There may also be less community contact, with reduced access to amenities. Despite its disadvantages, a home in the country serves to cultivate a relationship with nature that cannot be found in the city.

UNLIMITED VIEWS

The private space of a rural property provides unlimited access to the natural landscape, affording the home the greatest potential for views. And without the rigid constraints of designing a home in the city – blending into a streetscape or orienting toward a particular view – the location of a home on a rural block is ultimately flexible. It can capture views from anywhere.

Before the design process begins, the architect may identify particular views as focal points to be exploited once the home is built. A glimpse of a grove of trees might suggest the location of the bedrooms, while a vista that stretches cross the landscape would suit a living room. Taking advantage of such views could necessitate locating the home on a higher contour or building it on two levels.

LIGHT FOOTPRINT

If the site has no infrastructure and utilities in place, there may be an imperative to leave the existing landscape undisturbed, resulting in a home with a light footprint.

The home should merge with the landscape without unsettling the existing environment. A series of pavilions could be nestled into the descent of a steep incline, or an internal courtyard could be designed around an existing tree. Using solar energy or rainwater tanks instead of town supply further reduces the impact of the home on the environment.

A home in harmony with its natural surroundings still makes a statement on the landscape. This separateness can be expressed architecturally by raising the structure off the ground, making the lightest footprint of all.

ABOVE
Bowral House,
Glenn Murcutt

TOP RIGHT
Möbius House,
UN Studio

OPPOSITE
Chameleon House,
Anderson Anderson Architecture

NATURAL INFLUENCE

Ideally, the architect should borrow forms from the environment and replicate or reinterpret them in the design of the country home. If a home is built in a forested area, an exposed post and beam method of construction could echo the tall trees outside. A stone walkway could mimic a rocky outcrop, or an indoor plunge pool could be designed to look as if it is a natural part of the landscape.

PART OF THE ENVIRONMENT

A home in the country offers access to the natural environment, a private retreat from the outside world. Such a home should be designed to have a light footprint, with architectural details that echo the surrounding landscape.

Berman House JOADJA, AUSTRALIA

Harry Seidler & Associates

Constructed	2000
Home type	One-story, split-level home
Structure	Floors: concrete on steel support system. Walls: sandstone collected from the site and concrete blocks. Roof: steel framed with corrugated steel roofing

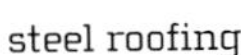

"The location was resolved after hours of exploring the many acres available. The final location was chosen because it combined magnificent views with generous, safe play areas for children, proximity to power, and a deep recess for a natural pool. This house is a culmination of Seidler's Modernist work, shaped as much by a global culture and technology as by the rugged Australian landscape and climate that it inhabits so compellingly."

Harry Seidler & Associates

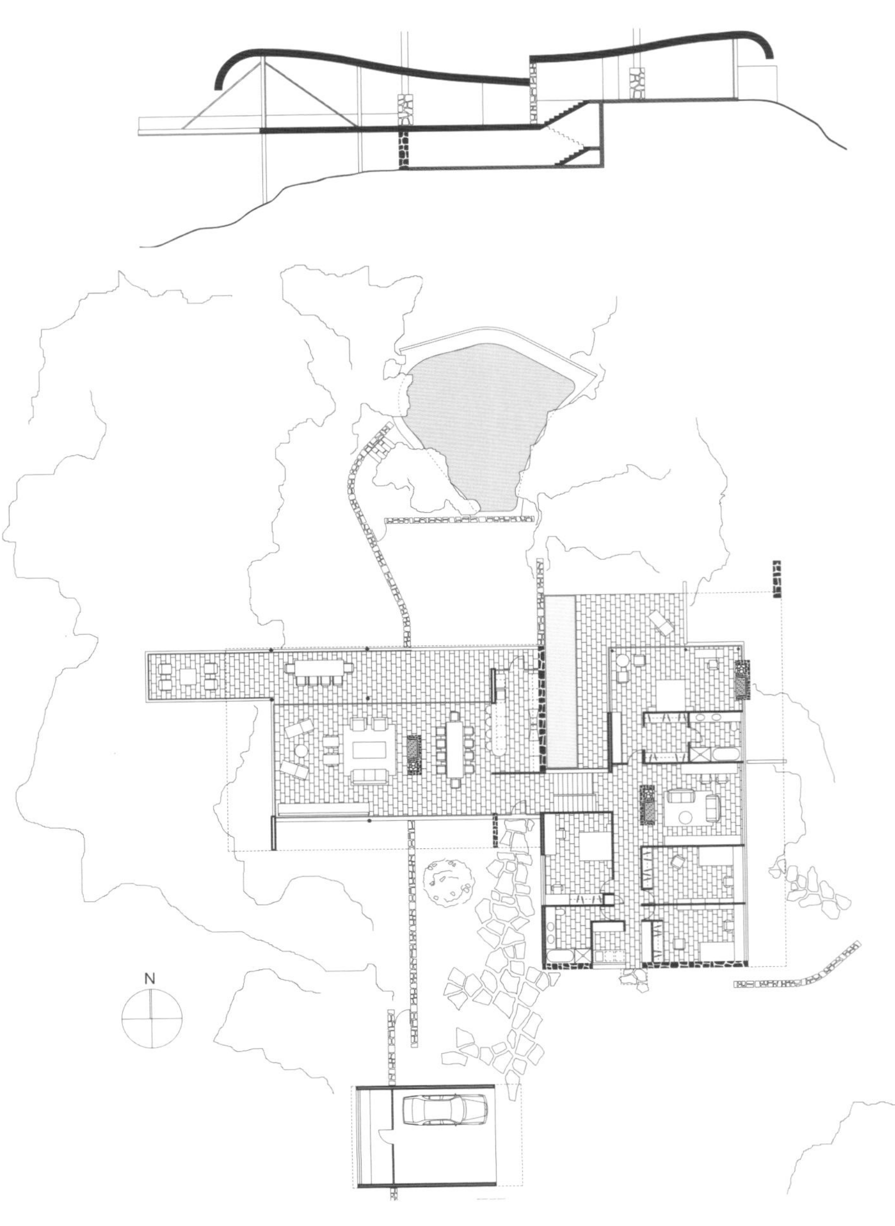

A HAVEN IN THE WILDERNESS

Berman House is situated in country New South Wales, on the crest of a rugged escarpment surrounded by a vast area of natural wilderness and overlooking a meandering river far below. The house itself is positioned against a large rock platform, so the living area is suspended and the balcony projects out from the home dramatically, taking full advantage of the beautiful natural setting. The vista from the living area is quite breathtaking.

The house is organized on two levels, with the enclosed bedroom area strategically placed above the generous living area. The living area is essentially a large pavilion with a preponderance of glass.

The main bedroom has been deliberately located on the northern end of the bedroom wing in order to take full advantage of sunlight, not to mention the splendid views to the northwest. An intimate view of a peaceful reflecting pool between the living and sleeping areas adds a dramatic contrast.

There are three other bedrooms, for children and for visitors. These are separated from the main bedroom area by a cosy living room that has its own fireplace. These three rooms share the main bathroom, while the main bedroom has its own large ensuite bathroom.

Following the natural topography of the site, the living room, kitchen, and dining areas are located half a level below the bedrooms. In order to suit the clients' casual lifestyle, and to maximize exposure to the spectacular outlook, these rooms are open plan, with a free-standing sandstone fireplace separating the living room from the dining room and kitchen.

TOP LEFT
Berman House with its swimming pool is seen here in its natural bushland setting. The pool is not just for cooling off and having fun, it is also a source of extra water when bushfires threaten.

FAR LEFT
Seen from below the cliff face, the home's protruding balcony looks like a springboard from which one might dive into the river below.

ABOVE
Diagonal braces and steel columns from the roof support the home's gravity-defying balcony, which is suspended over bushland and the Wingecarribee River.

FOLLOWING PAGES
The unique curved roofs, offset from one another, make the home a sculptural presence in the bushland surroundings. This view of the home's north elevation and pool shows the sleeping pavilion on the left and living pavilion on the right.

ABOVE
Floor to ceiling glazing on three sides of the living room gives spectacular panoramic views of the rugged Australian terrain and river below.

LEFT
View from the main entrance looking toward the dining and living areas. In an otherwise open plan space, the sandstone fireplace between the rooms gives some definition to the specific areas.

BOTTOM LEFT
Berman House's living and sleeping pavilions are separated by this stone paved courtyard and reflecting pool. The wall behind the pool is faced in sandstone hewn from the site.

STRUCTURE AND STYLE

The floor is constructed of concrete, and there are curved steel beams framing the extensively profiled roofs of the living area, the bedroom wing, and the garage. New developments in technology have made it possible to create these interesting profiles using a series of different radii.

The long balcony protrudes out over the edge of the cliff, making a stunning architectural and gravity-defying statement. It is hung from the steel columns of the roof and held in place with diagonal braces. The straight lines of the balcony complement the offset curved roofs of the dwelling.

ON THE GROUND AND IN THE POOL

To create a contrast with the suspended roof structure, the house itself is fixed to the ground – a very rugged landscape – by projecting rubble stone screen walls placed randomly on the site, as well as support piers and retaining walls. All of these have been built from sandstone, which is present in quite large quantities on the site. A welcome sense of continuity between the house and the garage is established by the unbroken sandstone retaining wall.

The long balcony protrudes out over the edge of the cliff, making a stunning architectural and gravity-defying statement.

The sandstone wall also embraces the swimming pool, which is located and maintained between two big rocky outcrops to the north of the house. Energy collectors have been positioned on the north-facing hillside right below the pool, allowing the water in the pool to be solar heated. As the area is also very susceptible to bushfires during the summer months, the pool has another very important function – it doubles as a water reservoir.

When the pool is switched to bushfire mode, water is pumped to sprinklers that are hidden under the eaves and projecting living areas. The house itself is bushfire resistant, built entirely of fireproof materials, including reinforced concrete floors, white block, stone walls, and a steel roof structure.

WATER FROM THE HEAVENS

The difficult site means that there is no access to the town water or the sewerage system. To counter this, rainwater is collected from the roofs and stored under the house in a large central storage tank. Waste water is recycled – it is chemically treated and then used for irrigation.

ENERGY RESPONSES

Stone fireplaces have been placed throughout the house, providing a means of energy self-sufficiency. The house is mostly open plan, so the fireplaces also function as effective dividers between specific areas. To further heat the house, radiant floor heating has been installed underneath the stone paving stones.

The landscaping around the home has been designed to recreate the natural bush environment. There are two grassed areas to provide play space for the owners' young children. The entry courtyard was sensitively designed by the owners using indigenous plants and stone paving collected from the site, all harmoniously relating to the pristine bushland surroundings.

ABOVE
Glazed walls and the curved roof "floating" over the 23-ft (7-m) ceiling in the main lounge area, create the impression of a graceful bird in flight.

Bowral House BOWRAL, AUSTRALIA

Glenn Murcutt

Construction	1997–2001
House type	Country house, single dwelling
Structure	Single level, reinforced concrete, timber frame, and structural steel on concrete slab

"The public and work entries of this house are both protected by a courtyard and a sloping wind-deflecting wall that houses the main access gallery serving all rooms. This wind deflector is a response to my observations and experience with pressure differential."
Glenn Murcutt

ABOVE
Viewed from the north, Bowral House's three major functional zones can be easily read: garage/tractor shed to the left, entry courtyard, and the main residential wing, with, at the extreme right, the veranda roof extending out over the terrace.

ABOVE RIGHT
The main facing of the house for walls and roof is corrugated galvanized steel. On the garage/tractor shed, there is a further layer of photovoltaic cells and inverter, which provides electric underfloor heating. The north face of the bedrooms is modulated by reinforced concrete blade columns.

RIGHT
At the western end of the house, beneath the Dutch gable roof, are two bedrooms that have external sliding timber screens for sun protection. To the right, behind a wind-protecting wall clad in slate, is the formal entry court and the homestead's front door.

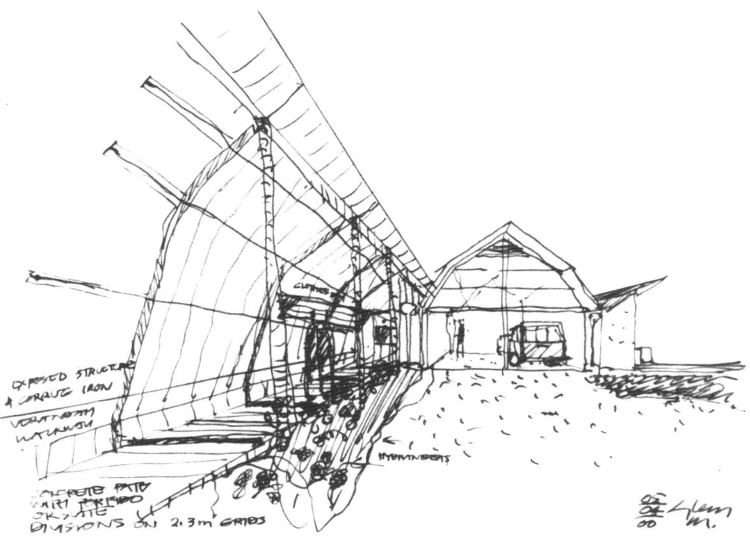

THREE LINEAR ZONES

Layers and lines define many of Glenn Murcutt's houses – not just his approach to climate. In Bowral House, one of his largest designs, Murcutt separated the house into three linear zones defined by the section, with each differentiated by its roof shape, and hence by a different internal volume.

RURAL IDYLL

Located at Bowral in the Southern Highlands of New South Wales, 125 miles (200 km) southwest of Sydney, the home is set amidst undulating and prosperous farmland, hedgerows, and expanses of green pasture. It is a beautiful place, but winter can be very cold. Winds from the southwest can be particularly fierce. At the same time, summers can be very hot. The design had to respond to these competing demands – to provide warmth and shelter, to open up to the sun and air, and at all times to maximize the dramatic panorama of an Arcadian rural landscape.

SILVER WINDBREAK

From afar, the house looks like a long silver windbreak. There are no windows in the west wall, which folds up and over toward the north sky. It encloses an entry gallery that shields the three major forms of the house: the garage/tractor shed; a small courtyard; and a large residential wing of five bedrooms and two living rooms.

FOLLOWING PAGES
From the south, the Bowral House appears as a giant silver windbreak, or a low-lying cloud that might be reflected in the reservoir pond. The only vertical line is that of the fireplace flue.

The main living/dining/kitchen space has an internal volume that rises 15 ft (4.6 m). This big airy volume is grand, almost baronial in scale; it's rather like occupying the nave of a church.

HALL AS CATHEDRAL AISLE, HOME AS NAVE

The most extraordinary space of Bowral House is the 230-ft- (70-m-) long entry hall, an aisle-like space of cathedral proportions with sunlight bouncing off curving plaster. It's this gallery-like space which gives access to every room of the home. Murcutt has observed that "the form of the main access gallery suggests the wind-shaped trees" outside. The main living/dining/kitchen space, by contrast, has an internal volume that rises 15 ft (4.6 m) and reflects the wind-deflecting Dutch gable profile of the main roof. This big airy volume is grand, almost baronial in scale; it's rather like occupying the nave of a church. To the north, in this same space, windows overlook a broad terrace and it's here that the roof profile changes again, lifting up like the brim of a hat to the sky, and broadening at its end to form the third linear zone, a cantilevering veranda roof to the terrace. Along this north face, there are sliding insect screens, timber slatted screens, and glazed doors, all part of Murcutt's tripartite system of climate, light, and ventilation control.

FADE TO GRAY

The materials palette is consistently gray throughout. Floors are insulated reinforced concrete and finished in porfido stone or carpet. Externally, walls are either lined with gray slate, or where concrete, they are painted dark warm gray. Reinforced concrete columns and all corrugated galvanized steel wall linings and roofs are left in their natural state. Structural steel elements are painted in a natural gray, protective metallic. Paving is gray slate and porfido stone. Inside, plaster walls and ceilings are painted white and joinery is lined in clear finish timber veneer.

ABOVE
From a distance, the north face of the house at sunset highlights the dramatic upturned sun-catching eaves. Emphasized also is the mass of the terrace and the line of concrete blade columns, which indicate the module of bedrooms within.

RIGHT
The largest interior space is the living/dining/kitchen space, separated from the main access gallery by a wall of storage cupboards and joinery units. This is a grand space, a magical barn made into an elegant living space, or the nave of a church made into home.

OPPOSITE PAGE
The view from the front down the 230-m- (70-m-) long access gallery is dramatic. It's like looking down the aisle of a cathedral. Light spills down the curved profile of the wind-deflecting south wall. On the floor is the warm porfido stone, which grounds this ethereal, other-worldly space.

BR House RIO DE JANEIRO, BRAZIL

Marcio Kogan Arquiteto

Constructed	2004
Home type	Two-story house
Structure	Concrete construction with timber stilts

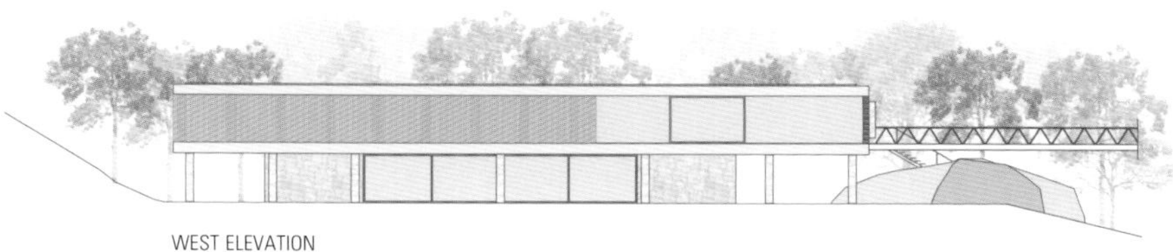

WEST ELEVATION

"In terms of an architectural proposition, BR House, located in the countryside, could not be more intriguing – the way the dense and impressive rainforest circumscribes and penetrates the area, and dominates all the senses. From the project's inception, the circumstances forced fundamental questions for our architecture: How can architecture present itself and how can it deliberately show itself as construction?"

Marcio Kogan & Gabriel Kogan

A RAINFOREST RETREAT

BR House is situated in a mountainous region of Rio de Janeiro – a particularly beautiful location. The challenge for the architect was to integrate the house with the forest landscape of creeks, towering trees, and brightly colored flowers. The architect wanted to create something that was not only in harmony with its surroundings, but was also comfortable and functional, stamped with his own particular style.

One source of inspiration for BR House came from another Brazilian house, Casa de Vidro (Glass House), designed by Lina de Bardi. That home is raised on stilts, seeking the same visual perspective as the crowns of trees; the use of glass blurring the distinction between the interior and exterior worlds.

Constructed as two monolithic cement blocks, BR House also stands on stilts. Raising the house in this way helps it to blend into its surroundings. The horizontal lines are visually distinct, while the vertical ones are designed to merge with the environment.

The thick wooden stilts or pillars of BR House are reminiscent of the trunks of the great trees in the rainforest, and give the effect of dimming the vertical lines, so the house seems to hover above the treetops. The beams and flagstones provide a contrast with the exposed raw concrete. In this way, the house proclaims its presence – it is not trying to hide in the forest; instead it affirms itself as a product of human endeavor and also as a place of shelter.

FILTERING THE LIGHT

The use of so much glass has created a transparent effect, and the house easily merges with the forest. This is because there are no frames – the glass is inlaid into the floor and the ceiling, creating an open, harmonious ambience.

The facade of the house is covered with a "skin" of vertical wooden laths or slats that create a light filter. When these slats are opened, they unfurl, turning outward as they open. A striking effect of the wooden facade is that in the evenings, the "skin" looks as if it is lit up.

SPACE FOR RELAXATION

The first level contains a heated swimming pool and a dry sauna, which has a large fixed glass wall, allowing an uninterrupted view of the landscape, the beautiful Atlantic rainforest. This area has been designed so that when one looks toward the pool, the glass wall acts as a frame to the scenery in the background. There is more than 70 ft (20 m) of door space on this first level, and a large rock sits half in and half out of the area, thus providing a link between the interior and the exterior.

The second level contains four bedroom suites, a guest bathroom, the kitchen, and the living and dining rooms. In the living room, the huge glass windows frame views of the surrounding forest, reducing to a minimum any visual barriers between the interior and exterior. Conversely, in the private part of the house, the wooden slats provide privacy for the bedrooms.

ABOVE
This view of the home's western facade shows how the bedrooms and kitchen on the upper level are faced with vertical wooden slats, which can be turned to admit more light. On the lower level is the leisure area, which includes a sauna, heated pool, and two bathrooms.

CENTER RIGHT
The inlaid floor to ceiling glass wall adjacent to the deck is virtually invisible, giving the illusion that one might step straight out into the forest. On the floor inside, the brown aluminum grid is the central heating duct.

RIGHT
This interior view shows the hallway that links the bedrooms with the living room. To the left, the entry deck "floats" among the rainforest trees. The thick wooden columns running alongside the glass wall are designed to echo the tree trunks outside.

FAR LEFT
A recycled wooden coffee table sits in front of the living room fireplace, which is faced with cinder limestone and topped by a stainless steel flue. The fireplace is flanked by a low wooden and cinder limestone closet housing the audiovisual system, designed by Marcio Kogan.

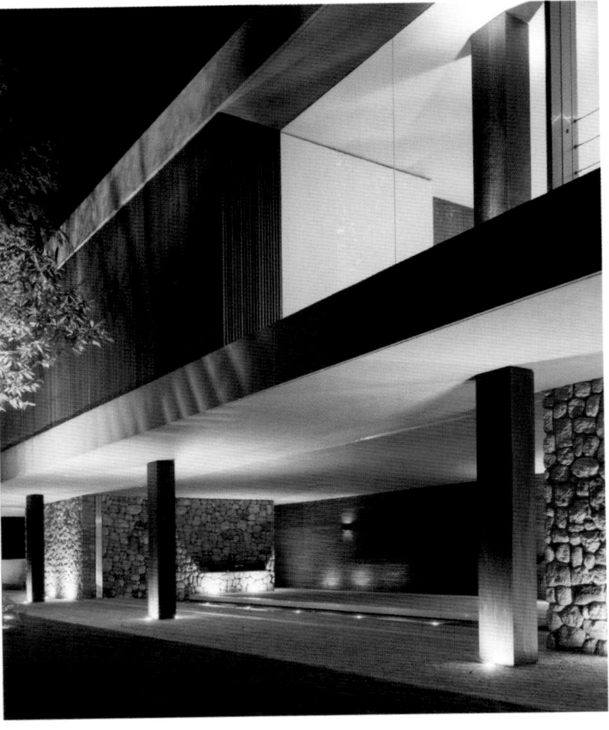

GETTING INSIDE

The terrain of the site made it possible to create something special. The house can be approached on both levels, but the formal entry is actually located on the second level, where the living areas are situated. (The first level houses the pool, jacuzzi, and sauna, and utility area.)

Instead of going up and down a staircase inside the house, one must go outside. On the second level, a bridge, or elevated walkway, passes over a small stream in the woods, and arrives at a wooden, tree-covered deck close to the entry door. Interestingly, this entry was built before the interior.

As night falls over the rainforest, the relationship between the interior and exterior of BR House acquires a completely new dimension. Once the trees disappear into the darkness, the house functions as a sort of flashlight. The interior light, filtered through the vertical slats in the private part of the house, or refracted through the expanses of glass in the living room, illuminates the surrounding forest, once again showcasing a house that is both a shelter and a form of artistic expression.

TOP
The elevated steel bridge connecting the parking area with the deck emerges out of the forest and leads to the second-level formal entry. The minimalist furnishings take nothing away from the breathtaking rainforest that surrounds the space.

ABOVE
Established rainforest trees "push" through the wooden deck, enhancing the impression that the house itself is part of the rainforest.

ABOVE RIGHT
A night view of the western facade of the house. On the lower level, the pool is lined with green glass pastilles. The pool area seems open to the elements but in fact it is protected by a glass wall.

FAR RIGHT
This view of the pool area is taken from the sauna. All the stone used for the wall facing comes from the property itself. To the left of the back wall is the end of an aluminum screen, which recedes into the wall.

FOLLOWING PAGES
Another view of the western facade of the house shows the mountainous terrain. The leisure area on the first level is inserted between two stone walls, while the second level houses the living areas and bedrooms.

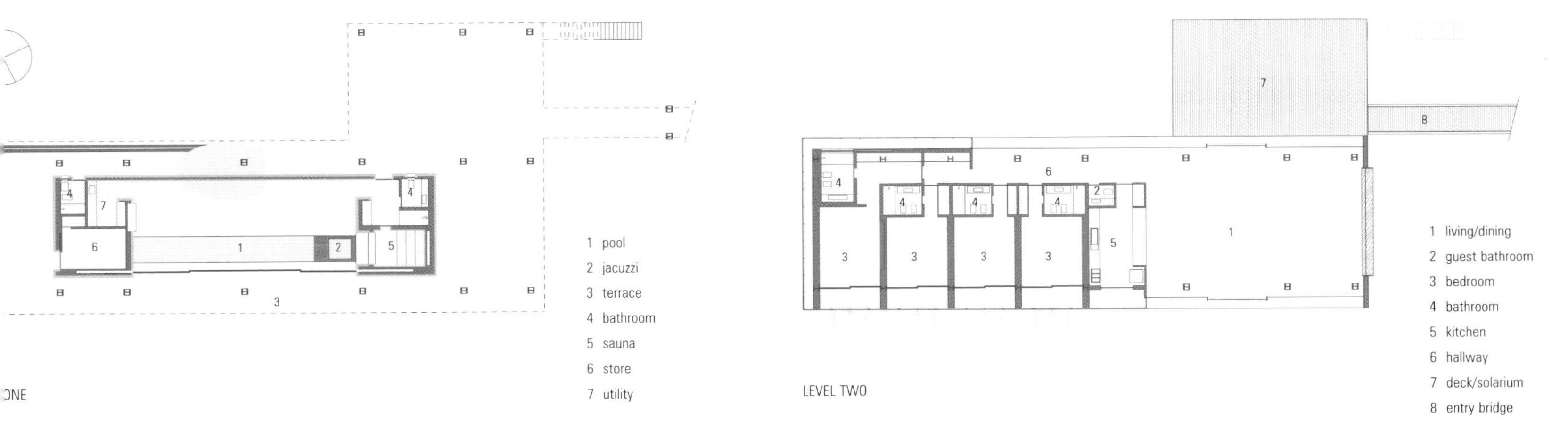

ONE
1 pool
2 jacuzzi
3 terrace
4 bathroom
5 sauna
6 store
7 utility
LEVEL TWO
1 living/dining
2 guest bathroom
3 bedroom
4 bathroom
5 kitchen
6 hallway
7 deck/solarium
8 entry bridge

Chameleon House MICHIGAN, USA

Anderson Anderson Architecture

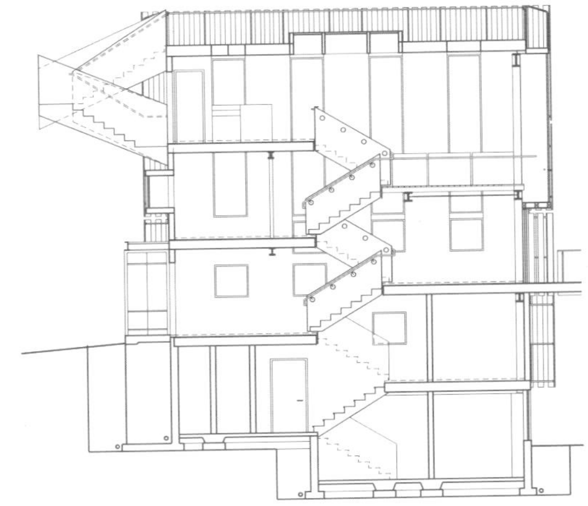

Constructed	2002
Home type	Family residence
Structure	Steel frame, prefabricated SIP panels

"A house would appear as an unsympathetic intrusion in this pure landscape, and with its singular vertical presence rising above the orchard, the tower is intended to reflect the austere, scaleless non-particularity of the occasional metal farm buildings dotted elsewhere on the hills."

Anderson Anderson Architecture

OPPOSITE
An exterior view in winter showing varied reflective surfaces of acrylic slats, glazing, aluminum window frames, and galvanized steel skin and stairs. This visual feast of textures extends into the steel-blue winter sky.

ABOVE
The cantilevered steel staircase that leads to the roof juts out from the main footprint of the building. This perspective is seen from the ground.

ABOVE LEFT
This view from the driveway approach shows the side of the house where the main entry is. Taken in spring, the surrounding grasses and rocks provide a lively contrast to the more subdued tones of the prefabricated materials.

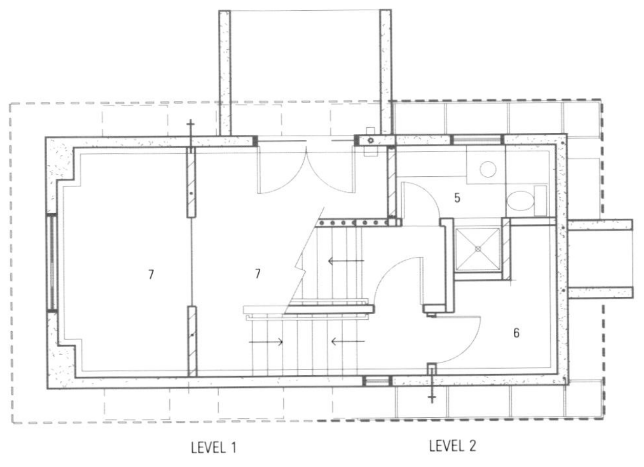

LEVEL 1 LEVEL 2

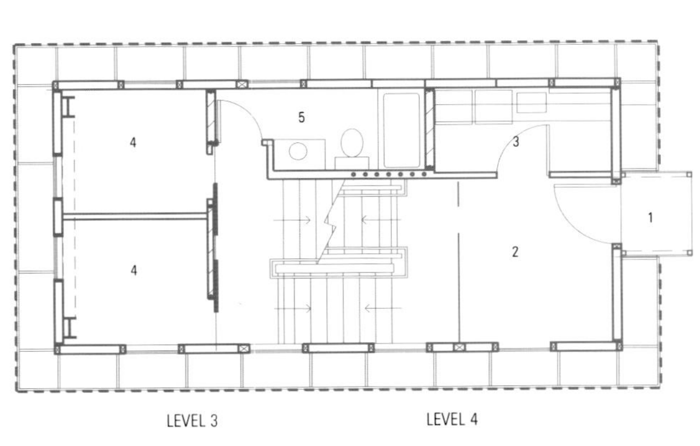

LEVEL 3 LEVEL 4

1 entry
2 playroom
3 laundry/pantry
4 bedroom
5 bathroom
6 work
7 storage
8 kitchen/dining
9 deck
10 main bedroom
11 main bathroom
12 living
13 guest/study
14 open to below

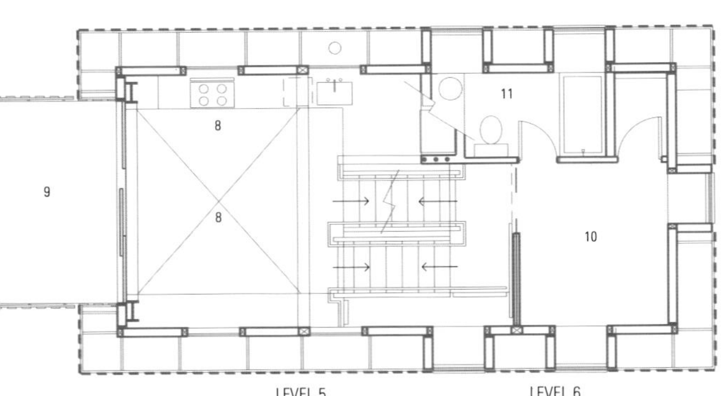

LEVEL 5 LEVEL 6

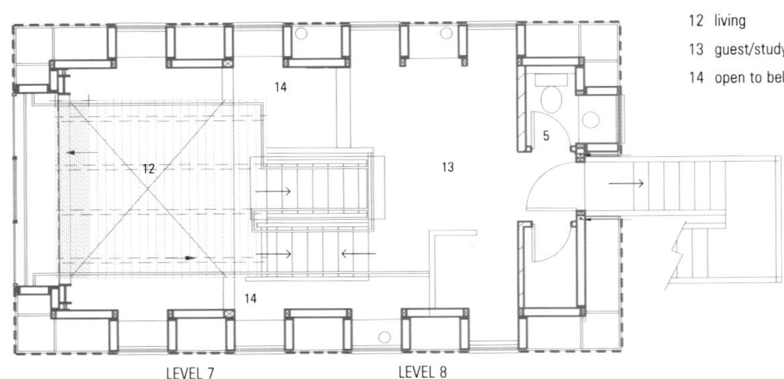

LEVEL 7 LEVEL 8

ABOVE
Every level of the house reveals another space for living; some are light and airy while others are more subdued. The assembly items for the prefabricated materials add points of interest as the eye scans the space.

ABOVE RIGHT
The harder surfaces and clean lines of the interior contrast with the organic shapes of the nearby cherry orchards that are seen through many of the windows.

OPPOSITE
Light, both natural and artifical, features largely in highlighting the impact of the varied levels of the house, using strategically placed spotlights as well as skylights that allow natural shafts of light to stream through.

LAKESIDE LIVING

Chameleon House is designed as a tower, standing tall in the beautiful rugged landscape on a peninsula that extends into Lake Michigan. The clients, a couple and their three children, wanted to use the house at weekends and during vacations, and they were keen to maximize the views across the lake and the nearby cherry orchards.

There were a number of challenges faced by the architects in designing the house. First, the site is environmentally sensitive, and the terrain imposed its own restrictions. As a result, the foundations of the house take up less space than would otherwise be expected, stepping up into the natural slope of the land. This reduces the footprint while simultaneously allowing for more expansive lake and orchard views.

LIVING LARGE

It may not look it, but the house is small – 1,650 sq ft (149 sq m) – comprising nine different levels, with a roof deck. The deck is accessed by a cantilevered staircase that hangs from the outside of the structure.

The natural inclination of the site means that the entry is on level four of the house. The children's bedrooms and bathroom are located downstairs, and the main bedroom with ensuite is on the sixth level. The spacious living area is on the top level to optimize the sweeping views. The owners wanted large, open, family living spaces and smaller bedrooms, to encourage more communal gatherings, both inside and outside.

THE RIGHT MATERIALS

The architects decided to use some low-cost, quality prefabricated materials in the construction of the house, because of their adaptability. These materials are suitable for a range of site conditions and have minimal impact on the surrounding environment. The decision had a positive effect on the budget, but also meant that the house could be built quickly. Prefabricated panels were used for the exterior walls, floors, and roof. The steel frame and narrow height created volumes of space in the main living area, encouraging plenty of natural light and cross-ventilation.

The home's energy-efficient materials include solar heating, incorporating photovoltaic collection, and water catchment on the roof. Corrugated acrylic slats form the outer skin of the house, giving it a unique "chameleon" effect. The inner skin is reflective galvanized siding, which reflects the differing seasonal colors of the landscape. The overall effect is that the house completely merges with its surroundings at some times of the year, while standing out like a beacon at others – a true statement of originality. The inner skin also permits privacy, and screens out the worst effects of the sun and wind. It also creates a cooling effect for the house, as the heated air moves upward, drawing cool air into the interior, and eliminating the need for air-conditioning.

With such innovative design, it is not hard to see why Chameleon House is an award-winning construction.

Desert House CALIFORNIA, USA

Marmol Radziner + Associates

Constructed 2005
Home type One-level single family residence
Structure Prefabricated steel modules

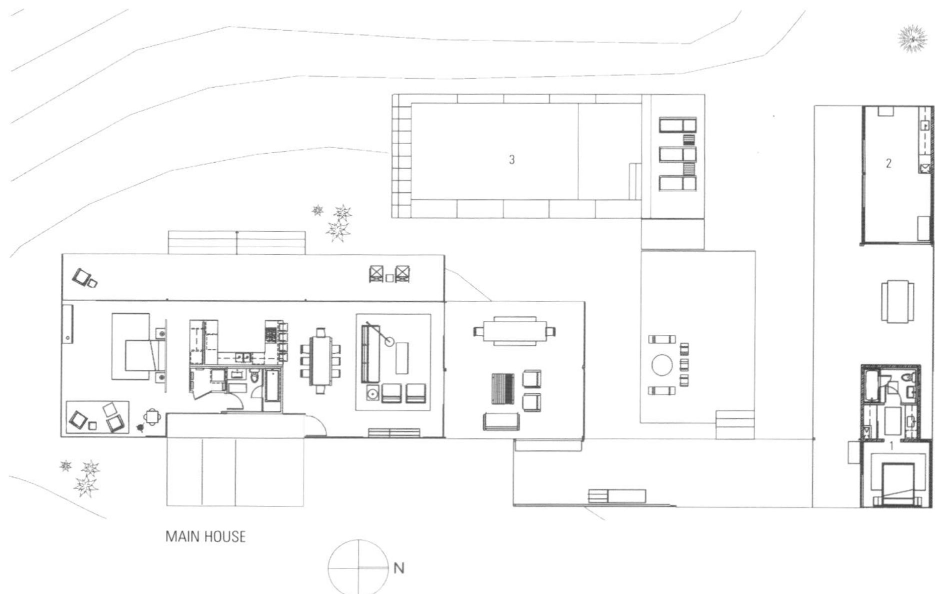

1 guest quarters
2 studio
3 pool

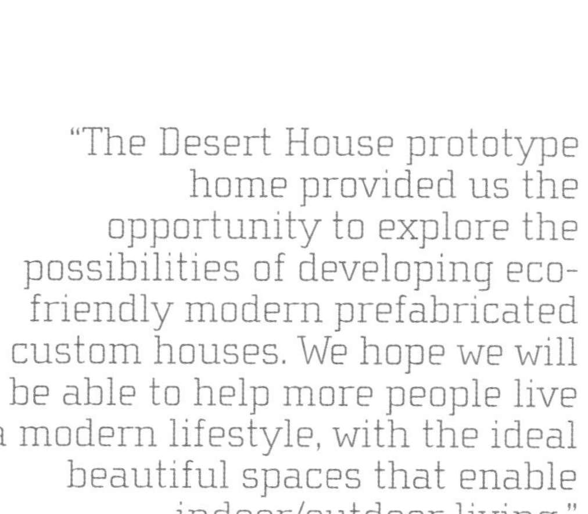

"The Desert House prototype home provided us the opportunity to explore the possibilities of developing eco-friendly modern prefabricated custom houses. We hope we will be able to help more people live a modern lifestyle, with the ideal beautiful spaces that enable indoor/outdoor living."

Marmol Radziner + Associates

BELOW
The Desert House stretches across the desert landscape in a series of enclosed spaces, covered walkways, and decks. The walls of windows and glass doors face the open environment and provide views to the San Jacinto Mountains.

AN OASIS IN THE DESERT

The Desert House prototype prefabricated home is oriented to best capture views of beautiful San Jacinto peak and the surrounding mountains. Located on a 5-acre (2-ha) site in Desert Hot Springs, California, the house extends through the landscape with covered outdoor living areas, which more than double the 2,100 sq ft (195 sq m) of interior space. A detached carport allows the owners to "leave the car behind" as they approach their home.

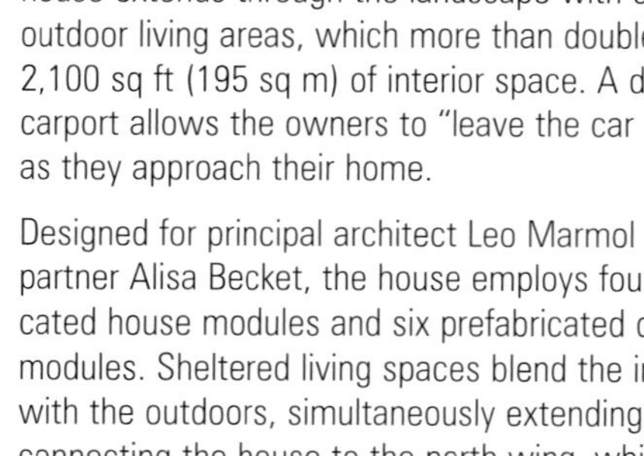

Designed for principal architect Leo Marmol and his partner Alisa Becket, the house employs four prefabricated house modules and six prefabricated deck modules. Sheltered living spaces blend the indoors with the outdoors, simultaneously extending and connecting the house to the north wing, which holds the guest quarters and studio space. By forming an L-shape, the home creates a protected environment that includes a pool, fire pit, and open terrace area.

AN ORGANIC APPROACH

While the walls facing the public dirt road are clad in metal siding to provide privacy for the owners, the walls facing the open terrace area are floor to ceiling windows and doors. This glazing floods the house with natural light, as well as providing extended views to the mountains beyond. The material palette of the home seeks to blend in with the surrounding natural environment. The zincalum metal siding provides both durable protection and a weathered finish color that recedes into the landscape. The use of vertical grain cedar siding on the front entry and guest quarters introduces a rustic brown color to the home.

Seeking to complement the modern esthetic of the architecture and the organic beauty of the desert surroundings, the interior design reflects great esteem for nature and obscures distinctions between indoor and outdoor living spaces. By combining vintage, contemporary, and custom pieces, the home has a feel of understated elegance that highlights a genuine connection to the earth.

USING PREFABRICATION TECHNOLOGY

The home was built in a factory with prefabrication technologies, out of two basic types of modules: interior modules comprising the living spaces, and exterior modules that define covered outdoor living areas and provide protection from the sun. Using steel framing, the 12-ft- (3.5-m-) wide modules extend up to 64 ft (19.5 m) in length. The modules employ different types of cladding, including metal, wood, or glass, or are simply left open to the surrounding landscape. The modular steel frame construction is sustainable and durable, while allowing for maximum flexibility in creating large expanses of open space and glass.

The modules were shipped to the site, as were many "pre-installed" finishes, such as the custom wood cabinets and concrete floors. First, the steel floors and roof frames of each of the modules were independently welded. Then, the floors and roofs were connected with steel columns. Once the full steel frame was prepared, the interior wall framing, plumbing, and electrical and mechanical components were completed. The finishes, cabinetry, appliances, and fixtures had been installed before the modules were shrink-wrapped for delivery. After being trucked to the project site, a crane then placed the modules onto the foundation, leaving minimal work left to complete the installation.

ABOVE
The Desert House is composed of ten prefabricated steel-frame modules. The design of the home places great emphasis on the merging of indoor and outdoor living spaces to create a modern retreat in the desert.

RIGHT
A long deck module runs the length of the main house, providing both outdoor living space and shade protection from the desert sun. The pool and studio, in the background, provide spaces for recreation at this weekend home.

FOLLOWING PAGES
Acting as a breezeway, a covered deck module connects the main house to the guest quarters and studio. Situated behind the vertical grain cedar siding, the guest quarters comprise kitchenette and full bathroom. As part of the prefabrication process, the concrete floors throughout the house were poured in the factory.

ABOVE
The wide concrete entry steps provide views to the deck module that connects to the guest quarters. In one day, a large crane placed all ten prefabricated modules on their concrete block foundation.

TOP RIGHT
Along the approach from the prefabricated carport to the front entry, a cutout section provides framed views of the San Jacinto Mountains and the guest quarters and studio wing of the house.

Since the house is located in the desert, the use of prefabrication provided an ideal way to ensure the high level of detail and precision for the less-developed location. In more remote locations, it can often be difficult finding a local contractor with the ability or the desire to build according to the exacting standards required by a Modernist design. Because the home's modules were constructed in a factory, it allowed for greater control over the details and finishes.

SUSTAINABLE DESIGN, SUSTAINABLE LIVING

Just as the spaces of the home embrace nature, so too do the designs and methods of fabrication. Because factory construction provides greater precision in cutting materials and increases the ability to save and reuse excess material, the construction of this home created significantly less waste than a home built on-site.

The factory-made modules employ renewable and environmentally friendly materials. For its primary structural system, the home is made from recycled steel rather than non-sustainable wood framing. Steel framing produces less waste because, unlike wood, the pieces are uniform in cut and quality. Steel also promises long-term endurance against natural elements, insects, and mold without requiring the chemical treatments necessary for wood framing.

To minimize energy consumption, the Desert House uses efficient materials and careful "green design." The home derives its electrical power from solar panels located on the roof above the bedroom, thus maximizing the benefits of the desert location. Deep overhangs shade the house from the harsh summer sun, and hidden pockets hold window shades that provide additional protection from the sun. In colder months, the concrete floors absorb solar energy during the day and release the stored heat at night, helping to make the home energy efficient. To increase insulation from the extensive use of windows and doors, triple-pane, low-emissivity (low-e), argon-filled insulating glass is used, which provides superior protection to standard glass. The floor to ceiling windows and doors supply ample natural night, thus eliminating the need for artificial light during the day.

As a prototype home, this house provided valuable design, fabrication, and installation lessons for the development of the architect's line of modern prefabricated homes. By combining Modernist esthetics, prefabrication technologies, and sustainable materials and design, the Desert House encapsulates a new potential for embracing a modern lifestyle that encourages indoor/outdoor living.

LEFT
The main house was prefabricated from two interior modules that are each 64 ft (19.5 m) long and 12 ft (3.5 m) wide. In the open plan, the living room, dining room, and kitchen all share a communal space, bound by the long wall of sliding glass doors.

ABOVE
The kitchen features custom-made teak cabinetry with cantilevered shelves and wall paneling – all constructed and installed in the modules prior to them being delivered to the site.

Gradman House CALIFORNIA, USA

Swatt Architects

Construction	2002–2005
Home type	Single dwelling, vacation retreat
Structure	Five-level, wood frame

"This design is a response to a near impossible site – a steep uphill parcel within a forest of towering cedar trees. The driveway switches back and forth, almost like threading a needle, to protect as many trees as possible, while the house has been designed with five ground-floor levels which 'tiptoe' on the land, providing access to the outdoors from every major space."

Robert Swatt

A FOREST LOCATION

The Gradman House is located on a steep up-sloping lot in Inverness Park, California, near the Point Reyes National Seashore. The site contains large mature cedar trees, and has beautiful filtered views of Tomales Bay to the northwest and the wetlands to the northeast.

LONG-TERM LIVING

The owners, a couple with grown children, currently live in Palo Alto, California, where they have been for more than 25 years. Through the years, the family vacationed in the area where the home is now located, and over time fell in love with the northern California coast. The new home is a vacation retreat for the short term, but will eventually become a permanent residence after the owners reach retirement.

The goals of the project are common to West Coast residential living – promoting enjoyment of the outdoors, maximizing views, and sensitively knitting the house to the land. It was important to provide access to the outdoors from all the major spaces in the home. The house and access road have been carefully situated to protect as many existing trees, most of them indigenous cedar, as possible.

USING TOPOGRAPHY

The house has been designed with multiple levels that "tiptoe on the land," minimizing grading and adverse effects on existing vegetation.

The dwelling includes five floor levels which gently step with the topography and create distinct zones for living. The entry and circulation space, located at the middle level, is designed as a light-infused central spine. It joins the "public" living and dining spaces at the lower level with the "private" bedroom areas at the upper levels. Each bedroom meets a natural grade and opens to its own private hillside terrace at the top of the site, whereas the living and dining areas open to expansive terraces with magnificent views to the bay and wetlands below.

ECONOMY AND STRENGTH

The building is a standard wood frame over a cast-in-place concrete pier and grade construction. The main living and dining area includes two levels of Douglas fir framing. The lower level includes glue-laminated beams that penetrate the space to create a low, wide overhang at the main terrace. Steel columns and beams have been kept to a minimum to keep the project economical.

ABOVE FAR LEFT
The front elevation, which shows the carport at the left and the kitchen at the right, features a stunning junction of textures including wood, glass, concrete, and stone. The construction is a standard wood frame over a cast-in-place concrete pier. Steel columns and beams have been minimized to help keep the project economical.

LEFT
Clean simple lines are the order of the day in this space with a color scheme to match. The openness of the upstairs corridor creates a connection with the living space below, ensuring one level of the house harmonizes with another.

ABOVE LEFT
The multi-level retreat features extensive floor to ceiling glass surfaces to maximize the surrounding woodland views. Warm natural timbers work hand in hand with sleek manufactured materials to create a perfectly balanced exterior.

The house includes five floor levels which gently step with the topography and create distinct zones for living.

ABOVE
From the glassed corner of the kitchen and breakfast space there are filtered views, through the large cedar trees that surround the site, of the wetlands to the northeast.

LEFT
The living and dining area features two levels of Douglas fir framing. The lower-level, glue-laminated beams penetrate the space to create a low, wide overhang across the entance.

FAR LEFT
In the bedroom wing, each bedroom opens out to its own private hillside garden at the top of the site, complete with viewing area to sit and contemplate the superb woodland vista.

House Lina LINZ, AUSTRIA

Caramel Architekten

Constructed	2004
Home type	Single-story family home
Structure	Timber, glass and steel, with fiberglass reinforced PVC-membrane

"The question here was how to build a fully functioning home, with an inadequate budget and only a few weeks in which to complete the construction. We had a small space and were building a small house, but wanted to create the appearance of much bigger home."
Caramel Architekten

SMALL SPACE, BIG PLANS

The biggest challenge for this project was how to build a practical, functional, self-sufficient home in a very short space of time and with very limited funds. Another consideration was that even though the house was small, the architect wanted to give the home the appearance of looking bigger by providing different rooms for different functions. This posed a number of problems because the house size is just 743 sq ft (69 sq m) and the budget was very small.

WHEN AN EXTENSION IS MORE THAN AN EXTENSION

The house is officially classified as an extension, but in reality it is an autonomous separate dwelling, for a mother and her child. The house is situated on family land in a pretty, partly wooded area on the south-western slope of Pöstlingberg, in the city of Linz. The design of the house takes full advantage of the beautiful panoramic views on offer, with extensive use of floor to ceiling glass. This also means the interior is bathed with natural light.

Though infrastructurally "docked" onto the extant building, the new unit includes all the necessary primary facilities, such as a full bathroom, kitchen, a heating system, and hot water. There is also a bedroom, a nursery, and a living room.

ABOVE LEFT
White walls and a cleverly placed floor to ceiling mirror give the small bedroom a spacious feel.

ABOVE
A glazed wall runs along the southern face of the home, flooding the interior with natural light. It also creates the illusion of a much larger home by making the room part of the wooded landscape.

STRETCHING RESOURCES

Because the architect was constrained both on a budgetary level and also because of the shortage of available construction space, the building's dimensions had to be very carefully determined. Through consistently rational planning, it was possible to reduce the duration and cost of construction. The proportions and the construction grid of the unit, for example, were designed in order to correspond with standard particleboard dimensions; and the building as a whole was planned using simple lightweight construction methods. The latter had the added bonus of providing an efficient system of thermal insulation.

Finally, it took only a few days to mount the partially prefabricated elements onto the completed steel framework, which is attached at regular intervals to the strip foundations of the dwelling. Because of the position of the building on the plot, it was not possible to use large prefabricated elements, so the architect decided to produce small elements, determined according to the size of the timber boards. These could easily be handled by two people.

A FLEXIBLE INTENTION

The dwelling is not intended to last forever, and this was a deliberate decision taken by the architect. It was designed so that it could be easily removed or extended, depending on the future living situation and differing requirements of the inhabitants.

ABOVE
Despite having a built area of just 743 sq ft (69 sq m), this compact home has all necessary primary facilities, including kitchen, living/dining, bathroom, and bedroom.

RIGHT
The veranda pulls out like a drawer from the main structure, the floor-level window representing the space left by the open drawer.

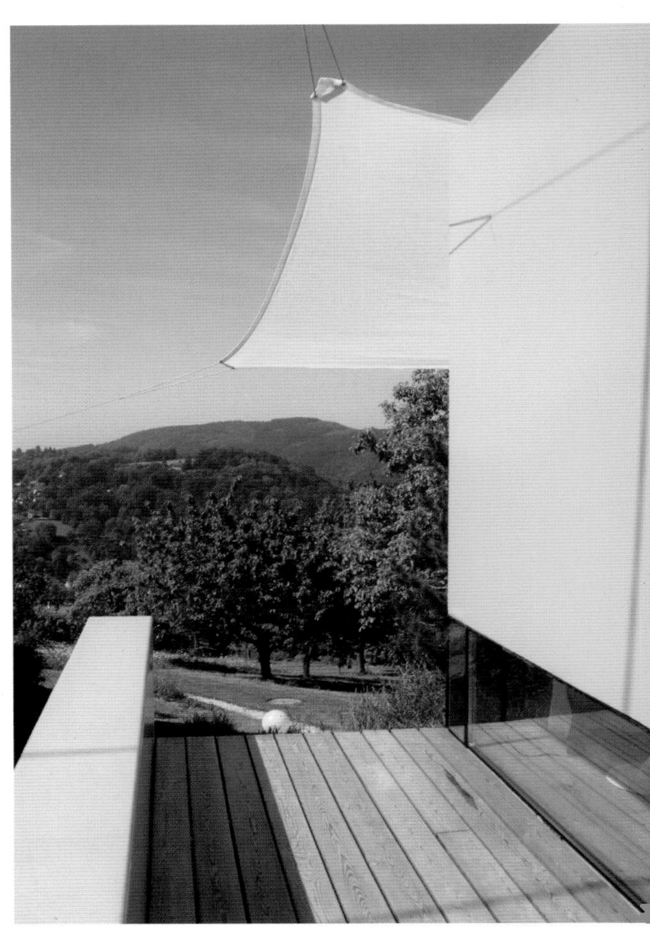

Jackson Family Retreat CALIFORNIA, USA

Fougeron Architecture

Constructed	2004
Home type	Two-story family home
Structure	Wood, copper, stucco, steel, and glass

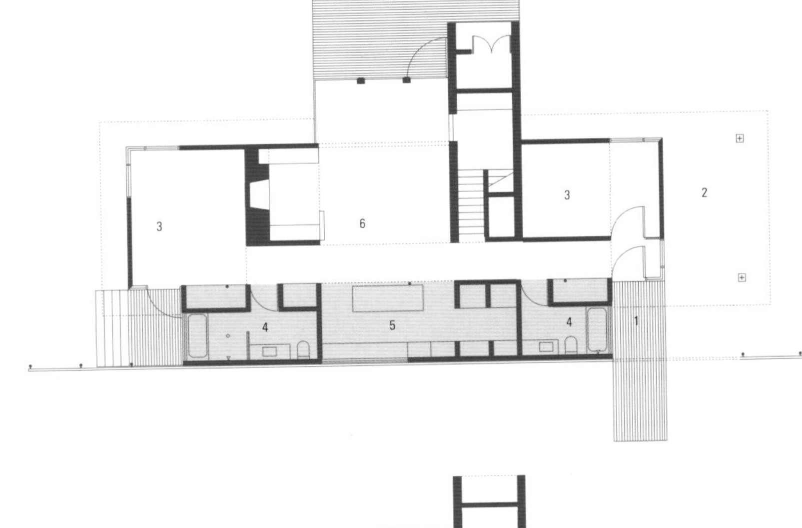

LEVEL ONE
1 entry
2 carport
3 bedroom
4 bathroom
5 kitchen
6 living/dining

LEVEL TWO
7 sleeping loft
8 library
9 deck
10 open to below

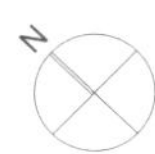

TOP
Fashioned after nineteenth-century conservatories, a steel and glass enclosure protrudes from the rear facade, stepping out from the living/dining area and offering views of the nearby creek. Steel columns delicately lift the Jackson Family Retreat nearly 3 ft (1 m) off the ground, to reduce its impact on the land and protect it from flooding or damp soil.

ABOVE
A small gangplank leads to the entrance of the home, where a buttery yellow screen of Alaskan cedar slats extends horizontally across the south wall to shield the kitchen from the sun's glare. Glass of varying translucency allows the lofty open-plan interior to be filled with light – even when it's raining.

"...wild natural beauty and strict environmental regulations to protect it; extreme variations of canyon light, weather, and topography; and living spaces for both family reunion and retreat – for three generations... Resolving these opposing tensions in a compact house that would respect the land, reach for the sky, and communicate the relaxed intimacy of a Big Sur cabin was my inspiration and challenge."

Anne Fougeron

BIG SUR RETREAT

Located in the Big Sur area of Northern California, this 2,500-sq-ft (232-sq-m) two-bedroom house was built for a family to enjoy together on the weekends and holidays.

Jackson Family Retreat is a Modernist structure that sits lightly on the land acknowledging the ecologically fragile nature of the site. It took working with ten different consultants for three-and-a-half years to satisfy all the requirements of the local governing agencies that would have preferred to leave the site as it was – overgrown and uninhabited.

The house is composed of four volumes, all made of different materials that are interwoven and interconnected to create visually and spatially complex exterior and interior spaces.

USING THE CANYON

The steep walls of the canyon dominate the wooded site next to a creek. The house holds its own in this tall and cavernous place – neither dominating nor being dwarfed by it. The main volume of the house runs parallel to the canyon, with a butterfly roof and glass corners that reach out to the sky and the light at the open ends. The thin roof sits delicately above a band of extruded glass, connecting to the roof structure with thin rods that are invisible on the exterior.

At the corners of the house, two-story clear windows frame the views of the majestic redwoods and the sky at the ridge of the canyon. This volume is clad in standing seam copper.

FUNCTIONAL BEAUTY

On the front, the second volume is a one-story structure that includes all the service functions for the house and acts as a buffer from the dirt road, which leads to the other houses in this old subdivision. It is clad in yellow Alaskan cedar that is turned in three directions acting as a rain screen, a fence, and a railing. The material is left untreated, and as it ages naturally will become silvery gray in color.

The back of the house is open to the views of the creek with a custom steel and glass volume. Finally, the fourth volume of the staircase is both the seismic structural brace for the house and a visual foil to the shimmering and transparent volumes around it. It is clad with gray integral color stucco that wraps inside and out.

ABOVE
This glassy haven grabs every sliver of canyon light, looking out and up to grand views of Big Sur redwoods, ridges, and sky. Night exposes the transparency of the house, the glazed living/dining area acting as a welcoming beacon in the surrounding nature preserve.

RIGHT
The 52-ft- (16-m-) long roof deck stretches the length of the kitchen and bathrooms below, and is accessed via the steel bridge that bounds the living area. The private deck faces a grove of redwood trees.

On the ground floor, two bedrooms at opposing ends of the house sit either side of a two-story communal living space, fireplace room, and loft library above the living area. The 15-ft- (4.5-m-) high windows in the bedrooms dissolve the corners of the spaces, bringing light and views into the bedroom and living spaces of the house.

THE EFFECT OF GLASS

On the second floor, the space is open. The library and communal sleeping loft are separated from the upper level of the two-story bedrooms by glass walls.

A combination of transparent glass and extruded channel glass reflects and dapples the light on the inside, creating an ever-changing interior with a warm play of light and shadow throughout the day.

ABOVE
The compression and release of space evoke the architecture of Frank Lloyd Wright. Two-story corner windows in the first-floor bedrooms that bracket the central communal space not only create a soaring quality, as in Wright's designs, they also make the house look less large in relation to the site.

TOP RIGHT
The double-height living area is bounded by a steel bridge that connects a multipurpose room and loft library on the upper level.

OPPOSITE
The main living/dining area provides different kinds of spaces in which to be separate, yet connected. The focal point of this "retreat within a retreat" is an aingre-paneled fireplace inglenook with built-in seating, an area that exudes warmth and intimacy within the lofty room.

Kangaroo Valley House KANGAROO VALLEY, AUSTRALIA

Glenn Murcutt

Construction	1996–1998
House type	Country house, single dwelling
Structure	Single level, reverse brick veneer on concrete slab, and steel frame roof

"The site is in a beautiful valley falling to the south. The house is sited as near as I could locate it along the contours, which provide a wonderful outlook to the escarpment. My clients wanted a very simple house, with living, dining, and kitchen together... It was very important to capitalize on the northern light to the rear of the house. The excavated earth was reworked to create a flatter terrace in front of the living space."

Glenn Murcutt

ABOVE
Facing south toward a national park but with the sun coming from the north, the Kangaroo Valley House captures the best of both orientations with its tilted roof and linear siting.

PROSPECT AND REFUGE

Located 120 miles (190 km) south of Sydney in New South Wales, between Nowra and Moss Vale, Kangaroo Valley House sits on a site of nearly 5 acres (2 ha). The site, which slopes to the south and faces and borders a national park, was formerly part of a large farm and includes grassland and "bush," the Australian term for untouched indigenous forest and shrublands. Pritzker Prize-winning architect Glenn Murcutt chose to locate the house relatively close to the road, and on part of the site that had previously been cultivated, so that the home's aspect would always include that of an untouched wilderness. As a weekender, this was to be an escape where one's view from the home would be a constant embrace of landscape – a classic description of one of Murcutt's favorite design themes: prospect and refuge.

TOUCH THE SITE LIGHTLY

Murcutt's next design strategy was to minimize the impact of the house on its site. He located the slim linear box with its single monopitch roof between two contour lines. The driveway came in from the east, also negotiating contours gently, so that on approach by car, the expanse and length of the valley was emphasized, and the presence of the car was made as unobtrusive as possible. Indeed the owner's car slips into and is hidden in one end of this linear block.

LINEAR PLAN

The plan of the house is a sequence of rooms laid along the contour. In line with, and following the garage are a studio, study/guestroom, bathroom, hallway (which splits the house in two), and then the true heart of the house – the refuge – a traditional farmhouse kitchen, which incorporates dining/living and a firebox, before the main bedroom, ensuite, and west-facing veranda/terrace. Murcutt is the master of the linear-planned house, and this plan form has been developed by him for more than thirty years. The single-room width plan (never more than 14 ft [4.3 m]) is also excellent for cross ventilation, and enables the capturing of sunlight and view, whatever the orientation.

TILTED ROOF, TILTED WINDOWS

The roof is tilted at 11° to parallel the slope of the land, and a continuous band of clerestory windows enables northern winter sunlight to penetrate the narrow plan. To the south, where the views are, large glazed sliding doors open up the kitchen/living/dining space entirely to the landscape. Elsewhere, there are tilted bay windows that serve a number of functions: shedding rainwater; incorporating ventilation flaps as sill panels; on the north side, external retractable venetian blinds for shade; while on the south, they have sliding timber screens to provide shade, privacy, and security. As Murcutt says, "It is one of my objectives to design openings to function in multiple ways."

SIMPLICITY IN MATERIALS

The materials palette for the house is understated, in contrast to the rich green of the surrounding pasture and soft gray-green of the distant landscape. Corrugated galvanized iron is used for roofing and for the four tanks that collect the home's drinking water. As winters can be cold in Kangaroo Valley, Murcutt chose to build the home in reverse brick veneer, with the internal brickwork walls clad in western red cedar. The double concrete floor has insulation between the slabs as well as cable heating. As a floor surface it was trowelled and given a latex finish. Elsewhere, joinery is painted white and benches are stainless steel.

ABOVE LEFT
The tilted bay window of the living/dining/kitchen space sheds water as well as acting as a shading device. External retractable aluminum venetian blinds can be closed to block out the summer sun. To the left is the front door. Above is the continuous band of clerestory windows and the repetitive series of tapering timber rafters.

ABOVE
In contrast to the openness of the living/dining/kitchen space is the enclosed refuge space of the main bedroom. A corner window frames a view of the escarpment landscape beyond.

TOP
A habitable veranda that can be completely closed or open is the theme of the home's major living space. Part traditional farmhouse kitchen, part elegant holiday pavilion, this is the sort of space that gives Murcutt's houses their universal appeal.

As a weekender, Kangaroo Valley House was to be an escape where one's view from the home would be a constant embrace of landscape – a classic description of one of Murcutt's favorite design themes: prospect and refuge.

RIGHT
The living/dining/kitchen space is the heart of the house. The proprietary firebox is built into a continuous stainless steel bench/joinery unit. The tilted bay window has as its sill, a series of ventilation flaps and insect screens, which can be opened and closed at will. Above, the tilted plane of the roof flies uninterrupted through the space.

Maison Goulet QUEBEC, CANADA

Saia Barbarese Topouzanov Architectes

Constructed 2003
Home type Private residence
Structure Steel-reinforced wood-frame construction, wooden frames, open wood metal trusses, and exposed plywood

"Maison Goulet is inextricably bound with its environment, designed in response to the site's topography, climate, and ecology. In planning and constructing in a dramatic landscape, isolated on a natural plateau, we noted the broader impact of design decisions on the local environment. Principles of sustainability formed an integral part of the design, informing every decision."
Mario Saia

ABOVE
At night the rooms throw a warm glow because of the reflected tones of the interior fir plywood paneling. The overall effect, from the outside looking in, is that of a sanctuary, secluded and safe from the extreme landscape outside.

TOP
Entry to the house is from the north, with stairs forming a buffer zone to the living areas situated to the south. On the north side, the facade remains closed to the harsh weather. The openings are few, and their dimensions reduced.

TOP RIGHT
The interconnected living spaces on the ground floor are extended into screened loggias at either end of the home. Seen here, the east loggia, which acts as a breakfast area. During the summer, the leaves of the trees filter the harsh southern sunlight.

RIGHT
A stone chimney terminates the western extension and signals the home's anchor point. The archetypal form of Maison Goulet refers to the traditional Quebecois rural residence, with its simple shape, practical roof form, and imposing chimneys.

A RETREAT FOR WORK AND LEISURE

A harsh landscape in the Quebec Laurentians and a steeply sloping site posed a challenge for the design of Maison Goulet. The slope runs from north to south toward a lake below. A sheer rock face forms part of the descent, acting as a retaining wall for the plateau upon which the house is situated. It is a long house, the shape being ordained by the projecting ledge that runs from east to west. Two chimneys, one located at the center, the other at the end of the house, anchor the steel-reinforced wood-frame construction. The zinc cladding provides an even finish.

THE WARMTH OF STONE

The house sits on a stone base. Prevailing winds are deflected by both trees and the walls of the house. The first level of the house, which lies on top of a 5-ft- (1.5-m-) deep stone core, covered by an irregular sawn-stone paving, serves to store the sun's heat. In the summer months, the foliage from the trees filters the sun's glare and heat. A ventilation system catches the warm air that has collected in the roof and then circulates it underneath the slab of the floor, keeping the house cool in summer and warm in winter.

The interior is lined with fir plywood, and the panels are placed horizontally, presenting a uniform continuous effect. There are no moldings or framing – there are simply openings, producing a dramatic outcome.

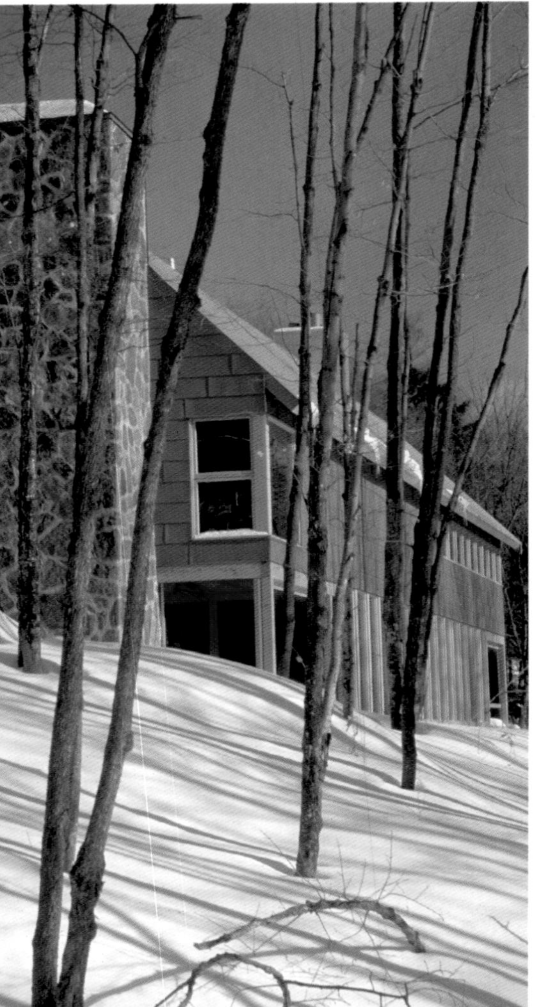

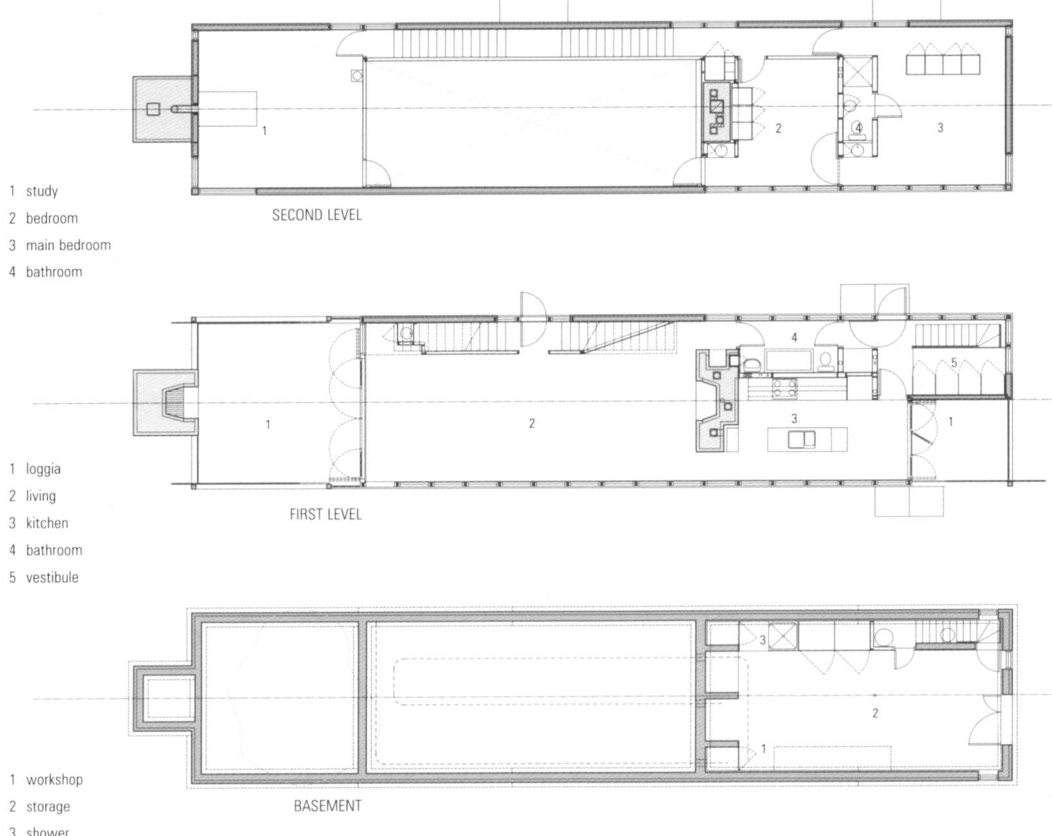
N
SECOND LEVEL
1 study
2 bedroom
3 main bedroom
4 bathroom
FIRST LEVEL
1 loggia
2 living
3 kitchen
4 bathroom
5 vestibule
BASEMENT
1 workshop
2 storage
3 shower

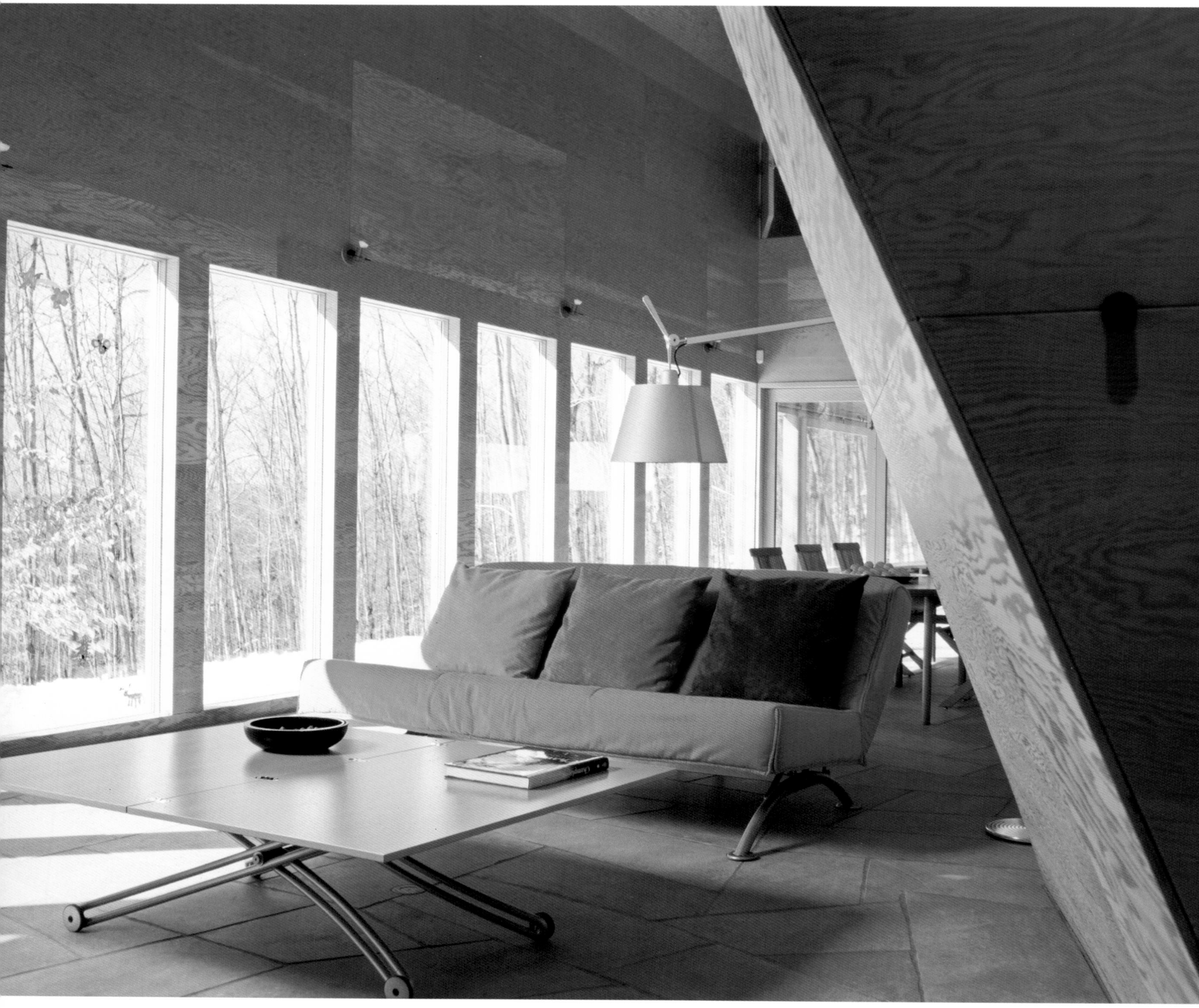

ABOVE
The floor to ceiling windows flood the room with light and much-needed warmth, and reveal views to the lake. One of the screened loggias is visible at the far end, to the west. In warmer weather, the large doors open to the outside.

THE SYMMETRY OF STAIRS

The central space extends to the full height of the house. Two independent staircases positioned symmetrically, face to face allow access to the second-floor bedrooms and the study. Although they are on the same level, the study is quite separate from the private area of the bedrooms.

The staircases are braced in parallel between the thick northern wall and the second wall, which extends to the level of the top plate, where the base folds at an angle. This gives the effect of a sculpted-out space for the living area below.

KEEPING THINGS IN PERSPECTIVE

In warmer weather, the large doors of the screened loggias open out. Because the walls appear to disappear, the outside area gives the impression of making the inside area much longer. On the second floor, a series of "enfilade"(aligned openings) create the perspective of length and continuity beyond the east and west gable walls. This reinforces the initial architectural concept and also orients the user toward the landscape.

Because the architect kept the topography of the site at the forefront of his mind, and also took into account the climate and the position of the sun in different seasons, the house is inextricably linked to its surroundings.

Although the house at first glance may seem to have many traditional characteristics, the simple lines and volume of the home remove any superfluous details. There is no ambiguity in the design and yet flexibility is evident – there are a number of areas that offer privacy and seclusion.

RIGHT
The central space occupies the full height of the building and looks almost church-like with its high ceilings and altar-like fireplace. The plywood skin lines the interior and produces a pictorial effect.

ABOVE
The private study and the bedrooms are located at opposite ends of the house on the upper floor, physically disconnected from one another with separate stair access.

TOP LEFT
In the winter, the sun is reflected in the snow, bouncing in through the windows and up to the ceiling. The intensity of the light makes the living area and the kitchen bright, as the windows are floor to ceiling. On a sunny day, changing patterns of light dance on the limestone floor.

Möbius House 'T GOOI, THE NETHERLANDS

UNStudio

Construction	1993–1998
Home type	Residential house
Structure	Glass and concrete on a concrete slab

"Möbius House represents a radical departure from long-held approaches to architecture that rely on traditionally aligned 'Platonic solids' in their design and construction."

UNStudio

GEOMETRIC GYRATIONS

This home was built using a principle of geometry known as the "Möbius Band" as the basis for its design. Imagine a strip of paper, turned once through 180° into a twisted figure eight, then attaching its two ends to produce one endlessly repetitive, non-orientable surface. Though not literally transferred to the building, the Möbius mathematical model can be found in architectural innovations throughout the house, including staircases, furniture, lighting, and in the way its occupants move through its interior. This endless repetition of the twisted figure eight is used in Möbius House purely as a design concept. It illustrates how two people can dwell together, yet be separate, while still sharing a common space. This premise lifts this residence out of the realm of architecture and into that of a provocative social experiment.

In an age where computers and computer modeling have become modern-day sketchbooks, experiments in constructing surfaces and solids based on pure mathematical formulas such as the Möbius Band are becoming increasingly common.

ABOVE
This view along the axis of the first-floor bedroom illustrates the profound relationship between the house and its surroundings. The project stretches over a 5-acre (2-ha) plot. The Möbius House is designed to provide an overwhelming sense of interconnection with the environment.

ABOVE LEFT
The clients' wishes for their two working environments to be sited at opposite ends of the house can be seen to great effect here in Studio 1, a bold, cantilevered mass triumphantly forming the western end of the elevated ground floor.

TOP
Glazed exteriors are in the ascendancy on the southern elevation. Internal concrete partitions are clearly visible through the glass, highlighting the Möbius concept. The elongated design begins at left with Studio 1, which leads via an interior ramp to the meeting room (center) and through to the living room at right. The upper-level windows frame a guest bedroom and bathroom.

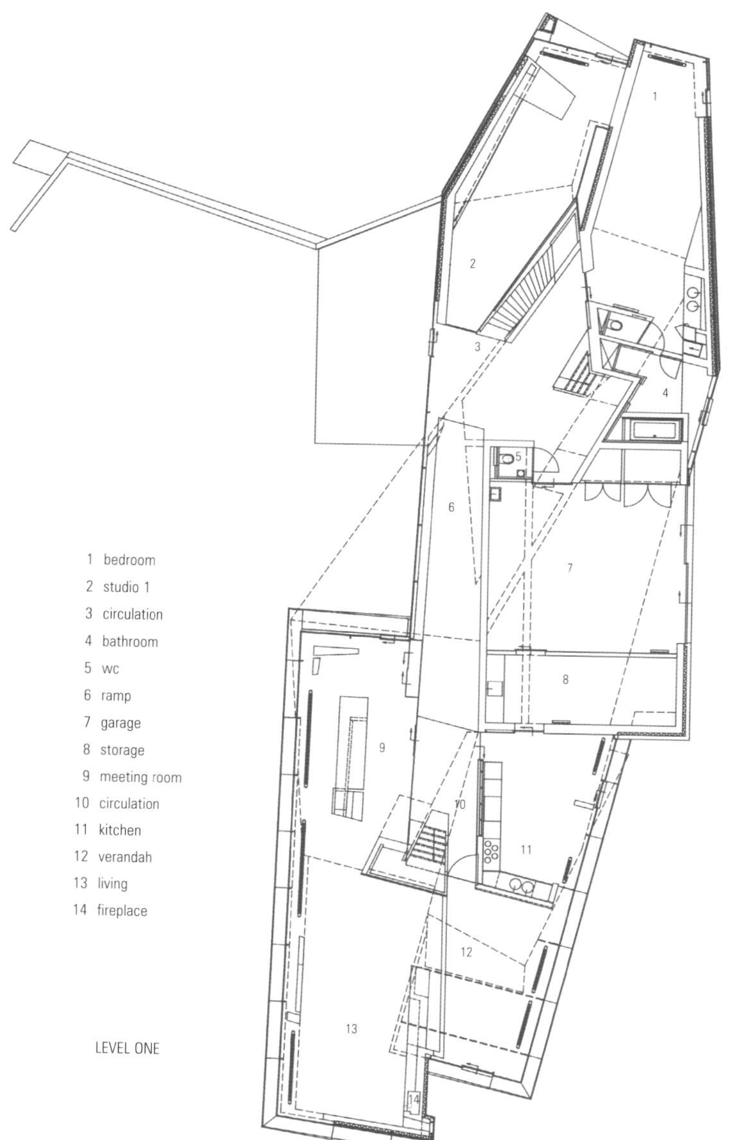
1 bedroom
2 studio 1
3 circulation
4 bathroom
5 wc
6 ramp
7 garage
8 storage
9 meeting room
10 circulation
11 kitchen
12 verandah
13 living
14 fireplace
LEVEL ONE

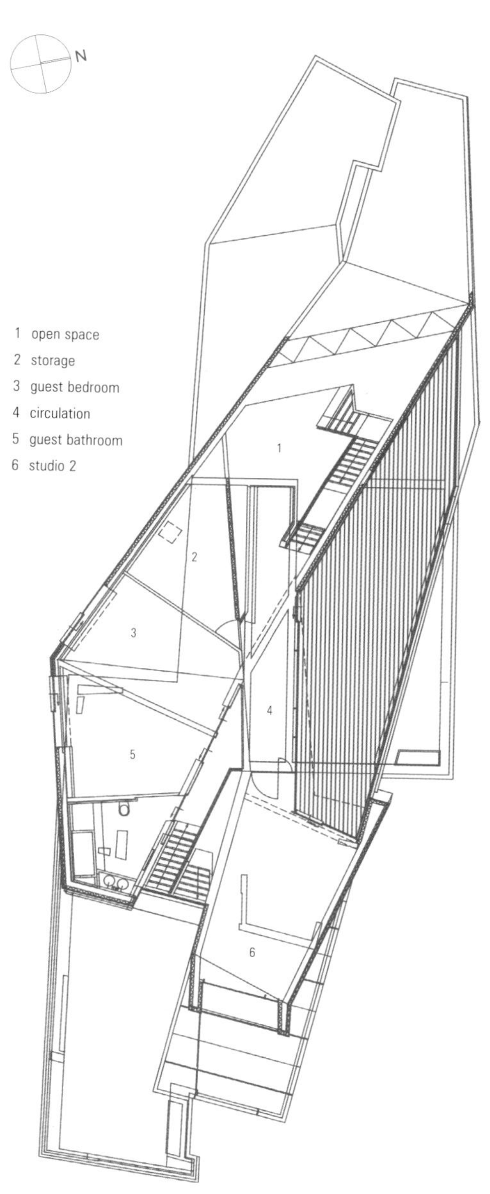
N
1 open space
2 storage
3 guest bedroom
4 circulation
5 guest bathroom
6 studio 2
LEVEL TWO

PREVIOUS PAGES
Even the structure's concrete slab has a part to play in the Möbius concept of intertwining elements. Extending beyond the building's perimeter, its role is transformed from the purely structural into the decorative and abstract, appearing to lift Möbius House serenely above its environment.

TRANSFORMING BOUNDARIES

Containing several interesting elements that can easily be applied to architecture, the Möbius Band's twist and continuity mean that, at least theoretically, floors can become walls, and walls can become ceilings. A design can be transformed so that the boundaries defining what is internal and external are so blurred that one can transmute into the other. This means it is possible to walk into an enclosed space and experience a spatial twist without having to walk upside down.

The exterior surfaces of Möbius House are so far removed from tradition that the glass is likened to a skin draped over concrete from one perspective, and a glass house framed in concrete from another.

The home's internal spaces represent a circular pattern of working, living, and sleeping, with the inherent deformation of the Möbius Band resulting in alternating forms and functions. The roles of glass and concrete structural elements have been reversed. Dividing walls are glass whereas tables are concrete. Furniture becomes a facade, a facade becomes a partition, a partition becomes furniture, and all simultaneously define and reveal spaces, culminating in an exciting sense of dislocation.

Unlike a traditional home with its clearly defined functional and social distinctions, the interior of Möbius House is akin to a continuous ribbon, where living areas, work spaces, and utilities all have their allotted place within the home's endlessly repetitious loop.

ABOVE
The concrete floor of Studio 2 on the upper level extends through the glass wall into the living area. Concrete forms such as this provide the necessary Möbius Band "intrusiveness" as well as adding dynamic points of reference.

RIGHT
Form and function stand as shoulder-to-shoulder equals in Möbius House's meeting room. Multi-layered planes are interwoven into structural columns to add a Modernist style of ornamentation. The cantilevered concrete surface provides bench space.

ABOVE
Carefully placed internal glass walls divide the central corridor on level one from the meeting room. A first floor window floods the innermost recesses of the house with sunlight, bringing warmth to the cold, neutral concrete surfaces.

TOP
Much thought was given to the orientation and siting of Möbius House prior to its construction. Nestling it among a grove of trees succeeds in applying texture and human scale to the project, and helps counter the impersonal scale of the concrete.

Rose House KIAMA, AUSTRALIA

Ian Moore Architects

Constructed 2000
Home type One-story family home
Structure Reinforced concrete, steel, and glass

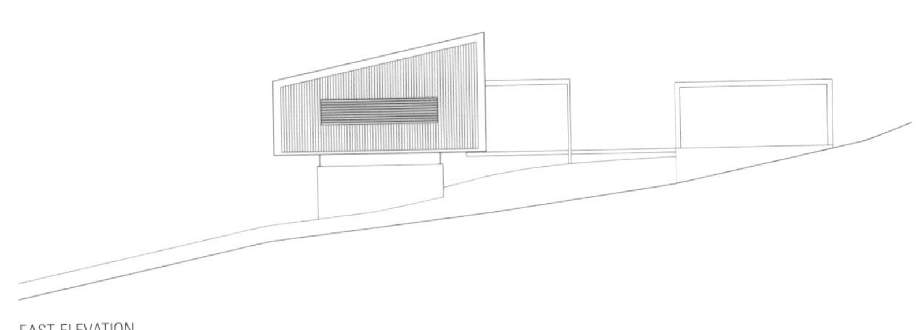

EAST ELEVATION

"The home is like a hovering viewing platform high on a mountain; its simple form and materiality inspired by the nearby utilitarian farm sheds – the external cladding forms an open-sided box, framing the view of the coast below. A simple subdivision of the plan, with parents at one end, children at the other, and the communal family space at the center create a comfortable living space."

Ian Moore

ABOVE
The north elevation of Rose House, showing the concrete entry bridge and the transparency of the living area, with a view of Seven Mile Beach to the south. A louvered roof over the entry bridge forms a shaded outdoor room.

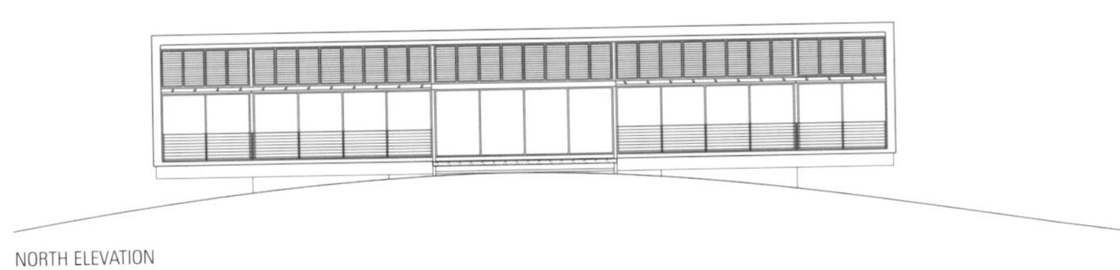

NORTH ELEVATION

ALL-ENCOMPASSING VIEWS

Saddleback Mountain is about a two-hour drive from Sydney, and the site for Rose House is the southern side of the mountain, some 165 ft (50 m) below the summit. There are spectacular views to Pigeon House Mountain in the south, the wooded hillside to the north, the coastal escarpment to the west, and the Pacific Ocean in the east.

To take full advantage of the views, the house has been built close to the road and centered on a north–south ridge, which also allows excellent views to the east and west. The site presented a challenge – the architect wanted to retain views to the south, yet still allow winter sunshine to permeate the house from the north, so he decided to design the roof to follow the natural slope of the site. This allowed for a clerestory with adjustable glass louvers to be placed in the northern part of the house. On the southern side, facing the prevailing winter winds, the glazing is lower in height.

THREE ZONES, THREE USES

The house is divided into three zones – the eastern zone is for the parents, the western zone is for the children, and the center of the home contains the kitchen, living, and dining areas. This not only allows private space for all the occupants, it also permits dazzling views from the central living space, with its floor to ceiling glazing.

TOP
View from the east, showing the house cantilevered above the concrete pods, which form the only contact with the ground. The profiled steel cladding and simple form recall the nearby farm sheds.

ABOVE
Night view from northwest, showing the single internal space subdivided into three zones by the bathroom pods, which pass through the floor slab to form the two concrete feet on which the house sits.

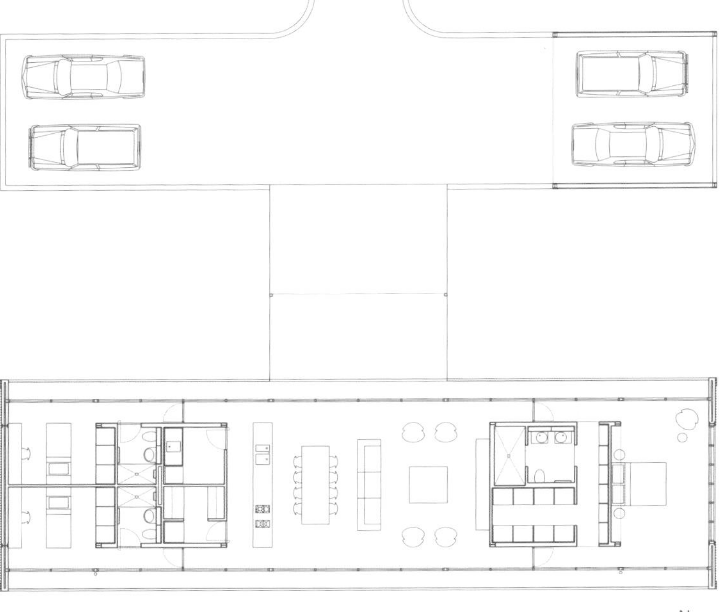

The eastern aspect is particularly inviting, looking, as it does, to the horizon – to maximize the vistas, a horizontal window was inserted in the main bedroom, so that the views can be enjoyed even while lying in bed. External aluminum louvers protect the room from the hottest sun.

To the north of the living areas, there is an open platform with an aluminum louvered roof. It functions both as the entry to the home, and as a shaded veranda. When the home is entered, the first sight is the view down the mountain to the south.

Narrow decks run down the length of the house on the north and south sides. They offer protection from the sun and wind. When the large sliding glass doors are open the entire living area becomes an open veranda space, permitting excellent cross-ventilation.

LOW IMPACT MATERIALS

Being attuned to environmental concerns, the materials for the site were carefully chosen. A light-weight steel structure was used, consisting of two trusses running along the length of the house. This was placed on reinforced concrete block storerooms underneath the house. This is the sole contact with the ground. The trusses allow the house to cantilever 12 ft (3.5 m) beyond the storerooms at the east and west extremities. Two service cores passing through the floor to ground level brace the entire structure. They also contain the plumbing.

The end walls and the roof are clad in gray-profiled steel sheeting, to harmonize with the farm sheds that are a common sight on adjacent properties. Windows and doors are sliding aluminum-framed glass.

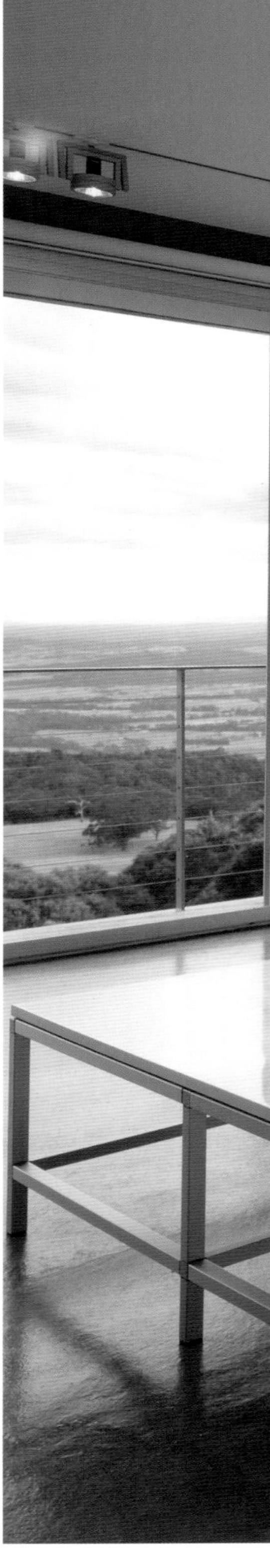

When the home is entered, the first sight is the view down the mountain to the south.

TOP LEFT
The living area showing the polished concrete floor slab and the patterns cast by external aluminum sun-control louvers. The artwork on the wall is by Australian artist John Coburn.

ABOVE
Living area and kitchen. The elevated position of the house affords dramatic views down the mountain and over farmland. The artwork behind the kitchen is by Australian artist Sydney Ball. The kit-set dining and coffee tables were designed by the architect.

Tea Plantation House NILGIRI HILLS, INDIA

Rahul Mehrotra Associates

Constructed 2001
Home type One-level family home
Structure Load-bearing masonry, steel, and glass

"The intention was to make the houses touch the landscape as lightly as possible and yet root them in the site. The combination of a local stone base with a lighter superstructure in steel was used to achieve both objectives simultaneously ... the buildings seem to want to dive into the spectacular surrounding views."
Rahul Mehrotra

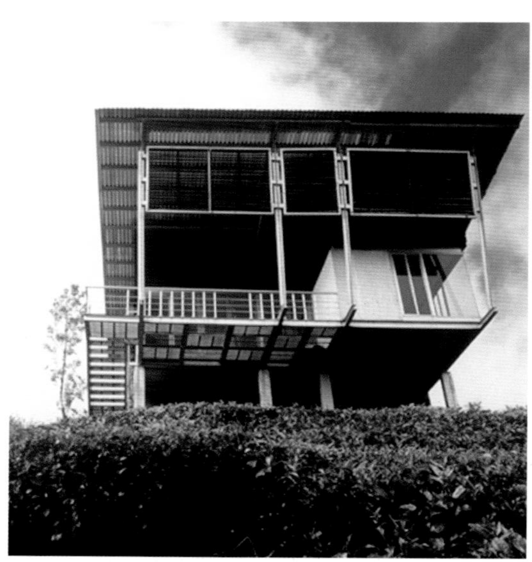

ABOVE
The home's front facade is fashioned in steel, accentuating the lightness with which the structure sits in the landscape. The tea bushes form a pleasant green border, framing each of the six individual homes in this rural hillside development.

TOP RIGHT
The corner windows in the main bedroom look outward to the viridescent "ocean" of tea bushes and the hills beyond. While the corner is made in fixed glass, the adjoining panels are movable, allowing for ventilation when required.

ALWAYS TIME FOR TEA

Overlooking an extensive tea plantation in the heart of the Nilgiri Hills in southern India, six identical contemporary houses sit on a hillside, marketed by the developer as "a few hours to a salubrious climate, clean air, amazing views, and a restful state." Set amid an emerald carpet of tea bushes, the Gurensey Estate homes lunge forward to embrace the spectacular vista. The house design combines metal, wood, and glass in a way that respects the land, while also achieving visual transparency to the views of the plantation. A cantilevered deck extends the usable space beyond the house and into the dramatic natural setting.

BORDERING ON COMMUNITY

Without the usual boundary fences, the arrangement of the houses on the site allows each owner a private yard, but also grants the residents the opportunity to become part of the community. Common infrastructure such as roads, electricity, and water are shared by community members, while a dense covering of tea bush helps unify the separate properties.

In this project, the architect attempts to address a contemporary issue facing tea plantations such as this, where adjacent existing towns are expanding rapidly and acquiring the cheap plantation land for development. It attempts to demonstrate how development can be accommodated in a fresh and innovative way, while still safeguarding the verdant ambience of the plantation. Achieving this kind of balance is a crucial issue for the burgeoning towns and settlements in the Nilgiris, where many South Indian tea plantations are located.

A HYBRID CONSTRUCTION

The method of construction employs both load-bearing masonry structure as well as lighter prefabricated steel frames. The choice of a hybrid construction stems from the difficulty involved in transporting materials to the site, coupled with the limitations of skills available in these presently remote locations.

Local stone was quarried partly from the site and partly from locales in close proximity. The stone was used to create a large plinth for each house, and also created an architectural platform on which the lighter structure could be situated. The clear advantage of this strategy was that the elevation of the form protected the living spaces, lifting them above the plantation so that the areas could embrace the stunning views that surrounded them.

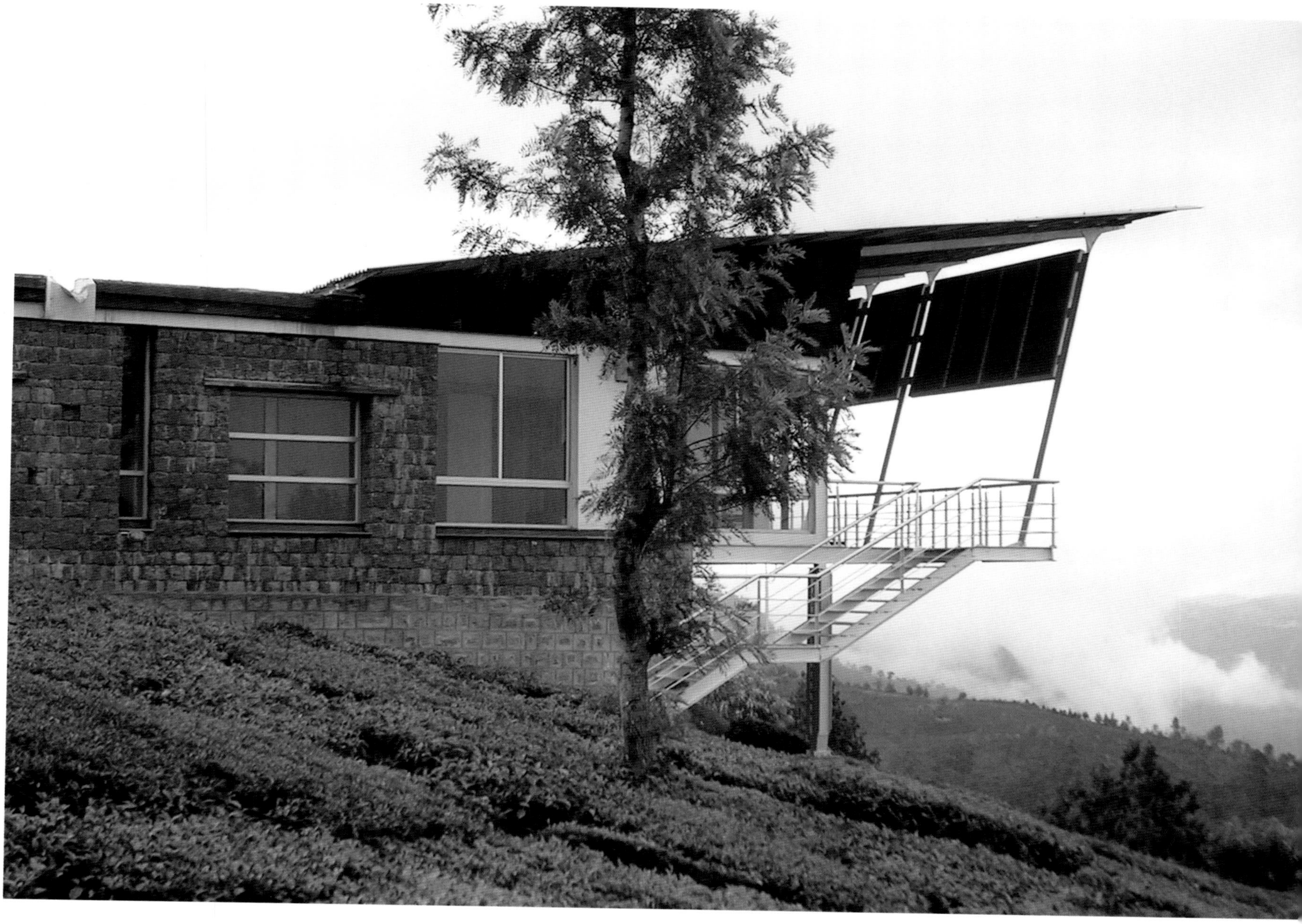

USING UNDERSTATEMENT

The houses were conceived as cool-climate retreats, far from the hot, crowded, and overwhelming cities. Architecturally, they were designed to be understated on approach, opening up dramatically to the wonderful vistas that are presented once the houses are entered.

The interiors received only minimal design treatment, allowing the views to take center stage. This also gives the occupants the choice to colonize the house according to their own tastes, and in keeping with standard development practices.

1 bedroom 2
2 bathroom 2
3 main bedroom
4 main bathroom
5 bedroom 3
6 bathroom 3
7 kitchen
8 living/dining
9 veranda

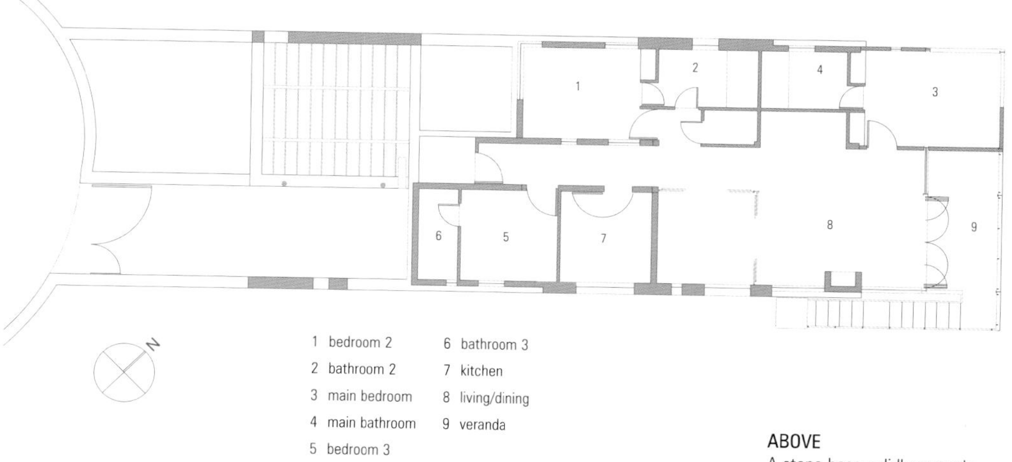

ABOVE
A stone base solidly grounds each house in the high-altitude site, while the upper steel portion lunges toward the landscape. The louver panels help ameliorate the effects of sun and rain, and protect the veranda space, which juts into the surroundings.

Tree House DELAWARE, USA

Sander Architects

Construction	2004–2006
Home type	Three-level family home
Structure	Timber, concrete, and glass

"The house is on a magnificent small site with tremendous trees. The 100-year-old flood plain carved a small buildable area into the site, and thus we decided to go 'vertical' with the house. The site really constrained us in this way – it really decided the form of the house. This led to the magnificent additional benefit of being 'in the trees' on the third level."

Whitney Sander

ABOVE
The house sits on a mature wooded site. The living area on the second level features 20-ft (6-m) windows with an open corner, allowing views into the protected woods to the northeast.

RIGHT
A bar grating staircase rises away from the facade, then turns and stops abruptly at the landing, which functions as a viewing platform.

OPPOSITE
The front stairs move away to the left, while the open deck canopy twists to the right. A spiral staircase leads from the ground level to the roof deck, which doubles as an outdoor living space.

A HOME IN THE TREE TOPS

The design and building of the Tree House was a labor of love. The architect, Whitney Sander, designed it for his sister. When their father died, he left sufficient funds for her to build her dream house. It is also her first house.

The Tree House sits on a cul-de-sac at the end of a mature subdivision in Wilmington, Delaware. It is filled with 100-year-old deciduous trees, which form a magnificent canopy 150 ft (45 m) high. A gentle stream runs around the house, and due to certain restrictions imposed by the Army Corps of Engineers and also because of the potential for flooding, the buildable area is quite small. The architect solved the problem by designing a vertical house. The main living area is on the second level, while the main bedroom and ensuite occupy the entire third level. These spaces give one the feeling of being in the trees, of being part of the canopy itself.

There is one other bedroom on the ground or first level, and one overflow bedroom, which doubles as a study, on the second level.

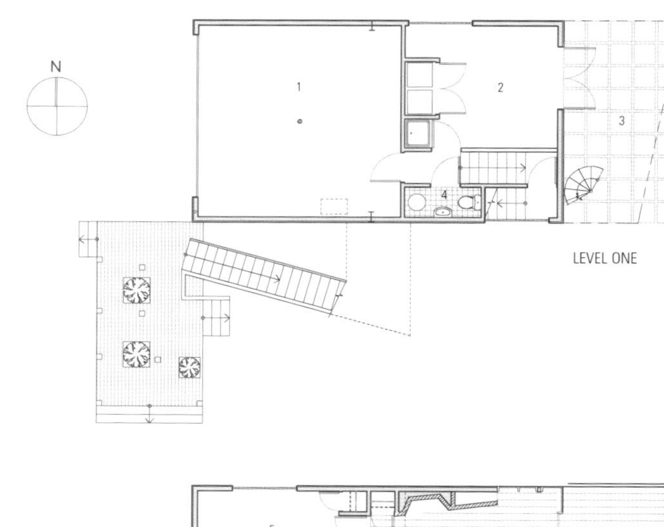

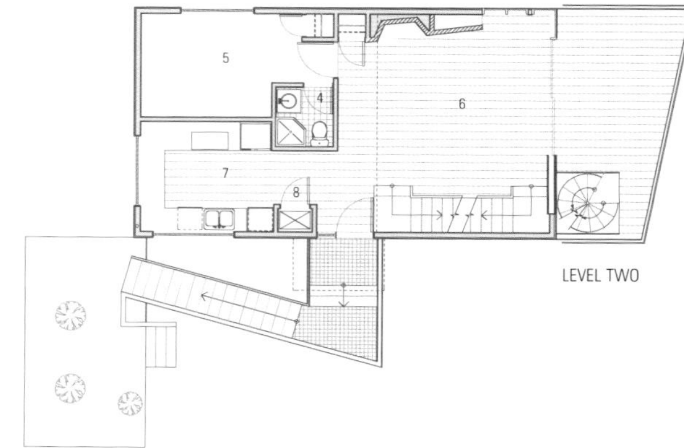

1 garage
2 bedroom
3 patio
4 bathroom
5 study
6 living
7 kitchen
8 pantry
9 hallway
10 main bedroom

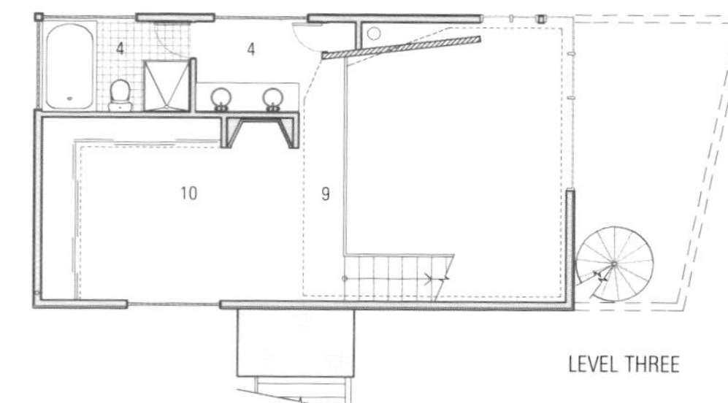

STRIKING STAIRS

From the grade outside, one ascends to the main level on a grand stairway. This wood structure has galvanized metal bar-grate treads that allow you to see the ground below as you walk up. A landing projects over the site and provides a viewing point of the stream, which carved out the building site. The stairs inside the house were made at the owner's place of work. With two treads in each unit, the stairs are made of ½ in (13 mm) aluminum plate.

Various shades of purple set the color scheme for the house – a gray-purple slate encloses the fireplace wall and the media storage area, and the walls are complemented by full length drapes in a darker shade.

WINDOWS TO THE WORLD

Horizontal windows encircle the house, and provide select views of the surrounding landscape. In contrast to these small views, a great wrapping window in the double-height living room provides a dominant diagonal focus for the house, and allows views into the deep woods to the north and east.

A 35-ft (10.6-m) roof deck provides a sweeping view in all directions, and also a space for outdoor entertaining among the tree tops.

ABOVE LEFT
The stairs are made of ½ in (13 mm) plate aluminum. Each pair of treads is one unit, twisted together like the stair and canopy elements outside.

OPPOSITE
With its suspended lighting and slate feature wall like a scenery flat, the double-height living room is reminiscent of a theater. The floor to ceiling drapes draw back to reveal the view into the woods.

Villa Kaleidoscope NAGANO PREFECTURE, JAPAN

Cell Space Architects

Constructed	2005
Home type	Two-story cottage
Structure	Reinforced concrete with timber frame

"With this building, we strived to achieve a sense of connectedness with the environment, amplifying the number of surrounding trees by reflecting them in mirrors in the home's interior. Its occupants are immersed in nature regardless of where they are and in what direction they are looking."

Mutsue Hayakusa

ABOVE RIGHT
Villa K's upper level juts out on all sides beyond its reinforced concrete base. The home's timber exterior perfectly complements its rural setting.

TOP RIGHT
This view of Villa K's galley-style kitchen extends through to the entrance hall where the central tatami room lies to the left. A mirror is used to reflect the landscape, providing a sense of depth to the narrow space. Behind the mirror there is a generously sized storage area.

ABOVE FAR RIGHT
The assemblage of rooms on the upper level, including a living/dining room, kitchen, and west-facing balcony, revolve around a traditional raised tatami room. A floor to ceiling mirror to the left of the picture creates a "virtual reality" – where a forest panorama is visible. The pre-dominantly cream-toned interior complements the changing seasonal colors outside.

Villa Kaleidoscope, also known as Villa K, is a family residence built as an occasional weekend retreat for a couple in their fifties and their daughter.

The aim of the project was to create a home that immersed its occupants in the natural environment through choice of site, extensive glazing, and a clever arrangement of internally placed mirrors.

A honeycomb-like arrangement of living spaces characterizes the upper level, which is cantilevered over the first-floor bedroom and its exterior of reinforced concrete and glass.

MOUNTAIN LOCATION

Located on a sloping, forested block in the popular mountain resort town of Karuizawa in Nagano Prefecture, the villa commands an enviable view looking toward Mt Asama.

Designed to appear as though it is transcending its surrounding stand of trees, the upper level contains all of Villa K's compact, functional living spaces – a living/dining room, generous west-facing balcony, kitchen, and bathroom, all constructed around the traditional raised tatami room. Carefully placed full-length mirrors serve to reflect the surrounding natural landscape, creating virtual perspectives of its forested environment and conveying them into every corner of the home.

Cooling breezes and dappled light from the surrounding trees bring relief from summer temperatures, with a fireplace in the living room a remedy for winter chills. An elongated external chimney echoes the verticality of the surrounding trees.

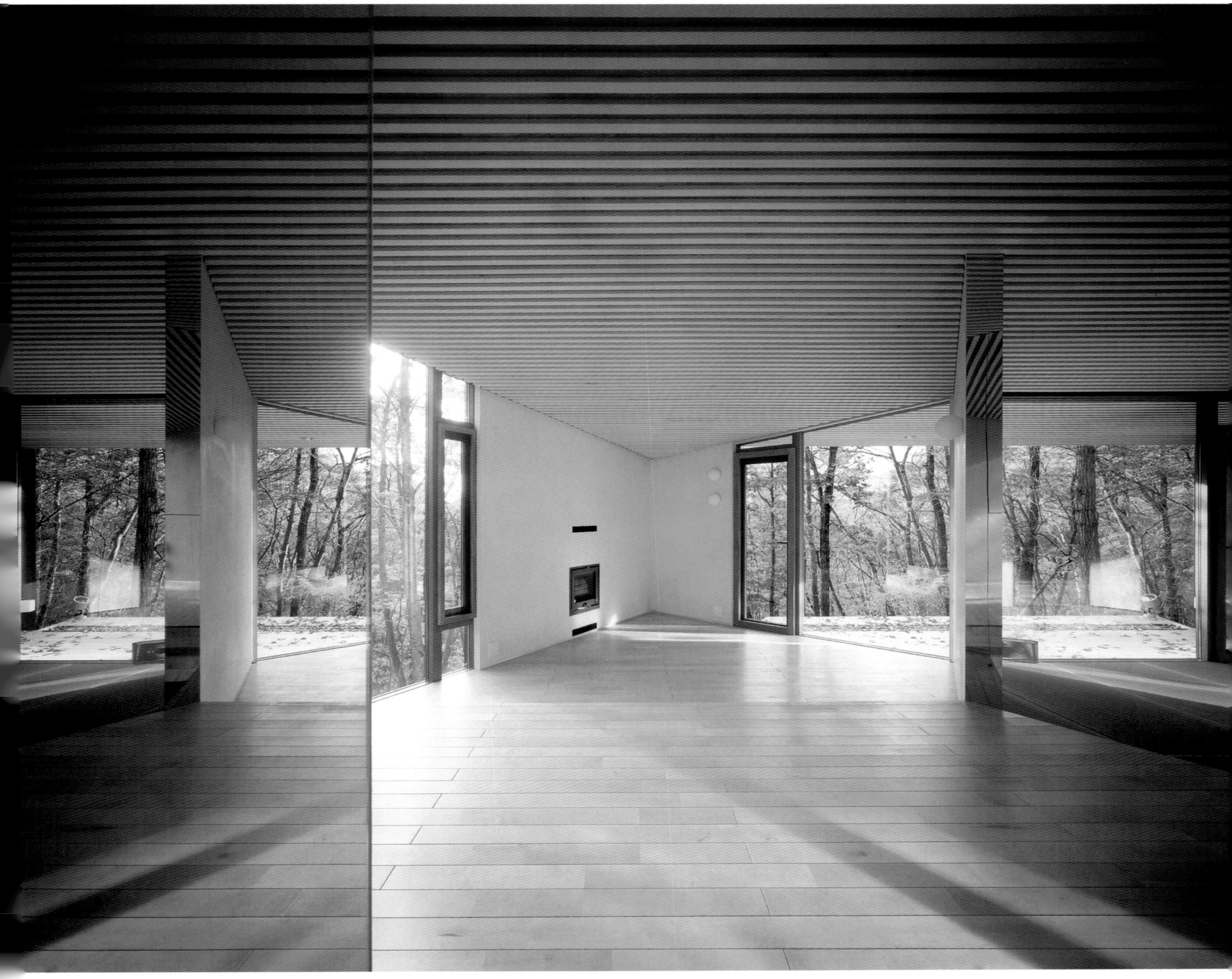

SMALL BUT SPACIOUS

The upper level's timber-clad exterior integrates the structure into its tranquil setting. Japanese cypress is extensively used throughout the interior and the pale, creamy color of its internal walls is a perfect accompaniment to the striking seasonal colors outside.

Although individually the rooms are small, Villa K's open design combines with its extensive glazed areas to give the impression of spaciousness. The mirrored walls add to the sense of openness and provide constantly changing perspectives of the house and its serene setting.

1 living
2 tatami
3 dining
4 kitchen
5 bathroom
6 bedroom

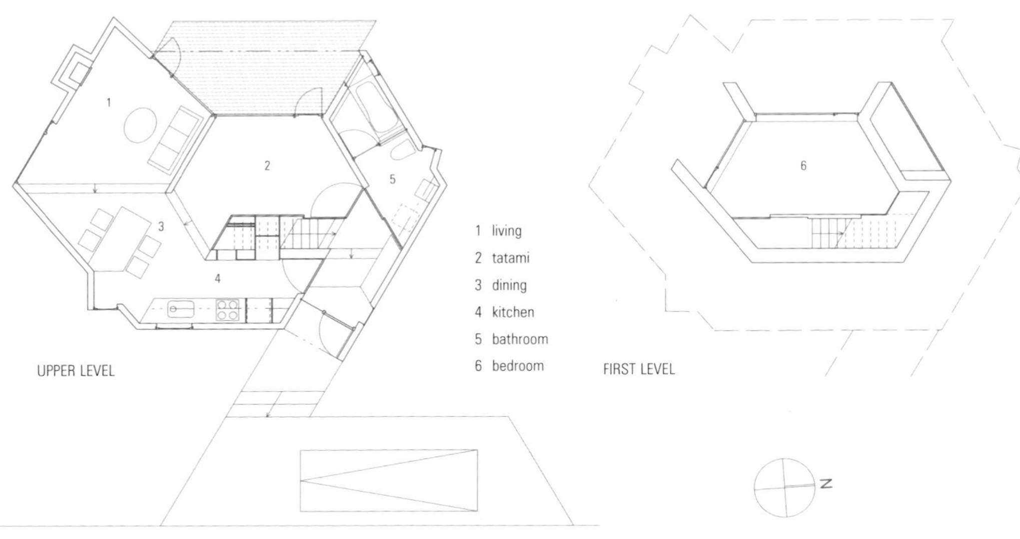

Chapter 13

By the Water

Water is a dynamic life force that evokes feelings of serenity and vitality. A home by the water should capture the views and create a sense of place.

The primary design objective of a home by the water – whether it is a cottage on a sandy beach or a house perched on a cliff overlooking the ocean – is to capture and enhance the view of the water.

A home oriented toward the water has a view to an enormous amount of space. No buildings encroach on the water-side of the property, which creates a sense of tranquillity and seclusion, even if there are neighbors in close proximity.

Working with the client, the architect may strive to "diminish" the structure, making it simple and compact taking nothing away from drama of the site. Alternatively, the architect may experiment with shape, form, and color so the building makes a contrasting statement against the natural backdrop.

WORKING WITH NATURE

There are several challenges involved in designing a home to capture views: the site may be difficult to access and build on; while seeking out the view, the ideal aspect may be compromised; or the home may be exposed to the elements, such as salt-laden winds or tropical storms, defining the structure and many of the finishes in the architect's repertoire. Often too, an orientation to the water can ignore the potential for ancillary views from the sides and back of the house.

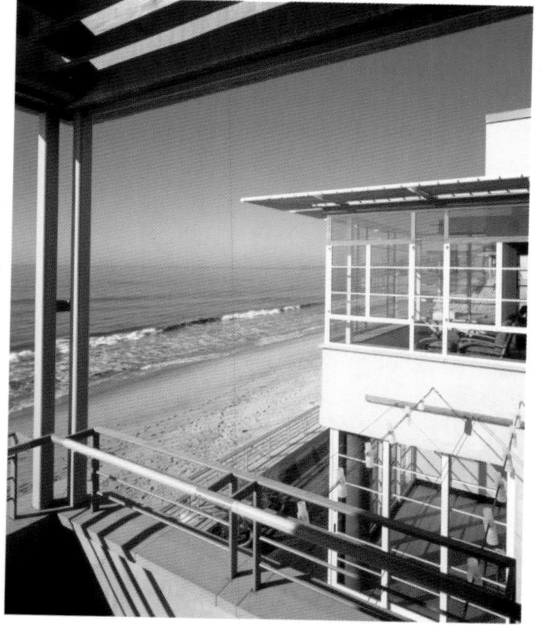

TELLING THE STORY

While maximizing the home's connection to the vista, the metaphorical challenge for the architect is to create variation for the occupants so they are not "saturated" by the views, rather like telling a story: the tale might begin with a strategically located window that captures a glimpse rather than a sweeping panorama; the story continues to unfold in the bathroom which admits an intriguing sliver of the outdoor scene; larger windows in the bedrooms and study further develop the plot, before the denouement in the living and dining areas, where panoramic views are revealed by a wall of glass.

CREATIVE SOLUTIONS

With so much on offer from the water-side, primarily solid walls may be the answer to other unattractive outlooks, where neighboring properties encroach, for example. On a rocky or steeply sloping site, a sensitive solution to the uneven building surface, may be a terraced footprint, rather than a cantilevered structure.

The terraced building fits the site like a waterfall collecting in pools as it spills down the slope. Connected by a series of stairs, each level of the home contains pavilions or a different set of rooms according to function – bedrooms on one level, living and dining on another, entertainment on the next.

OUTSIDE IS INSIDE

A home by the water should invite the outside in. Architectural ingenuity is put to the test to realize the clients dream: floor to ceiling "frameless" glass; a wrap of glass, angled and transparent at its edge; or walls of doors that vanish into a cavity, to create a truly indoor/outdoor space.

Balconies and exterior courtyards along the foreshore function as outdoor living spaces, bringing the occupant one step closer to the water beyond.

ABOVE
Peg Yorkin House,
Moore Ruble Yudell Architects & Planners

TOP RIGHT
Sea Farm House,
Stefan Antoni Olmesdahl Truen Architects

OPPOSITE
Rochman Residence,
Callas Shortridge Architects

Cape Schanck Residence VICTORIA, AUSTRALIA

Denton Corker Marshall

Construction	1997–1999; studio extension 2001–2004
Home type	Two-story holiday residence and separate studio
Structure	Steel frame, concrete floors, cement cladding

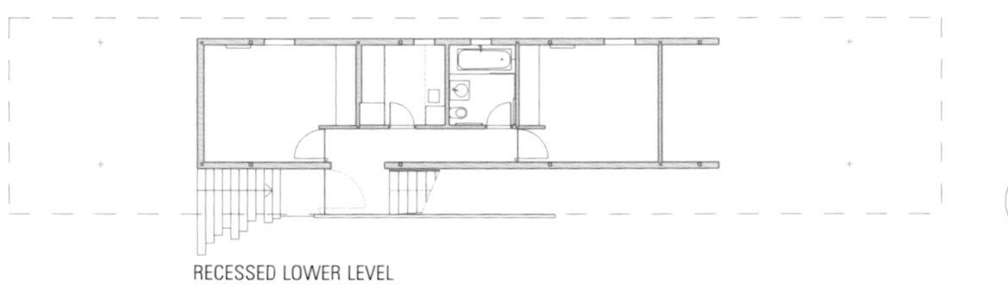

RECESSED LOWER LEVEL

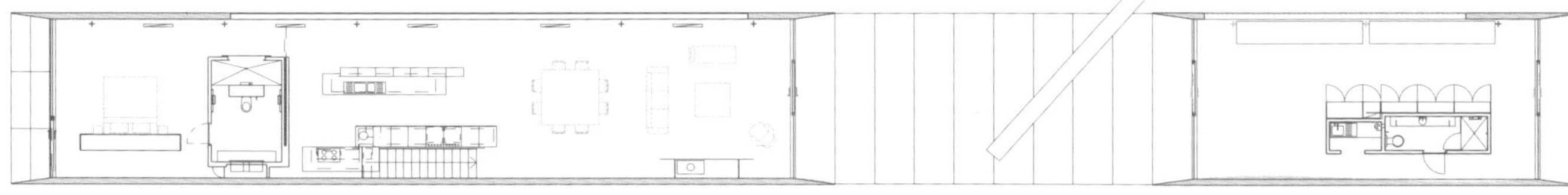

MAIN LIVING LEVEL

STUDIO

"Although we don't design many single houses, it was great fun to work with the owner – an old friend – because as a graphic designer who had worked with us on many projects, there was a close understanding of what might be possible on this difficult site. We worked to achieve the expression of a simple and clear idea of a southern Australian house."

Denton Corker Marshall

A RUGGED RETREAT

The Cape Schanck Residence is located south of Melbourne on the Bass Strait coast. Intended as a holiday home and work retreat for a city-based professional and his family, the site contains a two-story house and a separate studio pavilion. Set on a rather steep site, and encircled by a golf course, the main house is positioned to maximize the stunning panoramic views to the ocean. The form of the house is simple and elegant, but it has a unique and irregular shape. The tubular form is twisted, with the chimney materializing from the wall at a jaunty slant. The cladding is raked and the lower windows are cranked. The overall effect is of something other-worldly, of something that has been carefully placed on the land as a unique and complete entity. It is unquestionably a dramatic form.

The studio is located as an extension to the rear of the main house. This self-contained work space is long, with clear lines defining its shape. A paved courtyard, complete with a long concrete bench, sits between the two structures. To accentuate the unusual shape, the bench has been placed at an angle.

TOUGH MATERIALS FOR TOUGH CONDITIONS

The shores of Bass Strait – the body of water separating mainland Australia from Tasmania – experience intense weather conditions, and the architects kept this in mind when designing the home. The windows facing the sea are kept to a minimum and both buildings are constructed using a steel frame. The principal house sits atop the recessed lower level so that the second story rises above the local native trees. The exterior of the main house and studio is clad with gray cement sheets, while the lower level is colored a dull brown to merge with the coastal ti-tree vegetation. Entrance to this part of the dwelling is via a concrete staircase behind a glass screen.

FREEDOM IN LIVING

On the main level, the central living area looks west, out to dazzling views across the treetops, into the surrounding bushland, and out to the ocean. A fire-place sits in the eastern wall, set behind a stainless steel plate. Freestanding American maple-veneer cubes function as room dividers; these punctuate the length of the house, differentiating the living and dining areas, and the bedrooms.

The main bedroom and ensuite bathroom are hidden from the rest of the house by a concealed sliding door. There are two more bedrooms on the lower level, along with the laundry and a second bathroom.

The studio, which was constructed after the main house was completed, can be entered through sliding glass doors from the courtyard. It contains a comfortable sitting area, a kitchenette, and a bathroom. If necessary, the living space can double as guest accommodation.

ABOVE
The north-facing courtyard is cocooned from blustery winds by the dense and enveloping coastal vegetation. The living area and kitchen are separated from the main bedroom and ensuite by free-standing, timber-veneered boxes.

TOP FAR LEFT
The house sits atop a large sand dune like a twisted gray stick jutting out of the native ti-tree scrub. A slim slot window looks out to the sometimes tempestuous Bass Strait, its narrowness also buffering the occupants from the cold southwesterly winds.

FAR LEFT
The main house and studio are two buildings from the same extruded form, separated into two parts. As well as a spacious workspace area, the studio contains a sitting area, a kitchenette, and a bathroom.

ABOVE
Brightly colored contemporary furniture adds a quirky graphic focal point when placed against the gray, white, and silver backdrop of the living space and courtyard. The stainless steel fireplace on the right provides warmth during the colder months.

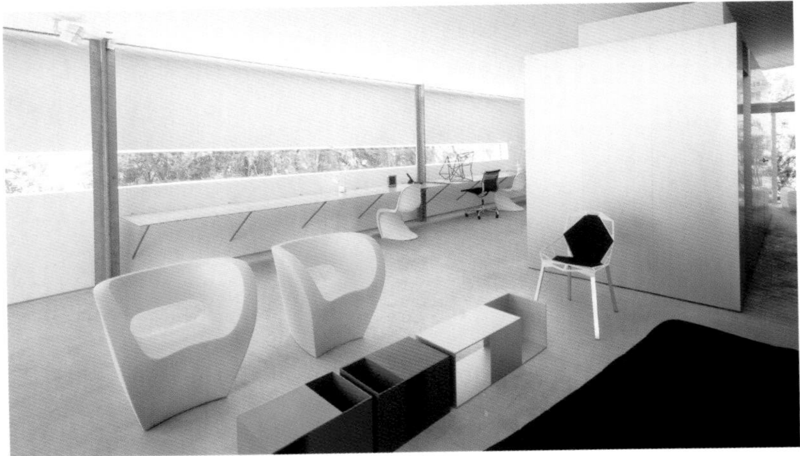

CENTER LEFT
The living, dining, and kitchen areas share the central streamlined volume of the house, with expansive views to the west across the treetops to the ocean. Beyond the kitchen is the ensuite box, which separates this area from the main bedroom. A further two bedrooms are incorporated into the lower level of the house.

LEFT
The bright white minimalist studio space includes a metal-clad bathroom box on the right. A sleek studio bench runs along the far wall, with a narrow slot window set above the bench providing glimpses to outside. The sitting area is used as a meeting place for clients, or it can be transformed into a guest bedroom when required.

ABOVE
The buckled form of the studio, and beyond it the main house, is accentuated by the raked cement cladding that forms the tough gray carapace of the buildings' exteriors. The sunny courtyard separates the two structures and is reached through the large sliding glass doors of both buildings.

Casa Fontana LUGANO, SWITZERLAND

Stanton Williams LONDON

Constructed	2000
Home type	Seven-level villa
Structure	Reinforced concrete

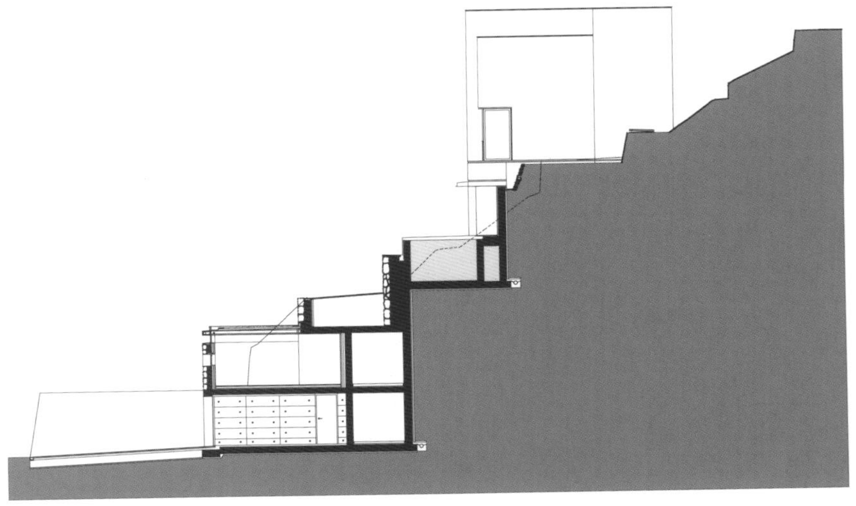

"Casa Fontana rises above the lake of Lugano in a series of terraces, each one boasting a different view. The house was carefully built around the views – exposing, protecting, or framing them, depending on the use of space."

Stanton Williams

TERRACED LAYOUT

Casa Fontana sits on a very steep, terraced slope above the city of Lugano in the Swiss-Italian county of Ticino. The biggest challenge for Stanton Williams was the panoramic view – of the lake, the mountains, and Lugano itself. He wanted his client to be able to escape the view from time to time so that he didn't become desensitized to it; and, at the same time, the architect didn't want the house to be overpowered by the landscape. The end result is a home that interacts with the landscape and the views so that the views are either concealed or revealed, depending on your location.

SEVEN LEVELS

The house is equivalent to a seven-story building and can be accessed from above and below. There are two distinct parts of the house. One part is intimate – set against the side of the mountain, shaded and cool in the summer, with a small fountain contributing to the calm and refreshing atmosphere. The other part is much more extrovert, looking out to the view.

The entry sits on a bridge, with light metal and glass stairs leading to the main bedroom and ensuite on the seventh level. Travertine stairs lead to the first level bedrooms, dining room, and kitchen. Across the bridge is the living room, a double-height space designed to maximize the impact of the 180° views. The room is overlooked by a minstrel gallery, and a slot in the ceiling allows light into the top part of the room.

ABOVE
The steep site was mapped by computer and terraced to support the garage, guest studio, pool, and main house. The safety shelter, a building requirement in Switzerland, was constructed in concrete and bedded deep into the hillside below the studio.

The living room furniture is positioned on a patch of American oak treated with white oil. It is surrounded by travertine, a traditional local material, which extends beyond the glazing, making the observer feel as if they are sitting on a ledge overlooking the lake. There are no balustrades or barriers to obscure the view. The large fireplace reflects traditional rural houses and provides cosy winter warmth.

Downstairs, tucked against the mountain, are the domestic rooms, such as the open-plan dining room and the kitchen, where the challenge was to hide the cooking area while entertaining without blocking the view. This problem was solved by a sliding wall.

The way the house "plays" with the view is apparent in the quiet meditation space at the top of the house. The view is revealed at one end only, surprising the observer with the architect's game of hide and seek.

COOL SHADE

Spaces are characterized by light and shade, and also by temperature. The granite slope is exposed to the full effect of sunlight and heat during the afternoon. The "compressed" space between the house and the rock is shaded during the day and acts as a cooling element overnight. Light is drawn down through this space into the living areas.

The open terraces are cooled with water – a cascade and pool are carved into the rock midway up the site. The mirrored surface of the pool stretches out to the surface of Lake Lugano in the distance.

ABOVE
Drawn along the hillside, the main terrace was carved out to form an infinity lap pool with its own cascade – a cooling sound on a hot day. The pool is lined in locally sourced stone, giving the water a tone reminiscent of Lake Lugano far below.

TOP RIGHT
The concealed glazing and the continuity of travertine dissolves the interior and exterior spaces, allowing uninterrupted panoramic views. One can enjoy the vista in Jasper Morrison's The Thinking Man's Chair, which complements the dramatic views of the lake and mountains.

ABOVE
The concrete structure allows glass to fold around corners without an obviously visible means of support. The main public areas of the house have no thresholds or doors, allowing one space to flow into another.

RIGHT
The dramatic nature of the living room is highlighted by its double height and the blonde wooden floor. A wall to wall ribbon window frames the view of the lake, while a carved light slot animates the envelope of the room. The cantilevered open fireplace is faced in unfinished travertine – a local material that is historically and culturally significant in the area.

OPPOSITE
By "folding" travertine up from the first-level wall to the next level, the architect has highlighted the fact that the house is carved into the mountainside. Key design elements and different spaces are connected by interlocking yet contrasting surfaces of unfinished and polished travertine.

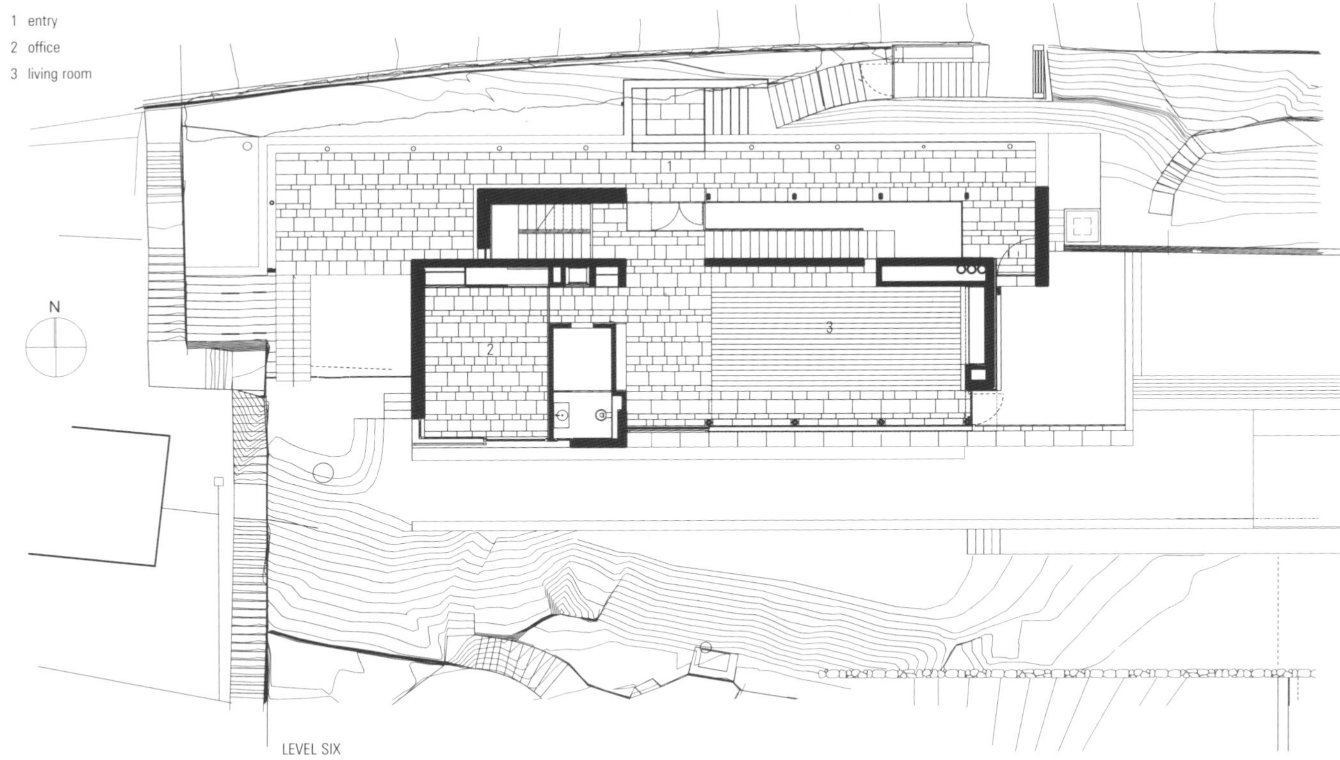

Glass House KYUSHU, JAPAN

Shoei Yoh

Constructed	1991
Home type	Single-story family residence
Structure	Glass curtain walls and steel-frame reinforced concrete, cantilevered from concrete slab

> "I call this house 'Another Glass House Between Sea and Sky' as it unites the built environment with the natural elements. I wanted it to almost disappear into the landscape."
>
> Shoei Yoh

THE PERFECT SITE

After an exhaustive ten-year search for the site of his own dream home, Shoei Yoh purchased the land for his Glass House on a high ocean bluff in the town of Shimomachi, 20 miles (32 km) from Fukuoka on the island of Kyushu in 1983. Yoh, his wife, and two children were to spend the next eight years visiting the site every month, visualizing a dwelling that would one day capture the full splendor of the northern vistas provided by its 450-ft (137-m) vantage point above the Sea of Japan.

CANTILEVERED GLASS BOX

Echoing Farnsworth House, Ludwig Mies van der Rohe's seminal glass box built in 1951, Yoh's straightforward single-story elevated glass and concrete creation is firmly anchored to its precipitous site by two vertical concrete slabs that extend dramatically southwards. Its living area faces north in a cantilevered space enclosed entirely in $\frac{3}{4}$-in (19-mm) glass curtain walls and railings. These are connected with silicone rubber and held in place by suspension rods that run down to the concrete base below in a complex network of tensioning. This results in a statuesque structure that seems to challenge the laws of gravity.

The glass provides an ideal barrier against the elements, integrating the home into its environment and connecting it to the outside world. The use of glass proved an ideal solution to Yoh's philosophy that architecture and nature should always strive to be integrated, never separate from one another.

AT ONE WITH NATURE

The region's heavy mists, harsh rains, and fierce winter winds, which once turned back the armies of Genghis Khan, combine to form wind pressures consistent with that of skyscrapers in typhoon-prone areas. Here, nature is confronted and absorbed by a house that was never intended to provide a sense of safety or security.

RIGHT
Silhouetted in Kyushu's early morning light, the Glass House boldly shows its majestic cantilevered north-facing elevation. The steel tensioning ropes almost seem a decorative afterthought, angling back to the two vertical concrete slabs that anchor the house to the site.

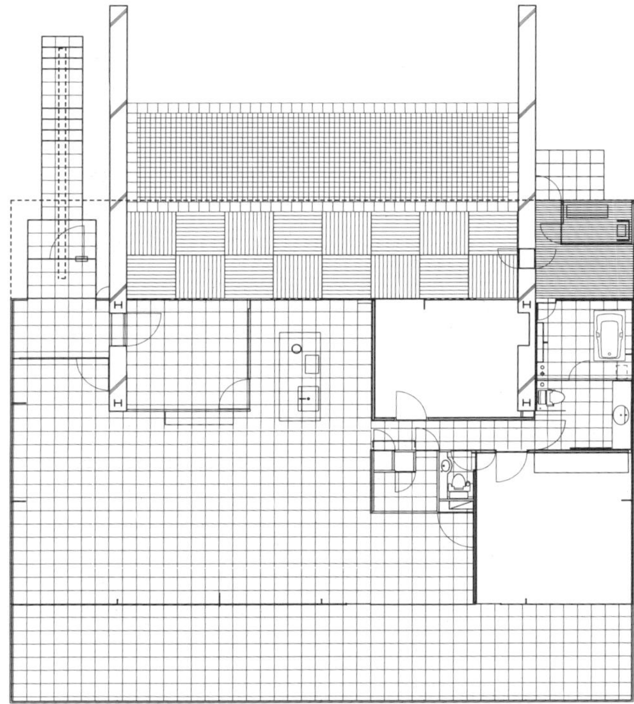

Yoh is very much at ease living in awe of nature and its destructive potential. The aim was to create a structure that would be as close to invisible as possible; one that blended into the landscape and became part of its fabric. Despite incorporating an array of Modernist materials in its construction, the home eventually came to reflect the age-old Japanese principles of transparency and flexibility. Like a traditional tatami room, its central living area has spaces that can be screened off. Inside the house, occupants are encouraged to go barefoot with the installation of heated white marble pavers that extend under the glass to the exterior deck. This also provides a striking sense of visual continuity.

From its inception, the sole determinant in Glass House's design was the extent to which the unfolding drama of nature could be witnessed. Its celebration of the struggle between humankind and nature led the architect to a refreshingly unorthodox use of transparent materials, resulting in a vulnerability that would not exist if he had designed the house for a client rather than for himself.

ABOVE LEFT
The glass curtain wall wraps itself around the house, providing 270° views of the Sea of Japan along with vast swathes of coastline. The wall is the architect's expression of the ancient Japanese notion that architecture and nature must always be in harmony with one another.

ABOVE
From inside, the ocean appears to be an extension of the house itself. The home's unadorned, minimalist interior offers few distractions, encouraging its occupants to focus beyond the humdrum of everyday life.

FOLLOWING PAGES
The architect's initial concept for the site was for a "watchtower," but this was impractical for a family of four. For all its outward sophistication, Glass House seems to embody the sense of isolation and singular purpose one expects from a lighthouse. Despite the setting, the bright lights of Kyushu's largest city, Fukuoka, are just 20 minutes away.

Gloucester House MASSACHUSETTS, USA

Charles Rose Architects

Constructed 2004
Home type Three-level residence
Structure Steel frame over concrete slab

"My clients expressed a desire for a home with expansive water views and abundant natural light. At the same time they wanted a house that would offer a protected landscape on the unexposed side of the home. As well as a place to get away to, the owners wanted the home to be appropriate for entertaining. The views, the pool, and the soaring, open plan living spaces all contribute to this."
Charles Rose

ABOVE
In a house that possesses two very distinct focal points, this view of the southern facade gives no hint of the grandeur of the views. Windows and internal partitions have been carefully placed to allow views through the house to the ocean beyond.

TOP RIGHT
The overpowering presence of the lead-coated copper roof is quite dramatic as it extends out over the south-facing elevation, providing early morning and late afternoon shade to upper level spaces. The formality and structure of the pool surround is in stark contrast to the granite foreshore beyond.

The architects' approach to unified concepts that create innovative environments with a focus on open spaces and natural light finds full expression in their design of Gloucester House in Massachusetts.

HISTORIC SETTING

On the outskirts of the historic whaling port of Gloucester, the house is situated above a granite ledge next to the Atlantic Ocean. Its L-shaped floorplan provides expansive ocean views through a wall of windows in the living area. This is made possible by the sail-like quality of its roofline, which responds in scale to the ocean and the craggy rock formations of the coast.

Two environments have been created by the home's distinctive shape. While the ocean's crenellated, granite foreshore graces its northern and western boundaries, softened by a selective planting of indigenous shrubs, this is juxtaposed on the property's southern boundary to a rather traditional expanse of lawn facing the street. The lawn is ringed by a planting of mature shrubs and small trees, which find shelter from salt spray and damaging ocean breezes in the embrace of a home that is in perfect union with its surroundings.

NEW FOOTPRINT OVER OLD FOOTPRINT

Technically a renovation, the 5,000-sq-ft- (464.5-sq-m-) dwelling was constructed over the footprint of an old, dilapidated bungalow, and burrowed into its sloping site with a scaled-down southern elevation presenting a modest, restrained view to the street.

Built over three levels, the uppermost level has a number of rooms that flow into one another creating a continuous space that opens onto the north- and west-facing balconies.

While the kitchen is an integral part of the surrounding space, it can be contained by closing off four sliding steel and glass doors.

NAUTICAL TOUCH

In catering to the client's desire for extensive water views, the sweeping roofline allows for the massive expanse of glass, which gives the ocean a palpable immediacy akin to being on the deck of a large boat. Lead-coated copper roofing and siding provide protection from the corrosive effects of the sea, while stainless steel railing and balustrade add to the home's nautical feel, as well as providing a low maintenance alternative to timber for the decking surrounds.

The home's patios, terraces, and walkways are made from a green-toned granite streaked with quartz, which ties in esthetically with the granite foundation upon which the home is built.

The architects' commitment to houses that have a sculptural quality is shown to full effect as Gloucester House rises from its surroundings beneath its spectacularly jagged, pitched roof. The home won the 2005 Boston Society of Architects Design Honor Award.

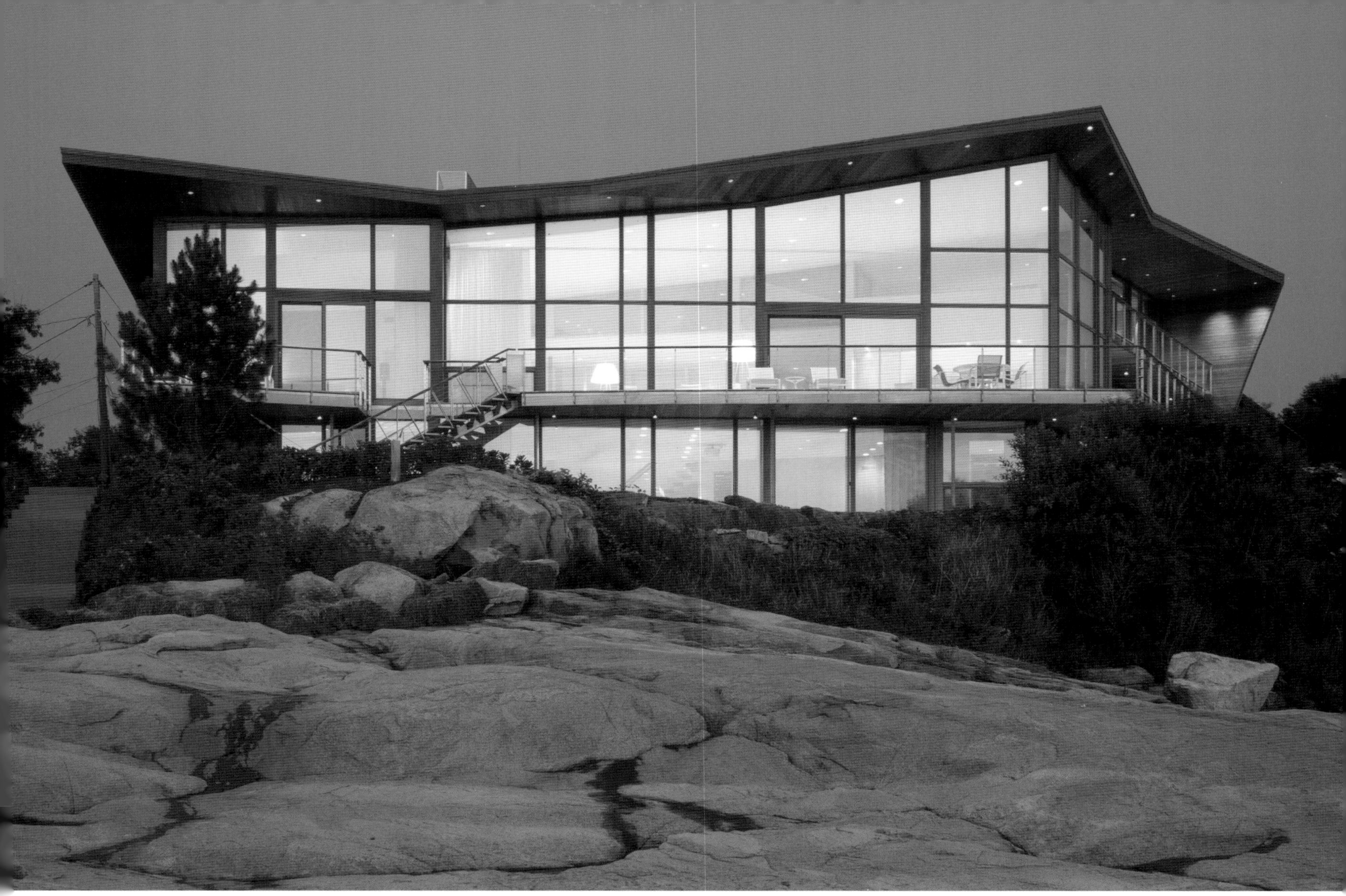

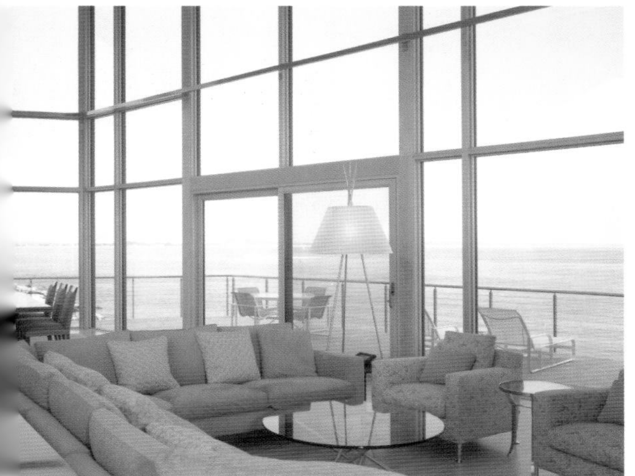

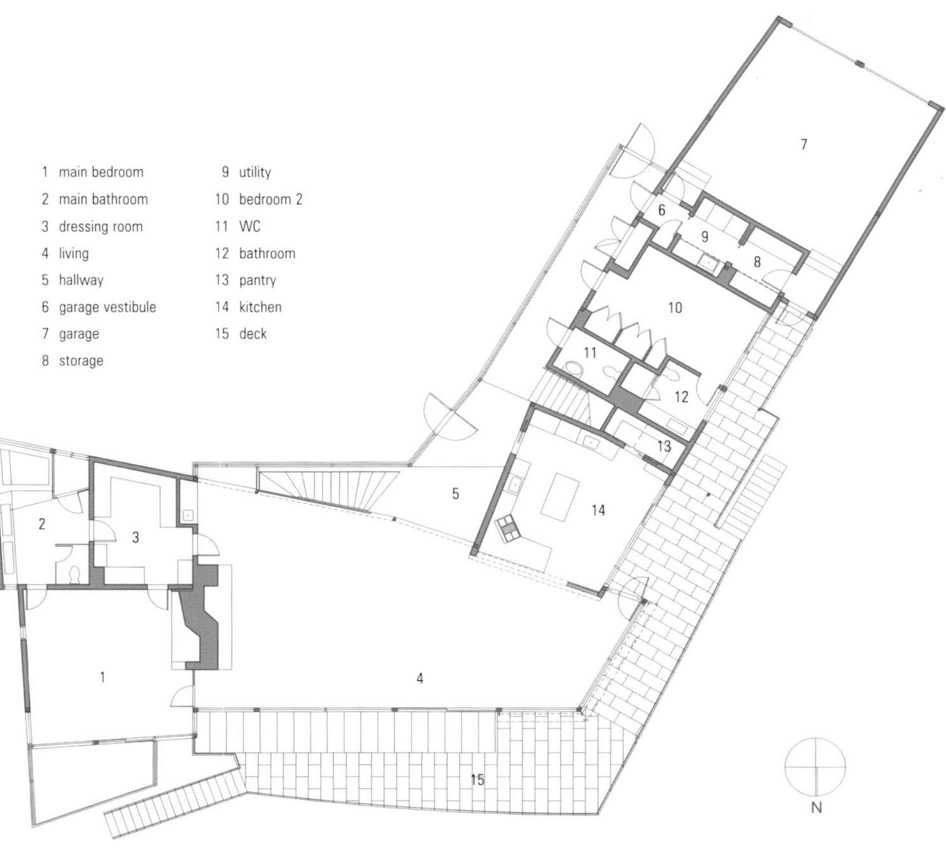

ABOVE
The panorama of the surrounding seascape is pulled in and fully exploited beneath this soaring wall of glass. Triple-glazed to minimize heat loss, the panes are set within an almost abstract framework of mahogany, bringing a much-needed sense of warmth and texture.

TOP
Gloucester House seems to raise a defiant wall of glass, where the proximity and relationship of the house to the ocean is obvious. Granite boulders fall away to an eroded shoreline below, presenting an intriguing mix of strength and fragility.

1 main bedroom
2 main bathroom
3 dressing room
4 living
5 hallway
6 garage vestibule
7 garage
8 storage
9 utility
10 bedroom 2
11 WC
12 bathroom
13 pantry
14 kitchen
15 deck

MAIN LIVING LEVEL

Island House ONTARIO, CANADA

Shim-Sutcliffe Architects

Constructed	2001
Home type	Single family summer house
Structure	Wood frame, steel columns and beams with concrete retaining walls

"Our agricultural landscapes are a diminishing resource. This new building project is inserted into a clover meadow and asserts a unified and integrated relationship between building and its pastoral agrarian landscape. Simultaneously, the metaphor of island and water is created and extended though one's physical experience from the site to water's edge."

Brigitte Shim and Howard Sutcliffe

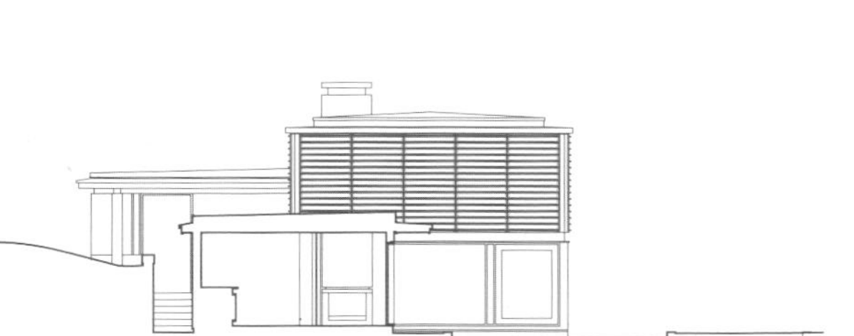

ABOVE
The lantern-like living room is visible above the wildflower-studded roof of Island House. The concrete walls and natural textures of this summer house complement the clover meadow that shrouds it from the road.

RIGHT
Both the living room on the left and the study beyond look out to the limpid reflection pool. Plantings of bulrushes, grasses, and water lilies add detail to the sweeping canvas of meadow.

ROOFTOP MEADOWS

Built on a pleasant pastoral island in the majestic St Lawrence River, this summer home both engages the existing landscape and creates its very own distinctive perspective. The house is approached from a quiet rural road and presents itself as a long low concrete wall set into the gentle slope that leads down to the river. Both of the low roofs have been planted with wildflowers and essentially become their own abstract meadows. Above these flat roofs, the lantern-like living room is clearly visible.

From the road the entry to the house is arrived at by walking along a path set between two gentle berms. These clover-covered berms serve two important functions – they obscure the road from the house, and they establish a seamless continuity with the meadow and the adjacent farmland.

SIMPLICITY THE KEY

The simple plan of this house spatially interlocks two linear flat-roofed bars around a cubic living room pavilion. Located six steps down from the entry and to the west side of the living room are the dining room and kitchen. The kitchen leads on to a west-facing wooden deck, which has been set into the gravel dry garden.

On the east side of the entry is the rectangular bar containing the study, the main bedroom, and the main bathroom. The block that contains the bathroom and dressing area forms a freestanding island, sitting adjacent to an exterior deck that overlooks the river. For visual continuity, the floor of the bathroom, dressing area, and external deck are constructed from the same timber. The thick north wall contains storage areas, stairs down to the basement level, and a water closet.

MAINTAINING THE PASTORAL

Ever mindful of the decreasing areas of natural vegetation, the architects ensured that the whole home maintained an air of unity and integration with the surrounding environment.

From the entry, one can look down through the living room pavilion – sitting like an island in a large tranquil reflection pool – across a meadow to the river beyond. The small rectangular island within the reflection pool has been planted with bulrushes. A freestanding fireplace acts as a pivot point between the living, dining, and entry areas.

The landscape and planting plan has attempted to reinforce both the meadow and the pastoral quality of the island in a more geometric form. Ornamental grasses have been set against natural field grasses, while large swathes of colorful wildflowers and clover form the bucolic palette, with water lilies and bulrushes acting as the detail elements. An attractive crushed limestone dry garden contains slabs of limestone that were removed during the excavation.

1 entrance
2 living
3 dining
4 kitchen
5 outdoor deck
6 dry garden
7 winter garden
8 study
9 bedroom
10 outdoor deck

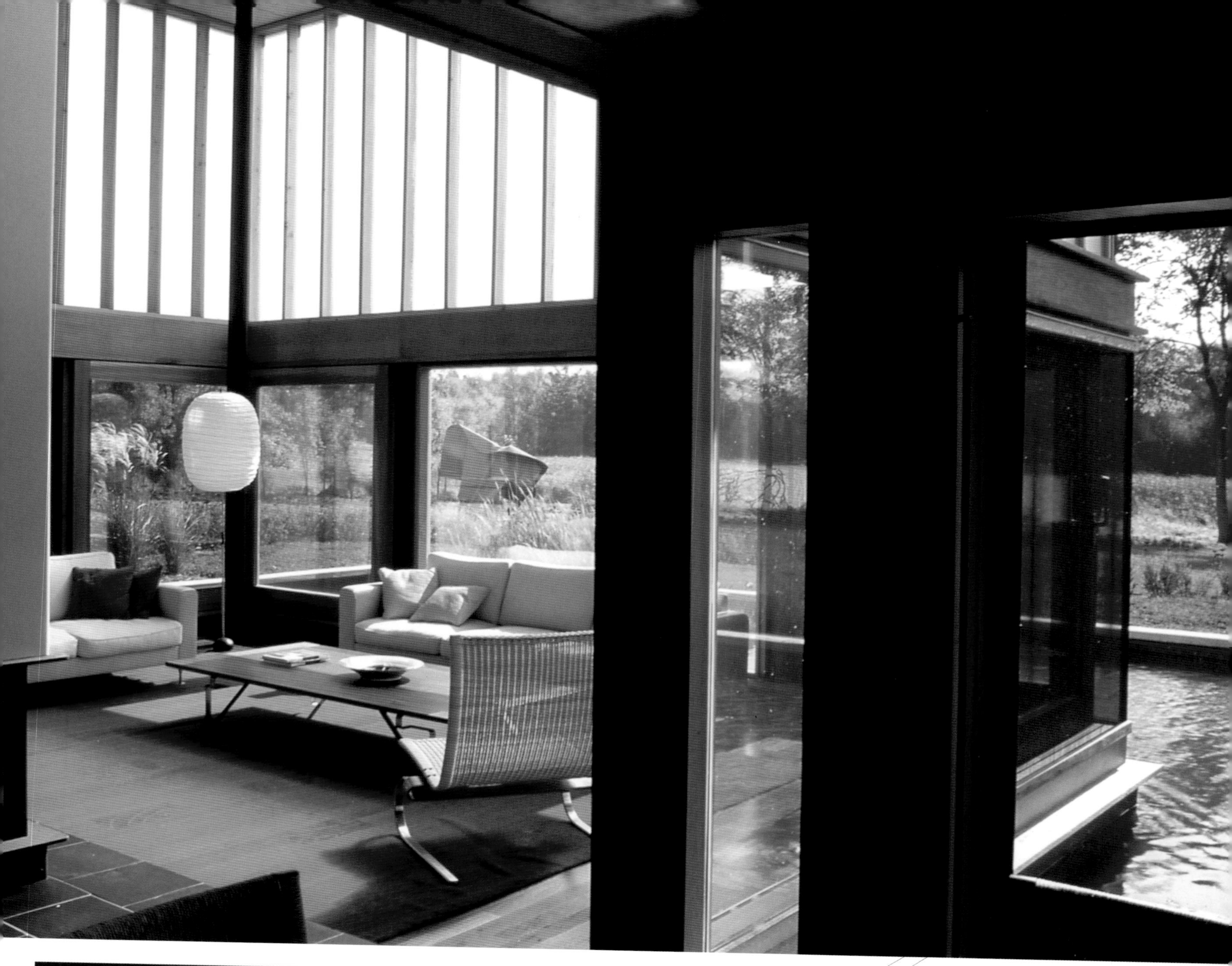

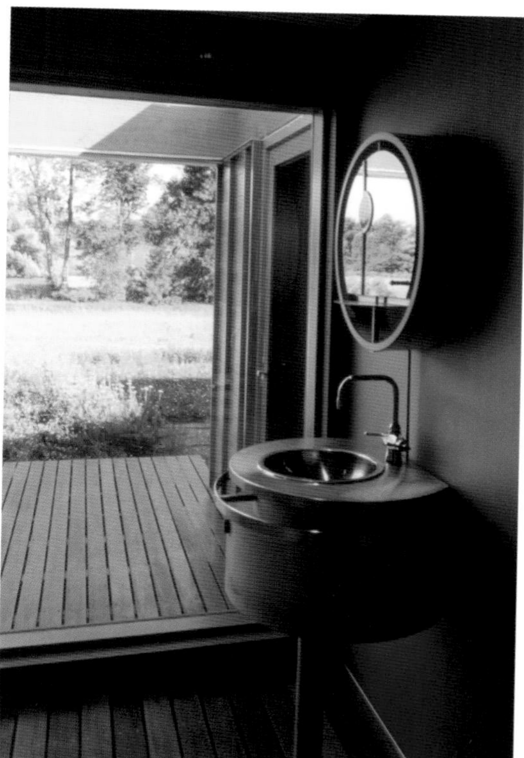

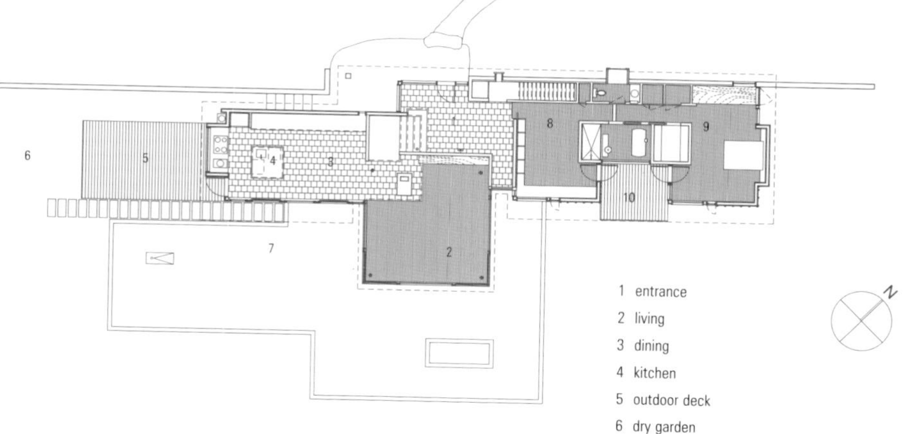

LEFT
A custom-built vanity and medicine cabinet add rustic charm to the home. The bathroom enjoys views across the verdant pastureland.

ABOVE
The view from the light-filled living room across the meadow is punctuated by the calming reflection pool and a Robert Murray sculpture beyond.

James-Robertson House SYDNEY, AUSTRALIA

Casey Brown Architecture

Constructed 2003
House type Two-pavilion family home
Structure Glass, steel, copper, timber, and stone

"The more you look at nature, the more intriguing is the relationship with the man-made. I prefer to look at shells, at rock overhangs, and the more that I see, the more I am attracted to an organic vision of form and to creating in harmony with the natural world."

Robert Brown

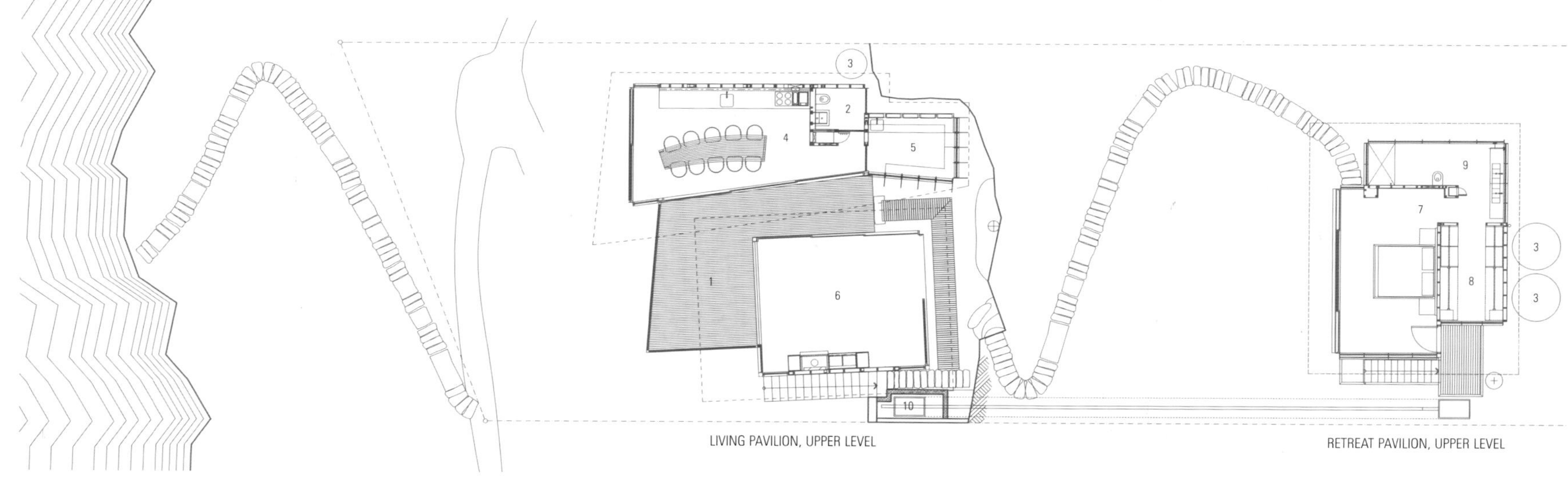

1 deck
2 bathroom
3 water tanks
4 kitchen/dining
5 pantry
6 living
7 main bedroom
8 walk-in wardrobe
9 ensuite
10 inclinator

ABOVE
The glass doors between the dining room and the deck can be folded back in warm weather, so that the indoor and outdoor spaces become one. Trees hug the building, but the house is high enough to overlook the treetops to the views of Pittwater beyond.

RIGHT
A view to the northeast, toward Palm Beach lighthouse at the end of the isthmus. The double-height living room has louvered windows that control the air flow through the house. An inclinator connects the main part of the house with the owners' retreat pavilion up the hill.

IDYLLIC LOCATION

This house is situated on a steep 45° slope on the western side of Pittwater, less than one hour's drive from the Sydney CBD. National park surrounds the site, and the views are unparalleled – sweeping from Pittwater and Palm Beach to the mouth of the Hawkesbury River where it enters the Pacific.

Mackerel Beach is a small community linked to the mainland by the ferry that travels to and from Palm Beach. After the boat trip, reaching the house involves a walk across the beach and a climb up the hill. Apart from dealing with the challenges of the site itself, the architect was briefed to design a home that kept guest accommodation separate from the living areas. In addition, a separate pavilion was designed to be the main bedroom hideaway.

IN HARMONY WITH THE LANDSCAPE

Because the natural environment is so spectacular, the architect designed the house to merge with the landscape. Glass, steel, and copper pavilions constitute the makeup of the dwelling. A large sandstone retaining wall was excavated from the site and used to anchor the lower structure. Not only is the natural sandstone a beautiful local material, it also stabilizes the slope.

Dark colors were chosen to help the house harmonize with its bushland surroundings. The form of the house, and colors complementing the native vegetation, have the effect of reducing the visual impact of the building; you can hardly see the house from the water.

ABOVE
The sandstone base, hewn from the site, anchors the house to the boulder-strewn slope. The main bedroom sits further up the hill in a separate pavilion, above the living areas.

ABOVE RIGHT
Essentially, the frame of the house was designed to be taut and lightweight. The roofs seem to float over each other like the sails of a yacht or the wings of a bi-plane.

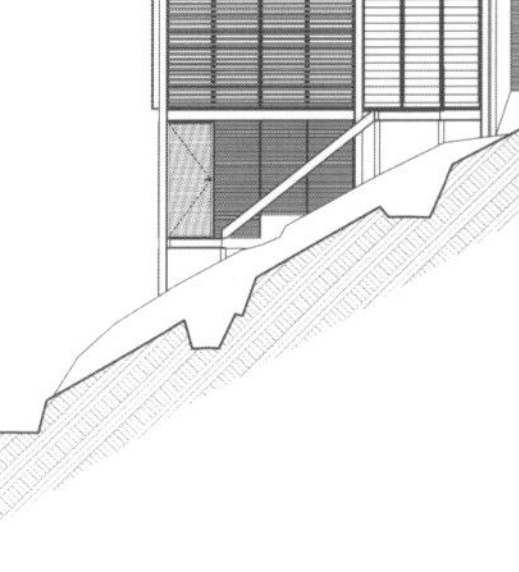

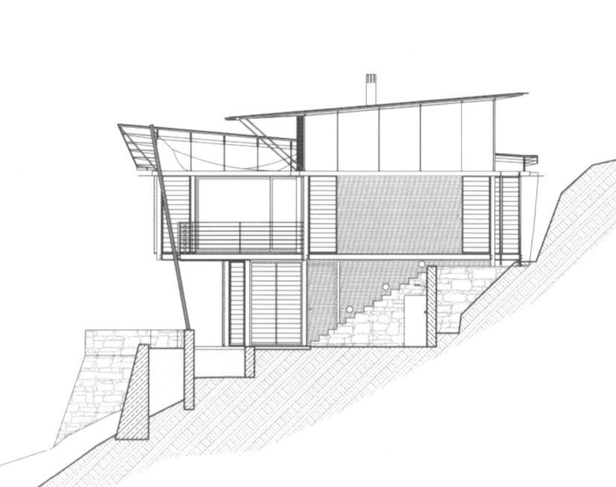

EXPERIENCING THE HOUSE

The lower level of the living pavilion contains a study, guest bedroom, and wine cellar. Above this is the double-height main pavilion, which contains the living areas. The floor-to-ceiling glass allows uninterrupted views of the natural surroundings. Directly outside the living area, the cliff face features a large Port Jackson fig tree, its distorted roots like a natural artwork. A timber boardwalk leads past this feature to the sandstone steps and the inclinator.

Copper's innate shine and the beautiful changes it undergoes over time made it the logical choice for the exterior walls and the roof. Its rich color also helps the home to be at one with its surroundings.

ADAPTING TO THE CLIMATE

The main exterior deck links the kitchen and dining area with the living area. When the glass doors are opened out, the inside extends to the outside. As the house is located in a mild sub-tropical climate, it was essential that the owners be able to use the outdoor space all year round. Interlocking layers of copper and steel hoods form the cover for this part of the house.

ABOVE
The house enjoys an intimate view of Mackerel Beach as well as grander ones such as those of Palm Beach to the northeast, and the Central Coast in the distance.

LEFT
The living room's stone and stainless steel mesh unit houses the entertainment system, as well as the floating fireplace. The floor is blackbutt.

ABOVE
View from the guest bedroom to the bathroom and study. The full-height, opaque, sliding glass walls and louvered exterior admit plenty of natural light but also provide these areas with privacy.

PERFECTLY PRIVATE

An inclinator connects the living pavilion with the retreat pavilion. Otherwise it's a steep climb, as this part of the house sits some 165 ft (50 m) up the incline. This separate building affords the owners the ultimate in private space.

Although the windows and glazed walls are large, generous overhangs and unusually shaped roof planes provide privacy from prying eyes and protection from the elements, while at the same time allowing light and warmth to enter.

SUSTAINABLE LIVING

A waste-treatment system and water-storage tanks that collect rainwater for drinking are featured. The design also allows the free flow of breezes through the pavilions, helping them to stay cool in hot weather. Steel hoods, which offer protection from heavy rain, conceal the mechanical blinds and outdoor lights. Minimal energy is used for heating – there is an open fireplace, and also radiant heating foils in the ceiling.

As well as being esthetically pleasing, the materials used in the construction – steel, glass, copper, timber, and stone – help keep the maintenance to a minimum. This is a must in an area that is subject to strong summer sun and salt-laden wind.

MATERIAL MATTERS

A major consideration in building this house was getting materials to the site, as there is no road access. Most materials had to be brought to the site by boat; some items even had to be brought in by helicopter.

Because of its resistance to bushfires and termites, steel was chosen as the major construction material. Durable corrugated copper sheets were used for the roof and walls. The copper will weather to a rich red-brown color, reminiscent of the iron colors in the Hawkesbury sandstone. The decks are teak, and the internal floors are laid with recycled blackbutt, another homage to the Australian bush.

The building fuses state-of-the-art computer design with tried-and-true traditional building techniques.

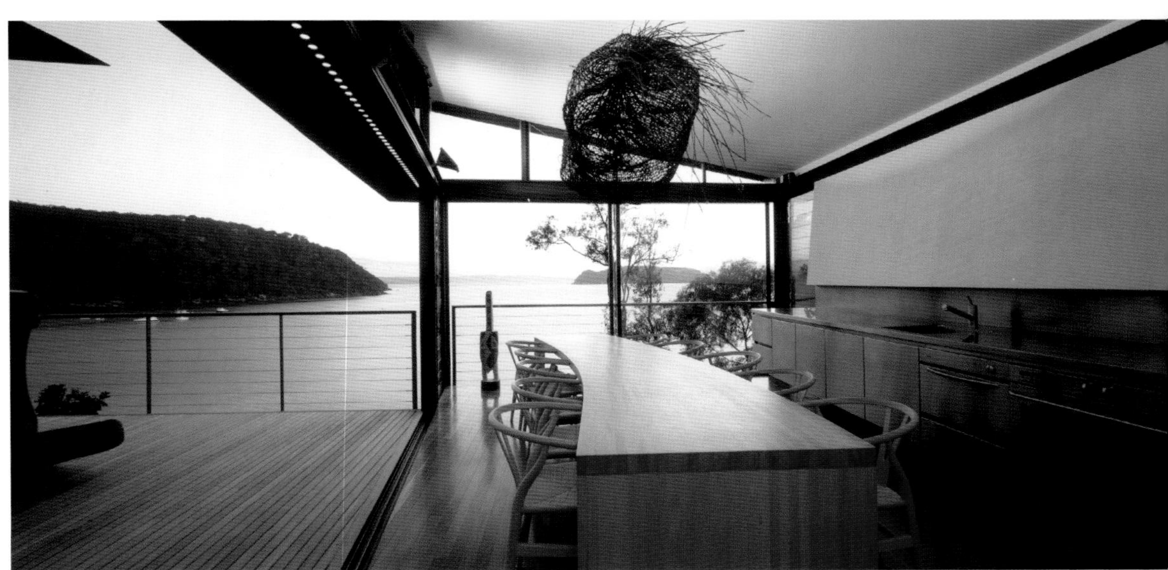

INVITING INTERIORS

To enhance the feeling of openness, the interior spaces were customized, just like the fittings on a boat. Because access to shops is difficult, adequate food storage facilities were necessary and a modern adaptation of the outback meat safe was custom-made for the home. Complete with louvered screens, the pantry adds charm as well as functionality.

THE LONG WEEKEND

The James-Robertson House is the owners' home, not just a holiday house. The flexibility provided by modern communications makes it possible to live almost anywhere. For some, the weekender, in a desirable seaside location, has become the permanent experience.

LEFT
A timber boardwalk links the living area with sandstone steps and the inclinator. The floodlit aerial roots of the Port Jackson fig tree form a natural artwork against the rock face.

ABOVE
The landscape, with its stunning views of Pittwater and Broken Bay, was the defining factor for this house. Even the table, designed by Caroline Casey, reflects the crescent curve of Mackerel Beach.

Killcare House KILLCARE, AUSTRALIA

buzacottwebber

Constructed	2003
Home type	Three-level home with flat below
Structure	Traditional timber frame, masonry clad, steel-frame roof, floor, and deck; timber, steel, aluminum

"What makes this house special is the large, dramatic, cool, light-filled living areas which allow views out in all directions. This space feels different from the typical suburban house and its openness gives this house its contemporary beach house feel."

Stephen Buzacott

TOP
From the beach the house is seen in its bush context, perched high on the ridge between the ocean and Brisbane Water. The original dark brick has been bagged with a colored render which sets off the bush tones; the off-white roof dissolves the roof line in the sky.

TOP RIGHT
The large, calm volume of the living area, featuring its raked ceiling, provides a sense of spaciousness, and the glazed eastern wall allows full contact with the ocean view. A double-sided steel fireplace sitting on a stone tiled plinth mediates the space and delineates the dining area. This calming space is large enough to hold a crowd yet intimate enough for smaller groups to sit and converse.

RIGHT
This beautiful view due east to the sheltered northern end of Putty Beach, Bouddi National Park, and the Pacific Ocean sweeps south along to Killcare Beach and to the headlands of northern Sydney as far as Manly.

OUT WITH THE OLD, IN WITH THE NEW

This house was designed for a professional couple (lawyer and production designer) with no children, who have a wide circle of friends and love entertaining. The house was also designed for holiday letting.

Situated on a high, steep ridge overlooking the Pacific Ocean, the house was an existing three-level masonry veneer 1970s project house with dark klinker brick and timberwork painted mission brown. The original house had fantastic views of the beach and down the coast to Sydney's Palm Beach and Manly, but was in a very dilapidated condition due to poor construction and maintenance, and required extensive repairs. The house was poorly laid out with small pokey rooms, giving little access to the exterior or the views beyond.

MAXIMIZING THE OUTLOOK

A large building that could not be replicated under prevailing design rules, the house was largely rebuilt within the existing envelope with strategic changes to allow the full potential of the view to be revealed. A major element of the redesign is a dramatic raking steel-framed structure that supports the three new deck levels and the redesigned glazed eastern facade. The structure is supported on cantilevered beams with the rake allowing for three decks, widening out to the main upper deck. The whole house has been oxide color-rendered and re-roofed. The pool area has also been completely redesigned with a smaller pool built within an existing pool and surrounded by new timber decks accessed from a veranda off the kitchen.

CONTEMPORARY LIVING

The house is entered from the existing drive court directly off the street via a new timber pergola. Inside the gate a smaller external vestibule space opens to the tall entry space at the half level between the two upper floors. This leads to an open steel and timber staircase that goes up to the living floor and down to the bedroom floor. The living area has been totally opened up as one large double-height space, overlooking the dramatic eastern view and, via the open kitchen, the pool terrace to the west. The kitchen windows look south to Pittwater and the Barrenjoey headland. A new loft/study space above the existing garage overlooks the living areas. A bathroom and laundry complete this level.

The middle floor was completely redesigned to provide four large bedrooms, three opening to the view. The main bedroom has a bathroom and walk-in wardrobe, and a new WC and bathroom complete this floor. The lower floor, previously unusable, has been designed as a self-contained flat with separate access.

BRINGING IN THE TWENTY-FIRST CENTURY

This project is an example of how to sympathetically renovate a mid-twentieth-century project home which had reasonably good bones but lacked the imagination for contemporary living. The innovative revision of internal spaces to minimize circulation and wasted space, while linking the new spaces with the exterior in a more direct manner, allows the outside to become part of the decoration.

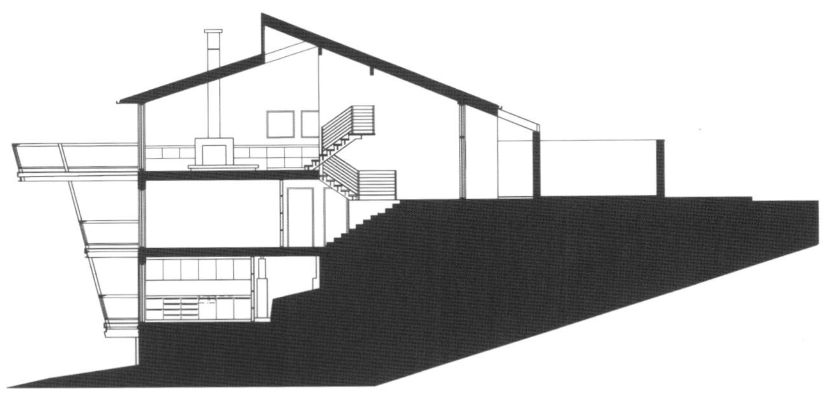

Lo House SINGAPORE

SCDA Architects

Constructed	2006
Home type	Three-level family home including basement
Structure	Timber, aluminum, granite, glass, and plaster

"'Sentosa' means 'tranquility' in the Malay language, and this house was designed and built with this in mind. Set in an exclusive residential part of Singapore, the house is a sanctuary against the hustle and bustle of the real world."

Chan Soo Khian

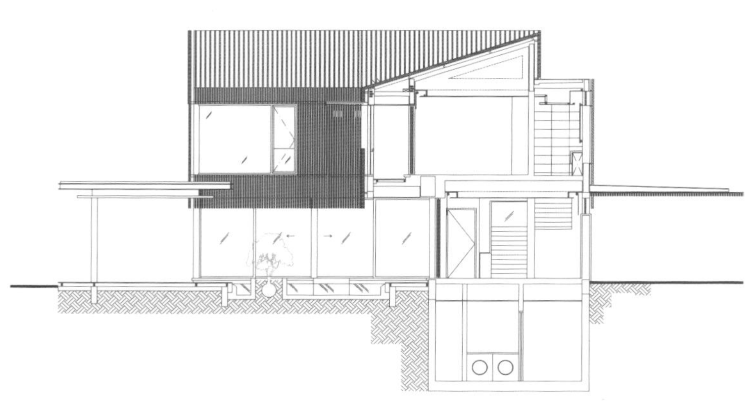

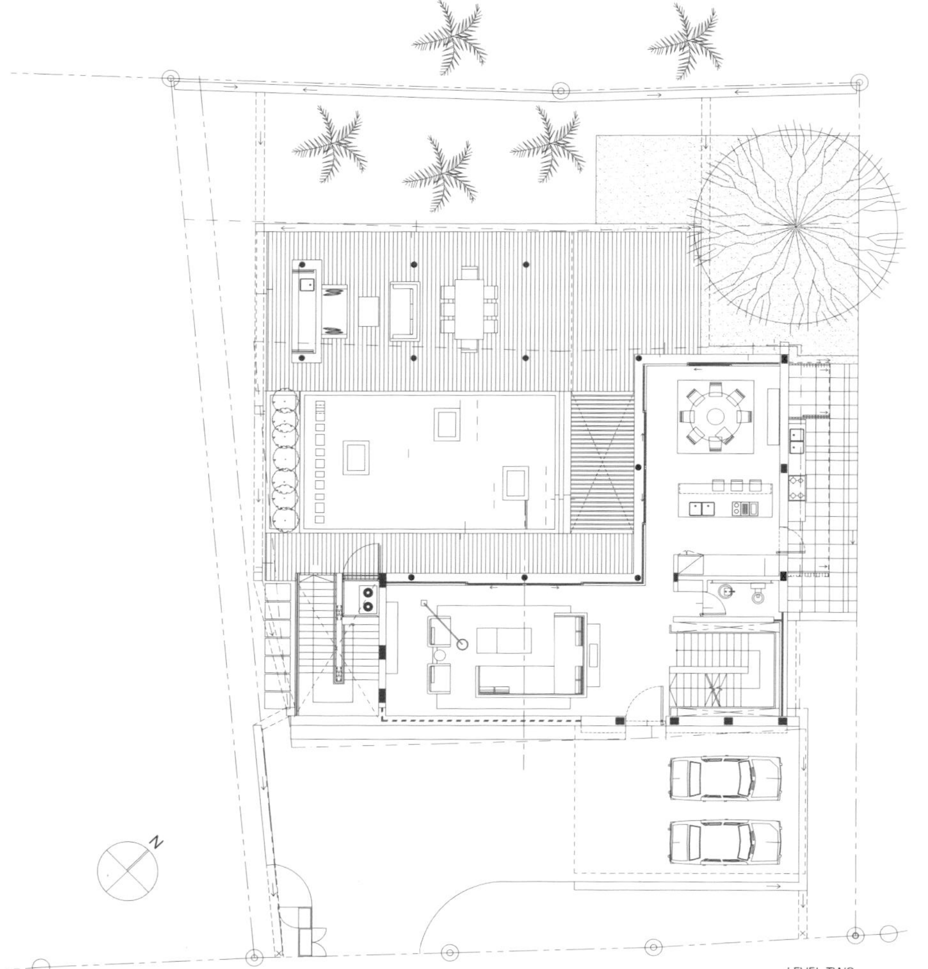

LEVEL TWO

SEASIDE LIVING

Singapore is a small island nation where space has always been at a premium. Many people live in apartments in the city, but there are also areas with lush gardens and glorious ocean views. This particular plot is part of a large tract of reclaimed land marketed as Sentosa Cove, only five minutes from the central business district. Sentosa is an elite resort island, most of which is covered with rainforest and teeming with wildlife. It has a villa community with marinas, golf courses, and a clubhouse.

Set in this beautiful location, the Lo House was designed using an L-shaped plan as the grid. The plan encompasses a carefully landscaped garden, which incorporates a peaceful reflection pool and an outdoor pavilion with views of the ocean.

ABOVE
This simple cantilevered carport, which doubles as a canopy over the entry area, has been carefully detailed using quality timber.

SEPARATING SPACES

The built form emphasizes the timber floor on the second level. It appears to float over the solid enclosure of the basement, and the whole effect provides a rather dramatic backdrop for the interior spaces that open out to the stunning ocean view.

A rough stone wall leads from the basement to the second level, and also separates the living areas from the road. On this side of the room the wall is topped by a long horizontal glass slit. The second story is lighter, wrapped in a "veil" of vertical timber battens.

The second level was conceived as an open plan, with strategically placed freestanding walls that screen the interior of the home from the road. The courtyard is a focal point, and the eye is automatically drawn there before moving on to the ocean beyond.

The third level of the home has a mono-pitched roof. This level has been interpreted as a kind of box that shelters the private areas of the house while keeping the views accessible, so the windows are openings cut into the facade. On this level there are four bed-rooms, one guest room, and six bathrooms.

SMOOTH TRANSITIONS

The entry and carport, both in the shelter of a huge cantilevered canopy, lead to the living and dining rooms, which are enhanced by the delightful view of the courtyard and pavilion.

ABOVE
In the living room a floor-to-ceiling glass wall allows plenty of natural ventilation and access to the wonderful view.

LEFT
The main staircase features a bright red load-bearing wall that contrasts with the color of the timber steps, the stone, and the pale walls elsewhere.

ABOVE
The main material used in the construction of the house is timber. When coupled with the reflection pool and the tropical plants, this natural material creates a resort-like atmosphere that suits the house's location.

RIGHT
Cooled by sea breezes, the house has been designed as an L-shape so that the courtyard and reflection pool face the ocean. At different times of the day, the pool mirrors sections of both the house and the landscape.

The living room looks out at the view across a tranquil reflection pool surrounded by a timber deck, then through a pavilion toward the sea. There is also a void that overlooks the basement. Adjacent to the kitchen is the dining room, which enjoys the same views.

The staircase is set against a striking bright red wall. This contrasts with the palette of gray and brown that leads to the more private spaces of the bedrooms, the bathrooms, and the basement.

CHOOSING THE RIGHT MATERIALS

The architects chose materials for the Lo House that would bring a genuine unity to the entire structure, and gave a great deal of attention to connecting spaces. The house expresses modern sensibilities but also captures the essence of relaxed seaside living in the tropics.

"The brief was to clad the house in timber. During the day, the house is solid yet elegant, but in the evening its interior is expressed behind the timber screens both at the front and rear ends. This creates an openness and a lightness of expression."

Malibu House CALIFORNIA, USA

Kanner Architects

Constructed	2004
Home type	One-story family home
Structure	Concrete, plaster, glass, and wood (teak, mahogany, and vertical-grain Douglas fir)

"The project was supremely rewarding because it was a second chance of sorts. Kanner Architects had designed the house in the 1990s after the original home was destroyed by fire. A new owner with more money and bigger plans bought the project in 2002 and invited Kanner to come back and completely make it over. Square footage remained constant, but walls came down and every surface was updated and upgraded. The resulting house was closer to what the original might have been if not for budget constraints."

Kanner Architects

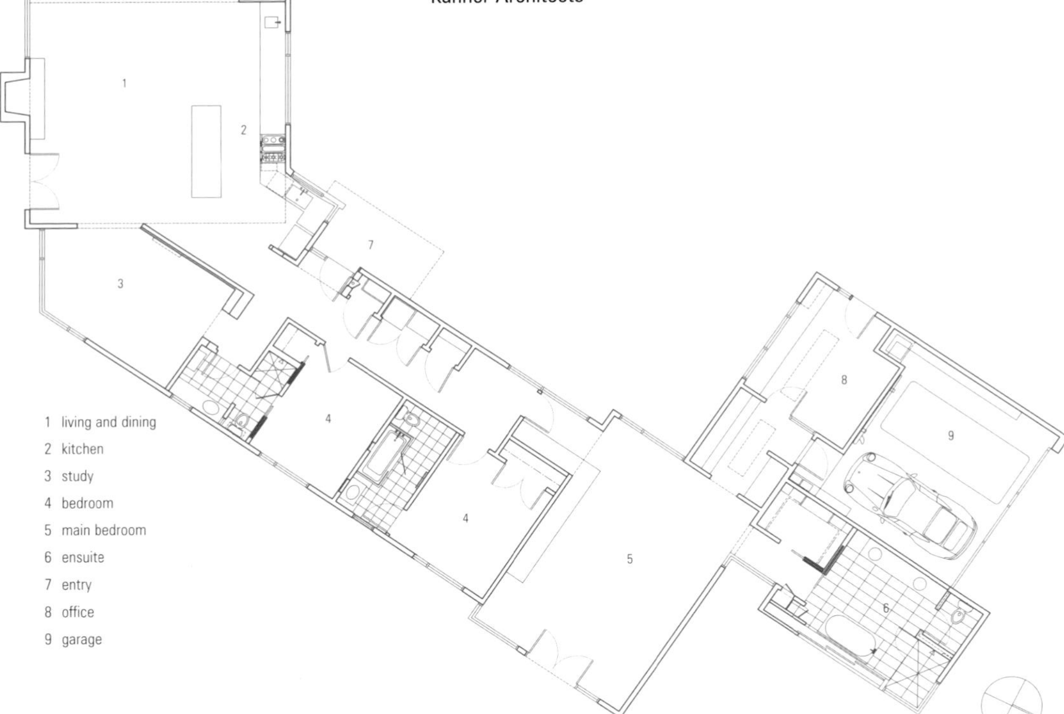

TOP
A courtyard is created by the U-shaped plan, which utilizes simple geometric forms. The white plaster shapes are strategically aligned in order to use the changing light of day and the resulting shadows to creative effect.

ABOVE
A look at the entry illustrates the varying heights of the home's different forms. Ceiling heights rise and drop throughout the house, creating a natural rhythm. The taller form at right includes the dining room, kitchen, and living room.

INSPIRED CHOICES

This house is inspired by the work of Luis Barragán, the Mexican architect, whose courtyard designs show a skilful use of light and space. Other influences are the houses of the Greek islands and the cubist work of Irving Gill, another specialist in internal courtyards.

FEEDING THE SENSES

The house is designed to take full advantage of its dazzling views of the Pacific. The stark white plaster exterior contrasts dramatically with the colors of ocean and sky. Inside, mahogany doors and cabinetry provide a warm complement to the austere exterior.

Varying ceiling heights create a ladder of space and volume, with vertical space being at its greatest in the living room, dining room, and main bedroom. The overall effect is one of compression and expansion, creating a bond between the rise and fall of room heights and the rolling Pacific Ocean.

OPENING TO THE WORLD

An interior courtyard doubles as the entry. When the glass walls are opened, the house extends out to the exterior spaces, and permits unencumbered views of the ocean and the mountains.

There are three bedrooms, three bathrooms, and a study. To increase the feeling of spaciousness without increasing the real space, the wall between the kitchen and the living and dining areas was removed, opening up views from all perspectives.

The main bathroom, which opens up to outside, is the gem of the house. It has stacked sliding glass doors and a butt-glazed corner in the shower. Black granite floor tiles are accented by a vertical-grain Douglas fir vanity and wall panels.

Another special feature of the 3,200-sq-ft (300-sq-m) house is the wall separating the pool area from the driveway and garage. A series of back-lit etched-glass panels stand on concrete bases in a reference to the simple geometric structures that compose the house. These panels create a glowing opaque barrier and light source for evening lounging or swimming.

JAPANESE TOUCHES

The owners are interested in Japanese art, so the architects chose a number of items that provide a distinct Japanese flavor to the home. Some of the most noticeable are the wooden shower fixtures in the bathrooms. The landscaping too, has an understated Japanese feel to it.

ABOVE
Retracting exterior glass walls fuse the inside and outside. Alder floors in the living area give way to a carpet of green grass outside. White walls trimmed in mahogany supply warmth for the open floor plan, which comprises the dining room, kitchen, and living room.

FOLLOWING PAGES
Malibu House's minimalist esthetic allows the natural beauty of the site and its views to dominate. With its retracting walls, the main bathroom opens to the pool deck. At right, a fence of translucent panels, which are 5 ft by 7 ft (1.5 m by 2.1 m), lines the driveway, hiding it from the pool area as well as creating an artistic sculptural element.

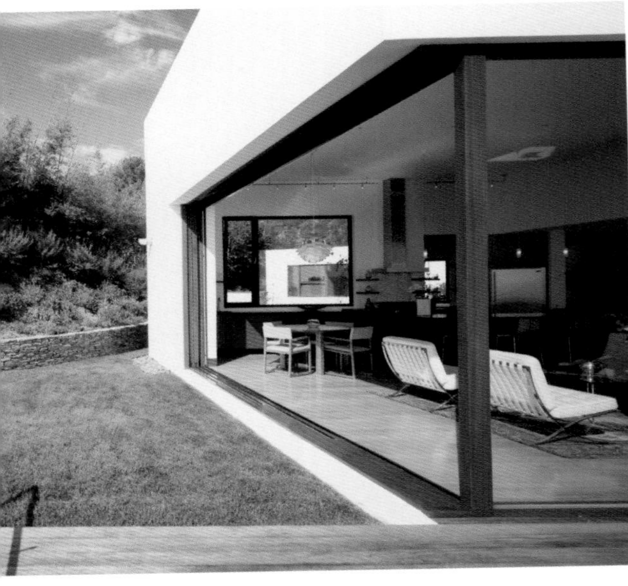

ABOVE
This view of the kitchen, dining, and living areas from the deck shows the spacious open floor plan. The home office at the rear of the garage can be seen through the dining room window.

TOP FAR RIGHT
Sliding mahogany-framed doors open the main bathroom to the pool deck, providing a stunning backdrop for bathing among ocean breezes. Both the floors and the tub platform are granite.

FAR RIGHT
The living room – with Mies van der Rohe's leather Barcelona chairs – opens to the deck and garden. The floors are alder and the wall panels are mahogany divided by stainless steel splines.

RIGHT
The island in the kitchen is mahogany – as are all the cabinets – and capped with granite. The vertical orientation of the stainless steel appliances interacts with the otherwise horizontal lines of the island, counters, and shelves. The ceiling height changes in the hallway to the right, and this change indicates the transition to another part of the house.

"Ceiling heights rise and fall throughout the house, creating a natural rhythm."

Martha's Vineyard House MASSACHUSETTS, USA

Architecture Research Office

Constructed 2005
Home type Country house
Structure Timber, steel, and concrete

"This house embodies qualities unique to the Chilmark shore. Its orientation and composition frame the passage from land to sea. The various shadows cast by the cedar siding allude to what occurs naturally on the site, where the scrub oak shadows change throughout the day."
Adam Yarinsky

TOP
The series of planes defining the entry court draw the visitor toward the entrance of Martha's Vineyard House, creating a sense of anticipation. Upon rounding the corner, an unexpectedly grand view of the ocean beyond is revealed.

ABOVE
A large fireplace of basaltina separates the living room from the dining room, while maintaining the openness of communal living spaces. The fireplace is complemented by oak floorboards, which have been laid in a staggered pattern in the living areas, as well as in the bedrooms.

AN ISLAND SANCTUARY

A peaceful hillside at the southern edge of a clearing in the woods is the site of this house in Martha's Vineyard, an island 7 miles (11 km) from the Massachusetts coastline. The home's elevation allows for expansive views across the water, and permits a blending of the home with the scrub oak trees that surround the site.

COMPACT FORM

To conform to stringent local code requirements and to stay within budget, the design of the home is compact and simple. Each of the three blocks composing the home have been arranged to define the world outside, making full use of the varying traits of the site. Entry to the house is through a protected, quietly landscaped entry court, which is formed by two of these blocks. From the entry, which looks through the living area, there is a view of the ocean and outlying islands in the distance. The main living block contains the entry foyer, living, and dining rooms. It offers views of a field and the water beyond. The main bedroom wing faces a densely vegetated gorge. The kitchen and guest wing faces out to the lawn and garden.

COMPLEMENTARY MATERIALS

Building materials were chosen to harmonize with the site. They also serve to delineate the interior and exterior areas. Two L-shaped cedar-clad walls, placed at a 90° angle, are the defining elements of the blocks. Cedar shingles are widely used in the Cape Cod region, and the architect varied the theme by alternating the widths of the siding, effectively creating something new and different. There is a genuine connection with the landscape here, emphasized by the parallel detailing on the walls. The architect chose zinc panels and wood windows, which achieve a bold contrast with the cedar. Zinc walls also feature in the living area.

SENSITIVE FINISHES

The cedar siding and cedar walls blend with the low stone landscape walls, all striking a chord of unity with the surrounding landscape.

White-washed ash has been used in the cabinetry; glass and marble tiles are the prominent elements in the bathrooms. Basaltina tiles run from the drive all the way into the foyer and stone is the defining feature of the kitchen and the outdoor dining terrace.

1 entry foyer
2 living
3 dining
4 kitchen
5 guest bedroom
6 main bedroom
7 study

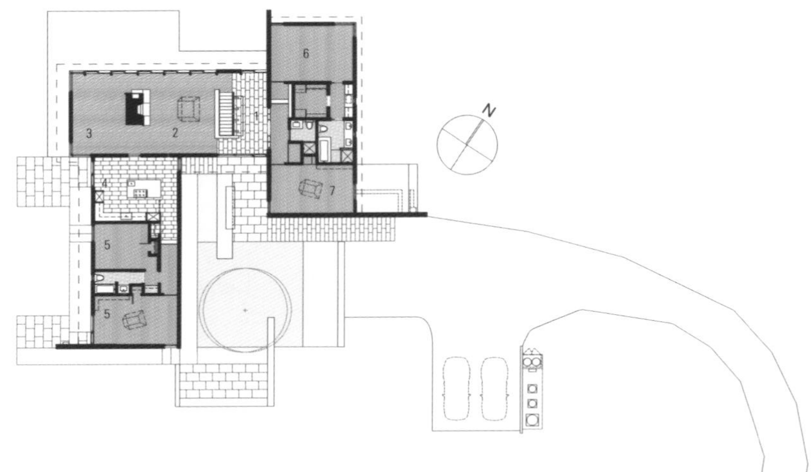

TOP
The south wing of the house interlocks with the main living block at the kitchen. It houses the guest bedrooms. Tucked back into the site's gentle slope, this living block intimately relates to the site in contrast to the main living block.

ABOVE
The main living block of the house is stretched across the shoreline with a panorama of the waterfront and distant horizon.

Orleans House MASSACHUSETTS, USA

Charles Rose Architects

Constructed	2004
Home type	Two-level family home with studio
Structure	Steel, timber, concrete, and glass

"The house is sited on a bluff overlooking a bay and the Atlantic Ocean to the east. The footprint traces a naturally occurring bowl in the landscape. The varying floor levels reflect the original rise and fall of the grade while providing spatial definition to the functional areas of the interior. The forms reflect the natural landforms and every effort was made to preserve the existing flora of the site."

Charles Rose

ABOVE
Granite stairs in the landscape provide an imposing access from the parking court to the main entrance of Orleans House.

TOP RIGHT
The two-level cabana sits on the western edge of the main house (in view, at left). The office on the upper level enjoys spectacular views of the bay and Atlantic Ocean.

ABOVE RIGHT
Floor to ceiling windows allow natural light to stream into the house, giving it a translucent quality. Generously sized overhangs and sunscreen trellises give the home plenty of shade and shelter from weather extremes.

COLOR, LIGHT, AND MOVEMENT

Orleans House is situated on a high bluff overlooking Pleasant Bay, Nanset Beach, and the Atlantic Ocean, and sits in a natural recess in the topography. The architects were briefed to design a house that would take advantage of the glorious water views, while still permitting comfortable living in all seasons. Winters get very cold in Massachusetts, so it was important that the design include adequate shelter and protection from the elements.

To take advantage of the views, large amounts of glass face the sea. This allows plenty of natural light and ventilation into the house. On the side away from the ocean, the house is covered with a low copper roof, which adds warmth and texture. The design encompasses the main house, an art studio, a self-contained guest apartment, and a separate cabana with an office above.

MASSACHUSETTS LIVING

The main house consists of a roomy single-story space. It contains the entry foyer, living room, dining room, kitchen, and gallery area. Although these spaces open into one another, they are separated by stepped floor levels and strategically placed walls.

Stepped exterior terraces emanate from the southern and western ends of the house. These are protected from the sun by roof overhangs and sunscreen trellises, bringing the outside into the inside and allowing more outdoor living.

The brief was to design a house that would take advantage of the glorious water views, while still permitting comfortable living in all seasons.

ABOVE
The entry to the house occurs along a natural rise in the landscape, and is framed by the architecture and the plantings.

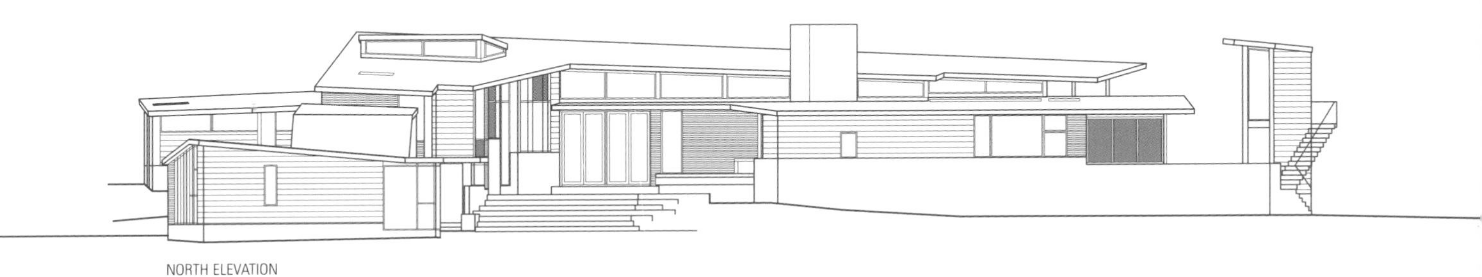

NORTH ELEVATION

The eastern side of Orleans House contains the library/media room. The south-facing, L-shaped master bedroom is also on this side. The intersection of the L is the spine of the house, and permits access to the guest bedroom level, the wine cellar, and an upper sitting room positioned underneath a roof window.

On the northern side of the house, the family room is linked to the main house by a covered walkway. Designed for a range of recreational activities, the family room was purposely set apart from the rest of the house. It has a charming aspect over the garden and surrounding landscape and also hides the parking court of the main house.

SEPARATE SPACES

On the western edge of the main house sits a towered cabana with a second-level private office. The room commands dazzling views to the bay and ocean beyond. It also contains a spa, shower, and toilet.

The separate guesthouse sits on the northern edge of the site. The first level of this space has large roller doors and contains an art studio. The upper level consists of the bedroom, a south-facing terrace, a small eating area, and a bathroom.

MATERIAL RESILIENCE

The materials used were chosen for their durability and practicality. The house has a conventional wood-frame structure, reinforced with steel columns and beams. On the exterior, exposed board-formed concrete foundation walls were used, as well as lead-coated copper walls and roofs, and cedar siding. The windows are framed in mahogany, and exterior stainless steel has been acid-finished to give it a brown color, making it blend with the outside.

Plaster walls and ceilings have been used inside. The doors are made of the exotic African wood anagre, while the floors are either jatoba wood or golden juperana granite.

ABOVE RIGHT
A view of the living area looking west. The client's artwork was considered in the development of each interior space.

LEFT
The stairs link the wine cellar on the lower level to a sitting area on the mezzanine level. The staircase is constructed from mahogany, acid-washed stainless steel, and glass.

1 cabana
2 jacuzzi
3 west terrace
4 dining terrace
5 screen porch
6 dining
7 sitting area
8 kitchen
9 pantry
10 gallery
11 living
12 pantry entry
13 south terrace
14 north entry
15 foyer
16 library/media room
17 WC
18 main bedroom
19 main wardrobe
20 main bathroom
21 utility
22 lower hallway
23 bathroom
24 bedroom
25 utility entry
26 breezeway
27 motor court
28 family/bunk room
29 bathroom

N

LEVEL ONE

Peg Yorkin House MALIBU, USA

Moore Ruble Yudell Architects & Planners

Constructed 1997
Home type Two-story family home
Structure Concrete foundation, pre-cast concrete, timber frame construction, and sliding glass and aluminum panels

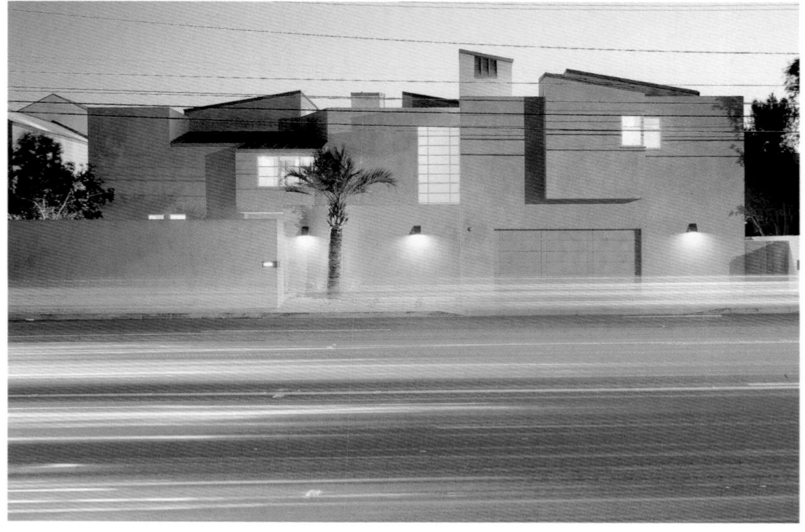

"The house evolved from understanding and embracing the complexities of the site and the social needs of the family. It is buffered and urban on the highway, transparent and transformable toward the water, and permeable and vertically connected to the animations of light and sky. It provides an urban refuge for three generations and can be shaped and tuned by them according to the season, or the needs of their varied social occasions."

Moore Ruble Yudell Architects & Planners

ABOVE
Toward the highway, the Peg Yorkin House is expressed as a collage of relatively solid forms of roofs and light-scoops that reach up to bring skylight and views into the house. Entry to the home is through a sequestered courtyard to the left of the palm tree.

LEFT
Facing toward the beach, the house is highly transparent giving it a "lightness" on the landscape. On the upper level, most bedrooms have a private, shaded balcony. At the lower level, sliding doors allow all major living spaces to open up to outdoor terraces and entertainment areas.

RIGHT
Toward the beach, the house is articulated to optimize views from individual spaces. Terraces and living spaces have varying degrees of shade, depending upon their requirements.

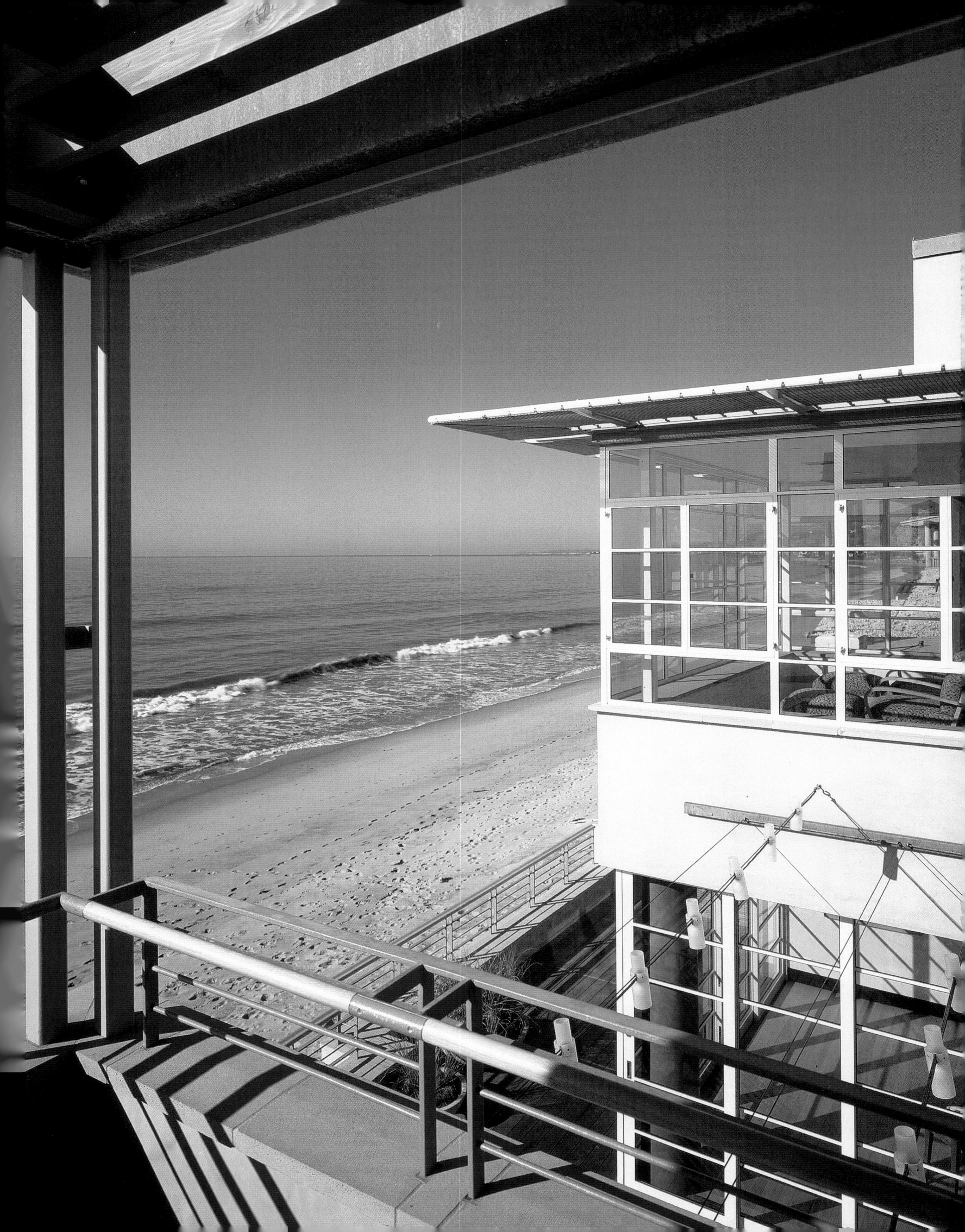

RESPONDING TO THE SITE

The Peg Yorkin House evolved in response to the tensions of its site. It is on the edge of the busy city of Los Angeles, where the Santa Monica Mountains and the Pacific Coast Highway meet the ocean, with its dazzling and infinitely changing panoramas. Sitting snugly between the highway and the sandy beach is the Yorkin site, which provides an urban-edge refuge for three generations of a family with creative and social commitments.

The house is a social and familial retreat for the owner, her two adult children, and their families. All of them were intimately involved in the design process. It was critical that the house be comfortable for the individual as well as the group, and that the range of activities – both formal and informal – of each family member could be accommodated.

OPENING TO THE ENVIRONMENT

The urban courtyard is used as the basic building form and typology. A system of sliding exterior and interior panels allows the occupants to transform the home, creating varying degrees of openness to the environment. As well, these panels provide privacy when required. This transformability is reminiscent of the shoji screen systems found in traditional Japanese houses.

LAYERS OF MEANING

The house unfolds as a series of layers. Entry to the interior is through a courtyard of native beach grasses and over a wooden boardwalk. Inside there are dedicated family living areas, most of which retain a correlation to the exterior through sliding glass walls that lead to an outside courtyard, terrace, and beyond that, to the beach. The glass walls also permit the entry of plenty of natural light.

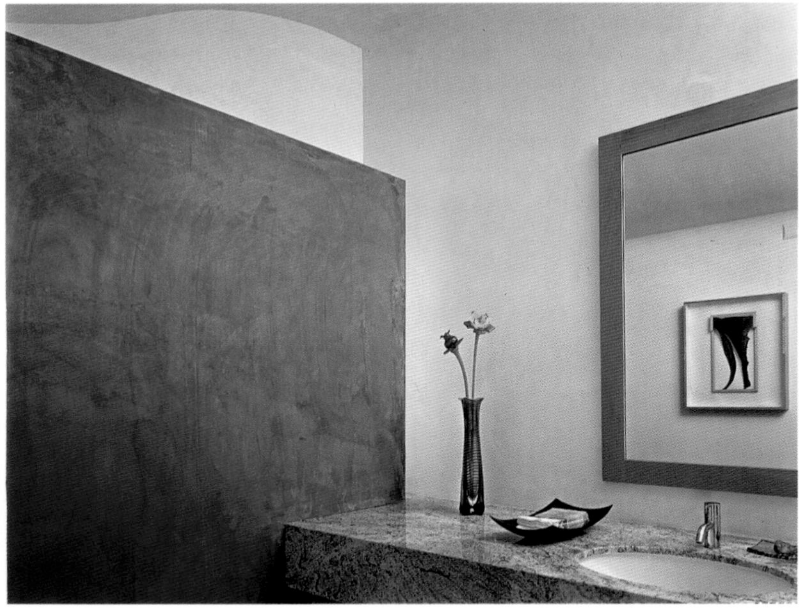

FAR LEFT
The primary staircase to the bedrooms is illuminated by clerestory light. Sliding color glass panels provide visual privacy, as well as "borrowed" light, to dressing areas of bedrooms. These panels can be moved to create an infinite number of abstract murals of colored light.

LEFT
A guest bathroom is animated by the simultaneous intensity and subtlety of integrally colored Italian plaster. Indirect light adds further richness to the spatial experience of this small room.

ABOVE
Highlighted by indirect lighting, the curve of the articulated ceiling in the main bedroom is reminiscent of the waves outside. To the left, a low bay provides a place for contemplation and viewing the everchanging panorama.

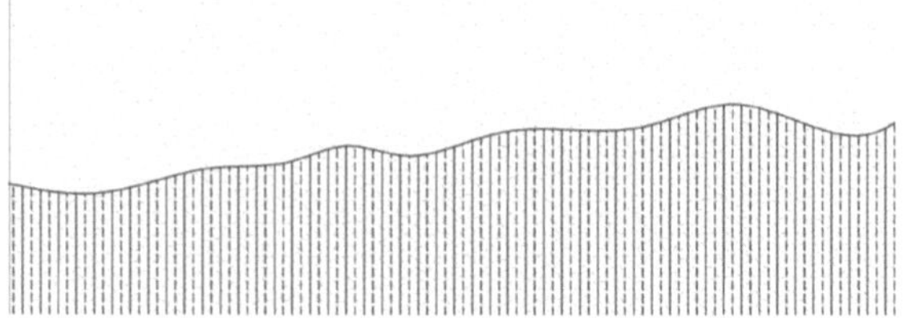

ABOVE
The dining room space is more than doubled when the sliding glass walls are opened to the exterior terrace. These sliding glass walls are used extensively throughout the home to invite light in, and to unite internal and external spaces.

RIGHT
The home's centrally located family room opens out to an expansive terrace, which is the focal point around which all the major living spaces revolve.

A central courtyard is the focus of the house – it serves as the pivot around which the major living spaces of kitchen, family room, dining, and media room revolve. The courtyard, which is partially covered, includes an outside dining area and fireplace, and can be used year round.

Most of the bedrooms, all of which are located on the second level, have an individual ocean-facing terrace, allowing plenty of light and air to penetrate the house. In spite of this, each bedroom is completely private from the outside. There are six bedrooms and six bathrooms upstairs.

COASTAL COLORS

The colors and the materials were carefully selected to maintain a strong connection with the coastal setting of the house. It was important that materials be strong and durable enough to withstand the force of salt, sun, and seawater.

The outside walls are integral cement plaster, with concrete and pre-cast concrete details. The windows and doors are powder-coated aluminum. The exterior wood is teak, and the sun shades are stainless steel woven fabric or aluminum lattice. The roof is zinc with a matt finish.

ABOVE
The doors of the living room disappear into a wall cavity, creating a room completely open to the surrounding terrace and sea. The continuous deck creates the sense of a promenade on a large ship's deck.

Pond House ARIZONA, USA

Will Bruder Architects

Construction	2003–2005
Home type	One-bedroom home
Structure	Concrete block, structural steel, and wooden frame

"Pond House runs along a creek bed outside the town of Cave Creek, north of Phoenix, Arizona, at the end of an isolated, unpaved road. As suggested by its solitary bedroom and isolated location, it was conceived as a place of reflection and contemplation for its owners."

Will Bruder

DRAMATIC ENTRY

Thirty miles (50 km) north of Phoenix, Arizona, is architect Will Bruder's carefully crafted and modestly scaled retreat, Pond House, embedded in a rock outcrop in the midst of the Sonoran Desert.

The house, nestled into the rock banks of Cave Creek and overlooking a natural, year-round swimming hole, is approached by a natural gravel road. A vast 7-ft (2.1-m) steel plate emerges from the ground and gradually arcs away from the natural stone of the home's anchoring wall. An opening in the steel reveals the funnel-like approach to the house, and draws the visitor inexorably toward the heavy, raw steel entry door.

A natural spring, collected in a concrete cistern, overflows and trickles down the natural flagstone stairs toward the entry under the house, before reaching the creek below.

THE ORIGINAL INHABITANTS

The arc of the natural stones in Pond House's northern wall echo the crumbling remains of nearby irrigation ditches and the foundations of small abodes left by the Hohokan Indians, who inhabited this area from 800 to 1400 CE. They used the waters of Cave Creek to irrigate their land.

MAXIMIZING THE VIEW

Once inside, a small set of stairs descends into the central living/dining area and kitchen, featuring exposed concrete floors and maple veneer millwork, accented with a complex mix of plywood, steel, and natural stone. A panoramic view of the lush vegetation along Cave Creek floods in through Pond House's articulated custom windows of raw plated steel, set in weathered steel cladding beneath thin, broad eaves of re-sawn plywood.

ABOVE LEFT
The warm glow of the entry door resonates with the soft trickle of water from a natural spring between embracing walls of stone and steel to create an invitation into the home. A small window is set into the eastern wall under a heavy stone lintel, introducing to the living space views of the lush vegetation along the creek below.

LEFT
The low roofline and natural materials of Pond House allow it to easily meld with its desert surroundings. It seems to sit naturally within the rocky outcroppings above the swimming hole, bridging the transition between the creek vegetation and the Sonoran Desert beyond.

TOP RIGHT
The view looking back up the flight of natural flagstone steps leading from the entry, past a concrete cistern to the garage beyond, typifies the integration of Pond House into the landscape. The design of the house, and its form, location, and materials attempt to resonate with, rather than impose upon, the serene surrounding oasis.

ABOVE RIGHT
The rocky banks of the swimming hole seem to be part of the home's foundations. Reflective glass further softens the impact of the home by mirroring the surrounding landscape, while the cantilevered deck creates a dialogue between Bruder's idyllic hideaway and the harshness of the Sonoran Desert.

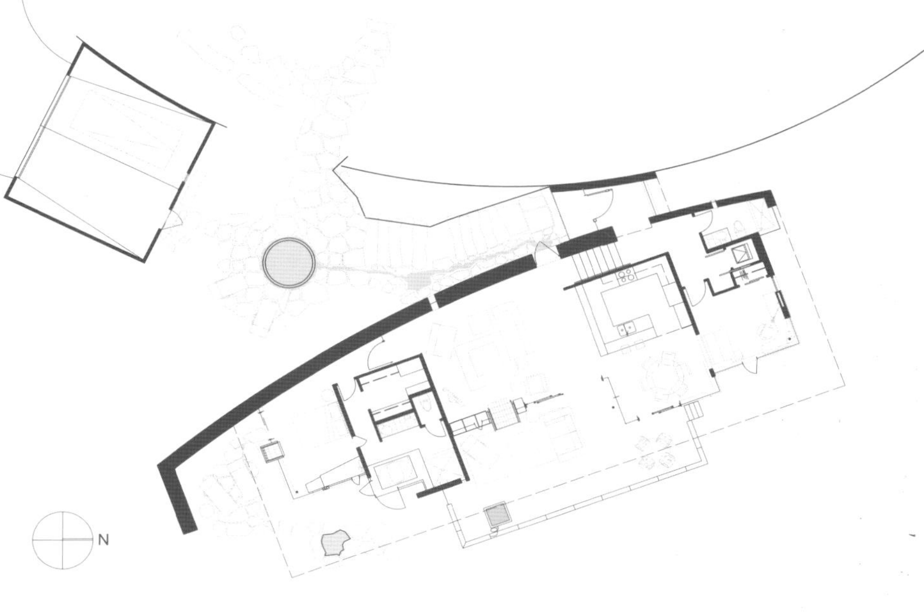

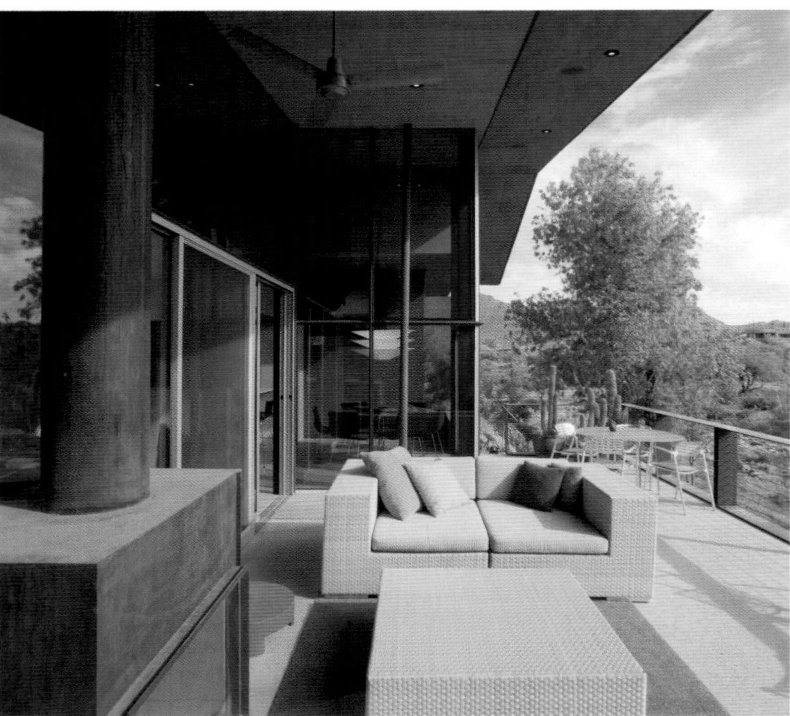

A cantilevered concrete deck, with minimal stainless steel guardrail, hovers effortlessly above its rocky escarpment, combining with large sliding glass doors to create a seamless transition between the interior and exterior spaces.

ATTENTION TO DETAIL

Native stone, rough-sawn plywood, and Venetian plaster characterize the home's interior, providing it with its warmth and scale. The eastern elevation is a fully glazed, intimate expanse of carefully selected textures and materials. This glazing offers views of the creek to each room, including the main living spaces, a large main bedroom, bathroom, and a home office, which can be converted to a guest room if required.

Pond House's natural stone western exterior doubles as an internal feature wall. This extends along the living/dining area and into the main bedroom, where a semi-frameless glass door permits the eye to follow the gentle arc of the wall. Beyond the bedroom, the stone wall turns east to define an intimate sunken garden. The bedroom faces southeast to enjoy this garden through large expanses of glass, complete with vent panels to allow natural ventilation.

PEACEFUL RETREAT

Pond House is replete with windows of glass and colored translucent resin that present a kaleidoscope of surprising, unexpected perspectives in a serene and peaceful setting.

ABOVE
The carefully chosen fabrics of the furnishings in the living/dining area combine with the natural stonework and woods to absorb, rather than reflect, the large volumes of diffuse light entering the east-facing windows. The small set of stairs from the entry on the left recede from the space, enhancing the peace of this desert oasis.

LEFT
Looking north along the generously scaled deck, one of the home's two slow-combustion wood fireplaces can be seen in the foreground. The wide overhangs of the roof help to shelter the deck, and filter early morning and afternoon light.

OPPOSITE
Echoing the building techniques of ancient communities across the southwest, from the abandoned Anasazi settlement of Mesa Verde in Colorado to the extensive ruins of Chaco Canyon in New Mexico, Pond House is both southwestern vernacular and desert modern.

Rochman Residence CALIFORNIA, USA

Callas Shortridge Architects

Construction	1998–2000
House type	Two-story family home
Structure	Wood frame construction with deepened foundation, stucco, steel

"The task at hand was to illuminate the inherent drama of the site and reflect that seamlessly in a natural architecture: as though the result of millions of years of geology and a human enterprise were logically intertwined."
Barbara Callas

IN CONSORT WITH NATURE

Precipitously perched above the curve of Pacific Coast Highway between the Palisades and Malibu, California, the Rochman Residence rises like an outcropping of angular granite, sculpted by the architects in consort with nature. The clients first approached Frank Israel to discuss the site; shortly afterward, the project was taken over by associates Steven Shortridge, David Spinelli, and Barbara Callas, who was the design principal.

Viewed from the roadway below, the home stands as a singular artefact and unique habitation. Large, thrusting parallel planes of eucalyptus-toned stucco jut from the upper reaches of the steep cliffs. The lines of the top level frame a wrap of glass, angled and transparent at its edge. This modern, mythic bird of prey stares silently out from its perch, sentient and all seeing.

The base of this expansive glassed room is the floor of the main bedroom below. Its face frames the ocean side of the structure as it bends crisply into a sharp, narrowing, structural support. The effect created by the acute angle of the column animates this essential function. The column seems to be a massive, mechanical knee, folded to brace itself into the substratum.

SHAPE AND FORM

A vertical wall of upthrust steel-trowelled plaster stands at the entry of the residence – both a practical and metaphorical subterranean anchor of Euclidian variation.

Adjacent to it, thin, elongated, and irregular concrete steps lead to the zinc-metal front door, which swings open to reveal a kinetic contrast between the muted exterior and a vibrant interior of color that is spontaneously enlivened by the transition. The geometry within becomes a subtle form of theater, where shifting shapes of angular walls and ceilings create visual intrigue against the endless panoramas.

LEFT
Indigenous vegetation was preserved, privacy heightened, and the naturally shallow-stepped site focused to give the structure a sense of lightness. Simultaneously, this achieved a solid anchoring into a perch that affords uninterrupted views of the coast from Santa Monica eastward to Malibu in the west.

ABOVE
Two non-native elements inhabit this western view – a eucalyptus tree included as a feature in the Spanish cedar deck, and the residence, which stands here like the prow of a ship heading out to sea. The deck is protected by steel and glass railings that provide increased solidity where previously there was only air. The mitered glass window leans in two directions to reduce the effect of enclosing the living area above.

ABOVE RIGHT
In contrast to the severe slope of the main residence, the entry is reached by climbing broad, slightly elevated, concrete steps that traverse the site, shifting axis while slipping through a displaced wall plane.

RIGHT
The drawings depict both a sectional elevation, through the axis of circulation, as well as a transectional axis, through the fireplace. In addition, reference is made, in the second vertical sketch, to the dining trellis that connects with the outdoor terrace.

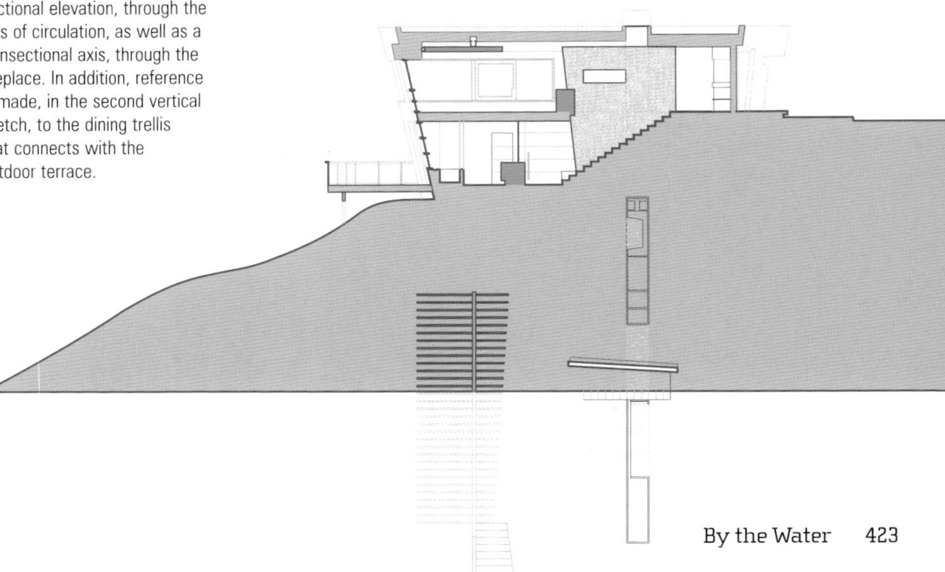

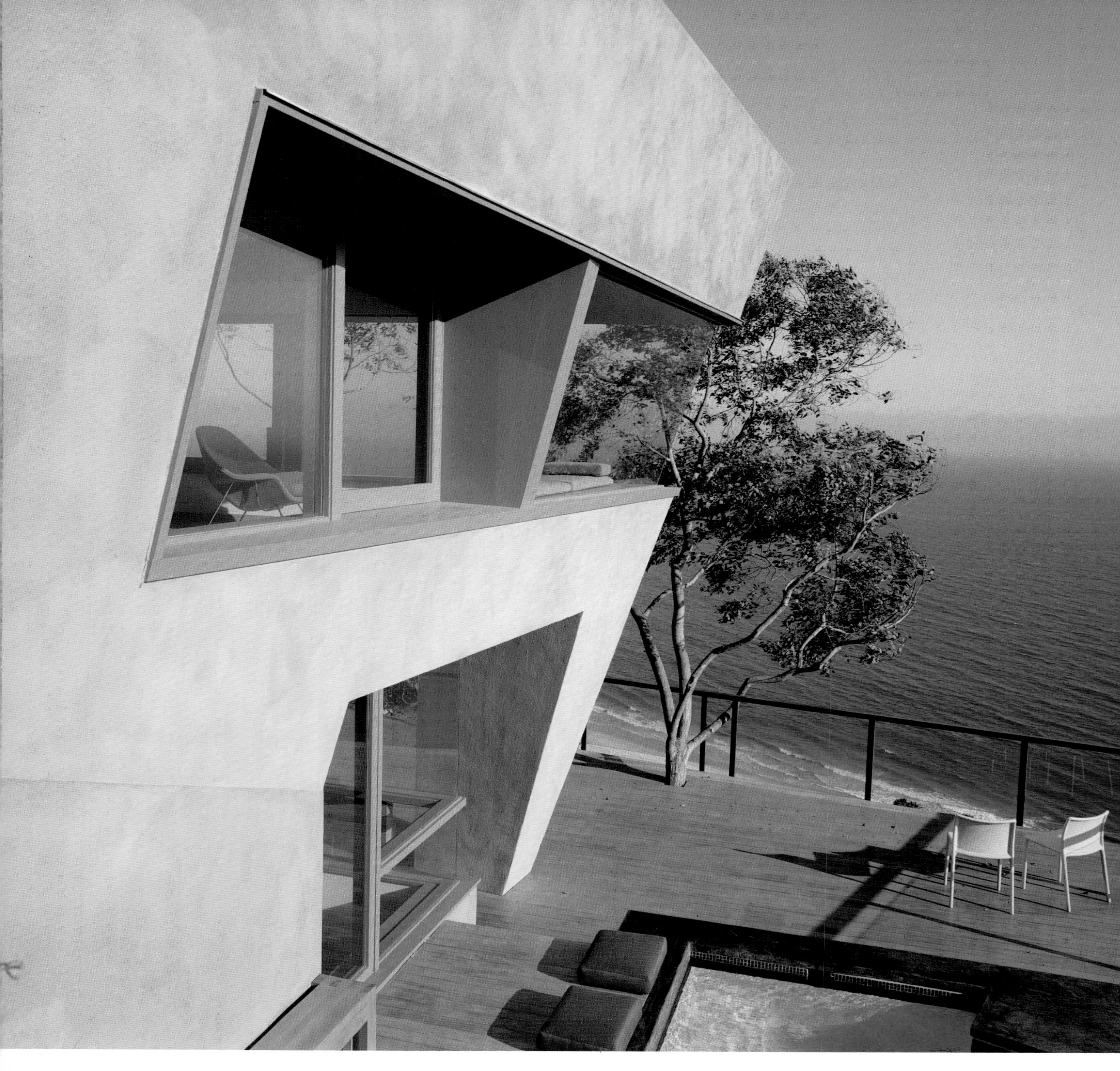

ABOVE
The structure's transparencies are choreographed to produce energy while thrusting vertically, wrapping horizontally, or tilting at various angles. Southern California climatology and the proximity of the ocean allow fenestration, both fixed and movable, to substitute for forced air-cooling.

A SPECTRUM OF HUES AND VIEWS

In part, this design evolved as an internal logic in response to code demands that restricted the height and flexibility of roof permeations. The varied shapes of the interior walls are saturated with color. The hues, ranging from eucalyptus to deep orange, create a three-dimensional effect.

The upper level encompasses an office, living, and dining space, where a cedar trellis cantilevers over the deck to carry it outside to sense-saturating views of the Pacific. The lower peripheries of the view include the beach and the ocean.

BEAUTIFUL BEECH

Natural light dances upon the upper level's beech wood floor, which sets off the black and chrome chairs of the mahogany-stained dining table and dramatizes other space that is introduced by pronounced, straight-edged materials in radically contrasting tones.

The entry level is divided by a central, internal stair that descends as the base of an angled wall. Its treads continue the beech wood motif until they change to walnut-stained concrete at a platform two steps above the lower floor. This poured, richly burnished element is the surface on all lower level living space, including the main bedroom, its ensuite, and the adjacent gym.

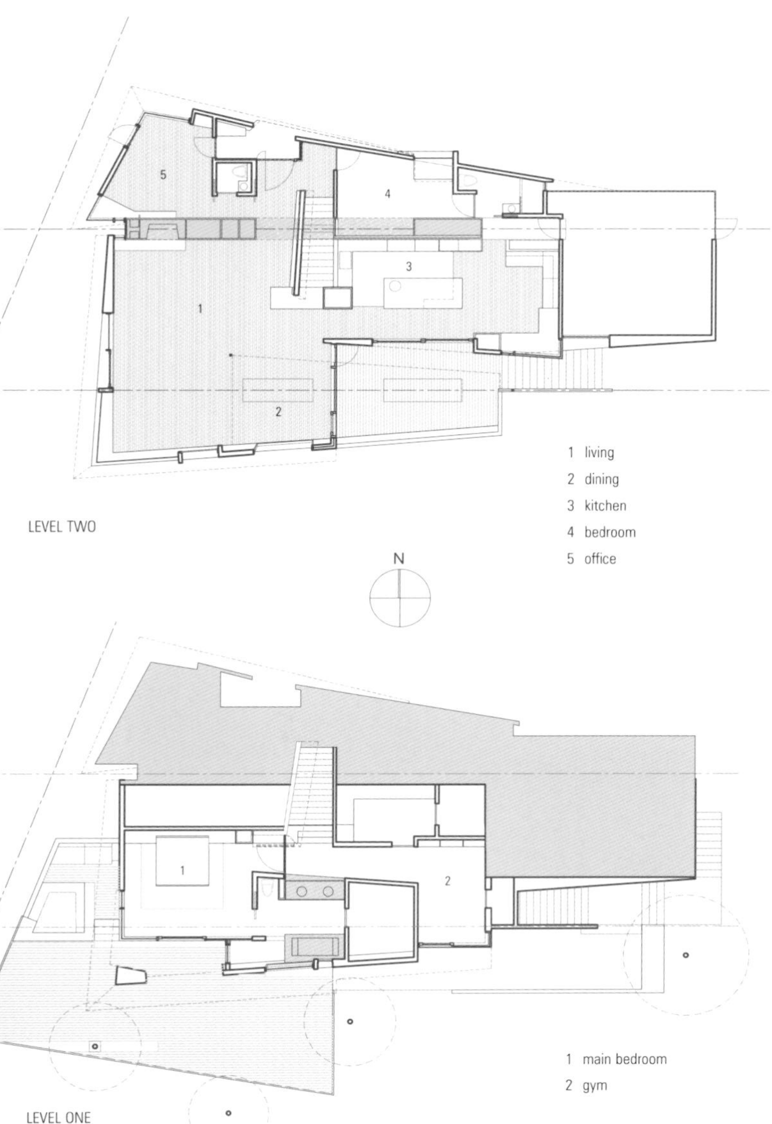

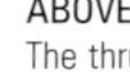

ABOVE
The thrust of a tilting plaster wall along the left flank of the entry procession carries the visitor into either the living room to the right, the dining room featured here, or beyond the dining room to the spaces that view limitless horizon. The ceiling is dramatized by ribs of Spanish cedar that pass by overhead to connect with the trellis, heightening the interior/exterior dialectic, ever present in the architect's design and implicit in California living.

LEFT
The base of the entry plaster wall functionally inverts in the lower spaces, providing privacy and separation between them and the main bedroom, seen beyond. The honeyed beech wood of the floor above continues as steps until they end at a stepped plinth of burnished concrete. The large section of Douglas fir pivots closed as a door, then comes to rest as a seamless wall.

LEFT
A 40-ft (12-m) continuous band of glass mitered at the corner of the living room contains a window seat that floats above the sea and mist. The ever-present eucalyptus softens the view and emphasizes the natural grounding of an otherwise incongruous site.

Sea Farm House HANGKLIP, SOUTH AFRICA

Stefan Antoni Olmesdahl Truen Architects

Constructed	2002
Home type	One-story family holiday home
Structure	Timber, stone, travertine, plaster

"The earliest inhabitants, the Khoisan, known as strandlopers ('beach walkers'), lived in caves or simple stone structures scattered along the coastline, living mainly on fish. Inspired by these simple dwellings, and the stone and lime-washed fishermen's cottages built later, the house has been designed to be very basic, virtually primal, and yet very sophisticated at the same time."

Stefan Antoni

RUGGED SETTING, STURDY STRUCTURE

This home is located on a rocky peninsula in a nature reserve, and is perched above a dramatic seascape with spectacular views of Hangklip Mountain. The area is home to indigenous fynbos and a vast array of sea life.

The walls are simple and heavy. The roof is thin and floats over voids created between the solid mass of stone and plastered wall, extending to form covered and open terraces tailored to the specific orientation of the space. The materials and finishes were chosen for their inherent qualities and relationship to the site.

LAYERING THE HOUSE

The linear homestead is layered horizontally, from the central living zones through the intermediate pause zone to the bedrooms and on to the bathroom areas that open out into the natural landscape.

To take advantage of the sea and surrounding views and to provide protection from the extreme coastal climate, the living spaces were designed with north–south orientations, resulting in an open, flowing space with sea and mountain terraces. The main living spaces form the link between inside and outside. The living area is on the sea side, and the dining room and kitchen, slightly raised and on the north, open out onto a deep-covered outdoor living terrace. This transparent center allows living to occur on either side of the house depending entirely on the prevailing weather conditions – in poor weather, the mountain-facing dining terrace is preferred; in fine conditions, living and entertaining takes place in the sea-facing area.

Natural colors and materials were used, including warm sandstone, ash-gray balau woodwork and a charcoal metal roof. There are large glazed areas with views from every room. Each aspect of the house has a private terrace or a deck.

ABOVE RIGHT
The holiday house, a linear single-story structure, is situated on the headland of a private nature reserve, surrounded by the Indian Ocean, indigenous fynbos, and Hangklip Mountain.

RIGHT
The doors to the bathroom slide back completely and open onto a private deck. A traditional timber "latte"screen adds privacy to the space. The bath is sunken, set on floor level to minimise its dominance in the space.

ABOVE
The lounge room opens up onto the front terrace, blurring the boundaries between inside and out. This space makes for easy living and stunning entertaining during fine, summery conditions. A Balau timber pergola frames the view and filters the natural sunlight, adding to the picture-perfect setting.

WITHOUT WALLS

The house appears to be "without walls." Nothing seems to contain the house, and its dual identity in terms of internal and external spaces is an integral part of the design: All the rooms, including the bedrooms and bathrooms, open up, extending beyond sliding glass doors onto decks with sweeping views to the horizon on all sides. Even the internal spaces trifle with the finality of walls – some do not meet the ceilings, yet they still fulfil their purpose of partitioning rooms.

Other spaces are subtly divided by contrasting surfaces, and elsewhere, heavy wooden beams are stopped abruptly by the sensual lines of a gentle arch which denotes a different zone.

The intermediate pause zones are enclosed in the stone walls and sculpted to create arched, cave-like, intimate, and cosy spaces. Each space contains a fireplace alcove on one side and the working part of the kitchen on the other. In contrast, the living spaces have high ceilings of thick timber beams and "latte," a material traditionally used in the construction of the thatched roofed houses of the Cape.

The result is a house with a strong yet understated character that is both elegant and timeless.

ABOVE
The dramatic view of the ocean, kelp, and rocks, which evokes a sense of seeing forever, is enhanced by the horizontal lines and expansive living room doors. The contrasting natural tones in the indoor space pick up on the coastal hues outdoors.

ABOVE LEFT
The bathrooms, situated at each end of the house, afford sweeping water views. The bathroom areas open out into the natural landscape.

ABOVE
An arched ceiling cove flanked by stone-cladded walls provides a private zone in the main bedroom. The texture of the stone work adds a warmth to the space. The ensuite bathroom and dressing area are situated behind the alcove.

LEFT
The ceiling is constructed of deep, exposed timber beams with "latte" infill panels (timber slats) between. Clerestory windows provide additional natural light and cross ventilation. The differing ceilings and split-level floors help to define the individual spaces.

Shaw House VANCOUVER, CANADA

Patkau Architects

Constructed	2000
Home type	Private residence
Structure	Reinforced concrete

"The Shaw House is an essay in light, water, and concrete in which the material character of each, both ephemeral and enduring, is revealed by the presence of the others. Time enters in through changing light conditions and the movement of water – seen against the unchanging backdrop of concrete – to create a dynamic environment within which the daily events of domestic life unfold."

John Patkau

SMALL SITE, BIG IDEAS

The site for this house is a small waterfront property that enjoys wonderful views across English Bay to the North Shore Mountains that tower above Vancouver's city skyline. The site is 33 ft (10 m) wide and 155 ft (47 m) deep. Side yard setbacks required by the local government meant that the building – a private residence for one person – was limited to a width of 26.4 ft (8 m). The client requested the usual living spaces, as well as a single bedroom, a study, a music room, and a lap pool.

ORGANIZED LIVING

The arrangement of Shaw House is very simple. Living spaces are on grade (ground level), the music room is beneath grade, while the bedroom, study, and the lap pool are above it all. The pool was placed above ground level because putting it elsewhere would have compromised the size of the living spaces. It sits along the west side of the house and is connected at either end to terraces that merge with the study and bedroom, providing a seamless sense of continuity.

The narrowness of the house means that spatial expansion is only achievable upward through the volume of the house and outward over the water. The ceilings are quite high, having the effect of making small spaces appear bigger. The dining room, for example, rises from ground level to the upper level to a clerestory. Because the lap pool is on the west side of the house, it allows daylight – as well as reflected light from the pool – into the central area of the home.

ABOVE
From the street, the view of the Shaw House reveals wood-louvered skylights combined with cast concrete, creating a compositional calm, while also establishing a sculptural quality through the interplay between complementary textures and planes.

RIGHT
This perspective of the home demonstrates how the architects surpassed the constraints of a tight site. Long, parallel concrete walls and a narrow lap pool are positioned to navigate lines of sight toward the impressive views of the bay, the North Shore Mountains, and the city beyond.

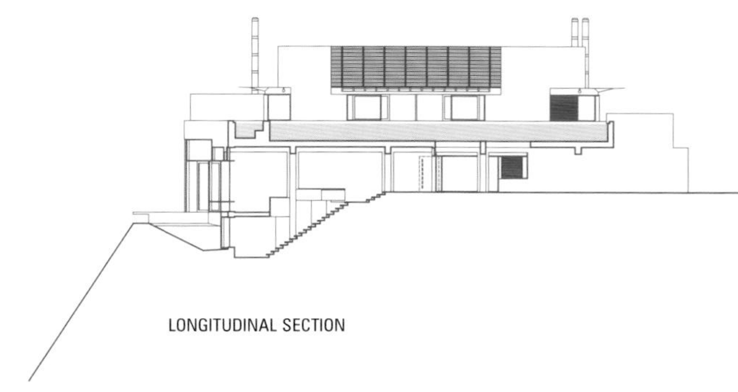

LONGITUDINAL SECTION

The entrance to the home is situated directly under the pool about halfway along the side of the house. The whole of this area is illuminated by the patterns of light that pass through the pool's glass bottom.

READY FOR ANYTHING

Vancouver, like many of the cities on the west coast of North America, is situated in an area of high seismic risk, so it was important to ensure that a strong structure was in place in the event that an earthquake should occur, particularly as the lap pool is located aboveground. The architect chose to construct the house almost entirely of reinforced concrete to provide resistance to any earthquake activity and its aftermath. White cement incorporated into the mix resulted in the house maintaining a bright external appearance even in wet weather, which is frequent in this part of Canada.

Inside the concrete exterior, the inside of the house is insulated and then clad with painted gypsum board. There are areas in the house that do not require insulation, and for these, the architect decided to leave the concrete structure exposed. The colors chosen for the interior are soft and muted, which allows natural light to make a real impact in the home.

TOP RIGHT
View from the living room toward the dining room and entrance to the home. Although the rooms are fairly narrow, a sense of space is achieved with high ceilings. This can be seen here where part of the dining/living room ceiling rises from ground level to the upper level.

RIGHT
Sunlight is refracted through the lens of the pool's water and filters into the entry space below. This not only provides a natural light source, but also causes the concrete-clad space to come alive with the ever-changing patterns of rippling pool water.

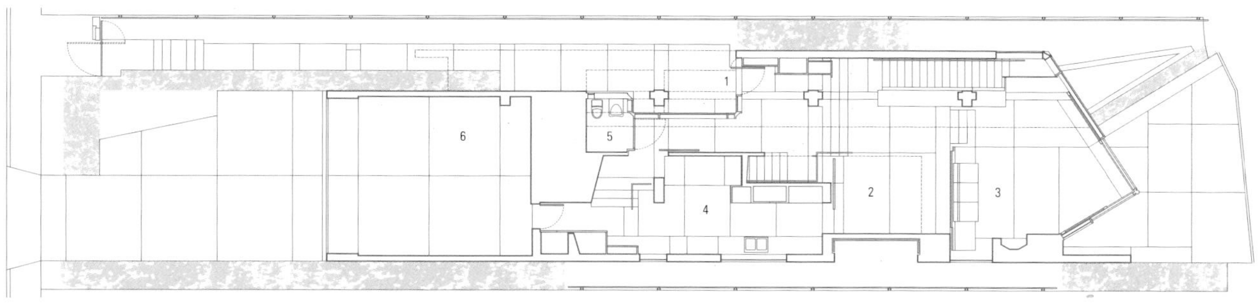

LEVEL ONE

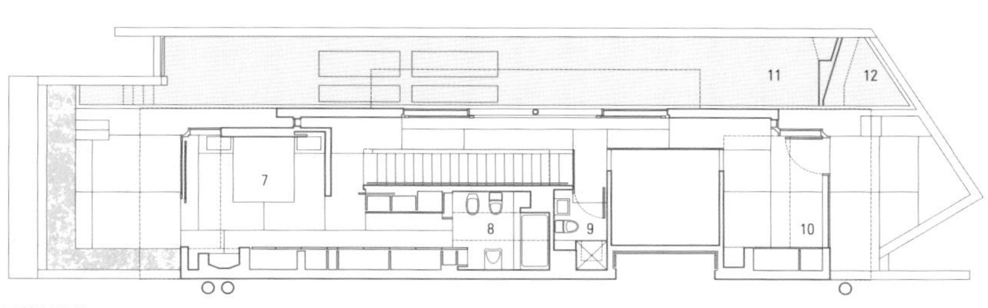

LEVEL TWO

1 entry
2 dining
3 living
4 kitchen
5 WC
6 garage
7 bedroom
8 bathroom
9 guest bathroom
10 study
11 lap pool
12 hot pool

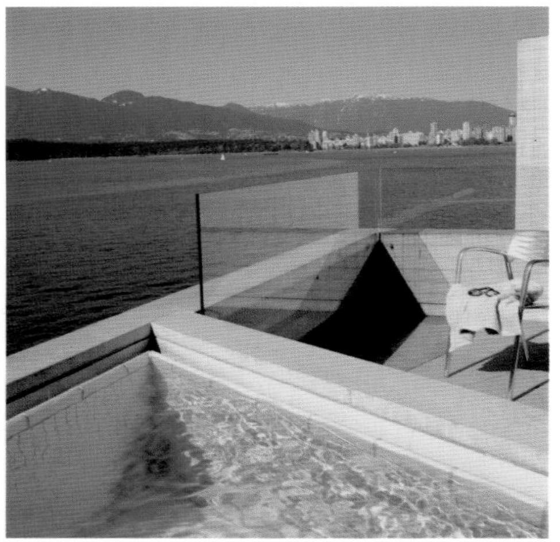

LEFT
Shaw House's well-situated terrace takes advantage of spectacular views of English Bay and the North Shore Mountains, as well as the beautiful city of Vancouver.

ABOVE
At night the white-tile-clad pool seems surprisingly shallow, and becomes almost like a light-box beaming against the darkened silhouette of the house.

Slat House CALIFORNIA, USA

David Hertz Architects

Constructed	2005
Home type	Three-level single family home
Structure	Concrete, typical wood framing, and some steel framing

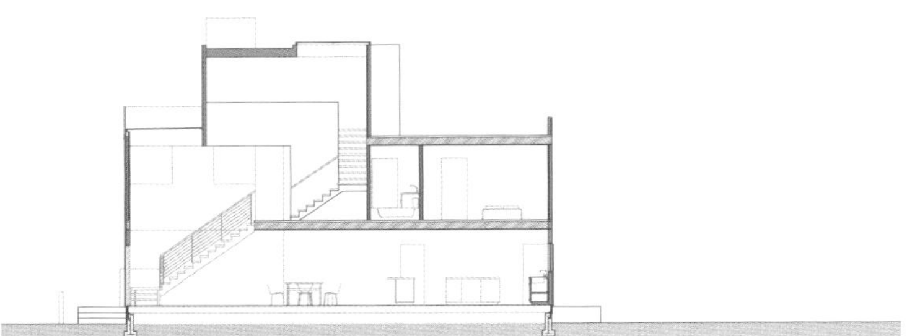

"The intent was to create a constantly changing facade on an existing elevation. Thin slats of Ipe wood provide a dynamic elevation defined by light and shadow...I've employed many environmental features – natural ventilation strategies, solar systems, solar hydronic radiant heating, and recycled content."

David Hertz

ABOVE
A clear view of the open kitchen/dining room area and the cantilevered Ipe wood stair is offered from the entry and living room. The double height volume and open plan provide a passage for natural ventilation and allow for an abundance of natural light.

SENSITIVE REVAMP

Built for an architectural lighting distributor and his young family, Slat House is an extensive remodel to an existing single-family residence. The client desired the new residence, located three buildings from the sand in Marina del Rey, to have the look and feel of a contemporary beach house while maintaining environmental consciousness.

The previous residence was an unsightly shingle-siding and mansard-roof structure; however, its position and proximity to the street, not allowed by today's code, made it essential to do a renovation rather than a rebuild.

A DYNAMIC EXTERIOR

Keeping the existing setback preserved the view of the ocean and allowed for more space within the dwelling. The proximity to the street did not allow for any extension of the facade. Within this limitation and in order to reinvent the exterior, the architect chose to integrate slats of Ipe wood, thus creating a front elevation that is both consistent with the building requirements, but also dynamic through its constant play of natural light and shadows.

The facade is designed to display an open or closed form through sliding panels at the corners and front door of the residence. By opening the corners, the ocean view can be enjoyed from inside, and at night, with the panels closed, the structure glows through veiled openings. The Ipe slats extend upward past the roofline, serving as an open railing for the roof deck.

During the renovation, the interior was stripped down to the studs and an extensive mold remediation completed. The remodeled interior consists of typical wood framing, steel framing, and solar hydronic radiant-heated concrete flooring.

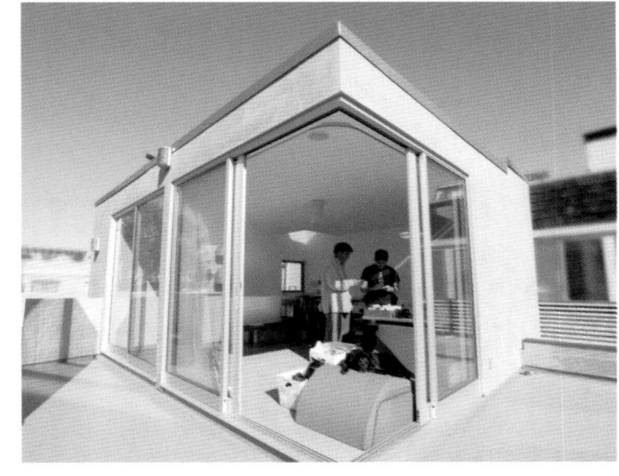

TOP LEFT
Building codes restricted a street-side extension, so the architect revitalized the facade with Ipe slats. The adjustable slats not only provide a more dynamic facade, they effectively modulate the passage of light and air into the interior.

TOP RIGHT
A home office, removed from the other areas of the residence, perches on the roof deck. The corner opens completely to the exterior, allowing fresh air to circulate through the space.

ABOVE
The structure within glows through the veiled openings, private without the need for draperies. The Ipe slats extend past the roofline, to become the railing for the roof deck.

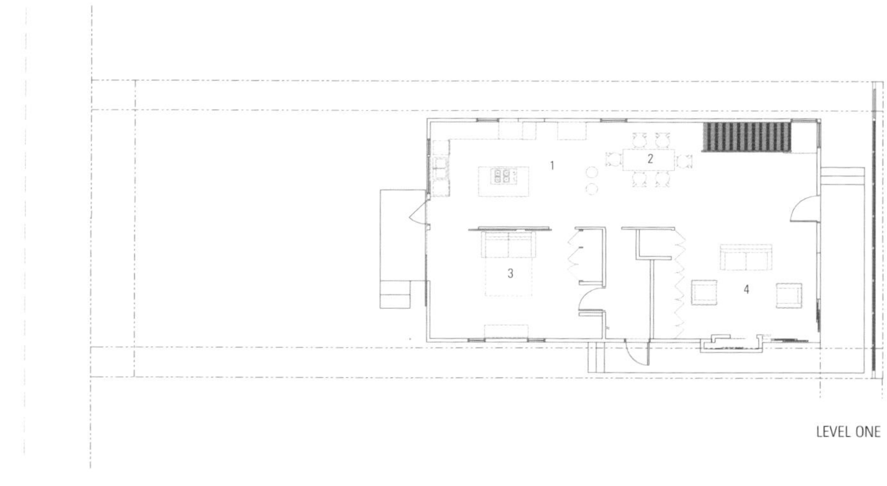

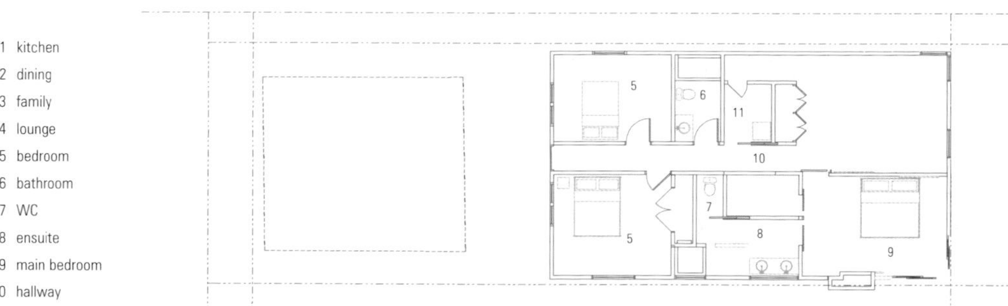

1 kitchen
2 dining
3 family
4 lounge
5 bedroom
6 bathroom
7 WC
8 ensuite
9 main bedroom
10 hallway
11 utility
12 office
13 roof terrace

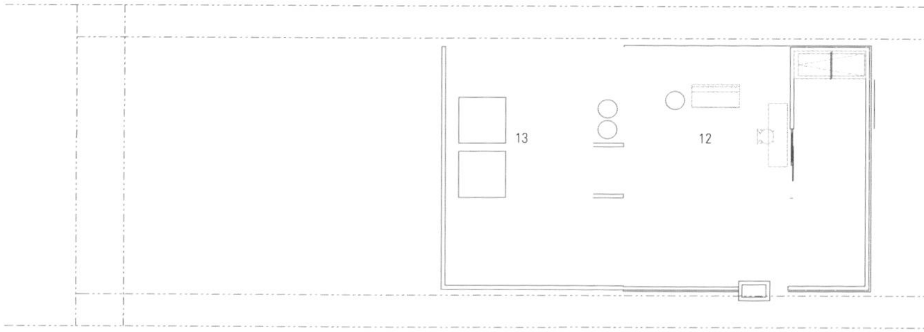

ABOVE
The Ipe slats of the facade create an interesting display of interrupted light bands that track the sun's movement.

RIGHT
This *Ofuro*, or Japanese soaking tub, is tucked away to provide a space both private and tranquil.

BEACHSIDE LIVING

On entry, there is a double-height living room space that seamlessly blends into the dining and kitchen areas toward the back of the house. The open space, clean finishes, and light-filled aspect of the first level is typical of beachside living. Notably, the kitchen counters are made of a recycled lightweight concrete developed by the architect.

The vertical circulation, a three-story sky-lit volume, hugs the south wall of the house. The stair treads from the first to second level are made of Ipe slats supported by cantilevered steel beams, and rest on a lightweight concrete plinth. The staircase from the second to third level has bamboo treads. The second level hosts the main bedroom and ensuite, two more bedrooms, a shared bathroom, and a utility room.

SEPARATING WORK AND LEISURE

An open-air office was added to the roof deck in order to separate the work area from the living areas. The roof deck is a gathering space with views of the beach and exposure to cooling ocean breezes.

LEFT
The cantilevered Ipe slat staircase, naturally lit by the skylights above, leads to the second-story living spaces. The second set of stairs, made from bamboo, leads to the roof deck and third-story office. Both staircases were made with sustainably harvested materials.

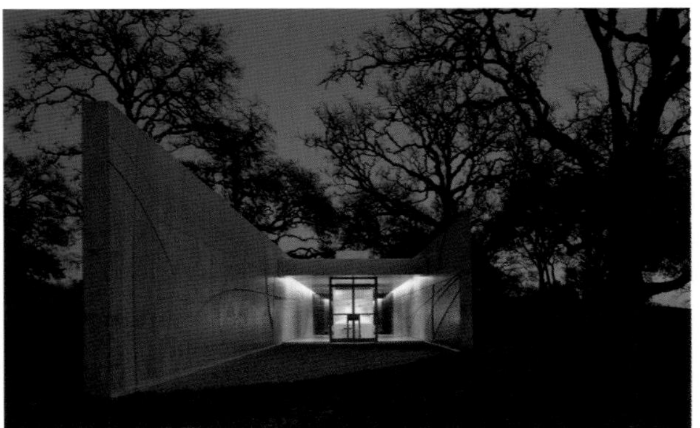

Chapter 14

In Your Dreams

The home of your dreams should be a unique form of self-expression. Its design and location are expressions of your lifestyle and personality.

Your dream home might be a luxurious penthouse in a vibrant city center, a cosy cabin in the woods, or an exhilarating place by the sea. Whatever your taste and lifestyle, the design of your dream home is a reflection of your preferred lifestyle. It is also informed by the location in which you build.

CAPTURING THE DREAM

The style of your dream home may be bold and vivacious or subtle and subdued. It may be organic in form, or have simple rectilinear shapes and clean lines. The interior could be a gallery that showcases a lifetime collection of treasures, or a stark and empty space, allowing the architecture itself to decorate your home.

It is the combination of the esthetic of your home and its surrounding context that truly reflects your personality – and the home of your dreams is the ultimate form of self-expression.

REFLECTS YOUR VALUES

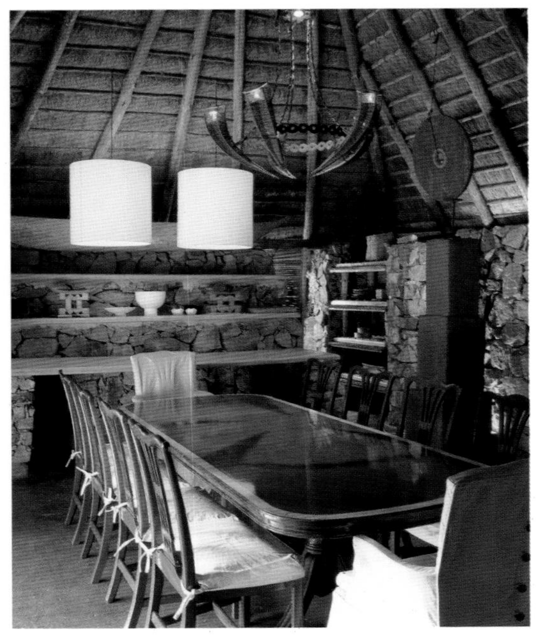

The functions of the internal spaces will reveal your ideals and dreams. Perhaps the bathroom is a simple basin and shower, a purely practical space. Or maybe it is a room where you can bathe in a deluxe spa tub while gazing out at a breathtaking view. The function of such a space is to soothe your body and re-energize your spirit.

Your belief system is further revealed by the spatial sequence and hierarchy of rooms. Is the parent's bedroom separate or adjacent to the children's bedrooms? Is the focal point of the living room an entertainment system or a fireplace? Is the kitchen spacious enough to accommodate a large dining table, or is it a compact area used for food preparation only?

The building process also illustrates your values. If you are committed to the ethos of sustainability, you will choose materials and construction methods that are environmentally sensitive, minimizing the impact of your home on the environment and the drain on natural resources.

REFLECTS YOUR LIFESTYLE

Your dream home should be situated in a place that is ideal for the lifestyle you wish to live, and this setting ultimately determines the appropriate architectural style. A tropical seaside villa might be open on all sides, inviting the environment inside, whereas the urban retreat may be a haven of calm within high security walls.

Unlike a project home that can be built almost anywhere to meet most people's needs, the dream home is tailored to suit the precise requirements of the owner, from concept to detail, be it an infinity pool that meets the horizon, creating luxurious quarters for guests, or using hand-crafted materials.

Although the location of the home will in some way inform the architecture, many of the defining elements will be custom built rather than bought off the shelf.

In extraordinary landscapes, architects have worked with their clients to explore new ideas about what "home" might mean with new materials and alternative construction techniques. Many of today's dream homes are limited only by the imagination.

ABOVE
House Westcliff,
Silvio Rech & Lesley Carstens,
Architecture & Interiors

TOP RIGHT
Visiting Artists House,
Jim Jennings Architecture

OPPOSITE
St Leon House,
Stefan Antoni Olmesdahl
Truen Architects

Casa Cusenza PUERTO VALLARTA, MEXICO

Van Tilburg, Banvard & Soderbergh SANTA MONICA, USA

Construction 2003–2005
Home type Two-story, single-family dwelling
Structure Cast-in-place concrete frame, with slab on grade and partially raised first floor structural slabs, masonry walls

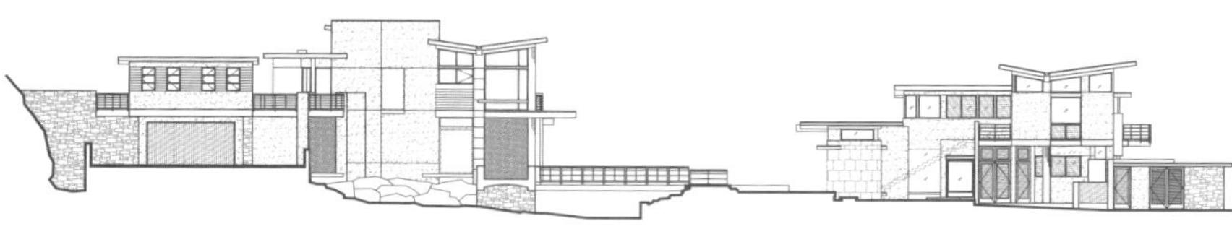

EAST ELEVATION – MAIN HOUSE AND GUESTHOUSE

"Nature was the catalyst for design, form, and function. From the moment I set foot on the site, three monumental higuera trees, towering well over 50 ft (15 m) above the jungle floor, became my focal point. Articulating design elements of glass, stone, and concrete beneath their protective canopy evolved into what is now Casa Cusenza."

Peter J Petraglia

ABOVE
An evening view of the guesthouse. The sloped concrete "butterfly" roofs add a sculptural element to the home. Strategically placed scuppers catch rainfall and create a series of waterfalls that cascade from roof to roof, and then drain into the natural stream below. The solid teak wood entry door was fabricated in Bali by Jerome Abel Seguin.

A TASTE OF PARADISE

The clients, successful business owners with an insatiable appetite for design and creativity, envisioned a contemporary oasis along the southern shores of picturesque Puerto Vallarta. They wished to create a Zen-inspired oasis embracing Vallarta's natural beauty, while at the same time pushing the envelope and redefining traditional construction techniques.

A lush tropical rainforest with mature specimen trees, natural waterfalls and streams, a private sandy beach, and breathtaking cobalt blue ocean vistas are just a few of the natural amenities to be found on the site.

WEAVING THE HOUSE INTO THE LANDSCAPE

After clearing the undergrowth, the main challenge was preserving the integrity of the land while at the same time creating the clients' dream home: This was to be contemporary with a minimum number of interior walls and a maximization of views – a home that seamlessly moved between interior and exterior spaces.

The next challenge was to incorporate the main house and guesthouse into lush hillside jungle, while preserving the natural beauty of the higuera trees, rambling streams, and a sandy beach. Landscaping the site and creating outdoor rooms became the primary design focus. Both architect and clients were acutely attuned to respecting nature and the gifts it had given them.

The main house was positioned beneath the large higuera trees, taking advantage of the shade from their canopy. Raising the foundation 10 ft (3 m) above the forest floor minimized the impact on the root structure and allowed the natural stream cutting through the site to run its course.

Smooth white plaster and concrete were the primary building materials, while limestone and natural rock veneers were used as accent finishes.

CONNECTING INSIDE AND OUTSIDE

Public rooms, including the main "gathering space," kitchen, and dining room are positioned on the first level to maximize a connection between inside and outside. Bedrooms are on the second floor to capture views and take advantage of natural ocean breezes. The guesthouse is across the natural stream facing the main house. A wooden bridge connects the guesthouse to the main entry, while a cascading terrace and lawn make the transition down to the edge of the pool.

Despite its soaring two-story volume, the main living space is the intimate heart of the house. Pocketing glass walls allow nature to flow through the space. Sheer fabric scrims and sliding glass panels create layers between interior and exterior – a design element echoed throughout the home. Sloped concrete "butterfly" roofs are a sculptural feature of the house. Rain scuppers are strategically placed to create a series of waterfalls that cascade from roof to roof, and then drain into the natural stream below.

ABOVE
Here the interplay between interior and exterior creates a "dreamy" ambience. The creamy white terrazzo slab floors seamlessly flow from the interior to the outdoor dining terrace, while the frameless corner glass panels, with floating concrete serving counter, redefine the lines between the spaces. A teak wood deck, punctured by the natural vegetation, extends out to the ocean's edge.

RIGHT
The two-story "gathering space" is the heart of the main house. All of the living spaces radiate from this central area. A living tree next to the floating wood slab staircase provides texture and contrasts with the contemporary lines of the space.

Creating seamless transitions between interior and exterior space, and blending the natural beauty of the oceanfront site with the clients' vision of their "dream home" presented challenges that ultimately became the genesis for the project.

1 main bedroom
2 main bathroom
3 bedroom
4 loft
5 employee quarters
6 terrace
7 roof
8 open to below

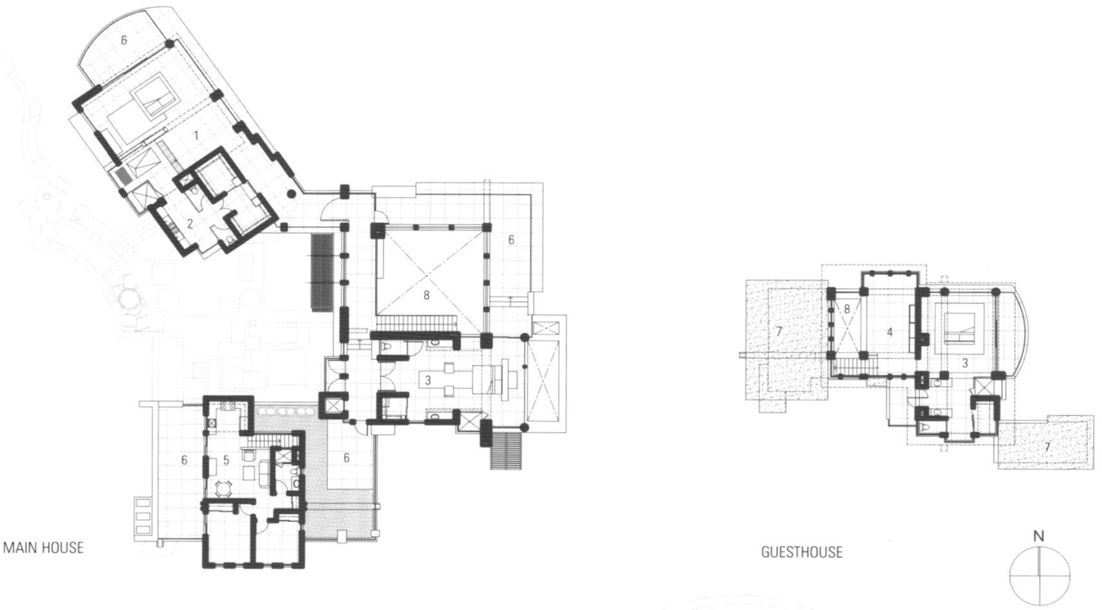

LEVEL TWO, MAIN HOUSE

GUESTHOUSE

N

1 entry
2 gathering space
3 media room
4 Zen garden
5 kitchen
6 dining
7 pantry
8 WC
9 outdoor pizza oven
10 teak bridge
11 terrace
12 pool
13 bedroom
14 bathroom
15 utility
16 laundry
17 storage
18 entry drive
19 garage
20 water feature

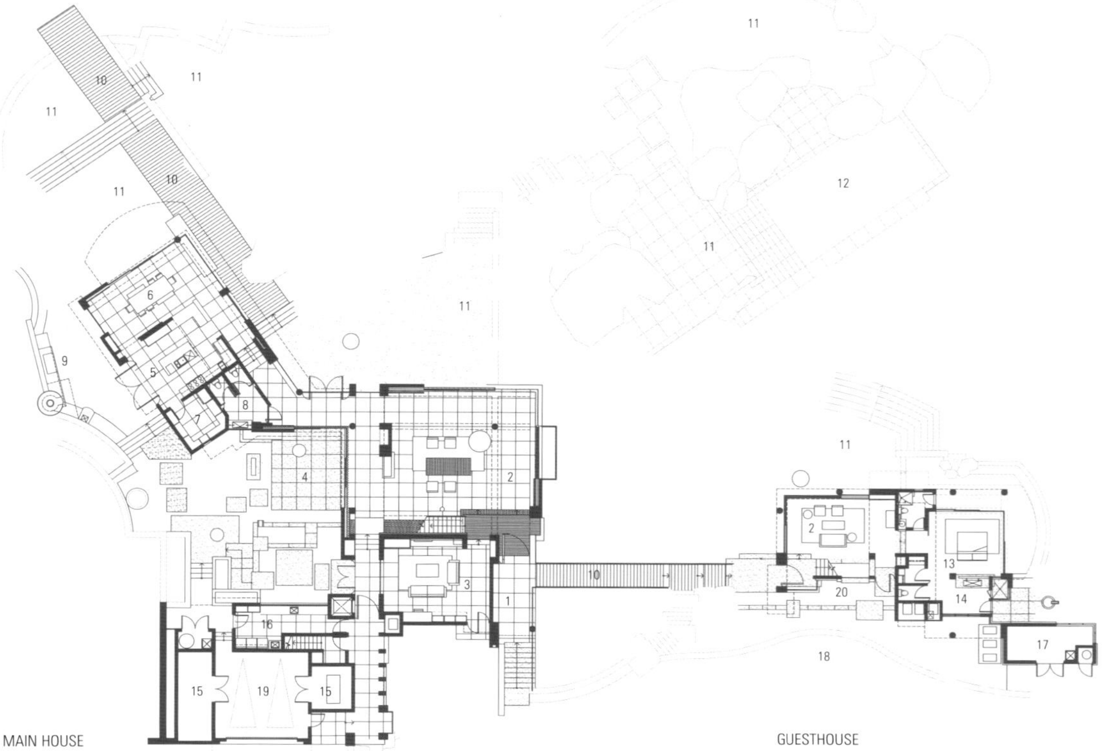

LEVEL ONE, MAIN HOUSE

GUESTHOUSE

ABOVE
The cantilevered floor slabs and frameless corner glazing of the main home's "gathering space" reach out and embrace the natural beauty of the site. The sheltering canopies of higuera trees provide a natural enclosure for the surrounding terraces.

FAR TOP LEFT
A natural clearing on the site provided the perfect location for the guesthouse. Cascading concrete terrace steps flow gracefully onto the wooded lawn, which meets the travertine-lined pool at the ocean's edge.

RIGHT
Natural stone finishes – the travertine slabs in the pool, granite boulder chairs, and limestone buddha – ground the Zen garden, which is located just off the gathering space of the main house. Ocean breezes naturally cool the space as they pass through the terrace doors.

Casa Marrom SÃO PAULO, BRAZIL

Isay Weinfeld

Construction	2003–2004
Home type	Four-level family home
Structure	Poured concrete and steel

"Our clients are very informal people who wanted a house that expressed their relaxed way of living. Bright, wide living areas open onto the garden, patio, and pool allowing for full integration of interior and exterior spaces."

Isay Weinfeld

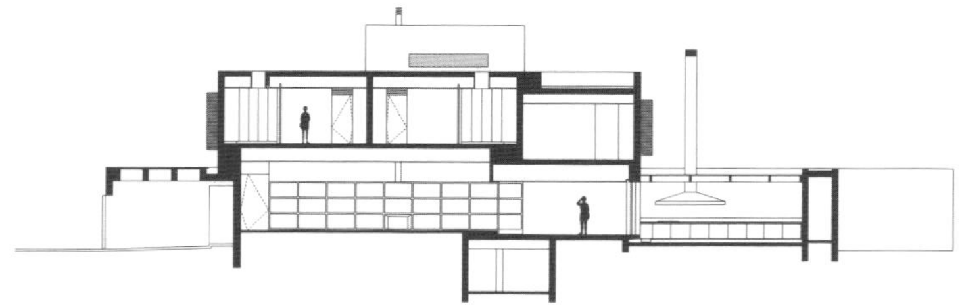

ABOVE
The three main elements of Casa Marrom can be seen in this view of the front facade – concrete, steel, and prefabricated plates made of cement and brown pebbles. These provide absolute privacy and a pleasing textural motif.

RIGHT
Timber was a logical choice for the external cladding on an upstairs bedroom because of its inherent ability to minimize heat. The living room below is oblivious to the vagaries of nature due to the presence of a large concrete overhang, which protects it from torrential tropical rains as well as providing much-needed shade.

NATURE-BASED RETREAT

In the teeming midst of the Brazilian city of São Paulo, with its 18 million inhabitants, a warm, comfortable residence has been conceived by architect Isay Weinfeld for his brother and his family.

Tropical trees stand in contrast to the muted grays of the property's high perimeter walls. The walls provide the home with an introverted focus and transform Casa Marrom into a retreat that helps reconnect its occupants with nature, and cocoons them from the city's tumultuous rhythms.

BEAUTY IN A BLIGHTED METROPOLIS

Weinfeld's engaging residences can be found spread across the city's wealthier neighborhoods, providing occasional glimpses of beauty and form in a metropolis the architect freely admits has no equal when it comes to ugliness.

His interest in design was first prompted by the city's high crime rate and population density, which, in turn, is forcing people to live in increasingly smaller spaces. São Paulian interest in design is a relatively recent phenomenon, with considerations of safety and economic well-being understandably taking precedence over mere visual esthetics.

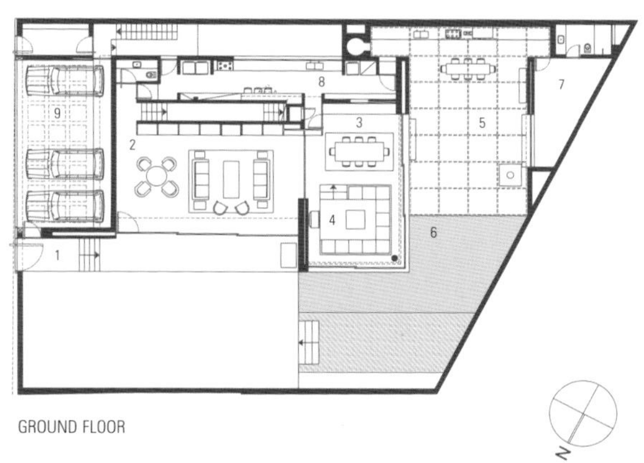

GROUND FLOOR

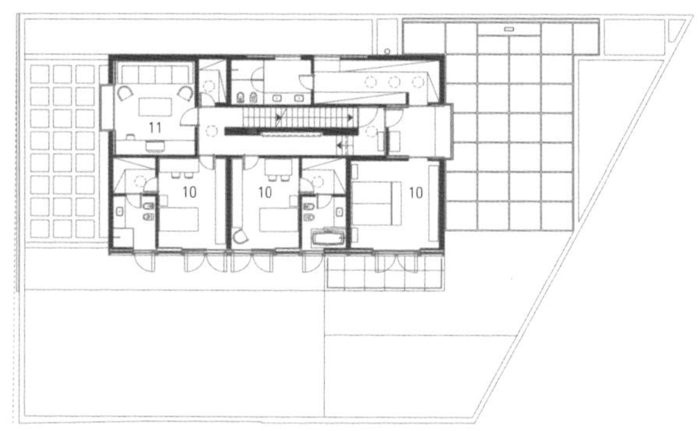

FIRST FLOOR

1 main entrance
2 living
3 dining
4 media
5 barbecue/dining
6 swimming pool
7 gym
8 kitchen
9 garage
10 bedroom
11 family

TOP
This view of the outdoor living area highlights its central role in the relaxed approach to life inherent in Casa Marrom. A kiln, a stove, and a grill are all to be found beneath the broad expanse of the glass-covered, wooden pergola. The swimming pool and living area combine to form a haven in the midst of the tumult of the city.

ABOVE
The entrance lawn on the building's northern facade, bordered by massed plantings of vibrant tropical foliage, abuts the main living room and its heavy concrete overhang. Glass doors slide into deep recesses in the walls to provide an exhilarating connection to this simple, elegant garden.

MATERIALS AND SCALE

Weinfeld's love affair with Brazilian raw materials yields an inviting tropical Modernism in Casa Marrom. Stone and timber have been used side by side to provide textual contrasts. A specially constructed design element involved prefabricated panels of cement and brown pebbles, used both as a facing on the street wall and facades, and as paving on the roof terrace. Steel and concrete also figure prominently. Experiments of scale are played out throughout the home where large sliding doors, when not recessed into the wall cavities, turn soaring, wide-open spaces into cozy, intimate nooks.

The 6,867-sq-ft (638-sq-m) house is constructed over four levels and begins with a step-up to the entry from street level. Wide living areas, designed in succession, open up to the garden, pool, and patio area creating a seamless integration of internal and external spaces. A large concrete overhang protects the living room from sun and rain.

Wooden siding and glass louvers characterize the upper level, while a rooftop terrace overlooks Casa Marrom's elegant L-shaped courtyard.

An outdoor swimming pool is connected to a deck via a stone pathway, before wrapping itself around the living room in its approach to the outdoor dining/barbecue area. This dining space is equipped with a kiln, grill, and a stove, all set beneath a large glass-covered wooden pergola, reflecting the clients' relaxed and informal approach to life.

The home also contains a basement level, complete with bedrooms and bathrooms for employees, a laundry, storage area, and a utilities room.

RIGHT
The exaggerated depth of the concrete overhang affords the living area a sense of separateness from the home's exterior even when its sliding doors are open. A pathway of stones creates an informal trail to the swimming pool deck.

Chesa Futura ST MORITZ, SWITZERLAND

Foster and Partners LONDON, ENGLAND
Küchel Architects ST MORITZ

Construction	2001–2004
Home type	Six apartments (with potential for 12) on three stories
Structure	Double-curved timber frame with wooden shingle cladding

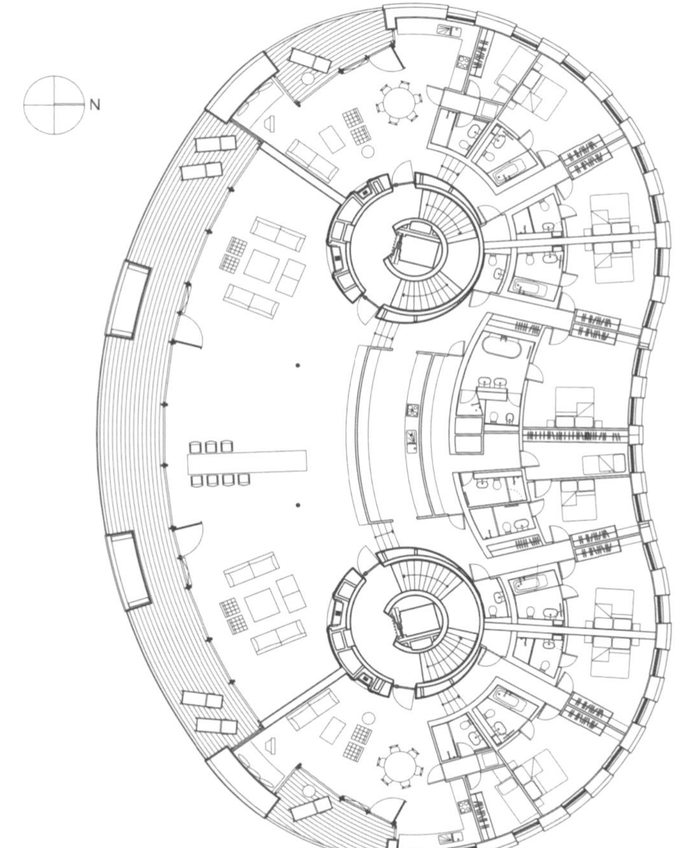

"Taken overall, Chesa Futura (literally, 'house of the future') might be regarded as a mini manifesto for architecture, not just here but in other parts of the world. Contrary to the pattern of sprawl that disfigures the edges of so many expanding communities, it shows how new buildings can be inserted into the existing grain at increased densities, while sustaining indigenous building techniques and preserving the natural environment."

Foster and Partners

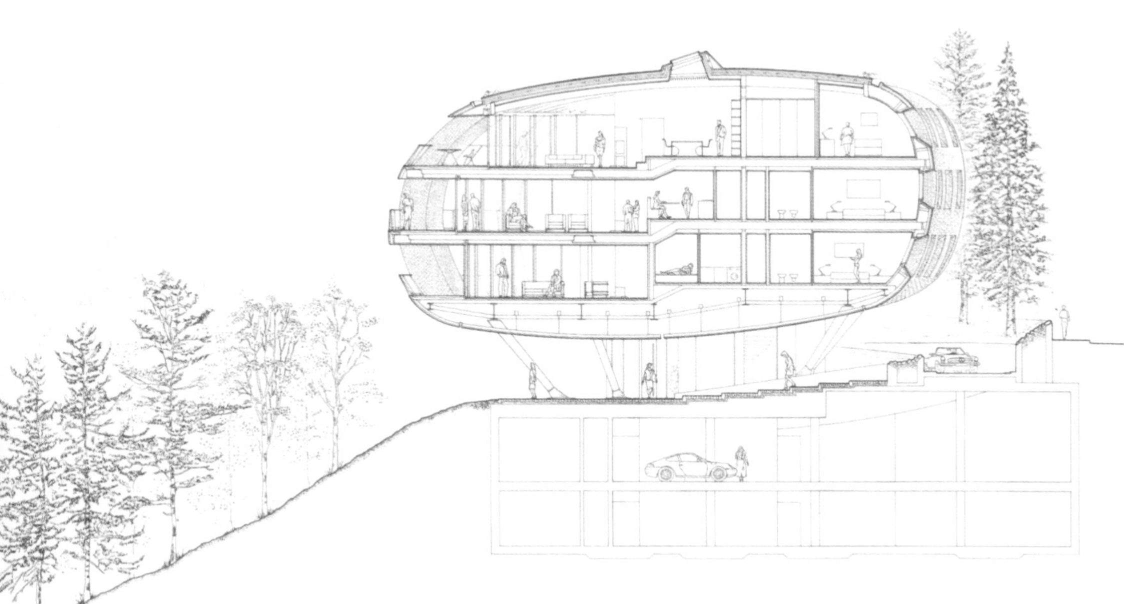

ABOVE
The building's facades curve in two directions and are reminiscent of a boat's hull. The bedrooms sit along the highly insulated northern facade, whereas the living areas with terraces, pictured above, are to the south and make the most of the sunlight and the views. There is no storage against the external walls, only on the internal partitions, which radiate from the cores.

ABOVE LEFT
Visible to the right of the church spire, Chesa Futura, with its unique fusion of modern design ideas and centuries-old construction techniques, is noticeably different from surrounding buildings, but at the same time sympathetic to the alpine landscape. The building does not appear bulky because of its rounded form.

Chesa Futura apartment building lies in the densely built town center of St Moritz – the popular skiing resort in Switzerland, 6,000 ft (1,800 m) above sea level in the Engadin valley. Although small, the site is spectacularly located on the edge of a slope looking out across the village toward the lake. The building fuses state-of-the-art computer design with "tried and true" traditional building techniques. Considered novel in form, it uses age-old timber construction – one of the most sustainable methods of building.

A CHALLENGING SITE

The kidney-shaped, three-story structure contains six apartments sitting above the ground on eight "legs" – the architect's creative response to the multiple demands of the site, the local weather conditions, and the planning regulations. (In Switzerland, where snow lies on the ground for many months of the year, there is a long tradition of elevating buildings to avoid wood rot due to prolonged exposure to moisture.)

The site has a height restriction of 51 ft (15.5 m) above its sloping contours. A conventional rectilinear building would have protruded over the specified height, whereas the raised, sculptured form complies with planning regulations without compromising the overall floor area.

LETTING IN THE LIGHT

Large south-facing windows and balconies literally wrap around the convexly curved facade of the building. This allows generous amounts of sunlight into the apartments and makes the most of the spectacular view. The north-facing concave aspect gives protection from the coldest mountain weather. The building also provides insulation through its own thermal mass – the structural frame creates a 16-in- (40-cm-) wide cavity filled with insulating material. Small windows are punched into the northern facade, echoing traditional Engadin windows with their chamfered surrounds, to allow maximum light penetration.

PREFABRICATION IS THE KEY

The structure was developed in close collaboration with two engineering firms: Arups in England and Toscano in Switzerland. Construction was restricted to less than eight months of the year because of the winter holiday seasons, so a high degree of prefabrication was important. The tight site, which could only be approached via narrow winding roads, coupled with the length and width of the construction equipment, meant that considerable time went into the sizing of individual components.

ABOVE
By raising the building on legs, each of the apartments enjoys a wood-framed alpine panorama. The small, densely populated skiing village of St Moritz, Switzerland, accommodates a resident population of 5,000 – a number that swells to 50,000 during the peak seasons.

STRUCTURE AND FUNCTION

The foundations consist of a sunken concrete box, which houses the plant rooms, car parking, and storage spaces. Above ground, the building is supported on a lightweight steel "table" approximately 65 by 130 ft (20 by 40 m) with eight steel legs. Two concrete cores, 6½ ft (2 m) in diameter, housing the elevator shafts and stairwells, provide further stability. The remaining structure is timber.

The total weight of the structure (steel columns and table, the concrete cores, and the timber frame) is 2,750 tons (2,500 tonnes). The timber load-bearing frame reduces the dead load of the building by as much as 40 per cent.

The timber frame is made up of a series of prefabricated elements. Each element is composed of glue-laminated beams (thin pinewood planks, 1 in by 10 in by 40 ft/25 mm by 250 mm by 12 m, glued together to obtain the various geometric shapes), a skin of plywood, and OSB timber (oriented strand board). By using computer-driven cutting machines in the factory it was possible to obtain precisely sized elements with up to ⅛ inch (3 mm) tolerance.

SHINGLES – SIMPLE AND SUBLIME

The larch shingles that make up the building's skin not only reflect local architectural traditions, but also combine harmoniously with the building's shape. Because local timber was used, little energy was expended in its transportation. The trees were cut during winter when the wood was dry and without sap, which helps prevent timber shrinkage.

By cutting the timber both laterally and radially, the wood was used in the most efficient way – 80 trees provided the required 8,500 cubic ft (240 cubic m) of shingles. The two different cuts combine beneficial water-draining characteristics with structural strength. They also provide an appealing variegated appearance.

The copper roof, chosen because copper is sufficiently malleable to be formed on site when temperatures drop below 12°F (-11°C), has long been used by locals and is sympathetic to surrounding buildings.

The building fuses state-of-the-art computer design with "tried and true" traditional building techniques.

ABOVE LEFT
Eighty larch trees, taken from the surrounding landscape, provided the required 8,500 cubic ft (240 cubic m) of shingles for the building. To eliminate shrinkage, the trees were felled during winter when the wood was dry and without sap.

LEFT
The shingles were cut by a local family firm (that has practised the craft for generations) and applied to the roof by hand using nails. Over time, and in response to the weather, the shingles will change to silver-gray. They will last without maintenance for about 80 years.

ABOVE
By sculpting the building into a rounded form, the architects were able to maintain the desired overall floor area, while at the same time complying with building regulations – a conventional rectilinear building would have protruded over the specified height. The curved form allows windows to wrap around the facade, providing panoramic views of the town and the lake.

TRADITIONAL MATERIALS MEET COMPUTER DESIGN

The building's curved form was refined using a specially written computer program which converted flat plans into a three-dimensional form. The computer model acted like a conventional spreadsheet, enabling any part of the building to be altered and instantly generating a new overall form. Also, this allowed numerous design studies to be tested in a fraction of the time required for conventional modeling techniques. The computer model could be cut through any section to produce drawings of any part of the building.

The digital information was directly exported to cutting tools to build physical models and then ultimately to the machines that made the timber building components.

Chicken Point Cabin IDAHO, USA

Olson Sundberg Kundig Allen Architects

Constructed 2003
Home type Two-level family holiday home
Structure Concrete block, steel, and wood

ABOVE
This spectacular glass and steel door pivots up, opening the living room area of the cabin to the lake and surrounding countryside. The pivoting door is operated by an innovative hand-cranked mechanism that might be regarded as quaint in this age of remote controls.

"The idea here was to create a little house with a big window, so that the interior became the threshold, or link, between the lake and the forest – literally opening the cabin to the natural landscape of northern Idaho."
Tom Kundig

NOT YOUR AVERAGE LAKESIDE CABIN

The shore of a lake in northern Idaho is the setting for this unique vacation home. While the concept is of a lakeside shelter nestled in the woods, Chicken Point Cabin is far more than simply a holiday house. At first glance, it may resemble a little box with an outsized window, but it is a forest retreat and an artistic expression all in one.

WINDOW TO THE WORLD

The front entry to the house is an unusually tall and wondrous steel door, 19 ft (5.8 m) high. It opens to a narrow hallway, which in turn leads to the spacious living room, designed as a seamless extension to the exterior environment.

The living room measures some 22 ft (6.6 m) high and contains the home's most dramatic and defining feature: An enormous glass and steel window-wall measuring 30 ft by 20 ft (9 m by 6 m), which opens out the entire living space to the lake and forest. Operated by a specially designed hand-crank mechanism, named "the gizmo" by the architect Tom Kundig, the window-wall opens out rather like a garage door. Outside, on the concrete terrace, the family – a couple and their two children – can enjoy the tranquil views of the lake from the hot tub.

STAIRWAY TO HEAVEN

Just inside the entry door, there is a huge wooden staircase that leads up to the main bedroom, which is essentially a simple plywood box that seems to hover over much of the ground floor of the house, and which looks out over the lake. The children's bedrooms are

more of a bunk style and the house can sleep ten people at any time. There are two bathrooms. The roof of the cabin tilts upward to optimize the amount of light coming into the interior.

MATCHING MATERIALS WITH THE SETTING

The design of the cabin is in three main parts – a concrete block box with a plywood insert and a 4-ft (1.2-m) diameter steel fireplace. The fireplace is a feature in itself. It is constructed from a large steel pipe, which has structural as well as esthetic importance. Directly in front of the fireplace is a rock that is similar to rocks found on the lake's edge. It adds a natural texture to the floor, which is concrete.

The materials selected for the house are all low- or no-maintenance, and were chosen because of the way they age. The concrete and steel were left unfinished, so that as they age they acquire the natural patina that merges well with the forest landscape – the steel oxidizes a reddish brown and the concrete gathers moss.

The internal finishes also maintain this theme, being stainless steel, timber, and concrete. The whole effect is one of warmth and welcome.

ABOVE
The main bedroom area, a simple wood construction, is seen here hovering above the ultra-modern kitchen. Another feature of the living room is the fireplace (on the right), which is housed in an impressive steel pipe that reaches 22 ft (6.6 m) to the ceiling.

TOP RIGHT
The roof's wide overhang tilts upward, allowing plenty of light to reach the interior, while at the same time protecting the living spaces from the hot sun.

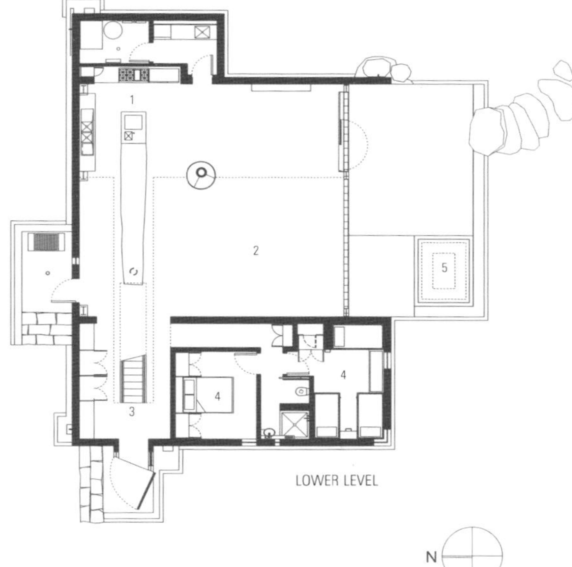

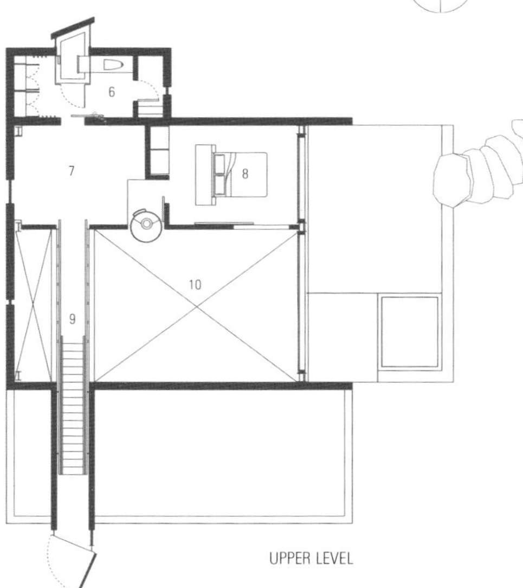

1 kitchen
2 living
3 staircase/entry
4 bedroom
5 sunken tub
6 main bathroom
7 sitting area
8 main bedroom
9 staircase/bridge
10 open to below

Coromandel Bach COROMANDEL, NEW ZEALAND

Crosson Clarke Carnachan Architects

Constructed	2002
Home type	Single dwelling
Structure	Timber-frame floor, walls, and roof with membrane roofing over plywoods

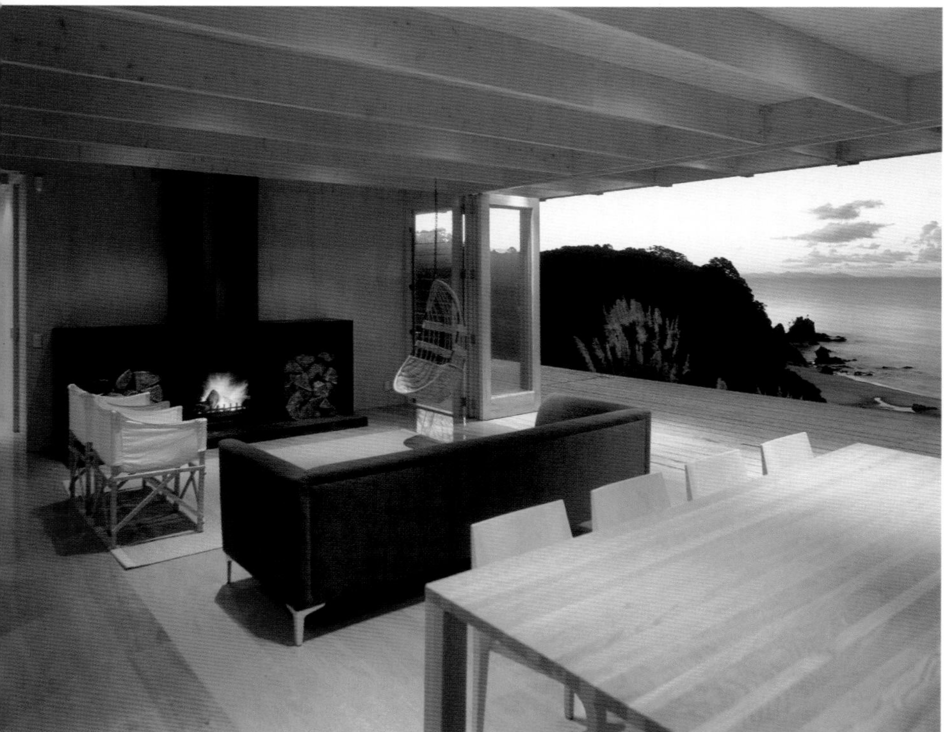

"I was interested in designing a building that contrasted with living in the city, a building with a naturalness and openness to the outside – the sun, sea breezes, and view. By dissolving the walls the experience of common rituals is reinforced – showering in the sun, bathing under the stars, cooking outside, and gathering around the fire."

Ken Crosson

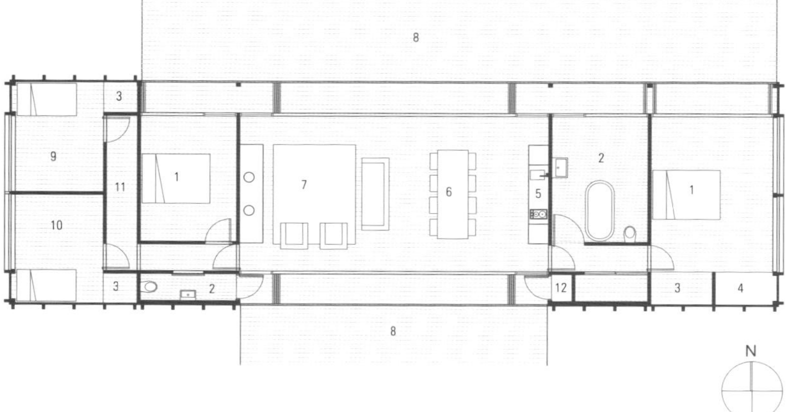

1 bedroom
2 bathroom
3 wardrobe
4 desk
5 kitchen
6 dining
7 family
8 deck
9 bunk 1
10 bunk 2
11 hallway
12 barbecue

ABOVE LEFT
The open fire burns while the living room remains open to the outdoors – giving the home a "camp-like" quality.

ABOVE CENTER
The perfect weekend cottage is a shut up "box" while the owners are away. On arrival, the decks are opened down on either side, providing a stage for living.

TOP
The architects conceived the structure as a "container" sitting lightly on the land. The rich yellow joinery and interior plywood contrast with the naturally weathered cladding on the exterior. The silver gray exterior merges with the gray trunks of the Manuka tree-covered ridge.

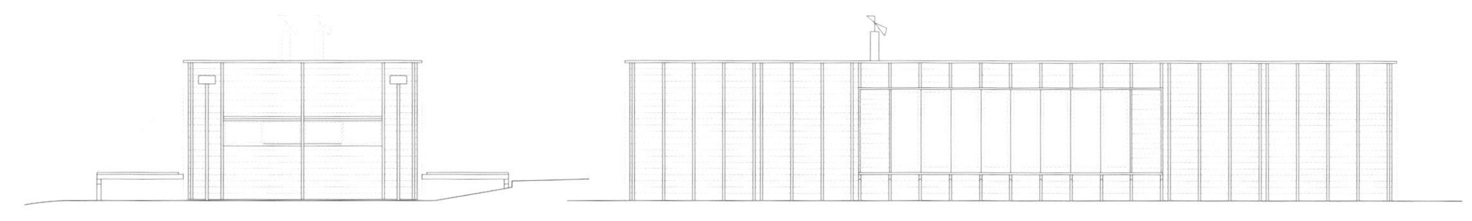

A PACIFIC HAVEN

The Coromandel Peninsula is just east of the North Island's biggest city, Auckland. It enjoys beautiful views over the Hauraki Gulf, and with its pristine beaches and stunning coastal scenery, is a favorite tourist and holiday destination for locals and international visitors alike.

REINTERPRETING TRADITION

The site is 26 acres (10.5 ha) and the house itself measures 1,378 sq ft (128 sq m). This house was conceived as a container sitting lightly on the land either for habitation or simply the dream of habitation. The intention was to reinterpret the New Zealand building tradition of the crafting of wood – the expression of structure, cladding, lining, and joinery in a raw and unique way. The construction is reminiscent of the "trip" or "rafter" dams that were common in the Coromandel region at the turn of the twentieth century. – heavy vertical structural members supporting horizontal boarding.

SUSTAINABLE MATERIALS, WARM RESULT

The structural posts of the house are Saligna, as are the exterior studs and joists. The cladding, decking, flooring, and rafters, as well as the bathroom gratings, are Lawson cyprus. This particular timber was chosen because of its durability and sustainability. The internal walls and ceilings are hoop pine plywood, as is the interior cabinetry.

The unadorned natural timber provides a connection to the natural environment. A simple mechanism to the deck allows the "box" to open on arrival, providing a stage for living, and to close on departure, for protection while the inhabitants are away.

SIMPLICITY AND STYLE

The house has a rectangular plan that sits across the contour in a patch of cleared bush, much like a rural shed, facing north and toward the view. The living room is open to the outside and the sun, acting as a metaphorical tent or campsite.

There are two main bedrooms with bifold doors that open the rooms to the outside. Additionally, two bunk rooms provide a shady haven from the hot summer sun with their small west-facing slot windows.

Further reinforcing the "camping out" experience, the bathroom opens to the outside. The bath itself is on wheels, thus providing the opportunity to bathe as one prefers – sheltered indoors, under the stars, or in front of the fire.

CAPTURING THE ESSENCE OF NEW ZEALAND

In New Zealand, "bach" describes a weekend cottage or house, usually located at the beach. With this bach, the architects have attempted to provide an environment that captures the essence of the New Zealand holiday spirit within its beautiful local landscape.

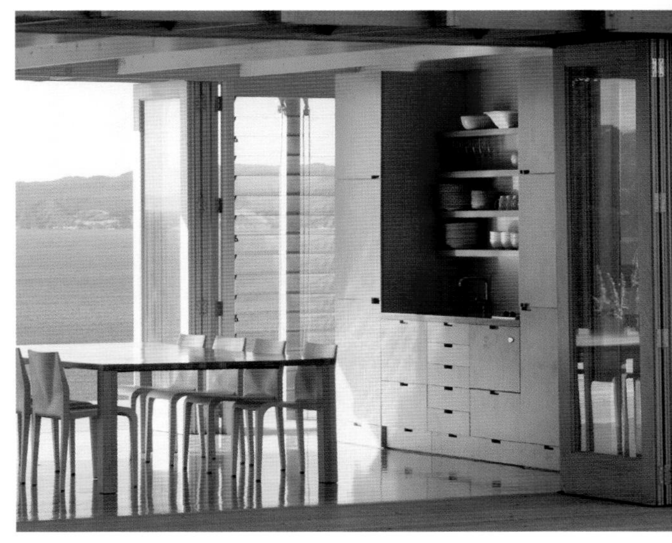

ABOVE
The dining table, designed by Ken Crosson, is an extension of the small kitchen. The kitchen is simple and open, unadorned and practical, with all crockery and utensils within easy reach. The plywood cabinetry has the same finish as the interior wall lining.

Crescent House CALIFORNIA, USA

Wallace E Cunningham

Construction 2000–2004
Home type Multi-level family residence
Structure Steel frame on concrete slab with cast-in-place concrete walls

"The clients required a residence that would provide a retreat from their active business lives as well as accommodate recurrent and extended family stays. An attempt has also been made to create a sense of isolation from the surrounding built environment."

Wallace E Cunningham

RAMP IT UP

Crescent House is a multi-story, concrete and glass residence situated on a clifftop in the southern Californian city of Encinitas. The area is known for its beautiful beaches, flat-topped cliffs, and steep mesa bluffs, and so the bedrooms, living areas, and terraces all boast expansive views of the Pacific Ocean.

From the street, a circular concrete ramp connects all three levels, wrapping around an overflowing crescent-shaped swimming pool that is surrounded by soaring walls of concrete and dominated by an expressive, triangular-shaped roof. This filters light into the interior spaces below.

GEOMETRIC FORMS

Because the home is perched on a clifftop, an extensive bluff retention system, which incorporated concrete tiebacks, was required to anchor it into the site. The building's opaque northern and southern elevations, closely bordered by neighboring properties, are punctuated by small, strategically placed openings designed to admit light into carefully selected spaces. A garage on the basement level has both a stairway and private elevator that serves the terrace and upper levels. The roof's complex geometric forms provide an exciting visual connection to the ocean while obscuring any views of neighboring buildings.

SURFACES AND FINISHES

The exterior surfaces of the home are a combination of cast-in-place concrete (which serves as both walls and facade), Portland cement plaster, clear frameless laminated glass with mirror-insulated glazing, and metal panels finished with a protective fluoropolymer coating that is stable in UV light.

The house's external decks are fashioned from metal, while the roof is constructed from a series of steel tube trusses that unfold across the house. In order to protect the exterior from the highly corrosive effects of the coastal surroundings, these elements (including integrated gutters) are also sheathed in flat-seamed fluoropolymer-finished metal panels for longevity.

TOP LEFT
Deeply recessed balconies provide shade from the afternoon sun on the western side of the house. From inside, the ocean views are dramatized through rectangular frameworks of cast-in-place concrete, the vertical slabs doubling as both internal walls and external facades.

ABOVE
Bold and complex geometric forms adorn the roof, angled to allow filtered light into various internal spaces in the home's upper level. These forms also act as a visual path to the horizon.

LEFT
A series of recesses – perhaps a Modernist version of Doric columns – provides an almost ornamental touch to the curved concrete wall. The sense of timelessness and classic strength is intensified by the water's reflection.

FOLLOWING PAGES
Surrounded by soaring walls of concrete, the three-level structure wraps around the overflowing crescent-shaped swimming pool that is the heart of this impressive house.

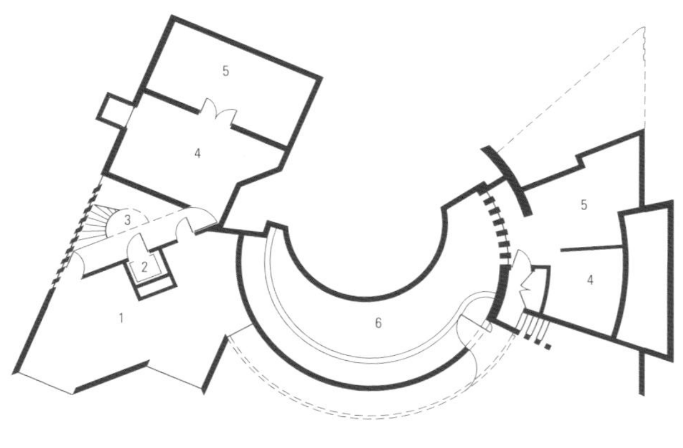

BASEMENT

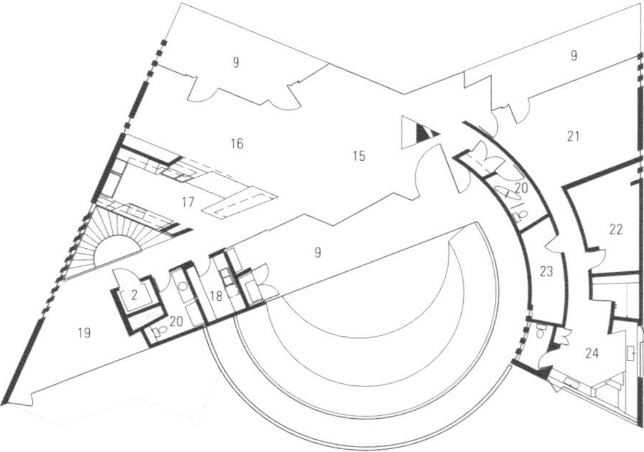

UPPER LEVEL (LEVEL THREE)

1	garage	13	closet
2	elevator	14	gym
3	entry foyer	15	living
4	storage	16	dining
5	utility	17	kitchen
6	pool	18	pantry
7	laundry	19	media room
8	office	20	powder room
9	terrace	21	main bedroom
10	hall	22	walk-in robe 1
11	bedroom	23	walk-in robe 2
12	bathroom	24	ensuite bathroom

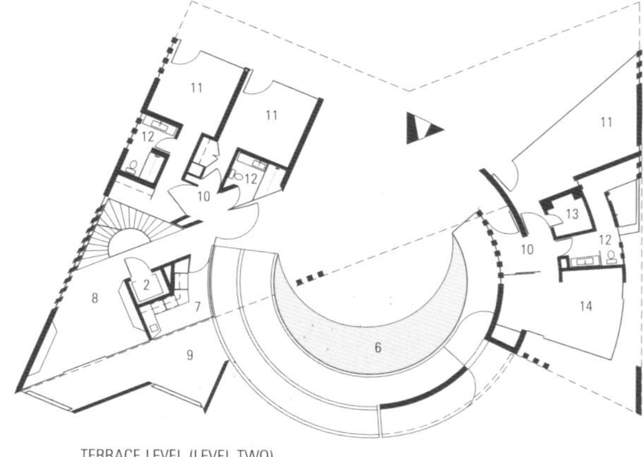

TERRACE LEVEL (LEVEL TWO)

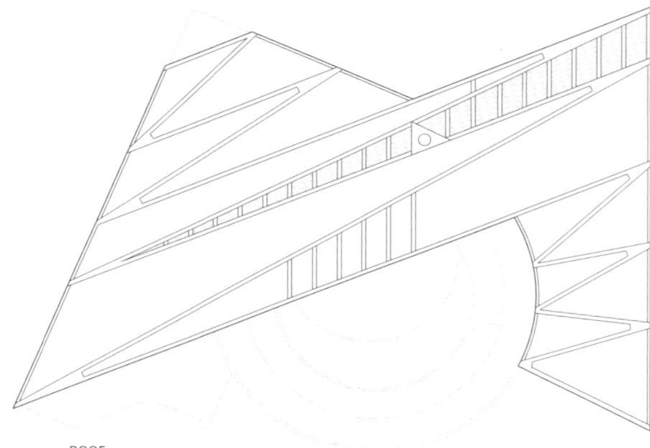

ROOF

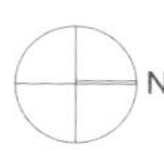

The interior walls are largely veneer plaster, architectural concrete, and fluoropolymer-finished metal panels; the internal stairs are stainless steel and glass. Throughout the 6,329-sq-ft (588-sq-m) home, the limestone flooring has an underlying hydronic heating system – hot water is pumped through a thermal mass floor, which absorbs the heat and radiates it to the living space.

SEA FOR MILES

Frameless glass panels in the capacious bedrooms on the terrace level afford expansive views of the ocean. On the upper level, the kitchen leads directly into the living room, where a spectacular triangular-shaped fireplace echoes the geometric forms found throughout the home.

LIGHT THE WAY

The innovative lighting design in Crescent House plays an important role in amplifying the home's geometric flow, particularly as sunlight fades. Recessed up- and downlights softly illuminate the generous interiors, producing dramatic wall shadows. Lights embedded in the concrete ramps and walkways direct and propel occupants through the different areas of the house.

The complex geometric form and scale of the house is tempered by its visually pleasing marriage of resolute Modernity and regal serenity. Crescent House's appeal goes beyond its architectural significance to encompass its pure and simple livability.

ABOVE
The main bedroom is a massive open space set amid a sea of glass and concrete. A minimalist approach to furnishing emphasizes the room's clean lines and functionality.

LEFT
The down-lit bar area is the perfect retreat for the owners from their busy city lives – a place to sit, relax, and relate the events of the day.

TOP
Lights embedded in the concrete ramp are an innovative alternative to ceiling lights. Slightly recessed, they provide an interesting wave effect – a nod of recognition to the home's waterfront location.

ABOVE
In the late afternoon light, the massed concrete forms of the interior generate bold and ever-changing shadows. The fireplace, perfectly positioned near the glass walls, is reminiscent of a Californian beachside bonfire.

House Westcliff JOHANNESBURG, SOUTH AFRICA

Silvio Rech & Lesley Carstens, Architecture & Interiors

Construction	1999–2001
Home type	Single dwelling for a family
Structure	African mud, thatch, and stone

ABOVE
The outdoor dining deck is built over the existing storm water run. The old pool pump house has been transformed into a conveniently positioned wine cellar. Its wooden doors with beaten metal spears were fashioned on site. Perched like sentinels above the doorway are temple birds from Java.

OPPOSITE
Reminiscent of a forest rockpool, the round-rim swimming pool features its own specially commissioned mosaic. Tumbled quarry tiles decorate the pool's perimeter; the retaining walls are constructed from local Magaliesburg rocks. A handhewn bed, purchased on a trip to Bali, sits on the deck outside the thatch-roofed dining room.

"We strive to make each project unique, handcrafting it down to the finer details so that the experience is a constant adventure in a cohesive whole."

Silvio Rech, Lesley Carstens

House Westcliff is situated in suburban Johannesburg and built on what was considered a difficult and challenging site. Storm water ran through it and the land was overgrown. Yet its spectacular view over Johannesburg motivated Silvio Rech and Lesley Carstens to create something unique and striking underneath the forest canopy.

AT ONE WITH THE ENVIRONMENT

The architects had been building exotic bush camps for clients over the previous five years and wanted to use the same concept for their own home. One idea they favored was a mud African dwelling, as Rech and Carstens had great resources and connections to craftsmen and builders from all over Africa – Malawi, Tanzania, Zimbabwe, and South Africa – and their builder, Patrick Jonk, did not build conventional homes. So the African route was taken.

Basing the design on an African village was an inspired idea. The home is comprised of a series of rooms that form a compound – much as a series of huts do in the village context – ordered and connected along various axes. Rech and Carstens favor this "natural" form of architecture, fitting, as it does, with the surroundings.

There was an existing circular thatched building (rondavel) on the site, and this was retained as the heart of the building. The thatched roof was raised using a truss work of gum poles (round eucalyptus poles stripped of bark), the floor was re-screeded with brown pigment, and the walls were plastered with brown mud from the site. Large windows were placed into the front of the rondavel, their shape inspired by

The spaces between rooms are circles, rectangles, or semicircles. These have niches carved into them in the classic African tradition, called "poche."

the windows of the Ngorongoro Crater Lodge in Tanzania, also designed by Rech and Carstens. Tanzanian artisans carved the entire 10-ft- (3-m-) high frame, which is flanked by two sculpted chimneys.

USING WHAT WAS THERE

The original rondavel contained a small altar and Rech and Carstens retained the suggestion of the altar and built a plastered bed 20 ft (2 m) above the floor in the center of the room. It is reached by a carved ladder. The architects' two young children sleep beneath their parents in a cosy little cube.

Because the room looks over the forest, a deck was added in front of the room to maximize use of the area. This steps down into the garden by means of a rock amphitheater, which gives a magical sense of drama to the garden.

One side of the room opens into a dressing room, which has a vaulted roof with handhewn wooden trusses. To the left lies a semicircular bathroom with sunken bath. The front of the bathroom is a large sliding window (with carved frames) that overlooks the vegetation, giving a sense of bathing in nature.

The spaces between rooms are circles, rectangles, or semicircles. These have niches carved into them in the classic African tradition, called "poche." The bathroom vanity is set into one of these niches – two white basins sit on top, much like an upturned lily pad.

The toilet room is conical shaped with a corbeled brick roof. A large steel screen with a metal cut-out motif sits behind the toilet. The basin, sitting on a mud pedestal, is a simple and elegant bowl hewn out of rock from Zimbabwe.

EVERYDAY LIVING

In the area between the bedroom and dining room a tree grows though the floor and roof. The dining room sits under a rough-thatched roof and the walls are built from local rock, packed tightly so the mortar joints cannot be seen. The room overlooks a stunning round pool, protected from street noise and prying eyes by dense vegetation and decorated with a mosaic of a man swimming – a calm and timeless image created by South African artist Clive van der Berg.

The separate kitchen has a vaulted roof made out of rough bricks and features a large curved glass window. The kitchen formwork was constructed from wires spanning the length of the room; rows of bricks were laid and then rubbed down with wire brushes to create a unified surface. The slight imperfections in the roof add to the home's handcrafted nature.

All the doors and window frames were custom made and designed for the house.

ABOVE LEFT
A temple bird sculpture from the island of Java is framed in a hand-packed rock wall niche, adding to the textural and handcrafted feel of this property.

ABOVE FAR LEFT
A network of stone paths and steps, as well as an extensive use of decking, help to link the individual huts in the complex. Glimpses across the shrub-filled garden, such as this one from the bedroom deck, reinforce the communal "village" ambience.

ABOVE
Light filters into the dressing room through a vaulted, sculptural roof. In front is the outdoor rooftop "sala", which affords a spectacular view across the garden. Constructed from gum poles, mass mud columns and a canvas roof, the sala is used as a sleeping retreat during the hot summer months.

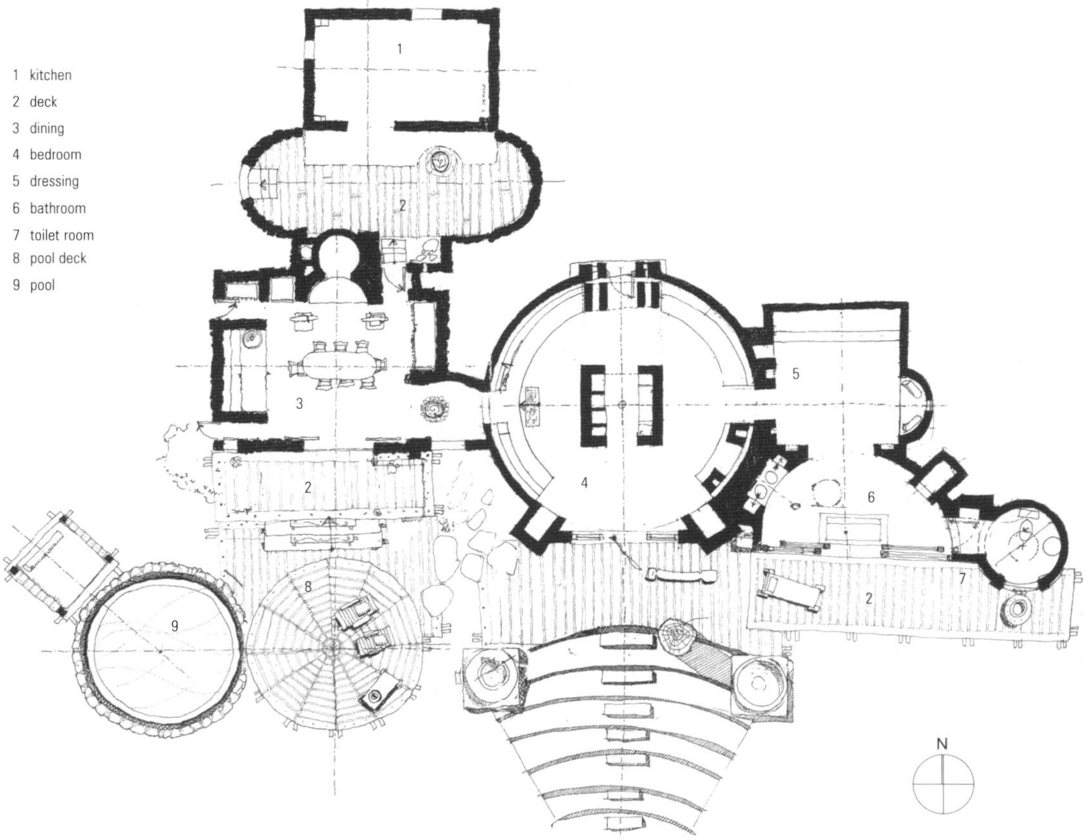

1 kitchen
2 deck
3 dining
4 bedroom
5 dressing
6 bathroom
7 toilet room
8 pool deck
9 pool

ABOVE
The rock steps lead up the side of the amphitheater toward the main bedroom. The sculptural chimney stacks are flanked by Javanese water vessels. Large, intricately carved merbau doors were crafted by Tanzanians who had worked with Rech and Carstens on their exotic bush camp projects. All doors and windows for the complex were made on site.

Most of the furniture, screens, and light fittings in the house were designed by Rech and Carstens. (These were often prototypes for items later used in the various lodges the team designed.) The house contains an eclectic mix of furniture, with materials chosen for their tactile qualities, and shapes derived from natural forms and inspired by the African landscape.

A NATURAL GARDEN PARADISE

The garden has been left wild. Exotic plants were removed and native trees and shrubs were planted, so bird life is prolific – resident hadedas, paradise fly-catchers, as well as owls and eagles. The property is in the city, yet the jungle-like atmosphere sets it apart.

The storm water that ran through the property was stemmed and a small stream now links the various outdoor areas. An old swimming pool has been turned into a pond and the pool's pump house converted into a wine cellar at the bottom of the garden near the outdoor dining deck. It is decorated with a baroque gilt-framed mirror handcarved by Rech's father.

Reminiscent of the rooftop living quarters seen in hot and arid areas, such as Zanzibar and Egypt, small outdoor rooms (salas) were built on the flat roofs to capture some of the Johannesburg views. These are accessed by a series of wooden ladders. In summer, it is mild enough to sleep in these "nests" in the sky.

A HARD ROAD TO COMPLETION

Building the house was not a smooth process, as the architects were simultaneously involved with other projects in the Okavango Delta and in the Seychelles.

Because their buildings are unique handcrafted lodges in extreme places, the team were required to live on site for the duration of the building process. Meanwhile, their own house, House Westcliff, remained in a semi-finished state for some two years. However, it was well worth the wait.

ABOVE LEFT
The huge altar-like bed with its carved steps dominates the main bedroom. Underneath is a safe sleeping haven for the children. This structure is surrounded by seating topped with simple white cushions; animal skulls found on various sites around Africa are displayed on the walls. The back of the bed is framed by a suspended rock "curtain."

TOP
The toilet room houses a handcarved stone basin from Zimbabwe, set atop a mud plinth. The metal frame on the mud walls is made from strands of metal rod studded with white quartz stones, and is used for holding soap and candles.

ABOVE
The dressing room niche, one of many purpose-built niches throughout the complex of huts, provides a comfortable place for repose while dressing and preparing for the day ahead. The large standing sculpture, made from giraffe vertebrae, was crafted by Rech, as was the sensuously curved table.

OPPOSITE
Packed rock walls in the dining room support counters and display shelves for practical items as well as artefacts. The walnut table and chairs were skilfully crafted by Rech's father. Suspended above the table is a woven copper chandelier – a prototype made for the Ngorongoro Crater Lodge, one of the architects' award-winning bush camp designs.

John Lee House PETALING JAYA, MALAYSIA

Jimmy Lim

Construction	1999–2002
Home type	Multi-level family home
Structure	Concrete frame with brick infill, timber, and rendered plaster

SOUTH ELEVATION

"The main consideration in tropical architecture is to minimize heat build-up and maximize the cross-ventilation. My aim is always to create an environment where the client can enjoy their home and live life to the full."

Jimmy Lim

ABOVE
Columns provide a imposing aspect to the house facade, while the prominence of the pool and its proximity to the living spaces demonstrate the architect's careful response to his clients' specific needs and lifestyle.

RIGHT
A traditionally pitched roof combines with spreading, decorative eaves to provide protection from torrential tropical rains and the heat of the sun. White rendered plaster walls also reflect the sun, while narrow and vertical box-like windows permit the strategic entry of light.

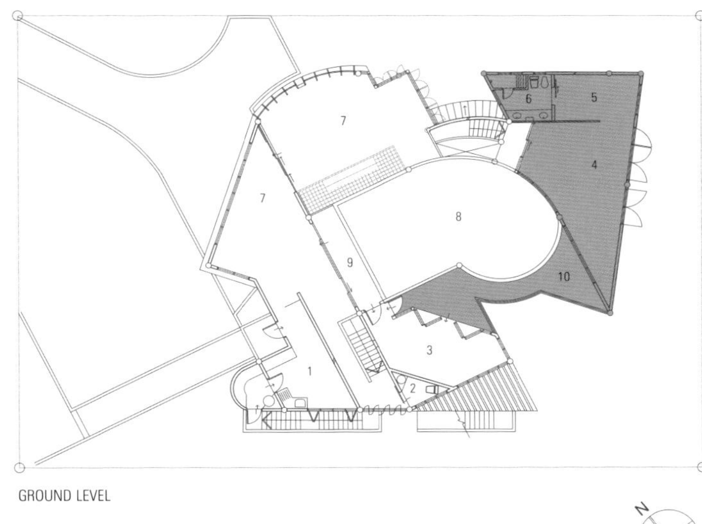

1 kitchen
2 toilet
3 dining
4 main bedroom
5 dressing room
6 main bathroom
7 living
8 pool
9 pool deck
10 main bedroom deck

TROPICAL RESORT

In the Petaling Jaya district, north of the Malaysian capital of Kuala Lumpur, architect Jimmy Lim has added to his already impressive residential portfolio with the vast 7,000-sq-ft (650-sq-m) John Lee House. Lim's fusing of traditional Malay architecture with the modern principles of design has resulted in a home that was conceived as a private resort, then planned around the needs and personal interests of his clients.

RECYCLED TIMBERS

The concrete-framed structure is raised on stilts, eliminating the need for expensive retaining walls and also allowing natural drainage during the heavy tropical rains. The pitched terracotta-tiled roof combines with both traditional and abstract stepped eaves to protect the interior from monsoonal rains and summer heat.

Recycled timbers have been used throughout the home. The exaggerated mortise and tenon joinery matches the workmanship of traditional craftsmen, resulting in a rough-hewn architectonic that expresses Lim's fondness for bold forms.

DIVE POOL

The heart of the home is a massive, 26-ft- (8-m-) deep kidney-shaped saltwater swimming pool, populated with tropical fish. It was purpose built for the clients, who wanted the luxury of being able to scuba dive without leaving home. The dining room's north-facing wall is a series of vertical slats that gently arc from east to west. They connect the external plate of the roof to the floor below. The slats draw in air, which then rises through the house and out through vents high in the walls, naturally ventilating the living spaces.

SEMICIRCULAR STAIRCASE

Forming a semicircle on the pool's northern side, the main staircase is a significant feature of the house. There is a study, and also a guest room on the ground floor. A further half-flight descends to two children's bedrooms and an audiovisual room, while another stairway leads beneath the lobby to an art gallery. The western end of the main stairway leads to an unusual, triangular-shaped main bedroom.

ABOVE LEFT
High ceilings are a natural defense against the build up of heat in the interior. Windows beneath the eaves permit the exit of warm air, while ceiling fans aid air circulation. Exposed beams provide both strength and an intricate web of ornamentation. Bi-fold doors lead from the generous living area to the kidney-shaped pool beyond.

ABOVE
This abstract collection of individual awnings rises in line with the arc of the main staircase leading to the main bedroom. Local chengal hardwood, known throughout Malaysia as the "king of woods," was chosen for its durability and water resistance, and is employed on both the supports and the awnings.

Mataja Residence CALIFORNIA, USA

Belzberg/Wittman Collaborative

Construction	1997–2000
House Type	Four-bedroom family home
Structure	Concrete with steel frame

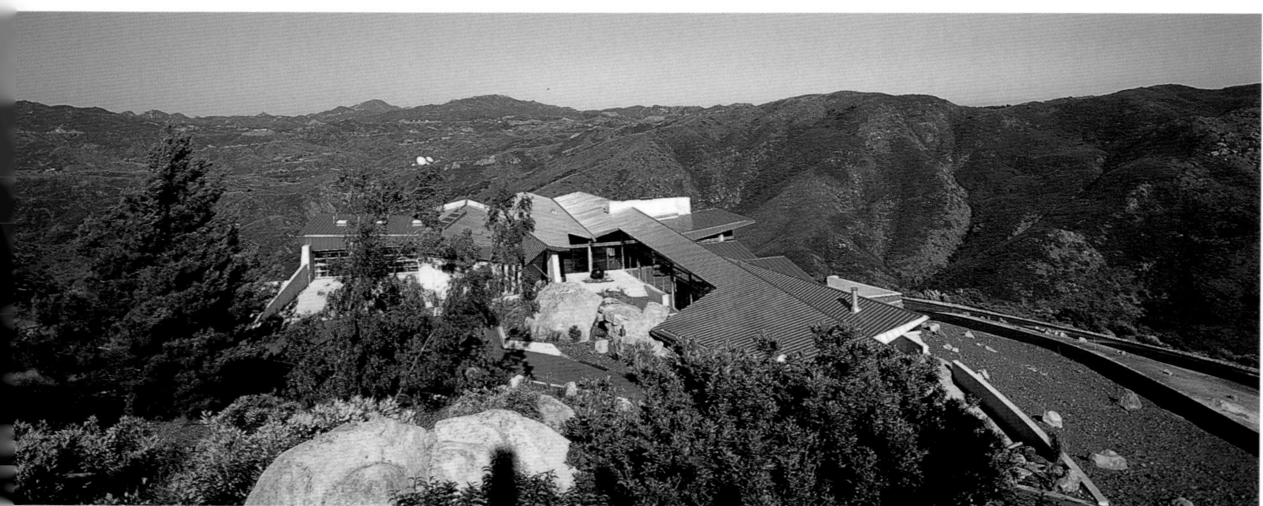

"When you watch the systematic construction of a building taking place, what you learn is freeing instead of controlling."

Hagy Belzberg

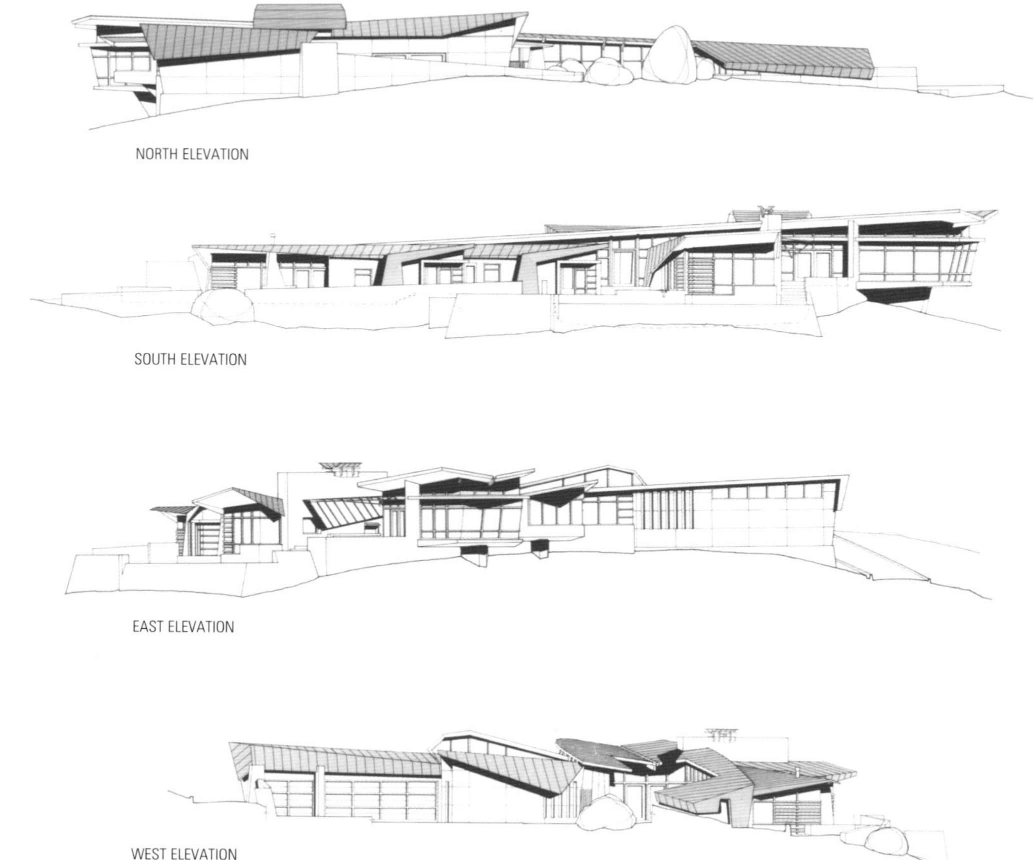

SENSITIVE SURROUNDINGS

Situated about 2 miles (3.2 km) from the Pacific coast, in an environmentally sensitive area covered with native vegetation (mainly chaparral and coastal sage scrub), is the site of the Mataja Residence. Local planning authorities, including representatives from national parks, only approve those building sites that have a low impact on the natural surroundings. As a result, there are few new buildings in the area. Projects that do gain approval have been through a rigorous proposal process.

National parks border the north and east of the site, which sits at the western end of the Santa Monica Mountains. There are sweeping and spectacular views to the mountains, as well as some rugged rocky outcrops in the northwest corner. The area also holds significant historical importance – Chumash Indians lived here for hundreds of years, and their rock art and burial grounds can be found throughout the mountains.

SENSITIVE APPROACH

The architects had two major issues to address. First, there was the challenge of designing an efficient family home on an environmentally delicate site. Second, they had to adhere to the client's wish that the architects themselves actually do the construction. This meant being involved at every stage, and with every single aspect of the construction, a process that took three years.

LEFT
One of the requirements of developing the site was the protection of sensitive coastal vegetation. The area also has important historical significance, with burial grounds and rock art of the Chumash Indians located nearby.

FAR LEFT
The stately arrangement of volumes and roof planes demonstrates the interplay between the canyon's distinctive topography and the home's wraparound form. Rather than remove an imposing granite outcrop, the architects melded it into the design as a buffer against prevailing winds.

ABOVE
The National Park Service requested "an articulated roof line." The architects addressed this by breaking down the building into smaller volumes and fragmenting the roof lines, resulting in a composition that both reflects and complements the terrain.

ABOVE
Spectacular vistas are on offer from every part of Mataja Residence. The paved entry courtyard boasts a view through the family room to the Pacific Ocean.

PREVIOUS PAGES
Perched high in its montane surrounds, the cantilevered dining room overlooks the magnificent, misty panorama of Mulholland Canyon below.

ENVIRONMENTAL WRAP

An existing granite outcrop on the site proved to be a source of inspiration – rather than remove it, the architects decided to wrap the house some 270° around it. This dramatic natural feature was thus incorporated into the architecture itself, providing protection to the courtyard and the house's interior from northerly winds and inclement weather. There was an added bonus – it helped to merge the house into its surroundings, effectively concealing it from visitors to the nearby national park.

MAKING MATERIALS MATTER

The architects believe composing and freely articulating the pattern and form of a building can be achieved without having to use gauged, manufactured products. They also developed novel ways to use standard materials and were able to achieve impressive results on site. Key segments of the roof face south and sit at a 32° angle. This orientation maximizes the house's solar heating system. The angulation also permits rainwater collection, thus reducing reliance on external water sources. The framework is rigid steel, and the windows have been double glazed, helping to keep the house warm in winter and cool in summer.

The architects selected pre-formed concrete "trombe" walls for the exterior, and installed honeycomb concrete slabs on the floor, both of which are insulated, allowing for maximum heat retention.

INTIMATE INTERIORS

The house measures approximately 6,500 sq ft (604 sq m) in area. It contains four comfortable bedrooms and a spacious gallery. A three-car garage is located on ground level, as are the lap pool and spa.

The hub of the house is the dining room and kitchen area. The two rooms are intertwined, creating a warm and welcoming ambience.

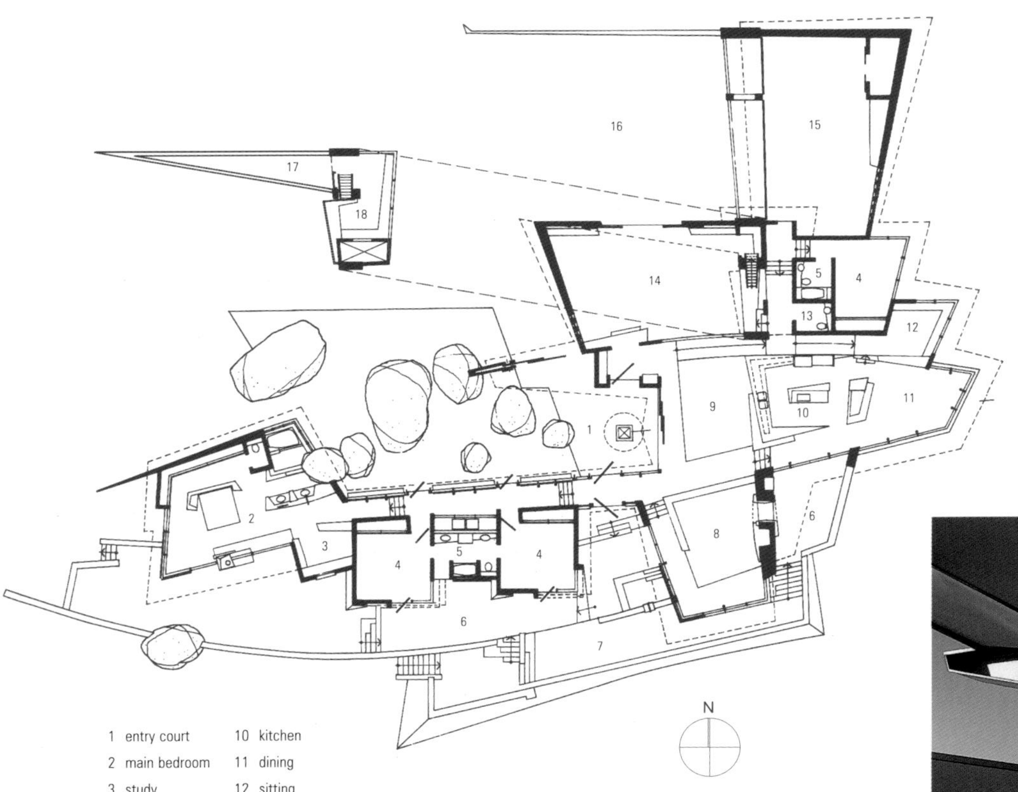

1 entry court
2 main bedroom
3 study
4 bedroom
5 bathroom
6 terrace
7 lap pool
8 family
9 living
10 kitchen
11 dining
12 sitting
13 powder room
14 car gallery
15 garage
16 auto court
17 deck
18 loft

An existing granite outcrop proved to be a source of inspiration – rather than remove it, the architects decided to wrap the house around it.

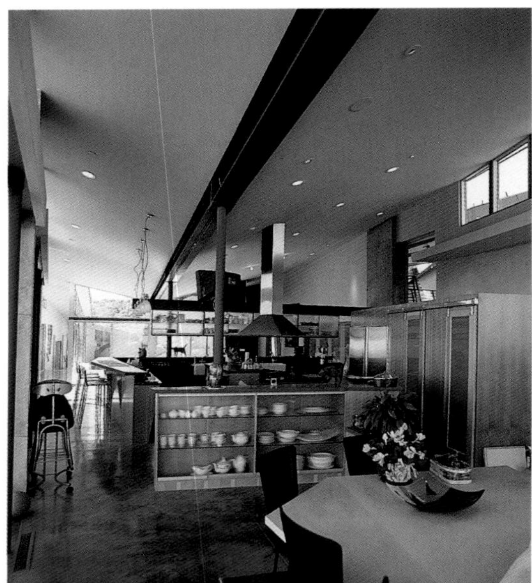

ABOVE
With breathtaking views over the canyon, the dining room's glass walls and vaulted ceiling bathe the space in day-long sunlight.

ABOVE LEFT
The family room intersects the integrated lap pool. The room's butterfly-shaped roof plays an important role in rainwater collection and solar heating.

LEFT
The dining room and kitchen interlink to create a continuous and harmonious flow of space.

Orchard House AHMEDABAD, INDIA

Rahul Mehrotra Associates

Constructed 2004
Home type Single family weekender
Structure Load-bearing walls clad in Porbunder stone, sand-faced cement plaster, and concrete

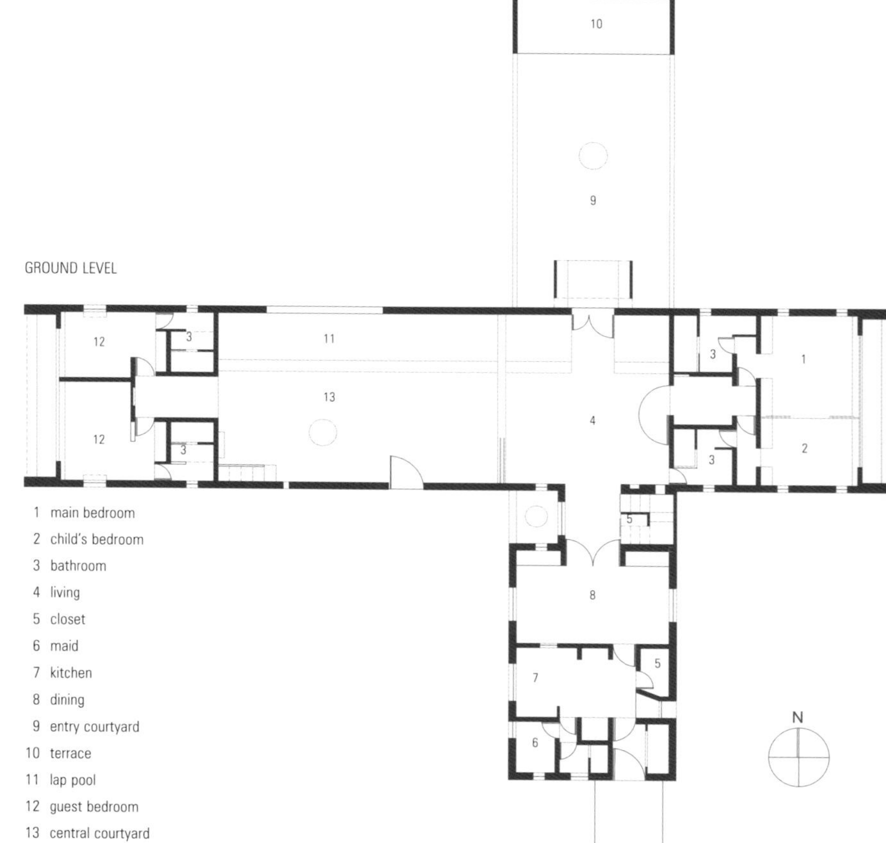

1 main bedroom
2 child's bedroom
3 bathroom
4 living
5 closet
6 maid
7 kitchen
8 dining
9 entry courtyard
10 terrace
11 lap pool
12 guest bedroom
13 central courtyard

"The house is designed like an oasis that one arrives at after driving through the orchard. On entering the house, the 'liquid' landscape of the water in the courtyard ... is a welcome contrast to the hot dry landscape the orchard is set in. The water also helps humidify and cool the breezes that blow through the house and work as effective air-conditioning in the semi-desert climate of Ahmedabad."
Rahul Mehrotra

HOT CLIMATE, COOL HOUSE

Orchard House is situated at the center of a mango orchard, just north of Ahmedabad in western India. Designed as a weekend retreat, the house is organized around a central courtyard, which contains a lap pool filled with fresh water. The water in the pool is used to recharge the wells on the property when the house is closed up during the week. The pool also harvests water during the monsoon months. Water management is critical in the hot dry climate of Ahmedabad, which is plagued by perpetual water shortages.

To further mediate the extreme climate, the house is sited in the center of the orchard rather than at the edge of the property. Besides being a naturally insulated location, the green canopy cover also provides visual relief in the summer months when the glare is uncomfortably intense. The terrace level, situated slightly above the treetops, gives wonderful views of the orchard. The use of terraces for recreation in the evenings or even for sleeping at night is a traditional practice in this region of the country.

AN OASIS IN SIGHT

Summer in this region is characterized by dust storms and extremely hot daytime temperatures. The house is designed as an oasis – a place to effectively escape the oppressive heat. The outer skin is local Porbunder sandstone, emphasizing the textures of a semi-desert landscape. Entering the house brings an instant relief. The sight of lapping water in the courtyard and the vibrantly colored plastered surfaces give solace from the searing temperatures outside. The pool itself enters the living room space, as does one of its blue walls, enhancing the connection between inside and outside.

COLONIZING WITH CONSCIENCE

The broader issue addressed in this design is appropriate building practice on the periphery of India's cities. Weekend houses such as this symbolize the colonization of rural landscapes by urban people. If not appropriately positioned and situated, architecture can create a polarization between urban and rural communities. Siting the house in the orchard's center was an important move – not only climatically and visually, but also socially and politically. Being in the center, the house becomes integral to the landscape.

Furthermore, the orchard can be accessed through a courtyard door and produce grown can be cleaned in the courtyard facilities. As the central courtyard is the heart of the house, the use of this space by farmhands symbolically helps to break down the implicit polarities between country and city. In creating a softer threshold between the orchard and the central courtyard, perhaps the tenuous relationship between the weekend house and the rural landscape on the city's edge can be dissipated by spatial planning and design.

FAR LEFT
The floor of the living area is a mirror-polished gray limestone from the Kotah area in the state of Rajasthan. The furniture is designed as a series of platforms, leaving the space clutter-free, tranquil, and inviting.

TOP LEFT
The staircase leading up to the terrace has a screen wall made from cast-in-form reinforced cement concrete in lieu of the standard handrail. Integrated into the wall is small pantry counter to serve the pool area. The imprints of the wooden planks on the wall impart a handmade feel.

TOP RIGHT
The walls of the front facade are clad in sandstone from the Porbunder area of Gujarat. They form a distinctive and impressive base for the house, as well as a visual connection to the textures of the semi-desert setting. The entry porch and terrace pavilion are made from concrete.

ABOVE
The pool penetrates the envelope of the house, the water creating delicate reflective patterns on the ceiling and walls. The door on the right leads into the orchard. This gives farm workers direct access to the center of the house and courtyard to wash and dry the harvested produce.

Quito House MIRAVALLE, ECUADOR

Carlos Zapata NEW YORK, USA

Construction 1998–2002
Home type Three-level family residence
Structure Steel, concrete, and glass

"The main intention with this house was to maximize its clifftop location to take advantage of its views across the Cumbaya Valley to Cotopaxi and the Andes Mountains to the south. Privacy is provided by the largely concrete, street-facing northern facade, which provides a secure, tranquil living environment."
Carlos Zapata

SPECTACULAR LOCATION

On a wooded hillside 30 minutes east of Quito, overlooking the Cumbaya Valley, stands the wing-shaped, glass and concrete Quito House.

The challenges the site presented to its designer, New York-based architect Carlos Zapata, were threefold – to maintain the privacy and security of the client; to integrate the residence into the surrounding landscape; and to maximize its unparalleled views over the Cumbaya Valley south to the Andes Mountains and Ecuador's Mt Cotopaxi, which, at 19,388 ft (5,909 m) high, is the country's highest active volcano.

A DRAMATIC RESPONSE

Dramatic vistas often demand a dramatic response in design. Quito House is wholly oriented toward the mountains, its southern facade faced with green-tinted glass, which not only provides views but also reflects the landscape, making the home all but invisible when it is seen from across the valley.

By contrast, a heavy band of reinforced concrete has been used on its street-facing northern elevation, which extends in a dramatic arc to form the external west-facing wall of the main bedroom and living room, providing a sense of privacy and insulating the home from noise.

The home hugs its clifftop location, the two main wings of the house opening in a wide angle, embracing the view and reaching toward it.

ABOVE
Despite its size, Quito House sits comfortably in its environment. Surrounding trees were not sacrificed in the pursuit of expansive views; the design contents itself with the vagaries of its hilltop setting.

RIGHT
The soaring glass facade of the living room and main bedroom are drawn forward in sensual communion with the panoramic mountain views. A cantilevered concrete terrace extends from the dining room, terminating in a small reflecting pool.

ABOVE
Massed volumes of reinforced concrete separate the living areas, their larger-than-life scale dwarfing the human figure but in keeping with the drama of the site and the scale of the living spaces,

TOP RIGHT
View of the home's entry and the underside cladding of the main staircase. Next to the stairs, the tilted wood wall continues up through the second level and pierces through the third level's glass facade.

SWIMMING IN SPACE

A cantilevered concrete terrace extends from the dining room at the extreme end of the main western wing; a deck and lap pool extend from the eastern wing providing balance and proportion.

Beginning inside the house and continuing outside, the pool runs along the home's eastern facade, then cantilevers over the cliff face. For the swimmer, this creates a sense of swimming in space.

GENEROUS LIVING

Within Quito House's sprawling 8,000 sq ft (745 sq m) of living space, there are four bedrooms, a kitchen with separate store, multiple dining areas, living room, playroom, family room, and an artist's studio, which is adjacent to the main bedroom.

Slabs of circular reinforced concrete in various sizes have been randomly placed within a manicured lawn between the home and the street, providing an unorthodox, visually stimulating alternative to a traditional driveway.

A SENSE OF PLACE

In Quito House, Carlos Zapata has simultaneously deferred to the drama of the site, as well as confronted it with the home's dramatic form. In making nature an intrinsic part of the home's environment, he has achieved a unique interaction between the landscape and the built elements of concrete and glass.

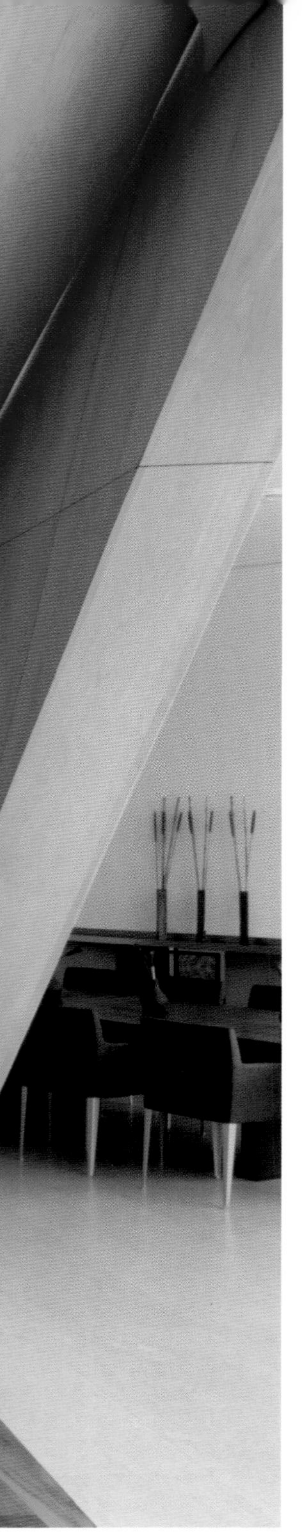

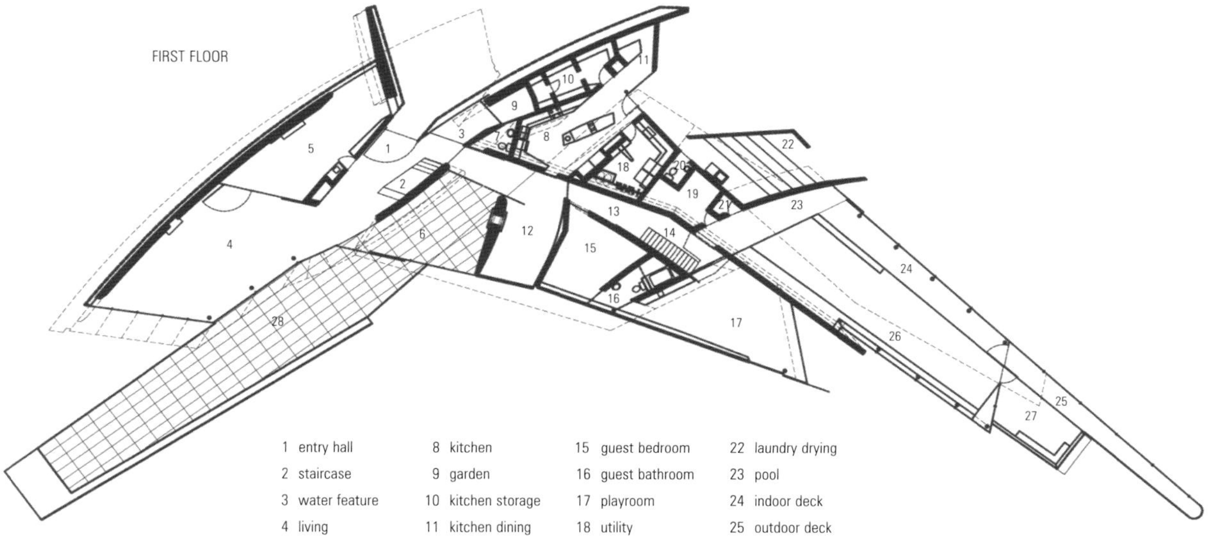

FIRST FLOOR

1. entry hall
2. staircase
3. water feature
4. living
5. family
6. main dining
7. WC
8. kitchen
9. garden
10. kitchen storage
11. kitchen dining
12. dining
13. rear hallway
14. staircase
15. guest bedroom
16. guest bathroom
17. playroom
18. utility
19. storage
20. WC
21. storage
22. laundry drying
23. pool
24. indoor deck
25. outdoor deck
26. lap pool
27. wading pool
28. dining terrace

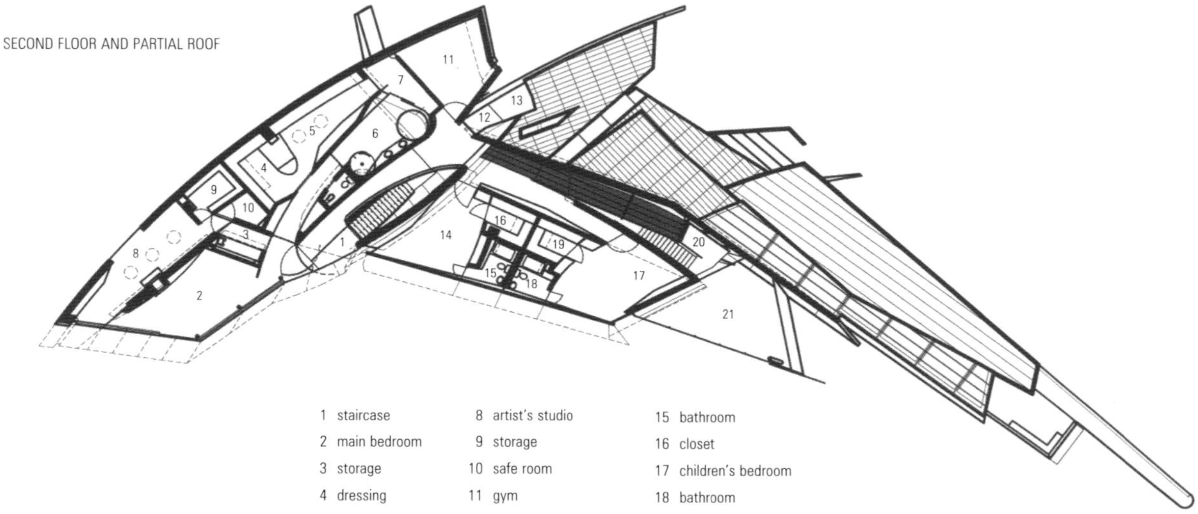

N

SECOND FLOOR AND PARTIAL ROOF

1. staircase
2. main bedroom
3. storage
4. dressing
5. dressing
6. bathroom
7. garden
8. artist's studio
9. storage
10. safe room
11. gym
12. glass sloping to below
13. open to below
14. children's bedroom
15. bathroom
16. closet
17. children's bedroom
18. bathroom
19. closet
20. hallway
21. open to below

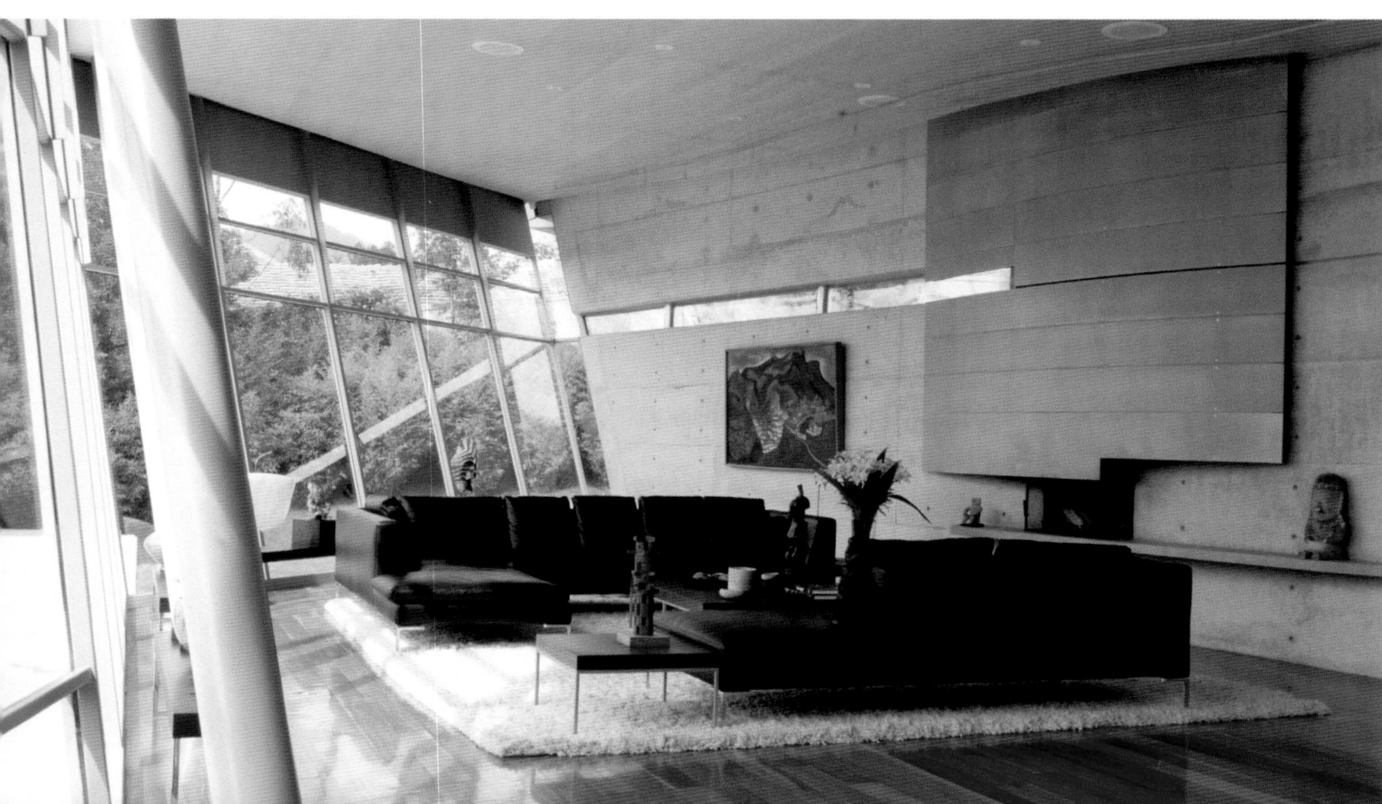

LEFT

The main living room is a functional, open space with ribbons of glass inset in the concrete facade, as well as large expanses of glass facing south and east to capture mountain vistas and early morning sun. The room also features several of the family's pieces of African and pre-Columbian sculpture.

TOP LEFT
The main bedroom has a curved, pivoting, solid timber door that closes away from the glass, extending the line of vision from the bed. The floor-to-ceiling angled glass reaches toward the mountain views.

LEFT
The lap pool begins within the confines of the house, continues to the outside, and is cantilevered over the cliff – for the swimmer creating a feeling of swimming in space. A deck following the pool extends further still.

ABOVE
This detail of the landing of the main staircase presents a kaleidoscope of overlapping geometric shapes. The handrail is recessed into the wall and lined with leather.

RIGHT
The base of the main staircase forms a powerful sculptural image, the curved wooden staircase anchored by its smooth concrete plinth.

Residence for a Sculptor CALIFORNIA, USA

Sander Architects

Construction 2001–2003
Home type Single residence and studio/gallery
Structure Steel and wood on prefabricated rolled-steel frame

"With this residence I had the chance to work with a billion-dollar view. I chose steel because it possesses strength in all directions. The clients admired the construction method, and understood truth in simplicity and in simple structures."
Whitney Sander

ABOVE
Built on the crest of a 4-acre (1.6-ha) allotment, the home from this rear perspective resembles a transport container, the steel girders like crane arms setting it in place.

HOME AND GALLERY

Whitney Sander's metal-clad Residence for a Sculptor is located 55 miles (88 km) north of San Francisco, perched on a wooded 4-acre (1.6-ha) hillside.

Situated in the midst of Sonoma County's 200 wineries with views extending over Jack London's Valley of the Moon, the house is an exciting mix of geometric shapes and curves. With its inherent qualities of adaptability and flexibility, metal lends itself well to the demands of the structure, which included a 22-ft (6.7-m) curved steel wall, and raised platforms for displays of the owner's pottery.

INDUSTRIAL APPEAL

The facade of Residence for a Sculptor is a mix of exposed structural framing and ribbed zincalume sheeting, the latter chosen for its durability, low cost, and quality of lightness, which seems to lift the home above its natural terrain.

The use of zincalume roofing as cladding for the home's external walls is a bold esthetic statement, complemented by a low-maintenance, uncomplicated exterior design. The sheet's recurrent, vertical ribbing, combined with the exposed steel girders that provide the home's structural framework, give the house an industrial appearance.

Galvanized high-tensile steel and, for lateral stability, a circular bolt pattern that does not require cross bracing, provide the home's stability, and meet all the state's seismic requirements.

HORIZONTAL OR VERTICAL?

The first impression of the house emphasizes its horizontal arrangement, suggesting an outward-focused experience might await. Paradoxically, the entry hall is stongly vertical and inward-focused, with a molded staircase along one side of a curving wall and a high curving, torqued steel wall on the other.

This entrance hall or "entry vessel" is an atmospheric space designed to capture some of the qualities of the sculptor's large clay pots. More than one third of the residence is dedicated to sculptural displays and the artist's studio.

The first level of the house contains the garage, a guest bedroom, a large, high-fire kiln, and two working studios totaling 1,500 sq ft (140 sq m). There is also an elevator for groceries and heavier loads.

STEPPING UP

The entry hall's curved steel staircase is anchored to the curved wall on one side but is free floating on the other. These stairs lead to the second level, containing the main bedroom with ensuite and dressing room. A bridge across the upper level of the entry hall leads to the home's expansive living/dining area with its exposed steel beams. The kitchen, family room, and study make up the remainder of the floor. It is here that the Valley of the Moon, bounded by the Maya-camas Mountains to the north and the Sonoma Mountains to the south, comes into full view through the home's large, metal-framed storefront windows.

LEFT
Zincalume's distinctive vertical ribbing defines the home's skin. The structural steel girders extend into the second level living areas. Both combine to form a durable, low-maintenance living space characterized by lightness and strength.

ABOVE
The unashamedly industrial facade is suggestive of the working space within. Modestly sized windows adorn the private living spaces to the left, whereas the kitchen, family room, and study at right of the balcony invite light and views within.

TOP
Large, metal-framed windows protrude from the facade and provide expansive views of the Valley of the Moon and the Sonoma Mountains. The balcony is accessed from the living room.

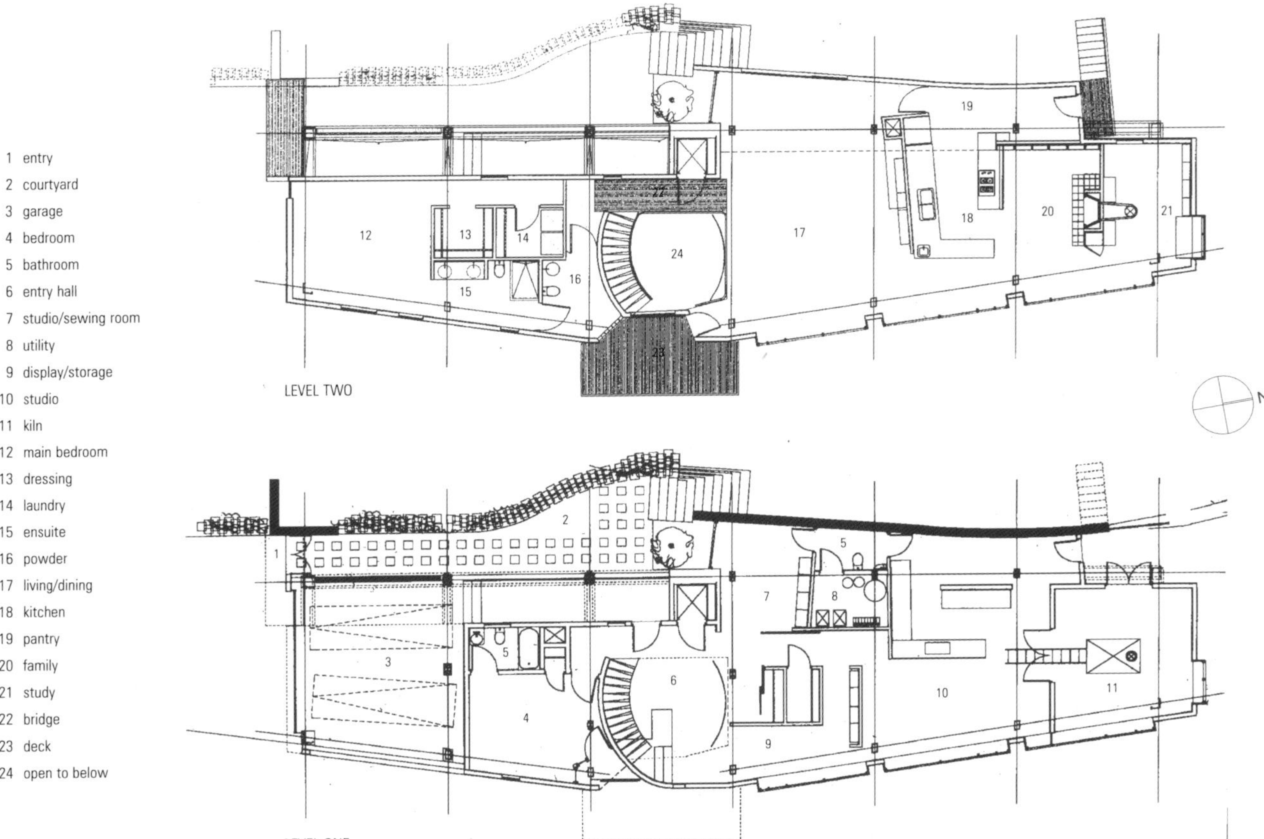

LEFT
The sculptor's pottery is superbly offset by the light and shade of the entry hall. The staircase, fabricated by Stockland Iron of Santa Rosa, is anchored to the wall on one side and free-floating on the other. It ascends from the entry level to the home's upper level, where a bridge connects the two sides of the home.

ABOVE
A profusion of geometric shapes and curves come together on the second-level of the entry hall. The penetrating light gives the shapes light and dark, creating its own work of art.

ABOVE
Softened by the dove-gray wall cabinet, furnishings, and sculpted forms, the hard-edged structural steel girders become an integral part of the gallery decor.

Sekeping Serendah SELANGOR, MALAYSIA

Seksan Design

Constructed	2000
Home type	Multi-level rainforest holiday retreat
Structure	Steel frame and concrete post foundations

"Buildings can be erected without resorting to the 'slash and burn' approach so common in Malaysia today. The 'sheds' of Sekeping Serendah have been sensitively integrated into the landscape and are a kind of glorified tent. Staying here is all about enjoying the great outdoors."

Seksan

One hour north of the Malaysian capital Kuala Lumpur, along winding dirt roads in the foothills of the Malayan Main Range, stands Sekeping Serendah, two contemporary structures designed by landscape architects Seksan and his partner Caroline Lau.

RAINFOREST RETREAT

Responding to the "slash and burn," "cut and fill" approach to construction normally associated with developments throughout Southeast Asia, these two multi-level, 700-sq-ft (65-sq-m) retreats rise above a sloping terrain of dense, pristine rainforest. Slender steel posts leave mountain streams to run their natural course, while effortlessly supporting the designers' light composition of glass, aluminum, and iron.

A COMMUNION WITH NATURE

Designed to represent a traditional *kampong*, the "sheds" contain no Balinese teak or travertine marble. There is no hint of pretentiousness here. The designers believe that materials transported over long distances tend to lose their "spirit" along the way. Instead, Sekeping Serendah reveals a communion with nature through the use of simple elemental materials that were carried to this 5-acre (2-ha) hideaway by hand, in order to minimize any environmental impact.

Materials used include construction chippings, corrugated iron, brick powder, asphalt, laterite mud, chicken wire, and old roof tiles – these buildings are as honest and uncomplicated as the landscape that surrounds them.

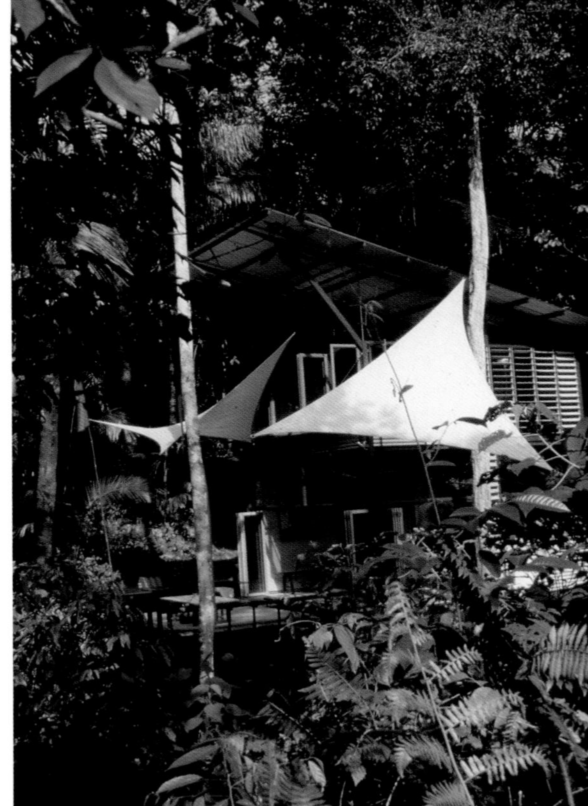

TOP
Strategically placed canvas awnings provide shade to the outdoor living area and day bed, where gaps in the rainforest canopy allow through the harsh rays of the tropical sun. They typify the approach used here – provide only what is necessary for the comfort of the users, unencumbered by unnecessary embellishments.

ABOVE
An elevated walkway protects a natural creek bed on the approach to Sekeping Serendah. From a distance the building is barely distinguishable from its dense tropical surrounds, achieving a sense of place rarely found in modern architecture.

LEFT
An absence of solid walls allows for 360° views of the rainforest, which itself is reflected in the building's glazed front elevation, further minimizing its visual footprint. Slender steel supports and an elevated floor plan are testimony to the environmentally sensitive approach to its construction.

1 living
2 kitchenette
3 shower
4 day bed
5 bench
6 balcony
7 bedroom
8 extended deck
9 outdoor living

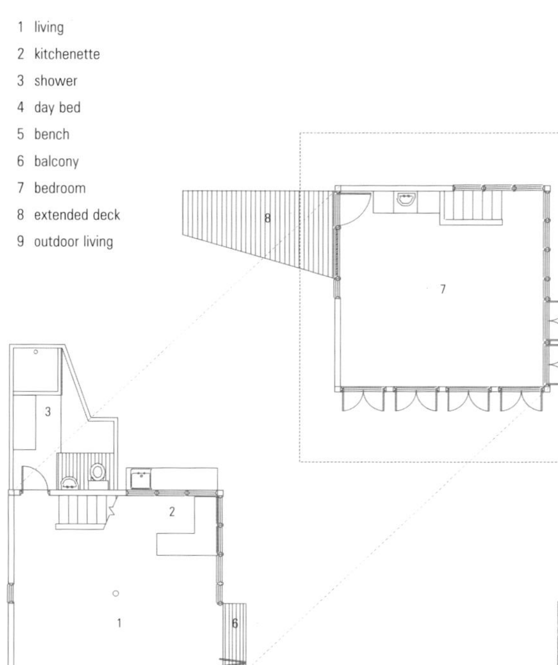

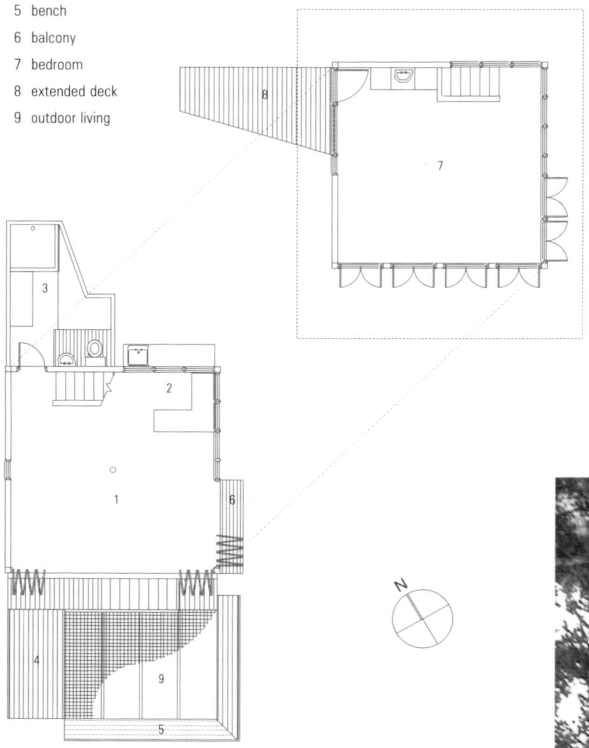

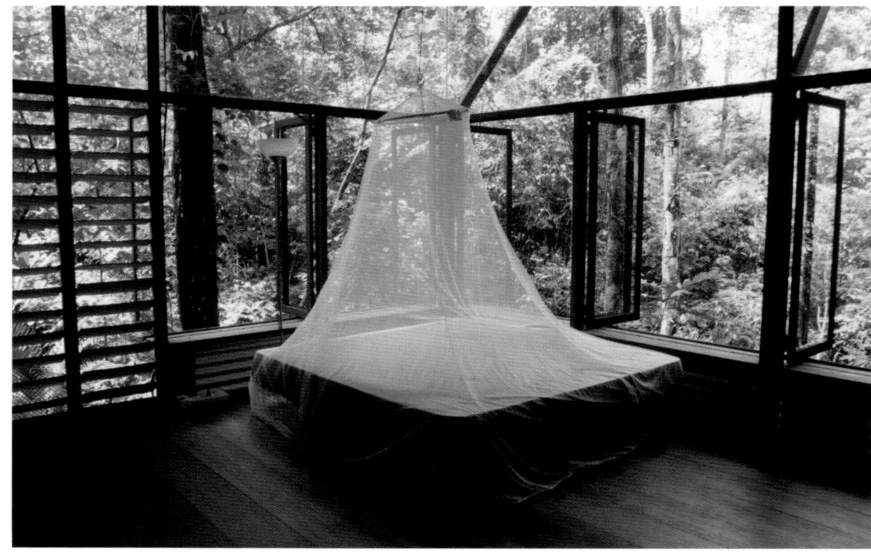

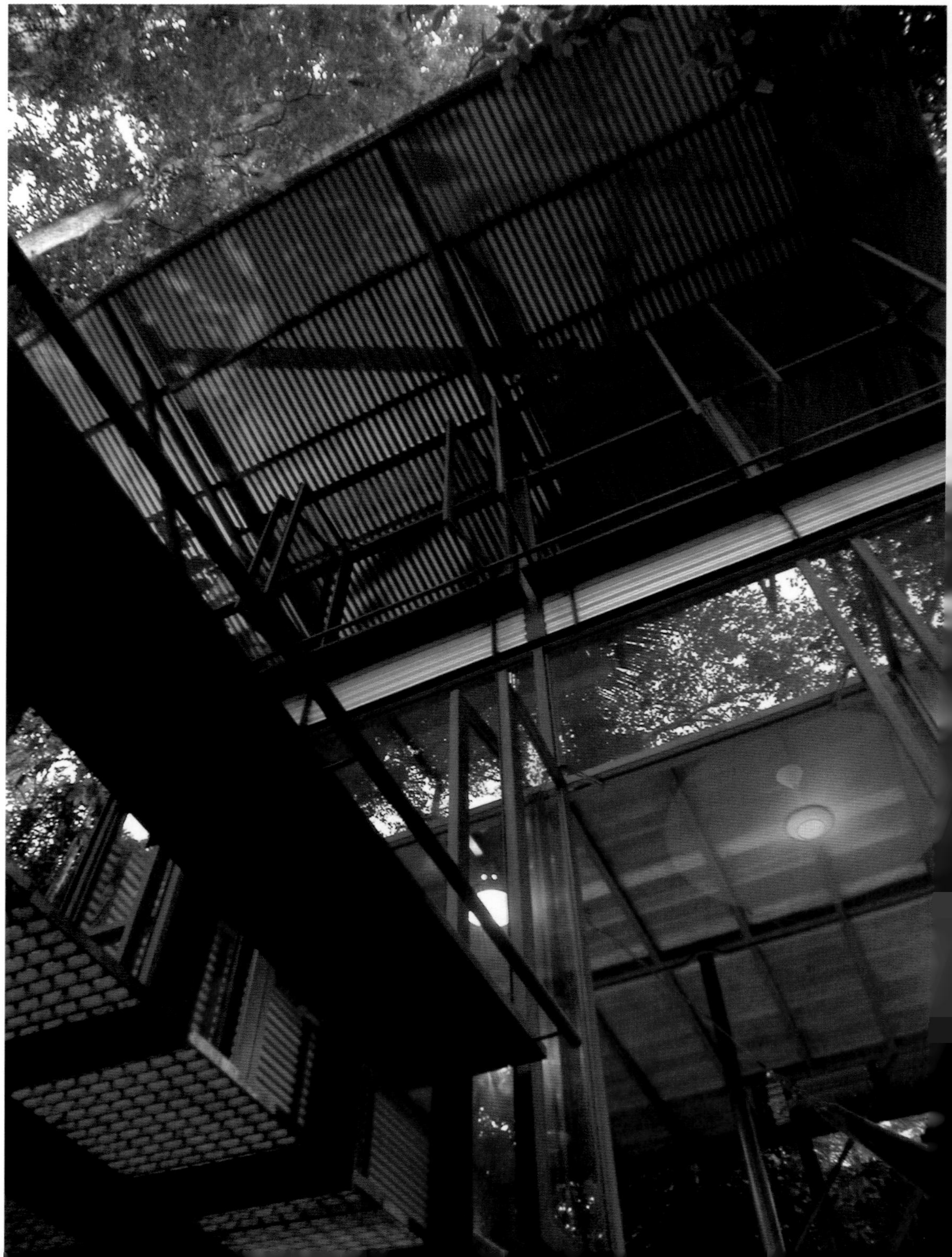

PRIMITIVE APPEAL

Sekeping Serendah is approached along a sinewy rainforest walking track, ending at a iron gate. The gate is flanked by gabion walls of local stones set in a framework of welded mesh. Past high mud walls thick with green moss, the track becomes a plinth that follows the terrain across a creek bed to where the glass and steel house rises up from the surroundings.

Mats and hammocks provide seating on the lower floors. A kitchenette with an unpainted zinc wall accentuates its primitive appeal. An outdoor living area, complete with a floor of industrial metal grating, a day bed, and seats that resemble a traditional *anjung*, flows out from the inside living area beneath the structure's cantilevered, corrugated iron roof.

Aluminum-framed bi-folding windows wrap around the internal spaces. Natural ventilation is provided by an extensive network of metal and glass louvers that eliminate the need for air-conditioning.

NATURE IS EVERYWHERE

Staircases lead to upper-level sleeping areas with mattresses laid on wire mesh bases, all set under a protective canopy that drenches Sekeping Serendah in day-long dappled light. There are no curtains. Transparency is everywhere, allowing the senses to experience the joy of nature in all its glory. A short walk along the valley is the spring-fed, cement-rendered swimming pool, set amid the rainforest

A cost-effective design respects the natural habitat and the traditions of surrounding communities, and triumphantly captures the intentions of its creators.

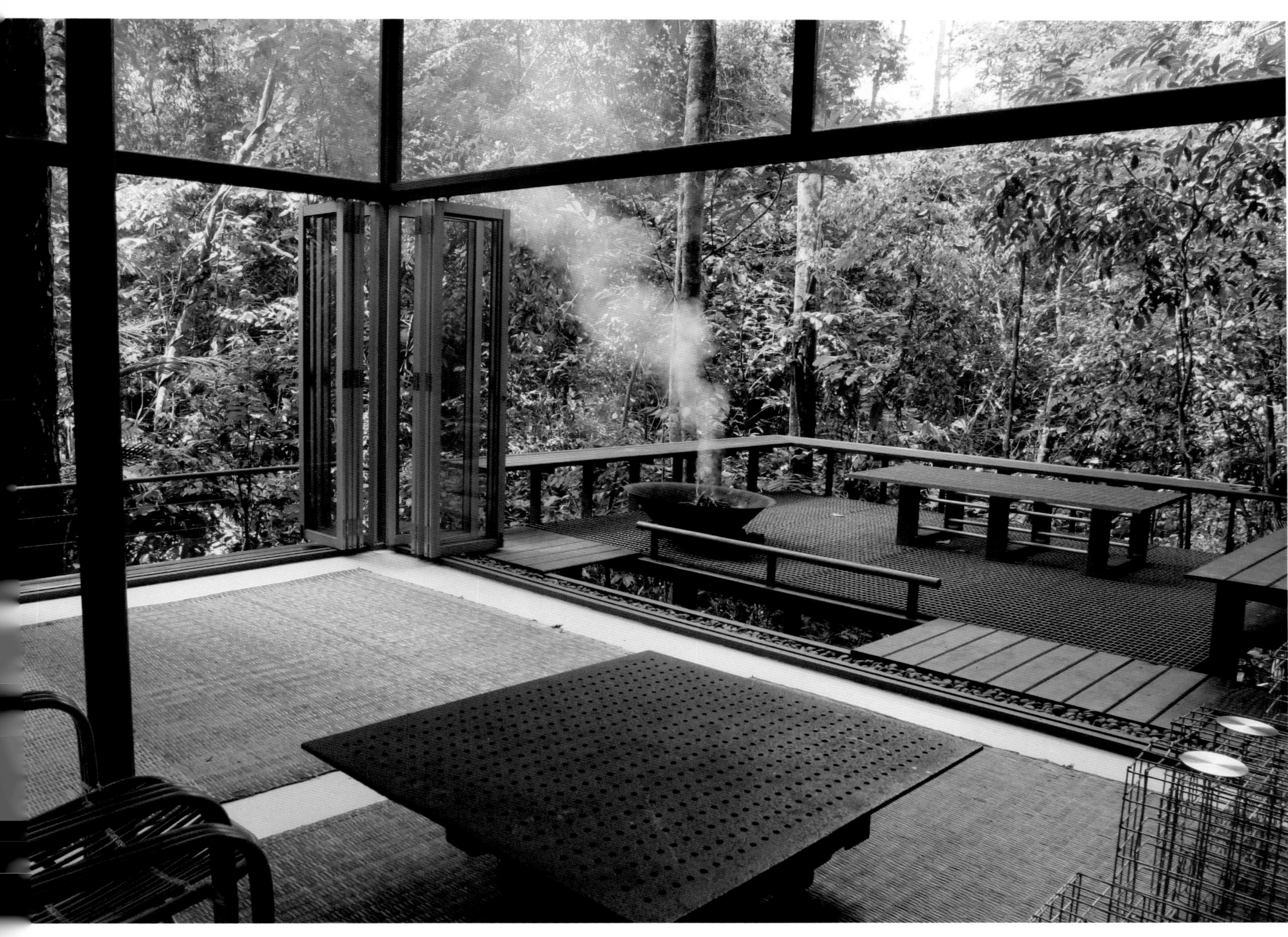

TOP LEFT
With its mix of louvers, casement windows, and wide timber floorboards, the bedroom strikes a contemporary pose. Glass and metal louvers are present throughout the retreat, allowing the regulation of natural breezes. With the absence of fly-wire screening on its windows, mosquito netting is essential.

LEFT
Aluminum, corrugated iron, and glass work together harmoniously to create a structure highly resistant to the corrosive effects of the harsh, tropical environment. The dominance of the surrounding rainforest and its penetration of the retreat help to soften the impact of the iron roof and metal walkways.

ABOVE
Rattan matting in the living area combines with the metal-meshed floor of the patio. A slender border of river pebbles and use of timber decking present a rich tapestry of textures. Bi-folding doors open the retreat to the forest, with Sekeping Serendah's splendid isolation ensuring privacy is not compromised.

Sky Arc Residence SAN FRANCISCO, USA

Will Bruder Architects

Construction 2003–2004
Home type Two-level family home and separate music studio
Structure Steel frame with concrete pier foundation

"The greatest charge at Sky Arc was to create a sensitive environment, an architecture rooted in this place. The house had to negotiate a challenging site – to engage the earth, recede into the trees. The simple volumes choreograph a pattern for living in an amazing landscape. The architecture amplifies the play of light and melts into the fog – a magical effect."

William Bruder

LEFT
The music room and studio is an 1,100-sq-ft (102-sq-m) haven, which is detached from the main residence. Constructed of board-formed cast-in-place concrete, it is set into the ground to minimize the intrusion of external noise. A suspended ceiling of origami-like fabric combines with walls of wood and fabric to enhance the room's acoustic properties.

ABOVE
The glassed living room glows at dusk, the suspended fireplace making a dramatic statement. The home is oriented to capture views that extend south from the Golden Gate National Recreation Area and eastward to San Francisco Bay.

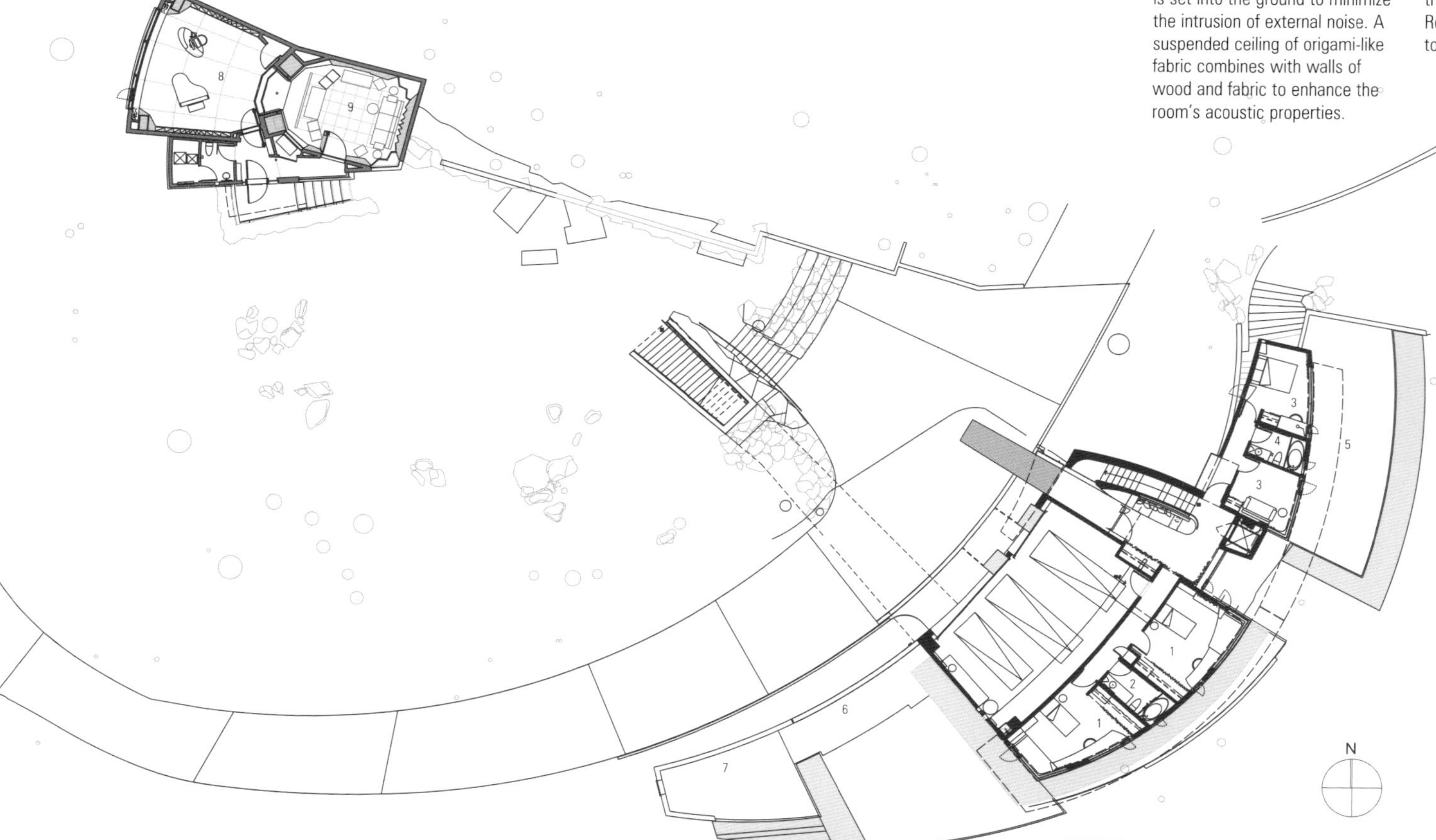

1 children's bedroom
2 bathroom
3 guest bedroom
4 guest bathroom
5 main bedroom below
6 gallery below
7 studio below
8 music room/ recording studio
9 studio control

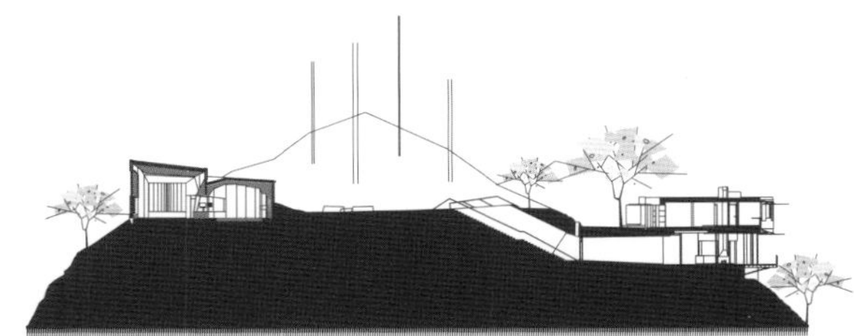

PART OF THE LANDSCAPE

In Kentfield, just north of the Golden Gate Bridge in San Francisco's Marin County, is William Bruder's crescent-shaped Sky Arc Residence, set on 1.5 acres (0.6 ha) of forested hillside. It has dramatic views east over San Francisco Bay and south to the redwood and oak slopes of Mt Tamalpais.

The house is a collection of simple volumes. Sheathed in an external skin of pre-weathered, pewter-gray zinc and "solex green" glass, it easily recedes into the texture of the surrounding hills. This merging with the landscape is aided by the zinc's vertical, random ribbing, which harmonizes with nearby redwood trees.

CRESCENT SHAPE

The home's crescent shape embraces the natural contours of a rugged site, with the main residence located on the steeper eastern portion, and the garden and children's play area to the west, safely removed from dangerous precipices.

PANORAMIC VIEWS

Translucent fiberglass awnings encasing gossamer-thin filters replace more traditional overhangs and provide shade for the home's extensively glazed exteriors.

The upper level contains the children's bedrooms and a guest suite with bay views. A staircase descends to the "great room," with its sweeping 180° views from the bay to the mountains. Floors of Norwegian slate and mahogany are combined with birch and madrone casework and Venetian plaster, and there is a spectacular perforated metal fireplace suspended from the ceiling. This room is filled with a complex interplay of radiant, reflective textures.

The living room opens out to a wooden cantilevered deck and lawn terrace that uses perforated metal balustrades to blur any boundaries between the structure and the vistas beyond.

MUSIC STUDIO

Across the garden and detached from the house is a music room and recording studio. It is constructed of cast-in-place concrete, and features a reverberant concrete floor, all set several feet into the ground to minimize the penetration of external noise. Origami-like fans made of fabric form a false ceiling and, together with walls of wood, fabric, and plaster, diffuse, absorb, and reflect sound.

ABOVE
Fiberglass awnings containing blue filters replace traditional overhangs and glow luminously on gray, overcast days typical of the San Francisco Bay area. The crescent shape of the cantilevered wooden deck derives its form from the gentle, curvaceous topography of the surrounding northern California hills.

RIGHT
An external skin of pre-weathered zinc, with its vertical, randomly placed ribs, is designed to help the house recede into the texture of the landscape. Inspired by its site and exposed to the whims of nature, Sky Arc Residence promises to continually challenge and dazzle the senses.

St Leon House CAPE TOWN, SOUTH AFRICA

Stefan Antoni Olmesdahl Truen Architects

Construction	2003–2004
Home type	Single-family dwelling
Structure	Reinforced concrete, glass, marble, timber

"While being totally luxurious, the house also has a raw and robust quality to it. Materials and textures have been carefully selected to enhance the layered and magical experience. It is a house that needs to be given time to reveal itself."

Stefan Antoni

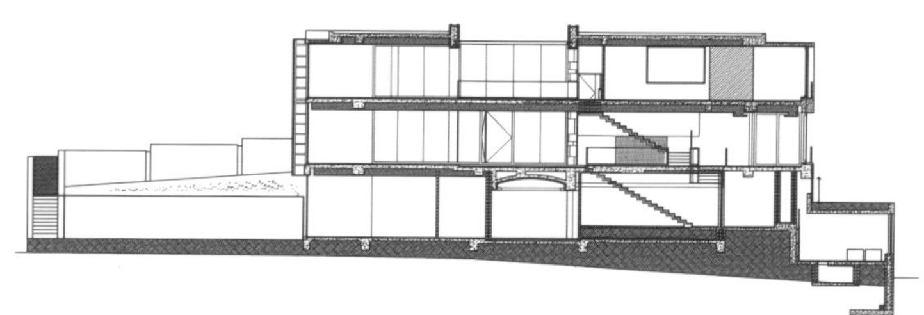

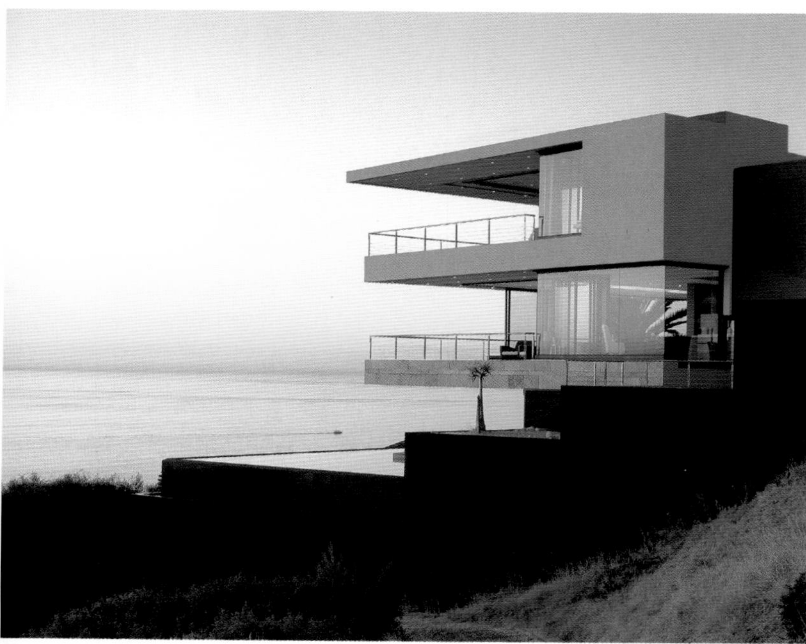

VIEWS TO DIE FOR

The magnificent site of St Leon House, nestled in a steep spur that separates Bantry Bay from Clifton, was the primary inspiration for architect Stefan Antoni's design. The property boasts breathtaking views toward the southwest, to the Twelve Apostle Mountains, across the beautiful Clifton beaches, and to the northeast over Robben Island toward the heart of Cape Town. Views from the back of the house frame Lion's Head.

The building is cut into the slope with approximately 50 percent of its rear face below the natural ground level. The engineers faced numerous challenges, the most critical being the large retaining walls that were required for the steep site, and the dramatic cantilevers, which were achieved by post-tensioning the beams. The third level of this imposing home floats over the extensively glazed southwest-facing second level, exaggerating the height of the building in relation to the adjacent first level.

CONTEMPORARY DESIGN, NATURAL FINISH

Although the design is uncompromisingly modern, the architects worked hard to soften the visual appearance by relying on the extensive use of natural finishes and textural elements.

Designed for a couple and their two children, the house also includes generous guest accommodation. The client, whose job requires him to travel between major cities, wanted a home that could cater for casual, intimate family occasions as well as large get-togethers with friends.

ABOVE
A dramatic view of the southwestern elevation at sunset highlights the home's elegant angular lines and cantilevered slabs and roof.

RIGHT
Seemingly adrift in the black quartz-fringed infinity pool, the spa, with its balau timber deck, epitomizes the luxury and meticulous attention to detail incorporated into the house design. The unparalleled views of the Twelve Apostles Mountains can be fully appreciated while languishing in the warm water.

1 pool
2 recreation/living
3 guest room 2
4 ensuite 2
5 gym
6 steam room
7 garden
8 garage
9 bedroom 3
10 ensuite 3
11 bedroom 4
12 ensuite 4
13 main bedroom
14 main ensuite
15 terrace
16 entrance
17 patio
18 dining
19 living
20 media
21 study
22 guest room 1
23 ensuite 1
24 kitchen

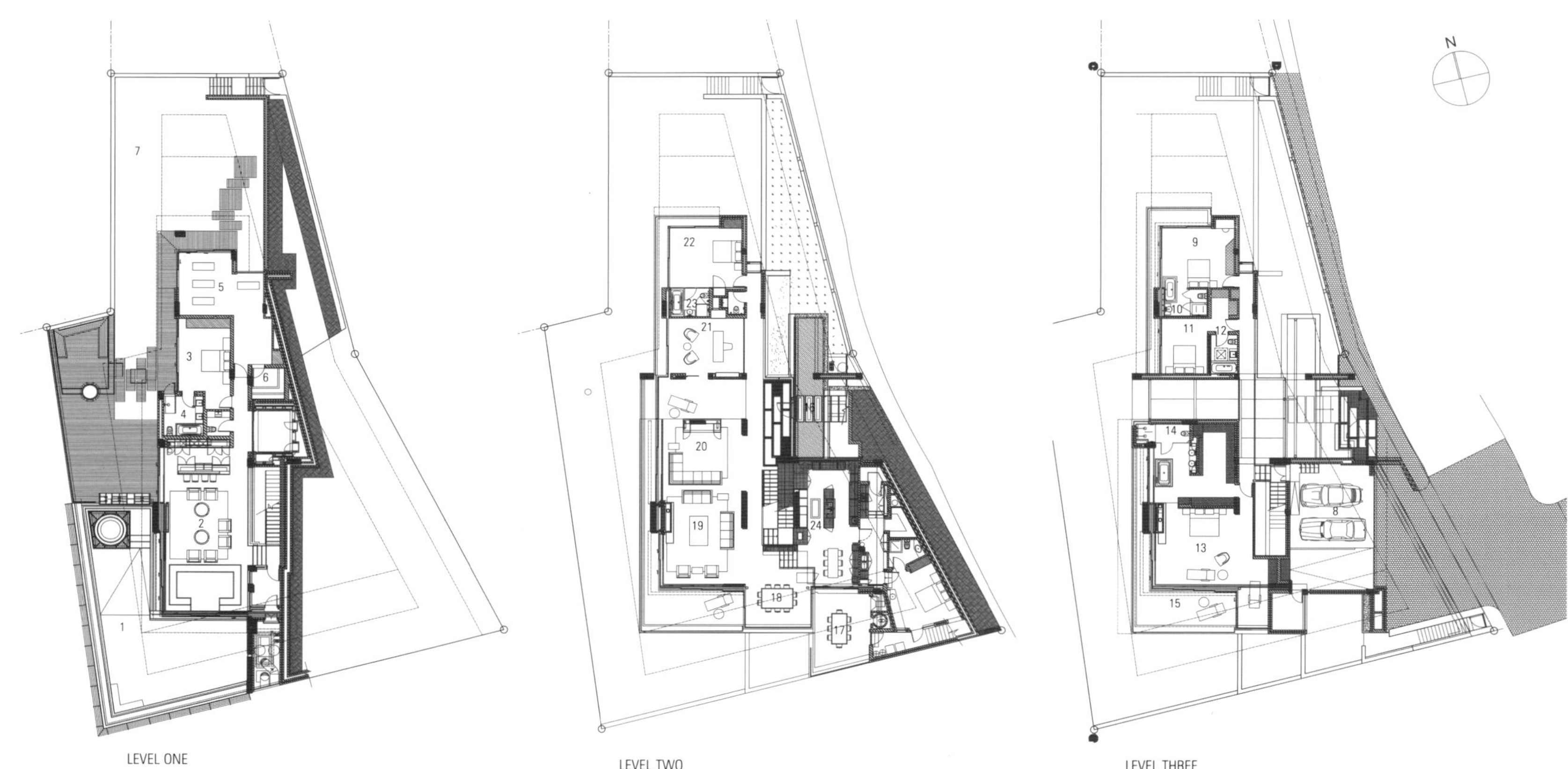

ABOVE
Balau timber screens and a quartzite feature wall create a crisp contrast in colors and textures on the home's northeastern elevation.

RIGHT
Travertine stepping stones lead to the entry. Light floods into the living room beyond, with its magnificent ocean panorama. A timber screen provides privacy for the bedroom level above.

FAR RIGHT
The double-volume entry atrium "punches" through the quartzite feature wall. Glass balustrades reinforce the external/internal flow of the design.

COMPLEMENTARY INTERIORS

The architects' selection of exterior and interior finishes are complemented by the interior decorating skills of Antoni Associates. The third level main bedroom and ensuite have a lime-washed, solid oak ceiling that extends through and over the external terrace.

The building relates to the site by creating outdoor terraces at the first and second levels as the house steps down the slope. The kitchen opens up onto an intimate dining area, which includes a barbecue and pizza oven. This terrace has expansive views over the greenbelt alongside the house and down to the Twelve Apostle Mountains.

The large entertainment room, guest room, and gym on the first level open onto timber decks, a tranquil sculpture garden, and the large infinity pool.

LEVELS FOR LIVING

There are two levels devoted to living space and one full third level containing bedrooms. The first level entertainment room and cocktail bar open onto a timber deck, and are surrounded on two sides by the expansive infinity pool, and. The second level accommodates the entry and dramatic double-volume hall, and also the majority of living areas, including the kitchen, dining, two lounges, a study, and a guest room. Staff accommodation and the garden are at the back of the property on this level, below the garage. The third level has three generous ensuite bedrooms as well as a triple garage.

LINEAR LAYOUT

The house is organized in a linear manner, so that all the rooms face the magnificent sea view. Volumes and circulation penetrate the spaces vertically. The rear of the house offers a great deal of privacy – there are no openings other than the glazed double-volume entry space, which is shielded from the rear neighbors by a steel-framed timber screen.

To access the house from the street, one passes between heavy timber gates, past off-shutter, concrete-finished garden walls, over stepping stones and a water feature and, finally, through a minimalist Zen garden.

The design plays with transparency and translucency...The first impression is powerful and magical at the same time.

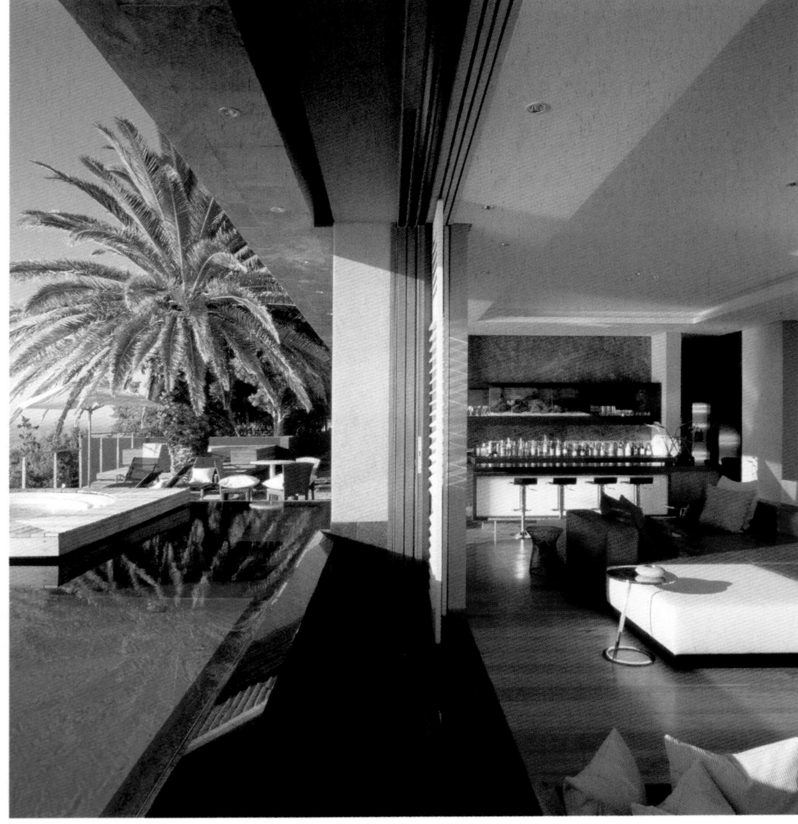

The main entry, at the rear of the second level, opens into a double-volume hall space framed by two stone walls. These cut perpendicularly through the main body of the building and frame a view of the sea and a sculptural palm tree. This space leads onto the main living wing of the house, which includes two lounges, a dining room, and a kitchen.

DRAMATIC LUMINOSITY

The design plays with transparency and translucency, with glimpsed views through timber screens into the entry, patterned voil curtains into the study, surprise glimpses into the kitchen, and views up to the bedroom bridge. The first impression is powerful and magical at the same time.

A sculptural stair leads up a triple-volume space from the entry to the third level. The west wing houses the main bedroom, which opens onto a terrace facing one of the most spectacular views of Cape Town. A bridge over the double-volume entry leads to the other two family bedrooms. Surprise glimpses of the distant views are revealed through the thin, tall end slots of the hallway, and between the timber screen and the face of the rear of the house. The bedrooms open up to provide sea views.

Accessed via the same stairwell, the first level includes a generous infinity pool, entertainment room, bar, and wine cellar. A gym and second guest room are also on this lowest level.

MAKING A STATEMENT WITH MATERIALS

The home is a reinforced concrete structure, and almost all the walls are full-height glass walls of either fixed frameless panels, or large sliding doors that slide into cavities. The wall and floor finishes are of natural textured plasters, silver-gray quartz cladding and natural timbers, and/or travertine tiling. The overall effect is warm and inviting.

TOP LEFT
Surrounded by panoramic views, the living room features textured plaster walls, lime-wash oak flooring, and a staircase clad in travertine.

ABOVE
The entertainment area boasts a bar clad in Marron Emperador marble as well as a tropical fish tank. To the left is an infinity pool flanked by palm trees.

OPPOSITE
Effective lighting creates a magical effect on the weathered balau timber deck, which leads to the infinity pool.

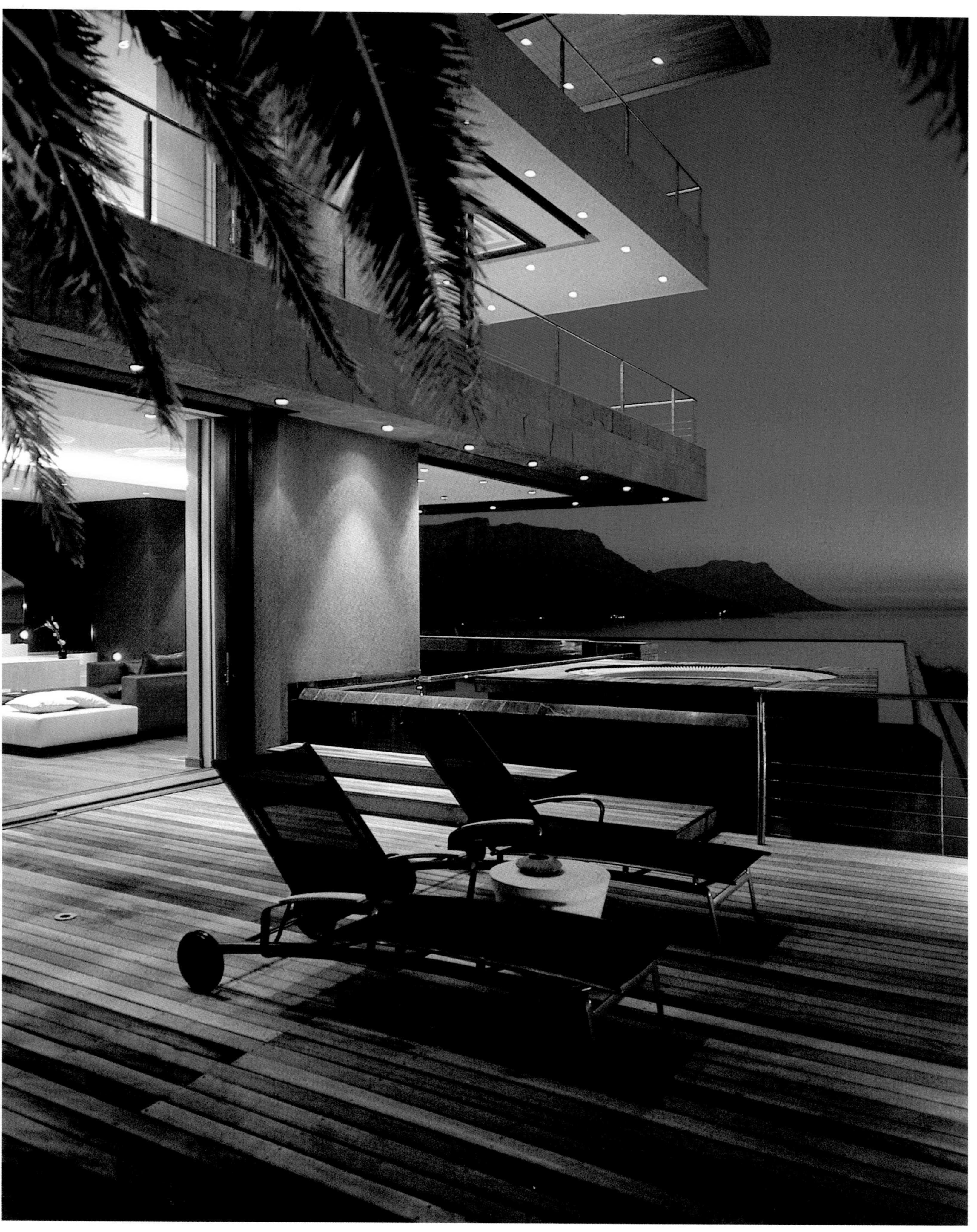

The Tree House CAPE TOWN, SOUTH AFRICA

Van der Merwe Miszewski Architects

Construction	1997–2000
Home type	Three-level family home
Structure	Steel, glass, and brick

"Trees are precious in Africa. They provide shelter for the elders at meeting time, for children from the midday heat, for all to shield against the elements. The building is an 'African folly' – immersed in, and inextricably linked with, the African landscape – a simultaneous dialogue between inside and outside, and outside and inside, neither taking precedence over the other."

Van der Merwe Miszewski Architects

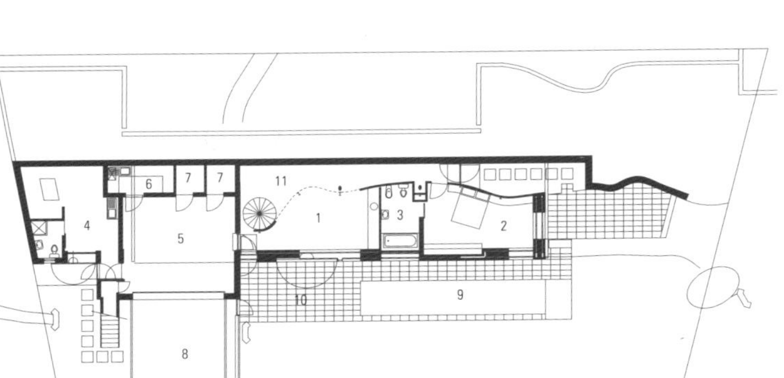

LEVEL ONE

1 study
2 bedroom
3 bathroom
4 bedroom
5 garage
6 laundry
7 store
8 driveway
9 pool
10 terrace
11 void over

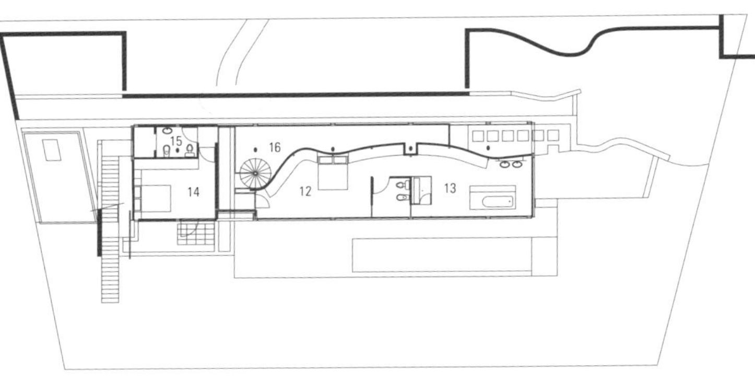

LEVEL TWO

12 main bedroom
13 main bathroom
14 bedroom
15 bathroom
16 void

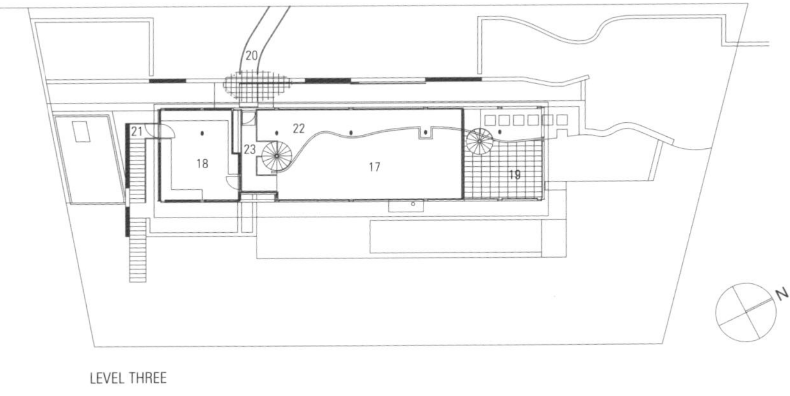

LEVEL THREE

17 lounge/dining
18 kitchen
19 terrace
20 main entrance bridge
21 service stair
22 void
23 access bridge

ABOVE
The north facade of the Tree House showing the heavy ground-level base with steel-and-glass structure above. Enclosed within the steel framework, the tree-like columns support the roof.

A NATURAL INSPIRATION

The majesty of the African landscape and the defining canopy of the surrounding umbrella pine trees form the setting and inspiration for the Tree House. Five tree-like structures root the house to the earth. Over this framework is an enclosure of transparent glass and steel, which opens the house to the trees outside.

SEPARATE ROOF, UNIFIED HOUSE

The structure supporting the roof – made of steel and timber – is completely separate from the actual enclosure, which consists of a base, a middle section, and a top section. The brick base is clad in black slate. The doors can be pulled back into the walls, and the security screens perform their utilitarian function while at the same time accentuating the weight of the base.

The middle part of the house is covered by the steel "shaft" of the structure. On the northern side, glass infill panels merge the boundaries between interior and exterior. On the southern side, timber infill panels create the kitchen and services spaces of the house. There is a timber theme here, the motif extending to the fireplace, which appears to hover above the floor.

A LAYERED EXPERIENCE

Layering is a theme that continues throughout the structure of the Tree House. A steel bridge connects the outside with the inside. A screen wall provides protection from the sun, and privacy from prying eyes.

The front entry door opens to the interior bridges. One bridge leads to the working spaces of the home, such as the kitchen. Another leads to the welcoming center of the home, where side panels of transparent grating create a sensation of being suspended above what lies beneath. The bridges have an inner lining of maple, which provides warmth and texture.

A cylindrical staircase wrapped in a metal perforated screen covering takes the visitor down to the lower levels. The maple motif continues with the triple volume curved wall that winds its way through the house.

The main bedroom, bathroom, and a self-contained staff flat are located on the middle level. The walls of the main bedroom are glass, with opaque spots for privacy. The guest bedroom and study are on the ground level and open onto the garden, the swimming pool, and the nearby river.

Natural shade is provided by the surrounding trees, and the internal temperature is kept reasonably constant because of the triple volume of the space.

THE BRANCHES OF THE TREE

The tree-like structure was carefully thought through. The "trunk" is constructed of two folded mild steel plates welded together and bolted to the base.

The top of the roof is accessible, providing a deck that hovers above the surrounding trees with magnificent views of the sea and mountains.

ABOVE
The upper level living room with triple volume void to the left of the tree-like columns. The undulating timber-clad wall separates the rooms below from the void space, while the spiral staircase in the foreground links the three levels vertically.

RIGHT
A circular skylight above the spiral staircase accentuates the cylindrical form of the expanded metal sheath that encloses the structure.

Visiting Artists House CALIFORNIA, USA

Jim Jennings Architecture

Constructed 2003
Home type Two joined, self-contained suites
Structure Concrete, steel, glass, and wood

"By the act of cutting through the hill, the long walls integrate into the curve of the land, in essence creating their own site. It is an architecture of containment and an architecture of connection. At its most subterranean, the building is most open."

Jim Jennings

ABOVE
The main gravel courtyard lies below ground level and joins the two units of the dual residence. At the north end, the transparency of the enclosed living area allows unobstructed views through to a small lake beyond. Glass curtain walls, steel crossbeams and metal roof decking contrast with the thick concrete walls.

CONTAINMENT AND CONNECTION

On the crest of a hillside that was once home to a northern California sheep ranch, this starkly minimalist building – consisting of two joined, self-contained suites for artists while on site – now boasts sculptures by Richard Serra, Bruce Nauman, Martin Puryear and others. Two seemingly parallel poured-in-place concrete walls cut through the hill, diverging at the north and converging at the south. Throughout the length of the structure, the stepped floor constantly reconfigures the horizontal and vertical planes, accentuating the perspective of elongation and foreshortening of space.

THE ART OF TRANSPARENCY

Jim Jennings conceived the building as an intervention in the landscape rather than as an object on top of it. His response to the program was the simple act of cutting through the hill and occupying a void in the landscape. He opened both ends, connecting the inside and outside, making the building a visual link between a small lake on one side and a major sculpture in the landscape on the other.

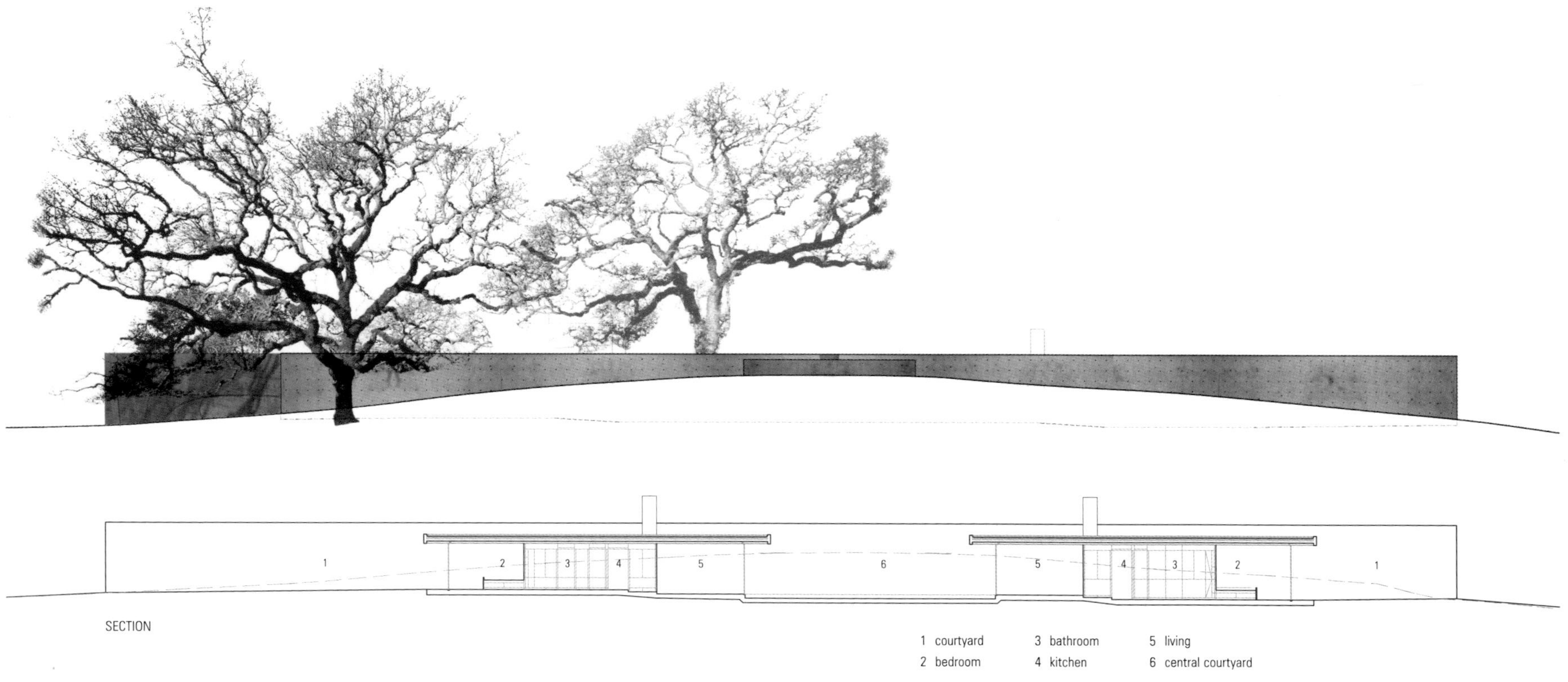

LEFT
The concrete walls cutting through the hill are unadorned on their exterior surfaces and are carved into a sculpture by David Rabinowitch on the inward-facing sides. The walls at the northern end diverge slightly outward, just as their counterparts at the southern end converge.

ABOVE
A gravel pad edged with steel forms an entry platform for the paired stairs leading to the courtyard below. The recessed entrance is situated at the top of a knoll on the vast property.

FOLLOWING PAGES
The transparency of the house at night is striking. A band of fiber optic light is buried in the ground at the base of the walls, leaving visible a 4-in (10-cm) strip on each side that illuminates the interior edges of the building from below. A light source hidden in the ceiling closely replicates the patterns of daytime light. Mechanical shades provide privacy when desired.

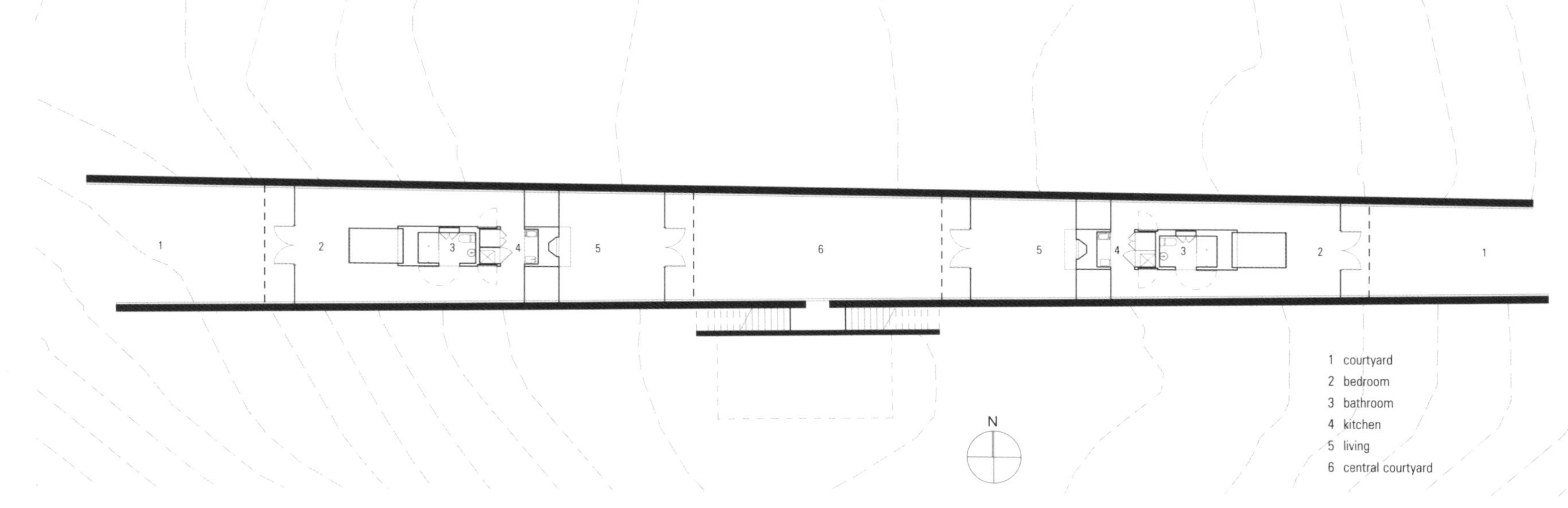

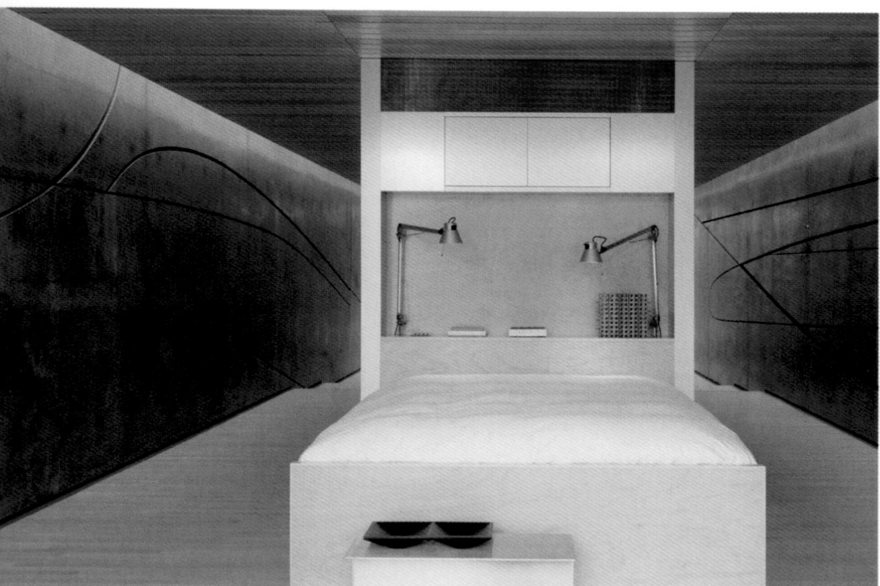

SEEING DOUBLE

The house is 1,700 sq ft (158 sq m) in area and is composed of two nearly identical suites that contain basic living functions. In each, the central core element – bathroom, kitchenette, and fireplace – is the same. The suites differ slightly in size, each offering a richness of spatial experiences throughout as the walls converge and the floors step down.

CARVING A DIALOGUE

A site-specific work by the New York artist David Rabinowitch is carved directly into the inward-facing surfaces of the concrete walls, in concert and in dialogue with the architecture. The sculptor's intent was not to ornament or define the spaces but to involve the architecture in a relationship of rhythm and shape. For his part, Jennings used a fine aggregate in the concrete and added a non-reinforced area of 4-in (10-cm) thickness to the 10-in- (25-cm-) deep structural walls as a "canvas" for Rabinowitch's work.

ART REFLECTS LIGHT

The house was designed for two artists to share at any one time, and the emphasis is as much on privacy as it is on communal living. Each pavilion opens from the living area to the central common courtyard as well as from the bedroom to a private graveled terrace whose outlook varies from its counterpart. Mechanical shades can be utilized to enclose and set off the pavilions; pocket doors pulled from the core structures out to the walls also allow a degree of demarcation if needed.

Narrow skylights fitted inside the walls wash the surfaces with light during the daytime; at night, lighting designed by Dan Dodt approximates the daylight effect. A band of fiber optic lighting runs the length of each side of the building – a unifying element that, even in the day (when it is far less dramatic than at night) adds a hint of pale blue color to the decidedly neutral palette.

ABOVE LEFT
Each of the two bedrooms, which are oriented to views of the bucolic landscape, has a maple and aluminum unit containing a built-in headboard and bed that abuts a private bath on the other side. The maple floor steps down toward the main living space.

ABOVE
A freestanding aluminum kitchenette is contained within the living area's fireplace wall. Steel and glass doors open to the central courtyard, designed as a meeting place for the artists in residence.

LEFT
Artist David Rabinowitch carved 4 in (10 cm) deep into the concrete walls' interior sides, which were then honed and sealed; 10 in (25 cm) of wall remains structural. It took four stone carvers eight months to execute the sculpture. The gravel continuing outside from the maple floor adds to the continuity of space and the indoor–outdoor character.

ABOVE
Furnishings were kept to a minimum throughout. Natural light washes the concrete walls to accentuate the carvings. Monopoint light fixtures project from the slatted-wood ceiling to provide multidirectional sources of illumination.

Yudell-Beebe House CALIFORNIA, USA

Moore Ruble Yudell Architects & Planners

Constructed	2001
Home type	Two-story, family holiday home
Structure	Concrete foundation, timber frame, and aluminum-frame glazing

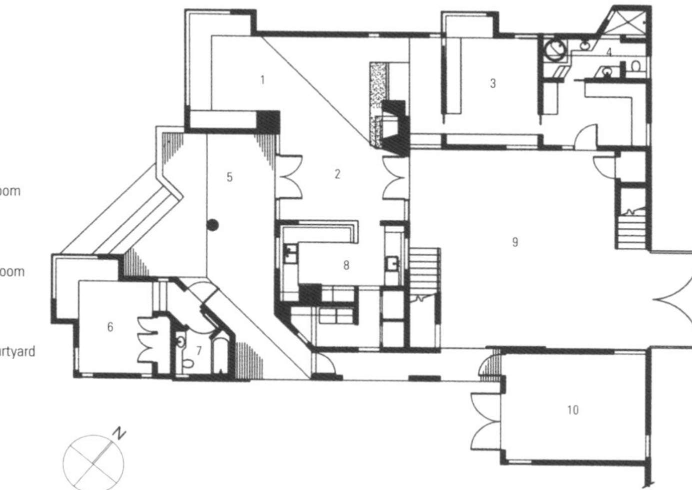

ABOVE LEFT
The exterior of the house, with its natural timbers and sympathetic color scheme, merges with the native landscape. From this perspective, the visual impact of the stepped roof line makes a bold statement, contrasting beautifully with the blue hues of ocean and sky.

LEFT
A courtyard of native plants, including mosses and grasses, catches the morning sun while offering protection from prevailing winds. The rocks mimic the formations of the local area and help the ground to drain well.

"In harmony with its environment, the house celebrates craft and materials and shapes a retreat for quiet contemplation or spirited social interaction. The house developed in close response to the rhythms and materials of the rugged coast of northern California."

Moore Ruble Yudell Architects & Planners

BONDING WITH THE SITE

This house at Sea Ranch was designed by and for its inhabitants, architect Buzz Yudell and colorist and painter Tina Beebe, who fell in love with a site near a dramatic cove on the rugged coast of northern California. They wanted to create an intimate house for work and play, where they could entertain friends and family.

Local planning authorities have imposed strict architectural guidelines in the area, and these were embraced by the owners, as they have a strong bond with nature and the environment. At the same time, they wanted their home to have an individual character.

RESPONDING TO THE SITE

Each part of the house responds to its specific site conditions. The north elevation presents a rugged entry, while the west elevation opens to the ocean with full or partial shading. The east screens the interior from houses across the meadow. The north is shaped as an intimate court with mountain views. The garden's native grasses and rocks reinforce the bond between ocean and mountain.

The interior design is elegant and simple with different feelings created by different internal shapes. The varying layers and levels offer a variety of views from various parts of the house.

FRAMING VIEWS

The windows frame the landscape and allow ample light into the house in this northern climate. The north-facing courtyard catches the morning sun and screens prevailing winds. The studio towers also collect light and serve as markers in the landscape. The house is arranged as a one-room deep array and all spaces have multiple exposures, optimizing both daylight and ventilation.

The main living space of the house can be seen either as one great room framed between the ocean and the courtyard, or as a sequence of spaces from kitchen to dining, living, and library. This provides intimacy for a small group or, conversely, accommodation of a larger gathering.

The main bedroom runs at an angle to this. Aligned on a north-south axis framed by the meadow and the courtyard, it has ocean views. A guest bedroom and bathroom are detached for privacy but linked by a south-facing protected porch.

Stairs in the courtyard lead to two small studios, which provide ideal work spaces. The studios are positioned as "tower" rooms, and have views to the ocean, meadow, mountains, and the home's courtyard.

NATIVE LANDSCAPING

The courtyard garden is populated with rocks, moss, and native grasses. In fact, the landscaping for the entire site contains predominantly native plants, mostly grasses and shrubs. The garden's rock pattern reflects the nearby natural rock formations, and also provides effective drainage for the outside.

COMPLEMENTARY MATERIALS

The materials used for the house are similarly inspired by the site and region. The external walls are redwood siding, from local sources. The windows are gray powder-coated aluminum, and the roof is a light matt gray powder-coated corrugated aluminum, which mirrors the varying conditions of the sky.

Inside, the walls are skim-coated, integral color plaster. The colors complement the native grasses and wildflowers. The exposed beams and window reveals are Douglas fir. The floors are end grain hemlock, and the built-in furniture and cabinets are beech.

TOP
The hearth provides an anchor for the major living spaces. The color scheme, reminiscent of native grass and wildflowers, counterpoints the natural timber and plaster. The cutout windows that sit flush on the main wall allow shafts of natural light to filter through, acting as organic spotlights on various surfaces in the space.

ABOVE
The aspect of this tower studio – one of two in the house – frames views of ocean, meadow, and sky. The essentials for a creative work space – natural light, clean surfaces, and an inspiring outlook – are well catered for.

Part 3

The Architects

The lives and work of architects who have shaped home design in the twentieth and twenty-first centuries

Alvar Aalto

Hugo "Alvar" Henrik Aalto (1898–1976) was born in a small village of Kuortane, Finland, in the depths of winter. His father was a land surveyor, but both sides of the family shared a love of rustic nature, the forest, and woods. In 1907, Aalto moved with his family to Jyväskylä in central Finland, where there was the first Finnish-language secondary school. He was brought up in a family which spoke Swedish, but he learned Latin at school, and his family maintained Humanist values. As a boy he sketched people, and although he was not particularly musical, he took piano lessons and wrote humorous articles. Aalto became a great storyteller. He liked to sing (out-of-tune), and at parties became a great favorite with the ladies. His need for human affection was strong, and this marked his architecture in the most human and gentle of ways.

Aalto graduated from the Jyväskylä Lyceum in 1916, and then attended the Helsinki University of Technology, where he had no difficulty adapting to the cultural life of the capital. At the University he was influenced by Armas Eliel Lindgren, who was a partner of Eliel Saarinen. Aalto graduated from the University as an architect in 1921. He established his practice in Jyväskylä in 1923, and from the earliest days Aalto and his partner Aino were involved in designing furniture. At this time, Finland was marked by "Nordic" Classicism. Not surprisingly, Aalto's first single-family houses carried this architectural language in function and form to perfection. His Villa Manner (1923), situated on the shores of Lake Ponnenjävi, and built for a land surveyor, has a Classic monumentality that is rare in Aalto's work. Villa Manner carries a complete Classical colonnade and pediment, with a strict symmetry maintained by its flanking wings. The interior has a free plan, rather than a central axis. The upper floor is built from exposed logs with vernacular furniture. This composition carries the dream of the Finnish manor house to perfection, especially when viewed in winter snow.

Aalto's transition from Classicism to Functionalism was a natural process – a direct product of the need for economy, accommodating the requirements of people, and following the spirit of the times. By the end of the 1920s he began to make contact with the leading figures of Modernism – Le Corbusier in France, and Erik Gunnar Asplund and Sven Markelius in Sweden. From these men he learned the architectural "language" of flat roofs and white walls. His best work of this period is the Villa Tammekann (1933) in Tartu, Estonia, built in brick and painted white, with open balconies, and a terrace in front. The kitchen was modern, complete with metal windows, but carried an open fireplace. Aalto was never entirely seduced by Functionalism, and was soon making architecture from a more human and Romantic point of view.

After building his own rural house and studio, in Helsinki by 1936, Aalto had the chance to design the Villa Mairea at the end of the 1930s. In Villa Mairea Aalto received a free hand from client friends, with no economic limitations. The result is a natural masterpiece among the pine woods of Noormarkku in Finland. Aalto combined the needs for formal entertaining with an L-shaped plan, using two and three stories including a sauna and a swimming pool, all set within a beautiful garden. The entrance has a free-form canopy, with an abundance of metaphorical references to spruce trees tightly bundled together. The suggestion to the forest landscape is Romantic, and this is carried through in the door details and the vertical poles lining the staircase. In an Aalto house, one is continually reminded of the aural and spiritual values of the forest.

While Villa Mairea is Aalto's finest house, he also created a very elegant French house called Villa Carré, between 1956–59, for Louis Carré, an art dealer in Bazoches-sur-Guyonne, France. This monopitched, white-painted villa carries a very rich timbered and spatial interior filled with sculpture and art. In 1996 it was made a *monument historique classé* (a historic monument).

The legacy of Aalto is his understanding of the psychological needs of human beings, the particular qualities of the Finnish milieu, and the use of the landscape, setting his houses among granite boulders. Aalto believed that the task of the architect was to give creative definition, in form and detail, to the aesthetic and technical direction of his time. His interiors are marked by the use of natural light, texture, and color. He used wood, brick, copper, and marble to provide textural contrasts. While his emotional vitality was provided by the women in his life, as a man he was a great charmer and a great architect who advanced architecture in Scandinavia.

David Adler

David Adler (1882–1949) was born in Milwaukee, Wisconsin, USA, and designed over 200 residences during the period known as that of "the great American house." After graduating with a degree in architecture from Princeton University in 1904, he traveled extensively overseas before returning to the United States of America in 1911, finding work with one of the pre-eminent "great house" architects – Howard Shaw in Chicago, Illinois.

Adler was elected to the prestigious American Institute of Architects in 1926, despite not becoming a licensed architect until 1929. He spent long hours on the fine details of his designs and had a love for symmetry, often creating doors in a room that served no purpose, simply to achieve a visual balance. The Crane House (1924–27), a 59-room Stuart-style mansion built for Mr and Mrs Richard Crane Jr in Ipswich, Massachusetts, was by far Adler's most ambitious project and came to embody the American Country Place Era with its landscaped gardens and diverse farm and estate buildings.

Adler was an intensely private man who gained the bulk of his commissions as a result of referrals from friends and clients. In 1925 he was made a trustee of the Art Institute of Chicago.

Gregory Ain

Gregory Ain (1908–88) was born in Pittsburgh, Pennsylvania, USA, and graduated from the University of Southern California in 1928. He first worked for Rudolph Schindler and Richard Neutra, whose Modernist ideas tempered his largely Classical training. In 1936 he started his own practice in Los Angeles, concentrating on private houses and developing his life-long interest in low-cost, yet dignified, public housing. Ain served as dean of the School of Architecture, Pennsylvania State University, from 1963 to 1967.

Ain's first Californian projects – the Charles Edwards House (1936) and Anselem Ernst House (1937) – reflect a strong Schindler influence with their asymmetrical planes. He followed with his renowned, Neutra-influenced, Dunsmuir Flats (1937–39), which comprises four staggered two-story white blocks, with private porches and patios, and ceiling levels defined by continuous ribbon windows. The panel-post construction limited building costs, while managing to successfully incorporate the conflicting needs for both privacy and exterior light.

In 1940 Ain was granted a Guggenheim Fellowship to explore methods of panel design for low-cost, high-density housing. In collaboration with the landscape architect Garrett Eckbo, he produced a series of housing units in garden settings, most notably the Park Planned Homes (1946) in Altadena, California, and two clusters in Los Angeles: The Mar Vista Housing complex, and the Avenel Housing complex for musicians at Silver Lake (both 1948). The latter features 20 attached units, broken into two blocks on a hillside site, with private patios off the living rooms facing the view.

Other notable Ain creations in California include the Brownfield Medical Building (1938) in Los Angeles, the Vorkapich Garden House (1939) in Beverly Hills, and the Hollywood Guilds and Unions Office Building (1948) in Los Angeles. In 1950, with Joseph Johnson and Alfred Day, Ain designed an exhibition house for the garden of the New York Museum of Modern Art.

Ain designed a large number of low-cost housing project plans, but many remained unrealized, largely because lending agencies opposed multiple ownership.

Tadao Ando

Tadao Ando (1941–) was born in Osaka, Japan. He is a self-taught architect with no architectural degree or training with a master architect. Ando attributes his development as an architect to extensive reading and a number of study trips to Europe, Africa, and the United States of America. In 1969, he established Tadao Ando Architects and Associates, in Osaka.

Most of Ando's projects have been in Japan, mainly in the Osaka area. In addition to a number of religious structures, he has designed museums and commercial buildings including offices, factories, and shopping centers. His professional career began, however, with residential projects including homes for single and multiple families, mixed commercial/residential buildings, and apartment complexes.

One of Ando's first commissions was in 1977 for a small row house in Osaka called Azuma House, which received the top prize of the Architectural Institute of Japan in 1979. The house is characterized by its interior courtyard, which attempts to integrate light, air, and rain into the Japanese lifestyle. The courtyard is also a spatial entity that compensates for the small site the house is built on.

One of Ando's most important housing projects is called Rokko Housing, which was completed in two stages: The first, of 20 terraced apartments, each differing in size and layout, in 1983, and the second, of 50 apartments, in 1993. While the apartments appear to be the same on the outside, each has a unique interior. The complex is built of reinforced concrete with a rigid frame and is imbedded in the side of a 60° sloping hillside. Each apartment has a panoramic view of Osaka Bay.

Ando's other residential projects include the three-story Ishihara House (1977–78) in Osaka – another concrete-bearing wall structure with a unique central courtyard surrounded by a glass block membrane – and the three-story Horiuchi House (1979), which uses a glass block wall as a freestanding screen between the home and street traffic.

Ando captured the imagination of the younger architects in Japan and became known worldwide for his beautifully rendered buildings. He has written, "I am interested both in Japanese aesthetics which places importance on parts and the application of reason which gives order to the whole. To give a stable order to the building as a whole, I use geometry."

Ando's use of geometric forms in themselves are derived by spaces and natural light. Patterns of shadow are thrown against the evenly finished concrete surface that softly envelops the space. He is always conscious of the nature of the times and the needs of human beings. His architecture is like that of Louis I Kahn's "Concrete and Light." However, the designs of some of his subtle houses have included stone, steel, and glass, to serve many intentions. The strength of Ando's very powerful building lies in the use of basic materials (usually concrete) and simple geometric shapes such as the square, rectangle, and circle.

Ando has received the Annual Prize of the Architectural Institute of Japan in 1979, the Japanese Cultural Design Prize in 1983, the Alvar Aalto Medal in 1985, the Annual Award from the Japanese Ministry of Education in 1986, the Mainichi Art Prize in 1987, the Isoya Yoshida Award in 1988, and the Gold Medal from the Académie d'Architecture in Paris in 1989.

Arquitectonica

The architectural firm of Arquitectonica – meaning "architectural" in Spanish – was begun in 1977 by Bernardo Fort-Brescia and Laurinda Spear. Laurinda Spear (1951–) was born in Miami, USA, and educated at Brown and Columbia universities and is the 1978 recipient of the prestigious Rome Prize in Architecture. Bernardo Fort-Brescia (1951–) was born in Lima, Peru, and is a master of merging formality with playfulness, always reminding us that architecture can be fun as well as functional. They are married with five children.

Arquitectonica came to international prominence in 1982, startling the design world with the flamboyant Atlantis – a condominium tower with a "hole in the middle" on Miami's Brickell Ave, which has become an symbol of both tropical Modernism and of the optimism of the "new" Miami.

Arquitectonica now has a staff of over 400 in offices throughout Asia, Europe, and the Americas. Their designs have been exhibited in museums throughout the world and their plans and philosophy have been featured in thousands of magazines and journals including *Time*, *Newsweek*, *Progressive Architecture*, and *Fortune*.

The unusual name of the firm was born from necessity. In 1977 a business name was required to formally bid on a large project in South America. With time of the essence someone asked, "How do you say 'architectural' in Spanish?" Arquitectonica was born, though now it is referred to simply and affectionately as "Arq."

At Arq the client is intimately involved in the design process – from the preparation of initial drawings through to completion – to avoid any miscommunication, with the style an unconventional Modernism that is at times dramatic, Romantic, and even whimsical. Projects range from luxury condominium towers, casinos, hotels, and resorts to schools, universities, and retail centers.

Arq is recognized for its excellence and innovation and its awards are too numerous to recount. Among them are the American Institute of Architects Test of Time Award, and it was named the 1998–99 AIA Florida Firm of the Year.

Their first collaboration was The Pink House (1976), a concrete, glass, and stucco residence on the shore of Biscayne Bay, Miami. Painted in five shades of pink, its sculptural elements are intimately connected to its use of color, which fade from a deep to a pale pink, heightening the sense of perspective. Its interior and exterior spaces are blurred by an extensive patio, pool, and oversized windows that maximize bay views. The Pink House won the American Institute of Architects Test of Time Award in 1998.

Their twin 43-story high-rise condominiums in downtown Miami, due for completion in 2008, is the first building in the city to utilize Sony's Intuitive Resident Information System (IRIS), allowing residents to access all services and amenities at the touch of a button and typifying Arquitectonica's reputation for employing cutting-edge technology.

Erik Gunnar Asplund

Erik Gunnar Asplund (1885–1940) was born in Stockholm, Sweden. He was the most outstanding Swedish architect of the first half of the twentieth century. Asplund was educated at the Royal Institute of Technology, Stockholm, from 1905 to 1909. His initial design preferences combined national Romanticism with Nordic Classicism, however, later in his career, he would become a Modernist both in thought and deed.

As a student he won a traveling scholarship which took him to Germany where he was influenced by the Classicism of Karl Friedrich Schinkel and Peter Behrens. On his return to Stockholm, with the help of fellow students, he founded the Klara School – an independent design academy under the tutelage of Carl Bergsten, Ragnar Östberg, Ivar Tengbom, and Carl Westman – where they favored a Romantic sensibility incorporating Scandinavian vernacular and craft design.

Asplund began private practice in 1909 mainly on small houses. His Snellman Villa (1917–18) at Djursholm, near Stockholm, shows the influence of the English architect Baillie Scott. He later traveled to Italy and Greece, where Classicism left a deep impression on his architecture.

Asplund's mastery of the vernacular and the classical – in collaboration with Sigurd Lewerentz – resulted in the winning entry for the Woodland South Cementery (1915) in Stockholm. Here Asplund's Woodland Chapel (1920) blends Romanticism and Classicism beautifully. Asplund used a Tuscan portico, which admitted mourners to a circular interior, articulated by white-rendered stucco walls with a timber and shingled roof. The top-lit interior was so arranged that mourners faced each other in the most personal of ways, so that their grief was open for all to see. Situated among the pine trees, this chapel marked Asplund as an environmentalist and a major Scandinavian architect with a sure sense of place and occasion. This combination of traditions was also worked through in the Villa Snellman and the Lister County Courthouse (1921) in Sölvesborg.

A second chapel was opened on the Woodland site in 1925, to the design of Sigurd Lewerentz. This famous forest cementery is on a gently sloping hillside covered with pines, heather, indigenous bushes, and wild grass. The landscape remains untouched as a Garden of Remembrance and repose.

Perhaps Stockholm's Public Library (1920–28) marked the end of Asplund's Nordic concerns with Romanticism and Classicism. In this masterfully conceived building, Asplund takes the library user on a clear progressive path of book borrowing. The layout of the building is positively clear, and its exterior drum form uses a simplified architecture of sensibility. However, by the 1930 Stockholm Exhibition, Asplund had begun to embrace Modernism as an instrument of social reform.

Asplund was commissioned to create a new crematorium in the Woodland Cemetery, where the increasing number of cremations required new facilities. This work became Asplund's final masterpiece. His beautifully articulated monumental portico faces directly towards a naturalistic landscape of heroic scale and sensitivity. His rectilinear loggia is a dynamic and emotional experience. It prepares mourners for the chapels behind. Returning from burials, mourners face directly out into a rolling landscape. The retreat for the mourner – down a long, gradual incline – encounters a huge granite cross, embedded in the landscape. Designed as the language of retreat, it is a consummate and compelling experience in human sympathy: Imaginatively conceived and sensitively detailed, this retreat is the ultimate Asplund experience.

Ian Athfield

Ian Charles Athfield (1940–) was born in Christchurch, New Zealand and trained at the University of Auckland School of Architecture under Charles Light and Richard Toy, completing a diploma in architecture in 1963. Athfield is one of Wellington's most controversial domestic architects. Even today, he still carries the identity of a defiant rebel, caring revisionist, and relaxed maker of architecture. But despite his rebelliousness, in May 2006 he was elected president of the New Zealand Institute of Architects. Throughout his career he has won many National Awards for Architecture, but at the same time never having anything to do with the tyranny of professionalism.

His personal vision of architecture is very much that of a practical person who believes in the process of building as an art form. As a practitioner Athfield regards architecture as a human community of flexible interaction. In this Ian Athfield has a high sense of humor and imagination, while at the same time adopting a "down-to-earth" directness and casual demeanor. He never misses a chance to tilt against city planners and the "establishment." As a domestic architect he is not a formalist, but blends Mediterranean white plasterwork with timber frame construction, while dealing sensitively with the needs of people. Athfield has a deep involvement in humanistic architecture. He realizes that people have hidden talents, and he likes to work directly alongside his domestic clients. His inclusive approach finds expression in the incorporation of movement, change, diversity, complexity, and ambiguity – an architecture for our time.

As a bruised misfit from several corporate offices, Athfield started private practice in 1968, and in a long series of houses and public buildings, he has become an important commentator on what it means to be a New Zealander operating in the South Pacific. During his career he has completed many houses. It all started with his own house – Athfield House – a white-painted, east-facing villa, set on a hillside overlooking Wellington Harbour – the subject of continuous tumbling-down development over the years. Other Wellington houses have followed in quick succession: The Cardiff House (1969) above Karaka Bay; the Porteous House (1969) using second-hand bricks; and the Cox House (1978) a hill-top cluster of the old and new, with a view to the western hills of the Hutt Valley. Athfield's Cox House is a particularly interesting experience in personal building.

According to its owner, Bart Cox, the Cox House has a high sense of order and workability – a heightened sense of visual freedom and spatial development – and a profound agreeableness which is present in the bathroom, the small-scaled bedrooms, the cosseted dining room, and the sense of enclosure and deep security in stepping down into the living room. Bart Cox, with little building experience, built this house in 18 months, working seven days a week. Athfield helped him to set it out, and a couple of builders put up the timber frame, but after that Cox was on his own. Cox thinks Athfield is a natural builder with an instinctive feeling for people and materials – a self-effacing architect who has the courage to put humor into his working life.

Athfield has also done many distinguished houses in other parts of New Zealand: The Logan House (1978) along the shoreline of Eastbourne, Wellington; the Buck House (1980) for a wine-maker in Havelock North; followed by bigger houses in Queenstown, the Bay of Islands, and the grape-growing region of Nelson.

Perhaps his social concern for architecture was best recognized by his winning of an international housing competition in Manila, the Philippines, when in the late 1970s the Marcos Government wanted to re-house squatters on the Tondo foreshore. Although the Philippine government reneged on the whole deal, Athfield's social concern positively marked his career with distinction. The ingenuity of Athfield has made him one of New Zealand's leading community-involved architects.

Mackay Baillie Scott

Mackay Hugh Baillie Scott (1865–1945) was born in Ramsgate, near Kent in England. His father was a baron of Scotland, who owned a sheep station in Australia. His mother came from a distinguished military family, and encouraged the architectural and cultural development of her son. Coming from an affluent family, Baillie Scott received a full education before he was articled to the City Architects of Bath – an unlikely choice for a student with Arts and Crafts and Romantic sympathies.

Baillie Scott was one of Britain's most distinguished domestic architects. Together with Charles Voysey, Charles Rennie Mackintosh, and Raymond Unwin, he altered the course of domestic architecture in England. In his long domestic practice, Baillie Scott was almost exclusively concerned with country houses. For inspiration he drew upon the work of Augustus Pugin, John Ruskin, William Morris, Philip Webb, and Norman Shaw. Rallying around the Arts and Crafts, these architects created domestic architecture that was widely accepted – it even spread to Germany and the United States of America, influencing the Prairie school.

We need to remember that in this matter there is a connection between the Arts and Crafts and the Gothic Revival. While Pugin inspired by doing, polemicist Ruskin's writings led to the Gothic Revival. Ruskin thought good art flowed from Gothic art and it was the craftsmanship of this artistic world that Baillie Scott absorbed.

Baillie Scott built his Red House on the Isle of Man in 1893, and it is full of quotations from the Romantic imagination. He used red brick and tile hanging – these were combined with the timberwork of Cheshire farmhouses. He carried this through into the wooden interior, where he delighted in opening up the social rooms. It was this wealth of vernacular inventiveness, and the way it related to the garden, which moved the heart of Baillie Scott. Like most architects of his time he promoted his ideas in the *Studio* magazine.

Around the turn of the twentieth century, Baillie Scott's architecture moved away from the half-timbered look of his early work to the broad simplicities – long green slate roofs over white-washed and buttressed walls marked his maturity. In these houses Baillie Scott retained his respect for the Arts and Crafts and their longing to live in contact with natural beauty. Examples of this include Blackwell House (1900) near Windermere, and Winscombe House (1902) in Crowburgh, Sussex.

Baillie Scott moved his family to Bedford, Hertfordshire in 1901 while he was gaining recognition in Britain and Germany. Bedford was a furniture center of like-minded artists. In 1906 he published *Houses and Gardens,* which marked the high point in his career. His book stood out because its argument defended the Arts and Crafts movement, and the illustrations were his own. His book presented a distinctive architecture of long low roofs, spacious hallways, and flowering gardens. In this Baillie Scott fused the vernacular characteristics of Edwin Lutyens' earliest architecture with Gertrude Jekyll's garden design.

His houses up to 1914 were simple, spacious, and self-assured – all significant places in which to live – where he used sliding screens to open up bigger rooms. In *Houses and Gardens*, Baillie Scott advanced planning concepts, integrating and subordinating other rooms in the house to the greater spatial glory of the living room, which was placed towards the garden. As an Arts and Crafts disciple, Baillie Scott thought furniture ought to be built-in wherever possible. In this respect he aligned himself with Frank Lloyd Wright, and even Le Corbusier.

Understandably Baillie Scott deplored mass housing with its lack of individual character. The miles of contemporary brick houses built in Britain in the later part of the twentieth century would have appalled him. Every house for Baillie Scott had to be personal and distinctive. Like Frank Lloyd Wright, Baillie Scott believed in "organic" architecture.

Baillie Scott worked all over England. He designed many houses in Cambridge. His book *Houses and Gardens* bought him many clients. He had a private income, so he could be selective in his choice of commissions. Unlike Lutyens, who refused to consider clients with less than £20,000 to spend, Baillie Scott maintained a relaxed attitude to fee gathering. Like Voysey he deplored Modernism. He hated the Modern movement in its naive disregard for location, sound construction, and materiality. Baillie Scott stood in the divide between tradition and Modernism. Far from marking the end of the Arts and Crafts, Baillie Scott's gentle domestic agenda still endures.

Shigeru Ban

Shigeru Ban (1957–) was born in Tokyo, Japan. He graduated with a Bachelor of Architecture from the Cooper Union School of Architecture in the United States of America in 1984, before establishing his own private practice in Tokyo in 1985. His influences would include the work of Arata Isozaki, with whom he worked in Tokyo prior to attaining his degree.

Ban has mastered the Japanese concern with impermanence both aesthetically and programmatically. He achieved fame within the architectural world with his innovative use of paper within built structures, including the Paper House (1995) at Lake Yamanaka, Japan. The Paper House consisted of an S-shape configuration comprised of 110 paper tubes that provide a colonnade dividing the space while supporting the roof. The uniqueness of the design is found in the use of cardboard in a structural role that would more commonly be provided by concrete. Such housing is both affordable and sturdy, proving Ban as somewhat of a Modernist with the intent of wanting beauty to be attainable by the masses. His paper structures have been provided to underdeveloped countries as a UN initiative. Outside of his paper houses, Ban has a myriad of commercial and domestic buildings. One of the most famous of these is the Curtain Wall House (1995) in Tokyo, located on a corner site within the city. The brief required that the house be as open as possible in order to maintain contact with its neighbors. Ban takes this idea with an adaptation of the *shoji* screen to spatially open up the corner of the house, leaving two horizontal slabs that appear to be supported by a single column. The facade, from the first to the second floor, is maintained by a huge curtain that is drawn back to reveal the living area.

Most of Ban's domestic architecture is found in Japan. All display an exceptional attention to detail and quality of space from the Double-Roof House (1993) in Yamanashi to the Wall-less House (1997) in Nagano, and the M Residence (1998) in Tokyo. Whether it be residential, commercial building, or a humanitarian project, Shigeru Ban does not hold back on innovation. A master of his craft, he has proven himself as a vision of invention and beauty, with the ability to marry these attributes with traditional architecture. Shigeru Ban constantly improves upon a Modernist ideal with a twenty-first century twist.

Edward Barnes

Edward Larabee Barnes (1915–2004) was born in Chicago, Illinois, USA. He was a leading exponent of the European Modern movement as expressed in the Harvard Graduate School of Design. After traveling through Europe on a fellowship, he established a private practice in New York. He has taught at the Pratt Institute in New York and Yale University in Connecticut. He has also served as vice-president to the American Academy in Rome. Described by the *New York Times* as an architect who cherished clarity and functionality, while at the same time devising novel approaches to houses, skyscrapers, and university campuses, he is probably best remembered for the design of IBM's New York Headquarters, which was completed in 1983.

Barnes adhered to the concept that buildings should appear to be anchored to the earth. Avoiding grandiose statements he, instead, pursued gentle, contextual architecture that seemed to reflect his urbane and gracious nature. His Walker Art Center in Minneapolis was completed in 1971 to much acclaim. Barnes' concern was more with the flow of the building rather than its form, intent on taking the visitor on a processional journey through the artworks and not to have the building be an artistic distraction from the art within. Barnes noted, "A museum is not a monument to the architect... it is part of the fabric of daily life."

Barnes was also a prolific designer of houses throughout his career, displaying a keen awareness of a building's relationship to the land around it. In 1994 he won the American Institute of Architects 25 Year Award for the Haystack Mountain School of Crafts, a collection of shingled cottages on the Maine coast. Designed to create a sense of community, all the cottages were connected by a raised platform "much like Main Street," Barnes once said in an interview.

Barnes had a modular approach to design using glass, stone, and pre-formed concrete to create beautiful and complex structures that reflected his own personal preference for simplicity and functionality.

Luis Barragán

Luis Barragán (1902–88) was born in Guadalajara, Mexico. He studied engineering and architecture in Guadalajara, at a time when, after centuries of colonial rule, Mexico's artists and intellectuals were seeking a new identity. In 1925 he attended the Paris Exhibition of Decorative Art, where he was exposed to Art Deco and the International Style creations of Le Corbusier and Charlotte Perriand.

Considered Mexico's most influential twentieth-century architect and urban planner, Barragán did not achieve widespread recognition until late in his career. A master of space and light, he incorporated colorful, sensuous, Mexican Modernism into the International Style. In the early 1930s Barragán met Le Corbusier and the landscape architect, Ferdinand Bac, in Paris. He then went on to establish his practice in Mexico City where he progressed his own ideas on Modernism. With a nod to the International Style, Barragán created a vibrant, sensual Mexican aesthetic by using vivid colors and textural contrasts, and emphasizing his buildings' natural surroundings.

In 1954 he built the superb convent at Tlalpan, an outer suburb of Mexico City. This highly influential building conveys monastic serenity with deftly positioned shafts of light. In 1957 he designed the much-acclaimed Torri Satélite, a clump of brightly colored towers in a chaotic traffic exchange in Mexico City. In an audacious departure from the norm, it is designed to be seen from a moving car, rather than the sidewalk.

Barragán once said that light and water were his favorite themes, and this is apparent in his Mexico City buildings like the Folke Egerstrom House and Stables (1966) built around a brightly colored, sculptured sequence of horse pools, and Francisco Gilardi House (1975), which frames an indoor pool. Like Brazilian architect Roberto Burle Marx, Barragán developed a personal approach to designing within a Modernist milieu, while harmonizing with the local terrain and foliage. His enormous influence on architecture belies his relatively small output.

Barragán's houses provide a retreat from contemporary life. Barragán House (1947), Prieto Lopez House (1950), and Galvez House (1955), all integrate interior and exterior spaces through the use of walls which create a private and tranquil ambience. Barragán uses the wall as sculpture: Doors, windows, and other wall features are placed with artful consideration. His walls create a secluded domestic enclosure, allowing glimpses of the sky but little else. Color is used on walls for spatial effect, or to express moods. A wall might be painted blue as a metaphor for the sky, yellow to give an impression of sunlight, or pink to reflect warmth into the house.

In 1977 Barragán achieved belated recognition when a retrospective of his work was held at the Museum of Modern Art in New York. In 1980 he was awarded the prestigious Pritzker Prize.

Geoffrey Bawa

Geoffrey Bawa (1919–2003) was born in Colombo, Sri Lanka. He graduated from the Architectural Association in London in 1956 and returned to Sri Lanka where he gathered together a group of talented young designers and artists who shared his interest in Sri Lanka's forgotten architectural heritage, and his ambition to develop new ways of making and building. The practice established itself as the most esteemed and prolific in Sri Lanka, with a folio that included religious, social, cultural, educational, governmental, commercial, and residential buildings, creating a catalog of archetypes. It also became the catalyst for a new generation of innovative Sri Lankan architects.

Geoffrey Bawa is considered Sri Lanka's most prolific and influential architect. His work has had enormous impact upon Asian architecture, and is unanimously applauded by connoisseurs of architecture throughout the world. One of Bawa's earliest domestic buildings – a Colombo courtyard house (1961) – was the first to blend elements of traditional domestic architecture with the Modernist concepts of open planning, demonstrating that an outdoor lifestyle may be created on a small urban plot.

The Bentota Beach Hotel of 1968 was Sri Lanka's first resort hotel, combining tourist conveniences with an awareness of place and tradition. During the early 1970s his series of buildings for government departments introduced innovative ideas for tropical city workplaces, culminating in the State Mortgage Bank (1976) in Colombo, hailed at the time as one of the world's first bio-climatic high-rises.

Bawa's growing prestige was recognized in 1979 when President Jayawardene invited him to design Sri Lanka's New Parliament at Kotte, near Colombo. A swamp was dredged to create an island at the center of a large artificial lake, with the Parliament appearing as an asymmetric arrangement of copper roofs floating above a series of terraces rising out of the water. Conceptual references to traditional Sri Lankan architecture were incorporated within a Modernist framework to create a potent image of democracy, cultural harmony, tradition, and modernity.

During the 1980s Bawa also designed the Ruhunu University near Matara, a project that demonstrated his mastery of external space and the harmonious incorporation of buildings into the landscape. The result is a pattern of pavilions and courtyards, arranged with a strong sense of theater across two rocky outcrops overlooking the Southern Ocean.

In the 1990s Bawa designed three ground-breaking hotels: The Kandalama, an austere jungle palace that snakes around a rocky outcrop beside an ancient tank in the Dry Zone; the Lighthouse at Galle, which precariously faces the Southern Ocean from a boulder-strewn cape; and the Blue Water, a pavilion in a sedate coconut grove on the edge of Colombo. All three demonstrate Bawa's self-stated aim to "consult the genius of the place in all," as well as his ability to integrate architecture with the landscape, and his panoramic management of space.

In 2002, after a severe stroke had ended his active career, Bawa was granted one of architecture's highest honors when the Aga Khan gave him a special Chairman's Award for Lifetime Achievements.

Peter Behrens

Peter Behrens (1868–1940) was born in Hamburg, Germany. Known as a designer and architect, he originally studied painting at the Karlsruhe School of Art and then in Düsseldorf under Ferdinand Brutt. While working as a painter, illustrator, and bookbinder, he moved in Bohemian circles and was interested in subjects related to the reform of lifestyles.

In 1899 Behrens was invited to become a member of the artists' colony founded by Grand Duke Ernst Ludwig II of Hesse. Behrens House, designed for the 1901 Darmstadt Exhibition, was created in its entirety by Behrens and signified a turning point in his style of design. Behrens designed every aspect of the house – everything from the structure to the cutlery. The house is organized around a dining room and music room on the ground floor with a kitchen in the basement. The main bedrooms and studio are on the top level. While this design was typical for a small bourgeois house, its combination of features was clearly influenced by the Arts and Crafts movement.

In 1903 Behrens was appointed director of the Kunstgewerbeschule in Düsseldorf and four years later established the Deutscher Werkbund, a German association of architects, designers, and industrialists and a precursor to the Bauhaus. As one of several collaborators, their objective was to generate social and industrial reforms through design. Best known for his design of the AEG Turbine Factory (1908–09) in Berlin, during his time as artistic consultant for the company, Behrens was able to synthesize art with industry, which was one of the first implementations of corporate identity of this kind.

Some of Behrens' other works of this period were firmly within the German Neo-classic tradition. Schroder House (1908–09) and the Cuno House (1909–10), both at Eppenhausen near Hagen, are prime examples. The Schroder House, which was destroyed during World War II, was a two-story geometric building characterized by a combined living room and hallway on the ground floor. Meanwhile Cuno House, built for the then mayor of Hagen, Willy Cuno, is distinguished by its spiral interior staircase, which rises from the entrance and is lit by long narrow strips of window. This feature determines the austere design of the external facade with its semi-circular central projection.

Behrens' students include such names as Ludwig Mies van der Rohe, Le Corbusier, and Walter Gropius. He accepted the position to teach at the Akademie der Bildenden Kunste in Vienna in 1922 and later became Director of the Architecture Department of the Preußische Akademie der Kunste in Berlin. He was an architect of the Modern movement who pioneered a functional architectural style upon which much industrial design, incorporating the materials of glass and steel, has been subsequently based.

Pietro Belluschi

Pietro Belluschi (1899–1994) was born in Ancona, Italy, and moved to Rome with his family in 1905. He received a degree in civil engineering from the University of Rome and in 1923 worked briefly as an inspector on a housing project before traveling to the United States of America to study at Cornell University in New York. At Cornell he took a course in architecture and continued his studies in civil engineering, obtaining his degree in 1924. Later that year he moved to Oregon and found work tracing drawings at the Portland architectural firm of AE Doyle. In 1927 he became head of the design department and in 1933 was made a full partner. During this period Belluschi was involved in the designing of many residential and commercial buildings in the emerging International Style, though personally a liking for regional styles and traditions began to emerge. He took over the firm under his own name in 1943.

In 1948 Belluschi designed the Equitable Building in Portland – America's first "steel box," sheathed in aluminum and the first office building to employ double-glazed windows. He also designed the Bank of America in San Francisco in 1949 and assisted in the design of the massive Pan Am building in New York, which opened in 1963.

However, his great legacy lies in his development of a Pacific Northwestern aesthetic in his residential designs. Joss House (1940–42) in Portland, Oregon, has an L-shaped floor plan opening the home's living areas to a view of the Tualatin Valley and the Cascade Range, with exteriors of unpainted rough-hewn spruce, and all natural wood interiors. The house possesses an informal relationship between public spaces, and the structural fir ceiling gives texture and warmth. Peter Kerr House (1941) in Gearhart, on the Oregon coast, is a simple beach house designed with a low-pitched roof and deep overhangs to shield it from the salt, rain, and wind. Its muted street facade protects the privacy of its residents. Belluschi wanted to create a low-maintenance house that would weather gracefully with the landscape. He clad the building in vertical spruce boards, adding an unfinished tree trunk to support the front porch's roof. The narrow floor plan ensures ocean views from almost every room in the house.

A noted educator and theorist, Belluschi lectured and wrote frequently, stressing the need to combine elegance and beauty at a time when commercial architecture was dominated by stale and emotionless Functionalism. During his tenure at the Massachusetts Institute of Technology's School of Architecture between 1951 and 1965, he was responsible for establishing a PhD degree in planning as well as co-founding the Joint Center for Urban Studies with Harvard University. In a career spanning 50 years, Pietro Belluschi designed over 1,000 buildings.

Julian Bicknell

Julian Bicknell (1945–) was born in Cambridge, England, and was educated at Winchester College and King's College before earning a degree in architecture at the University of Cambridge Department of Architecture. He taught at the Royal College of Art from 1972 to 1979, joined Arup Associates in 1979, and set up his own practice in 1983.

Bicknell became involved in the restoration and modification of historic buildings early in his career before moving on to the construction of new buildings in the Classical style. One of Bicknell's undoubted triumphs is the Henbury Rotunda (1984–86), his magnificent Palladian villa in Cheshire, England, which illustrates his flawless sense of proportion. He is part of the growing revival of Classicism, alongside architects of the caliber of John Blatteau and Demetri Porphyrios.

Bicknell's Upton Viva (1987–89) near Banbury in England was built for Mr and the Hon Mrs Waley-Cohen when the original seventeenth-century mansion passed to the National Trust. Hornton stone from local quarries, brick, and concrete dominate the structure. The interior sees typical, well-lit rooms enhanced by a wealth of features including bookcases, cupboards, and even hidden rooms that recreate the mysteries of the past. Walls forming sheltered gardens lead from the main house to various outbuildings. His Forbes House (1996–97) in southwest London is an all-brick building on a scale reminiscent of the grand manor houses of the eighteenth and nineteenth centuries, characterized by heavy timber surrounds to the windows and reconstituted stonework, a slate roof, and heavy ornamentation to the front facade.

Since 1990, Bicknell has worked extensively in Japan creating English-style buildings such as The Georgian Club Restaurant (1995) and the One Thousand Leaves Golf Club House (1992). With the high cost of land in cities generally requiring tall buildings to make them viable, Bicknell concedes his smaller, Classic structures are destined for the English countryside, the suburbs, and small towns. Big city commissions for Classicist architects remain rare. In any case Modernity, as seen by big business, often favors exciting technology and short-lived buildings, whereas Classicism raises structures that are meant to last hundreds, if not thousands of years, and are encouraged to do so with low elevations and the heavy use of load-bearing masonry.

Bicknell was heavily involved in the establishment of the Prince of Wales Institute of Architecture, and despite an ever-growing number of commissions, he has continued to teach in England and overseas.

Ricardo Bofill

Ricardo Bofill (1939–) was born in Barcelona, Spain. He graduated from the Barcelona University of Architecture and the School of Geneva. In 1963 Bofill gathered a group of architects, engineers, planners, sociologists, writers, movie makers, and philosophers and formed the Taller de Arquitectura – an international team, which for more than 40 years, has undertaken projects in urban planning, architecture, landscaping, interior design, furniture, and product design with a focus on design keeping in harmony with specific, different cultures. The studio has established an international reputation with urban planning for cities such as Paris, Luxembourg, Warsaw, Prague, Madrid, and Barcelona as well as projects in the United States of America, Asia, Africa, Japan, and China.

In the words of critic Christian Norberg-Schulz, Ricardo Bofill is a master at creating architectural stage sets in which the "experience of intimacy and protection is combined with a sense of a continuous, grand environment where zones of movement are juxtaposed with places of meeting and togetherness."

Bofill's buildings and architecture are gigantic models articulated by precise geometry and a three dimensionality. These reflect his predilection for designing from models and larger perspective drawings. Architecture critic David Mackay calls it "an indifference to detail that sometimes makes his buildings seem like full-size models with abundant redundancies."

Bofill's genre is mostly Classical, although he does borrow from the Baroque period, believing that intermediate spaces change the experience of light. He looks at the integration of spatial effects through expansion and contraction, subdivision and juxtaposition. He believes the mission of architects is to make a spiritual reaction in man. Bofill says that "man requires a context for social activities that cannot be defined solely in terms of use" – a notion turning away from the Functionalism of the Modern movement. His great concern is providing a common, public place by creating streets, squares, promenades, and forums. His architecture looks at the reinvigoration of iconic buildings into great pieces of art and pure geometry in urban planning.

Bofill's memorable housing projects include the 10-story Avenda Berna Housing Block (2005) in Lisbon, Portugal; the Beijing Huayuan Jidianyuan Project (2005) in Beijing, China; the Housing Complex in Manhattan (1988) in New York City, USA; The Lake Temples (1986) in Saint-Quentin-en-Yvelines, Paris, France; the Palace of Abraxas (1978–83) in Marne-La-Vallée, Paris, France; and Walden 7 (1975) in Barcelona, Spain. Walden 7 features a myriad of walkways, bridges, and arcades that cross five internal courtyards around which a 16-story cluster of buildings is grouped. Meanwhile, the Palace of

Abraxas is a dramatic complex with a monumental entrance. Classical in form, it features giant columns in prefabricated concrete, and glass attached to the facade. Despite its imposing design, the complex actually houses small, low-ceilinged apartments.

Bofill's private residences include his holiday home Casa Bofill (1975) in Montras near Girona in Spain; Can Mordenyach (1990) in S'Agaro in Spain; the Residential Complex in Luxembourg (2002); and the Oz House (2004) in Tokyo, Japan. Casa Bofill is a summer house set in a landscape of hills and woods. The complex consists of several pavilions arranged around a central exterior space occupied by a swimming pool and the main dining room, which stands as an independent pavilion. The three-story house features five independent modules with mezzanine for family and guests with all the built elements standing on a rectangular platform. The exterior cladding is a dark brown sandstone, and the interior has red ceramic cladding. The Oz House is a single-family dwelling on two levels, morphologically and geometrically creating an entrance garden and a glazed patio around which the living room, the bedrooms, and service areas are arranged.

Bofill has received the International Design Award from the American Society of Interior Designers in 1978, the Gold Medal from the Académie d'Architecture Paris in 1983, and he became an Honorary Fellow of the American Institute of Architects in 1983.

Gottfried Böhm

Gottfried Böhm (1920–) was born in Offenbach-am-Main, Germany. The only German to have won the Pritzker Prize (1986), he studied architecture at the Munich Technisch Hochschule (graduating in 1946), and sculpture at the Academy of Fine Arts, before taking over his father's architectural firm upon his death in 1955. It was during this period that he also worked with the Society for the Reconstruction of Cologne, which was severely damaged by the Allied air forces during World War II. In 1949 he designed the chapel of Madonna in the Ruins, created within the bombed-out ruins of Cologne's magnificent cathedral, and representing a sort of Gothic shelter for an unscathed Virgin.

Böhm's varied output included churches, houses, apartments, museums, civic centers, and office buildings, and he is generally regarded today as one of the most significant architects of the post-war era. An Expressionist and post-Bauhaus architect, his concern is always to create structures that form a bridge between the past and the future that are in keeping with the built environment around them. He believes the future of architecture lies not in filling up the landscape, but in bringing back life and a sense of order to the world's cities and towns.

Böhm seemed to reserve his greatest inspiration for his churches. His best-known building is unquestionably the Church of the Pilgrimage at Neviges (1960–64) in Germany, which is acknowledged as one of the great religious monuments of the twentieth century, with its soaring interior and long ceremonial approach.

Frederic Borel

Frederic Borel (1959–) was born in the southern French town of Roanne and graduated from the École Speciale d'Architecture in 1982. He established his own practice in 1985 and ever since has been creating unfailingly spectacular works; a living, reactive architecture steeped in autonomous components that "talk" to one another in a sort of scaled-down cityscape.

His apartment block for postal workers near the Place de la Bastille in Paris (1994) is a boldly unconventional building. Rather than beginning on the street with a typical facade, an opening was cut through the building's front with a passageway leading to an interior landscaped courtyard with curving mounds and narrow sidewalks, creating a spectacular interior space with housing units lining its periphery.

Borel's Pelleport Apartments (1996–99) at 15 rue de Pavillons in Paris was the latest in a series of three complexes designed in the Menilmontant and Belleville districts, the first of which, completed in 1990, won Borel the 1990 Le Moniteur Prize for the best first commission by a young architect.

Rue Pelleport's eight floors rise from a small, difficult corner site, employing a unique architectonic palette of form, color, and materials which Borel uses to challenge the accepted notions of apartment design. The building expands outwards from its base with the help of levitated planes, skewed fins and walls, canted blocks, and a mix of tilted, irregular forms that seem to grow upwards in a series of bright rendered colors rising to the tower's penthouse on the top floor. Borel's rue Pelleport Apartments, like his other signature apartments on the rue Oberkampf and the Boulevard de Belleville, punctuate the surrounding urban fabric, expressing a resistance to uniformity.

Mario Botta

Mario Botta (1943–) was born in Mendrisio, Switzerland. He trained as a technical draftsman before studying at the Liceo Artistico in Milan and then at the Istituto Universitario di Architettura in Venice between 1965 and 1969. During this period he worked as an assistant to Le Corbusier and Louis I Kahn. In 1970, he opened his own practice in Lugano, Switzerland.

Botta does not fit comfortably into a Modernist labeling, but it is easy to see the lasting influences on his design philosophy, and it is also clear that tenets of Modernism are brought out in his individual work. Botta was strongly influenced by Le Corbusier, Carlo Scarpa, and Louis I Kahn. He believed good architects allow their architecture to talk for them and was both articulate in his designs and written rationale. Although his later works increasingly accept existing forms and styles as the starting point of design, Botta still adheres to a philosophy of historical determinism in which architecture acts as a mirror of its times.

Botta's works characteristically show respect for topographical conditions and regional sensibilities and his designs generally emphasize craftsmanship and geometric order. Because he attempts to reconcile traditional architectural symbolism with the aesthetic rules of the Modern movement, Botta is often identified with the Italian Neo-rationalist group, the Tendenaz. Botta designed his first building at age 16 – a two-family house at Morbio Superiore in Ticino, Switzerland. While the layout in this structure is inconsistent, its relationship to the site, the separation of the living areas from the service spaces, and deep window recesses echo his stark, strong, towering style. His single-family residences, particularly his famous one-family house in Breganzona (1971) near Ticino, showcase strong geometric forms and a modeling of light that is a reflection of the lessons he learned from his three mentors.

His buildings are not tied to any single material. Many of them are of poured concrete and concrete blocks, with his later projects showing a skill with brick masonry, with no noticeable loss of quality or spirit of intentions. However, by the late 1970s, his houses became more Classical in plan and elevation.

His trademark style can be seen widely in Switzerland, particularly the Ticino region, and also in the Mediatheque in Villeurbanne (1988), a cathedral near Évry (1995), and the San Francisco Museum of Modern Art (1994). In 1998 he designed the new bus station for Vimercate (near Milan) – an impressive red brick building linked to many facilities, underlining the city's recent development.

In 2006 he received the Grand Officer award from the president of the Italian Republic, Carlo Azeglio Ciampi. He became an Honorary Fellow of the Bund Deutscher Architekten in 1983, and an Honorary Fellow of the American Institute of Architects in 1984.

Robin Boyd

Robin Gerard Penleigh Boyd (1919–71) was born in Melbourne, Australia. A notable practitioner of Modern architecture as well as a writer and publicist, he came from a literary and artistic family and was committed to Modernism, but was articled to the relatively conservative architect Kingsley Henderson. He became one of the founders of the Victorian Architectural Students Society, and as the editor of the society's journal, *Smudges*, he began his career as an uncompromising critic of poor and retrograde architecture.

After a period of war service in New Guinea he entered the partnership of Boyd Pethebridge and Bell, which had a small but significant output, but left the firm in 1946 to found the *Age* Small Homes Service, which opened the following year. The service was a joint enterprise between the *Age* newspaper and the Royal Victorian Institute of Architects, designed to bring modern domestic architecture within the reach of the ordinary citizen by selling sets of architects' plans at a moderate price. The designs by members of the institute, and many by Boyd himself, had a dramatic impact. So did Boyd's weekly articles in the *Age* on a variety of aspects of modern design, materials, planning, and architectural history.

Boyd left the service in 1953, and in that year the partnership of Grounds, Romberg and Boyd was formed with (Sir) Roy Grounds and (Professor) Frederick Romberg. In 1953 Boyd designed the first project house, the Peninsula House, and in 1954 devised the Stegbar Windowall for the Stegbar joinery company: This was a modular timber-framed window system which was structurally self-sufficient, and which did much to advance modern domestic design. The partnership foundered when Roy Grounds arrogated to himself the commission for the Victorian Cultural Centre in 1959, but Boyd continued with Romberg. Boyd complained of never receiving any real substantial public or commercial commissions, and his work remained overwhelmingly domestic.

Boyd's own houses were known in architectural circles but they were not publicly prominent, and certainly not nearly as influential as his writings. He progressed from a form of Modernism influenced by the Bay Region and other American movements, towards the International Style, but never strongly espoused a specific philosophy or style. In fact, his houses often seem to search for a theme, and those that do not find it, can appear somewhat thin and carboardy. The theme may be a response to the topography of the site, a structural device, a dominating functional element, or a combination of these. The Gillison House (1952) in Balwyn demonstrated both the thinness and the theme. It was of the lightest materials – timber, glass, and asbestos cement – but the main glazed walls were divided into diagonal squares, on the excuse that this braced the frame, but looking rather arbitrary and certainly demonstrating what Boyd himself would call "featurism." More robust examples included the Richardson House (1954) in Toorak, which crossed a gully and was therefore slung between two arches in the form of a rather unnecessary grand bridge; the Ken Myer "Pelican" House (1956) in Mount Eliza, which had a roof in the form of a platform floating free above it on giant timber girders; and his own house in South Yarra (1959), where he capriciously chose to suspend the roof from cables. The Featherston House (1967–68) in Ivanhoe, was more successful than these because the innovatory aspects – rooms turned into floating platforms and garden areas entering the interior – seemed less arbitrary because they more clearly related to Modernist philosophy.

Boyd's impact on domestic architecture was greatest through his authorship of a number of books, including *Victorian Modern* (1947), *Australia's Home* (1952) and *The Australian Ugliness* (1960). In it he coined the terms "featurism" and "Austerica" (the mindless imitation of America) and criticized the poorly designed sprawl of the Australian suburb. He died suddenly in 1971, and in 1973 was posthumously awarded the Architecture Critic's Medal of the American Institute of Architects.

Marcel Breuer

Marcel Breuer (1902–81) was born in Pécs, Hungary. In 1920 he dropped out of an art course at the Vienna Academy of Fine Arts, joining the recently-founded Bauhaus school in Weimar, Germany in 1921, and graduating in 1924. He became a protégé of Bauhaus director Walter Gropius, and soon produced his first piece – the throne-like, grandiloquent Romantic Chair.

Breuer is best known as one of the twentieth century's most influential furniture designers, but his designs of the UNESCO Headquarters in Paris, and a series of private houses on the East Coast of the United States of America after World War II, were no less influential. Although a prolific member of the Bauhaus, Breuer had little tolerance of the ubiquitous academic debates that characterized the school, preferring to work "without having to philosophize before every move." His work, as exemplified by the wood-slat chair, was increasingly influenced by the conceptual aesthetic of the Dutch art movement, De Stijl.

In 1926 he created his highly acclaimed steel club armchair. Remarkably light and easy to assemble, it was named the Wassily, after the Bauhaus teacher Wassily Kandinsky.

Breuer worked between Paris and the Bauhaus until 1928, when he resigned and set up an unsuccessful architecture practice in Berlin. When the National Socialists came to power in 1933, he abandoned Germany for Switzerland, and then London, before taking up a professorship alongside Gropius at Harvard University in 1937. Here Breuer taught the principles of European Modernism to students, including Paul Rudolph and Philip Johnson, who became important architects.

In 1946, Breuer left Harvard and opened an office in New York, where his first building was the Geller House (1945) on Long Island – an airy, wooden structure hailed by the media as "the house of the future." The house was described by Breuer as "binuclear." The design separates the living, dining, and kitchen areas from the bedrooms, with the two annexes of the house connected by an entrance hallway. The house and the adjacent guesthouse are positioned to create a semi-enclosed courtyard, which invites outdoor living.

For the rest of his career, Breuer concentrated on architecture, but occasionally designed furniture, including the pioneering Museum of Modern Art cut-out chair made from a single plank.

He designed dozens of private houses, many in characteristic H- and T-plans in New York, Connecticut, New Jersey, and Massachusetts. Examples include Robinson House (1947) in Williamstown in Massachusetts, and Breuer House II (1948) in New Canaan, Connecticut. Breuer used combinations of glass, gravel, and local wood, thus permeating the dwellings with the characteristics of their surroundings.

In 1952 he was part of the design team for the UNESCO Headquarters in Paris, and designed the Bijenkorf department store in Rotterdam. For these public buildings Breuer experimented with grandiose forms, which he christened "concrete sculpture," culminating in the mid-sixties with his design for the Whitney Museum of American Art in New York – probably his finest legacy.

Neave Brown

Neave Sinclair Brown (1929–) was born in Utica, New York, USA, and graduated from the London Architectural Association in 1956. He is renowned for successfully applying the principles of the London terrace house to the design of high-density public housing.

In 1975 Brown designed five connected terraces on Winscombe Street, London, for himself and his friends, and also began the Camden Town project at Fleet Road, consisting of over 50 dwellings organized in parallel rows. The latter features split-level, multi-unit sections – characteristics it shares with the typical London terrace house. Its design includes the placement of large two-story maisonettes above small one-floor units, upper balconies, and a narrow path which provides the entrance to the lower units.

In 1978, he completed the enormous and controversial Alexandra Road terrace housing project in Camden. The long, curved site is bounded by existing housing, major streets, and a railway. The need to reduce train noise and vibrations was a major consideration in Brown's organization of three parallel rows of terraced apartments made from cast-in-place concrete. Two rows are aligned along the tracks, with the higher, eight-story building designed to shield noise from reaching the interior of the site. A four-story block runs along a public sidewalk that serves both rows. The third row abuts another public sidewalk and defines a public park containing a community center, school, reception center, maintenance facilities, a heating plant, and an underground car park. The ground level of the buildings contain maisonettes with shared access, terraces, and gardens. The estate has a Mediterranean feel, and is an oasis of peace despite its noisy surrounds.

Neave Brown's work is dominated by strong ideals of social structuring, and an acknowledgment of the interdependent identity of all the separate components of a project.

William Bruder

William Bruder (1946–) was born in Milwaukee, Wisconsin, USA. A self-trained architect, he has worked out of his professional studio and residence on 10 acres (4.5 ha) in the Arizona desert north of Phoenix since 1974.

Bruder has received over 400 commissions ranging from commercial and mixed-use developments to residential and major cultural and civic projects, and his designs have been widely published in periodicals and books throughout Europe and the United States of America. A modern disciple of Frank Lloyd Wright, his philosophy has always been to search out a building's "poetic possibilities;" to sift away prevailing fashions and arrive at a basic human simplicity.

His Sky Arc House (2004) in Marin County, northern California, is a crescent-shaped home clad in pre-weathered, pewter-gray zinc that blends seamlessly into the surrounding landscape. Its abstract, contemporary shape defers to its siting on a heavily wooded slope. Employing a clever use of translucent fiberglass awnings and perforated metal railings on cantilevered wooden decks, all boundaries between structure and environment are minimized to the point of abstraction.

His Pool Residence (2006) in Reno, Nevada, consists of two bunker-like concrete cubes that display permanency, as well as being a strong sculptural element in defiance of its high-desert environment. Carefully placed windows frame the surrounding landscapes in a home where primacy has been given to providing a sheltered family retreat, humble in its materials yet grand in its scale.

In 1985 and 1995, Bruder received the Honors Award from the American Institute of Architects, Western Mountain Region and has been a lecturer and studio critic at the School of Architecture at the Tempe Campus of Arizona State University since 1971.

Beni Burnett

Beni Carr Glyn Burnett (1889–1955) was born in Mongolia. He was educated in China and Scotland and was articled to a British firm in Shanghai, and then worked for other British architects in China. He established his own practice in Tientsin (Tianjin), but departed for Malaya in 1930. Two years later he migrated to Sydney, Australia and after a brief period of private employment entered the Commonwealth service, first in Sydney and then in Canberra. In July 1937 he was appointed Architect Grade 1 and posted to Darwin.

Burnett created a Modern tropical house form in the Northern Territory of Australia, and in the town of Darwin in particular. There the hot humid climate had, even in the nineteenth century, encouraged the development of elevated open-plan houses enclosed only in slatted screens, and Burnett drew upon this tradition and upon his Malayan experience in his work. Five houses built for public servants at Myilly Point, Darwin, exemplify his work: They are raised on stilts, have the minimum of internal partitioning, and are encased in asbestos cement louvers and casement windows, so as to maximize possible cross ventilation. The government evacuated Darwin for Alice Springs in 1942, and when it returned to Darwin in 1945 Burnett resigned and entered private practice in Alice Springs. The report of the Commonwealth Housing Commission in 1944 illustrated a Burnett-style design on a 3-ft (0.9-m) module, and brought his work to a wider Australian audience. It was later to influence Troppo Architects and hence another generation of designers in tropical Australia.

Adam Caruso and Peter St John

Adam Caruso (1962–) was born in Canada and studied architecture at McGill University in Montreal. Peter St John (1959–) was also born in Canada and studied at the University College London and the Architectural Association in London before going to work for Florian Beigel and Arup Associates in London where he met Adam Caruso. Together they formed the firm of Caruso, St John in 1990.

In 1995 the pair won an international design competition for a new art gallery in the British midlands town of Walsall, which was opened in 2000, catapulting the young firm to national prominence. Other significant projects have included the Center for Contemporary Arts (1999) in Rome, and the Millennium Bridge (1996) in London. In 1999 the firm won a competition for the renewal of the historic city square around the Baroque cathedral of Kalmar in southern Sweden.

Their conversion of an old barn into a contemporary residence – Private Residence (1995) in Kent, England – maintained the original roof trusses in the ground floor, which was opened up into a continuous 72-ft (22-m) long living space. External elements were left undisturbed with the exception of a 30-ft (9-m) glazed expanse inserted into the southern facade framing a view towards distant apple orchards.

Caruso and St John's enjoyment of rural transformations is also seen in their Private Residence (1991–92) in the Isle of Wight, where they subtly altered the shell of an old barn to make it habitable, leaving the interior unaltered for the family to complete over time. Corrugated cement was laid over the existing oak roof, with a new first floor landing for the interior.

Recently the pair seem to have rediscovered the art of ornamentation in their extension to the Museum of Childhood in Bethnal Green (2002–06), exhibited in the British pavilion at the recent Venice architecture biennale.

Adam Caruso is currently the Professor of Architecture in the Department of Architecture and Civil Engineering at the University of Bath. Peter St John taught for 10 years at the University of North London and has been a visiting professor at the Academy of Architecture in Mendrisio, Switzerland, from 1999 to 2001.

Chamberlin, Powell and Bon

Peter Chamberlin (1919–78) was born in London, England, and educated at Pembroke College, Oxford, between 1938 and 1940. He signed up for an architecture course at the Kingston School of Art where he went on to head their School of Architecture. It was here that the three men first met. Christof Bon (1921–99) was born in Switzerland and studied architecture at the Swiss Federal Institute of Technology in Zurich. He moved to London in 1946 and taught architecture at the Kingston School between 1950 and 1952. Geoffry Powell (1920–99) was born in India and went on to study at the Architectural Association in London. In 1949, he began teaching at the Kingston School.

In 1951, the City of London launched a competition for designs for the proposed Golden Lane Estate. Chamberlin, Powell and Bon each submitted their own designs, but it was Powell who won the competition. The three decided to pool their resources and establish the firm Chamberlin, Powell and Bon to build the estate. The Golden Light Estate exemplifies their skill in planning urban spaces. With this integrated estate set in a pleasing environment, their ability to combine mass with void showed the trio could design "places" as well as a buildings.

However, Chamberlin, Powell and Bon are best remembered for London's Barbican Estate (1966–80), a residential estate featuring a labyrinth of concrete monuments consisting of over 2,000 units built on the site of the old northern walls of ancient London. It was to dominate the careers of these three men for nearly three decades, 1963 to 1976 and was constructed over five phases. Covering a 35-acre (14-ha) site, this enclosed enclave housed 6,500 people. Its Brutalist influences are seen in the extensive use of exposed concrete and wood-framed windows, and it was undoubtedly one of their most significant commissions.

The three became heavily influenced by the principles of Modernism and the designs of Le Corbusier, with their main focus being the designing and renovating of university campuses, among which was a scheme for the reconstruction of Leeds University campus that would include laboratories, libraries, and halls for student accommodation.

The firm received the Bronze Medal from the Royal Institute of British Architects in 1956 and 1957, and the RIBA Architectural Award in 1973 and 1974.

Pierre Chareau

Pierre Paul Constant Chareau (1883–1950) was born in Bordeaux, France. Studying at the École des Beaux-Arts in Paris from 1900 to 1908, he divided his time between painting, music, and architecture, though he never formally qualified as an architect. From 1908 until the advent of World War I, when he was drafted into the army, Chareau served an apprenticeship as a decorator in Paris. Surviving the drama of the trenches, he returned to this city to start his own design business. As Kenneth Frampton observed in his masterful book *Pierre Chareau*, "Chareau's career was in many respects inseparable from the life of a young couple, Jean and Annie Dalsace, who were in the end to be the clients of the Maison de Verre." These distinguished Parisians started Chareau on his design career, by entrusting him with the decoration of a two-room apartment at Saint-Germain-des-Près, which Chareau completed in 1918. Such a distinctive commission led towards the progressive design of prestigious furniture and experimental construction which he celebrated in the Salon d'Automne of 1919, and the 1925 Paris Exhibition of Decorative Art.

Chareau's best house is without doubt La Maison de Verre (1929) – a Modernist vision at 31 rue Saint-Guillaume, which was designed in collaboration with Dutchman Bernard Bijvoët – an expert in constructional problems. In this kinetic architecture, Chareau embodied the new spirit by using exposed steel framing for the structure, translucent glass blocks for the facades (allowing light to filter through into the interior) and Pirelli rubber tiles for the floor. He transformed three domestic floors by using perforated metal screens. On the ground floor he used glass partitions to the doctor's consulting room. The large double-storied living room on the second and third floors, lined with metal shelving for books, lent an air of Parisian delight.

By 1932, La Maison de Verre won international recognition as a forward-looking example of the new spirit in architecture. At the same time Chareau captured the dynamism of modern life and its need for unrestricted open space in a domestic situation. His forward thinking even attracted the interest of Le Corbusier, who was often seen visiting La Maison de Verre under construction. For him, La Maison de Verre exemplified the true expression of a "machine for living." On the strength of this house Chareau was asked to join the editorial board of the progressive Parisian journal *L'Architecture d'aujourd'hui (Architecture Today)*. Chareau's La Maison de Verre not only looked modern, it was a house with a difference because it had a strong technical basis. As an architect Chareau bridged the gap between the desire for Modernity and its achievement in technical terms. Clearly by 1932, Chareau's La Maison de Verre was the most advanced expression of Modernity in Paris.

By 1940 Chareau left France to work in New York. His last significant commission was a weekend house and studio for Robert Motherwell in East Hampton, on Long Island. In this commission Chareau adapted a military hut with a large barrel vault to suit Motherwell's domestic requirements. But as a work of architecture it was a pale imitation of the industrial promise provided by his Parisian masterpiece.

La Maison de Verre represents a single moment in Chareau's career when he stood apart from every architect in twentieth-century France. Chareau was an architect who could "make a jewel out of a pebble." As an architect he possessed that rare gift of Modernity. He listened to the needs of his clients and demanded perfection of things well made: He hated pomposity and superficial display. Chareau got on well with the craftsmen who were good with their hands. His furniture was a revelation – a modern synthesis in harmony with his time. And like Aalto, he needed the warmth of women. Chareau worked through the currents of the 1920s and 30s, when the decorative arts were undergoing a revolution in thinking. In this respect, he was a man with a building mission and a true disciple of the nineteenth-century French architect Eugène Viollet-le-Duc.

Georges Chedanne

Georges Paul Chedanne (1861–1940) was born in Maromme, France. He later moved to Paris where he studied architecture at the École des Beaux-Arts under the French architect and writer, Julien Guadet. Chedanne won the Prix de Rome with a gymnasium restoration in 1887, as well as winning notoriety for a series of restoration drawings of the Roman Pantheon. He was influenced by the Art Nouveau movement, characterized by highly decorative styles and a dedication to natural forms, which was at its peak from the 1880s through to 1910. Chedanne, however, was more interested in creating a modern art that was a combination of both Art Nouveau and more traditional Parisian architecture. His ornamentation often involved groups of sculptures that blended into his facades – the result of his highly collaborative approach to architecture.

Chedanne's desire for collaboration with a broad range of artists and artisans in order to create an opulent environment was first seen in his grand "fin-de-siecle" residence of the Hotel Dehaynin (1897) – a truly original and even courageous design which was likened to some of the great Parisian private residences of the seventeenth and eighteenth centuries. The sculptures on its facade included figures decorating the first floor windows by Paul Gasq with François-Leon Sicard supplying keystones in the form of heads.

Chedanne's buildings were highly individualistic. His commercial building (1905), at 124 rue Reaumur in Paris, has a facade made entirely of steel beams, which support the bay windows. Dwellings on the top floor are made from brick. Art Nouveau influences are seen in the delicacy of the ground floor entrance doors and curved brick arches beneath the bow window – a rectangular opening with an arched section of wedged-shaped panes on top.

Wells Coates

Wells Wintemute Coates (1895–1958) was born in Tokyo, Japan, and received Bachelor degrees in Engineering and Science at the University of British Columbia, Canada, before receiving a PhD in Engineering from London University in 1924. He set up his architecture practice in London in 1928.

His childhood experiences in Japan played a pivotal role in the aesthetic sensibility that he brought to his architectural work, and he found a fitting outlet in the Modernist movement. Coates' first commissions were to design shops for Cresta Silks, considered to be among the most distinguished, elegant examples of contemporary design. The doors featured a Coates invention – the D-handle – now in widespread use around the world.

Wells embraced Le Corbusier's concept that buildings should be "machines for living." This idea was clearly reflected in his London Isokon Building (1934) – also known as Lawn Road Flats. It was compared to an ocean liner by the novelist Agatha Christie, who lived there for a time. With simple, Japanese-style living spaces, and built-in Isokon furniture, the building was an experiment in collective housing, and became a haven for Germans escaping Nazi persecution, hosting many famous personages including the architects Walter Gropius and Marcel Breuer. The building was ahead of its time, exemplified by the fact that, in 1946, it won second place in *Horizon Magazine*'s "Ugliest Building Competition." It is now recognized as one of England's most important Modernist buildings.

Coates followed up with his only two apartment blocks: Embassy Court (1935) in Brighton; and 10 Palace Gate (1939) in Kensington. During this period he also had several private home commissions, which featured such Japanese influences as sliding walls and large, strategically-placed vases.

During World War II Coates served with the Royal Air Force, working on fighter aircraft development, for which he received an Order of the British Empire. He then contributed to the British post-war housing effort by introducing a pioneering scheme for modular housing, which he called Room Unit Production.

In 1955 and 1956 he taught at the Graduate School of Design at Harvard, then moved to Vancouver, Canada, where he designed a rapid transit monorail, dubbed the Monospan Twin-Ride System. Once again, he was ahead of his time – the project was abandoned, but would be revived years later in a similar form known as the SkyTrain.

Coates was an inventive genius across a variety of fields. The innovative design of his iconic radio, the AD 65, is frequently used to symbolize 1930s design. His blocks of units, shop and office designs, houses, interiors, radios, boats, and other industrial designs are evidence of his commitment to a practical aesthetic and high standards of construction. However, above all, Coates was an idealist. He believed it was necessary to formulate codes of behavior: What was to be done and how it could be done. This led him to a deep and sustained involvement in group activities of many kinds and to search for architectural principles appropriate to the modern world.

William Cody

The maverick Desert Modernist William Cody (1916–) was born in Dayton, Ohio, USA, and educated at the University of Southern California, where he worked for architect Cliff May. He arrived in Palm Springs in 1942, which had been a mecca for Modernist architects since the 1930s. Together with architects like Donald Wexler and Albert Frey, Cody created a new regional style called Desert Modernism using local materials such as rock, concrete blocks, and metal, leaving in their wake a rich legacy of mid-century Modernism at its most glamorous.

Desert Modernism meant clean lines, brash angles, the heavy use of glass, butterfly roof lines, and a dedication to function inspired by form. It came to reflect a lifestyle of elegance and informality and grew out of a desire to adapt modern materials and techniques to the uniqueness of desert living.

Cody's personality can be seen in the intensity of his designs, their energetic detailing, and polished compositions. His first project in Palm Springs was the Del Marcos Hotel (1947) and is one of the best examples of his architecture. Replete with private patios and large sliding plate glass windows, this composition of natural redwood and stone walls contrasts with a framework of angled doglegs that seem to lift the building out of the ground. This was followed by his conversion of the Thunderbird Dude Ranch to the Thunderbird Country Club, which led to later designs for the Tamarisk and El Dorado country clubs, as well as numerous commercial and residential projects.

Cody's elegant residential buildings in Palm Springs include the Cody/Urrutia House (1947), the May House (1951), the Pelberg Residence (1952), the J B Shamel Residence (1961), and Abernathy House (1962). In his designs, Cody strove to reduce roof slabs and beams to the bare minimum (the roof on his own house was only 4 in/10 cm thick). Reflecting his affinity for Scandinavian modern design, Cody used wood and stone to imbed his houses in the desert landscape. His homes were low-slung, glass-walled buildings, some with swooped or peaked overhanging roofs, ingeniously designed for the southern California desert. Their glass walls blurred the distinction between indoor space and the exterior landscape of beautiful desert and nearby mountains.

Today, more than 200 works of Cody, Frey, Wexler and others represent the largest single concentration of mid-century Modernism in the United States of America.

Connell, Ward and Lucas

Amyas Douglas Connell (1901–80) and Basil Robert Ward (1902–76) were two New Zealand-born architects who were in partnership with Colin Anderson Lucas (1906–84) in London between 1933 and 1939. Under the influence of Le Corbusier, their practice exerted considerable impact upon domestic architecture in England, and their white architecture was a critical part in establishing Modern architecture in Britain.

Amyas Connell was born at Eltham – a small town in the Taranaki district, and educated at New Plymouth Boys' High School. Basil Ward was born in Wellington and educated at Napier Boys' High School. In 1919, Connell became an articled student in Stanley Fearn's office in Wellington. Here he received a thorough Beaux-Arts apprenticeship – a course administered by the New Zealand Institute of Architects – passing his first professional year of study in 1921. Basil Ward trained in the Napier office of Louis Hay – a disciple of the Arts and Crafts architects Norman Shaw, Charles Rennie Mackintosh, and Frank Lloyd Wright. Ward completed his articles late in 1922, and moved to Wellington where he worked for William Crichton – a classical architect of stark contrast to the work of Louis Hay.

Connell and Ward most probably met at Wellington's Architectural Students' Association where they were keen members. Both young men needed to travel in order to widen their horizons, and in 1924 they worked their passage as stokers on a coal steamer to England. Here they became part-time students in a Beaux-Arts atelier of London University. As ambitious students they began to follow European developments, particularly the 1925 Exhibition of Decorative Art in Paris where Le Corbusier's L'Esprit Nouveau Pavilion was a major attraction. This pavilion stood out for its purity and wholesome expression of the modern world opening up before them. Both young men became avid Corbusian followers.

Although Le Corbusier was never a fan of the Rome Prize as an architectural education, Connell in June 1926 carried off the first prize with a Beaux-Arts design for a Royal Naval Academy. By the autumn of 1926, Connell and Ward were in Rome where they followed a Classical training, while at the same time absorbing the influence of Le Corbusier's *Vers une architecture (Towards a New Architecture)*.

As a student at the Rome school, Connell was asked to design a Modern villa for Bernard Ashmole, the director of the British School in Rome, on a site at Amersham in Buckinghamshire. After much battling over legal obstacles High and Over (1929–31) was built as a Corbusian-inspired reinforced concrete frame villa with ribbon windows. Designed with a flat roof, this house carried a cantilevered roof-deck, and its walls were shorn of decoration. While this white-painted Classical imagery shocked the district council traditionalists, High and Over became a stepping stone into British architectural practice.

Connell and Ward were joined by Colin Lucas, the Englishman in the group, in 1933. Lucas was educated at Cheltenham, then trained at the Cambridge School of Architecture. Lucas initially formed his own building company with his father to construct reinforced concrete houses. Then he joined Connell and Ward, and together they produced a whole new series of Modern houses around England. Most prominent among these were New Farm (1933) in Grayswood, Surrey, for champion client Sir Arthur Dickenson. At New Farm the architects were given a strict budget, but they had design freedom on a 17-acre (7-ha) site. Each of their houses came in for severe criticism, and none were built without battling with local council and town planning committees of which 66 Frognal, Hampstead (1935–38), London was a "white" classic. Today it still stands proudly among the Georgian brick villas of Hampstead – a minor triumph in reinforced concrete, steel windows, and glass.

Arguably the *cause célèbre* of Connell, Ward and Lucas is the magnificent clarity and formal confidence provided by Tarburn House (1937–38) in Moor Park, Hertfordshire. While Connell, Ward and Lucas worked well as a team of architects, many of their white houses aroused a good deal of conservative animosity from the establishment, who found it different to see these "foreign creations" as "homes" in England. World War II brought their practice to an end, and with the resumption of peace in 1945, the partners moved in different directions.

Coop Himmelblau

Helmut Swiczinsky (1944–) was born in Poland and educated at Vienna's Technical University and the Architectural Association in London. Wolf Dieter Prix (1942–) was born in Vienna and educated at the Technical University of Vienna. Together, they formed the firm of Coop Himmelblau in Vienna in 1968. Wolf Prix is currently teaching at Vienna's University of Applied Arts and is head of its postgraduate program "Urban Strategies." Helmut Swiczinsky is a permanent member of the European Academy of Sciences and Arts whose headquarters are in Vienna, Austria.

Coop Himmelblau's commitment to designs free from the constraints of any given style and possessing interiors of complex, undefined spaces can be seen in their Apartment Building Gasometer B (1995–2001) in Vienna. Their conversion of the building's shell into apartments and offices sees three new spaces created: Apartments in the interior of the shell itself; the addition of a distinctive "shield" office block outside; and a multi-function event hall on the ground level.

Other projects have included a master plan for the French city of Melun-Senart (1987), the SEG Apartment Tower (1994–98) and SEG Apartment Block Remise (1994–2000) in Vienna, and the Academy of Fine Arts (2002–05) in Munich. The 197-ft (60-m) high SEG Apartment Tower contains 70 apartments and an angular exterior designed to minimize wind velocities whilst maximizing light. The SEG Apartment Block Remise is a closed building block broken up and rearranged in an open and differentiated building volume to provide common spaces, public and semi-public spaces, and private terraces and gardens. Most of the apartments are maisonettes with a two-story living room and a glass facade.

Coop Himmelblau's UFA Cinema Center in Dresden has been the recipient of countless awards including the German Architecture Prize (1999), and the European Steel Design Award (2001).

Charles Correa

Charles Correa (1930–) was born in Hyderabad, India. He studied at the University of Michigan and the Massachusetts Institute of Technology in the United States of America, after which he established a private practice in Bombay in 1958. On his return to India he started a prolific career in writing, teaching, and building beautiful architecture. Although trained mainly in the West and frequently a lecturer at many American universities, Correa has never lost contact with the heart and soul of his native country.

Charles Correa is an architect from the Third World, and therefore faces a different set of conditions for designing humane and aesthetically pleasing environments than architects of more affluent or developed First World countries. The sheer numbers of people in India are an ever-present constraint, as is coping with the overwhelming influx of migrants from outlying rural regions to the urban centers. While the design of indigenous houses in climatic conditions is often an ally in solving a design problem – allowing for lighter, open-air structures and natural rather than mechanical ventilation – inadequate budgets are not, and require great imagination and skill to create durable and beautiful buildings. These challenges are always very daunting and few are able to achieve any international recognition where their work is subjected to some critical review without an understanding of the political and social circumstances under which the designs were created.

Correa's work in India shows a careful development, understanding, and adaptation of Modernism to a non-western culture. His early works attempt to explore a local vernacular within a Modern environment. Correa's land-use planning and community projects continually try to go beyond typical solutions to Third World problems.

Correa's buildings reflect a Modern attitude but are also totally in their place and culture. He has led his way out of British colonialism to an indigenous contemporary Indian architecture. His houses and group-housing projects, such as the Tube House (1961–62) in Ahmedabad, India; Previ Housing (1969–73) in Lima, Peru; Kanchanjunga Apartments (1970–83) in Bombay, India; and Gobhai House (1995–99) in Golwad, India, never lose sight of the special problems of population and climate that determine form. His houses never allow us to forget the actual living conditions of the people of Asia and their desperate struggle to meet a much better future.

From 1970 to 1975, Correa was appointed the chief architect for New Bombay – an urban growth center of 2 million people across the harbor from the existing city. In 1985, Prime Minister Rajiv Gandhi appointed him chairman of the National Commission on Urbanization.

In 1980 Correa was awarded an Honorary Doctorate by the University of Michigan. He received the Royal Gold Medal from the Royal Institute of British Architects in 1984, the Gold Medal of the Indian Institute of Architecture in 1987, the Gold Medal of the International Union of Architects in 1990, the Praemium Imperiale from Japan in 1994, and the Aga Khan Award for Architecture in 1998.

James Cutler

James Cutler (1949–) was born in the town of Wilkes-Barre, Pennsylvania, USA, and studied architecture at the University of Pennsylvania in 1973. The following year he studied under that great guru of architects, Louis I Kahn, who taught the young Cutler that architects don't build buildings, they create clothing that houses institutions. Under Kahn, Cutler developed a philosophy of reaching into the core of a work to search out its meaning amidst a fusion of emotions, materials, and setting. In 1977 he founded James Cutler Architects on his home island of Bainbridge in the San Juan island chain off the coast of Washington State. He has since won nationwide recognition for finely crafted buildings rich in detail and exhibiting a refined Pacific Northwest aesthetic.

James Cutler Architects have won four National Honor Awards from the American Institute of Architects, more than 30 regional and national awards, and have designed over 300 residential, commercial, and cultural projects around the world. Recent projects have included residences in Spain, California's Napa Valley, the Big Island of Hawaii, and the largest private home in North America – Bill Gates' family compound in the woods outside Seattle.

Always respectful of nature, Cutler's preferred materials are recycled Douglas fir, stone, concrete, and steel, producing structures that "sing" and reveal the true spirit of their constituent elements. His Long Residence (2003) on Orcas Island is a cabin that melds into its surroundings, supported on 18 sets of wooden tripods all connected by concealed steel plates to cedar log beams and finally to a series of graduated rafters that seem to defy gravity.

His Tanglefoot Residence (2001) in northern Idaho was built for privacy rather than expansive views and includes an enclosed outdoor entertaining area built to withstand mosquito-ridden summers. Its glass-enclosed exterior also serves to connect the home's winter wing to the summer wing, which includes a main suite and conference area.

The Schmidt Residence (2000) at Sequim in Washington State again demonstrates Cutler's sensitivity to the environment with the 4,500-sq-ft (418-sq-m) cabin being built along an existing clearing in the forest and along a ledge with views over Sequim Bay; the house is designed with a sensitivity to nearby trees, views, and prevailing weather patterns.

An educator and critic, Cutler has held teaching positions at the University of Washington (1978–87) and Harvard University GSD (1993) and was Artist in Residence at Dartmouth College (2004). His contributions to architecture were recognized in 1994 when he was elevated to the American Institute of Architects College of Fellows.

Howard Davis

Howard Davis (1907–) was born in New York City, USA. He is Professor of Architecture at the University of Oregon at Eugene and a specialist in vernacular architecture, low-cost housing, and community design. He has a Masters degree in Architecture from the University of California at Berkeley and co-authored *The Production of Houses* (1985) with Christopher Alexander. He is also on the faculty of the Center for Housing Innovation within the University of Oregon, the purpose of which is to advance expertise and knowledge in the design, planning, and construction of residential housing across North America.

Davis is best known for his studies in "vernacular architecture" – buildings constructed outside any academic traditions; their shapes and floor plans gleaned from centuries of old traditions and usually lived in by those responsible for their design and construction.

He has taught at Edinburgh University, worked professionally in the United States of America, England, India, and Mexico and is the author of *The Culture of Building* (1999), in which he examines how buildings the world over are a product of systems that involve not only architects but building inspectors, bankers, contractors, and many others, and that improvements in our built environment depend upon establishing structures and environments that foster and enable good design on an everyday basis. The book shows how building cultures reflect the general culture in which they are set, and focuses on the transformations that have occurred in architecture from the eighteenth century to the present day. In the book Davis encourages us to see buildings as belonging to one single system, and proceeds to analyze it and its ability to create for us a living world.

Davis' most recognized residential project is his own home, Davis House (1990) in Eugene, Oregon. A simple wooden frame house with thoughtful facades, the design optimizes both its indoor and outdoor space. Built on a limited site and with a limited budget, Davis understood that the beauty of materials, carefully chosen, would enrich the house. He covered the walls and roof in cedar shingles and avoided a monotone appearance by using a cool blue-green paint on the window, door, and rafter trims – a color that beautifully contrasted with the warm, reddish brown tones of the shingles. He embellished the entry by using smooth, fitted wooden boards for the porch roof, railings, and bench – which all complemented the paneling and wainscoting found inside the house. The interior is characterized by patterned natural oak floors and wooden ceilings of Douglas fir. Connecting these two horizontal surfaces are walls of smooth drywall, painted a light yellow.

In the early 1990s Davis collaborated with David Week of Pacific Architecture in Sydney, Australia, on a series of housing projects near Vellore in southern India, and recently has engaged in research centering on how commercial and residential uses can be combined in urban structures.

Charles Deaton

Charles Deaton (1921–96) was born into poverty and the Great Depression in the small town of Clayton, New Mexico. Too poor to attend college, he studied drafting in high school and was earning a living as a commercial artist at the age of 16. After working at a Lockheed aircraft factory during World War II designing aerodynamic shapes, he began his own architectural firm in New York in 1946 with no formal training. He moved to St Louis in 1949 and became a designer for the Bank Building and Equipment Company prior to moving to Denver, Colorado, in 1955, where he remained for the rest of his life.

Deaton's architectural concepts were in complete opposition to prevailing trends. Fascinated by the shapes he saw in nature, he pursued designs that reflected the graceful curves and arcs of caverns, river rocks, and canyons. He would start with a model, then draw out the plans based on the model's dimensions, rather than the traditional approach of drawing plans first, then constructing the model from the plans.

Despite a career dominated by commercial projects, Charles Deaton will be forever associated with his futuristic, outrageous Sculptured House (1963–66), set on 15 acres (6 ha) high up in the foothills above Denver. Believing that people were not squares so why should they live in them, Deaton constructed his first model of the house in 1960, obtaining his initial drawings by slicing through the model and measuring each individual segment to obtain its dimensions. Anchored to the mountainside by precast piers set deep into bedrock, steel posts support the curvaceous superstructure – a welded steel cage covered by wire mesh, pumped full of concrete, and finally sheathed in Hypalon (a synthetic rubber noted for its resistance to chemicals, high temperatures, and ultraviolet light), and finished in white pigment. The house appears to hover over the landscape, connected to the ground by a glass and aggregate cylindrical pedestal that led to its nickname, the "Flying Saucer" house. Completed in 1966, it was rapturously received by the media and captured the imagination of architects the world over, appearing in countless books and professional journals. Deaton's masterpiece is a stunning example of organic architecture executed with minimalist detail.

Michel de Klerk

Michel de Klerk (1884–1923) was born into a large Jewish family in Amsterdam and was heavily influenced by the work of Hendrik Berlage – the "Father of Architecture" in the Netherlands – as well as possessing an interest in the English Arts and Crafts movement.

A series of apartment blocks in the Spaarndammerbuurt area of Amsterdam was built following the adoption of the Housing Act of 1901, which ended the construction of slums. Built between 1913 and 1921, de Klerk's apartment block, famously known as The Ship, represents some of the most important examples of the Amsterdam School of Architecture of which he was a leading exponent. Its 102 apartments also held a meeting hall and post office. Buildings were five stories high and of brick construction with a facade on the top floor rather than a mansard roof. The post office has an arched, rectangular ceiling over an irregular, trapezoid surface, and today represents the only interior space of de Klerk's that has been fully restored in all its glory.

Though building for the city's working class, de Klerk included a degree of ornamentation unusual for such housing at the time. His apartments were considered palaces when compared to public housing in other areas of the city. The Expressionist painter Anton Martineau even referred to de Klerk's work as "bringing dead materials back to life." This "excess" ornamentation took many forms, including minarets and the art of "pinching" bricks together in places to produce a kind of rippling effect. Making his designs expensive drew criticism because it was thought inappropriate for municipally financed housing.

After de Klerk's sudden death in 1923, the strong, horizontal lines, lead-lighting and fanciful shapes of the Amsterdam School began to evolve into a more moderate Expressionism seen best in the work of Frank Lloyd Wright.

Jeremy Dixon

Jeremy Dixon (1939–) was born in the town of Bishops Stortford in the British Midlands and graduated from the Architectural Association in London in 1964. Dixon first came to international prominence in 1973 when he was selected with his firm's partners Fenella Dixon and Edward Jones to design the new County Hall at Northampton.

His first residential project was a studio house in Chelsea between 1975 and 1977 – a former dilapidated stables which was completely demolished, though retaining the street facade which was rebuilt with some revisions. From 1975 to 1979, Dixon designed St Mark's Road Housing in Kensington. He saw London as a city with streets of houses – not apartments. In keeping with the Victorian terraces in the area, the project comprised 12 large dwellings, each being two narrow houses over a unit. The houses are angled to the street to help maintain privacy between adjacent buildings. This allows a contrast in scale between the double-fronted street facade and the individual stepped form of the rear elevation.

In 1983 Dixon won the competition to redesign the Royal Opera House in Covent Garden. Avoiding the bombastic appearance of Parisian opera houses, both old and new, Dixon chose to create an urban village of buildings that radiated from the Neo-classical building fronting Bow Street and connecting with the shops, cafes, and street theater of Covent Garden. The reconstruction took 16 years to complete, occupies an entire city block, and is criss-crossed with walkways and two new auditoriums for the ballet and opera. Grand Classical details were reproduced in plastic to decorate the new fly tower in a successful marriage of architectural history and present-day practice.

In 2000 Dixon designed the sleek private residence Villa Jones above the French town of Bargemon in the Var region. The design fits neatly into the area's stepped terraces formed by dry stonewalls traditionally used for the cultivation of olives. The house is long in plan but narrow in section, open to the south but closed to the north, allowing for cross ventilation and access to the views from all the rooms. The monopitched pantile roof and stuccoed walls reflect the vernacular tradition.

Following on from their work on the Royal Opera House, the firm of Dixon Jones has gained a deserved reputation for sensitively and appropriately creating new public spaces within historical buildings. Jeremy Dixon received a Knighthood from Queen Elizabeth II in 2000.

Balkrishna Doshi

Balkrishna Vithaldas Doshi (1927–) is India's most respected architect. He was born in Poona, India, and completed his education at the Fergusson College in Poona and then the JJ School of Art in Bombay in 1950. Doshi worked with Le Corbusier in Paris between 1951 and 1956 and went on to become a senior designer on Le Corbusier's projects in Ahmedabad and Chandigarh. In 1956 he established a private practice in Vastu-Shilpa, Ahmedabad, and in 1962 he began the Vastu-Shilpa Foundation for Studies and Research in Environmental Design, which works towards developing low-cost housing and city planning. He also founded and designed the School of Architecture and Planning in Ahmedabad. Doshi has worked in partnership as Stein, Doshi and Bhalla since 1977. He has been a visiting professor at principal universities throughout the United States of America since 1958.

Doshi has assimilated western influences into a practice that was still connected to the cultural roots of his native country. His approach to architecture is based on the need to make the physical setting harmonious with the individual's social and cultural needs. Doshi says, "I believe that all designs should be based on community considerations." He believes it is always necessary to consider the family ties and local associations of older buildings – associations that one cannot give up. Buildings that survive in time have more than a material utility: They indicate a meaning in a building, as opposed to the present-day Functionalism, which has no meaning except in its craving for modernity.

Architects, students, writers, and critics alike believe that Doshi's built work is an architecture influenced by his deep interest in education. There is an underlying factor based on tradition, honesty, and truth. Doshi relies on using natural elements in an ingenious way, and above all being humane in every aspect. Architectural scale and massing, as well as a clear sense of space and community, mark most of his work.

Doshi is known for his Aranya Housing Project (1995) – a low-cost housing development designed to combat urban poverty. Aranya, 4 miles (6 km) from the city of Indore in India, will eventually have 6,500 dwellings on a planning area of 210 acres (85 ha). The master plan, completed in 1983, was designed around a central spine comprising a business district with six sectors surrounding it, each with populations of 7,000 to 12,000 to the east and west of the spine. Ten houses, each with a courtyard at the back, form a cluster that opens onto a street. The site accommodates and integrates a variety of income groups: The poorest are located in the middle of each of the six sectors, while the wealthier residents are along the peripheries of each sector and the central spine. The homes range from one-room shelters to spacious houses. The poorest have access to the cheapest accommodation – a plot with a concrete plinth, a service core, and a room. Brick, stone, and concrete are available locally, but owners are free to use any material they choose for the construction of their house. Aranya is seen as an innovative sites-and-services project that allows the integration of families within a range of poor-to-modest incomes.

Doshi is an Associate Member of the Royal Institute of British Architects. He received a Fellowship from the Graham Foundation in 1958; became an Honorary Fellow of the American Institute of Architects, as well as the Indian Institute of Architects in 1971; and received the Padma Shri Award from the Government of India in 1976.

Charles Eames

Charles Ormond Eames (1907–78), who was born in St Louis, Missouri, USA, liked to describe himself as a "Midwesterner." Like Frank Lloyd Wright, Eames' kindergarten experiences were based on the progressive Froebel system of elementary blocks of spheres, cones, and pyramids, and this may account for his life-long interest in structure. In 1921 he started his education at Yeatman High School in North St Louis, where he showed an aptitude for art, mathematics, and science. He was also a star athlete at secondary school, and from an early age wanted to be an architect. He studied at Washington University in St Louis from the summer of 1925, but found the Beaux-Arts curriculum narrow and dated, and in 1928 he was asked to leave.

Eames traveled to Europe in 1929 with his first wife Catherine Woermann, who was training to be an architect. She had a Bachelor's degree from Vassar, and together they visited the Weissenhof housing exhibition in Stuttgart – an experience which Eames later described as "having a cold hose turned on you."

On his return from Europe in 1930, Eames went into private practice with Charles Gary, but the Depression devastated this arrangement. Disillusioned by 1933, he left his wife and daughter and ran off to Mexico. Here Eames acquired an admiration for the "ethnic" objects which was to form an important aspect of his work.

In 1940 he got a job at the Cranbrook Academy of Art in Michigan. Here he met Ray Kaiser who was to become his second wife in 1941. Of critical importance at Cranbrook was the Scandinavian influence of Eliel Saarinen (the father of Eero Saarinen). Cranbrook was decisive in Eames' Modernist formation where he also reconciled the influence of Alvar Aalto's humanism. Joining forces with Ray Kaiser, the pair came to occupy a critically important position in post-war American design.

The reputation of Charles and Ray Eames depends upon two important case-study houses – the Eames House, and one for John Entenza – which share the same site in Pacific Palisades, less than 654 ft (200 m) apart. Both houses were built between 1945 and 1949. These houses are also renowned for their furniture. Together the Eames couple designed a series of beautifully fashioned objects, like the molded dining chair of walnut plywood (1946); and the lounge chair and ottoman in molded rosewood plywood and black leather cushions, which pivoted on a five-pronged base of black aluminum with polished top surfaces (1956). In these particular works they made their mark in furniture design.

While the two-storied Eames House and Studio was designed in collaboration with Ray Eames, the Entenza House was done in collaboration with Eero Saarinen. The Eames House is tall and open, spatially articulated, and structured of skeleton steel, with colored infill panels; the Entenza House is a flat metal box concealing its structure, emphasizing the horizontal by using free-standing screens and partitions.

The warm sunny climate of southern California is the home of the aeroplane, aerospace, and movie industries, and the Eames couple readily adapted to this environment. From these industries they studied the way aluminum and plastic, wood and steel are joined together, and they used this knowledge to make splendid furniture.

The Eames House is the more important of the two. It was spatially designed as a place for change. This reasoning was considered more important than the inclusion of a swimming pool or garage. Such design is not formal in a European sense (like the Greek temple) and their approach centers on addition – an assemblage of pieces added together which are capable of change. This theme represents a fundamental shift in the design of an architect's home, where everything has to be perfectly designed and positioned. This lack of permanence is part of the Californian scene, where the pristine position is not encouraged. In spite of this, the Eames House has a wonderful sense of spaciousness, and it is elegantly furnished.

The Eames approach to architecture is a cheerful acceptance of mass-produced materials using ready-made windows and doors. The Eames House provides a lesson in prefabrication, using delicate steel frames and translucent glass. Above all it is a product of lightness – like the Japanese tea-house.

The Eames House interior is spacious, light, and flexible, and it is crowded with flowers, toys, and furniture. It carries a cheerful sense of wellbeing, where nothing is covered up. This is a direct response to the "quick city culture" of California, which studiously encourages the ambiguities of life on the West Coast of America.

Karl Ehn

Karl Ehn (1884–1957) was born in Vienna, Austria, and trained at the Wagnerschule, under Otto Wagner. He graduated in 1907 as one of its most promising students, and from 1908 to 1914 worked for the City of Vienna as architect to the XXII district.

Ehn is best known for the immense Karl Marx Hof, the largest, and perhaps best, example of the ground-breaking public housing of the Red Vienna movement of the 1920s.

After Austria's defeat in World War I, Ehn returned to his city job, where social and housing issues dominated the construction program. He was necessarily drawn into the debate over the rival merits of low-density cottage developments, and those of high-density, high-rise edifices. In 1922, he planned a Neo-classical, restrained six-story block on the Balderichgasse, and the following year designed the Hermeswiese Siedlung, a low-density, mostly two-story suburban complex.

While others, including Ernst May, were experimenting with clusters of small, architecturally-radical dwellings, Ehn led the movement towards large perimeter block apartment houses. When Karl Marx Hof opened in 1930, it symbolized the hope of a better life for city workers living in squalid conditions. With its massive red front elevation and powerful arches – and its name – it immediately became a symbol of the power of the city's socialist government.

Uniquely for Vienna in the 1930s, each apartment had cold running water and a WC, and the rooms had balconies. All entrances into the apartments led from the courtyards rather than from the street. The courtyards featured laundries, bathrooms, playgrounds, and a school. The Expressionist buildings were characterized by a sculptural and holistic approach, and striking detail, with Cubist forms that recall Frank Lloyd Wright.

Ehn spent the remainder of his professional life as an architect and technical director, under various regimes, for the City of Vienna. Ehn's innovative concept of using block apartment houses with collective facilities to create a new urban culture has been copied all over the world, notably in New York.

Peter Eisenman

American architect, theorist, and educator Peter Eisenman (1932–) was born in Newark, New Jersey, USA. He received his Bachelor of Architecture from Cornell University (1955) and a Masters in Architecture from Columbia University (1960), before completing his postgraduate studies at the University of Cambridge in England between 1962 and 1963, where he studied under Colin Rowe. Eisenman also holds a number of honorary doctorates. Other influences on his work include Italian architect Giuseppe Terragni, on whom he wrote the book *Giuseppe Terragni: Transformations, Decompositions, Critiques* (2003).

Eisenman rose to prominence in the late 1960s and early 1970s as one of the "New York Five." He was the founder and director of New York's Institute for Architecture and Urban Studies (IAUS) – an independent research body of avant-garde architects (1967). He was also the editor of the institute's journal *Oppositions*.

Eisenman worked in partnership with architect Jacquelin Robertson during the 1980s and is now the principal of Eisenman Architects in New York. His distinguished academic career includes his current positions as the Louis I Kahn Professor of Architecture at Yale and the first Irwin S Chanin Distinguished Professor of Architecture at the Cooper Union, where he has taught for many years. He has also taught at Cambridge, Princeton, and Harvard universities. Eisenman has been involved in many forums, exhibitions, and competitions worldwide and is a prolific writer. His books include *Eisenman Inside Out: Selected Writings, 1963–1988* (2004), and *Houses of Cards* (1987).

In architectural theory, Eisenman is known for his use of models or concepts from outside architecture, particularly from linguistic theory. He is heavily influenced by the French literary critic and philosopher Jacques Derrida, exploring architectural applications of Derrida's concept of Deconstruction. Eisenman's focus is the process, rather than the product, of design – the exploration of grids, formal geometries, and ideas about syntax and underlying structure. Many of his projects have associated analytical texts which were developed as part of the process and assist the user to understand the project. His work has been described as both Post-modern, for its ambiguity, and Late-modern, for its visual relationship to the Modern villas of the 1920s.

Eisenman's most famous projects include the Wexner Center for the Visual Arts at Ohio State University (1980s); House I (1967–68) in Princeton, New Jersey; and House II (1969–70) in Hardwick, Vermont, which were featured in the 1972 book *Five Architects*.

While his more recent work is predominantly public buildings, it was these early houses, and the explanatory texts produced as part of the design process, which brought him to prominence. Built projects such as House VI: Frank House (1972–75) in Cornwall, Connecticut, and House III: Miller House (1969–70) in Lakeville, Connecticut, are distinguished by their model-like appearance, white exteriors, and layers of intersecting planes.

Eisenman's projects are intended to intellectually stimulate their user, and many feature unusual elements such as internal columns and beams which do not support any structural load.

The firm Eisenman Architects has won many design competitions, as well as other prizes including a number of American Institute of Architects National Honor Awards. Eisenman has also won many personal awards. He is a Fellow of the American Institute of Architects and a member of both the American Academy of Arts and Sciences and the American Academy of Arts and Letters, by which he was awarded the Arnold W Brunner Prize for Architecture in 1981. In 2001, he won the American Institute of Architects, New York Chapter Medal of Honor and the Smithsonian Institution's Cooper-Hewitt National Design Award for Architecture.

Craig Ellwood

Craig Ellwood (1922–92) was born Jon Nelson Burke in Clarendon, Texas, USA. He took his name from a liquor store on Beverly Boulevard, Los Angeles. He taught at Yale, yet never graduated as an architect, entrusting talented assistants to carry out his ideas. He lived a Hollywood lifestyle and raised eyebrows with his ambition, charm, and self-publicity, but it must be said that his achievements stand as undeniable proof of his originality and connoisseur's vision.

In the 1950s Ellwood emerged on the national and international scene through his award-winning and highly-acclaimed designs of three Case Study Houses in the Los Angeles area: Case Study House 16 (Salzman House) in Bel Air, 1951–53; Case Study House 17 (Hoffman House) in Beverly Hills, 1954–56; and Case Study House 18 (Fields House) in Beverly Hills, 1955–58. This series of dramatic, open, and elegant houses led to numerous commissions and launched him as a media star. His subsequent Californian residential designs, including the Hunt House (1955–57) in Malibu, Smith House (1955) in Los Angeles, Daphne House (1960–61) in Hillsborough, and Palevsky House (1968) in Palm Springs, demonstrated a lifestyle which was both inspirational and attainable.

He drove a red Ferrari with the license plate VROOM, and was named one of the "three best architects of 1957," along with Frank Lloyd Wright and Ludwig Mies van der Rohe. The output of his Los Angeles practice blended an informal California breeziness with the stark Germanic "International Style" Rationalism of Mies van der Rohe, and the austere, Modernist, steel cage-like structures of Charles Eames.

Ellwood obtained the commissions and provided the vision, leaving the technical details, plans – and authorized signature of a licensed architect – to Robert Theron Peters and other employees. He incorporated steel in thoughtful ways, and developed a trademark structural device of an exposed warren truss that used small, connected components to cover large distances.

In the 1970s he planned the Rand Corporation headquarters in Santa Monica, California, several IBM and Xerox offices, and the trademark "bridge building" which spectacularly spans an abyss and roadway at the Pasadena Art Center College of Design. Appreciation of his work has only increased since his death in Italy in 1992.

Arthur C Erickson

Arthur C Erickson (1924–) was born in Vancouver, Canada, and studied at the University of British Columbia and McGill University in Montreal. Long considered one of Canada's greatest architects, and credited with contributing to the rebirth of Modernism in this country, Erickson creates bold architectural forms and displays his unique skills designing and filling urban spaces with large-scale architectural images.

Erickson's philosophy is that a building is never just a solitary structure in total disregard to its environment, but should be designed in response to existing environmental and urban settings. His pre-eminent example of this philosophy is the Graham House (1962), built on an almost impossibly steep site overlooking Puget Sound in British Columbia. This multi-level residence descends down a rocky slope over 40 ft (12 m) in four stages, with each area opening onto a roof terrace above the level below. The Graham House delivered Erickson a lifelong reputation for design excellence on seemingly impossible sites.

Erickson is exceptional in designing houses that work within difficult terrain. His design solution is a series of platforms stepping with the grade. Fire Island House (1977) at Fire Island, New York, follows this principle. The wood frame structure is built on elevated wood decks firmly attached to concrete pilings. In the Catton House (1967) in West Vancouver, decks are incorporated into the framework of the building to give easier access to the dwelling. The Smith House (1964), also in West Vancouver, is situated between two rock outcroppings that are on a prominence that slopes down to the sea. The house was designed as a square spiral, built up by the lapping of the major beams around a courtyard. Erickson felt that reducing the number of materials and elements in the house achieved a certain strength and simplicity in the design. The beams and posts are the same size, with the flooring, roofing, and sidings made of the same material, but smaller in scale.

His Waterfall Building (2001), in a busy residential/commercial district of downtown Vancouver, necessitated the relaxation of rezoning laws in order to permit this innovative urban development that challenges conventional concepts of condominium living. Its five separate buildings cover 60,000 sq ft (5,574 sq m), comprising 38 artist's studios and 49 split-level units. Features include external steel spiral staircases and cantilevered walkways. The Waterfall Building gets its name from a waterfall of recirculated water that plunges down the middle of its main entrance. The building is typical of Erickson's ability to combine visionary architecture with the many restrictions and challenges imposed by medium-density living.

In 1986 he received the Gold Medal from the American Institute of Architects, the highest award bestowed by the AIA.

Ralph Erskine

Ralph Erskine (1914–2005) was a Swedish-British architect born in Mill Hill, London, England. A graduate of the Regent Street Polytechnic in 1938, he moved to Sweden just months prior to the outbreak of World War II, after being unable to secure work with any of the large English partnerships. Sweden had industrialized late, and Stockholm had some of the worst slums in Europe. In a push to modernize, architectural commissions were not hard to find there.

Erskine's early designs reflected his belief that buildings should conform to their climatic environment, with an early design for flats in Waxjo having clip-on balconies to prevent damage by frost. His practice began to grow in the late 1950s, and the 1960s saw him increasingly involved in the design of public housing with projects including the town center of Lulea and the mining town of Svappavaara north of the Arctic Circle. But it was his impressive Byker Redevelopment in Newcastle-upon-Tyne, England (1973–78) – one of Britain's first attempts to create a dialog between community and architecture – that brought Erskine international recognition. The Byker Redevelopment's famous patterned and modeled northern brick wall was built as a barrier to the noise of a motorway that never eventuated, and acted as a barrier for a huge network of terraces, gardens, and private and public spaces.

His design of The Ark (1990), an office block in West London, was seen as one of the first ecologically-sound office blocks in London, with materials such as glass, copper, and bronze giving it a distinctive nautical appearance. Its interior features bright, sky-lit spaces, a floor-to-roof atrium, scenic elevators, and white walls – a dramatic contrast to its dark exterior and to the design of most open-plan office spaces.

Erskine's initial concepts were often made in large freehand sketches not uncommon in children's books. He also preferred to work with other firms on large-scale projects, allowing them to look after the administrative details and thus keeping his own practice simple and compact.

In 1987 he was awarded the Royal Institute of British Architects Royal Gold Medal.

Aarne Ervi

Aarne Ervi (1910–77) was born in Forssa, Finland, and graduated from the Helsinki University of Technology in 1935. He was regarded as one of the most gifted and versatile architects ever to come out of Finland. After graduation, he went to work at the offices of Alvar Aalto prior to establishing his own practice in 1938.

Ervi is probably best remembered for his contribution to the Tapiola "Garden City" in the Finnish town of Espoo, built from nothing by the Finnish developer Asuntosaatio (The Housing Foundation). It was to be a Finnish society in miniature, and Ervi was one of five architects asked to contribute to the project.

Ervi's designs for Tapiola included a strip-model shopping center, a ten-story residential block, and cinemas, all connected along a pedestrian walkway that would serve as an axis for the entire project. Construction began in 1958 and Tapiola's development continued through various stages into the mid-sixties, by which time Ervi has become head of the newly organized Helsinki City Planning Department where he remained until 1969.

Located just 6 miles (10 km) west of Helsinki, Tapiola was considered one of the finest cityscapes in the world and a triumph of urban design. In Finland today, Tapiola is still considered part of the Finnish "national landscape" and an "area of national importance;" a sort of cultural national capital.

Joseph Esherick

Joseph Esherick (1914–98) was born in Philadelphia, Pennsylvania, USA, and graduated from the University of Pennsylvania with a degree in architecture in 1937. After serving in the navy during World War II, he began his own practice in San Francisco in 1946. His early work was primarily residential, building upon and refining what had become known as the Bay Area Tradition of architecture pioneered by Gardner Dailey and William Wurster. Hundreds of designs were to follow, all centering on an attention to regional traditions and all showing a barely disguised contempt for aesthetic theories of design. Esherick believed that form and function had to be addressed in buildings that needed to be designed for their specific purposes and the client's needs.

In 1952 Esherick joined the Department of Architecture at the University of California at Berkeley and taught there until his retirement in 1985, when he received the Berkeley Citation – a prestigious award for achievement and service to the university. Esherick was instrumental in bringing many world-renowned architects and theorists to Berkeley, the curriculum of which became a model for many institutions across America. His method of design studio teaching inspired generations of students in a free and open examination of how buildings are made.

An example of Esherick's adeptness at creating contemporary urban versions of rural vernacular architecture, his Cary House (1960) in Mill Valley, California, is a fairly simple box-like building ornamented by eyelash-like overhangs above windows that weren't merely holes in solid walls, but rather designed to collect light and act as portals to frame specific vistas. Each window's trellis-like overhang filters the incoming light, giving it a complexity rarely achieved with traditional windows.

Romano House (1972) in Kentwoodlands, California, again demonstrates Esherick's manipulative use of light, filtering it through vertical railings and trellises in a homage to the Californian barn. Its shingled exterior again features windows specifically located to juxtapose dark timbers in the ceiling, and white walls that create complex patterns of light and an interplay between large and small spaces that bring depth to what is essentially a very simple, understated space.

Goldman House (1957) in San Francisco explores and develops the idea of capitalizing on the north views of San Francisco and provides an elegant setting for living in this city. Esherick used a mix of materials and elements to design the house, blending the traditional with the industrial. Redwood siding and double-hung windows are combined with sonotube concrete columns and industrial light fixtures.

In addition to his countless residential designs, some of his more notable contributions to the built environment are The Cannery (1968) in San Francisco, the Monterey Bay Aquarium (1980), the Adlai Stevenson College (1968) at the University of California at Santa Cruz, and Wurster Hall (1964) at the University of California.

In 1982 he won the ACSA–AIA Topaz Medallion for Architecture Education, and in 1989 was awarded the American Institute of Architects Gold Medal.

Hassan Fathy

Hassan Fathy (1899–1989) was born in Alexandria, Egypt, and was his country's most important architect of the twentieth century. Throughout his life it was his belief that architects had a social responsibility to design affordable housing for the poor and disadvantaged. His great contribution to Egyptian architecture was his rediscovery of ancient design methods and materials, particularly clay. His buildings were built almost entirely of clay, and he trained ordinary Egyptians in long-forgotten methods of construction and maintenance, creating a virtual renaissance in archway and cupola construction techniques. He also contributed environmentally sound techniques such as wind-catchers, cooling towers, interior fountains, and courtyards, as well as reintroducing lost methods of roofing adobe buildings with vaulted ceilings crafted by hand from sun-dried bricks.

Fathy graduated from the High School of Engineering, Architectural Section, University of King Fuad 1 (now University of Cairo) in 1926 before designing his very first mud-brick project houses in Lower Egypt in 1937. From 1946 to 1953 he was delegated to the Antiquities Department to design and supervise the project of the New Gourna Village near Luxor – a hoped-for, cost-effective solution to the problem of relocating an entire community that had taken up residence over the ancient royal necropolis in Luxor. His design was based on the homes being constructed mostly out of mud-brick steps, walls, vaults, and domes. Despite Fathy's best intentions, the Gournis themselves preferred to stay where they were, plying their lucrative trade in archeological oddments. Thus the New Gourna Village came to embody the problem of how to create a community space without first allowing our subjective values to intervene and determine its suitability.

Despite a lifetime of opposition from authorities and architects throughout Egypt saying his style was anachronistic and bordering on the irrelevant, Fathy saw himself as the latest in a long line of master builders carrying on the proud legacies of Arabian building. Fathy has received the Union of International Architects Gold Medal in 1984, the Egyptian Government's National Prize for Arts and Letters, and the Aga Khan Award for Architecture in 1980. He is also author of the acclaimed 1973 book *Architecture for the Poor.*

Sverre Fehn

Sverre Fehn (1924–) was born in Kongsberg, Norway, and today lives and works in Oslo. In 1997 he was awarded the Heinrich Tessenow Gold Medal and architecture's highest honor – the Pritzker Prize – for "representing the best of twentieth-century

Modernism...a unique life's work of extraordinary richness." The leading Norwegian architect of his generation, Fehn graduated from the Oslo School of Architecture in 1948 and soon became a leading exponent of Modernism whose buildings, despite often displaying a rare simplicity, were imbued with an inspired use of light and subtleties of form.

International recognition came in 1958 for his design of the Norwegian Pavilion at the Brussels World Exhibition. What are generally regarded as his career highlights both emerged in the 1960s with his Nordic Pavilion at the Venice Biennale and the Hedmark Museum in the Norwegian town of Hamar.

One of the finest examples of his approach to design is the private residence Villa Busk (1987–90), constructed along a ridge near the Oslo Fjord in the town of Bamble. A seamless blend of regionalism and Modernism, it demonstrates his belief that humanity is subordinate to nature with it being built into, rather than on, the landscape. A rough concrete exterior gives the impression of it rising from the earth, though balanced by Fehn's extensive use of timber providing a human scale, texture, and intimacy. Villa Busk is a declared national landmark in Norway.

The 1990s saw some of his largest works come to fruition, in particular the Norwegian Glacier Museum at Fjaerland (1991), which sits "like a large, light-gray rock" in the midst of the rocky landscape left by the glacier's retreat. Almost aesthetic in his minimalist approach to ornamentation and detail, Fehn is both visionary and tradition-bound, where craftsmanship will always take precedence over technology.

Albert Frey

Albert Frey (1903–98) was born in Zurich, Switzerland. He gained his architectural diploma from the Winterthur Institute of Technology in 1924. After studying with the architect A J Arter in Zurich, he worked briefly for Le Corbusier before emigrating to the United States of America in 1930 and worked for various architects including A Lawrence Kocher, with whom he co-authored many essays on urban planning and modernity in the *Architectural Record*. Frey and Kocher also collaborated on the design of what is now generally regarded as America's first prefabricated home – the Aluminaire House.

First displayed at an architectural show in Manhattan in 1931, this 29 ft x 30 ft (8.8 m x 9 m) aluminum and glass cube was fastened together by nuts and bolts and featured such innovations as a drive-through garage with electrically operated doors. However, it was a commission for Kocher's brother in Palm Springs that first introduced Frey to southern California's stark desert landscapes. He found the combination of sun, pure air, and the desert's simple forms to be ideal conditions for architecture.

In the aftermath of World War II, peace and prosperity saw the population of Palm Springs nearly triple. Coveted by a new Hollywood elite with blank cheques for their residences, Frey and others began to establish a new aesthetic called Desert Modernism – low, sleek, horizontal homes constructed primarily of concrete, prefabricated wall units, aluminum, and vast expanses of glass to emphasize their natural surroundings.

Frey's Loewy House (1947), built for the industrial magnate Raymond Loewy, was a typical Palm Springs Modernist villa with low-slung pavilions incorporating floor to ceiling glass doors that provide striking views of the desert and mountains. A free-form swimming pool even dips under the doors to the house and into the interior, forming a small stream.

At just under 1,000 sq ft (92 sq m), his Frey House II (1963–64) was a typical Palm Springs steel and glass residence clad in corrugated metal. Following the site's topography, a small deck extends from the house to form the roof for a carport below and a deck for an adjacent swimming pool. Inspired by fellow Desert Modernist William Cody's love of placing boulders in a building's interior, a boulder was used by Frey as a headboard in one of the home's sleeping areas.

Frey's projects contributed significantly to establishing Palm Springs as a progressive desert mecca for innovative Modern architecture during the 1950s, '60s, and '70s. He produced designs for a wide range of architectural commissions, from custom homes to institutional and public buildings. But overall, Frey preferred to design homes, and his residential designs integrate into the surrounding landscape and draw from the local surroundings for color and metaphor.

Antonio Gaudi

Antonio Gaudi (1852–1926) was born in Reus, Catalonia, south of Barcelona in Spain. On June 10, 1926, aged 74, he suffered the indignity of being run over and killed by a tram. Although Gaudi was Catalan's cultural hero and a highly methodical architect, neither the tram driver nor the ensuing mob gathering around his body recognized him. Unfortunately, his work also went unrecognized in Pevsner's first edition of *The Pioneers of Modern Design* (1936), which meant the western world was late in its appreciation of Gaudi.

Gaudi was the conventional product of an architectural school, and on graduation he went straight into private practice. From the very beginning Gaudi was a maverick outsider who reacted against Classicism. This is obvious from his first major work – the Casa Vicens (1883–85) in Barcelona for a wealthy tile manufacturer. Here he used stone, brick, and brightly colored glazed tiles in his creation. Gaudi's work carried a deep nationalistic conviction, and the overall effect was one of dynamism, power, and richness. The interior of this house was no less rich, displaying an abundance of color and ceramic detail. These materials may sound strange, but we need to remember that Spain links Europe with Arab culture. One has only to examine the Alhambra in southern Spain to realize there is a good deal of difference between Mediterranean culture, and the more restrained products of northern Europe.

Before Casa Vicens was finished, Gaudi began to work for Count Eusebi Güell. Gaudi started with a porter's lodge, gate, and stables for Güell in the suburbs of Barcelona. Here Gaudi began to assert that structural and decorative individuality which marks his maturity. The stable was cylindrical in shape, built in brick with ceramic decorations recalling Casa Vicens. Between the porter's lodge and the stables, Gaudi built a broad and venturesome dragon gate in wrought iron. It represents the old Catalan legend of St George and the dragon, which guards the entrance to an enchanting garden.

Gaudi worked for Count Güell between 1900 and 1914, when his energies were occupied with the idea of developing a garden suburb for some 60 houses. Only two of the houses were ever built, and the rest of the land was developed into the municipal Park Güell. Its entrance is flanked by a gatekeeper's lodge whose roof carries a twisting spire and cross, while the public washroom has an elaborate ceramic roof.

A wrought iron entrance gate admits one to the Park Güell water garden, which is shrouded by ceramic banisters. Beyond this and upwards, a staircase beckons to an open terrace, surrounded by the most beautiful ceramic bench in Barcelona. This curvaceous bench, which surrounds the perimeter of the terrace, is supported from below by slanted columns, and forms a complete artistic circuit. It was chosen for its utility, and its facing material had to be smooth, comfortable, and able to withstand weathering. Its colors had to resist the sunshine, and finally the bench profiles had to accommodate the human body, shed water, and be hygienic. Gaudi's bench is a permanent masterpiece for the people of Barcelona.

Gaudi's domestic architecture is a product of sense and sensibility. To fully understand this architect, one must feel the sense of magic and the unmeasurable elements in the Catalan temperament. Against these vibrations, one must not forget Gaudi was a profoundly religious man and a practical stonemason. His work is deeply visual – the Villa Bellesguard (1902) is a battlemented exercise, romantically recalling the last monarch of the throne of Catalonia-Aragon. As Gaudi took on new domestic work his architecture became more expressive. The Casa Batllo (1905–07) and the Casa Mila apartments

(1905–10) exhibit an unrestrained use of free-form windows, curving balconies, and warped surfaces. These houses are all experimental works whose facades are in motion, contributing to the urban magic of Barcelona.

The work of Gaudi embraced the plasticity of "ruled surfaces." This system of building – which was borrowed three dimensionally from nature – was reconciled with his practical ability as a builder. Gaudi's architecture was never arbitrary. His unfinished Church of the Sagrada Familia (1911–), and the Crypt of the Colonia Güell (1915), provide Gaudi's last testament. They demonstrate the totality of his artistic methodology and practical convictions.

Gaudi's non-conformist buildings are strong, memorable, and persistent. They also demonstrate courage, generosity, and sustaining joy.

Frank O Gehry

Frank O Gehry (1929–) was born in Toronto, Canada. At the age of 17, he moved to California where he studied at the Los Angeles City College before completing his architecture degree at the University of Southern California. He went on to study city planning at the Harvard Graduate School of Design in Massachusetts. He established his private practice, Frank O Gehry and Associates, in 1963. In 1979, this practice was succeeded by the firm Gehry and Krueger Inc.

Gehry's style is influenced by late Modernism. The warped forms of his architecture are considered Deconstructivist – a style that de-emphasizes societal goals and functionality. Gehry's office is in the suburb of Santa Monica, not far from the studio of Charles Eames – an American architect whom he greatly admires – and Gehry has modeled his work around Eames' design of architecture and furniture.

Gehry first came to attention in 1972 with his "Easy Edges" cardboard furniture, and his deconstructed architectural style followed in the late 1970s when he, directed by a personal vision of architecture, created collage-like compositions out of found materials. Instead of creating buildings, Gehry created ad-hoc pieces of functional sculpture.

Gehry took many years to find his voice and feel comfortable with the aesthetic brought to the solution of architectural problems. His true architectural flare was never shown with corporate clients. The architect-cum-artist first emerged with his own outrageous house, Gehry House (1979) in Santa Monica. The building's explosion of shapes and forms is in keeping with Gehry's design logic. The house shocked everyone! His buildings are characterized by unconventional or distorted shapes that have sculptural, fragmented, or a collage-like quality. Gehry House introduced many "raw materials," chain-link fencing, corrugated metal siding, and unfinished wood surfaces into the Santa Monica residential district. As he was insulted by the architectural critics for this work, Gehry pulled away sections on the original house in 1987 and rearranged them in an artfully haphazard way like some mischievous giant.

Gehry's other notable Californian houses all demonstrate his Deconstructivist view. Ruscha House (1977) in Palm Springs, Norton House (1983) in Venice, the Schnabel Residence (1986) in Brentwood, the Venice Beach House (1986) at Venice Beach, and the Wosk Residence in Beverly Hills, all utilize concrete blocks, glazed tiles, stucco, and wooden logs, and various textures and colors reflect the chaos of the structures.

Gehry is regarded as much a sculptor as an architect: A three-dimensional collage artist who sculpts spaces and encases them more often that not in plywood and metal surfaces, he readily concedes this predilection for the visual arts and its influence on his work. Gehry more then any other architect eschews historicism as a source and precedes directly from the artistic.

His iconoclastic structures earned him the Pritzker Prize in 1989. Gehry was made a Fellow of the American Institute of Architects in 1974. He also received the Arnold W Brunner Memorial Prize in Architecture in 1974, the Gold Medal from the American Institute of Architects in 1999, and the Royal Gold Medal from the Royal Institute of British Architects in 2000.

Bruce Goff

Bruce Alonzo Goff (1904–82) was born in Alton, Kansas, in the heartland of the United States of America. Educated at Lincoln Public School, Tulsa, Oklahoma, he apprenticed at the age of 12 to the firm of Rush, Endacott and Rush in Tulsa. He was self-educated in architecture. As a Romantic Goff was certainly influenced by Louis Sullivan, Frank Lloyd Wright, and Antonio Gaudi. He worked in private practice in Chicago, Illinois (1936–42); Berkeley, California (1945–56); Bartlesville, Oklahoma (1956–64); Kansas City, Missouri (1964–69); and finally Tyler in Texas until his death. s

Goff was certainly one of America's most complicated personalities, and for most of the twentieth century he generated an idiosyncratic presence in architecture, doing highly individualistic and inventive family houses in rural and suburban locations throughout America. A wide range of influences nurtured his work, and throughout his career he remained closely attuned to the Romantic inclinations of Frank Lloyd Wright, whom he met at Taliesin in 1927. His first houses – like the Elin House (1938–39) – resembled the Usonian houses of Wright, but by 1940 he was beginning to come into his own with the angular Unseth House (1941) in Park Ridge, Illinois.

With the outbreak of World War II, Goff enlisted in the United States Navy. After the war he also spent time at the University of Oklahoma, where he became chairman of the architectural department until his resignation in 1955. Goff used spherical volumes, and unusual materials like goose-feathered and coil-rope ceilings. He was never confined by the rectangle or the square. In his Bavinger House (1950–55) near Norman, Oklahoma, he created one of his most distinctive houses – a logarithmically spiraling wall of stone complete with a continuous glass skylight, while the interior carried a three-dimensional flow of space uniquely divided by plants, carpets, and fishnets as opposed to regular doors. The steel-bracing cables supporting the roof were derived from oil-rig technology.

In 1956 Goff moved to Bartlesville, Oklahoma, where he made his home and office in Frank Lloyd Wright's Price Tower. Interested students and many clients soon followed. Prominent among the visitors was Joe Price. He became a client and a major supporter which resulted in the Price House (1956–58) – a hexagonal retreat with carpeted floors which were turned up into seating areas. This cosy environment was completed by a feathered ceiling, which created a great deal of comment. The Price House was twice expanded incorporating a glass-wall pool (1966–68), and a tower by 1978. Such a complex geometry of interlocking forms brought Goff many more clients. In 1957, for the Pollocks of Oklahoma City, Goff designed a house of nine interlocking squares. Each square was covered with a hipped roof, and a pyramidal skylight was placed at the peak of the roof. What was always at stake with Goff was the spatial organization of the house. His Bartlesville years brought much popular acclaim, as he continued to free himself from the right angle.

In 1964 Goff moved to Kansas City, Missouri, where he designed a series of prefabricated houses. By 1970, and in a state of restlessness, he moved again to Tyler, Texas, again in response to speculative work for commercial concerns. His Plunket House (1970) again showed his Romantic interest in decorative values.

During his life Goff designed at least 500 buildings, with a fifth of these being built, demonstrating astonishing individuality. Throughout his career Goff maintained an interest in complex geometries – squares, triangles, and circles – in a rich variety of compositions and use of materials. In maturity Goff demonstrated an extraordinary range of diversity and spatial organization. As an architect he had the spatial ability to respond imaginatively to the encouragement provided by his many clients.

Ernö Goldfinger

Ernö Goldfinger (1902–87) was born in Budapest, Hungary, and moved to Paris in 1920 with his family after the collapse of the Austro-Hungarian Empire. In Paris he worked with the French architect Auguste Perret and studied architecture at the École des Beaux-Arts. He spent the next 13 years in Paris before moving to London in the late 1930s, where he found commissions hard to come by, as did the majority of Modernists in pre-war Britain.

In 1939 he designed a Modernist house in Hampstead, North London, in which he and his wife would live in until his death. Three Georgian cottages were sacrificed to make room for it, which incurred the ire of local resident and author Ian Fleming, the creator of James Bond, who exacted vengeance by naming the villain in his 1959 novel after the flamboyant architect. Today, No 2 Willow Road is regarded as 1930s Modernism at its purest.

After World War II Goldfinger continued to struggle with commissions while at the same time beginning to champion high-rise apartment blocks as the solution to Britain's growing urban population. His most productive period began in the late 1950s and into the '60s and involved three projects that have come to form the bulk of his legacy: Trellick Tower (1968–72); Balfron Tower (1967); and the Alexander Fleming House (1959–63). Despite the fact that the Trellick and Balfron towers are now regarded as two of the ugliest buildings in Britain, representing a sort of "last stand" of what became known as Brutalism, they contained many innovations such as sound-proofing, windows that pivot to permit access for cleaning, and fan-coil units for heating. Goldfinger was also gaining a reputation for getting the best space out of a site.

In 1967 he won a civic trust award for the Alexander Fleming House in Elephant and Castle, in southeast London. Goldfinger's career suffered in the 1970s when the Modern movement fell out of favor, and Trellick Tower became synonymous with Modernist "folly." Goldfinger retired in 1977 and 11 years later Trellick Tower became a Grade 2 listed building and thus has been saved from the wrecker's ball.

Michael Graves

Michael Graves (1934–) was born in Indianapolis, Indiana, USA. He studied at the University of Cincinnati (1958) and Harvard (1959), and also won the Brunner Fellowship Rome Prize, to study for two years at the American Academy in Rome between 1960 and 1962. The influence of Italy's classical architecture can be seen in some of his built work. He is a Fellow of the American Institute of Architects, and a member of the Academy of Arts and Letters, and he has taught at Princeton University since 1962 and has been the Professor of Architecture since 1972.

Graves has been the principal of his own firm – Michael Graves and Associates – based in Princeton, New Jersey, since 1964. The office is involved in a diverse range of work, including architecture, interior design, furnishings, and graphic design. Graves has also become known for the design of consumer products for manufacturers such as Alessi and Baldinger, as well as his line of homewares commissioned for American Target stores.

Architectural projects include office buildings, hotels, libraries, museums, university buildings, and Walt Disney hotels. While his early residential work was predominantly extensions for private homes, such as the Benacerraf House (1969) in Princeton, New Jersey, more recent projects include multi-story apartment buildings: 1500 Ocean Drive (1994–99) at Miami Beach, Florida; and the Impala Residential Tower (1997–99) in New York City.

Michael Graves emerged in the early 1970s as one of the "New York Five," with the publication of *Five Architects* in 1972, making him famous for his early Cubist-influenced residential projects, such as the Hanselmann House (1967) in Fort Wayne, Indiana. These early projects were linked with the work of other architects who drew inspiration from Le Corbusier's white villas of the 1920s and 30s.

His work since the early 1980s is better described as Post-modern or Neo-historicist, in that it focuses on making new forms which respond to their unique context and take their place as part of a historical continuum. These buildings are shaped by a reinterpretation of the elements, forms, and compositions of existing architecture, of various styles, to create a form that relates to the site and to neighboring historical buildings, but which is considerate of human scale and everyday use. For example, the Alexander House (1971–73) in Princeton, New Jersey, is a light-filled extension to a colonial style home, which features a strong visual connection through glazing to the garden in which it sits, and incorporates sculptural elements which are visual plays on elements or features of the existing house.

Graves' built work is characterized visually by primary solids; the interpretive use of traditional, Classical, or vernacular elements, such as arches and pediments; and a muted palette of colors such as terracotta, mauve, off-white, and soft blue.

Graves was made famous internationally by the Portland Building (1983), a public services building in Oregon, for which he controversially won a design competition in 1980, and which has become known as an icon of Post-modernism. Portland, and the Humana office building (1982–85) in Louisville, Kentucky, like much of Grave's large-scale work, are characterized by simple forms adorned with color and features abstracted from historical architectural language.

Graves and his firm have been recognized with many awards from the American Institute of Architects including several National Honor Awards and the 2001 Gold Medal.

Eileen Gray

Eileen Gray (1878–1976) was born into a wealthy background and into a distinguished family home called Brownswood, which stood on the banks of the River Slanery, 2 miles (3 km) from Enniscorthy, in county Wexford, southeastern Ireland. Known as both an architect and a furniture designer, Gray studied drawing at the Slade School of Fine Arts in London from 1898 to 1902, lacquer-work in Soho, London from 1900 to 1902, drawing at École Colarossi and Académie Julian in Paris from 1902 to 1905, and finally furniture making with the renowned Japanese lacquer craftsman Seizo Sugawara in Paris from 1907 to 1914. She also drove an ambulance in the French Army between 1914 and 1915. All these experiences – particularly the new freedoms of Paris – were integrated into her architecture and furniture making. In France, however, as a woman designer, she was an exception. Gray distinguished herself because her approach was unprecedented among decorative artists. The simplicity of her forms, and the sensual impact of the materials she used, brought lacquer to the attention of Parisian artists.

Eileen Gray was a very talented artistic person. She was beautiful and independent. A woman with pale blue eyes, she cut a truly "Romantic figure." Gray dressed with elegance and loved hand-made shoes. As a person she was a great believer in decorum, and she despised familiarities. Although she was conventional as a human being in dealing with people, as a designer she exploited the sensual impact of surfaces and textures. In 1926 she began a six-year collaboration with Romanian architect Jean Badovici, which had a decisive influence on her involvement with architecture. In her search for synthesis, she distilled influences from Le Corbusier, Adolf Loos, and the Dutch De Stijl school, which turned her into a professional designer, and subsequently into designing a small number of distinguished houses.

Paris, of course, was bursting with new ideas about architecture. Le Corbusier and the painter Amédée Ozenfant launched their review *L'Esprit Nouveau* in 1920. It was through Badovici that Eileen met the French Cubist painter Fernand Léger and Le Corbusier. Badovici edited *L'Architecture Vivante* which covered the whole spectrum of modern design and architecture. In this way Eileen joined the creative edge of what was happening in Paris, the Netherlands, Germany, Russia, Belgium, and the United States of America. This was Gray's textbook.

In 1924 the Dutch magazine *Wendingen (Turning Point)* devoted a whole issue to the work of Eileen Gray, and described her work as, "A real joy to go from one piece of furniture to another." *Wendingen* also included Gray's first house – a model of a house for an engineer. It used Le Corbusier's architectural vocabulary (flat roof and white walls) – a roofed-over terrace supported on *pilotis* (poles). This house had two living rooms and a kitchen on the ground floor, and two bedrooms above. As a house for the Mediterranean it had a central staircase, and although Gray wanted to build this house, it does not appear to have been built. But it certainly provided the prelude to her own house that she began building at Roquebrune-Cap-Martin, in the south of France, in 1926.

About this time she also furnished a house for Badovici in the medieval town of Vézalay, in Burgundy. From here, it was but a short step to the south of France to the peninsula of Saint-Tropez and the little town of Roquebrune-Cap-Martin, on the coast between Menton and Nice. Next to the Mediterranean, she found a plot which determined the refuge that she was later to build – a villa she named E-1027: A cipher for the joint architect-design, hence the intertwined initials of (EJBG) reflecting the collaborative nature of the venture.

Most houses on the Côte d'Azur were derivative Provençal copies of local farmhouses, so Eileen's design was a calculated shock to the people of Roquebrune. Nevertheless, Gray's design was exhibited in the Salon d'Automne of 1929, and the Union des Artistes Modernes – a dissident group of designers of which she was a founding member. Badovoci published a special issue on the villa, which certainly attracted Le Corbusier's attention. The building work was hard, as access to the site was only by wheelbarrow. But the daily swim in the sea in front of the house was a spiritual liberation. This two-storied Modern house contained a large living room which was extended by a terrace facing the sea. It incorporated Le Corbusier's "Five Points of the New Architecture." Yet E-1027 was logically organized with a sound transition between inside and outside. An appropriate house for the Mediterranean, E-1027 was furnished with the proverbial care and abstract arrangement of a Gerrit Rietveld house. As far as Eileen Gray was concerned, her house was a place of freedom: A refuge for which, during her lifetime, she received little praise. Its classic beauty was a sustaining example of new architecture admired by many including Le Corbusier.

E-1027 was a vacation house. It was in every sense a Modern logical house, with an ideological difference, and it owed much to the thinking of Le Corbusier – whose cabin retreat was just next door beside the Mediterranean Sea.

Allan Greenberg

Allan Greenberg (1938–) was born in Johannesburg, South Africa, where he was trained in both Classical and Gothic architecture. Today he is America's foremost Classicist. He studied architecture at the University of Witwatersrand and moved to the United States of America at the age of 23. In a world of Modernity, Greenberg's reputation for keeping true to the Founding Fathers' desire for grandeur in the halls of government has seen him become the first American to be awarded the prestigious Richard H Driehaus Prize for Classical Architecture in 2006 from the School of Architecture at the University of Notre Dame.

Greenberg has lectured at Yale University's School of Architecture, the University of Pennsylvania, and the Department of Historic Preservation at Columbia University. The author of many articles and books on Classical American architecture, Greenberg has lectured extensively on the need not merely to replicate the past, but to make it relevant to our time. He claims that Modernism, despite its bold claims has, in fact, failed to create a viable vernacular tradition. Its buildings don't "talk" to those around them and therefore fail to fit into their environment.

With many Americans rejecting Modernism for its inaccessibility and austerity, Greenberg is at home in the midst of a conservative people who prefer the familiar forms of the eighteenth and nineteenth centuries.

Greenberg opened his own firm in 1972, designing courthouses and, eventually, residences. His first house project was an addition to a seventeenth-century home in Connecticut. He added a family room and kitchen, and he raised half of the attic for a studio. Next came the Farmhouse in Connecticut (1979–83), which launched his career as a master designer of large residential houses and their accompanying outbuildings. Modeled on George Washington's Mt Vernon home, the Farmhouse is a horse farm with a very grand house clad in wood, hewn and painted to look like stone, in an effort to make the house appear less formal.

Greenberg continues to practice in Washington DC, which he sees as the first city designed to give form to democratic principles.

Charles and Henry Greene

Charles Sumner Greene (1868–1957) and Henry Mather Greene (1870–1954) were a collaborative team of Arts and Crafts architects who practiced in the early years of the twentieth century. Charles and Henry Greene were both born in Brighton, Ohio, USA, now a part of Cincinnati. Moving to St Louis as teenagers, the two were enrolled by their father in practical education, in the field of machine-tool making and woodworking at the Manual Training School of Washington University between 1884 and 1888. This was followed by architectural training at the Massachusetts Institute of Technology in Boston between 1888 and 1891, and later in various Beaux-Arts offices around Boston. As disciples of Augustus Pugin and John Ruskin, the Greene brothers soon shook themselves free from Classicism, adopting Arts and Crafts philosophies.

In 1893, the Greene family moved to Pasadena, California. Working together, Henry and Charles began to produce some of the most sensuously timber-crafted houses in this State. Using timber as their expressive medium, the temperamentally different brothers brought a Romantic, yet practical identity, to the Pacific-rim of Carmel and Pasadena. Their work inspired the cultured and intellectual sensibilities of southern Californians.

Charles and Henry were utterly different as architects. Charles was an artistic, intellectual dreamer, while his brother Henry was more practical in the traditional sense of the working architect. Both minds and methods, however, were indispensable to the Greene and Greene synthesis. Artistic expression of structure was the basis of their working philosophy. Using beautifully grained wood (Honduras mahogany, Burma teak, Californian redwood, and Oregon pine), boldly detailed and finished to a beautiful sheen which exposed the sinuous timber grain, the Greene brothers astounded their "well-heeled" middle-class clients. The builders who worked with the Greene brothers were also seduced by the need to achieve high standards of craftsmanship and comfort to match the natural surroundings of southern California.

It is generally acknowledged that the best examples of their work are: The Robert Blacker House and Garden in Pasadena (1907–09); the David Gamble House, also in Pasadena (1907–09); the Charles Pratt House or "Casa Barranca" in Ojai (1908–11); and the William Thorsen House in Berkeley (1908–10). All these beautifully crafted houses carry the striking identity of Greene and Greene regionalism combining gabled over-hanging roofs, timber decks with pegged railings, spacious porches embracing nature, and delicate transparent Japanese-inspired screened interiors of elegant proportions to create the ultimate Arts and Crafts intensity.

The Blacker House and Garden site was large and gave ample scope for the Greene brothers to push their talents to perfection, providing sweeping landscaped views of a garden from the house's terracotta terraces. Using a limitless budget, the Greene brothers used the finest selection of timbers, identifying an expressive range of spaces articulated by exposed beams, rafters, and purlins with mortise-and-tenon jointing.

The David Gamble House used gabled elevations with deep horizontal eaves, sheltering large terraces, and sleeping porches, which embraced the outdoor life of Pasadena. Like the interiors of Mackintosh and Voysey, the Greene brothers delighted in inglenook spaces which were thoroughly detailed in redwood paneling. Currently the Gamble House is owned by the University of Southern Californian School of Architecture. It is the only Greene and Greene house open to the public. The Gamble House is also distinguished by the fact that it contains nearly all the original, architect-designed furniture.

The Charles Pratt House is less formal than either the Blacker or Gamble houses, though the synthesis of roofs, beams, rafters, and terraces continue to open out to nature. The last of the elaborate wooden houses built by Greene and Greene was the William Thorsen House (1911) in Berkeley, California, which was built to the highest standards. The Thorsen House represents the ubiquitous bungalow – the ultimate in Arts and Crafts sensibility – which was exposed to the world via the publications *Craftsman* and *Ladies Home Journal*.

Of all the houses by the Greene and Greene brothers, the Gamble House personifies the work of master Arts and Crafts architects working together for the greater glory of their clients, and in harmony with the topography and climate of southern California.

Walter Burley Griffin

Walter Burley Griffin (1876–1937) was born in Chicago, Illinois, USA, and graduated from the University of Illinois in 1899, after which he worked for various Chicago architects, including five years with Frank Lloyd Wright, before setting up his own practice in 1906. Influenced by Chicago's Prairie School, he developed a somewhat prismatic geometrical form of organic architecture, and did some work using terracotta block construction, which was to exert a continuing influence upon him. Marion Mahony, an MIT graduate more than five years his senior, joined him in 1911, and they were married in the same year. In 1912 they won the international competition for the design of Australia's new capital city, Canberra. In 1913 Griffin visited Australia and was appointed Federal Capital Director of Design and Construction, and in the following year the couple settled in Australia. They established a private practice in Melbourne and Sydney, which was to undertake major projects such as the Capitol Theatre and Newman College in Melbourne, and a number of reverberatory incinerators in both Sydney and Melbourne, but they always maintained an innovative domestic practice as well.

Their domestic work includes two distinctive strands. The first is the "Knitlock" – a form of concrete unit construction invented by Griffin in 1917, which is quite distinct from Wright's Textile Block, though there was to be some controversy about the relationship between the two. Griffin's system consisted of "tesseral" and "vertebral" wall elements, and a system of diagonal overlapping concrete roof tiles. Four curved units could be assembled to produce a section with flanges projecting at right angles like a vertebra, with a hollow core within which rods and concrete could be placed to create a structural column. The tesseral elements were square tiles with ridges and grooves on the back so that two could lock together, back-to-back, to create a vertical wall surface. The cavity could also be grouted and reinforced, and an assemblage of these units could be used to fill a bay between the vertebral columns. These standard elements were also used by other architects in a variety of works, but the typical Knitlock house of the Griffins was a square with a shallow pyramidal roof, over a single main living area surrounded by minimalist kitchen, bathroom, and sleeping compartments at the periphery. However, the promise of the system as a general solution for cheap housing was never realized.

More elaborate design, which reflects more of the Griffins' background in organic architecture, is seen in the Castlecrag development on Sydney Harbour. Griffin was a financial partner in a syndicate which bought 650 acres (263 ha) of ruggedly scenic land in 1921 and developed it with individual houses designed to blend into the landscape and to facilitate a communal lifestyle. More than 50 houses were designed for the estate, with 16 of them built, and the Griffins lived there for a period from 1925. The houses were mainly flat-roofed blocky shapes in rock-faced sandstone and concrete, sometimes Knitlock, and often named in keeping with the castle theme, as with the Embrasure and the Oriel. The roads had names like the Parapet and the Rampart, the park reserves names like the Gargoyle and the Buttress, and there was a network of pedestrian ways. Marion Griffin was particularly involved in promoting communal activities, which included boating, music, play-reading, and discussion groups. The Griffins designed an open-air theater for the estate in 1930, where anthroposophical festivals (a spiritualistic philosophical movement) were held after the Griffins joined the cult in 1930–31.

In 1935 Griffin received a commission for the Lucknow University Library in India, and after Marion joined him in the following year, about a hundred projects were designed, including some major houses. However, Griffin succumbed to peritonitis on 11 February 1937, and his widow returned to Chicago, where she died in 1961.

Walter Gropius

Walter Gropius (1883–1969) was born in Berlin, Germany, the son of an architect. He was educated at the technical universities in Munich and Berlin. The founder of the Bauhaus School of Design, Gropius initially worked in the office of architect Peter Behrens, who was one of his major influences in architectural design. In 1910, he started a private practice with Adolf Meyer, and a year later became a member of the Deutscher Werkbund, which encouraged the collaboration between creative designers and machine production. These methods were soon to be applied to the renowned Fagus Shoe-last Factory (1913) – a building incorporating glass curtain walls demonstrating the Modernist concern that form reflect function, as well as providing safe conditions for its workers.

As Gropius' career progressed, he was elected chairman of the Working Council for Art in 1919 and soon after was appointed director of the Bauhaus where his innovative approach incorporated both art and manufacture. When World War I commenced, he left the Bauhaus and resumed private practice in Berlin for a short period before being forced to immigrate to the United States of America.

After accepting a position as Professor at Harvard University, Gropius mentored such scholars as Paul Rudolph, I M Pei, and Philip Johnson. In 1938, Gropius built Gropius House in Lincoln, Massachusetts, which had a dramatic effect on American architecture and introduced International Modernism to the country. The design of Gropius House combined the traditional elements of New England architecture (wood, brick, and fieldstone) with innovative materials rarely used in homes at that time (glass block, acoustical plaster, and chrome banisters), along with the latest technology in fixtures. In keeping with Bauhaus philosophy, every aspect of the house and its surrounding landscape was planned for maximum efficiency and simplicity of design.

In 1945 Gropius established The Architect's Collaborative which, with an emphasis on teamwork, created plans inspired by modern technology to build practical designs. His belief in the importance of prefabrication and standardization incorporated innovative design with the new science of industrialized methods of building. Although they were initially condemned as "architectural socialism," today his ideas are recognized as a benchmark for construction.

Zaha Hadid

Zaha Hadid (1950–) was born in Baghdad, Iraq. She received a degree in mathematics from the American University in Beirut before deciding to study architecture at the Architectural Association in London. After graduating in 1977, she became a partner of the Office for Metropolitan Architecture, taught at the Architectural Association with Rem Koolhaas and Elia Zenghelis, and later led her own studio at the Architectural Association until 1987. Since then she has held the Kenzo Tange Chair at the Graduate School of Design at Harvard University; the Sullivan Chair at the University of Chicago School of Architecture; and guest professorships at the Hochschule für Bildende Künste in Hamburg, the Knolton School of Architecture in Ohio, and the Masters Studio at Columbia University, New York. She is currently Professor at the University of Applied Arts, Vienna.

In Zaha Hadid's work there is an architectural expression that deals with motion rather than the controversial language of static elements. It manifests itself in the work of architects like Coop Himmelblau and Mark Scogin, and in projects such as Bernard Tschumi's Parc de la Villette in Paris and in the visionary drawings of Lebbeus Woods and Daniel Libeskind. Zaha Hadid is a member of this group of practitioners who draw their inspiration from an age of speed, electronics, and dynamic forms.

Hadid creates extraordinary designs for buildings that strive for a sense of weightlessness, and she describes them through dense and elaborate multi-layered sketches. These drawings are unlike conventional architectural renditions and yet, like her buildings, are filled with the suggestion of movement. "They are sequential," Hadid says. "They move along. You really need to do a movie or a cartoon to show all these things in motion."

She believes that an architect's drawings should not only be able to show plans, sections, and elevations. Architects invest in codes of presentation, so why can't we change them? She bridles at any suggestion that her nearly abstract delineations are merely for illustrations. Her ideology, whether for houses or urban projects, shows some great promise for architecture that defies the accepted ideas about vertical and horizontal planes, and about weight and permanence. There is a very distinct adventure of technology, computerisation, planes, and a stark architecture that reflects purity and simplicity.

Hadid's built work has won her much academic and public acclaim. Her best-known projects to date are the Vitra Fire Station (1994) and the LFone Pavilion (1993–99), both in Weil am Rhein, Germany; a housing project for IBA-Block 2 (1993) in Berlin, Germany; and most recently the Mind Zone (1999) at the Millennium Dome, Greenwich, London.

She has also completed furniture and interiors, temporary structures, exhibition designs, installations, and stage sets. Hadid received the British Architectural Awards Gold Medal in 1982, was honored with a CBE in 2002, and became the first woman to receive the Pritzker Prize in 2004.

John Hejduk

John Hejduk (1929–2000) was born in New York, USA, and studied at the Cooper Union School of Art and Architecture where he was dean for 25 years. He graduated from the Harvard Graduate School of Design with a Masters in Architecture in 1953. In 1955 he was appointed a lecturer at the Texas School of Architecture in Austin, Texas.

One of America's most visionary and original designers, Hejduk largely eschewed conventional practice by creating buildings with little or no socially redeeming values, denying the accepted notion that architecture should have a role to play in social activism.

Hejduk was associated with several schools of architecture including The Texas Rangers and The "New York Five" – a group of architects including Richard Meier who shared a common allegiance to Modernism in its purist form with its roots in the 1920s and the works of Le Corbusier. Though his designs were largely theoretical works on paper, his influence upon the graduates at Cooper Union was immense. His early drawings began as more or less rigid lines but evolved over his lifetime into elaborate, soft sketches. In 1997 his collection of drawings were purchased by the Canadian Center of Architecture. In the final 15 years of his life students, teachers, and others inspired by his work collaborated to bring his drawings to life.

His model Wall House (1969) contradicted the Modernist obsession with Functionalism, with each room resembling an exposed internal organ against a backdrop of a square wall. Hejduk's Bye House (Wall House 2), designed in the early 1970s, was finally constructed on a lakeside site in the Netherlands in 2001. A purely theoretical concept, its 5 ft (1.5 m) thick wall rises well beyond the roof line bisecting the living area on one side and the entrance hall on the other, with both spaces literally hanging off it. To emphasize the wall's abstract nature, it remains detached from the house itself, there to be perceived visually though not structurally necessary.

Hejduk never lost sight of the importance of the relationship between the shapes and forms of buildings and their immediate environments. His earliest drawings were obsessively centered around the interrelationship of geometric shapes such as frames, cubes, and grids, though they evolved over time into sophisticated combinations of colorful, abstract planes and curved masses.

Herzog and de Meuron

Herzog and de Meuron were one of the most influential architectural firms of the 1990s and their work has been widely published internationally. Both being born in Bäsel, Switzerland, Jacques Herzog (1950–) and Pierre de Meuron (1950–) met during their studies at the Swiss Federal Institute of Technology (ETH) in Zurich where they studied under Aldo Rossi, who left an indelible mark on their architectural sensibility. Their partnership was established in 1978 in Bäsel, near the French and German borders. In 1991 Harry Gugger (1956–) became a partner of the firm and in 1994 Christine Binswanger (1964–) also became a partner. In 2001 the firm was awarded the prestigious Pritzker Prize for their achievements in architecture.

Often associated with ideas familiar to minimalism in art, Herzog and de Meuron's architecture is characterized by its elemental use of form, its precise attitude towards architectural detail, and the innovative use of materials. Emerging in the aftermath of the Post-modernist fascination with ornament, the work of Herzog and de Meuron was prescient in the 1990s for its reductive aesthetics and seductive materiality.

Having completed a number of small projects in Bäsel in the first decade of their practice, it was the commission to design a storage building on an industrial site for confectioners Ricola in 1986 (completed in 1987), that launched the career of the firm. The elegantly simple building is rectangular in plan and enveloped by a layered timber facade, building an architectural language from the logic of its construction. A similar austere attitude towards materiality was developed in subsequent projects, such as their Bäsel Signal Box (1989–94), Goetz Art Gallery (1989–92) in Munich, and the Dominus Winery (1995–98) in the Napa Valley, California, which uses a monolithic stone gabion wall around its external perimeter, allowing light to penetrate through the gaps in the stones.

As well as their more well-known public buildings, Herzog and de Meuron have completed a number of influential housing schemes, at a range of different scales. Their elegant urban apartment housing at the rue des Suisses (1998–2000) in Paris, France, uses operable steel shutters to create a textured facade to the building while creating simple but well-organized internal relationships. A similar strategy is employed in the Apartment and Commercial Building, at Schutzenmattstrasse in Bäsel (1984–93). The firm have used single-house projects to further explore concepts of materiality and architectural form in their practice. Their Stone House in Ligurie, Italy (1982–88), explores stone in a creative way while their House in Leymen, Ht Rhin in France (1996–97) explores the typology of the house and its traditional representation in architectural form.

More recent projects from Herzog and de Meuron, such as the Prada Epicenter (2003) in Tokyo, Japan, and their stadium in Munich (2006), have looked at the synthesis between skin and structure. Their commission to build the new National Olympic Stadium in China has allowed the firm the opportunity to explore these ideas of synthesis on an even larger scale.

Josef Hoffmann

Josef Hoffmann (1870–1956) was born in Pirnitz, Moravia (now the Czech Republic), and studied architecture at the Academy of Fine Arts in Vienna under Otto Wagner, whose innovative theories of a serviceable, Modern architecture profoundly affected his outlook. He won the Rome Prize in 1895, and established his own office in 1898. He taught at the Vienna Kunstgewerbeschule from 1899 until 1936.

In 1897 Hoffmann, along with artist Gustav Klimt and others, founded the Vienna Secession, a group of revolutionary artists and architects who aimed to reinvigorate the Arts and Crafts by applying abstract, pure, and decorative forms to the designs of buildings, furniture, glass, and metalwork.

In 1903, with Koloman Moser and Joseph Maria Olbrich, he helped found the Wiener Werkstatte, an Art Nouveau spin-off dedicated to the concept of "a total work of art" – that art and beauty should be essential prerequisites for all features of functional design. Their collaboration resulted in Moser House (1903) in Vienna, Austria – a large house featuring a stucco exterior in the Pre-modern style.

In 1905 Hoffmann and the Werkstatte artists designed the magnificent and influential Palais Stoclet in Brussels. Every surface, detail, and adornment, is an expression of harmony and beauty, from the gray marble facade and bronze fittings, to the graceful garden arrangement, and concert hall decorated in multi-colored marble. The crowning glory is the luxurious dining room, decorated with black-and-white marble, rare timbers, and gold-imprinted leather furniture. Hoffmann designed the silver table decor and silverware, while Klimt added the finishing touches of mosaic friezes with gold, white, and multi-colored tiles, featuring abstract patterns, spiraling, stylized trees and, famously, two figures embracing.

Following the Palais Stoclet, Hoffmann designed many other residential properties including the Skywa–Primavesi Villa (1913–15), and the house of Sonja Knips (1924), both in Vienna; and three Czech Republic dwellings – a "fairytale" mansion (1914) for the Primavesi family in Kouty nad Desnou; a house for Sigmund Berl (1919) in Bruntal; and a house for Franz Grohmann (1920) in Vrbno pod Pradedem.

Hoffmann's works combined practicality and simplicity of production with sophisticated and inventive ornamental details and geometric components. His functional, yet eye-catching interior designs were an important precursor of the Modernist and Art Deco movements. His later highly individualistic works, with their grids and squares, functional clarity and abstract purity, anticipated the Bauhaus movement.

Steven Holl

Steven Holl (1947–) was born in Bremerton, Washington, USA. In 1971 he graduated with a degree in architecture from the University of Washington and did postgraduate work at the Architectural Association in London in 1976. He founded Steven Holl Architects in New York in 1980. In 1989 he became a tenured professor at Columbia University and has taught at the University of Washington, Seattle; the Pratt Institute in New York; and the University of Pennsylvania, Philadelphia.

Holl's major residential works include the Van Zandt House (1982–83) in East Hampton, New York, and the Berkowitz-Odgis House (1984–88) on Martha's Vineyard, Massachusetts. His inspiration for Berkowitz-Odgis House came from a local Indian legend that involved stretching skins across the skeletal carcasses of beached whales. Holl's approach was to place the frame on the outside, which carries and anchors the home's veranda. Posts descending from the porch receive the island's naturally growing vines.

In 2005 Holl experimented with the principles of prefabrication with his glimmering, sculptural Turbulence House – a 900-sq-ft (83-sq-m) residence made from 31 digitally shaped pieces of unpainted aluminum which act as both the house's structure and skin. Built for his friend, the artist Richard Tuttle, on a wind-swept mesa in northern New Mexico, a breezeway beneath the structure allows cooling winds to pass underneath. Solar panels in the roof generate enough electricity to cover all the domestic needs in a day. Storm water is collected for recycling and the majority of its windows are north facing to minimize heat gain. Turbulence House reflects Holl's fascination with the potentials of modern science and what he sees as the poetic nature of space.

In 2001 *Time Magazine* voted Holl "America's Best Architect" and over the years his firm has collected countless accolades including the Alvar Aalto Medal in 1998 and France's 2001 Grande Medailles d'Or Académie d'Architecture.

Michael Hopkins

Michael Hopkins (1935–) was born in England and studied architecture at the Architecture Association in London where he graduated in 1964. After collaborating on the design of new halls of residence at Leicester University with Leonard Manasseh, he helped design an industrial estate in Yorkshire with Norman and Wendy Foster. He then founded his own firm in 1976, which has since earned numerous awards including the Royal Institute of British Architects Royal Gold Medal. Important commissions soon followed for the new headquarters of the Inland Revenue in Nottingham and the opera house at Glyndebourne.

Hopkins' use of high-tensile structures and a high-tech, industrial approach to architecture rarely results in purely functional designs. His Portcullis House (1998–2001), the offices designed to house 210 Members of Parliament in London's Westminster "Parliamentary Campus," remains one of his best-known works. Bombproof and built to last 200 years, the support within its perimeter is provided solely by six columns connected by huge concrete arches. Its impressive facade is topped by 14 oversized bronze chimneys, which line the top of its three-story-high roof, drawing used air from the building.

His own home, Hopkins House (1975–76) in Hampstead, is a residence of note. It is completely glazed on its northern and southern elevations in frameless glass, with silver profiled steel sheeting contributing to its industrial appearance. Cleverly sited, it is barely noticeable from the road.

Hopkins' designs are difficult to categorize due to their extremely varied nature. Contrast the perceived austerity and brooding nature of Portcullis House to his ethereal, tent-like curving grandstand at Lord's Cricket Ground (1987). His design for London's Evelina Children's Hospital (2003) contains innovations such as single-nurse stations scattered throughout instead of an all-in-one isolated and hard to find location, and an absence of long and depressing corridors. Pull-down guest beds in the wards allow parents to be close to their children.

His design for a new chemistry laboratory and surrounding structures at Princeton University (US) showcases his ability to create spaces that encourage interaction as well as accommodating the technical needs of a complicated research building.

Michael Hopkins was the recipient of a CBE in 1989 and was knighted for services to British Architecture in 1995. He also served on the council of the Royal Institute for British Architects from 1991 to 1994.

Arata Isozaki

Arata Isozaki (1931–) was born in Oita, Kyushu, Japan. In 1961, he completed his Doctorate in Architecture at the University of Tokyo under Kenso Tange, and in 1963 he established his own practice, Arata Isozaki and Associates. He has lectured at the University of Tokyo, the University of California in Los Angeles, Harvard University, and Columbia University as a visiting professor, and is active in lectures, symposiums, architecture exhibitions, fine arts exhibitions, and private exhibitions all around the world.

Isozaki's approach to architecture is successfully integrating both eastern and western ideas into a harmonious whole. He is a member of that small club of contemporary Japanese architects who have obtained widespread international fame for their inventiveness, boldness of form, and color. Geometric shapes – circles, triangles, pyramids, spheres, and cubes – are all very much the signature of Isozaki's work, as is his scrupulously careful detailing. His work in the late 1960s was influenced by the Metabolism school: A style of architecture focusing on creating a dynamic environment that can live and grow by discarding its outdated parts and regenerating newer and more viable elements. The Joint Core System that he developed in 1960 was essential to the Metabolism movement and was influential to Tange, his former teacher.

Arata Isozaki achieved international status as an architect when he designed the highly acclaimed Palladium Discotheque (1985) in New York City – an amalgam of flashing lights, high-rise television sets, grids that rotated and gyrated kinetically, and theater-set interiors for this vulnerable renovated movie house.

His residential projects are found in Japan and include Nakayama House (1964) in Oita, Yano House (1975) in Kawasaki, Hayashi House (1976–77) in Fukuoka, Kaijima House (1976–77) in Tokyo, Aoki House (1976–77) in Tokyo, and Iwata House (1985–86) in Oita. The houses are characteristically built of concrete and his use of glass and architectural forms such as barrel vaults, pyramidal skylights, and curved walls mark his designs. These are elemental forms that are commonly used in Isozaki's architecture. Sunken courts and yards are very distinctive of his style. His exterior designs are a rich palette of materials and forms and his interiors are minimalist with some rigorously geometric compositions of white walls, pure proportions, and neutral space. Primarily, Isozaki deals with each space as a place of contemplation.

Isozaki became an Honorary Fellow of the American Institute of Architects in 1983, and an Honorary Member of the Bund Deutscher Architekten in West Germany in 1983. He has received the Architectural Institute of Japan Design Prize (1967 and 1975), the Special Expo Prize (1970) from the Architectural Institute of Japan, and the Mainichi Art Prize in 1983.

Hugh Jacobsen

Hugh Newell Jacobsen (1929–) was born in Grand Rapids, Michigan, USA, and educated at the University of Maryland. In 1954 he received his architectural diploma from the Architectural Association in London and the following year earned a Bachelor in Architecture from Yale University. He has had his own practice in Washington DC since 1958, and in 1971 was made a Fellow of the American Institute of Architects.

Jacobsen earned a reputation for his historically faithful restorations of Washington DC townhouses. In 1963 he became intrigued with the American pavilion style of architecture. Though he certainly pays homage to vernacular forms, with many of his designs reminiscent of the barns and outbuildings of a bygone rural America, they nevertheless remain unmistakably modern.

An affinity for picturesque compositions can be seen in his Beech House (1963), with its pyramidal forms defining interior spaces and multiple roof apexes to break down its apparent scale. His Buckwalter House (1982) in Pennsylvania is a rectangular, telescopic design reminiscent of early Quaker homes, with each of its units diminishing in size at regular intervals. The main facade recalls a colonial farmhouse, but its mirrored sides, light-filled interiors, and completely glazed end gable exposing a steel-reinforced balloon frame, are clearly modern.

His awards and citations span four decades, from the American Institute of Architect's 1962 Award for Excellence for the Robert Shord House to the 1996 DuPont Benedictus Award for his extension of the West Terrace to the US Capitol building in Washington DC. He has won six National Honor Awards from the American Institute of Architects. Jacobsen has been a juror on over 50 AIA award programs, and is a contributor to periodicals such as the *Architectural Record* and the *Architectural Digest*.

Philip Johnson

Philip Cortelyou Johnson (1905–2005) was born in Cleveland, Ohio, USA, and was educated at Harvard University, Cambridge, Massachusetts. Johnson was a product of East-Coast money and political influence, and as Director of Architecture at the Museum of Modern Art, New York, from 1930 to 1934, and again from 1946 to 1954, Johnson became a major intellectual propagandist for bringing Modern architecture to the notice of Americans. His 1932 exhibition, Modern Architecture: International Exhibition, drew attention to the European masters of the Modern Movement, though this exhibition drew criticism for its attention to formalism. By 1934 Johnson's architectural career was side-tracked by his serving as an activist for right-wing causes. With the world at war, Johnson enrolled in Harvard's Graduate School of Design in 1940, then under the leadership of Walter Gropius.

His first built building was a Cambridge house he built for himself using Mies van der Rohe's courtyard principle. This was offered as his Harvard thesis in 1942. In 1947 Johnson curated an exhibition on Mies van der Rohe, and this returned him to the central position in architecture he occupied before Word War II.

Johnson's political and cultural development in New York was long and hard, and at the age of 43 he built his first major building – the Glass House for himself at New Canaan, Connecticut, in 1949. In one compelling sweep, this house displayed a geometric structure and a calm and aristocratic interior, which represents the heart of his intellectual preferences. The inclusion of a seventeenth-century Poussin entitled *Landscape with the Burial of Phocion* sums up his belief in architecture as a high art.

While his writings are also important, the Glass House was a total testament to the glory of great architecture. Johnson often said he was a historian first and an architect second, and perhaps this is the reason why he took the radical step of declaring his intellectual supports.

Johnson made his Glass House deliberately transparent, and it was built as a paradigm to his beliefs. In order to make the invisible visible, Johnson was prepared to acknowledge the fact that his Glass House was "frankly derivative." The historical references brought to bear are almost dazzling in their ancestry. From Le Corbusier's Village Farm Plan of 1933, he took his house approach along the diagonal. He arranged his Glass House into separate blocks, following the organizing influence of Mies van der Rohe. By using sliding rectangles as a compositional device, Johnson acknowledged the influence of Theo van Doesburg. Next came Choisy, who proved that the Greek architects restricted the angle of approach to their buildings by exploiting the oblique. But no Johnson synthesis is complete without the site relationships to the German nineteenth-century architect, Karl Friedrich Schinkel. The cubical form of his Glass House owes its absolute shape to the major and minor massing of Claude Nicolas Ledoux. At the time of design, Mies van der Rohe's Farnsworth House was under construction, and Johnson learned a good deal from this direction. In thinking about the plan of his Glass House, Johnson borrowed the supremist circle (which became his bathroom) from the abstract painter Kasimir Malevich. The brick cylinder which forms the main motif, was a memory source from brick chimneys standing alone after a fire. Johnson deliberately arranged his interior like a seventeenth-century framed landscape, while using nature as a visual backdrop. At the same time the Glass House was furnished as a plea for richness.

Johnson never again matched the memorability of his Glass House, and in the years that followed he left a trail of confusion taking New York and other American cities by storm. By the late 1950s Johnson became bored with Modernism, and set about undermining it with much joyous enthusiasm for Post-modernism and Deconstructivist architecture. Whatever history makes of his last years of flamboyance – the all-glass Crystal Cathedral (1980) in Garden Grove, California, and the AT&T Headquarters (1984) in New York with its "Chippendale" roof (now the Sony Building) – it will always find a memorable place for his Glass House at New Canaan. These structures provide the epitome of Johnson's concern for architecture as an intellectual activity demanding excellence.

Louis I Kahn

American architect and teacher Louis I Kahn (1901-74) is considered one of the foremost architects of the twentieth century. He was born in Estonia, and moved to the United States of America as a child in 1906. He received a Bachelor of Architecture in 1924 from the University of Pennsylvania, where he learned from Paul Philippe Cret the essential doctrines of the Beaux-Arts tradition, and where he would later become an influential professor himself. He also taught at Yale University in the late 1940s and early 1950s.

Kahn's Philadelphia-based office began with predominantly residential work, such as the monumental, thick-walled Esherick House (1961) in Philadelphia, but became better known for larger scale institutional buildings and urban planning work, including renewal projects and proposals for Philadelphia's city center in the 1960s which featured ideas about separating pedestrian and vehicular traffic. Other well-known houses include the Norman Fisher House (1960) in Hatboro, Pennsylvania, the form of which is generated by two cubes that intersect to form courtyards. Both this project and the Esherick House feature double height living spaces.

Kahn first gained international recognition for the Yale University Art Gallery (1951–53) in New Haven, Connecticut, which is characterized by its open plan, achieved through the use of an innovative concrete space frame ceiling. Other well-known projects include the Kimbell Museum of Fine Art (1967–72) in Fort Worth, Texas, which cleverly provides diffused natural lighting by way of internal courtyards and skylights in the vaulted ceiling.

Kahn believed that an architect must respect and facilitate the tendency of each building material to act or be constructed in a certain way. His reaction to the International Style's analytical approach was to consciously engage the instinctual or "feeling" element of his mind in the design process. His process involved identifying the essence or spiritual dimension of a building type, then developing the concept to respond to the site and functional constraints of the individual project. Kahn believed in monumentality only when it is appropriate to the building type. Many of his most significant buildings are museums, churches, and synagogues. For example, the form of his National Assembly complex (1962–74) in Dacca, Bangladesh, is simple and bold, with the associated prayer hall positioned adjacent to the central assembly building to reinforce what he considered the spiritual aspect of a community gathering place.

Kahn is known for his revolutionary concept of separating or distinguishing "served" and "servant" spaces, as in the Jonas Salk Institute for Biological Studies (1959–65) in California, which is a complex of laboratory and study spaces in which the services are piped through separate floors rather than conventionally concealed by suspended ceilings or visible ducts. This separation is expressed in a different way in the Richards Medical Research Building (1957–61) at the University of Pennsylvania, in which three laboratory towers are arranged around a central tower which houses services.

Kahn was recognized with many awards, most notably the American Institute of Architects Gold Medal in 1971, and the Royal Institute of British Architects Royal Gold Medal in 1972.

Frederick Kiesler

Frederick Kiesler (1890–1965) was born in Vienna, Austria. He was an architect, theater designer, artist, and theorist. Kiesler studied at the Technical University and at the Academy of Fine Arts in Vienna from 1910 to 1916. He had a creative European career as a theater and art exhibition designer in the 1920s, during which time he was a member of the De Stijl – a group of artists, sculptors, writers, and architects advocating greater geometric simplicity in art and architecture. Kiesler lived in the United States of America from 1926 until his death. During that time he collaborated with the Surrealists and knew most of the major figures in the avant-garde art world. Though he was an architect by trade, he built only one building in his lifetime: The Shrine of the Book (1965) in Jerusalem. For much of his career, economic circumstances forced him to work in window display design, teaching, writing, sculpture, and painting, often producing works in these fields radically ahead of his time.

Perhaps Frederick Kiesler's Endless House (1947–61) – a vision that did not reach fruition as a built form – should be raised to the status of twentieth-century icon. Kiesler who worked with Adolf Loos, was influenced by Functionalist theories and produced a concept for a house that predates the fluid and continuous forms of today. The Endless House proves to be a source for the imagination, constantly borrowed upon by architects of the last four decades. Kiesler is suggested to have developed his Endless House from Loos' Raumplan (space-plan). The Raumplan is simplified as an attempt to create an independent, flexible space within a continuous shell. Kiesler was a visionary, producing drawings on the Endless House that echo current ideas of continuity of space and open-ended process within design. Among architects that have been influenced by his designs, Ben van Berkel and Caroline Bos of the architecture firm UN Studio, appear to have applied, or adapted, some of Kiesler's ideas and research within their Mobius House (1993–98). A designer of furniture and architectural concepts, Kiesler's Endless House was exhibited within the Museum of Modern Art, New York. Whilst opposing the de-humanised apartment of the 1920s, Kiesler was able to begin somewhat of a revolution of architectural form, which manifested within the imaginary project that he called the Endless House.

Pierre Koenig

Pierre Koenig (1925–2004) was born in San Francisco, California, USA, and studied at the University of Utah's School of Engineering. He received his Bachelor of Architecture at the University of Southern California in Los Angeles. The architect, lecturer, and author James Steele refers to Koenig as one of the major figures of Modernity in the United States today, and *Time Magazine* recently lauded his minimalist steel and glass residences as sleek and glamorous.

Koenig first came to prominence in 1959 with his collaboration on the Case Study House Program – a USC initiative to bring the steel and glass of the Modernist school to southern California and to study the application of industrial principles and materials to residential design. Years of living in Los Angeles had given Koenig an understanding of its hilly terrain and arid climate. His historic Case Study House No 22 (1960), also known as the Stahl House, is said to be the most written about Modernist residence ever, appearing to hover over its site in the Hollywood Hills, made impervious to earthquakes by the steel in its walls, cooled by prevailing breezes and warmed by the summer sun thanks to an expansive use of glass. Its long, cantilevered roof and floor overhangs combine to extend the viewer's eye to the ocean and horizon beyond.

Koenig's abstract compositions, his innovations with steel framing, and his use of natural ventilation for heating and cooling which makes air-conditioning obsolete, earned him praise and countless awards. Sadly, Koenig's dream of bringing cheap, attractive, and economical housing to southern California never materialized. His innovative natural air ventilation failed to attract sufficient interest in the age of air-conditioning. While people around the world continue to spend fortunes on split-system and ducted air-conditioning, Koenig was able to significantly lower the temperature of his Brentwood home simply by opening a ground-floor door.

Koenig taught at the University of Southern California School of Architecture for over 40 years. In 1996 he received the American Institute of Architects Lifetime Award and in 1999 was the recipient of the Gold Medal from the Institute's Los Angeles chapter.

Rem Koolhaas

Rem Koolhaas (1944–) was born in Rotterdam, the Netherlands. Formerly a journalist and screenwriter, he found his true calling as an architect and studied architecture at the Architectural Association in London between 1968 and 1972. He went on to become the principal of the Office for Metropolitan Architecture and of its research-oriented counterpart AMO. He is also the Professor in Practice of Architecture and Urban Design at Harvard University's Graduate School of Design.

Rem Koolhaas expands our perceptions of cities and civilization. His most provocative view is expressed in his 1978 book *Delirious New York: A Retroactive Manifesto for Manhattan* – an examination of Manhattan and a "search in the influence of the metropolitan masses and culture on architecture and urbanism." Koolhaas found that architects of his era were obsessed with the historic centers of Europe, "much to the detriment of modern architecture." He believed their activity threatened to completely deny, ignore, and ultimately repress crucial aspects of the modern world. These included factors like scale, numbers, technology, and variance with their ideal of a "rediscovered" history. This has led to confusion between what some architects consider "real history" and "fabricating history."

Koolhaas' important housing work includes the Boompjes Apartment Building in Rotterdam (1981), and housing at Kochstrasse and Friedrichstrasse in Berlin (1980), which show that Modernism can co-exist with a New Urbanism that abandons harmony and coherence; attributes that tear a historical city apart. The Nexus Housing project in Fukuoka, Japan, consists of 24 individual houses, each three stories high, packed together into two blocks. Each house has a private vertical courtyard providing light and space into the center. Koolhaas describes the wall surrounding the Nexus Housing estate as cyclopic. "A closed cyclopic wall wraps around the exterior of the blocks; escaping from the walls are floating rooflines, which resonate with the mountains that define the bowl of the city."

Koolhaas has also designed a number of private residences, including the Villa Dall'Ava (1991) at Saint Cloud in Paris, France; the Dutch House (1992–93) in the Netherlands; and the Maison at Bordeaux (1998) in Bordeaux, France.

Villa Dall'Ava is a floating glass box capped with a rooftop swimming pool. The client wanted two separate apartments as part of the design: One for the parents and one for their daughter. They also wanted panoramic views of Paris and the Eiffel Tower from the pool. Koolhaas conceived the house as a glass pavilion containing living and dining areas with two hovering, perpendicular apartments, shifted in opposite directions to exploit the view.

The Dutch House, built in a pine forest on fine sand, contains facilities for two permanent residents – the parents – and amenities for three adult daughters who are regular visitors. A floating deck supports the glass-walled parents' quarters. At ground level, a wall wraps around the living quarters and patio for the visiting daughters.

Maison at Bordeaux was designed for a man confined to a wheelchair. Koolhaas describes the building as three houses because it has three separate sections layered on top of one another. The lowest part is "a series of caverns carved out from the hill for the most intimate life of the family." The middle section is a smaller glass room where the wheelchair-bound husband has his private living area. The entire room is an elevator platform which rises and lowers to other levels of the house. Bookshelves line one wall of the elevator shaft. The upper level, which Koolhaas calls the "top house," has separate areas for the husband and wife and for their children.

Leon Krier

Leon Krier (1946–) was born in Luxembourg. He is an architect and urban planner whose architectural style has heralded some of the most important Neo-classical designs of the twentieth century. One of his most noted projects is the Poundbury "village" in Dorset, which he was commissioned to draw up for Prince Charles of Wales.

Krier studied at the Technische Hochschule in Stuttgart, but left after six months, dissatisfied with its Modernist teachings. By the age of 20, he had developed a strong and enduring belief in the Classical ideal of architecture.

In 1964 he began work for James Stirling in London, after which he taught at the Architectural Association in London and the Royal College of Art. He eventually opened a private practice in London in 1974. His fascination with industrialization and the ways in which it affects urban planning inspired Krier to turn to the nineteenth-century Neo-classical models of spatial zoning, which he believed were more humanitarian than those used in the twentieth century. He reproduced these formulas in projects such as the Royal Mint Square Housing Development (1974), as well as Spitalfields market in London where laneways and Classical architecture were incorporated. For 17 years, Krier worked as Professor of Architecture and Urban Studies at the Architectural Association and the Royal College of Art in London, at Princeton University, the University of Virginia, and as a Davenport Professor at Yale University until 1991.

In 1988, Krier was appointed to head the 20-year project to build up to 2,400 homes in Poundbury – Prince Charles' dream of a model village on the western edges of Dorchester, England. Poundbury challenges Modernist theories on planning and design. The convergence of various building types, such as social and private housing, alongside commercial and light industry removes a reliance on cars by allowing residents to work close to home. The narrow streets of the town control and slow traffic through the area, and parking spaces behind the houses have, for this purpose, been designed to prevent cars from blocking the streets at night. Stone is the preferred construction material, which has been used to acknowledge the English vernacular style and heritage of the area. The development encourages community spirit and gives priority to people rather than their vehicles.

Krier has also developed master plans for Washington DC (1985), the town of Atlantis (1986–88) in Tenerife, and Pliny's Villa (1982) in Laurentum, Italy. Krier took on Pliny's large-scale reconstruction of a European city in order to deal with the pressing socioeconomic concerns of the times. The village development is dictated by site views and constraints, and consists of many separate buildings, the functional hierarchies of which are reflected in their scale and design. Krier's theories also form part of the urban development recommendations of the Organization for Economic Cooperation and Development, and the European Union. His awards include the Berlin Preis for Architecture (1977), the Jefferson Memorial Medal (1985), the Chicago AIA Award (1987), the European Culture Prize (1995), and the Silver Medal of the Académie Française (1997).

Robert Krier

The older brother of Leon Krier, Robert Krier (1938–) was born in Luxembourg and is a leading proponent of New Urbanism – the creation of entirely new architecturally designed towns and communities. A protagonist of Post-modernism and one of the leading thinkers in the theory and practice of town planning, Krier is an exceptional draftsman, whose colorful and precise drawings resemble architectural caprices, demonstrating his objection to the dominance of Rationalism and Functionalism in architecture. Krier has lectured at Stuttgart, Lausanne, and Yale universities and in 1975 wrote the book, *Urban Space in Theory and Practice*.

The partnership of Rob Krier and Christoph Kohl has been based in Berlin since 1993. They are advocates of a city architecture that meets the practical needs of its inhabitants and contributes to the enhancement of the environment. Krier's first attempt at New Urbanism was the Ritterstrasse project (1977–80) – a residential quarter of 23 houses in a Berlin suburb. Their design of the Kirchsteigfeld development (1991–97) in Potsdam resulted in one of the largest construction projects undertaken in the former East Germany since reunification in 1990. Schools, town squares, cultural amenities, a central market, churches, shops, and offices all combine to create a totally planned and seemingly ideal, if not idealized, community.

Critics have argued that the creation of projects such as Kirchsteigfeld in Germany, Poundbury in England, and Seaside in Florida, USA (the location of the fictional and utopian community in the film *The Truman Show*) are inherently flawed by aspiring to create a sense of community by harking back to the past. Proponents claim that New Urbanism is pragmatic, allows for differing solutions to urban development, and has been commonplace in Europe for centuries and can be seen today in its medieval hill towns cloistered behind protective ramparts and city walls.

Currently the Meander project is being realized on a former industrial site in Amsterdam with 11 buildings comprising 220 residential units and related infrastructure all held together by three imposing hexagonal towers.

Kengo Kuma

Kengo Kuma (1954–) was born in Kanagawa, Japan. He studied architecture at the Graduate School of Engineering at Tokyo University, where he graduated in 1979. In 1999 he established the firm of Kengo Kuma and Associates. Between 1998 and 1999, he was a professor at the Faculty of Environmental Information at Keio University in Japan.

Kuma's approach to architecture could almost be termed "unique." His stated aim is to make architecture "disappear:" To try and thwart the presence of architecture by using transient materials that dissolve into one another and into the landscape. His Water and Glass Villa (1995) on the Atami coast, in Japan, overlooking the Pacific Ocean, reflects this approach. An all-glass construction, its three living areas are linked by glass bridges, giving the impression that the building barely exists at all.

His Kitakami Canal Museum (1999) in Miyagi, Japan, also blurs boundaries. With half the building underground, a seamless interplay between landscape and structure has been achieved, with transparent walls merging interior and exterior spaces.

Kuma has also strived to reinvigorate traditional Japanese building methods. His Bamboo House (2000) outside Beijing, China, rediscovers Japanese architecture through its use of bamboo as both a structural and aesthetic element. Unlike other wood that is processed and has its shape altered, bamboo cannot be processed and is used by Kuma in its original form to transfer light and wind effortlessly from one part of the house to another, and to display a delicate quality where charm can be found in its inherent weakness. Local materials are often employed by Kuma, such as cedar and rice paper, and he possesses a gift for rendering heavy materials fragile. In his design for the Nasu Stone Museum (1999) in Nasu, Japan, Kuma left openings in the exterior stonework to create a passage through which light and wind could pass, causing the walls to appear light, even transparent.

His prime concern always is to create an "architecture of experience;" to preserve the landscapes in which he builds through a strict adherence to minimalism deeply rooted in traditional Japanese architectural principles. His awards include the 1997 Architectural Institute of Japan Award and the 2002 Spirit of Nature Wood Award in Finland.

Kisho Kurokawa

Kisho Kurokawa (1934–) was born in Nagoya, Japan. He graduated from Kyoto University in 1957 and went on to study at the Tokyo University School of Architecture under Kenzo Tange.

Kurokawa is one of the most ambitious and prolific architects of our time and has fashioned a career of extraordinary dimensions. He says that Modern architecture in the twentieth century has been dominated by western thought and reason, and that "The Modern movement sought an internationalism, a universalism that transcended its own personalities and regional characteristics."

Early in his career Kurokawa rejected orthodox Modernism and a western obsession with mechanical analogy. In the 1960s he founded a Japanese avant-garde movement known as the Metabolists to combat this western Modernism. The Metabolist movement in Japan was governed by the "chief" of the group, Kenzo Tange, who was their leader in the early 1960s. They believed architecture should not be static, but rather capable of evolving over time with a building's structural elements becoming interchangeable, like pods or capsules which can be attached or removed at will. The group consisted of Tange, Maki, and Kurokawa, among others. They were all following a similar path and philosophy.

Many of Kurokawa's buildings explore the notion of *engawa* – the "in between space" where public realm and private space co-exist in harmony. His design, even in housing, is very streamlined and futuristic. Metal cladding and aluminum in linear patterns (primary shapes such as circles, squares, triangles, and pyramids) are very much a part of his work. Examples of this are his Karuizawa House (1974) in Karuizawa, and the Nakagin Capsule Tower (1972) in Tokyo. The Karuizawa House is a modular vacation house with a concrete core with metal attachments, while the Nakagin Capsule Tower is a hostel with an exterior which resembles a molecular structure. The 14-story complex has 140 prefabricated "living capsules" stacked at angles around a central core. The capsule units are installed into the concrete core by four high-tension bolts, and are detachable and replaceable. Each unit accommodates one person and has a circular window, a built-in bed, and a bathroom.

Kurokawa has received many awards and also some prestigious commissions for major buildings in Japan and throughout the world. In 1989 he was awarded the Grand Prix Gold Medal (sponsored by the Union of International Architects) for his Hiroshima City Museum of Contemporary Art. He has also received the Gold Medal from the Académie d'Architecture in France (1986) and the 48th Japan Art Academy Award (the highest award for artists and architects in Japan, 1992). He was the first Japanese architect to become an Honorary Fellow of the Royal Institute of British Architects and the Union of Architects in Bulgaria.

In 1994, The Art Institute of Chicago named their architecture gallery the "Kisho Kurokawa Gallery of Architecture."

Lake | Flato Architects

Ted Flato and David Lake are natives of Texas, USA. Flato attended Stanford University where he received a degree in architecture, and Lake gained his degree in architecture from the University of Texas in Austin in 1976. Their tactile, Modern approach to design has been seen in a wide range of projects from private residences, universities, and museums to civic spaces and corporate headquarters. Since establishing the firm of Lake/Flato in 1984 they have gained a reputation for seamlessly blending high tech with regional traditions in a quest for a Modern vernacular.

Their Chandler Ranch House (1993), high above the Llano River in central Texas, is firmly anchored to its site by blocks of weathered limestone collected from the surrounding area that act as sturdy corbeled piers and minimize the building's appearance. A long, arching entry porch creates a wide seating area at the bedroom wing, and leads to the main octagonal pavilion that serves both as a living room and year-round lookout.

The Hill Country Jacal (1997), a Mexican version of a lean-to, is situated west of San Antonio, Texas, on an escarpment above Bear Creek. A stone wall on its northwestern side shields the occupants from fierce winter winds while the simple cedar pole structure faces the prevailing summer breezes with a screened living space and porch stepping down the hill beneath an elongated shed roof.

Lake/Flato have received over 100 national and regional awards including the American Institute of Architects Honor Award in 1992, 1997, and 1999, as well as the prestigious National Firm Award in 2004, given for producing distinguished architecture over a minimum of 10 years.

Noel Lane

Noel Lane (1955–) was born in Helensville, New Zealand. He began his working life as a drain-layer before becoming an architect. He trained at the University of Auckland School of Architecture, and in the office of Manning and Mitchell, where he "cut his teeth" on the Judges Bay, Gibbs House (1982) in Auckland, and the Auckland University School of Music. As a training ground this practical experience was essential to his three-dimensional development.

Noel Lane's architecture packs a powerful punch in light, space, and materials. His houses display an intuitive flare and expressive potential. His most sculptural work is the Brick Bay House (1988–98) at Warkworth, overlooking the Hauraki Gulf. While this expansive site of land, sea, and sky threatens to overwhelm the designer, Noel Lane responds with all the uncompromising confidence of a "lion tamer."

In plan and section the Brick Bay House is no ordinary statement of domesticity. Its enormous tapering brick-chimney is both fetish and an archeological demonstration rooted in the earth with a megalithic quality, while at the same time anchoring the house to its hillside. This house recognizes complexity. Its roof breaks apart, revealing a communicating bridge which spans across the roof space. The three-storied interior is a burst of energy – its forms laden with Arts and Crafts imagery. The huge brick inglenook identifies the monumental presence of the living room – a space which also carries a roof of demolition timber. Above the dining room is a copper-sheathed room which is held aloft by nikau-like columns, reminiscent of the only palm tree native to New Zealand. This spatial complexity is reflected on the exterior, which carries a broad roof with wide eaves sheltering the walls. The whole design offers a profound shock to the earthly paradise of New Zealand, as it opens up to a magnificent panorama of the vast Pacific Ocean.

In 1999 Noel Lane returned to this site to provide a tennis pavilion which doubles as an elegant guest-house. He used a surfboard roof-form of pine boards, which is supported on slender steel poles above glass walls. This pavilion is an exquisite spatial experience, immaculately detailed to a Constructivist perfection rarely encountered in New Zealand.

Denys Lasdun

Denys Lasdun (1914–2001) was born in London, England. One of his country's most eminent architects, his career spanned the entire Modernist era. Dubbed "the grandfather of Modernism" in his later years, Lasdun trained at the Architectural Association School of Architecture before earning an MBE with the Royal Engineers during World War II.

Lasdun was an unashamed proponent of concrete construction. His design for the Royal National Theatre on the South Bank of the Thames involved massive proportions of exposed concrete which he believed would weather over time, producing lichen and fungi growths that would ultimately make it a seamless part of the river; an extension of the Thames' riverbanks. However, the massive scale of the project combined with its exterior of thick, bush-hammered concrete slabs, brought Lasdun much criticism from public and peerage alike, with Prince Charles commenting it was "a clever way of building a nuclear power station in the middle of London without anyone objecting." Despite this, Lasdun nevertheless chose to have its terraces slope away from the River Thames, much like an embankment, thus draining it of the monumental presence it could so easily have possessed.

Lasdun strongly believed that architecture has a social role to play and was a proponent of the theory that buildings should foster a sense of belonging and of community. Concerned that Modernists were failing to follow the examples of successfully integrated communities, he designed Keeling House (1957–59) in the East End suburb of Bethnal Green in London. A cluster block of four towers surrounding a central courtyard, they were designed to face one another in the hope of encouraging social contact. Instead of corridors there were laundry areas between the entrances and the apartments to encourage socializing. Keeling House, however, soon exhibited many of the social problems that bedevil council estates everywhere and the social integration evident in more traditional housing failed to materialize. Despite this, Keeling House and other Lasdun landmarks illustrate his belief that Modernism properly applied can improve the lives of its residents.

Though many of his creations drew controversy, Lasdun is now regarded as a hero of Modernism, with a disproportionately large number of his works being listed as architecturally and historically important structures. Lasdun always claimed that his best works were imbued with a spirit that would see them through. In 1977 Lasdun received the Royal Gold Medal from the Royal Institute of British Architects.

John Lautner

John Lautner (1911–94) was born in Marquette, Michigan, USA. He was an influential American architect who built his reputation doing affluent residential buildings in the hills of Los Angeles, California. His architecture is characterized by its dynamic use of structure, free-flowing planning, and the integration of high-tech gadgetry. His work built upon the organic principles of Frank Lloyd Wright to develop an original and idiosyncratic architectural language that was instrumental in the evolution of the architectural identity of Los Angeles.

Lautner started his architectural career as an apprentice to Frank Lloyd Wright, having earlier studied to become a teacher. His time in Wright's studio, where he lived with his wife for six years, was highly influential and shaped his attitudes towards architecture. In 1938 Lautner left Wright to move to Los Angeles where he started his own practice. Among his most influential early work was the roadside cafe Googie's (1949) which used dynamic forms to attract the attention of passing motorists. However, Lautner is recognized principally for his residential buildings which have become iconic, particularly the UFO-shaped Chemosphere House (1960) which is perched above the Hollywood hills on the famous Mulholland Drive. Other Californian houses by Lautner include Garcia House (1962), the Silvertop House (1956–74), the Elrod House (1968), and the Stevens House (1968). Some of Lautner's most spectacular works occurred late in his career, demonstrating his mastery of materials and innovative construction methods. In particular the sculptural use of monolithic concrete in the vast Arango Residence (1973) in Acapulco, Mexico, and the complex geometries embedded in his Pacific Coast House (1979–90) in California are among his most enduring architectural statements.

Lautner's buildings have been widely disseminated in the popular media, appearing in a number of movies (such as the 1971 James Bond classic *Diamonds Are Forever*), TV shows such as *The Simpsons*, as well as *Playboy* magazine and *Gentlemen's Quarterly*. Despite its proliferation in popular culture, Lautner's work has not been widely recognized in the architectural media, and it is only after his death in 1994 that his work has been more broadly appreciated.

Jules Lavirotte

Jules Lavirotte (1864–1924) was born in Lyons, France. From 1888 to 1892 he studied architecture at the École des Beaux-Arts in Lyon and was a pupil of Antoine Georges Louvier. Immersed in the Art Nouveau movement that was sweeping France at the time, and inspired by the works of Charles Chedanne, Victor Laloux, and Edouard Niermans, Lavirotte began to develop a keen interest in ornamentation, particularly of doorways and facades, often depicting sensuous human figures intertwining with plants and each other.

Lavirotte decorated his first block of apartments at 151 rue de Grenelle, in Paris, with a colored enameled brick in a conservative design which held few clues of the eroticism to come. In 1899 he decorated another block of apartments at 3 Square Rapp, using a profusion of stonework on the doorways' interior sections with the exterior a profusion of stained glass and ceramic tiles adorned with sexually promiscuous figures. He was commissioned for this work by the apartment's occupant Alexandre Bigot, who wanted a facade that would bring him notoriety.

His masterpiece, however, is universally regarded to be the entry portal of 29 avenue Rapp, for which he won an international design award. Lavirotte won the Concours de Façades de la Ville de Paris three times including in 1905 for his work on 34 avenue de Wagram. His increasing maturity and complexity can easily be seen as nearly all his works appear in the same Parisian block, and his elaborate designs soon had many imitators. However, his unconvincing and, at times, banal arrangement of figures have failed to see him regarded alongside other masters of the Art Nouveau era.

Le Corbusier

Le Corbusier (1887–1965) was the spiritual leader of the Modern movement. Through his public buildings, he exerted the most powerful form-giving influence on the architecture of the twentieth century. His public creations have tended to overshadow his contribution to domestic architecture. While not as domestically prolific as Frank Lloyd Wright, his early contribution can be reduced to houses in the Purist tradition, while his more mature houses are the regional product of a Mediterranean sensibility.

Born in the watch-making town of La Chaux-de-Fonds in Switzerland, Charles Edouard Jeanneret-Gris (his birth name) achieved fame, at the age of 30, with his Villa Schwob (1916), which was called the "Turkish villa" by the locals. It was the first flat-roofed, concrete house for the elite of the Chaux clockmakers, and it was the last building he built in La Chaux-de-Fonds. It was also the only early house that he deemed to write about in his journal *L'Esprit Nouveau.*

Moving to Paris in 1917, he became determined to make his way as an architect. Under the tutelage of Amédée Ozenfant, Le Corbusier came to understand the eternal values and Purist principles found in the Modern tradition. According to this classical horizon, architectural value could only be measured against absolute timeless standards. These were the Classical principles that were to drive the ideology of the machine age. In his 1923 book *Vers une architecture (Towards a New Architecture)* he argued that a "house was a machine for living in." Through Purism, and through countless lectures, Le Corbusier sought to bring art and technology together in harmony, in order to relate to "the spirit of the age."

Le Corbusier's Parisian houses grew out of a desire to renounce the decorative effects of Cubism. This movement sought Classical values – logic, clarity, simplicity, and an ordered calmness. Poetically Le Corbusier wrote, "Architecture is the masterly, correct and magnificent play of volumes brought together in light." This was the force which defined his white-painted Purist villas. His best four are: The La Roche-Jeanneret Villas (1923–25) in Auteuil, Paris; the Villa Stein at Garches (1927), Paris; two exhibition houses at the Weissenhof Estate (1927), Stuttgart; and the Villa Savoye at Poissy (1928–29), outside Paris.

The Villa Savoye is a pristine house with a spatial richness. As a paradigm of Modernism, Villa Savoye is a horizontal white slab standing on *pilotis* (concrete poles). The plan of the building is an articulated square with a ramp passing through the middle of the villa. The kitchen, bathroom, and living quarters are grouped on the *piano nobile* (the main floor) around a roof terrace (which contained a solarium) open to light and sunshine. This was Le Corbusier's clearest statement of a Purist villa. It was a unique house for a rich Parisian banker, and it recalled the ridges and decks of an ocean liner. In other words it looks like a "machine for living in." The Villa Savoye was not lived in a great deal during the 1930s, and today, technically restored, it remains a listed building – a historic manifesto for Purism.

Following World War II, Le Corbusier came back to architecture a changed man. He renounced the smooth and precise values of his Purist years, and embraced plasticity in rough textured concrete and brickwork with a "primitive" vengeance. In the process he turned the Modern movement on its head. Gone were the sweet-pea colors of his early houses; gone were his Purist hymns to machine morality, and in came the force of a Mediterranean personality – the sea, sand, and sunshine – sustained by his summer visits to his log cabin at Cap Martin, in the south of France. His best family houses are: Sarabhai House (1951–55) in Ahmedabad, India; Shodhan House (1956) also in Ahmedabad, India; and the two Jaoul Houses (1954–56) at Neuilly, Paris. These houses all break with Le Corbusier's white villas of the 1920s. The difference between the two periods of work is pronounced by the Jaoul interiors, which used sculptural elements, plywood paneling, and the warm hue of brickwork and yellow and blue panels. The overall experience was rich and substantial – even sensual.

The three houses that Le Corbusier designed for influential families in Ahmedabad required a different approach. These Indian houses required shade and coolness of air for living. This opened up new creative opportunities in brick and concrete, where Le Corbusier robustly attempted to deal expressively with the Indian climate.

Arguably his three-storied Jaoul houses in Paris, built in concrete and rough brickwork, confirm Le Corbusier's regionalism. The construction was complicated by the need for two separate houses on a small Parisian site, and the budget was limited. Using concrete frames, Catalan vaults, and brickwork, these houses capture a sense of Parisian urbanity in primitive materials. The brickwork walls were left natural, while the interior walls were plastered to avoid condensation. The kitchens were incorporated into the living area. In these Parisian houses, Le Corbusier embraced the desire for urbanity, while providing a psychic refuge for the occupants.

Le Corbusier's domestic architecture commands our emotional and intellectual attention. His life and work provide a series of expressions defining his creative journey. If his architecture differs from the herd instinct, it is because he had the capacity to endure creative isolation. This irony may be complex, but the message is plain. His final houses were more human and personal than his houses of the 1920s, but the difference between the two periods is one of degree, not of kind.

William Lethaby

William Lethaby (1857–1931) was born in Barnstaple in Devon, England. When only 14 years of age he began working for a local architect before moving to London in 1879 to work under one of the most sought after architects of his day, Norman Shaw. Noted more for his writings and subsequent influence on the development of art education than for his abilities as an architect, he founded the Arts and Crafts Exhibition Society and in 1900 became the first Professor of Design at the Royal College of Art. In 1906 his concern for the preservation of old buildings saw him appointed Surveyor of Westminster Abbey.

In 1891 Lethaby wrote what was to become one of the most pivotal books ever written on architecture: *Architecture, Mysticism and Myth*. In his book, Lethaby argued that architecture could only be a valid pursuit if it assimilated symbolic imagery reflected in humanity's relationship to the environment. This idea profoundly influenced subsequent generations of architects, influencing the teaching methods of, among others, Frank Lloyd Wright and Walter Gropius. Lethaby's insistence on the use of ancient geometrical shapes in determining design in effect marked a resurgence of ancient temple design principles using a synthesis of circles, squares, and crosses.

From 1894 to 1918, Lethaby was art adviser to the London County Council where he helped to found the Central School of Arts and Crafts in 1896, of which he was Principal from 1902 to 1911.

Lethaby's Melsetter House (1898) on the Orkney Islands is one of the finest surviving examples of the Arts and Crafts movement, built for the Midlands industrialist Thomas Middlemore over an earlier building dating back centuries. It embodies all the movement's themes of strength, simplicity and of harmony with nature.

Lethaby was also a consummate furniture designer, producing many pieces that eschewed the principles of the Arts and Crafts style – minimal ornamentation and embellishment but with an emphasis on quality materials and construction.

Daniel Libeskind

Daniel Libeskind (1946–) was born in Lodz, Poland. He originally studied music in Israel but abandoned his performing career to study architecture at the Cooper Union for the Advancement of Science and Art in New York. He completed this degree in 1970 and in 1972 finished a postgraduate degree in the History and Theory of Architecture at the School of Comparative Studies at Essex University in England. He became an American citizen in 1965.

In 1989, Libeskind won a high-profile competition to design the Jewish Museum in Berlin, for which he received praise for his ability to fuse history, memory, and structure. From this venture he acquired many other distinguished projects such as the Imperial War Museum North (1997) in Manchester, England, where he produced the aluminum-clad east facade; the Graduate Student Centre at the London Metropolitan University (2004); and the most recently acclaimed commission to create the master plan for the reconstruction of the World Trade Center (the proposed Freedom Tower) in New York City. Libeskind was subsequently appointed Cultural Ambassador for Architecture by the US Department of State.

The practice of Daniel Libeskind has completed a range of building types, from major cultural establishments to residential schemes. His Deconstructivist architecture often integrates piercing shards with warping angles and sharp lines. His residential schemes include two high-rise housing developments in Sacramento, California (the Epic and Aura towers); and a condominium tower in Union City, New Jersey. The Epic development (2005–07), is a fifty-story tower specially positioned to take advantage of the best light and views to and from the residential units. The design of the building strives to reach a balance between the individual units (a private realm) and its presence in a city (a public domain). The Union City Condominiums (2008) are inspired by their unique location atop a 200 ft high (60 m) cliff of the New Jersey Palisades overlooking the Hudson River. The tower itself rises an additional 220 ft (67 m) and features a glass-and-steel curtainwall. Every unit is designed to take in the breathtaking views of the river. Private outdoor terraces are designed to integrate with each unit and complement the massing of the form.

Libeskind currently holds many positions including that of Professor at University of Pennsylvania, and holds the Frank O Gehry Chair at the University of Toronto and the Louis I Kahn Chair at Yale University.

Adolf Loos

Adolf Loos (1870–1933) was born in Brünn, Moravia then part of the Austro-Hungarian empire (now Brno in the Czech Republic), the son of a stonemason and sculptor. He was an architect and critic who condemned ornament, historicism, and those who attempted to nostalgically unify art with industry. Loos studied at the Royal and Imperial State College in Reichenberg, Bohemia 1887–1888, and then at the Dresden Polytechnick 1890–1893.

Loos was one of the first European architects to visit the United States of America, and from 1893 to 1896 he experienced New York, Philadelphia, St Louis, and Chicago, where he visited the World's Columbian Exposition of 1893.

On returning to Europe, Loos' field of critical thought encompassed the whole Viennese cultural life – a city rich in ambiguity and contradiction, where intellectuals turned art upside down. Loos was an architect opposed to all "styles." He believed that cultural progress was linked to the deletion of ornament from everyday objects, and to force builders and craftsmen to waste their time on decoration – that only hastened to render an object obsolete – was a crime. In 1908 he wrote an essay on the subject entitled, "Ornament and Crime."

As an architect he recognized the widening gap between the decorative arts and the practicalities of architecture. As an educator he founded his own school in 1912, though his program remained strongly influenced by Classicism. His students included Richard Neutra, Rudolf Schindler, and Paul Engelman – all were influenced by Loos' ideas.

As to be expected, his clients were mostly well-to-do intellectuals; people fascinated by the artistic world of Vienna. As an architect Loos believed in Humanism. He welcomed progress when it served people, and condemned it vehemently when it exploited them. Loos believed that "the Modern spirit was a social spirit." For him, using steel and concrete was not enough to become the basis of meaning and expression in architecture.

His Steiner House (1910) in Vienna – a "two-faced villa" – is his best-known residential work. It bears a certain visual relationship with his Michaelerplatz (1909–11) – a high-class store of "Goldman and Salatsch," and an important Viennese building which shocked the public with its flat, plain white walls and total lack of ornament. Loos thought the man who decorates his walls with erotic images was "a degenerate criminal."

Both works proclaim Loos' belief that ornament was a crime. The Steiner House was built for a wealthy textile manufacturer, whose wife was a graphic artist and painter. Viewed from the front, the three-storied Steiner House has a strangely curved metal roof attic, which was Loos' response to local building by-laws that required the street front to be no more than one story. Loos concealed the fact by having a two-storied attic which looked no more than a single story. The rear of the house was a very different story. The garden facade had a courtly *cour d'honneur* (principal court) but with its flat roof, smooth stucco-finished walls, and rectangular windows, it presented a very stark face to the garden.

Loos' image of Modernism was forthright and real because it anticipated the Purist revolution in architecture, which was just over the horizon. Yet, there is a distinct contrast in the Steiner House between its formal exterior and its much more humanly relaxed interior. This is an acknowledgement of how Loos viewed the public and private world. In retrospect, we can now see more clearly that the Steiner

House was a pioneering architectural effort evident in Loos' use of planar walls. His lack of traditional detailing was a valiant attempt to find a language of architecture nobly suited to the twentieth century. Loos argued that architecture would never move forward if it spent its energies in the copying of decoration. Loos condemned historicism and the educational methods in Viennese design schools that promoted these attitudes.

Berthold Lubetkin

The Russian-born architect Berthold Lubetkin (1901–90) was born in Tiflis, Georgia. He left for Moscow in 1917, just prior to the Russian Revolution, to enrol at a prestigious private art school. Under the influence of the Bolsheviks there emerged the concept of the "artist engineer," and a growing movement of these "Constructivists" such as Tatlin and El Lissitzy began an industrialized approach to architecture, the principles of which Lubetkin would remain an advocate of for the rest of his life. After studying architecture at the Warsaw Polytechnic in 1923 he moved to Paris and completed his studies at the École des Beaux-Arts.

His set design for a Parisian nightclub called the Club Trapèze Volant (1927), saw him emerge as a promising young architect. In 1931 he received a commission to design a house in London and within a year he had joined with architects Denys Lasdun, Maxwell Fry, Lindsay Drake and others to form "Tecton" – an abbreviation of the Greek word *architecton*, meaning architecture. Tecton's first commissions were for the Gorilla House and Penguin Pool at London Zoo. The Gorilla House contained screens to protect the primates from human infection, and the Penguin Pool had walkways for the penguins in the shape of a double helix – a Constructivist favorite.

Lubetkin and Tecton's design of the housing project Highpoint One in North London in 1935 predated Rob Krier's concept of New Urbanism by decades. The complex of luxury high-rise apartments contained everything its occupants could desire, with each apartment designed from the ground up with attention given to every detail, down to the hinges on its doors and the design of its tapware.

After World War II Tecton and Lubetkin continued to design public housing, notably the Spa Green Estate (1943–50) and the Priory Green Estate (1943–57), both in London, however, Tecton disbanded in 1948 when it became apparent the hoped-for commissions to rebuild post-war Britain would be hard to find in the conservatism of the time.

Lubetkin's great dream for the post-war years was Peterlee, a town to be designed and built on the Durham coalfields to house a 30,000-strong community. It was to be a brand new town in the midst of national austerity. When it became hopelessly mired in red tape Lubetkin resigned a bitter man; his career over but for a few scattered projects in the years that followed.

In 1982 he was awarded a Royal Gold Medal from the Royal Institute of British Architects, though he remained disillusioned about the state of architecture in Britain until his death in 1990.

Edwin Lutyens

Edwin Landseer Lutyens (1869–1944) was born in Surrey, England, and with the collaboration of Gertrude Jekyll, became the predominant English domestic architect of the first part of the twentieth century. Both Lutyens and Frank Lloyd Wright were acutely aware of the need of the house to engender feelings of shelter and security, and they made a compelling response to nature and the placement of the house within the garden.

The works of Lutyens were both original and complex. He had an almost mystical understanding of the architectural form in brick, tile, and timber. Lutyens is chiefly remembered because he built large houses with large budgets for rich people. While still a young man, Lutyens defined the conservative language of the "stockbroker belt" in Surrey. Here, Lutyens became an architect of flux and surprise, wit, anticlimax, and sheer delight. Today his houses are worth a small fortune.

In creating what was to become the domestic architecture of Surrey, Lutyens drew on the work of Philip Webb, William Lethaby, and Richard Norman Shaw. From these visionaries, Lutyens absorbed the ideals of honest craftsmanship, the timeless way of building, and the virtues of simplicity. In all of Lutyens' architecture the values of Gertrude Jekyll, along with picturesque sentiments inspired by Surrey lanes predominate. Indeed, in every grand house Lutyens designed, whether it was picturesque, Arts and Crafts, or Classically inspired, Lutyens made a complete personal statement about what a home should be in Edwardian England. In this designed equation, Lutyens' relationship with the house is proverbial. All his architecture evoked intuitive ideas and sentiments of home in England – the smell of lavender, the sight of hollyhocks, the taste of toast, the clunk of croquet mallets. Clearly, Lutyens knew a house had to be more than a mere building: It had to embrace nature and the garden, and it had to make an impression on the mind.

Lutyens was extremely fortunate early in his career to be introduced to Gertrude Jekyll, who was not only a woman of considerable culture, but at that time, the greatest gardening genius in England. Together they made magic at Munstead Wood, the Surrey home of Gertrude Jekyll (1893–97). By the end of the nineteenth century Lutyens, with the support of Edward Hudson, founder of the magazine *Country Life,* became the last great outstanding architect of the English country house.

Lutyens built Munstead Wood in a clearing, and paths were cut through the undergrowth so that the many thrilling aspects of the house were revealed as surprises at the end of leafy vistas. Lutyens also managed to ingeniously mask these paths, so that the approach through the shrubbery displayed a masterful integration of nature and traditional materials. One's response to Lutyens is almost instantaneous, for he managed to embrace everything that was considered essential to Edwardian splendor and upper-class domesticity.

As an architect he combined formality and naturalness. Natural materials and natural detailing were all brought together in a cosy, comfortable way, which supported – even enhanced – English "upper crust" domesticity. This was a very secure world, supported by servants, beauty, and class manners.

It would be difficult to find a more convincing example of his architecture than the Deanery Garden in Sonning, Berkshire, built between 1899 and 1902. Not only is it one of Lutyens' finest Romantic houses, but it was described by his biographer, Christopher Hussey, as a "perfect architectural sonnet." This house was completed in the dawning years of the twentieth century for Edward Hudson, a man who did more than most to promote the Edwardian dream. Hudson was the managing director of the magazine *Country Life* and one of Lutyens most influential patrons.

Lutyens as an architect was aware of the need for the house to provide a vision of shelter, privacy, security, and the way a house settles into its surroundings in nature. In this enviable task, Lutyens provided stability, order, wit, and spatial complexity.

His best houses and gardens are Munstead Wood in Surrey; The Deanery Gardens in Sonning, Berkshire; Tigbourne Court (1899–1901) in Witley, Surrey; Goddards (1899) in Arbinger, Surrey for Sir Frederick Mirrielees; The Hoo (1902), a garden pavilion, in Willingdon, Eastbourne, Sussex; the Garden at Plumpton Place (1928) in Plumpton, Sussex, for Edward Hudson; and The Viceroy's House (1912–31) in New Delhi, India.

Charles Mackintosh

Charles Rennie Mackintosh (1868–1928) was known as an architect, designer, and water-colorist and is considered one of the most talented and creative architects to have come out of Glasgow, Scotland. His architecture, interior design, and furniture came at the end of one architectural era and the beginning of another. As an architect he was more influenced by Charles Voysey than Edwin Lutyens. Mackintosh was a hard-headed architect. His buildings belong to the Northern tradition, in particular, his masterpiece, the Glasgow School of Art (1897–1909), is notable for the elegance and clarity of its spatial concept, its skilful exploitation of natural illumination, and the patient care that he lavished on detailing. For Mackintosh each design, whether for a chair, the interior of a room, or a building, was understood as a total work of art, and an endless source of delight. Nobody who has ever seen a Mackintosh chair would forget its visual enlightenment.

Mackintosh was the product of a wealthy industrial city, but he was born into a large family of 11 children in Glasgow. At an early age Mackintosh was determined to become an architect, and in 1884, aged 16, he was apprenticed to a local architect, John Hutchinson. Here he learned to draw and watercolor, and began to understand the design of furniture. On completion of a five-year apprenticeship he moved to the distinguished firm of Honeyman and Keppie, where he eventually became a partner. At the same time he completed his education at night school in the Glasgow School of Art, doing various drawing programs. From this rather pedestrian start, Mackintosh survived to become an architect deeply imbued with the idea of artistic freedom – a concept in harmony with the sensibility of Augustus Pugin, John Ruskin, and William Lethaby.

While he was with Honeyman and Keppie he did his best work – the Willow Tea Rooms (1902–04) for Catherine Cranston – where he designed not only the interior and furniture, but also the fabric. He also did two houses of real user-friendly importance: Windyhill (1900–01) for William Davidson of Kilmacolm; and the Hill House (1902–04) at Helensburgh for the publisher W W Blackie – which is the most distinctive of his domestic houses. Designed very much in the Scottish tradition, Hill House has a sculptured gable, battered chimney, and an asymmetrical grouping of elements: All traditional features which recall the Romantic work of Philip Webb and Charles Voysey.

Both these houses used logical plans, which were surmounted by traditional seventeenth-century Scottish forms, expressing the Romantic spirit of their time and place. In these houses Mackintosh made the house to form part of the landscape. He arranged the gardens to complement the long sweeping lines of the principal elevations. Each of these houses met the demands of their particular families, and they were beautifully detailed and furnished with meticulous attention, even the cupboards and linen-stores were heated by warming pipes. Mackintosh also used color through simple stencilled designs in delicate shades of green and rose, rhythmically repeated in his interiors. The drawing room of the Hill House was white with a bay window exhibiting a view that reached out to a panorama of the Clyde estuary. The bedrooms of both houses assembled beautiful pieces of individual furniture, with a dream-like reality. Mackintosh succeeded domestically because he received the full support of sympathetic clients who were willing to experiment.

To understand Mackintosh's contribution we must recognize his Scottish heritage – the baronial keep and use of solid walls with slit windows. He also used circular towers, corbels, and crow-stepped gables. This was Scotland's contribution to architecture, and Mackintosh absorbed this lesson, which he thought was appropriate to its cool climate. Mackintosh thought architecture was the synthesis of the fine arts and all the crafts – an idea which belongs to Lethaby's *Architecture, Mysticism and Myth* (1891).

Fumihiko Maki

Fumihiko Maki (1928–) was born in Tokyo, Japan, and studied architecture at the University of Tokyo, Harvard University, and Cranbrook Academy. His buildings are renowned all over the world for their fusion of eastern and western disciplines and incomparable technical precision, with Maki himself regarded a doyen of Japanese architecture. Maki is an Honorary Fellow of the American Institute of Architects and the Royal Institute of British Architects, and is a member of the Japan Institute of Architects and lectures widely throughout the world.

Maki returned to Tokyo after studying abroad in 1960, establishing his own practice and teaching at the University of Tokyo for 10 years where he served as Professor of Architecture. His design for Tokyo's Hillside Terrace Apartments (1969, 1973, 1976, 1992) – a unique, privately sponsored urban development that has been constructed in stages over thirty years – represents one of the greatest achievements in Japanese architecture in the post-World War II period.

In the 1960s Maki became a proponent of a new movement in Japanese architecture called Metabolism, believing architecture should not be static, but rather capable of evolving over time with a building's structural elements becoming interchangeable, like pods or capsules which can be attached or removed at will. Maki's concepts continued to evolve through the 1970s with designs of international civic projects of varying size and complexity. Award-winning large-scale projects include the Fujisawa Gymnasium (1984), the Wacoal Spiral Building Tokyo (1985), and the Tokyo Metropolitan Gymnasium (1990).

In 1987 he was the recipient of the Reynolds Award. In 1993 he was awarded the Prince of Wales Medal for Urban Design as well as the prestigious Pritzker Prize for a lifetime of achievement in architecture and buildings that are not merely expressions of the times in which we live, but are also destined to survive the vagaries of fashion.

Curzio Malaparte

Curzio Malaparte (1898–1957) was born Kurt Erich Suckert in Prato, Italy. He was an Italian writer, journalist, and social commentator who worked as a war correspondent in Finland and eastern Europe during World War II. In 1938 he designed what some commentators have described as "the most beautiful house in the world" – his sculpture in stone, the Villa Malaparte, on the isle of Capri.

Malaparte disliked what he saw as the "eclectic kitsch" that characterized much of what had been built along the rugged Capri coastline. His masterpiece in Punta Massullo, though born from sketches drawn by the famous Italian Rationalist architect Adalberto Libera, is now generally agreed among scholars to owe far more to Malaparte's own personal vision.

Villa Malaparte sits along a narrow ridge that points finger-like into the Mediterranean Sea and is famous for its lack of convention, seen in its ever-widening staircase that leads to a stunning roof terrace, its exterior color of Pompeiian red, and a fireplace with a glass backing so one can see the blue of the sea through the red of the flames. The house is now run by the Malaparte estate and has recently undergone an extensive restoration.

Robert Mallet-Stevens

Robert Mallet-Stevens (1886–1945) was born in Paris, France. He received his training from the École Speciale d'Architecture in Paris from 1905 to 1910. One of France's leading exponents of Modernism, his flair for architecture began to emerge in the 1920s after gaining initial notoriety for interior designs for houses and set designs for the Parisian theater scene.

Mallet-Stevens' first private house was his Chateau de Mezy in a wooded area west of Paris, which was intended to be a Modernist version of a traditional French chateau. Built from 1921 to 1923 for the couturier Paul Poiret, the pure white residence set on 11 acres (5 ha) boasted over 8,600 sq ft (800 sq m) of living area all built around a spectacular central staircase, complete with a 360° viewing platform overlooking the River Seine. Nine houses designed by Mallet-Stevens still stand in Paris today.

In 1926 Mallet-Stevens was commissioned to build the Villa Noailles at Hyeres, in the south of France. Extended over the years and decorated by Eileen Gray, Pierre Chareau, Francis Jourdan, and Theo van Doesburg, the villa boasts sea views, terraces, wrought-iron sunrooms and a Cubist garden. His Villa Cavrois (1929–32) in Croix, France, is a vast building with a series of terraces. Its yellow "briquettes" with stressed horizontal joints emphasize the general aspect of the house and led to its nickname, the "Cavrois boat." The interior is relatively traditional with detailed lighting and polychrome coloring. Villa Cavrois was partly altered from 1947 to 1955 by the architect Pierre Barbe and was classified as a National Historic Monument in 1990.

The bulk of Mallet-Stevens' architectural legacy stems from a 10-year period that includes hotel reception areas, cabins, private residences, and retail and commercial outlets. As a set designer he also collaborated with the painter Fernand Leger and others on Marcel L'Herbier's film *L'Inhumaine*, to which he contributed decor and furnishings in tubular steel with Art Deco overtones and upholstered in fabrics depicting Cubist imagery.

For the 1925 Paris Exhibition of Decorative Art, which has since become synonymous with the birth of Art Deco, he designed the entrance hall of the Ambassade Française and the Pavillon de Tourisme, on which he again collaborated with Leger and the musicians Francis Poulenc and Arthur Hunegger. The Paris Expo succeeded in establishing Mallet-Stevens as the archetypal avant-garde Modernist of his time, and in 1930 he was voted the inaugural president of the Union des Artistes Modernes.

Rick Mather

Rick Mather (1937–) was born in Oregon, USA, and educated at the Architectural Association in London, where he has run his own planning and urban design practice since 1973. He has designed numerous public and private buildings, specializing in the cultural and education sectors. All his designs, whether new buildings or renovations, pay particular attention to sustainable low energy.

Mather designed a Chinese restaurant which uses captured and recycled heat from the kitchen's woks to power the restaurant's hot water supply. He built a house without central heating for his sister in northern Canada, where temperatures drop to 40° below freezing. He commented, "That's done by energy conservation rather than solar power... We waste a lot of energy, that's what you want – to attack, rather than keep the waste, and have solar power to cover the waste. You design the problem out rather than applying therapy to the problem."

He uses such details as polished steel handrails, glass walls, and circular skylights in his highly original designs, and in his remakes of both heritage sites and tired urban streetscapes in Britain and the United States of America.

In 1992 Mather designed an extension in Hampstead, London, for an eighteenth-century cottage that was all glass – including the beams – after persuading local authorities that this was the best means of letting the integrity of the original structure shine through. This audaciously pioneering structure was designed to realize the client's desire for complete interaction with the garden. The almost external garden room, and new living, dining, and kitchen areas are flooded with light, and have transformed the way the residents use the house. Highly innovative in design, technology, and construction, the extension is built entirely of laminated glass columns, walls, beams, and roof, with heating supplied by a transparent layer applied to the glass.

Mather's Private House (1997) in Hampstead, London revolutionizes the concept of "house:" Its three stories extending outwards to sunny terraces and gardens on every level. Inside, double-height rooms with glass stairs, and floors over the swimming pool, allow natural light, and glittering reflections off the water to fill the house. Views to adjacent buildings are controlled by window placement, with translucent screens and strategic landscaping to provide privacy. The white exterior and interior walls set off the oak and slate floors, maple doors and wardrobes, blue glass pool tiles, and etched glass screens and railings.

As part of the regeneration of Glasgow's East End, Mather's "Homes of the Future" (1999), is a showcase residential development overlooking Glasgow Green. Mather designed the central 24-apartment block of the complex: A bold, sculptural facade of curving balconies facing south over the Green toward the river, with the rear overlooking a new landscaped urban square. Above the undulating balconies, a sky-deck with spectacular panoramic views connects to the neighboring building, and provides access to the two- and three-bedroom penthouses.

Mather has won many awards for projects such as the Wallace Collection (1995); the ARCO and Sloane Robinson Buildings at Keble College, Oxford (1995); London's National Maritime Museum (2000); and the extension of the Dulwich Picture Gallery (2002). Other award-winners include London's ZenSW3 restaurant (1987), *The Times* Newspaper headquarters in London's Docklands (1991), the University of East Anglia Climatic Research Unit (1994), Constable Terrace at the University of East Anglia (1995), and private residences in Hampstead.

Mather is a Trustee of the Victoria and Albert Museum, the Theatre Museum, and the British Architectural Library Trust. He has served on the councils of the Architectural Association and the Royal Institute of British Architects, and as a RIBA external examiner to several architecture schools. He has taught at the Bartlett University College, London, the Architectural Association, the University of Virginia, and the Harvard Graduate School of Design.

Bernard Maybeck

Bernard Maybeck (1862–1957) was born in New York City, USA, to German immigrants. After studying at the École des Beaux-Arts in Paris in 1882 he returned to the United States of America where he found work at the New York partnership of Carrere and Hastings. Seeing his opportunities there as limited, he moved to Kansas City and eventually to Berkeley, California. After an unsuccessful bid for the design of a new building at the University of California, Maybeck established an office in San Francisco where over 200 commissions were to follow for homes and churches.

In 1910 he defied all the rules of church architecture when the First Church of Christ Scientist was completed in Berkeley. The use of metal industrial windows, Gothic overtones combined with aspects of the Californian Craftsman style, and brilliant coloring of cast concrete have led some commentators to refer to it as the most significant ecclesiastical building in the United States of America.

After unsuccessful bids for the San Francisco City Hall and a courthouse in Dayton, Nevada, he was appointed the architect for the Palace of Fine Arts for the upcoming Panama-Pacific International Expo in 1913. Today, this is seen as Maybeck's great legacy to the city of San Francisco. The building is a kind of decaying Greco-Roman temple, with its magnificent domed rotunda, Corinthian columns, and semi-circular peristyle, all made from plaster of Paris and hemp fiber on a framework of wood and lathes. It was the cornerstone of Beaux-Arts Romanticism; an architectural triumph of unrivalled beauty.

Much of Maybeck's residential work before the 1906 San Francisco earthquake reflected his interest in Swiss, German, and English medieval styles. The house he designed for Howard B Gates in San Jose is Italian in design, yet its extended roof line, forming a cover for its elaborate Baroque balconies, gives the upper part of the house a Swiss feel. Natural light comes in from numerous rear windows and skylights. After the San Francisco earthquake, Maybeck looked to the villas of Pompeii for inspiration to create an earthquake-proof house of hand-mixed, poured concrete. The Andrew Lawson House (1907) became one of his most brilliantly colored buildings; its richness defined by the elaborate foliage design of the arches in the loggia.

Maybeck's homes conform to the northern California climate, and eliminate the distinction between indoors and outdoors. His Berkeley houses, such as Chick House (1914), Hunt House (1915), Whitney House (1915), and the Mathewson House (1919) make extensive use of balconies, rooms which open into gardens, and large cathedral-height windows that make the rooms seem larger than what they are. The lavish use of carved redwood and Gothic tracery windows characterize his homes. Like Frank Lloyd Wright, Maybeck believed that the home should blend in with its natural landscape.

In 1952 at 90 years of age, Bernard Maybeck was at last awarded the American Institute of Architects Gold Medal, mostly for works long since completed and in recognition of his uniquely Romantic, improvisational, and eclectic contribution to American architecture.

Thom Mayne

Thom Mayne (1944–) was born in Waterbury, Connecticut, USA. He was educated at the University of Southern California and Harvard University. Since 1972 he has run his own firm, Morphosis ("manner of formation"), which now employs over 40 architects. Also active in the academic world, Mayne is a founder of the Southern California Institute of Architecture, and is currently a professor at the University of California in Los Angeles.

Mayne has been called the "bad boy" and "angry young man" of American architecture, and is most renowned for his radical designs of numerous public buildings. Many of his buildings and precincts are multi-functional hybrids, and all aim to integrate the structure with elements of its environment.

Mayne's 6th Street Residence (1985) in Santa Monica, California, is a remodel of a former loft. It reflects its surroundings, while simultaneously resolving the opposing demands for privacy and interaction with society by using found objects. The foundations, floors, and external walls of the existing duplex are retained, while the wood frame, board, and cement composite structure of the renovation are left unconcealed. Ten remodeled steel pieces, made of discarded machinery, have been placed in the living space, forming the stairs, skylights, showers, and other functional elements. The exterior of the house is conventional, creating a facade of formality and protecting privacy, while the industrial discards on the inside reflect the reality of a high-tech world.

Some of Mayne's residential projects alter the concept of a traditional suburban home by blurring the boundaries between the interior and exterior. Crawford House (1990) in Montecito, California, has no obvious front or focal point, using a semi-circular arc to orient views toward the ocean and to enclose the house. The Blade House (1995) in Santa Barbara, California, uses an elliptical arc to the same effect, with an outdoor garden room that dominates the 4,800-sq-ft (446-sq-m) home.

The highly acclaimed Diamond Ranch High School, (1999–2000), on the outskirts of Los Angeles, is a succession of jagged shapes covered in corrugated metal, resembling troops marching up a steep chasm. The Hypo Alpe-Adria Center (2002) in Klagenfurt, Austria, combines office, bank, retail space, and a kindergarten, in a design that integrates both rural and urban qualities. Mayne comments, "...the bank headquarters itself erupts out of this pregnant, expectant form clad in sheet metal, declaring its status as a major cultural and civic institution and connecting the public forum with the street."

The Los Angeles Caltrans District 7 Headquarters (2004), blends, chameleon-like, with the exposed structural elements of the city, and evokes a feeling of being in and under the freeways.

Mayne is known for ignoring, or transcending, traditional limitations of materials and forms, and has been honored with numerous awards during his career. In 2005 he became the first American in 14 years to win the prestigious Pritzker Prize.

Richard Meier

American architect Richard Meier (1934–) was born in Newark, New Jersey and received his Bachelor of Architecture from Cornell University in 1957. His firm, Richard Meier and Partners, has completed an extensive body of work throughout the world, including museums, courthouses, and office buildings, as well as private and large-scale residential works. His best-known projects include the Getty Center in Los Angeles (1984–97) and the Frankfurt Museum of Applied Arts (1979–85) in Germany. Meier has taught at the Cooper Union, Princeton University, the Pratt Institute, Harvard University, Yale University, and the University of California in Los Angeles.

His work gained widespread attention with the publication of the book *Five Architects* in 1972, cataloging selected projects of the "New York Five." It was partly because of Meier's houses, such as the Saltzman House (1967–69) in East Hampton, New York, that this group of architects became known as the "Whites." Influences on Meier included Colin Rowe, as well as influential Modernist Marcel Breuer, for whom he worked in New York in the early 1960s.

Meier's signature style is characterized by the use of white enamel panels and glass, in combination with stucco, as in the Ackerberg House (1984–86) in Malibu, California, and the Giovannitti House (1979–83) in Pittsburgh, Pennsylvania. The Hoffman House (1966–67) in East Hampton, New York, is an illustrative example of Meier's explorations of geometry in planning. His work has been characterized as late Modernist, because of its pure white forms and ribbon windows, which are suggestive of Le Corbusier's villas of the late 1920s.

Several of Meier's projects, both residential and institutional, are shaped by the coding of spaces through the use of heavy solid walls with small windows for intimate spaces, and large expanses of glazing to designate more public areas. Examples of this approach can be seen in the Bronx Developmental Center (1976) in New York; the Smith House (1965–67) in Darien, Connecticut; the Douglas House (1971–73) in Harbor Springs, Michigan; and the Westchester House (1984–86) in Westchester, New York.

Meier was awarded the prestigious Pritzker Prize in 1984, the profession's highest honour. He is a Fellow of the American Institute of Architects, and has won many AIA National Honor Awards, as well as the Gold Medal in 1997. He also won the American Academy of Arts and Letters Arnold W Brunner Memorial Prize in Architecture in 1972.

Gerald Melling

Gerald Melling (1943–) was born in Liverpool, England. Known as an architect, critic, and poet, he trained in architectural offices in Liverpool, Toronto, and Oxford, before finishing at the University of Auckland in 1976. He was editor of *Architecture New Zealand* (1983–86), and an architecture columnist for the *National Business Review* (1986–88), where he gave these publications an energetic, critical edge. He is the author of *Joyful Architecture: The Genius of New Zealand's Ian Athfield* (1980); *Open School House* (1981); *Positively Architecture: New Zealand's Roger Walker* (1985); and *The Mid City Crisis and Other Stories* (1989), as well as the poetry books *Postcards from the Coast* (1992), and *b. 1943* (1999).

As an architect, Melling has practiced with Allan Morse since 1990. The best of their houses include the Tree House (1992) in Wellington; the Music Box (1992) for an international violinist (Pugh House), Wellington; Kew House (1993) in Ruamati; Otaki River House (2000) and Sky Box (2002) both in Wellington; and Samurai House (2004) in Upper Hutt. Their sustainable architecture maintains respect for people, is intimate in scale, while using low maintenance materials, such as unpainted timber.

Melling and Morse are consistent advocates of low-cost architecture, and encourage their clients to personally engage in the building process. The fashioning of the small and beautiful can be every bit as demanding as the complications of big budget projects, and their small, detached houses have a special, often experimental, place in New Zealand domestic architecture. The built dreams of Melling and Morse nest-making have made a significant contribution to the creative place of women in architecture – particularly through their ability to listen and sensitively interpret the client's point of view. From a professional perspective this architectural firm is relatively removed from the ego boosting syndrome. Together they believe that a functioning brain is a prerequisite to clear thinking. In their domestic architecture Melling and Morse make music together; a quintessentially New Zealand harmony.

As an architectural critic, Gerald Melling has a courageous record of social and civic consciousness. An intellectual with a poetic gift for words, he carves an individual path. As an architect he uses timber in a practical way – his sense of scale is both human and generous, and he is a model of integrity as a New Zealand architect. Gerald Melling believes in the human being in architecture, and for that reason he is often at odds with his profession.

Konstantin Melnikov

Konstantin Melnikov (1890–1974) was born in Moscow, Russia, and though born into a peasant family, he was able to attend the Moscow School of Painting, Sculpture and Architecture where he studied architecture from 1912 to 1917. In the 1920s Melnikov began to translate the visual arts into architecture, drawing inspiration from the art world with its emphasis on the expressive and the emotional, though in an era where buildings were still dominated by Functionalism and Rationalism. In 1925 he won the Grand Prix for his universally praised design of the Soviet pavilion at the 1925 Paris Exhibition of Decorative Art.

Melnikov built six worker's clubs in Moscow from 1927 to 1929, and in 1929 completed designing his family home, Melnikov House, consisting of two upright, interlocking concrete towers, one taller than the other and studded with rhomboid windows. It was a house with a total absence of right angles, and which Melnikov and his family were permitted to own and live in as private property, almost unheard of in 1930s Russia.

However, Melnikov's brazen individualism was short-lived, and by the mid-thirties Stalin had reinstated the Neo-classicists, ending Russia's brief indulgence with Modernism. Today the house is under serious threat of demolition in the face of a Moscow building-boom that sees city authorities deeply enmeshed with developers who have little regard for historic preservation. In April 2006 architects from around the world gathered in Moscow for the Heritage at Risk Conference to petition President Putin to put safeguards in place for the protection of historic structures.

In 1933 Melnikov became the chief designer of a Moscow studio, but his disenchantment of Soviet bureaucracy led to his expulsion from architecture in 1937. Although he was partially reinstated into the profession, he lived in seclusion, working as a portrait painter, until his death in 1974.

Erich Mendelsohn

German architect Erich Mendelsohn (1887–1953) was born in Allenstein, East Prussia (now Poland), and is considered a leading pioneer of Modern architecture. Beginning with a sculptural, Expressionist method, he later became more closely allied with the International Style. Mendelsohn studied architecture in Berlin and Munich, setting up private practice in Munich in 1912, and becoming associated with leaders of the German Expressionist art movement. Following military service in World War I, Mendelsohn held an exhibition of his Expressionistic and Modern architectural sketches.

His first major commission was the Einstein Tower observatory (1919–21), in Potsdam, Germany, constructed of brick rendered with cement. The building appears to flow upward from its circular base to its seven-story high domed observatory, and exemplifies Mendelsohn's interest in abstract Expressionism.

During the 1920s he became influenced by the formal lines of the International Style. His asymmetrical Schocken Department Store (1926) at Stuttgart, Germany, uses continuous ribbon windows separated by strips of brick. The Schocken store at Chemnitz (1929) features windows alternating with opaque white strips in an imposing curved facade, which nonetheless creates a feeling of light airiness.

The rise of National Socialism in Germany forced Mendelsohn to flee to London in 1933. He divided his practice between England and Palestine, most notably designing the De La Warr Pavilion (1935) at Bexhill-on-Sea in England; the University Medical Center (1934–39) on Mt Scopus, Jerusalem; and the hospital at Haifa in Israel (1937–38).

Cohen House (1934–36), at 64 Old Church Street, Chelsea, London, was designed in collaboration with Serge Chermayeff as part of a largely Classical urban renewal project next to Trafalgar Square. It brought continental standards of Modernism to a conservative neighborhood, and despite its uncompromising appearance in a Neo-regency environment, it was generally well received.

Mendelsohn emigrated to the United States in 1941. His American work included the 14-story Maimonides Hospital (1946–50) in San Francisco, which emphasizes the horizontal with its cantilevered balconies and curved protrusions. Mendelsohn also designed several synagogues and community centers in the American mid-west. The synagogue at Cleveland, Ohio, was the most ambitious, harmonizing the synagogue's dome and lines with the building's undulating site.

Mendelsohn forged new methods of construction, and made brilliant use of the advent of electric lighting. He pioneered a vibrant contextualism, and epitomized the best of German Modernism. His Schocken department stores became international models for that type of building.

Ludwig Mies van der Rohe

Ludwig Mies van der Rohe (1886–1969) was born in Aachen, Germany, but later moved to the United States of America in 1938, becoming naturalized in 1944. Initially he was known professionally as Ludwig Mies, but later he decided to splice his father's name with his mother's maiden name, Rohe, by adding the invented "van der." He came from a background of stonemasons, which accounts for the fact that all his life he was concerned to bring material order to the desperate confusion of our time. Although he finished trade school at 15, he did not continue with formal training. His early years were served with the designer Bruno Paul from 1906–08. During this time he did his first private house in Potsdam-Neubabelsberg which attracted attention. He made a trip to Italy in 1908 and began to come to terms with the Classical tradition.

From 1909 to 1910 Mies van der Rohe managed to spend time in the Berlin office of Peter Behrens, the industrial designer for AEG (Allgemeine Elektricitäts Gesellschaft). Behrens was widely known for his factories, but he also did domestic work where he demonstrated sympathy for Classicism. This experience certainly influenced Mies van der Rohe, and in 1912 he distinguished himself with an unrealized design for the Kroeller-Muller House for a Dutch Industrialist near the Hague. This design carried a certain monumentality of interlocking geometric forms, and like Schinkel before him, Mies van der Rohe spent energy understanding the difficult principles of composition. He continued to experiment in two modes of composition – one symmetrical and the other asymmetrical – with two country house prototypes, one in concrete (1923) and the other in brickwork (1924). Both designs embraced free layouts from a common core, and expanded the possibility of relating interior and exterior space.

The first part of his career in Germany saw him become the first vice-president of the Deutscher Werkbund, a German association of architects, designers, and industrialists and a precursor to the Bauhaus. He then became director of the Weissenhof housing estate in Stuttgart in 1927, which was one of the most significant housing exhibitions of the twentieth century, initiated by the Deutscher Werkbund and financed by the City of Stuttgart. The Siedlung houses carried unadorned facades and flat roofs – formal characteristics suggesting an agreed harmony among the designers. Mies van der Rohe designed a four-story block of terrace apartments, which formed the centerpiece of this progressive exhibition. Later he led the Bauhaus from 1930 to 1933. His most fruitful period of architecture was after World War II in the United

States of America, where he built meticulously proportioned buildings in steel and glass that won him almost universal praise.

In the domestic situation, Mies van der Rohe's contribution to the design of the house was critically challenged by Dr Edith Farnsworth from Chicago. Her house, built in Plano, Illinois, between 1945 and 1951 ranks alongside Frank Lloyd Wright's Fallingwater and Le Corbusier's Villa Savoye – three of the most beautifully designed houses of the twentieth century. Mies van der Rohe's domestic legacy, however, cannot just end on this note.

The Farnsworth House was built for an unmarried, upper-class doctor, who lived and worked in Chicago but sought a country weekend retreat. It occupies the middle of a grassy meadow on the banks of the Fox River, some 50 miles (30 km) west of Chicago. From a distance this house appears as a transparent glass box – two horizontal crisp planes supported on eight, white-painted steel columns hovering above the ground. To this oblong structure is added a low terrace and a ladder-like entrance staircase suspended above the ground. The composition is one of Platonic purity – a pure glazed pavilion, and a spiritual refuge of high abstraction situated in nature.

From the inside things begin to look different. Mies van der Rohe's lack of human association is inescapable. The awareness of this criticism has its roots in the problem that Farnsworth House is a single volume subdivided by a freestanding service core. The living room remains totally open, which is a challenge to human behavior itself. This conceptual problem caused a great deal of strife between what the client wanted and what the architect was prepared to compromise. In the end, Mies van der Rohe was determined to pursue his vision of high abstraction, which for the client began a retreat from serving the needs of a human being.

Dr Farnsworth was a well-traveled person with an affinity for European art and architecture. Being aware of Mies van der Rohe's Barcelona Pavilion (1929) and his Tugendhat House (1930) in Brno in the Czech Republic, Dr Farnsworth recognized Mies van der Rohe's single-minded devotion to high architecture, and while it appeared widely that they were romantically involved, nothing seems to have come of it. Yet Dr Farnsworth was clearly impressed by Mies van der Rohe's reputation, and when his model of Farnsworth House was exhibited in the Museum of Modern Art in 1947, the client-patron was proud of her role in this enterprise. Yet there still remained problems of a human nature.

The Farnsworth House became an abstract exercise in contemplative architecture, where Mies van der Rohe's universal ideals came before aspects of human activity. The final rupture between client and architect occurred over money, when it became apparent that the house cost more than twice the original budget. Such a battle was fought out in court, and certainly made the publicity charts, raising concerns over domestic departures, choice of furniture, matters of gender, and the general workability of the house.

In this whole enterprise Mies van der Rohe appears to have been unmoved by the unrelenting geometry of his creation. Dr Farnsworth lived in the house for 20 years, until she moved to Italy early in the 1970s, when it was finally sold to a Mies van der Rohe enthusiast who filled it with furniture designed by the architect. As a client, Dr Farnsworth challenged the Platonic principle, and found the architect's need for human universality wanting.

Charles Moore

American architect and teacher Charles Willard Moore (1925–93) was the senior partner of the Californian firm MLTW (with Donlyn Lyndon, William Turnbull and Richard Whitaker) in the 1960s and '70s. The office is known for its eclectic design, particularly of large-scale urban complexes. Well-known projects include Kresge College at the University of California at Santa Cruz (1973).

Moore graduated from the University of Michigan in 1947, and later received a PhD in architectural history from Princeton University. While he was educated at the height of Modernism, Moore rejected the idea of using architecture to promote the moralistic Modernist ideal, in favor of a more humanistic approach to design. He was concerned with memory and the establishment of a sense of place through a relationship to the site and visual links with the architecture of the past. Moore was influenced by the work of Louis I Kahn, and believed in engaging all the senses rather than just the visual. Together with Donlyn Lyndon and Gerald Allen, Moore authored *The Place of Houses* (1974) and with K C Bloomer, *Body, Memory and Architecture* (1977). He served as head of three architecture schools, teaching at Yale, the University of California at Berkeley, and at the University of California in Los Angeles.

MLTW came to prominence in the mid-sixties with their Sea Ranch Condominium project (1964–65) in California – a design for multi-family holiday housing consisting of units built around a common courtyard to provide a sense of community. It featured monopitched shingle roofs and timber siding as cladding – references to the vernacular architecture of ranch and cottage buildings. This project led to many other houses and other projects, especially in California.

Moore's houses tend to feature a variety of levels and spaces overlooking one another within the interior, in the form of indoor courtyards, platforms, and balconies, and multi-layered transitions between inside and outside. They often use unusual window positions and shapes, and create a range of more or less intimate spaces by varying the height and detail of ceilings. Well-known residential projects include the Burns House (1974) in Santa Monica Canyon, and the Moore House (1962) in Orinda, California.

Moore's approach to design was characterized by his commitment to active collaboration with each client and, through workshops, with the anticipated users of the building, to develop a personalized response to their taste and their needs beyond pragmatic requirements. For houses, he was concerned with understanding the memories a client needs their home to evoke. Each of his projects is unique in its relationship with the landscape and response to the historical associations suggested by its site.

Charles Moore was awarded the American Institute of Architects Gold Medal in 1991. The Moore Center for the Study of Place in Austin, Texas, has been established to continue the influence of Moore's teaching and writing through publications, conferences, and lectures, and to conserve a collection of his buildings.

Julia Morgan

Julia Morgan (1872–1957) was born in San Francisco, USA, and raised in Oakland, California. She pursued an undergraduate degree in civil engineering at the University of California, influenced by her mother's cousin, Pierre Le Brun, who designed the Metropolitan Life Insurance Tower in New York City.

In 1896 Morgan traveled to Paris to study at the École des Beaux-Arts, but was refused admission for two years, for no other reason than her gender. After graduating in architecture, Morgan returned to San Francisco, taking up a position with architect John Galen Howard. Together, between 1902 and 1903, they designed the Mining Building, and the Hearst Greek Theater, at the University of California.

In 1904 Morgan opened her own practice in San Francisco, securing residential commissions in Piedmont, Claremont, and Berkeley. She developed her signature California-vernacular style of architecture, with exposed beams, extensive use of shingles, horizontal perspectives harmonizing with the landscape, and California redwood and earth hues.

After the San Francisco earthquake and fire of 1906, Morgan rebuilt the Fairmont Hotel, and began to add more institutional work to her portfolio. She received commissions from numerous women's groups, including the Young Women's Christian Association (YWCA), for which she designed the Asilomar Conference Center in Pacific Grove, California, and a series of other YWCA centers in California, Utah, and Hawaii.

Her most acclaimed residential work of this period was Livermore House (1917) in San Francisco: An urban house that transformed simple Crafts origins into sophisticated, even daring design. Morgan designed a pied-à-terre on the family estate – a rectangular duplex with upstairs hall, bedroom, living room, and bathroom, and downstairs kitchen and dining room. In 1927 and 1930 Morgan added an L-shaped annexe to the upper side, with a bedroom, bathroom, and study space, giving the impression that the house is linked to the city by a footbridge.

In 1919 she was hired by newspaper magnate Sir William Randolph Hearst to design buildings for his California ranch, starting an association which lasted until the 1940s. As well as designing many structures for Hearst's numerous properties (including Hearst Castle in San Simeon, and Wyntoon [1924–39], a stone and timber villa set in the forest near Mount Shasta in northern California), Morgan continued to take on public and private commissions, including the remodeling of the *Los Angeles Examiner* Building (1915), and the Phoebe Apperson Hearst Memorial Women's Gymnasium at the University of California at Berkeley (1925–27).

Julia Morgan was America's first independent woman architect; a quiet revolutionary in her self-effacing way. She designed over 700 buildings, ranging from palatial ranches and major university buildings, to modest cottages. Her 1929 honorary Law degree citation from the University of California, lauded her as an "architect in whose works harmony and admirable proportions bring pleasure to the eye and peace to the mind."

Glenn Murcutt

Glenn Murcutt (1936–) was born in London, England, but spent his early childhood in New Guinea, until 1941 when the family settled in Sydney. He studied architecture at the Sydney Technical College (later the University of New South Wales), graduating in 1961, and spent two years in Europe, returning to Sydney in 1964 to be employed by Ancher Mortlock Murray and Woolley.

Murcutt founded his own practice in 1969, and ever since has worked mainly on private houses, almost entirely alone. His early works explored variations in Miesian Modernism, but it was in about 1974, after his return from his second overseas trip, that the distinctive Murcutt house began to crystallize, as in the confident coherent simplicity of the Marie Short House (1974–75) in Kempsey, New South Wales.

The houses at this stage of Murcutt's career consisted of one gabled unit, or two running in parallel, generally different in length or staggered in placing, but never with a hipped roof or an intersecting gable. The juxtaposition of a pair of parallel but staggered rectangles has been convincingly traced to Mies van der Rohe's Farnsworth House (1951) in Plano, Illinois. The majority of the wall area is of glass and/or louvers, and there are no verandas. The Murcutt roof is of corrugated iron, which at the Marie Short House continues in a curve over the ridge, so that no ridging is required. Later he was to use much more radical forms of the material, from complete barrel vaults to assemblages of curved segments. The building is raised on stumps and gives the impression of minimal interference with the ground below, like a mosquito that has just landed.

Murcutt has encouraged the perception that his buildings are environmentally friendly and "touch the earth lightly," although the thermal properties of structures with open subfloor space and extensive glazed areas are suspect. In fact, for all its air of rationality, it is a creative and intuitive architecture, rather than the outcome of a cerebral process. Although most of Murcutt's work was in Sydney, many of the urban projects did not proceed, and his country projects of the late 1970s and early '80s – commonly detached houses in spacious rural settings – were what made his reputation. From the mid-eighties Murcutt's work becomes harder to characterize, for it no longer employed his own unique vocabulary. He used increasingly elegant steel detailing, bringing him at times close to the work of contemporaries such as Philip Cox.

In the late 1980s Murcutt developed a concept even more basic than the earlier barn type. The Meagher House (1988–92) at Bowral, New South Wales, was essentially a simple long rectangle, roofed with a simple skillion detailed to a thin edge, almost like a piece of stiff card casually placed over the plan. At the Simpson-Lee House (1989–94) at Mount Wilson, New South Wales the form was simplified into two plain rectangular plates, one on each of the linked pavilions. These houses were integrated with substructures and landscaping rather than delicately perched above the ground, but Murcutt revived that concept in the Marika-Alderton House (1994) for the Yirrkala Community in Arnhem Land. While the planning was intended to relate to Aboriginal traditions and sensibilities, the overall form – a rectangle with a simple gabled roof and very broad eaves – had much more to do with European architectural traditions in the Northern Territory. It has been estimated that Murcutt had designed about 500 houses by 2002.

Murcutt's work was exhibited at the Paris Biennale of 1986 and the Venice Biennales of 1991 and 1996. He has received many Australian awards, as well as the Alvar Aalto Medal of the Finnish Institute of Architects in 1992, the Richard Neutra Award in 1998, the Danish Institute of Architects International Award for Ecology in 1999, the Thomas Jefferson Medal in 2001, and the Pritzker Prize in 2002.

MVRDV

The architectural office of MVRDV (Winy Maas, Jacob van Rijs and Nathalie de Vries), was set up in 1991 in Rotterdam, the Netherlands. The trio quickly gained international recognition with a series of relatively high-profile commissions, from the headquarters for the Public Broadcasting Company VPRO (1997) in Hilversum, to housing for the elderly (WOZOCO, 1997) in Amsterdam.

Alongside the practice of architecture, MVRDV express their own style of methodical research, which includes the shaping of space through the analysis of the enormous amount of data that accompany contemporary design. Within housing, MVRDV have explored their unique process of design and produced a series of dwellings that challenge the idea of space. A particular commission is The Double House (1995–97) in Utrecht, the Netherlands. The house occupies a single site, yet is for two independent families. Both families expressed their own specific needs and MVRDV set to work designing a double dwelling that allowed the desires of both parties to be accommodated while avoiding the traditional separation of space. Where many would believe that the co-habitation of two families on the one site would present many problems, the clever planning and respect for the space in-between the two, allowed MVRDV to produce what appears as an interlocking three-dimensional puzzle that accommodates the two families within the one residence.

The Dutch government and local councils invest large amounts of money into public space and housing, with the opportunity for young designers to gain notoriety through such commissions. MVRDV have a notable list of public housing commissions that promote individualization within large building masses. An example of this is found within Silodam (2002) in Amsterdam, which presents as apartment living with the distinct appearance of the compression and amalgamation of a series of different houses. Responding to the housing shortage in Amsterdam in the 1980s, MVRDV designed a rectilinear envelope to contain a series of apartments, business units, and public spaces. The apartments differ in size, shape, orientation, and color. Apartments may take up an entire block, half a block, or be split diagonally over two levels. The interior walls are flexible, and are able to be removed or replaced by future inhabitants. MVRDV are compelled to maintain an innovative approach, producing spatially dynamic commissions within their housing. This allows them to benefit from a position that late twentieth-century Dutch architects have enjoyed for many years as cutting edge in architectural design.

Richard Neutra

Richard Josef Neutra (1892–1970) was born in Vienna, Austria – a city rich in architecture and intellectual cross-currents. Educated at the Vienna Technical University between 1911 and 1915, and 1917 and 1918, where he was influenced by Rudolf Salinger, Karl Mayreder, and Max Fabini, he graduated with a Diploma in Architecture in 1918. While he did not study under Otto Wagner, he was deeply influenced by this architect–teacher. He served as a lieutenant in the Imperial Austrian Army, and later worked in Switzerland, before moving to Berlin to work for Erich Mendelsohn in 1921. Believing the future of Modern architecture lay in the United States of America, he emigrated there in 1923.

Arriving in New York, Neutra soon moved to Chicago, where he managed to get himself hired in Holabird and Roche's office – a large and prestigious firm that, along with Adler and Sullivan, had pioneered the development of the skyscraper. Sullivan died in April 1924, and at the funeral, Neutra met Frank Lloyd Wright who invited him to his home, Taliesin, where he stayed for three months with his wife Dione, who entertained them all with her cello. While he was with Frank Lloyd Wright, Neutra learned a good deal about placing buildings in the landscape. Neutra, however, never quite managed this integration as naturally as Frank Lloyd Wright.

Moving to Los Angeles in 1925, Neutra joined Rudolf Schindler – an old student friend from Vienna. Together they collaborated on a competition design for the League of Nations Building in Geneva. Apart from problems in personality, Neutra began to work towards a new architecture of prefabricated parts – he saw this as the only way of meeting the needs of the twentieth century.

The house that Neutra used to announce to the world that he belonged among the "greats" was Lovell House (1929) in Los Angeles. It was the first completely steel-framed prefabricated residence in the United States of America. After this classically composed house was finished, it was opened to the public on four successive Sunday afternoons – and an amazed 15,000 Angelenos poured through Neutra's vision of landscaped Modernism.

Determined to be a Messiah, Neutra went on to design and build a whole range of famous houses in California: Author Ayn Rand's House (1936) in the San Fernando Valley; the Kahn House (1940) in San Francisco; the Kaufmann Desert House (1946) in Palm Springs; the Tremaine House (1948) in Santa Barbara; and the Constance Perkins House (1955) in Pasadena. Out of this regional success in southern California, Neutra graced the front cover of *Time* magazine in 1949. Such an event almost made him a saint in his own eyes.

Be that as it may, Neutra's hallmark is the beautiful Kaufmann Desert House and the Tremaine House. These large family houses are all significant works of architecture, both being integrated into nature with swimming pools and lush gardens. Neutra's strength was his sensitive handling of indoor–outdoor space. He used large over-hanging flat roofs with exposed redwood beams that reached out into the mild climate and horticultural potential of California. His clients were mostly comfortable middle-class people who furnished their houses beautifully. Neutra used large areas of glass, and made splendid interpenetrations into a rich abundance of planting, affirming his houses in the landscape. Neutra had an ecological concern before it became fashionable.

Neutra combined a thrusting mind with technical competence, and in combination with his European background, this gave him an air of intellectual superiority. His work combined sophistication with sensitivity to the climate of southern California. He was a master of public relations, who had the energy to network and meet people like Charles Eames, Harry Bertoia, Robert Motherwell, and John Entenza, the publisher of *California Arts & Crafts*, who pushed Neutra's "Hollywood ego" to the skies. In this matter, Neutra was neither reserved nor reticent. He championed the aesthetic and practical values of unrestricted domestic interiors of steel and glass as the key ingredients of Modernism, celebrating the micro-climate of golden California.

He published *Mystery and Realities of the Site* (1951), *Survival Through Design* (1954), and *Life and Human Habitat* (1956). It was a tireless life determined to be heard, read, and architecturally vindicated by houses sympathetic to nature.

Oscar Niemeyer

Oscar Niemeyer (1907–) was born in Rio de Janeiro, Brazil. He is one of the most influential and idiosyncratic exponents of Modernism and Brazil's most celebrated architect. His work is characterized by the sculptural use of curves which, for Niemeyer, is inspired by nature and the seductive contours of the mountains which flank Rio. In 1929 Niemeyer began his studies in architecture at the National Art Academy, graduating in 1934. Following his graduation Niemeyer went to work for Lucio Costa, one of his teachers at the Academy, and together they formed an important and productive relationship. In 1936 Costa was asked to design the Ministry of Health and Education building in Rio, appointing Niemeyer to the team and inviting Le Corbusier to serve as a consultant on the project. Niemeyer heavily influenced the design of the final building, reworking Le Corbusier's ideas to suit the site.

The 1940 commission to design the Pampulha Club Complex in Belo Horizonte allowed Niemeyer the opportunity to develop his own language of architecture. The fluid curves of the building, the sculptural white walls, and its elegant free-form planning arrangement were all themes that dominated Niemeyer's architecture for the next 50 years.

The opportunity to do the architectural work for the new capital of Brasilia (1957–61), in collaboration with Lucio Costa, who produced the urban plan, provided Niemeyer with an unprecedented opportunity to test the ideas of Modernism at an urban scale. The buildings of Brasilia remain an enduring image of high Modernism, crystallizing its aesthetic purity as well as the vast and imposing monolithic scale that has been widely criticized.

Niemeyer joined the Brazilian Communist Party in 1945 – an affiliation which he maintained throughout his life, despite it indirectly causing his expulsion from Brazil in 1967. During this period Niemeyer lived in Paris, where contact with the existentialism of Jean Paul Sartre had a profound effect on him. During his period of exile he executed a number of important buildings, including the French Communist Party Headquarters (1965–72) in Paris, the Cultural Center (1972) in Le Havre, and the Constantine (1969) and Algiers university (1968) campuses in Algeria. Having returned to Brazil in 1982, some of Niemeyer's most refined buildings have occurred late in his career, such as the UFO-shaped Niteroi Museum of Contemporary Art (1996). In 2003, at the age of 95, Niemeyer completed the Serpentine Gallery Summer Pavilion in Hyde Park, London.

Jean Nouvel

Jean Nouvel (1945–) was born in Fumel, France, and graduated from the École des Beaux-Arts in 1972. He has operated his Paris practice since 1975. He treads a stylistic path between Modernism and Post-modernism, rejecting the stern obedience to Le Corbusier, which characterizes much contemporary architecture. Nouvel often borrows from traditional forms, but his designs extend beyond established conventions and constrictions. With an eye to site and surroundings, he nonetheless stamps his creations with a recognizable personal style, based on the interplay between shadow, light, and transparency.

Nouvel is perhaps best-known for his highly original Institut du Monde Arabe (1981–87) in Paris, one of President Mitterrand's *Grands Projets*. Situated across the River Seine from Notre Dame, this superb complex represents 19 countries, and is designed to foster knowledge of Arab culture by the exchange of information on the arts, sciences, and technology. It incorporates bright exhibition areas, a library, museum, restaurant, a 300-seat hall, and office space surrounding the glass-and-steel stairs, and elevator enclosure. Incorporating Islamic decorative influences, it features metallic "lenses" set in stamped-metal borders, which open and close in response to the available sunlight.

Nouvel is a master of trompe l'oeil. His sixty-story Dentsu Tower (1998) in Tokyo, with its crescent shape and glass skin, seems to float in mid-air, while the facade of the Foundation Cartier (1994) in Paris – a series of overlapping glass planes – makes it difficult to see where the building starts and ends. Lucerne's Cultural and Congress Center (2000) appears transparent when viewed from the lake.

Nouvel's numerous acclaimed works include Berlin's Galeries Lafayette (1995), the Conference Center and Deluxe Boutique Hotel (2000) in Lucerne, and the judicial complex (2000) in Nantes, France.

He has received numerous awards, including the Grand Prix d'Architecture for his entire body of work, and the Equerre d'Argent for his minimalist furniture designs (both in 1987). In 1991 he was appointed vice president of the Institut Français d'Architecture, and in 1993 received another Equerre d'Argent for the Opera House at Lyon.

Nouvel is now one of the few truly international architects, with recent projects in the United States of America, Czech Republic, Spain, Denmark, Mexico, and Japan. Nouvel purposely understates the material and construction qualities of building, in favor of aesthetic and surface effects. He has said, "Most architects want to make something exist...my problem...is to eliminate all I can...to make things non-existent..."

Nouvel's French public housing projects include the Nemausus social housing project (1981–87) in Nîmes, Pierre and Vacances housing (1991) in Cap d'Ail, and the ZAC Parmentier Housing (1993) in Bezons. The Nemausus complex has become so familiar that its radical qualities may now appear passé. Nouvel's use of industrial components (concertina garage doors for balconies, metalwork decking, aluminum open stairs) is radical, but not for its own sake. His design incorporates his definition of a "good apartment" – large, adaptable, and inexpensive. Minimal communal spaces, such as staircases and hallways, allow maximum apartment sizes. Adaptability was fashioned by dividing 17 different layout modules into the 114 apartments contained in the two blocks. The low-cost requirement was met by using prefabricated manufacturing components for interior and exterior fittings. The building shell is thin concrete cased in aluminum sheeting. The balconies provide for outdoor living, with full-width concertina doors allowing complete integration between the balcony and the main living space.

Liam O'Connor

Liam O'Connor is a British architect registered in the United Kingdom and a member of the Royal Institute of British Architects. He established his own practice in London in 1989, and has since become one of the country's most prolific designers. With a core staff of only four, his firm has recently completed a winery in Switzerland, two commercial and residential buildings in Brussels, and six terrace houses in the center of historic Bath in England. O'Connor specializes in the construction of new buildings within important conservation areas populated by listed buildings, enhancing these areas with new buildings that perpetuate and complement their aged surroundings.

In 1992 O'Connor co-organized the Vision of Europe exhibition in Italy. A non-profit association established by the University of Bologna, this annual three-week design workshop brings in architects from across Europe to discuss concepts and projects for the revitalization of Europe's urban environment. Much of the philosophy of Liam O'Connor is reflected in the Vision of Europe's stated goals: Urban architecture devoted to the promotion of the art of building traditional cities and Classical and vernacular architecture.

In 1999 he won the Invited International Competition for the design of the Memorial Gates near Buckingham Palace. Completed in 2002, the Memorial Gates represent, for the first time, the sacrifices made by volunteers from the Indian subcontinent, Africa, and the Caribbean during World War I and II. A monumental project, O'Connor's design has won the Stone Federation of Great Britain Stone Award with its Portland stone piers, balustrades, cast bronze streetlamps, and urns in a stunning Classical setting. O'Connor also won an international competition for the design of the Armed Forces Memorial to be situated in Staffordshire at the National Arboretum, with sculptural elements to be supplied by Ian Rank-Broadley.

J J P Oud

Jacobus Johannes Pieter Oud (1890–1963) was born in Purmerand, the Netherlands, and received his education at the Arts and Crafts School in Amsterdam and the Delft Technical University. He then found work with the architectural firm of Cuijpers and Stuyt in Amsterdam and was influenced by the work of H P Berlage and Frank Lloyd Wright. A pioneer of Modernism, he was as highly regarded in his day as Le Corbusier, whose influence declined after World War II when the focus of the movement shifted from Europe to the United States of America.

An interest in abstract paintings saw Oud align himself early on with the De Stijl movement – a group of artists, sculptors, writers, and architects advocating greater geometric simplicity in art and architecture. They were bound together by a belief in complete abstraction, straight lines, straight angles, and primary colors.

From 1918 to 1933 Oud was the Municipal Housing Architect of Rotterdam and became highly regarded for his use of reinforced concrete in housing schemes in expanding urban areas. Breaking away from the De Stijl school, he became a leader in the Dutch expression of the new International Style. His design for the facade of the Cafe de Unie (1925) in Rotterdam, destroyed in the German bombings of May 1940 and reconstructed in 1986, and some workers' housing quarters in the Hook of Holland Estate (1924–27), are now seen as representing the pinnacles of his career. The Hook of Holland development features two-story buildings run in low horizontal lines along new conventional streets, although the blocks appear as single entities from a distance. Close up each house is identifiable with its own entrance and walled garden. The buildings are characterized by rounded ends that contain small shops.

Oud's output declined significantly after the early 1930s. Though continuing to practice as an independent architect, the only buildings of note that followed were the Shell Building in The Hague (1938–42) and the Bio Health Resort in Arnhem (1952–60). Oud was awarded an honorary doctorate in 1955 from the Technical University in Delft.

John Pawson

John Pawson (1949–) was born in Yorkshire, England. He spent several years teaching English in Japan before returning to England to study architecture at the Architecture Association in London. He left in 1981 to establish his own practice, in which he has undoubtedly drawn upon his time in Japan.

Pawson achieved international status during the early 1990s as he concentrated on light, space, proportion, and materials, with a mastery that saw his career take off with a series of high-profile commissions from the Calvin Klein flagship store in Manhattan, New York, to airport lounges for Cathay Pacific in Hong Kong. His domestic commissions all express the thoughtfulness with which Pawson approached all his designs. Attention was always applied to the experience of arrival, heightened by the compression of space or the continuity of the extended wall: A theatrical device that builds anticipation. Of his domestic commissions, the common factor appears to be simplicity of the spaces combined with an astute attention to detail, from the Medina House (1995) in Tunisia, to the Baron House (2005) in

Sweden, and Tetsuka House (2005) in Japan. Within his domestic scale architecture Pawson's emphasis includes a study of how domestic architecture can be designed around the rituals of everyday life. His popularity grew due to the creation of the home as an oasis of calm within urban contexts. Within his exploration of space, light, proportion, and materials, Pawson avoids stylistic mannerisms, preferring to concentrate, with astute attention, on detail.

John Pawson is now recognized as one of the most influential minimalist architects of our time. The Neuendorf House (1989) in Majorca, Spain was designed with his former partner, Claudio Silvestrin. This commission provided an opportunity to move away from the inner-city oasis and develop a minimalist ideal that relates to the surrounding landscape, with large windows and an impressive entrance. No roof is visible, just a high concrete perimeter wall finished in terracotta stucco. The house contains an amphitheater courtyard flanked by stone benches, which leads to the dining room, which is at the center of the house. All the rooms use the same palette of materials – stone floors, wooden benches, and smooth, white concrete walls. Daylight enters the house through slits and chutes in the walls.

Pawson pays homage to the work of mid-twentieth century architect Luis Barragán. The extraordinary discipline, grace, and simplicity of Barragán's work is evident within the clean lines and appreciation of space and light that emanates from the architectural work of John Pawson.

Cesar Pelli

Cesar Pelli (1926–) was born in Tucuman, Argentina, and is known for designing some of the world's tallest buildings and major urban landmarks. He emigrated to the United States of America in 1952 and became an American citizen in 1964. He initially studied architecture at the Universidad de Tucuman in Buenos Aires in 1949, but later completed his studies at the School of Architecture at the University of Illinois at Urbana-Champaign between 1952 and 1954. In 1977 he became dean of the School of Architecture at Yale University and established the firm Pelli Clarke Pelli in New Haven, Connecticut.

The architecture of Cesar Pelli is very much the architecture of the modern skyscraper in America. His designs are very dignified and substantial, but still seem to be respectful of their surroundings without being overly conservative. His architecture is aesthetically pleasing and precisely executed. Pelli has said about his approach to urban architecture, "I strongly believe that if we are going to succeed in designing beautiful and coherent cities we, as architects, will have to be able to work within a great variety of design guidelines and constraints, where the individual buildings and vision of each architect will have to yield to the high purpose of the whole and those who are responsible for the whole."

His design of Herring Hall (1982–84) at Rice University, Houston, Texas, used contemporary materials, space configurations and detailing, but still conformed to traditional brick architecture. His Pacific Design Center (1975) in Los Angeles, California, is a stark and audacious urban centerpiece, which consists of a glass building and has been affectionately dubbed "the Blue Whale." It has been used for displaying design products. Pelli's housing projects include the Kukai Gardens Housing complex (1967) in Honolulu, Hawaii, and the 52-story residential tower on top of the Museum of Modern Art (1984) in New York. But he is perhaps, most famous for the Petronas Twin Towers (1998) in Kuala Lumpur, Malaysia, which were, for a time, the world's tallest buildings.

Pelli's private residences display his penchant for designing elegant buildings and include the Pebble Beach House at Pebble Beach, California; and houses in Maryland and the west of the country. Located on a steep hillside overlooking Carmel Bay, Point Lobos, and the Pacific Ocean, Pebble Beach House is organized around a central outdoor courtyard facing the bay and the southern sun. Three lines of circulation surround the courtyard and organize all of the functions of the house. The private residence in Maryland uses the spine of the building as the central public space that connects five pavilions organized by use and their unique relationship to the landscape. The private residence in the west of the country is a wood structure located in the woods. The house is organized around a spine. Common and public areas are situated to the west of the spine; bedrooms and other more private spaces are to the east. A small guesthouse shares the construction vocabulary.

In 1991, the American Institute of Architects listed Pelli as one of the 10 most influential living American architects. He has won numerous awards and is the recipient of the 1995 American Institute of Architects Gold Medal. He has also received the Arnold W Brunner Memorial Prize in Architecture, the National Institute of Arts and Letters in 1978, and became a Fellow of the American Institute of Architects in 1980.

Auguste Perret

Auguste Perret (1874–1954) is considered the father of Modern French architecture, who gave reinforced concrete an architectural expression. He was born in Brussels where his father, a builder, was sheltering after the Paris Commune. Along with his two brothers, he was educated at the École des Beaux-Arts in Paris between 1891 and 1895, before joining the family business. He designed and built his first house at the age of 16 at Berneval-sur-Mer, near Dieppe. Perret was a good student, but he never finished his diploma at the École des Beaux-Arts, however, the Vichy Regime during World War II gave him official recognition as an architect.

Auguste Perret trained in the atelier of Julien Guadet, who also taught Tony Garnier – the city architect of Lyon. French Classicism at this point maintained that the basic elements – column and architrave, post and lintel – were the most rational elements in architecture. The Classicists stressed the formal elements of architecture – to them architecture was more than the fulfilment of practical function, and construction and function were secondary to the classical vocabulary of form, proportion, and order. From this sort of training Perret was the first architect to give full architectural expression to the reinforced concrete frame: A structural system first patented by François Hennebique in 1892. But Perret took the development of reinforced concrete further – he believed deeply in reinforced concrete as the constructional means of the future.

Perret's first multi-story apartment building was constructed at 25b rue Franklin, Paris, in 1903. This was followed by his car garage in rue Ponthieu (1905) which was demolished in 1969. Next came his Théâtre des Champs Elysées (1911–13) based on the preliminary designs of Roger Bouverd and Henri van de Velde. All these buildings were in Paris, where his reputation as a builder in reinforced concrete became well established.

On the domestic scene Perret's next important building was an apartment he built at 51–55 rue Raynouard (1930–32), also in Paris. This was a speculative exercise that required innovative prefabricated work in reinforced concrete. Perret lived here in an apartment on the top floor, which shared a good view over central Paris. In this construction Perret relied upon vibrating the concrete to achieve maximum compressive strength; and his second technical process removed the thin film of mortar on the surface, to reveal the stone aggregate which was the basis of its structural strength. This sort of concrete work became known as *béton brut* (rough concrete).

As a building-architect Perret was an inspiration for the post-war work of Le Corbusier. In this we should remember the young Le Corbusier spent time in Perret's office as a young man. Perret, in fact, was a major tutorial influence on Le Corbusier. His ability as a builder, and the fact that he helped Le Corbusier, were factors that put him straight into books on the history of architecture. Perret's ability to build economically attracted the interest of the church. At Notre Dame du Raincy (1922–23) he built a war memorial to soldiers who fell in the tragic battles of World War I. He also built the Chapel of Saint Therese (1925–26) at Montmagny, and while these buildings were economically successful, their plans did not liturgically transform the faithful from "silent onlookers." His churches clearly expressed their concrete structure as an economic necessity, but that's where his innovative thinking ended.

Perret's work was restrained, rational, and Classical in thought and feeling. Intellectually, he continued the line of thought instituted by French Rationalism, which had begun with Eugène Viollet-le-Duc. What really mattered for Perret was the visual expression of the constructed frame and the durability of the structure.

Perret's design challenged traditional French architecture, which had reached a height of seven stories laid down by Napoleon I's legislation. If reinforced concrete was to be used, then Perret decided the frame was the true structural form for concrete. Perret applied this knowledge by teaching at the École des Beaux-Arts in 1940. In this we should never forget the tremendous influence of commercial energy on the birth of Modern architecture. Perret earned his place in history because he gave reinforced concrete a post-and-beam dignity of its own.

Renzo Piano

Renzo Piano (1937–) was born in Genoa, Italy, and studied at the Milan Polytechnic School of Architecture from 1959 to 1964, where he continued to teach until 1968. In 1970 Piano and the famous English architect Richard Rogers established the partnership of Rogers and Piano, designing several buildings throughout Europe including the groundbreaking Pompidou Center (1977) in Paris.

Piano's reputation as a commercial and civic designer is unquestioned. Football stadiums, museums, cruise ships for P&O, and the largest airport terminal in the world at Japan's Kansai International Airport in Osaka (1994), showcase his ability to apply advanced technology to large institutional buildings.

Piano is also capable of turning his expertise and innovation to the design of low-cost housing. His design for the rue de Meaux apartment complex (1991) in Paris saw him apply a strikingly new prefabricated system of glass-reinforced concrete panels (GRC) and terracotta panels to its exterior, taking the prefabricated panel to a new level of sophistication. His use of GRC technology is an innovative approach to low-cost housing, much of which is still constructed using conventional construction techniques and materials. The six-story-high street facade maintains a respect for the height and alignment characteristics of neighboring buildings. Forty differing styles are seen in the complex's collection of 220 apartments, including a row of duplexes on the top floors, and studio apartments with mezzanines. An inner landscaped garden court is filled with birch trees set among honeysuckle and narrow paved walkways, providing a private retreat for residents.

Renzo Piano is an Honorary Fellow of the American Institute of Architects and has won countless international awards including the Royal Institute of British Architects Royal Gold Medal (1989), the Neutra Prize (1991), the Erasmus Prize (1995), and the Pritzker Prize (1998).

Demetri Porphyrios

Demetri Porphyrios (1948–) was born in Greece and is one of the world's leading Classical architects and theorists. He studied at Princeton University, where he received a Master of Architecture and a PhD in the history and theory of architecture. Porphyrios is currently based in London and is principal of the firm Porphyrios Associates.

In an age of Modernism, Porphyrios has carved out a reputation as one of the world's leading Classicists who refuses to consign it to history, asserting Classic architecture is not a style but rather a philosophy; always relevant, always in search of perfection, and always flattered when the casual observer is unable to distinguish his buildings from their centuries-old neighbors.

His design of a new auditorium for Magdalen College (1994–98) at Oxford University fits seamlessly into its fifteenth-century surroundings. Porphyrios is also a proponent of New Urbanism – the total reconstruction or recreation of a community in a Classical setting, which he says is helping overcome the argument of relevance often used by critics of Classicism. One of his best-known examples of Classical urban planning is the extension of the Greek island town of Spetses along traditional urban lines. Seventy-two new villas with town squares replete with gardens have been built along topographical lines that maintain the long-established harmony of the old town.

Porphyrios' residential projects include the Bab Al Salam Palace (1994–96) in Amman, Jordan (built for Queen Noor and the late King Hussein); the Efthymiou House (1996–98) in Porto Heli, Greece; and the Leventis House (2001–03) in Spetses, Greece. The architecture of Bab Al Salam Palace is calm simplicity with its smooth local stone surface contrasting with timber pergolas, mashrabiyas, iwans, and kiosks, which help control light, temperature, and humidity in the building. Leventis House is built in a Classico-vernacular style, with a double peristyle pergola at its entry, and Classical references in its cornice profiles and in the capitals of its columns and pilasters. The interior rooms are arranged around a central courtyard atrium.

Porphyrios' commercial buildings are no less impressive. His red-brick office block at Three Brindleyplace (1996–98) in Birmingham, England, is a masterpiece of quasi-Romanesque arches with a glorious portico, wrapped around its base with a series of Doric columns creating a succession of pointed Gothic apertures.

In 2004 Porphyrios was awarded the University of Notre Dame's prestigious Richard H Driehaus Prize for his outstanding contribution to furthering the traditions of Classical architecture.

Christian de Portzamparc

Christian de Portzamparc (1944–) was born in Casablanca, Morocco. A French architect and Urbanist, he studied architecture at the École des Beaux-Arts in Paris from 1962 to 1969. After graduating he became involved with a group of sociologists studying how people interacted with their neighborhoods and why they liked or disliked the buildings in which they lived, developing an approach to design that treated the void surrounding a structure to be every bit as important as the structure itself.

De Portzamparc didn't open his first office until 1970. The following year he received his first commission – a water tower in the French town of Marne-La-Vallée. Portzamparc gave it an outer skin of trellis covered with vines; its mass bringing a striking visual statement to its nondescript location at the center of a crossroads. His design for the residential precinct in the thirteenth arrondissement of Paris, known as Hautes-Formes (1975–79), saw the construction of an arcade, a small square, and 210 apartments in what Portzamparc calls a "restitching" of an existing urban space. Its seven residential towers are situated in such a way as to open up a previously cramped site, assisted by carefully placed pedestrian thoroughfares and a centrally placed square.

Spain's *Interior Architecture & Design* magazine referred to de Portzamparc's design for the City of Music (1995) as possessing "lyric qualities:" Praise that was echoed in architectural journals around the world. Part of a new cultural center for music on a 55-acre (22-ha) site, it was designated by the French President as one of the country's *grande projects*. This self-contained village for over 2000 musicians consists of two wings that contain concert halls, an amphitheater, rehearsal halls, and dressing rooms, as well as accommodation for 82 students from the National Conservatory.

Christian de Portzamparc is the only Frenchman to have won the Pritzker Prize (1994).

E S Prior

Edward Schroeder Prior (1852–1932) became one of the leading figures in the Arts and Crafts movement, which originated in England in the second half of the nineteenth century. It then spread across the Atlantic to the United States of America, where it was also referred to as the Mission Style. Prior received his training in the offices of the London architect Norman Shaw. He was a theorist committed to the belief that local craftsmen using local materials should be employed in the building of a given structure.

Prior's crowning achievement was Voewood (1903–05), a country house in Norfolk, England, and one of the finest examples of the Arts and Crafts style to be found in Britain. Often compared in originality to Gaudi's stunning landmark buildings of Barcelona, the house was commissioned by the Reverend Percy Lloyd and designed by Prior whose design drew from the butterfly pattern of Lutyen's Papillon Hall. Work began in 1903 and included electric lighting throughout, hot running water, and cost a staggering 60,000 pounds to build. Voewood is now a family home but is available as a venue for private functions.

Prior's approach to architecture was total: From the initial sketches to the styling of door hinges and tapware. He believed not only in using painting and sculpture to decorate a room, but all of the decorative arts to mold the room and the furniture within it into one single purpose of design. His approach was therefore an intensely collaborative one, seemingly placing him at odds with the Arts and Crafts principle of the individual craftsman working alone, without the need of even an architect to guide him.

Gerrit Rietveld

Gerrit Thomas Rietveld (1888–1964) was born in Utrecht, the Netherlands, where he studied architecture and worked in his father's cabinet-making business. Rietveld was the designer of the delightful Red Blue Chair (1918–23), which made a colorful addition to the Bauhaus exhibition in 1923. Rietveld was a member of the De Stijl group, led by Theo van Doesburg, that shared his love of bright colors, rectangular sliding planes, and a search for honesty. While the Red Blue Chair has been published endlessly in the media, it is not too comfortable to sit upon, but it carried a clear aesthetic simplification between sitting and support planes, which were identified in bright colors, making it a delight to look at. The Red Blue Chair was a De Stijl construction using unadorned rectangles that architects were to use in building. While the chair was important, the house designed for Mrs Truus Schroder-Schrader had more spatial, intellectual, and artistic importance. Indeed, it is regarded as an icon of early Modern domestic architecture in the Netherlands.

The Rietveld-Schroder House (1924–25) in Utrecht, stands in marked contrast to its traditional dark-brick neighbors at the end of Prins Hendriklaan. Designed as a colorful asymmetrical composition, Rietveld used white, gray, black, red, and bright yellow to define roofs, walls, windows, and thin independent planes and lines. This house has often been compared to the paintings of Piet Mondrian, but the reality of it in light, space, and color is anything but a cerebral fascination of painted form. Rietveld originally wanted to build this house in concrete, but this proved too costly. While the foundations and balconies are in concrete, the walls were built in traditional brickwork and plastered over.

It is true that Frank Lloyd Wright broke open the Victorian box, but on the first floor of the Rietveld-Schroder House, Rietveld made a complete flexible space. He used screens to open and close this space at will, and windows to develop the spatial theme even further than what Wright managed to do. In Rietveld's need to liberate the interior, he was assisted by the use of the steel frame, and the encouragement of his client.

Mrs Schroder-Schrader was a young widow with three children when she moved into this house. She had a vision of family life far removed from the average Utrecht apartment – to which Rietveld responded wholeheartedly. There was a romantic attachment between the two of them, which helped both the personal and spatial development of this house. Passionate about each other, the Rietveld-Schroder House became a complete liberation – free from Victorian rules and values.

Entering this house one has no warning of the spatial development on the first floor. Climbing the stairs, the visitor emerges into a space of light and color. On the floor and walls rectangles of color in light create a coherent sense of family togetherness. Large expanses of glass de-materialized the boundary between interior and exterior. The first floor was furnished by Rietveld using retractable wooden partitions, which could be opened or closed. At the same time he rejected rich fabrics and conventional ornaments. His ideas about form and color produced a space that has a feeling of playfulness – an environment designed for human beings.

Rietveld's philosophy in furniture-making was a matter of assembling specific things and creating dynamic spaces. The work that Rietveld and Mrs Schroder-Schrader did together guided them towards the idea of a "user architecture" which was completely different to the Platonic purity used by Mies van der Rohe. Bourgeois notions of respectability, parental discipline, and containment gave way to a new sense of freedom and personal family openness. One could argue that in the Netherlands, the Rietveld-Schroder House helped people to rethink what a family home might and could be – it became a sort of human and personal laboratory for developing new ideas in living and architecture. Rietveld removed the solidity and space-enclosing nature of the walls. A new sense of space and freedom was achieved, which took Rietveld straight into the history books. Today the Rietveld-Schroder House is open to the public.

Jaquelin Robertson

Jaquelin Robertson (1933–) was born in Richmond, Virginia, USA, and was educated at Yale University, and earned a Rhodes Scholarship to study at Magdalen College in Oxford, England. He is the former dean of the University of Virginia School of Architecture. Arriving at Yale with thoughts of a career in the foreign service, it was the Bauhaus master Josef Albers' freehand drawing classes that first steered Robertson towards architecture.

Robertson founded the New York City Urban Design Group and now works as an urban planner in the firm of Cooper, Robertson and Partners. He has taught architecture and design at the Salzburg Seminar, and at Yale and Columbia universities. For three years in the 1970s he worked in Iran planning the then Shah of Iran's new capital center in Tehran, left incomplete when his client lost his throne. He has also been a Board Member of New York City's Architectural League and an adviser to the Aga Khan's Study of Islamic Art program at the Massachusetts Institute of Technology and Harvard.

Robertson's East Hampton Cottage (1996) in East Hampton, New York, draws upon long established traditions with its shingle roof, imaginative high Dutch gable, and wrap-around porches effortlessly projecting the romance associated with shingle-style architecture. While his design for a Barn Complex and Guest Lodge (2002) in Bedford, New York, combines twentieth-century elegance with the traditional Adirondack vernacular of rustic functionality. A fieldstone and timber-clad A-framed exterior encloses a soaring living area complete with an internal balcony set beneath massive exposed beams leading to the residence's five bedrooms, dining room, and gym. Outbuildings on the extensive property include barns for exotic animals and a greenhouse.

In recent times the firm of Cooper, Robertson and Partners has been involved in establishing a framework for the expansion of Yale University over the next 20 years. What began as a single city- block-sized university 200 years ago has grown to a collection of 340 buildings that has expanded into the surrounding town of New Haven, but not always in an organized fashion. Cooper, Robertson and Partners' long association with urban design in cities and on college campuses made them an ideal choice.

In 1998 Robertson was the recipient of the Thomas Jefferson Foundation Medal in Architecture and has been a consultant for government organizations and foundations such as the Ford Foundation and the government of Jamaica. Jaquelin Robertson is an author of *The American Institute of Architects National Growth Policy*, and in 2002 was awarded the Seaside Prize for his contributions to American Urbanism.

Richard Rogers

Sir Richard Rogers (1933–) was born in Florence, Italy. From 1954 to 1959 he studied at the Architectural Association in London, before achieving his Masters of Architecture at Yale University.

Rogers' design philosophy rejects Classicism, placing an emphasis on technical innovation, which he sees as not being merely an end in itself, but having to address existing social and environmental considerations. A leaning towards Functionalism can be seen in his penchant for large, uninterrupted interior spaces. Rogers believes that size is an irrelevant concept in architecture; that small buildings can be monumental in nature while large buildings can also be monumentally oversized.

In the early 1970s Rogers collaborated with Renzo Piano on the Pompidou Center (1977) in Paris. With moveable interior walls and its stunning exterior of exposed structural elements including staircases, elevator towers, and lavatories, it took Rogers five years to create and catapulted him from relative obscurity on to the world stage. The idea of placing internal elements on the building's exterior of course left interior spaces open and uncluttered, reflecting the architect Louis I Khan's concept of having both "served and servant" spaces.

Rogers is actively involved in urban regeneration, believing that a return to the concept of urban spaces built around piazzas is becoming increasingly vital in an era of ever-increasing urban "creep." With central London losing a third of its population over the last 30 years as people feel the city is fast losing its ability to provide a healthy, secure, and affordable lifestyle, Rogers has in recent years attempted to lure people back to the city. His Montevetro Residential Project (1999) in Battersea is a vertical village of over 103 apartments and is unapologetically modern. The apartments vary between 1,000 to 2,500 sq ft (93 to 232 sq m) and all have generous balconies. The east facade has panels of terracotta, while the west facade is heavily glazed, providing superb views over the River Thames, Chelsea, and west London. It is these views that echo Rogers' belief that the river holds the key to the city's revitalization. Other public housing projects of note are the Thames Reach Housing project (1984–87) in London, and the Daimler Chrysler Residential project (1993–99) in Berlin.

Rogers' most recognized house is Dr Rogers House (1968–69) in London. The house, situated on a long and narrow site, is designed to provide privacy and consists of two separate buildings facing an internal garden courtyard. The smaller building consists of a separate unit and pottery studio and acts as a sound barrier between the main house and the road. The steel structure of the main house is inside to eliminate maintenance and to simplify the junctions between the structure and skin. Eight welded clear-span steel portals permit demountability and the re-use of the enclosing envelope and internal partitions. Flexibility was a high priority in the design and most internal partitions are moveable. Maximum-sized, double-glazed, sealed units in painted steel frames have been used, and glazed, solar reflecting roofs enclose the bathrooms.

His numerous awards include the Royal Institute of British Architects Royal Gold Medal (1985), and the Royal Academy Summer Exhibition Gold Award Winner (1996).

Aldo Rossi

Aldo Rossi (1931–97) was born in Milan, Italy, and received his architectural qualification from the Milan Politecnico (1959) where he later became a professor. He also taught at several other architecture schools in Italy, the United States of America, and Spain. In 1990 Rossi was awarded the Pritzker Prize.

Rossi was an internationally influential theorist and historian, as well as a practicing architect and a sometime controversial critic. He was the editor of the journal *Casabella-Continuita* during the 1960s. His reputation was established in 1966 with the publication of *L'Architettura della Citta (The Architecture of the City)*; considered an essential text on architecture and urban theory, which reacted against Modernism by putting forward ideas about the role of monuments and collective memory in the city.

Rossi, along with Giorgio Grassi and Massimo Scolari, was part of a group of Italian architects and theorists in the 1960s that Scolari referred to as "La Tendenza." They challenged the Late-modernist tendency of self-expression of the designer, downplaying the subjective role of the architect in the design process, and rejected the idea of Functionalism in favor of a focus on form. Their discourse was described as "Neo-rationalist" and became associated with the work of other Rationalists throughout Europe, such as Leon Krier. Rossi's later work, including the ideas promoted in *The Architecture of the City*, embraced more subjectivity and expression of personal memory in design.

Rossi has completed a great deal of work worldwide including in Italy, Japan, the United States of America, Spain, the Netherlands, and the United Kingdom. Two of his most famous works are the Gallaratese 2 apartment complex on the outskirts of Milan (1970), and the Cemetery of San Cataldo in Modena, Italy (1971–84), for which he won a design competition with the architect Gianni Braghieri.

On Gallaratese 2, Rossi worked with Carlo Aymonino, with whom he had worked at the Instituto Universitario de Architettura in Venice. The project coincided with growing recognition for their theory from the international architectural community, but attracted criticism from the public, as it did not look like a typical apartment complex. Rossi's contribution to the project is one apartment building in the complex, characterized by its severe, monumental, undecorated appearance, in contrast with more traditional buildings in the area. Although for Rossi the design may have been a logical extension of the essential characteristics and meaning of traditional Italian arcades and streets, to the working-class community it may have recalled the bare mass housing of the 1930s.

Rossi's work is difficult to categorize, as his focus on historical precedent and traditional forms can be understood as Post-modern, yet the references are so abstracted in his built work that its appearance could be described as Late-modern, particularly with regard to the use of modern technologies such as concrete.

Among Rossi's projects are several notable houses, mainly found in Italy. His design (with Braghieri) for a Villa in Borgo Ticino (1973) explores the essence of European fisherman's houses, with long building wings supported on high poles. Rossi has also produced several designs for the Alessi family, which include not only his iconic range of coffee makers, but also houses such as the Villa Alessi (1991–93) at Lago Maggiore, which is an unusual combination of Classical and vernacular elements. It features a steel vault roof over a four-story building that is sandwiched between two smaller scale and visually heavy brick elements. Other well-known projects include houses in Broni (1973 and 1982–83) and the gable-roofed houses in Zandobbio (1979).

Paul Rudolph

Paul Rudolph (1918–97) was born in Elkton, Kentucky, USA, and graduated from the Alabama Polytechnic Institute in 1940. After serving with the US Navy during World War II, he entered Harvard's Graduate School of Design, where he graduated with a Masters in Architecture in 1947 and began his career designing houses on Florida's west coast in the early 1940s.

His 1,800-sq-ft (167-sq-m) Umbrella House (1953) in Lido Key, Florida, was named by *Architectural Digest* as one of the most remarkable houses of the mid-twentieth century. A pinnacle of the Modernist Sarasota School, it got its name from a sheltering parasol that extended from the main body of the house to create a grand entry on its west side and its pool deck to the east. Its horizontal articulation results in nine distinct levels. By elevating the house a foot off the ground, a floating effect against its surrounding lush, tropical landscape is achieved.

Rudolph's Revere House (1948) on Siesta Key, Florida, was one of eight prototypes commissioned by the *Architectural Forum Magazine* to demonstrate how attractive and affordable residential buildings could be constructed using industrial materials. With its 6 in (15 cm) thick slab walls, wide overhangs, non-load bearing walls, and a flat roof, it was billed as the house of the future.

From 1958 to 1965 Rudolph was chairman of the Department of Architecture at Yale University, bringing cohesion to a troubled department, brilliant insights, and facilitating connections to other respected architects. Architect George Ranalli credited Rudolph's teaching methods and influences as being responsible for creating one of the most significant bodies of architects in the United States of America. Rudolph's design for Yale's Art and Architecture Building (1963) made him a legend, and was immediately praised for its sense of balance in its interior and exterior spaces, and its horizontal and vertical planes. Critics began associating his name with the likes of Le Corbusier, Wright, and Kahn.

Moshe Safdie

Moshe Safdie (1938–) was born in Haifa, Israel. He received his architectural education in Montreal at McGill University between 1955 and 1961, and has become one of their famous architectural graduates. After working for two years in the office of Louis I Kahn, he started his own practice in Montreal. Later, he moved to the United States of America and established a private practice and taught at Harvard University.

When we consider architecture as a profession, we do so not for early fame and remuneration. Unlike music and mathematics, there are a few child prodigies in the profession. In fact, there are few who receive serious recognition before fifty, Moshe Safdie, however, is an exception. In 1967 he built a revolutionary prefabricated housing project at the World Expo and achieved world notoriety. It was known as Habitat 67 and while its promise of low-cost, humane housing was not fully realized, it was nevertheless a full-scale demonstration of the possibilities that precast concrete technology afforded. Safdie contended that the high costs, which eventually rivalled custom development prices, were due to the small number of units (158) produced for the Habitat site and program. This project inspired a larger proven housing project in Puerto Rico, which tended to validate the architect's thesis. Whether critics consider this a success or failure by economic measures, there is no question that Habitat 67 – a carefully ordered jumble of concrete boxes that formed a new urban silhouette on its spectacular Cité du Harve site in Montreal, Canada, surrounded by water – became an instant symbol throughout the world of modern, advanced technology in architecture.

Safdie's early talent and energy was borne out by a series of commissions that followed. His private residential project of note is the Callahan Residence (1978–81) in Birmingham, Alabama, USA. Designed to respond to the client's fantasy of living in the control tower of Dulles Airport, the wood-framed building contains three levels connected by a central staircase, and is an extroverted mass with a commanding presence over its surroundings. The south-facing roof contains large skylights that capture the sun during the winter, and are covered by a rolling white canvas screen during the summer.

Safdie's housing projects, such as David's Village (1972) in Jerusalem; the Ardmore Habitat Condominiums (1980–85) in Singapore; the Esplanade Condominiums (1986–89) in Cambridge, Massachusetts; and the Cairnhill Road Condominiums (1997–2003) in Singapore, all synthesize his approach to architecture: To create buildings that are cohesive expressions of their technology and construction materials, as well as their surroundings and purpose. The Esplanade Condominiums feature 206 luxury units; each with either a roof garden or an enclosed winter garden. To the south, the "hillside" facade features cream pre-cast concrete panels, while the northern elevation, by contrast, is in red brick. Cairnhill Road Condominiums are three semi-circular, twenty-story towers, each containing luxury apartments. Each tower has a solid masonry curved wall on its inward side and a glazed, sun-shaded wall on its outward side, with a circular glazed room protruding from the outward surfaces. In response to Singapore's tropical climate, exterior sunshades cantilever out from all the glass surfaces.

Safdie's architecture hit a low in 1987 with a project called The Columbus Circle. It was criticized by citizens and groups who protested over its environmental impact on Central Park, New York. Both groups cited the mass and height of Safdie's prismatic skyscraper would cast an objectionably long shadow over the park. There is little time to dwell on this setback, as Safdie received one of the most prestigious commissions available in Canada: The National Gallery of Canada. It was a triumph for him and a major architectural monument for Canada.

Safdie received the Canadian Massey Medal for Architecture in 1968, an Order of Canada in 1986, and the Prix d'Excellence in Architecture of the Quebec Order of Architects in 1988.

Hans Scharoun

Hans Scharoun (1893–1972) was born in Bremen, Germany. An avowed socialist, he received his architectural training at the Technical University in Berlin-Charlottenburg from 1912 to 1914. His work on reconstructing East Prussia (now Poland), devastated in the aftermath of World War I, continued until 1925.

In 1919 he joined the Expressionist circle led by Bruno Taut, becoming involved in their fanciful "Crystal Chain" network. Taut's elite group of architects would engage in whimsical correspondence, inventing imaginary identities and discussing ways of bringing about a revolution in architecture using words couched in rhetoric. This playful approach to design resulted in many futuristic and totally impractical concepts, such as genital-shaped Black Forest settlements and flower-shaped communities outside crumbling, decaying cityscapes. Many of Scharoun's own drawings possessed surreal and dreamlike structures that lacked practicality and, in fact, only a very few of his designs were built, despite his submissions to various architectural competitions eliciting reasonable degrees of consideration.

In 1927 Scharoun built a house in the Stuttgart Weissenhof Estate. He also gained the commission at the end of the 1920s for the development of the Siemensstadt housing estate in Berlin. Scharoun departed from Rationalism and from preformulated plans in order to develop buildings with a unique functional character, where the organization of the living spaces played a central role. He went on to design several public housing projects in Berlin, including the Apartments at Kaiserdamm (1928–29), the Apartments at Hohenzollerdamm (1929–30), as well as the Salute high-rise apartments (1961–63) in Stuttgart, and the Orplid high-rise apartments (1971) in Boblingen.

Scharoun also designed villas, like the Schminke House (1933) in Lobau, the Mattern House in Potsdam (1934), and the Baensch House (1935) and Mohrmann House (1939), both in Berlin. They were private commissions, with innovative interiors hidden by traditionally shaped walls and roofs. The Schminke House is considered one of the last great International Style buildings in Germany. This large, elongated country house is situated parallel to the street on a slightly sloping site. The street facade is relatively closed, while the opposite front has huge windows stretching from the floor to the ceiling. This gradual opening is reflected in the internal composition of the rooms: It starts at the entrance and continues through the main hall towards the living room with its winter garden and terrace. Scharoun's floor plan was based on diverse overlapping grids and building parts projecting outward.

Recently, Scharoun's importance as one of Modernism's leading figures has been re-evaluated. His dynamic interior spaces, use of non-rectilinear forms, and a sculptural approach to design are characteristic of his later years, and are probably best exemplified by the Philharmonie in Berlin (1963), which is generally regarded to be his masterpiece.

In the aftermath of World War II, Scharoun proposed a series of grand public spaces and civic structures to guide the consciousness of the people. Located close to the Berlin Wall, Scharoun intended the Philharmonie to be the nucleus of a cultural center for a reunited Germany. Designed from the inside out, the stage is surrounded by the audience who are seated in a tiered arrangement encouraging their appreciation of not only the orchestra, but of themselves, all wrapped together in a classic model of organic design.

In 1964 he won the Federation of German Architects Grand Prize, and was the recipient of the Auguste Perret Prize in 1965 and the Erasmus Prize in 1970.

Rudolph Schindler

Rudolph Michael Schindler (1887–1953) was born in Vienna, Austria, at a time when the city was marked by cultural pluralism. Schindler first studied at the Imperial Technical Institute in Vienna between 1906 and 1911, and later in Otto Wagner's school known as Specialschule dur Architekur, at the Academy of Fine Arts in Vienna. He immigrated to the United States of America in March 1914, and worked for the firm Ottenheimer, Stern and Reichert in Chicago until 1917. Here Schindler met Louis Sullivan, and later after a trial period he worked for Frank Lloyd Wright at Taliesin, in Spring Green, Wisconsin. Here he learned a great deal from Wright's Prairie architecture. Wright also sent him to Los Angeles where he supervised the completion of the Hollyhock House for Aline Barnsdall in 1921. After the Hollyhock House Schindler decided to stay on in Los Angeles. Wright's influence on Schindler is best seen in his own house, the Schindler House, built in 1922 in Kings Road, or the Schindler-Chase House in Hollywood (1921–22), which was designed for two couples, with common living spaces. This house was built from a series of concrete interlocking slabs. But Los Angeles, with its palm-tree dreams, was a big contrast from the public buildings and ancient monarchy of Vienna.

Yet it was in Los Angeles that Schindler was to find his own identity. His theory of "space architecture" is a direct product of Wilshire Boulevard with its sunshine and unclouded optimism. The building of the Schindler House set the seal in Schindler's attitude towards domestic architecture. In this house he used a prefabricated concrete system, where he combined Wright's "destruction of the box" with his own idea of "continuous space." Schindler used concrete construction up until 1928, when he abandoned it for cost reasons, in favor of the American balloon-frame principle of timber and plaster.

Perhaps the Lovell Beach House (1922–26) at Newport Beach, California, is Schindler's first real important work. Its design has often been linked to Walter Gropius' Bauhaus buildings in Dessau (1925–26), the Barcelona Pavilion at the World Fair in Barcelona by Mies van der Rohe (1929), and the Lovell House in Los Angeles by Richard Neutra (1929). In the Lovell Beach House (for the same client as Neutra's) Schindler took the family requirements of a vacation house, and used them to create a prototype in healthy living. This was an exercise in the use of a concrete frame, the inclusion of a roof garden for sunbathing, and the projection of cantilevered balconies – "space trays," as Schindler called them. It also included the creation of a spacious living room which absorbed two stories, and the use of a proportional system to achieve an overall sense of Classic harmony. At the same time Schindler achieved a sense of informality incorporating life at the beach with a positive idea of healthy living.

Schindler's ideas evolved out of a familiarity with the more casual and personal concerns of "golden California." And his work, therefore, contrasts with the impersonal approach of the Europeans during the 1930s. During this time Schindler built outstanding Californian houses, namely the Oliver House (1934), the Buck House in the same year, the Fitzpatrick House (1936), followed by the Henwar Rodakiewicz House (1937). In these houses he identified vertical and horizontal planes, while articulating his spatial concerns.

Schindler's ideas were a creative synthesis of his background and were shaped by the impact of Otto Wagner, Adolf Loos, Richard Neutra, and Frank Lloyd Wright. Above all, Schindler understood the needs of a family living a "Californian dream." As a person, Schindler was lively with a good sense of humor – a personality that followed its own path, and in the process rejected impersonal architecture.

John Scott

John Colin Scott (1924–92) was born at Haumoana, Hastings, New Zealand and was of English, Scottish, Irish, and Te Arawa ancestry. His family did not openly express their Maori heritage. He trained at the University of Auckland School of Architecture between 1946 and 1950, where he was influenced by Bill Wilson, the unpretentious leader of the Auckland Group Architects. Most of Scott's commissions were for private houses, though his Chapel of Futuna (1958–61) in Karori, Wellington, is his *cause célèbre.* Futuna is regarded as a major cultural landmark within New Zealand's history of architecture. It is arguably the first New Zealand building to creatively fuse European and Polynesian sympathies – a genuine creative synthesis of humane regionalism.

Yet for all of Scott's ability to bridge the cultural gap between Maori and *Pakeha* (white New Zealanders), he remains completely self-effacing. He was a "down-to-earth" architect who incorporated the *whare* (meeting house) and woolshed in his work, while also responding to the needs of people. For him architecture had to complement its purpose. Scott's distinguished domestic work is all about the earth, sea and sky, and he used light and materials as a generator of form. He built logically like a carpenter, and the technical performance of his buildings mattered. Scott's work is a poignant expression of what Pacific architecture might and should be.

Scott's earliest houses were both visually and spatially strong. His use of creosoted weatherboards and monopitched roofs came together with much conviction, which outpaced the Auckland houses of Vernon Brown and Bill Wilson. We only have to compare Brown's Auckland houses with what Scott built for the Hancocks of Arthurs Crescent, Takapuna in 1952 to realize that by this time, Scott had fully assimilated the work of the Auckland Group.

His best houses include the Anderson House (1956) facing onto Lake Taupo; the Pattison Farm House (1968), composed on a brow in the rolling landscape of Waipawa; the Rowe House (1979), with its magical entrance in Havelock North; and the Apu House (1985), set within the high country tussock of the Ngamatea Station, North Island. In all these North Island houses, Scott displayed a strong sense of place and sensitivity to the landscape.

Scott practiced architecture during a period obsessed with the social and political issues separating Maori and *Pakeha* New Zealanders. Though through his architecture, he envisaged a cultural fusion rather than division. Highly talented and arguably alone as a cultural synthesizer, Scott followed his own path. As an indigenous pioneer, he provided an amalgam of domesticity whose humane regionalism combined not only the best of both worlds, but his work was timeless, and this New Zealand example will prevail.

Denise Scott Brown

Denise Scott Brown is an architect and urban planner, and a principal of the firm Venturi, Scott Brown and Associates (VSBA), based in Philadelphia. She is also an influential theorist, writer, and teacher. She has participated in hundreds of forums and lectures and has taught at many architecture schools throughout the United States of America, including Harvard, Yale, and the University of Pennsylvania.

Scott Brown (1931–) was born in South Africa and studied at the University of Witwatersrand in Johannesburg, followed by the Architectural Association in London, and the University of Pennsylvania. She also holds several honorary doctorates. Scott Brown has collaborated with the architect Robert Venturi since 1960, and in 1967 joined the firm Venturi and Rauch, which later became Venturi, Rauch and Scott Brown.

The firm is known for architectural work which explores complexity, decoration, symbolism, historical references, and mannerist gestures such as distortions of scale. An unusual example of decoration in VSBA's work is the Brant House in Connecticut (1970), designed for a client who collected pop art and Art Deco pieces. It features a pattern formed out of green bricks over the facade, and elements inside that are also reminiscent of Art Deco, such as a black-and-white chequered entry floor pattern.

Scott Brown's approach to design is shaped by social concerns and a call for understanding between architects and social planners. Her more recent projects include several campus planning projects for universities throughout the world, including Brown University in the United States of America and Tsinghua University in Beijing, China.

Scott Brown is also well-known for the 1972 publication of the book *Learning from Las Vegas* (co-authored with Venturi and Steven Izenour) – a significant text on Post-modern design theory, now published in many languages. More recent books include *Architecture as Signs and Systems* (2004), also with Venturi.

VSBA, as a firm, has won a great many significant project-related awards in the United States of America and also the United Kingdom, particularly for their institutional work. Scott Brown has also been personally honored with many awards, including the Edith Wharton Women of Achievement Award for Urban Planning in 2002 and the ACSA–AIA Topaz Medallion for Architecture Education in 1996.

Harry Seidler

Australian architect Harry Seidler (1923–2006) was born in Vienna, Austria. He was of Jewish descent and following the Anschluss occupation of Austria in the late 1930s, he escaped to England where he was interned along with many other refugees before being transported to Canada. He gained release by being accepted to study architecture at the University of Manitoba, and later completed his graduate studies in the United States of America, before moving to Australia in 1948 to design a house for his parents.

Seidler was directly influenced by the Modernist leaders, particularly Walter Gropius, whose master class he participated in at the Harvard Graduate School of Design between 1945 and 1946, and Marcel Breuer for whom he worked as an assistant in New York between 1946 and 1948. On his way to Australia, he worked with Oscar Niemeyer in Brazil where Modern architecture was becoming dominant and was particularly flamboyant and sculptural. Seidler also attended painter Josef Albers' summer design course at Black Mountain College, which focused on visual perception.

Harry Seidler first gained public attention for his work when he was awarded the prestigious Sir John Sulman Medal in 1951 for the Rose Seidler House (1948) at Turramurra in Sydney – his first house in Australia. The Rose Seidler House was one of the first Modernist homes to be built in Australia, and many of the themes of this design can also be recognized in his later work. It is now owned and managed by the Historic Houses Trust of New South Wales.

The economy of planning evident in his early residential work throughout New South Wales, was the result of both the relatively limited means of his clients, and the shortage of building materials after World War II. These early houses utilized raw or white-painted natural materials, and explored responses to Australia's harsh local environment, particularly sun shading. Houses such as the Harry and Penelope Seidler House (1966–67), the Hannes House (1983–84), and the Mellor House (1950), all in Sydney, also feature split-level arrangements with open voids, spaces overlooking one another and connecting ramps and bridges for continuity, suggesting the influence of Le Corbusier's 1920s villas.

Seidler's later work was predominantly larger commissions and focused on exploring innovative planning for high-density multi-residential work, but still with an interest in novel details for sun control. Projects include the Condominium Apartments (1969–70) in Acapulco, Mexico; the Horizon Apartments (1990) in Sydney, Australia; and the Hochhaus Neue Donau (2001) in Vienna, Austria. Many of these later projects are also innovative in their use of concrete, developed in close collaboration with the office of structural engineer Pier Luigi Nervi. Examples include the design for Sydney's well-known Australia Square Development (1961), commended for its efficient and wind-resistant circular plan.

Seidler is well known for his many public buildings, including the Australian Embassy in Paris (1973–77), the Riverside Centre in Brisbane (1983), and the MLC Centre in Sydney (1972) which, like Australia Square, was developed to maximize the unbuilt open public space on the site. These projects explore curvilinear and elliptical geometries, in contrast to the rectilinear planning of his early houses.

Seidler was a committed Modernist despite being isolated in Australia from other architects producing leading Late-modern work internationally. He brought a Modernism to Australia that was more pure and uncompromised by historical and "colonial" influences than any other Australian work of the time. Many of his designs were controversial and perceived as futuristic, and met with resistance from local councils, in some cases having to be defended in court.

Seidler was awarded the Royal Australian Institute of Architects Gold Medal in 1976, and the Royal Institute of British Architects Royal Gold Medal in 1996, as well as several RAIA awards throughout his long career.

Josep Lluis Sert

Josep Lluis Sert (1902–83) was born in Barcelona, Spain, and educated at the Escuela Tecnica Superior de Arquetectura in Barcelona, where he graduated in 1929. Inspired by the work of Antonio Gaudi, and having worked with Le Corbusier, he opened his own practice and in 1937 designed the Spanish Pavilion for the World's Fair in Paris. From 1947 to 1956 he was president of the Congres Internationaux d'Architecture Moderne (CIAM) in Spain, and in 1953 became dean of the Faculty of the Graduate School of Design and Professor of Architecture at Harvard University. In 1959 he established Harvard's first professional degree program in urban design, which is now America's leading center for research, education, and information on the built environment.

The 1950s and '60s saw a reshaping of cities through localized interventions. Sert became influential in bringing together architects, landscape designers, and town planners, and integrating them at every level of the design process.

In 1968 he began construction of his own villa, Sert House, on the Spanish island of Ibiza, one of a collection of nine dwellings that reinterpreted the island's vernacular architecture and were built to resemble an indigenous village. Sert was a Functionalist who enjoyed combining the timeless features of Mediterranean architecture with the visual stimulation wrought by contemporary art. His houses are characterized by rectangular living areas that run parallel to a terrace with a view, so that one side is completely glazed. They all contain fireplaces accompanied by masonry benches that line the entire wall to which the chimney is joined – a feature found in traditional peasant homes in Ibiza. The walls and ceilings were painted white to allow accents to be introduced by the use of carpets, tapestries, and paintings. The placing of paintings and art pieces was strategic to provide the most visual impact.

Among his many commissions are the Science Center at Harvard University (1973), the Miro Foundation (1974) in Barcelona, and the Maeght Foundation (1959–64) in the southern French town of Saint-Paul-de-Vence.

Kazuo Shinohara

Kazuo Shinohara (1925–) was born in Japan. Educated at the Institute of Technology, Tokyo, he is considered one of Japan's most influential architects. Shinohara's philosophy is to design a whole edifice rather than just building a structure with walls, roof, and fittings for a particular practical purpose. As a professional academic, he only allows himself to build works that fit in with his intellectual concepts. He sees it as his duty to set an example as an architect and erect buildings that prove his theses and demonstrate them in lively fashion.

Contemporary Japanese architecture relies on traditional design as a starting point, but Kazuo Shinohara says, "It must be the point to which it returns." All the new wave of Japanese architects would agree. Shinohara's concepts are of particular interest to western architects because he started from basic Japanese architectural forms and further developed them. In this he found a new mode of architectural expression that was his own, but still owes a great deal to things "Japanese." He has always taken the "Japanese architectural tradition" as a starting point to find an expression for current design, thus preserving something of value for the contemporary period. But this does not mean that he is a "traditionalist;" he develops the possibilities of the Japanese view of architecture in order to extract something new from it and make this his own.

Shinohara's designs speak a rich minimalism and there is a conscious deliberation of hard-surfaced geometry in his work, reminiscent of the Modern architects, especially Le Corbusier. The primary shapes – cubes, cylinders, trilateral prisms, orthogonal grinds, or trabeated pergolas – are important in Shinohara's architecture. Geometry serves to focus the Genius Loci within their structures and the intention is to create a "spirit of places."

Shinohara's architecture has a bold purity in its elements. Botond Bognar in his book *Contemporary Japanese Architecture: Its Development and Challenge* states, "Shinohara's abstract and 'naked spaces' of transcendental purity are created for reasons beyond easy comprehension. They defy any rational expectation and explanation even if sometimes they are so explained. But while they leave the rational mind stuttering, they 'conform to the deepest levels of human emotions' in Shinohara's words, and promote spiritual purification."

Shinohara produced modernized versions of the traditional Japanese house in his early domestic work, but this changed with his so-called House with a Big Roof (1961) in Tokyo. Thereafter his houses tended to be identified by the single-minded image that was the basis of their design. He went on to create eccentric works with earthen floors and high-pitched interiors devoid of furniture. His obsession with an existential iconic architecture reached its climax in a series of stark concrete houses designed between 1970 and 1976: The Incomplete House and the House at a Crooked Corner, both in Tokyo; a house in Uehara; and one in Ashitaka. Together they formed a series that brought this phase of his work to an end.

Shinohara received the Architectural Institute of Japan Prize in 1972 and became an Honorary Fellow of the American Institute of Architects in 1988.

Heikki and Kaija Siren

Heikki Siren (1918–) and Kaija Anna-Maija Helena Siren (1920–2001) were a husband-and-wife team who practiced architecture in Finland for more than 50 years. While Heikki was born in Helsinki, the son of Professor J S Siren, Kaija Tuominen was born in Kotka. Both graduated in architecture in the 1940s from the Technical University in Helsinki. Today their practice is carried on by their son, Jukka Siren.

The Sirens became internationally famous for their distinguished Otaniemi Technical University Chapel (1951–57). This Lutheran chapel is described in Russell Walden's 1998 book *Finnish Harvest*, as a timeless creation: A work of veritable fidelity in brick, timber, and glass -- an architectural example of deep simplicity, faithfulness to the inner voice, and the genius of the Finnish soul.

A critical part of the Sirens' practice from the 1950s onwards was their work in private houses and public housing – particularly that of providing for university students. As dedicated architects, their domestic work created a "stage" for the nourishment of human beings in close sympathy with nature. Long Finnish winters and snow storms create the need for an intuitive and imaginative approach to disciplined and "balanced" work in architecture. Probably the words "clarity and restraint" best describe the plan- and section-making of Heikki and Kaija Siren. Their architectural creativity is marked by the vitality of an articulated plan as the basis of their spatial embrace with human beings. In this equation, the feminine and masculine values were held in a delicate harmony as a manifestation of built love.

Their domestic work began with the design of their own home in Lauttasaari, Helsinki, between 1951 and 1960. Entering their three-storied home, one is immediately entering a spatial world of fine art objects, flowers, sailing boat models, books and sculpture. This home accommodated their office. Both architects were art lovers, and became great sailors from their vacation hideaway and family gathering place on the sheltered side of the uninhibited island of Lingonso, in the outer Barosund Archipelago. Here they built their summer retreat – a series of log cabins (1966–69) for living and sleeping complete with the traditional Finnish sauna. These single-storied timber buildings were designed to face the setting sun. This domestic group was joined together by timber decking. On the other storm-centered side of the island, above a natural outcrop of ageless granite, the Sirens built a contemplative pavilion facing the open sea. Set against such an emphatic horizon, where the sea touches an endless sky, this glass pavilion enjoys a lonely landscape of glacial granite tumbling down into a mirroring sea. Of all the Siren buildings the "sea-pavilion" is a favorite.

Face-to-face with primeval nature in its purest form, the Sirens applied all the meditative lessons learnt in the design and construction of their Chapel at Otaniemi. Exploiting the simplicity of the horizontal and vertical, the Sirens' contemplative pavilion provides a supreme relationship with a landscape millions of years old. Here, before the Barosund Archipelago, the open sea is experienced alone. From this earthly paradise, Heikki and Kaija Siren became keen boat builders and architects of a maturing urbanity.

Sailing, like architecture, calls for ecological sensitivity, individual character, and teamwork. This was a potent reminder that everything in Finland is rooted in nature. Moreover, the sea is a source of sustaining strength. Not surprisingly, the Sirens' architecture echoes a totality of restraint and positive harmony. Combining competitive teamwork and depth of character provides the will towards authenticity in architecture. For this very reason, all the Sirens' architecture maintains a natural flexibility in harmony with the universal themes of humanity and the collective unconscious. In the end their creative labor quietly translates human dignity through the rhythms of nature and the rigorous harvest of winter. This particular reality – with its denial of summer light – opens up the humanized world of Finland as a dialog with nature.

Alvaro Siza

Alvaro Siza (1933–) was born in the small coastal town of Matosinhos in northern Portugal. Widely acknowledged as Portugal's greatest living architect, he studied at the University of Porto School of Architecture from 1949 to 1955. In 1954 he opened his own practice in Porto, and since then his body of work has comprised mass housing developments, museums, private residences, restaurants, and office buildings that display a unique understanding of spatial relationships, texture, and light that have led to some of the twentieth century's most sublime, balanced, and timeless structures, all testifying to his belief that "architecture is art."

Siza's first work was his Four Houses (1954–57) in Matosinhos. The organic design of these houses echoes the architecture of the region, while his subtle twisting of the geometry of the rooms gives each interior space definition. On the outside tall, narrow slits cut into a wall beneath an exterior staircase reveal Siza's fondness for Modernism. Siza's Alves Costa House (1964–68) in Moledo do Minho also reflects a sensitivity to the surrounding landscape, and the qualities of light. Featuring intersecting planes, an opening onto a small pine forest, and an almost naked street facade, the design of this house is characterized by carefully thought-out details, such as wood-leaf wainscoting painted a pale yellow, placed precisely where the sun penetrates the interior.

International recognition came in 1980 with his winning design for a large public housing block in Berlin – the Schlesisches Tor. Now known as the Bonjour Tristesse, it demonstrates Siza's contextual qualities and sensitivity to a project's surroundings. Other projects that followed included the restoration of the Chiada area of Lisbon, destroyed after a disastrous fire in 1988; the Setubal College of Education (1986–94); and Oporto University's Faculty of Architecture (1987–93).

Siza is also a participant in the Rolex Mentor and Protégé Arts Initiative, launched in 2002. Its aim is to seek out gifted young artists and align them with contemporary masters in their chosen fields, providing protégés with the opportunity to develop their talents and grow creatively.

Siza's fascination with common, everyday geometric forms, together with a controlled composition of interiors, and mastery in utilizing light to create new interior spaces all combine to see him seated comfortably in the company of the world's most acclaimed architects. He was the winner of the Pritzker Prize in 1992 for designs that "are a joy to the senses and which uplift the spirit;" a product of a philosophy in which architects are seen not as inventors, but rather as responding to and overcoming a series of prescribed challenges.

Luigi Snozzi

Luigi Snozzi (1932–) is a Modern architect from the influential region of Ticino, the Italian-speaking section of southern Switzerland. The area has played an important role in twentieth-century architecture and has developed its own idiosyncratic and highly influential architectural language based on Rationalist principles of design. Snozzi's work is characterized by its simple forms, its visual connection with the site, and the creative use of raw concrete which has become Snozzi's lifelong obsession.

Snozzi was born in the historical town of Mendrisio at the southern extremity of Switzerland. He studied classics in nearby Ascona before undertaking studies in architecture at the Swiss Federal Institute of Technology (ETH) in Zurich between 1952 and 1957. In 1958 he started his own practice in Locarno.

Snozzi's architectural career has shown incredible versatility, working at a range of scales including small residential alterations, free-standing houses, social housing, public amenities, commercial office buildings, and vast urban planning proposals. As well as its distinctive architectural vocabulary, Snozzi's work demonstrates a sensitivity towards the integration of Modern architectural forms with local cultures and history. One of Snozzi's most widely recognized works is the urban redevelopment of the small principality of Monte Carasso (1977–90). The outcome of a protracted political process, Snozzi's redevelopment of the township centered around creating a strong urban center from the remnants of a sixteenth-century monastery that was originally marked for demolition.

As well as his urban planning, Snozzi has designed a number of influential Modern houses in the small townships around Ticino. The Snider House (1964–66) in Verscio is one of Snozzi's first houses and explored, through simple forms, the house as a platform for orienting the individual within a broader contextual landscape. The visual relationship between a building and its site was further developed in subsequent houses such as the Kalmann House (1972–75) in Minusio, Casa Bianchetti (1975–77) in Locarno, and Casa Bernasconi (1989) in Carona.

Kalmann House is a concrete box situated on a hillside. Strict in geometry and the use of minimal materials and colors, the landscape provides all the color and decoration for the house. A bridge juts out from the house and leads to a pavilion from which the owners can enjoy views of the surrounding mountains, lake, and valley.

As well as his architectural practice, Snozzi has also been heavily involved in teaching and is a professor at the Federal Polytechnic in Lausanne.

Paolo Soleri

Paolo Soleri (1919–) was born in Turin, Italy. He attended the Torino Polytechnico in 1946 where he was awarded a PhD before going to the United States of America the following year where he studied with Frank Lloyd Wright. In 1956 he settled in Scottsdale, Arizona, where he established the non-profit Cosanti Foundation to further research and experimentation in urban planning.

In 1949, Soleri began the Dome House at Cave Creek in Arizona. Completed in 1952, the radical design includes the house being dug into a hillside and lined with masonry walls, making the interior warm in winter and cool in summer. Daylight and air enter the house through its glass dome. Mounted on rails, this feature reacts to heat and light, making the Dome House one of the first low energy and sustainable homes ever built.

But it is the Cosanti Foundation's current project, Arcosanti, designed by Soleri and under construction since 1970, that has cemented Soleri's commitment to sustainable urban planning. A futuristic community for 5,000 people, it is based upon Soleri's concept of "Arcology" – the minimal use of resources, land, and raw materials coupled with minimal waste and environmental degradation. Cars are banned in Arcosanti; electricity is generated by wind and solar plants; water is provided from a nearby river; and buildings serve multiple purposes with offices, residences, and storage areas all combined. Over 6,000 architecture students from around the world have visited Arcosanti since it opened in 1970 to learn its principles and the methods of applying them in urban planning. Students complete a series of workshops in architecture, learning the principles of design and "arcology," with the choice of staying on as volunteers or paid workers.

By 1970 Soleri had designed 30 such experimental communities, driven by his realization that the planet's population will double by 2050, and new methods of habitation and material consumption must be addressed and that architecture is at the forefront in the fight to find more environmentally sustainable lifestyles. Soleri sees cities as being three dimensional – neither flat as in suburbia nor outrageously vertical as seen in the modern metropolis. For his work on these communities Soleri is referred to not merely as an architect, but as a visionary and a pioneer of radically new forms of human habitation.

Raphael Soriano

Raphael Soriano (1904–88) was born on the Greek Island of Rhodes. After emigrating to the United States of America in 1924, he enrolled in the University of Southern California's School of Architecture from which he graduated in 1934.

By 1946 Soriano believed the extensive use of steel would be the answer to the post-war demand for housing and so constructed his first steel-framed house, a full two years before Ludwig Mies van der Rohe famously applied it to his Lake Shore Drive Twin Towers in Chicago.

In 1950 Soriano participated in the famous Case Study Program that sought to introduce industrial building concepts and materials to residential design, which culminated in Pierre Koenig's remarkable Case Study Houses No 21 and No 22. In the 1930s Soriano first began to experiment with lightweight steel trusses, columns, and beams, bringing credibility to the Case Study Program, which remained an unrealized ideal of industrialized building based on prefabrication and modularity. His Colby Apartments (1951) in Los Angeles were praised for their extensive use of steel and received the American Institute of Architects Award for Design and the VII International Pan American Congress Award.

In 1961 Soriano was made a Fellow of the American Institute of Architects. Although now regarded as one of the most inventive and pioneering architects of mid-twentieth century Modernism in California, he was also one of the least successful, and in all likelihood would now be forgotten were it not for his friendship with the photographer Julius Schulman who photographed and cataloged many of the 50 homes he built, only 12 of which now remain.

In 1986 he received the American Institute of Architects Distinguished Achievement Award.

François Spoerry

François Spoerry (1912–99) was born in Alsace, France, and studied architecture at the École des Beaux-Arts in Paris from 1934 to 1938. In 1945 he opened an architectural office in the Provençal town of Mulhouse.

Recognition came in the 1960s when he purchased land at the mouth of the Giscle River near Saint-Tropez with a vision to construct a network of canals so that every resident would have their own mooring right outside their door. Today over 2,500 homes have been built, with no two the same. Known as Port Grimaud, Spoerry's vision features squares, vernacular style houses, narrow streets, channels, and bridges and has proved a spectacularly successful example of New Urbanism. He wanted Port Grimaud to resemble Venice but with the colors of Provence.

Spoerry believed that architecture had to be human in scale, and had to impart beauty and uplift the spirit. His designs were very much a reaction to much of the architecture of the 1950s and 60s, such as the brutal nature of Modernism and the growth of the skyscraper. Spoerry's pioneering development provided the blueprint for countless other developments around the world such as the Port Agrilia project on Turkey's Aegean Coast, which has used Spoerry innovations, such as a mooring for every house, though few developers possess the courage to ban the automobile – one of the key aspects of Spoerry's design.

Although the architectural press denounced Port Grimaud as a "boring deception," in the climate of 1970s Post-modernism, there emerged a more favorable re-appraisal of his original intentions. Latter projects have included Port Liberty (1981) in New York, and Puerto Escondido (1986) in Mexico.

Robert Stern

Post-modern architect, historian, and educator Robert A M Stern (1939–) was born in New York City, USA. He received a Bachelor of Architecture from Columbia University in 1960 and his Masters degree from Yale in 1965. Stern worked in the office of Richard Meier in 1966, before becoming a principal partner of the firm founded in 1969 with John S Hagman. The firm became Robert AM Stern Architects in 1977, and while Stern made his name designing large houses, his company now undertakes a broad range of housing, commercial, institutional, and master planning projects.

A professor in the Yale School of Architecture, having also taught at Columbia University, Stern is an active promoter of architectural debate and criticism. Other architects whose work has influenced him include Paul Rudolph, Vincent Scully, Philip Johnson, Sir Edwin Lutyens, and Robert Venturi. As a student in 1965, Stern was the editor of the significant issue (9/10) of *Perspecta: The Yale Architectural Journal* that featured the essay, "Complexity and Contradiction in Architecture" by Venturi. This was one of the first publications on Post-modern architecture, and the essay was later included in Venturi's revolutionary book of the same name (1966).

Stern embraces tradition as well as innovation, and his work is based on the belief that a building should respect the cultural value of those surrounding it, and continue a dialog with the architecture of the past. His buildings are historically referenced using, in an interpretive manner, conventional elements such as moldings and arches. He is concerned with responding to the historical context of each site to preserve its unique sense of place, with particular attention to maintaining continuity in established places.

Stern does not characterize his own work as belonging to a particular movement and his buildings cannot be categorized as one distinct style. Many of his well-known designs for homes such as the Wiseman House (1967) at Montauk; the House in Quogue (1979–81) at Long Island, New York; and the Residence at Chilmark (1979–83), Martha's Vineyard, Massachusetts, are examples of Modern interpretations of the Shingle Style. They use the architectural language of traditional seaside houses of the area – for example, shingled hipped roofs and deep porches – and combine a variety of interesting circular, semicircular, and square window configurations. Many of his notable civic and commercial buildings, such as his award-winning Observatory Hill Dining Hall (1982–84) at the University of Virginia, Charlottesville, and the Point West Place office building (1983–85) in Framingham, Massachusetts, are re-interpretations of the language of Classical architecture.

Stern is a fellow of the American Institute of Architects, and was the president of the Architectural League of New York from 1973 to 1977. With a particular interest in the early twentieth-century architecture and urbanism of New York City, he has co-authored a series of books: *New York 1960,* with Thomas Mellins and David Fishman; *New York 1900,* with John Massengale and Gregory Gilmartin; and *New York 1930,* with Mellins and Gilmartin. His firm has won several awards from the American Institute of Architects, including a number of National Honor Awards and the Medal of Honor of the New York Chapter in 1984.

Peter Stutchbury

Peter Stutchbury (1954–) was born in Australia and was educated at Newcastle University in New South Wales, and has since gained notoriety as one of Australia's most innovative and dynamic architects, combining a keen sense of place with the need for sustainability in urban planning. He was the first architect to win both the Robin Boyd Award for houses and the Sir Zelman Cowan Award for public buildings in the same year.

Sitting atop sandstone cliffs overlooking Sydney Harbour is his marvelous residence Springwater (1992–2002) – an austere, frugal blend of concrete, glass, and timber forms a haven that runs parallel to the adjacent hillside with extensions that allow the house to be an eclectic mix of treehouse and residence.

Stutchbury is keenly aware that an integration of house and environment is still possible in Australia and needs to be pursued, unlike much of Europe where urban encroachment allows for little such experimentation. Very few of his designs incorporate air-conditioning, reflecting a belief that if all the commonsense approaches to heating and cooling are done, there should be no need for artificial environmental controls.

His experimental, stunning, award-winning Bay House (1996–2000) in the Sydney suburb of Watson's Bay represents a search for the ultimate in ecologically sustainable architecture. Natural ventilation is gained through the use of high louvers and sliding panels in the roof with the south side of the house a kind of thermal vault designed to trap heat.

In 2006 Stutchbury won a national competition to design the $10 million Learning Commons development at Charles Sturt University's Albury–Wodonga campus in which he plans to incorporate a massive rust-colored steel-and-glass feature wall, which is sure to become the University's "signature." The project is due for completion in 2008.

Thomas Tait

Thomas Smith Tait (1882–1954) was born in Paisley, Strathclyde, in Scotland. After receiving his education at the John Neilson Institution he became an apprentice to the Paisley architect, James Donald, winning a scholarship to study at the Glasgow School of Art under Eugene Bourdon in 1903. In 1904–05 he traveled throughout Europe before returning to London, where he became an assistant at the prestigious firm of JJ Burnet.

Tait's flamboyant vision and energy led to his collaboration on a number of significant projects including the Edward VII Galleries (1907–14) at the British Museum, and the glazed, metal-framed Kodak Building (1910–11), now regarded as a classic British example of Modern architecture. By 1919 Tait was a partner in the new firm of Burnet, Tait and Lorne, with Tait possessing a fervent determination to take them down the path of Modernism – a style that had made few inroads into Scotland prior to World War I. In fact, it wasn't until the 1930s and the 1938 Empire Exhibition at Bellahouston Park in Glasgow, that a display of New Architecture was ever seen in Scotland. Designed chiefly by Tait, the display covered 150 acres (61 ha) with over 200 pavilions dedicated to the celebration of the British Empire. Its crowning achievement was a stunning tower designed by Tait that rose to over 300 ft (90 m) in height, complete with elevators that took people to a series of observation platforms that could be seen from 100 miles (160 km) away.

The 1920s and '30s saw Tait at the forefront of British Modernism with successful designs for Adelaide House (1924–25) on the banks of the Thames in London; the Silver End Housing Estate (1928) in Chelmsford, England; Hawkhead Hospital (1936) in Paisley, Scotland; and St Andrews House (1939), on Calton Hill in Edinburgh overlooking Holyrood Park.

Tait's Silver End Housing Estate was a very English introduction to Modernism with the garden village comprising conventional brick villas with flat roofs, horizontal windows, and white exteriors. St Andrews House is a monolithic Art Deco-influenced building. Extensively renovated in 2001, it is now protected as a Category A listed building. These and other works have combined to see Thomas Tait now regarded as Scotland's pre-eminent inter-war architect.

Kenzo Tange

Kenzo Tange (1913–2005) was born in Osaka, Japan. He graduated from the University of Tokyo in 1938 and worked for four years with Kunio Maekawa, the pioneer of Modern Japanese architecture and a disciple of Le Corbusier. Tange studied city planning at the University of Tokyo, after which he assumed a position as an assistant professor of architecture. He received a degree in engineering in 1959. Two years later he established Kenzo Tange and Urtec, which later became Kenzo Tange and Associates. He served as professor of urban engineering at the University of Tokyo from 1963 to 1974, when he retired as professor emeritus.

The career of Kenzo Tange began with the master plan for the rebuilding of Hiroshima in 1946 and continued unabated until his death. No other architect of the twentieth century, with the possible exception of the Greek planner Constantinos Doxiades, has had such a global practice, ranging from Texas and Damascus to Singapore and Minneapolis. The sheer volume and scale of Tange's work places him in a category which few architects attain in a lifetime.

Tange's career can be divided into three more or less distinct periods. In the first, following the end of World War II, he was greatly influenced by Le Corbusier and attempted to steer Japanese architecture away from the traditional and slavish copying of European and American styles to a more Modern architecture that incorporated elements of an earlier Japanese stylistic vocabulary. This feeling is expressed in concrete in the Kagawa Prefectural Office (1958). This period of his career culminated and terminated with the now famous twin gymnasia for the 1964 Tokyo Olympic Games. These graceful buildings with their sweeping roof lines and artful siting represented a watershed in Modern Japanese architecture capturing, as they did, the spirit of the culture in original and contemporary terms.

The second stage of Tange's career seemed propelled by his visionary plan for Tokyo's future growth. In 1960 he proposed a daring overlay of the chaotic existing city plan with his own audacious scheme calling for extending the city into Tokyo Bay, thereby creating a new system of super highways and transportation routes. Metabolism advocated the organic growth of cities and the recognition of growth, decay, and rebirth in them as what occurs in nature. Like other utopian movements, the principal achievement proved not to be the realization of goals but instead the wider recognition of the participants. The Tokyo plan by Tange, however, was such a strong idea that it remains today as an influential factor in city planning. Other urban design and planning projects were begun in 1967 for the Fiera District of Bologna, Italy, and for a new town with residences for 60,000 in Catania, Italy.

The third stage of Tange's career advocated a new "architecture for an advanced information society." Among the far-flung commissions for Kenzo Tange and Associates are a master plan for Place d'Italie in Paris, a major banking plaza in downtown Singapore, the Al'Gassim Campus for King Saud University in Saudi Arabia, the redevelopment for the oldest section of Kuala Lumpur and a new capital there.

Tange's most famous residential project is the Ichinomiya Rowhouses (1961) – the eastern equivalent of the rowhouse. Set in a rural landscape, the individual units have a strong western influence in their grouping. Each unit has a garden defined by a low wall, and a higher wall separates every second unit.

Tange will be remembered for being able to demonstrate his theories of architecture for an information society – theories that make a distinction between the technical and the social aspects of communication, that is "the direct communication among men."

Tange has received the Annual Prize from the Architectural Institute of Japan in 1954, 1955, and 1958; the Royal Gold Medal from the Royal Institute of British Architects in 1965; and the Gold Medal of the Académie d'Architecture, France, in 1973. He also received the Pritzker Prize in 1987. He became an Honorary Member of the Academic der Kunste, Germany, in 1962; and an Honorary Fellow of the American Institute of Architects in 1966.

Bruno Taut

Bruno Taut (1880–1938) was born in Königsberg, Germany. Initially a painter and pastel artist, Taut went on to study architecture in Königsberg and Berlin-Charlottenburg prior to joining the firm of Theodore Fischer in Stuttgart. In 1910 he opened his own office in Berlin where he continued to practice until the outbreak of World War I.

Taut's commission for the Falkenberg housing estate (1912) in Berlin-Grunau was a collection of 128 flats and houses set in terraced rows that became known as the "Paint-box Estate," with Taut using primary colors to bring nature and harmony into the city, and to make one dwelling distinctive to its neighbor. It was Taut's bold use of color as an architectural tool that was to distinguish him in the years to come.

In the aftermath of war, large-scale residential estates were seen as the answer to the critical shortage of housing that existed throughout Germany. Bruno Taut was appointed chief architect for the trade union organization Gehag, and was commissioned to design and construct affordable housing for its members. The result was his famous Britz Horseshoe Estate (1925–33), constructed over seven phases in the Britz-Hufeisensiedlung district south of central Berlin. The heart of the Britz estate was a giant horseshoe-shaped ring of terrace houses built around a natural pond. The estate's 1,000 units were standardized with just four floor plans and were among the first examples of flat-roofed housing with overhanging eaves seen in Berlin. To avoid monotony, the houses were set forward or back and set on rows where color was used to provide each street with its own particular character. Diversity was also achieved by variations in height and exterior detailing.

His own home in Dahlewitz, Germany (1926–27) saw Taut use color to explore spatial perceptions and energy-saving techniques. The home's eastern facade was painted black to absorb the sun's morning light, whilst its westerly facade was white to reflect afternoon heat.

Known as the "Apostle of Color," Taut's legacy may well have been greater had he not lived in an age dominated by the pure, white facades of Modernity nor been held captive in a world where the architectural record was cataloged and preserved using black-and-white photography.

Giuseppe Terragni

Giuseppe Terragni (1904–43) was born in Meda, Italy. His career lasted an all-too-brief 13 years, yet in that time he left an indelible impression upon the world of architecture. Terragni first studied architecture at the Milan Polytechnic before going on to open an office in Como with his brother Atiilia in 1927.

From the late 1920s and into the 1930s, Como became the center of Modernity in Italy, and Terragni was hailed as the country's leading Rationalist architect. In 1926 he was one of several signatories to a series of articles on the state of Italian architecture, which represented the first treatise on Modernity in Italy. The group of architects, which included Gino Pollini and Luigi Figini, later became known as the Gruppo 7.

Terragni's masterpiece is universally acknowledged to be his Casa del Fascio (1932–36) at Lake Como – a Rationalist semi-cubed office building with each side displaying alternating filled and empty exterior spaces constructed in marble and reinforced concrete. Terragni used a local and elegant stone on the building's facade, discarding any slabs with imperfections in an attempt to achieve a kind of "dematerialization" in a design that is still regarded as a landmark of Modern European architecture.

Terragni, in association with Pietro Lingeri, formed a partnership to design several apartment buildings in Milan, culminating in Casa Rustici (1933–36); Casa Ghiringhelli (1933–35); and Casa Toniello (1933–35). Casa Rustici was designed to house luxury apartments, with spacious rooms decorated with the finest materials. Situated on a trapezoid-shaped lot, bound by crossroads, Lingeri and Terragni decided to divide the site into two distinct buildings, both with principal street facades. They then connected the two narrow "heads" across a courtyard using loggia-gantry walkways. The complex features different sized apartments ranging from three to seven rooms.

Terragni also designed the private residences Villa Bianca (1936–37) in Seveso, and Villa per un Floricoltore (1936–37) in Como. Villa Bianca was built for his cousin, Angelo. The family connection gave Terragni great creative freedom. He drew up many sketches and studies for the villa, exploring a new kind of one-family home. Terragni used an asymmetrical and harmonic arrangement of overhanging elements (the living room is connected to the main facade, the balcony, the access stairs, and the pensile roof-top areas). The villa is made from reinforced concrete and plastered with gray stone, and the iron window frames are surrounded by white marble, and the railings are also made of iron. Villa per un Floricoltore had a stricter brief, with its occupants wanting a small building and single living quarters. The design maintained the original structure on stilts with a rectangular layout. The villa features a continuous staircase which leads to the first floor, an asymmetric row of windows on one side of the building, a long cornice running the length of another side which frames the second-floor balcony, and a portico that appears to lift the building up from ground level without disrupting its continuity with the garden.

In 1939 Terragni was drafted into military service and was sent to fight in the Balkans. In 1941 he was sent to the Russian Front from which he returned in an ambulance in 1943, said to have been devastated by what he saw at Stalingrad, dying soon after his return to his beloved Como at the age of 39.

Quinlan Terry

Quinlan Terry (1937–) was born in London and educated at Bryanston School and the Architectural Association. His thesis was initially failed by examiners, but he was granted his degree after resubmitting a satirical folio of what he considered to be appalling Modernist designs.

Terry joined Raymond Erith's London firm at a time when Modernism ruled, especially among those who granted public commissions. His big break came in 1984, with the commissioning of his design for Richmond Riverside, today a popular tourist attraction. This harmonious collection of Classical buildings, including offices, restaurants, private dwellings, and community space, is regarded as an iconic model of urban design and illustrates Terry's underlying principle that traditional designs may, or should, be adapted to provide Modern architectural solutions.

Waverton House (1978–80) in Gloucestershire uses the style popularized by Matthew Brettingham in the eighteenth century, with its central staircase surrounded by rooms on both stories. It blends the traditional stone vernacular of the region with the bolder expression of Sanmicheli, most notably in the Ionic doorway.

One of Terry's finest works, Brentwood Cathedral (1989–91) in Essex, uses the Italian Renaissance style mixed with English Baroque. It also features, unusually, all five classical orders of architecture – Doric, Ionic, Corinthian, Tuscan, and Composite. Its portico is based on the south portico of Sir Christopher Wren's St Paul's Cathedral.

Terry received great acclaim for two buildings at Downing College, Cambridge (1987 and 1993), including the library, which was awarded "Building of the Year" by the Royal Institute of British Architects in 1994.

In the mid-nineties, Terry designed the restoration of St Helen's Cathedral in London, incorporating tenets of Protestant Reformation theology, after the church building was severely damaged by IRA bombings. He also designed three staterooms at No 10 Downing Street, and numerous private homes in the United States of America, including the Abercrombie Residence (1986–88). This mansion is based on Marble Hill House in Twickenham, England, and features a pediment supported by Corinthian columns.

Highland Park House (2002–04) in Dallas, Texas, is a large Palladian house, constructed from natural stone. The front and rear facades feature Ionic columns, porticos, modillions, and finials, while both sides use Doric porticos as exterior rooms, which form an intricate garden arrangement. The interior is ordered around a large central Corinthian hall, which accesses the living room, dining room, kitchen, and library. The living room is decorated in the Composite style, with a Baroque fireplace and overmantle of Statuary marble. The dining room is Doric, with a fireplace of Moleanos marble in Michelangelesque style.

Six private villas of varying Classical designs in Regent's Park, London (1988–2004), which Terry created for the Crown Estate Commissioners, recall the picturesque tradition established by John Nash in the early nineteenth century.

In 1982 Terry was awarded the Philippe Rotthier European Prize for the Reconstruction of the City of *Archives d'Architecture Moderne.* In 2002 he was honored with the Arthur Ross Award from the Institute of Classical Architecture and Classical America, and in 2003 he won the British Georgian Group's "Best Modern Classical House" award, for a private residence in Dorset.

Quinlan Terry is one of the most notable practitioners of Neo-classicism, and perhaps the most radical. During a 1987 Oxford Union debate, he said, "...let us take inspiration from the wisdom of our forefathers, so that our buildings will be signs and heralds of a more natural, more stable and more beautiful world."

Troppo Architects

Troppo Architects is a partnership of four Darwin practitioners who trained together in South Australia, before establishing a practice in the Northern Territory of Australia. Phil Harris, James Hayter, Justin Hill, and Adrian Welke, then architecture students at the University of Adelaide, decided at the end of 1977 to travel together around Australia. Their joint report *Influences in Regional Architecture* of May 1978 foreshadowed their interest in appropriate tropical design – a question relevant to a large area of Australia but only a small percentage of the population.

Work was scarce, but Welke ultimately took a position with Vin Kenneally and Associates in Darwin, where he was followed by Harris. In mid-1980 the two won a history grant to study housing in the area, and in February 1981 they opened their office as Troppo Architects. In Darwin they found a tradition of elevated open-plan houses, especially in the 1930s houses of Beni Burnett, the influence of which they acknowledge. They were also influenced by Glenn Murcutt, who was to work with them on the Bowali Visitor Centre, and whose lightweight elevated architecture is arguably better suited to tropical Australia than to those areas of New South Wales in which it is principally found.

Troppo's first significant house, known locally as the Green Can (1981) was a line of cross-ventilated rooms linked by a gallery, and roofed with straight and curved corrugated iron in the Murcutt manner. Six variants of this design followed for other clients. After 1989 Troppo received many commissions for larger and more varied projects all over Australia, and especially in northern Queensland. Examples include the Poole House near Kuranda in Queensland and Rozak House (2001) in Batchelor, Northern Territory. Their houses became more diverse in form and angular in geometry, but they were still commonly elevated, and they continued to maximize natural ventilation. Their forms and approach have influenced other domestic architects in tropical Australia generally.

Horace Trumbauer

Horace Trumbauer (1868–1938) was born in Philadelphia, USA. At the age of 16 he left school and ran errands for the architectural firm of GW and WD Hewitt. In 1890 he opened his first architectural office at the age of 22.

Trumbauer matured as an architect, harmonizing basic geometric forms and avoiding the cluttered ornamentation typical of the Victorian era. A refined sense of form and proportion saw him design hundreds of residences (suburban houses, Manhattan townhouses, and country estates), with Queen Anne, Romanesque, and Norman influences. In 1895 he began a lifelong association with two families that would provide him with the bulk of his work.

The Widener and Elkins families commissioned Trumbauer to erect the Ritz Carlton Hotel (1911) in Philadelphia, the Widener Building (1915) on Philadelphia's South Penn Square, and the Classical Widener Library at Harvard University (1915). However it was the grand mansions of America's elite for which Trumbauer is best remembered.

Lynnewood Hall (1900) was one of the most imposing residences in America upon its completion. A remarkable accomplishment for someone not yet 30 years of age, its 110 rooms were designed in the French Classical style complete with grand foyers, French-styled salons, and formal gardens replete with statues, fountains, and terraces. In addition to his many mansions and villas, Trumbauer also designed urban townhouses along New York's Fifth Avenue such as Duke Mansion (1909), built for the founder of the American Tobacco Company James B Duke. Typically designed in the French Classical style, it showcases Trumbauer's ability to bestow dignity and grandeur on a small, urban scale.

After World War I Trumbauer built fewer residences, shifting his emphasis to commercial and institutional buildings, although his last grand Manhattan residence – the forty-room Herbert N Straus Residence (1933) – remains one of the city's few remaining freestanding mansions.

Bernard Tschumi

Bernard Tschumi (1944–) was born in Lausanne, Switzerland. A contemporary French/Swiss architect, he was educated at the Federal Institute of Technology in Zurich, Switzerland. Between 1970 and 1979 he taught at the Architectural Association in London, and from 1976 at the Institute for Architecture and Urban Studies in New York and at Princeton Uni-versity. Between 1980 and 1983 he was visiting professor at the Cooper Union School of Architecture in New York.

Bernard Tschumi has been analyzed in many ways. People have cited his work as having many ideas and have compared his architecture to a river flow, which causes change whenever an errant current overflows its banks. Since the 1970s, Tschumi has asserted that there is no permanent relationship between architectural form and the events that take place within it. In Tschumi's theory, architecture is not to express an existing social structure, but to function as a tool for questioning that structure and revising it.

Tschumi made his mark with his masterpiece, the Parc de la Villette (1982) in Paris. It has been aptly described as a composition of intriguing pieces and parts, with each piece or part being very complex, red structures called "follies." It was intended that these bright red pieces or parts would house various events and groups related to the activities of the park. Regarded as an urban park for the new millennium and beyond, it broke away from the traditional English parks and gardens of the past.

Tschumi's architecture looks at a radical way of "disassembling" the traditional parts of buildings and takes into account "notions" of movement and activities as opposed to static and axial approaches. His work reflects that of the Russian Constructivist art. His residential designs follow this notion and include the apartment complexes West Diaoyutai Tower (2004–08) in Beijing, and the Blue Tower (2004–06) in New York. The Blue Tower is notable for its unusual angled geometry and its pixilated facade of blue glass, while the West Diaoyutai Tower features a dramatic cantilevered prow and an exterior of perforated metal plates, except at a cutaway corner where a cut surface features a glass curtain wall to emphasize the building's unique geometry.

Tschumi has been awarded the Grand Prix National d'Architecture and awards from the American Institute of Architects and the National Endowment for the Arts.

William Turnbull Jr

William Turnbull Jr (1935–97) was born in New York City, USA, and studied at Princeton University and the École des Beaux-Arts in Paris. In 1963 he became a partner in the architectural firm of MLTW (Charles Moore, Donlyn Lyndon, William Turnbull, and Richard Whitaker).

Turnbull's Allewelt House (1977) near Madera is an underrated Californian classic featuring extensive shading from its wrap-around porch and an inner courtyard set beneath a simple gable roof. However, he is best known for his Sea Ranch Village (1993), designed in a series of enclaves on the northern Californian coast. A collection of 15 units were set on several thousand acres of large open meadows and marshland, conceived as a response to the future need of affordable housing for employees of the nearby Sea Ranch Lodge. The basic timber-framed one-, two-, and three-bedroom units with exposed beams and shingle roofs sparked a generation of imitators, and placed Turnbull on the architectural map. The design became known as the Sea Ranch Style, considered by many as the closest thing to a vernacular northern Californian architecture. In 1991 the Sea Ranch Village won the American Institute of Architects 25 Year Award.

Turnbull was a Fellow of the American Institute of Architects and lectured throughout the United States of America and Canada. He taught at Stanford

University, the University of California at Berkeley, Yale University, and the University of Maryland. In 1998, a year after his death, the California Architectural Foundation initiated the William Turnbull Jr FAIA Environmental Education Grant for the purpose of fostering public education and awareness of the natural and built environment.

UN Studio

Operating out of Amsterdam in the Netherlands, UN Studio (United Net for Architecture) – the Dutch partnership of Ben van Berkel (1957–) and Caroline Bos – (1959) are responsible for some of the most innovative architecture of the past 15 years. Van Berkel studied architecture at the Rietveld Academy in Amsterdam and the Architectural Association in London, receiving a diploma with Honours in 1987. Caroline Bos was awarded a Bachelor of Arts in Art History from Birkbeck College in London.

Within the firm's repertoire is a wide variety of both civic and domestic scale buildings, outstanding among the domestic scale being the Mobius House (1993–98). Ben van Berkel appears to be concentrating on the redefining of organizational structures that apply to the architect's role within an environment of change. The organizational structure of the Mobius House is based on the question of how two people may live together, yet apart, meeting at certain points. Within this brief the house must accommodate a 24-hour cycle of leisure and work. The design of the project is dependent upon a mathematical approach in which the formal structure appears as a diagram of a double-locked torus: A figure eight that programs the daily cycle of the inhabitants. This provides a seamless integration of program, circulation, and structure. The plan is devised upon the diagram of a loop, a continual path that serves to provide individual working and sleeping places, separating the two inhabitants and subsequently drawing them together at the crossing point of paths. Materially, vertical elements of concrete and glass continually switch places at designated points in order to maintain the continuity of the concept. Not only has UN Studio provided a complex, yet clever, solution to the problem of cohabitation and the problem of work and leisure on the one site, but it has been able to produce an outstanding twentieth-century residence that shall serve to influence architecture for centuries to follow.

UN Studio excel at creating designs that challenge the traditional notion of home or office. Relevant examples of this spatial play lie in their domestic-scale work such as Villa Wilbrink (1994) in Amersfoot, the Netherlands, and Villa NM (2000–06) in New York. UN Studio have definitely cemented their position as pioneers in architecture and are a firm to watch in the twenty-first century.

Raymond Unwin

Raymond Unwin (1863–1940) was born in Rotherham, Yorkshire, in England. Rather than entering the Church of England as his father had wished, he chose instead to become involved in social activism and moved to Chesterfield in 1878. In 1881 he took a job as an apprentice engineer at the firm of Staveley Coal and Iron Company in Chesterfield. It was here that Unwin first made the acquaintance of his second cousin Barry Parker, his future partner in town planning.

From 1885 Unwin worked as an engineering draftsman in Manchester and became increasingly active in politics, becoming a branch secretary of the Socialist League and meeting Bruce Glasier who first introduced him to the world of architecture. In association with Barry Parker, he planned the New Earswick community (1902) on the outskirts of York, the Garden City at Letchworth (1903), and the Hampstead Garden Suburb (1907) near London. Due to intense lobbying by Unwin, the British Parliament passed the First Housing and Town Planning Act in 1909, allowing the regulation and design of new layouts for suburban subdivisions. That same year he published *Town Planning in Practice*, which remains one of the most influential texts on urban design ever published and has been translated into French, German, and Russian.

By now Raymond Unwin's life had departed entirely from traditional architecture and had become wholly consumed by town planning. From 1911 to 1914 he lectured at the University of Birmingham and published a revolutionary set of designs for traffic intersections. With open vistas framed with building facades, a hallmark of the picturesque planning tradition, their seemingly complex geometric shapes were considered too complex for "high speed" travel.

In 1928 Unwin became the president of the International Federation for Housing and Town Planning and in 1931 was elected president of the Royal Institute of British Architects. He was knighted in 1932 and in 1937 was bestowed an honorary doctorate from Harvard University in addition to being awarded the Royal Gold Medal from the Royal Institute of British Architects.

Ushida Findlay

Kathryn Findlay (1953–) was born in Scotland and graduated from the Architectural Association in London in 1979. Eisaku Ushida (1954–) was born in Japan and graduated from Tokyo University in 1976. The two established the firm of Ushida Findlay in 1987.

Ushida Findlay's commitment to improving their client's quality of life begins with the correct orientation of space and light and continues through to looking at a site's topography, and personal and communal lifestyles. They see their interiors as "inhabited landscapes," and architecture as the projection of the psychological desires of its inhabitants. Rather than imposing a structure upon the environment, this visionary husband-and-wife team, with a predisposition to "Daliesque" organic concepts, see their designs as the taming of technology, not of nature.

Their Japanese masterpiece Truss Wall House (1992–93) features ceilings merging with floors and a plasticity that allows for an outrageous degree of melding of structure and void. Soft and Hairy House (1992–94), also in Japan, includes floors covered by wild grasses native to the area all wrapped around an interior courtyard, together with a womb-like bathroom in a surreal rebuke to the rampant minimalism seen in much Japanese architecture at the time.

In 1994 Ushida Findlay won the Tokyo Journal Innovative Award for Architecture, and in 1996 they were the recipients of an Architectural Institute of Japan Commendation. Kathryn Findlay was both the first woman and the first foreigner to be made a professor in Tokyo University's Department of Architecture.

Jørn Utzon

Jørn Utzon (1918–) was born in Copenhagen, Denmark, though he spent his childhood in Ålborg, where his father was an engineering director of a local shipyard. He completed his schooling at Ålborg Katedralskole in 1936, and was accepted into the architectural school at the Royal Academy of Fine Arts, Copenhagen, from which he graduated in 1942. Between 1937 and 1942 he studied under Kay Fisker (renowned for housing and constructional logic) and the historian Steen Eiler Rasmussen (a town planner and author of *Experiencing Architecture*). Like his father, Utzon was also a practical man who liked hunting, fishing, and sailing.

During the war years Stockholm became a lively, cosmopolitan center, and it was a natural progression for Utzon to move there following graduation. While in Sweden, Utzon studied vernacular, Chinese, and Japanese architecture, as well as the architecture of Erik Gunnar Asplund. He worked briefly for Hakon Ahlberg, and Paul Hedquist (who continued Asplund's practice after his death in 1940). Towards the end of 1945, Utzon went to Helsinki and spent some weeks in the office of Alvar Aalto. Besides these mentors Utzon is an original architect. His architecture is profoundly sculptural, drawing his inspiration more from Europe and Hawaii, rather than from his Danish roots.

On his return to Denmark, Utzon entered several design competitions, and by 1952 was building a house for his family at Hellebaek. This was not the first long and low open-plan house in Denmark, but Utzon provided a fresh vision in terms of its spatial reality. This house sits on a brick base with the living space pivoting about a fireplace. Many of its features occur in the early work of Wright, Aalto, and Japanese architecture.

Utzon's Middleboe House (1953) in Holte, next to Lake Furesø, shows the steel and glass influence of Mies van der Rohe's Farnsworth House, but the scale is smaller and the family demands more complex. This flat-roofed, two-storied house is organized around a service core. Other houses he built at this time show the influence of Wright's Usonian vision.

Following his victory at winning the design competition for the Sydney Opera House in 1957, Utzon received two commissions for large private houses on the outskirts of Helsingborg in Sweden. These two houses were organized around courtyards – a principle which Utzon consistently adopted to explore light and shade, space and form. The courtyard, of course, had its roots in traditional Danish buildings as well as in Chinese, Japanese, and Islamic cultures. These ideas were developed in the Kingo Houses on the outskirts of Helsingör near Utzon's home in Hellebaek and they were widely followed in Denmark. This communal principle was further elaborated at Fredensborg (1965) in North Zealand, following Utzon's departure to Sydney to oversee the construction of the Sydney Opera House. These houses have a common core of kitchen and bathroom facilities. These communal buildings hold low walls and broad sheltering roofs, presenting an ease of naturalness to the landscape, with protection from the wind and sunshine.

Returning from Sydney, Utzon brought the courtyard principle to bear on his Church at Bagsvaerd (1968–76) in the suburbs of Copenhagen, and at Can Liz (1971–74) – his holiday home on Majorca, the largest of the Balearic Islands off the east coast of Spain. Arguably, Utzon's island retreat of five pavilions, built along a cliff edge facing the sea, is the clearest statement of what he regarded as a retirement home in light and shade. Instead of reaching up with skylights like Bagsvaerd, Can Liz's pavilions reach out to the horizon in five deep bay windows, which are angled to control direct sunlight, and to provide an unobstructed view of the landscape (in the manner of the Swedish architect Sigurd Lewerentz). Utzon's masonry architecture frames the sea and the passage of light, and with its deeply splayed window reveals, it clearly is a Corbusian inspiration from Notre Dame-du-Haut-de Ronchamp. Can Liz is a tiny community of buildings, a cliff-house, which provide a radiant experience in living above the Mediterranean. Like Le Corbusier, Utzon is very much his own man. Next to the influence of sunshine, light, and the magic of the sparkling sea, Utzon was content to be a recluse away from the media.

Theo van Doesburg

The painter, designer, and architect Theo van Doesburg (1883–1931) was born in Utrecht, the Netherlands. As a painter he was influenced by the Impressionists, later moving on to Expressionism and ultimately total abstraction. In 1917 he was one of the co-founders of the De Stijl movement, a sort of collective project or "enterprise" including the artist Piet Mondrian, and the architect J J P Oud. Despite rarely meeting as a group, they were all nevertheless closely in touch with each other's work and all shared the conviction that art and design had the power to transform society. Their common beliefs included a reduction of existing architectural forms into simple, basic geometric elements. Heavily influenced by the Dutch architectural theorist H P Berlage, the De Stijl movement decried ornamentation as irrelevant, emphasizing that only three architectural truisms existed: The importance of walls as creators of form, the importance of proportion, and the primacy of space.

In the 1920s van Doesburg stated that past styles of architecture were no longer appropriate and that the art he would create would be avowedly "style-less." Throughout this decade he slowly evolved from painter into architect, and in 1929 designed and built his artist's house in Meudon, which consisted of two interlocking cubes, one being his studio and the other containing the kitchen, living area, and garage. After living in the house for a month, asthma forced van Doesburg into a sanatorium in the small Swiss town of Davos in the Swiss Alps, where he passed away in 1931.

Aldo van Eyck

Aldo van Eyck (1918–99) was born in Driebergen, the Netherlands. He studied architecture at the Eidgennossische Technische Hochschule in Zurich, Switzerland, from 1938 to 1942 before moving to Amsterdam in 1946, where he found work as a designer in the town planning section of the Amsterdam Public Works Department from 1946 to 1951. From 1951 to 1954 he lectured in art history at the Academy of Art and Industry in Enschede. He lectured widely and became a fierce critic of the dearth of originality in a lot of post-war Modernism.

His reputation as an original designer is best seen in his Amsterdam Orphanage (1955–60). Stressing the need for a return to humanism in architecture, the building is a revolutionary synthesis that caters for the needs of the individual and the group by breaking up the spatial continuity usually associated with large buildings into a series of clearly defined intermediary spaces. It made his reputation and became an iconic building overnight.

His Sonsbeek Park Pavilion in Arnhem, the Netherlands, brought him further acclaim. Consisting of six parallel walls built from solid concrete blocks, all covered in transparent sheeting, it formed a street-like environment that encourages one to wander. Sculptures of people placed inside became pedestrians within van Eyck's artificial urban environment.

Van Eyck went on to lecture as a professor at the Delft Technical College until 1984, all the while continuing to propound a return to humanism within Modernism in his capacity as co-editor of the Dutch magazine *Forum*. Though not a prolific architect, he was one of the most influential with his seminal buildings shaping the approach of architects the world over.

Van Eyck received the Royal Institute of British Architects Royal Gold Medal in 1990.

Robert Venturi

Robert Venturi (1925–) was born in Philadelphia, USA. He studied at Princeton University, and also won the Brunner Fellowship Rome Prize to study at the American Academy in Rome (1954–56). As a young architect he worked in the offices of Louis I Kahn, Eero Saarinen, and Oscar Stonorov. His reputation and influence are the result of not only his built work but also his teaching and theoretical writing, particularly the book *Complexity and Contradiction in Architecture* (1966), which is now published in many languages throughout the world and has been recognized with the American Institute of Architects Classic Book Award. Among Venturi's many awards are the prestigious Pritzker Prize in 1991 and America's Presidential National Medal of the Arts in 1992.

Venturi is generally known for being a leading Post-modernist of the 1960s and '70s although the categorization is disputed by him. He was made famous internationally with the publication of *Complexity and Contradiction* and also *Learning from Las Vegas* (1972) with Denise Scott Brown and Steven Izenour, which were both controversial when they were released and have come to be regarded as the seminal texts on architectural Post-modernism.

The essential theory of the books is that building designs are more interesting if they develop out of a range of complex criteria. *Complexity and Contradiction* presents an argument for richness, complexity, ornamentation, symbolism, and ambiguity in architecture, in response to the International Style, which is characterized by purity, simplicity, and unity of design. It was in this book that Venturi famously challenged architect Mies van der Rohe's Modernist dictum "less is more" with "less is a bore." In *Learning from Las Vegas* he contends that architecture can draw on not only historical references but also popular culture, iconography, and the ordinary everyday environment.

Venturi's most recent book, *Architecture as Signs and Systems* (2004), co-authored with Scott Brown, illustrates the ideas they have advocated in past texts with their own built work.

Venturi worked in partnership for some time with John Rauch, and since 1967 with his wife, architect and urban designer Denise Scott Brown. The Philadelphia-based firm of which he is a principal, now Venturi Scott Brown and Associates (VSBA), gained its reputation with early residential projects, but has more recently completed many university commissions for both buildings and campus planning. Recent work also includes the Sainsbury Wing of the National Gallery in London.

Venturi's best-known project is the Vanna Venturi House (1962) in Chestnut Hill, Pennsylvania, for his mother. At a time when Modern design was still dominant, the house was unusual in its reference to vernacular domestic buildings, the use of decorative moldings applied to the facade, and Mannerist devices such as layering, and contradictions in its planning. It is considered a seminal work which has had a wide-ranging influence on other architects, and was honored with the American Institute of Architects 25 Year Award in 1989. Other well-known projects include the ghost structure of Benjamin Franklin's house (1996) in Franklin Court, and the Guild House apartment building for the elderly – an adaptation of vernacular apartment buildings – constructed in the 1960s and criticized for features such as its gold-anodized aluminum antenna.

Interesting houses include the shingled Trubek and Wisloski houses (1970–71) on Nantucket Island, Massachusetts, a pair of holiday homes inspired by local fishermens' cottages in the area. The Tucker House (1974) in Mount Kisco, New York (also shingled), and the tower-like House in Vail, Colorado, (1975) both feature steeply pitched pyramid roofs and large circular or semi-circular dormer windows with deep window seats.

Venturi was a lecturer at the University of Pennsylvania in the late 1950s and early 1960s, and later a professor at Yale University (1966–70). He has also lectured extensively at other universities in America and overseas.

Charles Voysey

Charles Francis Annesley Voysey (1857–1941) was born in Hessle, near Hull in Yorkshire, England, and was the son of an independent and unorthodox Church of England cleric. He grew up in London and became an exponent of Arts and Crafts architecture, being influenced by the spiritual leadership and writings of Augustus Pugin, John Ruskin, William Morris, and Philip Webb. By the late 1880s Voysey established his practice of moderately sized country houses for the upper middle classes. In this area Voysey created simple, white-stuccoed houses that encapsulated the values of English domesticity. Like Lutyens, Voysey was a provocative homemaker, with a fondness for rural England. Yet he also welcomed the machine for making furniture. As a traditionalist he used dowels, mortise, and tenon jointing. Simplicity marked all his design thinking.

Voysey made his name by creating architecture that served vernacular values. His favorite themes were a singular and rectangular two-story domestic volume contained by high-pitched roofs, which protected white rough-cast stuccoed walls. His roofs were timber framed and covered with slate. As an Arts and Crafts designer he exemplified the use of a fine abstract sense of formal containment using hips and gables, which rose up gracefully from their surroundings. His horizontal windows were framed in stone. In all his compositions Voysey maintained a fine sense of scale and attention to detail. Voysey was one who embraced the human dimension. His architecture expressed repose, cheerfulness, simplicity, warmth, economy of upkeep, a sense of protection, and above all, maintained a harmony with the landscape.

By 1895 Voysey had established a substantial architectural practice. He built a cottage at Bishop's Itchington, near Warwick, in 1888, which brought him to the attention of many people. It carries many of his trademarks – a steeply pitched shingled roof defined by prominent chimneys and horizontal strips of leaded windows which were tucked up under the eaves at first-floor level. The eaves themselves had deep overhangs, which carried gutters supported on metal brackets. The walls were slightly buttressed, and rendered with rough-cast sand and cement. The whole composition spelt "home" – a conservative home in England.

Towards the end of the nineteenth century Voysey's practice entered his busiest period (1898–1910). During this time he did his grandest work: Broadleys in Windermere (1898), his most important singular work; Moorcrag in Windermere (1898); Spade House in Sandgate, Folkestone, Kent (1899); and the architect's own house, The Orchard at Chorleywood, Hertfordshire (1900). All these houses, with first-floor bedrooms, look out onto natural settings and carefully landscaped gardens, emphatically maintaining the picturesque tradition.

Broadleys on Lake Windermere is a very distinctive house which fronts onto the lake. Its front elevation is Voysey's most published house, with deep, semi-circular bow windows and gabled and hipped roofs covering an L-shaped plan. Inside there is a strong sense of solidity and comfort, while containing a play of levels, which respond to its location.

The legacy and individuality of Voysey can be measured by the respect which was upheld by the younger generation of British and Commonwealth architects who followed him. Voysey's individuality was hailed by the British at home and abroad. Even the German critic and diplomat Muthesius in his 1904–05 book *Das Englische Haus*, *(The English House)*, understood Voysey's attempt to combine the forces of tradition, with those of Arts and Crafts individuality. Voysey, like Lutyens, played a major part in the domestic architecture of the late nineteenth and early twentieth centuries. While the Great War of 1914–18 effectively destroyed the world these architects knew, nevertheless, the principles and standards they believed in formed part of the spiritual legacy and intellectual culture of Arts and Crafts architecture, whose in-dividuality is timeless.

Perhaps the example of Lutyens and Voysey helps explain the reluctance of the British to wholeheartedly adopt Modern architecture in the 1930s.

Otto Wagner

Otto Koloman Wagner (1841–1918) was, in spite of his traditional training, the founder of the Modern movement in Austria. As Professor of Architecture at the Academy of Fine Arts in Vienna, he had enormous influence on students including the group which formed the Vienna Secession in 1887, and the later generation which formed the Austrian Werkbund in 1913. Both of these groups looked upon Wagner as a leader in the profession.

Otto Wagner was born into a wealthy bourgeois family in Penzig, near Vienna. After preparatory education in Vienna's Akademisches Gymnasium and a prestigious boarding school, Wagner received training at the Polytechnic Institute in Vienna (1857–59), and the Academy of Fine Arts (1861–63), where he was influenced by Vienna's Opera House architects August von Siccardsburg and Eduard Van Der Nüll. He also spent an intervening year at the Royal Academy of Building in Berlin where he came under the Classical influence of successors to Karl Friedrich Schinkel.

In 1894 he succeeded von Hasenauer as Professor at the Vienna Academy. His inaugural lecture, published as *Moderne Architektur* (1895), was a spirited attack against stylistic thinking in nineteenth-century architecture – a subject later elaborated by three of his significant students: Adolf Loos, Richard Neutra, and Rudolf Schindler. As a teacher, Wagner was inspired, and as an architect, he practiced what he preached.

Wagner was an enthusiastic supporter of the Secession movement, and after completing the Villa Hahn (1885–86) in Baden, Germany, he turned to his own summer house at 26 Hüttelbergstrasse (1889) in Vienna, for his family of two children. This villa was designed in the Classical tradition with a certain amount of applied decoration. His first house, built on an imposing site, was symmetrically approached using a double flight of stairs leading up to the front entrance. Wagner designed this pitched roof house on a spacious square plan, with a transverse axis including galleries which carried stained glass. The right-hand gallery was converted into a living room in 1895, and the gallery on the left into a studio in 1900. The interior of the left-hand studio carried a window *Autumn in the Wienerwald* – a stained-glass artwork by Adolf Böhm. The composition carried overtones of Palladio.

Wagner's houses for his personal needs helped him develop his thinking and provided a distraction from his municipal work. While his first house carried an entrance portico of four Ionic columns which carried colored porcelain, his front staircase carried a balustrade of curved wrought-iron railing. At the time, the intensity of this Palladian composition provoked the comment that this house was for a prince of the Imperial household. Certainly by 1886, Wagner had not shaken himself free from the portmanteau of Classicism.

By the time he came to do his second house, just along the road at 28 Hüttelbergstrasse (1912–13), Wagner's thinking had moved a good deal towards a more Modern approach. This house carried a flat roof and walls, with tall rectilinear window reveals. Decoration had almost disappeared with the exception of the white and blue Majolica tile dado at the mezzanine level. These colored tiles also identified the front entrance. In the white-walled purity of this villa, one senses Wagner's struggle to rid his work of stylistic thinking in architecture. All this is clearly visible in his most admired Viennese Postal Savings Bank Office completed by 1912, where Wagner made extensive use of metal materials new to building in Vienna.

The transformation of a radically new architecture, operating outside the formal confines of traditional practice, demonstrated a shortfall between theory and practice in Wagner's work. In his struggle for defining the variable aspects of a Modern architectural agenda, Wagner removed the traditional curriculum of the Hapsburg Empire from the Academy of Fine Arts, a premier academy of art. In retrospect this opportunity moved things towards a more Modern vision – a vision later adopted by Le Corbusier's *Vers une architecture (Towards a New Architecture)* of 1923. As an architect, Wagner celebrated the rational and geometric causes in which he believed. With Wagner, thought and action were always close together.

Roger Walker

Roger Neville Walker (1942–) was born in Hamilton, New Zealand, and graduated from the University of Auckland School of Architecture with Honors in 1967. He first worked for Wellington's mayor, Michael Fowler, who provided the opportunity for Walker to design the Wellington Club (1972). Walker's first building was a provocative low-rise cluster in the middle of Wellington's expensive Terrace area. After a prominent court battle over land values in 1985, the individualistic Wellington club was demolished.

Right from the very beginning Roger Walker's career has been controversial. But before he started his own practice in 1970, he did the Mansell House (1967), high up in the hills of Highbury, which celebrates the crown of a hill complete with yellow roof-fin metaphors. In this one house Walker's career had arrived. This was quickly followed by more Wellingtonian houses such as the Hyde House (1969), the Sotiri House (1970), and the much larger Johnson House (1971). Not to be outdone, Walker's Hingston House (1971), for a graphic designer, represents a broad vocabulary of glass pyramids, circular windows, and crisscross bracing.

From Walker's Romantic "butterfly breakout," where he used pyramidal roof forms over small children's bedrooms, Walker's work also carried circular drainpipe windows, and these characteristics marked this energetic counter-culture architect. By now Walker had established his Romantic language of design, and he began to spread his wings like the butterfly.

Walker's most distinguished butterfly was his energetic creation for the Brittens (1972–74). Built dramatically on a steep cliff face overlooking the inlet to Wellington Harbour, the Britten House defied all simplistic notions of what a house might be. His client was a television personality, who later became an Anglican priest, who encouraged Walker to break all the rules. So this colorful house spirals through eight levels around two sides of a courtyard. The Britten House includes sleeping caves, crisscross windows, light scoops, glass turrets, high-point snugs, and a cacophony of living spaces. His *cause célèbre* reads like a relentless vertical flower rising up from a steep hillside which brought him instant fame. He was the first imaginative architect from New Zealand to front the cover of London's prestigious *Architectural Review,* in February 1981. The Britten House was an evocation of fragmentation, encouraged by clients who delighted in celebrating their individuality. Clearly Walker's imaginative response was a product of a Romantic adventure celebrating the hills, the sky, and the sea below. A landscape which is different every day.

Walker's domestic architecture is user friendly, but from the 1980s onwards, he began to move into a great deal of commercial work and tourist architecture like the Whakatane Airport, the Masterton Retail Centre (1974), and the Rainbow Springs Tourist Centre, in Rotorua. His success at Rainbow Springs – a famous place for viewing rainbow trout – soon attracted the environmental interest of the Tourist Hotel Corporation, where he was invited to design tourist facilities for New Zealand natural wonders, the Waitomo Caves in 1981, and a Tourist Hotel in Queenstown. In all these buildings Walker maintained the joyful and imaginative approach of an attention maker in architecture.

Much of his skilful dexterity and individuality was shown on his own home in Thorndon (1999) in the suburbs of Wellington. He continued to use primary shapes and radiant colors – pink and green – which successfully shocked his more conservative neighbors. As an energetic innovator, Walker may have become a gray-haired architect, but his work continues to project the humanity of a visual communicator *par excellence.*

Frederick Warren

Frederick Miles Warren (1929–) is the Edwin Lutyens of New Zealand architecture. Both men began life doing small domestic houses; both are superb draftsmen delighting in detail; both are avid water colorists and garden lovers; both became architects of ambiguity, wit, and surprise; and both did chanceries abroad for their respective governments. As architects of Classic inclination, both ended up doing formal houses in beautiful gardens, mostly on large budgets to loose briefs, and both were knighted for their services to architecture.

Warren spent his postgraduate years in London in the London City Council, and bicycling around Denmark sketching family houses of masonry with gabled roof forms. Returning to New Zealand in the mid-1950s, Warren gave Christchurch a new sense of ordered domesticity with high-gabled roof forms in white-painted concrete blocks. These masonry overtures provided a sharp shock to the flat plains of Canterbury and the carpenter mentality of the timber-frame situation advocated by the Auckland Group Architects. Warren's early Christchurch houses include Ballantyne (1959), M B Warren House (1960–61), and Townhouses for Miss Broderick (1962–64). These carefully articulated and layered gabled homes show the influence of traditional houses in Copenhagen.

Larger developments in concrete block and tile include M J Foster House (1974), and Warren's *cause célèbre* D J Mulholland House (1985–1987) in the wilds of Managahu, Wanganui. The Mulholland House is Warren's celebrated statement of the grand country home reinforcing cultured values. This house is organized in the grand Palladian manner including a *cour d'honneur* (principal court) front entrance, which is formally composed on the central line of the house. This formal entrance leads progressively to the principal living rooms in the central block, with side pavilions embracing bedrooms, a swimming pool, and a billiard room. Prominent tiled roofs define the pavilions, organized spatially, with deeply recessed windows, and steeply timbered pitched roofs.

Arguably, no New Zealand house matches the rural and Classic grandeur of the Mulholland home, built formally above the Mangawhero River.

Architecturally speaking the Mulholland House belongs to a "horse and hound" society – a special group of people who have the money and the sense of grandeur to be able to live in the manner advocated by Palladio, and traditionally carried on by Edwin Lutyens in England. The Mulholland House is set in a rolling sea-green landscape, and identifies a farming scene with which the architect captivates in "high game" grandeur. This world-view may be old-fashioned in the twenty-first century, but it exudes dignity, imagination, and civilized behavior.

Frank Lloyd Wright

Frank Lloyd Wright (1867–1959) has the reputation of being America's greatest architect. He was born in Richland Center, Wisconsin, USA, the son of a Baptist preacher and musician, just after the American Civil War and died at the advent of the space age. During 70 years of practice he became a master of domestic architecture through his almost mystical veneration for the family. His designer's vision celebrated the notion from "within to without." Wright called this elusive principle "organic." He believed that an organically designed house combined the unique characteristics of site, the climate, the client, and the building process into a single unity – and this unique synthesis was totally integrated into nature. Wright believed that people who live in organic architecture were more spiritually alive in themselves. In this world-view, Wright continued the dream of a community of individuals advocated by American philosophers Walt Whitman, Henry David Thoreau, and Ralph Waldo Emerson. In short, Wright was a spiritual person with a Romantic disposition.

To the outside world Wright often seemed truculent and arrogant, strident and full of conceit. Yet, much of this was the mask he adopted as a sort of psychological shield. Beneath this defensive facade Wright was a Wisconsin country boy, who was intensely conscious of his clothes, and what people thought and said of him. He was deeply sensitive to criticism, but during his lifetime at least 600 houses poured from Wright's drawing board. Of these designs Wright used to say, "I just shake them out of my sleeve." While he proclaimed his genius loud and long, Wright produced at least 10 great contributions to American culture, which were defined by Prairie and Usonian worldviews.

Prairie houses are spatially defined, soul-bearing timbered living rooms, centered around large brick chimneys, endless ribbon-windows, long and low free-floating roofs covering outside decks which reach out horizontally. The Prairie house is above all a dynamic and serene refuge, spiritually rooted in the Emersonian belief that domestic bliss owed deep allegiance to nature. In the Prairie house Wright rejected the Victorian box. Examples of Wright's Prairie designs include the Ward Willets Residence (1902) in Highland Park, Illinois; the Coonley Residence (1907) in Riverside, Illinois; the Robie Residence (1908–09) in Chicago, Illinois; the Frank Lloyd Wright Residence "Taliesin" (1911–25) in Spring Green, Wisconsin; and the Herbert Johnson Residence (1937–39), the largest and best built Prairie house at Wind Point (near Racine) Wisconsin.

Wright called the Herbert Johnson Residence "Wingspread," because it has four wings which stretch out in cantilevered balconies embracing the prairie, while the roof over the central hall with three bands of skylights, soars skywards in a distinctive "crow's nest." The Great Hall with its high ceiling and massive fireplace is the center of this house – a spatial experience in light, combining the living, dining, and library areas. Wingspread's design created a sense of continuity between the indoors and outside. Wingspread was built with a red-brickwork base with exterior woodwork balconies of unfinished tidewater cypress weathered to a silver-gray. It is the largest of Wright's Prairie houses at 14,000 sq ft (1,300 sq m), and it includes a generous swimming pool. The Johnson family lived happily in Wingspread for 20 years. It is now The Johnson Foundation Conference Center, and was declared a National Historic Landmark in 1990.

The boom of the Prairie houses came to an end in the stock-market crash and Depression of the late 1920s and early '30s. Wright retired to revise and recuperate in the desert. For him this enchanting environment was a spiritual revelation in light – the brilliant sunshine heightened all perception. In the sharp mountains, rocks, and indigenous plants Wright observed triangular forms, and this began a new phase in his work. Gone was the desire for the heavily timbered roofs of mid-western domesticity. In its place Wright sought a new credibility serving and supporting the American dream through what he termed Usonian utility.

The Usonian house was Wright's answer to democratic America. This worldview resulted in a compact and geometrically organized plan. While the living room (still the largest space) dominated the design, the kitchen acquired a new functional importance as the workspace of the house. Wright also became more interested in creative detailing and modular building. Examples of Wright's Usonian designs include: The Kaufmann Residence known as Fallingwater, (1935–37) in Bear Run, Pennsylvania; the Hanna Residence (1936), also known as the Honeycomb House, in Palo Alto, California; the First Jacobs Residence (1936) in Madison, Wisconsin; Palmer House (1950) in Ann Arbor, Michigan, which was constructed of cypress and brick; the Hagan House (1954) in Kentuck Knob, Pennsylvania, which was constructed entirely of red tidewater cypress and native fieldstone.

Open floor plans, freedom from centralized spaces, geometric floor grids, walls of timber and masonry, copper roofs, and great expanses of glass artfully integrate the outdoor and indoor spaces in site-specific architecture. These are the marks of the Usonian synthesis. In these houses Wright rejected European Modernism. His idea of organic architecture revolved around nature and beautifully detailed building in a single unity, and this defined his human approach to domesticity. In all this activity Wright saw himself as a one-man revolution – added to this he relied upon charm and charisma to settle economic and technical difficulties. With a full heart he proclaimed himself the greatest architect of all time. To this flamboyance, British critic Reyner Banham replied that Wright "was the best domestic architect since Palladio."

Of all Wright's houses Fallingwater is his most celebrated and layered creation. Situated above a mountain stream, Wright took possession of a place in nature. It was the natural place which received him and sustained his vision for an elevated house in nature. Wright's Fallingwater is his *cause célèbre* of what he meant by the notion of organic architecture. Built as a symphony of sounds, Wright believed he had become the Beethoven of architecture.

Index

Picture Credits

Efforts have been made to contact the holder of copyright for each photograph. If any errors or omissions have occurred, Millennium House would be pleased to hear from copyright owners.

t = top; b = bottom; l = left; r = right; c = center; tl = top left; tr = top right

2–3 Erhard Pfeiffer; 4 Fawn Art Photography; 6-7 Nigel Young/F&P; 8–9 Undine Prohl; 13 Paul McCredie; 14–15 Mark Callanan.

Introduction (US edition)
16 t, John Edward Linden; 16 b, © Hester + Hardaway Photographers; 17 t, Leonardo Finotti; 17 c, John Edward Linden; 17 b, TEN Arquitectos; 18 t, Bill Timmerman; 18 b, 19 l, Undine Prohl; 19 t, Howard Sutcliffe; 19 b, Eric Staudenmaier; 20 tl, Kim Zwarts; 20 tr, Richard Barnes Photography; 20 c, Cesar Rubio; 20–21 b, Tim Griffith; 21 tl, Benny Chan/fotoworks; 21 tr Marvin Rand.

Introduction (South African edition)
16, 17 t & bl, 18 l, 'Ora Joubert; 17 br, Peter Rich; 18–19 t, Dook Photography; 18–19 b, Mario; 19 tr, Hugh Fraser; 19 tc, Wieland Gleich of Archigraphy; 20 tl & tr, Van der Merwe Miszewski Architects; 20–21 b, 21, Stefan Antoni.

Introduction (Australian edition)
16 t Patrick Bingham-Hall; 16 bl, John Gollings; 16–17, Anthony Browell; 17 tl, Ross Honeysett; 17 tr, Adrian Boddy; 18 tl, John Gollings; 18 tr, Stephen Varady; 18 c, Adrian Boddy; 19, Eric Sierins; 20 t, Anthony Browell; 20 b, Willem Rethmeier; 21 tl, Rocket Mattler; 21 tr, Shannon McGrath; 21 c, Adrian Boddy.

Introduction (New Zealand edition)
16 t, Patrick Reynolds; 16 b, Ken Crosson; 17 t Mark Smith ©; 17 br & bl, Patrick Reynolds; 18 tl, Mark Smith ©; 18–19, Patrick Reynolds; 18 b, Paul McCredie; 19 Ken Crosson; 20 l, Paul McCredie; 20 tr, Megan Rule; 20 cr, 21 t, Patrick Reynolds;
21 b, Mark Smith ©.

Introduction (All other editions)
16 t, Stefan Müller-Naumann; 16 b, Manuel Herz; 17 t, Leonardo Finotti; 17 b, David Pisani / METROPOLIS; 18 t, Stanley Chou/ ©Millennium House; 18–9, 19 t, Christian Richters; 19 b, John Gollings; 20 l, John Edward Linden; 20–21, Benny Chan/fotoworks; 21 tr, Caramel; 21 br, Eugeni Pons

Part 1 HOME IN THE PAST
Arcaid: 33 t, 33 b, 39 b, 49 b, 60 t, 65 tl, 68 b, 70 t, 70 b, 71 tl, 71 tr.
Alexander Cuthbert: 28 tl, 32 l, 45 b.
Getty Images: 24 b, 25 t, 25 b, 26 t, 26 b, 28 tr, 29, 30–31, 32 tl, 32 c, 34 b, 35, 37, 38 l, 39 t, 41 tr, 41 b, 45 t, 47 t, 47 b, 48, 49 tl, 49 tr, 50 b, 51 t, 51 b, 52–53, 54, 55 tl, 55 tr, 56 t, 56 b, 57 tl, 57 tr, 57 b, 58 t, 58 b, 59, 60 b, 61, 62–63, 64, 65 tr, 66 t, 66 b, 67.
Picture Desk: 24 t, 27, 34 t, 36 t, 38 t, 40 t, 41 tl, 42–43, 44, 46 t, 46 b, 47 r, 50 t, 55 b, 68 t, 69 tr.

Part 2 HOME TODAY

In The City
74, Richard Barnes Photography; 75 t, Manuel Herz; 75 b, Marvin Rand; 76–79, Benny Chan; 80–83, Richard Barnes Photography; 84–85, © Hester + Hardaway Photographers; 86–89, Adrian Boddy / Stephen Buzacott; 90–93, Alvaro Povoa; 94–97, David Pisani / METROPOLIS; 98–101, John Gollings; 102–103, Mark Smith ©; 104–105, Kouji Okamoto; 106–107, Eric Sierins; 108–11, ©TEN Arquitectos; 112–13, Willem Rethmeier; 114–15, Hugh Fraser; 116 l, 119 r & b, Seksan; 116–18, 119 l, Stanley Chou/©Millennium House; 120–25, Manuel Herz; 126, 127 tr, Nik Randall; 127 tl & b, Katsuhisa Kida; 128–31, Rocket Mattler; 132–35, John Edward Linden; 136–37, Keith Parry; 138–39, Stephen Varady; 140–41, Megan Rule; 142–45, Marvin Rand; 146–49, Patrick Reynolds; 150–53, Paul McCredie; 154–57, Marvin Rand; 158–61, Sharon Risedorph; 162–63, Patrick Reynolds; 164–65, Michael Awad; 166 tl & bl, James Dow; 166 r, 167, Steven Evans; 168–71, Mario; 172–77, Tim Griffith.

Outer City
178, Eric Staudenmaier; 179 t, K.L. Ng; 179 b, John Edward Linden; 180–81, Stanley Chou/©Millennium House; 182–87, Wieland Gleich of Archigraphy; 188–91, Cesar Rubio; 192–93, Benny Chan/fotoworks; 194–95, Eugeni Pons; 196–97, Van der Merwe Miszewski Architects; 198–99, Ali Bekman / Ozlem Ercil; 200–203, K.L. Ng; 204–205 l Michael Simmons; 205 r Andrew Blaxland; 206–209, Eric Staudenmaier; 210–11, 210, 211, tr & br, Rupert Steiner, 211 l, Paul Ott; 212–13, 214–15 c, 215 b, Stefan Müller-Naumann; 214 l, Nagler Architeckten; 216–17, © Hester + Hardaway Photographers; 218–23, John Edward Linden; 224–25, Suan Lim; 226–27, K.L. Ng; 228–29, Eresh Weerasuriya; 230–31, David Pisani / METROPOLIS; 232–235, Undine Prohl; 236–39, John Edward Linden; 240–43, Nelson Kon; 244–49, Mitsuo Matsuoka; 250–53, Tim Street-Porter; 254–55, James Macmillan / Nik Randall; 258–59, Thomas Jantscher, Colombier CH; 260–65, Benny Chan/fotoworks.

Future City
266, 267 t, Christian Richters; 268–69, Lawrence Anderson Photography; 270–71, 274–77, Christian Richters; 278–79, C3D Interactive; 280–83, ©TEN Arquitectos; 284–85, Ali Bekman / Ozlem Ercil; 288–89, Marks Barfield Architects; 290–95, John Gollings; 296 t, Aditi Shah; 296 b, William Gullette; 297, Wallace E. Cunningham, Aditi Shah & Geoffrey Uhl.

In The Country
304, Anthony Vizzari; 305 t, Christian Richters; 305 b, Anthony Browell; 306–11, Eric Sierins; 312–17, Anthony Browell; 318–23, Nelson Kon; 324, 325 r, Anthony Vizzari; 325 l, Jim Yochum; 328–33, Benny Chan/fotoworks; 334–37, Cesar Rubio; 338–39, Caramel; 340–43, Richard Barnes; 344–47, Anthony Browell; 348 tl & b, 350–51, Undine Prohl; 348–49, Frederic Saia; 352–57, Christian Richters; 358–61, Ross Honeysett; 364–67, Sharon Risedorph; 368–69, Takeshi Yamagishi.

By The Water
370, Undine Prohl; 371 t, Stefan Antoni; 371 b, Kim Zwarts; 372–75, Shannon McGrath; 376–77, Patrik Enquist; 378–79, Simon Phipps; 380–83, Shoei Yoh; 384–85, John Edward Linden; 386–87; James Dow; 388, 390–91, Patrick Bingham-Hall; 389, 390 l & r, 392–93, Anthony Browell; 394–95, Adrian Boddy; 396–99, Albert Lim K.S; 400–405, John Edward Linden; 406–407, Elizabeth Felicella; 408–11, John Edward Linden; 412–17, Kim Zwarts; 422–25, Undine Prohl; 426–29, Stefan Antoni; 430–33, Undine Prohl; 434–37, Fawn Art Photography.

In Your Dreams
438, Stefan Antoni; 439 t, Tim Griffith; 439 b, Dook Photography; 440–43, Mark Callanan; 444–47, Leonardo Finotti; 448–51, Nigel Young/F&P; 452–53, Undine Prohl; 454–55, Patrick Reynolds; 456 l, 460, 461 bl, Erhard Pfeiffer; 456 r, 457, 461 br, Wallace E. Cunningham; 458–59, 461 t, Holt Webb; 462–67, Dook Photography; 465 r, David Ross; 468–69, Stanley Chou/©Millennium House; 470, Tim Street-Porter; 471 t, Tim Street-Porter; 471 b, 472–73, 475 r, Hagy Belzberg; 474, 475 t & bl, Tim Street-Porter; 478–83, Undine Prohl; 484–87, Sharon Risedorph; 488, 490 b, Seksan; 489, 490 t, 491, Stanley Chou/©Millennium House; 492–93, Bill Timmerman; 494–99, Stefan Antoni; 500–501, Van der Merwe Miszewski Architects; 502–507, Tim Griffith; 508–509, Kim Zwarts.

ACKNOWLEDGMENTS

The publisher would like to thank John Aspinall, Jyhling Lee, William Lim, Anoma Pieris, and Space Craft Architects for their assistance.

Thanks also to Barry Stone for the preparation of project descriptions for pages: 104–105, 108–11, 180–81, 240–43, 256–57, 270–71, 274–77, 280–83, 296–97, 352–57, 368–69, 380–85, 418–21, 444–47, 456–61, 468–69, 478–93.

ADDITIONAL INFORMATION AND PROJECT CREDITS

204–205 Peter Downes Designs: www.peterdownes.com

240–43 Marcio Kogan Arquiteto: www.marciokogan.com.br Pacaembu House: Author: Marcio Kogan. Co-author Bruno Gomes. Interior Design: Diana Radomysler, Marcio Kogan. Project Architects: Lair Reis, Oswaldo Pessano, Paula Moraes, Regiane Lão, Renata Furlanetto, Samanta Cafardo, Suzana Glogowski. Landscape architect: Renata Tilli. Structural Design: Leão e associados. Engineer: João Rubens Leão. General Contractor: DP Unique.
318–23 BR House. Architect: Marcio Kogan. Co-architect: Bruno Gomes. Interior design: Diana Radomysler & Marcio Kogan. Project architects: Lair Reis, Oswaldo Pessano, Paula Moraes, Regiane Lão, Renata Furlanetto, Samanta Cafardo, Suzana Glogowski. Photographer: Nelson Kon. Landscape architect: Isabel Duprat. Lighting design: Maneco Quinderé & Associados - Maneco Quinderé, Eduardo Lemos. Structural design: Construções metálicas ltda. Engineer: Wilson Ramos da Silva Filho. General contractor: Tempore Engenharia ltda.

270–71 Living Tomorrow. Client: Living Tomorrow, Vilvoorde. Design, UN Studio: Ben van Berkel with Igor Kebel, Aad Krom, Martin Kuitert, Markus Berger, Ron Roos, Andreas Bogenschütz. Executive architect: Living Tomorrow, Vilvoorde.
352–57 Möbius House. Design, UN Studio: Ben van Berkel with Aad Krom, Jen Alkema, Matthias Blass, Remco Bruggink, Marc Dijkman, Casper le Fevre, Rob Hootsmans, Tycho Soffree, Giovanni Tedesco, Harm Wassink.

Produced by Millennium House Pty Ltd
52 Bolwarra Rd, Elanora Heights
NSW, 2101, Australia
Phone: (612) 9970 6850 Fax: (612) 9970 8136
Email: rightsmanager@millenniumhouse.com.au

Villa Rica Coca - Cola Delivery Wagon

Villa Rica Presbyterian Church

Villa Rica Train Depot

Kennedy Chapel West Ga.

Carrollton Presbyterian Church

Veal School

Bonner House

Roopville Baptist Church

Statue of Confederate Soldier

Replicate McIntosh House

Sprayberry's Barbecue

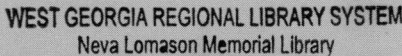

Carrollton First United Methodist Church

Mandeville Mills

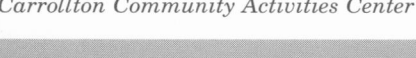

Carrollton Community Activities Center

Johnson's Sweet Potato House

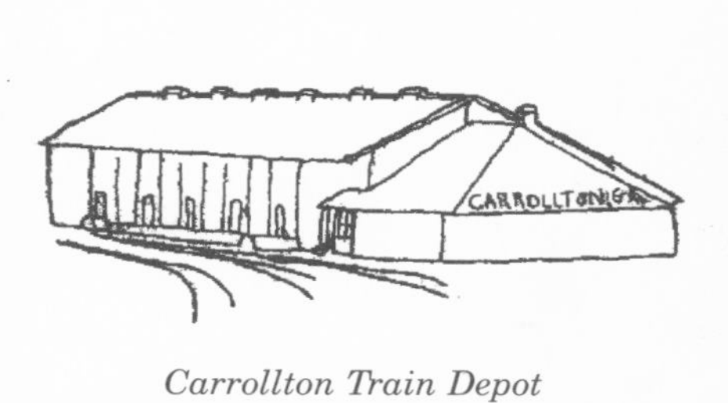

Carrollton Train Depot

THE HERITAGE OF CARROLL COUNTY GEORGIA

1826 - 2001

TABLE OF CONTENTS

DISCLAIMER

The Carroll County Heritage Book Committee disclaims responsibility for any erroneous statements presented in any article submitted by contributors to the Carroll County Heritage Book. Any questions should be referred to the person who submitted the article.

Printed in the USA by
Walsworth Publishing Co., Inc.

EXCLUSIVE AGENT:

www.countyheritagebooks.com

LC# 2002104095

CARROLL COUNTY HERITAGE BOOK COMMITTEE

L to R. Seated: Mary Florence Word, Chairman; Standing L to R: Myron House, Treasurer; Betty Jo Parsons, Family History Chairman; Violette Denney, Publicity; Gwen Chesnut, Adviser; Dr. David Wiggins, Topical Chairman

IN APPRECIATION

In May I was asked, by the executive committee of the Carroll County Heritage Book, to assume the chairmanship of the committee. The purpose of each member of the committee was to "make our book the best possible." Every committee member worked with this as their goal, making my task an easy one.

Betty Jo Parsons, whose interest in local family history dates back several years, was asked to serve as family history chairman. She dealt with the many families and their stories in a professional manner. Her typing and organizational skills have helped us to complete this enormous task in the allotted time frame.

Dr. David Wiggins, topical chairman, having worked on a committee such as this before, was able to guide us when questions arose about the publishing procedures. Although not a native of Carroll County, he calls Carroll County his home and he has pioneer roots here. Because of his knowledge and love of local history, the whole county has been well represented.

Violette Denney, publicity chairman, wore several hats. Because of her standing in the community we were able to have a very positive recognition. She provided us with original publicity, using her artistic talents to design the well placed notices. As you look through the book, pay special attention to the ads, tributes and memorials. These are the results of her dedication.

Gwen Chesnut, president of the Carroll County Historical Society, was able to advise us on the availability of resources and to provide us with a center for the storage and distribution of the completed books. We are very grateful that she shared her time with us.

Myron House, treasurer, is Special Collections Librarian at the State University of West Georgia. He has seen that all funds were deposited in a timely manner.

The results of the time and effort of the executive committee can be seen in this publication.

Mary Florence Arthur Word

SPECIAL THANKS

This book is dedicated to all those who have made it possible. It is dedicated to all who have spent many hours contacting people, encouraging them to submit materials, and to those who spent time compiling the book with endless hours of keeping records, proofreading, typing, and preparing articles for submission.

To those who have submitted stories for publication, we thank you. For all parties involved in this book, it has become an undertaking of devotion and love for our families and county. It has become an adventure in learning and sharing.

The executive committee of the Carroll County Heritage Book would be remiss in not singling out several key individuals who went beyond the call of duty to make this book a success. Special thanks to typists Cecelia Church and Charlene McDonald, to Judy Rowell, Mignon Wessinger, Jack Dorsey, Rebecca Merrell, Ruth Holder, Jan Bell, Earline Powers, and to Ozzie Binion for assistance with the end sheets.

INTRODUCTION

The Heritage of Carroll County Georgia 1826 to 2001 is a collection of materials — both fact and folklore — submitted for publication to preserve the present and past for future generations. It is compiled from information received from individuals who have submitted records of their families, heritage, churches, schools, organizations, businesses, along with the opportunities to include tributes and memorials.

Fifteen months have gone into this process, which was done completely by a committee of volunteers. Thousands of working hours have gone into the making of this book through processing, cataloging, editing, reading and proofing the submitted material.

While editing for error and space is a necessary aspect of publishing, we have tried to preserve the style and flavor of the articles as its author submitted them. Family stories containing more than 500 words were submitted by either an author having a pioneer ancestor in the county, or the author elected to purchase the additional space.

Our objective was to publish an accurate and factual account of the past and present heritage of Carroll County. There may be incorrect dates, misspelled names, or other errors that we can expect in a project of this magnitude. For any errors we apologize and say we did our best to present the material as it was given to the committee. The Carroll County Heritage Book Committee is not responsible for incorrect information within the publication. Each author is responsible for his or her submission. Any questions concerning information within an article should be directed to the author for clarification.

CARROLL COUNTY
BOARD OF COMMISSIONERS

423 COLLEGE STREET • P.O. BOX 338
CARROLLTON, GEORGIA 30117
PHONE: (770) 830-5800 • FAX (770) 830-5992
www.carrollcountyga.com

BOARD OF COMMISSIONERS:
ROBERT P. BARR, CHAIRMAN
TRENT T. NORTH, DISTRICT 1
J. RUSTY DEAN, DISTRICT 2
BILL HEAD, DISTRICT 3
ROBERT A. KENIMER, DISTRICT 4
RANDY G. SIMPKINS, DISTRICT 5
HERMAN K. AYERS, DISTRICT 6

March 14, 2001

"PROCLAMATION"

WHEREAS: *Carroll County does not have an up-to-date history; and,*

WHEREAS: *Carroll County recognizes a need for the publication of "The Heritage of Carroll County," Georgia, to pay tribute to our county and our citizens; and,*

WHEREAS: *Other Georgia Counties have successfully published such history books; and,*

WHEREAS: *Walsworth Publishing Company will invite all current and former residents of Carroll County to participate in the writing and production of a new history without financial risk;*

NOW THEREFORE: *I, Robert P. Barr, Chairman of the County Commission in Carroll County, Georgia, do hereby proclaim that WALWORTH PUBLISHING COMPANY shall be the official publisher of the "THE HERITAGE OF CARROLL COUNTY, GEORGIA," for delivery in late 2001.*

Whereupon, Robert P. Barr, Chairman, declared said resolution duly adopted; and it is therefore ADJUDGED and ORDERED said resolution be, and the same is, hereby adopted.

Robert P. Barr

Robert P. Barr, Chairman

Office of the Mayor

City of Carrollton

Proclamation

WHEREAS, Carroll County does not have an up-to-date history; and

WHEREAS, the City of Carrollton recognizes a need for the publication of ***"The Heritage of Carroll County"***, to pay tribute to our county and our citizens; and

WHEREAS, other counties have successfully published such history books; and

WHEREAS, Walsworth Publishing Company will invite all current and former residents of Carroll County to participate in the writing and production of a new history without financial risk; now

THEREFORE, I Gerald Pilgrim, Mayor of the City of Carrollton, Georgia, do hereby proclaim that WALSWORTH PUBLISHING COMPANY shall be the official publisher of ***"THE HERITAGE OF CARROLL COUNTY, GEORGIA"***, for delivery in late 2001.

In witness whereof I have hereunto set my hand and caused this seal to be affixed.

Gerald Pilgrim

Historic Carroll County Redwork Quilt

1. Description of the Endsheets of This Volume

When you are an organization with a lot of creativity and known for your unique Art Form, it is natural to make a quilt to raise funds for projects. The guild wanted to design something that would preserve some of our local history and knew that we only needed a limited number of blocks for a quilt. Guild members were asked to suggest one or two sites that they wanted to include. A committee selected 32 from these. Then members were asked to volunteer to embroidery a Redwork block. Some agreed to do two if needed. With a project like this there is a place for every member to participate from planning, shopping, designing, to finishing the edges! This Legacy in Stitches consumed a full year and it was an event to celebrate when Representative Tracy Stallings drew the winning ticket, which belonged to Guild Member Brent Hildebrand. Brent is pictured with the quilt on October 19, 1999. The following list is a brief description of the 32 drawings and the center map, which are featured in the end sheets of this book.

Endsheets

From top left:

#1 - Temple Train Depot by Nadine Cole. This depot was built in 1906 after the original one burned. It is 27 feet by 70 feet and served the area as a social center where visitors were met. The residents waited there for the mail train to arrive. It is located between Johnson and Sage Streets. The town was built around the depot.

#2 Round Barn at Hickory Level by Gloria Pope. Walter Dorough built the barn in 1917, after seeing a similar one in Arkansas. It was placed on the National Register of Historic Places in 1980.

#3 Cross Plains School by Mabel Walls. The schoolhouse was built around 1850 and closed in about 1937. The building, about 40 feet by 40 feet, housed all grades and it is located on the corner of Cross Plains Road and Old Four Notch Road.

#4 Villa Rica Coca Cola Delivery Wagon by Marilyn Clark. 1885 - 1889 Regular horse drawn wagons to fit requirements of delivering Coca Cola. Signs were painted and attached to the wagon.

#5 Villa Rica Presbyterian Church by Jane Brownlow. The church was established in 1855 in downtown Villa Rica, Ga.

#6 Villa Rica Train Depot by Lucy Walls. The first depot was built in about 1890 to accommodate the passengers who rode the train.

#7 Stewart house by Jane Kingsley. This 150 year old landmark was built about 1844 by John Stewart (Great Grandfather of Robert L. (Bob) Stewart). It was opened in October 1996 as a "Personal Care Retirement Living Home" by Ricky and Melissa Newbern, who are the present owners.

#8 Tabernacle Baptist Church by Juanita Davis. It was moved to Cottage Hill Road from Bradley Street in 1989

#9 Carroll County Courthouse by Inez Presnal. 1893 - 1928 It was located on Newnan Street where the present courthouse stands.

#10 Kennedy Chapel by Mary Bell Chandler. This chapel was built by the Episcopal Church, which was organized in 1892. This "Country Gothic" chapel was constructed on the corner of White and West Streets, and it was consecrated as Saint Margaret Episcopal Chapel on July 15, 1893. The new St. Margaret Church building, on Newnan Street, was built in 1953. The chapel was sold to the Catholic Church, which they quickly outgrew. The area churches raised $6,000 to move the chapel to the campus of the State Univ. of W. Ga. Robert Kennedy came for the dedication service of the Kennedy Interfaith Chapel in memory of John F. Kennedy on May 26, 1964.

#11 Carrollton Presbyterian Church by Vivian Fidler. The Church was founded in 1841 and this building was completed in 1902.

#12 Veal School by Liz Runyon. The school was established in 1899 and closed in 1949. It is now used for community singings.

#13 Abilene Baptist Church (1875) by Anita Thomas. The church was organized on May 8, 1875 and first met in a bush arbor. In 1892 the first small unceiled building was started near the road in front of the present building. It has grown considerably and is located on Hwy. 113 in Carroll County, Georgia.

#14 Statue at Carrollton City Hall by Genny Crawford. The "Farmer sitting on a Bale of Cotton" statue was commissioned by the Parks, Recreation & Cultural Arts Department from Henry Setter. The bale of cotton is a standard size - 54" long, 29" high, & 40" deep - and appears to be covered with burlap with steel bands. A bale of cotton weighed about 500 lbs. the statue of course weighs much more! If the man was standing straight up he would measure 6ft. 9ins. to the top of his hat. It was unveiled and dedicated May 4, 1997.

#15 Center - Map outline of Carroll County designed with cities and landmarks by Natalie Steinborn and embroidered by Marlene Uglum.

#16 Bonner House by Tommie Freeman. It was built in 1853 and is located at the State University of West Georgia. It is now used for Public Relations Offices.

#17 Roopville Baptist Church by Katie Wiggins. It was established in 1883. The building is located on Old Franklin Street in Roopville, Ga. Mr. Roop gave land for three churches.

#18 Shiloh United Methodist Church by Alma Bohannon. This church at Burwell was Chartered in 1856. The Camp Ground building is 140 years old.

#19 Appleton Mandeville home by Jennifer West. Mr. Mandeville (1802-1892) born in New York came to Georgia in 1821 and to Carrollton in 1833. He married Mary Ann Stewart (sister of John W. Stewart) from Vermont in 1835. Their home was on Maple Street beside the Mansion Restaurant. It was built in 1836-1841 and was a white house with boxwoods down the walk way. Appleton and Mary Ann Mandeville raised ten children.

#20 Statue of Confederate Soldier by Bette Ferreri. It was moved 6-6-1958 from Adamson Square to the hospital grounds on Dixie St., later it was moved to the courthouse on Newnan Street. It was placed there "IN PROUD AND LOVING MEMORY OF THE CONFEDERATE SOLDIERS OF CARROLL COUNTY 1861 - 1865" and it was "ERECTED BY THE ANNIE WHEELER CHAPTER UNITED DAUGHTERS OF THE CONFEDERACY, APRIL 26, 1910." "UPON THE ALTAR OF HOME AND COUNTRY, THEY PLACED THE OFFERING IN FULLEST MEASURE, OF ALL THEY HAD TO GIVE."

#21 Replica of Chief William McIntosh's home by Violette Denney. It is located on the site belived to be near where his original home stood in McIntosh Reserve, Whitesburg, Ga. The Abraham Baldwin Chapter, NSDAR, worked on this project for several years.

#22 Aycock House by Gaye Pollock. This was the home of Thomas Jack and Emma Lee Aycock, parents of Ed Aycock, who said they purchased a two-room house on Dixie Street and in 1900 enlarged it to the present size. Thomas Jack Aycock was the owner of the former Kytle-Aycock Funeral Home. "Miss Emma Lee" was a dedicated piano teacher and entertained with music from her concert grand piano.

#23 Carrollton First Christian Church by Violette Denney. The buff brick building is located on the corner of Ward & College Streets and that structure was completed in 1947. The church was established in 1872.

#24 Green Front Restaurant by Sandra Gowing. It was located on Bradley Street near the railroad tracks and across from the depot. The restaurant was owned and operated by Henry Lumpkin from about 1938 until his death in 1986. Then Charles Lumpkin took over and it was sold in 1990. College students who worked there were fondly called "The Green Front Flies."

Carroll County Historical Redwork Quilt with winner Brent Hildebrand

#25 Sprayberry's Barbecue by Sue Ellen Chandler. It was located on Hwy. 27 N., near Carrollton. There was a juke box in the back with a platform for dancing and needless to say that it was a popular spot on Saturday night.

#26 Carrollton First United Methodist Church by Nancy Hallden. The Methodist Church of Carrollton erected their first house of worship in 1847 at the corner of Alabama and N. Park Streets (where the cemetery is now). The church building at 206 Newnan Street was built in 1904 and the last renovation project on that building was completed in June 1989.

#27 Mandeville Mills by Ollie Wright. The Mandeville Cotton Mills began operation in July 1890. L. Clifton Mandeville (son of Appleton Mandeville) was President of Mandeville Cotton Mills. Joseph Amis Aycock built the county's first cotton gin in 1890 and helped organize the Carrollton Oil Mill in 1898. In August 1902 the Carrollton Oil Mill and the Mandeville Cotton Mills incorporated as Mandeville Mills, Inc. Lights were added in 1920 and water pipes were installed in 1921. Mandeville Mills, Inc. was believed to be the most important industry in Carrollton prior to Southwire, which opened in 1950. The Mandeville Mills, Inc. were liquidated in 1954.

#28 Bookmobile by Mildred Bennett. The Bookmobile of the W. Georgia Regional Library started in 1947 and served Carroll, Haralson, Douglas and Heard Counties. A station wagon was used until the late 1950's or early 1960's.

#29 Lovvorn Home, Bowdon, Ga., by Nancy Gilmer. This Queen Anne Victorian home was built by Dr. J.L. Lovvorn around the turn of the 19th Century. It has always been in the same family and is on the National Register.

#30 Bethesda Baptist Church by Erma Stone. The church is at 1539 Bethesda Church Road, Roopville, Georgia.

#31 Carrollton Community Activities Center by Sue Hardin. It was completed in 1921 and was the Carrollton High School and then the Carrollton Junior High School until April 1986 before later becoming the Activities Center.

#32 Johnson's Sweet Potato House by Norma West. It was built on Hwy. 27 S. in 1940 and used for sweet potatoes for 25 years. It is now a landmark and continues to advertise Coca Cola!

#33 Carrollton Train Depot by Gene Cooksey. This historic building is located on Bradley Street. The first train arrived in Carrollton from Whitesburg in 1874. The Chattanooga, Rome to Carrollton line was completed in 1888.

Submitted by: Violette Denney

Early History of Carroll County

2. Native American Housing – Pre-Contact

The Native Americans of the areas that later became known as Virginia, North Carolina, South Carolina, and Georgia lived in rectangular gabled thatched houses (wattle and daub) or in some areas, rectangular barrel-roofed houses (long houses). The wattle and daub, a pole framework intertwined with branches and vines, and covered with mud plaster inside and out, could be found in the Southeast. The long house was a gabled or vaulted framework with a door at each end and a variety of coverings, such as bark from various types of trees.

All of the men from a village would gather to build houses. A good-sized dwelling could be completed in one day. They would mark the dimensions of the house on the ground, then the timbers were cut and marked. They used plumb lines to align the walls. They set strong poles deep in the ground at regular intervals. These poles extended upward approximately six to seven feet. The posts were usually dried locust and sassafras for durability. The posts were notched at the top and wall plates fit into the notches. A large notched post was set in the center of each gable. The ridgepole ran the length of the house. It was tied at regular intervals using bark strips or splinters of white oak or hickory. The roof consisted of mat-like layers of split saplings or bundles (three large canes) that were tied together above the rafters or saplings. Sometimes, it was shingled with the bark of pine or cypress. The windows were about one square foot in size. Doors were of poplar planks covered with straps of shaved and wet buffalo hides, which tightened and strengthened when dry.

The Cherokee women furnished the houses. They crafted beds and seating from river cane, strips of maple and oak, and honeysuckle. They made dyes from bloodroot, butternut, walnut, and other plants to decorate the furniture and baskets.

Inside the house there was little more than stools, storage chests, and broad beds. The beds were about three-feet-high, made of boards and white-oak foundations. Each bed had cane-splinter mattresses covered with bear, buffalo, mountain lion, elk, and deerskins with fur intact.

Outside of each dwelling was a small "sweathouse" and another mud hut. Inside these sweathouses, the fire was kept burning. These were for purification and to cure diseases. The mud hut was used to store or smoke food.

Some lived in more than one type of shelter according to the season. In colder areas, each village had a large winter hothouse. The hothouse walls were plastered six or seven inches thick with clay and grass. These hothouses were usually built on high ground or mounds. There was a hole in the center of the roof to allow smoke to dissipate. These houses were windowless, lacked air, and were hot, smoky, and dark.

The Cherokee lived in villages. Some villages extended several miles along riverbanks. Each village had a council or town house and a plaza where everyone met to socialize, make decisions, or conduct ceremonies. These council houses were very large, circular, and sat on top of a mound. The private houses lay outside the plaza.

Submitted by: Cecilia Wood Church, 128 Brock Street, Carrollton, GA 30117, E-mail address: cechurch@charter.net.

3. Carroll County - Gateway to the Former Creek Nation

Indians belonging to the Creek Confederacy in early historic times occupied most of the area of what is now Georgia. The name "Creek" originated from a shortening of Ocheese Creek Indians, the name given by the English to the native peoples living along Ocheese Creek (Ocmulgee River).

The area that became Carroll County was occupied by the northern most tribes of the "Lower" Creeks (those living along the Flint and Chattahoochee Rivers). This part of Georgia was also just south and east of the "Upper" Creeks (those living along the Coosa, Tallapoosa and Alabama Rivers). The Lower Creek people were much more receptive to the white man and his culture than the Upper Creeks, due in part to the fact that the lower towns had been exposed for almost two hundred years to Spanish, French, and English traders and settlers. The biggest difference between the two Creek groups was the differences of language; the Lower Creeks were Muskogee speaking and the Upper tribes spoke various non-Muskogee dialects (primarily Hitchitis).

The Cherokee have long overshadowed the Creek tribes in Georgia history. This oversight exists in spite of the fact that over seventy-five percent of the state of Georgia was inhabited by the Creeks and that the first Native Americans to welcome James Oglethorpe near Savannah were the Yamacraw Indians (a part of the Creek Confederacy).

The Creek (Muskogean speaking) people are believed to be the direct descendents of the Mississippian Mound Builders (1000-1500 A.D.). This Mississippian culture arrived via a southeasterly migration through west and middle Tennessee. In some instances, the migrating Mississippians seem to have been a coherent culture group that split apart and respectively traveled into eastern Tennessee and Georgia. In other areas, they were apparently chronologically and culturally slightly different and thus represent separate migrations following the same general route.

When we study these mound builders the most frequently asked question is — Were these people Creeks or Cherokees? There were no groups called Creek or Cherokee in 1000 A.D. but the Creek would appear to be their descendents. There is evidence that the Creeks did not withdraw from the eastern Tennessee region until after the beginnings of trade relations with the English colonies. The various Creek groups withdrew from their more northern locations to avoid reprisals after the Yamassee War in 1715, which involved the Creeks as well as other southern Indian groups. The Yuchi remained along the Hiwassee River up to 1714 when the Cherokee destroyed the Yuchi town of Chestowa. These Yuchi abandoned the region and were incorporated into the Creek nation. Cherokee myths and ethnohistory indicate that they drove the Creeks further south out of north Georgia and the Etowah country about 1750. In many instances they preempted sites formerly inhabited by Creeks.

There is little doubt that the once powerful Mississippian chiefdoms in the interior Southeast described by the de Soto narrators were reduced to the small societies that banded together to form the Creek Confederacy by the early eighteenth century. By the time white men began to record the life of the Indian, the Creek Confederacy had appeared and the ancient powerful chiefs had been replaced by mikos. Theoretically, the miko was little more than the head of the tribal council and spokesman of his tribe. Furthermore, the miko acted only after conferring with his council. The miko governed a town or talwa. A province or complex chiefdom of the sixteenth century probably "devolved" into several Creek talwas by the eighteenth century. The fall of the chiefdoms was closely tied to depopulation from disease and famine and the loss of culture that ensued. It seems certain that the loss of manpower had much to do with the changes in political organization.

Remnants of the once-powerful chiefdoms now reduced to little more than small towns, banded together for mutual defense from incursions of armed Indians from the north and slave

traders from the east. Thus the Creek Confederacy was formed as a response to outside pressures. The Muskogee (Creeks) gradually brought into amalgamation the Apalachicola, Hitchiti, Okmulgee, Sawokli, Chiaha, Asochi, Yuchi, Alabama, Twasa, Pawolke, Muklasa, Koasati, Tuskegee and sections of the Shaunee, Guale, and Yamasee.

Tribal unity, communal solidarity, and internal harmony were paramount in the reasoning of the Creek, for they were not a single tribe ruled by a despot whose word was law, but a group of many small tribes who needed each other to survive.

The story of the Creek people is almost unknown to the public. Most people have heard of the Cherokee's "Trail of Tears" but almost no one is aware of the cruelty to the Creeks during their removal to the west several years earlier. Their estimated losses were the highest of all the removed tribes — between 4 and 5 thousand deaths. This tragic series of group removals could be called the "Creek of Tears" to reflect the great hardships endured by this once great, proud people. *Submitted by: Doug Mabry*

4. Chief William McIntosh

The most controversial figure on the American frontier lived and died in Carroll County — Chief William McIntosh. To the white man he was a great hero because he helped them gain more and more land; to many southeastern Indians he was one of the greatest traitors of all Native American history.

He was a half-breed chief of the Lower Creek Nation whose mother was a full-blood Creek from the very influential "Wind" clan of the Coweta tribe and his father was of the powerful McIntosh clan from Scotland. The chief's grandfather, John McIntosh came with James Oglethorpe to help settle and establish the state of Georgia.

Chief McIntosh was one of the most important figures not only in the history of Georgia but of the American frontier. He dined at the White House with President Thomas Jefferson; and later had meetings with President James Madison and James Monroe, as well as Secretary of War, John C. Calhoun. He fought for Andrew Jackson in the Creek Indian War along side Sam Houston and Davey Crockett. It was very rare for one man to have so much influence in two cultures. In the Lower Creeks Federation, he was a principal chief and conducted most of the important council meetings, in addition to being the signer of all the treaties between the Creeks and the government between 1805 and 1825 (½ the state of George — some 20 million acres — was gained for the state through the treaties signed by Chief William McIntosh). In 1821, there was a treaty signed at McIntosh's place on the Chattahoochee between the Creeks and Cherokees about the boundary between the nations. All the head chiefs of the Creek and Cherokee Nations were assembled at what is now the McIntosh Reserve Park.

In his white world, McIntosh was made a Brigadier General for his heroism in the Creek Indian War under General Andrew Jackson against the Upper Creeks and later the Seminoles. Both of these tribes were supplied arms by the British to cause trouble in the southern states. The chief was also a cousin to Georgia Governor, George M. Troup. In 1825, the governor was running for re-election on the popular promise to remove all the Indians to the western territories. This attitude toward all the native inhabitants not only helped Troup win his election but also was widespread enough across the southern states to later help Andrew Jackson win the presidency.

There was tremendous pressure on McIntosh from his cousin and the state government to sell more and more Indian land. The chief signed a total of five treaties with the government moving further west each time the boundaries of the Creek nation. Each time he was assured that the state's new land would be enough to satisfy arriving settlers. In the last treaty McIntosh signed at Indian Springs on February 12, 1825 his people not only got money for the land but the Creeks were also given an equal amount of land out west on which to live.

Some have said that McIntosh was a traitor for signing the treaties that sold the Creek land and moved his people out west. However, he knew the mind of the white man and their great desire for more land. This was reflected in a quote the chief made shortly before the Treaty of Indian Springs:

> "The white man is growing in the state of Georgia. He wants our lands. He will buy them now, but by and by he will take them and the little band of our people will be left to wander without homes — poor, despised, and beaten like dogs. We will go to our new homes and learn like the white man to till the earth, grow cattle, and depend on these for food and life. Let us learn to make books like the white man does and we shall grow again into a great nation."

To the non-Muskogee speaking tribes (Upper Creek and Seminoles) McIntosh was a cold-blooded killer who would sell out anyone or anything for money. The state and federal government leaders knew of McIntosh's quest for power and wealth and always knew they could get him to agree to anything if offered enough money. Every time the chief teamed up with General Andrew Jackson he received the spoils of war. He was given large tracks of land in Alabama for helping in the slaughter at Horseshoe Bend. In the Seminole Wars at the Negro Fort, McIntosh and his followers received the booty; 2,500 stands of arms, 500 carbines, 200 pistols, 500 swords, 1,062 kegs of powder, bars of lead, uniforms, and food.

McIntosh's periodic incursions into Florida netted captives that he and his partner, Creek agent David B. Mitchell, disposed of profitably. In a sense, Prospect Bluff (the site of the Negro Fort) had been transformed into a slave mart.

As McIntosh and his warriors charged into the Negro Fort, scalped Garcon (the leader) and the Choctaw chief, rounded up the people of diverse ethnic backgrounds classified as Negroes and put them in chains, they were sending a message to non-Muskogees. All Muscogulges (all tribes in the lower Southeast) must adopt the American scheme of civilization and acknowledge the leadership of McIntosh, his kin, and the National Council.

McIntosh's aversion toward those Indians in the opposite moiety (non-Muskogee speaking), whether they were called Creeks or Seminoles, was genuine and he had no qualms about profiting at their expense.

Chief McIntosh from 1910 Postcard

The chief was murdered on May 1, 1825 at his home on what is now the McIntosh Reserve by a large group of hostile Upper Creek warriors who claimed they did not want him to sell the Creek land to the government and have the people move west to the Oklahoma territory. These Upper Creek assassins were led by some of the same chiefs who McIntosh had helped defeat during the Creek Indian Wars. They possibly were using the treaty signing as an excuse for revenge against their old enemy.

Even though Chief McIntosh received payments and favors for his treaty signing (this was a very common practice in many deals during this time period) he was somewhat vindicated less than a year later when the same Upper Creek chieves who ordered McIntosh killed signed an almost identical treaty with the federal government (for less money than the original deal). At the time of his death McIntosh was living on his plantation on the Chattahoochee River where he operated a ferry, two taverns, a trading post, and an overnight lodge. He owned almost one hundred slaves who helped maintain the plantation and several hundred head of cattle and hogs. Chief McIntosh is buried where he fell on beloved, beautiful land at the river of the McIntosh Reserve. *Submitted by: Doug Mabry*

5. Transactions Found in Deed Book A and B Carroll County, Georgia

The land in Carroll County was originally distributed by a lottery held in Milledgeville, Georgia in 1827. 202½ acres were included in a land lot. Fortunate drawers paid $18 per lot. Carroll County at that time included parts of Heard, Troup, Campbell and Haralson counties as well as the present Carroll County. Lottery records, which have been published, are the earliest land records, and no deeds were recorded until the land was sold by the fortunate drawer.

Some of the lots were sold immediately, an example being the first deed recorded in Carroll County.

> Elbert County, 23 May 1827. Ealum Hill to Walker Horton, land lot #98, 5th district. $200.00.

Some of the land was leased.

> In January, 1828 William Rolls leased to William O. Wagnon, for the year, land lot #90, 5th district in consideration of Wagnon "putting up a hewed log house 16 feet clear, 9 feet high with a good chimney, clearing not more than 50 acres, but at least 30 with the owner having the right to take possession at any time after the year 1828".

Some of the land was sold to satisfy a debt.

> Chatham County, 7 Aug 1827. Abraham D. Lyon, Sheriff Chatham County to William Williams. $80.00. Land lot 149, 6th district. Drawn by Sarah Crim, sold for taxes in the name of her husband.

Profits were made when mining started in Carroll County.

> Georgia, 20 Jul 1827, George Smith to Ann Green. $100. Land lot # 238, second district Carroll (now Douglas) County drawn by George Smith.
>
> 26 Jun 1830 Ann Green, Mobile County, Ala. to John Childers, Bibb County. $100. Land lot #238, 2nd district of Carroll (now Douglas).
>
> Carroll County, 5 Aug 1830, Anne Green to Patrick B. Connelly and Robert Collins, $3000, land lot #238, 2nd district Carroll (now Douglas) reserving 10 acres on the south line on the north side of Sweetwater Creek, but granting mineral rights.

Other types of transactions were recorded.

> September 1829, William O. Wagnon appointed Isaac Wood his attorney to collect from the U.S. Government for provisions furnished to the McIntosh party of Indians during the year 1826.
>
> May 1831. Joseph Little's mark and brand. A crop off the left ear, a slit in the right ear, brand J&L for Joseph Little.
>
> May 1830. Benjamin Merrill, Henry Curtis, George Gibson, John Gibson, Aaron Jones, Hinchea P. Mabry and Levi Benson to Governor George R. Gilmer. Bond in the amount of $10,000. Term of office of Benjamin Merrill, Sheriff Carroll County.

The most common transactions were deeds to individuals who planned to make Carroll County their home for life.

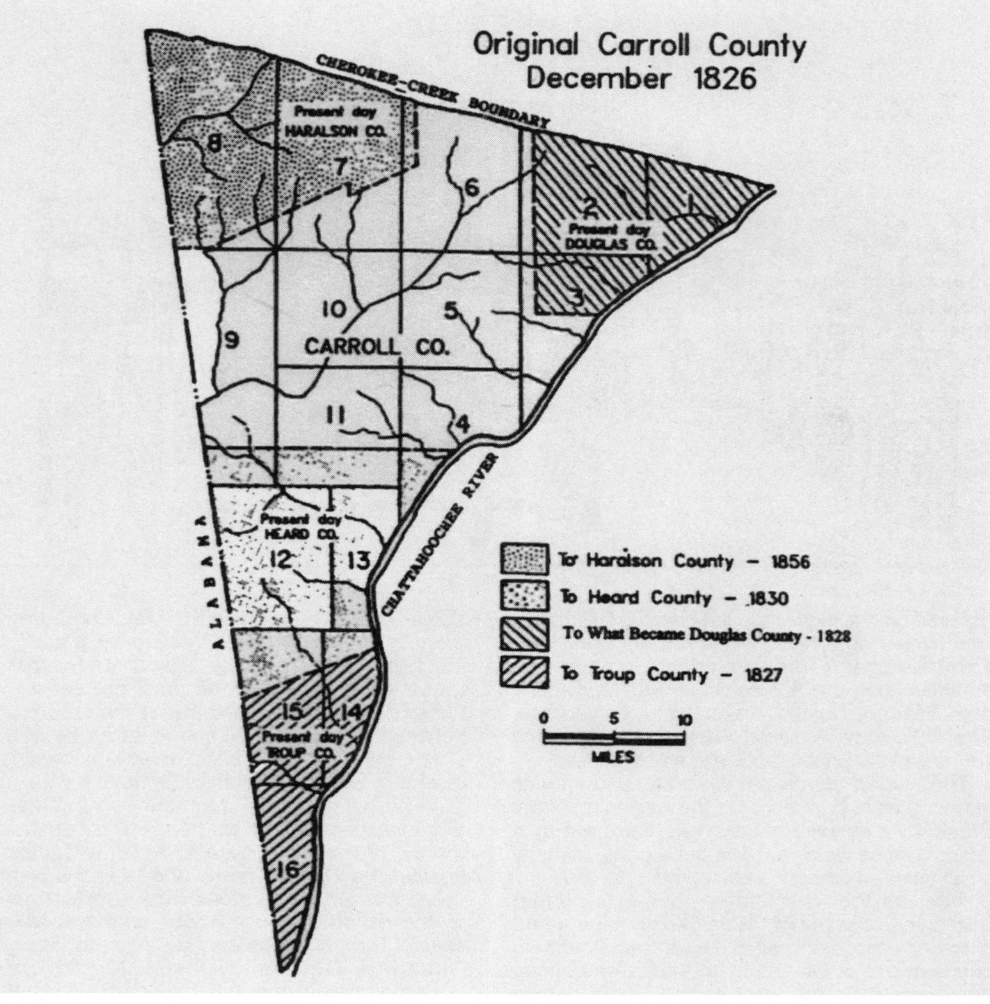

Original Carroll County December 1826

> Franklin County, Ga. 5 Jan 1836. John Banks to John B. Word. $800. Land lot #194, 11th district Carroll County.

Submitted by: Mary Florence Arthur Word.
Source: Abstract Deed Book A & B. 1827-1836.

6. Carroll County Wills

Recording in *Carroll County Will Book A* begins in 1852. Before 1852 some wills have been found recorded in the book *Carroll County Ordinary Inferior Court Records 1829-1845, 1848.* This volume also contains estate settlements and early marriages. A copy of an excerpt of the will of Richard Benson, written on 9 July 1828 and registered on 8 July 1829 is shown. He names his wife Sarah, a son Andrew Jackson Benson, and a daughter Elizabeth Oakley. The will was recorded with William G. Springer as the Justice of the Peace and Larkin Bell and George H. Cosper as witnesses. *Submitted by: Mary Florence Word*

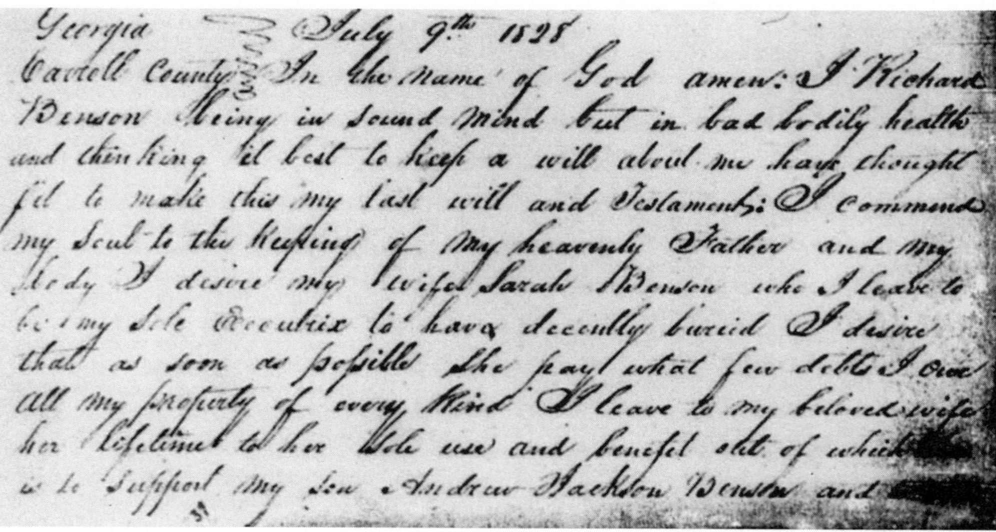
Georgia July 9th 1828
Carroll County In the name of God amen: I Richard Benson being in sound mind but in bad bodily health and thinking it best to keep a will about me have thought fit to make this my last will and Testament: I commend my Soul to the keeping of my heavenly Father and my body I desire my wife Sarah Benson who I leave to be my Sole Executrix to have decently buried I desire that as soon as possible she pay what few debts I owe All my property of every kind I leave to my beloved wife her lifetime to her sole use and benefit out of which is to support my son Andrew Jackson Benson and

Early Will for Richard Benson

Military History

7. Revolutionary War Soldiers in Carroll County

John Carmichael, born 1737. Served from Pennsylvania. In 1833 a John Carmichael purchased land with a Thomas McGuire in what is now Haralson County. He is not found in the 1840 census, Carroll County.

Peter Helton, born 1756, served from Surrey Co. North Carolina. Applied for pension while living in Carroll County.

Nimrod Jones, Revolutionary War soldier. Served from Georgia. His grave site is off Highway 27 south on Shadinger Road. The grave site was marked by the Abraham Baldwin Chapter DAR, September 1997.

Benjamin Parr, Revolutionary War soldier, b. September 1, 1760. Served from New Jersey, enlisted from North Carolina. Died 22 December 1842, Carroll County, Georgia. Marker placed at New Hope Methodist Cemetery. Researched by Ray Brown.

Jesse Peters born c1753, served from Georgia. Drew land in the 1827 land lottery, and received a pension for his service while living in Carroll County.

Levi Phillips drew land in the 1838 Cherokee Land Lottery from Carroll County as a Revolutionary War Soldier. Received a pension for his services.

John Robinson Sr. age 88 in the 1840 census Carroll County, living in 653rd district.

Jesse Rowell age 87 in the 1840 census, living 754th district of Carroll County. On 25 April 1834, Revolutionary War pensioner Jesse Rowell appointed his son, William Rowell, to take lawful means to obtain bounty land.

Gabriel Smith, Revolutionary War soldier. Served from North Carolina. His age is listed between 70 and 80 in the 1840 census, Carroll County. He is buried at Old Poplar Springs Cemetery, near Poplar Springs Church.

Zachariah Stedham listed in the 1840 census as a Revolutionary War soldier. He was living in the household of James H. Stedham, 729th district, age 89. According to pension records he served from South Carolina. *Submitted by: Mary Florence Arthur Word*

Sources: *Georgia Revolutionary War Soldiers Graves* Volume One, Appling and Lanier Counties, compiled by H. Ross Arnold Jr. and H. Clifton Burnham. *1830 & 1840 Federal Census of Carroll County, Georgia* compiled for the Carroll County Genealogical Society, 1998. *Carroll County, Georgia, Abstract of Deed Book A and B 1827-1836* Mary Florence A. Word, 1992. Abraham Baldwin Chapter, Daughters of the American Revolution. Ray Brown, Carrollton, Georgia

8. Camp Odum

There is a marble marker about four miles south of Carrollton off Blandenburg Road that marks the site of Camp Odum. On June 6, 1836, a military company, the Carroll County Guards, camped here. The company was raised out of fear that Cherokees in the north were to join with the Creeks and war was to be raised against the settlers. The volunteer company was raised on May 21 and consisted of 12 commissioned officers and 66 enlisted men. Captain of the Company was W.L. Parr; First Lieutenant was James H. Rodgers; Second Lieutenant was Emanuel B. Martin; and Third Lieutenant was Appleton Mandeville. The camp was named for Benton Odum, one of the men of the company.

The monument was erected on June 6, 1906, seventy years after the encampment. A picnic was held to commemorate the camp and while sitting under the shade trees, the crowd that had gathered was entertained by Captain J.B. Martin, Judge W.C. Hodnett, and the Honorable L.P. Mandeville. Many of the descendents of the men of the company were in attendance.

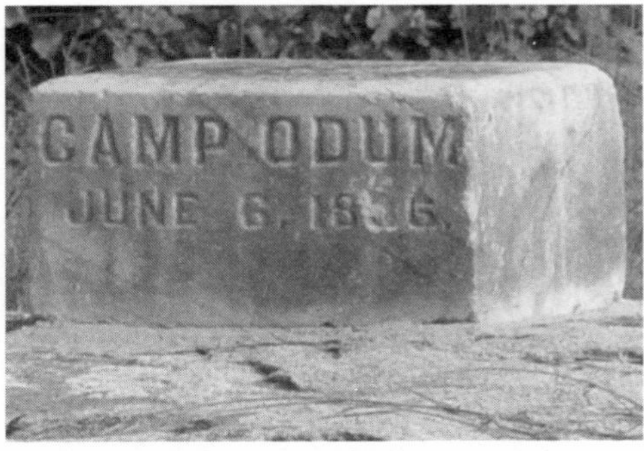

Camp Odum Marker

Sources: *Carrol County and Her People; At Home in Carrollton 1827-1994; Carroll County Historical Quarterly,* Spring and Summer 1968

9. Letter Home From the Front 1848

Tampico Mexico January 15th 1848

Dear Father & Mother

At length I have found an opportunity of writing to you and informing you of our situation. We left St. Joseph's Island on the 5th Inst. On board the steamer Ann Chase, after a stay of two months and four days on the island. We had pretty weather for two days and thought we would have a pleasant passage to Vera Cruz. But suddenly a storm came up from the north and continued until the evening of the 9th Inst. when it suddenly changed to the east. The wind blew so hard that it was impossible to keep the steamer on its course without it filling and sinking. The Captain of the steamer then turned her to windward and put her on the mercy of the waves (which never show pity in the time of a storm.) About half past eleven o'clock Sunday night the 9th Inst. we heard a crash like the ship had broken to pieces. And to our astonishment found it on the breakers, and then it was that we were really alarmed, as no one but one who has been shipwrecked in a dark night in time of a storm can imagine. The tide being very high soon carried us across the breakers and run us out on the shore when it stuck. We then waited in awful suspense till day and then got our horses and plunder on shore about fifty five miles below here in the heart of hostile Mexicans. A courier was immediately dispatched to this place with a letter to the Quartermaster informing him of our shipwreck etc., who immediately sent a steamship down after our dismounted men and baggage and with an order for the mounted men to come up by land. We staid there two days and marched up here by land and reached here the 15th Inst. We will stay here five or six days longer to recruit our horses and then start to Vera Cruz. We are all well pleased with what of Mexico we have seen and especially with this city. Then we can get any kind of fruit of the Temperate or Torrid Zone at all times. The cocoanut, the pineapple, oranges, lemons, figs, bananas we have seen growing around lakes in abundance. We have seen the Mexicans planting corn, chopping it over and gathering corn since we have been here. The weather is about as warm as it is there in May. I have had the pleasure of going to two Fandangos since I have been here. The Mexicans all dance well. It is worth coming all the way to Mexico to see them waltz. They waltz around near as fast as tops. This is a great place for amusement of any kind. Every Saturday night they have a masquerade ball and Sunday is their day for chicken fighting, horse racing, etc. The American soldiers all appear to be satisfied and healthy who stay here and had rather be here than in the United States. Capt. Wofford's company all look well and are in good health. The Carroll boys have no desire to return to the United States before two or three years at which time they think they can have money enough to do them. Joseph C. Benson will write today to A.J. Boggess and instruct the holder of his notes on Thos. Bonner to pay BD Thomasson eighty dollars and take up the note I gave him. I wish you to see that it is attended to and have the note taken up.

I am getting very anxious to hear from home as I have not heard anything from you since we left Mobile. We will probably receive your letters as soon as we get to Vera Cruz. I wish you to write often, to us. Direct your letters to Vera Cruz in charge of the Quarter Master. I hope you will never suffer any uneasiness about us being killed because we have been shipwrecked twice and got off safe and of course a Mexican cannot hurt us.

Your son

Benj. M. Long

Submitted by: Myron Wade House

Sources: From the B.M. Long album, courtesy of Frances McNamara, Annie Belle Weaver Special Collections, Ingram Library, SUWG

10. Confederate Units Formed in Carroll Co. Ga 1861-1865

Ga. Volunteer Infantry

These units were organized to serve for three years or the duration of the war.

Cobb's Legion Inf., Co. B. "Bowdon Volunteers"
Cobb's Legion Inf., Co. F "Carroll Boys or Cobb Invincibles"
Stovall's Battalion, 4th Brigade, Ga. Artillery "County Line Volunteers", later Co. C, 3d Battalion, Ga. Inf. and later Co. I, 37th Ga. Inf. (Carroll, Campbell, Coweta and Fulton Co's.)
7th Regt. Ga. Inf., Co. F "Iverson Invincibles or Carroll Rangers"
19th Regt. Ga. Inf., Co. F "Carroll Guards or Carroll Volunteers"
19th Regt. Ga. Inf., Co. I "Villa Rica Gold Diggers"
26th Battalion Ga. Inf., Co. C
34th Regt. Ga. Inf., Co. K (organized from Heard Co., also)
41st Regt. Ga. Inf., Co. G "Boggess Avengers"
41st Regt. Ga. Inf., Co H "Wool Hat Boys"
56th Regt. Ga. Inf., Co. B "Carroll Coasters"
56th Regt. Ga. Inf., Co. C
56th Regt. Ga. Inf., Co. H "Carroll Invincibles or Carroll Infantry"
56th Regt. Ga. Inf., Co. I

Ga. Volunteer Cavalry

These units were formed to serve for three years of the war.
1st Regt. Ga. Cav., Co. E
Phillip's Legion Ga. Cav., Co. F (also Coweta and Newton Co's.)
7th Regt. Ga. Cav., Co. B "Confederate Partisan Rangers"
7th Regt. Ga. Cav., Co. L "Confederate Partisan Rangers"
Ga. State Line Militia
Formed to served within the state of Ga. in Jan. 1863 to May 1865.
2nd Regt. Inf., Co. F, 4th Brigade "Carroll Guards or Volunteers"
2nd Regt. Inf., Co. I (Storey's) "Carroll Guards"
3rd Regt. Inf., Co. D "Carroll Coasters"
3rd Regt. Inf., Co. F "Carroll Invincibles or Carroll Infantry"
3rd Regt. Co. G "Carroll Grays or Carroll Rangers"
Ga. State Guards Militia

These united were organized for a period of six months or less to serve as home guards.
2nd Regt. Cav., Co. I "Carroll Defenders"
7th Regt. Inf. Co. I "Carroll Infantry"
10th Regt. Cav., Co. D "Carroll Cavalry"
10 Regt. Cav., Co. I "Carroll Guards or Cavalry Guards"
Beall's Battalion
Ga. Reserves Militia

The following units were organized in April and May of 1864 for a period of six months or less to serve as home guards.
1st (Fannin's) Regt. Inf., Co. F
1st (Fannin's) Regt. Inf., Co. I
1st (Fannin's) Regt. Inf., Co. K

Carroll Co. men served in other units as well. Some of these were 12th Battalion Ga. Artillery and 11th Ga. Artillery Battalion (Cutts) *Submitted by: Sam Pyle, 1471 Mandeville Rd., Carrollton, GA 30117*
Sources: Units of The Confederate States Army — J.H. Crute Jr.; Joe Brown's Army — W.H. Bragg; Roster of Confederate Soldiers of Georgia 1861-1865 — Henderson; Carroll Co., Ga. Souvenir-Historical Edition 1910; Paper compiled by T.O. Brooke from "Breakdown by County of Enlistment of Military; Companies from Ga. in Civil War" by J.H. Smith, Ga. Dept. of Archives and History, 1960.

11. The "Gold Diggers"

Gold Diggers was the nickname for the men of Company I, 19th Georgia Regiment during The War Between the States. This was an appropriate nickname since members of Company I came from the gold mining town of Villa Rica.

Company I was organized under a large oak tree in front of S.T. Haynes Home in old Villa Rica, with John T. Chambers serving as captain. The company mustered into the confederate cause in August 1861, as part of the Nineteenth Georgia Infantry. In 1863 the 19th Regiment was assigned to the famous "Colquitt Brigade".

In 1861 Company I was sent with the 19th to Virginia, where a measles epidemic spread throughout the regiment. In 1862 the 19th fought in the following battles: Seven Pines, Mechanicsville, Richmond, Cedar Mountain, Second Manassas, Antietam, Sharpsburg, Warrenton and Fredericksburg. In 1863 the 19th fought at Chancellorsville. 1864 saw the 19th and other Georgia Regiments headed south to Florida. It was in Northern Florida, where the 19th along with other battled-hardened Georgia Regiments earned for Brigadier General Colquitt the nickname of "Hero of Olustee" for defeating the Northern Troops at the Battle of Ocean Pond.

Later in 1864 the 19th was back in Virginia fighting at Drewry's Bluff, Cold Harbor and Petersburg. Near the end of the war the 19th was ordered to North Carolina and surrendered there at the end of the war.

Of the 133 men that served in Company I, 17 were killed in battle. 43 died from other causes such as diseases and 16 were wounded, giving a total casualty rate of 57% for the company.

Captain John Chambers exemplified the sacrifice of many Carroll County families during the war. One son died of illness and is buried in Richmond. One son was wounded in the leg and was disabled for life. One son was interned as a POW at Johnson Island, Ohio Prison Camp. Two sons died from wounds received in battle, one at Chancellorsville and one at Mechanicsville. After the war these two sons' remains were placed in a wooden box and sent by rail to Atlanta. Captain John went to Atlanta by wagon and brought his sons home. They are buried in a single grave in Hillcrest Cemetery in Villa Rica.

Having suffered physical and emotional hardships that war brings, Captain John Chambers (at the age of 60) resigned his commission and returned home. He outlived all five of his sons that fought under his command in Company I. He died August 04, 1890 at the age of 87. *Submitted by: T.C. Chambers, 6843 Tilton, Atlanta, GA 30360.*
Sources: Help of many Chambers Family Researchers

12. A Letter Home 1862

Camp Bartow
Manassas Road
Fairfax, Virginia
Sept'r 21st, 1862

My Dear Wife:

In haste, I drop you a few lines, I hope it may find you and my little boy well.

Write and give me all the news about Georgia. I wish I was there and could get a good cup of coffee and some biscuits, I am hungry.

There is a great sickness in camp, Typhoid fever, besides me having the mump's. It's a wonder more are not sick because we had a severe rainstorm, which flooded our camp, there was not a dry tent! Added to our misery, a heavy frost and considerable ice befell us. We had to sleep four days in wet blankets on the cold ground. Next week will do battle in Washington and I know there will be a tremendous amount of bloodshed. It makes the hart of the most savage shutter. I need not attempt to point out to you the horrors of the battlefield. Time appears long since we parted.

I hope we will soon be permitted to meet again on earth.

Your devoted husband

W. Britton Caple Duffey

In memory of all men great and small who did battle in the Confederate War, especially great granddad, W. Britton Caple Duffey, great uncle Samuel S. Sr. and Great Uncle James H. Duffey. *Submitted by: Sheila Smith, PO Box 1733, Douglasville, GA 30133*

Sources: Ga. Census Records of Heard, Carroll, Cobb; Registered Voter Returns; Personal Knowledge; Margaret Wood, Douglasville

13. Letter Home 1864

To Mary Hutcheson from
Joseph Hutcheson,
June 24th, 1864

In the trenches near
Marietta, Georgia
June 24th, 1864

Dear Mary,

I received your kind communication of late date day before yesterday and I was much vexed at the action of our excited cavalry in sinking the Flat which could not have been any material advantage to the enemy's cavalry had they come, which I hope will not occur. I hope the Flat can be raised.

Last night we returned from picket after 24 hours exposure to the continual heavy fire of the enemy during which time the artillery of both sides played furiously for a while-but fortunately for us we had but three of the regiment wounded.

Heavy skirmishing continued from day to day and scarcely a day passes but we have some killed and wounded in the Regiment. Friends are fast fallin around us and we are now experiencing one of the most trying campaigns of the war.

You speak of the noble Kendrick and the details(?) connected with his untimely death. I have written you something concerning it. He was on picket at the time he received his wound, in charge of the line of our brigade pickets. I was on the day before with Major Guthrie of the 20th Tenn and after pointing out the posts and position of the lines, left him. This was the last time I saw him in health and vigor. The next evening, I deeply mourn to say, I saw him bourne into camp on a gory litter. He asked for medical aid earnestly & was immediately carried to the ambulance train. I went down, talked with him for the last time during life. I told him I thought he would survive, but he was very doubtful of recovering and urged the Doctor to be candid and tell him his chance for getting over it. Soon after I assisted in getting him in the ambulance and there I gazed upon the nobel gentleman and zealous patriot for the last time. I loved him kindly and from long association have learned to appreciate his worth.

I don't think Mrs. Kendrick can survive the terrible shock long. He intimated that he regretted to die at this stage of the war-but said that he had ever endeavored to do his duty to his country and trusted God for the future. Mr. Jones came up too late to converse with him in his rational state of mind. Scarcely recognized him. And soon the sadly mourned patriot soldier took his exit to join the noble band of Southrons who have yielded all in the defence of those sacred rights for which we have fought so long. I hope he is among the blessed beyond the flood. Our position is unchanged for some time past and I believe all will yet be well. The Yanks don't advance very fast to the much-coveted rebel city, Atlanta. Your neighborhood is somewhat exposed to a raid from enemy's cavalry, but I hardly apprehend a successful one as we have a largely superior force of mounted men to them in this department. You all down there must not have become excited unduly, but bear up under the circumstances like heroines. Many are in worse condition.

Bill has gone to the hospital sick.

I received the Pants, Suspenders & Handkerchiefs and am much obliged to you all as they are greatly needed. Also two Presbyterians. I am anxious to hear from home now since the raid has been engaging the attention of this people. Write often. An always very glad to hear. Afew days ago I heard that Dr. Tatum was on the verge of death. Tell me about it. Does he still live? What has become of Mr. W. Write all the news.

And remember me as your Brother.
Joe Hutchinson

Joseph Hutcheson was the son of James Hutcheson who owned Hutcheson's Ferry. The flat mentioned in the letter is apparently the boat used at the ferry. Joseph rose to the rank of 2nd Lieutenant of Co I, 37th Regiment, GA Infantry, CSA. He was captured at Utoy Creek near Atlanta on August 7, 1864 and imprisoned at Johnson's Island, Ohio until June 16, 1865. He lived for a time in Carroll County. *Submitted by: Myron House*

Sources: Annie Belle Weaver Special Collections, Ingram Library State University of West Georgia

14. Carroll County's WWI Veteran's Who Died in Service

A book that can be found in the Neva Lomason Library's Special Collection in Carrollton is titled, *In Memory of the Gallant Sons of Georgia.* The 1921 memory book lists the gallant sons of Carroll County who died during military service for the nation during World War I. Featured in the book is a small description of how they died and a service picture. This book was the official record of the Military Department of Georgia.

Those listed who died from Carroll County were: Pvt. Charlie Mosley Barron, Whitesburg; Cpl. Herman E. Carter, Carrollton, Killed in Action (KIA) Argonne Forest; Pvt. Albert Milton Eidson, Clem; Lt. Robert Ellis Foster, Carrollton; Pvt. James Casper Holland, Villa Rica, KIA Cantigny, France; Pvt. Ben H. Jones, Banning, KIA Meuse-Argonne Offensive; Pvt. Benjamin L. McLain, Roopville; Pvt. Ronie S. McElroy, Villa Rica; Sgt. Damon Miller, Carrollton; Pvt. Joseph Glen Moore, Villa Rica; Pvt. George Albert Paschal, Roopville; Sgt. Charlie W. Payne, Bowdon; Instructor Charlie Douglas Rabun, Villa Rica; Pvt. James A. Robinson, Bowdon, KIA Meuse, France; Pvt. Samuel I. Rooks, Carrollton, KIA; Cpl. Jethro Shoemaker, Clem, KIA Battle of Cantigny, Somme, France; Pvt. Ira Smith, Villa Rica, drowned in sinking of the transport *Otranto;* Mechanic James Samuel Wallace, Carrollton; and Seaman Henry Leonard Yeager, Wylam. *Submitted by: Dr. David Wiggins*

Carroll County and Communities

15. Carroll County

Carroll County was created December 11, 1826 as Georgia's sixty-sixth county and the twenty-seventh of Georgia's thirty-two original counties. The land that became Carroll County had been Creek Indian land ceded under the Treaty of Indian Springs in 1825. It was for his role in this cession that Chief William McIntosh paid with his life.

On the first Monday in May 1827 an election was held at the house of William O. Wagnon on the McIntosh Reserve to select the first county officers. The first Inferior Court convened May 31, 1827 on Lot 115 in the Fifth District at a site which the court promptly designated as the county seat. This site is known today as Old Carrollton. The county seat remained at Old Carrollton only briefly. During this time it was known simply as Carroll Court House. One superior court session was held here. Tradition says the judge's bench was a pine log.

As early as March 1829 a new site for a county seat was being pursued. On November 14, 1829 the justices selected Lot 128 in the Tenth District as the new county seat. The original name chosen was Troupsville, in honor of Governor George M. Troup. However, the state legislature was controlled at that time by the Gilmer faction and they incorporated the new county seat under the name of Carrollton.

The early removal of the county site required only a minimum of physical changes. Apparently the only substantial building ever constructed at Old Carrollton was a log jail. This structure was removed in 1830 to the new county seat and reassembled on the west side of Rome Street two hundred feet from the public square.

In the meantime the county boundaries were changing. On December 20, 1828 Campbell County was created partly from the eastern portion of Carroll County. In 1870 the part of Campbell taken from Carroll became Douglas County. On December 22, 1830 all land south of the current county boundary was cut off into a new county named Heard County. In 1856 the northwest corner of Carroll County was cut off to form part of another new county, Haralson County. There have also been numerous smaller shifts in the county line.

During its first few years Carroll County was truly frontier. A band of horse thieves called the Pony Club for a time dominated local affairs until honest citizens, known locally as "Slicks," were finally able to band together and drive them out of the county.

By 1860 Carroll County was beginning to leave the frontier period behind. Ahaz Boggess from Carroll County had just been elected Surveyor General of Georgia and the county, which by then was the seventh largest county in the state in white population, was starting to exert some influence in state politics. Then came the Civil War.

Carroll County apparently sent more men into the Confederate Army than any other county in the state except Chatham County, despite the strong Unionist leanings of many of its residents. Although there was no significant fighting in Carroll County, many soldiers never returned, dying from wounds or disease on battlefields as far away as Kentucky and Virginia. The end of the war found the county impoverished. There were many widows and orphans and a lot of farms to be improved.

Carroll County did recover. By the turn of the century Carroll County was one of the leading cotton producing counties in the state, in some years leading the state in cotton production. Hutcheson's Factory at Banning offered an alternative to agricultural employment and by 1890 Mandeville Mills in Carrollton was also offering jobs to local residents. In education Carroll County could boast Bowdon College chartered in 1856 and in 1906 Carroll County was chosen as the site for one of the twelve agricultural and mechanical schools which were built in each Congressional District. *Submitted by: Myron Wade House*

Source: Condensed from James C. Bonner's *Georgia's Last Frontier: The Development of Carroll County*

Early Postcard View: Leading chicken and cotton growing county in Georgia.

16. Bowdon

Bowdon has a long, distinguished history. In 1814, Andrew Jackson's troops camped at the future site of Bowdon College on their way to Horseshoe Bend, Alabama. Their ensuing triumph over the Creek Nation forced the cession of most Creek land in Georgia and Alabama. Bowdon is near the geographic center of the last land in Georgia owned by the Creek Nation and ceded to the United States on November 15, 1827.

In 1847, Carroll County troops from this area fighting under General Winfield Scott defeated a large army under Santa Anna at Cerro Gordo, Mexico. The town of Bowdon was originally called Cerro Gordo to commemorate that victory. After Alabama Congressman Franklin Welch Bowdon assisted the town in securing a post office, the citizens honored him by renaming their town Bowdon in 1848.

In 1849, Nathaniel Shelnutt moved his family from Fairburn in Campbell County to Bowdon, and in 1853 he and about thirty other citizens selected the present town site. The owner of the land, W.F. Johnson, sold lots to highest bidders, with the most expensive lot selling for $10.50. The city grew quickly and by 1855, Bowdon had "five stores, two barrooms, several shops, a good primary school and a high school" (Rowell, 1990) Nathaniel Shelnutt's original home, a "dog trot" style structure with two rooms separated by a breezeway, survives today. The Bowdon Area Historical Society is in the process of restoring it as a museum.

Pvt. Joe Cobb, in his 1906 *Carroll County and Her People,* described Bowdon as "the educational center of a large territory in Georgia and Alabama," and there's no doubt Bowdon College is synonymous with Bowdon's history. Bowdon College was chartered in 1856. It was the fifth college chartered in Georgia and the State's first coeducational college. It continued to furnish opportunities for thousands of poor but ambitious young men and women to attain higher education until 1936. The people of this community "with little resources and the vision of dedicated educational leaders, displayed rare courage in establishing a college ... an achievement unmatched anywhere in Georgia at that time." (Bonner, 1971) In 1861, all seven of the graduating seniors "offered their services to the Confederacy and nearly 135 of the lower classmen volunteered, making a total of over 140 Bowdon boys who largely composed Company B, of Cobb's Legion." (Caswell, 1978) After the War, Bowdon College was one of five endowed by the State of Georgia for the purpose of educating wounded and disabled Confederate Soldiers in 1866-67. Over 200 were educated in that way.

The Bowdon Inn was a boarding house for travelling salesmen

By 1906, Bowdon had "twelve stores and businesses, a bank, a good hotel, Masonic Lodge, three churches, no bar rooms and ... a splendid weekly newspaper. *The Bowdon Intelligence*". (Cobb, 1906). It was "an outstanding cotton market, plus a flourishing lumber market. Cotton bales were hauled by wagon to Waco, Carrollton, or Heflin, Alabama, then sold by local buyers. Cotton and lumber had to be taken to where freight trains came by. Seeing the need for rail service, Dr. J.L. Lovvorn headed a drive to get Bowdon a railroad and succeeded in selling enough stock to make the railroad a reality in 1910". (Johnson, 1984) Dignitaries attending ceremonies at completion of the railroad included the Governor of Georgia, Hoke Smith, and U.S. Congressman William Charles Adamson who was born in Bowdon and was 1874 valedictorian of Bowdon College. The Bowdon railroad continued operation until 1964.

Warren Palmer Sewell attended Bowdon College from 1906 through 1908. In 1932 in the midst of the depression, Mr. Sewell built a clothing plant in Bowdon. Although the College had struggled to continue on citizen funding until 1936, State funding ceased in 1933. "The wounded and concerned Bowdon residents viewed the new Sewell plant as an affirmation of faith in the town, and they were proud of the new business" (Godbold). At his death in 1973, Warren Sewell Clothing was one of the ten largest manufacturers of men's clothing in the country.

Bowdon City Hall, built in 1948, as it looks today.

Today the City of Bowdon is a full service city and provides all basic municipal services. These include police and fire protection, water, sewage and natural gas services, streets, trash collection, and construction inspection. The city maintains a recreation department, senior citizens program and Warren P. Sewell Memorial Library. Each August Bowdon holds its annual Founders Day celebration. It is a time to recall a rich heritage of self-reliance and vision, and to build upon that heritage for future generations. *Submitted by Mignon Wessinger, P.O. Box 25, Bowdon, GA 30108*

Sources: Bonner, James. *Georgia's Last Frontier.* Athens, Ga.: The University of Georgia Press, 1971; Caswell, Render R. *The History of Bowdon College.* The Warren P. Sewell Library, 1978. (Orig. pub. 1952); Cobb, (Private) Joe. *Carroll County and Her People.* Sesquicentennial-Bicentennial Committee of Carroll County Chamber of Commerce, 1976 (Orig. pub. 1906); Godbold, Edwin C. *Diligent in His Business: Warren Sewell*; Johnson, J.L. (Jack). *Yesterday: A Trip Into the Past.* A Compilation of articles by the author from *The Bowdon Bulletin* ca. 1980-1984; Rowell, Judy Copeland. *Bowdon: The First Hundred Years.* Dallas: Curtis Media Corporation, 1990.

17. The Bowdon Junction Community

The Bowdon Junction community was not so named until the Bowdon Railroad was built in 1910. Before that it was called Harmony from the name of the Methodist church located across the road from the house shown in the picture of the entire community taken in 1900. The house is that of Steve and Kate Parker.

To the North was Holly Springs Primitive Baptist Church and to the South was Pleasant View Baptist Church. The community had a school and to the East was Miller's Academy at Walnut Hill. A high school was at Mt. Zion.
Submitted by: Wallace T. Lambert
Source: Myric D. Shaw's History of Bowdon Junction

18. Carrollton's Complex History

Like the people that populate Carrollton, the city's corporate identity is much more complex than it may appear to the visitor or new resident. With its old railroad depot, its quaint, bustling downtown square, its Confederate Soldier Monument and stately tree-lined in-town residential streets, Carrollton presents the appearance of Smalltown, Southland, USA. But the history of this "typical" town shows diversity, old-versus-new contrasts, famous people and a few genuine surprises — in short, not at all typical.

The Georgia Legislature created Carroll County on December 11, 1826. The name came from Charles Carroll of Maryland, the last living signer of the Declaration of Independence. The first Carroll Inferior Court (an early governing body exercising many of the same functions as today's county commission and a county or city court) met May 31, 1827, at a site near present day Sand Hill and designated this spot as the county seat. The "town" was known simply as Carroll Court House. Carroll County Superior Court met only once here (it is said the judge's bench was a pine log) and in March of 1829 the county justices ordered the purchase of a new lot for the county seat about two miles north of the current town square. However, when the county was unable to come to favorable financial terms with the lot's owner, the justices simply bought another site, the site of today's town square from Henry Curtis for $150.

The justices originally named their new county seat Troupsville in honor of the former Georgia Governor but when the State Legislature met December 22, 1829, under Governor Gilmer, that name was done away with. In another move to honor the old signer, the Legislature replaced Troupsville with the name of Charles Carroll's Maryland estate, Carrollton. Thus, depending on how you look at it, at the time of this writing the idea of Carrollton is 174 years old while the actual city of Carrollton, in this location and with that name, is 172.

The town square was cleared from the unbroken wilderness by Jiles Boggess who

Bowdon Junction community in 1900

Early Postcard Birds-eye View of Carrollton

erected a tavern on the north side of what is now Newnan Street. In fact, near the end of the 19th Century, there would be as many as seven taverns on the public square of this town so deep in the heart of the Bible Belt and that even today struggles with just how much Demon Rum it wants to allow within its borders. There were no official names to any of the streets in Carrollton until after the War Between the States. The northern road out of the square was known popularly as the Cedartown Road. The western road was known as the Alabama Road and the eastern route was Newnan Road.

Early Carrollton was essentially a Wild West town, a frontier village with an abundance of taverns, horse thieves, trading posts, and horse races. Sanford Kingsbury raised racehorses on his farm, Oak Lawn. His home still stands today on Rome Street. Longview Street was actually a racetrack in the earliest days, thus accounting for the long, straight configuration from which it gets its name. A notorious band of horse thieves called the Pony Club wreaked havoc upon the locals until just before Election Day of 1832 when some members of the community horsewhipped some known members of the Pony Club. In an effort to save face, Club members started a fight with two vigilante groups known as "Slicks" on the public square on Election Day. Jiles Boggess, by then county sheriff, led the Slicks into rock-throwing, stick-beating, hand-to-hand battle from which the law-abiding citizens emerged victorious. Hoping to capitalize on some of their members' place on the Grand Jury, the vanquished Pony Clubbers charged Boggess and the Slicks with assault with intent to murder. The majority of the Grand Jury, however, ignored the complaint, opting instead to officially commend the sheriff and the Slicks for providing the local criminal element with a good dose of come-uppance. Thereafter, the Pony Club was no longer a problem.

Despite the almost universally assumed view of American history that all small southern towns were chomping at the bit to secede, when Carroll County's delegates went to the state convention on secession, it was to vote against Georgia's pulling out of the Union. However, once the state at large chose a different course, Carrollton joined the fight and provided men and supplies to the Confederate effort. In 1911, the United Daughers of the Confederacy raised money and erected a monument to those Carroll Countians who died in the Civil War. The stone statue of a Confederate soldier was erected in the center of the town square facing northward, always vigilant against the Northern enemy.

Although there was no battle on Carrollton soil during the Civil War, an incident that happened just days after Lee's surrender in 1865 left a mark on the city that endures to this day. A group of Yankee raiders held the town's populace at bay with firearms while one quadrant of the square was set ablaze. Upon learning that a group of Southern soldiers were approaching from the south along the Roopville Road, the raiders hightailed it out of town. As the Southern soldiers marched into town, reportedly singing 'Dixie,' it was decided to rename the street in honor of the occasion. Thus, Dixie Street, which features some of the city's most beautiful historically significant private homes, was born.

Many small towns owe their founding or at least their livelihood to the coming of the railroad. In yet another example of Carrollton's diversity, this was never the case here. Founded by the government instead of springing up along a rail line, Carrollton was already a thriving, mostly self-sufficient little town for 50 years before the railroad came. Of course the coming of the railroad in 1874 improved the quality of life and commerce in Carrollton, making the town a lot less isolated. Although other means of transport for people and goods have largely supplanted trains, the tracks still run through here, trains still tie up traffic from time to time and the forlorn call of the train whistle still echoes across Carrollton. Two enduring reminders of Carrollton's past to the railroad still stand: the depot on Bradley Street and the Croft Street wooden overpass bridge. The depot was built in 1888 on what was then known as Depot Street (even before a depot was built there) and was the first sight many saw upon their arrival in Carrollton. At this writing negotiations are underway between the railroad and the city with plans to install a visitors center there being discussed.

The Croft Street wooden bridge was built sometime after 1874 by a Captain Croft. Croft was an official with the railroad and had built his home on the other side of the tracks from his family church. To avoid his family having to cross the tracks each day of worship, he bought a small piece of land from James Tanner for $65 and had the bridge built. After more than 100 years and a fair number of refurbishings, the bridge remains one of two routes (the other is the more modern underpass on US Highway 27) drivers can use to avoid train delays when traveling from one side of Carrollton to the other. The bridge is owned by the railroad and is part of the depot negotiations.

Another feature in Carrollton's complex identity is the high degree of industrialization present in this rural, small-town setting. Carrollton and Carroll County have been recognized agribusiness centers, being the top cotton, chicken and beef cattle producers in the state at various times through the years. Today's agribusiness giant, Southern States (formerly GoldKist), had its start as cotton cooperative in Carrollton.

But Carrollton has also been the birthplace or adopted home of several industrial giants over the years. Mandeville Mills, at one time the largest textile mill in the area, was started here in 1890 by Clifton Mandeville. The mill grew and was for most of its lifespan the number one employer in Carroll County. As its sun set in the late 1940s, a new industrial player was born. Southwire Corporation, founded in 1950 by Roy Richards, Sr., grew out of Richards and Associates, an electrical wire-stringing concern Richards had started in the late 1930s that had done REA work all around the South. Southwire's meteoric rise soon made it the largest wire and cable manufacturer in the world and the county's largest employer. Southwire is still one of the world's largest wire makers and has plants all over the globe. Its worldwide headquarters, however are still located in Carrollton. From 1978 until 2001, Sony Music (originally CBS Records) operated the largest recorded music manufacturing plant in the world in Carrollton. Although the company ceased its manufacturing operations here in 2001, its warehousing and distribution operations are still active. And as this new century dawns, retail giant Wal-Mart is

Early Postcard view of Maple Street looking East

building a mammoth distribution center just north of town, slated to open in early 2002. These businesses along with hundreds of others have allowed Carrolltonians, so close to the Goliath of Atlanta, to work where they live and forge an identity as something other than a bedroom community for a metro center.

Mandeville Mills circa 1902

The Fourth District Agricultural and Mechanical School, what we would today call a vocational high school, was created by the legislature in 1906 and construction began in 1907 on the former Thomas Bonner plantation on Maple Street. The school would survive for the next 26 years, instructing students on a variety of agricultural and homemaking endeavors until the state Board of Regents abolished A&Ms in 1933. Later that year, the assets and buildings of the defunct A&M were given to the newly created West Georgia College. West Georgia began as a two-year institution offering mostly courses in teaching and has grown in to the State University of West Georgia offering a wide array of courses up to and including some doctoral programs. West Georgia's location here was no accident. In fact, it was good old-fashioned pork barrel politics and family pressure that ensured Carrollton's place as educational center of West Georgia. Nettie Talmadge Tyus lived in a home (still standing on Centr Street) in Carrollton that she ordered from the Sears Roebuck catalog. Her brother was Georgia Governor Eugene Talmadge. Legend holds that when the Board of Regents was pondering the placement of West Georgia College and there was some thought to awarding the school to some other town, Tyus stormed into her brother's office and informed him, "Gene, I don't know where you think you are putting that school, but you're putting it in Carrollton!" To the eternal benefit of Carrollton and its people, the governor listened to his sister and followed orders.

Carrollton has been home to many nationally and internationally prominent people. At the dawn of the 20th Century, U.S. Rep. W.C. Adamson, for whom Adamson Square was named, sponsored legislation that created the eight-hour workday and was instrumental in the creation of the U.S. Department of Labor. Six decades later, West Georgia College professor Newt Gingrich was elected to the House where he remained a controversial presence for the next 20 years, eventually rising to the position of House Speaker. Oscar-winning actress Susan Hayward married Carrollton businessman Eaton Chalkley in 1957 and moved to a farm here, adopting Carrollton as her hometown. She moved to Florida and then back to Hollywood after Chalkey's death in 1966 but remained so attached to Carrollton that, according to her last wishes, her funeral was held here in 1975 and she was buried next to her husband in the cemetery of the Our Lady Of Perpetual Help RC Church, across the road from her former ranch.

Tanner Memorial Hospital came into being in 1949, the result of a long, hard-fought battle on the part of the community that ensued when local wholesale grocer C.M. Tanner offered in 1943 to support a hospital to the tune of $75,000 if the community would raise $25,000. The money was raised but due to the war construction had to wait. After the war, the new City-County Hospital Authority took advantage of federal matching grant money and the hospital began construction. It was dedicated October 30, 1949. Among those on the hospital's staff was the county's first black doctor, Dr. Samuel Thomas. Dr. Thomas' home is currently the subject of a community restoration effort.

Through each change in the landscape and population of Carrollton, the heart of town, Adamson Square, remained a constant reassuring presence. However, it too saw many changes and had its ups and downs. In its original form the square had taken the traditional shape of a courthouse square with three courthouses occupying its center. The last of these was built in 1857 by the Rodahan brothers and lasted until 1893 when a new courthouse was built two blocks from the square at the intersection of Newnan and Dixie Streets. The old courthouse was demolished and over the course of the next two decades the center of the square was basically an open expanse. The Confederate Soldier monument was erected there in 1911 where he remained until June 6, 1958 when the center of the square was cleared to make way for a four-way intersection. The statue was first moved to the lawn of Tanner Memorial Hospital then in the 1970's the nomadic soldier was assigned his current sentry post on the lawn of the Carroll County Courthouse.

From 1854 until the 1970s Johnson's Drug Store watched the parade of Carrolltonian life on the square. For the last several years of its existence, Johnson's enjoyed the distinction of being the oldest family-owned drugstore in the nation. Horton's Books and Gifts, still in business at the time of this writing, was opened by N.A. Horton in 1892. While it for many years has been the county's oldest business, Horton's was designated in 2000 by the American Booksellers Association the oldest bookstore in the state, the third oldest in the South and the tenth oldest in the nation. The original 1892 hand cranked cash register is still in use at Horton's. The oldest building on the square was built by Patterson G. Garrison in 1872-1873 and still stands today, home to the very popular Cake Shop Bakery.

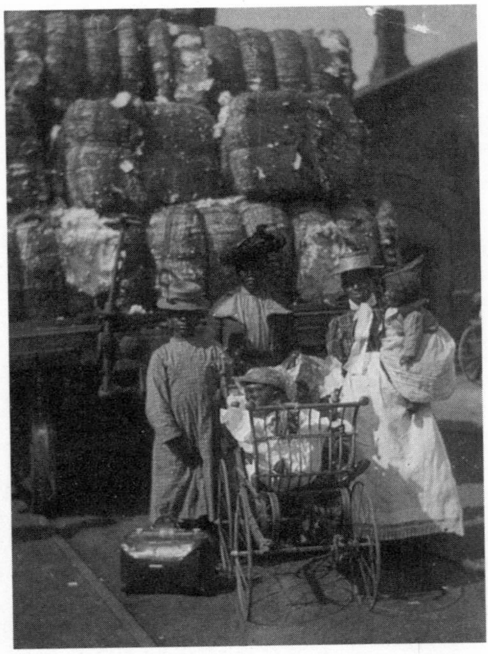

Early Scene at Carrollton Depot circa 1900 with cotton from the Mandeville Cotton Company

At the turn of this latest century, Adamson Square is reaping the crop of economic development sown by its designation as a Main Street district in 1985. The Main Street program spurs economic development in downtown areas. After many years of decline when strip centers and shopping malls siphoned off shoppers from downtown, the square and its surroundings are rebounding with new shops, renovated buildings, a new multimillion dollar Cultural Arts Center and bigger and better promotional events.

A visitor to Carrollton may be forgiven for falling victim to the surface impression of this city as just another small town in the South. But even a cursory scratching of the surface will reveal a town with a complex, colorful, at times contradictory but never simple history and a great deal of room to grow in the future.

This history is by no means comprehensive nor detailed. It is intended to serve as a road map with some points of interest of a trip through Carrollton's history highlighted. To get more of a complete picture of this remarkable town, the reader is encouraged to absorb all the family histories in this book and also seek out the following publications: *At Home In Carrollton, 1827-1994,* Griffith, The Carroll County Historial Society; *Georgia's Last Frontier,* Bonner, The Carroll County Genealogical Society; *Carroll County and Her People,* Pvt. Joe Cobb and the reference paper *The Square Root of Carrollton*, by Edith Foster, available at the Neva Lomason Library in Carrollton. *Submitted by: Jonathan Dorsey; Photos courtesy of Wayne Cook, Carrollton and Mrs. Susan Patton Hamersky, CA. from the Nell Mandeville Henderson album*

19. Clem Georgia

The little village of Clem is located about six miles southeast of Carrollton on the Norfolk Southern Railroad. Its beginning was when the railroad came through in 1874 on its way to Carrollton from Newnan. A depot was built with two waiting rooms, the station agent's office, a freight storage room and a loading platform to the rear. The railroad built its own telegraph line and telephone line. The station agent sold tickets, looked after outgoing and incoming freight, and had to know how to operate a telegraph machine. For a number of years, four passenger trains a day came through on their way from Griffin to Chattanooga or vice-versa. Four section houses were built about one half mile up the tracks toward Carrollton. The section foreman and railroad workers lived in these houses. When the Depression of 1929 hit, two passenger trains were discontinued, and the station agent's job was eliminated. The depot and section houses were torn down in the mid 1930's, and a little one-room building was erected in place of the depot. The last passenger trains were discontinued in 1952. Soon after that diesel engines replaced steam locomotives.

Soon after the railroad came through, houses were built in the area near the depot. Several stores sprang up in the area and a post office was established. In the late 1800's, John Henry Jones built a brick general merchandise store, and the post office was located in the front corner of the store. The first rural mail carrier was Ezekial Haynie. He delivered the mail in a buggy and traveled about 20 miles to his route. After his death, George Davenport delivered the mail in a little mail wagon. A while later, two mail routes were established and Manuel Fuller carried the second mail route. In the early 1920's, both mail carriers started carrying their mail by automobile. Mr. Davenport and Mr. Fuller retired in the early 1930's, and Dewey Reid took over both routes. He drove a little Austin automobile. Sometimes, when he stopped at the store in Lowell and got ready to

Lassetter's Store at Clem 1928. Jim Lassetter, store owner in the background with Lassetter and Davenport ladies in the foreground.

leave, devilish boys would pick up the back of his car and his back wheels would just spin around. The Clem mail route was eliminated somewhere around 1960. The post office operated until 1973 when the postmaster, Mrs. Mae Holloway Lassetter retired.

Other people who operated stores in Clem were Silas Harper, Bob Key, Joe McCarty, Tom Phillips, Carl East, Joe Head, and C.O. Bates. Jim Lassetter who operated it for over 30 years purchased the store operated by John Henry Jones. C.O. Bates operated a filling station and blacksmith shop on what was called "north Clem." Mr. Bates was the last of about four blacksmiths who operated shops in Clem. The other three were Arthur Swyert, John Will Webb, and Sam Jones. Mr. Bates operated his shop from 1933 until 1949. He would shoe a mule or horse and furnish the shoes for $.80. The current price for shoeing a horse today is between $40 and $50. He sharpened two medium-sized scooter plows for five cents and sharpened a cultivator tooth for two cents. He also repaired wagon wheels and other farm equipment.

A steam-powered cotton gin was located on a little stream near Lassetter's store. Around 1920 it was moved across the railroad tracks to its present site and was powered by a huge one-cylinder diesel engine. The children who lived nearby always enjoyed the starting of the engine because it blew out big smoke rings and was quite noisy in doing so. In fact, the engine could be heard as far away as three or four miles on a still, clear day. During the busy cotton-ginning season in the fall, it was fairly common for the gin to run all night. Laz Holloway was in charge on the gin operation until his death in 1933, and then Dave Jones was the supervisor of the gin until it closed down around 1950. There was also a sawmill, a gristmill, a garage, and a barbershop in the Clem area at one time.

A one-room school was built on the hill about one quarter of a mile north of the depot in the late 1800's. The school remained at that site until 1934 when the Clem Jr. High School was built on the Clem-Lowell Road. Whooping Creek School, Union School, and the old Clem school were all consolidated into the modern Clem Jr. High School, which went through the ninth grade. The school was closed in 1959 and the students from the area went to the Central School.

Three churches were organized in the Clem area before 1900. Mt. Pleasant Missionary Baptist Church was located abut one mile north of the depot in 1874 under the leadership of Rev. J.M.D. Stallings. It has been a fast growing church in recent years, and is now among the 19 fastest growing Baptist churches in Georgia. In 1897, the Clem Methodist Church was organized under the leadership of Rev. W.L. Davenport, a Confederate veteran. The church was located on Clem-Lowell Road about one tenth of a mile from the depot. A storm destroyed the church in April 1909, and a new church was built at its present site about 300 yards west of the original building. Antioch Baptist Church was established around 1900 about one half mile southeast of the depot and has been a fast growing congregation since that time.

The Clem Ladies Home Demonstration Club was organized in 1929 under the leadership of Mrs. V.D. Whatley, the home demonstration agent for Carroll County. Some of the first members were Mrs. Alice Fuller, Mrs. Lottie Davenport, Mrs. S.C. Gladney, and Mrs. Mallory Crews. For several years, they met in different members' homes, and later met in a little store building near the depot that belonged to Lewis Cook. The ladies sat on padded nail kegs for seats during the meetings. This club phased out after 65 years, and Mrs. Alice Fuller is the only surviving member of the original group.

A new clubhouse was built on the highway just above the Clem Fire Department around 1950. It was doubled in size in the mid-1970's. The Clem Community Civic Club was organized in 1976 and meets about nine times a year. This building is used as the Clem Voting Precinct and for family reunions, showers, birthday parties, etc.

Clem could boast of having a five-man brass band consisting of the Holloway brothers, who entertained the people of Clem and surrounding communities during the early 1900's.

Clem had three different doctors from the early 1900's until about 1920. These doctors were Dr. Andrews, Dr. Lewis, and Dr. W.A. Aderhold who finally moved his practice to Carrollton.

About 200 yards below the Clem Clubhouse is the Clem Fire Department. It got its start as a volunteer department under the leadership of J.T. Miles. It is now a county supported fire department with two fire trucks. Jerry Eason is its Chief.

Highway 16 was paved on the eastern edge of Clem in 1946. The first county road to be blacktopped through Clem was in 1951.

A wood-yard was built across the road from the old gin in the early 1970's. A house, a store, a barn, and a warehouse all stood on that property at one time.

When driving through Clem at the railroad crossing, the old Lassetter store where the post office was, is now covered with kudzu vines. The old warehouse that sat by the gin, the little brick store, and the old cotton gin, which is used as a hay storage barn, are all that's left. If one could reminisce back 50 or 60 years ago, Clem was booming on Sundays. That was the day that the north and southbound trains met. The northbound train brought the Sunday paper, and many people came to meet the trains and get their Sunday papers over at the post office. Today, like many other small communities, people simply pass through Clem and wonder what it looked like it is heyday. However, there is a growing housing development going on near the old Bates Filling Station and Blacksmith Shop.

The name Clem is said to have originated from the Coleman brothers, Jim and Allen, who had a gristmill and gin on Whooping Creek to the south. The Colemans were prominent in the community and it was suggested the depot be named for them. However, there was already a Coleman, Georgia, so apparently Mr. Croft, the first conductor serving the depot, picked four letters out of the name Coleman and Clem was born. *Submitted by: M.T. Fuller and Angela Fuller Thompson*

20. County Line

The Third District of Carroll County lies in the eastern corner of the county along the Chattahoochee River. Some of the earliest settlers came here before the county was created in 1826. One such settler was my great-great grandfather, Andrew Camp, and his son, my great-grandfather, Wesley Camp, who came in 1824. All these men were farmers who were attracted to the rich bottomland along the river and several excellent large creeks. In 1828 this area along the west side of the Chattahoochee River became part of Campbell County, where it remained until 1870 when Douglas County was created. It was part of Douglas County for only two years and then reverted to Carroll County in 1872.

According to Edgar Watkins, in an article in the *Carroll County Times* of October 13, 1927, the courthouse area in this district was originally called Lick Skillet, but no stories explaining this name can be found. The change to County Line was probably because it was so near the junction of Carroll and Campbell Counties. Court was held here before the Civil War.

Three large creeks called Snake, Wolf, and Hurricane run through this settlement. The original Old Five Notch Road also runs through here, along the path laid out in 1798 by Creek Indian Agent Benjamin Hawkins near the Chattahoochee River and named by the Creek Indians.

County Line Primitive Baptist Church was organized in the home of Wesley and Mariah Lassitter Camp in 1829. The first building was erected sometime in 1833. I have read all the old minutes of the church from the first conference on July 24, 1830, through 1878 and nowhere did they give the exact date when this building was completed.

In August 1839 the congregation voted to build an addition to the church, and on January 12, 1850, they asked permission to build a schoolhouse near County Line Church. After the school was built sometime in 1850-51, it was formally named County Line School. On October 30, 1851, County Line Masonic Lodge No. 159 was granted a charter, and held their meetings on the second floor of the school building.

Also in this area was the Mt. Pleasant Baptist Church near Hutcheson's Ferry. On August 27, 1886, the Baptist Association held its meeting at this church.

County Line Post Office was established December 19, 1879, with Henry Head named the first Postmaster. It was discontinued in 1903. Rhett Post Office was established May 19, 1881, near County Line and operated until 1905. Mrs. Lucy Russell was the first postmaster.

On December 28, 1883, Walter C. Camp was Postmaster at County Line, and the mail left Whitesburg for Campbellton via County Line every Friday at 7:00 a.m. In August 1884, the County paper reported that the mail now goes to County Line every Thursday.

Another settlement in the Third District, just below the County Line Community on the road to Whitesburg, was Buyer's Crossroads. Here near the Chattahoochee River, Holland's Meeting House was founded about 1825 by James H. Holland, another pioneer citizen of the area. This church later became St. Paul M.E. Church.

Also in the Buyers Crossroad area was the Watson School, a one-room log building. I don't know when it was built, but a picture of this school was published in the county paper of May 3, 1872. Some years later in the late 1800's or early 1900's, another school was built on the same property and was named New Watson. School was held here until 1921 when County Line and New Watson were consolidated. A large two-story building was erected halfway between the two schools on land donated by Jim Vines and Isham Burnett. This became Lucy T. Russell Institute, named after one of the first teachers at County Line, Mrs. Lucy Taylor Russell. This school opened its doors October 1, 1922, and later became Russell High School. The building for the New Watson School became Antioch Baptist Church in 1922.

Rock Springs M.E. Church was also in the Third District on Hutcheson Ferry Road. Mr. Joe Hutcheson had this school and church built on his farm.

There were two ferries across the Chattahoochee River in this area: Jones Ferry, near County Line, and, down the river, Phillips Ferry which later became Hutcheson's Ferry. This ferry was sunk June 24, 1864, during the Civil War because people were afraid the Union Army would use it to cross over into Carroll County.

Some of the pioneers of the County Line area were Major Stephen Neal, William Word, Hiram Embry, M.D. Watkins, Wesley Camp, F.M. Camp, John Bryant, W.B. Richards, Perry Richards, William Vines, Gaines Barron, James Head, Henry Head, Frank Morris, Benjamin Durette, Benjamin Lasseter, Lindsey Holland, and Joseph Hutcheson. There were many others.

During the Civil War, County Line was in Campbell County. A company of Confederate soldiers was formed here known as the Chattahoochee Volunteers, Company K, 30th Georgia Infantry.

The following is a partial list of men who served in this company: Capt. William B. Richards, 1st Lt. Henry Head, 2nd Lt. George F. Longino, 1st Sgt. Henry H. Smith, 2nd Sgt. Lewis Jones, 3rd Sgt. John L. Camp, 4th Sgt. Henry Summerlin, 5th Sgt. John Humphery, 1st Cpl. Benjamin L. Camp, 2nd Cpl. Alfred P. Bryant, 3rd Cpl. Benjamin J. Crutchfield, 4th Cpl. Andrew J. Richards, Pvt. John Perry Richards, Pvt. Andrew J. Camp, Pvt. Benjamin Durett, Pvt. William H. Hudson, Pvt. Oliver P. Owens, Pvt. William E. Vines, Pvt. Peter S. Wilson, and Pvt. Moses A. Duncan.

My ancestors, Andrew Camp and his son Wesley Camp, settled here in 1824 and since that time there has been a direct descendant living here in the County Line area, covering a period of 166 years and seven generations, as we live within a mile of where my great-great-grandfather and great-grandfather settled, and now our children and grandchildren live here.

Submitted by: Mrs. Thelma Pate, 199 Old 5 Notch Rd., Whitesburg, GA 30185

21. Horace

Horace was in the Centerpoint Community 6 miles southwest of Temple and 7 miles west of Hickory Level. The post office was established there in 1892. Charles W. Bonner was the postmaster in 1892, W.A. Almon in 1893, and Moses E.V.C. Spence in 1894. He served until 1899 when Imar D. Keyes took over. Mr. Almon returned in 1900 and served until the post was discontinued in 1902.

22. Lowell Community

Lowell, originally known as Trickum, is located eight miles southeast of Carrollton. The hardwood and pine forest that once dominated the landscape were removed in the early to mid 1800's and Lowell became a leading cotton farming community. The first post office, Trickum, was established February 18, 1854 and became the Lowell post office March 4, 1878 with Joseph M. Walker as postmaster. Around 1860 the Savannah, Griffin and North Alabama Railroad Company surveyed a route for the railroad near Lowell at Dorris Mill on Whooping Creek to continue on to Alabama. Work did begin before Carrollton won the battle for the railroad route. Evidence of a portion of the proposed railroad bed is still visible at the McIntosh Reserve. In 1889 when the Roopville District chose to outlaw open range, "liners" built a fence between Lowell and Roopville from the Heard County line north.

Lowell School 1910 to 1936

Sawmills were a vital part of early Lowell, as the homes were built from the heart pine that grew in the area. Also most farms had a few long leaf pine trees for gathering turpentine. In the late 1800's the Brown and Freeman sawmill cut much of the virgin timber in the area. J.T. Cowart operated a sawmill near Whooping Creek in the early 1900's. Mr. Robert Toombs Spearman operated one of the last sawmills in the area.

Two German Jews, Jake and Joe Shapiro operated a store around 1899 to 1901 in Lowell. Peddlers traveled the countryside carrying large bags with their wares. Walter Nix built and operated a store on the site where the Methodist Church now sits. The post office was also on this site until 1903 when it closed. The Nix store was moved across the road using large wooden rollers and stump pulls. Lee Jackson, Jordan Jackson, Ben Burns, Render Spence and Clay Chappell were among the early storeowners when the country store had all the necessary goods for living and farming. The store was the meeting place and men frequently challenged each other to a game of checkers around the potbelly stove. Mr. Jackson would make trips as far as New Orleans to pick up goods for sale. Reuben Williamson had a barbershop in a small store and Rolf Holder and Gus Duncan were local barbers. Joe Duncan was the village blacksmith and his son Roy took up the trade of shoeing the horses and mules and sharpening of the plows.

John C. Musick told of drawing a steer drawn cart with wheat for a two-week trip to Columbus to get their grain ground into flour. The need for local processing brought about a number of water mills in the area. The Lowell Water Mill on Yellow Dirt Creek was operated by millers including A.I. Morgan and J.M. Porter. This water mill was noted for grinding the grain into

Early Store in Lowell

superior flour. Lem Dean operated a gristmill on Whooping Creek near the present day Highway 5 bridge. A steam-powered mill was near Jackson's store in Lowell and was converted to electrical power after 1933 and Lem Dean was the miller through out the 1940's and early 50's.

In the late 1800's W.A. Coleman ran a cotton gin at Coleman Mill. There was also a gin north of Lowell at a site near a government-regulated distillery around 1890. J.C. Musick operated a gin south of Lowell on Gin Branch. In the early 1900's J. Harold Burns built a ginnery on property leased from Toombs Spearman. This was a coal-fired steam generator operated gin, but with the availability of electricity, the Burns ginnery was converted. Georgia Power Company ran electrical power down Highway 27 and Lowell Road to the gin in 1932. This gin operated until around 1950.

Lowell's earliest families included Echols, Stallings, Johnson, Upchurch, Spearman, Summerlin, Ward, Cowart, Taylor, Richards, Burns, Hollingsworth, Pentecost, Millican, Morgan, Fleming, Chappell, Smith, Duncan, Webb, Gray, Baughtman, Jackson, Spence, Williamson and Musick. Most all were landowners and farmed or ran a business that supported the farming community.

Drs. George Willis Hammond and D.S. Reese began their medical practices in Lowell. They were the doctors who were summoned to deliver babies and often operated on their patients in their homes on the kitchen table.

One of the early sawmills in the Lowell community around 1890

Short sessions of school were held at New Lebanon Church just west of Lowell prior to 1890. A rustic one-room school was built and served the community until around 1910 when it burned necessitating the construction of a new building. An 1897-98 class register of John R. Spence listed 80 students ranging in age from 7 to 18 years. The school day was from 8AM to 4PM for two sessions each year, one from November through April and a summer session from July to September. The school calendar was set around the farming activities. The two story school building had two large classrooms downstairs and one classroom plus the lodge room upstairs, which was used by Lodge #170, established October 1858.

In the summer of 1936 citizens of the community including M.T. Fuller and Charlie Jackson, who were young men, helped to tear down the old two-story school building. Materials were salvaged for a new larger brick school to be built on the same site. Classes were held in the Methodist church until the new building was completed in 1937-38. A smaller white building was added around 1940 for first and second grades and lunchroom. There was much community involvement in the building and landscaping of this new school. The four large classrooms and the bell room, which served as the office and discipline center, were along a long hallway from the large auditorium. It was a privilege to be allowed to pull the rope to sound the bell for the beginning and end of the school day. During the school year each child had an opportunity to perform on the large stage, which was complete with dressing rooms, a beautiful scenic advertisement screen and a maroon velvet curtain. The auditorium not only served for school events but also was a community-gathering place for plays, singings, entertainers and funerals. With the advent of bussing and improved roads it became easier to transport students and consolidation became the trend. The school was consolidated with Roopville in the fall of 1959.

Churches were established in this thriving community and include Liberty Congregational Methodist established in 1852 and New Lebanon Baptist organized July 30, 1870. Mt. Lowell Missionary Baptist began 1879. The Lowell Christian Church was founded in March 1914 under the leadership of Rev. Owen Still and J.W. Webb but no longer exist. Rev. W.A. Woodruff chartered the Lowell United Methodist Church August 3, 1919 as the Methodist Episcopal Church South. Rev. Milton Anderson started Lowell Congregational Holiness in 1954.

Jim W. Hollingsworth with workers in his cotton field in 1924

In the 1920's and 1930's Lowell was the number one cotton producing community in Carroll County. In 1937, 2700 bales were produced and it was said, "the hills looked like they were white with snow". One of the largest producers that year was the Larkin Staples Family. In 1944 Kenny C. Moore was recognized by the Soil Conservation Service as a successful farmer using improved farm machinery. In the late 1940's cotton production dropped as the boll weevil and economics of production reduced the profitability. Pimento peppers were grown for a short period during the 1950's but most of the land was converted to pasture land and timber.

Georgia Highway 5, originally known as McIntosh Trail, the major east west road, was re-routed around Lowell and construction and paving of the Lowell segment was completed in 1960. Construction of this new arterial was begun in 1958 from Roopville and Whitesburg, leaving a section in the middle uncompleted until 1964. Pete White built a store in 1963 at the new intersection of Highway 5 and Lowell Road and is the only store operating presently. In 1975 Fashion Star converted the old school building into a clothing manufacturing facility. Plant Wansley built south of Lowell in Heard County began operation in August 1976 and has its main entrance from the Lowell side, which impacts the community. The Southern company is continuing to expand this facility with two additional units under construction in 2001. Chattahoochee River Turf and greenhouses located at the confluence of Cavender Creek and Whooping Creek began operation in 1984 in a bottomland area once farmed by Ed Burns and later by Larkin and Larry Staples.

Staples Dairy began operation in 1959 and is one of the remaining five dairies left in Carroll County. Lowell remains a community of small farms with many raising cattle, hay, chickens and timber, however since 1990 the number of farms have declined with the addition of many residential sites. *Submitted by: Angie Hollingsworth Stober, 1071 Lowell Road, Carrollton, GA*

Sources: *A Look at Lowell Past and Present, Carroll County Times, Carroll Free Press* and personal interviews

23. Mandeville Community

Mandeville got its name from the Mandeville family from Carrollton who built a cotton gin at that location. The Mandevilles selected the site because it was one of the places where the railroad and the highway from Carrollton to Bremen came the closest to meeting. The location is one mile South of Bowdon Junction.

The photograph is looking South at a general store and location of the post office prior to its moving to Bowdon Junction. A schoolhouse was located to the North of the store and to the Northeast was a small depot where passenger trains stopped daily. A cotton storage building was located next to the depot. That building is still standing.

The general store was operated by the Adams family and the building shown was still used until the early fifties. When Franklin Adams returned from a career in the US Navy he married Ellen Putnam Stallings, widow of Horace Stallings and built a house just South of the building shown in the picture. He was the stepfather of Tracy Stallings and Charlcie Stallings. The store was torn down in the early fifties and vandals burned the gin in the late seventies. **See photo below.** *Submitted by: Wallace T. Lambert*

24. Mandeville, Georgia

Mandeville is located about six miles north of Carrollton on U.S. Hwy. 27. "In the early days Mandeville had two large warehouses, a cotton gin, one large General Store that had about anything you needed - clothes both dress and work, farm tools, groceries, seeds of all kinds for planting, fertilizer, etc. You could take eggs or live chickens to the store and barter for your needs with Mr. W.S. Adams, the owner.

Mandeville had two other grocery stores, a post office, a passenger depot, a freight depot, two medical doctors, and a two-story building with a one-room school downstairs and an Odd Fellow Hall upstairs.

The one-room school had a large Pot Belly Stove for heat. A water bucket on a table in one corner of the room supplied our water and two toilets, one on the north side for boys and one on the south side for girls.

There were eight passenger trains and several freight trains each day. They all stopped in Mandeville.

Mr. Dan Creel, a one-armed Confederate veteran was the Depot Agent and Telegraph Operator. My dad, Martin Earnest had charge of the gin and Uncle George Earnest was Mandeville Mills local agent; he took care of the warehouse, sold fertilizer, and feed stuff.

Mr. Cliff Mandeville and Mr. Appleton Mandeville were owners of most of the cotton gins in the county. They had a very large cotton mill and oil mill in Carrollton."

The Bowdon Railroad was built in 1910 to connect with the Central of Georgia Railroad at Bowdon Junction which is about a mile north. That was the start of Bowdon Junction and the end of Mandeville.

Source: From *My Life* by Zellie Clarence Earnest with permission to use by son, Zellie Guinn Earnest, Kingsport, TN

25. Mt. Zion

Settlers moved into the Mount Zion area as early as 1827, but most moved on to Alabama, Mississippi, and Texas. The first permanent settler was Hicks Martin and his family. Martin was born in York District, S.C., and later moved to Forsyth County, Georgia, where he married Margaret Casey. In the 1840's, he moved to Cherokee County. In the fall of 1852, he moved to Carroll County. Hicks Martin and his family cleared the land, built a two-story log house, and farmed his 202.5 acres. The site of the original Martin house is now occupied by the home of Mrs. Buena McClain.

Martin was a remarkable man for his day. He was a farmer, a Methodist minister, a medical doctor, a pharmacist, and a church and school

Mandeville community 1900

founder. He was the head of a large family whose children grew up to become doctors, ministers, teachers, developers, postmasters, etc. One of his grandsons, J. Roy Martin, was one of the oldest Peace Corps volunteers from Georgia.

Other settlers began to move into the Mount Zion area. Among the early Mt. Zion family names were: Alexander, Austin, Bryan, Bagwell, Bevis, Burrow, Chaney, Crawford, Davenport, Finley, Fielder, Harrison, Ingram, McBurnett, McCalmon, McRea, McPherson, Morrison, Posey, Price, Proctor, Reid, Roberson, Smith, Thompson, Trimble, Walker, and Windom.

After building their homes, the settlers started churches in the area. Some of these churches were: Bethel, Lenity, Mt. Pleasant, Mt. Zion, New Hope, New Salem, Old Harmony, Pinetuckey, Ramah, Shiloh, and Union. Later Bethel, Shiloh, and Union Campgrounds were established.

When the settlers needed flour, meal, and grits, to have lumber sawed, or to have cotton ginned, they visited the watermills operated by Bryan and Davenport, Leak and Putnam, Entrekin, Trimble, and Robertson. Trimble and Robertson also operated a tan-yard.

As the area began to be settled, enterprising young men began to operate general stores, as well as to farm. James M. Savitz, Entrekin and Shaw operated some of these stores in Mt. Zion, W.T. Morris, H.H. Morris, Fowler and Landers, D.P. Holmes, Gammon Brothers, Aubrey Martin, and Pope Garrett. Nearby stores were operated by J.G. Robertson and Floyd Harris (at Jake), J.B. Moore (at Plowshare), and George J. Creel (near Eureka Baptist Church).

In the early days of the Mt. Zion area, medical doctors made house calls and charged from twenty-five cents to two dollars for their services. Medicines made by the doctors were extra. Some Mt. Zion area doctors were: Hicks Martin, William H. Malone, James Rogers, and a bogus doctor named Lewis.

First Mt. Zion City Hall built in 1907 as seminary library

The earliest post office in the Mt. Zion area was called Loyal and probably was operated in the Trimble-Robertson Mill. The postmaster was Wiles G. Roberson. A few years later, the name was changed to Turkey Creek Mills and was located in Joseph Entrekin's Mill. Joseph Entrekin was postmaster. On May 21, 1876, the name was changed to Mt. Zion (after the church) and the post office continues to today. Since 1876 the post office has been located in various places. Some of the postmasters were: Wiles G. Roberson, John Entrekin, Joseph Entrekin, Belle Roberson who became Belle Morris, Anna Mitchell, Mamie Martin, J.W.B. Pharr, Julia Clark, Alton Smith, Opal Stokes and currently Opal Newman.

Mt. Zion Methodist Episcopal Church (North) was founded in April of 1865 by Hicks Martin and ten other couples. The first conference preacher was John Murphy (1812-1897). The present Mt. Zion pastor is Hammett Evans. The first church buildings for the Mt. Zion Church were a brush arbor and a log building. The present sanctuary was built in 1889 with additions made in 1944 and in the 1950's. The first parsonage for the church was built in 1889 and was used until 1953, when the present parsonage was built.

In 1876, Rev. James Mitchell, the presiding elder of Carroll Circuit, Atlanta District, Georgia Conference, met with 25 other preachers and laymen at Bethel Campground and organized and chartered the Mount Zion Seminary. The school was one of the first high schools and served students from first grade to college. The school began its operations on December 6, 1880. It is the oldest school in Carroll County in continuous operation. In 1974, the schools were divided into a high school and middle school under the principalship of Leon Golden at the middle-high school and Quentin Miles at the elementary school. The current principals are Tony Childers at Mt. Zion Elementary and Cynthia Clanton at Mt. Zion Middle-High School. The building for the current Middle School was built in 1976, and has served students in grades six through twelve.

Both before and long after the advent of motor vehicles, the blacksmith took care of all mechanical needs, metal work, woodwork, and repair work. Some early blacksmiths were J.M. Ellison, Ellison and Albright, T.G. Harrell, and others.

Cotton gins in the Mt. Zion area were owned and operated by J.A. Entrekin in Jake, Garrett near Eureka Baptist Church, Mandeville where the agent was W.T. Morris, Shaw at Mt. Zion, and others. In later years, W.G. Entrekin was a real estate agent with offices in Bremen and Mt. Zion.

Transportation for passengers and freight began in 1910, when the Bowdon Railroad began services from Harmony (now Bowdon Junction) to Bowdon, passing through Mount Zion, Burwell, and other places. The company built a station in Mt. Zion for the benefits of the Mt. Zion area citizens.

Mt. Zion was settled in 1852 and was chartered as a town in 1910. A fire destroyed the early city records in the 1950's. The mayors since 1953 have been: Hicks Ashmore, T.H. Gammon, Gene Ashmore, Mary Ward, Jack Dorsey, Donald Newman, Clyde McWhorter and currently John Griffin.

Since 1975, the city of Mt. Zion has grown by the hundreds in population. Improved services for the citizens have followed. The population in 1975 was 295 and the present population is 1395. The city limits were a one-mile square. In 1975, Mt. Zion had a tiny city hall that had been built in 1907, an antiquated water tank built in 1918 with leaking water lines that served about fifty customers, one store, a post office, and a clothing factory.

Since 1975, the following improvements have been made: Lake J. Ebb Duncan has been built; sidewalks were laid; and a police department, fire department, recreation department, public library, and the Mt. Zion Primary Health Care Center have been organized and continue to serve the citizens of Mt. Zion. Additionally, the city now utilizes the positions of recreation director, city manager, city planner, works director, and librarian. Recreation fields have been built at Dillard Field and Katy Lane. The water distribution system has been rebuilt and expanded. The city limits have been extended. Property has been purchased to be utilized as a community center. All city streets have been marked and streetlights have been installed. Two bridges have been replaced. Ten new streets have been paved. An old café building has been remodeled to house the city recreation department. A new city hall and post office have been built and the Mt. Zion-Carrollton Road was changed to state highway 16.

W.W. Robinson, Donald Dillard, Walker Earnest, Clyde McWhorter, and Donald Newman have established construction companies. Other businesses include a tax service, a recreation center, a hardware store, and a gun shop.

Present City Hall built in 1977

The county commissioners of Haralson and Carroll Counties founded the West Georgia Regional Airport over 30 years ago. It borders Mt. Zion on the east at Airport Road. West Central Technical College at Waco is located five miles from Mt. Zion and will help serve the needs of the area's population. A major state park, John Tanner State Park, is located near the city and helps to serve the recreation needs of Mt. Zion and the West Georgia area.

In the future, Mt. Zion wants to re-develop its downtown district, create a community transportation system, develop water treatment and sewage treatment systems, build a new community center, establish a branch bank, have rural mail delivery under the Mt. Zion name, expand the serves of the Primary Health Care Center and expand and improve the present library. *Submitted by: Jack Dorsey, City Planner, Mt. Zion, Georgia, P.O. Box 701, Mt. Zion, GA 30150*

26. Town of Roopville

Roopville is located on a high ridge in the southern end of Carroll County. It is situated on the old McIntosh trail, also known as State Highway #5.

Roopville was named in honor of Martin Roop by his sons. When the Roops settled here the area was very much undeveloped. Native timber had not been cut. Surrounding the rocky ridge were rich uplands and well-watered bottomlands.

In addition to the Roops, other early settler families included: Stalling, Wood, Webb, and Stillwell. They were followed by Garrett, Howard, Burk, Duffey, Alexander, Guthrie, Almon, Thomasson, Staples, Worley, Freel, Huff, Towns, Merrell, Storey, Nolen, Craven, Veal, Pentecost, Hayes, Warren, Steed, Blackwelder, Ware, Cammon, Gentry, Friddell, Phillips, and Key.

The village contained several dwellings, three stores, a sawmill and a blacksmith shop. By 1893, Roopville had an additional general store, post office, drug store, shoe shop, gin sawmill, planing mill, grist and wheat mill, blacksmith shop, school, Baptist and Methodist Churches, and a population of approximately 150. Roads had been built north and south, east and west. Located at the intersection of these roads, Roopville enjoyed early wagon trade. Just about everything that the residents needed was either produced on the farm or could be purchased in Roopville.

By the early 1900's, Roopville was a thriving business community. Farmers throughout the area could get better prices for their cotton in Roopville. They bought fertilizer and other supplies from the Roopville merchants, usually on credit.

John Warren operated a feed mill and gin near the Theo Bell spring. Jim Craven ran a blacksmith shop near the cemetery. Will Creel operated a grocery and general merchandise store. Lee Steed, Sr. had a grocery store and cafe. Other businesses were J.T. Veal and Sons, Veal and Company, Roop and Company Roopville Mercantile Company, P.P. Staples Grocery, and Garrett's Grocery. A garage was run by Bill Alexander and Olin

Howard. Adjoining the Roop Company was a drug store and soda fountain. Tom Broadwater operated a barber shop for many years. Roopville had its own bank, part of a chain, known as Witham Bank.

Several doctors practiced in Roopville including Thomason, Green, Blackwelder, Veal, Goodwin, Hammond and West. Two dentists, Dr. Bill Brock and Dr. Alton Hallum, practiced in Roopville. Dr. Fitts operated the drug store. Each day he rode his bicycle to and from Carrollton where he lived.

During the height of this thriving period, Roopville was an important regional center. Justice court was held here for many years. Roopville often had its own law enforcement. A small jail, located at 148 West Highway 5, built by George J. Towns, Bailiff, was used until about 1925.

After crops were laid by, the men played baseball. Roopville was well known for their good teams. Among players of note were Jimmie Parrish, Terrell Huff, Glenn Tuggle, Eric and Don Staples, Walter Key, Claude Tuggle, Tom Kidd, Alvin Ward, Jim Gibson, Sam Alexander, Earl Staples, Harris and Ralph Ashmore.

A community house, which was located south of the Roop home, was used as a "meeting house" where the ladies of the community would gather there to do sewing projects such as quilting. It was also a time that they could gather and enjoy each others company. Although there were churches in nearby communities, a need was felt for houses of worship in Roopville. The people soon saw a need to replace the meeting house with their own church. Pleasant Grove Baptist, Roopville Methodist, and Roopville Baptist Church were all built with the generosity of both land and money from John K. Roop.

Citizens were involved in providing fire protection for many years. The earliest protection was a hose which was transported on a cart that could be pulled to the fire site by volunteers and then connected to the town's water system. In 1957, $220 was donated by 20 individuals to purchased the fire hose, donations ranged from $5 - $25. This almost covered the cost of $272. In 1971 an army surplus truck was acquired and converted to the town's first fire truck manned by volunteers. In 1980, the county built a modern station which currently is manned full time and also has trained volunteers. Where the first protection was for the town only, the current station serves a larger area.

Some of the residents who have served as mayor are: Jim Merrell, Barney Garrett, Robbie A. Merrell, Sr., G. Terrell Huff, Frank Farmer, and R.A. (Bob) Merrell, Jr. Some who served as councilmen were: O.M. Garrett, J.W. Garrett, W.H. Brock, J.A. Veal, G.T. Huff, G.E. Pentecost, H.J. Lanier, Ray Hightower, Chambers Almon, F.F. Fridell, Verbon Lovvorn, Ralph Huff, Theo Bell, Hugh Dorsey Perry, Julian Freel, Lee Steed, Robbie Merrell, James Garrett, J.W. Wood, Hershel Howard, Judson Bell, John Hodge, Tony Mosley, Chris Bell, Don Vennable, Leigh Wooward, Jim Veal, Perry Hannah, James Jones, and Emanuel Reid. City Clerk has often been one of the councilmen but from 1982 to 1997 J.L. Dean served.

Roopville has a water system serving 112 customers. The early system was provided by several private wells belonging to Gifford Bell, Odie Garrett, and a spring belonging to Theo Bell. In 1955 donations for drilling a well were collected in amounts from $5 - $100. Drilling was done by J.M. Turner at a cost of $1,315. The first well was located on property donated by Robbie A. Merrell. Later a second well was drilled on property donated by Robbie Merrell's family, and a third well on Ronnie Vaughn's property.

Each year on the 3rd Saturday in September, the annual "Homecoming Festival" is sponsored by the Historical Society and the Town. The following reunion of the old Roopville High School graduates makes for a lively day.

Roopville Merchant's Association: Mr. Monroe, Ginner; Tom Broadwater, Barber, Olin Garrett, Frank Roop, Pelham Staples, Arthur Garrett, Jim Veal, merchants and Mr. A.L. (Gus) Ware

At the present time Roopville has become a quiet community where the residents enjoy rural life. The Roopville Archive and Historical Society was organized on December 1984. The Archive is located in the renovated Roopville Bank where many items of interest are on display. Following the removal of three dilapidated old stores the Town built a small city park next to the Archive. The construction in November 1997 of a four-lane by pass of US Highway 27 moved the heavy traffic east of the town. The citizens of Roopville remain very proud of their community. *Submitted by: Rebecca Merrell, President, Roopville Historical Society and Archive, 124 Old Franklin Street, Roopville, GA 30170*

Sources: Old city records and interviews.

27. Shady Grove

Shady Grove Community retains its original name and was given to the community because of a thick grove of trees that were trimmed high so horses and wagons could be tied there. At one time it boasted of having two stores with the post office located in one of them. In the past, Filmore Peek operated a gin and sawmill in the community. It burned and Oscar Muse erected a gin on his property. There was a gristmill built on the Burnt Mill Creek, which got its name from the mill that burned there. Later a corn mill was built near Shady Grove Store. The late Dr. Sheets came from that area. The old Shady Grove School was consolidated with the Sand Hill School. Beside the names of Muse and Peek, others of prominence included Morgan, Shadrix, Bell, Robinson, Harris, Horton, Hendrix, and Jordan. The first school was a log cabin built just south of Hog Liver Road. *Submitted by: Bonnie Wilson, 1347 Stewart St., Carrollton, GA 30117*

28. Temple, Georgia

Temple, Georgia, is located 40 miles west of Atlanta on the Bankhead Highway (U.S. Highway 78) and the Southern Railroad. The Interstate Highway (I-20) runs approximately one mile south of the city. State Highway 113 runs through the city. Temple is twelve miles north of Carrollton, seven miles east of Bremen, and six miles west of Villa Rica. The elevation is 11,000 feet. The population is approximately 2,250.

Temple was settled in 1882 alongside the Georgia Pacific Railroad as it was being built between Atlanta, Georgia, (then Marthasville) and Birmingham, Alabama. The railroad was a vital link between the commercial interests of Atlanta and the rich iron beds and coal fields of eastern Alabama. The town was chartered on August 28, 1893.

General John B. Gordon, a Civil War hero who later became governor of Georgia, was the organizer and president of the Georgia Pacific Railroad. Major Robert Henry Temple, a native of Virginia and a Civil War veteran, was the chief civil engineer of the railway. The town was named for Major Temple.

Before the town was settled, Temple was a remote spot marked by a single log cabin and known as Ringer's Cross Roads, which was named for Benjamin F. Ringer, an early settler. The crossroads were formed by the Atlanta to Jacksonville, Alabama, and the Carrollton to Cedartown roads. About three miles southeast of the crossroads was Simsville, a thriving

West Johnson Street Scene in the 1890's

farming community of about 200 people. A general store, post office, cotton gin, grist mill, flour mill, and a saw mill were located there. Doctors James F. Brooks and Richard L. Rowe practiced medicine there. In anticipation of the railroad being built, the doctors built a wood-frame store building at Ringer's Cross Roads in the winter of 1882. Within a year, ten stores had been built.

The small agricultural village became quite a bustling cotton market and was very progressive until the Great Depression, the boll weevil, and other factors played havoc with the economy. However, throughout the years it has remained a wholesome community offering jobs, schools, banks, churches, and other facilities.

Sage Street Scene

Temple is governed by a mayor and five council members. The city has its own water distribution system furnished by two lakes. The city offers sewage, garbage pickup service, county and volunteer fire protection with a fire station inside the city, and 24-hour police protection provided by eight full-time police officers. Recreational opportunities are provided.

Some Temple highlights include:

(1) Buckhorn Tavern, built in 1833, was a well-known stagecoach stop between Marthasville (Atlanta) and Jacksonville, Alabama.

(2) The Temple United Methodist Church, built in 1898, is the oldest brick church in Carroll County.

(3) The Temple Model School opened in 1904 and received state-wide attention. It not only concentrated on academic subjects, but it also had an outstanding agricultural and homemaking program, which later served as a model for the Agricultural and Mechanical Schools established in the state.

(4) The first school transportation system in the state was started at the Temple Model School in 1904. It consisted of four horse-drawn wagons.

(5) The Georgia High School Association had its beginning in Temple in 1905. It was started as the Northwest Georgia High School Association by Dr. Joseph Stewart of the University of Georgia and Laura J. Rozar, a teacher of the Temple Model School. It later became the Georgia High School Association.

(6) Samuel M. Cown was the first County Agent in Georgia and the second in the nation. He accepted the position of Carroll County Farm Agent in 1907.

(7) Hampton H. Sewell, an evangelistic singer, composed more than 100 hymns. One of these, "He Included Me," is included in many hymnals today. Mary Ella West Hamrick also had several songs published in the Stamps Baxter song books.

(8) Casper Lassetter, the first graduate of Temple Model School (1905), became an editor of *The Progressive Farmer,* a popular agricultural magazine.

(9) Dr. Guy Wells, a distinguished educator, served as president of Georgia Southern from 1924 to 1934. He became president of Georgia State College for Women in 1934 and held this position twenty years. He also organized the Georgia School Superintendents Association.

(10) Adrian Drew, a 1939 Temple High School graduate, set a world speed record in 1957, flying an Air Force F101A.

(11) Knox Walker, Sr., a native of Temple, became a well-known educator in the state.

(12) Phil Campbell, a teacher at the Temple Model School, became the Commissioner of Agriculture for the state of Georgia.

(13) Paul Cobb, a native of Temple, was the district director of the Internal Revenue Service for many years.

(14) Robert McBrayer, a graduate of Temple High School, recently retired as Mission Control Manager for the International Microgravity Laboratory for the National Aeronautics and Space Administration at Huntsville, Alabama.

(15) Lee Fabricators is the sole supplier of handlebars for Harley Davidson, the American manufacturer of motorcycles.

Temple celebrated its Centennial in the fall of 1983 with a week-long schedule of events. During this same year B.W. Holder published the book, *A Historical Sketch of Temple.* The 100th birthday of the Temple Post Office had been celebrated on April 24, 1983.

Today Temple is experiencing much growth as development pushes westward from metro Atlanta down Interstate 20, making it one of the fastest growing areas in the county. *Submitted by: Ruth Holder, P.O. Box 70, Temple, GA 30179*
Source: Temple Historical Records

29. Tyus

Tyus got its name in a most unusual way. Andrew Hallum and Jack Tyus tossed a coin and Jack won, hence, Tyus Georgia was named.

Tyus Post Office was established in 1892. Postmaster Andrew Hallum lived in the two-story home. W.D. Bass bought the home and built the first store in 1901. J.H. Barr bought the store and it was called Barr and Son and was operated by the Barr family for a number of years until 1968. Having changed ownership a number of times, the present store is called Luu's and is owned by Mrs. Brenda Eady.

Tyus Baptist Church was organized in 1902 and built on Stoney Point Road, south of the store. The church was moved to the present location facing Tyus Road in 1929. Sunday school rooms were added in 1939. The auditorium was remodeled in 1957 and in 1961 the pastorium was purchased. A new pastorium was built in 1966. The auditorium was again remodeled in 1977 and there presently is a building fund for a new Fellowship Hall.

The Methodist Church was moved from Highway 5 to Bowdon Road. It served the community for a number of years but was discontinued several years ago. The Primitive Baptist Church was a mile west of Tyus. It was disbanded in 1929.

Tyus Lodge was organized in 1919 and met in the schoolhouse for several years before the house was built in which they now meet. *Submitted by: Beatrice Joyner Burson, 4351 Tyus Road, Carrollton, GA 30117*

30. Victory Community

The lovely community of Victory was named for Victoria Hines McDaniel, the wife of one of Carroll Counties' highest-ranking officers, Colonel Charles A. McDaniel who was killed at the Battle of Perryville, Kentucky in 1862. It is located along the Little Tallapoosa River east of Bowdon. The area was first known as "Chandler Springs" before being purchased in 1866 by George Ambrose McDaniel.

Mr. McDaniel's nephew Warren Morris operated the mill, a store, and a blacksmith shop for ten years. Then in 1876 when Mr. Morris' health failed, Mr. McDaniel sold his store and farm in Bowdon and moved to the mill.

The first thing Mr. McDaniel did was to build a new dam and a three-story mill on the river. As the community grew and prospered Mr. McDaniel added a number of other mills and shops to his property; and it became known as "McDaniel's Mill". The mill operations included saw, shingle and planning mills; and a wood and blacksmith shop, and cotton gin - for cotton was the farmers' main money crops.

A general store was run by Mr. McDaniel's daughter Ella. The store supplied the needs of the workmen, as well as the surrounding farmers and their families. Ella also did the mill's bookkeeping and millinery work. A post office was established in a corner of the store on March 12, 1873 and its first postmaster was Henry Wyatt McDaniel.

In 1880 George McDaniel sold one half interest in the mills to James R. Barrow. In 1899, G.A. McDaniel died and the mills were sold to the Barns family who continued to run them until the 1940s when the three-story mill was struck by lightning and burned in 1945.

Grist Mill, Victory Community

In 1897 the congregation of Antioch Methodist Protestant Church, erected a new building, a beautiful country church with two spires on the hill overlooking Victory, and named it Victory Methodist Protestant Church. On August 12, 1999 the community was saddened by the loss of its church when it was struck by lightning. It was rebuilt to a structure that resembles the original.

Victory community continues to grace the landscape of Carroll County with some of its original homes and farms. These include the McDaniel/Striplin House, the Woods/ McDaniel/ Wadsworth House, the Tisinger home and farm, and the old Word Place located high above the river. Some of the descendants from the McDaniel, Tisinger, Causey, Smith, and Garrett families still live in the community. *Submitted by: Gwyn Chestnut, 185 Cottage Hill Rd., Carrollton, GA 30117*
Source: Jessie Hamrick

31. Whitesburg

The following is a history of Whitesburg written by Mrs. Benjamin Camp in 1928:

"Since Whitesburg proper was incorporated in 1874, Civil War stories do not properly belong on her history, although the surrounding area have many. We don't have the time or space for this, but the county surrounding Whitesburg gave unstintingly of her blood and brawn to the Confederate army as any other portion of Carroll.

The writer probably is not in possession of the full data of the young men who went from Whitesburg District to the World War I. Hubert Brantley of Whitesburg served in the army in France and among the soldiers who occupied Germany. He came home safely, married and now lives in Los Angeles, California. Benjamin Jones, son of Mr. and Mrs. Joe Jones and great grandson of Thomas B. Jones, a pioneer of Carroll County, laid down his life on the battlefield of France.

Benjamin L. Camp, the young son of Mr. and Mrs. Benjamin L. Camp, enlisted for service in the American Expeditionary Forces while in Chicago, Illinois, when he was only seventeen but before he got his papers of consent from his parents to headquarters, Congress passed an act to prohibit enlistment under eighteen. A year later, having reached the age of eighteen, he left from Whitesburg and enlisted March 1, 1917 at Fort McPherson, Georgia. On June 1, he landed at an English port and crossed over into France where he remained until April 1919. He returned home safely and is now a resident of Chicago, Illinois. He married Frances Luthardt of the city.

The following colored soldiers went to the World War I from the vicinity of Whitesburg: George Billings, Paul Rowe, Ellige Crumbie, Julius Houston, John Crumbie, Cube Wallace, and Paul Wilcoxin. The last three were the only ones who returned alive. George Billings was the first one to be sent back, his casket draped in "Old Glory." He was interred in the colored people's section of Whitesburg Cemetery. The sight of the flag draped casket in which his body lay being carried to its last resting place, gave Whitesburg its first real shock of war.

Dr. J.R. Strickland, Dr. C.A. Duncan and J. Albert Jones were all in the army, but none of these went to France.

John Graves, a son of one of the old colored families was drafted but received an honorable discharge due to physical disability. John still lives in Whitesburg and seems to be the prop and stay for his aged parents.

Whitesburg has had, among her citizens, a number of the Legislature. Mr. M.D. Watkins 1906-1908. W.C. Wright, a member of Congress from the Fourth District, spent part of young manhood in Whitesburg connected with the firm of E.S. Roberts. Whitesburg was once the home of Raymond Daniel, Grand Master of the Masonic Grand Lodge of Georgia. Solicitor Emmett Smith of Carrollton City Court claims Whitesburg as the beloved home of his boyhood. Benjamin L. Camp, rural letter carrier of Route No. 1, Whitesburg, is president of the Georgia Rural Letter Carriers Association.

It was in 1916, under the administration of T.J. Jones as mayor that Whitesburg installed an electric light system. With the advent of electricity the town soon had an electric corn mill. The late William Tyre Jones and his brother T.J. (Tom) and R.E.L. (Bob) Jones installed this mill. The equipment was destroyed by fire in 1926. Since then Rev. J.W. McLeod has installed another mill.

In 1925 C.D. Goodroe installed a mattress factory in the brick warehouse built by the Jones brothers some years ago. This business is known as The Lucile Manufacturing Company. New mattresses were made and old ones overhauled. Recently there has been a furniture shop added to this. About two years ago R.L. Huggins, a former employee of the Lucile Manufacturing Company, installed another mattress factory.

The youngest church organization in town is the Church of the Disciples or Bible Christians. This church was organized in 1920 by Reverend Owen Still, who ran a series of meetings in a tent on the school campus in early autumn of that year. Some of the charter members were Professor W.W. Swetnam, Mrs. Swetnam, George and Walter Swetnam, Mr. and Mrs. E.W. Stevens, Misses Edna and Bernice Stevens, and Mr. and Mrs. G.W. Rooks. Professor Swetnam and family were conducting the school here at that time.

The church grew rapidly and with some outside aide an attractive building was soon erected. Reverend C.C. Turner of Carrollton, a young minister of this church, has recently told the writer that at this time they have one hundred and fifty members in reach of the church beside a considerable number that live away and can't often get back.

Both the Baptist and Methodist Churches have had various young people's auxiliaries connected to them from time to time, and the women's missionary societies of both churches have been of much service not only to their respective churches but to the community welfare. The most faithful leaders of this work in recent years whom I feel deserve mention are Mrs. R.E.L. Jones of the Baptist and Mrs. T.W. Camp of the Methodist Churches.

In the early summer of 1926 fire of unknown origin started in the night and destroyed seven of the old business houses of the town. No residences were burned. The citizens of the town fought the fire with outside aid. The city of Carrollton was asked for help but for some reason help was not sent. Then Newman was appealed to and some help was sent but the fire had been controlled before it arrived. Had it not been for the cool determination of the people of Whitesburg, the entire town, residences, churches and all, would probably have been destroyed that night. Nothing has ever happened in the town in the quarter of a century that the writer has resided here, which brought to light the calm, cool fiber of the people as did this fire. Probably some of the very old records of Whitesburg School and other papers were destroyed in this fire.

Of recent years Whitesburg has lost some of its old landmarks. The town well, which for perhaps forty years was in the center of the Main Street of the town with watering troughs built around it where boys who are now grandfathers drove their oxen or rode their horses to water, was filled in 1926 when State Highway No. 16 was being built. Another well was dug in a more out of the way place, but the picturesque old town well standing in the center of the Main Street is gone forever. In its place is a beautiful stretch of broad highway unbroken by any group of thirsty cattle as in former days.

The steeple and tall spire, built onto the Baptist Church about 1875-76 and which seemed to point one to the skies, was the first object in the town to meet the eye of the traveler who approached Whitesburg. It was struck by lightning in the summer of 1927 and badly damaged but for a wonder did not ignite. When repairs were made, it was decided by the church officials to leave off part of the steeple and the spire, which was probably a point of wisdom, but it was with regret that the older residents who loved the old landmarks gave up the steeple and spire.

There was only one hotel ever built in the town. It was famous in the early history of the town and was kept by Captain W.W. Harris. Later it was used as an apartment house and later rented by individual families as a residence. Following the World War it was allowed to go to ruin. The ruins of the old building were torn down in 1927 and the material carried to Carrollton to use for building.

At this time there are five grocery stores, three general merchandise stores, one restaurant, one lunch house, two blacksmith shops, one automobile repair shop, one drug store, one barbershop, one soda fountain, and two or three homes that have meals and lodgings. In summer ice trucks come daily. A laundry wagon from either Newnan or Carrollton comes at certain seasons. A good highway connects the town with Newnan, Carrollton, Bowden, Atlanta, ect.

The colored people are for the most part the old Negro families who have been here for years: the Russels, Fishers, Welcoxins, Lyons, O'Neals, Calhouns, Wallaces, Kirks, Graves, Phillips, Dominiques, and Redleys. They have several houses of worship with regular meeting days and are trying as best they can to educate their children. A kindly feeling exists between the white people and those of the colored race."

Submitted by: Mrs. Thelma Pate, 199 Old 5 Notch Rd., Whitesburg, GA 30185

Arts and Music

32. Arts Alliance

In 1976, following dedication of the Bess H. Williamson Cultural Arts Center in the Neva Lomason Memorial Library, a call was issued to citizens interested or involved in the arts. A committee was formed and plans were made to form an arts guild. The committee met with Ruth Gasset, Art Consultant for the State Department of Education and later, John Bitterman, Director of the Georgia Council for the Arts and Humanities. Both encouraged forming an Arts Council, representative of both visual and performing arts. Committees were formed to draw up by-laws and nominations were made for a board of directors. On July 12, 1977, the fruits of many hours of work by these two committees were presented and the West Georgia Arts Council came into being, with Jay Cain, President; Estelle Condra, Vice-President; Penny Butterbaugh, Secretary; and Andrea Cordell, Treasurer. The council's purpose as stated in the by-laws: "shall be to encourage and stimulate the practice and appreciation of the arts among the people living in the Carroll County area.

In 1978, the Arts Council met with Ronnie Young, Director of the Carrollton Parks and Recreation Department and Jim McKinnon, Art Education Consultant for the Carroll County School System, about receiving local funding. Soon a joint effort between the Carroll County Board of Education and the Recreation Department formed the West Georgia Arts Council. Carol McWhorter was hired as the Coordinator of Cultural Arts for the Recreation Department.

July 1981, the Cultural Arts alliance merged with the Recreation Department to become the Carrollton Parks, Recreation, and Cultural Arts Department. In May 1981, Deloris Brown, now Deloris Covel, became the Executive Director of the Alliance. In 1982 Dr. and Mrs. Ralph Fleck hosted the first Arts Alliance Gala, which resulted in a large membership increase.

2000 Cajun Arts Gala

In addition to the annual arts gala, the Alliance serves as an advisory board for the arts. Programming includes spring and summer Art camps; Theatre camps for Primary Theatre ages 4 to 6, Children's Theatre for ages 7 to 12 and Teen Theatre; Adult Theatre; Community Chorus; Art in Education Programming; Adult painters; Gallery 118 exhibits, clothesline art exhibits; storytelling festivals; High School poetry/short story writing contests; High School juried art show and many other programs and special art events. *Submitted by: Penny Lewis, Box 532, Carrollton, GA 30117*

33. Mom and Fine Arts

The Mom and Tot Fine Arts Group began with a request by interested moms who wanted to introduce their little ones to the fine arts. Two classes were offered in the fall of 2000 to a group of enthusiastic preschoolers and their moms (sometimes grandmas and dads). Due to popular demand, a Mom & Kinder class was added for 4-5 year olds and their moms.

Mom and Tots 2000: Connor and Mom

A variety of instructors teach the classes which focus on different areas of the fine arts and involve both the child and the parent in creative play. Pottery, puppetry arts, paper making, painting, folk music, theatre makeup and performance are all included.

Mom's role in the class is to work side by side with her child to create art. She may assist when needed, but is encouraged to allow the child to explore his own creativity while she explores hers. If the child is making a clay pot, the mother will make one, too. The emphasis of the program is to enable young artists to explore

Primary Theatre: "Edgar and the Really Big Egg Plant"

and develop their inherent art talents. *Submitted by: Penny Lewis, Box 532, Carrollton, GA 30117*

34. Primary Theatre

Carrollton Parks, Recreation and Cultural Arts Department's Primary Theater has grown from 2 shows a summer to 7. That's 7 different plays produced with actors ages 4 to 6. The children rehearse an hour a day for 10 days ending with a staged performance. The goals of Primary Theatre are 1) To have fun. 2) To make the parents laugh and cry and 3) To have candy every single day. Though having a great show is not a goal, it is always accomplished anyway. After all, 4 to 6 year olds are natural stars the minute they step out on to the stage. **See photo above.** *Submitted by: Penny Lewis, Box 532, Carrollton, GA 30117*

35. Children's Theatre

Carrollton Parks, Recreation, and Cultural Arts Department's Children's Theatre is a program designed for 7 to 12 year olds. The children have, with a variety of directors, produced comedies, musicals, theatre improv and even an original play totally written by the actors themselves. The Children's Theatre produces 2 plays each summer. Past performances include: *Annie, The Hobbit, Alice in Wonderland, Peter Pan, Stewart Little,* and many more. *Submitted by: Penny Lewis, Box 532, Carrollton, GA 30117*

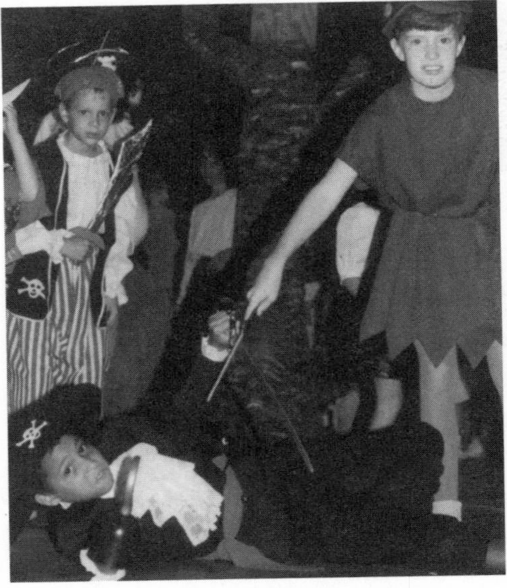

Children's Theatre, Scene from Peter Pan

36. Teen Theatre

Carrollton Parks, Recreation, and Cultural Arts Department's Teen Theatre has produced many shows over the years. The 2000 calendar included *Romeo* and *Juliet* and *Once Upon A Mattress*. The teens not only act, but they help

1999 Teen Theatre: Robin Hood

Richards, Lenaeus, Callahan, Cumming were part of Carrollton tradition.

build the set, make props, handle publicity and anything else they can do to make their show a success. The Teen Theatre Program runs all summer long and draws actors from all over the country and surrounding towns. *Submitted by: Penny Lewis, Box 532, Carrollton, GA 30117*

37. Dickens' "A Christmas Carol" A Carrollton Tradition

During the 1990s local theatre groups took turns presenting Charles Dickens' *A Christmas Carol* to a full house at the Townsend Center for the Performing Arts on the campus of the State University of West Georgia (formerly West Georgia College). Local psychotherapist Dr. Fred Richards played The Spirit of Christmas Present. With him are local actors who played Ebenezer Scrooge in three separate productions: Local businessmen and past president of the Carrollton Rotary Club, George Lenaeus; Father Jim Callahan, then minister of St. Margaret's Episcopal Church; and Joe Cumming, Carrollton resident, former *Newsweek* editor and a retired University of West Georgia journalism professor. **See photo above.** *Submitted by: Fred and Anne Richards, 301 Dixie Street, Carrollton, GA 30117*
Sources: Fred and Anne Richards

38. The Phil and Freddy The Rabbit Show

Between 1997 and 1999, *The Phil and Freddy the Rabbit Show* was featured on the State University of West Georgia cable television station.

Phillip DePoy, author, playwright and then Artistic Director of the Townsend Performing Arts Center at the University, played straight man to a philosophical, trickster rabbit played by local therapist, Dr. Fred Richards. In each show, the comedy-therapy team of DePoy and Richards explored a different topic of a psychological or philosophical nature. *Submitted by: Fred and Anne Richards, 301 Dixie Street, Carrollton, GA 30117*
Sources: Fred and Anne Richards

DePoy and Richards shared laughs, life lessons on cable program.

39. The Sacred Harp in Carroll County

Very soon after its publication in 1844 *The Sacred Harp* was in use in Carroll County, Georgia. Though *The Sacred Harp* was never officially endorsed by any denomination, it was a popular tunebook. The minutes of Bethesda Baptist Church show that it was in use there during the 1860's.

The Chattahoochee Musical Convention was organized in 1852 in Coweta County at Macedonia Baptist Church. This convention has continued until today and has always used *The Sacred Harp* solely. Today the regular home of the convention is Wilson's Chapel near Cross Plains. Wilson's Chapel was built by Matthew Wilson in the 1930's as a home for the Chattahoochee Convention. The first president of the convention was S.P. Barnett. He is buried in Carroll County. The first vice president was Oliver Bradfield. He lived for a time in Carroll County. Both Barnett and Bradfield wrote songs included in *The Sacred Harp*. Although Wilson's Chapel is now the regular home of the Chattahoochee Convention, in the early days it moved location almost every year. In 1854 the convention met at Bethesda, in 1856 at Wesley Chapel, in 1858 at Old Camp, in 1865 at Mt. Zion, in 1868 at Concord, in 1870 at Pleasant Grove, in 1873 and 1874 at Mt. Carmel, in 1878 at Macedonia, in 1880 at Mt. Zion, in 1885 at Temperance, in 1886 at Emmaus, in 1887 at Eureka, in 1892 at Salem, in 1893 at Powell's Chapel, in 1894 at Pleasant View, in 1898 at Flat Rock, in 1899 at Kansas, in 1900 at Pleasant View, in 1901 at Stripling's Chapel, in 1902 at Indian Creek, in 1904 at Oak Grove, in 1905 at Flat Rock, in 1906 at the Carroll County Courthouse, in 1910 and 1911 at Ramah, in 1912 and 1913 at Indian Creek, in 1917 at Villa Rica, in 1918 at Fairview, in 1919 at Sandy Flat, in 1920 at the Carroll County Courthouse, in 1921 at Indian Creek, in 1922 at Ramah, in 1923 at Stripling's Chapel, in 1924 at Sandy Flat, in 1926 and 1927 at Indian Creek, in 1928 at Ramah, in 1929 and 1930 at Poplar Springs, in 1931 and 1932 at Pleasant Grove, in 1933 at Bowdon, in 1934 at Union Camp Ground, in 1935 at Emmaus, in 1936 at Concord, in 1937 at Indian Creek, in 1938, 1939, and 1940 at Bethlehem at Cross Plains, from 1941-1945 at Emmaus, from 1947-1951 at the Carroll County Courthouse, in 1952 at West Georgia College, in 1953 at the Carroll County Courthouse, from 1954-1961 at West Georgia College, in 1962 at Holly Springs, and most of the years since then at Wilson's Chapel.

There were always many regular annual singings held in Carroll County besides the Chattahoochee Convention. Those remaining are at the State University of West Georgia on the first Sunday in January, Emmaus on the first Sunday in May, Holly Springs on the first Sunday in June and Saturday before and also the first Sunday in November, Mt. Zion on the 4th Sunday in July and Saturday before, and the Chattahoochee Convention at Wilson's Chapel on the first Sunday in August and Saturday before. In 2001 Carrollton hosted the Georgia State Sacred Harp Singing Convention at the Carrollton Community Center on White Street with approximately 200-300 attending from numerous states.

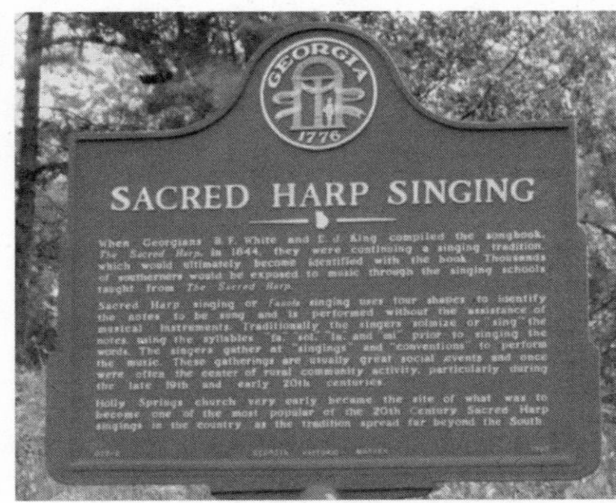

State Historical Marker in Carroll Co. for Sacred Harp singing

Several Carroll Countians authored songs included in *The Sacred Harp*. Among these are Jim Ayers, T.B. McGraw, H.N. "Bud" McGraw, H.M. Blackmon, Hugh McGraw, Charlene Wallace, Richard DeLong, Buford McGraw, Willis D. Jones, James R. Turner, S.P. Barnett, Oliver Bradfield, and A.J. McLendon. It would be impossible to even begin to mention all of the families who have sung or supported the singings over the years.

Among those singings not mentioned above which are no longer held are Antioch Primitive Baptist Church on the fourth Sunday in April and the annual picnic singing at Joe Warren's Lake between Bowdon and Tallapoosa which was held on the third Friday night in July. *Submitted by: Myron Wade House*

40. The Music Men Quartet

Following their 1991 performance in The Carroll County Community Theatre production of *The Music Man,* these four gentlemen put together a quartet for the sole purpose of having some fun. They never dreamed that they would have this many laughs.

The quartet's first event was in the small town of Buchanan, Georgia for the Spring Fling festival. Since then, the quartet has performed the national anthem at the Evander Holyfield Arena, Fulton County Stadium and Ted Turner Field. They have sung valentine songs to a newly wed couple in a doublewide trailer, to a waitress at Leather's Truck Stop and to hundreds of senior citizens at the VFW. They have performed in Rome, Tallapoosa, Montgomery, Rockmart, Stone Mountain, Daytona, Villa Rica, Douglasville, Fayetteville, Atlanta, Cedartown, Bowdon and LaGrange. They have performed in weddings, Fourth of July festivities, the Olympic Torch Run, Christmas parties, fund raisers, restaurants, golf outings and a summer concert with the Rome Symphony Orchestra.

Entertaining senior citizens and cruising restaurants tables has provided The Music Men Quartet with some very rewarding moments but their most memorable performance was to 400 teenagers camping out in Cedartown High School during the summer of 1999 for a church service project known as "Camp Build." They also performed for Ukrainian athletes and delegates during the 1996 Olympic Games.

The quartet started celebrating its tenth year together in the same way it got started — in a play! The members performed in the Encore Theatre Company production of *Forever Plaid* in January 2001.

41. Thomas A. Dorsey Birthplace Choir

On April 21, 1993, after the death of Mr. Dorsey on January 23 (please see Dr. Thomas Dorsey article), Mr. Evan Wilson and Shirley Marchman met to discuss the idea of a museum as a way of remembering such a great man, since he was born in Villa Rica. Sunday, February 14 was declared Thomas Dorsey Day, and a proclamation was read by the Mayor. The topic of discussion was about a birthday celebration for 1994. The Thomas A. Dorsey Birthplace and Gospel Heritage Festival Inc. were formed that year.

Shirley Marchman suggested a choir in his honor since his life was about music. The late Rev. Verlyn Styles and Shirley got their heads together and sent out a letter to the surrounding cities soliciting members.

On May 28, 1994, the Thomas A. Dorsey Birthplace Choir was organized with Verlyn serving as musician and director and Shirley serving as president. The first performance was held July 2, 1994 at the dedication ceremony of a Georgia Historical State Marker to honor Dr. Dorsey in Villa Rica. Our National President, Bishop Moales was in attendance and the marine Corp Band played music along with the choir. The National Organizer, Dr. Dorthy Grant inducted the choir into the National Convention of Gospel Choirs and Choruses on October 9th of that year.

The first Annual Dorsey Day Gospel and Blues Festival was held July 1, 1995, which would have been his ninety-sixth birthday. Verlyn died June of 1995 and his nephew Eic took over the job of musician and Brenda Williams became the director. The annual event is always held the Saturday on or before his birthday.

Some of our guests have been: Evangelist Dorthy Norwood, Dottie Peoples, The Associated Note Singers, Evelyn Turrentine-Agee, and noteworthy blues singers of the likes of Freddie Hughes, Cora Mae Bryant, and Cottie Starks. The Choir begins the festivals at Mt. Prospect Baptist Church in concert and then there is blues singing at Gold Dust Park.

Some of our engagements have included: Annual Gospel Festival at the New England Conservatory of Music in Boston Massachusetts, the Original House of Blues in Cambridge, Massachusetts for their Sunday Morning Gospel Brunch, the Martin Luther King Jr. Historic Site in Atlanta, and we sang with the Male British Choir from Britain at the State University of West Georgia. The choir received the Thomas Dorsey Award at the Gospel Choice Awards program at Morehouse College. The choir has served as backup for Dorthy Norwood and has been featured on a GPTV special *Georgia Back Roads.* Our goal is to always commemorate Dr. Dorsey and keep gospel music alive. *Submitted by: Shirley Marchman, 224 Sunset Dr., Villa Rica, GA 30180; Charles Hudson, 945 S. Lassitter Circle, Villa Rica, GA 30180-1421*

Thomas A. Dorsey Birthplace Choir

Business

42. Bank of Villa Rica

The Bank of Villa Rica was the first bank in Carroll County and the only bank in Carroll County that did not close during the 1929 depression. On February 1, 1899 a group of businessmen in Villa Rica met to discuss the establishment of a bank. Officers were elected and given the task of securing a charter and setting operations. The charter was approved May 4, 1899. Members of the first Board of Directors were W.B. Candler, S.O. Fielder, J.N. Wilson, F.A. Pritchett and W.A. Maxwell. The bank was chartered with a capital of $15,000.00 which by 1905 was increased to $30,000.00. The bank began operations in a store building in the middle of town. By 1974 it had outgrown these quarters so a new one story facility was constructed on Bankhead Highway. The original building in the middle of town became a branch bank. Capital had increased to $200,000.00.

Soon another expansion was needed and a four story building, constructed on adjoining land, was occupied in 1989. The branch bank in town was closed and the 1974 building was sold to the city for a City Hall. Capital had expanded to $55 million. The new building featured the first elevator in Villa Rica and had a Community Room for meetings.

In 1993 the bank merged with First National Bank of Gainesville that in 1996 merged with Regions Bank. The original Bank of Villa Rica is now Regions Bank of Villa Rica. It is interesting to note that through four generations there has always been a Candler on the board, from its inception in 1899 to the present Regions Bank of Villa Rica. *Submitted by: Randy Boyd, c/o Regions Bank, 1 Community Square, Villa Rica, GA 30180*

43. The Bowdon Railroad

Between 1910 and 1962, the Bowdon Railroad connected Bowdon to the rest of the outside world via the Central of Georgia mainline at Bowdon Junction. It was originally constructed under the leadership of Dr.J.L. Lovvorn. The Bowdon Railroad was a big factor in the economy of this area until railroads lost out to other forms of transportation. Mr. Will Roop owned the railroad from the early 1940's until abandoned.

The railroad was affectionately known in this area as "The Bowdon Dugan." It brought all types of commodities into and out of town. The railroad also hauled passengers. The Bowdon railroad originally owned two steam engines. In later years, engines were leased from the Central of Georgia Railway. After steam ended, the railroad bought a small Plymouth diesel.

Last Bowdon Railroad Steam Engine April, 2000.

Central of Georgia #349 was the last steam engine used on the line and is still with us preserved at the Tennessee Valley Railroad in Chattanooga on display. Old #349 has faired much better than her sisters. She is still displayed in Central of Georgia paint just like when she ran on the "Bowdon Dugan." The #349 still has her whistle, bell, major appliances, and even still has her wooden cowcatcher.

Today all that is left of the Bowdon Railroad are a few cuts and fills between Bowdon and Bowdon Junction. One can only tell where the railroad ran if he knows where to look and doesn't blink. *Submitted by: Richard Driver, 6154 Smithfield Rd., Bowdon, GA 30108*

Sources: Bill Barker and Joe Wheeler Barker

44. The Depot at Bowdon Junction

The depot at Bowdon Junction was built when the Bowdon Railway was completed in 1910. It was destroyed by a train wreck in the early seventies. The station was divided into a office for the station agent, a white waiting room, a colored waiting room and a freight storage room. There were two large hand trucks that the agent used to move freight from the train to the storage area.

Milard Parker was one of the first station agents. Another agent, Mr. Ansley (?) was there in the thirties and when it was cold would crank up his car that was equipped with a throttle and would run the car in idle at full speed for twenty or thirty minutes to warm it up. Drafton Earnest was the depot agent in the early forties. He had a brother who was a train engineer and a half brother Earnest Elder was also an engineer. The community knew when a train came through with one of them as the engineer because they blew the train whistle longer.

Waymon Aiken was the agent for a period of time and then M.L. Thomas was one of the last agents before the station was closed. During the thirties two passenger trains came through each day, one in the morning and one in the early evening. During WWII trains came through carrying men to and from Fort Benning.

The community of Bowdon Junction was developed because of the building of the railroad from Bowdon to the Central of Georgia Rail Line. The Bowdon Rail Road had a locomotive engine that pulled one or two box cars to haul freight. They also had a truck that had been converted to run on the rails. In later years this was used mostly when only small shipments were being hauled.

Telegraph lines provided communication between the stations. An American morse code was used that was slightly different from the international morse code. The depot agent was very proficient in using the telegraph key or the more advanced "bug" which was a key that permitted the agent to hold the key down and get several dots or dashes. The agent could tell by the sound of the clicking of the key which other agent was sending a message.

The accompanying picture was taken at the depot in about 1920 of the Lambert family reunion. In the background is the general store and post office run by Oscar Lambert.

In the early fifties Lester Lambert, the postmaster, moved the post office into what had been the colored waiting room. The waiting rooms had posters promoting automobile safety when crossing a railroad. The posters were from the twenties and were always of an automobile running into a train and never of a train running into an automobile.

The passenger trains had a mail car and when the passenger trains were discontinued the mail car was included in a train of boxcars each day. Lester Lambert, the postmaster, exchanged mail pouches with the mail car as the train stopped or slowed down enough for him to run along side the train to make the exchange. *Submitted by: Wallace T. Lambert*

Bowdon Junction Railroad Depot about 1920.

45. Carroll County Livestock Sales Barn

In 1941 discussion of establishing a livestock sales barn was initiated concurrent with organizing the Farm Bureau in Carroll County. At an organizational meeting held at the courthouse Mr. John Burson, Tax Commissioner, told the group about a livestock auction barn he had visited in South Georgia. The producers of cattle, hogs and mules depended on traders who traveled the county buying and trading livestock. The stockyards in Atlanta were not easily accessible for the farmers and an established local marketplace would insure that they received top price for their livestock.

Plans for the Carroll County Livestock Sales Barn were begun and stock was sold for $5.00 per share to raise funds to build the facility. There were about 25 original stockholders. Land was obtained on Fertilla Street at the end of Clifton Terrace and Hamp Chappell, road commissioner, had the county grade the land for construction. Plans were obtained from the Department of Agriculture and Claude Bonner agreed to build the barn for $3000. Joe Aycock, owner of Aycock Feed Mill, made arrangements for used scales to be installed. R.D. Tisinger filed the necessary papers with the Secretary of State for the charter.

The first sale was held on November 9, 1942 and sales were held every other Monday at 12 noon. Hubert Braswell, Fred Rutledge, Pace Craven and Charley Stallings worked the first sale, Claude Rigsby was barn foreman, C.L. Carden was ringmaster, and Pierce Smith of Hogansville was auctioneer. Mable Craven was bookkeeper and the price for all sales was figured using a Borough's adding machine and a calculator book. The commission was determined in a sliding scale basis of fifty cents to three dollars as a maximum and ten cents per head charged as insurance.

A sale of 200 to 400 head with the value of five to six thousand dollars and consisting of cattle as well as hogs mules and horses was considered an excellent sale. December 6, 1945 the sale disposed of 196 head of cattle and 20 hogs with a value of $7,034.14 with springer cows bringing $47 to $100 per head, pig shoats bringing $7.50 to $20 per head and steers bringing nine to twelve and one half cents per pound. The highest sale to date was on March 11, 1946 for a total of $10,394. with 44 buyers and 78 sellers selling 245 head of cattle and 55 head of hogs and pigs. By April 1, 1946 the farmers and buyers required that livestock sales be held weekly. The newspaper reported, "This is another indication of the success being enjoyed at these sales, which are attracting wide interest in this section of the state".

In first directors were of B.L. Garrett, F.L. Rutledge, A.L. Crook, C.J. Steed, A.R. Lovvorn, T.J. Lawler, secretary-treasurer and S.P. Craven, who served as President for 25 years. The general managers of the barn have been Pace Craven, Hubert Braswell, Lee Barr, Lillian Steed and Newt Muse with barn foreman being Claude Rigsby, Warner Muse, Hamp Jones, Hugh Brock and Rex Steed.

By 1968 the sales barn on Fertilla Street had under gone two additions and an office and lunchroom had been added. All of the improvements had been made without securing any loans. By 1955 the stock value had increased to $30.00 per share and under went a stock split with a value of $10 per share resulting.

With the increasing cattle industry in Carroll County there was a need for a new, larger barn. A new barn opened in 1970 on Highway 166 east of Carrollton. The Carroll County Livestock Sales Barn serves much of northwest Georgia and has sales every Monday, selling 41,513 head of cattle during the first 7 months of 2001.

The total 2000 sales were valued at 16 million dollars. Cattle farming remains a vital part of Carroll County's economy.

46. Early Carroll County Post Offices

Abilene, Allen's Mill, Banning, Barge, Bennie, Berlene, Billow, Birtha, Bonner, Bowdon, Bowdon Junction, Bowenville, Buckhorn, Buckingham, Buffalo, Burnt Stand, Burwell, Carroll Court House, Carrollton, Catie, Central Point, Cerro Gordo, Chanceville, Cheeves, Clem, Copper Hill, Coraxi, Corbett, County Line, Cross Plains, Curtis, Ditto, Dot, Elon, Emily, Fitts, Flint Hill, Genola, Gold Village, Gulledge, Harman, Henley, Hickory Level, Hodge, Holland's Mills, Horace, Hulett, Ithaca, Jake, Jet, Joel, Kansas, Katharine, Labor, Lairdsborough, Lang, Laurel Hill, Lilac, Lockville, Lowell, Loyal, Mabry, Mandeville, McIntosh Old Place, Mistletoe Bower, Moses, Mount Zion, Otto, Plowshare, Plug, Possum Snout, Ralterwood, Reavesville, Rett, Rilla, Roopville, Rotherwood, Sackville, Sand Hill, Shady Grove, Simsville, Sine, Siver, Sprewell, Stell, Stogner, Tall Pine, Tallapoosa, Temple, Tompkinsville, Trickum, Turkey Creek Mills, Tyus, Veal, Victory, Villa Rica, Whitesburg, and Wimberly. *Submitted by: Ruth E. McNinch, 801 College St., Carrollton, GA 30117*

47. Carroll Creamery and Dairying in Carroll County

Every farm had a milk cow to furnish the family with the essential milk and butter. Churning and ice cream making were the norm. Early dairies not only milked the cows but also bottled and delivered the milk to individual residents, schools, as well as stores.

As early as October 1944 there was talk of a milk processing plant for Carrollton. It was felt that it would increase the revenue and assist in stabilizing the farmer's income. Pet Milk Company was contacted and considered setting up a milk processing plant.

Bert Hobbs owned and operated Oak Lawn Dairy at the north end of Rome Street in Carrollton and was among the first to pasteurize milk and built a processing plant that was to later become the home of the Carroll Creamery Cooperative.

Dairying increased in popularity as the profitability of cotton production waned. Rogers Walker said August 16, 1945. "I had rather milk and feed 12 cows twice a day than chop or plant cotton ..." The idea that a dairy was easier work and paid three times as much as the average cotton farm resulted in many small dairies being built throughout the county.

A farmer with 24 cows could expect to gross $5000 per year and feed cost would vary depending on the forage the farmer provided, but would average around $1000. The barn and equipment cost around $2000. The average cow produced three gallons of milk per day compared to five that an average cow of today produces.

In 1951 a group of 36 local dairymen formed the Carroll Creamery Cooperative for the purpose of jointly producing, processing and selling dairy products. They purchased the facility that Bert Hobbs had built for his milk processing. Initially the individual farmers delivered their milk to the processing plant daily. Later refrigerated tanks were installed at each farm and the processing plant sent stainless refrigerated tank trucks to pick up the milk at the farm. The dairymen used automatic milkers and a laboratory quality control program ensured purity. T.J. Lawler was the first chairman of the Board of Directors and Troy Holcombe served as general manager and secretary treasurer of the co-op from 1952 to 1964.

The University of Georgia recognized the Carroll Creamery as a model for farm entrepreneurs and had field trips to inspect the operation. The Atlanta newspapers ran several articles extolling the success of this farmer enterprise. The total number of employees and owners grew to about 100. In 1967 Carroll Creamery Cooperative merged with the Atlanta Dairies Cooperative, which operated at the Carrollton site until 1984 as a distribution center and as a cheese plant to convert surplus milk to a cheese curd which was transported to a Kraft Foods plant in Marietta for making the finished product.

Early dairy farmers were Bert Hobbs, T.J. Lawler, M.C. Roop, Griffin Harris, Jubal Watts, Sr., James Burson, Sterling Stipe, J.C. Daniel, Bill Bagwell, Quinton Robinson, Charles Smith, J.O. McKenzie, Troy Buchanan, Lindsey West, Horrie Jones, Herman Brown, George Burns, Will Hammond, Robert Burns, Hamp Chappell, Tom Staples, J.R. Garrett, Opal Shirey, Grady Ayers, Rogers Walker, Ben Robinson, Ray Jones, Larry Steed, Felton Denney, and Alton McWhorter. Many of these were the original founders of Carroll Creamery. Some retired from dairying and others were bought out by a government-organized buy out in 1986. This program was solely financed by the dairymen who bought out competing dairies for five years. All the cows from the terminated dairies were sold for slaughter over a two-year period. This was an effort to aid in supply and demand while keeping the dairy industry profitable.

This buy out and the increased production and efficiency have resulted in only five dairies operating today in the county. These dairy farmers are Kenneth Robinson, Dan Warren, Steve and Larry Staples, Henry Windom and J.W. Bartlett. *Submitted by: Angie H. Stober, 1071 Lowell Road, Carrollton, GA*

48. Carroll EMC

Robert D. Tisinger, a prominent lawyer in Carrollton, filed a formal application to the Rural Electrification Administration in Washington, D.C. in May 1936. In a letter dated August 11, 1936, Morris L. Cooke, REA Administrator, said, "... I am glad to advise you that the application ... has been approved ..." Georgia Power in Atlanta was to furnish the power. Legal papers were filed in Carroll Superior Court on August 25, 1936, seeking incorporation of The Carroll Rural Electric Association. On September 21, 1936, Judge L.B. Wyatt signed the document, making the corporation official. On September 11, 1937, the charter of the Association was amended and the name was officially changed to the Carroll Electric Membership Corporation.

In the early days of the cooperative, only two linemen were needed to maintain the lines. These linemen were R.E. (Pedro) Muse and J.W. Bryce. W.L. Garrett served as chairman of the board and as temporary manager until L.L. Hardin, Jr., was named permanent manager in 1937. Mr. Hardin served until 1940 when W.G. (Chip) Foster was named as manager. Mr. Foster resigned in 1945 and R.E. Muse was appointed the job. During Mr. Muse's tenure, a new office building was constructed on Dixie Street and the office was moved there from its original Blue and White filling station location on Rome Street. Following as manager was Russell A. O'Neal who was appointed in 1955. James M. Hubbard served as manager from 1972 to 1978. At that time, Gary M. Bullock assumed the position of General Manager, and has been in that position since 1978. Another milestone for the cooperative came in 1969 when Carroll EMC became the first electric cooperative in the State of Georgia to be safety-accredited through the National Safety Accreditation Program.

Early into the decade, the energy supply picture became dismal. Georgia Power Company, the supplier of wholesale electricity to the cooperatives and cities, was having financial difficulty. This brought an uncertainty of adequate power supply for the cooperatives to meet the future needs of the member-owners. The forces, which helped organize many of the EMCs, were called upon again to form another cooperative to assure rural Georgia of having electric power when it was needed. In 1974, a generation and transmission cooperative was formed, by the name of Oglethorpe Power Corporation. Through Oglethorpe, the 39 member systems like Carroll EMC were able to move toward self-sufficiency and provide their cultures with reliable, affordable power.

In that first month of operations back in the summer of 1937, 344 customers were billed for electrical service. As 1987 got under way, there were some 25,000 member-owners with annual sales running more that 339 million kWh. In 2001, Carroll EMC serves over 40,000 customers and maintains over 4,400 miles of line in portions of several counties. The present Board of Directors includes: J.G. McCalmon, Chairman; Emmett Harrod, Vice-Chairman; Eddie Gore, Secretary-Treasurer; Donnie Brannon; J.P. Browning; Alvin Ginn; Max Goldin; W.S. Harman, Jr.; and Buddy Kimball.

49. Carroll Frozen Foods and Provisions Company

In June 1945 the Agricultural Panel of Carroll County Agricultural and Industrial Board began exploring the possibilities of utilizing funds from the War Protection Board to build a freezer locker near the Carroll County Livestock Sales Barn off Clifton Terrace. D.B. Blalock, Sr. of Newnan constructed the $85,000 facility to help provide a year around market for fresh fruits, vegetables and livestock produced in this county. On August 14, 1946 Carroll Frozen Foods and Provision Company formally opened to the public. A 57 by 120 foot locker plant was built in connection with a modern abattoir for the slaughter and processing of livestock.

At the opening D.L. Franklin, plant manager, said, "We are very anxious for everyone in this section to see our new plant and to find out for themselves the many advantages to be enjoyed from frozen foods." Carroll Frozen Foods was the most modern and complete facility of its kind in the south and expected to buy commodities on a large scale for processing and shipping to distant markets.

Individuals could rent one of the 777 locker spaces for $15.00 per year for 6 cubic feet storage space. A home economist, Mrs. Siebert, was employed to train and instruct homemakers in the skill of preparing foods to be frozen.

This plant eventually became the home of Duffey's sausage. Southwire bought the property in the 1980's and removed the building. *Submitted by: Angie H. Stober, 1071 Lowell Road, Carrolton, GA*
Source: *Carroll County Times*

50. Carrollton Hardware Company

The Carrollton Hardware Company was founded in 1900 and remained one of Carrollton's most popular businesses until 1980. Carrollton Hardware remained in the same building at 204 Adamson Square for the entire eighty years. The original stockholders in the business were W.W. Baskin, Iverson Coney Loftin, Charles Mabry Tanner, and Mr. Hughey. In the 1930's, Mr. Baskin, Mr. Loftin and Mr. Tanner

CARROLLTON HARDWARE COMPANY
Dealers in Builders and General Hardware.
Norman Buggies, Chattanooga Plows, and Majestic Ranges. See our Line.
Agents I. H. Co. Gasoline Engines and Thrashers.
John Deere Plow Co's Farm Implements.
We Sell Lime, Cement and all Kinds of Roofing. Come to See us.

Carrollton Hardware Company

bought out our Mr. Hughey's stock. In 1949, Mr. Baskin sold his stock to Mr. Ellis Merrell.

In 1940, Mr. I.C. Loftin died and left his stock to his wife Hilda who was the bookkeeper and became Chairman of the Board for Carrollton Hardware. Later on, in 1949, Mrs. Loftin gave the stock to her children, Tom Loftin and Lucille Loftin. Lucille Loftin kept her stock until the 1960's when she went to work for Sears & Roebuck. She then sold her stock to Henry Aldridge who became the bookkeeper of Carrollton Hardware Company

Marilyn Merrell at "Toyland"

Mr. W.W. Baskin died in 1954 and at that time, Ellis Merrell decided to buy Mr. Baskin's stock. After Tom Loftin died in 1969, Ellis Merrell bough the remaining stock that he owned. In 1973, Ellis Merrell sold his stock to Henry Aldridge and Mr. Aldridge continued with the business until 1980. Although there were other employees over the years that purchased stock in Carrollton Hardware, the names mentioned were the major stockholders.

Carrollton Hardware had the very first bridal registry in Carrollton and they kept a full line of china, crystal, silver, and all kinds of gift items at that time. In 1953, they opened the largest toy store that has ever been in Carrollton. Many remember the wonderful "Toyland" that Carrollton Hardware had in their downstairs, especially at Christmas time. Marilyn Merrell is pictured sitting on Santa's knee telling her all her Christmas wishes to Santa Claus. *Submitted by: Ellis and Eloise Merrell*

51. C.M. Tanner Grocery Company

The C.M. Tanner Grocery Company was originally begun in 1893 as a part of the Iron Belt Mercantile Company of Anniston, Alabama. Charles Mabry Tanner started out as a young man working as a salesman for this company. In 1895, the company was bought by C.M. Tanner and J.S. Stokeley and the name was changed to Carrollton Grocery Company. In 1898, C.M. Tanner bought the business and renamed it The C.M. Tanner Grocery Company — as it has remained ever since.

The business is the oldest firm in the West Georgia area and remains in the same location as it was in 1893 — next to the Central of Georgia Railway on Maple Street. However, a new building with more space was constructed in 1912 — which is the brick building still used today. It was constructed with deep wells in the loading docks for wagons, buggies, or Model-T Fords to pull into for loading of the groceries.

The trading area in the beginning of Tanner Grocery Company extended from Cedartown to Franklin and from Austell to Heflin, Alabama. Roads weren't paved in those years and the wagons would many times find themselves stuck in the slick red Georgia mud. Many a

Johnny Tanner is the fourth generation of his family to operate C.M. Tanner Grocery Company

kind-hearted Carroll County farmer has had to use his mules or oxen team to pull the wagon load of groceries out of the mud! The grocery company had to quickly upgrade from wagons to Model-T deliveries after those came into style — for the mules pulling the wagons would bolt and run if they met a Model-T coming toward them on the highway!

In 1993, the offices at Tanner Grocery were completely renovated making them more attractive and efficient. Johnny Tanner had already computerized the business and brought it up to 21st century technology. John W. "Johnny" Tanner, III now serves as President and CEO, the fourth generation of his family in the C.M. Tanner Grocery Company. First generation was C.M. Tanner, second generation, John W. Tanner, Sr., then third generation, John W. Tanner, Jr. Barbara Reed Tanner began to take a more active role in the business after the death of her husband, John W. Tanner, Jr.

Barbara Tanner came on board just in time to help plan the grand centennial celebration in 1993 to celebrate the 100th birthday of Tanner Grocery. On June 4, 1993, a Barbecue was held at John Tanner State Park for all the vendors. The next day, a trade show was held at the Park for customers of Tanner Grocery. Then, the next day, on Sunday — an Open House was held at Tanner Grocery where all community friends were invited to visit and tour the warehouse and offices and enjoy refreshments.

Many pieces used in the business 108 years ago were refinished and restored for the centennial celebration. Ed Lands beautifully refinished the old desk that C.M. Tanner had originally used in 1893. Johnny Tanner proudly uses it as his desk today. Portraits of the three previous company presidents now hang in the entrance hallway of the company.

An interesting point about this 108 year old firm is that there have been only five bookkeepers in a hundred years: N.N. Johnson, Luna Cook, Frances Jackson, Gwen Cocklereece, and Karen Buchanan. Luna Cook, as bookkeeper, and Julian Freel, as manager, gave many loyal years of service to Tanner Grocery Company. Also, later, too, did Frances Jackson. Katherine Lands has been with the firm the longest. She began working as soon as she finished high school in 1955. Brenda Carroll was with the firm for many years but died with cancer on 2 October 1997. The company also employs warehouse managers, Ed Lands and Bret Barnes, and out-of-town salesmen are David McDaniel, Jerry Weldon, Barrett Lawler and Gary Tallent. Gene Smith has been with the company since 1969 and handles all of the town orders.

Tanner Grocery Company has been with Carroll County since the old "horse and buggy days" of your ancestors of the past century and even struggled with the county through the food rationing years of World War II. Now the C.M. Tanner Grocery Company is ready to pioneer the new challenges of the 21st century! *Submitted by: John W. Tanner III, Tanner Grocery Company and Written by: Jan R. Bell*

52. Cook and Causey Building Supply

The year 1933 appeared to be a discouraging time for launching a new business in Bowdon, Georgia. The Great Depression gripped the land. Business in the town struggled to survive, and in the surrounding communities farmers' yearly income levels dropped to $200 to $400.

Prices for baled cotton, the single money crop, sank to 10 cents a pound or less. Production costs were higher than income produced.

Two farmers in outlying areas, Eugene Causey and Travis Cook, brothers-in-law, ventured to start a building supply company. For five or more years, little new building or repairs had been done. When a break in the depression came, demand should increase.

With a used planing machine for dressing lumber and little cash for purchasing lumber, the two men opened Cook and Causey Building Supply in 1933. Business increased, but a tornado ravaged the town in 1934, practically demolishing the rented building. The business operated briefly with no roof.

Eugene A. Causey, co-owner Cook and Causey Building Supply

Cook and Causey became a respected name in West Georgia and East Alabama. The business became the largest of its type in the immediate area.

Cook was bothered by illnesses during his last years and died in 1963. Causey had no heirs who could move to Bowdon and take over the business, and he sold the firm in 1964.

Gene Causey and Travis Cook served hundreds of customers during that period when the rural South was recovering from its most dismaying time since the Civil War. *Submitted by: O.B. Copeland, 383 Shades Crest Road, Birmingham, AL 35226*

53. Cottage Hill Greenhouses

Herman and Pansy Brown opened the Cottage Hill Greenhouses in 1945 when he built a greenhouse for her plant collection. They closed their ice cream shop, The Dari -Bar, as sugar was too hard to get during the War; and turned it into a flower shop. The only one who sold flowers for funerals, and other occasions at that time was Mrs. T.J. Robinson. She ran her business out of her house on West Center Street in front of Martin Funeral Home.

Cottage Hill Greenhouse was the only greenhouse business in the West Georgia area for many years. The Browns grew a wide collection of plants including houseplants, cacti, palms and orchids. Mr. Brown was especially known for growing geraniums as the business grew to five greenhouses. Seasonal plants such as poinsettias, Easter lilies, and hydrangeas were a beautiful sight. Many people would just walk through the greenhouses to enjoy the plants.

Cottage Hill became a landmark on U.S. 27 that brought travelers to tour the greenhouses as they made a point to stop on their way to or from Florida each year. Also, the goat man came by on his travels around the country. Loads and loads of cotton on the way to the gin came by from farms south of Carrollton.

The flower shop was a beehive of activity with flowers arranged for all occasions. Decoration Day at local churches required some kind of bouquet for every grave in the spring and summer. For Mother's Day, everyone in the family wore a red or white corsage or boutonnière according to whether their mother was living or not. On Easter, all women wore new outfits including hats and gloves, and of course a corsage of large purple or white Catalina orchids, gardenias, roses, or carnations. May Day at West Georgia College was a big occasion in the 40s and required the making of many corsages for the girls for the dance that night.

Cottage Hill was primarily a family operation run by Herman, Pansy, David and Gwyn Brown. Some of the designers who worked with the Browns were Mr. O.P. Baxter from Bremen, Hazel Whitman, Mozelle Jackson, Kathryn Lane, and Margaruite Steed. Mr. Bill Reese was their bookkeeper for many years.

They moved and rebuilt on the back of their property in 1975 when the Department of Transportation took the old site including all of the greenhouses, farm buildings, windmill and houses to widen U.S. 27 and build the south bypass. Houseplants, bedding plants, and many varieties of tomatoes, peppers, geraniums and ornamental peppers were grown at that time. The flower shop did not reopen; but the greenhouse business continued until 1985. Today the Crossroads Shopping Center is located on the former site of the greenhouses. *Submitted by: Gwyn Brown Chestnut*

54. Fisher's 5 & 10 Store

This is a picture of my daddy's store made about 1926. The location of the store was on the Carrollton Square. Currently, Sabrina's is located at the corner. Pictured left to right on the sidewalk: the first three are sales ladies

Plants inside greenhouse one at Cottage Hill

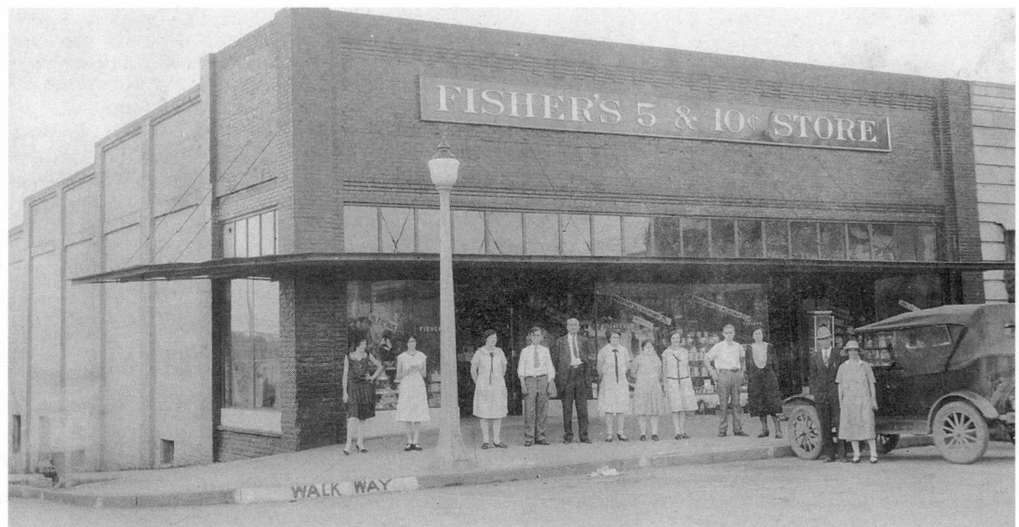

Fisher's 5 & 10

whose names are unknown, M.L. Fisher Sr. the store owner, an unknown drummer or traveling salesman, Kate Taylor, Tiny Taylor, unknown, Hollis Brisman, Beulah Kaylor Hayes, and the couple by the car are unknown. Any corrections, additions, or comments are welcome. *Submitted by: M.L. Fisher, Jr., 205 Camp Drive, Carrollton, GA 30117*

55. Georgia's Oldest Bookstore and Carrollton's Oldest Business

Horton's Books & Gifts, LLC, Carrollton's oldest business and Georgia's oldest bookstore was founded by N.A. Horton in March, 1892 in the northeast section of the public square. He originally operated a small book shop in the furniture store owned by Mr. Hughes which was in the two-story building in the corner of the square (404 Adamson Sq.). Later that year, finding he needed more space, he moved to the building next door. When the First National Bank completed its new building, N.C. moved into the space vacated by the bank. He stayed in this location until his death in 1917. In 1903, N.A. Horton was advertised in the Carroll County Times as an

> "undertaker and dealer in Furniture, Matting, Rugs, Coffins, Caskets, Robes, Slippers, etc. Books, Stationery, and School Supplies, Pictures and Frames. Frames made to order. Silver metal knives, forks, and spoons, china, etc. Musical instruments and strings; Estey and Peerless Organs and Pianos. Best goods and lowest prices. Northwest corner of the Public Square."

Horton's also supplied text books and school supplies to the local students until the state began supplying free books to the children. During one of N.A.'s trips to Atlanta to pick up his book stock, his car caught fire. Knowing that he had to salvage the books to save his business, N.A. managed to extinguish the fire without damaging the books.

N.A.'s son, Hap, who took over the business at his father's death, operated the business until his own death in 1969. During the next fifty years, Horton's adapted and changed to meet the customers' needs. Hap added gifts, tailoring, and office supplies to his stock of books. Once, during the Great Depression, money was so scarce that Hap had to go to the bank to get change for a customer's $5.00 bill. Doris Shadrix, just twenty and newly married, joined Hap in 1947. She remembers that when Hap moved Horton's to its present location at 410 Adamson Sq., the large oak display cases were taken apart and "rolled" up the street from the old location on Rome St. In 1978, when Hap decided he needed more time away from the store, Doris became a partner with an agreement that she would work full time and Hap would work when he wanted to.

Hap Horton - Horton's 75th Anniversary 1967

After Hap's death in 1969, Doris bought his share of the store from his estate and became the full owner of the business. After spending a total of 42 years at Horton's as an employee and owner, Doris sold the business to Larry G. Johnson. During his tenure, Johnson opened up the basement to add used book sales to the offerings of the store. In 1997, Johnson sold the business to Dorothy E. Pittman, a descendent of Carroll County pioneer Benjamin McFarland Long.

Recently the store's facade has been returned to its former "turn of the century" look while computers help in searching for book titles and take care of the accounting and inventory activities. Even so, the sales are still rung up on the same hand cranked National cash register that N.A. Horton used when he founded the store. *Submitted by: Leslie Stokes, 160 Edgewood Dr., Carrollton, GA 30116 and Written by: Dorothy Pittman*

56. Stories Told For Horton's Book Store

How many tales can be told by a bookstore
more than a hundred years old?
Who were the people who came through
the door
And browsed the shelves of this
quaint little store?
Merchants, bankers, farmers, and kids —
How was Carrollton when each one of
them lived?
Dirt streets and cotton, corn, and old men
Got to town on Saturday —
how's things at the gin?
History is made one day at a time —
Time passes slow in this town of mine.
Smiles through the window,
new faces at the door,
What tales can be told by
an old bookstore?

By Mark Kenneth Crawford, Printed with Permission - Copyright 1995 *Submitted by: Jan Bell*

57. Griffin's Department Store

Griffin's Department Store was founded in September 1899, under the name of Jackson, Perryman and Griffin, general retail store. The initial capital stock was $4,500 equally divided among J.W. Griffin, R.D. Perryman, and J.M. Jackson. Perryman sold his one-third interest and Jackson and Griffin purchased the lot and building, located on the corner of Alabama and Maple Streets. In 1912, J.W. Griffin became the sole owner and the name was changed to Griffin's, and he adopted the famous slogan "One Price House".

In 1919, the old wooden building was replaced with a new brick building at a cost of

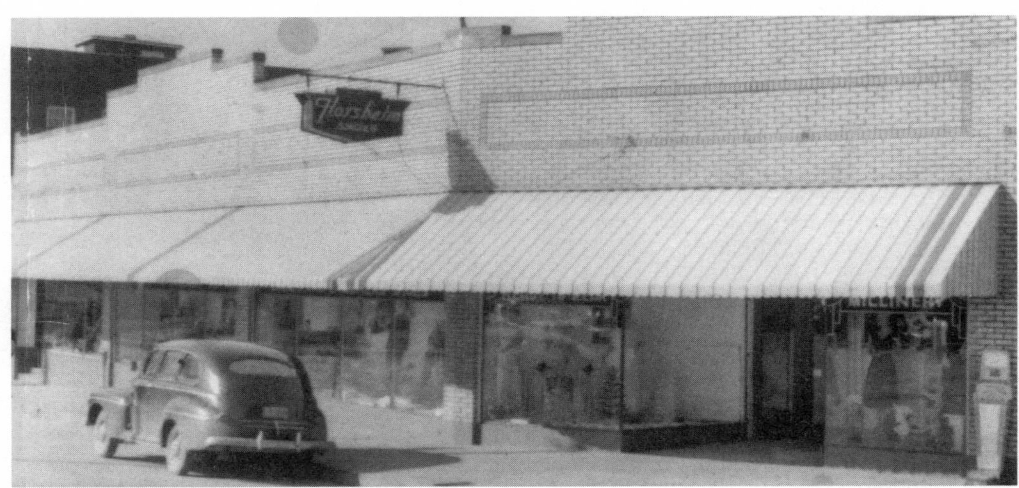

Griffin's Department Store 1950

$20,000. In 1926, an annex was added and a coffee shop installed, this was later replaced by a beauty shop. In 1940, the annex was remodeled making it a part of the main store.

Griffin's was incorporated in 1947 with J.W. Griffin as President and his son J. Hubert Griffin as Vice-President. On July 10, 1950 the 50th Anniversary Sale was held. Following the sale, J.W. retired and J. Hubert assumed management.

J. Hubert retired in the early 70's and the store was leased to a retailer from Alabama. The building was sold in 1981 after J. Hubert's death. Soon after it was torn down and replaced by a parking lot.

Some memories remain, the little change "cars" that ran all over the store, the magic shoe machine that x-rayed your feet, the bargain basement filled with dry goods and Lee overalls, and Mrs. Jesse's hat department. *Submitted by: Marion Griffin McIntosh, 244 N. Lakeshore Drive, Carrollton, GA 30117*

58. Johnson Auto Electric

Camped on the banks of the Elbe River in Germany, Edwin Snead Johnson learned the war was over in Europe; and soon he would head home. He had spent three and a half years in the Army, fifteen months in Europe with the 84th Infantry Division (Railsplitters). At home he found his brother, Aubrey, was rebuilding starters, generators, and electric motors. Wire for rewinding was hard to find; so Snead rebuilt batteries. Then new batteries came on the market. After working together for a while, his brother took the electric motor business; and Snead started a generator and starter business.

In 1947 Snead bought a place on South Park Street where Eckerd's is now; and in 1951 he rented the old Triangle Service Station on Bankhead where Georgia Power is located. He soon outgrew this building and in 1952 purchased a one-stall building at 159 Newnan Road, adding a center stall in 1964, and the truck stall in 1972.

Through the years Snead saved thousands of dollars making most of his machinery for rebuilding which should have been patented. Now son Ralph Edwin Johnson is owner and carrying on the family tradition; and Ralph's son, Seth Edwin Johnson, is learning the trade and hopes to carry on for a third generation.

At 79 and with failing health Snead looks back with pride. He remembers beginning in 1947 with one Ford starter and generator soon adding a Chevrolet starter and generator. He was on his way! When he sold one he took the old trade-in and rebuilt it. Gradually he was able to build his stock. It was a life of hard work but rewarding as he served west Georgia and east Alabama. *Submitted by: Marie Johnson, 205 South Street, Carrollton, GA 30117*

Source: Personal knowledge

59. Johnson Drug Company

In 1854, William E. Johnson, a doctor and pharmacist, sold Stone Mountain and moved his family by wagon to Carrollton. He opened Johnson Drug Company in the northeast corner of the public square where he sold patent medicines, paint, and cosmetics. Dr. Johnson also traded with the local Creek Indians to obtain roots and medicinal plants necessary for his pharmacy practice.

Johnson Drugs 100th Birthday Celebration - 1954

The drug store continued in business on the square for 117 years until 1972. In the 1950's it became "America's Oldest Drug Store" owned by the same family in the same location. Four generations of Johnson pharmacists worked in the store. They were: Dr. William E. Johnson Sr., William E. Johnson Jr., Edgar William Johnson Sr., and Edgar William "Billy" Johnson Jr. Jewell Johnson also worked at the store for over forty years. Ed and Jim Johnson are fifth generation pharmacists and practice in the West Georgia area today.

The old drug store added a soda fountain and offered free delivery. Jeff Powell was the delivery man and rode his bicycle through the streets of Carrollton for over thirty years, carrying Lemon Coca-Cola on a tray with prescriptions. The location of the store is where Cole's Jewelry stands today.

60. Lovvorn's Mill

Before the town of Bowdon was founded in 1853, W.F. Johnson built a mill on the creek north of town. When Col. W.D. Lovvorn bought it, the name Lovvorn's Mill stuck even though it was at one time Cook's Mill and Johnson's Mill. Sometimes the area around the mill was referred to as Mill Town for in addition to the mill itself, there was a store, a sawmill, a wool plant, a tannery and a gin.

Lovvorn's Mill, Bowdon, GA

During the harvest season, the mills operated day and night. The farmers waited in lines to process wheat, corn and cotton. Flour, meal, whole-wheat flour, grits, seconds and wheat bran were all ground at the mill.

The tannery was located across the creek from the mill. The branch which ran close by was called Tan Yard Branch. The tan yard had five or six "vats" dug four or five feet deep. Hides of cattle were laid in the vats and acid poured over them. They soaked in this manner until the hair separated from the hides.

The area around the mill provided a recreation area especially for young people and was a favorite spot for pictures. *Submitted by Judy Rowell, 1472 Garrett Creek Road, Bowdon, GA 30108*

61. Milk Business Evolves

Milk is an important, almost essential, item of diet. Farm people first produced milk for their own family, then some started producing enough for others. Early milk production was nothing like today.

My grandfather, John Worth Williams, established a dairy in 1892, when he finished his house on the Carrollton-Villa Rica road, two miles south of Villa Rica. The dairy was a major part of the family business for many years.

Grandfather built a very "up to date" barn, with metal stanchions and a concrete floor with drains. He also built a brick milk room. There they made butter and butter milk. At first, these were the main products sold from the dairy. They were shipped daily from the Villa Rica depot on the "Accommodation Train" to Grady Hospital in Atlanta. To my knowledge, this was the only commercial dairy in Villa Rica then or later.

John Worth started with a herd of 20 purebred Jersey cows — the number he could put in the barn for one milking. Their milk averaged about 6% butterfat, the ingredient used for butter. Grandfather also fenced a considerable amount of his land for pasture, over half of 365 acres.

Since Grandfather had five strapping sons, he had plenty of help for milking these cows, for growing feed for them, as well as cleaning after them. Besides, he had several tenant farmers who were available for extra work.

Unfortunately, Grandfather died young. The farm was inherited by my Grandmother, Martha Caldonia, "Callie" Williams. She turned the dairy business over to my Uncle Felix Williams, who operated it until the late 1960's.

Felix greatly expanded the herd. By the time I was born, in 1921, he had about 60 cows. These were served by a herd bull, and calves and heifers were raised to continue the herd, or for sale.

To handle this increased herd, Uncle Felix added to the barn, putting in an additional 10 stanchions. Still, he and his "hands" had to make two milkings each morning and afternoon to handle the numbers. By the time I was in high school, herding and controlling them had become a task, one which often fell to me.

Since men could milk faster, boys like me usually didn't start milking until they became older. The women in the Williams family worked in the milk house, bottling the milk. This was delivered door to door in Villa Rica and Carrollton. They also washed and cleaned all the cans and buckets.

Uncle Felix studied the business, and was always up-to-date. He bought and installed the first pasteurizer in this area about 1939. After WOW, he built a new milking parlor with a milking machine.

Though I was attending West Georgia College when the pasteurizer was bought, pasteurizing milk fell to me on vacations and weekends.

You'd pour 50 gallons of milk into a stainless steel vat, which was surrounded by a steam jacket. Then, you'd valve in steam, watching the thermometer in the milk, to get the temperature up to 160 degrees quickly. A motor driven agitator kept the milk moving so that it all remained at the same temperature.

The milk was held at that temperature for 30 minutes. A recording thermometer monitored this. It took some skill with the steam valve not to over-heat the milk or let it cool too much.

After 30 minutes "cooking" time, you valved out the steam and replaced it with cold water. The idea was to reduce the temperature as rapidly as possible. Otherwise, the milk acquired a "cooked" taste.

My stint on the pasteurizer ended when I joined the Air Corps in 1942. A new, and superior form of pasteurization came into use about the early 1950's. It was called Flash pasteurization. This machine was quite expensive, and small producers could not afford it. So my folks began to sell their milk to a large cooperative.

The dairy business became almost a factory operation, as it is today. A stainless steel milk truck came by the farm each day and picked up the production. This was taken to a central location, along with milk from other farms, to be processed and bottled.

Uncle Felix lost his herd to Brucelosis in the late 1960's. He and my Dad then put in beef cattle. So ended the era of the Goldworth Farm Dairy. Note: The Goldworth dairy supplied milk to the CCC Camp during the time it was active.
Submitted by: Bill Mitchell, 55 Goldworth Rd., Villa Rica, GA 30180

62. Oakland Improvement & Manufacturing Company

On 22 January 1894 C.B. Simonton, L.C. Mandeville, C.H. Stewart, E.C. Stewart, E.G. Kramer, and A.D. Harman purchased for $8,000.00 seventy-five acres of land (lots 98, 127) in the tenth district of Carroll County and incorporated the Oakland Improvement & Manufacturing Company. The property ran from Kramer's land on South Street up Bowdon Street [now Maple] to Franklin Road [now Hays Mill] and down Longview Street which was then known as the "race path" used for horseracing.

Two blocks of Longview, running from Tuggle Street [which becomes South Boulevard after it crosses Longview] to South Street, is the area residents and owners of the houses consider an historic district.

Seventeen of the houses in this block were built in the 1880's, only one being two stories. It is one of the oldest houses in the neighborhood. Several, including the house at 419 Longview, were built by Charles Williamson, who built other Victorian houses in Carrollton. The Williamson houses still standing bear the same gingerbread trim. Charlcie Williamson McElroy, daughter of Charles Williamson, owned the Longview house until the 1970s.

During the Great Depression, a family of seven who lived at 419 needed to supplement their income and took in a young girl from the country to live with them while she worked. One of the daughters had a single bed, which was extended with orange crates to provide sleeping accommodations for the new border. When the family decided to bring in a second boarder to share the make-shift bed, the young woman found another home.

Next door at 409 Longview, the house is said to have been built earlier. The family waited there for the man in the family to return from the Civil War. A descendant built a millinery shop in the yard [now a home]. There the owner made hats for the ladies of Carroll County and beyond.

Other houses in the two-block area date from 1900 to 1960. All of the older houses have weatherboard exteriors, while several newer houses are brick. Garages and rooms have been added to many, reflecting the changes from the 1890s.

Although the street is zoned for one-family residences, there are some multi-family houses that were grandfathered in. Longview is still a quiet street despite its use as a thoroughfare for people at the university or living on Hays Mill. Joggers and walkers find their way going to and from Longview Park. A few young families are rearing their children in the old fashioned atmosphere of the real estate venture begun by the Oakland Improvement & Manufacturing Company in 1894. *Submitted by: Douglass McFerrin Ruskell, 419 Longview Street, Carrollton, GA 30117-3709*

63. Old Perry Alford Farm

An old store sits on what was the Perry Alford farm on Alford Road off Bowdon-Tyus Road. The old road connected Tyus and Bowdon and was used by farmers and travelers. They brought their butter and eggs and traded for coffee, tea, and other goods.

The "store" was in the front part of the building, and the people lived in the back room. The wooden floor, plank walls, and ceilings are just as they were more than a hundred years ago. The fireplace, made from hand-made bricks, serves both the store side and goes through to the living quarters. Today, it shows signs of crumbling, but it must have been a source of warmth for the travelers.

The outside of the building has been covered with some type of asbestos siding, but the old original planks show through in many spots. Alongside the store is a large old oak tree that still has nails and other hardware in it where farmers tied their horses and mules when they stopped. It is believed this store was the oldest building on the property.

Old store between Tyus and Bowdon.

About one-fourth mile from the store the road crossed the Little Tallapoosa River. A ford was there, where the water ran shallow and the river bottom was rocky. The animals and wagons could cross the river here without any problems.

A well-known citizen of Bowdon, Ellie Bryant, was born in the house that now stands on the farm (where the old log home was originally). Ellie told us that her father first lived in Bowdon. He then went to Arkansas to learn to be a boilermaker, and was sent to Montgomery, Alabama. It was here that he had a heart attack and was no longer able to keep his job, so he came back to Bowdon in early 1932 and rented what was then called the Burson place. Harold and Lula Keith (called Mama Lou) were tenant farmers and their living quarters were the old store building. Mama Lou helped look after Ellie and her siblings. After about a year, the Bryants moved to the farm (along with the Keiths) where Ellie lives today.

In talking with Mr. Wayne Alford (whose father was Perry Alford), he said he thought some previous owners of this property were the Butlers (who might have been the man who ran the store); Bursons owned it before the Alfords; and a Mr. Gay owned the property at one time.
Submitted by: Rudy Parsons, 2085 Bowdon-Tyus Road, Bowdon, GA 30108

64. The "Olden Days" of the Grocery Business in Carroll County, Georgia

"Just Dial 5 — say charge it — and have your groceries delivered by bicycle."

From a 1935 advertisement of The Carroll Trading Company

Back in 1983, the people of Carroll County were in for a real treat when J. Edwin Copeland wrote a series of historical articles for the *Times-Georgian* newspaper about his experiences over nearly half a century in the grocery business. Ed Copeland had started out as a shipping clerk for C.M. Tanner Grocery Company in 1930. Ed's father, George T. Copeland, had originally had his own wholesale grocery business in Carrollton in partnership with Newman N. Johnson. Later Copeland and Johnson decided to sell their stock to C.M. Tanner Grocery Company and become a part of that business where both were Vice Presidents for many years. So, Ed Copeland was "born into the grocery business" on 13 May 1910 at the beginning of the twentieth century. Here we are now at the beginning of the twenty-first century — and Ed Copeland is still a dynamo at 91 years of age!

Ed Copeland managed the first supermarket in Carrollton, the Carroll Trading Company, which was owned by C.M. Tanner Grocery Company. This was in the days when you could buy salmon for 10 cents a can and coffee for 28 cents a pound. Even better — all you had to do was "Dial 5 — say charge it — and have your groceries delivered by bicycle." In those days, few people had their own automobiles, so delivery was an important part of the business.

From 1934-1954, Ed remained in this position until he decided to go into business for himself. He and his brother, Perry Copeland, opened Copeland's Supermarket on May 19, 1954, which was located at 199 Newnan Road. This was a modern brick building with — of all things! — air conditioning! Their business was an immediate success — and this was in the days when you could buy green cabbage for 3 cents a pound — and well, look at those prices in the window above!

Ed Copeland is the perfect person to write about his first-hand experiences in the grocery business — for he demonstrated an observant eye and a natural talent for writing at an early age. For those not familiar with *The Howler* of Carrolton High School of the 1920's era — this you should know. In the 1920's, Carrollton High School did not publish a yearbook — rather, in its place was a quarterly publication, entirely written and published by CHS students — and this was *The Howler*. This is more of a genealogical treasure trove than even a yearbook. There are pictures of students with full descriptions of what their interests, their achievements, their hopes and dreams etc. might be. There are original poems, cartoons, jokes written about themselves, and articles all written by the CHS students.

Ed Copeland was an All-Around American boy of that era — and he was the business manager of *The Howler* in his Junior and Senior years. He went out to Carrollton businesses to

Copeland's Supermarket

sell ads for the purpose of getting money to publish this quarterly. The CHS students subscribed to *The Howler* and kept up with all the happenings of the students there. If you find these old *Howlers* in attic trunks of your ancestors — don't toss them away! They are wonderful sources for genealogical research.

Ed Copeland was the President of his Junior and Senior classes at CHS and was the Captain of the Basketball team in 1928 year as well. He was selected "Best Sport" and "Boy with the Best Personality" by his classmates — and these qualities are still "shining through!" Ed continued his education at Emory University where he was a member of SAE — the social fraternity. Ed Copeland continued in leadership positions in civic affairs of the community throughout his life and was elected the fourth President of the Jaycees in 1942-43.

Ed was a charter member of the Sunset Hills Country Club and also is the last surviving charter member of the Moose Club in Carrollton (there were only six original members who organized the Moose Club). Ed says he has been a member of the First United Methodist Church since he was a "Crib Baby" in 1910. His wonderful sense of humor is sprinkled throughout the series of articles that he wrote — and these are printed here in their entirety — just as written by Ed Copeland himself in 1983. Ed enjoyed a thriving grocery business in Carrollton until his retirement in 1975. You can take a wonderful trip to the "olden days of grocery shopping" as experienced by our ancestors — and as remembered by Carrollton's own J. Edwin Copeland — still just as dynamic a personality as he was nearly a century ago!

Preface by Jan Robinson Bell

"Several Barrels of Flour Was no Unusual Purchase in 1930's"

First of a Series, "The *Daily Times-Georgian*", January 11, 1983

By J. Edwin Copeland

Gloom and doom seemed to be everywhere. Bread lines were forming and the dolers were doling but were short of funds. It seemed the economy was diving into a bottomless pit. The economic condition of the country was getting worse day by day and bankruptcies were increasing. It was the onset of the Great Depression and it was against this background that I started working in the food business. Jobs were hard to find but I was lucky. Through family connections, I got a job in the wholesale grocery business. In the fall of 1931, I took a job with C.M. Tanner Wholesale Grocery Company. They were the largest and oldest jobbers (wholesalers) in west Georgia, distributing groceries over a wide area since the business was founded in the early 1890's.

Their salesmen covered an area from Cedartown on the north, to Franklin on the south, to Austell on the east, and west to Heflin, Alabama. The sales had pioneered from "horse and buggy days" to the "Model-T" car. Travel was slow in those days, as the roads were not yet paved and on rainy days, sometimes cars would get stuck in the mud on the slick red hills of Georgia. Sometimes they would slide into a ditch and had to get a farmer with a pair of mules or oxen to pull them out. The salesman's day was long — he usually did not get home until late at night so he would go by the warehouse about 6 in the morning to turn in his orders.

When I first started working my main job was as shipping clerk. In those days, salesmen made a memorandum of the customer's orders on a sales pad and it was my job to write up the order on an invoice sheet and fill in the prices. Also, to get the truck loaded for delivery of orders to the retail grocery store.

In the "olden days" as they usually are referred to now, grocery stores carried items that are now obsolete or rarely ever seen. For example, before rural electrification, people used kerosene lamps to light their homes. They also had to buy lamp chimneys, lamp burners, lamp wicks, and kerosene.

Most cooking was done on a wood stove. Homemakers baked their own biscuits, bread, cakes and pastries and therefore used a lot of flour, sugar and pure lard. The grocer stocked these items in sizes seldom seen now — 48 and 96-pound sacks of flour, 100-pound sacks of sugar, and 50 pound cans of pure lard. These items were stocked in large quantities for they were staple items.

Large farm families would buy several barrels of flour at a time (a barrel of flour was 196 pounds or four 48-pound sacks.) Since so much flour was consumed, wholesalers had to stock large quantities. We received flour in railcars, called carload lots. A carload consisted of 40,000 pounds and up. Since I had to help unload these railcars, it seemed like we were getting a car in every few days.

All warehouse employees had to help unload the railcars during their spare time. Sometimes, several cars came in at once and we would hire extra people to help unload a car and if you went overtime, you had to pay "demurrage" — a penalty for each day overtime.

Besides flour, all heavy staple items were shipped by railroad cars such as roofing, barbed wire, poultry wire, fencing, sugar, lard, soap and soap powders so called because detergents were not compounded then. We sold lots of stock feeds and received carloads of hay, oats, sweet feeds cotton seed meal, corn, and beet pulp. These and many other items, too numerous to mention, were shipped by rail because motor carriers as such were not operating then.

Lighter merchandise was shipped to us on a drop shipment basis — that is, shipped to the local depot and we had to pick it up and bring it to the warehouse. The same policy applied to drop shipments as to railcars — we had a limited time to pick the merchandise up and being late again required paying demurrage.

Drop-shipped items included cigarettes, chewing tobacco, snuff, candy, chewing gum, shoe polish, school supplies, tea and coffee. At times it fell my lot of "clean out the depot" as we called it.

I mentioned that in my early work days we called them "olden days" — but we also referred to them "horse and buggy days." There were still lots of mules, buggies and wagons and very few cars. Horses and mules were afraid of cars and trucks back then. When you met a horse and buggy or a mule team hitched to a wagon on a country road, you had to slow down to a creep or stop completely or the animals wound run away!

It was before the gasoline tractor became popular and most farmers still plowed their fields with a mule. Therefore, the wholesale grocery store carried an inventory of items to sell to the country grocery — plowstocks, scooter plows, bolts and horseshoes. We sold lots of these popular items.

As the depression continued, business declined and merchants reduced their work force more and more. Our business was no different from the others. At one time, we were down to about seven employees and our usual work force was two or three times that many. This was before C.M. Tanner retired and he was still running the business. Our other employees were: Miss Luna Cook, bookkeeper and office manager, George Copeland and Percy Smith, traveling salesmen, and stockmen and deliverymen, Matt Phillips, John Lambert, and myself. In addition to shipping clerk, I was also given extra duties of warehouse manager and city salesman.

Being city salesman meant that after I had the trucks loaded with the traveling salesmen's order, I would call on town merchants and get their orders. Then I would come back to the warehouse, invoice and load a truck with the orders and most of the time, deliver them myself. Someone later asked me how I did all this in one day. My reply was that we had long work days — 12 to 15 hours. I'd go to work at 6 a.m. and lots of nights would get home around 8 or 9 p.m. This was long before the Wage and Hour Law.

Perhaps some of you will remember the following merchants in Carrollton during the 1930's: Cartwright Grocery, J.M. Harman, A.M. Thompson, W.F. Parker, A.T. Jackson Feed Store, M.W. Lovvorn's Shoe Shop, Ralph Turner's Fruit stand, Carrollton Hardware Company, Ogletree's Grocery, Jones Drug Store, Johnson Drug Company, Robinson and Walker General Merchandise, Fishers 5 & 10, Cecil Rutherford's Grocery, Hammond Grocery, Oaklawn Tourist Court, W.L. Smith Grocery, Banfords, Brooks and A.W. Alexander.

"Country Pulls Out of Depression, Economy Looks Up"

Second of a Series, "The *Daily Times-Georgian*", January 12, 1983

By J. Edwin Copeland

As the months passed, the depression continued to slow down business. This gave Mr. C.M. Tanner the opportunity to go to Daytona Beach for a week or two at a time. He had a second home there and it gave him a chance to get away from a busy schedule to rest and relax. He left "Miss Luna" as she was affectionately called by her fellow workers and friends, in charge of the front office and I was in charge of the shipping department and warehouse. And, of course, the salesmen kept the orders coming in.

This was a wonderful experience for me because it gave me the opportunity to deal with some of the largest food manufacturers and processors in the country — such companies as General Foods, General Mills, Standard Brands, Proctor and Gamble, Colgate-Palmolive-Peet, Hershey Candy Company, Coca-Cola Company, and many many more.

Many large companies that didn't have their own representative to call on us directly would operate through Food Brokers, as they were called. These Food Brokers would have their specialty salesmen call on us who brought sample bags loaded with a wide assortment of foods since they represented several manufacturers. They had samples of new food items they were introducing which they hoped you'd buy and place an order. Or, maybe you'd try the sample later and give them an order on the next trip around.

During this period of time in the wholesale grocery business there was a facet of food merchandising that I think, looking back on it now, was interesting. It was before the time of mass media and TV advertising and the large food companies had what we called "missionary Salesmen." These were special salesmen sent by the manufacturer to wholesale companies and his mission was to travel a week with the wholesaler's salesmen to promote a regular item to increase volume, or to introduce a new product. The "missionary" spent a week because each jobber's territory was so arranged as to take a week to cover it.

After the missionary had been with all the salesmen, he would total up the orders he had received from the retailers. The wholesaler would place the order to cover all the orders taken plus some extra of his stock to take care of re-orders. This arrangement was beneficial to the manufacturer and wholesaler alike. The manufacturer got his promotional and advertising work done and the wholesaler got extra business because an extra salesman was working for him.

During this period, Mr. Tanner was spending more time in Florida. He wanted to get onto a semi-retirement basis and decided to bring in his second son, John W. Tanner, Sr., (who was working in Florida) back to Carrollton to manage the company. This was a good move, for it gave Mr. C.M. Tanner more time to travel and relax, and it gave the company a full time manager.

John Tanner, Sr. ran the company with the same conservative policy that his father had, and it continued to show an extra good growth rate. The economy was gradually pulling out of the depression and John initiated new ideas and made improvements that increased sales and profit. The capital improvements he made were long-lasting benefits to the company.

I might note here that the company is now run by a third generation Tanner, the grandson of the founder, John W. Tanner, Jr. As president and chief executive officer, he is carrying on the same conservative administrative policies as his father and grandfather, and the company is continuing to show an extra good growth rate.

The years 1932 and 1933 were eventful years in our nation's history. In 1932, the nation's economy was at its lowest ebb. I believe it was in June 1932 that the depression hit bottom and it seemed a turn around was nowhere in sight. Then, in the fall, Franklin D. Roosevelt was elected President and was inaugurated in January 1933.

As soon as Roosevelt took office, he set into motion reforms that got the country on the road to recovery. He introduced in Congress legislation that set up reforms such as the PWA, CCC, RFC, and NRA. Some were stop-gap measures that lasted only a few years, but others, like REA are still active today.

Millions reaped benefits from the Rural Electrification Administration. The National Recovery Act was immediately helpful to workers during this period, many of whom were paid low wages. The act set the minimum salary at $13.75 per week and this raised the pay of millions and put millions of dollars into circulation. I know I liked it and it gave me a nice raise. Soil Conservation was another program that has had lasting benefits.

With the economy improving and our business increasing, John Tanner, Sr. and I started making plans to open a retail food store. The more we discussed the idea of entering the retail food business, the more excited we became over the prospects. We even discussed starting a small chain of retail grocery stores. The plan was to open a store in Carrollton, and also in the neighboring towns of Villa Rica, Bremen, Bowdon, and Newnan.

We opened a store in Carrollton and another in Villa Rica, but because of a number of events, the chain store idea was later dropped. For several weeks before the Carrollton store was to open, we thought we had a manager spotted to run the store. About a week before the "Grand Opening", he decided against taking the job — and John asked me to manage the store. At first, I was undecided but since a nice raise in salary came with the offer — and I was newly married and needed more money — I accepted the job. I thought I would be there a year at the most but it was a job that would last 19 years.

"Home Grocery Delivery in 1935 — Dial "5" and Charge it "

Third of a Series, "The *Daily Times-Georgian*", January 13, 1983

By J. Edwin Copeland

Tanner Wholesale Grocery Company had made the decision to open a retail food store in Carrollton and I accepted the job as manager. The retail grocery store then was much different than the large modern self-service stores of today. Now, stores have open-faced self-service display cases, tables and counters, with top side displayed foods. Back then, stores had closed glass display cases, arranged in different parts of the store, and wall shelving with a long counter in front. The clerk stood behind the counter and placed groceries on it as the customer called out his list.

It was necessary to have lots of top counter space because each customer had to have room to place his or her order. The cash register wasn't the adding machine type. It only registered the total sale so the clerk would then total it and ring that amount on the cash register. The paper sack containing the prices was packed with the customer's order so it could be checked at home. This was for cash sales only. Charge sales were listed on a sales pad.

We spent extra time and money to build a nice, up-to-date store — and for those days, it was just that. We bought modern fixtures and had equipment store planners arrange the layout. Now — what to name the store? Farm products in those days were a large part of a grocery store's business and we would be buying from farmers. We wanted to encourage them to bring their products to us and trade them for groceries. We decided to use the name "Carroll Trading Company" and the Grand Opening was held on June 14-15th 1935.

We bought lots of country eggs and country butter. Eggs were loose and counted out and placed in paper bags — no cartons back then. Country butter was molded in half pound and pound cakes and wrapped in plain butter paper. Margarine — oleo as some called it — was introduced about this time. We bought eggs and butter on the "barter system" — that is, they were traded for groceries.

Another interesting thing about the grocery stores of the 1930's and 40's was lots of customers charged groceries and also had them delivered. Our business was divided — about 65% was charged and 35% cash. We had a special section of the store set up for phone orders. Our phone number was 5. Several years later as business increased, we added another phone. Guess what the phone number was? It was 6. We had two easy to remember phone numbers — 5 and 6!

Our first delivery service was done by bicycle. We started with one bicycle and later added more. We bought our first delivery truck from Mr. Jim Webb, who was the International Truck Dealer for Carroll County. It was a new pick-up that cost us only $745. Our delivery service was very important. There were not many cars and a large number of our customers had their orders delivered.

Some customers would phone in their order and have it delivered; others would come to the store to shop and have their order delivered. There were some customers we seldom saw. They called their order in, we charged it, and delivered it, and sent them a statement at the end of the month. They mailed us a check. We did their shopping for them, so to speak.

The main part of the store was laid out for dry grocery items. We also had departments set up for produce and meats. The produce department had closed refrigerated display cases. This was very beneficial because it kept produce fresh for several days. Transportation was slower then, and truck deliveries were limited.

Our meat department had the latest refrigerated meat cases available. The display case was a long case with a glass window across the front to show the cuts of meat. The butcher served the customer from the back of the case, out of sliding doors. In addition, we had a large walk-in cooler for storing reserve meat cuts, and other cases for fish and poultry. John Fletcher was one of our early market managers and he was a top grade butcher who had many years of experience. He later founded Fletcher's Sausage Company.

Another employee who helped me in the early days of Carroll Trading Company was Carson Pritchard. He was real smart and a hard worker. We had been friends since boyhood days, grew up together, and worked together on several other ventures.

Still another employee who was much help to me was Donald Williamson. He was my assistant manager and was invaluable in the early days of Carroll Trading Company. Some of the other early employees were Elmer Kilgore, Kramer Broadnax, Clarence Vines, Bob Matherson, L.C. Harrison, Clyde Cartwright, Dudley Crosson, and Tommie Hubbard.

The grocery business back then consisted of hard work and long hours each day. We opened at 7 a.m. and closed at 8 p.m. through Thursday, stayed open until 9 p.m. on Friday, and on Saturday, stayed open until midnight or 1 a.m. Sunday. Carson Pritchard told me one Monday that he had his mother wake him up on Sunday at 6 a.m. I asked him why. "So I could have the pleasure of turning over and going back to sleep," he replied.

One of our market employees was a colorful old gentleman named Nath Astin. We called him our specialty salesman. He worked on the weekend selling fresh fish and poultry. He was one of those persons who seemed to know everybody in town and county. He had a strong booming voice that carried from our store on the corner of Newnan and Tanner Streets all the way to the square.

"Uncle Nath" would step out on our platform at the side of the building and shout, "Fresh Fish — come get 'em!" and come they did. His friends not only liked to buy his fish, they enjoyed his good human and salty stories. Nath said, "I'm a true Southern Democrat — ain't never been no farther north than Chattanoogee."

These were the days before World War II and things were still real cheap. Wages were low, but a dollar went a long way. We hired lots of high school boys and girls as clerks and the rate of pay was about $2 a day. Most of our business came on Friday afternoon and all day Saturday until midnight. We did as much business during this time as we did all the rest of the week.

The reason for this was most working people were paid either Friday night or Saturday night. Also, farmers worked all week and came to town on Saturday. The roads were not paved and they could not run into town in a few minutes like now. Many farm families also came to town in wagons, sometimes bringing farm products with them.

Prices were cheap for a number of reasons. Merchandise was plentiful. It was before the war inflated prices so much, and much food was sold in bulk, not in fancy packaging. Farmers with large families would buy their supplies in large quantities such as two or three barrels of flour (196 pounds to the barrel), 100-pound sacks of sugar, 50-pound cans of lard, 25 pounds of rice, and 10-15 pounds of coffee.

Farmers didn't get to town very often and another reason for stocking up was they bought their supplies when they sold some of their farm crops. Food remained relatively cheap during this time. Sugar, 5 cents a pound, coffee, 10-19 cents a pound, rice, 5 cents a pound, and streak o'lean, 7 cents a pound.

"War Years Bring Changes to Grocery Stores"

Fourth of a Series, "The *Daily Times-Georgian*", January 14, 1983

By J. Edwin Copeland

While I was running Carroll Trading Company, I had some odd experiences with my help. I remember one incident that happened on a busy afternoon. About the middle of the afternoon, when the store was full of customers, I noticed they were having to wait a long time for service. I noticed, also, that one of my male clerks was missing. I asked the other employees if they knew where he was and they didn't. About an hour later, he showed up.

I asked him where he had been and he said that he had gone home to take a bath. Shocked that he would leave his station at such a busy time of the day, I said, "Take a bath! If you don't hurry and get busy, you will have from now on in which to take a bath!"

Another incident was one not as serious and actually was just a prank. I had this boy who liked to play pranks on others. One day, he went next door to the Carrollton Building and Loan Association to use the phone to call our store. He asked to speak to a new boy who was very naïve. He gave the boy a grocery order and concluded by saying that his little son wanted a box of animal crackers but that he was afraid of lions. He asked the new clerk to please open the box and remove all the lions. The new clerk said that he would be glad to oblige. The prankster came back to the store and let the other clerks in on the joke. They took positions to watch the new boy fill the order. After he got the order together, he placed a piece of paper on the counter and emptied the box of animal crackers on it. He proceeded to pick out all the lions. Needless to say, all the other clerks stood by snickering. I never did know if they let the new boy in on the joke.

The war years brought on lots of changes in grocery stores and grocery shoppers. More and more foods were in short supply. After we entered the war, many foods were rationed. People who were accustomed to ordering their groceries and having them delivered found that if they didn't go to the store and shop that they wouldn't get some of the foods they needed. Many staple foods that were scarce sold out early and if the shopper wasn't there, he was left out.

Rationed items were cooking oils and shortening, pure lard, and all kinds of sugar. Nonfood rationed items included shoes and gasoline. I remember on one vacation where my wife and I went out west — out of Gerogia — because gasoline was not rationed in that part of the country. We went to New Orleans and had no trouble in getting gas.

Cigarettes were not rationed but were in short supply. When we received our regular shipment, we divided them among our customers on an allotment basis. Another big change in the grocery business during the war years was the make-up of the grocery store. The trend was toward cash and carry stores. The old way of charging and delivering foods was giving way to shoppers going to the store, selecting their foods, paying cash, and getting foods cheaper. The supermarket was beginning to be the popular way to merchandise groceries. As years went by, larger and larger stores were being built.

In 1950, we decided to change our style of business and go to a semi-cash and carry store. The plan was to reduce our markup enough so that customers who paid cash and carried their groceries would save money. We would charge a small fee of 5 percent if the customer wanted the order charged and delivered. This plan amounted to a savings of about 20 percent to the cash customer.

We closed the store and changed the layout to conform with the self-service type system. We marked down prices to the lowest level to still have a small profit. We owned a plot of land behind the store. We graded the lot, leveled and resurfaced it for parking. When the lot was finished and the store remodeled, we were ready for the modern trend of doing business.

We did fairly well for a while but then began to notice two things happening. Some of our regular customers thought we should not charge them a 5 percent fee for charging and delivering their orders. This was a small charge and it cost us money in the long run to give the service. The average monthly account then was only around $20 and the fee amounted to only $1. It was a bargain — but it resulted in dissatisfied customers. The other problem concerned the parking lot. It was not large but ample for our needs. If people who parked in the lot came in and bought groceries, and stayed half an hour, the turnover would have been great. But that didn't happen. Instead, people parked in the lot and went to work nearby or went shopping around town. The Carroll Theater was across the street and some went to the show.

There had been some discussion about closing Carroll Trading Company as I had been wanting to go into business for myself. I approached John Tanner about buying the stock of goods and fixtures. I would use them as a nucleus to start a store of my own. This was all right with John, so we made a deal.

The next move was to select a location. I knew that Hugh Richards had purchased a nice tract of land at the intersection of Newnan Road and West Avenue. About this time I ran into him at the bank and asked him about constructing me a building on this lot. He told me to draw up the plans like I wanted and he would build the store. I got busy on the layout and in a few days took him a rough draft of the store. He got his engineers to put my plans on blueprint and then started to work on the building. It was in January 1954 when I first approached Hugh and around the first of May 1954 that he had the building ready for use.

"Grocer Opens Independent Modern Supermarket"

Last of a Series, "The *Daily Times-Georgian*", January 15, 1983

By J. Edwin Copeland

During the time I was planning for a store of my own, I asked my brother, Perry, if he wanted to go into the retail grocery business. He had been traveling on the road as a manufacturer's representative for 20-odd years. He said he was tired of being on the road so much and accepted the offer. We set up a partnership business and called it Copeland's Super Market. Since the store was going to be twice as large as Carroll Trading Company, we had to buy many more store fixtures and much more inventory. This we did and had it all in place and ready for our Grand Opening on May 19, 1954.

After a very successful opening sale that ran for several weeks, our sales volume settled to a normal pace. Our business grew steadily for about five years as we were the only supermarket around. About five years after we opened, A&P opened a supermarket up the street from us on the corner of Newnan and White. It affected our sales for a few weeks, but we were soon on track again.

We wanted a nice up-to-date produce department so we bought modern refrigerated, open face display cases for staple vegetables such as potatoes, onions, turnips, etc. There were display cases for fresh fruit. Back then, most produce items were displayed in bulk — a few things were packaged — and the clerk waited on customers and weighed produce for them.

We tried to keep fresh good quality produce. We sent our truck to the Farmer's Market two or three times a week. The Atlanta Farmer's Market is a very interesting place. If one has never been there, it would be worth the trip just to go and ride around the market to see all of the activity. During the harvest season, farmers bring in their produce, rent a space called a stall, display their wares and sell to all comers, mainly independent grocers and chain store buyers. It is a very fast business as the merchandise is perishable and must be sold quickly.

I had two very capable produce managers — first Cecil Bohannon, and then Donald Williamson. They did a fine job of keeping the produce fresh and well displayed, were accommodating to the customers, and well liked by all. Another employee who worked during the 60's was Joe McGinnis. He was store manager and brought many fresh ideas and suggestions that were good for the business.

There were many changes in the style of merchandising in many types of businesses during the 1950's, 60's, and 70's — but I don't believe any changed as much as they did in the grocery business. In medium to large size supermarkets, the trend has been to go to self-service, especially in the grocery and market departments and recently in produce departments. However, all through the years we elected to stay with customer service except in the grocery department.

We did have an open-type self service meat display case in which to sell pre-packaged cold cuts and sausage items. All our fresh meats such as beef, pork, poultry, and fish were sold from closed display cases and served to the customer by the butcher. Most of our fresh meats were custom cut for the customer as they gave the order. (Remember pulley-bones?) Now, meat is sold from long rows of self service refrigerated meat cases.

And even the casual shopper has noted changes in the grocery department. Since there is a small mark-up, merchandise has to be turned over fast. Goods have to be attractively priced and displayed. In our business that required several part time stock boys, also carry-out boys to help the customer take the order to the car. We hired high school students to fill these jobs.

There have been vast changes in the grocery business during the last fifty years. Supermarkets of today are large, attractive store built with the shopper in mind. In the 1920's, and 1930's, the small corner grocery store was usually run by a husband and wife team called "Mom and Pop" stores, with sometimes the children helping out.

The modern supermarket is built with sanitation in mind. The building is a tight, air-conditioned structure that is practically free of dust. In the olden days, the wooden buildings with their wooden floors were dust collectors, and usually the doors and windows stayed open and let in more dust and dirt.

One of the greatest improvements in the distribution of food is the enormous progress made in the length of time stores can keep perishable foods. While we had refrigeration in the 1930's, this equipment was very crude in comparison with today's modern equipment.

You don't see brown paper bags in grocery stores now except in the cash and carry size. Years ago, that was all you did see since everything was packed in a brown paper bag. Prepackaged groceries are an amazing improvement.

Fast, automatic checkouts is another area of great progress. You would have had to be a checker in the old style store to really appreciate the modern automatic checkout. The old way was a back breaking chore, and very slow. The checker had to lean over the counter, get each item out of the cart, then ring it up. The old cash registers were not computerized and they did not multiply duplicated items. They did not give the amount of change the customer was to receive and they did not do half the work of the modern register.

Parking is much much better today. Most grocery stores used to be on a busy street or in the middle of a block on a busy street. Of course, most independent grocers charged and delivered so they did not have to depend on parking like the cash and carry stores. One of the first considerations for a location now is to be sure there is plenty of parking spaces.

One thing that has improved the food distribution business is the fast transportation that is available today. Decades ago, transportation was not only slow but very limited. Expressways are a big improvement and trucks are faster, larger and refrigerated so they can transport highly perishable foods long distances. I remember when we had fresh fish only on the weekend and then it was shipped packed in ice on non-refrigerated trucks. Friday was fish day for those families that enjoyed seafood — and now it's available every day.

When I think back about how long I was in the grocery business, I reflect on the hard work, long days, good times, and the bad times. Then I think about how lucky I was for I met so many nice people and had so many good customers. Then too, I think about how lucky I was in another way. When I retired in 1975, I had worked all the time for 45 years and I never did have to go out and look for a job. *Submitted by: J. Edwin Copeland, 530 Newnan Street, Carrollton, GA 30117 and Written by: J. Edwin Copeland*

65. Payton's Café

In 1926 William Walter Payton of Glenloch in Heard County gave to his son, Rufus Lee Payton, some land on which Rufus chose to plant cotton. After selling his cotton, he used his money to join his dad in starting a restaurant called "Payton's Café" on Bradley Street as shown in the photo. Two years later his brother, Winton Elvis Payton, given the same opportunity, used his "cotton money" to purchase his dad's share of the restaurant. Shown in the photo are Rufus and Elvis Payton with R.J. (Rip) Bonner in background.

Payton's Café on Bradley Street

Payton's Café remained on Bradley Street until the middle 1940s when it was moved to Newnan Street across from the First Methodist Church. The final location of Payton's Café was on the square in the Arcade building that had once been a movie theater. Payton's was always a popular gathering place in Carrollton to visit with friends and enjoy their good food. *Submitted by: Chip Payton, 505 Cedar Street, Carrollton, GA*
Source: Personal knowledge

66. Roopville Post Office

The area Post Offices had been located in the nearby communities of Needmore, Glenloch, Lineville, Lowell, Lurel Hill, and Laddsboro. In 1882 Roopville had a Post Office and Thomas M. Roop became Post Master, this was about three years before the community was officially named Roopville. At different times the Post Office was located in the Guthrie Shoe Shop, the Pentecost and Steed store, and the Mercantile Store.

Odus (Odie) Garrett delivering mail, 1904

Rural free delivery began in 1941. Some of the early mail carries were Odus O. Garrett, Henry Alexander, J.B. Merrell, Jack & Genevia Towns. Rural free delivery helped to put Roopville on the map. There were three routes to serve the area that would be one route later when roads and cars improved. The carriers struggled to find vehicles, whether horse drawn or motorized, that could take them over the country roads. The building known as the Roopville Bank served as the Post Office from 1925 to May 1, 1987. At that time the Post Office moved into a new building at 27 Old Franklin Street.

The following list of Post Masters may not be complete: Thomas M. Roop, James M. Alexander, David F. Pearce, John T. Veal, Uriel B. Pollard, George Ed Penecost, William Arthur Garrett, James Story, Margaret Hays, Eiler Mae Bates, Larry Atkinson, and currently Willard Burk. Early Post Masters were paid on a fee system. The fees received reflected the towns growth. Payment in 1883 was $10.37; in 1901 it was $139. *Submitted by: Rebecca Merrell, 124 Old Franklin Street, Roopville, GA 30170*
Sources: *My Small-Town Home Town Roopville, Georgia,* by Willis Huff, The Story of Carroll County by Her People, interviews.

67. Southeastern Motor Lines and Carroll County

Before the advent of the automobile, Carrollton and Carroll County were isolated from the rest of the world. Atlanta, the Capital, was a day or so away by horseback or buggy. The railroad ran north and south, connecting Chattanooga and Griffin, carrying one daily schedule each way, but other cities were inaccessible until the automobile came on the scene. Since farming was decreasing, cotton related industries were being established where the cotton was raised. Some type of public transportation was needed.

By the time of the 1929 depression, transportation was available between the smaller communities and industrial Atlanta, but it was a hit or miss proposition with different automobile operators being given state franchises to drive passengers to and from the city. In Carrollton, there was no bus station, and passengers were picked up on the town square, or along side the road on the way out of town.

The development of an integrated company, Southeastern Motor Lines, began when M.C. Roop, a Carroll County native, returned home after having been in the automobile business in another state. He purchased individual franchises from owners between Bowdon and Atlanta, and began to develop vehicles equipped to carry more passengers, beginning with a home made body on a truck chassis, then graduating to school bus type vehicles. He built a garage at the corner of Alabama Street and North Cliff Street, and later an impressive bus terminal building, where the company was headquartered until its termination.

It was during this beginning period that commuter traffic between the small western communities along Highway 78 grew, and Southeastern Motor Lines developed a strong allegiance from its many regular riders despite its inconvenient small buses and slower schedules. Loyalty developed between passengers and the regular drivers, and the passengers were allowed to embark along the side of the highway rather than to be required to go to a bus station.

In the meantime a route between Newnan and Griffin was acquired, and a line then began from Carrollton to Griffin, Georgia. By purchase of an additional franchise, a separate line was opened from Rome to Jasper, Georgia. Also, the line became interstate by extending service from Bowdon across the Alabama line to Heflin, which in effect provided service from Atlanta to that Alabama city.

During the war years the business expanded greatly with the shortage of gasoline, tires and automobiles, and the need for commuter services grew. Special runs were made to Bell Aircraft plant in Marietta, Georgia, and service was heavy between Carrollton and the larger communities, including for a time, service from Bowdon to La Grange.

Bus Terminal Southeastern Motor Lines

Eventually, in the late forties and early fifties, Southeastern Motor Lines expanded for a time to a service from Griffin, Georgia to La Grange and from Villa Rica to Cartersville and from Dalton, Georgia, to Cleveland, Tennessee, Dalton to Chatsworth and to La Fayette, Georgia. Other routes were attempted in conjunction with other companies, even from Chattanooga to Tallahassee, but most of these routes were unsuccessful, and as bus service demands were ever decreasing, other bus companies absorbed most of the routes, eventually leaving the company with only its one line to Atlanta.

In 1975, a move was made by other companies to eliminate all intrastate routes, and Southeastern Motor Lines was offered for sale. There were no takers so the franchise was abandoned.

Today, Carrollton and Carroll County are back in the same position they were before 1930, in that the public can only move from this area to another by the individual efforts of the citizens. It is fortunate that the automobile has replaced the horse and buggy as public transport in most of Carroll County lived and died with Southeastern Motor Lines. *Submitted by: Reuben M. Word, Carrollton, GA and Picture supplied by: Helen R. Foster*

68. Southwire Company

When Roy Richards, Sr. founded a wire and cable manufacturing business to help bring electricity to rural Carroll County, he had a particular customer in mind.

Fresh out of the U.S. Army, Richards sought to run power lines to his grandmother's home. Getting the lines there was no problem. Richards owned a construction company that erected poles and ran wire for utilities. At the same time, funding from the U.S. Rural Electrification Administration (REA) was bringing the promise and convenience of electricity to much of the South.

Roy Richards Sr.

The trouble was finding enough wire to carry current to rural areas. During a conversation with a wire manufacturer, Richards learned that it would be three years before the company could deliver wire to West Georgia. A company representative asked why Richards was in such a hurry, joking that farms in the area had operated for hundreds of years without power.

Richard's stern reply brought his vision into clear focus. "My grandmother is 85 years old, and she has never had the pleasure of sitting under an electric light in her own house," he told the manufacturer. "She's seen it two times she's been to Atlanta, but she's never had it."

That pivotal moment marks the start of Southwire Company, which has grown into one of the world's leading wire and cable manufacturers.

Southwire's roots extend to 1937, when Richards, then a young 25-year-old, started a company to erect power poles. Two years earlier, he had graduated from Georgia Tech. While the promise of jobs paying $80 a month lured 90 percent of his classmates to New York, Richards chose to stay in Carroll County, a commitment he kept even after Southwire grew into a leading player in the wire and cable industry.

During its first two and a half years, Richards and Associates strung 3,500 miles of cable, becoming the second-largest REA contractor. As World War II halted all REA construction, Richards joined the U.S. Army, eventually reaching the rank of captain.

Richards returned home to find that power poles put up by his company often stood wireless for months because of post-war shortages in wire. Seeing that a market existed, he decided the only way to ensure a steady supply of wire was to make it himself.

On March 23, 1950, Southwire Company started cranking out wire with 12 employees and second-hand machinery. Two years later, the company had shipped 5 million pounds of wire and had doubled its plant size.

Early Scene of Machine Operator at Southwire

But the process used in those days to make wire kept production at a dragging pace. Electrical wire was made by welding lengths of aluminum rod end-to-end. The brittle welds often broke in the process, causing production delays.

Frustrated by the inefficiency of traditional wire making, Richards sought a faster way to produce electrical wire of higher quality. He learned of an Italian industrialist named Illario Properzi, who developed a method of continuously casting and rolling rod.

The process had only been used for commercial-grade lead and zinc wire used in fences and baling wire. Properzi tried feverishly to convince Richards that it would not work with smaller electrical wire. Not to be deterred, Richards persuaded Properzi to sell him one of his machines and a team of Southwire engineers adapted the process to produce aluminum and copper rod.

Today, half of the copper rod for electrical wire and cable is made using Southwire's patented Southwire Continuous Rod (SCR) method.

The technology catapulted Southwire to the forefront of the industry. The company began selling SCR systems and wire and cable products around the world. In the eight years starting in 1967, Southwire opened six manufacturing plants, an aluminum smelter and a copper refinery. The company now had operations in Carrollton; Hawesville, Ky.; Osceola, Ark.; and Flora, Ill.

Southwire's Current Corporate Headquarters

In 1968, Southwire engineers created aluminum alloy building wire products with the development of TRIPLE E aluminum alloy. Seven years later, Southwire Machinery Division was founded to produce SCR system components, wire-making equipment and other machinery.

Southwire saw a change in leadership in 1985, when Richards died of bone cancer at the age of 73. Roy Richards, Jr., who had worked in Southwire plants since he was 10 years old, eventually became chairman and chief executive officer. Under a second generation of Richards, Southwire has concentrated on its core business of wire and cable manufacturing.

In 1987, Southwire opened a building wire and utility cable plant in West Jordan, Utah. Two years later, the company purchased Southwire Company Starkville Plant, a utility cable and building wire plant in Starkville, Miss.

Named for D.B. "Pete" Cofer, Southwire's first chief engineer, the D.B. Cofer Technology Center opened in 1992, providing a home for ongoing development in wire and cable design, metallurgy, and plastics compounding. The center provides scientists and engineers state-of-the-art facilities for research, improvement of manufacturing processes and product testing.

Forte Power Systems, in Heflin, Al., started production of medium and high-voltage utility cables in 1996. A year later, Southwire entered the voice and data communications cables market with the opening of Cyber Technologies in Peachtree City, Ga. Expanding into Mexico, the company opened Southwire Americana De Mexico, a building wire plant in 1998.

As the 20th Century came to a close, Southwire pioneered work in the development of the next generation of power lines - superconducting power cables. Together with Oak Ridge National Laboratory, the U.S. Department of Energy and a list of industrial partners, Southwire developed superconductor power cable technology and threw the switch on the first real-world application of superconductors on Feb. 18, 2000.

Nearly immune to resistance, superconductors carry three to five times the load of traditional cables, providing more power to urban areas with no new right of way for the construction of extra lines to serve a growing demand for electricity.

Fresh into a new century, Southwire hired Stuart Thorn in January 2001 as president responsible for all company operations. Roy Richards, Jr. remains chairman and chief executive officer of the company, which enjoys annual sales of $1.5 billion.

More than 50 years ago, Southwire was founded to help bring electricity to rural Georgia. Today, it supplies 135 of the nation's top power companies, plus dozens of utility companies abroad and is pioneering new technology to better serve all of its wire and cable customers. Nearly a fifth of all homes in the United States contain Southwire's building wire products.

"I believe in doing what one man can," Richards once said.

With a team of talented engineers and dedicated employees that continues to provide the best products and service in the industry, he has accomplished the works of thousands. *Submitted by: Southwire Company, One Southwire Drive, Carrollton, GA 30119*

69. Tanner Medical Center

During the first half of the 20th Century, Carroll County's medical needs were served only by a series of small clinics. C.M. Tanner, a Carrollton wholesale grocer, saw the necessity for a comprehensive hospital. In 1943, he pledged the first $75,000 toward building a $100,000 hospital and challenged the community to raise the remaining $25,000.

However, due to rationing and material shortages during World War II, hospital planning was delayed until 1946. Congress passed the Hill-Burton Act in 1946, which provided government funds to help rural communities build hospitals. Through promotion by Judge Bob Tisinger and hospital chairman Roy Richards, Carrollton became the first community in the state to be approved for Hill-Burton funding.

Movie actress Susan Hayward, center, breaks ground for a 1961 Tanner Memorial Hospital addition. Pictured with the actress are Bob Tisinger, left, Tanner board member, and Bill Warren, hospital administrator.

Tanner Memorial Hospital, named for Lydia and Mary Tanner, C.M. Tanner's wife and mother, officially opened its doors on Sunday, Oct. 30, 1949 in a public ceremony attended by hundreds of local citizens.

In 1961, a 26-bed addition was built after a fundraising drive led by Hollywood actress and Carrollton resident Susan Hayward. Overcrowding necessitated a second addition in 1965, which brought the hospital up to 119 beds.

In 1976, a major $7 million project added the Y-shaped west wing which now houses the 1-West and 2-West patient floors. A $14.1 million addition in 1985 added the 90,000 square foot, five-story east wing. After this construction, the original 1949 building and the 1960s additions were demolished. The name was also changed to Tanner Medical Center to reflect the facility's expanding role in medical care.

Over the years, several new services and locations have opened.

Tanner Women's Center opened in 1987 to provide services for women in a private, relaxed, homelike atmosphere. The Women's Center provides mammography, ultrasound, osteoporosis screening and educational programs designed especially for women.

The Tanner Radiation Center opened in 1987 to provide radiation cancer therapy. It was renamed Tanner Cancer Center in 1997 with the addition of full-time chemotherapy services.

In 1996, a $4.5 million renovation program began which created a new laboratory, expanded the Short Stay Unit and added a new patient registration area.

Tanner Home Health and Hospice Care became part of the Tanner organization in 1999. In the same year, a $2.7 renovation of the Maternity Center was completed. This project added six new birthing rooms, with adjacent family waiting areas; expanded the nursery and created new nursing stations.

Tanner celebrated its 50th birthday on Sunday, Nov. 7, 1999, with a gala event which was highlighted by outdoor speaking ceremonies and the unveiling of a new history exhibit and video in the Short Stay lobby area.

Tanner Medical Center/Carrollton today is a 202-bed, acute care hospital, part of Tanner Health System, which also includes hospitals in Villa Rica and Bremen. *Submitted by: Winston Jones, Tanner Health System, Marketing/Public Relations Dept.*

70. Tanner Medical Center of Villa Rica

Tanner Medical Center/Villa Rica is a 53-bed general care facility located at 610 Dallas Highway, Villa Rica.

Considerable community effort went into the planning and building of the Villa Rica City Hospital, forerunner of Tanner Medical Center/Villa Rica. The hospital was built under the federal Hill-Burton Act which required that one-third of funding be raised locally. Stockholders of the old Community Hospital, now the site of Westside Baptist Church, voted to sell its building and donate the funds to the new hospital building fund. These initial funds were supplemented by donations from local citizens. In addition, the new City of Villa Rica Hospital Authority issued revenue certificates for $45,000. This amount was underwritten by the City of Villa Rica, but the hospital itself pledged to pay off the certificates as they came due. Through careful management and conservation, the hospital was able to meet the obligations without city assistance.

Villa Rica City Hospital opened in July, 1955 as a 25-bed unit with one private room. Only eight months after it was dedicated, the Hospital Authority began making plans for an expansion that would almost double the floor space. Funding was again granted with assistance from the state and the Hill-Burton Act. The hospital underwent additional expansions in 1967 and 1973 to meet the community's needs.

The Villa Rica City Hospital was built in 1955 with federal Hill-Burton funds. The name was changed to Tanner Medical Center/Villa Rica in 1985 when it was purchased by the Carroll City/County Hospital Authority.

Villa Rica City Hospital was purchased in 1985 by the Carroll City-County Hospital Authority, making it part of the Tanner system. The hospital's name was changed to Tanner Medical Center/Villa Rica.

An $800,000 renovation project in 1990 enlarged the size of the Emergency Department and added 24-hour emergency service with a physician always on duty. The project also centralized the nurses' station and isolated some areas from public access for more privacy. The hospital's appearance was revamped throughout with new wallcoverings, paint, carpeting and furniture.

A three-story, 56,000-square-foot medical office building opened in October, 1998 in the new Tanner Medical Park, located on a 10-acre tract adjacent to the hospital campus. In addition to medical offices and other health-related businesses, the building houses Tanner's Outpatient Surgery Center, Women's Center and Physical Therapy Center. *Submitted by: Winston Jones, Tanner Health Sysem, Marketing/Public Relations Dept.*

71. Temple Banking

Banking had its beginning in Temple when the Temple Banking Company opened in 1903 at the corner of West Johnson and Rome Streets. J. Frank Durrett was the first cashier. In 1913 the bank built a brick building at the corner of James and Sage Streets. Temple Pharmacy now occupies this building. The second bank in Temple, Farmers State Bank, opened in 1912 on Sage Street. These banks flourished, as did the entire town, when Temple was the center of a large and prosperous cotton market. However, as business slowed in the 1920's and approached the depression of the 30's, the banks were forced to close.

Sketch of Temple Banking Company building (1913) now occupied by Temple Pharmacy

Temple was without a bank until November 25, 1946, when R.B. Manning, D.C. Williams, C.R. Hart, J.H. Thomas, G.M. Burns, E.S. West and A.B. Crews chartered the Bank of Temple with $25,000 in capital. The bank opened for business in the Farmers State Bank Building on Sage Street where it remained for twenty-four years. The bank brought to Temple the chance to locally finance homes, businesses, crops, and automobiles in addition to other types of loans. C.R. Hart was the first President, with G.M. Burns, Vice President and R.B. Manning, Secretary. In 1949 Dave Williams was elected President. L.G. Lyell began his banking career on July 11, 1950, with the Bank of Temple as Cashier and served as Vice President. C.R. Hart was elected President on July 13, 1954, to replace Dave Williams who had retired. J.H. Thomas was elected President on December 1, 1964, upon the death of C.R. Hart. Mrs. C.R. Hart was elected as President on November 25, 1969. Mrs. Hart and L.G. Lyell retired on September 25, 1970, when C.A. Roush, Jr. purchased the majority of the bank stock. Raymond Burrell was elected President at that time. The bank moved from its store-front building on Sage Street to a modern brick building (its present location) in October, 1971, and it became known as The Bank of Carroll County. The building is at the corner of Sage and Carrollton Streets on the site of the old Fowler Warehouse.

Truett Spivey was elected as President on January 1, 1974, and served until December 15, 1975, when Tom Rankin was elected President. In 1984 the bank joined the CB&T Bancshares, Inc. family electing James A. Gill as the new President on August 29, 1984. On October 1, 1985, the bank name was changed to Citizens Bank and Trust of West Georgia.

In recent years Citizen Bank and Trust has experienced tremendous growth with ten offices located in two counties and seven cities.

Recently, ground has been broken at the corner of Highway 78 and Carrollton Street for a new building in Temple.

The First National Bank of Georgia opened a bank at 184 Carrollton Street, Temple, Georgia, in the fall of 2000. This bank has continuously operated in Haralson County since 1909. It was chartered as the Haralson County Bank and was located in Buchanan, Georgia. In 1928, the Farmers and Citizens Bank merged with the Haralson County Bank. In 1976, the bank became the First National Bank of Haralson County. In 1992, the Commercial Bank of Tallapoosa merged with the bank. The First National Bank of Georgia is now located in each of the four towns of Haralson County plus the new branch in Temple and continues to operate as a community bank with local ownership and local management. *Submitted by: Ruth Holder, P.O. Box 70, Temple, GA 30179*

Source: Information from banks; Holder, B.W. *A History of Temple, Georgia*. Thomasson Printing Company, Carrollton, Georgia, 1982.

72. Temple Post Offices

Before 1900 there were approximately eighty-four post offices in the county. Many of them sprang up where there was a store, grist mill, or gin, or voting place. These small communities often had colorful names, although they frequently took the name of the postmaster. Many of them were discontinued after a short time. The postmasters received their pay on a fee system which usually amounted to only a very small amount.

Early post offices near Temple were Buck Horn, established September 16, 1856, east of Temple with Joseph L. Hart as first postmaster and discontinued in 1857; Simsville, established July 20, 1876, south of Temple with George W. Autry as first postmaster and discontinued in 1883; Birtha, established January 28, 1897, with June Waddell as first postmaster and discontinued in 1898; Berlene, established February 16, 1898, north of Temple with James K. Haney as first postmaster and discontinued in 1898; Coraxi, established June 23, 1899, north of Temple with John C. Hicks as first postmaster and discontinued in 1900; Horace, established September 1, 1892, at Center Point with Charles W. Bonner as first postmaster and discontinued in 1902; and Lilac, established April 18, 1900, south of Temple with Elijah M. Yates as first postmaster and discontinued in 1902.

Rural Free Delivery of the early 1900's made the small post offices no longer needed. The rural mail routes were formed by prospective mail carriers mapping a route and getting the people to sign up for mail delivery.

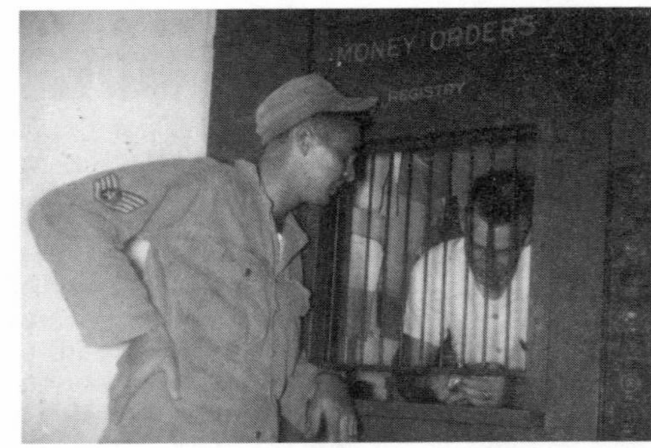

Postmaster Hugh Hudsputh and Donald Levans at Sage Street location.

The post office in Temple was established April 24, 1882, with James H. Allen serving as postmaster until October 15, 1887. From this date until about 1915 the following held the office: Richard L. Rowe (October 15, 1887), Miss Myrtie Craven (May 5, 1892), Van R. Davis (October 14, 1892), Thomas B. Griffin (June 17, 1893), and Walker M. Cobb (June 9, 1897). The post office was located on Sage Street in the building next to the Temple Pharmacy.

On January 22, 1915, Warner A. Entrekin was appointed postmaster. About this time the post office was moved to the building on the corner of James and Sage Streets. It remained there for approximately ten years before being moved to near the middle of the block on Sage Street.

From September 1, 1923, until the present date the following have held the position of postmaster or postmistress: Thomas E. Kirk (September 1, 1923), Maud E. Sewell (June 22, 1926), Morine Allgood McColister (February 27, 1931), Alvin B. Crews (April 15, 1942), William F. Lambert (August 4, 1949), Hugh W. Hudsputh (March 12, 1952), Johnny Muse (July 9, 1983), and John M. Frossard (September 3, 1998), until the present.

In 1959 the post office was moved into a new building built by Bill Steadham on Carrollton Street. On April 24, 1982, exactly 100 years from its beginning, the Temple Centennial Committee honored the post office with a huge birthday celebration. Featured speakers included Georgia Speaker of the House Tom Murphy and State Attorney General Michael Bowers. Representatives from the Atlanta District U.S. Post Office were present. Rick Palmer, postal service coordinator, presented a historical certificate to Postmaster Hugh Hudsputh. One hundred helium-filled balloons were released by the senior citizens of the town at the end of the ceremony. Replies were received from these Georgia cities: Duluth, Hull, Carlton, Dacula, Marietta, Powder Springs, and Roswell. One also came from Abbeville, South Carolina.

The present location of the post office is at 68 James Street. The building was built in May, 1991.

Rural Free Delivery was established in Temple February 1, 1902. In 1896 Senator Thomas E. Watson, a relative of James (Jimmy) F. Watson, Jr., a Temple rural carrier, pushed the bill through Congress to originate rural free deliveries. Today, there are seven rural routes serving 3561 deliveries and covering 380 miles daily. The post office also has 1300 post office boxes. *Submitted by: Ruth Holder, P.O. Box 70, Temple, GA 30179*

Sources: Holder, B.W. *A History of Temple, Georgia*, Thomasson Printing Company, Carrollton, Georgia, 1982; Post Office Records

Education

73. A & M School of Carrollton

The idea of the Agricultural and Mechanical Schools in Georgia originated with Governor Joseph M. Terrell in 1902. But the bill creating them was not passed until 1906. The citizens of Carrollton and Carroll County donated $39,000 with lights and water for ten years for the establishment of the Fourth District School. Of this amount, $9,000 was paid for 270 acres of land from B.A. Sharp that included the old Bonner plantation. The original Bonner House built in 1844 was moved several hundred yards east of its original location in 1913.

The first two buildings of the school were the boys dormitory and the academic building that were built by local contractors Mandeville and Aycock for $30,000. They erected the building at cost plus 1%. All furnishings for the buildings were supplied by the state at a cost of $1,500.

Each bedroom had a double bed, a combination dresser and a washstand, a study table, a washstand set, two straight chairs, a Hot Stuff Heater, and shades. The school opened January 8, 1908, with only the two unfinished buildings. Two classrooms were used temporarily as kitchen and dining room, and burlap and quilts were used in lieu of doors. One hundred and eight boys and forty girls enrolled the first day. Although snow and ice was everywhere that day, the water pipes frozen and only one cook, a luncheon was served for the student body, the eleven trustees of the school, and Governor Hoke Smith along with other prominent guests from Carrollton and the district.

The first faculty was composed of J.H. Melson, Principal; G.G. Daniel, Shop and Applied Agriculture; J.C. Britton, Science and Mathematics; Mrs. J.C. Britton, History and English; and Miss Leola K. Miller, Domestic Science. The first commencement was held in June 1909. The 1909 graduates were: Boyd Bishop, Mrs H.H. Boyd, W.H. Copeland, John Darden, Olney Meadows, Susie Nicholson, Eugene Spradlin, L.F. Stovall, and Wesley Veal.

Athletic competition began as early as February 9, 1908 with a baseball game against representatives from Carrollton High School. The

Academic Building October 1908

Early scene of student workers

boys acquired blue baseball uniforms trimmed in red, colors that had been adopted by the school. Football had its beginning in 1910 with Lander Lane as captain and student coach. O.K. David became the school's first experienced coach in 1913. They were first called the A&M Tigers but later were known as the Aggies.

McIntosh horse block cornerstone for Girls Dormitory 1916

With passing years the school grew and a larger faculty was employed. In 1915 the legislature appropriated $7,500 matching money for a girls dormitory. Judge Adamson was the single biggest contributor giving $1,500 and in 1916 the dorm was completed. Placed as the cornerstone with Masonic fanfare at the dedication ceremony was the old horse block of Chief William McIntosh from the McIntosh Reserve near Whitesburg. The landmark was moved to the school with permission from Preston Arkwright, President of Georgia Power Company, which owned the McIntosh land. Mr. Melson, Mr. Thomasson, and students Horace Shinn, Howell Robinson, and Lee Barr, along with a wagon hitched with Old Gray and Crap from the college moved the monument to the school. The monument has since been moved several times, but still stands at the State University of West Georgia. For many years its outline was used as the symbol for West Georgia College.

President Irvine S. Ingram

In 1919 Miss Martha Munro joined the faculty and in 1921 she became the bride of Dr. I.S. Ingram, who succeeded Mr. Melson as principal of the school in 1920. Miss Munro was the daughter of the Chairman of the State Board of Trustees that selected Carrollton as the site of the A & M School. Dr. Ingram served the school as principal till it closed in 1933 when the state withdrew support for the A&M School. The school then became a junior college under the name West Georgia College and in 1957 it became a senior college under President Irvine Sullivan Ingram. President Ingram served the school from 1920 to 1960, which was the longest administrative tenure in the history of the University System. *Submitted by: Dr. David Wiggins and photos courtesy of Mrs. Susan Hamersky, CA from the album of Nell Mandeville Henderson and Myron House, SUWG Special Collections.*

74. Black Schools of Carroll County 1939-1940

There were 23 black schools in the Carroll County School System in 1939-1940. Joe H. McGiboney was the County School Superintendent, while Mrs. Donetta Sanders was the supervisor for the black schools. The schools opened in mid October after the cotton-picking season was over.

The schools and their teachers were: Antioch, Leila Warren and Golden Thomas; Arnold, Lennie Wood; Bowdon, Mr. and Mrs. W.C. Hill; Bright Star, Bessie L. Hall and Jocelyn DeFoor, Fair Oak, Willie Lou Lester; Griffin's Chapel, Mary Alice Bailey; Hillside, Annie M. Cook; Mandeville, Lucy L. Bowen; McIntosh, Julie Simms and Corine Early; Mt. Airy, Clara Arnold; Mt. Olive, Robert Rhodan; Pate's Grove, Beatrice Parks Elliott; Pinetuckey, Grady North; Pineview, Mr. and Mrs. Hiram Bonner; Pleasant Grove, Jeannie Glanton; Poplar Springs, Rosa Mae Davie and Marjorie Lyle; Red Oak, Darthuba Arnold; Rock Spring, Annette Bowens; Rose Hill, Elivra Price Glass, Marie Mullins, and Martha Thomasson; Shady Dale, J.L. Wyatt and Earnestine E. Lee; Spence's Grove, Jessie Drummond; Temple, L.D. Spear, Donnie C. Wilson, Jessie B. Glissom, and Mattie Rice; Villa Rica, Lonnie Price, Minnie F. Harris, Mozelle D. Lee, Mrs. Agnes P. Smith Clarke, and Mrs. Thelma Vilato Carter. *Submitted by: Jack Dorsey, 228 S. Prospect Ave., Waco, GA 30182*

75. Bowdon College

William W. Fitts established a school in Bowdon about 1854 in "the old academy" on the west side of town. By 1855, he added another teacher, Charles McDaniel. Following Fitts' resignation, McDaniel teamed with John M. Richardson to open Bowdon Collegiate Institute. The Institute increased in numbers and McDaniel and Richardson were granted a charter by the Georgia legislature in 1857.

Encouraged by William T. Colquitt, who promised a tract of land and supported by the citizenry, a new two story building was erected. The downstairs contained three recitation rooms including a chapel, with three rooms for literary societies and a president's office.

When the Civil War began, students and volunteers formed a military company, commanded by McDaniel. As part of Cobb's Legion, they fought in key battles losing McDaniel at the Battle of Perryville in Kentucky.

After the 1866 legislature passed a law to aid veterans, Bowdon College reopened under the leadership of Richardson. The wooden building was replaced in 1901 by a large two story structure built exactly on the same spot. This structure included a laboratory, an auditorium, a museum and a music room in addition to classrooms.

Bowdon College's doors closed for a second time in 1915 following the drop in the price of cotton to five cents per pound and rendering patrons unable to pay the $3.50 per month. Following World War I, the citizens of Bowdon knew they would have to have an educational facility to meet the needs of the new industrial world. A charter was granted on August 12, 1919, creating Bowdon State Normal and Industrial College. The trustees donated the building and grounds to the state as a branch of the University of Georgia.

Early Postcard View of Bowdon College.

In 1933, when the Board of Regents voted to reorganize the University System of Georgia, West Georgia College in Carrollton consolidated Bowdon State Normal and Industrial College and the Fourth and Seventh District Agricultural and Mechanical Schools. Bowdon did not accept this decision easily and continued to operate under the 1857 charter until 1936 when the financial strain finally took its toll. Bowdon College closed and the trustees donated the property to the town.

Bowdon High School stands on this site today with the original bell and a historical marker denoting the College history. *Submitted by: Judy C. Rowell, 1472 Garrett Creek Road, Bowdon, GA 30108 and Photo courtesy David Wiggins*

76. Carroll County Schools 1918

A Call For School Restructuring

Mr. M.L. Duggan, Rural School Agent for Georgia, presented a preliminary report to the Carroll County Board of Education and the Citizens of the County. At the request of the Board of Education and the State Department of Education, Mr. Dugan was asked to make a careful survey of the schools of the county and make recommendations to the County Board, especially with reference to school districts. He found that within the county were eighty-eight schools, besides several private schools, and half a dozen county-line schools.

He concluded that there seems to have been no well-defined constructive policy of schools and that the entire system had become wholly inadequate to the educational demand of the children of the county. A strong and active central administration with a definite constructive policy and supported by a public sentiment willing to make many sacrifices in the interests of efficiency was the only remedy for the conditions. Georgia school law requires that each county shall be laid off into school districts of a minimum area of sixteen square miles with certain exceptions. It was his recommendation that the districts be reduced from 88 to 44 or less. "A little piece of ground, on which is a little house, in which is a little equipment, at which a little teacher, on a little salary, for a little while, is teaching little children little things, must no longer be the definition of our rural schools. When we come to realize that public interests and regard it as Big Business, then will our rural schools measure up to the demands of our children." The average value spent per child in Georgia in 1918 was $11 per child per year,

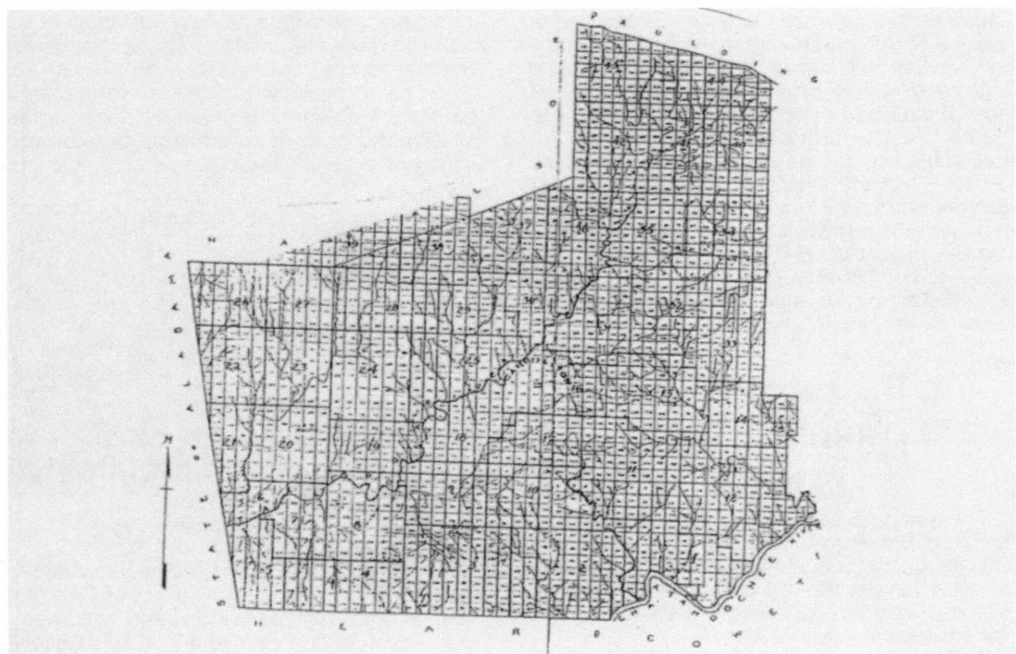

Proposed School District Map 1918

Bold Springs School 1918

which ranked Georgia 45th of the 48 states. The rural white schools of Carroll County spent an average of $7.50 per child for schoolhouses and equipment while the incorporated Carrollton City System was spending an average of $75 for schoolhouses and equipment per child. To accomplish this mission of restructuring would mean the closing of some schools in some districts and the building of new ones in other districts. The reduction of the 88 schools to 44 would increase efficiency and increase the amount of money spent on the children's education.

The preliminary report was submitted to a mass meeting of Carroll County citizens on May 8th, 1918 together with a map of the proposed new school districts. After a free discussion by the citizens, the Rev. W.W. Roop suggested that they adopt a resolution to endorse the report to the Board of Education. The plan was unanimously adopted. At a regular meeting of the Carroll County Board of Education on the same day, the map and school districts for the county were formally and legally adopted.

In 1918, the proposed districts and the schools that were located within the district were as follows: District #1 Rotherwood School, Shiloh School, #2 Lowell School, Liberty School, Star Point School, #3 Roopville School, #4 Veal School, Stony Point School, Belleview School, #5 Sardis School, Friendship School, #6 Midway School South, #7 Reavesville School, #8 Tyus School, Fairview School, Riverside School, #9 Bethesda School, Siver School, #10 Oak Ridge School, Rocky Mount School, #11 Whopping Creek School, Union School, Clem School, Center School, Westbrook School, Whitesburg High School, #12 Banning School, Lewis Chapel School, #13 New Watson, County Line School, #14 Little Bethel School, #15 Cross Plains School, Pleasant Hill School, Wayside School, #17 Stripling School, #18 Tallapoosa School, #19 Farmer's High School (a consolidation of Salem, Victory, and Antioch Schools), #20 Bowden High School, #21 Sandy Flat School, Melrose School, #22 Hill Crest School, Mount School, #23 Liberty Hill School, Indian Creek School, #24 White Oak Springs School, Burwell School, Sackville School, #25 Billow School, New Hope School, Beulah School, #26 High Point School, #27 Barge School, Kansas School, #28 Mt. Zion School, Maple Springs School, #29 Union Cross Roads School, Smyrna School, Bear Creek School, #30 Pine Grove School, #31 Midway (North) School, Shady Grove School, #32 Sand Hill School, Oak Ridge (East) School, #33 Hulett School, Little Vine School, #34 Boyd's School, Flat Rock School, #35 Hickory Level School, #36 Oak Grove School, Center Point School, Harmony Grove School, #37 Bold Spring School, Miller's School, #38 Bowden Junction School, Mandeville School, #39 Union Camp Ground, Pates School, #40 Villa Rica High School, #41 Pleasant Grove School, #42 Temple High School, Brooklyn School, Bethel School, #43 Mt. Carmel School, Taylor's School, #44 Wesley Chapel School, Union Grove School.

Not included in the district lists were the incorporated Carrollton City Schools but they were mentioned as being in #16. College Street School and Maple Street School of Carrollton were given as examples of quality schools. The end of the report encouraged the citizens of Carroll to impose a property tax for the education of their children at a county-wide local school tax of five mills, which was the rate levied by the communities of Carrollton, Temple, and Whitesburg for the benefit of their children. *Submitted by: Dr. David Wiggins; photos courtesy of Dr. Wilton Key and Judy Rowell*

Source: Report of Carroll County Schools 1918 by M.L. Dugan, June 20, 1918

Salem School 1914

77. Carroll County Schools

As the 25th largest school system in the State of Georgia, Carroll County Schools maintains the belief that its small community schools provide a personal approach that ultimately makes the difference. In this area where phenomenal growth is occurring, the school system has developed a ten-year comprehensive facility plan to continue the construction of state of the art facilities within the school communities. Quality learning environments support a refined curriculum and highly skilled teachers in order for every student to achieve success.

Approximately 13,000 students enrolled in Pre-Kindergarten through 12 grades attend five regular high schools, four middle schools, and ten elementary schools. Students within the West Georgia area may elect to attend the Open Campus High School, an evening high school designed to offer educational opportunities for those who desire to gain or extend required Carnegie units for graduation. The Carroll County Technical High School offers technical programs for all high school students in the system. The Crossroads Academy, the system's alternative school, is designed to help students get back on track. Additionally, the State University of West Georgia and the West Central Technical College offer dual enrollment programs to area high school students seeking post-secondary opportunities as they continue to fulfill graduation requirements.

"Putting Students First Through Quality and Excellence" is the mission of the Carroll County School System. **See photo at top of page 37.**

Submitted by: Dr. David Wiggins, Carroll County Schools, 164 Independence Drive, Carrollton, GA 30117, 770-832-3568

Sources: *Picture yourself in ... Carroll County, Georgia,* a publication of the Carroll County Chamber of Commerce and personal knowledge Carroll County School, 164 Independence Drive, Carrollton, GA 30117, 770-832-3568, www.carrollcountyschools.com

78. Carroll County Technical High School

The original name was the Carroll County Vocational High School. The school was acquired through the last Appalachian Grant

Carroll Co. Schools Administrative Team - 2001

issued to the State of Georgia through the efforts of former Superintendent Travis Edmondson and Assistant Superintendent W.S. Harman. The first administrator was Wendell Holmes and the original teaching staff was: Gary Lanier, Automotive; Barry Williams, Construction; Food Service, Allen Lawler, Jr.; Horticulture, Dr. James Garrison; Electro-Mechanics, Frank Foster; Health Occupations, Gerry Campbell; Graphic Arts, Trudy Duncan; RVI, Eddie Holz; and Kathy Lipham and Beverly Ellis served as secretaries. The school has a long history of articulating classes with Carroll Tech and West Georgia College.

Carroll County Technical High School

The fall of 1982 saw the doors open to serve students from all five county high schools in grades nine through twelve. Through this process, the high schools in Carroll County became comprehensive.

Listed are some of the schools highlights and milestones. In 1983, Graphic Arts student Lisa Todd (Yearta) won the state VICA title in graphic communications competition. In 1984 Health Occupations student Deborah Farmer won the state VICA title in Nurses Assistant Competition. Also that year, Dr. Jim Garrison became administrator and Gerry Gail Campbell was chosen as Carroll County Teacher of the Year. In 1985 Eddie Holz became the principal and vocational director for the school system. In 1988 the Construction program became industry certified. In 1989 Don Fussell became the principal and vocational director. In 1996 Food Service student Jody Huckeba won the state VICA title in Culinary Arts. In 1997 Don Fussell retired but remained as half-time principal along with former Assistant Superintendent Bill Shotwell and the school's name was changed to the Technical High School. In 1999 Automotive teacher Sonny Reeves was chosen as Carroll County Teacher of the Year. In 2000 Automotive Technology gained industry certification.

The staff of the school for 2000-2001 were: Administration, Don Fussell and Bill Shotwell; Automotive Technology, Sonny Reeves; Construction, Barry Williams; Food Service, Allen Lawler, Jr.; Horticulture, Johnny Mincey; Electro Mechanics, Tom Ballenger; Computer Aided Drafting, Dave Green; Graphic Communications, Trudy Duncan; RVI and Staff, Loretta Spear with aides Carey Lee and Charlene Reece; Parenting Program, Julie Burroughs; Health Occupations, Montes Kenerly; Youth Apprenticeship, Mike McClendon; CVAE, Lee Johnson, and secretary Beverly Ellis.

Over the years additional programs have been added to meet the needs of the students of Carroll County. These programs include: Parenting, CVAE, CAD, Law Enforcement, and Youth Apprenticeship. The Technical High School through hands on projects in their programs provides support for the students of Carroll County. These programs give the students practical experience while benefiting the county financially. *Submitted by: Carroll County Technical High School*

79. Carrollton's Child Development Center

The Carrollton's Child Development Center located at 115 Oak Avenue, Carrollton, Georgia began operation on September 1, 2000. Children are the future and we are committed to helping them receive the best head start in life. We provide a Christian atmosphere for early education. We serve our children as well as serve God. We have grown progressively in the few months we have been in business and we feel we can only continue to do great things as we strive to change a generation. We serve infants to 12 years of age. We have a staff of 5 and the Director is Carol A. Baker.

Carrollton Child Development Center

80. Carrollton City Schools – A Brief History

The award-winning Carrollton City School System continues the tradition of excellence that began with its founding in 1886.

Carrollton's first public school on College Street opened its doors in 1887 at the same location of its private predecessors, Carrollton Seminary and the Carrollton Masonic Institute. A new brick building for the school system was constructed on the same site in 1897. Its name was Carrollton Public School.

In 1913, another school was constructed on Maple Street and a school for African American children was built on Pearl Street. West View School, built by Mandeville Mills in 1910 to serve the children in its mill community on Lovvorn Road, was later rented by the Carrollton City Schools until the mill children were allowed to attend Maple Street School in 1922-23.

Carrollton High School was built in the 1921-22 school year and Carroll County Training School, which served Africal American children, opened in 1932 on Alabama Street.

Fire destroyed Maple Street School's original building in 1947. Students attended double sessions in the annex until a new school was built. College Street's original building fell into disrepair, was abandoned when a new school was built on the site in 1948 and was razed in 1954.

Early postcard view of Carrollton Public School

Also in 1954, Carver High School was constructed near the old Carroll County Training School, which became an elementary school. Both served African American children until desegregation in 1969.

In 1962-63, a new high school was built at the southern end of Oak Avenue. The old high school became the junior high. Westside Elementary was constructed on High Street in 1963-64 to serve African American children in grades 1 through 3.

With desegregation came change for all city schools. Children of all colors attended the schools under the following organization: City Kindergarten (formerly Westside Elementary); Maple Street, grades 1 and 2; College Street, 3 and 4; Alabama Street (former Carver High), 5 and 6; CJHS, 7 and 8; CHS, 9 through 12.

A new CJHS site was constructed near the high school in 1986. The former high school then junior high building became the Carrollton Community Activities Center.

In 1992, Carrollton's three elementary schools consolidated to create a new elementary school that today serves close to 1,800 students, making it one of the largest elementary schools in the state. The bell from the original Carrollton Seminiary building that warned townspeople of the proximity of Federal troops during the Civil War was pulled out of retirement and mounted in the cupola of this building.

All three former schools are in use today. Maple Street School houses the prekindergarten program and administrative offices. Alabama Street is home to the system's alternative school. College Street School now is administrative offices for Carroll County government and City Kindergarten serves the federally-funded HeadStart program.

Superintendents who have served the school system through 2001 are: Ronald Johnson, 1887-88; J.E. Witherspoon, 1888-89; W.W. Roop, 1889-90; T.E. Hollingsworth, 1890-97; J.L. Caldwell, 1897-1903; C.K. Henderson, 1903-07; H.B. Adams, 1907-20; J.N. Haddock, 1920-22; Knox Walker, 1922-27; W. Fred Gunn, 1927-33; M.C. Wiley, 1933-44; F.M. Chalker, 1944-66; H.M. Fulbright, 1966-81; Thomas S. Upchurch, 1981-94; Ronnie A. Williams, 1994-2001; and Thomas A. Wilson, 2001 to present.

The landscape of the school system and the student body it serves have changed dramatically over the years. Today, a 150-acre centralized campus located off Highway 27 at Trojan Drive and the 166 Bypass at Ben Scott Boulevard is home to all three schools and a massive athletic complex. More then 3,500 students are enrolled now, a far cry from the 752 recorded in an annual report published in 1904. *Submitted by: Julianne Foster and Photo courtesy: Dr. David Wiggins*

81. Central Elementary School History

Central Elementary School (CES) is located in Carrollton, Georgia, just 60 miles west of our state capital, Atlanta. CES is one of 11 elementary schools in the Carroll County School System. Throughout the years, the school has undergone many changes, from the grade levels it serves to the physical structure of the building.

Central Elementary School

Central Elementary School opened its doors for the first time in the fall of 1959. The school originally known as Spring View Elementary, served African-American children in grades K-7, while white children attended a K-12 school located at the present Central High School. During the early 1960's, Spring View Elementary became Central Primary School as a direct result of integration. As the years progressed, enrollment continued to increase, leading to the construction of additional classrooms and the placement of 20 portable classrooms on the campus. Central Primary School (K-3) and Central Middle School (4-7) shared the same facilities, which housed over 1800 children. In the fall of 1992, a new Central Middle School opened adjacent to this campus. Grades six, seven, and eight moved to the new middle school, leaving kindergarten through grade five on the present school campus. The vacated sixth and seventh grade classrooms allowed for the removal of 15 portable classrooms. At this time, the Carroll County Board of Education officially changed the school's name from Central Primary School to Central Elementary School. *Submitted by: Libba Conner, Central Elementary Media Specialist*

82. Cross Plains School

The one-room school house was built around 1850. It is forty feet by forty feet and it housed all grades. Students paid one cent a day for tuition, with upper-level students paying five cents a day.

In 1945 Norman Rockwell painted a picture of a similar school with the students and their teacher around an old, black, pot-bellied heater. He used pictures of the Oak Mountain School, which has since been torn down, for his painting. The picture appeared on the cover of the November 1946 *Saturday Evening Post* magazine. It is interesting that some of the students could recognize themselves in the picture and they have framed prints in their homes. For others it is simply a reminder of the way it was!

Mary Wilson Hackney attended the Cross Plains School many years ago. She remembers the school bell ringing and it could be heard for miles. The Cross Plains school had one teacher who taught grades one through eight. One grade at a time would go sit on the long bench at the front of the classroom to learn reading, writing, arithmetic, spelling, science and geography. The other students would spend time working on their assignments. Mary said the bell in the old one-room schoolhouse in rural southeast Carroll County has been silent for nearly 64 years now. The school closed in 1937. Mary was one of the last students. In fact she said this was the only school she ever attended. When the school closed the children were sent to other schools.

School was not all work and no play even back then. Mary remembers the games played were basketball, townball, jump board, jump rope, tag and stealing sticks. A merry-go-round was made by nailing a long board to a tree stump. Then the children would sit on each end and spin around.

The Cross Plains School - May 2001

In 1918 M.L. Duggan, rural school agent for Georgia, made a survey of the county's schools where he found many buildings either worthless or in extremely poor condition. He recommended consolidation, building new school houses, and repairs of others. He says new frame buildings were erected in several places including Cross Plains. This 1918 report listed 81 schools in the county operated by the County Board of Education.

After the school closed it was used for a store, a home for a destitute family, and then stood empty for several years. During the last few years former students and residents from the community have worked to repair and restore the building. Yard sales have been held to pay for a new roof and to install different doors. Their goal is to keep a piece of history alive by the restoration of this historic building. A visit to see the school house is a real history lesson! *Submitted by: Mary Wilson Hackney, 340 Hutcheson Ferry Rd., Whitesburg, GA 30185 and Written by: Sheri Taylor and Violette Denney*

Sources: from family information

83. Elizabeth Harris High School

The school was located east of Carrollton on Highway 166 about a quarter of mile beyond Old Airport Road on the left side of the highway. William Washington (W.W.) Harris gave a portion of his farm for the schoolhouse and it was named after his wife, Elizabeth Dixon Tyson Harris. W.W. Harris was born March 22, 1847, Coweta County, and Elizabeth Tyson was born September 10, 1847, Meriwether County. They were married in Carroll County, December 25, 1864. They had moved to Carrollton and lived on Stewart Street before her death on March 8, 1917.

Original picture has written on the window "Elizabeth Harris, H. 1921'S."

It was a two story building and the lower floor had four classrooms with an entrance hall and just inside the front door to the right were stairs going up to the auditorium. The upstairs was just one room with two small dressing rooms. This is where they had plays. Former teachers and students remembered the plays being very popular and the whole community would come to see them. They ordered a book and the students had to memorize their parts. If you had an important part with lots of lines, you were considered the "Star." The wall foundations and the old brown well curb are still there. The foundation measures 50 feet by 50 feet with an additional 12 feet by 12 feet for a front porch.

One of the teachers remembered living in one of the back rooms in the 1930's and that they didn't have electricity; they used an Aladdin Lamp. The room was divided into a kitchen, bedroom, and living room. She said that they had grades one through nine and she thought each teacher had about three grades. She said she couldn't be sure because after all she taught school for 33 years. Some students repeated the ninth grade because they didn't have transportation to high school.

The school was consolidated with Sand Hill in 1938 and in about 1940 the schoolhouse was disassembled and the lumber was used to build three or four small houses in Carrollton (probably on Sims Street). *Submitted by: Violette Harris Denney, (great-granddaughter of W.W. and Elizabeth Harris), 135 Maple Hill Road, Carrollton, GA 30116-7014*

84. Farmer's High School

The school known as Farmer's High became the first consolidated school in Georgia when the schools at Sackville, Victory, and Salem were combined in 1917. In 1918, Farmer's High School was built on what was known as the lower Bowdon Carrollton Road. Today the road is known as Farmer's High Road.

Farmer's High School

The school got its name because farmers built it, and because it was so tall. Mr. J.N. Hurst, father to Dr. Willis Hurst, famous heart surgeon from Atlanta was one of the early principals. The first teachers were Miss Nellie Tisinger and Miss Mattie Hearn. The first trustees were George Tisinger, Lee Morgan, and Bert Brock. There was one graduation class consisting of three members: Leah Garrett, Martha Bess Causey, and one male student.

From the *Educational Survey of Carroll County in 1918* comes this information:

> The new location is unimproved with ample playgrounds. The school gardens are not yet developed. There is only one toilet in average condition. The building is valued at $4,500. It is a two-story frame building with four classrooms and an auditorium above. There are no cloak rooms and lighting is barely sufficient. A good new building but the ceiling is not yet painted. There are shop-made desks, no teacher's desks, and poor blackboards. There is one United States history map, no carts, no globe, no sand-tables, no pictures, no reference dictionary, and no library. There are three teachers. The school lasts for eight months with eight grades. There are 130 students enrolled with an average attendance of 75 for the last three years. The school received $522 in maintenance from the county board.

Farmer's High Students, 1921

Farmer's High closed in the early 1950's and the building was abandoned. Students were then bused to Bowdon. Mr. and Mrs. R.E. "Red" Harman acquired the property. Their home, which is built on the original school site, displays bricks from the Farmer's High School chimney. *Submitted by: Judy Rowell, 1472 Garrett Creek Road, Bowdon, GA 30108 and Gwynn Chesnut, 185 Cottage Hill Road, Carrollton, GA 30117 and Dr. Wilton Key.*
Source: *Educational Survey of Carroll County 1918*

85. Teaching at Flat Rock School

This is an excerpt from a paper written in the 1970s by Madeline Hogue Boyd at the end of a teaching career spanning over 40 years. Madeline died in 1994.

I graduated from Villa Rica High [in 1928 or 1929] with a class of twenty-two, the largest in seven years. To prepare for teaching, I took two extension courses - "Introduction to Education" and "Methods of Teaching" - from Georgia State Teacher's College (now the University of Georgia). I taught with teachers who had only completed the seventh grade. In those days, no college was required if you passed a test given at the State Capitol and took a summer course every three years.

When I passed the State test in 1930, I applied to teach at Flat Rock Elementary and Junior High in the Flat Rock community about five miles south of Villa Rica. The chairman of the local school board - "Uncle Beverly" Harper - came to my parents' house to interview me. The other members of the board were Mr. Will D. Tyson and Mr. Wiley Gilland.

Members of the school board were not paid in a financial sense, but the position carried the respect of the neighborhood. These men were "pillars of the community" and were asked for advice concerning school and church matters. On occasion, they were even called upon to decide whether "this young man was good enough for that young woman".

I competed with over thirty other people for the job and was thrilled to learn that I would be the one to teach three grades - fifty students. No salary was mentioned at the time, but by the time school started, I knew that I would be earning $38 a month. When I came to school that next Monday morning, I also discovered that I was to "board" with Uncle Beverly and his wife Jenny five days a week, which cost $10 a month. At this point, my life changed from that of the daughter of a poor country doctor to that of a poor country school teacher.

Flat Rock school was divided into two large classrooms with a long hall across the front. Each of the classrooms was furnished with children's double desks, one "homemade" teacher's desk, a long recitation bench and a matching bench at the back of the room. There was a pot-bellied stove surrounded by chairs for the teacher and pupils to use in winter. The front hall was used as a cloak room; two water buckets and a wash pan were also kept here.

The children were allowed to choose their desk-mates; however, if there was too much whispering, I made them move to a different desk.

The recitation bench was for "reciting". With three grades, there was not time for grouping, so I would call the third grade Arithmetic class to the bench, then third grade Reading and so on. If a child disturbed recitation class - except to ask the teacher a word in Reading - that child had to go out to stand in the cloak room.

Flat Rock School

Flat Rock school was originally one room log building built in 1886. It was located near Allen's Mill on the stream flowing near "Five Acre Bald Rock." The mill was still in use when I began teaching there in 1930. A combination Post Office/country store was located next to the mill. At that time, the people of the community could have both wheat and corn ground, exchange stories, get their mail, all at Allen's Mill.

A few years after the log school was built, a frame building was erected just behind Flat Rock Baptist Church. Many years later it was moved to its present location about a quarter of a mile away by fastening a cable around the building and putting rollers under it. A cable attached to a pulley and pulled by a mule rolled the school house a few feet at a time. What a chore!!

No electricity! No water!
No central heating! No lunchrooms!
No indoor rest rooms!

The pot-bellied stove was our only heat supply. Parents would donate wood or sponsor a box supper to raise money to buy coal. These were Depression years and money was scarce. Funds for heating were not provided by the county. One year the very determined son of a sharecropper kept the fire for me for a nickel a week! I can still see his grinning face as I gave him that nickel every Friday!

Water was carried in two buckets from a spring beside Flat Rock Church, more than 500 feet from the school, straight up a hill. Everyone brought their lunch, usually a biscuit and sausage, jelly, or ham. Most had fruit in season and cake wrapped in butter paper or loose-packed in a "paper poke."

I began teaching at Flat Rock in 1930; at that time, the school year ran from July through August, skipped several months for the children to pick cotton, then resumed in the winter months. A typical school day ran from 8:00 until almost dark. Since most of the school year was during the winter months, I can remember seeing the sun go down many times as I came down the last hill to Uncle Beverly's.

By 1934, the Depression was at its height. At one time, banks, were ordered to shut down. The State Board of Education just did not have funds to pay us, so they issued "scripts" as a promise that we would get our pay. We could use these to borrow money from the bank. They kept their promise and we eventually were paid.

I had the privilege to teach with Homer Campbell, principal and teacher of the sixth through ninth grades at Flat Rock, Miss Ona Boyd, who taught first and second grades, and later Harold and Ann Burson. Harold Burson went on to serve for many years as head of the Georgia State Patrol.

I sure am proud of all the fine people who came through this school while I was there. For example, Verlyn Boyd went on to teach at Clemson University; H.L. Campbell went to Brazil as Vice-President of Southwire; Neal Wiliams became a preacher; Doris Tyson, Virlyn Hembree, and Fred Hembree made fine livings in the construction trade, and Ella Brittain was an excellent teacher and principal of Winston Elementary for many years. *Submitted by: David Hembree, 3560 Valley Hill Road, Kennesaw, GA 30152*
Source: Madeline Boyd

86. Liberty Hill School 1911

Mr. Awbrey Barrett, standing on the right, was the teacher at Liberty Hill in 1911. Identification of all students was made by Mae Warren on July 9, 1981. Several of the students shown here (Jesse Warren, Oren Warren, Albert Warren, Donie Lee and Otis McKibben) were already out of school, but when they heard the photographer was coming to take pictures, they showed up and wanted to be in the group picture.

Two of the students - Joe Warren and Mae Warren - decided to "punch" their faces out of the picture. Seventy years later, Mae could not remember the reason they did this except that she was following the example of her older brother, who was known to be a little "mischievous" at times.

Liberty Hill School, 1911

First row, bottom: Boyce Warren, Leonard Brock, Luther Warren, Berlin Thompson, Una Thompson, Alma Warren, Wilsie Warren, Jewell Kenerly, Nelah and Jewell Moore, Emma and Leona Pierce, Alma Moon, Winnie Rainwater.

Second row: Charlie Hollis, Lyman McKibben, Charlie Smith, Wayne Rainwater, Dewey Brown, Joe Adams, Lydia Brown, Alice Brock, Alice Moon, Margaret Warren, Mae Warren, Dussie Willingham, Sallie Hollis, Velma and Alma Robinson.

Third row: Oren Warren, Archie Smith, Marion Warren, Gus McKibben, Odus Bown, Aubrey Hollis, Minnie Lee Young, Viola Smith, Bertha Warren, Mae McKibben, Ollie Warren, Annie Warren, Johnny Rainwater (little boy).

Fourth row, top: Jesse and Joe Warren, Noah Warren, Albert and Robert Warren, Bodie Kent, Otis McKibben, Donie Lee, Ola Young, Hattie Hollis, Annie Brown, Lee Warren, Beulah Robinson, Dana Rainwater. *Submitted by: Betty Jo Carroll Parsons, 2085 Bowdon-Tyus Road, Bowdon, GA 30108*

87. Mt. Zion Schools

Mt. Zion Elementary School, along with her sister school, Mt. Zion Middle/High School, are the oldest schools in Carroll County, which are still in use. These two schools, which for almost one century were housed on the same campus, have been in continual service to the Mt. Zion community since 1880. The school was begun as a seminary school by Mt. Zion United (formerly Episcopal) Methodist Church. The Mt. Zion Seminary, like the other dozen plus seminaries in the state, was funded by gifts of land and investments from interested parties in the cause of educating young people from isolated districts. However, the financial condition of many of the Georgia communities in the post Civil War era was desperate, and all but two of the schools started by the Methodist Episcopal Church Conference (the governing body of the Methodist churches of North Geogia) were closed by financial problems by the turn of century. The school at Demorest remained open in 1900, but it has long since been shut down, leaving only the Mt. Zion school to continue its legacy as an educational facility. In 1937, the Mt. Zion Seminary was merged with the Carroll County School System, and became Mt. Zion School. In recent years, lack of classroom space at the school has required the higher grades to be served at other schools. In 1994, the seventh and the eighth grades were moved from the elementary school and placed into the campus of Mt. Zion High School. In 1996, the sixth graders of Mt. Zion Elementary were sent to the high school campus. Now the high school is called Mt. Zion Middle/High School. In 2000 Jonesville Middle School was opened. For the school year 2000-2001, Mt. Zion sixth and seventh graders attended Jonesville Middle School, which is located just outside the city limits of Bowdon, Georgia. As of the school year 2001-2002, sixth, seventh and eighth graders were given a choice of attending Mt. Zion Middle/High or Jonesville Middle School.

The original buildings from 1880, along with two additional buildings were all built by people in the community and were used until a "modern structure" was built in 1958. The modern building was the first to contain indoor toilet facilities. Before construction began on the 1958 building, the original building was moved across the road to the area where a gym now stands. This old building was torn down when the new one was completed. Until August of 1976, Mt. Zion School served its students from their first year of school until their graduation. At that time, Mt. Zion Elementary and Mt. Zion High School were made into two separate schools. The two schools shared the original campus until the nearby building for the new Mt. Zion High School was completed in March of 1977.

The photo taken at the dedication of the school on May 15, 1977, includes: back row left to right, Raymond Sherrill, Board Member from Temple; Ray Fulford, building contractor; Leon Golden, Mt. Zion High Principal, Dr. Travis Edmondson, Assistant Superintendent; Jack Dorsey, Mayor of Mt. Zion; and Roy Denney Jr., Architect. The front row from left to right includes: Paul Cooper, Board Member from Central; J.H. Gammon, Chairman of the Board, serving from the Mt. Zion School District; Spencer Teal, Superintendent; and Quinton Miles, Mt. Zion Elementary Principal. It should be noted that Leon Golden, long time principal of the school went on to serve the community faithfully as Superintendent of the Carroll County Schools and as a School Board Member for Mt. Zion.

Mt. Zion High School Dedication May 15, 1977

Mt. Zion Elementary still uses the two buildings, which were built in 1958. These two buildings are parallel halls, which run alongside Hwy. 16. In these two buildings, there are classrooms, administrative offices, the lunchroom, and the kitchen. In 1977, an additional hall was added. This classroom hall formed on L shaped at the end of the shorter, back hall. The media center was placed at the end of the hall. In 1983, another classroom hall was added. This hall is joined to the side of the 1977 addition. These two classroom halls are also parallel to each other. Mt. Zion Elementary now has a gym on its own campus, built in 1998, in the back area of the school. In addition to these permanent campus buildings, Mt. Zion Elementary must use several mobile classroom units.

The Mt. Zion High School football field is located closer to the Elementary School than it is to its own student body. The football field has been occasionally used by the students at Mt. Zion Elementary and by the local Mt. Zion Recreation Department. Likewise, what is now called "The Old Gym," built in the mid sixties, continues to be shared for various community events in Mt. Zion. This gym is located across State Highway 16 (Mt. Zion Road) from both the elementary school and the high school.

At its beginning, the Mt. Zion Seminary had 60 students and two teachers. The school has evolved through the years, chancing its classroom configuration to accommodate the students of the surrounding area. Currently, Mt. Zion Elementary has 660 students.

Plans now call for a new high school campus, a new middle school campus, and yet another elementary school to be built for the Mt. Zion area. These new properties have not yet been purchased, pending the passing of needed SPLOST funding for the costs of the buildings. The plan is for what is now Mt. Zion Elementary School campus to become a Pre-K through Grade 2 (Primary) school. Grades three through five (Elementary) are to be served in what is now Mt. Zion Middle/High School, which is located nearby.

Dr. James Michell, founder and first president of Mt. Zion Seminary, had come to the Turkey Creek community some time after the Civil War. Dr. Mitchell suggested the present name of the community, Mt. Zion, which replaced the name Turkey Creek. Mitchell had served on several committees supportive of slavery abolishment with Abraham Lincoln in Illinois. The settlers in this community were of like minds with Mr. Mitchell, and did not keep slaves before the Civil War. Mitchell and the community developed a mutual respect for each other. On cards sent to prospective parents in the vicinity, it was claimed that the community could not "be excelled for good morals." Indeed, throughout its history, Mt. Zion has earned a reputation for providing the best for its students. Very recently, in 1998, the elementary school earned designation as the winner of the national Reading Association's Exemplary Reading Program Award. That same year, State School Superintendent, Linda Schrenko, proclaimed Mt. Zion a "Georgia Dream School". In the school year 2000-2001, the Academic Team for Mt. Zion High School won the county championship and represented the school system at the Hi-Q competition. *Submitted by: Linda Smith, MZE, and Dr. David Wiggins, MZHS*

88. Mt. Zion Seminary 1880-1937

Rev. James Mitchell, presiding Elder of Atlanta District, Methodist Episcopal Church, from 1876-1880 had more to do in shaping and organizing the Seminary than anyone else. He was heartily seconded in all his movements by the leading citizens of Mount Zion. The Fall term of Carroll Superior Court granted a charter to Mount Zion Seminary Association. It was a joint stock association and provided for a Board of Trustees and the founding of a high school. Joseph Entrekin and Rev. William Culpepper Walker each paid $200 to fund the Association, and others according to their ability. Dr. C.W. Parker located the first building and paid in the first money.

The original stockholders of Mt. Zion Seminary were: Joseph Entrekin (President), S.J. Entrekin, H.A. Entrekin, Eli Entrekin, J.A. Entrekin, L.G. Entrekin, W.M. Ashmore (Bowdon), W.G. Jordan, Daniel McBrunett, James P. McKissack, Issac Price, William Walker, Hicks Martin, M.D., M.C. Trimble and Rev. James Mitchell.

Campus Scene 1935 at Mt. Zion Seminary L. to R. buildings: Academic, Methodist Church, Home Ec./Shop, Boy's Dorm.

The original campus contained five acres and was enlarged from time to time and in 1918 contained 20 acres. No Board of Trustees could have been more devoted to their trust than those of Mt. Zion sparing neither time nor money.

Mt. Zion Seminary Academic Building 1935

Professor J.E. Deacon was the first president, and in its first quarter of a century it had a dozen different principals. The most famous was Professor Rhonald Johnston. Professor Johnston was born in Scotland and graduated from the University of Edinburgh. Before the Civil War, he came to America and settled in Cass County, which today is Bartow County. At the invitation of his brother, Professor Johnston founded a private academy at Euharlee and taught there several years. One of his students was to become the world famous evangelist, Rev. Sam Jones.

Professor Johnston married in Paulding County while teaching there. After completing his work at Mt. Zion, he became the first superintendent of the newly formed Carrollton School System. After leaving Carrollton, he taught all over North Georgia and died about 1910 in Conyers, Georgia. The citizens from miles around had a just pride in the fact that the first County Board of Education, founded in 1870, recognized the good work that was done at Mt. Zion.

Scores of teachers were taught at the Seminary and many preachers were trained there as well as other professionals. Mr. Joseph Entrekin gave the land and Howard A. Pitts cleared the land where the Seminary was built which is the present elementary school site. Mr. J.A. Entrekin was the contractor and with the help of other men in the community built the first three rooms of the main building. In 1900, the auditorium was added and in 1924 the two-story addition was built. While the work was being done, the school was held in Mt. Zion Church, which was located on the current site of the parsonage. The original school had sixty pupils and two teachers, Mr. E.F. Entrekin and Belle Trimble.

In 1918 Lee Trimble, who was an alumnus, became the principal of the school and rechartered and updated the school.

In 1921, Herbert N. Howard (D.D.) a returned missionary from Zimbabwe was appointed President of the Seminary. In the summer of 1921, the community men donated about 700 hours of labor in grading the school campus, clearing and cleaning off the grounds, and repairing and painting the Seminary building. Mt. Zion began to grow under the administrations of Herbert and Estella Searles Howard. The vocational building was built in 1924 with an upstairs Home Economics room and a downstairs shop. Fuller Hall, the boy's dormitory, was raised and two stories were built underneath in 1924. The high school building was started in 1924. In the spring of 1925, Rev. Howard died and his widow, Estella Searles Howard, was appointed President of the Seminary. She served from 1925 to 1937. She was perhaps the greatest leader in the Seminary's history.

Fuller Hall - Boys Dormitory 1882-1937

Those serving as Mt. Zion Presidents were: E.F. Entrekin with Assistant Belle Thimble, J.D. Deacon with Assistant D.D. Entrekin, J.F. Palmer with Assistant Addie Thimble, Rhonald E. Johnston, R.H. Robb, J.F. Palmer, W.T. Morris, W.D. Stevenson, R.C. Bramlett, W.T. Morris, Perry Weston with Assistant Mose Weston, Alvis Craig, Foss Smith, J.L. Robb, R.H. Robb, H.A. Phillips, James Coleman, J.L. Robb, W. Williford, F.L. Bradley who died in WWI in France, Lee S. Thimble, P.L. Schneider, W.H. Howard and Assistant Estella Searles Howard, and Estella Searles Howard and Dean of Students Frank Argelandre.

In 1937 Mt. Zion Seminary merged with Carroll County School System and became Mt. Zion Elementary and High School. *Submitted by: Jack Dorsey, Mt. Zion Historian*

89. Open Campus High School

The Carroll County Board of Education and Superintendent Tim Wheeler created the Open Campus High School in 1989. The school was established to help reduce a high dropout rate among the students of Carroll County. The school was housed in the Central High School building for twelve years and offered evening

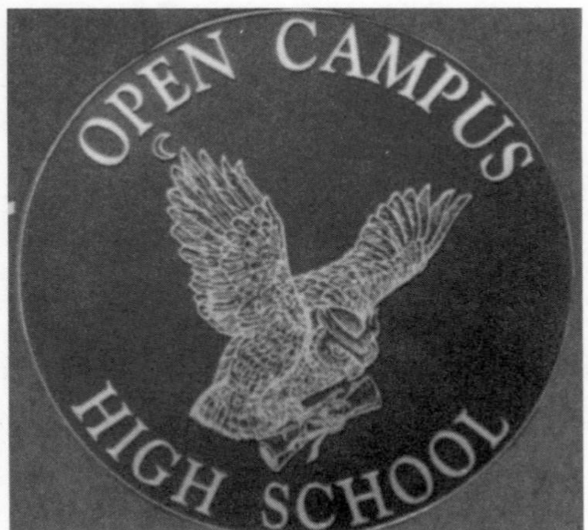

Seal of Open Campus High School

classes to both full-time students and students that needed to take additional courses for make-up or enrichment. The school has assisted students from over 16 different area high schools.

The school was established as a school of choice, in other words, students choose to be at the school. The school is run like a junior college with adult privileges with adult conduct. The school is noted as a model school by the State Department of Education as a continuation school.

The first staff consisted of: David Wiggins, Principal; Hildred Davis, Media Specialist; Virginia Wysong, Counselor; and Todd Farmer, Bookkeeper. Charter teachers included: Penny Ayers, John Beckvermitt, Jim Boyd, Penny Bradley, Joe Byrd, Nancy Clark, Debra Elarbee, Faye Gregory, Bobbie Howard, Chuck Joiner, Bonnie Robinson, and Lou Treadaway.

Charter Staff: David Wiggins, Virginia Wysong, Todd Farmer, Hildred Davis

In the fall of 2001, the school moved to Bowdon to the old Bowdon Primary Building. Sharing the same site as the Crossroads Alternative School, the Open Campus Educational Center was created. Hundreds of students have graduated from Open Campus High School and thousands have attended the school to make up work or seek enrichment. The school has had a very positive impact on the educational opportunities for the children of Carroll County. *Submitted by: Dr. David Wiggins*
Sources: *Alternative Education Programs: A Prescription for Success,* 1991 by Rhonda Hefner-Packer; personal knowledge

90. Reavesville School

Reavesville School was located south of Bowdon on Highway 5. In 1934 George Rogers was principal and the coach of the basketball team.

The Reavesville Basketball Team was the Carroll County Champion in 1934. The members of the team were Paul Chambers, Posey Wright, Ellis Word, S.Q. Chambers, Kirby Jackson, and Bruce Chambers. George Rogers was the coach. In May of 2001, only George Rogers remains alive. *Submitted by: Bobby Word, 624 Reavesville Road, Bowdon, GA 30108*

The 1934 Reavesville School Basketball Team and Coach Rogers

91. Rocky Mount School

The school is located on lot 32 two and one-half miles to Oak Ridge School. The area and titles are doubtful. The grounds are unimproved

Rocky Mount School

with large playgrounds, no school gardens and only one toilet. The grade for the grounds is average. The building is valued at $500. The building contains two rooms with no cloakrooms. The school is fairly well lighted, ceiled, unpainted and in good repair. There are shop-made desk, no teachers' desks, very poor blackboards, no maps, no globe, no charts, no pictures, no dictionary, and no library. There is one teacher. School last for six months. There are seven grades. The average attendance for the last three years is 43 pupils. The school received $300 in Maintenance from the county.
Submitted by: Wilton Key
Source: *Education Survey of Carroll County 1918*

92. Rocky Mount, Oak Ridge, and Rock Ridge Schools

I wish to give some history of three schools located south of Carrollton. Stripling Chapel was a two room school located on what was State Highway One which is now U.S. 27. Rocky Mount was located on the Franklin Road about four miles South of Carrollton. Oak Ridge School was located farther down on State Highway One, about seven miles from Carrollton. In the early 1930's the trustees of the three schools had an election to consolidate the three into one school. The building was to be located about four and one-half miles south of Carrollton on S R #1 across the road from the John Deere Tractor place.

The election didn't pass and the trustees of Rocky Mount and Oak Ridge planned another election to build a school about a mile further down S R #1, near Ringer's Store. The total property in the district tax assessment was $80,000. They voted to issue $3,000 dollars in bonds. They hired a builder, I think they paid him $5 a day. They paid a dollar a day to others to work on the building or to use their wagons to haul lumber.

They tore down both the old buildings and used the good lumber with the bond money, to build four class rooms and an auditorium and two out houses.

I think we were among the first families to do home schooling. We lived about a mile from Rocky Mount school on a dirt road with two creeks or branches to cross that had no bridges. There was nobody else for me to walk with in the community. My mother borrowed a book called a Primer and First and Second Readers from her mother and taught me to read. After two years other families moved in and I didn't have to go to school by myself. I started in the little room in the second grade. Let's think about the water supply for the school, the nearest water was at the farm house next door, which is now the Carrollton Manor Nursing Home. Two persons would go to get the water. They would use a stick about a yard long and hang the bucket between them and not spill a drop of the water. Each water bucket had a long handled dipper and some students brought a cup from home to drink from. Usually when a class was in session, at the front of the room some of the teacher's pets would ask to pass the water around so everyone could have a drink.

Now let us have a look at what was taught in school. Each grade had a reader and spelling book. Some grades had a grammar or English book. We had several history books and I remember when we studied the Confederate War I took a pencil and punched out General Sherman's eyes in my book. We had studies in Geography and I remember one summer when we didn't use the little room. We laid out a design of both North and South America using sand we toted from the branch. At least one year a class studied Latin, I think it was in the seventh grade. About all I remember is the word agreekla which meant a farmer.

The new building was ready the first of the year 1932. Since both old buildings had been torn down and materials used in the new building the school year began in the fall of 1931 in the Emmaus Primitive Baptist Church next door to where the Rocky Mount school had been. The Principal was Mr. Looney Martin who had taught at Rocky Mount and Stripling Chapel. The other teachers were Miss Ruth Shadinger, Miss Gladis Lambert and Miss Nollie Taylor.

Rock Ridge School, about 1939

The school bus owner and driver was Curtis Walker. He was paid $25 per month. The teachers were paid $25 per month and the Principal was paid $30 or $35. Rock Ridge had all grades including four years of high school, with agriculture time shared with Roopville School. Mr. H.H. Gibson taught agriculture in both places. Mr. Gibson was a builder and already had a carpenter shop and a steam canning plant. It wasn't long before Mr. Gibson had a canning plant behind Rock Ridge school. In addition to operating the canning plant, they would lay-out a new terrace in the farm land. They even went out and sprayed fruit trees.

Rock Ridge had two graduating classes. I'm not sure about the dates. After that they moved all high school students to Roopville High School. In the meantime, I had finished two years at West Georgia College in June 1933. There were no "Help Wanted" ads in the Atlanta newspapers. Mr. Gibson got me on a WPA project as an assistant in the agriculture classes. After Rock Ridge High School students moved to Roopville, Mr. Gidson had me transferred to Roopville to assist in all the agricultural operations.

In the meantime, Rock Ridge was growing, building classrooms and a kitchen to serve meals.

After Central school was built all pupils were transferred to Central, Rock Ridge was no more. I was gone for several years, but it seems like a church bought the building and it burned when the leaves got on fire and set the building on fire.

The students pictured at the school are: (front) Hazel Horsley, Fay Edison, Nell Wililamson, Barbara McLendon, Doris McLendon, Edna McWhorter, Nora Woods and Allene Denney, (back) unidentified, Percy North, Billy Thomas, unidentified, Buck Hollingsworth, and Harry Horsley. *Submitted by: Everette Denney, born in 1915; 105 Hubbard Springs Road, Carrollton, GA 30117*

93. Roopville Schools

Formal education began in 1851 when the early settlers decided they needed a "meeting house". This house was a one room log building with no windows, a large doorway and a large chimney at the other end for heat. It was located near the cemetery and was used as a church and school until 1871.

After the Civil War, citizens built another school building near the same location. This was a double log building with a rail fence and one of Martin Roop's sons served as teacher. This building burned in 1881, and a two room school was built. In 1885 the *Carroll County Times* newspaper stated:

> "The people of Roopville are prepared to enter life as good citizens. In the preparatory department they are preparing students to enter college."

The building stood until 1907 when the people decided they needed a better school. This time they built one of the best frame buildings in the county and it was called the Henry Grady Institute.

The new building was located on an acre lot on the main street. The title to the school was held by trustees. The two-story building had three classrooms, an auditorium on the second floor and a cloak room. It was well lighted and painted inside and out. It contained shop-made desks for the students, a blackboard and a few maps. It was lacking in library books, reference books, dictionaries and globes. This is easily understood considering that the people of the community were hard pressed to acquire these items and there were no state supplied books or teaching materials. The County School Board supplied the school with $800 but the bulk of this money paid the three teachers. In 1918 this two-story building was valued at $3600 and average attendance in 1918 was 91 students. The school met for an eight-month year.

In 1932 the people decided there was a need for a larger and better school for their growing community. In 1934 a brick building containing nine classrooms and an auditorium with stage which could be used as a gym was built. The cornerstone of this building, dated May 4, 1943, contains the names of the local trustees, J.B. Merrell, B.L. Garrett, C.G. Lanier, J.A. Veal, and W.B. Steed. The cornerstone is now located in the Historical Society's Archive. Mr. L.A. Ware of Roopville was a member of the County Board. The new school was named Roopville High School.

The Henry Grady Institute used until 1907.

Students graduated from Roopville High School from 1934 through 1959. During this time Roopville was well known for its winning basketball teams. In 1959 the high school was consolidated with other schools in the immediate area at Central High School located just south of the Carrollton city limits. Roopville continued to have an elementary school through 8th grade till 1994 when the 6th - 8th grades were moved to Central Elementary School near the high school campus south of Carrollton. Roopville now has an enrollment of 421, total staff of 63, and hold classes for 4 year old kindergarten to 5th grade students. *Submitted by: Rebecca Merrell, President, Roopville Historial Society and Archive, 124 Old Franklin Street, Roopville, GA 30170*

94. The Caswells and Roopville Basketball

In 1959, there was electricity in the air in Roopville as the high school basketball teams were off and running to yet another highly successful season. Render R. Caswell, Principal and Head Boys Basketball Coach, was a community fixtue having coached the Hornets for eleven years, and going into the tournament had a remarkable record of 322-17 in regular season games. An even more remarkable record, his wife Gladys, coached the girls teams and had a regular season record of 318-9 during her tenure.

The Roopville boys had enjoyed four undefeated regular seasons and the girls had won their district or region crown in all eleven years, had five undefeated regular season teams, and never lost an opener in the state tournament. This husband wife duo amassed a combined record of 614-26 in eleven years. During that time the boys average score was 52.5 points a game to 29.4 oppponent points. The girls averaged 48.5 points to opponents 23.6. Going into the state tournament, the boys of '59 had compiled a record of 28-2 while the girls recorded a perfect 30-0.

The Roopville boys team played Midville for the Class C Basketball crown and defeated them by a score of 42-39. It was described as a tremendously tough defensive battle with neither team seldom more than two or three points apart. Captain Emerson Lyle sank the basket that was the margin of victory with 1:13 remaining. The win was the first state title for any team in the Carroll County Schools. J.H. Horsley was high scorer for the tournament and for Coach Caswell, it was the crowning achievement of his 30 years as a basketball coach. Mr. Caswell was to move to the newly consolidated school, Central, to become Principal

Mrs. Gladys Caswell's girls team played in their tournament the following week. Like the boys the week before, they were inspired to win it all but had the added pressure of the boys winning it before them. The team romped through the tournament with a culminating victory over Yatesville by a score of 54-42. Glenda Williamson was high scorer for the championship

Mr. Render Caswell and 1959 State Champs

Mrs. Gladys Caswell and 1959 State Champs

game with 26 points. Both Render and Gladys Caswell were to be honored as Coaches of the Year in Class C by their colleagues. They coached Carroll County's first boys and girls state basketball titles and their wins became the first win titles by the same school in the state. They and their successes became legendary.
Submitted by: Dr. David Wiggins
Sources: Archives of Roopville History Center

95. Rotherwood School

Rotherwood School was located on land lot 84, three miles from Whitesburg, three miles from Lewis Chapel, and three miles from Shiloh. The land was in an uncertain area with doubtful titles. It adjoined the church lot. The grounds were utterly neglected with very small playgrounds and no school gardens or toilets.

Rotherwood School

The value of the building was $100. The building contained one small room, unceiled and unpainted. There was insufficient lighting and the building was in bad repair. The school had very rough homemade desks, no teacher's desk, no blackboards, no maps, no globe, one chart, no library, no dictionary and no pictures. There was one teacher. School lasted six months during the school year with six grades. The average attendance for the last three years was 40 pupils. The county supplied $258 for maintenance. *Submitted by: Wilton Key*
Source: *Educational Survey of Carroll County 1918*

96. Sand Hill School and Masonic Lodge

On 7 November 1889 John W. Carroll, a prominent citizen of Sand Hill, executed a deed in favor of school trustees John A.F. Broom, John T. Eady, and Phillip H. Garst for one acre of land in the northwest corner of Lot 82, 5th District. The purpose was to build "a good frame house upon the above land, two stories high, forty feet long and twenty-eight feet wide for the following purposes to wit: the lower room to be used as a school room for white citizens of the community and the upper story to be used by the Freemasons." At the time, the children of the Sand Hill community were attending school in a log structure built in 1858 which was across the road from the Macedonia Baptist Church building. This structure had replaced the original log cabin built in 1847 that was used for both the school and the Macedonia church.

Sand Hill School and Masonic Lodge

Work began on the building in the spring of 1890, with lumber coming from Hutcheson's sawmill on Snake Creek near Banning. The building was completed in the summer of 1890 and school classes began in the fall. In 1891, Masonic Lodge No. 350 was organized and occupied the second floor, with John A.F. Broom as first Worshipful Master. The building stands near the intersection of old State Road 61 and the Sand Hill - Hickory Level Road and is still home to the Sand Hill Masonic Lodge.
Submitted by: Alfred Turner, 6501 Peacock Boulevard, Morrow, GA 30260

97. Smithfield School

Memories by Roy Joe Moore and read at the 1996 Smithfield School Reunion

Nineteen hundred and thirty eight, oh what a treat!
Smithfield Junior High School is now complete.
The doors are all open so come on to school,
We are learning about life and the golden rule.
The men of our community have stood the test,
They built us a school house that is the very best.
Nathan and Marvin and oh what a crew!
Adams, Adamsons, Benefields, Brocks
and Browns,
Robinsons, Caseys, Garretts, Greys, Easons
and Downs,
Scales, Smiths, Styles, Sullivans and Spruells,
Williams, Williamson, Wilsons, Watsons
and Warrens,
McGuires, Moores, Nunnellys, Turners
and Hands,
All working together just to beat the band.
These supportive families and a few more it seems,
Have performed so diligently to fulfill our dreams.
Today! Let us honor with gratitude and pride,
These special people that decorated our lives.

The communities of High Point and Hill Crest joined together to build Smithfield School. Earnest Smith donated 5 acres of land. The land joined his property and the school was named Smithfield in honor of Mr. Smith. The men in the community agreed to work for $.10 an hour. The men too old to help with construction jobs used their wagons, mules, and wheelbarrows to haul the building materials. Nathan Robinson and Marvin Spruell contracted with the county to build the school for $5,000.00. Wagons hauled the fieldstones, an inexpensive durable building material, from surrounding farms. A 100-foot steel tape squared the building and mortar was mixed in a mortar box build on site.

Community men poured the foundation, erected the scaffold, and the walls came up. A rope, run through a pulley, was tied to a bucket filled with mortar or rocks. After climbing a ladder, Earl Grey put his foot into a loop at the other end of the rope and descended, pulling the bucket up to the scaffold. This procedure was done many times every day. J.B. Moore sustained the only serious injury, when he broke a bone as a board was thrown accidentally against his arm. He was unable to help finish building the school - J.B.'s only concern.

The building only took six months to complete. Before zoning, inspections, OSHA, and law suits projects moved much faster. The school opened in 1938 and closed in 1961. The first floor housed five classrooms, a lunchroom, and a small library (with very few books), while the second floor served as an auditorium. Smithfield held the honor of having the first lunchroom in the county. Miss Nell traveled

Smithfield School

once a month to the county office to pick up commodities. Delva Adamson, Dura Nunnelly, and Viola Robinson cooked for all the students and staff.

The building was used for adult education classes, and was also a community center. People came by bus every Friday night to see movies and other entertainment. Some of the activities included plays, movies, cakewalks, dinners, parties, and live entertainment. After the school closed, a clothing manufacturer came in and added a brick addition on the right side. The company stayed for approximately 8 to 10 years and provided jobs for the people of the community. After the clothing manufacturer moved out, various organizations tried to use the building, but the community did not feel that any of these operations would be good for the community. The building has been vacant since 1963.

Many people in the community regret the county did not give or sell the building back to the community. The walls are falling in, the roof has collapsed, but the memories are alive and will live on. *Submitted by: Myrtle Robinson Hearn, 228 Palo Verde Dr., Leesburg, FL 34748*
Sources: Nell Garrett Smith, Viola Robinson, Cordie Belle Green, Linda Lee Allen, Roy Joe Moore.

98. Smyrna School

Pictured at the top of page 45, is the Smyrna School on Highway 27 North about 1930. The teacher was Mildred Nixon. *Submitted by: Joe Earnest, 3500 North Highway 27, Carrollton, GA 30117*

99. History of West Georgia College

The State University of West Georgia was founded on August 18, 1906, as the Fourth District Agricultural and Mechanical School, one of twelve such institutions established by the State of Georgia between 1906 and 1917. Classes first started at the A&M School in January, 1908, under the leadership of Principal John H. Melson. Twenty-five years later, Carrollton's A&M School became West Georgia College, a junior college established by an act of the Board of Regents of the University System of Georgia. Dr. Irvine S. Ingram, who had been principal of the A&M School, was named the institution's first president.

In its early years, West Georgia College became one of the fastest growing institutions of higher learning in the South. From an enrollment of 576 in 1957, the institution's student body now numbers close to 9,000. In 1939, the College was authorized by the Board of Regents to add a three-year program in elementary education. In 1957, the institution was authorized to confer the B.S. degree in Education, making it a four-year senior college unit of the University System of Georgia. Two years later, West Georgia College added the Bachelor of Arts degree in the fields of English, history, and mathematics. In 1967, on the recommendation of President James Boyd, the Board of Regents authorized the initiation of a

Smyrna School about 1930

graduate program at the master's level. In 1996, the Board approved President Beheruz N. Sethna's recommendation to start a doctoral program.

The State University of West Georgia now offers 111 programs of study, including 59 at the Bachelors level, 51 at the Masters and Specialist levels, and one Doctoral program. Undergraduate degrees, with majors in 59 fields, include the Bachelor of Arts, Bachelor of Fine Arts, Bachelor of Science, Bachelor of Science in Chemistry, Bachelor of Science in Education, Bachelor of Science in Nursing, Bachelor of Business Administration, Bachelor of Music, Bachelor of Science in Recreation, Bachelor of Science in Earth Science, Bachelor of Science in Environmental Science, and Bachelor of Science in Environmental Studies. Masters degrees offered, with majors in 34 fields, include the Master of Arts, Master of Business Administration, Master of Education, Master of Music, Master of Professional Accounting. Master of Public Administration, Master of Science, and Master of Science in Rural and Small Town Planning. Also offered is the Specialist in Education degree with majors in 17 fields, and the Doctor of Education in School Improvement.

Dr. Beheruz Sethna, President, State University of West Georgia

In 1983, the Board of Regents approved the External Degree Program as a cooperative effort between Dalton College and West Georgia. Since its inception, close to 400 degrees have been conferred through the Center. The Board of Regents in 1988 approved opening the Newnan Center, a joint effort involving the Newnan-Coweta Chamber of Commerce and other business, civic and educational leaders in the area. With an enrollment of more than 200, the Newnan Center provides core curriculum and a possible degree in General Studies for residents in the Newnan/Coweta County area.

In June, 1996, the Board of Regents of the University System of Georgia officially changed the name of West Georgia College to State University of West Georgia. To accommodate the University's growth, a multi-million dollar building program has increased the value of the University's physical facilities to nearly $156 million. From a beginning of three small buildings, the University has grown to include more than 80 structures of learning, living, and recreation on its 394-acre wooded campus.

Dr. Irvine Sullivan Ingram served as West Georgia College's first president from 1933 to June 30, 1960, the longest presidential tenure in the history of the University System of Georgia. He was succeeded by Dr. William Hamilton Row, who served from July 1, 1960, until his death on March 15, 1961. At that time, Dr. Ingram was named acting president. He served in that capacity until Dr. James Emory Boyd was appointed president on August 16, 1961.

After a decade of service to West Georgia College as president, Dr. Boyd retired on March 30, 1971, to become vice-chancellor for academic development of the Unviersity System of Georgia. Vice-President George Walker served as acting president from April 1 to August 15, 1971. On August 16, Dr. Ward B. Pafford became the institution's fourth president. Dr. Pafford announced his resignation, effective June 30, 1975, in the fall of 1974. Dr. Maurice K. Townsend was named West Georgia's new president, effective July 1, 1975. Dr. Townsend served as the College's Chief Executive Officer until his death on May 16, 1993. Dr. Bruce W. Lyon, Vice President and Dean of Student Services, was named Acting President, effective June 1, 1993.

The University System of Georgia, following an extensive national search, named Dr. Beheruz N. Sethna to head West Georgia, effective August, 1994. At that time, it represented an historic decision, because Dr. Sethna was the first person of any ethnic minority in the State of Georgia to be named president of an institution other than an Historically Black one. When the Board of Regents officially changed the name of the institution to the State University of West Georgia on June 12, 1996, Dr. Sethna became the first President of the University. *Submitted by: Dr. Beheruz Sethna, President, University of West Georgia, 1600 Maple Street, Carrollton, GA 30118*

100. History of Temple High School

Temple High School has a long and interesting history. It was originally called the "Temple Academy" and was in operation at the turn of the century.

In 1903 a new school was proposed by Ira W. Williams, one of the teachers. The new school would be a model school, and was called the "Temple Model School". The new model school taught traditional classes and offered college preparatory courses.

Bonds were issued and a two story, brick building with four classrooms and an auditorium was completed in 1904. The innovative "Model School" was given publicity all across the state.

The Temple "Model" School also instituted the first school transportation system in the state. Wagons hauled children from surrounding areas to the new Temple school.

The Georgia High School Association also had its beginning in Temple in 1905. It was started as the Northwest Georgia High School Association, and developed into the present Georgia High School Association.

In 1907, the Temple Model School changed directions and became the Temple "Graded" School. The school offered more traditional courses. In 1914, the school became known as the Temple Public School.

In 1939, the High School was moved to its present location on Sage Street. The building was shaped like an "H" with the elementary school on the rear wing, the high school on the first wing, and an auditorium in the middle.

The first gymnasium was constructed in 1948 from an old army barracks transported from Fort Oglethorpe, Georgia. Billy Thomas was the basketball coach.

The twelfth grade was added in the 1951-52 school year.

During the summer of 1957, a fire destroyed the entire elementary section and most of the auditorium. The classrooms were rebuilt in an adjacent wing and the auditorium repaired.

Temple High School

A new gymnasium was built in 1960, and is now known as the "Stitcher" gymnasium. It was named for long time basketball coach, Donald Stitcher, who coached Temple's state championship girls basketball team. That gym is still in use today.

In 1965, Temple High School was integrated without incident. By 1968, all Temple schools were totally integrated and Providence Elementary, the black elementary school, became Temple Primary School.

The present Temple High School building was constructed in 1976.

In 1989, under principal Denzil Rogers, Temple for the first time played football. The current stadium was started in 1992 and completed in 1993. It was totally built by volunteers from the community and is known as "Rogers Stadium".

The people of Temple have maintained a tremendous loyalty to the school. Various attempts to consolidate Temple High School have been thwarted by local leaders and voters.

The Temple High School area is now experiencing tremendous growth. As Temple grows, it will build on the traditions started at the turn of the century at the Temple Model School. *Submitted by: Steve James, Principal Temple High School*
Source: *A Historical Sketch of Temple* by B.W. Holder, Ruth R. Holder, Caroline Hudsputh, Iva P. Levans, 1976.

101. Temple Model School

The Temple Model School of Temple, Georgia, had an influence on education in the state for many years. Agriculture was introduced at the high school level through this school.

After Temple was settled in 1882, students were schooled in a very traditional way for several years. More than one hundred students were being taught at Temple Academy by two teachers. The academy was filled and the building was not in good condition.

The destiny of the school lay in the hands of a man whose thinking in the field of education was years ahead of the times. The man who wanted to change all of this was a Carroll county teacher, Ira Wellington Williams, who held an A.B. Degree from the University of Georgia and later became state entomologist. He had a dream of expanding the educational opportunities of the farm children far beyond the areas of reading, writing, and arithmetic. Williams had previously taught at Sand Hill and developed some of his ideas there. His home was on a farm south of Villa Rica.

There were two main obstacles in the way of improving the school in Temple. One was the task of convincing the school patrons that completely breaking away from tradition and custom would bring about a better education for the children. The second, and just as difficult if not more so, was the job of raising the large amount of money necessary to build and operate a new school. These two hurdles seemed insurmountable to most people, but Professor Williams dared to try.

He wanted to include in his innovative educational program the children of farm families in the surrounding communities. This involved consolidation and a transportation system, both of which were almost unheard of then. His proposed program included a sound, varied curriculum taught by teachers who were trained, qualified, and willing to move to a small southern town.

The children were to be trained to use their hands and their minds. This training was to be closely related to farming, the children's way of life. A college preparatory course would also be offered.

Professor Williams diligently worked toward making his dream become a reality. He contacted both local people and prominent men throughout the state and in other states as well. He sold them on his idea and convinced them of the great need. Slowly many of those contacted began to open their pocketbooks and give to this cause. Among those who helped financially were the Honorable Hoke Smith and Clark Howell, Editor of the *Atlanta Constitution.* The new school in its formative stages was given much publicity.

It was proposed that a $5,000 bond issue be voted for building the new schoolhouse. There was much local support, but there was also disapproval as was brought out when the bond referendum failed more than once. Many people felt that taxes would increase too much and that the town would never be able to pay off the debt. Finally, in 1903 the voters approved the bonds.

The new school was to be a model school, "Temple Model School," whose graduates would be prepared for farming, to enter college, and to teach in the smaller, rural schools.

Hamp Sewell was the mayor of the town at the time. The town council members were M.E. Griffin, J.S. Dobbs, W.M. Cobb, G.W. Roop, and M.T. Marchman. The building committee was composed of E.L. Connell, E.H. Gober, G.S. Mathews, and W.A. Enterkin.

In the summer of 1903, they let the contract for construction of the new school. The structure was to be a two-story, brick building consisting of four classrooms on the ground floor and an auditorium on the second. The roof was to be covered with shingles of slate. The site chosen for the school was the corner of James and Griffin Streets.

Early in 1904 the new, brick building was completed. It stood majestically overlooking the town. The bell pealed clearly, announcing that the dream of a brave man had come true. An attempt to provide better education for rural children was finally awaking by way of leadership from a man who dared to have faith, confidence, and courage.

The Board of Directors of the new school were E.L. Connell, President; J.A. Griffin; W.P. Muse; T.M. Spruell; and C.L. Baskin.

At the opening of the school the faculty was composed of Ira Williams, Superintendent; J. Philander Campbell, Assistant Superintendent; Mrs. Laura Josephine Rozar, Wesleyan College, Principal High School; Miss Jessye Swope, State Normal School, Principal Model School; Miss Isabelle Thursby, Oread, Maryland, Domestic Science and Manual Training High School; Miss Evelyn Dimon, State Normal School, Fourth and Fifth Grades; Miss Ella Griffin, LaGrange Female College, First Grade; and Madam Dell Antonio, Vienna, Austria, Music.

A View of The School Building and Conveyances

The cornerstone ceremony was under the auspices of Temple Masonic Lodge, No. 322 F. & A.M. This occasion was attended by many local people on hand to share in the excitement and to hear the speeches of the day. Coins and other mementoes were placed behind the stone in a copper box. The second brick schoolhouse in the county was now complete.

Loyal Cobb (Mrs. Paul), a former student of the school, had a handbook produced by the Model School in 1904. The very informative booklet covers all aspects of the program of the school along with representative pictures.

One of the four Model School wagons

The transportation system was the first in the state. The buses were mule and horse-drawn wagons with covered tops and side curtains which were lowered in bad weather. Some wagons were equipped with small, coke heaters. The wagons would seat about twenty children on long benches built on each side. The driver of each wagon lived at the farther point along the route and stopped to pick up students along the way. There were two drivers for each wagon. The drivers either attended school or worked on the rented, school farm helping to produce feed for the animals. One early driver was Otis Camp who drove two beautiful, black horses called George and Dan by the scholars. Other drivers included Paul Astin, J. Phil Campbell, Sr., Henry Holcombe, Andrew Deese, Marvin Evans, Millard Nesselhunt, Charles Wynne, and Joe Biggers. Children were transported from Draketown, Center Point, Station 48, Hickory Level, District Line, Wesley Chapel, Mount Carmel, Brooklyn, and other surrounding communities. Other students boarded with local families for eight to ten dollars a month.

Parents of children living in Temple supported the school financially annually. Nonresident pupils were charged $1.25 to $3.00 per month tuition. The older students paid the larger amount.

John F. Brooks, who later became Carroll County School Superintendent, led in the development of the new and unique transportation system. With Mr. Williams' leadership and that of Phil Campbell, they expanded the school to ten grades. Casper Lassetter of near Villa Rica was the school's first graduate having attended one year. He later became an editor of *The Progressive Farmer,* a popular agricultural magazine.

Two courses of study were offered. A college preparatory program included English, Latin, Greek, botany, geology, physics, chemistry, physiology, algebra, geometry, trigonometry, history, geography, drawing, manual training, agriculture, farm engineering, surveying, and political economy. A college preparatory student could complete the fourth year of Latin and two of Greek by the end of the tenth grade. The terminal student, after completion of the seventh grade, took such courses as agriculture, farm engineering, drawing, and manual training for boys. The course for girls included sewing, painting, and domestic science. The primary graded school offered reading, writing, arithmetic, and geography. They also were involved in nature study, clay modeling, and paper cutting. American history, Georgia history, and government were included in the courses for the upper elementary grades.

All grades were involved in suitable manual training courses which were closely related to farming activities. The school rented a farm at which the principles learned in class were put into practice. Farming activities were mainly planned for the older boys. The younger students became involved in vegetable work. Local merchants supported the school by furnishing guano and farm supplies.

The Georgia High School Association had its beginning in Temple in 1905. At that time, Dr. Joseph Stewart was at the University of Georgia mainly to work with the high schools of the state. While performing his duties as high school inspector and high school representative, he and Laura J. Rozar organized the Northwest Georgia High School Association. This organization developed into the present Georgia High School Association.

Agricultural and homemaking education which was begun at Temple received statewide endorsement in 1906 when the law was passed establishing eleven congressional district agricultural and mechanical schools in the state.

The Temple Model School lasted only for a brief period. Though soliciting and receiving sizable gifts from people in Atlanta and elsewhere, the school made financial commitments that it was unable to meet. The community not only lacked the financial resources to maintain such a school, but the community's conservative outlook often clashed with the progressive ideas of Ira Williams and his staff.

At the close of the 1907 term the school resumed a more conventional program, but it remained one of the best village schools in the county. *Submitted by: Ruth Holder, P.O. Box 70, Temple, GA 30179*
Sources: *Temple Model School Booklet* 1904-05; Joiner, Oscar *A History of Public Education in Georgia 1734-1976;* Holder, B.W. *A History of Temple, Georgia*, Thomasson Printing Company, Carrollton, GA, 1982

102. Union School

Submitted by: Wayne Cook, 1298 Happy Hill Rd., Carrollton 30116. ***See photo below.***

103. Villa Rica Elementary School

Villa Rica Elementary School is located in downtown Villa Rica at the intersection of Peachtree and Dogwood Streets. This campus is also the site of the birthplace of Thomas Dorsey, "Father of Gospel Music." Over the years, this campus has housed various grade levels, including high school. This school currently has 572 students in grades three, four, and five. Villa Rica Elementary is SACS accredited and is a Title I School-Wide Program School. In addition to academic classes, students have physical education, art, computer lab, and music.

The friendly, caring staff of Villa Rica Elementary provides a quality education in a child-centered learning environment. The curriculum is enhanced with field trips and guest speakers. The vision of Villa Rica Elementary School is that "Students will see education as the means to shape their own future and achieve a better life for themselves and others."

104. Villa Rica High School Class of 1950

In 1990 all classmates were contacted and invited to be a part of the planning committee for our 40th year reunion. Plans were made to meet at the State University of West Georgia and a dinner was prepared by their food services. The committee decorated and planned the program. Several small groups had met before but this was the first time that all class members were contacted and encouraged to come. There were 54 students in the Class of 1950 and 37 attended this reunion. A cash contribution was given to the high school from the class.

Five years later in 1995 the planning committee organized a 45 year reunion and it was decided to have it in Villa Rica at the bank community room with Alice Fincher, caterer, preparing the hors d'oeuvre and dinner. The committee arranged the room and tables. It was a much more relaxed setting and everyone seemed to like this. 28 students were present for this gathering.

Next came the big 50! In 2000 the class planning committee decided to meet at the same bank community room in Villa Rica and asked the same lady to cater the food. Banners, decorations, and lots of purple and gold balloons were used to celebrate! This was an occasion to celebrate and express our gratitude to God for all His blessings. As a legacy from the class, 17 memory bricks were purchased to be placed near the Sam McIntyre Stadium, the new library and the new classrooms in an area called the courtyard. The bricks will be inscribed with "Villa Rica High, Class of 1950." 28 students came for this celebration! See page near the back - VRHS Class of 1950. See page near the back - Villa Rica High School Class of 1950. *Submitted by: Violette Harris Denney, and the VRHS Class of 1950, 135 Maple Hill Road, Carrollton, GA 30116-7014*

Union School in Clem 1901 or 1902

Betty Jeffers, Nancy Howell, Violette Denney, Carolyn Dodgen - 2000 Committee

105. Proud Villa Rica Wildcats

The following are proud Villa Rica Wildcat descendants and in-laws of Mamie McGraw Howell and James Asbury Howell. Serving in the senior store were Carlton Boyd and Harold Roberts 1949 and Johnnie Sue Carden 1958.

Basketball players were Betty Carden 1949, Joanne Hannah, Ray Barber and Anne Spake 1952, Frances Carden, Ted Carden, Charlotte Scroggins 1953, Jo Spinks and Sue Spake 1954, Jonnie Sue Carden 1958 who finished 2nd place in the State playoffs, Opal Carroll 1968, Phyllis Barber 1975, Terri Ward 1977, Margaret Sheppard 1999, and Lauren Sheppard 2001.

Cheerleaders were Anne Spake 1952, Charlotte Scroggins 1953, Jo Spinks and Sue Spake 1954, Terri Ward 1977, Jennifer Spake 1994, and Lauren Sheppard 2001.

Baseball players were John Wayne Sauls 1958-1959, Rick, Brian, Eric and Nathan Sauls 1980's, Jason Stitcher 1992 Coach's Award, Bryan Carden 1994.

Football players include Harold Roberts 1947, Ray Barber and Frank Green 1949-1952, Ted Carden 1949-1953, Wendell Stitcher 1955-1958, John Wayne Sauls 1954-1959, Richard Sauls 1956, Randy Carden and Scott Swafford 1969-1971, Tommy Ward 1970-1973, Steve Sheppard 1970-1974 Captain, Rick Sauls 1983-1985, Eric Sauls 1984-1985, Nathan Sauls 1986-1987, Curtis Sauls 1986 manager, Brian Sauls 1989, Jason Stitcher 1992 Golden Helmet Award Winner, Bryan Carden 1990-1994, Beau Swafford 1994-1998 Golden Helmet, Christian Athlete, Best Offensive Lineman, and Tyler Ward 1998-2001.

Participants in other sports were Hal Roberts 1976 horses, Steve Sheppard 1974 track, Jane Barber 1979 volleyball, James Rainwater 1981 tennis, Lara Jackson 1988 track, Jim Williams 1986-1987 tennis, Tina Jackson 1989 track, Jason and Casey Agan cars Pauling County.

Wildcat band members Rex Hannah 1958, Beverly Barber 1969-1972 John Phillip Sousa Award, Phyllis Barber 1971-1975, Susan Ward and Jane Barber 1974-1979, Dale Walker 1976-1982, Elizabeth Barber 1978-1982, James Rainwater 1977-1981 Captain, Jim Williams 1983-1987, Amie Barber 1984-1989 Best Drum Major, Anna Swafford 1988-1989, Lara Jackson 1988 Captain of Majorettes, Tina Jackson 1989. Future Wildcat band members are Katie Jiles, Joel Jackson, Andrew Rainwater, and Sara Jackson.

Contributing to the Wildcat tradition were *Golden Nugget* annual staff members. Reba Hembree 1949, Nancy Willis 1950, Ray Barber and Joanne Green 1952, Frances Carden, Ted Carden, Jo Spinks, and Charlotte Scroggins 1953, Johnnie Sue Carden 1958, Beverly Barber 1972, Phyllis Barber 1975, Jane Barber 1979, and Elizabeth Barber 7th grade.

Participants in Student Government included Frank Green 1952, Scott Swafford 1971, Beverly Barber 1972, Jane Barber 1979, Margaret Sheppard 1999, and Lauren Sheppard 2001. Class officers were Charlotte Scroggins 1952, Frances Carden and Ted Carden 1953, Jo Spinks 1954, Richard Sauls 1957, Wendell Stitcher 1958, Phyllis Barber 1975, Jane Barber 1979, Jennifer Sapke 1994, and Lauren Sheppard 2002.

Beta Club members were Joanne Hannah 1952, Sue Spake 1954, Phyllis Barber 1975, Beverly Barber 1975 Jr. Beta Club, Terri Ward 1977, Jim Williams 1987, Jane Barber 1987 Jr. Beta, Amie Barber (Jr. Beta), Anna Swafford (Irwin County and Gilmer County), Jennifer Spake 1994, Meg Sheppard 1999, and Lauren Shepard 2001. Governor's Honors Nominees included Beverly Barber 1972, Phyllis Barber 1975, Jane Barber 1979, Amie Barber 1989, and Anna Swafford 1993 Gilmer County. Who's Who in American High Schools nominees were Beverly Barber 1972, Phyllis Barber 1975, Terri Ward 1977, Jane Barber 1979, Dale Walker 1981, Elizabeth Barber 1982, Amie Barber 1989, Jennifer Spake 1994, Brandon Pritchett 1997, and Valerie Ward 1998.

Senior Superlatives included Carlton Boyd and Reba Hembree 1949, Anne Spake 1952, Ted Carden and Charlotte Scroggins 1953, Johnnie Sue Carden 1958, Randy Carden and Scott Swafford 1971, Steve Sheppard 1974, Phyllis Barber 1975, Amie Barber and Beau Swafford 1998.

Members of Homecoming Courts were Charlotte Scroggins 1953 Queen, Helen Wynn 1972, Phyllis Barber 1975 Queen, Terri Ward 1977, Jennifer Spake 1994, Valerie Ward 1998, Margaret Sheppard 1999, and Lauren Sheppard 2001. Those receiving the title Mr. or Miss VRHS were Joanne Hannah 1952, Charlotte Scroggins 1953, Jonnie Sue Carden 1958, Valerie Ward and Beau Swafford 1998 and Tyler Ward 2001. Members of the "Miss Wildcat" Court were Jane Barber 1979 finalist, Elizabeth Barber 1982, Amie Barber 1989, Jennifer Sae 1994 and Lauren Sheppard 1998 winner. Jennifer Spake 1994 was also crowned the first Miss Villa Rica Goldrush.

Participants in FFA were Charlotte Scroggins 1953 Sweetheart, John Stitcher 1981 State Winner, and Eric Sauls 1985 Greenhand. In FHA were Betty Carden and Hazel Roberts 1949, Charlotte Scroggins 1953 President, Jo Spinks 1954, Wendell Stitcher 1958 Sweetheart, Beverly Barber 1972 Betty Crocker Award, and Debbie Roberts 1972 Betty Crocker Award Carrollton. Members of the other clubs were Opal Carroll 1968, Terri Ward 1977, Jane Barber 1979, James Rainwater 1981, and Anna Swafford 1993 Gilmer County.

Teachers of Wildcats are Stephen Jackson 1974-2001, Scott Swafford 1983-1988, and Jane Jackson 1987-1995.

Wildcat mayors are Ray Barber 1986-1991 and currently Monroe Spake. *Submitted by: Betty Carden Boyd, Douglasville, GA*

106. "Ma's Girls"

The photo shows young ladies from Ann's past teams at the naming and dedication of the Ann Anders Gymnasium in Villa Rica, Georgia. The Lady Cats were her teams from 1942 to 1972. *Submitted by: Charlotte Barber, 524 North Ave., Villa Rica, GA 30180.* ***See photo at top of next column.***

Dedication of the Ann Anders Gymnasium

107. Wayside School

The old one-room schoolhouse stood on Wayside Road. It was not quite in front of where New Hope Baptist Church stands. A few years after this picture was made, a new two-room school was built across the road.

Pictured in the front row (L to R): Christine Crawford, Florene Horsley, Opal Farmer, Myrl Latimer, Eunice Young, Verna Fountain, Geneva Williams, Inez Morris, Mary Boatright, Teacher William Lambert, Floyd Herrin, Challenge Horsley, Willie Ray Fountain, Albert Chandler, Myrl Boatright, Alton Morris, Ray Latimer, John Boatright, Frank Chandler, Ernest Chandler, and Herman Boatright.

In the second row (L to R): L. Mae Chandler, Mildred Crawford, Madge Latimer, Lola Boatright, Lizzie Kate Morris, Elois Boatright, Annie Lee Boatright, Roberta Williams, Roy Elder, Harvey Boatright, Homer Webb, Harvey Herrin, and Everet Chandler.

In the third row (L to R): Bill Herrin, Paul Herrin, Lenord Young, Horace Boatright, Jewel Boatright, Ione Herrin, Euretha Herrin, Lola Morris, Lois Boatright, Lois Young, Clestell Horsley, Namon Chandler, Ralph Latimer, and Garland Young.

Back row (L to R): Emmett Morris, Raymond Boatright, and Eddie Young. *Submitted by: Randall Herrin.* ***See photo below.***

Wayside School circa 1917

108. West Georgia Regional Library

The West Georgia Regional Library System was begun in the summer of 1944. It was one of Georgia's three pioneer pilot regional library systems, which were originally funded under the wings of the State Department of Education. The original name of the library system was Carroll-Heard Regional Library. The Headquarters was in the basement of the Sanford Library on the West Georgia College campus. The beginning collection consisted of 1,000 books borrowed from the Extension Department of the State Department of Education. The first director of the library was Edith L. Foster.

Most of the library service during the early years of the library system was through extension services. This included delivery of books by truck to rural parts of the two counties. Local gathering spots in the counties, such as schools and stores, were given small deposit libraries to make available to citizens.

In 1946, the library system became West Georgia Regional Library, as Haralson County was added to the system. Seeing the need for a better book delivery system, local civic clubs and organizations raised funds to purchase a Ford station wagon to be used as the bookmobile. Through the work of a black-white planning committee chaired by Crogman Mullins, a branch library was set up to serve the black community in Carrollton. Leroy Childs joined the library staff to manage this branch library. In the late 1940's, Delta Sigma Theta Sorority cited the library system for its work with blacks and donated a bookmobile to the library.

In 1951, Douglas County joined the West Georgia Regional Library System and in 1958 Paulding County joined the region. Both Douglas and Paulding Counties had existing county libraries, but no bookmobile service for the outlying areas of the counties.

In 1963, Dixiesteel, Incorporated constructed an all-steel library in Tallapoosa. It was the first such library structure in the United States. Also in 1963, a library was opened in Lithia Springs in Douglas County.

In 1958, the Headquarters was moved to a small building on Maple Street in Carrollton with over 45,000 volumes available to the public. In 1967, the Headquarters Library moved into its current location on Rome Street in Carrollton. William Lomason gave $100,000 to provide local funding for two federal building grants for

Edith L. Foster

the construction of the building. In the early 1970's, branch libraries were built in Bowdon and Bremen. In the late 1970's and early 1980's, branch libraries were built in Heard County and Lithia Springs and a branch was opened in Villa Rica.

Edith Foster continually strived to develop library service throughout the five counties. School media centers were developed as well as the ever-evolving branch public libraries. Miss Foster worked with local government leaders, business leaders, educators, civic clubs and organizations to publicize and develop library services throughout the area. For her efforts, she was awarded the Georgia Library Association's Nix-Jones Award for outstanding library service and was named Director Emeritus of West Georgia Regional Library upon her retirement in 1977.

Leroy Childs became the second library director in 1977. Under his leadership, the library system opened new library facilities in Heard County, Lithia Springs, and Douglasville. Mr. Childs was very involved in discussing the importance of library services with state and federal legislators.

James P. Cooper became the third library director in 1987. Additional branch libraries were added in Paulding County in the communities of Hiram and New Georgia.

A courier service to provide more efficient delivery of materials to branch libraries and to school media centers began in 1987. Computer technology was utilized to circulate books beginning in the early 1990's. As computer technology advanced and the public became more aware of the Internet, all libraries in the system began to offer personal computers for the public to use to for a wide variety of computer applications and to access the Internet.

As West Georgia Regional Library entered the new millennium, the collection had grown to boast over 450,000 volumes in eleven facilities. Today, the library system continues to assess the communities that it serves to strive to provide needed information, resources and services to all citizens. *Submitted by: Roni Willis, Assistant Director, West Georgia Regional Library, 710 Rome Street, Carrollton, GA 30117*

LANDMARKS

109. ALICE PARK

In 1999, the city of Carrollton and a Dixie Street neighborhood committee joined forces to raise funds for the creation of a park in the city's downtown historic district. Roy Richards, then CEO of Southwire, purchased a lot on the corner of East Center and Tanner Streets and donated it to the city. An In-Town South Park Committee, made up of about 30 residents living in the historic district, raised money from tax-deductible contributions.

Park Committee Meeting at Barbara Tanner's home, September, 1999

Members of the In-Town South Park Committee included David Adams and Dorothy Pittman, Mae and Joe Aycock, Betsy Ayers, Jeanne and Eric Baret, Susan and Milton Berry, Frank Boozer, Barbara and John Burson, Carole and Ronald Burson, Andrea Fulford, Susan and Richard Ingle, Anne and Fred Richards, Ginna and Roy Richards, Carol and Roberto Rivera, Shirley and Tracy Stallings, Barbara Tanner, and Marjorie and Roy Templeman. Susan Ingle and Fred Richards served as co-chairs. Jane Carroll and Danny Mabry represented the City of Carrollton on the committee.

Two ground-breaking ceremonies for the park were held. Outgoing Carrollton City mayor Joe McGinnis presided over the first one, held December 31, 1999. Contents of the Carrollton Millennium Committee's time capsule (to be placed in the park) were on display and dedicated. On January 3, 2000, in-coming mayor Gerald Pilgrim joined co-chairs Susan Ingle and Fred Richards and consulting landscape architect, Christ Threadgill, in kicking off construction of the park, but an extended drought limited progress until Spring 2001 when the fountain became operational and a variety of native shrubbery and trees (e.g., azaleas, dogwood,

Committee co-chairs break ground with mayor and landscape architect.

hollies, hydrangeas, magnolias and rhododendron) was planted. Named Alice Park in honor of Alice Huffard Richards, the park was dedicated June 19, 2001.

Gold Level sponsors (contributing $5,000 or more) for park construction were the children of Alice Richards. Silver Level sponsors (contributing $1,000 or more) included Barbara and John Burson, Citizens Bank and Trust of West Georgia, Dixie Converting, Betty and Tommy Green, Kay and Mike Horton, Susan and Dick Ingle, J and S Electrical and Mechanical, McNaughton-McKay Electric, Polyamerica, Inc., Raven Wire and Cable, Inc., Anne and Fred Richards, Cornelia and Tom Richards, Barbara Tanner, C.M. Tanner Grocery Co., Woods Pallet Development. Bronze Level sponsors (contributing $500 or more) included Mr. and Mrs. Gary Aldridge; Meredith, Lindsay, Courtney and

Newlyweds Lynne and Phil Mengel dance under park arbor (2001)

Gordon Austin; Mae and Joe Aycock; Dr. Betsy Ayers, Mr. Jeff Ayers, and Tayler; Charles E. Beard; Susan and Milton Berry; Carole and Ronald Burson; Eddie Cole in honor of Woodfin and Marion Cole; Gail and Charles Lumpkin; Evalyn and Joe Parrish; Dr. and Mrs. Wililam J. Pottorf; Randstad Staffing Services; Carol and Roberto Rivera; Roush Family Foundation; Dr. and Mrs. F. Lawrence Rowley; Shirley and Tracy Stallings; Tisinger, Tissinger, Vance, and Greer; West Georgia National Bank; and an anonymous donor.

Four park benches were donated in memory of Jewell and Henry Burson, Louise and Buddy Green, Grace and Hugh Richards, and John W. Tanner, Jr. The park also features commemorative bricks and two arbors, one at either end. On May 20, 2001, the first wedding ceremony held in the park took place under the east arbor. Lynne Prince and Phil Mengel exchanged wedding vows in a ceremony conducted by the Reverend James Callahan (retired pastor of St. Margaret's Episcopal Church). *Submitted by: Anne and Fred Richards, 301 Dixie Street, Carrollton, GA 30117*

Sources: Anne and Fred Richards, Susan and Dick Ingle

110. BANNING MILL

Banning Mill, located in southeastern Carroll County, is situated on the banks of Snake Creek, "the Talullah of western Georgia". The mill has a long history and served as employer to generations of local residents. Through time, many of the company's records were lost so much of Banning's past has been reconstructed through family stories passed down through the years. The mingling of facts and folklore embody a rich heritage for the mill and its people.

Banning was originally built and operated by the Bowen brothers of Carroll County. The four brothers acquired the mill in the Georgia land lottery of 1842. By 1849, they were producing coarse yarns that were used in grain sacks. There are no records of the composition of the original workers at the mill. It is known however that Christopher Bowen, the oldest brother, owned a number of slaves. At the time, women and children were working in the textile mills. So the original workforce may have consisted of the wives and children of area farmers. The Bowens named their mill Bownesville Manufacturing although it was also referred to as Bowen's Mill. The area surrounding the mill became known as Bowensville.

The mill burned in 1851 and the Bowen brothers were forced to forfeit their business venture. In 1855, the mill was acquired by William Amis of Coweta County. Amis moved to the area of the mill and eventually built a new mill building. It is unclear whether he operated it during the Civil War. There is a persistent story that most citizens of the area are aware of from that time period. The residents believe that Sherman's troops, on his march to the sea, spared the mill because he could never find the isolated spot. This has never been conclusively proven but there was a skirmish fought not too far from the mill at Moore's Bridge in 1864. In that encounter, the Confederates held back the Union troops.

Hutcheson's Cotton Mill at Banning in 1885

Amis obtained a charter for his business, called Carroll Manufacturing, in 1866. By 1878 however, he was forced to sell it. The new owner was Arthur Hutcheson, an Irishman with family ties to Palmetto, and three of his business associates.

Hutcheson, after moving to the area of the mill, began making many improvements. Under his direction, two pulp mills, a grist mill and two dams were constructed. Additionally, he rebuilt the old paper mill which gained prominence, by becoming one of the first mills in the area that manufactured striped paper. The textile mill received new equipment and began production of cotton sheeting and shirting fabrics. Presumably, the mill houses were constructed at this time also with "a garden spot tree" for each. One of his best remembered accomplishments though was bringing electricity to the mill in 1889, one of the first in the region to make this claim.

When Hutcheson died in 1895, the mill property extended over 1,300 acres. The community was thriving as well. This prosperity continued after his death for the next two decades as the mill was run by different board members who had served with Hutcheson.

The name of the area was changed to Banning sometime after Hutcheson's death. The first time it appeared officially however was in court documents of 1921 showing Poncet Davis taking over ownership of Banning Cotton Mills. The new owners, Davis and Stokes, hoped for the prosperity of the Hutcheson years. They updated Banning through the addition of a rubber plant facility. They did not consider that the country's economy would change drastically during their ownership causing near disaster for the mill.

When the Great Depression hit America, the mill was forced to close on more than one occasion. The residents of Banning remained a close-knit community, but most were forced to seek work elsewhere. By 1940, with a world war looming, the mill was once again under new ownership. In an effort to cut costs, the rubber plant had been moved to Bowdon and a new electric motor was installed to replace the old water turbine. The workforce had been decreased also, there were now only 50 workers, 100 less than during the Hutcheson years.

The decades that followed brought changing ownership and diminished production. By the late 1940s the mill housing was offered for sale, many of the mill workers of the area bought the homes. In the 1950s Banning became associated with Carpet Manufacturers of Dalton and began producing carpet yarns. By the 1960s, with limited capital, unable to keep up with changing technology, the mill began the process of closing its doors for good. The final closure was in 1971.

Today there are still residents of the area that remember Banning with fond memories that they are sharing with students of the State University of West Georgia in an oral history project. For that reason, Banning Mill and its heritage will always be kept alive. *Submitted by: Arden Willams, 8536 Hwy. 54, Sharpsburg, GA 30277*

111. Banning Mill

Banning Mill was built as a textile mill sometime between 1855 and 1861 by William Amis, and was called Amis Manufacturing.

The first textile mill on this site was built in the mid-1840's by four Bowen brothers, Thomas T. Smith and William Humphreys and was called Bowen's Mill. It burned, resulting in bankruptcy of the owners, and the site was sold to Mr. Amis, who constructed a brick mill, a dam for increased water power, and Antioch Primitive Church, which still stands. This was the era of the war between the states. Locally it is still believed that Sherman's army could not find the (even now) secluded mill, thus it was spared the destruction experienced by the New Manchester Mill at Sweetwater, only 20 miles away. However, there is evidence that Union troops camped on the mill grounds, and that Mr. Amis sued the Union Army after the war for property damages. Many stories have circulated about the mill's survival. One has the workers hiding the machinery in the cotton fields and disappearing during the most dangerous period. In another, the machinery was loaded onto a train and taken off to some remote area until it was safe for it to return. After the war, Mr. Amis reorganized and updated the mill and renamed it Carroll Manufacturing.

In 1882, the mill was sold to Arthur Hutcheson, Robert McBride, Joseph Hayden and Thomas Bramlett, and they called it Hutcheson Manufacturing. Mr. Hutcheson made many improvements and built housing on the ridges around the mill for his employees. He increased the size of the mill from 17,500 square feet to 36,000 square feet, upgraded the machinery, and instituted many safety features, including a sprinkling system for fires. He also built a school in the building now housing Corinth Baptist Church on Banning Road. Electricity was introduced in the mill between 1885 and 1889, making it the first electrified business in Georgia and possibly the region. People came in buggies from as far as Atlanta to watch the lights come on at night. Mr. Hutcheson, who is buried in Roscoe in the Chapel Methodist Church graveyard, also owned the sawmill across the creek, two pulp mills, a paper mill, a sock mill, and a grist mill, all within a mile on Snake Creek.

In the 1920's, the mill was sold to Poncet Davis and Davis Stokes, who added a rubber plant facility and named the entire operation Banning Cotton Mills. The Depression forced the mill to close during the years 1929-1932 and 1936-1937. Around 1940 it was bought by Mr. Upchurch (first name unknown) and then by A.L. Fuller of Newnan. A huge flood in 1944 broke the dam (which has never been repaired) and washed away 100 bales of cotton and the former rubber plant facility in which it was stored.

Mr. Fuller sold the mill in 1948 to Charles Brown and Annie Fickett Senn who called it Fickett-Brown Manufacturing.

In 1953 the mill was purchased by Douglas Matthews, G.F. Freeman, H.G. Houseworth and Harry and Martha Allen.

In 1958 it was sold to C.E. Goodroe whereupon it was named C.E. Goodrow, Inc. When Goodrow became affiliated with R.L. Kimsey Cotton Mill of Floyd County, it was called Banning Yarn Mill, with a second yarn facility in Villa Rica called Banning Yarn Mill #2.

The mill closed in 1971, and was purchased by Mike McGukin of Carroll County. He established a restaurant and dinner theatre in the mill, now known simply as Banning Mill, and eventually built eight apartments which housed artists and students until 2000. In 1989 the mill and grounds were a site for the poker scenes, bridge scenes and creek-side scenes in the hit movie, *Fried Green Tomatoes.*

In early 1999 it was purchased by Banning Enterprises, LLC, owned entirely by Patricia A. Brown, Ph.D. and Nova Lee Simmons of Atlanta. They immediately began construction to transform the mill into a small conference center and retreat, expected to open in late 2002. They enabled the mill's eligibility for the National Register of Historic Places, and are preserving the historic aspects of the building for future generations. *Submitted by: Patricia Allen Brown, Ph.D., 3249 Teton Drive, SE, Atlanta, GA 30339*

Sources: Sanborn Insurance Maps from 1885, 1889, 1895, 1900, and 1911; • Census Records, County Records, Tax Digests; • Interviews by Arden Williams, Carey Tilley, Jennifer Sims et al of the State University of West Georgia History Department under the direction of Dr. Ann McCleary. Interviewees were people who lived and worked at the mill, or whose parents or other relatives lived and worked at the mill. Transcribed interviews can be read in the Special Collections, Ingram Library, SUWG; • Photos from 1885 forward. Stored in Special Collections, Ingram Library, SUWG; • Notes of Dr. Cope Goodwin, Associate Professor of History at the State University of West Georgia, Special Collections, Ingram Library, SUWG; • Newspaper archives, Carroll County, Coweta County, Fulton County; • Bonner, James C. *Georgia's Last Frontier: The Development of Carroll County,* Athens: University of Georgia Press, 1971; • Cobb, Private Joe. *Carroll County and Her People.* Privately published, date

Banning Mill and Rock Dam with mill workers, circa 1895

unknown; • Harris, Joel Chandler, *Memoirs of Georgia, Volume 1.* Atlanta: Southern Historical Association, 1895. [copy housed in Special Collections, Ingram Library, SUWG]; • Tilley, Carey. *Survey of Visible Cultural Resources on the Banning Mill Property,* January 29, 2001. Unpublished manuscript.

112. Log House - Bowdon Junction

John Stephen Earnest built the log house in 1860 just before the Civil War. He and his sister Nancy were orphaned as their family was on their way West. They went to live with relatives in Meriwether County (Gay), Georgia and were there in the census of 1850. The Earnest Family had substantial land holdings in 1850 but for some unexplained reason by 1860 they all had moved to Carroll County, lived in log houses and owned only nominal valued land.

John Stephen Earnest went to Atlanta to join the 7th Georgia Infantry Regiment on May 10, 1861. Although he had several major diseases he served the entire war. He came home and married Elizabeth Burrow. The Burrows lived about one half mile north of land lot 324 where John Stephen's log house was located. By 1870 they had two children ages 2 and 3. In 1877 they built another house on the Mt. Zion road and John Stephen Earnest died in 1880.

Log House being used as an office by Wallace Lambert

The orphans of the Revolutionary War veteran Abraham Miles won land lot 324 in the lottery but did not move onto the property. John Foster claimed the lot on October 4, 1848. Robert Amison sold the lot to Henry Bone (Boon) (Boone), son of Harvey Boon. Harvey Boon is shown in the area in the census of 1850.

Henry Boon sold the entire lot to John Stephen Earnest. The sale was not recorded until 1871 (deeds were not always given until full payment was made). The sale was recorded in Book AA page 466. This is the first recorded transaction on land lot 324 in the Carroll County records.

Thomas Entrekin, a Confederate Veteran of the 53rd Georgia Regiment purchased the house but was unable to make the payment and Elizabeth Earnest had to repossess the property. She then sold part of the lot to L.D. and L.P. Mandeville on February 26, 1889. They were buying land in the area to build a cotton gin. This was the only place in north Carroll County where the railroad and the road ran together for any distance. They built a gin south of the log house and the community of Mandeville was started.

Records show that part of the land lot was sold to W.M. Hendrix and J.M.D. Stallings purchased land from the Mandevilles and from Hendrix. J.M.D. Stallings was a veteran of the 56th Georgia Regiment.

In Myric D. Shaw's 1962 *Story of Bowdon Junction* she talked with Lilly Casey (the last to live in the house before it was moved) and found that Lilly had lived in the house as a little girl when her parents (John and Louisa Kierbow) rented the house in 1885.

Porch of Log House before it was enclosed.

In 1902 Oscar Lambert and his family lived in the log house and Lester Philip Lambert was born there. Oscar lived in the house again in 1910 while their house next door was being built and Oscar became Postmaster at Bowdon Junction. He had a general store, Presnell and Lambert, in which the post office was located.

Lester and his wife, Verdie, lived in a house across the field from the log house. Their house burned and they moved into the log house.

J.M.D. Stallings was the first pastor of the Harmony Baptist Church formed in 1916 in Bowdon Junction. After his death in 1920 his son L.M. Stallings administered his estate. The estate of J.M.D. Stallings sold the log house to Sol Davis in 1921 who ran a grist mill. Sol Davis sold the log house to Roland Akin. Roland had nine sons and several lived in the log house.

In 1947 the house sold to H.M. (Quill) and Lilly Casey. They did more to change the house than anyone to date. They added plumbing, an extra room, kitchen and bath facilities and placed dry wall on the living room's walls and ceilotex in the ceiling.

Most of the people who lived in the house were renters. Sol Davis rented to Rudy Key. When the house was being moved a board was found with Rudy's name and the date October 19, 1922. Roland Akin rented to R.M. (Marion) Reid and Mr. and Mrs. Pitman who were school teachers at the Harmony School. Mrs. Pitman was the first president of the Home Demonstration Club in 1924. Roland also rented to Mr. and Mrs. L.V. Lovvorn, Lewis Adams and Ed and Myric Shaw. Roland's sons, Larkin, Gresham and Reynold and nephew, Solan Akin also lived in the house. In 1941 Willie Williams and his family rented the house until they built a house across the road in 1947.

W.J. Wallace purchased the house in 1967 after the death of the Caseys and it remained uninhabited until it was moved in 1979. In 1979 the log house was purchased by Wallace and Charlcie Lambert and moved about 1000 yards North. It has been partially restored. *Submitted by: Wallace T. Lambert*

113. Buckhorn Tavern

Buckhorn Tavern was a famous stagecoach stop on the route between Marthasville (now Atlanta) and Jacksonville, Alabama, being about a day's journey from each. The tavern was located about one and one-half miles east of the present city of Temple. The log house was built in 1833 by William W. West, the father of William, George W. and Thomas H. West. Mr. West was the grandfather of G.H. West of Carrollton and the great-grandfather of Mrs. B.M. (Man) Long of Carrollton.

Isaac E. Cobb later bought the house, along with several hundred acres of forest-covered land. He had moved to Carroll County from Franklin County, Georgia, in 1928. After building a store and a house in Carrollton, he moved three miles outside of Carrollton before moving to Buckhorn Tavern. The Cobbs had eight sons and two daughters. All of the sons served in the Confederate Army. He was a member of the Legislature four times, three times in succession, and was sheriff of the county for several years.

Mr. Cobb was an energetic sportsman, and wild game was abundant. When he returned from his kills of wolf, deer, and bear, he nailed the horns of the buck on trees, under the eaves of the house, and along the entry or dog trot which ran through the middle of the house. The travelers used these as hangers for their hats, coats, and saddle bags. The horns also served as hay racks in the stables. Thus, it became Buckhorn Tavern.

The tavern was a welcome sight to the weary traveler. It is said that when a stagecoach was about a mile from the tavern, the driver would sound a blast on a hunting horn for each passenger he carried, and by the time it arrived the table was set for the exact number of guests. Attendants took care of the stagecoach, and the horses were fed and watered or fresh horses were hitched up and ready to go by the time dinner was finished. The stagecoaches were drawn by four and sometimes six horses. The seating capacity of the coaches was from eight to ten with the baggage piled on top. If guests spent the night, they slept in two large rooms — ladies on the ground floor and men in the attic.

Jack Ashmore's Interpretation of Buck Horn Tavern

Mr. Cobb is buried in the Old Bethel Cemetery about three miles southeast of Temple. The inscription on the marker of his grave reads "Isaac E. Cobb August 12, 1805 died August 5, 1852."

On September 16, 1856, a post office was established at Buckhorn Tavern, thereby becoming Buck Horn, Georgia. The first postmaster was Joseph L. Hart. The post office was discontinued in 1857.

John M. Walker, Sr. purchased the tavern and farm of 613½ acres from the Cobb estate in 1857. It consisted of land Lot No. 169, most of Land Lot No. 170, Land Lot No. 184, and part of Land Lot No. 151 in the Sixth District of Carroll County. John Walker's family included his wife, Margaret; daughters, Mary L., Elizabeth, Julia, Emma, Sevilla, and Margaret; and a son, John M. Walker, Jr., who bought the farm which consisted of 323½ acres in 1871. In 1895 he built an eighteen-room hotel in Temple and his wife, Lula, managed it. After her husband's death, she bought property in Villa Rica and ran a hotel there.

During the Civil War Confederate soldiers camped around the tavern and were extended hospitality by the innkeeper.

In 1925 the old log tavern was bought by J.P. Carnes, a section foreman for the Southern Railroad and great-grandfather of Mark and Scott Holder. He weather boarded it, painted it white, and it served as a tenant house.

In 1958 the tavern and farm were bought from the Carnes estate by Leon Lee of Villa Rica who enjoyed it as a cattle farm. Unfortunately, he lost his life on Highway 78 at the entrance to his farm.

The ruins of the foundation and framework of the old log cabin, which were held together with wooden pins, can be seen from Highway 78 today. The original road was on the opposite side of the tavern from the location of the present highway, and the tavern faced the road. The property is now owned by Three West L.L.C.

Lake Burkhorn, a large watershed facility, and the surrounding residential area take their names from the famous tavern. *Submitted by: Ruth Holder, P.O. Box 70, Temple, GA 30179*

Sources: Cobb, Joe *Carroll County and Her People,* Carrollton, GA, 1906; Cheney, George F. *Carroll County Souvenir-Historical Edition.* Carrollton, GA, privately printed, ca. 1906; Newspaper articles by Radford Hamrick, *Times-Free Press,* July 22, 1954 and Munroe (Monroe) Burns, *Carroll County Times,* May 2, 1935; Records of Jack Davis, Temple, GA.

114. Carroll County Historical Society

On June 19, 1975, a group of Carrollton citizens met to form a local Historical Society at the time that plans were being made to celebrate the United States Bicentennial. Mr. Leroy Childs was temporary chairman and Angie Cook was temporary secretary. It was decided that meetings should be held bi-monthly. Early historians included Miriam Merrell, Edith Foster, and Mrs. Jessie Hamrick. Dr. Steve Worthy was the first President.

The Curtis-Marlow-Perry house was given to the City for the use of the Historical Society, and moved to its present location in 1986. It is located on West Avenue and serves as headquarters. Being one of our oldest houses, it is used as a museum for special occasions.

Carroll County Historical Society Headquarters

Education and preservation of local history has been the emphasis. Residential, business and outstanding service awards have been given. A historical writing award was awarded for the first time in 2000.

Present activities include encouraging preservation, helping the community to rehabilitate the Depot, and developing our interpretative history through historical markers.

Activities include an annual dinner, speakers, books and field trips. Early accomplishments include establishing the In-town South Historic District, saving the old Carrollton High School, planning the use of McIntosh Reserve, oral histories, the play *Murder of Chief McIntosh*, and initiating the Cemetery Census.

2001 officers are Gwyn B. Chesnut, Edith Morehead, Jan Ruskell, Myron House, Sally Owen, Dutch Dreyer, Russell Lynn, Angie Cook and Carter Clay. *Submitted by: Gwyn Chesnut*

115. Carroll County Remembers Her Confederate Veterans

On May 28, 1910, the statue to honor the Confederate Veteran of Carroll County was dedicated in the public square. The original ceremony had been postponed from April 16, Confederate Memorial Day, due to the failure of the contractor to have the monument ready with only part of it on hand. The statue of a young soldier facing north down the old Rome Road to defiantly "keep the Yankees out" or so it has been said. The statue was a culmination of work by the Annie Wheeler Chapter of the UDC and the Veterans of the McDaniel-Curtis Camp. The monument cost $2000 and took close to ten years for the groups to raise the money. The granite shaft and marble soldier were made by the McNeel Marble Company, which was the largest monument maker in the South.

The Confederate Monument, Carrollton Public Square, 1912

Printed in 1910 as a fund-raiser for the monument, *the Carroll County, Georgia Souvenir-Historical Edition* best describes those responsible for the monument. "Since we are history, let us commend those who have so nobly wrought for the erection of a monument to the Confederate heroes of Carroll County. The United Daughters of the Confederacy deserve the first mede of praise. Had it not been for their incipient, as well as ultimate efforts, the grand shaft that now adorns the public square of Carrollton in commemoration of our Confederate Soldiers — living and dead — would not today be an accomplished fact. It was theirs to inaugurate the monument movement; and it remained for the Veterans and a generous public to perfect it. These noble women had pushed the work to what is known in mechanics, "as the dead point in the crank." It was at this juncture the Veterans of McDaniel (Curtis Camp) came gallantly forward and assumed the obligations so nobly prosecuted by the U.D.C. Their combined efforts and the generous contribution of a patriotic public overcame the financial hitch. No one individual has contributed more to the erection of the monument than has Commander George F. Cheney, who for the past year has devoted most of his time to devising ways and means for the erection of the monument."

The dedication ceremonies began in the packed county courthouse. Prayers by Rev. J.M.D. Stallings and the Rev. Jessie M. Dodd were given. The Honorable Sid Hoderness introduced the orator for the day, the Honorable H.A. Hall of Newnan. Captain "Tip" Anderson accepted the monument for the veterans. Hanging over the assembly was the flag of the 44th Georgia that had been torn from the hands of the dead flag bearer as he was defending it. The assembly then proceeded to the cemetery to decorate soldiers' graves and then returned to the public square where Miss Pauline Harris, the UDC president presented the monument to the city and county. Accepting was Mayor H.W. Long and Ordinary W.J. Millican. They responded by thanking all parties involved, especially G.F. Cheney, and promised to protect and preserve the monument. The old veterans were then given rides around town in automobiles and then ate dinner at Bradley's warehouse.

With time comes changes, in 1958 after a study of downtown Carrollton, it was decided that the monument should be moved from the public square to the lawn of the Tanner Medical Center where it remained for 18 years. During this move the monument "lost" four concrete cannonballs, which can be seen in the picture from 1912, and possibly some marble pieces. In 1976, the monument was moved again to the current location of the Carroll County courthouse.

The monument features a young soldier at ease holding his rifle, his Confederate uniform is believed to be inaccurate by some military scholars as the uniform appears to have patch pockets and resembles the U.S. uniform of a Spanish American veteran. The soldier may have been substituted in the delay. An article in the *Atlanta Constitution* of April 17, 1910, erroneously announced the dedication of the monument as the original date set. The article appears to show an artist's rendition of a soldier with his rifle over his shoulder, which of course is not the soldier on our monument.

Under the soldier stands a shaft and two slabs that rest on three steps. The monument is approximately 20 feet in height. The north side of the monument reads: "In proud and loving memory of the Confederate soldiers of Carroll County 1861-1865" and "Confederate Dead". The west side of the monument reads "How sleep the brave, who sink to rest By all the country's wishes blest! By fairy hands their knell is rung; by forms unseen their dirge is sung; there honor comes, a pilgrim gray; to bless the turf, that wraps their day." The East Side of the monument reads, "upon the altar of Home and Country they placed the offering in fullest measure, of all they had to give." The south side gives credit to the UDC and dates the erection as April 26, 1910. *Submitted by: Dr. David N. Wiggins, 1093 Oak Grove Rd., Carrollton, GA 30117*

Sources: *Carroll County Times,* 20 April 1910; *Atlanta Constitution* 17 April 1910; *Carroll County Times,* 3 June 1910; *A Souvenir History of Carroll County, Times Georgian* 11 June 2000, *The Standing Army* by Frank M. McKenney.

116. Chief McIntosh's Horse Block

In Chief McIntosh's yard stood an old horse block. It was the last remaining artifact of an era gone by. The Chief had chiseled steps out of a large piece of rock for the convenience of his guests when mounting a horse. Mr. J.H. Melson and Mr. J.J. Thomasson conceived the idea of making this horse block the cornerstone of the girl's dormitory at the new fifth district A & M College in Carrollton, Georgia which was to become West Georgia College and later the State University of West Georgia. (Note: Please see the Carrollton A & M article for additional information).

Chief McIntosh's Horse Block in 1916 before removal

After obtaining permission from Preston Arkwright, President of Georgia Power Company on whose property the horse block stood, Mr. Melson and Mr. Thomasson and several boys went to the reserve and moved the stone to the college. A few years earlier the McIntosh Reserve Chapter of the Daughters of the American Revolution, D.A.R. had gone to the reserve and placed a bronze marker on the horse steps to identify this important remaining artifact at McIntosh's home place. The Chapter protested the steps removal but to no avail. Today, the stone stands in a small park at the State University of West Georgia. *Submitted by: Doug Mabry*

117. Dixie Street

Dixie Street is part of the In-town South Historic District. The tree-lined street includes many of the finer old homes of Carrollton. In its earlier days there was a male academy at the corner of Dixie and Newnan Street where the present courthouse sits. The county's third courthouse built in 1893 of red brick was located on this corner. It burned in 1928. The lower part of Dixie Street has developed into a business and medical district. It is home to Southwire Company, and Tanner Medical Center. The upper part of Dixie Street is lined with azeleas in a revitalization effort to help make Dixie Street one of the city's most beloved streets.

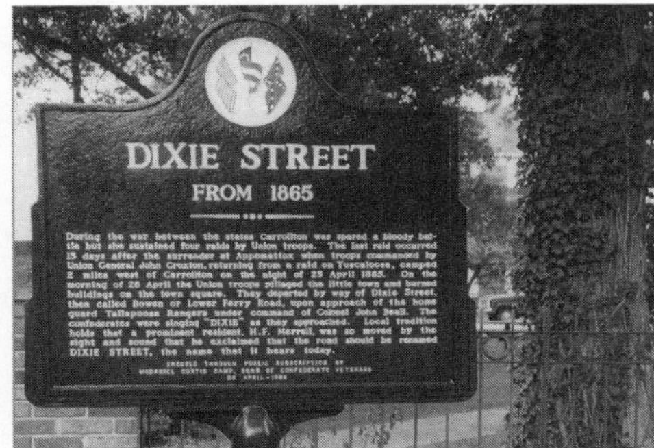

Dixie Street Marker located at the Merrell-Burson House

On April the 26th 1997 the McDaniel-Curtis Camp of the Sons of Confederate Veterans and descendants of H.F. Merrell dedicated a historic marker that tells the story of Carrollton and Dixie Street during the War Between the States. The marker is located on the front lawn

Early postcard view of Dixie Street (courtesy of Wayne Cook)

of the Merrell-Burson House. A small plaque with the history of the Merrell home is placed on the front of the house. The following is the contents of the Dixie Street marker.

During The War Between the States Carrollton was spared a bloody battle, but she sustained four raids by Union troops. The last raid occurred 15 days after the surrender at Appomattox when troops commanded by Union General John Croxton, returning from a raid on Tuscaloosa, camped 2 miles west of Carrollton on the night of 25 April 1865. On the morning of 26 April the Union troops pillaged the little town and burned buildings on the town square. They departed the way of Dixie Street, then called Bowen or Lower Ferry Road, upon the approach of the home guard Tallapoosa Rangers under command of Colonel John Beall. The confederates were singing *Dixie* as they approached. Local tradition holds that a prominent resident H.F. Merrell, was so moved by the sight and sound that he exclaimed that the road should be renamed Dixie Street, the name that it bears today. *Submitted by: H.M. Dreyer, 842 Centerpoint Road, Carrollton, GA 30117*
Sources: Sons of Confederate Veterans, McDaniel Curtis Camp #165

118. Hay's Mill and Buffalo Creek

In 1867, Mr. John Long willed a large tract of land and a water mill, which had been in operation for a number of years, to his daughter, Isabelle Long Hay, wife of David Reese Hay. The will specified that at her death the property would go to her four sons, one of which was William Robert Hay.

William Robert Hay, who was fondly known as "Uncle Billy", came into possession of a portion of the land and the old mill when he married. It was known as Hay's Mill after Isabelle inherited it. An interest in water mills among the Hay family dates back to 1748 when ancestors operated a similar mill with the same name on Hay's Mill Creek, S.C.

Hay's Mill was located a mile and a half from Carrollton on Buffalo Creek on the Old Roopville Road. It stood on a granite rock foundation, found to be the same vein of granite as Stone Mountain. The mill was powered by water from Buffalo Creek. A rock dam above the mill controlled the water that ran through a trace to the overshot wheel that furnished the power to operate the mill.

The building was tall and weather beaten, greyed with age, but striking to look at. Inside, a corner fireplace made of rock, warmed the huge room as best it could on cold days. The mill itself stood in the center of the room, its hoppers, stones, and other wooden mechanisms overpowering the otherwise bare room. The four huge mill rocks ground corn into meal, and wheat into flour. Farmers from Carroll and surrounding counties came in wagons, buggies, and on horseback to bring their corn and wheat to Hay's Mill to be ground.

"Uncle Billy" loved children and they were always welcome to come in and watch the mill grind the grain. They loved to watch him pour the grain into a huge overhead hopper, then watch the heavy millrock grind the corn into meal, which came pouring out a wooden spout into a hopper or big wooden bin. They especially like to catch the warm meal in their hands as it came out the wooden spout and lick it out of their palms.

Uncle Billy's sons took turns running the mill as they grew up, and kept it in operation after his death in 1923. On the 4th of July, 1954, vandals set the old mill on fire and it burned to the ground, but the old mill rocks were found in good condition the next morning. The site of the mill can still be located on Hay's Mill Road on Buffalo Creek where the rock dam still stands. (Hay's Mill Overlook is built on this property.)

Buffalo Creek was a popular place itself. Young people and older ones loved to picnic near its banks on the flat rocks or near a crystal clear spring up the hill. They would walk from town down a dusty road to Hay's Mill where the boys could dive into the old swimming hole. The girls and boys had a long rope swing that would glide over the creek, if one got a 'good' start from the old oak tree where the rope was tied to a limb. It was a favorite site for hot dog cookouts, marshmallow roast, and scouting trips.

Hay's Mill

Crossing over the creek was a swinging bridge that swayed sideways when the children and grown folks walked over it. It was lots of fun playing at Hay's Mill.

A more serious use of the creek were Sunday baptismal services. On many occasions during the summer, a group of people who had joined a church would line the creek bank. One by one, they would step into the creek and be dipped into the water by a preacher, similar to the way the early Christians were baptized.

It is easy to understand that Hay's Mill and Buffalo Creek are landmarks of Carroll County. *Submitted by: Jackie Talley, 230 S. Lakeshore Drive., Carrollton, GA 30117 and Written by: Sara Helen Hay in 1980.*

119. The Lovvorn Road

The Lovvorn Road, so long and slender
A lovely lady's arm,
Unwinding through the red clay hills
Like a mosaic length of yarn.

Dipper gourds and corn fields,
Old men in overalls
Pastures gleaming in the morning dew
Whitetails peering through the forest's wall.

Camp Creek Church and Ingram Road
In time like sentries stand
To greet the travelers ever passing
Down this western Georgia strand.

On this way a hundred times
The newness still the same
If eight or eighty summer
Make the vagabonds glad they came.

By Mark Kenneth Crawford
Printed With Permission
Copyright 1998
Submitted by: Jan Bell

120. Malone House

This is a picture of the George Malone House. Mr. Malone came to Villa Rica early in the 19th century. He followed the cotton and fertilizer business. He was associated with the Bank of Villa Rica and was promoter of Villa Rica Mills Inc. He had his house built around 1873 on Carroll Road in Villa Rica.

In the 1950s, Mr. R.R. (Doc) Richardson (George's nephew) owned the house and rented it out to people. Rush, Anna Lois and Charlotte Scroggins rented the house (1952-1957). Charlotte married Ray Barber (1953). She lived in the house with her daughter Beverly and parents (1954-1956) while Ray was in the army. Ray Barber was the mayor of Villa Rica (1986-1991). Monroe Spake and his mother Elsie rented rooms from Rush (1955-1957). Monroe is the present mayor of Villa Rica.

The Malone House

The Malone House was torn down about 1960 to make room for the Carroll Road Shoppette. *Submitted by: Beverly Swafford, Britton Drive, Villa Rica, GA 30180*

121. Moore's Bridge

During Sherman's famed march to the sea, Carroll County saw a small skirmish at Moore's Bridge between Confederate Brig Gen. Frank C. Armstrong and Union Gen. George Stoneman. Moore's Bridge was a 480-foot span over the Chattahoochee River near Whitesburg located just to the right of Alternate Hwy. 27. The bridge was built about 1855 or 1856 by Mr. Horace King, a master carpenter, for James D. Moore.

In 1864 Sherman was headed toward Atlanta in hopes of destroying all its railroad lines. On July 8, 1864, as Sherman was crossing Chattahoochee River, he ordered Stoneman's to follow the river to the south and destroy all factories and mills, and send the employees to Marietta as prisoners. On July 9, Stoneman's men burned the New Manchester Manufacturing Company, the 5-story cotton mill. As the Yankees continued down the west side of the river trying to find a place to cross, they learned of Moore's Bridge in Carroll County.

On July 13, Union Col. Silas Adams' 11th Kentucky was headed towards Franklin when they ran into Moore's Bridge. Dressed in captured Confederate uniforms they surprised Rebels guarding the bridge as they skinny-dipped in the river. These Rebels had stuffed the bridge with straw for burning. The Yanks opened fire and the rebels ran up the east side and across an open field. Sixteen men of the 1st Tennessee Cavalry were captured, including the bridge's owner James D. Moore. Stoneman ordered Col. Adam's men to guard the bridge and repair it. At nightfall the troops bivouacked on nearby Snake Creek, building many campfires to try and scare the Rebels away.

A rebel picket had escaped at the bridge and ridden to Newnan and warned that city of the Yankees. Newnan was located on the Atlantic & West Point Railroad and was the site of four Confederate hospitals.

On July 14th, about two miles up river of Moore's Bridge, rebel scouts reported a few Yanks on the east bank of the river. The Rebels' artillerymen sent two cannon shells over the river, scattering the Yankees. They began shelling back, but their shells did not explode. The Rebels later realized it was only a patrol unit they fired on. Stoneman had never shown much interest in crossing the river or striking the railroad and Armstrong's appearance thus gave him the excuse he needed to burn Moore's Bridge and keep the Rebels away for good. Braving a hail of bullets, Union Lieutenant William Ballard with the 1st Kentucky Cavalry was ordered to thrust the flaming torch that destroyed the bridge and it plunged into the river. Stoneman's troops continued on their raid of the Georgia countryside and destroying everything in their path.

The skirmish at Moore's Bridge was the only fighting that occurred on Carroll County soil during the War Between the States; but it helped save the Atlantic & West Point Railroad line, and the four Confederate Hospitals located in Newnan from falling into the hands of the Yankees. *Submitted by: John Carter Clay, SCV Camp McDaniel-Curtis #165.*

Source: Sherman's Horsemen

122. The Round Barn

The round barn located in the Hickory Level Community has been a well-known and talked about landmark in Carroll County since 1917. Walter Dorough built the large, unusual barn after seeing a similar one on a trip to Arkansas to visit relatives there. His plans were to begin a dairy on the family farm, therefore he adapted the design of the barn with that in mind. The dairy never came about, mainly due to the cost of building the barn. It has been described by some family members as, "the straw that almost broke the camel's back".

The barn was built with efficiency and convenience in mind. The design would especially be useful when tending to large numbers of animals. The ground floor was made up of many pens built around the entire outside wall. In the center of the barn around a large silo many cattle feeding troughs were located. Feed could be shoveled down from the second floor through troughs into the appropriate bins. The large second floor was also used to store hay. The many years of moving hay around left the wooden floor almost smooth as satin.

A huge silo was located in the exact center of the barn. It began under ground with a concrete bottom and sides that continued upward for about twelve feet. Narrow interlocking boards formed the silo wall from the concrete up to the rooftop. On the outer wall of the silo was a series of narrow iron and wood doors built one on top of the other for the entire height of the silo. These doors served as openings into the silo at any level and also the iron braces on the doors acted as ladder rungs so that the doors above ground level could be reached.

The house located on the Dorough farm was built in the 1800s by an ancestor who came to Georgia from Arkansas. The Dorough family has lived in the Hickory Level Community ever since and has been active in the community and in Concord United Methodist Church. The original house was a three room living area with a separate kitchen in the rear. Walter Dorough connected the kitchen to the house by enclosing the open space between the two and creating another room. Also, as his family grew in number, Walter added a second story to the house. The original walls were joined with wooden pegs.

The house served five generations of Doroughs with Walter's son and wife, Herschel and Elsie being the last to live there. The farm is still in the Dorough family with Ronnie and Brenda Hall, Herschel and Elsie's granddaughter and husband, and three daughters, Adecia, Whitney, and Breanna living there. *Submitted by: Brenda Dorough Hall, 3006 NE Hickory Level Road, Temple, GA 30179 and Photo courtesy Charlie Lott*

123. Walter E. Johnson Sweet Potato Curing and Storage Building

The year was 1940. This was one year after Walter and Ruth Johnson purchased a farm just north of Roopville on Hwy. 27.

An idea was projected to build a facility to cure and store sweet potatoes. The Johnson's would begin the practice of growing sweet potatoes for a cash crop, instead of relying totally on cotton. Crates would be assembled with slats for proper ventilation. The crates would hold approximately one bushel. The building was planned and constructed to hold 1,000 crates. After growing and curing the potatoes grown on the Johnson farm, the remaining space would be utilized by friends and neighbors. The cost for curing and storing for the public was $0.15 per crate. The building was constructed with 2' by 4' runners as the floor space, and these were spaced to take care of 4 runs of the slatted crates on either side of an aisle with a solid

Round Barn - Hickory Level

W.E. Johnson Sweet Potato Building

floor. The crates could be stacked 6 or 7 runs in height. Chalk was used to identify each crate with a number, corresponding with each person's name. This information was placed on a register reflecting the person's name and identifying number, and then the total number of crates for each person.

Heat was provided for the curing process with a wood furnace built just outside the front of the building. Twelve inch galvanized pipe came out of the furnace and down each side, coming together in a chimney in the rear of the building. The curing process was maintained at approximately 85 degrees for two to three weeks. Heat was controlled by vents in the bottom and top of the building.

As a side light, the potato house was designated bus stop for Southeastern Motor Lines, with a cost of a ticket one way to Carrollton of $0.15. *Submitted by: Horace A. Johnson, 30 Mashburn Rd., Roopville, GA 30170*

124. Wick's Tavern Museum

West Georgia's Oldest Commercial Structure

The year is 1826 and the gold rush is on in the western Georgia frontier. A small bustling town springs up to service the needs of the prospectors, travelers, and early settlers, whose descendants still inhabit the area today. The town was called "Hixtown" and was made up of many small storefronts along the road to the areas rich in the mineral which gives the town its' modern name, "Villa Rica", which means "City of Gold".

Among these early enterprises the only modern day survivor is the "Wick's Tavern". Built in 1830 by New York immigrant John B. Wick, it is a classic example of the "Dutch" style timber framing method. Constructed mostly of heart pine, its carefully cut and fitted wooden beams testify to an age of craftsmanship nearly lost to time.

After the arrival of the Georgia-Pacific Railroad in 1882, citizens began to roll homes and stores on large logs pulled by teams of horses and oxen from Hixtown to the site Villa Rica occupies today.

As Hixtown then became a residential area, the remaining commercial buildings were used for storage or barns until they passed into history. The Wick's Tavern structure (being too large to move) was converted to a private residence and served in that capacity for well over another hundred years.

The memory of "old Town" and its' Tavern has become legend in the West Georgia area. In fact few people remember the name being "Wick's", simply referring to the old home as the "Old Town Tavern".

Wick's Tavern

In 1998, due to the area filling with commercial development, the Tavern building became available for restoration. The Chastain family agreed to donate it to any group which would remove it from the property and restore it. A group of folks who are interested in the history of the Villa Rica area quickly formed a non-profit 501c3 corporation to take possession of the building, locate and purchase property suitable for its new home, relocate it, and begin restoration.

The name chosen for this corporation is "Friends of Wick's Tavern."

A suitable location was located at 212 West Wilson St., in downtown Villa Rica. From August to November, 1998, the Tavern was prepared for moving and its new home downtown was prepared to receive it.

In late November, 1998, the Tavern also made the journey to the downtown area. 116 years after the other "Hixtown" structures. Since that time the "Friends" have been busy completing the restoration on the Tavern, and completing a "service building" (which has the appearance of a barn) to house the rest rooms and the maintenance facility for the Tavern.

The Tavern now serves as a museum depicting life in this area from 1830 to the present.

Submitted by: Charlie Lott, P.O. Box 2, Winston, GA 30187-0002
Sources: *Carroll County and Her People* ... Pvt. Joe Cobb 1908

125. Windmills

Several windmills add interest and nostalgia to farms around Carroll County. They seem quaint today in our technical world; but they were a great invention back when most water was drawn from a well. One had to be very careful with water when they had to turn a windlass and pull a bucket up 50 to 60 feet. It was like a miracle when with a windmill, you could turn on the spigot and there was water right in your house. Back then, it was the fanciest farm tool around, and people came from all over to see how the process worked.

Herman Brown installed four windmills in the area around 1925-1930. The one that was built on the family farm is now located in a field behind the Crossroads Shopping Center on Highway 27 S. It had not been used to hold water in years; and baby white owls were found in the water tank when it was moved. Another one is located on the Tisinger farm at Victory. While installing this one, Herman met his future wife, Pansy Tisinger. A third windmill was built for Dr. Scales at Hickory Level; and a fourth one was built on the Lipham farm in Heard County.

There's something about windmills that continues to fascinate people. When the wind blows, the blades aim exactly into the changing wind by the ever-sensitive stabilizer device that changes direction to conform to that of the wind. Water is pumped into a tank until it is full. When the wind is not blowing, there is not much water or pressure; but once the tank is full, the law of gravity takes over, and alas - free water.
Submitted by: Matthew Clay, 106 Haberham Place, Carrollton, GA 30117
Source: family.

ORGANIZATIONS

126. ABRAHAM BALDWIN CHAPTER, NSDAR

The National Society Daughters of the American Revolution was established in 1891 to mend wounds caused by the Civil War, bringing families together with common bonds. The first President General, NSDAR, was Mrs. Benjamin Harrison.

The Abraham Baldwin Chapter, NSDAR, was organized in April 1953. Mrs. Ruth Brock Kramer was Organizing Regent. The Chapter was named for Abraham Baldwin, father of the university system (UGA) and signer of the US Constitution. Organizing and charter members: Ruth R. Alexander, Frances W. Astin, Mayne A. Aycock, Mary Jane Brock, Rebecca Brock, Nicie Burgess, Ruth H. Darby, Elma Fountain, Lenora C. Fountain, Francis F. Green, Lucia Massee, Ruth B. Kramer, Miriam C. Merrell, Irma H. Mitnick, Mary A. Patton, Marian S. Pritchard, Sarah H. Pritchett, Charlcie H. Stevens, Kathleen M. Thomasson, Wyolene M. Warren, Mary M. Wirsing, Elise Barr, Loraine P. Chalker, Inez A. Folds, Lonie R. Harris, Elizabeth W. Holderness, Martha M. Ingram, Dorothy D. Loftin, Frances C. Medlock, Mary Lou Munn, and Jamie T. Weaver.

Former Regents: Mrs. E.G. Kramer, 1953-55; Mrs. P.C. Astin, Jr., 1955-57; Mrs. Floyd Wirsing, 1957-59; Mrs. John Fountain, 1959-61; Mrs. J.H. Pritchett, 1961-63; Mrs. F.M. Chalker, 1963-65; Mrs. J.R. Hamrick, 1965-67; Mrs. Nolan Fletcher, 1967-69; Mrs. Jefferson Brock 1969-71; Mrs. Nat Hanna, 1971-74; Mrs. Jefferson Brock, 1974-78; Mrs. G.E. Lenaeus, 1978-84; Mrs. C.E. Hughes, 1984-88; Mrs. Victor Simpson, 1988-90; Mrs. G.E. Lenaeus, 1990-92; Dr. Nancy Mims, 1992-96; Mrs. Reuben Word, 1996-98; Mrs. P.C. Astin, 1998-2000; Mrs. James D. Denney, 2000-02. In 1994 Mrs. G.E. Lenaeus was named "Outstanding Chapter Regent" of the NW District by the Georgia State Chapter Regents Club. Chapter sponsored American History Scholarship winners were Harry Camp (2000) and Patricia Ballantyne (2001).

Pictured at top right are the 1986 Chapter officers: Mrs. F.M. Chalker, Mrs. Jane Jenkins, Mrs. Carl Stevens, Mrs. Nat Hanna, Mrs. Victor Simpson, Mrs. John Fountain, and Mrs. C.E. Hughes. *Submitted by: Susan Lenaeus, 311 Briarwood Dr., Carrollton, GA 30117-4132*

Source: DAR Chapter records.

The 1986 Abraham Baldwin Chapter, NSDAR, officers in Carrollton.

127. ALICE'S HOUSE

It is the mission of Alice's House — Community Children's Home mission to: provide a safe and secure environment for children so that emotional healing and development of personal and family living may occur; maximize the potential of children who are experiencing social and emotional difficulties; provide a safe home designed to meet the special needs of the children in our community.

Concerned for the welfare of abused, neglected and foster children, in 1993 local community activists in Carroll County, Georgia organized the Community Children's Home, Inc. This 501.c3 nonprofit organization recognized the need for children to have a safe shelter, protected from abuse and neglect. Named in honor of a longtime community leader, Alice Richards, Alice's House received its first child in March of 1997.

Located just east of Carrollton, Georgia Alice's House is a six thousand square foot home resting on three acres of land. It provides services to children from six to seventeen who live in Carroll and the surrounding metropolitan counties. The home has eight beds designated for long-term care and two beds set-aside for short-term or emergency needs. Priority is given to children in the protective custody of the Department of Family and Children Services or those children referred by the Juvenile Court. Guidelines allow private placement from families with costs based on a sliding scale.

The program operates with four group leaders working a rotating schedule. The program coordinator and administrative assistant complete the staff on site with technical, administrative, and supervisory help. Volunteers attend a training program before contact with children in the home. Twenty local volunteers have completed this training.

Alice's House receives the per diem for each child referred by the Department of Family and Children Services. The DFCS reimburses some cost of care. The Community Children's Home, Inc. is responsible for the remaining cost of direct services. Major funding gifts received in the past 12 months include $10,000 from Warren P. and Ava Sewell Foundaiton, $4,000 from the Viva Foundation, and $2,000 from the Thomas H. Lanier Foundation.

Georgia Baptist Children's Home, Inc. manages the home providing professional expertise and services. The Community Children's home, Inc. owns the building and carries the financial responsibility for operation and ownership of the properties and associated services. Each day, Alice's House provides direct services to a variety of children in need. Our annual personnel, food, clothing, utilities, supplies, vehicle lease, furniture, education and general administration totals over $170,000.

A beautiful home, quality management, and daily operation all demand that our local volunteers spend many hours per month in fundraising activities. The continued operation of this program hinges on our efforts to marshal support from our community and concerned foundations. Please consider joining hands with our organization, as we serve neglected, abused or abandoned children. *Submitted by: Evelyn Parrish*

128. THE ARTS STUDY CLUB

The Arts Study Club was organized February 12, 1946 by twenty young matrons at the home of the Rev. and Mrs. H.B. Benson with Mrs. Bill Harris as the first president. The purpose was to learn more about the arts. Today membership is limited to thirty-six and is by invitation only.

The charter members were Mrs. George Adams, Mrs. Howard Benson, Ms. Marie Campbell, Mrs. Glenn Elliott, Mrs. Alton Estes, Mrs. James Griffin, Jr., Mrs. T.R. Griffin, Jr., Mrs. William E. Harris, Mrs. T.A. Herndon, Jr., Mrs. Perry Huff, Mrs. Billy Johnson, Mrs. Paul Patton, Mrs. Hugh Richards, Mrs. George Kerry Smith, Mrs. Earl Staples, Mrs. Leon Tatum, Ms. Annie Belle Weaver, Mrs. Thomas Williams, Mrs. Steve Worthy, and Mrs. Robert Waters.

Arts Study Club

In the early 1950s the club sponsored a concert series at West Georgia College, which was inaugurated by a hometown artist, Mildred Miller Davis. In the early years the club gave several prints of famous paintings to Carrollton High School in order to foster the art of painting. A major club project has been funding two scholarships at the State University of West Georgia — one in music and one in art.

The club meets, usually in the home of a member, the first Thursday of each month excluding July, August and January. Each year a theme for study is selected, including such recent ones as "Great Cathedrals of the World," "Going East: The Road Less Traveled," "Museums of the World," "A Wealth of Southern Writers," and "Music in Our Community."

Submitted by: Jewell Johnson, 329 N. White St., Carrollton, GA 30117

129. "AS YOU LIKE IT" CLUB HISTORY

The "As You Like It" club was started in October 1947 as a spin-off of a couple's club which began in 1942 during wartime and gas rationing. As a means of entertainment, the Lod Matthews, Roy Merrills, Clyde Rowlands and

Perry Digbys formed a supper club meeting monthly for dinner. Realizing the pleasure of this, the ladies decided to invite four other ladies and form an afternoon club.

Bowdon already had three active clubs, Stitch and Chat, Blue Stocking and Hobby Club, thus it was agreed to invite non-members of other clubs. This rule continues today.

With new members Leila Arrington, Lilly Moon, Metta Rae Burroughs and Izora Kent, the ladies had their first meeting at Mrs. Arrington's consisting of games, refreshments and social hour. Names were suggested for the club and "As You Like It" was chosen because of its literal meaning and admiration of Shakespeare's play. The purpose of the club was to promote friendship, usefulness and cultural and spiritual growth. Each members' birthday was to be celebrated and the Christmas meeting would be special with husbands invited.

"As You Like It" Club Circa 1960

Over the years, membership increased to twelve and it changes as death, health and other reasons causes members to discontinue. Membership has included: Ara Matthews, Flossie Merrill, Nell McCarley, Jessie Digby, Leila Arrington, Lilly Moon, Metta Rae Burroughs, Izora Kent, Marguerite Johnson, Annie Davis, Sarah Barker, Jessie Roop, Adelle McCarley, Gracie Collins, Margaret Copeland, Naomi Lovvorn, Virginia Barrow, Ethel Russell, Connie Edwards, Margaret McCaghren, Louise Holland, Neva McWhorter, Nellie Blackwelder, with current members being Lilly Moon, Jessie Roop, Adelle McCarley, Margaret Copeland, Estelle Johnson, Edna Huey, Doris Davis, Betty May, Jean Burns, Peggy Boyd, Virginia Cramer and Betty Smith.

The "As You Like It" members have always found joy in participating as a wholesome, dedicated group. The current members are no exception. They are continuing the tradition of happily mingling, serving and sharing as important representatives of Bowdon. *Submitted by: Betty M. Smith, 124 Forest Hill Rd., Bowdon, GA 30108*
Source: "As You Like It" Club History by Jessie Digby - 1985

130. Blue Stocking Club

Bowdon, Georgia

The idea of forming a club for young matrons of similar interests was conceived at a meeting held in Bowdon, Georgia in April 1947. Present: Madian Witt, Billie Anne Ozier, Jean Barr, Frances Plunkett, Bonnie Barrow, and Mildred Lipham.

On June 23, 1947 an organizational meeting was held at the Community Clubhouse, a log structure located in the park in the center of Bowdon. The name "The Blue Stocking Club" suggested by Francis Plunkett, was adopted. This name is derived from clubs formed in England in the 1700's where women were allowed to participate in conversation with literary and ingenious men. The most eminent member, Benjamin Stellingfleet, always wore blue worsted stockings. So great was his influence that in his absence it was said "We can do nothing without the Blue Stockings". The term

Officers of Bowdon Blue Stocking Club, 1947/48.

thus came to denote women with a taste for learning and intellectual pastimes.

With funds donated by Lamar Plunkett, the club built Bowden's first supervised playground on the campus of old Bowdon College. They started a "Playschool", held "Honor Teas" for Bowdon graduates, sponsored Girl Scouts and supported Founder's Day and other civic endeavors.

Their 50th anniversary, June 1997, was celebrated with "High Tea" at the Ritz Carlton.

As of 2001 the club still meets every two weeks. Though activities are limited, the members still support every endeavor toward the betterment of Bowdon.

Bowdon Blue Stocking Club, Christmas Party 2000.

Members through the years: Jean Barr, Mary Ella Beam, Lucille Bishop, Bessie Coley, Margaret Durham, Edna Earle Eason, Jean Fuller, Mary Ruth Landers, Mildred Lipham, Nell Smith, Wilma Smith, Luta Vance, Peggy Warnock, Madian Witt, Jo Barrow, Billie Anne Ozier, Frances Plunkett, Katherine Merrill, Rosalie Bannister, Ruth Bailey, Velma Landers, Sara Joyce Yates, Bonnie Barrow, Edna Barrow, Mae Hawkins, Claire Taylor, Carol Martin, Posey Nell Arthur, Angie Swofford, Azilie Halverson. *Submitted by: Jo Garner Barrow and Madian Witt.*
Sources: Minutes and scrapbooks stored at Bowdon Library.

131. Bowdon Canasta Club

Twelve young women who enjoyed both the game and the fellowship with each other organized the Bowdon Canasta Club in 1955. Once a month they met at the home of one of the members. The original members were Lucille Bishop, Wilma Smith, Nelva Roop, Betty Smith, Dot Godwin, Cecilia Padgett, Janelle Smith, Annie Ruth Cook, Audrey Jones, Catherine Smith, Wynell Crawford, Edna Huey, and Posey Nell Arthur. Through the years some members moved away or dropped out of the club for various reasons, but the club remains strong, still experiencing the camaraderie and fellowship for which it was founded. Three of the charter members are deceased: Posey Nell Arthur, Annie Ruth Cook, and Martha Lou Holmes. Membership today includes the following ladies:

The Bowdon Canasta Club 2001

Ruth Ayers, Peggy Crawford, Edna Huey, Audrey Jones, Louise Meigs, Margaret Ozier, Nelva Roop, Betty Smith, Janelle Smith, Jeannie Steed, and Gwen Williamson. The meetings are still monthly. However, the group has added community projects and fund raising activities to its agenda, a wonderful way of extending its outreach to the community. *Submitted by: Nelva Garrett Roop, 400 Ellenwood Dr., Bowdon, GA 30108 and Janelle Warren Smith*

132. The Bowdon Area Historical Society

The Bowdon Area Historcial Society is the oldest historical society in Carroll County. Its purpose is fourfold: 1) to promote a greater appreciation of sites, structures, events, personalities, and all other matters pertaining to the establishment of Bowdon, Georgia; 2) to preserve, develop, and restore sites and other structures of historic and architectural interest; 3) to promote tours, establish educational venues and museums; and 4) to further the History of Bowdon, Georgia. Past presidents include: Wayne Copeland (1986-88); Diana Henson and Jackie Jackson (1988-91); Jean Barr (1991-93); Marcia McGahee (1993-95 and 1997-99); L.E. and Eddie Witt (1995-97); and Carol Ann Barr (1999-present).

The Meeting Place, formerly Bowdon Methodist Protestant Church

The Bowdon Area Historical Society organizes the annual Bowdon Founders Day held the first weekend in August. The Society also has begun restoration of the historic Shelnutt-Wessinger house, a "dog trot" type structure which was the original home of Bowdon founder, Nathaniel Shelnutt.

In 1997 the Society undertook renovation of the former Bowdon Methodist Protestant Church building, now called "The Meeting Place," which serves as the Bowdon Historical Society Headquarters. The church, organized under the leadership of Reverend John Thurman in 1855, was originally part of the Bowdon College campus. The first church was housed in a log cabin, and the second building was destroyed by the cyclone of 1934. The building that exists today was erected in 1938. The

The Shelnutt-Wessinger House is being restored

Meeting Place is located behind the Bowdon High School gymnasium. It's available for educational programs, classes and exhibits as well as community gatherings. *Submitted by: Judy Rowell and Mignon Wessinger on behalf of Bowdon Area Historical Society, P.O. Box 227, Bowdon, GA 30108*

133. Bowdon Junction Home Demonstration Club

In a picture dating from the twenties members of the club are shown with some husbands and neighbors. In the background is the home of Rev. S.B. Duncan, minister and school teacher at the Bowdon Junction School.

Mrs. Pitman a teacher at Bowdon Junction was the first president and Bertha Parker, wife of Millard Parker was its first secretary. The club started a library in 1927 with 74 donated books. Their exhibit at the Carroll County Centennial in 1927 won a twenty five dollar prize. They also had a float in the parade.

Bowdon Junction Home Demonstration Club

Mrs. H.M. Parker was the winner in a home beautification contest in 1929. Mrs. Tom G. Silvey, mother of Aubrey Silvey was selected club lady of the year for her outstanding club work in 1951.

The club owned and first used a small clubhouse and when the school was consolidated with Mt. Zion used the larger schoolhouse for activities. At a cake contest in 1928 the club had twenty-eight contestants. Mrs. H.H. Boyd won first place and Viola Wallace won second place. *Submitted by: Wallace Lambert*
Source: From the History of Bowdon Junction by Myric Shaw

134. The Camellia Garden Club

Bowdon, Georgia

The Camellia Garden Club was founded by Pearl Fowler in January of 1960. The membership was constituted of employees of Sewell Manufacturing Company, and meetings were held once a month after work, usually at the company day room.

The purpose of the club was to promote interest in gardening, to promote friendship among neighbors and to encourage civic beauty. The club motto was "Beautify as we go."

The club sponsored an annual flower show held in late summer/early fall. On special occasions or for special programs, meetings were held in the members homes.

The October 20, 1960, meeting of the Camellia Garden Club

The membership roster for 1961 included Mrs. Alvin Batchelor, Mrs. Rhudy Batchelor, Mrs. Milton Batchelor, Mrs. Hugh Benefield, Mrs. Hollis Chambers, Mrs. Ralph Fowler, Mrs. Frank Gilley, Mrs. Harold Garrett, Mrs. Doc Harris, Mrs. Curtis Holcombe, Mrs. Ray Holloway, Mrs. Hoyt Hosey, Mrs. Ewell Johnson, Mrs. Levi Jackson, Mrs. Ben Martin, Mrs. Homer Mize, Mrs. Whit Marlow, Mrs. Lunie Preston, Mrs. Claude Rowland, Mrs. Garfield Rainwater, Mrs. Robert Rampey, Mrs. Lois Whitehead, Mrs. Clyde Williams, Mrs. Bobby Word, Miss Floy Widner, Miss Lola Mae Wright, Mrs. Myrtie Wise, Mrs. Walter Smith, Mrs. Emmett Hanson and Mrs. Hollis Wortham.

The Camellia Garden Club remained active for several years. *Submitted by: Mrs. Sara Nell Word, 624 Reavesville Road, Bowdon, GA 30108.*

135. Carroll County Alzheimer's Support Group, Inc.

A small group of concerned individuals from various organizations met in the fall of 1986. A need was felt to exist for family members of Alzheimer's victims to have the opportunity to share experiences, learn more about the disease and to promote awareness of the disease to the public. Letters were written to physicians, nursing homes, community agencies and family members to inform them of the development of a support group. Information packets were developed for distribution and plans were made for the first meeting. The support group was sponsored by the Carrollton Senior Adult Center and Tanner Medical Center Social Service Department.

In addition to creating the support group, a grant through the Area Agency on Aging was submitted by Tanner Medical Center for an in-home Respite Care program for individuals with Alzheimers' disease and their family. The first year for the grant began in the fall of 1989 and has continued to the present time.

From the support group an Alzheimer's Task Force was also formed to increase membership and serve as an advisory board. The Task Force continues to meet on a monthly basis and works to assist Alzheimer's families with support, education, referrals, medication assistance and identification bracelets. The current Task Force officers include Camilla Stevens-Cooper; president, Dr. Fred Richards; Vice-President, Lisa Deming; secretary, John Matheson; treasurer, Tina Robinson; Goals Chair. Other board members include: Carla

Alzheimer's Board members recieving donation from Hog Wild Motorcycle.

Bryant, Gail Carnes, Amy R. Carroll, Bob Harris, Danielle Jenkins, Jack LaFoylette, Teresa Marlow, James Pienta, Linda Pope, Bibbi Ransom, Joy Shirley and Butch Woodsmall.

The group has been fortunate in the past couple of years to receive funding from HogWild Motorcycle in Temple and the Zacharian Foundation along with memorial contributions and proceeds from the annual fall benefit dinner. *Submitted by: Lisa Deming (secretary), P.O. Box 2465, Carrollton, GA 30117. Alzheimer's Board members receiving donation from HogWild Motorcyle.*

136. Carroll County Association For Retarded Citizens

The Carroll County Association for Retarded Citizens (CCARC) is an advocacy and support organization that works with and for persons with mental retardation in Carroll County. Members are committed to securing for all people with mental retardation the opportunity to choose and realize their goals of where and how they learn, live, work, and play. The CCARC is further committed to reducing the incidence and limiting the consequences of mental retardation through education, research and the support of family, friends and community.

The members of the CCARC believe that people with mental retardation are people first and should receive attention in a respectful manner. The Association also believes that any discrimination or the denial of needed services should be fought by all legitimate and effective means.

The movement toward the establishment of the CCARC began when Wesley Estes, the son of Frances Floyd and Alton Estes, was born. Frances and Alton Estes were married in 1941. They had two children, a daughter, Celeta and a son, Wesley. Wesley was born with Down's Syndrome. In the fall of 1961 Mr. and Mrs. Estes realized if Wesley was to have any educational services other than those provided at home, they would have to begin a program, since at that time, the Carrollton City Schools did not offer educational services to children with mental retardation.

The Rev. Howard Benson, pastor of the First Baptist Church, and the deacons approved the use of a room in the church as a classroom for persons with mental retardation. Five families organized the "Parent Group" and the School of Hope was founded. The parents paid for the teacher and provided all the materials for the classroom. The "Parent Group" was the forerunner of the Association for Retarded Citizens.

Eventually, the School of Hope outgrew the church facilities, and the Carroll County Training Center was opened in March of 1973 at 109 S. White Street. By the end of the first year the center had 58 clients. At this time the center was providing infant stimulation, education for school aged children, as well as education for adults. In 1980 the need for more space was so great, a new training center was built on Airport Road through the generosity and help of the people of Carrollton City and Carroll County. Airport Road was later named Alton Estes Drive to honor Mr. Estes, one of the original founders of the CCARC.

Following the building of the Training Center, the CCARC began studying the needs of the citizens with mental retardation and their families. The members of the organization determined that with the movement toward deinstitutionalization, there was a need for community housing. Through the generosity of a member of the CCARC, initial funds were provided for the building of two group homes, one for gentlemen and one for ladies. Later, a group of concerned citizens of Carroll County donated land and with another generous monetary donation from the CCARC, the Richards Respite House was built.

In 1992 the "Friends of the ARC" was organized for the purpose of raising funds for the CCARC. These funds have been used to buy vans, remodel existing buildings, and award scholarships to the State University of West Georgia for students preparing to be special education teachers or speech language pathologists. In 2000, the CCARC began an endowed scholarship in memory of Moselle Chappell, a founding member of the CCARC and the first special education teacher in Carroll County. The first scholarship was awarded in April of 2001. Other financial support for the CCARC is derived from contributions from firms and organizations, memorials, membership dues, and member pledges.

Through years of concern and support of the community, the Carroll County Association for Retarded Citizens continues to be an advocate for all persons with mental retardation. One of the original five members of the "Parent Group," Mrs. Frances Estes continues her loyal support and active membership in the CCARC. The theme of the first organizational meeting of the ARC was "They need you now." It is as true today as it was at that time. *Submitted by: Virginia Presley, Executive Director, Carroll County Association for Retarded Citizens, 200 Alton Estes Drive, Carrollton, GA 30117.*

Source: Information provided by Mrs. Frances Estes.

137. Carroll County Genealogical Society

In 1976 a group of genealogists met at the home of Mrs. Mary Florence Arthur Word to discuss the possibility of organizing a local Genealogical Society. Charter members were Clarice Cox, Mr. L.A. Foster, Mary Reeves, Evylyn Morrow, Mr. & Mrs. Elmo Roberds, Mary Rowell, Deborah Ivey, Mr. & Mrs. Curtis Harrison, Juanita Davis and Mrs. Word, who served as the first president. The society was organized for the purpose of preserving local records and evaluating and sharing with interested genealogists.

L-R Wade Dorsey, Mary Florence Word, Betty deVane, President

The first edition of the Carroll County Genealogical Society Quarterly was edited in 1980 by Jan Robison Bell. In 1985 Mrs. Shirley Gardner became the editor of the quarterly, a position which she continues to fill in a very professional manner.

At the present time there are about 200 members located over the United States. The society has published the 1830-1880 census of the United States. Three local histories have been republished by the society, along with *A History of Haralson County,* by Lois Newman, and the newspaper clippings of the V.D. Whatley. The society joined with the historical society in 1983 to publish *Carroll County Cemeteries.*

A very popular project of the society is a spring workshop. In the year 2000 officers of the Ulster Historical Foundation in Belfast conducted the workshop. In 2001, Wade Dorsey from the South Carolina Department of Archives and History was the presenter. *Submitted by: Mary Florence A. Word*

138. Carroll County Historical Society

On June 19, 1975, a group of Carrollton citizens met to form a local Historical Society as plans were being made to celebrate the United States Bicentennial. Mr. Leroy Childs was temporary chairman and Angie Cook was temporary secretary. It was decided that meetings should be held bi-monthly. Early historians included Miriam Merrell, Edith Foster, and Mrs. Jessie Hamrick. Dr. Steve Worthy was the first President.

Henry Curtis House, Carroll County Historical Society Headquarters and Museum

The Curtis-Marlow-Perry house was given to the City for the Headquarters of the Historical Society; and moved to its present location in 1986. It is located on West Avenue. Being one of our oldest houses, it is used as a museum and on special occasions.

Education and preservation of local history has been the emphasis. Residential, business and outstanding service awards have been given. A historical writing award was awarded for the first time in 2000 to Dr. Mac Martin. Present activities include encouraging preservation including saving the Carrollton Depot, and developing our interpretative history.

Activities include an annual dinner, speakers, books and field trips. Early accomplishments include establishing the In-town South Historic District, saving the old Carrollton High School for community activities, planning the use of McIntosh Reserve, oral histories, the play "Murder of Chief McIntosh", and initiating the cemetery census.

Officers are Gwyn B. Chesnut, Edith Morehead, Jan Ruskell, Myron House, Sally Owen, Dutch Dreyer, Russell Lynn, Angie Cook and Carter Clay.

The society is a non-profit group, and you would be welcome to join, or visit any of our meetings. We meet six times a year on fourth Tuesdays. Field trips are sometimes planned. Write us at P.O. Box 1308, Carrollton, GA 30117. *Submitted by: Gwyn Chesnut*

Sources: Historical Society's records

139. The Carroll Service Council Twenty Years Later

The Carroll County Service Council is a unique organization. The fact is that it is one of the most unique community organizations that I have ever known. When it was organized back in the early forties the city of Carrollton and Carroll County apparently did not know how to solve their own problems. Consequently they organized panels designated as Industrial, Religious, Information, Education and Recreation, and Public Welfare.

The Service Council had the support of Carrollton's leading business and professional men. They elected Dr. L.J. Brock chairman of the board of directors. At that time he was a member of the state senate and was perhaps one of the most influential men in the entire county. Dr. Brock enjoyed the confidence of the people as perhaps no other man in the county experienced.

With such interest and leadership, there was a wave of enthusiasm and as the group worked together, people came here from not only Georgia but literally from over the United States and in some instances, other sections of the world.

The Industrial Panel later became the Carrollton Chamber of Commerce. From the panel on Education and Recreation came our present excellent program which we know as a board which handles the very wide recreational activities in the city.

There were in those days only one or two industries. They were the old recognized businesses such as yarn and cotton mills. Today one of the largest industries is Southwire, internationally known, whose annual value of sales amounts to more than eighty million dollars. There is a variety of other types of industry which came into Carrollton. I do not know a town and county that has such a wide diversity of industry as does Carroll County. In the city of Carrollton alone there are 35 industries or processing plants which employ many people.

The Recreational Panel evolved into a constituted city commission of recreation in charge of a director paid by the city. This director's program involves four to five thousand participants. The director, who is a competent organizer, enlists four or five hundred adults who supervise baseball, basketball, and scores of other activities.

In my judgment, this is one of Carrollton's most constructive organizations. It is a character building organization in that it keeps youngsters busy and involved in doing worthwhile things.

The first activity of the Panel on Religion was to secure the services of a theological scholar working on his doctorate. As a result of his connection surveys were made of church and nonchurch members in Carroll County. Out of this study he was able to have a dissertation for his doctorate and to produce a unique study of the religious life of the county. The carry-over of this is now found in a strong Carroll-Haralson Ministerial Association, which coordinates the church activities of the area.

One of the most far-reaching humanitarian aspects of the Service Council was dealing with the emergencies in homes of the indigent sick and hungry. Pending such a time as the welfare agencies were able to take over, the Service Council saw that these needy people had medical help and food supplies. *Written by: Irvine Sullivan Ingram*

140. The Carrollton Brass Band

Carrollton had just organized a brass band in time for the Reunion of the 7th Georgia Regiment

(CSA) on July 20, 1889. Resplendent in their new uniforms, they were ready for the occasion[i]. During the first two decades of the 20th century, before the days when radio was common in Carroll County homes, Carrollton took great pride in its new brass band. During the early period in Carrollton history, one of the notable Carrollton Bands was also known as the Carrollton Zouaves, directed by George Gray.[ii]

During a recent visit with my cousin Mary Gray Searcy and her husband Frank, lifelong residents of Carrollton, they shared an original photograph of one of the early Carrollton bands with my brother, Steve Phillips (Fayetteville, GA), and I. Mary's father, George Gray, is seated, second from the right in the photo. We never knew Aunt Dovie Phillips Gray's husband, Uncle George, was a musician. It looks like he played a Cornet. Uncle George was born in Carrollton, on August 19, 1875, and Aunt Dovie Mae Phillips Gray, George's wife, was born in Carrollton on March 17, 1884. Both were lifelong residents of Carrollton.

Carrollton Band, George Gray, Director

We were fascinated by the photograph Mary Searcy shared with us. It was only later when we were scanning the photo into the computer that we noted the indentations on the back. It appeared to be handwriting, but the ink or pencil lead has long since faded away. We scanned and enlarged the backside of the photo in an attempt to read the writing, and determined it to be the names of the band members. The scanning made some of the names readable, but it was only after my brother, recommended sprinkling talcum powder on it and rubbing the powder into the scratches that most of the names became legible. Even then, however, we were unable to read one of the names completely.

Our deciphering of the names appear to be as follows: Howard Smith; Hugh Lee Griffin; Mark Long; W.G. Campbell; George Gray (Director); Dan Hearn; Ben New; Hap Horton; ??? Latham; and Vernon Torey.

Carroll County's CENTENNIAL CELEBRATION was held in February of 1927. It was reported that about 35,000 visitors attended this celebration and square dance on the public square.[iii] Some of the men in this photograph undoubtedly played in the band on that occasion. Those old enough to recall this occasion would be in their eighties now, but I and the Carroll County Historical Society would certainly like to hear from you.

A contemporary event which occurred in about 1889 is also interesting. WILLIAM C. and DOCK F. NEW ordered machinery for making window blinds, adding this activity to their blacksmith and wagon shop in Carrollton.[iv] *Submitted by: Rodric M. Phillips (born in Carrollton in 1937), 8325 N.E. 140th, Edmond, OK 73013-8717,*

Sources: [i]*Georgia's Last Frontier, The History of Carroll County*, James C. Bonner, 122; [ii]Ibid,, 174; [iii]Ibid,, 716; [iv]Ibid,, 100.

141. Carrollton Civic Woman's Club

After ten years' active membership in the Carrollton Junior Woman's Club, eight women met on September 28, 1968, to form the Carrollton Civic Woman's Club. Through its service projects, the Club has made a significant impact on the Carrollton and Sixth District Area.

Officers for 2000-2002 are President, Karen Hartley; First Vice President, Nina Chaffin; Second Vice President, Martha Ann Saunders; Recording Secretary, Jean Clements; Corresponding Secretary, Edith Coley; Treasurer, Helon Styles; Chaplain, Eugenia Johnson; and Historian, Helen Fay Lewis.

The six departments and Chairmen that make up the Club in 2001 are — Arts, Anna Fazio and Gwyn Chesnut; Education, Clemmie Walker; Conservation, Idys Overton; Home Life, Cathy Poston and Sandra Law; International Affairs, Ginny McGee; and Public Affairs, Elaine Shivers and Mary Ann Smith.

Monthly meetings are held on fourth Wednesdays at Sunset Hills Country Club. Club projects include supporting Tallulah Falls School, Neva Lomason Library, Emergency Shelter, Carroll County Children's Home - Alice's House, International Students at the State University of West Georgia, and various other organizations.

The Club was chartered on November 14, 1968 with eighteen members: Tommie Lou Batchelor, Inez Benson, Juanita Cobb, Gayle Cowart, Gloria Daniel, Lois Davis, Billie Ekman, Mary Feagle, Billie Fletcher, Helen Harman, Evelyn Hogan, Ann Holladay, Johnnie Hutchins, Jewell Johnson, Frances Lawrence, Ruby Perry, Doris Trinkner, and Mary Walsemann. Charter members who are still active are Jewell Johnson, Johnnie Hutchins, and Juanita Cobb. *Submitted by: Helen Faye Lewis, Historian*

142. Early Carrollton Fire Department

My father, Raymond Lewis "Dutch" Phillips was a firefighter most of his adult life, beginning in Carrollton. Because of the family ties, I have always treasured this photo. My dad is sitting in the right truck holding the child. I do not know who the child is, nor can I identify the men in the photo. Judging from other photos of my dad in my possession, I would estimate it to have been taken during the 1930's.

Carrollton Fire Department, Circa 1930's

Carroll County sent a total of twenty-eight Companies into the Civil War in addition to hundreds of individuals.[i] Carrollton sent many of it's own men among that number. While Carrollton was spared much of the direct involvement in the battles of the war, it was raided by Federal Troops in 1865. Union General John T. Croxton, with a brigade of Federal Troops, fought skirmishes around Tuscaloosa, and crossed the Coosa River near Talladega, entering Georgia west of Bowdon. They marched through Carrollton, Newnan, and Zebulon. On April 26, 1865, the Federal Troops camped two miles west of Carrollton. Croxton's men set fire to buildings on the north section of the Carrollton public square, and cordoned off the area with guards to prevent citizens from extinguishing the flames. No one knew why.[ii] During this early period in Carrollton history, since no brick buildings appeared in Carrollton until after the Civil War[iii], the wood frame structures, lack of available water and a ready supply of volunteers must have made such fires difficult to deal with.

Who were the Carrollton Citizens that the Federal Troops had to prevent from trying to put out the fire? Store owners? I suspect at least some of them were the owners of the stores being torched. Who were the rest? Well, based on Carrollton's history of community support, I also suspect it must have been a large crowd. Organized or not, they responded as Carrolltonians have always responded, such that it took Federal Troops to hold them back.

It was not until after the Civil War, in 1872, that efforts were made to form a hook and ladder company with a bucket brigade. The project lagged, however, and was still lagging some 20 years later[iv] and no brick buildings appeared in Carrollton until after the Civil War. It was not until 1916 that the first Fire Truck appeared on the scene in Carrollton. Then Chief, J.S. Dempsey, proudly announced the abandonment of the horse-drawn fire wagon.[v] As you can see in the photo, by about 1930, there were two modern, state-of-the-art Fire Trucks, and at least ten Firefighters. *Submitted by: Rodric M. Phillips, 8325 N.E. 140th, Edmond, OK 73013-8717*

Sources: [i]Georgia's Last Frontier: The History Of Carroll County, James C. Bonner, 82; [ii]Ibid,,86-87; [iii]Ibid,,28; [iv]Ibid,,153; [v]Ibid,,187

143. The Carrollton Rotary Club

The Carrollton Rotary Club had its organizational meeting on June 6, 1939, at the Clifton Hotel on Maple Street, at which time officers were elected. Thirty-five men were charter members. Irvine S. Ingram, president of West Georgia College, was the club's first president with Radar S. Stewart as secretary-treasurer and P.L. Shafer as sergeant-at-arms. The club began inducting women in 1987.

Since Rotary is service orientated, its motto being "Service Above Self," the Carrollton club over the years has participated in a large number of worthy enterprises, including the following: in the 1950s helping inaugurate the midget football program, which formed the nucleus of the Carrollton Recreation Department; in 1975 contributing $625 to the Tanner Hospital Auxiliary for a concession operation that by the year 2000 had made over $100,000 in profit; aiding in the eradication of polio worldwide through contributions to the Rotary Foundation; since 1951 bringing fifty international students to Carrollton through the Georgia Rotary Student Program; inaugurating in 1958 the career guidance program in local high schools; hosting several group study exchanges of businessmen from abroad and sending several local persons to other countries. Every year the club makes substantial monetary contributions to many local institutions and charities and to humanitarian causes abroad.

Membership in Rotary, which is by invitation only, is based on the vocational classification system, insuring a diversity of members, both male and female. The Carrollton club meets every Tuesday at noon at Sunset Hills Country Club. *Submitted by: James Matthews*

144. Carrollton Swimming Association

The Carrollton Swimming Association was formed in 1968 by an interested group of parents who wanted their children to enjoy the benefits of competitive swimming and good health. Mr. John Bowles of the Forest Park Swim Team was instrumental in assisting the

Carrollton parents, among which were Margaret and Doyle Garrett, Nina Johnson, Dott Cofer, and Sherry and Theron Jennings. In the beginning, the team was a summer-only effort, with practices held at the old City Park pool. Coaching was handled by Ed Lambert and Lyndon Huckeba for the first three years, with state champion Nancy (Tykac) Chandler being the outstanding swimmer.

In 1971, Laurence Smith was hired as head coach, and the program evolved to an eight-month season. During Smith's twelve-year reign, many outstanding swimmers were developed. Eventually the team moved to an eleven-month season, with practice scheduled four times weekly during the winter and five times weekly during the summer. The West Georgia College Pool was utilized by the team for year-round practices and meets. This continued cooperation between the college and the CPRCAD has been a major influence on the success of the team.

In 1978 the Lakeshore Pool was opened, which was funded jointly by the City of Carrollton and federal funds. The pool was designed with competitive swimming in mind, and many major events have been held there.

Coach Weeks enters his 16th season as head coach of the Carrollton Bluefins. During his tenure, he has coached numerous GRPA (Georgia Recreation and Parks Association) and USA state champions. He has also seen several of his swimmers placed into the top 16 rankings, which certifies him level 3 in the ASCA (American Swim Coaches Association). Beginning in 1994, David began serving as the GRPA state swim meet director for the B classification. He has served in that position for 6 years.

Coach Weeks started high school swimming in Carrollton. Four different high schools in Carrollton now offer swimming as a letter sport. Recently, junior high swimming has begun in the area.

David's next big project is to move the Bluefins' permanent home into the new Lakeshore pool facility. The new indoor structure is scheduled to be completed in the fall of 2001.

145. The Chattahoochee Sacred Harp Singing Convention

The oldest continuous convention since 1852, is held annually in the small community of Cross Plains, Ga., six mile east of Carrollton, at Wilson's Chapel, on the first Sunday and Saturday before it in August. In the year 2002, the convention will celebrate its 150th anniversary of singing the shape-note songs that were brought to America with the Pilgrims in the early 1600s. Enthusiastic singers throughout Georgia and Alabama and as far away as Chicago come together to sing songs, some of which were composed in England between 1690 and 1810, of their forefathers who have passed this tradition down to the 21st century. *Submitted by: Donna S. Duke, 120 Mink Hollow Drive, Carrollton, GA 30116*

146. The Civilian Conservation Corps

Recently, a call from Sam Roberts, Jr., of Villa Rica, set me thinking about old times. He asked me if I remembered when the road to Carrollton from Villa Rica was paved. I do remember. As a child will, I watched the work carefully.

But I was pretty young then. Children tend to be casual about exact dates. So I don't remember if the road was paved in 1933 or 1934.

I do remember quite a bit more about another signal local event — the coming of the Civilian Conservation Corps Camp. This camp was built on our farm, (then the Williams farm) 2 miles south of Villa Rica, in the summer of 1937.

The 30's in this country were the Great Depression days. Economic conditions were desperate. People could not get jobs. All over the whole United States, men searched for work, even offering to work for food. Hobos flocked onto the railroads, moving here and there, searching employment.

Franklin Delano Roosevelt was elected in the fall of 1932, promising to do something about the desperate situation. He instituted something called the New Deal, and set about proposing initiatives designed to end the Depression.

One of the first agencies created for this New Deal was the Civilian Conservation Corps. Set up in March 1933, the CCC was specifically charged with providing relief for unemployed young people.

Sam tells me that his father, Sam Roberts, together with my uncle, Felix Williams and other county leaders, worked hard to get a camp established here. The first contingent rolled into the farm about this time in the late spring of 1937. Sixteen young men, under the leadership of an Army sergeant, came in an olive-drab painted Chevrolet 2 ton truck. They set up tents in the pasture where the camp was to be laid out, and went to work.

First Leroy Williams house on Goldworth Farm built in 1832.

An army Caterpillar bulldozer was delivered. The "boys" laid out and built a road from the Carrollton-Villa Rica road, through our farm to the new site. Then carpenters and more CCC boys arrived to put up buildings.

Since this was summer, I was out of school. I got the first job I ever held with the camp construction crew. Never mind that it was the most lowly of jobs — that of water boy — it was a real, salary paying job. Very rare in those days. It paid $1.25 per day — a wonderful rate. I brought cool, fresh water to each man on the crew once every hour and a half.

The majority of the 30 buildings which made up the camp were Army designed, prefab buildings. They consisted of floor panels in sections, wall panels, also in sections, both of which were bolted together on the site. The walls were stained on the outside, but were not sealed on the inside. Roof trusses were prebuilt, and erected on the finished walls. Then decking and tar paper were applied to the roof.

First, the location for each building was leveled by the bulldozer. Then, the floors were placed on up-ended timbers which were treated with creosote against rot. The installation was never meant to be permanent. The Army style buildings were the eight barracks, a large mess hall, a recreation building, a school building, and the camp headquarters.

A number of storage sheds, truck garages, a blacksmith shop, a truck repair building and other small buildings were built on the site in the conventional manner, but using Army plans. All were stained green, A 4", 450 ft. well was drilled.

About two hundred men found jobs in the camp, plus several specialists in the type of work the men did. The camp was organized and headed by the U.S. Army. A Captain was in overall charge, with a Lieutenant under him. A top sergeant was a part of the contingent, as was mess sergeant and a supply sergeant.

The men "fell out" each morning on a parade ground in front of the Administration Building, where they witnessed the raising of the United States Flag, standing at attention. Then the men were free to go to the Mess Hall for breakfast. A Retreat ceremony was held each evening as the Flag was lowered.

This camp was primarily engaged in soil conservation work — building and maintaining terraces, planting ground covers which would slow soil erosion, and planting crops to encourage wildlife. The men build stone gully mouths, reinforcing dams in badly eroded gullies, and planted trees. Unfortunately for those of us remaining, the CCC's also planted kudzu — it was great for stopping erosion. No one knew, then, that it would eat Georgia.

John A. Salmond, writing in a book, *"the Civlilian Conservation Corps"*, says the federal government placed nearly three million single men from 17 to 25 years of age on a wide variety of conservation tasks throughout the country. This number included 250,000 veterans of World War I and 90,000 American Indians.

Salmond says reforestation was the most important task, and adds that more than half the tree-planting ever done in the United States was done by the CCC. The "enrollees" were paid $30 per month (and room and board, of course), $25 dollars of which was sent home to their families.

The Department of Labor, working with the states, selected the men; the Department of War administered the camps; the departments of Agriculture and the Interior were responsible for organizing an direction the work projects.

Salmond says the CCC was probably the most widely accepted of the New Deal agencies. Certainly, President Roosevelt thought it was among his most important achievements. It was disbanded in 1942, when full employment preceding WW II made it no longer necessary. Many of the "enrollees" went into the armed services.

We see little evidence now of the CCC camp which was once on Goldworth Farm. A few foundations which happened to be poured concrete are still visible. The old stone chimney and fireplace which once were a part of the Rec. hall are still standing. The well, and its pump house of stone still exist. And the roads the "boys" built are still in use as farm roads.
Submitted by: Bill Mitchell, 55 Goldworth Rd., Villa Rica, GA 30180

147. Forrest's Escort Camp #1239

Sons of Confederate Veterans

Organized in April, 1998 with 16 charter members, this Camp has in the past three years grown to be the largest Camp in West Georgia.

From its headquarters at Wick's Tavern Museum, 212 West Wilson Street, Villa Rica, Forrest's Escort reaches out to all areas of Carroll County. In addition, we also serve western Douglas, South Paulding, and a portion of Haralson Counties.

Our mission is the location, care and preservation of the graves of the Confederate Veterans who rest in this area and to pay them the honor they so richly deserve.

To this end we have thus far documented the locations of the final resting places of 840 Confederate Veterans in Carroll County. These rest in 118 different cemeteries. In western Douglas County, we have documented 117 Veterans in 13 cemeteries, and an additional 41 in Paulding and Haralson Counties.

Honor Guard: L.A. Burns, Gene Moore, Roger Denney, Robby Robison, Rick Pope, Ed Daniell, Tony Gonzales.

Our Honor Guard is acknowledged to be one of the best in Georgia. We have two full scale Artillery pieces, an 1861 6 pounder, and a 3 inch ordnance rifle. With them we travel extensively, holding Ceremonies at different Church homecomings. We also clean and restore abandoned cemeteries which contain the remains of even one Confederate Soldier.

At the death of Mr. Franklin Garrett, the "Official Historian of Atlanta", we furnished the Honor Guard for his funeral.

Forrest's Escort Camp S.C.V. Artillery

Each year we place approximately 550 "Battle Flags" on the graves of our Veterans. These we leave from year to year. So all who pass will know of their sacrifices, and their service.

We have the records of "all who served the Confederate armed forces. Approximately 1,500,000 total, including American Indian, Hispanic, Black, White, Jewish, etc. If you need help locating information regarding your Confederate Ancestor, we're happy to help.

Our phone number is (770) 456-0201. Our Email is woolhatboy@mindspring.com, and our Web Page is: *http://members. tripod.com/~car-OlescOtt/forrest.htm1* *Submitted by: Charlie Lott, 212 W. Wilson St., Villa Rica, GA 30180*

148. The Friendship Force of West Georgia

The Friendship Force of West Georgia is a branch of Friendship Force International (FFI), a nonprofit organization active in more than 60 countries, headquartered in Atlanta, Georgia. A 1992 nominee for the Nobel Peace Prize, FFI was founded by Wayne Smith and introduced in 1977 by U.S. President Jimmy Carter at a White House gathering of state governors. Mrs. Rosalynn Carter accepted and still holds the office of Honorary Chairperson, serving on the Board of Trustees. Chip Carter as FFI President succeeded Dr. Smith in 2000.

The FFI mission is to bring together the people of the world promoting friendship, understanding and goodwill through homestay exchanges. Our travelers are called Ambassadors of Friendship.

The local organization started when long-time Friendship Force of Atlanta members, Mary and Russ Sarner, moved to Fairfield Plantation. Hosting was difficult since most activities took place in Atlanta. After involving local friends in a highly successful "day hosting" experience for German Ambassadors, the Sarners decided to form the West Georgia club. Following an enthusiastic organizational meeting our club was chartered in 1987, and now boasts members from Carrollton, Bowdon, Villa Rica, Franklin, Newnan, Roopville and Whitesburg. During 14 years we have hosted, or sent Ambassadors to Argentina, Armenia, Austria, Australia, Azerbaijan, Greece, Belgium, Brazil, Canada, China, Colombia, England, Estonia, Georgia, Germany, Ghana, Holland, Hungary, India, Ireland, Israel, Italy, Japan, Kazakhstan, Kenya, Korea, Mexico, Mongolia, Nepal, New Zealand, Russia, Scotland, Singapore, South Africa, Taiwan, Thailand, Turkey, Ukraine, Uzbekistan, Vietnam and Wales making lasting friendships everywhere. **See photo below.** *Submitted by: Mary Acland Sarner, Founding President, FF of West Georgia*

149. Girl Scouts

Council-wide Girl Scouting began in Carroll County with the organization of an Executive Council, sponsored by Beta Sigma Phi Sorority, on August 18, 1950, at the Crepe Myrtle Hotel. The council was named the West Georgia Area Council and included Carroll, Douglas, Haralson, and Heard Counties. Mrs. Frank (Minnie Ann) Lovvorn was the driving force behind this organization. Officers of the first Executive Council were Mrs. Griffin Harris, president; Mrs. C.P. Tigner, vice-president; Mrs. Tom Reeve, secretary; and Mrs. Cal Parker, treasurer. By the end of that year there were 43 intermediate Girl Scouts registered.

In February, 1952, the first Court of Awards was held at the First Methodist Church in Carrollton, with 19 girls receiving 77 badges. Also on March 12 of that year the West Georgia Area Council became part of the Pineland Council, serving 6 counties: Carroll, Haralson, Heard, Troup, Meriwether, and Upson. Mr. W.T. (Buddy) Green was elected first president of Pineland Council.

The first day camp was held in 1953, directed by Mrs. C.P. Tigner and Miss Opal Beck. In 1957 Pineland Council merged with other counties to form Pine Valley Girl Scout Council with headquarters in Griffin, GA. Carroll County is still a member of Pine Valley Council, which now encompasses 13 counties in Georgia and Chambers County, Alabama. Since becoming a part of Pine Valley Council, Carroll County has supplied the council board of directors with a number of board members and officers, too numerous to mention in this space. *Submitted by: Martha A. Saunders, 25 Pine Meadow Circle, Carrollton, GA 30116, marthasaun@aol.com*

150. Goshen Lodge #71 F. & A.M.

In the early 1870's the two story building of Goshen Methodist Church was shared with the Goshen Masonic Lodge. Goshen Lodge #71 was chartered November 1, 1877 with W.L. Craven first Worshipful Master.

Goshen Lodge later moved to Roopville. Meetings were held upstairs over Roop Mercantile. In 1989 a new Lodge Hall was built on property donated by J.W. Wood on Main Street in Roopville. This is the site of the present Lodge. Goshen Lodge serves Roopville and the surrounding community.

Hester, Lewis, Bell, Stephens, Adams, Burt, Goshen Lodge #71

Past Worshipful Masters include: W.L. Craven, John K. Roop, S.W. Millican, J.R. Roop, D.L. Pearce, W.J. Millican, B.F. Roop, W.T. Freel, H.J. Goodwyn, A.H. Johnson, G.E. Pentecost, W.H. Brock, J.B. Merrell, T.F. Friddell, C.L. Towns, Jack Towns, J.K. Brown, T.J. Woodard, Wm. Theo Bell, F.P. Gentry, G.T. Huff, Wm. Roy Stephens, H.A. Dean, D.D. Staples, Lee Steed, Horry F. Denney, Wm. Raymond Griffin, Julian Charles Freel, Fred Lewis, Alton Fleming, John Vincent Todd, Jimmy M. Gentry, Steven George Dean, Curtis James Wilson, Jr., Donald E. Hester, Dillard Todd, Marion O. Jordan, Lloyd G. Hester, Edward Garland Bell, Ted Holloway, Raymond Walden,

First West Georgia Friendship Force Ambassadors Hosted in New Zealand.

Jesse Gilford Bell, Jason Hester, Chris Duncan, Donald Duncan, Kevin Newborn.

The officers of Goshen Lodge at the present time are: Worshipful Master - Jesse Bell; Senior Warden - Jeremy Milam; Junior Warden - Jason Hester; Treasurer - Fred Lewis; Secretary - Eddie Bell; Chaplain - Donald Hester, Senior Deacon - Raymond Walden; Junior Deacon - James Stephens; Senior Steward - Steve Whitlock; Junior Stewart - Danny Adams; Tyler-Lloyd Hester. *Submitted by: Jesse Bell, 500 Welcome Rd., Roopville, GA 30170.*

151. The Kiwanis Club of Carrollton

Kiwanis International began in 1915. The Newnan Kiwanis Club started the Carrollton club in 1947 with 32 charter members; 2 remained active at the turn of the century in a club which approached 100 members. It is one of 8,500 such clubs in 80 nations. Clubs are grouped into divisions; divisions, into districts. The members of each club are a cross section of local business and professional men and women. Guided by a locally-elected board, each club undertakes projects to improve its community and serve residents with special needs ranging from children ("Priorty Number One") to senior citizens. Members meet together weekly for lunch and an informative program. Over the years, the Carrollton Kiwanis Club has sponsored high school Key Clubs and Circle K for university students. Other projects have included aid to underprivileged children through "Unorganized Cheerful Givers" and Alice's House, contributions to the emergency shelter, expansion of recreational facilities, promotion of little league football, support for 4-H and scouting, sponsoring nursing home beauty pageants, providing various scholarships, hosting an annual Farm-City Banquet, and establishing new clubs in neighboring communities. Locally-raised funds and club members' volunteered time and labor support these projects. The Carrollton Club's revenue activities over the years have included Pimento Queen competitions, radio days, selling Vidalia onions, and the sale of program advertising and refreshments for youth football games. *Submitted by: Robert H. Claxton, POB 404, Carrollton 30117, Rhclax@bellsouth.net*

152. League of Women Voters of Carrollton / Carroll County

The local league was provisionally organized in October of 1960 and became operational in early 1961. It has played an active role in the community life of Carrollton and Carroll County through the sponsorship of studies on solid waste, water, and the multi-member county commission. A special election monitoring project in Carroll County was conducted by Georgia Simons. The league has been active in the League of Women Voters of Georgia with Lee Wash, 1983-85, Ruth Strausser, 1987-89, and Martha Ann Saunders, 1995-97, serving as state president and others as state board members.

For forty years the league, a non-partisan organization, has consistently provided the public with information to assure an informed electorate. The LWVCCC has published printed voter guides and political directories over the years. The league has sponsored political forums and voter education in the schools. The Dora Byron Award for citizenship has been given since 1982 alternately to league members and local citizens.

The LWVCCC initiated its first Great Decisions program in 1994. This program is provided by the Foreign Policy Association which encourages a careful study of all sides of international questions affecting the United States. The late Floyd Hoskins served as moderator of the program for the past six years. In recognition of Hoskis' leadership the program will be called the Floyd Hoskins Great Decisions Program beginning with 2001. The LWVCCC is the only local league out of 14 local leagues in the state to offer the program.

The LWVC/CC Board of Directors sitting in the front row Joyce Reid, Mattie Wilson, Martha Ann Saunders, Sue Jones, and Lucy Garmon. Standing in the back row Dottie Abbott, Joyce Alford, Tom Carrere, Jan Ruskell, Lucille Townsend, Rosemary Winter, and Mary Jo Alexander. *Submitted by: Jan Ruskell and Tom Carrere, Co-Presidents LWVCCC, Box 1014, Carrollton, GA 30117*

153. Lit-Mu Club

Organized in 1905, The Lit-Mu Club of Carrollton is this area's oldest literary music society. Celebrating its 95th anniversary in October 2000 with a performance for the community by the Emory Chamber Music Society of Atlanta, this group is continuing a long and varied tradition of study in the areas of art, music, dance, drama, opera, architecture and literature.

The charter group, organized by Mrs. W.C. Adamson included the following: Misses Aline Bradley (who later became Mrs. Buford Boykin), Eugenia Mandeville, Cora Mae Simonton, Susan Simonton, Kate Reese and Marion West. Mrs. Adamson subsequently served three consecutive terms as president.

Meeting monthly from October through May, each hostess was initially instructed to invite her neighbors. The objectives were to foster an interest in the best literature and music, as well as to promote the extension of the public library, by presenting "as many books as possible" with a focus on children's literacy.

There is a tradition in Lit-Mu that any member is on her honor to perform any duty assigned and that they research and present their own programs. From the early years members produced beautiful yearbooks as well as artistic and elaborate program booklets for each member at the monthly meetings.

The group currently provides an annual music scholarship and also supports the Opera Workshop at the State University of West Georgia. It also holds membership in the Carroll County Cultural Arts Alliance.

Most members make a lifetime commitment to Lit-Mu. Current members with the greatest longevity (including active as well as associate standing) are Mrs. T.E. Reeve, Jr., with 51 years; Mrs. Frank Cook with 42 years; Mrs. H. Lamar Knight with 41 years; and Mrs. James Griffin with 40 years.

Officers for 2000-2001 are: President, Mrs. Peter Worthy; First Vice-President, Mrs. Lawrence Alligood; Second Vice-President, Mrs. Ralph Fleck; Secretary, Mrs. Frederick Martin; Treasurer, Mrs. James Rash; Historian, Mrs. Harrell Fountain.

Other members include: Mrs. James Callahan, Mrs. Robert Coe, Mrs. Frank Cook, Mrs. Joseph Cumming, Mrs. Kirk Dortch, Mrs. Clarence Finleyson, Mrs. John Fletcher, Mrs. Wayne Garner, Mrs. Bogan Gist, Mrs. Robert Graf, Mrs. David Griffin, Mrs. James Griffin, Mrs. John Henderson, Dr. Anne Ingram, Mrs. Tony Johnson, Mrs. Howard Jones, Mrs. H. Lamar Knight, Mrs. George Lenaeus, Mrs. Louis Maier, Jr., Ms. Sue Medeiros, Mrs. Allen Murrah, Mrs. Lem Norrell, Ms. Susan Ogletree, Mrs. Robert Ogletree, Mrs. Robert Pitts, Mrs. Paul Quinn, Mrs. T.E. Reeve, Jr., Mrs. Thomas Richards, Mrs. Vann Saunders, Mrs. Rodger Smith, Mrs. John Tanner, Jr., and Mrs. J. Carter Wright. Mrs. Mac R. Morgan holds honorary membership. *Submitted by: Phyllis Fountain (Mrs. Harrell), Historian, 120 West Fairlawn Dr., Carrollton, GA 30117.*

154. McDaniel - Curtis Camp #165 Sons of Confederate Veterans

Carrollton, Carroll County, Georgia

The McDaniel-Curtis Camp #165, Sons of Confederate Veterans was chartered at Carrollton, Georgia on October 18, 1989 under the leadership of Sam Pyle. Mr. Pyle was a former member of the James Longstreet Camp in East Point, Georgia; and has served this Camp as commander for several terms.

The camp's name was inherited from the former camp of the United Confederate Veterans in Carroll County that was active in the late 1800's. The UCV camp ceased to exist with the death of its members. Both camps were named for Charles A. McDaniel and William E. Curtis, successively colonels of the 41st Georgia Volunteer Infantry in which many of Carroll County's men saw service. Both Colonel McDaniel and Colonel Curtis received mortal wounds while fighting for their country. Col. McDaniel is buried in the cemetery of the Methodist Protestant Church in Bowdon, GA. (of which he was the pastor), and Col. Curtis is buried in the Carrollton City Cemetery, facing north.

This Camp holds an annual Confederate Memorial Day service at the Confederate Monument in

Lit-Mu Club's Ninety-fifth Anniversary Celebration - Emory Chamber Music Society, Atlanta

Carrollton, works to clean up and place stone markers on the graves of Confederate Veterans, sets up living history demonstrations and participates in many of the county's local parades and festivals.

Some of its more active members have been Sam Pyle, Dutch Dryer, Darrell Smith, William Maddox, Robert Richardson, John Carter Clay, John McPherson, John Wright, Bill Deegan, Butch Lamb and Alan Trapp, who has served several terms as the Georgia Division Commander.

McDaniel-Curtis Camp at Confederate Monument in Carrollton

This camp is proud to bear the names of Colonels McDaniel and Curtis, and to honor the service and sacrifice of all Confederate Veterans.

The camp meets the third Monday night of each month at 7:00 P.M. at the Carrollton Community Activities Center in Carrollton, on S. White Street. *Submitted by: H.M. "Dutch" Dyer, 842 Old Centerpoint Rd., Carrollton, GA*

155. Mt. Zion Community Optimist Club

Mt. Zion Community Optimist Club was founded in 1992 with the sponsorship of the Carrollton Optimist Club. Charles Jetmore served as our first President and currently Jack Dorsey presides over the club.

For the past eight years the Mt. Zion Community Optimist Club has sponsored the following projects and services: highway clean up (2½ miles along Hwy 16), annual fishing rodeo with John Tanner State Park, annual bicycle rodeo, essay contest, oratorical contest, sponsors Mt. Zion High School Octagon Club, annual fall festival, welcome back breakfast for area teachers, quarterly cookouts for extracurricular students, assists churches, schools, and clubs in obtaining private foundation, state, and federal grants, and the club awards college scholarships.

The Mt. Zion Community Optimist Club meets on the 1st and 3rd Tuesday nights of each month at 6:30 a.m. for supper and then at 7:00 p.m. for the regular meeting. The meetings are held at the Mt. Zion High School Media Center.

Although small, the Optimist Club is an active force in the community working for the youth of the Mt. Zion Community. Visitors are encouraged to visit with us and learn about opportunities to serve area youth. *Submitted by: Jack Dorsey, Mt. Zion City Historian*

156. Optimist Club of Carrollton

The Optimist Club of Carrollton was chartered in December 1969 with 42 members. Four of those original members remain in the club today. Since 1969 the Club has been actively involved in community youth projects. Members participate in a wide range of Optimist programs designed to provide opportunities for youngsters to learn, grow, and serve.

Many members carry their commitment to youth service into their daily lives outside the Club. Optimist Club members are involved in scout leadership, youth-league sports, mentoring, tutoring, counseling programs, and a host of other services.

Throughout its history, the Carrollton Club has been a leader among area civic organizations. In 1975 the Club became the first civic club in Carrollton to integrate. The first female admitted to an all-male Carrollton civic club occurred in 1987 when Optimist International, our governing body, changed policy to admit female members. Since that time, three women have served as president of the Carrollton Club.

The Carrollton Club is associated with Optimist International, a federation of more than 4,200 clubs with approximately 150,000 members. Optimist International was established in 1919 to promote optimism as a philosophy, promote interest in good government and civic affairs, to inspire respect for law, patriotism, international accord and friendship among the members and among the youth of the community.

The Carrollton Club serves youth through many locally based programs. Through selective participation in a variety of Optimist International recommended projects, and creation of its own projects to better address local needs and interests.

Optimist International sponsored projects in which Carrollton Optimists participate include: essay and oratorical contests, respect for law, youth appreciation week, just say no! and youth groups. The Carrollton Optimist Club's local projects include: Christmas food baskets, playground improvements, student revolving loan fund at State University of West Georgia, youth of the month, and safe summer.

Optimists support these programs by conducting a variety of fund-raising activities that also provide an opportunity for member fun and fellowship. As a major source of funding, the Club provides concessions for State University of West Georgia home football games. A portion of the proceeds helps the West Georgia Athletic Department. Other fund-raising events are conducted as needed. Recent projects have included an annual circus and concessions at state recreation department basketball tournaments and track meets. Each year the Optimist Club returns an average of $20,000 to the Carrollton and Carroll County community through its youth oriented projects.

The Optimist Club of Carrollton promotes the purposes of Optimist International: To develop optimism as a way of life; To promote an active interest in good government and civic affairs; To inspire respect for law; To promote patriotism and work for international accord and friendship among all people; and To aid and encourage the development of youth in the belief that the giving of one's self in service to others will advance the well-being of humankind, community life and the world. *Submitted by: Dick Folk, Club Editor and Director, 218 Hidden Lakes Drive, Carrollton, GA 30116*

157. Carrollton's Chapter #28

Order of the Eastern Star

Prince Hall Affiliated Jurisdiction of Georgia

Carrollton Chapter #28 history can be traced back to the 1930's with this Chapter being in the Newman District. We know that we received our number from a Chapter that was no longer in existence. Carrollton Chapter was very active in the 50's and 60's. Sister Annie Mae Wilson served as Worthy Matron during this time. Members were Sister Willie Mae Watkins, Inez Brinkley, Sister Maggie Hearn, Sister Eva L. Shackleford, Brother Ernest Watkins, Sister Mattie Johnson, Sister Nadie M. Kendrick, and Sister Kathryne Ramsey. During these years our Chapter met regularly at First Baptist Church on Church Street. Membership began to drop around 1972, Sister Elayne Billingsley served as Worthy Matron. Sister Annie Mae Wilson never gave up even after the Chapter was labeled inactive in 1976. With the help of Brother Harold Mullins, Brother James Daniel, and Brother James Reid permission was granted to reorganize Carrollton Chapter on April 23, 1986.

The reorganization began with the submission of applications. Carrollton Chapter was now a part of the Atlanta District. Over 40 women and men were initiated into the Order. Past Matrons are: Sister Betty Newell, Sister Bonnie Thomaston, Sister Anne Sheppard, Sister Deaidra Wilson, Sister Mary Graves, and Sister Kathi Henson. Our Chapter continues to grow and do community service in the Carroll County area. We give scholarships annually to graduating seniors. We feed our Senior Citizens in the month of November. We give to the less fortunate during the year and especially during the holidays. We continue to visit the Sick and Shut-Ins.

We have a current Sisterhood of over 30. Our Current Matron is Sister Kimberly Kendall. We can be contacted at P.O. Box 2063, Carrollton, Georgia 30117. *Submitted by: Deaidra Wilson*

158. The Rebecca Martin Home and Garden Club

The Rebecca Martin Club was organized on May 16, 1924, under the leadership of Mrs. Berta Whatley, Carroll County's first Home Demonstration Agent. Miss Vera Driver, later Mrs. Glenn Moore, suggested the name "The Rebecca Martin Club" in honor of the oldest charter member. A number of the present members are descendants of the charter members.

Rebecca Martin

The County Board of Education gave the Stripling School ground for a building site. Through fund raisers the members planned for a club house; however, the club's funds were wiped out in the 1929 Great Depression. Never giving up the dream, the clubhouse was built in 1940. For many years the club was under the guidance of the County Extension Agents, but has been operating on its own for several years.

Some of the past service projects have been: packages to Viet Nam, sponsoring 4-H members, Alice's House, Tanner Hospital First Steps Program, and always remembering members who are shut in. Educational or Entertaining programs are planned for each club meeting and refreshments are served. The Club continues to hold monthly meeting at the 1940 site that is now the fellowship hall of the

Stripling Chapel United Methodist Church. Currently the oldest member is ninety-one years old. *Submitted by: Anita Smith*

159. Roopville Historical Society and Archive

The Roopville Historical Society's first meeting was September 1982 and it incorporated in 1984. Willis Huff, a former resident was instrumental in assisting in this venture. Officers elected were: President - Rebecca Merrell, Vice President - Audie Causey, Secretary - Emily Huckeba, Treasurer - J.L. Dean, and Historian - Frances Freel, Chaplain - Judson Bell. Willis Huff - Honorary Archivist, other members of that early meeting were Bob Merrell, Marie Merrell, Marie Dean, Nancy Bell, and Rachel Bell.

Roopville Historical Society members on a field trip.

Willis, an avid collector of memorabilia of Roopville history, donated numerous pictures, books, and other collectable items. Willis owned a building, formerly a garage, that he leased to the town for $1 a year. The Mayor and Council voted to renovate the block, brick front building. The inside was sheetrocked, carpeted, painted and soon ready for use as an archive and meeting room.

This building was used for many years as an archive and city hall. Later Willis offered to sell the city the building used as the Whitham Bank, 1912-1927, post office 1927-May 1, 1987, an antique shop, flower shop, and bail bondsman office. The city bought the building to use as a more appropriate location for the archive. The renovation committee consisted of Nancy Bell, Rebecca Merrell, and Jim Veal. The front room was restored in 1995.

An airlock front door and suspended cellotex ceiling tiles were removed. The windows were restored to their former size. The wooden ceiling was in bad shape due to many years of roof leaks. New baseboard to match the old was installed. The vault, which had been used a cooler for the florist, was restored to its original appearance. A modern heat/air central system was installed. Herman North, Kyle Holloway, Joe Garrett, Jimmy McGuire, Daniel Denny, Richard Bates, and Bobby Hosey were hired to do various portions of the work for renovating the front room.

In 2000 renovation of the back room began. Bobby Holcombe and Sherril Fordice repointed the brick on the front of the building. Work on the inside was done by Bobby, Sherril, and Rebecca Merrell. The tongue and grove ceiling and plaster walls had water damage but were repairable. The floors were tiled to match the front room and the bathroom was also renovated. Old windows were removed and replaced with windows to match the front room. A metal door was installed at the rear with a new window above the door.

New lights and bath fixtures were installed and the painting completed. Work began improving the displays inside. There are many items of special interest - school annuals, pictures and trophies, farming and carpentry tools, old store and doctor records, 100 year old quilt and coverlet, personal histories, many pictures, etc.

We're proud of this facility and we encourage you to come visit and bring something to add to the collection. *Submitted by: Rebecca Merrell, 124 Old Franklin Street, Roopville, GA 30170*

160. The Villa Rica Garden Club

In 1936, the Villa Rica Garden Club was organized with Mrs. A.A. Parker president and 39 charter members. The club assumed the responsibility of civic beautification as well as the study of flower and plant cultivation. In 1938 the club was federated in the Garden Clubs of Georgia.

From 1936-1943 the club's monthly meetings focused on beautification projects, flower and plant cultivation, flower arranging, preservation of cut flowers, the annual flower show, establishing city parks, and the upkeep of the city's cemetery and parks.

In 1943, the club adopted as a project to make surgical dressings for the Red Cross. Mrs. J.H. Kilgore's store building was used for a workroom. All regular activities stopped to concentrate on the war effort. Regular meetings resumed in March of 1946 with projects to beautify: Hillcrest Cemetery, town parks, and the school and hospital grounds. The club continued to study horticulture and continued the flower show until 1971 then the flower show was discontinued.

From 1971-1999 the club has: helped landscape the hospital grounds, planted roses and shrubbery at the local schools, planted shrubbery along the steps at the railroad, put a bird feeder outside the children's wing of the library, and placed barrels filled with flowers along Main Street. The club worked with the Department of Transportation and planted Bradford pear trees in the median along Highway 61 and Forsythia along the I-20 exits. In 1999 the club turned the maintenance of the cemetery over to the city.

In 2000-2001 the club planted a tree at Gold Dust Park in honor of Mrs. Vassie Hixon's one hundredth birthday. The club has looked at zoning ordinances regarding greenspaces, trees, and landscaping: along the streets, highways, residential and commercial developments. Villa Rica's mayor and council members declared Forsythia as the official flower for the city as suggested by the garden club. Forsythia was chosen because of its golden color and Villa Rica being known as the city of gold.

The club presents the Beautification Award each month to a home owner who has worked to improve their environment. It is hoped that this recognition will encourage others to beautify their property. Our goal is to do our best to preserve our environment as a club and as a citizen. *Submitted by: the Villa Rica Garden Club*
Source: Villa Rica Garden Club's scrapbook located at the Villa Rica Library

161. Early Villa Rica Mail Carriers

This old photo shows five early postal carriers from Villa Rica. The back row includes Charles Leathers, Route 1, T.P. Matthews, Route 4, and Oscar Payne, Route 2. The front row includes John Stalling, Route 5, and John Leathers, Route 3. *Submitted by: Wallace Lambert, PO Box 14, Bowdon Junction, GA 30109*

Villa Rica Mail Carriers

162. West Georgia Quilter's Guild

Pictured below is the "Historical Redwork Quilt of Carroll County, Georgia". It was made by the West Georgia Quilter's Guild. It contains drawings of 32 buildings and a county map. It was raffled and given away on October 19, 1999 to Brent Hildebrand. Pictured (Back L. to R.): Gloria Pope, Jane Brownlow, Sue Chandler, Sandy Gowing, Glen Kingsley, Tommie Freeman, Nancy Gilmer, Genny Crawford, (Middle) Sharon Snow, Alma Bohannon, Ollie Wright, Gaye Pollock, Gene Cooksey, Vivian Fidler, (Front) Juanita Davis, Jean Ashmore, Marilyn Clark, Liz Runyan, Nancy Hallden, Mary Bell Chandler, Ann O'Hearn, Sue Hardin, Jane Kingsley, Violette Denney, and Marlene Uglum.

The West Georgia Quilter's Guild first met in October 1987 at the Carrollton Community Archives Center with President Carol Kelley presiding. Organizational plans were made by Carol Kelley, Tommie Freeman, Betsy Scheufler, Brenda Kelley, and Brenda's neighbor. The "Georgia Block" was selected as the Guild Logo and modified to serve as name tags. The purpose is as follows: "We organized to bring people together with a common interest in quilting, to promote quilting as an art forrm,

West Georgia's Quilter's Guild

and to recognize its place in our heritage. We hope to educate and exchange knowledge about quilting by personal exchange, guest speakers, and instructional programs. To promote communication concerning quilting events locally, state-wide, and nationally. We believe, by meeting together, we will gain personal fulfillment, encouragement, and enthusiasm to grow as individual quilters and guild members."

Other guild presidents were Jeanette Bernhardt, Ollie Wright, Violette Denney, Sue Hardin, Jennie Dewberry, Nancy Hallden, Marilyn Clark, and Sandy Gowing. An annual February Quilt Show is held at the Neva Lomason Memorial Library, Carrollton, with quilting demonstrations. Charity quilts have been donated to many local organizations as well as numerous "ABC Quilts" for at risk babies and quilts for the Children's Home. In 1996 the guild members made 11 quilts for the Olympic Games as part of the Gift Quilts for the participating countries. The guild joined other Georgia Quilters and made enough quilts for Habitat for Humanity to build a house. In January 2000 the guild made 25 quilts to be shipped to Kosovo. *Submitted by: Violette H. Denney, 135 Maple Hill Road, Carrollton, GA 30116-7014*
Source: Guild records

RELIGION

163. ABILENE BAPTIST CHURCH

On May 8, 1875 a group assembled at the home of Mr. Sef Muse and Abilene Baptist Church was formed. The church later met under a bush arbor and then later under an 18 x 20 foot covered area. This took place on the land where the church now stands. Mr. J. Muse Sr. was pastor from 1875 to 1877. In the summer of 1892, members who gave trees to be sawed into the lumber for the church built the church. In 1902-03 the church was sealed and new benches and an organ were purchased. In 1940-48 the church was remodeled and the outside of the church was bricked. New pews, floors tiled and memorial windows were bought. In 1953 the church held its first Vacation Bible School. From 1953 to 1962 four Sunday School rooms were built, a water fountain was added, and separate restrooms for men and women were built. In 1962-63 a pastorium was built. In 1967 the church was again remodeled and more Sunday School rooms were added. In July of 1969 the parking lot was blacktopped and in 1971 a Fellowship Hall was built and the church bought 5 acres of land from Mrs. Burl Bivins.

Abilene Baptist Church

In 1973 the church was air-conditioned and additional Sunday School rooms were built upstairs. The church was remodeled again in 1979. The 1980's brought a number of improvements with the ball field dedicated in memory of Debbie Kierbow Yates in 1985. Also that year a recreation building in memory of Jimmy Couch was built. In the fall of 1987 the church bought an acre of land from Maxine Spence where the walking track is and began play in basketball and volleyball leagues. The spring of 1988 brought a new bus shed and a remodeled church added two new Sunday School rooms and bathrooms. The radio program was started in the Summer of 1989 which also saw the addition of new parking, a men's fellowship breakfast, tile for the Fellowship Hall, and an annual mission trip to Houston was begun.

In 1990 the church saw two morning services began in the spring and chimes beginning to ring in the summer. In August of 1991 the BBQ shed was built and in the fall a committee was elected for adding to or building a new sanctuary. In the spring of 1992 the kitchen was remodeled and the walking track was opened. In the summer the Ora Bivins Teen Center was started.

The 4th Sunday in August each year features an all night cooking of BBQ with dinner and is a tradition that has been done since the men came home from the war.

164. ANTIOCH BAPTIST CHURCH

Antioch Baptist Church on E. Highway 5 four miles north of Whitesburg was established in 1922 in a small building which was formerly New Watson School. Antioch was the center of a small farming community in the third district. In later years Sunday School rooms were added to the church and a small fellowship hall was built.

1983 Sanctuary

In 1982 we began building a new church. Our first service was held in the new church Easter Sunday 1983. Our small community grew and our membership grew. We then built a new Fellowship Hall.

We are still a country church but as one of our former pasters said, "We are a small church with a big heart".

165. BETHANY CHRISTIAN CHURCH

In September of 1883, a group of men and women met to form a congregation of Christians, dedicated to restoration of simple Bible truths. The first services were held in a brush arbor, located near the present location of the church. A few years later, a frame building was erected in a beautiful grove and was call Black Gum Christian Church. The name came from a very large black gum tree which stood just across the road from the church, and which many animals were hitched to while their owners attended church.

In the early years of the church, preaching services were only held once a month, as the preacher rotated duties between four congregations. Sunday School was held each week, however.

In 1921, Etta and Cliff Jordan gave one acre of land to build a new brick church. This land was at the church's present location at 2868 Carrollton-Villa Rica Highway. The building was begun in1927 and dedicated in 1928. When the congregation moved, the name was changed to Bethany Christian Church. Further donations from the Jordan family provided land for a cemetery. Carl and Thelma Jordan also gave land for the parsonage, and future expansions.

Bethany Christian Church

For almost 118 years now, Bethany Christian Church has continued a legacy of Christians dedicated to "simple Bible truths." Allen Howard has ministered with the congregation since 1983, and invites anyone looking for a church home to come and be a part of the Bethany family.

166. BETHEL METHODIST CAMPGROUND

The annual Bethel Camp Meeting services began in a brush arbor in 1858, meeting on Thursday night before the third Sunday in August and continuing through the following Thursday evening. Services were cancelled during the Civil War. In 1868 Rev. John Murphy, Bill Lambert, S. Ashmore, Bill Crumbly and others dragged brush to make a new arbor in the middle of the eight acres of property. This structure was used until 1905. In 1906 the men went to the woods, cut logs and had then sawed into lumber. The main timbers were drilled and put together with huge wooden pegs. This new arbor, covered with wood shingles, was completed in one week for camp meeting that year. Annual services were held under this arbor until 1987. The current arbor was built in 1989. The first dining hall, built in 1965, was used until the current dining hall was built in 1981. In 1984 a block structure (preacher's tent) was built for the visiting preachers to use the week of camp meeting.

Bethel Camp Meeting services were cancelled for 2000 due to lack of water — the spring was dry. Work is in progress for Carroll County water lines to be in service for the 133rd session of Bethel Camp Meeting to be held July 19-26, 2001. Services will be held beginning July 19 at 7:30 p.m. and continue daily with services at 11:00 a.m. and 7:30 p.m. The Campground is located off Bethel Church Road on Evergreen Road, Carrollton. *Submitted by: Bobby L. Smith, 368 New Hope Church Road, Carrollton, GA 30117*

167. Bethesda Baptist Church

Bethesda means "House of Mercy". Bethesda Baptist Church of Carroll County, Inc., was organized in 1846 with 15 charter members, meeting in homes or under a brush arbor until the first building was built on the Larry Grice property. This was Lot 61 and 68 of the eleventh district, presently Grice Road and Bonner Goldmine Road. The current location of the church is two miles west of the original site, and is Lot 125 in the eleventh district. It was purchased in 1859 for one dollar. A frame building was built and on March 19, 1860 the first meeting was held. According to early minutes, they were known as the "Church of Christ at Bethesda."

Bethesda Baptist Church

The church continued to thrive after the Civil War and added many new members. Bethesda public school was located across the road from the church until 1931.

During a flower dedication service at the church in 1922, members gathered at the altar and the floor gave way, so it was time to build a new building, which is the present structure. A financial statement dated Thursday, June 7, 1923 appearing in the *Carroll Free Press* lists numerous individuals and businesses who contributed money and work toward the new building, totaling $3,407.72.

Bethesda is the second oldest church in the Carrollton Baptist Association. A pastorium was completed in 1983, a new fellowship hall in 1987 and the sanctuary was remodeled in 1989, adding a baptistery. Services have been held without interruption for 155 years. *Submitted by: Tim Barnes, 2088 U.S. 27 South, Carrollton, GA 30117*

168. Beulah Baptist Church

In 1881, a Sunday School was organized and held in the schoolhouse, which was situated at the rear of the present cemetery at the top of the hill. It was then called Union Grove, but later called Beulah.

On a Sunday afternoon Brother W.W. Roop from Carrollton came out to preach. Other preaching services followed, which led to the constitution of Beulah Baptist Church on November 17, 1882. Services were held in the schoolhouse for the first year, except during the annual meeting for which a bush arbor was built to take care of the crowds.

On March 24, 1883, J.R. Marlow and J.K. Griffin agreed to give land for the church building. In February 1884 it was decided to build a church building, size 30 feet by 40 feet. There were 14 charter members plus 25 new members the first year.

Since the constitution of Beulah Baptist Church in 1882 until the year 2001 we have had 31 different Pastors. Three Pastors, Rev. W.W. Roop, Rev. Roy King and Rev. Herbert Cole served at two different times as Pastor.

Beulah Baptist Church

Brother Herbert Cole served the longest time, he led our Church as a loving Pastor for 21 years. He retired in 1994 due to ill health, and lost his battle to cancer March 19, 2000.

The original church built in 1882 is still a part of our church, which has been enlarged several times to what it is today. The church, Sunday School Rooms, and Fellowship Hall all have central heat and air and carpet. We also have a nice pastorium on Andrea Lane, not far from Beulah Church in Carrollton. *Submitted by: Ezma Thomas (church clerk), 1065 Beulah Church Road, Carrollton, GA 30117.*

169. Bowdon Baptist Church

In 1860, a group with the help of Eden Church and others separated themselves to begin the Bowdon Baptist Church. A building was erected and the Rev. G.W. Tumlin became the first pastor. By 1874 the church membership was 100.

The first WMU in Carroll County was organized at Bowdon Baptist Church in 1889. In 1894, a new building was erected on the same site. Between 1924 and 1933, the third sanctuary was erected on this site.

Through the years, the church has expanded and acquired additional properties and facilities. In 1937, a pastorium was build adjacent to the sanctuary. In 1950 the first educational annex was dedicated, and during that decade the sanctuary was remodeled, the parking lot was paved, and an electric organ was installed. In 1960, a new educational annex with a kitchen and social hall was completed.

Bowdon Baptist Church

The decade of the 1970's saw numerous additions. In 1971 a new pastorium was built on Frances Street, in 1972 a pipe organ was installed and a youth center built. In 1973, a steeple with a carillon as well as hand bells were dedicated, and in 1976 a deaf ministry began. A weekday kindergarten program began in 1978. In 1979, a Senior Adult Minister was employed and a van was given to that Ministry.

In 1982 an elevator was installed. In 1983, the sanctuary front was remodeled followed the next year by the remainder of the sanctuary and the addition of a playground. The gift of a Steinway Grand piano was made in 1992 and in 2000 the present sanctuary, social hall, and music suite were erected and dedicated. *Submitted by: Betty Jane Alford Landers, 335 W. College St., Bowdon, GA 30108*

170. Bowdon First United Methodist Church

Before Bowdon was a named community, Nathaniel Shelnutt began in 1850 what is now First United Methodist Church. In 1860 the congregation became a part of the Methodist Episcopal Church South. Also part of our roots were the Methodist Protestant Church established in 1855, closely associated with Bowdon College, and the Methodist Episcopal Church started in 1911. The three congregations merged in 1939 when their denominations, separated since before the Civil War, were reunited. The resulting "Methodist Church" continued to meet in the facilities of the Methodist Episcopal Church South. In 1968 the Methodist Church merged with the Evangelical United Brethren Church.

First United Methodist Church

The present brick sanctuary was constructed in 1909. An educational building-annex was added. Later additions included Sunday School rooms and a social hall in 1955 and more classrooms in 1962. The current parsonage is a spacious and beautiful home at 213 McElroy Street, purchased in 1991.

The Church continues a history rich in worship, nurture and education, evangelistic and social service outreach, and community leadership. In recent years our youth have been involved in gleaning crops with the Society of St. Andrew and repair and maintenance of homes through the "River of Life" ministries. The United Methodist Women have been a primary outreach arm of the church and now supports a Girl Scout unit. The United Methodist Men have enjoyed mission trips and support our Boy Scout units. Carroll Tech conducts its GED classes in the church. *Submitted by: Rev. Darrel Hessel, Bowdon First United Methodist Church, PO Box 187, Bowdon, GA 30108*

171. Bowdon Junction Methodist Church

The grandson of Thomas and Harriet Entrekin, who came to Bowdon Junction in 1874, tells of attending his first school at the Old Harmony Methodist Church in 1880. It was a small log building and was used for both a school and church. The church was relocated in about 1914.

Church, Lela Mae Lambert White and Verdie Wallace Lambert

Near the end of 1913 Oscar Bruce Tally, just out of the US Navy, organized a Sunday school at Harmony Methodist Church. In 1914 Mr. Lovvorn of Bowdon, one of the owners of the Bowdon Railroad, gave a lot to the church to build a new church building. The pastor at that time was Rev. Thomas M. Luke. The church was built in an octagon shape.

In 1920 a tornado destroyed the schoolhouse that was just under construction and damaged the church. A new building was constructed with a belfry, which was later removed. *Submitted by: Wallace T. Lambert*
Source: *History of Bowdon Junction* by Myric Shaw

172. Bowdon Methodist Episcopal Church

At the Georgia Methodist Conference held in 1911, W.E. West was appointed to serve the four churches making up the Mt. Zion charge. Some members of the Methodist Episcopal Church living in Bowdon saw a need for a church in Bowdon to care for the members moving into the growing town.

The first service was held on the fifth Sunday night in March 1912. In August, the pastor of the Methodist Protestant Church offered the use of his church to the new congregation. This facility was used from the second Sunday night in September 1912 until the completions of the M.E. church structure in 1914.

On January 2, 1913, a lot on the corner of College and McElroy Streets was purchased by E.J. Hammond and D.S. and W.E. West from Shelly Sewell. The building committee consisted of G.S. McElroy, J.G. Groover, F.A. Martin, John W. Hamil and C.M. Johnson.

Although the five families of McElroy, Martin, Hamil, Mrs. Wesley W. Johnson, and C.H. Griffith took on the responsibility of financing the building, in the spring of the same year, a subscription list was circulated in Bowdon to raise money for the church. On the first day, $1,233 was collected.

Bowdon Methodist Episcopal Church

In October the ground was broken for the foundation with J.R. Hammond of New York as builder and contractor. The building was completed in February 1914.

Reverend Newt T. Crumpton was the first minister with an initial membership of 45. Preaching services were held twice a month.

The cream-colored brick edifice served the community for 25 years. Services were discontinued in 1930 after unification of the Methodist Episcopal Church South, the Methodist Protestant Church and the Methodist Episcopal Church.

The steeple was removed and the structure served as a private residence for a number of years. Dr. and Mrs. J.W. Watts lived there adjacent to Jubal Watts Memorial Hospital for a number of years.

Pews and stained glass windows from this structure were relocated and incorporated into the current Bowdon First United Methodist Church where they are used today. *Submitted by: Judy Rowell, 1472 Garrett Creek Road, Bowdon, GA 30108*

173. Carrollton First United Methodist Church

Methodism began in Carroll County, Georgia, in 1828 through the efforts of Methodist Circuit Riders serving rural preaching places known as Campgrounds. Worship was carried on at the Courthouse until 1847 when Methodists erected a framed, unpainted building, located on the north side of Alabama Street and Highway 27, as a place of worship for Methodists, Baptists, and Presbyterians.

As the congregation grew, it was decided to build another wooden building more centrally located in town at 206 Newnan Street where the church now stands. Carrollton became a station church in 1875.

To serve the growing congregation, the wooden building was dismantled and a larger stone building was constructed. Bishop Warren Candler preached the dedication sermon for this building in 1906.

This stone building has been remodeled and additions added many times. In 1940, a three storied education building was constructed to meet the need for extra classrooms. The chapel was built in 1954. Major expansion was completed in 1989 which included the renovation of the sanctuary, the doubling of the size of the educational facilities, a fellowship hall, kitchen, and gathering room. Recently, buildings surrounding the church have been purchased to house the expanding children and youth ministries. As the congregation continues to experience growth (the membership at the close of 2000 stood at 1538), additional space will be needed.

Carrollton First United Methodist Church is a Daring, Caring, Serving Congregation of Faith and looks forward to the future with great hope. *Submitted by: Eugenia Johnson, 203 Griffin Drive, Carrollton, GA 30117*
Sources: An article written by Miss Nell Meadows, *The Carrollton Methodist Church* and the *Church Album Pictorial Directory for 1999.*

174. Carrollton Presbyterian Church

This church with its beautiful stained glass windows stands in the heart of downtown Carrollton proclaiming God's love to the community and to the world. The church was organized in 1841 when Flint River Presbytery sent two members to Carrollton to meet with the following people: Horace Smith, Paschal Grow, Mary Ann Kingsberry, Elmirea Grow, Elizabeth Baxter, Mary Springer, Eliza Baxter, Cathrine Rogers and Delia Wicks. At this meeting the church was organized.

The first pastor was J.T. Alexander who served until 1856. Other ministers include William Dimmock, James Stacey, W.W. Nesbit, W.E. Dozier, J.B. Gordon, E.L. Barber, J.L. McGirt, Richard O. Flinn, James Wafford, Tom Ballard, Jerry Patton and David Shelor.

Carrollton Presbyterian Church

The present church structure was erected in 1902, the building committee was composed of L.C. Mandeville, J.A. Aycock, A.A. Simonton with Rev. Dozier ex-officio member. In 1926 the "Little White House" was built to provide Sunday School space. Westminister Hall, the three-story addition to the original church was built in 1952 and was dedicated to Richard O. Flinn on June 22, 1986. Flinn served the church 38 years. On April 25, 1985 the church purchased the home of Howard Thomasson next to the church, first used as a manse and now as youth center and annex.

Carrollton Presbyterian continues to grow, from nine to over three hundred today. It provides various workshop opportunities, sponsoring Girl Scout Troop 179 since 1922, and serving mankind as Jesus taught. *Submitted by: Tommie Bandy Freeman, 1486 Pleasant Hill Rd., Carrollton, GA 30116*

175. Clem United Methodist Church From 1897 to 2001

Clem United Methodist Church is located in Clem, Georgia which is located in Carroll County. Clem is located about five to six miles south of Carrollton. The little community of Clem was built up in 1874 around the railroad. The little country church named Clem was established in 1897 by Rev. W.L. Davenport. Rev. Davenport was a chaplain in the Confederate Army. After the Civil War, he became a circuit rider in the Methodist Church traveling by horseback from church to church. Some of the early founding families included the Davenports, Ogletrees, Fullers, Haynies, McCartys, Daughterys, Coopers, Springers, Knotts, Turners, Gastons, and Crews.

The little church suffered a severe setback in April of 1909 when it was blown away in a windstorm. The church only faltered, it did not fail. The church was rebuilt onto its present site 300 yards from the original location. Revivial services were held at the new location by late summer/early fall.

Along with everyone else, the church went through some tough times during the Great Depression. It became somewhat rundown. The roof leaked and did some damage to the inside of the church. But yet again, the little church fought back. In 1937, Rev. Mattison wired the church for electric lights. In 1938, the church received a much needed new roof. The church began with a foot pedal organ and finally acquired a piano in the early 1940's. In 1947, the church purchased more land to expand the cemetery.

Many improvements have been made to this little church. In the early 1950's, an annex was added to the back of the existing building. This annex consisted of two Sunday school rooms upstairs and a kitchen downstairs. The Watkins family deeded three parcels of land to the church. Around 1980, a well was bored on one of those deeded parcels. Stained glass windows were installed into the church around 1985. Individual families purchased these windows in memory of loved ones. In 1991, another addition was made to the existing structure. The kitchen area was expanded to include a dining hall. A cornerstone was placed on the church in 1994. This little country church is yet still charging into the new Millennium with still more improvements. In the year 2000, we have installed new carpeting, purchased new pews, built a beautiful brick outdoor sign with the church name, installed a new sound system, and installed two new stained glass windows in loving memory of two special church families.

Clem United Methodist Church

Clem Church was always part of a circuit. We had always shared a minister with either Stripling Chapel or Lowell UM Church. Our little church is too small to provide for a parsonage, so we graciously shared our pastor with another church. However, in 1991 we were finally blessed enough to have our own full-time pastor, Rev. Jimmy Bryan. Since that time, we have been able to support having our own minister. At the present time, we are pleased to have Rev. Tom Howson serving as our pastor. Our church membership is presently at 35.

The road to Clem United Methodist Church has not always been a smooth one. We have had our ups and downs just like every other church. We have suffered through some adversities, but we have always pulled together to overcome them. *Submitted by: M.T. Fuller and Melissa Warren*

176. Concord Primitve Baptist Church

Concord Baptist was established 22 December 1834 by act of the Georgia House and Senate, Thomas Glascock, Speaker; Jacob Wood, President of the Senate; and Wilson Lumpkin, Governor. Trustees representing the church were Thomas Barnes Williams, Thomas P. Wilkins, and Isaac E. Cobb. The church is located on Hwy 113 between Carrollton and Temple.

Concord Primitive Baptist Church

The first church and cemetery, often referred to as Old Concord, was located about one half mile north of Spence Road. The old church burned and there are about 130 graves in the old cemetery. Descendents of those buried there have spent the last four and one half years trying to gain access to the land locked cemetery. We have, this year completed a new road to the cemetery with much help coming from the Carroll County Commissioners, a lot of hard work by prison laborers on the new road, and many thanks to the Forrest Escort Camp of Villa Rica for their hard work on this project. Concerned individuals for the gravel for the road raised some four thousand dollars. A special thanks to our senior citizens, and descendants that attended almost every commission meeting and would not accept "NO" as an answer to their pleas. Thanks also to the county attorney that spent many hours trying to find a solution and getting all the paperwork in order. Out of this came something special from our elected officials and county attorney, a new set of laws that protect cemeteries in Carroll County.

Isaac E. Cobb, the trustee noted above, was also the Sheriff of Carroll County, but probably was better known as the owner and operator of Buckhorn Tavern, a stage coach stop in Carroll County, between Marthasville (now Atlanta) and Jacksonville, Alabama. Mr. Cobb was also elected three times as a state legislator. He had eight sons that served in the Confederate Army.

Jeremiah Cole, buried at old Concord, served as a state troop soldier. He also built the second jail in Carrollton just off the Square for $749. It was a two-story log structure with each log being hewn 1 foot square (1837-1839). *Submitted by: Dennis W. Williams, 326 Rockmart Road, Villa Rica, GA 30180*

177. Concord Primitive Baptist Church Observed its Centennial

On the 15th of December 1934, Concord Primitive Baptist Church celebrated its one hundredth anniversary. After the assembling of the congregation and opening exercises, Joe Jackson gave an interesting talk. At eleven a.m., Elder W.O. Jennings, the pastor of the church gave the sermon. At noon, an adjournment was made for forty minutes for a bountiful and sumptuous dinner on the church grounds.

After the noon recess, the church went into its usual conference for the transaction of business of the church. G.H. Cole, the church clerk read from an old minute book, the original constitution, and the original decorum of the church. Judge W.J. Millican of Carrollton was introduced by the pastor and delivered a thirty-minute address.

The speaker stated that when the church was constituted Carroll County was only eight years old; that the population of the county was only 3500, both white and black, though the area of the county was considerably larger than at present; that Jonathan Walker and Dr. James H. Rogers were Carroll's representatives in the Legislature and that Giles S. Boggess was in the State Senate; that Wilson Lumpkin was Governor of the State, Thomas Glascock Speaker of the House, and Jacob Wood President of the Senate; that John P. King and Alfred Cuthbert were in the United States Senate from Georgia; that George M. Troup, John McPherson Berrien, Elijah Clark, and William H. Crawford were the leading statesmen in Georgia; that Andrew Jackson was President of the United States and John Forsyth of Georgia was Secretary of State in Jackson's cabinet; that Thomas M. Benton, Henry Clay, Daniel Webster, John C. Calhoun, Robert Young Haynes, and William H. Crawford of Georgia were the most conspicuous statesmen in the United States; that the population of the United States was only 13,000,000; and that Texas, New Mexico, Arizona, and California belonged to the Republic of Mexico.

Judge Millican further stated that when the church was constituted and for four years after,

Concord Primitive Baptist Church Marker

the Indians roamed the forest; that the fish and useful game were abundant and that the beasts of prey kept the pioneers alert by day and disturbed their repose by night; that it was the era of the ox-cart and the log cabin; of the loom, the reel and the spinning wheel; of the skillet, the trivet, the pot-hooks and pot-racks; of corn-shucking, house-raising and log-rolling; of dirt floored churches and puncheon seated school houses, the one the nestor of old time religion and the other the shrine of the "three R's" immortal.

The speaker stated further that in 1834 there were only four or five organized religious bodies in Carroll County and but few schools, these being one room, one teacher, and practically no equipment except such as was thought to be necessary for the maintenance of discipline; that there was $332.00 appropriated to Carroll County by the state for educational purposes; that there were no cook stoves, no sewing machines, no carriages or buggies, no railroads, no telegraphs, but few public roads and these were mere trails through the forest. In concluding his address, the speaker stated that practically the only thing in common with us and the people of that day is a sense of justice and an appreciation of the fundamental virtues; honesty, integrity, veracity, and patriotism, those elements which make up the spiritual compound that alone can save us and our civilization.

After the conclusion of Judge Millican's address, Deacon J.B. King, Hon. J.H. Burson, and John T. Eady gave addresses. The day was truly a celebration of Concord Baptist Church and Carroll County. *Submitted by: Dennis W. Williams, 326 Rockmart Road, Villa Rica, GA 30180*
Sources: excerpts from an article by Nancy Williams Gilmer, *Carroll County Genealogical Quarterly*, Summer 1997

178. Concord United Methodist Church

Concord United Methodist Church is located nine miles North of Carrollton, Georgia, in Carroll County, and six miles south of Villa Rica and Interstate 20. In 1828 Carroll County was constituted. The first settlers came to the area in the county known as Hickory Level in the early part of the same year. In 1828, John Quincy Adams was President of the United States and it was a good year at Hickory Level. Settlers built log homes, cleared land for crops and built fences for their livestock.

In the fall of 1828, thirteen families came together and Concord Episcopal Church was organized. They called the church Concord because of their desire to live in accord with one another. In 1828 the original house of worship was built of logs and was 18 ft. square. In 1836, a second house of worship was built and it was 24 ft. square. In 1854 a frame type house was built at a cost of $500, it was 40 ft. x 36 ft. In 1891 a fourth house of worship was built at a cost of $1000, it was destroyed by a tornado in 1909. That same year, 1909, the present church was built at a cost of a $4000 and is 60 ft. x 33 ft. It was dedicated to Christian service in July of 1909.

The first Sunday worship was by Bishop Warren Candler. Bishop Candler was the brother of Asa Candler, founder of Coca Cola. Both were from Villa Rica, Georgia. Bishop Candler and Asa Candler were instrumental in the establishment of Emory Hospital and University at its present location.

In 1939 the Methodist Episcopal Church South united with other Methodist Churches. In 1968 the name was changed to the United Methodist Church and that is how it is known today, Concord United Methodist Church.

Concord United Methodist Church

Concord United Methodist has had a duly appointed pastor every year except 1864 during the Civil War. Rev. William Francis Powell and Rev. David Stripling, members of Concord, organized and nourished Methodist Churches in Carroll County. Examples of their labor are Stripling Chapel United Methodist Church on Hwy. 27 and Powell Chapel United Methodist on Flat Rock Road.

In 1966, the North Georgia Conference gave Concord Church the citation of being the oldest Methodist Church in the Rome-Carrollton District and carries the honor of being Carroll County's oldest organized church.

The current church has an education building that was built in 1955. A fellowship hall was added in 1984 and is equipped to serve meals and have church and related activities. There is also a parsonage on the church grounds. The present pastor is Linda Hessell, who along with the Concord family serves the Hickory Level community.

With Concord's rich history, nestled in its quaint country setting of hickory and pine trees, and with its friendly members, visitors are welcomed with open arms and a warm smile. *Submitted by: Rick Waller as told by Bob Baskin, Rick Waller, 80 Pine Haven Court, Carrollton, GA 30116*

179. County Line Primitive Baptist Church Records

The Church of County Line was established in the home of Wesley and Mariah Lassetter Camp in the Third District in 1829 in what was then Campbell County. Mariah Camp was one of the charter members. Wesley did not join as he was a devout mason and the church did not believe in secret orders. This area was created in 1826 in Carroll County; in 1828 Campbell County was created from parts of Carroll County. In 1870 Douglas County was created from part of Campbell County. In 1872 the area again became Carroll County. After being in Campbell County for 41 years, County Line Church spent 2 years in Douglas County, back to Carroll County where it stands today.

Although the church has been enlarged and remodeled, the huge hand hewn sills are still the originals. We do not know when this was built. In minutes Nov. 26, 1830: "selected a place for meeting house. Resolved that we build our meeting house on lot 67 in the Third District of Carroll now Campbell Co., Ga. Also agreed to build one 20 by 27 ft." In the minutes of Oct. 13, 1832 the Church met in conference and "agreed to move her meeting house to a fracture of land lot 65 belonging to Bro. Wise. He promised to give two acres of land in the northeast corner of said lot." Jan. 12, 1833: "appointed Wise and Hendon to see Mr. McGill to procure a place for a meeting house, if we fail to accept Bro. Wise propersition." Feb. 9, 1833: "the committee report that the place selected to build a meeting house on a part of Mr. McGill's land ... Appointed Bros. Hendon and Wise to measure land for the meeting house and procure bond for the same as title." On Apr. 6, 1833: "request granted that Bro. Lassetter & Wise make a bargin to build the meeting house and agree to abide by the bargin that they may make." May 4, 1833 "Bros. Hendon and Wise came forward with deed to the land to build the meeting house which was approved of. Bros. Lassetter and Wise reported they had made the bargin with Brother Hendon to build it." The land was purchased at a cost of $6.00 (six).

I do not have a record of when the church was built, where services were held in the interim, or when they began having services there. The deed dated Oct. 6, 1934 is for "2 acres on the west side of Land Lot 89 in the Third District of originally Carroll County now Campbell being eighteen rods square."

The first ministers I have seen recorded were in 1831 when they would head their conference. In 1832 they started the conference, Ga Campbell Co. The Baptist Church of Christ at County Line. Also in the minutes of Apr. 23, 1831 moved and seconded by church: decided that "ordinance of foot washing shall be practiced in the church after communion." In July 1835 they started calling it the Primitive Baptist Church of Christ. In Conference Aug. 33, 1839 Bros. Lassetter, T. Duke and D.B. Head were appointed trustees to superintend the building of the addition to the meeting house. Jan. 23, 1850 church met in conference. Bro. Lassetter asked leave to build a school house at County Line which was granted by the church. Conference, Jan. 1863, Bro. James H. Lassetter delivered the deed whereon County Line Church is built to the church. On motion the church agreed for the same Brother Lassetter to keep said deed.

County Line Primitive Baptist Church

Conference Oct. 29, 1878 met in conference appointed Bro. R.B. Jones to fence graves in churchyard.

I mentioned before about the counties that had changed names over the years. The first conference there is a record of was held July 24, 1830 headed as follows: Ga. Campbell Co. In Nov. 1870 conference was held and began: Conference was held at Ga. Douglas Co. Baptist Church of Christ. Feb. 17, 1872 conference was held at County Line Baptist Church of Christ Ga. Carroll Co.

Services are still held here in Carroll County, Ga. on North Highway 5, Whitesburg, Ga. 30185 on the fourth Sunday of each month.

Submitted by: Imogene Frazier
Sources: Research by Thelma Pate and Imogene Frazier from Church Minutes and deed record

180. Cross Plains Christian Church

Cross Plains Christian Church was organized in 1926. There were 19 charter members. They were from the following families: Treadwells, Davis, Keys, Gladneys, Stichers, Hinesleys and the Boatwrights. The building at its present location was built in August and September of 1929.

Cross Plains Christian Church

The building is located at 1356 Cross Plains Road. Throughout the years the building has taken on several different looks. During the years of 1999 through 2001, a new fellowship hall and gym were added and some remodeling was done to the original building. Though the look of the building has changed through the years, we continue to put God first in our plans here at Cross Plains. As of the year 2001 our minister is Jason Nix. The church board consists of Elders: Wendell Stitcher, Junior Key, and Nelson Collins; Deacons: Chuck Barron, Larry Bishop, Camp Billey, Joel Hubbard, Tom Engle, Billy Horton, Jeff Pate, and Al Wallace. God has blessed our church with many blessings and we want to give Him all the praise and glory for the success since 1926 and we pray that He will continue to bless us and may He bless you as well. *Submitted by: Cross Plains Christian Church, 1356 Cross Plains Rd., Carrollton, GA 30116*

181. Eden Primitive Baptist Church

The first Baptist church in western Carroll County was Eden Primitive Baptist Church incorporated in 1835 under Rev. James Barrow's leadership. The church was located south of Bowdon near Lake Clyde and the Little Tallapoosa River where converts were baptized. James Reeves served as pastor from 1835 to 1845. Strongly Calvinistic the church brought charges against members who were either cleared or excommunicated for offenses including "pilfering, intemperance, and contemptible and profane language." Saturday services were held with footwashing part of each communion service. Deacons and deaconesses were appointed.

In June 1859 plans were made to build a new meeting house 30 by 45 feet, and the August 1850 minutes state, "our meeting much frustrated by rain, not having our house covered." In 1850 there were 60 members, four of whom were slaves. The August 1853 revival saw 40 added to the church "two by letter, one restored, and 37 by experience." The progressive congregation organized a Sunday School in 1853 and allowed Methodists to use their facilities.

In January 1857 the pastor was compensated $6.75 for the previous year's service. February 1860 thirteen members were granted their letters to form a new church in Bowdon, the current Bowdon Baptist Church. Minutes of

September 18, 1862, state, "By order of a proclamation by President Davis, President of the Confederate States of America, the church met and determined our thanks to the Almighty God, God of battles for the victories of our troops on the field of battle."

For the remainder of the century the little church in the woods "preached in the Spirit, communed in love, and dismissed in order." *Submitted by: Jan Rowland Johnson, 442 E. College St., Bowdon, GA 30108*

182. Ephesus Christian Church and its forerunners Enon and Enon Grove

In the mid-1800s about a mile east of the present Ephesus Christian Church, there was a congregation of non-denominational believers called Enon. This church was located on, or near the Arbor Hill, just off the present south Little NewYork Road. In March of 1884 a tornado blew this building away, down to the sills. It is said only the Bible, minus its covers, was found in the nearby woods.

Ephesus Christian Church 1962

A short time later some of these members started meeting in a building on property owned by Jimmy Webb, about 1 and ½ miles west of our church today, on what is now called Shoemake Road. This congregation was called Enon Grove or New Enon. They met here for nearly 10 years, until trouble arose.

About this time a man named Matt Rooks from this community, journeyed across the Chattahoochee River to a little nondenominational church in the edge of Heard County called Antioch Christian Church. He heard the word of God, repented and was baptized. Soon after returning home, he made preparations and sent for Mr. Zack Hardigree (the preacher from Antioch, who rode horseback and preached at many area churches) to come and preach a two-week revival in a brush arbor on the hill at the present location. This was 1894 and was the beginning of the Ephesus Christian Church.

Ephesus Christian Church 2001

In the early days of the church, the building was used as a combination school and house of worship. The cemetery was started here in May of 1871, at the death of John T. Clark, about 23 years before the church was established.

The following is a list of known ministers who have served Ephesus Christian Church starting with the founding minister: Zack Hardigree, Tumbling, Carter, Miller, Young Hardigree, W.R. Morgan, Eli (E.S.C.) Webb, Maude Webb, Fraily, Coley Turner, Bill Palmer, Coy Bass, Ted Jones, Donald Weldon, Robert Gibson, and J.C. Cook who has served from August 1958 to the present.

Today, as our church grows in building size and with new members, we offer Sunday School for all ages at 10 a.m., Sunday morning worship at 11 a.m., junior church for ages 5-12, nursery for ages 0-4, and monthly youth group activities. Everyone is welcome. *Submitted by: Minister J.C. Cook, Ephesus Christian Church, 280 Davis Road, Carrollton, GA 30116*

183. Eureka Baptist Church

In 1880, about six miles west of Carrollton, both Baptists and Methodists joined together to build a brush arbor as a place of worship. Some of the people who organized and helped with this work were Rev. E.E. Robinson, who was the first pastor of Eureka, Mr. and Mrs. Melvin Dingler, Mr. and Mrs. James Monroe Windom, Mr. Tommie Holmes, Billie and Tommie Baxter and Bill Crumbley. Land for a church cemetery was set aside across the road from the church building.

Later, a small wooden building was built. Some years later a larger wooden building was erected and served as a place of worship until 1946. This building was then torn down and a larger brick building was erected with four Sunday School rooms. A baptismal pool was built beside the church. This new building was built by members and friends who supplied logs for lumber, cut and dragged from their land by mules, and anything else they had to contribute to the building of this church so they would have a place to worship.

Eureka Baptist Church

Over the years several additions, including a baptistery, have been added. A fellowship hall was erected beside the church building and a parsonage was built in 1962.

Since 1925, Eureka Baptist Church has had 24 different pastors, including Rev. Gordon Willingham, who served as pastor and interim pastor several times. *Submitted by: Ellen H. Windom, (Church Clerk), 450 Eureka Church Road, Carrollton, GA 30117*

184. The First Baptist Church of Carrollton - Dixie Street

The First Baptist Church of Carrollton, which has met for worship and study on the corner of Newnan and Dixie Streets since 1875, has not always had the same name and location for the church. The records available indicated that the Church had its beginning in the home of William and Nancy Beall on Buck Creek, four miles north of Carrollton. On Monday, August 9, 1847, the Upper Tallapoosa Baptist Church was constituted by presbytery made up on James Reeves and Leroy McWhorter, with eight charter members. William Beall was chosen church clerk and six months later the Rev. James Davis was called "to the pastoral care of the Church." Services were held in the Methodist meeting house and in local school buildings. In 1851 the congregation would move to a new building at the intersection of what are now Lee and Bradley Streets. Twenty years later the coming of the railroad would make it necessary for the church to move to its present location on the corner of Newnan and Dixie Streets.

First Baptist Church of Carrollton

During those early years it was customary for the Church to hold services on two days of the month, a Saturday and the following Sunday. At that time there were both white and black members of what had come to be called Carrollton Baptist Church. In those years not only did the races seat themselves separately, the sexes did also, with men on one side and women on the other.

In September 1873, all black members except two asked for their church letters. The group that left would eventually become a part of the black congregation known as First Baptist Church, Church Street.

The Carrollton Baptist Church had a leading role in the formation of the Carrollton Baptist Association, which took place on October 24, 1874, with 17 Baptist Churches represented. The Rev. J.M. Muse was elected moderator and Dr.W.W. Fitts of the Carrollton Baptist Church became treasurer.

The decade of the 1890s was an eventful one in the life of the Church; a unit of the Woman's Missionary Union was organized in 1890; in 1892 the Church began to have preaching each Sunday; schism centering around pastor J.C. Wingo resulted in a number of members leaving the Church to form Central Baptist Church, now known as Tabernacle Baptist Church. After the division the Church located at the corner of Newnan and Dixie Streets came to be called First Baptist Church.

A new house of worship, located on the same site, was completed in 1908 with Tiffany stained glass windows on the north side of the sanctuary. A new pipe organ was installed prior to the formal dedication service that took place in 1910.

The early part of the twentieth century saw the Church grow steadily in numbers, finances, and influence in the community. Average Sunday School attendance in 1928 was 175, in 1938 it was 265, and in 1964 it was 345.

In 1944 Howard Benson was called as pastor, serving until June of 1975, the longest tenure of any pastor in the history of the Church. Organizational financial growth in the Church as well as leadership in the life of the community marked his years of service. In recognition of his lengthy tenure the Church made the pastorium on Dixie Street available for the Bensons for their lifetime.

The years Brantley Harwell served as pastor, 1976-1988, were marked by enthusiasm, growth, construction of an educational building, involvement in missions, a series of staff changes, and sadly, division within the Church. This schism led to the formation of the Trinity Baptist Church in 1988.

In September of 1995 Dr. Steve Davis was called as pastor. Under his leadership there has been growth in numbers, financial support, and personal involvement. A thorough renovation of the church's facilities has been completed, the project being called Vision 2000. Dual worship services on Sunday mornings were begun in March 2001. *Submitted by: C.D. McCollum, Historian, First Baptist Church, Carrollton*

Sources: Article taken from *A History of First Baptist Church* by James David Griffin

185. First Baptist Church of Temple

Temple, Georgia, was settled in 1882, alongside the Georgia Pacific Railroad as it was being built between Atlanta, Georgia (then Marthasville), and Birmingham, Alabama. Major Robert Henry Temple, a native of Virginia and a Civil War veteran, was the chief engineer of the railway. The town was named for Major Temple, and it was chartered on August 28, 1883.

First Baptist Church of Temple

Temple Baptist Church had its beginning on November 1, 1884. Four men and eleven women submitted their church letters on that date. These charter members were J.M. Daniel, S.B.L.J. McClung, J.M.D. Stallings, J.Y. Riggs, Martha Daniel, Deborah McClung, Mary E. Stallings, A.V. Riggs, Sarah Crockett, Amanda Jones, Sophronia Stallings, Hariette Vandergriff, Margret Vandergriff, Anna Vandergriff, and Susan Phillips. J.M.D. Stallings was the first pastor.

The first church building was a wooden structure located several yards west of the present church site. The present brick building was constructed in the early 1900s.

In 1939 four wooden Sunday School rooms were added to the east side of the building, and stained-glass windows were added to the auditorium. A Sunday School annex, baptistery, and vestibule were built in 1951, and another Sunday School annex was built in 1967.

In 1974 the church voted to change its name to First Baptist Church of Temple. In 1979 the sanctuary was remodeled again, and in 1995 a renovation project of existing space was undertaken. The present church membership is 325 and Reverend Larry Boswell serves as pastor. *Submitted by: Ruth Holder, P.O. Box 70, Temple, GA 30179*

186. First Baptist Church of Villa Rica

"The History of the Carrollton Baptist Association" sites the origin of First Baptist Church of Villa Rica back to 1845 where the church was organized in a little log schoolhouse in old Villa Rica. However, according to the minutes of the Tallapoosa Association, Villa Rica Baptist was listed as a new member in 1843.

Sometime later, a two-story house was built as the first church building. The first floor was used for school and the second floor served as the church.

A large landowner named Jack Jones deeded the site at 405 Main Street to the Baptist Church for 99 years. In 1885, a wooden structure was built on the heavily wooded land, where water was obtained from a well in the front yard. This building cost $6000, of which $2000 was raised by the WMU ladies.

First Baptist Church of Villa Rica

In 1878, the 45-member Villa Rica Baptist withdrew from the Tallapoosa Association and joined the Carrollton Association. One of the reasons the Carrollton Association was formed was to get a fresh start in mission work. It is with much praise and glory to God that the First Baptist Church sent out missionaries to foreign lands to serve and witness for the Lord. In 1920, Edna Earle Teal was sent to China where she served until her retirement in 1943. Judy and Gary Tapp left for foreign missions in 1980 and have served in the East Africa region, Northern Africa, and the Middle East.

As membership grew over the years, additional facilities were added at the Main Street location. The church's first brick building was built in 1935. Fifteen years later, a 2-story Sunday School annex was added. In 1960, an education building was added with Sunday School rooms and a choir room. The sanctuary was enlarged in 1964. The Marchman residence was purchased in 1977 for additional Sunday School and educational space. After the purchase of the Marchman building, First Baptist occupied the block surrounded by Magnolia Street, Rockmart Hwy., Dallas Road and Main Street. In 1983, the Family Life Center was completed, housing the nursery, a kitchen and a large multi-purpose gymnasium. A youth room and storage room were later added to this building. While buildings do not make a church, they do reflect a love for a great God and a desire to fulfill the spiritual needs of the community.

Relocation or renovation became a topic of prayer and discussion during the late 80's. After many years of prayer and seeking God's will, the decision was made to relocate. Forty-four acres of land was purchased at 1483 W. Highway 78 and erection of a multi-purpose building began at the new location. A final worship service was held at the Main Street location on November 22, 1998. Four weeks later, the first service at 1483 W. Highway 78 was held on December 20, 1998. In late 2000, the church began the next phase of the building program at its new location.

Many pastors, ministers of music, education and youth have faithfully served First Baptist Church throughout its history. Each pastor and minister has been influential in shaping the spiritual lives of the members of First Baptist.

Jesus tells us in John 15:16-17 "You did not choose me, but I chose you and appointed you to go and bear fruit that will last. Then the Father will give you whatever you ask in My name. This is my command: Love each other". The First Baptist Church of Villa Rica has obeyed this command by being a source of love, spiritual inspiration, and encouragement to its community. *Submitted by: Kerry Mote Burross, 8805 Hwy. 166, Winston, GA 30187*

187. First Christian Church, Carrollton

The staff at First Christian Church includes Senior Minister Fred Skinner. He serves as minister, evangelist pastor, and oversees the staff. His approach to ministry is two-fold. First, he has been called to spread the Gospel (good news) to our community and the world. This is accomplished through messages from the pulpit, Bible studies and personal visits. Secondly, to nurture the congregation into spiritual maturity. The message about the love and forgiveness of God draws men and women into a personal relationship with Christ and His Church. It is truly a blessing to see the lives of people as they grow in the Lord.

Dwayne Hicks is Youth Minister and he claims as his life verse for ministry Colossians 1:28, "So we continue to preach Christ to each person, using all wisdom to warn and to teach everyone, in order to bring each one into God's presence as a mature person in Christ." He tries to help young people grow physically, emotionally, spiritually, intellectually and socially. He says that he feels responsible for the spiritual teaching they receive while in his care. He programs Bible studies, worship times, conventions, retreats and even crazy events that are pure and plain fun! He enjoys seeing the students experience the joy-filled life that is available to everyone who has Jesus in their heart and life!

Dwayne Hicks, Fred Skinner, and William "Skip" Broome, FCC Ministers, 2001.

Children's Minister William "Skip" Broome oversees the spiritual development of the children ages birth through fifth grade. He is assisted by an advisory council. He is convinced that this is the most important ministry in a church because most people come to Christ before the age of 18. He says that he has 11 years to be able to form a relationship with them and help them grow. Some say that Children are the future church but he says that they are the church now! Because they are the future leaders, he feels the children's ministry is a top priority. He reserves the lunch hour two days each week during the school year for the children to make arrangements for him to have lunch with them and their friends at school. Also, he has organized a MOPS (mothers of preschoolers) group to address the needs of every preschool mother.

In addition to the three ministers, the church employs a Youth Intern, student from the Atlanta Christian College, to work part-time with the youth and children's ministers to gain experience.

For more information about First Christian Church, Carrollton, please refer to the article near the back of this book. The church website is www.1stchristianchurch.com. *Submitted by: Violette Harris Denney, 135 Maple Hill Road, Carrollton, GA 30116.*

Special covered dish dinner, Sept. 1986

Bible School 1990

Interior View

188. First United Methodist Church of Villa Rica

Our church was first laid out in 1830, four years after gold was discovered, in the oldest town in north-west Georgia. Early church records cannot be found and information must be secured from fragments gathered from the oldest inhabitants, scrapbooks, and church records of the late 1880's.

First United Methodist Church of Villa Rica established 1830's, this building 1906.

The first church was a log building located on the Willoughby farm, the only church in the community. Around 1845 an attractive wooden structure was erected in what is now called Old Town. The Methodist shared the pulpit with Baptist and Presbyterians, the strong Union Sunday School was attended by all denominations for years.

In 1883 a new town, called Villa Rica, was laid out a mile south of the old town and in 1886 a new church was built on the site of the present church at a cost of about $1200. The charge then was composed of Old and New Villa Rica, Temple and Concord. Sunday School was still conducted at the Old Town Church.

In 1890 the old church was abandoned, then sold by the trustees in 1896. The first parsonage was purchased in 1901. The white frame church was used until the present brick structure was completed for services in July 1906. In 1949 the main sanctuary was remodeled and redecorated and in 1940 a ten room annex was added for Sunday School classes. In 1985 construction was completed on a Family Activitiy Center and in 1998 we added an additional building named the Moore Christian Life Center in honor of Miss Ruth Moore. The church's address is 206 North Avenue, Villa Rica, GA 30180 *Submitted by: Reba Hembree Rainwater, 361 Bay Springs Rd., Villa Rica, GA 30180*

189. First Presbyterian Church PCA of Villa Rica

First Presbyterian Church PCA of Villa Rica is a very old and historic church. It was organized in 1855. All early records were destroyed and services were suspended during the Civil War, but services were resumed in 1867. The first building, constructed in 1855 was a white frame building on Candler Street. Mr. William B. Candler became Clerk of Lessons in 1880 and continued until 1921. At his death in 1928 his children gave to the church his home and the property on Main Street where the church now stands. The fifth generation of Mr. Candler's family still worships there. When the church was moved to this property, it was bricked and a basement added for Sunday School rooms. Mahogany pews and pulpit and stained glass windows, purchased from old Wesley Memorial Church of Atlanta, were added. The formula for the colors in the windows has been lost, making them irreplaceable. The sanctuary today looks much as it did then when the cornerstone was laid in 1930.

Mr. Candler's home directly behind the church was first used for a manse, later for Sunday School rooms and in 1998 was torn down to make room for Sunday School rooms and recreation activities. The basement was completely renovated for offices, a nursery and a library.

First Presbyterian Church PCA of Villa Rica.

Various ministers from the area served the church in the early days. Later in the 1940s through 1960s, the church was served by students and ministers shared with other congregations. The first full-time minister served the church from 1973 until 1982. In 1986 the name of the church was changed from Villa Rica Presbyterian Church to First Presbyterian Church of Villa Rica. In 1991 the congregation voted to withdraw from the Presbyterian Church in the United States and join the Presbyterian Church in America. The church's first full-time PCA minister was George F. Ganey. Today, the First Presbyterian Church PCA is a small friendly mission-minded congregation of 100 members under the leadership of Reverend Todd Allen. *Submitted by: First Presbyterian Church PCA, 519 Main St., Villa Rica, GA 30180*

190. Flat Rock Baptist Church

The Church was organized in June 1881 when Ephraim M. Allen gave two acres of land in Lot No. 34 in the Sixth District, and Willis Reynolds gave full privilege of drinking water for the use of the church from a spring near his house on Land Lot 33. The church was called Harmony Baptist Church and later changed to Flat Rock Baptist Church.

The Church joined the Good Samaritan Association in 1897 where it remained until 1963 when it joined the Carrollton Baptist Association.

In 1959, Mrs. Wiley G. Gilland gave an additional acre of land for the location of a pastorium that was completed in 1961.

The church records were lost in a fire in 1941. Although there is no list of charter members, the Allen, Boyd, Couch, Gilland, Hardin, Hembree, Noles, Payne, Reynolds, Samples and Tyson families have been long-standing members.

The following is a list of pastors since 1897: T.A. Colson, J.R. Cole, Billy Samples, J.M. Williams, Joe Davidson, John Crider, Milton Parish, J.T. Layton, Tom Connell, J.W. Womack, Andrew Eason, Lawrence Akin, S.B. Duncan,

Flat Rock Baptist Church, Villa Rica

W.L. Standridge, L.D. Palmer, Harold Freeman, John Allen, Horace Wilson, Hugh Formby, Eddie Morgan, Robert Startup, Wayne Jenkins, Howard Benson, William Updike, Ed Wix, Gary Ashley, William Clinton, and Ronnie Puckett. The church is located at 961 Flat Rock Road, Villa Rica. *Submitted by: Erlene Camp Boyd, 1539 Flat Rock Rd., Villa Rica, GA 30180*
Sources: Deeds and Church Records

191. Flint Ridge Baptist Church

The Flint Ridge Baptist Church, located on Highway 100 South, where Rev. E.L. Stewart is the pastor, was organized in the year 1927.

Flint Ridge Baptist Church, Bowdon, GA.

This church was located near Lovvorn Mill on Lovvorn Road on the other side of Bowdon with Rev. J.D. Dunson as the pastor. He had a membership of 250 there. In 1929 some of the members felt that the church should be moved to a better location.

The church was torn down and moved to Wedowee Road, its location today. With the cooperation of a sister church, church services were able to continue.

During the fall of 1929 a plain farm church was built. During the years between 1930 and 1939, a choir stand, usher's room and pastor's study were added, along with brick siding for the outside of the church.

During the 1940's white shingles were put on the church.

During the 1950's and 1960's bathrooms were built, gas was put in the church and the floors were carpeted.

During the 1970's, we bricked our church and purchased additional parking space.

Finally, in the year 2000, land was purchased adjacent to the church for Phase II of the Flint Ridge Baptist Church.

Leaders such as the late Rev. J.D. Dunson, the late Rev. C.B. Johnson, Rev. Harvelle Smith, Rev. Titus Robinson, Rev. R.L. Miller, our current pastor, Rev. E.L. Stewart and members helped make this church what it is today. *Submitted by: Shirley L. Shackleford, 57 Huey Drive, Bowdon, GA 30108*

192. Holly Springs Primitive Baptist Church

Holly Springs Primitive Baptist Church is considered one of the oldest Primitive Baptist churches in Carroll County. According to Church records, services have been held on a regular basis since 1840. The first meetings were held in a hunter's lodge that sat where the cemetery is now located. In 1848, Holly Springs became part of the New Hope Primitive Baptist Association. In 1853, Mr. William Rooker donated three acres of land to give the church a permanent home.

Holly Springs located near present Carroll/Haralson County line.

In 1864, The New Hope Association met at Holly Springs for the first time. In 1891, H.M. Reid donated five acres for a cemetery.

The third church building, the present one, was moved to its present location from the Buddapest area, now Haralson County, by a team of ten oxen. This memory was related by Paul (Bill) Howard who died in April 1998. He watched his family help move the building.

After I-20 and Highway 27 moved into the area, about four acres were left for the church. When the last member died, Holly Springs was kept alive by the help of Shiloh Primitive Baptist Church in the Buncombe, Haralson County area. The Elder (preacher) for the last 37 years has been Homer Benefield. Prior to that, Elders Holcombe and Parrish served Holly Springs. Before them, Elder R.T. Speight served Holly Springs for 49 years.

Today, Holly Springs is best known for its annual Sacred Harp Singings held each June. Presently services are held the fourth Sunday in each month. *Submitted by: Orlando Driver, 6154 Smithfield Road, Bowdon, GA 30108*

193. Kansas Baptist Church

On June 24, 1897, a group of people met at Kansas schoolhouse for the purpose of drawing a Constitution of Kansas Baptist Church. The meeting was called to order by Rev. W.J. Lovvorn, Rev. J.W. McLeod presided. The charter members were Charles Smith, Thomas Smith, Alford Smith, Asa Bearden, F.W. Rainwater, D.S. Haynes, Will E. Abercrombie, Mrs. S.J. Smith, Nancy C. Smith, Lucindy E. Smith, Mary G. Bearden, Julia Annie Bearden, and Sadie E. Abercrombie.

On August 13, 1897, the building committee met and agreed to bear an equal part if not built by the people. It was decided that the church should be 40 feet wide and 60 feet long. People hauled donated logs with mules and wagons to the sawmill and with free labor the house was completed and all expenses paid in full in the year of 1898. An organ was bought in 1908 for $45. Due to lack of money among the members, the church remained unpainted for nearly twenty years.

The original building was blown down by wind on Sunday May 30, 1937, about four o'clock in the afternoon. On June 5, 1937, a building committee was elected: W.B. Johnson, chairman; J.H. Teal, treasurer; M.A. McKibben, D.S. Warren, and Gilbert Cole. Rev. J.E. Eason was employed to supervise the building, and on June 29 sixty men met and roofed and floored the new building. The women served lunch to the workmen. The cost of the building was $497.61, and new benches were made by J.A. and C.L. McIntire. The first regular meeting was held in the new building on July 3, 1937.

Since that time, many other improvements have been made — extra rooms, the outside was bricked, memorial windows installed, benches and floors refinished, central heat, a Baptistry, choir loft, and a pastorium was purchased. Today, the church continues to be a stronghold to the surrounding community.
Sources: Excerpts from *The Records and History of Kansas Baptist Church* by Eva Mae King, Bowdon, GA

194. Lowell United Methodist Church

Rev. W.A. Woodruff, pastor of the Roopville Circuit of The Methodist Church made a survey of the Lowell area in his first year on that circuit. He found J.T. Cowart leading a community Sunday School and he continued as superintendent of the new church for several years. In the summer of 1919, Rev. Woodruff was able to get twenty people to be charter members of the new church. During the last days of August, 1919, a large tent was erected where the church now stands and a revival began. This resulted on September 10, 1919, with forty-five members being received by profession of faith, two by vows, and seventeen by certificates, bringing the total membership to 84.

Property was purchased from J.A. Jackson and another plot from W.L. Nix in September. J.T. Cowart began sawing the lumber for the church at his sawmill in the Whooping Creek community. Clarence L. Jackson, from Alabama, was employed as foreman. Most of the work was done by free labor in and around Lowell. The church was 60 by 40 feet, with a large balcony on the north end. It was dedicated in the spring of 1920. The old building was taken down carefully in 1945, in order to use the lumber, and a new church was constructed. It had some Sunday School space, and construction was led by Grady and Claude Lyle.

Those who have gone out from this church as ministers are: Luther Grandbury Cowart, 1921; William Powell Rowe, 1932; and William G. Cowart, Jr., 1950. *Submitted by: William G. Cowart, Jr., 235 Carroll Street, Carrollton, GA 30117-3703*

195. Lowell United Methodist Church

More than one effort was made to organize a Methodist Church at Lowell, but not until Rev. W.A. Woodruff made the attempt in 1919 was the effort successful. Lowell Methodist Episcopal

Church South was chartered August 2, 1919. Rev. Woodruff, pastor for the Roopville circuit gathered 22 charter members including Eula Spence, Lizzie, Etta and R.T. Spearman, Lula Hollingsworth, Mr. and Mrs. R.J. Chappell, Sallie Duncan, Mr. and Mrs. J.S. Williamson, Rev. A.H. Thompson, A.H. Thompson, Jr., Mr. and Mrs. E.T. Baughtman, Mr. and Mrs. J.T. Cowart, Vera Stanley, Lizzie McElroy, Maggie Smith, Lela Smith, Tempie Duncan, and Bertie Long. During late August a large tent revival was held and 62 members were received into membership of the new church, on September 10, 1919.

Mr. Jordan A. Jackson gave a lot and an additional lot was purchased from W.L. Nix for the new church building to be built adjacent to the already present Christian Church. The new church was centrally located in the community on McIntosh Trail. Mr. Clarence L. Jackson of Edwardsville, Alabama prepared the architectural drawings and aided Gus Lyle and other local people in erecting the building. Rich heart pine timber was cut from near Whooping Creek by Joe T. Cowart and hauled by Luther Rooks and Guy Cowart to Spearman's sawmill in Lowell. The commanding structure had two front doors, and a steeple giving the building 50 feet in height; the steeple bell hangs outside the church today. Professor Joseph A. Sharp, President of Young Harris College, led the dedication exercises in the early spring of 1920.

Lowell United Methodist Church

A severe storm December 1, 1942 during the funeral service for Jewel Ashmore, caused some structural damage. In 1945 the old building was torn down and much of the timber from the old building was used to construct the present building with stained glass windows. The altar rail and prayer bench from the original church were refinished by church members and used in the new building. In 1963 a fellowship hall and more Sunday school rooms were added. *Submitted by: Angie H. Stober, 1071 Lowell Road, Carrollton, 30116*
Sources: Church records

196. Macedonia Primitive Baptist Church

Macedonia Primitive Baptist Church was organized 24 September 1840 in Carroll County Georgia. It was part of Carroll County for fifteen years before being annexed into Haralson County in 1856. New Hope Primitive Baptist Association met at Macedonia on October 12, 13, and 14, 1940 for their 100-year celebration.

Members organizing the church were: Samuel Jordan and his wife Martha Jordan, Aaron Weatherby and his wife Mary Weatherby, McKinney Scott and wife, Pollyan Maner, Sciota Morris, Mary Wreay, Isabella Aldridge, Nancy Smith, William Jordan, Ann Rowell and Milly J. Stevens.

Ordained ministers before 1940 were: Henry Haynes, James Majors, Jonathan Holcombe,

Macedonia Primitive Baptist Church

and Richard Chandler. Elders serving the Church before 1940: Jonathan Holcombe, E.B. Stephens, R.T. Speight; William Robinson, J.J. Pope, J.R. Robinson, W.H. Hamrick, T.G. Layton, L.P. Daniell, W.E. Nix, C.A. Clemmons, and I.M. Patty.

My ggg grandfather James Hendricks donated part of the land for Macedonia. *Submitted by: Dennis W. Williams, 326 Rockmart Rd., Villa Rica, GA 30180*

197. Mars Hill Baptist Church - Hulett

On August 8, 1898 the Mars Hill Baptist Church was constituted with 18 members and 2 deacons. Rev. J.J. Shadrix was elected first pastor. Reuben Stitcher and D.N. Bateman were elected the first deacons with Reuben Stitcher elected as treasurer. The services were held in the schoolhouse and summer revivals in the brush arbor.

In 1900 the people erected a frame building on one acre donated by Mrs. Zachary Lumsden. Each male member was appointed to the building committee. In 1921 the church purchased two acres of land for a cemetery. In 1923 Rev. George W. Jones is the longest tenured pastor to date serving for 25 years. In 1935 the church adopted the half-acre plan to help with finances. It rented 6 acres to cultivate. Hoke Wilkens was elected treasurer and served almost 50 years. In 1937 the church was wired for electricity. In 1956 the church voted to erect a new church sanctuary and education building. During construction of the church, services were held in the Hulett School.

In 1962 Inis Jones was elected church clerk and served many faithful years. She is the oldest current member of Mars Hill Baptist Church. In 1989 Rev. Terry Wofford was elected as the first full time pastor. In 1994 the church voted to construct a new sanctuary and ground breaking was held in 1995 and construction was finished that same year. In 1998 the church reached its centennial on August 9, 1998 and celebrated by retiring its debt by burning the note. *Submitted by: Libbie Moss, 5440 E. Hwy. 166, Winston, GA*

198. Midway Macedonia Baptist Church

On July 14, 1847, five men and six women met and formed a new church for the "Glory of God". These people were Leroy McWhorter, William F. Jordan, Johnston H. McWhorter, William L. Neely, Isaac Kinney, Mary McWhorter, Rebecca Neely, Margret McRea, Elizabeth Jordan, Ann Jordan and Tabitha Poulstan. This group of people wrote the Articles of Faith for their church. They set the first church service to be held on July 15, 1847. They voted to meet once a month, thus the Baptist Church of Christ at Macedonia was born in a log cabin in the Sand Hill Community. This building served as a school and church. The log cabin was located across the road from the present church.

And so we grow!

The congregation outgrew the log house and saw the need of a larger building. A Methodist man, Thomas Willis stated he had no land for sale but would give them nine acres on which to build a church and in 1858 a building was erected on the opposite side of the road from the log house. In 1863, Pastor John M. Muse left the church to serve as a chaplain in the Confederate States Army. He returned to resume as the pastor in 1865. During his ministry from 1865 to 1876 another church was built, making this the third time Macedonia has built.

In 1894, the Sunday School was organized. In 1897, the first organ was bought and in 1898, we adopted the Biblical plan of systematic giving. In 1900, we had the first women on church committees. In 1924, the community used our church for singing school. In 1946, the members voted to meet twice monthly. In January 1947, a census was taken and mailed to Washington. And, in 1947 six more Sunday School rooms were added.

Second Church Building 1858

1947 marked Macedonia's 100th Anniversary and was celebrated on July 20, 1947. In 1952, while Rev. W.C. Lane was pastor, a new pastorium was built on the church property. In 1954 the auditorium was refurbished. In 1957, a two story Sunday School building was completed. In 1957 a two story educational building was completed. In 1974, the Constitution, bylaws, and Articles of incorporation of Macedonia Baptist Church were passed. In 1987, the McGuire family gave land to the church. On June 27, 1988, the name of the church was changed to Midway Macedonia Baptist Church. In 1992, a gazebo was built and named the "Royal Place" in honor of the Walter Royal family who built it and did ground work. In 1997, Mrs. Louise McGuire donated land to the church. In July 1997, the 150th year celebration. In 2000-2001, the new church was built on the hill.

In the years of this church there have been forty-one pastors serving God and the people. At least four church members have become missionaries, Miss Edna Tea, Miss Hattie Langston and the Rev. and Mrs. John Laramore. *Submitted by: Jerry Crumbley, Carrollton, GA*
Sources: Information obtained from the booklet printed for the 150th year celebration of Midway Macedonia Baptist Church.

199. Mt. Avery Missionary Baptist Church

Taking a glance back to the year of 1916 when a group of four men: Bro. Isom Allen, Deacon Henry Willis, Bro. W. Willis, Bro. Rob Perkins began thinking and planning to build a church. The plan continued for a year, and then in 1917 the church was completed under the name of "Gennings Grove".

On the Third Lord's Day of April 1917, they had their first service led by Rev. H.D. Dickerson, Protestant Pastor. Later they called Rev. Isiah Reid, who served the congregation for a year. Rev. J.C. Smith was then called as Pastor.

After serving as "Gennings Grove" for three years, the church was moved from Gennings Grove spot of ground in 1919 to Carroll County. Deacon Isom Allen dreamed a new name for the church after it was moved. He then presented the name "Mt. Avery (Aria) Baptist Church", to the Board meeting of Deacons and the members accepted the name.

In 1926, Rev. S.W. Woods was selected and served for a few years, following him was Rev. W.M. Covington who served for a few years. Later Rev. E.W. Willis served for a few months and Rev. W.M. Willis served a few years also.

In the year 1949 and 1950, all the members came to an agreement to move the church to Whitesburg at the site where it now stands. The land was purchased from Deacon Luther Marchman. The few members that Mt. Avery had left worked hard to keep things moving. They had their first revival in July 1951 under the leadership of Rev. J.H. Pullin who served as pastor for a number of years.

Later Rev. Davis served a term. He then presented Rev. McGhee and the church accepted him as our pastor and loved him dearly. He served for about eight years till his death in April 1964. Shortly afterwards, Mt. Avery was blessed with the leadership and guidance of Rev. L.C. Young whom we all loved. Under the leadership of Rev. Young, a Junior church was organized which included Junior Deacons, Junior Choir, and Junior Ushers. The Mother's Board and Young Adult Choir were also organized during this time.

Thank God for our former pastor, Rev. L.C. Young and his family who did great work on this building. In April 1973, the question of building came up among the church. The solution to the question was remodeling the building. The building was completed and rededicated to God by Rev. Young and the members of the Mt. Avery Baptist Church on November 23, 1973.

Mt. Avery Missionary Baptist Church

In September 1983, under the authority of Rev. Young, two Junior Deacons were ordained, Deacons Ronnie and Donnie Houston. On February 16, 1984, Deacon Luther Marchman resigned his position as chairman of the Deacon Board due to his health and age. Deacon John L. Houston, Jr. was appointed as his replacement for Chairman of Mt. Avery Deacon's Board and Deacon Melvin Brown was appointed Assistant Chairman of the Deacon Board. Deacon Brown served us until his death.

During the family night meeting in September 1986, it was voted to include Second and Third Sundays as days of worship. In June 1987, again, several junior deacons were ordained, Deacons Eddie Jones, Danny Allen, and Tommy Allen. In December 1988, Rev. L.C. Young resigned as pastor due to his health. Rev. Lois Anderson (his daughter) had been called as Associate Pastor in 1984. She served until 1989. Much progress was accomplished under their leadership. In 1989, Deacon Eddie Jones was elected as Assistant Chairman of the Deacon Board.

We were blessed once more in October 1989, when Rev. Milledge Mitchell and his wife, Sister Minnie Mitchell were called as Pastor and First Lady of the Mt. Avery Baptist Church. Under the leadership of Rev. Milledge Mitchell, the Word of God was continued to be preached, a Youth organization (SOS) was organized, Youth Ministry was inducted into the worship service, Bible Study was held on Wednesday nights, Annual Vacation Bible School as well as other betterments for our church family were held.

In 1991, Brother Hollis Pittman was ordained as Deacon. In June 1992, Rev. Brooklyn Smith, a son in the Ministry, joined the Mt. Avery family members. In June 1993, Sister Mildred Houston was licensed as Minister of the Gospel. In May of 1994, our beloved Chairman of the Board, Deacon John L. Houston, Jr. was called home for his reward. In November 1994, Deacon Ronnie Houston was elected Chairman of the Deacon Board. In January 1995, our faithful choir and church member, Sister Lizzie Kate Pittman was called home for her reward.

We, the members of the Mt. Avery Missionary Baptist Church family have had our ups and downs, some to go and others to come, we have withstood the passing of loved ones and we in turn welcome the coming of all new members.

In 1997, a vision of faith was planted in the hearts and minds of the Mt. Avery members. This vision from God is to build a new and improved sanctuary. We have been nurturing this vision by carefully planning, researching, fundraising and most of all praying. Philippians 4:13 says, "We can do all things through Christ which strengthens me." We Thank God that as of October 1999, we have a Building Consultant who has completed the blueprint design for this building and we are preparing for the next steps in this process.

Today, we give Thanks to the Lord for the many, many blessings He has poured through the window. Thank God for our faithful supporters of this ministry over the years. We continue to pray for physical, mental, and spiritual strengthening that our faith will grow stronger in the name of our Lord and Savior Jesus Christ. *Submitted by: Mildred Houston, Box 32, Whitesburg, GA 30185*

200. Mount Carmel Baptist Church

Mt. Carmel Baptist Church is located at 235 Mt. Carmel Church Road in Temple, Georgia. Within the past fifteen years, the church has been bricked and enlarged three times. At present the membership is over three hundred, and a five-acre youth facility located on Morgan Road is being completed. Dr. Corky Addison is pastor.

It is believed that Mt. Carmel Church was first established between 1871 and 1878 as a Methodist Church. It also served as a schoolhouse. It was later changed over to a New Hope Baptist and then to a Missionary Baptist which it is today. The building burned in the early 20's and was rebuilt in 1926. It was still used as a schoolhouse. Mr. and Mrs. Leonard McBrayer were among those who taught there in the 30's.

Mr. McBrayer's grandfather, Andrew E. McBrayer, donated the land for the church site. Mrs. McBrayer's grandfather preached the first sermon in the church. In 1925 Brother Palmer, a New Hope Baptist preacher, became the pastor. It is not known when it was changed to Missionary Baptist.

Among the charter members after the church was reorganized in 1929 were: Mr. and Mrs. Y.B. Ragsdale, C.B. Shirah, W.L. Adcock, Mrs. Lula Rainey, Mr. and Mrs. Leonard McBrayer, Sharon Ragsdale, Louise Ragsdale, Mrs. Rena Chance, C.B. White, Elma Ingram, Nannie Ingram, George Hansen, Fannie Hansen, S.M. Rutledge, J.D. Braswell, E.W. Ivey, T.J. Womack, Olin Johnson, Verlie Chance, Clyde Holloman, W.R. Shackleford, Carrie L. Womack, Martell Rutledge, Ovie Hansen, Mamie Bentley, W.T. Durrett, Ralph Durrett, Felton Chapman, Mr. and Mrs. W.Z. Shackleford, N.R. Shirah, Mrs. Vivian Chance Norton, G.O. Carroll, and Lottie Bell Chance.

Mt. Carmel Baptist Church

Other pastors have included: Y.B. Ragsdale, W.O. Cook, E.J. Cain, J.W. Womack, J.C. Pace, Roy Stanford, Tag Holland, Cliff Tyson, W.J. Jenkins, F.L. Carter, Artis Busbin, Grover Sheets, Thomas Garner, Charles Williams, C.L. Lyles, Clarence Agan, Curtis Cole, Jesse Robinson, Hiram McKenzie, Carlin Phillips, Dr. Calvin Brown, and Tim Stephens. *Submitted by: Wanda Addison, 309 N. Smith St., Bremen, GA 30110*
Sources: Church records

201. Mt. Pleasant Baptist Church

Mt. Pleasant Baptist Church, located in southeast Carroll County in the Clem Community, was constituted October 3, 1874. It is one of the oldest churches in the county. According to the church's original minutes, these families were some of the charter members - Brown, Burks, Davis, Cumbie, Cox, Tant, Jones, Hollaway, Mathews, Moran, Godsby, Edwards, Robinson, Rivers, Burnham and Wilson.

The first pastor was J.M.D. Stallings. He served until October 10, 1878. In the 127 year history there have been only 14 pastors. During the 79 year period between 1917 - 1996, Mt. Pleasant only had four pastors - C.L. Matthews, Irvine Phillips, Enver McKenzie and Vann Dempsey. The present pastor is Dr. Douglas

Mt. Pleasant Baptist Church Clem, GA

New, who has been at Mt. Pleasant since May, 1997. Also in 1997, Brother Shane Roberson began serving as our first full time associate/youth pastor. In 2000 Brother Donnie Muse became a full time Minister of Music & Education.

The first building was completed in 1874. A new building was constructed in 1900 at a cost of $100.25. Electric lights were installed in 1942. In 1950 it was voted to erect a new church building. On April 11, 1999 a dedication service was held for the new 22,000 square ft. Worship Center, library and Sunday School rooms.

Sunday School was organized in 1945 with Irvine Phillips elected superintendent. AWANA (Approved Workman Are Not Ashamed), which is a Bible memorization program for children, was started in 1987 with Mark Edwards as Commander.

Mt. Pleasant was recognized by the Georgia Baptist Association as one of nineteen Churches, out of 3,480 in the state, with consistent Sunday School and church growth between 1996-2000. *Submitted by: Joan Bush, 537 Roy North Rd., Carrollton, GA 30117*

202. The Mt. Prospect Baptist Church

The Mt. Prospect Baptist Church was established July of 1887. Records show land was purchased from Mr. Beecher Smith and six members held the first church meeting. From that meeting, Rev. J.M. Hindsman was elected pastor. He suggested the name Mt. Prospect. The present Church building still sits in the same location in the historical city of Villa Rica, Georgia. The city is the place of the first gold strike in Georgia, and is the birthplace of Thomas Dorsey. Mt. Prospect is his birthplace church.

Mt. Prospect Baptist Church, pastor James E. Potts established 1887

The first church building was erected in 1888-1890. The log cabin building was replaced by a brick veneer building in 1928. The brick building was destroyed by fire February, 1945, but reconstructed by July, 1945.

Rev. James E. Potts is the present pastor. The church embraces its rich history with annual events like the Hindsman's Day Note Singing Concert (held second Sunday in March), The Good Friday Concert and The Thomas Dorsey Birthplace Choir Concert (held on Thomas Dorsey's birthday July 1, or the Saturday before).

Many celebrities, i.e., Dottie Peeples, Dorothy Norwood and the Associated Notesingers, sing at these concerts. Many famous preachers have graced the pulpit, such as Rev. Jasper Williams, Rev. Ron Sailor, Rev. Earl T. Shinhoster and Dr. Watson from Atlanta. Rev. Dumas, from Macon, and Rev. McGowen, from Winston-Salem are among many who preached Revival during the fourth week of July. Worship Service is every Sunday at 11:15 am. Sunday School starts at 9:30. *Submitted by: Charles Hudson, 945 S. Lassetter Circle, Villa Rica, GA 30180-1421*

203. Mount Zion United Methodist Church

Mount Zion, Georgia, a small town in northwestern Carroll County with a population of approximately 1500 people, is located about eight miles east of the Alabama line. The landscape is mostly rolling, hilly pasturelands, interspersed with oak and piney woods and bubbling creeks. Yeoman farmers settled the area in the 1840's. The town itself consists of a Post Office, a City Hall/Library, a Primary Health Care Clinic, a fire department, a closed country store, and two schools.

Nestled right behind the elementary school at the corner of Church Street and North Prospect Avenue is Mount Zion United Methodist Church, a stately church with white exterior, beautiful stained glass windows, a lofty steeple, and a carillon that wafts beautiful music throughout the community, a church rich in tradition and heritage.

The church was founded on April 20, 1865 by a group of people led by Rev. Hicks Martin, M.D. This group broke away from the New Salem Methodist Episcopal Church (South) over the subject of slavery (most people of the community did not agree with slavery).

Joseph Entrekin gave the land on which a church, cemetery, and eventually a seminary were built. A new church was formed, belonging to the Methodist Episcopal Church (North). For a few months, the congregation met in a brush arbor. However, with winter approaching, a log church building was erected. Both the brush arbor and the log church were located where the parsonage is today.

Dr. Hicks Martin suggested that the church be named Mount Zion after Mount Zion in the Holy Land. Later, a town and a school grew up around the church and assumed the name of the church, Mount Zion.

A cemetery was established in 1866. It is located behind the present-day church. In the cemetery are the graves of the first Carroll County World War II casualty, James Brock, several Confederate soldiers, a Mexican War soldier, and a Texas Ranger. Eight former pastors are buried in the cemetery. As of this date, the oldest person buried in the cemetery is Mrs. Nan Earnest at 100 years old.

In 1876, Dr. James Mitchell, a personal friend of Abraham Lincoln and presiding elder of the Carroll Circuit, made his headquarters in Mount Zion. He is buried in the cemetery right behind the church. Dr. Mitchell and a group of men formed a corporation to build a boarding school, first grade through Junior College, in the community of Mount Zion. On December 6, 1880, Mount Zion Seminary opened its doors, educating students and training preachers. Later, a two-story dormitory for girls was built where the present day parsonage stands.

In the fall of 1889, the present church building was erected and occupied. Members of the church cut timber off their lands and had it sawed into lumber at a local mill. The men of the community built the church building and fashioned, by hand, pews and other church furniture. Carrollton merchants donated nails, hinges, etc. A bell was purchased from a foundry in Atlanta for $16.

Mount Zion Methodist Church 1920's

The original building was rectangular, unceiled, and had two front doors, one for the men, and one for the women. The men and boys, twelve and older, sat on the left-hand side and women, girls, and children below twelve sat on the right hand side.

In December of 1912, Mount Zion M.E. Church founded the first Boy Scout Troop in Georgia, Troop I.

In 1939, after the merging of the Methodist Episcopal churches, North and South, and the Methodist Protestant churches, the church became Mount Zion Methodist Church.

In 1944, the church was expanded by adding to each side, three Sunday School rooms and a pastor's study. Later, a narthex was added to the front of the church.

In the 1950's, a church annex with a basement was built, housing a kitchen, fellowship hall, restrooms, nursery, and Sunday school rooms. Recently, the church sanctuary was remodeled, adding a choir loft, new carpet, and new padding on the pews. Through donations, a new baby grand piano was bought for the sanctuary.

Mount Zion Methodist Church 2001

In 1968, after merging with the United Brethren Church, the church became Mount Zion United Methodist Church.

Having a rich heritage of professional people, the church had six medical doctors and eight ministers on its membership rolls at one time. Since its inception, over twenty members have answered the call to ministry. Today, the church is heavily populated with educators.

Presently, the church sponsors and/or hosts a food bank, helping-hands assistance, missions programs, Operation Santa Claus, a senior citizens luncheon, Vacation Bible School, the Last Supper Drama, Easter and Christmas musicals, Cub Scout, Alcoholics Anonymous (Alanon), youth groups, a women's organization, a men's organization, Memorial Day, Sacred Harp weekend once a year, and Bowling Green Men's Choir every two years, and many other activities.

The church, schools, city government, and service organizations work hand-in-hand to improve God's beautiful world in this small community of rolling hills, pastures, and creeks. *Submitted by: Sara and Jack Dorsey*

204. New Brooklyn Baptist Church

The New Brooklyn Baptist Church of Temple, Georgia, was organized on September 6, 1931, with forty-seven charter members. The Church Council was composed of the following men: Rev. W.M. Williams, Rev. S.T. Gilland, Rev. Willie Ayers, Rev. J.V. Hart and deacons J.T. Hixon, J.T. Davis, R.J. Hardin, J.T. Gallman, B.A. Harrison, J.B. McBrayer, Glenn Gray and Walter Johnson. Church was held in the old Brooklyn School building. Land was donated by G.T. Williams, and a new church was built in the mid-30's. Since then Sunday School rooms and a large fellowship hall have been added, and the church has been bricked. There are approximately 156 members.

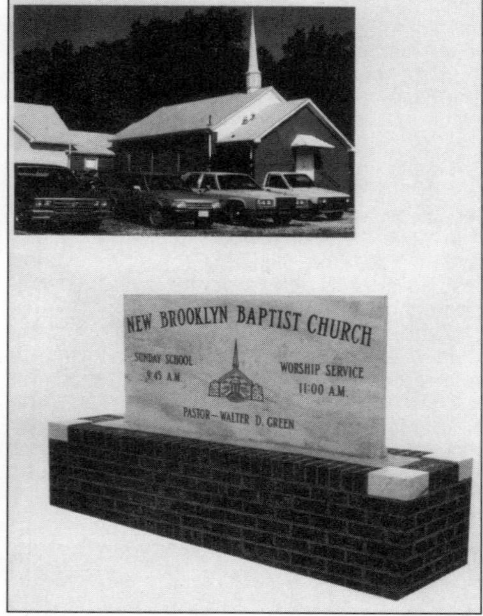

New Brooklyn Baptist Church

Pastors have been W.M. Williams, J.W. Holland, W.F. Lassetter, James Crabb, Grover Cook, Buddy York, Ralph Tapley, L.D. Palmer, Ray King, C.L. Lyles, Willie Hammond, Thomas Garner, J.O. Weaver, Thomas Garner, A.M. Ballenger, Aaron Johnson, Charles Monroe, Aaron Johnson, Walter D. Green, Aaron Johnson, and Michael Smith. *Submitted by: Roscoe Stephens, 462 Taylors Gin Road, Temple, GA 30179*
Sources: Church Records

205. New Hope Methodist Church

Halfway between Carrollton and Mt. Zion, there is a community that was named "Plowshare". The name originated because Bill Moore made plowstocks and wagons, shoed horses, and sharpened plows for farmers. He built a store at the crossroad and it was called Plowshare Store. There was also a blacksmith shop, a school, a syrup mill, and a grist mill in the community. In 1858, Mr. Moore deeded land for New Hope Protestant Church. The first structure was a brush arbor. The first building was a log cabin, as was the second building. A cemetery apparently began earlier than the church, and the first grave was in 1835, belonging to a child.

The present church building was built in three different stages. The present sanctuary was the first to be built. It was little more than a box structure. It is believed that the structure is over 100 years old. The narthex and entrance were added in 1927 or 1928. Sunday School rooms and bathrooms were added to the back

New Hope Methodist Church, New Hope Community (off Mt. Zion Rd.)

of the sanctuary in 1947. The Fellowship Hall was built in 1956. It consisted of a kitchen and one large room. In 1962, four Sunday School rooms and a basement were added. A parsonage was built and dedicated in 1984.

Numerous pastors have led the congregation of New Hope Methodist Church. It has gone from having one worship service each month, to numerous services and activities each week. It remains a meeting place of spiritual nourishment for the New Hope/Plowshare community. *Submitted by: Bobby L. Smith, New Hope Church Rd., Carrollton, GA 30117*

206. New Hope Primitive Baptist Church

Villa Rica

Often overlooked as a Carroll County landmark, New Hope was organized in Carroll County on the fourth Sabbath of December 1828. The first 42 years of service were conducted in Carroll County before being annexed into Douglas County in 1870. The county line literally runs through the church building. Bozeman Adair, a Carroll County representative, served as deacon of the church. James Majors was probably the first official preacher at New Hope and the Jonathan and Henry Haynes families were early members.

New Hope Primitive Baptist Church in Villa Rica

In the *History of Villa Rica* by Mary Talley Anderson, it is said that New Hope Primitive Baptist Church was the first church established west of the Chattahoochee River in Georgia, although Concord Methodist at Hickory Level may be older.

What we do know about New Hope Baptist is that it was surely a part of the local activity in the Villa Rica area with good preaching, the sacraments, and foot washing being the order of business followed by sacred harp singing and dinner on the ground. From church records we know the church also had a number of Black members.

Although the church was organized as a Baptist Church, the term Primitive or Hard Shell Baptist were labels applied by some in the community, because of their supposed narrow ways. Once becoming a member of the church, they expected you to live a Christian life, or they would simply turn you out of the church.

New Hope has recently discontinued services and the old building has been sold. It is currently the temporary home to a Methodist church.

The New Hope Cemetery has hundreds of graves, some marked and many with only fieldstones. There are at least 28 known Confederate soldiers buried there. Forrest Escort Camp, Sons of Confederate Veterans of Villa Rica, has hosted several, "Christmas with the Soldiers" ceremonies at the cemetery. This is a moving experience. Church records are on microfilm in the special collections room at the Neva Lomason Library in Carrollton and hard copy records can be found in the Summer 1984 and Fall 1985 Carroll County Genealogical Quarterlies. *Submitted by: Dennis Williams, 326 Rockmart Road, Villa Rica, GA 30180*

207. The New Hope United Methodist Church

New Hope Methodist Episcopal Church was organized in the 1860's at the site of the present Bowdon Community Cemetery on Highway 100, South. The first services were perhaps held in the school house. In 1899, records show that Fed Hudson, Austin Veal, and Thomas Cokely gave land and a permanent church building was erected. In 1905, a new church was built under the guidance of the Reverend J.H. Arney.

New Hope United Methodist Church

In 1926, the 1905 church building was destroyed by a storm. A new structure was built north of the 1905 structure. The new structure was destroyed by fire in 1959. Plans for a new building were begun under the guidance of Reverend A.C. Cobb, and it was completed in July 1961 through the supervision of Reverend G.W. Ransom. The mortgage was burned under the leadership of Reverend J.C. Neal in 1968. A new sanctuary was added and dedicated in 1987 under the leadership of Reverend J.D. Grier, Jr.

Since the beginning of New Hope Methodist Church, we have been spiritually guided by numerous pastors. In addition, we have enlarged our facilities and we feel fortunate to have come from a small, inadequate facility to an adequate, up-to-date facility as one of the oldest churches in the Bowdon Community. *Submitted by: Billie Ann Buchanan, Lay Leader, New Hope United Methodist Church, P.O. Box 81, Bowdon, GA 30108*

208. New Lebanon Church

New Lebanon Baptist Church is located at the intersection of the Lowell Road and Highway 5. It is over 130 years old and one of Carroll County's oldest churches. This church was established on July 30, 1870 with the Rev. S.B. Little being the first minister. Mr. T. Phillips was the first moderator and Mr. J.M.D. Stallings the first clerk. Mose Taylor was the assistant clerk.

In the beginning, services were held once a month, the third Saturday and Sunday of each month. According to the old church minutes, the following people were charter members: T.L. Ward, Sara Ann Ward, Reason Balew, Theresa Balew, Harriett L. Ballew, Leuna B. Balew, Arena J. Balew, Lucy Ann Balew, Arnalda Neely, J.M.D. Stallings, Mary E. Stallings, C.T. Richards, M.W. Richards, Mose Taylor, Mary Taylor, Alexander Burke, and Tabitha Burke. In 1878, E.S. Davis was the moderator.

In 1961, six Sunday School rooms were completed and major repairs were made to the church. Pastors of the church from 1870 to 1970 were: S.B. Little, W.W. Roop, H.B. Bartlett, J.M.D. Stallings, W.N. Carson, J.W. Hood, U.H. Clark, E.E. Robinson, W.J. Lovvorn, H.H. Connell, J.W. McLeod, R.M. Lovvorn, J.T. Roberts, W.T. Cumbie, G.W. Jones, Monroe Burns, Price McClung, P.B. Moore, R.J. Alexander, W.M. Chatham, C.M. Stallings, W.O. Wallis, Eugene Brock, C.W. Williams and interim preacher Pat Johnson. The current minister is Dr. Quinnion Duncan.

New Lebanon Church

At the time of the Centennial Celebration of New Lebanon that was held in 1970, the pastor was Frederick A. Delk. The active deacons were: Roy Little, J.M. Perry, Charles Steed, and Charlie Steed. The Sunday School Superintendent was Fred Lewis. The Pianist was Mrs. Margaret Steed and the Music Director was Clyde Synder. The two favorite Baptist hymns that were sung at the Centennial were *Blest Be the Tie That Binds* and *Leaning on the Everlasting Arms.* Psalm 84 was read.

The Centennial Committee that worked so hard to organize a nice celebration for the 100th birthday of the church was: Sara Perry, J.M. Perry, Margaret Steed, Roy Little, Fred Lewis, and Winston Mashburn.

My parents, James Frederick Hollingsworth and Cleo Morgan Hollingsworth were members of New Lebanon Church and are buried in the church cemetery. Many of the other family names that you find in the old church cemetery are: Burns, Stallings, Wards, Flemings, Steeds, Walkers, Milligans, Taylors, Yeagers, Jacksons, and others that includes a man who lived during the American Revolution. *Submitted by: Caroline Hollingsworth Chappell*

Source: 1870-1970 Centennial Program of New Lebanon Church

209. Oak Grove Baptist Church

The Oak Grove Baptist Church is located approximately 2.5 miles south of Carrollton at 2829 Oak Grove Church Road.

The Oak Grove Baptist Church was organized in the home of Mr. and Mrs. Jim Griffin in 1877. The land on which the building was located was given by Mr. Griffin. The first building was a cottage type building with a wide door in the front side and one end door. Rev. J.M.D. Stallings served as the first pastor.

In 1902, the church agreed to disband by granting letters to the entire membership. Three members did not take their letters.

In July 1903, a meeting was held to re-activate the church and erect a new building. In less than thirty days the old building was torn down and the new structure was completed enough for services to be held in it. Rev. W.S. Hubbard was pastor.

Oak Grove Baptist Church

The original building is now part of the present sanctuary. With building programs through the years, Sunday School annexes, Fellowship Hall, Church Offices, Library, Nursery, Choir Loft and Baptistry were added. In 1999 there were church and Sunday School room renovations, including the addition of a new alcove to the sanctuary and a new Youth Department. The church has a brick pastorium on land adjoining the church that was built in 1964.

When the church organized, services were held once a month until 1950 when services were held twice a month. In 1960 the church voted to have services every Sunday. Rev. W.L. Collins was the first full time pastor.

Sunday School was organized in 1910. Other church organizations were added at different times and presently the church has opportunities for all ages in Bible Study, Mission Study, Mission Projects, Mission Trips, Church Music and Discipleship Training.

Vacation Bible School has been held every year since its beginning in 1951.

Since the constitution of the church in 1877 until the year 2001 there have been 35 different pastors. Rev. Jerry Wolfe served the longest tenure, 1987-1997. Rev. Michael Owenby is the present pastor. *Submitted by: Rudene Hollingsworth (History Committee Chairman) 2272 Hwy. 27 South, Carrollton, GA 30117*

Sources: a) History of Oak Grove Baptist Church, Centennial Publication, 1877-1977; b) Church Minutes 1978-; c) History of the Carrollton Baptist Association, 1873-1973, Centennial Edition, by William Wyatt Givens. P. 150-151; d) Carrollton Baptist Association Annual & Directory

210. Our Lady of Perpetual Help Catholic Church

The first Catholics in the West Georgia area were 200 Hungarian families who settled near Tallapoosa in 1893 to grow grapes and make wine. They had a thriving community including a church, but the State Prohibition Act of 1907 ended their enterprise, and most of them left Georgia. Those few who remained were served by priests from Atlanta or Rome who came to say Mass once a month. Eventually their numbers began to grow again. In 1952, the Diocese of Savannah assisted local Catholics in purchasing the Episcopal Church in Carrollton. Our Lady of Perpetual Help Catholic Church was

Our Lady of Perpetual Help Catholic Church.

dedicated June 14, 1954. There were fewer than a dozen families, but they had a full church life. By the early Sixties, the parish had begun to outgrow its church. In 1962 a new church was built on land donated by F. Eaton Chalkley and his wife Susan Hayward (both are buried in the church cemetery). The church, a granite structure, is located on Old Centerpoint Road, convenient to the two counties (Carroll and Haralson) that it serves. The white frame building used from 1954 to 1962 was moved to the State University of West Georgia campus in 1964 and named Kennedy Chapel, an interfaith chapel. The parish grew by leaps and bounds in the last quarter of the 20th century. Two large buildings housing classrooms and a parish center were built. Today Our Lady of Perpetual Help Church serves 750 families with four Masses every weekend. *Submitted by: Carol Nelson*

211. Pleasant Grove Baptist Church

Bowdon

The church is located at Highway 5 and Blackwelder Road in Bowdon. Constitution of the Baptist Church of Pleasant Grove was on the Saturday before the second Sabbath in April 1886. Twelve ordinances for the church were agreed on and adopted. Brethren N.W. Moore and W.S. Tweedell met a few other brethren, and a presbytery was formed. A decorum was drawn up and adopted numbering twenty-four parts. One month later the band of brethren met again, went into conference after preaching by Brother Tweedell. Brother J.D.H. Robinson was elected clerk and Brother W.W. Carter assistant clerk. Brother W.S. Tweedell was elected Pleasant Grove's first pastor. Some of the surnames of the first members were: Carter, Holloway, Stewart, Robinson, Pate, Roberts, Beneford, Barr, Word, Norton, Johnson, King, Bachelor, Beck, Bloodworth, Sprewell, Brook, Morris, Warren, and Dowdy.

Pleasant Grove Baptist Church - Bowdon

The current church building, dedicated April 1962, stands as a memory to the late Mr. and Mrs. Willie Stewart, whose life savings paid for the entire building. It was erected at a cost of

$26,000. The dedication was by the Rev. Willie Harris with the opening speech by the Rev. Guy Rogers.

The church still has communion and feet washing as they did the first year the church was constituted. Brother Ridley Herren is the present pastor. *Submitted by: Bobby Word, Church Clerk, 624 Reavesville Road, Bowdon, GA 30108*

Source: original church minutes and *Bowdon Bulletin* April 26, 1962

212. Pleasant Grove Baptist Church

Villa Rica

Pleasant Grove Baptist Church was constituted in July 1849 by Preachers Parker M. Rice, James Reeves and LeRoy McWhorter. Some of the first members were the Harts, Greens, Davises, Dobbs, Hogues and Burtons. The first church building was constructed of logs. In later years there was a second, then a third and fourth, or present building. On March 13, 1913, the church building, which was a frame one at that time, was completely demolished by a cyclone. The roof and all the walls were swept away. The floor was moved several inches on the pillars. The pulpit stand, on which there was a Bible, and a small table that stood just in front of the pulpit were left. The Bible and water pitcher and drinking glass, which were on the table, were not disturbed. A Building Committee was elected immediately consisting of the deacons of the church and the church was replaced by a brick structure, completed, paid for, and dedicated on August 5, 1913, only five months after the destruction. Since that time memorial windows have been installed, Sunday School rooms have been constructed, and later more Sunday School rooms have been added.

Pleasant Grove Baptist Church - Villa Rica

Through special donations in 1961 an organ was purchased. In 1965 the auditorium was completely remodeled, including new pews. In 1970 central heat was installed in the Sunday School rooms and air conditioning installed in the Sanctuary. In Feb. 1958 final payment was made on the pastorium. On May 7, 1969 the deacons recommended that the church set up a Trust Fund to be deposited in a local institution and the interest be used for cemetery purposes, which is still in effect. This cemetery fund is supported by contributions. Our present pastor is David Marshall and Associate Pastor is Joel Grubbs. *Submitted by: Margaret Durrett, Age 96, Member Pleasant Grove*

213. Pleasant Ridge Baptist Church

Before the turn of the last century the means of travel was at best slow and arduous. For most people it was walking or mule drawn wagon or buggy. This is one of the reasons a church was started at Pleasant Ridge. There were already churches close by in todays travel. Abilene is a short distance and so is Pleasant View, but by yesteryear's means, a bone-jarring ways away. In 1893 the Pleasant Ridge community was known as Mandeville. The Mandeville Mills are a well remembered business. Mr. L. Cliff Mandeville owned the land where the present church stands. The people of the Pleasant View and Abilene churches held a brush arbor revival on the land where the church now stands. The next year, 1894, another brush arbor revival was held, and the Pleasant Ridge Baptist Church was organized. In 1895, Pleasant Ridge was admitted to the Carrollton Baptist Association with 17 charter members. In 1899, the land was donated to the church by Mr. Mandeville and a plank building was erected. The first pastor was Rev. Blake Drew, who is the ancestor of some of the present members. The first building was replaced in 1912 and is still standing. Actually it took about 3 years to complete the structure. There was a rail down the center isle as was the practice of those days. There were no extra rooms and no bathrooms. The first Sunday School was organized on the fourth Sunday of September in 1926. One person who was instrumental in starting it was Clara McGukin. She realized the importance of organized Bible study for all ages. Her husband, Russell, also believed it was important and he served as the first superintendent. They would serve the church in many other capacities for the next 70 years.

Pleasant Ridge Baptist Church

In the early years the church practiced foot washing. They also did not have a regular pastor all the time, so preachers who didn't have a church would come to preach. Some times more than one would preach and take up much time. Also sometimes the preacher would stay with members who lived close, so he didn't have to walk so far. When you hear an older person say something about the preacher staying for Sunday dinner, it was because he had a long trip home. Today he's lucky to get a McDonalds burger on his trip home.

Thru the years many names have appeared on the rolls of Pleasant Ridge Church. In 1921 the pastor was John Crider, clerk was W.E. Bowen who served the church for many years. Some of his family members are still active in the church today. In 1931 Brother Milton Parrish had begun to preach and also Brother Kierbow. These are ancestors of members today. Rev. Levi Bates was pastor in 1931 and served many churches in the area over a long period of time. A legend says that when it was rainy and muddy as it was on dirt roads, that he would walk to church barefooted and wash his feet after he arrived to keep his shoes clean. It must have been true because his granddaughter's husband has written and recorded a gospel song about it. The title is *Brother Levi* and tells the story of a country preacher that does the same thing. In 1931 2 elected deacons were F.J. Thompson and B.B. Brand. The later was my grandfather. The year 1932 was a growth year for the church and revival that year had many names listed as new members. Some of them were: Jessie Hudson, Aubry Brock, Ollie Shadrix, Sam Winkles and Harold Drew.

Some other names mentioned in the next years were: Grant Finnell, who went on to pastor many churches in the area, Barney Akin who was also a well known pastor, Carl Tapley, Dewey Robinson and Jessy Robinson who are Pastors in the area today.

If you look at Pleasant Ridge you don't see a great big church. We may never be a great big church. But if you look at the names of the people who have been touched by this church you will see that it is a growing place for pastors, teachers, singers, musicians and other workers for doing God's work. Names like Dewey Caldwell who for more than 50 years led the music for Abilene Church, who always told the story of how he went to his first singing school at Pleasant Ridge and Rick Hurst, who is a pastor and writer for the *Christian Index,* and attended Pleasant Ridge during his young years and married Joy Jones, a descendant of Brother Kierbow who was a pastor mentioned earlier. It is amazing what the Lord has done thru the people who have been called out of this small country church that was started under a brush arbor with 17 devout members and others who saw a need for a church at Pleasant Ridge. *Submitted by: Brenda Morris, 115 East Mill St., Tallapoosa, GA 30176*

214. Pleasant View Baptist Church

In the summer of 1876, Pleasant View Baptist Church was organized by J.M.D. Stallings and a small group of believers. It is believed there were seventeen charter members. J.M.D. Stallings was the first pastor, and he would return as pastor two more times. The group had no suitable place to meet, but Smyrna Methodist Church offered its arbor as a meeting place. Later a log house was used for services. On September 22, 1877, Pleasant View joined the Carrollton Baptist Association.

R.F. Miller and Elisha Creel gave two acres of land for the church. The original deed was dated June 15, 1878. A portion of land was set aside for a cemetery. In October 1878 the one-year-old son of Mrs. C.J. Edwards was buried in the cemetery. In 1897 the original part of the present church was built. The first record of a Sunday School was in 1898. A total of one dollar was spent for Sunday school expenses that year. Training Union was organized in 1922; however, it was discontinued for a time, but reorganized in 1938. In 1928 the front entrance with a steeple was added to the building, and during this same year the first piano was purchased at a cost of $125. In 1936 the church signed up for electricity. The first Sunday School rooms were built in 1948. The first Vacation Bible School was held in 1949. During the pastorate of E.J. Cain, the building was bricked and the twelve memorial stained glass windows were installed. In 1950 services started being held twice each month instead of once, and in May 1956 the church began having a worship service every Sunday. In 1958 construction began on five additional Sunday School rooms and two restrooms. Later the church would begin construction on a pastorium. It was ready for occupancy in June of 1966.

In 1974 the renovation of the church sanctuary included the installation of a baptistry. In earlier church years baptismal services were held outdoors in local ponds, lakes, creeks or baptismal pools. Sites of two outdoor baptismal pools are known. One pool was located on the property of Percy Johnson and was used at various times between 1919 and 1942. In August of 1942 the first baptismal service was held in a small cement pool which was fed by a spring in the wooded area behind the church. This pool was on the property of M.T. Earnest.

In November of 1976 a senior citizens group was organized. On September 22, 1977 the church cemetery became a perpetual care cemetery. On June 22, 1986 a groundbreaking ceremony for a new fellowship hall, kitchen, restrooms, church offices and additional Sunday School rooms was held. This addition was dedicated on Sunday, June 25, 1989. In 1995 the church sanctuary was renovated, Also during the pastorate of Jay Sutton, the pastorium has been renovated and a second Sunday morning worship service has been added. A children's church program began on April 22, 2001.

Pleasant View Baptist Church

During Pleasant View's 125-year history, twenty-five pastors have led the congregation. Their names are: J.M.D. Stallings 1876-1882, T.H. Higdon 1883-1884, H.B. Bartlett 1885-1887, J.M.D. Stallings 1988, J.W. Davidson 1889-1904, J.M.D. Stalling 1905-1914, W.W. Roop 1915-1918, S.J. Parrish 1919-1920, W.J. Lovvorn 1921-1923, J.R. Cole 1924-1926, W.P. Cumbie 1927-1932, G.W. Jones 1933-1938, H.L. Hanie 1939-1941, Monroe Burns 1942-1948, E.J. Cain 1948-1953, L.P. Lambert 1954, Gus Young 1955-1957, Allen Martin 1957-1959, George Stuart 1960-1963, Grant Finnell 1964-1970, Carl Tapley 1971-1972, Donald Voyles 1973-1977, Kenneth Holt 1978-1979, John Whetstone 1980-1984, Hugh Barrett 1984-1988, Tommy Wright, 1988-1991, and Jay Sutton 1992-

Pleasant View Baptist Church is located about six miles north of Carrollton just off North Highway 27. *Submitted by: Gail H. McEwen* (church clerk), *724 Smyrna Church Road, Carrollton, GA 30117. From materials compiled by: Gladys Foster (former church clerk)*
Sources: Pleasant View Cemetery compiled by Inez Earnest and Horry and Eunice Johnson.

215. Poplar Springs Primitive Baptist Church

The first church of Poplar Springs was a log structure across the road from the old cemetery. It was near the old Benjamin King home place. The church built near the one standing at this time was planked up and down as in older structures. The current church building is over 100 years. It still has the original oak floors, ceilings and benches, and has no electricity or plumbing, in keeping with the traditions of the Primitive Baptist beliefs.

Charter members were: Gabriel Smith, Deacon, Richard and Parks Chandler, Jesse Jenkins, and Beriah Hays. Female members were: Charity and Lucinda Chandler, Frances Jenkins,

Poplar Springs Primitive Baptist Church, established September 25, 1849

Polly Hays, Nancy and Sarah Smith. Beriah Hays was the first clerk. First Elders were Jonathan Holcomb, Peterson Black and J. Maze. Enoch Phillips served as moderator for many years beginning in 1866. Some of the clerks who kept records were Beriah Hays, Ransom Smith, Mark Smith and Richard Smith. The membership in 1859 was in the nineties. In 1899 it was still about the same.

Elder Floyd Horsley is the current preacher and has served in that capacity since September 14, 1963. Currently there are 5 members: Elder and Mrs. Floyd Horsley, Elder Bethel Bearden, Mrs. Lillie Robinson, and Mrs. Frances King Bearden Smith. Mrs. Robinson and Mrs. Smith are the oldest living members at 92 years old. Mrs. Smith served as clerk from February 1955 to September 1968 and from 1992 to 1998. The current clerk is Elder Bethel Bearden.
Submitted by: Dorothy Patterson, 327 Kensington Circle, Bremen, GA 30110
Source: Church Records

216. Powell Chapel United Methodist Church

According to oral history, this Church was established in 1850. It was built of logs on a hill in a grove of trees. In 1882, Alexander Tyson, a primitive Baptist, gave an acre of land apparently where the log church had been located to the Methodist Church, and a new wooden structure was built. At the same time, Fayette Edge also gave an acre of land to provide ample space for the Church and the adjoining cemetery.

Powell Chapel United Methodist Church

The Church was named Powell Chapel in honor of its first minister, Rev. William Francis Spaight Powell. B.F. Harper, G.W. Hall, James B. Aderhold and J.W. Carroll were the first appointed Trustees. A Sunday School was organized around 1900 with Bill Boyd as the first Superintendent. In March 1852, Women's Society of Christian Service was begun with Mrs. Candler Hembree as President.

Many changes have been made over the years to provide an up-to-date structure for worship, Sunday School rooms, a parsonage, and a fellowship hall.

A Memorial Day Service is held on the fourth Sunday in April each year for a homecoming and to commemorate those in the Community who have died during the previous year.

Some of the families in the Church have been: Harper, Hembree, Langston, Boyd, Wallace, Fortner, Mayfield, Williams, Richardson, Bivins, Sloan, Morrow, Hudgins, Dobbs, and Shadrix. The church is located at 1296 Flat Rock Road, Villa Rica. *Submitted by: Erlene Camp Boyd, 1539 Flat Rock Road, Villa Rica, GA*
Source: Deeds and Church Records

217. Rocky Mount Baptist Church

Rocky Mount Baptist Church, 583 Buffalo Creek Road, Carrollton, Georgia, was chartered as a Southern Baptist Church on Sunday, October 27, 1985. Sixty-six charter members signed the original charter that established the church.

Rocky Mount Baptist Church

The church is located on nine acres on Buffalo Creek Road. The land was donated to the church by Felton and Josephine Denney who farmed the land in the 1950's. Prior to that, the land belonged to Henry Nelson Stipe, the father of Dr. John Gordon Stipe who served Emory University for forty-two years, including four years as Vice-President.

Rocky Mountain Baptist Church was named after Rocky Mount School, a public school that was located on Oak Grove Church Road just north of Emmaus Primitive Baptist Church, which was the site of the fist meeting of the Rocky Mount Baptist Church congregation. The first verse of Scripture read in the newly constituted church was Psalms 133:1, "Behold, how good and how pleasant it is for brethren to dwell together in unity."

The interior of the church sanctuary is lined with knot-free heart pine, and each piece was sanded by Carl North, a well known and much loved member of Rocky Mount who also constructed the church pulpit.

Three pastors have served Rocky Mount Baptist Church. Larry Pearson served as pastor from December 1, 1985 until July 1, 1987. W.O. Wallis served as interim pastor in 1987. Jerry Little was called as pastor on December 9, 1987 and continues to serve in that position.
Submitted by: Chester Gibson, Rocky Mount Baptist Church Moderator

218. Roopville Baptist Church

The citizens first had church in the "meeting house", a one room, log building used for school which was located near the cemetery. Plans were soon made to build on a lot donated by John K. Roop. Mr. Roop also donated funds for half the cost of construction. The members worked to cut, haul, and saw the native pine for construction. Oxen hauled the logs to the Roop's gin house. With a cooperative, willing spirit, the members soon had the church finished. Pews were made from the same native pine. Beautiful but simple construction, planks wide enough for one plank to make the seat and another for the back. These pews are still in use by the church today.

Charter members were: Mr. and Mrs. T.H. Garrett, E.S. Garrett, Mr. & Mrs. W. A. Howard, J.H. and Susan O. Burks, J.K. and Eliza A. Roop, D.W. and Martha Stallings, J.A. and Mollie Roop, E.F. and Sarah Duffey, W.H. Alexander, J.I. Hendrix, Florida Roop, Elizabeth Roop, Susan Guthrie, Mary E. Roop, Sarah Hall, M.J. Almon. W.H. Alexander was elected clerk, J.W. Hood was first pastor.

On September 29, 1883 the first service was conducted in the new church. E.B. Barrett was elected moderator and preached to a happy congregation. Mr. Barrett, L.B. Little and W.W. Roop sat at the recognizing council in the organization of the Missionary Baptist Church at Roopville. Sunday School was organized and the church had preaching services once a month on Satuday and Sunday.

Members of the day took church work seriously and performed their Christian duties with love. There were times when members were called on to answer for absence or some offense. The customs at that time were very strict but mixed with compassion, love and forgiveness.

A pastorium was built in 1919. The church and pastorium were wired for electricity in 1930. In 1938 the pastorium burned.

Roopville Baptist Church 1883-1940

Members began planning for construction of a new church in 1939. The building committee consisted of J.B. Merrell, O.O. Garrett, J.A. Arial, B.F. Roop, C.H. Merrell, Jimmie Parrish, Walter Key, Jack Towns, Ed Pentecost, B.L. Garrett, and H.C. Hightower. Work soon began with willing members contributing generously and volunteering willingly. Funds ran out before completion and the church borrowed $1000 to finish the building. Since the old building was torn down to provide some of the timbers for construction of the new building, services were held in other places. Sometimes in the school house and at other times in the Methodist Church. The first service in the building was on November 3, 1940 in the basement. It was a day of celebration. Rev. J.S. Edwards preached the morning message and the people happily sang songs of praise. On December 5, 1943 the final payment on the note was made and the church had a mortgage burning to celebrate. By 1945 the pastor received a salary of $100 per month.

On November 1946 a decision was made to build a new pastorium to replace the one which burned in 1938. On September 6, 1953 the members decided to build additional classroom space and a Brotherhood Hall in a new annex on the back of the building. The church voted to name the fellowship hall the Frank Roop Memorial Hall and $2000 was borrowed to complete the annex. In January 1957 the stain glass memorial windows were installed. In 1957 the church voted to go to full time services, the decision was made to begin in June.

Roopville Baptist Church 1940 - present

On November 11, 1977 the members made decision to build a new pastorium below the church on 2 acres at 126 Old Franklin Street purchased from Bob and Rebecca Merrell. Half the selling price was returned to the building fund by the Merrells. A bid of $51,988 was accepted from Hammock and McLeroy to build the house. The members had $32,450 in the building fund and were proud to be able to build the new home borrowing $13,500. There was a balance due on the house of $7,918.58.

In 1978 Mrs. Audie Causey made a donation to cover all cost for the construction of a church steeple with chimes. In 1980's new chandelier lights, carpet and pew cushions were installed in the sanctuary. In the years following a fire alarm system, carpet in classrooms and brotherhood hall, and new sound system were added.

The church celebrated its first 100 hundred years in 1983. An Old Fashioned Day on September 25, and Homecoming on October 2. Patricia Jones, Church Choir Director, wrote a song titled *"The House We Built With God"* to help celebrate the event. The final sentence of the song says, "Folks may come and folks may go, but the Lord remains the same, Through all the years, through all the changing years it's still the house of God."

Pastors who have served the church were: J.W. Hood, W.W. Roop, Amos, W.J. Lovvorn, E.C. Smith, I.R. Walker, R.M. Lovvorn, J.T. Gibson, J.T. Roberts, J.J. Milford, J.M. Cook, Gilbert Dobbs, J.M. Flowers, J.S. Edwards, Pat Johnson, Gordon Ezzell, P.B. Moore, Gordon Willingham, Don Hazel, Charles Reitz, Joe Porter, Carl Tapley, C.R. McCutcheon, Larry Johnson, Grady Walden, Jimmy Brown, Lane Sanders, and currently Fred Cooke. *Submitted by: Rebecca Merrell, Church Clerk, 124 Old Franklin Street, Roopville, GA 30170*

Sources: Church Minutes, Church History 1983, and The Carrol County Story as told by The People.

219. Roopville Road Baptist Church

Roopville Road Baptist Church was established in February 1978. Fifteen men sat at a kitchen table and wrote down what they would be able to give toward purchasing land. When counted, it came to the exact dollar amount for the land acquisition.

The first building was a two-story building, 40 feet by 90 feet with Sunday school rooms and a fellowship hall in the basement. Soon, more room was needed for Sunday School classrooms due to growth. A new fellowship hall was built on the south side of the church and was quickly overcrowded. Therefore, the space was doubled in size in order to accommodate the congregational needs.

In the early 1990's, we again were pressed for much needed educational space. An education wing was added across the backside of the auditorium, adding 8,000 square feet. The auditorium was extended twenty feet in length as well to accommodate worship space.

In the late 1900's a Christian Life Center was started. The facility is approximately 32,000 square feet. It also houses a new Fellowship Hall that was dedicated November 19, 2000. Construction is currently underway on the remaining portion of this facility which has a full-size basketball/volleyball court, multipurpose event floor, exercise facilities, indoor walking track and additional education space. This facility is to be used for the Lord's honor and glory and to bring souls to a saving knowledge of Jesus Christ.

Roopville Road Baptist Church

Roopville Road has had six pastors and interims before our present pastor Stephen Peeples. The church now has 550+ members having grown from 55 charter members. The purpose of Roopville Road is "To invest in things that are eternal as we forever seek to love God" (Matthew 22:37-39 / 28:18-20). The fellowship of Roopville Road is "A Place For You to Call Home!" *Submitted by: Rev. Stephen Peeples, Roopville Road Baptist Church, 835 N. Hwy 27, Roopville, GA 30170*

220. Shady Grove Church History

In September 1886, Shady Grove Baptist Church was organized. Charter members were J.W. and Georgia Bell, William and Georgia Hendrix, J.W. and Mary Lawing, Sally Hendrix, Margaret Horton, R.A. and Georgia Rooker, B.F. and Matilda Rigsby, James and Tabetha Smith, Elizabeth and John Smith, Louiza Smith, and James and Mary Simms.

In October a committee of five was appointed to build a Church. They moved in the building in February 1887. The first offering was $1.00. In March of 1887 Sunday School was organized. The church moved to the present location in 1889.

In 1953 six Sunday school rooms were added. In 1956 the inside of building was remodeled by senior men of the church. In the mid 1950's R.W. Johnson was the first full time pastor. Additional Sunday school rooms and bathrooms were added in 1960. In 1961 the parsonage was purchased. The fellowship hall, nursery, baptistery, central heat and air was completed in 1972. In 1977 the library was added. In 1981 additional Sunday school rooms were built and the church purchased a van. In February 1989 the new sanctuary and fellowship hall was completed.

Shady Grove Baptist Church

The church has been blessed with twenty-eight great men of God to serve as ministers. The first pastor was Rev. W.M. Cason. The church boasts a choir for all ages, brotherhood, W.M.U., Bible study, and Awana program.

The present pastor is Rev. Jerome Mitchell. Under his leadership several programs have been added, Masterlife, CWT, Faith Training, and Awana. In 1999 Ricky Shadrix was named associate pastor and a larger bus was purchased. The current budget in $175,257.00, Sunday school enrollment is 250, training union enrollment is 100, and the current membership is about 630.

In the 114 years, Shady Grove Baptist Church has made a lot of changes not only in the building but in the lives of people bringing Glory To Our Lord Jesus Christ. *Submitted by: Bonnie Wilson, 1347 Stewart St., Carrollton, GA 30117*

221. Shiloh United Methodist Church and Campground

Ten members organized Shiloh Methodist Church in 1856 in a small log schoolhouse located between J.W. Kuglar's home and Kuglar Spring. Shiloh's members continued to worship in that location for several years. During that time, land was donated and more was purchased for its present location. In 1866, the Methodist Episcopal Church was organized in Mt. Zion. Loyalties over the Civil War caused a division in another area church, New Salem. A portion of New Salem's members went to Mt. Zion while the others, and later the church building, moved to Shiloh.

Shiloh United Methodist Church

The first camp meeting was held in 1867. A second camp meeting was held the following year in a brush arbor just east of the present one. Families loaded their wagons with clothing, food, pots and pans, tied their milk cow to the back, and headed to Shiloh. There they camped or "tented" during camp meeting.

The present church was constructed in 1881, and the other building was "rolled" to a new location for use as school. Shiloh became a full-time charge in 1952. Until then, Shiloh was part of the Bowdon/Shiloh Charge, sharing a pastor with Bowdon Methodist Church. Shiloh Church was the center of the Burwell Community, and was blessed with forward-thinking God-fearing leaders.

Rich in history and still nestled in a rural setting, Shiloh is an active and growing church whose focus is bringing others to Christ. Shiloh offers an opportunity for all ages to learn God's word and worship, and everyone is welcome. Sunday services begin at 9:30 with prayer and assembly, followed by Sunday School at 10:00, and morning worship at 11:00. Bible Study is at 6:00 in the evening on Sunday.

The United Methodist Men's and Women's Clubs meet regularly for devotion and fellowship. They are involved in special community projects and UM missions. The youth and children, under strong leadership, are actively involved in weekly Bible Studies, Children's Choir, Youth Retreats, and other seasonal activities. The Young at Heart Club is an active close-knit group of friends who enjoy one another's company while participation is a different outing each month. Our annual camp meeting is still held in August and families still camp on the grounds. Running concurrently, the Youth Camp serves youth grades 4-12. They spend a few days together having fun and, more importantly, getting to know God. Camp meeting is a peaceful time to just slow down and enjoy good preaching and the company of friends and family in the beauty of the outdoors.

Shiloh also has a well-maintained walking trail whose main attraction is a covered bridge. It's a beautiful place to meditate and listen to God. *Submitted by: Denise Crumbley, 2075 Davenport Mill Rd., Bowdon, GA 30108*
Source: From writings of Dr. J.C. Griffies

222. Smith Chapel Methodist Church

Around 1850, John Thurman bought land and erected a church where the road from the Thurman house crossed Buchanan Road. It had a rock chimney and logs covered with hand hewn boards. Logs for the floor, which was leveled with an adz, had holes in each end for hickory pins. No nails were used. Posts on each side of the pulpit held tallow candles.

Smith Chapel Before Restoration

Admitted to the Methodist Protestant Conference in 1852, it was named "Mount Pleasant" by Rev. Thurman's wife, Martha Ann McDaniel Thurman. Membership included: Thurmans, Parkers, Gambles, Davenports, Jeters, Stamps, Holmes, Alexanders, Moons, McCrays, Robinsons, Brown, Ragans, Crawfords, McBurnetts, Thompsons, Upchurches.

In 1875 a more modern structure using iron nails replaced the original. Pastor Anderson Smith renamed it "Smith Chapel" honoring his deceased son, Rev. Seaborn Smith. It also became a school. Nannie Thurman, wife of John Nance, was teacher.

Eventually, people attended other churches reducing membership. Descendants of early

Smith Chapel After Restoration

members comprise the present Memorial Association. James L. Thurman, son of Rev. John Thurman, directed construction of the existing structure in 1896.

Rev. Anderson Smith, pioneer of Christianity in Western Georgia, and Rev. John Thurman, distinguished early Georgia Methodist minister who organized Methodist Protestant churches across Georgia, are buried here. Rev. Thurman preached the first sermon in Marthasville, now Atlanta. Reportedly, he moved to Carroll County to avoid rearing his family near the railroad's negative influences.

Emory and Wilma Marlow purchased and restored Smith Chapel in 1988. *Submitted by: James Emory Marlow, 575 N. Jonesville Road, Bowdon, GA 30108*
Sources: Papers of Dr. J.C. Griffies, Rev. Seaborn D. Campbell, tradition, and memories of older citizens.

223. Smyrna United Methodist Church

Smyrna United Methodist Church was located on Highway 27 North five miles north of Carrollton. The exact date of its organization is not known, but the deed dated August 8, 1853, is recorded.

The Reverend David E. Stripling, organized the church according to local tradition. His membership was at Smyrna at the time of his death on August 13, 1882, and his grave is in the church cemetery. The "Register of Pastors" in record begins with A.J. Hughes, appointed in 1881.

The earliest record of church membership available in 1858 contains: S.B. Hays, William Eggnew, William Harper, Ishan Helton, Ira G. Jackson, Benjamin Crowel, James M. Harper, L.S. Thomas, Frances Butran, McEley McKissack, William ??, William Mote, R.L. G. ??, Snytha Helton, Elizabeth Broughron, A. Jackson, Mary McKissack, S.W. Williams, Julia A. Broughtron, Harret Harper, Malissa Harper, Georgia A. Jackson, M. McKissack, Emely Sewel, N.E. Whitehorn, Catharine E. Williams, Rachel I. Crowel, Elisabeth Gosden, Elisa Gosden, Savina M. Harper, Jane Hays, Sarah Butran, Mary M. Hays, Tersa W. Williams, Zelny Boyd, Elisabeth Nichum and Margaret Mote.

The first church building was used for both church and school. Also, when a number of Baptists in the community desired to organize a church but lacked a meeting place, the Smyrna building was offered and used for that purpose. That church became Pleasant View Baptist Church.

Smyrna United Methodist Church declined in membership during the 1980s and disbanded in the early 1990s. *Submitted by: Jackie Bagwell Pate, 3094 East Highway 5, Whitesburg, GA 30185*

224. Southern Hills Christian Church

Southern Hills Christian Church was the first new Christian church started in the area in the past 15 years in Carroll County. This church was a dream that turned into reality for the group who envisioned a new church with contemporary worship services to reach the unchurched and those who had strayed away from traditional worship and were no longer going to church. As a result of this dream, Minister John Latimer set a personal goal to reach unchurched "Baby Boomers".

The church began meeting at Sportsplex and as they out grew that facility, moved to Carrollton High School Auditorium. During this time the former Maranatha Church building was given to Southern Hills with 4 acres of land. This has been used for a Teen center and the church offices. The Lord has indeed blessed and on Sunday, June 3, 2001, Southern Hills held their first worship service in the new church facilities at 1103 N. Hwy. 113, Carrollton, GA. Adults, teens and youth enjoy the casual atmosphere. With upbeat music, drama, and practical messages we believe the service helps us have a greater awareness of God's presence through His Spirit in our lives.

Southern Hills Christian Church, 1103 N. Hwy. 113, Carrollton, GA

225. Saint Andrew United Methodist Church

Services were first held in Saint Andrew Methodist Church on October 12, 1954. This service was the culmination of the decision of the membership of Dodson Memorial Methodist Church, located on Burson Avenue, and the Mission and Church Extension Board to organize a new church in the western section of Carrollton. The goal was to continue to serve the membership of Dodson Memorial while making available a convenient place of worship for the students and faculty of West Georgia College.

The name Saint Andrew was decided upon because of the nature of the disciple, Andrew. In each instance of the New Testament that he is mentioned, he is bringing someone to Christ.

St. Andrew Methodist Church

The first pastor, appointed by the Annual Conference in June 1954, was the Reverend John Lindsey. Reverend Lindsey was followed by the Reverends Russell Taylor, Kenneth Diettle, C. Herman Smith, Charles Sineath, Walton Peabody, Don Harp, Mike Cordle, Albert C. Mahaffey, Edward L. Boye, Tim Holbrook, Joel Purcell, Rick Maesser, Jean Jones, Micheal Boen, Gail Hubbard, Arnold and Karen Kagiyama.

Reverend Kagiyama's many talents, including her musical talent and her compassion for all people, have made her an inspiration to the entire congregation. Through her leadership, the membership of Saint Andrew continues to strive to become active disciples of Christ.

Saint Andrew United Methodist Church, located on Maple Street at Hay's Mill Road, is continually expanding its growth within as well as in community and mission support. *Submitted by: Mrs. Beatrice Parker, South Boulevard, Carrollton, GA*
Source: A History of Saint Andrew Methodist Church

226. St. Paul Methodist Church

St. Paul Methodist Church in Whitesburg is so beloved by those with ties there that they speak of it with easy familiarity as "Paul". In fact, the roots of Paul took hold even before the beginnings of Carroll County. In 1823, two years before Chief William McIntosh and the Creek Nation ceded the territory to Georgia, James H. Holland settled on a tract of land near Byers Cross Roads. In 1825, he erected a one room log building that was used as a religious meeting place, a school, and a community gathering place. Known as Holland's Meeting House, it served its purpose for thirty years.

St. Paul Methodist Church, Whitesburg, Georgia

In 1853, when James Holland moved onto Land Lot 212, he built a large one room log house that he again made a place of worship for the neighborhood. It too was called Holland's Meeting House. In 1867, five years after the death of James Holland, five trustees purchased land located one and a half miles south of its second location near Wolfe Creek. Those trustees were F.W. Hilley, G.W. Camp, J.R. Bunt, William Peek, and Thomas E. Camp. Robert L. Richards, Carroll County Ordinary, donated land for the cemetery.

It's likely that the log building was moved from its former site at Little Bethel to the new site at Lickskillet. There it became St. Paul's Church. In 1898, Paul began having its annual homecoming day, an event that continues to the present. Jim Young was chairman 1898-1938. Rev. Charles Allen, one time pastor of the largest Methodist church in the country, preached his first sermon at Paul. It served the community and the Methodist Conference until 1964 when the Conference gave instruction to "eliminate Whitesburg Circuit .... "

However, there was an irrepressible spirit about the place and seven members rallied to save the little church. They were Lillie Hilley Hamilton, Mrs. C.B. McClendon, Mrs. Eugene Dukes, Mrs. Ruby Saylors, Mrs. Hugh Richards, Grady Crews, and Emma Driver. St. Paul's plight became a statewide — and beyond — concern that earned its reputation as "The Church That Would Not Die". *Submitted by: Mignon Wessinger, P.O. Box 25, Bowdon, GA 30108*
Source: "Legend of a Church That Would Not Die" monograph by Edith Foster

227. Stripling Chapel United Methodist Church

The Stripling Chapel UMC is located on highway 27 S below Crossroads Shopping Center. The first gathering place was a brush Arbor. In March 1857 eleven names were entered as members. Records show that 5 members died during the Civil War.

The first building was constructed of logs, which was near the present church building. It

Stripling Chapel United Methodist Church

was given the name in "Honor" of a local Preacher, David Stripling. Rev. Stripling was instrumental in organizing Stripling Chapel United Methodist Church and many other Methodist Churches in the county. The first frame building was erected near the present location. It was used as a schoolhouse during the week and for Worship on Sunday. As the membership increased, about 1890, a larger building was constructed. In 1926, a Woman's Missionary Society was organized, when Rev. B.N. McHan was Pastor. In 1949 Rev. & Mrs. C.L. Harris and Mrs. B.N. McHan organized the Woman's Society of Christian Service. It has remained active for 51 plus years and now has 13 members which are now called United Methodist Women. This group of Ladies does many things for the local church and community projects.

On December 16, 1951, the Church's frame building was destroyed by fire. The present building was dedicated November 1952. Around the early 1960's a Sunday School Annex was added.

History was made in June 1977, as the Church Services began as a "Full Time" Church. The first Homecoming was held in April 1978 with more than 200 people in attendance. Traditionally Homecoming is held the last Sunday in April each year. The Fellowship Hall was consecrated in March 1996. The Rebecca Martin Garden Club meets regularly in this building. The church pastorium is located on Stripling Chapel Road. We have an active choir and youth program. *Submitted by: Homa Archer, 3198 Oak Grove Church Road, Carrollton, GA 30117*

228. Tabernacle Baptist Church

The "runaway" known as Tabernacle Baptist Church, is well lit and is faithful in guiding every "plane" to a place where all people will experience the love given by the Savior and Lord of life, Jesus Christ.

The basis for all we do is centered on the conviction that God is interested in every part of our lives. Each Sunday, Tabernacle Baptist Church meets to worship together and fellowship in small groups. In worship, we celebrate the greatness of God. In small groups needs are met and friendships are formed. There is no better time than now to begin to experience personally what God has planned for you.

This is who we are. All we do is for the love of people. We invite you to join in this legacy and experience the joy of flying with other like-minded people. We look forward to seeing you.

Do you remember what it was like to be a child, replete with the fantasies, expectations and wonders unique to that time of life? Those were the days where you would get the "special towels" reserved for guests, tie one around your neck and find the highest launch pad around and jump. You honestly believed that flying was possible.

Life is different now. You woke up one morning never to wear a cape again, and the wonder of living had lost its luster. Perhaps it's the

Tabernacle Baptist Church

demand of daily living, juggling a hectic schedule and the ever-changing tempo of life. Change and its inevitable tension seem to be the driving force behind daily living.

Wherever you find yourself today, you can still come home and experience the wonder of daily living. *Submitted by: Tabernacle Baptist Church, 150 Tabernacle Dr., Carrollton, GA 30117, www.tabernacle.org*

229. Temple Church of Christ

Family worship service in the home of George Scott in 1946 was the beginning of the Temple Church of Christ. Hedric Laney and his family joined the Scotts in 1949. In 1952 a tent meeting was held by Minister Homer L. King. The Joe Bass family joined at this time. The group of worshipers started holding meetings in the old Temple Theater building on Johnson Street.

Temple Church of Christ

The modern brick structure at the corner of Griffin and James Streets was built over a period of time as funds became available. There are approximately fifty in regular attendance today. Trustees are Joe Bass and Steve Sampler. Among the ministers have been Homer A. Gay, Gillis Prince, E.H. Miller, Alton Bailey, T.J. Parker, Barry Owens, and Dennis Smith. *Submitted by: Lera Ivey, P.O. Box 237, Temple, GA 30179*
Source: Personal Knowledge

230. Trinity Baptist Church

Trinity Baptist Church was conceived in December of 1987. The Carrollton Baptist Association building on Stewart Street was the first meeting place for the new congregation. The Reverend Bob Skelton was called as interim pastor.

On April 3, 1988, Trinity Baptist Church was officially chartered and accepted 84 people as charter members. January of 1989 marked the beginning of a new phase for Trinity Baptist Church. In June, members of the church called Reverend Woodrow Hudson to become its first full-time pastor.

On October 14, 1990 Trinity Baptist held a dedication service and open house for the community

Trinity Baptist Church

at its new home on Northside Drive. In August of 1995, Trinity Baptist Church called Reverend Larry D. Insko as its second pastor. In addition to Reverend Insko, other staff of Trinity Baptist Church have included Audrey Culpeper, Charles Allen, Doug Davis, Dale Hendrick, John Gentry, Donna Hill-Spivey and Jimmie Allen. *Submitted by: Jimmie N. Allen, Church Secretary*

231. Union Campground

Open air religious services known as Camp Meetings were popular during the 1800's and prominent within the Methodist denomination. The popularity of this type worship swept through West Georgia, and in 1876, a brush arbor was built in the Jake community. In the 1930's, when three major Methodist conferences united, Union Campground became interdenominational.

In 1884 land was donated by W.A. McBurnett, Shade Thompson, and Nick McBurnett for the campground. On October 4, 1889, the 9.91 acres was bought and deeded to the trustees of Union Campground for $45.00.

A wooden arbor was built in one day under the supervision of Rev. Bill Walton, a carpenter. Rev. John Anderson, President of the Georgia Methodist Protestant Church was a great help in the organization of the campground. A preacher's cottage was built in his honor, and he served as the camp director for many years.

The Arbor as it appears where annual services are held.

The first lights for the night meetings were log fires outside the arbor. Oil lamps that sat on a shelf updated this practice. After that, generator lights and gas lanterns were hung from the arbor's rafters. Finally, in the 1930's electric lights were installed.

Early campers were supplied with water from a spring. In 1975, a brick wall was constructed around the spring with a canopy roof above it. Today the spring supplies much of the camps water.

Today Camp Meeting is held the Wednesday before the first Sunday in August through the following Wednesday. *Submitted by: Orlando Driver, 6154 Smithfield Rd., Bowdon, GA 30108*

232. Victory United Methodist Church

Victory United Methodist Church was built in 1897. It is located in the Victory community between Bowdon and Tyus. On June 1, 1997 the church celebrated its 100th Anniversary Homecoming.

The church began as a Methodist Protestant Church in 1897 with Rev. W.J. Causey as its first minister. George A. McDaniel gave 10 acres for a church for the congregation from Antioch because they did not have room for a cemetery. The church sits on a knoll where it has served as the center of community activity. Other than homes, the church is the last remnant from the past.

Historic Victory United Methodist Church

On August 12, 1999, the church was struck by lightning and burned. With support from near and far and the Joiner family from Tyus as builders, the congregation has rebuilt a similar white country church with steeple and pagoda located on the site where the old church stood. The new church added a fellowship hall and kitchen. Services are held on first Sundays. Jessie McDaniel Hamrick, whose father built the original church, and Robert D. Tisinger were two of its most faithful members.

Members of the church are Naomi Tisinger, Mildred Garrett, Eula Tisinger, Alvin and Virginia Chambers, Jerry and Martha Striplin, Judy and Joe Dixon, Jim Rowell, Cindy Saxon, Lillian Wheeler, Velma Hearn, John Carter Clay, Richard and Jimmie Kay Wadsworth Allen. Many friends of the church come to hear the pastor Tommy Greer. Many members from the founding families are buried in the cemetery beside this little country church in the wildwood.
Submitted by: Gwyn Chesnut
Source: They Called It Victory

233. Welcome Hill Baptist Church

On August 6, 1950 the following Ministers and Deacons composed a presbytery and met on the grounds of the Welcome Hill Church for the purpose of constitution of a Missionary Baptist Church.

Ministers were: Rev. Monroe Driver, Tommy Thompson, W.O. Johnson, Eddie B. Clay and I.V. Phillips. Deacons were Lonnie Neighbors, Buddy Pike, Kary Oliver and Vassie Shirey, from Antioch Baptist Church in Hogansville, Ga., John Carroll, Johnnie McClendon, Buford Thacker, Clarence Burnham and Fred Phillips from Happy Valley Church, near Newnan, Georgia. Rev. Monroe Driver was chosen as Moderator and I.V. Philipps, Clerk.

The following people were present at the constitution of this body: Sisters Mamie Morris, Mary Jo Wallace, Erma Stone, Geneva Wallace, Lorene Driver, Vera Lester, and Mrs. Marvin Gray.

Brothers: Pete Allen, Anderson Daniell, Frank McCravy, Charles Wallace, Willie Thompson, Comer Morris, Floyd Lester, Tommie Driver and George Stone.

Floyd Boice, Hulett Rooks, and Gaynelle Rooks came under watch care. Solona McCravey came upon statement.

It was moved and seconded to adopt the usual Missionary Baptist Church Convenant as ours and moved and seconded to name the church: Welcome Hill Baptist Church.

Brother Bud Wallace was nominated for pastor and Brother Tommnie Driver as ordained Deacon. The following spoke at the constitution: Tommy Thompson, W.O. Johnson, Eddie B. Clay, I.V. Phillips, Clerk, and Monroe Driver, Moderator.

Welcome Hill Church was first located at Avenue C., Carrollton, Georgia. The following men were ordained while at this location: Rev. Melton Jiles, August 19, 1951: Rev. Jackson Chambers, June 16, 1957: Rev. Spurgeon Powers, October 22, 1961 and Rev. Joseph Walker, December 31, 1961.

Welcome Hill Baptist Church

In 1966 a new church was built on Lovvorn Road, Carrollton, Ga. and the first services were held on August 27, 1966. Dedicaton of Welcome Hill Baptist Church's new building was held September 25, 1966. The opening song was by Brother Hulett Farmer. Brother Melton Jiles gave the prayer and Brother Tommie Thompson gave the dedication sermon.

After the sermon, the church gathered around the alter in prayer. Dedicating the church building to our Lord and Savior Jesus Christ.

The first wedding in our church was on October 5, 1966. Miss Lillian Daniel and Mr. Rayford Hightower were united with Minister Rev. Guy Rogers officiating.

The first funeral was held on October 16, 1966, Mrs. Mattie Mae Collin, with Rev. Melton Jiles officiating.

Our Present Pastor, Reverend Keith Jiles, was ordained at Welcome Hill on June 27, 1999. He is the youngest Pastor to ever serve our church, and is doing a wonderful service. Rev. Keith Jiles, his wife Shellie and three children are a wonderful dedicated family, loved by every member of our church. *Submitted by: Christine Collins, 118 Park Lane, Carrollton, GA 30117*

234. Westside Baptist Church

The founders of the Westside Baptist Church in 1969 were: Pastor W.E. Roberts, Deacon James Kight, Deacon Randolph Reynolds, Deacon James Dallas, Deacon Jessie Dallas, Deacon Roy Daniel, Deacon Amos Farmer, Deacon Eddie Garrison, Deacon Willie Frank West. On the first Lord's Day in July 1969 we purchased our church building, which is located at 719 Aycock Street. The church officers were: Pastor W.E. Roberts, Chairman Deacon James Kight, Assistant Chairman Deacon Randolph Reynolds, Sunday School Superintendent Deacon Amos

Westside Baptist Church

Farmer, Sunday School Teacher Deacon Frank West, Treasurer Sister Omie Dallas, and Church Clerk Sister Annie Boykin.

Since that time we have grown tremendously in the last 31 years. Today we are a community outreach church under the leadership of our pastor, Overseer Walter J. Kight. Our goal as a church is to reach into the community and answer the people's need in the West Georgia area. We feel that because we are in the community, we can assess the needs by reinvesting back into the community through our ministries in the church socially, economically, and spiritually. We are now members of the Full Gospel Baptist Church Fellowship and our Internatioal Presiding Bishop is Bishop Paul S. Morton. We are thankful to our founders. They have blessed the west side of Carrollton, Carroll County and the State of Georgia.

235. Whitesburg Baptist Church

Whitesburg was settled around 1860 when John Gilbert owned and operated a cotton gin in the area. In that same year New Providence Baptist Church was established and named.[1] Very little is known about the formation of the church, but historical sources include the church minutes dating from 1871; the original building burned prior to 1876. Church minutes reveal that the present structure was built in 1875 as the conference minutes, of May 13, 1876, state that the following conference was to be held at the "next church house." The first conference was held in the present building on June 10, 1876.[2]

Whitesburg Baptist Church, April 2001

In 1874, Whitesburg was incorporated with five councilmen elected to govern; the following year, the membership of New Providence Baptist Church changed the name to Whitesburg Baptist Church. From existing records, it is apparent that the Church has always been very clear on what it believes. As early as 1874, the membership adopted the *Articles of Faith and Rules of Decorum* which, with some minor modification, are the statement of the Church's beliefs today.[3]

Several major changes have occurred in the church structure over the years, with considerable improvements being made after 1960. Some changes include additions of Sunday School rooms, a baptismal pool, and a Fellowship Hall; all of which were completed in 1965. Previously, the Church's baptismal ceremonies were performed at Jones Mill on Snake Creek.[4] The stained glass windows were added to the building in 1973. Another major change involved the 1987 replacement of the original steeple, which was destroyed by high winds.[5]

Today, the Church stands solidly on its beliefs and has since the mid-19th century. The membership continues to be committed to serving their "living Saviour and Christ" faithfully as well as the people of the community and surrounding areas. *Submitted by: Helen Morek Chambers, 102 West McIntosh Circle, Whitesburg, GA 30185*

Sources: [1]Carroll Publishing Company, *The Carroll County Story as Told by the People,* (Carrollton: Thomasson Printing Company, 1976), p. 71; [2]Church Records, Folder 2; Whitesburg Baptist Church 1874-1878 Minute Book, N.P.; [3]Ibid, N.P.; [4]Church Records, Book II: January 17, 1920 - Third Sunday, Steptember, 1956, p. 165.; [5]Bulletin, N.P.

236. The Whitesburg Christian Church

The Whitesburg Christian Church began in one man's mind over 80 years ago. George W. Rooks, better known as "Uncle Bob Rooks" by those who knew him, wanted to see a Christian Church in Whitesburg. He began searching for others who had a similar desire.

Whitesburg Christian Church

"Uncle Bob Rooks" contacted Preacher Dodson of Atlanta, in search of a preacher. Owen Still and Curtis Hayes, an evangelistic team, were urged to go to Whitesburg to hold a meeting. After securing the loan of a lot through Professor W.E. Swetnam, they set up their tent, and began a three-week evangelistic meeting in October 1920.

Owen Still's preaching and Curtis Hayes' singing, moved the capacity crowds every night. Following this tent meeting, the church had 32 charter members.

They continued to meet in the Whitesburg School building, while searching for a desirable lot for a permanent house of worship, Mr. and Mrs. Harry Love gave the land for the church building site.

People immediately began offering shingles, two-by fours, and other lumber for the building. Volunteers labored hard to complete the wood framed building by October 1921. It cost $2,000 and was paid in full.

The church outgrew the original building, and built a new modern building on Highway 5. A new sanctuary in 1961, parsonage in 1962, educational building in 1972, and forty feet of additional sanctuary space and a covered drive-under in late 1970s. *Submitted by: Charlotte Posey, PO Box 535, Whitesburg, GA and Researched by Susan M. Gatlin, 132 Leland Sr. SW, Mableton, GA 30126-1839*

237. Whitesburg Methodist Church

Our church was organized in the year of our Lord, 1887. The land was purchased from R.E. Morrow. The following Trustees were elected: W.F. Story, J.E. Merk, J.W. Gilbert and J.M. Newton. J.O. McCullen and John Pentcost witnessed the deed before D.M. Gordon, Notary Public on November 30, 1887.

The original building was a wooden structure, and was destroyed in a fire in June of 1912. The present building was built between 1912 or 1913. Our church had a membership of about 200, and was very active for the next 45 years. It had a good Sunday School, a Wednesday Night Prayer Meeting, and an active Epworth League.

Whitesburg Methodist Church

The Fellowship Hall was built in 1950 with love and support of devoted members. Improvements have continued in the church through the years, due to the same love and devotion. Many of our loved ones worked hard to keep the doors of the church open, and hopefully their spirit has been instilled in those of us left, so that we may keep striving to preserve our precious church. *Submitted by: Camilla Stevens Cooper, 620 Main Street, Whitesburg, GA 30185*

238. Whooping Creek Primitive Baptist Church

Whooping Creek Primitive Baptist Church was constituted Saturday, April 29, 1852: Thomas B. Jones, Thomas Long, Richard Changler and James Jones, with Brother Chandler and James Jones as Deacons, being called on by scattered brethren at or near the place called "Holloway Meeting House", constituted the church. According to records found, Thomas Long, Moderator, Miles Pate, Church Clerk.

Deeds were recorded in 1891 to church by Sam Holloway and Obe Cook. Deeds was made 39 years after the church was constituted.

The following is from an article in the newspaper, *"Law & Grace"* by Rev. T.H. Edison.

In a woodland setting, accented with Honeysuckle and Mt. Laurel, the Oak and Hicktory trees extend their limbs as arms caressing the old Church with soft shadows. The church was named for a nearby creek that was once the sight of many Indian villages, which were widely known for their unusual summoning of their neighbors, when traders came with their wares.

Whooping Creek Primitive Baptist Church

Many of the church pews were the former pews in the Counties first courthouse, and the pulpit was the judge's bar. Many times the judge sounded the gavel and justice was placed in the balances and meted out with rigor. Perhaps many of the accused stood before the bar defiant, others stood pleading for mercy, while family and friends sat in those same pews weeping as sentences were pronounced according to the law of the land.

When the old courthouse was torn down, it was quite ironic, that the pews and judge's bar, should be placed in a church, continuing to be a part of the place of judgment. The gavel, continued to sound and the Supreme Judge of mankind, announced, "Let whosoever will, come." Justice was placed in the balances, on one side, "The wages of sin is death" on the other side, "But the gift of God is eternal life through Jesus Christ our Lord."

Many have stood before that bar guilty, but praying, "Father forgive me, a sinner." While family and friends sitting in those same pews, joyfully sang "Amazing Grace, how sweet the sound, that saved a wretch like me. I once was lost but now I'm found, was blind but now I see." The plea was made, evidence was heard, the law was read, and justice was administered, through grace and sentences were pronounced, "I forgive, I forgive."

The sparkling stream still flows peacefully, just as it did when Indians fished in its waters. The cemetery continues to grow with every passing year, and the old church still keeps a silent vigil, from stately courtrooms the law of the land is still meted out without favor or respect of persons. God still holds court daily, in homes, in great cathedrals, and little churches, throughout the land, administering justice without favor or respect of persons, to all that come boldly, unto the throne of grace, that they may obtain mercy and find grace to help in time of need. (Research by T.H. Edison)

My mother Mattie O. Jones Davis, was the last living member, when she died on January 13, 1983. Later, more people have joined. They still hold services once each month. Carlton Robinson is the Pastor. *Submitted by: Rudene (Davis) Daniel, 102 Myrtle Street, Carrollton, GA 30117*

239. Wilson's Chapel

The Wilson's Chapel, located in the Cross Plains community, was built by Matthew Hardy Wilson, across the road from his home. He started the church in 1937 and finished it in 1938. Mr. Wilson had extensive land holdings and cut the timber from his land to build the church. After his son, Samuel, ran the timber through his sawmill, it was then planed. No other finishing was ever put on the lumber. Mr. Wilson also built the benches, which are still used today. Mary Hackney, his daughter and my aunt, remembers holding the posts for her daddy when the foundation was being formed. The church still remains the same inside, just the way Mr. Wilson finished it except for a new floor and windows. Today you can stand in the doorway of Wilson's Chapel and gaze over the land and see the original 'gin' house and 'wood' house that Mr. Wilson built. Across the road you can see the 'homeplace,' which was bought by Mr. Wilson's grandson Matthew Wilson, his namesake. Matthew restored the house for his son, Douglas Wilson.

Services were not held on any regular basis, but Mary Wilson Hackney remembers hearing Ministers Jimmy Lee Shadinger and Roy Avery preach there.

Matthew Hardy Wilson (b. 2-4-1870 d. 3-13-1940) married Ada Ward on December 20, 1894 and they were blessed with a large family of six sons, Willie "Bill," Samuel Matthew, Frederic, Henry, Moses and Thomas, and six daughters, Clidie, Kathleen, Annie, Arrena, Naomi and Mary.

Wilson's Chapel

Mr. and Mrs. Wilson were great supporters of Sacred Harp music. Also he built the church so singers of Sacred Harp music would always have a place to come together and sing the four part harmony of Sacred Harp. Every year, the first Saturday and Sunday of August, the Chattahoochee National Sacred Harp Convention is held at Wilson's Chapel. At lunch time they fill the tables with wonderful homemade foods of all kinds and the meals are shared like any other large family. A covered pavilion with lots of tables stand ready for the occasion each year. There is a sign near the top of the pavilion "Wilson's Chapel, home of Chattahoochee Convention." My mother, Naomi, and my Aunt Mary, probably have never missed a single session of the convention held there. It is the oldest convention in Georgia. In 2002 it will meet for the 150th session.

The children of Mr. and Mrs. Matthew Hardy Wilson have kept the church in superb condition in their memory. They bricked the little white church in about 1958. A marble marker was placed on the church yard by Mary Wilson Hackney and Matthew B. Wilson, in 1990.

Matthew Hardy Wilson died in March 13, 1940 and his funeral was held at the church he had built. His body was laid to rest in the church yard, which has now become a family cemetery. Ada Ward Wilson died November 11, 1942 and her funeral was also held at Wilson's Chapel. Three sons, Bill, Moses, and Thomas, and two daughters, Annie and Kathleen Wilson Denney, as well as two sons-in-law, Loomis Hackney and Earnest Sailors, and two daughters-in-law, Celia Thomas Wilson, Vern Bill Wilson, are all buried in the family cemetery. Four of the ones buried there are Veterans and the U.S. flag files over their graves.

The little church has seen three weddings in recent years, all great-grandchildren of Mr. and Mrs. Wilson: Laura Webb Frey, Chasity Wilson Moreland, and Douglas Wilson. *Submitted by: Diane Sailors Smith, 750 Stewart Street, Carrollton, GA 30117.*

240. Early Coca-Cola Bottling Company Memories

My dad, Raymond Lewis "Dutch" Phillips worked for the Coca-Cola Bottling Company in Carrollton during the mid to late 1930's. I was born in August of 1937, and have distinct memories of two men carrying dad into our house on Rome Street after his Coke truck was involved in an accident. Both his legs were broken and in casts such that he could not walk, and the men sat him in a chair and pulled an ottoman up under his legs, so I place the accident at circa 1939 or 1940.

Compared to other photos of dad, I would judge the Coke photos as circa 1935-37. One photo was taken inside the Coca-Cola Plant, dad with four other men. The other photo is of dad standing in front of what appears to be a Coca-Cola Company display, sale or parade float. I don't know who any of the men in the photos are, but strongly suspect that the man with dad in the float photo was Bay Hay. Bay was one of dad's best friends, and we visited Bay before we left Carrollton.

Coca-Cola Bottling Company

I still have an early electric sewing machine that my dad won for my mother as "top Coca-Cola salesman". I spent countless hours watching mom (Myrtle Phillips) sew on that machine. I have a scar on my left index finger from my solo use of the machine. The needle went completely through the finger joint and stalled. The scar came from my panic as I unsuccessfully tried to pull my finger loose. Mom saved me by backing the needle out. I still loved that machine.

Coca-Cola Company Display Float

As a youngster, I spent summers with my Aunt Dovey Gray at her Sims Street home in Carrollton. Her son Buster, who had recently returned from WWII, worked for the Coca-Cola Company. I loved to ride the Coke truck with Buster, struggling so hard to carry one case of Coke into a store, while Buster would carry at last four each trip.

The summers were hot, and the Coke truck was not air-conditioned, so I would exchange a lot of hot Coke off the truck for a cold one from the store. The Coke Boxes were ice boxes, with several big blocks of ice chilling the water in which the Cokes sat. Oh my, how wonderful those Cokes tasted on a hot day. When I failed to eat much supper one evening, Aunt Dovie had Buster watch how many Cokes I drank the next day, and that night I heard Aunt Dovie's shocked response when she asked Buster how many I drank. "21? No wonder that child isn't hungry". I only got three the next day.

Many of the stores we delivered Cokes to were only reached by traveling dirt roads. I have read that most of the major county roads were paved by then, and to that I can only reply that many of Buster's customers were not on major county roads. I know we went throughout the area of Villa Rica, Draketown, Newnan, Temple, Douglasville, and other places I can't remember. We stopped at a lot of factory mills, and I often got a bundle of socks from some of the kind people we saw.

To this very day, I feel a little guilty if I ever drink anything other than Coke. Mom always said my baby bottle was a Coke bottle with a nipple on the end, and I believe that to be true.

Submitted by: Rodric M. Phillips, 8325 N.E. 140th Street, Edmond, OK 73013-8717

241. Crime and Punishment

The old Carroll County Courthouse was no exception to the penchant of pigeons for such an edifice; Carrollton's boys often had a great time trying to catch pigeons in the loft. However, there was an irrevocable rule: they should never go in the loft when Court was in session.

About 1913 or 1914-the exact year is unknown-five boys, ages 10 and 11, watched the Courthouse pigeons, speculating on how many were actually in the loft. Their speculated number became more, and more, until they were totally convinced there must be hundreds; and that was something they just had to see. They were sure, if they just looked and came right back down, it would be all right. In minutes they were climbing a ladder on the second floor of the Courthouse.

No one knows the number of pigeons in that loft, but it was certainly more than those youngsters had ever seen up that close. The proximity of five boys and all those birds? Some, perhaps just beyond arm's reach? It was too much. All thoughts of looking, the rule, whatever, vanished into thin air and the Chase was on.

In the Courtroom below, the reverberation of shouts, laughter, pounding of ten running, jumping feet; brought proceedings to a standstill. Two men in the Courtroom, recognizing their sons' voices, were the first to reach the loft ladder, and shouted to their sons, "COME DOWN HERE! NOW!" There was a dead silence. Five very scared boys peered over the edge of the entrance to the loft. Standing at the foot of the ladder was Wiley Garrett, Sheriff of Carroll County, and Judge John Norman of the Carroll Superior Court.

Nothing has ever been told about a trial, but punishment for two of the culprits was sure and swift—bent over the Judge's bench. Temporary baliffs were appointed to escort the others to their respective fathers for a like punishment; and Court resumed.

The old Courthouse burned in the mid-twenties. Our present Courthouse stands on the same site. Pigeons have never seemed to like it as much; or maybe they just keep a lower profile.

Of course, this "Family Tale" was the source of a lot of fun for Fred Garrett and his family; he often told it himself. However, if one of his brothers or sister was just a little exasperated with him, they invariably said, "Aw, Fred! Go chase a pigeon!" My Uncle Fred died in December 1969. As long as he lived, when he told his "most memorable childhood experience" he subconsciously rubbed his backside.

That licking must have been a good one.

Submitted by: Jackie Hughey Pritchard, 957 Brill Rd. No. 62, Mobile, AL 36605

242. Tragic Flood of 1882

Thomas M. Roop, B. Josephesus Roop and Family

The following information comes from an article in the *Times* newspaper, January 18, 1972, from an article originally printed in the *Times* newspaper on Feburary 22, 1883.

On a cold, stormy day on April 22, 1882 brothers Thomas (Bud) Roop and B. Josephesus (Ceph) Roop, brothers of John K. Roop, founder of Roopville, sat together in the home of Ceph, his wife, and three children at Merrell's Mill. Ceph's wife was the daughter of Mr. Robert Merrell, Sr. who owned a large plantation, corn and wheat mills, gin, blacksmith shop and store. After the Civil War some slaves remained with the Merrell family, including Aunt Flora and her son, Charles. Mr. Merrell's three sons (Joseph, William, and Robert) as well as Bud and Ceph Roop were becoming more involved with the family business.

This community began in Antebellum days and was located on Hillabahatchee Creek, once part of Carroll County that later became a part Heard County. Whooping Creek and Town Creek come together to form this larger creek.

Thomas Roop spent weekends at his home in Roopville. On Monday he returned to stay at the mill during the work week. On this weekend, he had decided to return on Sunday, probably because of the expectation of bad weather. At about 3:30 a.m. Thomas awoke and found water had reached the floor of his room. He called to his brother who first thought that the roof was leaking but once he lit a lamp, discovered the terrible truth.

A young black girl stayed with the family to help with the three young children. She, along with Ceph's wife and children were all terrified. As his wife's screamed in terror, her father, Robert Merrell, heard her and tried to come to help. His home, about 250 yards away, was the only building located on higher ground. He was unable to reach the house, ran back home to get a canoe but found it gone, swept away with the terrible force of the racing waters. The rapidly rising creek, foamed as it rushed down stream. Mr. Merrell ran back toward Ceph's home in time to see the store-house lifted from its foundation begin to wash away and fall to pieces. Ceph, sat on the edge of a window and tried to get his wife to come and save herself, she refused choosing to remain in the house with her children. Suddenly the house was lifted from its foundation and with a great force threw Ceph from the window. As he swam along, trying to stay near the family, the house was thrown against a huge bluff and exploded into pieces. The occupants of the house could be heard screaming. Ceph was forced under water. When he surfaced there was no sign of the family or servants. Huge timbers, uprooted trees, and other debris rushed by. For the next few minutes Ceph battled the rushing torrents, repeatedly being forced below the surface. As he tried to grab onto something to save himself he was forced against a tree and was able to hold on to the tree till dawn.

Although this horror lasted no more than ten minutes, he had traveled 3/4 of a mile downstream. As he clung to the tree, most of his clothes gone, in the cold, dark night, he called out but heard no one. At the first break of day he looked around the area but there was no sign of his lost family. He was able to swim to a spot of land about 80 yards away from the tree he had clung to during his hours of horror. He felt that he had little reason to live having lost all.

Bud was last seen on the store-house porch just before the waters lifted the building. He was never seen alive again, his body was found later.

When Charles, Aunt Flora's son, reached Roopville to relay the bad news later that morning, brother J.K. Roop hurried to the scene and found the horrible story to be true.

What had caused this terrible tragedy? Some said it was a "water spout" other call it a "freshet".

What happened to the survivors of the flood and their families? Ceph Roop went to Texas, remarried and raised a second family. Bud's orphan children, Mae Roop married Mr. Dorsett and moved. Frank Roop continued to live in the home place, he never married. Bud's widow, Florida Alexander Roop, later married Dr. Francis Marion Brock, MD. They had two children Mrs. Harry Sheets and Mr. Henry Brock. Mrs. Florida Roop Brock remained in Roopville in the Roop house till her death.

The members of the Roopville Historical Society have visited the site of the flood. The once self-sufficient village is now very peaceful, grown up with native vegetation. The graves of most of the victims, located on the hilltop, overlooks the peaceful stream that flows through the area. Many of the headstones are broken or have fallen over.

Many Roop family pictures, the reprinted news article, pictures of the area today, etc. can be viewed at the Roopville Archive and Historical Society building, in the center of town on Old Highway 27 in Roopville. *Submitted by: Rebecca Merrell, President of the Roopville Archive and Historical Society, P.O. Box 285, Roopville, GA 30170.*
Sources: *Times* Newspaper articles of 1883

243. Madstone Usage

The absence of readily available medicinal treatment in early Carroll County brought out many innovative local medicinals and cures. Being bitten by a rabid or supposedly rabid animal was a major concern. A fairly common treatment was the use of a madstone which is defined by *Webster's Third International Dictionary* as

> "a stony concretion (as a hairball taken from the stomach of a deer) supposed to counteract the poisonous effects of an animal (as one affected with rabies)."

People bitten by dogs thought to be rabid (maddogs) would travel a day's journey without hesitation to the home of someone known to possess a madstone for treatment. A madstone was kept in the home of Henry Martin Hanson (1857-1940) of the Hulett-Whitesburg area of Carroll County. Of unknown origin it was passed on to John R. Hanson, then to Maynard Hanson and Velma Hanson Bailey, and then to Verne Hanson Borders.

A very good account of madstone usage is recorded in the *History of Heard County* and described by Mrs. Mary Brett Ridley:

> "After the madstone was boiled in fresh sweet milk, it was taken up with a spoon and let stay in the spoon until you could hold your hand on it. When it got cool enough to put to the place, it would stick just like a magnet. If it stuck it meant it was a mad dog bite. The stone had little tiny holes that let the poison go up into it, and when it got full of poison it fell off. It was boiled in milk again and applied until it no longer stuck."

Madstone from Hanson Family; Key shown for comparative size

In 1999, Mrs. Jenny Crews Landry told that as a child in the 1930's, she was bitten by a small dog at her home near St. Paul's Methodist Church south of Hulett. As a precaution she was taken by her father to have the madstone applied by Mr. "Mart" Hanson, who lived nearby. Mr. Hanson's daughters, Effie and Bama, actually performed the evidently successful treatment. *Submitted by: Verne H. Borders, 1273 Blandenburg Rd., Carrollton, GA 30116*
Sources: Personal Knowledge and *History of Heard County* and Webster's Third International Dictionary

244. Plane Crash at Burwell

The Atlantic Southeast Airlines plane that crashed in a field at Burwell on August 21, 1995 was the worst aviation accident in the history of Carroll County. This unexpected tragedy changed the lives of those involved forever. The plane was an Embraer turboprop bound from Hartsfield airport in Atlanta to Gulfport, Mississippi, when the left propeller broke causing failure in the left engine. In 91/2 minutes the plane had been maneuvered into the field of Paul Butler in Burwell by pilot, Ed Gannaway, 45, of Dublin, who was killed on impact. He was called a hero by those who survived.

Within 70 minutes of the first call, hundreds of emergency professionals converged on the scene and removed the victims to hospitals. The 26 passengers showed great courage and selflessness in their rescue. Despite the quick response and courageous efforts of neighbors, local citizens and emergency personnel, two were killed on impact and two died later. Many suffered from traumatic burns. Flight attendant Robin Fech was also a hero. She saved several passengers despite her own severe injuries, but struggled with doubts that she should have done more. Robin returned to the scene in later years in her own search to heal.

There were many bonds formed between victims and those who assisted them through the ordeal. Visits to the hospital and keeping in touch through the years developed into lasting friendships much like family. It was truly a day to remember for all Carroll Countians and those involved. *Submitted by: Gwyn Chesnut*
Sources: *The Time Georgian*

245. Reminiscences of Nell Meadows

Some time in the first part of the 1900s, a family of black people lived in a house on Maple Street, near the railroad and back of 328 Maple Street.

They wanted something from a store on Dixie Street, so Ralph Bridges, a young man in the family, was going to get it. He started walking on the railroad tracks instead of the sidewalk, as he should have. A train was just starting in the direction the man was going, so he tried to jump on it and ride to Dixie Street, but he was thrown under the train and both of his legs were cut off.

One day, many years ago, when the train stopped in Carrollton at noon, a man got off and was talking to some men at the depot. He talked too long, and when the train started he ran and tried to get on, but was thrown under the wheels and both of his legs were cut off. He was carried to the little hospital on Maple Street, the only one in Carrollton at that time. People up and down the street could hear him screaming. His wife was called from their home in Cedartown. He died before she got here.

In the early 1900s, a story was told of a woman walking to church one rainy day, holding an umbrella over her. When she got to the church, she had difficulty getting the open umbrella through the door. She worked and worked, and finally succeeded, and then walked down the aisle holding the open umbrella over her.

There were four medical doctors in Carrollton in the early 1900s. Dr. Lee Fitts lived on Dixie Street (where Mr. and Mrs. Richard Ingle now live); Dr. Hamrick lived on corner of Depot (now Bradley) Street and West Center Street; Dr. J.B. Camp lived on Maple Street where Mr. Barnes, the lawyer, now lives; Dr. Goodwin lived on Dixie Street where Dr. Fitts had lived.

In the days before people had electric refrigerators, there was an "ice plant" in Carrollton. It was located just off West Center Street and near the railroad. Ice would be cut into blocks and sent around to sell to people to be put in their refrigerators. Norwood Weems was the manager of the Carrollton plant. He wanted a light in front of the plant. The Georgia Power Company told him that it would be dangerous to put a light on a pole that was there and they refused to do it. Norwood was determined to have a light there, so he and one of his helpers climbed the pole to try to do the job themselves. They were both electrocuted and died. *Submitted by: Nell Meadows, Maple Street, Carrollton, GA*

246. A Retelling of the Story of Eugenia Dubignon Burke

Miss Neil Meadows, a retired schoolteacher, recalls an interesting story her mother told her as a child when they would take leisurely walks on Carrollton's Spring Street near the City Park.

During the mid 1800's, Carrollton became the home of a reluctant coastal aristocrat, Eugenia DeBignon Burke, whose wealthy family helped settled Jekyll Island. She married Archibald Burke in 1853, and the couple moved to Carrollton, where he opened a law practice. They built a typical plantation-style home on a 300-acre tract that boasted a broad avenue connecting the home to Alabama Street near downtown. Behind the house was a free-flowing spring where Spring Street got its name and where the City Park visits would spark the recollections.

Meadows, who is now 102, and one of only a few Carroll County natives to live in three centuries, says her mother would point to a spot near an old oak tree and say, "That is where Eugenia DuBignon Burke is buried." She would then launch into her account of Eugenia's story:

> Eugenia, the daughter of a wealthy rice plantation owner, was the only Catholic in Carroll County and was looked upon curiously by the aristocracy of this area at the time. She stayed at her home, rarely venturing out. She bore

Archibald Burke three children, including a son who died at an early age.

After the Civil War, the family moved to Texas like many other families of the defeated South. But Eugenia was not with them. She died in Carrollton, but not before a Catholic priest from Savannah came to administer the last sacrament. Legend says the rites were performed at midnight with only the priest in attendance. She was buried on the plantation property alongside her son.

Miss Meadows's knowledge of the story came to be significant many years later when development along Spring Street turned up a tiny coffin with a glass front, revealing the remains of a little boy. "His hair was parted neatly and he looked well preserved." recalls Miss Meadows.

No one knew who the little boy was. The city had him re-interred in the pauper cemetery near the old Alms house. When Miss Meadows read about this, she contacted City Hall officials and told them that he had to be Eugenia DuBignon Burke's son.

"I also let them know she was Catholic and that he should be buried in the Catholic cemetery (Our Lady of Perpetual Help Catholic Church off of Highway 113 north of Carrollton)." He was.

But among the newer homes (compared to an 1850s plantation) Eugenia Burke still lies, buried in a town that she found unfriendly, or one with which she did not want to associate, causing her reclusive behavior. Either way, her story deserves to be a part of Carroll County's rich history. *Submitted by: Julianna Foster*

Some Special Citizens

247. Judge William Charles Adamson: A Big Man Who Did Big Things

The man for whom Carrollton's downtown square is named was a lawyer, judge and congressman whose influence can still be seen on street signs and buildings across the county. His home on Carrollton's West Avenue is marked on city maps as a site of historical interest and is still occupied by a distant relative. Although he was an influential congressman and was referred to as Judge Adamson by most, to many of his relatives, he was simply "Uncle Charlie."

Mary Lovvorn, 89, remembers Judge Adamson as a dinner guest on many occasions at her parents' home. "We had a big rocker, what they called a Morris chair," remembered Lovvorn. "It was a great big leather chair you could lean back on and take a nap. He had dinner with us and he would recline in that chair and talk. He was a great big fellow." Indeed, W.C. Adamson was a big man who did big things.

He was born in 1854 in Bowdon to John Whitfield Adamson and the former Mary Ann McDaniel, who had moved to Carroll from Clayton County shortly after their marriage. John Adamson was both a merchant in Bowdon and a farmer, so the future Judge Adamson was reared in a split environment, part town and part country.

Adamson was the product of a Bowdonian education. He graduated from Bowdon High School and received both a bachelor's degree and a master's degree from Bowdon College where he was valedictorian of his undergraduate class. It was John Adamson who convinced his son to study law. W.C. Adamson studied under Judge Sampson W. Harris and was admitted to the bar in 1876.

Although he loved Bowdon and continued to be a champion of Bowdon College for the rest of his life, Adamson moved down the road to Carrollton to hang up his shingle. He practiced law in the county seat as an attorney and judge for the next 20 years. He was known to discourage litigation except when he believed strongly in his client's case.

Adamson married Minna Reese in 1885. Minna was the daughter of the Rev. A.C. Reese who had served as president pro tem of Bowden College during the Civil War. The pair had three sons: Reese, Ernie, and Charles. The Adamsons were members of the Methodist Protestant Church. Judge Adamson was also a fan of Sacred Harp singing, an acappella singing style that has roots in Carroll County.

In 1896, the people of the Fourth Congressional District decided to send Judge Adamson to Washington. Judge Adamson gave up his law practice and devoted the rest of his life to public service. He remained a Congressman until 1917.

During his time in Congress, Adamson was instrumental in the construction of the Panama Canal and was Chairman of the Committee on Labor. He was pivotal in the creation of the U.S. Department of Labor and authored an act that established an eight-hour work day for railroad workers. His efforts also resulted in a broader exploitation of water power and water transportation in the South.

In 1917, President Woodrow Wilson appointed Adamson to a U.S. Customs judgeship, a position he held for the next decade. Ill health forced him to resign in 1928. He died in Carrollton, January 3, 1929. Judge Adamson is buried in the Carrollton City Cemetery.

Although he had seen the fast-paced Washington life and made his home in Carrollton, Judge Adamson always remained faithful to his Bowdon roots. In addition to serving as a Bowdon College trustee, he attended each academic year's opening and closing ceremonies. The last time he addressed the students of his alma mater, he offered them some advice, culled from a life in the spotlight that had begun years before in the same place those students were sitting.

"Never lose any time," he counseled them. "Read, talk with intelligent people, form no habits but to work, to pray, to save money and respect and love your fellow men." Jonathan Dorsey first published this article in the *Times Georgian* newspaper, May 11, 1997.

248. Jiles Sanford Boggess

Jiles S. Boggess is a name that stands out among Carroll County's earliest pioneers. He was a citizen of Carroll County, Georgia from 1824 until 1842 and during those years, he made valuable contributions to the county's early growth and development. In 1842, Jiles S. Boggess did migrate farther west and eventually settled down in Rusk County, Texas— where he lived to the ripe old age of 84 years. But the effects of his influence had left its mark on Carroll County, Georgia. What was written of him about his effects on Rusk County, Texas in his obituary in *"The Henderson Times"* at the time of his death—19 April 1881—could have also been said of him in his life and times in Carroll County, Georgia.

> "The name of Boggess has long been a household word in Rusk County, Texas ... Having settled here when it was a comparative wilderness, he had much to do in shaping her political and civic affairs. He was a man of great public spirit and enterprise, and on occasions, he took the lead in those things that resulted in good to the people. His kindness of heart, his honor and integrity, his strong conviction of right, backed by firm and good judgment, gave to him the great influence that he always exerted in our midst ... and there are many men among us today whose course in life he had much to do in shaping ... He will always be remembered as a most successful leader and patriot." (Abstracted from *"The Henderson Times."*)

Jiles Sanford Boggess was born 25 April 1797 in Greene County, Tennessee. At the age 15, he enlisted in the War of 1812 under General Andrew Jackson and took part in the Battle of New Orleans. In 1813, there is a record of Jiles S. Boggess on a Muster Roll as a Private in Captain Simeon Perry's Company of Mounted Infantry, East Tennessee Volunteer Militia, Col. Samuel Wear's Regiment. Boggess received pay of $60.80—$8.00 per month plus 40 cents per day allowance for his horse.

At the age of 18 years, he took part in the famous Battle of the Horse Shoe Bend in Alabama. As a volunteer, he served with distinction all through the Creek War. In his pension application of 22 March 1852, Jiles Boggess told of many of his experiences in the savage wars against the Indians. At the close of the war, Jiles Boggess was 20 years old and he married Sarah Bryan in Sevier County, Tennessee on 29 April 1817. Sarah, having been born 8 December 1799 was 18 years old at the time. Sarah was the daughter of Peter and Elizabeth Bryan.

Shortly after their marriage, Jiles and Sarah Boggess moved to Huntsville, Alabama, but by 1824 they had moved to Carroll County, Georgia which was just opening up. Georgia Archive records state that Jiles Boggess built the first house, a log cabin, in Carrollton. Jiles S. Boggess immediately set about trying to tame this wild and wooly frontier of Carroll County—which had just been created out of Indian lands.

The treaty with the Indians made at Indian Springs 12 February 1825 stated that the last of the Creek Indians were to have vacated the land now known as Carroll County by September of 1826. So, Jiles Boggess was among the first white settlers who had moved into this area while the Indians were still here. In the five years surrounding the time of the purchase of Carroll County from the Indians, there are records of about 100 families who lived here. In addition to Jiles S. Boggess were: John Long, E.B. Martin, Needham Jarnigan, Sloman Wynn, A.M. McWhorter, John Robinson, Isaiah Beck, Hiram Sharp, W.M. Stewart, Major W.D. Jones, and the Bonners—Zadock, Thomas and John. Also, William Boone, Thomas and Lindsey Chandler, John Chambers, Joe Little, Levi Benson, William F. Smith, N. Aderhold, Appleton Mandeville, Sanford Kingsberry, William Washington Merrell, James S. Baskin, William Beall, Isaac E. Cobb, Benjamin Merrell, Lee Bird, and many others.

Unfortunately, there was a lawless element in the county and they banded themselves together in what was called "the Pony Club". This club was expressly for the purpose of stealing horses and slipping them out of the county. They had established a system whereby one man stole the horse and quickly turned it over to another member. Then the horse thief would return home where another member of the "pony club" would help him to establish an ironclad alibi. The other man would quickly transfer the stolen horse over to the person paying for the horse—and then, too, he could return safely home with another "pony club" member vouching for his perfect alibi.

This made it very hard on the law abiding citizens— and horses were quite valuable in those days. To steal a man's horse was a terrible crime indeed. Finally, the citizens banded themselves together into a club they called "The Slicks". They set out to try to get rid of the lawbreakers and the horse thieves. In 1832 the "Pony Club" members became engaged in a desperate street fight with "The Slicks" on the public square in Carrollton. Fists, rocks, and clubs were used. Sloman Wynn was the Captian of the Slicks but in this battle, the representatives of law and order were led by Jiles S. Boggess who was then the Sheriff of Carroll County. "Might for right" was victorious. At the next session of the Grand Jury, some members of the defeated "Pony Club" charged Boggess and his associates with assault and intent to murder. Instead of bringing true bills, however, the jury expressed its gratitude to Boggess for his efforts to banish crime in the community. Jiles Boggess was re-elected to serve several terms as Sheriff of Carroll County.

It was the following year in 1833 when all the militia companies in the counties of Carroll, Coweta, and Campbell were designed as the 2nd Brigade of the 9th Division of the Georgia Militia. Carroll County's contingent became the 74th with Jiles Boggess as its Colonel. This militia was organized to move the Indians from the Georgia lands to Arkansas.

Jiles S. Boggess was elected to the Senate from Carroll County three different times serving between 1834-1837. He is said to have made a brilliant record as a leader of democracy in the State Legislature of Georgia. Boggess also constructed a tavern on the square in Carrollton which had become the center of commercial life in the county. This tavern faced the square at the north side of Newnan Street. Later, Boggess erected the first hotel which was later managed by John Long. Jiles S. Boggess was one of the seven members of the Board of Education along with Appleton Mandeville.

Jiles Boggess and Emmanuel Martin purchased a lot on the town commons of LaGrange on 5 November 1835 for $250.00. This was only one of many land purchases—which was sold later for a profit. Then, between 1836-1845, Jiles Boggess obtained a U.S. government mail contract to carry express mail by stage from Milledgeville, Georgia to Columbus, Georgia to Montgomery, Alabama. Later on, Boggess would operate a stage between Augusta, Georgia and Montgomery, Alabama. In the 1842 tax list of Carroll County, Georgia, Boggess is listed as owning in excess of 6000 acres of land in various parts of Georgia. By 1844, Boggess had sold about 2000 acres of this land—now listing 4800 acres.

During these years, Jiles and Sarah Boggess watched their family grow along with Carroll County. Their first child was Ahaz J. Boggess b. ca. 1819 in Tennessee. Bennett Boggess was b. 29 June 1820. Jane Evaline Boggess was born 29 September 1821 d. 29 September 1900 in Kaufman County, Texas. Mary Elizabeth Boggess was born 1822 and married William Henry Benson. Nicholas R. Boggess was born 12 February 1825 d. 8 October 1835, buried Meigs County, Tennessee. Jiles Sanford Boggess, Jr. was born 16 July 1827 m. Elizabeth and buried in Rusk County, Texas. Milton Marion Boggess was born 20 September 1830 in Carroll County, Georgia. Vashti J. Boggess was born about 1834 in Carroll County, Georgia and married James William Parr on 29 April 1869 in Rusk County, Texas. (J.W. Parr was born 29 August 1839 in Kentucky, d. 17 October 1906 in Texas). William Fannin Boggess was born 22 January 1836 in Carroll County, Georgia, died tragically when shot by a stray bullet at a circus in 1857 at the age of 21. Ruth E. Boggess was born about 1839, buried in Rusk County, Texas. Brazilla Bryan Boggess was born 27 September 1842 in Carroll County, Georgia.

William Fannin Boggess' wife's name is unknown, but he was the father of a little daughter named Adelia Eglentine Boggess. This little girl was adopted by her grandfather, Jiles S. Boggess on 7 January 1881. This was only a short time before his death since Jiles Boggess died on 19 April 1881.

About 1842, Jiles S. Boggess moved his family from Carroll County, Georgia and briefly settled in Goldville, Tallapoosa County, Alabama. For about three years, he was involved in a mining venture. From Goldville, the Boggess family moved to Wetumpka, Alabama but stayed there only long enough to settle up affairs. In 1847, Jiles Boggess moved to Henderson, Texas which is in Rusk County. He was elected Assessor of Taxes twice and was appointed by Governor Pease to lead a company of cavalry for frontier purposes. There at the age of 48, Jiles Boggess led the Texas Rangers against the wild Commanche Indians of the southwest. Boggess remained in command of this company until it was mustered into the service of the U.S. Cavalry.

At the time the Civil War came along, the Boggess family continued to live in Henderson, Texas on a plantation which was located about 5 miles west of the Courthouse. Jiles S. Boggess was about 67 years old by then. In 1864 when it appeared that the invasion of Texas was imminent, Boggess raised a company of old men volunteers and went in command of the company to Mansfield, Louisiana. He was described as "a man of powerful physical endurance who retained up to a late period of his life a strong mind and sound judgment."

All the Boggess sons—Jiles, Jr., Milton M. and Brazilla— "made news" during the Civil War. Milton was a Captain of a Company organized in Rusk, County and Jiles, Jr. was a Lt. Colonel during the war. According to family history, a daughter, Ruth Boggess even served the Confederacy as a spy. Another daughter, Mary Elizabeth Boggess, was married to a Confederate soldier, William Henry Benson. The son Bennett Boggess became a leading man in Henderson, Texas and owned the first livery stable there. By the 1880 census, Jiles Boggess is shown as 83 years old and is serving as "the County Constable." He was given a title of respect and called "Colonel Boggess" in his later years. In 1998, several of his descendants were still living on his original property in Texas.

Jiles Sanford Boggess died on 19 April 1881 and was buried in the old city cemetery in Henderson, Texas. His wife, Sarah, had preceded him in death as she had died on 27 January 1875. Many other members of the Boggess family are buried in this same cemetery in Texas. Jiles Sanford Boggess— a name of importance to be remembered in the history of early Carroll County—"a mover and a shaker wherever he lived"—and a patriot devoted to his country from a very early age indeed.

He married Sarah Myriam Bryan on 29 April 1817 in Sevier County, Tennessee. Sarah was born 8 December 1799. *Submitted by: Jan Robinson Bell*

249. Susan Hayward Chalkley

One of the most exciting chapters in the history of Carrollton was during the years 1957-1966 when the beautiful and vivacious movie star, Susan Hayward Chalkley, lived here with her husband Floyd Eaton Chalkley. When Susan Hayward Chalkley returned home to Carrollton in 1959 after winning the Academy Award for her performance in the movie "I Want To Live", she made this statement: "I've never really had a hometown before, but I do now." Mrs. Chalkley, as she preferred to be called, always said that the people of Carrollton were "her kind of people."

Susan's son, Timothy Barker, would later say that his mother had loved Carrollton so much because the people here were sincere and honest. "People here say what they mean, and that's the way my mother was—she was a straight-shooter—" Tim said in his interview with the *Times Free Press* of March 18, 1975. Mrs. Chalkley didn't put on any airs about being one of America's most famous movie stars. She could often be seen dressed in her pedal pushers, hair tied up with a scarf, driving around in her pick up truck. But Susan was still beautiful—she didn't need the makeup men of Hollywood to create any illusions about that!

Tim went on to say in his interview that his mother had grown up in poverty of the Depression years herself so she really identified with the hard working people of Carrollton. She enjoyed being away from the flash bulbs and the fanfare of Hollywood—and here she could just be a simple housewife and mother to her young children. Her twin sons, Timothy "Tim" Marrenner Barker and Gregory "Greg" Marrenner Barker (born on February 17, 1945) spent some of their most formative years growing up in Carrollton. Susan Hayward Chalkley much appreciated the fact that Carrollton never tried to take advantage of her fame to "use" in some way for the community. People just let her be herself and enjoy her privacy.

Susan Hayward was born Edythe Marrenner June 30, 1919 in Brooklyn, New York, the third child of Walter and Ellen F. Marrenner. The new baby had a shock of beautiful red hair that would become her famous trademark. Ellen F. Pearson's family had migrated to America from Skane, Sweden and Ellen was the daughter of Theodore Pearson, an enterprising businessman of Brooklyn, New York. Ellen F. Pearson was born 10 October 1888 and she had three brothers and six sisters—Theodore, Jr., Oscar, Guy, Lillian, Alice, Jenny, Emma, and twin girls who died in infancy.

Walter Marrenner was the son of Joseph Marrenner and Katherine Harrigan, Irish Catholics who also lived in Brooklyn. When Ellen Pearson first met Walter Marrenner, she was working as a stenographer and Walter was a dashing red-headed Coney Island barker. Apparently, Ellen and Walter met with some family disapproval — due to the differences in religion—so Walter Marrenner and Ellen Pearson eloped to be married on 14 August 1909. Their first child was a daughter named Florence born 29 May 1910. A son, Walter Marrenner, Jr. was born on 8 December 1911. The third child, Edythe, made her appearance on 30 June 1917—and shortly after birth, someone placed a shiny new dime in the baby's little hand—in keeping with family tradition.

When Edythe was seven years old, she was hit by a car and suffered a broken hip. She was confined to bed for many months and had to hobble about on crutches for even longer. Edythe would say in later years that it was this early experience that probably helped to develop her into an actress. Lying in bed for so long, she had to use her imagination in order to entertain herself. When Edythe was ten years

Picture of Susan Hayward receiving the key to the city from Mayor Stewart Martin

old, her teacher, Miss Rappaport, gave her much encouragement for her acting abilities in the school play. One of the young boys that Edythe struck up a friendship with in school play at her grammar school was a young man named Ira Grossel. He would later gain fame in Hollywood as the movie star "Jeff Chandler".

Edythe continued to be encouraged by teachers for her acting abilities and she would always take the parts that nobody else wanted—like the toothless old hag—that might have more opportunities for developing dramatic skills. At the time, Barbara Stanwyck was Edythe's movie idol—partly because "Barbara Stanwyck" had been Ruby Stevens of Brooklyn. And Edythe felt if Barbara could rise to stardom above a background in Brooklyn, that she could do the same. Edythe would practice talking like Barbara Stanwyck to try to lose her Brooklyn accent. Edythe didn't really want to be "just a movie star"—she really wanted to be known as a "movie actress." When she graduated from high school in 1935, her yearbook noted that she had achieved honors in math, sciences, and arts and in Dramatic Club she was—"one of our prize actresses."

Shortly after high school, Edythe began her modeling career—she was a stunning beautiful girl. In this way she earned money to pay for attending Drama School. Edythe's flaming red hair turned out to be a real advantage to her as a model since color photography was just becoming popular. That flaming red hair really made her stand out. Edythe appeared on the cover of the magazine, *"The Saturday Evening Post"* and this was certainly a feather in her cap. Edythe would often model hats since they were the fashion rage of that era.

Edythe had a lucky break when Walter Thornton chose her to represent the Thornton Modeling Agency in a Vitaphone movie being made about girls looking for jobs as models in New York. This was the very first time that Edythe Marrenner had been placed before the movie cameras. This one opportunity was enough to convince her that this was exactly where she needed to be—and that her future lay in Hollywood. She saved every penny she made to try to build up a tasteful wardrobe—one that would help make a good impression when she went to apply for a job.

By 1937, Edythe had acquired an air of sophistication and the wardrobe to go along with it—and photographers remembered her and would ask specifically for her on modeling jobs. One early photographer said of her, "It was her self-confidence that made you remember her—she swept into the studio as if she owned the place." It was this characteristic that would help propel Edythe Marranner to fame in Hollywood.

When Edythe was 19 years old, she boarded a train to go to Hollywood to do a screen test for the part of Scarlett O'Hara. She didn't win the part, but Warner's gave her a contract. They changed her name to Susan Hayward—and the rest is movie history. During her long movie career, she appeared in more than 50 major films and was nominated for Best Actress five times. In 1959 she won the coveted Oscar for Best Movie Actress for her portrayal of a woman convicted of murder and sent to the gas chamber in "I Want To Live". Susan became the "box-office queen" of Twentieth-Century Fox. Even after she lost the title in 1952 to Marilyn Monroe, Susan's movies continued to be top-moneymakers. Susan's last motion picture was made in 1971 but she did continue to make some movies for television.

In 1943, Susan Hayward had met Jess Barker, also a Hollywood actor, whom she later married on 23 July 1944. Together they would have the twin sons—Tim and Greg—and no other children. Their relationship seemed to be rather stormy from the beginning and the marriage ended in divorce about ten years later. The boys kept up a good relationship with both mother and father—and both Jess and Susan continued to make films in Hollywood.

Susan Hayward met Eaton Chalkley about 1956 when they were introduced by Harvey Hester, the owner of the famous Atlanta restaurant "Aunt Fanny's Cabin". Chalkley was a native of Virginia and had worked for the FBI at one time. He was divorced and had two daughters and a son. In 1956, Chalkley had been living in Carrollton about three years and was the owner of the Chevrolet-Oldsmobile-Cadillac dealership in town. (At that time, it was located next to the old Carroll Theatre on Newnan Street.) Susan and Eaton became close friends and in 1957, Susan made her first trip to Carrollton to visit with Eaton and his family—his mother, Alma, and his sister and brother-in-law, Margaret and Matthew Irwin. On February 8, 1957, Susan Hayward and Eaton Chalkley married in Phoenix, Arizona.

When they returned to Carrollton, the Chalkleys were feted with a reception at the Carrollton B&PW Club, hosted by Margaret and Matthew Irwin. Mrs. C.L. Zachry, Mrs. Otis Smith, Mrs. W.T. Green and Mrs. Dick Newell presided over the silver services. Others assisting in entertaining were James Upchurch, Tom Martin, Bill Warren, Cal Parker, Robert Griffin, Frank Rose, Ned Blackman and Mrs. Hadley Allen of Bremen. (*The Times Free Press*, Tuesday, March 5, 1957.)

The Chalkleys built a beautiful home located about seven miles north of Carrollton just off the Temple Road. The lakeside home was filled with awards that Susan had received over the years for her dramatic art. Many will remember the beautiful black fences which enclosed the rolling green hills that surrounded the Chalkley property. Both Susan and Eaton loved horses and the horses were often seen grazing in the pastures there.

The Chalkmar farm in Heflin, Alabama had about 225 head of cattle and the farm was ably managed by Guy Carrington. Susan once bought a white faced bull for about $30,000. That bull's calf, named "Susan's Pride", and a thoroughbred Palamino named "Texas Sunset" were Susan's personal pets. Susan had always said that some of her favorite movies to make were westerns. She also loved to make movies about the South.

Susan's twin sons, Tim and Greg Barker, would often visit the Chalkley farm at Heflin. "It's wonderful there for them," Susan would say in a newspaper interview. "They have horses to ride, woods to explore, streams and lakes to fish in." Tim and Greg would spend time on the farm when they were not at school, which was the Georgia Military Academy. As for future plans of their lives, Tim seemed to favor going to Hollywood to study cinematography while Greg was more interested in becoming a veterinarian. Eaton Chalkley's son, Joseph, from a previous marriage, tragically died in a plane crash in West Virginia in 1964.

The Chalkleys would later donate land and funds towards the building of a new Catholic Church—the same one we have today—located not far from the Chalkley home. Since 1953, the Catholics had worshipped in an old 1893 church building—really inadequate to the needs of the growing congregation—until the Chalkleys donated the land for the new Our Lady of Perpetual Help. The first service was held at the new Our Lady in 1962. In 1964, after the assassination of President John F. Kennedy, the old 1893 church building was moved to the West Georgia College campus to be used as a chapel for all faiths—and it was named in honor of the slain 36th President. Kennedy Chapel remains on the campus today—and many students have been married in the quaint old church. Robert F. Kennedy came to Carrollton on 27 May 1964 for the dedication of the chapel in honor of his brother.

Mrs. Eaton Chalkley became an important part of the community of Carrollton during the years that she spent here. Of course, she still spent time in Hollywood because she was still under contract to continue making movies—but then she'd be "home again" to Carrollton. She shared her time and talent in helping to fund the new addition to Tanner Memorial Hospital, and took part in the promotion of the Neva Lomason Library Festival—Tournament of Books. Edith Foster, Director of the Library, adored Susan Hayward and especially when she allowed Edith to come into her home after the death of Eaton Chalkley and select any books and records that she might want to add to the library collection.

Susan Hayward also made a film—"Susan Hayward Invites You to Georgia"—to promote the state and its scenic attractions. Even though J. Ebb Duncan—who was the Senator from our district at that time, and Alpha Fowler of Douglasville, offered Susan Hayward $100,000 to star in the film—she would not accept one penny. The $100,000 went towards financing the movie instead. "Very few people are aware of the great favor that Susan Hayward did for the State of Georgia in making this film" said Senator Duncan. "She traveled all over the state of Georgia—at her own expense—and furnished her own hair-stylist and makeup artist to travel with her." The film premiered at J. Ebb Duncan's Carroll Theatre in Carrollton which used to be located where the Confederate Monument now stands.

The film showed Susan Hayward touring such places as Callaway Gardens, Stone Mountain, the Okefenokee Swamp and other places of interest. The film was shown continuously at the Georgia exhibit at the World's Fair in Seattle. After the film made the tour of theatres around the state, it was then shown to more than 1700 school and civic groups. For donating her time and talent in this generous way, Susan Hayward Chalkley was honored by the Georgia General Assembly, the Southeastern Theater Owners, and Georgia Theatre Owners.

The Chalkleys also formed a corporation which would handle a variety of business ventures—one of them was to make movies and records. One of their very first projects was the making of the 1958 movie that won Susan Hayward the Oscar—"I Want To Live." The other actors competing for the award that year were Shirley MacLaine, Deborah Kerr, Elizabeth Taylor, and Rosalind Russell. Twentieth Century Fox also sponsored the movie along with "Carrollton, Inc." which was the name of the Chalkley corporation. Eaton Chalkley's sister, Mrs. Margaret Irwin, also owned a part of the corporation. Winning the Oscar gave the movie an extra bonus of one million dollars.

Upon the Chalkley's return to Carrollton from the 31st Academy Awards in Hollywood, a delegation of local citizens of Carrollton went to the Atlanta airport to greet them. A brief ceremony was held at the airport and then the motorcade accompanied the couple all the way back to Carrollton and to Chalkley Motor Company. There, Carrollton Mayor, Stewart Martin, as master of ceremonies, presented the beautiful Susan Hayward Chalkley with the key to the City of Carrollton.

In 1959, Eaton Chalkley sold his automobile dealership to Joe Whit Walker and Willard Moore and it became known as the Walker-Moore dealership after that. The Chalkleys continued to enjoy their 200 acre farm in Heflin and also maintained a winter home in Ft. Lauderdale, Florida as well as the home in Carrollton. It was during a visit to this winter home that Eaton Chalkley died on January 9, 1966. He was brought "home" to Carrollton and laid to rest at Our Lady of Perpetual Help Catholic Church cemetery. His gravestone faced the home that he and Susan had shared.

Though Susan Hayward had loved Carrollton, after Eaton's death, the memories were too painful to continue living in the home where they had been so happy together. So, Susan sold the cattle ranch and the Carrollton property in 1966 and then moved to her residence in Ft. Lauderdale. She lived for many years very quietly there. Her son Tim served as a Green Beret in Greece, Turkey, and Cambodia. Her son Greg graduated from Auburn University in 1969 with a degree in Veterinary Medicine.

In 1971, Susan finally took note of the popular "Movies of the Week" that were coming into vogue. She also noticed that many of the older movie actresses were being given starring roles in them. She liked the idea of a comeback—and was happy to accept when she was asked to replace Barbara Stanwyck in a "Movie of the Week" that was in production. Soon, she'd signed a contract to do several of these movies for television. But she only lived long enough to complete one of them—"Say Goodbye, Maggie Cole" was her last movie. Susan learned that she had multiple inoperable brain tumors and that she only had a few months to live.

Still, Susan kept her same courage and spirit—and even attended the 1974 Academy Awards to be a presenter of the Oscars. She was elegant in her green sequined gown and would be remembered this way—it was to be her last public appearance. On March 14, 1975, Susan Hayward Chalkley died exactly 37 years to the day from when her own father had died. She was laid to rest alongside her husband Eaton Chalkley (1909-1966) in the Our Lady Catholic Cemetery—in the red clay of Georgia—on the properly she and Eaton had donated to the Catholic Church many years ago.

Her tombstone reads simply "Mrs. F.E. Chalkley 1917-1975." In later years, someone placed a little wooden marker on the grave to read "Susan Hayward Chalkley" because so many people came to the cemetery trying to locate the grave and could not find it. The people of Carrollton will always fondly remember the beautiful and vivacious Susan Hayward Chalkley—and though she was not born a Southerner—she did have the fire and the spark—and the heart of a Southerner. She was a very great lady indeed.

Submitted by: Jan Robinson Bell

Sources: *Susan Hayward: Portrait of a Survivor* by Beverly Linet; *Time Free Press* newspapers; *The Washington Post* and *Times Herald* newspaper, November 19, 1958 and April 7, 1959; The *Evening Star* newspaper February 10, 1959; Interview with Margaret Chalkley Irwin and Matthew Benedict Irwin *The History of Virginia*

Picture of Susan Hayward at Anne Warren's birthday party in 1958

250. David Clopton, Carroll County Gold Miner

The following is an excerpt from *The Clopton Chronicles, the Ancestors and Descendants of Sir Thomas Clopton, Knight & Dame Katherine Mylde.* The Clopton Family Genealogical Society holds the copyright on this material.

The early part of nineteenth century found three high spirited sons of David and Mary Ann Clopton in Georgia. The early years were good to Alfred, David and Albert Clopton. Gold was discovered as early as 1826 in Villa Rica, Georgia, and David was among Carroll County first gold miners and settlers. A Clopton Goldmining Company was still operating as late as 1895, producing gold and quartz.

It isn't clear who owned this gold mining company in 1895. *"The Carroll Free Press,"* on September 6, 1895, reports that the Clopton Goldmining Company had finished and put into operation a large Huntington mill, 5 stories high. In an 1896 geological survey of Georgia it is reported that the Clopton property is in the vicinity of Villa Rica. It was located on lot 194, 3rd district and was in the hands of a Boston Company. It had recently completed some work, including a new mill of recent patent. In *Gold Deposits of Georgia*, by S.P. Jones, a 1909 geological survey of Georgia, quotes Mr. Clarke Watkins, of Villa Rica, who was familiar with the history of most of the gold mines of that portion of the Carroll County belt, about thirteen hundred pennyweights of gold were obtained at this locality from a cut of comparatively insignificant size. The mine was located on lot 194, 6th district, "a short distance to the northeast of the Chambers mine." David Clopton earned his first fortune from this gold mine.

In 1850 only ten percent of the population of Georgia owned slaves. David owned nineteen, which is one indication of his wealth. Although the gold mine may have produced the funds necessary to initially purchase slaves, mining was back breaking and no doubt David worked very hard. In her *History of Villa Rica*, [8] Mary Talley Anderson describes the process used in Georgia. (Mary Talley Anderson, *The History of Villa Rica (City of Gold)*, Villa Rica, Georgia Bicentennial committee, 1976, p. 4)

> "From 1830 to 1840 the prospectors worked extensively. It is said that for the first ten years not less then 20,000 pennyweights were taken out annually.
>
> All mining was done until around 1840 by simply panning. A vessel was used, generally shaped like a long-handled skillet. It was imperative that the vessel be free from all grease, so it is not likely that the miners good wife was permitted to use it for cooking purposes, no matter how short she may have been on cook utensils. Into this vessel the sand, gravel, and gold was poured together with water. Grasping the vessel firmly with both hands, back and forth, the miner worked, as though he were sifting meal, with the water, sand and gravel spilling over the sides of the vessel. Again and again, he renewed the water until nothing remained but the gold dust which settled to the bottom of the vessel ...
>
> The next method of mining employed was the "Rocker Process." Rockers were made of hollowed out logs and lined with copper in which holes so small as to appear almost negligible were made. Into this rocker the sand, gravel and gold were poured together with water. Two men caught either end and rocked it back and forth, very much as women used to rock their babies in cradles. Again and again they replenished the water until the gold was thoroughly washed and

adhered to the copper lining of the rocker. This method was favored over the Sluice Box process as it was difficult to obtain sufficient water to operate these boxes, since dams had to be built on elevated ground to catch rain water for washing the gold."

Little mining was done after 1844, and it appears that David had moved to Polk and Paulding Counties and became a planter. Polk and Paulding Counties were swept up in the fight for Atlanta. Marauding rogue Yankee soldiers plagued the area for months. Richard J. Lenz, *The Civil War In Georgia*, Infinity Press, Watkinsville, Georgia, 1995, p. 33 notes that on May 27, 1864, the Yankees suffered a humiliating defeat against the Confederates at Pickett's Mill Creek in Paulding County.

"In the Battle of Picket's Mill, Sherman ordered three brigades to attempt a flank attack of the Confederate line. Johnston anticipated the Union move and placed Confederates under Patrick Cleburne at the end of his line. The attacks were poorly coordinated and the Yankee brigades got lost in the dense forest and deep ravines."

When they emerged the Confederated engaged them, and

"the Rebel fire swept the ground like a hailstorm."

Pickett's Mill is considered one of the best preserved Civil War battlefields in the nation and represents one of the few Confederate victories in the Atlanta Campaign.

By the beginning of the War Between the States, approximately forty-four percent of the entire population of Georgia was composed of slaves. While much has been made of the sacrifices and hardships of white women in protecting the plantations, far too little attention has been paid to the sometimes courageous roles played by loyal slaves who risked life and limb for their masters. It has become fashionable in some circles to poop-pooh the very notion there existed mutual feelings of love, loyalty and devotion between master and slave, however, several letters written by David Clopton to a friend brilliantly illustrates a complex and trusting relationship between himself and a slave named Edy. As Sherman's troops pushed into Georgia, David, entrusting his plantation to his loyal slave, Edy, went to hiding. With the Yankees breathing down her neck and her master gone, Edy displayed remarkable calm and forethought as she went about attempting to hide valuables.

Although David Clopton was an elderly man, the Yankees were rounding up any male who was able bodied enough to put up a fight or intelligent enough to organize new companies, albeit composed of the very young and the very old.

The following letters written by David Clopton were sent to Fanny Hargrove Carson. She was the daughter of Bright W. Hargrove of Villa Rica. He was one of three Carroll County delegates to Georgia's 1861 Secession Convention. These letters are part of the Hargrave Family Papers, Annie Belle Weaver Special Collections, Ingram Library, State University of West Georgia.

March 21st, 1865
Dear Fanny;

Your letter of 12th of last month came to hand a few days back, and as Mr. McClure is with me and will leave in the morning for the low country I will send this by him. If I mail it here it is very uncertain whether you will ever get it. I will not attempt to give you a history of my ups and downs since I saw you; it would take a volume. I will only say I left home Saturday before the Yankees came on Monday. I did expect they would get here on Sunday morning from what I had heard.

They robbed my house, took a part of my meat and corn, and broke up things generally. They found the box containing your bedclothes, etc. and took most of your things, scattered your books all over the yard, robbed Edy of her money and the most of her fine clothes and took many things from the rest of the Negroes. Your box was under Edy's bed. She thought, and was told that Yankees would not rob Negroes. Edy sent Mr. Pentecost's trunk to Patience's house and had it hid, but they found it and took out all his clothes.

I camped out in the woods for five or six weeks, thinking the Yankees would be driven back. I then left the country and landed down in Chambers County, Alabama, where I staid until sometime in September when I thought I would come home and see if I had anything left.

I found the Negroes had not worked one week all put together. They did cut a little wheat but let it get spoiled. I had been but a short time at home when the Yankees moved up from Stilesborough and for weeks they were camped on this side of the Van Wert and raiding through here every day. They passed my house many times but paid no attention to me. They stripped my house again of everything they wanted and left me almost without anything to keep house on. I have but two old broken knives and forks and would have been without bedclothes to sleep under had not Edy patched up a comfort or two.

The Yankee army has passed twice through here and our army once. The deserters and stragglers of our army have been in here all the summer and all together they have left this country almost destitute of anything for the people to live on.

They have taken five horses from me, about 80 heard of hogs, and everything in the shape of a cow I had on the place and fully half of what little corn that was made. I am now without syrup, without milk, and have only corn and meat enough to last me half the summer.

But I am better off than some of my neighbors. There is poor Kingsbury had every pound of meat, and every bushel of corn, every horse, cow, hog, and chicken taken; the house stripped of everything they could carry off and he and his family left with only the clothes they had on, without one mouthful to eat. And he is not alone. Dodds and some others here left in the same fix.

The Negroes I took off with me, I left in Alabama working for their victuals and clothes. I could not feed them if I had them here. The families of Seaborn Jones and Geo. Rentz have just reached home. I don't know where they will live. I was at Seaborn's a few weeks since and he and Mr. Rentz were living on two scanty meals a day and as for their Negroes, they did not taste of meat.

I have lost four Negroes since you left. Jesse and Big Joe sickened and died. Adaline took fire with her child in her arms and they both got burnt so badly that she died the second night after.

I am glad to know you have got a good place among kind and friendly people. You have ample means to pay your way and I would advise you to stay there, and not think of coming to this destitute country. It is not the country it was when you left — everything wears a gloomy aspect — everyone stays at home and we see nobody passing unless it some poor refugee slowly wending his way to his devastated home.

How is it, Fanny, you bear your misfortune with so little fortitude so little patience? There are many who have been equally, or more, unfortunate than you have been whose situation is far worse than yours and they became reconciled after the lapse of time.

It is useless, Fanny, to attempt to resist the degrees of Providence — you can't do it. We all have to submit to fate and it is well for us if we can do it cheerfully.

I have received a letter from Martha — that first I've received in twelve months. They all seem to be getting on well — everything quiet there.

Your friend,

David Clopton

Nineteen days later, on April 9, Lee surrendered to Grant at Appomattox Court House, Virginia. The last Confederate forces in Georgia would surrender at Kingston May 12.

However, Martha was apparently an adopted daughter. David Clopton of Polk County on February 20, 1854, adopted Martha Jenkins Ellington and changed her name to Martha Jenkins Clopton. The 1850 Georgia census shows David, aged 53, living with Martha, aged 13.

Daugertype of Fannie Hargrave, GA, seated on left, Clopton's letters were to her

Unfortunately for Fanny, by fleeing to Ogtelhorpe, she jumped from the frying pan into the fire. Ogtelhorpe, located in Macon County, is just north of the infamous Andersonville Prison. On March 22, one day after David had penned this letter, Union General James H. Wilson led the Civil War's largest cavalry force, Wilson's Raiders, in a raid against the heart of Georgia and Alabama.

Finally the long War came to an end. Approximately 130,000 Georgians answered the call. By war's end, over 11,000 of Her sons, husbands and fathers lay dead. Life went on as the South as people attempted to pick up the pieces. Everything was pretty much in shambles throughout Georgia, and David plodded through the days and tried to maintain the plantation as best he could.

July 15th 1866

Dear Fanny

Don't be uneasy I will send your things in a short time. I have been a little careless about sending of them, but I knew what the Yankees left were all safe and did not expect you stood in need of them. Besides you have no conception of the difficulty of getting any little job done in this country — (that is at a fair price). I don't suppose I could get a box hauled from this place to Van Wert only one mile for less than two dollars and if I had have sent your box off before this I should have had to hire a two horse wagon at five dollars a day to haul it. Now I can send it by the State Waggons at 50 cents pr. Hundred. The first man I can find who can or will make a box I'll hire him and send you things off — One Box will hold them — I have got Mr. Carson's clothes & watch from Cedar Town.

I have heard nothing from your people for a long time, got a letter from Martha dated 12th May, all well — looking for another —

In haste your friend

David Clopton

Write me how you are etc.

Van Wert Sept. 7th 1866

Dear Fanny:

I have sent the Box containing your Bed and Bed Clothes to Cartersville expressed to you, sent word to Alfred Williams to see it off right. I had the Box fixed up without knowing exactly what you had to send —there is less than I thought and consequently the Box is too large but I hope they will not injure on that account. Your Bed has certainly been robbed. Edy says she thinks it was done by some of the Negroes on the place and not by Patience, but I don't know I did not like the answer Patience gave when Edy asked her about the Bolster & pillows. It remained in Patience's hands a good while after the Yankees collected their Negroes on the place. I ought to have been more particular and got the Bed out of P's care before I came away from the old place. But if you could know Fanny the trouble and care I have labored under you would excuse. The fact is I have lost & lost until I looked upon everything as lost. You may live to see things come right again, and get over the troubles that have been on us for the last five years but I never can. I have saved enough to live on in my plain and saving way if I can keep it — but there is the rub, I feel that nothing is safe, and what may yet esall me in my old age, heaven only knows. I am truly glad Fanny that you are married and to a man that will in all probability take care of you, and amidst your many sources of grief you can feel that Providence has not entirely forsaken you. I see by your last letter that you have noticed in some of my previous letters that I did not request you to write to me or answer my letters. I am sorry you are so particular — for I did think you knew me well enough to know that I would be at all times glad to hear from you. You also know my careless way of writing letters - Don't Fanny, give me any reason to believe you doubt my friendship.

I heard from Martha a few days since, her letter was dated the 17th of last month, she was well but one of her children had the chills. She says the crops are almost a failure in that section and that the Negroes who are working on our place will make but little if anything over a bare support but our crop is as good as any in the neighborhood. Martha appeared to be in rather lower spirits than usual when she wrote. Do you ever hear anything from Mollie these days. Perses Kingsbury told me day before yesterday she had just received a letter from Mollie and said she did not know what to make of her — there was several by, but the next time se Perses I will make her tell me all about it. Perses & Bate Jones is very friendly and I think Mollie writes to her thinking she may yet hear something from Bate favorable. There is nothing stirring in the neighborhood, no life, but little visiting, everybody and everything seems down, down, nobody has any money and the little crop that is making has cost the people more to make it than it will bring after it is made. The general cry is what are the people to do the next year. The Negroes have to be fed, and horses furnished them and fed in making another crop and most or many of the farmers will not have the means of doing it, either in provisions or money. And many of the poorer people who has been rationed by the government this year seems to think that government will feed always and have made but little effort to provide for the next year. What then is to become of the Negroes & poor whites is the great question of the day.

I said everybody was dull, there [was] a party at Bob Jones a short ago. The Miss Mores from Alabama has been staying with Mrs. Rentz a week or two, they did not seem disposed to stay with Bob & Malisa although their father had done them many flavors & was very kind to Bob & Malisa when they refugeed to Ala. So Malisa concluded to give them a party and invite the neighborhood. There was some 15 to 20 at the party. Malisa spread herself — had everything in great stile — everything done up according to the latest stile & fashion, but from what I have been told the thing passed off rather dull. Bate says they went before they got their suppers and when the supper came on it consisted of nothing but cake, candies etc. etc. and it was ill suited to the apatites of a hungry crowd -no coffee, no tea, no meats, but it was all very fine and that suited Malisa — Yes & Bob. I was not invited and I am glad of it for I know Bob's feelings are quite cool toward me and I should not have felt easy had I been there. You see I hold a note on Hems estate for about five thousand dollars and as they would not make any satisfactory arrangement about it I sued Bob and ever since he has appeared cool. I am glad of it, for it always kept me under a strain to keep in with him.

Well, as Edy wants the table to set for dinner I must stop — write me when you get this & believe me your friend

David Clopton

We hear no more from David. He was to die only a few years after the War ended. Nothing is known about his adopted daughter nor the fate of his devoted Edy. *Submitted by: Carol Elizabeth Scott and Suellen Clopton Blanton*

251. Pvt. Joe Cobb

Joseph L. Cobb was the sixth son and eighth child of Isaac E. Cobb. Isaac moved to Carroll County in 1828 and is reported to have built the first store in Carrollton on the north side of the square. He later moved to the Buckhorn Tavern area near Temple. He died in August 1852 and was buried at Old Bethel Primitive Baptist Church.

After the war, Joe Cobb came home and married Augusta Grow in 1868. They had two children, Hugh B and Joseph. Joe is best known for writing a series of articles for the *Villa Rica Star* and then later publishing a history, *Carroll County and Her People.* Along with Leon P. Mandeville, he is responsible for saving much of the county's early history.

Although known as Pvt. J.L. Cobb, he became Sergeant Major in Camp A. Wheeler's United Confederate Veterans. He was very proud of his roots and his heritage. From *Carroll County and Her People* he recalled,

"I was with General Wheeler on his celebrated raid from Atlanta through the mountains of Georgia, east and middle Tennessee in 1864. For six months I was a courier for General Wheeler and carried dispatches for him. At one time, I remember, near Philadelphia, Tenn., I was sent with a verbal message to General Wheeler that cavalry was about to capture a wagon train. Going through the clover fields on my horse I rode up to the side of Gen. Wheeler and delivered the message. He was sitting on his horse in the square near the courthouse. He gave the command and the bugler sounded the summons for the 2nd Georgia, which was held in reserve, and the regiment charged the enemy, General Wheeler leading the charge, and I, a sixteen-year-old boy had the honor of charging by his side. We saved the wagon train. I was with General Wheeler in all the campaigns in Georgia, Tennessee, Alabama, South Carolina and North Carolina until Greensboro, when we surrendered. After the surrender my regiment, the First Georgia cavalry, was formed in a square. General Wheeler rode to the center of the square, dismounted from his horse and taking off his hat said: "My brave boys, you did your duty. The war is over. I beg you to return to your homes and live quiet peaceable citizens."

Private Joe Cobb

Pvt. Cobb returned home and became a highly respected citizen. Pvt. Joseph L. Cobb deserves a great gratitude from the citizens of this county for preserving much of our early history. If you are interested in the early history and flavor of Carroll County, please read his book, *Carroll County and Her People.* *Submitted by: Dr. David Wiggins, 1093 Oak Grove Rd., Carrollton, GA 30117*
Source: *Carroll County and Her People*

252. Dr. Thomas Andrew Dorsey

Dr. Thomas Andrew Dorsey was born July 1, 1899, in Villa Rica, Georgia, to Rev. and Mrs. Thomas Madison and Etta Plant Dorsey. It is said that they were married sometime between 1894 and October 1895. Rev. Dorsey was an itinerant preacher traveling from community to community. Etta was a respected member of the Black middle class of Villa Rica. She purchased a two-acre lot, which sits where trailers are now at Villa Rica Elementary School, and an interest in a nearby 50-acre farm. One of her Christian attributes that she was so admired for was feeding the hobos who found their way to her door from the railroad tracks. She never turned any away. Thomas Andrew was born about this time. Etta mortgaged part of the farm property to move to Atlanta. After realizing that preaching was not going to support his family, in 1903 Rev. Dorsey moved his family back to Villa Rica to try farming. Wanting to help his ministry, Etta purchased an organ, which Dr. Dorsey later said played an important part in his music career. He was known to play on the floor under the organ as his mother played in church; he also played at preaching under the porch at home imitating his father.

Dr. Thomas A. Dorsey

In 1908, the Dorseys again moved to Atlanta where Thomas heard his first blues singers like Gertrude "Ma" Rainey and Bessie Smith and didn't know what type of music he was listening to. By the age of twelve, he was playing the piano. His first blues song was, "A Good Man is Hard to Find". He earned the name "Barrelhouse Tom" and "Georgia Tom". Dorsey also attended Morehouse College.

Dorsey moved to Chicago in 1916 where he worked in the steel mills and attended the Chicago Musical College. He never forgot his Christian upbringing and in 1920, he wrote, "Stand By Me" and "If I Don't Get There". He continued to write blues. These were the first of what he called "Gospel Songs", but he found he was not welcomed in many churches with what they called that bluesy kind of music.

In early 1932, Dr. Dorsey along with Theodore Frye and Magnolia Butts formed the National Convention of Gospel Choirs and Choruses, Inc. This year was the turning point in his life. On August 26, he went to St. Louis to preside over the National Convention of Choirs and Choruses and received a telegram that his wife had died in childbirth. He hurried back to Chicago and on the next day, his son, Thomas Andrew Dorsey Jr. died.

A few day later he let his fingers browse over the keys of a piano. He said, "I found myself playing a melody I'd never heard or played before, and the words came into my head." Although it contains less than 100 words, "Take My Hand Precious Lord," has been translated into 32 languages, sung in 80 countries, recorded by over 500 artists, recited by the Governor of Tennessee at the Democratic Convention of 1956, sung by Mahalia Jackson at Dr. King's funeral in 1968, and by Aretha Franklin at President Lyndon Johnson's funeral in 1973. It is still popular to this day. He never wrote another blues song.

He was the first Black to be awarded the Nashville Songwriters Association International Hall of Fame Award in 1979. He received a Grammy Award for Lifetime Achievement in 1992, Illinois Governor's Award for the Arts in 1985, Songwriters Hall of Fame in New York in 1982, Georgia Music Hall of Fame 1981, Gospel Music Association Living Hall of Fame 1982, and Doctor of Humane Letters from Fisk University, Selma, and Howard University in 1982. He served over 32 years as the President of the National Convention of Gospel Choirs and Choruses.

Dr. Dorsey died Saturday, January 23, 1993 in Chicago, Illinois. Sunday, February 14, 1993, was declared Thomas Dorsey Day in Villa Rica with his niece, Mrs. Velma Johnson attending and a proclamation was read by the Mayor of Villa Rica. *Submitted by: Shirley Marchman, 224 Sunset Dr., Villa Rica 30180*

253. First President's Wife Began Landscaping Design That Remains Today on College Campus

Since the days that Martha Munro Ingram poured her labors into the soil on the campus of West Georgia College, the institution has been known for the attractiveness of its grounds. Students from the days of the old A & M school and early junior college still describe how they were first stricken by the beauty of Mrs. Ingram's flower gardens.

And though much has changed at the college since the days of Mrs. Ingram, front campus still retains the same design, as planted and nurtured by WGC's first landscape gardener.

"We have made every effort to keep front campus as it was. She had a beautiful design and there is no way we can improve it," says Troy Holcombe, the college's landscaping director for the past 15 years.

"There's no doubt about it, she did it for love," Holcombe adds, speaking of the 40-acre garden campus single handedly cultivated in the college's early days.

But Mrs. Ingram passed away and as the college was converted to senior college status, there became more and more campus land to maintain with less and less attention to the college's old gardens.

By the time President James Boyd lured Holcombe in 1965 to become the college's first trained professional to landscape the campus, the grounds had admittedly deteriorated.

"When I first came here, the grounds were in exceedingly bad shape. To be frank, it looked like Tobacco Road," Holcombe laughed. But he wasn't laughing in 1965.

The college president had ordered a program of "professional landscaping and maintenance upkeep" and as an Ivy League trained scientist, Holcombe says, the president would not allow any "scientific boo-boos."

In those early days, Holcombe didn't have an office except for the back seat of his car. And he only had a broken down old tractor for heavy equipment. He had only six men to help him shape up the grounds and he quickly was hit with a 100 acre campus expansion soon after he arrived on the job.

Not only did Holcombe have the job of catching up on several years of neglect, but the explosive growth of the campus had begun. Holcombe would be in charge of landscaping all the new buildings that were to be built in the next 15 years, as well as the new ball fields and track facilities.

Most of the college's $10 million physical plant was built in that tune and Holcombe looks back on those busy times with relieved nostalgia.

"It's been terrific. We've had to plan out all those buildings and plant all those trees. I couldn't have done it without some good people here."

Since 1965, Holcomb's crews not only returned the campus to its former beauty, but took several steps further. The campus has won numerous local and national awards among professional landscapers and once was named by a national organization as a model campus landscape design.

How did Holcombe do it?

While Mrs. Ingram had started the college's early gardening with a lot of love, Holcombe's crew mixed a little science in the soil. And though Holcombe, a trained agronomist from the University of Georgia would probably disavow the connotation, the mixture produced a little magic.

"When I first came here, the plants were all disease ridden. The plants were all covered with insects. And the holly and the flowering shrubs weren't producing flowers because they were all pruned at the wrong time," he says with the disgust of a frustrated artist.

It didn't take Holcombe long to turn things around on the college campus. Every hoe, shovel, and other gardening tools were soaked in bleach and water overnight to sterilize them from spreading plant diseases. He showed the landscaping crews how to spray dogwoods in the spring in a way that would produce what Holcombe calls "rampant blossoms." He showed people how to prune azaleas, camellias, and spirea in the fall so they will produce more flowers in the spring.

Holcombe also showed the college gardeners how to prune holly, pyracantha, and forsythia in the early spring to produce maximum blossoms on those plants. *Author: Bob Holding, Georgian Staff Writer*

254. Keith Jackson

"Whoa, Nellie!" This was one of many expressions that you might hear from the dean of college football announcers. He brought the excitement of football into our households and his down to earth Georgia mannerisms and comments were music to our ears. To many of us who grew up listening to his play-by-play and color commentary, he became college football.

Keith Jackson's childhood began on a dirt farm about eight miles from Carrollton. He attended junior high at Tyus and attended Roopville High where he played basketball for Rudy Maxwell and graduated in 1946. From 1946-50 he served in the Marines. In 1950 he enrolled in Washington State University and graduated with honors in broadcasting in 1954.

Keith Jackson

Jackson took over the play-by-play duties at Washington State's radio station in 1952. His first job out of college was as a news anchor with the ABC affiliate in Seattle. He spent ten years there calling games for the U. of Washington and Seattle University. His television debut was with NBC in 1957 on the Dave Garroway's Wide Wide World program. He joined ABC Radio Network in 1964 as a news correspondent and sports director of ABC Radio West.

Assignments for ABC-TV have included the Olympics, NBA, NFL, MLB, auto racing and the events that took him to 31 countries. He is best known for his coverage of college football. His achievements include being the only person to win five consecutive Sportscaster of Year Awards from 1972 to 1976. He was the first sports announcer to receive the Amos Alonzo Stagg Award from the American Football Coaches Association. He won an Emmy Award

for best play by play in 1994. He was inducted into the American Sportscaster Hall of Fame in 1994 and the National Sportcasters and Sportswriters Association Hall of Fame in 1994.
Submitted by: Dr. David Wiggins
Sources: Villa Rican Dec. 16, 1981; Atlanta Journal Constitution Jan. 3, 1999; Roopville History Center

255. First Female College Graduate in Georgia

Bowdon College was the fifth chartered college in Georgia but the first in the State to confer degrees on coeducational students. Miss Mary Malinda McDaniel was the first female student to be awarded a college degree in Georgia. She graduated from Bowdon College in 1874 with an Arts degree to teach. Mary was the daughter of George A. and Martha Jane Lavendar McDaniel, and the niece of Charles McDaniel, founder of the college. She taught school in Griffin, where

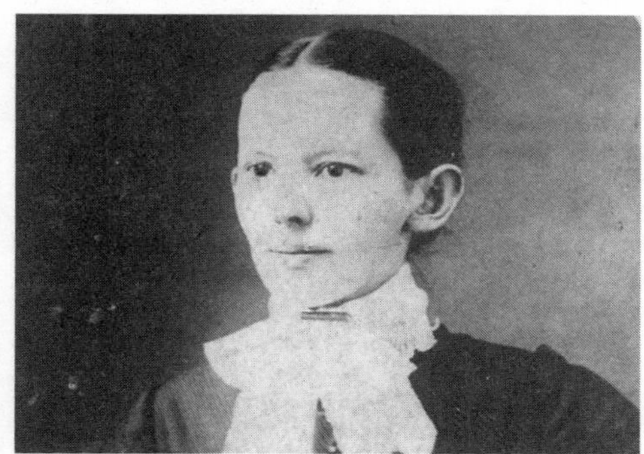

Mary M. McDaniel

she met and married Mr. N.A. Horton. She died during childbirth on August 25, 1884. She and the child are buried at the Methodist Protestant Cemetery located on the old college campus in Bowdon. Mr. Horton remarried and his son, Mr. Hap Horton opened Horton's Bookstore on the square in Carrollton. Horton's is now owned by Dorothy Pittman, and is considered the oldest bookstore in America. *Submitted by: Gwyn Chestnut*
Sources: Family history and *The History of Bowdon College* by Render R. Caswell.

256. Chief William McIntosh

Way out in Oklahoma, the story is told
about Chief William McIntosh, and
how the land was stole;
He died then for his treachery, oh how
the land did bleed!
It's healing now — can't you hear? You can
help to plant the seed.

At a place called Lochau Talofau,
the story is told
about a man who was caught between
two fires — a leader so bold.
On the banks of the Chattahoochee, Menawa
did lead,
Creek warriors moved on through the night, and
sent their chief to history.

Tustunugee Hutkee went down to Indian
Springs,
he signed his life away in blood, and
died along the stream.
Some people call him hero, some people
say he lied,
A wealthy man, with all his land, and
house on the riverside.

Governor Troup and McIntosh, together,
had a plan
To make themselves a fortune, and
send the Creeks to the western lands.

McIntosh from Indian Tribes of North America by McKenney & Hall

The Upper Creeks were furious, and
wouldn't give up without a fight,
From Alabama, they came to punish,
and killed on on that night.

In the red clay hills of Georgia, on the
banks of a mighty stream,
Greed took the life of a stalwart chief,
and stole away his dream.
He had more than most men wanted
and more than was his share,
Red Stick warriors burned his home
and laid his farmland bare.

Menawa came to ambush, on the
first day of May
Many warriors made the trip, two
hundred or more they say.
Acorn Bluff was set on fire and he was
forced to flee,
Death came that night for McIntosh, on the
banks of the Chattahoochee.

In Carroll County, Georgia the story is told
About Chief William McIntosh and how
the land was stole;
He died for his treachery — oh, how
the land did bleed!
It's healing now, can't you hear? You can
help to plant the seed.

By Mark Kenneth Crawford
With permission Copyright 1997

Submitted by: Jan Bell

257. Erby "Erb" Morgan

Roopville's Inventor

The son of Joseph and Elizabeth Morgan, brother to twins, Grace Morgan Smith and Grady Morgan, Erb lived in the home most recently occupied by Clark and Audey Causey. He was a gun smith, a machinist and all 'round "do it yourselfer". He submitted the fender with spring and was granted a patent for it during the "King Cotton" era. The fender was used in combination with the scooter and scrape on the plow stock powered by a mule. The fender protected the young cotton plants while the scooter and scrape plowed up the grass in the middles (between the rows). We are told that he also invented and was granted a patent for a cotton chopper. Cotton was planted with so many seeds that a continuous row was the result. After it grew to an inch or so it had to be tinned by chopping. This was usually done with a hoe and by hand. It was a slow process as was the later chore of "hoeing", which was done with a hoe to loosen the soil around the plants and to dig up the grass which, if left grow, would sap the nutrients needed by the cotton plants. Erb's mechanized chopper probably was also a labor saver, but it never became popular as did the fender.

The plow stock, singletree, heel bolt, plow handles, scrape and scooter along with the fender were donated to the Roopville Archive and Historical Society by Erb's nephew, Gwynn Smith. **See photo at top of next column.** *Submitted by: Rebecca Merrell, President of Roopville Archive and Historical Society, Roopville, GA 30170 and Written by: Mr. Willis Huff.*

LR: Fred Levens and Erb Morgan

258. The Story of Roy Richards and Southwire

The Roy Richards story is one that the people of Carroll County, Georgia have the deepest sense of pride in sharing with others. It is the story of a young farm boy who grew up here among us and — even after achieving international fame and wealth — he remained one of us throughout his life. As an article about him in the *New York Times* of August 4, 1968 reported, "Roy Richards never had to write home to tell the folks back there of his great success — they already knew about it because he never left from there!"

Because Roy Richards never left his hometown, he made the people of Carrollton and of Carroll County, Georgia a very big part of his success story. He is our "favorite son" and at the end of the twentieth century, Roy Richards was named as Carroll County's "Person of the Twentieth Century" for all that he had achieved in his lifetime in our community. The story of Roy Richards is an American success story that serves as an inspiration to young men and young women everywhere.

Roy Richards achieved international fame and became a millionaire many times over — and he could have made his home anywhere in the world that he wanted. But he was not a man who desired castles in France nor mansions displaying untold wealth. One person has said of him that "the only thing greater than his wealth was his humility." Roy Richards was humble — and deeply interested in "just being a good neighbor." He was always trying to better everything he could for all of the people of his community right here. "I believe in doing what one man can," Roy once said — and that was the philosophy on which he based his life.

And the things that Roy Richards left behind as his legacy are a monument to exactly what one man can do. However, Roy Richards was never one to take all the credit for himself — he always recognized the many people who had inspired or encouraged him along the way, or who had worked beside him to help him achieve his goals, And, too, Roy always gave credit to the greater power of us all who was responsible for the many blessings of his life — and Roy was a thankful man who really tried to give back as much as he had received.

Another defining characteristic of Roy Richards would be that when he was told over and over again in his life that "it couldn't be done" — he would never give up. Whenever faced with such "Doubting Thomases" and negative reactions to his "wild ideas," Roy never wasted time in debate over the issue. He simply went out and he did it. Like his ancestors before him, Roy Richards was a man who had true pioneer determination — and once he'd set his mind to a task, he was going to accomplish it.

Yet, he was not a ruthless man. He was not the kind of man who would trample over others in pursuit of his goal. He was not a man who would compromise any aspect of his own code

Picture of Roy with coils of wire at Southwire

of honor or moral conduct — nor one who would try to make the ends justify the means. Roy was a decent man, a good man, and a fair one. This is what the people of his own generation would tell you. Also, Roy was a great believer in the freedoms of America and in the free enterprise system of America.

Each new generation faces some new kind of frontier — whether it be wilderness to conquer or space to explore. Whether it be how to make fire — or how to make wire. There will always be some new technology to invent. It is interesting to trace the journey of the ancestors of Roy Richards in this book down through the generations to see exactly how these same "family traits and characteristics" — of remaining on the cutting edge of technology — prove themselves out in each new era.

Roy Richards was a man who certainly met his destiny on his own terms and in his own time and place. His time was the twentieth century — and his place was his hometown of Carrollton, Georgia. Carrollton began as just a tiny town in Georgia — about fifty miles west of Atlanta. It used to be mainly rural, but Roy Richards is the man who changed all of that. Roy Richards grew up in an era of the South when "Cotton was King" and just about every family around here made their living by planting cotton in the red dirt fields of Georgia.

But then in the 1930's the boll weevil began its journey eastward from Texas into Georgia. And that one little insect toppled the entire booming cotton economy of the rural South. Cotton farming virtually came to an end after the boll weevil disaster. The Great Depression of the 1930's was already in full swing — and this added to the poverty and caused an even greater loss of jobs.

Roy Richards was a young man just graduating from the Georgia Institute of Technology "right at the time that King Cotton had been dethroned" as Roy himself would later say. Roy was a brilliant young engineer nearly bursting at the seams with all kinds of new ideas about ways to make things better for people. But at that time in 1935, about 90% of his graduating class was having to go North to find jobs — there were no engineering jobs available in the South. Carroll County, Georgia economy had always been geared towards farming and as Roy said some years later, "If you told folks you were an engineer, they wanted to know what railroad you worked for." That was the only kind of engineer the South had ever known.

Roy himself had received a good job offer from General Electric in New York but he didn't want to move North. Roy loved the South, loved his home and the people in Carroll County, Georgia. Roy was from the Hulett community and this really was "home sweet home" to him. Roy's ancestors — the Richards and the Stovalls — had first come to Carroll County as early pioneers in the 1850's and they had put down deep roots here.

Roy had grown up on a farm and had done his share of plowing and planting — for every family had to farm to produce their own food. But the Richards family also had another business — a sawmill — which was their livelihood. Many of the farmers around Carroll County sold timber off their land to the Richards Sawmill. Roy had worked at the sawmill since the time he was a boy — and he wanted to stay in Carroll County to help build up his family's business — as well as to help to make the community a better place, too.

Roy always said that his family had wanted him to "grow up to be a good neighbor". And so, after graduating with honors from Georgia Tech in 1935, Roy Richards returned home to Carroll County — and went back to work in his family's sawmill — working six days a week sunup to sundown. "In a way, I was right back where I'd started from" — Roy said later on.

But this wasn't exactly true — for there were all kinds of events about to unfold which would come together in this one time and place to shape this young man's destiny. One of Roy Richards' favorite quotes was that of Victor Hugo who said, "Nothing is as powerful as an idea whose time has come." And it was this one spark of an idea — in the mind of Roy Richards — that would lead him forth into what he would call "his great adventure in life." It was a powerful idea that would sweep him along over the next half century. And it was an idea that would change his own life, his community, his county, his state — and America — and then even the whole world — into a better place. And what this idea had to do with was electricity.

In the mid 1930's electricity was an idea whose time had come. Of course, all of us have heard the story as school children of how Benjamin Franklin flew the kite and proved that electricity was out there. It's just that it took about a hundred years for people to figure out exactly what to do with it. Then in 1879, Thomas Alva Edison had invented the light bulb. Roy Richards would say later on he always knew that when Edison had invented that light bulb that he was onto something very good, very big — something that could revolutionize the world.

In fact, Roy would say that the idea "grasped his imagination" that he would like for his mother, who was Myrtice Stovall Richards, and his grandmother, who was Armendie Ayers Stovall of Hulett, to enjoy the pleasure of an electric light bulb in their homes. "Just to be able to turn a switch and for a light to come on" — in those days, an idea such as this was incredible.

It is something that in the fast-paced world of technology of today we hardly give a thought to — until perhaps an ice storm comes and we are without power for a brief time. Then we begin to appreciate being able to turn that switch and for a light to come on! But in that era of the mid-1930's, Roy's mother and grandmother lighted their homes with kerosene lamps, just like everyone else in Carroll County. Kerosene was 20 cents a gallon and most families tried to make a gallon of kerosene last for a month.

However, in 1925 something had already happened in New York — a far distance from Georgia — that would be the first event in a series of events that would lead towards lighting that electric light bulb in the Richards and Stovall homes. Franklin Delano Roosevelt — who would later become our 32nd President — had been stricken with polio. As a part of his therapy, Roosevelt had begun to make journeys to Warm Springs, Georgia where the warm mineralized waters had a healing and beneficial effect to his paralyzed legs. A few towns had begun to have electricity by then and in fact, Roosevelt did have electricity at his "Little White House" — the name given to FDR's home in Warm Springs when he visited there. Many Georgians remember FDR's trips to Georgia by train — and his little Scottie dog, Fala.

One day President Roosevelt looked at a power bill that he had received for his "Little White House" and realized that electricity in Georgia cost about four times what it cost him for his home back in New York! He was shocked at this discovery and that's when Roosevelt decided that something needed to be done about making power more affordable and more available to everyone. Even though a few towns had electricity, the entire rural South was as much in the dark as their own ancestors had been for hundreds of years. Roosevelt would later say that the ideas for the REA — the Rural Electrification Administration — was first born at "The Little White House" in Georgia.

By May of 1935, Roosevelt had issued an executive order that created the REA. A year later, Roosevelt signed into law a lending agency that would lend the money for the building of the power lines. Attorney Robert D. Tisinger of Carroll County petitioned the REA to bring electricity to this county — and by August 11, 1936, he had received word that Carroll County was approved. A meeting was held at the courthouse and hundreds of people signed a petition to establish the Carroll Rural Electric Association. The right of way for the initial project was going to be 108 miles and years later, Tisinger laughed when he remembered that it cost a grand total of $2.50 for the easements. "And only that because one man complained that his cherry tree had to be cut down," Tisinger had said.

And so this was the beginning — and when Roy Richards had first heard that plans were about to be made for bringing electricity to the rural South — he saw many great opportunities there. For one thing, he saw a business opportunity for himself — because at the sawmill he immediately began converting trees into "power poles" instead of lumber. He also saw that such a project would bring many jobs to men who needed work badly in this Great Depression.

And Roy saw that this was his opportunity to bring that electric light bulb to his mother and his grandmother's homes — and to his whole community. And to everyone in the whole South. It was a way to make things better. Roy Richards borrowed $856 and established a construction company called Richards' Brothers — for Roy's brother, Hugh, also came in with him on this business — in order to be able to bid on projects for building power lines throughout the South.

Fifty years later when the REA celebrated its Golden Anniversary, Roy Richards was the honored Pioneer and Guest Speaker for the occasion. He shared many of his memories about those early days of REA:

"My father's birthplace, and the home I grew up in were heated by a fireplace. My mother cooked on a wood stove. We used kerosene lamps, drew water from a well, and our bathroom was an outhouse. It was very primitive by today's standards, but it was the only way of life that we or any of our neighbors had ever known. A lot of people were afraid of electricity and my own Mother was very concerned about making a commitment to pay a two dollar a month electric bill ... In August of 1937 I bid on the job to build the first power line. I was 25 years old. I'd had no experience in this, but I took a train to Washington, D.C. to plead my case. I had memorized the contract so every question I was asked, I could quote chapter and verse."

In February of 1937, it was announced that Richards' Brothers had won the contract for building that first power line at the low bid of $80,863. People all along the route of the proposed power line began wiring their home so they'd be ready when the first electricity was delivered to them. And the rest is history. It was on July 31, 1937 at 10:15 am. when the first electrical current was turned on — and the lights came on in rural Georgia.

The first power line was 108 miles long and served 344 families. Roy had set the very first power pole beside his parents' home in Hulett community. The REA had loaned Carroll County $118,000 to build the whole line. Roy built 121 miles of line for $95,000. In August of 1938, the second REA loan came through and this time $110,000 was given to build 135 miles of line.

When this line was completed in 1939, 1500 farm homes had electric lights in Carroll and surrounding counties. At completion of this line, this historic occasion was marked by a gala REA Power Festival. People in Carroll County came from miles around to be entertained with music, speeches, and demonstrations of what electricity could do for your home. The Carroll County system was only the fourth in Georgia — and it was the 19th in the nation. Roy Richards had achieved something very special.

Roy's record of achievement in Carroll County was so impressive that he was asked if he could take on the Hart County, Georgia project and complete it in six months instead of a year. When Roy said that he could, he was then asked, "And what if we asked you to cut that in half?" Roy replied he thought it might take some planning and organizing, but he said it could be done. Roy doubled and tripled his work crews — now he had 80 men and 12 trucks for the job. Roy Richards came up with some very innovative ideas about how to speed up the progress of building these power lines. He structured his work crews on an assembly line basis — which had not been done before.

Roy continued in his work towards bringing electricity to the rural South — and the world — until the beginning of World War II brought a halt to any and all types of REA work throughout the USA. Actually, at that very time, Roy had been working on a contract in the Caribbean for Western Electric to lay an undersea cable to St. Croix in the Virgin Islands. He had just left from the islands when he received news of the bombing of Pearl Harbor.

Like all of his ancestors before him, when his country called — Roy stopped what he was doing and answered the call to country first. So, Roy had to postpone his important work for the duration of World War II — as did many American men. But what Roy had already accomplished in his pioneering efforts in electrification of the rural South was incredible. During the time that Richards served in the U.S. Army, he came to know two men under his command — Lt. Frank Watson Rose, Jr. and Lt. James Albert Feagle — whose work ethic and brilliance in the field of civil engineering would impress him greatly. Roy invited both these men to come join his business of Richards & Associates after the war was over. Both men — Frank Rose, Jr. and Jim Feagle were graduates of Georgia Tech like Roy. Frank Rose, Jr. was a native of Cohutta, Georgia and married to Ellen Nooe of South Carolina. Jim Feagle, was a native of Atlanta and his wife Mary Heatherly, was a descendant of one of the First Families of Campbell County, Tennessee.

The Roses and the Feagles moved to Carrollton after the war had ended to join Roy Richards in his plans to bring more electricity to the rural South. Both the Roses and the Feagles are good examples of the fine quality people that Richards always encouraged to become a part of his business family — and the kind of people who accepted his invitation to come here and have added so much to our community over the years.

So, Roy Richards' company had began setting poles in the ground again — just as they had done before the war. Roy merited Margaret Samples with "holding down the fort" for him in his business while he had had to be away for three years during his military service. Margaret had been a childhood friend of Roy's and had come to work for Richards Brothers in 1938 working as a secretary and bookkeeper. Later she became Margaret Braswell, Corporate Secretary-Treasurer supervising the flow of millions of dollars. "Mainly I was the watchdog," Margaret would say later. And she was that as she watched where every penny was going. Employees were asked to not throw away rubber bands and paper clips were bent back into place to be used again. Margaret was one person who had known Roy from a very early age and who always told her mother that Roy was destined for greatness in some way.

There was one story of an early experience Roy had had while attending Berry School at Rome in 1928 which seemed to show him having a brush with his own destiny. One day Roy had been repairing a tractor in a field at Berry when a long sleek automobile drove up and a well-dressed man stepped out of the car to have a conversation with Roy. After a few minutes, the man explained that he had noticed the young man was repairing the tractor — and stated that he was an inventor himself and might be able to help in some way. So, he worked with young Roy there in the field and helped him to repair the tractor. They enjoyed a conversation together — and then the man drove away.

It was not until later that Roy had discovered that the man had been Henry Ford, inventor of the automobile and one of the major benefactors of Berry School. It was an interesting meeting — one the inventor-industrialist who had already achieved great things — and the young boy who was about to become just as great an inventor and industrialist himself — though he did not know it yet ...

One rather humorous example of Roy's business frugality occurred some years later when his valued manager, James H. Griffin, had to make a sudden emergency trip to New York City. Griffin had had to take the only seat he could get — which turned out to be in first class. He flew to New York, tended to his business, and returned to the airline for his flight back to Carrollton. As he was seated in his first class seat again, who should be coming down the aisle towards him but his own boss, Roy Richards? Richards greeted Griffin and then continued on his way down the aisle towards his own seat in the economy section. After they'd gotten back to Atlanta, Griffin tried to explain to Roy what had happened, but Roy had said he didn't want to hear it. "It'll make a good story I can tell for a long time," Roy had said laughingly.

So, after Roy had returned to Richards & Associates after the war, the power poles were being set for miles and miles, but there was something wrong. There was no wire to string on them — and with no wire there could be no power delivered to the many rural customers hoping that it would soon come. Roy was finally told by one wire company in the North that it might be nearly four years before any more wire could be delivered. The man had said to Roy, "What's the big hurry? Those folks have not had electricity for a hundred years — they can wait a little longer ... "

Roy did not see the humor in this remark and had replied, "My grandmother is 85 years old and she has never had the luxury of an electric light bulb in her home ... " And that's when Roy Richards decided that if no supplier could deliver him the wire he needed, then he'd have to just find a way to make it himself. He'd have to build his own wire mill. And he decided he wanted to build it right here in his hometown of Carrollton, Georgia. Not only was that a good idea for him, but it would be good for the community, too. There were many men returning home after World War II who were in need of good jobs.

Of course, everybody told Roy it couldn't be done. There were many good arguments about why Carrollton was not the proper location for such an industry. In the first place, it was "out in the middle of nowhere" — it would cost a lot of money to transport in the supplies needed. And because of the recent war, supplies were hard to come by sometimes. The town was landlocked — there was no major waterway for delivering the goods by water routes. All Roy's trucks had been confiscated by the government during the war to use towards the war effort — and Roy was still trying to build back his truck fleet. The whole thing sounded like a risky venture — and who knew how to even make wire anyway?

But one of the strongest arguments against Roy's plans came from his old mechanical engineering professor at Georgia Tech, Major A.A. Case, "You can't do it, Roy," he'd told him. "The only tools most of those people over there ever used were an axe handle and a plow stock" Case explained. And it was true — Carroll County, Georgia was an area that was geared towards farming almost completely. The only real industry the town of Carrollton had ever known was Mandeville Mills, which was where the cotton produced on the farms was spun into yarn. And Mandeville Mills was even about to close down, because the cotton era had ended.

But Roy would not take no for an answer. Roy knew that Major Case was anticipating his retirement from the faculty of Georgia Tech and he told him, "You can teach them." Roy promised that he would provide whatever tools Case needed to teach his people the ways of manufacturing and the intricate skills of the machinist. And as Roy said in later years, "As was always true with the Major, when the challenge was passed to him, he approached the problem with the enthusiasm of a youngster. He rolled up his sleeves and set about making journeymen machinists of men fresh from the cornfields. The Major's enthusiasm was infectious with West Georgians and we are extremely proud of the craftsmen in our shops who carry on with his training."

Major Case had moved to Carrollton, built a shop in his backyard, and had begun teaching the young farm boys of Carroll County how to enter the world of industrial production. The People's Bank of Carrollton wouldn't lend a dime towards this risky venture which they predicted would fail. Roy had to go to a bank in Newnan, Georgia to find any financial support for building a wire mill in Carrollton. Years later, when Roy had become the President of the Peoples Bank, he changed the lending policies to be more friendly to people starting out on new business ventures.

Next for his wire mill, Roy sought out a plant manager who would have experience in the manufacture of wire. He found his man in Roger Schoerner who was working for Anaconda Wire and Cable in New York in 1948 when Roy went there to purchase wire for an electrification project in St. Croix. And Schoerner accepted the position offered to him by Richards to manage his new Southwire Company. The Schoerners moved here just in time to help select the site for the location of the building. And they stood watching the red dirt being moved around in a cow pasture that would soon become Southwire.

So while all this was going on — in the way of getting the wire mill called Southwire started — Roy Richards had yet "one more iron in the fire" at the very same time. And this concerned the building of a hospital in Carrollton. The 40,000 people of Carroll County were being served by three tiny clinics — and these were not adequate for the peoples' needs at all. All serious cases had to be transported about fifty miles to Atlanta — and it was too long a ride for critical patients. And many people died because of the primitive conditions existing in the old Carrollton Clinic.

Roy had been called home during the war in 1943 because of his father's illness and he had visited him there in the old makeshift Carrollton Clinic. There was only one nurse to tend all the patients and the small cots used had no safety rails on them. Consequently, Wiley Richards had fallen out of his bed and broken his arm. He subsequently developed pneumonia and unexpectedly died on July 28, 1943. A new hospital was needed badly.

Dr. Tom Reeve, the son of missionaries to Africa himself, played a vital role in the early days of the new hospital which opened in 1949 and was the first surgeon to practice there. Dr. Reeve said, "Bricks and mortar are one thing — but you have to have a staff that goes with a hospital. You've got to have nurses and a laboratory, and an x-ray department, and an emergency room. It was scary in those early years when we had only one room, one doctor, and one nurse. The old clinic did a remarkable job for what resources it had — but it really was quite primitive."

Picture of Roy with first power pole set by his parents' home

Roy Richards had made a silent vow to himself that if there could be a way to build a better hospital, he wanted to find it. Roy always wanted to do anything he could to help better the community — and a hospital was definitely needed. When a Carrollton benefactor, Mr. C.M. Tanner, called Roy in 1946 to ask if he would be the pioneer chairman of the Hospital Board — and spearhead the drive to get the funds to get a hospital built — Roy accepted. Mr. C.M. Tanner was donating $75,000 and asking for the community to give $25,000. Mr. C.M. Tanner had told Roy that he felt that the Hospital Authority would need a very strong leadership in order to accomplish their goals — and Mr. Tanner had seen something in this young businessman that had convinced him that Richards was the one to "get the job done."

Also, too, Roy was just as respected in the black community as in the white — and he wanted to include all the people of the community in the fund drive from the beginning. Roy quickly gained the support of Crogman Mullins, the Owner of the Royal Funeral Home, who realized a hospital would benefit blacks as much as whites. "Germs don't recognize color," Crogman had said to Roy. And the black community raised more than $5,000 towards the hospital drive.

Roy Richards, Ebb Duncan, and Bob Tisinger had also started up a radio station in Carrollton — which was WLBB — and they donated much free airtime on the radio to spread the word of the hospital fund drive and encourage support. By May of 1947, over $145,000 had been pledged to the hospital. Then, on January 22, 1948, Tanner Memorial Hospital became the first hospital in Georgia to obtain state approval and qualify for funding under the Hill-Burton Act. The hospital construction was completed and open for business on October 30, 1949. Only one day after the dedication of the new hospital, Roy Richards opened up his new wire manufacturing mill in Carrollton —Southwire. Both Tanner Memorial Hospital and Southwire became the major employers of the people of this community from that time forward.

Roy Richards was recognized for many great achievements throughout his lifetime. In 1962, President John F. Kennedy awarded him the "E for Export" Award for export relations in 17 countries. Then, Roy was awarded The American Success Story in 1964 for a career symbolizing the success possible under America's free enterprise democracy.

On May 6, 1966, Roy Richards was inducted into the rolls of the American Newcomen Society — and this was a great honor. This society recognizes founding leaders of organizations who "by the pattern of their lives have furnished outstanding examples of vision, determination, hard work, and abiding faith.... Their struggles and success have laid the foundations of what have become great organizations who reputation for character, integrity, workmanship and quality has traveled into far-distant lands.... " This was only a part of the introduction of Mr. Roy Richards by Mr. John A. Sibley, upon his induction into the Newcomen Society.

Another factor which Newcomen noted about Roy Richards was that "he has brought wealth and prosperity into his own community." Roy could have easily brought in engineers from any part of the world to staff his Southwire Company. But, as Mr. Sibley noted, "He did not draw from other communities the skilled labor that his business required, but rather he developed the necessary skills in the untrained workers of his own community." Further, "He did not limit his efforts to things that were accepted in the range of possibility — but rather through the application of technology, he created products that others said, 'could not be done'." Mr. Sibley continued, "The story that will be unfolded will inspire and enchant all of us who believe that our economic system of free enterprise is the foundation of our prosperity and freedom."

Then Roy Richards himself gave a most eloquent speech in acceptance of his induction into Newcomen. And he told them the story of Southwire — and how the first wire was produced from there on March 23, 1950. He concluded his remarks in this way: "At Southwire, we feel that our adventure in free enterprise has been rewarding as well as challenging; and we hope that future chapters may be written with more telling emphasis on the application of those principles which we hold to be the very heart of the American way of life and the American way of business and technology."

In 1973, Roy was named a "Giant of the Electric Century" by *Electrical World* magazine; he received the "Golden Plate" award from the American Academy of Achievement in 1977. In 1984, Roy Richards was named Man of the Year by the Copper Club and he was honored as an REA pioneer on the 50th anniversary of the Rural Electrification Act by the Georgia Electric Membership Corporation.

Also, in 1983, Roy Richards was honored along with five other men of Carroll County with a Georgia state historical marker as one of the six industrial giants of the county. The marker also honors Asa Candler, the founder and first president of Coca-Cola, Sam Candler Dobbs and Arthur Acklen, both Coca-Cola presidents, Warren Sewell, the "father of the men's clothing manufacturing of the South", and D.W. Brooks who founded the Georgia Cotton Cooperative, which later became Gold Kist. Posthumously, Roy Richards was honored with the Modica Memorial Award by the Wire Association International for a lifetime of technical contributions to the wire industry. The Roy Richards story is a fascinating one that shows what vision, energy, hard work and determination can accomplish.

Roy Richards was a man who always believed in America and what she stands for. "He was a true Patriot of America," Judge Lamar Knight said, "I will remember Roy for his faith, his love and respect for his country,.... This is evidenced by the fact that he insisted upon the 4th of July Celebration for Southwire employees even when patriotism seemed to be falling. He also gave up his time to be in World War II."

The employees of Southwire had the greatest respect for their boss, Roy Richards. When Georgia Tech began a project to fund the building of a new Intercollegiate Athletic Center, Southwire employees pitched in and donated over $100,000 to their boss' old Alma Mater. The Richards family have always been "big Georgia Tech fans." That's one time when Roy would take a Saturday off — to go to a Tech game. Otherwise, he pretty much worked six days a week according to his family. And never missed a day.

"My father — and the men and women that worked with him in the beginning to establish Southwire — are people of extraordinary work ethic," Roy Richards, Jr. has said. "Those values are the values we will need in the future to succeed and it is important that we look back at pioneering people in our own company's history and apply in the future what we've learned from our past. These pioneers — Richards, Case, Schoerner, Cofer, Samples, Griffin — are people of great courage and fearlessness about trying new ideas and carrying them out. If we're to see ahead in the future, we've got to stand on the shoulders of the giants who brought us here," Richards said in *The People and Events That Shaped Carroll County* in the *Times-Georgian Horizons 2000*, January 30, 2000.

Roy Richards put our community of Carrollton, Georgia on the map with his Southwire Company. Southwire became the nation's largest privately-held producer of copper and aluminum rod, and electrical wire and cable products. Roy Richards along with D.B. "Pete" Cofer and his Southwire engineers in 1953 revolutionized the wire industry with new methods for continuous casting of copper wire. Using some ideas from an Italian industrialist by the name of Illario Properzi, Richards and his engineers developed a whole new technology for making wire. All the time they were doing it, Properzi himself was telling them that it was impossible and could not be done!

Now we have a much stronger, much better quality of wire. It is the kind of "superconductor wire" that will "light our way into the new millennium." And as more things become computerized — more of this kind of wire will be needed. That was one thing about Roy Richards — he was never just in the business to try to make money. He was always trying to find a better product and "build a better mousetrap". Southwire recently celebrated its 50th anniversary and the motto was "Southwire — 50 years of quality people bringing quality service." Today Southwire's products are available nationwide and a third of all the homes built across this country are built with the company's wire.

Our community prospered greatly in the twentieth century because of Roy Richards. Many fine families moved here looking for jobs and became a part of the Southwire business family — and they proved to be the kind of people that a community needs for growth. When buyers were doubtful of the "new kind of wire" that Roy Richards had to sell — he just invited folks to come to Carrollton and see how the wire was made. Roy Richards wrote the book on Southern hospitality and people did "come and see" and it became a part of the tourism of our town. Since "company was coming," naturally our community put on its shining best.

People liked what they saw — and they went back home and placed many purchase orders with Southwire. And then Southwire's fine fleet of trucks zoomed down the road to deliver the products. Whenever there was a disaster in some part of our nation, Roy Richards would make available these same trucks to our community so that we could fill them with donated items to send to the people left homeless by floods or hurricanes.

When a schoolboy in the new millennium of Carroll County, Georgia asks: "Who was Roy Richards?" — this is the legend he should be told. Roy Richards was a young man who went out and "captured the lightning bolt." He harnessed it — and he tamed that "bolt from the wild blue yonder" — and he delivered it right into our homes. He brought a new and magical force into our lives called electricity. And it changed our whole world for the better.

Can any of us of today's world even imagine what life would be like without computers or telephones or answering machines? Without modern luxuries like microwave ovens, television or air-conditioning? Our families of the past had none of our modern electrical conveniences of today. And many of them — the women especially — died at a very young age. Roy Richards changed our world forever when he "captured the lightning bolt" and brought us electricity by means of a tool called wire.

And his Southwire Company is keeping up with the growing demand for more power in the future. Southwire has just been recognized for making history with their new "superconductor" cables that will increase our energy efficiency. U.S. Representative Bob Barr likened the effects of this new technology to importance of the Internet. On February 18, 2000, Georgia Governor, Roy Barnes, and U.S. Secretary of Energy, Bill Richardson, were on hand to "flip the switch" and turn on this new superconductor cable energizing Southwire's three manufacturing plants in Carrollton.

Roy Richards, Jr., the CEO and son of the founder of Southwire, spoke at the dedication ceremony. He said, "A hundred years from now, who knows what changes our descendants will see in the world of electricity?" The poles that were set along Georgia's country roads by Roy Richards and strung with wire for electrification of the South in the 1930's may soon become antiquated in this new century — and may disappear with the appearance of new technology.

But the effects of what Roy Richards did for the people of our community will not disappear — and will not be forgotten for many generations to come. We who lived as his contemporaries in Carroll County, Georgia — of the century just past — are proud to have known him and call him "our hometown boy." The people of Carroll County, Georgia are very proud to have been a part of the American success story of Roy Richards and Southwire. *Submitted by: Jan R. Bell*

259. Martin Roop Family

Martin Roop was born in South Carolina, the son of John and Phoebe Roop. In 1845, he migrated to Georgia with his wife, the former Elizabeth King, to whom he was married in 1839. They settled first in Jackson County, later in Coweta, and in 1855 moved to the vicinity of Roopville. To this family were born ten children: John K., William W., Robert H., Benjamin J., Thomas M., Henry O., James G., Sarah Elizabeth, Savannah, and George W.

When the Roops settled, the area was very much underdeveloped. Native timber had not been cut. Surrounding the rocky ridge were rich uplands and well-watered bottomlands. Before the area was further settled, the Roops had to be self-sufficient. Mrs. Roop carded, spun, and wove all their clothing. She also made clothes for the soldiers in the Civil War. The Roops ate from pewter dishes.

Martin Roop was one of the most important figures in the development and prosperity of the entire region. He was a Mason and an influential and respected man. Mr. Roop's eldest son, John K., became the dominant figure during the early years of the settlement. John K. was born in 1839 before his parents left South Carolina. In 1861, he enlisted in the Confederate Army and served in both Company D of the First Regiment of Georgia Infantry and in the Phillips Legion Cavalry. In 1872 he was married to Eliza Moore of Henry County, GA. To this union were born five children: Nora L. (wife of Dr. Benjamin J. Veal and later wife of L.A. Ware, Henry A. Judge Charles E., Bessie (wife of Dr. H.J. Goodman) and Fanny (wife of W.C. Veal).

Upon returning to civilian life, John resumed farming. He became the owner of over 2000 acres of land, much of which he donated to enhance the growth of the area. He would often establish a business or build a residence and

The home of J.K. Roop and family.

sell it to new people coming into the area. He built a gin near Theo Bell's spring, hired a Negro to run it, and later sold it to Charlie Wood. He established a blacksmith shop where Mr. Jim Merrell's home is located and sold it to Jordan A., Wood. In 1882, Thomas M. Roop became Post Master and at that time the city was officially named Roopville.

Mr. Frank Roop, son of Mr. Thomas M. Roop and Mrs. Florida Alexander Roop Brock was the last of the Roop family to live in Roopville. He served in the Roopville Baptist Church for many years holding many positions including deacon, teacher and clerk. Frank never married and had no heirs. His picture can be found in both the archive and the Frank Roop Brotherhood Hall at the Baptist Church.

There are no Roops in Roopville today but many people still have fond memories of the Roops and an appreciation of their contributions. Descendants frequently come to Roopville searching for information on their ancestors. *Submitted by: Rebecca Merrell, 124 Old Franklin Street, Roopville, GA 30170.*

Sources: Roopville Baptist Church History, 1983; The Carroll County Story as told by Her People, 1976.

260. Judge Robert D. Tisinger

Mr. R.D. (Bob) Tisinger was more than a leader; he was a pioneer and visionary in the fields of rural electrification, soil conservation, communications, and public service. He was born October 20, 1909 to Ida Bibb McDaniel and George Washington Tisinger in the Victory Community. He attended Bowdon High School, the Fourth District A&M School; and received his law degree from the Atlanta Law School.

He met and married Naomi Evans in Atlanta, and returned to Carroll County where he became an important part of the county's history as a driving force for progress. He joined his older brother Harvey to form the Tisinger & Tisinger Law Firm located on the second floor of the Peoples Bank building. Later he formed the Tisinger, Tisinger, Vance, and Greer law firm with his sons David and Richard (Dick). Dick's son, Richard joined the firm later.

Bob Tisinger was involved in all aspects of community growth and development. He helped incorporate the Carroll Electric Membership Corporation, the Georgia Electric Membership Corporation, West Georgia Soil and Water Conservation District, Carroll Broadcasting Co., which was the first Carrollton radio station with the call letters of WLBB, and Carroll County Livestock Sales Barn, Inc. He also served as general counsel to the Carroll Electric Membership Corporation from 1936 until his death, Georgia Electric Membership Corporation from 1940, National Rural Electric Cooperative Association from 1943, Carrollton Federal Savings and Loan Association from 1932, and the Carroll County Livestock Sales Barn.

He was active in the judicial systems of Carroll County where he served as solicitor of Civic and Criminal Count for the county, and judge of Criminal and Civic Court. He served as vice-chairman of the Carroll County Hospital Authority from 1947-1972, and a member of the Board of Trustees for the West Georgia College Foundation, Victory United Methodist Church, Scottish Rite Hospital, and Georgia Bar Association. He was active in numerous civic organizations serving as president of the Carrollton Lions Club, president of the Carroll Service Council, and past Worshipful Master of the Carroll Masonic Lodge No. 69. As a Mason, he also belonged to the Shrine, Yaarab Temple, Atlanta, 32 degree KCCH, Scottish Rite Mason, Royal Order of Scotland, York Rite Mason and Knight Templer.

He was awarded the Man of the Year Award in Soil and Water Conservation in 1978, Georgia EMC Pioneer Award in 1986, Citizen of the Year from Carroll County Chamber of Commerce in 1978, and the Distinguished Service Award from the National Rural Electric Cooperative Association (NRECA) in 1986. Other recipients of this award were Franklin D. Roosevelt and Harry Truman. West Georgia College renamed The Red Clay Debate Tournament for Mr. Tisinger where he was a former debater at the Fourth District A&M School. The State Department of Transportation renamed Highway 5 in Carroll County the Robert D. Tisinger Highway. Lake Tisinger at Bowdon was named for him.

Robert D. Tisinger died on December 21, 1991. He certainly left an impact on our county and our lives; and as he said "paid a little rent on his time on earth." *Submitted by: David Tisinger, 322 East Club Drive, Carrollton, GA 30117*

Sources: Personal knowledge and family records

Judge Robert D. Tisinger

261. Lillian Murlene Williams

On Sunday, October 22, 2000, we marked the passing of one of our truest pioneers in the struggle for equal human rights in Georgia, Lillian Murlene Williams. She was born Lillian Murlene James on Sunday, January 5, 1930, the daughter of Jesse and Emma Ware James in Floyd County, Georgia. Lillian was the 5th child in a family of three sons and three daughters: Luke, Annie Paul, Robert, Eddie, Lillian, and Betty James.

In addition to growing up in the Deep South, Lillian James also grew up in the years of the 1930's Great Depression. This certainly left its mark on her in that there were so few jobs available for anyone and everyone suffered great poverty. Lillian hoped to increase her chances for a good job and a better life by gaining a good education. She was educated in the public schools of Rome, Georgia, and then went on to pursue a college education at Albany State College in Albany, Georgia. Of course, at that time, in the late 1940's, all schools in the state of Georgia were either all black or all white. There was no such thing as a mixture of races or colors of people in public schools or colleges. Albany State College was such a school and was an all black college.

Lillian Murlene Williams in action

It was here that Lillian would meet and fall in love with her husband-to-be, Clarence A. Williams, Sr. Clarence was pursuing a degree in Science and also hoped to become a coach in high school sports one day. Lillian James and Clarence Williams were married in 1948 and continued their education at Albany State. The year 1949 was a year of great beginnings for them for they welcomed their first child, Clarence A. Williams, Jr. into the world. Also that year, Clarence A. Williams, Sr. graduated from Albany State College. He accepted a position as a teacher in the Carrollton Public School System.

Here, Clarence Williams, would pursue his career as a teacher of Science and become one of the leading coaches in the area. He was the football, basketball, and track coach at Carver High School, which was the all black high school in Carrollton. During those years, Lillian was a homemaker and a mother. Three more children were to follow, a daughter, Faye in 1951, a son, Dumont in 1953, and another son, Eric in 1957.

During those years of early motherhood, Lillian would sometimes work as a substitute teacher. Still, Lillian longed to finish her education someday and become a teacher. Lillian and Clarence Williams started planning early and saving for their children's education. They hoped and believed that education was the key that would unlock the door to equal rights for all African-Americans.

In 1964 when I entered my freshman year at West Georgia College in my hometown of Carrollton, Georgia, it was an all white campus filled with thousands of students. But Lillian Williams was soon to change all of that. Lillian had made her decision to go after her dream. Being a mother of four, there was no way she could travel to attend an all black college. There was a perfectly good college right where she lived and Lillian intended to go there. Lillian put in her application to West Georgia College. There had never been a black student at West Georgia College and she was to become its first.

I wish now that I could look back on those years and say that there were many white students at West Georgia College who tried to make Lillian's student experience a pleasant one. But this would not be the truth and it would quite honestly, take away from what Lillian achieved.

I witnessed times when Lillian was jeered and times when there were whispered threats or names called behind her back as she passed by. Sometimes students would not give her the right of way if she attempted to go up a flight of stairs or pass through a door. There might be students to gather in an intimidating manner to stand at places where they could terrorize Lillian. Yet there were many of us who silently admired this black woman in her attempts to pursue her education in an all white school. But even if we began to admire her, most of us kept our thoughts to ourselves for we did not have the same courage that Lillian had. So, Lillian continued to face her daily hecklers and those who would discriminate against her, day to day, all alone.

There were times so hard for Lillian that she had to call her husband Clarence away from his job to escort her as she walked from class to class. Sometimes we would see the security guards of the campus actually escorting Lillian to her classes. There were times when the Williams family would awake in the morning to find that the yard of their home had been completely vandalized or trashed. There even came a time when one radical group on campus was supposedly plotting to kill Lillian. At this time the Mayor, Council, and local police fearing for her safety became involved. As for Lillian, she tried hard to keep these kinds of worries away from her family and she would speak little about the dangers to anyone, especially them.

Lillian Williams receiving her Founder's Day Award from Dr. Maurice Townsend, WGC, 1985

Lillian Williams, in the true tradition of Rev. Martin Luther King, was a completely non-violent person. Lillian was a soft-spoken person with exquisite manners. She was a very kind and forgiving person. She never reacted to the discriminations against her. Lillian just kept on going, head held high, with her eyes never taken away from the goal she meant to achieve. She was a mother of four and she wanted a good education for all of them.

Lillian Williams made one of the greatest contributions to the Civil Rights movement of the 1960's that I know, for she traveled her path to equality all alone. Any lesser person would have given up at the beginning, but Lillian was not that person. I do not think the word "failure" was in her vocabulary.

I had married in 1967 and given birth to a baby boy, Joe, in 1968 and I learned that Lillian had also had a son born that same year, Travis. They would grow up to attend the public schools of Carrollton together and they would become best friends in high school. Lillian had great hopes for this youngest son. Lillian's dreams for her oldest four children would come true, Clarence Jr. earned his B.A. in Chemistry from Albany State, and he later earned a M.A. as well. Faye earned her B.A. and M.A. at West Georgia College. Durmont followed his older brother to Albany State where he earned his B.A. Eric received his B.S. degree in Criminal Justice from Savannah State College.

Lillian achieved her own dream of becoming a schoolteacher. She taught at Sand Hill Elementary School and at Hudson Elementary School for a total of 31 years. Unfortunately, Lillian had to experience much heartbreak in her life. She became a widow in 1977. Her husband served the community at Carver High for 28 years. The whole community mourned his loss, but everyone admired her for her courage in going on alone. Tragedy struck her family when her youngest son, Travis, as a senior at Carrollton High School was involved in an automobile accident that severed his spinal cord. But we had forgotten that Travis was his mother's son. Travis became a pioneer well known in the medical field for his participation in medical experiments for those with spinal cord injuries. Travis has helped to give hope to many who did not have hope, as his mother did almost forty years ago. Travis did not let any kind of physical handicap keep him from getting his education. He graduated from high school and he received his B.B.A. with a major in Finance from West Georgia College. He has gone on to have a remarkable career with the Internal Revenue Service in Jacksonville, Florida.

Lillian Williams was the first black student to attend West Georgia College. She began the lonely process of integration into an all white school system by herself and she never gave up. No one ever heard anything negative from Lillian herself, for she was never one to hold a grudge. She would always say in later years that her college experience had been a good one. The only reason it was "a good one" is because she herself absolutely refused to allow it to be anything but that.

In her own era, Lillian Williams was a part of the blowing wind that brought to us the changing times from the 1960's to the present day. That wind brought change to our community, to education, and to civil rights for all. I will never forget Lillian Williams and her single black face among a sea of white students almost forty years ago. I have heard some people say that one person cannot make a difference, but for those of us who live in Carroll County, Georgia, we can say that the life of Lillian Murlene Williams did make a difference in our community, and our own lives have been enriched for having known her. *Submitted by: Jan Robinson Bell*

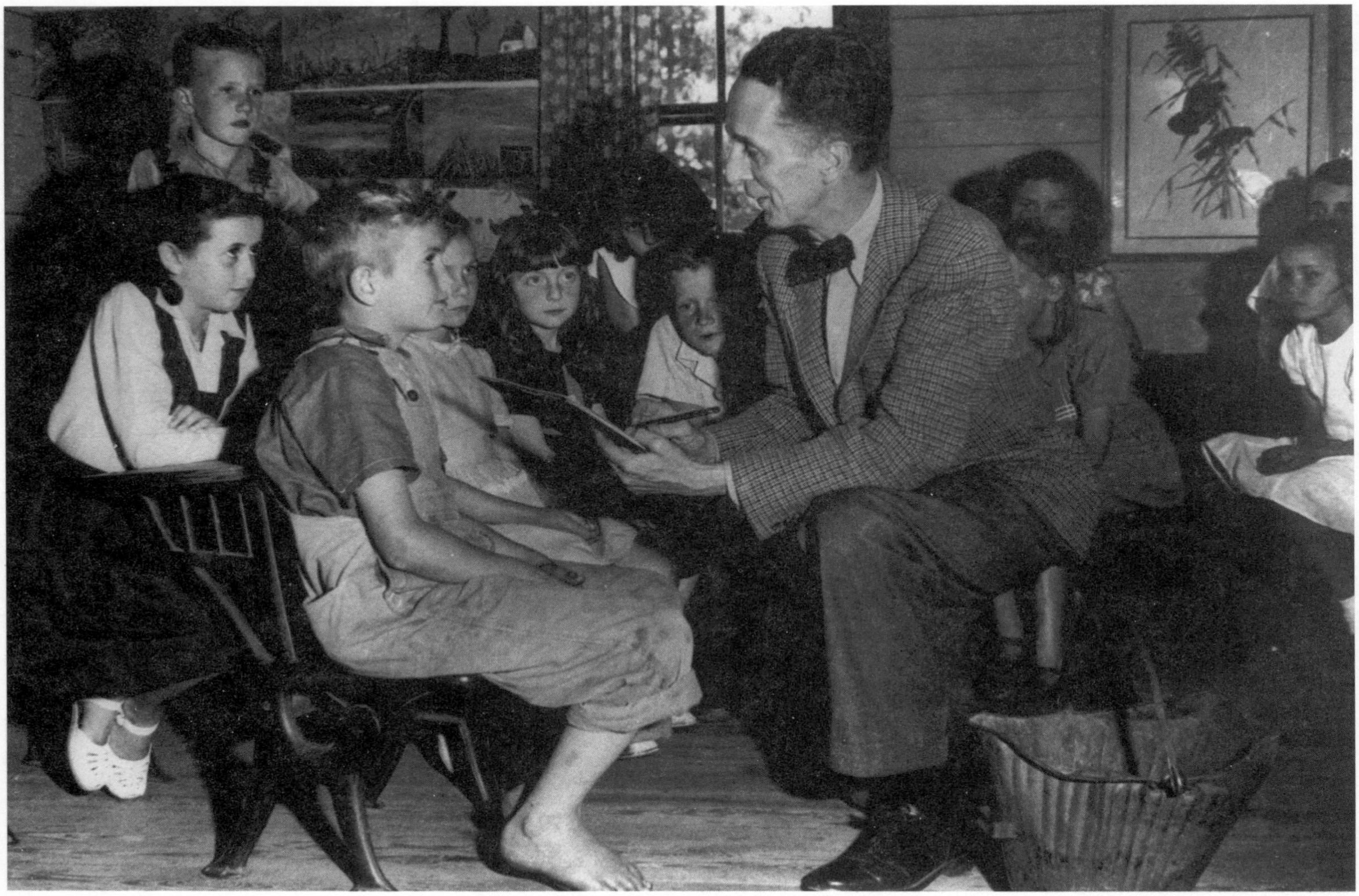

Norman Rockwell at Oak Mountain School for his famous Country School Illustration
(Courtesy SUWG Special Collections)

Old Carroll County Courthouse
(Courtesy of Dr. David Wiggins)

262. The Henry Acree Family

The Acree Family legend states that we Acrees owe our entry into Carroll County to the kindness extended by one man to our grandfather. The story says that in the fall of 1878 or 1879 the father of former Carroll County sheriff, Denver Gaston, had taken a wagon load of cotton to Sand Mountain, Alabama. On his return home he found a young Henry Acree sobbing as he walked down the road. Upon talking with this child, Mr. Gaston discovered his cuts and bruises. Henry told that he was plowing a field when his drunken stepfather came to the field and began to throw rocks at him; dropping the plow, Henry ran. Being evident that Henry was abused, Mr. Gaston brought Henry back to Carroll County. He and his wife fixed him living quarters in a building on their property. They provided meals and a small allowance in exchange for his help with farm chores. He lived under these conditions until he was old enough to support himself. Henry became a farmer, renting a small farm on Whooping Creek Road in the Clem community.

Henry and Lizzie Acree and five of their children.

In August 1886 he married Elizabeth Pate (Lizzie), whose complete name was Susan Sarah Jane Woodston Elizabeth. She was the daughter of Henry Pate (born 1829, died 1908) and Mary Jane Holloway Pate (born 1834, died 1913). Both are buried at Whooping Creek Primitive Baptist Church, Clem, Georgia. This same church is the resting-place of Henry and Lizzie Acree.

Henry and Lizzie raised seven children to adulthood, losing one daughter at age four. Mollie Mae was born 1888, died 1972, married William Gladney. They had four children Inez, Raymond, Christine and Bernice. Another daughter Myrtie Lee was born 1888, died 1893. Tura Velma was born 1893, died 1992, married Lewis Cook. They had two sons, Herman and Durwood. Later she married Mr. Francis Mote. Clifford Davis was born 1896 died 1978, married Ruth Davis. They raised two sons and one daughter, Davis, Leroy and Cliffine. Henry Delvous was born 1899, died 1964, first married Ethel Bracknell. They had two daughters who died at birth, then their son Johnny was born. Later, Delvous married Eunice Merrell. They had one daughter, Oleria. Paul Wilson was born 1902, died 1971, married Myra Lewis. They had two sons, Lewis Harold and Dennis. Samuel Frank was born 1905, died 1983, married Gladys Ergle. They had nine children, raising eight to adulthood, Margaret, Robert, Betty, Nell, Brenda, Carol, Sammy, Rickey and Linda June who died as a baby. Ralph Pate was born March 1908, died 1974, married Emma Vaughn. They had one daughter, Joyce, and two stepchildren Margaret and Kenny Vaughn.

The only knowledge Henry shared with his family prior to living in Carroll County was that he was born February 9, 1867. He lived in Alabama with his mother, called Babe, and stepfather, a Mr. Lankford or Langford. Life was hard.

Some descendants of Henry and Lizzie still reside in Carroll County, others live throughout Georgia and all across the United States. *Submitted by: John P. Acree, 1744 South Highway 27, Carrollton, GA 30117*

263. A.L. Adair Jr. and Esther McBrayer Adair

Both the Adair and McBrayer families have roots in Carroll County and have many descendants here now.

Most of the Adairs are descended from William Adair who fought with Elijah Clarke's unit in the Revolutionary War. William's grandson, James Lee Adair, was the first postmaster in Villa Rica in January 1831. Four years later James Lee's father, Bozeman Adair, was a delegate from New Hope Baptist Church in Villa Rica to form the Tallapoosa Baptist Association. The church still stands.

The McBrayers came from the area in Scotland that was near the scene of the Lockerbie plane sabotage some years ago.

A.L. Adair in mid-1940s

The first generation McBrayer in America was William McBrayer, born in 1696 and died in 1795. His great-grandson John H. McBrayer married Susannah Leathers in 1836 in Carroll County. John H.'s brother Andrew married Nancy Leathers. There are many relatives of the McBrayer and Leathers marriages in Carroll County at present.

The Adair-McBrayer union came to fruition when, in 1931, James Lee Adair's great-grandson A.L. Adair Jr. married Esther McBrayer, great-granddaughter of John H. McBrayer.

A.L. Adair Jr. had been a school teacher in Paulding County in the 1930s. After joining the Gulf Life Insurance Company, he was promoted to Carrollton as a manager around 1940. His office was upstairs in the old People's Bank Building.

Esther McBrayer Adair Dodson around 1970

Many have said if it had not been for him, they would not have had any insurance when they lost their spouses and other family members. This is because he made many trips over Carroll County roads to visit clients.

A.L., Esther, and by now, their son Billy, lived in four different locations in Carrollton. The longest duration saw them live in Dr. Steve Worthy's house. This home was directly across the street from the ball park where Billy developed his love for baseball.

A.L. died of a heart attack in Decatur, Alabama, at the age of thirty-seven in 1947.

Esther and Billy moved to Paulding County and lived with her brother Clyde McBrayer and his family for four years.

In 1951 Esther and Billy moved to Villa Rica. Esther worked at Berry's Pharmacy, a department store next door, and at Herman Newell's store.

In 1957 shortly after Esther's second marriage to John Henry Dodson, two of the three businesses where she had worked, were destroyed by a gas explosion that killed twelve.

Many became acquainted with Esther as the first nurse for Dr. Larry Boss in Villa Rica. She spent ten years greeting patients, giving them shots and preparing them for Dr. Boss.

Esther died on March 1, 1999. She and A.L. are buried at New Georgia Baptist Cemetery in Paulding County.

A.L. and Esther's son Billy finished school at Villa Rica, West Georgia College, and Georgia State University. He later taught school and coached basketball in Paulding County for thirty-three years.

Billy Adair still resides in Villa Rica. *Submitted by: Billy Adair, 217 Westview Drive, Villa Rica, GA 30180*
Sources: Personal knowledge and family records

264. Adams Family From Pennsylvania

William Adams, born 1793 in Pennsylvania, and his wife Sarah came to Georgia in the early 1800s. They moved to Randolph Alabama before 1850.

Isaac and Mary Jane Copeland Adams

Robert Adams, son of William, moved to Georgia between 1850 and 1860. Robert was born October 11, 1811, in Georgia. He married Martha Ann Jones in Carroll County, Georgia, on August 31, 1841. Robert and Martha had seven children: James, Isaac Marion, Nancy, Augustus, George, Sarah, and Martha. They lived in the Bowdon area and are buried at Old Camp Methodist Church.

Isaac Adams, son of Robert, was born in Randolph County, Alabama, June, 26 1845. He was married twice, first to Rachel Copeland who died, and then to Mary Jane Copeland, daughter of William and Mary Margaret Copeland. The Copelands came to Bowdon from Laurens, South Carolina. Rachel and Mary were cousins.

Robert Adams, Martha Ann Jones, Nancy Adams Tillman

Isaac was in the Civil War, Company B, 1st Georgia Glenn's Cavalry. He and his company received their parole on May 1; 1865, in Atlanta.

Children of Isaac and Mary were James, Robert, William, Walter, and Olen. Children of Isaac and Rachel were Martha, Ola and Lisa. Isaac, Mary, and Rachel are buried in the Bowdon Methodist Church Cemetery. Isaac helped build Shiloh Methodist Church and he was a blacksmith.

Members of the Adams family still live on the original home place in Bowdon today. *Submitted by: Joe Adams, 558 West Jonesville Road, Bowdon, GA 30108*

265. Absolom Adams

Absolom Adams, the son of William and Sarah (Blankenship) Adams, was born on February 15, 1810, in Blount County, Tennessee. William Adams was born in Virginia on March 31, 1777, and settled in Blount County, Tennessee, where he married Sarah Blankenship about 1797. Sarah Blankenship was born in Virginia on March 24, 1779, and was the daughter of Isham and Edith (Lane) Blankenship Jr. William and Sarah Adams moved with their family to Carroll County, Georgia, in 1829. Absolom took care of his parents in their later years. William Adams died on September 8, 1856, and Sarah Adams died on September 30, 1856. William and Sarah are probably buried at Old Bethel Primitive Baptist Church Cemetery on Bar J Road near Temple, Georgia.

Absolom Adams

Absolom Adams' first wife is unknown, and they had two sons.

1) Edmund Hunt Adams, October 18, 1828 - 1899, born in Tennessee, married Amanda J. Ballard on September 6, 1846, in Carroll County. Edmund was a farmer and moved to Fannin County, Texas, where he is buried.

2) William B. Adams, October 7, 1830 - December 17, 1899, born in Carroll County, Georgia, married Josephine Bonapart Riggs on July 21, 1853, in Carroll County. William was a farmer. He served in the War Between the States as a private with Company D of the 10th Georgia Cavalry, State Guard. Sometime after 1880, William moved with his family to Cullman County, Alabama, and Josephine and he are buried at Emeus Baptist Church Cemetery near Logan, Alabama.

On November 28, 1833, in Carroll County, Absolom Adams married Elizabeth Reid, daughter of Henry Martin and Edith (Harrison) Reid of Carroll County. Henry, the son of George and Margaret (Martin) Reid, was born on February 3, 1773, in Rowan County, North Carolina, and died March 27, 1853, in Carroll County. He served in the War of 1812 and was shot in the stomach with the ball passing through his body. The story goes that a silk handkerchief was drawn through the hole, and he recovered to live many years afterward. Edith Harrison, the daughter of Davis and Phoebe (Hood) Harrison, was born in Rowan County, North Carolina, in 1781, and died in Carroll County, in 1853.

Absolom Adams was a farmer and lived near Temple, Georgia. Absolom served as a private in the Creek Indian War of 1836 with the Carroll Rangers. Absolom Adams died on August 23, 1875, in Carroll County. Elizabeth Adams died on July 23, 1885, in Carroll County. Absolom and Elizabeth Adams are buried at Old Bethel Primitive Baptist Church Cemetery on Bar J Road near Temple.

Absolom and Elizabeth had seven children born in Carroll County, Georgia.

1) Mahala Jane Adams, September 17, 1834 - October 7, 1919, married William Smith West on March 23, 1856, in Carroll County. William was a farmer. Mahala and William are buried at Concord Methodist Church Cemetery in Carroll County.

2) Edith C. Adams, January 19, 1837 - January 12, 1898, married William M. Williams on December 13, 1855, in Carroll County, Georgia. William was a farmer. Edith and William are buried at Bethel Baptist Church Cemetery in Carroll County.

3) Phoebe Elizabeth Adams, September 18, 1839 - September 14, 1885, married first William B. Stripling on March 25, 1858, in Carroll County, and after his death married Henson Clark Dempsey on January 5, 1865, in Carroll County. Henson was a farmer. Phoebe and Henson are buried at Concord Methodist Church Cemetery in Carroll County.

4) Gilbert Marion Adams, about 1842 - June 26, 1862, unmarried, served in the War Between the States, enlisting on June 11, 1861, as a private with Company F Carroll Guards of the 19th Georgia Volunteer Infantry. Gilbert was killed in action at the Battle of Mechanicsville in Virginia.

5) Zachery Taylor Adams, October 3, 1845 - September 26, 1916, served in the War Between the States, enlisting first as a private with Company D of the 10th Georgia Cavalry, State Guard, and next enlisting as a private with Company B of the 63rd Alabama Volunteer Infantry. Zachery married first Rebecca Catherine Coleman on September 6, 1864, in Carroll County, and married second Rosa Brown on May 30, 1912, in Carroll County. Zachery was a farmer. Zachery, Rebecca, and Rosa are buried at Asbury Cemetery in Temple, Georgia.

6) Sarah Ann Adams, October 13, 1847 - July 5, 1931, married James Prince Griffin on February 13, 1868, in Carroll County. James was a farmer. Sarah and James are buried at Asbury Cemetery in Temple.

7) Margaret D.H. Adams, August 20, 1854 - June 9, 1890, married Charles W. Griffin Jr., on January 12, 1876, in Carroll County. Charles was a farmer. Margaret is buried at Concord Methodist Church Cemetery in Carroll County. Charles is buried at Asbury Cemetery in Temple. *Submitted by: Betty Rose Shope, 104 Rolling Rd., Gaithersburg, MD 20877*

266. Frank and Vick (Lovvorn) Adams

Francis Marion Adams was born in Carroll County, September 18, 1871. He was the son of William Adams and Polly Ann Blackman, buried at Smyrna Church Cemetery. He married Queen Victoria Lovvorn, born August 9, 1874 at Mt. Zion. She was the daughter of Talton Washington Lovvorn and Nancy Catherine Shelnutt. They were called Frank and Vick. They lived in this area all their lives and raised eight children. Their children were Ollie, Edgar, Carl, Roxie, Flora, Ruth, Jessie, and Cleo Adams. First they lived at Mt. Zion, and by 1896 they lived at Tallapoosa, and by 1907 were living at the state line near Macedonia church where they lived until Vick's death March 29, 1941, and Frank's death May 3, 1952. Their daughter, Jessie Wiggins, still lives in the same location.

Frank was a farmer and also operated a sawmill. They made wood shingles at the sawmill, and wood shingles are on the roof in the 1938 photo. Some of their children became storekeepers. Ollie had a florist in Carrollton, Flora and Millard had a grocery store in Tallapoosa, Carl and Eula had a grocery store in Carrollton and then Clem, and Ruth and Frank had a store in Ranburne and then Edwardsville. The house Vick and Frank lived in was a log cabin that had two rooms and a porch added. They hung sheets across the middle of a room to make sections and provide privacy for the children. In this home they raised eight children and also made room for Vick's three brothers Joe, Jim, and John Lovvorn, and later her three nephews Herman, Frank and Spence Lovvorn when they needed a home. They were very active in Macedonia Baptist Church and often held socials in their home for the young people, serving ice cream, lemonade, or watermelons. This family had a life full of love, sharing, fun and hard work.

Frank and Victoria Lovvorn Adams Family about 1907

(I) Ollie married Charlie Skinner and had two children who lived: (1) Q.P. married Georgia Leathers, and (2) Eartis married Ralph Norwood.

(II) Edgar married Barbara Robinson and had ten children: (1) Garland married Christine Skinner. (2) Paul married Leila Anderson, (3) Ralph married Maudie Pollard, (4) Ruby married Winton Warren, (5) Edna married Coy McClain, (6) Avis married Loyd Spence, (7) Roy, (8) Fred married Odette Adams, (9) Nellie married Harry Duke, (10) Clifford married Martha Walker.

(III) Carl married Eula Webb and had five children: (1) Marvin married Corine Warren, (2) Lois married Stanley Hughes, (3) Ray, (4) Dorothy Jean, and (5) Margie married James Crawley.

(IV) Roxie married Tom Robinson and had ten children: (1) Buford married Helen ____, (2) Bernard married Orie Smith, (3) Nina married Amos Hendrix, (4) Doyle married Sarah Robinson, (5) Eva married Phillip Teel, (6)

Frank and Victoria Lovvorn Adams Family about 1938

Ottis married Betty Catlett, (7) Curtis married Addie Whaley, (8) Coyce married June Strickland, (9) Martis married Jean Stapler, (10) Billy married Fay Smith.

(V) Flora married Millard Skinner.

(VI) Ruth married Frank Lowery and had five children: (1) Merrill married June Traylor, (2) Audrey married Julian Jones, (3) Ava Jean married Ambers Hanson, (4) Shirley married Pete Howell, (5) Ray Talton married Sarah Vaughn.

(VII) Jessie married Roy Wiggins.

(VIII) Cole married Vonnie Palmer and had two children: (1) Jeanette married John Babb and (2) Randy married Kathy ____.

The older lady in the 1907 picture is Vick's aunt, Sarah Lovvorn Hazel Whitaker, sister to Wash Lovvorn. The 1938 picture shows front row in chairs: L-R Roxie Robinson holding Martis Robinson with Eva Robinson and Dorothy Jean Adams standing behind her, Carl Adams with Margie Nell Adams, Edgar Adams with Nelle Adams, Ollie Skinner, Frank Adams, Victoria Lovvorn Adams, Cleo Adams, Jessie Adams, Ruth Lowery holding Shirley Lowery, Audrey Lowery with Ava Jean Lowery in front, Flora Skinner. Boys on ground: Ottis, Coyce, and Curtis Robinson, Roy Adams, Fred Adams, Merrill Lowery. Second row: Tom Robinson, Lois Adams, Eula Adams, Ruby Adams, Barbara Adams, Clifford Adams, Avis Adams, Eartis Skinner, Nina Robinson, Edna Adams, Vonnie Adams holding Jeanette Adams, Paul Adams, Frank Lowery, Spence Lovvorn, Millard Skinner. Back row: Marvin Adams, Bernard Robinson, Garland Adams, Ralph Adams, Q.P. Skinner, Buford Robinson, Ray Adams, Doyle Robinson.
Submitted by: John Lovvorn Camp, Bowdon, GA
Sources: Family record information acquired from all the families by Jessie Adams Wiggins, 1977. Childhood memories of Spence Lovvorn.

267. Genie Mae Adams
Lee Otis Westbrook Ancestors

William and Sarah Blankenship Adams, both born in Virginia, moved with six of their seven children to Carroll County prior to the 1830 federal census. Their eldest son, Elijah, did not move to Georgia with his parents. They were enumerated as Carroll County residents from the 1830 through the 1850 censuses. The Adams family lived in the Villa Rica area and were early members of the New Hope Primitive Baptist Church. William and Sarah were married about 1797 in Tennessee.

William and Sarah, according to the will of William witnessed on the 4th day of September 1852 by Hiram Spence and Starling T. Sims, had the following children: John, Elijah, Nathaniel (Nathanel), Absolom, Elizabeth, Anna and Susannah. William and Sarah both died in 1856 in Carroll County.

John Adams, born 8 February 1801 in Tennessee married Rebecca Mitchell about 1822 in Tennessee. Rebecca was born about 1800 in Tennessee. John died 20 August 1852 in Paulding County, Georgia, while Rebecca died in 1885 in Carroll County. She is buried in an unmarked grave in Pleasant View Cemetery. John and Rebecca had the following children: Laura Lucretia (Cressia), William, James, Sarah, Jefferson Moore, Alfred, John J., Nathaniel, Jesse Carroll and Henry Roberts.

William was born in 1824 in Tennessee and died on 12 December 1885 in Carroll County. His first wife was Millie Hooper born 1846. It is unknown to this author as to the parentage of Millie or her place of birth. They were married before 1857. Millie died in 1868 and William married Mary Ann (Polly) Blackmon that same year. Polly's father was Daniel Blackmon and her mother was Nancy Hartley. William and both of his wives are buried in Smyrna Methodist Cemetery on Highway 27 in Carroll County. William and Millie had two known children: William Stansel and William Ceborn, who were both born in Clay County, Alabama.

William Stansel Adams married Sarah Frances Woodard on 20 December 1877. Sarah was born on 23 July 1867 in Cherokee County, Georgia, and died on 21 July 1914. She was the daughter of Jesse Woodard and Elizabeth Kilgore. Jesse was a native of North Carolina and Elizabeth was born in Coweta County, Georgia. Sarah is buried in Concord Primitive Baptist Church in Carroll County.

After Sarah's death, William married Lennie B. Ethel Folds, who was called Effie. They were married on 13 May 1915 in Carroll County. She was born 7 November 1893 in Carroll County to King Daniel Folds and Mary Frances (Molly) Easterwood. William died 6 November 1928 and Effie died 3 October 1988 in Bremen, Haralson County. William and Effie are buried in Concord Primitive Baptist Church.

William and Sarah had ten children: Charles Thomas, Emma E., Ella L., Jessie Lee, Ana C., Pearl E., Genie Mae, Leonard Cliff, James "Harvey" and Marvin E. Adams. William and Effie had two children: Aubrey Lee and Laura Juanita Adams.

Genie Mae Adams was born 10 May 1890 in Carroll County. She married Lee Otis Westbrook, son of William Augustus and Martha Louise Morse of Bremen, Haralson County. He was born 7 July 1889. Lee was first married to Hallie T. Allen. Hallie died tragically after slipping and falling into a creek. She gave birth to a child shortly after the accident and they both died within the following week.

William Augustus Westbrook was first married to Martha Louise Morse who died 23 April 1891. They had the following children: John L., Ada J., Anna G., William A., Oscar A., Elander E., Lela E., Martha A., Lee Otis. William is said to be the son of Champion and Elvira Westbrook, however, the 1860 federal census for Haralson County lists Augustus W. Pond living in the household of the aforementioned. He is the same age as the William A. Westbrook shown in the 1870 census and living in the household of Champion and Elvira. After Martha's death, William married Mary Eliza Garrett. They had one child, Joseph Earle Westbrook.

Genie Mae and Lee were married on 1 March 1914 in Carroll County. They had the following children: Herman, Eula Mae, Otis S., Paul Otis, Edna Louise and Elna Elizabeth (twins), and Byron Lee Westbrook. The family left Carroll County and moved to Tifon, Georgia, and then to Miami, Florida, in 1924.

Genie Mae was affectionately called Mamaw by all her grandchildren and great-grandchildren. Lee was called Papaw. My childhood memory of Mamaw was that she was always sickly. She succumbed to uterine cancer after suffering from it for ten years. At the time of her death, she had fourteen grandchildren and twenty-nine great-grandchildren. She and Lee are buried in Southern Memorial Park Cemetery in Miami, Dade County, Florida. After her death, Lee married Mollie Faircloth, an old family friend.

When Genie and Lee's daughter, Elna, was asked about how her parents met, she recalled that they met in the post office where Genie was working. The post office was owned by Genie's father, William Stansel. It is said that he owned the post office, a drugstore, a rooming house and some land in Carroll County. However, that has not been verified by the author of this article. At the time of this writing, there are two surviving children of Genie and Lee, Elna and Byron.

Paul Otis, my father, was born on 28 November 1914 in Bremen, Haralson County. He married my mother, Evelyn Michella June, on 1 October 1935. She was born 11 January 1917 in Elyria, Lorain County, Ohio. They met in Miami where both of their families removed to. They had two children, Paul Howard and June Patricia Westbrook. Paul Howard has two children and three grandchildren. June has four children and five grandchildren. *Submitted by: June Westbrook LaVernway, 511 Mission Arch Drive, Roswell, NM, E-mail: JuneLaVernway@aol.com*

268. Gilbert Edmund Adams

Gilbert Edmund Adams, son of Zachery Taylor and Rebecca Catherine (Coleman) Adams, was born October 30, 1872, in Carroll County, Georgia. Zachery Adams' parents were Absolom Adams, who was born in Blount County, Tennessee, and Elizabeth Reid, who was born in Gwinnett County, Georgia. Rebecca Coleman's parents were Henry Allen Coleman, who was born in Putnam County, Georgia, and Sarah Ann Barnes, who was born in Georgia.

Adams Brothers - William, Newton, Gilbert, and Zachery

Gilbert Edmund Adams married Beulah Almon in Cullman, Alabama, on December 2, 1900. Beulah was born January 16, 1880, in Whitesburg, Carroll County, Georgia, and her parents were Hezekiah Gilford and Emily Teresa (Davis) Almon of Heard County, Georgia. Gilbert was a farmer and resided in Temple on Carrollton Street. His house still stands. Gilbert died October 11, 1962, and Beulah died December 5, 1938. They are buried at Asbury Cemetery in Temple.

Gilbert and Beulah had four children.

1) Edith Catherine "Katie" Adams, August 31, 1901 - June 14, 1926, married Clem Robertson on August 14, 1921. Katie and Clem are buried at Asbury Cemetery in Temple.

2) Emma Mildred Adams, June 7, 1905 - March 12, 1995, married Earnest Samuel Brown on June 15, 1929, in Atlanta, Georgia. Mildred retired as a bookkeeper from the First National Bank of Atlanta, and Earnest retired from Western Electric after forty years. Mildred and Earnest resided in Decatur, DeKalb County, Georgia, and they are buried at Westview Cemetery in Atlanta.

3) Hugh Gilbert Adams, August 22, 1907 - July 22, 1946, married Bessie Estelle Watkins on May 21, 1927, in Temple, Georgia. Hugh was an accountant, banker, and businessman, and Estelle was a retired school teacher. Hugh and Estelle resided in Atlanta, Fulton County, Georgia, and they are buried at Westview Cemetery in Atlanta.

4) Mary Clyde Adams, August 29, 1912 - January 4, 2001, married Josiah Bub Padget on April 4, 1936, in Atlanta. Clyde retired as a keypunch operator from the Southern Railway Company, and Bub retired as a rate clerk from the Southern Passenger Association. Clyde and Bub resided in Decatur, DeKalb County, Georgia, and they are buried at Westview Cemetery in Atlanta. *Submitted by: James E. Padgett, 115 Cupit Close, Alpharetta, GA 30022*

269. William "Bill" Adams Family

William "Bill" Adams was born September 9, 1840, son of Robert and Martha Adams. On July 15, 1861, Bill volunteered for the army. There were a total of 140 young men from Bowdon, Georgia, who volunteered. They formed a military company and elected their college president, Charles McDaniel, as their captain. During June and July, Captain McDaniel drilled his company daily. When Cobb's Legion was organized near Atlanta, McDaniel offered the services of his volunteers and the Bowdon group became Company B of Cobb's Legion.

On July 27, 1861, the volunteers assembled in the chapel for a devotional service attended by many people. After they were dismissed, the company assembled in front of the administration building and began the thirty-five mile march to the nearest railroad in Newnan, Georgia. Within a few months, Company B arrived in Virginia.

Bill Adams was wounded at Gettysburg on July 2, 1863, with gunshot wounds and entered Chimborazo Hospital No. 2 in Richmond Virginia. Then on August 15, 1863, he was transferred to Jackson Hospital in Richmond. He was severely wounded again at Gettysburg on September 14, 1862. Records show he had three gunshot wounds.

He was sent home on furlough on October 6, 1862, until January 28, 1863, because of wounds received on September 14, 1862. He was home 112 days on furlough. His army records show he received thirty-three cents per day while home. He received a check showing this was for 112 days @ .33 = $36.96. He then returned to duty and was there when General Lee surrendered on April 9, 1865, at Appomattox Court House, Virginia.

William Adams met and married a lady by the name of Ms. Ford in Augusta, Arkansas. They had two children, Georgia Ann and Martha Elizabeth "Mattie" Adams. His wife died March 28, 1871, and is buried in the north east subdivision of Augusta Cemetery in Arkansas. He then brought the little girls home to his parents near Bonner Goldmine. The girls lived with their grandparents while growing up. Georgia Ann Adams married K.W. Anderson. Mattie Adams married William Martin Thomas.

Jess Whitehead, Mattie Thomas and Martin and Morris

William Adams then married Melissa Yarborough on December 3, 1873. They had four boys, Ambros, Bob, John, and Charlie Adams, and three daughters Sally, Jess and Dovey. Ambros married Sallie Powell and they are buried in Carroll Memory Gardens. Dovey married G.W. Wilkerson. Jess married a Mr. Whitehead.

William Adams applied for disability at the age of sixty-two. He was suffering with rheumatism, severe bronchitis and general disability and was unable to work. He received $60.00 per year. He died August 18, 1913. His wife then drew her widow's pension. She was born October 30, 1855, and died June 19, 1936. They are both buried at Old Camp Methodist Church, Carrollton.

Shown in the photograph is Jess Adams Whitehead, standing. Seated are Mattie Adams Thomas and her children Martin and Morris. Picture made in 1903. *Submitted by: Larry D. Thomas (great-great grandson of William Adams), 1065 Beulah Church Road, Carrollton, GA 30117*

270. Zachery Taylor Adams

Zachery Taylor Adams, son of Absolom and Elizabeth (Reid) Adams, was born on October 3, 1845, in Carroll County, Georgia. His grandparents, William and Sarah (Blankenship) Adams, born in Virginia, moved to Blount County, Tennessee, and in 1829, settled with their family in Carroll County, Georgia. Absolom was born in Blount County, Tennessee, and settled in Carroll County, where he married Elizabeth Reid on November 28, 1833. Absolom and Elizabeth are buried at Old Bethel Primitive Baptist Church Cemetery on Bar J Road near Temple, Georgia.

Zachery Taylor and Rosa (Brown) Adams, 1912

During the War Between the States, Zachery Taylor Adams served as a private with Company D of the 10th Georgia Cavalry, State Guard, enlisting at Hickory Level, Georgia, on July 27, 1863, and discharging at Camp Mobley near Rome, Georgia, on January 17, 1864. He enlisted on August 15, 1864, as a private with Company B of the 63rd Alabama Volunteer Infantry. He was captured at Fort Blakely, Alabama, on April 9, 1865, imprisoned at Ship Island, Mississippi, and was received by the Confederate agent at Camp Townsend for exchange on May 4, 1865. He surrendered on May 6, 1865, and he was paroled at Meridian, Mississippi, on May 11, 1865.

On September 6, 1864, Zachery Taylor Adams married Rebecca Catherine Coleman. Rebecca was born on March 19, 1843, in Georgia, and she was the daughter of Henry Allen and Sarah Ann (Barnes) Coleman of Carroll County, Georgia. Henry Allen Coleman was the son of George Coleman of South Carolina and Nancy Bufford. Henry was born in Putnam County, Georgia, January 28, 1814, served as a private in the Indian War of 1836, farmed, served as a bailiff, served as a major of militia in Cobb County, Georgia, and he was a prominent member of the Missionary Baptist Church. He died on October 27, 1890. Sarah Ann Barnes was the daughter of James and Sarah (McKenzie) Barnes. Sarah Ann was born in Georgia on August 27, 1807, and died on October 4, 1880. Henry Allen Coleman, Sarah Ann (Barnes) Coleman, Nancy (Bufford) Coleman, and Sarah (McKenzie) Barnes are buried at Bethel Baptist Church Cemetery on Carrollton Highway near Temple, Georgia.

Zachery and Rebecca had six children born in Temple.

1) William Marion Adams, November 14, 1865 - August 19, 1933, married Martha Ann Amanda Johnson on December 2, 1886, in Carroll County, and moved to Cullman, Alabama. William was a farmer. He and his wife are buried at the Cullman City Cemetery.

2) Henry Thompson Adams, January 12, 1868 - December 7, 1917, unmarried, taught school in Texas, served with the Atlanta Police Force in Atlanta, Georgia, and was killed in the line of duty.

3) David Newton Adams, July 11, 1869 - November 5, 1939, unmarried, ran a general mercantile store in Temple.

4) Gilbert Edmund Adams, October 30, 1872 - October 11, 1962, married Beulah Almon, daughter of Hezekiah Gilford and Emily Teresa (Davis) Almon of Heard County, Georgia, on December 2, 1900, in Cullman, Alabama. Gilbert was a farmer and resided in Temple, on Carrollton Street.

5) Zachery Taylor Adams Jr., November 22, 1876 - December 1, 1948, married Annie V. Chandler on October 14, 1900, in Carroll County. Zachery Jr., was a farmer and resided in Temple, on Carrollton Street.

6) Bessie Lee Adams, February 10, 1884 - March 21, 1973, married Caro Wilson Henderson on June 26, 1904, in Carroll County. Bessie and Caro resided in Villa Rica, Georgia, and are buried at the Villa Rica Cemetery.

Zachery Taylor Adams was a farmer and resided in Temple, Georgia, on Carrollton Street. After his wife Rebecca died on November 28, 1911, Zachery Taylor Adams married Rosa Brown in Temple on May 30, 1912. Rosa was born on December 16, 1872, and died April 7, 1964, at the Confederate Soldiers' Home in Milledgeville, Baldwin County, Georgia. Zachery Taylor Adams died on September 26, 1916, in Carroll County. Zachery, his two wives, Rebecca and Rosa, Henry Thompson Adams, David Newton Adams, Gilbert Edmund Adams and his wife Beulah, and Zachery Taylor Adams Jr., and his wife Annie are buried at Asbury Cemetery in Temple, Georgia. *Submitted by: Jane Ethridge, 4665 Hawkins Academy Road, Social Circle, GA 30025*

271. Judge William Charles Adamson

A Big Man Who Did Big Things

The man for whom Carrollton's downtown square is named was a lawyer, judge and congressman whose influence can still be seen on street signs and buildings across the county. His home on Carrollton's West Avenue is marked on city maps as a site of historical interest and is still occupied by a distant relative. Although he was an influential congressman and was referred to as Judge Adamson by most, to many of his relatives, he was simply "Uncle Charlie."

Mary Lovvorn, 89, remembers Judge Adamson as a dinner guest on many occasions at her parents' home. "We had a big rocker, what they called a Morris chair," remembered Lovvorn. "It was a great big leather chair you could lean back on and take a nap. He had dinner with us and he would recline in that chair and talk. He was a great big fellow." Indeed, W.C. Adamson was a big man who did big things.

William Charles Adamson

He was born in 1854 in Bowdon to John Whitfield Adamson and the former Mary Ann McDaniel, who had moved to Carroll from Clayton County shortly after their marriage. John Adamson was both a merchant in Bowdon and a farmer, so the future Judge Adamson was reared in a split environment - part town and part country.

Adamson was the product of a Bowdonian education. He graduated from Bowdon High School and received both a bachelor's degree and a master's degree from Bowdon College where he was valedictorian of his undergraduate class. It was John Adamson who convinced his son to study law. W.C. Adamson studied under Judge Sampson W. Harris and was admitted to the bar in 1876.

Although he loved Bowdon and continued to be a champion of Bowdon College for the rest of his life, Adamson moved down the road to Carrollton to hang up his shingle. He practiced law in the county seat as an attorney and judge for the next twenty years. He was known to discourage litigation except when he believed strongly in his client's case.

Adamson married Minna Reese in 1885. Minna was the daughter of Rev. A.C. Reese who had served as president pro tem of Bowdon College during the Civil War. The pair had three sons: Reese, Ernie, and Charles. The Adamsons were members of the Methodist Protestant Church. Judge Adamson was also a fan of Sacred Harp singing, an a cappella singing style that has roots in Carroll County.

In 1896, the people of the Fourth Congressional District decided to send Judge Adamson to Washington. Judge Adamson gave up his law practice and devoted the rest of his life to public service. He remained a Congressman until 1917.

During his time in Congress, Adamson was instrumental in the construction of the Panama Canal and was chairman of the Committee on Labor. He was pivotal in the creation of the U.S. Department of Labor and authored an act that established an eight-hour work day for railroad workers. His efforts also resulted in a broader exploitation of water power and water transportation in the South.

In 1917, President Woodrow Wilson appointed Adamson to a U.S. Customs judgeship, a position he held for the next decade. Ill health forced him to resign in 1928. He died in Carrollton, January 3, 1929. Judge Adamson is buried in the Carrollton City Cemetery.

Although he had seen the fast-paced Washington life and made his home in Carrollton, Judge Adamson always remained faithful to his Bowdon roots. In addition to serving as a Bowdon College trustee, he attended each academic year's opening and closing ceremonies. The last time he addressed the students of his alma mater, he offered them some advice, culled from a life in the spotlight that had begun years before in the same place those students were sitting. "Never lose any time," he counseled them. "Read, talk with intelligent people, form no habits but to work, to pray, to save money and respect and love your fellow men." Jonathan Dorsey first published this article in the *Times Georgian* newspaper May 11, 1997. *Submitted by: Sally Owen, Carrollton, GA and Written by: Gwyn Chesnut, 185 Cottage Hill Road, Carrollton, GA 30117*

272. Samuel Davis Akers

Samuel Davis Akers, born January 13, 1892, died June 20, 1947, son of Samuel A. and Lula Viola Phillips Akers. On March 23, 1913, he was married to Mamie Beatrice Huckeba, daughter of Green Issac and Savanah Carroll Huckeba. She was born May 1, 1898, died December 5, 1918. They had three children, two children died in infancy. Their only child living is Savannah Viola Akers. She married Stephen P. Denney and their children are Alvin, Rudene, Phylis, and Beatrice.

On April 6, 1919, Davis married Dona Lee Huckeba, daughter of Green Issac and Savanah Carroll Huckeba. She was born March 31, 1904 and died June 29, 1965. Their children are: (1) Roy Franklin Akers born June 1, 1921, died October 17, 1939. (2) Mamie Lucille born June 1, 1923. She married Gerald Pete Thomas and their children are Fred, Lewis, Jean, Patsy, Ricky, Tommy, and Darlene. (3) Delia Christine born February 9, 1925. She married Luther Reeves Collins and their children are Miriam, Jerry, and Ronald. (4) Ellen Florence born April 12, 1927. She first married Lemuel Tyson (deceased) and their children are Linda, Billy, David, and Debbie. Ellen is now married to Buck Yates. (5) Eula Mae born October 17, 1929. She first married Edward Tyson (divorced) and their children are Gary, Charlsie, and Randy. Eula Mae is now married to Alton Stitcher. (6) Ezma Lee born August 30, 1932. Ezma married Clarence Thomas and their children are Roger, Larry, and Jane. (7) Doris Rudene born August 3, 1934, and died July 1, 1938. (8) Gerald Davis born and died August 21, 1938. (9) Harvie Reubin born November 28, 1940. He married Brenda Wilson and they had one child Patricia.

Samuel Davis and Dona Lee Akers

Davis had five brothers: (1) James Wilson born 1894, married Mae Irvin and their children are Homer, Grover, Opal Mae, Irvin, Rayford, Eugene, Faye, and Remona. (2) William Hampton born 1896, married Sudie McCarty. Their children are Effie, Thelma, and Dorothy. (3) Amos Nathaniel born 1898, married Millie McCarty and Delia Webb. Their children are Fao, George, Charlie, Junior, and J.C. (4) George Allen born 1903, married Bessie Adams, Maude Bradshaw, and Ruth. Their children are John D. and Edward. (5) Charley Leon "Lonnie" born 1907, married Pauline Akin. Their children are James and Myrene.

A sister Mahala Delia was born February 22, 1901, and died March 10, 1901. One half sister, Sarah Jane Akers, married James L. Carroll. Their children are Claude, Early, Eva, Myrtle, Reubin, Reese, Verna Mae, Kirby and Warren.

Samuel Davis Akers, born in 1892, was a Primitive Baptist preacher and a farmer. His father Samuel A. Akers, born 1878, and his grandfather Samuel Akers, born 1855, were also Primitive Baptist preachers. He had two brothers, Amos N. and Charley Leon Akers, who were Missionary Baptist preachers.

Davis was born in Cleburne County, Alabama, but as a young boy they moved to Carroll County and lived here the rest of his life. He is buried in Antioch Baptist Church Cemetery near Banning, Georgia, between his two wives (who were sisters) and four of their children. *Submitted by: Ezma Akers Thomas, 1065 Beulah Church Road, Carrollton, GA 30117*

273. Akin

John Akin was a sergeant in the Virginia Regulars in the Revolutionary War. In 1830 he was in Pike County, Georgia. In the 1835 list of living Revolutionary War Veterans he was seventy-five. His son John Akin Jr. married Elizabeth C. Dingler in 1823 in Jasper County. By the time Isham Akin (married Emaline Manard) was born they lived in Pike County. John and Elizabeth also had Mary Ann (married Henry Helms), Frances (married William Evans), James J. (wife Mary), William G. (married Sarah Parker), Millie S. (married James W. Leach), Rhoda E.

(married Asa Reeves), John T. (married Sarah Reeves), and Sarah J. (married Henry Adams).

William and Frances Evans had moved to Carroll County by 1860 and were neighbors of George R. Lambert, John Burrow, Henry Reid, and George Reid.

During the Civil War, Isham and William were in the 53rd Georgia Infantry Regiment, John was in the 27th Georgia Infantry Regiment. Isham enlisted at Haralson, Georgia. William died of typhoid fever at Richmond, Virginia, in 1863. Asa Reeves (Rhoda's husband) was in the 41st Georgia Infantry Regiment and died in 1862. Isham's wife, Emaline, and William's wife Sarah moved to Carroll County in 1861 and Emaline purchased two hundred acres of land near William and Frances Evans for two hundred dollars. Rhoda had two children, John and Elizabeth Jane. She went to live with her sister Frances during the war. There she met and married George R. Lambert who was recently widowed.

Children of Isham and Emaline Akin

Isham and Emaline had sixteen children. They were Sarah Elizabeth, William Henry Harrison (married Mary E. Dean), Nancy Christeanna, James Emmett, Eldridge Gibson, Upson Smith, Anderson Beverly (married Nancy Jane Adams and later Cora Jane Holcombe), Albert Thomas (twin of Anderson Beverly), Isham Anderson (married Margaret Alice Maddon, Amanda Emeline Orleans, Roland Jackson (married Susan E. Reid), Jeremiah Ditson (married Mattie Cook), Joseph Meredith (married Mary Elizabeth Bishop), Mary Ann, Edmond, and Benjamin Franklin. In the census of 1900, nine of their children were living.

The accompanying picture is of (back row left to right) Isham Anderson, Amanda E. and Joseph M. (front row left to right) Jeremiah (Jerry), William Harrison, Allison Beverly, and Roland.

Isham and Margaret's children were Fletcher, Leona, Homer, and Nora. Jerry and Mattie's children were Mary, Emmet, Barney, Milford and Dorsey. William and Mary's children were Mae, Emma, Alice, Joe, John, and Maggie. Allison and Nancy's children were Solan, Grady, Effie Lou, Paul, Clarence, Ola, Addie, Corvis, Opal, Mildred, Albrey, and Edgar. Roland and Susan's children were Reynold, Larkin, Palm, Ralph, Lawrence, Luna, Harmon, Woodrow, and Gresham.

Most of the Akin family in Carroll County have been concentrated in the Bowdon Junction area. Barney, Woodrow, and Lawrence were Baptist ministers. Palm operated a general store and service station. Several Akins have worked at Sewell Manufacturing Company. At one time there was an Akin singing quartet and several were active in the Sacred Harp singing at Holly Springs Primitive Baptist Church. *Submitted by: Charlcie Akin Darracott*

Sources: Information from Myric Shaw's *History of Bowdon Junction* and from Wallace T. Lambert

274. June Widner Aldridge History

My name is June Frances and I was born June 3, 1930, to Joseph Alton and Dovie Dean Barrow Widner. I am one of a set of twins. My twin sister was named Ela Joan. My mother's (Dovie Barrow) ancestry has been traced back to Thomas Barrow Sr. He came from Lancaster, England, to Northern Neck, Virginia, in 1680. He lived to be 100 years old. He had a son Thomas Barrow Jr., who was born in South Hampton County, Virginia, in 1698. Thomas Barrow Jr., and his first wife Mary came to Edgecome County, North Carolina, and purchased land there about 1747. Mary and all their children except one, Hosia, died. After her death Thomas Barrow Jr., married Elizabeth Atkinson, who was originally from Virginia, and had four children. The third child of Thomas and Elizabeth was Moses Barrow. Moses moved to Onslow County, North Carolina, in about 1759. He died in 1801 when his son was three days old. It was his son, Reverend James Barrow, who brought the family to Georgia. He was a very devoted Baptist minister. As he grew older he was stricken with arthritis to the point that he was unable to walk without crutches. Reverend Barrow died in 1884. One of his sons, William Henry Barrow (born 11-12-1842 in Carroll County, died 6-10-1901) married Ella Height (born 11-19-1853 died 9-19-1934) and had six children, one of whom was my mother, Dovie Dean, born February 24, 1890. They lived outside of Bowdon on a large farm. He served in the Confederate States Army and a marker has been placed on his grave in the Bowdon City Cemetery.

William Henry Barrow was tax collector for Carroll County. One of my mother's brothers, Bernard Bert, helped him when he was only six years old (and still wearing dresses, as they did back then!). He later became an engineer and helped build the Golden Gate Bridge in California. My grandfather died and was buried in the Bowdon City Cemetery when my mother was twelve years old.

Dovie (my mother, born 2-24-1890 died 6-20-1973) married Joseph Alton Widner (born 10-15-1882 died 4-8-1957) on September 3, 1905, when she was sixteen. The marriage ceremony took place in a buggy. They farmed during the first years of their marriage near Jonesville. They moved to Bowdon in the early 1900s. My mother and father bought the home of Dr. Wilson, one block from town. It was once a changing post for horses on stagecoaches during the early years. There were six girls born to them: Montie May, Margie Lydia, Floy Mildred, Ivey Geraldine and the twins (Ela Joan and June Frances).

Joseph Alton Widner's father was A.A. Widner of Bowdon (born 3-27-1843 died 3-27-1915) and this was my grandfather. My

Joseph Alton "Joe" Widner

grandmother was Sara Frances Blair of Bowdon (born 12-12-1846 died 1-14-1920). Their children were: James Oscar, born 10-24-1865 died 9-17-1867, he choked to death at the dinner table; Flory Hiburneir Elizabeth, born 3-4-1868; William Thomas, born 8-26-1870, died 2-6-1890; Sara Pursis, born 4-22-1873; Kathy Dora, born 3-3-1875, died 5-15-1899; next was my father Joseph Alton; Martha Jane and Mary Caroline were twins, born June 14, 1905. My father's brothers never married.

Dovie Dean Barrow Widner

My mother and father were God-fearing and wonderful people. They were loved very much by their children and grandchildren. My mother also had a strain of arthritis, which has run through the Barrow family. In later years my father worked at Bowdon Water Works and died while working there on June 18, 1957. His ancestors came from South Carolina, but they were originally from Germany.

Caroline, Ingrid, Joe, Will and June Aldridge, Susan with Bobby, Flynn, and Emily Nance

Bobby and his brother, Frank Aldridge, in Hawaii

I married Robert Graves Aldridge on October 21, 1951, at the age of twenty-one at the Bowdon Baptist Church. Bobby served in the U.S. Navy. He enlisted at the age of fifteen. Four of his brothers were already in the service and he could not wait to join. Bobby served on the *USS Mimosa (AN-26)* in the Pacific. He later worked at Lockheed as a data processor. We had two children, William Joseph "Joe", born September 27, 1955, and Susan Diane, born June 12, 1957. Joe was married to Ingrid Ortiz on August 18, 1978. They had two children: William Joseph Jr., born May 5, 1988, and Caroline Natalie born December 17, 1985. Our daughter Susan Diane was married August 14, 1981, to Robert Flynn Nance from Jacksonville, Florida. Susan and Flynn have three children: Emily Widner, born August 17, 1986, in Jacksonville, Florida; Robert Flynn Jr., born March 19, 1990, in Conyers, Georgia; and Elizabeth Grace, born April 29, 1991, in Conyers, Georgia.

June and Bobby Aldridge

Robert (Bobby), my husband, was born October 12, 1927, in Carrollton. He was one of thirteen children born to Jeff and Dura Aldridge. He died September 19, 1973, at the age of forty-five. He was loved very much by his family and friends. He is buried in the Carroll Memory Gardens and this is where I will eventually be buried, too.

The first born to my mother and father was Montie and she taught school for forty-two years. She was married to William Harold Jeter of Bowdon. They had no children. She was born in 1907 and died in 1997.

Zucchine (the dog), Susan with Grace, Bobby, and Emily.

The second born was Margie Lydia and she died in an accident while mother was mopping with hot water. She fell into the tub of hot water and died three days later of shock. Margie (4-13-1909 to 12-18-1912) was only three years old and she is buried in the Bowdon City Cemetery.

Floy was born July 24, 1913, and is still living but requires around the clock care. She is eighty-eight years of age.

Ivey was married to Henry Grady Muse. She was born August 16, 1918, and she died in April 1991. They had one daughter Peggy Ann. She married Charles Edmonds of Birmingham. They have three boys, Greg, Kevin and Charles.

Joan, my twin (born 6-3-1930 died March 1999), was married to Alvin Bert Chandler (born 12-29-1924 died 4-3-1981) of Carrollton. He was a WWII veteran and they are buried in the Carroll Memory Gardens. They have two children: Kathy Joan, born 1952 and Alvin Bert Jr., born May 1960. They have no grandchildren.

A highlight of our family was when we would all get together, eat and have fellowship. My sister, Montie, was an excellent cook and loved to do it. She was always inviting someone to eat with her. She was an excellent seamstress and liked sewing for the nieces and nephews. The clothes were well made and passed down to the next generations. *Submitted by: Mrs. June W. Aldridge, 210 Tuggle Street, Carrollton, GA 30117*

275. William Jefferson Aldridge Family

The Aldridge family has been traced back to the American Revolution through at least one family line. Family records show Carroll, Haralson and Heard County residents as far back as the early 1800s. Many family members have been traced to surrounding counties as far back as 1827 with William Jefferson Head from Fayette County.

William Jefferson (Jeff) Aldridge, born 1884, was the son of James William McDonald (Mac) Aldridge and Sarah Elizabeth Head. Jeff was married to Mary Dura Nix, both originally of Buchanan, Haralson County, Georgia. Mac Aldridge was a Confederate Veteran.

Jeff and Dura Aldridge had thirteen children. Their last Carrollton home was 810 Bankhead Avenue known as "The Hill." Those who have settled in Carroll and surrounding counties include the late Claude "Henry" and Bobby Aldridge, co-owners of Carrollton Ace Hardware on the square; the late Frank Aldridge of Cedartown; Ruth Aldridge Jackson Hewitt of Rome; Dura Aldridge Dyer and James Aldridge, both of Union City, formerly of Atlanta and Newnan respectively.

Jeff Aldridge devoted his career to textiles starting in 1900 with Mandeville Mills doing odd jobs and working in the oil mill and gins. He was elected secretary in 1914, director in 1926, secretary/treasurer in 1945 and vice-president in 1949. At one time he was president of Cunard Mills Inc. He was also one of the original directors of Carrollton Federal Savings and Loan.

Jeff Aldridge was also very active in three other particular fields of endeavor. Those were Masonry, scouting, and religion, though they do not cover all his activities of service.

Jeff was very prominent in Masonry, having risen to the higher branches of this honorable and respected organization. He served as Worshipful Master of Carroll Lodge No. 69 in 1919-20, and thrice as Illustrious Grand Master of the Grand Council of Royal and Selected Masons of Georgia, as well as Marshall of Masons in 1948.

In the field of scouting, he held just about every position there was to hold in his endeavor to make the program successful in Carroll County. This included vice-president of the Atlanta Area Council and member of the executive board for more than ten years and at least

Dura and William J. Aldridge, 50th Wedding Anniversary, July 14, 1957

two terms as chairman of the West Georgia Scout District. In recognition for this service he received the Silver Beaver Award in 1961.

No less prominent was Jeff Aldridge in his religious service. He was one of the pillars of the First Christian Church of Carrollton having served as secretary of Bible School, as a trustee, treasurer, chairman of the Board of Deacons and as an elder for more than fifty years.

Jeff Aldridge was a charter member of the Carrollton Rotary Club and a very active member serving on various committees and in leadership positions. He was also active with Woodmen of the World.

Of the more than twenty-five grandchildren, only one — Gary Aldridge — has lived in Carrollton all of his adult life. Gary and his wife Kara live in the Oak Mountain area. *Submitted by: Gary L. Aldridge, 525 Oak Mountain Road, Carrollton, GA 30116*

Sources: *Carroll County Georgian,* Georgian Spotlight, Tuesday April 13, 1950. *Centennial History 1872-1972 First Christian Church, Carrollton, Georgia.*

276. William Henry Alexander Family

Looking back to 1883 we find a few families had chosen their settling place on the beautiful ridge of U.S. Highway 27 called Roopville. The Roop family was the first to settle here. William Henry Alexander and his wife Allie Patterson Alexander came from Grantville, Georgia, and chose this as their home. Just south of them was W.H.'s sister Lilla and husband Jim Merrell, across the road was brother O.N. and wife Atta, still south but within sight was sister Elmira and husband Arthur Garrett. About a half mile north lived sister Florida and husband Dr. Marion Brock. Florida's deceased husband was a Roop and in the family for whom Roopville was named.

W.H., Allie, Roy, Geneva, and Jimmie Lou Alexander

The families recognized the importance of worship and education and they had a mind to work. Donated land, lumber, and labor enabled them to fulfill their dream for a school and both Baptist and Methodist Churches. W.H. Alexander helped to construct the Baptist Church and was the first church clerk. He and Allie were faithful members until their deaths. Allie was church pianist and collapsed at the age of forty-nine while sitting on the piano bench after the invitation hymn.

W.H. was the rural mail carrier for Roopville until his retirement. After that, Geneva and her husband Jack were mail carriers until their retirement. They were also faithful members and great contributors of Roopville Baptist Church. Their support continues even in death in the form of a trust fund.

W.H. and Allie lost two sons as infants. The oldest son Roy, daughter Geneva, youngest son William Henry Jr. are all deceased. Daughter Jimmie Lou Huff is 101 years old and lives in the home her daddy gave her when she married Willie Huff. She served her church, Roopville Baptist, faithfully as long as she was able and is now the oldest member.

Our ancestors left us a great heritage. Their example of loving and serving God, loving and supporting family, showing love and compassion to all, and being good citizens is a challenge for us all. *Submitted by: Joan Huff Bell McWhorter (granddaughter of W.H. Alexander), 74 Old Franklin Street, Roopville, GA 30170*

277. The Alford Family

Jeptha Alford was born in 1797 and he married Jane Scoggins on July 30, 1820. They had four children. James Richard "Dickey" Alford was born in 1821 and died in 1894. He married Jane Piper, and to this union was born Clarence Juhan Alford in 1859. Clarence married Allice Wessinger, and they had five children. They were James Richard Alford (1888), Ima Alford (around 1890), Alonzo Juhan Alford (1893), and Euna Alford (1896). Perry Calvin Alford, their youngest child, was born on April 28, 1899. Three days before Perry was a year old, Allice died. She is buried in the Bowdon Baptist Cemetery. Clarence died in 1936, after his marriage to Lenora Wessigner (Allice's younger sister) and is buried in the Tyus Baptist Church Cemetery.

Alonzo Juhan Alford married Frances Edel Barnes from the Bowdon area. Looking for a brighter future, they left the area and settled in Mexia, Texas, being a farmer. Their children were Alice Frances Alford (1917), Alonzo Juhan "Jay" Alford Jr. (1919), Ima Merle Alford (1922), Wilford Otis "Bill" Alford (1924) who later received the Silver Star in World War II, Jesse Henry "Buddy" Alford (1929), and Joel Max Alford (1933). Perry Calvin Alford first married Myrt Barnes. They had four children; Perry Calvin Alford Jr. (1923) who received the Distinguished Flying Cross in World War II, Wayne B. Alford (1925), Margaret Sula Alford (1928), and Mary Nell Alford (1930). Myrt died in 1930.

In 1935 Perry married Sara Josephine (Jo) Raven, born on April 17, 1910, in Clayton County. At the time of their marriage, Jo worked as a designer for the American Hat Factory in Atlanta. Perry and Jo were farmers and their home was located three miles south of Bowdon on what is now Alford Road. Initially, the farm raised cotton, corn and wheat, but like many in this area, they changed to cattle farming in the 1960s. Perry died in October of 1965 and Jo moved to Bowdon in 1966. She was an avid gardener and especially enjoyed raising a large variety of daylilies. In 1993, the *Jo Alford Lily,* a hybridized variety, was patented in her honor. Jo died on July 12, 1993. Jo and Perry Alford are buried in the Tyus Baptist Church cemetery.

To Perry and Jo were born one daughter, Betty Jane Alford, on June 16, 1946. Betty Jane Alford married Roger Preston Landers Jr., on June 10, 1966. Their first child, Paul Judson Landers, was born on June 11, 1972. Their daughter, Sally LeAnn Landers was born on February 20, 1978. Sally married Bryan Lewis Carden on June 17, 2000, and in her bridal bouquet was a *Jo Alford* daylily *Submitted by: Betty Jane Alford Landers, 335 West College Street, Bowdon, GA 30108*

278. Allen

Part 1

Alcimus Harris Allen was headed for Carroll County when he was only a "twinkle in his father's eye."

His father, Harris Allen, migrated from Anson County, North Carolina, to Milledgeville, Baldwin County, Georgia, in the early 1800s. He had two brothers, John and David. David once owned and operated a ferry on the Chattahoochee River in Carroll County.

Harris and Cynthia Kilgore Marcus were married 2 March 1807. They had eleven children between 1808-1828. John Marcus married Elizabeth Jane Ball, Elizanne married Thomas Shinholster, Allison married Rebecca Reynolds, Martha Early married Malichi Josey, Mary Frederick Freeman married Henry Ledbetter Threadgill, Adeline Marcus married Thomas A.H. Sledge, Alcimus Harris married Jane Moore McCain, Cynthia Elizabeth married James Sledge, William Gaston, William Boler (no further record), and Abner Bowen who died young.

Alcimus Harris Allen, Civil War soldier 1861-1865

In 1820, Harris was an Inferior Court Judge in Milledgeville, Georgia.

Harris named his daughter, Mary Frederick Freeman, for his superior army officer Frederick Freeman, who promoted him to second lieutenant in the War of 1812.

Harris died 30 August 1828 and was buried in Clinton, Jones County, Georgia, in the cemetery at the Methodist Episcopal Church where he was a member.

After settling her husband's business affairs in Jones and Baldwin Counties, Cynthia moved with her minor children to Troup County, Georgia, where she had relatives. She died and was buried in Troup Country in 1840.

Alcimus Harris married Jane Moore McCain in Troup County on 19 December 1844. He is found in Carroll County Tax Digest in 1853. Their children are as follows: William Marcus married Georgia A. Davis; James Harris married Ida Almyra Williams; Cynthia Elvira married John Wesley Brooks; Martha Jane (Mattie) married Thomas Jefferson Steele; Margaret Adeline, John A. (Johnny), and Robert H. (Bobby) died young. They settled in the Hickory Level community of Carroll County.

Alcimus served the full four years in the Civil War, having been in three different divisions during that time. After the war, he was accidentally killed while on a deer hunt on 28 July 1868. His wife, Jane, lived at the home place with her oldest son, William Marcus, until her death on 24 May 1894. The Allen home place is located about four and one half miles southeast of Temple, Georgia. Alcimus and Jane reared their children, as did William Marcus and Georgia A. Davis, at the old home place in Carroll County.

They were members of and attended Concord United Methodist Church in Hickory Level community. Four generations of my ancestors are buried there in the church cemetery. They are Alcimus Harris and Jane Moore McCain Allen, William Marcus and Georgia A. Davis Allen, Alcimus Harris and Susan Avery Allen, and George Parker and Elfie Chance Allen (my parents).

Alcimus and his dutiful wife Jane, at the death of his sister, Mary F.F. Threadgill, and her husband, Henry L. Threadgill (who died one day apart in July 1853) took the four children, one boy and three girls, the boy being named Alcimus H. Threadgill (evidently for his uncle) and raised them as their own. *Submitted by: Dorothy Allen Seals, 131 Harland Lane Road, Villa Rica, GA 30180*

279. Allen

Part 2

William Marcus Allen was born 9 August 1847, the eldest son of Alcimus Harris and Jane McCain Allen. He married Georgia A. Davis, daughter of John Jefferson Davis and wife, on 15 April 1869. Both grew up in Carroll County.

William Marcus was fifteen years old when his father, Alcimus, entered service of the Civil War and served the entire four years of the war, William Marcus assumed responsibility of the family until his father returned home.

Ten children were born to William Marcus and Georgia during their marriage: Alcimus Harris married Susan Avery; Elizabeth Jane married Elihu Thomas Abercrombie; Mary L. married Thomas Edgar Wynn; Martha A. married James Monroe Avery; J. Will married Cora Garrett; Cynthia Viola married Milton Harper; James Thomas married Georgia Garrett; Ann Talulah married Oscar Preston Henry; Ida Eugenia married Samuel Horatio Tyson; and Margaret Nesbert married William Madison Townsend.

All these children reached maturity and most married in Carroll County. After marrying, Mary migrated to Texas with her husband. Tom and his family moved to Tennessee. Will, Cora, and their children moved to Alabama. Alcimus and Susan lived in Carroll County area until all their children were born, then moved to south Georgia (Dooly County) where they farmed the beautiful, sandy soil, raising peanuts, cotton, corn, wheat, and various other crops.

Children of William Marcus and Georgia A. Davis Allen

William Marcus died 30 January 1916. Georgia died 20 October 1913. They are buried at Concord United Methodist Church Cemetery at Hickory Level. However, after Georgia's death, William Marcus and youngest daughter, Margaret, continued to live at the home place until feeble health caused him to move with another daughter, Annie Lou Henry, where he died.

Alcimus had extensive farm lands in Dooly County, Georgia, which he, his sons, sons-in-law, and other tenants farmed until his death on

15 March 1944. Upon his death, however, he was brought back to "Dear Old Carroll County" and laid to rest beside his parents and grandparents, the William Marcus and the Alcimus Harris Allens in his beloved church cemetery at Concord United Methodist Church at Hickory Level. Susie also joined him there in her final resting place in 1952.

Shown in the photo are Ida Allen Tyson, Ann Talulah, Allen Henry, Tom Allen, Mattie Allen Steele (their aunt), Alcimus Allen, Jane Allen Abercrombie, and Mary Allen Wynn. *Submitted by: Agnes Lamanac, 3040 Batesville Road, Woodstock, GA 30188*

280. Allen - Chance Part 3

George Parker Allen was born 18 January 1896 near Temple, Georgia. He held a fierce loyalty and love for Temple and Carroll County. He moved from Temple in 1921 with his father, Alcimus Allen, to Dooly County in south Georgia.

He was the oldest son of Alcimus H. and Susan Avery Allen. His grandparents were William Marcus and Georgia A. Davis Allen. Great-grandparents were Alcimus Harris and Jane Moore McCain Allen. His maternal grandparents were the Thomas Averys of Hampton, Jonesboro area in Henry County.

Elfie Chance was born 25 November 1897. She was the daughter of John Cannon and Martha Frances Lee Chance. Her paternal grandparents were William H. Chance and Mary Ann Merritt Chance. Her maternal grandparents were Green and Julia Lee. She and her parents were longtime residents of Carroll County.

George and Elfie were married on 9 January 1916. Incidently, Elfie's brother William Adolphus Chance and George's sister Lula Eanes Allen were married 19 December 1915.

George Parker Allen. Temple, Georgia, 1916

Elfie's grandfather, William H. Chance, was killed in the Civil War at Shepherdstown, West Virginia, on 28 September 1862. In 1998, 136 years after his death, a memorial stone was placed in the District Line Cemetery next to his faithful wife's grave.

George and Elfie had three children born in Carroll County — George Albert, Earnest Luther, Frances Elizabeth — then they moved with their parents to Dooly County, Georgia, where they had four children, Dorothy Estelle, Charles Edward, Agnes Lillian, and Sarah Ann. Sarah Ann died in 1936 at the age of two and a half years from malaria fever. That was the year George and Elfie decided to move back to Carroll County. They spent the rest of their years here and are buried at Concord Church at Hickory Level.

Albert married Willie Mae Cole and they had three children, Sarah, Malcolm, and Joy. Luther married Helen Womack and they had five daughters, Annette, Norma Jean, Alice Faye, Sandra, and Tina. Frances married Virgle Barber and they had two children, Peggy and Douglas.

Dorothy married first Grady Parrish and they had one son Julius, Dorothy married second to Max Seals and they had two daughters Judie and Susan. (see Julius Grady Parrish/Parish article for more on the Parrish Family. Also see memorial page in back of book for memorial to Judie Seals Bailey who died 30 October 1969 from a brain hemorrhage. She was twenty-one years old.) Charles married Mary Kate Bailey and they have two sons, Charles E. (Eddie) and Dennis Lee. Agnes married Lee Lamanac and they have no children. *Submitted by: Susan Seals Wix, 120 Hunters Pointe Drive, Villa Rica, GA 30180*

281. Allen - McCain Descendants Part 4

Alcimus Harris and Jane Moore McCain Allen left many descendants in Carroll County. Perhaps some of whom we are not aware. Many who are still living gather each year on the second Sunday in August at the dear old church and the sacred cemetery at Concord United Methodist Church at Hickory Level just to keep in touch, enjoy good food, and the fellowship of our Allen heritage. It seems very fitting that this is the place to gather because of the heritage and history that are here.

The Allen Children, about 1914

Some of the families still attending (in no particular order) are Bruce and Carlton McCain; Fred, Marcus, and Robert Tyson; Irene (Henry) Baxter; Nettie (Townsend) Hill; Evora (Tyson) McGuire; Albert, Luther, and Charles Allen and families; Frances (Allen) Barber and family; Dorothy (Allen) Seals and family; Agnes (Allen) Lamanac and husband; Jeanette Edleman; Douglas Barber and family; Peggy (Barber) Fincher and family; Eddie and Dennis Allen and families; Annette (Allen) Crook and family; Sarah (Allen) Crook and family; children of Joy (Allen) Padgett; Julius Allen Parish, children and grandchildren; descendants of Will and Cora Allen of Alabama; Susan (Seals) Wix and family; descendants of Jane (Allen) Abercrombie; descendants of Martha (Allen) Avery; descendants of Cynthia Viola (Allen) Harper; family of Cynthia (Allen) Brooks; Elizabeth (Heath) Smith and family; James Heath; Gloria (Heath) Hancock; Ellen (Heath) Chase, Virginia (Allen) Camp and family; Lucille (Allen) Smith; Vida (Allen) Stidd; Grace (Tyson) Lane's family; Louise (Tyson) Bently; Elsie (Henry) Dorrough's family; Inez (Henry) Barronton's family.

Some of our Texas and Tennessee cousins make it sometimes. It is good to see everyone that comes. Life is so short. This is one way we have to keep in touch.

Shown in the photograph are (back row from left) George Allen, Minnie Allen, and Hallie Allen. On the front row are Maureen Allen, Hubert Allen, and Lula Allen. *Submitted by: Dorothy Allen Seals, 131 Harlan Road, Villa Rica, GA 30180*

282. James Fred Allen

James Fred Allen was born 13 October 1867 in Alabama to James J. Allen and Cynthia E. Powell. James J. Allen was born about 1836 in Georgia and died, according to family legend, in Arkansas. His wife was Cynthia E. Powell born about 1844 in Alabama and her death date or the burial location is unknown. Family legend is that she and James separated, with James taking some of the children and going to Arkansas and she took some of the children to raise. Cynthia has not been found in the census after 1880 when she was living with her husband James.

James Fred had two known brothers and one sister: Arthur born 29 February 1872 married Lugenia Wortham on 30 December 1906 in Coweta County, Georgia, and their children were Maude, Janie, Mittie Lou, Annie, Lizzie, Elma, Agile, Leonard, Virgil, and Maggie. Arthur and his family lived in Meriwether County, Georgia; Alonzo, born about 1878 in Alabama, nothing else known; Maggie Viola born 13 May 1874 in Alabama, married Richard Morgan Pace on 21 November 1892 in Carroll County and their children were Claude, Stella, Ruthie Arthur, Lewis, Maybelle, Paul, Oscar, Avis, and Joe. Maggie's family lived in Carroll County and she and her husband are buried in the Veal Baptist Church Cemetery.

Another family member reported that James and Cynthia had two more children, but they have not been documented.

Jim married Ada Folds 23 February 1896 in Carroll County. Ada was born 13 December 1879 in Carroll County, the daughter of King Daniel Folds and Mary Frances Easterwood. Jim and Ada were members of Pleasant View Baptist Church. Jim's occupations were saw milling, farming, and he was working at Mandeville Mills after the age of seventy. Jim and Ada had celebrated sixty-five years of marriage when Jim died 19 March 1961, and Ada died three months later on 6 June 1961. They were laid to rest in the Carrollton City Cemetery.

James Fred and Ada had fourteen children with five living to be grown. There is a row of nine baby graves at Pleasant View Baptist Cemetery in Carroll County. The five children are McCurdie born 15 September 1902, married Martha Ellen Williamson on 2 May 1925 in Carroll County, and he lost his life in a house fire on 22 February 1977. Their children were Charles (Eva Mae Muse), Wilbur (Martha Jo Johnson), Ray (Sandra Estes), Elizabeth (Radar Roberts, Nevin Smith, H.L. Bonner, Joe Sims), and Ruth (John Williams and Mark Anthony); Theodore born 29 April 1905, died 5 February 1924, never married; Carlene born 10 September 1910, married Callie Edwards 18 May 1934 and had one daughter Jeanette (Austin Hammond); Lorene born 12 December 1912, married Vol Smith on 28 June 1929, Clyde Floyd and Otis Burgess. Lorene and Vol had two children Jenny Smith (Milton Marlow), and Freddy Smith (Pearlie Newborn); Clovis, born 18 March 1917, married Ruth Cole on 24 February 1946 and had no issue.

Many descendants of this family live in Carroll County. *Submitted by: Scott R. Allen, 30738 Highway 48, Graham, AL 36263. sloua@aol.com*

283. John Allen Sr. Harris Allen Alcimus Harris Allen

John Allen Sr. is a forefather of the Allen family in Carroll County, Georgia. His marriage to Sarah Thomas produced the following children (perhaps more): (1) John Jr. born 5 March 1766, died 12 August 1828, married Elizabeth Inman; (2) Harris born 13 March 1779, died 31 August 1828 or 17 December 1828 (both found as death dates); (3) Richard married Elizabeth Williamson; (4) Ava married David Inman. This information found in *The Family Heads of Georgia.*

Harris Allen, who served as a judge in Inferior Court of Milledgeville, Baldwin County, Georgia, married Cynthia K. Marcus on 2 March 1807 either in Georgia or South Carolina. Cynthia, the daughter of John Marcus and Hannah Kilgore, was born 24 July 1787.

Harris and Cynthia had the following children: (1) John Marcus born 8 March 1808, died 1 October 1836, Houston County, Georgia, married Elizabeth Jane Ball on 23 December 1829 in Jones County, Georgia; (2) Elizanne born 8 February 1810, married Thomas Shinholster on 12 January 1826; (3) Allison born 28 December 1811, married Rebecca Reynolds on 21 July 1833/35, Jones County, Georgia; (4) William Gaston born 28 June 1814; (5) Martha Early born 7 November 1815, married Malichi Josey on 30 April 1833; (6) Mary Frederick Frances born 15 September 1817, married Henry (Harry) Ledbetter Treadmill; (7) Adeline Marcus born 8 December 1819, married Thomas A.H. Sledge on 17 September 1831; (8) William Boler born 23 June 1823; (9) Alcimus Harris; (10) Cynthia Elizabeth born 24 August 1826, married James Sledge; (11) Abner Bowen born 7 July 1828; (12) Sylvanus Benjamin born 15 June 1829.

Alcimus Harris Allen is the first of the Allen family that records show in Carroll County, Georgia. He was born 10 October 1824 and died 28 July 1868. He married Jane Moore McCain on 19 December 1844 in Troup County, Georgia. Jane, the daughter of William Baskin and Margaret N. McCain and granddaughter of Hugh McCain Jr. and Isabel Baskin, was born 19 December 1826 in South Carolina and died 28 May 1894. Alcimus and Jane are buried in the Concord Methodist Church Cemetery, Hickory Level, Carroll County, Georgia.

Alcimus and Jane had the following children: (1) William Marcus born 9 August 1847, died 30 January 1916, married 15 April 1869 to Georgia A. Davis born 3 June 1841, died 20 October 1913, both buried in the Concord Methodist Church Cemetery; (2) Cynthia Elvira born 2 July 1851, married John Wesley Brooks on 24 March 1870 in Carroll County; (3) James Harris born 26 March 1849, died 23 September 1887, married Ida Alymra Williams; (4) Mattie Jane (Martha) married Jefferson Franklin Steele on 25 November 1876 in Carroll County; (5) Margarett (died age 12); (6) Johnny born ca. 1854 (died young); (7) Robert H. "Bobby" born ca. 1854 (died young); (8) Adeline born ca. 1857.

Alcimus Harris Allen is mentioned in the book *The History of Carroll Camp* by Joe Cobb, as a good citizen and a devout Christian. When Alcimus' sister Mary Frederick Frances and her husband Henry Threadgill both died one day apart, Alcimus and Jane took their four children into their home and raised them as their own.

Ironically, Alcimus, who had served four years in the War Between the States, was killed in a deer hunting accident. *Submitted by: Paula Allen Brock, 1590 Welcome Road, Cullman, AL 35058.*

284. Charles H. Almon

Charles H. "Chick" Almon was born January 21, 1915, the son of the late Henry Martin Almon and Maude Martin Almon. He died at his residence on February 12, 2001, at the age of eighty-five, after serving a lifetime devoted to funeral service and leadership to Carroll County.

His father, Henry M. Almon, was born November 27, 1881, and died November 6, 1943. He was a lifelong resident of Carroll County where he engaged in farming and other business activities. From 1925 to 1928, he operated a bus line between Carrollton and Atlanta. In 1928, he assisted in the organization of the Martin-Almon Funeral Home and was actively associated with funeral service until his retirement in 1942. He was a member of Oak Grove Baptist Church. His parents were Samuel D. Almon and Banie Roop Almon.

On December 19, 1943, Chick married Virginia Colquitt in Thomaston, Georgia. After serving in the United States Army during World War II as a dental assistant, he came home to work at Martin-Almon Funeral Home. Chick Almon was a licensed funeral director and embalmer. He received his education from Gupton Jones College of Mortuary Science in Nashville, Tennessee. In 1950, he established Almon Funeral Home which he owned and operated for fifty years, until his death.

Chick and Virginia Almon

He also graduated from the Fourth District A & M School in 1933 where he played on the basketball team, and in 1998 received the Outstanding Alumni Award. He was a deacon of the First Baptist Church, charter member and past president of the Carrollton Jaycees, member of American Legion Post 143, Sand Hill Ruritan Club, Carrollton Rotary Club, receiving a Paul Harris Fellow, and received the Farm City Business Man of the Year Award in 1998.

Virginia Colquitt Almon was born September 29, 1917. She graduated from R.E. Lee High School in Thomaston in 1934, attended West Georgia College in 1936, and in 1938 received her B.S. in home economics from Georgia State College for Women in Milledgeville, now Georgia College.

She was a member of the First Baptist Church and the Loyalty Sunday School Class. Virginia belonged to several civic clubs where she held many offices and served on the board of directors. She was a member of the Arts Study Club, Annie Wheeler Chapter of United Daughters of the Confederacy, American Legion Auxiliary, the Carroll County Historical Society, Carroll County Cultural Arts Alliance, Abraham Baldwin Chapter of the Daughters of the American Revolution, and Tri Delta Sorority. In 1992, she received the West Georgia College Alumni Loyalty Award. She was a licensed funeral director and secretary of Almon Funeral Home which she and her late husband owned and operated for fifty years.

Wendy, Ron, Charlie, Sissy, and seated are Virginia and Chick Almon

Descendants of Chick and Virginia Almon are Ronald C. Almon and William C. Almon. Ronnie married Wendy Jean Siekman of Memphis on November 19, 1977. Charlie married LaRita Rae (Sissy) Brumbelow on December 5, 1992. They all currently reside in Carroll County.

Ronnie is a graduate of the Business School of the University of Georgia. He was a member of the Sigma Nu Fraternity and is a veteran of the United States Air Force. Wendy attended Wagner College, Staten Island, New York, and is a graduate of the University of Memphis. She served as "cheer girl" for Twigs for Egleston Hospital. She volunteers for Hospice and is a member of the Fine Arts Club and Administrative Council for the First United Methodist Church. She is a flight attendant for Delta Airlines.

Charlie joined his parents at Almon Funeral Home in 1976, after graduating from West Georgia College with a bachelor of business administration. In 1978, he graduated from Gupton Jones College of Mortuary Science. Charlie is a past member and president of the Carrollton Jaycees becoming the first father and son presidents. He is a member of the Rotary Club of Carrollton, Carrollton Evening Sertoma Club, and the West Georgia Alumni Council. Sissy graduated from Mt. Zion High School in 1977 and attended West Georgia College before going to work full time for West Georgia Internal Medicine in 1981. She is a member and serves on the board for the Association for Retarded Citizens. She and Charlie are members of the First Baptist Church and play in the handbell choir. *Submitted by: Charlie Almon, 322 Cedar Street, Carrollton, GA 30117*

Sources: Virginia C. Almon, Violette Harris Denney, Ron and Wendy Almon, and Charlie and Sissy Almon.

285. Zachariah P. Almon

Zachariah P. Almon (23 April 1827-26 December 1907) married first to Mary Antoinette Babb (7 January 1833-28 November 1881), daughter of Mercer Babb and Mahala Echols. Almon married second to M.A. Roop of Carroll County, by whom he had several children. Zachariah is buried at Bethel Primitive Baptist Church in Heard County, and Mary in the Echols Cemetery near Plant Wansley, also in Heard County.

Zachariah Almon and Mary Antoinette Babb Almon were the parents of: (1) Samuel D. Almon (23 August 1853-19 July 1924, Carroll County, Georgia), married Martha Savannah Roop; (2) Susan DeLaney Almon (4 March 1858-27 July 1935) married Franklin David Pearce; (3) Mary E. Almon (1859-1860); (4) Eliza E. "Lydia" Almon (1861-1939, Carroll County, Georgia), married George W. Roop; (5) Lou A. Almon (1864-1882); (6) Frances Lee Almon (1868-1870).

By his second marriage, Zachariah P. Almon had several children: (1) Z.P. Almon (living 1924); (2) Blake Almon (1884-); (3) Ruth Almon Pullen (1886-living 1924); (4) Philip Almon (1887-); (5) Henry Grady Almon (1891-1961); (6) Bryant Almon (living 1924); and (7) a daughter who married J.J. Holloway (living 1924).

Samuel D. "Darl" Almon and wife Martha Savannah "Bana" Roop (1860-1930) lived most of their lives in Carroll County; both died there and are buried in Oak Grove Baptist Church Cemetery. They were the parents of Bana Almon (1879-1948), wife of Joel R. Burnham (1878-1933); and Henry M. Almon (1881-1943), husband of Maude Martin (1885-1974). Henry M. Almon and Maude Martin were the parents of: Samuel Wilbur Almon (1906-1975) married Margaret (1910-1969); Mary Beatrice Almon, married C. Earl Garner; Evelyn M. Almon (1909-), married Raymond Riggs; Ima Lee Almon married Loy P. Kelley; Charles H. "Chick" Almon (1915-2000) married Virginia (1917-2000); Verna M. Almon (born 1919) married Serena (born 1921).

Susan DeLaney Almon and husband Franklin David Pearce were the parents of: Eddie Lee Pearce (1879-1916) who married

Blanche Carroll Roop; Zachary Buren Pearce who moved to Texas; and Lurlie Lou Pearce Murrah (1889-1991); and two children who died as infants. Susan DeLaney and husband Franklin David Pearce moved in their later years to Webster County, where they lived near their daughter Leslie Munah and are buried.

Lydia Almon and G.W. Roop (1858-1936) were well known residents of Bowdon. G.W. Roop was a merchant in Bowdon, Temple, Carrollton, and Lineville, Alabama. Both he and his wife Lydia were remembered for their faithful leadership within the Bowdon Baptist Church, and their community more generally. Both are buried in Bowdon City Cemetery. They were the parents of five children: Abel Roop (1883-1883); Senator Martin Cleveland Roop (1884-1985) who married Alma Barfield; Quannah Parker Roop (1888-1971) who married Winnie David (1887-1953); William Carver Roop (1891-1988) who married Mabel Lovvorn (1898-1983); and Mildred Elizabeth Roop (1905-1992) who married George Raymond Burson.

The descendants of Zachariah P. Almon and Mary Antoinette Babb have been active in business, civil and political activities in Carroll County for more than a century. Henry M. Almon operated a bus line between Carrollton and Atlanta in the 1920s and then in 1928 helped establish Martin-Almon Funeral Home in Carrollton, which is today known as Almon Funeral home. Likewise, the manifold activities of Q.P., M.C., and W.C. Roop are testaments to the family's importance in Carrollton and Bowdon and in all of Carroll County more generally. *Submitted by: Thomas Daniel Knight, 2485 Cameron Mill Road, LaGrange, GA 30240*

Sources: T.D. Knight, *McGee and Allied Families* (2001); G.F. Whatley, *Whatley-Fields-Roop-Person;* Carroll County newspaper obituaries; Carroll County marriage and cemetery records.

286. George Washington Anderson

George Washington Anderson was born March 28, 1892, and lived his entire life in Carroll County. He died September 21, 1973. His wife, Lula Bell Eason, was born August 27, 1895, and died April 2, 1961.

Lula Bell was the daughter of John T. and Mattie E. Eason who are buried at Indian Creek Baptist Church in Carroll County. After Mattie's death, Lula Bell's father married M. Lottie Anderson. Lula Bell's siblings were Charlie, Ella, and Dura. Her half-siblings were Harold, Emory, John Thomas, Robert L., Henry, Vesta, Georgie, Inez, and Merle.

George was the son of Newberry Anderson and Georgia Ann Warren who are buried at Indian Creek Baptist Church in Carroll County. George's siblings were Blanchard, William, Verdie, Lottie, Jim, Ada, Bertie, Etta, Vergil, and Margie.

George W. and Lula Bell had five children: Lavada Elizabeth (born July 27, 1911; died September 4, 1986; married Buford Bradley), Bernard Clarence (born July 8, 1913; married Mary Moon), Robert Lee (born November 25, 1918; married/divorced Ruby Smith; married Nelle Robinson), James Cliffie (born January 26, 1921; married Marie Ada Grizzard), and William Joyce "Joe" (born June 21, 1933, died October 3, 1992; married/divorced Kathryn Woods). The family lived in the Indian Creek and Kansas communities where George farmed and ran a cotton mill, a grist mill, and a blacksmith shop. They are buried at Kansas Baptist Church, Carroll County. *Submitted by: Jim Anderson, Carrollton, GA 30117*

Sources: Ret. Major James Cliffie Anderson and other family members

287. John Priar Anderson's Children

John Priar Anderson and Martha Fincher have many descendants living in Carroll County today.

They had the following children:

(1) Cynthean Josephine (February 8, 1850-December 26, 1903), married John Nails and had one child, Jeffrey.

(2) Thomas Wesley (June 7, 1852-December 3, 1920) married first Lovina Washington and had children: James, Thomas, John, William, George, Mary, Martha, Lovie, Joseph, Emma, Parmer. Thomas married second Viola Murphy and had one daughter Jewell. Most of Thomas' descendants live in Bell County, Texas.

(3) Lucinda Elizabeth is covered separately.

(4) Jeptha Mason (May 2, 1856-February 20, 1944) married Elizabeth Hewey (1861-1947). Their children were: Cora married Jim McManus; Martha married Percy Lott; Lonnie married Emma Shaw; five infants died; Belma married Alton Deese.

(5) Marion Jefferson (May 15, 1858-August 31, 1925), married Sarah Cordelia Traylor (March 1863-August 28, 1926). Their children were: Luther married Lula Reaves; Mattie married Tinc Walker; Corrie married Gaines Lovvorn; Floyd married Minnie Strain; Charlie married Ermis Tomlinson.

(6) Frances Cyndonia (February 17, 1860-June 27, 1937), married John Knowles (Apr. 15, 1852-September 15, 1936). Their children were: Rmettie married Charles Lipham; Theoria married Jessie Smith; Morris; Eddie married ____ Nolen; Attie married John Otwell; Geneva married Sam Otwell; Chester married Pearl Robinson; Charter married Jewell Chaple.

(7) James Henry (December 28, 1861-January 25, 1908), married Louella Kite. Their children were: James Warner; William married Emma Maden; Carrie married Jim Fletcher; Dovie married Bud Smith; Flora married John Roberts.

(8) John P. (August 31, 1864-January 6, 1927) married Fannie Cottle (December 25, 1864-July 2, 1939). Their children were: James married Anna Bradbury; Cedora married Walter Jackson; Hattie married Luther Bradbury; John Carroll married Nelia Langley.

(9) Zachariah Harris, (October 12, 1866-July 15, 1959), married Maggie Burdett (October 13, 1872-February 15, 1957). Their children were: Math married Luther Bradbury; Minnie married Austin Adcock; Beulah Leona married Tom Cash; Linus married Mattie Baker; Glover married Bert Estes; George married Bessie Pirkle; Tom married Dura White; Tinna married Herbert Alewine.

(10) William Gardner (February 13, 1870-died March 21,1926), married Alice Williamson (June 23, 1875-October 5, 1932). Their children: Clementine married Jim Weathington; William Matthew died in Arp, Texas, married Linnie Weathington; Nettie married Will West; Marietta married Newman Williams; Sarah Anderson married Jessie Wisener; Lennie married Johnnie Chandler; Lillian married Roy Lambert; Lena married William Warren; John Hugh married Ada Louise Mayfield and went to Cherokee County, Texas.

(11) Lydia May Doner Anderson (February 17, 1877-September 8, 1943), married John Hartford Daniel, and had these children: Essie married Lonnie Beddingfield; Velton married Viola Beddingfield; Henry Grady married Eugenia Shelnut; Mark married Christine Fraser; William married Wimbreth Wright; Eva married Will Smith; Buster married Mary Steward. *Submitted by: Amanda Chase, Sargent, GA and Written by: LaRelia Camp*

Sources: Anderson Family Bible and family information sheets.

288. Ariail Family

Joseph Albert Ariail Jr. was born in Banks County, Georgia, 14 November 1908, the son of Joseph Albert Ariail Sr. and Orpha Elizabeth Garrison. He married Geneva Lucille Ritchie on 14 June 1937 at her home in Commerce, Georgia. She was the daughter of Frank Telford Ritchie and Susie Lillian Evans of Jackson County, Georgia.

The Ariail Family. Albert, Ritchie, Joseph, Geneva. Eagle Scouts, 1959.

Albert Ariail graduated from Maysville High School and the University of Georgia. He became a high school teacher of vocational agriculture in South Georgia, moving to Carroll County in 1936.

Geneva was born 14 August 1914 in Commerce, Banks County, Georgia. She graduated from Cornelia High School and North Georgia College and became a teacher of primary children.

Two sons, Joseph Albert Ariail III and Frank Ritchie Ariail, were born in Roopville before the family moved to Villa Rica in 1945. Both sons became Eagle Scouts, graduated from Villa Rica High School and attended the University of Georgia.

Albert and Geneva Ariail retired from the Carroll County School System after having taught a total of 68 years.

Albert died 6 July 1996 and is buried in Villa Rica City Cemetery. Geneva Ariail continues to live in Villa Rica. Their descendants are two children, seven grandchildren, and thirteen great-grandchildren. *Submitted by: Geneva Ariail, 313 Sylvan Drive, Villa Rica, GA 30180*

289. "Miss Leila"

Miss Leila was an important part of the Bowdon community for many years. This talented lady taught piano and organ lessons, started an orchestra, and served as pianist and organist for Bowdon Baptist Church for many years.

Miss Leila was born Nancy Leila Moore on June 10, 1902, in the Plowshare or New Hope community. Her father Joseph Brown (J.B.) Moore was a farmer and the community postmaster. Her mother was Georgia Ann Smith Moore. The Moore family, which included children Olin, James, Minnie, and Leila, moved to Bowdon in 1906 into the historic home which stood until 2000 on College Street. Leila started school at age six in the old Bowdon High School building and attended there through the eighth grade at which time she entered Bessie Tift Academy in Forsyth. After graduation, Leila entered Bessie Tift College, graduating with a degree in music in 1923. Leila taught music at Tift until Christmas when she returned home to marry Fonzy E. Arrington on December 24. Fonzy and Leila moved to Flint, Michigan, where they lived for about a year before returning to Bowdon where they also lived in the home on College Street.

Miss Leila began teaching music for a charge of fifty cents per lesson. Leila and Fonzy were blessed with three children, Mary Jo, Wallace, and Edwin. Miss Leila's mother and sister helped to care for the children while she taught her music lessons at home and at the high school and elementary school. Miss Leila began playing at Bowdon High School graduation in 1924 and continued until the 1970s. During the 1930s, she started an orchestra. Some of the original members were Mauguerite Johnson, Blanche Duncan, Cliff Lipham, Bub Smith, Hugh Ayers, Roy Dobson, Martin L. Johnson,

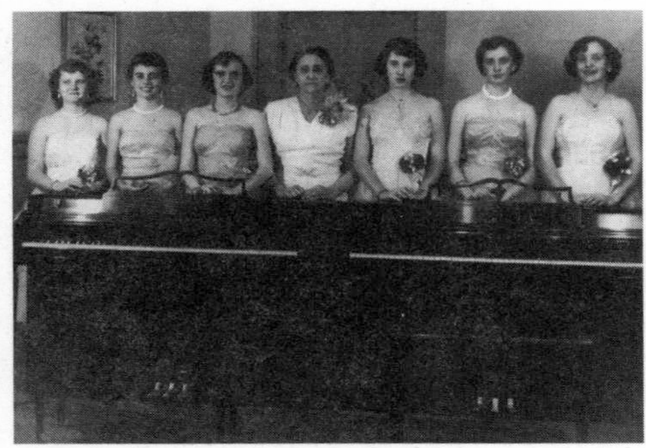

Senior Recital, Students of Leila Arrington, 1953

Merrell Warren, Harold Johnson, Mary Jo Arrington, and Roy Hancock.

Miss Leila also played for numerous revivals and other community events. She became pianist at Bowdon Baptist Church in 1935, a job she would hold for fifty-one years, eventually moving to the position of organist when the church acquired an organ. Her students then served as pianists. She retired as organist in 1986, but remained as the Keyboard Coordinator until around 1990 at age eighty-eight. She continued to give music lessons in her home until the age of ninety, never charging more than $1 per lesson. Many of Miss Leila's students became professional musicians and church organists and pianists. She had eight grandchildren, who all took piano lessons, of course. One of her numerous great-grandchildren, Ben Chambers, now serves as part-time organist at Bowdon Baptist. Leila Moore Arrington passed away on January 7, 1996, at the age of ninety-three. Miss Leila has truly left a wonderful musical legacy in the Bowdon community. *Submitted by: Sara Nell Word, 624 Reavesville Rd., Bowdon, GA and Written by: Deborah Dobson Ivey*

290. Arthur - Holland

Arnol Arthur was born June 25, 1896, in Point Pleasant, Mason County, West Virginia. He died December 2, 1979, in Carrollton, Georgia. He was the son of William Arthur and Mary L. Bates and the grandson of Lafayette Arthur and Lemuel Bates. Lafayette was a Union soldier in the Civil War, enlisting from Coalsmouth, Virginia (West Virginia). Lemuel was a Confederate soldier, having enlisted in Craig County, Virginia. At age twelve, Arnol moved to Huntington, West Virginia, with his parents. His father owned a grocery store and a livery stable in Huntington.

Arnol and Mary Holland Arthur, 1939, Huntington, West Virginia

Mary Abigail Holland was born December 3, 1895, in Marion County, West Virginia; she died November 7, 1971, in Carrollton, Georgia. She was the daughter of James Shaw Holland and Florence Musgrave. Her father died in 1912, not long after the family moved to Huntington. Her great-grandfather, John Holland, was born in 1788 in Staley, Cheshire, England. He settled in Preston County, West Virginia, where he owned a small woolen mill. The Musgrave family migrated from Ulster about 1680. They were Quakers and settled first in Philadelphia, Pennsylvania.

After serving in World War I, Arnol Arthur returned to Huntington. He married Mary Holland on July 1, 1922. Their only child, Mary Florence, was born May 10, 1923. Before the birth of Mary Florence, Mary Abigail had been a first grade teacher in the Huntington schools and Arnol had traveled the mountains of West Virginia selling tobacco and shoes. They had met in the seventh grade. For ten years after his marriage Arnol was an office manager, but his first love was traveling and selling. In 1935 he returned to selling and traveled in Kentucky. Many of the roads were unpaved then and he was particularly careful to make sure that his customers knew he was not a "revenuer."

In 1940, Arnol Arthur moved with his family to Carrollton, Georgia. He was employed by the E.J. Brach Candy Company selling in Florida and Georgia. During World War II he again had to leave the road because of the lack of sugar, tires, gasoline and new automobiles. He and his family left Carrollton and lived in Raleigh, North Carolina, and Mobile, Alabama. He returned to Carrollton in 1947, and in 1950 he became sales manager for the Runkle Candy Company in Kenton, Ohio. In 1952 he accepted a position with Southwire as their Alabama salesman and returned to Carrollton.

Mary Florence Arthur attended public schools in Huntington, West Virginia. She graduated from high school in 1940, and her family immediately moved to Georgia where she enrolled at West Georgia College in Carrollton and met her future husband, Reuben Word. After completing her junior year at West Georgia College, she and Reuben were married. He had received his officers commission and pilot wings in the spring of 1944. They were married in Newburgh, New York, July 15, 1944, they returned to Carrollton in 1947. Reuben completed law school in 1951. Mary Florence graduated from West Georgia College in 1961 with a B.S. in education. Reuben and Mary Florence have three children, David Arthur Word, Gerald Patrick Word and Susan Gayle Word Kypreos. *Submitted by: Susan Word Kypreos, Pensacola, FL*

291. Harris Allen Ashmore Family

Harris Allen Ashmore moved from Heard County to Carroll County's Bethel community during the Civil War. According to family stories, Harris was a slave overseer in Heard County at the time of the war and refused to fight, saying he owned no slaves so he saw no reason to get involved. He supposedly hid in a cave to avoid being drafted. One of Harris' sons, Joseph Tucker, told his children that he smuggled food, salt, and clothing to Harris and others who were "in seclusion."

Harris's property in the Bethel community was described at his death as "a large estate of real and personal property worth the sum of $2500, including 50 acres off a lot of land No. 150 in the 10th District, commencing at the public road near Bethel Church running north to Kilgore line south to public road at bridge southwest to F.M. Harrison's corner."

Harris was born June 15, 1826, in Henry County. Harris's first wife and the mother of all his children was Harriet J. Lambert, born December 25, 1833. She died September 12, 1898. Harris married Samantha L. "Babe" Chappell on October 19, 1899. Harris died August 18, 1915. All are buried at Smith's Chapel Methodist Church.

Calvin Reed, great-grandson of Harris, compiled this list of Harris's children. (1) William Monroe, born October 23, 1850, and died October 19, 1931, married Mary Carrie Boyles, born September 29, 1853, and buried at Smith's Chapel. (2) Joseph Tucker, born September 1, 1852, died February 3, 1944, married Sarah Elizabeth Boyles in 1871. She was born June 17, 1849, died October 29, 1923. Joseph donated the acreage for Bethel Methodist Church and cemetery. (3) Frances, born March 29, 1856, married Edward Garrett, buried at Smith's Chapel. (4) Hezekia ("Is") Ashmore, born April 1, 1857, died May 13, 1939, was trustee of Mt. Zion School and Seminary. On November 4, 1880, married Lou Cindy Ingram (born April 13, 1858, died November 2, 1907, buried at New Hope Methodist). He married Emma (born October 11, 1873, died December 18, 1942), and is buried at Mt. Zion Methodist Church. (5) Harris Bunk Ashmore born 1861, died October 3, 1881. (5) Thomas Henry, born May 17, 1862, died April 16, 1945. Married Eleanor Jackson on December 1889. Buried Shiloh United Methodist. (6) James Sanford Ashmore, born December 7, 1863, died March 1, 1921. In 1884 married Frances Elizabeth "Fannie" Baker (born December 12, 1863, died April 26, 1935). Buried Mt. Zion United Methodist. (7) George Washington, born November 11, 1870, died July 12, 1956, buried at Roopville Methodist. He married Mary Addie Watson, born October 18, 1870, died May 30, 1963. (8) Sarah born May 13, 1872, married Will Musick, died August 6, 1958. (9) Dora Jane Ashmore was born 1873 and died as a child on October 3, 1879. (10) Mattie Harriett Ashmore Phillips, born August 29, 1875. Married William Thomas Phillips, born October 14, 1872. They both died on February 24, 1934, when a tornado destroyed their home in the Bethel Community. Buried at Bethel Methodist Church. *Submitted by: Dulcie Ashmore Bagwell, 77 Little River Road, Carrollton, GA 30117*

Sources: Petition for Letters of Administration filed in Carroll County, GA on September 7, 1915. Carroll County Court of Ordinary October term 1915 (October 4, 1915). Information regarding children compiled by Calvin Reed, grandson of Joseph Tucker Ashmore and great-grandson of Harris Allen Ashmore.

Harris Ashmore with his children and second wife. Made in 1913.

292. Astin Family

The Astin family name is a misspelling of Austin from England in the 16th century (University of Georgia Library). There were three families of Astins who lived 30-40 miles up river from London. After a series of crop failures due to too much rain, they sold their farms for three gold pieces. They floated to London on a barge and took the first ship to Virginia. This was in the early 1700s. We know all this because my great-great-great-great grandmother was born in 1800 and lived until 1902. She knew some of them who came over.

My father was born 1892 and he heard these stories and passed them on to his family. They were farmers. The local Astins arrived around Newnan and Greenville in the late 1700s. They were Loyalists during the Revolutionary War. We have a copy of the old family Bible that Aunt Dora Astin Stamps has. I met her in 1934.

Phil Carroll Astin Sr. 1914

Grandpa Elijah McPherson was in the Battle of New Orleans, 1814. He brought back some rice seeds and tried to grow them at the Double Branches of Carroll County. The experiment was a failure. At that time there were no native wild pecans here and he supposedly planted some around his house. They were destroyed in the ice storm of the 1960s.

In 1830 they organized a Militia Cavalry in Newnan, Georgia, to fight the Creek Indians. My great-times-two-grandfather was in it. They were cut off and had to eat horses. That band of Indians was never defeated and retreated to Florida to become the Seminoles.

Joseph Hilsman Astin and his brother Samuel Astin joined the Confederate States Army as musicians playing coronet, but were transferred to the Calvary in 1863. They fought in five or six battles around Atlanta. Grandfather was wounded in the Battle of Atlanta in the behind. They said he was running from the Yankees. He never denied it. He was sent by an ambulance train to West Point. He recovered and returned to his Georgia Militia Company camped around Palmetto, Georgia, about 500 yards from the Astin Farm on Cedar Creek.

The house, which they built in 1848 of chestnut hand hewn logs, has been remodeled with white clap board siding and is now owned by a Delta pilot. There is an airstrip in the pasture. Great-great-grandmother nursed a blind baby on the front porch of this house while watching flashes and hearing the heavy guns in the battles occurring around Atlanta.

At that time in the Confederate States Army, a company commander could write out an honorable discharge. They were camped 500 yards from home. They went to the company commander and asked for an honorable discharge on the grounds of long, honorable service and wounds. He turned them down with an oath, cursing — an unwise thing to do to two six-foot hardened soldiers armed with rifles lethal to 600-800 yards, and four-feet sword bayonets. They put the bayonet to his throat and he said "I have reconsidered." This was after the Battle of Jonesborough. Joseph and Samuel went up the road and started the Astin dynasty. Samuel Astin was a part-time Primitive Baptist preacher. They were supposed to have apologized and shook his hand. We are a courtly, formal people.

My great-great-grandfather William (Uncle Billy) Spence (1845-1941) was in the Battle of Atlanta. He was knocked down in the railroad cut as pictured in the painting of the Battle of Atlanta. He had three day's battle rations. He picked up the shell fragments that hit him and when it got dark he started for Carrollton, arriving in three days, and never went back. He told me all of this in 1940. I saw the shell fragments. It was from a British Wentworth Rifle Cannon and had the fuse hole in it.

Soon afterwards, Joseph Astin bought 275-plus acres two miles northwest of Villa Rica on Astin Road, Astin Creek, Astin Creek Road, and Astin Bridge. He and his troop were supposed to have waylaid a lost U.S. Army Paymaster and "borrowed his gold." They apologized, shook his hand, mounted him on a good horse (they were Calvary), and gave him three-day's emergency ration consisting of three large hard-baked pones of cornbread, and they pointed the way to the Yankee lines. There was a big beaver swamp in 1868, which has returned, proving what goes around, comes around. The farm was sold during the depression to a pulp wood company.

My grandfather rented and sharecropped the land after 1914. They moved to Carrollton so the seven children could attend Carrollton High School and the old A&M. The farm was lost during the depression. Grandpa ran a small convenience store at Rome Street and West Chandler. Grandmother summoned him to lunch every day by blowing a shofar, rams horn, like the Jews blow on Passover.

Phil C. Astin Sr., who died at age eighty-seven, was a farmer, merchant, policeman, and sold insurance during the depression — this was very difficult, try it. My mother, Delphia Wester Astin, died at age ninety-two. She was a schoolteacher, landscape architect, bank cashier and interior decorator specializing in custom-made drapes. In other words, "she took in sewing" to send me to medical school. Tuition in 1946 was $180 per year; for room and board at a fraternity house it was $45 per month.

My wife of fifty-four years is Frances Wilkes Astin, whom I met here in West Georgia. Her people were in Middle Tennessee before Daniel Boone. I have three sons who are physicians: Phil Astin III, Internal Medicine; George Astin, General Practice/Family Medicine; and David Astin, General Practice/Family Medicine. I also have five grandchildren.

The Astin Family is doing very well. All of this is an oral family history of Missy Barton Astin from 1700-1902 passed on to seven of her great-great-great-grandchildren to me Phil C. Astin Jr.

As in the old Army marching song "I don't know, but they said so." *Submitted by: Phil C. Astin Jr., M.D., 702 Dixie Street, Carrollton, GA 30117*

293. James Calvin Austin

James Calvin Austin was born in Florence, Alabama, in 1821. He married Mary Ellen Richardson (daughter of William Richardson and Zepha Turner) in Henry County on December 25, 1842. In 1850 James and Mary Ellen were in Coweta County and their children were Zepha A., Mary N.E., James H., and Martha. In 1858 they had William Green Austin. They moved to Heard County and James joined the 34th Georgia Infantry Regiment on May 13, 1862. He was captured and paroled at Vicksburg and was in battles in Georgia and Tennessee. He was captured at Franklin, Tennessee, on December 17, 1864, and was sent to Camp Chase at Columbus, Ohio, where he stayed until June 12, 1865. He was described as being five feet, nine inches tall with dark hair and dark complexion.

Marshall and Dora Austin Putnam

William Green Austin married Mary (Polly) Parker on January 23, 1879, in Carroll County. Their children were Jimmy, Charlie, Elmus, Jossie, William Luster, and Dora. Elmus' son was Rayford who lived at the falls in Mt. Zion. His daughters are Betty Austin Grey and Martha Lannett Austin Horton. Jossie married Walter Bailey. William Green and Mary (Polly) Parker Austin are buried at Union Camp Ground Cemetery.

Dora married Marshall Nathaniel Putnam and their daughter was Mary Ellen Putnam. Dora and Marshall operated the Entrekin Grist Mill at the falls in Mt. Zion and the Davenport Grist Mill before moving to Carrollton. Mary Ellen married Horace Stallings and their children are Tracy Stallings and Charlcie Stallings Lambert. (See related articles, Stallings in Carroll County, Green Berry Hammock and James Parker and Henry Parker) *Submitted by: Lannett Austin Horton*
Source: Information furnished by Wallace T. Lambert

294. Ayers Family 1880-1976

Stephen Kirkland Ayers and Maude Fountain Ayers

S.K. and Maude Ayers, referred to as "Papa and Mama Ayers," were married on October 14, 1906 in the Hulett Community by Rev. Ed Robertson. Prior to their marriage, S.K. traveled to Texas to work. Before his trip he told Maude that he had something to ask her when he returned. Two years later upon his return he asked her to marry him. They recited their vows while sitting in a horse and buggy. That was the beginning of a marriage that lasted for sixty five years.

The S.K. Ayers Family

S.K. was born January 8, 1880, in the Hulett Community. He was the son of David A. and Cosby Stovall Ayers. His mother died in childbirth with her third child. S.K. had one brother John Allen. His father later married Mary A. Bagget. S.K. was raised by his uncle and aunt, Willie and Etta Barton. Maude Fountain was born in June of 1892 in the Tyre Community,

Douglas County. She was the daughter of Greenberry and Lula Fountain. S.K. and Maude had one daughter Inez Cosby who was born March 15, 1913, in Hulett. Inez married Buford Author Boggs on March 12, 1931. (See related Boggs Family article.)

S.K. and Maude moved from Hulett in the 1930s to the Five Points community on Highway 61 after S.K. bought a farm from a Smith family. He raised cattle and farmed the land. He even had his own blacksmith shop. Maude was a wonderful cook. She would always have fresh baked pound cake and apples. She held several quilting parties at her home over the years. She also invited young women attending West Georgia College to board with her. Maude was a devoted wife and mother. S.K. and Maude attended Macedonia Baptist Church, Sand Hill, for many years where S.K. served as a deacon. In 1953, S.K. attended "College in the Country," a community education program, where he studied family living. He also received several senior citizen awards from the Sand Hill Ruritan Club for devotion, love, and outstanding service to the Sand Hill community. He was also given an award by the American Legion, Carroll Post No. 143, for eighty-five years or more of superior, constructive, and inspiring service to his neighbors, community, state and nation.

After ninety-two years of being a devoted husband, father and community member, Papa Ayers died at home in his feather bed on March 7, 1971, following a short illness. Mama Ayers lived five years after Papa's death. She died at the age of eighty-four in May of 1976.

Photograph information: Back row, left to right, Buford Boggs, Inez Ayers Boggs. Front row, left to right, Larry B. Boggs, Maude "Mama" Ayers, Brenda Boggs Bostwick, S.K. "Papa" Ayers. *Submitted by: Larry B. Boggs, grandson, 71 Garst Road, Carrollton, GA 30116 and Compiled by: Lori Bostwick Leo, great-granddaughter, 2835 NE Hickory Level Rd., Temple, GA 30179*

295. Doris Emma Jones Ayers

Jake Cancelor Jones was born October 7, 1881, in Douglas County and died in Carroll County in 1957 at the age of 75. Jake was the son of Nath Jones and Jennie Cancelor Jones. Nath and Jennie's other children included five brothers Ben, Tom, Ob, Burnett, Wid, and three sisters Salley, Maggie and Alice. Jake moved to Carroll County when he married Ada Pope. Ada suffered with asthma and died in 1951 at the age of 68. Ada's parents Jefferson Pope (born 1856) and Emma Wilson Pope farmed the land before Jake and Ada. Jefferson and Emma had three other children: Ida, Rula and Burney. Jefferson Pope's father was Henry Pope (born 1810) who settled in the Villa Rica area in the 1840s. Jake and Ada later moved to Newnan Road in Carrollton where they operated a dairy farm.

Doris Emma Jones Ayers (June 30, 1912) was the only child born to Jake and Ada in the home her mother Ada was born in on Villa Rica highway. Although the house has been demolished, it stood above what is now Bay Springs Middle School. Jake and Ada worked the farm on the Villa Rica Highway for most of their lives.

Doris married Rhudy Guy Ayers (January 11, 1911). Doris was a homemaker, community volunteer and helped her husband Rhudy with the dairy farm. They lived next door to Rhudy's parents and his only sister Vola and her husband Curtis Waddell. Doris' husband Rhudy attended Carrollton city schools and was a 1930 graduate of the Fourth District A&M School. He worked at Lawler's Hosiery Mill as well as running a dairy farm. He worked his way up to foreman and was in this position when he retired. During World War II, Rhudy and Doris and Vola and Curtis Wadell worked building airplanes in Baltimore, Maryland, and at the Bell Bomber plant in Marietta. Rhudy died on February 13, 1990, and Doris died August 15, 1995. Both Doris and Rhudy died after extended illness resulting from Alzheimer's disease. They are buried at Midway Macedonia Baptist Church at Sand Hill with their parents and other family.

Rhudy and Doris had three children. Their first child, Allen Jones Ayers, died at birth. Sons Rhudy Ralph Ayers (January 29, 1947) and Roy Jasper Ayers (April 22, 1952) both reside in Carroll County not far from where they grew up.

Doris Jones with parents Jake Jones and Ada Pope Jones

Ralph married Vesta Garrett Gentry in 1975. Ralph and Vesta had two boys Ryan Garrett Ayers (May 7, 1978) and Russ Robert Ayers (August 31, 1980). Ryan married Andrea Wilson in Athens, Georgia, on November 19, 2000. Ralph is an Animal Health Inspector for the USDA and Vesta is an art teacher at Central Middle School. They reside outside of Carrollton on a cattle farm.

Roy married Valerie Duffey. Roy and Valerie had two daughters Jennifer (July 25, 1973) and Janet (October 21, 1976). Roy is employed by Georgia Power Plant as an electrician and Valerie is owner of the Classy Cricket gift shop in Carrollton. They also reside outside of Carrollton on a cattle farm. *Submitted by: Vesta G. Ayers, 288 Bull Run Road, Carrollton, GA 30116*

296. John B. Ayers

John B. Ayers was born 16 December 1795 in Richmond County, Georgia. He died on 23 March 1858 in Carroll County, Georgia. He married Mary Ayers about 1815 in Georgia. She was born on 20 August 1792 in Georgia and died on 8 April 1856 in Carroll County. Both John B. and Mary Ayers are buried in the family cemetery about three miles north of Whitesburg off Jones Mill Road near the top of a hill overlooking Snake Creek. John B. Ayers was the son of Elizabeth Blanton and Thomas Ayers, and the grandson of Abraham Ayers, a captain in the Refuge Regiment of Richmond County during the Revolutionary War, who was wounded at the Battle of Long Cane, South Carolina in December 1780.

John B. Ayers came to Carroll County in January 1850 from Meriwether County, Georgia where he had lived for about fourteen years. He purchased land in the 3rd District of Carroll County and built a home there. The home was located about one-quarter mile north of Snake Creek at the crest of a hill adjacent to Jones Mill Road. He was a farmer with ninety acres under cultivation, growing corn and wheat and raising cattle, hogs and sheep.

John and Mary Ayers were the parents of nine children. They were: William B., born in Columbia or Lincoln County in 1817, married Sarah Parker in 1851 in Carroll County. (See related William B. Ayers article). He died in Carroll County in 1899; James B., born in 1819 in Columbia County, married Mary Martha Houseworth in 1855 in Carroll County. He was in 5th Georgia Battalion during the Mexican War of 1846 and was also a Confederate soldier in the 26th Georgia Infantry Battalion. He died in 1901 in Douglas County; Thomas N., born in January 1820 in DeKalb County, died in May 1862 at a Confederate Army hospital in Lauderdale County, Mississippi. He had enlisted at Carrollton in March 1862 in Company G, 41st Regiment, Georgia Volunteer Infantry; an unnamed twin to Thomas who died at birth in 1820; Abraham J., born in 1822 in DeKalb County. He was a Confederate soldier in Company I, known as the Villa Rica Gold Diggers, 19th Regiment, Georgia Volunteer Infantry. He married Elvira Chambers in 1867 in Carroll County and died in 1908 in Carroll County; Elizabeth S., born in 1825 and died in Carroll County in 1864. She was married to William Morris; Rebecca J., born in 1829 and died in 1895 in Meriwether County. She was married to David York; John P., born in 1827, married (1) Susan Houseworth in 1850 in Carroll County and (2) Leah Benford in 1872, also in Carroll County. He was a Confederate soldier in the 26th Georgia Infantry Battalion. He died in Coweta County in 1911; and Mary A., born in 1833 and died about 1872 in Sebastian County, Arkansas. She was married to Franklin McFarland. *Submitted by: Jim Turner, 2914 Maple Circle, Grimesland, NC 27837; and Researched by: A.E. Turner*

297. Rhudy Guy Ayers

Rhudy Guy Ayers was born to John Allen Ayers and Minnie Charlotte Fountain Ayers in the Hewlett community in Douglas County on January 11, 1911. John Allen Ayers' parents were David A. Ayers and Cosky Stovall. His great-grandfather used a different spelling: William B. Ayres.

The family moved when Rhudy's parents bought a farm on Newnan Road in Carrollton. Growing up, Rhudy helped with the farm and dairy. The family bought another farm not far from there on Burns Road and grew peanuts, cotton and butterbeans. Rhudy met and courted Doris Emma Jones (born June 30, 1912). They were married on Christmas Eve in 1933. Doris was the only child of Jake Cancelor Jones and Ada Pope. Doris was a homemaker, community volunteer, and helped Rhudy with the dairy farm. On Newnan Road Doris and Rhudy lived next door to Rhudy's parents and his only sister Vola and her husband Curtis Waddell. John Allen Ayers built six houses on that side of Newnan Road, which is now inside Carrollton city limits.

Minnie Fountain Ayers, John Ayers and Minnie's mother "Granny" Fountain

Rhudy was a 1930 graduate of the Fourth District A&M School. He operated a dairy farm from 1947 through 1968. In addition, he worked at Lawler's Hosiery Mill. He worked his way up to foreman and was in this position when he retired. During World War II Rhudy and Doris, and Vola and Curtis Waddell worked building airplanes in Baltimore, Maryland and at the Bell Bomber plant in Marietta. Rhudy died on February 13, 1990, and Doris died August 15, 1995.

Both Rhudy and Doris died after extended illness resulting from Alzheimer's disease. They are buried at Midway Macedonia Baptist Church at Sand Hill with their parents and other family.

Rhudy and Doris had three children. Their first child Allen Jones Ayers died at birth. Sons Rhudy Ralph Ayers (January 29, 1947) and Roy Jasper Ayers (April 22, 1952) both reside in Carroll County not far from where they grew up.

Ralph married Vesta Garrett Gentry in 1975. They had two boys Ryan Garrett Ayers (May 7, 1978) and Russ Robert Ayers (August 31, 1980). Ryan married Andrea Wilson in Athens, Georgia, on November 18, 2000. Ralph is an Animal Health Inspector for the USDA and Vesta is an art teacher at Central Middle School. They reside outside of Carrollton on a cattle farm.

Roy married Valerie Duffey. They had two girls Jennifer (July 25, 1973) and Janet (October 21, 1976). Roy is employed by Georgia Power Plant as an electrician, and Valerie is owner of the Classy Cricket gift shop in Carrollton. They also reside outside of Carrollton on a cattle farm. *Submitted by: Ryan Garrett Ayers, 730 Cherokee Road, Winterville, GA 30683*

298. William B. Ayers

William B. Ayers was born in Columbia County or Lincoln County, Georgia, on 15 December 1817. He died on 2 January 1899 in Carroll County, Georgia. He was married to Sarah Parker on 26 March 1851 in Carroll County. Sarah was born on 4 September 1833 in Campbell County, Georgia, to Nancy and Allen Parker. She died on 18 September 1904 in Carroll County. Both she and William B. Ayers are buried in the Little Vine Baptist Church Cemetery in Carroll County. William B. Ayers was the oldest son of John and Mary Ayers and came to Carroll County from Meriwether County in January 1850.

Sarah Parker and William B. Ayers

William Ayers was injured in a childhood accident that left him crippled and consequently required the use of a crutch for walking. Being unable to perform many of the manual tasks of farm life, he was sent to school and studied to become a physician. He was a practicing physician in rural Carroll County from before 1860 until his death in 1899. He owned a farm east of Sand Hill in the Hulett community of Carroll County where he oversaw the cultivation of corn, cotton, and wheat and the raising of hogs, poultry, and sheep.

Sarah Parker and William B. Ayers were the parents of eleven children, all born in Carroll County. They were: John Creed, born in 1852, married Louise Hembree in 1872 in Carroll County, and died in Carroll County in 1852; Alonzo, born in 1853, married (1) Millie Ann Hembree in 1871 and (2) Nola Norris in 1928. He died in 1935 in Carroll County; Julia Ann, born in 1855, married James Henry Chastain in 1873 in Carroll County and died in 1929 in Brown County, Texas; David Allen, born in 1856, married (1) Cosby A. Stovall in 1879 and (2) Mary Ann Baggett in 1890. He died in 1935 in Carroll County; Nancy Marietta, born 1858, married William K. Barton in 1879 in Carroll County, and died in 1938 in Carroll County; Evan A., born 1859, died before 1870; Sarah Jane, born 1862 and married Reese Watkins Neal in 1878 in Carroll County. She died in 1949 in Brown County, Texas; Jabus Abraham, born in 1864, married (1) Lorane R. Stovall about 1890 and (2) Ethel L. Houseworth in 1909 in Carroll County. He died in 1937 in Carroll County; Thomas, born and died in 1864; Arminda Elizabeth, born in 1866, married Elisha Thomas Stovall in 1884 in Carroll County. She died in 1957 in Carroll County; William Lloyd, born in 1868, married Georgia Ann Robinson in 1887 in Carroll County and died in 1934 in Taylor County, Texas. *Submitted by: Tony Knott, 58 Dixon Street, Newnan, GA 30263; researched by A.E. Turner*

299. Babb

Eldest son of Rev. Joseph Edwin Babb and his first wife Mary Mercer Babb was born about 1793 in Laurens County, South Carolina. His ancestry was varied and represented an important strain of the pioneer stock that peopled the Southern colonies in the later eighteenth-century: English Anglicans who had settled in Maine; English Puritans who had settled in New Hampshire and Massachusetts in the 1630s; and English and Irish Quakers who had settled in Pennsylvania and Delaware between 1680 and 1730. Leaving Frederick County, Virginia, the Babb and related families came to South Carolina in the 1760s and 1770s.

Mercer Babb purchased property in Hall County, Georgia, in 1821 but sold it as a resident of South Carolina. In 1828, he first purchased Carroll County tracts. He is mentioned in several Carroll County deeds between 1828 and 1832, and on 9 August 1830 he was paid $350 as first payment for building a court house in Carrollton. A prominent contractor who was also involved in the lumber trade, Babb participated in similar projects in Coweta and other counties.

Babb married Mahala Echols, daughter of Judge Samuel D. Echols and Elizabeth Wood, on 9 August 1830 in Coweta County. Babb sold his Coweta County lands in 1835 and married 8 February 1837 in Troup County, Georgia, to Lodiskey McGee (1819-circa 1842), daughter of John C. and Nancy Hood McGee. He was enumerated in Russell County, Alabama, in 1840 but returned to Georgia where he married Lodiskey's sister Concord McGee (1824-1889) in Harris County in December 1842. Babb lived the rest of his life in Harris County, where he was deceased by 2 February 1867.

By his three wives, Mercer Babb fathered thirteen surviving children: nine daughters followed by four sons, the youngest of whom was an infant when Mercer Babb died. Of these children, his eldest daughter Mary Antoinette Babb, first wife of Zachariah P. Almon, left many descendants in Carroll County. Her half sister Eliza Babb, with husband Edward Solomon Hand, lived in Carroll County in 1880 but later settled in Cleburne County, Alabama. *Submitted by: Christi K. Smallwood, 6295 Hogansville Road, Hogansville, GA 30230*

Sources: Jones and Reynolds, *Coweta County, Georgia, Chronicles; History of Carroll County; Carroll County Genealogical Quarterly,* Winter 1988; Troup, Harris, Coweta, and Carroll County courthouse records; T.D. Knight, *McGee and Allied Families* (2001).

300. J.L. Bailey Family

Lem Bailey was married to Leila Hardy of Heard County. Their three girls were Carrie Dean, Minnie Ennis, and Francis Bailey.

Beatrice (called Beat) Barr was married to Hez Cumbie and had four boys: Johnnie Cumbie, Lynn, Bruce, and Jim. Their spouses died at an early age. Lem and Beat were married in 1907. They owned the Phillip Almon place where Mae, Sarah, Bunie, Kate and Winfred were born. They moved to Tyus in 1915 where Jessie and Stanley were born.

Most of the children moved out of Carroll County. Those making their homes here were Bruce Cumbie who had a general merchandise store in Bowdon, later moved to Carrollton on City Hall Avenue. A daughter, Virginia and Singleton Jackson owned a hardware store with son Tom until retirement. Lynn's son, Aubin Cumbie, lived in Carrollton and was a rural mail carrier. Daughter, Helen and Herbert Walker owned Maryon Mill. Doris and Hoyt Lee were also residents of Carroll County. Jim Cumbie was a car dealer in Bowdon, but later moved to Florida. Sarah married Hoke Barker. They had Barker's Gift Shop in Bowdon until retirement. Kate and Hiram Lanier made their home in Roopville where he was in the store business and car dealer. Gary Lanier and Mary Jim Veneble are still living in Roopville. Winfred was a State Trooper, later sheriff of Troup County for twenty-eight years. Jessie was born at Tyus in 1916, married Lloyd Joyner in 1935. Their children are Jack, Beatrice, and Lynn. Jack and Lynn are owners of J & R Construction in Carrollton. They are living on the original farm and purchased adjoining farms, having gone from row crops of corn and cotton to cattle and poultry. Jack is married to Judy Grey of Clem and Lynn married Lucy Sherrill of Bowdon. Beatrice married G.W. Burson of Bowdon and are living on an adjoining farm. They owned Burson Printing for twenty years. G.W. is now with Steed Sales in Bowdon. Beatrice just retired from Bowdon Manufacturing and they, too, are cattle farming. Stanley Bailey lived in Birmingham all his married life.

Having forty-six grandchildren and too many great-grandchildren to count, there were many wonderful Christmases, birthdays, and reunions. Beat died in 1938 and Jessie moved in with her father Lem until 1955 when he died. She still lives on the original farm and is the last living member of the family of fourteen.

This was a mixed family of "mine, yours, and ours" but never permitted to say half-brothers or sisters. This was one big, happy family with many good memories. *Submitted by: Jessie Bailey Joyner, 4144 Tyus Road, Carrollton, GA 30117*

301. William Henry Baker

William Henry Baker was the first son of William C. and Mary Baker. He was born September 19, 1825, in South Carolina. William Henry was a farmer, wagon maker, writer, and postmaster at Plowshare (Carroll County, Georgia). He married Mary Elizabeth Thomas on November 8, 1853, in Fulton County, Georgia. William Henry wrote short stories, poems, riddles and a news column for the *Carroll County Times* newspaper in 1883 and 1884. The column was called "Furrows from Plowshare" written under the nickname "Champion." He helped organize a school at Plowshare and arranged for several teachers to come to the school. William Henry and Mary had seven children: William C. (9/5/1854-2/25/1923), Margaret J. (3/23/1860-1/4/1942), Julie Clementine (1/24/1862-8/26/1943), Francis Elizabeth (11/18/1864-1935), Thomas R. (7/30/1866-3/10/1926), Henry L. (1868-1917), and Albert Wesley (5/26/1871-11/30/1903).

Julie Clementine married William Jefferson Segler on February 16, 1889, in Carroll County, Georgia. After their marriage, Julie and William moved to the Cullman/Blount County, Alabama, area. They began their family in 1890. It has been passed down that everyone met at Julie's home for her cooking of black beans. She would cook big pots of them with hamhock and fatback. It has also been told when she would

William Jefferson and Julie Clementine Baker Segler

visit her relatives in Georgia, she would smoke her corn cob pipe in the sitting room after dinner. Julie also served as a midwife when needed. She would help her husband deliver mail by buggy and help in the fields with crops. It has been noted that Julie's heritage was of Cherokee blood through her mother's family. Julie and William Jefferson had five children: Mittie Ann (2/19/1890-1/01/1982), Lillie Mae (3/21/1892-3/09/1978), Henry Hayden (4/02/1894-6/07/1971), Terry Lee (10/09/1896-5/23/1979), Willie Esther (6/08/1898-10/12/1976).

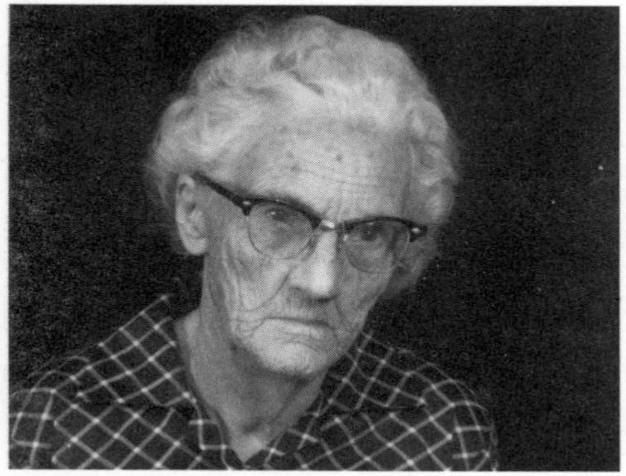

Mittie Ann Segler Alldredge

Mittie Ann married John Thomas Alldredge on December 25, 1906, in Cullman County, Alabama. Mittie Ann was born and raised in the Cullman/Blount County area. In her early years, she was a cook at the Eurika Hotel in Cullman. She was well known for her biscuits! John Thomas passed away in 1936 and Mittie Ann moved to Birmingham in the 1960s. She lived near her children and their families until her death in 1982. Mittie Ann and John Thomas had three children: Marvin Wilson, Florine and Euel Essnel (Buddy). *Submitted by: Barbara Duffel, 321 Jacqueline Dr., Birmingham, AL 35217*

302. William Henry Baker

William Henry Baker, a farmer, wagon maker, writer and postmaster, lived in Plowshare between Carrollton and Mt. Zion. He wrote short stories, poems and a news column for the *Carroll County Times* in 1883/1884 - "Furrows from Plowshare" under his pseudonym Champion. He helped organize a school at Plowshare and operated a livery stable and a stage business.

He came to Carroll County from Fayette County, Georgia, purchasing land from William M. Ingram on December 16, 1862, 100 acres in the west half of Lot 185 in District 10, for $400.

Baker was born September 19, 1825, in South Carolina and died September 14, 1897. He was married November 8, 1853, in Campbell County, Georgia, to Mary Elizabeth "Polly" Thomas (born September 4, 1829, in Georgia, died January 23, 1899). They are buried at New Hope Methodist Church.

Mary Elizabeth Thomas was the daughter of L.S. Thomas (born 1806/Georgia; died January 11, 1883/Waller County, Texas) and Julia (born 1802/Georgia and died July 6, 1883/Waller County, Texas). In 1868 they moved from Carroll County to Texas where they farmed and ranched. Both are buried in Waller County.

Baker described his family: "My great-grandfather was William; married to Mary Frost not far from London, England. I do not know how many children was the fruit of their union, but grandfather John Baker was one. He married Mary Cannon; to them were born three sons: John, Joseph and William, the last named was my father. I do not recollect hearing but of three girls, Aunt Faitha married Enoch Night, Aunt Betsy married Jesse Adams who was my mother's brother, the other one whose name I do not recollect, married a Mr. Wallace. Father moved from South Carolina when I was five months old ... "

William Henry Baker was the son of William C. Baker, born 1803 in South Carolina, and Mary Adams, born 1803 in South Carolina. They lived in Fayette County, Georgia where William C. was a farmer and mechanic.

The children of William Henry and Mary Elizabeth "Polly" Thomas Baker are: (1) William S. Baker, born 1855; (2) Mary A.B. Baker, born 1858; (3) Margaret Jessaline Baker Garrett, born March 23, 1860 (died January 4, 1942); (4) Julia C. Baker, born 1862 (died April 26, 1935); (5) Frances Elizabeth "Fannie" Baker, born December 12, 1863, married James Sanford "Jim" Ashmore in January 1884 Carroll County and died April 26, 1935, buried at Mt. Zion United Methodist Church, Mt. Zion, Georgia; (6) Thomas Richard Baker, born July 30, 1866, married Bertha Esther Sabina Cash (born June 1, 1879, died January 6, 1971), died March 10, 1926 and buried at Mt. Gilead United Methodist Church Cemetery on Fairburn Road, Atlanta; (7) Henry Taylor Baker, born 1868, married Lola (last name unknown, born 1883, died 1957), died 1917 and buried at New Hope United Methodist Church; (8) Albert Wesley Baker, born May 26, 1871, died November 30, 1903, buried New Hope United Methodist Church. *Submitted by: Jackie Bagwell Pate, 3094 East Highway 5, Whitesburg, GA 30185*
Sources: *Carroll County Times, Georgia's Last Frontier* by James C. Bonner, letter from William Henry Baker to Dora Baker.

303. Robert W. Ballard Susan A. Childs Lela Ballard Kuglar Robert Lee Ballard

Born in North Carolina on 25 August 1829, Robert W. Ballard migrated with his parents to Pike County, Georgia in 1832. Robert's parents were Miles and Evelina (Billingsley) Ballard. Robert had nine brothers and sisters. They were (1) Lucy A. born in 1834, (2) Powell F. born in 1835, (3) Henry J. born in 1842, (4) Miles L. born in 1844, (5) James P. born in 1846, (6) Amanda S. born in 1848, (7) Susan E. born in 1849, (8) Sarah A. born in 1852, (9) John H. born in 1854.

On 16 December 1849 Robert married Nancy H. Turner. They had four children: (1) John born in 1851, (2) Job born in 1854 (married Elizabeth "Lizzie" Jane Bevil), (3) Mary born in 1858, and (4) Walter born in 1860 (married to Sarah Caroline "Carrie" Bevil). Robert and Nancy were my great-grandparents. Their son Job and his wife "Lizzie" were my grandparents.

Robert enlisted in H Company, 44th Infantry Georgia Regiment, Army of Northern Virginia, on 4 March 1862 as a private. He was wounded in the back and hip at Ellison's Mill, Virginia, on 26 June 1862. He was promoted to full first lieutenant on 15 April 1863 and resigned on 12 October 1863 due to his injuries and illness.

At some point during the war, his first wife Nancy died. On 20 December 1864 Robert married Mrs. Susan A. Childs. This marriage took place in Pike County, Georgia. They had two children — Lela and Robert Lee — both born in Pike County. According to a pension deposition Robert gave for his friend, James Lafayette Buckelew, Robert and Susan and their children moved to Carroll County in the fall of 1875. They are listed on the 1880 Carroll County census in the Turkey Creek District G.M. District 1240.

According to Carroll County marriage records, Lela Ballard, born in 1866, married Jesse L. Kuglar on 26 August 1889. They had at least three children who lived to adulthood — Kate, Paul and Bonnie. Kate married Joseph Tom Broadwater. Robert Lee Ballard, who was born in 1871 married Ida L. Walker on 3 January 1899.

Robert W. Ballard died 4 March 1897 and Susan died 29 June 1911. They are buried in the New Hope United Methodist Church Cemetery in Carroll County. Lela, who died in 1955 and Jesse Kuglar, who died in 1937 are buried in the Shiloh Methodist Church Cemetery also in Carroll County. *Submitted by: Lynn Ballard Cunningham, 847 Scott Lane SW, Marietta, GA 30008-4069*
Sources: census records, marriage records, cemetery records, military/pension records and land records

304. Hattie Holcomb Bandy

Hattie Holcomb Bandy was born in Murray County, Georgia, on April 27, 1908. She was the only daughter born to John William Holcomb (9/5/1872-9/3/1918) and Cora Malinda Whittemore Holcomb (6/9/1872-5/22/1960). Hattie's brothers included Charles Luther, John Russell, Oscar Maine, Arthur Osburn, Mack Eakes, Robert William, Melvin Benjamin, Mitchell Andrew, and Joseph Dunn.

Hattie's paternal grandfather was William Andrew Holcomb (born in Murray County, Georgia 10/8/1846). William Andrew married Louisa Swisher (2/7/1837-12/12/1912), daughter of Rev. William Henry Swisher. Rev. Swisher was also the postmaster, and as a young woman Hattie's grandmother Louisa carried mail from Red Clay, Georgia, to Apison, Tennessee, while her brothers were away in the Civil War. After Louisa's death, William Andrew remarried W.A. Nicholson and moved to Ardmore, Oklahoma, where he died on March 9, 1933.

Hattie Bandy, Tommie with Vesta (and Cora Holcomb in background)

Hattie was named for her maternal grandmother Harriet Augusta Putman (5/22/1837-1/18/1917) wife of Melvin Warren Whittemore (5/22/1846-1/15/1911).

Hattie married Wilbur Earl Bandy (9/1/1911-10/22/1952). Their only child was a daughter, Tommie Lee Bandy (born 5/3/1931). From 1941, Hattie lived as a single parent working hard to provide for Tommie. She farmed with her brothers and during World War II worked in a factory sewing pup tents. She helped with all the household responsibilities for her brothers and later spent years caring for her mother after her health failed.

Eventually, Tommie came to West Georgia College in Carrollton where she met and married Bobby William Garrett (born 8/10/1928). Bobby was the son of Edgar Henry Garrett (8/18/1905-1/1/1993) and Mildred Inez Robinson Garrett (12/1/1911-7/15/1975). Tommie and Bobby had three children: Vesta Melinda (2/4/1951), Robert Lyle (11/25/1952) and Celia Leigh (4/15/1955). In 1959 Hattie moved from Murray County, Georgia, to Carrollton to help care for Bobby who died from a brain tumor on March 6, 1960 at the age of thirty-one.

For six years Hattie worked as a saleslady for a dress shop in Cleveland, Mississippi, where Tommie lived with her second husband Rev. Lee Gentry (7/29/26-5/19/69). Tommie had two children with Lee: Mimi Harriett (6/18/1961) and William Lee (4/18/1967). After Lee's death of heart failure, Tommie moved back to Carrollton where Hattie helped Tommie with the five children.

Vesta married Ralph Ayers (children: Ryan (married Andrea Wilson) and Russ). Lyle lives and works in New York City. Celia married/divorced Dwayne Leatherwood (children: Katie (married Brandon Fehring; children: Layne and Haley) and Chad. Celia subsequently married Ken Miller. Mimi married/divorced Martin Legant and subsequently married Jay Altree. Bill lives and works in Atlanta. Vesta, Celia and Mimi still live and work in Carrollton. In 1979 Tommie married Wilson Cleveland Freeman (11/17/1924).

Hattie lived and worked on the family farm in Carrollton where she particularly enjoyed sewing, quilting, gardening, and working in her yard. She was proud of her independence and fiercely devoted to her family. She was a member of Oak Mountain Presbyterian Church.

Hattie died in Carrollton surrounded by her family on May 13, 2001. *Submitted by: Tommie Bandy Freeman, 1486 Pleasant Hill Road, Carrollton, GA 30116*

305. The Banks Family

Drury (Drewry) Banks, one of seven children of David and Elizabeth Banks, was born in 1754, in Brunswick County, Virginia, and died in May of 1834, in Coweta County, Georgia. Because of his service in the Continental Forces during the Revolutionary War, he drew land in Henry County, Georgia. The county was later divided, creating Fayette and Carroll Counties, the latter being the location of his land grant.

Thomas Mercer Banks (1828-1912) and wife Sarah Chambers Banks (1828-1900)

In 1831, he sold the Carroll County property and sometime between 1832 and 1834, he moved to Coweta County to be closer to his son William, and daughter Sarah (wife of Abram Carmichael) who had settled there.

William Banks, born in 1782, in South Carolina, married Elizabeth Banks, daughter of Charles Banks Jr., in 1802. William owned property, Lot No. 59 in the second district of Coweta. This was about two miles from Bailey's Crossroads, toward Senoia. They had twelve children. The eleventh child, Thomas Mercer Banks, was born on July 6, 1828.

Thomas Mercer Banks married Sarah Chambers on 4/4/1850. The census of 1870 shows them living in the Glenlock area of Carroll County with their children, Texas, Benjamin, Louisa, Bass, Edward, Caldwell, Mary and Jane. His occupation is listed on the census as a farmer. Records show that he served the Confederacy in the War Between the States, enlisting as a private on February 14, 1863. He was wounded the following July but returned to duty, serving until he surrendered in Greensboro, North Carolina, on 4/26/1865. He was awarded the Southern Cross of Honor by the Annie Wheeler Chapter of the United Daughters of the Confederacy. His wife died on 7/20/1900 and Thomas died on 2/19/1912. They are buried at the Centralhatchee Baptist Church.

Caldwell Banks, seventh child of Thomas and Sarah, was born on 2/16/1865. On February 24, 1884, he married Lucy Emma Huckeba, born 2/7/1867. They resided in the Star Point community and had four children: Maude, Luna Grady and twin sons, Hoke Smith Banks and Joe Brown Banks.

Luna Grady and Maude Banks, children of Caldwell Banks

The twin brothers were named after two politicians who were running for governor of Georgia. Caldwell died 3/3/1947 and Emma died 3/9/1949. Both are buried at Glenlock Baptist Church.

Maude Banks, born 6/11/1885, married William Mitchell "Sank" Andrews, born 11/25/1881, and died 11/27/1910. They had two children, Willie Lee, born October 1904, and Lloyd Caldwell, born about 1910. Maude later married Edgar Lee Eidson, with whom she had two children, Millard Houston, born 9/17/1914, and Travis Henry, born 9/22/1916. Maude died 5/10/1965.

Luna Grady Banks, born 1/28/1887, was married to Amanda Lela Armstrong, born 12/17/1891. They married on 12/9/1907, in Carroll County and lived most of their lives in the Glenlock community, where they farmed. They had two children, Winfred Grady, born 2/14/09, and Thomas Wayne, born 1/25/11. Luna died 1/17/75, and Lela on 10/13/85. Both are buried in the Carrollton City Cemetery.

Hoke Smith Banks, born 10/14/08, married Gladys Waldrop and they had one daughter, Bonnie Lynn. Hoke was a career employee of the Montag Company in Atlanta, where he retired as comptroller. He died in Douglasville on 9/3/74 and is buried in the Sunrise Memorial Gardens in Douglasville.

Joe Brown Banks, Hoke's twin brother, married Inez Morris on 7/6/30. They resided in the Roopville area and had four children, Mary Jo, Sarah Inez, Alan and Gloria. Joe was a farmer and also worked for Belks Department Store for 20 years. He died 11/30/98 and is buried at Glenlock Baptist Church.

Descendents of the Banks family are currently living in Carrollton and Carroll County. *Submitted by: Carole Banks Riddle, 5 Club Drive, Newnan, GA 30263*

306. Barber

George W. Barber was born December 25, 1866, and raised in Murray County. He married Mary Caylor. They had three children, Daniel Richard, Mattie, and Minnie. Mary died, and George married two more times, but we do not know those women and families. Minnie B. Elliott married and moved to Michigan, then to Macon, Georgia, where she died. Mattie B. Bradley married and moved to Ashburn, Georgia.

Lovie, Daniel, Claudis, Jewell, and Clarence Barber.

Daniel Richard moved to Villa Rica with his wife, Odessa Dukes Barber, and four children, 1928. Clarence, Lovie, and Claudis worked at the Villa Rica cotton mill (off and on for fifty years) with "Dan" and "Ode" but Jewell worked at the Villa Rica hosiery mill for fifty years. Dan's son, Clarence, married Jewell Cole 1931. They had one son, Ray, who served in the Army Signal Corps from 1954-56, reaching the rank of Specialist 3rd Class. Later, Ray owned and managed B & A Lumber Supply in Winston, Georgia, and served as the mayor of Villa Rica from 1986-1991. Ray married Charlotte Scroggins in 1953, who was a Carroll County school teacher. They had five daughters, Beverly Swafford, Phyllis Sheppard, Jane Jackson, Elizabeth Rainwater, and Amie Williams. They all live in Carroll County.

Clarence and Jewell Barber, 1985.

Lovie served during World War II in Salt Lake City, Utah. Lovie married Mary Waddell of Bremen. They had no children. Claudis married Mozelle Campbell of Villa Rica. They had one

Anna Lois and Rush Scroggins, 1984.

Ray and Charlotte S. Barber and Amie B. Williams, 1989.

daughter, Sandra. She lives in Douglasville. She had a boy and a girl. They all live in Carroll County. Jewell married O.E. (Bill) Wilkins in 1939. They had one daughter, Sue. Sue married L.W. (Bud) Wix in 1960. They adopted a boy Timothy, and a girl Tara. Tara lives in Douglasville.

Beth, Beverly, Amie, Phyllis, and Jane Barber, 1993.

Andrew Rainwater, Meg Sheppard, Lauren Sheppard holding Riley Williams, Beau and Anna Swafford, in wagon Hannah and Daniel Rainwater, Joel Jackson, and Sara Jackson.

Odessa died February 1957. Dan married Pearl Rainwater. Pearl was the only great-grandmother that the children knew. Dan and Pearl lived to know six of Clarence's great-grandchildren. There were five generations living for eight years. *Submitted by: Jewell Barber Wilkins*

307. The Barkers

Following graduation from Georgia Medical College in 1912, Dr. Homer Lumpkin Barker came to Carrollton and established the practice of medicine in which he continued until his death September 1963. Arriving with him from Heard County in 1912 were his mother, Mrs. John William (Ida) Barker, sister Zema who later married Joe Martin, a Carroll County native, and a niece Dester Barker whom he reared. Before coming to Carrollton, Mrs. Barker was postmistress at the Elery Post Office and was the first woman in Heard County to vote. The Barkers are direct descendants of John Bonner, early settler in Carroll County, and his wife Martha.

Dr. Homer Barker, Zema, Mrs. Ida Barker, Dester

Dr. Barker was born in Heard County in 1884. He, his wife, and daughter Betty are buried in the old section of the Carrollton City Cemetery. Also in this plot is Dr. Barker's grandmother, Mrs. Ida Tumlin who died in 1913.

A veteran of World War I, Dr. Barker served as first lieutenant in the Medical Corps.

Demmy Barker, Homer Barker, Zema Martin, Glimma Denney, Bea Marshall

In 1919 Dr. Barker and Bessie Treadaway of Tallapoosa were married. From this union were three daughters — Angelene Barker, Joyce Barker Robertson (deceased 1987) Betty Barker (deceased 1993). Bessie Treadaway graduated from Piedmont Hospital School of Nursing circa 1917.

Angelene, Mrs. Bessie Barker, Joyce, Betty, and Dr. Homer Barker

Dr. Barker was active in community affairs until his death. He was selected Man of the Year by the Chamber of Commerce in 1942, served eighteen years on the Carrollton City School Board, was a 50-year member of the Masons, served on the State Appeal Board during World War II, an International Director of the Lions Club, and was active in the First United Methodist Church. *Submitted by: Angelene Barker, 115 Spring Street, Carrollton, GA 30117*

308. Barlow

Emmett Virgil Barlow was born September 19, 1838, in Laurens County, Georgia, the son of James and Ellen Jones Barlow. While he was still a boy, Virgil moved with his family to Butts County, Georgia, where he grew up on the Barlow Plantation. The Barlows of Butts County were prosperous land and slave owners during the time leading up to the War Between the States.

Shortly before the outbreak of this war, Virgil moved to Carroll County where he met and married Susan A.C. Burrow (1837-1920) on February 14, 1861. They initially lived just a few miles west of Carrollton in GMD 714 where Virgil owned one hundred acres, and in the decades after the war they would live and raise their family near Mt. Zion and Jake in the Turkey Creek district and also near Tallapoosa in Haralson County.

Grave of Emmett Virgil Barlow, near Tallapoosa, Georgia.

On May 8, 1862, Virgil joined Company B of the 56th Georgia Infantry, C.S.A., and would fight with this Carroll County unit in the western theater of the war. He and his company were involved in all the campaigns to try to control the vital Mississippi River which would culminate in the Yankee's siege of Vicksburg where Virgil was eventually captured, along with thousands of other Confederate soldiers, on July 4, 1863. After being coerced into signing the so-called "oath" Virgil was released by the Union Army and reenlisted with his Confederate unit and would go on to see action in the battles of Chattanooga and Atlanta. Virgil served faithfully through the close of the war and was present when Gen. Joseph E. Johnston surrendered the Confederate Army of Tennessee in Greensboro, North Carolina, on April 26, 1865.

In 1909 Virgil and Susan Barlow moved to Atlanta to live with their daughter Mary S. and her husband William H. Chapman. Virgil died on August 15, 1911, and was buried in Tallapoosa, where Susan was also laid to rest in 1920.

Virgil and Susan Barlow had the following children: (1) George V., born May 8, 1862, (2) Amelia M., born October 1, 1866, (3) Francis or Fannie, born June 9, 1869, (4) William S., born July 30, 1871, (5) Nancy Laura, born September 2, 1873, (6) Mary S. or Mollie, born February 6, 1876, and (7) Arthur W., born September 27, 1879.

William Sylvester Barlow (1871-1948), son of Virgil and Susan Barlow, was a saw miller setting up and running saw mills in western Georgia and Alabama. He married Claudia Nichols (1883-1949) and they raised a large family in Carroll County near Jake. Sylvester's saw milling kept him and his family on the move and they eventually ended up settling in Upson County near Logtown where Sylvester ran a saw mill. In the late 1930s and 1940s, Sylvester and his wife lived just south of Thomaston and were both buried in the Zions Chapel Methodist Church Cemetery. *Submitted by: Clinton D. Barlow, PO Box 2064, Clayton, GA 30525*

309. The Barnes Family

Part 1

Many Barnes families of Carroll County trace their roots back to Jethro Barnes Sr. and his wife Nancy Pender of Edgecombe County, North Carolina. The Barnes of Edgecombe had migrated south from Isle of Wight County, Virginia, where they were early pioneers, having immigrated there from England about 1635. Jethro's children, named in estate papers filed after his death in 1812, were Jesse, Jethro Jr., William P., Enos, Michael, and Elizabeth Marchman. All of Jethro's children migrated to Georgia before his death.

Of these children, only William Pender Barnes lived in Carroll County. He was listed in the 1870 census living in Bowdon. He ran a boardinghouse and was age 65 at the time. William left Carroll County sometime before 1880, possibly for Coweta County.

Enos W. Barnes

William's brother, Enos Barnes, was the ancestor of most of the Carroll County Barnes, although he never lived here. He moved from North Carolina to Baldwin County, Georgia, by 1815 and married Bersheba Allen, daughter of Harrison Allen. Enos and his family moved frequently. They were in Jasper County in 1820, Henry County in 1830 and 1840, and moved to land Enos won by lottery in Lumpkin County by 1847. At one time or another, Enos was a merchant, a farmer, and a judge (Lumpkin County 1847-1852). He was quite likely a gold prospector as well, having lived in Dahlonega during that period; plus, in 1852 at age 62, he became a "Forty-niner." He outfitted and led a small company across the Plains to California to mine for gold. He died of pneumonia soon after his arrival there.

Enos's son, Allen Barnes, lived close to his parents following his marriage to Lucinda Ann Moore. He was a Lumpkin County Clerk of Court during the same time his father was a judge. Allen died suddenly in 1858, reputedly on a trip to visit a brother in Fayette County. His widow and mother-in-law held an estate sale, bought property in the Laurel Hill area of Carroll County and moved there in 1858/59. Bersheba, Lucy Ann, and three of Lucy's daughters joined the Bethesda Baptist Church in 1860.

Allen Barnes' children were Martha, Jesse Mercer (who married Eliza Brown), Lizzie (who married Columbus W. Worley), Mary J., Enos Washington (who married Fannie Hunter), Harrison Allen (who married Mollie White), Eliza, Benjamin Franklin, Sarah (who married Seaborn McGarity), and Corinthia. Many descendants of Enos W. Barnes and Harrison (Hat) Barnes are still active members of Bethesda Baptist Church. Allen's brother, James Thomas (Jim) Barnes, also moved to Carroll County, originally working as a farmhand for his sister Sallie and her husband Harrison W. Moore. Jim Barnes was a great-grandfather to Carl Barnes, founder of Barnes Freight Lines/Van Lines. Jim Barnes, Jesse Mercer Barnes, and Jethro H. Barnes of Carroll County were Confederate soldiers.

Jethro H. Barnes moved to Carroll County about the same time as Lucy Ann Barnes, Sallie Barnes Moore, and Jim Barnes. Although most of the Barnes settled in the Laurel Hill area, Jethro settled in the Hickory Level community. He had married Mariah Allen (probably a relative of Bersheba Allen Barnes) in Baldwin County. He moved to Carroll from Fayette County (he was possibly the brother that Allen Barnes went to visit on his fateful journey).

Many of the descendants of Allen Barnes, Jim Barnes, Sallie Barnes Moore, and possibly Jethro H. Barnes (grandchildren of Jethro Barnes Sr.) still live in Carroll County and are active in church, business, and civil service. *Submitted by: J. Brett Barnes, 70 Colonial Drive, Carrollton, GA 30117, bbarnes@healthwest.org*

310. The Barnes Family

Part 2

Enos Washington Barnes, born in Lumpkin County, Georgia, on December 2, 1846, came to Carroll County around the age of thirteen. His parents, Allen and Lucinda (Lucy) Ann Moore Barnes named him after his grandfather Enos Barnes. On the 1850 census, the family lived in Dahlonega. A receipt from 1857 shows that Enos's tuition was ninety-seven cents for sixteen days of school. After his father died in 1858, Enos's mother moved their large family to Carroll County. This included Enos's widowed grandmother, Bersheba Allen Barnes, and Lucy's ten children, ages three to twenty-one. They settled in Laurel Hill on 202 acres along the McIntosh Trail. Today, this is on Highway 5 between Roopville and Tyus.

Enos was fifteen at the start of the Civil War. He told his grandchildren they had to bury the silver and hide their cows from the Union troops. Soldiers raided their farm, took what they wanted and broke all of their dishes. Enos's brother, Jesse Mercer Barnes, was on the muster roll of Company K in the 34th Regiment, Georgia Volunteer Infantry, Army of Tennessee. He enlisted when he was twenty-three on June 27, 1862, and surrendered at Greensboro, North Carolina, April 26, 1865. In 1870, Jesse and his wife and child lived next door to Enos. Enos was single, twenty-three years old, and worked the farm with his siblings, his mother and her second husband, Henry Wyatt McDaniel, who was the first postmaster of Victory.

Enos married Mary Frances (Fannie) Hunter on February 2, 1871, in Carroll County. Fannie was born 1857 in Troup County, Georgia, the daughter of Wiley Brooks Hunter and Susan Laurana Duke. Enos's farm was in the Bethseda community. They attended Bethesda Baptist Church where Enos was chorister and deacon. Fannie is remembered as a very good cook. She would spin her own wool to weave cloth on her loom. They made their white oak baskets and built rail fences. The whole family worked hard to square the farm in operation. They went to square dances, candy pullings and corn shuckings. Their children were Henry, Coat, Perry, Ance, and Della. In his will Enos left all his possessions to his "beloved wife Fannie." Enos died in 1927 and Fannie in 1939, they are buried at Bethesda.

Henry Lee Barnes, born 1871, married Minnie Perdue, born 1877. Henry was a farmer. Their children were Otice L., Benjamin Franklin, Robert Jefferson, Roy, Kate Bouchillon, James (Loyce), Clara Hasting, Ellis (Duke), and Garfield (Buck). Henry died 1956, Minnie died 1966, they are buried at Bethesda.

James Coatsworth (Coat) Barnes, born 1874, and Georgia Amy Eason, born 1878, were married in 1897. Coat was a farmer. Their children were Mae, Horace, Elgie, Annie, Howard, Ethel, Grace, Charlie, Myrtle, Dumah, Estelle and Arnold. *(See Barnes Family Part 3)*

Luvic (Perry) Barnes, born 1877 and Sula Benford, born 1877, were married in 1898. Perry operated a cotton gin. Their children were Eva Bishop, Howell B., Myrtis Alford, Howell (Alton), Erma Striplin, Reba Burson, Mary Miles, Herman Enos, Ann Burson and Jackie Fuller. Perry died 1945, Sula died 1968, they are buried at Tyus Baptist.

Georgia Della died young in Carroll County.

Anderson W. (Ance) Barnes, born 1882, married Arvella McGuire in 1901. He was a grist miller. Ance died 1968, Arvella died 1958. Their children were Belle, E. Marshall, Myers M. and Austin.

Coat and Georgia Barnes and family around 1907

Hundreds of descendents of the Allen Barnes family still live in Carroll County. *Submitted by: Lee Barnes, 2051 Arnold Road, Hoover AL 35216.* Sources: Carol Barnes McWhorter.

311. The Barnes Family Part 3

James Coatsworth (Coat) Barnes, born January 18, 1874, married Georgia Ann Eason on February 4, 1897. She was born April 1878, the daughter of George Washington Eason and Sarah Jane (Sallie) Carroll. Coat and Georgia were both born and married in Carroll County. Their land in the Bethesda community had belonged to Coat's father. They were active in Bethesda Baptist Church. Their children were: Mae, Horace, Elgie, Annie, Howard, Ethel, Grace, Charlie, Myrtle, Dumah, Estelle and Arnold. They have all recounted happy childhood memories. They attended the one-room school at Bethesda. They raised almost everything needed on their farm. Cotton was their cash crop. Half of the year they worked planting, raising and picking cotton to sell in the fall. The trip to town by horse and wagon to sell the cotton was a major event. They had cows, mules, chickens, geese, pigs, and guineas. They harvested their own honey. Their place was famous for the ride hill and wagons the boys built. Children would come from miles around to take a turn. Coat could play the harp and fiddle very well and many in the family inherited musical and creative talents. Coat died in 1935, Georgia in 1951, and they are buried at Bethesda.

Willa (Mae) born March 9, 1898, died November 8, 1908. She is buried at Bethesda.

James (Horace), born January 14, 1900, married Mary Dixson, their children are: Sybil, James, Harold, and Peggy. Horace was a Bible scholar and carpenter. He died January 9, 1977, and is buried at Antioch Baptist near Bowdon.

Eldred (Elgie) McKinley, born November 10, 1902, married Grace Sprewell, their children are: Tyler, Jeanette, and Sarah. Elgie was a farmer and carpenter. He died December 6, 1984, and is buried at Salem Baptist with Grace and daughter Jeanette.

Annie Laura was born May 6, 1904. She was a seamstress and the backbone of the family. Annie died suddenly October 29, 1948. She is buried at Bethesda.

Howard was born and died in 1906. His grave is at Bethesda, marked infant. His name is in Coat's memorial in church records.

Ethel Susie, born July 5, 1907, married Davis Walker. Their children are: Larry, Bonnie, and Ann. Ethel was a homemaker. She died July 23, 1981, and is buried with Davis at Bethesda.

Grace Vera, born January 21, 1910, married Garford Rooks. Their children are Zonna, Maureen, and Steve. Grace is an artist, a poet, and has written a book about life on the farm.

Charlie Marvin, born October 11, 1913, married Ellen Striplin who died in childbirth, their daughter is Charlene. Charlie then married Helen Tarpley and their children are Sharon and Deborah. Charlie was a farmer and metal worker. He died September 3, 1992, and is buried at Mt. Harmony Gardens in Cobb County.

Myrtle, born August 17, 1915, died June 7, 1917. She is buried at Bethesda.

James (Dumah), born September 11, 1918, married Eljein Duke. Dumah served in the Army during World War II. He was a mechanic and saw miller. Their children are: Brett and Tim. Brett married Vicky Jo Traylor, their daughter is Houston Sonja Marlene Barnes.

Lucille (Estelle), born November 8, 1920, married Dumah Morris, their daughter is Nan. Estelle is a homemaker. Dumah died in Haralson County.

Arnold Carl, born May 12, 1922, married Bette Phillips. Arnold was a truck driver and Bette was the Carroll County tax commissioner. Their children are: Carol, Lee, Scott, and Phil. Phil died in 1979, Scott in 1997, and they are buried at Antioch Baptist. Lee married Bridgett Gilbert, their children are Philip Gilbert and Aaron Kyle. Carol married Don McWhorter, their children are Arielle Autumn McWhorter and Alex Hayden McWhorter.

Today there are over 150 living descendents of Coat and Georgia Barnes and many are still in Carroll County. *Submitted by: Arnold and Bette Barnes, 570 Old Antioch Road, Carrollton, GA 30117* Source: researched by: Carol Barnes McWhorter

312. The Henry Marquis Barnes Family

James Thomas (Jim) Barnes and his wife Susan Jane McGarity were farmers in the Blackjack Mountain area of Carroll County (U.S. Census 1860-1900). They had five children, James B. (born November 1, 1863), Enos W. (born April 29, 1866), William "Bill" Jackson (born December 27, 1867), Henry Marquis (born December 22, 1869) and Mary "Mollie" Bersheba (born February 22, 1872).

Henry Marquis grew up on the farm but as a teen-ager went to west Texas to work on a horse ranch. He was called back to Georgia to fulfill a battle field pledge by James Thomas Barnes and James Henry Lamar Benford to seal their friendship by the marriage of one of their future off-springs. As time passed, only one unmarried child remained in each family so James Thomas called for Henry Marquis to return to Georgia to "help on the farm." A large camp gathering with many neighbors attending was held to welcome Henry home. It was by a carefully arranged "accident" that Henry met Ada Perdue Benford. Shortly after that, on February 15, 1896, they were married and began a relationship that lasted for sixty-six years.

The newly weds continued to live in the Bowdon area as farmers and raised Francis Edel (1896), Susan Ethel (1898), Ima Estelle (1902), Sterling Benjamine (1903) and Ola Eugenia (1906). The family moved to Halesville, Alabama, where James Henry Kermit (1909) and Vera Inez (1911) were added to the family.

Henry M. and Ada Perdue Barnes. 1943

In 1914, Henry loaded the family into covered wagons and migrated to west Texas to begin farming in the Big Springs area. Dry land farming in this area was non-rewarding and strictly dangerous to your health, as this was primarily cattle country. After threats by cattlemen to "burn them out," the hand writing was on the wall. In 1917, the family moved to Mexia, Texas — this time by car — where he continued farming. When oil was discovered in Mexia in 1920, he began building houses for the "oil boomers" and became a successful developer and investor in land and oil ventures. During World War II, he served in various civic capacities including head of the Gasoline Rationing Board. He and Ada Perdue were active members of the local Baptist church. Their lives came to a tragic end December 25, 1953, when both were killed in an auto accident while visiting grandchildren in west Texas.

All of their children married and remained in Texas but at this writing only James Kermit survives. At family gatherings, discussions always included concerns of uncles, aunts, and cousins back in Bowdon, so in many respects they all had Georgia on their minds. *Submitted by: James A. Cox, 7918 Oxfordshire Drive, Spring, TX 77379*

313. William Jackson "Billie" Barnes and Lula Delone Hughey Barnes

James Thomas "Jim" Barnes, born 1837, was the youngest child of Enos and Bersheba Barnes and a brother to Allen Barnes. He moved to the Laurel Hill community of Carroll County in 1860. At age twenty-three he married Susan Jane McGarity. He served in Company C, 56th Georgia Infantry, during the Civil War. They had five children: James "Jim" B., Enos W., William Jackson "Billie," Henry Marquis, and Mary "Mollie" B. Barnes.

William Jackson "Billie" stayed in the Blackjack Mountain area and married Lula Delone Hughey in 1893. It was told that they had never dated. They had seen each other in church and one day he drove up in his buggy and asked for her hand in marriage. The marriage lasted fifty-eight years. Billie and Lula purchased a farm just east of Tyus and there they had six children: Carrie Lee, Mittie Belle, William Stacy, Benjamin Carl, and Jessie Louise. Billie became a successful farmer and landowner in Carroll County, scanning several hundred acres of farm land and also a couple of store buildings in Bowdon. He also was a successful trader on Trading Days and became a cotton buyer from those farmers having their cotton ginned in Bowdon.

Lula became a well-known seamstress in the area. She owned the only hemstitching machine around and the ladies from all around brought their work to her. As they were lifelong residents of Carroll County, so were some of their children.

Carrie Lee married James Richard "Jim" Alford and they had nine children. Most of their life was spent in Alabama.

Barnes Family Reunion 1994

Mittie Belle married William Durwood Jenkins of College Park, Georgia. They had two children. The second child died at six months and Mittie Belle died of tuberculosis three months later.

Stacy William remained in Bowdon and married Clyde Paula Copeland. They were childless but were industrious business people. They were insurance agents and at different times owned a small business.

Benjamin Carl "BC" married Nellie Kate Rainwater in Bowdon in 1926 and had two children. In 1930, BC entered the business world as a partner in the grocery business. In those days, most merchandise for the local merchants came out of Atlanta. Since there were no commercial carriers to bring that merchandise to them, they had to go get it for themselves. BC borrowed money to start a commercial carrier line from Atlanta to Carroll County. That was the beginning of Barnes Freight Line. It became a very successful part of the Carroll County economy for more than fifty years. Their youngest son is still active in business in Carrollton.

William Jackson "Billie" Barnes and Lula Delone Hughey Barnes

Jessie "Jett" Louise married Bill Roop and had three children. The Roop Wholesale Grocery Company was a major part of the Carroll County economy. Bill's grandfather founded the company and it was passed down through the family to Bill. After Bill passed on, Jett and her children remain active in the business and social world of Carroll County today. *Submitted by: William D. Jenkins Jr., 16907 Waycreek, Houston, TX 77068*

314. Barr

Joseph Barr was born in 1787 and married Eliza Houston in Abbeville County, South Carolina, in 1808.

Josiah Kanady (Kennedy) Barr (1817-1889). Josiah Barr was the Barr who brought the Barr name to Carroll County by Cobb County. Born in Abbeville, South Carolina, he died in 1889 and was buried in Lebanon Baptist Church near Roopville. He married Jane Owen Griffith in 1834. Jane was born in Cobb County in 1816, died in 1901 and was buried in New Lebanon. During Josiah's days, he and Jane not only grew their food but also spun their cloth and made their clothes, including the men's hats and shoes. J.K. Barr was instrumental in organizing New Lebanon Baptist Church. He and Jane were charter members of Bethesda Baptist Church in 1849. At the second meeting of the Bethesda congregation, Josiah Barr was elected clerk. In 1851 he was asked to serve as a deacon at Bethesda. J.K. was a farmer by then. He and Jane had eleven children: Maranis Caroline (1835), George Alexander (1837-1862) died in War of Aggression in Virginia, Clementine Gammon (1839-1923), Elizabeth Catharine (1841), Eliza (1843-1927), Nancy Emaline Chambers (1845-1917), Martha Ann Chambers (1847-1922), Louisa Jane Chambers (1849-1930), Judson Cook (1852-1948), Josiah Towers (1855), and Dr. John Houston (1860-1914).

Four generations of Barrs. John Barr II, John Barr holding John Bar III, and Judson Cook Barr.

Judson Cook Barr (1852-1948). Judson Cook Barr married Sally Lewis. Judson was buried in Roopville Cemetery. He was a master carpenter and cabinetmaker. Judson made bonded whiskey near Roopville. He lived to be ninety-six years old and outlived five wives. It is said that the last time he got married, he went to the courthouse to get a marriage license. He sent someone in from the car he was in to get the license for him. They said he would have to come in to get it himself. The person sent in for the license said, "Judge, he is too old to come in." Judson and his first wife Sally Lewis had eight children: George, John, Seab, Joe, Jim, Beatrice Bailey, Alice Taylor, and Millie Perdue.

John and Myrtle Barr's children and spouses, and John Barr's mother.

John Houston Barr (1876-1958). John H. Barr was married to Myrtle King (1880-1960). J.H. Barr was called "Uncle John" by most of the people around Tyus and Bowdon. He was a banker, saw miller, cotton ginner, store owner, and mule barn owner. J.H. and Myrtle had eight children: Lee Houston Barr (1898-1966), Owen Price Barr (1901-1979), Clara Gert Barr (1903-1996), Zelma Barr (1905), Ara Barr (1908-1964), Avis Barr (1911), Grace Barr (1912-2000), and John Barr Jr. (1915-1998). J.H. Barr Sr. had seventeen sawmills and was in the lumber business with Zuber Lumber in Atlanta. Around the turn of the century, John Barr would take lumber to Atlanta by ox and wagon. It would take more than a day to get there so he would sleep on the wagon of lumber. Cotton was big in Carroll County at that time, so John Barr had several cotton gins. Barr opened a general store in Tyus in 1911 that later became Barr and Sons (with son Lee). John Barr was also president of the Commercial Bank of Bowdon, a bank he helped organize. Mules were also a big business in Georgia and in Carroll County. There were over one-half million in Georgia in 1925. Many of those mules passed through John Barr's mule barns in Bowdon, Georgia. He started a mule business shortly after the turn of the century. Having lived forty-four or forty-five years, he brought many mules from Texas, Oklahoma, Tennessee, and Missouri. He left home at age thirteen because his father wouldn't let him go to school to learn to read and write. He made him work in the crop fields and whiskey stills. John Barr went to Texas and learned to read and write while living with his uncle. You've heard the term "self-made man." John Houston Barr was truly that kind of man.

Lee Houston Barr (1898-1966). Lee married Dura Simonton (1903-1977). They had two children: Lee (Sonny) and Fred Barr.

Owen Price Barr (1901-1979). Owen was married to Elise Lovvorn (1900-1983). They had twin daughters: Joan Hendrickson and Jane Clinton.

John and Myrtle Barr with their grandchildren.

Clara Gert Barr (1903-1996). Clara was married to Malcolm Yates (1894-1986). They had two children: Rob Yates and Mary Lynn Yates (1931-1990).

Zelma Barr (1905). Zelma was married to Luther Harman (1900-1959). They had two children: Nan Kent and Ned Harman.

Ara Barr (1908-1964). Ara was married to Lod Matthews (1907-1980). They had two children: Mike and Tim Matthews.

Avis Barr (1911). Avis was married to Dr. Charlie Eberhart (1908-). They had two children: Charles and John Eberhart.

Grace Barr (1912-2000). Grace was married to Bill Smitha (1908-1992). They had two children: Betty Eubanks and William A. (Chic) Smitha.

John and Myrtle Barr, with their children, spouses, and grandchildren.

John Barr Jr. (1915-1998). John married Virginia (Jean) Barrow (1918-). As you will notice from above, J.H. Barr Sr. had eight children. The first seven children had two children each. John Jr. and Jean had four children: John Barr III, called Johnny (1938-1976), Carolann Blackweilder, Gini Braiden, and Robert Barr. *Submitted by: Ned Harman, 18845 Highway 27, Roopville, GA 30170*

315. Benjamin Franklin Barrett and Texanna Awbrey

Benjamin Franklin (called B.F.) Barrett, the son of Francis M. Barrett and Amanda Prudence Johnston, was born February 23, 1860, in Heard County, Georgia.

Texana Awbrey, known as Texie, was the daughter of James Jackson Awbrey and Lucy Ann Catherine Jones. Texie was born on April 11, 1861.

B.F. and Texie were married February 23, 1883, and moved to Carroll County around 1890 to a farm on Salem Church Road near the Little Tallapoosa River. They lived there for some time and then moved to Bowdon on old Rome Street. Benjamin was a member of Bowdon Methodist Church and was on the building committee when the church was built in 1909. At one time, Benjamin was a merchant in Bowdon near the site of the present post office. Benjamin and Texie had seven children — four daughters and three sons.

Benjamin Franklin and Texie Awbrey Barrett Family. About 1897.

(1) Marion Awbrey was born June 27, 1885, and died October 12, 1946, in Bowdon, Georgia. He married Ammie Crews (1894-1946) on March 12, 1922. Ammie was the daughter of Charles Berry Crews and Lela Edna Jackson. Marion and Ammie had four children, Athie Mae, Gladys, Texie, and Glenn. Marion Awbrey graduated from Bowdon College in 1910 and was the recipient of a medal from his mathematics class. He taught a number of schools in the Bowdon area (see related topical article *Liberty High School 1911*) for many years, but when his health got bad he chose another livelihood — selling fruit trees around Bowdon and the surrounding areas. Marion Awbrey and Annie are both buried in the Bowdon First United Methodist Church cemetery.

(2) Leah was born December 2, 1887, died March 11, 1967, and is buried in the Bowdon First United Methodist Church Cemetery. Leah and James Clark McWhorter (1883-1952) were married December 24, 1905. Their six children were Ralph, Ben, Hugh, Inez, Thelma, and Fred.

(3) Lucy Eula was the third child. She was born July 21, 1891, and died October 30, 1969. Eula is buried in the Bowdon First United Methodist Church Cemetery. She and W. Homer Tarpley (1889-1925) were married September 13, 1914. They had two children, Harold and Marion.

(4) James Tensey was born October 26, 1894, died March 10, 1943, and is buried in the Bowdon First United Methodist Church Cemetery. James married Leda Joy McGraw (1903-1934) on February 4, 1932, and they had one child, Barbara. James remarried after the death of Leda Joy in 1934.

(5) Lura Ann was born August 3, 1897, died March 12, 1949, and is buried in the Bowdon City Cemetery. On October 20, 1920, she married Jim Smith and they had three children, Margaret, Julian, and James Robert (Bobby).

(6) Joe Frank was born September 19, 1899, and died from diphtheria on May 5, 1901. He is buried in Old Camp Cemetery, Carrollton.

(7) The last child in this family was Tempie Amanda Barrett, born June 14, 1902, and died March 25, 1982. She married Grady Jeter on October 7, 1920, and they had one child, Earlene. Tempie is buried in West View Cemetery in Atlanta. B.F. Barrett and Texie moved to a large house on Carrollton Street East on the outskirts of Bowdon and he began to sell fruit trees for a living.

Texie Awbrey died on February 24, 1926. During and after this time, B.F. went to North Alabama to pick up his stock (fruit trees). He met and married Ida Luther there (no issue from this marriage). He moved to Albertville, Alabama, and lived there until his death on February 11, 1936. He is buried in the City Cemetery in Albertville. Most of his family stayed in Carroll County and Georgia.

The Barrett family photograph taken about 1897 shows (from left) Eula, J.T. Benjamin Franklin, Awbrey, Texie, Lura and Leah. *Submitted by: Glenn Barrett, Bowdon, GA 30108*

316. The Barron Family

In December 1975 Charles Barron moved to Carroll County to start work at Southwire Company as a draftsman. Born 9-4-57 he was the middle child of Earl and Willene Barron of Habersham County. Earl Barron was a carpenter by trade until his death on 11-24-87. Willene was a housewife and mother of three children, Ouida, Charles and Dale, and still resides in Habersham County. Charles is a graduate of Habersham Central High School and North Georgia Tech.

On 7-28-78 he married Julie Shackelford the daughter of Lee and Janice Shackelford of Carroll County. Lee Shackelford was owner/operator of Shackelford Auto Supply in Carrollton from 11-21-63 until its closing in 1992. He now runs a Mobile Locksmith Service. Janice was a housewife and mother of two children, Greg and Julie. They both still reside in Carrollton.

Charles worked at Southwire until December 1978, when he went to work for Julie's father in the Auto Parts business. He worked there for thirteen years, then went to Auto Parts Company and worked three more years. He is now employed at Mike Bell Chevrolet as parts manager.

The Barron Family

Julie born 4-15-60 is a graduate of Carrollton High School. She also worked for her father in his parts store for twelve years. She worked at Sportsplex Health & Athletic Club from 1987-1997. She is now employed at B & T Sales in Carrollton. They have two daughters, Trish and Hope. Trish was born 6-25-81 and Hope was born 10-21-85 in Carrollton. Trish now resides in Fayetteville, North Carolina, with her husband Airman Michael Engle. Hope is now attending Central High School. *Submitted by: Charles and Julie Barron, 256 McKinnon Trail, Carrollton, GA 30116*

317. The Barrons of Carrollton

Part 1

Our family moved from Terre Haute, Indiana, to Carrollton in June of 1983 and brought our then thirteen-year-old son Joseph Rodney with us. Rod had been laid off from his job at CBS Records (now Sony Music). We decided to take a chance and move to Carrollton where the new plant had relocated. Rodney had just finished eighth grade in Terre Haute and was about to start his freshman year at Carrollton High School. I worked as a private nurse while waiting to take the board examinations.

In August of 1983, CBS rehired Rod. We then bought a house the following month. Rodney enjoyed his first year of high school as a member of the Trojan soccer team, and I passed the boards in January of 1984. I felt we were back to normal again.

During his high school years (1983-1987), Rodney enjoyed three years on the soccer team with Coach Alex Miccachione, three years as a writer for the Gold and Black (newspaper staff) with editor Mrs. Terri Minish, and two years as an actor and dancer with director Mrs. Brenda Sue Knapp (now Holcomb) and the Performing Arts Director.

Rodney graduated from Carrollton High in May where they awarded him the trophy for Best Actor 1987. I was not too keen on his decision to become a professional actor, so I told him that he could major in drama if he won a Speech and Theater Arts scholarship to West Georgia College. On the recommendation of Mrs. Holcomb, Dr. J. Oliver Link granted him a four-year scholarship. Rod and I never missed a performance during both his high school and college years.

After performances in *Native Son, The Diary of Anne Frank,* and *Minnesota Moon* with college buddy and fellow Thespian Tony Pearce, Rodney decided to join the WGC Concert Choir, where he was a member of the 1990 choir group that toured and sang in Austrian and Hungarian cathedrals on a ten-day Eastern European tour.

Also that year, I was listed in the Who's Who in American Nursing and two years later in the Who's Who Among Human Service Professionals (1992-93) for my contributions as a nurse, nursing educator, and nursing administrator in the Philippines, Canada, and the United States.

In 1991 I attended a conference and reunion of nursing in Manila, Philippines, where I saw some of my classmates for the first time since graduation. During that same trip, I also attended a one-week nursing convention of the Philippine Nursing Association. I was so happy and excited to see my old mentor, Herminia Reyes, again. She was my favorite teacher. If it wasn't for her continued encouragement and support, I would have quit nursing school. Later she encouraged me to teach nursing. She continued to send me advice from India and Nairobi where she was a World Health Organization nursing consultant; I was a Philippine Nursing School principal at the time.

During Rodney's Junior year at WGC, he auditioned for and garnered a spot on the Position One Dance Company, where he, along with four other males, was a member of the 30+ female-laden dance company. For three years, Rodney learned jazz, modern, and hip-hop dance alongside former Miss West Central Georgia, Deanna Harper-Doherty, and former Atlanta Falcons cheerleader and current owner/director of the Dance Company of Carrollton, Shannon Tillman-Boss. *Submitted by: Puring Barron, 103 Kristy Lane, Carrollton, GA 30117*

318. The Barrons of Carrollton

Part 2

In 1992 Rod and I attended a conference and reunion of the St. Luke's Alumni Nursing Foundation in Orlando, Florida. The foundation's purpose is one of fellowship and fundraising for the St. Luke's School of Nursing in the Philippines.

In 1994 Rod was honored at a country club dinner by Sony Music for twenty years of service. We enjoyed a very special evening out. I was beaming with pride while we sat at the table with the president of Sony Carrollton, Mr. Robert Myers. Rod proudly displayed his gold and ruby ring which I had given him to commemorate the occasion. Mr. Myers then got the idea of giving a silver ring to all employees who had devoted fifteen years of service to the company. In appreciation of his contributions to the company, they gave Rod a plaque and a $500 Sony gift certificate, and his picture and a write up were published in the Sunday *Times-Georgia.* Soon after that, Rod received his fifteen-year silver ring.

Two years after graduating from WGC with a B.A. in speech and theater, Rodney moved to Atlanta. While living the bachelor's life and working as a Sportslife Health Coordinator, Rodney danced with the Position One Dance Company and appeared in episodes of the WB television series *Savannah,* the motion picture *Fled,* and various industrial videos for Turner Productions and the Atlanta Committee for the Olympic Games. One of his most enjoyable roles was that of "John" in the Actor's Express Olympic production of the *Harvey Milk Show.* He also hosted game shows in White Water and in Six Flags. In 1997, Rod took an early retirement from Sony and found time to rest and relax for about a year.

While attending a Filipino-American Association of Atlanta Spring Picnic, Rodney met his future wife, Evelyn Prudencio, on the volleyball court! After creating the Hotlanta Pride Basketball, Volleyball, and Dance teams, attending the Atlanta Olympic Games, and numerous outings to see the Braves, Falcons, Glory, Hawks, Ruckus, and Thrashers play, Rodney and Evelyn finally tied the knot on July 25, 1998.

Evelyn and Rodney, Puring and Rod Barron. 1999

With about 180 guests, the two were wed at the Catholic Church of St. Ann in East Cobb County, where Mrs. Holcomb was asked to play the organ. The ceremony was a combination of a traditional church wedding with some Filipino customs to honor our proud heritage.

Just last summer, Rodney and Evelyn celebrated their new home with a house blessing/warming in Austell, Georgia. They then accompanied me in October as we journeyed to San Francisco for the Golden Wedding Anniversary of my Uncle Joe and Aunt Pat. Rodney was the master of ceremonies for the reception and Evelyn was the official photographer.

Currently, Rod is working again, this time for Southwestern Color, a printing company in Villa Rica. Rodney is now in his third year with Verizon Wireless in Alpharetta, where he is a member of the Internet Response Team. Evelyn is also in her third year as a member of the radiology department of Northside Hospital in Dunwoody. As for me, I have been a nursing supervisor for both Pine Knoll and Bagwell Nursing Homes here in Carroll County.

Our community activities include fund raising for cancer research, Humane Society, March of Dimes, and AIDS Walk Atlanta.

Rodney and Evelyn are looking forward to starting their own family, just as Rod and I are looking forward to becoming grandparents, hopefully in the very near future. *Submitted by: Rodney Barron, Austell, GA*

319. Barrow Family

James R. (Reeves ?) Barrow, youngest child of the Rev. and "Lucy" Barrow, was born in Bowdon, Georgia, on 31 October 1844. He was a student at Bowdon Collegiate Institute when the Civil War began and became a member of Company B, Cobb's Legion Infantry. Charles McDaniel who was president of the institute and a Methodist preacher formed the unit in Bowdon.

The company took part in most of the major battles in Virginia and suffered tremendous loss of life and limb. Private James R. was wounded in left ankle and foot during the Battle of Crampton's Gap Maryland on 14 September 1862. They captured him and his left leg was amputated by Yankee surgeons. He recovered and was sent to prisons in Maryland, was exchanged, and returned home to Bowdon. He served in some capacity in the army around Atlanta drawing pay at least into 1864. He returned to Bowdon and married Martha S. "Mattie" Holmes on 10 December 1865. Mattie was the daughter of Thomas F. and Mary J. Holmes of Bowdon. Holmes was a local blacksmith. He never drew a Confederate pension but did receive money from the state for the purchase of an artificial leg.

James became a very prosperous merchant in Bowdon and was half-owner of Victory Mills, a complex consisting of a gristmill, cotton gin, saw mill and tannery, on the Little Tallapoosa River east of Bowdon. This mill boasted of having the first circular saw in western Georgia. He and Mattie had a son John William, a daughter Georgia who was born on 3 September 1868, and an infant born January 1 and died 1 February 1872. Mattie died the following June 10th and on 5 December 1876 little Georgia died. Four years later on 11 July 1880 James R. died, leaving fourteen year old John William an orphan. James died testate and his brother William was named guardian for his young son. James, Mattie, Georgia, and the infant are buried in the Bowdon Baptist Church Cemetery. It is said that James R. died from TB contracted in the Yankee prison camps.

John William Barrow was born in Bowdon on 5 September 1866 during the reconstruction era of the beaten South to a disabled Rebel soldier father. He was orphaned at age fourteen and went to live with his Uncle William whom they appointed his guardian. He attended school in Bowdon and then entered Mercer University. He did not finish, but returned to Bowdon to enter business. He traded his inherited half-interest in Victory Mills for a store in Bowdon and established a mercantile business on the north side of the main street. He later built several brick buildings on the south side of the street and expanded into a general store and even later specializing in hardware. The store became one of the largest and most successful in the area. He was a director of the local bank, director of the railroad and oil mill and was a part owner of an unsuccessful pickle factory venture. He was also a trustee of Bowdon College and active in the Baptist Church, the Masonic Lodge, and other civic organizations. He became wealthy, only to lose everything during the great depression of the 1920s and 1930s. With all the disappointments, he maintained his great love of Bowdon and his fellow man, many of whom owed him money which was never repaid. He started several smaller businesses after the hardware store closed and in his last years he could be found on the streets, especially on "Second Tuesdays," Bowdon's Trade Day, swapping and selling knives. He was great fun to be around and was Bowdon's greatest booster.

"J.W." married Martha Ellen Lovvorn on Christmas Day 1887 in Bowdon. Ellen was the daughter of the prominent citizen, W.D. Lovvorn, owner of the Lovvorn Mill complex on Indian Creek a mile or so north of Bowdon. Their children were Otis who married Alice Walker, Roy, Hugh Witt, infant Guy, Gladys who married Mallory "Bubba" Rumble, and Frances who married Henry Jackson. To make ends meet after the business failure, "Miss Ellen," as we knew her, turned the Barrow house, which they had built around the turn of the century, into a boarding house. It was known for the great food and for a clean and safe home away from home for travelers and many of Bowdon's college students and school teachers. Ellen died in December 1943 and J.W. lived with his beloved Hugh and Virginia in the Barrow house until his death on 29 July 1951. He and Ellen are buried in the Bowdon City Cemetery.

Hugh Witt Barrow was born in Bowdon Friday the 13th of January 1894. He always said that this was bad luck and maybe it was. He attended Gordon Military Academy in Barnesville where he was a close friend and classmate of his distant cousin, future Georgia governor and Senator Richard Russell. He returned to Bowdon and worked in the family hardware store and was in charge of their two White trucks, hauling all types of goods from Atlanta. After the store closed, he took the trucks and hauled material for building highways in Alabama. Soon the trucks were also taken. He then was a shop supervisor at Folds Motor Company in Carrollton and later a furniture salesman in Rockmart. He returned to Bowdon and worked at Sewell's for many years and later was a rural mail carrier.

Hugh married Virginia Mae Trammell, daughter of Thomas Appling and Lelia Johnson Trammell of Bowdon and Five Points, Alabama, on 28 October 1917. They were the parents of Virginia Ellen (Jean) who married John H. Barr Jr., infant Sue, Hugh Will (Bill) who married Bonnie Jeanne Spruill, and David Trammell who married Josephine Garner and later Linda Allen. "Gin" worked at Sewell's for many years, and after the death of Hugh on 10 November 1950 continued to care for his dad until his death. She then struck out on her own and became a housemother at The Church's Home for Girls in Atlanta where she became the trusted "mother" and friend to hundreds of young girls who were coming to the big city to find jobs. She retired and returned to live out her life in her "little house" in Bowdon next door to the Barrow House and to enjoy her children and grandchildren, her church and Sunday School, her "As You Like It" club, and her many friends. She died on 21 May 1963 and is buried with Hugh in the Bowdon City Cemetery. *Submitted by: Carol Ann Barr, Bowdon, GA*

320. John Henry and Lucy Holmes Bartlett Family

John Henry Bartlett was born December 18, 1884. Lucy Viola Holmes was born August 7, 1888, the daughter of Will Holmes and Mary Elizabeth Sigler. The Holmes family had lived in Carroll County for years, and many of their descendants still do.

Lucy and John married in 1918 and raised eight children: Newton Henry Bartlett, born October 13, 1918; Vassie Maude Bartlett, born September 11, 1917; Mary Idella Bartlett, born July 3, 1920; James Lewis Bartlett, born January 31, 1922; Edward Barney Bartlett, born December 13, 1923; Elizabeth Bartlett, born February 22, 1925; Margaret Marie Bartlett, born November 17, 1927; and Sarah Nell Bartlett, born July 14, 1929.

John had lived in Bowdon Junction, Georgia before marrying Lucy. He then moved to Carrollton, where they raised their family. It was actually in the county — mostly in the New Hope community (near Mt. Zion.) The children attended Mt. Zion School and the family was active in New Hope Methodist Church. They tell stories of walking on dirt roads to school and to church. Many of their dates were to church services and social functions.

Lucy and John's children married the following: Newt married Opal Broom; Vassie married Buford Crutchfield; Mary married James Steed; Lewis married Kathleen Williams; Ed married Dorothy West; Marie married Edward Smith; and Sarah married J.W. Daniell. These children produced nineteen grandchildren and forty-two great grandchildren — many of whom still live in Carroll County with families of their own.

John died in 1938. Lucy died in 1971. They, along with their son Lewis (who died in 1983) are buried in the New Hope Methodist Church cemetery off the Mt. Zion Road. Newt died in 1977, and is buried in the Sunrise Memorial Gardens in Douglasville, Georgia. Vassie died in 1980, and is buried at Oak Grove Baptist Church at Carrollton. Ed died in 1999 and is buried at the Carrollton City Cemetery on Alabama Street.

John and Lucy Bartlett Family in 1946.

The children tell of how difficult it was to live during the Great Depression, but also how close it made them feel to each other and neighbors. Farmers helped each other harvest crops and kill hogs. They "serenaded" neighbors at Halloween. (I think we call it "trick or treating" today.) They tell of "taffy pullins," church box suppers, home-made toys to play with, and home-made decorations for celebrations such as Valentine's Day and Christmas. Before electricity, they didn't have lights for Christmas trees, so they strung popcorn, and made paper chains for decorations. They baked many cakes and stored them in trunks weeks before Christmas. Then when Santa Claus came he brought maybe an apple, an orange a stick of candy, and maybe a top, a doll, or a pop gun. Even though times were hard economically (especially for Lucy when the children were young and John had died), they thrived with love and respect for their fellow man.

Submitted by: Marie Bartlett Smith, 112 Eureka Church Road, Carrollton GA 30117

321. Mary Pennington Bartlett

Mary Pennington Bartlett was the daughter of Rev. Ephraim Pennington and Lucy Brown Pennington. She was born and lived in Campbell County where her father was a Methodist minister and performed many marriages there. She was born 10 March 1827 (Bible) married 28 January 1855 as third wife to Reuben S. Bartlett born 1817 in Virginia. He had a daughter by his first marriage and a daughter by his second marriage.

Mary Pennington Bartlett

The family moved to Cleburne County, Alabama, for a time, where he joined the Masons. After the death of Reuben there in March 1870, Mary moved to Carroll County, where Henry Bartlett was a tax collector. He was her brother-in-law. Reuben Bartlett was a maker of fine carriages and buggies and was often paid in deeds rather than cash.

Children: 1. Marietta Bartlett married in Cleburne County, Alabama, first to an Allen and second to Angus McEachern as his second wife. She was called "Alabama Auntie" by the family. 2. John Henry Bartlett born 15 January 1859 married (1) Idella Wester (2) Clark McClendon, mother of Mary Bartlett Word. 3. James Ephraim Bartlett born September 1860 married Ella Spence 22 February 1881. 4. William P. Bartlett born 2 April 1863 married Addie Trimble, no issue. 5. Joseph S. Bartlett born September 1866 married four times; lived in Texas for many years; family reunion about 1955 at Center Point. 6. Thomas Edward Bartlett born 12 September 1867 died 14 March 1949 married 8 February 1888, Martha McCollister born 15 August 1869 died 9 January 1957 buried Center Point Cemetery. 7. Lucy Armeda Bartlett born 30 November 1869 died 14 January 1958 married 16 December 1890 James Daniel Wester born 22 March 1866 died 5 December 1948 buried Center Point Cemetery.

After moving to Carroll County, Mary Bartlett applied to be appointed natural guardian to five of her minor children ... 1 May 1882.

Although a relationship is not known, one Nathan Camp of Douglas County applied for permanent letters of administration on the estate of Reuben Bartlett. He was granted such and asked to sell lands belonging to the estate for the benefit of heirs. He evidently sold such lands but the family did not receive monies. He sold 101 ½ acres of Lot #144, District 2 of Carroll and many others.

Family tradition tells us that the Widow Bartlett and her children had a very hard life, and her sons worked to make a living. On October 21, 1885, the family brought suit in superior court against the administrator asking to recover some of the monies from the sale of real estate. The administrator appealed, on account of his poverty he was unable to pay cost. Family tradition tells a sad tale of this family. Family research has found many relatives and many families have been joined by it. The Bartlett family had come from Patrick County, Virginia, to Georgia. *Submitted by: Mildred Parrish, Temple, GA; written by June Hart Wester, 133 Mountain Crest Drive, Canton, GA 30114*

Sources: County records of Campbell and Carroll, Cleburne County, AL; Cemetery search Lecta Churchyard, Alabama.

322. Bass and Argo Families

John C. Bass was born 1825 in Meriwether County, Georgia. He was the son of William and Lirla Bass of North Carolina. He married Mary Ann Williams, the daughter of Jalla and Joanna Williams. John and Mary had three children, all of whom were born in Carroll County. William J. born April 13, 1853, Cindy J. born 1857 and John Henry born January 8, 1860. It was shortly after the birth of John Henry that John C. Bass enlisted in the Civil War. He was in the 41st Georgia, Company G. According to his military records, he was last listed as being in the hospital. As far as I know he died in 1863 from wounds received in the war. The following year Mary Ann married Matthew Campbell of Carroll County. It is not known where John C. Bass is buried. Mary Ann is buried with her second husband Matthew in an unmarked grave in Providence Cemetery in Douglas County, Georgia.

John and Mary's son William J. married Texas A. Johnson, the daughter of Joseph John and Elizabeth Velvin Johnson. Texas's father Joseph died as a prisoner of war at Camp Douglas, Illinois, on November 3, 1864. He enlisted in the Civil War on April 24, 1864 as a private in Company K, 1st regiment Fannin's Georgia Reserves. He was captured by Union Troops on August 13, 1864, while at home on sick furlough.

William and Elizabeth Bass had seven children, all of whom were born in Carroll County; John Jackson, Vesta Jane, Mary Elizabeth, Florance, George O., Emily Frances, Eliza Savannah, Julia A., Celia A., Dora, and William David. Their daughter Emily Frances (called Fannie) married William Thomas (Tom) Argo. Tom was the son of George W. and Sarah E. George Argo. Tom's grandparents were Simeon and Nancy Miller Argo. Tom's grandfather Simeon was in the 5th Alabama Calhoun County Sharp Shooters. He died May 17, 1862, of disease while in camp. Simeon and Nancy Argo had three children, Martha E. (Sis), who married Robert Harden, John W., died at a young age, and George W. born July 11, 1861. After Simeon's death Nancy married Tom J. Wallace. They lived in the Whooping Creek area of Carroll County. It was here that George grew up with his brother and sisters. Although George lived most of his life in Coweta County, he always considered Carroll County as his home. George W. Argo married Sarah E. George on November 24, 1878 in Cleburne County, Alabama. George and Sarah's son Tom was born August 25, 1882. Sarah died in 1884 in Carroll County. George W. Argo then married Susan A. Dorsey and they had five daughters, Georgia A., Fannie B., Ethel M., Lizzie and Lillie. George and both of his wives are buried at the Old Camp Ground Methodist Church Cemetery in Carroll County.

William Thomas and Emily Frances Argo had six children. Charlie G., Ernest W., George J., Eunice, Evelyn and Thomas Watson.

Emily died in 1920 and William died in 1921. Emily's sister Dora Bass Crider and husband John H. Crider took William and Emily's children to live with them. This was a house full, because John and Dora had six daughters of their own. When John died, Dora was no longer able to take care of that many children, so Thomas and Emily's children went to live with their grandparents William and Texas Bass. Thomas and Emily are buried in the Oak Grove Church Cemetery in Carroll County. Thomas Watson Argo, the youngest of Thomas and Emily's children, was born July 4, 1916. He married Lemma L. Davenport, daughter of Cleveland and Dece Davenport of Blue Ridge, Georgia. Thomas and Lemma lived all of their life in Polk County, Georgia. They had seven children, Thomas Watson Jr., Linda, Richard, Thomas George, James Clyde, Patricia and Wanda.

Thomas W. Argo died Aug. 24, 1988 and is buried in Rose Hill Cemetery in Rockmart, Georgia. *Submitted by: Patricia Argo Williams, 111 Brackett Road, Rockmart, GA 30153*

323. John Alan Batchelor

John Alan "Paw" Batchelor (15 April 1867), the third child of William and Susan Walton Batchelor, was born in Carroll County, Georgia. William was born in Cobb County, Georgia. John married Eveline Stewart (27 March 1867), daughter of Cyrus and Jane Smith Stewart. William and Susan Batchelor homesteaded at Sally Creek. They cleared the land for their crops and pastures for their livestock.

John farmed the land at Sally Creek that he inherited from his parents. He raised corn, cotton, and syrup cane. He would raise the cane and Newell Gay, his future son-in-law, would cook the cane squeezings into syrup at his syrup mill. Newell could have earned seventy-five cents per day digging ditches, but he chose to work for John making fifty cents per day sprouting (cutting sprouts off stumps). This choice was made so he could be close to William's daughter, Mary Ellen, his future wife. After their affection grew, Newell kidnapped her at school at the age of fifteen. They were in such a hurry to make their getaway that the horse fell down, causing the buggy to dump everyone out. They made it to a preacher, were married, and raised nine children. They were married for more than seventy-five years.

John A. Batchelor and Sons

Pa and Ma Batchelor moved to the ridge near Fortner's School in about 1924. When Sunday came, Pa would hitch up the horse and buggy for church. Pa and Ma Batchelor and their nine children (five boys and four girls) attended the Salem Methodist Church near Union Hill. He served as a steward and sang in church. Raising a large family and farming took a lot of time. Whenever there was extra time, Pa enjoyed being a comedian, telling funny stories, playing a fiddle, and playing a French harp.

There was always a lot of work to be done on the farm. The children had their chores of feeding livestock, fetching water to the house for cooking, and scrubbing clothes. Ma Batchelor would cook the family's meals on an old iron stove. The children would study at night by the light of the fireplace and oil lamps. Clothes were often homemade by Ma and the older girls.

Pa enjoyed horses. He traveled by horse and buggy until he was too old to drive. He took pride in keeping his buggy clean and shiny. He always saw that his horse was well cared for. He never owned an automobile. Pa died in 1963 and Ma Batchelor died in 1961. They are buried in Union Hill Cemetery. *Submitted by: Bessie Barnes (granddaughter), 7989 County Road, 49, Ranburne, AL 36273*

324. Bates Family
William Bates and Sarah Hembree

William Bates was born June 14, 1802, in South Carolina. He married Sarah Hembree on September 26, 1833, in Carroll County, Georgia. Sarah Hembree was born in 1802 in South Carolina. Their children were:

(1) Eliphus William Bates was born August 31, 1830, in Georgia. He died September 11, 1923, in Cullman, Alabama. He married Mary Elizabeth Chandler on June 12, 1853, in Carroll County, Georgia, Sarah Elizabeth Hayes on June 8, 1871, in Carroll County, Nancy Elizabeth Burges (no date), and Nannie Elizabeth Hornsby in 1912. He served in the Confederate States Army. More information in the following articles.

(2) Henry A. Bates was born in 1836 and married Allissey C. Barber on December 26, 1855, in Carroll County.

(3) William Bates born 1837 (no other information).

(4) Willis W. (Willie) Bates was born in 1839. He married Ammanda Melvina Easterwood on April 26, 1859, in Carroll County. Willis enlisted in the Confederate States Army on May 13, 1862, in Carrollton. He was a private in Company H, 56th Georgia Infantry. He appears on the list of wounded prisoners admitted to the prison hospital in Champion Hills, Mississippi, from May 17 to May 23, 1863. No further records on Willis.

(5) Nathan S. Bates was born 1841, died September 9, 1864, in Washington, D.C. He was a private in Company I, 19th Georgia Infantry. He enlisted June 22, 1861, in Carroll County. He was captured December 13, 1862, at Fredericksburg, Virginia, paroled for exchange in December 17, 1862. He was admitted to Chimborozo Hospital #4, Richmond, Virginia, on August 19, 1864. His arm was amputated at Union Field Hospital, City Point, Virginia, on August 20, 1864, and transferred to Lincoln U.S.A. General Hospital, Washington, D.C., where he died from his wounds. He is buried in Arlington National Cemetery, Confederate Circle in Arlington, Virginia.

(6) James W. Bates was born in 1843, and married Mollie T. Lassiter.

(7) Martha Rebecca Bates was born in 1846. She married Marshal Sparkes on December 12, 1866, in Carroll County.

(8) Charity Bates (no other information).

All children of William Bates and Sarah Hembree were born in Carroll County, Georgia. *Submitted by: Clay Smith*

Sources: Census, land, marriage records researched by Jerry Crumbley

325. Bates Family
Part 1
Eliphus William Bates and Mary Elizabeth Chandler (First Marriage)

Eliphus William Bates was born August 31, 1830, in Georgia, died September 11, 1923, in Cullman, Alabama. He married Mary Elizabeth Chandler on June 12, 1853, in Carroll County, Georgia. Mary Elizabeth Chandler was the daughter of Ambrose Chandler and Jerusaha White Chandler. Their children were: (1) William Ambrose (Billy) Bates was born in 1854, and died in 1941. He married Sidney Belzora Patterson on September 14, 1875, in Carroll County. They had twelve children. (2) Charity Bates was born in 1858. (No other information). (3 Hiram Bennett Bates was born February 22, 1860, and died April 8, 1917. He married Nancy Carolyn Thompson on January 10, 1879, in Carroll County. They had twelve children. (4) Mary Josephine (Phenie) Bates was born June 21, 1864, and died May 10, 1931. She married Henry Clay Smith in 1882 in Muscadine, Alabama. They had seven children. (5) John Robert Bates was born in 1867. He married Martha Jane Singleton on October 26, 1892, in Carroll County. They had six children.

Jerry Crumbley said she had the great pleasure of knowing Savannah Smith York, the daughter of Mary Josephine Bates Smith. She said Savannah was an amazing lady and could remember Eliphus William Bates, her grandfather. She told her stories and gave her information about the family. Her mind was very clear until several months before her death. She died at the age of ninety-nine in Alabama. *Submitted by: Avil York*

Sources: Census, land, marriage records and personal information researched by Jerry Crumbley.

326. Bates Family
Part 2
Eliphus William Bates and Sarah Elizabeth Hayes (Second Marriage)

Eliphus William Bates was born August 31, 1830, died September 11, 1923, in Cullman, Alabama. He married Sarah Elizabeth Hayes on June 8, 1871, in Carroll County, Georgia. Their children were: (1) Eliphus Buriah Bates was born April 24, 1872, and died November 27, 1941, in Addison, Alabama. He married Mary Odesser Baggett. They had one child. (2) Rebeckah Lucinda Caroline Bates was born July 9, 1874, and died January 13, 1962, in Cobb County, Georgia. She married Charles Hampton Willis in July 1893. They had ten children. See Willis Family for picture and more information. (3) Martha A. Bates (twin of Mary F.) was born January 1, 1877, died March 28, 1918. She married Silas Fawn Green. They had nine children. (4) Mary F. Bates (twin of Martha A.) was born January 1, 1877, died in 1932. She married James F. Dutton. They had one child. (5) Hester Bates was born 1881 (no other information). (6) Julia Bates was born November 19, 1884, and died January 17, 1936. She married William L. Morgan. They had ten children.

Eliphus William Bates Family

Eliphus W. Bates was a private in Company F (Iverson Invincibles) 7th Georgia Infantry, Confederate States Army. He enlisted May 10, 1861, in Carrollton, Georgia. He fought in twenty-five battles and was released from Appomattox Confederate Hospital in Virginia on April 9, 1865.

Shown in the family picture on the front row are unknown man, Eliphus Buriah Bates, Eliphus William Bates, Sarah E. Hayes Bates. On the back row are Mary, Martha (twins), Hester, names unknown for the last three ladies. *Submitted by: Mrs. Jewel Hampton*

Sources: Census, land, marriage records and personal information researched by Jerry Crumbley.

327. Samuel J. Bates

and Descendants

Samuel J. Bates was born November 11, 1816, in North Carolina and came to Carroll County, Georgia, in the early 1840s. He married Martha Chance on October 20, 1842. She was born January 25, 1824, and died December 12, 1905, and is buried at Concord Methodist Church in Hickory Level. Samuel and Martha had children: twins Simeon Franklin and Simpson Smith, Mary Ann Elizabeth, John Wesley, Isaac Walker, and William Augustin, who died in infancy.

Samuel and sons, Simeon and Simpson, were in the Confederate Army. Samuel was in Company F, Cobb's Legion, Georgia Volunteers. He died of "camp" fever in Richmond, Virginia, around December 25, 1862, and is buried in the Confederate Cemetery there. Simeon died of severe wounds received in a charge at Fort Harrison, Virignia. He died in Richmond on October 24, 1864, at eighteen years of age. Simpson Smith was a guard at Andersonville Prison. After the war, he was determined to go west until he ran into Indians. He did, settling at Callaham, Texas.

C.O. and Lilla Bates outside older Bates Store in Clem.

John Wesley Bates, born 1854, and wife Martha Ann Smith Bates moved to Marshall County, Alabama, in the late 1800s. He was said to be a merchant around Hickory Level at one time.

Mary Ann Elizabeth Bates was born July 7, 1849, and married William J. Defreese in 1869. Mary Ann died in 1929, and is buried at Pleasant Grove Baptist Church near Villa Rica.

Isaac Walker Bates was born June 26, 1858, and died about 1902, He married M.P. "Mollie" Lassetter in 1885. She was born April 21, 1863, and died in November 1944. They had seven children: Cuyler Otto, George, John, Mary, Verna, Vera, and Mattie Lou. Isaac was a farmer in the Cross Plains area. Isaac, Mollie, and most of the children are buried at Cross Plains Baptist Church Cemetery.

Only two of Samuel J. Bates children, Isaac W. and Mary Ann Elizabeth, have descendants known to be currently living in Carroll County.

Cuyler Otto "C.O." Bates was born June 15, 1887, on Horsley Mill Road near Carrollton. He died June 15, 1966. He married Lilla Wiles in February 1910. They had seven children: Horace (died in infancy), Pauline, James H., Charles Alvin, John Wilton, Jewell, and Forrest. C.O. Bates and family lived in several locations around the county including Cross Plains, Hutcheson Ferry Road, County Line, and Clem. In January 1930 they moved to Clem, where C.O. was a farmer, blacksmith, and a store operator until 1954 (see photograph). While at County Line, he helped to build a school, the Lucy Russell Institute, and served on the board. He had also operated a small store at County Line.

One of his sons, Forrest, took over the newer store at Clem in 1954, and operated it until 1986. He was born in 1926, married Margie Heath in1947, and had one son, Dennis.

Another son, Jewell, was born in 1922, and died in 1987. He married Doris Morrow, and they had three children, Richard, Steve, and Lawana. Jewell served in the U.S. Navy during World War II as a ship's cook. He was also a well known insurance agent in the Carrollton area, and served on the county school board at one time.

Daughter Pauline was born in 1912, and died in 1999. She married Tom T. James of Sand Hill, and had two children, Elizabeth and Charles.

James H. "Buddy" Bates was born in 1914, and died in 1981. He was married to Mary Nell Nixon, and they had one daughter, Joyce. Buddy operated a furniture business in Clem for many years.

Charles Alvin was born in 1917 and died in 1989. He married Helen Kemp, and they had four children, Linda, Wanda, Charlene, and Nicki. Charles served in the U.S. Army during World War II, and later worked at Lockheed in Marietta until retiring.

John was born in 1920 and died in 1989. He served in the U.S. Air Force during World War II. He was married to Jeanette Gilley, and had four children, Jerri, Barbara, Johnny, and Alan. Shortly after their marriage, they moved to Dallas, Texas, where they reared their family. *Submitted by: Dennis Bates, P.O. Box 1935, Carrollton, GA 30117*

328. The Bearden Family History

Richard Bearden was born about 1753, possibly in Caroline County, Virginia. He died in 1831 in Clarke County, Georgia. In Ruth Blair's *Some Early Tax Digests of Georgia-Wilkes County: 1793,* Richard Bearden paid taxes in Wilkes County, District #2, Capt. Smith's District, on 200 acres of third-grade lands adjoining lands of "Kinsman."

Of this I am positive, our Richard Bearden is probably close kin of the Revolutionary War Richard Bearden, who went into South Carolina and many of his descendants are found in South Carolina and Tennessee. They seem to have been contemporaries and probably cousins.

Richard Bearden (about 1753-1831) married unknown, and they had Solomon who married a Robinson. Solomon's son, Edward D. (1829-?), married Elizabeth Boatright (1835-?) in 1856 in Carroll County. Edward D. and Elizabeth's son, William Lewis (1859-1921) married Rhody Missoury Smith (1862-1925) in 1885. William and Missoury had Alsia Munrow (1886-1887); Henry Elbert "Doc" (1887-1958) who married Nancy Everlina Moore (1855-?) in 1904; William Albert "Bert" (1889-1955) who married Frances King; Mary Ida (1891-1946) who married James Thomas Wood (1890-1965); James Aron (1893-1948) who married Pricilla Louvina Bates (1894-1966) about 1912; Jesey (1896-1898); David (1898-1899); Besie (1900-1900); and Lincon (1901-1903).

Doc and Everlina had four children. They are (1) Lovie (1906-); (2) Dovie (1908-); (3) Berlin Eugene (1912-1984) who married Ila Belle McGuire (1913-) in 1931; and Arvella who married William Emesley Lee in 1937.

Berline Eugene and Ila Belle had (1) Hulett, who had Alan, David, Jeff, and Tim. Tim married Triska and had Brantley; (2) Jean married a Jones and had Gregg; and (3) Ronnie (1942-1970) had Johnny, Elizabeth, and Rhonda.

Arvella and William had (1) William Barry who married Sarah Bass in 1961 and had Mark Emesley and Suzanna: (2) Donnie Adron who married Joane Wells (1943-1993) in 1965. They had Lorri Dawn who married Paul Marcus Hammond in 1987 and had Matthew Guy; and Lisa Dianne, who married a Steed in 1998; and (3) Larry Eugene who married Pamela Wells in 1985 and had William Chandler.

Bert and Frances had Dorothy Mae who married Neal Ray Patterson in 1951, and had Paula, who married Johnny Richard Golden, Sr. Paula and Johnny Richard had Johnny Richard Jr. and Justin Ray. Bert and Frances' second child, Billy John, married Bertha Mae Williams in 1955 and had Billy Randall and Tracy John. Billy Randall married Sharon and had Jeremy. Tracy John married Kim and had Jonathan and Macy Ann.

Ida and Tom had the following children: (1) Eunice (1910-1944) who married Jim Smith and had Bonnie, Lewis, and Betty; (2) Carl (1912-1993) who married Ruth and had Anna Lee, John, Tom, and Carlotta; (3) Lillie Mae (1914-1916); (4) Harvey (about 1916-about 1973) who married Ruth and had Douglas and Larry T. (1946-1966). Larry was a casualty of hostile fire in South Vietnam; (5) I.V. (circa 1918-circa 1995) who married Frank Hicks, and had Sonny, J.R., Dorothy Jean, Cletus, Donald, and Earlene. She later married Joe Conway and had Joe Marvin; (6) Clifton Q.P. (1920-1990) who married Bamah Lanette Sprewell in 1941 and had Cecilia and Dr. Morgan Clifton; (7) Olivia (March 9, 1922-April 1992) who married Johnny Patterson (January 19, 1925-May 1983); and Infant (about 1924-about 1924).

This family is first seen in Carroll County in 1856 and many members of this family still reside here. Many of the family are buried at Poplar Springs Primitive Baptist Church Cemetery, Bowdon, Carroll County, Georgia. *Submitted by: Paula Patterson Golden and Written by: Cecilia Wood Church, 128 Brock Street, Carrollton, GA 30117, cechurch@charter.net.*

329. The Beasley Family

William Cornelius (Bill) Beasley was born in June 1899 in Troup County, Georgia. At the age of seven, his father Cornelius C. Beasley moved his family to Bremen, Georgia, where he raised his family.

In 1911, William (Bill) began working for a cotton buyer and moved to Bowdon, Georgia. He married Miss Hattie Rosetta McDaniel and they settled in Bowdon. Bill was a farmer and he also operated several restaurant businesses. Miss Hattie was a beautician, educator, midwife, and housewife. Miss Hattie kept accurate records of local births.

They were the parents of three boys: James (Ruby "Granny") Beasley, Sidney (Carrie) Beasley, and Amos (Lindy "Louise") Beasley, and one girl Billie Ann Beasley(Judge) Buchanan. The descendants of the late Bill and Hattie Beasley are distributed throughout the country — Georgia, Ohio, Tennessee, California, New Jersey, and Florida. The Beasley grandchildren, one daughter-in-law Ruby, the youngest child Billie Ann, and their children and grandchildren continue to reside in and around Carroll County. *Submitted by: Billie Ann Buchanan, PO Box 81, Bowdon, GA 30108*

330. Isaiah Houston Price Beck

Isaiah Houston Price Beck was born February 17, 1862, in Heard County, Georgia. He died June 30, 1938, in Bowdon, Georgia. He was married to Mary Ida Jeter on January 8, 1885, in Carroll County, Georgia. She was the daughter of Amanda Elizabeth Robinson and Richard Dudly Jeter. Mary Ida was born April 20, 1867, in Carroll County and died November 23, 1940. They are buried in Bowdon City Cemetery.

Isaiah Houston Price Beck was the son of Isaiah Springer Beck and Martha Mathias Davis. His grandfather Isaiah Beck Jr. and his grandmother Elizabeth Tanner are both buried in Pleasant Grove Cemetery, Carroll County. Isaiah Jr. was born in South Carolina, son of Isaiah Becky Sr. and Ruthie Youngblood.

I.H.P. Beck and Mary Ida Beck on 50th Anniversary

When his son was three weeks old, Isaiah Springer Beck enlisted in Heard County Rangers as third sergeant, Company I, 41st Regiment, Georgia Volunteer Infantry, Army of Tennessee, C.S.A. He died in Lauderdale Springs, Mississippi, when his son was just over three months old. Price and his mother moved to Carroll County and lived in the Tyus community with her father, John Davis. His education came from reading and the educated men of the community.

Price Beck became a member of Bowdon Methodist Episcopal Church South in 1876. In January 1885, he was approved by Methodist Episcopal Church South, LaGrange District, North Georgia Conference to preach the Gospel according to the teachings of said church. In 1912 he was made a deacon of said church. He taught the Men's Bible Class for fifty years and served as chairman of Board of Stewards for a number of years.

In 1885, Price Beck began his career as schoolteacher in Carroll and Heard counties until 1907.

He entered the general mercantile business in Bowdon. In 1912 he started I.H.P. Beck Company, dealing in fertilizer and cotton. He continued until bad health forced his retirement in 1935. His son, Larry Price Beck, became a partner in 1920. Price Beck retained farming interest in the Bowdon area and was a director of the Merchants and Planters Bank and the Georgia State Bank, all in Bowdon. They lived in several houses around Bowdon and lived in the Shelnut house while his new house was being built on Wedowee Street.

In 1893 he became leader in the Populist Party of Carroll County. In 1910 he was a candidate of the Georgia Legislature and served in Lower House from 1912 to 1928. He was state Senator from the 37th Senatorial District, 1930 to 1932.

In 1919, his bill in the legislature made Bowdon College a branch of the University System. He served as secretary and treasurer of Board of Trustees of Bowdon State College 1929 to 1933.

Price and Mary had eight children: Martha Amanda, Larry Price, Lola Frances, Lovie Vesmal, Lula Helen, Lake Jeter, Evie Lee and Mary Ida. *Submitted by: Joe Beck Moore, 356 Rome Street, Bowdon, GA 30108*

331. Isaiah Beck Jr.

Isaiah Beck Jr. was born April 18, 1803, in Randolph County, North Carolina, and died December 31, 1896, in Carroll County, Georgia. He married Ruthy Youngblood. She died about 1828, possibly in Rabun County, Georgia. They had two sons, Jeffrey Youngblood Beck (1826) and Samuel Barker Beck (1828), who were born in Georgia and lived to a very old age. On January 7, 1830, Isaiah married Elizabeth (Betsy) Tanner, daughter of Matthew Tanner Jr. and Alsey Langley. She was born October 31, 1812, probably in Hall County, Georgia. They had seventeen children.

Isaiah Beck Jr. was the son of Isaiah Beck Sr. and Dorothy Barker. His grandfather was Jeffrey Beck Jr., who was in the Revolutionary War. He served in North Carolina. After the war they moved to South Carolina. His family, along with Isaiah Sr.'s brothers, moved to Rabun County, Georgia. After a few years, Isaiah and his two boys and his father had possibly moved to Fayette County, Georgia. From there, he drew Lot 120, 9th District in the Carroll County Land Lottery. Tom Sherrill has the original land grant deed. He later sold this and bought Lot 207, 9th District. After coming to visit the area, he went back and brought his father and two sisters and their families to Carroll County. It is not known for sure whether they came by pack mule or covered wagons. After reaching their chosen site he made settlement and, having planned for the future, returned to get Betsy Tanner for his wife. Isaiah Jr. was Justice of the Peace for several years.

Isaiah Beck Jr. built Beck's Mill, one of the first in the that part of the country. He built a cabin just up the creek from the mill. A few years later he built a log house at the crossroads of Old Columbus Road and Highway 5. He first built a rock chimney, eight feet across at the base. It could burn four-foot cordwood. He then built a two-story log house to the chimney. Most of the chimney and house still stand today and is owned by Mrs. Don Farr. He deeded four acres east of land Lot 207, 9th District for a church to be called Bethlehem, of the Primitive faith.

Isaiah and Betsy's seventeen children are: Semore York born December 11, 1830; Avington Tanner born March 17, 1832; Rudah Caroline born March 13, 1833; Isaiah Springer born June 16, 1834; Arah Ann Safrona born January 29, 1836; Merium Marilza born October 4, 1837; Barzilla Eluerana born March 14, 1839; Drucilla Bethana born March 14, 1839; Elizabeth Dorcas born March 15, 1841; Thomas David born June 15, 1842; Mary Adaline born January 8, 1844; Luzana Marrilla born April 12, 1845; Martha Jane born July 31, 1847; Susanna Mavell born February 26, 1849; Joseph Langley born March 29, 1852; Whit Heron born July 16, 1853; and Delana Indiana born May 24, 1855. *Submitted by: Joe Beck Moore, 356 Rome Street, Bowdon, GA 30108*

332. Isaiah Beck Sr.

Part 1

Isaiah Beck Sr. born September 2, 1778, in Randolph County, North Carolina. He died in 1854 in Carroll County, Georgia. He married Dorothy Barker, parents and birth date unknown. She died at childbirth about 1803. They were married about 1801 in North Carolina and they had one son, Isaiah Beck Jr., born April 18, 1803, in Randolph County, North Carolina.

Isaiah Sr. married Dorcas York, daughter of Semore and Sylvania Aldridge York. Dorcas was born in 1780, also in Randolph County, North Carolina, and they were married there November 16, 1804. They had two daughters, Dorcas Beck born 1809 in South Carolina, married John Holloway; Mary Polly Beck born 1812 South Carolina, married William Stewart.

Isaiah Sr. was the son of Jeffry Beck Jr. and Mary McDaniel. His father, Jeffry Beck Jr., was in the Revolutionary War in North Carolina. Isaiah Sr. and Jeffry Jr. families moved to South Carolina in 1802. Isaiah Beck Sr. was deeded 200 acres on the water of Little River, Oconee County, South Carolina, January 7, 1807. Isaiah Sr. and his family lived a short time in Rabun County, Georgia. At the time of the land lottery for Carroll County land, he was in Fayette County. He drew Lot 221, 9th District, Carroll County, Georgia.

Isaiah Beck Sr. was one of the first Justices of the Peace in the 9th District in Carroll County and his name appears often on early records and jury lists. He also performed many weddings. He was one of the leading citizens of Carroll County. *Submitted by: Martha Smisson, 189 County Road 670, Ranburne, AL 36273*

333. Larry Price Beck Family

Part 2

Larry Price Beck was born April 20, 1891, in Carroll County Georgia. He died August 26, 1946, in Bowdon, Georgia. On June 12, 1919, Larry married Nannie Maude Hearn, daughter of James Abner Hearn (1858-1930) and Mary Elizabeth Hutcheson (1873-1966). Maude was born July 19, 1892, and died August 7, 1975, in Atlanta. They are both buried in Bowdon City Cemetery.

Larry Price Beck

Larry Price Beck was the son of Isaiah Houston Price Beck and Mary Ida Jeter. His grandfather, Isaiah Springer Beck, died in the Civil War in Mississippi. His grandmother was Elizabeth (Betsy) Tanner, daughter of Mathew Tanner and Alsey Langley.

Larry received his early education at different schools in the area and attended Bowdon College.

He worked on the Bowdon Railroad, then on the Central of Georgia. He worked about ten years in different positions, including conductor. He was a member of the Brotherhood of Railway Trainmen.

During World War I, he enlisted at Camp Gordon, Georgia, and held the rank of sergeant in the 384th Infantry but was never sent overseas. In World War II he was organizer and head of the Home Guard and chairman of O.P.A.

Larry, Martha, Maude Beck

In 1920 he joined I.H.P. Beck Company, a large warehouse dealing in fertilizer and buying and selling cotton, owned by his father I.H.P. Beck. Larry developed the "Beck's Big Boll Cotton seed" that sold throughout the Southeast.

He was a councilman and mayor of the town of Bowdon, a trustee of Bowdon School District #20 and a director of the Commercial Bank of Bowdon.

He joined the Bowdon Methodist Episcopal Church South in his youth and served as Superintendent of Sunday School and member of Board of Stewards and Trustees. In 1936 Larry was elected to the Georgia General Assembly from Carroll County where he served for two terms.

Larry belonged to both the Independent Order of Odd Fellow and the Free and Accepted Masons and in the Masonic order was affiliated with the Lodge (past master), the Royal Arch Chapter (past high Priest), Knights Templar Commandery and Yaarab Temple Ancient Arabic Order Nobles of the Mystic Shrine.

Larry and Maude had one daughter, Martha Larry, born February 24, 1928, Bowdon, Georgia. Martha graduated from Bowdon High School in 1944. She attended West Georgia College for two years and graduated from Georgia State College for Women in 1948 with degrees in chemistry and biology.

She trained and worked as a medical technologist at Piedmont Hospital in Atlanta, Georgia. On May 16, 1953, she married Louis E. Smisson Jr. of Peach County, Georgia, a captain in the U.S. Air Force. They served in Texas, Illinois, France, Virginia and Georgia where he retired in 1966. In 1980 they moved to the country outside Ranburne, Alabama. They have two children, Louis III born April 23, 1959, in Athens, Greece, and Larrie Maude born December 1, 1959, in Athens, Greece. *Submitted by: Martha Smisson, 189 County Road 670, Ranburne, AL 36273*

334. Sidney Harrison Beck

Sidney Harrison Beck and his family are found in Carroll County, Georgia, in the 1920 census. Sidney was born in Georgia on December 4, 1889, the son of David Milton Beck Jr. and Sara Ann Criswell. Sidney's first marriage was on October 12, 1913, to Lemma Lou Adams, the daughter of Claud Duvall Adams and Mary Mahaley Braswell. Lemma died on October 19, 1931, and Sidney died on October 8, 1940. Both are buried at Tallapoosa East Cemetery in Haralson County, Georgia. To this marriage were born four children: (1) Milton Claud, born on July 31, 1914, in Laurens County, Georgia. He died February 10, 1986, and is buried at Tallapoosa East Cemetery in Haralson County. On October 3, 1931, in Haralson County he married Myrtle Virginia Hudgins, daughter of James Hudgins and Ida Hopkins. They had eight children: Datha Marie, Jessie Elisha, Theron Gannoway, Mary Lou, Milton Harris, Jimmy Roger, Virginia Lorraine and Donnie Ray. (2) Alvin Sidney, born March 3, 1920, in Carroll County. He died on January 10, 1983, and is buried at Tallapoosa East Cemetery in Haralson County. His first marriage was in 1941 to Hester Lou Frances Brown, daughter of William Ervin Brown and Minnie Lee King of Calhoun County, Alabama. They had four children: Margaret Gwendolyn, Ina Frances, Wayman Theodore and Alvin Terry. Second marriage was in 1996 to Helen Faye Leatherwood. They had three children: Lesia Maria, Julia Florine and Sidney Thomas. (3) Lora Mae, born August 13, 1925, in Haralson County. On May 27, 1944, she married Rush Ollie Gipson in Calhoun County, Alabama. They had two children: Patricia Gail and Darrell Edwin. (4) Emerson Shaler, born in December 1927 and died November 23, 1931. He is buried at Tallapoosa East Cemetery in Haralson County. Sidney Harrison Beck's second wife was Ora Summerville Adams. They had three children: Sara, Perry and Levie.

Sidney Harrison Beck Family

Shown in the Sidney Harrison Beck family photograph are: (Standing) Alvin Sidney, Sidney Harrison and Milton Claud. (Seated) Emerson, Lemma Lou, and Lora Mae. *Submitted by: Gwen Thigpen, 6156 Queens Road, Douglasville, GA 30135*

335. Mr. and Mrs. Alonza David Bell

Alonza David Bell was born in Roopville, Georgia, October 9, 1887, the first of eleven children, to David E. (Sonny) Bell and Sarah Warren Bell.

Alonza was married to Cora Dell Stephenson of Bowdon, Georgia. Sonny built a one-room school house near his Roopville home called Bellview so his children and neighboring children would not have to walk miles to school. He hired the beautiful and eligible Cora Stephenson as teacher. Cora and Alonza met and it was love at first sight. Shortly afterward (in 1910) they were married. This union produced six children: Fred, Garland, Harold, Lewis, Wenona, and Hubert.

Alonza was a big man, not only in stature, but in character and integrity as well. He was loved and respected by all who knew him. To most of his younger siblings he was fondly known as "Brother." He was a farmer by trade and was an ordained deacon at Tyus Baptist Church, Tyus, Georgia.

Cora finished high school and college in Bowdon and taught school several years before their marriage. She was equally loved and respected by all who knew her. She could quote the Bible and knew a verse for every occasion. Her cooking skills were top notch.

Cora and Alonza David Bell

The five boys were always bringing friends home and she never knew how many she would be feeding at their large farm house table. But no one left hungry.

All of the children married. Fred married Lorene Lovell and had two children, Mary Jewell and David; Garland married Evelyn Eason and had three sons, Eddie, Randy and Kim; Harold was married and had no children; Lewis married Mary Ann Harper and had one daughter, Sandy; Wenona married Alexis Klamke, who had two sons, Stephan and Alexis; and Hubert married Joan Huff and had two daughters, Jan and Nan.

Alonza David Bell on left; Theo Bell driving tractor.

Alonza died November 6, 1949, and Cora died October 17, 1961. All of their children are deceased except their daughter Wenona who resides in Roopville. Most of the descendants of Alonza and Cora are currently living in Carroll County.

The farm picture shows Alonza D. Bell on the extreme left, and according to family information Theo Bell is driving the first tractor in Carroll County. *Submitted by: Sandy Bell Mosley, 122 Old Franklin Road, Roopville, GA 30170*

336. Ben and Donna Rivers Bell Family

Robert Benjamin Bell was born on 8 March 1971 in Coweta County, Georgia, the son of Joseph Terrell Bell Jr. and Jan Robinson Bell. Ben was born in the old historic Newnan Hospital. Ben's father, Joe Bell Jr., was a native of Newnan, Georgia, and at the time of Ben's birth, Joe Bell Jr. was the assistant city manager of Newnan. When Ben was about a year old, Ben's father accepted a position with Carrollton Federal Savings and Loan, later becoming a vice president and comptroller. Joe Bell Jr. would remain with Carrollton Federal for twenty years.

The family moved to Carrollton, Georgia, in 1972 and made their home in Southgate, which at that time was a brand new subdivision. Good friends and relatives already living there were Dr. and Mrs. E.V. (Lucy) Patrick and Bobby and Betty Morgan family. Bobby Morgan was Ben's grandmother's brother, and Bobby's youngest son,

Jimmy Morgan, (who was stair step in age next to the Bell boys) grew up with Joe, John, and Ben.

Ben's maternal grandparents were John and Melba Morgan Robinson, the owners of Robinson Drug Company in Carrollton, Georgia. Melba died 23 January 1996. Ben's paternal grandparents, Joseph Terrell Bell Sr. and Annie Louise Godard Bell, were natives of Spalding County, Georgia, but had moved to Newnan about 1935. Joe Bell Sr. attended Georgia Tech and played football there from 1922-1925. He was a 1926 graduate of Georgia Tech with a degree in commerce and was employed by Bankers Health and Life Insurance for more than thirty years. Louise Bell worked for many years as a secretary for Hollis Lumber Company in Newnan before her retirement. The Bells were members of the First United Methodist Church of Newnan. Joseph Terrell Bell Sr. was born 30 January 1900, married Annie Louise Goddard 15 February 1934, and he died 5 May 1973. Annie Louise was born 3 February 1908, and died 26 May 1994. Both are buried at Forest Lawn Cemetery in Newnan.

Robert Benjamin Bell, always called Ben, grew up in Carrollton. He attended Oak Mountain School in early years and then the public schools of Carrollton. Two of his special teachers were Betty Loosier in first grade, and Beth Parkman (now Mrs. E. Tom Johnson) in second grade. The old Maple Street School where Ben attended was also the same grammar school that his mother had attended when she was growing up. The old school used to be surrounded by maple trees that were ablaze with yellows and reds in the fall of the year.

Ben played football for the Trojans under Coach Charlie Grisham and Coach Ben Scott. Ben graduated from Carrollton High School in 1989 and attended West Georgia College where he was president of his Sigma Nu fraternity. While in college, he met his bride to be, Donna Lynn Rivers who was born 9 June 1971, grew up in Roswell and graduated from Rosell High School in 1989.

Ben graduated from West Georgia College in 1993 with his degree in finance. Donna was a member of Delta Delta Delta while in college and served as chaplain of her sorority. She graduated with a major in history and a minor in secondary education from West Georgia College in 1994. After graduation, Ben Bell and Donna Rivers married on November 19, 1994, and made their home on Lake Lanier for a few years. They lived with Donna's grandparents who had a wonderful retirement home and a separate apartment for them there. Later Ben and Donna moved to Douglasville, where Donna had spent her early childhood. Ben and Donna are active in the First Methodist Church of Douglasville.

Since graduation, both Ben and Donna have earned their licenses in real estate. Donna is now employed by REMAX in Douglasville. Ben worked as a branch manager of Regions Bank from 1994-1997 and now works as manager of the sales division of Atlanta Metal Products.

Donna Lynn Rivers is the daughter of John Joseph Rivers Jr. (born 15 February 1946) and Brenda Carolyn Pitts (born 28 May 1947). Both Joe and Brenda Rivers grew up in Atlanta and attended Southwest DeKalb High School. Joe graduated in 1964, and Brenda graduated in 1965. Joe Rivers then attended Auburn University where he graduated in 1968 with a B.S. in business administration. Joe Rivers Jr. went into banking and has spent over thirty years in that profession. Brenda Rivers is office manager for Alpharetta Internal Medicine where she has been employed for many years. Brenda and Joe Rivers Jr. are active in the Northbrook United Methodist in Roswell. Joe Rivers is the son of John Joseph Rivers Sr. (died 21 November 1993) who was married on 29 December 1943 to Frances Williford Bailey (born 15 October 1923).

Joe Rivers Sr. worked at downtown Rich's in Atlanta. Naturally, Donna's grandmother, Frances Rivers, has taught her family the art of shopping at Rich's — and it's still a family tradition.

Brenda Carolyn Pitts is the daughter of Curvin Thomas Pitts (born 23 September 1922, died 14 October 2000) and Helen Loree Landrum (born 4 June 1926). For most of their lives, Curvin and Helen Pitts made their home in Atlanta, but upon retirement they moved to Lake Lanier in Forsythe County, Georgia. Curvin Pitts was in the newspaper business, serving as district supervisor for *The Atlanta Journal and Constitution.*

Helen and Curvin met at West Fulton High School. Curvin joined the Army after graduation — as World War II was raging — and Helen did her part for the war effort in that she worked for the Army Air Force at the Atlanta Airport where they were modifying airplanes to be used in the war. Helen remained at this job about three years and then became a secretary for the C&S Bank where she remained until her retirement.

Ben, Donna, and Cooper Bell

The parents of Helen Loree Landrum were Lillie Belle Payton (born 30 January 1896) and Thomas Coy Landrum (born 10 March 1896). Coy Landrum worked for the Atlanta Transit Company back in the days when there were trolley cars in the streets of Atlanta. Coy was a driver and he happened to notice a pretty young lady riding his trolley car to work every day. This was Lillie Payton. Lillie had come to Atlanta from Orrick, Missouri. Lilie had a sister whose husband was in the Army stationed at Fort McPherson. So Lillie had come to Atlanta to be close to her sister and she'd found work as a seamstress. Lillie's parents were Letsie Belle Jefferies, a native of Missouri, and Lee Roy Payton, a native of Kentucky. After Coy Landrum married Lillie Payton, they made their home around Lithia Springs. They are both buried at Union Grove Baptist Church near there.

Thomas Coy Landrum was the son of John Daniel Landrum, a native of Douglas County, Georgia. The home place, no longer standing, was once in "walking distance of Union Grove Church." John Daniel Landrum's wife died when Coy Landrum was only three years old, and though John Daniel Landrum lived to be about ninety years old, he never remarried.

Curvin Thomas Pitts was the son of Roy Thomas Pitts and Elizabeth Irene Sullivan (born 6 August 1903). Roy Pitts worked for Georgia Power at the Atkinson plant on the Chattahoochee River for all of his life. Curvin had one brother, Roy Clifton Pitts who also worked for Georgia Power, but lived at Rome, Georgia. A baby sister died as an infant. When the boys were in grammar school, the Pitts family moved to Tallulah Falls. One of Roy Pitts' children has done extensive work on the Pitts family tree, linking it to the Candler-Reed genealogy.

Curvin Pitts was a veteran of World War II in the 102nd Infantry Division known as The Ozarks. He was injured while fighting in Germany and was left with a back disability that affected him for the rest of his life. By 1985, he was getting about with his "scooter" and he and Helen made the trip to Europe in 1989 for the reunion of the 102nd. They visited all the countries where the 102nd had fought — Germany, Belgium, Holland, Austria, Switzerland, Italy, and France. The 102nd had regular reunions and the Pitts attended them all until Curvin Pitts died at age seventy-eight.

Donna Rivers Bell is also proud to have in her family tree one of Georgia's most illustrious genealogists. Her grandmother, Frances Williford Bailey Rivers, had a brother named William Williford Bailey. Since the Williford name was going to die out, William Bailey legally adopted his mother's maiden name of Williford. His son Lawrence Williford now carries on that name. Many genealogists are familiar with *Williford and Allied Families.* Donna's Williford family tree is traced back twenty generations to Sir Thomas Williford and Margaret Sandys of England.

William Bailey Williford was a writer and publisher who owned Cherokee Publishing Company in his lifetime. He wrote other books of importance to those of us who climb the family tree: *The Early History of Cuthbert and Randolph County, Georgia,* which he compiled, *Americus Through the Years, Peachtree Street, Atlanta,* and that wonderful book about the antebellum homes of Covington, *The Glory of Covington.* Mr. Williford and his wife lived in the oldest home in Covington, Georgia, which is known a Swanscomb.

Three Bailey brothers, William, Thomas, and Patrick came to Colonial America in 1768. They were descendants of a general of William the Conqueror who was entrusted with the King's treasures. Patrick Bailey settled in Virginia and married a Miss Wise. They had a son named Henry "Harry" Bailey who moved from Brunswick County, Virginia, to Oglethorpe County, Georgia. He acquired many thousands of acres of land on Long Creek there. They granted some of this land to him for his service in the American Revolution. Harry Bailey died in 1843.

Frances Williford Bailey was the daughter of William Francis Bailey, born 5 December 1884, who married Frances Elizabeth Wiliford (born 29 May 1894) on 22 September 1919. William Francis Bailey was the son of William Douglass Bailey who married 26 September 1882 to Annie Louise Ansley (born 26 July 1859). Annie Louise Ansley was the daughter of Thomas Wesley Ansley (5 February 1815 - 29 December 1898) and his third wife whom he married on 13 March 1856 in Stewart County, Georgia, Mary Jane Elam (16 January 1833 Cuthbert, Georgia - 27 November 1893 Americus, Georgia). Mary Jane Elam was the daughter of Hodijah Elam and Mary Davenport

The Ansleys trace their family tree all the way back to Dr. Samuel Annesley of England who was the brother to the Earl of Anglesca. Dr. Samuel Annesley was the father of Susannah Annesley who married Rev. Samuel Wesley. Susannah and Samuel Wesley were the parents of Rev. John Wesley (1703-1791) who helped to found the Methodist Church. Also, John Wesley was a brother to Rev. Charles Wesley who authored many religious hymns and was secretary to James Edward Oglethorpe, the founder of Georgia.

Charles Jackson Bailey was born 16 June 1799, the son of Henry and Sarah Jackson Bailey. Charles received his medical training at the University of Pennsylvania and then set up his medical practice in Jackson, Butts County, Georgia. Dr. Charles Bailey married third to Amanda M.F. Smartt (12 September 1817 - 6 November 1888). Dr. Charles Bailey died 4 May 1850. Charles and Amanda's son was Francis David Bailey born 31 November 1834 in Jackson, Georgia. Frank Bailey (as he was known) attended Princeton and later graduated with a degree in law from the University of Delaware. He engaged in law partnership with his cousins at Cuthbert in Randolph County, Georgia. Frank Bailey married Narcissa Weakly Douglass of Butts County, Georgia, a girl with a rich Scottish heritage. Frank Bailey enlisted in Company H, 51st Georgia Regiment, C.S.A., as a private. He died during the war on 28 November 1864 and was buried at Rosedale Cemetery in Cuthbert, Georgia. The son of Francis David Bailey and Narcissa Weakley was William Douglass Bailey, Donna Rivers Bell's great-great-grandfather. William Douglass Bailey was the father of William Francis Bailey (born 1884).

Donna Rivers Bell has one brother, Michael Thomas Rivers, born 15 October 1975. Michael attended the University of Georgia where he was a member of Sigma Nu fraternity. Michael graduated from the University of Georgia in 1999 with a degree in consumer economics. He is presently employed as a recruiter for Fortune 500 Companies.

Ben and Donna Bell have one son, Cooper Benjamin Bell, born 27 October 1999. It looks as though Cooper Bell might be another ballplayer like the original Bell boys before him. As Cooper's Uncle Joe likes to say, "He came out of the same cooky cutter," also making reference to our famous gingerbread men we make at Christmas time which have been a family tradition for many years. Donna Bell, an excellent cook, mastered our family recipe for gingerbread men long ago. We are also predicting that Cooper Bell may have the height of the Bell men in earlier generations. Many of them reached 6.6 feet. Cooper is already very tall for his age and has feet the size that older generations used to say would foretell the future height. We'll have to wait and see. Donna and Ben Bell and Cooper make their home in Douglasville. *Submitted by: Robert B. Bell, Chapel Heights, Douglasville, GA 30135 and Written by: Jan Robinson Bell*

337. Jan Robinson Bell

As my contribution to the Heritage Book, I would like to share my poem about the old Empire Five and Dime that many people have enjoyed over the years. This poem was written in memory of Lonie Reese Harris. Her husband, Mr. J.C. "Red" Harris, had this published in the newspaper shortly after her death. The response to this poem has been overwhelming to me over the past fifteen years. Are you ready? Let's take one more trip to that wonderful spot of our childhood ...

Taylor Christian Bell graduates from kindergarten

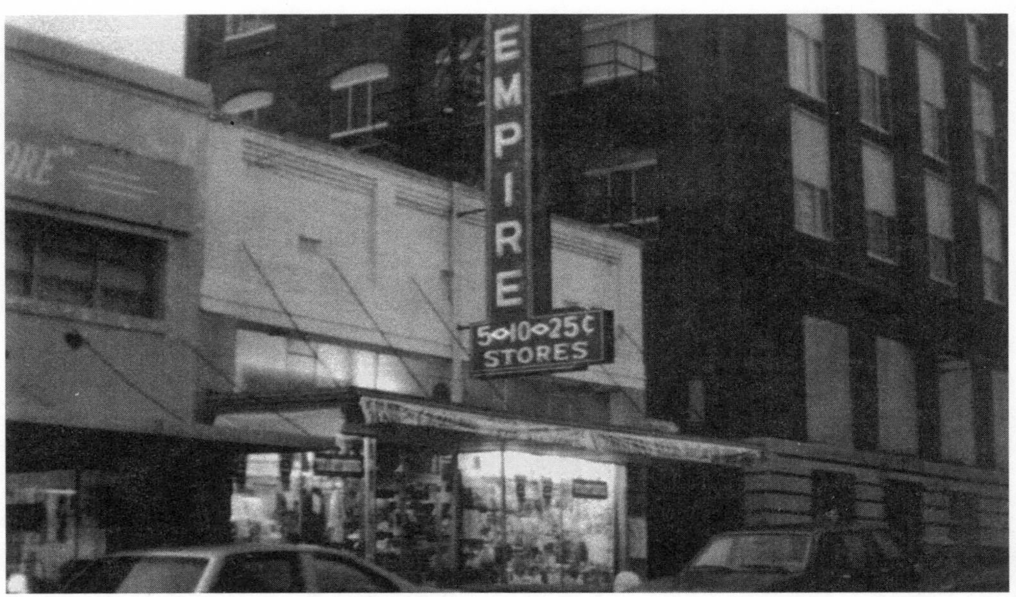

The Empire Five and Dime

THE EMPIRE FIVE AND DIME

Sometimes when I sit in my rocking chair
And the fire glows warm and bright —
I remember the scenes of my childhood
And the places of a child's delight.

I lived in Carrollton — the folks were nice
And they said, "How do you do?"
And they all shook hands when we met on the street
And even hugged me a time or two!

This town — it had the usual things
That any town ought to own —
The stores surrounded a neat little square
That had a monument made of stone.

The soldier statue firmly stood
With his musket so straight and tall —
And he seemed to dare anyone to change
The tranquility of it all.

The old men played their checkers
And the ladies bought brand new hats —
And the bus went by to Atlanta —
Now can you imagine that?

The shoe shop smelled of leather —
Newspapers came twice a week —
Coca-Colas were made in bottles
(Through the window you could take a peek!)

Merrell's Dress Shoppe had the latest —
Polka dots are here to stay!!
And Miss Miriam would whistle you a pretty tune —
Before you went along your way.

The hardware store was another place
Where they greeted you with a smile —
Tom Loftin would show you how to measure nails
As he scooped 'em up in great big piles!

McGee's Bakery — ahhhh! That aroma!
Close your eyes and it would carry you away!
Pink sugared roses on the cake squares —
Freshly baked for you that day!

And you never had to worry when you
bought new shoes
That they'd ever pinch or be to tight —
'Cause at Griffin's they would ask you a million times
If the size of the shoe was right!

Then, standing with your feet in a brown machine
That x-rayed all the bones in view,
You proved to your mother (and to God up above)
That what you said about the shoe was true!

There were other great lessons in town to learn
Such as "Don't grow up to be a cheater!"
'Cause you always knew if you parked on the square
You put a penny in the parking meter.

Now right around the corner was the best of all —
Just a few paces off the square —
I could hardly wait for the light to change!
Cross the street and skip over there!

The name of the store suggested something grand —

Taylor and Jack Bell

Cooper Benjamin Bell

Tall building that touches the sky —
They called it The Empire Five and Dime —
Though as a child, I didn't know why.

The store was friendly — that's for sure!
Folks called you by your name!
They treated you like a special guest —
And said how glad they were you came.

Excitement sparked the very atmosphere
And to a child it was quite exotic —
A black myna bird sat perched in a cage —
When he talked, you thought you'd gone psychotic!

Mr. Red was the boss — we all knew that —
He ruled the Empire like a King.
He made the laws — "No running in the aisles!"
And he watched over everything.

Mr. Red made you think of "Stars and Stripes"
And he was really big on Local Pride
'Cause the Empire sold a tiny cedar chest
With the name of the town inscribed.

His soft-spoken wife with the shy sweet smile
Always helped him in her quiet ways —
Miss Lonie Reese was the special touch
Of those grand and glorious Empire Days.

If you came into the store anticipating
Buying candles for a birthday cake,
She'd ask you lot of questions all about it —
Like the kind of cake you'd like to make.

And she didn't just sell you the candles —
I'll tell you what she would do —
She'd really hope those birthday candles
Would make your every birthday wish come true!

Now the Empire Store was a child's delight —
A treasure chest opened wide!
You just can't imagine the things you'd see
— Once you really got inside!

Flags and popcorn, pickup sticks
Balloons and modeling clay,
Lincoln logs and hula hoops,
Paper dolls for a rainy day!

Batons and cat's eye marbles,
Tambourines and kaleidoscopes,
Pop beads, skates and whistles,
Crazy Eights and jumping ropes!

There were big Green Rubber Lizards
That you'd purchase with a wicked grin!
And those funny "Chinese Fingers"
To trick friends to stick their fingers in.

Miss Lonie Reese would help you choose
From this treasure trove galore!
You could always find the perfect gift
At the Empire Five and Ten Cent Store!

If your Grannie had a birthday coming up,
You could buy her a crochet hook —
Or if your little sister had a real bad cold,
You could take her home a comic book.

For Daddy there were all kinds of useful things
Like chains for his important keys —
And hankies that he'd keep in his pocket
Waiting for that — Ah Choo! — sneeze.

Gadgets and gizmos, spatulas and spoons
Lined the shelves in a gleaming array —
It was hard to decide just which one was best
For a special gift on Mother's Day.

There were Valentines for your classmates —
And sandbuckets for the beach —
And frightful masks at Halloween
That were sure to make your neighbors screech!

At Eastertime there were baskets filled
With chicks and a chocolate bunny —
And pretty hair clasps and hairbands, too —
To keep your hair from looking funny!

But Christmastime was the best of all —
Jingle bells and Christmas trees!
And if you were good and waited your turn —
You could even sit on Santa's knees.

There were icicles, sparklers, and tinsel —
Yes! The Empire had it all
No matter the season of the year —
Summer, Winter, Spring or Fall!

I remember the day with the high school band
When I marched through the streets of town —
It was the year that I would graduate —
Soon to wear a cap and gown!

First class of nurses to graduate from West Georgia College, 1976.

Jan Robinson Bell

The folks in the Empire Five and Dime
Turned out to watch this grand parade —
They stood right there till we were out of sight
And cheered us all on — and waved!

They'd known us from our pacifiers
To our crazy teenaged fads —
And they'd cheered us all on since childhood
Towards the special hopes and dreams we had.

Those simple things that I used to buy
At the Empire Five and Ten Cent Store
Have disappeared now — like my childhood —
Gone for forty odd years or more.

But I still can see them — oh, so clearly!
Almost like it was yesterday —
My childhood's dearest treasures
When I was a child at play.

I think I know the grownup answer now
To the Empire Five and Ten Cent Store —
They didn't just sell any ordinary thing —
No, it was something more.

The things they sold at the Empire Store
Were the simple things that make life Grand!
Why, a child with one harmonica
Was Alexander's Ragtime Band!

And a girl gazing on her reflection
As she chose a satin ribbon for her hair
Was imagining herself on Prom Night —
And the ribbon made her really seem there!

Yes, the merchandise in the Empire Store
Was the stuff of which dreams were made —
And they kept us all stocked for years and years
As we marched along through Life's Parade.

The seasons come and the seasons go
And the times — they have really changed —
In the places so dear to my childhood
Are things that are new and strange.

The old parking meters are gone from the square
And so is the soldier of stone —
And here I sit in my rocking chair
A penny for my thoughts alone.

Now some folks will tell you — and maybe it's true
That nothing in life is free —
But when I think back on what a penny bought
It really just amazes me!

Just a penny in a parking meter
To park on the old town square
Bought a visit to the scenes of my childhood
And all the friendly faces there.

Oh, a million pennies or more I'd give
To turn back the clock tonight —
And visit once again that friendly town —
The places of a child's delight.

Why, the Empire Store had the perfect name!
Tallest building in the World!
'Cause that's the way it is in the memories
Of all little boys and girls.

Let's give three cheers for the Empire!
And all the dreams that we purchased there
When we put a penny in the parking meter
And parked on the old town square.

By Jan Robinson Bell

Carrollton, Georgia. The Square 1950

James Charles "Red" Harris was born 24 July 1912 and died 24 May 1985. Lonie Reese Couch Harris was born 23 June 1913, and died 8 February 1985 (DAR).

I'll tell my own grandchildren about the old Empire Five and Dime. Pictured here are Taylor Christian Bell, John Robinson "Jack" Bell Jr., and Cooper Benjamin Bell. My grandchildren call me Trixie.

The first graduating class of nurses from West Georgia's College in 1976 is shown here. Front row left to right; Miriam Hammock Musick, Bonnie Rebecca Barr, Deborah M. Muse, Jacqueline Randitt Esslinger, Terry Hall Coursey, Janet Denise Teague, Alice Allene Hammock, and Jan Robinson Bell. Second row: Orice Edison Brannan, Barbara Ann Meeks, Josephine Smith Hancock, Sharon Smith Hancock, Angela Steed Strickland, Martha Garrett Huff, Linda Liner Wood, Nancy Lee Gardner, and Bruno Emile Marlier (from Belgium). Back row: Virginia Lee Gott, Sherry Malinda Wiggins, Gail Belinda Stanford, Barbara Harris Auble, Robert Bruce Chandler, Sharon Jean Lewis, Annette Berla Sasser, Jaqueline Smith Hargrave, Sara Eason Miller. All received the associate of science degree in nursing on Sunday morning June 6, 1976, at West Georgia College. All of us became registered nurses. The speaker at our graduation was the Honorable Sam Nunn, United States Senator. *Submitted by: Jan Robinson Bell, 315 Kramer Street, Carrollton, GA 30117*

338. Jessie Bell and Doris Walker Bell

Gilford Bell (December 13, 1990-October 3, 1965) was born to David Ephram Bell (May 3, 1864 - April 30, 1930) and Sarah Warren Bell (January 29, 1870 - November 26, 1935). On February 13, 1921, Gilford married Amanda Pearl Brown, daughter of Miles A. Brown (April 11, 1867 - September 26, 1931) and Retha Jackson Brown (October 10, 1865 - March 2, 1955). Pearl was born February 5, 1905. She celebrated her ninety-sixth birthday on February 5, 2001. She lives in Roopville.

Pearl and Gilford had one child, Jesse Gilford, born February 15, 1926. Their home was previously Bellview School. When Jesse was six months old, Gilford moved his family to Roopville. Gilford owned and operated a general merchandise store, grist mill, blacksmith shop, and saw mill. He sold the grist mill during World War II. Later, he operated Armstrong Grist Mill and a dairy in Heard County. Gilford and his brother Theo installed the first water system in Roopville.

As a child, Jesse lived in Roopville. He spent two years in the Navy on the *USS Case* in the Pacific. Jesse bought the grist mill when he returned home from the Navy. Jesse operated the grist mill and built and operated a dairy in Roopville.

On June 5, 1947, Jesse married Doris Walker, daughter of Floyd Curtis and Mary Lousie Shadinger Walker. Curtis was born June 21, 1904, to Daniel Lee (July 9, 1875 - September 8, 1964) and Maude Eugenia "Jeanie" Kelly Walker (October 5, 1884 - April 1, 1971). Mary Louise was born July 19, 1904 to William "Billy" Carroll Shadinger (July 8, 1857 - December 7, 1926) and Burma Moore Shadinger (December 20, 1869 - April 30, 1948).

Doris and Jesse Bell

Curtis worked at the Goodrich Rubber Plant in Akron, Ohio. He returned to Carroll County in March 1925 and married Mary on April 25, 1926. They owned and operated a grocery store in Carrollton. When their daughter Doris (born April 22, 1927) was three months old, Curtis sold the store and moved his family to Akron, Ohio. This time he worked at the Goodyear Plant. Later, they returned to Carrollton. He bought a farm, built a school bus, and drove the bus to Rock Ridge School and A & M School. He was employed with Tanner Grocery and retired after twenty-five years. After retirement, he built several houses in Walker Woods, south of Carrollton. Curtis died October 29, 1995. Mary died September 26, 1997.

Most of Doris's childhood was spent near Carrollton in the Oak Grove Community. Doris has two sisters: Burma Joyce and Nina Carol, and one brother, Curtis Wendell. Jesse and Doris have two children, Linda Kay and Jesse Don, and three grandchildren. In 1952, Jesse began work at Lockheed Aircraft in Marietta, Georgia. He moved his family to Marietta and lived there until his retirement, when they moved back to Roopville. *Submitted by: Doris Bell, 500 Welcome Road, Roopville, GA 30170*

339. Joe Bell III and the History of The Thomas Bell Family

When my brother, Ben Bell, was in second grade at Maple Street School, his teacher, Beth Parkman (Mrs. E. Tom Johnson), gave an assignment one day for the class to write about. She said: "If a flying saucer landed in your back yard and little green men got out — what do you think your family would do?" Ben wrote, "Well, this might not sound like much fun to you, but in our family, we'd load them up in the station wagon, go get a bucket of Kentucky fried chicken, and head out for the grave yard!" Mrs. Parkman called us up to find out just what exactly was going on at our house. It was genealogy.

The Bell boys are pictured, Joe #86, John #84 and Ben #69. They played football for Carrollton High School. The picture was made at Grisham Stadium by Carrollton photographer, Glenn Holmes.

Joseph Terrell "Joe" Bell III was born 7 March 1968 in Carrollton, Georgia and named for his father — and also for his grandfather who was Joseph Terrell Bell Sr. of Newnan, Georgia. Joe's great-grandfather was named Joseph Brown Bell — and he was named for the Civil War Governor of Georgia — Joseph Brown. Joe's great-grandfather decided to carry on the tradition of naming a son for a governor — and Joseph Terrell was another favorite Governor of Georgia who was a personal friend to Joseph Brown Bell. Joe B. Bell knew Gov. Terrell during the days he served in the Georgia State Legislature from Spalding County, Georgia 1898 -1899. So that is how the names of Georgia governors came to be a part of our family heritage.

Our Bell family history is an exciting one — especially when we turn back the centuries — all the way back to the very beginning of our family name. This story is told here especially for Taylor and Jack (daughter and son of John Bell) and Cooper (son of Ben Bell). Those are the descendants that we presently have in the year 2001 — and it is also for any new little "twigs on the family tree" that might appear in the future.

It was in 1413 that King Henry V passed a law in England that every person should take on a surname that had something to do with his "place of abode or his calling." And so it was that some names came from the places where people lived — Greenfield, Brooks, Chappell, Woods, Atwater, Hillyard, to name a few.

Some names developed from actual physical characteristics of people: Golightly, Armstrong, Treadwell (must have been a good swimmer), Longshanks (meant long legs) and Stout, Truelove, Jolley, or Swift. Many other names came from the occupations that people held: Farmer, Miller, Baker, Cook, Weaver, Glover (who made the gloves), Fletcher (who made the arrows), Hunters, Skinners and Tanners (important when our ancestors had to find their supper or their winter coat in the woods!)

Also, Smith — for the blacksmith who shod the horses and made the plows and other farming tools, and so forth. The Cooper was the barrel-maker — and barrels were quite important in the era before there was such a thing as boxes. Just about everything was stored or shipped in barrels — and there was quite an art to barrel-making. And the Tailor or Taylor was one who traveled about the countryside mending people's clothes or sewing brand new ones for them. We actually have one tailor in our family tree who reportedly invented the thimble! Except that he called it a "thumble" since he wore it on his thumb. A name like Robinson developed from "Robin's son."

By the 1500s names had become a birthright and a matter of family pride. Names were not changed from one generation to the next, but instead stayed the same. For example, even though a person no longer held the occupation of Glover, the name remained the same. This is why so many of our names today reflect the life and occupations of the Middle Ages that are no longer in existence. Eventually a name like Robinson was passed on down even though the boy was no longer Robin's son.

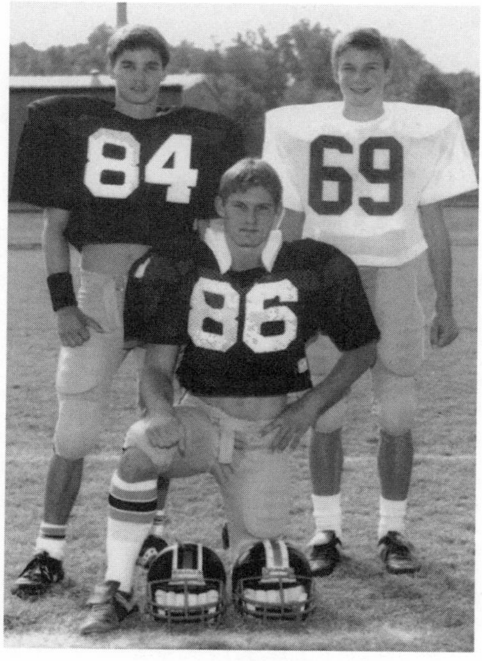

Joe Bell #86, John Bell #84, Ben Bell #69

A young boy of the 1500s would often enter into a trade and work as an apprentice under the guidance of an experienced craftsman. By the time he came of age, he would thus have a trade himself and could join one of the craftsman's guilds. This gave him the status of a free man and other special privileges. So this is why young boys would flock to become apprentices to learn one craft or another. And one of these important crafts involved the making of bells.

We must think back to an era that knew no electricity, no telephones, no televisions, no computers, no fax machines, and no cell phones, no beepers. It is hard for people of our era to think of a time that had none of these means of communication — since we live in the Age of Communication at its finest. (That's what we may think now, but who knows what our descendants a hundred years from now might know! Our methods of communication may look as old fashioned to them as a horse and buggy looks to us today!)

So, how did people communicate in the 16th century? Why, with bells, of course. Bells were used as one of the very earliest means of communication. Bells were used to announce important events — the town crier of London would wander the streets ringing his bell to announce who would be beheaded at the Tower on Tuesday next! The town crier was a practice in England for centuries. Town Bells in towers were used to give warning of danger — such as to call in the men from the field to help put out a fire in the village. Or to call people together for any important announcement. Perhaps there was revolution or war!

In the Middle Ages after the Norman Conquest of England — and after the French influence had impacted the English language, a bell was rung in the evening to announce it was time to "cover the fire" and go to bed. (Hopefully, a reminder given to keep houses from burning down). This time of night came to be known as "curfew" which came from the French "couvre feu" or "cover fire". In a later era, the curfew simply came to mean that it was time to be off the streets and home in bed. The practice of curfew remained in Carroll County, Georgia as late as 1900 when a law was passed that no person under 18 years old could be out in the town after 9 p.m. — penalty of being caught was "$2 or spend the night in the calaboose." So, the curfew bell has only disappeared from our traditions in the last century or so.

Bells were often used as a signal of when to start and when to stop work. Mr. Son Carter who worked our family farm for about half a century used to tell us a story of how on another farm the laborers were "saved by the bell" one hot July. A stern new overseer had taken over and he had decided that the farm laborers were not to be given a lunch break.

Well, as usual, the noon bell rang which signaled noon and time to stop work for lunch break. And the foreman insisted that the black men keep on plowin' those fields. But the mules would not budge. The mules had learned that that noon bell was the signal for THEM to stop and rest awhile. And you know how stubborn a mule can be — so the farm laborers got their lunch break after all.

Nautical bells were used on ships to mark the time — "Two bells was two o'clock." Bells were used on buoys to signal danger to ships coming too close to a reef or dangerous coast. In England, there was actually a "pudding bell" that was rung at a certain time of day to remind cooks it was time to "cool the pudding." And bells have long played an important part in religious occasions since early Christianity. Bells would ring from church steeples to call people to worship. Bells in towers would ring to announce the time of day. Bell choirs had members who held one bell in each hand — ringing it with mathematical precision to create beautiful chords and chiming music. When my grandmother, Louise Bell of Newnan, Georgia, was still living, she loved being a part of a bell choir such as this in her First United Methodist Church in Newnan, Georgia.

Sleigh bells were put on horses, tinkling bells were hung around cow's necks, and bells were placed on the fingers of dancing girls, such as Esmeralda in *The Hunchback of Notre Dame.* Of course, there were also people who climbed the bell tower (like the Hunchback of Notre Dame) to actually ring the bell. That was an occupation involving bells in itself as well. So, the Bell Ringer himself — could have been named Bell. He had followed the King's order and taken the name of his occupation.

Bells have been of importance from earliest times — and especially important were the craftsmen of the 16th century who knew how to make the bells. The Bellmaker was the one who knew exactly what to do to create a perfect bell. He knew that the most resonant bell was made of 13 parts of copper to 4 parts of tin. He knew how to mold the bell so that the bell would be thicker at the rim to create the best resonance. In early times, bells were shaped more like beehives. There were two clay molds — an inner one and an outer one — and the bellmaker would pour the molten metals in between the two.

The making of a new bell in a community was a matter of great importance. When the Bellmaker was ready to pour the hot metals for the mold, he would call together the whole community — and the priest would come to bless the bell. All would pray that no cracks or other unusual defects would appear in this bell. People of this era were extremely superstitious and they wanted their town bell to be known for its good luck and beautiful sounds. The very sound of the bell could have an impact on the fortune of the whole town and its people.

People would seem to imagine certain words or phrases in the ringing of the bell. Indeed, every bell seemed to have its own personality. For example, it would be bad luck for the town if the people seemed to hear in the rhythm of the bells ringing: "You owe me five farthings ... Say the bells of St. Martin's" or "When will you pay me? Say the bells of Old Bailey" This could cause people to have a feeling of foreboding — and they might just drive on to the next village to peddle their wares.

It was often a matter of great discussion in the taverns of the town as to just exactly what the bells of a town were saying. Some bells just had a happy feeling about them and chimed out cheerful messages: "Good market today, fair weather to stay." — which would bring out townspeople in droves — and the town would prosper.

And so it was that whenever a new bell was about to be cast for the town, the townspeople would try to think of some precious metal they might own — a silver bracelet, or a golden ring perhaps—that they might throw into the melting pot — just for good luck. The townspeople had gathered — and the priest had said his blessings — so it was now a moment of great anticipation.

But just before the Bellmaker was about to pour the hot metals, there was suddenly a great commotion heard — someone running down the street hollering "Wait, wait!" They all turned to see who it was — and it was the Great Lady of the Manor herself. In her apron she was carrying something that seemed to be heavy. And as she approached the pot with the molten metals, the townspeople saw that their Lady had her apron full of sterling silver spoons! Into the pot they went — and all the spoons melted down with the other metals.

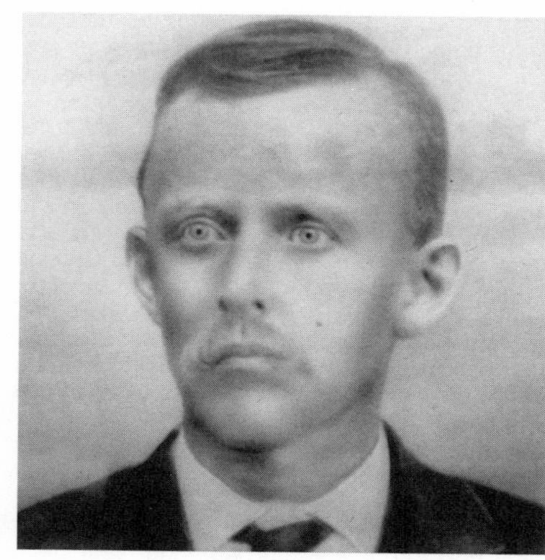

Joseph Brown Bell

Everyone laughed and smiled at this gracious gesture. Surely this was a good luck sign that meant their bell would ring out beautiful silver chimes one day. Once the bell was cast into the mold, there was much rejoicing and merrymaking in the town that day. We have always had much rejoicing and merrymaking in our own family when a new "Bell" (boy or girl) is cast in the mold and born!

So, it is very likely that our earliest ancestor was one who was a craftsman of bells. Or certainly, he was a ringer of bells in some way. As for the town with the newly cast bell, there was much talk in the taverns of the Lady of the Manor and her kindness. And her gesture did bring good luck to the bell because for many hundreds of years, the people of that town would say: Our bell says: "Lady Lady Silver Spoons — Rings Our Bell in Silver Tunes!"

There is one other bell story that pertains to a more recent generation in Carroll County, however — and that would be a story about my Grandmother's (Melba Morgan Robinson's) brother, Bobby Morgan. When he was a little boy growing up on the Whooping Creek Church Road in the 1920's, there was a hugh "dinner bell" on the Morgan farm. It hung on a large frame in the backyard so that it could swing back and forth. That bell was used for communication between the farms and the farm workers mainly. It was rung at beginning and end of work day — if it rung at an odd time, most folks interpreted it to mean that the house was on fire.

David Miller Bell

Bells were used between farms in other ways of communication, too, in early Carroll County. And one of these was to notify neighbors of a death in the family. The way in which this was done was to ring the bell once for a man — then his age. Or, it was twice for a woman, then her age. Three times meant a child had died — and then the age. If a man in the neighborhood was elderly and expected to die — and if the bell on that farm rung once and his age, for instance, eighty times — then it was a sure sign that person had died. And neighbors would prepare accordingly. There were very few telephones.

Well, it so happened that one sunny day in the summer of Bobby's boyhood about 1928, he felt a streak of mischief coming on that was a mile wide. All the rest of the family was out in the fields or otherwise occupied — and Bobby was left to his own designs. And Bobby had decided to ride the bell. It had not been done before, of course, but it looked like something fun to swing on. And so, Bobby decided to ride the bell. And just by coincidence, there was a neighbor on a nearby farm who had been ill, and was old, and might be expected to die any time.

Bobby — little fella he was — got on that bell and ride it he did! Ding! Dong! Ding! Dong! And his family in the field heard it and began running towards the house. But Bobby was going good now and it was fun riding that bell! Ding! Dong! Ding! Dong! The family kept on running and the bell kept on ringing. In fact, it rung about 75 times before they could reach Bobby and pull him off that bell. Of course, Bobby got a switching with an old hickory for his mischief. But little did the Morgan family know then exactly what kind of chaos Bobby had created.

Other neighbors out in the fields in the distance had heard the bell and counted the number of times it rang. Yes, it had rung 75 times — poor old Mr. North — he must have passed on. And folks went out in the yard and killed a chicken and pretty soon there were chickens frying in skillets all over the Clem-Lowell neighborhood! That evening everybody (except the Morgans) showed up in their Sunday best clothes with a platter of fried chicken for the North family. Of course, Mr. North was seated in a rocker on the front porch — and gleefully took the news of his death all in stride! The news of his death was "greatly exaggerated" he said, but the fried chicken was quite delicious.

After the Morgan family had heard of this commotion that Bobby had caused, they took the clapper out of the big bell. And from that day forward, they had a big gong stick that they used to ring the bell instead. And the gong stick was always hidden very well — in a high place where children could not reach — on top of the pipe that vented the old wooden stove in the kitchen. And I'm not saying that maybe Bobby didn't *ride* that bell again — but at least it didn't ring. (With a name like Bell, we have a lot of "Bell stories" in our family.)

Our Bell ancestors originated from Scotland — where they were Lowlanders. There was a great difference in the Lowlanders and Highlanders of Scotland. The Highlanders were mostly descended from Vikings who had migrated south to settle in the north of Scotland in mountainous terrain. The Highlanders had their own customs — kilts, bagpipes, speaking Gaelic, and so forth. Our Robinson ancestors originally were Scottish Highlanders, descended from the Celts and the Vikings.

However, the Lowlanders were more like the English people. They lived in the area that was mostly south of a line drawn from Edinburgh to Glasgow. Many of the early Bells were stonemasons who lived in the area around Fife. They helped to build the five major castles in Fife — and their names are chiseled into the castle walls as the builders. Ian Bell was one of the most famous stonemasons.

The Lowlanders had developed into a people of hardiness and durability. While the Highlanders were largely Celtic in origin — the Lowlanders were a mixture of many peoples — Britons, Romans (soldiers during the Roman occupation), Saxons, Teutonic Angles, and the original people who had come from Ireland to populate Scotland in the first place. This is why — when the English King wanted to try to "tame the Irish" into being more like the English, he sent thousands of Lowland Scots in 1610 to the plantations of Northern Ireland.

Of course, this plan did not work for the simple reason that Lowland Scots were staunch Presbyterians — and the Irish were mainly Catholic. So, they did not intermarry and mix together as the King had hoped. But this is how it happened that our Lowland Bells were transported from Scotland to Ireland. Though several generations of Bells may have been born in Ireland, they still considered themselves to be Scottish — not Irish. One Ulsterman tried to explain himself in this way: "Just because a man be born in a horse stable, would ye think him a horse??" So, our Bell ancestors were Ulstermen, born in Northern Ireland — yet, they clung to their Scottish origins and traditions fiercely. It was only about 12-20 miles across the Irish Sea from Scotland to the province of Ulster in Northern Ireland. So, they really hadn't moved that far from "home" in Scotland. The Bells had been a part of the McMillan Clan.

It was about 1761 when a large number of Ulstermen began to migrate from Ireland to South Carolina. A treaty had been made with the Indians that they would move west of Abbeville, South Carolina — and this opened up a large amount of land. The King of England wanted to fill up this area so South Carolina passed The Bounty Act on July 25, 1761. This act provided that the King would pay for passage to South Carolina if the immigrants were "poor and Protestant." Payment was four pounds for each adult and two pounds for each child under fourteen.

The Act also provided that they would help to pay to transport the immigrants from Charleston to the interior of South Carolina and assist with food and in helping them become established. And freedom of religion was promised. So, this enticed many of the hardy Scots of Northern Ireland to make the journey to South Carolina. This Bounty Act would play an important part in the reasons why so many of our early "Scotch Irish" ancestors would populate the South. There have been at least nine major Bell families identified in Ulster — and approximately 500 Bell families emigrated from Ulster Plantation between 1707 and 1729 to North America where they now thrive.

Our first Bell ancestor that we know about is Thomas Bell who was born on 1 July 1801 in Northern Ireland and whose father was a Scottish soldier in Her Majesty's Royal Forces. By the time Thomas was about fourteen years old, he was working in a tannery to help make the leather armor and leather saddles used by the British soldiers. A fateful battle was about to be fought by the British against the French in a little place called Waterloo near Brussels, Belgium in June 18, 1815.

The fighting was so violent in this great battle that nearly 45,000 soldiers lay dead — in just an area of three square miles — when it was over. Victor Hugo wrote of this historic battle in his book *Les Miserables.* Waterloo was fateful day for Thomas Bell because his father was killed in that battle while fighting under the Duke of Wellington against Napoleon. The story passed down in the family says, "He was killed on the last day of the last battle in the last hour with the last bullet fired." We don't know if Thomas' mother had already died, but we think she might have — because Thomas Bell — and his younger brother, George — decided to stow away on a ship and come to America.

We believe that they may have been planning to try to find some of their family that had gone on ahead to America some years before — because there had been a story left behind of how to find them. The relatives who sailed away promised they would name their church in America for the ship that they sailed away on. And this ship was believed to be the "Hopewell" because that's what the Bells named their churches in America.

Elizabeth Caroline Henderson Bell

It was actually in 1793 when a Reverend Martin had led a great migration of Ulster Scots from Northern Ireland to America — five shiploads of people — and one of the ships was named the "Hopewell." Some of these family names were Orr, McCaw, Chestnut, McCrackin, Gardner, Nesbit, Cowan, Stewart — and also possibly, Miller, Bell, and McDill, we believe. These were also the names of people who later migrated together from Chester County, South Carolina to Georgia.

Thomas Bell and his little brother stowed away on a ship headed for Charleston, South Carolina in 1817. By the time the ship was out to sea a ways, the boys were discovered. The captain told them they'd have to work on the ship to pay for their passage to America. So, they were made "bound boys to the ship." This would mean they'd have to work on the ship virtually as slaves for years.

Mary Hartsfield Banks Bell

However, once the ship had arrived in Charleston Harbor, the boys jumped overboard and swam for shore. It was in 1819 that Thomas Bell later took his naturalization oath in Chester County, South Carolina. He married a young lady by the name of Mary Stewart in South Carolina on 22 September 1819. Mary, who was born 3 October 1794, was the daughter of Archibald Stewart — however, there are about a dozen by this name to sort out. We believe Mary is related to the set of Stewarts who are related to Archibald Barron b. 1734 in Ireland who marries Elizabeth Ingram in 1755 in Ireland.

This family had a daughter, Elizabeth Barron, born 1756 in Londonderry, Ireland who married Alexander Stewart born 1744 also in Londonderry and who died 1823 in Morgan County, Georgia. Alexander and Elizabeth married in 1774 in York District, South Carolina. This Alexander had three brothers killed in the American Revolution — but we believe one of his other brothers is the father of Mary Stewart Bell. Alexander had a son named Archibald Oliver Stewart born 25 November 1781 — so he is not the right age to be Mary's father. Mary was born in 1794. So the Stewart research continues ...

We believe that Thomas Bell's relatives already in America may have been named Miller as well as Bell. Possibly, Thomas' mother had been a Miller before her marriage. There is a strong connection of our Thomas to the Bells of Buncombe County, North Carolina, and the Millers there, too. Both were large landowners around Asheville, North Carolina. Hendersons also intermarried a lot with the Millers and Bells in this area. Thomas Bell purchased property in Buncombe in 1834.

In later years, the Bells of Bumcombe sold much of their property to the land purchaser for the Vanderbilts who was buying up beautiful property for a grand estate. And that is where the Biltmore House stands today in Asheville — on what used to be original Bell property. The David Miller of Buncombe, N.C. — may possibly be an uncle of Thomas and George Bell. We know that Thomas named a son David Miller Bell. And this was our ancestor. There was a migration of people back and forth between Chester County, S.C. and Buncombe Co., N.C. — other researchers have noted this, too.

Later on, in the 1850 census, Thomas Bell appears with three sons who are born in N.C. — and this was in a time period after Thomas had moved to Georgia. So, there still seems to be some evidence that Thomas went back and forth to Buncombe, N.C. Perhaps he was checking up on an elderly relative — perhaps an uncle like David Miller — who might have been the one who helped him when he first came to America as a young boy.

Thomas and Mary Stewart Bell moved into Newton County, Georgia about 1823 when there was a large migration of people from the Chester County, South Carolina area to there. Their good friends, the Thomas McDill family moved with them to Georgia. They settled at Snapping Shoals — where the water made a snapping sound as it went rushing over the smooth rocks.

Thomas and Mary Bell were founders of the old "Hopewell" A.R.P. (Associate Reformed Presbyterian) Church there and the old published minutes of that church are filled with the history of the Bell family. The first church was built of hand hewn logs. One of their churches in Chester County, S.C. had also been called "Hopewell" and this reinforces the old story that the church was named for the ship.

Thomas Bell did not register his first deed until 1831 when he bought 45 acres in Lot 239 16th District on Snapping Shoals Creek for $125. He later bought more property #9 and #24 in the 8th District. Thomas participated in the 1832 Land Lottery from Chesnut's District in Newton County and drew Lot #3 in 26th District, but probably did not occupy this land. Such lots were often sold.

Before Thomas and Mary Stewart Bell had moved to Georgia, one daughter named Nancy Boyd Bell had been born. Then, a son named Archibald Stewart Bell was born 6 January 1825 in S.C. There was another daughter, name unknown. After they'd arrived in Georgia, a son name David Miller Bell was born. He was always called "Miller." A daughter, Mary Ann was born in 1832, and then a son named Thomas Jefferson Bell was born 13 February 1834. He went by J.T. Bell instead of T.J. Bell. There is a Lucy Caroline baptized on 2 April 1834, daughter of "T.A. Bell" and this could be Thomas Bell. If so, we have his middle initial. The three sons born in North Carolina were Matthew Bell born 1836, William Bell born 1838, and John Bell born 1840. We have not ever known anything about the descendants of these last three sons. But we believe Thomas had returned to Newton County, Georgia from North Carolina in time to be counted in the 1840 census here. Some researchers have theorized that the three sons born in N.C. are actually sons of George Bell — but this is only a theory.

As the Bell sons grew into adulthood, they established large farms of their own. David Miller Bell owned about 3000 acres in Spalding County. He also operated a general store at Patillo which was located almost on the Lamar, Butts, and Spalding County line. Other Bell properties were in Jasper County which was not far from Snapping Shoals. Archibald Stewart Bell married Sarah Lucy McClelland and had Mary Jane, Carrie, George, and William Bell. Secondly, he married Margaret Weir and had Nancy Euphemia, and Josiah Thomas Jefferson Bell. Thomas Jefferson Bell married Emma Janie McNair and had Livingston Quigg Bell, Margaret Beatrice, Ernest Lawson, Robert Glenn, and Walter Stewart Bell. We believe the Bob Bell who ran for Governor of Georgia in 1981 was a descendant of A.S. Bell. The Bell brothers of Carrollton — Joe, John, and Ben — had their picture made with Bob Bell when he campaigned in Carrollton.

When the Civil War came along, all the Bell men served in the Confederacy. The names of the wives of A.S. and J.T. Bell can be found on the "salt lists" of Newton County in 1863. Salt was a benefit provided to those who were wives or widows of Confederate soldiers.

Mary Stewart Bell died on 20 September 1846 and was laid to rest in the cemetery of Hopewell Church that she had helped to found. Next to Mary at Hopewell is a tombstone that says:

> "In memory of James Stewart born 3 September 1797 died 18 July 1878, aged 80 years, 10 months, 15 days."

We believe this must be Mary's brother.

On 29 April 1847, Thomas Bell married a second time to Ellender Etheridge (or Deathridge as some records say.) Thomas and Ellender had several children together: Sarah Elizabeth born 1848, Frances Ellender born 1849, a son named Solomon Bell and a daughter named Elsie Jane. We believe the Solomon Bell is the same "Thomas Solomon Bell, son of Thomas Bell, baptized at Hopewell on 28 July 1855." Possibly there is a child named Alley? also baptized in 1855. This could be a nickname for an Elizabeth.

Thomas Bell died on 10 October 1857 and was laid to rest next to Mary at Hopewell Church. After Thomas's death, Ellender Bell moved with her children to Clayton County settling at Jonesboro. One of Thomas' daughters by his first wife also moved with her. A will of S.T. Bell in 1918, Clayton County, bequeaths to son Benjamin Thomas Bell, daughter Mary Annie Ellender Bell Callaway, daughter Lora Ruth Bell, son Jesse Bealer Bell, and sister Elizabeth Williams, and son Rufus Bell.

Joseph Terrell Bell Sr. and Louise Godard Bell

Thomas Bell's son, David Miller Bell, was born 11 March 1828 and died 22 January 1908. He lived most of his life in Spalding County and Lamar Counties, Georgia. He married Elizabeth Caroline "Ann" Henderson born 5 September 1832 and died 6 December 1893. "Ann" was of the Hendersons of Jasper County, Georgia. She married David Miller Bell on 6 March 1851. Ann was the daughter of Joseph J. Henderson and Kissiah Perry who had married in Jasper County, Georgia on 10 March 1831. The Hendersons later moved to Spalding County.

Ann's mother, Kissiah Perry, was the daughter of James Perry (1759-1843) who had married Elizabeth Valentine (19 September 1768-1853) in 1783 in Tarboro, N.C. The Perrys and Valentines were of French Hugenot descent. James Perry was a soldier in the North Carolina line of the American Revolution and many of the Bell daughters have joined the DAR on his American Revolutionary record. Kissiah Perry Henderson appears on the "salt lists" of Newton County, GA as mother of a Confederate soldier.

David Miller Bell was a Confederate soldier who fought in many of the major battles of the Civil War. He enlisted at Griffin, Georgia, on 28 April 1862 in Co. A 53rd Regt. Infantry under Col. L.S. Doyal. He was made Sgt on 12 December 1863. His regiment became a part of Longstreet's Corps of Lee's Army of Northern Virginia. He was in the battles of Second Bull Run, Antietam, Fredericksburg, Chancellorsville, Wilderness, Cold Harbor, and the sieges of Petersburg and Richmond. Longstreet's Corps was detached briefly for service in Tennessee where it was engaged in the battles of Chattanooga and Knoxville in which Miller Bell also fought.

Miller Bell was captured and wounded at Gettysburg on 23 July 1863 and sent to a hospital at David's Island, New Jersey. He was exchanged on 28 August 1863 at City Point, Virginia. The 53rd Georgia Infantry, a part of Semmes Brigade at Gettysburg, was located near the Confederate right flank and took part in some of the heaviest fighting of the battle in the Peach Orchard, Wheatfield, and Devil's Den in front of Little Round Top. Longstreet attacked Little Round Top on July 2nd and 3rd and the regiment was badly shot up. Miller Bell was wounded at Gettysburg and the mini ball that went into his back was never removed. It was lodged too close to his spine and the doctors were afraid to remove it. Miller Bell was later furloughed to Griffin after another wound which he received at Richmond.

At the time that Miller Bell was furloughed home, this was when Sherman was making his march to the sea across Georgia. The siege of Atlanta took place from July 23rd to August 25th, 1864. Sherman's armies passed through the Bell homestead around 17th and 18th of November. There was a skirmish on Towaliga Creek not too far from the Bell homeplace on November 15, 1864. We believe Miller Bell was home on furlough during this time and may have even participated in this fight. Miller Bell carried the mini-ball — "his souvenir of the Battle of Gettysburg" — in his side until he died. He received a $50 per year pension for the rest of his life for this war injury.

David Miller Bell and Elizabeth Caroline Henderson had the following children: (1) Thomas Perry Bell born 7 February 1852 died 9 September 1919; married Nannie E. Harper; buried at Rock Springs Church in Lamar County (2) John Colin Bell the well known author born 9 January 1854 died 12 May 1917; married Mary Matilda "Minnie" Harper, sister of Nannie; buried at Rock Springs (3) Joseph Brown Bell born 20 March 1859 died 5 August 1942; married Mary Hartsfield Banks; buried at Rock Springs. Joe Bell owned land in Spalding and Butts County and also owned a general merchandise store in Butts County. (4) Mollie Bell married Hardy Ogle tree (5) Sarah Ella "Sallie" Bell born 23 August 1861 married Alfred McKinney Watkins in 1880, buried in Watkins Cemetery, Butts County, Georgia (6) Ida Bell born 3 September 1866 married William Parks Walker, buried at Union Church in Spalding County.

At the time of Miller Bell's death, his estate consisted of a store in Patillo, the Bell ginnery at Patillo, stock in Griffin banking company, various parcels of land, and livestock. Miller Bell died on 8 January 1908 and was buried at Rock Springs Church. Elizabeth Caroline Henderson died on 6 December 1893 and was also buried at Rock Springs.

Joseph Brown Bell, son of David Miller Bell, was our ancestor. He was born 20 March 1859 on a farm at Orchard Hill that was then situated in Pike County, but later on became included in Lamar County. Joe Bell was educated in the schools of Liberty Hill and afterward became associated with his father and brother, Thomas P. Bell, in merchandising. In 1893, they organized a company and his father, D.M. Bell, remained at the head of the business until his death. The sons, Joe and Thomas then continued the business for many years. "They were always prepared to meet the needs of the customers and were known as up-to-date businessmen of thorough reliability." After the death of Thomas P. Bell in 1919, the business was discontinued and Joe Bell engaged in farming. He owned a large plantation at Spalding County, Georgia.

From the *History of Georgia Vol. III,* published 1926:

> "Joe Bell is one of the most influential Democrats in Georgia and he has been closely identified with political affairs since he was 21 years of age. He has been a delegate to various congressional conventions and has an extensive acquaintance among governors, U.S. Senators, and other men of prominence in the arena of politics. He numbers Henry W. Grady and General Fitzhugh Lee among his friends. In 1887, Mr. Bell moved to Spalding County and in 1898 was elected a member of the Georgia Assembly. He took a strong stand for prohibition and was recognized as one of the most progressive members of the House ... he was a candidate for state senator in 1912 but was defeated due to the fact that the prohibition cause was unpopular at that time. In 1917 he was appointed a member of the Spalding County School Board ... and during his tenure, many school buildings were erected and the standard of education in the county materially advanced. He has been a deacon of the Liberty Hill Baptist Church for 35 years ... is a Knight Templar Mason and Noble of the Mystic Shrine ... His influence on the life of his community has been of the highest order."

Joseph Brown Bell married Mary Hartsfield Banks on 27 February 1887. She was the daughter of John Larkin Banks (a Confederate soldier) and Mary Hartsfield. Mary Hartsfield Banks has a family tree that fills several books — and she is descended from the same set of Hartsfields that produced Mayor William B. Hartsfield, one of Atlanta's best loved Mayors. Many people will also remember "Willie B" — best loved gorilla of Zoo Atlanta. He was named for Mayor William B. Hartsfield of Atlanta. Also, the Hartsfield International Airport of Atlanta is named in honor of Mayor Hartsfield.

Joe and Mary Hartsfield Banks Bell were the parents of: (1) Thomas Grady Bell born 23 December 1887, educated at Dahlonega, married Mary Sue Wallace 1919; died 1964 (2) Miller Bates Bell born 29 May 1889, educated in Gordon Institute at Barnesville, married Emily Emogene Maddox 1919; died 6 October 1962 (3) John Banks Bell born 15 January 1891, a successful planter and saw miller in Spalding County, married Lois Fisher in 1932; John served in France in WWI; died 1971; he was tallest of the Bell brothers — about 6'7" — what a great sense of humor in this family (4) Annie born 23 September 1892 married Willis L. Biles 1919; the Biles family is another "book" in our genealogy; Willis was a cousin to my Grandmother, Louise Godard Bell, who was the daughter of Frederick Luther Godard and Annie Lee Biles (5) Robert Strickland Bell born 1895 became a captain attending the Gordon Institute; "won fame as a football player at Georgia Tech, a member of the team that defeated the Carlisle Indians and the Washington and Lee players"; he played in the Tech game in the Rose bowl when the player ran the "wrong way" for a touchdown; served as a Marine captain in WWI in France; married Edna Hearn of Carroll County, Georgia in 1926; died 12 May 1972 his namesake is Robert Benjamin Bell, son of Jan and Joe Bell, Jr; (6) Roger Hardy Bell born May 1897, a graduate of Mercer, became Principal of the high school at East Point; in U.S. Navy during WWI; he was on the ship that escorted the world flyers around the globe, became an attorney in Atlanta, married Floy Etheridge of Milner, lived at Decatur; died 1970; our cousin, Russell Allen, grandson of Roger Bell by daughter, Janie Pearl Bell Allen, does genealogical research on this line; Russ is a graduate of West Point (7) Ida Lou Bell born April 1899, graduated State Normal College in Athens, Georgia and taught home economics at Cordele and LaGrange, Georgia, never married; "a great beauty" of the family who lived to be 100 years old — all the Bell family were noted for their longevity. "We are like great old oak trees," Aunt Ida once said. She was dearly loved. (8) Joseph Terrell Bell (Sr.) born 30 January 1900, spent summer of 1925 at McClelland Training Camp, graduated from Georgia Tech in 1926 with degree in Commerce; worked in Insurance for over thirty years; married Louise Godard of Spalding County, lived at Newnan, Georgia; died 5 May 1973; he was 6'4" tall — adored his grandchildren and especially "The Bell boys" (9) Mary Lillian born 1 December 1903, graduated Georgia State Normal College; became a doctor of osteopathy, practiced in LaGrange and was much loved in the area around Lakemont, Georgia where she practiced osteopathy for many years; married William Hinrichs in 1948.

The Bells were a loving and close-knit family whose habit of "little notes" posted several times a week to each other kept them in touch. And they loved to have "Cousin's Day" in the Spring. The family reunion was always held at Thanksgiving each year at the old Joe B. Bell homeplace on the High Falls Road in Spalding County, Georgia. The old homeplace is still occupied by descendants of the John Banks Bell family. Though we have names of all the descendants of the Bell brothers and sisters of this family, it just was not possible to list them all.

After the death of his first wife, Joseph Brown Bell married Miss Laura Morgan of Macon, Georgia on 5 January 1925.

On 20th March 1924, Joe B. Bell sat down and penned these words which he placed in his Family Bible.

> "These things I remember — my homeplace contained 200 acres. Thirty seven years ago when I moved here, this was a fresh place — good land and big crops were made every year. Since 1888, I have added 800 acres to the place — as valuable a land as has ever been in Georgia ..."

Joseph Brown Bell home place, Griffin, Georgia

Joseph Brown Bell who was born 20 March 1859 died 5 August 1942. He was laid to rest beside his wife, Mary Banks Bell, at Rock Springs Church in Lamar County, Georgia. Mary Hartsfield Banks Bell was born 27 October 1864 and died 22 May 1920.

My grandfather, Joseph Terrell Bell Sr., married Annie Louise Godard on 15 February 1934. Louise Bell has one of the most fascinating of family trees — she is descended from English and Scottish stock. Many of her ancestors were the early settlers of old Spotsylvania County, Virginia. One of her most interesting ancestors was Thomas Bloodworth who was Lord Mayor of London during the time of the "Black Death" and "The Great Fire of London," too. We have almost a full accounting of all her ancestors for six generations back.

Louise and Joe Bell Sr. lived in Spalding County about a year before moving to Coweta County, Georgia where they lived the remainder of their lives in Newnan. They were much respected and well loved members of their community and active members of the First United Methodist Church during their lifetime. They were the parents of: (1) Jane Louise Bell born 2 June 1936 m. 4 August 1957 Dr. Fred Donald Bass, lived at Newnan — children: Katherine & Carolyn (twins), Julia, and Jane Morgan Bass; owner of "Jefferson House Antiques" in Newnan; Dr. Bass a respected surgeon in Newnan many years. (2) Martha Lee Bell born 2 March 1938 m. Luther Coleman Lewis on 17 April 1965, lived in Atlanta; children: Claire, Coleman, and Beth Lewis; Martha a teacher of History and Latin; Luther, Director of Georgia Building Authority (3) Mary Lillian Bell b. 22 May 1942 m. Melvin Strickland, lived in Royston; Mary, a teacher and owner of "Wilder Flowers Florist Shop", children: Patie and Joseph Strickland; Melvin died in 1995 — he had the greatest sense of humor (4) Joseph Terrell Bell, Jr. b. 28 December 1946 m. Janice Trixie Robinson on 25 August 1967 lived in Newnan and Carrollton; children: Joe III, John, and Ben Bell. Jan and Joe Bell, Jr. divorced in 1987 after twenty years of marriage; Joe married 2nd Patricia Driver McWhorter in 1989. Patricia has two children by a previous marriage to Dale McWhorter: (1) Brooke McWhorter married to Michael Harvey, one daughter "Kate" and (2) John McWhorter.

Joe Bell III played football under Charlie Grisham and was co-captain of the Trojans in his senior year. He was named Outstanding Offensive Lineman and Outstanding Defensive Lineman in his senior year in Trojan football; Joe was named Outstanding Latin Student as well. As a senior superlative, Joe's classmates named him "Most Dependable." He won a scholarship to Georgia Southern upon his graduation from Carrollton High School in 1986. Joe graduated from Georgia Southern in 1990 with a degree in business administration. Joe has been employed with Delta Airlines since 1990. He loves to take advantage of his flying privileges and has traveled extensively with Delta. Like his grandfather, John Robinson — Joe has an interest in aviation and he took up a hobby of flying for a few years, earning his pilot's license.

There is much interest in the Bell genealogy today and we have presented our lines as much as we know them. So many people have asked if our set of Bells are related to the many Bells who live around Roopville or Bremen. The answer is that we really do not know. As you can see from this genealogy — there are many Bell lines that we have not followed down. Certainly, we have many Bell men who could have migrated from the areas of Newton, Spalding, Lamar, and Clayton Counties to Carroll County, Georgia. And don't forget about Thomas Bell's brother, George Bell. Though we know little about him, he was in nearly all the same places as Thomas Bell — and we know from census records that he also had many sons. But this is a complete accounting for the male descendants of the Joseph Brown Bell line out of Spalding County, Georgia. Joe B. Bell had six sons — but all those sons had daughters except for my grandfather, Joe Bell Sr., who had one son, Joe Bell Jr. And then Joe Bell Jr. had three sons — Joe III, John, and Ben Bell. We will be glad to hear from others who research the Bells of these areas of Georgia and the Carolinas. *Submitted by: Joe Bell III, Davis Mill Drive, Dallas, GA and written by: Jan Robinson Bell*

340. The Joe Bell Jr. Family

Joseph Terrell "Joe" Bell Jr. was born 28 December 1946, the son of Joseph Terrell Bell Sr. and Annie Louise Godard Bell of Newnan, Georgia. On 25 August 1967, Joe married Janice Trixie Robinson. She was the daughter of John Talmadge Robinson and Melba Angeline Morgan. Together, Joe and Jan would have three fine sons — Joe, John, and Ben Bell.

Joe Bell Jr. would work for over twenty years in his wife's parents' drug store, Robinson Drug Company, on Dixie Street in Carrollton. He assisted them by keeping the books for the drug store, preparing tax reports, etc. Joe also worked for Carrollton Federal Savings and Loan as a V.P. in this same time period. Joe and Jan divorced in 1987 and Joe married Patricia Driver McWhorter in 1989. Patricia had two children by a previous marriage to Dale McWhorter — Brooke and John. Brooke is now married to Michael Harvey with a daughter, Kate. The Bell genealogy is being submitted through Joe's sons for this book, but Joe would like to present more of his mother's side of the family here. Through his mother, Joe Bell Jr. is a descendant of many Revolutionary War soldiers and patriots.

Through Louise Godard Bell's paternal line of Frederick Luther Godard (b. 9 June 1876 d. 24 June 1963) the Revolutionary War Ancestors are as follows: John Thornton who was born in 1718 and died in 1787. He served in Am. Rev. from Virginia — his wife was Elizabeth and he died in Franklin County, North Carolina. Larkin Johnston was born 1 May 1727 in Spotsylvania County, Virginia. Larkin died in Jasper County, Georgia, on 16 March 1816. He was an American patriot in North Carolina. Larkin's wife was Mary Rogers (2 Jan 1728-25 October 1800). Larkin Johnston's mother was Anne Chew, a descendant of Joseph Chew. There is a famous painting of the American Revolution which took place at the Chew House in Pennsylvania. The painting is by Alonzo Chappell and it hangs in the Chicago Historical Society now.

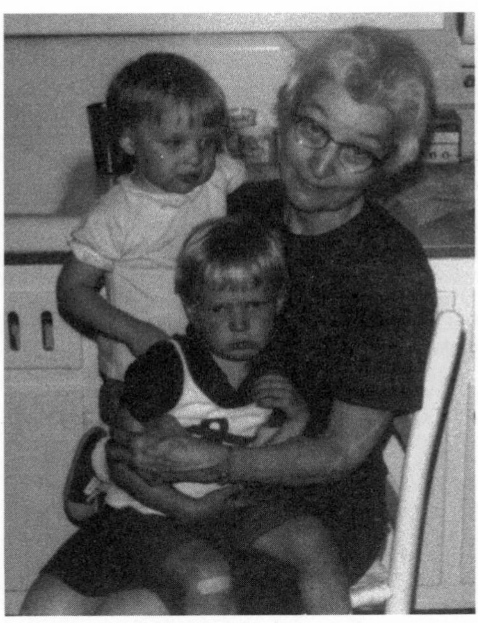

Ben sitting in Grandmama Bell's lap, and Jane Morgan Bass

Littleton Johnston was born 1761 in North Carolina and died in 1842 in Jasper County, Georgia; he was an American Revolution Sergeant. His wife was Lucy Childs — and she was the daughter of Nathan Childs who was born 1730 and died 1809 in Georgia, an American Rev. Patriot of North Carolina. John Bloodworth was born 1730 in England and died 1808 in Georgia. John Bloodworth was an Am. Rev. Lt. in North Carolina; his wife was Tamsa Axon whom he married in 1748. Thomas Bloodworth was born 1755 in North Carolina and died in 1836 in Georgia. Thomas was an Am Rev. Colonel, Civil Service, North Carolina and his wife was Tamsa Proctor.

Through Louise Godard Bell's maternal line of Annie Lee Biles (b. 21 Feb 1881 — d. 28 Dec 1962), my Revolutionary War Ancestors are: Daniel Biles born 1755 PA died 1835 North Carolina, Am. Rev. Pvt NC, married Jean Conger 1775 the daughter of John Conger Jr. b. 1751 NJ d. 1806 NC, Am Rev Ens NC, married Mary Ross daughter of John Ross born 1726 in Scotland and died 1800, Am. Revolution Patriot, Rowan County, North Carolina. John Conger Sr. was born 1710 in New Jersey, died 1793, American Revolution Patriot, wife, Zipporah. Anthony Cozart III born 1739 in New Jersey and died 1817 in North Carolina. He was a

Frederick Luther Godard and Annie Lee Biles

American Rev. Pvt. And his wife was Winifred Bumpass. Solomon Ewards was born in 1756 in Virginia and died 1844 in Clarke County, Georgia; Am. Rev. Pvt in Virginia, his wife was Sarah Mathews who is believed to be the same Sarah Mathews daughter of the famous gunsmith of the American Revolution, Moses Mathews of Lincoln County, Georgia. Joseph Wise born 1745 in Brunswick Co, Virginia and died 1804 in Oglethorpe Co, Georgia, Am Rev Patriot Virginia, married 1765 in North Carolina. Margaret Patton daughter of Jacob Patton born 1720 died 1783 Wilkes Co, Georgia, Am Rev Pvt Wake County, North Carolina, wife Jane Pickrell. He fought under Elijah Clarke.

Louise Godard Bell shared mutual ancestors of Francis Thornton (1651-1726) and Alice Savage with two American Presidents, James Madison and Zachary Taylor. Also, through Louise Godard Bell's paternal line, through Daniel Godard b. 1793 who m. 1819 in Jones Co, Georgia to Elizabeth Rogers, our family can trace its ancestry back to Thomas Rogers who first came to America on the Mayflower.

We have a humorous picture to share — it's of Ben Bell when he had first found out that he had to share his Grandmama Bell with his first cousin Jane Morgan Bass. Boy was he mad!

Submitted by: Joe Bell Jr., Star Point Road, Carrollton, GA 30117 and written by: Jan Robinson Bell

341. John and Christi Padgett Bell Family

John Robinson Bell was born 1 May 1969 in Carrollton, Georgia, the son of Joseph Terrell Bell Jr. and Janice Trixie Robinson Bell. John is named for his maternal grandfather John Talmadge Robinson, pharmacist and owner of Robinson Drug Company in Carrollton for over fifty years. John's maternal grandmother was Melba Angeline Morgan (born 28 May 1922 — died 23 January 1996).

Joe, Ben, and John Bell

John's father, Joe Bell Jr., is the son of Joseph Terrell Bell Sr. and Annie Louise Godard Bell of Newnan, Georgia. Joe Bell Jr. was a 1964 graduate of Newnan High School and he received his degree in business administration from West Georgia College in 1968. Joe was employed by Carrollton Federal Savings & Loan for over twenty years, serving as vice president and comptroller. From 1975-1995, Joe Bell Jr. had the largest number of market shares of IRAs in Carroll County at Carrollton Federal. Joe is presently employed by CB&T Bank of Carrollton.

Joe Bell Jr. has always been active in civic affairs of Carrollton, serving as president of the Carrollton Kiwanis Club and as president of the Carrollton Booster Club. Joe Bell Jr. was the president of the Carrollton Booster Club the year that Carrollton High School celebrated its 150th anniversary, and many people remember the grand parade held that year. It included many of the former majorettes (who marched the distance of the parade route once again after many years!) and former homecoming queens from the previous fifty years.

Bell family at christening of Taylor Christian Bell, 1995.

At the homecoming game there were cheerleaders from as far back as the 1920s who turned out to go onto the football field and even do cartwheels for the halftime show, cheering "Go Trojans!" Edith Foster wrote about this as one of the grandest celebrations ever held in Carrollton and it was quite memorable! Joe Bell Jr. also participated in the community play — "White Warrior" — held in 1976 about Chief William McIntosh. Joe has always had an interest in history of the community. He has long had an interest in his genealogy and his family history will be presented in this book under the heading of his son Joe Bell III.

Another of Joe Bell Jr.'s lifelong interests has been in the sports and sports facilities for the youth of Carroll County. He has worked diligently with different civic clubs in Carrollton over the years to help establish playing fields and other recreational facilities for softball and baseball teams. Joe's father, Joe Bell Sr., was a 1926 graduate of Georgia Tech, and Joe has carried on his family's tradition of being a "Tech fan." Also, Joe Bell, Jr. has been one of the most loyal of Carrollton Trojan football fans, especially so since he had three sons to play football for the Trojans.

Jan Robinson Bell was a 1964 honor graduate of Carrollton High School, and she received her A.B. in English from West Georgia College in 1968. Later she graduated with an A.S. degree in Nursing with the first class of nurses to graduate from West Georgia College in 1976. It was Jan's class who had the honor of designing the first nursing pin that all West Georgia nurses have worn since that time. Jan's career in nursing has spanned over 25 years during which her specialties as an R.N. were Operating Room and Intensive Care nursing. She was employed for over 15 years at Tanner Medical Center in Carrollton. She has also worked at Newnan Hospital and other hospitals and home health agencies in the areas of Carroll, Heard, and Coweta Counties.

Jan is a creative writer who probably best known for her poem *The Empire Five and Dime* which can be seen in this book. It has touched Jan deeply over the years to visit in so many homes in Carroll County, as a home health nurse, to see that many people have this poem framed on the wall or under the glass of their coffee table.

"We all share something special in our memories of The Empire Five and Dime,"

Jan has said. Mr. J.C. "Red". Harris, the owner of the store, had loved the poem so much that he had it published in the newspaper just after Mrs. Louise Reese Harris had died in 1985. The poem was written in her memory.

Jan Bell has had a lifelong interest in genealogy, and she served as the first editor for the Carroll County Genealogical Society's Quarterly. "So many people have an interest in the genealogy of Carroll County because this was the jumping off place for people going west," Jan says. She has written many family histories for her grandchildren to enjoy one day and hopes to one day write a history of other early Carroll County families. Jan also writes mini-biographies of early Carroll County people and places them on the internet in the "Biographies" section of the Carroll County, Georgia, site of the U.S. GenWeb. After twenty years of marriage, Jan and Joe Bell, Jr. divorced in 1987.

Joe Bell Jr. married Patricia Driver McWhorter on 4 February 1989. Patricia's children by a previous marriage to Dale McWhorter are Brooke McWhorter (M. Michael Harvey — one child — Katherine "Kate" Harvey, and (2) John McWhorter. Patricia is the daughter of Louis Cary Driver and Nevelle Walls Driver of Carroll County, both now deceased. The Driver family history is presented in this book by Patricia's sister Carol Driver. Patricia Bell has been a wonderful stepmother to her Bell stepsons and is much loved and appreciated. Patricia Bell is employed by Community Federal Bank in Carrollton. Joe and Patricia Bell are members of Stripling Chapel Methodist Church.

Stripling Chapel church cemetery is one of the oldest in the community and many of the ancestors of Jan Bell are buried there including the Morgans and the Chambers. It is also the church where John and Christi Bell have had their children, Taylor and Jack Bell, christened. In the family group picture of Taylor Bell's christening in 1995 are left to right: Jan Bell, Brooke Harvey, Donna Bell, Christi Bell holding Taylor Bell, John Bell, Joe Bell III, Patricia Bell, Joe Bell Jr. Back row: Michael Harvey, Ben Bell, John McWhorter.

John Robinson Bell married Mary Christian Padgett at the First United Methodist Church in Carrollton, Georgia, on July 31, 1993. John received his BBA in finance from the University of Georgia in 1991. Christi received her degree in journalism from the University of Georgia in 1992. John was a member of Sigma Nu Fraternity and Christi was President of her Phi Mu Sorority at Georgia. Christi is the daughter of Dr. Thomas C. Padgett and Joy Hilliard Padgett of Carrollton, Georgia. (See the separate heading for this family.)

Christi Padgett was born 21 May 1970 at Vandenberg AFB in Santa Barbara, California during the years that her parents were in the Air Force. Christi attended Carrollton High School and graduated in 1988. John Bell and Christi Padgett first became sweethearts when Christi was in the 8th grade and John was in the 9th grade at Carrollton High School. Christi and John dated in high school and then dated other people for a few years. They got back together when they were both students at the University of Georgia.

After their marriage, John took a job as a stockbroker for Olde's in Atlanta and Christi went into advertising. Christi then began to handle one specialty account which was for the Coca-Cola Company in Atlanta. The Coca-Cola Company liked Christi so much that they decided to hire her fulltime for The McDonald's Account. Christi worked in this capacity for several years and did a lot of traveling for Coca-Cola. Currently, she does consulting work for The Coca-Cola Company.

Christi loves to decorate her home with the paintings of Thomas Kincaid, who incidentally gives all his children a middle name of Christian. Mary Christian Bell was named for her Aunt Joyce whose name was Joyce Christian Wilkes Mayo. Christi was also named for her paternal grandmother, Mary Gillingham Padgett. Christi has the beautiful oil paintings done by her grandmother, Mary Padgett, who was a very talented artist. Mary loved to paint in oils the ocean scenes and lighthouses of Savannah where she lived. A family favorite is also the portrait that Mary painted of Christi with her wonderful orange and white cat, Ali. John Bell likes to tell people, "I married into a cat family."

John and Christi Bell, Jack and Taylor

John and Christi Bell make their home in Lawrenceville, and John is a v.p. for First Union Bank Securities in Atlanta. He is also working towards a degree in financial planning and will graduate in October 2001. Christi travels a few times a month with her consultant work for The Coca-Cola Company.

John and Christi Bell have two children: Taylor Christian Bell born 9 February 1995 and John Robinson (Jack) Bell, Jr. born 12 November 1998. Taylor Bell enjoys making A's in school, learning to play the piano, and likes to win swimming medals. Jack Bell likes preschool, and his favorite movie is "My Dog Skip." It appears that Jack Bell is going to be a ballplayer like all the other Bell boys. He does love a ball of any kind.

The Bells are very active in their church which is Cannon United Methodist Church in Snellville, Georgia. Christi Bell has a beautiful voice and is often asked to sing for weddings. She also sings in the church choir and often sings solos. The family loves to go visit their church for her solos and the Christmas program is especially beautiful. Christi is now taking piano lessons along with Taylor since she wanted to brush up on her piano skills so she can play for her church when needed. Christi and Taylor get up early in the mornings so that they can play the piano together before beginning their day. What a beautiful way to begin the day!

Jan Bell thinks she is the lucky one. "I have the most wonderful daughters-in-law. Both Christi and Donna Bell are like the daughters I never had," she says. "We are looking forward to this Heritage Book so that the grandchildren can see in a real book the stories of all their ancestors. Both Christi and Donna Bell are such wonderful mothers to read to their children. I have always loved the old poem that says:

> "You may have tangible wealth untold ...
> Caskets of jewels and coffers of gold ...
> But richer than I you can never be ... For
> I had a mother who read to me."

(From *ChildCraft Encyclopedia,* Author unknown.) "This is only one of the many sterling qualities that I find in my lovely daughters-in-law," Jan Bell says. "My sons are my finest achievement in my life — and Christi Padgett Bell and Donna Rivers Bell are the crowning glory for the whole Bell family. We are so lucky and so proud of them all."

Submitted by: John Robinson Bell, 3397 Remembrance Trace, Lawrenceville, GA 30044 and written by: Jan Robinson Bell.

342. John David Bell Family

My paternal great-grandfather, John David Lee Bell, was born April 5, 1827. He married Margaret Elizabeth Campbell (Peggy), born December 27, 1824. They came from Saluda, South Carolina, sometime between 1840 and 1849. I was told that John D. Bell was a private in the Confederate Army, which might have influenced him to migrate further south because of the land lotteries. The Bell family attended Liberty Christian Church which is located between Temple and Bremen, Georgia, and they are buried there.

According to a deed on file in the Douglas County courthouse, John David Bell bought land from K.C. Mobbs of Douglas County for $300 being 50 acres in the 2nd District (originally Carroll County, now Douglas), dated September 24, 1875. I believe the old house was located on Banks Mill Road.

The families seemed to have been very close. Sometime later, John and Peggy lived next to the Campbell farm, located now on Mandeville Road in northwestern Carroll County. Later the property was called the Bell Campbell farm. It is now owned by Joe Bass, the great-grandson of John David Bell. Joe still does some farming and has some cattle. There is a barn on the property that was built by my grandfather, Hugh B. Bell, and his brothers when they were teenagers. It is still in pretty good shape. (See photograph.)

Many of the descendants of John David and Margaret E. are still in and around Carroll County. Their children are Thomas William Jefferson Bell, Sarah Jane Bell Bass, Hugh Boyd Bell, and John S. Bell.

My grandparents, Hugh Boyd Bell and Mary Martha Awtrey Bell, lived in several places in and around Carroll County and Haralson County. One place they lived was a two-room cabin over near Bell Road near Buck Creek, and another was in Mt. Zion. This property is still owned by their granddaughter Opal Ashmore Stokes Harrison. She was the postmistress at Mt. Zion for a number of years.

Shortly after World War I, my grandparents decided to sell the farm and move into Bremen and go into real estate. They made their living that way for the rest of their lives. When I was small, they had a house on Highway 27, a couple of blocks south of town, and one north of the railroad.

John David Lee Bell and Margaret Elizabeth Campbell Bell.

Granddaddy had been married before, and had a daughter by his deceased wife. This daughter's name was Bertha. He and grandmother had ten more children. Their children were: (1) Bertha Bell, born 1883, (2) Walter D. Bell, born 1887, (3) Harvey A. Bell, born 1889, (4) George A. Bell, born 1895, (5) Ieulah Bell, (6) Beulah Bell, (7) Horace Grady Bell, born 1901, (8) Iva Mae Bell, born 1904, (9) Buna Clark Bell, born 1906, (10) Bernard Clay Bell, born 1908, (11) Lewis Gordon Bell, born 1912.

Of these children, five met untimely deaths. Walter was drowned at about age eighteen. Harvey was killed in France in World War I. Iva Mae was killed by a stack of stove wood falling on her when she was four years old. Clark and Bernard were killed in separate automobile wrecks.

My father, Horace Grady Bell married Edna Jeanette Howell in 1924. He met her at church at Harmony Baptist Church near Waco, Georgia. She was about sixteen years old, he was about eight years her senior, but apparently they were both smitten immediately. I think she was seventeen when they were married and they had two children, James Hugh Bell and Gradyne Bell (me). We lived in a lot of places due to my father pursuing better work. Most of my life he worked as a railway postal clerk. Our last move was to Lithia Springs, where we have lived since 1948.

Barn built by John D. Bell's sons when they were teenagers.

When my dad retired, he found his avocations. He organized, founded, and was president of the Bartram Trail Society. The society was responsible for marking many miles of William Bartram's travel through Georgia. He was a botanist and artist, who traveled through the Southeast cataloging the plant life of the area in the 1700s.

A historical marker in Thomaston, Georgia, marks the place where the Bartram Trail Society's charter meeting took place. He was also instrumental in the effort to get the Factory Shoals area of Douglas County made into Sweetwater State Park, and was a happy camper with the Spring Lizards Camping Club, which my family and I still enjoy.

Lewis Gordon Bell, youngest of the family also made a name for himself. He was a state patrolman, who rose to the head of the first Police Academy, and then to the position of deputy director of the Georgia State Patrol.

Submitted by: Mrs. Gradyne Myers, Lithia Spring, GA

343. W.T. Bell Family

"I remember it well, the first time I ever laid eyes on Theo. We were introduced at a small gathering at a home in Roopville, and I knew right away that I loved him. When I got home that night I told Mama that I had met the man I was going to marry, if he felt the same way I did. I was almost 17 at the time, but I knew he was the one!"

These were the words of Rachel E. Hipp of Hogansville, Georgia, spoken to her mother after she and William Theodore Bell of Roopville had met for the first time in 1930. At this time, Rachel was a junior in high school, and Theo was a graduate of Carrollton High School, had attended Oglethorpe University, and finished business school in Carrollton.

After dating for two years, they did get married on a beautiful Indian summer afternoon on October 1, 1932, at Tyus, Georgia. Brother W.P. Cumbie married them at his home.

Following a short honeymoon to Stone Mountain, Georgia, the couple moved in with Gilford and Pearl Bell, for about a year until their first child, William Theodore Bell Jr., was born on September 25, 1933. For a short time, they also lived at the Bell home place where they enjoyed hearing about old true stories that had happened during the Bell family's younger days.

Rachel and Theodore Bell, shortly after they were married, October 1932.

One winter evening, while residing there, Mrs. Sally Bell (Theo's mother) told about an Uncle Russ Bell, who was running a government still at the spring where they lived. (This is where the Bell family reunions were held for many years.) She said she went to see Aunt Liz (his wife), and she pointed her finger towards the closet, and told her that those piles of flour sacks stacked full with money would never do them any good! And, she said, "It didn't, either."

She remembered that on each Sunday afternoon, the buggies would come out from the spring, with women so drunk they would almost fall out of their buggies. She said she prayed that God would wipe the still off the map. But the big showdown came when Uncle Russ asked Mr. Bell (David Ephram, but affectionately known as "Sonny") to help him at the still. Mrs. Bell told Mr. Bell that if he did, he could take half of the children and she would take the other half, and that she meant business! And, she said, "That was the end of that subject!"

Children of Rachel and Theodore Bell. Judson, Rachel, Linda, and William.

Rachel Bell says she also learned a lot from both Mary (Theo's sister) and Mrs. Bell, and remembers that they had the first carbide lights that she had ever seen.

After almost a year, Theo and Rachel moved into their new home in 1934 on a windy hill in Roopville, Georgia. Theo began farming and operating a store and mill with his brother, Gilford, and later he became the owner of the store where he sold general merchandise, fresh ice cream, home grown beef, etc. He also ran a peddling truck in the area, and sold produce in Atlanta weekly. During this time period, Theo also supplied a large number of citizens in the area with water from his spring, for $2.50 per month.

Rachel spent her time enjoying the pleasures of being a housewife and mother and was and still is an active member of the Roopville Baptist Church in her community. She served as a Sunday School teacher for seventeen years and is "still there" for others.

During earlier years, Rachel cooked for all of the farm crews each day, and it wasn't long until they had a second son, Judson David Bell, born May 2, 1935, a daughter Sarah Linda Bell, born April 13, 1938, and their last, a daughter, Rachel (Trudy) Bell, born December 31, 1941.

Theo believed in keeping his children busy on the farm with crops of cotton, a garden and cattle. He also had a smoke-house, where he smoked his hams and sausage, and did some trucking on the side. He said he enjoyed being his own boss and working with the earth and he would often come home from quail hunting with his vest filled with quail.

Active in supporting the local Roopville High School, Theo was a member of the board of trustees and later served as school county board member for most of the 1950s. He also served as a deacon at the Roopville Baptist Church.

Both Theo and Rachel helped to take care of their daughter Linda's two children, Lee and Rachel Markham, after their own children left home. This was a very happy experience for them.

Rachel still lives in their original home in Roopville, where she enjoys frequent visitors from all ages who come to see her for inspiration. Her family also visits her regularly and she is enjoying life to the fullest at age eighty-seven. Her memory is still excellent and she especially likes to recall the first time she met Theo.

1. William Theodore Bell (October 1, 1905-September 12, 1978); son of David Ephram Bell (May 3, 1864-April 30, 1930) and Sally J. Bell (January 29, 1870-November 26, 1935) and grandson of William L. Bell (February 28, 1824-November 30, 1883) and Mary F. Bell (August 28, 1827-March 15, 1914), all of Roopville.

2. Rachel E. Hipp (October 9, 1913) daughter of Mr. and Mrs. Gus Hipp of Hogansville, Georgia.

3. William Theodore Bell Jr. (September 25, 1933). William is married to Judith Hewitt, daughter of Mr. and Mrs. Lewis Hewitt, of Carrollton, is retired from Lockheed and resides in Marietta.

4. Judson David Bell (May 2, 1935). Judson is married to Nancy Beavers, daughter of Mr. and Mrs. Dalton Beavers of Carrollton; retired from Georgia Power, and resides just down the hill from the Bell house in Roopville.

5. Sara Linda Bell (April 13, 1938-April 19, 1990). She had been a registered nurse for twenty-seven years, and was married to Albert Markham of Richmond, Virginia. Linda and Albert had two children, Albert Lee Markham (February 20, 1970) and Rachel Ann Markham (March 25, 1975).

6. Rachel (Trudy) Bell (December 13, 1941). Trudy is retired from West Georgia College, and is married to Donald N. Healy of Seattle, Washington. They reside in Ponte Vedra Beach, Florida. *Submitted by: Rachel B. Healy, PO Drawer 2539, Ponte Vedra Beach, FL 32004-2539*

344. Zadoc Russell Bell and Melissa Davis Bell

Russ and Liss Bell lived their early life at Bell Spring on Veal Road.

Their children were: Dover, 1886-1996, married Katherine Driscoll. Ida, 1888-1968, married Drew Watson. James L., 1890-1952. Frieda Elma, 1896-1970, never married and worked for 40 years for the telephone company in Carrollton. Roy, 1899-1947. Walter Clarence, 1900-1964. Mary, 1905-1979, married William Kulp. Hoke Smith, 1907-1991, married Mildred Thomas. Russell, died in infancy. Hoke Smith Bell was inducted into the Carrollton High School Trojan Hall of Fame in 1977 and into the Oglethorpe University Athletic Hall of Fame in 1988. He was very proud of the fact that while he was playing football at OU, the football team defeated Georgia Tech and the University of Georgia.

Melissa Davis Bell was a daughter of James Monroe Davis of Randolph County, Alabama, and Heard County, Georgia, who served in the Confederacy. Her mother was Mary Elizabeth Pearce. James Monroe Davis was a son of Chesley Davis and Elana Menelus Green of Randolph County, Alabama. Melissa's brothers and sisters were Nancy Davis Veal, William Davis, James Wyatt Davis, Samuel Augustus Davis, Mariah Davis Howard, Walter Jackson Davis, and Carrie Davis Steed.

Zadoc Russell Bell was a son of William L. and Mary Bell. Russ, 1859-1917, and Liss, 1869-1953, are buried at Carrollton City Cemetery.

Bell Family at home at Bell Spring.

In the photograph, left to right: Three household helpers. The woman is holding Walter Clarence Bell. James Monroe Davis. Mary Elizabeth Pearce Davis. Dover Bell. James Wyatt Davis, son of James Monroe Davis. Zadoc Russell Bell. Melissa Davis Bell. John Howard, husband of Mariah Davis Howard. Mariah Davis Howard, daughter of James Monroe Davis. Samuel Augustus (Gus) Davis, son of James Monroe Davis. Another brother of Melissa Davis Bell.

Four children in front: Ida Bell, Frieda Elma Bell, James L. Bell, Roy Bell. *Submitted by: Mildren Thomas Bell, 374 Lynnhurst Rd., Smyrna, GA 30082.*

345. Hester Bennett and Lela Hogan Bennett

Hester Bennett was the youngest of nine children with only a ninth grade education. Many say he was "fifty years ahead of his time." He was born in Cleburne County, Alabama, May 1900 and worked as a laborer on Highway 78 construction. He and his wife, the former Lela Hogan, a devoted and supportive wife, lived in Edwardsville, Alabama, and had a boarding house for many years. They grew most of the food served there and provided housing for many co-laborers.

Hester and Lela Hogan Bennett

The Bennetts had three daughters, LaRuth the oldest, and twins Betty Hester and Lela Esther. Living at several locations in Heflin and Anniston Alabama, they finally expanded to Carrollton,Georgia, in the late 1940s. Hester had numerous sawmills in Alabama and the west Georgia area, and supplied lumber and wood pallets for government use during the war when barracks were near the now University of West Georgia. At about this same time, Hester Bennett had two large lumber yards in Carrollton and employed a number of people. One yard was located off Adamson Avenue near the now Southwire Plant, the other was off Roop Street where the McIntosh Plaza is now. He maintained his office on Dixie Street for many years. Hester began to invest in timber and land, building numerous rental homes in the Sunset Hills and Bennett Circle areas of Carrollton, as well as in other parts of Carroll, Haralson, and Heard Counties.

In 1953, he opened a ladies ready to wear store in Carrollton called Bennett's. The shop was managed at first by Avis Evans, and later by his daughter LaRuth. The shop remained in operation for thirty years and was considered a top fashion store in the area.

All three of Mr. and Mrs. Bennett's daughters graduated from West Georgia College with degrees in elementary education. LaRuth married Talmadge Ayers from Bowdon in 1954, and they have three daughters, LaDonna, Elizabeth and LeeHester. Talmadge was a brickmason originally. In 1963 he became part owner of Ayers and Smith Motor Company in Carrollton where he is presently. The twins both moved to Cobb County Georgia, and taught in area schools for several years. Betty Hester married Bobby Cosper from Carrollton and have one daughter Pamela, and three sons, Rolin, Robert, and Roderick. Bobby Cosper passed away in November 1998. Lela Esther married Travis Denney who was also from Carrollton. Lela Esther passed away in January 1998 after a battle with cancer.

Throughout his entire life, Hester Bennett's focus was on his family and the church. He and his wife Lela continued to support their original home church, Harmony Grove Baptist in Cleburne County, Alabama, and later Tabernacle Baptist in Carrollton where he served as deacon for many years. His wife Lela preceded him in death in December 1977. Hester passed away in September 1981, both are buried in the Carrollton City Cemetery. *Submitted by: Mrs. LaRuth Bennett Ayers, 125 Sunset Blvd., Carrollton, GA 30117*

346. Birdsong

Mr. and Mrs. William E. Birdsong of Carrollton celebrate an anniversary. The Birdsongs owned and operated a photography studio on Rome Street for many years. He was also the photographer for several Georgia governors, including Sanders, Carter and Maddox. **See photo atop of the next column.** *Submitted by: the committee*

Mr. and Mrs. William E. Birdsong

347. Blackmon Family

Edmond/Edmund Blackmon (1787) and Mouren Massengill Blackmon were born in North Carolina. They were in Fayette County, Georgia, by 1810 census records. Their sons were Daniel born 1810; George born 1808; Cullen born 1818; Daniel born in North Carolina.

Fayette County, Georgia, marriage records show George married Martha Hartley 2 February 1834, Daniel married Nancy Hartley 18 August 1836, Cullen married Harriett Hartley 29 October 1837. The Hartley sisters were the daughters of James and Mary Lee Hartley.

Daniel Blackmon was listed in the Henry County, Georgia, census in 1840. By 1850 he and Nancy were in DeKalb County, Georgia, with James, Mary A., Edmund, Adeline, Redding, and Simon. In the 1860 census, Daniel and Nancy were in Haralson County with Emanuel, Redding, Simon, Nancy E., Martha, Mary A., Adeline. Adeline married William Speight who was killed in the Confederate States Army (CSA). Mary A. (Polly) married Elijah Folds who was also killed in the CSA.

The Blackmon Family

Edmon/Edmund Emanuel was married three or four times and never divorced. He was married to Ann and Christina. His wives are buried beside him in the Piney Woods Cemetery in Haralson County, Georgia. He served in Company G, 40th Regiment of Georgia in the CSA.

Daniel and Nancy's other children, James married Margaret, Reding married Elizabeth, Simon married Mary E. Bradley, Nancy Elizabeth married Ewel Uriah Victor Posey. It is not known to whom Martha and Tabitha married.

Daniel was a farmer and the census listed him as a miller. He and his family attended the Holly Springs Primitive Baptist Church. They sang Sacred Harp music. Most of the family are buried in Holly Springs Primitive Baptist cemetery at the corner of I-20 and U.S. Highway 27. Most of their lives were lived in the Waco-Bremen area. Daniel served in one of the Indian wars. *Submitted by: Virginia Kelley, 921 Chesterfield Drive, Marietta, GA 30066*

Sources: Census records, cemetery markers, county marriage records, Holly Springs Primitive Church records, family and other public records.

348. Daniel Blackmon

Daniel Blackmon was born 19 November 1810 in North Carolina, probably Johnson County. Daniel was one of nine children born to Edmund Blackmon and Mouren Missouri Massengill. Edmund migrated from Johnson County, North Carolina, to Henry County, Georgia, where he and Mouren died. Edmund is listed as an elder in the Flat Shoals Primitive Baptist Church in Henry County. The nine known children of Edmund and Mouren are: George born 1808; Daniel born 1810; Cullen born 1812; Mouren born 1820; John born 1822; P. born 1825; S. born 1829; and I. born 1832.

At the age of twenty-five, Daniel married Nancy Hartley 17 August 1836 in Fayette County, Georgia. Nancy was born 11 December 1815 in Georgia and was the daughter of James Hartley and Mary Lee of North Carolina. Nancy had seven brothers and sisters: Coleman born 1810; Drewery born 1812; Martha born 1814; Harriett born 1817; Emmerine born 1819; Mary born 1820; and Elizabeth born 1824. Three Hartley sisters – Martha, Nancy and Harriett – married three Blackmon brothers – George, Daniel, and Cullen. Daniel drew a pension from serving in the Cherokee Indian War and was a miller by trade. In the census, Daniel is found 1860 in Haralson County, 1870 in Carroll County, and by 1880 in Haralson County. In 1871 Daniel returned land in Haralson County, but was listed as a non-resident. He is listed on the 1890 tax digest of Haralson County.

Daniel and Nancy were married fifty-eight years when Daniel died 29 March 1889 at the age of seventy-eight. He was laid to rest in the Holly Springs Primitive Baptist Cemetery, north of Carrollton. Ten years later Nancy died 9 August 1899 at the age of eighty-three and was laid to rest beside her husband Daniel.

The nine known children of Daniel and Nancy Blackmon are: (1) James F. born 1838, married Margaret ?. Children were James, William, and Mary; (2) Edmund born 1841, married Christina Ann Waldrop. Children were William L., Robert Daniel, John Grier, Sarah F., Nancy Luvenia, Henry James, George Washington, Arthur Clemens and Joseph Simeon. Edmund married second to Jane F. Carroll. No known children. (3) Adaline born 1844, married William R. Speight. Child was Sarah Jane. (4) Redding Taylor born 1846, married Eliza Jane Williams. Children were Nancy Caroline, John W., Amanda E., Matthew, Laura Ann, Rosetta, Emma, and Idora. Redding married second Bell Bledsoe.Children were Buford, Carl Gillespie, Calvin, and Julia. (5) Mary Ann (Polly) born 1848, married Elijah Folds. Child was King Daniel. Mary Ann (Polly) married second William Adams. Their children were Sarah Cordelia, Frank Marion and John R. (6) Simeon Daniel born 1849, married Mary E. Bradley. Children were William Edward Columbus, Nancy, Robert Tobias, Martha Jane, Polly A., Newton Daniel, Henry Martin and Volley Estelle. (7) J. Nancy Elizabeth born 1852, married Ewell Victor Posey. Children were Daniel, Dovie Iona, Pink, Francis, and Charter. (8) Martha J.T. born 1854. (9) Tabitha Lilitha born 1855. *Submitted by: Charles Allen, 4348 Cook Place, Decatur, GA 30035. sloua@aol.com*

349. Robert Arthur Blakemore

I moved to Carroll County in 1972 with my family. Born in 1955 at the Anniston Regional Medical Center in Anniston, Alabama, I had two older brothers and two younger brothers. Our father, the late Jack C. Blakemore Sr., was employed with the Plantation Pipe Line Company. This employment resulted in five moves along the eastern coastline, to North Carolina, Louisiana, Virginia, Texas, then Georgia. Georgia would become our home.

After graduating from Carrollton High School in 1974, I married the love of my life Becky B. Blakemore in 1975 and moved to Bowdon. She is the daughter of the late Carlos E. Brown and Beatrice Brown. I was not sure how they would received the "city boy" in the country. They are very loving and supportive "parents" and took me in and finished "raising" me.

I attended Carroll County Technical and Vocational School taking the electrical and construction course, and was employed by Douglas and Lomason in Carrollton from 1974 to 1981. I began my career at CBS Records in 1981 after sending a resumé to the company headquarters in New York. The company forwarded the resumé to the Carrollton plant. I must have been the only maintenance applicant to interview in a suit, as my supervisor Fred Dunajek later commented that " ... he looked so I couldn't help but hire him." In 1994, Mr. Dunajek nominated me for the Sony Music Spirit Award. I was honored to receive this award, and later the Carroll County Spirit Award.

I worked as an electrical technician, working my way up to "plant manager." This was my favorite joke, as being in the Facility Maintenance Department we did any and everything. It became my assignment to water the plants each Monday morning and manage them.

Becky and I raised four children in our home in Bowdon: Tanya Watson, Tiffany Blakemore, and the twins Bobby and Robby Blakemore. All of our children attended the Bowdon School system. Tanya is married to Vince Williams and they have four children, Megan Williams, Taylor Jones, Alli Williams, and Brooke Jones. They reside in Bowdon. Tiffany Blakemore graduated in 2000 from the State University of West Georgia with a degree in human resource. Bobby and Robby Blakemore are attending State University of West Georgia and plan to graduate in the fall of 2001 with a finance degree.

Carroll County is an absolutely wonderful place to live and raise a family. There are a number of good-hearted people willing to share their life with you that you might have a great experience here. There is also a receptiveness, allowing you to contribute your resources and make it a better place or maintain the quality of life here. *Submitted by: Robert Blakemore, 454 Adamson Road, Bowdon, GA 30108*

350. Blalock

It is thought that the first Blalocks in America came from Ireland, and that the word "Blalock" means "blue lake."

Some of the Blalocks who came to Georiga settled in Fayetteville and Jonesboro.

James Marion Blalock (1825-1872) came to Carrollton. He married Mary Gresham (1826-1872). He was the first Ordinary of Carroll County from 1853 to 1868.

During the War Between the States, he was a captain in the Confederate Army.

Mr. Blalock had a general merchandise store on the public square. It was a wooden building. When some Northern soldiers came through Carrollton, they set the store on fire. Mr. Blalock's young son, Jesse, ran through the burning building, and in trying to save what he could, he threw things, including dishes, out the door!

The Blalocks had ten children, five boys and five girls. The boys were: Jesse Young, James (Jimmy) Edward, Samuel (Sammie) Anthony, Willie, and Robert (Bob) Lee. The girls were: Margaret (Maggie), Emily (Emma) Lewis, Amanda (Manda) Frances, Katherine (Katie) Gresham, and Mary (Mollie) Caroline.

Jessie Y. Blalock married Mary Benson. Their children were: Ed, Albert, Lewis, Claudie (Mrs. Doss Summers), Alma (Mrs. Edgar Harmon), Mary Jessie (Mrs. Maxwell and later, Mrs. Schroder), Grace (Mrs. Homer Millican), and Mary (an adopted child).

Ed Blalock married Fannie Butler. They moved to Newnan. They had four sons: Marion, Edwin, Taylor and Benson; and three daughters: Katherine, Mary and Nell.

Mr. and Mrs. Summers lived in Newnan, but later moved to Houston, Texas. They had three daughters: Louise, Alma Fay, and Mabry; and two sons: Frank and Harmon.

The Maxwells had one daughter, Mary Maxwell.

James Edward Blalock married Emma Reese, and moved out west. They had at least one son.

Sammie Blalock (May 10, 1857-June 11, 1896) married Mollie Daniel (July 30, 1861-June 1, 1892). Their children were Marie Louise, Lizzie Maud, Jim and Dan.

Sammie Blalock later married Mrs. Sophronia Hopson Coleman.

Louise Blalock married R.F. (Robert Franklin) Hyatt. Their first child was born dead and is buried in Carrollton. They had two more children, Mary and Bob.

The Hyatts moved to Gainesville, Florida in 1922.

Mary Hyatt married Russell McCaughan, a lawyer. They had two children, Louise and Ralph.

Bob Hyatt married Doris Young. Their children were Helen and Robbie.

Lizzie Maud married Louis Geeslin. Their children were Louis Jr. and Virginia.

Willie Blalock died when he was nearly four years old.

Bob Blalock died in early manhood. He never married.

Margaret (Maggie) Blalock married Jimmie Tanner. They had six daughters: Mary, Emmie, Beulah, Annie, Minnie (Mrs. Louis Heaton), and Maggie (Mrs. Willis King); and one son, Gene.

Mr. and Mrs. Heaton had one daughter who was stillborn.

Gene Tanner married Zelma Hamilton of Bremen, Georgia. They moved to Charlotte, North Carolina. Their children were Eugene Jr., Jack, Margaret and Ann.

Emma Blalock married B.F. (Ben) Brown. They had four sons: Frank, Sam, Paul and Hugh; and two daughters: Eula and Kate.

Frank Brown married Ola Jackson. They had three sons: Griffin, Ernest and Olen; and two daughters: Willie (Mrs. John Robertson) and Ethel (Mrs. J.E. Daniel).

Sam Brown married Louise Crenshaw. They had one daughter, Elizabeth.

Paul Brown married Gussie Young. Their children were Emma Earl (Mrs. Elon Perry), Awilda, Hugh and Paul.

Sam and Hugh were pharmacists. Hugh had a drug store in Atlanta.

Eula Brown married Henri Honrath (a German). Their children were Walter, Katherine, and Jack.

Kate Brown never married.

Amanda Blalock married James (Jimmie) Jefferson Thomasson. Mr. Thomasson was editor and publisher of the *Carroll County Times.* They had ten children, listed according to their ages: Eva, Katie Lou, Sada, Beverly (Bev), Will, the twins (Jessie and Evan), Toombs, Frank and Mary.

The family moved to Arkansas but later came back to Georgia. Little Mary died in Arkansas

Eva taught at College Street School. She later married William Scott Campbell. They had two daughters, Sarah and Frances; and one son, Beverly.

Sarah married M. Earl Davis. They have one daughter, Sally (Mrs. Coleman White).

Frances married Walter Reeves. They live in Bainbridge, Georgia.

Beverly graduated at West Point, and was a general in the U.S. Army. He married Blanche Evans of Tallapoosa, Georgia. They had three sons, Bill, Jim and Bob.

Katie Lou Thomasson married Joe Harris.

Sada Thomasson married Clifton Thomas. They lived in LaGrange, Georgia.

Beverly (Bev) Thomasson died soon after starting the practice of law.

Will Thomasson was a medical doctor in Carrollton. He married Howard Bradshaw. They had one daughter, Sarah (Mrs. Luther O'Hearn).

Jessie and Evan Thomasson were twins. Jessie married Florence Harris. They had two daughters, Beverly (Mrs. Edward Gnehm) and Lula (Mrs. David Garrett).

Edward Gnehm Junior has been a U.S. Ambassador to several foreign countries.

Jessie later married Marion Royston.

Evan married Betty Clay and had one son, James. They moved to Newnan, Georgia and became editor and publisher of a newspaper.

James Thomasson married Emmaline Cheney of Carrollton. They had one son, James, who became a medical doctor in Newnan; and one daughter, Emily.

After Emmaline's death, James married Ida Askew. They had one son, Billy Thomasson, who is now owner of the *Times Herald.*

Toombs Thomasson married Clair Downs of Bowdon. They had one son, Toombs Junior. Toombs was a lawyer. They lived in LaGrange.

Frank Thomasson married Kathleen McLean. Their children were Frank Junior and Kathleen.

Katherine (Katie) Blalock married Albert Sharp. They had four sons and two daughters: Emory, Ernest, Eugene, Tom, Eva, and Nelle.

Emory Sharp died when he was a young man.

Ernest Sharp was in the U.S. Army during the Spanish American War. He never married.

Eugene (Gene) Sharp married Ida Itjen of Jacksonville, Florida. They had one daughter, Margaret Katherine Sharp.

Tom Sharp married Inez Nugent of Jacksonville, Florida. They had no children.

Eva Sharp died when a small child.

Nelle Shar married Nat Clemons. They lived in Plant City, Florida. They had no children.

Mary Caroline (Mollie) Blaclock married Warren Marion Meadows. They had one daughter, Nell Katherine Meadows.

Before her marriage, Mollie Blalock worked in the Carrollton courthouse copying records.

Mrs. Meadows was an active member of the Carrollton First Methodist Church. She wrote a history of the church. She was a member of the Women's Missionary Society (later called the Women's Society of Christian Service), and served as secretary for about fifty years. She was also secretary of the UDC (United Daughters of the Confederacy) for many years. She sometimes wrote obituaries for friends who had died. *Submitted by: Nell Meadows, 327 Maple Street, Carrollton, GA 30117*

351. Blandenburg History in Carroll County

Olin Alexander Blandenburg and his wife Lydia Isabel Whitfield Kempson married December 7, 1877, in Meriwether County and moved to Carroll County, Oak Mountain area, in 1881.

Olin was born February 3, 1853, in Meriwether County. Parents were Lewis and Ann Hatton Brandenburg. (Olin chose Blandenburg as an adult.)

Lydia was born January 27, 1854, in Meriweather County, daughter of Peter and Mary Long Kempson.

Their first home in Carroll County was a dirt floor, sawmill camp one-room building, with an open fireplace for cooking. Water was from a nearby spring that still serves the home place dwelling.

While living in the sawmill house, they had two children. In order for the children to be safe, Lydia would set the bedpost on the dresses while she went to the spring.

The original house they built was three rooms. Later the two story colonial front addition was built to provide space for their ten children, five boys and five girls.

Claude Elmer was probably born in Meriwether County. The others born in Carroll County are: Lewis Alvin, Peter Harmon, Mary Ann (Mamie), Emmette Alexander, Margaret (Marguarite) (Maggie), Hubert R., Orrie Kate, Dora Isabel, and Susan Beartice.

Ten children of Olin and Lydia Blandenburg.

Olin developed a traditional farm operation — cotton, corn and other crops. Lydia, in addition, ordered fruit trees and vegetable seeds from H.G. Hastings Company in Atlanta and grew fruit and vegetables, along with egg and milk production. She, and later the daughters, made regular deliveries to the homes of many prominent Carrollton citizens. As a result, Dora Shackleford pursued this business from the middle 1930s until the early 1960s, producing eggs, chickens and vegetables marketed by the same methods.

Blandenburg House on Blandenburg Road.

Family traditions and a sense of heritage were significant. Sundays were a special family time for the cousins to get together playing, while the parents visited. August was reunion week; the out-of-towners came and daily noon time dinner rotated to the homes of local brothers and sisters. This tradition is still important. The grandchildren and great-grandchildren meet in September at a local restaurant for lunch, then homemade ice cream and cake at the home place on Blandenburg Road. This provides time for sharing memories, old photographs, and catch-up of current family news.

Nat and Louise Shackleford (son of Cicero and Beatrice) bought the home place when the estate was sold in 1950. They renovated the house keeping the original structure in tact. Through their hard work and love of family the traditions are continued. *Submitted by: Madelyn Morgan, 811 Sand Hill, Shady Grove Road, Carrollton, GA 30116*

352. Boatright / Williams Family

Joseph Benjamin Boatright (1859-1935) and Martha Susann (Susie) Williams (1864-1952) were married in Carroll County on November 29, 1883. They lived in several different places in the Wayside community, eventually owning over 2,000 acres of land. In early 1906 Ben purchased a house in Hodge, which he and his family moved into in early 1907. The house was built in 1881 by Charles Williams, a relative of Susie's. Ben lived in this house for the rest of his life. The house has since been renovated and still remains in the Boatright family.

Ben Boatright was an old fashioned entrepreneur — farmer, country store owner, and cotton market speculator. Ben and Susie had one of the first home generators in the area for electricity. Their surviving children were daughters Bertie Horsley (1885-1975), Pearlie Crawford, (1886-1969), Lena Young (1888-1956), Buna Morgan (1893-1968), Cassie Harris (1897-1992), Elois Embry (1902-1980), and Jewel Bowen (1906 to present), and sons Worley (1890-1971), Raymond (1899-1951), Horace, (1904-1948), and Myrl (Pat, 1909-1977). When the children married, Ben and Susie gave them either a house with 50 acres of land or $500. During the Great Depression Ben sold much of his property to repay debts incurred from cotton speculation. All the children spent most of their lives in Carroll County except for Pat who moved to Florida. Jewel, a hair stylist, owned and operated Jewel's Beauty Shop in Carrollton for forty-five years. Ben and Susie are buried in the Cross Plains Baptist Church Cemetery along with a number of their descendants.

Ben Boatright was the son of James A. Boatright (1818-1890) and Mary C. Bell (1820-1909). James' family came to Carroll County from South Carolina around 1825. Mary's family came from Tennessee. James and Mary were married on December 29, 1847, in Coweta County. They soon relocated to Carroll County. Their other children were Hiram W., D. Melvin (Doc), John T., Willis M., Martha, Elizabeth, and Amanda. John T.'s son, Dr. Homer Boatright (1883-1912), was a physician in Carrollton. The graves of James, Mary, and Amanda are in the Jordan Cemetery on Highway 61.

Susie Williams Boatright was one of seven surviving children born to Joel Casper Williams (1821-1872) and Mary Barbara Kiser (1828-1907). Joel and Mary were married on December 31, 1846. Susie's six siblings were Rebecca Catherine Reese, Amanda Elizabeth McKee, Mary Ann, Moses, George Thomas, and Joseph Johnson. Mary Kiser's family had come from North Carolina. Joe's family arrived in Carroll County around 1825 from Laurens County, South Carolina. Joel, Mary, and two of their children are listed in the 1850 Carroll County census. Joel and Mary are buried in the Stitcher/Kiser family cemetery in Carroll County. Also, listed in the Kiser Cemetery records at the West Georgia Regional Library are George and Rebecca Kiser (born 1797 and 1798 respectively in Lincoln, North Carolina) who may be Mary Kiser Williams' parents. Joel's parents were Thomas Barnes (Barney) Williams (1790-1856) and Hannah Pinson (1875-1868). Hannah was the daughter of Isaac Pinson, a member of a prominent family in Laurens County. Barney and Hannah are believed to be buried in the Williams family cemetery in Carroll County.

Joseph Benjamin Boatright and Martha Susann Williams Boatright about 1920

Ben and Susie Boatright have many descendants in Carroll County. Most of the above information came from notes compiled by the late James D. Embry, one of Ben and Susie's grandsons. Other sources include the late Robert K. Williams of Memphis, Tennessee, and local resident, Violette Harris Denney.

This article was submitted by Ruth B. Fuller and Teresa B. Ausburger, daughters of Jewel Bowen. *Submitted by: Teresa B. Augsburger, 193 Hampton Way, Carrollton, GA 30116*

353. Buford Author Boggs and Inez Ayers

Buford and Inez Boggs were married March 12, 1931, in Carroll County. Buford, the son of Author and Bessie Johnston Boggs, was born September 7, 1911, in Carroll County. Inez Ayers Boggs was born March 15, 1913, in the Hulett community. She was the daughter of S.K. and Maude Ayers of the Sand Hill-Five Points community. (See related Ayers family article.)

After their marriage, Buford and Inez lived with her parents on their farm for approximately seventeen years before building their home in the Five Points community where Buford ran a Texaco grocery store for thirty years. Inez was a homemaker. She was a wonderful cook, who was well known for her chocolate pies and fresh coconut cakes. She and Buford entertained frequently, and Inez loved to garden. She was well known for her flower gardens with beautiful roses, gladiolas, and iris and also for her bountiful vegetables she grew in her vegetable garden. Buford and Inez attended Macedonia Baptist Church where he was a deacon and Inez taught Sunday School.

Buford and Inez had three children, Billy, Larry and Brenda. Billy was born in 1932, but only lived one day. Larry was born on November 5, 1935, and Brenda was born on August 12, 1946.

Larry graduated from Villa Rica High School and attended the University of Georgia where he graduated with a B.S. degree in 1957. As a teen, he helped his grandfather S.K. Ayers around the farm and he helped his father with his store and moving business. He once moved a family to Texas. Larry married Elizabeth Farlowe on March 29, 1958. They have three children Lisa, Kirk, and Stephen. Larry served in the United States Marine Corp. Reserves where he retired as a lieutenant colonel after twenty-two years. Larry and Liz started Benchmark Homes, Inc. in 1971. The company builds homes in all of metro Atlanta. All three of their children are affiliated with Benchmark Homes. Larry and Liz also have eight grandchildren: John, Lauren, Charles, Lawrence, Mallory, Holly, Olivia and Caroline. Larry and Liz built their home on the family farm in the Five Points community on Highway 61 in 1974.

Brenda graduated from Villa Rica High School and West Georgia College where she earned a bachelor's degree in early childhood education. She taught at Sand Hill Elementary School for four years before she became a homemaker. Brenda married Lanny Ivan Bostwick, originally of Grove Park, Atlanta, on August 7, 1966. Lanny moved to Carroll County with his family who bought the old Kinney farm in the Five Points community. She and Lanny have four children, Lori, Julie, Ivan, and Kara. She and Lanny live on the family farm that her grandfather S.K. Ayers owned. Brenda and Lanny have five grandchildren: Taylor, Alex, Katie, Ty and Kylie.

Buford and Inez lived her entire lives in Carroll County. They were greatly loved by both family and friends. Buford died after a brief illness on December 23, 1969. Inez passed away after an extended illness in January of 2000. Both Buford and Inez are buried at Macedonia Baptist Church. *Submitted by: Brenda Boggs Bostwick, daughter, 4930 Carroll-V.R. Hwy., Carrollton, GA 30116 and Compiled by: Lori B. Leo, granddaughter, 2835 NE Hickory Level Road, Temple, GA 30179*

The Buford and Inez Boggs Family

354. Bohannon

This was told to me (Patty Wampler) by Carrie Bohannon Odom. This is the story of four Bohannon men. The Bohannons came from Scotland very early in American history. They settled in Massachusetts, Virginia and North Carolina. This family of Bohannons came to Georgia early in 1800 after the Indian lands opened up. The first Bohannon that we can find was Alexander Bohannon. He was born November 20, 1769, died March 20, 1833, and is buried in Coweta County, Georgia. There has been a Bohannon family in Georgia from 1800 to present day. Alexander was Carrie Bohannon Odom's g-g-great-grandfather.

James Elmer Bohannon

Joseph Alavia Bohannon born April 20, 1841, married Elizabeth Jane Moore on October 17, 1865. Joseph Alavia Bohannon was g-great-grandfather of Carrie Bohannon Odom.

John Dooley Bohannon is Carrie Bohannon Odom's grandfather. John Dooley Bohannon married Carrie Eugenia Hughes. They have five sons and four daughters. They are Claude Eugene Bohannon, Homer Bohannon, John Glover Bohannon, Joseph (Joe) Hughes Bohannon, James Elmer Bohannon, Jennie Chloe Bohannon, Gladys Elizabeth Bohannon, Annie Maude Bohannon, and Bernice Gertrude Bohannon.

Claude Eugene Bohannon married Bessie Mae Morrow on November 7, 1920. They have ten children — five sons and five daughters: Cecil Eugene, William Carl, Donald Norman, Bobby Joe, John Franklin, Nellie Maude, Ruby Inez, Carrie Mae, Billie Chloe, and Mary Janez. Claude Eugene Bohannon raised his large family in Carroll County. He worked in a cotton mill a few years. Then moved back to Carroll County. He worked at a sawmill and while working there he lost the ends of two fingers. After that he sharecropped on a farm for a long time.

Homer Bohannon married Nellie Lessetter. They have two daughters, Janice and Janette.

John Glover Bohannon served in military service in World War II. John Glover married Lois Brown. They have two sons, John Brown Bohannon and Gary Richard (Ricky) Bohannon. When he came back to Carrollton, he had a store on Bradley Street named Bradley Street Grocery Store.

Joseph Hughes Bohannon married Alma Fuller and had one daughter, Martha Sylvia Bohannon, and one son Joseph Selby Bohannon. Joseph Hughes Bohannon had a grocery store on Rome Street named Bohannon's Grocery for a few years; then he had one on the corner of Highways 27 and 113. First it was called Clover Farm. Then it was named Bohannon's Grocery Store for a number of years.

James Elmer Bohannon married Lillian Thompson. They have two sons, James (Jimmy) Charles Bohannon and David Arlin Bohannon, and one daughter Jane Ann Bohannon. James Elmer Bohannon worked in the Economy Auto Store in Carrollton for a few years. Then he was Justice of the Peace in Carrollton. He was also in the realty business for a few years.

Annie Maude never married. She worked in Five and Ten Cent Stores in Carrollton and in Alabama.

Gladys Elizabeth Bohannon never married. She was in bad health.

Bernice Gertrude Bohannon married Herschel Miller. They have two sons and one daughter, Ray Allyn Miller, Stephen (Steve) Elbert Miller, and Elizabeth (Libby) Miller.

John G. Bohannon and Ricky Bohannon

Cecil Eugene Bohannon married Virginia Essie Fuller. They have one son, Randy Willis Bohannon. Cecil Eugene Bohannon worked at J.B. Warren's Furniture Store in Carrollton. Then he worked for R & A many years. Cecil Eugene and Essie Bohannon moved to Crystal River, Florida, for seven years where he worked for R & A again. Then they moved back to Carrollton in 1986. Cecil Eugene Bohannon died January 16, 1988. Essie Virginia Bohannon died September 26, 1998. They have two grandchildren. Cecil Eugene Bohannon is Carrie Bohannon Odom's brother. *Submitted by: Carrie Odom, 35 Valley Drive, Carrollton, GA 30117*

355. Thomas, John and Zadock Bonner, Jr.

Thomas, John, and Zadock Bonner Jr. came to Carroll County in 1829 shortly after the county opened up for settlement with their parents Zadock Bonner Sr. and Susan Johnson.

Zadock Bonner Jr. was born 18 Oct 1804 on Powell's Creek in Greene County, Georgia. He died in 1891 in Carroll County. On 28 December

John Bonner

1825 in West Point, Georgia, he married Lucy B. Ridgeway Jackson, widow of Drury W. Jackson. She was born 1 June 1806 in Elbert County, Georgia, and died 7 April 1872 in Carroll County. He was the second largest slave owner in the County. Zadock's property had gold mines that were worked by slave labor. During the Civil War he put three quarters of a million dollars of gold into Confederate bills and lost it!

Thomas Bonner was born 11 November 1807 in Georgia and died 11 November 1881 in Clay County, Alabama. In 1829 he married Lucinda Ridgeway who was born 11 November 1808. Thomas had a 700 acre plantation on the Little Tallapoosa River. Thomas sold the plantation to the B.A. Sharpe family in 1866, at which time he moved to Clay County, Alabama. In 1906, the house was purchased with 275 acres for the Fourth District Agriculture and Mechanical School, which was the predecessor to West Georgia College. The house is still standing on the Campus of West Georgia. Officially known as the Bonner-Sharpe-Gunn House, it was selected in 1966 as the site of a historical marker representing West Georgia College. Also in 1966 the house was put on The National Register of Historic Places by the United States Department of Interior.

John Bonner was born 2 February 1817 in Fayette County, Georgia. He died 24 August 1893 in Carroll County. He is buried in Old Camp United Methodist Church Cemetery. He married first on 15 November 1835 Martha M. Gillespie who was born 15 November 1815. She died 9 March 1857 in Carroll County. He married second on 3 September 1857 in Carroll County Martha Ann Upchurch. She was born 18 May 1833 in Georgia and died 13 January 1881 in Carroll County. He married third on 7 August 1881 in Fulton County, Georgia, Lucy J. Wood. She was born 1 August 1844 and died 14 April 1935 in Carroll County. John's first two wives are buried in Old Camp Church Cemetery. Lucy J. Wood is buried in Asbury Cemetery. In 1880 he owned a 1200 acre farm which was well diversified, a gin, and a grist mill around Buffalo Creek which is now Oak Grove Road between Carrollton and Roopville. He was elected county commissioner several times. John was a member of the Georgia House of Representatives 1882-1883. His name is on the cornerstone for the 1893 courthouse. He was a founding member of Old Camp Methodist Church. John was ordained on 28 July 1870 as a Methodist Minister. He fathered twenty-three children of which seventeen survived him! *Submitted by: Teri Bonner, 310 Emory Lane, Columbus, SC 29212*
Sources: Migration Pattern of Thomas Bonner by James C. Bonner; Virginia Moss; Cecil L. Bonner; *At Home in Carrollton*; Public Relations/Visitors Center of West Georgia College

356. John Robert Borders and his Mules

John Robert Borders, born in Carroll County in 1874, was a well known mule dealer in the county from the 1910s to the 1940s. Often called Uncle John by his peers, he had a reputation as an honest dealer, a good farmer and successful businessman. He was my Grandpa Borders.

My grandfather's great-grandfather had moved from Pennsylvania to North Carolina while very young, had married there and moved to Pike County, Georgia, shortly after 1800. In the early 1830s the first Borders moved into southeastern Carroll County.

Evidently the family never acquired land and Grandpa was a tenant farmer himself as he began his marriage to Anne Dukes in 1897. Soon he did own a good farm and somehow became involved in mule trading by working for the firm of Mr. Fleming in Carrollton. Grandpa was a stout and determined young man and many times walked the ten miles to Carrollton, worked at the mule barns all day, and walked back home after dark.

In a few years he was doing extremely well with the mule business and farming. One mark of a successful farmer was having good, well-kept livestock. On his own farm, Grandpa used the best, slickest, handsomest mules available. Horses were not very important to most farmers.

Once Grandpa bought a new fringed surrey and hitched two of his finest mules to it. The family sat high in the tandem seats with John and Anne in front and the three children, Otis (my father), Emmett, and Agnes in the back. After starting down the road, an excited puppy ran and yelped alongside. The mules were spooked and ran away, taking the new surrey with its terrified passengers across the cotton field. No one was hurt much, but the surrey did not survive.

John Robert Borders and Anne Dukes Borders

Mule men were a fraternity and the Atlanta stockyards was the favorite meeting place. Business was conducted there but the camaraderie was special. Sometimes called the "Jim Dandies" of the stockyards, the fellows would talk and walk through the pens of mules carrying their prodding stick, a six foot ash wood straight staff about an inch in diameter and tapered gradually to a larger head for a handle.

A wealth of verbal expressions defined the mule trading world. If my grandpa was showing a mule to a prospective buyer and he said "There's not a blemish on 'er," it was a good one.

In late winter, Grandpa would travel by train to Ft. Worth, Texas, to buy a carload or so of mules for sales in the spring. Texas mules, by his belief, were superior to Tennessee mules.

When the shipment reached the Carrollton depot, a bridled horse was brought nearby, the doors to the rail cars were opened and the mules exited unharnessed and followed the one horse as it was led up Depot (Bradley) Street into the barn. It was quite a sight and a sure sign that spring was near. *Submitted by: Verne H. Borders, 1273 Blandenburg Rd., Carrollton, GA 30116*
Sources: Personal Knowledge

357. Bowen / Brock Family

The Bowen/Brock family came from the marriage in 1887 of Thomas Henderson (Tom) Bowen (1861-1935) and Sarah Elizabeth (Betty) Brock (1857-1942). The Brock side of the family can be traced back to Rubin Brock I

Sarah Elizabeth Brock Bowen, Circa 1887

who emigrated from Ireland to Virginia circa 1750. He later moved to North Carolina. His son, Rubin Brock II (1754-1842), was born in Orange County, North Carolina, and served in the colonial army during the Revolutionary War after which he moved to Anderson District, South Carolina. He married Elizabeth Kemp (date unknown) with whom he had a son, William (Billy, 1792-mid 1860s). Circa 1815 Billy married Temperance Ann (Tempie) Gay (1796-1869), the daughter of Allen and Abigail Castleberry Gay. Billy and Tempie had seven children to include James Daniel (1830-1864) who on December 26, 1850, married Frances Rebecka Hogan (1827-1911). James and his parents are listed in the 1850 Coweta County census and the 1860 Carroll County census.

James and Frances had eight children, one of whom was Sarah Elizabeth (Betty). Their other children were George Mack, William Horry, James Robert, John Thomas, Francis Marion, Mary F., and Daniel Richmond. James Daniel fought for the Confederacy during the Civil War and died on June 2, 1864, from a "minnie" ball wound to his head received during the battle of Cold Harbor (just north of Richmond, Virginia). James Daniel and Frances' last child, Daniel Richmond, was born on August 6, 1864. Frances named him after his father and the place that his father had died. Richmond Brock would later author a Masonic manual that is still used today. Frances and three of her sons are buried in the Pleasant View Baptist Church cemetery which is located off U.S. Highway 27 in Carroll County just west of Carrollton.

Thomas Henderson Bowen and daughter Evie Oliver Bowen, Circa 1887

By the 1880s, Frances and some of her children to include Betty were living on a farm in the Pleasant Ridge community of Carroll County. Frances advertised in a local newspaper (referred to as a tri-weekly constitution) for a man to help with her farm. Thomas Henderson "Tom" Bowen (1861-1935) of Henry County answered the ad and was hired for the position.

At the time Tom began working for Frances he was a widower with a daughter named Evie Oliver (1881-1935) who later married Sam Cook. Nothing is known about his first wife.

Tom and Betty were married on December 22, 1887. Following their marriage, Tom and Betty acquired a farm near her mother Frances' property. Tom's vocations were farming and bee keeping. He is remembered as a sweet, gentle man, who loved children and animals. Tom and Betty's three surviving sons were: Walter Emerson (1889-1952), Henry Lee (1892-1959), and Charley Henderson (1897-1974). Walter, a farmer, married Mary Ruth Hurst (1898-1928) in 1921, and had three surviving daughters: Sarah Elizabeth, born 1922; Mary Frances, born 1925; Gussie Lee, born 1928. Ruth died in childbirth and in 1933 Walter married Leila M. Jordan (1897-1976). There were no children born to this marriage.

Henry Lee, a mail carrier, married Jewel Boatright (1906 - present) in 1925 and in 1928 they adopted Gussie, and changed her name to Ruth Lee. They had one other daughter, Teresa Ann, born in 1947.

Charley Henderson, a farmer, never married. All three sons served in World War I. Tom, Betty, their sons Walter and Charley, Betty's brother Richmond, Mother Frances, and many more Brock relatives are buried in Pleasant View Baptist Church Cemetery. Henry Lee and other family members are buried in the Carrollton City Cemetery. Tom and Betty's farm remains in the Bowen family.

Ruth Bowen married Wilmer Carlos Fuller (born 1925) in 1949 and their children are David George, born 1953; Joseph Frank, born 1957; Nancy Susan, born 1958; and Jon Alan, born 1961.

Teresa Bowen married Grayson Terry Augsburger (born 1941) in 1974 and they have a son named Grayson Lee, born 1987. *Submitted by: Ruth B. Fuller, 1701 Pleasant Ridge Road, Carrollton, GA 30117 and Researched by: Teresa Augsburger and Ruth Fuller, granddaughters of Tom and Betty Bowen.*

Sources: Records at West Ga. Regional Library and family members.

358. Boyd

Joseph Boyd was born June 25, 1791, in Newberry County, South Carolina, and died June 2, 1877, in Carroll County, Georgia. He was the son of Robert Boyd and Rosannah Stewart. He married Jane McMillan around 1824. Jane was born in 1801 in South Carolina and died in 1863 in Carroll County. Both are buried in the Powell Chapel Cemetery in Carroll County.

Joseph was a very successful farmer and bought 202-1/2 acres in Land Lot 35 in the Sixth District of Carroll County on January 26, 1855, from Abel Embry at a cost of $2,217.00. By 1858 he owned 507-1/2 acres.

Their children, all born in Meriwether County, Georgia were:

Rosannah Frances Boyd, born February 5, 1826, and married to Alexander Tyson on March 12, 1846 in Meriwether County. Both are buried in the Powell Chapel Cemetery. They had two children, Elizabeth, born 1849, and William H., born 1851.

David Boyd was born June 29, 1827, and died August 30, 1900, in Carroll County. He married Joanna A. Williams on September 18, 1855, in Carroll County. Joanna was the daughter of Jala Williams and Joanna Providence. Both David and Joanna were buried in the Powell Chapel Cemetery. Their children were: (1) John Henry Boyd, born July 27, 1856, died October 11, 1882, married to Susan Ada Tyson on December 9, 1891. (2) James Robert Boyd, born December 14, 1858, died February 7, 1938, married to Amanda Louiza Lizabeth McBurnett on December 6, 1891. (3) Joseph Jaley Boyd, born in 1861, married to Eliza Caldonia Hanson on December 9, 1888, and moved to Lauderdale County, AL. (4) Sara Elizabeth Boyd was born January 1864, died in 1939, and was married to Thomas Sherman Boyd on January 2, 1887. (5) William Franklin Boyd, born September 1866, married Effie B. Chambers on December 14, 1893, and moved to Cullman County, Alabama. (6) Thomas Jefferson Boyd, born December 25, 1868, died January 16, 1955, married Mary Bamma Richards on October 27, 1895. (7) David Monroe Boyd, born September 1871, died in 1952, married Phoebie Elizabeth Harper on September 18, 1904. (8) Ephraim M. Boyd, born July 17, 1874, died August 19, 1988. (9) Rutherford Hayes Boyd, born May 1877, died 1951, married Venie Florence Wheeler.

Richard L. Boyd, a physician, born 1830, died before 1872 probably in Gwinnett County, married Nancy Elizabeth Austin on January 10, 1855, in Carroll County. Their children were Mary Jane Boyd who married John Steele Collins, Georgia Ann Boyd who married T.A. Hall, and Sarah Frances Boyd who married Jacob Quickle Carpenter. Nancy Elizabeth's second marriage was to George Hopkins, and the family moved to Floyd County, Texas.

Elizabeth Boyd, born September 15, 1834, died March 26, 1891, was married to William Thomas Richards on July 11, 1861. Both are buried at Powell Chapel Cemetery. Their children were (1) Josephine Elizabeth Richards born August 19, 1864, who married Joseph Peek. (2) Charles Forest Richards born August 16, 1867, who married Helen May Hammond. (3) Thomas Wiley Richards, born May 21, 1870, who married first Mary Houseworth and secondly Myrtice Stovall. (4) Ella Jane Richards, born April 4, 1873, who married George Chance.

Mary Emily Boyd, born March 16, 1836, died February 18, 1920, married John R. Pope on December 17, 1857. They are buried in Hillcrest Cemetery in Villa Rica, Georgia. Their children were Mary E. Pope, Alston Pope, James M. Pope, John H. Pope, Rufus L. Pope, William Charles Pope, Occia Pope, Nancy Pope, and Rilla A. Pope who was born July 26, 1873, and married Charles E. Smith.

Rebecca Boyd, born March 7, 1837, died in 1864. Probably buried in Powell Chapel Cemetery.

Robert Milton Boyd, born around 1840. He was handicapped and died before 1880. He is probably buried in Powell Chapel Cemetery.

Eliza C. Boyd, born around 1842, married James M. Laguin on February 19, 1865, in Carroll County. Their children were Lot Monroe Laguin born in 1867, Samuel J. Laguin born in 1873, and Elizabeth Laguin born in 1875.

Joseph Boyd had two brothers who also moved to Carroll County around 1855.

One was William who was born June 27, 1789, in Newberry County, South Carolina, and died in 1857 in Carroll County where his estate was settled. He moved to Carroll after his wife Martha died. They had two children, Malinda J. Boyd who married Lewis D. Groce, and Hugh H. Boyd who married Martha C. Pyron and moved to Texas.

The second brother was Hugh Boyd, a farmer and landowner, who was born December 16, 1797, in Newberry County, South Carolina, and died before 1880 in Carroll County. He was married to Nancy Hopper about 1826 in South Carolina. Their children were (1) Rosana Boyd, born October 19, 1823, in Newberry County, South Carolina. (2) Robert B. Boyd, born May 27, 1827, in Newberry County, South Carolina. (3) William M. Boyd, born June 25, 1829, in Meriwether County. (4) Martha Ann Boyd, born November 26, 1830, in Meriwether County, died July 30, 1904, in Marshall County, Alabama. She was married to John Marcus McRae. (5) James Boyd, born February 13, 1832 in Meriwether County. (6) John David Boyd, born August 27, 1834, in Meriwether County, died March 30, 1903, in Carroll County. He married Mary L. Williams on February 16, 1849. (7) Marion O. Boyd was born February 24, 1840, and died in the Civil War. (8) Joel Wesley Boyd, born October 13, 1842 in Meriwether County. He married Martha J. Richards on October 13, 1842. (9) George White Boyd, born February 17, 1845, in Meriwether County, died January 26, 1914, in Carroll County. He married Mary E. Pope. (10) Lewis Dudley Boyd was born January 29, 1849, in Meriwether County, died April 16, 1922, in Carroll County. He married Vianna Hunt on September 21, 1882.

The majority of this Boyd family is buried in the Powell Chapel Cemetery, in Carroll County, Georgia. *Submitted by: Edna Boyd Helton, 3037 S. Van Wert Road, Villa Rica, GA 30180*

Sources: Family Bible, Census, Marriage and Cemetery, Records Researched by Erlene Boyd

359. Robert Boyd and Sarah Ann LeGuin

Robert Boyd was born May 27, 1827, in Newberry, South Carolina, son of Hugh Boyd and Nancy Hopper and grandson of Robert Boyd and Rosannah Stewart. The Boyds came from Ireland to South Carolina in the 1700s and moved to Meriwether County, Georgia, in the 1840s. Many members of this family came to Carroll County between 1850 and 1860 and settled near Villa Rica.

Robert married Sarah Ann LeGuin in Meriwether County February 19, 1846. Sarah was born December 30, 1848, and died February 19, 1907. They had four children: Christopher Columbus, born March 29, 1847, died December 29, 1940; Melvina V., born May 29, 1850, died January 6, 1902; Louisa Elizabeth, born February 1, 1858, died March 23, 1950; and Nancy Ann, born September 30, 1863.

Robert Boyd and Sarah LeGuin with baby Louisa Elizabeth

Christopher Columbus ("Lum") married Sarah G. ____ October 18, 1868. (Information from family Bible. Marriage record has not been found.) Lum and Sarah had ten children: LaFayette Randolph S., born November 14, 1870, married Mollie Heath; Albert H., born November 23, 1873, died August 30, 1907; Martha A.L., born October 1875; Charles S., born July 1878, married Florence Martin; George Robert, born August 9, 1881, died August 13, 1911, married Mary Couch; Wiley A., born December 1883; Columbus Braswell, born July 10, 1886, died September 22, 1962, married Artie Lee Chandler; Hugh S. born January 1889; Edgar E., born February 1891, married Annie M. Marchman; Lalina B., born November 1897.

Melvina married her second cousin, David Sloan, December 26, 1867. David was born July 20, 1842, died May 21, 1909, the son of Rosannah Boyd and Richard Sloan. They had nine children: Sarah Florence, born February 4, 1869; died August 6, 1927; Ulysses Sidney, born 1872, married M. Ellen Cook; William Fan, born March 12, 1874, died 1955; Emma Lourena, born February 28, 1879; Georgia A. born February 1878, died 1968; Walter R.G., born April 1882, died 1950, married Dora Couch; Lucrecia, born June 1884, died 1959, married George Allen Huff; Florida Oregon, born March 8, 1888, died March 30, 1987, married Thomas Couch; and Ida Mary, born May 1892, married Reese Smith.

Louisa married Joseph Joshua Payne December 15, 1877, son of William Jasper Payne and Mary "Polly" Ann Wood(s). Joseph was born January 20, 1854, died May 1862. They had five children: Coie Lonzo, born September 9, 1878, died February 21, 1962, married Annie Hyde, daughter of William Hyde and Laura Beula Long; Robert Stephen, born April 9, 1882, married Delia McPherson; Milie Ann, born May 13, 1885, married Will White 25 February 1906; Sarah Jane, born April 6, 1888, died June 13, 1952, married John Allen McWhorter August 19, 1906, son of William Leroy McWhorter and Eliza J. Wren; and Gooly Ross, born January 1891, who died at five months.

Nancy married George Groce December 11, 1879, son of Lewis and Malinda Groce. Robert died March 5, 1894, and is buried at Powell's Chapel, along with Sarah. *Submitted by: Marjorie McDuffie McIntosh, great-granddaughter of Louisa Elizabeth Boyd, 101 Tinsley Mill Road, Peachtree City, GA 30269*

360. Boyd - Willingham

William James Boyd was born in April 1832 in Meriwether County, Georgia, and died September 5, 1908, in Carroll County, Georgia. He was the son of Alexander Boyd and Sarah Ann Hinton who moved to Randolph County, Alabama, before 1840 where they made their home and lived the remainder of their lives.

Around 1850, William James married Nancy B. Willingham, the daughter of John C. Willingham and Sara A. Brown of Randolph County. Nancy was born January 9, 1831, in Walton County, Georgia, and died April 14, 1905, in Carroll County. All their children except the last one were born in Randolph County, Alabama.

Their children were:

1. John Griffin Alexander Boyd was born December 27, 1851, and died February 2, 1929, in Carroll County. He married Celia Saxon Johnston on December 23, 1873, in Carroll County. They are buried in Powell Chapel Cemetery in Carroll County.
2. Sara Elizabeth Boyd was born August 28, 1853, and died January 29, 1934, in Palm Beach County, Florida. She married Ephraim Mostiller Allen on January 27, 1876, in Carroll County. They donated the land on which Flat Rock Baptist Church was built. They are buried in Concord Methodist Church Cemetery in Carroll County.
3. William Washington Boyd was born in October 1855 and died after 1920 in Cullman County, Alabama. He married in Carroll County first to Julia A. Aderhold on October 21, 1875, and second to Claudia Lambert about 1915.
4. James F. Boyd was born in December 1857 and died after 1920. He married Eliza Jane Johnston on October 3, 1882, in Carroll County. They are buried at County Line Baptist Church Cemetery in Carroll County.
5. Cash Boyd, was born in February 1860 and died before 1880.
6. Jarrell Joseph Boyd was born in June 1862. On September 3, 1882, in Douglas County, he married Marietta Cohen.
7. Thomas Sherman Boyd was born February 19, 1864, and died June 15, 1928, in Douglas County. He was married to Sara Elizabeth Boyd on January 2, 1887, in Carroll County. They are buried in Powell Chapel Cemetery.
8. Robert Ulysses Boyd was born April 4, 1868, and died November 25, 1950, in Carroll County. He was married to Margaret Frances Edge on September 8, 1887, in Carroll County. They are buried in Powell Chapel Cemetery.
9. Samuel Alonzo Boyd was born in November 1870 and died in 1950 in Douglas County. He married Annie Lee Cansler on May 21, 1899, in Douglas County. They are buried in Pray's Mill Baptist Church Cemetery in Douglas County.
10. Nancy Leila Boyd was born in April 1874 in Carroll County. She married James C. Bice on December 14, 1893, in Carroll County.

William James and Nancy Boyd are buried in Powell Chapel Cemetery. *Submitted by: David Boyd, 47 Parks Avenue, Newnan, GA 30367*
Source: Research by Erlene Boyd, (ecboyd@bellsouth.net)

361. Boykin Family

Samuel Jefferson Boykin Sr. (1862-1918) and his wife, Ida Wilkinson (1862-1951), moved to Carrollton in the 1890s from LaGrange, Georgia. He set up his law practice in what is known as the Boykin building on Adamson Square in Carrollton. Samuel served as a federal judge in Washington, D.C.

Samuel and Ida had four sons: Buford Francis (born October 4, 1884, died February 2, 1964); Fuller (lborn 1886, died 1889); Shirley Caffee (born December 18, 1889, died June 1, 1963); Samuel Jefferson Jr. (born May 10, 1901, died September 20, 1972).

Buford married Aline Bradley (born February 12, 1885, died 1968), They had one daughter, Caroline, who married John Beury. They had two children, John Jr., and Frances Wakely, both of whom live in Florida.

Shirley Caffee married Helen Long (born September 21, 1894, died May 8, 1986). They had no children.

Samuel Jefferson Jr. married Miriam Stone (born July 8, 1903, died December 21, 1994). They had one daughter, Martha Alice. She and her husband, Thomas Matthew Robertson, her daughter Miriam Ann Threadgill, and granddaughter, Meagan Alexandra, still live in Carroll County. Alice's son, Samuel Thomas, lives in Colorado.

Samuel and Ida had three daughters: Luta Wilkinson (born December 4, 1892, died October 3, 1978); Elma (born January 15, 1895, died June 4, 1981); Martha Elizabeth (born September 10, 1903, died May 15, 1965).

Luta married Thomas Ambrose (T.A.) Herndon (born December 23, 1888, died August 26, 1950). They had two children, Luta and Thomas Ambrose Jr. (Tom), who became a lawyer. Tom married Helen Kinsey. His daughter, Karen McWilliams, and her family live in North Carolina. Luta married Lewis Vance. They had two children, Joseph Thomas, who is a lawyer in Carrollton, and Shirley Anne Hughes, who lives in Texas with her family.

Elma married Pomp Shaefer (born September 14, 1893 died November 13, 1956), who started and owned Carroll Mills on Bradley Street. They had no children.

Martha Elizabeth (Libby) was a physical education teacher at West Fulton High School in Atlanta. During retirement she lived in Carrollton with Elma.

Buford first became a dentist before becoming a lawyer. Buford, Shirley and Sam became lawyers and part owners of Lawler Hosiery Mill. Their law offices were in the Boykin building. They could be found Sunday afternoons gathering at Buford's home or Luta's home and engaging in their favorite pastime — arguing points of the law. Samuel Jr. later served for twenty years as the judge of the Coweta Judicial Circuit and as president of the Judges Association in Georgia. He was the presiding judge in the case which is told in the book, *Murder in Coweta County.*

Pomp, Samuel Jr., and Lewis were instrumental in the founding of Sunset Hills Country Club. Pomp started and owned Carroll Mills on Bradley Street. T.A. owned Long and Herndon Insurance Agency. All of the Boykins, Herndons, and Shaefers are buried in the Carrollton City Cemetery. *Submitted by: Alice Robertson, Carrollton, GA*

362. Bracknell - Carroll

J. Richard Bracknell (born 1949) and Lauren Diane Carroll Bracknell (born 1949) were married March 20, 1971, and have resided in Temple since 1972. They have one son, Timothy Sean Bracknell (born 1973), who married Stacey Nell Blackman (born 1971) of Temple, and a foster son, Dimitri Magradze (born in the Republic of Georgia in 1979). Sean and Stacey have a daughter Molly, born 1996; a son Kendal, born 1997; and are expecting another son in fall of 2001. They currently reside in Bremen.

Richard is a native of Temple. He graduated from Temple High School in 1967. He earned three degrees, including his six-year at State University of West Georgia, formerly West Georgia College. Lauren, a native of Cobb County and 1967 graduate from Wills High School, also attained her bachelor's degree at West Georgia, then went on to attain her master's degree at Georgia State University.

Richard is the son of Jesse Monroe Bracknell and Myrtle Wallace Bracknell, both from Carroll County. Richard's brothers and sisters are Geneva Prichard (Haralson County), Bill Bracknell, (Carroll County), Wallace Bracknell (Haralson County), Jean Frost (Carroll County), and Debra Langley (Haralson County.)

Lauren is the daughter of Alvin Brennan Carroll (1921-1967) from the Temple area and Kathryn Scott Carroll (1920-1993) from Cherokee County. Lauren is an only child. A.B.'s brother and sisters were Fred Carroll, Lorene Lyle, and Mildred White.

Richard teaches special education and successfully coaches the debate team for the Carrollton City School System. He holds the office of president of Georgia Forensic Coaches Association and Southern District Debate. He has been named STAR teacher eleven times and was inducted into the Georgia Forensic Coaches Hall of Fame in spring of 2001. He previously taught government and social studies at Temple High School, Carrollton High School, and Haralson County High School.

Lauren retired from teaching in 2001 after thirty years. She taught eighth grade during 1971-1972 at Rockmart Junior High, English from 1972-1980 at Temple High, and vision education from 1980-2001 at Carrollton City Schools. As a vision educator, Lauren was an active member of the West Georgia Vision Educators Consortia. While teaching at Temple, Lauren sponsored the annual staff and Richard sponsored the student council. In addition, they co-sponsored the junior class and hosted several exchange students from Brazil and Mexico. Their interest in different cultures eventually led their long-standing relationship with Dimitri who came to their home while he was in high school during a time of political instability in his own country.

Richard and Lauren, their children, and their grandchildren, along with many family members, worship at Liberty Christian Church in the Temple area. Richard is a deacon. Lauren participates in numbers ministries at the church. *Submitted by: Lauren Bracknell, 175 Lakeview Drive, Temple, GA 30179*

363. George Washington Bradley

George Washington Bradley was born 15 June 1864 in Randolph County, Alabama, the son of Caroline Freeman Bradley (1835). George's family came to Carroll County in the late 1860s to live. His siblings were Emeline (1852); Newt (1856) married Mary C. Kittle; William Tom (1860); and John J. married Elizabeth Warren.

George Washington Bradley married Annie Jones on 17 November 1895 in Carroll County. They lived in the Stripling Chapel/Lowell area in the early days and finally made their home in the Tyus area. Children of George and Annie Bradley are William Bryant (1899) married Vera Pitts; Era Pearl (1901) married first to Roy Shinn and second to Claude Eason; Earmer Lee (1902) married Viola Duke; Winnie Myrtle (1904) married Young Marshall Johnson; Alton Allen (1912-1965) married Ruby Phillips; George Grady (1909-1993) married Avis Key. They had three sons and a daughter who died in infancy.

Annie Jones was born 5 January 1870 the daughter of John and Rebecca Sarah (Chappell) Jones. In 1880 after the death of her mother, Annie Jones lived with the Gray family and later she lived with the Copeland family. It is known she had two sisters: Ellie Jones who married George Washington Gray and Jane Jones who went to Cullman, Alabama, to live. Annie died 4 October 1926 and is buried at Pleasant Grove Baptist Church at Tyus, Georgia.

My grandmother, Era Pearl Bradley, first married Roy Shinn and had one child, Hugh Lee Shinn. In 1924 she married Claude Eason and raised a large family of ten children. She was a homemaker and a very Christian woman. Pearl Eason died in September of 1970 after an extended illness. Her children were Myrl who married Robert Meigs; Ruel married first to Glady Harden Moore and second to Inez Jackson; Wendell married Jane Dockery; Jean married Billy T. Lowery; Joanne married Randall Buchanan; Claudette married James Harold Smith; Susie married Donald Farr; Patricia married Quinion Robinson; Tracy married Janice Calhoun; and Terry married Maxine Smith. She is buried beside Claude at Pleasant Grove Baptist Church at Tyus, Georgia.

My mother is Jean Eason (1931) who married Billy T. Lowery on 20 March 1948. Mother worked as a lunchroom worker until she retired. I have one sister Vicky Lowery (1950) who married Steve Sheffield; and three brothers — Tommy (1959) married first to Dixie Norrell and second to Carolyn White Coggins; Bradley (1962); and Wayne (1964-1998) married Christine Thornton. I was born 20 December 1952 and married Judy Gibbs on 24 May 1975 and later we divorced. We have a set of twins, Jason and Jeremy Lowery, who were born 13 June 1977. *Submitted by: Steve Lowery, 1501 Smithfield Road, Bowdon, GA 30108*

364. William Edward Brett Jr.

Born on May 29, 1929, in Haralson County and raised in Haralson County, William Edward Brett married Flora Duke, formerly of Cullman, Alabama, on November 27, 1951.

After making a home in Waco, Georgia, for one year, they moved to Carrollton in 1955 so Edward could work at the supermarket. Buying a house one block from the Carrollton square, Edward worked at the A & P Supermarket located on the square. The supermarket moved to Alabama Street, then to Maple Street. Edward worked at all three locations until 1973 when he became a self-employed refrigeration specialist.

The William Edward Brett Jr. Family

Four children were born: Shirley Rae, January 1953; Jacquelyn Elaine, September 1955; William Edward Brett III, March 1958 (died at birth); and Steve O'Neill Brett, April 1959. Descendants of Edward and Flora who are currently living in Carroll County are children: Shirley Gray, Jackie Caldwell, Steve Brett; grandchildren: Matthew Gray, Carrie Gray Tarpley, Nathaniel Gray, Ami Caldwell Madden, Benjamin Caldwell; great-grandchildren: Brett Madden, Beau Madden, Allyson Tarpley, Erin Tarpley, Austin Gray.

Edward and Flora joined the First Christian Church in 1957. They, along with their children, grandchildren, and great-grandchildren, still attend today.

Edward served in the U.S. Marine Corps from July 1947 to July 1950.

In 1983 Edward Brett, Bill Gray, and Mike Caldwell purchased a portion of the old W.A. Spence home place located on Temple Road where today all enjoy a large garden and orchard. *Submitted by: Edward and Flora Brett, Carrollton, GA*

365. The Bruce Brewer Family

The Bruce Brewer family moved to Carroll County in the fall of 1981. Bruce had taken a job at West Georgia College and was charged with setting up the Cooperative Education Program at the institution. Bruce and his wife, Patricia Lumley, his two stepsons (Frank and Patrick Hollifield), and their one-year-old daughter, April, moved to Carrollton together.

Brewer Family in the 1980s

Over the years, Bruce became director of the Department of Career Services of the State University of West Georgia (UWG), completed his Ph.D. at Georgia State, worked to establish the Existing Industry Committee of the Chamber of Commerce (receiving Outstanding Volunteer Award in 1993), assisted in establishing and eventually serving as president of both the West Georgia Personnel Association and the West Georgia Industrial Leaders Association, and assisted in continuing the scouting effort in the Carroll Haralson District of the Boy Scouts of America where he served as district commissioner and then as district chairman.

Patricia completed her undergraduate degree in mass communications from West Georgia College. In her career, she has served as a field executive in the Pine Valley Girl Scouts program for Carroll and Haralson Counties, was on the founding board of Alice's House, was the original executive director of the CASA program (Court Appointed Special Advocates' Program), serves on the Alumni Board of UWG, and currently works as a field agent with a staffing agency (Randstad).

All three children were educated in the county and city school systems. Frank, who was active in debate and band at CHS, went on to eventually complete his undergraduate, graduate and law degrees at the University of Alabama. He served his country in Desert Storm and is currently a captain with the Judge Advocate General's office in the Air Force. His wife, the former Dana Holliday, and he will be relocating to Wyoming during the summer of 2001. Patrick graduated from Carrollton High School and, after serving his country in the Marines (avionics), works for one of the largest independent insurance firms in Georgia. He is engaged to be married to Kimberly Potter. April was a varsity cheerleader at Carrollton for both basketball and football. She was a Thespian with the high school theater department. At present, she is a Hope Scholar and a sophomore at the State University of West Georgia majoring in business. She will perhaps be remembered by many as being the first fencer from Carroll County (at the age of fourteen) to participate in the Junior Olympics, which was held in Louisville, Kentucky (1995). The Fencing Club was started at Carrollton Junior High by Coach Shawn Lawrence.

The family was one of the charter families of King's Way Presbyterian Church (PCA), though their church membership is at First Baptist Church on Dixie Street. Bruce is a Sertoman, a deacon, a Gideon, faculty sponsor of UWG's Campus Outreach, and has played an instrumental role in bringing the field of job placement into the Internet age. He designed one of the Internet's first job search web sites (jobNET), created the first ever e-fairs (virtual career fair) in Georgia and the Southeast (2001), and assisted in creating Georgi-Hire.com (an Internet job search system). *Submitted by: Bruce Brewer, Carrollton, GA*

366. The James Wilburn Jesse Britt Family

James Wilburn Jesse Britt was born in Ireland in 1820. He came to the United States and settled in North Carolina. He later moved to west central Georgia. James was a farmer and he and his wife had ten children. The family is listed in the Carroll County census books of 1860 and 1870. During the Civil War, James fought with the Confederate Army, and after being wounded in battle was sent home. He was shot through the chest and the doctor caring for him cleaned his wound by sticking a rifle cleaning rod through his body. He was forty-four at the time of his injury, he recovered and lived to be ninety-three years old. He died in 1913 and he and his wife are buried at the Little Vine Baptist Church in Tallapoosa, Georgia.

Beverly and Bill Britt, Barbara, Will, Johnny and Alex Waters

A son, William Luther "Bud" Britt was born in 1850 in Carroll County. Bud was underage during the Civil War, but from his home he saw Sherman's men going by and could hear the cannons in Atlanta. Bud and his mother walked to Atlanta to get food; it was the nearest place to get anything to eat. Many women walked to Atlanta to get food, but they seldom got home with anything, they were so hungry they ate it all on the way home. Bud helped lay the Georgia and Pacific Railroad, now the Southern, running from the Chattahoochee River to Birmingham, Alabama. Bud moved to Sapulpa, Oklahoma, and lived to be 108 years old. At the age of ninety-seven, against his family's wishes because of his age, he traveled to Bowdon to visit his brothers there.

Another son of James Jesse Britt was named Robert Ridley "Bob" Britt. He was born in 1865 in Carroll County. Bob was a tenant farmer and worked for shares of the harvest. One fall a land owner he worked for claimed all the crops and household items for himself. Bob had other ideas, so one night he placed his family, his home furnishings, and the cotton seed from his share on their farm wagon. He placed a shuck inside the cow's bell so its ringing wouldn't wake the landlord, tied bossy to the back of the wagon, and when dawn broke the family was in Randolph County, Alabama. Bob and his first wife had eleven children. Her name was Mary Elizabeth Philips and she died in childbirth. He later married Sophie Berry and they had five more children.

The youngest son of James Jesse Britt was Andrew Jackson "Jack" Britt,, born in 1881. He died October 24, 1955, in Carroll County and is buried in Alabama. Jack was thirty-one years younger than the oldest brother Bud, but they had the same mother.

Robert Ridley "Bob" Britt's youngest son, William Oneal "Bill" Britt was born in Lanett, Alabama. After serving in the Army and winning a Purple Heart, Bill traveled to Missouri to attend college. There he met his wife, Beverly Jackson, and they were married in 1948. They lived in Kansas City; Houston, Texas; Tampa, Florida; and then moved to Georgia in 1969. In 1988 they moved to Carroll County. Bill died June 11, 1998. Beverly Britt is active in various civic organizations in Carrollton, and dances with a senior ladies group in Atlanta.

Their daughter, Dr. Barbara Waters, is a radiologist. Her husband Johnny Waters is chairman of the geology department at the State University of West Georgia. Granddaughter Emily Alexandria "Alex" Waters graduated from Carrollton High School as valedictorian of her class and attends Harvard University. Grandson John William Edward "Will" Waters attended Carrollton Junior High School and then transferred to Woodward Academy in Atlanta.

Bill and Beverly Britt's other daughter Belinda lives in Seattle, Washington with her husband Jim, and daughters Tracy and Leslie. *Submitted by: Beverly Britt, 223 Plantation Walk, Carrollton, GA 30117*

Sources: *The Britt Kin* by Vera Carson Wilder, and personal knowledge.

367. Bob and Drucilla Brock

James Robert "Bob" Brock was born February 23, 1857. He was seven years old when his mother, Frances Hogan Brock, received word that his father James Daniel Brock had been in the Battle of Cold Harbor, Virginia, on June 2, 1864. James Daniel died from wounds received during the battle.

Post Civil War times were very difficult for the family but determination and hard work brought them forward. Bob and Drucilla Josephine Mote married December 15, 1878. They had ten children, nine of whom lived to adulthood. Leon married Flora Thorton; Emma married Malcolm Evans; Sara Frances "Fannie" married Newt Blackmond; Pearl married John Edgar Matthews; Wiley married Effie Lucille Matthews, then Iree Smith; Estelle married Herschell Hendrix; Della married Martin Blackmond; Grady married Avice Parker; and Ruth married Eli Whitney, then Ervin Snyder. Their daughter Estelle lived 101 years. The nine children had forty-four children who lived past infancy. Their grandson James S. Brock was the first World War II casualty from Carroll County. He was killed in a plane crash in Natal, Brazil.

Bob and his family were farmers. When Wiley's wife Lucille died, leaving him with five small children, he moved in with Bob and Drucilla so they could help care for the children. About 1920, a runaway boy came by the Brock house wanting a job and a place to live. Bob gave the

The Brock Family in 1904

boy a job and a place to sleep. A little over two months later the boy's grandfather Gilbert came from Anniston, Alabama, looking for his grandson. The family hated to see the boy leave because he was a good worker and a joy to have around. Bob died April 24, 1927, and Drucilla February 17, 1933. They are buried in Pleasant View Baptist Church Cemetery.

I'm one of Bob and Drucilla's seventy-two great-grandchildren. My grandparents, Pearl and Edgar Matthews, moved to Bear Creek Road adjacent to Bob and Drucilla's place in 1916 and remained there until their deaths. Papa Matthews was a farmer, as were his sons Clarence and Wiley. He knew how to grow delicious watermelons. Edgar was born December 30, 1886, died January 26, 1976. Pearl was born November 25, 1888, died February 27, 1983. They are buried in Pleasant View Baptist Church Cemetery.

The family photograph shows the Brock family in 1904. Seated from left are Bob Brock and Drucilla Brock holding daughter Ruth. Others in the picture are Leon, Emma and Malcolm Evans, Fannie, Pearl, Wiley, Estelle, and Della. *Submitted by: Horry Johnson, 3391 N. Highway 27, Carrollton, GA*

368. Brook

The roots of the Brook family go back several generations in Carroll County. Wiley Venson Brook, a Civil War veteran, was a farmer in Tyus, Carroll County. The farm remains in the Brook family today, and some of Wiley's descendants still reside in Tyus and surrounding areas. Wiley Venson Brook, also known as Dock, was the eighth child of fourteen children born to Henry and Sarah Brook (nine sons and five daughters). He was born June 4, 1837 in Wilkes County, Georgia. The family migrated from Wilkes County to Coweta Co. and about 1871, on to Carroll County.

Wiley married Sarah Elizabeth Moore on December 18, 1860 in Coweta County. Sarah, the daughter of Willis B. Moore and Hepsibah Adams, was born August 7, 1840 in Coweta County.

Wiley Venson Brook with grandson Millard Lee Brook about 1920

Wiley and five of his brothers served the Confederacy during the Civil War. They all served in Company C of the 34th Georgia Infantry. The two eldest brothers, William Henry and James, were killed. Wiley enlisted in Captain Jordan Rowland's Company K, 4th Regiment, Second Brigade, Georgia State Troops October 25, 1861 and was appointed second corporal. He mustered out in April of 1862. On May 13, 1862, Wiley was appointed first corporal of Company C, 34th Regiment Georgia Infantry. Wiley and three of his brothers were captured at Vicksburg, Mississippi on July 4, 1863, and paroled there July 8, 1863.

Wiley and Sarah Brook had three children: Emma, Ella, and William Thomas Edward. Emma Wiley Brook was born August 9, 1862 in Coweta County and died May 22, 1907. She married Rev. John Thomas Layton. Ella G. Brook was born June 11, 1864, in Coweta County and died February 22, 1908. She married Jesse E. Wade. William Thomas Edward, "W.T.E.," was born August 12, 1871 in Carroll County and died April 18, 1938. W.T.E. married Mary Ann "Annie" Elizabeth Stewart. Wiley and Sarah were members of Pleasant Grove Baptist Church at Tyus in Carroll County, and they and their children and some succeeding generations are buried at the Pleasant Grove Baptist Church Cemetery. Also buried at the church are some of Wiley's brothers and families and their descendants. Sarah died March 16, 1908 and Wiley died March 19, 1921.

Andrew Venson and Dovie Brook on their farm about 1919

William Thomas Edward Brook, "W.T.E.", married Annie Stewart on November 13, 1892 in Carroll County. Annie was the daughter of Andrew Jackson Stewart and Martha "Mattie" Ann Elizabeth Bishop of Carroll County and was born December 2, 1871, and died March 27, 1958. W.T.E. was a farmer like his father, on the land that had belonged to Wiley. He and Annie had two sons. Andrew Venson Brook was born June 24, 1894, in Tyus and died August 22, 1976. William Ozmo Brook (Uncle Dock) was born December 21, 1898 in Tyus and died August 1978.

Andrew Venson was known as A.V. or Mr. Venson to those who knew him well and loved him and was the third generation to farm the land, which had been split between him and his brother. Andrew married Dovie May Brown on January 2, 1916, in Carroll County. Dovie was the daughter of Miles A. Brown and Retha Jackson of Heard County and later Carroll County. She was born May 5, 1894 and died June 13, 1929. Andrew and Dovie had two children, Millard Lee and Miles Garland Brook. After Dovie's death, he married Bessie May Boyd on September 24, 1933. Andrew and Bessie had two children, Willie Kenneth and Martha Ann Brook. After Dovie had passed away, Andrew left his children with his parents for a while, taking a job at the A&P Food Store to pay hospital and doctor bills. During World War II, he joined the war effort by working in a box factory at night in Bowdon, manufacturing wooden bomb crates. He still worked his farm by day. At some time in his life, he also worked for Callaway cotton mills in LaGrange. Farming was in his blood and was what he loved to do most. Andrew was once offered a deal to sell his produce on credit, with interest. This took place during a time of drought, when everyone's crops were failing. Andrew was blessed with a bountiful harvest, due in part to a natural spring on the farm. He refused to exploit his friends and neighbors and chose instead to share what he had with others. Andrew died in 1976 and is buried alongside both his wives at Pleasant Grove Baptist Church in Tyus, next to his parents and grandparents. The old home place still stands on the farm.

Andrew V. Brook was my Papa, my grandfather. This was written to honor him and the heritage he left to me. *Submitted by: Michael E. Brook, 1313 Viola Drive, Yukon, OK 73099*

Sources: Information from cemetery, census, military and church records; data from Ted Brooke, a descendant of Henry Brook; family interviews.

369. Dr. W.L. "Bud" Brooks

W.L. "Bud" Brooks was born 23 October 1870 in Randolph County, Alabama. He died 1 March 1948 in Bowdon, Georgia. He married Dora Landers on 15 January 1914 in Heflin, Alabama. She was born 7 September 1874 and died 22 December 1928. They are buried in Corinth Cemetery in Randolph County, Alabama. His grave is no longer marked. They had no children.

W.L. Brooks was the son of William D. Brooks and Mary L. Brooks. His grandfather, Daniel A. Brooks was a miller in Randolph County, Alabama, and his grandmother's name was Elizabeth Brooks.

W.L. Brooks became an orphan in 1880 at the age of ten. He moved from home to home until he was old enough to support himself. He held numerous jobs and was later offered a chance by H.D. Landers Sr. to go to school. Afterward, he taught at Flint Ridge, Alabama. Later he worked in Heflin, Alabama, and opened a grocery store there. By 1913 he had completed his degree in pharmacy at the School of Pharmacy at Macon.

In 1913, W.L. Brooks moved to Bowdon, Georgia, and purchased the Bowdon Drug Company-The Rexall Store owned by Dr. W.P. Smith. He later sold the store to Charles Emory Downs and Olen Downs. On 26 September 1926, The Commercial Bank of Bowdon was organized on the corner of Main and Rome streets with W.L. Brooks as president.

W.L. Brooks spent his last years residing at the Bowdon hospital where he eventually died. *Submitted by: Melinda Shelton, 4605 7th Court South, Birmingham, AL 35222*

Sources: *Dr. W.L. Brooks, Outstanding Citizen, Claimed by Death* by Mrs. H.M. Bird. *The Bowdon Bulletin* v.58 March 4, 1948. *Bowdon the first hundred years, 1853-1953* by Judy Copeland Rowell and Mary Dobson Rowell.

370. Joseph Harrison Broom

Joseph Harrison Broom was born on 20 August 1834 in Taliaferro County, Georgia. He married Mildred Wood on 6 October 1853 in Warren County, Georgia. Mildred Wood was born on 25 November 1817. In 1838 she had married John Linn of Warren County and there were five children by this marriage: James, Drucilla, Joseph, Sarah, and Emily. John Linn died in 1851. Joseph and Mildred Broom had two children, both born in Warren County. They were John Augustus Franklin who married Margaret Carroll, and Alice Almira who married Joseph Hicks.

Joseph Harrison Broom was the son of Moses Broom and Loediske Harrison Broom of

Mildred Wood Broom

Taliaferro County. Joseph Harrison and Mildred Wood Broom moved to Carroll County by 1858 with their two children and the five Linn children. The obituary of his son gives the date as 1860, but it was before 7 October 1858, for on that date Mildred's daughter, Drucilla Linn, married Labon Jackson Smith in Carroll County.

Joseph Broom purchased a house on the corner of Cedar and College streets in Carrollton and established a shoe manufacturing business. In 1861, as men went off to war, there was a shortage of qualified men for judges so Joseph Broom was recruited to be a justice of the Inferior Court. He filled the position until April 1862 when he enlisted in Company E, 1st Georgia Regiment of Cavalry, Wheeler's Corp. He was detached from Company E and appointed assistant quartermaster for the Regiment. In his service record there is a requisition in his handwriting made at Knoxville, Tennessee, dated June 17, 1862, which is a request for one hundred and fifty pounds of horse shoe iron and twelve pounds of horse shoe nails. The requisition states

> "A good number of horses in the command are without shoes and can't travel". It is signed "J.H. Broom, A. Qm. Det., 1st Regt Ga Cav".

He was with the regiment at the battles of Murfreesboro and Chattanooga, Tennessee, and during the Atlanta Campaign. While the regiment was near Newnan, Georgia, on 30 July 1864 he came home to Carrollton on leave, then returned to his unit near Acworth, Georgia, about 19 August 1864. He was last heard from in November 1864 and presumed killed in one of the actions as Wheeler's Corp was harassing Sherman's Army in southeast Georgia and into South Carolina.

In early 1864 Joseph Harrison had sold the property in Carrollton but his wife and children continued to live there. After the war, Labon Smith bought the property and Mildred Broom lived there with her daughter, Drucilla Linn Smith, until the death of Labon Smith in 1876. Mildred Broom then lived with her son, John Broom, in Carroll County and with her daughter, Alice Broom Hicks, in Floyd County. She received a Confederate Widow's pension from 1890 until her death in Floyd County on 6 June 1906. She is buried in the Sand Springs Baptist Church Cemetery in Floyd County. *Submitted by: Alfred Turner, 6501 Peacock Blvd., Morrow, GA 30260*

371. Moses Broom

Moses Broom was born on 28 January 1806 in Warren County, Georgia. He married Loediske Pulaski Harrison on 23 June 1831 in Taliaferro County, Georgia. Loediske Pulaski Harrison was born on 18 September 1810 in Wilkes County, Georgia, to Joseph and Elizabeth Harrison. Joseph Harrison was a Revolutionary soldier, first in the Virginia Continental Line, then a lieutenant in Salter's Company of Continentals at Wilmington, North Carolina, and was captain of the same company at the siege of Savannah, Georgia, under General Pulaski in whose honor he named his daughter. Joseph Harrison never lived in Carroll County but drew land in the county in the Lottery of 1827.

Moses Broom was the son of Solomon Broom and Elizabeth Mims. Solomon Broom was a shoemaker and farmer in Warren and Taliaferro counties, occupations that he taught his son. He was a private in Captain Heath's Company of Infantry, 3rd Regiment Georgia Militia during the War of 1812. In addition to Moses, Solomon and Elizabeth Broom had three more children, Celia, Leroy, and Ann, and the latter two were also residents of Carroll County.

Moses Broom was a farmer and shoemaker in Taliaferro and Greene counties but in the fall of 1853 moved to Carroll County, purchasing farm land about two miles southeast of the Sand Hill community on the Sand Hill-Hulett Road. In January 1854 his brother, Leroy Broom, purchased an adjoining lot. In October the following year, their sister Ann and her husband, William O'Neal, purchased nearby land. The Broom and O'Neal families were members of the Macedonia Baptist Church in Sand Hill. Leroy Broom and his wife, Selethia Stephens Broom are buried in the Macedonia cemetery but their graves are not marked. Ann and William O'Neal are also buried there in marked graves. The will of William O'Neal even specifies that he be buried in the Macedonia churchyard.

Moses and Loediske Broom had eight children, the first seven born in Taliaferro and Greene counties and the last born in Carroll County. They were: Joseph Harrison born in 1834 and married Mildred Wood in Warren County; Sarah Ann Elizabeth born in 1837 and never married; Mary E. Celia born in 1840 and married Alexander Bobo in Floyd County; Emily born in 1842 and married to Henry J. Hicks in Floyd County; Alexander H. Stephens born in 1845 and married to Mary Caroline Turner in Carroll County; John William Pulaski born in 1850 and married Susan Reynolds in Floyd County; James Francis born in 1853 and married Mary McCoy in Chattooga County; and Seaborn Moses born in 1857 and married Ollie A. Weaver in Chattooga County.

Moses Broom grew corn, cotton, oats, and wheat and raised sheep and swine on his land in Carroll County. He sold this land to his brother, Leroy, and moved to Floyd County, Georgia, after 1866. He died in Floyd County on 19 July 1870. Loediske Broom died in Floyd County on 20 February 1898. *Submitted by: Elizabeth McIntosh, 2800 Old Carriage Dr., Marietta, GA 30060*

372. Broom - Carroll

John Augustus Franklin Broom was born on August 1854 in Warren County, Georgia. He married Margaret Ann Temperance Carroll on 9 August 1872 in Carroll County, Georgia. Margaret Ann Carroll was born on 14 February 1852 in Carroll County, the daughter of John Workman Carroll and Rachel Stidham Carroll. Margaret Ann's father was a prominent citizen of Carroll County, operating a hat manufacturing business and farm in Sand Hill, a Representative in the State Legislature, a Justice of the Peace for the Fairplay District, and Postmaster at Sand Hill. Margaret Ann attended school in the old log structure near the Macedonia Baptist Church and was a member of the Temperance Methodist Church in Sand Hill, which was adjacent to her father's home. She was baptized by the Reverend James Baskin from the Old Concord Methodist Church in Hickory Level, one of the original settlers of Carroll County. It is no coincidence that one of her given names was Temperance and also the name that was given the church. Her father and grandfather, Moses Carroll, were deeply committed to the Temperance movement of that time. (See related Carroll and Broom articles).

John A.F. Broom came to Carroll County from Warren County in 1858 with his parents, Joseph Harrison Broom and Mildred Wood Broom. His father operated a shoe manufacturing business in Carrollton until his enlistment in the 1st Georgia Cavalry in 1862 and subsequently lost his life in the cause of the Confederacy. John A.F. Broom served Carroll County in an official capacity for many years. He was justice of the peace and postmaster at Sand Hill, county tax collector, and Commissioner of Roads and Revenues at various times. He was co-founder of the Carrollton Telephone Company, a black smith, a farmer, and a charter member of the Sand Hill Masonic lodge.

John and Margaret Broom surrounded by grandchildren.

All of the children of John and Margaret Broom were born in Carroll County. They were: James Robert; Earskin Augustus who married (1) Leila Reese and (2) Susan Edna Cooke; Jerusha Elizabeth who married Samuel Reese James; Lura R. who married Willie Gerald Gray; Irvin B.; John Moses; Buvo Buren who married Mary Parks; Charles Roland who married (1) Emily Agerton and (2) Lettie Ann Broom; an unnamed son who died at birth; Mary Alice who married Buren Robert Turner; and Velma G. who married Lowell A. Muse. All of these children are buried in the Temperance Methodist Church cemetery except Earskin (Oak Hill cemetery in Coweta County) and Velma (Pleasant Grove Baptist Church cemetery in Villa Rica.)

John Augustus Franklin Broom died on 1 May 1928 in Carrollton, Georgia. To accommodate the many mourners, services were held in the new, more spacious Bethany Christian Church near Sand Hill. The Masons had charge of the graveside services at Temperance Methodist Church cemetery. Margaret Ann Temperance Carroll Broom lived for years with her daughter, Jerusha Broom James, before she died on 12 January 1949 in Sand Hill. She is also buried in the Temperance cemetery. *Submitted by: Charles James, 458 Cove Drive, Marietta, GA 30060*

373. Broom - James

Samuel Reese James was born on 8 August 1875 in Oconee County, South Carolina. He married Jerusha Elizabeth Broom on 6 May 1896 in Carroll County, Georgia. Jerusha Elizabeth Broom was born on 24 October 1877 in Carroll County, Georgia, to John A.F. Broom and Margaret Ann Carroll Broom. (See related articles on Moses Carroll and John Workman Carroll.) Jerusha Elizabeth grew up in Sand Hill, attending school in the log cabin schoolhouse adjacent to the Macedonia Baptist Church cemetery on State Highway 61, known at the time as Ridge Road. She was a member of the Temperance Methodist Church.

Samuel Reese James was the son of Theodore Perry James and Harriet Caroline Rowland James of Oconee County, South Carolina. Harriet Caroline was descended from several Revolutionary War soldiers. She was the granddaughter of Peter Rowland who was at the Battle of Kings Mountain, South Carolina; the great-granddaughter of John Harris who was at the Battle of Cowpens, South Carolina; and the great-great-granddaughter of General Andrew Pickens. Theodore Perry James was a farmer and miller in Oconee County, South Carolina, and served the Confederacy in the 27th Regiment, South Carolina Infantry. Samuel Reese James came to Carroll County about 1890 with his cousin, William T. Rowland, seeking a fortunate in the gold mines of Carroll County. Finding the mines in decline he made his way to Sand Hill where he found employment with John A.F. Broom.

Samuel and Jerusha James' children were Nettie, Jesse, Earl, Kie, Tom, and Henry. Nettie Roena was born in 1897, married Coleman Clay Turner in Carroll County in 1918 and died in 1975 in North Carolina. Jesse Braswell was born in 1899, married Dora L. Hogan in Carroll County in 1919, died in 1938 and is buried at the Temperance cemetery. Earl A. was born in 1905, married (1) Tessie Portwood in Carroll County in 1927, (2) Avis Thompson in 1937 in Carroll County, and (3) Leona Ricks in Wedowee, Alabama, in 1960 He died in 1974 and is buried at the Bethany Christian Church cemetery. Kie Lewis was born in 1906, married Mary Burzelle Gordon in Carroll County in 1924, died in 1991, and is buried at Carroll Memory Gardens. Thomas Theodore was born in 1909 and married Mamie Pauline Bates in 1931 in Carroll County. He died in 1993 and is buried at Cheatham Hill Cemetery in Cobb County. Henry Roland was born in 1913 and married Edna Naomi Sticher in 1932 in Carroll County. Henry was in the 28th Infantry Division during World War II, was taken prisoner in Luxemburg during the Battle of the Bulge and died in a German prisoner of war camp in 1945. He was later re-interred at the Temperance cemetery.

Sam and Jerusha James

Samuel James was a farmer in Sand Hill and Clem and also operated a gristmill in Sand Hill. Jerusha Broom James died in Carroll County on 8 May 1966 and Samuel James died on 11 January 1969. Both are buried in the Temperance cemetery. *Submitted by: Ruth Knott, 1689 Roscoe Rd., Newnan, GA 30263*

374. The Daniel Brown Family

One of the pioneer families of Carroll County was Daniel Brown and Sarah "Matilda" Jones who came to the Centralhatchee area of Heard County from South Carolina between 1836-1838. Daniel was born in 1791 in Virginia and died in 1869. His wife Sarah was born in 1800 and died sometime after 1870. They are buried in the Yellowdirt Church cemetery in unmarked graves. This church is located on property in Carroll County now owned by the Georgia Power Company at Plant Wansley.

On 30 November 1844, their son Robert Jones Brown bought 202 ½ acres; land lot 105, in the 4th District of Carroll County; and on 24 November 1849 bought 100 adjoining acres on Notched Road from Eliza Baxter. Descendants from the Willie Taylor family who bought this land from the Browns still own the original 300 acres.

Daniel was a sheepherder and farmer. They had ten children: Robert Jones, George S., an unknown child, Sarah, Lucille Francis Jane, Josephine E., Samuel, Lewis H., Ira A., and Mary A.

Robert J. was born in South Carolina and came with his parents to this area. In 1841 he married Elizabeth Jane Stuart, daughter of Margaret Corry Stuart. The children of Robert and Eliza Brown were Mary A., Elizabeth Jane, Sarah Margaret, James S., Robert, Mary Ann Eliza, Robert William, and Gustavuas. They lived near Rotherwood, on the McIntosh Trail. A cemetery is located on this property that has eleven unmarked graves of the Brown family including Margaret Corry Stuart who lived to be 106 years old.

J.R. and Georgia Brown with son Herman

During the Civil War, Private Francis Cicero Ray served in Company K, 30th Regiment Georgia Infantry. Sarah Margaret corresponded with him while he was in Savannah. She began a quilt made from cloth that she had spun and dyed into beautiful colors of brown and orange. This quilt remained in the Brown family with her niece, Lorene Musick Eiss. Cicero and Sarah Margaret "Aunt Peggy" were only married for four months in 1863 before he died of pneumonia while home on furlough. He is buried in the Brown cemetery. Aunt Peggy lived to the age of ninety-four and never remarried. She is buried at Liberty Methodist Church.

Times were hard, so many of Daniel's children moved away. Robert J. and his family plowed the land with an ox and raised sheep. They spun cloth from wool and cotton to make their clothes and linens. Many of this family died early from diseases and fevers; so several generations lived together. James S. Robert and Elizabeth "Neally" Holsomback, parents of Lewis, James Robert and Sarah M. Brown, died with fevers in 1872, leaving the children to be raised by their grandfather.

James Robert "J.R." worked at an early age by using the family oxen to help pull wagons up the steep hill on the McIntosh Trail (now Highway 5) at Whooping Creek. He was sometimes called "Trader Jim" as he was known for trading mules - always knowing a good mule by its teeth. He sometimes drove herds of cattle from Carroll County to the stockyards in Atlanta to be shipped to market. In 1929, he bought a house and farm on the Carrollton Roopville Road in Carrollton. He married Georgia Texas Yeager on February 2, 1889. Their son Fredrick Vernon died at the age of thirteen. Their son Herman Franklin worked at a soda fountain in New York City; and was there the day the Stock Market crashed in 1929. He worked at drug stores in Jacksonville, Florida and Rome, Georgia, before coming back to help farm and raise cattle on the family farm.

Herman F. Brown put up four windmills in this area and met his wife, Pansy Tisinger, while installing a windmill at the Tisinger farm near Bowdon. She was a graduate of the first nursing class at Emory University in 1926. Together they ran the Cottage Hill Farm and Dari-Bar ice cream shop, and later the Cottage Hill Greenhouses and Florist.

Their son David Robert Brown moved to Newnan with the Soil Conservation Service. He owns a large cattle farm in the Haralson community. He first married Martha Pettway and later Rita Bruner Geddings. His daughter Amanda married Scott McDonald, Stephanie married Mark Bolier, and Abigail married Henry Cole from Newnan. Her daughter Kirsten married Bryan Beard. Abigail and Henry's children are Jordan and Madeline.

Their daughter Gwyn married Neal Clay and later Charles Chesnut. She worked as a home economist for Martha White Mills and Atlanta Gas Light Company. She had two sons John Carter Clay and Matthew Clay. Matthew married Melanie Nunnally Hill. Their children are Britanny Hill and Austen Neal Clay. *Submitted by: Matthew Clay, 106 Habersham Place, Carrollton, GA 30117*
Sources: *William Corry and His Descendants* by Mildred Seab Ezell; and Gwyn Brown Chesnut, personal knowledge.

375. Franklin Brown and Agnes Stipe

Franklin Brown, about 1820-1880, was born in North Carolina, and was a son of Isaac Brown, born in Virginia. Isaac's will in Coweta County, Georgia, names other children: Jane, Caroline, Martha, Henry, Oliver, and Madison.

Franklin married Agnes Stipe in Coweta County, Georgia, in 1840. Agnes was a daughter of John Henry Stipe, who was born in Germany in 1775. His parents were John Christian Steup and Arma Rubsamen, who migrated to America from the German Palatinate. John Henry Stipe married first Margaret Lawler in Culpeper County, Virginia. He married second Elizabeth "Betsy" Lumpkin in 1800, also in Culpeper County. Other children of this couple were Lewis Luther, John, Christian, Nancy, Lucy, Elizabeth Mary, Henry Jr., Ephraim, Jane, and Mary "Polly." John Henry and Betsy lived for a time in North Carolina and migrated via Oglethorpe County, Georgia, to Campbell County, Georgia. Betsy's place of death and burial are unknown. John Henry Stipe is buried at Antioch Cemetery in Campbell County.

Franklin and Agnes lived in Coweta and Campbell counties in Georgia, in Talladega County, Alabama, and returned to settle in Carroll County by 1870. Their children were Susan Ann Brown; Mary Jane Brown, believed to be the Jane Brown buried at Old Camp Methodist Cemetery near Russells, apparently never married; Elizabeth Lucie Brown, who married Moses Richard Russell (see that family's article); John H.T. Brown; Marcus A. Brown; Tabitha Brown; N. Brown; James M. Brown; and Francis B. Brown (male). Great-grandchildren of Franklin and Agnes remember an Aunt Bithy (Tabitha?) and an Uncle Bartow. Possibly Francis B. was Bartow.

Franklin and Agnes Brown apparently died after 1880, and their burial places are unknown, but it is possible that they are buried in unmarked graves at Old Camp Methodist Cemetery. *Submitted by: Nancy E. Williams, 701 Wind Grove Rd., Marietta, GA 30067. nelizw@aol.com*

376. James R.T. Brown

James R.T. Brown (born 1832) and wife, Elizabeth (born 1831) were born in South Carolina and spent most of their adult lives in Carroll County, Georgia. Their children were Benjamin H. (married Amanda Stephenson); Alpha Eugenia (married John Warren Jackson); Susan Elizabeth (married Llewyen Smith); John M. (married Salina Ray); Joseph (married Mrs. Ophelia Holmes); Thomas H.; and Martha Elizabeth (married Fredrick T. Pentacost).

Around 1850 at an early age, he began his career founding and pastoring many of the area churches, one of the first being First Baptist Church in Villa Rica, the next being New Providence Baptist Church, now known as Whitesburg Baptist Church.

On May 27, 1861, he entered the Civil War as part of Company G, 7 Georgia Infantry for a one year period. In August 1861 he was elected third lieutenant, and was discharged on May 18, 1862.

Around 1880 he lost his wife, Elizabeth, and in 1882 he married Mrs. J.R. Roberts in Paulding County, Georgia. She was originally from Carroll County, and together they had two sons.

While giving what would be his last sermon at Pleasant Grove Baptist Church, James R.T. Brown suffered a heart attack and retired to his home and bed, going home to his Lord on January 31, 1891. His body was interred at his beloved Pleasant Grove Baptist Church. *Submitted by: Florine Hallmark, P.O. Box 837, Boaz, AL 35957 fthlmark@aol.com*

377. John Burks Brown

The Brown family has lived in Carroll County for over 125 years, but it is not known exactly when they came to Carroll. The first record of John Burks Brown is the 1878 Carrollton tax digest. He and his family moved to Carroll between 1873-1877 from Monroe County. John and family were listed in the 1880 census in Carrollton. According to that and later census records, John was born in Alabama and his parents in Georgia. John may be the son of William and Martha Brown of Carroll County. They lived next door to John's family in 1880. His family may have moved to Carroll by 1845 before moving to Alabama for a short time. John married Eliza Jane Trapp (born November 1, 1847, Johnstonville, Monroe County). She and her sister Mary were orphaned as toddlers and were raised by different families in Monroe County. In 1870 John, Eliza, and John's older sister Francis were all living in Johnstonville, which was where their first children were born.

John and Eliza Brown, about 1920.

In 1883, The Browns moved to Chulafinnee, Cleburne County, Alabama, and by 1891 to Clay County where they remained until about 1915. John and Eliza finally moved to Alexandria in Calhoun County where Eliza died on November 3, 1922. John died 1923-5. Both are buried at Mount Zion Baptist Church, but no death date was inscribed on John's tombstone. John served in the Confederate Army. According to his granddaughter, Era Faulkner, he said that the warmest night he ever spent was under brush packed with snow. After Eliza died, John stayed with some of his children, including Luther and Beulah.

John and Eliza had eleven children, two of whom died before 1900. The other nine are:

Henrietta Hill (November 16, 1871-December 20, 1947) married William Columbus Striplin (1858-1924). They both died in Roopville, Carroll County, and are buried at Bethesda Missionary Baptist Church there. They had nine children: Edgar, Allen, Viola Barnes, Hugh, Jesse, Houston, Alma Denny, Newman, and Velma Denny.

William Robert (February 03, 1873-May 12, 1948). He married Uphamie (1869-1955). They are both buried at Mount Zion. Bud, as William was known, died in Jacksonville, and Uphamie in Alexandria. They had seven children: Addie and Lucy Feazell, Mae, William Jr., Leola and Alice Hammond, and Nonnie Shelton.

Ella F. (February 1874-1920/40) married Joel Houston Wade (1861-?) in Clay County October 01, 1892. In 1900/1920, the family lived in Cleburne County, but for sometime lived in Delta, Clay County, where they ran a general store. They had five children: Leona, Russell, Garrett, Stephen, and Joel.

Sarah Jane (March 1876-September 01, 1949 Heflin, Alabama) married Thomas P. McLeroy (1871/2-?) in 1895-6. In 1900, they were living in Randolph County, but by 1910 were in Clay. They had nine children: Myrtle, Henry, Ire, Ina, Estice, Ogden, and Lawrence, Florence, and Albert.

Mary Mag (1877/8-before 1940) married George W. Wilf (1873-?). They had no children. In 1920, they were living in Jackson County, Alabama, where Mary died in February 1935.

Minnie (November 21, 1880-January 19, 1951 Wellington) married John Anderson Key (1880-1951) November 23, 1902 in Clay County. They lived in Randolph County in 1920, but spent most of their life in the Friendship Community of southern Calhoun County where they are buried. They had eleven children: Milton, Martha, Clifford, Delilah, Dervey, William, Franklin, John, James, Christine, and Clyde.

Luther Washington (August 12, 1882-August 20, 1946, Oxford) married Ida Florence Newsome (August 02, 1880-May 17, 1957, Oxford) December 11, 1902, in Clay County. Ida is a first cousin to George Wilf and John Key. Luther and his family moved often, including Delta, Jamback, Pleasant Ridge, and Choccolocco. Around 1910, they moved back to Carrollton for a few years. They are buried at Bethlehem. Luther had nine children: Lois Clark (1903-1961), Ligon (1905-1990), Infant (about 1906), Era Faulkner (1908-), Cleo Bannester Cadenhead (1912-), Homer (1915-1992), Alma (1919-1989), Carl (1920-), and James (1922-1966).

Ida (September 20, 1884-January 31, 1940 Ohatchee) married Emmett Lee Pate (1883-1968) July 27, 1902 in Clay. They both are buried at Mount Zion. They had six children: Aaron, John, Etta Black, Austin, Louisa Medders, and Calvin.

Beulah Estelle (June 06, 1886-December 02, 1979 Oxford) married William Northern Strickland (1885-1967) November 1, 1905, in Clay. They are buried at Oxford, Alabama, Memorial Gardens. They had five children: Janie Miller, Grace Houston, Edna Hubbard, Bernice, and Earnest.

Era Jane Brown, born August 15, 1908, in Delta, Clay County, Alabama, is the granddaughter of John Brown by his son Luther. Era was raised in Clay, Talladega, and Calhoun Counties. On December 13, 1925, Era married Charles Walton Faulkner in Choccolocco Road in Choccolocco, Calhoun County. They raised five children in Choccolocco until January 1, 1936, when Charles was killed in a hunting accident. Their children were: Howard (1927-), Frank (1928-), Lois (1930-), Eloise Lloyd (1931-1999), and Jack (1933-). Era raised her children alone, but with a strong will and

Era Faulkner's 90th birthday, with daughter Lois and her daughters.

hard work they all made it and have families of their own. She now has four living children, fifteen grandchildren, about twenty-five great-grandchildren, and four great-great- grandchildren. Era lived at her home in Choccolocco until 1999, when she moved into the Oxford Senior House where she has her own apartment. At 93, Era walks two or three miles a day, regularly attends church, cooks for many of the disabled (and even younger) neighbors of hers, and enjoys visiting her children. Howard lives in Oxford, Frank in Birmingham, Lois in Marietta, Georgia, and Jack in Winter Haven, Florida.

Audrey Lois Faulkner Glosson is my grandmother. After my grandfather Ralph Spencer Glosson (1926-1998) retired from the Navy in 1970, they moved to Marietta, where she has remained. They have three children: Joan Melhaff (1950-) of Glendale, Arizona; Karen Williams (1959-) of Smyrna, Georgia; and Cherri Garrett (1960-) of Powder Springs, Georgia. I am the son of Karen. The Brown family, as easily seen, still flourishes across the South and the United States, me just being one of the hundreds of proud descendants.

Submitted by: Chad S. Williams, 486 Hurt Road, Smyrna, GA 30082. tw5@prism.gatech.edu

Sources: Tax and census records, tombstones, Bible abstract, family stories.

378. Brown - Angle

Fannin Brown, born in 1785 and died 9 December 1852, is buried in an unmarked grave at Clifton Methodist Cemetery in the Panthersville community of DeKalb County, Georgia. He was in the militia and taught school, and served on the Grand Jury on at least two occasions. He and his first wife were the parents of William S. Brown (Tinzy S.?). The family had lived in Gwinnett and DeKalb Counties, Georgia, through the 1860 census.

William was born about 1805 and died about 1870. Tinzy is buried at the Neal Cemetery in Carroll County, Georgia, on property now owned by Charles Freeman. A Confederate monument has been placed for William. Tinzy's grave is marked with a marble monument. She was born 16 February 1811, they married 11 February 1830 in DeKalb County, Georgia, and she died 16 October 1869. Their children were J. Peter, a Confederate soldier ("Eranny" Arena Carlisle); John W., a Confederate soldier; William A., a Confederate soldier; Martin, a Confederate soldier; Mary; Denson, a Confederate soldier; Joshua, a Confederate soldier; Robert B., a Confederate soldier (Julie E. Angle, daughter of Charles Winston Angle, a Confederate soldier, and his first wife); Emily; Sarah; Martha A.; and Thomas J. Brown.

Robert B. Brown and Julia E. Angle are both buried at Mt. Zion Baptist cemetery just over the Carroll County line in Douglas County, Georgia, on Highway 5 from Whitesburg. Robert B. served with the Wool Hat Boys in the 41st Regiment Infantry, Company B. He fought in the Atlanta campaign. He was a Mason and member of Flint Hill Lodge #371 of Douglas County. They lived in the County Line community. Robert B. was born 15 December 1844 and died 18 May 1916. Julia E. Angle Brown was born 28 March 1852 and died 3 August 1916. They were married on 30 July 1868 in Carroll County. Their children were Sidney "Sid" (George Long), William Winston (Hattie Smith), Joseph Patrick (Annie Bell Houston), Margaret "Mag" A. (Robert Quillon White), Charles T. (Della?), Julia Annie, Mark (Agnes Ivey), Vero (William Wiley Cagle), and Sarah "Sally" Nancy (Allen David Giles).

Joseph Patrick Brown and Annie Bell Houston (second great-granddaughter to Revolutionary War soldier John Houston) were married in Carroll County on 22 December 1895. Joseph Patrick was born 17 June 1871 and died 14 May 1927. He was a Mason and belonged to the Rotherwood Lodge #618 and also a member of the Independent Order of Odd Fellows. Annie Bell was born 7 September 1869 and died 30 November 1942. They both are buried in the Whitesburg, Georgia, cemetery. Their children were Cora Bell (Cicero Elmer Holloway), Seals Askew (Fannie Lucy Moore), Robert Gustus (Lillie Mae Thurman), Evelyn Lee (James Walter Wright), Emma Sue (J. Coy Morrow), and Joe Waymon Brown (Adie Blanche Hubbard).

Robert B. Brown and Julia E. Angle Brown

Joe Waymon Brown was born 19 March 1910 and died 28 November 1963. Addie Blanche was born 6 May 1912 and died 28 February 1998. They were married on 8 June 1928. Both are buried in Oak Hill Cemetery, in Newnan, Georgia. They resided in Whitesburg community until his death. Then she moved to Bay County, Florida, in 1975 where she resided until her death. Their children are Joseph Donald (Mary Lou Green Ridley Hicks), Peggie Ann, Jerry Wayne who married (1) Martha Pope and (2) Norma Jean Whisenhunt Harris, and Ray Elliott Brown (B. Kay Crawford). Ray Elliott Brown and B. Kay Crawford reside in Carrollton and their children are Jennnifer Rebecca, Jonathan Marc (Christina Michele Randles), Joshua Aric, Jasper Kohlby, Jordan Christia (deceased) and Jared Paul Brown.

Jonathan Marc Brown and Christina Michele Randles are the parents of Jacob Marc Brown.

Submitted by: Rebecca Brown, 1319 Crossings Drive, Lithia Springs, GA 30122. Researched and Written by: Ray Elliott Brown

379. William and Mary Orr Bryce / Brice

William Bryce was named a member of the Grand Jury for the first court in Carrollton, Georgia. William is mentioned in the book *Georgia's Last Frontier* by James C. Bonner as being appointed a Commissioner for the Town of Carrollton on 22 December 1829.

William Bryce and Mary Orr Bryce married 13 April 1793 in Ayr, Ayr, Scotland. Their daughter, Agnes was christened 9 February 1794 in Ayr, Ayr. They moved to Lanark, Gorbals, Scotland, and had three more children: Mary born 18 October 1795, Thomas Jimison born 23 July 1797, and Elizabeth christened 19 June 1799.

In 1799 William, Mary and daughters Mary and Elizabeth departed Scotland for the United States, leaving Agnes and Thomas Jimison in Scotland (reason unknown). They settled in Union District (now Columbia), South Carolina and had either eight or nine more children: William, James, John, Robert, Joseph, Ellen/Eleander, Sally/Sarah, and Emily. In October 1808, William filed a petition for citizenship.

In 1825 William and Mary were in DeKalb County, Georgia. They settled near Decatur, Georgia, in a village later called Ingleside. On 29 October 1825, they were co-founders of the present day Decatur Presbyterian Church.

In 1827 William and Mary were in Carroll County, Georgia. In the *Carroll County Abstract of Deed Book A and B 1827-1836* there are numerous entries indicating William was a Justice of the Peace. Five of their sons were with them in Carroll County — Thomas Jimison (who had been left in Scotland), William, James, Robert and Joseph. John Bryce married and remained in Decatur. He apparently visited his family and purchased Land Lot #200, 5th District, on 22 November 1830. *Carroll County and Her People* by Private Joe Cobb states that William and Mary's son James was one of the early white settlers in the county. On 14 May 1829 James and Eleanor Ray Sharp(e) were issued the first marriage license from Carroll County. James, later in life, became an ordained Methodist minister. Five of James' sons became Methodist ministers.

In the 1840 census for Carroll County, the five Bryce brothers — Thomas J., William, James, Robert and Joseph — are all shown as living in Militia District 649, Land District 6. Joseph is listed as head of household and in the home with Joseph is a male between the ages of 70-80 and a female between 60-70. It is suspected this was William and Mary.

Inferior Court minutes in Carrollton indicate that William's will dated 12 August 1837 was recorded 4 January 1841. It is believed William passed away in late 1840.

My search for their final resting place, with the help of cousin Dick Chambers of Villa Rica, led me to the Brice Cemetery in Bremen. I located the graves of Thomas Jimison and his wife. Close to their graves, sunk in the ground, are two plain unmarked stone slabs. I do believe these are the graves of my GGG-grandparents.

Submitted by: Mary Bryce Wilding, 13648 Gordonia Court, Jacksonville, FL 32224

380. Joel Colley Burnham Family

Joel Colley Burnham was born 9 December 1828 in Walton County, Georgia. His parents, Thomas and Frances Manning Burnham, drew land in the 1821 Land Lottery and moved there from Pulaski County, Georgia. While in Walton, Thomas served as road commissioner and Frances was listed as a charter member of the Gum Creek Primitive Baptist Church. They had several children: James Early, William W., Thomas Jefferson, Joel Colley, David and Benjamin.

The Burnhams moved to Heard County, Georgia, some time in the 1830s and settled in the area known as Red Bone to farm the land. Thomas died, leaving Frances a widow. Frances and Joel Colley continued to live in the area in the household of William W. Burnham who had married.

Joel Colley had joined the Baptist Church at Centralhatchee and soon thereafter felt the call to the ministry and was ordained to preach. His first churches were Centralhatchee in Heard County and Enon Grove in Coweta County. He served in the Confederate Army, Company D,

9th Regiment, Georgia Volunteer Infantry, Army of Northern Virginia, C.S.A. He enlisted 11 June 1861 was appointed fifth sergeant and Regimental Chaplain February 1863 and served to the surrender at Appomattox, Virginia, 9 April 1865.

After the war ended, Joel Colley Burnham rejoined his mother in Heard County and shortly afterward married Mary Caroline Jackson, daughter of Reuben and Mary Elizabeth Jackson. At this time they came to Carroll County, according to the 1870 census. He purchased Land Lot Number 2 in the Eleventh District and built a house which was occupied by the Burnham Family for about 150 years. The house was built where the Carrollton to Roopville travel route crossed with the Clem-Lowell-Hubbard Springs travel route. This crossroads made a good place to stop, rest, and water horses at Hubbard Springs which was a short distance west of the route. It became known as "The Burnham Place." As travel increased and modes of travel changed, this travel route was improved and became major thoroughfare for north to south traffic and is today known as U.S. Highway 27.

Joel Colley Burnham with John Shadinger and Isaac McLendon organized Emmaus Primitive Baptist Church in 1871. Mr. Burnham served as the first pastor and was pastor for a number of years. This church is located about two miles west of the Burnham home.

The Burnham House in 1990

The children of Joel Colley and Mary Caroline Burnham were: Viola Frances (North), Robert Lee, Derah Idella (Morgan), Reuben Jackson, Joel Rufus, Sampson, Walter Leonard, Joseph Claudie, Winnie May (Crews). The family farmed and grew cotton, corn, wheat, swine and cattle. After the children were married, all stayed in Carroll County except Reuben Jackson Burnham who went to Alabama to farm.

Joel Colley Burnham died 4 April 1907. Sampson and Joseph Claudie Burnham bought the farm, lived in the house and cared for their mother until her death 26 January 1919. Joel Colley, Mary Caroline, and his mother Frances, who was more than 100 years when she died, are buried at Emmaus Primitive Baptist Church Cemetery.

Sampson, who never married, and Joseph Claudie Burnahm, who married Minnie Moore, continued to farm until Sampson's death 17 October 1948. Joseph Claudie farmed for ten more years until his health declined. He died 20 April 1964.

Joseph Claudie's widow, Minnie Moore Burnham, kept the home place and family members lived there until she died on 22 June 1998 at the age of 102 years, nine months and six days. The three daughters of Joseph Claudie and Minnie Moore Burnham kept the farm until construction project of four laning U.S. Highway 27 and widening and relocating the connecting roads were completed. The farm was sold in December 2000. This closed the era of "The Burnham Place." *Submitted by: Rudene B. Hollingsworth, 2272 Highway 27 South, Carrollton, GA 30117*

Sources: Family Bible, family papers, census records, church records, *Wayfarers in Walton* by Anita B. Sams, *History of Heard County 1830-1900* and *Roster of the Confederate Soldiers of Georgia.*

381. Burns Family

Carroll County census of 1850 is the first listing found for James W. Burns, (teacher, later becoming a farmer) Bowdon, Carroll County, Georgia. Also listed were: Samuel Burns, farmer (father) age 51; Jane (Morris) Burns (mother) age 39; James W. Burns, teacher age 21; Mary J. and Martha (twins) age 18; Jubey E. Burns age 14; Samuel T. Burns age 12; Benjamin F. Burns age 10; Joseph T. Burns age 8; Marion W. Burns age 6; Ezeckiel C. Burns age 4; Margaret B. Burns age 2; Charles H. Burns age 5/12.

Son of Samuel and Jane (Morris) Burns, born in Florida on December 19, 1838. His grandfather on his father's side, James Burns, came from Ireland to the United States early in 1800s, settled in North Carolina and was a soldier in the War of 1812. He was a near relative of the poet Robert Burns. In 1835, he came to Georgia, settled and cleared a farm in Henry County. Some years subsequently, he came to Carroll County, Georgia, and settled. Mr. Burns' father was born in Ireland in 1804, came to this country with his father James, and with the family from North Carolina to Georgia. His grandparents on his mother's side, William and Hannah Morris, were natives of Virginia. They came to Georgia and made their home in DeKalb County, being among the county's earliest settlers. Mr. Burns was reared on the farm, received only a limited education obtainable between "laying by" and "fodder-pulling time" at the old-time schoolhouse two and one-half miles away. In early manhood he taught school for two years.

In 1861, he enlisted in Company E (Captain James Blalock) 1st Georgia Calvary. For a while he was with General Forrest and afterward with General Wheeler. To have been with either of these generals means he saw as much continuous, hard service and bore a part in as much hard fighting as anyone during the war. He was in the battles of Perryville, Murfreesboro, Chickamauga, Missionary Ridge, and Franklin; was with Johnston and Hood all the way to Atlanta; under Wheeler made the raid all the way to Nashville; was with the forces that harassed Sherman when he marched through Georgia. While in the service, he was sergeant of his company. After the war, he returned to Georgia.

Mr. Burns was married 1865 to Miss Elizabeth F. Moore, born Henry County, Georgia, daughter of Harrison Moore, a native of Georgia who moved from Henry to Carroll County and who, though starting poor, lived to be rich. To the happiness of this household eleven children were added — nine of whom are living — Sarah J., Lula, James M. Jr., Beulah, Benjamin L., Samuel Harrison, Ed, Katie and Joseph. After his marriage, he began life without a dollar but by hard work, economy, and good management he has accumulated a fine property, including 1,000 acres of excellent land with an improved farm and a delightful home in Bowdon. He is solid, substantial and popular. Mrs. Burns is a member of the Missionary Baptist Church.

Samuel Harrison Burns, my grandfather, and son of James W. and Elizabeth F. Moore, was born October 8, 1878, died February 12, 1970, buried Carroll Memory Gardens, Carroll County, Georgia. Married Susan Harriett Sewell (Susie) daughter of Milton Newton Sewell and Nancy Delaney Watson, born October 1, 1880, in Cherokee County, Alabama, died August 13, 1968, Carroll County, Georgia.

Of this union, eight children were born: (1) William (Roy) born December 22, 1904, died May 3, 1994, in Augusta, Georgia. (2) Robert Milton Burns Sr. (my father) born July 4, 1906, in Carroll County, Georgia, died December 22, 1974, Carroll County, and buried Carroll Memory Gardens. December 1, 1935, Robert was married to Buvena Holder of Carroll County. (3) George Harris Burns born 1907 in Carroll County, died 1980 in Carroll County, buried Carroll Memory Gardens. On December 31, 1933 in Carroll County, he was married to Mary Chappell. (4) Nell Burns born in Carroll County, and died in Carroll County, buried Carroll Memory Gardens. (5) Sarah Burns born Carroll County and is now living in Carroll County, married to Walter McGarrity. (6) Miriam Burns was born January 11, 1914, in Carroll County, died August 1, 1999, Carroll County, married to Lewis H. Hamm. (7) Racheal Burns born Carroll County, died July 1998 in Ohio, married John S. (Rich) Richardson. (8) Howard Millard Burns born 1922 Carroll County, and November 1974 buried Carroll Memory Gardens. On July 2, 1952, he was married to Dorothy (Helen) Pentecost in Carroll County.

Some of my fondest childhood memories revolve around visits to my grandparent's home and having my granddaddy come for a visit at the dairy farm on which I grew up. I recall spending the summer with my grandmother, along with my sister Sylvia and my cousin Marie, during my grandfather's stay in the hospital.

Robert Milton Burns Sr. and Buvena Holder Burns (born October 15, 1910, Carroll County, Georgia, daughter of William Ludie and Ida Beatrice Holder, died March 29, 1997, in Carroll County, buried Carroll Memory Gardens) (my parents). Their children were: (1) Judith Marie Burns born November 27, 1936; (2) Steve Benton Burns born March 3, 1939; (3) Robert Milton Burns Jr. born May 12, 1941; (4) James Donald Burns born December 4, 1942; (5) Carol Dianne Burnes born March 11, 1945; (6) Sylvia Joan Burns born December 16, 1946; (7) David Harry Burns born February 1, 1949.

My children are Melissa Dianne Woodard born September, 1964, and Eric Gerald Woodard born May 27, 1970.

My granddaughter Kayla Whitney Gilbert born June 27, 1988 to Melissa Dianne Woodard Gilbert and Kyle Clarence Gilbert born June 20, 1963. *Submitted by: Carol Dianne Burns Whitley*

382. The Burns Family

James W. Burns was born 19 December 1838 in Florida, the son of Samuel Burns and Jane Morris. The paternal grandfather of James W. Burns came from Ireland to America early in the 1800s, settling in North Carolina, and served as a soldier in the War of 1812. This immigrant ancestor was a near relative of the poet Robert Burns. In 1835 James W. Burns' grandfather came to Georgia settling in Henry County where he established a large plantation. He came to Carroll County in 1880.

James W. Burns' maternal Grandfather Morris was born in Ireland in 1804 and came to America with his father, settling in North Carolina. Later, the family would migrate to Georgia. William and Hannah Morris, the maternal grandparents of James B. Burns, were natives of Virginia who were some of the earliest pioneer settlers to DeKalb County, Georgia.

James W. Burns was reared on the farm and received only limited education obtained between the "laying by" and "fodder pulling" times of the crops. The old-time schoolhouse that he attended was about two and one-half miles from his home. But he must have received a good education because he returned in his early manhood to teach at the same school that he had attended as a child. He was a farmer most of his life, but he taught school for two years as well.

In 1861, James W. Burns enlisted in Company E, 1st Georgia Cavalry, under the command of Captain James Blalock. He was given the rank of sergeant. Later, Burns served under Forrest and Wheeler. To have been with either of these generals meant that he saw as much continuous hard service and bore a part in as much hard fighting as any soldier in the war. Burns was engaged in battles of Perryville, Murfreesboro, Chickamauga, Missionary Ridge, and Franklin. He was with Johnston and Hood all the way to Atlanta and was with the forces that harassed Sherman when he made his march across Georgia.

After the war, James W. Burns returned to Georgia and married Elizabeth F. Moore in 1865. Elizabeth was born in Henry County, Georgia, and was the daughter of Harrison Moore, a native of Henry County. It was said of Elizabeth's father that even though he started out poor in life, he worked hard and lived to obtain great wealth.

James W. Burns Famly, 1900

Eleven children were born to James W. Burns and Elizabeth F. Moore. They were Sarah J., Lula, James M., Beulah, Benjamin L., Samuel H., Ed, Katie, and Joseph. Two other children must have died early and the names are unknown.

Of James W. Burns, it is said that he "started life without a dollar, but by hard work, economy, and good management, he accumulated a fine property." The Burns owned a farm of one thousand acres at Bowdon, Georgia. Mrs. Burns belonged to the Missionary Baptist Church at Bowdon. In 1886 at a meeting at the old courthouse in Carrollton, James W. Burns and Lindsley Holland were elected to be candidates for the Georgia House of Representatives. *Submitted by: Gayle Burns, 607 Burns Road, Carrollton, GA 30117*

383. John J. Burrow

John J. Burrow was born April 6, 1806, in Wilkes County, Georgia, to Phillip Burrow Sr. and Leah (unknown). His siblings were Elizabeth, Nancy, Mary, Priscilla, Sarah, William, Leah Celia, Phillip Jr., Martha Lucinda, and Cynthia.

John married Amanda Frances Fretwell, daughter of William and Ann Fretwell, on December 6, 1832, in Pike County, Georgia (See related Phillip Burrow Sr. article). Children born to John and Amanda were Elizabeth Leah (October 19, 1836, married John Steven Earnest); Phillip J. (1839, married Mary Sophonia McKissack); Julia A. (1843, married Elisha C. Coleman); Francis Ann (1845, married Elijah H. McPherson); Martha Jane (1848, married Walter S. Entrekin); John William (March 22, 1849, married Ophelia Hill Overton); James Daniel (1851, married Eliza Jane Weir); and Amanda (August 5, 1854, married Oscar Freeman). They lived between Carroll County, Georgia, and LaFayette County, Mississippi, from 1836 to 1853. John is recorded as an attestor on a deed in Carroll County in 1837. After his mother died in October 1849, John's father married John's wife's mother, Ann Fretwell, on November 18, 1850, in Carroll County. When his father died in July 1853, John and his brother William acted as administrators of their father's estate. These papers state:

> "Advancements made to John J. Burrow: 202 ½ acres of land @$250.00; one horse @ $60.00; 2 cows and calves @ $20.00." He received a male slave, Warren, as his share of the inheritance. The slave was valued at $1,050.74.

In 1860-61 the husband of John's daughter, Elizabeth, built a large log house in Bowdon. (This house was moved to Bowdon Junction; it still stands and is owned by Wallace Lambert). John's son Phillip J. served in Company H, 56th Regiment, Georgia Volunteer Infantry Army during the Civil War. Phillip J., a private, was captured at Baker's Creek, Mississippi, on May 16, 1863. Died at Fort Delaware, Delaware, November 26, 1863. John moved to Alabama and died there April 20, 1888, in Randolph County. *Submitted by: Grace Presswood Light, 508 Turner Avenue SE, Apt. 218, Fort Payne, AL 35967 and Written by: Elizabeth Light. lightelizabeth@hotmail.com*

384. Phillip Burrow Jr.

Phillip Burrow Jr. was a descendant from a family line that first came to America about 1660 with the arrival of Philip Burrow. Phillip was born on January 13, 1812, the son of Phillip Burrow Sr. and Leah Burrow, in Jones County, Georgia. He was married to Theresa J. Morris on April 30, 1832, in Pike County, Georgia. While in Pike County, Phillip was listed in the 1832 Cherokee Land Lottery. In the mid 1830s, Phillip and Theresa moved with his family into Carroll County where they made their living as farmers. In the 1841 Carroll County Tax Digest, Phillip was listed as being in the 9th District and 754 Military District. Phillip was also listed as having 202½ acres; Lot 174.

Phillip and Theresa had eight children: Matilda born April 26, 1835; Savannah born February 2, 1837; Phillip born March 6, 1839; Sarah born April 9, 1841; Banks born March 9, 1843; William born May 23, 1845; John B. born December 27, 1847; and Augustus born September 7, 1850.

Phillip died on May 8, 1850, at the age of thirty-eight and is buried in Carroll County, Georgia, leaving his wife and children. Theresa continued to farm the property under the security of James G. Davenport, a relative. *Submitted by: Jerry Burrow, 237 Skyline Drive, Russellville, AL 35653. jeedbu@aol.com*

385. Phillip Burrow Sr.

Phillip Burrow/Burrough Sr. was born in 1770 in Dinwiddie County, Virginia, to Phillip Burrow and Martha Littlefield. His siblings were Ismael, Sterling, Ephraim, Frances, Martha (Patsy), Mary (Polly), James, and Banks Burrow. Phillip married Leah Unknown (thought to be Banks, Burr or Jones) about 1793, possibly in North Carolina. Leah was reported to have been born circa 1774 in Maryland, parents unknown. Deed records show Phillip owned land there in South Guilford County on Stinking Quarter Creek. Born to them through the next twenty-five years were Elizabeth (1792) who married James W. Kelley, Nancy (1796) who married (? Green) Berry Hammock, Mary (1797) who married William McKissack, Priscilla (circa 1799) who married William Turrentine, Sarah (1804) who married Reuben Phillips, John James (1806) who married Amanda F. Fretwell (see related John J. Burrow article), William Burrow (circa 1808) who married Eliza Unknown, Leah Sewly (1810) who married Dennis McClendon, Phillip Jr. (about 1812) married Theresa J. Morris, Martha Lucinda (1816) married Archibald McKissack, and Cynthia (1820) married Isham Helton.

They moved to Wilkes County, Georgia, about 1805 where Phillip is listed as testator for John Bush on March 10, 1805. Deed records show Phillip Burrow in Jones County, Georgia, in 1809. They are on the 1820 census there. There are five deeds for him, acres not stated. Six deeds show his disposal of his property, with a total of 317 acres (acreage is not cited on one deed). They soon moved to Pike County, Georgia, where Phillip Sr. appeared on a list of the land lot grantees for the western half of Monroe County, which became Pike County in 1822. Deed records between 1830 and 1838 show Phillip Sr. selling a total of 1,586 acres of land in Pike County. His name begins to appear in Carroll County, Georgia, by 1837. He was sixty-eight years old that year. He and his wife are on the 1840 census in Carroll County in District 714, ages 70-80 and 60-70. They owned seven slaves and considerable property. His married sons, John, William, and Phillip Jr. are also found in records there. In 1847 he sold three acres of land in land lot 179 in the 10th District to the trustees of the Methodist Episcopal Church South and was remembered in a son-in-law's history as an elder in the Methodist Church. Two interesting deeds were found between Phillip and his daughters, Sintha Helton and Nancy Hammock, which shows concern for them. On March 9, 1846, Sintha was given three slaves

> "in consideration of the love and goodwill that I bear for and towards my beloved daughter ... and her children ... without any contract or management of the slaves by her present or any future husband or any incumbrances, benefit or sue to the same by or on account of her present or future husband."

On February 28, 1848, Nancy was given land lot 206 in the 10th District

> "for and in consideration of the love and good will which I bear to my beloved daughter ... and her son-in-law James Davenport ... to hold in trust ... during her natural life and for her use and benefit during that time, and at her death the same to go to ... James Davenport and his heirs ..."

Phillip's wife, Leah Burrow, died in October 1849 at age seventy-five. Phillip shows up on the 1850 census alone. However, he married the widow Ann Fretwell on November 18, 1850. One tradition says that Phillip sent his son John to Mississippi to get John's mother-in-law to come marry him. Carroll County court records show entries for medical expenses in March, April, and May 1853 for Ann. May 21st purchases indicate she had died. According to doctor visits and medicines recorded in these same court documents, he died about July 21, 1853. Phillip Burrow Sr. and his wives were buried in Carroll County, Georgia, "out near Mt. Zion and I have seen this grave," according to an eyewitness (1961). They are thought to be in the same church yard he had deeded to the Methodists in 1847. The congregation had ultimately split and went two ways. The building was moved to Shiloh in Burwell. All that remains are the graves and it is now called the Holmes Cemetery, located on north Davenport Mill Road. Phillip Burrow Sr. was a well-to-do farmer in his day with considerable property including a gristmill and nine slaves when he died. The slaves went to his children along with other property and money. His estate papers show that his children, Elizabeth and Phillip Jr., preceded him in death. Phillip Burrow Sr.'s father, Phillip Burrow, and the rest of the family settled in Carroll County, Tennessee. This Phillip Burrow died November 11, 1829, in Carroll County, Tennessee. Only Phillip Sr. and his children lived in Carroll County, Georgia. *Submitted by: Elizabeth Light, 508 Turner Avenue SE, Apt. 218, Ft. Payne, AL 35967 and Written by: Pauline McConkie Derhak from Elizabeth Light's research. LightElizabeth@hotmail.com.*

386. Aubrey Drayton Callaway

My grandmother Emmaline Catherine Gaston born April 2, 1883, in Carrollton, Georgia, married first Zebedee (Dee) Frank Rooks on March 30, 1902. He passed away about 1904 and is buried at Old Camp United Methodist Church Cemetery. She married second time to William David Gaston on April 13, 1913. Among their children was my mother, Lena Brilla Gaston, who married Aubrey Clarence Callaway. They had only one child, me, Aubrey Drayton Callaway.

Drayton married Susan Carol Boleman, daughter of William Desmond and Nell Mae Hicken Boleman Sr. Carol and I moved to Carroll County in 1974 after my parents and uncle moved here. Carol's brother, William Desmond (Bill) Jr. and Maxine Boleman moved here in 1982. Her parents moved here in May 1985. I continued to work for the City of College Park Fire and Police Departments until I retired in 1996. At this time, I went to work for Carroll County Board of Commissioners Magistrate Court as a constable. I also worked for the City of Bowdon Police Department as a dispatcher. Carol worked at T.G.&Y. Department Store and West Georgia Micrographics. She is now a homemaker. We were foster parents for Carroll County from January 1977 until October 2000. We fostered many children, seven of whom we adopted. Those adopted were Glenn, David, Robin, Christina (Christy), Crystal, Charlie, and Kelly Callaway. Glenn passed away at the age of thirty on May 26, 1997. He had one child Nicholas Cody. Robin has three children, Austin, Sebriana, and Briteny.

Bill and Maxine Boleman's daughter, Anna Michelle Shoemake, lives in Carroll County. Lisa Marie Hinson lives in South Carolina.

Desmond and Nell Boleman commuted to Atlanta until they retired. Nell has a half-brother, Ferney Hicken, who lived in Carroll County for several years.

Our fathers, Aubrey C. Callaway and William D. Boleman Sr., served in World War II. Bill Boleman and I served in the Vietnam conflict. *Submitted by: Drayton and Carol Callaway, 120 Hilley Road, Whitesburg, GA 30185-2226*

387. Cammon Family

The Cammon Family came to Roopville, Georgia, from Coweta County, Georgia, after 1880. Robert and Joe Cammon are listed in the 1880 Coweta County census, Hurricane District, with their mother Sarah. Three sons are all that are known: John P. married Jane Ellen Phillips, Joseph Isaac married Margaret Elizabeth Phillips (sister of Jane Ellen), and James Robert married (1) Emma Black, (2) Nannie Widner. All three brothers were farmers and listed in the 1910 Carroll County census.

James Robert, born 1851 and died 1919, was married to (1) Emma Black and (2) Nannie Widner. Their children were Ezra who married Ethel Williamson, Glenn B. who married (1) Alice and (2) Margarette, Otis who married Kate Wynn, John R., Ollie M., Joseph Young who married Eula Belle Thornton, Wymon Seal who married Charlotte, James who married Nancy Lois Puckett, Bessie P. who married Nicholson, Estella, Emily, and Leonard L. who married Pearl Farmer.

John P., born 1852 and died 1919, married Jane Ellen Phillips 3 January 1878. They had Robert L. who married Nora Freel, Julie M. who married Samuel E. Carroll, Jennie Lee who married Allen L. Striplin, Eafrom F. who married Emma Freel, Orange (Dock) who married Cora Wymen, Ray B. who married Grace Hammond, and Howard who married Doshie Shelnutt.

Joseph Isaac, born 1856 and died 1923, married Margaret Elizabeth Phillips March 1888. They had Ella who married Luther Beck, Nellie Sue who married Claude Carroll, Arrie M. (died young), Elizabeth (died young), William David who married Claucie Kelley, Geneva who married L. Gaines Kelley, and James Herman who married Lenora Rogers.

These family members are buried in local cemeteries. The husband of Sarah is not known. Tennessee Land Grants have been located in Tennessee under the names of Isaac and Samuel, but no evidence of descendancy exits.

Joseph and Margaret Elizabeth Cammon family

Shown in the family picture are David, Joseph Isaac, Ella Cammon Beck, Margaret Elizabeth and baby Nellie Sue, with Elizabeth standing in front. *Submitted by: James Kelley, 485 Buncombe Road, Waco, GA 30132*

Sources: Coweta and Carroll County censuses, cemetery and marriage records, tax records, and personal acquaintance.

388. Camp Family

Andrew Camp born 1779, and his son Wesley born 1804, came to what is now Carroll County in 1825 while the Creek Indians were still here. They settled land when Carroll County was created in 1826. They were in the land lottery. They settled several hundred acres on the Chattahooche River. Wesley built a large house overlooking the Chattahooche River in 1869.

Andrew married Nancy Maddox of Henry County. She was born 1780. He died in 1853 in Carroll County. Nancy died after 1850 and is buried in Camp Family Cemetery in Carroll County.

Wesley Camp, Andrew's son, married Mariah "Molly" Lassetter, daughter of Benjamin and Elizabeth Lassetter, in DeKalb County in 1823. She was born in 1805 and died in 1893. Wesley died in 1873. Both were buried in Camp Family Cemetery in Carroll County. (see related Lassetter article).

His six sons were all in the Confederate Army. All returned, but one.

Walter Camp, youngest son of Wesley, was born in 1847 died in 1904. He married Mary Jane Barron, born in 1851 and died in 1919. She was the daughter of Oliver Gaines and Clementine Barron. They are both buried in Camp Family Cemetery.

Eunice Camp, seventh child of Walter and Molly, was born in 1883 and died in 1946. She married Ernie Rooks, son of Allen Jackson and Ellen Edgeworth Rooks, in 1912. Ernie was born in 1878 and died in 1943. Eunice died in 1946. Both are buried at Mt. Zion Baptist Church in Douglas County.

Thelma Rooks, born 1913, is the only child of Eunice and Ernie. She married Jack Pate, born in 1918 in Carroll County. He is the son of Will and Viola Clark Pate. They married in 1940. They have three sons: (1) William, born 1943, married Jean Smith Barn in 1948. They have two daughters, Jodi Pate Foster and Brook Pate; (2) Danny Pate, born 1946, married Judy Holloway Moore. They have one son, John Pate, born in 1985; (3) and Larry Pate, born 1951, married Jackie Bagwell.

Our sons and their families live near us. There has not been a time since the Camps settled here in 1826 that a direct line of mine has not lived within a mile of the Camp home place. *Submitted by: Thelma Pate, 199 Old Five Notch Road, Whitesburg, GA 30185*

389. L.J.M. and Henrietta Yeager Camp

Our grandmother was Frances Marcell Camp Lyle and this is background on the Camp family which dates back to Nasing County, Essex, England. Frances (Fanny) Marcell Camp Lyle was married to Gus Tavus Lyle. They lived in the Lowell community and had six children. The children were Irving Lyle, Lester Lyle, Claude Lyle, Willie Maude Lyle Mote, Eunice Lyle Duncan, and Elsie Lyle Jackson.

Frances was the only child of Louis Jefferson Mordica Camp and Henrietta Yager (Yeager) Camp. (see Elisha Yeager Family).

Louis Jefferson Mordica Camp was born in Randolph County, Alabama, in 1843. He enlisted in the Confederate Army on July 19, 1863, at Carrollton, Georgia, and served as a private in Company B, 7th Confederate Cavalry which later became Company B, 10th Georgia Cavalry, C.S.A. under General Wade Hampton. He received his parole in May 1865 at Greensbourgh (Greensboro), North Carolina, in accordance with terms of military convention of April 26, 1865.

L.J.M. and Henrietta Yeager Camp

L.J.M. Camp was the son of Seaborn Moore Camp and Agnes Grace Nolen. Seaborn was born in 1810 in Jackson County, Georgia, and died in 1888 in Arab, Alabama, at the home of his daughter Sarah E. Rigsby. He married Agnes Grace Nolen, born in 1814 in Georgia, daughter of George Nolen of Henry County, Georgia. They settled in Henry County, Georgia, and later moved to Butts County, Georgia. Thirteen children were born from this marriage. While a young man, Seaborn lived in Henry County and farmed for a while, but later served as overseer for the famous W.H. Grier, author of Griers Almanac. He named his third son William Harrison Grier in honor of his employer. In his later years Seaborn moved to Heard County where he was a millwright, a cabinet maker of rare accomplishments, and with his own hands, without the aid of machinery, manufactured wagons, buggies, farming tools, tables, chairs, tubs, and almost any article used in homes in that age that could be made of wood.

Seaborn was the son of Burwell (Burrell) Camp and Elizabeth (Betsy) Moore who were married in 1799. Burwell was born in 1784 in South Carolina. Betsy was the daughter of Signor Moore of Laurens County, South Carolina. Burwell and Betsy had four sons and two daughters. From the records at the National Archives Burwell Camp served in the War of 1812 under General Jackson when he met and defeated Lord Packingham at New Orleans, Louisiana. He received 40 acres under the Act of September 28, 1850, and 120 acres on April 26, 1856, under the Act of March 3, 1855, for his service in the War of 1812. He died in 1862 at the home of his son Seaborn Camp in Carroll County, Ga.

Burwell Camp was the son of Thomas Camp and Nancy Anne Tarpley. Thomas was born in 1747 in Orange County, Virginia, died in 1811 in what is now Walton County, Georgia, and was buried in Old Bethlehem Cemetery in an unmarked grave. He married his cousin, once removed, Nancy Anne Tarpley, daughter of James Tarpley and Mary Camp. They had seven children. Records on file in the National Archives show that Thomas Camp enlisted in the 4th Artillery Regiment of South Carolina on February 14, 1776.

The descendants of Frances and Gus Lyle were as follows: (1) Irving (Ruth Crews). They had one daughter Rachel (Richard St. John). (2) Lester (Gwynne Meigs). Their children are Mary (Elbert Wood), Bill (May Holland, deceased), Kenneth (Betty Kenerly), and Elton (Virginia Webb). (3) Claude (Ruby Entrekin). Their children are Winton (deceased) (Syble Parker) and Jimmy (Janice Rooks). (4) Eunice (Brown Duncan). Their children are Opal (Price Lewis, deceased), (Wood, deceased), Brownie (Chuck Shelly), Clarice (Jimmy Alexander), Charles (Joyce Patterson), Gloria (Benny Eidson), Roy Irvin (deceased), Calvin Sewell (deceased). (5) Willie Maude (Oscar Mote). Their children are Harold (Norma Dorsey), Sybil (Guy Landers), Vivian (Roy Shuman, deceased), Hazel (Max Grist), Joyce (Sheldon Brown, deceased), and Selby (deceased). (6) Elsie (Render Jackson). Their children are Martha (Harry Hughes), Charlotte (Sam Ashmore, deceased), Nevin (Roberta Jones), and Grace (Jimmy Redding). *Submitted by: Charles Duncan (grandson) - Member SCV - McDaniel Curtis Camp 165, Carrollton, GA and Researched by: Sherilyn Ashmore Sarff (great granddaughter); Compiled by Grace Jackson Redding (granddaughter)*

390. Samuel Charles Candler

Samuel Charles Candler was one of the original settlers of Carroll County. He was born in Columbus County, Georgia, in 1809. He died in Villa Rica, Georgia, November 13, 1873. He first came to Carroll County in 1828 as the local representative of a gold mining company. He left briefly to go to Cherokee County during the gold rush there. He met Martha Bernetta Beall, married her on December 8, 1833, and brought her back to Villa Rica where they lived the remainder of their lives.

He soon gave up prospecting and opened the first store of general merchandise in the new town. He bought land and laid it out in lots for sale to prospective residents. Over the years he acquired a great deal of land and was a very successful farmer. He served as state senator from Carroll County several times. His wife Martha was a feisty little woman who used a shotgun to keep the Yankees from invading her home.

Samuel and Martha had eight sons and three daughters. Historians say that these were the most outstanding children produced by one family in the history of Georgia. Milton and Ezekiel were well-known lawyers. John was a judge of the State Supreme Court of Georgia. Warren became a Bishop in the Methodist Church and president of Emory College at Oxford which later was moved to Atlanta and became Emory University. Probably the most widely known of Samuel's sons was Asa who founded the Coca-Cola Company.

Of all Samuel and Martha's children, only two stayed in Carroll County. One was Samuel Charles Jr. who started out as a large scale planter in Carroll County, but in the early 1900s moved to Florida where he died.

The other son who stayed in Carroll County was William Beall Candler, commonly known as W.B. He was born January 1, 1847, and died April 6, 1928. He is buried in Hillcrest Cemetery in Villa Rica. He was the eighth child and fifth son of Samuel and Martha. W.B. married Martha Elizabeth Slaughter on January 19, 1891. She was the daughter of Dr. John Thomas Slaughter. They lived in Villa Rica all their lives.

Eight sons of Samuel Charles Candler. 1891

At the death of his father in 1873, it fell W.B.'s lot to look after the family estate. He not only looked after it, but expanded it. He became a merchant, farmer, banker, undertaker and a large land owner in the Villa Rica area. He credited farmers for seed and fertilizer in the spring and collected when the crops came in. Much of his time was spent driving his horse and buggy from farm to farm to visit his clients.

W.B. was instrumental in founding the Bank of Villa Rica in 1899, the first bank in Carroll County. He became its first president. While buying cotton from farmers, he saw the need of processing it at home and was a leading factor in organizing cotton gins, an oil mill, and a cotton mill. Later with the addition of a hosiery mill, these were combined into Villa Rica Mills, Inc. W.B. was president of this corporation until his death.

W.B. was an elder and Clerk of Session of Villa Rica Presbyterian Church from 1885 until his death in 1928. On Sunday afternoons he traveled out into the countryside to teach Bible stories to groups of children. He believed in keeping the Sabbath Day holy. One Sunday on his way to church, he saw carnival workers setting up their tents for a show. He stopped, told them, "We don't work in this town on Sundays," and he spoke with enough authority that they waited until Monday to set up!

W.B. and Elizabeth had three daughters and a son. The daughters moved away after they married, but their son William Beall Jr., known as Will, remained in Carroll County. Will was born May 26, 1879, in the Old Town section of Villa Rica. He died November 21, 1972, and is buried in Hillcrest Cemetery in Villa Rica. At his father's death, Will sold the store for he disliked the merchandise business. He kept the land and farmed it until World War II when the lack of laborers forced him to sell it. He followed in his father's footsteps in the other businesses. He became president of Villa Rica Mills Inc. and chairman of the board at the Bank of Villa Rica. He also became clerk of Session of the Villa Rica Presbyterian Church.

Will married Margaret Cobb in 1900 and they had five daughters and one son. Three of the daughters married and moved away. Two, Anne and Lucy, became teachers at Villa Rica High School. Anne Candler Anders was well known in Carroll County and beyond for her winning girls basketball teams and the gym at Villa Rica High School is named Anne Anders Gym in her honor.

Will and Margaret's only son William Cobb Candler, known as Bill, was born in Villa Rica in 1914. Bill still lives in Carroll County. He is a veteran of World War II and has been active all his life in community affairs. He has been an active supporter of all phases of athletic programs in the schools and community. He is a charter member of the Villa Rica Lions Club. He also was chairman of the board at the Bank of Villa Rica (now Regions Bank of Villa Rica). He is an Elder Emeritius of the First Presbyterian Church PCA of Villa Rica and still participates in church activities.

He married Elizabeth Hairston in 1941 and they have two daughters and one son, all of whom live in Carroll County. Their only son, William James Candler, has three daughters so he is the last direct male descendant of Samuel Charles Candler living in Carroll County who carries the surname Candler.

The accompanying photograph made in 1891 shows the eight sons of Samuel Charles Candler. Standing are John, Charles, Asa, and William. Seated are Warren, Milton, Mrs. Candler, and Ezekiel. *Submitted by: Elizabeth H. Candler, 3062 East Highway 166, Carrollton, GA 30116*

391. Sarah and Harriett Cannon

George W. Cannon married Mary Elliott in Pike County in 1832. Their children were Stephen, Margaret, Sarah, Harriett, Benedia, Augustus, Benjamin Franklin, and George W. George W. Jr. was in the 53rd Georgia Infantry Regiment during the Civil War. Sarah married Henry Parker and Harriett married Thomas N. Entrekin who was also in the 53rd Georgia. Sarah and Henry Parker, along with Harriett and Thomas Entrekin, moved to Carroll County after the Civil War. Thomas and Harriett lived near Henry and Sarah in the Holly Springs, Harmony Methodist Church area and then moved on the Mt. Zion - Jake Road. Thomas and Harriett's children were George W., John F., Augusta, Jones B., Sallie, and Henrietta.

Sarah Cannon Parker, daughter Lela, grandchildren Homer and Verdie Wallace

Henry and Sarah's children were Harriett who married Wilbur Wallace (parents of Homer and Verdie pictured with Sarah and Lela), James, Mary B., Henry Steve who married Kate Casey (they were parents of Avis who married Grady Brock), George H., Sarah E., Ella, Lela (pictured with her mother) who married Van Kierbow (their sons are Glenn and Carlos), and Martha.

Harriett died in 1904 and Homer and Verdie Wallace, her grandchildren, lived with her much of the time until their father Wilbur Wallace remarried Harriett's first cousin, Molly Prince.

Van Kierbow was killed by a falling tree. Carlos lives on the land that Sarah and Henry farmed. Henry had lost a leg during the Civil War and Carlos remembers playing with his wooden peg leg when he was a young boy. *Submitted by: Wilbur Wallace, Mandeville Lane, Bowdon Junction, GA*
Source: Wallace T. Lambert

392. The Cantrell and Couch Families

David Cantrell was born about 1810 at Greenville, South Carolina. David and two sons, Merrick (born 4 August 1840) and Perry (born 1843), were living at Sand Hill, Carroll County, per 1860 census. Merrick served as a private in the Confederate Army, Company D, 14th Battalion, Georgia Light Artillery.

After the Civil War, Merrick married Ellen Couch (born 29 December 1846), daughter of John Couch (born 8 July 1815) and Nancy Manly (born 21 March 1818). They farmed near Macedonia Baptist Church near Smithfield community in Carroll County. John was the second pastor at Macedonia Baptist Church. Merrick and Ellen raised ten children. Thomas T. Cantrell (born 31 January 1883), their ninth child, is my granddad.

Jeanette Cantrell Capes and Christine Cantrell Gay, granddaughters of Merrick Cantrell.

Farming was a major part of their lives, but his first job was driving a freight ox wagon. He and the other drivers would haul lumber from Pull-Tight Ridge to the rail head at Carrollton, Georgia. They would leave early Monday morning, then camp at a spring just east of the Tallapoosa River for the night. When they reached the rail head, they would unload the lumber and start home. Once home, they would load for the next Monday's trip.

Big Papa and Violia Harris (born 19 February 1888) were married 20 November 1904, and he returned to farming. They bought their home with fifty acres near Pleasant Grove and remained there the rest of their lives. There they raised two children, Pauline Martin and Christine Gay, and helped to raise three grandchildren, Sybil Batchelor, Ruth Batchelor, and Tommy Martin, when Pauline died at a young age.

They raised cotton and corn until the early 1950s. Of course, as the practice was in those days, T.T. would follow a mule from sunrise to sunset to get his crops planted and harvested. Everyone joined in for fall cotton picking. Besides raising enough food in the garden for canning, T.T. gathered honey and had a blacksmith shop.

T.T. contracted with Elmer Cason to build a commercial chicken house. Dewey and Clyde Gibbs supplied them with chickens and feed until 1960. If anyone ever remarked about the odor from the chicken houses, Violia would comment, "Oh, that just smells like money to me."

Violia was the third child of James Monroe Harris (1859) and Elizabeth Ann Phillips (1861). The story was told that J.M. was kidnapped in Atlanta, Georgia, as a lad of nine and brought to Cleburne County to work on the farm. J.M. liked Cleburne so well that he never returned home. My grandmother (Violia) was one of the nine charter members of the Crumbleys Chapel Church of God (1909). She, with her sisters (also charter members), Hattie Williamson and Essie White, sang together as the Harris Trio. Violia exhibited her faith in God on the day she was swinging her twin grandchildren, Betty Ann and Billy Joe Gay, on the front porch. The swing broke dumping everyone out and breaking Violia's arm in the fall. She wrapped the broken arm in a Church of God Evangel, never sought medical treatment, and the arm healed without complications. Violia always cooked a big breakfast, enough for the household and visiting grandchildren who would stop in for midmorning buttered biscuits with jelly. Besides the great love for her grandchildren, she had a special love for flowers and potted plants. Passers-by would see pots lined up on the front porch in summertime. She planted azaleas around her front porch that they brought from Foley, Alabama.

Both T.T. and Violia are buried at Crumbleys Chapel cemetery near Ranburne, Alabama. *Submitted by: Wallace D. Gay (grandson), 1907 County Road 1843, Arab, AL 35016*

393. Capes

James C. Capes was born November 9, 1849, in Georgia and died July 29, 1919, in Carroll County, Georgia. He married Louisa Lewis about 1872 in Heard County. She was born November 1, 1853, in Georgia and died January 5, 1924, in Carroll County. Both are buried in the Abilene Baptist Church Cemetery in Carroll County. Their children were:

Florence Capes, born April 30, 1875, died March 30, 1912, who married William Tidwell on November 24, 1895, in Carroll County.

Parthenia Capes, born August 16, 1873, died June 2, 1956, who married Elijah F. Ward on March 4, 1900, in Carroll County. Both are buried in the Abilene Baptist Church Cemetery.

Lewis Joseph Capes, born in January 1880, died in 1945, who married Fannie P. A marriage record has not been found. Both are buried in the Abilene Baptist Church Cemetery.

Mary J. Capes, born in March 1884.

William C. Capes. born October 30, 1885, died December 5, 1975, in Coweta County. He married Esther Dingler. Both are buried in the Forest Lawn Memorial Park in Newnan, Georgia.

James W. Capes, born in October 1887.

Henry W. Capes, born in November 1889, died August 3, 1956, in Carroll County. He married Viola Sudders on December 25, 1910, in Carroll County. Both are buried in the Abilene Baptist Church Cemetery.

Samantha Capes, born in July 1892.

Ola L. Capes, born January 9, 1894. She married Olin McClung on December 6, 1913, in Carroll County. Both are buried in Abilene Baptist Church Cemetery.

Homer Brinkley Capes, born October 14, 1896, died August, 31, 1971, in Carroll County. He married Hattie Mae Wren on November 12, 1922, in Carroll County. Both are buried in Hillcrest Cemetery in Villa Rica, Georgia.

Fletcher Elbert Capes, born November 17, 1898, died December 20, 1972, in Carroll County. He married Elsie Collins on September 16, 1923, in Carroll County. Both are buried in Abilene Baptist Church Cemetery. *Submitted by: Sonya Capes Shelton, 2409 Lovvorn Road, Carrollton, GA 30117*
Sources: Census, Marriage and Cemetery records researched by: Erlene Boyd

394. Carden Family 1770-1929

Part 1

John Carden Sr. and Cartha Jane Davis

John Carden Sr., born about 1770, married Cartha Jane Davis, November 25, 1791, Buckingham County, Virginia. Census records in Pike County, Georgia, show John Carden living there in 1830, 1840, and 1850. He died after 1850 in Pike County.

John Carden and Cartha J. Davis had six children: (1) David, born about 1793 in Goochland County, Virginia, died September 28, 1869, in Pike County. (2) Elizabeth A., born about 1795. (3) Benjamin, born about 1800. He and Elizabeth Scrougs, born between 1800-1810, married December 21, 1825, in Henry County Georgia. (4) Mary A., born about 1804 in Jasper County, Georgia, died after 1860 in Pike County. (5) John Jr., born about 1806, Jasper County, died after 1850. (6) Andrew Jackson, born about 1814, Jasper County, died after 1880 at Liberty Hill in Pike County.

Their first son, David, married Elander "Nelly" Deadwilder on May 2, 1814, in Jasper County. She was born 1800 in England and died after 1870 in Pike County. David fought in the War of 1812 and records show that Nelly applied for a widow's pension from this war.

David and Elander Carden's children were: (1) Christopher, born August 30, 1821, in Jasper County, married Willie Parker on December 19, 1843, in Pike County, and died there on September 5, 1910. (2) Thomas Jefferson, born August 15, 1825, in Jasper County, married Permelia Ann Moore on October 28, 1850, in Pike County, and died 1910 Campbell County, Georgia.

(3) George Washington was born May 29, 1827, in Jasper County, married Eleanor Jane Willoughby on February 4, 1852, in Campbell County. He was a private in Company H, 44th Regiment, Georgia Volunteers Infantry, Army of Northern Virginia, C.S.A., and was wounded at Spotsylvania, Virginia, on May 10, 1864. He farmed while living in Pike and Fayette counties, and died February 13, 1900. (4) Sarah Ann Barnes, born 1833, also in Jasper County, died 1901 in Lamar County. She is buried in Hickman-Abbott Cemetery, Hog Mountain, Barnesville, Georgia. (5) Mary J., born 1835 in Pike County. She and Jordan Abbott were married there on January 4, 1857. Jordan Abbott was born about 1828 in Georgia and died May 16, 1865, at Camp Chase, Ohio. (6) Martin Van Buren, born September 25, 1837, in Pike County. He was a private in Company H of the 44th Georgia Regiment, Doles Brigade, and lost a leg while in active combat during the war, was captured at Spotsylvania, Virginia, on May 10, 1864, and released at Fort Delaware June 16, 1865. He lived many years after the war in Pike County. He married Almedia Frances Duncan. (7) John Milner, born November 5, 1840, in Pike County. He served as a private in Company H, 44th Regiment, Georgia Volunteer Infantry, Army of Northern Virginia, C.S.A., and was wounded and captured at Spotsylvania, Virginia, on May 10, 1864. He was paroled at Fort Delaware in January or February of 1865 and received at Boulware and Cox's Wharves, James River, Virginia, on March 10-12, 1865. John Milner married Nancy Ann Elizabeth Teal on September 7, 1870, in Campbell County, Georgia. He died January 23, 1929, in Carroll County and is buried at Concord Primitive Baptist Church Cemetery in Carroll County. *Submitted by: Mrs. J. Sue Carden Sticher, and Compiled by: Nancy Anne Willis Howell based on census research by Erlene Boyd.*

395. Carden Family 1827-1955

Part 2

George Washington Carden and Eleanor Jane Willoghby

George Washington Carden was born on May 29, 1827, and died February 4, 1852, Pike County, Georgia. He married Eleanor Jane on February 4, 1852. She was born June 23, 1833, in Pike County and died November 14, 1879, in Fayette County, Georgia. They are buried at Antioch Cemetery, Fayette County.

They had eleven children. (1) John Christopher Carden, born November 1852, Pike County, died July 25, 1936, Carroll County. He married Temperance Louisa "Lou" Hodges about 1870. (2) Sarah A. Carden, born 1854, married January 4, 1888, to J.T. Jacobs, Fayette County. (3) Phoebe S. Carden, born 1856, married May 9, 1875, to W.E. Driggers in Fayette, County. (4) David Carden, born 1858, married Carrie Adams, November 3, 1876, in Campbell County, Georgia. (5) George Washington Carden Jr., born March 1860 in Georgia, married Martha F. (unknown). (6) Solomon C. Carden, born February 1862, Pike County, married Millie A. Cook March 4, 1882, Campbell County. (7) Noland Franklin "Noah" Carden, born 1864 in Georgia. He married Henrietta Adeline Jacobs. (8) Martin Van Buren "Mart" Carden, born December 25, 1867, died October 8, 1960, Crisp County, Hatley, Georgia, married Mary Frances (unknown). (9) Dalitha Carden "Sis," born May 1870, Fayette County, married F.M. Pope, September 6, 1891, Fayette County. (10) Jesse W. Carden, born May 18, 1870, died September 29, 1946, married Martha Ella Slaton, September 6, 1891, Fayette County. (11) Lillie Belle Carden, born 1872 in Georgia, married W.J. Slaton, Fayette County. She died in Hialeah, Florida, July 16, 1955. Obituary states: Mrs. Lillie Belle Slaton of Hialeah, Florida, formerly of Atlanta, died July 16, 1955. Surviving are her daughters Mrs. Elvira Frye, Hialeah; Mrs. Sally Ruschmeyer, Chamblee; sons, Mr. G.S. Slaton, Mr. H.M. Slaton, Mr. H.S. Slaton all of Hialeah; Mr. R.D. Slaton, Miami; Mr. G.B. Slaton, Camilla, Georgia; brother, Mr. Mark (Mart) Carden, Hatley, Georgia.

Children of George Washington and Eleanor Jane Carden

The photograph shows the eleven children of George W. and Eleanor Jane Willoughby Carden: Seated: John Christopher, Sarah Ann, Phoebe, David, George, Saul. Standing: Noland, Martin, Jesse, Dalitha called "Ellen," and Lillie. *Submitted by: Mr. and Mrs. Chris Carden, Villa Rica, GA, based on census research by Erlene Boyd and Compiled by: Nancy Anne Willis Howell, Douglasville, GA*

396. Carden Family 1852-1971

Part 3

John Christopher Carden and Temperance Louisa "Lou" Hodges

John Christopher Carden, born November 1852 in Pike County, Georgia, died July 25, 1936, in Carroll County, Georgia. He married Lou Hodges, from Butts County, Jackson, Georgia, near Indian Springs, about 1870. Lou was born January 1846 in Fayette County, Georgia, and died August 9, 1929, Carroll County. Both are buried in the Mt. Zion Cemetery, Douglas County, Georgia.

Lou's parents, Jesse Hodges (born in 1807) and Elizabeth West (born in 1811) had eleven children: John A., Bluford, Simon, Susan, Jesse W., James, Martha, Mary, Temperance Louisa "Lou," Francis, and Patie Ann Hodges.

John and Lou made their home in the Whitesburg community, attended Mount Zion Baptist Church and are buried in the cemetery there.

Lou H. Carden and John Christopher Carden

They had five children: (1) William Frank Carden was born June 15, 1871, died December 8, 1935. He married Nicholas "Nickie" A. Thompkins. They are buried at Mt. Zion Cemetery. (2) Solomon David Carden was born May 15, 1873, died July 16, 1944, and married Mary Evelyn "Mollie" Lassetter on December 24, 1896. Mollie died January 2, 1926. They are buried at Mt. Zion. (3) Annie B. Carden was born about 1875 and died December 10, 1971. She married Sidney A. Camp, March 28, 1895. They lived between Mt. Zion Baptist Church and Whitesburg and are buried at Mt. Zion Cemetery. (4) Lizzie Carden was born July 1879 and died 1961. She married William Thomas "W.T." Richards of Whitesburg, April 28, 1901, in Carroll County. They are buried at Whitesburg Cemetery, near the Methodist Church where they attended. (5) John Henry "Dick" Carden was born November 19, 1882, and died September 17, 1917, in Douglas County. He married Frances "Fannie" Cosby, born 1883, died February 23, 1964, in Coweta County. They are buried at Mt. Zion Cemetery.

John Christopher and Lou Hodges Carden were remembered well by my mother, Dorothy Carden Willis, and all the aunts and uncles. Aunt Nancy said, "We all loved Granny Carden, she was always a good sport with us children." She preceded grandpa's death by about seven years, and though he stayed more with Sam and Mollie and their daughter, Annie and Sid Camp, he visited all his children after his wife died.

A wonderful memory from Aunt Nancy about her Grandpa Carden was, "He was a good man, though depressed after Granny died. He knew the Bible almost by heart. When we kids went to Sunday School, we had cards with pictures on the front and a verse from the Bible. He would ask and we would say the verse for him. He would tell us from what book in the Bible it came, the chapter and the verse. He said he started reading the Bible and praying when he was quite young."

The Bible speaks the truth when it says that God's Word will not return void. Her Grandpa Carden died in 1936, Aunt Nancy died in 1983, all of his children, grandchildren and a few great-grandchildren are with him in heaven now, but those still living in 2001 continue to be told what God's word and prayer meant to our ancestors, in the good times and the hard times. *Submitted by: Ken Richards, Jonesboro, GA*
Source: Personal knowledge of Nancy Lou Bartlett, compiled by Nancy Anne Willis Howell.

397. Carden Family 1873-1926

Part 4

Solomon David "Sam" Carden and Mary Evelyn "Mollie" Lassetter

Sam and Mollie Carden — called Mama and Papa Carden — married in Coweta County, Georgia, December 24, 1896.

Sam Carden was born May 15, 1873, to John Christopher and Lou Hodges Carden. He died July 16, 1944, with a gangrenous leg from diabetes at the home of his son, C. Lewis Carden, Carroll County. Mollie Lassetter was born October 15, 1878, to William J. Lassetter and Nancy Jerusha Holland. She died on January 2, 1926, with heart dropsy (congestive heart failure). Both are buried at Mt. Zion Baptist Church Cemetery, Douglas County. An article in the *Douglas County Sentinel* following her death in 1926 gives tribute to her life and states, "She was a member of Mt. Zion Church and was 47 years old on October 15, 1925."

Mama Mollie Carden with twins, Dorsey and Dorothy

Sam and Mollie had nine children: Ora Corine, Nancy Lou, John William, Joseph Weyman, George Washington, Claude Lewis, Jesse Cedric, and twins Clarice Dorothy and Clarence Dorsey. (See individual articles).

Nancy Lou Carden Bartlett, daughter of Sam and Mollie, had an excellent memory and shared many stories of their growing up years. She recalled "how it was back then." Her parents were tenant farmers or sharecroppers and they lived in many different places around Carroll and Douglas Counties, helping farmers in need to raise their crops. The farmers in turn gave them a place to live and shared the harvest of the crops.

Papa Sam Carden and his nine children

When they lived at Byers Cross Road, Georgia Highway 5, Papa rode a pony twice a week to Whitesburg to pick up mail for his family and the neighbors. Aunt Nancy dated this time around 1906 and said, "It was a pretty good ride to go on a pony." She also remembered Papa's brothers coming for a visit from South Georgia by horse and surrey. They were Noland and Martin Van Buren Carden, referred to as Uncle Noel and Uncle Mart. The Martin Van Buren Carden family has written an interesting history about their family in the *Hatley/Crisp County, Georgia* history book. (More about Sam Carden's family in Part 5.)

The first photograph, made about 1915, shows Mama Mollie Carden with twins, Dorsey and Dorothy. The group photograph shows Papa Carden and his nine children: Front row, from left are Dorothy Carden Willis, and twin brother Dorsey Carden, Papa Carden, Corine Carden Richards, Nancy Carden Bartlett, and John Carden. Back row, left, Jesse, Lewis, George, and Weyman Carden. *Submitted by: Mrs. Frances Banks, Douglasville, GA*

Sources: Personal knowledge of Nancy Lou Carden Bartlett compiled by Nancy Anne Willis Howell.

398. Carden Family 1873-1944

Part 5

Sam and Mollie Carden

Though the Sam Carden Family worked hard in the cotton fields, Nancy and her brother Lewis told of how Papa loved sports and playing with his boys. He liked playing marbles and wrestling. Lewis said with a chuckle, "He loved to wrestle, until one day we got big enough to throw him and when we would outwrestle him, that's when the game stopped."

Papa Carden and his sons.

Aunt Nancy remembered the places they lived with such accuracy. She would say, "Corine was born in Douglas County at the Old Brooks place near Hannah, Fairplay community, I [referring to herself] was born at the Old Nicks place. John and Weyman were born when we lived at the Russell farm, County Line, below the Mt. Zion Community. We attended our first school at County Line-Watson School, at Byers Cross Road." (At present, Antioch Baptist Church is at this location). Thelma Pate, a Lassetter family member and historian, living on Old 5 Notch Road in Whitesburg community, says that the County Line School and New Watson School were consolidated and called Russell High or Lucy T. Russell Institute. (See the school picture of Russell High taken about 1926.)

Aunt Nancy continues: "We lived one year at the Molly Camp place," this was Thelma Pate's grandmother. "George was born at the Frank Camp place (Uncle Sid Camp's brother)." Uncle Sid Camp married Papa Sam Carden's sister, Annie Carden. "Lewis was born when we lived at the Will Richards place, between County Line and Byers Cross Road. Jesse was born at the Isom Burnett place." She said they lived four years in the same community and the twins, "Doc and Dot were born near the Byers Cross Road community. In 1918 we lived a year at Grandma Lassetter's place." (Author's note: Grandma Lassetter, Nancy Jerusha Holland Lassetter, died in 1920. She was Mollie's mother, and I imagine they needed to live near to help out.) (See related Holland/Lassetter stories).

Russell High School, Whitesburg, about 1925/26

"In 1919 we lived near McWhorter at the Gaines Holland place," located near the Flint Hill Methodist Church on Highway 5. "In 1920, Papa bought the Bud Pruitt place, (Aunt Sara Ann's husband's) they were there until 1922." This is near the Bill Arp Community, Poole Road. Aunt Nancy Carden married Dewey Bartlett in 1920. They lived part-time with Mama and Papa until Mama Carden died in 1926. In 1928, Papa and his children moved back to the Will Richards place, to the Johnson home place and then to the Watkins and Ed Harper's place."

How hard this must have been for our family, yet they survived! All nine children worked alongside their mother and dad. The closeness that bound this family together for as long as they lived was, and is, a blessing to their offspring. They helped one another, they stood by one another, and they loved one another.

The photograph taken in 1943 shows Papa Carden and his sons. Standing from left to right: Dorsey, Papa, Lewis (back), John, Jesse (back), Weyman, and George in uniform. Papa died in 1944 at age seventy-one. *Submitted by: Mrs. Ted Carden, Powder Springs, GA*

Sources: Personal knowledge of Nancy Lou Carden Bartlett, compiled by Nancy A. Willis Howell

399. Carden Family 1897-1955

Part 6

Ora Corine Carden and Clifford Richards

Corine Carden, Sam and Mollie Cardens' first, was born on November 9, 1897, in Carroll County, Georgia, and died on her birthday November 9, 1955, in LaGrange, Georgia. She married Clifford Benton (Big Boy) Richards on August 22, 1915. Big Boy was born July 13, 1889, and died February 18, 1958. Both are buried in Shadowlawn Cemetery in LaGrange. Their children were Jack Milton Richards and Mary Evelyn Richards. Jack married Violet Hines (nicknamed Pete) from Hogansville, Georgia. Jack and Violet had two children, Jacquelyn Ann and Kenneth Richards. Evelyn married Hubert Dorrough from LaGrange, no children.

Corine Carden Richards and Gray Boy

Corine was like a mother to her younger brothers and sisters when their mother died, and like a grandmother to her nieces and nephews who never knew their Grandmother Mollie. Our Aunt Corine had the heart of a "nurse," a compassionate, loving spirit, and a way about her that made you want to do and be your very best. We knew she would be by us and on our side if we ever needed her. Her love for us was shown in so many ways — by correspondence, post cards, birthday and get well cards, by invitations to their home during school breaks at Christmas and summer, and by pampering and babying us, making us all feel very special. Her husband — called Big Boy — was a barber for years in Villa Rica and LaGrange. He loved us and was also interested in our well-being. He loved Coca Colas, his cigarettes, and their big German Shepherd dog named Gray Boy, who scared us but we knew he was part of their family.

Big Boy and Corine Carden Richards and children, Jack and Evelyn

Daughter Evelyn and daughter-in-law Violet lived with Corine and Big Boy while their husbands, Hubert and Jack, were away during World War II. Hubert, Evelyn's husband, was the one we worried about most. He was in the heavy battles in Germany and France. He fought in Patton's army in the Battle of the Bulge and suffered from horrible nightmares for a very long time.

Corine loved spelling, reading and reciting. I believe Grandmother Nancy Jerusha Holland Lassetter's family may have been instrumental in teaching a love for this. Nancy J. was Lindsey Holland's daughter and James H. Holland's granddaughter. (See related Holland-Lassetter story). James started the Holland Meeting House which was active in the Whitesburg community for many years. It was a church, school and community log building, moved twice, and is now the St. Paul's United Methodist Church. Edith Foster of Carrollton records information about spelling bees and recitations being held in the Holland Meeting House. I remember stories of how Corine won many spelling bees in her day and how she read books to her younger brothers and sisters when they were growing up. At Christmastime, we nieces and nephews liked nothing better than to sit by the fire while Corine recited from memory *Annie and Willie's Prayer* by Sophia Tucker. She taught it to me, and it remains a tradition in our family. The Carden family was truly blessed to have a "Corine" given to us. *Submitted by: Nancy A. Howell, 9049 Allison Court, Douglasville, GA*

400. Carden Family 1900-1983

Part 7

Nannie "Nancy" Lou Carden and William Dewey Bartlett

Nancy Carden Bartlett was born August 27, 1900, in Carroll County to Sam and Mollie Carden. She died March 30, 1983, in Douglas County, Georgia. She married William Dewey Bartlett on February 1, 1920, in Carroll County. Dewey was born December 10, 1900, and died July 12, 1965, in LaGrange. Both are buried in the Shadowlawn Cemetery in LaGrange, Georgia.

Dewey and Nancy Carden Bartlett - Bartlett's Superette

After leaving Carroll County, the Bartletts moved to Atlanta and then to LaGrange in the 1930s, where he went into the grocery and café business.

Scenes in the café during World War II might picture the nieces and nephews perched on a stool at the counter eating one of Aunt Corine's hamburgers. She ran the café for several years. The typical 1940s jukebox played the favorite tunes of that time — the Andrews Sisters, Bing Crosby, Frank Sinatra, etc.

Ten members of our large Carden family lived in LaGrange, therefore we never lacked for attention. Going to visit them was so special, and we continue to reminisce more than sixty years later. Their homes were only a few blocks apart, so after supper family members gathered in living rooms and sat until bedtime. We talked, listened and laughed at their many funny stories. There was no television; had there been, we would have missed so much! We were encouraged to talk about our interests, and they were interested in our lives.

In addition to good books, there were large jigsaw puzzles to work on, and in the summer they took us to the local baseball games and Callaway's swimming pool. We could walk to the playgrounds, parks, and movies. When Aunt Nancy knew we were coming, our favorite dishes were prepared and her Brunswick Stew became a tradition at our Carden reunions.

Her home was always neat. Even now, I can almost smell and feel the clean, ironed sheets and starched pillowcases, embellished with her embroidery, crochet, or cut-work edging. Many valuable lessons regarding homemaking were given to us. The boy cousins enjoyed helping in the store, delivering groceries, and occasionally pushed the old fashioned lawn mower.

After her husband died, I visited Aunt Nancy and slept on the twin bed next to hers. She shared her prayer time with me. Every night she prayed out loud and named all the family members, one by one, including the in-laws of each of our mates. She named all the children of her nieces and nephews and did not miss a single one.

Our ancestors were certainly not free of stress, heartaches, worries or pain. But, we were mentored without even knowing what that meant. There were nine children in Papa Carden's family, but it was these older sisters, Corine Carden Richards and Nancy Carden Bartlett, who set the pace and standard for the tie that bound this great family and their offspring together. Maybe they learned it from the Hollands and the Lassetters before them, maybe it was because their mother died young and they learned early what it meant to need the support of one another. I don't know, but one thing I do know, genuine love was given and that love lives on. *Submitted by: Valerie Howell, Douglasville, GA*

Source: Personal knowledge of Nancy Anne Willis Howell

401. Carden Family 1902-1973

Part 8

John William Carden and Dora Easterwood

Son of Sam Carden and Mary Evelyn Mollie Lassetter Carden, John was born September 12, 1902, in Carroll County and died September 4, 1973. He was married first to Daisy Irene Cook of Carroll County, second to Beulah Hendricks of Atlanta, and third on September 11, 1966, to Dora Easterwood of Villa Rica, Georgia. He is buried in the Hillcrest Cemetery in Villa Rica.

John William Carden and Dora Easterwood Carden

He served in the U.S. Army during World War II. After the war, he went to work with Georgia Power Company and worked until his retirement. His office was downtown Atlanta and he enjoyed his years with the power company. Though he lived in Atlanta, he purchased a farm in Carroll County in the 1950s. He and his wife enjoyed spending weekends and vacations at the farm, where he raised cattle, hay, and held many family reunions. He really loved getting back to the "country" after his retirement. The kids loved going there to play in the creek, ride his horse Polly, or even better, ride in his surrey with the fringe on top.

Uncle John's surrey was used several times in Villa Rica's Wagon Train event from Douglasville to Villa Rica via the back roads, and to Midway Macedonia for homecoming and other events. However, his most famous ride was in 1969 escorting Senator Jimmy Carter, who was running for governor, in a Villa Rica Saddle Club parade.

Uncle John had a stroke in the early 1970s that left him unable to talk, and was followed by a fatal heart attack in 1973. He was also one who was thoughtful to his family! *Submitted by: John and Jason Sticher*

Source: Personal knowledge of Nancy Anne Willis Howell, Douglasville, GA

402. Carden Family 1904-1976

Part 9

Joseph Weyman Carden and Clemmie Black

Weyman was born June 13, 1904, in Carroll County to Sam and Mollie Carden. He died June 11, 1976, in Georgia Baptist Hospital, Altanta, Georgia. He married Clementine "Clemmie" Black on December 26, 1925. Clemmie was born April 11, 1905, and died February 21, 1973, in the Villa Rica Hospital. Both are buried in the Hillcrest Cemetery, Villa Rica, Georgia.

Clemmie and Joseph Weyman Carden

Weyman and Clemmie lived in Villa Rica in their early marriage and ran a café on Main Street there. In the mid to late 1930s, Weyman went to work with Colonial Bread Company and worked there until he retired. They moved to Atlanta in the 1930s and back to Villa Rica in the early 1950s.

Weyman worked long hours, getting up in the wee hours of the morning to deliver fresh bread on a large bread route. As soon as his two sons, Ted and Earl, were old enough, they helped their dad. Mother Clemmie took care of the household, and being the good cook she was, worked more than ten years at the Villa Rica School cafeteria.

Children of Weyman and Clemmie were: (1) Joseph, a stillbirth, December 15, 1927. (2) Ted Norman Carden, born September 27, 1934, in Carroll County and died March 20, 2001, in Cobb County. He married first Peggy Annette Land, and second Phyllis Robinson in Cobb County. (3) Earl Wayne Carden, born October 29, 1938, in Fulton County, married Jacqueline Ann Camp in Carroll County.

Ted followed his father in the bread business, working with Colonial Bread Company for thirty-four years after his tour of duty in the U.S. Army. After his retirement from Colonial, he went to work with the Georgia State Patrol Governor's

Staff in the State Security Division where he worked until his sudden death March 20, 2001. Ted and Annette Land Carden had four children: Sherrie, Angie, Chris and Scott Carden.

Earl followed his Uncle John Carden in going to work for Georgia Power Company after his tour of duty with the U.S. Army. He worked for Georgia Power for thirteen years and then started his own Electrical Sub-Station company for a number of years. He now works for Silvey Enterprises, Incorporated in Carrollton. Earl and Ann Carden have two sons, Ken Obukuro and Joseph Wayne Carden, and two daughters, Wendy Melissa and Heather Rebecca Carden.

In addition to going to LaGrange in the summer, we loved going to Aunt Clemmie and Uncle Weyman's house in Atlanta. Uncle Weyman would take us on excursions to the zoo at Grant Park, swimming, and the movies at Little Five Points, plus we played Monopoly for hours on their front porch. Aunt Clemmie was so jolly and happy and cooked the best fried chicken we ever ate. We country kids ate vegetables, cornbread, and biscuits all the time, so it was a real treat having Colonial loaf bread sandwiches and hot dogs on 'good ole' fresh buns. Uncle Weyman — The Bread Man — kept them stocked with good bread products, and we hungry kids were happy. *Submitted by: Earl Wayne Carden, Villa Rica, GA*
Source: Personal knowledge of Earl Carden and compiled by Nancy Anne Willis Howell

403. Carden Family 1907-1990

Part 10

George Washington Carden and Martha Elizabeth McDonald

George was born April 15, 1907, in Carroll County to Sam and Mollie Carden and died November 9, 1990, in Douglasville, Georgia. He married Martha Elizabeth McDonald on December 20, 1941. She was born on February 1, 1910, in Montgomery, Alabama, and died September 12, 1990, in Melbourne, Florida. Martha is buried in Montgomery in the McDonald family plot and George is buried in the Hillcrest Cemetery, Villa Rica, Georgia, and his brother, Weyman Carden's family plot.

George Washington and Martha McDonald Carden

He and Martha lived in Florida for over forty years but after the death of his wife (only two months before his own) he returned to Georgia to reside with his niece. George and Martha had no children together but Martha had a daughter by her first marriage, Annette Boyd (Bohlin). For a short period of time, and due to declining health, the Cardens lived with Annette and her family prior to Martha's death. Annette and Harold Bohlin, their children and grandchildren were very special to George and Martha.

George retired from the United States Air Force with twenty-five years of service. He enlisted May 6, 1939, and served in many Air Force Bases, stateside and overseas. During World War II he was in Guam and the Philippines. He rose to rank of master sergeant and received numerous awards during his years in the United States Air Force. In Florida, he and Martha attended the Church of Christ and he was a Mason.

Aaron Hodge, retired chaplain of the U.S. Air Force, visited George the day before his death. George had lung cancer and was very short of breath, but a soldier to the end! It was during the Persian war buildup in 1990, and Aaron, who was about the same age as George, asked, "George, if you were told today you had to go to the Persian Gulf, what would you say?" George, in a weakened voice said, as he gave the soldier's perfect salute, "Reporting for duty, sir."

Aaron officiated at George's funeral and he used this last statement George said to him, adding these words: "God has called George home and I can hear him saying, 'Reporting for duty, sir.'

He was a true soldier and ready for service anytime he was called. My husband and I counted it a privilege and were blessed to minister to him the last two months of his life. *Submitted by: Bryan and Sylvia Carden (Vietch), Villa Rica, GA. Written by: Hancy Anne Willis Howell.*
Source: Personal knowledge of niece, Nancy Anne Willis Howell, 9049 Allison Court, Douglasville, GA 30134

404. Carden Family 1908-1982

Part 11

Claude Lewis Carden and Eva Louise Howell

Lewis Carden was born December 7, 1908, to Sam and Mollie Carden, and died January 23, 1982. He married Eva Louise Howell on September 27, 1930. Louise was born March 14, 1910, and died November 23, 1998. They are buried in Hillcrest Cemetery in Villa Rica, Georgia.

The Lewis Cardens lived all their married lives in Carroll County. They had four children: Mary Elizabeth "Bette" (Boyd); Doris Frances (Banks); Johnnie Sue (Sticher); and Randy Lewis Carden.

Lewis was a farmer and livestock dealer. They lived on Highway 61 in a two story historical home about forty years. The home and old barn were noted in several articles for their historical significance. The house was moved and is being renovated but the old barn was torn down to make room for a new bank and some future businesses planned for the site. This is near Ithica Gin and Van Wert Roads at Highway 61. Lewis' son Randy, and his grandson Bryan continue to operate the cattle business in the Hulett area of Carroll County.

The grandchildren of Lewis and Louise Howell Carden are Hugh and Jeff Boyd, Reneé Banks, Lisa Sticher Thompson, John and Jason Sticher, Sylvia Carden Vietch, and Bryan Carden.

Lewis was one of the best "story tellers" in the Carden family. He could take an ordinary story and have you in stitches before he finished. When our large family gathered, it was pure entertainment for the young and old to sit in a circle and listen to tales of "growing up." All the stories were interesting and funny, but it seemed that Lewis and his youngest brother, Doc, knew how to enhance what they told.

One trick pulled on every little kid was going to watch Lewis milk the cow. He could milk so fast. I can still hear the sound as it would begin filling the bucket — one quick stream and then the other. All of a sudden, Lewis would stop and look at the child, knowing he had his full attention and he would say, "You want to see where this milk is coming from?" Of course the child would say, "Yes." He would then hold the utter up and tell them to bend over and look at the little hole, and then he would give a quick pulse and you got a little splash of milk right in your face. I think every child in our family was initiated with the "milk in the face trick" as long as Lewis continued to milk cows.

Lewis and Louise Carden Family. Randy, Louise, Frances, Lewis, Sue and Bette

Aunt Louise was like the other women in our family, always busy in the home. She also loved yard work and quilting. She churned and sold butter and was a very good cook. When we were teenagers, their house was often the gathering place for the teenage parties. Her children were good to help her, but she was self sufficient in managing her home and affairs for nearly fifteen years after her husband died. *Submitted by: Randy Carden, and Compiled by: niece, Nancy Anne Willis Howell.*
Source: Personal knowledge, Bette Carden Boyd and Frances Carden Banks

405. Carden Family 1911-1981

Part 12

Jesse Cedric Carden and Eva Bentley

Jesse was born October 6, 1911, to Sam and Mollie Carden, in Whitesburg, Georgia, and died June 24, 1968 in Atlanta. He married Eva Mae Bentley, born December 1, 1914, in Carroll County, and she died October 10, 1981, in Atlanta, Georgia.

They had two sons, Franklin Dewey Carden and Sammy Dennis Carden. Dewey married Marjorie Kim and they have no children. Sam married first Janice Hardy and they had one son, Barry Carden. His present wife is Paula Carden.

Jesse worked as a lineman for Georgia Power Company for about twenty-five years. He retired following a stroke in the early 1960s. He and Eva lived in Atlanta most of their married life, with the exception of two years in Winston, Georgia.

Jesse was a real baseball fan. Like all the Carden brothers, they kept up with the Atlanta Crackers until the Braves moved to Atlanta. Then, the Braves became their team. Jesse especially enjoyed his rabbit dogs and hunting, with fishing coming in a close second. His son Dewey told of seeing him catch fish out of a creek, and he loved fishing at Lake Carroll.

One of the Carden traditions was for Jesse to bring his rabbit dogs to the Carden Thanksgiving gathering at Tom and Dorothy Willis' home. All the men and boys went hunting, mostly for rabbits. The hunting was a sport but also provided meat on the table. Many times the women fried up a good rabbit and served it with biscuits and gravy.

Eva was a good cook and I learned to cook many dishes while talking to her on the telephone. She loved serving others. I stayed with them for a few months when I first came to

Jesse and Eva Carden and Family. Dewey, Marjorie, Eva and Sammy, Jesse sitting.

work in Atlanta. After Jesse died, she moved to Lithia Springs near her son Sammy. As the years moved on, and her needs increased, several of us counted it a blessing to return the many things she had done for us.

Jesse and Eva kept our son for about six months when I [Nancy Anne Willis Howell] needed to work. It was a pleasure to know they were taking care of our little boy. David began calling them Mama Eva and J.C., and to this day he still refers to them that way. They also loved our son. Jesse gave him the nickname "Crockett" for the popular series "Davy Crockett." He called David "Crockett" as long as he lived. When I lived with them, Jesse called me "Little Daughter" and that stuck too. I loved and appreciated Uncle Jesse and Aunt Eva, as did all our family. They were special and were there for us when we were young, so we were willingly there for them when they needed us.

Dewey and Sam called their mother "blessed," and their dad "loving" and a "good sport" as they remember the years of wonderful love and support given to them. *Submitted by: Franklin Dewey Carden, Hampton, GA and Written by: Nancy Anne Willis Howell*

Sources: Personal knowledge of Franklin Dewey Carden and Nancy Anne Willis Howell

406. Carden Family 1914-1952

Part 13

Clarence Dorsey Carden and Eva Phillips

As mentioned in the previous article about these twins, Clarice Dorothy and Clarence Dorsey (nicknamed Doc) were born May 8, 1914, in Carroll County to Sam and Mollie Carden.

Dorsey and Dorothy Carden, 1914

Dorsey lived in Carroll County until moving to LaGrange when his two older sisters, Corine Richards and Nancy Bartlett, and their families moved there in the mid to late 1930s. He met Eva Phillips in LaGrange and they married about 1942. They had a wonderful life together, though brief. They had no children, but just like the other family members in LaGrange, gave plenty of attention to their nieces and nephews. Doc was full of good humor and fun and enjoyed teasing his wife, whom he loved dearly, as well as us kids, making our visits to LaGrange even more fun through our young years.

Dorsey had rheumatic fever in his late teens, which left him with a weakened heart. He suffered a fatal heart attack and died January 9, 1952, at age 37. Eva Phillips Carden died in a LaGrange nursing home in the late 1990s. They are buried in the Shadowlawn Cemetery, LaGrange, Georgia.

See picture of Doc with Papa Carden and his brothers and sisters in the Carden Family Part 4 and 5 in this Carden Family series. *Submitted by: Scott Carden, Carrollton, GA, and Written by: Nancy Anne Willis Howell, 9049 Allison Court, Douglasville, GA 30134*

407. Carden Family 1914-1984

Part 14

Clarice Dorothy Carden (Willis) and Clarence Dorsey Carden (Twins)

Dorsey and Dorothy were the last children born to Sam and Mollie Carden on May 8, 1914. In those days twins were rare, and there were no tests (like in 2001) to prepare you for more than one child. The Cardens had a big surprise when they got two instead of one.

The family was thrilled and excited over the two little ones. Having two older daughters surely helped. However, Nancy (fourteen at the time) said she had to work on being happy due to all the extra work. Corine, the oldest daughter got married the following year (1915) so she was not there for long.

Son Donald with Tom and Dorothy Carden Willis

The extra stress on Mama Mollie began to show up after this pregnancy and by the time the twins were age six, she had more and more heart problems. In those days they called her condition heart dropsy. Today they call this illness congestive heart failure. She also had a large goiter on the thyroid. The country doctors came to their home often to care for Mollie, once sending her to Emory Hospital in Atlanta, which was quite a journey from Whitesburg in the early 1920s. (See Carden Family, Parts 4 and 5 for Sam and Mollie's story).

Clarice Dorothy was my mother and by the time her mama died, her sister Nancy had also married and left home. Mother, (Dorothy) had many sad stories about being the only little girl at home with no mother. Her papa loved her, as did her brothers Dorsey, Jesse, Lewis, and George, who were still at home, but she spent many lonesome days, especially the first years after her mother died. As mother got older, the highlights of her young life were visiting her sister, Corine, who was beginning her own family by then, and Nancy, her other sister, who had moved to Atlanta. She had many interesting stories to tell of "the way it was" in Atlanta during the mid to late 1920s.

Dorothy Carden met and married my father, Tom M. Willis, in 1931. They lived in Carroll County most of their lives. Tom's parents, Charlie and Rebecca Bates Willis, lived in the Sand Hill Community, close to the Midway Macedonia Baptist Church.

My brothers and I were so blessed by having our mother with us as we grew up. She expressed many times and in so many ways how she missed not having her mother as a young girl. She wanted to be there for us. I can still picture the happy look on her face as she would watch us happily open a flour sack full of tea cakes or a plate of chocolate fudge that she had made just for her kids. There are hundreds of remembrances of my mother's love. The most important to me was her love for God's Word, the Bible, and prayer. Dorothy died on December 9, 1984, from a massive heart attack. She and her husband Tom Milton Willis are buried at the Midway Macedonia Cemetery, Carroll County, along with their two sons, Donald M. and Thomas "Tommy" D. Willis. (See their story in the Willis section, and their memorial page with my brothers and nephew.) *Submitted by: Brett Willis, grandson, and Written by: Nancy Anne Willis Howell, daughter*

408. The Doll C. Carden Family

Doll Chris Carden descends from John Carden who was born about 1770 in Virginia (probably Goochland County), and died after 1850. He married first Cartha Jane Davis, born November 25, 1791, in Buckingham County, Virginia; date and place of death unknown. John's second wife was Elizabeth, name unknown, who was born after 1840, death unknown.

John Carden and Cartha Davis' children were David Carden, born about 1793, Goochland County, Virginia, died September 28, 1869, Pike County, Georgia; Elizabeth A. Carden, born about 1795, death unknown; Benjamin Carden, born about 1800, death unknown; Mary A. Carden, born about 1804, Jasper County, Georgia, died after 1860, Pike County; John Carden Jr., born about 1806 in Jasper County, died after 1850; Andrew Jackson Carden born about 1814, Jasper County, died after 1880, Liberty Hill, Pike County, John Carden and Elizabeth Carden's child was Eliza, born about 1842 in Georgia.

Andrew Jackson Carden was born about 1814 in Jasper County, died after 1880 in Liberty Hill, Pike County; married on March 4, 1838 in Pike County; Adeline Crawford who was born in October of 1816 in Georgia, and died after 1910 in Liberty Hill, Pike County. Andrew Jackson Carden died on the creek bank while fishing.

Andrew Carden and Adeline Crawford's children were Catherine E. Carden, born in December of 1840 in Pike County, death unknown; Rebecca J. Carden, born about 1843, Pike County, death unknown; Andrew Jackson Carden Jr., born July 21, 1848, in Pike County, died June 27, 1914, Paulding County; Nancy Ann Carden, born October 18, 1848, in Pike County, death unknown; John W. Carden, born about 1852 in Pike County, death unknown; Henry Carden, born about 1854 in Pike County, probably died September 29, 1934, in Fulton County, Georgia; James Buchanan Carden, born about 1856, Pike County, died before 1920 in Paulding County; Thomas John Carden was born in 1862 in Pike County, death unknown; Mary Frances Carden was born April 12, 1862, in Pike County, and died March 16, 1950.

Henry Carden was born about 1854 in Pike County and died September 29, 1934 in Fulton County, Georgia, married Marian B. (Molly) Blisit, born December 15, 1854, in Monroe County, Georgia and died November 6, 1941, in Paulding County. Marian (Molly) married in Alabama and she was the daughter of William Blisit and Mary Burt.

Henry and Marian B. (Molly) Carden's children were David Jackson, Doll C., Samuel Tilton, Carrie Adeline, Henry Matthew, Mamie A., Annie Mae.

David Jackson Carden was born April 10, 1874, in Monroe County, and died April 22, 1946 in Wood County, Texas; first married on August 26, 1900, in Paulding County, Georgia, Amanda Ada Hinman, born April 22, 1882, and died March 13, 1917. David Jackson married on January 19, 1920, in Harmony Community, Hopkins, Texas, Opal Azilee Smith, born December 3, 1890, in Winnsboro, Wood County, Texas; and died March 9, 1983, in Ft. Worth, Tarrant County, Texas. She was the daughter of Samuel Smith and Etha Patilla. David Carden and Amanda Hinman's children were Delia, Lucile, Julia, Mary, Nettie Alfa, Vernon Wesley, Ollie David and Joseph Leonard. David Carden and Opal Smith's children were Elba Rowena and Jackie Mareba.

Doll C. Carden was born September 21, 1875, in Monroe County, GA, and died April 29, 1959, in Carroll County.

Samuel Tilton Carden was born September 26, 1879, in Monroe County and died August 18, 1951, in Georgia; married on February 18, 1906, in Paulding County; Emma Hinman, born August 30, 1887, and died June 1, 1953. Samuel Tilton Carden and Emma Hinman's children were William Robert, Eva Etay, Homer Levi, Ida Mary Estell, Benny Lee, Nettie Molly Pauline, Emma Ethel, Carmon, Myrtis Moline, Clara Lillian, Lucille, and Clarence Everett.

Carrie Adeline Carden was born September 26, 1880, in Monroe County, Georgia and died September 2, 1931; first married on November 25, 1900, in Cedartown, Polk County, Georgia; Walter Levi Parker, born July 23, 1875, death unknown. Carrie married her second husband on September 6, 1921, Marvin Wall. Carrie and Levi Parker's children were William Levi, an infant Parker and Hubert Milton. Carrie and Walter Wall's child was Annie.

Henry Matthew Carden was born September 7, 1886, in Pike County, Georgia and died November 11, 1961, in Cobb County, Georgia married on December 28, 1912; Lillian Louise Gay, born June 26, 1893, in Floyd County, Georgia and died February 28, 1918. Matthew and Louise Carden's children were Maggie Lee and Roy Matt.

Mammie A. Carden was born March 26, 1889, in Monroe County and died June 14, 1974, in Fulton County; married on September 27, 1907, James Oscar Morgan, born July 18, 1890 in Pike or Paulding County, and died July 31, 1977. Mamie and Oscar Morgan's children were James Emmett, Mary Irene, Thomas Watson, Myrtle Lucendy, Ruby Lee, and Mamie Louise.

Annie Mae Carden was born April 26, 1890, in Monroe County and died February 25, 1981, in Fresno, Fresno County, California; married her first husband on May 3, 1908, in Polk County, Georgia, Calvin Edgar A. Atkins, born April 11, 1886, and died September 13, 1918, in Georgia. Annie Mae married her second husband on November 29, 1917, in Tulsa, Oklahoma, John Olin Krantz, born May 10, 1892 in Tennessee and died April 16, 1954 in Fresno, California. Annie Mae and Calvin Atkins' children were Ola Mae, Claudie Calvin, Maggie Rene, Callie Lee, Cecil Jessie Bill, and Myrtle. Annie Mae and John Krantz's children were Johnie Mae, Mary Rhoda, and William Euben.

Doll C. Carden married Ella Mae Carden, daughter of Andrew Jackson Carden and Nancy Annette Blisit. Nancy's parents were William Blisit of Butts County and Mary Antionette Burt of Monroe County, GA. William Blisit fought in the Civil War, Company C, 13th Regiment. He was killed in line of duty about August of 1862 and he is buried at Lynchburg, Virginia.

Andrew Jackson Carden Jr. and Nancy Annette Blisit's children were Sarah Bradley, Nancy Ann, Della Ray, Ella May, Albaines, Mary Odessa, Leona, and Andrew Jackson III.

Sarah Bradley Carden was born about 1873 in Georgia and died December 31, 1958, and is buried at Hillside, New Jersey; married her first husband on July 23, 1891, in Paulding County, William R. Cole, born in October 1869 in Indiana and died September 13, 1900, in Paulding County. Sarah married her second husband, Christopher Columbus Fuller, born after 1900 in Alabama. Christopher is buried at Hillside, New Jersey, no death date. Sarah and William Cole's children were Bert, Paul and Eric. Sarah and Christopher Fuller's children were Foster, Elizabeth Mable, Tommy Jack, and Effie Antionette.

Doll and Ella Carden, Smyrna Methodist Church, 1941.

Nancy Ann Carden was born October 18, 1875, in Georgia and died January 11, 1906 in Paulding County; married on August 11, 1894, in Paulding County, Walter A. Cole, born August 10, 1874, in Columbus, Ohio, and died April 12, 1969. Nancy and Walter Cole's children were Charlie Louis, Clarence B, and Oscar H.

Della Ray Carden was born September 13, 1877, in Paulding County, and died in 1950 in Paulding County; married on December 27, 1892, in Paulding County, Marcus E. Caldwell, born in 1867 and died in 1935 in Paulding County, Della and Marcus Caldwell's children were Cora, Eula, Calvin, Homer L. Annie, Deedie, Ollie, Nora Gennell, Claude, Audie Mae, Florence and Ernest.

Ella Mae Carden was born September 13, 1877, in Paulding County and died November 15, 1949, in Carroll County.

Albaines (Ab) Carden was born January 18, 1880, in Paulding County and died January 7, 1950, in Paulding County; married on August 5, 1900, in Paulding County, Vilor Carter, born May 15, 1879, in Paulding County and died May 30, 1960. Albaines and Vilor Carter's children were William Lloyd, Cleora, and Ola Ethel.

Mary Odessa Carden was born in 1882 in Paulding County, and died in 1959 in Calhoun County, Alabama, married on January 6, 1907, in Paulding County, Charlie Smith, born in 1885 in Paulding County, and died in 1938 in Calhoun County, Alabama; Mary Odessa and Charlie Smith's children were Alfred, Andrew Jackson, Charles Leo, Annie Odessa, Florence Elizabeth, Paul, and Silas.

Leona Carden was born July 31, 1884, in Paulding County, and died March 16, 1967, in Paulding County; married W.L. Hutcheson, born July 11, 1885, and died August 14, 1980, in Polk County. Leona and W.L. Hutcheson's children were Ruth, Ruby, and Luther.

Andrew Jackson Carden III was born March 5, 1887, in Paulding County, and died May 16, 1971, in Polk County; married on January 2, 1910, in Paulding County, Susan Louise Elder, born January 8, 1888, and died June 30, 1973. Andrew Jackson and Louise Carden's children were Clarence, William Euell, Ralph Orie, James Carl, Fletcher, and George Lee.

Doll C. Carden married Ella Mae Carden on December 24, 1901, in Paulding County. Doll and Ella's children were Clifford Anderson, Eunice Lee, Lillie Nan, Ida Gertrude, Marten, Andrew Jackson Huie, and Myrtle Ruth.

Clifford Anderson Carden was born August 16, 1903, in Paulding County and died May 30, 1974, in Carroll County; married on December 1, 1923, in Carroll County, Janette Florence (Nettie) Hicks, born on December 31, 1900, and died February 9, 1976, in Carroll County. Nettie was the daughter of Elizabeth Pace and Denmon Hicks of Paulding County, and the granddaughter of John B. Pace Jr. and Missouri Fuller of Paulding County. Clifford and Nettie Carden's children were Emma Pauline and Robert Gene (Bob) Carden.

Eunice Lee Carden was born April 15, 1905, in Paulding County and died on August 15, 1941. She never married.

Lillie Nan Carden was born December 26, 1907, in Paulding County and died May 17, 1991, in Carroll County; married on December 23, 1923 in Carroll County, William Chester Thomas, born July 12, 1901, in Paulding County, and died August 22, 1987. Chester Thomas' parents were Sam Thomas and Ella Shead of Paulding County. Lillie and Chester Thomas' children were Frank, Ernest, William Curtis, Hugh Jack, James Hoyt, Tommy Howell, Geraldine, Windell Wayne, Charles Douglas and Joel. Note: Ernest, Frank and Joel were stillborn.

Ida Gertrude Carden was born July 2, 1910, in Paulding County and died October 16, 1989, in Douglas County; married on December 24, 1927, in Carroll County, Lonnie Bragg, born September 30, 1905, and died March 16, 1972, in Douglas County. Lonnie Bragg's parents were Henry Bragg and Frances Shead of Paulding County. Ida and Lonnie Bragg's children were: Trudie Mae, Morine, William Lovie, Myrtle Dean, Juanita, Louis, and Judie. Note: Morine and Juanita were stillborn; Judie lived about one year.

Marten Carden was born September 28, 1911, in Paulding County and died February 24, 1915, in Paulding County.

Andrew Jackson Huie Carden was born February 19, 1914, in Paulding County, and died on January 10, 1993, in Cobb County, Georgia; married on December 19, 1936, his first wife, Katie Clay, born July 1, 1909, in Paulding County and died June 20, 1966 in Cobb County. Katie was the daughter of Warner Clay and Fannie Land. Huie and Katie Carden's children were David DeWayne, and two stillborns.

Myrtle Ruth Carden was born March 18, 1916, in Paulding County and died December 21, 1995, in Cobb County, first married on May 2, 1931, in Douglas County, Sam Hugh Hodges, birth and death unknown. Ruth married her second husband, John Frank McCoy, born May 6, 1916, probably in Oklahoma and died July 8, 1981, in Carroll County. Ruth and Sam Hodges' child was Evaril Gloria.

In the early 1900s, Doll Carden relocated from Barnesville, Pike County, Georgia, to Union Community in Paulding County. While in Paulding County, he owned a farm, a grocery store, a syrup mill, and a grist mill which were located near Smyrna Methodist Church in that area.

Most of the Carden family attended church and were members of Smyrna Methodist Church in Paulding County, and most of the Carden relatives are buried in this cemetery. Doll's wife, Ella Carden's, grandmother, Mary Antionette Burt Blisit, wife of William Blisit, gave three and one-half acres of land for the Smyrna Methodist Church and Cemetery in Paulding County on August 19, 1896, which is noted in a Paulding County court document.

Sometime before 1922, probably in 1919, after the Carden children had finished school at Union in Paulding County, Doll relocated his family to Villa Rica in Carroll County. Because of uncollectible debts in his business, the family was forced to seek employment elsewhere. Since textiles were a going concern in this area at that time, most of the family were employed in textiles. Doll also farmed after he moved to Villa Rica. He leased tracts of land and grew cotton and corn for many years.

Later, Clifford, Huie and Ruth were employed with aircraft companies; Clifford and Huie worked for Bell Aircraft during World War II; Ruth worked for an aircraft company in Aurora, Illinois. Clifford and Huie were both excellent carpenters and later Huie was employed at Lockheed as an aircraft model builder. He retired from Lockheed with twenty-eight years service time.

In the 1930s, the Cardens bought a house with three acres of land west of Villa Rica on Highway 101, removed the old house, and built a new one. While they were building their new house, Doll bought a new 1933 green, four-door Chevrolet sedan from Kinney Motors in Villa Rica on August 7, 1933. He paid $465 for this automobile.

When the house was finished, they planted all kinds of flowers, shrubbery and trees. Doll planted many pecan trees, and even an English walnut tree which produced nuts. Pecan trees line both sides of the house. These trees were enjoyed until Highway 101 was widened and paved, at which time most of them were taken out by the Highway Department. This house also had a wide brick walkway, and on either side of the walk were large beds of red verbena which looked like red carpet when it bloomed.

D.C. Carden's children - Huie, Clifford, Ida, Ruth, and Lillie.

Some of Doll's closest friends were the Reids, the Raburns, and Dr. Hogue. Since Doll knew most of the people in Union community, Dr. Hogue would always stop by and ask Doll to go with him to visit his patients in that area. He always enjoyed these visits with Dr. Hogue, as well as getting to see his friends and relatives around Union.

Doll and Ella Carden had relatives located in Texas, California, New Jersey and South Georgia. These relatives visited periodically. I remember how all the family cleaned and cooked for about a two-week period in preparation for their arrival.

In 1954 some Texas relatives came to Villa Rica for a visit. They asked Doll to go with them to Smyrna Methodist church to visit the cemetery. Doll Carden was eighty years old at the time and he gave them an interview about our descendants. The following is the interview that he gave the Texas relatives:

"There were seven Carden boys that came to America from Ireland. Andrew J. "Jack" Carden came to Georgia while the Indians were still here - was one of the first settlers. He had a home in Pike County and was a farmer. This was where all of his children were born and some of his grandchildren, too. He was section foreman on the Southern Railroad, the first railroad built in Georgia - from Atlanta to Savannah. He was living at the home place during the Civil War. There was fighting on the old home place during the war. They derailed a train there. The cars were filled with dried peas and we were trying to get to our men down south. They were starving, just about. When those railroad cars turned over, dried peas went everywhere and our cows ate them. Those cows burst when those dried peas swelled. Killed all 'em and left the family without any milk. Grandpa, Jack Carden, wasn't killed in the war. He dropped dead at the creek, a'fishing. He is buried at Liberty Hill, in Pike County, in the old Carden Cemetery. His wife, Adeline Crawford Carden is buried in the same place. That's near the new Goggins Station on the railroad. Adeline and Jack Carden had eight children: Tom, John, Henry, Buck, Catherine, Becky, Mary and Andrew. Henry Carden, my father, married Molly Blisit, my mother. He was born in Pike Co., and she was born in Monroe County. He was buried in Monroe County, Georgia (Uncle Doll had previously said that his father died and was buried near Atlanta??) Molly, my mother, was buried at Smyrna Cemetery, up near Dallas, Paulding County. Mammie was 12 years old when our father died. I don't know my parents' birthdays; they were about the same age. They had seven children. They were: Dave J., Doll C., Carrie, Sam, Mamie, Matt and Annie. Grandfather, William Blisit, married Nettie (Mary Antionette) Burt. He was a Baptist preacher, educated and wrote a beautiful hand. All of his brothers (4) enlisted at the start of the war, but he preached a year before he enlisted. He went to Griffin, Georgia, and had his Confederate suit tailor-made. Molly was a baby when he left home for the war. They had 4 children: Sally, Bud, Molly and Annie. They were all born in the same house, same as all of Molly Carden's children (that is me and my brothers and sisters) - in Monroe County. Duirng the war, Grandmother Blisit buried her meat under the smokehouse to save it, when the Union soldiers came. They killed all the stock and burned the outhouses. William S. Blisit died in Virginia and is buried there. Aunt Nan's sister lived with her. They were Burt's. Bud Blisit married Liza (Maddock?). Sally married John Carden, Nancy Annette (Annie) married Andrew J. Carden; Molly (Marian B.) married Harry Carden. The Cardens were brothers, sons of Jack (Andrew J.) and Adeline. Aunt Annie and Uncle Andrew had eight children: Della and Ella were twins. I married Ella and Della married Marcus E. Caldwell; both are buried at Smyrna Cemetery. Nan Carden married Walt Cole. He is still living in Anniston, Alabama. Jack Carden lives at Rockmart, Georgia. Bradley Carden married Will Cole, then re-married a Mr. Fuller and lives in New Jersey. Ab Carden is buried at Smyrna. Mary Carden married Charlie Smith. He is buried at Smyrna and she lives in Anniston, Alabama. I have told this the best I can remember it. Doll C. Carden, July 1954."

In the early 1900s, while he was still in Paulding County, Doll lost an eye while cutting wheat in one of his fields. He was using a scythe, it hit a rock and a piece of the rock bounced into his eye and completely destroyed it.

Doll Carden was a great outdoorsman. His greatest enjoyment in life was to hunt and to fish which is true of most Cardens that I have known throughout my lifetime. Doll not only liked to hunt and to fish, he liked to eat fish and wild meat. He also like to gather a group of family members or friends on his porch and tell hunting and fishing stories for hours at a time.

Doll was also known as a stubborn man. Once he set his mind to do something, there was no changing it. After he became elderly, he had the tendency to slip off from the family and go fishing and hunting with his little dog, Corky. Even with one eye, he would walk foot logs, climb trees, and he would try anything else that crossed his mind. Many times the family waited and worried until he returned from one of these trips. Usually, he would stay all day and late into the evening. I think that anyone who knew my Grandpa Doll could truthfully say that he liked to hunt and to fish more than anyone in this world!

Many of Doll Carden's descendants hold degrees from schools of higher learning. Two of these descendants hold doctorates; one is a medical doctor, and one is a laboratory director over Kiel Laboratories; one has two masters and is a librarian over five-county area of the Public Library System in Georgia. Several hold bachelor degrees; others graduated from business schools and attended colleges. One is a technical writer; one is a Spanish teacher in Cobb County Schools, one is a computer specialist, one is an accountant; one is legal secretary; one was a dental hygienist; one was the founder and owner of J. Hoyt Thomas Funeral Home in Villa Rica, Georgia; and one is Chief of Fire and Rescue for Carroll County; one retried as a construction representative from the Federal Bureau of Prisons, Department of Justice, with twenty-one years service time; and three were employed with Lockheed Aircraft and two retired. One was employed fifteen years until he died of cancer; one retired as a secretary in engineering program management with almost thirty-six years of service; and one retired as an aircraft model builder with twenty-eight years service time. Others have retired from Southwire Company, Motor Convoy, Electric Storage and Battery Company, and Villa Rica Mills. One married a farmer, cattleman, and landscaper who owned a 140-acre farm in South Georgia. One is married to a dentist in North Carolina; one is married to an engineer with Martin-Marietta in Huntsville, Alabama; one is married to psychologist in Atlanta; and one is married to tax specialist with the State of Georgia, Department of Revenue. *Submitted by: Geraldine Forrester, 626 Rockmart Road, Villa Rica, GA 30180, and Written by: Pauline C. Roberts, P.O. Box 461, Villa Rica, GA 30180*

Sources: Personal knowledge, family relatives, and Mike Collins, Pickton, TX. castron72@hotmail.com

409. Carden - Hicks

Clifford Anderson Carden was born August 16, 1903, in Paulding County, GA and died May 30, 1974, Carroll County, GA. He married on December 1, 1923, Janette (Nettie) Hicks who was born December 31, 1900, in Paulding County, GA, and died February 9, 1976, in Carroll County, GA. They are buried at Sunrise Memorial Gardens, Douglasville, GA.

Clifford Carden's family roots have been traced to John Carden, born about 1770 in Virginia (probably Goochland County), and died after 1850. He married Cartha Jane Davis in Buckingham, Virginia, on November 25, 1791.

Clifford descends from John Carden, Andrew Jackson Carden, Henry Carden, and Doll C. Carden.

Clifford Carden's parents were Doll C. Carden, born September 21, 1875, in Monroe County, GA and died April 29, 1959, in Carroll County, GA; married on December 24, 1901, to Ella Carden who was born September 13, 1877, in Paulding County, GA, and died November 15, 1949, in Paulding County. She was the daughter of Andrew Jackson Carden Jr. and Nancy Blisit of Paulding County.

In the early 1900s, Doll Carden owned a farm, a grocery store, a syrup mill, and a grist mill in the Union Community, near Smyrna Methodist Church in Paulding County. Most of the Carden family attended church and were members of Smyrna Methodist Church and many of these relatives are buried there. Clifford Carden was a member of this church. His mother's grandmother, Mary Antionette Burt, wife of William Blisit, gave three and one-half acres of land for Smyrna Methodist Church and Cemetery on August 19, 1896, which is noted in a Paulding County court document. Clifford Carden's wife, Nettie, was a member of Fullerville Baptist Church, Villa Rica, GA.

After Clifford and the other children finished Union School in Paulding County, Doll and Ella relocated to Villa Rica in 1922, and built a new home on Highway 101, west of Villa Rica, GA.

Nettie Hicks Carden's parents were Emma Elizabeth Pace who was born in 1862 in Paulding County, GA and died on May 27, 1931, in Haralson County, GA; married on March 3, 1881, Denmon A. Hicks who was born in 1861 and died March 17, 1921, in Paulding County, GA. Her parents were farmers. Elizabeth Hicks' grandparents were John B. Pace Jr. and Missouri Fuller of Paulding County and Isaac Crayton Hicks and Eliza Jane Richards of Paulding County, GA. In late 1861, John B. Pace Jr. joined the Confederate Army, went to a training camp in Knoxville, TN, took the measles, and died in late 1862. He is buried in the Confederate Cemetery in Knoxville, TN.

Nettie and Clifford Carden at their 50th Wedding Anniversary Celebration on November 25, 1973.

In 1816, Nettie's great-grandfather, John B. Pace Sr. married Nancy Camp in Gwinnett County and relocated to Cobb County, GA. He owned a plantation on Sandtown Road, near Noses Creek in Marietta, GA; he served one term as Justice of the Inferior Court; and he was one of the Justices who helped select Marietta as the County Seat and caused the courthouse and other public buildings to be constructed in Marietta. In 1819, John relocated to Paulding County, where he served two terms as Associate Justice of the Inferior Court during the 1850s until he retired to tend his plantation full time. His plantation was located three miles south of Dallas, GA. The Paces were all landowners.

Nettie Hicks' roots have also been traced to Matthew Hicks who was born in 1795 in NC, and died March of 1868. (Note: His tombstone states his death as March, 1868, but he was shown on the 1870 census roll in Cleburne County, AL.)

Matthew Hicks married Sarah (Sally) Green, born about 1790 in NC. Matthew bought two tracts of land on the west bank of the Pigeon River near Richland Creek, Haywood County, NC in 1828. He sold this land and moved to Carroll County, GA about the time Sara Green's brothers relocated to Carroll County (Hickory Level community). After Sarah Green died, Matthew married Louisa McElroy and relocated to Cleburne County, AL (Muscadine area) where he lived on his approximately 500-acre farm and tended his store with the help of his son, Moses, until his death. He is buried at Bethel Cemetery, Cleburne County, AL, Road 80.

During his lifetime, Clifford Carden was employed in textiles; he was employed at Bell Aircraft, Marietta, GA; he was a farmer; and he was a finish carpenter. He suffered all his life with lung problems — asthma, emphysema and lung cancer. Later in life, he farmed briefly, and he was employed as a finish carpenter in Atlanta, Georgia for a number of years. He enjoyed this kind of work because he could breath better when he worked outside in the air.

Nettie Hicks Carden was a homemaker and a wonderful cook, and she had a "green thumb" because she could grow anything. She always had beautiful flower and vegetable gardens every year. They owned four homes in their lifetime: a beautifully landscaped home across the road from Belmont Hill Shopping Center in Smyrna, GA; a 15-acre farm that had a large peach orchard in Tallapoosa, GA; one house that they built in Villa Rica, GA; and later, they bought a small house in Villa Rica because it was convenient to the school. They lived in this house until they died.

Clifford and Nettie Carden's children were: Pauline and Robert Gene (Bob).

Pauline Carden was born February 27, 1930 in Haralson County, GA, and married Robert Glenn Roberts who was born July 2, 1926 in Carroll County, GA.

Robert and Pauline Roberts were both employed at Lockheed Aircraft Company, Marietta, GA for almost 36 years. During that time, Robert was a supervisor over several manufacturing shops for many years, and later, at retirement, he was a Leadman over the Propeller Shop.

Pauline finished two business schools and attended West Georgia College for two years. She lacked one quarter completing an A.S. in office administration. She was employed at Lockheed during the day and went to West Georgia College at night, and she could not get all the classes at night that she needed to graduate. She was a secretary and was employed in the Engineering Test Pilots' Organization, in Manufacturing Planning, and in Engineering Program Management at the time of her retirement.

Robert and Pauline Roberts had one son, David Paul.

David Paul Roberts was born August 6, 1949, in Carroll County, GA, and married on April 28, 1972, Sherry Roberta Norvell who was born July 21, 1953, in Ft. Worth, TX. Her parents are Robert and Joyce Norvell of Ft. Walton Beach, FL.

Sherry and David Roberts have two children: Brian David and Jennifer Sherry.

Brian David Roberts was born August 13,1983, in Fulton County, GA; and Jennifer Sherry Roberts was born June 29, 1988, in Fulton County, GA.

Brian will graduate from Woodstock High School, May 26, 2001, and he has been accepted at Georgia Tech; Jennifer will be in the eighth grade at Woodstock Middle School, fall of 2001.

David attended West Georgia College and Southern Tech. Later, he returned to Southern Tech and audited college-level technical writing courses. He holds a certificate in technical writing from Southern Tech; and a B.S. in business administration from Shorter College, Rome, GA. David also served four years in the Air Force in Electronics-Navigational Systems during the Vietnam War.

Sherry holds an A.S. in data processing degree from Oklaloosa-Walton College in Ft. Walton Beach, FL; and a bachelor's in business administration from Georgia State University.

David Roberts is a technical writer with ADP in Alpharetta, GA; and Sherry is a management analyst with the U.S. Department of Agriculture, Food and Nutrition Services in Atlanta, GA.

Robert Gene (Bob) Carden in the early 1950's.

Robert Gene (Bob) Carden was born April 15, 1934, in Haralson County, GA and died August 6, 1970, in Carroll County, GA. Bob first married Martha Banks of Douglasville, GA. Martha was the daughter of Lawton Banks of Douglasville, GA. They divorced while he was in the Army and they did not have any children.

Bob's second wife was Katherine Shirley Brown who was born on July 27, 1958 in Douglas County, GA. Bob and Katherine were married on July 27, 1958 in Douglas County, GA. Katherine's parents were Newt and Blonnie Vansant Brown of Douglasville, GA.

Bob was employed by Lockheed Aircraft in 1953 shortly after he graduated from Villa Rica High School. He was soon drafted into the Army and served two years, the last part of this time being spent at the Savannah River Nuclear Project at Aiken, SC. After he was discharged from the Army, he returned to Lockheed where he worked for fifteen years. He was a manufacturing research technician in Manufacturing Research until his death of lung cancer on August 6, 1970. Bob made many contributions to Lockheed with his ideas, and he was written up in the *Lockheed Star* several times during his years at Lockheed. He only lived three months after he was diagnosed and had surgery, and he was thirty-six years old when he died. His hobbies were antique cars and guns. He is buried at Sunrise Memorial Gardens, Douglasville, GA.

Katherine Carden received an A.S. in nursing from West Georgia College, and she has worked as an RN in various hospitals, and Home Health Care Services. She resides in Wedowee, AL, and she is employed at Traylor's Nursing Home in Roanoke, AL as a staff development coordinator.

Bob and Katherine Carden had one child: Christopher Robert.

Christopher Robert Carden was born October 3, 1961, in Fulton County, GA.

Chris first married Penny Ann Henry who was born February 14, 1980. They had one daughter, Bethany Amber Carden, who was born June 26, 1983, in Cobb County, GA.

Amber will be a senior at Central High School, Carrollton, GA, fall of 2001.

Chris married his second wife, Candice Cornn. Candice and Chris Carden had one son, Christopher Chance, who was born September 6, 1995.

Chris and Candice Carden divorced. Chris is presently employed in the parts department at the Douglas County Dodge, Lithia Springs, GA. *Submitted by: Katherine Carden, 471 First Avenue, SE, Wedowee, AL 36278 and Written by: Pauline C. Roberts* Sources: Court Records, Family Records, and Personal Information

410. John Workman Carroll

John Workman Carroll was born on 31 August 1821 in Orange County, North Carolina, to Moses and Elizabeth Workman Carroll. He moved to Carroll County, Georgia, with his parents in January 1844. He had been taught the hat manufacturing business by his father who had established a hat factory at Sand Hill. He assisted his father and brothers in the enterprise and later assumed control of the business. In addition to operating the hat factory, he had about fifty acres of land under cultivation.

John Workman Carroll

John Workman Carroll was married to Rachel Stidham on 9 April 1847 in Carroll County. Rachel, born 20 March 1829 in Walton County, Georgia, was the daughter of James Howard Stidham Sr. and Rachel Steedman Stidham. The children of John and Rachel Carroll, all born in Carroll County, were: Elizabeth Rowena, Margaret Ann Temperance, Elizabeth Ruth Jerusha, James Moses, Sarah Jane Frances, Mary Susan Martha, a male infant who died at birth, and Lydia Estridge Pearce. James Moses is buried in Marshall County, Alabama, and the rest are buried in the Temperance Methodist Church cemetery in Sand Hill. Their mother, Rachel Stidham Carroll, died on 28 October 1880 in Carroll County and is buried in the Temperance Methodist Church cemetery.

During the War Between the States, John Carroll manufactured wool caps for Confederate soldiers and a local unit, Company H, 41st Regiment Georgia Infantry, took the name "Wool Hat Boys" in honor of these hats. In 1863 the citizens of Carroll County petitioned the governor of Georgia for an exemption from military service for John Carroll due to the nature of his work of manufacturing hats for soldiers. In 1874 he applied to the Southern Claims Commission for reimbursement for mules taken by Union cavalry in July 1864, but was denied.

On 5 June 1881 John Carroll married Mary Antoinette Cooke in Carroll County. She was born on 3 December 1856 to Rowland Cooke and Francis King Cooke. Their children, all born in Carroll County, were Thomas Workman, Bishop Marvin Burrus (a female), and Benjamin Franklin. Thomas Workman Carroll is buried in Jefferson County, Alabama, and the latter two are buried in the Temperance cemetery.

John Workman Carroll owned 400 acres of land in Sand Hill, property in Haralson County, and a town lot in Carrollton. He was Postmaster at Sand Hill, member of the Georgia House of Representatives, Justice of the Peace for the Fairplay District, a member of Sand Hill Grange Number 285, and a Mason. In 1889 he deeded the land for a schoolhouse in Sand Hill with the deed specifying that the second floor of the building be used by the Freemasons. This building stands near the intersection of State Road 61 and the Sand Hill - Hickory Level Road and is still used as a Masonic lodge.

John Workman Carroll died 8 February 1897 and Mary Antoinette Cooke Carroll died 3 November 1907 in Carroll County. Both are buried in the Temperance Methodist Church Cemetery. *Submitted by: Deloris Lynch, 110 Brooks Rd., Brooks, GA 30205*

411. Moses Carroll

Moses Carroll was born 13 November 1789 in Orange County, North Carolina, the only child of Michael Carroll and Bettey Estridge Carroll. On 10 February 1810 he married Elizabeth Workman who was born 2 July 1791 to John and Silvia Cates Workman of Orange County. Moses was a farmer in Orange County, however his primary occupation was that of hat maker, a trade that he also taught his children. Seeking a new source of raw materials and a market for the product, he brought his family to Georgia in about 1834.

The family settled first in Floyd County, near Rome, Georgia, and remained there until January 1844 when Moses' son, Michael, purchased an acre of land that was part of Lot 111, 5th District of Carroll County. The family built a house and a log building for the hat factory on this property that is immediately south of the site of the Temperance Methodist Church in Sand Hill. Michael Carroll transferred the title to his brother, John Workman Carroll, in 1846. There is no deed evidence that Moses Carroll actually owned property in Carroll County but the 1870 Federal Population Census indicates otherwise and he was known to have several acres of land under cultivation. In January 1850 the brothers, Thomas, John, and Archimedes Carroll, purchased a portion of adjacent Lot 82 and relocated the hat factory about one-half mile east toward the business section of Sand Hill.

Moses Carroll

Moses and Elizabeth Carroll were the parents of fourteen children, nine of whom have been identified. All were born in Orange County except the two youngest who were born in Floyd County, Georgia. The children were: Michael, born 1811, died after 1880 in Pike County, Arkanas; Mary, born 1818, died 1897 in Carroll County; John Workman, born 1821, died 1897 in Carroll County; Thomas Marion, (see related Thomas M. Carroll article) born 1826, died 1908 in Haralson County, Georgia; Archimedes M., born 1827, died 1901 in Sevier County, Arkansas; Susan E., born 1830, died 1917 in Haralson County, Georgia; Ann Jane, born 1833, died 1894 in Carroll County; Frances V., born 1835, died 1911 in Baldwin County, Georgia; and James M., born 1840, served in the 1st Georgia Cavalry for the Confederacy and died 1920 in McLennon County, Texas.

Frances V. Carroll married Tilman Muse in Carroll County in 1858 and they had one child, Athalona Muse, who is believed to have been the first person buried in the Temperance cemetery. Tilman Muse had enlisted in the 1st Regiment, Louisiana Infantry and died in Richmond, Virginia, in 1862. Frances Carroll subsequently married James Lawing, the widower of her sister, Mary, and after his death she married Michael Sailors. The latter marriage occurred in 1910 and they were reported to be the oldest couple ever to marry in Carroll County.

Moses Carroll died on 28 January 1874 and Elizabeth Workman Carroll died on 19 April 1874. Both are buried in the Temperance Methodist Church cemetery along with four of their children and numerous other descendants. *Submitted by: Ruth Knott, 1689 Roscoe Rd., Newnan, GA 30263*

412. Rachel Lydia Carroll Hubert Charles Anderson

Rachel Lydia Carroll was born in 1908 in Carroll County, Georgia, the daughter of Roderick Wallace Carroll and Josephine Rebecca Hamrick. She grew up in Tallapoosa, Georgia, and graduated from Tallapoosa High School. She died in 1947 in Atlanta, Georgia.

Rachel Lydia Carroll, About 1927

In 1927 she married Hubert Charles Anderson. He was born March 21, 1902, in Waco, Georgia, and died August 5, 1970, in Atlanta, Georgia. He was one of four children of Methodist minister and circuit rider, John Wesley Anderson and Mary Louise Wright. Reverend Anderson was known for his powerful voice and sermon delivery. His family was present at every church service. A family story about him concerns his youngest child, our late Aunt Marie. As a very small child, she lay down in the pew and fell asleep during one of his sermons. When Papa Anderson saw her sleeping, he interrupted his sermon and said firmly, "Marie, sit up!" Sundays were observed as a day of worship and rest. Grandmother did not even cook on Sunday, the meals having been prepared on Saturday.

Hubert Charles Anderson, About 1927

As a single young man, Daddy lived at the YMCA in Atlanta. While there, he became an amateur boxer for a time, and loved the sport all his life.

Rachel Carroll and Hubert Anderson had two daughters, both born in Atlanta, Georgia, Rachel Carroll, June 16, 1933, and Reba Charlene, September 6, 1939. One of the few memories of Mother is that during World War II, she worked in the Commissary at Ft. MacPherson, Georgia. As she was an employee, we were allowed to buy groceries at the Commissary. As a small child, I remember standing, for what seemed like hours, at the meat counter waiting for our meat to be cut to order. I also remember the white oleo margarine that came with a little envelope of orange powder, which was mixed into the oleomargarine to give it a yellow color. Mother would press the oleomargarine into a round wooden mold. When it was released from the mold, it had a pretty flower design on top. Milk was not homogenized then, and I loved to taste the cream that rose to the top of the glass milk bottles with their cardboard lids. Mother would sometimes skim the cream off to make whipped cream.

My sister Carroll remembers when we were children she would sometimes be assigned the task of bathing me. So, she bathed me in the most efficient way she could think of, which was to soap me up really well and then towel me dry without rinsing off the soap! Mother did discover this eventually.

Descendants of Rachel and Hubert Anderson currently live in Atlanta, Marietta, Georgia and Boston, Massachusetts. They include two daughters, a granddaughter, Lisa Carroll Ball Remaley, five great-grandchildren, John-Paul Rubadou, Jesse William Remaley, Anderson James Remaley, and twins Julie Rachel Remaley and Joseph David Remaley. Their grandson, James Matthew Ball, lives in Boston and is on the staff of the Harvard University Law Library. *Submitted by: Reba Charlene Anderson Kruse, 310 Lamplighter Lane, Marietta, GA 30067 and Rachel Carroll Anderson Ball, 2112 Palifox Drive, Atlanta, GA 30067.*

413. Roderick Wallace "Rod" Carroll

Old Carrollton was situated in the vicinity of Sand Hill in the original Carroll County. Moses Carroll (1789-1874), an early Carroll County settler, is buried at Sand Hill with his wife Elizabeth Workman Carroll, (1791-1874). Roderick Wallace "Rod" Carroll, grandson of Moses and Elizabeth, was born to Dr. Thomas Marion Carroll (1826-1908) and Isabella Anne McAllister (1833-1906) on July 14, 1869. Dr. Carroll served in the Confederate Army during the Civil War, and of his war years later confided to Rod's brother, James M.B. Carroll, "We had to do some terrible things in the war."

Rod had a twin brother, Oscar Bruce Carroll (1869-1948). Rod's other siblings were James Moses Blackburn Carroll (1862-1955), Ida Anaballe Carroll (1865-1919), Thomas Oree Carroll (1870-1957), and A. Dewitt Carroll (1876-1921). Rod's father, Dr. Carroll, owned a hotel in Waco where he maintained his medical practice on the first floor, and Rod's mother Isabella managed the hotel and the books for the medical practice. (*See related Carroll article.*)

Rod married Josephine Rebecca "Josie" Hamrick (1872-1919) on November 25, 1891. Josie was the daughter of James T. and Rebecca Hamrick. Surviving children were: Thomas R. Carroll, Ross H. Carroll, Anna Belle Carroll (Chapman), Roderick Mitchell Carroll, Myrtle Pauline Carroll (Phillips), Rachel Lydia Carroll (Anderson), and Edgar Carroll.

Rod and Josie owned a farm in Tallapoosa bordering on the old Lithia Springs Hotel property. Many family stories I remember centered on the hotel and farm. The hotel was completed in 1892, cost $100,000, was of wood-frame construction, had a large dining room, a ballroom, 130 bedrooms, steam heat, electric lights and an elevator. I have an *Atlanta Journal* newspaper article dated August 10, 1985, which describes "The Great Gathering" for the 125th Anniversary of Tallapoosa, originally called 'Talapouchie' by the Creek Indians.

Roderick Wallace Carroll with daughters Anna Belle, Myrtle Pauline, Rachel Lydia

One day, Rod (Pop to me) parked his wagon on the town square in Buchanan while delivering milk. The old courthouse was at the center of the square with steps to a raised level above the rest of the square and additional steps into the courthouse. After making his delivery, the wagon was gone. Pop first thought it stolen, but heard laughter coming from the area of the courthouse. His horse had pulled the wagon up the first level of steps, up the second steps leading into the old courthouse, and had wedged the wagon in the courthouse door. It was only recently that I saw the old courthouse, and recognized it immediately as the very location of Pop's story.

Grandma Josie died on March 16, 1919. Pop stayed on at the farm for a time, but eventually lived with members of his family, including us, until his death October 29, 1956. Rod is buried beside Josie at the Waco Cemetery in Waco, Georgia, not far from his parents. *Submitted by: Rodric M. Phillips, 8325 N.E. 140th, Edmond, OK 73013-8717*
Sources: *Georgia's Last Frontier,* family records, *The Atlanta Journal/Atlanta Constitution*

414. Thomas Marion Carroll and Isabella Anne McAllister

Thomas Marion Carroll was born in Orange County, North Carolina, on February 26, 1826. His parents were Moses Carroll and Elizabeth Workman who moved to Floyd County, Georgia, around 1834. When Thomas was about fourteen, his parents moved to the Sand Hill community in Carroll County. His father was a hatter by trade and several of Thomas's five brothers worked in this occupation. Thomas chose not to follow the hatter profession. Instead, he became interested in the field of medicine.

Isabella Anne McAllister (see McRae-McAllister article) was born December 27, 1833. We know she was born in Georgia and think she was born in the Hickory Level community of Carroll County. Sometime around 1832 to 1833, her parents had moved from Tennessee to Georgia.

The Rev. James Baskin married Thomas and Isabella in Carroll County on October 27, 1857. Before 1860, they moved to Haralson County near Waco where they are listed twice on the census records. On one entry Thomas is listed as a farmer, and on the other entry as a physician. They appear on the 1870 census in Carroll County and the Haralson census for 1880 and 1900.

Six children were born to this union — five boys and one girl. (1) James Moses Blackburn (our grandfather) was born July 2, 1862. (2) Ida Annabelle was born April 20, 1865. She was married first to Samuel Newman on August 11, 1881, and second to Jim Nickels on January 17, 1892. Ida had no children by either marriage. (3) Next were twin boys. Oscar Bruce born May 11, 1869. He married Mary Fannie McBurnett on May 11, 1890, and they had fourteen children. (4) Roderick Wallace was born on May 11, 1869, Roderick married Josephine Rebecca Hamrick on November 25, 1891 and they had nine children. (5) Thomas Oree was born in July 1870. Oree never married and he lived with his brother James for several years after his parents died. After losing his eyesight, he then lived in a home for the blind in Valdosta and later in a nursing home. (6) A. Dewitt was born in May 1876 and died August 4, 1921, in Chatham County, Georgia. He was married to Pearl Parker in 1904; this marriage ended in divorce around 1915. There were no children born to Dewitt and Pearl.

Thomas and Isabella lived in the Waco area for many years. Records show Thomas sold to the city part of the land for the first city cemetery. The price received for this property was $5.00. For many years, Thomas and Isabella owned the old hotel in Waco where the present Post Office is located. Based on family stories, Thomas maintained his medical office there and Isabella ran the hotel and kept books for both the hotel and Dr. Tom's medical practice. Many death records can be found in both Haralson and Carroll that show his name as the attending physician. However, no one has yet to ascertain what formal schooling Thomas Marion went through for his medical training. His obituary reads that he was a well-known medical practitioner in that part of the state. Only a few of his personal belongings have ever been found. Family tradition relates that many of his records were probably burned when the family was preparing to move from the old home place. Isabella died in Waco on April 11, 1906. Thomas Marion died in Buncombe at his son's home on May 7, 1908. Both are buried in the Waco City Cemetery.

James Moses Blackburn Carroll, our grandfather, was born July 2, 1862 in Haralson County and spent most of his ninety-two years in the western parts of Carroll and Haralson County as a farmer and a saw miller. Friends frequently called him "Uncle Jim," but to many he was simply "Grandpa." Some family members addressed him as J.M.B., a name that he liked to be called. The source for the name Blackburn remains another family mystery. Grandpa was very proud of his name and he generally emphasized the Blackburn part when telling his name. One existing theory on his name was that his parents added Blackburn to serve as an identifier since there were already two, and possibly three James Moses Carrolls in the broader Carroll family.

According to the family Bible, which belonged to her parents, Lucinda Indiana McBurnett was born October 29, 1872. The family always thought her name was Minnie Lee McBurnett and that she was born on October 29, 1870. Another family mystery is why and when Grandmother decided to alter her name and birthday, but she did and not one of her ten children was aware of this fact.

Minnie was the oldest of thirteen children born to Jefferson McGee McBurnett and Sarah Ann Elizabeth King (see related McBurnett-King article). The McBurnett family, minus Minnie and one sister, moved to Texas around 1892.

J.M.B. Carroll and Minnie Lee McBurnett were married in Haralson County on October 15, 1890. Ten children were born to this union: (1) Willie Belle was born March 12, 1891, died April 24, 1988. Married Marvin Brown March 5, 1911. (2) Eucleod McAllister was born June 23, 1893, died October 12, 1976. Married first to Ollie Melvina Warren January 13, 1918 (our parents), and second to Lillian Styles Sims October 4, 1974. (3) Irwin Jefferson was born March 25, 1895, died November 19, 1934, resulting from exposure to poisonous gas during World War I. Married Annie Lee Leak on August 31, 1919. (4) Lillie Gayce was born December 7, 1896, died September 6, 1998, at a nursing home in Carrollton. She lived longer than any other known Carroll. Married Lee Otis Barrow on February 13, 1913. (5) Cecile Fern was born March 9, 1898, died June 1, 1992. Married first to William Ambrose Cooke on August 27, 1913, and second to Chester Myers on January 24, 1953. (6) Henry Lawton was born September 23, 1899, died November 8, 1989. Married Lallie Lee Morris on June 15, 1919. (7) Jimmie Lou was born March 27, 1902, died January 30, 1920. Married Eldridge Love on June 15, 1916. Jimmie died at age eighteen and is buried at Union Camp Ground Cemetery near Waco. (8) Johnnie Beatrice was born March 21, 1904, died March 18, 1995. Married Andy Ray Kite on October 20, 1920. (9) Thomas Marion was born May 9, 1906, died October 5, 1987. Married Bessie Lou Slaton on December 14, 1930. (10) Charles Barrett was born September 21, 1909, died February 27, 1969. Married Jimmie Ruth Cole on October 2, 1932.

Minnie Lee died in an Atlanta hospital on September 7, 1950. J.M.B. died in the Bremen Hospital on June 22, 1955. Both are buried in the Waco City Cemetery. *Submitted by: Charles E. Carroll, Bremen, GA, based on research by Stanley N. Carroll and Betty Jo Carroll Parsons.*

Sources: Family Bible records, personal knowledge, U.S. Census Records, Carroll County marriage records

415. William Wesley Carroll

William Wesley Carroll was born May 16, 1881, in Carroll County, Georgia. He was the oldest child of Pleasant Ance Carroll and Emma Adkins Carroll. He was the grandson of Pleasant L. Carroll and Cynthia Trawell Carroll who were married in Carroll County in 1849. He grew up in Carroll County and married Rhoda C. White on February 16, 1902. From this union there were six children, Amy, Omie, Ance, Carrie, Abbie, and Verdie.

He was a share cropper, always farming someone else's land. He never stayed more than two or three years on one farm. He was a strict disciplinarian and perfectionist. He expected the job done well; if not, it was to be done again. At one time the children were to clean a new ground. After they thought they had finished, it wasn't as clean as he wanted it, so they had to sweep it. This was in the New Brooklyn community near Temple, Georgia. He lived from the north end of the county to the south end, even one year in Turin, Georgia which is in Coweta County.

Pleasant A. Carroll Family

Rhoda died in 1916 leaving the children, all under the age of thirteen. On July 2, 1922, William married Katie Ann Reese. He continued farming and the children left home to marry or work elsewhere. Omie married Roy Muse, Carrie married Andrew "Jay" Rigsby, Ance married Georgie Alexander, and Verdie married Willard Muse. Amy later married Lawson Reese, Katie's brother. After spending some time in the army in Panama, Abbie married Vera Compton of Ninety Six, South Carolina.

William still did not own any property but continued farming. To friends and neighbors he became known as Mr. Will and his wife as Miss Katie. To his eleven grandchildren, they were "Papa Carroll" and "Granny Kate."

After living on so many different farms, in 1947 he finally settled on two acres which he bought on what is now known as Maple Hill Road, just east of Carrollton. There he had a little three-room house with front and back porch, huge pecan trees, lots of fruit trees, and a large garden. Each year there was an abundance of fresh vegetables of every kind and he enjoyed planting and weeding the garden. Grass or weeds didn't have a chance. He kept it clean and raked, even to backing out and smoothing out his tracks. The garden was fenced and he used this fence to grow anything that made vines. No space was wasted. On the outside of the fence which was along the driveway, was the flower garden with old-fashioned plants, especially zinnias, dahlias, and four-o-clocks. Nothing was lost; everything was canned, dried, or in some way preserved including all kinds of fruits, apples, peaches, and pears. The bounty was also shared with family and friends. There were also blackberries and strawberries. These were made into jams and jellies, but he also made wine. He said it was for medicinal purposes. Blackberry wine was especially good for upset stomach and for the digestive system. If you visited during the time watermelon and cantaloupes were ripe, you didn't leave until you had eaten at least one slice. They were placed on the shelf on the back porch to be cut and you were always filled before you left.

The Carroll Family Reunion was always held at his home on the second Sunday in August such a happy time! All the family would come home and we looked forward especially to seeing the youngest son, Abbie and his family from South Carolina. The day started early and there was always a bountiful table at lunch time and then all the visiting and catching up as we sat under the large trees. There was a little store on the Carrollton-Villa Rica Highway, now known as 166 East. It was owned by Virgil Carmichael. He walked to the store most every day, early in the morning, not necessarily to buy anything, but just to visit. He and "Granny Kate" also walked to Amy's house which was about two miles away to get milk and butter. On these walks he was always on the look-out for any objects he might find along the road, such as nails, nuts, bolts, unusual rocks, or maybe some bits of string. There was a little basket which sat on the cabinet just inside the kitchen door. That's where it was all collected. He was always showing some of these "special finds" to family and friends. In the summer time, late in the day you would find them both sitting on the front porch in the swing. He would be barefooted and holding the fly swatter. He said if you went barefooted in the summer, you wouldn't have corns.

In 1960 he moved into a little house near his oldest son, Ance. He only lived there a couple of years before he moved into an apartment in Carrollton. He died March 27, 1965. Granny Kate lived to be 103. She died in 1986. Both are buried in Shady Grove Baptist Church Cemetery. Pictured in the photograph of the Pleasant A. Carroll Family are: Front row: Vassie and Audie Carroll. Second row: John Lewis, holding Lomie Lewis, Rose Carroll Lewis, Pleasant Ance Carroll holding Obie Carroll, Emma Carroll, holding Bewie Carroll, Della Carroll Morris, holding daughter Gladys Morris, Frank Morris, Island Morris, and Mary Adkins, mother of Emma Carroll. Third row: Ida Carroll, Bell Carroll, Lovie Carroll, Dock Carroll, Lela Carroll, William Wesley Carroll, Olin Carroll, and Rhoda Carroll. *Submitted by: Carrie Carroll Rigsby, 530 Northside Drive, Carrollton, GA 30117 and Written by: Louise M. Petty*

Sources: Family stories and personal experiences.

416. The James Richard Carter Family

The first historical record we have of the Carters in America dates back to 1748 when King George II of England ceded to Thomas Carter three-million acres of land on Cape Fear River in North Carolina. From that time, we have authentic and reliable history of the Carter family and their migration into Virginia, South Carolina, and Georgia. The head of the South Carolina Carters was Charles Carter of Edgefield District, South Carolina. He and his wife, Lydia Scurry Carter of Ireland, came to Edgefield District between 1750 and 1800.

Between the years 1845 and 1848, one group of their children left the Edgefield District and settled in Coweta County, Georgia. The others remained in Edgefield. At this time, Lydia Carter, their mother, was still living. Those who migrated to Georgia consisted of four brothers (Martin, Daniel, Thomas, and John) and two sisters. Both sisters married, one to Oliver Bradfield, and the other to a Mr. Trotter. Daniel Carter bought land nine miles west of Newnan. John's place was ten miles west of Newman on the banks of the Chattahoochee River. The Bradfields settled on land six miles northwest of Newnan, Georgia.

James Richard Carter Family

Daniel Carter was born March 4, 1795, and died in 1861. He was married to Eliza Williams, born August 15, 1801. Their children and their birth dates are as follows: Charlotte Temple Carter January 29, 1819; William Williams Carter October 5, 1820; Enoch Carter November 10, 1822; Eliza Elisha Carter January 7, 1825; Caroline Elizabeth Carter October 12, 1826; Elva 1829; Lydia Ann Amanda Carter September 18, 1831; Charles Warren Carter July 2, 1833; S. Ann Matilda Carter September 3, 1835; James Richard Carter February 12, 1838; and Arthur Holland Carter March 6, 1840.

James Richard Carter was nine years old when his parents came to Coweta County. Stories of his happy childhood in South Carolina and how he loved his Carter cousins that he left behind have been passed down to us through the generations. His father, Daniel, was a first cousin to Ann Hill Carter, who married Henry (Light Horse Harry) Lee, the famous general in the American Revolution. Ann Carter Lee would visit the Carters in Edgefield and bring her young son, Robert E. Lee. James Richard told many stories to his grandchildren about these visits and how years later he would fight for the Confederacy under Lee's leadership in the Phillips Legion Company F, Cavalry Battalion of the Georgia Volunteers. He was discharged in Atlanta, Georgia, in 1865.

James Richard Carter married Leander Frances Friddell on December 12, 1858. She was the daughter of Joseph and Matilda Friddell. Joseph was born in 1793 and died on November 26, 1886, at the age of ninety-three. Matilda was born in 1797 and died on August 26, 1885, at the age of eighty-eight. They are buried in Whitesburg, Georgia, in the Methodist Church cemetery.

The Carters spent most of their married life in Carroll County and the Whitesburg area where they farmed. Their children all lived within a few miles of each other in Carroll, Coweta, Douglas, and Campbell (now Fulton) counties. Their children are as follows: Dawson Richard (January 16, 1866-October 12, 1942); M. Loula Sims (July 27, 1866-December 23, 1950); Della (October 9, 1871-1955); M. Robert L. Holloway (January 31, 1869-April 15, 1918); Exa Leander (December 15, 1873-December 17, 1953); M.J.P. Morris (August 30, 1873-April 4, 1911); William W. Carter (March 5, 1876-July 6, 1950); M. Ollie Bell (December 27, 1876-July 16, 1940); Rev. Daniel W. Carter (January 31, 1878-May 10, 1943); M. Ida E. Barefield (June 17, 1883-January 21, 1961); Hattie Mae (July 2, 1883-October 31, 1960); M. Joseph Benjamin Lassetter (September 1, 1880-August 26, 1928); and Amellia Carter.

At the time of their deaths, James Richard and Leander Frances were living in Palmetto, Georgia, with their youngest daughter, Hattie Lassetter. They are buried at Ramah First Baptist Church Cemetery in Palmetto. A Confederate marker shows his death as 1916. Her birth and death dates are unknown.

These are the names of those shown in the picture: front row, Vivian Carter, Eula Carter, twins Ella and Stella Carter, Loula Carter, Amellia Carter, Exa Morris, Willie Frank Morris, Frances Friddell Carter, and Hattie Carter; back row, Clif Carter, Arthur Carter, Dawson Carter, Dan Carter, Will Carter, Joe Morris, and James Richard Carter. *Submitted by: Thomas W. Harper, Jr., 510 Bradley Drive, Palmetto, GA 30268 and Written by: Carole Lassetter Harper.*

417. The Son Carter Family

Willie Ben Carter (known as Son Carter) was born 11 March 1898 in Troup County, Georgia. His mother was Mrs. Emma (William) Carter who was the daughter of Hardy and Lucy Lynch. Lucy Lynch was descended from slaves. When Son Carter was twelve years old, his family, including his mother and four younger sisters, Ocie, Lucy, Johnnie Mae, and Lou Ella, moved from Troup County to Carroll County. This included the Lynches, and also Emma's sister who was called Sweet. The story was told in the family that a terrible flu epidemic had swept over the county about 1914 and nearly wiped out the entire Carter family. Son's father died in this epidemic.

Son Carter grew up in Carroll County and quickly rose to a position of responsibility as overseer for a large farm near Clem-Lowell. Son knew just about everything there was to know about farming in Carroll County, and he was a great believer in planting by the signs of the zodiac. Whatever he did seemed to be right because his crops were some of the finest in the county.

Son was married first to Willie Mae Hogan on 30 April 1921, but this wife died giving birth in 1927 to their only child Thelma (who later married J. Bassett). However, it was this tragic event that brought Son Carter into the lives of the J. Horry Morgan family. In the wee hours of the morning, Horry Morgan heard a tap-tapping at the windowpane. He looked out and there in the moonlight stood Son Carter. Horry knew Son worked for another farm farther down the Whooping Creek Church Road. Son apologized for disturbing their sleep but his business was urgent. Son told Horry Morgan that his young wife had died in childbirth and that he had no money to pay for a coffin to bury her in. He had appealed to everyone else he knew, but no one would advance him this money. He told "Mister Horry" if he would pay for his wife to have a coffin, he would come work for him and would be a loyal and hard worker for the rest of his life. Son had said to him, "I loved her so, Mister Horry, I just can't put her in the cold ground without a coffin."

Son Carter knew that Horry Morgan had a reputation for kindness to black people in the community and Horry Morgan knew that Son Carter had the reputation of being a hard farm worker and a man of his word. Horry advanced Son the money to have not only a coffin for his wife, but a funeral as well. Their deal was struck and it was the beginning of a friendship that would turn to gold over the next seventy-five years. Son Carter became the right hand man of Horry Morgan on his farm and in many of his business enterprises, including his sawmill. Son was especially proud of the responsibility of keeping all the Morgan cars — 1920-1940 vintage — in tune. Also, Son would chauffeur "Miss Trixie" around since she did not drive.

After Horry Morgan died at the age of forty-six, it left his aged mother, Derah Morgan, and his widow, Trixie Morgan, on the home place alone. This was just after World War II and had it not been for Son Carter who stayed on to work the farm, they would have lost everything.

The Morgans bought Son a tractor and with that he was able to manage to keep the farm producing cotton and other crops. Son Carter prided himself on his cotton crops and was often the first one to have a boll to bloom, or the first one to get his cotton to the gin. Prizes were given for these county honors and Son loved to win prizes, and he often did.

On 13 April 1930, Son Carter married a second time to Charlcie Mae Chivers who was born 29 July 1911. She was the daughter of Talston and Ludie Bonner Chivers. Charlcie Mae had four brothers: Edward, James, LeRoy and Talston Chivers. Her sisters were Edna and Jeannie Chivers. The Chivers family have long been a part of Carroll County and are greatly respected in the community. Elbert Chivers, a cousin, worked many years as the custodian of Carrollton High School and is well remembered by the students of CHS in the 1950-1960 era.

Son and Charlcie's first child was Wilbert Edward Carter born 18 November 1931. Wilbert worked for J. Carl Dry Cleaners many years. He never had children. A second son was Benny Hearly Carter, born 19 October 1933. Benny was for many years employed as a cook at Tanner Memorial Hospital. Benny Carter served in the U.S. Army in the Vietnam War. Benny Carter died 12 November 1966. Benny had one daughter named Diane.

The third child was Ocie Lee Carter, born 28 January 1938. Ocie Lee worked many years as a nursemaid for the children of John and Melba Morgan Robinson and she was Jan's special nursemaid. (She caught a million butterflies for Jan.) There were no schools for black children when Ocie Lee was young and she spent most of her young life picking cotton. But Ocie Lee wanted to learn to read and write. Jan's mother, Melba Robinson, was a teacher of home economics at Roopville High School. After her official work day ended at Roopville, Melba would come home and teach Ocie Lee, and Ocie Lee did learn to read and write. "The purpose of education is not to earn your bread, but to make every mouthful sweeter" was an old saying in the black community in this time period. When Ocie Lee was about thirteen years old, she was able to enroll in Oakridge School where she caught up with the other children in her class. Ocie Lee was ever grateful to Melba for teaching her how to read and write. Later, Ocie Lee married Ernest Henson and they had a daughter named Patricia Ernest born July 13, 1958. Patricia's children are Shantana Renice Green and Herman White III. Ocie and Ernest's son, André Henson, was born 16 October 1959 and he married Twyla McPherson. They had one daughter, Patrice Ladrea.

The fourth child of Son and Charlcie Mae was Lucy Mae Carter who was born 28 December 1941. Lucy Mae was as "pretty as a picture" and was named Miss Carver High School. Lucy Mae also worked for the John Robinson family. Lucy Mae was the mother of Michael Buchanan born 17 June 1961 and Gregory Buchanan born 28 January 1963. A third son, Stephon Dimone Carter was born 15 August 1966. Later, Lucy Mae married Joe Castleberry, also a graduate of Carver High School, and they had three more children, (1) Jacqueline Castleberry born 14 September 1968 and now married to Afton Lee, one son Afton Lee Jr., (2) Sharon Castleberry born 17 February 1970, and (3) Connie Castleberry born 8 July 1971. Lucy Mae Castleberry died on 3 February 1999.

The fifth child of Son and Charlcie Mae Carter was Irma Jean Carter, born 30 November 1943. Irma Jean graduated from Carver High School in 1961. Her children are Breshaun Lee Carter born 25 July 1969 who married Catesia Powell and has two children: America Sierra Carter born 12 December 1990. Also a son, Terrell Breshaun Carter born 9 September, 1996. Irma Jean's daughter is Shameka Dionne Carter born 13 March 1973. Shameka has a son Dajour Faizon Brewer born 6 November 1996. Shameka and Shaun Carter both graduated from Carrollton High School. Irma Jean Carter worked at Goldkist briefly but worked many years as the caretaker for the many nieces and nephews in her family who needed a good caretaker while their parents worked. Irma Jean became the caretaker of her parents in their old age as well, so she has served in this capacity for her family for many years. She later married Willie B. Joiner who is employed in construction and they make their home in Woodland, Alabama.

The sixth child of Son and Charlcie Mae Carter is James Robert Carter, born 29 July 1945. James Robert always had a natural knack for mechanics and worked for over thirty years for Robinson Drug Company in Carrollton. He repaired hospital beds, wheelchairs, and also worked on the farm and kept the farm equipment running smoothly. James Robert Carter served his country in Vietnam as Specialist E4 in the U.S. Army. He was stationed at Bien Hoa and part of the 500th and 100th Baileybridge Engineer Corps that built landing strips and bridges in Vietnam. James Robert Carter married Saundra Sue Rock and they later divorced. James Robert has one son, Kimberly deWayne Carter born 1 March 1966. He also has a daughter Shanta Carter. James Robert Carter received his disability from the exposure to Agent Orange while in Vietnam.

After Horry Morgan's death, Son Carter became devoted to Horry's daughter, Melba, who had married John Robinson. When the Robinsons moved to Carrollton in 1954, the Carters moved as well and the Carters settled on the Robinson farm (previously known as the Julian Kaylor farm) on Kingsbridge Road. Son managed this farm capably in addition to performing many duties for Robinson Drug Company.

In the early 1960s, the Robinson daughters owned horses and Son Carter built them a riding ring so they could practice for their horse shows. John Robinson also had a number of Hereford cattle which he highly prized and Son took care of all the farm animals. There was a beautiful lake on the property with a cabin and both Son and Charlcie Mae loved to fish there. The pecan groves around the house supplied both the Carters and the Robinsons with all the pecans they could shell for pies and cornbread dressings at Thanksgiving.

"Miss Charlcie" was a great storyteller and could scare the living daylights out of you with some of the ghost stories she used to tell. She once told a story about a rope coiled up in a barn that turned into a rattlesnake! James Robert Carter and Jan Robinson (who were playmates as children and spent early years together on the Morgan farm) have never spent more than three shakes of a lamb's tail around a coiled up rope since then. And don't even mention coach whip snakes to us.

One rather humorous experienced occurred in the 1970s when America was facing a severe gasoline shortage because of the oil embargo with Iran. It looked like we were about to be completely out of fuel and John Robinson was worried about how he would have the gasoline to deliver medicines to his customers of Robinson Drug Company. Son Carter reassured John that he had once worked for an old sea captain who had a recipe for a type of alcohol that might run a tractor engine and it might work for a car, too. (And some folks drink it!) John launched headfirst into this project, hoping to save his community from his gasoline crisis, for John Robinson had been mayor of Carrollton and always wanted to find solutions to city problems.

So Son began with his recipe of "a handful of corn kernels wrapped up in a burlap bag, tied with string, and buried in the ground yea deep at a certain phase of the moon." After a few days, the kernels would sprout and then had to be added to a hogshead (barrel of certain size) and filled with water and more corn. And so forth, until the sign of the moon was just so again and then you would have a combustible alcohol type fuel. (Or moonshine, however you look at it.) All this was going along pretty well until suddenly Son realized that he was — in fact — about to put John Robinson in the gasoline business which would be in direct conflict with Betty and Bobby Morgan's Amoco stations that dotted the country. Suddenly, Son was facing a dilemma, for he adored both of Horry Morgan's children and their spouses, Melba and John and Betty and Bobby, and for once in his life, he was caught up in a conflict of loyalties here.

And so what happened was that Son stalled again and again saying the phase of the moon wasn't quite right yet, or that the hogshead was not the right size, or that the kernels didn't sprout just so, ad infinitum. And that's how it happened that John Robinson never went into the gasoline business! As it turned out, the gasoline crisis was soon resolved and this became yet just one more interesting and rather unbelievable chapter in our family's history.

Son Carter became the first black man to drive a white school bus in Carroll County. This was in the days before integration and sadly the black children had to walk to school. Only the white children could ride. But Son was a wise and patient man and a peaceful one, too. He was willing to make that one small step each day toward the journey of thousands of miles in achieving civil rights for his race. He listened to the speeches of Rev. Martin Luther King and he knew that changes would come "a blowin' in the wind" as that great old song would later predict.

Son Carter knew it might take his whole lifetime to ever effectively bring about the changes, and it almost did, but Son did live to see a new era throughout the South before he died. The signs on rest rooms and water fountains that said "Colored Only" would disappear in the 1970s. But in the 1930s, these signs were still in place and very much enforced.

One of the scariest experiences that Son ever had was about 1930 when he drove Horry's wife, Trixie Patrick Morgan, back home to visit her family in Cullman, Alabama. It was a matter of great pride to Son that he would be entrusted to capably manage the automobile, the entire road trip, and to escort Trixie safely to and from home. One thing that was unusual about Cullman was that it was a town with no black people in it. In fact, in those days, it was a matter of pride to some townspeople who would boast "no Negroes live here." So when Son Carter would appear driving Trixie into Cullman, it always caused a bit of a stir and people would come to stare at this oddity, a black man chauffeuring a white woman.

One fateful thing happened just before Son and Trixie left on what was to be their last trip to Cullman together in 1930. Horry Morgan came home with a new license tag for the car that Son would be driving to Alabama. He asked Son to put it on the car before leaving and Son had gone out to do this. But in those days, Son had not had any schooling yet and he could not read the license plate. (He did learn to read and write in years later.) Son did not know that he had put the plate onto the car upside down. And no one else noticed it either. And off Son and Trixie went down the dirt road with dust a boilin' behind them on the "trip back home."

Shortly before arriving in Cullman, the car had needed gas, so Son pulled into a tiny Alabama filling station. A gang of unruly men gathered to stare at this unusual sight, a black man driving toward Cullman. They began to heckle and jeer at Son and then accused him of trying to be some kind of smart-aleck because his license plate was on upside down. Son had apologized for this error and said he had not known it was upside down. He said he'd change it if they would loan him a screwdriver.

Willie Ben "Son" Carter and Charlcie Mae Chivers Carter

They wouldn't, and said he was going to change it right now anyway and that he could unscrew the screws with his fingers. And that's what they made him do. Son's fingers were raw and bleeding by the time he'd accomplished changing around the license plate. A bigger crowd was gathering to watch Son try to unscrew the screws with his bleeding hands. Trixie sat in the car, terrified and crying, and so upset thinking perhaps these men were going to do even worse to Son. The tone of the crowd had grown mean and angry. Unfortunately, this is the way times used to be. But Son had managed to change the plate and then drive them safely away from the filling station before any further incident. But after that time, Son never had to drive Trixie or anybody else to Cullman, Alabama, again. "We'll never put you at that kind of risk again, Son," Horry Morgan had told him. "You mean too much to us and we don't want to lose you." After that, Trixie would ride the train from Atlanta to Cullman for her trips back home to visit her family. And it would be several decades later before the signs would come down that said "No colored allowed."

Son Carter had his own secret way of making sausage and curing hams and whenever he brought these as gifts to friends and neighbors they had quite a tasty experience. Son Carter was a deacon in the Antioch Clem Baptist Church and taught Sunday School there for many years. One of his devoted Sunday School pupils who is a well established citizen of our community of today is Joseph Jones, who is an electrician and a plumber, too. Joe can tell you what a great influence Son Carter was on him in his youth. Son loved Sacred Harp singing too.

Son also had a hobby of being a barber, and he had a real barber chair he'd set up in his home. Son always maintained he wanted to "wear out, not rust out" and he continued to work for Robinson Drug Company until shortly before his death at the age of ninety-two. When John Robinson's grandsons became teenagers and old enough to work at Robinson Drug Company, it was Son who trained them in the business and mechanics of how to deliver and assemble hospital beds and wheelchairs.

Son Carter had a great influence on the lives of many people in this county — black and white — and will long be remembered. He died on 26 August 1990 and his funeral was preached by Rev. Covington. The eulogy was given by Jan Robinson Bell. In years previous, Son had asked Jan to write a poem about his early years on the Morgan farm when he always prided himself on the beautiful fields of cotton he produced. Jan wrote a poem for Son called *Cloud Cotton* using the imagery that Son had loved his cotton fields so much that now he had "gone to tend God's cotton clouds." The church was packed for Son's funeral and many people requested a copy of this poem afterward. In part this is what the poem said:

The years they rolled by swiftly
Just as clouds roll in the sky
And the Lord looked down from Heaven
As Son's days were drawing nigh

And He smiled to know that Heaven
Would soon be very proud
To call home a real hard worker
Who could tend those cotton clouds.

Oh, to go plant clouds in Gloryland!
And plow to his heart's content!
And that is why when Son was called,
Off with a smile he went.

And it makes me smile to really think
Instead of a harp of gold
The Lord gave Son a golden plow
In his strong hands to hold.

To help make Heaven beautiful
With crops of snow-white clouds
There's plenty enough of Angels
With harps a singin' loud!

Oh, the Lord's work is never finished
And this is why I know
That Son is plantin' and plowin' now
Makin' clouds for us below.

Yes, Son was called to Gloryland
To work a different sod,
To help keep our eyes toward Heaven
And the greatness that is God.

One of the most loving traditions that Son Carter always had for the Robinsons was that in his belief it would bring good luck for the New Year if a man of color was first to knock on your door. For sixty years, Son Carter got up at crack of New Year's Day to come and knock on the Robinsons' door so he could bring them good luck — and he always did, all year round. We loved him so.

Son Carter was buried at Antioch Clem Baptist Church. "Miss Charlcie Mae" survived him by a few years and she died on December 11, 1994, being laid to rest beside her husband. Their son, Benny Hearly Carter rests beside them. Also, Lucy and Hardy Lynch and members of their family are buried there.

Son and Charlcie Mae Carter would be proud to see the many fine accomplishments of their descendants in Carroll County today. Their granddaughter, Sharon Castleberry, is the office manager for Dr. Karen Avery at her Pain Clinic on the Bremen Highway in Carrollton. Carrollton is so lucky to have this wonderful neurologist and we are proud that Dr. Avery has put down deep roots here. And Dr. Avery prizes having not one but two of the Carter granddaughters, Sharon and Shameka "Meka," to assist her in her office. Shaun Carter has worked for Southwire for many years. Gregory Buchanan works in concrete and construction. Michael Buchanan and Stephon Carter have continued to work for Robinson Drug Company in various capacities. Michael has been especially appreciated by Jan Bell since her disability and he has been her right-hand in helping with so many projects at home. The Carter family has meant a lot to our family. But as Son Carter would probably say (since it was a favorite old saying of his anyway), "Oh, that's too much sugar for a dime and not enough for fifteen cents." *Submitted by: Ocie Lee Henson, 3601 Highway 100 South, Bowdon, GA 30108 and Written by: Jan Robinson Bell*

418. Benjamin Butler Cassels

Benjamin Butler Cassels (1824-1901), the son of Henry Cassels and Charlotte Jones, was born in Georgia and died at age 76 in Banning, Carroll County, Georgia. He married Harriet Parazette Mathews of Georgia. She was born in 1831 and died in 1905 at age 73. She was the daughter of Moses Mathews and Sarah Welch. Harriet, or Parry as she was called, is buried beside Benjamin in the Antioch Primitive Baptist Church Cemetery, Whitesburg, Georgia.

Benjamin and Parry each had eight brothers and sisters. Benjamin's brother Robert Henry married Parry's sister, Sarah Jane Mathews. His sister Rebecca married Parry's brother Henry Jasper Mathews and moved to Angelina County, Texas. With the two families being so closely related, their letters from the late 1800s and early 1900s usually mentioned both families. These letters were beneficial in establishing relationships within the family as well as places of residence.

The other children of Henry and Charlotte Cassels were Avington who married Winnie Ann Waldrop and moved to Angelina County, Texas; Absolum who married Ellenor Linville and remained in Georgia; Mark C. who married Martha Linville; William Harrison who moved to Angelina County Texas, became a medical doctor and married (1) Mary Ellen Dearmond (2) Clara Edna Waddell; and Alfred L. who married Martha Talley and moved to Arkansas.

Benjamin Butler and Harriet P. Mathews Cassels, after Civil War

Moses and Sarah Mathews' other children were George, Lawyer, James, John and Zebulon.

Benjamin's grandfather was John Cassels who was born about 1744. According to John's will, his children were Henry, Absolum, Levi, Rebecca, Elizabeth and Sarry or Parry. In his will, John left Benjamin's father, Henry,

> "the lower half a lot of land lying on the waters of Little River in the Nineteenth District of Baldwin when drawn, now Jasper #131."

Today this land is in Morgan County, Georgia. Benjamin's grandfather John won this land in the 1807 lottery. He was a Revolutionary War soldier listed in Georgia's Roster of the Revolution. The certificate of Colonel Greenbury Lee dated 21 February 1784 certified that John Cassels was entitled to a bounty of 250 acres of land.

In Carroll County, Benjamin made his living as a farmer. He and Parry already had six children when he enlisted for the Confederacy as a private in Company K, 56th Georgia Infantry over in Franklin, Heard County, Georgia, on 12 May 1862 as a substitute for R.J. Beasley. The following August, his brother Robert Henry died from wounds sustained at Cedar Run and was buried in the Confederate Cemetery at Charlottesville, Virginia.

Alfred and Susie Cassels

While serving in Stevenson's Division, Benjamin was at the fall of Vicksburg, Mississippi. He was captured 04 July 1863 when his right hand was either seriously injured or partially severed during the conflict. He was paroled on 08 July 1863 and was discharged to this disability later that year.

Four more children were born following the war years. Their ten children were Frances, Alfred Eraster, Richard, Virgel, Monroe, Absolum A., Mollie Belle, John, Myrtie and Judson.

Three of their children married in Carroll County during the late 1800s. Virgel married Josie Langford; Judson married Alice Pike; and Alfred married Susie Elvie Langford. Alfred's daughter Delia Elvira was living in Carroll County in 1918 when her young son and her husband John William Lovvorn died during the influenza epidemic. She was listed on the 1920 Carroll County census with her six children — Eula, Herman,

Eunice, Frank, Spencer and Bernice. Descendants of Benjamin Butler Cassels and Harriet Mathews still live in Carroll County today.

Note: Other variations of the Cassels surname used by family members include Cassell, Cassel, and Castle. *Submitted by: Shirley Hutcheson, 2535 Cardinal Lake Circle, Duluth, GA 30096*

419. Edward Clark Causey Family

Edward Clark Causey was born in the Victory community on October 16, 1902. He was the son of William Randolph Causey and Emma Blanche Causey. He graduated from Fourth District A&M School in 1922 and later attended Bowdon College and North Carolina State College. He was a farmer and a successful brick mason. He retired from Southwire in 1981. Clark was also a member of Victory United Methodist Church. With a passion, he supported and loved his church. While he was a quiet man, he possessed a great wisdom.

Edward Clark Causey

Audie Farmer was born in Haralson County on December 13, 1912, the daughter of George and Lavonia Harper Farmer. After her parent's death, she and her brother Todd were sent to live with an aunt, Mrs. Emmie Farmer West, at Roopville.

She attended Roopville School and graduated from Bowdon High School. She attended Berry College, West Georgia College, and graduated from North Georgia College in Dahlonega, Georgia. Having a strong desire to teach, Audie made a commitment to Miss Martha Berry: if Miss Berry would accept her as a student, she would give back to society all that was given to her.

Audie Farmer Causey

Audie began a very successful teaching career that spanned forty-three years. She taught at Farmer's High School, Oak Mountain, Tyus School, and Roopville. It was while teaching at Farmer's High that she met Edward Clark Causey. On August 7, 1937, they were married in Carrollton, Georgia. Four years later on August 26, 1941, a baby girl was born to bless this union, Emily Nan. She was born at the Carrollton Clinic.

During her career, she influenced many lives. She taught her son-in-law, daughter and granddaughter. She was named the first Teacher of the Year for Roopville School and for Carroll County. She retired in 1979.

She was always active in Roopville Baptist Church whether it was teaching Sunday School or Bible School or arranging flowers from her garden for the church and also Roopville School. She was active in the Roopville Historical Society and a volunteer at Bagwell's nursing home for eighteen years. She was loved and respected by all who knew her.

Mr. and Mrs. Causey purchased the Alexander-Morgan home place and moved to Roopville in 1947 from Tyus. This home is 153-years old. Clark Causey died on November 24, 1986, and Audie Causey died on April 21, 1997. Both are buried at the Roopville Cemetery. *Submitted by: Catherine Huckeba, 160 Hennon Drive Apt. H. Rome, GA 30165. Researched by: Emily Huckeba*

Sources: Family interviews, Family Journals and Familly Bible

420. Joseph Franklin Causey

Joseph Franklin Causey was born in Georgia 13 March 1833, son of Allen Causey and Martha McBride, and married Susan "Nancy" Elizabeth Pruitt on 3 June 1860. Nancy was born 7 April 1844. Joseph resided in Campbell County when he enlisted 4 March 1862 in the Confederate Army and served in K Company, 41st Infantry Regiment of Georgia, as a private. Joseph and his family moved from Campbell County to Cobb County and then appear in Carroll County at the time of the 1880 census enumeration. Joseph and Nancy had thirteen children: William S. (1861), Elmira (1863), Samuel and Margaret Ann (1865), Benjamin Whitaker O. (1867), Mary Ann (1869), Frances (1872), Simon Allen (1874), Georgia Ann (1876), Sanford Leak (1877), John (1878), Joseph Russell (1883) and Van Buren (1889). Margaret Ann and Georgia Ann died in infancy, and Mary Ann died as a relatively young woman in 1908. Joseph and Nancy both died in 1909.

Their seventh child, Simon Allen, was born 9 January 1874 in Georgia and married Exer B. Perren 29 October 1893 in Carroll County. Exer was born 5 September 1871, daughter of Banister and Catherine Archer Perren. Banister and Catherine were married 17 May 1849 in Carroll County. Sim Allen and Exer had five children: Charles Gordon (Charlie) (1894-1973), Serena Catherine (Rena) (1896-1983), John Thomas (1899-1950), Homer Lee (1901-1972) and Jamie William (1912-1976). All of these siblings lived and had families in Carroll County, where many descendants still reside. Sim Allen died 23 June 1934, and Exer died 27 February 1941; both are buried at Wesley Chapel Cemetery.

Charlie married Cora Alvin Williams (1897-1966) on 26 July 1914 in Carroll County, and they had seven children: Verdie Mae, Ora, Sarah, Maurine, Thomas Watson, Nora Lee and Ruth. Charlie and Cora are buried at Hillcrest Cemetery, Villa Rica.

Rena married Sidney Arthur Chance (1889-1958; son of John Cannon and Martha Frances Lee Chance) in February 1915, and they had seven children: Virlie Chester, Presley Martin, Mary Alma, Jesse Cannon, Buford Levi, Otis Prince and Alice Ruth. Most of this family is buried at Hillcrest Cemetery, Villa Rica.

John married Stella Mae Dewberry (1906-1996; daughter of Benjamin Franklin and Annie Missouri Eady Dewberry) 17 May 1927, and they had eight children: John Thomas, Mona Mae, Jesse Ray, Betty Joyce, Lucy Jeanette, Janice Exer Ann, Frank Allen and Sandra Jewel. John and Stella are buried at New Brooklyn Cemetery, Temple.

Homer first married Mobell Johnson and then married Eunice Geneva Williams (1924-1989). Homer and Eunice had seven children: Brenda Joyce, William Earl, Glenda Diane, Jerry Wayne, Dura Lee, Mary Jane and Dorothy Jean. Homer and Eunice also are buried at New Brooklyn Cemetery.

Jamie married Eva Bee Dobbins (1916-1998: daughter of Henry Quiller and Sally Clayton Turner Dobbins) 1 September 1951 in Carroll County, and they had one son: Jamie William (Jimmy) Causey Jr. Jamie is buried at New Brooklyn Cemetery, Temple, and Eva is buried at Bethany Christian Church Cemetery, Paulding County. *Submitted by: Jimmy Causey, 511 Pate Dr., Villa Rica, GA 30180*

Sources: *Roster of Confederate Soldiers of Georgia 1861-1865, GA Roster C,* published 1955 by Longino & Porter; Causey Family Bible; 1880 Carroll County Census; Carroll County Marriage Index; Family Interviews

421. William Jasper Causey

William Jasper Causey who moved to Carroll County, Georgia, in the early 1880s, was born in Randolph County, Georgia, August 1, 1841. He was a descendant of a line of four Phillip Causeys, beginning in Dorchester County, Maryland, in 1724.

The generations gradually migrated down the southeastern coast. Phillip IV was born in Edgecomb County, North Carolina, January 16, 1795, and died in Randolph County, Georgia, October 22, 1855. Philip Causey IV had one son, John R., who was the father of William Jasper.

William Jasper Causey had one brother and five sisters. John moved to Texas; Evelyn married a Cox; Irene married a McEarchin and moved to Carroll County; Fannie married a Perkins and remained in Randolph County; Louisa (Aunt Lou) lived her last years in the Victory community of Carroll County and is buried at Victory Methodist Church; Jane died in 1887.

Causey Family; L to R: John, Sim Allen, Charlie, Exer B., Rena, Homer

During the Civil War, William Jasper Causey fought for the Confederacy and was taken a prisoner by Yankee troops. He spent some months in a U.S. Prison Camp near Chicago. During imprisonment he assisted two southern friends in escaping the camp, and they later described him as "one of the finest men we've ever known."

When William Jasper returned to Randolph County in 1865 after military service, he discovered that his Randolph County sweetheart had married someone else. In 1867 he married Mrs. Martha Jones who had two children, Fannie and Eddie. William Jasper and Martha Jones Causey had four children: Simeon, Homer, Lena and William R. All these children migrated to Carroll County as adults.

Following the death of Martha Jones Causey in 1873, William Jasper married Patience Gay in Randolph County in 1877. Mrs. Gay had a daughter, Emmie. William Jasper and Patience Gay Causey had a daughter Mamie, who was born in Carroll County on May 28, 1883, and died in 1964. Mamie married Murray Smith and lived in the Victory community all her life.

Rev. and Mrs. William J. Causey, 1889.

William Jasper moved to Carroll County in the early 1880s to afford his children high quality schooling offered at the time by Bowdon College (or Bowdon Institute). With the help of John M. Richardson, this college had been founded in 1856 by a young, well-educated Georgian, Charles A. McDaniel. Through their leadership, they enlisted the keen interest and strong financial support of Bowdon citizens for the new institution in the West Georgia wilderness. The college attracted students from a half dozen Georgia counties and an area of East Alabama. Patience Gay Causey died January 30, 1887. William Jasper married Martha Frances McDaniel, December 5, 1887.

William Jasper, a circuit-riding Methodist minister, immediately became active in Methodism upon his move to Carroll County. He eventually became president of the Georgia Conference of the Methodist Protestant Church.

He found in Martha Frances McDaniel Causey a strong supporter of Victory Methodist Church. Her father, George Ambrose McDaniel, gave the land on which they built the church. He was a prominent farmer, land owner, and rural business leader. In the Victory community he operated a water-powered cotton gin, saw mill, grist mill, blacksmith shop, tannery and country store. He was an older brother and mentor to Charles A. McDaniel, founder of Bowdon College.

The marriage of William Jasper Causey and Martha Frances McDaniel Causey forged a dynamic Methodist team. William Jasper preached the first sermon in the newly built (1897) Victory Methodist Church and served as the first pastor. Martha Frances was a chief financial supporter of the church through many years and she counseled young ministers assigned to the church through recitations in Sunday School, singing church hymns, and memorizing Bible verses. Well educated, Martha Frances attended what is now North Georgia College in Dahlonega and became the first female graduate. She traveled part-way from the Victory community to Dahlonega by covered wagon.

Descendants of William Jasper and Martha Frances Causey are Eugene Ambrose Causey, born October 21, 1888, died January 27, 1979; Norman Henry Causey, born February 11, 1892, died October 1959; Martha Elizabeth Causey Hill, born May 1, 1902, died October 22, 1988; and Victor H. Causey who died as an infant.

William Jasper Causey and Martha Frances McDaniel Causey are buried in the Victory Methodist Church Cemetery. *Submitted by: Barry Copeland, 1459 Kendall Court, Birmingham, AL 35209*

422. The William Randolph Causey Family

William Randolph Causey was born January 6, 1873, in Randolph County, Georgia. He was the son of Reverend William Jasper Causey and Martha Lewis Causey. In 1885, Rev. Causey moved his family to Bowdon after serving in the Civil War. He served as the first pastor of Victory Methodist Protestant Church and later was president of Georgia Methodist Protestant Conference.

Emma Blanche McDaniel Causey was born May 19, 1873, in Bowdon, the youngest child of George Ambrose and Martha Lavender McDaniel, a pioneer family of the Bowdon-Victory area. Blanche was the niece of Charles McDaniel, the president of Bowdon College. Her father, George Ambrose McDaniel, donated the land and was instrumental in the building of Victory Methodist Church in 1897.

William and Blanche were married on January 1, 1898. They were blessed with seven children: (1) William Lewis was born September 10, 1898, and died July 5, 1969. He attended the University of Georgia. He married Evelyn Atkins in 1930. (2) Florence was born March 31, 1900, and died July 4, 1900. (3) Harold Bates was born April 4, 1901 and died November 16, 1971. He graduated from the University of Georgia. He married Elizabeth Burgess in 1936. They were blessed with two daughters, Martha and Susan. (4) Edward Clark was born on October 16, 1902, and died November 24, 1986. He graduated from the Fourth District A&M School and he attended Bowdon College and North Carolina State College. He married Audie Farmer in 1937. (5) Lula Mabel was born August 7, 1904, and died January 21, 1994. She graduated from Bowdon High School. She married William Dahlman in 1946. (6) Francis Catherine was born June 23, 1906, and died December 26, 1936. She graduated from Bowdon State Normal and Industrial College. She married Frank Fletcher in 1928. They were blessed with a son, Joel. (7) Kenneth Klein was born on February 4, 1909, and died January 15, 1992. He attended West Georgia College. He married Jewel Cunningham in 1939. They were blessed with a daughter and a son, Nancy and David.

Victory Methodist Church played a vital role in shaping the religious beliefs of this family. William and Blanche's signatures were found on documents when the cornerstone of the church was opened in 1997, celebrating one hundred years. Blanche was an accomplished pianist. She played for church as long as health permitted. William assisted by leading the singing.

Blanche delighted in preparing for family gatherings in her Victory home. She hosted the first McDaniel-Causey Reunion in her yard in 1936. She was thrilled to play the piano for her grandchildren. She also taught piano for the children in the community.

Descendants of William and Blanche still reside in Carroll County. They are often found attending reunions and homecomings at Victory United Methodist Church. William died on March 17, 1920, and Blanche died on May 7, 1954. They are buried at Victory Church Cemetery. *Submitted by: Emily Causey Huckeba. and Researched by: Emily Huckeba and Joel Fletcher.*

Sources: Family notes written by the late Audie Causey, Family Bible records, and family interviews.

423. F.M. and Loraine Chalker

Loraine Pickens Chalker was born March 28, 1911, in Martins Ferry, Ohio, and moved to Fitzgerald, Georgia, on March 23, 1914, with her parents, Robert Clark and Maud Clifford Pickens.

She married Fussell Marion (F.M.) Chalker on March 23, 1929. F.M. Chalker was born June 30, 1904, in Fitzgerald and he died on August 18, 1982, in Carrollton. He was the son of James and Alice Barrentine Chalker. He was a classroom teacher at Fitzgerald High School and West Georgia College. He served as principal of Douglas and LaGrange high schools and as superintendent of Carrollton City Schools.

Their children are Frances Marion, b. 4-3-1933 in Douglas, Georgia, d. 12-29-1999 in Atlanta, James Robert, b. 1-13-1935 in Douglas, and Clifford Michael, b. 7-4-1943 in LaGrange, Georgia. Loraine is a charter member of the Abraham Baldwin Chapter, NSDAR, and received her membership papers on February 1, 1954.

William Randolph Causey Family. Lewis, William, Blanche, Mabel, Clark, and Bates

Mr. F.M. Chalker

She is a descendant of Revolutionary Soldier James Alexander who served in Pennsylvania during the war. James Alexander, b. 1723 in Scotland, arrived in America in Pennsylvania and then moved to Ohio where he died in 1817. He was married to Margaret Clark (1743-1809). Their son was William Pickens (1762-1841) and he married Agnes Nancy Alexander (1769-1815). William and Agnes had a son John Clark Pickens (1806-1887) and he married Martha McConahey (1807-1831). John and Martha's son was Samuel Alexander Clark Pickens (1848-1925) who married Mary Jane Finney (1853-1930), and, Loraine is the daughter of their son Robert Clark Pickens (1878-1928) and Maud Clifford (1875-1916).

Loraine is a housewife and mother. She did a lot of school and community work. She taught three-year-old children in Sunday School at First Methodist Church for 46 years. The Chalkers grew up in the same church in Fitzgerald and were involved in youth activities which resulted in their dating. At first they were together in groups and double-dating with another couple in a Ford with a rumble seat. They would take turns driving and riding in the rumble seat.

In the January 28, 2001, *Times-Georgian* newspaper, Stanley Parkman's article says that F.M. Chalker became superintendent of Carrollton City Schools from 1944 to 1966. Parkman's son, David added "I can tell you how much the school children admired him. We always looked forward to his visits to each classroom around holiday time to draw seasonal scenes on the boards and throw in some stories. I think that my high school class of 1956 might have been a little special to him since we were the first to follow him all the way through school; but he spent time with all classes several times each year." In retirement years, he wrote the book *Pioneer Days Along the Ocmulgee* which he published in 1970, traveled a lot to see family and friends, and explore the back roads and rivers of Georgia. *Submitted by: Mrs. Loraine Chalker, 314 Dixie Street, Carrollton, GA 30117-3311 and Written by: Violette H. Denney*
Source: Family records

424. Floyd Eaton Chalkley

Floyd Eaton Chalkley was born 19 June 1909, the son of Floyd Albert Chalkley and Alma Noel Callenberger Chalkley who were natives of Chesterfield County, Virginia. Eaton Chalkley grew up near Richmond, Virginia, and received his first college degree from Mount St. Mary's in Emmetsburg, Maryland. He then earned his law degree from Columbia University. Eaton worked for some years as an attorney and then became a member of the Federal Bureau of Investigation. Later, he became a member of the investigative legal team for Southern Railway and General Motors.

Though he lived in Virginia, where he had many horses and a beautiful home called Malbrook, Eaton fell in love with Carrollton, Georgia, in the early 1950s while on a business trip there. By 1953, Eaton had settled in Carrollton and had become a prominent businessman. He was the owner of the Cadillac-Chevrolet dealership in town.

Eaton loved Carrollton so much that he encouraged his sister and brother-in-law, Margaret "Peggy" and Matthew Irwin, and his mother Alma Chalkley, to also move to Carrollton. They had become active members of the community and Peggy Irwin and Alma Chalkley served as Grey Ladies, as the Tanner Memorial Hospital Auxiliary used to be called. Then in 1957, the Chalkley family was suddenly propelled into the national spotlight when Eaton married the beautiful and talented movie actress, Susan Hayward. Susan and Eaton Chalkley made their home in Carrollton until Eaton's death in 1966.

Eaton Chalkley's father, Floyd Albert Chalkley, was born 22 August 1882 and married on 16 August 1904 in Richmond, Virginia, to Alma Noel Callenberger. Alma was born 25 March 1884 near Richmond. Floyd Albert Chalkley was a cabinetmaker and eventually moved his business to Washington, D.C. where he and his wife spent most of their lives. They were parents of six children: The oldest was Ruth Noel born 3 January 1908. Second was Floyd Eaton born 19 June 1909. William Aurelious was the third child born 11 May 1911. Charles Albert was born 13 January 1918. The fifth child was Marvin Cary born 5 August 1919, and sixth was a daughter Margaret, who was always called "Peggy," born 24 January 1922.

Floyd Eaton Chalkley

The Chalkleys were an old Virginia family that dated back to Colonial times. Achilles Chalkley had served in the American Revolution from Chesterfield County, Virginia. The family of Achilles Chalkley had come from England to Virginia during the times of Colonial America. Spencer Chalkley had served in the War of 1812 and reared a large family of sons and daughters. The Chalkleys sent many sons to fight for the Confederacy. It was from this stock that Floyd Eaton Chalkley came. The Chalkleys of this era also intermarried with the Washington family of Virginia.

Eaton Chalkley's sister Margaret "Peggy" Irwin and her husband Matthew Benedict Irwin also made their home in Carrollton for seven years, moving here first in 1953. They later returned to their home in Washington, D.C. where they lived the next thirty years, but after retiring they returned to live in Carrollton. Matthew Benedict Irwin was born 8 July 1918, the son of Matthew Williamson Irwin and Agnes Roberta Jarboe who were natives of Charles County, Maryland. Both of Matthew's parents are buried there in Chapel Point at St. Ignatius Catholic Church.

Matthew Irwin and Margaret Chalkey married 11 March 1942 during World War II. Matthew had to leave immediately after the wedding for the war. He served in the U.S. Navy as a part of the construction battalion — the SeaBees — who constructed the many air strips, barracks, hospitals, etc. that were required by the thousands of servicemen stationed on the islands of the South Pacific during the war. Peggy didn't get to see her husband for over two years until the end of the war.

Matthew and Margaret "Peggy" Irwin have two sons. The first, Matthew Wayne Irwin, was born 14 April 1949. Thomas Eaton Irwin was born 22 November 1951. The Irwins make their home now in the Cottage Lane community. Peggy Irwin is a member of St. Margaret's Episcopal Church and Matthew Irwin is a member of Our Lady of Perpetual Help Catholic Church. Matt Irwin has served as treasurer of the Knights of Columbus for several years and is a member of Kiwanis K. *Submitted by: Matthew and Margaret Chalkley Irwin, Plantation Walk, Carrollton, GA 30117*

425. Jesse Harrison Chambers

On October 27, 1835, Jesse Harrison Chambers was the fourth of fourteen children born to John and Lucinda Hawkins Chambers. In 1834 John had moved his family from the western mountains of North Carolina to (old) Villa Rica, Georgia, seeking the gold that was discovered there in about 1827. Jesse lived with his parents until he was twenty-five years old, helping them farm and work the gold mines. On April 11, 1861, he married Tabitha Sarah Jane McCarley of Villa Rica, daughter of Moses McCarley and Lydia Yates McCarley. Jesse and Sarah farmed for a living. They lived out from Villa Rica in Carroll County which was changed to Douglas County in 1870. They lived in the Conners Militia District in the 1880 census of Douglas County.

Eight children were born to Jesse and Sarah while they lived in Carroll/Douglas County. They were: Elizabeth Cornelia, born 1862, married 1880 to William Thomas Arnold and lived near Brownsville, Paulding County; Mary Louvenia, born 1864, married 1886 to Jacob Newton Meadows and lived in the Sweetwater Church community of Paulding County; John Moses, born 1866, married 1887 to Mary Louella Seals in Cullman County, Alabama, and lived in Joppa, Alabama; Thomas Franklin, born 1869, died 1870; James Andrew, born 1871, married 1891 to Willie Louisa Barber in Marshall County, Alabama; Robert Pinkney, born 1875, married 1896 to Corah Baker in Cullman County, then in 1949 to her sister Mary Baker in Winston County, Alabama; Walter Harrison, born 1877, married 1898 to Addie Pearl Martin in Cullman County.

In 1886, Jesse H. moved his family to Cullman County, Alabama, except for the two oldest daughters who had married and were living in Paulding County, Georgia. After retiring from farming Jesse and Sarah moved back to the Sweetwater Church community in South Paulding County. Late in his life, Jesse had a cancer appear on his face near his eye. He used arsenic to treat the cancer and was successful in stopping the cancer, but he lost his sight in that eye and wore an eye patch for the rest of his life.

Jesse Harrison Chambers and Tabitha Sara Jane McCarley

His obituary in the Douglas County *Sentinel* in 1918 stated that he died at the home of his son-in-law, J.N. Meadows, at Brownsville. He and Sarah are buried at Sweetwater Baptist Church Cemetery.

After Jesse died in 1918 Sarah lived with her daughter and son-in-law, Louvenia and Newt Meadows, in the Sweetwater community. She would ride the train from Douglasville to Haleyville, Alabama to visit her son, Walter H. Chambers, and his family. Sometimes she would bring her grandson Roland Meadows on the train with her. Roland said when the train crossed the Tallapoosa River coming back to Georgia, Grandma would say, "Roland, we're crossing the Tallapoosy and it won't be long now." Those who knew Sarah said she had a knack for saying what she thought and had a lot of devilment about her, all in good fun. Her sense of humor was passed to her son Walter. She died in 1932 at the age of ninety-two. *Submitted by: Benny Roger Smith, 7343 Dogwood Hills Drive, Douglasville, GA 30134*
Sources: Family Bibles, U.S. census records, personal knowledge.

426. John Thaddus Chambers

John Thaddus Chambers was born April 25, 1803, in Buncombe County, North Carolina, died in Villa Rica, Carroll County, Georgia, August 4, 1890, and is buried in what is now Hill Crest Cemetery in Villa Rica. He was the first child of Joseph and Sarah Moody Chambers. John T. married Lucinda Malvina Hawkins on April 2, 1829. She was born April 25, 1809, in Buncombe County, North Carolina, died in Villa Rica on April 3, 1880, and is buried in what is now Hill Crest Cemetery in Villa Rica. She was the daughter of Benjamin and Hanah Hawkins.

John Chambers drew land in the 1827 Land Lottery, in District 11, Lot 13, Carroll County. John T. Chambers was listed in the Carroll County census in 1840, 1850, 1860, 1870, and 1880. John T. Chambers (known as "Honest John") was listed as an early white settler by Pvt. Joe Cobb in his book *Carroll County and Her People.* John T. Chambers was appointed clerk of the New Hope Primitive Baptist Church, Villa Rica, on August 25, 1839. He and his wife Lucinda M. Chambers were "Excumicated April 5th 1845 for Communing with the Missionary Baptist."

John T. served in Company I, 19th Regiment, Confederate States Army, during the first part of the Civil War. He joined on June 22, 1861, and was appointed captain of the unit. They nicknamed his unit "Villa Rica Gold Diggers." Four of his sons served under his command. Two of his sons died in Virginia during this war. He resigned on October 8, 1862, because of failing health.

John T. Chambers and Lucinda Hawkins Chambers had fourteen children. They were:

(1) Nicholis Franklin Chambers born March 13, 1830, in Haywood County, North Carolina.

(2) Joseph Washington Chambers born October 20, 1831, in Haywood County. He married Mary Jane Elsberry on April 2, 1855, in Carroll County. She was born about 1832 in Georgia. She was the daughter of John Elsberry and Sarah Oliver.

(3) Sarah Ann Elizabeth Chambers, born December 29, 1833, in Haywood County, died in the Fairview community, Cullman County, Alabama, on July 6, 1906, and is buried in the Fairview Methodist Church Cemetery. She married Benjamin Jackson Garrison on December 7, 1854, in Carroll County. He was born March 2, 1817, in York County, South Carolina, died in the Fairview community, Cullman County, on June 1, 1904, and is buried in the Fairview Methodist Church Cemetery. He was the son of William Garrison and Mary "Polly" Hall Garrison.

(4) Jessie Harrison Chambers born October 27, 1835, in Villa Rica, died in Brownville, Paulding County, Georgia, on March 10, 1918, and is buried at the Sweetwater Baptist Church Cemetery, Paulding County. He married Tabitha Sarah Jane "Puss" McCarley on April 11, 1861, in Carroll County. She was born November 5, 1839, in Villa Rica, died in Brownville, Paulding County, on February 17, 1931, and is buried at the Sweetwater Baptist Church Cemetery, Paulding County. She was the daughter of Moses McCarley and Lydia "Lida" Yates.

John T. Chambers and Lucinda Hawkins Chambers

(5) William Posey Chambers born October 2, 1837, in Villa Rica, died in Carroll County on August 23, 1885, and is buried in what is now Hill Crest Cemetery in Villa Rica. He married Emily Margrette Bryce on September 12, 1866, in Carroll County. She was born November 15, 1846, in Georgia, died in Carroll County on March 13, 1899, and is buried in what is now Hill Crest Cemetery in Villa Rica. She was the daughter of James Bryce Sr. and Eleanor Ray "Nelly" Sharp.

(6) Robert W. Chambers born August 20, 1839, in Villa Rica, died in Villa Rica on May 1, 1840, and is buried in what is now Hill Crest Cemetery in Villa Rica.

(7) James L. Chambers, born May 20, 1841 in Villa Rica, died 25 March 1875. He married Mary Mote on February 15, 1872. She was the daughter of Levi and Elizabeth Mote.

(8) Benjamin D. Chambers, born August 20, 1842, in Villa Rica. Wounded at Mechanicsville, Virginia on June 26, 1862. He died at the 4th Georgia Hospital in Richmond, Virginia, on July 28, 1862.

(9) Merrill Columbus Chambers born November 28, 1844, in Villa Rica. Died near Camp Winder, Richmond, Virginia, on May 31, 1862. Buried there in Hollywood Cemetery.

(10) Doctor Porter "Doc" Chambers, born October 30, 1846, in Villa Rica, died in Carroll County, February 17, 1929, and is buried at Pleasant Grove Baptist Church Cemetery, Carroll County. He married Sarah Josephine "Josie" Yates on December 31, 1868, in Carroll County. She was born November 18, 1849, in Carroll County, died in New Mexico GMD of Carroll County on December 1, 1934, and is buried at Pleasant Grove Baptist Church Cemetery. She was the daughter of Joel Pinkney Yates and Martha Jane Stewart Yates.

(11) Milton Rice Chambers, born June 2, 1848, in Villa Rica, died in Carroll County on October 28, 1927, and is buried at Pleasant Grove Baptist Church Cemetery in Carroll County. He married Georgia Ann Carolina Yates on February 22, 1872, in Carroll County. She was born February 18, 1852, in Carroll County, died in Carroll County on February 12, 1890, and is buried at Pleasant Grove Baptist Church Cemetery. She was the daughter of Joel Pinkney Yates and Martha Jane Stewart Yates. Milton Rice Chambers married second to Martha Kansas "Mattie" Stephens in December of 1891. She was born December 19, 1860, in the Kansas community of Carroll County, died January 19, 1944, in East Point, Fulton County, Georgia, and is buried at Pleasant Grove Baptist Church Cemetery.

(12) Francis M. Chambers, born May 4, 1850, in Villa Rica, died in Carroll County on November 13, 1920, and is buried at Pleasant Grove Baptist Church Cemetery near Villa Rica. He married Mary Rosanna "Rosie" Sykes on November 12, 1871, in Carroll County. She was born June 28, 1855, in Georgia, died July 25, 1938, and is buried at Pleasant Grove Baptist Church Cemetery near Villa Rica. She was the daughter of Darling. F. Sykes and Sara Ann Cochran Sykes.

(13) Hannah Minerriva "Minerva" Chambers, born June 27, 1852, in Villa Rica, died in Morgan County, Alabama, January 18, 1891, and is buried at Pleasant Grove Church Cemetery, Morgan County, Alabama. She married James Knox Polk McCarley on July 27, 1872, in Carroll County. He was born September 17, 1849, in Villa Rica, died in Los Angeles, California, April 5, 1911, and is buried at Inglewood Park Cemetery, Los Angeles, California. He was the son of Moses McCarley and Lydia "Lida" Yates McCarley.

(14) Nelson Josephus Chambers born March 29, 1855, in Villa Rica, died in Carroll County in 1938 and is buried at Pleasant Grove Baptist Church Cemetery in Carroll County. *Submitted by: Peggy S. Chambers, 6279 County Road 51, Newell, AL 36270-4803*
Sources: Many Chambers Family researchers

427. Joseph Chambers

James Chambers was among the first settlers on the Pigeon River in Rutherford County, North Carolina. He probably came from Virginia. He secured large grants from the state some years after the close of the Revolution and was living upon his grant prior to 1790. According to the best information obtainable, he died during that year. In 1791, Buncombe County was formed from this area of Rutherford County. This area would be split into another new county in 1808. They would name the new county Haywood County. James settled on the west side of the Pigeon River where the present town of Canton, Haywood County, North Carolina, is now located. James had three sons, Elihu, William, and Joseph.

Elihu was almost a giant in stature, a man of great strength and morals and physical courage. He remained in western North Carolina all his life. William was a man of adventure. He went to the northwest, engaged in the Indian Wars in that early period but finally settled down in the Midwest and made his home there. Joseph was perhaps the best known of them. He was a member of the North Carolina State Legislature four terms, 1813, 1815, 1819, and 1820. He was a faithful and patriotic representative of the county during those years. Joseph also served in the War of 1812. He was mustered out of service in May of 1815. Joseph Chambers was listed in the 1800 census, Asheville Town, Buncombe County, North Carolina.

Joseph Chambers was probably born in Virginia about 1778. He died between June 17

1839, and July 23, 1840. He was buried in the family cemetery in Villa Rica, Carroll County, Georgia. This family cemetery was renamed Hill Crest Cemetery in the 1930s when the City of Villa Rica started maintaining the cemetery. He married Sarah C. Moody about 1800, probably in North Carolina. Sarah was born on December 20, 1782, in South Carolina. She died on September 5, 1860, in Villa Rica and is buried in what is now Hill Crest Cemetery in Villa Rica. She was the daughter of Jesse Moody and Dinah Hollingsworth Moody.

Joseph and Sarah Moody Chambers had eleven children. All of the children were born in North Carolina before Joseph and Sarah moved to Carroll County. They were:

(1) John Thaddus Chambers born April 25, 1803, in Buncombe County, North Carolina, died in Villa Rica, Carroll County, Georgia, August 4, 1890, and is buried in what is now Hill Crest Cemetery in Villa Rica. He married Lucinda Malvina Hawkins on April 2, 1829. She was born April 25, 1809, in Buncombe County, North Carolina, died in Villa Rica, Carroll County, Georgia, April 3, 1880, and is buried in what is now Hill Crest Cemetery in Villa Rica. She was the daughter of Benjamin and Hanah Hawkins.

(2) Jessie H. "Jepe" Chambers born March 13, 1805, in Buncombe County, North Carolina, died in Tyler, Smith County, Texas, November 29, 1881. He married Catherine Steed on January 7, 1837, in Columbia County, Georgia.

(3) Nancy A. Chambers born June 25, 1807, in Buncombe County, North Carolina, died in Chattooga County, Georgia, August 9, 1869, and is buried in the Garrett Cemetery, Chelsea, Chattooga County, Georgia. She married Nelson A. Allman on August 2, 1827, in Haywood County, North Carolina. He was born December 14, 1806, in Buncombe County, North Carolina, died in Chattooga County, Georgia, May 1, 1864, and is buried in the Garrett Cemetery, Chelsea, Chattooga County, Georgia. He was the son of Gideon and Margaret Allman.

(4) Nicholas F. "Nic" Chambers born August 23, 1809, in Haywood County, North Carolina, died in Villa Rica, Carroll County, Georgia, October 7, 1859 and is buried in what is now Hill Crest Cemetery in Villa Rica.

(5) Hannah Chambers born March 10, 1810, in Haywood County, North Carolina, died in Acworth, Georgia, October 3, 1882. She married Abel Hill Harrison on January 6, 1835, in Carroll County, Georgia. He was born March 31, 1808, in North Carolina. He was the son of Joseph Harrison and Margaret Hill Harrison.

(6) William K. Chambers born in Haywood County, North Carolina. He married S.C. Holloway in Carroll County on October 28, 1848.

(7) Elizabeth Chambers born in Haywood County, North Carolina.

(8) Mary Chambers born in Haywood County, North Carolina. She married Clayton Williams on December 6, 1832, in Carroll County.

(9) Sarah L. Chambers born about 1814, in Haywood County, North Carolina. She married Merrell C. Autry on September 4, 1842, in Carroll County. He was born July 18, 1816, in Walton County, Georgia. He was the son of Jacob Autry and Nancy Hill Autry.

(10) Martha Ann Chambers born February 13, 1820, in Haywood County, North Carolina, died July 23, 1858, in Luling, Caldwell County, Texas, and is buried in the Lone Oak Cemetery, Luling, Texas. She married Leonard Corder Huff in Carroll County on April 12, 1835. He was born July 10, 1811, in Cocke County, Tennessee, died in Luling, Caldwell County, Texas, July 29, 1873. He was the son of John Huff and Mary Elinor Corder Huff.

(11) Joseph W. Chambers, born about 1822, in Haywood County, North Carolina. He married Sarah L. on September 4, 1842. She was born about 1823 in Georgia.

Joseph first appeared in Carroll County when he attested the sale of land between Thomas Ruben and John Brooks on October 29, 1832. A few days later on November 25, 1832, Joseph and his son Jesse H. Chambers purchased land lot #195, 6th District in Carroll County, except 60 feet sold to William Dixon, John Sheppard and Allen Tolbert.

Joseph Chambers' will was dated June 17, 1839. His will was recorded on July 23, 1840. He was not listed in the 1840 census of Carroll County but his wife Sarah Chambers was listed. Therefore, we summarized that he died between the above dates. In his will he listed a minor son Joseph W. Chambers and a minor daughter Sarah L. Chambers. His will also states "My lawful heirs: John T. Chambers, Jepe H. Chambers, Nancy A. Chambers, Nicholas F. Chambers, William Chambers, Elizabeth Chambers, Mary Chambers, Hannah Chambers, and Ann Chambers. Grant Sarah Chambers my wife free access to dig or cause to be dug in the gold mine on Lot One Hundred and Ninety Five, in the 6th district."

Chambers Mine: This mine on Land Lot 195, 6th District, adjoins the Jones tract and is about a mile northwest of Villa Rica. Considerable mining has been prosecuted on an auriferous quartz vein at this locality and surface washing, covering an area of a number of acres, has been done. An open cut was made before the Civil War on the vein referred to and was enlarged in the course of more recent mining operations. Some shafts were also sunk on the vein. The cut is about a hundred and fifty yards long. At one point where a small portion of the ground was left standing for passage way of limited exposure of the vein is to be seen. At this point it shows a thickness of about four feet. No work has been done on the vein for a number of years and it could not be ascertained what gold was obtained when mining operations were being carried on. The date of this written description is unknown. The author is unknown. *Submitted by: Sanford D. Chambers, 6279 County Road 51, Newell, AL 36270-4803*
Sources: Many Chambers family researchers

428. Milton Rice Chambers

Milton Rice Chambers was born 2 June 1848 in Carroll County and died 28 October 1927 in New Mexico, Georgia. He married first Georgia Ann Carolina Yates, born 18 February 1852 in Carroll County, died 12 February 1890 in New Mexico, Georgia. Children of Milton Rice and Georgia Carolina Yates Chambers are as follows:

(1) Warner Avery, born 14 October 1872 in Villa Rica, died 6 December 1902 in Carroll County.

(2) Martha Loutelia, born 20 April 1874 in Villa Rica, died 3 July 1915 in Carroll County.

(3) Mary Etta, born 11 September 1875 in Villa Rica, died 28 August 1952 in Macon, Bibb County, Georgia. What I remember most about Aunt Etta was when she came to visit us. I would sit by the fire on the floor at her feet. She would tell me stories in the Bible about Heaven and Hell. It was scary for a small child like me.

(4) John Pinkney, my father, was born 26 March 1887 in Villa Rica, and died 30 May 1953 in Carroll County. Papa, as we children called him, was quiet and a good man. He loved his church, and on homecoming he would go into the woods and gather wild flowers for the graves. He would help Nezzie dress us kids. I remember him getting a hot biscuit and shining our patent leather Sunday slippers. Papa was a farmer. One day, he asked Nell and me to plant peas in between the corn. After a while we got tired, so we devised a plan. Every time we got near the ditch, we would throw a handful of peas into the ditch. When time for the peas to come up, there were more pea vines in the ditch than in the corn field. Papa didn't say a word.

(5) William Milton, born 25 April 1879 in Villa Rica, Carroll County, died 22 December 1945 in Tyus community.

(6) Nora Valina, born 29 June 1881 in Carroll County, died 16 July 1952. I can remember Aunt Nora and her family coming to visit us in a wagon and stayed several days. There was lots of cooking to be done. Nezzie was glad when they left, but we children had a wonderful time.

(7) James Odis "Ode," born 27 July 1883 in New Mexico, Carroll County, died 24 April 1954 in Franklin, Heard County, Georgia.

(8) Ophelia Myrtle Chambers, born 16 December 1886 in Carroll County.

(9) Joseph Frank Chambers, born 16 February 1888 in Carroll County, died 12 May 1943 in Atlanta, Fulton County, Georgia. I loved for Uncle Frank to visit us. We lived on a big river, in fact, it was almost in our back yard. He would put fish baskets in the river. One time he came and it had come a storm and it rained so much that the river was out of its banks. But Uncle Frank was not afraid to dive in and pull up the baskets to see what he had caught. A few fish, a great big eel, and also a turtle. We had fried turtle, biscuit and gravy for supper.

(10) Myrtle, born 6 February 1890 in Carroll County, died 31 December 1890.

Milton Rice married second to Martha Kansas Stephens. Their children were:

(1) Alberta, born 17 October 1895 in Carroll County, died in East Point, Georgia.

(2) Robert Benjamin, born 18 December 1892 in Carroll County, died 4 January 1975 in Jonesboro, Clayton County. Robert never married.

Shown in this family photograph are standing left to right: John Pinkney, William "Will," Otis "Ode," Frank, and Robert. Seated are Nora, Telia, Grandpa, Grandma, Nora, and Alberta. *Submitted by: Elzador Morris, 104 Stewart Street, Carrollton, GA 30117*

Chambers Family

429. William Posey Chambers

William Posey Chambers was born October 02, 1837, in Villa Rica, Georgia, died in Villa Rica August 23, 1885, and is buried in what is now Hill Crest Cemetery in Villa Rica. He was the fifth child of John Thaddus and Lucinda Malvina Chambers. William married Emily Margrette Bryce on September 12, 1866, in Carroll County, Georgia. She was born November 15, 1846, in Georgia and died in Carroll County on March 13, 1899. She is buried in Hill Crest Cemetery. She was the daughter of James and Eleanor Ray "Nelly" (Sharp) Bryce. James was born January 18, 1806, in South Carolina and died February 23, 1880, in Carroll County. Eleanor was born in Georgia on November 25, 1812, and died February 17, 1879, in Carroll County. They are both buried in the Old Town Cemetery, Villa Rica.

James was a Methodist minister in Carroll County. His parents, William and Mary Ellen (Orr) Bryce, arrived in the United States from Glasgow, Scotland, about 1799. They settled in South Carolina, along with Mary Ellen's parents, James Orr Sr. and Agnes (Fulton) Orr. In 1825, William and Mary Bryce were in DeKalb County, Georgia. On October 29, 1825, they were two of eight co-founders of the present day Decatur Presbyterian Church.

Lt. William Posey Chambers was a member of the Gold Diggers, Company I, 19th Regiment, during the War Between the States. William was wounded in the leg and after a brief medical leave, served throughout the war with the 19th Regiment.

William and Emily Chambers had seven children. They were (1) Ira William "Willie" Chambers, who was born in 1868 in Villa Rica and died in 1948. He married Mary E. Newell December 29, 1898, in Carroll County. She was born in 1875 and died in 1948. She was the daughter of Ben and Mary Teal Newell. William and Emily are buried in Prays Mill Cemetery, Bill Arp community, Douglas County, Georgia. Their children were William Ben "Will," Ruby Ann (Calhoun), Maggie May (Dukes), Annie Ruth (Dahrymple), John Thomas, and George.

(2) Perthenia Melvina "Mallie" Chambers was born May 13, 1870, in Villa Rica and died January 01, 1957, in Cullman County, Alabama. She married James William "Will" Keaton on November 06, 1890, in Carroll County. He was born September 29, 1867, in Carroll County and died October 6, 1942, in Cullman County. He was the son of John D. Lafayette Keaton and Sarah M. (Williams) Keaton. Mallie and Will are buried in Fairview Methodist Church Cemetery, Cullman County. Their children were Florence (Blandenburg), Ella Ruth, William Lafayette, Emily Sara, Warren H., Charley G., and Erie (Key).

(3) Eleanor Mervina "Ella" Chambers was born on May 13, 1870, in Villa Rica and died in 1959 in Georgia. She married Benjamin Alonzo "Ben" Murdock. He was born in 1868 and died in 1951. He is buried in Hill Crest Cemetery. Their children were Ben Jr., Mary E., Charlotte (Lawler), Margaret Emily (Warren), and Ethelyn Bryce (Chambliss).

(4) Effie Bryce Chambers was born February 16, 1872, in Villa Rica and died August 20, 1935, in Cullman County, Alabama. She married William Franklin "Billy" Boyd in Villa Rica. He was born September 1866 in Carroll County and died November 22, 1951, in Villa Rica. William was the son of David and Joanna Williams Boyd. Effie and William Boyd are buried in Fairview Methodist Church Cemetery, Cullman County. Their children were Maggie (Boyd), Ray Lenton, Joseph Carl, William W., Etcyel Burrell, and Casper Brice.

(5) Ryburn Harrison Chambers was born July 11, 1873, in Villa Rica and died November 19, 1949, in Cullman County, Alabama. He married Nannie Ruth Pope on January 24, 1896. She was born July 16, 1877, and died May 19, 1938 in Cullman County. She was the daughter of John and Emily (Boyd) Pope. Ryburn and Nannie Ruth Chambers are buried in Simcoe Cemetery, Cullman County. Their children were Clyde Harrison, Archie Clay, Fern Pope, Hugh Harold, and Nannie Ruth (Brock).

(6) Eugene Nelson Chambers was born December 25, 1876, in Villa Rica and died September 25, 1964, in Villa Rica. He married Mollie Mae McGuire on February 06, 1902, in Carroll County. She was born October 20, 1886, and died August 20, 1966. She was the daughter of J.P. and Ida (Kilgore) McGuire. Eugene and Mollie Mae Chambers are buried in Hill Crest Cemetery. Their children were Agnes and George Amos.

(7) George Alvin Chambers was born January 09, 1879, in Villa Rica and died June 24, 1958. He married Nell Tisinger on December 24, 1922, in Carroll County. She was born November 25, 1889, in Carroll County and died February 9, 1983. She was the daughter of George Washington and Ida Bibb (McDaniel) Tisinger. George and Nell are buried in Hill Crest Cemetery. Their children are George, Alvin, and Eugene. *Submitted by: Richard Chambers, P.O. Box 297, Villa Rica, GA 30180*

Sources: Many Chambers Family Researchers

430. Chance Family

Henry Smith Chance was born in 1797 in Georgia, and died in 1870. He was married to Sarah Streatman and they had ten children, Isaac S., Martha, Labisa, Arminda, Augustus Smith Clayton, Nancy, Sarah H., William E., Mary and George.

In May 1836 Mr. Chance was a member of the Carroll Rangers, a company that was raised by volunteer enlistment from the 74th Regiment of Georgia Militia at Carrollton, Carroll County, Georgia. This was during the time of the Creek Indian uprising in West Georgia.

In July 1857 the Chanceville Post Office was established in an area southwest of Villa Rica. H.S. Chance was the first postmaster.

His son Augustus Smith Clayton Chance was born April 1, 1835, and died Aguust 7, 1889. He is buried in the Kiser Cemetery near Horsley Mill in Carroll County. He was married to Martha Mary Wilson in 1857. She was born in North Carolina on February 28, 1837, and died September 10, 1911. They had seven children: Hester Jane, Ephriam James, Sarah, Marcus, Warren, George, and John. A.S.C. Chance was a blacksmith and farmer and also taught school in the Cross Plains community. He served in the Confederate Army, Company B., 7th Calvary Regiment, Confederate Partesan Rangers. It is fortunate that several letters survived that were written to his wife and children in 1862-1863. These were written from camp at Sycamore Church, Virginia and from the First North Carolina hospital in Petersburg, Virginia. They give an interesting account of the trials and details of daily life in the army.

Ephriam James Chance son of A.S.C. Chance was born November 25, 1865, and died March 16, 1937. He married Seleta Evie Laird from Hiram, Georgia, in Paulding County on January 29, 1885. She was born January 21, 1867, and died September 2, 1943. They are both buried in the Carrollton City Cemetery. They had nine children: Thomas B., Andrew Barton, Lena Hester, twins Lora Mae and Marcus Luther, Clarence Clayton, Vera Ione, Estelle and Nellie Pearl. E.J. "Jim" Chance was a blacksmith at Cross Plains and in Carrollton. He also operated a grocery store at one time on Newnan Street just off the square on the left where Little Gem Barber Shop was at one time. He was a member of the Mt. Carmel Methodist Church near Horsley Mill. In 1900 he was granted a patent for new and useful improvements in wagon brakes. He was also a Justice of the Peace in Carrollton.

His daughter Nellie was born February 13, 1903, and died October 2, 1972. She was married to John Dewey Nixon and they had one child, Mary Nell. Nellie was widowed when Mary Nell was two years old. She later married B.B. Stanley and they had one daughter, Martha Jo. During the years of World War II a great number of young women, including Nellie, joined the work force. She worked at the Bell Bomber Plant in Marietta as a riveter. Due to her small size, Nellie was often held by her ankles and lowered into tight spaces to complete a task. Artist Norman Rockwell later immortalized this nontraditional workforce in a famous painting entitled "Rosie the Riveter."

Mary Nell Nixon was born August 12, 1921, and died March 26, 1993. She married James H. "Buddy" Bates. He was born September 7, 1914, and died February 13, 1981. They had one daughter Barbara Joyce. She is married to Rayford Edwards and they have two children, James Mark and Amy Katrina, all currently living in Carroll County. Some other descendants of E.J. and Evie Chance currently living in Carroll County include granddaughter Betty Jean Chance Mullins, daughter of Clarence Clayton

E.J. Chance Blacksmith Shop - 1905

and Lola Morris Chance. Clarence was a blacksmith in Carrollton for over fifty years, until the early 1970s. His shop was just off Rome Street on Ward Street. He served in the United States Marine Corps in World War I.

Other grandchildren, great-grandchildren and great-great-grandchildren are currently residing in Carroll County. *Submitted by: Joyce Bates Edwards, 1545 Clem Lowell Road, Carrollton, GA 30116*

431. Chance Family In Early Carroll County

Cannon Chance, born 1784 in Duplin County, North Carolina, was the son of Nathan Chance and Abigail Canaday. He died in Carroll County prior to the 1880 census. He and his wife Nancy settled in Carroll County with at least two of their children: Warren and George William.

Warren was born in North Carolina, married Smithy Strickland in Henry County, and died 2 July 1894 in Carroll County. They had nine children: O. Eveline (married Mr. Birch), Francis Marion (married Martha Estes), Martha J. (married Charles Vines), Mary Elizabeth (married Joel A. Higgins), William E. (married Barbara Wilson), Sarah A. (married James Whitley Bryant), Nancy Catherine, Serena Louisa (married William W. Lee), and Warren E.A. Four of these marriages are recorded in Carroll County between 1861 and 1874.

George William Chance was born 30 November 1813 in North Carolina, married Eliza Bryant (some records indicate "Briant") 15 January 1835 in Henry County, and died July 1888 in Carroll County. Eliza was born 15 July 1818 in Indian Territory that later became Carroll County. They had ten children: William H. (married Mary Ann Merritt), Cannon B., Nancy Arcena (married Jacob Merritt), Mary J.F., Lucyann R., James W. (married Martha Cochran), Nathan Talley (married Sarah Cochran, then Margaret Jane Nesbert Hill), Elizabeth E., Sarah Ellen, and Josephine (married Charles Crawford Cochran). Little is known about Cannon B., Mary and Lucy; Elizabeth died at age 82 in Cullman County, Alabama; Sarah died in infancy; and the remaining five children married in Carroll County between 1 April 1855 and 26 November 1874.

Eldest son William H. was born 30 December 1835 in Henry County and married Mary Ann Merritt 27 May 1853 in Carroll County. William and Mary had three children prior to his joining the Confederate Army: George R. (1857), Arcena (1859), and John Cannon (26 January 1862). Seven weeks after John Cannon's birth, William joined Company I, 19th Georgia Regiment. After admission to hospital in Richmond, Virginia, 17 August 1862, William returned to duty 2 September 1862 and suffered mortal wounds in the left side of his head at the Battle of Shepherdstown 19 September 1862. He died nine days later. Captain T.G. Abercrombie reported this to Mary, when John Cannon was eight months old. (See related John Cannon Chance article.)

William was "buried" 136 years later, when two of his great granddaughters, Dorothy Allen Seals and Agnes Allen Lamanac, researched and proved to their own satisfaction and that of the Sons of Confederate Veterans, that no record existed of William's having been afforded that honor or religious rite of passage. No grave, marker nor other record was ever identified in or around Shepherdstown and other sites. On 7 November 1998, however, proper services were conducted and a marker placed beside that of his widow in the District Line Methodist Church Cemetery, Haralson County.

Tradition tells us that Mary Merritt Chance was terrified of storms and requested John Cannon to build a shelter over her grave. He did this sometime after her death in 1905; and in the middle of District Line Cemetery is a small shelter with a bright, white and charming picket base, under which William and Mary now "rest." *Submitted by: Andy Chance, 600 South Park Street, Apt. 2, Carrollton, GA 30117*

Sources: Research of Sherry Mize; Research of Dorothy Allen Seals and Agnes Allen Lamanac; Carroll County Marriage Index; Chance Family File, Special Collections, Neva Lomason Memorial Library; Chance, George and Eliza, Family Bible.

432. Ann Louise Hanson McCullough Chance

Ann Louise was born 1 May 1924 in Haralson County, daughter of George Martin and Dora Ophelia Harper Hanson. She began her education at the age of four at the Mount Carmel School and then attended Brooklyn School, Concord School and Union School where she was on the basketball team. In 1938, farmwork took precedence over her formal education, so Louise worked with her parents and younger siblings until striking out on her own in 1940.

Ann Louise Hanson McCullough Chance, 1942

That year George moved his family to his birthplace and father's farm in the 5th District of Carroll County, Louise joined Concord Baptist Church in May, and by the end of that year she moved to Rockmart to work in the Goodyear Mill. In October she met her first husband, James Ira McCullough (son of Love Mason and Sarah Idella Johnston McCullough); and they married 10 May 1941 in Paulding County. In 1942, Louise returned briefly to her parents' farm for the birth of her first child, Joseph Ira, on 21 October 1942. Joe married Janice Cheryl Costley 15 June 1963, daughter of Ulvie and Joyce Clayton Costley, descendants of Pierce and Caroline Lee Costley of 1850 Carroll County. In early 1943, she and Joe returned to Rockmart, where Louise continued work at Goodyear.

In 1944, Louise moved to Villa Rica with Joe. They lived first on Peachtree Street behind the Cleghorn home and then in the Kilgore house on North Avenue. In Villa Rica, Louise married second Presley Martin Chance (son of Arthur and Rena Causey Chance) on 7 April 1946. Presley and Louise had four children between April 1947 and July 1953: Joan Sherrie (married Hayes), Freida Diann (married Windell "Ted" Thomas, son of Chester and Lillie Carden Thomas), Donald David (married Beverly Ann Sowell, daughter of Maurice and Eleanor Bankston Sowell) and Andy Martin.

In 1958, the family settled into their home at 428 Old Town Road in Fullerville, where they attended Fullerville Baptist Church and the children were educated in the Villa Rica schools. Joan, Freida, Donald and Andy became members of Fullerville Baptist Church 1961-1963.

Between 1968 and 1979, Louise had seven grandchildren: Joseph Ira Jr., Cynthia Joyce, Susan Yvonne, and Joel Glen McCullough; Christopher Derrick Hayes; Windell Chadwick Thomas; and Clint Marshall Chance. Grandsons Joe Jr. and Christopher died in infancy. Oldest son Joe Sr. was killed in a boating accident on Lake Lanier in 1974. Between 1988 and 2001, the McCullough grandchildren presented Louise with four great grandchildren. They reside in Henry County. Grandsons Chad and Clint live in Carroll County.

Louise's main occupation always has been her family. She spent many hours crocheting, sewing her children's clothes, piecing and framing quilts, canning and freezing fresh food, and working long hours outside the home to provide for her family. Two of her favorite avocations are health care and gardening. In earlier years Louise worked with local doctors who would refer patients to her for informal care and assistance outside their medical practices. In later years, she has given much of her time to friends and neighbors who are elderly or in need. Presently, Louise has enjoyed living at 614 Spring Street for the past seven years, right up the road from her stepmother and father's former residence adjacent to Jones-Wynn. She loves working in her yard and often smiles and tells her children, "I've got the prettiest little house in Villa Rica." *Submitted by: Donald Chance, 100 Estates Drive, P.O. Box 323, Villa Rica, GA 30180*

Sources: Personal Interview with Ann Louise Hanson McCullough Chance; Family Records; Personal Experience

433. The James W. Chance Family

James W. Chance b. 22 August 1845, son of George W. Chance and Eliza Briant m. 19 Oct. 1865 to Martha Teresa Cochran, daughter of Jacob F. Cochran b. 1817 South Carolina and "Betsy" Endsley b. 1829.

The 1880 census of Carroll County, GA gives 7 of the 10 children of this family. These children intermarried with other families in the Temple area. James W. was a large landowner and allowed his children to have 50 acres of land, pay rent and then it was theirs "free and clear."

The father and older boys raised mules and took them to Atlanta to market, camping along the road overnight on the way there.

James W. and Martha Teresa Cochran Chance

Today in 2001 there are descendants living on the acreage which James W. Chance owned.

Children: 1. William F. Chance b. 5 Sept 1866 m. Anna Evans 19 Feb 1888. 2. Charles C. Chance "Uncle Coot" b. 20 March 1868 m. Della Nabors. 3. Noel E. Chance b. 9 May 1870 (1) Della Brown (2) Beadie ____ . 4. Preston Chance b. 12 August 1872 d. 18 Sept 1872. 5. Elizabeth Teresa Chance b. 2 July 1874 d. July 1957 m. Alcimus Allen McCain 31 Dec 1896 b. 5 Dec 1874 d. 26 Jan 1966. 6. Talulah Chance

b. 9 Sept 1876 m. Moses Spence. 7. Thomas Walter Chance b. 28 Nov 1878 m. Minnie Bonner: to Alabama. 8. Bishop Marvin Chance b. 2 Nov 1881 m. Delia Brown bur. Fla. 9. Mary M. Chance b. 21 Oct 1884 "Mamie" m. Wiley McCain. 10. James W. Chance b. 6 May 1890 d. 1980 m. Ruby Brown. *Submitted by: Mac Hamil, Temple, GA; Written by: June Hart Wester, 113 Mountain Crest Drive, Canton, GA 30114*

Sources: Census records; Carroll County court records; Granddaughter Ruby McCain Wester's memory.

434. John Cannon Chance

and Descendants

John Cannon Chance was born 26 January 1862 in Carroll County, son of William H. and Mary Merritt Chance. He married Martha Frances Lee (daughter of Green and Julia Lee) 19 December 1886 in Carroll County. They lived, farmed and raised their family in the northern portion of Carroll County. They had eleven children between 1887 and 1910: Claudie Prince (married Myrtice Garrison, then Lula Carroll Rainey), Sidney Arthur (married Serena Catherine Causey), Rilla (married W. Richard Shackleford), William Adolphus (married Lula Eanes Allen), Elfie Alene (married George Parker Allen), Myrtie Lee (married Sherman Johnson), Johnny, Loyd, Roy, Lula, and Omie Elsada (married William J. Davis). Johnny, Lula, and the twins, Loyd and Roy, died in infancy. Claudie, Rilla, William, Elfie and Omie's marriages are recorded in Carroll County between 8 January 1911 and 19 February 1955.

John Cannon died in 1936 and Martha Frances died in 1939; they are buried in the District Line Methodist Church Cemetery beside the white picketed shelter that protects his mother's grave.

The second son of John and Martha, Sidney Arthur, was born 28 June 1889 and married Serena Catherine Causey in February 1915. Arthur and Rena had seven children between December 1915 and 1932: Virlie Chester (married Inez McCurdy), Presley Martin (married Ann Louise Hanson McCullough), Mary Alma (married Alton Crews, second Cecil Leathers), Jesse Cannon "J.C." (married Sybil Rainwater), Buford Levi "Shorty" (married Ethel Swafford), Otis Prince (married Mary Hartley) and Alice Ruth (married Robert Garner, second Harold LePert). The marriages of Virlie, J.C., and Mary's second are recorded in Carroll County. Presley married Louise in Paulding County. All of these children made their homes in Carroll County, except Mary, who lived mostly in Haralson County, and Alice, who made her home in Atlanta.

Sydney died in 1958, following an extended illness; Virlie died in 1969 from heart failure; Otis died in 1979;' and Rena died in 1983. The remainder of the children died between 1984 and 1995. All of them are together in the Chance plot of Hillcrest Cemetery in Villa Rica, except Virlie, who is buried beside Inez in the McCurdy-Chance plot of Hillcrest, and Mary, who is buried beside Alton in the Bethany Church Cemetery in Paulding County.

Presley Martin Chance Family. L to R: Joe McCullough, Joan, Freida, Presley, Donald, Louise, Andy

The second son of Arthur and Rena, Presley Martin, was born 22 April 1918 and married 7 April 1946 to Ann Louise Hanson McCullough, daughter of George Martin and Dora Harper Hanson. Between 28 April 1947 and 24 July 1953, Presley and Louise had four children: Joan Sherrie, Freida Diann, Donald David and Andy Martin.

Presley worked in commercial transport for many years with Barnes Freight Lines in Atlanta. He was gifted with great manual dexterity and could whistle melodically. His children remember a tiny wagon replica he made, and a common fond memory is one of him sitting on the back porch steps, polishing his shoes while he whistled.

This entire family is remembered for their ability to work hard and to play hard. All of them were loving, affectionate and generous. Many of their descendants still make their homes in Carroll County. *Submitted by: Andy Chance, 600 South Park Street, Apt. 2, Carrollton, GA 30117*

Sources: Chance Family Bible (John Cannon and Martha Frances Lee); Carroll County Marriage Indices; Family Records and Interviews

John Cannon Chance Family. Front L to R: John Cannon, Myrtie, Martha Frances, Loyd or Roy, Elfie, Mary Ann. Back L to R: Claudie, Adolphus, Arthur, Rilla

435. Thomas Chandler

Carrollton's First Lawyer

Thomas Chandler moved to Carroll in 1827 from Franklin County, Georgia, where he married Polly Jackson. General William Beall, Benjamin Merrell, and Isaac E. Cobb married Chandler's sisters. He was the first lawyer in Carroll. They lived at Old Carrollton until 1830, when he moved to the present county site where he died in 1890. He bought Land Lot 129 in the 10th District, upon which part of Carrollton is situated. He paid forty dollars and a small pony-horse worth thirty-five dollars, which his wife's father gave to her. He built a small cabin near a spring which is in the park now. Later, they enlarged the house on West Chandler Street. The spring, called Chandler Spring, was near the old city gym.

The house had a puncheon floor and was very rough. He went to work farming and practicing law, and early on was elected tax receiver of the County. His duties required him to ride from one end and one side of the county to the other and travel Indian trails, which were almost the only roads then. He rode from the line of the Cherokee country to West Point, Georgia, and from the Alabama line to the Chattahoochee River. This area was forty miles by one-hundred miles. His annual salary was thirty dollars. There were only about six-hundred voters in the county and the population was 3,400. He became well acquainted with the people and soon began to make money and accumulated a competency. He owned a considerable amount of land and several slaves when the Civil War began in 1861.

Lovie and Buford Holmes

He raised three sons — Marion of Mississippi, Newton J. who died in Bowdon, and Thomas H., who went to Texas in 1866. There were five daughters — Dorothy Wright, Rhoda Bledsoe (afterwards Baskin), Martha Mathews, Mary Ann Thrower, and Hattie Baskin, widow of Thomas W. Baskin.

"Uncle Tom" Chandler died in 1890 at the age of eighty-six years. He was always a temperate and moral man. He was a member of the legislature in 1843, where he served with General Robert Toombs. They were close friends ever after that time.

Rhoda Chandler, born October 14, 1835, married William H. Bledsoe on January 27, 1852. They had five children: Dorothy E., Bailey F., Oscar Marion, Thomas Chandler, and William H. Bledsoe.

Thomas Chandler Bledsoe, born November 24, 1859, married Capitola B. Gardner, born February 10, 1859. They had four children: Robert I., Ellis C., Bessie, and Hilda L. Ellis C. married Glenn Merrell Holmes on November 6, 1901. They had three children: Charlcie, Buford, and Robert. Buford married Lovie Thaxton in Clearwater, Florida, in 1925. They had three girls: Charlcie, Jeanette, and Brenda. *Submitted by: Lovie Holmes, 112 Spring Street, Carrollton, GA 30117*

Sources: *Carroll County and Her People*, by Joe Cobb

436. Chandler - Baskin

On November 13, 1867, Thomas W. Baskin married Hattie Chandler. Thomas was the son of Rev. James Baskin, who founded Concord Methodist Church in Hickory Level. Hattie Chandler was the daughter of Thomas Chandler and Mary (Belle) Polly Jackson. Thomas Chandler was one of the early settlers in Carroll County (1827). He came to Carroll County from Franklin County with his wife. He was the first lawyer in Carroll County; he helped make the treaty with the Indians so Carroll County could be open for settlement. He bought land in the new 10th District (lot 129, which is part of Carrollton today). In 1830, he was elected tax receiver and in 1843 was a member of the legislature. During the Civil War, he served with General Robert Toombs. Thomas was from a long line of pioneers, his great-great-great-great-grandfather and grandmother came to America in 1609 on the second Jamestown Ship. Jamestown was the first English settlement in America.

Thomas and Hattie Baskin had four children: William Jasper, Wright, Weems, and Charles. Dr. Charles Baskin was one of the early doctors in the Temple area. W. Jasper married Lydia Gray. They had three children: Irene, Hurbert, and Esther.

Cleve and Esther Morris and Kenneth Truitt, grandson

Esther married Grover Cleveland Morris on March 3, 1912. Cleve was the son of Thomas Harris Morris of Haralson County and Mary Raburn of Carroll County. Cleve was one of ten children: Claude (lived in Temple and owned a café), Robert, Lebanon, Ovie, Ida, Merdice, Lonnie, Loyd, and Ruth. Cleve and Esther made their home in Temple. Cleve was a farmer. They had two daughters: Mable and Hattie. Mable married Griffin Truitt. They lived in Temple many years. Griffin worked for Southern Railroad as a conductor. Griffin and Mable had three children. Hattie married Raynor Potate. Raynor worked for Southern Railroad. He was the son of James Andrew Potate and Lula Smith. James Potate came to Temple when he was thirteen years old from North Carolina. His father served in the North Carolina 57th Regiment and was captured at Gettysburg. He was sent to Fort Delaware. He managed to escape and return to North Carolina. James and Lula had five children: James Andrew Jr. lived in Temple; Martha married and moved near LaGrange; Mary married Frank Singleton of Draketown; Harold lived in Temple; Raynor and Hattie had five children: Larry married Polly, they live in Temple; Sandra married John Whorton, they live in Centre, Alabama; David lives in New Orleans; Gail married Doug Keith, they live in Powder Springs; and Peggy married Earl C. Dunaway.

Earl Dunaway is the son of Jesse Dunaway and Genobie Hendrix of Bartow County. Earl and Peggy had a fishing tackle shop in Temple for many years. Earl also worked for the City of Temple before moving to Florida. They had two daughters, Joann and Susan. Joann married Lester Harmon. Lester is from Alabama but has made his home in Temple. They own a dental lab in Temple. Lester is a deacon in the First Baptist Church and serves on the Temple City Council. Lester and Joann have two daughters, Carol and Crystal. Carol married Barry Shumake of Carrollton. They live in Temple with their two sons, Gerald and Taylor. Barry works for King Packaging and is a deacon in the First Baptist Church. Both Barry and Carol are active in the church. Carol works for West Georgia Crown and Bridge Dental Lab. Crystal works for the City of Temple and is going to college.

Susan married Jimmy Tidwell from Villa Rica. Jimmy is the son of Buford and Jennie Bea Tidwell. His sixth great-grandfather served with Francis Marion, the Swamp Fox, in the Revolutionary War. His fifth great-grandfather served in the Civil War. His third great-grandfather helped found Newnan. Jimmy and Susan live in Temple. Jimmy owns and operates a garage door company. They have four children: Eric (married Spring), Stacy, Candi, and Jessica. *Submitted by: Susan Tidwell, 651 Spiva Road, Temple, GA 30179*

437. The Chappell Family

The Chappell family has been in Carroll County at least since the early 1840s. Reuben Jefferson Chappell was born 10 November 1844. He was married to Dicie Ellen "Pinkey" Neil who was born on 30 December 1850. He moved his family from the old Bowdon Junction home place to Lowell in the south district of Carroll County because of better farming conditions there.

Reuben Jefferson Chappell enlisted in Company E, 53rd Regiment, Georgia Volunteers Infantry, Army of Northern Virginia, C.S.A. He enlisted as a private on 30 April 1862 during the War Between the States. He was appointed third corporal in October 1863, and first corporal in February 1864. He was captured at Burkeville, Virginia, on 6 April 1865 and released at Point Lookout, Maryland, on 10 June 1865. Reuben Jefferson Chappell died on 31 December 1932.

The children of Reuben Jefferson Chappell and Dicie Ellen Neil Chappell were: Charles Oscar, Mildred Jewell, Wade Hampton (who was sole commissioner of Carroll County for eight years during the 1940s), Custus Fitzhugh Lee, Emma Mae, Lula, and Rosa Chappell.

Reuben Jefferson Chappell and Dicie Ellen "Pinkey" Chappell

Some of the descendants of this family living in Carroll County today are Berta Hollingsworth, Alma Eastling, William J. "Bill" Chappell Sr., William "Bill" Chappell Jr. (who is co-owner and publisher of *Carroll Star News*), Reba deGaris, James Levi Hollingsworth, Cathy Hearn, Linda Hanney, Mike Chappell, Don Chappell, Danny Chappell, Hamp Chappell, Harley Chappell, Bryan Chappell, Wade Chappell, Jamie Bishop Chappell, Peggy Irwin, Ann Carter, and Hildred Page. *Submitted by: Caroline Hollingsworth Chappel, 428 Hamp Chappell Road, Carrollton, GA 30116*

438. Carrie Maria Faver Chappell

July 10, 1888-August 11, 1988

Carrie Maria Faver, one of twelve children (ten sons, two daughters) of William Andrew and Maria Jane Merrill Faver, was born at home in Heard County, July 10, 1888. She received her schooling at Riverside School, a one room schoolhouse established by her parents. Her family was very active in the Centralhatchee Baptist Church, where she played the organ and taught several of her nieces to play.

Carrie Faver Chappell

Carrie, a remarkable, caring, patient, loving lady, spent her life caring for others. In her late teens, she assumed the enormous responsibility of caring for the family home and her mother during her mother's lengthy illness before her death

The Chappell Family

on June 18 1909, due to cancer. That same year, on October 20, she married Wade Hampton "Hamp" Chappell, of the nearby Lowell Community in Carroll County. She and Hamp lived in Lowell the remainder of their lives. Most of their years were spent in a large white house built on Hamp Chappell Road where their large family was reared. Hampton Chappell was commissioner of Roads and Revenues of Carroll County from 1937-1945.

Carrie and Hamp enjoyed their large family of five boys and five girls. He was a successful businessman, farmer, and dairy farmer on the large acreage he owned. The Chappell family was very active in the nearby Lowell United Methodist Church.

As a busy homemaker, mother, and grandmother, Carrie was adored by her children and grandchildren. After thirty-eight years of marriage, Hamp died on December 25, 1947. Besides her busy years of rearing a large family, she reared a grandson, Danny Chappell, after her husband's death.

Wade Hampton's granddaughter, Carol Chappell Dalton, born after her grandfather's death, remembers her mother telling her that he was a kind and wonderful man and was very proud of his children. These were some words of wisdom he quoted to Carol's mother when she was a bride: "Be patient, men do not grow up until they are over 45," and "In-laws are at their best when they are over 230 miles away." These were repeated to Carol, as a bride, by her mother.

Carrie's greatest legacy was that of being a loving, patient, caring mother and grandmother. She lived almost eighty years in Lowell, the area she loved, where her ten children were born and reared. She appreciated the privilege of being able to remain in her home with Minnie, her long time companion, and her daughters who cared for her until her death.

Carrie Marie Faver Chappell celebrated her 100th birthday on July 10, 1988, with a large number of her six children, thirty-six grandchildren, and one great-great-grandchild present for this very special day. She received two cards from The White House and many from family and friends. These cards were placed in a special memory book presented to her children, Bill and Ray Dorlon, by Shirley Adams at the May 22, 1988, Faver Reunion. NBC TV's Today Show also recognized Carrie.

As far as our records reveal, Carrie Maria Faver Chappell, a genteel, loving person, lived longer than any of her lineage; she died on August 11, 1988, and is entombed beside her husband in the Lowell Cemetery, Carroll County, Georgia. Her four sons, Hoke, Clay, Hugh, and Wade, are also buried in this cemetery. *Submitted by: William J. Chappell Jr.*

439. James Henry Chastain

James Henry Chastain was born on 3 October 1848 in Carroll County, Georgia. He died on 14 August 1927 in Brown County, Texas, and is buried in the Pendergrass Cemetery, Sidney, Comanche County, Texas. He married Julia Ann Ayers on 9 January 1873 in Carroll County. Julia Ann was born on 14 January 1874 in Carroll County, the daughter of Sarah Parker Ayers and Dr. William B. Ayers, a physician in rural eastern Carroll County and western Campbell County. Julia Ann Ayers Chastain died on 3 August 1929 in Brownwood, Texas, and is buried in the Pendergrass cemetery in Comanche County.

James Henry Chastain was the son of Mary Dewberry and William Chastain who had come to Carroll County from Spartanburg County, South Carolina, in 1844, settling in the Hulett community east of Sand Hill. James Henry Chastain worked on his father's farm and attended school at Sand Hill. After his marriage, he farmed in the 3rd District of Carroll County. He was a member of the Chattahoochee Musical Convention, which is a Sacred Harp singing convention. He joined the convention in 1869 with his brother, Thomas, and was a composer of Sacred Heart music. He was also a member of the Macedonia Singing Society. James and Julia Chastain moved from Carroll County to Comanche County, Texas after 1900 along with two of their children and some of Julia's Ayers relatives.

James and Julia Chastain

Julia Ann and James Henry Chastain were the parents of six children, all born in Carroll County. They were: Ephraim A., born in 1874, married Missouri C. "Dossie" Johnson in 1892 in Carroll County. Ephraim died in Brown County, Texas in 1948; Idella, born in 1876, married Edmund Lee Turner in 1892 in Carroll County (See related Coleman Clay Turner article). Idella died in Carroll County in 1942; Malachi, born in 1878, married Ora H. Fountain in 1902 in Douglas County and died in Carroll County in 1931; Mary Francis, born in 1880 and died in 1884 in Carroll County; William Benjamin, born in 1883, married Demma Stovall in 1905 in Douglas County. William died in 1979 in Crosby County, Texas; and Sarah Jane, born in 1886, married Jesse W. Hendrix in 1906 in Carroll County and died in 1918 in Cullman County, Alabama. *Submitted by: Anne Childs, 12451 N. Shawdee Drive, Huntsville, AL 35803*

440. William Chastain

William Chastain was born on 3 February 1815 in Haywood County, North Carolina. He died on 13 February 1899 in Carroll County, Georgia. He married Mary Dewberry about 1840, probably in Spartanburg County, South Carolina. Mary Dewberry was born on 6 March 1812 in South Carolina and died on 10 March 1894 in Carroll County. Both are buried in the Little Vine Baptist Church cemetery in Carroll County.

Mary Dewberry was the daughter of Elizabeth Cole and William Dewberry, and her maternal grandfather, Thomas Cole, was a Revolutionary soldier in Colonel Benjamin Roebuck's Regiment of South Carolina Militia that was at the battles of King's Mountain and Cowpens, South Carolina. On the other hand, her paternal grandfather was Giles Dewberry, a fierce Loyalist (Tory), who was captured and executed by Colonel Roebuck's men. This was not an uncommon occurrence in the South Carolina upcountry where allegiances were evenly split. William Chastain's parents have eluded positive identification but there is little doubt that he descends from the patriarch of North American Chastain's, Pierre Chastain, the French Huguenot refugee who arrived in Virginia in 1700.

William Chastain

William Chastain came to Carroll County in the fall of 1844, settling in the eastern part of the county close to the old Campbell county line and near the Little Vine Baptist Church. He appears on the 1844 and 1847 tax digests and the 1850, 1860, and 1880 Federal Population censuses of the county. He was a farmer, growing corn, cotton, peas, sweet potatoes, and wheat and raising hogs and sheep. In 1874 he filed a claim with the Southern Claims Commission for mules taken by marauding Union troops following the Battle of Atlanta. The claim was denied. On 25 June 1867 he signed the voter registration oath allowing him to vote for delegates to the state constitutional conventions in accordance with the Reconstruction Acts. He signed his name "William Chesteen." His wife's brother, Tilman Dewberry, signed on the adjacent page. Also signing on that day was his neighbor, William B. Ayers.

William and Mary Chastain had seven children, the first two being born in Spartanburg County, South Carolina, and the rest in Carroll County. They were: Sarah Malinda, born in 1842 and married James T. Robinson in 1867 in Carroll County. She died before March 1899 in Carroll County; Lewis W., born in 1844, married Sarah Elizabeth Johnson in 1866 in Carroll County and died in 1925 in Douglas County. He was a Confederate soldier in Cobb's Georgia Legion; Susan M., born in 1845, married Ethaniel McWhorter in 1866 in Carroll County. She died before March 1899; James Henry, born 1848, married Julia Ann Ayers in 1873 in Carroll County and died in 1927 in Brown County, Texas; Thomas N., born in 1851 and died before 1910; William, born in 1852 and died before 1860; and Mary Catherine, born in 1853, married Joseph T. Richards in 1873 in Carroll County and died in 1920 in Carroll County. *Submitted by: Alfred Turner, 6501 Peacock Blvd., Morrow, GA 30260*

441. Cecilia Wood and Leo Gene Church

Cecilia Wood was born in the Farmer's High community of Carroll County in 1943. She was born in a house her parents, Bamah Lanette Sprewell and Clifton Q.P. Wood, rented from her great-grandparents, Leon Davis Morgan and Elizabeth Eugenia Jordan. Leldon Bobby Sprewell has since built a house there. As a child, Cecilia moved with her parents to Caruthersville, Missouri; Mt. Pleasant, Tennessee; Elizabethtown, Kentucky, Hopkinsville, Kentucky; Memphis, Tennessee; Milan, Tennessee; Atlanta and College Park, Georgia, as well as back and forth to Carroll County. When she began high school, the family settled in College Park.

Cecilia's roots run very deep in Carroll County. Her grandparents were Clarence B. Sprewell, born April 24, 1902, and died January 15, 1978, and Dula Mae Morgan, born June 6, 1904, and died August 18, 2000. They were both born in Carroll County and are buried in Carroll Memory Garden, Carrollton, Georgia. Clarence's parents were Caleb Marshall Spruell, born October 1, 1866, at the old Veazey home place in Carroll County and died February 10, 1928, and Sarah Amanda Walker, born May 11, 1870, in Campbell County and died February 5, 1931. Both died at home in Carroll County. Caleb's parents were John F. Spruiell, born 1837 in Fayette County, Georgia, and died May 3, 1883, on the Veazy home place, and Martha Frances Veazey, born December 25, 1843, in Carroll County and died August 5, 1927, at the home of her son Rufus Spruiell in Douglas County, Georgia.

Even though Cecilia's roots are immersed in Carroll County, she met and married Leo Gene Church, a career military man. He fought in World War II with the U.S. Navy. He earned the bronze star, two purple hearts and many other medals. Leo was born July 3, 1925, in Wichita Falls, Texas, and died May 4, 2000, in Carrollton, Georgia. He was buried in the National Cemetery at Arlington, Virginia. After they married, May 18, 1963, they moved to Dallas, Texas, and then on to San Jose, California. They lived in California for about twenty-five years. Cecilia earned her Certified Public Accountant's license while in California. She worked for Cooper, Collins & Pors, a professional corporation, in San Jose, California, as a senior accountant until 1990, when the family moved to Georgia.

Leo Gene, Michael Leo, Cecilia, and Robin Gayle (standing) Church. About 1982.

Cecilia and Leo have two children: Robin Gayle born 1965 in Atlanta, and Michael Leo born 1975 in San Jose, California. Robin has a son, Kyle Thomas Church, born 1989 in Santa Clara, California.

When Leo retired from TCI in Mountain View, California, they decided that costs were just too expensive for them to live comfortably, so they returned to Carroll County. *Submitted by: Robin Gayle Church, 255 Riviera Drive, Carrollton, GA 30116 and Researched by: Cecilia Wood Church, 128 Brock Street, Carrollton, GA 30117, and Mary Clarice Spruell Cox, compiler of Gabriel Spruill of Carroll County: Descendants and Allied Families, 1984.*

442. Clancy Family

The Jerome Clancy family moved to Carroll County February 28, 1969. Jerry's great-grandparents emigrated from Ireland and Jane's great-grandparents came from Baden, Germany. Jerry (July 31, 1926-November 29, 1995) was born and raised in Wisconsin and

Clancy Family, Jerry, Jane, Karen, Patty and John. 1988

Jane Marie Simon (October 21, 1937) in Pennsylvania. They met and married (November 28, 1959) in Birmingham, Alabama. Jerry accepted employment with E.F. Houghton & Company in Carrollton, which prompted the family's move from Birmingham. The Clancy children were born in Birmingham; John Emmet (December 7, 1960), Patricia Jean (February 28, 1962), and Karen Marie (February 14, 1966).

Carrollton is a wonderful place to grow up and the family thrived here. John graduated from Auburn University and is making his home in Jackson, Mississippi, where he is employed by Sherwin Williams. Patty was a member of the U.S. Coast Guard for ten years and now resides in Carrollton and is employed by Trent Tube. Karen graduated from Georgia State University, is a C.P.A. and married Brad Tuggle on November 28, 1988. They have three children, Parker Scott (March 24, 1992), Clancy Elizabeth (August 2, 1993), and Nicholas Kie (2001) and live in Carrollton.

The Clancy roots are not deep in Carroll County, but have been lovingly treated and hope to bloom here for many years. *Submitted by: Jane Clancy, 547 North White Street, Carrollton, GA 30117*

443. John Carter Clay

John Carter Clay, a descendant of several of Carroll County's pioneer families was born July 7, 1965, at Piedmont Hospital in Atlanta, Georgia, to parents Neal M. Clay Jr. of Winchester, Kentucky, and Gwyndolyn Brown of Carrollton, Georgia. At an early age Carter developed hearing problems from severe ear infections. He spent his elementary school years overcoming his problem before undergoing several ear surgeries to repair the inner ear damage. His father was transferred with his young family to Augusta as local telephone company manager in 1966, and there Carter was given a brother Matthew Neal Clay.

John Carter Clay

In Augusta, Carter was active in scouting and spent many weekends with his family on their houseboat on Lake Clark Hill. He enjoyed coming to his grandparent's farm in Carrollton. In 1975 when the home place was moved to widen U.S. 27 and build the Carrollton Bypass, his mother brought her sons back to Carrollton.

While growing up in Carrollton, he received his education from county and city schools. He marched in the Tournament of Rose Parade with the Carrollton High School Band his freshman year, and attended the National Citizenship Conference in Washington D.C. and the National Cooperatives Convention at Ohio State University with the 4-H Club.

After high school he attended West Georgia College, West Central Technical College, and Southern Union in Wadley, Alabama. Here he studied business and computer applications. Since school he has helped the family manage and maintain several apartment complexes near the college.

Being born in Atlanta, and living in the South all his life helped him foster a love for Southern History. He became a member of the McDaniel-Curtis Camp #165, Sons of Confederate Veterans; the Carroll County Historical Society; and active supporter of the city's revitalization effort. As a member of the SCV, Carter has served on the camp's board of officers, as historian, and scrapbook person. He is a member of the camp's reenactment unit, been active in marking the graves of Confederate soldiers, and has attended many State and National SCV Reunions.

Carter is also a member of Victory United Methodist Church; and helped in the rebuilding efforts of the church after it burned in August 1999. *Submitted by: John Carter Clay, 179 Cottage Hill Rd., Carrollton, GA*
Source: Personal knowledge

444. Charles A. Clayton Jr.

It would be hard to say which love was the greater — the love that Charlie Clayton had for Carrollton or the love that Carrollton had for him. Charlie lived to be one hundred years old and was quite independent and active right up to the last. He was a character — one you might frequently see as the subject of a sketch in the local newspaper. The picture of Charlie with his gun and his Bible (taken by his son Al) appeared with an article about Charlie in the *Carroll Star News* on March 2, 1997.

Charlie and his wife, Rena, moved to Carrollton in 1979 when Charlie was eighty-one years old, and a cancer survivor at that. He'd had a malignant myeloma removed in 1949 and had had radiation therapy for it. Charlie and Rena lived at Copperhill, Tennessee. Rena was a

Charles A. Clayton Jr., age 99

retired principal from Delano Schoolhouse in Polk County, Tennessee, and Charlie was retired from the L. & N. Railroad. As they advanced in years, however, they wanted to be closer to their children. Both sons, David and Al, lived in Atlanta, and their daughter Alice lived in Carrollton. Alice was the wife of Dr. Jerry C. Robinson and they lived on Horsley Mill Road with their two young sons, Jason and Joe Robinson.

Charlie and Rena bought a lovely red brick home on Cedar Street and settled down for their sunset years, but somehow there didn't seem to be anything about sunset in Charlie! He was more of a sunrise kind of guy. The Claytons immediately started getting to know their neighbors and became best friends with Francis and Amelia Sullivan who lived just next door to them. Only four years after they moved to their new home, Rena Clayton died of cancer on 21 February 1983.

The Claytons. Charlie, Rena, Al, David, and Mary Alice

Charles A. Clayton, Jr.

Charlie was the most outgoing person you'd ever want to meet, as friendly as the day is long. He took a daily walk to the post office on Cedar Street. He'd find a comfortable place to perch outside and greet everybody going in and out of the post office. He came to know the folks who were the regulars and made many friends this way, people who would sometime stop by to visit at his house. Charlie was a great conversationalist and had many things he could talk about. After all, he had lived almost one hundred years. When the movie about the Titanic came out, Charlie said, "Oh, I remember that."

Varena Witt Clayton

People, both young and old, found Charlie fascinating. Sharon Clower, who wrote a column for the local newspaper, was one person who'd made a friendship with Charlie and she and her husband would regularly invite Charlie out to eat Sunday dinner at Kroger with them. In spite of his age, Charlie was certainly no shut-in and there were lots of people who stopped by his home for a brief visit or take him for an afternoon ride. Charlie and his grandson, Joe Robinson, enjoyed going to the flea markets together. "Let's go get us some cans of corn," Joe would say to Charlie. And his daughter Mary Alice stopped by for frequent visits, too. Charlie also found a lot of friends in the Businessman's Sunday School class at First Baptist Church. Someone had asked Charlie once what was the secret to his longevity and what would he advise people to do if they wanted to live to be a hundred. His reply was, "Always go to Sunday School." Sometime after that, if asked the question, he'd also answer (with a chuckle) " ... and eat lots of banana pudding." Everybody knew that Charlie loved bananas and people would frequently be seen leaving a bunch of bananas on his screened-in front porch.

Charles A. Clayton Jr. was born 29 December 1898 in Tate, Georgia, the son of Charles A. Clayton and Cora Threalkill. Charlie was born second in a family of four sons and four daughters. Charlie was the son of a railroad man. His father had started with the railroad when he was but a boy of fifteen. Charlie started even younger than that. He began as a messenger boy when he was thirteen years old at the same railroad station where his father worked as a ticket master. Charlie started making $6 a month, and then he went to work in the freight department where he made about $10 more a month. Later, he began working as ticketing the passengers and the baggage. So, Charlie Clayton spent nearly all his life working for the Louisville & Nashville Railroad.

Charlie remembered the very first time he ever laid eyes on Rena Witt. "She walked into that depot and she looked like an armful of roses to me," Charlie said. "I'd had four or five sweethearts by then, but she sure busted an egg in me," was his memorable comment about their first meeting.

For some reason, Charlie's father was opposed to the match. Possibly, it was because he thought someone who'd paid no more attention to schooling than Charlie had could not find happiness with a schoolteacher. Charlie admitted that all he'd ever really studied was hunting, fishing, and girls. Charlie's father arranged a job interview in Florida for him. Charlie did go to Florida, interviewed for the job and was hired. As Charlie would later tell it, he was walking toward the train for his first day on the job; the train was about to leave the station, and suddenly he stopped in his tracks, turned around, headed back to the hotel, picked up his suitcase and went straight back to Tennessee and to Rena. Charlie gave up his drinking and his wild ways in 1926.

Fifteen months later, on 11 June 1927, Charlie and Rena secretly married. Charlie said, "I went plumb under the suds and it stayed that way." They were happily married for fifty-five years until Rena's death in 1983. "We only had three or four spats," Charlie admitted later, "and only then because it was three o'clock in the morning and one of the teenaged boys hadn't come in yet. A mother will imagine anything."

Charlie Clayton (far right) working for L. & N. Railroad

Charlie used to talk a lot about the Great Depression of the 1930s, and how hard those times were. He remembered in 1927 seeing forty or fifty men riding on top of the trains "like birds on a wire." They'd be riding from town to town looking for work. Sometimes men who had not eaten for four or five days would knock on the door of his home. Rena would always find some way to give them a plate of food. Charlie remembered that in those times he worked for a dollar a day himself. He worked from 1:00 p.m. until 6:30 a.m., a fifteen and half hour day.

Something happened during the Great Depression that made a great impact on Charlie and his belief in the power of prayer. Charlie said that in the 1930s he'd gotten a notification there would be some cutbacks made at the railroad and his job was on the line. A new man was coming to take over Charlie's office, and renovations were already underway at the office to suit the new man's specifications. On the day the new man arrived, Charlie showed him around. Then Charlie took a break and went outside behind the boxcars on the track and knelt down in prayer. Charlie prayed to God that he would not lose his job, for how would he support his wife and children? How would they eat? When he returned to the railroad office, he finished showing the new man around and thought that this would be his last day. But something miraculous happened.

Charles A. Clayton Jr. and Rena Witt Clayton

The next day, they told Charlie they had made a change and the new man was not coming back; Charlie was to be kept on in his job after all. Charlie had no doubt it was an answer to his prayer. He always said it was his miracle. Later, Charlie would say that although the Great Depression was the hardest time of all to live in, it held some of his favorite memories. "People stuck together back then and would help each other," Charlie would say.

It was when Charlie was ninety-eight years old that Alice had asked if cousin Jan could listen out for Charlie while Alice went to California to help her son Jason set up his apartment out there. Charlie was still living all on his own, just like he wanted to do. Jason was going to school at Berkeley, California. Jan had said that sure she'd be glad to help and so Alice had flown to California. No sooner had the jet taken off from Atlanta than something happened that never happened to Charlie before — he took a tumble down his back porch steps.

His neighbors, the Sullivans, had come to his immediate rescue and had notified Dr. Robinson of the fall. Consequently, Charlie had been hospitalized at Higgins General Hospital where Dr. Robinson worked as a radiologist. Jan went to the hospital to spend as many hours as she could every day to keep him company. Charlie was not seriously injured, but had required some

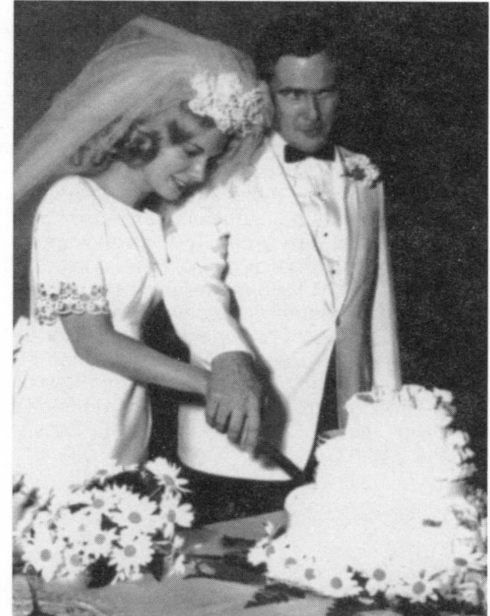

Dr. and Mrs. Jerry C. Robinson, June 3, 1967

stitches and had quite a bump on his head. The whole event had left him a little confused, which Charlie was never that.

"The thing that worried me most," Jan later said, "was that Charlie's hospital room was not that far away from the railroad tracks next to the hospital in Bremen. And Charlie was an old railroad man — his ears were tuned to the call of the railroad whistle. He kept thinking he was a young man again and that it was his train tooting that whistle. He kept trying to get out of the bed and get to that train. I was afraid that as spry as he was that he'd actually manage to get to where the train was and hop on!"

So when Jan had to leave for the day, Charlie's grandson, Joe Robinson, would stay with him through the night. "I never saw a sweeter relationship between a grandpa and a grandson," Jan said. There was no generation gap between them, even though Charlie was ninety-eight and Joe was about twenty years old at the time. "They both liked to talk about pretty girls," Jan noticed. They had the greatest conversations. "And it was incredible the number of visitors that Charlie had," Jan said. "There were people of all ages, too. I remarked about this one day to Charlie and admitted my surprise at how many young people came to visit him." "Well, you know, Jan" Charlie had said, "I'm almost a hundred years old. I used to have friends my own age but they kept on dying. I had to get new friends because all my old friends died."

And among those young people who Charlie had such special relations with were his own two grandsons — Jason and Joe — and his two granddaughters, Al Clayton's children, Jenny and Hope. Charlie would always say how richly blessed he had been throughout his life and he'd always give the good advice, "Always go to Sunday School and read His Word. Always just talk to the Lord and ask Him to help you understand."

Jason, Joe, and Dr. Jerry Robinson

Charlie Clayton died on 3 March 1999 and was taken back to the hills of Tennessee where he had loved to go hunting. They laid him to rest in the old Benton Cemetery alongside his beloved wife Rena. In the words of Robert Louis Stephenson, "Home is the sailor, home from the sea, and the hunter, home from the hill." *Submitted by: Joe Robinson, 211 Cedar Street, Carrollton, GA 30117 and Written by: Jan Robinson Bell*

Hope and Jenny Clayton

445. Emory Russell Cleghorn

Emory Russell Cleghorn was born in Flowery Branch, Georgia, on September 4, 1880.

He learned a trade as a leather worker and was employed at the age of eighteen by Southern Oak Leather Company. He later worked for Bona Allen in Buford.

After living in several locations, he moved to Villa Rica from Hoschton on December 5, 1906. It was in Villa Rica that he settled, putting down roots and helping the little town grow and prosper.

When he moved to Villa Rica, it was a town of some 300 people and had little more than an oil mill, ice plant, and Coca-Cola bottling plant.

The gold mine was in operation and the sulfur mines in full production outside of town.

Soon after his arrival, he and his brother Frank L. Cleghorn, also from Hall County, went to work for W.F. Strickland and Son — a harness shop.

In 1908, he and Frank bought the Strickland shop, and the name of new business became Cleghorn Brothers. Several years later, their brother Benjamin R. Cleghorn joined them.

With the demand for leather harness down due to the emergence of the automobile, the brothers branched into hardware, furniture, and building materials and supplies.

Quite the entrepreneurs, they were also funeral directors for many years and bought the first motor-driven hearse in Villa Rica. A hearse/ambulance was purchased later. This part of the business was sold in 1940.

The brothers built the block of buildings in which the Masonic Hall is currently located. The hosiery mill was also situated here.

They contracted to build houses for others, and Russell was responsible for one of the first subdivisions in Villa Rica. He owned some land on the edge of town on which he laid out streets and sold lots. The main street was named Cleghorn, and the other streets were named for his children. The area is now known as Cleghorn Village.

Cleghorn Brothers furnished materials, hauled by mule dray, to the Sewell Manufacturing Company #1 building in Bremen.

And, true to their roots, the brothers also bought hides, which were stacked on the ground level below the store.

Russell served on the school board and on the board of directors and as secretary of the Villa Rica Community Hospital.

He belonged to the Villa Rica Masonic Lodge #72 F. an A.M., the Order of the Eastern Star, and several other Masonic organizations. He was a member of Yaarab Shrine Temple and a charter member of the Civitan Club.

He had belonged to the United Brotherhood of Leather Workers.

Soon after moving to Villa Rica, Russell joined the First Baptist Church, where he remained a member until his death.

Emory Russell Cleghorn died on September 10, 1976, at the age of 96. *Submitted by: Russell O. Cleghorn, 595-13 Eaglescrest Village Lane, Roswell, GA 30076*

446. The Jacob F. Cochran Family

Jacob Franklin Cochran b. South Carolina d. Carroll County Oct. 1879 m. Elizabeth Jane "Betsy" Endsley b. 1829 d. 1917, buried Asbury Cemetery, Temple.

"Betsy" Endsley was the daughter of John Bluford Endsley who died in the west. She gave power of attorney

> "August 11, 1881 to trusted friend Isaac M. Dempsey to do all things necessary in the settlement of the estate of my father John Endsley (late) who died in Cass County, Texas."

The affidavit is in Miller County, Ark.

The Cochran family lived for a time in the Campbell/Coweta Counties area before moving to Carroll where they lived in the 6th land district in the 1860 census. Jacob F. Cochran (written Cockrell) served in Company F, Cobb's Legion, Georgia Volunteers.

After the war they moved to lots 214 & 215 of 6th district. The obituary of Jacob Cochran is in the *Carroll County Times* 24 Oct 1879 where it was reported he had been confined to his house for 2-3 weeks with a cut from an axe on his knee from which he died. Dr. Brooks reported the details on the 1880 mortality census.

Grandpa Cochran entertained the grandchildren with stories of his being born in Scotland and coming to America with a brother to live with an uncle who was cruel to them. They ran away and the brother was never heard of again. However, he told the census takers he was born in South Carolina. An intriguing mystery!

J.F. Cochran and Betsy Endsley Cochran

Elizabeth Cochran mother of three minor children at his death applied as natural guardian to her children giving bond of $2400. An appraisal was required for a year's support for herself and the children; she gave annual reports to the court until 1889 when she was discharged.

Land lots #214 and south ½ of #215 district 6 were subject to widow's dowery during her lifetime. "Betsy" told her grandchildren she was one-fourth Cherokee Indian.

Children: 1. Martha T. Cochran b. 1847 d. 1915 m. James W. Chance b. 1845 d. 1921. Buried Asbury Cemetery. 2. Sarah E. Cochran b. ca 1849 d. before 1880 m. Nathan Chance. 3. Charles J. Cochran b. ca 1853 d. 1902 m. Josephine Chance, moved to Cullman County, Alabama: known descendants. 4. Frances Cochran. 5. Thomas J. Cochran b. 7 May 1858 d. 5 Dec. 1910 m. Lemma ____ bur. Asbury Cemetery. 6. Georgia Cochran, minor 1879. 7. Elizabeth Talulah Cochran m. ____ Allgood. 8. Wilton John Cochran b. Dec. 1867 m. Estoni Brown Carroll MB G. *Submitted by: Bob Hamil, Palmetto, GA; and Written by: June Hart Wester, 133 Mountain Crest Drive, Canton, GA 30114*

Sources: Family memories, family research in Coweta and Carroll Counties.

447. The Cole Family

The Cole family began its life in Carroll County when Jeremiah Cole and his wife Mary Pinson arrived in a covered wagon in the year of 1831. They apparently sailed down the eastern coast from Providence, Rhode Island, to Charleston, South Carolina, and began their land trip to Laurens, South Carolina. From there, they made their way westward into Georgia until they finally settled near the present-day Old Concord Primitive Baptist Church in northern Carroll County.

The family has been traced definitively to seventeenth-century France and England, with some sources linking them to Old King Cole, King of Ireland.

Jeremiah and Mary had thirteen children. Their second, Gilbert Cole, was twelve years old when his family arrived in Carroll County. He married Elizabeth Haynes, born in Carroll County in December 1843. The two raised twelve children and farmed the tract of land given to them by his father. Before dying in 1903, Gilbert handwrote his last will and testament. He bequeathed $150 to each of his children and all remaining property to his wife. By handwriting his will, he demonstrated a high level of education for the early 1900s.

The fifth child, William Pinkney Cole, an attorney, married Mary E. Crutchfield on October 21, 1874. Both were natives of Carroll County. They had two children together. Mary died at age thirty-one and William soon married Rebecca Caroline (Cally) Reid, who later bore him four children: Grady Woodfin Cole, born March 25, 1889, married Lela Williams; Belva May Cole, born August 20, 1894, never married; Horace Reid Cole, born August 1, 1899, married Mary Astin; and Charlsie Cole, born November 15, 1905, died during childbirth in 1936.

Grady Woodfin had one son, Earl Woodfin Cole, known as Woodfin. His brother Horace Reid had a daughter, Jane Cole Walker. His sister Charlsie died at the birth of her son, Charles Nunnalley-Cole. Grady and Lela took responsibility of raising Charles.

Grady was a sports fan and played baseball for the A&M school that later became the State University of West Georgia. He died before ever seeing a major league game, but his son Woodfin would later name the university's baseball field for him.

Grady and Horace became Carrollton bankers. However, after the government mandated a separation of insurance from banking, Horace transferred to Carroll Realty and Insurance (CR&I), which had been established in 1913. Today, CR&I is located on College Street in Carrollton.

The Cole Family

In 1940, Grady's son, Woodfin, joined his uncle at CR&I after graduating from the University of Georgia. It was during his college days that he met Marion Allene Lanier, a former Miss Carroll County, who had graduated from both West Georgia College and the University of Georgia. She was born in Roopville, Georgia, on May 19, 1919. By August 1942, Woodfin was stationed in Utah for World War II. Until then, Marion had never traveled outside of Georgia. She boarded a train in Chattanooga for the first time in her life and rode alone to Salt Lake City for their wedding. The two had four children: Charles Edwin (Eddie) Cole, born April 18, 1945, married Sally Gilliland; Belva Carole Cole, born January 30, 1948, married Bart Hickman; Grady Woodfin (Woody) Cole, born April 18, 1952, married Kathy Beaty; and Marion Connie Cole, born November 13, 1958, married Randy Jones.

Woodfin would become influential in the commercial development of Carrollton. He was the organizing president of the Chamber of Commerce, built the Tower Apartment complex (the first of its kind in Carroll County), the strip mall on Rome Street where Sears is now located, and was an original founder of the Carrollton State Bank in 1972. He died in 1991.

His sons purchased Carroll Realty and Insurance in December 1988 and run it today. They are the sixth generation of Carroll Countians and entrepreneurs.

Several members of the Cole family are buried at Concord Primitive Baptist Church on Highway 113 between Carrollton and Temple. But when the family discovered that the patriarch, Jeremiah, was buried in an abandoned cemetery less than a mile away, they resolved to restore it. With the help of Carrollton's Pete Rowe and others, public access to the weed-covered cemetery was finally gained. A fence was erected around its perimeter and grave markers were located. The resting place of their forefather, a pioneer of Carroll County, is considered sacred to the Cole family. *Submitted by: Mrs. Misty Doxey, Carrollton, GA.*

Sources: Researched by: Sandra Allen and Eddie Cole of Carrollton, and Donald Levans, Chicago, IL, formerly of Carroll County. Edited by: Eddie Cole.

448. George and Narrie Cole

George Henry was born 7 July 1871 in Carroll County, Georgia, to Henry Lee and Eliza Anne Reeves Cole. Siblings were Mary, Margaret Ann, Melton, Franklin, Gilbert, Robert Lee, William Counce, Veleta, Steller, Emmer Inez, Emmely, Quill, and Minnie Lola.

On 16 August 1892 George married Narcissus (Narrie) Jones, daughter of Lindsey Jackson and Elizabeth Clarice Hogan Jones. Narrie's siblings were John, William Smith, Joseph Tyre, Maude, Tempie, Ben Hill, Lloyd Camp, Seley, and Lizzie Mae.

George and Narrie made their home on Miller Academy Road. They were highly respected people and enjoyed relatives and friends visiting their home. Narrie did beautiful hand sewing and quilting. She had many beautiful flowers and a large vegetable garden.

George and Narrie Cole

George and Narrie's children were: (1) Rilla Myra 1893-1973; husband Clyde Edward Stephens; buried Concord Primitive Church Cemetery, Carroll County. (2) Lillie Maude 1895-1900; buried Pleasant View Church Cemetery, Carroll County. (3) Mary Lou 1898-1984; husband Emit Miller; buried Pleasant View Church Cemetery, Carroll County. (4) Roy Huston 1900-1971; first wife was Thelma Bell, second wife was Lula Stamps; buried Forest Lawn Memory Gardens, Haralson County. (5) Ruth 1902-1993; husband Walter Johnson; buried Carroll Memory Gardens, Carroll County. (6) Raymond Ellis 1906-1988; wife Avis Louise Reese; buried Pleasant View Church Cemetery, Carroll County.

George and Narrie lived their lives in Carroll County. George died 29 March 1939. Narrie died 16 October 1946. They are buried in Concord Primitive Baptist Church Cemetery, Highway 113, Carroll County, Georgia. *Submitted by: Stewart Strickland, 107 Venetian Way, Bardstown, KY 40004*

449. Jeremiah and Charlotte Cole

My first ancestors to come to Carroll County were Jeremiah and Charlotte Cole. They rode into Carroll County in covered wagons in 1833 or 1834. They lived in the wagons until they could cut logs and build a cabin. They settled near Old Concord Church and Sharps Creek. Jeremiah homesteaded enough land for his twelve children to have a home. The children attended Framville School.

Jeremiah, born 1 August 1793 in Laurens County, South Carolina, was the son of Solomon and Mary Pinson Cole. About 1815 he married Charlotte Martin who was born 1795 in North Carolina.

Primarily a farmer, Jeremiah was active in Carroll County. On June 20, 1834, Jeremiah was commissioned first lieutenant of Carroll Company, Georgia Militia. In 1837 he got the bid to build the second jailhouse. It was completed in 1839. From 1845-1847, Jeremiah served as one of four justices for Carroll County. He was one of the four justices who presided over the first murder trial held in Carroll County. He also served as deputy sheriff.

Jeremiah and Charlotte never left Carroll County. They are buried in marked graves in the Old Concord Cemetery on Spence Road in Carroll County. This is an old grave yard in the woods. Jeremiah died 10 October 1873 and Charlotte died 1 March 1880. They were devoted to their family, church, and community. They were of the Baptist faith.

Jeremiah and Charlotte's children were: (1) Luduska 1816-1873; husband Daniel Jones. (2) Gilbert 1819-1903; wife Elizabeth Haynes; Gilbert was commissioned ensign of Carroll Company Militia in 1838. In 1849 he was elected justice of Inferior Court of Carroll County. In 1877 he was elected coroner. He served as first sergeant, Company 2, Georgia Militia, Carroll County Unit, during the Cherokee Indian removal. Gilbert and Elizabeth were of the Primitive Baptist faith. They remained in Carroll County. They are buried in marked graves in Concord Primitive Church Cemetery, Highway 113, in Carroll County. Gilbert is my great-great-grandfather. (3) Susannah 1822-?; husband Henry Haynes. (4) Henry Morland 1823-1905; wife Elenor Matthews; died in Craighead County, Arkansas. (5) Eli Franklin 1825-1885; wife Clementine Burke; died in Craighead County, Arkansas. (6) William A. 1829-1862; wife Martha McLendon; died in Civil War in Lauderdale, Mississippi. (7) Aaron J. 1832-1906; wife Rebecca Filder; died in Craighead County, Arkansas. (8) Seaborn Vandiver 1835-1897; wife Marietta Mary Wright. They remained in Carroll County. (9) Jeremiah Martin 1836-1906; wife Elizabeth Johnson. They remained in Carroll County. (10) Young Alonzo 1836-1910; wife Sarah Stephens, died in Craighead County, Arkansas. (11) Mary Ann 1840-?; husband Jacob Williams.

My Cole ancestors came to America from Devonshire England. They were in America by 1650 in Anne Arondel, Maryland, and then in Baltimore County, Maryland. *Submitted by: Margaret Cole Strickland, 1229 South Georgia Avenue, Bremen, GA 30110*

450. Raymond and Avis Cole

Raymond Ellis Cole, born 31 October 1906 in Haralson County, Georgia, died 3 February 1988 in Carroll County, was the son of George Henry Cole (1871-1939) and Mary Narcissus (Narrie) Jones (1871-1946). Grandparents were Henry L. Cole (1848-1918) and Eliza Anne Reeves (1851-1948), Lindsey Jackson Jones (1850-1906) and Elizabeth Clarice Hogan (1851-1926). Great-grandparents were Gilbert Cole (1819-1903) and Elizabeth Haynes (1826-1908), Aquilla Reeves (1829-1899) and Mary Edison (1829-1919), Thomas B. Jones (1806-1880) and Celia Velvin (1809-1890), Hamilton Hogan (1820-1911) and Jane Watson (1830-1905).

Raymond's siblings were Rilla Myra (1893-1973), husband Clyde Edward Stephens; Lillie Maude (1895-1900); Mary Lou (1898-1984), husband Emitt H.L. Miller; Roy Huston (1900-1971), first wife was Thelma Bell and second wife was Lula Stamps Cole; Ruth (1902-1993), husband Walter Johnson.

On 11 August 1928 Raymond married Avis Louise Reese in Carroll County, Georgia.

Raymond and Avis Cole.

Avis Louise Reese was born 23 November 1911 in Carroll County, died 7 July 1998 in Carroll County. She was the daughter of Fred Ball Reese (1877-1926) and Susie Olive Pye (1886-1959). Grandparents were Samuel Russell Reese (1849-1922) and Margarette Louise Ball (1846-1920), Willard Taylor Pye (1848-1899) and Julie Ann Elizabeth Wellborn (1857-1947). Avis's siblings were Fred Bailey (1905-1958), wife Jannie Oglesby; Robert Lee (1909-1985), wife Lucy Hayes; Willard Taylor (1914-1991), wife Evelyn Bradley; Harmon Russell (1916-1919).

Raymond and Avis's children were Mary Evelyn (1930-2000), husband Raymond William Langford; Margaret Edna, husband Ralph Franklin Strickland; Frances Imogene, husband Richard Garland Dodd; Rebecca Ann, husband Alvin Capes; Mainnon Gerald, wife Debbie Melton.

Raymond attended Union Crossroads School. He and Avis lived on Miller Academy Road in the Walnut Hill community. Avis was active in the Walnut Hill Home Demonstration Club. She was a cheerful and outgoing person, always concerned about her neighbors. Avis always had something good to eat — popcorn balls, syrup candy, and tea cakes. She was a good seamstress and made clothes for all the children.

Raymond joined Concord Primitive Baptist Church in Carroll County on 7 September 1957. He loved his church, family and neighbors. One of his greatest joys was Sacred Harp singing.

Raymond and Avis are buried in Pleasant View Church Cemetery in Carroll County. *Submitted by: Susan Strickland Johnson, 3851 North Highway 113, Temple, GA 30179*

451. Robert Lewis Cole Family

Robert Lewis Cole was born April 26, 1899, in Carroll County, Georgia, the son of Franklin Joseph Cole and Maude Jones Cole.

He married Jessie Pearl Stamps on January 18, 1927. She was born February 15, 1908, the daughter of Robert Brooks Stamps and Laura Pamelia McLeod. They raised a family of thirteen children, seven boys and six girls: Robbie, married Lawrence Akin Jr. and has two children, Edwin and Edie. Herbert, (deceased) married Clarice Adams and had two sons Randy and Ricky. C.E., married Wilma Patterson and has one daughter, Beverly. Betty Ann, has two children, Tony and Tammy (deceased). Houston, married Merial

Johnson and has two daughters, Cindy and Carla. Peggy, married Chester Reid and has two sons Steven and Mark. Michael, married Charlsie McDaniel and has four children, Keith, Kay, Shelia and Greg. Dwayne, married Beth Simonton and has two children, Kimberly and Kevin. Charlotte, married Sherron Muse and has two children, Sherri and Ricky. Wendell, married Brenda Henderson, and has one daughter, Debbie. Janice, married Donnie Kittle and has three children, Neil, Susan and Julie. Barry, married Fredia Pritchard and has two daughters, Lori and Lisa. Bonnie, married William Jenkins, and has three children, Tonya, Matthew (deceased) and Doug.

Robert and Jessie have a total of twenty-eight grandchildren, thirty-one great-grandchildren, and five great-great grandchildren. The family tree grows bigger each year.

Robert and Jessie were members of Pleasant View Baptist Church in Carroll County. They both taught Sunday School for many years. The joy of a close and loving family was shown, as one by one they saw all thirteen of their children come forward and join Pleasant View Baptist Church. Eight of their children and their families are members of this church today. Three sons are ministers of the gospel, Herbert (deceased); Dwayne, a doctor of theology; and Barry.

Mr. and Mrs. Robert Lewis Cole. – 60th Wedding Anniversary, 1987

Robert was a watch and jewelry repairman and taught many family members this trade. He traveled and worked in different towns until he went to work with his brother, Reeves Cole at Cole's Jewelry in Carrollton. He worked there until his retirement in 1962. He loved to fish and after his retirement he had a lake built behind his farm on Mandeville Road in Carrollton.

Robert and Jessie farmed and raised a garden to help support their family. Robert also had a syrup mill on his farm for many years.

The example they set as loving parents and grandparents will live on for many generations to come.

Robert passed away on March 14, 1987. Jessie passed away on January 4, 1991. They are buried in Pleasant View Church Cemetery in Carroll County. *Submitted by: Bonnie Jenkins, 120 West Lake Drive, Carrollton, GA 30117*

452. Hoke Collins

Joe Hoke Collins was born April 22, 1897, died April 2, 1958, and was son of William Wright and Lou Meeks Collins. On May 14, 1916, he married Lula Puckett who was born November 28, 1901, died January 29, 1983, daughter of John and Lonie Ham Puckett. Hoke and Lula are buried at Stripling Chapel Church, Carrollton, Georgia. They had twelve children: Lena, John, Luther, Inez, Homer, Otis, Ophelia, Lewis, Eva, Herman, Ray and Rayford.

Lena married Bob Hickey and their children are Wesley, Evelyn, Syble, Donald, and Melba. Wesley married Freida Gray and they have two children, Dale and Sue. Evelyn married Howard Baughn and they have two children, Steve and Joann. Syble married Wayne Williamson and

Lula and Hoke Collins

they have two children, Donna and Sherri. Donald married Faye Rice and they have two children, Bobby and Jason. Melba married Kenneth Ashley and they have four children, Ken, Angie, Gina and Patrick. Lena later married Otis Brown.

John married Odell Lewis and their children are Shirley, Calvin and Carl. Shirley married Donald McIntosh and they have two children, Tracy and Tammie. Calvin married Connie Bailey and they have five children, Victor, Vincent, Terry, Tommy and Shawn. They divorced and Calvin later married Merlene Liner and they have two boys, Brian and Derrick. Carl is a Catholic Priest and not married.

Luther married Christine Akers and they have three children, Miriam, Jerry and Ronald. Miriam married Frank Chapman and they have four children, Mike, Tim, Greg and Christi. Mike married Susan Exley and they have three children, Sarah Beth, Anna, and David. Tim married Leah Hudspeth and they have four children, Josh, Amy, Loriann, and Hannah. Greg married Rebecca Gunn and they have two children, John Michael and Daniel. Christi married Wayne Hammock and they have no children.

Jerry married Janice Golden and they have three children, David, Deneen and Don. David married Michelle Rayburn and they have two children, Santana and Jamie. Deneen married Ronnie Rush and has two daughters, Kelley and Kristin. Don married Ammy Lance they have two children, Garrett and Sarah.

Ronald married Brenda Chambers and they have two children, Joey and Lisa. Joey married Debra Strowhebker and they have two children, Amanda and Danna. Lisa is not married.

Inez married Dave Henry and they have five children, Charlsie who died in infancy, Harold, Virgil, Sandra, and Susan. Harold married Judy McGraw and they have two children, Mark and Karen. Virgil married Faye Rice and they have three children, Angie, Amanda, and Tony. Sandra married Joel Frost and they have two children, Tim and Sandy. Susan married David Warren and they have three children, Jeff, Matt, and Tara.

Otis married Mary Lou Wessinger and they have three children, Mary Ann, Danny, and Ray. Mary Ann married Jim Barr and they have one child Renee. Danny married Ruth Warren and they have one daughter, Paige. Ray married Debra and they have two children, Isaih and Malea.

Ophelia married Paul Hambrick and they have two children, Willard and Pam. Willard married Grace Davis and have three children, Keith, Alicia, and Ricky. Pam married Terry Stookey and they have two children, Chris and Emily.

Lewis married Blanche Rivers and they have two sons, Nelson and Nathan. Nelson married Mary Lovell and they have two sons, Jason and Brad. Nathan married Debra Yates and they have two daughters, Jennifer and Melissa.

Eva married Charles Gilley and they have three sons, David, Gary, and Randy. David married Cindy Warren and they have two children, Heather and Blake. Gary married Janet Hyde and have two children, Amanda and Mitchell. He is now married to Tina Quarles. Randy married Donna Braswell and they have a daughter Lindsey.

Herman married Freddie Ruth Hudson and have one daughter Nelda. They divorced and he married Jane Broom and they have two children, Wade and Amy. They are divorced and he is now married to Phyllis Rains.

Homer, Ray, and Rayford all died in infancy. *Submitted by: Christine Collins, 118 Park Lane, Carrollton, GA 30117*

453. William Terry Colquitt

William Terry Colquitt's ancestry can be traced to St. Sampson Parish, Isle of Gurnsey, Channel Islands, as early as 1540. W.T.'s grandfather was brought to Virginia as a small child. It is unknown as to just when the Colquitts moved from Virginia to Oglethorpe County, Georgia, then on to Russell and Lee Counties in Alabama.

Seven of the nine children of William Terry and Mary Ann Stringer Colquitt.

William, the son of Thomas Colquitt and Elizabeth Franklin, was born September 28, 1816, in Oglethorpe County. He married Ann Stringer on February 28, 1836. Ann Stringer was born April 16, 1815, in Edgefield District, South Carolina. Ann was the daughter of William David and Mary Franklin Stringer. Nothing more is known to this writer of the ancestry of Ann Stringer.

It is not known exactly when the Colquitts moved to Alabama. William's grandfather, John Terry Colquitt, died August 3, 1865, and is buried in Russell County, Alabama. His father, Thomas, died 1865 in Lee County, Alabama.

William T. Colquitt was a great believer in education. In 1858 he moved his wife and nine children to Bowdon, Georgia. He wanted his children to have more educational opportunities. He later donated a tract of land on Main Street for Bowdon College. He was one of ten men directly responsible for the building of Bowdon College.

William and Mary Ann had eight daughters and one son. His daughters were: (1) Martha Elizabeth (Mattie) married A.B. Mitchell. They had four children. (2) Mary Ann (Sis) married F.H.M. Henderson. They had no children. (3) George Washington, the only son in the family, married Mary Fannie Word and they had four children. (4) Frances Abigail was married first to Joseph B.E. Brown who died in the first year of their marriage. She then married Joseph Brown's brother, Henry Clay Brown. They had five children. (5) Harriet Virginia married John Humphrey Word. They had no children of their own. (6) Susan Isbella married W.T. Johnson and they had three children. (7) Charlotte Candace married Samuel J. Brown and they had eight children. (8) Sallie Beatrice married W. Tommie Johnson and they had no children. Sallie Beatrice died in 1883 at the age of thirty. (9) Savannah Georgia married Joseph Posey Little and they had five children. Savannah died at age thirty-eight, leaving four small children. At least two of Savannah's children went to live with John H. and Harriet Word.

William died September 4, 1874. Ann died ten years later on November 30, 1884. Both are buried in the Bowdon Baptist Church yard. *Submitted by: Joe Mosley, 116 Cherry Street, Bremen, GA 30110*

454. William Terry Colquitt 1816-1873

Born in Oglethorpe County, Georgia, in 1816, William Terry Colquitt was one of seven children of Thomas Colquitt and Elizabeth Betsy Franklin of Halifax County, Virginia, and later of Russell County, Alabama. In 1858 William Terry Colquitt moved from Alabama to Bowdon to give his ultimately nine children better educational opportunities. They had known the hardships of the frontier, and when William T. Colquiutt and Ann Stringer were married [in 1836], they began housekeeping with only a frying pan and two old chairs. By the time they moved to Bowdon, they were quite prosperous, devoted members of the Missionary Baptist Church and liberal contributors to all worthy causes. (1)

"As described by Professor John Manley Richardson [President of Bowdon College 1867-70], Colquitt was a 'plain and silent man, tall and strong, and rugged of aspect; stern and lofty in principle, yet gentle and generous in heart; liberal of hand, and broad in educational views. Never was man more devoted to education than he was'. (2)

"Colquitt observed the good work that Professors McDaniel and Richardson were doing [in founding Bowdon College] and suggested that they sell the log schoolhouse and the land connected with it and put all the means in the erection of a new college building. He promised to give a tract of land on Main Street, just west of then-President McDaniel's home, for the location of the college. Both readily agreed, and the people of Bowdon entered wholeheartedly into the enterprise ...

"[They] began plans for building the college edifice ... on December 22 1857 ... and when spring came, they began to build on the land that William T. Colquitt had given.(3)"

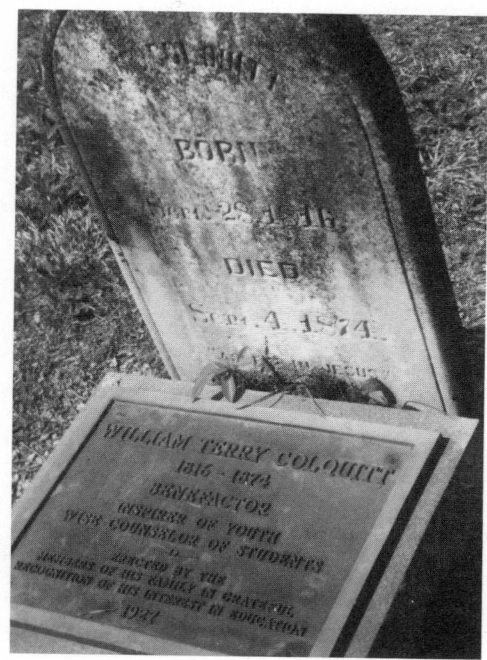

Grave marker for William Terry Colquitt

The bronze monument on his grave reads "William Terry Colquitt, 1816-1874 - Benefactor, Inspirer of Youth, Wise Counselor of Students — Erected by the members of his family in grateful recognition of his interest in education, 1927." He and his wife are buried in the old cemetery beside First Baptist Church, Bowdon, Carroll County, Georgia. *Submitted by: Walter Judson Eldredge, 1245 Pasture View, Baton Rouge, LA 70810*

Sources: (1) From *Memoirs of Georgia,* Vol. I, pp. 448-449, Atlanta, Georgia, The Southern Historical Society, 1895. (2) John Manly Richardson, *A Tribute to the Memory of my Friend, Charles A. McDaniel* in *Catalogue of the Officers, Alumni and Students of Bowdon College 1890-91,* Atlanta, Georgia: V.P. Sisson Publishers 1890, p. 18 (3) From *Memoirs of Georgia,* Vol. I, p. 449." Above excerpted from *The History of Bowdon College,* pp. 7, 16-20, 39 by Render R. Caswell, 1978.

455. Cook

James Monroe Cook was born in Carroll County on September 19th, 1929. His father was James Madison Cook and his mother was Clara Maggie Chambley. He has one brother, Joseph Luther Cook and one sister, Gladys Cook Shoemake. His grandfather was David "Dave" Cook and his grandmother was Hattie Lee Phillips. His great-grandfather was Francis Marion Cook and his great-grandmother was Hester Ann Clark. His great-great-grandfather was George Washington Cook and his great-great-grandmother was Nancy A. Rooks. His great-great-great-grandfather was Robert Cook and his great-great-great-grandmother is unknown. Robert's second wife was Anna Holder George.

George Washington Cook was a private in Company B 7th Regiment Confederate Cavalry until July 1864 when he was assigned to the 10th Regiment Georgia Cavalry. He enlisted in October 1861. According to records of the Annie Wheeler Chapter of the United Daughters of the Confederacy, G.W. Cook was awarded the Southern Cross of the Legion of Honor on January 18, 1902. He died on November 3, 1904, and is buried at Ephesus Christian Church in Carroll County where most of the Cook and related families are also buried.

Johnny Cook, Margie Bonnell Pyles, and James Monroe Cook

On December 17, 1947, James Monroe Cook married Margie Bonnell Pyles in Cobb County, Georgia. Her father was John William "Willie" Pyles and her mother was Geneva Anna Gray. She has one sister, Mattie Lou Pyles that was first married to Thomas Cowart and after his death in 1986 she married Garvie Word. Bonnell's grandfather was W.E. Pyles and her grandmother was Martha Moseley. Her great-grandfather was John P. Pyles and her great-grandmother was Mary M. Pyles. Maiden name unknown. John William Pyles and Geneva Anna Gray were of Carroll County, but his parents and grandparents were from Heard County.

John "Willie" Pyles was known as a "Jack of all trades." He worked on guns and clocks in his shop. He made a guitar, which he sold, and a fiddle which I, Johnny Cook, still have. On June 14, 1914, John "Willie" Pyles lost his father, two brothers and grandfather, John P. Pyles, when a boiler that was being used for threshing wheat and oats in the upper portion of Heard County exploded and instantly killed John P. Pyles, his son, Ed Pyles and two sons of Ed Pyles. According to the newspaper article that was found in Geneva Pyles papers

> "the affair is one of the most shocking that has happened in our county in many years."

James Monroe and Margie Bonnell Cook had two children, four grandchildren and seven great-grandchildren. Their children are Johnny Mitchell Cook, who was born in Carroll County in 1950, and Sheila Regina Cook who was born in Atlanta, Georgia, in 1952. Johnny Cook, his wife, Angie Howard Cook, and family lives in Fannin County, Georgia, and Sheila lives in Carroll County. James Monroe Cook retired from Mead Packaging in Atlanta, and he and Margie Bonnell now lives in Eatonton, Georgia on Lake Sinclair. *Submitted by: Johnny Cook, 2494 Old Dial Rd., Morganton, GA 30560*

456. Cook Family

My great-great-granddaddy, George Washington Cook, was born 1 January 1829 in Jackson County, Georgia. He later moved to the Rotherwood District of Carroll County. He married Nancy A. Rooks Stone and had ten children.

In the fall of 1861, he enlisted in Company B, 7th Regiment, Confederate Cavalry Partisan Rangers. He survived the war and returned to Carroll County. On 18 January 1902, he was presented with the Southern Cross of the Legion of Honor, along with several other veterans, by the Annie Wheeler Chapter of the United Daughters of the Confederacy. After the war, he drew a pension for some health problems he suffered as a result of his service. An 1895 pension application lists him as married with ten children, ages twenty to forty years, supported by their own labor on the farm. George W. Cook's first wife died in 1868. He married his second wife, Hester Ann Dover Rooks, on 31 October 1869. From that marriage came my great-granddaddy, Jacob Brown Cook, born 30 March 1875.

J.B. Cook lived in Clem. He was a farmer and fertilizer salesman. He married twice. He and his first wife, Mary Jane Phillips, were married 9 April 1893 and had four children. One was my granddaddy, A.B. Cook, born 3 February 1896. J.B.'s first wife died 23 February 1918. He married Susie Ethel Tinney on 30 September 1920. J.B. Cook died 26 December 1949.

A.B. Cook married Ruby Lizziebeth Burks on 24 December 1917. They had six children. Granny Ruby was born 5 February 1901, the daughter of W.A. Burks and Manda Pate Burks. A.B. was a farmer, bee keeper, fiddle player, and also made cane syrup. He owned and ran a little country store from the late 1940s to the early 1970s. Some of my fondest memories are of that little country store, especially around Christmas time. The wood stove would be hot and friends and relatives from the community would be sitting around it talking and telling stories. PaPa Noot (don't know how he got his nickname "Noot." but that's what a lot of folks called him) would have those good Christmas things in the store like stick candy, gum drops, and oranges. I miss those times. Granny Ruby died 24 August 1986 and PaPa on 29 December 1987.

George Washington and Hester Ann Dover Rooks Cook

My parents are Harold Aubrey Cook and Myrtle Margaret Wood Cook. They live in Carroll County and recently celebrated their fiftieth wedding anniversary. They had four children counting me. Mother is the daughter of John W. Wood Sr. and Effie Estelle Maxwell Wood.

My name is Alfred Wayne Cook born 6 April 1953. I am married to Janice Marie Watson Cook. We reside in Carroll County with two of our three daughters. I am a member of Sand Hill Lodge #350, Wool Hat Boys Lodges #1, Sons of Confederate Veterans Camp #1239, and Teamster's Local #728. *Submitted by: Wayne Cook, 1298 Happy Hill Road, Carrollton, GA 30116*

457. William Frank Cook Jr.

William Frank Cook Jr. (1925-1987) and Angie Luck Cook moved to Carrollton in the spring of 1951. He came to work for Southwire Company, a very new company at the time.

Frank was the son of William Frank Cook Sr. and Bessie Williams Cook of West Point, Georgia. He was born in Newnan, Georgia, lived in Savannah, Georgia, in early childhood, then in West Point where he graduated from high school. He graduated from Auburn University. While living in Carrollton he worked for Southwire and Daniel Construction Company, operated Cook's Hardware, and taught at Carrollton High School. He served on the city council and was mayor pro-tem, was a member of the Carrollton Rotary and the First United Methodist Church, where he taught Sunday School.

Angie was born in Carrollton in the house where her mother still lived when she died in 1986. She graduated from Carrollton High School, West Georgia College, the University of Georgia (where she was a member of Delta Delta Delta Sorority) and Emory University (M.A. in librarianship). She taught school for five years in Georgia, Alabama, and North Carolina and worked at the West Georgia Regional Library. She has been a member of the Carroll County Historical Society, Carroll County Cultural Arts Board, Civic Woman's Club, Lit-Mu Club, League of Women Voters, Friendship Force of West Georgia, Spade and Trowel Garden Club and the First United Methodist Church.

Front: Jane, Tom, Luck and Bill Cook. Back: Frank and Angie Cook.

Their children are: Jane Williams Cook, Carrollton; William Frank Cook III, Carrollton; Luck Singleton Cook, Marietta; and Thomas Hobgood Cook and his wife, Terri Goss Cook, Acworth. *Submitted by: Bill Cook, 422 North Lakeshore Drive, Carrollton, GA 30117*

458. Cooke Family

Great-great-grandfather Rowland B. Cooke was born 1805 in North Carolina and educated in Oxford, North Carolina. When he was about twenty years old, he moved to Fayette County, Georgia, and was married first to Catherine Moseley in Fayette County. Rowland was married second to Martha (last name unknown). Rowland had seven known children by 1850. Martha died in early 1851 and afterward Rowland moved to Carroll County, Georgia. He was married third to Frances Jane King, daughter of Benjamin King. Rowland remained in Carroll County where he served as Baptist minister, moderator and clerk pro-tem at Poplar Springs Primitive Baptist Church until 1866, when he moved to Giles County, Tennessee.

One child born to Rowland and Martha Cooke was called P.A.J.M. Cooke, or more commonly known as John Moses Cooke. He was born June 19, 1845, and married Amanda Jane O'Neal who was born March 27, 1847. John Moses and Amanda had twelve children, among them my grandfather, George Washington Cooke.

George Washington Cooke was born in Carroll County on April 11, 1864, and died in 1949. He was married three times: first to Mollie King in Carroll County on September 7, 1880. Mollie was the daughter of Thomas Hiram King and Charity Matilda Chandler. George W. and Mollie had ten children. The youngest son in that family was my father, William Ambrose Cooke. Mollie died in 1905 and George W. married Samantha Gammon (1870-1912) on September 29, 1910, in Carroll County. After Samantha died in 1912, George W. married Meda McLear on July 27, 1913.

My father, William Ambrose Cooke, was born November 6, 1894 in Carroll County. He met my mother Cecile Fem Carroll (daughter of James Moses Blackburn Carroll and Minnie Lee McBurnett Carroll) at a Union Camp Ground meeting near Waco and they were married on August 27, 1913. As newlyweds, they lived in a small house on the Carroll farm in Haralson County. Their first daughter Sara Frances Cooke was born July 15, 1919. The family later moved to a house down the hill from the Carroll home where their second daughter Lois Moselle Cooke was born February 4, 1923.

William Cooke farmed until he got a job in Atlanta with a roofing company. He and Cecil lived in Atlanta until he was seriously injured and was unable to continue in his job. They moved to Tallapoosa about 1928 and their third daughter Elynor Carol Cooke was born there July 20, 1928. My parents raised chickens for a while and then moved to a farm behind the old Lithia Springs Hotel in Tallapoosa. After a year there, they moved to the Dodge farm east of Tallapoosa where they lived for about two years. They then moved to the Hansard farm west of Tallapoosa. In 1932 they bought a home on the hill back of the Lithia Springs Hotel. While living there, Daddy farmed and worked as a mechanic and was a rural mail carrier.

In 1940 they bought a cafe in Atlanta, Georgia, in the same block as the State Capitol. Daddy had a massive heart attack in 1945. When he could return to work, the City of Atlanta employed him as a night watchman. After a few years, they sold the cafe and were in the midst of building a new home in the southern part of Atlanta when Daddy had a fatal heart attack on July 22, 1948. He is buried in West View Cemetery, Atlanta.

My mother Cecil, and sister Carol and her husband, John L. Abbott, lived in the new house for a year or so, but sold it and bought a home on Beecher Street in Atlanta. Mama came to Birmingham in 1951 and lived with Frances for a year or so. She returned to Atlanta in late 1952 and married Chester A. Myers, a retired mechanic from Seaboard Railroad, on January 24, 1953. They soon sold the Beecher Street home and bought a two-story house there in West End, Atlanta.

Four generations of the Cooke family

About 1960 they sold their home and moved to Birmingham near Frances. They lived there until 1964 when they moved to Bremen, Georgia. In January of 1976 they moved back to Birmingham and lived in the Club View Apartments. Chester died on April 14, 1976, and is buried in West View Cemetery, Atlanta. Mama continued to live in Birmingham until she died on June 1, 1992. Rev. Pete Furio conducted her funeral in Bremen, Georgia, and she is buried in West View Cemetery, Atlanta, Georgia.

This picture shows four generations of the Cooke family. From left are George W. Cooke and his second wife Meda McLear, William Ambrose Cooke, Frances Cooke Batts holding daughter Cecile Batts, Cecil Carroll Cooke, and Orlan G. Batts. *Submitted by: Frances Cooke Batts, 307 Sunbrook Avenue, Birmingham, AL 35215*

Sources: Personal family knowledge, *Many Cookes and their Broth*

459. Copeland Family

George Prangle Copeland came from Ireland to Pennsylvania in the 1750s. Family researchers picked him up in Pennsylvania about 1755 when he moved to Laurens County, South Carolina, a sparsely settled area. The Copelands, and possibly three or four other families, traveled the hundreds of miles in covered wagons. Among the others was the Blakely family. George P. Copeland's son, John, seven years old during the trip later married Margaret Blakley.

It is uncertain if George, the son of John and Margaret, moved on to Georgia, but George's son Samuel showed up in Newton County, Georgia in the 1840s. A merchant, he moved to Carroll County around 1850 or 1851. He is said to have opened one of the first two stores in the Bowdon area in 1851.

Eleven children were born to the Samuel Copelands. James Robert was the seventh child. He entered the Civil War at age sixteen and following the war suffered from poor health the remainder of his thirty-five years. He married Emma Augusta Stephenson and together they had seven children before his death. The family grew up in the Blackjack Mountain area. A physician never came to the home when the children were young. One and two room schools offered the only educational opportunities.

In spite of difficulties, those grandchildren of Samuel and children of James Robert became worthy citizens. A large majority of them settled in Carroll County. Generations later, we find in this group teachers, farmers, merchants, dentists, physicians, ministers, pharmacists, lawyers, PhDs, bankers, administrators, nurses, military officers, and other outstanding individuals.

Sons of James Robert Copeland

Children of Samuel Copeland (1811) and his wife Elizabeth (1812) were: S.E. 1831; W.G. 1834; J.C. 1836; R.A. 1839; M.E. 1841; M.C. 1843; James Robert 1847; J.E. 1848; L.J. 1848; Elizabeth or Eliza 1850; Sally 1852; Tallie 1854; and Texas 1857.

Children of James Robert Copeland and Emma Augusta Stephenson were: Robert Lamar 1869; William E. 1871; Laura E. 1873; John W. 1876; Marietta 1879; James Pleas 1881; Joseph Bryant 1884; and Thadeus S. 1886.

Shown in the picture are sons of James Robert Copeland. Pleas and Robert L. are on the front row, and Joseph Bryant and Thadeus are on back row. *Submitted by: O.B. Copeland, 383 Shades Crest Road, Birmingham, AL 35226*

460. "B" and Annie Lee Copeland

Joseph Bryant "B" Copeland was born near Bowdon (Blackjack Mountain) on the McIntosh Trail on February 17, 1884. He was the fifth son of James Robert Copeland and Emma Stephenson Copeland. Annie Lee Jackson was born on September 10, 1884, in Carroll County. She was the daughter of James Henderson "Happy Jim" Jackson and Laura Celestial Marlow Jackson.

"B" attended school in a one room, dirt floor cabin near Bucktown outside Bowdon. Annie Lee attended the small community schools near where she lived. "B" lived for a while with his eldest brother, Robert Copeland, and for a year in the home of Henry McDaniel near the Victory community. This was about three miles from the farm where Annie Lee was growing up. They met during this period, courted in a buggy and in the little Salem Community School both attended. They were married September 18, 1904, on the back porch of the Jackson farm near Salem Church while witnesses stood in the yard.

The first year of their marriage, they lived with his mother on the Copeland farm near Blackjack Mountain. Within a short time, they bought a small farm in the same community. During their marriage and while the family was growing, they moved a number of times. Their last home was on Salem Church Road outside Carrollton.

"B" and Annie Lee Copeland

"B" and Annie Lee had five children. Bessie Lee Copeland was born on October 15, 1905. She married Oscar L. Nixon. Reba Celestial Copeland was born on October 30, 1907. She married Hoke Lancaster. James Millard Copeland was born on July 2, 1911. He married Lerlie Traylor. Otis Bryant Copeland was born on August 7, 1916. He married Dorothy Causey. Jimmy Bryant Copeland was born on December 9, 1924. He married Barbara Bargeron.

In addition to buying and selling farms, "B" was a farmer, bought and sold livestock, operated a mule barn and was a cotton buyer. Like the women of her time, Annie Lee's career was family and home. She helped to start the first home demonstration club in Carroll County (the Tallapoosa Community Club). She served as president of this club several times. In her later years, she wrote the Tallapoosa Community News for the Carrollton paper.

They celebrated their golden wedding anniversary in the fall of 1954. "B" died on October 26, 1958. Annie Lee died on December 27, 1964.

"B" and Annie Lee joined Tallapoosa Primitive Baptist Church in the early 1920s. They are buried in that church cemetery on the Carrollton-Tyus Road. *Submitted by: Carol Copeland, 5 Willow Tree Run, Asheville, NC 28803*

461. Millard and Lerlie Copeland

James Millard Copeland was born on July 2, 1911, in Carroll County, the son of Joseph Bryant Copeland and Annie Lee Jackson Copeland. He was the middle child in a family of five. Bessie and Reba were older sisters and Otis and Jim were younger brothers.

Lerlie Evelyn Traylor was born on November 26, 1911, on what is now Brock Road near the Farmer's High community. She was the older daughter of Albert Tony Traylor and Myrtie Maybell Smith Traylor. Her father died when she was five and her mother, who never remarried, raised Lerlie and her sister, Louise, at the home of her parents Arch and Marih Smith.

Millard had an uncle, John Copeland. Lerlie had an aunt, Adella Smith. John and Adella married and Lerlie and Millard first met when he and his parents gave her and her mom and sister a ride home.

Lerlie attended Farmer's High School and was a boarding student attending Bowdon High School. She graduated from Bowdon Normal and Industrial College in 1928 and began a teaching

Millard and Lerlie Copeland, November 1985

career that spanned forty-two years. She retired from Tyus Elementary School in 1972.

Millard attended schools near his home, including Salem and Tallapoosa and for a while the Agricultural and Mechanical School, before going to work. His work history included Mandeville Mills, building power lines for Roy Richards in North Georgia and Tennessee, a lineman for Carroll EMC, and at the time of his retirement he was parts manager for Richards and Associates. During the 1960s, he owned and operated a retail clothing business — Copeland and Lancaster — in Carrollton. He was a cattle farmer and a member of both the Carroll County and Georgia Cattleman's Association. He was a director of the Carroll EMC and the Carroll County Livestock Sales Barn in his later years.

On November 18, 1934, they were married in Bowdon and after living in several communities following Lerlie's teaching career, they purchased a home on what is now Salem Church Road where they lived for the remainder of their lives.

On July 1, 1945, their only child, Judy Carolyn Copeland, was born. She married James Lovvorn Rowell Jr. on June 12, 1966. Jim and Judy had two children. Julie Carol Rowell was born on October 1, 1971 and on August 1, 1998, she married Derick Nelson Steed. Copeland James Rowell was born on May 19, 1980.

Lerlie died on July 9, 1985, and Millard died on July 14, 1985. They are buried in the Bowdon City Cemetery. *Submitted by: Judy Copeland Rowell, 1472 Garrett Creek Road, Bowdon, GA 30108.*

462. J.T. Cowart Family

There is much information about the Cowart family. It has been gathered from the four winds of the earth. Robert J. Robinson, one of the descendants, has researched for information for over thirty years. The first knowledge of Cowarts was in Virginia, then North Carolina, and from there to South Carolina.

The story of the Carroll County, Georgia, family begins with Lewis Grandberry Cowart, born in Sumter County in the middle of the nineteenth century.

The story is told that from near Americus, Georgia, my grandfather, Joseph Thomas Cowart, tried to follow a stolen mule as far north as Summerville, Georgia. He liked Carroll County — the land, climate, and all general conditions that would enable him to make a living as a farmer.

Grandfather became a circuit-rider minister of the Methodist Church. He preached in Carroll County at Rotherwood Church near Whitesburg. It was very difficult to make a living here. He walked many times from Lowell to the church at Rotherwood on Saturday. If not invited to spend the night, he would walk back to Lowell that day, then back in the same way the next day.

To try to better take care of his family, he moved to Alabama near Guntersville, continuing to try to provide for family by farming and preaching. He died and is buried in Alabama.

In the meantime, he lost two wives and two children. Of the four children who lived, one was my father. He had met and married a Carroll County girl who lived at Lowell. Her name was

The Joseph Thomas Cowart Family

Amanda Julie Katherine Smith, born at the top of Doris Hill on Georgia Highway 5.

They, along with my mother's entire family of fourteen brothers and sisters, went to Texas for a while. My dad hurt himself pulling big sacks of cotton; so he, Mama, and the two oldest children (Susie and Beatrice) came back to Georgia. Only one of my mother's sisters, Lizzie Roberts, came back to Georgia. She settled near Fayetteville.

The children of Joseph Thomas and "Mandy" Cowart were eleven in number, not including a stillborn baby. All of the eleven were born near Lowell in Carroll County. These eleven children, from oldest to youngest, were Susan Eliza Rooks (Jones after the death of her first husband), Beatrice Elizabeth Cowart Dorough, Luther Grandbury Cowart (a preacher), Ida Cowart Musick, Lillian C. Taylor, William Guy Cowart, Orban Jewel Cowart, Gladys C. Baughtman, Vera Cowart Pyron, Euel Cowart and Opal C. McWhorter.

To these eleven children, fifty-two grandchildren were born. The number of descendants now would be over three hundred.

Lowell was a small place. However, I remember a blacksmith shop, a grist mill, two country stores, a school two-stories high that cared for children through the ninth grade and had room for a Masonic Lodge in one room upstairs, two churches, one of which was a Methodist that had a small balcony upstairs with four Sunday School rooms.

My father helped with the lumber that he sawed, and with the building of that church. My parents had belonged at Liberty Methodist before becoming charter members at Lowell. At that time, we were on a "circuit" with other churches so we had preaching on one Sunday a month at each of the circuit churches.

Children mostly walked to school when possible. Sometimes they were brought in buggies or wagons. We carried lunch from home — maybe sausage and biscuit, or fried okra, depending on the season or what we had at home to eat.

Six years ago, in 1995, the living blood-kin descendants from Joseph Thomas and Amanda Smith Coward were 362. The Cowarts have made history in Carroll County. *Submitted by: Opal McWhorter, 515 Dairy Drive, Franklin, GA 30217-3431*

463. Lewis Grandbury Cowart Family

This branch of the Cowart family has been traced to Somerset, England, and to one William Coward who fathered James Coward in 1660. James Coward moved to the Virginia Colony about 1687. Later a part of the family moved to North Carolina. The name was changed to Cowart about the time of the Revolutionary War. Soon after that some of the family moved to South Georgia. Lewis Grandbury was born in Sumter County in 1847 and married Mary E. Speight in 1871. He served in the Civil War, was a railroad worker and Methodist minister. Their child, Joseph Thomas Cowart, was born in 1872 in Summerville, Georgia, and Mary Speight Cowart died about 1878, is buried there. He married Exah Matilda Stephens in 1879. One son, John, died when three months old. John's mother died soon after he was born. He married Mary Jane McRae in 1886 in Alabama. They moved to Carroll County and had three children: Lewis Nathaniel 1888; Mary Exah 1889; and Lillie Alice (Mattie) 1893. Mary Jane Cowart died in 1924 and Lewis Grandbury Cowart died in 1925. Both are buried in Marshall County, Alabama.

Joseph Thomas Cowart married Amanda Julie Smith in 1891. Except for a short time in Texas, they lived in the Lowell community for the rest of their life. Joseph Thomas Cowart accumulated a great deal of land in his lifetime and worked as a farmer, and both were very active in their community and, when it was established, Lowell Methodist Church. They had twelve children: Susan Eliza 1892; Beatrice Elizabeth 1894; Luther Grandbury 1896; Ida Gertrude 1898; Mary Lillian 1901; William Guy 1903; Orban Jewell 1905; Amanda Gladys 1908; Vera Mable 1910; Gene 1912 (died as infant); Euel Milton 1913; Josie Opal 1917. Luther Grandbury became a Methodist minister and Opal worked in a Savannah shipyard and later became a teacher and librarian.

William Guy Cowart started working at a sawmill when he was thirteen. He later worked in the construction of the Allatoona Dam. He worked at the Farmer's Mutual Warehouse in Carrollton until retirement. He married Zula Beatrice Crawford in 1920 (died 1932). They had five children: Thomas Franklin 1922; Verdie Mae 1925; Julian Eugene 1927; Mandy Elizabeth 1929; and Virginia Evelyn 1932. Guy worked as a sharecropper on land owned by his father. He married Mary Elizabeth Haynes in 1932 and they had five boys: William Guy Jr 1934; Earl Rex 1937; Jerry Travis 1942; Terry Kenneth 1944; Don Ellis 1949. Julian Eugene finished high school at Whitesburg. Elizabeth, Evelyn, W.G., and Rex graduated from Roopville High School. Still remembered by W.G. is the time in the early 1940s when Guy and J.T. Cowart leaned against the front porch and Guy arranged to buy the property he lived on from his father - thus going from a sharecropper to a landowner. Eugene served in the Army Air Force, W.G. finished college and seminary and served in the USMC and then as a chaplain in the U.S. Navy. Rex served in the U.S. Army Reserve until retirement. He worked at the Carrollton Post Office and as the postmaster at Franklin until retirement. Travis spent a career in the Air Force and then worked at Sears and the postal service after retirement. Don served in the Navy and then Army National Guard until retirement. *Submitted by: William G. Cowart, Jr., 235 Carroll Street, Carrollton, GA 30117-3703*

464. Benjamin Franklin Cox

Benjamin Franklin Cox (Uncle Ben) was born in Henry County 16 February 1829 to Henry Cox and Maria Pace. He came to Carroll County via Heard County, Georgia, early in 1857. He bought forest land on Whooping Creek between Clem and Lowell and cleared part of it on which to farm and build a log house.

In May 1857, he went to Fulton County, Georgia, to claim his bride, Sarah Emeline Wellborn, daughter of W.E. and Charity Brogdon Wellborn. It is thought that he met her while visiting his uncle, Hardy Pace, who lived in a seventeen-room house in what is now Vinings in Cobb County overlooking Paces Ferry, which he operated on the Chattahoochee River. He brought Emeline to Carroll County in a wagon. They lived in the log house and reared a family of seven children to wit: (1) Cicero Cox born circa 1858 and died 8 August 1884 in Modesto, California, where he is buried. He never married. (2) William Alexander Cox (Alec) born circa 1859. He married Fannie Pander in Atlanta, Georgia, in 1882 and died in Atlanta Alms House 12 April 1918.

Mr. and Mrs. J.T. Cowart, children and in-laws, August 29, 1948

Benjamin Franklin Cox

He is buried in the single grave section of Westview Cemetery, Atlanta. (3) Charity Maria Cox born 1 December 1862 and died July 1960 at age ninety-eight. She married J. Tom Coleman in Carrollton, Georgia, in 1882. He died in 1941. Both are buried in the Carrollton City Cemetery. They had children: Minnie, Nettie, Roy, Purl, Lurline and Verra. All are deceased. (4) Sallie Cox born 1866, married Marshall Love in June of 1889 (divorced). They had two daughters, Eula Love Harwell and Ollie Love Putman. Sallie died in 1941 and is buried in Thomaston, Georgia. (5) Henry George Cox born 1868, married Olive Magdeline McKnelly in 1896. Henry died of cancer in 1912. He is buried in the single grave section at Westview Cemetery. Their children were Gladys, Herman, and Cuva. Olive M. Cox died in November 1965 and is buried in Forest Park, Georgia. (6) Benjamin Hardy Cox born 11 May 1872, married Gillie Gordon 24 December 1907 in Carroll County. Gillie was born in 1886. She was the daughter of Millie P. Tomlin and William Davis Gordon. Their children were B.H., Kermit, Millicent Eugenia (Jean), and Gordon. Gillie died January 1921, and Benjamin H. Cox died October 1933. Both are buried in Stripling Chapel Cemetery, Carrollton, Georgia. (7) Stephen E. Cox, born 11 November 1873, married Martha Burns in 1900. Both are buried in Westview Cemetery, Atlanta. He died in 1956.

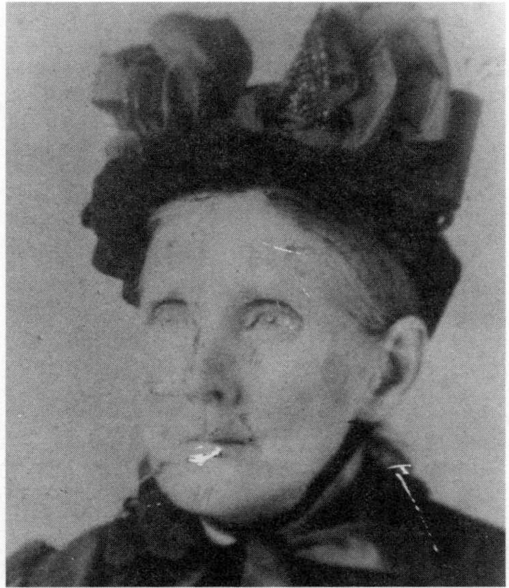

Sarah Emeline Wellborn Cox

All these children of Benjamin F. and Emeline Wellborn Cox were born and reared at the home place that he bought in 1857. Emeline died of pneumonia while on a visit to her daughter, Sallie, in Griffin, Georgia, in February 1909. Benjamin F. died of "old age" at the home of Stephen E. Cox in Atlanta in 1916, age eighty-seven. He never belonged to a church, but Emeline was a staunch Methodist and is thought to have been a charter member of Stripling Chapel Church. *Submitted by: Carol Cox Mock, Hayesville, NC*

465. Charlie Lee Cox

Charlie Lee Cox was born February 10, 1872, in Georgia. Vianna Elizabeth Arrington was born December 1, 1872, in Clay County, Alabama. They were married in 1889. Charlie's parents were David and Frances Cox. Frances's maiden name is unknown, but believed to be Lee. Miss Lizzie's, as grandmother was affectionately known, parents were John J. Arrington, born May 15, 1849, and died November 28, 1903. Mary Catherine Prestridge was born November 7, 1850, and died November 15, 1942.

Charlie and Miss Lizzie had nine children: Elbert Brittian (November 14, 1892-September 15, 1948); Eunice Emmett (March 10, 1894-June 8, 1851); Warner David, known as "D" (1896-April 27, 1962); Claudia Lee (August 30, 1898-May 22, 1974); Wade Johnson (January 4, 1901-October 4, 1985); James Aubrey (April 11, 1903); Mary Annice (August 24, 1905-May 9, 1993); Marvin Jefferson (May 24, 1908-May 13, 1928). Marvin was found dead from a massive heart attack a few days after graduating from high school; Hoyt Owen (September 27, 1910-November 3, 1963).

Elbert married Florrye Ophelia Thornton on December 25, 1922. They had three children: Ernest Edward (October 19, 1923-March 28, 1973); Charles (September 3, 1925-May 21, 1927); and Howard Glen (July 11, 1929-uncertain).

Eunice Cox married Ena Traylor and they had two children: Margaret Bernice (February 24, 1928-September 30, 1989), and Annie Ruth (born August 10, 1930).

David Warner married Grace Moore. They raised one child, Charles William, their dearly beloved and cherished adopted son, born May 16, 1932.

Claudia Lee married Murdock Duke Holcomb on October 5, 1919. They had three children: Charlie Lee (C.L.), born August 30, 1920; Harold, born October 14, 1923 and died the same day; and Doris Elizabeth, born March 1, 1927 and died (date uncertain).

Wade Johnson married Stella Mae Wessinger on October 1, 1922. They had three children: Viola Elizabeth, August 19, 1924; Emmette Johnson, December 8, 1926; and James Clement, November 6, 1927. Wade was the fourth son, born January 4, had a stroke on March 4, and died October 4, 1985.

James Aubrey Cox married Winnie Lee Caswell on December 9, 1928. They had one child, Mignon Elizabeth, born September 25, 1929.

Mary Annice married Leon Jewell Pitts in November 1923. They had five children: Geraldine Frances, born September 22, 1924; William "Bill" Leon Pitts, August 4, 1926; Gwynnelle, October 13, 1928; James Truitt, November 26, 1930; and Lewis Trenton, born December 16, 1933, and died June 27, 1934.

Hoyt Owen Cox married Annie Yarbrough. They had two children: Eleanor Joan, stillborn on March 28, 1940; and James Jerry, born October 16, 1942. Ann died one week later on October 22, 1942. On June 8, 1946, Hoyt married his childhood sweetheart, Dicie Ineze Chambers, and they had one child, Roger Hoyt, born February 17, 1948.

Charlie Cox was a strong, stern, loving, and devoted family man. He believed in God, family, himself, the Ten Commandments, Golden Rule and working. *Submitted by: Viola Elizabeth Cox Robinson, 3881 N. Cooper Lake Road, Smyrna, GA 30082*

466. Charlie Lee and Vianna Elizabeth Cox

Charlie Lee and Vianna Elizabeth, known as "Miss Lizzie" moved their family to Bowdon around 1910. Charlie Cox was a man of vision. He wanted his children to attend the best schools. Bowdon had a college. His sons could attend college and stay at home. Equally important to him was Bowdon's elementary and high school because of their excellent academic reputation.

Grandfather Charlie was a successful farmer, merchant and cotton broker. He served as city councilman and policeman in Bowdon 1916-1917. He loved buying and selling land and real estate. He bought and sold several places before he traded for Frank Fuller's farm off the Bowdon-Tyus Rd., known to us as the Cox home place.

Charlie Cox was proud of his name and of who he was. He only had a fifth grade education but was constantly reminding his children there was nothing a Cox could not accomplish if they wanted to. He was proud of the fact there was a Female Seminary in La Grange, first known as Cox College and also a Cox College in College Park. I don't know if Charlie was related to the founders of those two colleges or not, but he held the name and their accomplishments in high esteem and tried to inspire his children to set their goals in life high and be the best that they could be. Granddaddy believed that anyone bearing the name of Cox could be proud of their heritage and the many outstanding contributions made by people bearing the name of Cox to the development of our country. He often told his sons their most important mission in life was to find someone worthy of sharing their name.

My sister and I were doing some research on the Cox family. Since Charlie and "Miss Lizzie" had lived in Heard County, we were at the court house in Franklin one day going through their

Charlie, "Miss Lizzie," and their first seven children

record books when my sister suddenly announced, James, listen to this, and I told her the story. It was not at all unusual in those days for the doctor to stay over night while waiting for the arrival of a new baby. After I arrived and Dr. Kirby had checked mama and me out good, he packed his things and returned to Bowdon. He registered my birth but forgot to ask Mama and Dad what they wanted to name me. So Dr. Kirby recorded my name as Wade Jr. I had a hard time straightening that out when I enlisted in the Navy during World War II.

Charlie and "Miss Lizzie" had seven boys and two girls. All the boys played basketball in high school and college and Dad (Wade) and Uncle Eunice coached basketball. Granddaddy Cox appreciated the importance in owning real estate. He was a firm believer that no one could accumulate anything until he owned his own home.

The day we were in the court house in Franklin, checking their records for family information, we found another surprise. Records show that grandmother Cox bought and sold real estate in her name. This was really exciting to us.

Dad told us that one of our ancestors came to America on the Mayflower in 1620 along with two brothers. Unverified. However, records show Coxes living in America as early as 1659. *Submitted by: James Clement Cox, 1142 Hilldate Ct., Villa Rica, GA 30180*

467. John Craven

John Craven was born 1799 in North Carolina. He moved to Carroll County, Georgia, before 1850. The family shows up in the 1850 Carroll County census and John is age 51. John was married to Elizabeth. John separated from his wife sometime in 1853. We have not been able to discover what happened to him from that time on. The 1853 Tax Digest shows him living in Alabama.

Elizabeth (1800-1881) remained in Carroll County and is buried in the Craven Family Cemetery near Roopville. Her tombstone inscription reads

> "The first one buried here. Mother, Grandmother and Great Grandmother of all who are buried here."

John and Elizabeth had the following children: 1. William S. born 1820, married Eliza Ann Wood. William Craven was a notary public of the 1111th District. He was also a Mason and belonged to Goshen Lodge No. 71 in Heard County. Later it was moved to Roopville. He was the first Worshipful Master. The Gentrys were members also. William was called Squire Craven at times in the paper. On Indigent Soldiers Pension Roll, W.L. Craven is listed as having been paid from 1903-1911. 2. Sarah Annis (Sally) (1821-1904) married Young Hutchens in Coweta County, Georgia. Sarah and her children always lived with her mother. Daughter Catherine married William Hallmark. We have never located Young Hutchens in any census records nor have we found any war record for him. 3. Samuel M. (1826-1912) married Louisa Adaline Walden, daughter of William Henry Walden and Martha Harrison. Married second to Rebecca A. Griffin. Samuel is buried at Shiloh Methodist Church Cemetery. Indigent Soldiers Pension Roll of Carroll County shows S.M. Craven, Company B, Regiment 2nd Georgia, paid 1898-1910. He died June 25, 1912. Sam and Louisa had a daughter named Lula Craven who married John Mercer Strickland. Lula and John had a daughter named Verdie (my great-grandmother) who married James Andrew Ivey. 4. Barsilla Jane born 1827, married Enoch W. Smith. This is the notorious Smith line of Heard County, Georgia. Enoch died before his son was hanged 1887. We do not know when or where Barsilla was laid to rest. 5. John S. (1828-1910) married Martha C. (Patsy) Henderson. John S. Craven was listed as a private May 12, 1862, captured at Vicksburg, Mississippi, July 4, 1863, paroled there July 8, 1863. 6. Andrew Jackson (1833-bef 1870) married Mary E. Nix. Andrew may have died during the Civil War. I have not been able to confirm this. 7. Wilson L. (1835-1923) married Louise E. Gentry. Wilson L. Craven was listed as a private May 13, 1862, appointed sergeant, captured at Vicksburg on July 4, 1863, paroled July 8, 1863. Pension records show he was wounded at Nashville, Tennessee, on December 16, 1864, and was home on wounded furlough at close of war. He was in Company K, 34th Regiment, Georgia Volunteer Infantry, also known as Company F., W.A. Walker, Captain. After Louise died, he married Rebecca E. Gentry. 8. Elizabeth A.L. born 1830, married Seaborn W. Walden. 9. James K.P. born 1843, married Annie A. Stewart. *Submitted by: John Ivey, MBIGJ@aol.com, P.O. Box 31051, Clarksville, TN 37040*

468. Archie Crawford Family

Archie H. Crawford was born October 18, 1852. He came from Meriwether County as a young man to Carroll County. Arch was a bridge builder and built the first covered bridge over Whooping Creek. He met Miss Sophie Thompson, born June 22, 1850, married her and settled in Carroll County. Arch died May 13, 1915, at the age of sixty-two. Sophie died September 8, 1930, at the age of eighty. They are buried at Whooping Creek Baptist Church.

Family of Laura and Henry Crawford

Sophie's and Arch's son, William Henry Crawford, was born in Carroll County on September 18, 1876. Henry married Laura Beatrice Godbee on December 25, 1898. Laura, daughter of William Talley and Ada Phillips Godbee was born on August 28, 1879.

Their children were Abbie, Jesse, Hyacinth, Earle, Tommy and Dewey. Henry died October 12, 1950, at the age of seventy-four. Laura lived to be 101 years old, dying on November 17, 1980. Henry and Laura are buried at Whooping Creek Baptist Church.

Jesse, born March 13, 1903, married Bertha Mae Davis on May 22, 1922. Bertha, daughter of Samuel and Elizabeth Tant Davis, was born July 20, 1893. Jesse and Bertha had three sons, James Curtis, Joseph Kenneth, and Verlyn Davis Crawford. Jesse was a barber and owned and operated The Little Gem Barber Shop for fifty-two years. Bertha died at the age of eighty-one on November 23, 1974, and Jesse died June 6, 1986, at the age of eighty-three. They are buried at Carroll Memory Gardens.

Joseph Kenneth Crawford, born January 22, 1927, married Charlotte Ann Creel on February 10, 1952. Charlotte, daughter of Earl Delone (Jack) and Mamie Grizzard Creel was born on June 20, 1933. Their children are Joseph Dave, Mark Kenneth, Lisa Ann and John Jeffery. Kenneth died on April 2, 1988, and is buried at Carroll Memory Gardens next to his mother, father, and brother Verlyn.

Shown in the Laura and Henry Crawford family photograph made in 1951 are Hyacinth, Laura, and Earle on the front row, and Abbie, Jesse, Tommy, and Dewey on the back row. *Submitted by: Mark Kenneth Crawford, 521 Dixon Street, Bowdon, GA 30108*

469. Henry Franklin Crawford

Henry Franklin Crawford was born 21 August 1846 and died in Carroll County on 6 February 1915. He married Nancy E. Lee who was born 13 January 1846 and died 4 July 1925. Six children were born to them, Robert Lee Crawford, Joe Arthur Franklin Crawford, Alice Crawford Cantrell, Rilla Margaret Crawford, William Hampton Crawford and Cassie Ovelia Crawford Smith, all of whom are now deceased.

The Crawford family was of Scottish-Irish descent and came to this country and settled mainly in North Carolina and Texas. They were pioneer settlers in Carroll County. Mr. Crawford served as a private in the Phillips Legion Calvary CSA during the Civil War. The Crawfords had a sixty-acre farm south of Temple on Crawford Road, now known as Venable Road, where they grew corn, cotton, vegetables, fruits, and raised cattle which the family drove to Atlanta to sell, usually taking two days walking and spending the night in someone's pasture en route. They had a huge barn, crib, chicken houses, cider and syrup mills, and a large country home with a porch all the way around, and lightning rods. The yard was shady with a picket fence and covered with large gardenia bushes and blooming shrubs and flowers, and several tenant houses on the property.

Mr. Crawford was authorized and paid by the U.S. Government to make liquor. The Crawford family attended school in a one room school house at old Bethel Church which they later attended as a church family. Most of the family are buried in the cemetery there on Carrollton Road south of Temple. *Submitted by: Ruby Crawford, 102 Lakeview Dr., Temple, GA*

470. The J.N. Crawford Family

It all began when a gentleman named Jefferson Newton Crawford married a gentlewoman named Georgia Lee Treadwell. They made a life together on a farm bordering the Little Tallapoosa River on South Highway 100. Georgia was of Irish descent, as evidenced by her red hair. She was also a descendant of Chief McIntosh. Geat, as he was nicknamed, was a farmer, carpenter, and blacksmith. Georgia was a housewife and the local community nurse. Since hospitals were few and far between, she was often called upon to sit with sick children or adults. Both Geat and Georgia were active in the Midway Methodist Church located on Dot Road, where Geat was a steward and Georgia was the organist. The original Midway church was built by Geat's great-grandfather.

Geat and Georgia had nine children, beginning with a boy, Loy. Loy married Fay Cosper and had three sons: Loy Jr., Jerry, and Larry Joe. Loy was a farmer who lived in Pine Hill, Alabama. Loy was the humorist of the family. He entertained children with his story telling and buck dancing. Next born was Lois who married Kermit Johnson and moved to Akron, Ohio. They had three sons, Dwane, Harland and Buddy, and an adopted daughter, Junie. Next was Eula Mae, who married Clint Holliday. They had three children, Barbara, Sara, and Michael. They lived in Marietta. Sara and Michael continue to live in Marietta. Barbara lives in St. Petersburg, Florida. Next, another daughter Elsie was born. She married Grover

Herren and lived in Newell, Alabama. Grover and Elsie had three children, JoAnne, Bill, and Paul. Elsie continues to live on her farm in Newell with all three children close by.

Next born was my dad, Howard Steve, better known as Jack. Daddy married Pauline King, who was also from a family of nine. Together they had two children, my older brother, Steve, and me. My dad was a well-known carpenter and could build a house from start to finish. People knew a "Jack Crawford house" might cost more to build but they knew it would be built right. My mom was a stay-at-home mom while we were young and later worked at the local LaMar Manufacturing Company. My brother is the only descendant who lives on land that was once part of the old Crawford home place.

Geat and Georgia Crawford

Next comes Mildred, who married Clarence Butler. Clarence was the postmaster of Graham, Alabama and the director of the local community bank. Mildred always tended flowers. Together they had a daughter, Jane. Mildred continues to live in Graham. Then another daughter, Lou, was born. She married John Johnson, who served four years of military service during World War II and then worked at Roop Wholesale. Lou was also a housewife and tended gardens of flowers. John and Lou had two daughters, Rebecca and Jenny. Lou continues to live in Bowdon.

Dorothy was born next. She married W.G. Strickland of Carrollton. They have a boy, Alan. Dorothy died from bone cancer during the 1960s at a very young age.

Last born was another daughter, Claris. Claris married Thomas Durward Norton. They lived in Atlanta and had two children, Teresa and Rick. Durward worked for and retired from Georgia Power Company. Claris was a stay-at-home mom while the children were young and later worked as a substitute teacher for the local school systems. Claris continues to substitute as needed and lives in Atlanta.

Geat and Georgia were prominent citizens in early Bowdon history. Geat was born May 26, 1885, and died August 10, 1961, at the age of seventy-six. It has been said that Geat's "word was as good as gold." Georgia was born October 28, 1887, and died September 26, 1968, at the age of eighty-one after a long extended illness. Geat and Georgia, along with their nine children, were good country people, simple, honest, and well thought of in the early community of Bowdon. Today, the descendants of the early Crawford family include educators, artists, builders, printers, bankers, machinists, musicians, and other professions. *Submitted by: Wynelle S. Crawford, 463 Sally Ann Circle, Bowdon, GA 30108*

471. William Crawford

William Crawford was my great-grandfather. They called him Uncle Billy and he was a peddler. Most people remembered him because he had a parrot that he carried around with him. He married Sarah Powell. They lived near Bowdon, Georgia, in the Smith Chapel community. They are buried there at Smith Chapel.

William came to Georgia with several brothers. Uncle Joshua Crawford, one of his brothers, lived in Atlanta and owned a lot of property around the country. After his first wife died, he went to Florida where a woman by the name of Favage got him drunk and got him to marry her. He was seventy-four at the time. After only three weeks of marriage, she poisoned him and took off with all his money. William and his brothers went to Atlanta to get help. The court had him dug up and found that he had been poisoned. The police tried to find the Favage woman but only found that she had a living husband when she married Joshua. She was never found and brought to justice.

William had Joshua brought back to Smith Chapel and buried by his first wife, Nancy.

William and his wife had ten children. His oldest, August, had a store. My grandmother was Samantha Josephine Crawford. She married James M. Entrekin. My mother was Eula Entrekin Adams. *Submitted by: Isabelle Lovvorn, 26 North Jonesville Road, Bowdon, GA 30108*

472. William Hampton Crawford

William Hampton Crawford was born 16 August 1879 and was the son of Henry Franklin and Nancy E. Lee Crawford. He married Elizabeth Lois Gray on May 5, 1907, and to them were born four children, Dayton Hampton Crawford, deceased, Mary Joan Crawford of Douglasville; and twin daughters, Ruth and Ruby Crawford of Temple and Atlanta, who are attorneys, accountants, bankers and realtors, and who have won national and international distinction in their professions.

Mr. Crawford was the oldest merchant in Temple until his death 20 June 1968, starting out as a young boy with a small café selling homemade ice cream, milkshakes, (shaken by hand) parched peanuts, and sandwiches. He walked to work each day several miles carrying the milk to make the milkshakes and ice cream after arising early to milk the cows. He also ran a "jitney" (known as taxis today) in a T Model Ford, being the second car owner in Temple, transporting "drummers" (salesmen) who had arrived by train and spent the night at the Temple Hotel across from the depot, to Bremen, Villa Rica, or Carrollton areas.

Ruth, Mary Joan, Mr. and Mrs. Crawford, Ruby, and Dayton

From this small beginning, and operating two farms, his business emerged into a restaurant and grocery store which he, assisted by his wife, Elizabeth Gray Crawford and his twin daughters, helped him operate. The restaurant was well known for its delicious food, including great hamburgers and chili, and salesmen from other areas would notify them in advance of their next arrival date so they would be sure to have chicken and dumplings, or their favorite entrees, the world's best chili, fried or home baked delicious coconut or other pies, whatever their preference might be. He also operated a restaurant in Villa Rica in 1933 and 1934.

Mr. Crawford, as a young man, laid some of the brick on the Temple Methodist Church, having gone by while brick masons were on their lunch break and, in their absence, proceeded to lay a few bricks, which they let remain.

Mr. and Mrs. Crawford were married over sixty-one years. Mr. Crawford died 20 June 1968 and Mrs. Crawford died 26 November 1968. Both are buried at Asbury Cemetery in Temple in the lot occupied by her parents, Mr. and Mrs. Zachary Taylor Gray, and several aunts and uncles of the Williams family. Their surviving daughters, Mary Joan Crawford resides in Douglasville and the twins, Ruth and Ruby, live in Atlanta and still maintain a home in Temple. *Submitted by: Ruth M. Crawford, 3745 Narmore Drive NE, Atlanta, GA 30319*

473. Crawford - Brown

Gallant Garland Crawford, was born October 16, 1916, in Henry County, Georgia. He was the son of William T. Crawford, soldier in the War of 1812 (son of Thomas Crawford and a ? Reed), born 7 March 1778 in Abbeville, South Carolina, and Mary Shanklin (daughter of Thomas Shanklin), born 25 December 1788 also in Abbeville, South Carolina. Gallant came to Carroll County, Georgia, from nearby Pike County. He and his first wife Carion ("Katie" or "Carrie") Riland are buried in the County Line Cemetery in the Center Point community of Carroll County. Gallant was also married to Sarah Ann West who is buried in a family plot at Concord Methodist Cemetery in Carroll County. Gallant and Sarah had no children. Children from the union of Gallant and Carrie were: Mary Jean (Willis W. Holloway), William D., George W., Mahala, Henry F. (Nancy N.E. Lee), Amanda, John James (J.J.) (Georgia Ann Gilley), Wyatt Jefferson (married first to Ember Ann Wester, and second to Martha L. Morris), Julia A. (R. Fletcher Otwell), Carra (W.L. Pattrson) and Hiram S. Crawford (Melissa Wright).

Gallant was a soldier in the Creek Indian War. Three of his sons were Confederate soldiers — George W. (killed at Savage Station, Virginia, on 28 June1862), William D., and Henry F. Crawford. Gallant was a member of the Carroll County, Georgia, Superior Court in 1864.

John James (J.J.) and Georgia Ann Gilley are buried at the Gilley Cemetery in the Cross Plains community. Their children were: Grant, Belvia, James "Jim" Blalock Crawford (Lena Mae Long), L.B. "Lem" (Emma Lou Long), Birdo M. (married first to Burrus Carroll and second to Amelia ?), Letha, S. Jackson "Jack" (Pearle Boatright), William Lee M. (Maude Carroll) and Eddie Crawford.

James "Jim" Blalock Crawford and Lena Mae Long are buried at the Cross Plains Christian Church Cemetery. Their children are: Lora Mattie Lee Crawford, Pauline "Polly," James Dewey Crawford Sr. (married first to ? Phillips and second to Effie Mae Hennings), Ruby (Price Ford), infant son #1, Wyley Buford, Leona G. (John T. Eason), Homer Lyle (Eunice Lee Johnson), infant son #2, and Clara Belle Crawford (Jack Thomas Chandler).

Homer Lyle Crawford and Eunice Lee Johnson and a daughter Peggy Lee are buried at Carroll Memory Gardens, Carrollton, Georgia. Other children to them are: JoAnn (Garry L. Baughtman) and B. Kay (Ray Elliott Brown).

Ray Elliott Brown and B. Kay Crawford reside in Carrollton and their children are: Jennifer Rebecca, Jonathan Marc (Christina Michele Randles), Joshua Aric, Jasper Kohlby, Jordan Christia (deceased), and Jared Paul Brown.

Jonathan Marc Brown and Christina Michele Randles are the parents of Jacob Marc Brown. *Submitted by: Ray Elliott Brown/Patriot Treasures*

474. Creel Family

In 1729 John Creel was living in Virginia. He had a son named Thomas, who named his son John. John named his son George. George was born in what is now Monroe County, Georgia, in 1816. While still a young man, he moved to Fayette County, becoming one of its earliest settlers. He settled in the woods and cleared a farm.

George married Harriet Belcher, daughter of William Belcher, a Clayton County, Georgia, pioneer and a soldier in the War of 1812. George and Harriet's children were George Daniel, born 1844; Elisha and Elijah, born in 1847 (Elijah died at birth); Mary Mahalia; Joseph born in 1850; and Jackson.

In 1866, Elisha married Mary Ann Miller, daughter of Jefferson and Eliza Eidson Miller, early settlers of Campbell County. Their children were George Jefferson, Joe, Wiley, Robert, Alice, Alva, Hattie, Mary (Mae) and Anna (Annie).

Elisha was reared on a farm and received only a limited education but by 1895 (according to the Atlanta Southern Historical Association) due to hard work, economy, and careful management, he owned a 750-acre farm and was recognized as one of the best farmers in Carroll County. The home of Elisha and Mary Ann still stands (but with recent renovations) about one mile south of Bowdon Junction on Highway 27. They were early founders of Pleasant View Baptist Church.

George Jefferson Creel was born October 4, 1871. On January 8, 1891, he married Margaret Angeline (Liney) Ingram, born July 10, 1871, daughter of Mary McBurnett and Isaac Newton Ingram, early founders of New Hope United Methodist Church.

George and Liney were the parents of Oliver, born January 9, 1892, died December 26, 1960; Austin, born October 23, 1893, died September 4, 1894; Mary Myrtle, born July 9, 1895, died August 28, 1896; Earl Delone (Jack), born July 17, 1897, died December 2, 1964; twins Gladys and Glenn, born March 2, 1900. Glenn died July 30, 1900, and Gladys died October 14, 1900; Allie Ruth, born July 30, 1901, and died December 31, 1989; Georgia Ellen was born May 7, 1905, and died August 5, 1988; Lillian Pope (Polly) was born December 27, 1907, and died June 12, 1972.

The Creel Brothers and Sisters, 1952

George and Liney lived in Mount Zion, Georgia, and operated a store there. He owned the first buggy in Carroll County in 1889. Liney died May 23, 1938, at the age of sixty-six. George lived to be eighty-two years of age and died January 26, 1953.

Pictured left to right on the front row are Hattie Creel Johnson, Mae Creel Carter, George Jefferson Creel, and Georgia Ingram Pierce (sister-in-law). Standing are Annie Creel Cook and Wiley Creel. *Submitted by: Charlotte Creel Crawford Cowart, 235 Carroll Street, Carrollton, GA 30117*

475. The Creels

Elisha Creel was born June 10, 1848, the son of George and Harriet Belcher Creel. His maternal grandfather, William Belcher, was a Clayton County pioneer and a soldier in the War of 1812. Elisha's father was born in what is now Monroe County in 1816, but while yet a young man he moved to what is now Georgia Highway 314, south of the Atlanta airport. Elisha was born there and spent his single life there.

Elisha was too young to fight in the Civil War but he, along with many young boys south of Atlanta, were "rounded up" to go to Atlanta and burn Atlanta before Sherman got there. What a scene — a frightened young lad running feverishly with a lighted touch in hand setting buildings on fire.

Elisha and Mary Miller Creel

Elisha married Mary Ann Miller February 22, 1866. They moved to Carroll County in 1869 and settled about six miles north of Carrollton on Highway 27. They had thirteen children and nine lived to adulthood. The children were: Alice, who married H.M. "Bud" Harper and they had eight children; Alva married George Earnest and they had seven children; George married Linnie Ingram and they had five children; Joe married Alice Ivey and they had two children; Harriet married J.M. "Jim" Johnson and they had seven children; Mary "Mae" married J.L. "Bill" Carter and they had five children; Wiley married Carrie Shanks and they had no children; Robert "Bob" married Bessie Bledsoe and they had no children; Anna "Annie" married John Cook and they had no children.

In the 1920s and 1930s, the Creel name was very prevalent in Carroll County. Due to most of Elisha and Mary Ann's descendants coming from their daughters, the name isn't heard often. Nevertheless, there are many descendants in Carroll County.

Ollie Byrd Carter, age ninety-one, is the only grandchild presently alive. Byrd served in the Navy during World War II.

Mary Ann died January 25, 1918, and Elisha February 13, 1920. They are buried in Pleasant View Baptist Church Cemetery. *Submitted by: Bill Johnson, Newnan, GA*

476. Caswell Berry W. and Lela Edna Jackson Crews

Caswell Berry W. Crews, my husband's grandfather, was born 6 June 1873 in Meriwether County, Georgia. Out of ten children, he was the only surviving son of James "Jimmy" Monroe (born 16 March 1846, died 28 October 1904) and Sarah Jane Darrington Crews (born 27 March 1842, died 23 April 1926).

Berry, as he was known, married Lela Edna Jackson, the daughter of Jesse and Athie A. Barker Hill Jackson, on 22 October 1893, her twentieth birthday.

Their children were Athie Aimee, born 5 October 1894. She taught school as a young woman and married M. Awbrey Barrett, a 1910 graduate of Bowdon College and also a teacher. They married on 12 March 1922 and were parents to Athie Mae, Edna Gladys, Texie Aubrey, and Robert Glenn. Aimee died 12 October 1946 and is buried at the First United Methodist Church in Bowdon.

Emmie J. was born 7 February 1896 and was a teacher. She married Homer Middlebrooks and had one daughter, Lanelle. Emmie died 23 January 1977 and is buried at Union Hill Baptist Church in Cleburne County, Alabama.

Eula B. was born 14 January 1898 and followed her sister's footsteps as a schoolteacher. She married Pierce Ballenger and had three children: Buford, Kirby and Grecilda.

James Virgil was born 3 September 1900. He married Maude Cosper, a music teacher in Carrollton, then wanderlust took over and he joined the Merchant Marines. His second marriage was to Edith Elizabeth MacPherson from Boston, Massachusetts. They had two children, Eunice, who along with her husband, V.C. Curtis, operates a ferry from the mainland at North Haven, Maine, and Vernon who still lives in Boston. Virgil married a third time to Rose, a native Hawaiian of Hilo, Hawaii, and they have a daughter named Eunice who still lives on Hilo.

Evna Mae was born 3 December 1902 and married Charles Arthur Spier and had two children: Hannah and Charles Jr.

Alvin Mermon was born 10 December 1904. He married Dura Estes and their children were Alvin Jr., Charles G., Eura E., Winford and Etha C. Alvin died 18 October 1965.

Henry Gordon was born 3 May 1907. He was barely three when the family moved to Carroll County where they were listed in the 22 April 1910 census as being on Blackjack Road in the Tyus District.

Henry Gordon married Narma Ruth Walker, daughter of John Emmett and Jerusha Bradberry Walker on 29 May 1932. Their children were Gordon Wallace, Sherwin Donald, Helen Ruth, Narma Laqueata, and Malinda Daphine. Henry died 8 September 1965 and is buried at Union Hill Baptist Church in Cleburne County, Alabama.

Berry and Lela Crew's home place on Dot Road, Bowdon.

Barnie L. was born 20 July 1910 and married Avis Walker, sister of Narma Ruth. They had seven children: Lovonne, Carla, James, Donald, Amelia, Jerry Lee, and Sarah. After Avis' death on 26 July 1948, Barnie was unable to raise his young family and they were placed in the Methodist Orphanage in Atlanta.

Myrtice Alice was born 11 October 1912. She married Carl Abraham Christian and had two children, Dorothy Ann and Buddy Gene.

Berry and Lela are interred in the cemetery at the First United Methodist Church in Bowdon, Carroll County, Georgia. *Submitted by: Evelyn J. Crews, 110 Walker Woods Drive, Carrollton, GA 30116*
Sources: Crews family Bible; courthouse records from Carroll, Meriwether, Heard, and Cleburne (Alabama); death certificates, tombstone records; and family knowledge.

477. Henry Gordon and Narma Ruth Walker Crews

Henry Gordon Crews was born 3 May 1907, the seventh child of Caswell Berry and Lela Edna Jackson Crews. His paternal grandparents were James 'Jimmy' and Sarah Jane Darrington Crews, originally from Meriwether County, Georgia. His maternal grandparents were Jessie and Athie Barker Hill Jackson of Heard County.

On 29 May 1932, he married Narma Ruth Walker in Cleburne County, Alabama, county of her birth on 20 June 1909. She was the daughter of John and Jerusha Bradbury Walker.

Henry Gordon and Narma Ruth Crews

When Henry was barely three, his family moved to Carroll County where the 1910 census listed them as being on Blackjack road in the Tyus District. He attended school at Veal where some of his sisters taught, then later moved to Dot Road where he attended Midway School where Eula, his sister, taught.

The couple lived in Cleburne County for several years then moved to Carroll County. They eventually bought a farm house surrounded by acres of farmland from John Barr. The house had a separate kitchen and a wide hall in the center of the house when they bought it.

They had five children: Gordon Wallace was born 30 August 1933. He married Helen Joan Richardson and their children are Clark Gordon and Mira Joan.

Sherwin Donald was born on 14 March 1935. He married Evelyn Jean Ledford of Hayesville, North Carolina and they have four children, Laura Hope, Donna Ruth, Stuart Blane, and Marcia Jan.

Helen Ruth was born 27 April 1936 and married John Ray Moore. They had no children. Helen died 1 January 1969 and is buried at Salem Baptist Church Cemetery in Carroll County.

Narma Laqueata was born 10 November 1939 and married Jack Henderson of Graham, Alabama. They have three sons and one daughter: Jackie Dwain, Kenneth Mark, Gregory Alan and Emily Karen.

Malinda Daphine was born 4 July 1942. She was first married to Orbie Larry White, and second to Don Inman. Both husbands are deceased. She has no children.

Henry and Ruth farmed, along with running a country store, barber shop and driving a school bus. After they quit farming, he worked with the City of Bowdon Water Department, the Bowdon Fire Department and Police Department serving as police chief for several years. He had one of the first police dogs on a local police force. For a brief period before his death, he worked as a security guard at West Georgia College.

Ruth worked at Sewells as a seamstress for some years and told of how she would milk cows, strain the milk and fix breakfast before the children went to school and she clocked in for work at the plant. After she quit Sewells, she operated a nursery for the children of mothers working at the local plant. After reaching adulthood, several of her children returned to see "Mama Crews."

Henry and Ruth's final resting place is Union Hill Baptist Church Cemetery, Cleburne County, Alabama. *Submitted by: Laura Lowery, 362 Kuglar Road, Bowdon, GA 30108*

Sources: Death Certificates; tombstone records; census records, Courthouse records Carroll County, Interviews with family members.

478. Sherwin Donald and Evelyn Jean Ledford Crews

Sherwin Donald was born 14 March 1938, the son of Henry Gordon and Narma Ruth Crews. He was their second child and one of five: Gordon Wallace, Helen Ruth, Narma Laqueata and Malinda Daphine.

Just barely into the twelfth grade at Bowdon High School, Sherwin quit school, ran away to Atlanta with his cousin Winfred and eventually joined the Army were he got his GED and spent time in France and Germany. After his tour of duty, he came home and worked at the Chevrolet plant in Atlanta until the early 1960s recession hit and he was laid off.

Sherwin and Evelyn Crews; Stuart, Laura, Marcia, Donna

While he was in Atlanta, he met Evelyn Ledford from Hayesville, North Carolina, who worked at Southern Bell. Her parents were Willard and Mattie Kitchens Ledford in Clay County, North Carolina. They married in 1958 and have four children.

Laura Hope was born 26 November 1958 in Atlanta. She married Ronald Dale Lowery and they have one son, Brandon Dale who attends UWG. Laura is a school teacher and Dale is an electrician at Southwire. They live between Bowdon and Carrollton.

Donna Ruth was born 17 April 1960. She married Stevie Eugene Harper and they have a daughter, Shanda Lae and a son, Jacob Matthew. Donna works as a para-professional at Jonesville Middle School and Steve at the Wellness Center at Southwire. They live at Bowdon.

Stuart Blane was born 28 February 1962. He married Carol Jean Swayngham and they have three children: Ginger May, a student at UWG, Brian Stuart, and Levi Harold. Stuart works at West Georgia Aerial Lift and Carol is a CPA and comptroller at Tanner Medical Center. They live outside Carrollton.

Marcia Jan was born 3 September 1964 and is married to Gilbert Delmar Iverson. They have three children, Dustin Adam, Cierra Nichole, and Devin Alexander. Gilbert works for Randolph County, Alabama, and Marcia works in the photo lab at Wal-Mart in Carrollton. They live in Woodland, Alabama.

Sherwin is retired from Southwire and Evelyn is retired from the State University of West Georgia. They live in Carrollton. *Submitted by: Carol J. Swayngham Crews, 1695-A Carrollton-Tyus Rd., Carrollton, GA 30117*

Sources: Family knowledge

479. Crews, Sparks, Richards, Horsley Families

This is a very precious picture made in May of 1916 of people I loved. This photo of four families was made by Jim Byers at the Joe Thomas Crews house near Paul's Church on Jones Mill Road. I am the only one living today. I am the little girl (age four) third from left on front row between my two little aunts, Mama's sisters. I am not smiling in this picture; the photographer put me on the end of the row and I left and went back to stand by my little aunts. I was mad, and Mama's stern look was because she didn't like the way I acted. My little aunt said to me, "Melba, don't worry, Sister won't be able to find you. We will climb up in the biggest apple tree." We did and by that time Mama had cooled off! My mama and daddy, Vivian and Bartow Sparks, are on the back row. My brother Alton Sparks was born two years after this picture was made.

Thirty-six grandchildren descended from this group and twenty-four of them are still living.

On the first row, from left to right, are Harold Horsley, Allene Crews, Melba Sparks, Ione Crews, Manola Horsley. Second row shows Martha Huff, Grady Crews, Joe Lee Crews, Purn Crews, DeLouvia Crews, Irma Crews, Joe T. Crews. Third row, Frank Richards, Marion Richards, Eva Richards, Bartow Sparks, Vivian Sparks, Leila Horsley, and Herman Horsley. *Submitted by: Melba Sparks Leggett, PO Box 1002, Villa Rica, GA 30180*

Crews, Sparks, Richards, and Horsley Families. 1916

480. Crook - Haynes Family

William A. Crook was born in April 1866 and was married to Alice Haynes (who was born in October 1867), on December 7, 1890, in Coweta County, Georgia. William was the son of Lewellyn Crook and Sarah E. Pennington of Coweta County.

Alice was born in October 1867. She was the daughter of James M. Haynes and Susan Caroline Stevens of Coweta County and was one of sixteen children. James died when he was only fifty, and Susan provided for their children alone. She lived to the age of eighty-four.

William and Alice were the parents of the following children, all born in Coweta County: 1. Albert Lee Crook was born October 22, 1891, and died March 2, 1968, in Carroll County. On December 19, 1910, in Carroll County, he married Maude M. Ivey, the daughter of Martin Ivey and America Kuglar. Maude was born November 24, 1890, in Carroll County and died September 25, 1975. Albert was a farmer. He and Maude are buried in the Tyus Baptist Church Cemetery, Carroll County. Their children were Hugh L., Robert Weyman, Mildred Frances, Joseph Max, Kate, Helen B., and Betty Sue. Hugh L. married Mary Campbell; Robert Weyman married Pauline Lee; Mildred Frances married Arrie Williamson; Joseph Max married Dorothy Stevens; Kate married Ira Winford Lee; and Betty Sue married Lawton Elbert Samples. 2. Elbert George Crook was born December 17, 1892, and died February 23, 1970. He is buried in Antioch Baptist Church Cemetery in Carroll County. On May 9, 1914, in Carroll County, he married Elizabeth Cammon. He served in World War II. 3. Luie Crook was born September 21, 1895, and died August 27, 1980. On December 30, 1931, in Carroll County, he married Evie Lee Holcombe. They are buried in Antioch Baptist Church Cemetery in Carroll County. 4. Nora S. Crook was born in February 1897. 5. Annie L. Crook was born in July 1898. 6. Will L. Crook was born in 1903 and married Mildred Rigsby on February 15, 1925, in Carroll County. 7. Vannie Crook was born in 1904.

William died August 3, 1944, in Carroll County, and Alice died June 16, 1951, in Carroll County. Both are buried at Old Camp United Methodist Church Cemetery, Carroll County, Georgia. *Submitted by: Render Crook, Villa Rica, GA*
Sources: Personal knowledge, census, marriage and cemetery records researched by Erlene C. Boyd

481. Crumbley Family

Anthony Crumbley Sr.

Anthony Crumbley Sr. was born in 1760 and died January 1, 1786, in Henry County, Georgia. He married Mary Elizabeth Adeline Lee Armstrong in 1786 in Stewart County, Georgia. They had seven children: (1) George B. Crumbley was born in 1787 and died November 17, 1872. He married Tabitha Mackey. (2) John Crumbley was born in 1790 and died in 1874. He married Orpha Neal in 1820. (3) Anthony Crumbley II was born in 1792 and died November 4, 1869. He married Zephyha A. Grooms. (4) Nancy Crumbley was born about 1795. She married Joseph O. McKindley (McKinley). (5) Alexander Crumbley was born about 1800 and died before 1870. He married Nancy Castellaw on January 17, 1835. (6) Catherine Crumbley was born February 12, 1802, and died March 29, 1984. She married William Elias House on November 17, 1826. (7) William Crumbley was born about 1803. He married Grace Ann (Gracey) Moore.

George B. Crumbley: George B. Crumbley was born in 1787 in Washington County, Georgia, and died November 17, 1872, in Henry County, Georgia. He married Tabitha Mackey in 1812 in Washington County. Tabitha was born in 1790 in Virginia and died October 14, 1846, in Henry County, Georgia. They had twelve children: (1) Anthony C. Crumbley was born 1813 and died February 19, 1890, in Carroll County, Georgia. He married Martha Ferrell and Nancy Mary Lester Sowell. (2) Jordan Crumbley born about 1814 and died about 1851. He married Sarah S. Levedle. (3) Rebecca Crumbley was born November 20, 1817, and died October 31, 1903. She married William Ferrell. (4) Catherine (Katie) Crumbley was born November 20, 1818, and died January 1, 1912. She married George Washington Castelaw on February 26, 1845. (5) Nancy Crumbley was born 1820 and died in 1835. (6) Emmeline (Emmie or Emmy) Crumbley was born in 1822. (7) William H. (Bill) Crumbley born January 6, 1822, and died March 26, 1911. He married Frances (Fannie) A. Walker. (8) Alexander Crumbley was born March 4, 1824, and died May 4, 1907. He married Mary Elizabeth Johnson, Nancy Elizabeth Walker Bryans and Elizabeth Pierson. (9) Mary Ann Crumbley was born 1830. She married Sam A. Fleetwood. (10) Barbara Crumbley was born February 11, 1835, and died May 25, 1913. She married Jonathan Jackson Brannan. (11) George M. Crumbley was born August 6, 1834 and died January 29, 1915. He married Nancy McCully (McCullough) and Emmaline Brown. (12) Elizabeth (Betsy) Crumbley was born May 4, 1840. She married Edmond LaFayette Elliott and Sam Ferrell. George was found in Carroll County in 1847.

Joseph L. and Mary B. Crumbley

Anthony C. Crumbley: Anthony C. Crumbley was born in 1813 in Henry County, Georgia, and died February 10, 1890, in Carroll County, Georgia. He married Martha Ferrell on February 4, 1836, in Henry County, and Nancy Mary Lester Sowell on March 8, 1860, in Henry County. He had ten children: (1) Samuel J. Crumbley was born October 13, 1836, and died June 28, 1908, in Carroll County, Georgia. He married Licinda Selena (Seleny) Mitchell on December 20, 1861, in Henry County. (2) Caroline Crumbley was born about 1843 in Georgia (no other information). (3) George Thomas Crumbley was born March 5, 1845, and died February 6, 1927, in Carroll County. He married Mary Jane Lambert on December 25, 1870, in Carroll County. (4) James Crumbley was born in 1852 (no other information). (5) William (Will) Crumbley was born June 15, 1852. He married Nancy Jane Walker on November 15, 1870, in Carroll County. (6) Sarah Ellie (Ella) Crumbley was born January 1863 and died May 12, 1938. She married Archibald (Archie) Preston Robinson on November 18, 1877, in Carroll County. (7) Emmeline (Emma) Victoria Crumbley was born April 6, 1867, and died May 14, 1936, in Carroll County. She married Ira John Francis (Frank) Cantrell on December 27, 1883, in Carroll County. (8) Anthony Franklin (Frank) Crumbley was born July 12, 1868, and died January 19, 1948. He married Cynthia Alberta (Berta) Marlow on December 11, 1886. (9) Joseph (Joe) L. Crumbley was born March 29, 1872, and died February 6, 1936. He married Mary Beattrice (Bettus) Spruell on November 24, 1895. (10) Infant 18??.

Joseph L. Crumbley: Joseph L. Crumbley was born March 29, 1872, and died February 6, 1936. He married Mary Beattrice (Bettus) Spruell on November 24, 1895. Mary B. Spruell was born July 13, 1881, and died December 4, 1921, in Carroll County. They had twelve children: (1) Maggie Mae Crumbley born September 8, 1898, and died January 24, 1903, in Carroll County. (2) Minnie Lee Crumbley was born May 20, 1901, and died March 7, 1903, in Carroll County. (3) Luther Grady Crumbley was born April 7, 1903, and died August 29, 1905, in Carroll County. (4) Freddie Claude Crumbley was born September 24, 1904, and died August 11, 1905, in Carroll County. (5) Joseph Dura Crumbley was born October 28, 1906, and died January 27, 1990, in Rome, Georgia. She married John Dewey Gann on January 18, 1925, in Carroll County. (6) Blanch Jewell Crumbley was born September 7, 1908, and died April 15, 1996. She married Jasper Grady Short on September 24, 1928, in Rambon, Alabama. (7) Henry Clarence Crumbley was born April 29, 1910, and died January 26, 1962, in Fulton County, Georgia. He married Minnie Marie Ellis in Fulton County. (8) Griffin C. Crumbley was born November 2, 1911, and died December 15, 1988, in Cartersville, Georgia. He married Florence Gillispie on August 14, 1937. (9) Carl Rufus Crumbley was born August 2, 1913, and died May 12, 1988, in Cobb County, Georgia. He married Velma Louella Proctor and Mary Weldon. (10) James Roy Crumbley was born July 2, 1915, death date unknown. He married Mary Lou Adams on September 24, 1932, in Carroll County. (11) Reece Calab Crumbley was born April 24, 1918, death date unknown. He married Lucille Black on August 15, 1937. (12) Ethel Merinda Crumbley was born April 29, 1920, and married Henry Grady Farmer and Edgar Bertice Pitts.

Henry Clarence Crumbley: Henry Clarence Crumbley was born April 29, 1910, in Carroll County and died January 26, 1962, in Fulton County, Georgia. He married Minnie Marie Ellis in Fulton County. They had four children: (1) Clarence Lee Crumbley was born September 10, 1935, and married Carolyn Beckham, (2) Bobby James Crumbley was born March 9, 1937, and married Clarice Gentry, (3) Robert Daniel Crumbley was born February 9, 1940, and married Jerry W. Cleveland on July 28, 1962 in Fulton County. (4) Joe Walter Crumbley was born August 2, 1942, and married Diane Shackleford in Fulton County. *Submitted by: Mrs. Ethel Pitts*
Sources: Census, land, marriage records and personal information researched by Jerry Crumbley.

482. Crutchfields

By 1870 two families of Crutchfields were in Carroll County. Both Phillip Crutchfield and Jesse Crutchfield were thirty-five years old. Jesse's wife was Caroline and their children were Joseph M., Sarah E., John, Mary, Jesse Oscar, and Frank. Phillip lived near the Sharps and McKenzies. His wife was Sena and their children were William, Mary, Martha, Sarah, Jesse, and Ida B. Octavia. The accompanying photograph is left to right standing, Joseph, Earl, Oscar, and Frank, sitting are Orvil and John.

Jesse Oscar Crutchfield (born 1866) married Texas Octavia Cole (born 1867). Their children were Inez (married Sam Johnson and then Arthur Bentley when Sam died), Paul married Dura Shell, Lee P. married Ester Weathers, Bessie married Robert McKenzie, Evie married Duma Sharp, Lula married Johnny Skinner, Lloyd (Sam) married Anna, Carl married Fern Brooks, Florence married Wilburn (Jack) Jackson McKenzie. Both Jesse and Texas are buried at Concord Primitive Baptist Church.

The Crutchfield Brothers

Their house is still standing off Center Point Road. It was purchased by the Bearden family and remodeled.

Florence Geneva Crutchfield and Wilburn (Jack) Jackson McKenzie were married in Carroll County in 1906. They lived on McKenzie Bridge Road. Their children were Iva Novell, Gladys Modell, Ruth Mozell, Jackson Oswell, Willard Oliver, and Joseph Alvin. See related article on the McKenzie family.

Gladys married Hershell Allen who was a farmer and had a mule named "Rhodie" and participated in covered wagon type exhibitions in the eighties long after other farmers no longer had a mule.

Ruth married John Daniel (Dan) McDowell and moved to Bowdon Junction where Ruth still lives. *Submitted by: Kathryn McDowell Hughes*

483. William Curtis Daniel Family

Curtis Daniel, June 3, 1920-February 13, 2001, of Carroll County, Georgia, Kingsbridge Road, Carrollton. He was the son of William Rufus Daniel, August 8, 1870-November 28, 1950, from Randolph County, Alabama, and Ella Buckanan Daniel, February 28, 1875-May 2, 1952, from Heard County, Georgia. Curtis was the youngest of nine children: Macy Daniel Hughes, Avie Daniel Sewell, Lois Daniel Chandler, Ivaleen Daniel Stephens, Garland Daniel, Dewey Daniel, Joe Wheeler Daniel, James Grady Daniel, William Curtis Daniel. Curtis' grandparents were John Anderson Daniel, November 8, 1841-October 23, 1931, and Emily Wilson Daniel, March 26, 1846-June 28, 1925, who lived in Heard County, Georgia, near Antioch Road on a 300-acre cotton plantation. Later, he gave land to build Salem Methodist Church off Highway 100 South. The deed is displayed in the church.

Curtis married Emily Windom, born November 24, 1920, of Burwell, Carroll County, Georgia. Emily, daughter of Edward Alton Windom and Dora Cantrell Windom, grew up on a farm. She is one of four children: Roy Windom, Christine Windom Upchurch, Emily Windom Daniel, Betty Windom Hendrix. Emily was employed by Sears Roebuck and Company in Carrollton from 1951 to 1983.

Curtis grew up on their farm during the depression, producing vegetables, poultry, hogs, cotton and sugar cane. They owned and operated a syrup-making business on Kingsbridge Road from early fall to late winter. He enjoyed sharing his depression year's experiences, such as making toys in his daddy's shop; dating girlfriends (riding them on his bicycle handlebars); driving his daddy's Model-T at age twelve to Rome, Carrollton, Newnan, and LaGrange where they sold produce from the farm; plowing his mule all week, and on Saturday riding her to Carrollton to see a western movie (twice), buying a hamburger, RC Cola, and a box of Prince Albert tobacco — with change left from 50 cents. A World War II veteran, 1942-1946, Army Air Corps from Milney Bay, New Guinea on the Island of Okinawa, he was stationed on Luzon, Philippine Islands, when the first atomic bomb dropped on Hiroshima, Japan. He stood on Okinawa and watched while planes with Red Crosses on top and underneath landed and took off on Tashima on the way to Manila with government officials to sign Armistice. After World War II ended, he attended West Georgia College and passed the GED, receiving his high-school diploma at age fifty. Curtis was a 32° Scottish Rite Mason, Shriner, member Yaarab Temple. He worked for and obtained the charter for the Carrollton Shrine Club in 1983. He loved children and worked to raise money for the Masonic fraternities to help deprived, crippled, and burned children have a better life.

Their direct descendant is Dr. William Douglas Daniel, OB-GYN at Bethesda Navy Hospital in Bethesda, Maryland. He has lived on the island of Guam, in New York City, and in Buckhannon, West Virginia. He married Marsha McCormick of Akin, South Carolina. Grandson William Rufus Daniel, II was born July 7, 1972, in Bethesda Navy Hospital. He graduated from West Point Military Academy in 1997. Now he is a captain in the Army, and married to Brook Willow. Grandson Douglas Blaine Daniel was born July 23 1976, in Guam. He graduated Wesleyan Methodist College and now works as a public relations media coordinator at Snowshoe Ski Resort International, Snow Shoe, West Virginia. *Submitted by: Emily W. Daniel, 110 Lake Point Drive, Carrollton, GA 30117*

484. David and Clare Dannenberg

David Randall Dannenburg, was born on March 8, 1970, in Santa Clara County, California, the son of Robert Alan Dannenberg and Nancy Kathleen Robinson Dannenberg. David was a fifth generation of California, based on his paternal grandmother's ancestry. In 1970, this was rare.

David's maternal grandparents were Walter Hill Robinson Jr., born in Fulton County, Georgia, on January 19, 1923, died November 20, 1996, in Carroll County, Georgia and Mercedes del Socorro Figueroa Robinson, born September 21, 1914, in Metapan, El Salvador. They were long-time residents of Palo Alto, California, having settled there after World War II until they retired in Carrollton on forty-four acres on Jones Mill Road. Walter prided himself in having built his retirement home himself, and growing his own vegetables organically on his 2000 square foot garden.

David's father, Robert Alan Dannenberg was employed by Raychem Corporation in Menlo Park, California, at the time of David's birth. He was an early employee of the company and was employed there for over almost thirty-five years, specializing in inventory control management.

David's paternal grandparents, Robert Efraim Dannenberg and Marian Coomber Dannenberg, were both natives of California, having attended Lincoln high school. Robert graduated from UC Berkeley, after serving in World War II, and received a master's degree in aeronautical engineering from Stanford University. He was a researcher at the NASA Ames Research Center in Mountain View, California working on the wind tunnel. His mother, Anna Lorenzo Dannenberg Hill was a native of Spain, having come to the U.S. as a young child and settling in San Francisco after marrying Efraim Dannenberg, who fled Odessa, Russia, in the early 1900s. He was of Jewish heritage and fled when the Jews were being persecuted in Russia. He lived in Argentina for a while and entered the U.S. through either New Orleans or Boston, Massachusetts. Anna and Efraim had only the one child, Robert Efraim Dannenberg, born in July 1923 in San Francisco.

Marian Coomber's grandfather emigrated to California in the 1800s and settled in North Columbia, California, where he ran a grocery store, near the Malakoff diggings (a hydraulic mining area closed down many years ago. The family story has it that they came around Cape Horn — or at least their box piano did. His son, David Dannenberg's great-grandfather, was a gold assayer in Nevada City. David's great-grandmother on his paternal grandmother's side, Irma Louise English Coomber, was raised in Nevada City. Her brother was Holden English, a school principal in the Willows or Arbuckle area of Northern California. Irma settled in San Francisco when she married Robert Coomber in the early 1900s. Robert and Irma had three children, Marian (born December 4 or 7, 1923 (?) in San Francisco), Robert, and Charles. Charles had no offspring. Robert had four children, Robert, William, Caroline and Marilyn.

David's maternal grandparents, Walter Hill Robinson and Mercedes Figueroa Robinson had three children, Nancy Kathleen, born November 17, 1948, at the French Hospital in San Francisco (now a Kaiser hospital), Walter Ernest Robinson born September 18, 1950, and Jacqueline Carmen Robinson born January 10, 1952, in San Mateo County, California.

Nancy Kathleen Robinson married Robert Alan Dannenberg on March 17, 1967, in Palo Alto, California. In addition to David, they had another child, Ross Alan Dannenberg, born at Stanford Hospital, Santa Clara County, California. They lived in Menlo Park, California until 1975, moving to Palo Alto, California. They were divorced in 1979. Nancy Kathleen married Thomas Melvin Adams on May 20, 1979. They had no offspring.

In 1981, the family moved to Stone Mountain, Georgia, then Lilburn, Georgia, to be near Walter and Mercedes who moved to Carrollton in 1979. David graduated from Parkview High School in Lilburn, playing on the varsity soccer team. He attended Young Harris College in North Georgia mountains and Maryville College in Maryville, Tennessee. He was on the soccer team at both schools and graduated with a degree in outdoor recreation. He married Clare Jacobs (born November 4, 1969), of Maryville on November 21, 1991 in Maryville. After working at Young Harris for two years, they moved to Garner, North Carolina. David received a master's in outdoor recreation from North Carolina State University and Clare a doctorate in sociolinguistics from University of North Carolina at Chapel Hill. They currently reside in Blacksburg, Virginia, where David telecommutes as a technical writer and trainer for The Nature Conservancy and Clare is a professor of linguistics at Virginia Tech. David is an active soccer coach and recently completed the Nashville Country Music Marathon, raising over $3000 for children with cancer. He and Clare are also on the leadership board for Fieldstone Methodist Church. They have one child, Houlton Alexander Dannenberg, born November 5, 2000 in Blacksburg, Virginia. *Submitted by: David Dannenberg, 3416 Deer Run Road, Blacksburg, VA 24060*

485. Nancy Kathleen Robinson Adams and Robert Alan Dannenberg

Nancy Kathleen is the eldest daughter of Walter Hill Robinson Jr. (19 January 1923-20 November 1996). His father was Walter Hill Robinson of Carroll County and Jacqueline Zora Harris Robinson.

Nancy was born in San Francisco at the French Hospital, now a Kaiser hospital. She has been known as Kathy her entire life. She was raised in

Palo Alto, California, graduating from Cubberly High School in 1965. To know her Georgia roots, she, her mother and siblings took the train to Atlanta, Georgia, to visit with her uncle, J.D. Robinson, and his family in 1957. They drove to Melrose, Florida, to meet their grandparents, Jacqueline and Walter Hill Robinson. This was a most memorable summer vacation.

Nancy's mother, Mercedes, spoke almost no English when she married Walter. Walter had been studying Spanish since junior high school and was active in his school's Pan-American club. Mercedes and Walter always spoke Spanish to each other. Nancy Kathleen spoke Spanish fluently as her mother spoke so little English. This was an invaluable asset when Nancy Kathleen entered the job market, as it enabled her to work in Latin America and communicate effectively.

Nancy attended San Jose State University, graduating summa cum laude in 1969 with a major in French. On 17 March 17, 1967 she married Robert Alan Dannenberg, a fourth generation Californian, born 16 November 1943 in San Francisco. They had two children, David Randall Dannenberg (born 8 March 1970) and Ross Alan Dannenberg (born 3 August 1972). In 1978, Robert and Nancy were divorced and Nancy married Thomas Melvin Adams, born 10 October 1946 in Philadelphia, Pennsylvania, and raised in Palo Alto California. Nancy was active in Santa Clara Valley as president of Nursing Mothers Counsel, a group dedicated to supporting breast-feeding. She was also acting director of the Mothers Milk Bank, part of the Northern California Transplant Bank, for a short time.

In 1981, Nancy and Thomas moved their family to Georgia to be near Walter Hill Robinson Jr. and his wife who had retired to Carrollton. Nancy worked for Management Science America from 1981-1983, implementing accounting systems and then became an independent software consultant. She worked in Latin America at start-up wireless telephone companies, often Bell South properties, managing the installation of billing systems. She and her husband currently reside in Fairfax, Virginia, where Nancy continues to consult and lead projects in implementing billing software for communications companies.

Nancy has been an avid quilter for many years. It was through her love of sewing that she was introduced to the Kuna Indians in Panama who make a reverse applique called "Molas." After meeting these Indians, Nancy has returned to Panama annually to donate school supplies to the schools. She and her husband are always warmly greeted by the shouts of children calling out "Senora Kahty" as their canoe arrives at the islands to see what the schools need.

David Smith Harris and Nancy Alice Smith

David Smith Harris was the father of Jacqueline Zora Harris of Carroll County. David was born 15 November 1857 in Carroll County and died 14 March 1925 in Carroll County. He married Nancy Alice Smith (born 26 June 1859, died 22 December 1930) on 6 May 1877. Both were born, married, and died in Carroll County.

David Smith Harris' father was David Smith Harris as well. The elder David Smith Harris' wife's name was Letitia or Leticia Jackie Dwyer. The elder David Harris Smith died in the Battle of Gettysburg.

Nancy Alice Smith's parents were John N. Smith born 29 March 1809 and died 9 June 1884. We believe he was born in Carroll County. We know he died in Carroll County. Nancy's mother was Sallie Watson, born 19 July 1815 in Carrollton and died 2 December 1892 in Carrollton. *Submitted by: Nancy Kathleen Robinson Adams, 11614 Fairfax Meadows Circle, Apt. 18211, Fairfax, VA 22030*

486. Ross and Elizabeth Dannenberg

Ross Alan Dannenberg was born on 3 August 1972 in Santa Clara County, California, the son of Robert Alan Dannenberg and Nancy Kathleen Robinson Dannenberg. Ross was a fifth generation Californian, based on his father's mother's ancestry.

Nancy Kathleen Robinson graduated from Cubberly High School in Palo Alto, then majored in French, graduating from San Jose State College, suma cum laude in 1969. She married Robert Alan Dannenberg on March 17, 1967, in Palo Alto, California. In addition to David, they had another child, Ross Alan Dannenberg, also born at Stanford Hospital in Santa Clara County, California. They lived in Menlo Park until 1975 and then moved to Palo Alto. They were divorced in 1979. Nancy Kathleen married Thomas Melvin Adams on May 20, 1970. They had no offspring.

See David Dannenberg for paternal information.

David's maternal grandparents, Walter Hill Robinson and Mercedes Figueroa Robinson had three children, Nancy Kathleen, born November 17, 1948, at the French Hospital in San Francisco (now a Kaiser hospital), Walter Ernest Robinson born September 18, 1950, and Jacqueline Carmen Robinson born January 10, 1952 in San Mateo County, California.

Ross Dannenberg and Elizabeth Derting's wedding day.

Ross lived in Menlo Park, California from the time of his birth until 1975, moving to Palo Alto. In 1981, his mother and stepfather moved to Stone Mountain, Georgia. They later settled in Lilburn, Georgia where Ross graduated from Parkview High School. He attended Georgia Institute of Technology, receiving his bachelors of science in computer science in 1994. After working for Carnival Cruise Lines for two years as an Information Systems Manager on cruise ships, he moved to Alexandria, Virginia. He graduated from George Washington University Law School in 2000. He is a member of the Virginia State Bar, practicing law at Banner & Witcoff in Washington, D.C., specializing in intellectual property rights.

On May 13, 2000, Ross married Elizabeth (Libby) Kate Derting of Johnson City, Tennessee. They were married in the boyhood home of Robert E. Lee in Alexandria, Virginia. They met in law school and reside in Alexandria, Virginia, with their dog Bailey. Libby, also a member of the Virginia State Bar, works for the Alliance of Automobile Manufacturers, where she practices trade association, antitrust, and dealership franchise law. She was born April 18, 1972. Her parents are Pauline Lois Meade and William Isaac Derting. Pauline was born October 14, 1946, in Gate City, Virginia. William was born November 28, 1930, in Hiltons, Virginia.

Elizabeth attended Daniel Boone High School, and the University of Tennessee, where she received her bachelor's of arts in economics in 1994 and her master's of English in 1997. She graduated from George Washington University Law School in May, 2000.

Shown in the photograph on back row are (L to R) Pauline Lois Meade Derting, William Isaac Derting, Robert Alan Dannenberg and Thomas M. Adams. Front, Elizabeth Derting, Ross Alan Dannenberg, Nancy Kathleen Robinson Adams. *Submitted by: Ross Dannenberg, 1200 Braddock Place #502, Alexandria, VA 22305*

487. Darsey

The earlier ancestors of the Darseys have been traced back to Denmark in 400 A.D. The Darsey ancestors were Vikings. The Vikings attacked all over Europe and the New World. One such Viking was Rollo the Dane who conquered Western France. The land that he and his followers conquered became Normandy (land of the Northmen).

Rollo made a treaty with the King of France, married a daughter of the king, became Christianized, and became Robert I (Duke of Normandy). One of his sons became the grandfather of William the Conqueror and William Deareci. William had married Pavia Deareci and took for his title William I (Count Deareci which became D-Arcy).

William D'Arcy accompanied William the Conqueror to England in 1066 and became the ancestor of all the Darsey/Dorsey families. One descendant, James Darsey, came to Maryland in 1660 and settled in Calvert County. His son James (died 1759) had fourteen children. One was named Joseph Dearcey (1720-1781). Joseph settled in Lunenburg, Virginia, where he probably married Catherine Corbet. Later they moved to North Carolina, and still later (1762) to St. George Parish (Burke County) in Georgia. He and his family lived in what is now Jefferson County from 1762 until 1825. Joseph and Catherine had five sons. They were Joseph Jr., settled in Columbia County, Georgia; Joel Darsey, settled in Decatur County, Georgia; William Darsey, settled in Washington County, Georgia; Benjamin and James settled in Laurens County, Georgia. Joseph (private) and all sons fought in the Revolutionary War. Joseph Jr. (private), William (major), Joel (private), Benjamin (private), and James (lieutenant) served in Burke County militia units.

In 1819 James and his family settled in Laurens County, Georgia. James was married twice. He had two sons by his first wife and one son, Seth, by his second wife. Seth (1770-1847) is the ancestor of Jack Dorsey of Mt. Zion.

Seth married Edith Peacock in 1811. They had eight children. One child was David Jackson Darsey (1832-1897). David married a widow, Mary Ann Braswell, with eight children. David and Mary Ann had five children. Charles Eldridge Darsey (1866-1948) was one of their five. Charles married Catherine Bridgers and had eight children. One of these children was Samuel Jackson Dorsey (1902-1974) who married Berdia Swearingen (1916-1947). They had one child, Striblen Jackson Dorsey.

Striblen Jackson "Jack" Dorsey was born in Hawkinsville, Pulaski County, Georgia, on December 6, 1934. Jack attended public school in Alabama and Georgia. In December 1951, he enlisted in the United States Marine Corps. He served in various places including Korea. In Korea, he served as a platoon sergeant in "B" Company, 1st Battalion, 1st Regiment, 1st Marine Division. Dorsey received six medals and was discharged in July 1956.

Jack entered Reinhardt College in 1957 and attended five colleges and universities. He earned two undergraduate and four graduate degrees. Jack was an educator for thirty-one years, councilman (one term), mayor (four terms), magistrate (one term), and has been a local preacher since 1974.

During Dorsey's four administrations as mayor, he founded the Mt. Zion Fire Department, Police Department, library, Recreation

Department, Health Care Center, built the present City Hall, Lake J. Ebb Duncan, and Dillard Recreation Field. Since 1974, he has obtained $1,000,000 in federal, state, and private foundation grants for all organizations of the Mt. Zion community. He also founded the Burwell Psycho-Educational Center. Dorsey is a Methodist, "Yellow Dog" Democrat, Optimist, and community volunteer.

Dorsey was married to Sara Jo Bookhardt on December 24, 1961, by Rev. Horace Williams in the Excelsior United Methodist Church in Snipesville, Jeff Davis County, Georgia. Sara Jo was born on July 23, 1940, near Denton in Jeff Davis County. She was the eldest of seven children born to Edward Lee Bookhardt (1905-1984) and Evalou Walker Bookhardt (1909-1999). Sara's father was born near Dorchester, South Carolina, and was descended from the Bookhardts who settled in South Carolina in 1740. Sara's mother was born in Alston, Montgomery County, Georgia, and was descended from the Walkers who left Pitt County, North Carolina, and settled in Washington County, Georgia, in 1819. Sara graduated from Hazlehurst High School in 1958. She was the class valedictorian. She entered Reinhardt College in 1958 and received two undergraduate and two graduate degrees from Reinhardt and West Georgia College. Sara retired in 1998 after serving thirty years as a first, second, and third grade teacher in Cobb, Douglas, and Carroll counties. Sara is a Methodist, Democrat, homemaker, and an active church and community worker.

The Dorseys have two sons: (1) Wade Hampton Dorsey, born in 1964 in Marietta, Cobb County, Georgia, and (2) Jonathan Jackson Dorsey, born in 1968 in Carrollton, Carroll County, Georgia. Wade was married to Sheila Roth (born in 1962 in Ohio and grew up in Charleston, South Carolina) on September 9, 1990, at his parents' home in Mt. Zion. The official was Rabbi Stephen Lebow. Wade and Sheila have a daughter named Sarah Mariah Tzipporah, born 1998. Wade was an honor graduate from Mt. Zion High School (1982), received his B.A. degree (West Georgia, 1986) as a cum laude student, and M.A. degree (University of South Carolina, 1988). He is an archivist in the State Department of Archives in Columbia, South Carolina, a member of the Blythewood, South Carolina Zoning Board, a Democrat, a Methodist, a member of Sons of Confederate Veterans, and a community leader. Sheila was an honor graduate from Charleston College (B.A.) and the University of South Carolina (M.A.). She is a political activist, media specialist, Democrat, Jewish, and a community leader.

Jonathan was married to Caroline Jane Reid (born in Philadelphia, Pennsylvania and grew up in Tyrone, Georgia) on July 13, 1991, in the Mt. Zion United Methodist Church. The official was Rev. James Callahan (Episcopal Priest). Jonathan and Karrie have two sons: (1) Joshua Reid Jackson Dorsey (born 1995) and (2) Jesse Edward Reid Dorsey (born 1999). Jonathan was an honor graduate from Mt. Zion High School (1986) and received his B.A. degree (West Georgia College, 1990). He is director of the Carrollton Visitor and Tourism Bureau, member of a popular band (BackStreet), Optimist, Democrat, Episcopalian, writer, and community leader. Karrie graduated from Fayette County High School (1986), graduated from West Georgia College (B.A., 1991), and is working on her master's degree at West Georgia. She is a political activist, community and school activist, Methodist, Episcopalian, homemaker, and writer.

Jack came to Mt. Zion in 1956 and Sara came in 1965. *Submitted by: Jack Dorsey, PO Box 701, Mt. Zion, GA 30150*

488. Marvin Daugherty and His Ancestors

After a life of traveling all around the world, Marvin Daugherty has only lived in Carroll County since 1985, but his roots in this area go back many generations

His great-great-great-grandfather Thomas Daugherty was born in Ireland in 1779. Upon arriving on these shores, he served in the War of 1812 and married Sarah Tomlin of Morgan County. He became a landowner in Upson County and died there in 1834. In 1814 Dennis Daugherty became the first of nine children born to Thomas and Sarah. At age twenty-one, Dennis married Eleanor "Nellie" Hudgeons and moved to Carroll County.

Chief Warrant Officer Marvin G. Daugherty, 1966.

Dennis and Nellie Daugherty had five children, of whom the second, born in 1838, was named Thomas for his paternal Irish grandfather. In 1866 Thomas L. Daugherty married Sarah Phillips. Their seventh child (of ten) was Charlie Marion, born in March 1879 in Carroll County.

At age twenty-three, Charlie married Nancy Bates and they settled on a farm in the Jake community of Carroll County. Charlie and Nancy had eight children: Gladys (1903), William (known as "Roy") (1904), Lawrence (1906), Floyce (1907), Curtis (1911), Addelene (1917), and twins Johnny Milton (known as "Bud") and Mildred (1918).

Charlie's wife Nancy died in 1922, leaving him with the daunting tasks of farming his land and raising the children alone. His eldest daughter Gladys helped to look after the children and keep the house until she herself married. Charlie married in 1930 to Jennie Farrow. They lived in Jake until Charlie died in 1959. Charlie, Nancy and Jennie, as well as Charlie's parents Thomas and Sarah, are all buried in the Poplar Springs Primitive Baptist Church Cemetery.

In 1926, Charlie's oldest son Roy married the fifteen-year-old Ruby Lorena Roberts of Gadsden. Roy followed work in the cotton mills until the great depression, when he found work in the WPA. Being the only man in his outfit with a driver's license, he was given the job of driving a dump truck! Roy and Lorena moved to Newnan after the war, where he sold insurance.

Roy and Lorena Daugherty's children were Lettie (1927), Marvin (1929), Harold (1931) and Ken (1939). As a child, Marvin spent summers on his grandfather Charlie's farm in Jake. "We'd pick a watermelon before working in the fields," he recalls, "and tote it to a creek to keep it cool until we were ready to crack it open. Later, I'd take a bar of soap and get a bath in that same creek!"

Marvin joined the U.S. Navy in 1946. He served tours of duty in the Mediterranean, the Philippines, and Japan, and bases throughout the United States. He served on the U.S.S. Franklin Roosevelt during the Vietnam War, then retired in 1968 and went to work for Lockheed in Marietta. He later taught at Chattahoochee Tech.

Marvin and his wife, the former Wyolene Douglas of Carrollton, moved from Powder Springs to Carrollton in 1985, and they live here to this day. *Submitted by: S.R. Daugherty, 220 Don-Rich Drive, Carrollton, GA 30117*

489. James Gillam Davenport

James Gillam Davenport was born December 16, 1818, in Newberry County, South Carolina, to Raymond Davenport and Martha "Patsy" Adams Davenport. His older sisters were Elizabeth (ca. 1808), Lucresire (ca. 1810), Catherine (ca. 1812), Artemesia (1814-md. Lewis W. Hammock in Jones Co. GA; d. aft 1860), Matilda (ca. 1816-md. Robert Mitchell in Jones Co. GA), and one younger brother, Charles J(?onathan) (ca. 1821 GA-md. Elizabeth Gibson in Columbus, Muscogee Co. GA 1850).

The family left Newberry and moved to Georgia after the 1820 Census had been taken in January 1821 in Newberry, but before Charles was born, for they are listed there without him. James' mother is said to have died soon after. They were in Jones County during 1829-1837 when the two girls were married there. James was "bound out" as an apprentice while still a boy, and worked "like a slave." James' father Raymond Davenport was living in Marion Co. GA between 1838 and 1846, and one newspaper notice mentioned his name along with James G. and a brother-in-law, Allan Adams, as persons having mail at the Tazewell Post Office.

James G. and Sarah F. Davenport at their home. About 1890.

At age 20 James G. married Rachel Cicely Hammock, on September 5, 1838, in Coweta County, GA. She was the daughter of (?Green) Berry Hammock and Nancy Ann Burrow Hammock and was also 20 years old. They had 1.) Joseph Raymond (1840-1840), 2.) Charles James (1841-1862); md. Susannah Kelley in Coweta County), 3.) Martha May Ann (1843-1931; md. John Newton Roberson), 4.) Nancy Caroline (1845-1920, md. Henry Wyatt Reid), 5.) Susan Catherine (1849-1932; md. John Albert White), 6.) Lucinda E. (1850-1935; md. Samuel J. Parker). Even though Martha was born in Pike Co. and Nancy was born in Meriwether Co., there are evidences James and his family were in Carroll County before 1850.

1.)- James' first son Joseph Raymond was born in 1840 and died a month later. In the little cemetery where James' family plot is located is a headstone with RAYMON inscribed on it. 2.)- Mr. Jerry Harper, owner of James' home in 1999, said he was told the house had been built in 1840. James built the home himself, with hand-hewn stones in the two chimneys, and hand-made pine shingles on the roof. 3.)- On February 28, 1848, James was named trustee for a land lot for his mother-in-law, Nancy Hammock. Her father Phillip Burrow Sr. gave a piece of his land in Carroll County for her support and livelihood, and James was listed as her trustee on the county tax rolls. 4.)- James and family are listed on the 1850 Census for Carroll County, though Rachel is listed as "Ruth" and baby Lucinda is listed as "Lewis", with Nancy not listed at all.

James' wife Rachel died July 28, 1853 at age 35, leaving him with 5 young children to raise alone. He married Amanda E. Johnson on December 14, 1855, and their children were: 1.) Twins, Thomas Franklin and Mary F. (1856-Mary died 1857), Green Washington (1859), Theodora S. (Dora) (1861), and Margaret E. (1864-1864). After the War Between the States began, James' oldest son Charles joined up with the Company F, 19th Regt. Georgia Volunteer Infantry, Army of Tennessee CSA. Carroll County GA. Charles married his second cousin, Susannah Kelley in Coweta County December 19, 1861, then the following June he was killed in a skirmish at Vicksburg, a year before the great siege there. It was written of James. G. Davenport that during the War he was exempt from soldiering because he had the gristmill — "He befriended many people to help them." He had his mother-in-law, Nancy Hammock, in his home in 1860, and was also trustee for his wife's aunt Teresa Burrow, whose husband Phillip had died young. He acquired many acres of land, and had slaves to work the fields. One old slave shanty still remains to the west of the old house he built so long ago. After the slaves were freed, some of them stayed with him. "Uncle Jimmie" was also named as a relative of "Old Greenberry Hammock, the father of the more eccentric man of the same name" in the county, who died of dropsy when very old. He brought the coffin for Old Mr. Hammock's burial.

James' wife Amanda died November 1, 1867, and he married for a third time on April 24, 1868. She was the widow Sarah Francis Bailey Moses 1840-1920) who had a small child by her first husband, William Neal Moses, named Alston LaFayette Moses (1859-1951, md. Mattie M. Jackson). James treated him as his own, and he and Sarah had Mary Jeannette (1872-md. James A. Bryan), William Neal (1875-md. Hattie Owens), and Dicey Eliza (1876-1970; md. Nelson C. Steed).

The history of the Smith Chapel Methodist church in north Carroll County not far from James G. Davenport's home, contains a reference to him:

> "Uncle Jimmie Davenport was a faithful man of God and his wife; both were loyal to the community and church friends; together with their children they had a home of prayer and thanksgiving."

Some of his descendants recalled hearing him spoken of as a firm man, a "pistal ball". He was also remembered in writings of the Shiloh Methodist Episcopal Church as a mighty fine speaker and one who supported the annual Camp meetings. He lived a long and productive life, and died at age 88 on June 20, 1906. He is buried with his wives and three of his children in the Holmes Cemetery just north of his gristmill, found on a hill on north Davenport Mill Road near the Delia Pease Road intersection, just north of Turkey Creek bridge. *Submitted by: Pauline McConkie Derhak, 1375 West 4505 South, Taylorsville, UT 84123.*

490. Davis

Samuel Allen Davis born January 25, 1885. Mattic O. Jones born August 4, 1888. Married November 1905. He died April 1, 1961, and she died January 13, 1983. They had eleven children.

Estelle born November 24, 1906, died November 21, 1973. Married January 16, 1937, to Render Webb, born August 5, 1907, died February 2, 1984.

Ruth born June 22, 1908, died February 2, 1989. Married Bill Taylor in 1927, died October 16, 1969. Their children were Lucille, Rudolph, Shelby, Virginia, Shirley and Annette.

Samuel Allen Davis and Mattie O. Jones Davis

Gladys born November 24, 1910, married Paul Duncan, January 18, 1932. Their children were: (1) Donald born September 21, 1935, married Judith Burns August 1, 1953. He died May 22, 2000. Their children were: (a) Mark born December 5, 1955, died March 15, 1983, married Lisa Dowd. Two children: Christina born November 11, 1977, and Daniel born, August 17, 1981. (b) Michael Scott, born December 27, 1958, married Violet Elliot June 3, 1978. Two children: Gabriella born December 23, 1978, and Joshua born September 21, 1985. (c) Christopher born March 31, 1969, married Rebecca Light, August 15, 1987. Three children: Levi born December 24, 1987; Ethan born November 8, 1993; and Isahel born June 20, 2000. (2) Janice born July 31, 1940, married Jimmy Walker November 24, 1956. Their children were: (a) Susan born July 11, 1957, married Horace Garrett April 17, 1975. Two children: Andrea born June 15, 1983, died January 8, 1999, and William born April 30, 1992. (b) Kathy born June 24, 1959. (c) Richard born September 28, 1961, married Julian Collins April 4, 1992. (d) Charles born December 15, 1969, married Rebecca Henry March 18, 2000. (3) Bobby born May 21, 1943, died January 29, 1981, married Betty Turner. Their child: Lori Duncan.

Durward born May 18, 1914, died October 15, 1991.

Dorsey born December 1, 1916, died September 23, 1938.

Kathleen born August 3, 1919, married Roy Henderson August 7, 1937. He died November 29, 1983. Their children were James, Dillard, Retha, Wayne and Clipper.

Martha born March 5, 1921, married Howard Wilburn August 19, 1939. He died November 14, 1992. Their children were Jerry Ann, Linda, Allen, Rodney, Debbie.

Billie born July 17, 1924, married Miriam Driver. He died April 3, 1960.

Willene born October 23, 1927, married William Prescott May 3, 1947. Their children were: (1) Terrell born June 12, 1957, married Diana Robinson July 14, 1979. One child: Jason born April 8, 1981. (2) Marty born February 18, 1962, married Patrice Jones. One child: Matthew born August 12, 1989.

Rudene born October 23, 1927, married Jack Daniel on November 26, 1947. Their children were: (1) Belinda born June 23, 1960, married Steve Rowlette September 23, 1978. Two children: (a) Cancace born July 9, 1981, and (b) Danille born April 27, 1984. (2) Gregory born February 22, 1963, married Melinda Kilgore March 22, 1986. Three children: (a) Joshua born December 19, 1987, died March 24, 1990; (b) Sierra born September 27, 1989; and (c) Tyler born November 20, 1990.

Joyce born May 8, 1931, married Thomas Jiles December 23, 1946. Thomas died May 19, 1997. Their children were Ronnie, Sue, Sheila, Anthony, Mark, Tim, Sammy, Enoch, Robin, and Patsy. *Submitted by: Rudene Daniel, 102 Myrtle Street, Carrollton, GA 30117*

491. Drusilla Warren Davis

Drusilla Warren was born May 31, 1888, in Bowdon, Georgia, to Drury Melvina and William Gabriel Warren. She and a sister married brothers making their children "double first cousins." Her brother-in-law and future husband, James Leon Davis (born July 27, 1885, Bowdon) knew early on that he would "marry that little Warren girl." Dru proved harder to convince. She had another marriage proposal and that suitor owned a surrey. Jim's 1905 marriage license expired. Two years later, second license in hand, he told Dru she could marry him now or he was headed for Texas never to be seen again. They married March 10, 1907, two months before her nineteenth birthday.

Early in their marriage, Jim and Dru farmed in Carroll County like their parents. Their first son died at birth in 1910. Girlilee was born July 22, 1912, the first of six daughters. Son Harold Jesse was born April 29, 1914. Daughter Jimmie followed on June 3, 1916.

Drusilla Warren Davis, early 1940s

Jim's older brother, Charlie, taught him the machinist's trade and in July 1916, the young family moved to Newnan for Jim to work at the cotton mill. Six more children were born in Newnan: daughter Willene October 18, 1918, son Warren G. July 3, 1921 (died of diphtheria April 1924), daughter Mildred July 29, 1923, daughter Frances July 31, 1925, daughter Wawena August 18, 1927, and son James Leon August 13, 1930.

By all accounts, Jim Davis was a man who could do almost anything. Anything that broke at the mill or village, he fixed — even redesigning machinery. He made furniture, played any musical instrument he picked up and doted on his children. They watched for him coming home and Jim usually finished the walk with children dangling from him. On Christmas Eve 1929 he worked on a burst water pipe. When he came home his clothes were frozen to his body. Pneumonia developed. On New Years Day 1930, he died. Drusilla was 41, pregnant, with 7 children under age 17 at home. The Great Depression gripped the nation and families in the community offered to raise the younger children to help the young widow. She refused, determined to keep her family together.

Dru lived strength and determination leavened with humor and love. She understood the importance of family and hard work and didn't dwell on sadness. In 1935 Dru and the youngest children returned to Bowdon with Girlilee, now an R.N. Later she moved back "to the country" and cared for her mother, then her brother, Jesse. In 1967 Dru bought a small house from Jesse's estate. She was so proud. She had her own home which she kept until her death on May 8, 1981, three weeks before her 93rd birthday.

After Jim's death she and the children worked in the fields and whatever jobs were available for the joy of living together as a family. And it was a joyful family as evidenced by their annual Thanksgiving reunion dubbed "the gathering of the nuts." It is a tribute to the love and loyalty she taught that her family continues this tradition in a new millennium. *Submitted by: Laura Davis Taylor, 3132 County Highway 5, Hayden, AL 35079*

492. Enoch Davis

Enoch S. Davis was an early pioneer of Carroll County. He was listed in the 1840 census of Carroll County. On an early deed dated November 11, 1843, in Carroll County, he bought 202½ acres in the 4th District of Carroll County. Witnesses on his deed were David Gray and William Rooks, J.P.

The following is part of an article that appeared in the *Times Free Press* on January 11, 1911, following Enoch's death. It was submitted by the Committee of Carroll Lodge #69. Enoch was a member of this lodge at his death. In 1859 he joined the Masonic fraternity at Rotherwood, Georgia. In 1905, he joined the Carroll Lodge and was a member until his death.

> "'Resolution of Respect' your committee in offering this tribute of respect to our deceased brother, Enoch S. Davis, cannot but feel our inability to do the subject justice. Brother Davis, always greeting you with a smile, was never out of humor. Brother Davis was just a man. His youthfulness never grew old, but simply matured, his heart was always young. He was faithful to every duty devoted to every obligation.
>
> "Brother Enoch S. Davis was born in North Carolina on the 1st day of Sept. 1818, moved to Georgia in 1828, and married Miss Sarah P. Walker of Coweta Co. in the year of 1837.
>
> "In 1864 he went from Carroll Co. to the War between the States and was a faithful servant of the Confederacy. He returned to his home after the unpleasantness and lived an honorable upright citizen, serving his community as miller at Coleman's Mill near Clem, Ga. for more than 30 years. In 1898 his beloved wife was chilled by the icy hand of death, leaving him and several children to morn her loss.
>
> "On December 3rd 1910 there came an Angel of Death from o'er the fields of Glory, over the Jasper Sea, calling for his spirit at the ripe old age of ninety-two years three months and three days. And, as the working tools of the Craft fell from his grasp forever, and his eyes closed in sleep, Brother Davis was no more. Respectfully submitted by J.D. Hamrick, W.J. Millican, J.T. Norman, Com."

Enoch S. Davis

Enoch's wife Sarah was born January 28, 1817, in Georgia. They are buried in the Davis Family Cemetery located next to their home. The cemetery was started in 1864 after the death of their son Bud. He died from wounds he received at a battle near Dalton, Georgia. After he was wounded, he was sent to a hospital in Marietta, Georgia. According to a descendant, Louise Gaines, his mother Sarah went to Marietta to get his body with a horse and wagon. He was buried not far from their home. She planted a cedar tree at the head and foot of his grave.

His father Enoch surrendered at Appomattox, Virginia, on April 9, 1865. He had to walk home and, according to Louise, he picked up rocks along the way home. At one time, she had the musket ball and a piece of bone from Bud's wound. Bud served in Company B, 56th Regiment, Georgia Volunteer Infantry, Army of Tennessee, Confederate States Army (CSA), Carroll County. Enoch served in Company I, 10th Regiment, Georgia Volunteer Infantry, Army of Northern Virginia, CSA, Campbell and Fayette Counties, Georgia (Fayetteville Rifle Greys or Fayette Grey Guards). According to pension records, he drew a pension from 1896 to 1909. He was listed as being blind.

. Enoch and Sarah had seven known children: (1) Susan Emily born about 1839 in Carroll County, married Thomas Hanvey, a Civil War veteran, on August 18, 1856; (2) Tiney C. born November 18, 1840, in Carroll County, died June 4, 1902, in Carroll County, buried in Davis Family Cemetery; (3) Sarah A. born October 17, 1842, in Carroll County, died May 13, 1898, in Carroll County, married H.W. Holloway, a Civil War veteran on June 28, 1865. Both are buried in Whooping Creek Primitive Baptist Church Cemetery, Carroll County; (4) William A. (Bud) born about 1845 in Carroll County, died 1864 during the Civil War; (5) Hannah born about 1848 in Carroll County, no dates on her death; (6) Samuel M. born May 28, 1851, in Carroll County and died March 31, 1920, in Carroll County. On August 12, 1869, married first to Mary Elizabeth (Betty) Tant. She was born May 17, 1851, in Georgia and died from smallpox on March 16, 1901, in Carroll County. She was the daughter of Kinyard, a Civil War veteran, and Josephine Jarrett Tant. Samuel married second to Etha Langley; (7) F.M. (Frank) born about 1859 in Carroll County married Lula Coleman on January 11, 1882.

Enoch and Sarah and Samuel and Betty were members of Whopping Creek Primitive Baptist Church. Numerous descendants of Enoch and Sarah are still living in Carroll County.

The Davis Cemetery is located on the property of the late Donald Davis Duncan, the great-great-grandson of Enoch and Sarah. Donald used Enoch as his Confederate ancestor to join the Sons of Confederate Veterans (SCV). At his death, he belonged to Forrests Escort Camp, SCV, Villa Rica, Georgia. He also belonged to the Woolhat Boys, a group of Masons that wanted to help other Masons or anyone who needed their help. Donald was a Mason and he belonged to the Roopville Lodge. Not long before his death, he learned that Enoch had also been a Mason.

Donald Davis Duncan, 1935-2000

Samuel M. and Betty Tant Davis were Donald's great-grandparents. Samuel Allen and Mattie Ophelia Jones Davis were his grandparents. His parents were the late John Paul and Gladys Lovdell Davis Duncan. He was married to Judith Marie (Judy) Burns Duncan, daughter of the late Robert and Buvena Burns. Their children were (1) the late Mark Howard Duncan who married Lisa Gail Dowd. Their children were (a) Christina Beth Duncan who married Kenneth Richardson. Their children were

Betty Tant Davis, Bertha Mae Davis, Dean Davis, and Kate Davis.

Alexus Victoria (Lexi) Manning and Haley Lynn Richardson and (b) David Mark Duncan; (2) Michael (Scott) Duncan who married Violet Dennise Elliot. Their children were Gabriella Sue (Gabby) Duncan and Joshua (Josh) David Duncan; (3) Christopher Brad (Chris) Duncan married Karen Rebecca Light. Their children are Justin (Levi) Duncan, Ethan Blake Duncan, and Isabel Jordan Duncan.

Most of Donald's family still live on Davis Road on the property that once was owned by Enoch. *Submitted by: Chris Duncan*

Sources: Researched by Judy Duncan, 1177 Davis Road, Carrollton, GA 30116, and other family members.

493. Farrell J. Davis Family

The Farrell J. Davis family located in Carroll County in April of 1964 on fifty acres of land at 875 Pleasant Ridge Road. Family members were Farrell (born November 19, 1924) son of Andrew Jack Davis and Azzie Ann Roe of Cherokee, Pickens and Bartow Counties; Juanita (born August 9, 1924) daughter of Henry and Lillie Elliott of Fisk, Missouri; Gregory F. (born December 24, 1949); and Barry E. (born May 20, 1951). Farrell and family members constructed the 3000 square foot residence and two out-buildings located there.

Farrell graduated from Martha Berry School at Rome and radio schools in Missouri, South Dakota, and Atlanta. He was employed by Trans World Airline, Eastern Airlines, and Delta Airlines. Farrell was a communication officer in the Air Force Reserve and retired from Delta. Juanita graduated from West Georgia College and was a librarian at West Georgia Regional Library. She then completed her M.A. in library science from West Georgia College and served until her retirement as librarian at Sand Hill School in the Carroll County School System. Gregory joined the family in June 1964 after his ninth grade year at Berry Academy in Rome. He graduated from Carrollton High School in 1967. Barry graduated from Carrollton High School in 1969. The family have been members of Tabernacle Baptist Church of Carrollton since 1964. Juanita served as librarian and deacon of that congregation.

Farrell J. Davis Family

Gregory married Jeannine Walker (born June 24, 1949) daughter of Novyce and Grady Walker of Carrollton. They both graduated from West Georgia College in 1971 and the University of Georgia in 1974. Gregory also attended the University of South Carolina for postgraduate study and taught for seven years at Midlands Technical College in Columbia, South Carolina. Jeannine taught for ten years at Columbia College and served as secretary of South Carolina Music Teachers Association. Their two sons Evan G. (March 30, 1980) and Benjamin W. (June 21, 1982) were born in Columbia. Evan graduated with honors from Cartersville High and is a Charter Scholar at the University of Georgia majoring in economics and languages. Benjamin graduated from Interlochen Center for the Arts in Michigan, winning the President's Achievement Award in Theatre and attends the Julliard School of Acting in New York. Presently, Gregory is Financial Consultant for the Robinson-Humphrey Investment Center at West Georgia National Bank in Carrollton and in Douglasville. Gregory formed Davis Rental Management in 1983 and owns buildings which he rents for stores and offices in Cartersville, Rockmart, Summerville, Canton, Carrollton, and Bremen. He served on the Cartersville City School Board for ten years where he was elected president of the board. Jeannine taught at Rome City, Bartow and Carroll County Schools and was named "Teacher of the Year" twice.

Barry married Nancy S. Patterson (born June 14, 1952) daughter of Raymond and Mable Patterson of Carrollton. Barry graduated from Carroll Technical College and worked for Gifford-Hill in Atlanta as a draftsman. He was also production scheduler for the MARTA construction. Barry founded Rapid Rents in 1982 with stores in Carrollton, Bremen, and Rockmart. He also founded the Mr. Movie stores and Photos to Go store. Barry is currently owner of North American Numbers Inc., an aerial photography company and an aircraft/watercraft graphics company. Nancy graduated from West Georgia College and worked in her family's business, Patterson Television Company. She was also an officer and co-owner of Rapid Rents. Later, Nancy went to real estate school and graduated in 1999. In 2000 she was the "Rookie of the Year" at Duffey Realty with over two million dollars in sales. Jonathan B. Davis (born Juned 14, 1971) married Kristie Freeman and they have a daughter Rebecca E. Jon graduated from Atlanta Technical College in avionics/airframe/communications and works for Gulfstream Aerospace Corporation. Kristie graduated from West Georgia College and works as a banker and mother. Jennifer S. (born September 11, 1981) was the 2000 Carrollton High School salutatorian and received a scholarship to Georgia Tech. She is majoring in aerospace engineering and has signed a co-op job agreement with Gulfstream Aerospace. James Davis (born February 25, 1984) is the Carrollton High School Band Captain for the 2001-02 school year and will be a senior at the high school. *Submitted by: Gregory Davis, Carrollton, GA*

494. Henry Madison Davis and Elizabeth Frances Cockrell

Henry Madison (Mat) Davis, 1848-1928, was the eighth of ten known children of Chesley Davis and Elana Menelus Green. The Chesley Davis family lived in Monroe and Fayette Counties in Georgia and were in Heard County in 1850. By 1855 the family had crossed over into Randolph County, Alabama.

Mat saw five of his brothers leave home to serve the Confederacy. He must have had a lot or responsibility as the oldest boy at home during the time of the war. Two of the brothers, John Toliver and Robert A., died in service. Other children of Chesley and Elana Davis are William Thomas, Green Jackson, James Monroe, Nancy A., Eliza Ann, Emily, and Noah Augusta.

Thomas and Martha Garner Cockrell moved from Heard to Randolph also, settling near the Davises, and around 1869 Henry Madison Davis married Elizabeth Frances (Beth) Cockrell. Other children of Thomas and Martha Cockrell are: Borden (Barton? Brittain?), Allan, Louisa, Mary Penelope, Martha Ann, Amanda, Brazoura (Tuck, Tucky), twin, Missouri (Tink, Tinky), twin.

Mat and Beth moved back to Georgia by 1870 and were in Carroll in 1910 before moving on to settle in Bremen. Both are buried in the Bremen City Cemetery.

Henry Madison Davis and Elizabeth Frances Cockrell Davis

Children: Martha Menelus (Nealie), 1870-1959). She never married and loved to garden. She is buried near her parents. Thomas (Tommy), about 1871-1875. Lucy Theodocia (Docia), 1875-1942, married Marshall M. Duke. The couple moved to Phil Campbell, Alabama, where Marshall was the postmaster, and later settled in Tennessee. They had no children. Mary Elizabeth (Mollie), 1878-1951, married John Marvin Bonner. Mollie and Marvin settled in Phil Campbell, Alabama, where he owned and operated a cotton gin. Their children: Thomas Cohen, Augusta Elizabeth, Madison Davis, Emma Menelus, William Martin, Oscar Milton, John Marvin Jr., and Loyce Smith. Mollie played the organ for the Baptist church she attended and loved Sacred Harp music and playing dominoes. She was known for her bread and tea cakes. Marvin hunted fox and quail. They are both buried at Shady Grove Cemetery in Phil Campbell. Eliza Leola, 1881-1966, married Abner R. Harman. They lived in Carroll all of their lives. Their children: Vernon, Spurgeon, Sophie Mae. Nancy Louthella Florence, 1884-1978, married Grover Cleveland Russell. Their children: Henry Moses, Frances Willard, Annie Belle, Mignon, and Edwin. Nancy and Grover are buried near Nancy's parents in the Bremen City Cemetery. Velona Belle, 1888-1960, married Herbert G. Monroe. Their children: Twins, a boy who died shortly after birth, and Elizabeth Vashti (Betty). Velona and Herbert are buried at Crest Lawn Cemetery in Atlanta. Henrietta, 1891-1968, married Fred Head. Their children: Frederick I., Cora Beth, James Stanley, and DeLois. Henrietta and Fred settled in Tallapoosa, Georgia. *Submitted by: Kathy Moore Fambro, 122 Morallion Hills, Peachtree City, GA 30269*

495. John Davis Family

There was a tradition of seven John Davises in direct line of descent. My story will begin with the first American ancestor John Davis born in 1720 in Wales where he was reared and married. He migrated to the colonies with his brother Richard about 1745 settling in King William County, Virginia, near the fork where the Paminkey and Mattapony rivers make the York River and not a great distance from Yorktown. He was wealthy, owning several properties.

It is not known who he married; only that he married in Wales and all of his children were born in America.

Little is known about his life except he seemed to have some taste and aptitude for frontier life. After his children were grown, he left on a trip and was never heard from again. County authorities assumed he had been killed by a band of Indians or slain for his money. We have the name of only one of his children who was also named John.

John Davis son of the above John was born 1756 in King William County. He lived with his father but when the Revolutionary War broke out he shouldered his musket and marched off in defense of his country enlisting at Culpepper, Virginia and served under Captain Rucker and Colonel Pendleton until its close. When the war was over, he migrated to Amherst County, Virginia, and settled in the bend on the James River. There he married Miss Sally Ann Ham of Irish descent in 1781. They had several children. Sally died in 1812 and John in 1843 in Elbert County.

John Davis, of whom I write, was born January 5, 1787 in Amherst County, Virginia, to parents Sally Ann Ham and John Davis. At the age of three his family moved to Elbert County, Georgia, where he was raised principally on the farm. He also taught in one or two schools.

He served in the War of 1812. After the war he engaged in wagoning, going into nearly every state of the Union at that time.

He took Ms. Lucy Ham as his bride January 31, 1817 in Madison County, Georgia. Lucy was the daughter of Elizabeth Pendleton and Reuben Ham. They started their family and had four boys: William Pemberton married Sarah Hearn, Reubin Jackson married Elizabeth Parilee Bailey, John Jones married Rebeckah A. Sims, Littleton Early (my gggrandfather) married (1) Harriett Amanda Gillespie, (2) Elizabeth King (my gggrandmother); and one daughter Martha Mathas married Isaiah Springer Beck.

Two of his sons were in the C.S.A. Reubin Jackson Davis was killed only a few months after volunteering. John J. returned home to his wife Rebeckah Sims Davis in Randolph County, Alabama.

In 1829 after the Coweta Purchase was drawn, he settled in the part of it that became Campbell County, then in 1856 moved to Carroll County after the death of his wife Lucy in 1848. He built a log cabin which in later years was torn down and was the location on which the Tyus school was built.

John moved back to Campbell County in his aging years to live with his son until his death April 29, 1879, at the age of 92. He is buried at the old cemetery at New Hope Methodist church in Fayetteville, Georgia, where his son John Jones Davis was pastor for a number of years.

The following description of him was given to me: He had a full head of black hair, his eyes were keen and bright as an Indian's, his hearing unimpaired, possessing all of his faculties to a remarkable degree, large luminous eyes, beautiful teeth and was a man of fine intelligence.

Lucy and John Davis were my ggggrandparents. *Submitted by: June Brown Hayes, 6955 Lockridge Dr., Doraville, GA 30360*

Sources: Notes from a family history by W.P. Davis son of John and Lucy Ham Davis but was not put in permanent form because the courthouse in Warrenton, Georgia, including the record vaults where both the original and copies intended for the printer were burned about 1908. The final draft was fully complete but much of the information was burned, therefore lost.

496. John Benjamin and Arizona (Zonie) Key Davis

John Benjamin Davis and twin sister Clara Isabelle were born November 27, 1865, to parents Littleton E. and Elizabeth King Davis in the Laurel Hill community of Carroll County.

Other children included Adeline S. and Melissa A. There was also a half-sister Lucy Louella and half-brothers Benjamin F. (who we think died in infancy) and Henry C. Davis. Their mother was Harriett Amanda Gillespie.

Clara Isabelle married J.T. Statham and had several children. Melissa married R.L. Buchanan and had one child Clyde. Adeline married E.T. Gordon and thought to have had one child. Lucy had one child Ida Elizabeth who died at the age of twelve. No marital information for Henry C.

Davis Family. Etta and Nora (back), Ben, Dovie, Arizona (front)

Littleton taught in common schools, farmed, and was a Methodist minister.

Arizona Samantha Uneta Key Davis was born June 8, 1869, in the Victory community to parents Samantha Nancy E. Farmer and Burrell J. Key (see article on Burrell J. Key).

Ben and Zonie had known each other for several years and on April 11, 1889, they were married and set up housekeeping in the Tyus/Laurel Hill area. While Ben was farming, Zonie was happy housekeeping and in 1894 they started their family with daughter Mary Etta, Nora Samantha in 1899, and Dovie Lee in 1904. Death took two other children in infancy.

In 1912 Ben moved the family to Bowdon where, for twenty-six years, he delivered mail from the post office to the train depot, making three trips a day. His transportation was a wagon and a mule named Maude. Both were familiar and known by all.

Ben Davis and Maude the mule

They moved their membership to the Bowdon Baptist Church in 1914 from the Tyus Baptist Church where both had been members for more than thirty years.

As the daughters reached adulthood, they married. Mary Etta married John B. Smith, Dovie Lee married J. Loyal Bates, and Nora Samantha married William Farmer. One child (a daughter) was born to each Etta and Dovie. Nora never had children.

Sunday evening February 25, 1934, a tornado swept through Bowdon destroying their home at the corner of Rome Street and Grammar School Drive. One wall was left standing. Ben was taken to the Carrollton Clinic and released several days later. Others in the family were not seriously injured. Maude the mule was found grazing two pastures over. No fences were down so it was presumed the force of the wind picked her up and set her down in another pasture.

Zonie was closely confined to her home for several years due to illness. She passed away November 13, 1940, at the age of seventy-one. The funeral service and interment were at the Pleasant Grove Baptist Church near Tyus.

Less than two years later, on March 30, 1942, at the age of seventy-six, Ben joined his beloved Zonie at the Pleasant Grove Cemetery. His only surviving sibling was his twin sister Clara Isabelle.

V.D. Whatley quoted in Ben's obituary:

> "My old friend has paid the debt that all will have to pay. In Pleasant Grove Cemetery he will sleep, undisturbed by the wars of man or the storms of nature. Eternal rest to his soul."

Ben and Zonie were our great-grandparents. Unfortunately, I was too young to remember either of them. Mary Etta Smith was the researcher's grandmother. Dovie Lee Bates was the submitter's grandmother. *Submitted by: Pamela Stephens, Carrollton, GA* and Researched by: June Hayes, 6955 Lockridge Drive, Doraville, GA 30360

497. John Jefferson Davis

John Jefferson Davis was born 1825/26 in Tennessee. He died in 1901 and is buried in Old Bethel Primitive Baptist Cemetery in Temple, Georgia. He married Elizabeth McAllister on 6 January 1847 in Carroll County, Georgia. John served in the Civil War in Company I, 5th Georgia Infantry.

John and Elizabeth had seven known children as follows: (1) Georgia Ann born 3 June 1849, died 20 October 1913, married 15 April 1869 to William Marcus Allen born 9 August 1849, died 30 January 1916, Carroll County, Georgia; (2) John Thomas (Bud) married Kate Chambers 25 October 1877, Carroll County; (3) John Jefferson, Jr. born 3 March 1865, died 18 August 1929, married Florence Jane Hebisen; (4) Hannah married William (Bill) Wallace; (5) Sally first married (?) Raines, second married John Wallace; (6) Jane married (?) McLaughlin; and (7) Ann Kate married (?) Herrin.

John Jefferson Davis is buried in the Old Bethel Primitive Baptist Church Cemetery located between Highway 20 and Highway 78, southwest of Holly Creek in Temple, Georgia. *Submitted by: Paula Allen Brock, 1590 Welcome Road, Cullman, AL 35058*

498. Hubert Arlin (Bud) Dean and Dora Ethel Towns Dean

Arlin, better known as Bud Dean, son of Mann and Carrie Dean, born May 4, 1915, died March 30, 1970. Dora, daughter of George J. and Maiden S. Towns was born December 29, 1916, and died February 12, 1995. Bud and Dora were married November 11, 1937. They attended Roopville High School where Bud was a star basketball player. He was a tall, six-foot, slender young man and easily won the heart of Dora. The high school then consisted of ten grades. Following graduation from Roopville, Dora chose to attend Tyus since the school was extended to eleven grades. She was always a good student and enjoyed studying.

Following their marriage, November 11, 1937, they lived in Bowdon where Bud worked in Aubin Cumbie's store and also drove the "peddling truck." Bud was suffering from typhus fever and unable to work so the couple moved in with her parents till he was stronger.

Their first child, Vivian Rebecca was born April 8, 1940. The couple lived for a while in the upstairs apartment of the Roop home in Roopville. Mrs. Florida Roop Brock and Henry Brock were living downstairs. Rebecca celebrated her first birthday here and also took her first steps. (Years later, Mrs. Henry Brock and other ladies would be hosting her bridal shower in this same house.) Bud soon found work at the Atlanta Prison Farm and the family moved to a basement apartment in her sister's (Velma Johnson) home, and later to a small house on Gresham Avenue. While in Atlanta, Linda was born, October 3, 1942.

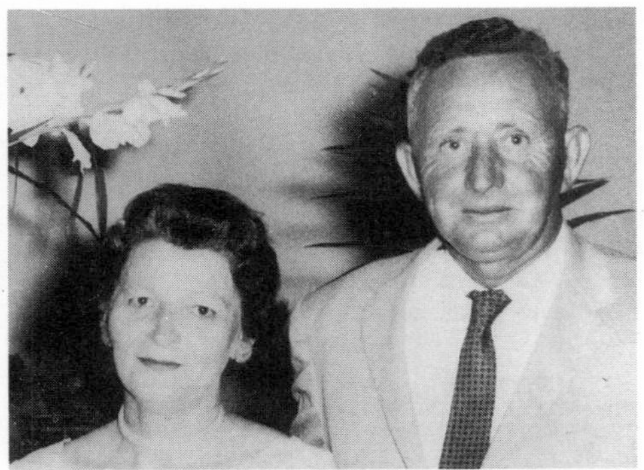

Dora E. Towns Dean and Hubert Arlin (Bud) Dean

Bud was drafted into the Army during World War II. Soldiers were badly needed, even though he had two children and was over the age limit. The government changed the age requirements to draft the older men. Bud was called 'Pop' by the younger men in his unit because he was the oldest. Times were difficult, Dora and the girls continued living in Atlanta until Bud returned from overseas. He was aboard ship enroute to the war zone when peace was declared.

In December 1946 Bud purchased a farm on Old Carrollton Road and the family moved into an old frame house that had once belonged to Dora's Uncle Charlie Wood.

Bud farmed for awhile and drove a school bus route for Roopville. Later they decided to buy a store in Roopville and had a successful gas and general merchandise business for several years. Cotton was no longer a cash crop and for a few years pimento peppers were grown on the family farm. Later the farm was fenced and Bud had cows, then built a chicken house, eventually building two more houses. They raised fryers and also had layers.

Bud and Dora were happy when their third child, a son, Steven James Dean was born on May 26, 1948, and then a daughter Beverly Elaine on June 1, 1950. A fifth child, Deborah Ann died at birth.

Bud suffered from rheumatoid arthritis for several years before his death from agranulucytosis at age fifty-four. Dora continued to grow chickens and cattle for several years and remained on the family farm. Dora was seventy-nine years old when she died from emphysema.

Of the four children, Rebecca D. Merrell and Steven live in Roopville, Linda D. Elkins in Jonesboro, and Beverly D. Kruse in Carrollton. Bud and Dora had six grandchildren and six great-grandchildren. *Submitted by: Nancy Merrell Edmondson, 74 Oswegatchie Road, Waterford, CT 06385*

Sources: Research by Rebecca Merrell, family Bible, family interviews.

499. William Byron Dean and Carrie Belle Bailey Dean

William Byron (Mann) was the oldest son of Joseph Green Dean and Mollie Taylor Dean. Mann was born March 15, 1891, died September 3, 1984.

Carrie, one of six children of Judge Lemuel (Lem) Bailey and Leila Beatrice Hardy Bailey, was born April 1, 1893, died May 22, 1966. Her mother Leila died October 2, 1903; Lem married Lilla Beatrice Barr Cumbie. Lem and Lilla had six children.

Mann and Carrie had three sons and one daughter. Clyde Edward was born August 30, 1913, died February 7, 1932; Hubert Arlin (Bud) Dean was born on May 4, 1915, died on March 30, 1970, married Dora E. Towns on November 11, 1937; Ruby Senus Dean was born on June 2, 1917, married Homer Boyd on September 3, 1938; and Joseph Lemuel (J.L.) Dean was born April 30, 1926, and died March 6, 1997, married Marie Perry, August 31, 1946.

Mann and Carrie first lived in Heard County, later moving to Tyus, and then Roopville, buying a farm on Highway 5. Life was not easy in the 1900s. Carrie had been the oldest child of the family and responsible for her siblings after the death of her mother. (Carrie was nine years of age.) Her father's second family and her children were about the same ages. Mann and Carrie struggled to provide for their family farming the property in Roopville. Mann and the boys were in the field early while Carrie and Senus prepared food for the day and then joined the men in the field. The family food came from the farm, vegetables from the garden and meat from the chickens, pigs, and/or cows they were able to raise each year.

Back: Dora, H. Arlin (Bud), J.L. Dean, Senus Boyd Front: Rebecca, Carrie, Linda, W.B. (Mann) Dean, Peggy Boyd

Clyde, the oldest son, had finished school and was helping his parents on the farm when in 1952 at the age of nineteen he died of appendicitis. This was an extremely difficult time for the family. Bud was seventeen and Senus fifteen and they continued to help their parents, leaving home when they married.

Bud and Dora remained in Roopville except for a few years when they lived in Atlanta, later coming back to Roopville to raise their four children, Rebecca, Linda, Steven, and Beverly. Senus and Homer moved to Sand Mountain, Alabama, and raised their two children, Peggy and Stewart.

In 1961 they decided to sell their farm and build a smaller home on the east side of their property. Judson Bell bought the farm and lives there today. Carrie and Mann called on Bud to build them a smaller two bedroom home. They prepared to celebrate their 50th wedding anniversary, which was September 26, 1962, in their new home. The proud couple welcomed their family and relatives to their home.

Following the death of Carrie, Mann remained in Roopville until 1969 when he moved to Lowell with his second wife, Minnie Baughtman, whom he married on November 21, 1969. He remained in Lowell until his death in 1984. *Submitted by: Steven G. Dean, 264 Old Carrollton Road, Roopville, GA and Researched by: Rebecca Merrell*

Sources: Family Bible and family interviews

500. Denney Family History 2001

In 1794 Edward Denney and his family moved to Elbert County, Georgia. It is believed that he was born about 1747, and that he came from Pennsylvania to Union County, South Carolina, in about 1772 before coming to Georgia. He married Jean Armstrong, daughter of Thomas and Sarah Armstrong. Edward served in Thomas Brandon's Second Spartan militia regiment during the Revolutionary War. He also operated the Denny Ferry from about 1799 until 1821 when he died. His descendants continued to operate the Denney Ferry across the North Fork of the Broad River which separated Elbert and Madison Counties.

Mary Elizabeth "Mollie" Yates (5-11-1866 - 4-21-1939) and Cullie Mitchell Denney (1-20-1860 - 12-3-1934).

Edward and Jean had the following children: David, Edward, Thomas, Robert, Jane, Catherine, and Margaret. Their first son, David, was born about 1785 in Georgia and he married Polly Ruff, December 21, 1807, in Elbert County, Georgia. The children of David and Polly are: Margaret, George Washington, Allen F., Stephen M., Nancy, William, James A., Mary A., and Dorcus F.

The seventh child of David and Polly was James A., born 1832, DeKalb County, Georgia, and he married Martha Angeline (Mary Ann) Patterson (born 7-12-1835) at Christmas time in 1852. James was 6'4" tall, 240 pounds and wore a size 16 shoe. His father died when he was 16 so he had to work hard in the family business (in Troup or Meriwether County) which included farming, milling, blacksmithing, and cattle raising. By 1861 James and Mary Ann had three children, Frank, John, and Cullie.

In 1862 James joined Company B of Cobb's Legion of the Confederate forces, leaving his beautiful, large house, wife and children. Because of his size and experience, he was given the duty of carrying a bellows on his back. He was shot in the abdominal area at the Battle of Perrysville. The only treatment he was given was a vinegar soaked handkerchief placed on the ramrod of a rifle and pushed through his body. He remained with the army until 4-13-1865, when the Southern forces surrendered at Appomattox Courthouse. When he left for home, he had no money, no shoes, and threadbare clothes. It took him three months to get home and then he found his house and mill destroyed and his farm had been sold by carpetbaggers for delinquent taxes. His wife hid with the children and a cow (for milk) in a cave during part of the war to escape the Yankees. Mary Ann killed small animals like rabbits and squirrels for food.

After the war they started over and bought a 202½ acre farm in Heard County (with gold that Mary Ann had managed to keep while James was away at war). They had six more children: James (born during the war), Lonnie, William, Charlie, Buna Vista, and Joseph Benjamin.

In October 1984 a ceremony was held to honor his memory and place a Confederate marker on his grave at Hopewell Primitive Baptist Church, Heard County. Cullie Mitchell Denney, born 1-20-1860, Troup County, married Mary Elizabeth (Mollie) Yates on 5-20-1881 in Heard County. Their children were: Arminda Elizabeth, William Eddie, Lewis Garvey, Bessie Cleo, Jefferson Franklin, Berta Zeola, Zelder Veno, Annie Belle, Lola Aline, Carey Nolan, and four infants who died.

Lewis Garvey was the third son of Cullie and Mollie. Garvey was born on 3-20-1890 in Heard County. He moved to Carroll County with his parents in 1910. He married Susie Mae Shadinger on 8-2-1914, Carroll County. Their children are: Lewis Everette, Merlin, Bernard Awtry, Annie Maureen, Garvey Melvin, Allene, James Donald and Millard Fillmore. Garvey was a farmer and he supplemented his income by working at the cotton gin and at the Bell Bomber Plant during World War II. He had a genuine interest in schools and he enjoyed Sacred Harp singing immensely. He was dedicated to his church, Emmaus Primitive Baptist Church, where he was ordained as a deacon in 1934. He depended on his faith, especially when his wife died in 1929 and during World War II when he had four sons in the Navy and one son-in-law in the Marine Sea-Bees. He married Kathleen Wilson in 1935 and they provided a good home for their children and the grandchildren spent many happy times with them.

Garvey Melvin was born 11-3-1923 in Carroll County and he married Doris Truitt on 1-6-1951. Doris (1926-1991) was the daughter of Archie and Annie Truitt. Melvin and Doris had two sons: Kenneth Melvin born 1957, and Russell Keith born 1958. They were both born in Carroll County. Melvin married Iva Robinson Benefield on 3-5-1993 in Newnan, Georgia, and he is retired from Southwire. *Submitted by: Melvin Denney, 156 Hubbard Springs Road, Carrollton, GA 30117 and researched and written by: Donald and Violette Denney*
Source: Family records

501. The Denney Home Place

No one stops anymore at the branch that runs across Denney Road to water their mule or wash their car. Denney Road is a little winding dirt road south of Carrollton, where descendants of Denneys and Shadingers have lived for the past century. The "Home Place," as it was called, is a fifty-acre farm down the road from the branch on Denney Road. The road had no name until the county decided a few years ago to put road signs on all county roads. It was simply Rural Route #3.

The Home Place consists of half of a 100-acre plot purchased in 1916 by William C. Shadinger (1857-1926), father of Bertie Shadinger Denney (1897-1994). Bertie S. and Jefferson (Jeff) Denney (1894-1977) became owners of this land shortly afterward; Jeff's brother, Garvey, and wife Susie Mae Shadinger Denney, became owners of the other half of the plot.

Jeff and Bertie grew cotton on their farm, as well as most of the family's food. Cotton brought three cents a pound and they were lucky to make three bales a year ($15 a bale). Four of their children (Howard 1917, Horry 1919, Hazel 1921, Herman 1923) were born at the Home Place.

The year Howard was born, December 1917, a freeze came before the cotton had opened well enough to pick. So Jeff pulled the cracked bolls and brought them into the house. By Christmas the cotton was dried and open enough to pull out, so they spent Christmas Day in front of the fire picking cotton. Bertie rocked the cradle holding her three week old baby with her foot while she picked cotton.

Bertie Shadinger Denney and Jefferson Denney, about 1913.

About 1925, Jeff and Bertie decided to move about a mile away on Highway 27, in order to have electricity. The remainder of their children were born here: Frank in 1925, and Frances in 1928. They still farmed the Home Place land, and Jeff's mother and father, Cullie (1860-1934) and Mollie Yates Denney (1866-1939) moved into the house.

After the death of Cullie and Mollie, Jeff and Bertie's son, Horry and his wife Nell, moved to the Home Place and farmed the land for awhile. Their son, Kemp (1939) was born in the old house, just as his father before him.

Jeff died in 1977. Granddaughter Diane Denney (Howard's daughter) and Allen Rooks continued the family tradition of farming the land. Corn was grown for awhile for use on their dairy farm, but it is now fenced in for cattle. Bertie gave her permission for the old house to be taken down before her death in 1994. The Rooks built a new farm house on the same site.

Today, in addition to the Rooks family, Joan Collins, and Laura Edwards, granddaughters of Jeff and Bertie, have homes on property adjoining the Home Place. Jane Denney Cooper owns part of the land near the branch, and great-grand children Jeff Rooks, Greg Denney, Salita Denney Parker, own adjoining land and homes. Sons of Garvey Denney (Everette, Bernard, Melvin) still live on Garvey's land.

The branch still runs across the road without a bridge covering it, and although Denney-Shadinger descendants no longer water their mule here, their children enjoy playing in its clear water. *Submitted by: Diane Denney Rooks, 321 Denney Road, Carrollton, GA 30117*

502. James Donald Denney Family

Once a country boy, always a country boy! My father, James Donald Denney, and mother, Violette Harris Denney, lived in Carroll County until they married. After marrying on February 24, 1951, in the little country church Bethany on Highway 61 they lived and worked in the Atlanta area. Actually they raised us in Chamblee and we graduated from Chamblee High School.

However, in the early 1960s when the Harris farm was sold to close the estate of W.S. and Mattie Harris, my parents (Donald and Violette) bought the section with the old family farm in which Violette's grandparents had lived since 1894. After renovating the house Terrell, the youngest son of W.S. and Mattie Harris, and Elma Harris (Violette's parents) made this their home until my grandmother died in 1982. Besides week-end visits, my brother Jeff and I usually spent a week with our grandparents during the summer. It was wonderful to have this time with Mama and Papa Harris.

Brandon, Joseph, Michael, and Zachary Denney - Thanksgiving 1997 in the country.

During our summer visits we heard a lot about "the good ole days" and how things used to be. We received special treatment but we knew to behave or we would wish we had when our parents came. Mama Harris liked to play Scrabble and Rook and she wanted to win, so we spent many hours playing and talking.

In the late 1960s we built a cabin on the farm. Daddy taught us how to build - we learned many valuable lessons which continue to help us maintain our homes today. In fact I built a room on our house in Roswell and my

Judy, Jeff, Violette, Donald, Tony, and Karen Denney, 2-24-2001.

son Michael helped me. Michael is eight so he couldn't handle some of the jobs and tools, but at least he was introduced to them.

We learned to drive in the country and it is very interesting to hear my brother Jeff talk about the trees moving when the pine needles on the ground are wet early in the morning. Before we got a well, we had to haul water. Actually Jeff hit a tree with Daddy's 1965 Chevrolet pick up truck. That old truck is still Daddy's favorite. He had it completely rebuilt during the late 1990s and still drives it.

Daddy and mother added some rooms to the cabin and moved back to Carroll County in 1983. And that made it possible for our children to go spend weeks with their grandparents. My oldest son died in 1976 as the result of an accident. He was named Scott and he was only seventeen months old. He is buried in Carroll Memory Gardens in Carroll County. My next son Joseph was born in 1979 and he now lives in Macon. I live with my wife Karen and our son Michael in Roswell.

Jeff and his wife Judy have two sons - Brandon and Zachary. They live in Lawrenceville. Brandon (13), Zachary (7), and Michael (9) still enjoy weeks in the country. Because my mother quilts, they always want to make something. So they come home with little wall quilts, towels with appliqué, etc. which we all enjoy. Seriously, we all like mother's quilts and we all have quilts on our beds and our walls! They also come home with things from daddy's garden or a flip made from a tree limb. Daddy lets them play cowboy and chase his cows. They really enjoy climbing in the trees and playing in the barn loft.

This year my daddy and mother celebrated their 50th Wedding Anniversary and we hosted a reception for them. This was a memory making experience for all of us. *Submitted by: Tony Denney, 915 Laurel Mill Drive, Roswell, GA 30076*

503. William Ray and Elizabeth Gore Dial Family

William "Ray" Dial was born March 2, 1938, in Floyd County, Lavender, Georgia. He married Elizabeth Ann Gore on July 27, 1956, in Carroll County at the home of Rev. Marvin George. Ray's parents are Earl Eugene Dial born December 11, 1912, in Haralson County, Georgia, died October 6, 1989, in Carroll County. He is buried at Star of Bethlehem Baptist Church in Paulding County, Georgia. Annie Grace Powell Dial born July 25, 1916, in Carroll County, Temple, Georgia. Ray has three brothers, Rev. Charles Eugene Dial, Donald Norton (deceased), Jerry Wayne, and one sister Glenda Sue Miller.

Elizabeth Ann "Liz" Gore was born July 27, 1941, in Cobb County, Georgia. Her parents are Wesley Lee Gore born February 18, 1909, in Douglas County, Georgia, died November 2, 1967, in Douglas County, and Julia Long Gore was born May 15, 1910, in Pickens County, Georgia, died November 16, 1997, in Carroll County. They are buried in Barber Cemetery, Mableton, Georgia. Liz has two sisters, Mary Helen Perryman (deceased) and Era June McCleary, three brothers, Wesley Lee Jr., Jackie Lenley, and Jimmy Lee Gore.

Ray is retired from the Automobile Repair Business which he owned and operated for many years. He and Liz attend Christ Cathedral Church in Winston, Georgia. Ray is an ordained minister and taught Sunday School for many years. He loves writing poetry. He and Liz love doing genealogy. They are always going to libraries and archives or to meet new cousins they have found. They have a great love for preserving family history so they can pass it down to future generations.

William Ray and Elizabeth Gore Dial

Ray and Liz have five daughters, Cindy Renae and Melinda Sue died shortly after birth. Cheryl Lynn married Douglas Merlin Braswell and they have two children, Jason and Jennifer. Donna Jean married Samuel P. George and they have three children, Brandon, Brent and Bryan. Melissa Anne married Perry Vance Hardegree and they have two children, Casey and Cary.

We are very proud of our families, parents, and grandparents. *Submitted by: Daughters Cheryl Braswell of Carrollton, GA, Donna George, 1073 Old Draketown Trail, Temple, GA, and Melissa Hardegree of Carrollton, GA.*

504. Samuel Carter Dickson Family

Samuel Carter Dickson (1817-1904) was a son of Stephen Dickson and Nancy White, who were born in Virginia and came to Georgia through South Carolina. Stephen Dickson's parents were Thomas Dickson and Martha Adams of Virginia. Nancy White's parents were William White and Mary Hooper. The Stephen Dickson family lived for a time in Franklin County, Georgia, and then migrated to Coweta County. Other children were Thomas Greene Dickson (1804-1845), married Elizabeth Herron; William White Dickson (1807-1881) married Lucinda Beadles; Wiley Pope Dickson (1809-1848) unmarried; and Stephen Light Dickson (1811-1880) married Elizabeth Jane DeVane.

Sam Dickson married Martha Matilda Neely, daughter of Jackson Neely and wife Sarah of Coweta County. Jackson and Sarah Neely migrated to Coweta from York District, South Carolina. Other children were Eliza W. (1813/14-1880) married James W. Carson; Sarah Jane (1815-?) married Charles J. Lyle; James Jackson (1818-1889) married Eliza Jane Mackey; and George W. (1829-?).

All the children of Samuel Carter Dickson and Martha Matilda Neely settled in Carroll County. Sarah S. (1849-1898) never married, and is buried at Midway Macedonia Church. Mary Virginia (1853-1921) married William Allen Eady; she is buried at Smith's Chapel. Wiley Pope (1856-1941) married Lula L. Brown; he is buried at Macedonia. Frances Elizabeth (1859-1935) married John Thomas Eady (see related article about this family). Lora Codova (1866-1947) married Thomas Galloway Johnston; she is buried at Macedonia. The Sam Dickson family lived in the Sand Hill area. Both parents are buried at Macedonia. *Submitted by: Brenda Harper Green, 417 Sand Hill-Shady Grove Road, Carrollton, GA 30116*

505. The Dobson Family

Family history alleges that the first Dobsons of the Carroll County line came from England on a ship carrying seven barrels of gold. Pirates boarded the ship, taking the gold, but leaving the passengers unharmed.

The Dobson family has been in Carroll County since 1837. John Ferdinand Dobson, born in Macon County, North Carolina, on June 8, 1808, purchased 135 acres from James McElrath on January 16, 1839, for $750. This land is located in the 6th District, lot 168. John F. Dobson continued to buy and sell land in Carroll County until his death in 1883.

John F. married Elizabeth (born 1814) on January 22, 1832, in North Carolina. They began their family in North Carolina with Joseph, Nancy (born 1836, married John Keese on July 27, 1856, in Carroll County) and Sarah (born 1838, married John T. Hawkins on October 13, 1857 in Carroll County). Their last child William Leander (or Lee Andrew) was born in Carroll County on March 10, 1845. John and his family appear in the Carroll County census beginning in 1840 and continuing through the 1880 census when John was listed as 72 and Elizabeth as 66. John F. died on August 27, 1883. His obituary notes that Reverend Dobson was licensed to preach in July 26, 1867.

William Leander (Lee Andrew) Dobson, son of John F. Dobson, continued to live in Carroll County. William enlisted in the Confederate Army on May 4, 1864, in the 1st Georgia Reserves, Company F, as a corporal under Col. Fannin. He served the Confederacy as a guard at Andersonville Prison and was discharged on May 6, 1865, in Albany. His children said that his unit had to retreat to Jacksonville, Florida, when Sherman invaded Georgia and that William had to walk all the way back home. He married Isabella Victoria Vinson on November 2, 1865, in Carroll County. They had ten children: Sarah Amanda (born November 26, 1866); Joseph A. (born November 22, 1868, died November 3, 1873); Martha Ophelia (born June 14, 1871, married Harrison); Andrew F. (born April 13, 1873, died August 15, 1958); Elmira (born February 27, 1876, married Thornton); Elizabeth (born August 21, 1881, died October 8, 1921); Benjamin (born March 21, 1881, died 1966), John Leander (born October 6, 1883, died July 18, 1966); George Washington (born May 25, 1886, died June 2, 1960) and Ida Nancy (born December 11, 1889, died May 14, 1925). Isabella Victoria (or Elizabeth) died January 30, 1891.

George and Adren Dobson, about 1913

William Leander (or Lee Andrew) Dobson married Annie Swint on June 4, 1891. They had four children: Alonzo Brooks (born June 14, 1892); Isabella Victoria (born January 6, 1894, married Brooks, died 1968); Emmett Sedone (born January 15, 1896, died 1901) and Albert Earl (born December 28, 1897, married Jewel Cook). After Annie's death William married Julia Logan Moncrief in 1907. William Leander (Lee Andrew) Dobson died on June 22, 1926, and is buried in Rockmart City Cemetery. Julia died on September 25, 1939.

George Washington Dobson, ninth child of William (and Isabella Victoria), was well known in the Bowdon community. Known as "Mr. George," he was soda jerk at Dr. Lovvorn's drugstore. Later he ran numerous restaurants including The Bowdon Cafe and Dobson's Cafe until his retirement. He returned to his original job as soda jerk at Dobson Rowell Drug until his death on June 2, 1960.

George Dobson married Adren Delaney Saxon of Randolph County, Alabama, on January 12, 1913. They established a home on Mill Street in Bowdon. Adren (born March 11, 1895, died April 11, 1977) was the daughter of Alfred Allen Saxon (born December 5, 1865, died May 2, 1922, in Carroll County, buried at Bowdon City Cemetery) of Randolph County, Alabama, and Mary Elizabeth Disharoon of Georgia. George and Adren had three children: Mary Elizabeth (born March 4, 1914, married James Lovvorn Rowell on June 12, 1936; G.W. Jr. (born December 5, 1917, died December 12, 1920); and Roy Edward (born January 21, 1925, married Mary Jo Arrington on December 23, 1945, died May 3, 1984).

Mary Dobson Rowell and James Lovvorn Rowell had two sons: James Lovvorn Rowell Jr., "Jimmy," (married Judy Carolyn Copeland) and George Edward Rowell, "Eddie," (married Jennifer Mount). Roy Edward Dobson was a Bowdon pharmacist and owned Dobson Rowell Drug and later Dobson Drug for many years. He and his wife, Mary Jo Arrington had three daughters: Deborah Lynn (married Bill Ivey); Jacqueline Anne (married Michael Chambers) and Mary Elizabeth.

Descendants of the Dobson family still live in the Bowdon area. *Submitted by: Jackie Dobson Chambers, 1234 Reavesville Road, Bowdon, GA 30108 and Written by: Deborah Dobson Ivey*

506. Dr. Thomas Andrew Dorsey

July 1, 1899 - January 23, 1993

Dr. Thomas Andrew Dorsey was born July 1, 1899 in Villa Rica, Georgia, to Rev. and Mrs. Thomas Madison and Etta Plant Dorsey. Rev. Dorsey was an itinerant preacher and Mrs. Etta was a respected member of the black middle class. She purchased a two acre lot, located where the Villa Rica Elementary School trailers now sit. After Thomas was born, the family moved to Atlanta. In 1903, when Rev. Dorsey realized that preaching alone was not going to support his family, they moved back to Villa Rica to again try farming. Etta, wanting to help her husband's ministry, purchased an organ. Dr. Dorsey said later that this played an important part in his music career.

In 1908, the Dorseys again moved to Atlanta where Thomas first heard blues singers like Gertrude "Ma" Rainey and Bessie Smith. By age twelve, he was playing the piano. His first blues song was *A Good Man is Hard to Find.* Dorsey attended Morehouse College, but received the nicknames "Barrelhouse Tom" and "Georgia Tom" by playing on the blues circuit.

Dorsey moved to Chicago in 1916, where he worked in steel mills and attended Chicago Musical College. Never forgetting his Christian upbringing, he wrote *Stand by Me* and *If I Don't Get There* in 1920, the first of what he called Gospel songs.

In early 1932, Dr. Dorsey along with Theodore Frye and Magnolia Butts formed the National Convention of Gospel Choirs and Choruses, Inc. On August 26, he went to St. Louis to preside over the convention and received a telegram that his wife had died in childbirth. He hurried back home, but the next day his son, Thomas Andrew Dorsey Jr., also died. A few days later he let his fingers browse over the keys of a piano and he said "I found myself playing a melody I'd never heard or played before, and the words just came into my head." The song was *Take My Hand, Precious Lord* and is the most popular Gospel song ever. It has been translated into thirty-two languages and recorded by over five hundred artists.

This Villa Rica native, whose boyhood church was Mt. Prospect Baptist church, was the first Black to be awarded the Nashville Songwriters Association International Hall of Fame Award in 1979. He also received a Grammy Award for Lifetime Achievement in 1992 and the Illinois Governor's Award for the Arts in 1985. He was inducted into the Songwriters Hall of Fame in New York in 1982, The Georgia Music Hall of Fame in 1981, and the Gospel Music Association Living Hall of Fame in 1982. He received Doctors Degree of Humane Letters from Fisk University, Selma, and Howard University in 1982.

Dr. Thomas A. Dorsey died Saturday, January 23, 1993, in Chicago, Illinois. Sunday, February 14, 1993 was declared "Thomas Dorsey Day" in Villa Rica. Each year a festival is held in Villa Rica, the Saturday on or before his birthday, to honor and commemorate Dr. Thomas Dorsey. *Submitted by: Zelma McKinney, Villa Rica, GA 30180 and Written by: Charles Hudson, 945 S. Lassetter Circle, Villa Rica, GA 30180*

507. Douglas - Jennings Family

Charles Morrow Douglas, son of Joseph Douglas (born 1833) and Sarah Morrow Douglas (circa 1848-1888), was born 2-28-1886 and died 3-5-1954. He married Clara Irene Jennings, daughter of Henry Grady Jennings (1849-1931) and Edith Frances Young Jennings (1866-1938). Clara Jennings Douglas was born 2-16-1894 and died 9-1-1932. All of them, except Charles' parents, are buried in St. Paul Methodist Church cemetery in Whitesburg.

Hoyt, Doris, Wyolene, and Charles Douglas in a Hoover Cart

Family tradition has it that Charles Douglas' father, Joseph, emigrated from Scotland at the age of twelve by stowing away on a boat bound for America. He died when Charles, his younger son, was an infant, and his wife died soon thereafter. Charles and his brother Joseph Lang Douglas (1883-1921) were raised in Carroll County by their mother's sister, Elizabeth Strickland. Charles' brother Lang died at age thirty-eight while he and another man were cleaning a well. The well filled with methane gas and the other man was overcome. When Lang went into the well to rescue him, he perished also.

In 1864, when Gen. Sherman issued an order to seize and burn New Manchester Manufacturing Company in Campbell (now Douglas) County, Clara Jennings Douglas' grandfather, Gideon J. Jennings (born 1819), was among those arrested and deported to Indiana. None of the women captured by the troops ever found their way back home after the internment and only a handful of the men, though Gideon, a machinist, was one of the few who did. Clara Jennings Douglas' father, Henry Grady, then a teenager listed on the militia census of 1863 as not yet drafted into military service, was also working at the mill. He recalled hiding from the soldiers, thus avoiding capture. The destruction of New Manchester is a little known wartime atrocity, an act of senseless violence against civilians.

Charles Morrow Douglas suffered repeated loss and disappointment in his life. He never remarried after Clara's death. He sacrificed to keep his family together and raise his children to adulthood. Although he had little formal education, he tried to keep himself informed and always had reading material in the home. Clara Douglas was a kind, happy person, always thoughtful of others. Charles and Clara Douglas provided for their family by farming. On the day before her death, Clara Douglas was digging sweet potatoes and piling them on a wagon, despite advanced pregnancy.

Charles and Clara Douglas had eight children. Henry Joseph (1912-1973) married Margie Morris. Sarah Josephine (1914-1990) married Curtis Lambert. Winnie Mae (1915-2000) married Ralph Burson. Grady (1917-1918) died in infancy. Mary Ruth (1919-1995) married Edgar Johnson Wessinger Jr., Hoyt Hill (1920-1978) married Vivian Nix, Doris Helen (1922-1938) died at age fifteen, Wyolene (born 1932) married Marvin Daugherty. *Submitted by: Wyolene D. Daugherty, 75 Fuller Drive, Carrollton, GA 30117*

Sources: *The Destruction of New Manchester, Georgia,* monograph by Monore M. King

508. George L. Downs (1871-1940)

"Reviewing Thirty Years Service as a Rural Mail Carrier"

From *Bowdon Bulletin,* Thursday, August 13, 1936

"My Service as a Carrier for R.F.D. No. 4, Bowdon, Ga., started August 1, 1907; the Star route was 24 miles long and carried me in two states and three counties six days a week. At first I survived using my faithful mule and buggy, but the mule had farmed so long she never realized the importance of getting letters to their destination quickly. I traded her for two good horses to whom I must pay tribute here: John and Mack.

"Soon, volume demanded a modern U.S. Mail Wagon, painted white, with oil lamps on either side. I traveled at the astonishing speed of six miles per hour. Next the Ford car was commandeered and my route lengthened to 40 miles, growing to 62 miles these last two years. Change has been tremendous. The road with its many creeks to ford became a paved highway with concrete bridges; I have memories of pick and shovel, chains and mule teams to pull the mail vehicle out of the ruts and the ditches.

"My mileage for the thirty years was 390,000 miles, or enough to have driven around the earth at the equator about twelve and one-half times. I delivered 3,228,000 pieces of mail. In the 30 years I served about 45,000 individuals. The grim

George Downs, Mail Carrier R.F.D. No. 4, Bowdon. 30 years.

reaper took its toll, and I am made sad. The faces from my first rounds have all been removed except six, but in death there is life. Boys and girls who greeted me in the early days have grown up, wooed and wed; now their children's children turn smiling faces and offer cookies in return for their mail.

"There was much of human interest, such as delivering messages by the grapevine method. Sickness must be reported, and sweethearts' dates have to be made. All marriages are told to the mail carrier and have you heard the news? Doctor is sent for, and stork reports do not necessarily go by mail. Public meetings, road workings, pound suppers, and raising money for the church organ may be announced by the mail man — for he passes there anyhow.

"In 1916 when the call to arms came, I delivered the official letters which called the boys to service. Later came messages from 'somewhere in France', and for some the sad news that no more messages would ever come.

"I clearly recognize the blessing of the Father above in giving me strength to carry on. There were hailstorms, lightning, thunder, cyclones, tornadoes, and snow but the mail must go. I lost but two days during my time because of my own sickness, and for this I am thankful. I appreciate the friendships made. They stand out as flowers to brighten my pathway the rest of the journey. I pray that my life may have touched yours and made someone's way happier."

Submitted by: Betty Lou Crocker, 3020 Pinehill Rd., Montgomery, AL 36109

509. The Living Room

A Story About the Home of George L. Downs 1930-1990

Why did they call it the living room? Well, Grandmother Downs did call it the parlor instead of the living room. "If you children don't stay out of there, you'll be sorry!" was heard by me and my cousins from all the adults. We certainly could not LIVE in the living room.

The Downs house, the home of George Luna Downs and Hettie Lipham Downs at Bowdon, Georgia, was a wonderful place for all the Downs grandchildren - ten offspring of four of the six Downs children. It was a large house with four bedrooms, living room, dining room, a huge kitchen and a wide front-to-back hall. Each bedroom had two double beds, except the "little room" that was Grandmother and Grandpa's bedroom, which contained a double bed, dresser, trunk, wall pegs and storage boxes. The "little room" was another semi-off-limits room. A cot was in the hallway, enough room for everyone. Porches extended across the front and rear of the house and two porch swings were out front.

Evie Lee, my mother, was the oldest Downs girl and married the oldest Johnson boy, William Johnson Jr., who lived across the road (College Street). My daddy was named for Will T. Johnson Sr., his father, who owned Johnson's Store (College and Johnson Street) where you could buy anything that was needed for life or death, so I was told. It was all gone before I was born and the store had become Bowdon Auto Supply, owned by Jim Smith, who later married Mother's sister Mary Downs.

Mother, Daddy, Isabelle and Eleanor were all born in Bowdon but I was born after they had moved to Atlanta, Georgia. I'm glad they liked to go back home to visit in Bowdon.

During my early childhood, I thought I was unfortunate enough to have two older sisters - Isabelle, nine years my senior and Eleanor, five years older than me. They loved me dearly but most times seemed to be against what I wanted to do. Small wonder, I was always getting into something. Actually, they were nice to have around to clean and doctor my scrapes and bruises and they read me stories and taught me neat songs that are still sung to me by my own grandchildren.

We Johnsons were three of the ten cousins that went to Grandmother's during the summer vacations. Aunt Ruth Downs Wilson, married to William Rhudy Wilson, a railroad track and signal foreman, had three girls. Carolyn was a few months older than I and Eloise and Betty Lou were "little" girls. I remember at an early age when Aunt Ruth was giving baby Betty Lou a bath, I was allowed to watch and I found out what girls were and what they weren't too. I was fascinated, until I was shooed out of the kitchen. Uncle Charles Emory Downs and his wife, Aunt Ruby had two girls, Laura Helen was a few months younger than I, and Sylvia who was the youngest of all my cousins.

Uncle Olin Downs and Aunt Mary Downs did not get married until later in life and their marriages did not produce children.

Aunt Mildred Downs married what Grandmother at first referred to as "That Yankee from up North." Uncle Warren Steele did talk funny but he was a great guy. Later after their twin boys, Ulyssis and Novice, were born and old enough, he would take all of the cousins down to Lovvorn's Mill and we got to go swimming in the Indian Creek. Of course Ulysses and Novice, just a little older than Sylvia, were too young to be fun to play with. They always wanted to tag along and tried to do what we did. That meant they got hurt or felt left out and in either case always ended up crying. Guess who always got blamed? We were!

By this time, my sisters were young ladies and the "we" that I'm talking about are Carolyn, Laura Helen, Eloise, Betty Lou and me. Sometimes even Eloise and Betty Lou were left out. Not so for Carolyn, Laura Helen and me. We were the closest three of the bunch. After all we were all practically the same age. PALS! Then things began to happen for us that we did not like or understand. Aunt Ruby and Uncle Charles Emory moved to Silvertown, Georgia, when we were ten years old. What happened? We did not see Laura Helen much and she seemed almost like a stranger when they did come back home. We never really got to know Sylvia due to that move.

When Laura Helen visited, at least we got to see her and the younger cousins were growing old enough to be more compatible with what we liked to do. Some neighbor friends would come over and we had great times playing Fox and Hounds, Hiding Seek, Monopoly, Kick the Can, Hop Scotch, Jacks and many others. If the girls started playing paper dolls I quickly lost interest and turned to other pursuits. If we got tired of playing the active games we made "frog houses" in the sand pile or took turns on the plowrope swing that hung on a limb of the big oak tree between the house and driveway. What a carefree, happy time we had during those days.

Pals. Cousins Laura Helen, George, and Carolyn. About 1939.

It always has to rain at some time or other. This was a rural community and the farmers had to have rain. Even though they lived in town, both Grandmother and Grandpa had farms. Grandmother's was "down on the creek" and Grandpa's was "over in Alabama" (I never really knew where). I'm sure the days when the children were indoors were harder on the adults than us but we didn't know that then. Sometimes we even got to play in the living room.

There was a wind-up Victrola that played thick seventy-eight speed records, a piano with four pedals (one gave it a real tinny sound that Grandmother said sounded cheap), also a soft carpet to sit on and play indoor games. On occasion we would sneak in some roughhousing (if we didn't get too loud), like bouncing on the sofa or a "quiet" game of tag. Did you ever get a switching for just playing some dumb game? Well I did, because it was not allowed in the living room.

When I was nearing thirteen, the living room became something quite different to me. It became a place of death. My mother died in Atlanta but her beautiful casket was brought to Bowdon and placed next to the three front windows of that room. She looked so pretty and just asleep. I wanted her to talk to me, even more I wanted to tell her things I should have said last week, but didn't. Like, "I love you!", "I'm sorry I haven't been a better boy," and other thoughts that now I only could think - not expressing to anyone because my throat was too tight and dry. I knew that she was in Heaven, and she knew that I would join her there because I had accepted Jesus the past spring. Still the big question, "Why did you die?" The knowledge that I would see her again did not stop the pain of a twelve year old boy, nor did it help me to see the others that I loved feel the same pain that hurt them like it hurt me. Mother died from pneumonia in 1938, the year before sulfa drugs became available. The memories of happier times did help me some and the newness of time's passing experiences have softened what I felt, but even now some hurt is still there.

In quick succession, other members of our happy group followed my mother in death. After Mother's funeral, I heard Grandpa Downs say "I've outlived one of my children. I guess I'm next." He was! Grandpa also died of pneumonia. Next was Aunt Ruth, who was most like Mother's gentle loving personality. She died of an epileptic seizure during her sleep. These three deaths occurred during the time span of March 15, 1938, Mother's death; May 5, 1940, Grandpa's death; and July 27, 1940, when Aunt Ruth died. All of them lay in state in the living room.

These deaths had a profound effect on my life. I wish I could say I was strengthened and improved by them but the opposite was true, for a time at least. Mother's absence from our family life was felt deeply by Daddy, my two sisters and me. My daddy never recovered from the loss of his cherished wife and it caused an outlook of melancholy, combined with the feeling of his not having been able to protect her from her sickness. My older sisters seemed to be more resilient and tried to help all of us to still be a family, even as their interests outside the home were expanding.

How could I console my cousins and grandmother when all I could feel was that they, like me, were left alone and would have this area of aloneness for the remainder of our lives. We could cry together, but I knew this would not solve any problems that our daily lives were faced with - the void of Mother's love at every moment of need. How could I console when I felt it was me who needed to be consoled! My grief was trapped inside. Subsequent visits to Grandmother Down's were still a time of happiness and closeness but not carefree like before when we were small children. Some of the time on these visits was always spent in remembering what we did in earlier years. These returns to happier times were good for us all and helped bridge the gap of growing older and its diverse interests.

One of these diversities was an interest in the opposite sex, girls for me and boys for my girl cousins. For me, another consuming hobby was building model airplanes. What a challenge to build something that would fly - sometimes up and away enough that the plane would disappear forever. I did not know if it had ever come down, at least in one piece. The varieties of interests, being active teenagers, kept us from visiting Grandmother as often as we could and should have. Now as a grandfather myself, I see what a visit would have meant to Grandmother in her later years, especially after Uncle Olin and Aunt Mary had married and moved away from home.

I did work for Uncle Olin in his Bowdon Rexall Drug store one summer (1943) and lived at Grandmother's once again. Working from seven o'clock in the morning until six in the evening, on week days and seven until nine on Saturdays, kept me pretty well occupied. Still I had time to do some plumbing) a water line out to the horse trough) and rebuilding of the front porch flooring. It made me feel good when Grandmother would ask "George are you sure you can do that?" and then brag on me for good job I did when it was finished. Uncle Olin gave me good training too. He taught me the importance of doing a good job, even if it was a menial task. He was a great fox hunter and liked to hunt rabbits too. He made me very proud when he took me rabbit hunting and his one quick shot got the only rabbit among the five of us hunting together. Sitting around the camp fire and listening to the fox hounds "talk" was an experience that I still recall.

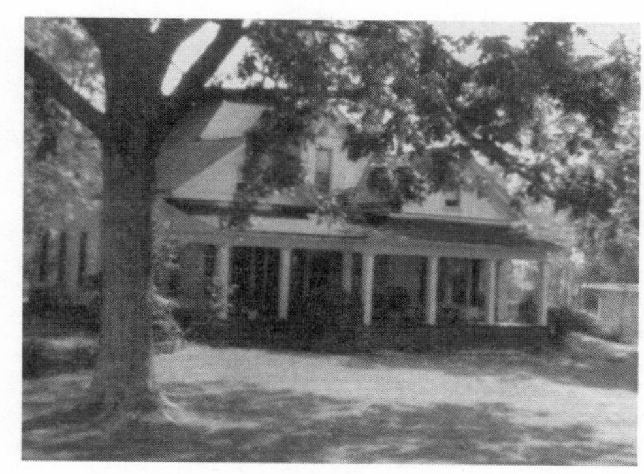

The Downs House, Bowdon, GA 1907-1952

The years of World War II (Air Force service), marriage, finding work and housing after the war, added schooling, my own three sons, and daily living, all took time and held my interest over years that were passing faster than I realized. Limited visits and a few phone calls were made, but the passage of much time flew by. Many changes took place in all our lives. After an extended illness on October 11, 1952, Hettie Lipham Downs died. Hers was a life given in loving and guiding her children and grandchildren and working so others could have what she had to give - herself. Suddenly it was gone! Grandmother's house in Bowdon was to be sold!

Others, too, are now only in our memories - a long list - Daddy, Uncle Charles Emory and Aunt Ruby Downs, Uncle Olin Downs, Uncle Jim Smith and Aunt Mary Downs Smith, Uncle Rhudy Wilson, Tommy Bolan (Carolyn's husband), cousin Laura Helen Downs Newbern, brother-in-law Paul J. Eldredge (Eleanor's husband), Norman Downey (Eloise's husband), cousin Novice R. Steele, and brother-in-law Sam and sister Isabelle Johnson Whatley. Deaths in our spouse's families could be added to our list but are not related to this story of the living room except by being our loved ones. All were important pieces of life's jigsaw puzzle.

The house containing the living room, the Downs house, has been sold out of the family. It is now known as the "Downs/Hicks" house. On one visit to Bowdon, the Hicks family said I was welcome to visit, which I have done on several occasions. It is as if they now have an interest in continuing the tradition of keeping love of one's family as part of their living - at this place where we all spent times in our lives being guided and loved.

On my last visit to Bowdon, we drove out on the bank parking lot now next door to Grandmother's house, and saw a small girl playing in the side yard. What a pleasure it was to realize that this girl, the Hicks's little daughter, without even being aware of what was happening, was in an expanded "living room." Not just one house but a time of her life, not meaningful until later in life when the mind expands and better understands what is stored forever in the heart. Thank you God for my "Living Room"! *Submitted by: George William Johnson, 355 Saddle Lake Drive, Roswell, GA 30076*

Sources: Personal experiences and Downs/Johnson family history

510. Hettie B. Lipham Downs

John Monroe Lipham and Sarah Sophronia Davis, daughter of Joshua Davis and Martha Trammel Davis, married in Heard County, Georgia, on October 10, 1854. By the time the 1870 census was taken, they were living in Randolph County, Alabama, and had six children. The oldest was my great-grandfather, William Franklin Lipham.

The Liphams were close neighbors in Randolph County to Isham Bailey Lee, son of John Lee and Temperance Knight Lee, and Mary Alice Weathers Lee, daughter of Jessie Weathers and Elizabeth Reeves Weathers. One of the Lee daughters, Sarah Vida Lee, married William F. Lipham on October 22, 1874. Both were eighteen years old at the time.

Their daughter, Hettie Beatrice Lipham, was born the next year near Rock Mills, Alabama, on September 27, 1875. The young mother did not recover from childbirth. Ten days later, on October 8, Sarah V. Lee Lipham was dead. She was buried in the Lee family cemetery behind the farm home of her parents near Rock Mills.

Hettie's grandmother, Sarah Sophronia Lipham, also had a new baby girl and she nursed Hettie along with her own child. Hettie told her children many times about living with her Lipham grandparents until she was about three years old. She felt close to them as if they had been her real parents.

On September 23, 1877, William F. Lipham married Charlotte Stewart (Merrill) Reeves. She was the widow of C.J. Reeves, and had one son Herman J. Reeves, who was born April 16, 1872.

Around 1878, the John W. Lipham family and the William F. Lipham family left Randolph County, Alabama, to settle in Haralson County, Georgia, on Tallapoosa River farmland. By 1880 Hettie was living in the home of her father and stepmother.

On October 25, 1889, at the age of thirty-four, William Franklin Lipham died of pneumonia. He is buried near Tallapoosa, Georgia, near Pleasant Hill Cemetery along with five infant children. Hettie, the oldest of his six surviving children, was twelve years old at the time. She remembered that she was not allowed in the sick room but through the window glass could see her father lift his hand and wave to her.

In January of the same year that he died, William Lipham had bought Carroll County farmland near Bowdon, Georgia. He and Charlotte had made the trip from Haralson County by buggy many times during those months, working on the house and farm preparing to move. Some months after his death, Charlotte finished the house and brought their children to live there.

On June 26, 1893, Hettie Lipham married George Luna Downs of Bowdon, Georgia (born July 29, 1871) He was the son of James Wesley Downs Sr. (born July 24, 1831, died October 11, 1900, Bowdon) and Hettie Jane Cockrell Downs (born June 10, 1832, died November 9, 1911, Bowdon).

William Franklin Lipham

James W. Downs was one of the seven Bowdon citizens who suffered financial hardships in 1872 by the failure of the Savannah, Griffin, and North Atlantic Railroad Company to come to Bowdon. The others were John B. McDaniel, George A. McDaniel, John W. Adamson, Nathaniel Shelnutt, W.F. Johnson and J.B. Merrill. They had jointly signed a note for money to assure the building of the tracks to Bowdon. This did not materialize. The note was called and the seven were left with ruinous debt during the height of reconstruction and with nothing to show for it. This caused the whole town to suffer a staggering blow. Hopes were dashed for a booming economy.

On October 9, 1871, James W. Downs was granted a patent on an improved plow. There was an advertisement in the August 2, 1872, *Carroll County Times* stating that orders for this plow could be left at Mr. Down's store.

Hettie and George Downs had six children, all born in Bowdon. They were: (1) Evie Lee Downs born August 6, 1894, died March 16, 1938, Atlanta, Georgia. She married William Thomas Johnson of Bowdon who was born November 15, 1884, in Bowdon and died February 11, 1943, in Atlanta. They had three children: Charlsie Isabelle Johnson born October 25, 1917, in Bowdon, died February 4, 2001, in Marietta; Eleanor Johnson born March 22, 1921, in Bowdon, and George William Johnson born February 6, 1926, in Atlanta.

(2) Edna Ruth Downs (my mother) who was born March 21, 1897, died July 27, 1940, in Montgomery, Alabama, married on June 8, 1921, to William Rhudy Wilson who was born May 14, 1898, in Randolph County, Alabama, and died April 15, 1977, in Montgomery, Alabama. Rhudy Wilson was a descendant of William Calhoun of Ninety-Six District, South Carolina. William was a Revolutionary soldier and uncle of John C. Calhoun, the great Southern statesman. William Calhoun was also a survivor of the Long Cane Massacre by Cherokee Indians in 1769 near what is now Abbeville, South Carolina, but his mother Catherine Montgomery Calhoun and two of his daughters were killed. A third daughter, five year old Anne Calhoun, was captured and held prisoner for a number of years. Years later (the number is uncertain), she was returned to her people during a treaty with the Cherokees signed by General Andrew Pickens.

On October 12, 1784, Anne married Issac Mathews who later became a Revolutionary soldier. Anne Calhoun is listed on the D.A.R. Patriot list for her contribution to the war effort. She and Issac had four children, one of whom was Joseph Calhoun Mathews. One of his daughters, Martha Lorine Mathews, married Samuel Sheals Wilson. They were the parents of George Albert Wilson, father of Rhudy Wilson. Ruth and Rhudy Wilson had three children: Carolyn Jeanice Wilson who was born June 18, 1925, in Bowdon; Eloise Wilson who was born December 18, 1929, in Bowdon; and Betty Lou Wilson born April 25, 1932, in Century, Florida.

(3) William Olin Downs born January 9, 1899, died October 21, 1961, in Bowdon, married Lucille Wyatt Alexander of Centralhatchee, Georgia. They had no children.

(4) Charles Emory Downs born June 14, 1901, died August 8, 1972, Thomaston, Georgia, married Ruby Barwick who was born April 3, 1899, in Soperton, Georgia, died September 10, 1981, in Thomaston, Georgia. They had two children: Laura Helen Downs, born February 16, 1927, in Bowdon, died January 18, 1989, in Valdosta, Georgia; and Sylvia Gay Downs born September 18, 1936, in Thomaston, Georgia.

(5) Mary Jeanice Downs born September 2, 1906, died October 23, 1990, married Jim Smith, who was born December 17, 1893, in Wedowee, Alabama, died September 26, 1972, in Bowdon. They had no children but Jim and his first wife, Lula Barrett Smith, had three children — Margaret Smith, Julian Barrett Smith, and James Robert Smith.

(6) Mildred Helen Downs born January 23, 1912, died May 7, 1998, at Ft. Walton Beach, Florida, married the Reverend Warren Hugh Steele, an educator and Episcopal priest. Steele was born April 7, 1909, in Nauvoo, Pennsylvania, and died February 4, 1983, at Ft. Walton Beach. They had twin boys, Ulysses "Lis" Moody Steele and Novice "Nobby" Richard Steele born February 4, 1934, in Wellsville, New York. Nobby died August 25, 1997, at Ft. Walton Beach.

George and Hettie Downs lived in Bowdon for all their married life. They each had a farm and he was a rural mail carrier for thirty years. His route was into Alabama through Ranburne. George died of pneumonia on May 5, 1940, and Hettie died on October 11, 1952. Both are buried in the City Cemetery in Bowdon. Their home was a happy place, bursting at the seams with aunts, cousins, children, friends, and friends of friends. Everyone was always welcome. Many of the Downs children and grandchildren spent every summer in Bowdon during the 1930s and 1940s and also every holiday possible. To me, it will always be home.

Hettie B. Lipham Downs, about 1887.

Through her father's family, Hettie Lipham Downs' ancestors can be traced to John, King of England, who granted the Magna Carta in 1215 and also to nine of the twenty-five barons who became sureties for its execution. This line is traced through the Davis family. One of Hettie's ancestors, Col. William Davis of Dinwiddie County, Virginia, a Revolutionary soldier, married Agnes Lanier of the Virginia Laniers. Her grandfather, Samson Lanier Sr. married Elizabeth Washington of Surry County, Virginia, who had a mutual ancestor with George Washington. He was Lawrence Washington of Sulgrave Manor, Northampton, England. Through Lawrence Washington's marriage into the Butler family, the descent from King John and nine of the barons of Runnymede is traced.

Hettie Lipham Downs' granddaughter, Laura Helen Downs Newbern, joined The Descendants

Olin, Evie, and Ruth Downs (seated) 1900.

of The Knights of the Garter and The National Society of Magna Carta Dames through this line. Hettie Downs' descendants are also eligible for the D.A.R. through Col. William Davis, and for the Colonial Dames of America in the Commonwealth of Virginia through Samson Lanier Jr., John Washington of Surry County, Virginia, and John Flood.

John Flood came to Virginia in *The Swan* in 1610. He was a Burgess, Flowerdewe Hundred, Weyanoke, and Westover, 1632; Burgess, James City, 1643, 1645, 1646, 1652, 1656; Captain, Militia 1643; Lieutenant Colonel 1652; Colonel, 1653. John Flood was the father of Mary Flood Blunt Ford who married John Washington.

Several Downs descendants have joined the Huguenot Society through the Laniers who had been musicians in the courts of Henry II of France, Elizabeth I of England, King James I, and Charles I of England. Their art collections were legendary. The Laniers were Royalists during the English Civil War, and when Cromwell came into power their fortunes fell drastically. Many, including our ancestor John Lanier, became immigrants to America. There are thousands of these Laniers in the South today. In fact, they are said to cover Dixie like the dew. *Submitted by: Eloise Wilson Downey, 403 Thorn Place, Montgomery, AL 36106*

Sources: Family records, census records, D.A.R. papers of Mary Downs Smith; *Descendants of Knights of the Garter;* papers of Laura Helen Downs Newbern; *Register of Ancestors - The National Society of the Colonial Dames of America in the Commonwealth of Virginia; Lanier* by Louise Ingersoll; *Liphams — Old, Young, and In-Between* by Clarice S. Cox; *John C. Calhoun: American Portrait* by Margaret L. Coit; *Calhoun, Hamilton, Baskin and Related Families* by Lewis Dwinell McPherson.

511. A Grandchild's Remembrance: Hettie Lipham Downs The Years 1945-52, Bowdon, GA

It was summer at Grandmother Down's house. The kitchen was hot near the great iron woodstove but cool as I entered the dining room and halls. The whitewashed fireplace, clean-smelling, felt good to my touch, and every morning Grandmother sat there to comb her white hair, pinning up the long strands finally with twin pearl combs.

On those sultry days, I would take long drinks of water from the tin dipper, cold water, drawn not from a tap but from the porch well. And since then I've not had such satisfying gulps again.

Sometime the stove was hot because teacakes were baking. It was at these times the

1950 - Jeanne Whatley age 11, Hettie Lipham Downs age 75.

kitchen assumed a different and promising fragrance. Some of Grandmother's cookies would turn out thin and crisp, others a little softer, and I never knew for sure which I liked best.

My favorite seat was in the dining room, near the fireplace and her chair. From this throne I could spy the muscadine jungle out the side window and watch Grandmother's pet sing his canary songs. I could admire for the hundredth time the plates and pitchers in the bowfront china cabinet and keep watch over the handsome black and walnut crank phone, in case someone called on the party line. If so inclined, I could even mount a chair and proudly ring my aunt Mary, the town's lone telephone operator, just two blocks away in town.

This place, so many years ago, had a specialness about it: a rarity (for didn't I come from a very different world?). These people cared, they worked, laughed and talked together. Family was the key: who you were, who your folks were.

At Bowdon cemetery: "Do you think they know we're here?"

Mostly, though, there was time — a child's sense of timelessness — and a non-city style of communication. There was time for afternoon naps, for evenings passed on the wide front porch with both swings creaking to the rhythm of cousinly stories and harmless gossip.

There was food too, enough always for one more or five more. Maybe I wanted to invite my friend Peggy (Roop) to spend the night. Peggy and her friend and maybe her friend's friend were welcomed as well.

We were rich, though not in dollars. Didn't Grandmother always have a nickel in the sugar bowl for a grandchild to "go to town"? Convinced that she, as least, was rich, I accepted her gift like an heiress and banked heavily on our family name with the local merchants, somehow bolstered by being known as Miss Hettie's grandchild.

> "Isn't she getting big! Why I remember her mama about that age. I tell you, years sure do get by, and the older I get the faster they go."

Submitted by: Great-grandchild Jeanne Whatley Baldwin, 2400 Carrington Way, S.E., Marietta, GA 300367

512. Downs - Wilson

One of the beautiful social fairs of the season was the wedding of Miss Ruth Downs and Mr. W. Rhudy Wilson at the Baptist church Wednesday, June the 8th, at 6 o'clock in the presence of a host of friends and relatives.

The church was beautifully decorated in pink, green, and white for the occasion.

A musical program was rendered just before the ceremony by Mrs. Talmadge Martin and Miss Myrl Whatley.

Entering before the bridal party, a group of the bride's pupils came singing the bridal chorus and took their places forming a lovely background for the bride and her attendants.

Just before the ceremony, Miss Cleo Stone sang "Because".

The ushers came first, two abreast, down the side aisles taking their places outside the large improvised columns. The Rev. W.W. Roop came next, then the attendants, Misses Ela and Odessa Johnson and Messrs. Luther Johnson and Griggs Swann.

The maid of honor, Miss Mary Downs, sister of the bride, entered alone followed by the little flower girls, Misses Katherine Wilson and Addie Morris.

The bride was given in marriage by her brother, Mr. Olin Downs, and was met at the altar by the groom and his best man, Mr. Taylor Wilson.

Little Isabel Johnson, niece of the bride, was ringbearer.

Rev. W.W. Roop of Carrollton read the very impressive double ring ceremony .

The bride and groom left immediately for a short stay in Atlanta before going to Wedowee where they will make their home.

This article, from my Grandmother Ruth Downs Wilson's scrapbook, is from the June 1921 edition of the *The Bowdon Bulletin.*

Ruth was the daughter of George Luna and Hettie Lipham Downs of Bowdon, Georgia. She met William Rhudy Wilson in 1918 while teaching in the New Hope Community near Rhudy's home in Randolph County, Alabama. She lived in Wedowee and made the trip to New Hope daily by horse and buggy.

Rhudy Wilson and his brother Taylor had a mercantile firm, Wilson Brothers, in Wedowee. It proved to be unsuccessful due to selling on credit. Rhudy eventually went with the Louisville and Nashville Railroad and they lived in many

Ruth Downs Wilson, 1916

south Alabama towns and in New Orleans before finally setting in Montgomery, Alabama.

Ruth and Rhudy Wilson had three daughters: (1) Carolyn Jeanice Wilson, my mother, was born June 18, 1925, in Bowdon. (2) Eloise Wilson was born December 18, 1929, in Bowdon. (3) Betty Lou Wilson was born April 25, 1932, in Century, Florida.

Ruth Wilson died unexpectedly in her sleep at the age of forty-three on July 27, 1940, in Montgomery, Alabama. She is buried in the Bowdon City Cemetery.

William Rhudy Wilson, 1921

William Rhudy Wilson married second to Irma DeLoach, born March 31, 1906, in Vida, Alabama. They had one son, William Rhudy Wilson Jr., born September 25, 1945, in Montgomery, Alabama.

Rhudy died on April 15, 1977, in Montgomery, and is buried there in the Masonic section of Greenwood Cemetery. Irma DeLoach Wilson is ninety-five years old (May of 2001) and lives in Montgomery. *Submitted by: Maureen Bolan Carroll, 314 East Wyngate Drive, Augusta, GA 30907*

Sources: *The Bowdon Bulletin,* Family Bible, cemetery records and personal knowledge.

513. Doyal Family

The Doyal family of Villa Rica, Georgia, has operated a general store in this area for five generations. People come by every day to see one of the remaining family stores left in the area and to swap stories, some of which are true.

William S. Doyal was born September 10, 1810, place of birth unknown. He died in 1878 and is buried in the City Cemetery at Griffin, Georgia.

Leonard Thompson Doyal, son of William S. Doyal, was born in the Chattanooga, Tennessee, area May 17, 1845, and he died October 18, 1928. He was part Indian. He volunteered for the Civil War at the age of seventeen. He married Francis Mae Davis who was born October 22, 1849, and died in 1898. He moved to the Paulding County area of New

E.T. Doyal's Store, 1938 – J.L. Doyal, Herman Newell, E.T. Doyal

Georgia where he was a farmer and a merchant. He later married Belle Jeffers, who was the oldest living Civil War widow at one time.

John Leonard Doyal, son of Leonard Thompson Doyal, was born August 9, 1878, and died April 30, 1941. He married Lillie Eugenia Steed on October 16, 1891. She was born September 12, 1879, and died of pneumonia on December 26, 1913. He helped his father in the New Georgia business until his father started businesses in the Hulett and Jake communities. John Leonard continued in the New Georgia community until 1925 when he moved to Villa Rica, Georgia, and opened a store. He married Effie Mae Hayes (1884-1967) of Bremen, Georgia, on August 25, 1915. John Leonard was a director of the Bank of Villa Rica when one million dollars was posted on the window as surplus. This bank survived the depression.

John Leonard and Lillie Steed Doyal's children included a son, Emmett Thompson Doyal, six sisters, and two half-sisters.

Emmett Thompson Doyal, was born in Paulding County on August 24, 1899 and died December 26, 1982. He married Ida Beulah McBrayer from Paulding County, Georgia. She was the daughter of Mr. and Mrs. Andrew (Andy) J. McBrayer. She was born February 3, 1901, and died March 25, 1965. Emmett attended Draughn's Business College after which he worked at Villa Rica Feed Mill and the Bank of Villa Rica. He then started working with John Leonard at the New Georgia store, and in 1925 they moved the business to the corner of Highway 78 and Carrollton Highway in Villa Rica, and the business was known as J.L. Doyal and Son. The location, with a hitching ground and a blacksmith shop behind the business, was ideal. The warehouse is their present location. Emmett was very active in community and church affairs. Included among these were: member of Villa Rica City Council, director of Bank of Villa Rica, president of Villa Rica Mills, Inc. for many years, which included Villa Rica Hosiery Mill, Cotton Mill, pants factory, Villa Rica Feed Mill (which was about the only employment in Villa Rica until after World War II) and about eight cotton gins in a large area, on the board of directors for the Villa Rica Hospital, Board of Education, Masonic Lodge No. 72, delegate to the 1960 Republican Convention in Chicago, listed in Marquis' *"Who's Who - South and Southwest,"* deacon of the First Baptist Church of Villa Rica, and he was on the building committee for the church in 1936. Emmett and Beulah had two sons, Buna Eugene and Wilbur Joe. Emmett later married Allie Bell Walker, who was the daughter of William Matthew and Mary Lenora Bell.

Eugene was born in 1923 in Villa Rica, Georgia. He served in the U.S. Navy in the Pacific Zone during World War II, graduated from Auburn University, and entered into the business with E.T. Doyal. The store later became known as E.T. Doyal and Son. He married Robyn Wall and they had three daughters. Robyn Ann, who was born July 12, 1947, married William Smith. They have a son, William McBrayer (Bray), who was born February 21, 1973. Pamela Doyal Bruce was born July 24, 1951. Jane Allison Doyal was born May 12, 1955. She married Eric Vandiver, and they have a son, Wesley Dillon, who was born September 7, 1995. Eugene has been on the board of directors of the Villa Rica Mills, Inc. and president and chairman of the board. He is now running Villa Rica Knitters.

Joe was born in 1927 in Villa Rica, Georgia. He graduated from Auburn University and entered into business with E.T. Doyal in March 1948. He married Charlotte Moon of Loganville, Georgia, who was a home economics teacher. Joe has been president of the Jaycees, Lion's Club, and Band Boosters. He has also been Scout Master and Sunday School teacher, and he still helps Jerry in the business. Joe and Charlotte had three children: Sonay Marie, Jerry Lamar, and Dr. Linda Elaine Doyal. Sonay, who was born May 31, 1953, and had worked in the family business, died June 8, 2001. Jerry, born March 6, 1956, graduated from West Georgia College, married Alisa Matthews and they have two children, Allison Leigh, born June 4, 1987, and April Leigh, born December 11, 1992. Jerry has been active in the Lion's Club, Football Booster Club, Downtown Development, Villa Rica Gold Rush activities, and the annual parade each September. Dr. Linda Elaine Doyal, born September 10, 1957, married Robert Currie. Their children are Amanda Doyal Currie, born July 18, 1992, and Kevin Doyal Currie, born July 2, 1994.

Many members of the Doyal family are buried in the New Georgia Cemetery, Paulding, County. The family home place was located at the present site of the New Georgia Library. *Submitted by: Joe Doyal, 39 Post Oak Trace, Villa Rica, GA 30180*
Sources: Family records and personal knowledge

514. Earl William Driver

Earl William Driver, son of William Hubert Driver and Elizabeth (Priest) Driver was born in Carroll County on November 8, 1907. After growing up here, he moved to Florida for a short time. After moving back to Georgia, he met and married Katie Jane Rush on November 17, 1935, in Draketown, Georgia. She was born July 14, 1915, the daughter of Walter and Virgil (Ross) Rush. They initially settled in Draketown, but in 1936 they moved to a small log cabin near Asbury Cemetery in Temple. After several moves, sometime between 1942 and 1944, they moved to the home place in Temple where they lived in an older home until Earl built the home in 1951-1952 that presently stands.

Earl and Katie Driver, November 1935.

For many years, Earl and Katie, along with their children, ran a small farm. They grew everything from cotton to vegetables, along with cows, chickens, and other assorted farm animals. Earl was also, at times, employed by the railroad and Manning Cabinet Shop that was in Temple then. He also worked at Bell Bomber Plant (today Lockheed) during World War II, installing windshields in bombers. For many years, Earl was a carpenter who traveled all over what is now known as the metro area building houses. Katie was a mother, homemaker, and ran the farm when Earl was working elsewhere. Earl was a lifelong member of the Temple Masons and was also a Temple council member for many years.

Earl died in April 1994, Katie in January 1985, after an extended illness. Both are buried at Shady Grove Baptist Church Cemetery in the Shady Grove community in Carroll County.

Earl and Katie had eight children during their life together. Joseph Edward (Ed) born November 15, 1936, in Draketown; James William (J.W.) born March 15, 1940; Sherman Wayne born July 25, 1942; Larry Earl born September 24, 1944; Jerry Jerome born March 17, 1947; Brenda Gail born May 23, 1950; Lynda Kay born July 22, 1952; and Connie Jane born July 7, 1956. All the children grew up in Temple, with four of them graduating from Temple High School.

The Driver Children in April 1994.

Ed is a retired Georgia State Trooper, lives in Armurchee near Rome and has four daughters and ten grandchildren. J.W. is retired Navy, with three daughters and four grandchildren. He lives in Elizabeth City, North Carolina with wife Sally. Wayne is a retired government employee with three children and five grandchildren, along with two great-grandchildren, and he lives in Carrollton with wife Helen. Larry is a retired Delta employee and lives in Fayetteville, Georgia, with wife Carolyn. Jerry works in Carrollton and has four children and eight grandchildren. Jerry still lives in Temple with wife Mary in the home that Earl built. Brenda is a computer graphics designer, has two sons and three grandchildren. She lives in Villa Rica with husband Doug Gray. Lynda is a travel agent in Carrollton. She has three sons and lives in Temple with husband Lamar McBurnett. Connie works full time as a Mom with two young sons. She lives in Villa Rica with husband Barry Land.

The Drivers are long time residents of Carroll County, settling in this area sometime in the late 1700s or early 1800s. Along with this family, you will also find Drivers in Carrollton, Villa Rica, Sand Hill, the Clem and Huelett communities, and spilling over into surrounding counties. *Submitted by: Brenda Gray, 523 North Avenue, Villa Rica, GA 30180-1314*

515. Louis Cary Driver and Nevelle Walls

On June 22, 1945, Nevelle Walls and Louis Cary Driver were united in marriage.

Louis Cary Driver was born in Carroll County on August 22, 1917, to Henry Albert Driver and Lola Ida Gentry Driver. His family included Guy Fletcher Driver, Vera Mae Driver Moore, Roger Glynn Driver, Robert Fredrick Driver, Lila Inez Driver Walker and Vachel Vane Driver.

Nevelle Walls Driver was born in Heard County on October 24, 1917, to Alvin Lindsey Walls and Cordia B. White Walls. Other children were Evelyn Walls, Howard Leonard Walls, John Oscar Walls II, and Candler Lindsey Walls.

Louis Cary and Nevelle Walls Driver

They became self-employed partners in an agri-business that eventually became a 150 acre cattle farm. Poultry was the foundation of the farm that also included the production of corn, wheat, oats, soybeans, and cotton. They were the first cotton producers in Carroll County to yield two bales per acre. This was announced on WLBB Radio by Tal Duvall, a good friend and the Carroll County Extension Service Agent. In 1980, they were awarded the Outstanding Hatching Egg Producer of the year by Gold Kist. Cary and his farming techniques were featured in several articles in the *Carroll County Times,* and in the 1950s was featured in *The Progressive Farmer.* With three freezers and a large pantry, "The Garden" was a labor of love and necessity. With mouths watering, the family still remembers the sugar cured hams and suppers of fried ham, red-eye gravy, scrambled eggs, and made-from-scratch biscuits that only mother could make. And who could forget the sweet potatoes cured, of course, at Johnson's Potato Curing House.

They were members of the Stripling Chapel United Methodist Church. Serving in various leadership roles, as choir members and teachers, the church was an integral part of their lives.

Two daughters were born to the couple. Carol Elaine was born December 23, 1947, and Patricia Ellen was born December 9, 1950. It seems there was always a project in the home. The girls remember many nights when they went to sleep to the sound of the Singer sewing machine and the banging and buzzing of a hammer and saw!

On August 16, 1969, Patricia was married to Dale Alan McWhorter (born July 11, 1950). They presented Granny and Papa with their two grandchildren. Caryn Brooke McWhorter was born on August 8, 1972, and John Alan McWhorter was born on November 29, 1974. Brooke was married to Michael David Harvey (born December 30, 1971) on August 6, 1994. Katherine Anne Harvey, the first great-granddaughter was born on December 12, 1999. On February 4, 1989, Patricia was married to Joseph T. Bell, Jr. (born December 28, 1946) Joe and his sons (Joseph T. Bell II, John Robinson Bell, and Robert Benjamin Bell) were welcomed to the family.

Sadly, the family lost Nevelle Walls Driver on October 20, 1991 and Louis Cary Driver on December 21, 2000. They left a legacy of faith in their God, strength of character, a devotion to family, and service to their church and community.

They will forever be remembered in our hearts. *Submitted by: Patricia Bell, and Carol Driver, 350 Star Point, Carrollton, GA 30116*

516. Duffey - Duffie - Duffey

Over the years, we were told stories about the children of our Duffey family. One story tells of parents who left their children sitting on a wood box at a store in Carrollton. The parents told the children that they would be back to get them. Another story says that the parents left their children in a wagon yard in Carrollton, and never returned to get them. Still another story claims that a farmer came by their home soon after their mother died. The farmer took the children and distributed them to a number of farms throughout the valley in the Chambers County, Alabama area.

Mary E. Cantrell Hale, granddaughter of Vassie Lee and Cora Lee Nix Duffie, located information about two of the children of Franklin Duffy Duffey. They are Charles Thomas Duffey, who went to the home of Joseph H. Cleaveland of Troup County, Georgia, and Elisha Franklin Duffey, who went to the home of W.H. Thompson of Troup County. Franklin died before October 10, 1865. Family stories say that they were from a large family. However, at this time, we do now know of any other children.

Charles T. Duffey died in 1928; his spouse died in 1918. Their known children are Tommy, Beulah, Willie, Trudra, Gladys, Orn, Claude, and Bertha. We have been told that the family moved to Texas.

Elisha F. Duffie (August 1, 1858-July 9, 1909, on Bowdon-Tyus Road in Roopville, Georgia) married Sarah Agnes Perry (Feburary 20, 1861-February 14, 1937, in Roopville, Georgia) on October 13, 1878. They raised their family in the Roopville area. Their children are: (1) Luther Martin Duffey (1879-1965) married Ledonia Noles (1884-1966) and had Perlonia in 1903, Cora in 1903, and Grady in 1906; (2) William Thomas Duffie (1881-1967) married Mary Pellie Grower (1883-1981) and had Henry in 1903, Molly in 1905, Perry in 1909, Clarence, Bainor in 1914, Kermit in 1918, and Holmer in 1920; (3) Mary Olar Duffie (1883-1967) married C.D. Henson

Elisha and Sarah Duffey-Duffie Family. About 1900

(1875-1957) and had Vera who died 1969, Alma, Bill who died 1968, Josie, Homer who died 1957, Colie, Bernard who was born 1917, and Bud; (4) Mary Bell Duffie (1885-1966) married Charles Madison Levens (1890-1964) and had Ellie in 1917 and Leon in 1920; (5) Perry Easborn Duffie (1887-1963) married Marilla Francis Burt (1896-1968) and had Olen in 1917, Mary in 1921, Oscar in 1924, Rachel in 1925, Garfield in 1927, Lillar in 1930, Zann in 1934, and Milton in 1938; (6) Ruth Jane Duffie (1890-1979) married Robert Franklin Nelson (1888-1954) and had Robert in 1908, Aaron in 1912, Hurtlie in 1913, Arthur in 1915, Sarah in 1917, and William in 1928; (7) Dillie Duffie (1892-1939) married Harvey Brannon and had Willie in 1909 and Dovie in 1912; (8) Lula Duffie (1896-1929) married Calip Hardy Nelson (1895-1967) and had Edward in 1919, Agnes in 1920, Sylvia in 1922, and AZ in 1923; (9) Vassie Lee Duffie (1899-1980) married Cora Lee Nix (1902-1954) and had Mary in 1926, Ollie, Johnny in 1928, Betty in 1931, Harold, and Dorothy in 1937; and (10) Allie Kate (1901-1936) married James Verner Nix and had Allivee.

Both Elisha F. and Sarah Agnes Perry Duffie are buried at the Roopville City Cemetery. *Submitted by: Mary E. Hale, 1802 Briarwood Lane, Opelika, AL 36801*

Source: Patricia Nelson, 1789 Kellogg Creek Road, Acworth, GA 30102

517. Duffey

Dreamers from the Emerald Isles

In 1830 my great-grandad John M. Duffey lived in Carroll County, Georgia, with his wife Mary B. Duffey and children Eliza, W. Britton Caple, Elizabeth, John M. II, James H., and Samuel Smile.

(1) Eliza, believed to have lived in Heard County in 1850-1870. (2) W. Britton Caple was in 2nd Cavalry (State Guards) Company G. In 1870, W. Britton Caple and wife Quenn Mary Heptinstall lived in Carroll County in the Bowdon Laurel Hill area (which is today between Roopville and Tyus) with children Samuel S., Sarah Catherine, David Albert — all born in Carroll County. John Thomas, Dollie Henrietta, William Caple, and Jessie Daniel were born in Randolph County, Alabama. John Thomas Duffey was my dad. His children were (by first wife Minerva), Jessie James, John Tallmadge, daughter born and died, Lena Pearl, Corbett, Alice Henrietta, Nancy Leo, and Frankie Catherine. Children by his second wife Roberta were Lottie Leo, Margaret Irene, E. Johnny Jr., Kathryn Ruth, and son born and died. Most of my family moved on into Randolph County, Alabama, and then settled in Attalla and Aurora, Alabama. (3) Elizabeth lived in Heard County in 1850-1870. (4) John M. also lived in Heard

James Smiley Duffey holding child, and W. Britton Caple Duffey

County in 1850-1870. (5) James H. was in 41st Infantry, Company I, and was wounded at Kennesaw Mountain, Georgia, on June 27, 1864, in the Battle of Big Shanty. James H. and wife Mary had children Susan E., William, John V., Mary C., James A., Charles, Ilsa A., and Lucy. (6) Samuel S. was in the 7th Infantry, Company G, and was wounded at Bull Run, the second battle at Manassas, Virginia, on August 30, 1862. He was wounded and captured at Knoxville, Tennessee, on November 30, 1863, and on disabled furlough from March 4, 1865, to close of war. Samuel Smile Duffey Sr. and wife Mahulda drew a pension which they filed for in Carroll County. Their children were Elizabeth Leonora, John M., James Smiley, Levi J., Lillian, William, Lydie, Sammy, Arzie Britton, Sadie, Rufus and Mary Effie. Mary Effie Duffey McGuire was a teacher first at Ephesus School in Heard County, Georgia, and then at Oak Mountain in Carroll County. She is in the Norman Rockwell picture for *Post Illustration* November 2, 1946, called "Norman Rockwell Visits A Country School." Samuel S. Sr. lived in Carroll County and is buried at Stripling Chapel.

All three of the brothers — W. Britton Caple, James H., Samuel S. — who served in the Civil War were also registered voters.

The many Duffey descendants from Samuel S. Sr. and W. Britton Capel are well known in Carroll and Heard Counties. They are hard working law abiding citizens, doing the duties of their county and country. They served and suffered for our country as is shown. Many served in the military and other occupations and professions. They were mechanics, machinists, farmers, doctors, nurses, secretaries, poets, lawyers, judges, and are living in several states, from coast to coast.

Duffey Family

Shown in the small group picture is Quenn Mary Heptinstall Duffey (wife of W. Britton Caple Duffey) in center. On the left is Mrs. Hill and Benjamin F. Hill. William Denson Hill is on right. *Submitted by: Margaret Wood, 7009 Berea Road, Douglasville, GA 30135*

Sources: Census records, Registered Voters and Returns, personal knowledge.

518. Samuel Duffey Family

Samuel Smiley Duffey was born in Heard County on May 1, 1845. On Samuel's sixteenth birthday, he volunteered to fight for the Confederate Army. It is known that at one time he fought at Richmond, Virginia. During his service, he was wounded many times. The last few years of his life, he drew a pension of $25 a year.

He later married Mahulda Maxwell Duffey, who was born August 21, 1851. The Duffey family moved from Heard to Carroll County sometime during the early twentieth century to a place "three miles south of Carrollton." they had eleven children: Leonora, John, Smilie, Lillian, Will, Sadie, Lida, Sammy, Rufus, Effie, and Arzie. Many of these continued to live in the Carrollton area. One daughter, Effie Duffey McGuire, grew up to be a teacher and was painted by Norman Rockwell in his portrait, "One-Room Schoolhouse."

Rufus Russell Duffey

Rufus Russell Duffey, born December 12, 1890, had an accident on his way to school at the age of seven. He fell from a footbridge into icy water while walking to school. He became unable to make it back home before his legs and clothing were covered with ice. From this accident, he was stricken with an illness similar to polio. After the age of thirteen, Rufus never walked again. He was confined to a wheelchair. When his father died in 1913, he left a widow and two younger sisters. Rufus provided for the family by buying and selling cattle and other livestock. During the year of 1923, Rufus married Carrie Mangham Duffey, born January 25, 1903. They lived in the family home, Mountain Oak Farm. They had three sons, Charles, Donald, R. Lee, and two daughters, Jane (Foster), and Vauncille (Barnes). Many of the Duffey descendants still live in and around the Carrollton area.

From a diary kept by Rufus, it is known that he corresponded with two Indian princesses and Orville and Wilbur Wright. Norman Rockwell was also a visitor to the Duffey home while staying in Carrollton.

R. Lee Duffey (1931-1998) married Earline Casey of Cedartown and continued to live on the family land. He and his wife later owned and operated Mountain Oak Florist until shortly before his death. R. Lee's children and grandchildren continue to live on the family land. *Submitted by: Becky Duffey Sailors, 90 Whooping Creek Road, Carrollton, GA 30116.*

519. The Duke Family

The Duke families of Carroll County share a common ancestry and an uncommonly deep sense of duty and devotion to their land and beliefs.

John Taylor Duke Sr. was the first Duke to arrive in Georgia. His father was Virginia Militia Capt. Henry Duke Jr., son of Col. Henry Duke Sr., a member of the Virginia House of Burgesses. Col. Duke's father was the immigrant, Thomas Duke, who came to America from Kent, England in 1637. Duke University is named for Washington Duke, its chief benefactor, a great-grandson of John Taylor Duke Sr.

Most of John Taylor Duke's sons and grandsons served in the Revolutionary War. This includes his sons Robert and Thomas Sr. and grandson, Lt. Taylor Duke, son of James. These three patriots were the forefathers of the Duke families of Carroll County.

Rev. Thomas Duke was probably the first of the family to settle in Carroll County, arriving before the 1830 census. He was a son of John P. Duke, son of Taylor Duke. Rev. Duke was a Baptist Minister (possibly the first in the county) and served in the Old Carrollton and Sand Hill area.

Thomas' uncle, Charles Duke Sr., was another early settler. He appears on the 1840 census, along with Thomas, Charles E., Edmund, John T., William, John, and William R. Duke. Charles was born 1780. He married Nancy Bonner, daughter of Thomas Bonner (ancestor of the Carroll County Bonners). Charles' brother, Edmund Duke, married Nancy's sister, Mary Bonner. The Duke and Bonner clans of western South Carolina in the late 1700s formed a deep friendship and migrated westward across the state together to Carroll County.

Edmund Duke's son, James H. (Jimmy) Duke moved from Troup County to the Laurel Hill District of Carroll County by 1860. His farm was just south of Bethesda Baptist Church, adjoining his uncle Judge Zadoc Bonner's plantation. James was an early member of Old Camp United Methodist Church. He and his wife, Kezziah, are buried there.

Clifford T. Duke and Blanche Thompson Duke

Another branch of the family moved to Carroll from Heard County about 1890 when Robert Ferdinand Duke, a great-great-grandson of Revolutionary War soldier Thomas Duke Sr. arrived in the Tyus community. Robert (Bob) Duke married Ada Lydia Wessinger. Their children moved back to Heard County, but son Clifford T. Duke, his wife Blanche Thompson Duke, and their children — Eljein, Doris, Bobby, and Zelda — later moved to Carrollton, settling here in 1958.

A third branch of the family also moved to Carroll from Heard County. Paul Duke of the Kansas community moved there from Centralhatchee. Paul Duke is a great-grandson of Willis W. Duke of Heard County who joined the Confederate Army in 1863 at age 45 after receiving word that a son had been killed in action. Willis was a great-grandson of Robert Duke, son of John Taylor Duke Sr. Paul Duke married Estelle Whitman.

Their children are James and Sarah. Another branch of this family settled in the Whitesburg area where many descendants still reside. *Submitted by: Eljein Duke Barnes. Research compiled by Brett Barnes, Carrollton, GA*

520. Harold Dunaway Family

It was 1927 when the Dunaway family first moved to Carroll County, Georgia. They had long been residents of Clark County, Georgia, prior to then, but the country was in the grips of the Great Depression and people had to move where jobs were available. My grandfather, Beeler Dunaway, owned a combination furniture store and funeral parlor in Athens, Georgia.

Beeler Dunaway and his wife Lenora Wigley had five sons and one daughter: Clarence, Artie, Ira, Edgar, Alva, and Bertha. Clarence Jackson Dunaway, who was my father, was the oldest son. Clarence Dunaway was born in 1898 in Clarke County, Georgia, and he had grown up to learn the occupation of his father. In 1927, Clarence accepted a job offer from Mr. Aycock in Carrollton to become the funeral director of Kytle-Aycock, which was the first funeral home in Carrollton. My grandfather, Beeler Dunaway, died in 1931. He and his wife are both buried in Oconee Heights, the city cemetery of Athens, Georgia.

Clarence Jackson Dunaway had married Annie Elizabeth Young in Clarke County, Georgia. Annie was born 31 January 1899, the daughter of James Lewis Young of Clarke County who was a farmer and a cattleman. My grandfather Young died when Annie was thirteen years old in 1912. He is buried in the Gateway Methodist Church Cemetery in Clarke County. The wife of James Lewis Young, who was Fannie Lou Lane Young, sold her farm on the Jefferson Road after her husband's death and moved to Kirkwood in Atlanta, Georgia.

The Young children were Annie, Louis, James, Herbert, Charles, and Paul. One of these brothers, even though he did not live in Carrollton, wanted to be buried in the City Cemetery of Carrollton anyway. That brother was Charles Young. He and his wife, Thelma, are buried there. My parents, Annie and Clarence Jackson Dunaway are also buried in the City Cemetery at Carrollton. Annie died on 30 December 1979 and Clarence Jackson Dunaway died 26 April 1949.

During her lifetime, Annie Dunaway worked for many years at the old Carroll Theater which used to be on Newnan Street where the Confederate Monument now stands. She was the lady who sat in the box office selling tickets to the "picture show" as we called it back then. The Confederate Mounument used to be in the center of the Square in downtown Carrollton when I was growing up there. Annie and Clarence Dunaway were the parents of three sons.

Harold Milton Dunaway was born 9 July 1921 in Athens, Clarke County, Georgia. He moved with his family to Carrollton in 1927 and grew up there. He married Jeanne Sims who was born 7 October 1922 and a native of Meriwether County, Georgia. Her father was Otis Raymond Sims, a farmer in Meriwether County, and who is buried at the Hogansville City Cemetery. Jeanne's mother was Nannie Sue McKoy who was born in Coweta County, Georgia, and grew up there. Jeanne Sims was an only child.

Harold and Jeanne Dunaway have three children. The oldest is Harold Alan Dunaway born 2 November 1947 in Atlanta. Harold grew up in DeKalb County, Georgia, and graduated from Southwest DeKalb High School. In 1969 he graduated from North Georgia College. He was commissioned as a second lieutenant and spent two years in the U.S. Army. He served with the 1st Air Cavalry Division in Vietnam. Harold Alan Dunaway now works as the Regional Claims Office Manager for State Farm Insurance in Duluth, Georgia. He is married to Jerri McNeal, a native of Jackson County, Georgia and they have two children.

Children of Harold Alan and Jerri McNeal Dunaway are: (1) Joshua Alan Dunaway who was born 20 April 1976 and attended Gwinnett College. He is now employed by Gwinnett Medical Center in Lawrenceville. (2) Kari Lynn Dunaway was born 18 February 1979 and is a 2001 graduate of North Georgia College with a degree in psychology.

The second child of Harold and Jeanne Sims Dunaway is Larry Sims Dunaway who was born 1 November 1950 in Atlanta and graduated from Southwest DeKalb High School. He attended Southern Tech. Larry spent twenty years in the Air Force Reserve. He was married to Amy Clifford, but later divorced. They had one child Melody June Dunaway, born 7 October 1971. Melody is married to Don Matagi.

The second son of Clarence and Annie Young Dunaway was Robert Edward Dunaway who was born 22 May 1923 in Athens, Georgia. Robert Dunaway married Charlotte Bailey and they had three children: John Edward, Diane, and Suzanne. Suzanne Dunaway Morris still lives in the Dunaway home place in Carrollton. Suzanne teaches school in Douglasville. Robert Dunaway died 13 December 1993 and is buried at Carroll Memory Gardens.

The third son of Clarence and Annie Young Dunaway was James Clarence "Boots" Dunaway born 5 July 1926 in Clarke County, Georgia. Boots Dunaway married Carolyn McCurdy in Walker County, Georgia. Boots is remembered as the manager of WLBB, the first radio station in Carrollton. Boots and Carolyn had two children: David and Julie. Boots Dunaway died on 22 December 1970 and is buried in the Carrollton City Cemetery. *Submitted by: Harold Dunaway, 1866 Barber Court, Ellenwood, GA 30049 and Written by: Jan R. Bell.*

521. J.A. and Sally Moore Duncan Family

Joseph Alexander Duncan was born in 1858 in Whitesburg, Georgia, son of John Duncan and Judie McDonald Duncan. He married Sally Melinda Moore (born 1863 in Whitesburg) on February 12, 1882. She was the daughter of George W. Moore and Minerva Hagen Moore. They lived in the Whitesburg and Lowell communities. He was a farmer and blacksmith in Lowell. She was a charter member of the Lowell Methodist Church and a loving mother concerned for all her children and grandchildren. They were a hard-working family of fourteen children. The following are their children and their spouses. Pearl married Walter Scudder; Travis married Exa Treadwell; Thomas married Kate Houston; Katie Lou married Richard Parks; Brown married Eunice Lyle; Roy married Eunice Shadinger; Gus married Tempie Brown, after her death Gladys Lovvorn; Hattie married Grady Nix; Annie married Ernest Nix; Oly married Mae Trammell; J.P. married Sallie Hollingsworth; Jewell married Charles Craven; Ruth married Alfred Bonner; and Marjorie married Robert Lightburn. J.A. died in 1928 and Sally died in 1952. They are buried in the Lowell Cemetery.

Travis, Thomas, and Katie Lou all settled in Coweta County; Annie in West Point, Georgia; Marjorie in Panama City, Florida; and all the others stayed in Carroll County. Brown and Gus were farmers in Lowell. Ruth, Pearl, and Hattie were homemakers and lived in Carrollton. Jewell worked as a sales clerk at Moore and Cline in the early 1940s and later at Griffin's Department Store. J.P. farmed and worked in the grocery business with his brother-in-law, Alfred Bonner. His wife Sallie worked in the cafeteria at Rock Ridge School. Roy continued as a blacksmith in Lowell and later in Carrollton. He served as a blacksmith during World War I in France.

Oly farmed the home place in Lowell. He served on the Board of the Carroll County Membership Corporation in the 1950s and 1960s. His wife, Mae, taught school at Lowell until consolidation in 1959 when she transferred to Roopville Elementary School. She taught first grade and kindergarten until she retired in 1971, after more than forty-five years. They, along with J.P. and Sallie and Roy and Eunice, were longtime and loyal members of Lowell United Methodist Church. Oly was a much-loved adult Sunday School teacher and devoted many hours preparing his lessons during the week for the following Sunday. Mae was the pianist and children's Sunday School teacher for over forty years. She worked in Bible School each summer and led the women of the church in the mission programs. They are all buried in the Lowell Cemetery. *Submitted by: Faith Duncan McLendon, 150 Honeysuckle Lane, Temple, GA 30179*

522. Joseph Elvin Duncan

Joseph Elvin Duncan (1909-1980) was the son of John Raymond and Pearl Perkins Duncan of Douglasville, Georgia. Ebb's father was the first Ford dealer in Douglasville. In 1931, Ebb married Antionette Talmadge Tyus (1909-1996) of Carrollton, Georgia. Antoinette's parents were Hilton Morgan Tyus and Nettie Talmadge Tyus. Nettie was the sister of Eugene Talmadge, former governor of Georgia for four separate terms of office. His son, Herman, later became governor and then United States Senator from Georgia.

Ebb and Antoinette lived for three years in Jacksonville, Florida. They joined the Methodist Church while there. They both stayed active in the Methodist Church for their entire lives. Their first son, Robert Tyus, was born in Jacksonville in 1937.

J.A. Duncan Family, 1916

Sen. and Mrs. Duncan's first house on Bowdon highway built by Hugh Richards.

They moved back to Carrollton in 1939. Ebb and Roy Richards formed Duncan-Richards Theaters which grew to a sizable chain of theaters in small towns and cities in Georgia and Alabama. Later, Mr. Richards sold his interest in the theaters to Ebb and established Southwire Company with headquarters in Carrollton.

Ebb and Antoinette had Hugh Richards build their first home on the Bowdon highway across from West Georgia College (a two year college at that time). In 1947, their second son, Richard Allen, was born. A year later, a third son, Joseph Elvin Jr. was born.

He later sold off the various movie theaters and became a life insurance broker. He was so successful in this new occupation that the Wall Street Journal ran a front page article on his mercurial rise to become one of the top life insurance produces in the country.

Ebb Duncan, Roslyn Carter, President Jimmy Carter, and Antoinette Duncan.

Ebb honorably served the people of Carroll County and the state in general as a member of the Georgia House of Representatives for sixteen years. Later, he was serving a third term as state senator from Senatorial District 30 (Carroll County and part of Douglas County) when he passed away in 1980. He served on and was chair of many important committees in both the House and Senate, with keen interest in education, appropriations, mental health and mental retardation, banking and finance, and the University System of Georgia, to name a few. For his continued work in support of the Democratic Party, he was elected Whip of the Senate majority party in 1978. The Georgia General Assembly approved the naming of Georgia highway 166 from the Alabama line to the Douglas County line the J. Ebb Duncan Memorial Highway.

His other civic duties included president of the Jaycees, president of the Methodist Men's Club, and president of the Young Men's Bible Class. He was a Mason, Rotarian, and active in the work of the Carroll Service Council.

He was active in organizing and promoting midget football.

Antoinette was a long time active member of the Allie Beall Sunday School Class of the First Methodist Church of Carrollton. She also belonged to the Lit-Mu Society and served with the Grey Ladies at Tanner Memorial Hospital. She was a loving mother, as her three sons would quickly agree. Without her love and devotion to Ebb, he might never have achieved so much in his lifetime. She knew how to laugh and have fun as her bridge playing friends will testify. Many people will verify that she was the southern lady personified. *Submitted by: Robert Duncan, 200 Azalea Drive, Roswell, GA 30075*

523. The Gospel According to "Conkie"

My grandmother, Ola Blanche Smith Duncan, born November 4, 1904, in Bowdon, Carroll County, Georgia, was the second child of Sarah Elizabeth McDonald and Emory Eli Smith. She and her siblings, Mozelle, Roy, and Iris, grew up in a loving family. In recalling childhood, she told of being excited getting an orange and apple for Christmas; being devastated when Mozelle, wearing their mother's bifocals, stepped on and shattered her favorite doll; trying their grandmother's snuff and getting sick. Typical kids!

Her first encounter with an automobile was scary. Walking along the road one day, she and some friends heard a strange roar. Suddenly, a "monster" approached. The girls hid under a bridge. Imagine their horror when the vehicle rumbled over their heads!

Education was important to my grandmother: a degree in home economics in 1925 and a bachelor of science in 1929 from Bowdon State Normal and Industrial College; a master's degree in education from the University of Georgia in 1951. First, she taught in Florida schools. About 1931, she returned to Bowdon, teaching in the Carroll County School System until she retired in 1969. Among the subjects she taught were home economics, English, algebra, math, and world history. Hugh Ayers said he was later able to skip algebra because of her thorough instruction.

With her quiet manner, students sometimes thought they were "getting away" with improper conduct. I knew better. She loved and understood youth, aware of everything that was going on. I remember her telling my mom, Janice, "You see and hear too much!" To her, some things should be ignored.

Mother told of crying and "pitching fits" to get her way. My grandmother simply said, "No!" Nothing else, which was also her way in the classroom. At school and at home, punishment was doled out quietly but consistently. One of her students, Debbie W. Richardson said, "I think I was mean in school, but Miz Duncan told the other teachers that I wasn't mean. I was just mischievous." That was her way: understanding, consistent, firm.

Her other love was music. At Bowdon High School, she organized the Glee Club. Yearly, under her direction, students presented lively programs of music, dance, and drama. She was the choreographer and costume designer for all productions. She sang in the adult choir, often as soloist, at Bowdon Baptist Church, her home church since her baptism May 14, 1916. In the community, she played the xylophone in the Bowdon Orchestra. At home, she encouraged her daughter to excel in music, especially piano.

Divorced when my mom, Janice Adelia, was six, she raised this only child with the help of her mother and father. Honesty was important in the family. My mom, Janice, tells the following story: "At age nine, I went with a friend to a local carnival. When I bragged, 'There wasn't a fence. We slipped in and didn't pay,' Mother said, 'Janice, that was wrong. You go back and pay the money. And apologize!'" What a lesson!

Janice married James Vernon Warren in 1954. To this union were born three children: Janet Vernelle, Nanette Janiece, and me, Vincent Eugene.

Ola Blanche Smith Duncan, "The Gospel According to Conkie"

We adored our grandmother. Janet's "Ga-ga" for "Grandma" soon translated to "Conkie," the name she was lovingly called by all who met her. We were very special to Conkie and she to us. She passed along the understanding that love was more important than material goods; we looked forward to her summer visits.

Conkie's life motto was "Others." Many people received her attentions and love: her daughter and grandchildren; her students; her mother and father whom she cared for until they died; her widowed Aunt Edna who needed a home; friends. My grandmother was remarkable woman with a truly "big heart."

Conkie developed Parkinsonism about 1965, but her zest for life never diminished. Needing living assistance, September 1975, she came to live with us. Spring 1976, a broken hip never mended because of spastic hamstring muscle, rendering her bed-ridden the last years of life. Through all suffering, she remained the patient, quiet, caring woman we loved so dearly. Although her death saddened us, her funeral was one of celebration of a life lived to the fullest. She died September 25, 1981, leaving her descendants a legacy that far surpasses wealth and fame. She taught us how to live, to love, and to die! Even though Ola Blanche Smith Duncan, our "Conkie," was buried in the Bowdon City Cemetery, we know she lives, walks, and sings! *Submitted by: Vincent Eugene Warren, grandson, 119 Rebecca Morris St., Bowdon, GA 30108*

524. Senoia Baltimore Duncan: A Man of Versatility and High Ideals

Senoia Baltimore Duncan was the first born of six to Levi Brantly Duncan and Lucy Ann Dobbins on 27 November 1877, in Douglas County, Georgia. S.B.'s father later moved the family farther west settling in Union, Paulding County, Georgia.

In 1898, Senoia joined the New Georgia Baptist Church in Paulding County, Georgia. It was during this time that he worked in the copper mines in Villa Rica, Georgia. Family members believe that S.B. had little formal education. However, the pursuit of education was important to him, a tenet that was to play a major role in his life. When still a young man, he became a rural schoolteacher. By 1903 Senoia was teaching school in the community of Indian Creek in western Carroll County, Georgia. On December 27, 1903, he married his former student, Arabelle Warren, the daughter of Charles Marion Warren and Josiphine Robinson. As Senoia and Arabelle's family grew, they moved east to the community of Mandeville in Carroll County. Around 1912, S.B. moved his family one mile north to the new house he had just built in Bowdon Junction, Georgia.

In 1916, Senoia and Belle became charter members of Harmony Baptist Church in Bowdon Junction, Georgia. On the 26th of November 1922 Senoia was ordained a Baptist minister at Harmony Baptist Church. After his ordination, S.B. served many rural churches in the West Georgia area; including Bethany in Haralson County, Eureka and Flat Rock in Carroll, Concord and New Georgia in Paulding, Mt. Zion, Ebenezer, County Line and Union Hill in Douglas, Yellow Dirt in Heard and Mills Chapel and East Newnan in Coweta County.

In addition to being a miner, a schoolteacher, and a Baptist minister, Senoia was also a farmer. He had a two-mule farm raising crops on about 100 acres around Bowdon Junction. On the farm he and Belle brought up their nine children. His other occupational pursuits, for a time, were as railroad agent for the Central of Georgia Railroad and proprietor of a mercantile business both at Mandeville and Bowdon Junction, Georgia.

Senoia Baltimore Duncan, Arabelle Warren Duncan, son Amon. Fall, 1904

Even though S.B. had limited education, and was mostly self-taught, he instilled in his children a need to pursue higher educational opportunities. Seven of S.B. and Belle's children attended the University of Georgia and six graduated Phi Kappa Phi. Two of the daughters attended the A&M Normal State Industrial College in Bowdon, Georgia, majoring in home economics. Eight children of S.B. and Belle's became teachers. Senoia himself taught school for twenty-five years in Georgia in Paulding, Carroll, and Douglas Counties.

Senoia was a man who was known and respected far and wide in the West Georgia area. Senoia Baltimore Duncan passed away on February 20, 1953, at his home of forty years in Bowdon Junction, Georgia. The values and morals that he gave to his children have been passed on to his grandchildren. His legacy lives on! *Submitted by: Timothy Douglas Duncan, Grandson and preserver of the Duncan legacy, HCR-1 Box 86, Kelso, CA 92351*

Sources: Death certificates/US censuses; Duncan Family Bible; tombstones, family lore, land deeds; news articles.

525. Durrett Family

Part I

Joseph Francis Durrett and Penelope Cocks

Joseph Francis Durrett, born 1775 in Virginia, was the son of Thomas Durrett (1750) Powhatan County, Virginia, and Agnes Alice Goree (1750-1822). Joseph Francis Durrett was very young when his father Tom Durrett died, and his mother Agnes married Lt. James

James Durrett and Martha Ross, 1842

Kelly of Newberry, South Carolina. He never accepted Lt. Kelly. They argued, he stabbed Lt. Kelly, got on his horse, and rode away to his grandfather's home and never went back. Agnes Alice Goree and Lt. James Kelly settled her first husband's (Thomas Durrett) estate, so they must have married soon after his death. Thomas Durrett, son of Francis Durrett and Rebecca Winn, died in Newberry County, South Carolina, before 1789.

Agnes Alice Goree was born March 10, 1750 and died before 1822 in Newberry, South Carolina, daughter of Daniel Goree of Powhatan County, Virginia, who died in 1801 in the Newberry District of South Carolina, according to his will. Daniel Goree married first Sarah, and then married second to Elizabeth Britton. Cladius Goree, born 1684 in France, died 1736 in Goochland, Virginia, and his wife Jeanne were the parents of Daniel Goree. Cladius Goree was the son of Jean Gaury, born 1645, and his wife Mary Rue, born 1660 in Soubise Saintonge, France.

Martha Ross, possibly a member of Chief John Ross' Family - Cherokee Indian

Thomas Durrett married Agnes Goree in 1768. They had four children: (1) Benjamin (Benedick) Durrett, born 1769 in Virginia, married Margaret Hogg (1789-1839) circa 1788. (2) Lucy Durrett, born 1771, married Edmund Rice. (3) William Durrett, born 1773, married a Kelly, daughter of his step-father, Lt. James Kelley. (4) Joseph Francis Durrett, born 1776, married Penelope Cocks, June 23, 1807. Penelope Cocks was the daughter of Andrew Cocks and Penelope Ward. Andrew Cocks gave sixty-five acres of land "to my daughter Penelope Durrett and her husband Francis Durrett," in 1817 in Franklin County, Georgia. Francis and Penelope were in the 1827 Land Lottery. In 1830 they were in DeKalb County, Georgia. They were already on the move to "Lost Creek" and settled on the Georgia/Alabama Stateline Road, known as the "Crossroads" between Bowdon, Georgia, and Ranburne, Alabama, near what became known as Sandy Flat. Francis Durrett died before 1848 and is buried in an unmarked grave, probably in the Ranburne, Alabama area. His wife Penelope moved to the Black Warrior River with her son, Peter Frank Durrett, and died there. This couple has been credited with many children. Known ones are: (1) Nancy Jane Durrett, born in Virginia. (2) Mary Ellen Durrett, born in Virginia, married Mr. Hogg, moved to Eagle Pass, Texas. (3) William Thomas Durrett, born 1814 in Virginia, lived in Carroll County, Georgia. (4) Sarah Elizabeth "Sally" Durrett, twin to William Thomas, born 1814 in Virginia, married James Francis White on May 28, 1837, in Carroll County, Georgia. He is the son of William White and Nancy Hooper (see William White Family History). (5) James Francis Durrett, born 1816 in Virginia, married Martha Ross in 1840. He died in 1885 and is buried in Ranburne First Baptist Church Cemetery, "Lost Creek Church," (See James Durrett Family History). (6) Benjamin Durrett, born December 26, 1817 in Franklin County, Georgia, married Jane Emeline Barron (1826-1878) in 1841 in Carroll County. He died September 13, 1887, and is buried at County Line Cemetery near Whitesburg, Carroll County. (7) Peter Frank Durrett. (8) Daniel Stone Durrett. (9) Mary "Polly" Durrett. (10) John Durrett. (11) Agnes "Aggey" Durrett married Matthew Jackson White, son of William White and Nancy Hooper (see William White Family History). (12) Andrew Jackson Durrett, born March 18, 1808, married first to Elenor Prater, and second to Mrs. Jane Lankford Benge.

Penelope Cocks was the daughter of Andrew Cocks, granddaughter of John Cocks and Penelope Ward (Clifton) Cocks, great-granddaughter of Thomas Ward (listed on her marriage bond) and Mildred Walden, great-great-granddaughter of Major John Ward and Anne Chiles from Bedford County, Virginia, and Richard Walden and Candace Hubbard, descended from Lord John Walden who came to America in 1715. *Submitted by: Kay Cosper, Atlanta, GA and Written by: Peggy Jackson Hughes, 1550 Tyus Road, Carrollton, GA 30117*

526. Durrett Family

Part 2

James Francis Durrett and Martha Ross

James Francis Durrett, born 1816 in Virginia, married Martha Ross about 1841. He is buried in the Lost Creek Cemetery in Ranburne, Alabama. He was an infant when his father Joseph Francis Durrett and mother Penelope Cocks Durrett moved from Virginia into DeKalb County, Georgia, then into "Indian Lands" in Carroll County, Georgia. By 1828-1830 they settled in the Crossroads section known as Lost Creek. What brought them so far from Grayson County and Bedford County, Virginia, the home of Penelope's ancestors? No one knows, but it must have been the promise of the newly opened Indian Lands of Western Georgia and Eastern Alabama. The 1840 census records show that Francis Durrett lived next to a James Ross and his wife Chloe. However, the *Pirkle Family* states that

> "the parents of Martha Ross were Frederick Ross and his wife, Nancy."

Frederick and Nancy Ross are buried on their plantation near Heflin, Alabama.

James Francis Durrett was the grandson of Thomas Durrett (1750-1784) and Agnes Goree Durrett (1750-1822), and great-grandson of Francis Durrett and Rebecca Winn. He owned enough land along the Stateline Road to leave his sixteen children approximately ninety acres each when he died. He was a farmer, owned and operated a gunsmith shop, a blacksmith shop, and operated a government still in the Sandy Flat Crossroads area during the period before and following the Civil War. He sent his older sons away to the Civil War and lost two of his daughters to fever in the period between 1861-1864.

Many sources claim that Martha Ross had Indian blood and perhaps belonged to the Chief John Ross Family. She was born about 1822 in North Carolina. There has always been a story in our family that she was somehow connected to Betsy Ross. We know that she and many descendants of James and Martha Ross had dark hair and high cheekbones.

The children of James Durrett and Martha Ross Durrett are: (1) Mary Jane Durrett, born 1842, married Thomas Jefferson Snow in 1859 (CSA, Company B, 7th Calvary). They had ten children. (2) Reuben Durrett, born December 1, 1842, died January 1, 1910, (CSA), Company B, 7th Cavalry) married Caroline Alewine December 5, 1867. They had thirteen children. (3) Sarah Durrett, born 1845 (listed in the 1850 and 1860 censuses), died between 1861-1870, buried with her parents in the Lost Creek Cemetery in Ranburne, Alabama. (4) George Washington Benedick Durrett, born 1846, (CSA, Company B, 7th Cavalry) married Addie Humphries in 1874. There are no further reports about George, except that he and his family left on one of the two wagon trains that left the area in the 1880s. (5) Nancy Durrett, born 1847 (found in 1850 and 1860 census), died during the Civil War from fever, buried with her parents. James and Martha Durrett have been credited with two daughters named Nancy, one born in 1847, the other born in 1863. (6) Julia Durrett, born May 14, 1848, died February 13, 1922, married John Tanner Pirkle, son of Jacob Floyd Pirkle and Nancy Alewine Pirkle.

Martha Caroline Durrett and Stephen P. Hanson

They had five children. (7) James Francis Durrett, born 1849, (CSA, Company B, 7th Cavalry) married Amarilla Ridgeway. This couple also left on one of the two wagon trains for Texas in the 1880s. (8) Martha Caroline Durrett, born 1851, married Stephen P. Hanson, August, 5, 1879. (9) Susannah Durrett, born April 20, 1852, died June 4, 1939, married James Martin "Jim" Hill, February 25, 1868, (CSA, Company B, 7th Cavalry). He was the son of Rev. Martin Hill and Sarah Ann Tomlin. They had ten children. This couple is buried in the cemetery at Lost Creek, Ranburne, Alabama. (10) Andrew Jackson "A.J." Durrett, born 1854, married Mary L. Alewine in December 1874. "A.J." and family left for Texas sometime in the 1880s. (11) Frances "Fanny" S. Durrett, born 1855, married Benjamin Franklin Snow (his second wife), July 20, 1875. They had five children and he had two children from a previous marriage. (12) Thomas Jefferson Durrett, born 1857, died August 20, 1888, married Virginia C. Ridgeway, March 1, 1883. Jeff also moved to Texas and died there. (13) Joseph Columbus "Lum" Durrett, born 1859, married Virginia Farmer October 5, 1882. This couple moved to Texas. (14) Nancy Durrett, born 1863, married Marion D. Whitman. (15) Cora Penelope Durrett, born April 6, 1865, married George Mandeville Pirkle December 31, 1885. He was the son of Jacob Floyd Pirkle and Nancy Alewine Pirkle. They had twelve children. (16) Alice Durrett, born 1868, married Theron Andrew "Doc" Lands (his second wife) July 17, 1886. "Doc" born February 23, 1855 in Bowdon, Georgia, was the son of John Land and Elizabeth Rutledge. "Doc" married first Eliza Jane Sudderth, January 21, 1883. Eliza died October 1, 1884. Alice Durrett Land died in 1892 of tuberculosis. "Doc" had a "falling out" with Alice's father, and brothers, so he left in the middle of the night and they never saw the four little children again. "Doc" married his third wife, Zelphia Wood, 1900 in San Saba, Texas.

Joseph Columbus "Lum" Durrett

The sons and sons-in-law of James Durrett were all in the Confederate States Army, Company B, 7th Cavalry Regiment, Confederate Portesan Rangers (State Line Troops made up of Randolph, Alabama and Carroll County men.

Submitted by: Patricia Hughes Edwards, Columbia, SC and Written by: Peggy Jackson Hughes, 1550 Tyus Road, Carrollton, GA 30117

527. Durrett Family Part 3

Lost Creek - Sandy Flat Area

This western area of Georgia and eastern area of Alabama that extended from Bowdon, Georgia, through Trickum Valley into Heflin, Alabama, truly made up the last frontier and the early settlers did not really know if they were in Georgia or Alabama. The early settlers of the Lost Creek area were frontiersmen and Indian traders and were wholly dependent upon their own efforts to provide for their families.

The Lost Creek area was wedged between the Cherokees on the north and the Creeks on the west. These tribes were hostile at times. In 1828 there was considerable tension with the Indians and many families moved east to Carrollton, Georgia. Often the families were not sure if they were in Georgia or Alabama because the state lines, as well as the county lines, were moved several times.

William White and his eleven sons, along with the Hooper, Durrett, Alewine, Crumpton, Smith, Skinner, Word, Mabry, Pirkle, Jackson, and other families, were constantly on guard against Indian hostilities. They fought in the 1836 Indian Wars.

Indian trails had been used long before the settlers arrived. The most famous of these was the McIntosh Trail from Georgia through the Indian towns in Alabama. This trail became a public road in 1829 and was called the Alabama Road. We now call it Highway 5. This road brought the Lost Creek families into the western Georgia and eastern Alabama area.

The nearest post office in 1840 was Cerro Gordo (Bowdon). This was another strong link that bound these early settlers together. The Stateline Road included that area of land between Bowdon, Georgia and Heflin Alabama. Many of these settlers owned land in both Georgia and Alabama.

The area of Sandy Flat emerged after the Civil War and the Cross Roads became the intersection that divided Georgia from Alabama.

The John Tanner Pirkle and Julia Durrett Family

The last raid of the Civil War occurred a few days after Lee's surrender. It was part of the famous raid of General James H. Wilson from north Alabama to Macon, Georgia. General John T. Croxton, with his entire brigade, was sent by Wilson to make a raid from Tuscaloosa back to Macon. It was during this raid that the Yankees, entering Georgia west of Bowdon by way of James Durrett's farm, destroyed his gunshop. They camped at Lost Creek on April 24. Susannah Durrett and her sisters hid their best horses in the woods all night to keep the Yankees from stealing them. The Yankees then crossed over into Georgia and raided Carrollton where they were chased down Dixie Street by the Home Guard. *Submitted by: Doris Granger, 47 Dot Road, Bowdon, GA and Written by: Peggy Jackson Hughes.*

The George Mandeville Pirkle and Cora Penelope Durrett Family

528. Allen Hill Eady Family

Allen Hill Eady was born in Wilkinson County, Georgia, about 1824. He was a son of Henry Eady and Elizabeth Gay (daughter of Revolutionary soldier Allen Gay). Henry Eady is the only proven child of John Eady who immigrated from Ireland prior to the Revolutionary War. John received bounty land for service in the Revolution. John Eady was a fervent Baptist, even getting into fist fight with a preacher over missions. He and his son Henry settled in Wilkinson County.

Henry Eady and Elizabeth Gay were parents of nine known children: (1) Margaret (1809-1881) married Hansford Davis. They settled in Wilkinson. (2) John (1810-1880) married Many Weatherby, Frances Murphy, and Martha Johns. (3) Martha (1812-1858) married James Daniel Pittman. (4) Temperance (about 1813-1843) married Oren Davis. (5) Mary married Samuel Pittman. (6) Henry H. married Nancy Caldwell. (7) Harriet Deborah (1825-1889) married William Coalson.

Although Allen Hill Eady has not been located on any census of 1850, it is known that he was in Carroll County by that time. He and his mother Elizabeth are shown as charter members of the Upper Tallapoosa (Baptist) Church in 1847. He also gave the land for the Temperance Church at Sand Hill. Allen married Edna Hampton West in Carroll in 1851 (see article on the William West family).

Allen Eady served in the Confederacy and was mortally wounded at the Battle of Petersburg. He was taken prisoner and treated at Lincoln General Hospital, where he died April 10, 1865. His burial place is unknown but is probably Arlington Cemetery. He wrote his will on the battlefield.

The Eady family lived in Wilkinson County during the war, but after the war their home burned, which may have caused them to return to Carroll to be hear Edna's family and remain there. Allen and Edna Eady had five children. (1) Thomas Allen Eady (1852-1909) married Mary Virginia Dickson and settled in the Bowdon area. He is buried at Smith's Chapel. (2) John Thomas Eady (1854-1937) (see the article on his family.) (3) Mary Elizabeth Eady (1856-1883) never married and is buried at Macedonia. (4) Martha Ann (1858-?) married Tampton Hulsey. (5) Robert (1860) died in infancy. *Submitted by: Mary Nell Pesnell, 453 Sand Hill-Shady Grove Road, Carrollton, GA 30116*

529. John Thomas Eady Family

John Thomas Eady was a son of Allen Hill Eady and Edna Hampton West (see the article about that family). His early years were spent in Wilkinson County, Georgia. However, after his father was killed in the Civil War he returned with his mother and sisters to Carroll County where he lived the rest of his life in the Sand Hill area. Without their father, the family faced many hardships but managed to survive and prosper.

John married Frances Elizabeth Dickson, daughter of Samuel Carter Dickson and Martha Matilda Neely, in 1876 at the Dickson residence in Carroll County. To this couple were born ten children. (1) Effie May Eady (1877-1941) married B.O. Johnston; (2) Liberia Eady (1881-1882); (3) Maynard Bracewell Eady (1883-1973) married Hardy Walker Dyer, son of James Walter Dyer and Amelia Morgan. The Dyers had two daughters, Mary Nell Dyer Harper Pesnell and Louise Dyer Smith; (4) Jessie Delva Eady (1886-1969) married Thomas W. Brasher; (5) Willie Patience Eady (1888-1962) married William Samuel Williams. Willie and Will had three children: Clara Elizabeth, who married William Grady Hamrick; William Harold, who married Annie Belle Russell; and Dickson, who never married; (6) Martha Albertine Eady (1891-1947) married A.A. Parker; (7) Harry Stephens Eady (1894-1896); (8) Thomas Frank Eady (1897-1898); (9) Marshal C. Eady (1899-1900); and John Thomas Eady Jr. (1902-1984) married Maud Harris.

John Thomas Eady Family

John and Fannie were lifelong Baptists and were members at Hopewell Primitive Baptist (Old Carrollton) and at Macedonia. They are buried at Old Carrollton.

In the photo, left to right, John Thomas Eady holding Marshal C. Eady, Frances Elizabeth Dickson Eady, Samuel Carter Dickson, Jessie Delva Eady, Willie Patience Eady, Martha Albertine Eady, and Maynard Bracewell Eady. They are standing in front of their home on today's Lake Connie Road. *Submitted by: Mary Nell Pesnell, 543 Sand Hill-Shady Grove Road, Carrollton, GA 30116*

530. The Eason Family

The many branches of the Eason family of Carroll County are apparently all descended from one patriarch, Thomas Eason Jr., who came to Carroll from Coweta County about 1853. Thomas was a son of Thomas Eason Sr. and Martha "Patsy" Welch. The elder Thomas was a War of 1812 soldier. He was closely related (possibly a brother) to Rice and Abraham Eason of Oglethorpe and Morgan Counties in the early 1800s.

Thomas Eason Jr. married Nancy Briant. Their children were: (1) John, born about 1834, who married Sarah E. Johnson. (2) James, born about 1838. (3) William, born 1840, who married Rachel M. Johnson. (4) Jefferson, born about 1841, who married Mary Ann Fulton. (5) Augustus "Guss," born about 1844. (6) Thomas III, born about 1847, who married Sophronia Jackson. (7) Jasper, born about 1852, who married Susie A. Carroll. (8) Henry Harrison, born about 1853. (9) George Washington, born 1855, who married Sarah Jane "Sallie" Carroll. (10) Benjamin Franklin, born 1859, who married Sarah Jane Wiggins.

Of Thomas and Nancy Eason's ten sons, five served as Confederate soldiers. Of those five, four died during the war. John Eason was wounded at Seven Pines, Virginia on May 31, 1862, and died soon after. James Eason died May 3, 1863. Jefferson Eason died just weeks after enlisting, on April 21, 1862. Augustus "Guss" Eason, a member of the Carroll County Wool Hat Boys, died July 16, 1862. William Eason was (along with John, James, and Jeff) a member of the Bowdon Volunteers of Cobb's Legion. Williams was the only one of these five brothers to survive the war. He was wounded and taken prisoner but made his way home after the war. Unfortunately, he only lived to age 40, passing away "after a short illness" in 1880.

William and his brother John were the patriarchs of the "Indian Creek Baptist Church Easons." William is buried at Indian Creek.

Harrison Eason also died young, in 1883. A memorial to him proclaiming his

> "pious life that had gained the love and esteem of all who knew him" was recorded in the Bethesda Baptist Church minutes.

Jasper Eason left Carroll County, moving to Louisiana, where many of his descendants still reside. Jasper and George W. married sisters, Susie and Sallie Carroll, daughters of Edmon and Martha Dyer Carroll. George and Sallie moved into Edmon's house on Oak Grove Church Road. The house still stands today and is owned by Mickey Eason, a great-grandson of George and Sallie.

The George W. and Sallie Eason Family

George Washington Eason was a charter member of the Antioch Baptist Church on Highway 166 between Carrollton and Bowdon.

George and Sallie Eason's children were: (1) Georgia Ann who married James Coatsworth Barnes, (2) Nancy Ada who married J. Bryant Garrett, (3) Milton Perry who married Ida Johnson, (4) Emma who married a Mr. Towns, (5) Jesse M. who married Lilla Broadwater, (6) Alonza "Lon" who married Dussy Carroll, (7) Leon who married a Nora B.

After Sallie's death in 1933, George Eason spent much time at the home of his daughter, Georgia Barnes. Georgia's son, Dumah Barnes, remembers many an evening spent listening to Grandpa Eason's fine fiddle playing and hearing his stories of the "old days" in Carroll County.

The accompanying picture shows (front row from left) George W. Eason, Sallie Eason, James Coatsworth Barnes, Georgia Eason Barnes with infant. Back row from left are Emma, Jesse, Lon, Leon, Perry, and Ada Eason. *Submitted by: Brett Barnes, Carrollton, GA*

531. Jasper Eason Family

Jasper Eason was born 17 May 1849 in Coweta County, Georgia. On the 1860 Carroll County census records, Jasper is found in the household of Thomas Eason in the 9th District (Bowdon) and is eleven years old. On 9 October 1875 in Carroll County, Jasper Eason married Susan/Susie Ann Carroll, daughter of Edmond and Martha (Dyer) Carroll.

Jasper and Susie Carroll lived in Carroll County until the late 1890s when they took the younger children and went west to Louisiana. He died 10 January 1929 in Leesville, Louisiana. He was the son of Thomas Eason (1808) and Nancy Bryant (1815) who married 1833 in Oglethrope County, Georgia. Jasper's brothers were John (1834); James (1838); William (1840) married Rachel Minerva Johnson; Jefferson (1841) married Mary Ann Fulton; Augustus (1844); Thomas (1847); Henry (1851); and George Washington (1853) married Sarah J. Carroll.

Jasper and Susie had the following children: Hamy; Alvin (1892); Lonnie (1897); Addie; Bernie married Gus Brown; Fulton; Bessie married Francis Martin; Bud; Martha (1879); Walter Jasper (1881-1966) married Martha Eugenia Word, daughter of James Madison and Hannah Yates Word.

Walter Jasper Eason chose to make his home here in Carroll County when his parents traveled west. He met and married Martha Eugenia Word on 27 October 1901 in Carroll County. They had Claude Matthewson (1902) married Pearl Bradley; Carl (1904) married Myrtle Odell Richardson; Hannah (1905) married James Monroe Hilton; James Edward (1909) married Sara Lee Riddle; Fulton Robert (1912) married Thelma Hall.

After Hannah's death in 1912, Walter Eason married Corilla Willingham on 26 March 1913. They had two children: Burl Harvey (1917) married Grace Hightower, and Ernest Leonard (1919) married Syble Phillips. In 1942 after Corilla's death, Walter Jasper Eason married a third time to Lizzie Foster.

Several of Walter Jasper's descendants still live here. Claude Matthewson and Pearl Bradley Eason, daughter of George Washington and Annie Jones Bradley, married on 8 April 1925 in Carroll County. Claude worked the mail train from Atlanta to Savannah until he retired. Their children are Myrle (1925) married Robert Meigs; Walter Ruel (1927-1988) married Gladys Harden Moore, and Inez Jackson; Claud Wendell (1929-1983) married Thelma Jane Dockery; Dole Imogene (1931) married Billy T. Lowry; Joanne (1933) married Randal Buchanan; Claudette (1935) married James Harold Smith; Ellen Susie (1937) married Donald Morgan Farr; Patricia Hilda (1940) married Quinion Robinson; Robert Tracy (1944) married Janice Lana Calhoun; and Jasper Terry (1946) married Maxine Smith. *Submitted by: Jean Lowery, 194 Sandy Flat Road, Bowdon, GA 30108*

532. Milton Perry Eason

My grandfather, Milton Perry Eason — known as M.P. — was born May 18, 1880, and died March 16, 1971. He was the pastor of Abilene Baptist Church in 1907 and 1908. His parents were George Washington Eason, born April 28, 1855, and died November 20, 1938, and Sarah J. (Sallie) Carroll, born May 4, 1856, and died March 10, 1933. We were told growing up that her family settled in Carroll County. Also, a large number of related Easons settled in Carroll County. My mother, Bonnie Lucille Eason McCurdy, remembered a lot of second and third cousins when she was a child. George Washington Eason and Sallie Carroll Eason had seven children.They were Jesse, Lon, Leon, Georgia who married a Barnes, Ada who married Bryant Garrett, Emma who married Minton Garrett, and Milton Perry who married Ida Savannah Johnson. Ida was born October 1, 1886, and died January 7, 1921. They were married December 9, 1908. Their eight children were: Bernice who married John Beckom; Eunice who married Cleophas Gilbert and died at age twenty-four; Ruby who married George Nelson; Preston who died at twenty-one; Nelle who married Clyde Sloan; Ida Mae and Perry Jr., twins, who died as infants; and Lucille who married Jim McCurdy of Atlanta.

Milton Perry Eason

Ida's parents were Joseph Albert Johnson, born June 13, 1865, and died March 30, 1950, and Cassie Rilla Lee Johnson, born October 1, 1866, and died February 28, 1929. They had eleven children and lived in Bowdon.

George Washington Eason had two brothers, Will and Frank, who were killed in the Civil War and also another brother named Jeff who married Sallie Eason's sister in his middle years. Any others were not known.

Sallie Eason had a younger brother in Texas and a brother John in Carrollton. Both George Washington Eason and Sallie Eason were charter members of Antioch Baptist Church. He was Sunday School superintendent 1922-1924. He was also a deacon. Their son, Milton Perry Eason, was the first man to be ordained there in 1907. The church was constituted August 14, 1903.

George Washington Eason was a farmer. Both were very neat, industrious, hard-working people. The house the Eason's finally owned after moving around for many years was the center of many acres. There were four tenant houses and numerous out-buildings, a barn with corral, adjacent space for buggies, surrey, wagons and large farm equipment. There was a crib, chicken house, wash house, smoke house, outside toilet and another barn for milk cows and a lot for hogs. Also, there were fruit orchards across the road from the house. He had a blacksmith shop and shod his own mules and horses. She cooked on a wood burning range and scrubbed her kitchen floor with a corn shuck mop. Yards were swept every Saturday with a brush broom. They would pick cotton by moonlight when it was "ripe." They got up at 3:00 a.m. in the summertime and 4:00 a.m. in the wintertime. Most household chores were done by daylight. A "country store" would come by the house periodically from which she would buy household items that they didn't raise, such as cloth, thread, toilet soap, etc. For this, she traded chickens, eggs, and other items. *Submitted by: Beverly M. Oeser, 2078 Lavista Circle, Tucker, GA 30084*

533. Fayette Edge Family

Morgan Lafayette Edge was born June 10, 1841, in Meriwether County, Georgia. He died December 2, 1892, in Carroll County, Georgia. On February 12, 1867, he married Elizabeth Jane Tyson, the daughter of John Dixon Tyson and Nancy Sasser. She was born October 19, 1849, in Carroll County and died March 29, 1926, in Carroll County. Both are buried in the Powell Chapel United Methodist Church Cemetery, Carroll County.

Morgan Lafayette Edge, known as Fayette, was the son of Joseph Edge and Margaret Flynt. On August 15, 1861, he joined Company F, Infantry Battalion, Cobb's Legion, Georgia Volunteers of the C.S.A.

In 1926, the final report of his estate showed a value of $1,594.67.

Fayette and Elizabeth Jane had seven children all born in Carroll County: Robert C., Margaret Frances, Zillia C., Joseph A., Julia A., and Henry H. Edge.

Robert C. Edge, born July 4, 1868, married Mary Ann Keaton, born March 13, 1865, on October 3, 1886, in Carroll County. Robert died October 1, 1899, Mary Ann died February 23, 1942. Burial was in Powell Chapel United Methodist Church Cemetery. Their children were Allen Oliver Edge who married Hattie Lee Payne, and Venie M. Edge who married Chalmers W. Couch.

Margaret Frances Edge, born July 1, 1870, married Robert Ulysses Boyd, born April 4, 1868, in Randolph County, Alabama, on September 8, 1887, in Carroll County. Margaret died May 28, 1947, and Robert died November 25, 1955. Burial was in Powell Chapel United Methodist Church Cemetery. Their children were Joseph Clarence, Leona Velia, Ethel Florence, and Elbert Clinton Boyd. Joseph Clarence, a minister, married Zillia Williams. Leona Velia married Lindsey Hamilton Phillips. Ethel Florence married Moses Monroe Samples. Elbert Clinton married Mary Flurnoy Langston.

Zillia C. Edge, born January 20, 1873, married W.E. Williams on December 18, 1892 in Carroll County. Zillia died October 7, 1894. She is buried in Powell Chapel United Methodist Church Cemetery.

Joseph A. Edge, born April 7, 1875, married Lela E. Boyd, born April 10, 1880, on January 13, 1897, in Douglas County, Georgia. Joseph died November 30, 1903, Lela died September 1, 1900. Burial was in Powell Chapel United Methodist Church Cemetery.

Julia A. Edge, born July 1877, married John W. Loyd, born April 1872 on October 6, 1894, in Carroll County. Their children were Lizzie, Zillie, Claude F., and Ola.

Henry H. Edge, born December 1879, married Elizabeth E. Rainey, born October 1883, on May 22, 1898, in Carroll County. Both died in Cullman County, Alabama. Their children were Henry Olen, Vennie J., Herman B., Mamie K., Cora I., Venice M., Loyd E., and Essie B. Edge.

William Samuel Edge, born 1887, married Sarah Pauline Ayers, born August 31, 1891, on December 12, 1909. She died and is buried in the Little Vine Baptist Church Cemetery in Carroll County. They had one child, Wilma, born in 1911. On May 10, 1942, he married Kittie Smith. *Submitted by: Charles C. Boyd, 1496 Flat Rock Road, Villa Rica, GA 30180, and Researched by: Erlene C. Boyd.*
Sources: Personal knowledge, census, marriage and cemetery records.

534. Edgeworth

This is a history of the Edgeworth family from England and Ireland. The numbers below indicate the generation number. 1. John, no date, 2. Francis (son) married an O'Cavanagh. He died in 1627, 3. John (son of Francis) married Anne Cullum. He died in 1668, 4. Sir John, born 1638, died 1696, married Anne Bridgman,, born 1642, died 1714, 5. Francis, born 1657, died 1709, married Mary Bradston, 6. Richard, born 1701, died 1770, married Jane Ormond, 7. Richard Lovell Edgeworth, born 1744, died 1817. He lived at Edgeworthtown, Ireland where he raised his family. 8. Richard, his oldest son, came to America in 1783, married Elizabeth Knight in 1788 in Richmond County, South Carolina, 9. Richard Edgeworth, son of Richard and Elizabeth, was born 1795, married Anna Knight, 10. Their son Richard, born 1821, married Maria Knight. He came to Georgia from South Carolina after 1863. He came to Carroll County in 1870. He invested largely in Carrollton property including building the Kramer building. At the time of his death he had been engaged in farming. He died January 14, 1887. 11. His daughter, Ellen Kaziah, was born 1854 in South Carolina, married Allen Jackson Rooks, born 1851 in Carroll County. 12. Their oldest son, Ernie Jackson Rooks, born 1878, married Eunice Camp, born 1883. They married in 1912. 13. Their only child was Thelma Jackson Rooks, born 1913, married John Thomas (Jack) Pate on November 16, 1940, in Carroll County where they lived sixty years. Their children were: 14. William J. Pate married Mary Jean Smith and their children are Jodi Pate Foster and Brooke Pate; John Daniell Pate married Judy Holloway and their child is John Daniell Pate Jr.; Larry M. Pate married Jackie Bagwell and they have no children.

All three sons of Thelma Jackson Rooks and Thomas Pate live on the family farm on land given to them by their father when they married. *Submitted by: John D. Pate, 132 Old Five Notch Road, Whitesburg, GA 30182*

535. The Elam and New Families of Carrollton

Irena Jane Austin and John Elam, both from South Carolina, married about 1835. They were in Carrollton, Georgia, by 1850. The three youngest of their nine children (George, Mary Ann, Sarah, Elizabeth, Armida, Wiley Cumbia, William, Frank), including my great-grandmother, Josephine Alice Elam (b. March 16, 1855, d. May 10, 1912) were born in Carrollton. Both Irena Jane (d. June 6, 1880) and John (d. June 1, 1888) are believed to have died in the Rome Street home of Alice and her husband, D.F. New.

On December 4, 1877, Alice Elam married Dock Franklin (D.F.) New. D.F. was born in Chatooga County, Georgia, on February 14, 1852, the son of Elizabeth Lawrence and Ansel New of Virginia. He was very active in the Carrollton community. He owned a local lumberyard and helped build the First Baptist Church of Carrollton. He is recognized for this with his name on a plaque in front of the church. The home on Rome Street was solidly built for his family with the best lumber from his lumberyard. He also owned the local ice company and the first Buick agency in Carrollton (see photograph of two granddaughters Alice Mary and Miriam New with friend Sarah Burnett). D.F. and Alice had nine children (Ben, Irene, Mary Lou, Joseph Howard, Robert Paul, Annie Maude, Myrtis, Elam Coleman, and Judge), all born, raised, and buried in Carrollton.

Miriam New (front), Alice New (forward, rumble seat). About 1927.

My grandfather, Robert Paul New, born July 21, 1889, married Mamie Lee Snead, daughter of Nancy Marietta Woolsey and John Adams Snead. Mamie was also the great-niece of Rev. Isaac Gray Woolsey for whom Woolsey, Georgia, is named. "Daddy Bob" and Mamie lived in the house next door to his parents on Rome Street. The couple had four children before Mamie died on November 24, 1931, at the age of thirty-nine from complications of pregnancy. The family lost both Mamie and the baby. After the death of their mother, the New children — Rob, Alice Mary, Miriam, and Linda — were raised with the help of their paternal aunts, Irene, Mary Lou, and Annie Maude, in the large rambling home of their grandparents, D.F. and Alice Elam New.

For many seasons after my brother, cousins and I were born, our mothers would take us to visit Aunt Rena, Aunt Boo, and Annie Maude. Aunt Rena would bring out her wonderful pecans gathered from the trees in her back yard. She toasted them better than anyone else so they literally melted in our mouths. We children loved to play on the wonderful wrap-around front porch and spend hours in the porch swing, activities surely enjoyed by the two generations of children before us. *Submitted by: Gail Simmons Hammond, 2770 Jo Beth Drive, Lawrenceville, GA 30044*
Sources: Alice Mary New Simmons, Vickie Elam White, and personal knowledge.

536. Eleanor Johnson and Paul J. Eldredge

Eleanor Johnson, middle child of William T. and Evie Lee Downs Johnson, was born March 22, 1921, in Bowdon, Georgia. She married Paul Judson Eldredge September 1, 1940, in Atlanta, Georgia, at West End Baptist Church. Paul was the son of William Judson and Emma Binns Eldredge. He was born October 14, 1915, in Atlanta, and died July 23, 1994, in Baton Rouge, Louisiana. Paul served as captain in the U.S. Army 1942-45 and retired from Exxon Company after a long career. They had two sons, Walter Judson (1946) and Michael Paul (1949).

Eleanor and Paul Eldredge, 1979 Exxon Retirement Gala, Houston, TX.

In 1992 Paul Eldredge wrote the following in his *Life Writing Journal,* describing how he met Eleanor:

> "It was 1936 and I was a sophomore at Georgia Tech. One afternoon, my friend Sam Whatley came to our home on Gordon Street in Atlanta saying that I'd been studying too hard, and if I could use the family car that night he'd like to arrange a blind date for me with a girl he knew. Incidentally, he'd come along with a date also.
>
> "I was ready, the car was available, and it was a deal. Now Sam had been dating Isabelle Johnson for a long time. I learned later that the reason he did not date Isabelle that evening was that he had kept her out too late the weekend before. She was in nursing school at Georgia Baptist Hospital and curfew for the student nurses was 11 p.m. For violating curfew the prior weekend, Isabelle was restricted to quarters.
>
> "To keep himself safe with Isabelle, Sam arranged a date with her younger sister Eleanor that evening, and she in turn lined up her friend A — as a blind date for me. Now A — was an attractive and pleasant date, but I must confess I hardly noticed. From the time she got into the car with Sam,

my real attention was riveted on Eleanor Johnson. The next week I asked her for a date, and in 1940 we were married.

Moral: A blind date need not be with the 'right' girl to have lasting results.

Submitted by: Michael P. Eldredge, 225 Alex D. Owens Drive, King's Mountain, NC 28086

537. Elliott, Tolbert, and Morgan Families 1858-2001

Robert Elliott and Frances Russel were from Wilkes County, Georgia, and Oglethorpe County, Georgia. Their son, George Elliott (August 7, 1785, Wilkes County-1870, Fulton County), married Susannah Susan A. Martin (about 1800, Georgia-after 1870, Fulton County) on November 7, 1815 in Oglethorpe County. Robert is buried in the family cemetery on Bankhead Highway, Atlanta.

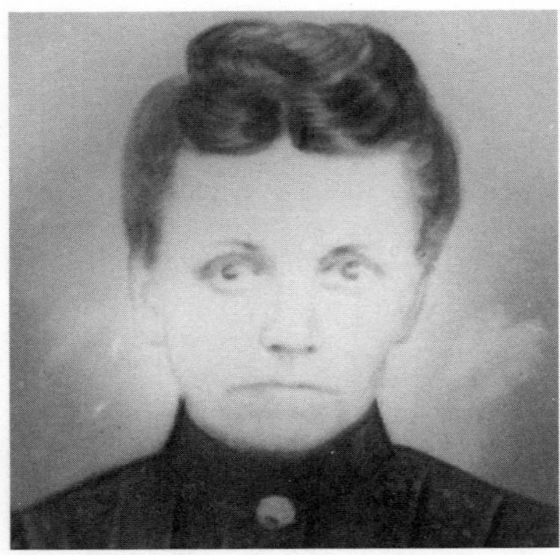

Nancy Susan Elizabeth Elliott Tolbert. 1859-1914

George and Susan had the following children: Henry in 1817, Edmond R. on November 24, 1818, Marshall Milton on October 5, 1820, Lucinda Ann on August 4, 1822, Charles Wesley on August 30, 1824, William H. on August 11, 1827, Doctor Ewell, Hopson H. in 1833, Jesse Herd in 1834, Irvin J. in 1837, Nancy E.S. in 1838, Walter in 1840, and Narcisa C. in 1841.

Doctor Ewell Elliott (April 29, 1829, Jackson County, Georgia-about 1902, Georgia) married Rose Eiseman (August 27, 1834, Prussia, Germany-November 24, 1898, Acworth, Georgia). Rose's mother was Harriett Jacobs Eiseman. Rose's siblings were Benjamin Aliece Eiseman (August 22, 1839, Prussia, Germany-July 4, 1904, Bartow County), Jacob Eiseman (July 26, 1842, Georgia-March 13, 1920, Atlanta), and Elizabeth Eiseman (March 1845, born and died in Georgia). Doctor Ewell and Rose had the following children: Edwin Jackson, Nancy Susan Elizabeth, Viney Armindy, George Benjamin (1866-1937), Beulah (1870-1943), Lucy (1871-1903), and John J. (1875-1939).

The Elliott children arrived in Carroll County in the 1870s.

Edwin Jackson Elliott (November 21, 1856-February 1, 1907, Atlanta, Georgia) married Mary Jane Mollie Tolbert (March 8, 1858. Villa Rica, Georgia-June 13, 1937, Atlanta) on January 10, 1878 in Carroll County.

Nancy Susan Elizabeth Elliott (September 18, 1859, Fulton County, Georgia-January 31, 1914, Atlanta) married John Thomas Harrison Tolbert (December 7, 1860, Villa Rica-February 8, 1947). John Thomas Harrison Tolbert is the brother of Mary Jane Mollie Tolbert. Nancy and John Tolbert are buried in Hillcrest Cemetery, Villa Rica.

Viney Armindy Elliott (August 13, 1862-March 27, 1890), married Columbus Green Morgan (February 22, 1866, Randolph County, Alabama-December 12, 1922, Spalding County, Georgia) on November 21, 1886 in Cobb County, Georgia. *Submitted by: David Nelson, P.O. Box 2195, Woodstock, GA*

Source: Patricia Tolbert Nelson, 1789 Kellogg Creek Roada, Acworth, GA 30102

538. Amanda Moses Entrekin

David Moses was the oldest son of John and Anna Moses. He was born in Pulaski County, Georgia, around 1806. He had one sister Nancy and one brother Hirman and several half brothers and sisters.

David married Martha McCrary on November 30, 1826, in Baldwin County, Georgia. They had two children: Leander Goodman Moses born 1830, and Amanda Moses (Entrekin) born in 1828.

In 1835 David went to Columbus, Georgia, and joined the 1st Company of the Georgia Battalion under Capt. William A.O. Wadsworth for the Texas cause. First Sergeant Hutchins M. Pittman preserved a copy of Lewellen's Company roster which (with his own notations as to the fate of its members) he filed in the office of the Adjutant General. The second name on the roll is David Moses, killed at Goliad. David Moses was with Dr. Grant and twenty-six others about twenty miles west of San Patricio gathering horses for the army and warning the settlers of the impending danger. They came upon a party of Gen. Urren's army at Agua Dulce. Sixteen of Grant's men were killed and four captured, including Grant. Six men escaped. David Moses was one who escaped. David Moses rejoined Fannin. On March 20, 1836, after trying to leave Goliad with his men and being surrounded by the Mexican army, Fannin surrendered to Gen. Urren. Fannin and his men were marched back to Goliad. Fannin and the soldiers were led to believe that they were to be marched back to the coast and loaded on ships and sent back to the States. These men were cruelly mistreated and finally on March 27, 1836, they were marched out at Goliad and surrounded by the Mexican army and killed. At the last battle when the Mexicans were defeated, the battle cry was "Remember Goliad and the Alamo." Later, the men's remains were gathered up and buried with full military honors by General Jefferson Rusk of Georgia.

Entrekin and Adams Families

Leander Goodman moved to Texas and married America May. They are buried in Refugio County, Texas.

Amanda married David Entrekin, son of Thomas Entrekin of South Carolina, on January 8, 1851, in Coweta County, Georgia, and moved to Mount Zion, Georgia, during the 1870s. The Entrekin family started a Methodist Church and a school in Mount Zion. Amanda and David donated the land. Both the school and church still stand today and are in use.

David and Amanda had nine children: Nancy, Leander, James, Sarah, Martha, Clifford, Luther, Irena, and Ewell. David and Amanda are buried at the Mount Zion Methodist Church.

James Melvin Entrekin was born in Coweta County, Georgia, July 26, 1854. James married Symantha J. Crawford on November 2, 1876, in Carroll County. They had four children: Eula, Lewn, Cora, and Lily. James and Symantha are buried at the Mount Zion Church cemetery. My grandmother was Eula Entrekin Adams, wife of Robert Reese Adams of Bowdon.

The photograph shows James Melvin and wife Symantha and daughter Eula Adams seated. Standing are Robert Adams holding baby Cora Entrekin, Lily Entrekin, and Lewn Entrekin. Children are Lewis Adams and Zelma Adams *Submitted by: Linda Austin, 995 Beulah Church Road, Carrollton, GA 30117*

539. Oscar Malvie (O.M.) and Lilla Bell Williamson Entrekin

Oscar Malvie (O.M.) Entrekin (31 August 1907) was born in Heard County, Georgia, to Oscar Loyd Entrekin (23 March 1886) and Naomi Beatrice Walls Entrekin (11 November 1884). He was the oldest of seven children. His family moved to Carroll County near Bowdon Junction, Georgia, when O.M. was young. They farmed several acres there.

Oscar Malvie and Lilla Williamson Entrekin, about 1975.

Lilla Bell Williamson Entrekin (3 August 1911) was born in Carroll County in the Dashboard Community near Tyus to James Buren Williamson (6 July 1872) and Janie Farmer Williamson (25 December 1874). She and her twin, Lillie Nell, were the ninth and tenth of twelve children. Her family moved near the Entrekins in the Bowdon Junction area around the 1920s.

O.M. and Lilla were married by the Rev. Grover Bell on 27 December 1933 in Bremen, Georgia. They began their lives together as farmers. They continued to farm in Bremen until 1940 when O.M. began working for Plantation Pipe Line. After a short transfer to Macon, Georgia, they moved to Bowdon in 1947. They were members of the Bowdon Baptist Church.

O.M. enjoyed the outdoors. He was an avid fisherman and especially looked forward to trout fishing in North Georgia streams. He kept registered bird dogs and enjoyed hunting with family and friends. He liked being with people and retired from Bremen-Bowdon Investment Company.

Lilla was an excellent cook and looked forward to having family members join them for meals. She had a brilliant sense of humor and felt very close to the friends she made while working at Bremen-Bowdon Investment Company. She retired early because of health problems and spent many hours embroidering and crocheting items for family and friends.

They had two children. Sara Nell (11 November 1934) married Bobby Dwight Word (26 July 1930) on 8 November 1953. Both retired from Blossman Gas Company. Peggy Ann (10 December 1943) was married first to Larry David Musick (22 January 1946) in 1968 and then on 1 July 1990 to Bob Ross Young (12 December 1939). Peggy retired from Carroll County Schools and Bob owns B&G Machinery in Ranburne, Alabama.

O.M. and Lilla's only grandchild, Penny M'Nell Word, arrived on 9 February 1962. She spent many hours in their home. Penny married Gregory Scott Akins (6 April 1958) on 14 December 1985. Greg is a senior vice-president with Citizens Bank and Trust of West Georgia. Penny is an administrative assistant with Carrollton Eye Clinic. Their children are Gregory Scott Akins Jr. (16 October 1988) and Ashley Elizabeth Akins (10 May 1993).

O.M. passed away 5 September 1975 and Lilla on 17 January 1976. They are buried in Pleasant Grove Baptist Church Cemetery on Highway 5 near Bowdon. *Submitted by: Peggy E. Young, 1163 County Road 440, Heflin, AL 36264*
Sources: Family Bible records

540. Estes Family

Elizabeth Mathews was born September 23, 1916, the oldest child of the late Mr. and Mrs. Lunie Mathews. A Temple High School graduate, she married Ray Estes, a Haralson County resident, on December 30, 1944. After his discharge from the United States Navy at the conclusion of World War II, the couple moved to Atlanta, where Mr. Estes pursued a career in commercial construction from 1948 until his retirement in 1984. During this time period, Steven Ray, their only child, was born March 19, 1953.

Mr. Estes' retirement presented an opportunity for the family to return to Carroll County. For the next ten years, they shared a renewed love for gardening. Meanwhile, Mr. Estes became a member of the Temple Lions Club, serving as club president during the 1992-1993 fiscal year.

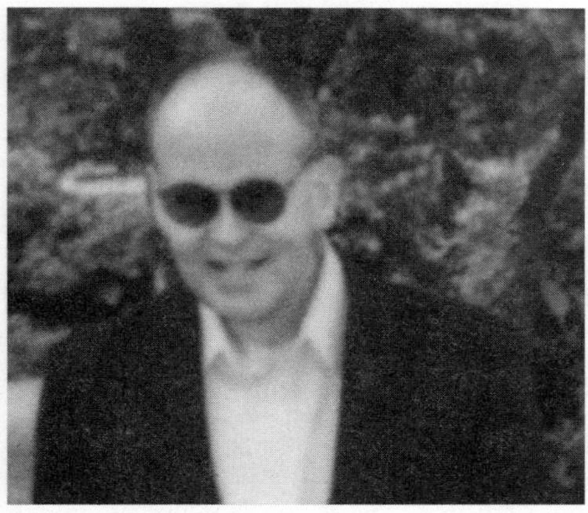

Steven Ray Estes

Since Mr. Estes' death in March 1995, Steven has continued to take an interest in Carroll County activities. He is a member of the Temple United Methodist Church, where he participates in the choir, as well as in many church leadership roles. With the dissolving of the Temple Lions Club in 1995, Steven transferred to the Villa Rica Lions Club. For the past five years, he has served on its board of directors. He eagerly awaits the challenge of serving as club president for the 2001-2002 fiscal year. Lionism is an opportunity for him to combine two of his interests — helping persons with disabilities and improving community life in the Temple/Villa Rica communities. *Submitted by: Steven Estes, 59 Carrollton Street, Temple, GA 30179*

541. Kimbrel Estes

Kimbrel Estes was born about 1815 in North Carolina. At this time, his parents are unknown. Kimbrel migrated to Georgia and was found in the 1840 and 1850 census of Troup County. He listed his occupation as a farmer. We find Kimbrel taking a bride 2 May 1837 in Troup county, Rebecca Caldwell, daughter of Matthew Tanner Caldwell and Mourning Satterwhite. Rebecca was born 10 March 1818 in Jasper County, Georgia, and had nine siblings: James, John, Elizabeth Ann, David Satterwhite, Nancy, Martha, Amy, Lucy and George W.

Kimbrel is found purchasing land lot 66 in the 10th District of Carroll County on 5 December 1850. The cost is $1200, but we find Kimbrel selling this same land to James B. Estes of Meriwether County on 24 September 1851. James B. is the right age to be Kimbrel's father but this has not been proven. Kimbrel's name was not found serving in any war but his name did appear on the 1860 mortality schedule as being killed in a combat. In the 7 February 1860 edition of the *Columbus Enquirer* on the front page is an article telling of Kimbrel being shot and killed by another man while working in his field. At press time the man had left the county. The date of death is listed as 25 January 1860 in the estate papers and his burial location is unknown. When the 1860 census was taken, Rebecca was located in Troup County in O'Neil's District. Before the 1870 census was taken, Rebecca had relocated to Cleburne County, Alabama, and by 1880 was in Cherokee County where she remained till her death on 28 May 1897 and was buried at Providence Cemetery at Forney. Her name was found on the church roll of Providence Church.

Kimbrel and Rebecca were the parents of ten children: Andrew Jackson born 1839, married Vernon Malissa Clark, Milly Tanner and Viola Greer, lived in Cheorkee County, Alabama, and Haralson County, Georgia, and had twenty-three known children; Joshua born 1840, married Frances Hart, lived in Troup County and had two children; Lucy Ann born 1845, married J.W. Whitten, lived in Troup and Carroll Counties and had five children; Isaiah born 1847, married Sarah Allen, lived in Cleburne County, Alabama,and had nine children; John Wesley born 1850, married Nancy Teague, lived in Cleburne, Cherokee and Dekalb Counties, Alabama, and had ten children; James born 1852, married Betty Patty, lived in Cherokee County, Alabama, then moved west and they one baby; Martha Ann born 1855, married Francis N. Patty, lived in Cherokee County, Alabama, and had seven children; Buchoner born 1857, married Carrie, lived in Polk County, Georgia, and had three children; Elizabeth born 1857, married John Ed Simmons, lived in Polk County, Georgia, and Cherokee County, Alabama, and they had six children; and Sarah Lorraine born 1858, married James Meadows and William King, lived in Polk County, and had seven children.

Many descendants of this family now reside in Georgia and Alabama. *Submitted by: Sandra Allen, 160 E. Greenwood Drive, Carrollton, GA 30117 sloua@aol.com*

542. Evans

William Evans, a Revolutionary War veteran, and his wife Andelen were in Jasper County, Georgia, in 1810 and in Pike County by 1850. Their children were Joshua (wife Rebekah R. Smith, daughter of Abraham and Sarah Rosser Smith), Lee L. (wife Charity), David (wife Anna Knoles), and Evan in Jasper County with eleven children in 1820.

The children of Joshua and Rebekah were Benjamin Franklin (wife Sophronia A. Futrell), William H. (wife Frances Akin), Isaac E. (wife Mary Young), J.M. (wife Manerva), and Joseph H. (wife Pheriba R.T. Futrell). Lee and Charity's children were Mary J., David U., Martha C., Catherine A., Susan C., and Lee R.

William H. and Frances Akin Evans moved to Carroll County just after 1850 and lived near Holly Springs and Reid Mountain. Their children were David Americus, Benjamin Franklin, Mary P.C., Georgia, Samantha, and William H., (wife Annie). Most of the other Evans, Akin, and Futrell families later moved to Carroll County during the Civil War.

Benjamin Franklin Evans - Killed at Battle of Cedar Creek,Virginia

The Evans and Futrell families were blacksmiths, woodworkers, shoemakers and farmers. In the census of 1860 Benjamin F. Evans was a blacksmith and had property valued at $850. He and Sophronia's children were Phereba Caroline (married Thomas William Wallis), Benjamin H., and Louisa A. (married John T. Kierbow).

Joseph H., Benjamin F., and William H. Evans were all in the 53rd Georgia Infantry Regiment during the Civil War. Joseph H. was wounded during the battle at Cold Harbor and died in a Richmond, Virginia, hospital in 1864. Benjamin F. Evans was killed at the Battle of Cedar Creek in 1864. William H. Evans was wounded through the chest and shoulder at Cold Harbor. Furloughed home for the rest of the war.

After the war Phereba Caroline and Thomas William Wallis moved to Carroll County and settled near their Uncle William H. and Aunt Frances Evans. John T. and Louisa A. Evans Kierbow also moved to the same area in 1885 and lived in the log house built by John Stephen Earnest for a while. See related article on log house. Their children were Effie, Lilly (married Quill Casey), Edgar, Van (married Lela Parker), William and Henry. Van was killed by a falling tree. Quill and Lilly's children were Vera (married Tom Pettigrew), Leona (married Larkin Akin), Willie Mae (married Kaylor Norton), Rudy (Doc) (married Mary Day) and Lucille.

Phereba Caroline and Thomas William Wallis' children were Manuel, Walter, Viola, and Wilbur. See related article on the Wallis family. *Submitted by: Mary Casey Finnell*
Sources: Wallace T. Lambert

543. Evans Family

The fourth son of William Evans and Frances Akin, Moses Jefferson Evans was born about July, 1855, probably in Carroll County, Georgia, where his parents had recently settled near relatives after moving from Pike County. Moses was enumerated in his father's household in Carroll County in 1860 and in the home of his widowed mother Frances in 1870. Six years later, on 13 January 1876, he married Nancy P.G. Williams in Carroll County and headed his own household at the time of the 1880 Carroll County census.

Nancy P.G. Williams Evans was born 31 July, 1862, also in Carroll County, and died 22 April, 1940 in LaGrange, Troup County, Georgia. She was buried there in Hillview Annex Cemetery.

Nancy was the only surviving child of Perry G.J. Williams, a Confederate soldier who died in 1863 in Lynchburg, Virginia, and his wife Priscilla Coleman, whom he married 13 May 1861 in Carroll County. Perry's parents were Wyatt and Nancy (Williams) Williams, who had married 12 March 1829 in Meriwether County. Priscilla's parents were Humphrey Coleman, son of Samuel and Sarah Evans Coleman (natives of Virginia who married in 1805 in Greene County, Georgia), and Nancy Earnest. Nancy Earnest Coleman's parents were Elisha Earnest (1797-1892) and Priscilla Williams (1795-1860) who settled in Carroll County in the early 1850s. The Williams and Earnest families had come together from Clarke County (where Elisha and Priscilla married on 22 January 1818) to western Georgia. It seems likely that Elisha's wife Priscilla was a sister of either Wyatt Williams or his wife Nancy. George Earnest (1762-1840), a Revolutionary soldier, and his wife Catherine White (1761-after 1845) left Louisa and Hanover counties (Virginia) and settled in Georgia at the end of the eighteenth-century. When the Creek lands to the west opened for settlement by white settlers, they were part of a migration of several allied families from Clarke County into Meriwether and Carroll counties. Descendants of the Earnest and Williams families remained in Carroll and Meriwether counties into the twentieth-century, and several members of the Earnest family continued to intermarry with Evans family members.

In the 1880s, Moses and Nancy Evans moved with several of Moses siblings and his mother into Randolph County, where they lived in Burson's Precinct. Moses was enumerated there in 1900. He afterward moved to Coweta County where he died 15 September 1916. By 1920, Nancy and her children had settled in LaGrange. Her obituary described her as a beloved resident of the Dixie Mill Village where she had lived on Georgia Avenue for more than two decades. Moses and Nancy had several children who died as infants or young adults, including a daughter Frances. Surviving offspring were: Ophelia Evans Spivey (1883-1947); Alice Evans Cummings Roberson (1888-1969); Jesse Green Evans (1890-1962) who married Josie Bearden and Luna Mae Sheppard; Eldridge Evans (1896-1941) who married Eddie Blake; and Joseph Bernard Evans (1901-1964) who married Jessie Cash.

Submitted by: Kathryn H. Knight, 64 North Cary Street, Wood Glen Apartment D-17, LaGrange, GA 30240

544. John Henry Evans

John Henry Evans, born 17 April 1852 in Spalding County, Georgia, died 18 April 1906 in Randolph County, Alabama. John Henry was the son of William Evans and Mary France Akins. When John Henry was three years of age, the family moved to Carroll County, Georgia, in 1855 and settled in the seventh district. When John Henry was only thirteen years of age, his father, serving in the Civil War, died of smallpox as a prisoner of war in Alton, Illinois. William Evans was buried on Small Pox Island at Alton, Illinois.

John Henry Evans, the oldest child in the family was forced to accept the responsibility as the head of the family. When John Henry was twenty years of age he returned to Spalding County, and married his cousin, Lucinda C. Helms, 4 March 1873. A short time later they returned to Carroll County where their first child was born 9 March 1874. John Henry purchased farm land from Chief McIntosh. His primary occupation was farming; however, he also owned and operated a grist mill. The 1880 Carroll County census gave his occupation as a miller. It was related that he was known for his willingness to assist others in his community in various activities.

Lucinda C. Helms, John Henry Evans' wife, was the daughter of Henry Helms and Mary Ann Akins. She was born, 22 October 1855 in Spalding County, died in Randolph County, Alabama. John Henry and Lucinda are both buried in the Rocky Branch Baptist Church Cemetery in Randolph County. During their thirty-three years of marriage they were blessed with fourteen children.

John Henry and Lucinda Evans survived several difficult years. Only eight of their fourteen children reached adulthood, six died before they reached their teen-age years. One of the saddest days of their lives must have been when their thirteenth child, George Washington passed away, for on that same day their fourteenth child was stillborn.

John Henry and Lucinda C. (Helms) Evans with 5 of their 14 children. L/R: Ivadell, Robert, John Wesley, Thomas Henderson, and Elisha Cleveland.

John Henry and Lucinda Evans' eight children who reached adulthood gave them eighty grandchildren. Their children and spouses are as follows:

William Henry Evans, born 9 March 1874 in Carroll County and died 25 October 1930 in Carroll County. He married Annie Helms on 2 August 1894. She was born 7 July 1874 in Spalding County, and died in Griffin, Georgia. They had seven children.

James Franklin Evans, born 1 December 1875 in Carroll County and died 16 May 1937 in Carroll County; he was married twice. His first wife, Sarah Maggie Miles, born 3 November 1895 and they had three children. The second marriage was to Violet Valerie Garrison, born 1896 in Tallapoosa County, Alabama. They had three children.

Mary France "Mollie" Evans, born 11 November 1877 in Carroll County and died 5 December 1957 in Randolph County, Alabama. She married Elisha Henry Rollins on 26 December 1897. He was born 13 May 1867 in Randolph County and died 1 August 1949 in Randolph County. They had nine children.

Martha Lucinda "Lull" Evans, born 8 October 1881 in Carroll County and died 11 March 1952 in Carroll County. She married George Albert Huey on 11 December 1898 in Randolph County, Alabama. He was born 26 May 1879 and died 4 April 1974 in Carroll County. They had nine children.

John Wesley "Wes" Evans, born 11 December 1884 in Carroll County and died 10 November 1945 in Carroll County. John Wesley "Wes" was married twice. His first wife was Hosanna Camp, born 1891 and died in 1917 in Randolph County, Alabama. John Wesley "Wes" and Hosanna Evans were married 24 September 1905 in Randolph County. They had five children. John Wesley "Wes" second wife, Bertha Lou Garrison, born 31 January 1901 in Chambers County, Alabama, and died 11 August 1973 in Atlanta, Fulton County, Georgia. John Wesley "Wes" and Bertha Lou Evans are buried at Pleasant View Baptist Cemetery, Carroll County.

John Wesley "Wes" and Hosanna Evans children were all born in Randolph County, Alabama. They are as follows: Lera Ethel Evans married Charles M. Dean; Nora Clyde Evans married Clarence Crammer; Lonnie Leo Evans married Eula Mae Gable; Eva Mavodean Evans married Euclid Moon; Charles Evans, stillborn.

John Wesley "Wes" and Bertha Lou Evans children, all born in Carroll County, are as follows: Minnie Lee Evans married James Edward Lewis; Ruby Mae Evans married James France Vaughn; Mary Eloise Evans married Ralph McDonald McCain; Eva Christine Evans married Lynwood L. Hubbard; Evelyn Floriene Evans married John W. Eason and Dorothy Marie Evans married Waymon Hasten Kierbow.

Thomas Henderson Evans, born 5 April in Carroll County and died 29 May 1972 in Randolph County, Alabama. He married Mary Angeline Bailey, born 19 January 1893 and died 27 November 1985. Thomas Henderson and Mary Angeline Evans were married 24 August 1910 in Randolph County. They had three children.

Robert N. Evans, born 5 May 1888 in Carroll County and died 13 January 1908. It is said that he married a Nettie (last name unknown) and they had children but no record can be found.

Elisha Cleveland "Cleave" Evans, born 8 December 1892 in Carroll County and died 2 December 1951 in Greenville, South Carolina. He was married twice. His first wife, "Sallie" George, born about 1891 and died 28 November 1973 in LaGrange, Troup County, Georgia. They had nine children. His second wife, Minnie Lemerle Manley. They had five children.

Ivodell Evans, born 23 August 1895 and died 1 April 1925 in Randolph County, Alabama. She married James Robert Rollins who died 16 September 1954 in Randolph County. Ivodell and Robert Rollins was married 14 August 1911 in Randolph County. They had five children.

Submitted by: Mrs. Christine Evans Hubbard, 1079 Ball Park Road, Thomasville, NC 27360, kurakai@nr.infi.net

545. Thomas Henderson Evans

Thomas Henderson Evans was born on 5 April 1886 in Carroll County, Georgia. He died 29 May 1972 in Randolph County, Alabama, and is buried at Union Hill Baptist Church Cemetery in Randolph County. He married Mary Angeline Bailey, daughter of Solomon Henry Jeremiah Bailey (born 28 May 1867, died 13 March 1946) and Martha Odelia Henry (born 19 February 1872, died 6 January 1938), on 24 August 1910 in Heard County, Georgia.

Henderson (pronounced Hennichson by friends and family) was the seventh of fourteen children born to John Henry Evans and Lucinda Helms. His brothers and sisters were: William Henry, James Franklin, Mary Frances (Rollins), Joel P., Martha Lula (Huey), John Wesley, Robert N., Mattie Mabel (died young), Elisha Cleaveland, Ivadell (Rollins), Ola Pearl (died young), George W., and an unnamed brother who was stillborn. John Henry and Lucinda moved their family to Randolph County, Alabama, when Henderson was a young boy.

Though Henderson was a farmer most of his life, he also worked in textile industries on several occasions and briefly owned and operated a café in Roanoke, Alabama. He was of the Baptist faith and served as a deacon for many years in several Randolph County churches, including Union Hill Baptist Church and Union Baptist Church. He possessed a good basic knowledge in music and was often asked to lead the congregation in singing and occasionally taught singing school.

Three sons were born to Henderson and Mary: (1) Doris Leon Evans born 6 March 1912, died 7 April 1982, married Eulette Electra Fincher born

Thomas Henderson and Mary Angeline Evans, with sons Thomas Dewey, Doris Leon, and John Henry.

25 March 1916; (2) Thomas Dewey Evans born 26 September 1914, died 14 June 1998, married Alma Bailey Evans born 22 March 1918; (3) John Henry Evans born 11 October 1916, died 12 November 1989, married Izetta Matthews born about 1916.

Henderson's wit and keen sense of humor won him many friends and made him a favorite among nephews, nieces and grandchildren. The writer, a grandson, fondly remembers the children's games that he played with us and the many occasions that we walked down to the creek to either fish or swim. Visiting our grandparents was something that my brother Barry and I always looked forward to, especially during summer school breaks when we could stay for a week or two at a time.

Mary performed her role as a homemaker, wife, mother and grandmother as well as anyone could. She possessed wisdom and knowledge well beyond that obtained in her few years of schooling. Both she and Henderson played prominent roles during the formative years of their grandchildren, helping to teach us to know right from wrong and being good examples for us to follow. They were salt of the earth people. *Submitted by: Jerry W. Evans, 225 Inland Circle, Newnan, GA 30263*

546. William Evans

William Evans was born in 1827 in Jasper County, Georgia. He died from smallpox on 9 March 1865 at Alton, Illinois, where he was a prisoner of war. He married Frances Akin, a daughter of John Akin and Elizabeth Dingler, on 7 February 1847 in Pike County, Georgia. Frances was born ca. 1824 in Jasper County and she died ca. 1889, probably in Carroll County, Georgia. Her place of burial is unknown but she may be buried in an unmarked grave in the Linity Methodist Church Cemetery where her brother Isham Akin is buried which is located only a few hundred yards from where she lived for more than thirty years.

William Evans was the son of Jesse Evans and Lucinda Dingler who were married on 16 April 1826 in Jasper County, Georgia. Jesse was born ca. 1788 in Wilkes County, Georgia and died in July 1869 in Clay County, Alabama. Lucinda was born ca. 1805 in Georgia and died before 1860 probably either in Troup County, Georgia or Randolph County, Alabama. Additional children by Jesse and Lucinda were: Elisha J., Frances (Green), Elijah T., Dennis Pascal, James H., and George W. Jesse had several children from an earlier marriage to Nancy (Polly) (?). Jesse and Nancy were members of Antioch Baptist Church in Morgan County, Georgia, at the time of her death in 1824.

William and Frances moved their family from Spalding County, Georgia, to Carroll County around 1855 and settled in the 7th District. About 1862, Frances' parents John and Elizabeth Akin and brother, Isham Akin, also moved from Spalding County to Carroll and settled on adjoining properties to William's, but which was in the 10th District. About the same time, another brother, William G. Akin, purchased property from William Evans and moved his family to Carroll County. William G. Akin died of typhoid fever at a hospital in Richmond, Virginia, on 20 June 1863.

William Evans, a farmer, built a one-story frame house in Carroll County in the 1850s. (See accompanying picture.) This house was later renovated by a successor owner, and the attractive white, now two-story, house located on Meadowbrook Road near the intersection with Bowdon Junction Road is still occupied. Children of William and Frances were: Elisha J., John Henry, William Alexander, Moses Jefferson, David Americus, Benjamin Franklin, Mary P.C. (Entrekin), Georgia Anne, and Eliza Samantha (Helms).

William Evans served as a Confederate soldier in the Civil War in Company C of the 26th Regiment, Georgia Infantry. He was enlisted by Captain N. Estes on 1 September 1863. It was following the first battles of the Atlanta campaign fought at Resaca, Georgia, on 14 and 15 May, 1864, that William was captured at Calhoun, Georgia, on 16 May 1864. He was transported by rail to Nashville, Tennessee, then to Louisville, Kentucky, and arrived at Alton, Illinois on 25 May 1864.

Following is a letter that William wrote to his wife Frances dated 28 November 1864 only a few months prior to his death. It reveals that William was a compassionate man who trusted in God, loved his family, and was concerned for the well-being of all that were a part of his life. Of such heritage this writer, a great-great-grandson, is proud to claim.

Thomas D. Evans, great-grandson of William Evans, standing in front of house that William built.

Alton Illinois

November the 28th 1864

My Dear wife, it is with pleasure that I am permitted this day to right you A few lines which will inform you that I am well at the present-time and it is my sincere desire that those lines may reach you in due time and find you and the children enjoying the best of health. I hav nothing verry important to right to you at this time more than I wood be extremley glad to see you and the children and all my friends but we are so distantly situated that it is impossible fore me to see you at the presant but I oftimes see you in my night visions but then I awake and you are not present then sleepless hours pass by and trouble banish all my immaginary happiness. But I still hav A hope that we will meet again this side of eternity to spend our latter days together as we once hav done in laboring to raise our dear little children to those ends let us continue to pray to our heavenly Father who is willin to heare and answer our petitions. The health of the people here are not as good as it has previously bin E.W. Peace Died on yesterday evening at sun set W.H. Steed is well R.F. Thurman is in the Horspitle though not much sick he says tell his Father to continue to pray for him the wether is verry cold here at times send me word when you hav herd from your brothers and mine giv my respects to your Father and Mother and Jane Tiney Babe Mare Sarah Voley and Lue and all inquiring friends right as often as you can and I will pay the postage here Direct to Alton Military Prison Illinois. Fairwell Williams Evans

Submitted by: Jerry W. Evans, 225 Inland Circle, Newnan, GA 30263

547. Robert Edward Falls Family

Robert Edward Falls Sr. was born near Double Springs (Winston County), Alabama, and moved to Gainesville, Alabama, to work as a carpenter. He was a supervisor with the CCC and retired from the Soil Conservation Service. He lived briefly in Carrollton prior to his death at age eighty-four.

Mattye Annie Turner grew up in Mount Sterling (Choctaw County), Alabama. After attending college in Livingston, Alabama, she accepted a teaching position in Gainesville, Aabama, which is situated on the Tombigbee River. There she met and married R.E. Falls. To this couple were born a daughter and two sons: Robert Edward Falls and Joseph Benjamin Falls. In her later years she moved to Carrollton to live with Laura and Ross Miller until her death in 1979. She is buried with her husband in the Odd Fellows Cemetery in Gainesville, Alabama.

Laura F. Miller was born in Gainesville, (Sumter County) Alabama, at home on Yankey Street on May 2, 1929. She was the second of three children (the only girl) born to Robert Edward Falls and Mattye Annie Turner Falls. Laura graduated from Livingston High School in 1947. In the fall of 1947 she entered college at Alabama College, Alabama (then an all girls school, the equivalent of GSCW in Georgia), located in Montevallo, Alabama (Shelby County). In college she prepared to be a high school teacher with a major in history and a minor in mathematics. Upon graduation in 1951, Annie Laura Falls accepted a position as math teacher at Valley Vocational High School in Langdale, Alabama (Chambers County). Laura Miller continued her education by attending summer session at the University of Alabama and Emory University and later by taking several courses at West Georgia College. The following year she moved to LaGrange High School in LaGrange, Georgia (Troup County) where she taught until her marriage to Ross W. Miller in 1962. Ross was an elementary school principal in West Point, Georgia. Approximately a year later they moved to Carrollton, Georgia (Carroll County) where they have lived since that time, with one exception. Ross took leave from West Georgia College in 1966 to study at the University of New Mexico where he received his EDD degree. Robert Walter Miller was born on June 27, 1964 before they went to New Mexico in August. Eliza Anne Miller, daughter of Ross and Laura, was born on September 9, 1965 during their stay in Albuquerque. *Submitted by: Laura Falls Miller, 155 Greenwood Lane, Carrollton, GA 30117*

548. Sarah Emma Ferrell Family

Samuel Ferrell was born around 1808 in South Carolina and died around 1884. Elizabeth Crumbley was born in Henry County, Georgia, around 1810. She was the daughter of George Crumbley of Henry County and Tabatha McMacky Crumbley. Samuel was a farmer.

During the Civil War, Sam took clothes and food to his sons who were in battle and became sick with the fever. When the northern troops came to Henry County, they came to Sam and Elizabeth's house. They wanted all their food. Elizabeth was sick in bed and the girls had put the food in bed with their mother so the soldiers couldn't find it. When one soldier started toward the bed, the oldest daughter Tobatha told him if he touched her mother she would beat him with the stick of stove wood in her hand. The soldier said he believed she would and turned and left.

Sam and Elizabeth are buried at the Old Tallapoosa Primitive Church in Carroll County, Georgia. Samuel and Elizabeth had eleven children: (1) William H. Ferrell born March 5, 1839, (2) Tobatha E. born January 17, 1840, (3) Samuel A. Ferrell born November 7, 1842, (4) Anthony M. Ferrell born November 5, 1844, (5) Mary R. Ferrell born September 16, 1846, (6) Martha C. Ferrell born January 13, 1849, The twins (7) Nancy Kate and (8) Sarah Emma Ferrell born September 30, 1856, (9) Glory T. Ferrell, (10) Joseph F. Ferrell born 1856, and (11) Mary E. Ferrell born 1860.

According to the Henry County marriage records, Tobatha Ferrell married Allen Johnson in 1886. Sarah Emma Ferrell married George Washington Williamson in Carroll County, Georgia, on February 20, 1881.

Sarah and George W. Williamson had four children: Henry, Robert, Elizabeth (Sissy), and Nanny Kate, Sarah died January 19, 1939, G.W. Williamson died on October 15, 1920, after a surgery had gone bad. They are buried in the Carrollton City Cemetery.

The Ferrell family picture includes Sarah, Nancy, Mary and Tobatha on the front row, and Sissy, George W. Williamson, Tom Walker, and Robert Williamson on the back row. *Submitted by: Sarah McEwen, 1016 Beulah Church Road, Carrollton, GA 30117*

Ferrell Family

549. Marion Lafayette Fisher Family

In May 1923, Marion Lafayette Fisher with his wife Beatrice Taylor Fisher, formerly of Rome, moved to Carrollton from Cedartown to open Fisher's 5 Cent and 10 Cent Store. Born in Murray County, he attended school in Rome and became a protege of Martha Berry who recognized his potential. Through Miss Berry's influence, M.L. attended Dwight L. Moody's School at Mt. Herman, Massachusetts.

His first store in Carrollton was on Newnan Street (where Tisinger Law Firm is now located). Later he moved his successful business to the corner of Adamson Square and Rome Street. His wife and children, Taylor, Marion Jr., Beatrice, and Helen, often helped in the store.

Mr. Fisher early became involved in life in Carrollton. He was a member of the Carrollton Board of Education, a founder and president of the board of directors of Carrollton Federal Savings and Loan, a director of the Peoples Bank, member of the Rotary Club, Civitan Club, a steward in First Methodist Church and president of the Men's Bible Class.

After selling his fleet of stores in West Georgia, M.L. Fisher became a Realtor, building houses on Bankhead and Dixie Streets and his home place on the corner of Spring and Rome Streets (now occupied by grandson Jim Dye and his wife Martha, an ordained "United" Methodist minister).

Marion L. Fisher Jr. also became a Carrollton merchant after selling his 5 and 10 Cent stores in West Georgia. A graduate of UGA and a Naval officer during WWII when he attended Harvard Business School, he established Fisher's Hardware on Newnan (across from the United Methodist Church). He was chairman of the Carrollton School Board, a charter member of Sunset Hills Country Club, a director of the Merchants Association, a member of the Methodist Church Board of Stewards and the Men's Bible Class. He was married to the late Sally Clodfelter and has two daughters, Marena and Jane, and four grandchildren. He married second Douglass McFerrin Ruskell. Marion worked for the Georgia State auditor for sixteen years after selling his store. *Submitted by: Marion L. Fisher Jr., 205 Camp Drive, Carrollton, GA 30117*

550. James Monroe Fletcher Family

Part 1

James Monroe Fletcher was born August 31, 1816, in Morgan County, Georgia, and moved to Carroll County in February of 1860. He died December 25, 1904. He was married to Sarah Haynes of Henry County, Georgia, on November 16, 1841. Their children were James, Elizabeth, Robert, Celia, Mary, Theresa, Margaret, Amanda, Rabe, Rufus and John.

James Monroe Fletcher, 1816-1904

James was a successful farmer of the Burwell community and a founder of the Shiloh Campground. He was a member of Salem Baptist Church where he served for many years as a deacon, Sunday School teacher and superintendent.

James was a militiaman in the Indian Wars of the 1830s and also served in the Confederate Army. He is buried at Salem Baptist Church cemetery. *Submitted by: Joel Franklin Fletcher, 2207 Windsor Drive, Snellville, GA 30078*

Sources: Reba Tarpley Morgan and Delia Fletcher Langley

551. John Stell Fletcher Family

Part 2

John Stell Fletcher was born February 12, 1865, and died May 28, 1936. He married Martha Ann Kuglar (1869-1925) and they had eight children. One child, Fred, died in infancy. John, known as Johnny, was the eleventh child of James Monroe Fletcher and Sarah Haynes. (See related James Monroe Fletcher story.)

John Stell Fletcher was an outstanding citizen of the Burwell and Farmer's High communities. He was a successful farmer and gifted carpenter, beloved by all his children who called him "Papa." The family was struck by tragedy on May 30, 1925, with the sudden death of beloved wife and mother, Martha Ann.

These were the years of the boll weevil and during this period John was forced out of farming as were so many Georgia farmers. After losing his wife and farm, he followed three of his children, Frank, Eva, and Margie, to College Park, Georgia, where he lived for a time. During this period he stayed with several of his children for extended visits.

The legend is that he was much admired by the widows of College Park. He had brought with him from the farm his mule, Old Nell, and he and Nell were kept busy plowing the gardens of College Park. Once Nell fell into a deep hole and the fire department helped pull her out.

John was a life-long Baptist and is buried beside his wife at Antioch Baptist Church Cemetery in the Antioch community. By all accounts he was deeply loved and respected by his large family and many friends.

John Stell and Martha Ann Kuglar Fletcher Family

His children were Ruth, Alma, Willie Mae, James, Frank, Eva and Margie Fletcher. Their children number thirteen and their grandchildren twenty-eight. We, his grandchildren, cherish the life and legacy of this good and kind man.

Shown in the family photograph are John Stell and Martha Ann seated in front. Standing from left to right are Frank, Ruth, Alma, Margie, Willie Mae, Jim, and Eva. *Submitted by: Joel F. Fletcher, 2207 Windsor Drive, Snellville, GA 30078*

552. King Daniel Folds

King Daniel Folds was born 1 May 1861 in Haralson County, Georgia, to Elijah Folds and Mary Ann (Polly) Blackmon. Elijah was born 1837 in Georgia, the son of King Tyre and Maranda Folds and married Polly 13 June 1860 in Haralson County. In the 1860 census of Haralson County, Elijah and Polly are found living in the household of her parents, Daniel and Nancy Blackmon.

We found Elijah listed on a Civil War muster roll of the militia of Haralson County with commanding officer Col. John Dean. King Daniel, the only child of Elijah and Polly, was sixteen months old when Elijah lost his life in the Civil War at Bean Station, Tennessee, on 19 September 1862. Six years later, Polly married William Adams and had three children, Sarah Cordelia, Frank Marion and John R. Adams.

King Daniel married Mary Frances Easterwood (parents unknown) 23 September 1879 in Carroll County. King Daniel and Molly were members of Pleasant View Baptist Church and made their home in the Mandeville area of Carroll County. King Daniel listed his occupation as a farmer, saw miller and horse trader.

Nine children were born of this union: (1) Ada married James Fred Allen. Their children were McCurdy, Carlene, Lorene, Theodore and Clovis. (2) Nora married James T. Lovvorn. Children were Dolly, Ralph, Bertha, Loyce and Melton (Punk). (3) Elijah Daniel married Vertie Anderson. Their child was Lawrence William. (4) Laura Mae married Thomas Avian Lott. Their children were Reese, Cleola, and Roberta Evelyn. (5) Wyley Thomas married Dessie Dingler. Their children were Lowell, Paul, Hoke, Odie, Nolly, Dolly, Voncee, Hulett, and Ossie Ree. (6) Minnie V. married James Hudson. Their child was Nol. (7) Lennie B. Ethel (Effie) married William Stansel Adams. Their children were Aubrey Lee and Laura Juanita. (8) Ila Leona married George T. Lankford. Their children were Louise, Grafton, Hosea, Mary, Christine, Homer, Ellis, Hadley, and George Jr. (9) Abner R. married Minnie Crews. Their children were Ima Jean, Horace, Dura, Cora, Wynelle, Barbara Marie, Billy Ray, Raymond, and Clifford.

Molly and King Daniel were married twenty-five years when Molly died in 1904 at the age of forty-two and was laid to rest in Pleasant View Cemetery.

On 3 August 1916 we find King Daniel marrying his second wife, Missy Rudy, and in 1920 they obtained a divorce; reason unknown at this time. On 3 July 1921 King Daniel is found marrying his third wife Ora Hutson. From this union one son was born 16 July 1933, Franklin D., married Jeanette Nicholson, without issue. King Daniel died 20 October 1933 at the age of seventy-two and was laid to rest along side Mary Frances at Pleasant View Cemetery, north of Carrollton. *Submitted by: Wilbur Allen, 318 Ingram Road, Carrollton, GA 30117. sloua@aol.com*

553. John McEver Forbes 1800-1895

Who best to tell a story, but the man who lived it?

"Mr. John M. Forbes, better known as Uncle Johnnie Forbes .... The deceased was well known in this and adjacent counties and was held in the highest esteem ... a most excellent man, an elder in the Presbyterian Church and his life and influence was for the elevation of his fellow man and the betterment of society. He was one of the most devout and consistent Christians the writer has ever known ...

"Some two or three years ago, the deceased ... came into the *Carrollton Free Press* office ... this writer wrote down the following sketch of his life at his dictation:

> I was born in Jackson County, Georgia .... Jackson County at that time was a frontier country, joining the Indian Nation. Mother was a good woman and I was carefully raised in accordance with the teachings of Scripture ...
>
> At the age of twenty-three I moved to Henry County. While in this county I served as clerk of the Superior Court for one term and ... I surveyed the ground upon which McDonough now stands ... I went back to Jackson County and married ... moved to Fayette County where I lived a number of years ... I farmed.
>
> I also built a saw mill on the Flint River. I served as Justice-of-the-Peace two terms while in Fayette County. I moved to Benton, now Calhoun County, Alabama, where I farmed. I lived there til after the War. Served two terms as Justice-of-the-Peace while in Alabama. Moved to Carroll County, Georgia in 1868, where I have resided ever since.
>
> In 1829 I joined the Presbyterian Church and have been a member since. At the age of twenty-four I married Azubah McNeas, who died in 1844. Unto us were born five children: Ralph; Margaret, who married James Carlyle Schackelford; James Arthur, who married Frances Jennings; Michael Dixon married Joanna Jordan; William Patton married Sarah McCully.
>
> I was afterward married to Ann Davis. She died in 1877 ... no children.

John McEver Forbes was the son of Arthur and Catherine McEver and the grandson of Colin Forbes and Mary Hawthorne and John McEver and Margaret Collins. He and Ann are buried in Bonner Cemetery in Carrollton. Their descendants are scattered throughout Alabama, California, Georgia, Florida, Texas, and Oklahoma. *Submitted by: Mr. and Mrs. Durward Forbes, 410 North Avenue, Villa Rica, GA 30180*

Sources: Documented in a book in the Villa Rica library, *Colin Forbes, His Ancestors, Descendants and Related Lines.*

554. George Washington Foster

George Washington Foster was the son of William Sims and Mary Ellen Arnold Foster. William Sims' parents were Richard and Nancy Ward Foster from the Jasper/Wilkes County, Georgia, area. George W. was born 16 July 1854 in Carroll County. He married Victoria Adeline Eady in 1873. Her father, Jackson J. Eady, was a CSA veteran.

George W. and Victoria A. moved to the Flint Corner of Carroll County early in their marriage. They tended 200 acres of land and ran a general community store. They raised ten children: James (Jimmy), born 1888, married Delia McWhorter; John T., born 1877, married Phoebe Reeves; William J. (Billy) married Lonie; George M., born 1891, married Mary Ellen Farmer; Emory L., born 1880, married Effie Bowling; Lula Jane, born 1882, married John W. Stevens; Temperance Amanda, born 1877, married John W. Finley; Callie married Lonnie McWhorter; Idela S., born 1880, married Jackson Bates; Sarah Elizabeth, born 1878, married (1) Lorenzo Bates, (2) Thomas, (3) Bivens, and (4) Lowe.

George W. Foster was a Methodist and a Mason. He was believed to be an honest man with high moral character. According to the memoriam published by the Carroll Mason Lodge, he was held in high esteem. A story told

Family of William Sims and Mary Ellen Arnold Foster

by his family: he began dressing for an appointment when the children asked if they could harness the horse. He replied, "No, they have paid their debt, this one is one I promised to pay today." George W. promised to pay a debt by Saturday. On his honor, he walked to Carrollton Saturday afternoon and returned Sunday morning before daybreak.

The family members own the George Washington home on Five Points Road, Waco, Georgia, today. George and Victoria are buried at Old Camp Methodist Cemetery. George was a member of that church for many years. After Victoria died in June 1922, George W. married Amanda Holcum. George's health failed and he spent the last few months in the home of some of his children who cared for him.

Front, George W., and Victoria Foster. Back, George M. and Victoria Callie.

The second picture shows George W. Foster and Victoria Adeline Eady Foster with their two youngest children, George M. and Victoria Callie McWhorter. *Submitted by: Jinnie Kelley, 485 Buncombe-Waco Road, Waco, GA 30132*

Sources: Carroll County, Georgia marriage records, census, newspaper articles, cemetery markers and family recollections.

555. Robert Sinclair Foster

Robert Sinclair Foster and his brother, Thomas Allison, migrated to Gwinnett County, Georgia, about 1831 from the Spartanburg District of South Carolina. Robert was married to Margaret Allison and he became a deputy sheriff for Gwinnett County. They had the following children: William Green born ca 1831; Thomas A. born ca 1834; Margaret born ca 1836; Kinchen Rambo born ca 1838; Robert born ca 1840; Matilda born ca 1842; Moses 1845; John Cunningham ca 1852.

Robert R. and Hugh Blair McGee sold their property on the Black Bluff Road in 1863-1888 to George G. Thomas, William G. Foster, Foster and Brothers. The McGees owned fifteen forty-acre land lots for a total of 600 acres. Legendary stories say there was gold in that area and that is why the land lots were in 40 acre lots in the southwestern part of the county.

A beautiful two-story colonial home facing the Black Bluff Road was the residence of the Fosters.

William Green Foster and Kinchen Rambo Foster married Mayo sisters, the daughters of Micajah Mayo, who built the Mayo lock and dam. William Green joined the 65th Georgia Regiment and was promoted to colonel before the war was over. He was in line for a promotion to brigadier general when the war ended. He never received that commission.

He and his wife, Sarah Adeline Mayo, had the following children: Mary Alice, Rachel Brooks, Margaret Elizabeth, William Preston, Barbry, John Henry Lumkin, Robert Edgar Lee. William Preston Foster married Ida Tarpley Waters and they had the following children: Addie Lou Foster, Wyatt Holmes Foster, Mattie Belle Foster, William Green Foster, Margaret Elizabeth Foster.

William Green Foster married Gena Mae Herrin and they had a son, William Green Foster, who is my father. *Submitted by: Dr. Vicky Foster, Allens Park, CO and Written by Helen Foster, 1924 Victory Church Road, Bowdon, GA 30108.*

556. Freeman

Ah, the secrets the box holds. It is of simple construction. A plain wood box, just over three inches tall, with a checkerboard top. "Razor + strap brought to America about 1800," reads a hand-scrawled note inside. The razor and strap are long gone. Only the box remains, and the unspoken memories it carries.

It once belonged to Robert Hugh Freeman. While family lore says he left Ireland in 1848 during the potato famine and came to America as an indentured servant, the note in the box suggests he was second generation. He first lived in the Lumberton, North Carolina, area, then moved to Henry County, Georgia, and married Georgia McCollough. They each spoke Gaelic, the ancient Irish language. The couple moved to Carroll County, Georgia. Robert farmed until his death around 1914; Georgia lived until 1920 or 1921. They had ten children: Robert Jr., Dave, Wilbur, Lloyd, Grover, Julia, Jessie, Lula, Etta and Lily.

Grover Cleveland Freeman (1889-1972) was the youngest son. He served in the 82nd Division in World War I and fought in France. When he returned, he married Betty Lou Presnal of Randolph County, Alabama, and began to farm near Smith's Chapel in western Carroll County. They had five children: Louise (1923), Wilson Cleveland (1924), John Griffis (1926-1982), Milton (1935-1937) and Martha (1938-1988).

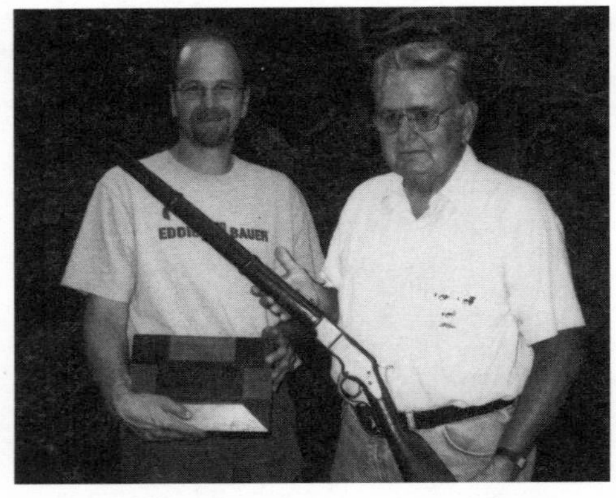

Scott and Wilson Freeman with the box brought from Ireland

By 1929, Grover owned a cotton farm outside Bowdon. Cotton prices rose above 40 cents a pound that year, and he elected to hold on to his crop until they hit 50 cents. The price reached 49 cents in late October. The next day the stock market crashed and he lost almost everything. In the end, all he had left was his prized 1866 Winchester buffalo rifle and an iron-gray buggy horse. The rifle remains in the Freeman family.

Grover became foreman of a peach orchard in Coweta County. He later farmed on Lovvorn Mill Road outside Bowdon. Of his children, Louise, Martha and Griffis married and had families in the Bowdon area. Wilson served in World War II, as member of the 82nd Airborne Division and the Screaming Eagles of the 101st Airborne Division, and helped liberate the concentration camp at Dachau. Wilson was the first member of the family to graduate college, and became an educator. He married and later divorced Joy Elizabeth Prince (born 1928) and they had one son, Scott Wilson Freeman (born 1958). Wilson served as Haralson County Superintendent of Schools, and retired in 1989 as a school principal in Paulding County. In 1979, he married Tommie Bandy. Scott Freeman is now a magazine writer and author of two books.

The box remains in the Freeman family. It is the keeper of family heirlooms. There is a necklace pendant carved from an ancient peach pit, carefully placed inside. Why is it there? The old box knows the secrets. And though it will never tell, the comfort is in knowing they are there at all — held in the modest little box brought here generations ago from Ireland. *Submitted by: Scott Freeman, 2228 Rigby Avenue, College Park, GA 30337*

557. The H.M. Fulbright Family

Norma and H.M. Fulbright came to Carrollton from Warner Robbins, Georgia, in 1966 when H.M. accepted the position of superintendent of the Carrollton City Schools. The family put down roots quickly as Norlydia, age six, began first grade at College Street and Max, age four, was to follow close behind. Norma Fulbright, herself an educator with a degree in early childhood education, began employment with the Central school system as a teacher in their kindergarten program doing what she loved — providing young children with a strong foundation for the life ahead of them.

Dr. and Mrs. H.M. Fulbright

Through nearly two decades, the Fulbrights offered capable guidance as imaginative and effective changes were made on behalf of the children of Carrollton which have resounded far beyond the Fulbrights' tenure. With Dr. Fulbright's dedicated and gentle leadership, the Carrollton schools eased, without turmoil, through the racial desegregation of Georgia schools in the 1960s. In 1969, Norma Fulbright joined her husband in the Carrollton school system and with his help established one of the first public kindergartens in Georgia, one which would focus on the total child. City Kindergarten, according to the State Department of Education, was a "crowning achievement of preschool education" and was one that was used as a model for many school systems in our state and beyond.

In keeping with his commitment to education, Dr. Fulbright received his Ph.D. in educational administration from Georgia State University in 1973 and in 1981 received the Department of Education's first Distinguished Alumnus Award. After spending fifteen of his thirty-five years of education to that point in outstanding and dedicated service to the Carrollton schools, Dr. Fulbright retired as superintendent in 1981. In 1981, he became the first full-time executive director of Georgia Association of Educational Leaders (1981-1986), a group that he had helped to form six years earlier. In 1986, he began serving as the president of Truett-McConnell College (1986-1992), helping to reestablish this Baptist College in Cleveland, Georgia, as a valuable resource to education in North Georgia. Norma Fulbright retired in 1985 after having devoted sixteen years of her life to holding both small faces and small lives in her very capable hands at Carrollton City Kindergarten. After so many years of lending their considerable talents to the cause of education in Carrollton and the State of Georgia, the Fulbrights left with the admiration and devotion of those with whom they had worked. Their leadership, always a partnership, was characterized by vision and integrity.

Dr. H.M. Fulbright, Presidential Inauguration, Truett-McConnell College, 1987

Dr. and Mrs. Fulbright served Carrollton in many capacities. Dr. Fulbright held numerous positions of leadership, among other things he served on the Board of Deacons, as Sunday School director, and as music director at Carrollton First Baptist; was a member and past president of the Rotary Club; served in Europe during World War II and participated in the D-Day invasion of France; was an adjunct professor at West Georgia College; served as chairman of the Carroll County Heart Association; was chosen to serve on the Governor's Task Force on Education twenty-six times, and was the Georgia Coordinator for the Southern Baptist Convention's Laity Abroad Progam. Likewise Mrs. Fulbright has been a full participant in her community, holding active memberships in Delta Kappa Gamma and Art Study Club, as well as coauthoring a book for kindergarten instructional staff and conducting educational workshops throughout the state. Their social and educational activities brought numerous honors, such as the Distinguished Educator Achievement Award from the Southern Association of Colleges and Schools honoring Dr. Fulbright's achievements in educational leadership and the Teacher of the Year award given twice to honor Mrs. Fulbright's educational contributions. However, their true fulfillment was in enriching the lives of the youth of Georgia, which they did with humility and integrity.

Dr. Fulbright died in August 1994 at the age of seventy-two. Leslie Nevois, a counselor at Carrollton Junior High School for many years, wrote of him,

> "His influence will be timeless, and we are the beneficiaries of his accomplishments. He graces our lives with quiet eloquence. His was a grand journey."

As for their children, after graduating with an engineering degree from Georgia Tech in 1983, Max married Sherrie Shoemake and they continue to reside in Carrollton as they raise Amanda, Max III, Brooke, Ryan and Rhett. Norlydia married Charley Smith of Atlanta, Georgia, in 1982 and remained happily so until Charley's death in 1995. He is missed greatly by everyone one who knew him. Norlydia received her Ph.D. in clinical psychology in 1993 and returned to Georgia to live in 1998. In 2001, Norlydia married Brian Stamper of Atlanta, Georgia, where they now reside. Norma Fulbright still lives in Carrollton where she continues to contribute and to watch her grandchildren thrive. *Submitted by: Dr. Norlydia Fulbright, 3788 Harris Boulevard, Kennesaw, GA 30146*

Sources: Personal recollection, information from those involved, and numerous articles from the *Times Georgia* spanning thirty years.

558. Barney Lee Garrett and Gussie Hay Garrett

Barney Lee Garrett was born August 18, 1900, in Roopville, Georgia. He was the only child of James Lee (4/19/1878 - 9/20/1960) and Ophelia Hayes Garrett (7/4/1881 - 1/27/1933). Barney started life large weighing in at 13 pounds and was a large man all of his life — both in size and deed. He did not finish school, but was self-taught in the ways of business. He married Gussie Hay in 1921. As a young man he was a farmer and merchant. In approximately 1931, he went to work for International Mineral and Chemical Corporation as a salesman for their fertilizer and retired in 1965 as Southeast Sales Manager. Because of this promotion, Barney and Gussie had to leave their beloved Roopville and move to Atlanta until his retirement. Barney took great pride in his work and often spent his own money for incidentals such as telephone calls, gas, etc. His legs were severely burned while inspecting fire damage at the Atlanta plant and though he was offered a new car to help him get around, he said his secretary needed a raise instead. As a community member, Barney was known for his heart. He helped many families in need (especially at Christmas) by leaving groceries where they could be found without the recipient knowing who they were from. Once he managed to sneak a milk cow into a family's pasture when the children needed milk. Barney served on the Board of Education for several years and was its chairman part of that time. He was a Mason and a Shriner as well as being a member of the Lions and Civitan Clubs. He died October 3, 1986.

Barney Lee and Gussie Hay Garrett, 50th Anniversary.

Gussie Hay Garrett was born April 14, 1896, in Bowdon, Georgia. She was the oldest daughter of Will and Della Duke Hay. Her siblings were: Claire, Marian, James W., Shelton Earl, Charles and Harold Hay. Prior to marriage, she taught school in Carroll County. After her marriage, she was known as a gracious hostess. She never knew how many she would feed for a meal, but always had plenty. She was also an outstanding seamstress, often making clothes for her family and others from pictures in the latest style magazines or from clothes seen in stores. She painted china as well as pictures and modeled at Rich's as a member of the Grandmother's Club. She died June 28, 1971.

Barney and Gussie Garrett were members of Roopville Baptist Church where both were active in the work of the church. Barney served many years as a deacon while Gussie played the piano and organ, when needed, and sang in the choir. They enjoyed the young people of the church and often entertained them in their home.

The Garretts had one daughter, Frances L. Garrett, who was born and raised in Roopville. Frances married A. Powers Goodson from Franklin, Georgia, and had two children John Powers and Judy Garrett Goodson. *Submitted by: Judy G. Farmer, 380 Newnan Street, Franklin, GA 30217*

559. Edgar Henry Garrett

Earlier generations of this branch of the Garrett family came to Carroll County originally from Leicestershire, England, by way of Laurens County, South Carolina, and Muscogee County, Georgia.

Elisha Garrett (8/9/1788 - 4/15/1853) married Nancy Madison (children: Serena, William Buford, Wesley Robinson, Chaney Alfred, Charles Madison, John Robert, E. Frank, Elizabeth, unknown female, and Schemirie Yarbouragh.

Edgar Henry Garrett, Bobby Garrett, Mildred Robinson Garrett with Judy

John Robert Garrett (5/5/1824 - 8/11/1904) came to Heard County and later to Carroll County. He married his cousin Martha Ann Garrett (9/27/1830 - 2/20/1917) and lived in house below Eureka Church (children: Andrew, Martha Liza, Edgar, Henry, James (son Wiley was sheriff; Hosea was a minister whose last sermon at Shiloh was at 80 years of age), John (died as child), Levi, Elisha, Joseph, George W., Martha Lula, and William Issac Newton "Newt". Before the war, John Robert paid $6.00/acre for 500 acres where Tanner Park is today. The bottoms where the lake is located today were then pasture and corn fields.

William Isaac Newton "Newt" Garrett (8/25/1875 - 2/18/1930) farmed and ran a cotton gin and sawmill. He was instantly killed in a tragic sawing accident. Newt married Emma Othello Holmes (1/1/875 - 10/31/1957) (daughter of Thomas Holmes and Edie Bird McCray (children: Fred (10/4/1896 - 9/16/1901) died of malaria, Horry (7/21/1898 - 5/23/1909) died as a result of kidney damage sustained in a fall from a tree at Bethel Church (diabetic), Jimmie Lou (10/20/00 - 8/11/1994), Mary (2/2/1903 - 6/15/1984), Edgar (8/18/1905 - 1/1/1993), John Ray "Runt" Garrett (1/5/1908 - 2/20/99), Buford (11/22/1910 - 10/10/1911) died of diptheria, Ray (9/30/1913 - 4/20/1924) (died at age 11 with complications of diabetes), and "adopted" son Frank Jones, a young child left behind by slaves after the Civil War.

Edgar Henry Garrett married Mildred Inez Robinson (12/1/1911 - 7/15/1975) (children: Bobby William (8/10/1928 - 3/6/1960) married Tommie Lee Bandy (5/3/1931); Juliette (8/19/1931) married Joe C. Rainwater (1/29/1927) and lives in Goodman, Missouri (children: Cathy, Ellen, Jearan); Earl Holmes (9/30/1936) married Margie Nell Daniell (2/5/1936) (children: Lance, Joey and Sheila (twins) and Nancy); and Joan Elaine (7/11/1949) married/divorced Robert Herrin (1/26/1947 - 6/15/1999) (children: Kelly and Adam).

In 1928 while Mildred and Edgar Garrett were at her parents home on Mandeville Avenue in Carrollton, Mildred gave birth to Bobby. He was five years old when his parents bought the farm on what is now Pleasant Hill Road in Carrollton. Edgar and Mildred grew cotton and corn, and were some of the first chicken farmers in Carroll County. They worked hard on the farm and also worked at the Bell Bomber plant in Marietta during World War II. They sold the home farm to Bobby and Tommie in 1955. The farm is still maintained by Tommie and their children: Vesta married Ralph Ayers (children: Ryan (married Andrea Wilson) and Russ); Lyle who lives and works in New York City; and Celia married/divorced Dwayne Leatherwood (children: Katie (married Brandon Fehring, children: Layne and Haley)) and Chad. Celia subsequently married Ken Miller. *Submitted by: Lyle Garrett, 77 West 104th Street, Apt. 9C, New York, NY 10025*

560. John Roy Garrett Family

John Roy Garrett, known as "J.R." and "Runt" in the Bowdon area, was born on January 5, 1908. He was the son of William Issac Newton (Newt) Garrett (b. 8/25/1875; d. 2/18/1930) and Emma Othella Holmes (b. 1/1/1875; d. 10/31/57). Their families were closer than most for Newt Garrett's sister married Emma's brother, making their children what is commonly known in the South as "double first cousins."

There were eight children in J.R.'s family, but four died at an early age. Newt was a farmer and ran the community sawmill. Emma was a strong Christian lady who taught her children Biblical lessons including regular worship, neighborly love, and Christian caring.

J.R. attended the Bowdon schools where he excelled in math and played all the sports. He played on the Bowdon College football team while still in high school, although his favorite sport was baseball. During a time that the average weekly earnings for a man were $3.00, J.R. earned $2.00 a game playing semi-pro baseball. He would spin a lot of yarns for listening ears about a naïve country boy, touring the Southeast with older, more experienced ball players. His career as a baseball player ended when his father was killed in a tragic sawmill accident in 1930. J.R. returned home to help his mother on the family farm.

J.R. and his sisters, Mary Garrett Wilson and Jimmie Lou Garrett Craven, all attended Bowdon College. While there, J.R. met Elma Heard from Heard County, fell in love and married her in 1931. He was a devoted husband for sixty-seven years, always speaking lovingly of his sweetheart and never fully recovering from her death in 1998. J.R. died in 1999.

During the early part of their marriage, both J.R. and Elma taught school. In fact, at one time, Elma and J.R.'s two sisters were the only three teachers at Smithfield and Unity, strong Carroll County schools. J.R.'s only brother Edgar had a farm east of Carrollton.

Always a farmer, J.R. and Elma purchased a 150-acre farm east of Bowdon in the Jonesville Community where they reared their four children: Nelva (Roop), Doyle, Roy, and Randy. There he managed a cow operation, broiler house, dairy farm, cotton and corn crops, and enough vegetables to feed his family and extra to sell.

Like a lot of people who experienced the fall of cotton in the South, J.R. continued to farm but supplemented his income through entrepreneurial adventures. He operated the first Tastee Freeze in the area. He also had a produce business, a trucking company, a memory garden, and various other projects that allowed him to invest in real estate. After thirty-seven years of teaching, Elma retired.

At the time of this writing, all four of J.R. and Elma's children live in Carroll County as do most of their children and grandchildren. Nelva and David Roop have three sons: Craig, Lance, and Keith. Doyle married Margaret Smith and their four children are Dana Garrett Diment, Greg Garrett, Kelly Garrett Glanton, and Ben Garrett. Roy married Lumis Hopkins. They are the parents of Bryan Garrett and Michelle Garrett Patrick. Randy is married to Shirley Duncan Garrett. His sons are Scott, Kevin, and Matt (sons of Becky Lee Zenefski).

J.R.'s greatest joy was his grandchildren and great-grandchildren. In addition to his twelve grandchildren, the family has grown to include twenty-five great-grandchildren, and most were at his 90th Birthday Celebration. J.R. took great pride in "starring" in a family video that chronicled his life.

It was always important to J.R. that something of significance remain where he and Elma raised their family. As a man of great faith, he took enormous pride in the fact that his son, Roy, would build Community Church on the exact site of their home. His oldest son, Doyle, uses part of this site for his produce business. And most importantly, J.R. and Elma are now buried in the Memorial Garden that was once a part of their family property.

J.R. and Elma Garrett contributed to the growth of Carroll County through years of service to the Democratic Party, membership in Bowdon Methodist Church, and teaching thousands of children in the West Georgia area.

His legacy lives on through his children, grandchildren and great-grandchildren who loved him dearly. *Submitted by: Nelva Garrett Roop, 400 Ellenwood Dr., Bowdon, GA 30108*

90th Birthday Celebration of J.R. Garrett

561. Wiley A. Garrett

In December 1908, Georgia Governor Hoke Smith appointed Wiley A. Garrett sheriff of Carroll County for the 1909-1910 term of deceased incumbent sheriff A.D. Hagen. Mr. Hagen died only a few days after he took his oath of office. Wiley A. Garrett became one of the most respected peace officers; his record of active service in law enforcement unparalleled in the history of Carroll County.

Wiley A. Garrett was born 25 September 1881; the son of James Madison and Elizabeth Woodard Garrett. His grandfather, John R. Garrett — the first Garrett child of their line born in Carroll County — was born 05 May 1824, in a small community in West Carroll County, twenty-five years before it was named Bowdon, Georgia. He was the son of Elisha and Nancy Madison Garrett, who moved from Laurens, South Carolina, to Carroll County in 1821. John and Martha Ann Garrett were married 08 March 1847. Eight of their twelve children made their homes in Carroll County near the communities we know as Mount Zion, Burwell, Bowdon, and Roopville. They were farmers and lifetime residents of Carroll County. John Garrett died 11 August 1904. Martha Garrett died 20 February 1917. They are buried in Smith's Chapel Church Cemetery. Today, in 2001, six generations of their descendants have lived in Carroll County.

W.A. "Uncle Wiley" Garrett

James Madison (Bud) Garrett was born 26 November 1855. He married Elizabeth Woodard 13 December 1877. They had eight children. Elizabeth was born 09 May 1859 and died 27 December 1900. She was buried in the Mount Zion United Methodist Church Cemetery. James Madison Garrett died 30 June 1933. He was buried in the Old Camp United Methodist Church Cemetery.

Wiley A. Garrett was their second child. Wiley went to school at Mount Zion, Georgia. His future father-in-law, William Tileroe Morris was the schoolmaster. He worked on the family farm with his father and brothers until his marriage to Lena Morris 18 January 1903. Lena was born 24 May 1885. They moved to Carrollton, Georgia, where Wiley was employed in Griffin's Department Store. They were members of the First United Methodist Church of Carrollton. Over the next eighteen years they had five children: Fred, Lewis, W.A. (Dub), Harry Lee, and Mara.

In January 1909, Garrett, his wife, and two young sons moved into the sheriff's quarters in the Carroll County Jail. The Garrett family lived there for over a decade. Wiley A. Garrett was sheriff of Carroll County from 01 January 1909 thru 31 December 1924; elected six consecutive times for the longest continuous service of any Carroll County sheriff to date. The tenure of his last term was four years, as the tenure is today.

Garrett returned to farming in 1925. However, much of his time was spent as investigator for private individuals, sheriff or police departments in the area. In 1927 he sold some of his land in the south side of Carrollton for development. City Councilman Bob Wynn named two of the new streets, Garrett Street and Mara Street, for Wiley Garrett and his then six year old daughter. Garrett, a master carpenter, built the first two houses in the new subdivision.

Wiley Garrett was then deputy sheriff in 1933 through 1936 with Sheriff J.L. Webb. In those days sheriff and deputies ran as a team and were elected together. Garrett was appointed deputy sheriff by the Carroll County Commissioner in 1937. However, he was drafted by the Carrollton mayor and council for chief of the Carrollton Police Department. He served in that capacity until 1941. In his last active service, 1941 through 1944, Wiley Garrett was Chief of the Carroll County Police Department.

Wiley A. Garrett was a man of integrity and dignity, whose word was his bond. He was affable, courteous, and completely impartial. He handled all situations with equanimity; he was never known to lose his temper; and few, if any, ever heard him raise his voice. He was a superb marksman with pistol and rifle. However, he believed guns and force should be a last resort. Garrett had a photographic memory, and his investigatory abilities proved to be phenomenal. He attained the reputation of "best detective" over a large area of northwest Georgia. He received many life threats during his career. Five actual attempts were made on his life; the first, in his third year as sheriff; the last, in 1943 while he was chief of the Carroll County Police Department.

Wiley Garrett had a good sense of humor; he was generous and charitable; and he sincerely liked and enjoyed people. He was devoted to his family, and regardless of the stress of his work, he was never too busy or too tired for time with his children. He was always concerned for the welfare of all children. Through his years of service, if a prisoner had children, Garrett felt those children were victims too, and never failed to check on their welfare. Many a Carroll County child had needed food, clothes, or shoes, and the money came from his pocket.

In the early years, Wiley Garrett was respected because of his office, but it became more and more respect for the man himself. People began calling him "Uncle Wiley," not as a familiarity, but an indication of their respect. Over the years, that respect grew until he was known as "Uncle Wiley" throughout Carroll County.

Wiley A. Garrett died 28 March 1949, in Carrollton, Georgia. Lena Garrett, always a source of strength and support for her husband, faced the danger of his work equanimity equal to his own. She died 01 January 1968. Wiley and Lena Garrett are buried in the Carrollton City Cemetery. *Submitted by: Mara G. Hughey, 219 West Chandler Street, Carrollton, GA 30117*

Sources: Census, probate, family records, Sheriff's Certificates of Commission.

562. The William Garrison Family

William Garrison b. 1785 South Carolina m. 16 May 1792 York County, S.C. to Mary "Polly" Hall b. 16 May 1791 York County. His father was Benjamin Garrison, mother Nancy Agnes Paris.

He moved from Coweta County to Carroll between the 1840-1850 census. According to the 6th land district map owned by the family of Samuel Hart, he owned lots 190, 140 and parts of lots 118 and 139. The estate in Carroll County, Georgia, courthouse at his death when he died 29 Oct. 1860, and 1861 probate of his will required that the estate be kept intact until the death of the widow, leaving sons William H. Garrison and John Galespi Garrison as executors. This estate is in the records until 1880 when Polly died. They are both buried at Concord Methodist Church.

Using the census and the estate records the children were: 1. Martha Catsey Garrison b. ca 1812 m. Wm. H. Brashier in Coweta. 2. Nancy Hall Garrison b. 25 Jan. 1814 m. Alexander M. McCain between 1821-1836. This family moved to Cullman, Alabama and no stones have been found there. 3. Benjamin J. Garrison b. 2 March 1817 m. 7 Dec. 1854 (1) Sarah A.E. Chambers, he d. 1 June 1904 m. (2) Mary ____ . 4. Martha Garrison m. ____ Hogan. (May be Margaret). 5. Prudence J. Garrison b. 1823 m. (1) Peter R. Hogan (2) ____ Davis. 6. William Hall Garrison b. 23 July 1823/stone 1827 d. 9 July 1921 m. 5 Nov. 1857 Mary Charlotte Gray. Their son, Zachariah moved to Texas, known descendants. 7. John Galespi Garrison b. 1832-34 moved to Arkansas about 1878 when he was serving as co-executor of his father's estate with brother William according to estate records. *Submitted by: Ned Hamil, Ponte Vero, FL and Written by: June Hart Wester, 133 Mountain Crest Drive, Canton, GA 30114*

Sources: Research in county records of Coweta and Carroll Counties.

563. The Garst Family in Carroll County, Georgia 1826-1963

Christopher Garst was born in Botetourt County, Virginia, in 1804, the son of Jacob Garst and Sally Frantz. Jacob's grandfather, Theobald Garst, came to Philadelphia from Pfalz, Bavaria, aboard the *Patience,* 11 August 1750.

The family story is that Christopher ran away from home when he was fourteen because his father beat him. Where he went and what he did is a mystery because there are no records at all for him until his marriage to Sarah Coltharp in Jefferson County Tennessee, 11 December 1825. Shortly after their marriage, they moved to Carroll County, Georgia, with Sarah's brother, James Coltharp. After ten years, James Coltharp moved to Texas, but Christopher and Sarah Garst remained in Carroll County where three more generations of Garsts were born and raised. Many of them are buried at Macedonia Baptist Cemetery in Sand Hill.

Mary Hager Garst and grandchildren Jarvis and Janie B. 1911.

The Garsts had a number of properties between Villa Rica and Carrollton, but the home place was a two-story brick built before the Civil War. It burned down in 1949, but was replaced by Ira and Pearl Garst with a white bungalow, built from the homemade bricks of the original house.

Christopher and Sarah Garst had fourteen children born in Carroll County between 1826 and 1854: Martha who married Isaac Kinney, Frances, James, Joanna, William Eli, John, Jacob, Susan who married John Richards, Mary who married Stephen J. Pyron, Anabelle, Eliza, Robert, Philip, and Nancy.

In 1861 four of the Garst brothers enlisted in the Confederate troops. James served in the 10th Regiment of the Georgia State Guards; Eli and John served in the 7th Georgia Volunteer Infantry; Jacob served in Cobbs Legion. Eli died in Charlottesville, Virginia, November 1862. Jacob died at Richmond, Virginia, 11 May 1863. James and John survived the war and returned home, but John was weakened by two years as a prisoner of war at Rock Island, Illinois, and died 22 January 1870. James died in the veteran's home in Atlanta, 5 March 1916.

James had three children. Christopher, born in 1860, tried his hand at farming in Carroll County, but about 1889 he moved to Marion County, Alabama, where a number of his descendants still live. Arthur, born in 1865, lived in Carroll County all of his life, dying in 1953. He had four children, Grover, Pearl, Leola, and Bessie (Boyd). James' daughter Carrie married William Aderhold in 1883. They lived in Paulding County, Georgia.

Phillip Garst and the old house built from homemade brick before the Civil War.

Sarah Coltharp Garst died 6 April 1877, age seventy. Christopher Garst died July, 1881, and his funeral was held at Macedonia Baptist Church. Although the old tombstones are unreadable, both Chris and Sarah are buried in the old part of the Macedonia Cemetery.

After Christopher's death, most of the land went to the youngest son, Philip Hinkle Garst. Philip was born in 1851 in the house built by Christopher, and he died in that same house in May, 1937. About 1875, Philip married Mary Hager, a school teacher ten years older than he was. The family joke was that he married her for her books, not her looks. The Hagers had moved to Carroll County before 1830 from Lincoln County, North Carolina. Mary's father, Jonathan Hager, was as German as Christopher Garst. Jonathan's grandparents, George Hager and Crete Killian, were both born in Germany in the 1730s.

Mary Hager died in 1911, and in 1915 Philip married Miss Emma Brooks. They had no children.

Philip and Mary's only son, Ira Clifton Hinkle Garst, was born in Sand Hill, 17 November 1880, but unlike his father and grandfather, Ira was no farmer. He went to Atlanta Medical School and graduated first in his class in 1902. He married Pearl Viola Moon in Decatur, 30 March 1903, and they came back to Carroll County where Ira started his medical practice and Pearl learned to cook. She was a city girl, just seventeen years old, daughter of a widow who ran a boarding house near the medical school. Pearl's mother, Minerva Mason Moon, told her two girls to sit on the porch and look pretty so they could "catch" doctors. Both did.

Pearl actually met Ira at a dance in Decatur. The first thing he said to her was "Cold hands, warm heart." He was a pretty good judge of character.

Doc Garst (even his grandchildren called him "Doc") opened an office in Sand Hill before World War I, and he made his rounds on a motorcycle. He said it was better tempered than a horse and didn't wander off.

Dr. Ira Garst, Pearl, son Jarvis. About 1935.

Doc and Pearl Garst wandered a lot before they returned to Carroll County for good about 1940. In 1904 they went to Colorado because Doc had "weak lungs." He bought a practice in Pueblo, but soon after that their office/home burned to the ground. Philip wired them the money to come home, so once more Doc Garst practiced in Carroll County, in Sand Hill. During World War I he enlisted in the Army medical corps. After he was discharged in 1919, he took a job in Texas with the state public health system, living first in the Rio Grande Valley, then in Austin, where he was the director of mental hygiene for the state of Texas. But Doc never sold the farm. After he retired, he and Pearl moved back to Carroll County, back to the house that Christopher Garst had built before the Civil War. At the beginning of World War II they still had no running water or electricity. The house was still much the same as it had been when Christopher and Sarah lived there. Doc Garst died 11 March 1954, and Pearl sold the house, but she had a small house built for herself at Five Points, behind Boggs' store. She lived there part of the year, but also lived in Houston with her daughter, Janie B. Pearl Moon Garst died 10 December 1963 in Houston. Both Doc and Pearl Garst are buried at Macedonia.

Doc and Pearl had three children, all born in Sand Hill. Christopher died at age four, in 1909. Jarvis was born 27 April 1908, and is still living on his own in Austin, Texas. Janice Beatrice — always known as Janie B. — was born 29 March 1910. She died in Larkspur, Colorado, on 15 September 1997.

Author's note: Although they grew up elsewhere, the grandchildren of Doc and Pearl Garst spent a great deal of time at the farm in Carroll County, beginning in 1942, when Janie B. and her two children moved to Georgia to stay with her parents while her husband was overseas, and continuing in visits until Pearl Garst died in 1963. Each of those grandchildren has fond and specific memories of a very old house, a natural spring, corn fields, a team of mules called Toby and Mary, a farm hand named Rufus, pine woods, Cousin Arthur roasting peanuts, an old gold mine, a close-knit, rural community, a small white church, and a cemetery where many of their ancestors are at rest. *Submitted by: Karen Lewis Dale, 6737 Perry Park Boulevard, Larkspur, CO 80118*

564. Garvin - Morehead

Years ago, five Garvin brothers left England and came to North Carolina. Here the five brothers separated and as far as is known, never saw each other again.

Dr. Gabby Garvin came to Tennessee where he met and married Temperance Burnett, born Statesville, North Carolina, in 1841 and died 1918. They had one son, Hilary Joseph Garvin (Joe). Dr. Gabby Garvin died in Memphis, Tennessee, during the yellow fever epidemic. His young widow met and married Captain William Winston who was a conductor on the Chattanooga and Cincinnati Railroad run. They lived in Chattanooga, Tennessee. During this time Captain Winston purchased the Silk place in Chattooga County, Georgia, which included about 250 acres of land. He and Temperance continued to live in Chattanooga.

Hilary Joseph Garvin was born May 29, 1868, and died July 6, 1946, at Menlo, Georgia; buried in Forest Hills Cemetery, Chattanooga, Tennessee. Hilary Joe was raised in Fayette County, Tennessee. He attended Lebanon College where Edith Bradley Dunham from Mt. Vernon, Ohio, was enrolled. She was born 1868 in Mt. Washington, Ohio, died August 15, 1929, in Menlo and is buried in Chattanooga. Her father was W.E. Dunham, druggist and pharmacist in Mt. Washington, Ohio. While Edith and Hilary Joe both were attending college, the two met and were married. They moved to Chattanooga where Mr. Garvin was employed with the Southern Express Company. While living in Chattanooga, he also ran H.J. Garvin Publisher of Standard Works and was half owner of the Garvin & Tatum Feed and Grain Company.

In 1901, Hilary Joe, Edith, and their three sons (Hilary, Norman and Judson) moved to the farm in Georgia that Captain and Mrs. Winston had bought and never lived on. Hillary Joe and Edith wanted a place in the country where the air was clean and fresh. In Chattanooga the smoke from the coal and the odor from the outhouses, which also caused mosquitoes, was very unhealthy. The house in Georgia originally had two rooms but Hilary Joe added four more and several large porches and hallways. There were three tenant houses. They raised strawberries, peaches, cotton and corn. The strawberries and peaches were shipped by the car lots to Ohio. Two Garvin girls, Dorothy and Betty, were born on the farm. The children walked three miles to school each day. When the girls were about ten and twelve years old, they hitched up "Bob" and drove the buggy. The corn was ground at the grist mill on the farm and the family sawmill provided lumber for the barns and other buildings as well as furniture. Mrs. Garvin was very active in the Presbyterian Church.

Norman Winston Garvin in World War I uniform.

Norman Winston Garvin was born October 24, 1895, and died May 22, 1983, at Summerville, Georgia. Norman attended the Menlo schools and studied agriculture in Knoxville, Tennessee. He served with the 31st Field Artillery in France during World War I. After the armistice was signed in 1918, Norman arrived back in Georgia on February 3, 1919. At the time of his return, Reva Louise Hawkins was teaching school in Menlo. She, along with other teachers, was invited to the Garvin home for dinner where she met Norman. They were married on November 15, 1925. Louise was born August 11, 1902, died June 11, 1979, at Menlo, Georgia. Norman and Louise are buried in the Alpine Cemetery near Menlo.

Norman and Louise had two children, Julie Ann Garvin and Edith Dunham Garvin. Norman and Louise lived on the farm near Menlo for the remainder of their lives where they raised Julia Ann and Edith. Julia Ann was born March 3, 1932, in Chattooga County. She married James Regan Hicks on April 19, 1956. James was born May 23, 1930. They reside in Thomson, Georgia. Their children are James Regan Hicks Jr. and Norman Garvin Hicks.

Edith Dunham Garvin was born September 30, 1935, Summerville, Chattooga County, Georgia. Edith married Marcus Billy Morehead (Bill) on August 17, 1957. Bill was born in Gastonia, North Carolina, on April 25, 1933, died May 19, 1992, in Weymouth, Massachusetts. Bill and Edith both graduated from the University of Georgia in 1957. Their graduation speaker was John F. Kennedy who was a young senator at that time. Bill and Edith lived in Atlanta, Georgia, and Chapel Hill, North Carolina, for a number of years while Bill continued his graduate studies. Edith taught school in DeKalb County, Georgia, while they were in Atlanta. Later they moved to Boone, North Carolina, where Bill taught geology at Appalachian State Teachers College. Edith and Bill had two children: Pauline Garvin Morehead, born August 18, 1958, in Summerville; and Marcus Winston Morehead, born November 15, 1963, in Watauga County, Boone, North Carolina. Marcus resides in Anniston, Alabama.

Bill, Edith and family moved to Carrollton in 1966 where Bill was chairman of the Geology Department and later division chairman of math and science. Bill and Edith divorced in 1977 and Bill moved away. Edith remained in Carrollton where she served as children's librarian at the West Georgia Regional Library from 1967 until her retirement in 1998. *Submitted by: Edith G. Morehead, 95 West Lake Drive, Carrollton, GA 30117*

565. James Monroe Gaston

James Gaston born 30 September 1793 in Chester, South Carolina; died 8 April 1860 in Roanoke, Alabama; married 25 November 1818 in Chester, South Carolina, to Elizabeth Burns born 7 September 1798 Ireland, died 20 May 1831 Newton County, Georgia. James married second about 1832-33 to Harriet Hulda Johnson, born 3 March 1808, died 27 July 1889, buried Old Sylacauga Cemetery, Alabama.

Children of James and Elizabeth were: (1) William B. born 1 May 1821 in South Carolina; (2) Samuel Burns born 19 October 1823 in South Carolina; (3) James Monroe born 23 February 1825 in Newton County, Georgia; (4) Robert born 5 May 1829 in Newton County.

Children by Harriet Hulda were: (1) David McClesky born 26 December 1835 in Newton County; (2) Daniel Allen born 21 January 1838 in Newton County; (3) Martha A.L. born 24 December 1839 in Newton or Heard County; (4) Sarah Ware born 22 July 1841 in Heard County; (5) Missouri Virginia born 1844 in Heard County.

All sons and one son-in-law in Civil War.

James Monroe Gaston died 13 July 1890 in Georgia; married 1851 to Emmaline Catherine Barker, born 17 August 1833 in South Carolina, died 17 May 1904. Both are buried in Old Camp United Methodist Church Cemetery, Carroll County. Her parents were William and Sarah (unknown) Barker. Emmaline C. had three brothers and one sister. The Barkers moved from South Carolina to Troup County, Georgia, then to Heard County about 1851. That is when they met and married. James M. and Emmaline C. lived in Heard County 1850 and 1860, 1870 in Roanoke, Alabama, in 1880 census were living Carroll County. They could have moved to Carrollton in early 1870s. He owned 100-plus acres. James M.'s occupation was farmer and mill wright. He was in Civil War. Children were: (1) William Burns born 12 October 1854 Heard County. (2) Sarah Elizabeth born 17 November 1856 Heard County.(3) James Lafayette born 17 June 1859 Heard County. (4) Robert Barker born 24 June 1867 Heard County. (5) George Washington (Toby) born and died between 1870 and 1880, age 7, buried beside his parents.

(1) William Burns Gaston died 21 January 1929, Ben Hill, North Georgia, married about 26 December 1880 to Alice Lillian Carter, born 16 February 1863, died 8 April 1933 in Hapeville, Georgia. Both are buried in Hill Crest Cemetery, East Point, Georgia. Alice Lillian's parents were Isaac Washington Carter born about 1830, died 6 July 1879, was in Civil War, married 14 September 1859 to Threasa Ann Spears, born 13 March 1843 in Georgia, died 7 June 1904, buried Ebenezer United Methodist Church Cemetery, Fayetteville, Georgia. Isaac was a landowner in Carroll County. Threasa and children, Alice L., Maggie, Victoria, and Claudie, living in Carroll County (1880 census). William B. and Alice Lillian's children were: Emmaline Catherine born 2 April 1883; Bessie born 15 January 1885; Tessie Theresia born May 1887; Dea Cleste born 25 December 1888; Willie Bell born 9 January 1891; Sarah Ruth born 9 December 1892; Allie Lillian born 30 July 1896; Johnnie Inez born 5 January 1898; Lena Leola born 24 May 1899; died 20 August 1912 (these nine children all born in Carrollton); James Monroe born 12 April 1901; Isaac Carter born 30 November 1902; Georgia Eugenia born 31 July 1905, died 22 March 1910 from burns (last three children born in Cartersville).

William David Gaston and Emmaline Catherine Gaston, May 1918

Emmaline Catherine died 3 January 1936, married first on 30 March 1902, Carroll County, to Zebedee (Dee) Frank Rooks, born about May 1876 in Alabama, died about 1904 in Carroll County, buried unmarked grave at Old Camp United Methodist Church Cemetery. Children were: Hattie Emmaline born 6 November 1903 in Carrollton; married Joseph Terrell Coggin 6 October 1923 in Coweta County. Hattie E. died 8 December 1983. Joe born 10 August 1902 at McCollum, Georgia, died 20 June 1985. Both are buried at College Park Cemetery, College Park, Georgia. Children: Joseph Terrell Jr. (J.T.) born 19 March 1925 in Madras, Georgia, died 24 March 1996 in Texas; Frank Edward born 2 October 1927 in Madras, Georgia; Mary Ann born 12 September 1938, died 31 January 1998; Patrick Howard born 12 February 1940. Sarah Dee born about 1905, died 20 June 1918, Coweta County, buried Hill Crest Cemetery, East Point, Georgia. Emmaline C. married second on 13 April 1913 to William David Gaston in Fulton County, Georgia. He was born 24 February 1865 in Alabama, died 31 March 1932, buried College Park Cemetery, College Park. William was son of Robert and Mary Burrilla Smith Gaston (see Robert Gaston). Emma and W.D.'s children were: Samuel Monroe born 7 May 1914 in Palmetto, Georgia, died 21 July 1990 Pompano Beach, Florida, buried at Consolation Baptist Church Cemetery, Carroll County. Married first to Ruth Mangum, divorced. Married second to Marie Brooks Turner, born 12 October 1926 in England. Sam and Marie adopted a son Anthony Spencer Gaston, born 23 July 1965. Josephus Eugene born 7 August 1915 in Palmetto, Georgia, died 5 February 1976, VA Hospital, De Kalb County, Georgia. Married in 1935 to Martha Louise Wallace, born 15 December 1917, died 30 November 1971 in College Park. Both are buried in College Park Cemetery, College Park. Children: Betty Louise born 8 November 1935; Josephus Ernest born 27 December 1937; Martha Ruth born 22 October 1939; Emma Lee born 27 December 1941. Lena Brilla born 13 December 1917 in McCollum, Georgia, married 8 April 1939 to Aubrey Clarence Callaway, born 13 September 1918 in Clayton County, Georgia, died 31 January 1995 in Whitesburg, Georgia, buried Consolation Baptist Church Cemetery, Carroll County. Child was Aubrey Drayton born 20 February 1945 in Fort McPherson, Fulton County, Georgia. He married Carol Boleman on 17 June 1966 in Fort Carson, Colorado, born 7 January 1947 in Atlanta, Georgia. Willie Catherine born 22 January 1919 in McCollum, Georgia, died 25 October 1964, buried Hill Crest Cemetery, East Point. Married first to Robert Bennett, divorced. Married second to Ralph Lloyd Mickey. Children by Bennett were Constance Catherine born 10 February 1939; Joan Ethel born 23 July 1942, died in accident 24 June 1964, buried Hill Crest Cemetery, East Point; Robert James born and died 1944, crib death, buried Hill Crest Cemetery, East Point. Children by Mickey were Samuel Monroe born 20 August 1954; Ralph Lloyd born 28 May 1956, died 22 February 1981, suicide, buried Hill Crest Cemetery in East Point. Jewel (man) born 20 May 1922 in Madras, Georgia, married 20 January 1941 to Clara Eugene Baker, born 7 April 1921 in East Point. Children were Jewell Eugene born 26 June 1942; Robert William born 10 April 1944, died 7 July 1966, auto accident; Clara Marie born 23 January 1946; Emma Louise born 8 November 1950; Deborah Sue born 14 September 1955; a stillbirth; Molly Darlene born 30 July 1965 (all born in Fulton County, Georgia). Emma's stepchildren under Robert and Mary.

(2) Sarah Elizabeth born 17 November 1856, died 24 September 1938, married 20 February 1879 in Carroll County to John Thomas Boatright, born 1 January 1857 in Carroll County, died 18 March 1934. Both are buried in Carrollton City Cemetery. Children were: Eva died in infancy; Homer M.D. born 30 June 1888, died 4 June 1912, died in sleep, buried in Carrollton City Cemetery; Katherine born and died unknown, married 29 January 1910 in Carroll County to Wilbur Wester West, born 1 September 1884, died 24 June 1952, buried with Boatrights.

(3) James Lafayette died 26 March 1924, married 30 January 1887 in Carroll County to Eula Beatrice Flemming, born 14 April 1870, died 10 May 1931. Both are buried in Old Camp United Methodist Church Cemetery. Children were: Lena Lillian, James Henry, Eva Beatrice, and Walter. All born and died in Carroll County.

(4) Robert Barker (see Robert Barker Gaston).

Submitted by: Lena G. Callaway, 128 Hilley Road, Whitesburg, GA 30185

Sources: Census, obituaries, marriage records, newspapers, family records, and personal knowledge.

566. James Monroe Gaston

James Monroe Gaston, possibly the son of James Gaston, married Emmaline Catherine Barker in Heard County in 1851. James Monroe Gaston was born February 23, 1825, and died July 13, 1890. Emmaline Catherine was born August 17, 1833, and died May 17, 1904. Both are buried at Old Camp Methodist Church in Carrollton, Carroll County, Georgia.

James Monroe had five children. He was living in Heard County, Georgia, in 1850 and 1860 census. By the 1880 census he had moved to Carrollton. His son William Burns Gaston was born October 12, 1854, and died January 21, 1929, in the alms house in Ben Hill, Georgia, of pneumonia. He married Alice Lillian Carter, the daughter of Isaac Washington and Thersia Ann Speer Carter. She was born January 16, 1863, in Fairburn, Fulton County, Georgia. She died April 8, 1933, in Hapeville, Fulton County, Georgia. Both are buried in Hillcrest Cemetery in East Point, Fulton County, Georgia. They had twelve children whom they raised on Horsley Mill Road in Carrollton. Their second daughter was Bessie Gaston.

Bessie Gaston Raven and George Elmer Raven

Bessie Gaston was born January 15, 1885, in Carrollton and died July 9, 1973, in Fayetteville, Fayette County, Georgia. She is buried in College Park, Fulton County, Georgia. On June 5, 1904, at the age of nineteen, she married George Elmer Raven. George was born August 20, 1867, and died October 28, 1948, in Atlanta. He is buried at Ebenezer Methodist Church in Fayette County, Georgia. George was a farmer. They lived in Shake Rag District of Fayette County. George Elmer was first married to Victoria Carter who died February 28, 1904. She was the aunt of Bessie Gaston Raven. At the time of George and Bessie's marriage, he had five children at home from his marriage to Victoria. Bessie helped raise these children and eight of their own.

George Logan Raven, the fifth child of George and Bessie Raven was born in Plains, Sumter County, Georgia, on October 19, 1919. They moved to Hapeville when he was seven years old. He was a charter member in 1928 of North Avenue School and graduated from Russell High School in East Point. He served in World War II in the Army as a private first class in Iran. He married Margaret Cromer Davis on November 1, 1939. Margaret was born July 20, 1918, in Greenwood, Greenwood County, South Carolina and died April 23, 1973, in Hapeville, Georgia. She is buried at West View Cemetery, Atlanta. George was employed by the *Atlanta Journal* until Margaret became pregnant with twins. He then began to work on the Nashville, Chattanooga and Saint Louis Railroad. He was an engineer for forty years. In 1971, he drove the last daily train — The Georgian — to Atlanta. Since his retirement, he has worked full time raising flowers for commercial sales.

The first child of George and Margaret was Carol Celeste Raven, born August 21, 1940, in Atlanta. Carol married Thomas William Haynes on November 9, 1958. On May 15, 1942, George and Margaret had twin daughters named Bessie Georgianna and James Frances Raven. They were born in Atlanta. Bessie Georgianna was married to James Hugh Maddox on March 19, 1961. She died on September 10, 1983, in Warner Robins, Houston County, Georgia, and is buried at Cedar Rock Methodist Church Cemetery, Jackson, Butts County, Georgia.

George and Margaret Raven and children, Georgia, Carol, and Jimmie

James "Jimmie" Frances Raven married Jeramiah "Jerry" Eugene Hosey on June 27, 1963, in Atlanta. Jerry was born July 12, 1944, in Lakeland, Polk County, Florida. They had three children whom were all born in Atlanta.

David Dwayne Hosey was born June 4, 1964. He married Patricia Ann Strain on June 15, 1991, in Carrollton. She was born on January 24, 1964, in Wedowee, Randolph County, Alabama. Their children are Zachary Logan Hosey, born July 15, 1993, and Mallory Caitlin Hosey, born April 18, 1996. Both children were born in Carrollton.

Deborah Denise Hosey was born July 15, 1966. She married Michael Ray Parmer on June 9, 1990, in Franklin, Heard County, Georgia. He was born on April 20, 1961, in Carrollton. Their children are Meaghan Elizabeth Parmer, born April 27, 1991, and died May 10, 1991. Meaghan is buried at Gray Hill Church of God in Woodland, Randolph County, Alabama. Tyler Ray Panner, born April 22, 1992; Hunter Blake Parmer, born December 16, 1995; and Mikaela Grace Parmer, born April 25, 2001. All four of their children were born in Carrollton.

Charles "Chuck" Edward Hosey, the third child of Jerry and Jimmie Hosey was born January 14, 1971. *Submitted by: Jimmie Hosey, 282 Jackson Road, Franklin, GA 30217*

567. The James Monroe Gaston Family

James Monroe Gaston was born in Carroll County Georgia on December 4, 1898. He was the firstborn of Robert Barker and Ida Rosanie Hesterlee Gaston. Monroe worked on the family farm as a young child. When his family moved to a farm near Smarr in Monroe County in 1910, he helped drive the livestock with his dad and brothers. He rode the train each day to Monroe County Public School No.20. Monroe learned the work ethic quickly as his father met the train with axes, picks, shovels, and mattocks each day so he and his brothers could work on the farm until dark. He quit school before graduating.

In 1918, he volunteered for the U.S. Army for World War I. With only six weeks of training he went to France. He was discharged on July 9, 1919, after touring and teaching in Italy. Monroe returned to his parent's farm, now in Sumter County. His love of travel and adventure took him to jobs in Florida, Michigan, California, and elsewhere. When his father died on December 31, 1925, Monroe returned to Sumter County to operate the family farm for his mother and younger siblings.

On January 25, 1935, he married Mary Louesa English. She was born on August 15, 1910, in Sumter County. Their marriage license is filed in Lee County. They had three children: Dorothy Louesa, born August 22, 1941. She married Verren Wilson Lee, born August 24, 1939. Their children are: Lance Wilson, born September 15, 1969; Charlotte Louesa, born June 5, 1972; Margaret Eugenia, born July 15, 1974; Virginia Ruth, born March 6, 1976; David James, born September 2, 1978. Monroe's second child, James Monroe Gaston Jr., was born: January 2, 1945. James married Nancy Carol Wesson, born March 12, 1950. Their two sons were: James Monroe III, born September 4, 1976; and Wesson Dalton, born December 5, 1980. Monroe's third child was Corrie Ida, born April 22, 1946. She married Thomas Harold Richburg born December 30, 1939. They had three daughters: Amy Louesa, born September 20, 1976; Melanie Suzanne born May 23, 1980; Sara Elizabeth, born June 16, 1982.

During the 1940s, Monroe and Louesa bought the Gaston Farm from his siblings. He farmed until 1959. He was known as an innovative farmer and leader in conservation. Monroe was a member of the Sumter County USDA-AAA Committee, the Farm Bureau, the VFW, American Legion, and Sons of Confederate Veterans. He was active in Concord Methodist Church. A political Conservative, he was active in political and public affairs in Sumter County and the Third Congressional District. His keen interest in history and family motivated him to take his family throughout the South.

James Jr., James III, James Monroe Gaston

Monroe believed that a man's word was his bond and exemplified the Proverb etched on his tombstone, "A good name is rather to be chosen than great riches."

On August 26, 1992, Monroe died at home. He and Louesa, who died on February 13, 1989, are buried at the Friendship Baptist Church Cemetery in Sumter County. *Submitted by: James Monroe Gaston, Jr., 2220 GA Hwy. 30 West, Americus, GA 31709*

568. Paul Jones Gaston

Paul Jones Gaston, the fourth child of Robert Barker Gaston and Ida Rosana Hesterle, was born July 4, 1903, in Carroll County, Georgia. The family moved to Smarrs Station, Monroe County, in 1909. Another move was to Sumter County, Georgia, in 1916.

Paul graduated from Plains High School in 1923. During his high school, he enjoyed maintaining the Model T school bus, which he also drove.

After graduation, he worked in Buffalo, New York, returning home at his father's death. Two years were then spent in Tampa, Florida. All his jobs, until this time, were in the automobile business. Back to Atlanta in 1927, he met and married Paralee Whitehead (Polly) of Bogart, Georgia, born April 6, 1906. To them were born Richard Paul (6/4/28) and Mildred Louise (6/21/32).

In 1931 he bought a movie theatre in Atlanta. Having success in the theatre business in Atlanta, he bought another one in Griffin, Georgia, and moved there in 1933. He operated this theatre until 1960 at which time he purchased the local Chrysler dealership that he ran until his retirement in 1965. Paul passed away in October 1982 and Polly passed away in September 1985.

The son, Richard Paul, married Jane Lee. Three daughters were born to them: Nancy Jane (1956), Janet Ellen (1958), and Beth Ann (1960). The daughter, Mildred Louise, married Edward Handley. They were blessed with three children: James Edward (1955), Mary Catherine (1957), and Richard David (1959).

Submitted by: Richard P. Gaston, 1809 Maple Drive, Griffin, GA 30224

569. Robert Gaston

My grandfather Robert Gaston, fourth son of James and Elizabeth Burns Gaston, was born 5 May 1829 in Newton County, Georgia, died 2 June 1901 in Coosa County, Alabama. He married Mary Burrilla Smith on 28 April 1854. Mary was born 29 December 1831 in Georgia, died 11 February 1875 in Heard County, Georgia. Robert's occupation was millwright. Their children were:

(1) Samuel Clinton born 18 March 1856 in Alabama, died unknown, married first on 5 September 1880 to Lucinta Haines in Coweta County, Georgia, born and died unknown; married second on 5 July 1885 to Catherine R. Nestlehut in Coweta County, born about 1853 in Heard County, died unknown; married third on 10 April 1898 to Nannie J. Williams, Douglasville, Georgia, born about 1871, died about 1959, buried Hill Crest Cemetery, East Point, Georgia. Known children: Sara E. born about 1889, died about 1979; H.C.; Samuel Ithamar born 12 May 1899; Willie Petty born 10 June 1900; N.J. born 1909, died 13 May 1932, buried College Park, Georgia.

(2) Frances Montery Harriet Elizabeth born 29 March 1857 in Alabama, died 25 July 1858 in Alabama.

(3) James Robert born 28 January 1860 in Alabama, died 14 June 1918 in Egan, Georgia (now East Point), married 11 January 1885 in Coweta County to Emily Argo, born 1860 in Coweta County, died 23 May 1921 in Egan. Both are buried at Oak Hill Cemetery Newnan, Georgia. Known children from 1910 census and obituaries: E.T.; John Clinton born 26 December 1890; Jett Miller born 9 January 1895; W.N. born about 1898; Daniel H. born about 1902; daughter born about 1893.

(4) Amarintha Burrilla born 13 September 1862 in Alabama, died 14 July 1864 in Alabama.

(5) William David born 24 February 1865 in Alabama, died 31 March 1932 in Egan (now East Point), buried College Park Cemetery, College Park, Georgia. He was a farmer and carpenter. Married first on 23 May 1886 to Mary Ellen Nestlehut in Coweta County, born 17 March 1866 Heard County, died 3 January 1910 in Egan, buried New Labanon Church Cemetery, Sargent, Coweta County, Georgia. Married second to Emmaline Catherine Gaston (Rooks) 13 April 1913 in East Point. Children by Mary Ellen were: (a) William Dovert born 31 March 1888 in Coweta County, died 3 October 1952, run over by a city bus in Atlanta, buried in College Park. Married first to Mollie unknown, divorced. Married second to Willie Baker unknown, divorced, childless. (b) Mary Berilla born 21 September 1889 in Coweta County, died 26 March 1959 in East Point, married 24 December 1910 to William Claude Hudson, born 13 July 1880 in Douglasville, Georgia, died 9 May 1961, East Point. Both buried in College Park Cemetery, College Park, Georgia. Children: William Clemon born 1911, died 20 November 1977; Mary Ellen born 12 March 1914, died 28 April 1966; Esther Naomi born 25 August 1917; James Dovert born 22 October 1919, died 1965; Florence Cornelia born 10 July 1924. (c) Hattie Lou born 1 November 1892 in Douglasville, Georgia, died 16 December 1980 in East Point, married 24 December 1910 to William Malcomb Dunagan born 29 July 1884, died 30 March 1972. Both buried in

College Park. Children: Willie Geraldine born 5 October 1911; Mary Ellen born 11 November 1914, died 3 June 1999; Robert Milton born 4 November 1917; Janette H. born 28 June 1919; Verna Wynelle born 13 December 1921; Naimo Elizabeth born 26 April 1924, died 22 April 1928; Thelma Lee born 7 July 1926, died 15 October 1995. (d) Robert F. born 13 April 1894, died 6 November 1916 in Florida, was an electrician, killed, and is buried with mother in Coweta County. (e) James Harlin born May 1897, died 31 September 1984, married to Beulah Hadaway, born 1 September 1901, died 9 December 1992. Both are buried in Fayetteville, Georgia. Children: James Harlin born 30 January 1927; David George born 1930. (f) Ollie Elizabeth born 4 October 1900, died 24 November 1967, married 22 October 1927 as second wife of Robert B. Johnson, born 31 August 1886, died 8 July 1954. Both buried in College Park. Stepchildren: Tommy, Oddie, Edna Ray. Children: Frances Wynelle born 11 September 1934, died 14 August 1999; Betty born 12 September 19??; Robbie Elizabeth born unknown. (g) Harrison Clinton born 1 September 1901, died 16 September 1951, married Opal Parks born 25 February 1913, died 18 December 1985. He is buried in College Park, she is buried in Charlotte, North Carolina. Children: Sara Berrilla born 1 March 1932, died 14 August 1988 in Charlotte, North Carolina; William Clinton (Buddy) born 11 December 1934; Robert Lewis born 6 May 1938, died 23 June 1999, buried Charlotte, North Carolina; Mary Ellen born 2 May 1946; Wilburn David born 25 October 1949. All children born in East Point, Georgia, and now live in Charlotte, North Carolina. (h) Homer Lee born 22 September 1905, died 21 August 1955, married 14 September 1929 to Melba Irene Brown, born 20 December 1913, died 21 August 1988. Both are buried in College Park Cemetery. Children: Sarah Lillian born 18 December 1931, died 6 September 1995, buried in West View Cemetery, Atlanta, Georgia; Robert Lee born 16 March 1934; Carole Cornelia born 5 July 1938; Homer Lamar born 13 September 1941; Mary Ruth born 6 November 1944.

Children of William David and Emmaline C. and stepdaughters with Emmaline C. under James Monore;

(6) Daniel Harlen born 25 April 1867 in Alabama, died 29 December 1926, married 28 December 1887 in Coweta County to Idella Dial, born 14 May 1869 in Coweta County, died 8 August 1930 in College Park. Both buried at Ebenezer Baptist Church Cemetery, Douglasville, Georgia. They lived in Coweta County, Villa Rica, and Douglasville, Georgia. Children: Cora born September 1889; Oscar Burnett born 25 January 1891, died 4 August 1958; Mattie Delthia born 28 October 1894; Willie Harlen born 6 December 1897, died 9 June 1947; Lora A. born 1908.

(7) John Fletcher born 25 January 1870 in Alabama, died 23 September 1958, married 26 April 1881 in Coweta County to Margaret Lula Argo, born 15 October 1871, died 13 January 1962. They lived in Coweta, Carroll and Fulton Counties. Both are buried in Rico Cemetery, Rico, Georgia. Children: Clara born 1894; Lula Burrilla born 31 January 1897, died 18 April 1988, buried Rico Cemetery, Rico, Georgia; Joe Cephus born 1902, died unknown, married 27 November 1921 to Ruby Marie Jordan in Carroll County, she was born 1904, died unknown, buried Jordan Cemetery, Carroll County; Emily born 27 March 1904, died 9 February 1988, married 26 March 1922 in Carroll County to Ed Couch, died in World War I; Robert N. born about 1906, died 13 February 1999, buried Holly Hill; Wiley Morgan born 3 June 1908, died 23 November 1972, unm., buried Rico, Georgia.

(8) Olive (Ollie) Elizabeth born 29 September 1872 in Heard County, died 18 February 1951 in Moreland, Coweta County, married 20 May 1888 to John Thomas Wallace in Coweta County, born 7 August 1866 in Coweta County, died 1 January 1953. Both buried Oak Hill Cemetery, Newnan, Georgia. Children: Marvin Dent born 20 December 1890, died 22 March 1952; Willie Bruce born 9 June 1893, died 20 November 1976; John Robert (Bobby) lived in Gadsden, Alabama, born 24 January 1908.

(9) Josephus S. Gaston born 17 November 1874 in Heard County, died 13 August 1939 in LaGrange, Georgia, married about 1899 in Weoka, Talladega, Alabama (now Coosa, Alabama) to Jossie Sizemore, born July 1875, died 16 April 1970 in La Grange. Both buried in unmarked graves in Hill View Cemetery, LaGrange, Georgia. Child: Jossie (Little Jossie) born unknown, died 29 November 1973, buried with parents, married Riley Rosemond, born unknown, died 17 March 1980, buried Hill View in La Grange. *Submitted by: Jewell Gaston, Newnan, GA and Written by: Lena Callaway, 128 Hilley Road, Whitesburg, GA 30185.*

Sources: Bible, obituaries, cemetery, census, and marriage records, family and personal knowledge.

570. Robert Barker Gaston Family

Robert Barker Gaston spent much of his childhood and adult life in Carroll County, where he farmed and was involved in community, civic, and church affairs. He was born on June 24, 1867, in Randolph County, Alabama, as the fourth child of James Monroe Gaston, a Confederate soldier, and Emeline C. Barker. Robert married Ida Rosaine Hesterlee on January 12, 1896, in Carroll County. She was born on April 23, 1875, to Melvin S. and Elizabeth Jane Boatright Hesterlee.

Robert Barker and Ida R. Hesterlee Gaston

Robert and Ida lived with his mother on the family farm until her death. By 1910, six children had been born to Robert and Ida in Carroll County. James Monroe, a World War I veteran and farmer, born December 4, 1898. He married Mary Louesa English of Sumter County, Georgia. Robert Benton, a farmer was born February 4, 1900. He married Marjorie Smith, of Terrell County. George Washington, a businessman, was born April 21, 1901. He married Nellie Mae Gunn of Crisp County. Paul Jones a business man, was born July 4, 1903. He married Paralee (Polly) Whitehead of Oconee County. Florence Lenora (Nora), a teacher, was born December 19, 1907. She married Leroy Sewell Stevens Sr. of Sumter County. Otis Lee, a World War II veteran and college professor, was born July 28, 1909. He married Catherine Clardy of Randolph County, Alabama.

Before leaving Carroll County, Robert Gaston was a delegate to the National Presidential Convention in Cincinnati, Ohio. He was a strong supporter of Congressman Thomas Watson and the Populist views. Robert attended the Cotton Expo in New Orleans where he bought a beaded Indian necklace for Ida.

Sometime during 1910, Robert and his family moved by mule, wagon and train to a 600-acre farm near Smarr in Monroe County. His two older sons, Monroe and Robert Benton helped him clear the land after school each day. During the eight years in Monroe County, they had two daughters. Ida Louise, a teacher, was born August 17, 1911. She married George Washington Mosely of Jacksonville, Florida. Ruth Elizabeth, a teacher, was born February 16, 1916. Each of the three daughters graduated from Georgia State College for Women. Otis Lee, their fifth son graduated from Georgia Tech and the University of Georgia.

Robert and Ida's work ethic and involvement in community, civic, and family responsibilities were nurtured in all of their eight children.

In 1918, the Gastons sold their farm in Monroe County and moved to Sumter County, where they bought the Crawford Plantation in Concord community. There Robert farmed until he died of a heart attack on December 31, 1925. Ida continued to live on their farm and in Americus until her death on September 9, 1970.

Both Robert and Ida and their children, Monroe and Ruth, are buried in Friendship Baptist Cemetery, one and a half miles from the family home.

The old Carroll County Gaston home built by Robert's father, James Monroe Gaston, is presently used by the Carroll County Fire, Rescue, and Emergency Management Agency at 501 Old Newnan Road. *Submitted by: Mrs. Dorothy Gaston Lee, 6991 Lee Road 390, Opelika, AL 36804*

571. George Washington Gay Sr.

George Washington "Wash" Gay was born January 17, 1846, in Coweta County, Georgia. His grandfather, Allen Gay, a Revolutionary War soldier, was a pioneer of Coweta County. Family tradition has it that Allen's first wife was the daughter of Samuel Elbert, an early governor of Georgia. However, I have not been able to confirm that claim to fame.

George Washington's parents were Gilbert and Sarah Stamps Gay. George Washington was the eleventh of thirteen children. Gilbert and his family moved to the Indian Creek area of Carroll County in 1850 where they settled near several other related families from Coweta County. They joined the fellowship of Indian Creek Baptist Church as a deacon and deaconess. After several official church-related trips to help the newly established church at Macedonia, Gilbert and his family moved to Cleburne County to be near the fledgling church.

George Washington Gay entered the Confederate military service as a private in Company B, 56th Georgia Volunteer Infantry in January 1864 at Dalton, Georgia. According to a deposition found in 1900 Confederate pension application, he "fought from Dalton to Atlanta. After the July 24 and 25, 1864, fighting at Atlanta, I was sent to hospital sick in Macon and then to Augusta, Georgia, and was never able to go to service anymore." The National Archives does not have his compiled military record. However, a family member has a copy of the medical register of May Hospital in Macon that includes his name and unit.

Several family members believe that Wash was married twice. Indeed, his 1900 U.S. Census enumeration indicates that he was married twice. However, I have found no record of a first marriage. The only known marriage record shows that Wash married Margaret C. Southerland on July 29, 1869, in Carroll County, Georgia. She was the daughter of Philip Smith and was born June 1833 in Tennessee. Her first marriage was to Jacob Southerland on June 6, 1852, in Benton County, Alabama. They had at least one child and possibly two others. The known child was John Albert Southerland, born July 14, 1853. He married Eliza Jane Gay, Wash's sister, on August 24, 1871. John died March 30, 1914, and is buried at Macedonia Baptist Church. The two other children were conceived either from Wash's supposed first marriage or were brought into the union from Margaret's preceding marriage, inasmuch as they were both born before Wash and Margaret were married. Sarah Ann Southerland (Gay) was born circa 1865. She married J.H. Martin. I have found no further record of her. Andrew Jackson Southerland (Gay) was born about 1867. Family members have related that his last known address was in Florida. I have not discovered the reason why Jacob and Margaret's marriage ended.

George Washington and Margaret Smith Southerland Gay had five children that we know were their own. They were: (1) Eliza A. Gay was born circa 1870. I have found no record of her. (2) George Washington Gay Jr. was born November 3, 1871. He married Ola Izora Skinner on January 4, 1891, in Cleburne County, Alabama. Ola Izora was born May 8, 1873, daughter of Andrew Jackson and Rebecca Ann McElroy Phillips Skinner. George Washington Gay Jr. died of a gunshot wound on March 3, 1915, and Ola Izora died April 6, 1950. George and Izora are buried at Pleasant Grove Methodist Church. George Washington Jr. and Ola Izora had ten children: Newell Franklin married Mary Ellen Batchelor; Belzie Arizona Gay married Dock W. Stewart; Horace Mack Comer Gay married Sadie Higgins; John W. Gay married Eriene Skinner; Eldora Gay married Harbard Ivey; Ethel Gay married George W. McKensie; Arleavy Gay married Monroe Benefield; Etta Gay married Joseph Teal; Bertie Gay married Rector Price; and Vela Mae Gay married first to Alonzo Brown and second to Enoch Smith. (3) Gilbert Gay was born May 14, 1873. He married Viola Texas Skinner on November 2, 1890, in Cleburne County, Alabama. Texas was Ola Izora Skinner's sister. Gilbert and Texas had two children. Robert Newton Gay married Mattie E. Handley, and Enos Farlow Gay married Rena Stewart. Gilbert died June 16, 1952, and Texas died May 6, 1957. Gilbert and Texas are buried at Pleasant Grove Methodist Church. (4) Absolam Columbus Gay was born in 1877. First he was married to Beulah Shelton and second to Almeda Stewart. Absolam died in 1935, Bulah died August 24, 1909, and Almeda died in 1960. All three are buried at Macedonia Baptist Church. (5) Ida A. Gay was born about 1878. I can find no further record of her.

George Washington Gay Sr. died April 14, 1915, one month following the death of his son, George Washington Gay Jr. Margaret died about 1918. They are both buried at Macedonia Baptist Church. *Submitted by: Larry F. Morrison, P.O. Box 26, Woodland, AL 36280*

Sources: Census records, marriage records, Southerland Family Bible, 1907 census of Confederate Veterans Living in Cleburne County, Alabama, Confederate pension application, and family interviews.

572. Gilbert Gay, Sarah Stamps and Allied Families

Gilbert Gay was born May 1803, in Hancock County, Georgia, the son of Allen Gay and Abigail Castleberry. Allen Gay was a Revolutionary War soldier who migrated to Georgia from Franklin County, North Carolina, about three years after the war ended, according to his Revolutionary War pension application filed in September 1832 in Coweta County, Georgia.

Gilbert Gay married Sarah Stamps in January 1829 in Coweta County. Sarah Stamps was born November 1809 in Georgia, the daughter of Moses Stamps and Ann Eason. Gilbert Gay and Sarah Stamps moved to Carroll County, Georgia, by 1850, where Sarah's brother Eason Stamps had also settled. Gilbert Gay and Sarah Stamps had the following children: (1) Anna Abigail Gay born 1830, married Joseph Webb. (2) Allen Moses Gay born 1831, married first to Martha Stamps, and second to Betsy Williamson. (3) Gilbert Gay born 1832, married L.E. Gays. (4) John R. Gay born 1834, married Ann Jacobs. (5) Mary M. Gay born 1835, married Manning Brown. (6) Sarah E. Gay born 1838, married James L. Hill. (7) Martha Ann T. Gay born 1839, married first to Francis M. Stamps, and second to James Thomas J. Skinner. (8) James Thomas Gay born 1841. (9) Eliza Jane Gay born 1844, married John Southerland. (10) George Washington Gay born January 1846, married Margaret C. Smith Southerland. (11) Susan E. Gay born 1848, married John Gibson Skinner. (12) Francis Marion Gay born 1850, married Mary Abbie Allen. (13) Georgia Rebecca Gay born 1853, married Joshua David Smith. (14) William Leonst Gay born December 1855, married Pelly Mylenda Langley.

Gilbert Gay family moved to Calhoun and Randolph County, Alabama, by 1860, with some of his descendants moving on to Cleburne County, Alabama, by 1870s. Gilbert Gay and Sarah Stamps moved back to Carroll County, Georgia, by 1880, where Gilbert Gay is shown in the census as "working in a wood shop" at the age of 77 years.

Gilbert and Sarah Gay's son, George Washington Gay, was born January 17, 1846, in Coweta County, Georgia. George Washington Gay married Margaret C. Smith Southerland in 1869 in Carroll County. George and Margaret Gay were residing in the Bowdon area of Carroll County in the 1870 census.

George W. Gay and Margaret Gay's son George Washington Gay Jr. was born November 3, 1871, in Carroll County. He married Ola Izora Skinner in January 1891 in Cleburne County, Alabama. Ola Izora Skinner was born May 8, 1873 in Cleburne County, the daughter of Andrew Jackson Skinner (1851-1908) and Rebecca Ann McElroy (1844-1902).

George Washington Gay Jr. and Ola Izora Skinner's daughter Etta Ophelia Gay was born February 22, 1896, in Cleburne County, Alabama. She married Joseph W. Teal in December 1911 in Hightower, Cleburne County. Joseph W. Teal was born June 1892 in Cleburne County, the son of Jesse T.C. Teal and Sarah (Sallie) Ashley. Jesse T.C. Teal was born December 1851 in old Campbell County, Georgia, the son of Joshua Teal and Polly Mary Wallace who migrated to Georgia about 1830 from Anson County, North Carolina. Jesse T.C. Teal died in 1936 in Carroll County.

The children of Jesse T.C. Teal and Sarah (Sallie) Ashley were: (1) Henry Newton Teal born July 1881, married Beulah Scott. (2) Cleveland Teal born October 1888, married Mary Etta Thomason. (3) Jepp R. Teal born April 1890, married Martha M. McClain. (4) Joseph W. Teal born June 1892, married Etta Ophelia Gay. (5) James I. Teal born May 1893, married first to Essie King, and second to Nellie Owens.

Sarah (Sallie) Ashley was born May 14, 1854 in Heard County, Georgia, the daughter of Reuben Ashley and Minerva Amanda Dunlap. Reuben Ashley was born October 1817 in South Carolina and died June 1888 in Heard County, Georgia. Reuben Ashley was a Civil War veteran, enlisting in Company A of the 1st Georgia Reserves, Fannin's Regiment, on May 1, 1864. His service record shows that he enlisted at the age of 46 years, was 5 feet 9 inches tall with ruddy complexion, blue eyes and gray hair. The muster rolls note that he was assigned to Andersonville, Georgia, for duty during the war. His widow Minerva Amanda Ashley received a widow's Civil War pension in Cleburne County, Alabama, in 1899. Reuben Ashley's tombstone is placed with a Confederate marker at the Salem United Methodist Church Cemetery in Heard County, Georgia. Reuben Ashley and Minerva A. Dunlap's children were: (1) William Ashley born May 1851, married Sarah Thompson. (2) Martha A. Lillie Ashley born April 1853, died 1916 in Randolph County, Alabama. (3) Sarah (Sallie) Ashley born May 1854, married Jesse T.C. Teal. (4) Mary Ashley born 1856. (5) Charlotte (Lottie) Ashley born May 1857, married Bill Bozeman. (6) Reuben Ashley Jr. born September 1860, married Martha E. Thompson. (7) Elizabeth Ashley born January 1863, married Young Gill Norton. (8) Joseph George Washington Ashley born March 1875, married Lucanda Frances Armstrong. (9) Phillip Thomas Ashley born December 1876, married Emma E. Harper.

Reuben Ashley Sr.'s parents are undocumented. From extensive research, it appears most likely that he is related to the Abbeville County, South Carolina, Ashley families, some of whom migrated to Georgia and Alabama before 1850. Reuben Ashley's known siblings from Ashley family Bible records, census and probate records were: (1) Martha A. Saleste Ashley born March 1816 in South Carolina; died January 1897 in Heard County, Georgia. (2) James Ashley born September 1819 in South Carolina. (3) Phillip Ashley born December 1823 in South Carolina. (4) Harriet Matilda Ashley born September 1827 in South Carolina, died 1908 in Heard County, Georgia. (5) Thomas Ashley born November 1829 in South Carolina, died July 1862 in the Civil War, married to Elizabeth Cox. (6) Elizabeth Ashley born December 1832 in South Carolina, died October 1908 in Heard County, Georgia. (7) Mary Ann Ashley born November 1834 in South Carolina or Georgia, married to Francis Marion Screws. *Submitted by: Candace Teal Gravelle, PO Box 3, Albany, OR 97321*

Sources: Family records, Bible records, census and probate records.

573. Newell Franklin and Mary Ellen Gay

George Washington "Wash" Gay was born January 17, 1846, in Coweta County, Georgia. His grandfather, Allen Gay, a Revolutionary War soldier, was a pioneer family of Coweta County. George Washington's parents were Gilbert and Sarah Stamps Gay. George Washington was the eleventh of thirteen children. Gilbert and his family moved to the Indian Creek area of Carroll County, in 1850 where they settled near several other related families from Coweta County. They joined the fellowship of Indian Creek Baptist Church as a deacon and deaconess. After several official church-related trips to help the newly established church at Macedonia, George Washington Gay Jr. and his family moved to Cleburne County to be near the Macedonia Baptist Church.

Newell Franklin "Big Papa" Gay was grandson of George Washington Gay Sr. of the Indian Creek community. Newell was the first born of three brothers and seven sisters. He was the son of George Washington Jr. (1871-1914) and Ola Izora Skinner (1873-1950). George Washington and family farmed just north of Sally's Creek. Newell farmed there the first year after his marriage to Mary Ellen "Big Mama" Batchelor, born July 12, 1895.

Big Papa stole Mary Ellen away from the Faulkner school on January 21, 1911. Born to this marriage were four boys — Rudy, Rubie, Fred, and Earl — and six girls — Bessie Barnes, Blanch Morgan, Wavelen Vison, June Jordan, Katy Crosson, and Shirley Noles. This marriage ended in 1990 at Big Mama's death. Seventy-nine years of marriage is quite a record. She said that Newell never got mad and stomped off without breakfast and she never got mad and didn't fix his breakfast. She said, "I like that."

Children of Newell and Mary Ellen Batchelor Gay. Bessie, Katy, Rudy, Shirley, June, Wavelen, Blanch, and Earl

Big Papa borrowed about a thousand dollars in 1920 to buy a seventy-seven acre farm at Pleasant Grove. They lived there until 1947. He bought another farm (181 acres) near Macedonia School and built a house. They lived there the rest of their lives. He mostly raised cotton, corn, syrup cane, hogs, and cows. I remember Big Papa going to the cotton gin before sunrise to get a place at the front of the line. Sometimes he would let some of the grandsons go along.

From a very young age, Big Papa made sorghum syrup for the family and others in the community at Sally's Creek. This produced syrup for the winter months and cash. Big Mama always hated the syrup mess of canning and cleaning. Well, the story goes that Big Papa was traveling in the wagon to Woodrow Wilson store at Hopewell to buy farm supplies. He met a stranger on the road in a wagon. About four hours later, Big Papa returned with his supplies and found that his syrup mill was gone. He just went about his farm chores and never said anything about the mill. Several years later, Big Mama asked who bought the syrup mill. It turned out that neither knew what happened to the mill other than a stranger loaded it on a wagon and hauled it away.

At the age of ninety-one, Big Papa said he was not going to plant a garden and corn patch next year, because he could not get off his tractor. This was the tractor that the grandsons learned their mechanical skills on. He always wanted his tractor to be ready for spring planting. Big Papa died in 1991, living only one year after Big Mama's death. Both are buried at Pleasant Grove Cemetery. *Submitted by: Billy Gay (grandson), 990 County Road 96, Heflin, AL 36264*

574. Rudy Bill Gay and Christine Gay

My granddad is Rudy Bill Gay, grandson of G.W. Gay of Indian Creek of Carroll, County, Georgia. This remembrance of a man who was a loving husband of fifty-three years, a supportive dad of three children, a kind and gentle Papaw to seven granddaughters and four great-grandsons, bring our hearts together with memories of Rudy Bill Gay. He was born January 20, 1919, to Newell Franklin Gay (1891) and Mary Ellen Batchelor Gay (1895). He survived his twin brother Rubie at birth. He was the oldest son of nine younger siblings with one older sister.

He spent his life on the hills of Pleasant Grove near Ranburne. His father's homestead connects to the land where he raised his own children and lived until 1994 at his death. The land he owned gave him great pride. On warm sunny afternoons he would take his children and grandchildren on walks across his land. He showed us the land that would someday be ours. The details of trees, rocks, and creeks were mapped in his mind to perfection.

His wife, Christine Cantrell Gay (1919), was always by his side. They were married in 1941. Their firstborn was Wallace Douglas Gay (1943) and their second were twins, Billy Joe Gay and Betty Ann Gay Hodge (1946).

They spent many years poultry farming, logging timber, and raising cattle. When each grandchild was born, he would sell a cow and put the money earned away to draw interest until the child's eighteenth birthday. The jobs worked away from home, the Rubber Plant, Lee Brothers, and assisting the commissioner of Cleburne County, succeeded in removing Papaw from his favorite responsibility, the farm.

His son Wallace had two daughters, Christy Lane Gay Osbome (1967) and Kendra Deann Gay Poirer (1973). His son Billy had three daughters, Lora Beth Gay Merrill (1976), Lisa Lanett Gay (1980), and Ashley Ellen Gay (1985). His daughter Betty had two daughters, Tonya Deann Hodge Hay (1972) and Anita Lynn Hodge Whiten (1976). Papaw always called us his "Gay Girls."

The Rudy Bill Gay Family

Spending time at Papaw and Grandma's for the grandchildren always ensured a trip to the store for candy and rides on the tractor. Their house was always open to playing, laughing, and a few tears. I remember picking strawberries on a hillside now covered with old growth pines. Those simple events gave us many memories to keep in our hearts. Rudy Gay was a strong, hard-working man with a humble heart. He always would tell us "I love you grown girls." Even in his last days he would hold Grandma's hand and kiss it. Our family was blessed to have been given him as a husband, dad, and Papaw. We all miss his voice and touch but we look forward to seeing him again in heaven. We love you Papaw and thank you for your love. *Submitted by: Christy Gay Osbone, 1545 Alkea Grove Lane, Arab, AL 38016*

575. The Aubrey W. Gilbert Family

John Luther Gilbert was born in Talladega, Alabama, in 1873 and his family eventually migrated to Clarksdale, Mississippi. He married Nora Lee Wilson who was born in Macon, Georgia, in 1877. They had seven children. Nora died in 1939 and was buried in Clarksdale. John Luther Gilbert died in 1958 and was buried beside his wife. Both had ties to Georgia and Carroll County.

The ancestors of John Luther Gilbert had arrived in Georgia with James Edward Oglethorpe when Fort Frederika was established. Many Gilberts still live in Brunswick, Georgia. After Nora's death, John L. Gilbert visited her relatives and the Confederate Cemetery in Macon where members of both families killed in the Civil War were buried. His brother, Osceola Pinkney Gilbert in Atlanta, was the editor of the Baptist Christian Index. John visited his daughter Inez, the wife of Reverend Howard Benson, and his grandson Aubrey Warden Gilbert and family in Carrollton, Georgia. Over the years John as well as other members of the Gilbert family spent time or lived in Carrollton.

John's daughter, Inez G. Benson, was born in 1912 in Clarksdale. She and Howard Beck Benson were married in 1938. They came to Carrollton in 1944 when he was called to pastor the First Baptist Church. Inez taught Sunday School and Howard remained as pastor until his resignation in 1975. While pastor, Howard was alerted to the welfare of "challenged" children, and he, Alton Estes, and others were instrumental in forming the Carroll County Mental Health Association. Howard died in 1978 and Inez in 1986, both are buried in Carrollton. The Bensons had no children but helped raise many.

Hazel G. Williams, another daughter of John L. Gilbert, visited her sister Inez in Carrollton often. Among other nieces and nephews, Hazel's son Clint Doss lived with the Bensons and graduated from Carrollton High School and later became an anesthesiologist. He now lives in Toccoa, Georgia.

Aubrey Wilson Gilbert, a son of John Luther, born in 1901 in Clarksdale, joined the United States Marine Corps after World War I, and later served in World War II. While in the Marine Corps he met his wife, Mary Ella Warden. Aubrey Wilson died after an illness in Carrollton, Georgia, in 1952. Ella, who had been born in 1901 in Virginia, moved to Macon, Georgia, where she lived until she died in 1997. They had two daughters, Jeune, and Joyce, and a son Aubrey Warden, who later lived in Carrollton.

Aubrey Warden Gilbert was born in Clarksdale in 1926, and died a resident of Carroll County in 1978. He came to Carrollton after serving in the Marine Corps during World War II. He graduated West Georgia College and married Rebecca Lawler, the daughter of Mr. and Mrs. T.J. Lawler. "Becky" was born in 1929, and grew up in Carrollton. They had five children. Aubrey then attended and graduated the Law School at Mercer University in Macon. After serving in the Korean War, Aubrey returned to Carrollton and practiced law. He served as the county attorney, and several times as judge in the various courts in Carroll County, as well as being active in many private and civic organizations. He remained in the Marine Corps Reserve until his death and had achieved the rank of colonel. Becky continued her education through the years and received her degree in accounting from Georgia State University in 1985, while working for the City of Atlanta. She later retired and returned to Carrollton, where she currently resides.

Of the Gilbert children, all grew up in Carrollton and graduated from Carrollton High School. The oldest, Howard, lives in Atlanta, as does the youngest, Claire, with her sons. The middle sons, Ward and Jack, and their families live in Carrollton. Both served in the Marine Corps. Jack served in the Persian Gulf War and retired from the Reserve as a lieutenant colonel. The youngest son Carl and his son live near Roopville *Submitted by: Jack Gilbert, 206 Ridley Dr., Carrollton, GA 30117*

576. John Griffin Giles and Elizabeth Ann Proctor

John Griffin Giles was born about 1830 in Georgia, married Elizabeth Ann Proctor on 9 September 1850 in Coweta County, Georgia. She was born about 1835 in Georgia and died about 1870/80 in Carroll County, Georgia. Griffin Giles served as a sergeant in Company G, 51st Regiment, Georgia. He was admitted to United States General Hospital, Point Lookout, Maryland, from prisoner of war camp on 28 June 1865. His diagnosis was chronic diarrhea. He died 2 July 1865 and is buried in the adjacent cemetery.

The children of Griffin and Elizabeth Giles were:

(1) Andrew J. "Jack" born 13 August 1851 in Carroll County, married first to Sarah Frances Lenderman (see Lenderman Family). He married second to Mary Jane Lewis, born 6 November

Sarah Frances Lenderman and Andrew J. Giles

1861, died 20 June 1940 in Cullman County, Alabama, buried at Hebron Church of Christ Cemetery, Hulaco, Morgan County, Alabama. Children of Jack and Sarah Frances Giles were: Malona H. "Lonie," born 21 November 1873 in Carroll County, married Mary Wallace; Minna Lee born 6 March 1875 in Carroll County, died 21 December 1942 in Morgan County, Alabama, married Benjamin Lee Earwood; Henry Oliver born 21 February 1877 in Carroll County, married Ludie Bell Roberts; Joseph Abner born February 1880 in Carroll County, married Lizzie Broom; Lucy E. born May 1883, married Millard Tanner; Nellie Frances born 16 May 1885, married Isaac Newman Nunnelley; Cornelius Walker born 21 October 1888 in Cullman County, Alabama, died 1973 in Jefferson County, Alabama, married Elvira Rodriquez in 1918 in Jefferson County, Alabama; Tempie Anna born 21 April 1890 in Morgan County, Alabama, died in Cullman County, Alabama, married William Oscar Hanes on 21 December 1910 in Cullman County.

Mary A. Giles Lenderman

(2) Tempie Janie, born 12 August 1858 in Georgia, died 6 December 1905 in Morgan County, Alabama, buried in Hebron Church of Christ Cemetery, Hulaco, Morgan County, Alabama. She married Robert Matthew Able Warnick (See Warnick family).

(3) Sarah Elizabeth, was born 11 March 1862 in Carroll County, died 15 October 1919 in Winston County, Alabama, buried in Upshaw Friendship Baptist Cemetery, Winston County, Alabama. She married William A. Wheeler on 28 December 1878 in Carroll County. He was born December 1857 in Georgia, died January 1929 in Winston County. Children of Sarah Elizabeth and William A. Wheeler were: Molly born April 1881 in Georgia, married on 4 March 1900 in Winston County, Alabama to W.M. Bryant, born December 1876 in Georgia; Liller Margaret born 18 May 1883 in Georgia, married Joseph Martin Hightower; Hannah born 16 June 1886 in Georgia, married Warner F. Pope; Tempa Alice born February 1892 in Alabama, married James Tigg; Ester born June 1899 in Alabama, died between 1910-1920.

(4) Mary A., born 11 October 1866 in Carroll County, Georgia, died 3 April 1920 in Morgan County, Alabama, buried in Hebron Church of Christ Cemetery, Hulaco, Morgan County, Alabama. She married Jacob Moses Lenderman on 3 January 1884 in Carroll County (see Lenderman Family). *Submitted by: Ranelle Gray, 1942 Poplar Drive SW, Cullman, AL 35055*

577. Gilland - McWhorter

Marcus Granville Gilland was born April 5, 1852, probably in Gordon County, Georgia, and died February 29, 1928, in Carroll County, Georgia. He was the son of Osburn Gilland and Lettey Turbyfield. His siblings were James W. Gilland who married Mildred Jones, Mary Gilland who married Burrell Huff, and Andrew Jackson Gilland who married Alice Ann Adaline Wrenn and moved to Cullman County, Alabama.

On January 1, 1874, in Carroll County, Marcus married Julia Angeline McWhorter. Julia was the daughter of Moses Allen McWhorter and Sarah Kinney. She was born August 17, 1855, and died April 29, 1931. Both are buried in the Powell Chapel United Methodist Church Cemetery.

Marcus was a farmer and owned a large amount of land. It has been said that he was an exceptionally smart businessman. In their later years, Marcus and Julia moved into Villa Rica and Marcus gave a parcel of land to the First Baptist Church

Their children were: 1. Sarah Florence Gilland was born October 18, 1876, and died December 3, 1932. She married Samuel Ratice Harper in 1896. They had three children: Walter, Rilla and Ruby. 2. Josephine Gilland was born May 1, 1879, and died January 17, 1945. She married Thomas Jeff Harden on January 26, 1896, and there were seven children: Linton, Annie Mae, Rosco, Myrtice, Owen, James and Carl. 3. Ila Irena Gilland was born July 13, 1880, and died August 4, 1957. She married Herschel Jordan Boyd on November 5, 1899, and there were two children: Minnie A. and Marvie Jordan. 4. Wiley Granville Gilland was born October 17, 1882, and died November 9, 1956. He married Nellie Grover Stovall on November 12, 1905, and there were five children: Zuma, Grover, Ella, Innis and Dorothy Mozelle. 5. Owen Oscar Gilland was born July 5, 1886, and died February 11, 1973. He married Emma Tyson on September 6, 1908, and there were five children: Leroy, Emily, Aubry, Lucille, and Osnie. 6. Claude Allen Gilland was born January 11, 1887, and died April 22, 1928. He married Causby Ethel Ayers on January 2, 1910, and there were six children: Lovelia, Ordel Ausburn, Edna Maureen, Willard Vernon, Claude Ovis, and Nelson Vonell. 7. Ralph Waldo Gilland was born August 8, 1891, and died July 13, 1975. He married Julie Mae Byram on April 22, 1917, and there were three children: Ralph Byram, Reginald Waldo, and Edna. 8. Cliff E. Gilland was born May 8, 1894, and died August 7, 1943. He married Mamie L. Cornett and there were two children: Marie and Cliff Duane. 9. Lillie Mae Gilland was born July 14, 1896, and died in March 1982. She married Gwendolin E. Merritt on July 3, 1921, and there were two children: George and Ray. *Submitted by: Neal Gilland, 970 Flat Rock Road, Villa Rica, GA 30180*

Sources: Personal knowledge, census, marriage, and cemetery records researched by Erlene Boyd.

578. William Bailes "Judge" Gilley

William Bailes "Judge" Gilley was born July 12, 1809, in South Carolina. He and his family moved from South Carolina to Tennessee where he spent his childhood. Then, he and his brother Jordan started out on their own. William Bailes Gilley married Matilda Roper Raiper from Tennessee on April 28, 1830, in Carrollton, Georgia. He finally became a large land owner. He owned many slaves and had some freed on him. He raised cattle, cotton and whiskey (legally) for the government. He had his own shoe cobblers, tanned his own leather, and made his own saddles on his plantation. At one time he owned land from Newnan Road in Carrollton to Cross Plains, approximately five-thousand acres. It was at Cross Plains that the old Gilley homestead was built of hewn logs in 1843. After being restored, it still stands today. It was here that he donated a plot for Gilley Cemetery. There is a Gilley Reunion held there the first Saturday of August each year. William Bailes "Judge" Gilley died May 19, 1886. His wife, Matilda, died February 13, 1888. Both are buried at the Gilley Cemetery on Gilley Road.

These two had ten children, one of whom was Thomas McDonald Gilley, the ninth child, born in 1850. He was married to Nancy Rebecca "Becky" Winkles on August 3, 1873. She was one-quarter Cherokee Indian. She died in 1921 and he died November 30, 1924. Both are buried in the Gilley Cemetery. They had eleven children with Cliffton Homer Gilley, born November 17, 1893, being the ninth child.

Cliffton Homer Gilley married Charlsie Cooper on January 2, 1916. She died in 1922 and was buried at Cross Plains Baptist Church. They had three children: Robert Denver, Paschael Henry, and twin "Pal" Gilley who died shortly after birth. Cliffton Homer Gilley married Jewell Clementine Smallwood on December 23, 1923. They had five children: Dorothy Alene "Dottie," Virginia, Frank, Camp H., and Patricia Elaine.

Front: Wyly, Mark, Lillie, Julia, and Owen. Back: Ralph, Claude, and Cliff.

Original Gilley Homestead House (restored) on Gilley Road

He was a farmer and still lived on part of the original Gilley plantation. Frank and his wife Barbara, and Camp H. and his wife Martha Ann and their children, Sandy and Rhonda, and their families still live on some of the original Gilley Plantation. *Submitted by: Camp H. Gilley, 799 Cross Plains Road, Carrollton, GA 30116*

579. Hale Gipson and Mary Dean

Hale Gipson was born June 1849. His name may have been George Hale, possibly George Washington Hale Gipson. Hale married Mary Dean on January 16, 1870, in Carroll County Georgia. She was born about 1848 (date of birth calculated from 1880 census records; however, this differs from date of birth shown in 1900 census.) Their children were: (1) William Jonathan Green Gipson, born September 13, 1874 or 1875, (probably in Carroll County), died June 16, 1948, in Albertville, Alabama. (2) Mary Emily Virginia Gipson, born July 05, 1891 or 1892, in Georgia and died September 24, 1975, Georgia.

William Jonathan Green Gipson, son of Hale Gipson and Mary Dean.

1880 census, Carroll County, Georgia:

Hails Gibson, white male, age 30, farming, born Georgia, father born Georgia.

Mary, white female, wife, age 32, keeping house, born Georgia, father born Georgia.

William, white male, son, age 5, born Georgia, father born Georgia.

Next household on census (possibly related to Mary):

Martha Dean, white female, age 45, widow, farming, born Georgia, father born Georgia.

Maronda, white female, age 30, daughter, single, at home, born Georgia.

Joseph, white male, age 20, son, single, at home, born Georgia.

Dania, white female, age 18, daughter, single, at home, born Georgia.

1900 census, Heard County, Georgia:

Hale Gipson, head of household, W,M, born June 1849, married 25 years, born Georgia, parents born Georgia.

Mary, wife, W,F, born 1860, age 40, 2 children, born Georgia, parents born Georgia.

Emma, daughter, W,F, b 1891, age ?, single, born Georgia, parents born Georgia.

William Gipson and wife Mattie, daughter Alma Jane, and son Conard. About 1907

William "Billy" Jonathan Green Gipson married Martha "Mattie" Moore about 1898 (possibly in Heard County, Georgia), daughter of Archibald Judge Moore and Rebecca (maiden name possibly Bonds).She was born May 03, 1877, in Randolph County, Alabama, and died April 03, 1963, in Albertville, Alabama. On the 1900 census, Heard County, Georgia, two households from Hale Gipson was the household of B.J. Sears and wife, Georgia. Georgia was an older sister of Mattie. My grandmother says that her mother, Mattie, lived with Georgia after their mother died. I believe this is how William and Mattie met. William and Mattie were in DeKalb County, Alabama, on the 1910 census with three children, and later moved to and raised a large family in Marshall County, Alabama. Both are buried in Asbury Cemetery in the Asbury Community outside Albertville, Alabama, as are most of their children. They have said that William was a very "well read" and knowledgeable man. He was always reading a book or newspaper.

Children of William Gipson and Martha Moore were (1) Johnny Gipson born before 1910 and died before 1910. (2) Alma Jane Gipson born January 25, 1903, died March 24, 1986, married Robert Luther Thomason. (3) Conard Vinson Gipson born February 24, 1906, died June 16, 1980, married Connie O. Thrash. (4) Buena Vista Gipson born May 03, 1908, died August 22, 1969, married William Dilmos Thrash. (5) Mollie Bell Gipson born January 25, 1911, married Julius Filmore Thrash. (6) Cleates Ruth Gipson born February 26, 1913, died December 27, 1996, married John Houston Thrash. (7) Homer Merle Gipson born April 9, 1916, died March 8, 1960, never married, no children. (8) Buford York Gipson born May 31, 1919, married Dora Lee Simmons. (9) Mary Emily "Emma" Virginia Gipson married Jessie "Jett" Hugh Franklin Ledbetter, born March 15, 1876, died April 19, 1947. Both are buried in Welcome All Cemetery, College Park, Georgia.

Children of Jett Ledbetter and Emma Gipson: (1)Ethel Ledbetter born April 06, 1906, deceased, married Adger Gossett, (2) William Harvey Ledbetter born September 29, 1907, died January 24, 1997, in East Point, Georgia, married Mary George Huey. (3) George Orrie Ledbetter born July 01, 1909, died January 08, 1987, in Fairburn, Georgia, married Elsie Phillips. (4) Garvie Lee Ledbetter born October 08, 1913, died January 03, 1998, in Jonesboro, Georgia, married Ivy Jean Burke. (5) Etta Mae Ledbetter born April 16, 1916, died September 17, 1917. (6) Vesta Virginia Ledbetter born October 14, 1918, Georgia, deceased, married Chester Rady King. (7) Artis Record Ledbetter born July 16, 1925, died April 07, 1984, in Riverdale, Georgia, married Edna M. Creel. (8) Ezelle Ledbetter born March 20, 1928, married John Doodle Thrower. (9) Billie Ledbetter born May 01, 1933. *Submitted by: Pamela T. Morring, 2754 Dug Hill Road, Huntsville, AL 35811*

580. Mollie Bell Gipson and Juluis Filmore Thrash

Mollie Bell Gipson was born January 25, 1911, in or near the Martling community in Marshall County, Alabama. Her parents were William "Billy" Jonathan Green Gipson and Martha "Mattie" Moore. William Jonathan Green Gipson is believed to have been born in Carroll County, Georgia, on September 13, 1874 (or 1875), son of Hale Gipson and Mary Dean, who married in Carroll County on January 16, 1870. He owned and operated a cotton gin in the Martling community for many years. He also operated a sawmill and a grist mill. When Mollie Bell was about nine years old, the family moved across the Tennessee River somewhere near where the Guntersville Dam is now located so her father could cut timber on another man's land. They had to be taken by barge across the river and Mollie Bell was "scared to death," in her words. She attended a one-room school in Upton. It took three years to cut all the timber. They then moved back across the river to the Martling community.

Mollie Bell Gipson Thrash with her great-grandson Carl Morring. About 1998.

Mollie Bell married Julius Filmore Thrash, son of William Andrew Jackson Thrash and Sara Minnie Dollar. They were married by a Preacher Childress in the preacher's home near the Martling and Poplar Spring communities in Marshall County, Alabama. Filmore was born July 24, 1910, died May 05, 1983, and is buried in Asbury Cemetery, Asbury community near Albertville, Alabama, as is their son Paul.

Mollie Bell and Filmore raised their family on Martling Road outside Albertville, Marshall County, Alabama. They farmed and worked hard all their married lives. They were doting grandparents. Mollie Bell is now ninety years of age (the last surviving of William's children) and still lives alone, her mind sharp as ever.

Children of Mollie Bell Gipson and Julius Filmore Thrash are (1) Charles Raybern Thrash born November 1, 1930, and (2) Paul Venson Thrash born January 4, 1934, died November 2, 1955. Paul never married and had no children. He was going hunting one day and tripped on a piece of barbed wire sticking out of the ground. His gun went off, hitting him in the chest, and he died three days later.

Charles Raybern Thrash married first to Betty Sue Rice, daughter of Robert G. Rice and Lorena Dobbins. Betty Sue was born February 15, 1933, in Grant, Alabama, and died June 7, 1972, in Center Point, Alabama. Cause of death was cancer. She is buried Marshall Memory Gardens, Albertville, Raybern married second to Darlene Holderfield.

Children of Charles Raybern Thrash and Betty Sue Rice are Pamela Gaye Thrash and Sheila Joy Thrash. Pamela Gaye Thrash married Carl Augustus Morring III on February 26, 1983, in Church of Christ, Guntersville, Alabama. Child of Pam and Gus is Carl Augustus IV.

Sheila Joy Thrash married Jerry Allen Duckett on July 21, 1978. Their children are Jenna Danielle and Jamie Michelle, twins. *Submitted by: Sheila Joy Duckett, 144 Duckett Place, Albertville, AL 35951*

581. The Family of John Ellington Godard, M.D.

In July of 1976, Dr. John Ellington Godard moved his family to Carrollton, Georgia, and opened the Carrollton Eye Clinic, P.C., to begin his practice of ophthalmology.

Dr. Godard was born on November 23, 1942, in Moultrie, Georgia, the son of Joncie Bryan Godard of Goggins, Georgia, and Frances Dorothy Baker of Madison, Georgia. After graduating from Moultrie High School, he completed his undergraduate degree at Emory University and received his doctor of medicine degree from the Medical College of Georgia in Augusta in 1968. In 1973 he completed a tour of duty as a physician in the United States Air Force serving a year and a half at a small base in Hof, West Germany, and two years at Upper Heyford Air Force Base in England. He and his family then lived in North Augusta, South Carolina, while he completed a three-year residency in ophthalmology at the Medical College of Georgia.

Dr. and Mrs. Godard had been married on June 10, 1967, at the Trinity Baptist Church of Moultrie, Georgia. Mrs. Godard was the former Mildred Peniston Fokes ("Bunny") of Moultrie and a graduate of Hollins College in Roanoke, Virginia. Her parents were Dr. Robert Engram Fokes Jr. of Montezuma, Georgia, and Catherine Romanz Cook of Newnan, Georgia. Their sons were John Ellington Godard Jr., ("Ellis" - born February 20, 1971, in Nuremburg, West Germany) and Robert Fokes Godard ("Bob" - born May 18, 1974, in Augusta, Georgia). On October 15, 1978, the Godard family welcomed the arrival of a daughter, Mary Louise.

At that time they lived in Colonial Estates just off Tyus Road. In January of 1981 the family moved to 100 East Club Drive, the site of the new Georgian home they had copied from the George Wythe House in Williamsburg, Virginia, originally designed by one of Mrs. Godard's ancestors, architect Richard Taliaferro. The architect for their home was Alex Roush, and the builder was Carrollton native Thomas T. Richards. All of the brick work in and around the home was the craftsmanship of Robert Hampton ("Hamp") Sullivan of Carrollton.

The Godard family was very active in the life of Carrollton and the West Georgia community. They were members of St. Margaret's Episcopal Church and Sunset Hills Country Club. Both Dr. and Mrs. Godard were Rotarians - he in the Dawnbreakers Club and she in the Carrollton Noon Club. Dr. Godard was on the Board of the State University of West Georgia Foundation. For seven years, Bunny Godard was a co-owner of Red Carpet Travel. For several years she wrote articles for the local newspaper, *The Times-Georgian.* She was a member of the Carroll-Haralson Medical Alliance, the Board of the Carrroll County Cultural Arts Alliance, the Spade and Trowel Garden Club, the Carroll County Community Theatre, and Lit-Mu and was a co-founder of the Encore Theatre Company. In 1991 she served as chairperson for A Day For West Georgia. Between 1976 and 1996, the family participated in many of the activities of Oak Mountain Academy, which the children attended.

Ellis Godard received two bachelor's degrees, a master's degree, and a PhD. degree from the University of Virginia and married Kristen Ann Ciarrocchi of Springfield, Pennsylvania, on June 18, 1994. Bob Godard graduated from the School of Architecture at the Georgia Institute of Technology; married Robin Suzanne Teets of Riverdale, Georgia, on June 24, 1995; joined the commercial development profession in the Atlanta area; and, on November 26, 1999, became the father of Lauren Suzanne Godard. Mary Godard graduated from Agnes Scott College in 2000. *Submitted by: Bunny Godard, 100 East Club Drive, Carrollton, GA 30117*

582. Golden

Caleb Golden born 1780, died 1855, married Elizabeth Beasley. Elizabeth born 1785, died between 1860-70. She was not found in 1870 census. Both buried in Old Union Hill Cemetery.

Caleb and Elizabeth had eleven known children. The oldest one was William Timothy C. (T.C.) born 1808 in Georgia. His will was dated February 1879 in Haralson County. On 27 April 1832 in Carroll County he married Elizabeth Ann White. Seven children. In 1850 census, T.C. and children were farming. Elizabeth was missing in the census.

T.C. owned a lot of land and in his will gave Union Hill Cemetery two acres of land in Haralson County. Haralson was taken from Carroll and Paulding Counties and became a county in 1856. T.C. did not move from Carroll County to Haralson County. T.C. and Elizabeth are probably buried in Union Hill Cemetery in unmarked graves.

Sarah E. Gallimore, born 4 July 1865 at Draketown, Georgia

On 12 November 1855 in Carroll County, T.C. married Armanda Catherene Turner born September 1831 in Georgia. Seven known children.

Amanda Elizabeth Golden, the fifth child of T.C. and Elizabeth White Golden, born July 1844 Georgia, died 1902-04, probably in Etowah County, Alabama. On 31 March 1859 in Haralson County Georgia, married Peter Alford (P.A.) Gallimore born 13 April 1836 at Dallas, Paulding County, died 5 May 1909 in Blount County Alabama, buried Oak Grove Cemetery, Blount County, Alabama. HIs grave has a Civil War marker. He enlisted 11 February 1862 at Etna Georgia, 40th Georgia Regiment, Company G. He was shot in the arm and also wounded in the hip at Cumberland Gap, Tennessee. His arm was amputated between his wrist and elbow by M.J. Medows, surgeon. He was discharged on disability 15 October 1862 and began getting a pension April 1899. P.A. was the son of J. Asapth and Mary Hobbs Gallimore.

P.A. and Amanda moved to Etowah County Alabama about 1880. P.A. was a farmer, watchman, waiter, and laborer. In 1900 they had eight living children.

Sarah E. Gallimore, the second child, born 4 July 1865 at Draketown, Haralson County, died 7 October 1936 Blount County, Alabama, buried Oak Hill Cemetery, Blount County. In 1883 in Lawrence County, Alabama she married Joseph J. (J.J.) Hobbs born December 1835 in Georgia, died 15 February 1906 near Altoona, Alabama, buried Altoona-Walnut Grove Cemetery Etowah County, Alabama.

J.J. enlisted in the service 7 March 1862 at Ball Play, Etowah County, Alabama in Company E, 30 Alabama Regiment of Volunteers. He was wounded at Salisbury, North Carolina. I have placed a Civil War marker at his grave. He was a miner. Nine children.

Lillie Hobbs (my Mom), the second child, born 26 December 1889 in Blount County, Alabama, died 22 May 1959 Etowah County. On 23 August 1914 in Etowah County she married Worthy Monroe Littleton Bradley born 13 June 1881 in De Kalb County, Alabama, died 16 August 1966 in Etowah County. Both are buried at Macadonia No. 2 Cemetery, Crossville, De Kalb County, Alabama. Eight children. Three died as infants.

Sarah E. Bradley born 3 March 1928 in De Kalb County, Alabama, married Elbert H. Garner. *Submitted by: Sarah Garner, 29 Sommersworth Avenue, Gadsden, AL 35904*

583. Gordon

Beginning with Silas Gordon, born 1796 in North Carolina, and Sarah Cook, born June 1801, who were married in 1820, the daughters of Brice and Mary Nell James Scott have traced their heritage back further than needed for qualification for the Daughters of the Confederacy.

Silas and Sarah's second child, William Davis Gordon, and his wife Millie Priscilla Tomlin are buried in the Stripling Chapel Methodist Church Cemetery, Carroll County. According to Civil War records on file in the Atlanta Archives, William Davis Gordon was a private in Captain H. Carmical's Company A, 7th Regiment, Georgia Volunteers. His pay was $49.60 less $6.00 owed for Confederate clothing. He was discharged on May 31, 1861, but reenlisted in the Georgia Calvary in 1863. He was wounded near Marietta, Georgia. Some say that he never had the bullet removed and carried it to his grave.

Their eight child, Burr Gordon, born April 17, 1880, in Coweta County, married Susan Stitcher, born November 17, 1889 in Carroll County. Burr and Susan's daughter, Mary Burzell Gordon, born February 2, 1909, married Kie Levis James (born February 15, 1906) in December 1924. Mary and Kie's daughter, Mary Nell James (April 15, 1926-June 8, 1991) married Brice Virgil Scott on May 8, 1941 in Carroll County. Brice is the son of John Calvin Scott (March 29, 1889-December 6, 1965) and Nora Estella Morrow Scott (June 5, 1897-October 12, 1973). Brice was drafted in 1942 and served at Army bases all across the States teaching troops on tank destroyers.

Leroy Wiley Riley Scott, a man of mystery, always rode a horse and introduced himself as Leroy Wiley Riley "by God" Scott. He was born in Georgia in August 1833. He and his wife, Elizabeth (Lizzie) Harrison made sure their children learned to read and attended some schooling each year. John Scott, father of Brice Scott, was a son of Leroy Wiley Riley "by God" Scott. It is said that John could stand on his head on a brick. Another of Leroy's sons was a caretaker of Cave Springs.

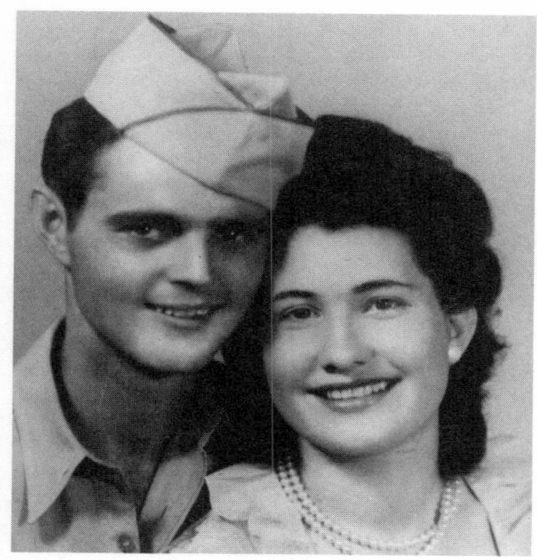

Brice and Mary Nell Scott

Brice Virgil and Mary Nell Scott had four daughters: (1) Sherry Marie, born November 29, 1942, married Jerry Austin Tuggle on March 3, 1961. He was born October 13, 1939, and died April 28, 1991. Their first child, Bradford Scott Tuggle, born January 26, 1962, married Karen Clancy on November 26, 1988. She was born February 14, 1966. Bradford and Karen's children are James Parker, born March 24, 1992, and Clancy Elizabeth, born August 2, 1993. Sherry and Jerry's second child, James Phillip Tuggle, born April 5, 1964, married Lori Johnson on June 12, 1993. She was born July 10, 1967. James and Lori's children are Jamie Ann, born May 1, 1996, and Samuel Johnson, born August 22, 1998. Sherry and Jerry's third child, Amanda Leigh, born April 30, 1973, married Mark Anderson on December 14, 1996. He was born on July 19, 1972. Amanda and Mark's children are Rachael Kylie, born February 14, 1999, and Ryan Austin, born August 3, 2000. (2) Gail Annette, born August 14, 1946, married Wyndel Richard Carnes on May 22, 1965. He was born July 2, 1942. Their children are (1) Mary Kathleen, born August 11, 1977, who married Chris Farmer, born March 9, 1971, on May 2, 1998 and (2) Holly Nicole, born December 16, 1980. (3) Vicki Ann, born November 13, 1954, married Richard (Bud) Scudder, born August 2, 1953, on March 22, 1982. Their children are James Camp, born October 27, 1985, and Haley Anna, born November 11, 1987. (4) Connie Michele, born October 29, 1956, married Johnnie Melvin Smith, born November 26, 1954, on March 25, 1974. Their daughter is Lyndi Michele, born July 26, 1974, married Mike Mashburn, born November 28, 1971, on September 28, 1996. *Submitted by: Gail Scott Carnes, P.O. Box 18, Whitesburg, GA 30185.*

Sources: *Gordon's Young and Old* compiled by Clarice S. Cox; Family history compiled by Michael Robinson on Jerusha Broom Family; and Nora Estella Scott's Family Bible.

584. The John Henry Gordon Family of Carroll County, Georgia

John Henry's family originally immigrated from the British Isles in the 1740s to Virginia and later about 1760 into Franklin County, North Carolina. Here the family split, some migrating to Spartanburg County, South Carolina in the 1810s, others migrated to Morgan County, Georgia, in the same time frame. One of these individuals was Silas Gordon, the great-grandfather of John Henry. Silas met and married Sarah Sally Cook, daughter of John Drury Cook and Mary Heard, and later moved with the Cook family to Coweta County, Georgia, where he served many years as Justice of the Peace. Here John Henry Gordon was born on May 24, 1870. He died March 22, 1936, in Temple, Carroll County, Georgia. He married Elizabeth Mae Gurley, the daughter of Joseph Gurley and Sally Garner. Elizabeth was born October 7, 1874, and died August 6, 1954, living all her life in Carroll County. They were married August 25, 1898, in Carrollton and both are buried, along with her parents, in the Abilene Baptist Church Cemetery, Carroll County, Georgia.

John Henry Gordon was the son of William Davis Gordon, who served during the Civil War in Company B, First Georgia Cavalry, and was wounded at the battle of New Hope, the bullet was never removed. His mother Millie Priscilla Tomlin, was the daughter of Jason Tomlin and Elizabeth Miriah Costley, both of Coweta County. John's parents migrated to Carroll County late 1880 from Coweta County. Both are buried in Stripling Chapel Methodist Church Cemetery in Carroll County. His grandfather, John Wesley Gordon served in the Civil War in Company B, First Regiment, Georgia Volunteer Cavalry. His grandmother was Mary Banks, daughter of William and Elizabeth Banks of Coweta County. They lived for many years in Haddock, near Milledgeville, Georgia.

The John Henry Gordon Family of 1913

John Henry Gordon since 1886 was an active member of Temple Masonic Lodge #322, a member of Mount Carmel Church where his children attended school, and in later years of his life a member of Draketown Baptist Church until his death. His land on Rainey Road (near Temple) was 100 acres, of which the family farmed 60, the rest was in hardwoods. He was known as a "little man with a big voice," who enjoyed playing the harmonica.

The couple had eleven children all born in Carroll County; Minnie Lorena, Bersie Mae, William Rayford, Joseph Carl, Ione, Elma Sally, Earl, Guy Walter, Addie Jane, Joe, and Willie Ruth. Of these only Addie Jane, Joe and Willie Ruth are living today. *Submitted by: Betty Jo Schultz, POB 165, Blairsville, GA 30514*

Sources: *Gordons, Young and Old;* Compiled by Clarice S. Cox, 1978 *Carroll County and Her People;* by Private Joe Cobb; U.S. Federal Census; Military records

585. Gray and Allied Families

Isaac Gray, born 1750 in South Carolina and died 1831 in Franklin County, Georgia, was a soldier in the Patriot Army throughout the Revolutionary War. He had eleven children. A son, Johnson Gray, born December 6, 1805, died in 1879, married Amelia Jenkins, born April 29, 1808. Johnson fathered seven children, Isaac J. born 1830, Jonathan born 1833, Elinder born 1835, Thomas born 1838, Rachel born 1839, Lydia, Sarah, and Sally. Johnson and his wife were buried at Hiram, Georgia.

Isaac J., born 1830, married Sara Elizabeth White on September 1, 1853, in Franklin County, Georgia. She was a daughter of Charles Carter White and Martha C. Speed Dortch. Isaac and Elizabeth's children were (1) William Johnson, born July 1860, married Nancy A. Nix; (2) Thomas Carter, born June 16, 1864, in Carrollton, Georgia, married Wilmer Drusilla Puckett, daughter of William Douglas and Sarah Francis Garner Puckett, (3) Liddy, (4) Margaret, (5) Louesa (Lou), and Martha.

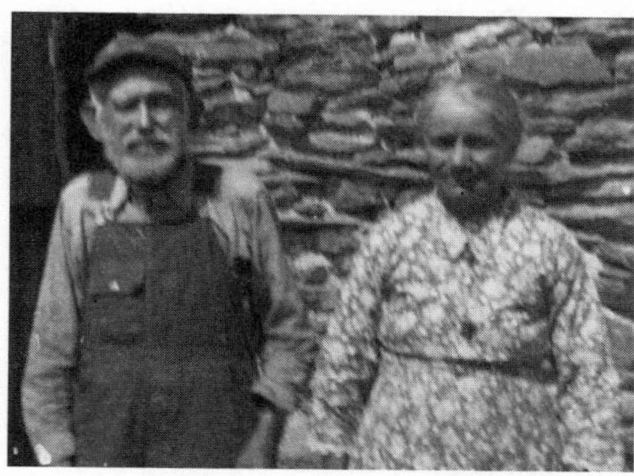

Thomas Carter and Drucilla Puckett Gray

Sara F. Garner Puckett was a daughter of William Garner and Sarah McGraw. They, along with Sarah McGraw's mother and family, were included in the Carroll County censuses of 1860 and 1870. William Garner was a son of Presley and Margaret Hinson Garner. Presley was born between 1766 and 1771 in Virginia. Presley's father was Charles Garner.

Carter White, father of Elizabeth White Gray, was a son of William White, born 1778, and Nancy Hooper. William was a son of William White Sr. and Mary Hooper. Mary was a daughter of Obediah Hooper, born about 1720 in Virginia, and Masilvia Brooks Hooper.

Thomas C. and Drusilla's children were (1) Thomas William Robert, born 1895 in Randolph County, Alabama; (2) George Washington, born April 14, 1896, married Odessa Morrison; (3) Minnie Lee, born July 19, 1900; (4) Martha Salona Ann, born October 18, 1901, married Rev. Minus A. Gann. She was his second wife; (5) John Carter, born January 5, 1903, married Bertie Lee Craft; (6) Charlie Lee (Jack), born December 25, 1904, married Minnie; (7) Virgle Savannah, born 1906 and died September 22, 1978, in Carroll County, married Lela Mulkey. He lived at Mt. Zion and owned and operated a barbershop; (8) James Parker, born July 30, 1909, married Ana Bea Pruett; (9) Lena, born December 22, 1910, married Lemuel Holloway; (10) Douglas, born February 7, 1913, married Vicie Holloway; (11) Isaac Jenkins, born May 3, 1916, (12) Odessia married Earl Bolt; and (13) Rachel married J.C. Cotton.

Martha Gray and Rev. Minus A. Gann had seven children who lived. They were (1) Rev. George H., born May 18, 1920, in Alabama, married Christine Daugherty; (2) Rev. Monroe A., born April 5, 1922, married first Ruby Lee Gore and second Ruth Pepper; (3) Rev. James Thomas (Jimmy), born July 28, 1924, married Mary Francis Daugherty, sister to Christine; (4) Nora Mae, born October 22, 1927, married John D. Harris on February 7, 1948. He was born in Bowdon, Carroll County; (5) David Elijah, born August 26, 1931, married first Joyce Ivey and second Persilla; (6) John Franklin, born June 18, 1934, married first Hattie Thomas, second Rose Mary Norton; and (7) Annie Lee, born May 23, 1939, married first H. Ivey, second Rev. Thomas Graham, and third George Nix.

Nora and Annie Lee and their families have lived in Carroll County for many years. Nora and John D. Harris had three children: Jimmy D., Michael J., and Rhonda M. Both Jimmy and Rhonda live in Carroll County now. Annie Lee had one daughter, Patricia, who, along with her children, Michael and Kelly and their families reside in Carroll County. *Submitted by: Nora Harris, 209 Rome Street, Bowdon, GA 30108*

586. DAVID AND REBECCA ROOKS GRAY

On December 31, 1837, in Carroll County, Georgia, David Gray was married to Rebecca Rooks, daughter of William and Sarah Rooks. David Gray was listed as a witness on Enoch Davis' deed dated 1843 in Carroll County, Georgia. David was born February 6, 1815, in North Carolina and died January 2, 1895, in Carroll County, Georgia. Rebecca was born June 29, 1820, in Georgia and died April 26, 1900, in Carroll County. They are buried in the Gray Family Cemetery, District 4, lot 23, in Carroll County.

They had ten known children: (1) Sarah E. Gray, born April 30, 1840, in Georgia, married John B. Bird on August 28, 1865, in Carroll County. He was born about 1831 in South Carolina. Sarah died July 30, 1898, and is buried in the Gray Cemetery. John was in the Civil War, Company H, 56th Georgia Infantry; (2) Samuel Gray was born about 1841; (3) Mary M. Gray, born June 30, 1845, in Georgia, married Nathaniel (Nathan) Jefferson Jones on December 16, 1865. He was born July 3, 1848, in Georgia. Mary died November 12, 1942, in Carroll County. Nathan died September 15, 1933, in Carroll County. They are buried in Whooping Creek Primitive Baptist Church Cemetery. They were members of the church; (4) Isabelle Gray was born about 1848 in Georgia; (5) Elizabeth Ann Gray, born October 9, 1850, in Georgia, married John B. Driver on December 12, 1868. He was a Civil War veteran, Company K, Georgia Reserves. She died March 15, 1922, in Carroll County. He was born May 24, 1853, and died January 20, 1918, in Carroll County. They are buried in Cross Plains Baptist Church Cemetery, Carroll County; (6) George W. Gray, born March 21, 1853, in Georgia and died April 24, 1911, in Carroll County. He was married to Susan Seagraves, born April 20, 1854, and died February 28, 1931, in Carroll County. They are buried in the Jordan Cemetery, Carroll County; (7) Susannah H. Gray was born about 1855 in Georgia; (8) William O. Gray, born about 1857 in Georgia, married Mattie H. Walker on November 28, 1878. She was the daughter of Captain William A. Walker and Mary A. Hanvey Walker; (9) Miriam R. Gray was born about 1859 in Georgia; (10) Lucinda J. Gray was born February 5, 1864, in Georgia and died February 5, 1938. She married Samuel Pate. She is buried in the Gray Family Cemetery.

David Gray served in the Creek Indian War of 1836. His name is on a list of the commissioned and non-commissioned officers and privates of a volunteer company raised by volunteer enlistment from the 74th Regiment of the Georgia Militia at Carrollton, Carroll County, Georgia, on May 21, 1836. His brother-in-law, James M. (Matt) Rooks, a pioneer of Carroll County, also served in this company during the Indian War. Matt Rooks is the brother of David's wife, Rebecca Rooks Gray.

They left Carrollton about sunset and camped the first night on a rocky outcropping on Blandenburg Road near the Clem community. Seventy years later, on the anniversary, a group of descendants of these men met at this site for a picnic. A block of marble was erected as a memorial, and the site was named Camp Odum in honor of Benton Odum, a member of the company. History does not record the deeds of the Carroll County Guards, but one of the speakers, Judge W.C. Hodnett, stated that they were "going on a perilous journey to fight a fearless and treacherous foe in his native wilderness." Another speaker, Leon P. Mandeville said the fact that they "all returned alive does not detract from their meed of glory." George Gilmer, former governor of Georgia, visited Carrollton when the uprising began. He found everyone ready and alert against an Indian attack. In the county, he had seen panicked people in flight and many cabins abandoned because of rumors that Indians in war paint had been encountered. James Bonner wrote, "Despite all this excitement, not a single cabin in the county was attacked in this uprising."

David Gray also served in the Civil War in Company H, 56th Georgia Infantry.

David's daughter, Mary M. Gray, married Nathaniel Jefferson Jones and had a daughter, Mattie Ophelia Jones. Mattie married Samuel Allen Davis. Their daughter Gladys Lovdell Davis married John Paul Duncan. Their son, Donald Davis Duncan married Judy Burns Duncan. They were my parents.

David Gray was my father's great-great-grandfather. Rebecca Rooks was my mother's great-great-aunt. James M. "Matt" Rooks was my mother's great-great-grandfather. *Submitted by: Michael (Scott) Duncan*

Sources: Researched by: Judy Duncan, 1177 Davis Road, Carrollton, GA 30116, and other family members.

587. DESCENDANTS OF ROBERT AND SARAH CAROLINE GRAY

Mattie Lou Pyles, born March 11, 1913, was the daughter of John William and Geneva Gray Pyles. Mattie married Thomas F. Cowart December 14, 1937, and lived in Carroll County. They have two daughters, Shirley and Rebecca.

Geneva Gray Pyles, was born September 10, 1902, the daughter of Robert D. "Bob" and Arranna Holloway Gray. She married John William Pyles on May 12, 1918, and they had two daughters, Mattie Lou and Bonnell. They lived in Carroll County. Geneva died November 13, 1996, and is buried beside J.W. in the Lowell Cemetery, Carroll County, Georgia.

Robert D. "Bob" Gray was born September 10, 1868, the son of Robert W. and Sarah Caroline Gray (maiden name unknown). Bob married Arranna Holloway on November 27, 1887, and they had the following children: Samuel, Emanuel, Melvin, Geneva, Dovie, and Mamie. They lived in Carroll County. Bob died on March 25, 1955, and is buried beside Arranna in the Whooping Creek Primitive Baptist Cemetery, Clem, Georgia.

Robert W. Gray, was born March 4, 1844, the son of Robert and Lucy Richardson Gray. He married Sarah Caroline (maiden name unknown) On December 22, 1865. They had children including Liza, Robert D., Lula, William, Lonzo, and Mollie. Robert is buried beside Sarah in the Whooping Creek Primitive Baptist Cemetery, Clem, Georgia. *Submitted by: Rebecca Cowart Chambers, 2820 Clem Lowell Road, Carrollton, GA 30116*

588. ZACHARY TAYLOR GRAY

Zachary Taylor Gray was born 1 January 1846 and died 10 October 1919. He was married to Mary Jane Williams who was born 15 November 1848 and died 1 February 1915. To them were born five children: William C. Gray 5 March 1877, Carrie E. Gray Williamson 26 June 1878, James H. Gray 20 April 1879, Mary J. Gray Threadgill 28 November 1882, Elizabeth Lois Gray Crawford 23 November 1884. All are now deceased.

Mr. Gray farmed and raised corn, cotton, and vegetables and had a great number of fruit trees on a forty acre farm south of Temple. His parents, Mr. and Mrs. Jesse Gray, had slaves who helped work the farm and during the Civil War they hid their horses and buried their food to prevent the confiscation by Sherman's troops. After the Civil War was over Mr. and Mrs. Gray continued to provide a place for all the slaves to live for their lifetime.

Zachary Taylor Gray

Mr. and Mrs. Gray are buried at Asbury Cemetery in Temple in a plot with their daughter, Elizabeth (Mrs. Hampton) Crawford. *Submitted by: Joan Crawford, 4009 Castle St., Douglasville, GA*

589. ROBERT A. GREEN

Robert Alberta Green was born 5 May 1826 in Buncombe County, North Carolina. Robert A., known as Bert, was one of twelve children born to William Mercer Green Jr. and Nancy Porter. Siblings were Ambrose C. (Frances H. Maria Russell); Rebecca (Jacob Cansler); Alexander Porter (Elizabeth Ann Chappell); Mary E. (Helburm Hulsey); Nancy (Joseph Wynn); Thomas Walter (Eleanor Caroline McClain); William Mercer (Sophronia Adeline Coltharp and Ella Ford); John Young (Margaret Janie Youngblood); unidentified sister; Martha Isabella (Wiley Gould Pope); and Martin Lafayette (Jiminey Elizabeth Wright). William Mercer and Nancy rest in the Old Bethel Cemetery located between Temple and Villa Rica. Bert married Elizabeth Adams on 23 January 1848 in Carroll County, Georgia, one of seven children born to Nathaniel and Mary Margaret Steele Adams. Her siblings were Peter; Sarah (Dr. Reuben Henry Holcombe); Mary (Isaac M. Abercrombie); Robert; Eliza (Harvey Gray); and Joseph. Nathaniel and Mary Margaret lost all three sons to the Civil War. Nathaniel died in 1847 in Carroll County and may be buried in the Old Bethel Cemetery. Mary Margaret moved with three of her daughters to Gothenburg, Nebraska, and is buried there. The Greens moved to Carroll County in 1832 and settled close to the Adams in the Villa Rica-Temple area. The Adams had moved to Carroll County before 1830 from Tennessee.

In 1862 Bert enlisted at Buchanan, Georgia, in Company G, 40th Georgia Infantry, and was captured and paroled at Vicksburg in July of 1863. From November 1863 to 1865, Bert was on extra duty as General Stovall's teamster, according to pension records. Bert was admitted to the Confederate Soldier's Home in Atlanta, Georgia, in 1903, and discharged 30 April 1904 by his request. Bert and Elizabeth were separated and living apart during the last years of their lives. This was indicated in Civil War pension records and the 1900 census. Bert, living in Draketown and Elizabeth near Bremen and next door to son William N., Elizabeth listed her occupation as Capitalist. Bert died 5 February 1905, and is buried in Pineywoods Cemetery. Elizabeth died 28 March 1915 and buried beside her husband. Robert A. and Elizabeth Adams Green were the parents of ten children: Sarah E. born 1848, married J.M. Ellis; William Nathaniel born 1850, married Elizabeth Catherine Kite and their children were Cathy, R.M. "Judge," Robert, Josephine Florence, Mahala Idella, Charlie, and Grady; Joseph T. born 1852; James J. born 1854, married Nancy Ann Brooks, daughter of Elijah Marion and Sarah

Atkins Brooks. Their children were Ida, Sarah Elizabeth, William Eligie, Norah, Cora Bell, Alex, Leila, Lula, George Lee, Lonnie and Richard. James married second Georgia Womack and their children were Margaret and Sarah; Robert Sim born 1857, married Irene Jane Baldwin; Mary E. born 1859; Nancy F. born 1861, married W.H. Sanford and their children were Reeney L., Alice D., James, and Annie. Nancy married second to George Wyley Davis and their children were Floyd, Lucinda, Frances, John W., George R., Lula, and Viola; John W. born 1862, married Mattie Peugh House and their children were J.E., Pearl, Joseph Simeon, James Moman, Vester, Lula, Oscar, and Jessie; Georgia Nora born 1866, married John Edward Baldwin and their children were Grover, Louella Elizabeth, Luther, Eva Judson, Versie, Beulah, Foster, William Thomas, Vera Estella, Robert Edward, and an infant; Rueben M. born 1868, married Mary Angeline Bishop and their children were Stella Mae, Lemma, Della Eugenia, Ida, Ester and Walter.

Many descendants of this family now reside in Haralson and Carroll Counties. *Submitted by: April Harris, 708 Twin Brook Court, Marietta, GA 30060. sloua@aol.com*

590. Widow Green's Place

Hiram Bray wrote this article for the *Carroll County Georgian* on June 8, 1978. Part of it (starting at the fourth paragraph) is a direct quote from an unknown source.

In 1864, Alexander Porter Green became ill while serving in the Confederate Army in Atlanta and was sent home to be with his wife and ten children. "Home" was near Villa Rica. He got as far as the Chattahoochee River and died.

His wife, the former Eliza Ann Chappell, was notified of his death. She and her oldest son, who was fourteen, drove to the Chattahoochee in a wagon and brought the body back to Pleasant Grove Cemetery for burial.

The Greens were grandparents of Frank Green, a prominent Villa Rica citizen. The story of his amazing grandmother and how she raised those ten children was told in a newspaper article in 1884. It was entitled, *"A Model Farm,"* and it gives me pleasure to share it with you. The author is unknown.

"In the 6th district, near Villa Rica, there is a cozy little home that deserves the title given this article. It is known throughout the county as the "Widow Green Place." About 20 years ago, Mrs. Green's husband died leaving her with a large family of little children too young to help her much.

Most women would have despaired and accepted the aid offered by kind neighbors but she did neither. She went to work, and made everybody around her work. She saved, pushed, managed, gave intelligent direction to all labor employed by her. She early adopted the rule of buying nothing, from a horse to an ax handle, that couldn't be raised or made at home and has adhered to that rule ever since. It was the writer's good fortune to spend a day on this farm last week and he wants the farmers of Carroll to know what a woman can do in 20 years on a Carroll farm.

Instead of the log cabin left her then, she lives in a handsome frame dwelling furnished with all the modern conveniences, and surrounded by a large yard that is itself as neat as a parlor.

Hundreds of chickens are scattered about the place; turkeys strut around, ready for the Christmas holidays; a large pen was filled with fat hogs averaging 200 pounds each; in a corner of the barnyard is a huge barn, its lower floor honeycombed with stalls and the upper one filled with feed and looking more like a livery stable than a country barn. Fine young colts were racing each other; sleek, well-fed cattle were quietly gathering as the evening shades came on, looking as though they would never need any of the corn stacked in an immense crib. Within a stone's throw is her gin house, thresh and evaporator; good houses wherein are sheltered the buggy, carriage and all farming tools.

Back of the dwelling stretches 300 acres of land, all the cleared portion in the highest state of cultivation. No complaint there of hard times. All years are good, all crops bountiful. Everywhere there is smiling peace, plenty and happiness. It looks like living when you go there and they do live like kings. The sons raise the food, the daughters cook it and it is needless to say that it is well done. They entertain a great deal of company and their fare blends the purity and sweetness of home victuals with the variety of a hotel. But this noble woman has done more than live well.

She does not owe a dollar, has money, at interest, has raised all those children, taught them how to work, given them a good education and sent them into the world honored, useful, prosperous men and women. One son is still at home and looks after the farm. The youngest daughter, just blushing into glorious womanhood, is also at home and graces alike the cook room and parlor, her rare beauty being equaled only by her varied accomplishments."

Submitted by: Evelyn Green, widow of Frank Green, Villa Rica, GA

591. William Green Jr.

William Green Jr. was born about 1786 in Burke County, North Carolina. He died 24 March 1847 in Carroll County, Georgia. He married Nancy Porter 29 October 1811. She was born about 1794 and died 06 March 1847. Their crypt-like tombstones in the Old Bethel Cemetery between Villa Rica and Temple were unmarked until two grandchildren, Bitt Parker and brother Frank Green, had granite slabs attached to them in the 1980s.

William Green Jr. was the son of William Green, born 06 February 1762 in Prince Edward County, Virginia and died 02 March 1837. His mother was Kizziah Stroud, born 1762 and died 01 August 1849. His father was a soldier in the Revolutionary War from North Carolina. William Green Jr. had eight brothers and sisters: (1) Thomas S. Green (born 24 October 1781) lived briefly in Carroll County; (2) John Green (born about 1784); (3) Sarah Green (born about 1790) married Matthew Hicks in North Carolina and moved to Carroll County; (4) Silas M. Green (born about 1796); (5) Martha Green (born about 1801); (6) Elizabeth (born about 1803); (7) Anderson Green (born about 1806) followed William Green Jr. and lived in Carroll County, Georgia, before moving on to Texas; (8) Tillman Green (born about 1810). The parents separated in the 1830s with the father remaining in Haywood County, North Carolina and the mother moving to Carroll County with son Anderson.

William Green Jr. moved to Carroll County in 1831 and bought land on the west side of the Little Tallapoosa River a few miles from Villa Rica. He built a log house on a high rise overlooking the river near the road from Villa Rica to Temple and called his home Sugar Hill. He prospered at farming to such an extent that he was able to make several additional land purchases, own a number of livestock and secure several slaves. At his death his estate was appraised at over ten thousand dollars which was a considerable amount for that day and time.

William Green Jr. and Nancy Porter Green were the parents of twelve children: (1) Ambrose C. Green, born about 1813 in Burke County, North Carolina, married Frances H. Maria Russell on 21 Dec 1837 in Carroll County. Family legend indicates that he left his wife and children and followed one of the Gold Rush Trails to California and was never heard from again. The Robinson family of Carrollton are among his descendants. (2) Rebecca Green, born about 1816 in Burke County, North Carolina, married Jacob Cansler on 05 June 1838 in Carroll County. The Jones and Keaton families of Villa Rica and Carrollton are some of her descendants. (3) Alexander Porter Green, born 19 May 1818 Haywood County, North Carolina, married Eliza Ann Chappell on 23 November 1843 in Carroll County. While serving in the 40th Georgia Infantry during the Civil War, he became ill during the fighting around Atlanta, was sent home but died at the Chattahoochee River. Eliza and her oldest son brought his body home to be buried in the Pleasant Grove Baptist Church Cemetery west of Villa Rica. Bitt Parker and Frank Green were two of his grandchildren. (4) Mary E. Green, born about 1820 in North Carolina, married Hilbern S. Hulsey on 15 February 1838 in Carroll County, but had moved to Alabama by 1860. (5) Nancy Green, born about 1822 in North Carolina, married Joseph Wynn on 05 February 1838 in Carroll County. A son, Charles, operated a country store near Draketown in Haralson County as late as 1900. Some descendants of daughter Martha, who married John W. Cash, live in Haralson County as well as descendants of daughter Frances, who married Harvey W. Green. (6) Robert A. Green, born 05 May 1825 Haywood County, North Carolina, married Elizabeth Adams on 23 January 1848 in Carroll County.

Graves of William and Nancy Green, Old Bethel Cemetery

He was living in that part of Carroll County that became Haralson County in 1856. He also was a Civil War veteran. Sandra Allen of Carrollton is a descendant. (7) Thomas Walter Green, born 16 January 1827 in Haywood County, North Carolina married Eleanor Caroline McCain on 21 September 1865 in Van Zandt County, Texas. He spent his youth in Carroll County but went to Texas in the early 1850s with brother William. He enlisted in the 12th Texas Cavalry (Parson's Brigade) at the beginning of the Civil War, was captured during the Battle of Mansfield, Louisiana, and released on 08 Jul 1864. The Maynard family are his descendants. (8) William Mercer Green, born 05 November 1929 Haywood County, North Carolina, married Sophronia Adeline Coltharp on 30 November 1853 in Van Zandt County, Texas. She had probably been his sweetheart in Carroll County and he simply went looking for her when her family moved to Texas. He was conscripted and served in a Cavalry unit in Arkansas where he was taken prisoner; serving time in Camp Douglas, Illinois and Camp Chase, Ohio before being exchanged during the Civil War. (9) John Young Green, born 16 Oct 1831 in Haywood County, North Carolina, married Margaret Janie Youngblood on 13 December 1866 in Van Zandt County, Texas. He enlisted in the Confederate Army at Atlanta in 1861 and served mainly in Virginia throughout the war. He was in the army that surrendered at Appomattox. He went to Texas shortly after the war and eventually became a successful businessman and farmer in the Concord Community near Chandler, Texas. (10) Martha Isabella Green, born 07 May 1835 in Carroll County, married Wiley Gould Pope on 08 October 1857 in Carroll County. He enlisted with friends in the 56th Georgia Infantry and was left sick in Lexington, Kentucky, where he died. He is buried in the Confederate National Cemetery there. Martha remained a widow. She was originally buried in the Old Bethel Cemetery, but a son later moved her body to the Pleasant Grove Baptist Church Cemetery. The White family of Villa Rica are among her descendants. (11) Unidentified Daughter Green, born about 1833, is probably buried in an unmarked grave in the Old Bethel Cemetery. (12) Martin Lafayette Green, born 31 August 1836 in Carroll County, married Jiminey Elizabeth Green on 22 Mar 1859 in Carroll County. He enlisted in the 56th Georgia Infantry in 1862 and was captured and paroled at Vicksburg Mississippi, in July 1863. He was living with sister, Martha Pope, in Carroll County in 1870, but had moved to farm just south of Dallas, Paulding County by 1880. One grandson said he dressed and acted like a "Southern Colonel," apparently leaving the farm work to be done by his large family of fourteen children: *Submitted by: Lawrence W. Maynard, 2821 West Boyce Avenue, Fort Worth, TX 76133-1503*

592. Griffin Family

J.W. Griffin was born near Carrollton in 1875, the son of J.K. Griffin and Molly Shackleford Griffin. He attended Carrollton schools and upon graduation taught school for several years. He joined with partners to establish the retail store later known as Griffin's Department Store. Mrs. J.W. Griffin was the former Virginia Hale of Griffin, Georgia. Their only son, J. Hubert Griffin, was born in 1907. He attended city schools and Emory University. He returned to Carrollton in 1928 to go in business with his father

J.W. Griffin

J. Hubert was a civic leader for many years. He served as mayor (1949-1951) and as city councilman (1944-1948). He was a past president of the Carrollton Lions Club, member of the Board of Stewards of the First Methodist Church, first president of the Highway 27 Association, chairman of the West Georgia Regional Library Association, and a director of the West Georgia National Bank.

J. Hubert was married to Elizabeth Stewart of Douglasville in 1933. They were parents of a son Charles Hubert and daughter Marion Elizabeth.

Hubert died in 1980 and his son passed away in 1998. Elizabeth lived with her daughter in Dalton, Georgia, until her death in 2000.

J. Hubert Griffin

After her mother's death, Marion and her husband Otis Mac McIntosh moved back to Carrollton, after an absence of thirty-seven years. They have two married children, John Hubert McIntosh and Christi McIntosh Crocker, and grandchildren Jake and Mallory McIntosh, and Ashley and Carley Crocker. *Submitted by: Marion Griffin McIntosh, 244 North Lakeshore Drive, Carrollton, GA 30117*

593. James Humphries Griffin Sr. James Humphries Griffin Jr.

James Humphries Griffin Sr. (1890-1956) moved his family from Cedartown, Georgia, to Carrollton in January 1937, when he was transferred as district manager of the Georgia Power Company. He served as district manager until 1955. He was born in Graniteville, South Carolina, son of Samuel C. Griffin (1832-1899), a Quaker born in Philadelphia, and Mattie Anderson (1852-1913), born in Milledgeville, Georgia.

Samuel C. Griffin was a Yankee soldier in the Civil War. Marching through Milledgeville, Georgia, he saw a beautiful, young girl swinging on her garden gate and announced that he was coming back after the war to marry her, which he did. His parents are buried in Cane Hill Cemetery, Louisville, Kentucky.

James H. Griffin Sr. was married to Lula May Turner (1897-1978) in Macon, Georgia, where they lived for seventeen years. Their three sons were born in Macon: James H. Jr. (1920-), Clarence Edwin (1925-), and Seaborn Sloan (1930-2001).

James H. Griffin Jr. received a B.S. degree, summa cum laude from Boston University. He became vice president of sales and later senior vice president of Southwire in Carrollton. He worked there for a total of thirty-three years. He served as chairman of the board of directors of Carrollton Federal Bank, now known as Community First Bank. He served as a captain during World War II with the 1881st Aviation Engineers in New Guinea and the Philippines. He was awarded the Silver and Bronze Stars and a Purple Heart. James H. Sr. and James H. Jr. became the first father-son presidents of the Rotary Club. James H. Jr. married Ruth Maret Meeks (1920-, A.B. degree in journalism from the University of Georgia) in Carrollton in 1941. This family raised Catherine (Kitty) Ruth Griffin Barr (1943-, Mary Baldwin College), and Allen James Griffin (1951-, Presbyterian College). Catherine's children were Maret Catherine Barr (1972-) and Lane Camille Barr (1977- University of Georgia). Their father was Alfred Kyle Barr, who was born in Virginia in 1942. Allen's children were Mason Allen Griffin (1978-) and Blakeley Ann Griffin (1982-). Their mother was Lisa Ann Messersmith Griffin (1951-) of Miami, Florida. Later, Allen married Ann Mechile Collins (1968-) of St Louis Park, Minnesota.

Clarence served in the Navy in World War II. He married Lillian Marie Davis in Macon, Georgia. Their son, James Bryan Griffin (1962-), married Colleen Bruner (1962-) in Atlanta. Their daughter is Alexis Lillian (1999-).

Seaborn graduated from the University of Georgia. He married Carolyn Blake (1930-). Their sons were Eric (1966-). and Mark (1969-). Mark married Laura Spuroock (1970-). Their children are Josh (1986-), Sierra (1989-), and Jake (1994-). They live in Ft. Myers, Florida. *Submitted by: Ruth M. Griffin*

594. Grizzard History

My great-grandfather's name was Jack Grizzard and his wife's name was Polly.

He was in the Civil War, but not because he wanted to be. He had to leave his wife and children, one of whom was my Grandpa Rufe. Rufe was captured by the Yankees when he was fourteen years old. The Yankees thought he was a spy. He weighed 210 pounds and was 6 feet tall. They took him to Nashville, Tennessee, and were going to execute him. Six hours before he was to be shot, orders came through that he was not a spy. He said he was so afraid, he could not speak when they told him he would not be killed.

The Grizzard Brothers in Carrollton, 1909.

Rufe was nineteen years old when he married seventeen year old Mary Jane Nolen. They had a daughter Della and then eight sons, Edd, Will, Claude, John, Jess, Horace, Earnest, Cliff, and then two more daughters, Lillie and Fanny.

The eight brothers shown in this picture met in Carrollton in the spring of 1909 and decided to have their picture made. Will had a patch on one knee of his pants but he said he would just cross the other leg. He forgot and crossed the wrong one. On the front row from left to right are Edd, John, Claude and Will. On the back row are Earnest, Cliff, Jess and Horace.

The Jess Grizzard Family in 1924, Minnie, Jess, Luther, Arnold, Mamie, Beatrice

All of their eleven children were good men and women and all lived to marry and have a family. God was good to them but Papa Jess was the very best because God picked him out to be my earthly father.

Jesse A. Grizzard, born October 2, 1881, married Ella Beatrice Powell, born January 2, 1888, on October 26, 1902. They had two daughters and three sons. Thomas Henry only lived two months. Their other children were Mamie Grizzard Creel Ashmore, Minne Grizzard Reeves, Luther C. Grizzard, and Arnold P. Grizzard all lived to have families of their own. *Submitted by Mamie Grizzard Ashmore, 305 South Boulevard, Carrollton, GA 30117*

595. Earl Thomas Grizzard

Earl Thomas Grizzard, who was usually called Tom Earl, was born on June 30, 1897, and died on May 27, 1975. He married Jessie Bell Geneva Holcombe on April 5, 1919, in Haralson County, Georgia. Jessie was born on July 12, 1901, and died on February 11, 1986.

Jessie's parents were Thomas Nicholas Holcombe and Margaret "Maggie" Elizabeth Mayfield who owned and ran a store in the Hightower, Alabama, area. They are buried at Union Hill Baptist Church in Hightower. Jessie's paternal great-grandmother was an American Indian, and because of her father's Native American heritage, he was offered an opportunity to reside on the Indian reservation. Jessie's siblings were Charlie, Alvin, John, and Emmie.

Tom Earl's parents were Emmitt Eugene Grizzard and Sabra Gentry who lived at times in Waco, Georgia, and in Muscadine, Alabama. They are buried at Concord Baptist Church in Muscadine. Tom Earl's father farmed and ran a store in Waco. Siblings of Tom Earl were Karl, Estelle, Sylvesta, Vera, Alton, Buren, Florence, Madelene, Era, Addie Lou, Euel, Neal, and Webster, who died as a child. Tom Earl and Jessie lived in Oxford, Alabama, where he ran a cotton gin, a sawmill, a grist mill, and a blacksmith shop. During World War II, he took a job at Anniston Ordinance Depot as a driver for U.S. Army officers. They had seven children: Marie Ada (born January 15, 1920; married James Cliffie Anderson), Jewell Sabra (born December 30, 1922; married Robert Entrekin), Louise Magdelene (born June 9, 1925; married Barney Lee), Myrlene Kathryn (born March 16, 1929; married Otis Brooks), William Thomas (born May 19, 1931; married Mildred Lindsey), Benjamin Eugene (born July 22, 1932; married Martha Warren), and Mary Frances Elizabeth (born May 26, 1935; married Glenn Pruitt). After living much of their lives in Alabama, Tom Earl and Jessie moved to Carroll County to be closer to their daughters and their families who live in the county.

Tom Earl and Jessie are buried at Concord Baptist Church in Muscadine, Alabama. *Submitted by: Gail Anderson, 65 Beauchamp Road, Carrollton, GA 30117*
Sources: Family members; a family Bible

596. Walter Neal Groover Family

Walter N. Groover and his wife, Sarah (Sallie) Catherine Slaughter, came to Carroll County in 1910. He was born in Cleburne County, Alabama, in 1891 to Lee Grant and Lula Belle Harris Groover and died in 1975. Sallie was the daughter of William E. Slaughter, a dentist, and Elizabeth Walton Slaughter. She was born in Haralson County in 1893 and died in 1986. Walter and Sallie were married in Haralson County. They are both buried in the Carrollton City Cemetery.

Sallie S. Groover and Walter N. Groover

Lee Groover was born in Abernathy, Alabama, in 1871 and moved to Tallapoosa around 1905. He lived in Bowdon and then settled in Tallapoosa where he served as city clerk, member of the city council, and mayor. At one time he lived with Walter in Carrollton. He died in 1965 and is buried in Tallapoosa.

Walter was one of five children. He has a sister, Jewell Groover Plunket born 1906, who lives in a nursing home in Carroll County. Jewell never had children.

The W.N. Groovers had two daughters, Madeleine and Haysel. Madeleine was born in 1913 and died in 1993. She married J.R. Newell, son of Camilla Mandeville Newell and John Oliver Newell. They had two sons, Richard Newell and Bob Newell. Richard and his wife, Lee, currently reside in Carrollton as do Richard's two sons, Glen and Scott Newell, and their families. Bob and his wife live in South Carolina and they have no children.

Haysel was born in 1918 and died in 1994. She married Ed M. Smith from Coweta County. He is the son of C.M. Smith and Mae Bynum Smith of Newnan. They have two daughters and a son, Sally Smith Miles, Laddie Smith Carter and W. Ed Smith.

Sally is married to Rodger A. Miles, son of R.N. and Nellie Robinson Miles. They, along with their children and their families — Cathy Miles Stewart married to James P. Stewart of the Horace Stewart family, and Rodger A. Miles Jr. married to Connie North from Carroll County — reside in Carrollton. Cathy has a son, Shane Jones, and a daughter, Andrea Stewart. Rodger Jr. has a son Coby, and a daughter, Jenna.

Laddie Smith Carter is married to Bill Cole Carter, son of the late Votice and Frances Cole Carter also of Carrollton. They have two sons, L. Brett Carter married to Marianna Michael, and Matthew Groover Carter. Brett and Marianna and their daughter Katherine Elizabeth reside in Carrollton. Matthew currently lives in Tampa, Florida.

W. Ed Smith resides in Chattanooga, Tennessee. He had three sons, Wes, Colin, and Evan Smith.

After coming to Carrollton, Walter Groover worked at several jobs, one being with Kytle and Aycock. At one time he was driving an ambulance, but gave that up after going to a train accident and having to retrieve a child's body. In 1932 he and Mr. Mather opened Mather-Groover furniture. He later bought him out, establishing Groover-Smith Furniture Company.

W.N. and Sallie were members of the First United Methodist Church where they were active for many years. Mr. Groover was a sound businessman and bought and sold real estate.

He built the brick house on the corner of Cedar and College Street known as the Lovvorn home, and several of the houses on Groover Circle just off College Street. He later bought the English Tudor house now owned by Tanner Medical Center from John Stewart adding considerably to its original size and building several additional houses on the property now known as Groover Drive.

When he purchased the house and property, it was considered as being out of town. They had a barn, a chicken house, and a smoke house. They also had a clay tennis court and a house in the woods known as the "Juke" where they entertained. It was later used for Boy Scout meetings. This is now part of the Tanner Walking Trail.

Mr. Smith, the Miles, and the Stewarts still reside on Groover Drive. Laddie and Bill live in the county and own and operate Groover-Smith Furniture Company and Antique Mall. (See Business Histories). *Submitted by: Laddie Smith Carter, 100 Green Acres Drive, Carrollton, GA 30117*

597. Ezra Thomas Guthrie Family

In 1800 Matthew and Nancy Dewberry Guthrie married. They had eight children — Frederick, Mary, Nancy, Julia, Susan, Samuel, Sarah, and Edward.

Frederick was born March 30, 1836, and died April 4, 1908. He married Ophelia, who was born May 16, 1853, died June 9, 1934. Their children were John Edward and Morinda Ora.

John Edward (J.E.) married Effie Moran on October 4, 1903. They had one child, Ezra Thomas born June 27, 1907. Ezra married Bessie Mae Pate on August 22, 1926. They had four children, Imogene, Lois, Blanche, and J.R. Imogene and J.R. died in infancy.

Lois married Byron Bradley and their children were Arlin, Brenda, Gerald, Michael, and Christie. Arlin died in infancy, Bryon died in 1986, Lois married Aubrey D. Pruitt who died in 1994.

Appreciation Plaque for J.E. Guthrie

Blanche married Charlie Neese and their children were Vivian, Barbara, Nancy, Debra and Charles. Nancy died in infancy. Charlie died in 1999.

In 1928, John and Effie Guthrie owned and operated Guthrie's Store for several years; then they sold tickets for the Greyhound Bus Line and changed the store name to Little New York. The location of the store was on the Old Newnan Highway, but because of the name change of the store the road name was changed to The Little New York and still goes by that name. They sold Gulf Oil products, groceries, and kerosene, and ran the store full time. After his death, his wife continued to keep the store until the early 1960s.

Their only son, Ezra Thomas Guthrie, was a member of the Sylvan Lodge No. 429 F. & A. M., Sargent, Georgia. After his death on May 24, 1975, this memorial was presented to his wife.

> This memorial is dedicated to honor the memory of Brother Ezra T. Guthrie whom death hath taken from us on May 15, 1975. There is calm sorrow for the absence of our brethren who has gone before us; earnest solicitude for our own eternal welfare; and a firm faith and reliance upon the wisdom and goodness of God.

Brother Guthrie was recommended for Masonry by Brother A.E. Holloway

John Guthrie, Ophelia Guthrie, Frederick Guthrie, and Ora Guthrie

(deceased) and Brother J.T. Millians on August 27, 1938. Passed to the Fellowcraft degree on November 12, 1938, and raised to the Sublime degree of a Master Mason on January 14, 1939. He served as our Senior Stewart in 1940, and as the Junior Deacon in 1941 and 1942.

A 25-year pin was presented to Brother Guthrie on October 10, 1964. On May 18, 1975, the brethren of Sylvan Lodge consigned Brother Guthrie's body to the grave after his many fruitful years which began June 27, 1907, in Carroll County, Georgia. His memory which will forever survive the grave should keep us reminded that our bodies shall someday be clothed in death and deposited in the silent tomb. Lovingly submitted: Lamar B. Meadows, Secretary; J.E. Brown, Senior Warden; P.L. Henson, Senior Stewart.

Submitted by: Lois Guthrie Bradley Pruitt, 2071 Mt. Zion Road, Carrollton, GA 30117

598. Kirby Dow Hamil

Kirby Hamil was born in 1937 to L.D. and Berma Hamil. He graduated from Roopville High School where he played on the basketball and baseball teams. He attended North Georgia College in Dahlonega, Georgia, for two years where he played on the varsity basketball and baseball teams. He transferred to Georgia Institute of Technology and received a degree in civil engineering in 1960. He received his master's degree in civil engineering in 1974.

Kirby Dow Hamil

He worked for thirty-two years for Georgia Department of Transportation in Atlanta. For sixteen years he was Assistant Urban Design Engineer in charge of the design of the rebuilding of the freeway system. This included the major interchanges of I-75 and I-285, I-85 and I-285 North and South, I-20 and I-75, and I-75 through downtown Atlanta, I-85 from downtown Atlanta to I-285 North, and Georgia 400.

The last two years of his career he was State Highway Transportation Planning Engineer, where he was in charge of gathering data and developing transportation plans for future projects all over Georgia. Mr. Hamil is a licensed professional engineer and is currently serving on the Carroll County Water Authority Board. He lives in the northern suburbs of Roopville.

Submitted by: Aubrey Kaylor, Carrollton, GA

599. L.D. and Berma Hamil

Lorenzo Dow Hamil (1907-1991) was born in the Mount Zion community to John W. and Tennie Earnest Hamil. The family moved to Bowdon when John Hamil received a rural mail carriers job, and from 1913 until his retirement he carried the mail for the rural area around Bowdon.

L.D. Hamil

L.D. attended school in Bowdon, except for one year when he attended Berry High School in Rome, Georgia. He attended Old Bowdon College where he was a star pitcher for their baseball team. L.D. is remembered for pitching a double header and winning the game after another pitcher was unable to pitch. He pitched against Johnny Mize when Mize played for Piedmont College in Demorest, Georgia. In 1934, L.D. entered the University of Georgia and in 1937 he received a degree in vocational agriculture. He taught agriculture at Roopville School from 1951 to 1959. In the 1950s he entered Auburn University where he received his master's degree.

Berma E. Kirby (1908-) is the daughter of Dr. Ellis G. and Lena Pearl Tomlison Kirby. Dr. Kirby practiced medicine in Carroll County from 1914 until his death in 1941. Berma attended Old Bowdon College. In the 1950s she attended the University of Georgia in the summers and received her degree in education in 1956.

In 1933 L.D. and Berma were married in Chattanooga, Tennessee, by L.D.'s uncle and namesake, Lorenzo Dow Hamil. He was a Methodist preacher in the Holston Conference at the time.

Most of L.D. and Berma's teaching careers were spent in Carroll County. L.D. taught in the following schools in Carroll County: Oak Ridge, Indian Creek, Elizabeth Harris, Roopville and Central. When he retired he had taught forty years. Berma taught in the following Carroll County Schools: Indian Creek, Temple, Elizabeth Harris, Villa Rica, Mount Zion, Rockridge, Clem and Roopville. Berma retired with thirty-two years of teaching.

Berma Hamil

L.D. and Berma have two children, Kirby Dow, who lives in Roopville and Mary Ann Barnes, who lives with her husband Mack, in Orlando, Florida. They have two granddaughters, Elizabeth Ann Barnes Quigley and Leah Emily Barnes. *Submitted by: Berma Hamil, Roopville, GA*

600. Green Berry Hammock

Green Berry Hammock married Nancy Burrow, daughter of Phillip Burrow Sr., who died in Carroll County in 1853. Records show that Green Berry Hammock purchased some of the items from the estate of Phillip Burrow which among other things included a shot gun valued at $7.35, a bay mare valued at $76.50 and 933 pounds of cotton valued at $9.79. Phillip Burrow had previously purchased Lot 175 in the 10th District of Carroll County. In 1847 Green Berry Hammock purchased Lot 178 in the 10th District of Carroll County for $53.37 and in 1856 purchased Lot 175 in the 10th District. This area is between Mt. Zion and Burwell along Davenport Mill Road. One of Green Berry and Nancy's children, Rachel, married James Davenport, who purchased adjacent land. Another of their children was Green Berry Hammock Jr. Green Berry Sr. was said to be eccentric and his son Green Berry Jr. was said to be even more eccentric even to the point of being a recluse. Articles were written in the *Carroll County Times* newspaper in the 1920s about the strange behavior of both.

Green Berry Hammock Jr. married Susan Ann Parker in Pike County in 1834. In 1838 he purchased land in Pike County from Phillip Burrow for $400 indicating that the Burrow family, Nancy's parents, were neighbors of the Hammock family in Pike County. Mary (Polly) Hammock, daughter of Green Berry Sr. and Nancy Hammock, married James Parker in 1834 in Pike County and moved to Carroll County with the rest of the Hammocks, Burrows and Parkers. Their daughter, Mary (Polly) Parker, married James C. Austin and one of their sons was

Green Berry Hammock

William Green Austin. William and Mary's daughter Dora Austin married Marshall Putnam who with his father James D. Putnam ran the Entrekin Mill at Mt. Zion (located at the falls where Lanett Austin Horton's parents lived). After the first World War, a returning veteran worked for the Putnams and against the advise of the Putnams tried to clean vines and leaves out of the mill's water mill while it was turning and was caught and killed. Dora and Marshall Putnam are the grandparents of Tracy Stallings and Charlcie Stallings Lambert.

Tracy Stallings has a letter written to Nancy Burrow Hammock by her son James from Newnan, Georgia, in 1855. He describes a trip he had just made to visit a sister, Matilda, and her husband James Thompson in West Point, Georgia. He discusses a nephew who worked for the Atlanta and West Point Railroad as a mail guard and made $25 a month, and also that the whole family had just recovered from the fever.

Nancy Burrow Hammock

Tracy has another letter written by Mary Parker in 1885 to some of her children in which she is concerned about where she will be living. She says that Bill McKissicks (her spelling) will let her stay in the house in which she is living as long as she wants to but asks her children to come visit her. This is in sharp contrast to Susan Hammock, Green Berry Hammock Jr.'s wife/widow who was buying land all over the place in Carroll County and Carrollton just a few years earlier and was referred to as that "rich Hammock woman." *Submitted by: Pam Stallings Almon*
Source: Wallace T. Lambert

601. Nancy Ann Burrow Hammock

Nancy Ann Burrow was born in 1794 (age 66 on 1860 Census) in Guilford County, North Carolina, to Phillip and Leah Burrow. She was one of eleven children — 8 girls and 3 boys. By 1805 the family was living in Wilkes County, Georgia and soon moved to Jones County, Georgia. It was very possible Nancy was married in that county about 1812. Her husband was (?Green) Berry Hammock, about whom little is positively known. They had a large family, many of whom are "circumstantially" linked to them, for documented proof has been hard to find. A list of the children known or believed to be theirs includes: (1.) James (born ca 1814 married Vianna Simms), (2.) Green Berry (born ca. 1815; married Susannah Parker), (3.) Matilda/Matildas (born ca. 1816; married James Thompson), (4.) Mary (Polly) (born ca. 1817; married James Parker), (5.) Rachel Cicely (born September 23, 1818; married James Gillam Davenport), (6.) Martha Ann (born December 5, 1819; married George Pendleton and Abner A. Hasty), (7.) Joseph T. (born May 1, 1821; married Mary Jane Land), (8.) Alethia Ann Eunice (born 1824; married Joseph Dolittle Land).

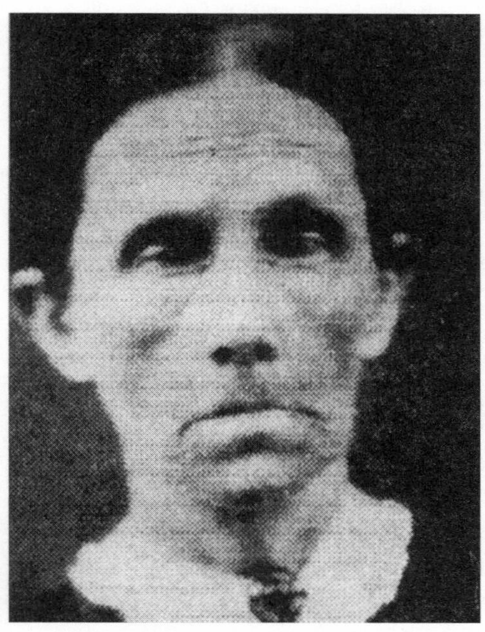

Nancy Ann Burrow Hammock 1794-1861

Not much is known of Nancy until 1848, when on February 28, her father Phillip Burrow Sr. made out a deed to "my beloved daughter Nancy Hammock and her son in law James Davenport". The deed was for LL# 206 "in the Tenth originally Ninth District" of Carroll County, Georgia, consisting of 202 ½ acres, with James as trustee for this land "for the said Nancy Hammock during her natural life and for use and benefit during that time, and at her death" the land would become James Davenport's for his own use. Nancy was listed on the County tax lists in the 1850s until 1857, when the lists record "J.G. Davenport agent for Nancy Hammock." In her father's estate papers in 1854, Nancy was given the slave named Prince, valued at $1,100. Nancy Hammock was living in James Davenport's home in 1860, even though her daughter Rachel had died in 1853. By 1861, Nancy's land was listed as James' property, indicating she had died. It is believed by some that Nancy Ann Burrow Hammock is buried in the Holmes Cemetery, on land her father gave to the New Salem Methodist Church in 1847. *Submitted by: Jennis McConkie Betts, R.R. Box 3326, Myton, UT 84052-9605 and Written by: Pauline McConkie Derhak.*

602. Thomas McCoy Hammond

Thomas was born to Elijah and Ester Green Hammond in 1828. Children of Thomas and unknown first wife were James Marion born 1851; Rhody Ellen born 1853; and William born 1855. When she died, Thomas married Mary Jane Davidson in 1858. In 1862 Thomas enlisted in Company C, 1st Regiment, Confederate Army. Wounded 22 July 1864 in Atlanta, he served as assistant enrolling officer for the rest of the war. Thomas died in 1891, buried in Oak Grove Baptist Church Cemetery in Carrollton. Mary received a Confederate widow's pension 1901 to 1911 in Carroll County. Her burial location is believed to be in Providence Baptist Church Cemetery, Tallapoosa.

James Marion, Malinda Ballard Hammond, Francis and Myrtie Hammond

James Marion Hammond, son of Thomas and first wife, married Melinda Ballard, (see John Thomas Johnston story) daughter of Abraham and Delana Jane Maderis Ballard and had Minnie, Levi Ballard, Frances Elizabeth, Lela Louvenia and Myrtie Hammond. James and Melinda Hammond are buried in Providence Baptist Church Cemetery in Rico, Fulton County, Georgia; William A. Hammond, married Ella Jones.

Thomas McCoy Hammond and Mary Jane farmed and raised ten children: Elijah Washington born 1859, died 1939 in DeKalb County, Alabama, married Georgia Hale, had Bell, Addie, William Ervin, Milton, Brillie, Robert L., Lue and Homer Hammond; John Thomas born 1860 was a merchant, married Texas Elizabeth Marlow, daughter of J.R. and Mary Carter Marlow, had son Otis. John died in 1935 and Texas died in 1938, buried in Carrollton City Cemetery; Nancy born 1863 married Columbus Garner, had Leila, Alice, Thomas, Oscar, Albert, Alvin, Harry, Cora, Olla, Jesse and Erma Garner; Noah Irvin born 1866 married Mary Elizabeth Davison, had Viola, Ida, David Lea and Luther Hammond. Noah and Mary died in Haralson County and are buried in Providence Baptist Church Cemetery; Julia born 1867 married John Hendrix, had John, Minnie Lee, William H. and Pearl F. Hendrix; Robert Wesley born 1869 married Mattie Louella Warren, had Gladys, Josie, Ella, Alma, Myrtle, May, John Marvin, William Roy, Dewey W. and Hubert Hammond. The second wife of Robert Wesley was James Anna B. Daniel. Robert died in 1960, is buried in Oak Grove Baptist Church Cemetery in Carrollton; Tazwell Milton born 1870 was a school teacher, married Cora Lee Hardegree in Heard County, had Edgar L., Mercer Milton, Elgin, Vester Rodgers, Mary, Sarah, and Louise Hammond. Tazwell and Cora Lee are buried in Oak Hill Cemetery in Newnan, Georgia; Joseph David born ca. 1874 married Ada Kalley Bradley, had Bennie Lee, Carl B., Grace, Joseph Oren, Warner Griffis Glen, and Florence Hammond; Mary Annie born ca 1874 married Charley R. Hendrix, had Maggie F., Mary Maude, Myrtle F., Mamie and Wilbur Hendrix. Mary Annie died in 1936, buried at Stripling's Chapel; Susan Drucilla born 1877 married John P. Warren. Susan and John have four infant sons buried in Oak Grove Baptist Church Cemetery in Carrollton. *Submitted by: Patricia Johnston Yates, 105 West Knight Rd., McDonough, GA 30252*
Sources: Personal research of Carroll, Campbell, Coweta and Fulton county records and cemeteries; federal census records; Confederate records at Georgia Archives; descendant Dennis Whitcomb.

603. George W. Hamrick Family

George Washington Hamrick was born 5 August 1841 in Carroll Co., GA. He was the son of Rebecca (Keith) and Harrison Hamrick. Harrison was a preacher and a farmer with large land holdings. Harrison was born 7 May 1803 in Jasper Co. GA to Margaret (Signor) and James Hamrick. Rebecca (Keith) Hamrick was the daughter of David Keith and Rebecca Whitton. She was born 8 December 1805. Rebecca and Harrison are both buried in the Stripling Chapel Cemetery, Carrollton, GA. George Washington Hamrick married Texas Annabel Rebecca Jones, daughter of Nancy (Calloway) and Orren Jones. Texas was born 4 September 1850 in Carroll Co. Orren Jones and his family were members of Stripling Chapel Church in March of 1857, according to *The Carroll County Story as Told by The People,* The Sesquicentennial-Bicentennial Edition.

George and Texas Hamrick's daughter, Martha Louisa, married Henry Louis Williams on 17 December 1905 in Winston Co. AL. Henry and Martha were both born in Carroll Co. Henry 23 May 1883, and Martha 15 of April 1877. They later moved on to Mississippi. Henry Louis Williams was the son of, Luradene "Lou" (Swords) born 27 August 1858 Carroll Co., and Joel Hood Williams born 9 June 1857 Carroll Co. Luradene's parents were Priscilla (Smith) and Henry H. Swords. Henry and Priscilla were married in Carroll Co. on 12 November 1857. Henry was killed in one of the closing battles of the Civil War near Marietta, GA. Joel Hood Williams was the youngest of five boys born to Henry Roland Williams and Elizabeth "Betsy" (Osborn). Joel Hood's four brothers were John T. Williams born 1849, died 1865; Charles Benjamin Williams born 1851, died 1909, married Susan Ella Haynes; George L. Williams born 1853, died 1875, married Amanda Boatwright; and Henry W. Williams born 1854, died 1855. These boys were born in Carroll Co. and all but Joel Hood are buried in Carroll Co. Joel Hood Williams is buried in Winston Co. AL. Henry Roland and Betsy were both born in Lauren Co. SC and died in Carroll Co. GA. They are buried in the Jordan Cemetery. Thomas Barnes Williams (born about 1795 in SC) was Henry's father. His mother Hannah (Pinson), born about 1795 in SC, was the daughter of Isaac Pinson. Hannah and Thomas Barnes Williams are buried in the Williams Family Cemetery, Carrollton.

Thomas Barnes and Hannah (Pinson) Williams raised a large family: daughter Hannah Williams married a Hendrix; James H. Williams married Sarah Davidson; Joel Casper married Mary Barbara Kiser; Henry Roland (mentioned above); Nancy Catherine married John Jefferson Hinesly; Elihu married Mary Hineslee; Mary A. married Duke Nail; Lucinda Williams; Martha Jane married a Cook: and Moses Williams married Mary Adams. With this article is a picture of the Williams family reunion taken in Carroll Co. around 1870. The third couple from the left is Henry Roland and Betsy Williams. The first young man on a horse (from the left) is Joel Hood Williams. If you can recognize any of your ancestors, please let me know. **See photo at upper right.** *Submitted by: Sharelle K. Williams, 920 Lake Circle, Magee, MS 39111. skw@c-gate.net*

Williams Family reunion, Carroll County, GA ca. 1870

604. William Grady Hamrick Sr.

William Grady Hamrick Sr., his brothers James Vester and Andrew Harrison, and his sisters Lillie Mae (Mrs. Walter Otwell), Ellie (Mrs. W.O. Wester) and Ruth (Mrs. J.W. Witcher), were the children of David Harrison Hamrick, (born in Carroll County in 1870) and Martha Baxter Hamrick. Grady's grandfather, James David Hamrick Sr. served in Company F, 19th Georgia Regiment, during the Civil War. His great-grandfather was Harrison Hamrick.

Grady, born in 1899 near Center Point, operated a Standard Oil service station at the corner of Newnan and College Streets in Carrollton, and in 1924 became the wholesale distributor for Standard Oil (later Chevron) products for the Carrollton area. After his death in 1966, his son William G. Jr. operated the business. In 1981, they sold the business and William practiced law in Carrollton, later served as district attorney of the Coweta Judicial Circuit, and later as deputy director of the Prosecuting Attorney's Council of Georgia until his retirement in 2001.

Grady was married to Clara E. Williams in 1926. Clara, also of Carroll County, was the daughter of Samuel William Williams and Willie P. Eady. Clara was the granddaughter of Charles Benjamin Williams and Susan Ella Haynes, and the great-granddaughter of Henry Roland Williams and Elizabeth Osborne. Grady and Clara were the parents of two sons, William and James Robert (Robbie). Robbie, who served as director of the Georgia Bureau of Investigation, and his wife, Linda Poole Hamrick, live in Forsyth County, Georgia. Their son, Brent, his wife Donna, and their three children live in Atlanta.

In 1961, William married Dottie Francis Sullivan, now a retired City of Carrollton school teacher. She was originally from Sumner County, Tennessee. They have four sons. William III (Bill) is an attorney with a private practice in Carrollton and serves as senator from the 30th Senatorial District representing Carroll and part of Douglas Counties. Thomas Ramsey (Bo), married to Courtney B. Gunter Hamrick, originally of Dallas, Texas, works for SYBASE, a computer company. They reside in Denver, Colorado. Andrew Sullivan (Andy) served in the Peace Corps in Costa Rica and now is living and working for NCR Corporation in Atlanta. James Harrison (Jamie), lives in Atlanta and works for Tatum Law Firm. *Submitted by: William G. Hamrick, 37 Lynda Circle, Carrollton, GA 30117*

Grady Hamrick (center) in front of Standard Oil Distributorship.

Back, Jamie, Dottie, Andy, and Bo. Seated, William, Amelia Sullivan (Dottie's mother), and Bill. 1997

605. George Martin Hanson

George Martin Hanson was born 11 November 1893 and lived most of his life in Carroll County. He was the eleventh child of James Frank and Cynthia Josephine Gore Hanson. George married Dora Ophelia Harper (born 25 March 1897, daughter of Patrick Henry and Georgia Ann Holcombe Harper), 28 February 1915 in Haralson County. During their courtship when George was traveling to visit Dora, a runaway horse and buggy accident left George crippled. And the difficult life of a farmer was made even more so.

George Martin and Fannie Womack Hanson

George and Dora settled in Haralson County and had four daughters: Ovia Odell (married Roy Lee Steadham, son of John and Eva Jordan Steadham), Eunice Inez, Dorothy Annie Mae (married Wilburn Nalley "Waddy" Farr, son of John and Evie Sewell Farr) and Ann Louise (married James Ira McCullough, son of Love and Sarah Johnston McCullough, second Presley Martin Chance).

On 14 March 1926, Dora died with pneumonia, and George married Fannie Lou Womack (daughter of J.C. and Della Greenwood Womack of Paulding County) 13 December 1926. George and Fannie had five children: George Martin Jr., Edna Gladys (married Render James "Doc" Collins), James Harold (married Laura Rudene Newell, daughter of Alton and Gladys Driver Newell), Charles Franklin (married Reba Chandler, daughter of Namon and Opal Cook Chandler) and Robert Mervin (married Ruth Orine Truitt, daughter of Marvin and Frances Adams Truitt). George Jr. died in infancy; and after the birth of daughter Edna in 1929, Inez died in 1930, age twelve, from pneumonia and spinal meningitis. Dora, George Jr. and Inez are buried at Little Vine. The remaining children made their homes in Carroll County. But in 1954, Annie Mae and family moved into Douglas County.

Ovia, Louise, Annie Mae and Inez Hanson

In 1940, George inherited his father's farm in the 5th District where he and his family lived and worked for some years. George, who found it increasingly difficult to farm due to age and health, sold the farm in 1954 after the children

Edna, Harold, Charles and Robert Hanson

were married. He and Fannie moved to Villa Rica where they lived on Wilson Street for two years. In 1956, they purchased a home on Spring Street beside Jones Funeral Home, where they lived until George's death 19 March 1963. He is buried at Little Vine.

After extended illness, Edna died on 4 April 1974 at age forty-five and Annie Mae died with cancer 25 March 1995 at age seventy-three. Edna is buried at District Line Methodist Church Cemetery, and Annie Mae is buried at Hillcrest Cemetery in Villa Rica. Fannie continued to provide many grandmotherly years to her family until her death 17 March 1988 at age eighty-nine. At age eighty-one, daughter Ovia died 22 December 1997.

Louise, Charles, Harold, Robert and their families reside in Carroll County. The brothers all have histories as farmers, in the tradition of their Hanson ancestors, and have worked as independent businessmen as well. Louise is the oldest living member of this line and is a symbol, along with her brothers, of the Hanson tradition of hard work and endurance. *Submitted by: Freida Chance Nalley, P.O. Box 28, Villa Rica, GA 30180*

Sources: Ann Louise Hanson McCullough Chance; Various documents in possession

606. Reuben Crawford Hanson, Jr. James Frank Hanson

Reuben Crawford Hanson Jr. (called Dock) spent most of his life farming in Carroll County. He was the ninth child born to Reuben Crawford and Margaret "Peggy" Jones Hanson on 15 May 1834 in Fayette County. In his obituary, written by son-in-law Rev. Willis Dallas Jones, is found one of the few records of his marriage to Caldonia "Donia" Bearden in 1852. Caldonia was born 1837 in Fayette County, daughter of Solomon Bearden and sister of Richard who married Nancy Hanson, Dock's sister. Dock was a Confederate Soldier, served as sergeant under Captain Hanley, Company F, 25th Regiment, Alabama Volunteers, and was wounded 22 August 1864 in the Battle of Atlanta. In 1897, Dock applied from the Emily Post Office in Carroll County for a Confederate Veteran's pension under the 1894 State Pension Act, although he had served in an Alabama regiment. At this time, Dock and his family had been living in Carroll County for nine years continuously. With relatives in both states and living at various times in both states, Dock's approval was made difficult. With assistance from G.W. Merrell and Willis Jones, Dock did finally receive his well-deserved pension, as his wounds had taken a great toll on his health. At least by 1903, he was finally awarded $60 per year, with the last record in that file dated 1907.

Dock and Donia's children include: James Frank (married Cynthia Josephine Gore, then Sarah Mattie Farmer), Margaret Jane (married Willis Jones), Reuben F., William W., John Edward, Elizabeth Caldonia (married J.J. Boyd), and Rosanna Augustus. Reuben F., Rosanna and one unnamed child died in infancy. Donia died 1872 shortly after Rosanna's birth, and Dock married Nancy Wilder 22 April 1874. Dock was living with his and Nancy's daughter, Mary Hanson Wilkins, in Newnan when he died 11 September 1909. Dock was buried at Pauls Church, with the Rev. S.E. Wilson officiating. Nancy died 29 February 1928, after many years of providing care for her older, injured husband and their family.

Dock and Caldonia's oldest son, James F.M. (Frank), was born 15 December 1852 and married Cynthia Josephine (Josie) Gore (born 2 April 1858, daughter of Manning and Malissa Malone Gore) 1 December 1874 in Douglas County. What became known as their "home place" near the Douglas County line in Carroll County was near the home place of Frank's grandfather, Reuben Sr.

Frank and Josie had thirteen children: Lela, Emmett (married Sarah Elizabeth Jones), Lora (married Leman Cansler), Dora Mary (married Homer Byrom), Callie (married Charles Peace), Maggie E. (married Alva Broome), Reuben C., James M., Richard J. (married Louise), George Martin (married Dora Ophelia Harper, then Fannie Lou Womack), Lula B. (married James Thompson), and Bernice C. Lela, Reuben, James, Bernice and an unnamed child died in infancy. Lula died at age nineteen.

Josephine died 4 August 1901, twenty-one days after Bernice. Frank then married Mattie Farmer, and they had one son, Willie Frank (married Ruby Mae Holland). Frank died 2 October 1934; and he, Josephine, Mattie and several children are buried in the Jones family cemetery near Consolation Baptist Church. *Submitted by: Joan Chance Hayes, P.O. Box 65, Villa Rica, GA 30180*

Sources: Margaret Hanson Hill (copy of her original text); Reuben Crawford Hanson Bible (cited in M.H. Hill's text); James Frank and Josephine Gore Hanson Bible (in possession); Ann Louise Hanson McCullough Chance.

607. Hansons

Chesapeake to Carroll

Ancestors of the Hansons in Carroll County originated in the Chesapeake Bay area of Maryland and Virginia, with progeny in surrounding Georgia counties and western Alabama. The name is sometimes spelled Henson and Hinson in records that document this migration.

Jesse Hanson is among the first of this lineage to arrive in Carroll County, Georgia, by the circuitous route of Wild Cat Creek in Jackson County, then Morgan, Walton, and Fayette Counties, landing in the Carroll County tax records in 1832. Jesse was born 24 July 1761 in Fauquier County, Virginia, son of Robert Hanson, and had nine siblings: Robert Jr., Elizabeth (married Whitten), Ann (married Dialls), James (married Ann Quisenberry), Tapley (married Elizabeth Holder), William, Haney (married Martin Dye), Margaret (married Presley Garner) and John. The eldest son, Robert Jr., applied for a Revolutionary War pension in Fauquier County in 1846 at the age of 95. In that application he stated that brothers Tapley and James were residing near the 96th District Courthouse in South Carolina.

Jesse married Elizabeth Crawford (born 1765), daughter of Reuben Crawford, on 28 November 1787 in Fauquier County. Their ten children include: Jane (married Phillip Phelps), Reuben Crawford, Sarah (married Edwin Lambert), Thomas, James (married Betsy), George W. (married Jerusha Lambert), William (married Sarah Lambert), Catherine (married Allen Lambert), Jesse Jr. (married Ms. Murphy), and Margaret (married Lewis Davis).

When Elizabeth died in 1840, she was living with her youngest daughter and son-in-law in Fayette County. In 1841, Jesse married Mary Murphy in Morgan County. They eventually moved to Randolph County, Alabama, where Jesse died on 7 February 1852.

Jesse and Elizabeth's children established more roots in Carroll and surrounding counties. Their son, Reuben Crawford Hanson, born 1793 in Fauquier County, married Margaret "Peggy" Jones 16 January 1818 in Morgan County. Although the identities of Margaret's parents are not known, tradition indicates that she is a relative of Thomas B. Jones who lived near them in Carroll County; and they are buried in that Jones family cemetery without markers. Reuben and Margaret were in Campbell County when their sixth child was born (1828); in Fayette County when their ninth child was born (1834); and finally in Carroll County when their twelfth child arrived in 1840.

Reuben and Margaret had thirteen children: Nancy (married Richard Bearden), Jane (married Jesse Silvey), Sally, Elizabeth, Mahala (married Lewis Odom), Henry Butler (married Sarah Stuart), Mary (married Martin Boon), Margaret (married E.Z. Lambert), Reuben Crawford Jr. (married Caldonia Bearden), (See related Reuben Crawford Hanson article), William Wallace, Amanda (married A. Tompkins), John Jesse (married Sarah Vines) and James Francis Marion (married Almedia Bailey). Sally and Elizabeth died in infancy. All five sons were Confederate Soldiers; and miraculously, all five returned home - but not without serious injury.

Reuben Sr. owned land in the 4th District on Whooping Creek called Hanson's Mill Place. What eventually became known as "the Home Place" was located in the 5th District on Snake Creek in the Cross Plains area. Much Hanson and Jones family history associates with this area.

Reuben Sr. died 20 November 1848 in Douglas County. Margaret died in 1870 in Carroll County. *Submitted by: Joan Chance Hayes, P.O. Box 65, Villa Rica, GA 30180*

Sources: Blair Jones (cited in M.H. Hill's text); Margaret Hanson Hill (copy of her original text); Reuben Crawford Hanson Bible (cited in M.H. Hill's text); Carroll County Marriage Records.

608. The Hanvey Family in the Civil War

The Civil War was a bitter time for the Hanveys. The family were avid supporters of the Southern cause and all of its men served and many died in its service. In fact one son, Capt. George McDuffie, is said to be the first person in Georgia to volunteer his service to Governor Brown of the state and even before that he had offered his service and that of his militia company, the Newnan Guards, to the governor of South Carolina. Ultimately, George's company did become the first to be accepted in the service of Georgia - Company A, 1st (Ramsey's) Georgia Infantry.

The following letter written by Susan Carter Hanvey just three months before her death in Carroll County, details some of her feelings about the war. In the letter, Susan speaks of the many deaths in the family and it is ironic in that the tragedy was not complete, because her son Thomas and son-in-law, Capt. William A. Walker, both of whom she speaks were to be killed later in the war. The letter is presented here just as it was written with no changes either in spelling or punctuation:

Georgia, Carroll Co.
January 14, 1863

Dear Son,

I take the pleasure of answering your kind letter that came to hand some time since though sickness and death has kept me from answering it sooner. I was proud to hear from you and family though grieved to hear of Susans death but believe me we have nothing but trouble in our land.

I also have the painful task of chronicling the death of your bother William. He died the 7th of the month after lingering for several months he had been in service some 19 months. Ned my children are nearly all dead and I am left hear to see all the trouble of this unholy war. That is four of my boys dead in 4 years Teague died at Richmond. Thos. wife is dead and he is married again his boys are all in the war. Your connection here are all gone Siss old man is gone he is the Capt. of his company and is a great deal thought of by all his men and officers. He has been home on sick furlough though has gone back again and is now at Vicksburg, Miss. Siss is left with three little children though William left her plenty to live on. He hired a Negro woman to stay with her she has a good home to stay at & is doing well he hopes. I am living as Thos. the connexion are all well She sent her best love to you & children & says write to her. I want you to write to me soon with all things this leaves me in tolerable good health & hope it may find you & children in good health and doing well. Excuse a short letter as I had no news to write. Write to me soon and often & be sure to come to see me one time more but my best love and wishes for you & children.

Your mother until death
Susan Hanvey

to E.L.H. (Edward Lain Hanvey) Abbeville District, South Carolina

PS- direct your letters to Enon Grove, Heard City, Ga. and I will be sure to get them as that mail is taken to Sisses house.

S. Hanvey

There is no doubt that the deaths of her children weighed heavily on Susan. The additional blow of her oldest son Thomas being killed on 4 April 1863, probably hastened her death, which occurred on 26 May 1863. Susan is buried in Carroll County, Georgia, but as of this writing the location is not known.

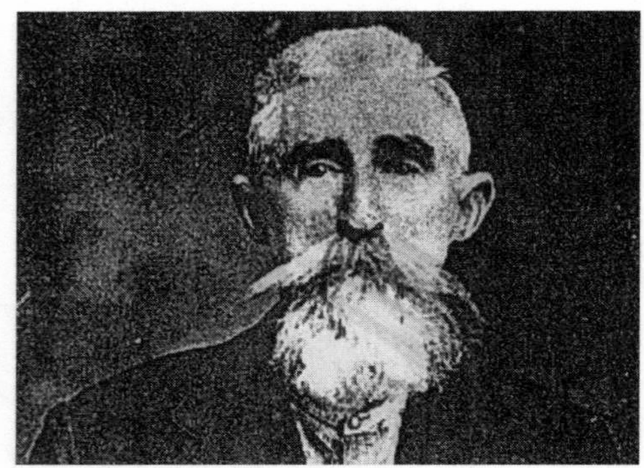

Grandson Thomas Hanvey (11-30-1838 - c. 1911), Company B, 56th Georgia Infantry.

The following are just a partial listing of sons and grandsons who fought for the Confederacy: (1) son - Thomas Wright Hanvey - killed - 4 April 1863; (2) grandson - Sherod P. Hanvey - Carroll Guards, Co. F, 19th Georgia Regiment and Co. D, Phillips Legion Georgia Volunteers and 2nd Co. A, 12th Battalion Georgia Light Artillery - survived; (3) grandson - Lt. Thomas Hanvey - Co.'s B and H., 56th Regiment Georgia Volunteer Infantry, Army of Tennessee, C.S.A. - severely wounded - survived; (4) grandson - William "Wid" H. Hanvey - Co. G., 3rd Regiment Georgia State Troops and Co. H., 56th Georgia Regiment Volunteer Infantry - survived; (5) grandson - James Edward Hanvey - Captain Long's Cavalry Co. and Co. D/K., Calvary Battalion, Phillips Legion, Georgia Volunteers - survived; (6) grandson - George W. Hanvey - Co.'s D and K., Calvary Battalion, Phillips Legion, Georgia Volunteers, Army of Northern Virginia, C.S.A. - survived; (7) son - James Thomas Hanvey, Sr. - Co. H., 19th South Carolina Infantry - killed - Salirsa, Kentucky - 9 October 1862; (8) grandson - George Alexander Hanvey - Co. G., 14th South Carolina Infantry - wounded - survived; (9) grandson - James Thomas Hanvey, Jr. - Co. G., 14th South Carolina Infantry - killed at Drury's Bluff, Virginia - 28 July 1864; (10) Son - Edward "Ned" Lain Hanvey - Co. I., 1st Regiment South Carolina State Troops - survived; (11) grandson - Thomas D. Hanvey, Co. G., 14th South Carolina Infantry - killed - Culpepper Court House, Virginia - 18 June 1862; (12) son - William C. Hanvey - 2nd Co. A., 12th Battalion Georgia Light Artillery - died of wounds - 7 January 1863; (13) grandson - Samuel "Sam" Teague Hanvey - 2nd Co. A., 12th Battalion Georgia Light Artillery - survived; (14) son - Maj. George McDuffie Hanvey - Newnan Guards, Newnan, Georgia and Co. A., 1st (Ramsey's) Georgia Infantry and 2nd Co. A., 12th Battalion Georgia Light Artillery, and Commander 12th Battalion Georgia Light Artillery - severely wounded - survived; (15) son - Wright Joshua "Josh" Hanvey, Co. B., 3rd Battalion South Carolina Infantry, Kershaw's Brigade, Army of Northern Virginia, C.S.A. - wounded at least twice - survived; (16) Son - Samuel Teague Hanvey - Co. E, 1st Georgia Regulars - killed near Richmond - 10 December 1861; (17) son-in-law - Capt. William A. Walker - Co. K., 34th Georgia Infantry - killed in action Jonesboro Crossing, Georgia - 31 August 1864. *Submitted by: Monteen Allie Hanvey Hart, 106 Sylvania Avenue, Greenville, SC 29609*

609. The William Hanvey Family

The Hanveys were a pioneering family in South Carolina. William Hanvey (circa 1740) and his wife, Sarah (circa 1741) arrived in Charles Town on the ship *Earl of Hillsborough* that left from Belfast in the Kingdom of Ireland on 30 November 1766. They were Protestants who had come on the encouragement of the bounty and were granted 250 acres of land on the waters of Long Cane Creek, near Belfast Township.

Then Hanveys remained in the old Ninety-Six District of South Carolina where a son James was born circa 1771 and died after 1796. James had several children, including William (born 7-20-1791 - died 3-14-1849) who married Susan Carter born 4-18-1794, died 4-26-1863) on 31 March 1815.

William had a family of eleven children, all born in Abbeville District: (1) Thomas Hanvey (born 3-23-1816, died 4-4-1863) who was born in Abbeville and died in the Civil War. Thomas is known to have had at least six children. (2) James Thomas Hanvey (born 3-19-1818, died 10-9-1862) who was killed in the Civil War. James married Matilda Ann Conner (born 10-2-1819, died 12-27-1981) on 19 December 1839. They had five children. (3) Edward "Ned" Lain Hanvey (born 3-12-1820, died 9-3-1977) who was married first to Susan J. Lindsey and second to Sarah Jane Wiley (born 4-15-1829, died 1-15-1913). Edward and Sarah Jane are buried at Buffalo Baptist Church in McCormick County, South Carolina. Edward is known to have had at least nine children. (4) William C. Hanvey (born 9-19-1822, died 1-8-1863) died in Carroll County, Georgia, of wounds received in battle in the Civil War. He was married twice, first to Isbella Wilson who died circa 1850, and second to Nancy M. He was buried in Carroll County. William C. had six children. (5) George McDuffie Hanvey (born 11-2-1824, died 11-16-1900) who died in Atlanta of a wound received thirty-six years earlier during the Civil War. George married Diana Hill (born 1830, died 9-22-1913) and both are buried at Oakland Cemetery, Atlanta.

They had five children. (6) Paten Hanvey (born 12-20-1826, died 9-14-1827). (7) Oliver N. Hanvey (born 12-16-1828, died 9-9-1860). (8) Wright Joshua (Josh) Hanvey (born 11-11-1831, died 12-23-1913. Wright married Mary Elizabeth Campbell on 18 April 1858 and they had thirteen children. (See related Hanvey story.) (9) Maryann "Siss" Tabitha Hanvey (born 2-8-1834, died 1896) is buried at City Cemetery in Bremen, Georgia. Maryann married on 5 November 1854 William A. Walker (born 1835, died 9-31-1864) who was killed at Jonesboro Crossing (Georgia) during the Civil War. Capt. Walker was buried on the battlefield. They had four children. (10) Benjamin Dudley Hanvey (born 3-11-1836, died 3-29-1850). (11) Samuel Teague Hanvey (born 12-29-1840, died 12-10-1861) who was killed in action on 10 December 1861 near Richmond, Virginia, during the Civil War. Samuel was married about 1859 to Martha (born 1842). They had one daughter.

Many members of the Hanvey family left South Carolina after William Hanvey's death in 1849. His sons, Thomas and William, were already in Carroll County before his death and William's widow Susan, with her three younger children (Wright Joshua, Maryann, and Samuel Teague) were living in the 11th District by the time of the 1850 Carroll County census. *Submitted by: Monte Arthur Hart, 105 James Street, Easley, SC 29642*

610. The Wright Joshua Hanvey Family

Wright Joshua Hanvey (November 11, 1831-December 23, 1914), the eighth child of William and Sarah Carter Hanvey, served in Troop F of the 3rd U.S. Dragoons in the Mexican War and lived in the 11th Division of Carroll County with his widowed mother in 1850. He remained in Carroll County with his relatives for several years before returning to South Carolina. There, in Laurens District on April 18, 1858, he married Mary Elizabeth Campbell (April 28, 1841-September 11, 1909). Wright served in the Civil War in Company B, 3rd Battalion of South Carolina Infantry. He was in many battles and was wounded twice, once at South Mountain and again at Gettysburg. He was a mechanic and miller most of his life. Wright raised a family of thirteen children and spent all of his later years in Oconee County, South Carolina. Wright and Mary are buried there at Cross Road Baptist Church. Their fourth child was Thomas Wright Hanvey (March 15, 1867-October 30, 1983).

Thomas Wright was born at Clinton in Laurens County and came to Oconee County before 1880 with his family. He married, circa 1844, probably in Spartanburg County, Susan Alma Nix (December 22, 1862-March 21, 1938). They raised a family of ten children. They were Methodist and he farmed in many places. In his later years, he was a carpenter and mill worker at Lonsdale Mill in Seneca. Both are buried at the Wesleyan Methodist Church near Oakway, South Carolina. Their first child was William David Lee Hanvey (July 29, 1885-January 28, 1937).

William David was born in Spartanburg County, but spent almost his entire life living at various places in Oconee County. His early years were spent as a farmer, but later he was a trader and merchant and owned several small general stores in and around the Cross Roads community. He married Margaret Eugenia Cole (January 22, 1884-February 11, 1951) on December 27, 1905. They had nine children. William is buried at the Wesleyan Methodist Church near Oakway and Margaret is buried at Woodlawn Memorial in Greenville, South Carolina.

Monteen (Teen) Allie Hanvey, born July 23, 1912, the fourth child of William David and Margaret Eugenia, was born in Oakway. She spent her early years attending school in Cross Roads, Oakway, Seneca, and Newry. She went to work at age thirteen at a mill in Westminster, running silk winders. Monteen continued to

Mary Elizabeth Campbell Hanvey and Wright Joshua Hanvey, ca. 1900

work in various mills until she married Guy Henry Hart, born November 24, 1908, in Greenville on March 25, 1929. Guy is the son of Charles Martin Hart (January 9, 1884-September 5, 1956) and Ellen Sarah McAbee (July 23, 1878-April 21, 1935). Guy is a World War II veteran. He served in the Philippine Islands. Today, they are in fairly good health and live in Greenville. Their third child is Monte Arthur Hart, born December 8, 1936.

Monte married Lois Kay Spear (born July 17, 1937) on January 19, 1961, in Newport, Rhode Island. Monte was born in Greenville, South Carolina. He is a retired naval officer with over twenty-three years of service. Monte and Kay are members of the Episcopal Church and have two sons: Monte Arthur Hart II born April 4, 1965, and Charles Martin Hart II born July 11, 1973. *Submitted by: Monte Arthur Hart, 105 James Street, Easley, SC 29642*

611. Alvin Vernice Hardeman Family

My mother, Mary Elizabeth Jordan Hardeman, was born May 27, 1923. Her parents were Ulysses Walker Jordan and Ammie Reese Jordan, who were married in May 1922. She was born in the Jordan home which still stands on Pleasant Hill Road. She had four half brothers and one half sister: Reese, Weems, Blanche, Harvey, and Harold.

Mother attended school first at Elizabeth Harris High in 1929 until she transferred to Villa Rica in 1937. She saved all of her report cards and can name all of her homeroom teachers. These names in order are Mrs. R.P. Maxwell, Miss Bulah Crews, Mrs. J.D. Vines, Mrs. Minnie L. Earnest, Mrs. L.D. Hamil, and Mrs. Gladys McClendon (who taught fifth, sixth and part of the seventh grades). Her teachers at Villa Rica were: Mrs. Neal, Mrs. Beuna Taylor, Mr. J.J. Hagood and Mrs. Reba Roberds. She remembers very well walking to Elizabeth Harris High and stopping by neighbor houses to pick up friends. All kids had to walk to school back then, even when it rained or the roads were covered with snow. She rode the school bus to Villa Rica.

After finishing school, she went to Carrollton NYA War Production Center to work. It was here she learned to sew. She was a wonderful seamstress for many years until eye surgery caused poor vision in 1999. Mother transferred from Carrollton NYA to Savannah to work in a bomb factory. It was on this job that she met Ruth Page, who still remains a friend, and who would later introduce her to her future husband. Her next job was at Bell Aircraft in Marietta (1943-1945), where she worked as a spot-welder. Several small jobs later, she was living in Atlanta with Frances, Doris, and Sarah North, working at Arrow Shirt, when she accepted an invitation to Ailey, Georgia, to visit her friend Ruth Page. Here she met the love of her life! At a "Peanut Boiling" she was introduced to Alvin Vernice Hardeman. This led to an ice cream supper, a movie, many love letters, visits from Ailey to Carrollton and vice versa, and a wedding on September 16, 1946.

My daddy, Alvin Vernice Hardeman, was born in Ailey, Montgomery County, Georgia, on November 6, 1917. His parents were Eligh and Barbara Page Hardeman. He lived in Ailey all of his single life except for three years that he served in the US Air Force. His tour of duty took him to Africa, Italy, and Germany. He was discharged in November 1945. Daddy was a tobacco farmer before and after he entered the Armed Services.

After meeting Mother, Dad made a statement to one of their friends "This is the girl I am going to marry." They were married September 16, 1946, in Mount Vernon, Georgia. Their first home was shared with Daddy's sister, Frances, and her husband, who were also newlyweds. Daddy and his brother-in-law, Uncle Barney, worked in the tobacco fields. They did very hard work and received very small pay.

Frances, Barbara, Mary, Martha, Vernice, Walter, and Lucy Hardeman, Christmas 1967.

I, Walter "Walt" Vernice Hardeman, was their first child and I was born January 26, 1948. We lived in Ailey just a short time until Dad decided Carrollton must have more and better jobs. So we moved to Carrollton! I graduated from Villa Rica High School, attended West Georgia College, and served my country in Vietnam during the war. I met Kay Browning from Glenwood, Georgia, and we were married on December 22, 1979. Our first son, Judson Walt, was born September 15, 1983. Another son, Jordan Thomas Hardeman was born July 1, 1988. Our home is located on the Jordan home place.

Mom and Dad's second child was Barbara Marie and she was born December 30, 1949. She graduated from West Georgia College in 1971. Barbara taught school until her sudden accidental death on June 4, 1975.

Child number three is Martha Louise, born March 6, 1952. She received her master's degree from West Georgia College in 1994. After a few teaching jobs and serving as assistant principal at Villa Rica Elementary, she accepted her current job as principal of Sand Hill Elementary. She married Bruce Shade.

Frances Elizabeth, child number four, was born December 20, 1955. She married Mike Brown on December 18, 1982, and their son Jeffery Michael was born September 19, 1986.

Mother and Dad's last child was Lucy Ann, born February 27, 1959. She was attending Carroll Technical School, pursuing a business degree, at the time of her sudden, accidental death on November 3, 1979.

Our parents worked very hard to support us and even though we all shared extreme sadness at the death of our two sisters, our lives remain full of love. Daddy had a tractor accident in April 1953 and was confined for nine months. Mother and all of us, with help from the neighbors and church, took care of him. Daddy never complained. In 1960 he started working at West Georgia College. He remained crippled until his death, but he never felt handicapped. We had a wonderful life. Daddy died January 12, 2000, at home, with all three children and mother at his side. He is buried with his two daughters at the Bethany Church Cemetery. *Submitted by: Walt Hardeman, 157 Holly Tree Road, Carrollton, GA 30016*

612. Harman

The first post office at Farmer's High was named Harman in 1894. The first postmaster was William Harman, son of A.D. Harman Sr.

Zachariah Harman (1740-1808): Zachariah Harman, of German descent, left Holland and came to America where he settled in Virginia. Later he moved to North Carolina where he married an English woman, Rebeka Petty. Zachariah was a farmer and tax collector. They had nine children: Hezekiah (1763-1832), Frances (1765-1822), John (1760-1831), Catherine (1762), Polly (1764-1836), Elizabeth (1779-1850), Merriman (1784-1850), Zachariah Jr. (1769-1846) and Rebekah (1792-1851). Zachariah served in the Revolutionary War and fought in the battles of Cane Creek and King's Mountain, among others.

Merriman Harman (1784-1850): Born in Pittsboro, North Carolina, in 1784, Merriman died in 1850 and was buried at Cedar Hill Plantation in Meriwether County, Georgia. He married Nellie May in 1803. They had seven children: William May (1805-1862), Calvan (1806-1865), Emeline (1811-1891), Harriet Kitty (1812-1877), Martha (1814), Luther Merriman (1816-1892) and Mahala (1820). Merriman was among the earliest settlers of Meriwether County. He traveled over the Indian Trail Oakfuskee. From there, he blazed his own trail to the land upon which he built his log cabin with a dirt floor. His blazed trail became an early road to Greenville.

Harman Homeplace

William May Harman (1805-1862): William married Nancy Dillard in 1830. They had five children: Eliza (1831), Arthur Dillard (1832-1902), Emiline Elizabeth (1841), Nancy Ann (1842-1918), and Martha Frances. William Harman was a farmer until his death in 1862.

Arthur Dillard Harman Sr. (1832-1902): Arthur married Jane Isabella Fincher in 1857. They moved from Meriwether County in 1872 to Carroll County's Bethesda Church community. In 1892, they moved to Maple Street in Carrollton. During the War of Aggression in 1861, A.D. fought in Petersburg, Davis Farm, Blow Up, Wilderness, Deep Bottom, Turkey Ridge, Hatcher's Run, and Suffolk. After the war, he returned to his farm. Later he was a cotton ginner and miller. A.D. was a Sunday School teacher and deacon at Bethesda Baptist Church starting in 1872 after having been a deacon at the Church of Christ in Meriwether County. In 1873, A.D. gave four acres across the road from the church for a school. A.D. and Jane had eight children: William Isac (1859-1926), A.D. Jr. (1861-1921), John Abner (1864-1913), Beula (1867-1943), James Robert (1870-1911), Luther Merriman (1872-1926), Edger (1875-1940) and Anna (1878-1944).

William Isac had eight children: Abener, Virgil, Luther Calvin, Lilla, Irene, George, Ethel, and Beulah.

A.D. Jr. (Pony) (1861-1921): A.D. Jr. married Adella Amanda Wood at Roopville in 1892. They moved to Farmer's High in 1892. They later moved to Carrollton in 1902. They had five children: Nell Loftin, Bess Williamson, Luther M., Annie Upshaw, and Hildred Thompson.

John Abner had nine children: Kate, Myrl, Bertic, Luther Hubert, Annie Mae, and Robert Willard. *Submitted by: Ned Harman, 18845 Highway 27, Roopville, GA 30170*

613. Luther M. Harman 1900-1959

Luther married Zelma Barr of Tyus, Georgia, in 1929. Zelma was born in 1905. Luther and Zelma had two children: Nan Kent (1936) and Ned Harman (1944). Luther was the son of A.D. Harman Jr. (Pony) who married Adella Amanda Wood in Roopville (1892). They moved to Farmer's High in 1892 and later moved to Carrollton in 1902.

Luther Harman and Zelma Harman

Luther attended Carrollton Schools and graduated from the University of Georgia in 1922 with a master's in agriculture. He taught school at the 4th District A&M school under Dr. I.S. Ingram until 1933. He was also a farmer. In the 1930s and 1940s, he farmed, ran a cotton gin and sawmill on the Carrollton-Tyus Road at the river. In the 1940s and 1950s, he farmed with 50 mules and raised 350 acres of cotton, 200 acres of corn, 200 head of hogs, 150 head of Angus cattle, and 60 head of Holstein springers. He also bought and sold timber. He farmed over 2,000 acres. He was a director of the People's Bank, Commercial Bank, Soil Conservation, and Cotton Producers Association (Gold Kist). He was also on the Tanner Hospital Board. In 1933, he helped D.W. Brooks start the Cotton Producers Association (Gold Kist). D.W. Brooks and Luther Harman attended the University of Georgia at the same time and they became friends. While Luther taught agriculture at the A&M School, he raised cotton where Sunset Hills Golf Club is now.

Luther and Zelma were the clay court tennis champions when they were at the A&M school. Zelma graduated from the A&M school and Bowdon College. She was Dr. Ingram's private secretary at the A&M school and West Georgia College until 1937. She ran the post office at the school as well. After Luther died in 1959, Zelma ran a big farm, farming over 300 acres of cotton and 150 head of Angus cattle. She was in the first group of Pink Ladies at Tanner Hospital (were called Gray Ladies when group started). Zelma was the first woman director of a bank in Carroll County starting in 1959 at the Commercial Bank and later at the Trust Company Bank. Zelma taught Sunday School for many years at the Tabernacle, Salem, and Bethesda Baptist Church. Zelma will be 96 in September 2001. *Submitted by: Zelma Harman, Stewart House, South St., Carrollton, GA 30117*

614. Ned Harman Family

John Ned Harman (1944-). Ned Harman married Karen Marlow in 1964. They had five children Dawn Harman Wilborn (1965-), Luke Harman (1968-1984), Shane Harman (1974-) Holly Harman (1976-2000), and Josh Harman (1980).

Ned farmed cotton, corn, soybeans, wheat, cattle and hogs. He grew 150 acres of cotton in the 1970s. To contrast, there used to be over

Back: Shane, Ned, Dawn, and Holly Harman. Front: Josh Harman, Barr Wilborn.

100,000 acres of cotton in Carroll County and over fifty cotton gins. When Ned quit growing cotton, he was the last cotton grower in Carroll County and he had to haul the cotton fifty miles to get it ginned. At one time, Ned had over 300 brood cows and a 500 capacity hog parlor. He grew 350 acres of corn, 200 acres of soybeans, and 200 acres of wheat. He had the first center pivot irrigation system in Carroll County. He was president of the Georgia Young Farmers in 1981, president of the Carroll County Young Farmers twice, and he has served on the board of Gold Kist and Farm Bureau. He farmed 750 acres at the Bethesda community and at Whitesburg on the River Bottoms.

Clockwise: Ned, Shane, Holly, Josh, and Patty Harman.

In 1985, Ned married Patty Phillips Harman. Patty has one daughter Rachel Phillips Robinson and one grandson Samual Robinson.

Dawn Harman lives in the Harman home place at Bethesda with her three children - Barr, Dustin, and Christena. Dawn is a school teacher.

Shane Harman married Kim Clauss (1977-) in 2001.

Shane and Josh Harman work with Ned at Harman & Sons Farms. They have eight 500' x 40' chicken houses. They grow 1.75 million chickens a year. They also have 300 acres of pine trees and a pine straw business, as well as hay and pasture. *Submitted by: Dawn Harman, 1641 Bethesda Church Road, Carrollton, GA 30117*

615. Harper Family of Roopville

My Harper ancestors descended from Patrick Harper, born about 1653 in Ireland and died about 1680 in Gloucester County, Virginia. George Harper, son of Patrick, and his descendants were landowners in several Virginia counties. Benjamin Ingram Harper distinguished himself as a captain in the Revolutionary War. His brother, William Peterson Harper

William A. Harper Family, about 1904.

Sr., was born 3 February 1785 in Dinwiddie County, Virginia, and died 3 June 1825 in Morgan County, Georgia. He was a veteran of the War of 1812, which entitled his widow, Mary S. "Polly" Dennis Harper, to a war pension. Several of Polly and William Harper's sons settled in various Georgia counties and in Randolph County, Alabama. In the 1880 census, Polly lived with her son Green R. Harper, a mill owner in Rock Mills, Alabama. At that time, she was ninety-two years old.

Andrew Shirah and Theresa Harper, Wedding Day, 13 November 1901

Green R. Harper, born 1809 in Morgan County, Georgia, married Catherine Farrer on 1 March 1831 in Morgan County. They eventually settled in Rock Mills, Alabama, where a son, Winston W. Harper, was born in 1838.

Green R. Harper is mentioned in the book, *Sherman's Horsemen,* by Davie Evans. Apparently some of Sherman's troops lost their way when they reached West Georgia and ended up in Rock Mills. They pillaged the little town, even stealing the "silver-mounted rockaway carriage" owned by a Mr. Stephens, the town's most eminent citizen. When the troops left Rock Mills, Rousseau (the troop commander) took Green Harper along as a guide, hoping to avoid another potentially fatal error in direction. Green Harper led the troops to Carrollton. One civilian was reportedly killed when someone took a shot at the rear of the brigade and Sherman's troops returned fire. When the troops turned toward Villa Rica, Green Harper began the long ride back to Rock Mills.

Winston W. Harper, son of Green and Catherine, married Martha Ellen Formby on 15 November 1855, in Troup County, Georgia. She was the daughter of George Washington Formby and Phereby Coffman. Winston and Martha had three children when he enlisted in the Confederate Army in 1861 in Troup County. He never returned from the war. Martha had two brothers who enlisted on the same day as her husband. One brother, Aaron Formby, was also lost in the war.

William Aaron Harper, son of Winston and Martha Ellen, was born in 1857 in Heard County, Georgia, and died 1 December 1903 in Carroll County, Georgia. He married Buelah Jane Jones on 31 December 1879 in Troup County. They settled in Carroll County in the little town of Roopville. They had eight children; the eldest was my grandmother, Theresa Mozelle Harper. Grandmother married grandfather, Andrew Jackson Shirah, on 14 November 1901. My grandparents settled in Carroll County and had a family of six children. My father, William Ralph Shirah was the eldest. He was born in Heard County on 20 September 1902 but lived most of his early life in Carroll County near Roopville and Tyus. *Submitted by: Bonnie Shirah Johnson, 5136 Lexington Avenue, Stone Mountain, GA 30087*

Sources: *Early Immigrants to Virginia (1623-1666)* by Michael J. O'Brien, *The Journal of the American Irish Historical Society,* Land Office Patents and Grants, marriage records, tax digests, and census records.

616. Patrick Henry Harper

Patrick Henry Harper was born 7 June 1857 in Georgia and married Georgia Ann Holcombe 7 January 1877 in Haralson County. She was the daughter of John Martin Holcombe and Nancy Howard. Georgia was raised by grandparents due to death of her father in the Civil War and her mother had died the year before. Georgia was born 1 September 1861 and died 9 February 1923. Henry died sixteen years later on 8 August 1939 and both rest in Little Vine Cemetery close to Bremen.

Patrick Henry was the son of James M. Harper born 29 May 1818 in Butts County, Georgia, and died 31 January 1887 in Haralson County. His mother, Lavonia Head, was born 7 January 1820 in Georgia and died 24 December 1900 in Cullman County, Alabama. James M. was living in the Kansas District of Carroll County in 1860 and in Haralson County in 1870. James M. is resting beneath the apple tree on his farm where he requested to be buried. His grave, surrounded by a wire fence, is found on Harper Lane off Georgia Avenue, east of Bremen. James M.'s name appears on a muster roll of the militia of Haralson County under Col. John Dean.

Henry had seven brothers and sisters: Elizabeth Rebecca (19 June 1844) married Robert M. Reid; William Thomas (1 June 1846) married Annie; Nathaniel William (22 December 1848) married Elizabeth Coleman; James M. Jr. (21 November 1850) married Georgia Ann Reid; Georgia Ann Lavonia (28 September 1852) married R.A. Rooker; Annilla Matilda Jane (21 July 1855-1856); Francis Marion (16 March 1859) married Nancy Lera Pate.

Henry and Georgia Ann Harper homesteaded in the 7th District of Haralson County, Georgia. Their names appear on the membership roll of Liberty Christian Church. In 1900, when the sanctuary was added to the church, Henry volunteered to help with the labor along with other members.

Henry and Georgia Ann were the parents of thirteen children: James Martin, (8 March 1878) married Ella Mayer; Nancy Lavonia (18 June 1880) married J.D. Smith and had a son Homer. Nancy married second to George Farmer and their children were Audie and Todd; Thomas Franklin (26 June 1882) married Leila Lavonia Green and their children were Fred and Luciel; George William Henry (13 February 1884) married Mary Ritter and had a son Lee; Leola Elizabeth (17 June 1886) married John Waston and had children Loyce, Roy, Eula, Margaret and Herman; Ella Jane, (20 November 1888) married Harvey Long and had sons Ralph and Rayford; Mary L. (25 April 1890) married Thomas Tillman and had sons Claude and Leonard; Reuben Matthew (20 October 1892) married Dora Mae Louey and had daughter Billie; John David (17 March 1895) married Mattie Theabold and had a son Jack; Dora Ophelia (25 March 1897) married George Hanson and had daughters Ovie, Inez, Annie Mae, and Louise; Lloyd Lucious (26 December 1898) married Thelma Stanford and had a daughter Lena Zan; Hattie Estell (13 January 1901) married Thomas Long and had children Maurine and Ross; Lowell Baskin (17 April 1904) made a career in the Navy.

Martin, Lavonia, Thomas, Ella, Mary, Dora, Lloyd, Hattie, and Lowell rest with their parents in Little Vine Cemetery. *Submitted by: Sandra Allen, 160 Greenwood Drive, Carrollton, GA 30117. sloua@aol.com*

617. Harris Family

John D. Harris, born October 24, 1925 in Bowdon, Carroll County, Georgia, was the son of Marion Bradford Harris and Evie Annie Wilson Harris. Marion was a son of George Washington Harris and Mary E. Nichols. George was a son of Green Berry Harris and his wife, Sarah, in 1850 Randolph County, Alabama, census.

John D. married Nora Mae Gann, February 7, 1948 in Calhoun County, Alabama. She was the daughter of Rev. Minus A. Gann and Martha Ann Gray of Cleburne County, Alabama. John D. and Nora lived in LaGrange, Georgia, for a while. They had two sons, Jimmy D. born November 27, 1948, and Michael Jerome, born July 18, 1952, in LaGrange, Troup County, Georgia. They moved to Carrollton in 1954. Rhonda Maria was born at Carrollton, January 27, 1956.

Jimmy D. married Rebecca Owens. They have two children: John Andrew, now in the Marines, and Laura Kate, now living in Texas with her mother and attending college in Austin, Texas. Jimmy is living in Carroll County.

Nora, Rhonda, Jimmy, Michael, and John D. Harris

Michael J. married Angeline Hyatt. They have two daughters, Courtney and Hillary. Courtney is married to Richard Roberts and lives near Fayetteville. Hillary is in high school in Coweta County. Michael and Angie lived in Carroll County, but now live in Coweta County.

Rhonda M. married Randy Steve Daniel of Carroll County. They have two children, Misty Suzanne and Kyle Steve. Misty is married to Russell Smith and lives in Carroll County. Kyle is working and attending college.

John D.'s father was Marion Bradford Harris. He was born March 7, 1890, in Alabama. He died August 8, 1973, in Carrollton. John D. died of cancer December 12, 1972. Both are buried at Pleasant Hill Church.

Marion B. Harris married first to Elvie Cox, and second to Evie Anne Wilson, and third to Velma Bentley. Marion had four daughters by Elvie: Bernice, Velma, Elizabeth, and Boyce. He had seven children by Evie: John D., Sarah, Hulet, Dean, Marion B. Jr., Frank, and Edward. Three children are still living — Sarah Hendley, Frank, and Marion B. Harris Jr.

We do not know who the father of Green Berry Harris was. He was born about 1808 in Georgia. We believe he had at least two brothers, Micajah and Elbert. Green Berry was in Randolph County, Alabama, in 1850. His children were Elbert born in 1834; George Washington born 1836; Francis M. born 1838; Lazarus H. born 1840; Sander born 1844; Mary born 1846; Henry born 1848; and James M. born 1850.

George Washington's first wife was Mary Elizabeth Hill. Their children were Emma C., born in Carroll County; Mary Elizabeth born 1868 in Alabama; Robert W. born in 1870. Green B. born 1873; Sarah A.; and Georgia Ophella. Mary died and he married second wife, Mary Elizabeth Nichols. Their children were Marion Bradford born March 7, 1890, Lora Cumie, and Silven Grady. *Submitted by: Nora Harris, 209 Rome Street, Bowdon, GA 30108*

618. Jimmy and Kimberley Harris Family

On July 18, 2000, our little triplet miracles arrived three months early. First came Britney Paige (2 pounds, 13 ounces), next came Justin Noah (2 pounds, 15 ounces), and following her sister and brother little Calli Anne (2 pounds, 3 ounces) arrived last and least in size! It was and still is one of God's greatest gifts. The weeks and months that followed were hard and required enormous faith as our babies slowly gained the required weight and strength to be able to come home. One by one we brought them home and with the help of family and friends we spent part of our time with the ones still in the hospital. After months we finally were all at home together.

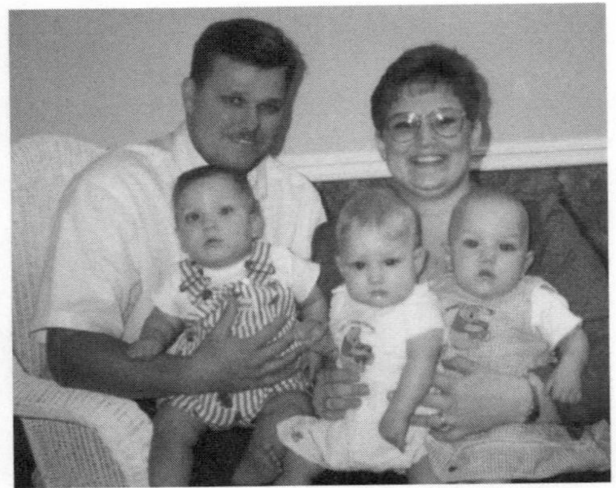

The Harris family Jimmy, Kimberely, and the triplets

My name is Kimberly Cannon Harris and I was born April 20, 1970, in Newnan, Coweta County, Georgia, and my husband is Jimmy Harris. We were married on May 18, 1996, at the Whitesburg Christian Church. My parents are Ronald and Shirley Altman Cannon of Hogansville. Ronald and Shirley were married August 20, 1975, at Happy Hill Baptist Church in Carroll County. Jimmy was born August 10, 1968, in Carroll County, Georgia, and he is the son of Joe Brown and Mary Alice Cooper Harris. Joe and Mary Alice were married on December 31, 1963, in Carroll County.

Joe Brown was born December 2, 1911, and he died on August 24, 1988. He is buried in the Carroll Memory Gardens. Joe Brown Harris was the son of Alexander Cliff (September 15, 1874-February 13, 1958) and Lucy Helton Harris (December 22, 1877-September 1, 1964). Cliff and Lucy were married November 17, 1895, in Carroll County. Alexander Cliff was the fourth child of William Washington (March 22, 1847-June 3, 1941) and Elizabeth Dixon Tyson Harris (September 11, 1847-March 8, 1917). William and Elizabeth were married December 25, 1864, in Carroll County.

Mary Alice Cooper is the daughter of Noah Washington and Susie Brack Cooper. Noah and Susie were married on March 16, 1919, in Carroll County. Mary Alice was born August 27, 1924, and still resides in Carroll County. Noah was born September 25, 1873, and died February 7, 1945. He is buried at Mount Pleasant Baptist Church. Susie died about 1968 and is buried at Mars Hill Cemetery. *Submitted by: Kimberley Harris, 325 Timber Ridge Trail, Carrollton, GA 30117-8884*

619. Simeon Harrison

Simeon Harrison was born October 27, 1807, in Greenville County, Virginia. He was the ninth of ten children born to John and Rebecca Dillehay Harrison and probably a ninth generation Harrison born in this nation since their arrival from England in the early 1800s.

The family moved to Rutherford County, North Carolina, in 1817 where many members of the family remain today.

Simeon Harrison is known to have been in Carroll County in the 1850s. He owned a farm of several hundred acres a few miles south of the community of Mt. Zion on what is now known as Harrison Road. His land abutted what are now the lakes of Tanner State Park.

On January 30, 1859, at the age of 51, Simeon married Nancy Jane Jones, barely 17 years old. They were blessed with six children: John Simeon Harrison, James Willie Washington Harrison, Rebecca Jane Harrison, Martha Dora Harrison Smith, Sarah Emma Harrison Crawford, and Fletcher Martin Harrison. The accompanying photograph shows the youngest of these children, Fletcher, with his wife Ida Crumbley Harrison and the first of his eight children: Curtis Harrison, Floyd Harrison, Guthrie Harrison, Glee Harrison, Mose Harrison and Prince Harrison. Simeon and Nancy now have over 290 known descendants.

Until the Second World War, most of this branch of the Harrison family lived within ten miles of the old home place. Since that time, members of the family have spread all over this country. A large number of descendants still live in Carroll County and part of the original farm is still in Harrison hands.

Simeon Harrison died October 27, 1880, and Nancy Jane died April 20, 1913. They are buried at Smith's Chapel Cemetery, a couple of miles north of the Burwell community. *Submitted by: Dan Harrison, PO Box 1558, Englewood, FL 34295-1558*

620. The Charles Arthur Hart Family

Charles Arthur Hart born 21 December 1877, son of Charles Stillwell Hart, grandson of Samuel Hart Jr., native of Carroll County, Georgia. Married Bertha Lee Powell born 13 February 1882 in the Hickory Level Community to John William Powell, son of Levi Thomas Gardner Powell and Frances Louellin Green Powell, was orphaned at age four. Bertha was raised by her Powell relatives and lived with various ones. Her Uncle Buna Columbus Powell was her guardian and that of her brother William Buna Powell until they came of age. Charles Arthur Hart's mother had died in 1891 leaving a large family.

Charles Arthur Hart and Bertha Powell Hart. Wedding, October 1901.

Bertha and Arthur were married in the Powell home on #90 of the 6th land district and the first grandchild to be married there. Their first child Charles Raymond Hart was born 4 October 1902. He was loved by all the kin when he was a tot. A photograph of him age two was made, seated on the seat of a Coca Cola truck in Villa Rica. His uncle "Uncle B" had the ice plant and delivery was made around the area.

When Raymond Hart was old enough to go to school the family moved to Dallas, Georgia where Arthur had bought a drugstore. After the 1910 census which shows them in Douglas on the edge of Carroll, they moved so Raymond could go to school there. The couple never forgot their Carroll County roots and relatives. *Submitted by: Frances H. Elliott, Niceville, FL and Written by: June Hart Wester, 133 Mountain Crest Drive, Canton, GA 30114*
Sources: Family Bible and personal knowledge

621. The Charles Raymond Hart Family

In the fall of 1924 Charles Raymond and Irma Ragsdale Hart moved to Temple, Georgia. He had purchased the stock and trade of the Connell Drugstore in the block of stores facing

The family of Fletcher Harrison, ca 1915.

the railroad. The infant daughter of the Harts, June, had been born in Albany where he had worked for the Albany Drugstore. The distance from the Paulding County relatives and the malarial climate brought them north.

After the closing of the Farmer's Bank, the federal bank sold the yellow brick building to C.R. Hart and he moved the alabaster fountain and the two milkglass tables with all the cabinets to the bank building.

A baby brother was born in 1926 but died in 1927 to the sorrow of all the community. However, in 1931 a baby sister, Elaine, was born. That year June contracted typhoid fever and was sick for six weeks. That event made such an impression on C.R. Hart he vowed to see that Temple obtained a filtering water plant.

In 1936 the Connell home was also sold to the Harts.

1935 saw the organization of the Major Temple Garden Club and Mrs. Hart was a charter member. After the birth of their fourth child, Carole, in 1933 their family was complete.

C.R. Hart and Irma Ragsdale Hart. 25th Anniversary 1947.

C.R. Hart served as the clerk of the Temple School Board when students paid tuition. His records survive. The students were from Hickory Level community and later from other nearby communities.

In 1935 when C.R. Hart was mayor of Temple a bond referendum was passed to build a water system. The Webster Creek was the site of the pumping station. So, he had been able to fulfill his vow when his daughter was sick with typhoid fever and people were dependent on wells at each house.

In 1939 a new school building was built on the loop when C.R. Hart was on the school board. It is no more and has been replaced, but at that time it was a needed expansion.

The Major Temple Garden Club, in cooperation with the Bremen and Villa Rica clubs, planted roses along the banks of Highway 78 which connected the towns. Many years later they are still seen in the spring.

Irma Hart was busy growing and arranging flowers for the Baptist Church. At the commencement each year at the Temple School, she provided wicker baskets of roses. One special project the club was proud of was the building of a brick shelter for persons at Asbury Cemetery. Much effort was expended to contact persons who had family buried there.

C.R. and Irma Hart were active in many organizations of benefit to the community. *Submitted by: Lee Clifton, Moultrie, GA and Written by: June Hart Wester, 133 Mountain Crest Drive, Canton, GA 30114*

622. The Charles Stillwell Hart Family

Charles Stillwell Hart, son of Samuel Jr., born 1850 married (1) 21 Nov 1872 to Mary Antionette "Nettie" Chambers, daughter of Josiah Chambers born South Carolina.

Hattie, Joanna, Arthur, Beulah, John, Mae, Leona, Ethel, Rufus, Sammy

"Nettie" bore eleven children to Charlie Hart and died 26 December 1891 leaving nine children. The couple lived on the road from Villa Rica to Wesley Chapel Methodist Church.

After the death of Samuel Hart Jr., the settling of the estate found its way into Charles Stillwell's hands. So many of his brothers had died in the war as had several brothers-in-law, he inherited the copper box of family papers. This is the basis of a microfilm at the Georgia Archives Drawer 227, Box 64, which many descendants have obtained for their research. It is available for purchase. Miscellaneous file #360 June Hart Wester Collection of Bible Records to be seen upon request. The Samuel Hart Jr. collection ms collection #76-93.

Children: 1. Mary Beulah Hart b. 21 Dec 1873, m. J.T. Camp, no children. 2. John Vernon Hart b. 8 Nov 1874 m. Annie Mae Beavers 12 Sept 1897 Carroll County, Marriage Book H. p. 583. He died 2 July 1960. 3. Charles Arthur Hart b. 21 Dec 1877 m. 6 Oct 1901 Carroll County MB 1, p. 342 Bertha Lee Powell dau. of John William and Frances Louellin Powell. She b. 1882 d. 1979. He d. 1970. 4. Martha Joanna Hart b. 4 March 1880 d. 26 May 1899 bur. Pleasant Grove Baptist. 5. Bobby Lee Hart b. 9 July 1882 d. 20 July 1882, Pleasant Grove. 6. Harriet Emily Hart b. 1 July 1883 m. Voss Pope; 4 children lived, Lakeland, Fla. 7. Infant, no name in Bible. 8. Susan Leona Hart b. 7 Feb 1886 d. 29 Feb 1960 unm. 9. Sammie Stillwell Hart b. 6 Mar 1888 d. 3 Dec 1911. 10. Celia Ethel Hart b. 27 Jan 1890 d. 1975 m. John B. Newbern who d. 13 Nov 1985; several children. 11. James Rufus b. 25 Nov 1891 m. (1) Era Chambers in Carroll County, MB L, p. 292, pharmacist in Atlanta, moved to Kerrville, Tex. when wife became ill. m. (2) Glea from Oklahoma, 2 children. Charles Stillwell Hart m. (2) Elizabeth Smith nee Pennington ("Bess Hindsman"). He was living in Villa Rica at his death, bur. Pleasant Grove. *Submitted by: Randy Elliott, Atlanta GA and Written by: June Hart Wester, 133 Mountain Crest Drive, Canton, GA 30114*

Sources: Family Bibles, Carroll County court records, personal knowledge from family

623. The Samuel Hart Jr. Family

The house known as Samuel Hart house in Harttown west of Villa Rica was probably built by his brother, William, who was here for the 1830 census. Samuel was militia captain of G.M.D. 608 of Hancock County in 1819. His father, Samuel Sr., who was a Revolutionary soldier, died in 1807 leaving a family of grown children and some minors.

Samuel Jr., drew land in Monroe County and his mother, Susannah Borin, drew land in Henry. It was registered and returned for tax until 1830. He moved over the county line into Talbot County and bought the lot known as Hottley's Grocery. His brother Eli died and he took care of his estate, selling land Eli had drawn in Lee County. Selling his land in Talbot, he moved to Carroll in 1843. Brothers James and William had by then moved to St. Claire County, Ill., where James died.

Samuel Hart Jr. and Martha Veazey Hart

Samuel Hart Jr. married Martha Veazey 11 October 1826. She was the daughter of John Veazey who was a founding member of the Powelton Church. They were married by Jesse Mercer and were close to the Mercer family. They became founding members of the Pleasant Grove Church. Samuel Hart Jr. obituary was carried in the *Carroll County Times* 15 August 1879 giving his age as 82 years.

At the Georgia Archives and History, available for family research, is the Samuel Hart Jr. collection, Microfilm Drawer 227, Box 64, and the ms collection #76-93. June Hart Wester donated the Bible Collection Miscellaneous File #360 ms 71-23. These are available for research and some family members have bought copies.

1939 NSDAR marker for Samuel Hart Sr., C.R. Hart Family

Children: 1. Joseph Lemuel Hart b. 6 Nov 1827; served Co. I, 56th Reg. Georgia Infantry, C.S.A. He m. Catherine ? and moved to Texas after the war. Known descendants. 2. Harriet Ann Hart b. 16 Jan 1829. Never married. d. 18 Feb 1885. 3. Sarah Jane Hart b. 3 Nov 1830; m. William W. Cobb who d. 1864. She d. 3 Feb 1909. He served Co. E. 1st Ga. Regiment, Cavalry, bur. Pleasant Grove Baptist Cemetery. Descendants lived in the county; 1880 census lists Isaac, Eldorado and John G. Cobb living with her. 4. John Thomas Hart b. 23 July 1832 m. Lundah ____. He served in the Civil War, d. 1 July 1862 at Richmond after the amputation of an arm. Children: Charles A., Cain Olin and George A. Hart. The mother remarried to James Redus, either in Georgia or Texas, where they moved, Pittsburg, Texas. ("Villa Rica Gold Diggers"). 5. Susan Hart b. 17 Aug 1834 m. Lindsay Dobbs (1831-1862). She d. 21 Jan. 1908. Bur. Pleasant Grove Baptist Cemetery. in 1871, Samuel gave power of attorney to his son, James M. Hart, giving bond to his daughter, Susan, to be appointed guardian of her children: Mary, Willard and Frances Dobbs. Served Co. E, 1st Georgia Regiment Cavalry. 6. Mary Elizabeth Hart b. 2 Dec 1836 m. ____ Parker, who probably died in the war, as she and two children (Atlanta, age 8 and Willie, age 6) are living with her father in 1870. Later she moved to Texas and died there. 7. William Hart b. 20 Dec 1838 d. June 1862, "Villa Rica Gold Diggers." 8. Martha Ann Hart b. 19 Dec 1840 m. 1 Sept 1859 Robert W. Mason. She d. 14 Aug 1909 and is bur. Old Enon Church, Old Campbell County, Georgia with husband and children. 9. Samuel Hart b. 19 Feb 1843 d. 7 Oct 1843. 10. Francis Eugenius Hart b. 17 Aug. 1844 d. 23 May 1862 bur. Hollywood Cemetery, Richmond, Virginia. 11. James Madison "Doll" Hart b. 3 July 1846 m. Vella ____ 1875. He served in the war and has descendants in Paulding County today. 12. Louisiana Hazeltine Hart b. 17 March 1848 d. 19 Dec 1857. 13. Charles Stillwell Hart b. 6 Mar 1850 d. 20 Mar 1929, m. Mary Antionette Chambers b. May 1853 in the Jonesboro area, daughter of Josiah Chambers and Mary Jane Andrews. "Netty" d. 26 Dec 1891 leaving eleven children. This family has many descendants living in the area today. 14. Ella Hart b. 2 Aug 1852 d. 13 Oct 1911, m. Rufus W. Walker and had three children: Charles R., Mollie and Samuel L. Walker.

The Hart family today is grateful to the John Long family for keeping the story of their first white child, B.M. Long, being born in the Samuel Hart house, to all subsequent families who have lived there: Leathers, Brooks, Hixon, and especially the John Johnstons, who restored it about 1989, to Guy H. Wells who compiled *Wells and Allied Families* and whose wife's NSDAR (Nancy Hart) Chapter placed the marker at the grave of Samuel Hart Sr. attended by the C.R. Hart family of Temple who motored down in their A-model; to Lilma and Joe Godsey who came from Pittsburg, Texas, visiting cousins and cleaning tombstones of family; to Grace Hart Ragsdale, who allowed the contents of the copper box to be microfilmed by the Georgia archives; to all descendants who have preserved family Bibles and shared with other families; yes, to descendants of someone who was probably the sweetheart of Francis Eugenius Hart, whose picture has surfaced publicly, but was not in our Bible; to those who continue the Hart Reunion and are known for their family closeness — Thank you! *Submitted by: June Hart Wester, 133 Mountain Crest Drive, Canton, GA 30114*

Sources: Personal research based upon *Wells and Allied Families* in state and county records.

624. Hay Family

William Hay came to South Carolina from Virginia in 1748. On October 8, 1750, he purchased a tract of land and named it Hay's Mill Creek, because of his water mill built on the site. William Hay married Mary Howell. They had eight children, including Hardy Hay, who served as a private in the American Revolution.

Hardy Hay's son, William Howell Hay, was born January 24, 1781, and came to Georgia in 1803. He drew land in 1803 in Wilkes County. He also lived in Meriwether County. He married Nancy Wooten and became a farmer. One of his eight children was David Reese Hay, born in 1808.

David Reese Hay married Susan Cole on February 29, 1832. They lived in Carroll County. Susan and David Reese Hay had no children. In 1851, Susan Hay died. Seven years later, David Reese Hay married Isabelle J. Long on May 20, 1858. Isabelle was the daughter of Judge and Mrs. John Long (Nancy).

In 1867 Mr. John Long willed a large tract of land and a water mill, which had been in operation for a number of years, to his daughter Isabelle Long Hay. The will specified that at her death the property would go to her four sons, one of whom was William Robert Hay, born in 1860. Isabelle Long Hay died June 28, 1906.

"Uncle Billy," as he was fondly known, came into possession of the old mill and farm when he married. He and his wife, Ida Fomby Hay, lived on the farm owned by his father. Like his father, William Robert Hay, became a prosperous farmer and miller. The land and mill became known as Hay's Mill.

Born to William Robert Hay and Ida Fomby Hay were six sons: David William Hay, Benjamin Verne Hay, Horace Euclid Hay, Kyle Forrest Hay, James Fomby Hay, and Charlie Hay who died as an infant.

Horace Euclid Hay married Bernice Nixon from Jacksonville, Alabama. They had three children: Anita Frances Hay, Horace Edgar Hay, and Eugene Hay. Horace Euclid Hay was born August 13, 1894, and died June 5, 1940. Anita Frances Hay married Charles Lawrence. Their daughter, Anita Lawrence, married Thurman Douglas Jones of Carrollton and still resides in Carroll County. They have two daughters, Katrherine Frances Jones and Laura Elizabeth Jones.

James Fomby (Bay) Hay, born May 31, 1898, married Sara Helen Shaw, born October 16, 1906. They lived on a portion of the original Hay's Mill farm for their entire fifty-year marriage and had three children: Margaret Ida Hay, Jacqueline (Jackie) Elizabeth Hay, and James David Hay. Their son, James David Hay, still resides in the home built by his father. James Fomby Hay died June 2, 1975, and Sara Helen passed away October 13, 1993.

Margaret married Nick Dobson of Philadelphia, Pennsylvania. They adopted one son, Michael Hay Dobson. Jackie married Bill Ray Talley of Carrollton. They have one daughter, Jody Elizabeth Talley, who married Danny Butler of Lineville, Alabama. They reside in Carroll County where she teaches at Carrollton Elementary School. David Hay married Ginger Ione Creech of Metter, Georgia. They have two children, James David Hay Jr. and Melanie Ginger McNair, and three grandchildren, Carrielee Crenshaw, Karen Crenshaw, and James Conner Hay. *Submitted by: Jackie Talley, 230 S. Lakeshore Drive, Carrollton, GA 30117*

625. William Franklin Hayes

Son of William L. Hayes

The Hays family was in Carroll County way before 1882, when my great-grandfather William Franklin Hayes and my great-grandmother Amanda Cathrine Ferrell were married at the home of her parents, John Thomas Ferrell and Melissa A. Holder, in Bowdon, Carroll County, Georgia. Although William Franklin was raised Baptist and was married by G.M. Burson, a Baptist minister, they attended the Midway United Methodist Church at Bowdon. Their twelve children were all baptized in that church and are documented in the church register. They are as follows: (1) Mary Malissie Hayes, born 21 July 1883, died 8 June 1887 in Bowdon. (2) Sarah Jane Serena Hayes, born 14 August 1886, married John Wiggins on 26 December 1903 in Bowdon. (3) Milton Franklin Hayes, born 8 June 1888. (4) Dura May Hayes, born 14 July 1890, married Wesley Ward. (5) John Wesley Hayes, born 11 March 1892, married Hattie Vance on 18 October 1915. (6) Nancy Elizabeth Hayes, born 8 February 1894, married on 26 December 1911 to James E. Leflar, born in 1872. (7) William Sappington Hayes, born 10 November 1896, married Sarah Ann (Annie) Campbell, born 25 March 1886. (8) George Washington Hayes, born 27 September 1897, died 2 June 1889 in Bowdon. (9) Albert Cearcy Hayes, born 10 June 1899, married Ola Loyd/Lloyd in 1924. (10) James Morris Hayes, born 27 March 1901, married Ernestine Cowdry in 1925. (11) Homer Reeves Hayes, born 13 November 1904, married Gladys Amanda McAdams on July 19, 1924. She was born 13 January 1906. (12) Loyd Elbert Wilson Hayes, born 22 September 1907, married first to Sammie Jackson in 1924, and second to Ethel Helfley Jones in 1937.

The Hays family operated a sawmill near Bowdon and did some farming on the side. They moved back and forth across the border of Georgia and Alabama, sometimes residing in Arab or Dime, Alabama.

William L. Hays and Mary E. Turner Hays

The coming of railroads about 1875 assured more lumber was needed to lay the track. The railroads also made it easier for the farmers to ship their farm crops to other areas for better pay. In the early 1900s, farming in the Carroll County area was being replaced by manufacturing, so after the death of William Franklin Hayes' parents, William L. Hays and Mary E. Turner, in June of 1911, William Franklin relocated his family to Haskell County, Texas. He lived there only three years as a Texan before his death in 1914 at age fifty-three. William F. had siblings in the Carroll County area, one of whom was Cathrine Ferrell. George relocated his family to Holland in Bell County, Texas. Another sibling, Cloie Emeline (Emma) Hayes, born 1855, married William Allen Craft. They were married before 1844 and several of their children were baptized and documented in the Midway United Methodist Church in Bowdon. Cloie Hayes and William Craft are buried at the Midway United Methodist Church Cemetery. Somehow the name has been changed from Hays to Hayes. Descendants in Texas are still farming. *Submitted by: Lorrie Hayes Willis, PO Box 171, Eden, TX 76837 and Written by: Emily Hayes Willis*

626. The Head Family

James M. Head, born in 1762 in Virginia, bought lot #100 in Carroll County, Georgia, in 1833. James married Margaret Roberts, born 1775, daughter of William and Mary Williams Roberts, on February 4, 1795, in Oglethorpe County, Georgia. They had several children. My ancestor, Daniel Baldwin Head, born January 20, 1803, was one of them. Daniel married Harriet Pearson on November 28, 1822, in Jasper

County, Georgia. Their children were James R. (1823), William Jefferson (1827), James M. (1830), Nancy Elizabeth (1832), Henry C. (1839), Charles P. (1845), Harriett Lucinda (1847), and Arteminia A. (1848).

After Harriett died, Daniel B. married Malissa (family tradition says she was an Arrington), born May 30, 1819 in Georgia. No proof has ever been found to the effect that she was an Arrington. Their children were Virginia Pocahontas (1853), Benjamin Franklin (1853), Bonita Ann (1856), and Jobie Lee (1862).

Virginia Pocahontas "Poky" married Quintus Cincinnatus Lycurgus Bailey, born November 1846, son of William Hubbard and Cynthia Adaline Chandler Bailey, on October 29, 1869, in Haralson County, Georgia. Their children were Leona (1871), Abbie May (1876), Myrtle Ivanonnan (1878), Dannie (female) (1881), and Douglas Head (1887). Quintus Cincinnatus Lycurgus was a farmer, public school teacher, and inventor. He died from heart trouble on August 15, 1902. He is buried at Posey's Mill Cemetery in Winston County, Alabama, where the family was living at that time.

James M. Head died April 23, 1848. His wife died June 1, 1852. Both are buried on lot #100 in Carroll County, Georgia. Both were members of the County Line Baptist Church.

Daniel Baldwin Head was a farmer and a physician. Around 1875, he moved his family from Georgia to Aurora, Marshall County, Alabama. They lived in the area until their deaths. Dr. Head, Malissa, Poky, Benjamin Franklin, Bonita Ann, and Jobie Lee are all buried at Buffington Memorial Cemetery, Aurora, Alabama.

Dr. Head died August 16, 1881, according to the date on his tombstone. Malissa's death was unusual according to the *Guntersville Democrat,* dated June 3, 1896. Benjamin Frank was bringing his mother, age seventy-eight, to Guntersville, Alabama, to have a sevile cataract removed from her eye. When turning the corner near the Southern Hotel, the buggy became tilted and Mrs. Head was thrown out. She struck on curb stones and sustained painful bruises on the head and back. The next morning, even though she was suffering, she asked Dr. Sullivan to proceed to remove the cataract, which was done. She went into a coma and about eight o'clock Sunday night passed away.

Abbie May Bailey, daughter of Quintus Cincinnatus Lycurgus and Poky Head Bailey, married Clarence Miller Taylor, son of John Dykes and Virginia Patton Taylor, in November 1894 in Guntersville. Their children were Quintus Donovan (1878), Jennie Lorene, Clarence Douglas, Katherine Myrtle, and Leo Miller.

Quintus Donovan Taylor married LoRee Grant, daughter of Charles M. and Minnie Lee Mayne Grant, in September 1924 in Guntersville. Their children are Betty Jean Taylor, retired public school teacher, and Quintus Donovan Taylor Jr., photographer. *Submitted by: Ms. Betty Taylor, 344 Hill Avenue, Guntersville, AL 35976-1114*

Sources: Census records, cemetery records, *Head History* by Garland Jr.; *Memories of Georgia.*

627. Head - Barron

William Head Sr., born about 1745 in Orange County, Virginia, and died in 1808 in Putnam County, Georgia, married Mary Williams in 1771. His family was first found in Georgia in 1786. He was a Revolutionary War soldier. They had three sons and two daughters.

James Head, son of William Head Sr., born in Lunenburg County, Virginia, in 1762 and married Margaret Roberts in Oglethorpe County, Georgia, in 1795. He moved to Elbert County, Georgia, in 1795. James was a farmer and a Primitive Baptist minister. They had seven sons and six daughters. In 1833, James bought land lot 100 in Carroll County, Georgia. Land lot 100 consisted of 202½ acres for which he paid $400. By 1838 they had built a home here. This became known as the Head Mill place which was a large two-story house with double decked porch supported by Corinthian columns situated at the top of a wooded hill looking down on a three-story merchant mill on Wolf Creek. James died in 1848 and Margaret died after 1849. Both are buried in the family cemetery on land lot 100 near their home.

Polly Head, daughter of James and Margaret, was born in 1796 and died in 1877 in Carroll County. She married John Barron, son of Samuel Barron who came to America from Ireland prior to the Revolution and settled in Virginia. I don't know when John came to Carroll County.

Oliver Gaines Barron was John and Polly's oldest son. He was born in 1817 and died in 1904. He is buried at Mt. Zion Baptist Church in Douglas County. He married Clementine Brown, daughter of John and Sarah Curruthers, who lived in Carroll County. Oliver Gaines Barron had four children by Clementine. Clementine died in 1855. Their daughter, Mary Jane, married Walter Camp in 1868. She was born in 1857 and died in 1919. She is buried in the Camp Family cemetery on Camp home place. The rest of this family history will be in the Camp line. *Submitted by: Jodi Foster, 603 Lovinggood Tr., Woodstock, GA 30179, and Written by: Thelma Pate*

628. Charles S. and Mabel Worthan Heard

Charles Spurgeon Heard was born June 14, 1897 in Omaha, Randolph County, Alabama. He was the son of John Lanier Heard and Ada Jane Camp. He was a teacher and a Baptist preacher. He received his BA degree from Mercer University and his ministerial training in Louisville, Kentucky. He died May 28, 1977. After the death of his first wife, Lucille Huffman, by whom he had one son, Charles Heard Jr., he married Mabel Wortham. They were married 14 May 1933.

Mabel and Charlie Heard

Mabel Wortham was born 3 March 1909 in Centralhatchee, Heard County, Georgia. She was the oldest of the five children of Dr. Albert Glenn Wortham, and his wife Ora Leberta Miller. Other children were Fannie Gordon Wortham Owen, Albert Glenn Wortham, Sara Wortham Yeates and Hollis Chilton Wortham. Dr. Wortham was born 23 August 1874 in Coweta County, Georgia, died 22 October 1957, Ora Leberta Miller was born 11 November 1885, died 1 July 1966. Dr. Wortham practiced medicine in Centralhatchee for 52 years. He was a graduate of the University of Georgia. His daughter remembers him making house calls in a horse and buggy before he purchased an automobile. He was often called out at night to treat his patients.

Reverend Heard preached at Beulah in Carroll County, Glenlock in Heard County, Union Hill in Randolph County, Alabama, as well as at Big Springs, Omaha, Alabama. T.J. Freeman, a former resident of Omaha, remembers him as a teacher at Omaha High School. He also taught at Glenlock in Heard County and Tyus in Carroll County.

Three sons were born to Charles and Mabel. Wortham Lanier Heard, Philip Spurgeon Heard, and James Lee Heard, now deceased. Philip Spurgeon Heard taught at Mt. Zion High School in Carroll County, Wortham Lanier Heard retired from Titusville High School, Titusville, Florida.

Mabel is still an active church member. She attends Beulah Baptist Church where she plays the piano when needed. She also plays the piano for rest homes. She has twelve grandchildren and 12 great grandchildren. *Submitted by: Mabel Wortham Heard, 45 Dixie Meadow Lane, Carrollton, GA 30117*

629. Hembree Families

After the mid-Atlantic states were settled and the population began to grow, many families moved from South Carolina to western Georgia seeking opportunities for their children and grandchildren to have farms of their own. This same desire brought several Hembree families to Carroll County in the 1830s and 1840s.

Able Owen Hembree (born 1807) headed one family. In November 1836, he acquired property in the sixth district (land lot 176); later, he purchased property in land lot 94. A.O. served the community as a member of House of Representatives from Carroll County in 1857-1858.

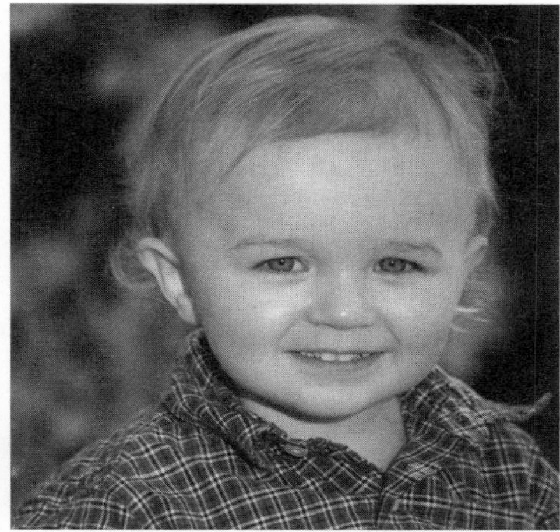

Tucker Jameson Hembree, g-g-g-grandson of Isaiah Hembree Jr.

Isaiah Hembree Sr. (1781-1853) and wife Mary "Polly" Brock (1788-1872) headed another family. In January 1841, they sold land in Spartanburg, South Carolina, and moved to Carroll County with grown sons Washington, William James Jasper, and Isaiah Jr. Isaiah Sr. was a son of William W. (1754-1821) and Orinah Hembree. He was a farmer and a veteran of the War of 1812. His family settled in the second and sixth districts, including areas later ceded to Campbell County. Just before his death in 1853, Isaiah Sr. transferred his property to Isaiah Jr. in return for "love and affection and reasonable support of my wife Mary."

Isaiah Sr.'s son Washington Hembree (1813-1862) was a Justice of the Peace in Carroll County and appears in numerous county records. He later served as captain, Company G, 41st Regiment, Georgia Volunteers, Army of Tennessee. Washington died of fever in Columbus, Mississippi in June 19, 1862.

William James Jasper Hembree (1821 South Carolina-died after 1870) married Emily "Millie" Bice (1824 South Carolina) before moving to Georgia. They arrived in Carroll County between the births of sons Milberry (1839) and Asberry (1842). William James Jasper and his wife survived the Civil War and cared for his aging mother and his wife's parents in the hard times that followed.

Isaiah Hembree Jr. (1828-1864) married Mary Long (1833-1881). Isaiah Jr. supported his mother until volunteering for military service

Fred Hembree, g-grandson of Isaiah Hembree Jr., and son James David

in August 1861. He served as first sergeant; Company E, 35th Regiment, Georgia Volunteer Infantry. His regiment fought in many of the great battles of the war including Mechanicsville, Second Bull Run, Harpers Ferry, Antietam, and Gettysburg. Isaiah Jr. was critically wounded on May 6, 1864, during the Battle of The Wilderness and died two days later.

Back home, the Hembree families struggled to survive. According to family stories, "Yankee soldiers were going house-to-house looking for food and valuables during Sherman's march to the sea. Isaiah Jr.'s infant son William was thrown to the floor when the soldiers flipped the mattress over to look for hidden money. They took everything that could be eaten, except a sack of salt."

Descendants of these original Hembree families continue to live in Carroll and surrounding counties. A family reunion is held each year on the second Sunday in April at Flat Rock Baptist Church on Flat Rock Road south of Villa Rica. All family and friends are invited. *Submitted by: David Hembree, 3560 Valley Hill Rd., Kennesaw, GA 30152*

630. The Charles Kennon Henderson, Jr. Family

Charles Kennon Henderson Jr. was born to Charles Kennon Henderson and Gertha Leary Long March 18, 1877, in Cedartown, Georgia. Graduating Emory 1900, he came to Carrollton as superintendent of schools. In Carrollton, he met Eleanor "Nell" Louise Mandeville (1880-1956), daughter of the Leroy Clifton Mandevilles. Charles and Nell married August 20, 1908, in Carrollton Presbyterian Church, where for many years thereafter he served as elder and Sunday school superintendent, and she played the organ. For a few years Charles was Newnan School superintendent. When they returned to Carrollton, Charles managed Carroll Realty and Insurance Company twenty years.

Twice he represented Carroll County in the Georgia State legislature. While in office, Charles worked to establish a college in Carrollton. This goal was realized in West Georgia College, but he did not live to see it. During his second term, Charles became suddenly ill. Leaving the session early, he returned home to Carrollton. He was diagnosed with pneumonia that evening and died the next day February 15, 1931, age 51. Charles, Nell, and daughter Janet are buried in Carrollton Cemetery.

The Hendersons had three children: Mandeville (1909-1992), Janet (died at birth, 1915), and Kennon (born 1918). Kennon recalls starting Maple Street School when she was not quite five. Being younger than six meant she had to take a $2/month tuition payment to the teacher. However, due to crowded conditions, after only three weeks, Kennon, Glen Hogan, Etta Williamson, and Mary Scott, were transferred to College Street School, returning to Maple Street for second through sixth grades.

Several years after her father died, Kennon and her mother built a home at 105 Rome Street. Kennon attended Carrollton High School where she played basketball and debated, graduating 1933. She remembers the home economics students prepared wonderful, hot lunches for fifteen cents. Pastimes included meeting friends at the square to walk, talk, and perhaps buy a five-cent Coke. Also, there were prom parties at the high school in which girls would fill a card with names of boys who asked them to walk. Each walk consisted of a round trip between two designated lampposts, one at each end of the school block. Of course, teachers were on hand to chaperon!

Charles and Nell Henderson, son Mandeville, 1912

Kennon attended Agnes Scott College, then the University of Georgia, graduating 1938 in journalism. While at GAB Business School in Macon, she was asked by Mr. Ingram, the president of the A & M, to teach physical education during summer and afterwards to be secretary to Mr. Gunn, Dean of Men. She did this, later becoming secretary to Mr. Ingram.

December, 1942 Kennon entered the WAVES. An ensign after training, she became a full lieutenant by war's end. Working in communications (cryptography), she was stationed in Charleston and Pearl Harbor.

November 23, 1946, in Carrollton Presbyterian Church, Kennon married E. Douglas Patton, son of Ezra Dillon Patton, from Laurens, South Carolina. They had met several years earlier through a blind date arranged by Doug's brother Henry Patton and his wife Mary who lived in Carrollton. Kennon and Doug eventually settled in Greenville, South Carolina, where they owned

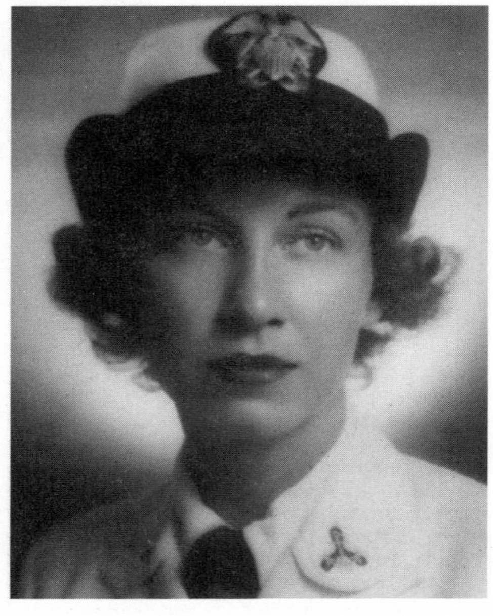

Kennon Blair Henderson, 1943 - WAVES

Patton Farms and later Patton Company Realty. They had three daughters: Blair (Mrs. Tom Greene of Lincoln, Rhode Island), Jean (Mrs. Kriss Preston of Huntsville, Alabama, and Susan (Mrs. Kaarel Hamersky of Woodland Hills, California). Widowed in 1993, Kennon still resides in Greenville. *Submitted by: Mrs. Blair Patton Greene, 14 Anna Sayles Rd., Lincoln, RI 02865-3812*
Source: Interview with my mother Kennon Henderson Patton

631. The William A. Hendon Family

William A. Hendon b. 1804 Oglethorpe County, Ga. m. Mary "Polly" Lassister, daughter of Benjamin Lassister, the first marriage recorded in Campbell County 29 Mar 1829. After moving to Carroll County he was elected Ordinary of the county 27 Jan 1852 and served until his death in 1853, Aug. 10. He is buried in the old original part of the Carrollton City Cemetery.

His estate was administrated by Rev. Israel Hendon, thought to be his father. They were members together at County Line Primitive Baptist Church in the 3rd district of Carroll near the county line. The property on South Street in Carrollton was sold and Mary "Polly" Hendon moved to old Carrollton near Sand Hill, where she is buried in the Old Carrollton Primitive Baptist Cemetery.

Children: 1. Eustalia Hendon b. 1836 m. William M. Jones 22 Dec 1857, both are buried in the old part of Carrollton City Cemetery. 2. Melissa Ann Hendon b. 1836 m. 9 Feb 1854 in Coweta County, to James Madison Wester, bur. County Line near Center Point. 3. Benjamin Hendon b. 1839. 4. Elizabeth J. Hendon b. 1842 m. Penn Watson, a landowner in Douglas County. 5. Susan Mariah Hendon b. 1843 m. Valentine B. Dale, moved to Calif. 6. Jackson Polk Hendon b. 1844 m. Mary Clark Powell 12 Aug 1867, Carroll County, Ga. 7. Mary Malvina Hendon b. 1846 m. John T. Norman 20 June 1867, Carroll County, Ga. He was a Justice of the Peace and Confederate veteran. 8. Emma Hendon, twin b. 1850 m. J. Thomas Upshaw 28 Apr 1870. 9. Ellan Hendon, twin died before she was 10 years old. *Submitted by: Charles Wester, Cumming, GA and Written by: June Hart Wester, 133 Mountain Crest Drive, Canton, GA 30114*
Sources: Ruby Wester Middlebrooks research material; Bible records of Lassister family; state records; Ted O. Brooke research.

632. Jesse Herman Hendrix and Eula Mae Hammonds Hendrix

Jesse was born Feb. 5, 1902 in the Roopville community. His parents were George Pendleton "Penn" Hendrix and Minnie Flora Carden. Penn was born in 1881 Coweta County. Penn's parents were Jim and Rosie Fuller Hendrix and they moved to Carroll County before 1898. Minnie was born in Paulding County in 1883 to Issam and Barbara Pritchet Carden. Her parents also moved to Carroll County before 1898. Penn and Minnie were married in 1898 in Carrollton and were parents of eight children who lived to adulthood: Jesse, Render, Grady, Elmer, Aubrey, Winfred, Fannie, and Pearl.

As a young man, Jesse and his parents attended Bethesda Baptist Church. Eula, born 1903, and her parents, Noah and Lizzie Davidson Hammonds who lived in Randolph County, Alabama, attended many church revivals together. This is where Jesse and Eula met. They were married in 1920 by Justice of the Peace, Lee Steed, while sitting in a buggy on Bethesda Church Road at Bonners Gold Mine Road. Joe L. Veal was the witness.

Jesse was a farmer for many years. He later began to work in the mills. They had nine children, eight who lived to adulthood: Vella died young and is buried in the Bethesda Cemetery along with Penn and Minnie, Herman, Jesse "Buddy," Ruby, Robert Milford, Betty, James Alfred, and the twins Elsie and Ellen.

Jesse and Eula shared fifty years together. At any gathering of their children there is a discussion on the great memories of their mother's wonderful biscuits, fried chicken, banana puddings and orange slice cakes. Jesse died in Columbus where they had later moved, just days after celebrating their 50th wedding anniversary. Eula moved back to Carroll County where she died in 1987. They both are buried in Parkview Cemetery in Columbus.

Hendrix Family

Jesse was a Deacon at Yellow Dirt Baptist Church and Pleasant Hill Baptist. He also was a representative from these churches to the Baptist Association. While living in the Whitsburg and Roopville area, he became a Third Degree Mason.

Their children and descendents today extend from coast to coast. Herman and Jesse live in Carroll County, Ruby lived in Oklahoma and is buried there, Robert is buried beside his parents in Columbus, Betty lives in Florida, James Alfred in Oregon, Elsie in Alabama and Ellen in Columbus. They had twenty grandchildren and many great and great-great-grandchildren. *Submitted by: Jesse Thurman "Buddy" Hendrix, 36 Lakeshore Drive, Temple, GA*
Sources: Family records and personal knowledge

633. James A. and Anna (Wynn) Henry

James A. Henry (born March 5, 1849, Carroll County) is the youngest of five children born to William Thomasson Henry (born ca 1820) and Eleanor "Leah" Turner (born ca 1826, Georgia). James is shown on the 1850 census of Carroll County as approximately six months old. Ten years later on the 1860 census of Carroll County he is nine years old and shown with his older four siblings: Samuel H. 18, Thomas Larkin 18, William Riley 14, Amanda 12, living with his paternal grandmother, Lucy Henry 60, in Whitesburg.

What happened to his parents, William T. and Eleanor (Turner) Henry is unknown. James and his brothers and sister lived with Lucy until they married and left home, with the exception of his brother Samuel H. who enlisted in the Confederate army on July 17, 1861, joining Company F, 7th Georgia Regiment. He died in a hospital a month later on August 22, 1861. He was only eighteen or nineteen years old.

James A. Henry married Anna Wynn (born May 4, 1855, South Carolina) on November 17, 1872, in Carroll County, Georgia. Anna was the daughter of Josiah Wynn (born November 15, 1827) and Sarah (born ca 1829, South Carolina). Josiah and Sarah are buried at St. Paul's Methodist Church on Jones Mill Road outside of Whitesburg.

Anna Wynn Henry

James was a farmer and lived all around Carroll County during his life. In 1870 he was nineteen years old and still living with his grandmother Lucy in Whitesburg. The 1880 census shows James and Anna married with three children living in the 642 Militia District. In 1890 they were most likely in Alabama where their eighth child and only daughter, Effie Loovela Henry, who was born February 10, 1892. They were back in Carroll County by 1895. In 1900 they were living in the 713 Militia District of Carroll County and had ten children by this time.

The census taken on Janaury 8, 1920, shows James and Anna with their youngest son, Paul L., living in Banning. They both passed away within six months. James died March 1, 1920, and Anna died June 3, 1920, both at Banning where they were living. They are buried in the Whitesburg Cemetery beside their youngest son Paul L. Henry and great-granddaughter, Shirley Ann Henry.

James A. Henry

James and Anna had ten children, at least forty-eight known grandchildren of whom approximately ten are still living in the Whitesburg area along with their children and grandchildren. James and Anna's children were: (1) William Thomas, (born October 9, 1873, died November 24, 1933, Carroll County) married Missouri I. (Albright?) ca 1892 in Alabama (?) They are buried in the Carrollton City Cemetery, Section C. (2) Edgar "Ed" G., (born June 1876, died unknown) married Berta Bliss Bonner on February 14, 1901, in Carroll County. He moved to New York. Place of burial unknown. (3) Robert Frank, (born November 1879, died unknown) married Lila Conner on November 23, 1902, in Carroll County. They are buried in LaGrange, Georgia. (4) Loon Clifford, (born May 15, 1881, died June 6, 1924) married Maud Idella Merrell on March 29, 1903, in Carroll County. They are buried at Macedonia Baptist Church in Carroll County. (5) John Chandler, (born December 21, 1883, died March 4, 1969) married Nora Bradberry on January 7, 1907, in Carroll County. They are buried at Bethany Christian Church in Carroll County. (6) Grover Cleveland, (born July 17, 1886, died November 28, 1967) married Susie Bass on September 27, 1908, in Carroll County. They are buried at St. Paul's Methodist Church in Carroll County. (7) Barney Pounds, (born April 9, 1889, died October 29, 1944) married Eva Bass on December 6, 1908, in Carroll County. They are buried at Mt. Zion Baptist Church in Dallas, Georgia. (8) Effie Loovela, (born February 10, 1892, died June 24, 1962) married Paul Tolbert on September 10, 1911, in Carroll County. They are buried at Banning Church of God in Whitesburg, Georgia. (9) Alva O., (born May 12, 1895, died June 11, 1988) married Eva Watts on November 29, 1914, in Carroll County. They are buried at Banning Church of God in Whitesburg. (10) Paul L., (born April 9, 1898, died May 4, 1923) never married. He served in Europe in World War I. He is buried in the Whitesburg Cemetery beside his mother and father. *Submitted by: Rev. Jimmy O. Henry, 304 East McIntosh Circle, Whitesburg, GA 30185, and Written by: Evelyn Henry Green.*

634. Lucy (Thomasson) Henry

Lucy Thomasson, fifth child of William Pollard and Mary Ann (Reeves) Thomasson, was born April 27, 1794. She was born in Granville County, North Carolina, before her parents moved to South Carolina. She was reared in York District where she married Samuel Henry on August 17, 1814, when she was twenty years old. Samuel was the son of James Henry and Lydia Neely and the brother of Jane Henry who had married Lemuel Thomasson five years earlier.

About 1832, Samuel and Lucy moved into Georgia along with other members of the Thomasson family. The first record we have of them in Georgia is in Coweta County. Their home was located in Land Lot 41 in the Fifth District of Coweta. This land lot consisted of 101-¼ acres.

Adversity soon struck when Samuel died in June 1841. Lucy was forty-seven years old at the time of her husband's death, and Samuel would have been a few years older — a man in the prime of his life. Samuel's handwritten will is still on file at the Coweta County Court House. Only two children are mentioned in Samuel Henry's will and, as far as is known, these are their only children: (1) Mary Ann Henry (born circa 1815 in York District, South Carolina) married about 1830 in York, South Carolina, to William W. Moore (born 1810 North Carolina). (2) William Thomasson Henry (born circa 1820) married September 12, 1841, in Carroll County to Eleanor "Leah" Turner (born circa 1826 Georgia), daughter of Larkin Turner (born 1778 in South Carolina) and Leah Turner (born 1783 in Maryland).

Soon after her husband's death in June of 1841, Lucy moved to Carroll County. She probably wanted to be near her son and daughter who had settled here. She first purchased a tract of land identified as Land Lot 149 from George Millen in the Sixth District of Carroll County, but she sold this property in 1853 to Zadock Blaylock. In 1852 her son-in-law, William W. Moore, sold Lucy and his son, George A. Moore, one hundred acres of Land Lot 17 in the Fourth District of Carroll County, what is now in the city of Whitesburg. Five acres of this tract was recorded in Lucy Henry's name. This is where Lucy lived until she died in 1879 at the age of eighty-five. Her grandson, George A. Moore, looked after her as long as she lived.

What happened to Lucy's son William T. Henry is not known; he was in Carroll County in the 1850 census. It is interesting that the census taker described William's occupation as "loafer!" It is possible that something happened to William and his wife after 1850 as Lucy Henry raised his five children. One of a set of twins, Samuel H.

Henry, enlisted in the Confederate army on July 17, 1861, joining Company F, 7th Georgia Regiment. He died in a hospital a month later on August 22, 1861. Lucy Henry was appointed administrator of Samuel's estate with William W. Moore as security. His parents would have been the ones to settle his estate if they had been living. There is no record of Samuel's twin, Thomas Larkin Henry, serving in the Confederate army. The other grandchildren, William Riley Henry, Amanda Henry, and James A. Henry, lived with Lucy until they married and left home.

It is unknown at this time exactly when Lucy died or where she might be buried. It is thought she might be buried at the Whitesburg Cemetery close to where she probably lived.

Submitted by: Evelyn (Henry) Green, 273 East McIntosh Circle, Whitesburg, GA 30185

Sources: Narrative from *Thomasson Traces Vol II* written by Curtis H. Thomasson and Marjorie B. Malloy, 1995.

635. William Thomasson Henry

William Thomasson Henry, born about 1820 possibly in South Carolina, was the only son of Samuel Henry and Lucy Thomasson. Samuel and Lucy married on August 17, 1814, in York District, South Carolina, and came to Georgia around 1832 with other members of the Thomasson family. On September 12, 1841, in Carroll County, Georgia, William Thomasson Henry married Eleanor "Leah" Turner, born about 1826 in Georgia. Eleanor was the daughter of Larkin Turner, born 1778 in South Carolina, and Leah Turner, born 1783 in Maryland.

William had one sister, Mary Ann, born about 1815 in York District, South Carolina, who married William W. Moore (born 1810 in North Carolina) about 1830 in York District, South Carolina. Mary Ann and William Moore also came to Georgia around 1832 and settled in Whitesburg and raised a large family.

It is interesting to note that the 1850 census lists Williams' occupation as "loafer!" Something must have happened to William and Eleanor between 1850 and 1860, because the 1860 census shows their five children living with William's mother Lucy Henry. It is unknown where or when William and Eleanor died or where they might be buried. The children lived with Lucy until they married and left home.

The five children born to William Thomasson Henry and Eleanor (Turner) Henry are: (1) Samuel H., born 1843 in Carroll County, enlisted in the Confederate Army on July 17, 1861, in Company F, 7th Georgia Regiment from Carroll County. He died a month later, on August 22, 1861, in a hospital; (2) Thomas Larkin, born 1853 in Carroll County, married Emma C. Pollard on August 18, 1868, in Carroll County; (3) William Riley, born 1846 in Carroll County, married Mollie J. "Mary Lou" Duncan on November 14, 1868, in Carroll County; (4) Amanda, born 1848 in Carroll County, married James G. Crouch on September 12, 1870, in Carroll County; and (5) James A., born March 5, 1849, and died March 1, 1920, in Carroll County, married Anna Wynn on November 17, 1872. Anna was born May 4, 1855, and died June 3, 1920. James and Anna are buried at the Whitesburg Cemetery. *Submitted by: Jason O. Henry, 310 East McIntosh Circle, Whitesburg, GA 30185 and Written by: Evelyn Henry Green*

636. The Hesterlee Family at Sand Hill

My mother's parents were Melvis Simeon Hesterlee and Elizabeth Jane Boatright Hesterlee. Melvis Simeon was born August 5, 1832, and died June 3, 1912. Elizabeth Jane was born January 27, 1849, and died August 14, 1918. They were married on October 3, 1867, and had thirteen children. My mother, Cora Lee Hesterlee Morgan, was the eleventh child of this marriage. I never knew either of my grandparents and am the youngest living Hesterlee grandchild. Both are buried at Jordan Cemetery. For some reason, this family changed the spelling of their name to Hesterlee from Hesterly.

Melvis Simeon Hesterlee was raised in Arkansas. He enlisted in the Confederate Army in Camden, Arkansas. My mother always said that he was raised an orphan. Evidently, he was sent to Georgia and after the war he decided to stay, get married, and raise a family here in Georgia at Sand Hill.

The original home place for the Hesterlee family was located on what is now known as Lake Connie Road. It is now demolished. Their home place was very near where the creek crosses the road to form the lake.

Elizabeth Jane Hesterlee's parents were Boatright. They are also buried in the Jordan Cemetery near Sand Hill on Highway 61, just south of Bethany Christian Church. It is not known where the parents of Melvis Simeon Hesterlee are buried. Elizabeth Jane's parents were James A. Boatright and Mary C. Bell Boatright. He was born 1826 and died 1890. She was born 1827 and died 1909. Mary C. Bell Boatright's mother was Mary Bell and she lived to be one hundred three years old. She is buried at Jordan Cemetery.

Melvis Simeon and Elizabeth Jane Boatright Hesterlee

Melvis Simeon Hesterlee and Elizabeth Jane were members of Macedonia Baptist Church at Sand Hill. They raised their family in the church. This church is now known as Midway-Macedonia Baptist Church. I have one uncle, Walter Lee Hesterlee, and Aunt Ara who are buried at Macedonia. My Uncle Dalton and Aunt Pearl Hesterlee are buried at Bethany Christian Church Cemetery. I have five aunts and uncles who are buried at Jordan Cemetery: John V. Hesterlee and his three wives, James David Hesterlee and Medie Crook Hesterlee, William Preston Hesterlee, Elizabeth Evaline Hesterlee (died in infancy), Lula Jane Hesterlee Smith, who was the wife of Claude Smith. Lula Jane was killed in a tragic accident when she was only twenty-one years old. The rest of the Hesterlee children are buried in locations away from Sand Hill. Mollie Emily H. Smith is buried at Cullman, Alabama. Ida Rossania H. Gaston is buried at Friendship Baptist Church near Americus, Georgia. Othello H. Knight was buried at Hillcrest Cemetery in Villa Rica, Georgia. Marzee McCain H. Jordan is buried at Greenwood Cemetery in Atlanta, and my mother and dad, Charlie Clifton Morgan and Cora Lee Hesterlee Morgan, are buried in the Masonic section of Westview Cemetery in Atlanta, Georgia. Bessie Mae H. McCord Daniel is buried at Hillcrest in Villa Rica by her first husband, Virgil McCord. *Submitted by: Bob Morgan, 4005 Pittman Road, College Park, GA 30349-1438*

637. Matthew Hicks and His Descendants

Matthew Hicks was born in 1795 in North Carolina and died in March of 1871 in Cleburne County, Alabama. He first married on January 27, 1814, in Burke County, North Carolina, Sarah (Sally) Green who was born around 1790 in North Carolina and died in 1840 in Carroll County, Georgia. Sally was the daughter of William Green who was born on February 2, 1762, and died on March 2, 1837, and Kezziah Stroud who was born in 1763 and died on August 1, 1849, in Carroll County. William Green was a soldier in the Revolutionary War from North Carolina.

Sally's father, William Green, sold Matthew two tracts of land on the west bank of the Pigeon River near Richland Creek in Haywood County, North Carolina, in 1828, a sale that was approved by Sally's siblings. Matthew sold this land about the same time Sally's brothers moved to Carroll County. He was shown in the census as being a farmer and living in Carroll County in 1850 and living in Oaklevel, Calhoun County, Alabama, in 1860, and living near Edwardsville, Cleburne County, Alabama, in 1870. His tombstone says he died March 1868, but he was on the 1870 census roll for Cleburne County, Alabama.

Matthew and Sarah Hicks' children were: Louisa, Green, James, Malinda, John A., Isaac Crayton, Alfred, Amanda M., Nancy, and William.

Louisa Hicks was born about 1814 in North Carolina and married Abner Goodson on November 6, 1832, in Carroll County.

Green Hicks was born about 1817 in North Carolina and died between 1858 and 1859 in Carroll County, married Mahala Upton who was born in 1826 in Tennessee and died after 1870 in Texas. They were married on March 13, 1839, in Carroll County.

James Hicks was born about 1818 in North Carolina and married Caroline McElroy on December 21, 1843, in Carroll County.

Malinda Hicks was born about 1821 in North Carolina and married on July 25, 1839, Leroy Hartsfield who was born about 1816 in North Carolina.

John A. Hicks was born about 1824 in North Carolina and died between 1874 and 1880 in Alabama. He married on December 25, 1846, in McDowell County, North Carolina, Susannah Biggerstaff who was born about 1827 in North Carolina.

Isaac Crayton Hicks was born April 22, 1830, in Haywood County, North Carolina.

Alfred Hicks was born about 1832.

Amanda M. Hicks was born about 1833 in North Carolina and she married Francis M. Little on October 18, 1849 in Carroll County.

Nancy Hicks was born about 1834.

William Hicks was born about 1837 in North Carolina, and he married Virginia Watson on August 18, 1854, in Carroll County.

After Sarah (Sally) Green died, Matthew married his second wife, Laura Louise (Louisa) McElroy on December 21, 1843, in Carroll County. She was the daughter of William McElroy and Nancy Johnson. Louisa McElroy was born January 4, 1818, in Georgia and died December 24, 1902, in Cleburne County, Alabama. Matthew and Louisa relocated from Carroll County to Cleburne County, Alabama, where he lived on his approximately 500-acre farm and tended his store with the help of his son Moses until his death. Matthew and Louisa Hicks and several of their relatives are buried at Bethel Cemetery, and other relatives are buried in the Mars Hill Primitive Baptist Church Cemetery. Both cemeteries are located in the Muscadine, Alabama, area.

Matthew and Louisa Hicks' children were Thomas Edwin, Jasper A., Andrew Jackson, Eliza Jane, and Moses.

Thomas Edwin Hicks was born June 9, 1844, in Carroll County and died February 16, 1908, in Cleburn County, Alabama. Thomas Edwin married Sarah J.N. (last name unknown) in 1866 in

Hicks - John, Eliza Jane, Lula, and Esta at 1897 Leatherwood Reunion

Cleburne County. Thomas Edwin Hicks enlisted as a private in Company H, 1st Georgia Cavalry in Kingston, Tennessee in August 1862 and served until April of 1865, CSA, Civil War.

Jasper A. Hicks was born May 1846 in Georgia and married about 1868 to Jane (last name unknown) who was born about 1839 in Alabama. Jasper married about 1890 his second wife, Susan (name unknown).

Andrew Jackson Hicks was born in February 1848 in Georgia and married M.K. "Haley" Williams about 1867. Andrew Jackson married about 1896 his second wife Barta S. (last name unknown) who was born in 1873 in Georgia.

Eliza Jane Hicks was born in 1858.

Moses Hicks was born March 22, 1859, and died October 3, 1941, in Cleburne County, Alabama. Moses married about 1876 to Dicey Shealy who was born January 1858 in South Carolina and died March 2, 1929.

One of Matthew and Sarah Hicks' children was Isaac Crayton Hicks who was born April 22, 1830, in Haywood County, North Carolina, and died May 4, 1887, in Carroll County and married on December 10, 1848, in Carroll County Eliza Jane Richards who was born in Febraury 1831 and died in 1910 in Carroll County. They are probably buried at New Georgia Baptist Cemetery in Paulding County, Georgia.

Eliza Jane Richards had a brother, John Richards, who owned a circus. From time to time, they came across country and put the circus down in a clump of trees on the south side of New Georgia Church in Paulding County. All the relatives looked forward to their coming because they were given free tickets to the circus. On one of these trips across country, the Richards stopped for the night and sent their two daughters, Mary and Gould, to a spring to get water. Mary saw some flowers above the spring and told her sister she was going to pick a bouquet to take back to the campsite. Suddenly, Indians came out of the bushes and captured her. It has been told that her father befriended the Indian chief and he was allowed to attend an Indian festivity. One of the Indians had Mary back of him on his horse. John quickly rode by and swung her back of him on his horse. As they were escaping, one of the Indians shot Mary in the hip. They managed to get away and Mary recovered from her injury, but she was left with a bad limp the rest of her life. Family members said that she later wrote a book that told of her horrible experiences while she was held captive by the Indians.

Isaac Crayton Hicks was a farmer and lived next door to his brother Green Hicks, and cousins Nancy Green Wynn and Rebecca Green Cansler in Carroll County in 1850. He lived in Hickory Level in Carroll County in 1860 and he was a farmer and lived in Paulding County in 1870 and 1880. His farm was located south of New Georgia Baptist Church on Highway 61 in Paulding County.

Isaac Crayton entered the Civil War on May 1862 as a substitute for Newton Roberts, private in Company I, 56th Regiment, Georgia Volunteer Infantry, Army of Tennessee, CSA. He received a disability discharge on November 25, 1863.

*Isaac Crayton and Eliza Jane Hicks' children were Mahala Elizabeth, Francis Marion, James (Jim), Amanda, Denmon A., John Columbus, Albert, Allas (Alice), and Julie.

*Mahala Elizabeth was born about 1851.

*Francis Marion Hicks was born January 22, 1853, in Carroll County and died on March 20, 1925, in Cullman County, Alabama, married about 1875 Nancy C. (last name unknown) who was born May 11, 1849, in Georgia and died November 22, 1931. Francis Marion and Nancy C. Hicks' children were Ovelia Hicks, Ardelia, Minnie, Victoria, L. Adison, Radford and Lizzie L.

Ovelia Hicks was born in June of 1877 in Georgia and married on June 14, 1903, in Cullman County, Alabama, Leon J. McCravey who was born in 1867 in Texas. Ovelia and Leo McCravey's children were Dewey, Lola, Myrtle, Loyd, Ruth and Eva.

Ardelia Hicks was born about 1879.

Minnie Hicks was born in September of 1881 and she married Elmer E. Suggs on October 30, 1902, in Cullman County, Alabama.

Victoria Hicks was born in 1883 and married George E. Suggs on January 11, 1903, in Cullman County. George E. Suggs was born about 1882 in Alabama and he was a general merchandise merchant and lived in Vinemont Beat in Cullman County in 1920. George and Victoria Suggs' children were Alma L., Floyd B. and Jewel C.

L. Adison Hicks was born March 17, 1886, in Georgia and died October 12, 1918, in Cullman County.

Radford Hicks was born April 14, 1888 in Georgia and died on November 2, 1919, in Cullman County.

Lizzie L. Hicks was born in January 1894 in Alabama and married John Bagwell who was born about 1891 in Georgia. They were married on December 1, 1912, in Cullman County. Lizzie L. and John Bagwell's children were James T., Lillie M. and Faye.

*James (Jim) Hicks was born February 22, 1854, in Carroll County and died July 8, 1915, in Paulding County, Georgia. He married Sarah Cole who was the daughter of Tillman Cole and Mary Francis Fuller of Paulding County. Sarah was born about 1859 and died about 1936 in Paulding County. Both are buried at New Georgia Baptist Cemetery in Paulding County. According to Etta Hicks Hitchcock of Paulding County, Sarah Cole Hicks' great-grandfather, a Mr. Fuller, gave the land for New Georgia Baptist Church and cemetery. New Georgia Baptist Church was named for Mr. Fuller's wife, Georgia. Sarah Cole Hicks' brother was Jeff Cole, who was an attorney in Villa Rica, Georgia for many years. Jim Hicks was a farmer. James (Jim) and Sarah Hicks' children were John, Ada Ann, Henry Datson, Bertis (Bert), Samuel Walker, Velma, Emmett Gordon, Olma Lee, and Etta May.

John Hicks was born on April 1, 1879, and died October 6, 1938. He married Savannah Miller who was born on September 12, 1881. Her death is unknown. They are buried at Union Church Cemetery in Paulding County. John and Savannah Hicks' children were W. Luther, Howard, Dolly, Oko, Jimmy and J.C.

Ada Ann Hicks was born on April 8, 1881, and died May 19, 1954. She married James Frank Browning whose birth and death are unknown. They are buried at New Georgia Baptist Cemetery in Paulding County. Ada and James Frank (Bud) Browning's children were Francis (Fannie), Annie Mae, and James Aubrey.

Henry Datson Hicks was born in 1882 and died in 1967, married Mattie Pithey Cole who was born in 1888 and died in 1984. They are buried in Melrose Cemetery in Paulding County. Henry Datson and Mattie Pithey Hicks' children were Birma, Jeff, Eutah, Etta, Wilburn H. and Ezell.

Bertis (Bert) Hicks was born in 1887 and died in 1968. Bert is buried in New Georgia Baptist Cemetery in Paulding County. Bert never married and she reared her brother Emmett's children after his wife died.

Samuel Walker Hicks was born on February 11, 1890, and died on January 31, 1951, married Elsie Louisa Matthews who was born on October 6, 1895, and died October 16, 1975. They are buried at Concord Baptist Cemetery in Paulding County. Walker and Elsie Hicks' children were Fred Eugene, Ezma, Agnes, Jewel, and Jesse Bell.

Velma Hicks was born March 24, 1892 and died January 29, 1986, married Zack Wix who was born August 24, 1893, and died November 1, 1942. Zack Wix was a private first class in the U.S. Army in World War I, and he is buried at New Georgia Baptist Cemetery in Paulding County. Velma Wix is buried at White Oak Cemetery in Paulding County. Velma and Zack Wix's children were Ralph and James.

Emmett Gordon Hicks was born August 27, 1894, and died August 13, 1983. Emmett first married Ada Bethany Roberts who was born April 4, 1901, and died May 17, 1941. Emmett and Bethany Hicks' children were Ernest Guy, Sallie Faye, Ila Mae, Ima Ree, Lillie Bea, Minnie Lee, Willie Tee, Reba Nell, Lyndal Vinnie and George.

Emmett Hicks married his second wife, Mary Nell Morris who was born May 10, 1924. Emmett and Mary Nell Hicks' children are Mary Maxine and James Gordon.

Olma Lee Hicks was born November 16, 1896, and died October 3, 1953, married Nathan C. Roberts who was born on September 2, 1896, and died June 7, 1981. They are buried at New Georgia Cemetery in Paulding County. Olma and Nathan Roberts' children were Hugh M. and Violet Mae.

Etta May Hicks was born on November 20, 1901, and died on January 29, 1908, in Paulding County. She is buried at New Georgia Baptist Cemetery.

James (Jim) Hicks' descendants hold degrees from schools of higher learning: Two of these descendants hold doctorate's degrees; one is professor in the School of Nursing at the University of North Carolina in Charlotte; and one holds a doctor of jurisprudence and a CPA status. She is an attorney and is a co-owner in a law firm in Atlanta, where she practices corporate and real estate law. Others hold bachelor's degrees; one is a R.N. at Dallas (Georgia)

Hospital; one is a senior accounts coordinator for Blue Cross/Blue Shield Insurance; and one was a teacher in Villa Rica High School; one is a director of Cooper-Green Hospital Foundation in Birmingham, Alabama; one is an engineer with United Airlines in San Francisco, California; one holds an A.S. degree and is a manager of an auto leasing company; one graduated from Gupton-Jones College of Funeral Service in Atlanta, and he is a mortician with Almon Funeral Home in Carrollton; one retired as a respiratory therapist from Tanner Hospital in Villa Rica, Georgia, with thirty years service time. One is the city manager of Bowdon, Georgia; three are teachers and two accountants. One is a minister; one is a gospel singer, two are married to ministers; many own businesses; one owned a flower shop and presently owns a carpet business; one owns a well drilling company; one is a residential builder; one owns an asphalt paving company; one owns a real estate business; one owns a mortgage business; one owns an antique business; several owned poultry businesses; and one is chief of police for Dallas, Georgia.

*Amanda Hicks was born April 20, 1858, and died October 4, 1901, in Paulding County. Amanda married General Marion Cole who was born December 4, 1856, and died April 7, 1944, in Paulding County. General Cole was the son of Samuel Craton (S.C.) Cole who is buried off Marshall Fuller Road in Paulding County. General and Amanda Cole are buried at New Georgia Baptist Cemetery in Paulding County. According to Clyde Cole of Paulding County, General Cole was a farmer and he owned a 250-acre farm, and at that time, the New Georgia Store and a sawmill in Paulding County. Amanda and General Cole's children were Samuel Craton, James Henry (Bud) and Savannah.

Samuel Craton Cole was born on January 21, 1879, and died March 24, 1956. Samuel Craton married Nancy Leatherwood who was born on December 26, 1880, and died June 12, 1963. They are buried at Hill Crest Cemetery in Villa Rica. Samuel Craton and Nancy Cole's children were William Clifford, Herman E., Walter Raleigh, Fred Watson, Clara, Lillie, Pauline and Lee.

James Henry (Bud) Cole, was born June 4, 1881, and died May 19, 1959, in Paulding County. James Henry married Pearl Land who was born November 21, 1886, and died December 1, 1972 in Paulding County. They are buried in New Georgia Baptist Cemetery, Paulding County. James Henry (Bud) and Pearl Cole's children were Price, Clyde, Roy Preston, Floy Tee, Mary Ruth, Dennis Oather and Billy.

Savannah Cole whose birth and death unknown, married P.B. (Bob) McAdams, whose birth and death unknown, of Powder Springs, Georgia, and they divorced. Savannah is buried at Westview Cemetery in Atlanta, and P.B. McAdams is buried at Smyrna Methodist Cemetery in Paulding County. Savannah and P.B. McAdams' children were Maud, Clarence, Beulah, Louise and Wallace.

Amanda Hicks Cole's descendants hold degrees from colleges and universities. One holds a doctorate's and is a medical doctor in California. One holds a master's and was employed at Thomas A. Eidson Industries in Atlanta in duplicating machines, and later held the position as counselor of Villa Rica High School for many years. Others hold bachelor's degrees. They include teachers, and a residential and commercial builder. One of her descendants was a bookkeeper for a fertilizer company in Atlanta, a farmer and a cattleman. He and his wife owned an 870-acre farm, southeast of Villa Rica. Another one is ninety-two years old and still raises cattle and tends his 110-acre farm in Paulding County. His wife taught school for thirty-four years in Paulding County. One was employed with gas companies for more than thirty-five years; one owned a cement business; another owned a jewelry business in Atlanta for many years; one owned a small hosiery mill and lawn mower business in Villa Rica; one was employed at the Bank of Villa Rica for thirty-three years; one was a master sergeant in the USAF, and one served in the Army.

*Denmon A. Hicks was born in 1861 in Paulding County and died on March 17, 1921, in Carroll County; married on March 3, 1881, in Paulding County, Emma Elizabeth Pace who was born in 1862 in Paulding County, and died May 27, 1931, in Haralson County. They are buried at New Georgia Baptist Cemetery in Paulding County.

Emma Elizabeth Pace Hicks' roots have been traced to Richard Pace who married on October 5, 1608, Isabella Smith, sister of Captain John Smith in St. Dunstan's, Stepney, England. They were the Original Planters in the Jamestown Colony. Elizabeth Pace was the daughter of John B. Pace Jr. who left his wife and three children under five years of age to join the Confederate Army in late 1861. He died of measles in a training camp in Knoxville, Tennessee, on May 12, 1862, and he is buried in the Confederate Cemetery in Knoxville. Elizabeth's mother was Missouri Fuller. Elizabeth and her two brothers, William (Bill) and John Pace, were born and reared in a log house located on Marshall Fuller Road in Paulding County. This house had a very large fireplace and wooden shutters for windows.

L-R, Denmon Hicks' seven sons: Edgar, Wallie, Lonnie, Hershel, Carl, Enoch and Elbert.

Emma Elizabeth's great-grandfather was John B. Pace Sr. who was born in 1797 in Spartanburg County, South Carolina, and married Nancy Camp of Gwinnett County, in 1816. They moved to Cobb County and lived on a plantation on Sandtown Road near Noses Creek in Marietta. The first Cobb County elections were held in John B. Pace Sr.'s home in March 1833. He served one term as Justice of the Inferior Court, and he was one of the justices who helped select Marietta as the county seat and caused the courthouse and other public buildings to be constructed in Marietta. In 1819, John B. Pace Sr. moved his family to Little Pumpkinville in Paulding County where he served two terms as an associate justice of the Inferior Court during the 1850s until he retired to tend his plantation full time. His plantation was located three miles south of Dallas, Georgia.

Denmon A. and Elizabeth Hicks' children were John Edgar, O'Desser (Desser), Walter Jackson (Wallie), Dora, James Lonnie, Leila, Hershel Monroe, Eugene Carl, Janette Florence (Nettie), Enoch Irving, and Elbert Eulas.

John Edgar Hicks was born on November 7, 1883, in Paulding County and died on June 18, 1950, in Haleyville, Alabama. Edgar married Ethel Elizabeth Abercrombie who was born on August 20, 1884, and died March 31, 1945. They are buried at New Georgia Baptist Cemetery in Paulding County. Edgar and Ethel Hicks' children were Uller Wesley, Clunnie Irene, Rilla Elizabeth, and Carl Eugene.

O'Desser (Desser) Hicks was born in 1884 in Paulding County and died in 1966 in Cobb County, Georgia. Desser married Levi Samuel Lawler who was born in 1880 and died in 1938. They are buried at New Georgia Baptist Cemetery in Paulding County. Desser and Levi Lawler's children were Minnie Florence, Dollie Elizabeth, Hubert G., Bessie, Ruby and Jesse C.

Walter Jackson (Wallie) Hicks was born on April 16, 1888, in Paulding County, and died in August 8, 1961, in Corbin, Kentucky. Wallie married Anna Alma Townsend who was born on March 23, 1897, in Paulding County and died on February 19, 1958, in Corbin, Kentucky. Wallie and Alma Hicks are buried at Rest Haven Cemetery in Corbin. Wallie and Alma Hicks' children were Flossie, Ezel, Ulas, Willard, Raymond, Marvin, Edward, Bobby, Billie, Lula Belle and Barbara.

Alma and Effie Townsend married brothers, Walter Jackson (Wallie) and Hershel Hicks. Their parents were Henry J. Townsend who married Martha E. Taylor. Henry J. Townsend was the son of Menerva Pace who married James Marshall Townsend. Menerva Pace's parents were John B. Pace Sr. and Nancy Camp who were Wallie and Hershel Hicks' great-grandparents.

Dora Hicks was born on April 16, 1891, in Paulding County and died on December 2, 1913, in Paulding County. Dora married on December 12, 1912, T. Elmo Parson who was born on May 13, 1888, in Paulding County and died on December 23, 1940, in Paulding County. Dora died at age twenty-two of Bright's disease. They did not have any children and they are buried at New Georgia Cemetery in Paulding County.

James Lonnie Hicks was born on January 4, 1892, in Paulding County and died on December 18, 1957, in Fulton County, Georgia. Lonnie served in World War I (85th Depot Svc. Co. ASC). He never married and he lived with his youngest brother, Elbert Hicks, most of his life. He died of heart problems in the Veteran's Hospital in Atlanta. He is buried at New Georgia Baptist Cemetery in Paulding County.

Leila Hicks was born on February 28, 1895, in Paulding County and died on February 12, 1965, in Carroll County. Leila's first husband was Zannie Wix of Paulding County who was born August 24, 1893, and died November 9, 1942. Leila is buried at New Georgia Baptist Cemetery in Paulding County. Leila and Zann Wix's child was Gladys.

Leila's second husband was T. Elmo Parson who was born on May 13, 1888, and died December 23, 1940, in Paulding County. Leila and Elmo Parson's child was Elmer Glenn.

Hershel Monroe Hicks was born May 9, 1897, in Paulding County and died December 7, 1960, in Haralson County, first married Mattie Matthews on October 31, 1918, in Paulding County. They divorced. On February 17, 1923, he married Effie Viola Townsend who was born on June 2, 1907, in Paulding County and died January 7, 1961, in Haralson County. They are buried at New Georgia Baptist Cemetery in Paulding County. Hershel and Effie Hicks' children were Annie Ruth, James Eugene, Adell Elizabeth, Thomas Ervin, Florence Janette, and Shelby Jean.

Eugene Carl Hicks was born on July 7, 1898, in Paulding County and died on June 5, 1954, in Carroll County. Carl married Jeanie (Jean) Austin who was born on May 2, 1898, and died January 3, 1983, in Carroll County. Jean Austin's parents were Amanda Croker and James M. Austin of Paulding County. Carl and Jean Hicks are buried at Hill Crest Cemetery in Villa Rica, Georgia. Carl and Jean Hicks' children were Horace Wilbur and Harold Denmon.

Janette Florence (Nettie) Hicks was born on December 31, 1900, in Paulding County and died February 9, 1976, in Carroll County. Nettie Hicks married on December 1, 1923, Clifford Anderson Carden who was the son of Doll C. and Ella Carden of Carroll County. Clifford was born on August 16, 1903, in Paulding County and died May 30, 1974, in Carroll County. They are buried at Sunrise Memorial Gardens in Douglasville, Georgia. Clifford and Nettie Carden's children were Emma Pauline and Robert Gene (Bob).

Enoch Irving Hicks was born on April 10, 1902, in Paulding County and he died on March 6, 1986, in Cobb County. Enoch married Mary Margaret Burdett who was born on July 23, 1903, and died on November 2, 1982, in Cobb County, Georgia. They are buried at Mountain View Cemetery in Marietta. Enoch and Margaret Hicks' adopted child was Patsy. Patsy died as a result of a tonsillectomy at age six. Margaret Hicks had one son by a previous marriage, Charles Herbert Jenkins.

Elbert Eulas Hicks was born February 19, 1907, in Paulding County and died February 24, 1967, in Haralson County. Elbert's first wife was Jessie Southerland who was born on June 9, 1900, and died September 26, 1934, in Haralson County. Jessie is buried in Hollywood Cemetery in Tallapoosa, Georgia. Elbert and Jessie Hicks' child was Martha Elizabeth (Betty).

After Jessie died, Elbert married Carrilla Dobbs who was born on September 22, 1914, and died on April 12, 1978, in Haralson County. Elbert and Carrilla are buried at Bethany Cemetery in Tallapoosa. Elbert and Carrilla Hicks' children were Elbert Jr., Inez and Earnest Dean.

All of Denmon and Elizabeth Hicks' children were born and reared in the New Georgia Community of Paulding County. For many years, they lived in the area where the Georgian Resort is presently located. They were farmers and they lived on a farm that had a large fruit orchard and a hand-operated water pump that all the visiting children liked to operate. Even though, the Hickses had plenty of fruits, vegetables and meats for their large family, periodically Denmon would take the two-horse wagon to Villa Rica to his brother John's store and bring it home full of supplies, such as hoops of cheese and stalks of bananas. The children all looked forward to these trips and to their surprises.

Later, the family relocated to a large, attractive, white house which is located south of New Georgia Baptist Church on the right-hand side of Highway 61, House No. 8400, in Paulding County. The family lived at this place for many years until the boll weevil "hit," and in 1922, they relocated to Villa Rica to seek other means of livelihood. Some went to work in textiles; others sought employment elsewhere. Carl Hicks was foreman of the Villa Rica Mills for thirty-five years. One son, Wallie, relocated to Corbin, Kentucky where he retired from L&N Railroad as a car inspector with thirty-two years service time. Wallie inspected and assessed train wreck damage.

Lonnie Hicks served in World War I, and Enoch Hicks was a master sergeant in the Army and served in World War II. He retired from the Army with twenty-three years of service time. Many of Denmon and Elizabeth Hicks' descendants served in the military. A total of twenty-nine descendants served in all branches of the military; four of these descendants retired from the military.

Around 1921, Denmon suffered a stroke that paralyzed his legs and left him bedridden. Dr. J.E. Powell decided to use electric shock treatments to try to revive the feeling in Denmon's legs. Once a week, he would come out to visit him, and he would have the children encircle his bed and hold an electrical wire that would send electricity through his body. The current was so strong that it would lift them off the floor. These terrible treatments continued for awhile, but they did not help. He died in March of 1921.

Two of Denmon and Elizabeth's children were almost killed in their early years. Edgar, the oldest son, was employed as some kind of boss in one of the mines located around Villa Rica years ago. An employee was trapped when a cave-in occurred in the mine. Edgar went in to rescue him and just as he got into the mine, a big rock slid in on him. My mother told me that when they finally got Edgar out of the mine, he did not have any skin left on his body, nor fingernails, nor toenails. She said that Edgar had to be "turned in a sheet" and they thought he would surely die for many months. He survived his accident and evidently he never got over his lust for gold because in later years he relocated to Horse Shoe Bend on the Tallapoosa (Georgia) River where he panned for gold in his free time. Over a period or time, he collected a large bottle of gold nuggets which he readily displayed to any one who might be interested. During his lifetime, he farmed, was employed at a gold mine, worked for a railroad, and owned and operated a restaurant in Cedartown, Georgia.

Another son, Walter Jackson (Wallie) was almost killed in the early years. He and his brothers decided to make some firecrackers one Christmas. Wallie was holding the fireworks when it exploded and almost killed him. He lost one eye and most of a hand. That is when his father decided to send him and his brother Enoch to live with his brother, John Hicks, in Villa Rica, so they could finish school. They lived in Villa Rica and attended school during the week and went home on the weekends to help with the farm chores.

Emma Elizabeth Pace Hicks, wife of Denmon A. Hicks

Many of Denmon Hicks' descendants hold degrees from colleges and universities. One holds a master's in education specialist in instruction technology and a bachelor's in music theory and composition, and he is in Network Service Supervision for MCSi. One holds a bachelor's in business administration and has CPA status and owns an accounting firm in the Vinings, Georgia, area; and one holds a bachelor's in business administration and a technical writing certificate and is a technical writer for ADP in Alpharetta, Georgia. One holds a bachelor's in environmental science and is an environmental engineer for Water Plant Systems in the Montgomery, Alabama, area; one holds a bachelor's and is in supervision for Pac-Car in Atlanta, Georgia; one holds a bachelor's and is employed in Electronics Data Systems in Richmond, Kentucky. Two hold bachelor's and are teachers. One teaches special classes at Eastern Kentucky University. One holds a bachelor's and is employed with an investment company. Others have held high-level management positions with large companies. One was an assistant manager for the Sears, Roebuck & Company Parts Distribution Depot which serviced 600 stores and kiosks in the Southern states, Puerto Rico and Spain. Another one is district manager over fourteen K-Mart stores in the Puerto Rico area. One is an assistant manager of Computer Networking for a large school district in the Dallas, Texas area. One owns fifteen security companies in three states; one holds a heavy equipment business in Jacksonville, Florida; one owns a mobile home company in Berea, Kentucky; several are residential builders, and several own construction companies. One was a beautician and owned a beauty shop; one owns a Muzak Company. These descendants also include medical personnel, teacher's aides and bank employees. One graduated from two business schools and attended West Georgia College and retired as an engineering secretary from Lockheed Aircraft with almost thirty-six years service time. Others have retired from Lockheed Aircraft Corporation, Southern Bell, L&N Railroad, CSX Railroad, Sears, Roebuck & Company, Philco Corporation, Frigidare Corporation, Quadgraphics, Motor Convoy, Cluett-Peabody, and Associated Rubber Company.

*John Columbus Hicks was born on May 6, 1865, and died June 1, 1924, in Carroll County. He married Lizzie Lelia (Doyle or Doyal or Steed?) on February 26, 1886, in Paulding County. Lizzie Lelia was born on November 12, 1870, and died on December 8, 1893. John and Lizzie Lelia Hicks' child was Enoch Grady. Lizzie Lelia and Enoch Grady are buried at New Georgia Baptist Cemetery in Paulding County.

After Lizzie's death, John Hicks married his second wife, Mary Winnie Lula Leatherwood, daughter of Ben and Naomi Leatherwood, who was born on October 9, 1877, and died on January 26, 1961, in Atlanta. John and Lula Hicks were married on March 15, 1896, in Carroll County by S.T. Gilland. They are buried at Crest Lawn Memorial Park Cemetery in Atlanta. John Hicks was first buried at New Georgia Baptist Cemetery in Paulding County, but in October of 1947 his wife had John's body moved to Crest Lawn Cemetery in Atlanta.

John and Lula Hicks' children were Lillie Estha, Lennie Carl, Effie Jane, Wallace B., Ernest Lewie, Mary, Helen Eugenia, and Robert.

Lille Estha Hicks was born February 6, 1897, and her death is unknown. She married Albert Peevy and they did not have children. Estha was a teacher at New Georgia School in Paulding County in 1915.

Lennie Carl Hicks was born in October of 1898 and died in 1954. He married Lillian Durham. Lennie was a manager of a hosiery mill and later, president of Excello Battery Company in Columbus, Georgia.

Lennie and Lillian Hicks' children were Lennie Jr. and Marion.

Effie Jane Hicks was born on February 1, 1901, and died August 29, 1902. She is buried at New Georgia Baptist Cemetery in Paulding County.

Wallace B. Hicks was born about 1904 and his death is unknown. He married first Teresa (last name unknown). They did not have children. Wallace married his second wife, Margaret (last name unknown). They did not have children. Wallace was a bookkeeper for a fertilizer company in Atlanta in the early 1900s and later he relocated to Jacksonville, Florida, to become president of a large fertilizer company in that area. He is buried in Jacksonville.

Ernest Lewie Hicks was born on August 19, 1908, and died on December 18, 1912. He is buried at New Georgia Baptist Cemetery.

Mary Hicks was born on November 1, 1911, and she married Carl Caldwell whose birth and death are unknown. They did not have children. Mary was employed as a secretary for the *Atlanta Journal* and later promoted to an accounts executive at the *Journal*. Her husband was general manager of the *Journal*. After retirement from the *Journal*, they relocated to Radium Springs and managed the Radium Springs Resort. Mary presently resides at an assisted living facility in Fayetteville, Georgia.

Helen Eugenia Hicks was born about 1915 and her death is unknown. Helen first married a Hicks, whose first name was unknown. She later married a second husband, Leon Johnson. Helen Hicks Johnson did not have any children. Helen was employed at St. Joseph's Hospital as an office employee.

Robert Hicks was born about 1916 and his death is unknown; married Ruth Wells. Robert and Ruth Hicks' child was Linda.

Robert was a Buick salesman in Columbus, Georgia. He is buried in Columbus.

John Hicks owned a store in Villa Rica, Georgia, during the early 1900s, and he was also a landlord who lived on College Street in Villa Rica, (presently known as North Avenue). He was also involved in politics as he was shown in a group picture of the mayor and city councilmen of Villa Rica, in 1909 in the book, *History of Villa Rica.* A story has been told by one of our relatives that years ago court was held upstairs over Berry's Drug store in Villa Rica. They stated that from time to time, John would yell from the upstairs window for the next witness to come upstairs and testify.

John was also involved in other functions around town, both social and otherwise. He and his son, Wallace, helped the local doctor when he performed surgery on patients by holding down his patients during surgery. It was told that Wallace Hicks would often become very sick from this experience.

John Hicks relocated to Atlanta about 1921 to become a manager of a department store in that area.

Most of John and Lula Hicks descendants hold bachelor's degrees. One holds a bachelors in geology and she is a geologist for the State of Georgia; one is a nurse; one is a medical technologist; and one is a teacher; one is a banker; and one was a residential builder.

Bert Hicks, daughter of James (Jim) and Sarah Cole Hicks

*Albert and Alice Hicks were born about 1868 in Paulding County.

*Alice Hicks married J.L. McCravy on January 2, 1886, in Paulding County.

*Julie Hicks was born about 1869 in Paulding County. Julie married A.J. Brown on April 8, 1888, in Paulding County.

The group picture on page 267 shows L-R, Back row, 1st. and 2nd. Two men were visitors; 3rd., William C. (Bud) Ford; 4th., Nan Leatherwood; 5th. F. Marion Leatherwood and child, Ed; 6th., William G. (Will) Matthews; 7th., Naomi Leatherwood; 8th. W. Ben Leatherwood; 9th., John Hicks; 10th., Charles Adkinson; 11th., (Cotton) John Matthews; 12th., Willis Leatherwood; 13th., his wife, Addie. Second row, L-R 1st. Eugenia Leatherwood Adkinson and child, Maud; 2nd., Elizabeth Leatherwood, wife of Marion, and child, Naomi; 3rd., Bell Leatherwood Matthews and baby John; 4th., Eliza Jane Richards Hicks, John Hicks' mother; 5th., Lula Leatherwood Hicks and baby, Estha; 6th., Alice Leatherwood and baby, Fred; 7th., Amanda Leatherwood Ford and baby, Willis. Front row, L-R - 1st., Homer Leatherwood; 2nd., Lena Leatherwood; 3rd., Lillian Leatherwood, daughter of F. Marion; 4th., Hattie Leatherwood; 5th., Ida Leatherwood; 6th., Laura Matthews; 7th., Elsie Matthews; 8th., Lucy Matthews; 9th., Pete Matthews; 10th., Tom Matthews; 11th., Claud Leatherwood; 12th., Ben Ford; 13th., Florence Ford; 14th., Zenna Ford; and 15th., Emma Ford. There are three empty chairs for the three Leatherwood children who are missing from this picture. They are Benny who died in 1882 and W. Monroe who died in 1891. Jesse Leatherwood was also missing because he married in Texas in 1896 and still lived there at that time. One grandson B. Frank (Dook) who was born in August 1897 and probably died while asleep in bed. *Submitted by: Carl Hicks, 8610 Florence Road, Douglasville, GA 30135 and Written by: Pauline C. Roberts, P.O. Box 461, Villa Rica, GA 30180, rgroberts@mindspring.com*

Sources: Census, courthouse, and cemetery records; *Paulding County Heritage Book;* Family Relatives; Personal Knowledge; Lawrence Maynard, Dallas, Texas; and Charlie Collins, Muscadine, Alabama.

638. Robert Young Higgins Family

Robert Young Higgins (1810-1864) and wife Elizabeth (1812-1880) moved their family from McDowell County, North Carolina, to Carroll County, Georgia, in 1840. They settled in the Wesley Chapel Community near the Paulding County line. Their children were: (1) Nancy who married Thomas Cheeves, and their children were Jessie, Thomas, William, Lola, Elizabeth; (2) Sarah who married Riley Haynes and moved to White County, Arkansas; (3) William (1835-1847); (4) Mills (1837-1913) married Emily Wright, and their children were Mary, Robert, Novella, Thomas, Oscar, Ola, Velar, Tommy, Ows, Molly; (5) Rebecca (1840-?) married Richard Bowling, and their children were James, Charles, Oscar, Hattie, Della; (6) Joel (1843-1875) married Mary Elizabeth Chance; (7) Thomas (1846-?) joined the 26th Georgia Infantry at age sixteen; (8) John (1851-?) married Mary R., and their children were Agnes and Robert.

When the Civil War called, R.Y. Higgins was fifty-three years old. He joined the Georgia Infantry, Company D. This was the Provost Guard. This company was composed mainly of the older men and younger boys who guarded the supplies and rounded up deserters, etc. In the Higgins Family Bible on the Death page it is written:

> "Robert Young Higgins was taken off by the enemy on August 11, 1864."

His wife Elizabeth died of paralysis in 1880.

R.Y. Higgins was the ninth child of Mills and Elizabeth Young Higgins of Youngs Fork of North Muddy Creek, McDowell County, North Carolina. His siblings were Elizabeth, Annie, Rachael, William, John, Mills Jr., Sallie, Joel, Polly, James and Alberto.

The Joel Alexander Higgins Family

Joel was born Janaury 17, 1843, in Georgia and died August 24, 1875. He is buried beside his wife Mary Elizabeth Chance at District Line Church in Temple, Georgia. They lived in the Hickory Level Community. He served with Carroll County's Company D, 10th Georgia State Guards Calvary. They furnished security for New Manchester Mills in Sweetwater, Douglas County, Georgia.

Joel's children included: (1) Sarah (1862-?) married Rally Boyles; (2) William (1863-1939) married Sara Jordan and their children were Octavia who married Lonnie Harrod; Sarah; Martha who married Lenny Kaylor; Boyd who married Meburyn McIntyre; Loyd who married Ethel Hendrix; Ella who married Herbert Kaylor; William; Wordie who married Willie Lanier; Emma who married Sanders Ward; and Clara who married Lewis Hendrix; (3) Marchal (1864-?) married Frank Horsley, and their children were Joseph, Marion, Oscar, Amos, William, Nancy, Mary, Robert; (4) Robert Young (1865-?) married Nancy Jane Laney; (5) John M. (1866-?); (6) Tallulah Mollie (1870-?) married Van Chaney; (7) Thomas (1871-?) married Bessie Shinn, and their children were Agnes, Arthur Barney; (8) Cynthia (1873-1947) married Lee Chaney and their children were Chester, Henry, Louis, Ray, Bertha, Gertrude, and Hattie.

The Robert Young Higgins Family (Son of Joel Higgins)

Robert married Nancy Jane Laney in 1885. She is buried at Union Hill Cemetery in Randolph County, Alabama. Children were Emma (1866-?) married Willie Farlow; Etta (1888-1923); Robert Lee Higgins (1892-1957) married Zora Lindley; Joseph Marion (1900-1958) married Cora Waters. *Submitted by: Herbert Higgins, 567 Wedowee Creekview Drive, Wedowee, AL 36278*

639. Hightower Family

The Hightower family was established in Northwest Georgia when Robert P. Hightower, a native North Carolinian, moved to Heard County during the 1850s and purchased land along the Georgia-Alabama border. He and his wife Elizabeth were the parents of Robert Asbury, Angeline, Louisa M., James, and Pollie. A typhoid fever epidemic during the 1870s claimed many members of the family, including eight-year-old Louisa, two-year-old Pollie, and their young stepbrother, Jesse Knight. They are buried at Salem United Methodist Church in Heard County.

James Hightower, son of Robert P. and Elizabeth Hightower, was the first of the family to move to Carroll County, which he did around 1910. He, like his father, was a farmer. He and his wife had five children: Lola, Robert W., Martha, Pearl, and William Cleveland.

Robert Asbury Hightower, another son of Robert P., was a farmer living near the Georgia-Alabama border. He was married twice and was the father of William Henry, Minnie, Sallie, James, and Luther.

William Henry Hightower, son of Robert Asbury Hightower, moved his growing family to Carroll County around 1915. He established a farm near the Victory community. He and his wife, Maudie, raised nine children: Alton, Lora, Lera, Hoyt, Ohmer, Ella Mae, Geneva, Stacy W., and Willie Maude.

Many of the Hightower descendants still live in and around Carroll County. *Submitted by: Kathryn Kruse, 11 Silver Leaf Court, Savannah, GA 31406 and Researched by Dennis M. Crews*

640. Jackson LaFayette Hill and Isabella Baskin McCain Family

Jackson LaFayette Hill was a pioneer of Carroll County arriving around 1848-1850. He was born August 26, 1826, in Harris County, Georgia. On August 1862 at the age of thirty-five he enlisted in Company I, 19th Georgia Infantry, private, Georgia Volunteers Infantry (Villa Rica, Georgia) Confederate States of America. He died December 25, or 28, 1862, from wounds received in battle during the Civil War. He died at the Institute Hospital in Richmond, Virginia, and is buried in grave No. 32 in Hollywood Cemetery there. His parents were Isaac Abner and Isable Cox Hill.

Jackson L. married Isabella McCain on October 28, 1847, in Troup County, Georgia. She was born August 26, 1828, in South Carolina and died March 6, 1898, in Carroll County. She was the daughter of William Baskin McCain and Margaret Nesbet McCain (they were cousins). Isabella and her parents are buried at Bethel Baptist Church in Temple, Georgia.

Jackson L. and Isabella Hill had seven children. (1) Isaac Sion born October 19, 1848, married Sarah E. Brooks. (2) Margaret Jane Nesbet born February 8, 1851, married first to Thomas S. Brooks and second to Nathan Talley Chance. (3) James Alexander born July 17, 1853, married first to unknown and second to Celesyia Windsor. (4) William Henry Hill born October 9, 1855, married first to Frances Ella Foy and second to Mollie Arnold. (5) Ellen Pamelia born March 8, 1858, married John William Powell (Methodist minister). (6) Benjamin Newton born October 9, 1859. (7) Isabella Virginia born November 4, 1862 (Isabella was pregnant with this child when Jackson L. went off to war, was wounded and died of injuries. He never got to see her), married William Albert Chambers.

Margaret Jane Nesbet McCain was Mrs. Ruby Middlebrooks' grandmother and she told this story. She said Margaret never talked about the Civil War, the only thing she ever spoke about was that her mother (Isabella) made her take the little children and spend the day with "Aunt Harriett and Uncle John," one of the two black families living on the farm, with the hope that the children would take the mumps from Aunt Harriett's children and keep the Yankees from taking and destroying all they had to live on, as they marched from Atlanta. None of the children came down with the mumps.

Jackson LaFayette Hill

Jackson L. and Isabella Hill are my great-grandparents. Their daughter Ellen Pamelia married John William Powell on December 19, 1887, in Carroll County, Georgia. They had three children. Their son John Howard Powell born December 21, 1891, died October 9, 1963, in Floyd County, Georgia, married Lois Irene Payne on March 21, 1913, in Carroll County. They had five children, Mary Ellen, Annie Grace, Virginia Ruth, John Howard Jr., James Roy and Peggy Nell Powell. *Submitted by: Annie Grace Powell Dial, 1008 Old Draketown Trail, Temple, GA 30179*

Sources: Carroll County census and marriage records, pension and war records, and family records.

641. James Martin "Jim" Hill and Susannah Durrett

Jim Hill was born April 7, 1846, in Carroll County, Georgia, and died December 17, 1905. He was the son of Rev. Martin Hill and Sarah Ann Tomlin. He was the grandson of Greenberry Hill and Martha Ivey Hill. Martin Hill and his family came to the Crossroads area of Carroll County, Georgia, and Ranburne, Alabama, from Fayette County, Georgia, sometime around 1845. Rev. Hill preached both in Carroll County and Randolph County, Alabama, during this time. Sarah Ann Tomlin was the daughter of William Tomlin and his wife Mary. William Tomlin was born 1784 in Pittsylvania County, Virginia, and died between 1860-1870 in Randolph County, Alabama, in the Stateline area of the section between Bowdon, Georgia and Ranburne, Alabama.

Susannah Durrett Hill, 1937, widow of James Martin "Jim" Hill.

James Martin "Jim" Hill married his neighbor, Susannah Durrett (April 20, 1852-June 4, 1939), February 25, 1868. She was the daughter of James Durrett and Martha Ross and the granddaughter of Francis Durrett (1775-1848) and Penelope Cocks Durrett, great-granddaughter of Thomas Durrett (1750-1784) and Agnes Goree Durrett (1750-1822), and great-great-granddaughter of Francis Durrett and Rebecca Winn.

James Martin "Jim" Hill was only seventeen years old when he fought for the South, CSA, Company B, 7th Cavalry Regiment Confederate Portesan Rangers (Stateline troops made up of Randolph (Cleburne), Alabama and Carroll County men).

Jim Hill only lived 59 years and left Susannah a widow with several children. Susannah Durrett Hill lived to be 87 years old and was living with her daughter, Ethel Hill Smith, during the period before her grandchildren became adults. She told many stories about her family and how they were always afraid of the Yankees during the Civil War years. The Yankees paid her father, James Durrett, and his gunsmith shop a visit during the last days of the war in July 1865. General John T. Croxton, with his entire brigade, entered Georgia (west of Bowdon) and destroyed James Durrett's gun shop. They made him wrap his guns around the trees and took his horses. They didn't get them all, though, because Susannah and her sisters hid some of them way off in the deep woods on the Georgia/Alabama state line. The Yankees left their worn out old mules and headed for Carrollton where they were chased down Dixie Street by the Home Guard.

Susannah Durrett Hill and her children in 1937.

The children of James Martin "Jim" Hill and Susannah Durrett are: (1) Rosella Hill born 1870, married Bill Lambert, two children. (2) John R. Hill born 1873, died about 1925 in Texas. (3) Zachariah Hill born January 3, 1875, died June 15, 1945, married Nancy Elizabeth Overton. (4) James Martin "Buck" Hill born 1876. (5) Julia A. Hill born 1878, died young. (6) Nettie Hill born December 1878, married Bill Rigsby, lived in Knoxville, Tennessee, and had several children. (7) William "Will" Hill born February 1880, married Daisy, moved to Texas, three children. (8) Alabama "Bam" Hill born August 1884, married Mose Abercrombie, died in Boaz, Alabama, and had four children. (9) Dovie Hill born February 1889, married Lum Gravett. (10) Lillie Ethel Hill born May 9, 1894, died January 6, 1964, married Seaborn Rufus Smith on May 19, 1912.

The Georgia/Alabama Stateline Road is located along the southwest boundary of Carroll County near the Tallapoosa River where Carroll County and present-day Cleburne County, Alabama, join.

Jim Hill and Susannah Durrett Hill are buried in the churchyard of the Ranburne, Alabama, cemetery. The family picture of Susannah Durrett Hill shows Dovie, Susannah, and Ella seated; and Will, Nettie, Ethel, and Zack Hill standing. *Submitted by: Sandra Jackson Beavers, 531 Tyus-Carrollton Road, Carrollton, GA 30117 and Written by: Peggy Jackson Hughes.*

642. Hinesley

Thomas A. Hinesley, born 1761 in Queen Anne County, Maryland, his wife Franky, and their sons: Alford born 1794; James M. born 1809; Miles P. born 1814; William born 1815; Alexander H. born 1820; and David S. born 1821, lived in several Georgia counties before settling in Carroll County around 1826. There were traces of the family found in Tattnall, Jasper, Henry, and Early Counties of Georgia. Thomas was a Captain in the Revolutionary War, enlisting from Chatham County, North Carolina.

While in Jasper County, Alford (the eldest son) married Nancy Phillips in 1821. Their children were John Jefferson born 1822; Thomas H. born 1825; Frances E. born 1831; Charles Marion born 1833; Nancy Ann M. born 1836; Permelia A. born circa 1837; Caroline Elizabeth born 1837; Owen T. born 1838; Mary Ann born circa 1839; Alford born 1842; John M. born 1844; Sarah born 1846; Morris born 1849.

Alford's first child, John J., married Nancy Catherine Williams about 1846, probably in Carroll County, Georgia. Their children were Malinda W. born 1848; Thomas Alford born 1850; Permelia E. born 1854; John Wesley born 1856; Jackson Monroe born 1857; Jefferson Davis born 1862; Mary Jane born 1865; and Martha Matilda Melissa born 1867. All were born in Carroll County. This family moved to Walker County, Alabama, and eventually to Stone County, Arkansas. The descendants of John Jefferson (known to them as "Grand Sir") have a reunion each June.

Alford's second child, Thomas H., married Rhoda Elizabeth Lambert in 1846 in Carroll County. Their children were Mary A. born circa 1847; Nancy born circa 1849; Frances born circa 1856; John F. born 1853; Alexander H. born 1856; Sarah Georgia born circa 1858; Julia Isabella Permelia born circa 1859; Thomas born circa 1861; William A. born circa 1864; Charles M. born 1866; Robert E. Lee born 1870. They were born in Carroll County, Georgia.

Alford's fourth child, Charles Marion, married Mary L.D. Lambert, daughter of William and Mary Lambert, in 1850 in Carroll County. Their children were John, George, James, Buddy, Missouri, Frances, Tom, Mary, William Alfred, Charles Monroe. All were born in Carroll County. This family moved to the Walker County, Alabama area.

Alford's fifth child, Nancy Ann M., married Robert R. Horsley in 1856 in Carroll County. This family moved to Florida.

Alford's sixth child, Permelia, married Jerolin/Julian Nail in 1842 in Carroll County. Their children were Sarah born 1845; John born 1846; and Alfred born 1849; all were born in Carroll County.

Alford's ninth child, Mary Ann "Polly" married Elihu M. Williams, son of Thomas B. and Hannah

Pinson Williams, in 1848 in Carroll County. Their children were Octavia I. born circa 1849; John Henry Crentillion born 1851; R.T. born 1855; James W. born circa 1859; all were born in Carroll County. This family moved to Texas with a short stay in Arkansas on the way *Submitted by: Neta Jane Doris, PO Box 670, Satanta, KS 67870; njdoris@pld.com*

643. Alexander Hogan 1801-1878

Alexander Hogan was born about 1801 in North Carolina. He moved his family to Carroll County in 1827. By the 1830 census, his father-in-law James Upton (see related James Upton article) had followed him, as well as his brother Emsley P. and his mother Ellis with his five unmarried sisters. By 1840, Alexander's sisters were either married (Polly married Edward Dyer in 1831 and Matilda married Miles Mosley in 1833) or were living elsewhere. His brother Emsley had left the county and his mother was living with him. Just before the 1850 census, Alexander moved his entire clan out of Carroll County and took them to Upshur County in East Texas where they settled near Soul's Chapel. Both Alexander and Anna died sometime in 1878 and are buried in unmarked graves in Upshur County, Texas.

The children of Alexander and Anna Upton Hogan were: (1) William Hogan was born 1827 in Tennessee, died ca. 1868 in Texas. He was married first on 18 November 1846 in Carroll County to Sarah Franklin and they had two children: Jane Irene "Rene" who married William Murphy, and Thomas Edward who married Elizabeth Germany Darden (my line). William Hogan was married second to Mary Margaret Green (daughter of Anderson Green of Carroll County) and they had four children: James A. (d. unm.); Austin A. married Sarah J. Bowles; Sarah Anna married John M. Taylor; and Ann M. married Mr. Goode. After William died, Margaret married second to Joseph Puryear Bowles and they had one son, Thomas P. (2) James Hogan was born 1828 and died 10 September 1872 in Upshur County, Texas. He married in 1854 to Elizabeth Nixon Porter and they had seven children: Benjamin Alexander married Maude Baine; Finas E. married Mary Jane Darden; Laura Eugenia married William Lee Stith; James Albert married Emily Leona Duffy, married second to Julia Frances Lovellette; Ella Ione married John Mitchell; Anna Dorothy married Robert Seaborn Darden; and Lula Cora married Charles Goff. (3) Sarah Elizabeth Hogan was born 1832, married 19 July 1849 in Carroll County to Irwin W. Ayres, and they had seven children: William Alexander who married first Adelia C. Ingram and second to Rosa Bell Allred; Marion Wilson who married Rosa Bell Cockburn; James Monroe who married Annie Jule Armstrong; Anna Paralee who married Simon Bush; Mary Ellen who married Will Armstrong; Sarah; and Emma who married first H.C. Armstrong, second to Crosby, and third to Henry Luker. (4) Daughter born 1830/35 and died 1935. (5) Thomas L. Hogan was born 25 June 1838, died 17 September 1901 in Upshur County, Texas, married Lavonia Villers Elizabeth Rosser, the widow of Ethelred J.A. Floyd, and they had seven children: Eugenia V., John W., Benjamin A., Arethy Ann, Martha Belzora, Lee Alphonso, and Ethelred James. (6) Son born and died 1839. (7) Bennett Hogan born 1842, died 1920 in Grayson County, Texas, married first to Elizabeth Villers McWaters and they had seven children: Annie E. (died unm.); Fannie Paralee who married Emsley Cherry; Emma A. who married Hill Morris; Alexander Houston who married Pearl Barnes; Bennett Luther who was married first to Annie Tennessee McDonald and second to Jenny Hemby; James Marvin who married first Ola Pate and second to Hattie McQuarry; and Minnie V. who married Preach Britt. (8) Emily Hogan was born 12 July 1844, died 8 February 1915 in Camp County, Texas. She married John Corly Porter and they had six children: Dorothy, Ione, Susan, Benjamin J., Della, and William. *Submitted by: Carol A. Hogan, 440 NW 23rd Street, Grand Prairie, TX 75050*

Sources: Census records of Carroll County and Upshur County, deed records, tax records, marriage records, personal memoirs of the grandchildren of Alexander and Anna Hogan and *The Pioneers Were Our Ancestors,* by Irwin A. Watson, privately published.

644. Emsley P. Hogan

Emsley P. Hogan, 1804-1840, presumed brother of Alexander, settled in Carroll County before the 1830 census with his wife Mary, two sons or stepsons, and a daughter. Also there were Ellis Hogan, probable mother of Alexander and Emsley. The family came from North Carolina and Tennessee, and possibly were in the Cherokee lands of Sequichee Valley, Tennessee, around 1813.

Emsley and Alexander had at least three sisters: Polly married Edward Dyer in 1831 and had a son, Alexander. Polly died before 1838; Matilda married Miles Howard Mosley and settled in Paulding County. Their children were Sarah Jane, Benjamin, Emsley P., Alexander Y., Moses Lafayette, Margaret M. Augustus N., Myles Thomas, William Calvin, and John Griffeth; and Nellie who never married.

Eventually, Emsley and Mary's family included (1) Elcanah D., born 1825 in Tennessee; (2) Peter B., born 1827 in Tennessee; (3) Susan, born about 1828 in Georgia, married a Davidson; (4) Infant son, born about 1829 in Georgia; (5) Nancy A., born about 1833 in Georgia; (6) Thomas Graham, born about 1834 in Georgia, married Martha E.; (7) Sara Elizabeth, born 1839 in Alabama, married George Morrow, and had William Thomas, Delura Alice, George Emsley, Mary Ann Teresa, and John Owen.

Elcanah D. and Mary Winningham Hogan

Mystery surrounds Emsley's whereabouts during the tumultuous years from 1836 through 1840 as the Indians were forced from their lands onto the Trail of Tears. A possible explanation is Elcanah's description of going west with the Cherokee. He told of a large amount of stars falling one night which lighted the whole elements. They went without bread for days, having nothing but parched corn and wild game. We cannot find Emsley's family on the 1840 census, yet by January 1841 Alexander Hogan (with James B. McCallister and Andrew McMullin) posted bond as guardians of Emsley's children. What would explain the family's return? Tradition says that Emsley was a minister, which suggests that he could have been a missionary traveling with the Cherokee; he died on the journey and his family returned to Georgia.

In 1842, Elcanah D. Hogan married Elizabeth Collins, daughter of Lydia. Their children were (1) Emsley P., born 1842 in Georgia; (2) Julia Ann Samanthia (1843-1916); (3) Dora Ann, born about 1848 in Georgia; (4) Thomas G., born about 1849 in Georgia; and (5 and 6) twins, George (1850- circa 1861) and Thomas Jeffeson (1850-1923).

Emsley's widow, Mary, married James Trammel in 1844. The marriage dissolved and Mary moved to Texas. By 1850, Alexander led the large Hogan clan, including most of Emsley's children, to Upshur County, Texas.

Elcanah and family went west shortly afterward. Elizabeth apparently died sometime after the birth of the twins in Tennessee. In 1853, Elcanah married Mary Winningham in Sevier County, Arkansas. Their children were (7) John Wilson (1854-1928); (8) Peter Bronson (1855-1912); (9) Mary Elizabeth (1857-1933); (10) William, born about 1859; (11) Telitha Idella, born in 1860; (12) Joshua Elcanah (1864-1942); (13) Isaac D., born about 1867; and (14) James Marion (1868- after 1904).

In 1853, Nancy A. Hogan married Andrew Jackson Ayres in Carroll County. Their children were William, Mary Frances, Martha, John, Orville, Lucius E., and Ada Ann. After some time in Alabama, they joined the other Hogans in Texas.

In 1863, Peter B. Hogan enlisted in the 14th Texas Cavalry, was wounded and sent to Dalton, Georgia. He married Prudence H. Harrison. As they awaited the birth of a child, he wrote,

> "Georgia, Carroll County, Jan. 15, 1865
>
> Dear Mother: ... we will try to get to Texas next fall, but I can't tell what will be, for we have had the Yanks through here and they have taken all the stock out of the country near here ... and they are still in the state. They are at Dalton and they have gone through the states and we can't tell what will be next. I do not think it is any use to think of Texas in the next four years ... not until all the men is killed and everything destroyed ... I would like to hear from you all to know what the war is doing in Texas. Have not heard from you in eighteen months .... "

By the time the war ended, the Hogans were essentially gone from Carroll County, though many ties remained. In 1865, Emsley's granddaughter, Julia Ann Samanthia married Alexander Whisenhunt, son of Henry and Sarah Collins Whisenhunt of Carroll County. The Whisenhunts had migrated to southwest Arkansas. Of the Carroll County families closely associated with the Hogans, the Bryant/Briants — Alexander, Peter S., William, David, and Emsley — are of special interest. *Submitted by: Jeanette Bismark, 2613 Regency Street, Magnolia, AR 71753. bismark@arkansas.net*

Sources: Census records, marriage records, court and land records, family Bibles, memoirs, documents, and generous contributions from other Hogan researchers.

645. Hamilton Hogan

Hamilton Hogan was born March 1, 1820 in Pendleton District, South Carolina, the son of James and Elizabeth Spraggins Hogan. James Hogan was the son of Irish immigrantes, William and Nancy Dillard Hogan.

Hamilton moved with his family to Habersham County, Georgia, in 1822 and in 1825 to Coweta County, Georgia. In 1846 he was teaching school in Carroll County, Georgia, and that year he purchased Land Lot 177 in the 3rd District of Carroll County. On August 13, 1846, he married Jane Watson, daughter of Tyre and Clarissa Sockwell Watson. He built their home on Jones Mill Road which is still occupied.

Hamilton enlisted in Company H, 66th Georgia when the War Between the States began and after two years he was released due to health reasons. He remained at home for a short period and enlisted in Company H, 3rd Georgia. He was captured in Decatur, Alabama, and imprisoned at Camp Douglas, Illinois. At the end of the war he was paroled in Richmond, Virginia.

Hamilton and Jane Hogan's Fiftieth Wedding Anniversary

Hamilton was elected to the Georgia Legislature in 1876 and served two terms. He was elected and served two terms on the Carroll County Board of Commissioners. The board appointed him to oversee the construction of the new courthouse which was situated on the site of the present one. This building was occupied March 1894 and burned February 3, 1928.

Hamilton Hogan died in Carrollton, Georgia April 29, 1911 at the age of 91.

Hamilton and Jane Hogan were the parents of nine children. Their daughter, Helen, married my great-grandfather, John T. Jones, the son of Thomas B. and Celia Velvin Jones. John T. Jones with four of his brothers was in the Confederate Army. John T. and Helen were the parents of twelve children. One of their children was Nancy Emiline, who married my grandfather, John W. Wilkins, the son of Joseph and Mary Richards Wilkins. Joseph was the son of David L. and Sarah Sparks Wilkins. Mary was the daughter of R.L. Richards and Elizabeth Elrod Richards. R.L. Richards was an attorney and served in the Georgia Legislature for two terms and as Ordinary of Carroll County for two terms after he was discharged from the Confederate Army. He and five of his brothers were in the war.

John and Emiline Wilkins had seven children, one of whom was my father, Hoke S. Wilkins Sr. Hoke married Mabel Beatrice Smith, daughter of John and Annie Burch Smith of Gordon County, Georgia. Hoke and Mabel had two children, Anthony and me. I married Doris Windom, daughter of William Clarence and Katrina Wood Windom. We have two sons, David Michael and Phillip Dean Wilkins. Phil married LaJuana Knowles and they have two children, Kaela and Kevin.

Most of my ancestors in Carroll County were farmers. *Submitted by: H. Smith Wilkins Jr., 315 Highland Avenue, Carrollton, GA 30117*

646. Bobby George Holcombe and Joy Elaine Shadrix Holcombe Family

Bobby George Holcombe was born September 16, 1940, near Roopville at the home place of his grandparents, George Washington Key and Permelia Jane Blackwelder Key, located off Highway 27 South, across from the famous Johnson landmark, the "Sweet Potato Curing House." It was a hot September afternoon and most of the family was in the cotton patch picking cotton. One of Bobby's aunts walked by the bedroom window on her way to milk the cow and someone ran out and told her that the baby had arrived. Bobby was delivered by Dr. Wortham from Centralhatachee in Heard County and was what in those days considered a "blue baby." He was wrapped in a blanket and placed in the cookstove oven to warm him up (pre-incubator). At age five, Bobby moved with his parents, Jeff Holcombe and Etha Key Holcombe to downtown Roopville next door to the "Uncle Gus Ware" home place and later moved two miles south of Roopville on Highway 5 to his great-uncle John Blackwelder's home place. He attended school at Roopville, graduating second in his senior class in 1958, then attended Berry College and West Georgia College. Bobby worked at Service Supply in Carrollton, Richards & Associates, and retired from Southwire in 1999 with over thirty seven years of service in Sales Administration.

Joy Elaine Shadrix Holcombe was born August 6, 1944, at the Villa Rica hospital. It was a rainy day and several bridges had been washed out causing her parents to make several detours to the hospital. She was the third of four children and only girl born to Henry Moses Shadrix and Mattie Ellen Peek Shadrix. Elaine grew up on a farm near Abilene Baptist church on Hog Liver Road. She attended school in Temple and graduated with honors from Temple High School in 1962 as valedictorian of her class. Elaine worked as a dental assistant for Dr. Bill Moore and in the late 1960s began working for Carroll County in the office of Clerk of Superior Court, celebrating thirty three years of service in 2001 as Deputy Clerk.

Bobby and Elaine were married by Rev. Elwood Cline on September 29, 1962, at Abilene Baptist church. They built a house on Hog Liver Road in 1964 and a new home at Lakeside Cove on Sharp Creek reservoir in 1999. They have three children: Scott Anthony born April 30, 1963, Kimberly Elaine born January 23, 1965, and Lisa Ellen born July 12, 1967.

Scott lives with his parents and works at the Carroll County Training Center. Although challenged by Down Syndrome, he and his family have overcome the condition with his involvement in the community and work place. Scott's outgoing personality and the love shown by family and friends has made his condition invisible.

Kim is married to Wendell Keith Carroll from Bremen (parents are Wendell and Virginia West Carroll) and is employed by Southern Therapy as the administrator. Keith is director of sales for King Packaging in Bremen. They have two children: Sarah Elaine born November 22, 1994, and Adam Keith born April 5, 1999. They live on Hog Liver in the house built by Kim's parents when she was six months old.

Lisa is married to Raymond Frances Walton and resides in Grapevine, Texas. Lisa is employed by Delta Air Lines and Ray is vice president of Harbor National Insurance Group. They have two children: Melissa Kristine, born March 8, 1987, and Tyler Raymond born July 14, 1997. *Submitted by: Kim Carroll, 3443 Hogliver Rd., Carrollton, GA 30117*

647. Reuben Holcombe III

Reuben Holcombe III was born 23 August 1814 in Laurens, South Carolina, to Reuben Holcombe II and Mary Ann Kellett. In the 1827 Land Lottery, Reuben II drew land in De Kalb County and in Cherokee County in the Gold Lottery of 1832. The Holcombe family moved to Carroll County but not before Mary Ann died in De Kalb County.

Reuben III has seven siblings: Clara (Shadrack Lewis), Martin 1809 (Phoebe Reid), John Kellett 1810 (Rachel C. Morris and Elizabeth Jacobs), James 1817 (Elizabeth Linchens), Luvina 1819, Hannah 1820, and Jonathan C. 1823.

Reuben II later married Elizabeth Felton Gentry and Reuben II may be buried in the Holcombe Cemetery in Haralson County. Reuben Holcombe III married Elizabeth Lewis 22 October 1835 in Carroll County and was found in Carroll County in the 1840 and 1850 census records. Elizabeth was born 25 September 1816 in Georgia and was one of eight known children born to Benjamin and Nancy Lewis. Elizabeth's siblings were: Jason, William, Henry L., Charity, Mary 1811 (Thomas M. Hogan), Shadrack 1811 (Clara Holcombe and Patsy Patton), John B. 1822 (Elizabeth ?). Benjamin and Nancy Lewis may be buried in the Holcombe Cemetery along with the Holcombe family.

Bobby Holcombe family (L to R), Bobby, Scott, Elaine, Lisa Walton, Ray Walton, Kim Carroll, Keith Carroll

Reuben III was in the military service removing Cherokee Indians from North Georgia for which he drew a pension. In 1877 Reuben III kept a post office in his home, which was served by weekly mail delivery on horseback from Campbellton, Georgia, to Tallapoosa, to Bremen, and possibly other towns. The Liberty Christian Church was begun under an oak tree on the Holcombe farm where a few Christians had gathered to hear the Gospel in 1870.

Reuben III and Nancy were the parents of fourteen known children: John Martin 1836 (Nancy Ann Elizabeth Howard) lost his life in Civil War; Mary Ann Elizabeth 1838 (George Fleming Reid); James Davis 1842 (Elizabeth Amanda Reid and Miranda Ann Casey); Martha Jane 1843 (Henry Reid and John W. Driver); Hannah Isabelle 24 March 1844 (Matthew Reid II and James Dallas Raburn); Reuben Kellett 1846 (Lydia Katherine Reid, Sarah Evaline Lovell, and Ester Angeline Lovell); Phoebe Catherine 1948 (David O. Nix); Nancy Ann Selina 27 January 1850-12 August 1854; Rhoda Luvina 5 November 1851-9 August 1854; Jonathan Shadrack 11 September 1853-13 August 1854; Robert Madison 15 March 1855-15 October 1856; William Joseph 1856 (Mary Ann Elizabeth Watson and Nancy Ann Idella Williams); Clara Lucinda 1858 (James Moses Nelson); General Jackson Longstreet Hill Lee 1862 (Mary Jane Farmer). Nancy Ann Selina, Rhoda Lucian, Jonathan Shadrack died within four days of each other during an epidemic and are buried in the Holcombe Cemetery with Robert Madison being buried two years later. Nancy and Reuben celebrated fifty years of marriage before Nancy died 12 December 1885 and is laid to rest with her four children in the Holcombe Cemetery. Three years later on 3 September 1888, Reuben married Elizabeth Ann Futral Kierbow. Reuben died 7 January 1894 and was laid to rest beside Nancy at one o'clock p.m. the next day. *Submitted by: Scott R. Allen, 30738 Highway 48, Graham, AL 36263. sloua@aol.com*

648. Holcomb(e), (Holcum)

The name was spelled "de Holcombe" in England in the early 1300s. The immigrant, William Holcomb (Harcum) of Pembrokeshire, Wales, Great Britain, was in Virginia in 1680 and had dropped the final "e" from his fine autograph, but his descendants soon restored it. William probably married in Wales before immigrating to the "Northern Neck" of Virginia.

His son Richard Holcomb II was in Prince Edward County, Virginia, in 1730 with five sons, and in 1754 the four youngest, including Richard III, moved to Granville County, North Carolina. They served in Capt. Shugan Jones Company of Col. William Eaton's Regiment and later were joined by their cousin Grimes. The five moved to old Ninety-Six District, South Carolina, within the Fairforest Baptist Church Association before 1771.

Richard III was granted 200 acres on Tyger river in Cravens County, North Carolina, and recorded in the 1790 census with wife Sarah. He signed his will on June 22, 1794, reciting "being very weak in body" giving Sarah "25 acres on Middle Fork of Durbin's Creek." They had eight children, and a son Johnathan became a large landowner and served in the American Revolution under Col. Thomas Brandon. Johnathan is listed on the membership of Padgett's Creek Baptist Church in 1805. His descendants remember him as the father of Cynthia Ann Eliza Jane Holcombe (wife of Aaron Jones of South Carolina, DeKalb and Carroll Counties, Georgia), Reuben II, and nine other children.

Reuben II married first in Laurens District, South Carolina, probably as early as 1805, to Mary Ann Kellett. She died in DeKalb or Carroll County in the late 1820s. They had ten children — four girls and six boys. Reuben moved in a horse-drawn wagon, to DeKalb County not later than 1823 and drew lot 246 in DeKalb County in the Georgia Land Lottery of 1827. He drew in the Georgia Gold Lottery of 1827, receiving land in the 16th District of Cherokee County. Reuben took deed June 6, 1834, for lot 201 in the 5th District of Carroll County. He married the second time in Carroll County to Elizabeth Felton Gentry and is recorded in the 1840 census of 714 District of Carroll County. He signed an oath in Carroll County on January 17, 1853, that he witnessed the marriage in South Carolina in 1799 of his sister, Cynthia Ann Eliza Jane Holcombe to Lt. Aaron Jones. Reuben died in Haralson County about 1872 and is buried in the family cemetery near Little Vine Primitive Baptist Church.

The Holcombe Family

James Holcombe, the seventh son of Reuben II, was a farmer in Carroll County and married Elizabeth Ann Lincens on March 28, 1839, and they had seven children. On July 17, 1846, he enlisted as a private in H. Seymour's Battalion, Georgia Infantry, U.S. Army at Columbus, Georgia, was promoted to sergeant, became sick at Jalapa, Indian Territory, and mustered out in Mobile, Alabama, on July 12, 1848. Elizabeth Ann died in 185? and he married a second time in 185? to Caroline Christine Holder, born in Georgia in 1837-38 and died in Cullman County, Alabama, on December 6, 1920. James and Caroline are recorded in the 1860 census of Calhoun County, Alabama. They had seven children, two of whom were twins, Phoebe and Robert Ahaz Boggess, born March 23, 1865.

Robert Ahaz Boggess Holcombe was a farmer in the Bowdon, Georgia, area in the early 1920s. He was married to Cynthia Sophronia Cole, born in 1864 and they had eight children. The youngest child, Jefferson, was the father of Bobby Holcombe. Ahaz moved to Albertville, Alabama, in 1922 where he died on March 3, 1936. He was a farmer and had an apple orchard. He is remembered by his granddaughter, Mavis Holcombe Denney Mashburn, as a kind and gentle old man who loved children. She remembers his apple barrel that he kept upstairs filled with sand and the best apples in the world. Mavis remembers that you had to ford a creek to get to his house from the main road.

Jefferson (Jeff) Holcomb was born in Carroll County January 1, 1897, near Black Jack Mountain. He worked on the farm and attended Sardis Baptist Church. He was drafted into the Army on August 13, 1918, served in France during the war, and was discharged on March 9, 1919, by reason of demobilization, returning to Carroll County to marry Lessie Hardigree on December 7, 1919. There were three children: Carlos Jefferson, and twins Mavis and Marvis. Jeff farmed near Whooping Creek off Lowell road and later moved to Albertville/Boaz, Alabama, where he farmed and painted. He and his family moved back to Carroll County in 1928 and he attended barber school in Atlanta. Lessie died October 12, 1929, and Jeff married a second time on December 25, 1937, to Eather (Etha) Key, daughter of George Washington Key and Permelia Jane Blackwelder Key. Jeff and Etha had two children: Linda Louise and Bobby George. Jeff was considered one of the smoothest "Buck" dancers in Carroll County and said that he learned to dance on an old pine stump. He could dance across a room holding a glass of water and not spill a drop. His dancing skills helped entertain fellow servicemen in France during the war. Jeff is remembered in Carrollton as a barber at Elm Rose Barber Shop. He had a reputation of giving a great shave and could shave a man in two minutes flat. Jeff was always pulling a prank and one day told a customer that his fellow barber Bunt Kilgore was running for sheriff of Carroll County. He later talked Bunt into running; Bunt won and served several terms as sheriff. As a young man, Jeff joined Mt. Pleasant Baptist church and was a member there at the time of his death on April, 28, 1954. He was buried in the Whooping Creek Primitive Baptist Church Cemetery. Pallbearers were Horrie Jones, Ralph Shirey, Preston Pentecost, Ambus Holloway, E.P. Seals, and Cliff Palmer.

The family photograph shows Jefferson and Eather Holcomb on the back row, and Bobby and Linda in front. *Submitted by: Bobby Holcombe, 125 Lakeside Cove, Carrollton, GA 30117*

649. The Holder Family

The Holders came to this country from England. It is believed that the Holder surname was found in America as early as 1638.

Luda Holder was born in South Carolina in 1827. He is listed in the 1850 census of Carroll County, Georgia, as "Lewdy," with his wife Martha Cook Holder, along with their sons James and Robert. They were also in the 1860 census of Carroll County as L. Holder, farmer, 33 years; wife Martha, and children James, Robert, Sarah Ann, Susan, George M., and Mary. Luda and Martha were married on November 15, 1846, in Carroll County, Georgia. Luda died July 1862 in a hospital in Atlanta from wounds sustained at the Battle of Chattanooga, Tennessee. He is buried at the Oakland Cemetery in Atlanta. Martha was born February 10, 1828, in Georgia. She died March 2, 1883, and is buried at the Dorris Cemetery in Carroll County, Georgia.

Robert and Catherine Holder

Their son Robert L. was born May 1, 1850, and died February 21, 1916, in Carroll County, Georgia. He married Georgia (Catherine) Dorris, the daughter of Lt. William C. Dorris and Eliza Ann Cosper, on August 2, 1868, in Carroll County. Catherine was born May 15, 1853, and died May 11, 1915, in Carroll County. Both are buried at the Liberty Methodist Church Cemetery in Carroll County. Their children were: (1) Martha Elizabeth (Lizzie), born ca. 1869. (2) Mary (Susie) born ca. 1871. (3) Georgia C. born and died in 1874 and is buried at the Dorris Cemetery in Carroll County. (4) Emily Rebecca (Beckie) born May 12, 1876. (5) William Ludie (Bud) born January 18, 1878. (6) Lucy Ann born May 30, 1880. (7) A.G. born November 14, 1882, and died July 7, 1884. (8) Lottie May born November 14, 1884. (9) J.M.

born September 18, 1886, died October 6, 1888, and is buried at the Dorris Cemetery in Carroll County. (10) Beulah Naomi born January 5, 1890. (11) John R. born August 1892. (12) Pearl E. born April 1895. All were born in Carroll County, Georgia.

William Ludie (Bud) Holder, fifth child of Robert and Catherine, was born January 18, 1878, and died December 14, 1945, in Carroll County, Georgia. He married Hester (Ida) Beatrice Rooks, daughter of George and Alice Walker Rooks, on November 5, 1899. She was born on May 26, 1879, and died November 25, 1953. They are both buried at the Lowell Cemetery in Lowell, Carroll County, Georgia. They had six children. (1) Amison (Ralph) born June 9, 1902, in Carroll County and died November 22, 1969 in Coweta County, Georgia. He was married on October 16, 1921, to Sarah (Ruth) Musick. They are both buried at the Forrest Lawn Cemetery in Coweta County, Georgia. (2) George (Rolfe) born March 15, 1904, and died May 3, 1984. He married Rozell Shoemake on November 11, 1923, in Carroll County. She was born February 28, 1907 and died November 10, 1992, in Carroll County. They are buried at the Lowell Cemetery, Georgia. (3) Robert (Clarence) born November 2, 1907, died September 7, 1937, and is buried at Lowell Cemetery. (4) Willie May born 1909, died 1909, and is buried at Ephesus Christian Church in Carroll County, Georgia; (5) Buvena born October 15, 1910, and died March 29, 1997. She married Robert Milton Bums Sr. on December 1, 1935. He was born on July 4, 1906, and died December 22, 1974. They are buried at Carroll Memory Gardens in Carroll County; (6) James M. Holder born 1912 and died 1916. He is buried at Ephesus Christian Church.

Bud and Ida Holder. Made in early 1940s.

Buvena and Robert Burns were my parents. Granddaddy Holder died when I was eight years old but I remember him well. We would spend the weekend with them a lot when my brothers Steve and Bob and I were young. We really enjoyed going there. Grandmother Holder always had cakes and pies cooked. She was a very good cook and always had lots of pretty flowers growing in the yard. In the fall I remember when they would pick cotton their front and back porches would be full of it. They would let us play in it and it was so much fun. They always spoiled us, too. Every time we went over there, they would have something for us. One Christmas, I received a child's glass baking set and I still a few pieces of it left.

I remember in the winter after we had had supper, we would sit around their fireplace and I would sit in Grandaddy Holder's lap while the grown-ups would talk. After Granddaddy died, Grandmother came to live with us. I am the oldest of seven children and we all loved having Grandmother with us. But I really missed Granddaddy a lot after he died. Grandmother Holder's sister, Etta Rooks Spence, lived in Alabama and would visit us while Grandmother lived at our house.

In the summer we would sit on the porch and I would encourage Grandmother to talk about when she was young. She would recall her mother, Alice Walker Rooks, telling of the hard times they had as a child. Alice's father, William Walker, was a captain of Company K 34th Georgia Regiment of the Confederate Army during the War Between the States. She remembered Union soldiers who were passing through Carroll County coming to their door looking for food. The soldiers did not harm anyone, but it was still a frightening experience. Captain William Walker was killed August 31, 1864, in the Battle of Jonesboro, Georgia, and is buried there. Earlier in the war, he was in the Battle of Vicksburg, Mississippi.

Grandmother Holder died on November 25, 1953, about three months after I married Donald Davis Duncan. I have a lot of good memories of Grandmother and Granddaddy Holder.

My parents, Buvena Holder and Robert Miton Burns Sr., had seven children. (1) Judith Marie (Judy) born November 27, 1936, in Carroll County. (2) Steve Benton born March 3, 1939, in Carroll County. (3) Robert Milton Jr. (Bob) born May 12, 1941, in Carroll County. (4) James Donald (Don) born December 4, 1942, in Carroll County. (5) Carol Dianne born March 11, 1945, in Coweta County. (6) Sylvia Joan born December 16, 1946, in Coweta County. (7) David H. born February 1, 1949, in Carroll County.

There are numerous descendants of the Holder family throughout Carroll County and the surrounding areas to this day. *Submitted by: Judy Duncan*

650. Isaac Jasper Holder Family

Isaac Jasper Holder was born May 7, 1894, in Floyd County, Georgia. He died July 21, 1975. On November 2, 1912, he married Edith Marie Carnes, who was born May 14, 1897, in Carroll County, Georgia, and died February 27, 1951. They were married at the famous four-story, one hundred-thirty bedroom Lithia Springs Hotel in Tallapoosa, Georgia. The hotel was the largest wooden structure ever built in the South and was known as the "Queen of the South." They are buried in the Carrollton City Cemetery.

Marie Carnes was the daughter of John Peter (Uncle Pete) Carnes (December 28, 1877-December 15, 1946) and Annie Williams Carnes (March 19, 1875-August 13, 1958). J.P. Carnes was a section foreman for the Southern Railroad. Annie Williams Carnes was the daughter of Burl W. Williams (July 4, 1838-June 26, 1908) and Janie Steele Williams (November 9, 1845-January 9, 1921) of Temple, Georgia. An infant sister preceded her in death. She is buried in the Old Bethel Primitive Baptist Church Cemetery which is located on Bar J. Road between Interstate Highway 20 and Highway 78 in Temple. In 1925, J.P. Carnes purchased the old log house which had been the Buckhorn Tavern. He weather boarded it and painted it white; then in 1958 he sold it to Leon Lee of Villa Rica. J.P. and Annie Carnes are buried in Asbury Cemetery, Temple.

Isaac Jasper, the second of fifteen children, was the son of James Marion Holder (January 6, 1870-June 3, 1938) and Rilla Rebecca Brock Holder (October 7, 1876-May 21, 1944), who were married December 6, 1891. They lived in Floyd County, Georgia, until 1910 when they moved to Fruithurst, Alabama, where he operated a general merchandise store for several years. While in Fruithurst, he also served as mayor, trustee of the school, and as mail carrier. Returning to Floyd County in 1918, he worked as superintendent of the Arrington Seed Farm on the Coosa River until failing health forced him to retire in 1927. Upon retirement he moved his family from Turner's Bend to his home on the Alabama Road, where they lived until they died. Other children included: Octavia (October 13, 1892-December 29, 1892), Linnie Lee (January 6, 1896-August 18, 1976), Thomas Curtis (December 13, 1897-February 5, 1992), William Roy (November 1, 1899-February 24, 1972), Agnes Ola (July 1, 1901-June 25, 1984), Aaron James Marion (May 22, 1903-April 15, 1989), Ella Mae (April 8, 1905-July 12, 1992), Vesta Irene (January 22, 1907-January 30, 1995), Lillian Lorene (October 25, 1908-May 20, 1985), Carlton Fletcher (October 14, 1910-February 29, 1912), Woodrow Wilson (January 7, 1913-December 15, 1946), Robert Gilmore (February 5, 1915-August 23, 2000), Gladys Rebecca (April 20, 1918), and Edward Julian (September 23, 1920-November 14, 1989).

Isaac Jasper Holder

Isaac Jasper Holder was a Roadmaster for the Seaboard Railroad in Montgomery, Alabama, when he retired in 1939 and moved his family to Temple, Georgia, where he farmed. On October 2, 1955, he married Nannie Lee Venable Horton. Children of Isaac Jasper Holder and Marie Carnes Holder were: Floyd Odell, Hazel Elizabeth, Hoyt Hoover, John Marion, Harold Lamar, and Burl (Burell) Williams.

Floyd, who was born in Cleburne County, Alabama, on August 22, 1914, and died July 15, 1995, married Claire Flynn. During his Navy career, Floyd served on the USS New Mexico, the USS MacLeish and the USS Bennington. Their children are Floyd Odell (Dell) Jr. and Janice Marie. Janice (October 27, 1943) is married to David L. Shumaker (July 25, 1945) and they live at Port Charlotte, Florida. The children are: Deborah A. Nutwell (March 15, 1963) of Bremerholder, Germany; Lisa M. Capone (March 12, 1964) of Port Charlotte, Florida; and Diane M. Boyt (June 15, 1968) of Dacula, Georgia. Dell (November 2, 1948) married Cheryl Bagley (November 26, 1950), who is the daughter of Calvin Coolidge Bagley of Cumming, Georgia, and Merceles Helmey Bagley who was from Savannah, Georgia. Their children are Lindsey Ann and Valerie Leigh. Lindsey (October 19, 1980) is a junior at Florida State University majoring in merchandising. Valerie (April 24, 1984) will be a senior in high school this fall. They live at Tampa, Florida.

Hazel, who was born March 25, 1916, in Cleburne County, Alabama, married James Robert Trawick on October 23, 1937. They moved to Carrollton from Montgomery, Alabama, in 1946. James owned and operated Trawick's Auto Top and Seat Cover business for many years. Their children are James Floyd (Jim), John Holder, Cheryl Marie, and Dana Gayle. Jim (August 22, 1938) was born in Montgomery and married Marsha Sullins (November 18, 1946), on March 21, 1976. They live in Terrell, Texas. Their children are Chase Harrison (October 1, 1985) and Chance Ronald (May 1, 1987). John (March 31, 1943), born in Dothan, Alabama, married Dondra Marks (August 9, 1943) of Carrollton on September 8, 1963. Her parents were Garvie and Sara Thompson Marks. John and Dondra have three children: John Holder Jr. (Jay), Mindi Marks, and

Elizabeth (Beth) Alane. Jay (April 22, 1969) was born in Macon, Georgia. Mindi (June 1, 1971) was born in Montgomery, Alabama. She is married to John Randel Cody, and they have two children: Sara (July 9, 1997) and Jacob (June 14, 2000). They live in Bowling Green, Kentucky. Beth (July 18, 1973) was born in Carrollton and lives in Atlanta. Cheryl (March 11, 1946), born in Dothan, Alabama, married Larry Vines. They live in Seattle, Washington. They have three children: Chris James (October 25, 1968). Todd Andrew (October 23, 1974), and Shea Marie (March 15, 1981). Dana (August 22, 1951) is married to Michael Duggan Hodges. They have two sons: Michael Duggan Jr. (April 22, 1986) and Matthew Trawick (January 2, 1988) and they live at St. Simons Island, Georgia.

Front, Hoyt, Burell, Lamar. Back, Isaac, Floyd, Marion, and Hazel Holder Trawick.

Hoyt, who was born August 15, 1918, in Calhoun County, Alabama, and died July 17, 1995, married Eloise Hester. He served in the Air Force during World War II. Their daughter, Lisa Marie (September 22, 1954), married Keith Creeden (January 5, 1951). They live in Longwood, Florida, and they have one son, Craig (January 8, 1991).

Marion, who was born February 2, 1921, in Douglas County, Georgia, lives in Temple. He started an upholstery business in his father's chicken house in 1946 and later moved it into a cotton warehouse in town and retired in 1978. He served in the Army Air Corps during World War II in the South Pacific and was at Iwo Jima. He is known locally as "Barnyard," a nickname he received as the result of a high school play.

Lamar, who was born July 9, 1923, in Douglas County, Georgia, lives in Clarksville, Tennessee. He retired from the Navy in 1963. He married Mary Lou Pace who was born June 17, 1926 and died July 9, 1986. Their children are Linda Marie and Ronald Lamar. Linda (July 1, 1959) married Jeff Douglas, and they live in Irmo, South Carolina. They had three children: Lauren Marie (September 25, 1989), Hannah Brooks (June 12, 1993) and Kathryn Hunter (November 20, 1995-December 11, 1996). Ronald (September 21, 1960) lives in Clarksville.

Burell was born February 21, 1927, in DeKalb County, Georgia, and died February 24, 1984, and he is buried at Meadowbrook Memory Gardens, Villa Rica, Georgia. He served as a pharmacist's mate 3rd Class in the Navy during World War II. On August 22, 1952, he married Eva Ruth Roberts, daughter of Samuel Watson and Claire Otwell Roberts of Villa Rica, Georgia. They had two children: Kerry Mark and Scott Roberts. Mark was born August 27, 1954, in Villa Rica. He lives in Atlanta, Georgia, and is a pharmacist in DeKalb, County, Georgia. Scott was born September 9, 1958, in Villa Rica. He lives in Atlanta and is self-employed as a securities trader.

At one time, all five of the Holder sons served in the armed forces in World War II at the same time. *Submitted by: Ruth Holder, P.O. Box 70, Temple, GA 30179*

Sources: Personal knowledge and family records.

651. Russell William Holder

Russell William Holder was born at Hoopins Creek near Clem in Carroll County, Georgia, on November 29, 1867. Margaret Eugenia Smith (daughter of Barnett Smith and Mathilda White Smith) also from Carroll County became his bride October 13, 1889. Russell William Holder was an engineer, engaged in road contract work for the A.B. & A. Railroad. He lived and worked in several surrounding areas including Troup, Meriwether, and Coweta Counties. He later moved with his family to LaGrange, Georgia, and in 1899 was elected to the Lannett school board. He was re-elected the following year on June 30, 1900, and was also appointed to the library committee. His wife, Margaret Eugenia (Smith) Holder died March 30, 1907, at the age of thirty-five and was survived by her husband and five children. Russell William Holder was working in Manchester, Georgia, helping to map out the streets when he developed pneumonia. He died the same year as his wife on December 26, 1907.

Russell William Holder's father, James M. Holder was born in Carroll County, Georgia, in 1849. He was married to Susan F. Jones in Carroll County, Georgia, January 3, 1866. James died in 1877. His wife Susan died when her clothes caught fire in 1912. They are both buried at Antioch Church Cemetery in Banning near Whitesburg, Georgia. Eugenia (Smith) Holder's parents, Barnett Smith and Mathilda (White) Smith are also buried at Antioch.

Russell William Holder – 1867-1907

Russell William Holder's grandparents were Luda H. Holder and Martha (Cook) Holder. They were married in Carroll County November 15, 1846. Luda enlisted with the Volunteer Infantry, 56th Georgia Regiment, Company B, during the Civil War. He was wounded June 1862 when the Union Army attacked Chattanooga, Tennessee. He was transferred to a hospital in Atlanta, Georgia. He died there from his wounds on July 31, 1862. He is buried in the Confederate Section of Oakland Cemetery in Atlanta, Georgia, along with approximately two thousand five hundred other Confederate soldiers, where they now rest beneath the beautiful dogwood and magnolia trees. The War of Northern Aggression left Martha (Cook) Holder a widow with six children ranging from two to thirteen years of age. Martha died March 2, 1883, and is buried in the Dorris Cemetery in Carroll County, Georgia.

Luda H. Holder and Martha (Cook) Holder's son James and their grandson Russell William are only a few of their descendants. Today, Luda and Martha Holder's descendants from Carroll County, Georgia, number more than one thousand. Other families that are related to them from Carroll County include Askew, Burns, Camp, Cook, Derris, Duncan, Gable, Griffith, Lee, Morgan, Phillips, Rooks, Smith, Stitcher, Taylor, Webb, White, and Williams. *Submitted by: Becky Holder Buck, 240 North Harris Street, Sandersville, GA 31082*

652. James H. Holland

Our grandfather, James H. Holland, was born in 1879. He was the son of James E. Holland and Mary Vines Holland. His father was a well-known sawmill man. The family home was in Bowdon. He had three brothers. They were Jordan (who was killed at an early age in a sawmill accident), Mose (who was a farmer in Bowdon), and Richard (who left the sawmill business and moved to Carrollton). There were also four sisters. There was Mary, who owned a ladies dress shop in Bowdon. The other sisters married and moved away. They were Hattie of Doerun, Bertha of College Park, and Myrtie of Springfield, South Carolina.

Holland home place in Bowdon

Our grandfather married Jackie McCord and moved to East Point where he was connected with the Smith and Simpson Lumber Company until retirement. They had three children and they were Vera (our mother), Elbert (Dutch), and Richard (Dick). Our grandfather was also a preacher in the Primitive Baptist Church. They traveled around quite a bit on Sundays because he preached at several churches and they often took me and my two sisters with them.

Jim and Jackie Holland

After retirement in 1946, our grandparents moved back to Carroll County. They bought a farm on Shady Grove Road in Carrollton and raised some cotton and had a dairy cow or two. They lived happily there until our grandmother became ill and passed away. Our grandfather lived there a few more years. He passed away at the age of ninety in East Point, Georgia. *Submitted by: Dorothy Wheeler Coogler, 50 Frasier Drive, Brooks, GA 30205, Martha Wheeler Thompson, and Jackie Wheeler Wallace.*

653. John J. Holland and Cardis E. Lenderman

John J. Holland was born 25 December 1847 in Georgia and died 2 December 1915. He married Cardis E. Lenderman (see Lenderman Family) on 26 May 1864 in Coweta County, Georgia. She was born 4 March 1843 in Greenville County, South Carolina, and died 22 April 1914. Both John J. and Cardis E. died in Morgan County,

Alabama, and are buried at Hebron Church of Christ Cemetery, Hulaco. Shortly after their marriage, John and "Card" moved to Carroll County. When the New Bethel Church of Christ was organized in 1872, John and Card were on the membership roll. They grew strong in the work of the church and became a lasting influence on their children and grandchildren. In 1882, John and Card moved with their nine children to Morgan County, Alabama, to a small community called Hulaco. After their move, three more children were born to them.

At the time the Hollands settled in Hulaco, Card's sister, Sarah, with her husband Andrew J. Giles also made the move. These two families became influential in the church and community. In the coming years, Hulaco was to become the home of more of the Lenderman and allied families.

John and Cardis were instrumental in the organization of the Hebron Church of Christ. John donated the land for the building and the adjoining cemetery. A large percentage of this cemetery is made up of Lenderman and allied families. John and Cardis are buried there with at least three of their children.

John J. Holland and Cardis E. Lenderman

The following were the children of John J. and Cardis E. Holland: (1) George David Holland, born 30 March 1866 in Carroll County, married Harriet Montrose (Monty) Waldrop; (2) Mary Frances Holland, born 18 July 1867 in Carroll County; (3) William (Bill) J. Holland, born 14 September 1869 in Carroll County, married first to Nancy S., and second to Mattie; (4) James (Jim) H. Holland, born 10 July 1871 in Carroll County, married Alice Cornelia McCarley; (5) Lula Ann Holland, born 10 August 1873 in Carroll County, married Ollie Pinckney Garrett; (6) Thomas B. Holland, born 3 June 1875 in Carroll County; (7) Cornelia C. Holland, born 26 June 1876 in Carroll County, married Wylie Waldon Garrett; (8) Walter W. Holland, born 22 April 1878 in Carroll County, died 30 March 1914; (9) John Foster Holland, born 22 February 1880, in Carroll County, married Almedia Edmondson; (10) Susan B. Holland, born 16 January 1882 in Morgan County, died 12 March 1884 in Morgan County, buried in Hebron Church of Christ Cemetery; (11) Ida Cora Holland, born 8 March 1883 in Morgan County, married John Alonzo (Lon) Seals; and (12) Bertha M. Holland, born 30 May 1886 in Morgan County, died 12 November 1902, buried in the Hebron Church of Christ Cemetery. *Submitted by: Joe Hamrick, 1112 Monte Vista Drive, Gadsden, AL 35903*

654. The Lindsey Holland Family

Lindsey Nathaniel Holland, son of Talton and Susannah (Susan) Shelnut Holland was born March 12, 1839, in Fayette County, Georgia. He married his first cousin, Rebecca Saphronia Shelnut, on July 10, 1860, probably in Haralson County, Georgia. Rebecca was the daughter of John and Edna Shelnut. John was the brother of Susan Shelnut Holland. Rebecca was born December 4, 1844, in Campbell County, Georgia. Lindsey's and Rebecca's parents moved to Carroll County, Georgia, about 1850 or 1851. They settled just north of what is now Waco, Georgia. This part of Carroll County later became Haralson County.

Talton Holland's and John Shelnut's families were very close, and there were several marriages between members of the two families in addition to Lindsey's and Susan's marriage. The Holland and Shelnut families helped to establish what is now the Bethlehem United Methodist Church, and Lindsey was the first preacher. Most members of the families attended the church. The first church building was also used as a school building and was called Holland's school.

Lindsey and Rebecca had nine children. They were John Talton Martin born February 24, 1865; James Marion (Jim) born May 26, 1867; Jefferson Andrew Washington (Jeff) born October 5, 1868; Joseph Henson born September 28, 1870; Mary Samantha (Daught) Holland born November 10, 1872; Nancy Elizabeth born October 20, 1874; Harriet Saphronia born October 3, 1877; Joshua Nathaniel (Nat) born October 8, 1879; and Jasper William Christopher born February 19, 1881. Nancy, Harriet, and Jasper never married. Daught Holland married Doxey Wilburn Holloway September 16, 1888, and Jeff Holland married Mary Ann (Molly) Felton the same day. Following his parents' example, Martin Holland married his first cousin, Mandy Miller, November 8, 1888. Mandy was the daughter of John William Miller, Edna (Unknown) Miller Cochran Shelnut's son, and Elizabeth Jane Holland Miller, Lindsey's sister. Jim Holland married Soloma A. Felton September 18, 1889. She was the sister of Molly Shelnut who married Jeff Holland. All these marriages were in Haralson County, Georgia.

In 1894, Lindsey and Rebecca Holland moved their family to Jackson County, Alabama. All of their married children also moved their families to Jackson County at the same time. Rebecca Holland's sister's family, James Martin and Mary H. Shelnut Adams, had already moved to Jackson County, Alabama, a few years earlier. Several other neighboring families from Haralson County, Georgia, moved to Jackson County, Alabama at the same time using twenty-two covered wagons. One was William Riley LovvornLovvorn's family. His wife Nancy Malinda Lavvorn, is believed to be Lindsey Holland's aunt, sister of Talton Holland. Another of the families was Seaborn Holloway, Doxie Wilburn's father.

The move to Alabama proved costly for the Holland family. Martin and Mandy Holland lost three daughters, and Jeff and Molly Holland lost a son within a two-week period in November 1897. Seaborn Holloway donated land for a cemetery. It is now a large cemetery, Pleasant View Cemetery, where many of the Holland, Lovvorn, and Holloway family members were buried. *Submitted by: Larry W. Holland, 222 County Road 383, Dutton, AL 35744*

Sources: Census, land, marriage, cemetery, and court records in Fayette, Carroll, and Haralson County, Georgia, and Jackson County, Alabama; *Histories of the Holland and Shelnut Families* by Fred Simpson; *The Shelnutt Book of Records* by Jane (Cobb) Shelnutt; and *The Miller Family Tree* by Brett L. Whiteside.

655. The Talton Holland Family

Talton Holland was the son of Rebecca Holland. It is not known for sure who his father was. In 1830 Rebecca was living in Fayette County, Georgia, near what is now Fairburn, with two sons and four daughters. Lindsey and James H. Holland, thought to be Rebecca's sons, were living nearby. The two sons living with Rebecca were probably Talton and Eli. One of the daughters is believed to be Nancy Malinda Holland who later married William Riley Lovvorn. The names of the other three daughters are not known.

On April 13, 1838, Talton Holland, born January 15, 1809, married Susannah Levina (Susan) Shelnut, born November 6, 1811, in Fayette County, Georgia. Susan Shelnut was the daughter of Andrew and Elizabeth Gentry Shelnut. Near the end of 1850 or early 1851, Talton and Susan sold their land in Fayette County and moved to Carroll County between Waco and Buchanan, Georgia. They lived near what is now the Bethlehem United Methodist Church building. Susan's mother, Elizabeth Shelnut, was already living in Carroll County with her son Andrew J. Shelnut. Her brother Nathaniel (Nat) Shelnut also moved to Carroll County. Nat was one of the earliest settlers in the town of Bowdon and was a judge in Bowdon. James H. Holland also moved to Carroll County and lived near Dallas, Georgia.

Talton and Susan Holland had four or five sons and two daughters. They were Lindsey Nathaniel born March 12, 1839; Elizabeth Jane born November 10, 1840; Andrew J. born August 18, 1842; Rebecca M. born August 25, 1844; Isaac Washington born December 15, 1847; Eli Thomas born March 13, 1852; and possibly William E. born December 3, 1854. William E. may have been the son of Lindsey Holland who was living in the household of Susan Holland in the 1860 census. He was listed after Lindsey as if he were Lindsey's son, but he was still living in Susan's household in 1870.

Lindsey Nathaniel Holland married Rebecca Saphronia Shelnut, his first cousin. She was the daughter of Susan Shelnut Holland's brother, John Shelnut and Edna (unknown) Cochran Miller Shelnut. Lindsey and Rebecca had six sons and three daughters. They were John Talton Martin, James Marion (Jim), Jefferson Andrew Washington (Jeff), Joseph Henson (Joe), Mary Samantha (Daught), Nancy Elizabeth, Harriet Saphronia, Joshua Nathaniel (Nat), and Jasper William Christopher.

Elizabeth Jane Holland married John William Miller, who was Edna Shelnut's son by a previous marriage. They had three sons and seven daughters. They were Edna Susana, Mary Elizabeth (Polly), Amanda Rebecca (Mandy), Nancy Jane (Nan), Sarah Ellen (Sally), John William Jr. (Bud), James Nathaniel (Jim), Harriet Marial (Hattie), Andrew W. (Andy), and Saphronia Clementine. Mandy Miller married John Talton Martin Holland who was Lindsey Nathaniel and Rebecca Shelnut Holland's oldest son.

Andrew J. Holland was a Confederate soldier and died April 27, 1862, at Knoxville, Tennessee. William E. Holland died August 3, 1872. *Submitted by: Marja Brock, 1606 Oscar Patterson Rd., New Market, AL 35761*

Sources: Census, land, marriage, cemetery, and court records in Fayette, Carroll, and Haralson County, Georgia; *Histories of the Holland and Shelnut Families* by Fred Simpson; *The Shelnutt Book of Records* by Jane (Cobb) Shelnutt; and *The Miller Family Tree* by Brett L. Whiteside.

656. Holland - Lassetter 1776-1862

Part 1

James Hodson Holland

The genealogy line to our Carden family goes like this: William Holland Sr. has a son James H. Holland, who has son Lindsey Holland, who has daughter Nancy Jerusha Holland who marries William Jackson Lassetter. Their daughter Mollie marries Sam Carden.

William Holland was born in 1776 in Nansemond, Virginia. He married Rebecca (unknown) Holland. They had a son James Hodson Holland who was born October 21, 1801, in Greenville,

James Hodson Holland

South Carolina. James died March 4, 1862. He married Mary Smith 1821 in Madison County, Georgia. She was born October 17, 1805, in Kentucky and died September 9, 1855, in Georgia. James moved from Fayette County to Carroll in the 1820s, settling near Whitesburg at Byer's Cross Roads.

Excerpts about James Hodson Holland are quoted below from Edith Foster's booklet entitled, *St. Paul Methodist Church, Legend of a Church That Would Not Die.*

> His one-room church, known as Holland's Meeting House, became St. Paul Methodist Church. It was in the fall of 1823, two years before the signing of the famous Treaty at Indian Springs whereby General William McIntosh, Chief of the Cowetas, and other Creek Chiefs, sold much of the Creek Territory to Georgia, a section of which was to become Carroll County, that James H. Holland moved from Fayette County, Georgia to the Third District of the area to be laid out in 1826 as Carroll County, settling on a large tract of land near the Chattahoochee River. Here he established a river farm on Land Lot No. 96 nearby a small settlement later to be known as Byers Cross Roads.
>
> Two years afterwards, in 1825, prior to the formation of the county, Mr. Holland, a devout Christian, follower of the Methodist doctrine, and a leader among men, constructed on his land a one-room log building accessible to the surrounding neighborhood as a religious meeting place, a school for the children, and a friendly gathering point. It was called Holland's Meeting House, and the predecessor of St. Paul Methodist Church. For the next thirty years Holland's Meeting House continued to service its good purpose.
>
> In 1853 James Holland sold his river acreage on Land Lot No. 96 in the Third District, purchasing another farm seven miles to the northwest on Land Lot No. 212, located in the vicinity of Little Bethel Community. Upon settling down at his new location, Mr. Holland built a large one-room log house, which he again made available as a place of worship for the neighborhood. It too received the name Holland's Meeting House. In addition to serving as a church, the building was used as a schoolhouse and a center for community social gatherings.
>
> For over thirty-five years, James Holland was the patriarch of his community, serving not only as religious leader but also as public relations proponent of coming together, old and young, to share a variety of activities of helpful import. Not only was he a participant in these functions, but as has been noted, he also provided the Meeting House. Here the rafters doubtless rang with laughter during sewing bees and quilting parties. Here, from all around the area, the people gathered to have a part in or to observe the periodic spelling contest (which literally came of age in such rural communities). Here the families met to plan corn shuckings and log rollings.
>
> From eight to four Monday through Friday, the Meeting House was an educational institute during the winter months and for a month or so during the summer. The children generally walked to school, carrying their slates and their lunch pails (which might have contained cold baked sweet potatoes, sausage and biscuit, or fried ham), to study and recite under the tutelage of one teacher chosen by local trustees, who after something of an examination, deemed the pedagogue capable of handling such rudiments of learning as arithmetic, spelling, and reading. On Friday afternoons, the time was given over to recitations and singing and turning down spelling matches.
>
> James H. Holland died in 1862 while the War Between the States was just settling into a devastating pace. Measured by modern consideration, he did not die an old man; however as a farmer and the operator and owner of a grist mill, the father of a large family of four boys and eight girls, an outstanding example of fine community leadership, the pillar and sustainer of church worship, he made his lasting mark upon his fellowman, leaving behind him a rich heritage." *(See note)
>
> As was the custom of the pioneer settler, as the children married, setting up their on home places, they usually established themselves in the vicinity of their father's home, so that ties remained strong. Such was the case of the Holland progeny; thus there resulted the development of good Christian character and good citizenship, which sterling qualities were handed down to the third and fourth generations.
>
> For example, James H. Holland's, oldest son, Lindsey, was a farmer, a miller, a postmaster, and a member of the Georgia Legislature. Lindsey's son, Frank, as a young man taught school in Florida, where he married a young woman from Virginia. There they made their home. Frank's son, Spessard, served for a number of years as Governor of Florida and for 25 years as a distinguished United States Senator from the State of Florida, serving his state and nation.

Note: Research indicates that James H. Holland was married twice to wives named Mary. His first, born 1805, died in the early 1850s. He married Mary A. Christian on November 25, 1855, in Carroll County. Two of his sons served in the Civil War. When James Hodson Holland went to see Lindsey (captured in the war), he caught pneumonia from the cold and dampness of the train and died a few days later on March 4, 1862. James H. and his two wives are buried at St. Paul Methodist Church (formerly Holland's Meeting House at Whitesburg, Georgia). Children of James H. Holland and Mary Smith are: (1) James H. Holland Jr., (2) Lindsey Holland, 1824-1912 (See next article), (3) Jordan S. Holland, (4) Tyree W. Holland. *Submitted by: Sherie Carden, Douglasville, GA*

Sources: Portions copied from *The Church That Would Not Die,* by Edith Foster; researched by Erlene Boyd, Villa Rica, GA, and Nancy Anne Willis Howell, Douglasville, GA

657. Holland - Lassetter 1824-1912

Part 2

Lindsey Holland

Lindsey Holland was a miller at Holland's Grist Mill on Wolf Creek in Whitesburg and may have served as postmaster at one time. He served in the Civil War and is buried at Lone Wolf Cemetery (apparently near his old home place or business). His brother, Jordan S. Holland, also served in Civil War and is buried there. Though Lindsey was captured in the war, neither brother died in the war.

Aunt Nancy Bartlett was twelve years old when her great-grandfather Lindsey Holland died, and again I quote from her remembrances, "My great-grandfather, Lindsey Holland, was the father of my grandmother Nannie Holland Lassetter (See her article later). He ran a grist mill on Dog River and was a very religious, kind, and friendly man. He was always ready to give a helping hand to any and everyone. He always had time for all of us children. He would talk to us and say, 'Love people and they will love you, Be kind to old people for you will be old one day.' He died when I was small, but I've never forgotten his talks. One day a man and his family stopped by the mill with all their worldly goods on their wagon. He asked grandfather for enough meal for his family. Of course, grandfather gave him a bushel of meal. The man then asked if the people in Georgia were friendly and good neighbors, and grandfather said, 'Yes, the best.' The man then said he was glad, for he had no neighbors from where he was coming. Grandpa then replied, 'Well brother if you had no neighbors in _____ , I'm afraid you won't in Georgia, as you have to be a good neighbor to have them.' "

Lindsey Holland

Aunt Nancy continued, "His first wife was part Indian. I did not know her, but their daughter was my grandmother "Nannie" Nancy J. Holland." She ended her story by saying, "He was the best Christian man I ever knew."

Lindsey was born July 28, 1824, married Elizabeth Lassetter, December 16, 1841, and died January 13, 1912. He was the son of James H. Holland (see previous article) and the grandfather of Spessard Lindsey Holland, former governor and senator of Florida. (See Spessard article.)

Lindsey's first wife, Elizabeth Lassiter, was daughter of Benjamin and his first wife Elizabeth Doris Hill Lassiter (sometime spelled Laciter, Lassiter, Lassetter).

Note: Research has shown in older records that names are often spelled several different ways in the same document. Benjamin's father, Tobias Lassetter, first appears when he is mentioned in his father's (John Laciter) will. John Laciter's will is dated January 15, 1759, in Chowan County, North Carolina. It is believed that one of the Lassiter men from North Carolina married a Cherokee Indian girl and Tobias Lassetter was one of their descendants (whether son or grandson is unclear).

A legal document written by Lindsey Holland at age eighty-three gives an account "in the matter of the Cherokee origin of Benjamin Lassetter." Lindsey Holland states how "Benjamin Lassetter, father of Elizabeth, (Lindsey's first wife) served in the Grand Jury Box of Henry County, Georgia." And how "honesty was a prominent virtue in his make up. He was faithful to his friends, his promises, and the truth." Lindsey goes on to tell when he asked Benjamin for his daughter, he said, "Lindsey, I have but one objection. You both are most too young." Lindsey agreed but told the father they were suited to each other and could get along, etc. Benjamin then said, "There was another fact, if he gave his daughter he wanted me to know that I was marrying a girl with right smart Indian blood in her veins and now was the time for me to find out. He further stated he told everyone who wanted to marry his daughters this fact." Lindsey told him "she suited him, Indian blood or no Indian blood, and so we were happily married, and I never had reason to regret my choice."

Lindsey and Elizabeth Lassitter (1824-1855) had several children. She died at age thirty-one. Their children were: (1) Sarah "Sallie" Holland married James Hollis. (2) Benjamin Franklin "Frank" Holland married Fannie Virginia Spessard (Governor Spessard Lindsey Holland comes from this line). (3) Harriet Ann "Hattie" Holland married John Houseworth (Dr. Delvas Houseworth in Douglas County comes from this line). (4) Elizabeth Holland, marriage unknown. (5) Mary Holland married Dr. Isham N. Brown. (6) Nancy Jerusha Holland married William J. Lassetter.

Our family line comes from their daughter Nancy Jerusha Holland, who was only two years old when her mother Elizabeth died. (See article and continuation in Nancy J. Holland and William J. Lassetter article). Nancy J. Holland, whose mother was a Lassiter, married a Lassetter. The genealogy does not make a connection between the two Lassetter families.

Lindsey outlived his three wives. He married Elizabeth (part Indian) when they were seventeen. The 1850 Carroll census, #599, shows Lindsey age 25 and Elizabeth age 25, children were Sarah 6, Benjamin 4, Harriet 2, Elizabeth 3 months (born June). Mary was born in 1852 and Nancy Jerusha was born in 1853. Their mother, Elizabeth, died in 1855. Lindsey married Martha Jordan in Carroll County in 1856. They had a daughter Martha (called Mattie) Holland, 1857. The 1870 census shows Lindsey living in Coweta County. Carroll County census in 1880 shows Lindsey and third wife Sarah Ballard and father-in-law William Ballard in the same household. Lindsey and Sarah had two girls, Lettie Ora born 1869, and Kate Holland born 1871. Lindsey was postmaster and miller at Holland's Mills, and JP is mentioned in one writing. It was stated "He operated a corn mill and was a very prominent man in the community, especially in Masonic circles" His mill on Wolf Creek in Carroll County is south of the Douglas County line. The 1879 *Georgia Gazetteer* lists the population there as less than twenty-five with I.N. Brown and George W. Camp as physicians, Walter C. Camp as constable, W.B. Richards as J.P., John R. Smallwood as carpenter, Lindsey Holland postmaster, Jordan S. Holland (Lindsey's brother) millwright, etc.

Many of these ancestors are buried at Mt. Zion Baptist Church, Highway 5, and St. Paul Methodist Church in Carroll County. *Submitted by: Reneé Banks, third-great-granddaughter.*

Sources: Research by Erlene Boyd, Villa Rica, GA, and Joe Baggett, Douglasville, GA; personal knowledge about family from Nancy Anne Willis Howell, Douglasville, GA

658. Holland - Lassetter 1892-1971

Part 3

Spessard Lindsey Holland

Spessard Lindsey Holland was born in 1892 and became Florida's twenty-eighth governor and served as senator of the state for twenty-four years. He died in 1971. Spessard's father was Benjamin Franklin Holland, his grandfather was Lindsey Holland, (Part 2 of this series,) and great-grandfather was James H. Holland (Part 1 of this series). James H. settled in Carroll County in 1823.

Spessard Holland

Lindsey Holland was Nancy Jerusha Holland's (Lassetter) father. Also, Nancy J. was Mollie Lassetter's (Carden's) mother. Again, I am trying to make the genealogy line clear for these Holland-Lassetter-Carden families.

I have taken most of this information on Spessard from a biographical sketch from the Internet. He is said to be one of the top ten governors of the state of Florida. You will enjoy reading this article. He loved baseball, too.

He had the stuff to pitch professionally for the Philadelphia Athletics in 1916, but the 24 year old University of Florida all-star athlete turned down the offer. With his law degree intact, Spessard Lindsey Holland returned to the mossy oaks and magnolias of his native Bartow. For the next 54 years, he pitched a different game — major league politics — without resorting to curveballs, spitballs or sliders.

Holland was born in Bartow, Florida, in 1892. He invigorated Florida politics with an integrity instilled by his schoolteacher mother and the sort of homespun ideals a boy learns early on by milking the family cow.

At the onset of WWI, he abandoned his Bartow law practice and traveled overseas as an Army Air Corps aerial observer in a cloth-winged aircraft. He survived the downing of his plane during combat. His political career was equally charmed. He never lost an election.

Appointed Polk County, Florida, prosecutor after the war, Holland was elected county judge in 1920. Eight years later, he returned to private practice and formed a partnership that would evolve into Holland & Knight, an international law firm.

As governor during WWII, Holland turned the influx of military and industrial employees into a cash bonanza. He imposed taxes on cigarettes and gasoline to obliterate a $4 million debt that was incurred by the previous administration, to buy school textbooks and to build more than 1,500 miles of highway. A man obsessed with the outdoors, he also was instrumental in creating Everglades National Park and the Florida Game and Fresh Water Fish Commission.

The office he once compared to a political graveyard served as a steppingstone to Washington and a 24 year career as a U.S. Senator, serving under Presidents Truman, Eisenhower, Kennedy, Johnson and Nixon. The man whose calm but commanding presence twice backed down angry lynch mobs in Lakeland and Tallahassee succumbed to a weak heart in 1971, just one year after leaving office. His wife, Mary Groover found him slumped over a radio at their home in Bartow. He was 79. Holland never regretted letting his law practice take a back seat to politics.

Submitted by: Lisa Sticher Thompson, Carrollton, GA, third great-granddaughter of Lindsey Holland, and compiled by Nancy Anne Willis Howell, Douglasville, GA

659. James Wesley and Lula Burns Hollingsworth

The Carroll Free Press reported in 1929 that James Wesley — known by his family and fellow farmers as Jim — was one of the biggest and most diversified farmers in Carroll County. He was born in Heard County April 16, 1860, and the fifth child of Levi and Betsy Ann Echols Hollingsworth who had settled along the Chattahoochee River and established Hollingsworth's Ferry, had a wool carding mill, furniture factory, gristmill and farmed. Jim was educated in the rural schools, and as a boy and young man worked on his father's farm in Heard County.

J.W. "Jim" and Lula Burns Hollingsworth with daughter Lunette

On January 16, 1890, he married Lula Burns who was born October 20, 1868, in Carroll County to James W. and Elizabeth Moore Burns. When teachers were not available at New Lebanon School, Lula's parents moved to Bowdon during the school year so the children could attend school. Jim and Lula lived in Heard County until the later part of 1892 when they moved to Carroll County and lived with Lula's parents while Jim sawed timber from his new farm to build his family a new home just north of the Lowell community. Expecting her fourth child, Lula was anxious to move into the new house, and in January 1900 she summoned the helpers and wagon, moving before Jim had planned. Annie, the oldest daughter walked behind the wagon carrying the clock so as not to disturb the balance.

Jim cultivated 700 acres "operating seven plows" with sharecroppers, growing cotton, potatoes, corn, oats, hogs, cattle, truck vegetables and sorghum. In the fall the "smell from the syrup mill would make your mouth water." He owned a threshing machine and would contract to thresh oats for other farmers. Cotton was the major crop and in 1914 they proudced 1800 pounds of seed cotton per acre. It was not unusual for one worker to pick 400 pounds of cotton per day. In 1920 the cotton sold for four cents a pound.

The six children walked one mile to Lowell School and attended A&M School in Carrollton for high school. The 1916 Grant automobile was a welcome replacement for the surrey and the two hour round trip to Carrollton. The Delco system for power brought the radio and lights in 1924.

Jim and Lula gave each of their children one hundred acres of land to farm. Annie, born November 5, 1890, and Lunette born March 4, 1894, remained on the home place until their deaths January 17, 1986, and May 29, 1983, respectively. In addition to the two daughters they reared four sons; James Fredrick born February 27, 1896, and died July 9, 1980; John born February 16, 1900, and died April 11, 1986; Benjamin Levi born February 11, 1902, and died January 10, 1983; and Charles Wesley born November 23, 1911, and died January 9, 1973. Jim was deceased on January 15, 1944, after years of declining health and Lula, a founding members of the Lowell Methodist Church, died at home February 2, 1952. All are buried in the Lowell Community Cemetery. The immigrant ancestors of the Hollingsworth came from Ireland to Delaware in 1682 and migrated to Virginia and South Carolina and into Georgia in 1815. *Submitted by: Jonathan M. Stober, Route 2, Newton, GA 31770*

Source: *Carroll Free Press, Decendants of Valentine Hollingsworth Sr.*, personal records

660. John and Angeline Spence Hollingsworth

John Hollingsworth, born February 16, 1900, and Flora Angeline Spence, born July 21, 1906, were life long residents of the Lowell community. They were married November 2, 1924, in Newnan, Georgia, by the Rev. J.E. Hannah and honeymooned in Atlanta. They built their home in a cotton patch just north of his parents, planting many trees and an orchard of fruit trees. Their parents, Jim and Lula Hollingsworth and John R. and Eula Spence, were among the early settlers in Lowell. John and Angeline attended school at Lowell and John continued to A&M School in Carrollton.

John and Angeline Spence Hollingsworth

As a young man John worked at Jackson Store for $50 per month plus board. A daily ledger was kept, as most business was a trade or credit. During 1934-39 he farmed and drove a school bus. He also worked in the fall during cotton harvest for the Farmers Mutual Exchange grading cotton for the co-op. John and Angeline farmed their 250-acre farm with help from the sharecropper families of Luke Cosper, Hershel Bonner, and Lamon Strickland until the boll weevil made cotton farming unproductive. Lamon remained on the farm until his death but Luke and his family moved north in 1948. John served on the Carroll County Board of Education for fifteen years from 1938 to 1953. When Bell Aircraft opened, he, along with many other local men and women, traveled to Marietta to work until the plant closed after World War II. In 1946 Carroll Frozen Food and Provision Company opened and he became a buyer of hogs and cattle for slaughter. Lockheed Aircraft opened in 1951, where he worked as a tool and die maker until his retirement in 1965.

Angeline, named for her grandmother Angelina Cheney Spence, ran the farm during his absence on his long work days in Marietta. She was an avid rose gardener and had a garden of more than 150 bushes at the time of her death August 31, 1984. She was a member of the Sallie Duncan Home Demonstration Club and a skillful seamstress, winning local and state dress review competitions.

John was among the first in Carroll County to convert his cropland into pasture and acquired a herd of Hereford cattle. He raised many prize-winning bulls and ran a cow-calf operation until his death April 11, 1986. They were both active members of the Lowell Methodist Church and are buried in the Lowell Community Cemetery. Their son John Mark was born March 9, 1929, married Helen Ray June 19, 1954, and tragically died in a boating accident on Lake Altoona July 10, 1965. Their children are David, Jane and Mark. A daughter Angie Nell, born August 6, 1938, married Jerry Stober on December 26, 1965, and together with their children Jonathan and Alyson continue to operate the family farm on Lowell Road. *Submitted by: Alyson C. Stober, 1071 Lowell Road, Carrollton, GA 30116*

Source: Personal records

661. The Larry Hollingsworth Family

If you were a traveler in the mid-nineteenth century-in a horse and buggy or in a wagon with a mule team-you would eventually find the need to cross the Chattahoochee River at a place known as Hollingsworth's Ferry. This old ferry was originally built by my great-grandfather, Levi Hollingsworth, at a point which was downstream from where an old wooden bridge used to cross the river.

The bridge was made of hand-hewn pine logs and spanned 70 yards across the river. A story in our family says the bridge had stood until the Civil War when word had reached Levi Hollingsworth that Sherman's troops were advancing closer and closer to the Yellowdirt community where he lived in Heard County, Georgia.

When Levi head of the advancing Yankees, he and some of his slaves went out to destroy the bridge so that it would not be of advantage to the Union troops. So, the bridge was not there when Sherman's troops arrived — and neither was anything left of the community after the Yankee troops had passed through and torched everything. All was gone — the woolen mill, grist mill, brick kilns, furniture factory, cotton gins. All these had been in full operation until General Sherman passed through. All these mills had been powered by the first dam ever built across the Chattahoochee — 10 feet tall — built by the first Hollingsworths to come into this area.

The bridge was never built back, instead, after the war ended, Levi Hollingsworth established the ferry about 100 yards down stream from where the old bridge had been. Hollingsworth's Ferry was located 14 miles from Whitesburg and 19 miles from Franklin, about where Plant Wansley is located now. In the era before interstate highways and concrete bridges, the ferries were the only means of crossing the river. The ferries transported livestock, horses, mill workers, travelers, families, mules, wagons, buggies, tractors and later on (after they were invented) even automobiles.

The ferry relied on the river's current to take the people across. The ferryman had to know just how to angle the direction of the ferry to get it across the river. In the early days, the ferryman had to pull on the rope to take the ferry over. Later on, a big reel was used to wind up the rope and carry the ferry to the other side. "Sometimes it could be dangerous," Larry Hollingsworth explained. "Once when my own father, Rob Hollingsworth, was a young man working the ferry, some mules hitched to a wagon bolted and they jumped off the ferry into the river. Since they were hitched to a wagon, they were immediately weighted down under the water. My father had to jump into the river and cut the hames traces in order to keep the mules from drowning." Many of the Hollingsworth men captained the ferry over the years — and later on, Joe Stephens, Ed Wright, Walter, Coot, and Pink Webb.

A man wanting to cross the river would ring a bell to alert the ferryman that he was needed. Sometimes the ferryman would wait until he had several people wanting to cross before taking the ferry over to the other side. For a hundred years or more, Hollingsworth's Ferry was an important mode of transportation for people who had business in Carroll, Coweta, or Heard Counties.

Larry Wingo Hollingsworth was born 23 October 1929 in Carroll County, Georgia, the son of Robert Allen "Rob" Hollingsworth Sr. (1899-1978) and Ozelma Cornelia Wingo (1903-1949). Larry was about ten years older than his only brother who was Robert Allen "Bob" Hollingsworth. After Robert Allen Hollingsworth's first wife had died, he married a second time to Nellie Ruth Shadinger, daughter of William "Billy" Carroll Shadinger and Burma Alberta Moore.

Both Larry and his brother Bob grew up in Carroll County, Georgia, and graduated from Carrollton High School and Southern Technical Institute, majoring in building construction. Larry Hollingsworth began in 1954 with a construction company that built many schools, hospitals, and churches. He also built the Carrollton High School football stadium, named in honor of Charlie Grisham. Larry and Patsy Hollingsworth started Redimix Concrete Company in 1959.

Bob and Peggy Hollingsworth were the owners of Masonry Products, Inc. Bob Hollingsworth was tragically killed when he and his sons were involved in an airplane crash in 1998. Bob's son, Allen Hollingsworth, also died in this terrible accident and Stacey Hollingsworth was badly injured, but survived. Stacey is now a veterinarian in Haralson County. Bob Hollingsworth's widow, Peggy Carroll Hollingsworth, survived him by only about a year. Bob and Peggy also had a daughter named Cornelia Ann Hollingsworth.

Larry W. Hollingsworth married Patricia Ann Smith, daughter of W.M. and Flonnie Smith of Carrollton, Georgia, on December 21, 1952. Patsy Hollingsworth was born 27 March 1933. Both Patsy and Larry have been active in civic affairs. Larry Hollingsworth served as a member of the board of Tanner Medical Center for nine years. Patsy has been active as a member of the Civic Woman's Club and has also been a member of Beta Sigma Phi social sorority. The Hollingsworths are charter members of Trinity Baptist Church. Patsy and Larry Hollingsworth are the parents of five children: (1) Larry Wingo Hollingsworth Jr. born 3 May 1956 who now owns Cowart's Plumbing and Septic Service (2) Walter Allen Hollingsworth born 18 July 1957 who graduated from Auburn in 1981 with a degree in landscaping design and now runs the Hollingsworth Concrete plant (3) Ray Smith Hollingsworth born 20 July 1959 and died 20 July 1959, buried Carroll Memory Gardens (4) Joseph Patrick Hollingsworth born 3 October 1962 and graduated from Georgia Southwestern in Americus (5) Patricia Anne "Patti" Hollingsworth born 3 December 1967. Patti Hollingsworth graduated from Auburn University and was an Auburn majorette during her college years. Patti married Russ Carreker of Americus, Georgia, and they have one daughter, Patricia Avery Carreker born 18 January 1992.

Larry and Patsy Hollingsworth, Patti, Larry Jr., Walt, and Joe 1967

The Hollingsworths have an extensive family tree that traces back twelve generations to Valentine Hollingsworth Sr., the Irish Quaker who first came to America in 1682 at the invitation of William Penn. The Hollingsworths were originally an old Saxon family who took their name from the grand holly trees that surrounded their estates in England. Patsy and Larry Hollingsworth visited this old ancestral estate of the Hollingsworths in England in 1978. Much of the original Hollingsworth Hall is in ruins now, but the dairy farm still exists. And the people who live there have an entertaining history to tell about the Hollingsworths who once lived there.

It was in the 17th century that the Hollingsworths had begun to migrate from England into Ireland in an attempt to escape the religious persecution the Quakers were suffering at that time. On 7 April 1655, Valentine Hollingsworth married Ann Ree, daughter of Nicholas Ree of County Armagh, Ireland. Ann Ree was the mother of Thomas Hollingsworth who became the progenitor of the Hollingsworths of Carroll County, Georgia. However, Ann Ree Hollingsworth never lived to see America since she died in Ireland in 1671 before the family's migration to the New World. Valentine Hollingsworth married a second time to Ann Calvert, who was related to the Lord Calvert who first established Maryland.

In 1682, Valentine Hollingsworth and his family sailed from Belfast, Ireland, arriving in America only a few months after William Penn. They arrived on the ship *Antelope*, one of William Penn's fleet bringing Quakers to America. The Hollingsworths landed at New Castle, which was then a part of the Province of Pennsylvania, but is now Delaware. Their estate was a plantation of a thousand acres near Brandywine Hundred. The Hollingsworths named their property "New Work" and this later became the thriving town of Newark, Delaware.

Valentine Hollingsworth became a man of great influence in political and religious affairs. He became a member of the First Assembly of the Province of Pennsylvania and also was a signer of Penn's Great Charter. Early meetings of the Quakers were held in the Hollingsworth home and Valentine Hollingsworth also donated property to the Friends to be used as a burial ground. In 1711, Valentine was buried there, alongside his second wife, Ann Calvert Hollingsworth.

The Hollingsworth family can be traced for a dozen generations and has been extensively documented in the book called *Valentine Hollingsworth* written in 1906. Those generations will not be repeated here, but instead we will begin with Joseph Hollingsworth born 22 September 1765. Joseph married in 1789 to Rosannah Nichols who was born 15 January 1767. Their son, Joseph born 10 April 1797, married Elizabeth Jane Carr Rogers who was a descendant of Thomas Rogers who first came to America on the *Mayflower*. Elizabeth Jane was born 14 February 1795. Joseph Hollingsworth Sr. and his wife Rosannah Hollingsworth are buried at Smyrna Church Cemetery in Rockdale County, Georgia. Joseph died 8 April 1844. Rosannah died 10 March 1839.

Joseph and Elizabeth Jane Hollingsworth were the parents of a large family including the son named Levi born 1822. About 1825, Joseph Hollingsworth moved his family to Newton County, Georgia. Joseph served as a member of the Georgia State Legislature there. Joseph Hollingsworth died 13 June 1859 and was buried at Hollingsworth's Ferry at Heard County, Georgia. Elizabeth Jane Hollingsworth died 4 February 1881 and was buried alongside her husband.

Levi Hollingsworth was born 25 December 1822 in Laurens District, South Carolina. He married Betsy Echols of Heard County on 19 December 1844 in Coweta County. Betsy was born 21 April 1828 and died 4 January 1917. Levi Hollingsworth died 23 May 1899 and both he and his wife were buried at Hollingsworth Cemetery in Heard County near the old Hollingsworth's Ferry.

The son of Levi and Betsy Echols Hollingsworth was Robert Stacey Hollingsworth born 18 March 1868, died 8 November 1927. Robert S. Hollingsworth married Anna Elizabeth Lane. Their son, Robert Allen Hollingsworth was born 2 May 1898. Robert Stacey Hollingsworth was actually the last member of the Hollingsworth family to be buried in the Hollingsworth Family Cemetery. Anna Elizabeth Hollingsworth died September 1905.

Robert Allen Hollingsworth married Cornelia Ozelma Wingo who was born 9 August 1903, the daughter of Ollie V. Wingo and Anolda Nelson Vineyard. The Wingos were a prominent old family of Petersburg, Virginia, and Spartanburg, South Carolina. The Wingos were descended from Abner Wingo Sr. and his wife Elizabeth Seay of Petersburg, and from Abner Wingo Jr. (born 8 July 1810) and his wife Missouri McCrory (born 25 October 1815) of Spartanburg. Abner Jr. and Missouri had married in Spartanburg on 1 December 1831 and shortly afterward, they had moved to Heard County, Georgia. Abner Wingo had followed in the tradition of his family and become a hatter. He especially made felt hats which were popular with men of that era. According to family Bible records, we know that Ollie V. Wingo died 13 March 1908. Cornelia Ozelma Wingo Hollingsworth died 5 September 1949. Robert Allen "Rob" Hollingsworth died November 1979.

Larry Hollingsworth is also descended from one of Carroll County's earliest pioneers Samuel Dorrell Echols. He was the father of Betsy Echols who married Levi Hollingsworth. Samuel Dorrell Echols was born in Wilkes County, Georgia, and married Elizabeth Wood in Clarke County, Georgia, in 1808. Elizabeth was the daughter of Richard Wood and Tabitha Glass of Clarke County, Georgia. Richard Wood was the son of William Wood, a Revolutionary war soldier.

The parents of Samuel D. Echols were Milner Echols and Susannah Samson, both of whom were born in Virginia. In 1785, Milner Echols had moved to Wilkes County, Georgia, with his father James Echols, also a Revolutionary war soldier. James Echols wife was Elizabeth Milner Palmer. James Echols had built new wagons for his family's journey overland to Georgia. The Echols had settled in the historic area of Kettle Creek.

Samuel D. Echols and his new bride, Elizabeth, moved in 1808 to Newton County, Georgia. Later, the Echols family migrated to Carroll County, Georgia, where Samuel D. Echols purchased land on 7 March 1843 "from Ezekiel S. Candler in the 4th district, land adjoining that of J.P. Cosper, belonging to John M. Walden," Deed Book E p. 45. Samuel D. Echols was also present in August of 1837 when he witnessed a deed of Joseph Sentall to Samuel's son, Winston M. Echols for Land Lot #99 in 4th District of Carroll County as well.

Samuel D. Echols purchased a hotel in Coweta County, Georgia, about 1835. He decided to also build a home in Coweta County and his family lived in the hotel during the time that the new home was being built. His home was built on Land Lot 29 of the 2nd District in Coweta County. Sam Echols became a major land investor in Carroll, Coweta, and Heard Counties. Sam Echols organized the first Baptist Church in Newnan, Georgia, in 1828 and he is still today credited with being the pioneer of the First Baptist Church of Newnan. He served as a State Senator from Coweta County for nine years between 1829-1841. He also served four terms as Judge of the Inferior Court. It was about this time in 1841 that Sam Echols decided to sell all his properties in Coweta and move to Heard County. It was said that his total amount of property at this time was 2888 acres. The Echols are buried in their own family cemetery in Heard County. *Submitted by: Larry Hollingsworth, 920 Kingsbridge Road, Carrollton, GA and Written by: Jan Robinson Bell*

662. Descendants of Miles Solomon Holloway

Mattie Lou Pyles was born March 11, 1923, the daughter of John William and Geneva Gray Pyles. She married Thomas F. Cowart on December 11, 1937, and they lived in Carroll County. They had two daughters Shirley and Rebecca.

Geneva Gray Pyles was born September 10, 1902, the daughter of Arranna Holloway and Robert D. Gray. She married John William Pyles on May 12, 1918, and they had two daughters Mattie Lou and Bonnell. They lived in Carroll County. Geneva died November 12, 1996, and is buried beside J.W. in the Lowell Cemetery, Carroll County, Georgia.

Arranna Holloway was born April 27, 1866, the daughter of Samuel Hopkins and Sophrania Davis Holloway. She married Robert D. "Bob"

Gray on November 27, 1887, lived in Carroll County, and they had the following children: Samuel, Emanuel, Melvin, Geneva, Dovie, and Mamie. Arranna is buried beside Robert D. in the Whooping Creek Primitive Baptist Church Cemetery, Clem, Georgia.

Samuel Hopkins Holloway was born February 22, 1840, the son of Miles Solomon Holloway and Jane M. Cash. He married Sophrania Davis Holloway on January 18, 1859, and lived in Carroll County. Samuel died, date unknown, and is buried at Sand Mountain, Alabama (location unknown). They had the following children: Levi, William, Miles Solomon, Elizabeth, John B., Samuel, and George.

Miles Solomon Holloway was born November 2, 1825, the son of Solomon and Felicia Jane Mabry Holloway. He married Jane M. Cash on December 17, 1845, and died November 8, 1855. He and his family lived in Carroll County. He and Jane had the following children: Miles Solomon Jr., Elizabeth Catherine, John James, George Washington, Lucy Campbell, Sarah Jane, Frances Marion, Levin Solomon, Samuel Hopkins, Seaborn Jackson, Willis Warner, and Louisa Dorcus. *Submitted by: Rebecca Cowart Chambers, 2820 Clem Lowell Road, Carrollton, GA 30116*

663. Myron and Jan House

Myron Wade House came to Carrollton in 1980 to be Special Collections Librarian at West Georgia College. In 1988 mutual friends, Daniel and Ellen Butler, introduced him to Janyce Elaine Rohde and they were married on November 25, 1988 at Holly Springs Primitive Baptist Church in Carroll County. The wedding music was provided by a group of their Sacred Harp singing friends. Both Myron and Jan continue to love Sacred Harp music and try to attend as many singings as possible. In fact, their first date was to a Sacred Harp singing at Edwardsville, Alabama.

Myron was born June 14, 1951, in New Albany, Indiana. He attended Jonesboro Junior and Senior High Schools in Jonesboro, Georgia. In the fall of 1969 he was a member of the inaugural freshman class at the newly established Clayton Junior College, graduating from there in 1971. In 1972 he received an A.B. in history from Georgia State University. His Georgia History professor, Henry Malone, urged him to enter Emory University in order to study with Dr. Bell I. Wiley, who would soon be retiring. House was one of Wiley's last graduate students, completing his master's thesis on the First Georgia Volunteer Infantry (Olmstead's) and graduating from Emory in 1973. After teaching two years at Mundy's Mill Junior High School in Clayton County, Myron entered Atlanta University, graduating with a M.S.L.S. in 1979.

Myron has been active in the Carroll County Historical Society (past president), the Carroll County Genealogical Society (past president), the Bowdon Area Historical Society (charter member), and recently joined the Haralson County Historical Society while serving as a consultant to the society under a Georgia Humanities Council grant. He has helped with several book projects, doing the copy photography for *Bowdon, The First Hundred Years 1853-1953,* editing V.D. Whatley's Bowdon newspaper columns in a volume entitled *The March of Time,* doing the copy photography and serving as photo editor for *At Home in Carrollton: A History Illustrated 1827-1994,* and once again doing the copy photography as well as co-authoring *From A&M to State University: A History of the State University of West Georgia.* He has also helped edit and compile other indexes and supplements and produced a video history of Sacred Harp music entitled *'Til Gabriel Blows His Horn: The Survival of the Sacred Harp Tradition.* House has served on numerous university committees and was president of The Society of Georgia Archivists in 1999.

Jan was born in Johnstown, Pennsylvania, December 1, 1952, and grew up in Hanover, Pennsylvania. She graduated from the University of Pittsburgh in 1974 with a B.S. in health information management. During her senior year at Pitt she took part in a nationwide study to develop diagnostic data on pediatric care in physicians' offices under the auspices of the American Medical Association and the American Academy of Pediatrics, traveling to Texas and California. Upon graduation she found employment on the central California coast and worked for five years as director of Medical Records in two healthcare facilities.

Myron and Jan House

Jan moved to northwest Georgia in 1979 to work at the Wildwood Lifestyle Center and Hospital, a preventive healthcare facility near Chattanooga. For nine years she directed the Medical Record Department, taught in health education programs and served as assistant to the president of Outpost Centers, Incorporated, an organization coordinating international health and education institutions including vegetarian restaurants, lifestyle centers, agricultural training programs, and schools operated by Seventh-day Adventist Christian lay people in forty-one countries.

After Jan and Myron married, she worked in medically-related employment until completing her master's degree in biology at State University of West Georgia in 1999. In December 1999, Jan was employed as science instructor at West Central Technical College (formerly Carroll Tech), a position she currently holds. She teaches anatomy and physiology, microbiology, chemistry, and biochemistry for Allied Health students.

Myron and Jan are active members of the Cedartown Seventh-day Adventist Church. Myron is organist and treasurer and co-teaches with Jan the primary class. Jan also serves as Sabbath School superintendent and co-teaches an adult class. The Houses love to travel when they have time. During the first year of their marriage they traveled to every state except Alaska and Hawaii. They enjoy their log cabin home in the Smithfield Community of Carroll County. *Submitted by: Myron House, 1400 Highpoint Road, Bowdon, GA 30108*

664. James Asbury Howell and Mamie McGraw

James Asbury "Jim" Howell, born 1883, died 1921, was a well-known, well-liked barber in Anniston and Oxford, Alabama. It was said that he could shave you smoother than any barber in Calhoun County at the time.

Jim Howell's grandparents were John Jr. and Elizabeth Howell. They came out of Laurens County, South Carolina, in the year 1825 and settled in Gwinnett County, Georgia, near Duluth. They had fourteen children; six were born in Laurens County, South Carolina, five were born in Gwinnett County, and three were born in Cleburne County, Alabama.

In 1835, after living in Gwinnett County ten years, John Howell moved his family to Alabama. They settled in the Rabbit Town community, Choccolocco Valley, four miles above White Plains in Benton County (now Calhoun County). They lived there three years and moved to Camp Creek, later known as Howell's Chapel and today called Oak Level. John Howell Jr. was a Methodist minister and the tenets of Methodism have remained strong among his descendents.

Ryal Madison Howell (writer's great-grandfather), one of John and Elizabeth Howell's fourteen children, married Nettie Bell in 1877. James Asbury "Jim" Howell (writer's grandfather) was one of Ryal and Nettie Howell's children.

Jim Howell married Mamie Elizabeth McGraw, born 1884, died 1942. They had seven children — one son Forrest Hubert Howell (my father), and six daughters, Edna Jeanette, Eva Louise, Esta Elizabeth, Elsie Mae, Eloise AnnaLois, and Edythe Virginia.

Shortly after Jim Howell died on April 1, 1921, Mamie Howell brought her family to live near her parents in the Bremen/Waco area. Later they moved to Carroll County in the Fullerville Community of Villa Rica. Many of Jim and Mamie Howell's descendants live in Carroll County today.

Forrest went into the Marine Corps in 1923 and stayed until 1930. He sent his Mother $10 each month from his pay of $28 per month. All six of the girls worked in the Fullerville Mill at one time or another earning $3 per week. Times were very hard for the young widow with six girls at home. Mother Howell and the girls lived in the Mill Village and someone from the mill would bring socks for her to darn. When she finished, they picked them up and left more.

James Asbury Howell and Mamie McGraw Howell

Forrest Hubert Howell born November 22, 1907, died July 7, 1975, married Myra Lela Medlock born March 28, 1909, and died February 27, 1978. Both are buried at Bryce's Cemetery in Bremen, Georgia. Forrest and Myra had two sons, Walter Asbury "W.A.," and Jimmy Ronald. W.A. married Nancy Rebecca Anne Willis on July 20, 1952. They have two children, Walter David and Valerie Ellen Howell. Walter David married Julie Ruth Wiens on May 14, 1996.

Jimmy Ronald Howell married Barbara Jane Huckaby on August 22, 1957, and they have one daughter, Edyth "Edye" Jane Howell. Edye married James Maxwell on May 27, 1989. They have twins, James Zachary and Courtney Christine. *Submitted by: Walter David Howell, Lithia Springs, GA and Written by: W.A. Howell*

665. The John Bunyon Hubbard Family

John Bunyon Hubbard was born on January 28, 1880, in Hall County, Georgia, to Albert Ellis and Frances Harriett Hubbard. John was one of eight children. His siblings were twin brothers, Alfred and Albert, Julia, Elizabeth, W. Decatur, Lee, and Lula. John moved with his family from Hall County to the Smyrna Church Community.

John Bunyon and Alice Parrilee Fields Hubbard

John and Jemima Creel Fields

Albert Ellis and Frances Harriett Hubbard

John Hubbard married Alice Parrilee Fields on December 4, 1910. Parrilee was born on June 11, 1889, to John and Jemima (Creel) Fields. John and Parrilee were blessed with three children: Theron Edwin, Clarice Mae, and Lola Louise. John Hubbard was a Christian, devoted father, and husband. He had an interest in photography and his jobs included surveying, school bus driver, and farming.

He moved his family from the Smyrna Church Community to the Oak Grove Community, south of Carrollton, around 1918. Upon his move, John became an active member of Oak Grove Baptist Church, where he served as clerk for several years. Later, he moved his membership to the First Baptist Church in Carrollton.

Parrilee Hubbard was a devoted wife and mother. She was a charter member of the Rebecca Martin Home Demonstration Club.

John died on August 21, 1967, and Parrilee died on May 7, 1982. They are both buried in Carroll Memory Gardens. *Submitted by: Timothy Scott Reeves, P.O. Box 342, Carrollton, GA 30117*

666. The Dale Huckeba Family

Dale Malloy Huckeba was born in Tyus on January 27, 1938, to J.T. and Juliette Huckeba. He was the only son and oldest of two children - he and his sister Sharon. He attended Tyus School and later moved to Roopville School in 1954. After graduating from Roopville High School in 1957, he joined the U.S. Army where he served a three-year tour of duty. He was stationed at Ft. Benning and in Germany. Following the army, Dale worked at Southwire in Carrollton. He retired in 1999 after thirty-four years of service.

Dale is active in the Roopville Baptist Church, serving in many capacities. He has served on the Board of Deacons for thirty years. He also plays an active role in the community. He is a Mason of forty years and a Gideon.

While attending Tyus school, he met Emily Causey. He then informed her mother, Audie Causey, that he would one day marry her daughter. And that he did, on August 26, 1961. The wedding was held on a special Sunday afternoon. It was reunion day for the McDaniel, Causey, Tisinger Family. The family was in attendance. Reverend Gordon Willingham performed the ceremony at Roopville Church. It was also Rev. Willingham's birthday.

Emily Nan Causey was born at the Carrollton Clinic on August 27, 1941, to Clark and Audie Causey. She lived in Tyus until the family moved to Roopville in 1947. She attended Roopville School. She graduated in 1959 as salutatorian of the last graduating class of Roopville High School.

Following high school, she attended West Georgia College. In 1962 she received a bachelor of science in elementary education and later a master's of education. Emily taught with her mother for thirteen years. She retired in 1999, having taught for thirty-five years, twenty-nine of those spent at Roopville. She began teaching piano at home. She continues to support Roopville Elementary School through substitute teaching. Emily is a member of the Alpha Delta Kappa teacher sorority. During her teaching career, she was listed in the *Who's Who Among America's Teachers* three times.

Emily began playing piano at Roopville Baptist Church when she was sixteen years old. She still continues to play both piano and organ after forty-four years. She, along with Dale, is an active member of the Roopville Historical Society.

Dale and Emily were blessed on May 25, 1971, with a daughter, Catherine Nan. She was named after her grandfather's sister Catherine Fletcher. She attended Roopville Elementary School. She went to Central High School of Carrollton and graduated in 1989.

Dale Huckeba Family, seated L to R - Emily, Dale; standing, Catherine

After high school, Catherine attended Shorter College in Rome, Georgia, on a scholarship. She was a member of the world-renowned Shorter Chorale, Delta Sigma Tau, and Mu Phi music sorority. In 1993 she received a bachelor of science in early childhood education. She taught at the Montessori School for a few years. She received a master's of education from Berry College in 1996.

Although Catherine still lives in Rome, she remains loyal to the Roopville Baptist Church and to the Roopville community. She is active in the Roopville Historical Society. She continues to play the piano and perform solos for wedding and special occasions around the North West Georgia area.

Dale and Emily still reside in Roopville on the property purchased in 1947 by Emily's parents. *Submitted by: Dale Huckeba, 1135 Highway 27 South, Roopville, GA 30170* and Researched by: Catherine Huckaba.

667. The John Thomas Huckeba Jr. Family

John Thomas "J.T." Huckeba Jr. was born on June 17, 1913, in the Mexico community near Bowdon. He was the third child of John Thomas and Cora Edna Cater Huckeba.

J.T. was a carpenter. He was well known for intricate finish work. He was a Mason at Tyus Lodge. He attended Bowdon School.

Juliette Willingham was born February 5, 1917 in Wedowee, Alabama, to Wyatt Seay and Zula Itura Yates Willingham. She was the second oldest of four children. She attended Centralhatchee School and Tyus School. She enjoyed playing basketball.

The J.T. Huckeba Jr. Family - Sharon, Juliette, J.T., Dale

J.T. and Juliette were married on November 15, 1936. They had two children. Dale Malloy was born on January 27, 1938, and Sharon Elicia was born on December 17, 1944.

Dale attended Tyus and Roopville School. On August 27, 1961, he married Emily Causey at Roopville Baptist Church. They have a daughter, Catherine Nan, who lives in Rome, Georgia.

Sharon attended West Georgia College. She received a bachelor of science in psychology from Berry College. She married Roy Stocks Philpot from Cedartown, Georgia, on June 21, 1964, at Tyus Baptist Church. They reside in Cedartown. They have two daughters, Deidra and Nancy. They also have two granddaughters, Katey and CeCe.

Juliette Huckeba was a graduate of a business school at LaGrange College. She taught commercial courses at Roopville School for several years. Later she was a legal secretary for Earl Staples.

J.T. and Juliette were avid gardeners. They were active members and supporters of Tyus Baptist Church, often serving in many capacities.

Juliette died December 26, 1979, and J.T. died on November 12, 1985. Both are buried in Tyus Cemetery. *Submitted by: Sharon Huckeba Philpot, P.O. Box 208, Cedartown, GA 30125* and Researched by: Emily and Catherine Huckeba.

668. Fed Hudson

Fed Hudson was born in 1839, according to his monument at his burial site in Villa Rica at the junction of Cole Road and Liberty; however, in the 1880 census report, he is listed as being 39. His wife, Amanda, was born in 1847 and was 32 on the 1880 census report. The main importance is what he did that made history. In 1869, Fed Hudson, freedman, felt the need for a "colored children school." He was intent on having a school, so he cut the trees to be used in the construction of the building. Before the end of the year, 1869, thanks to Fed and other enthusiastic citizens, the Fed Hudson High School of Bowdon was ready to serve the community.

Fed and Amanda Hudson's final resting place.

In 1878, according to courthouse records, Fed paid taxes on 178 acres of land. In 1880 the land for the school was officially donated to the Carroll County School system with the stipulation should the school become extinct for any reasons the property would revert to Fed Hudson or his estate.

After the Supreme Court decision in the 1942 Dred Scott Case, separate but equal became the law of the land for the school system. Fed Hudson High School was subsequently abandoned. A new school was built, which retained the name of the original benefactor. The school became the Fed Hudson Elementary School. At this point, Blacks of Carroll County were bussed to Carver High School, fourteen miles away in Carrollton.

Sometime between 1880 and 1900, Fed and his family moved to Villa Rica, where he and others started another school. In 1905 an acre of land was secured for ten dollars, with the expressed purpose for the construction of a school for "colored children." This school became known as the Midway School. There are a few people alive today who attended this school. The foundation and bricks where the chimney stood are still at the site today. The place is now a cemetery where there are many unmarked graves. But there is one site boldly marked with a six-foot marble stone, the graves of Fed and Amanda Hudson, which reads "Gone but not forgotten."

Many Hudson descendants live in Carroll County today. The family reunion is held the second Saturday in August at Gold Dust Park in Villa Rica. Many of the descendants attend the Founder Day Parade in Bowdon, for Fed was truly a pioneer in Bowdon, even though he was the son of a slave and slavemaster.

Many of Fed and Amanda Hudson descendants became teachers, i.e., Mrs. Dannie Hudson, Mrs. Flannie Hudson. Mr. Luther Gibson, a great-grandson became a principal of a major school in Columbus, Georgia. Dr. Roy Davage Hudson, a great grandson, became the dean of Hampton Institute and also dean at Livingstone College. All of Fed's descendants became productive American citizens and he can be proud of each one. At last count there were more than five hundred descendants and seven generations. *Submitted by: Charles Hudson, 945 S. Lassetter Circle, Villa Rica, GA 30180-1421*

669. Clifford M. Hudsputh Family

Clifford McCamey Hudsputh (June 3, 1892-March 24, 1969) was born in Polk County, Georgia, and is buried at Asbury Cemetery, Temple, Georgia. He was the son of Eli M. and Charlotta Hayes Hudsputh. He had two brothers and a sister: Harvey, who is buried in Birmingham, Alabama; Lonnie, who is buried at Antioch Cemetery in Polk County, Georgia; and Neeley, who is buried at Rockmart, Georgia. He moved to Haralson County as a young man and in 1913 he married Velma Gertrude Massey (March 24, 1897-April 6, 1939). They moved to Temple, Georgia, around 1925. To this union were born two children: Hugh Watson Hudsputh and Cecile Hudsputh.

Cecile Hudsputh (July 13, 1915-June 9, 1986) married Roy D. Otwell. They had an appliance and furniture store in Temple from 1948 until the late 1970s. It was located at the corner of James and Sage Streets. In mid-1959 their business became a collection agency for Carroll Electric Membership Corporation. They also collected for the phone company. They buried Cecile in the Asbury Cemetery at Temple.

Clifford M. Hudsputh, ca 1900

Hugh Watson Hudsputh was born February 24, 1921, in Temple. He attended West Georgia College where he was on the basketball team. During World War II he was in service from 1942-1946. He served in the European theater. It is interesting to note that he and a group of his buddies have continued throughout the years to contact each other during the Christmas season. He enjoyed playing baseball earlier in his life. He served as postmaster at the Temple Post Office from March 12, 1952, until his retirement in 1983. He married the former Mary Caroline Banks of Griffin, Georgia. She taught in the Temple schools for many years. They have two daughters: Marilyn (Bart) Etheredge of Trenton, Tennessee, and Laura Jo Parks of Temple. Marilyn is a middle school teacher in Trenton, Tennessee, and Jo is a registered nurse at Higgins Hospital in Bremen, Georgia.

Hugh and Caroline have five grandchildren, two step grandchildren, and three great-grandsons. *Submitted by: Hugh Hudsputh, P.O. Box 36, Temple, GA 30179*
Sources: Family records, Personal knowledge

670. Johnnie B. Huey Family

Johnnie B. Huey was born December 23, 1928, in Cleburne County, Alabama. He was the second of five children born to Vera Langley and Horace Benjamin Huey. Johnnie attended the Cleburne County schools until his parents moved to Carroll County, Georgia, when he was fifteen. There he completed his education. He then began his career in Carroll County, working in various textile mills. He worked in management for many years in the position of cutting room supervisor.

In the spring of 1947, Johnnie met Edna Pace, a native of Center, Jackson County, Georgia. She was the eleventh child of John Pat and Ida Collins Pace. After graduating from Young Harris Junior College and West Georgia College, she became an elementary teacher in the Carroll County school system. The young couple was married on April 2, 1948, at the home of a minister friend in Carrollton. Bowdon, Georgia has been their home since their marriage.

The Johnnie B. Huey Family: Johnnie, Edna, Mike, Chuck

To Johnnie and Edna Huey were born two sons. Their first child, Johnnie Michael Huey, was born October 24, 1950. He became a professional drummer and record producer in California. Their second child, Charles (Chuck) David Huey, became a cattle farmer and rural mail carrier in the Carrollton area.

Johnnie is now retired from Woolworth Company. However, he stays quite busy. He and wife Edna are very active in the Bowdon First United Methodist Church where he has served in many capacities. He is also on the Bowdon City Zoning Appeals Board and the Bowdon Area Hospital Authority. As a member of the Bowdon Area Historical Society, he volunteers his time for work in many of its activities. In his "free" time, he is a cattle farmer. *Submitted by: Edna and Johnnie Huey, 508 E. College St., Bowdon, GA 30108*

671. William Levi Huff

William Levi Huff married Lena Elizabeth Bonner in 1890. They lived on a farm given to Lena by her father, George T. Bonner, on the Roopville-Glenlock road. The farm was located in the Providence Church, Cainey Springs community. In 1916 they moved to a farm purchased by Levi about a mile from Roopville on the Veal Road. Levi and Lena had twelve children — eight boys and four girls. Their sons were Bryan, Willie, Terrell, Gertis, Herbert, Glen, J.T., Mellin. Their four daughters were Floy, Mary, Fannie, and Helen.

William Levi Huff Family. 1901.

Bryan died prior to age twenty of pneumonia; Willie operated a poultry business; Terrell had a retail store in Roopville; Gertis had a furniture and hardware store in Ellijay; Glen had department and shoe stores in Cedartown; J.T. worked for a farm implement dealer in LaGrange; Mellin retired from International Harvester Company in 1978 after forty-two years. He is the only surviving sibling as of May 2001. Mellin was the only sibling who had military service. He served in the Navy with Sixth Naval District at a base in Southport, North Carolina, with Seventh Fleet Service Force in Southwest and Western Pacific areas, Australia, New Guinea and Philippines, with Naval Air Stations at Dallas, Texas, and Atlanta, retiring after several years in the Naval Air Reserve with rank of LTCDR.

Levi was one of the better farmers of the community and held responsible positions in the Methodist Church and the community. He began teaching Sunday School classes at age twenty. He served as steward and Sunday School Superintendent, chairman of Board of Education, member of Odd Fellows and Masonic Order. He served many years as Justice of the Peace. After Levi's death in 1937, Lena sold the farm and moved to Roopville in a four-room house she had built for $750 on a lot purchased from Julian Freels for $50. Floy operated a kennel for small animals in Asheville, North Carolina. Helen was a registered nurse, retired from work Valdosta State College.

Pictured in the photograph is the William Levi Huff family in 1901. From left to right is Mary, Fannie, Bryan, Levi, Willie, Floy, and Lena.

Submitted by: Mellin C. Huff, 832 Sycamore Drive, Decatur, GA 30030

672. John Henry Hughes and Peggy Ann Jackson Hughes

John Hughes was born in Bremen, Georgia, July 22, 1939. His parents were William Howard Sr. and Gladys Marie Harper Hughes. They were with a large group of people associated with Sewell Manufacturing Company who had moved to the Bremen area from Roswell, Georgia, in 1929. William Howard Hughes soon bought a farm in Carroll County in the Waco-Jake community. This farm became known as the "Howard Hughes Shetland Horse and Pony Farm." It was located across the road from Camp Waco which, although a former Civil War training camp, was now a YMCA camp that operated all summer.

William Howard was the son of Henry Clay Hughes (1857-1940), born in South Carolina. Henry Clay's family moved to Roswell, Georgia, to escape the Civil War. However, they were caught there when General Sherman came through with his Union Army. Henry Clay was only a little boy but his mother, Lucy Ann Reeves Hughes, was desperately trying to get out of the way of the approaching army. Although traveling with several of her sisters, cousins, and many young children, young Henry Clay Hughes became separated from everyone else and was thought to have been drowned while crossing the Chattahoochee River. Lucy Ann and the rest of her family walked back to the Anderson County, South Carolina, farm of her father (Noah Riddle Reeves) and Henry Clay never saw her again. His father, Edward Jackson Hughes, died in an accident circa 1859 when a tree fell on him. His older brothers were away fighting the North so little Henry Clay was literally an orphan. He was raised by a minister, grew up, and married Josephine Daniel (1862-1951) and lived in Roswell, Georgia. One day, a few years after the Civil War, James "Jim" Hughes (Henry's older brother) came through Roswell and heard about his little brother. The brothers and their families were never separated again. Two other brothers, Edward and William, had migrated into the Rio Grande area of Texas and Henry Clay did not establish contact with them again. Two older sisters, Elizabeth and Mollie, had married and lived in the Marietta-Roswell area. Lucy Ann, the widow of Edward Jackson Hughes, had stayed in the Abbeville-Anderson area of South Carolina with her father, Noah Riddle Reeves. She remarried to John W. Guest.

Henry Clay Hughes married Josephine Daniel (1862-1951). She was the daughter of Rev. Joseph Kelsey Daniel (1830-1894) and Elizabeth Jane West (1833-1909). Henry Clay and Josephine Daniel Hughes moved to Bremen with several of their children and grandchildren. Their son, Clifton Eugene, was the plant manager of Sewell's and William Howard became head machinist. He was working with Sewell's and his horse and pony farm, but his wife Gladys Marie Harper Hughes was operating the family store — Hughes General Merchandising — located in Bremen.

John Hughes, the youngest child, was busy helping his mother with the store, helping his father with the horse and cattle farm, working at Camp Waco in the summers (his father supplied the horses and ponies for the young campers to ride and John had to look after them), attending Bremen High School, playing football and enjoying other high school events. However, the love of his life at this time (other than horseback riding events with the Villa Rica and Bremen Horse and Saddle Club) was flying. Every chance when he could slip away, he would go over to the airport to take flying lessons.

John Henry Hughes and Peggy Ann Jackson Hughes

John graduated from Bremen High School in 1958 and left for Southern Tech. He transferred to West Georgia in the summer of 1959 and met Peggy Ann Jackson, born June 23, 1939. They married December 26, 1959, and moved to Atlanta, Georgia, where John continued his classes at night school at Georgia Tech. He went to work with the NCR Corporation as a field representative.

The young couple was soon sent to Dayton, Ohio, for training on computers. Their son John Clay was born May 25, 1961, and daughter Judith Suzanne followed December 2, 1962. They built a home, settled in, and their last daughter, Patricia Dianne Hughes, was born January 20, 1965. Every time John was sent back to NCR for training — either in Dayton, Ohio or Denver, Colorado — they would close their home and go with him.

Wedding of Patricia Hughes to Robert McAlhaney Edwards in 1996.

John moved his family to Norcross, Georgia, in 1969, and Peggy went back to Georgia State University and earned her teaching degree. She began to teach the third grade at Rockbridge Elementary. John moved up fast with NCR and became field manager in 1969. The young family moved back to Carroll County in 1973 and settled down on Tyus Road in Carrollton. Peggy taught school at Central High School and later Central Middle School. Their children grew up in Carrollton and went to West Georgia College.

(1) John Clay born May 25, 1961, married Deborah Lynn Anderson, daughter of Harry and Penny Anderson. They have one daughter, Christine Hughes.

(2) Judith Suzanne Hughes born December 2, 1962, married first to Timothy Paul Fitz-Simons, son of Ted and Mary Jane Fitz-Simons. Judith and Timothy Fitz-Simons have two children, Amy Elizabeth Fitz-Simons and Timothy Paul Fitz-Simons. Judith Suzanne married second Amory Earling "Skip" Osborn Jr. (Skip had a daughter Elizabeth Osborn) and they had Andrew Harrison Osborn and Patricia Katherine "Kati" Osborn, Skip was the son of Amory E. Osborn and Hellen Harrison Osborn of Redbank, New Jersey.

(3) Patricia Dianne Hughes born January 20, 1965, married Robert Eugene McAlhaney Edwards, son of Dr. Robert M. and Miriam Smook Edwards of Columbia, South Carolina. Their child is Alexa.

Peggy Ann Jackson Hughes was born on June 23, 1939, in the home on the Georgia-Alabama Stateline Road where four generations of her family had been born. The old Durrett home place burned when Peggy was a year old. Her roots run deep in Carroll County. She is the descendant of many early Carroll County pioneers: Francis (1775-1848) and Penelope Cocks Durrett (1775-18??), William (1778-1875) and Nancy Hooper White (1783-1837), Joseph Elbert "Joe Turk" Smith (1859-1919) and Edna Skinner (1860-1904), Capt. Richard Brooks (1756-1840) and Elizabeth Adams Word Hooper (1753-1833), Isaac Skinner (1800-?) and Mary Ann Harley (1808-?), William Jasper Skinner (1827-1862) and Mary Arthur (1825-1887), Ira Jackson (1813-?) and Artemesia Aloma Haywood (1810-?), John Wesley Jackson (1856-1899) and Amanda White (1853-1938), and James Francis (1813-187?) and Sarah Elizabeth "Sally" Durrett White, and too many others to mention. (See related histories on the Whites, the Jacksons, the Skinners, the Smiths, the Durretts, and the Hills.)

Peggy is a history teacher. She dearly loves genealogy and anything to do with the Civil War. Both John and Peggy are now retired, but enjoy being together. The family picture shows the John Hughes family at the wedding of their daughter Patricia to Robert McAlhaney Edwards in 1996. *Submitted by: Amy Fitz-Simons, 1550 Tyus Road, Carrollton, GA 30117 and Written by: Peggy Jackson Hughes.*

673. William Howard Hughes Sr. and Gladys Marie Harper Hughes

William Howard Hughes Sr. married Gladys Marie Harper May 20, 1923, in DeKalb County, Georgia. This couple and four of their six children came to Bremen, Georgia, in 1929 from Roswell, Georgia. William Howard was the son of Henry Clay Hughes (1857-1940) and his wife Josephine Daniel (1862-1951). William Howard was born November 25, 1899, and died September 20, 1979. The Hughes family moved from Roswell because of Sewell Manufacturing Company. Howard's older brother, Clifton Eugene, was plant manager of Sewell's. He moved his family first. He soon sent for his younger brother, William Howard, and made

William Howard Hughes and Gladys Marie Harper family.

him head machinist of Sewell's. The brothers also brought along their parents and other members of the large Hughes family.

William Howard was the grandson of Edward Jackson "Jack" Hughes of Abbeville, South Carolina, and Lucy Ann Reeves, daughter of Noah Riddle Reeves (1799-1880) and Dorothy Deliah Kay (1803-1854), all of South Carolina. He was the great-grandson of Revolutionary soldier, William Reeves (1756-1842), and his wife Nuttie White (1755-1840). He was also the grandson of Joseph Kelsey Daniel (1830-1894) and Elizabeth Jane West (1833-1909). He was the great-grandson of Jessie Daniel and his wife, Sarah, and John West (1785-1869) and his wife Margaret Irene Porter. He was the great-grandson of Edward Hughes and Elizabeth Elgin.

In the early 1950s, Howard bought a farm in Carroll County across the road from the old YMCA camp called "Camp Waco" in the Waco-Jake community. He raised Shetland ponies. His farm became known as "The Howard Hughes Shetland Pony Farm." He supplied horses and ponies to the young men who came to Camp Waco. His son, John, was a youth counselor at Camp Waco and looked after his father's horses during his teen-age years. Camp Waco dates back to the Civil War when it was a training camp for Confederate soldiers.

John Hughes, circa 1948-50, driving his pony at Camp Waco.

Marie Harper Hughes was born April 8, 1906, in DeKalb County, Georgia, daughter of John Henry Harper (1876-1962) and Lillian Eldora Amerson (1879-1950). She was the granddaughter of James Wyatt Harper (1838-1922) and Elizabeth Speed Long (1840-1926) of Morgan County, Georgia, and Barnabas S. Amerson (1854-1939) and Mary Virginia Walker (1856-1923) of Putnam County, Georgia. Marie Harper owned and operated Hughes General Merchandising Store in Bremen.

The children of William Howard Sr. and Gladys Marie Harper Hughes were: (1) William Howard Jr., born March 5, 1924, died 1988, married Oreta Jordan. They had four sons: William Howard III, Henry, Keith, and Paul. (2) Gladys Marie (a twin) born July 21, 1925, married Charles Lee Mote. They had three children: Johnny Kyle, Nancy Jean, Charles Lee "Chuck" Jr. (3) Margie Lee (a twin) born July 21, 1925, married Michael Adam Semanchick Sr. They had two sons: Michael Adam Jr., Gary Lee. (4) Mildred Louise, born January 11, 1929, married Garland Jones. (5) Charlsie Jean, born May 5, 1933, married Malcolm J. "Mack" Walton. They had three sons: Joseph Mark, Malcolm Douglas, William Lewis "Billy." (6) John Henry, born July 22, 1939, married Peggy Ann Jackson on December 26, 1959. They had three children: John Clay, Judith Suzanne, and Patricia Dianne.

The family photograph shows Margie, William Howard Hughes, Marie, and Gladys on the back row. On the front row are Mildred, John, and Charlsie. Missing from the picture was Howard Jr., who was away in World War II. *Submitted by: Charlsie Hughes Walton, 3266 Shady Grove Road, Carrollton, GA and Written by: Peggy Jackson Hughes.*

674. William Arthur and Yvonne Physioc Humphries

Arthur married Yvonne on June 6, 1945, and moved back to Villa Rica, where he was born on May 16, 1895. He was the son of John Wiley and Ada White Humphries and the grandson of Captain Nathaniel Harbin Humphries, who was elected the first mayor of Villa Rica in 1884.

Arthur retired from the Life Insurance Company of Georgia where he worked for about forty years. He served as divisional manager for Georgia, Florida, Alabama, and Kentucky. As state manager of Kentucky, he opened up the state for the company. He was a life member of the Life Underwriters Association.

Arthur Humphries and Yvonne Physioc before their marriage.

As a conservationist he was always interested in progress and development. He had lots of information about the Sweetwater and Manchester Mill where his grandfather was superintendent, and he gave a speech about the mill one time. The 74-acre Lake Payne was donated to Carroll County by him. It is interesting that part of the Humphries land (corner of Conner Road and Pumpkintown Road) was sold to Roger Schoerner which later was developed into the first Industrial Park in Villa Rica. Mr. Schoerner and his son were the main developers of this project. Arthur served as president of the Little Tallapoosa Watershed and won "Man of the Year," a National Award in 1968. Mr. Robert Tisinger flew with Arthur to Sioux City, Iowa, to accept the award, which they both felt was an outstanding accomplishment. Part of the Mirror Lake Development is also on former Humphries property. In fact, the Welcome Center was dedicated to Arthur Humphries on April 6, 2000 - refer to the picture of Yvonne and Sam (Arthur's son) standing beside the plaque which reads:

"This facility is dedicated in memory of
W. Arthur Humphries,
loving husband to Yvonne, father to Sam,
William, John, and Helen,
Outstanding Citizen and grandson
of Villa Rica's first mayor."

Gray Ladies of Villa Rica Hospital in mid-1950s.

He was a longtime member of the First United Methodist Church in Villa Rica and served on the board and in various other church offices. For many years he was a member of the Carroll County Cattlemen's Association.

Yvonne and Sam Humphries Welcome Center dedication, Mirror Lake, 4-6-2000.

Yvonne was born in Americus, Georgia, on July 25, 1916. She is the daughter of Otis M. and Loulee Salter Physioc. Yvonne was a charter member of the Gray Ladies (now they are called Pink Ladies) at the Villa Rica Hospital. The Gray Ladies were organized in the mid-1950s and they are pictured from left to right: Lois McPherson, Estelle Conner, Bitt Parker, Yvonne Humphries, Pearl Vaughn, Lorene Williams, Doris Pope, Sara Holloway, Myra Smith, Floye Meek and Ina Hixon. Yvonne is a member of the Daughters of the American Revolution NSDAR. She joined and was admitted on December 12, 1969, as a descendant of Captain Simeon (Simon) Salter, a South Carolina soldier. She is active in the Garden Club and is a member of the First United Methodist Church in Villa Rica.

Arthur, her wonderful husband for 47 years, died on January 13, 1992 and he is buried in the Hillcrest Cemetery, Villa Rica, Georgia. *Submitted by: Yvonne Humphries, 622 S. Dogwood St., Villa Rica, GA 30180 and Written by: Violette Denney* Sources: Family records

675. Hurst - Bell

The Hursts sailed from England and settled in the Shenandoah Valley of Virginia in the eighteenth century. From there they migrated to Kentucky, Tennessee, Georgia, Indiana, Texas, and neighboring states. My grandfather Christopher Hurst, who was a lawyer, lived in Fentress County, Tennessee. He married Lucy Miller and had four boys, one of them was my father John Millet Hurst. My father's parents died when he was twelve years of age and he was reared by his aunt Faith Miller in Wayne County, Kentucky. My father became a teacher. He came to Georgia before World War I and traveled to Roopville, Georgia. It was there that he met the Bells.

The Bells, who were from Ireland, had settled there many years earlier. My grandfather David Ephram Bell married Sally Warren and owned a large tract of land. They had eleven children — six girls, one of whom was my mother Verna Bell, and five boys. As years passed, my grandfather became a rather successful farmer and landowner. There was a sufficient number of children in the area to justify the creation of a school. The schoolhouse was built. It was called Bellview. My father, John Millet Hurst, taught at that school and lived in the "big house" with the Bell family. He taught my mother, Verna Bell, in the eleventh grade. Eventually, several of the Bell children built houses on the land owned by my grandfather. The cotton gin and general store in Roopville were owned and operated by three of the Bell children.

My father continued his schooling at Bowdon College and Carrollton Agricultural and Mechanical School (old A and M). This school later became West Georgia College and still later it became the State University of West Georgia. He was then drafted into the Army in World War I. After his tour of duty in Washington, D.C. he returned to Roopville and married my mother.

They chose to settle in Wayne County, Kentucky. They lived in a little village by the name of Copper which was on the outskirts of Monticello. My father ran a general store there. I was born there on October 21, 1920. Later, Cooper became part of growing Monticello.

We moved to Carroll County from Kentucky when I was eleven months old. My father taught school in many of the little towns that surrounded Carrollton. His major contribution was to lead the way toward building a modern school building in Whitesburg. We lived in a large two-story dormitory-like building on the grounds of the school where he was the principal.

We moved to Cedar Street in Carrollton in 1932 when I was twelve years of age. My father gave up teaching at that time and was a major force in developing the Carrollton Federal Savings and Loan Association. None of my father's immediate family are alive now. None of David Ephram Bell's immediate family are alive, but Theo's wife Rachel and Gilford's wife Pearl live in Roopville. *Submitted by: J. Willis Hurst, M.D.*

676. Hutchins

Fred and Johnnye Hutchins, both University of Georgia alumnus, came to Carrollton from Winder, Georgia, in 1957 when Fred was made assistant vice president of the Peoples Bank. He became president in 1961 and remained with the bank until his retirement in 1988.

They and their four daughters, Rita, Marcia, Sheila, and Andrea, soon became members of Carrollton First Baptist Church where Fred served as deacon, Sunday School teacher, department director and was on various committees throughout the Baptist Association.

Their only son Fred "Chuck" Hutchins III was born at Tanner Memorial Hospital in 1967 but later died of cancer in 1993. He was a Sigma Nu and a graduate of Emory University.

The girls graduated from West Georgia College where Marcia received her master's degree in social studies. Andrea received her M.A.A. arts masters from North Georgia College, and Sheila received her master's degree at Candler School of Theology at Emory.

Fred Hutchins is a past president of Carrollton Kiwanis, member of Sunset Hills Country Club, Hospital Authority, and West Georgia College Foundation. He served three years with U.S. Army Military Police in the European Theatre of Operations during World War II.

Johnnye is a former school teacher and a former award-winning society editor of the local newspaper. She was organizer of Carrollton Junior Woman's Club in 1958 and charter president of Carrollton Civic Woman's Club in 1968, serving sixteen years on the Board of Trustees at Tallulah Falls School, 6th district president, GaF.W.C. in 1970-72, including many volunteer service hours for over fifty-five years in Georgia Federation. *Submitted by: Mrs. Fred Hutchins, 113 Lakepoint Drive, Carrollton, GA 30117*

677. Maurice Ingle Family

Maurice Bertrand Ingle was born October 14, 1864, in Darke County, Ohio, to Morris and Isadora Douglas Ingle. His dad was a Union soldier who was killed in the Civil War just before M.B.I. was born. His mother, Isadora, later married a Confederate veteran who had been released from a Civil War prison camp in Ohio. From this union, M.B. Ingle had a half brother named Isaac Brown, who settled in Indiana.

Hazel and M.B. Ingle, Lois, Richard, and Maurice

M.B. Ingle graduated from Kansas Christian College and completed additional studies at the University of London and Victoria Institute. He became a Christian minister and educator. Before settling in Carrollton in 1931, he had served the First Christian Church of Jacksonville, Florida, Columbia, South Carolina, and Olive Branch Church of Christ in Indianapolis, Indiana, and as state evangelist in Kansas, South Carolina and Florida. In 1918 he married Alida Hazel Prusman, who was born in Pawnee City, Nebraska, and was educated in the public schools of Nebraska and Highland Park College in Des Moines, Iowa. She was working as part of a Christian Evangelistic team when she met M.B. Ingle. They had three children: Maurice Dale, born January 8, 1919, in Kissimmee, Florida, Lois Nell, born October 20, 1920, in Eustis, Florida, and Richard Bertrand, born August 28, 1924, in Johnson City, Tennessee. From 1921 to 1928, M.B. Ingle taught at Milligan College, Johnson City, Tennessee. In 1928, he was called to be academic dean at Atlanta Christian College, East Point, Georgia. He later served as president. When the college closed due to lack of funds during the depression years, he was called to preach in Carroll County. He preached at First Christian Church in Carrollton, and also served a circuit of Carroll County churches including Bethany, Lowell, and Whitesburg.

M.B. Ingle's youngest son, Richard, attended Georgia Tech and joined the Marines during WWII. He was killed in 1944. Daughter Lois was educated at Carrollton High School, Cincinnati Bible College, and Auburn University. She lived in Carroll County for a number of years before settling in Tampa, Florida, where she was on the faculty of the University of South Florida. Oldest son Maurice received his education at Carrollton High School, Marshall High School in Minneapolis, Minnesota, West Georgia College, and Emory University.

Maurice Dale Ingle remained in Carrollton, where he started working for Lawler Hosiery Mills in 1938 and retired more than 55 years later as production manager of the company. During WWII, he served in the U.S. Army. While at Malden Army Air Base in Malden, Missouri, he met and married Marietta Swanagon. Maurice and Marietta have one daughter, Carol, and three sons, Richard, William, and Robert. Carol married Doug Mabry and settled in Carrollton. They have two married daughters, Lynne and Meredith. Richard married Susan Reeve and settled in Carrollton. They have three daughters, Kimberly, Deborah and Betsy, and one son, Reeve. William is single and also lives in Carrollton. Robert married Melanie Long. They have a son, Zachery, and a daughter, Emily, and reside in Acworth, Georgia. *Submitted by: Maurice D. Ingle, 1156 Rome Street, Carrollton, GA 30117*

678. Richard Ingle Family

Richard Maurice Ingle, first son of Maurice and Marietta Ingle, was born July 2, 1946. He was delivered by Dr. H.L. Barker at the old Carrollton Clinic on College Street. He graduated from Carrollton High School in 1964 as valedictorian of the first graduating class from the new CHS on Trojan Drive. This was the first class of baby boomers and class size doubled to a 3-digit number for the first time at CHS. He completed the BA degree in math and physics from West Georgia College and the MS and Ph.D. degrees from Georgia Tech. Richard (Dick) had been named for his uncle, whose education at Georgia Tech was interrupted by World War II. Ironically, Richard also had an interruption in his education at Georgia Tech to serve as a USAF captain during the Vietnam War. On August 20, 1967, one week after graduating from WGC, Richard married Susan Ellis Reeve, first daughter of Dr. and Mrs. Tom Reeve Jr. Susan was born October 27, 1948, in Atlanta and her family moved to Carrollton in 1949.

Richard Ingle Home

(Another interesting coincidence: When they married, Susan and Richard learned that as babies they had both slept, with a two-year time lag, in the same baby bed borrowed from Dr. and Mrs. Davis S. Reese of Dixie Street. In 1985 the Ingles bought the old Reese-Goodwyn-Fitts home on Dixie Street.) Susan graduated from CHS in 1966 as salutatorian. She attended Oxford College of Emory University and graduated from Agnes Scott College in 1970.

Susan and Dick have four children, Kim, Debbie, Betsy, and Reeve. Kim, a CPA, is married to John P. Culwell. They have two sons, Carter and Thomas. Debbie, a computer scientist, is married to William G. Esslinger Jr. Betsy, an industrial and systems engineer, is engaged to wed Richard Jason Perry in June 2002. Reeve is in the eleventh grade at CHS. All of these children and grandchildren live in Carrollton, with the exception of Betsy, who lives in Atlanta.

Richard Ingle Family

Dick's career has included university teaching and research on the faculties of the State University of West Georgia, Georgia Tech, and as a consultant to NASA from the beginning of the Space Shuttle program. He is currently head of the Systems Technology Branch of the Georgia Tech Research Institute and serves as a consultant to the USAF and a number of high-tech companies. Susan is bookkeeper for The Stewart House Retirement Living. Both are active in leadership at First Christian Church and in a number of community activities. *Submitted by: Richard M. Ingle, 305 Dixie Street, Carrollton, GA 30117*

679. Anne Gayle Ingram

Anne Gayle Ingram, educator, was born April 24, 1924 in Carrollton, Georgia, in the principal's house on the campus of the A & M School. Her parents were Irvine Sullivan Ingram, principal of the school, and Martha Munro-Ingram, who taught English and dramatics on the faculty and coached the debate team.

Mrs. Ingram's father, George Munro, previously had been chairman of the Board of Trustees that selected the land on which the A & M School was established, that later in 1933 became West Georgia College. He was a graduate of Emory at Oxford and became an attorney and judge.

Anne Ingram graduated from West Georgia Junior College and attended the University of North Carolina, Chapel Hill, graduating in August 1944. She was a member of the Alpha Delta Pi Sorority. She earned an M.A. degree, University of Georgia, 1948, and an education degree, Columbia University, New York City, in 1962. She lived two years in the International House of Riverside Drive while attending Columbia University Teacher's College.

She did post-graduate work at the University of Oslo, Norway, summer of 1965, her specialization being in physical education and dance. She was employed as an instructor at Louisiana Polytechnic Institute, Ruston, Louisiana, from 1950 to 1951. She was an assistant professor at the University of Mississippi, Oxford, from 1951 to 1954.

Anne Gayle Ingram

When her mother died on April 19, 1955, Anne Ingram returned to Carrollton to keep house for her father. She opened a studio, Dance Workshop, and taught dance and exercise classes to many different age groups.

During the summers of 1954 and 1955, she was a cast member of Unto These Hills, Cherokee, North Carolina, a production that portrayed the sadness of the forced march of the Cherokee Indians residing in the Smoky Mountains to Oklahoma. In 1960, her father received a grant to travel around the world to visit foreign educators who had been routed by the State Department to visit West Georgia College, and Anne accompanied him.

On her return, she taught at Western Illinois University, 1960 to 1961, George Washington University, Washington D.C., a year, and the University of Maryland, 1962 to 1988. She authored, with Dr. James H. Humphrey, *Education for College Students,* 1949; *Moving With Music: A Syllabus for Teaching Dance and Rhythms,* and contributed many articles to professional journals. She also served as the president of the University of Maryland chapter of the AAUP and was active in the woman's equity movement on the campus of the University of Maryland. She taught as an assistant professor, an associate professor, and professor, and retired in June 1988.

She received the West Georgia College Founders Award on September 24, 1983. *Submitted by: Anne G. Ingram, Carrollton, GA 30117*

680. Irvine Sullivan Ingram

First President of West Georgia College

Irvine Sullivan Ingram was born 11 November 1892, at Tunnell Hill, Whitfield County, Georgia, the oldest son of George Conley Ingram, a Methodist minister and teacher, and Annie Lee Irvine. He married Martha Lewis Munro. They had one child, Anne Gayle. He died 27 December 1981, in Carrollton, Georgia.

Irvine S. Ingram started his teaching career at the age of fifteen in Crawford County, Georgia. His father had hoped that he would become a minister, but after the death of his father in 1912 he assumed the responsibility of supporting his sisters. He continued to teach and took college courses as time permitted. In the 1919-1920 school year he became superintendent of schools in Chipley, Georgia.

Irvine Ingram was called to meet the trustees of the A&M School in Carrollton in April of 1920. Although he had no college degree, was not married, had no agriculture experience and was considered too young, he was selected as the new principal of the Agricultural and Mechanical School in Carrollton, Georgia.

While attending the trustees meeting in April, Irvine Ingram met his future wife, Martha Lewis Munro. Her father, Judge George Pierce Munro, was chairman of the Board of Trustees that founded the Fourth District A&M at Carrollton. Martha was a staff member at the school. They were married 11 June 1921. Shortly after his appointment, he was given a leave of absence to continue his education. His wife served as acting principal of the school during his absence. In the summer he attended the University of Georgia and in 1928 he earned his A.B. degree. He served as principal of the A&M for thirteen years.

At the time that he became principal of the A&M School, the state was reconsidering the entire A&M concept. Federal subsidies for high school agricultural programs and rural school consolidation made the A&M schools less attractive. In 1933 the newly established Board of Regents of the University System abolished the A&M schools and voted to establish a junior college in western Georgia. Carrollton was chosen as the location, using the old A&M buildings. Irvine Ingram became the new president of West Georgia College. He received his A.M. degree from Emory University the same year.

Irvine Sullivan Ingram

Irvine Ingram secured a grant in the amount of $250,000 from the Rosenwald Foundation to strengthen the credentials of the faculty. The foundation also helped fund a third year teacher training program. In the late 1940s, under his leadership the "College in the Country" program was begun. Members of the faculty went into local communities and conducted classes on topics of interest to the citizens. In 1952, Oglethorpe University conferred on him an honorary doctor of education degree. In 1957 the Board of Regents authorized West Georgia College to become a four year unit of the University System. Irvine Ingram remained as president until his retirement in 1960. His other affiliations included serving as Georgia Governor, Rotary International; teacher of the Young Men's Bible Class, First Methodist Church, Carrollton for seventeen years; president, Carroll County Chamber of Commerce; weekly column in the *Times Free Press.* *Submitted by: Anne Gayle Ingram, Hill Crest Drive, Carrollton, GA 30117*

Sources: Coleman, Kenneth and Curr, Charles Stephen, editors, *Dictionary of Georgia Biography,* University of Georgia Press, Athens, Georgia, 30602, 1903 Vol I., p.504 *Irvine Sullivan Ingram: A Personal Biography 1892-1981,* Nell's Composition and Printing, Carrollton, Georgia 30117, December 1, 2000

681. The Larry D. Insko Family

The Larry D. and Diane Case Insko family moved to Carrollton from Dayton, Ohio, in 1983. Larry came to Carrollton to serve the Tabernacle Baptist Church as associate pastor. Larry and Diane, natives of Kentucky, grew up as childhood sweethearts and were married on May 25, 1968. Their children, Lee Andrew, Laura Diane, and Lucy Case, were born in Kentucky.

Larry is a 1968 graduate of Georgetown College in Kentucky, and he received his M.A. degree from the Southern Baptist Theological Seminary in December of 1974. He did graduate work at the University of Kentucky and the University of Louisville. Diane received her degree from the University of Kentucky. Larry served Tabernacle Baptist Church until September of 1995 when he became the pastor of the Trinity Baptist Church in Carrollton. Diane worked in the Division of Continuing Education at the State University of West Georgia, where she was assistant director of Conference Services from 1984 until 1997.

All three of the Insko children graduated from Carrollton High School and received degrees from Samford University in Birmingham, Alabama. Lee graduated from Samford in 1992 and then married Cynthia Alice Williams also in 1992. Lee and Cynthia are the parents of two daughters, Caroline Grace born in 1997 and Sarah Glenn born in 2000. Lee, Cynthia, and the girls live in Birmingham. Lee received his M.A. from the University of Alabama and Cynthia received her M.A. from Beeson Divinity School. Laura graduated from Samford in 1995 and married Jack Barry Snyder, Jr. in 1996. Laura received her M.S. from Georgia State University and Barry received his M.A. from McAfee Divinity School. Laura, Barry, and their cocker spaniel Lacey Gator Snyder live in Atlanta. Lucy graduated from Samford in 1999 and serves as a Child Life Specialist at Huntsville Hospital in Huntsville, Alabama.

The Insko family lived at 75 West Lake Drive until 1992 when they moved to 24 Wynridge Drive in Carrollton. Both Larry and Diane are involved in many community and church activities in Carrollton. Larry has officiated at sixty-five weddings and conducted 280 funerals since being in Carrollton. Carrollton will always be considered the hometown of the Insko family.

The photograph shows the Insko family at the wedding of their daughter Laura Diane to Jack Barry Snyder Jr. on August 17, 1996. From left to right are Cynthia Williams Insko, Lee Andrew Insko, Lucy Case Insko, Laura Insko Snyder, Jack Barry Snyder Jr., Diane Case Insko, and Larry D. Insko. *Submitted by: Larry D. Insko, 24 Wynridge Drive, Carrollton, GA 30116*

The Insko Family

682. Harold and Janice (Jackson) Ivester

Harold and I have moved back to my hometown after thirty-six years of marriage. We love it! Whether we are sitting on the side porch of our Dixie Street home listening to the church bells, pulling the old wooden wagon full of grandchildren to explore the square and various parks, or eating out at Billy Bob's, Carrollton living is great.

Dixie Street holds many memories - time was when I knew every crack in the sidewalks. My sister Carolyn, brother Johnny and I grew up on Harmon Avenue, walking to schools, church, theater; skating around the block, playing kick-the-can or hide-and-seek with the neighborhood kids.

Janice, Johnny, and Carolyn Jackson

Lash LaRue came to town in the late forties. My best friend, walking home with me from College Street School, double-dog-dared me to go into the Crepe Myrtle Hotel to get his autograph. She stood guard over our books on the sidewalk while I marched bravely in and asked for his room number. Surprisingly the clerk allowed me to go upstairs and knock on the door, which opened slightly to reveal a tweedy, glaring man with cigarette dangling from beneath his short-clipped mustache. My voice sounded small and scared: "My I please have Mr. LaRue's autograph?" He removed his cigarette and growled, "Beat it, kid!" I ran down the stairs and all the way home. That staircase is now in our house, having been salvaged from the hotel's demolition.

Our grandfather, on his Saturday business trips into town, could always locate us; our dog Scraps usually slept on the sidewalk outside the theater while we took in the usual Saturday morning cowboy or Tarzan movie.

Mother, a stay-at-home housewife who kept an eagle's eye out for us, allowed us some freedom to roam our neighborhood. Daddy was a half-block away at Jackson Brothers Garage.

Knowing that not much escaped the eyes of relatives, neighbors and other adults all around us, we had a safe, secure childhood.

Mr. L.J. Hendricks ran the neighborhood grocery; we spent our pennies with ponderous consideration. Jawbreaker? Cup of ice cream with a movie star's picture under the lid? Candy machine prize? Crackerjacks? Mr. Hendricks was patient and respectful of our small purchases.

We had a mule on our back lot! We sold rides to the neighborhood kids; I think we told them it was a horse. We kept cows; Carolyn and I pulled the little red wagon around the block to deliver fresh milk to our customers.

Our neighbors were longsuffering: we sold Grits Magazine, Cloverine Salve, chances on punchboards; we went trick-or-treating, cut across back yards, walked fences, eavesdropped on party lines. But we were expected to help our neighbors when they needed help, without pay of course; a lesson in neighborliness.

I was graduated from high school in 1958, leaving for college that fall, like every young person never suspecting that an era was ending. Returning for summers, weekends, weddings, reunions, funerals, I vaguely noticed Carrollton changing: the square re-arranged, the Crepe Myrtle Hotel demolished, the cotton gin silent and empty, the theater gone, the Confederate Soldier relocated. My life was changing, too - that's the very definition of life.

Happily, some things don't change; something of the character and personality of Carrollton and its people remain. I gratefully acknowledge my debt to Carrollton's people past and present. *Submitted by: Janice Jackson Ivester, 205 Dixie Street, Carrollton, GA 30117.*

683. Jackson Family

Daniel Jackson was born November 29, 1782. Sarah Bowen was born March 22, 1780. They were married in Greene County, Georgia, on January 15, 1805.

Warren Henderson Jackson, the third son of Daniel and Sarah, was born on June 24, 1812. He served in the Civil War and was back home when Sherman's raiders came. Warren exchanged a secret masonic handshake with an officer who ordered the farmstead left intact.

Warren married Sarah Jackson. James Henderson Jackson was born on July 8, 1853. He grew up in Coweta County and married Laura Celestial Marlow, moving to Carroll County.

Typhoid struck in 1903, killing Laura Celestial. Only two children in the eight person family were well enough to attend the funeral. During typhoid attack, neighboring men gathered on the farm in the Salem Community to plant crops and gardens for the stricken family. James Henderson Jackson later married Nancy Adams.

The children, and many of the grandchildren, of the Jackson clan remained close. During the days of travel by horse and buggy, and later by Model-T Ford, overnight visits were a tradition. A reunion began in 1912 and this tradition continued until the 1980s.

Children of James Henderson/Laura Celestial Marlow were: Beulah, born September 16, 1880, (married Avis Horton; Jim Butler); Lamar, born January 10, 1882, (married Willie Josephine Horton; Myrtie Jackson); Annie Lee, born September 10, 1884, (married Joseph Bryant Copeland); Mildred (Millie), born April 19, 1889, (married Ovid Lee); Errie born May 20, 1891, (married Charles Yates) and Theo, born February 21, 1899, (married Willa Garrett).

Children of Warren Henderson Jackson/Sarah Jackson were: James Henderson, 1853; George Thomas (married Rigsby), John W. (married Brown and lived in Coweta County, Georgia), Mary (married John Stroud), Susan (Lizzie? married Charlie Sewell, lived Roscoe, Georgia), Martha (married Pony Morris, lived in Carrollton), Angeline (married Duke) and Ezekeil (died as a youth).

Children of Daniel Jackson, born November 11, 1782 and Sarah Bowen, born March 22, 1780, were: William, born December 3, 1806; Colby, born November 17, 1808; James born February 6, 1810; Warren Henderson, born June 24, 1812 (married Sarah Jackson) died Coweta County, Georgia, buried Macedonia Baptist between Roscoe and Newnan, Georgia; Elizabeth, born December 2, 1814; Henry, born February 28, 1817; Sussanah, born May 30, 1819; Daniel Andrew, born September 22, 1822; John Washington, born September 11, 1825; and Aletha, birth date unknown. *Submitted by: J.B. Copeland, 1012 Keystone Lane, Clemson, SC 29631*

684. Andrew and Clelia (White) Jackson

Andrew Jackson, born December 10, 1878, in Cleburne County, Alabama, to John Wesley and Amanda White Jackson, proposed to Mary Clelia White (2/21/1887-6/4/1986, daughter of William Christopher and Mary Catherine Norris White) in a buggy going home from Washington's Birthday celebration; he was twenty-five and she was one day past her sixteenth birthday. They married December 25, 1903.

There was never a dull moment! Clelia was small, lively and full of fun. Andrew had assumed quite a lot of responsibility due to his father's untimely death leaving his mother with six minor children. Andrew brought Clelia home to his Sandy Flat, Carroll County log cabin. Clelia cooked her first meal, and used soap powders instead of soda in the biscuits. Her husband and her brothers Bob and Will White, who had come along for the unpacking, never let her forget it.

Soon Andrew and Clelia moved to their house on Brickmill Road, and there they lived the rest of their lives. Eleven children: Robert Loyd (1904-1989, married Alice Mae Rooks); Edna Belle (1906); Leo Clifton (1907-1976, married Eva Dell Smith); Mattie Lee (1909-1910); Roma Eloise (1910-1998, married Harold Eugene Allums); Woodrow Wilson (1913-, married Sybil Verlie Smith); Van Buren (1916-1999, married Mary Lee Whitman); Minnie Willene (1921-,married Roy Webster Griffin); infant son 1924; James Ray (1928-1991, married Esther Cicelia Weaver); Lessie Lurlene 1930-,married Grady Alton Robinson).

Brothers Woodrow and Van Jackson, 1916

When Van was five (1921), he rode with his parents to Atlanta to the dentist and to visit relatives. Arising before dawn, and driving across the Carrollton square, Van saw electric street lights for the first time.

Van remembered sitting with his mother on the woman's side of the church. He misbehaved; she finally got up, led him firmly across to the men's side of the church, and deposited him with his father. This was serious trouble.

Leo and Van caught a skunk one night; they were waiting in a ditch for the moon to go down so that they could "borrow" a watermelon from a neighbor's patch. Van caught a "rabbit," or so he thought for one brief moment. Andrew and Clelia insisted that they shed and burn their clothes before coming into the house that night. But Van was fortunate; he was wearing Woodrow's pants.

Clelia, sociable and neighborly, once said that often after dinner, with chores finished, she cleaned up the children and visited neighbors. She loved the County Extension Club meetings, hosting them yearly. She and her sisters-in-law drove door to door in a buggy collecting money to build Sandy Flat Baptist Church.

Andrew was content with farm and family. He rode horseback to church meetings on Saturdays; drove a buggy into town to conduct business. He drove a car once; backed it out of the barn and straight into the house chimney, yelling "whoa," "gee," and "haw" all the way. After that, he kept a car for his boys, but he himself stuck to horses and buggies.

Andrew and Clelia are buried at Sandy Flat Baptist Church. *Submitted by: Carolyn Jackson Crews, 1522 Stripling Chapel Road, Carrollton, GA 30116.*

685. Daniel Jackson Family

Daniel (Dan) Andrew Jackson, the son of Ezra and Estelle Loftin Jackson, was born December 24, 1892. On November 26, 1916, he married Lola Wright, daughter of Pleasant and Beatrice Stewart Wright. Dan died February 23, 1972, and Lola died July 25, 1987. Dan and Lola Jackson lived in the Tyus and Rock Ridge areas until moving to the Abilene community in 1939 with their five sons, Nathaniel, Archie, Stewart, D.A. Jr., Searcy, and four daughters, Peggy, Videra, Ivee and Marie.

The eldest son, Nathaniel, married Ezelle Cook. They had one daughter, Eileen. Nathaniel died October 30, 1955. The second son Archie was first married to Willie Maude McClung. They had one daughter, Glenda. Willie Maude died August 30, 1951. In 1953, Archie married Edna Rooks. They had one daughter, Theresa. Stewart, the third son, married Lucile Nixon. They had one daughter, Patricia.

Jackson family reunion, 1912

Peggy, the oldest daughter, married Bill Leopard from Auburndale, Florida. There were four children from their marriage: Alice, Jane, Vickie, and Rodney. Bill died August 17, 1990. Videra, the second daughter, married Lester Gray. They had three children: Melba, Roger, and Carol. The fourth son, D.A., Jr., married Hellen Jackson from Hartsville, South Carolina. There were no children from this union. The fifth son, Searcy, married Nell Griffis from Villa Rica. They had three children: Danny, Jan, and Jeff. Ivee, the third daughter, married Gene McGukin. They had two children, Douglas and Donna. The youngest daughter, Marie, married Ted Ragsdale, who died February 4, 1996. They had two children, Mitch and Laura Leigh.

During the 1940s, Dan began growing sweet potatoes, along with young plants which he sold to other farmers in the area. After harvest, he made his potato curing house available for other farmers in the area to cure their potatoes as well.

In August 1946, when the young men in the community returned home after serving in the armed forces of World War II, Dan and Lola honored them and their families with a barbecue dinner. This became an annual tradition and is still carried on by Abilene Baptist Church. Two of the Jackson sons, Archie and Stewart, and sons-in-law, Lester Gray and Bill Leopard, served in World War II. D.A. Jr. served during the Korean War. Ted Ragsdale served in the Army Reserves from 1962 to 1969. Gene McGukin served in the Air National Guard from 1953 to 1961.

Dan Jackson Family

Dan was ordained as a deacon at Veal Baptist Church as a young man. All of the sons and sons-in-law have served as deacons except Searcy Jackson, who was ordained as a minister, serving churches in the Newnan area. Gene McGukin serves as minister of music at the First Baptist Church in Temple.

The home place where the family was raised is owned by Videra and Lester Gray. They host a family barbecue reunion annually in the month of September. *Submitted by: Ivee McGukin and Hellen Jackson*

686. Henry Arnold Jackson

Henry Arnold Jackson was born in Spalding County in 1841. When war broke out in 1861 Jackson enlisted in what would become Company F, 30th Georgia Regiment of Infantry, C.S.A. The regiment first went into camp at Fairburn, Georgia. Later, it was sent to Griswoldville, Georgia. While at Griswoldville, a measles epidemic broke out. Here the 30th suffered their first casualties of the war, from disease not battle. At this time Jackson was listed as "Present, sick in quarters." The next two months showed him "Absent, without leave." It is believed he went home to recover. Jackson returned to the unit in time for the battle of Chickamauga. His regiment was in some of the hardest fighting of the battle. The 30th lost thirty-one killed in action, with many more wounded. The regiment remained with the Army of Tennessee until the end of the war in 1865. At the surrender, the regiment that numbered about 1200 men in 1861 had less than forty left.

Henry Arnold Jackson, 30th Ga. Vol. Inf. Co. F.

William David Jackson and Mary Elender Teague Jackson.

After the war, Jackson came back to Carroll County where he married Mary Brown. Mary was the sister of W.H. Brown who served with Jackson in Company F. They raised three sons: William David Jackson, Jerry T. Jackson and Benjamin Jackson.

Around 1888 the family moved to Delta, Alabama. It was here that W.D. Jackson married Mary Elender Teague on October 10, 1889, at the home of her father Levy B. Teague. After a few years they moved back to Carroll County.

Lonnie and Henry Jackson

Arnold received The Southern Cross of Honor from the Annie Wheeler chapter of the United Daughters of the Confederacy. He was a member of the McDaniel-Curtis Camp of Confederate Veterans in Carroll County. In 1895 Arnold applied for his pension from the State of Georgia for indigent soldiers. At this time he was disabled due to throat and lung conditions that had rendered him unable to work for the previous eight years. On his application he listed his total property as one cow, which he had sold to pay his debtors. In his application for 1901, Arnold listed his property value at $11.50. This included his belongings valued at $10 and one shoat valued at $1.50. In March 1901, Arnold's wife Mary died. On October 20, 1903, he married a widow, Sarah Jane Hardigree. Arnold died in 1917. Sarah died in 1936.

William and Mary had eight children, most of whom were born in Carroll County. The children were: Sarah 1890, Henry 1892, Lonnie 1895, Carrila 1898, Etoy 1901, Arnold 1904, Edith 1908, and Maimie 1911. Between 1910 and 1920 William moved his family to Coweta County.

Lonnie Jackson had five children: Dewey, Radford, Edna, H.A. and Harvey. These were all in Coweta. Harvey has two sons, Scott and Ray. Scott moved to Carrollton in 1974 and married Reggie Riggs in 1978. In 1987 Daniel Lee Jackson became the first of this branch to be born in Carroll County in over seventy-five years. *Submitted by: Scott Jackson, 589 Gilley Road, Carrollton, GA 30116.*

687. John Wesley and Amanda White Jackson

John Wesley Jackson, born May 19,1856, at Sand Hill, Carroll County, was the son of early Carroll pioneers Ira and Artemisa (Haywood) Jackson. John was a minor at his father's death, and the court appointed as his guardian James Francis White, whose daughter Amanda he married on September 12, 1875. They lived in a log cabin on the Macedonia Road in Cleburne County, Alabama; today known as the county's oldest cabin. Into this cabin, son Andrew came home late one night to find a hound sleeping in his loft-bed, put there by his mischievous brothers. Andrew opened the shuttered loft window and threw the dog out.

John Wesley and Amanda (White) Jackson

In 1891 John swapped his Alabama land plus a shotgun for property across the Alabama/Georgia line in Carroll, at what is now the Sandy Flat/State Line crossroads, living in a log cabin until the house was built. In 1898 John rented out his farmland and bought a house in Bowdon, so that his children might attend Bowdon College. Unfortunately the well at the town house was contaminated, and John died with typhoid fever on January 20, 1899, at age forty-two. His wife and children moved back to the farm.

John and Amanda (8/2/1853-9/28/1938) had eight children: James Ira (1877-1931), married Verda Johnson 1881-1982); Andrew (1878-1964, married Mary Clelia White 1887-1986); Sarah Frances (1891-1969, married first Charlie Woodard, second William Martin Groover); Alabama (1883-1927, married Alonzo Levi Johnson); Henry McDola (1885-1886); John Rufus (1887-1974, married Rubie Belle Mitchell); Minnie Lee (1890-1968, married Oliver J. Stallings); and Eva Eunice (1894-1984, married William Martin Wright.)

Six of these children were minors at John's death. As these children became adults and married, a pattern developed: usually each couple lived their first year of marriage in the old log cabin behind the house. Then Amanda gave each a sixty acre tract of land in their Sandy Flat community, so that these close-knit siblings became close neighbors as well. Most of the houses remain; Andrew's home place and farm is still in the Jackson family.

Amanda's children and their spouses were instrumental in founding Sandy Flat Baptist Church. The church still continues to play a large part in the lives of the descendants. I remember in the late 1940s riding to the church on a summer evening in my grandfather's (Andrew's) buggy, tying "Doll" to one of the oak trees, and hearing the singing through the open windows carrying far over the countryside.

Children of these brothers and sisters (there were at least forty-four cousins) have lots of stories: the time Minnie, Bam, and Eunice cut their long beautiful tresses into stylish bobs; reunions (held at homes of the siblings until the 1990s, always on Amanda's August birthday); the harsh death of Frances' husband in 1912; the birth of twins to Rufus and Rubie in 1914 and again in 1921; the sudden death of Bam on Christmas Eve 1927; quilting bees, spring plowing, the swimming hole, the sound of the dinner bell across the fields, cotton-picking, late summer revivals, gospel singings, baptisms. There are only eleven of these cousins living today.

Amanda lived with Jim and Verda until her death in 1938. She is buried beside John at Macedonia Baptist Church, Ranburne, Alabama.
Submitted by: Willene Griffin, Route 2, Box 71, Ranburne, AL 30273

688. The Three Sons of Samuel Jackson

Seaborn, Hiram, and Ira Jackson, sons of Samuel and Mary Jackson, have descendants in Carroll County today.

Samuel Jackson (born South Carolina - died 1830 Warren County, Georgia) is supposed son of David Jackson, County Antrim, Ireland, immigrant to South Carolina. Samuel lived in 1790s Warren County, Georgia. His 1820 lottery draws were divided by Mary and sons.

Levi Newton Jackson; his father Seaborn Jasper Jackson; CSA veterans.

Seaborn Robert Jackson (born 1799 Warren-died 1886 Carroll, married 1819 Anne Holder), removed to Cherokee County 1844; to Carroll County 1878. His son, Seaborn Jasper (born 1821 Warren) married 1843 Martha Ann Newton; moved to Carroll County 1870. Jasper's son Levi Newton (1844-1916), married Delilah Ann Thrower (1846-1928). Children: Ira Barney (1875-1862); Mary Jane (1877-1952 married John A. Duke); James Warner (1877-1953 married Susan F. Long); Aliph May (1889-1952 married Feaster Alexander Thomas); Martha (1880-1924 married Pink Chambers); Ella Aline (1883-1930 married Walter Lee Powell); Seaborn Joseph (1882 married Minnie Burkham); and Angus Bruce (1890-1961 married Naomi Duke). Another son of Jasper Jackson is James Franklin (1850-1934 married Lula Agnes Duke). Jasper, sons Levi and James, and many descendants are buried at Pleasant Grove Baptist Church, Carroll. Jasper and son Levi fought in the Civil War: Jasper in the Cherokee Riflemen; Levi having run away from home at sixteen to join the Tate Guards. Descendant Jessie Thomas Pearce remembers several family stories: At war's end, Levi and company were far north, free to go home as best they could but with no provisions.

They walked all day, camping in the snow at night. At second day's end, they found a campsite used by previous soldier-travelers, and packed in the snow a freshly slaughtered beef, with note attached: "Eat what you need of this beef, and leave the rest for others behind you." Another story: Levi and his family were the first to move from Canton in Cherokee to Tyus in Carroll. Father Jasper rode horseback from Canton to visit Levi. Upon Jasper's leaving, daughter-in-law Delilah filled his pack saddle with corn pones, and sewed his money into his coat lining, guarding against highwaymen. In later years Jasper's pack saddle was kept in an upstairs room of the old house still standing between Tyus and Veal.

Hiram M. Jackson (born c. 1800 Warren, died Texas, married a Johnson). Their presumed children: Seaborn (1825-1866 married Julia Ann Bowen, settled in Newnan); Thomas Jefferson (settled in Columbus); Welborn; Julia (married Joseph Musgrove); Clarkie (female child kidnapped in 1835 and never found.) Hiram became guardian for younger brother Ira in 1830. Hiram was postmaster and owned property on the square in Griffin (1832). Hiram fought in the Indian Wars of 1836 from Houston. Hiram has been found in Warren, Coweta, Houston, Henry, Cherokee, Pike and Carroll (1843) Counties in Georgia, finally settling in Texas. Hiram left descendants in Georgia, Alabama, Texas.

Ira G. Jackson (born 1813 Warren -died 1874 Randolph now Cleburne, Alabama) married 1838 in Henry County Artemisa Haywood daughter of Thomas and Mary Haywood. There still exist papers dating 1836: Ira's account with a Warren County firm listing purchases: 4 vials folsom copenia, silk, casimers, tobacco, homespun, soap, gloves, coarse shoes, summer coat, watch, silk cravat, hair brush, watch crystal, etc. Ira bought property in Carroll 1843 becoming a pioneer settler. Ira and Artemisa had eight children: Samuel Lawson (1838-1899, married Mary Alexander, settled in Cleburne County, Alabama): Georgia Ann (1841-before 1875, married William W. Robinson); Thomas Aulsey (1842-1890s, married Martha E. Wright); Joann (1843-, married Isaac H. Robinson); William (1847-); Sophronia (1849-, married Thomas Eason); Mary Ellen (1853-, married Thomas Alexander Martin); John Wesley (1856-1899, married Amanda Francis White 1853-1938, daughter of James Francis White and Sarah "Sallie" Durette; settled near Bowdon). Ira appears often in Carroll County land records. In 1853 Ira was trustee of Smyrna Methodist Church; the family appears on that church's earliest record book. They then moved to Jonesville community north of Bowdon, joining Indian Creek Baptist. Ira, who lived briefly in Cleburne County before his death, is buried at Indian Creek Baptist. *Submitted by: Janice Jackson Ivester, 205 Dixie Street, Carrollton, GA 30117.*

689. Van and Mary Lee (Whitman) Jackson

Van first saw Mary when he was two and she a newborn; they lived in the same community (Sandy Flat Crossroads) although he was on the Georgia side of the line, and she on the Alabama.

Son of Andrew and Clelia (White) Jackson, Van Buren (7/6/1916-8/1999) was born in the Jackson house on Brickmill Road. Mary Lee (11/20/1918-6/2000) daughter of John Edward and Fannie Jones Whitman, was born in Cleburne County, Alabama.

They had three children: Joan Carolyn (7/25/1936, married Jack Lamar Crews: children: Jack Jr., Beth, Amy); Janice Louise 6/6/1940, married Jesse Harold Ivester; children: Andrew, Philip, Michael); Johnny Van (3/28/1947, married first Cathy Carnes: child John; second Phylus Smith Reid who already had Jeff by a former marriage.)

Van and Mary Jackson, 1936

There are now eleven Crews, Ivester, and Jackson great-grandchildren. Jack Lamar Crews Junior married Jody Jason: children Samuel Wilson, Kathryn Scott. Carolyn Elizabeth Crews married first Christopher Slade: child Thomas Jackson; second Keith Hardin: children David Alexander, Mary Elizabeth; third James Patrick Berzsenyi: child James Jackson. Amy Lee married first Peter Alford; second Cliff Hughes; she teaches in LaGrange.

Andrew Harold Ivester married Heather Lynn Peterson: children Wesley Andrew, Anna Kate, Rachel Grace Ivester. They live in Tyus. Philip Lloyd Ivester married Laura Lanier Adams; they live in Smyrna. Michael Van Ivester teaches in Germany.

Johnny Van Jackson Junior married first Shannan; second Diana Roach: children Ethan, Kyle; they live in Norfolk, Virginia. Jeffrey Scott Reid married Tina Dortch; they live in Birmingham.

Van and Mary Jackson's 50th anniversary, 1986.

Van moved the family to Carrollton (1942) and started Jackson Brothers Garage on Dixie Street (the building once housed Drury Buggy Works) with brothers Loyd and Woodrow. Mary's brother Orin Whitman joined them a few days after returning from Japan and World War II. The Jacksons bought the old Harmon place on Harmon Avenue, still in the family although the old house burned in 1962. (Mary even infused that tragedy with humor: a few days after the fire, when the young man who came to treat the house for termites stood in shocked silence surveying the gutted ruins, she explained, "Those termites just ate us out of house and home.")

Van loved the family farm, buying it from the other heirs, adding acreage as he could. He cleared and sowed for pastures, built fences, lakes, roads and bridges, and raised cattle. He and Mary lived in the farmhouse for their last years. Nothing made them happier than for grandchildren to come to fish, hunt, cut wood, bush-hog or explore with Van, and to enjoy Mary's home cooking, flower garden, and homemade ice cream.

Van and Mary are buried at Sandy Flat Baptist Church, within two miles of their birthplaces.

Submitted by: Andrew Harold Ivester, 785 Attaway Road, Bowdon, GA 30108.

690. Woodrow Wilson Jackson and Sybil Smith

Woodrow Wilson Jackson, born May 30, 1913, is the son of Andrew Jackson and Mary Clelia White Jackson. He is the grandson of John Wesley Jackson and Amanda White and William Christopher "Billy" White and Mary Catherine "Molly" Norris. He is the great-grandson of Ira G. Jackson and Artemesia Aloma Heywood, James Francis White and Sarah Elizabeth "Sally" Durrett, John "Jethro" Norris and Mary Johnson, and Henry Alan White and Elmina Suggs. "Woodzy," one of eleven children, was born exactly in the middle of Andrew and Clelia's large family on the Andrew Jackson farm. The farm is on the western side of Carroll County on land that bordered the Georgia/Alabama State-line Road. This family had settled there in the 1840s when Francis Durrett and William White had brought their large families into the Crossroads area of Carroll County, between Bowdon, Georgia, and Ranburne, Alabama.

Woodrow and Sybil Smith Jackson. Wedding day, Mary 13, 1933

Andrew Jackson and his two brothers, Jim and Rufe, cut the logs and built Sandy Flat Church (which also was Sandy Flat School during the week). When Andrew decided that it was too far for his children to walk, he built the Melrose School on his land behind the orchard for his large family and a few of the neighboring families, such as the Smith family and many other Jackson and White children. Andrew Jackson was on the school boards of both these schools. Woodrow Jackson married a neighbor and distant cousin Sybil Smith on May 13, 1933. She was born April 11, 1918, oldest daughter of Seaborn Rufus Smith and Lillie Ethel Hill. "Rufe" Smith had swapped farms with Jim and Verda Jackson, who at that time owned the John Wesley Jackson home place. Rufe moved his large family of eleven children from Bowdon to the Sandy Flat community into the big old sprawling John Wesley Jackson home place with its porches covering three sides. This farm was on the land originally owned by Francis Durrett and Penelope Cocks who were the ancestors of both Woodrow Jackson and Sybil Smith. Thus they were fourth cousins.

Sybil Verlie Smith is the third child and oldest daughter of Seaborn Rufus "Rufe" Smith and Lillie Ethel Hill. She is the granddaughter of Joseph Elbert "Joe Turk" Smith and Edna Skinner, James Martin "Jim" Hill and Susannah Durrett, and the great-granddaughter of William Enoch Smith (who died in the Civil War) and

Woodrow and Sybil Smith Jackson, 50th Wedding Anniversary, and their children, Peggy, Sandra, and Ernie. 1953

Sarah Couch, William Jasper Skinner (who also died in the Civil War) and Mary Arthur, and Rev. William Hill and Sarah Ann Tomlin.

Sybil Smith was born on the old Francis Durrett and Penelope Cocks Durrett home place, the home that her ancestors had built when they came from Virginia. Four generations of her Durrett families had been born there. She was also the great-great-granddaughter of Greenberry Hill, a drummer in the War of 1812, and his wife Martha Ivey. Greenberry Hill had received two land grants for his military service and had brought the Hill Family from Fayette County, Georgia, into Carroll County, and into the old Randolph (now Cleburne) County, Alabama, area. His descendant, Randal Turner, a grandson of Rufe Smith and Ethel Hill, now owns all this land. Greenberry Hill's son, Rev. Martin Hill, preached in both Carroll County churches and Randolph-Cleburne County, Alabama, churches before, during, and after the Civil War. He preached the first sermon in the Ranburne Baptist Church and is buried in the Ranburne Cemetery. His father, Greenberry Hill, is buried in the old Gold Ridge Cemetery with a War of 1812 marker on his grave. Sybil Smith baked two cakes on the morning of her wedding day as many family members and friends gathered into the Rufe and Ethel Hill Smith home for the great occasion. They both came from large families and the large old house, with its porches on three sides, was overflowing with the many guests who came to celebrate. After the death of her father, Seaborn Rufus Smith, in 1940, Sybil and Woodrow Jackson owned and lived in this large old home and raised their three children there. In the 1950s, they remodeled the old Melrose Schoolhouse and moved there.

Woodrow Jackson was a farmer for many years on the land of his ancestors. He then became a part of Jackson Brothers Garage with Van and Lloyd, his brothers, and Orin Whitman in Carrollton. He spent his later years affiliated with the maintenance of the Carroll County prison systems and served as a prison guard. He is now retired and lives on Brickyard Road with his wife of sixty-eight years and their son Ernie Jackson.

Sybil Smith Jackson worked for many years at Sewell Manufacturing Company and is now retired. She is known for her "doll making" and many beautiful quilts that she made for her children, grandchildren, and now great-grandchildren.

Woodrow and Sybil Jackson have three children, five grandchildren, and ten great-grandchildren. They are: (1) Peggy Ann Jackson, born June 23, 1939 who married John Henry Hughes on December 26, 1959. He was born July 22, 1939 in Bremen, Georgia, son of William Howard Hughes Sr. and Gladys Marie Harper Hughes. Peggy Ann is a graduate of the Bowdon Schools, the State University of West Georgia, and Georgia State University. She taught school for many years at Central High School and later at Central Middle School in Carrollton, Georgia. John Hughes is a graduate of the Bremen Schools and Southern Tech. He was Field Manager of the NCR Corporation for many years and worked out of the Atlanta office. He also had the Rome and Columbus, Georgia areas. Both John and Peggy are now retired. John's father owned and operated the Howard Hughes Horse and Pony Farm in Waco, Georgia, and he was head machinist of the Sewell Manufacturing Company. Gladys Marie Harper Hughes owned and operated Hughes General Merchandising in Bremen, Georgia. Peggy and John's children are (1) John Clay Hughes, born May 25, 1961, married Deborah Lynn Anderson, daughter of Harry and Penny Anderson, divorced in 1996, one daughter Christine Hughes born 1994; (2) Judith Suzanne Hughes born December 2, 1962, married first to Timothy Paul Fitz-Simons in 1980, divorced, two children Amy Fitz-Simons born 1980, and Timothy Paul Fitz-Simons born 1982. Suzanne married second to Amory E. "Skip" Osborn, son of Amory E. Osborn Sr. and Helen Harrison Osborn of Red Bank, New Jersey, three children, Elizabeth Osborn, born 1984 (Skip's daughter from a previous marriage), Andrew Harrison Osborn born 1988, Patricia Katherine "Kati" Osborn, born 1990; (3) Patricia Dianne Hughes, born January 20, 1965, married Robert Eugene McAlhaney Edwards on June 15, 1996. He is the son of Dr. Robert Marvin Edwards and Miriam Smoak Edwards of Columbia, South Carolina, one daughter Alexa Grace Edwards.

(2) Sandra Hope Jackson, born October 6 1941, married Ted Mack Beavers on June 10, 1962. He was born September 16, 1940, son of Mack Beavers and Julia Ann Bailey Beavers of

Great-great-great-grandchildren of William White and Nancy Hooper.

Carrollton, Georgia. They are the parents of two daughters: Kimberly Hope Beavers, born September 13, 1963, married William Burton "Burt" Grisham, son of Charles Louis "Charlie" and Yvonne Combes Grisham, one son Charles Gavin Grisham; Kristen Kay Beavers, born April 20, 1968, married William Walda "Bill" Stone, son of Robert and Tish Stone, two children Wesley Andrew Stone and Sydney Hope Stone. Sandra is a graduate of the Bowdon Schools and the State University of West Georgia. She taught many years in the Central Primary and Elementary schools. Ted Beavers is a graduate of the Bowdon Schools. He worked for many years with Sewell Clothing Company in Bremen, Georgia. He is presently employed by the State University of West Georgia as a locksmith in the Public Safety Department.

Peggy Ann Jackson, 1959. Descendant of early Carroll County pioneer families.

(3) Archie Ernie Jackson, born April 3, 1945. Ernie is a graduate of Bowdon High School.

The great-great-great-grandchildren of William White, descended from James Francis White, Amanda White Jackson, and Andrew Jackson's children are shown in the group picture. They are, seated, Bill Jackson, Ernie Jackson, Lemmie Griffin, Charles Griffin, and Harold Gene Allums. Standing are Shirley Griffin, Sandra Jackson, Janice Jackson, Kenneth Jackson, Peggy Jackson, and Carolyn Jackson. *Submitted by: Peggy Ann Jackson Hughes, 1550 Tyus Road, Carrollton, GA 30117*

691. Jeter

The Old Home Place

Have you ever heard the phrase, "the old home place?" Well this is a story of how I, Debra Jeter, moved back to "the old home place."

It all begins with my sixth great-grandfather, John Jeter, who was born in Suffolk County, England. As a teenager in the early 1700s, John moved to Carolina County, Virginia, where he met and formed an acquaintance with Elizabeth Vaughn whom he married in 1708.

John and Elizabeth's seventh child, my fifth great-grandfather, Samuel Jeter, was born in 1715 in Essex County, Virginia. In 1751, Samuel married Mary Dudley, also from Virginia, and fathered five children.

The second son of Samuel and Mary was my fourth great-grandfather, Dudley Jeter, born on September 20, 1754, in DeKalb County, Georgia. After the death of his first wife Sarah Jones, Dudley married a second time to Rebecca Wynn on November 22, 1797. Dudley had ten children between both marriages.

Nine sons of John Robert Jeter

Dudley's sixth son, my third great-grandfather, William W. Jeter, was also born in DeKalb County, Georgia. In 1808, William married Sara Thurman and had eight children. Living in a town that was growing quickly and in the process of building railroad tracks near the Jeter home, William decided it was time for a change. William decided to move his family away from the big city, hoping to find a more suitable and safer environment to raise children. With his possessions and family packed, William said goodbye to friends and family and moved to Carroll County. On October 23, 1852, William W. Jeter purchased Lot #133 in Carroll County, which was located in what is now known as the Burwell community. William worked hard as a farmer and at his death had a real-estate value of $1,800 and a personal estate value of $2,985.

William's third son, my great-great-grandfather, Richard Dudley Jeter, born in November 1841, married Amanda Elizabeth Robinson on May 6, 1866, and later had four children. Amanda Elizabeth died in December 1874, so Richard Dudley married her sister, Mary Lavonia, on March 25, 1875, and they, too, had four children.

Billy J. Jeter

Richard's second child by his first marriage was John Robert Jeter, who was my great-grandfather. John Robert was born May 2, 1868, in the Burwell community of Carroll County. He married Mary Elizabeth Craven and had ten children. Working as a sharecropper, John moved his family from Burwell to Lovvorn Mill Road, and from there to anywhere work was available in the county.

John Robert had two sons who were drafted and served in the United States Army. Gordon, the eighth son of John Robert, fought in Europe during World War II. John Robert's seventh son, Albert, also served in World War II, but he was killed in July 1945. After returning from France, an army buddy of Albert's shared the unfortunate experience with the family. It seems that Albert and his friend were walking down the streets of St. Lo, France, after the battle was over when the Germans fired a shell into the city. A piece of shrapnel hit Albert, almost slicing his body in half.

My grandfather, Joe Lee Jeter, the fourth child born to John Robert, was born on December 24, 1904. Joe married Annie Gertrude Ferrell from Cullman, Alabama, where they lived until November 5, 1930. Joe and Annie decided to move back to the Burwell community on November 5, 1930, when Annie was nine months pregnant with their third child. After arriving at the new home place around 7 p.m., my father, Billy Joe Jeter was born at 9 p.m.

Billy married Polona Joyce Jackson on August 4, 1956, and has four children: Tony Ray Jeter, Jerry Wayne Jeter, Kenneth Russell Jeter, and Debra Joyce Jeter. At the age of twenty he joined the United States Air Force where he served for the next twenty-four years. During that time, he served in Southeast Asia during the height of the build up of the Vietnam conflict. While there, he earned the Air Medal for combat missions, the Airman's Medal (which is the highest medal for non-combat service), the Vietnam Service Medal, the Republic of Vietnam Medal with two battle stars, the National Defense service Medal with a Bronze Star, Air Force Commendation Medal for outstanding performance, the Air Force outstanding unit with "V" for Valor, and several other decorations. He was also in twenty-two countries and forty-two states during his time in the military.

In 1970, Billy purchased ten acres of land in the Burwell community, anticipating his future retirement and wanting to settle his family in a good community near both his and Polona's family. Billy retired on May 31, 1974, packed the family's belongings and moved back to Georgia. It wasn't until years later while researching the Jeter family history that we discovered Billy had purchased part of the original Lot #133 bought by William W. Jeter in 1852.

When Billy decided to move his family back to the old home place, he didn't realize he truly was moving back to "the old home place."

John Robert Jeter's nine sons are shown in the family picture. On the front row are Albert, Bob, and Row. Second row shows Joe, John, and Gordon. Lloyd, Cirero and George are on the back row. *Submitted by: Debra Jeter*

692. Johnson Family

Campbell (Cam) Johnson and his wife, Emily Bennetta, moved from middle Tennessee to Georgia in the late 1800s. Most of their children were born in Tennessee but the youngest of nine siblings, Walter Earl, was born July 28, 1896, in Fayette County, Georgia. The family later moved to Carroll County. The nine children were: Mollie (Laster), Robert (Bob), Hugh, John, Earnest, Albert (Al), George, Myrtle Lou (Coats and Daniel), Charles and Walter.

Walter met a young girl, Ruth Cole (born November 28, 1903) and they were married on January 20, 1920. Ruth was the daughter of George and Narcisus (Narrie) Cole. There were five siblings in this family, Rilla (Stephens), Mary (Miller), Roy, Ruth (Johnson) and Raymond.

The remaining part of this story will be centered around Walter and Ruth Johnson. They had three children, Horace (1921), Wendell (1927) and Reba (1928).

Walter was a well known citizen of Carroll County. Always a farmer by trade, but met and made many friends. He was asked by many Baptist churches in the 1930s and 1940s to lead the music for summer revivals. His wife was always ready to stay home and care for the family needs while he was carrying out this responsibility. Ruth was a more reserved person than Walter, but supported him in every way possible.

Walter worked and cared for his family as a sharecropper until 1939. He always wanted to own his own farm and was much elated to purchase a farm, consisting of 125 acres, about two miles north of Roopville. He devoted the remaining years of his life, along with his wife, Ruth, with a great feeling of thankfulness in working and paying for this farm and home. Their oldest son, Horace, married Mary Key on February 22, 1942. This union produced three children, Angelin (1943) Larry (1944) and Dale (1950) Wendell married Mae Roberts and they had one daughter, Jeanette. Reba married William (Bill) Upshaw and they had two children, Debbie and Jeffery.

The following year (1940) after the purchase of the farm, a sweet potato curing house was constructed. Another story will cover this project. (See Johnson Sweet Potato Barn) With fifty years of a wonderful marriage, Walter and Ruth observed the joyous occasion with a reception in January of 1970. This was followed by a reception for their 60th anniversary in 1980. Then a lot of heartache was experienced due to an unbelievable situation with problems within the family. Walter died on May 22, 1985, with a broken heart. Ruth continued her life with much sorrow and declining health. She died on June 23, 1993. Thus the remaining members of the Johnson family continue to carry on in an adjusted lifestyle. *Submitted by: Horace Johnson, 30 Mashburn Road, Roopville, GA 30170*

693. The Allen E. Johnson Family

Allen E. Johnson was born in Henry County, the second son and youngest child of John G. and Mary Johnson Johnson. As a young man he served with the Confederate Army as a guard at Andersonville Prison. He happened to be on furlough when the war ended. His oldest brother, John, left Henry County for Alabama before the war. Stories are that he later went to Texas but nothing else is known. Several sisters were born between John and Allen E. All married and settled in Henry County.

Allen Franklin Johnson and Cornelia Roberts, November 9, 1899

After the war, Allen E. married Tabitha Ferrell of Henry County. His parents died in the early 1880s, and were buried on the family farm near Stockbridge. After their death, Allen E. and Tabitha loaded their six young sons and meager possessions on a wagon and headed for Carroll County, taking three weeks for the journey. He was a farmer and lived until 1909. They are buried in the Beulah Baptist Cemetery. His widow received a small pension for his service in the war.

Their six sons were: William (Bill) who died at the age of twenty-nine from burns; John Samuel (1871-1962); James (Jim 1824-1951); Allen Franklin (Frank 1876-1964); Earnest (1879-1957); and Lee (1885-1969). All sons grew up and married in Carroll County, became farmers, made good citizens, and left many descendants.

Allen Franklin, better known as Frank, was named after his father Allen E.; the name Franklin came from his mother's brother, James Franklin Johnson, the first state senator from the newly created Clayton County. James Franklin's wife was Martha Holiday, the aunt of the infamous Doc Holiday! Martha Holiday's mother was a Fitzgerald, ancestor of Margaret Mitchell.

Frank Johnson married Cornelia Roberts in 1899, a marriage that lasted fifty-nine years (see picture). They were blessed with eight children: Mercer (1900-1924); Aubrey (1902-1996); Buvena Eason (1905-1948); Ophelia Pearce born 1908 and still living at the age ninety-five; Winnie Ruth who died of an epidemic at the age of two; Theron (Gill, 1917) still living at the age eighty-four; Snead born 1921. Snead married Marie Dean of Roopville in 1942 and they have three children — a daughter Aloma Streetman, sons Randale and Ralph — six grandchildren, and two great-grandchildren.

After service in World War II, Snead started Johnson Auto Electric. Upon retirement, his son Ralph took over the business with his son Seth. Three generations have served the fifty-four-year-old business. *Submitted by: Marie Johnson, 205 South Street, Carrollton, GA 30117*

694. Allen E. Johnson Family

Allen E. Johnson was born January 12, 1846, in Henry County, Georgia. He was very young but he served in the Confederate Army as a guard at Andersonville Prison. He, along with the Union prisoners, almost starved because so little food was available.

Allen E. and Tabitha Ferrell Johnson

He and Tabitha Ferrell were married November 12, 1866. In 1880 Allen and Tabitha discussed leaving Henry County. They planned to move westward to Carroll County with their five sons — William T. "Billy" age 13; John age 9, Jim age 6, Frank age 4, and Earnest age 1. They packed their furniture and personal belongings in a two-horse wagon with side planks. Their cow and other animals were tied together with ropes for the journey. They had to cross the Chattahoochee River to arrive in Carroll County. Unfortunately, their milch cow had other plans in mind. About midway across the river their milch cow jumped ship and swam back to the east bank. Finally, they got her back on the ferry and to the west bank. They settled in the Beulah community and on May 23, 1885, another son Lee joined this family.

Allen E. Johnson died on February 15, 1909. His beloved wife Tabitha departed on June 2, 1920. Also, their son William T. "Billy" departed this life November 5, 1896, as a result of lockjaw.

Billy was married to Lena Hale and they had two children. John married Mollie Harper and had seven children. Frank married Cornelia Roberts and they had eight children. Earnest married Ezma McCray and had six children. Lee married Katie Coats and had seven children.

Jim married Harriet "Hattie" Creel. They had seven children: Era, Jewell, Mamae, Miller Ferrell "Caps," Percy, Gomer, and Gladys. Jim and his daughters Era, Jewell and Mamae sawed trees. He and Mr. Mart Earnest built them a new house in 1907 on Hog Liver Road near Pleasant View Baptist Church. They lived in this house about fifteen years. After Hattie's parents death, they moved to the Creel home place on Highway 27, north of Carrollton (presently Wal-Mart) and this was home until they went to their heavenly home.

My grandfather Jim played with us grandchildren. Son Gomer and family of Ohio visited in August so we enjoyed a week to ten days of playing and eating together. Grandpa grew watermelons, apples, pears, grapes, muscadines, etc. We would see who could eat the most of Grandpa's food. Then we had to go to the creek, with Grandpa as our leader, and use up some of our energy. We all enjoyed the Graphophone and Grandpa let me play my favorite record "Get Along Little Doggie" every time I visited them. When all twenty-two of the grandchildren visited our grandparents at the same time, the young ones played hide and seek and the older ones played Rook.

Jim died on February 28, 1951, and Hattie on June 29, 1959. They are buried in Pleasant View Cemetery *Submitted by: Earline J. Powers, 1002 West Highway 78, Villa Rica, GA 30180*

695. The Collus Johnson Family

Collus O. Johnson and his wife, Eugenia, native Tennesseeans, came to Carrollton with their children, Tom, Gene, and Colleen, at the invitation of Dr. Irvine S. Ingram, president of West Georgia College in September, 1951. Collus came having been on the faculty of Murray State College, Murray, Kentucky, working in the fields of Resource Use and Community Education Development. At the college, Collus was to teach education courses and work in the Continuing Education Department.

Collus found here a program to bring knowledge and information to the people of Carrollton and Carroll County. He became deeply involved in the evolution of this program, College in the Country, so named because the college worked in local communities on topics about which the communities wished to learn more. No tests or grades were given though the college did have a graduation day when certificates were given to the participants who had finished the course of study. Some of the participants valued these certificates so highly they framed them and hung them in their homes.

Eugenia and Collus Johnson

The Smithfield Community was one of the first groups to take advantage of this free instruction. In 1958, the Union Community had completed its seventh year of College in the Country. Lithia Springs had a long association with College in the Country. By 1958, the number of persons who had participated in this program was 3508 and of this number 2251 were rural people.

Ralph McGill, former editor of *The Atlanta Constitution*, said of the College in the Country program, "The College let it be known that its teachers, its library, and its facilities were at the service of all who wanted to learn."

Another program which became popular with the people of the area was the studycades which the Continuing Education Department took to satisfy the need of the people to "go and see" far places. Collus conducted many of these. Tour members would do advanced study and discussion of the place they were to visit. Then they would meet with the people visited and learn first-hand the history and outstanding features of the place.

Collus continued working in the field of continuing education until he retired in 1973. He was honored that year by the Georgia Adult Education Association with their Annual Adult Education Award. He worked part-time in continuing education in five counties surrounding Carrollton for ten years following his retirement. He died on December 20, 1990, and is buried in the Carroll Memory Gardens.

Eugenia was the homemaker, but due to her master's degree from Northwestern University with emphasis on Christian Education she became a certified Director of Christian Education by the United Methodist Church. She worked for many years as Director of Christian Education at the Carrollton First United Methodist Church and taught in numerous Christian Enrichment Schools in North Georgia Conference of the United Methodist Church. She continues to live in the family home on Griffin Drive, Carrollton.

The children are grown, married, and each has a daughter and son. All work in some field of education. *Submitted by: Eugenia Johnson, 203 Griffin Drive, Carrollton, GA 30117*
Source: Book by Mildred E. English, *"The College in the Country."*

696. Earnest and Ezma McCray Johnson

I, Mozelle Johnson Hughes, am the youngest child of Earnest Johnson and Ezma McCray Johnson. My father's family moved from Henry County to Carroll County in the late 1800s. Neither he nor his brother Lee were born at that time so they are Carroll County natives. My mother is a descendant of a McCray family who came to the United States from Ireland. My siblings are Lois Adams, Clovis Johnson, Willie Mae Akin, Mildia Akin, and Hazel Harden. All are deceased except for the latter two.

School, education, and learning have always been an important part of my life. When I started school in 1927, community schools were in existence such as Bear Creek, Beulah, Bowdon Junction, Burwell, Pine Grove, Jake, Walnut Hill, etc. I first attended school in Smyrna, a small community between Carrollton and Bowdon Junction. After a couple of years, I transferred to Mt. Zion Seminary which was supported by the Methodist Episcopal Church until 1937 when it became state supported. Mt Zion Seminary had a dormitory for faculty and boarding students. My sister, Mildia Akin, lived there during her senior year. She literally "worked her way through" by cleaning, cooking, and serving meals to faculty and students.

These community schools had no lunchrooms, indoor toilets or planned recreational activities. They were usually staffed by two teachers. A female teacher instructed and nurtured the younger students. A male teacher was employed for the older students and was responsible for discipline and sports activities. The boys often played basketball or baseball while the girls watched and cheered. The younger children entertained themselves with games of hop scotch, ring-around-the-roses, tag, and drop-the-handkerchief.

Since there were no lunchrooms at school, students brought lunch from home in a paper sack. My lunch usually consisted of a ham, sausage, or jelly biscuit which had been wrapped in newspaper, along with a jar of water.

Due to a scarcity of cars, transportation to school was primarily by foot, making travel particularly difficult during inclement weather. Occasionally, I was afforded the luxury of riding to school by way of mule and buggy, driven by my sister. I can recall many events, both pleasant and unpleasant, surrounding my travels to school in the buggy.

I attended Bowdon Junction School for a short time before completing my high school career at Mt. Zion High School. In 1938, I was one of the twelve members of the first graduating class of Mt. Zion High School.

Despite objections from my parents, I pursued my college career first by attending West Georgia College. There three other roommates and I occupied one room of the "Dial" house. In a very confined space, we ate, slept, and studied together for two years. From there I transferred to the University of Georgia in Athens. At that time, it was very rare for a woman to attend college, much less one so far away. Again, despite my parents concerns about finances, being so far from home, and in general, "being able to make it on my own," I moved to Athens and fulfilled my goal by graduating in 1942 with a degree in home economics.

I utilized my knowledge of home economics by teaching at my alma mater, Mt. Zion High School, in the late forties and early fifties. At that time, I ended my teaching career to become a full time wife and mother.

I am grateful for the educational opportunities which I was provided in Carroll County. My life has been positively influenced by many teachers for they helped me realize how valuable an education is and that it is a lifelong process.
Submitted by: Mozelle Johnson Hughes, 125 Old King Street, Carrollton, GA 30117
Sources: Family members and personal school records

697. Joseph Albert Johnson Family

Joseph Albert Johnson (born June 13, 1865, died March 1950) and Cassie Rilla Lee (born October 1, 1866, died February 28, 1929) were my great-grandparents but I never knew them. They were married December 23, 1884, and lived in Bowdon. What I do know about them was written in my mother's diary. My mother was Lucille Eason McCurdy, daughter of Milton Perry Eason and Ida Savannah Johnson Eason. My mother's mother died when she was five years old. Her grandmother Cassie was a mother to her.

Joe and Cassie Johnson had thirteen children. They were Albert (Cap), Elbert, Olin, Fred, Lee (Jack), Ewell (Shorty), Annie, Donie, Minnie, Ida, Alice and one daughter who died early. The following is from my mother's diary.

> "Grandpa was a miller. He always lived on a large creek or river. He also farmed. I don't know where he came from originally. Grandma was a Lee. She was related to the Virginia Lee's. General R.E. Lee visited Grandma's home before she was married. My happiest days as a child were spent at Grandma Johnson's house. She was my mother, I loved her as such. Grandpa was more reserved, he did not spend as much time with us. We spent every summer at their house, except for a couple of weeks at Grandma Eason's house. The three youngest brothers of my mother, Fred, Lee (Jack), and Ewell (Shorty) were unmarried and living at home at that time. They played games with us as if they were our age. They were very loving, gentle and caring. I always thought my mother's people were the greatest in the world. They were so kind and thoughtful of each other. Some of them always lived within walking distance of Grandma and nearly always visited on Sunday afternoons and often at night. Then we children would play in the big kitchen that was separated from where the adults were by bedrooms and a long porch. My grandmother died when I was thirteen years old. I thought I couldn't live without her. I felt completely lost. She always came when I needed her and often took me home with her where she could look after me, I still miss her."

Submitted by: Joanne Mann, 1925 Wynfield Point Drive, Buford, GA 30519

698. Percy V. Johnson

Percy V. Johnson, the fifth child of James M. and Harriet Creel Johnson, was born November 27, 1901. He married Avice Matthews, the oldest daughter of Edgar and Pearl Brock Matthews, on December 18, 1926.

Percy was one of seven graduates in the class of 1923 Mt. Zion Seminary. He was a full time farmer until 1936. He helped build the bridge over the Central of Georgia Railroad tracks on Highway 27 North and the bridges over Buck Creek and the Little Tallapoosa River. Also, he worked on several projects in the Buford and Norcross, Georgia, area.

In 1942, Percy started working in the sponging department of Sewell Manufacturing Company in Bremen, Georgia. He earned forty cents per hour as a beginner. The family sold forty quarts of sweet milk per day to the Dairy Queen for many years. Percy delivered butter, eggs, and other farm products to the Dr. Homer Barker family every Saturday for years. He grew acres of corn for the purpose of selling it by the dozen. Every customer received thirteen ears for each dozen sold, so hopefully everyone had twelve full ears.

Percy and Avice had four children: Earline 1930, Horry 1934, Donald 1940, and Bill 1944. Avice was a homemaker. She spent hours in the yards and garden. She canned, dried, and froze everything grown on the farm.

The Johnson reunion after Grandma and Grandpa were gone.

Percy and Avice Johnson

Percy and Avice joined Pleasant View Baptist Church in the 1920s and all four children grew up in the church and were very active. Percy was the caretaker at Pleasant View Cemetery for twenty-seven years. He was thrilled when the cemetery became a perpetual care cemetery in 1973. Presently, son Horry is the caretaker.

Percy served as a school board member from the Mt. Zion district for eight years during the 1960s. They had ten grandchildren: Tim and Greg Powers, Dennis, Dale, Carole, Rodney, Laura, Julie, Kelli, and Kris Johnson. Plus twelve great grandchildren: Cherri, Michael, Molly, and Rebecca Powers; Adam, Kristan, Paige, Whitney, Meredith, Mallory, and Gus Johnson; and Melanie Hollis. Percy died July 11, 1983, and Avice September 11, 1997. *Submitted by: Cherri Powers, P.O. Box 10670, Carrollton, GA 30118*

699. W.T. Johnson Sr., W.T. Johnson Jr., and the New Johnson House

Excerpts from *The Bowdon Bulletin,* "The March of Time" by Professor V.D. Whatley.

June 1944: PEOPLE AND EVENTS. Among recent former residents to visit recently was Mr. Will T. Johnson Jr. [1884-1940] of Atlanta, who is most pleasantly remembered by our people. Willie was not only a splendid business man, standing by and working for Bowdon, but he was active in every good cause. A Christian gentleman whose everyday life and talk and walk challenged all to higher levels of thinking and living. Better blood never pulsated in human veins. He is one of our dearest friends.

THE YEARS BRING CHANGES. There were several Johnson children. All attended our school. All lived in Bowdon. Now the family is scattered. THAT IS LIFE. I wish the children and grandchildren knew the history of the Johnson and Colquitt families. They were graduates in the art of gracious living. Want of space forbids my going into details, but I must say this: W.T. Johnson Sr. [1858-1917)] was our neighbor in Troup County and moved to Bowdon at or near 1880. Tom, as I always called him, my former patron and trustee of Old Bowdon College, was a successful business man known far and wide, owning valuable town and rural property, a member of the Bowdon Baptist Church for years, public spirited and active in every worthwhile movement, who reared a family that's honored wherever known. Our conversations were "many times many." Of course I esteemed him highly. A man of integrity, deep in faith and great in friendship. Words could scarcely measure his love for Bowdon.

"His home, still owned by some of the children, is a credit to the town. Somehow we cherish the hope of its remaining in the family. The old childhood home never completely fades from the memory. The room that each one occupied is a shrine where dreams bloomed and ambitions budded and lessons studied."

May 24, 1945: "Mrs. J.A. Waller (the former Miss Nell Johnson) recently bought the home that her father W.T. Johnson Sr. built and loved so much. This home is conveniently located and is one of the more desirable places in Bowdon. It faces College Street on the south and Johnson Avenue (named for her father) on the east. The building is imposing and presents a magnificent view. It is indeed commendable that this dear daughter bought the childhood home so full of sacred memories, and at some future date Mr. and Mrs. Waller expects to occupy it." - Professor V.D. Whatley

January 8, 1970:
Advertisement in *Bowdon Bulletin*

FOR SALE at AUCTION. COLONIAL JOHNSON HOUSE on Main Street, Bowdon McCarley Chevrolet Co. Time - 2 o'clock, Sat., Jan. 31st. This House has 10 Rooms, 5 Upstairs - 5 Downstairs and 2 large Halls. This is extra good lumber - hand picked. House is in good condition.

A REAL BARGAIN!

Johnson Home Place in Bowdon, built about 1901, dismantled 1977.

William T. and Susan Isabella Colquitt Johnson, about 1890.

1989: Requiem by George W. Johnson,
Grandson of its Builder and Owner

"Members of the Johnson family lived in this house on and off over the years until it was dismantled in 1977. The last occupant was my Aunt Nelah Johnson Alsobrook [1889-1981)] and her son Thomas. Aunt Nelah taught in the elementary grades at Bowdon for many years. The house was last known as the Johnson-Alsobrook House. At an earlier time, the first hospital in Bowdon was in this house. Dr. W.W. Watts lived there with his family and had a few patients stay there too. He later moved across from the former Bowdon College site, the current location of Bowdon High School.

"Later, the Johnson House property was sold to the Bowdon Chevrolet dealer by my Daddy's half-sister's (Aunt Nell Johnson Waller 1894-1964) husband, Uncle Amos Waller, of Bradenton, FL, after Aunt Nell's death. The house was razed, the large magnolia trees cut down, and a used car lot with a Butler building was put in its place. Now a small manufacturing plant is located there.

"This part of Georgia small town history, as well as our family history, has been replaced. Even memories of it will be gone as each of us who lived there, or saw it, are replaced by new generations. Soon the awareness of these events will not be there because even the telling about it will cease."

Note: W.T. Johnson Sr. married first Sarah (Sallie) Beatrice Colquitt in 1877, daughter of William T. and Ann Stringer Colquitt, born 1853. He then married her sister Susan Isabella Colquitt in 1883, born June 6, 1848, died April 10, 1892. They had three children: William Thomas Jr. (1884), Henry Colquitt (1887) and Nelah Belle (1889). In late 1892 he married for a third time to Charlsie Edna Vance, daughter of John C. and Delila Beavers Vance. Their children were Nellie Witt (1894), Ruth (1897), Dorothy (1901), Maude (1903), and Mary Elizabeth (1907). *Submitted by: Great-grandson Jeffrey Alan Johnson, 1206 Hickory Creek Court, Woodstock, GA 30188.*

700. William T. Johnson Jr. and Evie Lee Downs

William Thomas Johnson Jr. was born November 15, 1884, in Bowdon and died February 11, 1948, in Atlanta, Georgia at the home of his daughter Isabelle in the Kirkwood community. He married Evie Lee Downs December 20, 1916, in Bowdon. His great-uncle George Washington Colquitt officiated. Evie Lee, daughter of George L. and Hettie Lipham Downs, was born on August 6, 1894, in Bowdon and died March 16, 1938, of pneumonia in Atlanta at Georgia Baptist Hospital.

William T. Johnson, Jr. about 1915, around age 26

In 1895 Will T. Johnson Jr. attended the Piedmont Exposition in Atlanta and saw the great John Phillip Sousa band perform. This fostered his love of music and he consequently played trombone in the Bowdon band at the turn of the century; about 1915, he played in the Bowdon College Orchestra. Between 1900-1905 Will was cashier for the new Bank of Bowdon, located at the corner of Main and Wedowee Streets. Between 1921-1923 he was named Bowdon postmaster by the administration of President Warren G. Harding, as he was one of the few Republicans in the county at that time. Upon moving his family to Atlanta in 1925, Will worked as an auditor for Georgia Railway & Electric Company, which provided the streetcar system for the city.

Evie Lee Downs, age 19, 1913 Graduation, Bowdon College

Will and Evie Lee had three children: Charlsie Isabelle born in Bowdon October 25, 1917; Eleanor, born March 22, 1921, in Bowdon; and George William born February 6, 1926, in Atlanta at home near Grant Park.

George enlisted in the U.S. Army/Air Corps in 1943 before turning seventeen, but his father made him wait until his eighteenth birthday to join. In 1948 he attained the world record for a model airplane Class D, freeflight. George followed this early interest in model planes by making a 31-year career with Lockheed Georgia Corporation, and during that time earning five patents in his name and several national awards.

George wed Evelyn Annelle Stevenson, daughter of William Lewis and Catherine Tarrance Stevenson, on December 19, 1944, in Atlanta. They have three sons: William Michael (1946), Philip Thomas (1948) and Jeffrey Alan (1954).

Isabelle Johnson, age 18, 1935 Graduation, Girls' High School, Atlanta

From The *Bowdon Bulletin,* Feb 27, 1948: *"Tribute Written To Will Johnson One of Bowdon's Best Boosters* on the occasion of his death, by W. Otis Barrow

"I never had a better friend than Will Johnson. Only the old, original Bowdon people realize how much FREE work Will Johnson did for Bowdon. Every time there was any money to raise for charity it fell his and my lot to get out and collect the money. I think it got to the point when anyone in their stores would see Will Johnson and Otis Barrow coming together they knew to get out their pocketbooks, as they were promoting for some cause. I also remember him as clerk of the church, back when we had Saturday meeting. I was secretary of the Sunday School for years, while Will Johnson was superintendent of the Sunday School. I well remember him as he would use his slide trombone to help in the music while I tried to lead the singing.

"I remember also when we headed the drive for War Bonds during WWI, and we would build a stand in the center of the Bowdon square and sell bonds until we 'went over the top.'

"And how could I forget him when we both backed up the Lyceum Attractions at the college. We would move the piano from the Baptist Church to the college, lug it up those winding steps, and then have to carry it back the next day. Will was the first Fire Chief when we went to Carrollton and bought from them a hand-pulled cart which we used for years before Bowdon bought the fire truck. Although Will had not lived in Bowdon for several years, he still loved old Bowdon and enjoyed his return visits. I was glad that the family thought enough of the original Bowdon Band to ask them to be his pallbearers."

Excerpt from *Bowdon Bulletin,* March 24, 1938: *The March of Time* By Professor V.D. Whatley

" ... The death of Mrs. Evie Lee Downs Johnson removes one of our dearest pupils; from our hands she received her diploma; under our jurisdiction she taught in our schools. Learning and religion were stars that shined in the galaxy of her soul.

Eleanor Johnson, age 15, 1936 Graduation, Girls' High School, Atlanta

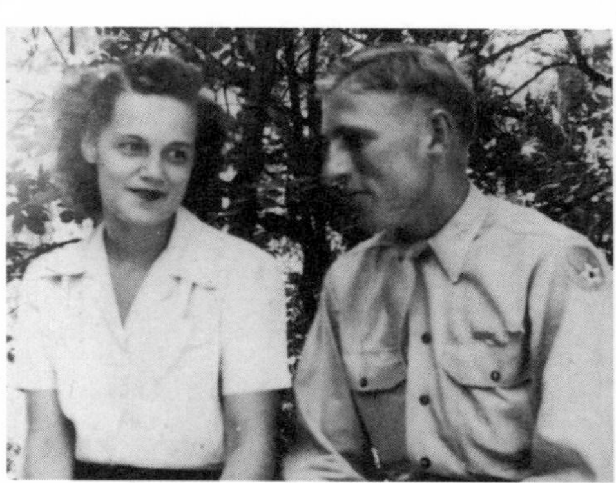

George Johnson and Evelyn Stevenson about 1944.

" ... Joined the Bowdon Baptist Church in August 1907; graduated from Bowdon College in 1913 with the degree of A.B. Taught at Barge, Liberty Hill, Rockmart, Kansas and Atlanta, and when taken sick was teaching 4th grade in the I.N. Ragsdale Elementary School.

"In 1932 she received a Normal Diploma from Bowdon State College and a Life Certificate from Georgia. In June 1938 she would have received her A.B. degree from Oglethorpe University. Her passion for learning remained with her until the sunset glow grew dim."

Submitted by: William Michael Johnson, 748 Iron Mountain Road, Canton, GA 30115

701. Joseph John Johnson / Johnston

Joseph John was born 1817 in Halifax County, North Carolina, to Dempsey Johnston and unknown first wife. Dempsey and second wife, Elizabeth Pritchett Moore came to Coweta County, Georgia, in 1825. Dempsey's story is told in *The Heritage of Randolph County Alabama,* published by Walsworth Publishing Company. Joseph John married Elizabeth Velvin, daughter of Robert and Frances Kilgore Velvin in 1839. In 1847 Joseph bought the west half of lot 201 in Carroll County from Joseph Beddingfield, both residing in Carroll County. Joseph and Elizabeth farmed at

County Line, attending County Line Primitive Baptist Church. In April of 1864, Joseph joined Company K 1st (Fannins) Georgia Reserves, Confederate Army and was promoted to sergeant. His service records state he was forty-eight years old, five feet ten inches tall, had blue eyes and a fair complexion, a farmer who resided in Carroll County, Georgia. While home on sick furlough, 13 July 1864 he was captured by federal raiders, taken to Camp Douglas, Illinois, where he died 26 October 1864 and was reburied in the Confederate Mound at Oak Woods Cemetery, Chicago, 3 November 1864. Elizabeth received a pension for his service in Carroll County 1891 through 1904, the year of her death. She is probably buried in an unmarked grave in County Line Primitive Baptist Church Cemetery.

Their twelve children were: Rebecca Emily born 1841, Carroll County, married William A. Williams, lived at Fairplay, had Francis, Elizabeth, David, Sarah and Media Williams; Mary born 1843, married Thomas Jefferson Fields, censused 1870 in the Fifth District of Carroll County, 1880 in Heard County, and in Fairplay District, Carroll County in 1900, had John, Elizabeth, William, Mary, Thomas, and Robert Fields; James P. born 1846, died 1869; Willis M. born 1847 married Mary "Polly" Beddingfield, lived in Fairplay, had John Edgar, Minnie, Lillian, Josie Eva, Willie V., Carl, Bertha, Elizabeth May and Lucille Johnston; Robert born 1848, died about 1862; Sarah E. "Sallie" born 1850, married Lewis Chastain, lived in the Third District in 1880 and Hulett District 1542 in 1900 of Carroll County, had William, Julia, Catherine, Beulah and Richard Chastain; Celia Saxon born 1851, died 1939, buried at Powell's Chapel Cemetery, Carroll County, married John Griffin Alexander Boyd, lived in the Third District in 1880 and were in Douglas County in 1900, had Sarah Ophelia, John William, Herschel Jordan, Elizer Vesta, Marilla, Thomas Allen, Jordan, Callaway Smith, Julia and Lunie Forsyth Boyd; Kiziah Texas born 1853, married William J. Bass, lived in Fairplay, had Jackson, Vesta, Mary, Florence, George, Emily Frances, Eliza Savannah, Julia, Celia, Dora and William David Bass; Vesta born 1855, died 1947, buried County Line Primitive Baptist Church Cemetery, married David Morris Truitt, had Carrie, George, Earnest and David Morris Truitt Jr.; Eliza Jane born 1857 married James F. Boyd, lived in Carroll County, had Mary Idella, Linton Emory, Oscar, Leona Pearl, James Monroe, Bessie, Nora and Elizabeth Boyd; John Thomas born 1860 married Sarah Florence Richards. See their story in this publication. *Submitted by: Laquita Vice, 477 Laurel Ridge Dr. # 4203, Ellijay, GA 30540*

Sources: *Our Johnson Family* by Willis Ezra Johnson, published privately, records of descendants, Patricia Yates, Erlene Boyd and Lucy Moye.

702. Johnson - Lambert Family

Mack Raymond Johnson of Duluth, Georgia, and Sarah Jane Lambert of Carrollton, Georgia, were united in marriage 11-19-1961 at the Tabernacle Baptist Church. Rev. Lewis H. Brazell, pastor, officiated.

Mack Johnson, son of Ralph Raymond Johnson (1917-1993) and Nancy Turner Johnson (born 6-17-1918), was born in Lawrenceville, Georgia 9-2-1942. He graduated from Martha Berry School for Boys, Rome, Georgia in 1960.

Jane Johnson, daughter of Curtis Newton Lambert (1911-1957) and Sarah Douglas Lambert (1914-1990), was born in Carrollton 7-13-1942. She attended College Street School and graduated from Carrollton High School in 1960. Mack and Jane met while freshmen at West Georgia College. After their marriage, they resided and worked in Atlanta. Later they returned to Carrollton, Jane assisted her mother in operating Toddler's Corner Nursery and Kindergarten. Jane is a homemaker and enjoys spending her time with her grandchildren and doing volunteer work at her church, New World United Methodist Church. Mack was employed by Southwire Company in inside sales. Southwire transferred him to Birmingham, Alabama, and later to Arlington, Texas, where they have resided since 1977. Mack is presently a manufacturer's representative of electrical products. They make visits home to Georgia each year to visit family and friends. Mack enjoys playing golf. They enjoy traveling to new places.

Mack and Jane have two children: Mark Newton Johnson, born 10-16-1962, and Todd Raymond Johnson, born 4-6-1968. Both boys graduated from Lamar High School and reside in Arlington with their families.

Mark graduated from the University of Texas at Arlington with a BBA degree and a MBA degree. He is employed by Verizon as a marketing research manager. On 5-9-1987 he married Cheryl Geiser, born 5-20-1963. Cheryl graduated from the University of Texas at Arlington with a BSN degree. She is employed by Dr. Frank DeLaTorre as a registered nurse. They have two children: Courtney Elise Johnson, born 7-22-1988, and Mark Tyler Johnson, born 9-28-1990. Courtney attends Boles Junior High School and Tyler attends Corey Elementary School.

Todd graduated from Sam Houston University in Huntsville, Texas with a BA degree. He is employed as a fire fighter/paramedic with the Grand Prairie (Texas) Fire Department. On 11-20-1993 Todd married Amy Campbell, born 6-19-1971. Amy graduated from Sam Houston University in Huntsville with a BA degree. She is employed by the Irving (Texas) Independent School District as a cable TV specialist/photographer. They have two children: Jake Raymond Johnson, born 9-3-1997, and Zane David Johnson, born 2-1-2000. *Submitted by: Mrs. Jane L. Johnson, 2512 Radcliffe Drive, Arlington, TX 76012*

703. John Thomas Johnston

John Thomas Johnston born 1860 in Carroll-County to Joseph John and Elizabeth Velvin Johnson/Johnston married 1879 Sarah Florence "Missie" Richards, born 1858 to William B. and Sarah H. Moseley Richards. John Thomas and Sarah farmed in the County Line community, attending County Line Primitive Baptist Church. Sarah Florence did beautiful handwork as did most of the ladies of her generation. John and Sarah Florence are buried in Ramah Primitive Baptist Church cemetery in Palmetto, Georgia.

Sarah Florence Richards Johnston and her children.

Their nine children were: Willis Dempsey born 1880, married Susan Frances "Fannie" Richardson of Palmetto. Their children were: Fred Hill married Christin Lucille Ekman, Roy Thomas married Cecil Watson, Willis Dempsey Jr., killed in action during World War II, married Elaine Long. Willis and Fannie are buried in Ramah Cemetery; William Homer born 1882, farmer and sawmiller, married Lela Louvenia Hammond, daughter of James Marion "Jim" and Melinda Ballard Hammond of Campbell, now Fulton County (see Thomas McCoy Hammond story). Their children were: Clarice Mildred married David Stith Kearns, Gordon Marion married Rosa Lee Davis, John Homer "J.H." married Eva Mae Martin, William Harold married Virginia Moulton. William Homer and Lela are buried in Floral Hill Cemetery in Palmetto, Georgia; John Gordon, spelled his name Johnson, born 1886 married Martha Talulah "Mattie" Hudson, daughter of William H. and Lucy Rebecca McCoy Hudson of Douglas County, moved to Camilla, Georgia. Their children were: Lois May married William Hall and Olin Hodnett, Gladys married Roy Vick and Guy Nicholson, John William married Alice Marie Ritchie, Robert Lamar married Martha Gardner; Henry Grady born 1890, married Lucy Victoria Landrum, daughter of Columbus Franklin "Lum" Landrum, lived in Newnan, had Sarah Ellen married Charles Allen Moye, Henry Landrum married Dorothy Quinn Thigpen. Henry Grady served in the Marines in World War I. He and Lucy are buried in Ramah Cemetery; James Moseley Johnston born 1892, married Dora Mundy served in World War I, lived in Atlanta, had Eleanor married George Traylor Thiesen, James Moseley Jr. married Connie. James Moseley is buried in East View Cemetery in Atlanta; Lula born 1895 married Virgil Quillian Shannon, lived in Atlanta, had Sara Barbara married Harry Oliver Dean, James married Carolyn Ward. Lula and Virgil are buried in Ramah Cemetery; Joseph Ezra born 1897, married Elizabeth Andrews, lived in Fairburn and Palmetto, had John Thomas born 1931, died 1934, Florence Clementine married Clifford Johnson, Joseph Olin, Jere Eugene, Hardy Stanton married Beverly Elaine Grubbs, Kenneth Andrews, Elizabeth Ann married Clyde Hufsteler, Katherine Elaine married Gerald Coleman, Joseph Howard "Jack," William James married Susan Jeanette Thomas. Joseph Ezra and Elizabeth are buried in Ramah Cemetery; Hardy Stanton, spelled his last name Johnson, married Eloise Sewell. They lived in Newnan, Georgia, had no children and are buried in Oak Hill Cemetery in Newnan; Elizabeth Florence born 1902, married Dewey Phillips, lived in Palmetto, had a daughter, Sara Juanita, born 1923, died 1933, buried at Ramah, Dan married Elizabeth. Elizabeth "Lizzie" Florence and Dewey Phillips are buried in Holly Hill Cemetery in Fairburn, Georgia. *Submitted by: Patricia Johnston Yates, 105 West Knight Rd., McDonough, GA 30252*

Sources: Personal research of records of Carroll, Coweta, Campbell, and Douglas counties, Federal census records, *Douglas County, Georgia Who Was Who Volume I* by Joe Baggett, *Our Johnson Family* by Willis Ezra Johnson, published privately, *Palmetto a Town and Its People,* Barbara Crisp, Teresa Daugherty, Editors, published privately, Johnston descendant Lucy Moye.

704. Jones Family of Whitesburg

Our earliest known ancestor at this time is Thomas B. Jones, Minister of Gospel, 1808-1880, married Celia S. Velvin 1809-1890. He was of Welsh descent and was a Primitive Baptist. They had nine children.

Their son Robert Benjamin Jones, born May 24, 1830, in Whitesburg, Georgia, died April 19, 1897, married Frances Jane Christian born January 24, 1839, died February 13, 1903, in 1853. Settled a home and reared a family of thirteen children near Lick Skillet, a famous Justice Court Ground about two miles from the present Douglas County line. This area was in Carroll County, then Campbell County, now Douglas County. I have heard my father, Jethro Gordon Richards Sr., say many times that he lived in three counties and never moved.

Their daughter, Cecelia Sexton Jones (my grandmother), was married by her grandfather, Elder Thomas B. Jones, to Robert Washington Richards in 1874. Cecelia and Robert W. Richards had ten children, all of whom lived in Carroll County.

My father, Jethro Gordon Richards, was their seventh child. I, Imogene Richards Frazier, am his daughter.

My grandmother's uncle, Jethro Jones, and three of his sons are the subjects of the remainder of this oratory.

James Jethro Peter Jones, born June 18, 1837, died November 29, 1907, was fifth child of Thomas B. Jones; married November 20, 1856, Mary P. Holland. Second wife was Cecelia Ann Watson, born March 12, 1836, married December 20, 1866, died November 24, 1899. Jethro had three children with his first wife, and seven children with his second wife.

Jethro Jones was a prosperous plantation owner of several hundred acres a few miles from Whitesburg off State Highway 5 North in the Byers Crossroads area near Antioch Baptist Church, and owned Black Dirt farm.

Whitesburg's first bank was organized in 1907 and was a safe institution. The Hon. Jethro Jones was the first president. He was murdered in 1907 by a band of cotton thieves whom he apprehended in the act of carrying off his cotton. Sadly, they were his renters. Jethro Jones' oldest son, William Tyre Jones, succeeded him as president of the bank.

In 1916 under the administration of T.J. Jones as mayor, Whitesburg installed an electric light system. With the arrival of electricity, the town soon had an electric corn mill. William Tyre Jones and his brothers (T.J. "Tom" and R.E.L. "Bob" Jones) installed this mill. Fire destroyed the equipment in 1926. Rev. J.W. McLeod installed another mill.

They have told me that the Jones Brothers were cotton brokers. When cotton was selling at about 40 cents per pound, they bought and were holding cotton for an increase when the price of cotton dropped to 3 cents per pound, That was a devastating blow.

Each of the three brothers built fine homes in Whitesburg. At this time, I am living in the home built in 1918-20 by Tyre Jones in Whitesburg at 710 Main Street. They tell me that Tyre carefully selected all material that went into the building of the home. He and brothers and sister Mattie are buried in the Whitesburg Cemetery. Tyre Jones died in 1923 of pneumonia. In 1936, R.E.L. (Bob) Jones was standing on the burning bridge across the Chattahoochee River on Georgia Highway 16 near Whitesburg when an automobile, whose driver tried to jump the area as it burned, hit Bob Jones. He died a few days later from the injury.

I do not know a lot about the rest of Jethro's children, but these three brothers made an impact on the town of Whitesburg in a very positive way. *Submitted by: Imogene Frazier, P.O. Box 124, Whitesburg, GA 30185*

705. Houston Nimrod Jones 1765-1849

Nimrod Jones was born 1765 in Orange County, North Carolina. He was listed on the muster call in Columbia County, Georgia, in 1793. He married Charlotte Bullock and she died before 1812.

They had five children: (1) Charlotte Jones, born in Columbia County Georgia, married unknown (Davis). (2) Feraby Jones, born 1795, married James Reynolds February 10, 1829, in Henry County, Georgia. (3) William Long Jones, born in Columbia County. (4) Permilia Jones, born 1798 in Columbia, County, died after 1883

Nathan J. Jones and Mary M. Gray

in Carroll County. She married Nathan Breed February 25, 1817 in Warren County, Georgia. (5) Louise Jones born 1804, died 1878 in Spalding County, Georgia, she married John Breed, November 18, 1823 in Henry County.

Nimrod then married Elizabeth Carmicheal on March 15, 1812. Her mother was Mary Carmichael. Elizabeth was born 1774 and died 1819.

Nimrod and Elizabeth had four children. (1) Richard Jones, born December 13, 1812, in Columbia County, died April 7, 1898, in Carroll County. He married Caroline Missouri Jarrett on September 20, 1835. She was born February 11, 1819, and died April 7, 1898. They are buried in Whooping Creek Primitive Baptist Church Cemetery. (2) Emaline Jones, born December 2, 1814, in Columbia County, and died June 28, 1884, in Spalding County. She married Etheldred Futral, October 29, 1834, in Henry County. (3) Elizabeth Ann Jones, born about 1817 in Columbia County, died 1896 in Cleburne County, Alabama. She married John B. McElroy, November 24, 1837, in Carroll County. (4) Mary Elinor Jones, born 1819 in Columbia County, died after 1880 in Lamar Beat, Randolph County, Alabama. She married John Stillwell January 9, 1840, in Carroll County.

The children of Nimrod and Rebecca White: (1) Rachel Matilda Jones, born 1822 in Columbia County, died 1914 in Georgia. She married Richard Webster Hicks, May 4, 1837, in Carrollton, Carroll County.

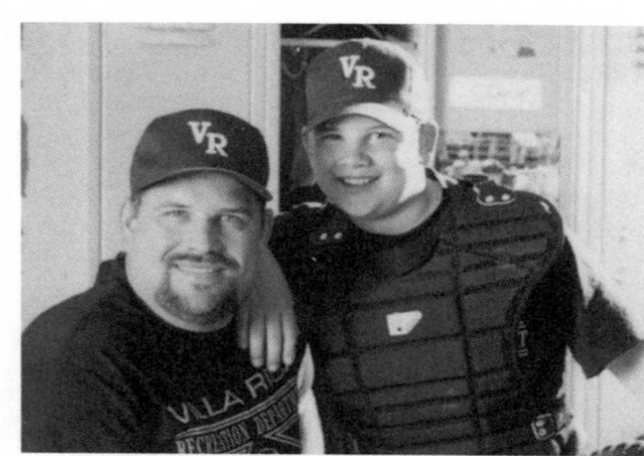

Elic Gregory Daniel and Tyler Matthew Daniel

The Children of Richard Jones and Caroline M. Jarrett are: (1) William Thomas Jones, born August 15, 1836, in Carroll County and died April 16, 1913. He married Susan Ann Afford. She was born August 24, 1840, and died November 7, 1907. They are buried in Whooping Creek Primitive Baptist Church Cemetery. (2) Mary Elizabeth Jones, born July 1, 1838. She married Wiley Hiram Nail on November 10, 1854, died January 15, 1928, in Carroll County. They are both buried in Whooping Creek Primitive Baptist Church Cemetery. (3) James M. Jones, born 1840 in Georgia. (4) Alonzo Jones, born 1842 in Carroll County. (5) Susan Jones, born 1844, Carroll County. (6) Permelia Ann Jones, was born April 2, 1846, in Carroll County. She married September 20, 1860, to Seaborn H. Scoggins in Carroll County. He died October 5, 1918, was buried at Whooping Creek Primtive Baptist Church Cemetery, Carroll County. (7) Nathaniel Jefferson Jones, was born July 3, 1848. He married December 17, 1865, to Mary M. Gray. She was born June 30, 1848, died November 12, 1924. Nathaniel died September 15, 1933. They were both buried at Whooping Creek Primitive Church Cemetery, Carroll County. (8) John Henry Jones, born October 12, 1854, in Georgia, died July 7, 1921. (9) Lewis Warren Jones, born 1855 in Carroll County, died August 16, 1875. (10) Richard Augustus Jones was born March 1, 1858, in Carroll County, died April 20, 1926.

Nathaniel Jefferson Jones and Mary Gray Jones, son of Richard and Caroline, had seven children: (1) George Jones married Sallie Irene Thornton and their children are Jewell, Ruby, Lloyd, Fred, J.B., and Doris. (2) Strawder married John Spence and they had three children: Athela married Earnest Young; Grady; Alma married John Cook they had one child, Avis. (3) Lou married Gene Burns and they had one child, Aubrey. (4) Rebecca married three different times, first to John Cosby and they had two sons, John Isom and Carl; second to Willie Farmer; and third to Jack Driver. (5) Dave Richard married Laula Hancock and they had seven children: Lester, Dewey, Ethelene, Jeanette, Susie, Nell, Dave Richard Jr. (6) Sam married Hattie Hendrix and they had four children: Roy, Lovern, Frances, and Betty. (7) Mattie Ophelia married Samuel (Sam) Allen Davis and they had eleven children: Estelle, Ruth, Gladys, Kathleen, Durward, Dorsey, Martha, Billie, Willene, Rudene, and Joyce.

In the early land lottery of 1820, Nimrod Jones received land in Columbia County, Georgia. He received land lot #256, 5th District of Carroll County, Georgia. It was awarded December 20, 1830. At the time of the 1830 census, Nimrod and his family were in Henry County, Georgia, but in 1840 they were living in Carroll County. In 1843 he was elected coroner of Carroll County.

Nimrod and Rebecca joined the Tallapoosa Primitive Baptist Church on February 2, 1842. On March 21, 1846, Richard Jones (a son of Nimrod) joined the church and later was one of the founders of Whooping Creek Primitive Baptist Church.

The will of Nimrod Jones was recorded January 8, 1849. He named all ten of his children in his will. He is buried with other family members on his plantation in the Clem District of Carroll County, now known as the Shadinger Farm on Shadinger Road, in Carrollton, Georgia. The National Society of Daughers of the American Revolution, Abraham Baldwin Chapter, did a dedication of the grave with a marker on September 13, 1997. *Submitted by: Belinda Rowlette, 102 Myrtle Street, Carrollton, GA 30117*

Source: Researched by Rudene Daniel.

706. Jones

In the Beginning, Everybody was a Jones

A beloved Jones minister always said that in the beginning, everybody was a Jones.

Our Jones family goes back to William Thomas and Susan Ann Alford Jones, daughter of Jeptha and Jane Scoggins Alford. William Thomas and Susan Ann married 20 September 1855. William was born 15 August 1836 and died 16 April 1913. Susan Ann was born 24 August 1840, and died 7 November 1907. They are buried at Whooping Creek Primitive Baptist Church.

William Thomas and Susan Ann were born, married, and died in Carroll County. Their children were Mary A. born 1858; James Thomas born 1860; Julia born 1868; Mansy born 1869; Alice born 1872; Lou born 1873; Mattie born 1874; and Augusta born 1876.

James Thomas Jones married Lucinda Rooks, daughter of William and Hester Ann Dover Rooks. James Thomas "Jim" was born in 1860 and died in 1923. Lucinda "Cindy" was born about 1862 and died in 1924. They are buried at Mt. Pleasant Baptist Church, Clem, Georgia. Their children are: William Albert born 18 April 1882, died 6 November 1957; Effie born March 1884, died September 1970; Ed born about 1888, died about 1918; Era born about 1890, died about 1920; Jack born about 1900, death unknown.

William Albert Jones married Earline Elizabeth Johnson, daughter of James Andrew and Willie Sapheria Cooper Johnson. Will and Earline married 25 November 1906 in Carroll County. She was born 16 September 1886 and died 9 July 1929. Their children were Margaret Willene born 10 October 1912; Mabel Catherine born 4 May 1914; Ray Madison "Bill" born 3 September 1916, died 6 February 1996 in Virginia; Kenzie Andrew born 30 November 1919, died 1 February 1996 in Georgia; Bennie Whitfield born 17 February 1922; Evelyn Irene born 19 September 1925.

Effie Jones married J.T. "Tom" Phillips. Their children are Vassie, Grady, "Tee," and Opal Lee.

Ed Jones married Maude Daugherty. Their children are Joe and Lois.

Era Jones married Ed Heard. Their children are James Zeddie, Eris, and Gladys.

Jack Jones never married.

Hester Ann Dover was born in South Carolina about 1831. After William Rooks died in the Civil War, Hester married George Washington Cook in 1869. They had a son, Jacob Brown Cook.

We have no information about the sisters of Lucinda, A.Y. (Anne?) born 1855, and Sarah born 1859.

Our Johnson grandparents are buried at Whitesburg Methodist Church. Grandpa Johnson ran a ferry across the Chattahoochee River. Their children are Maggie, Earline, Hall, Orlando, Mitchell, Marvin, Johnny, Eugene, Annie Ruth, Eva Mae, and Cecil.

My memories are vague at best, but have been kept alive and well by two older sisters who have the most vivid and entertaining memories of their happy childhood in Carroll County. As a child in Clem, I remember the Laz Holloways, especially the daughters Mildred, Blanche, Mae, and "Mutt." I thought their house was the biggest house in the world, not knowing my "world" was very small at the time. Neighbors I remember were the Keyes, Crawfords, Denneys, Cooks, Lassiters, Jones, Davenports, James, Rooks, and Bates. The post office and store were the fun place to go, as we kids could climb up the metal poles out front and slide down.

I will always be grateful for the short time in my life that God saw fit to plant me in Clem. My roots grew strong and healthy there. Forevermore, the memories I have of those times and people will touch my heart. *Submitted by: Evelyn Jones Mooney, P.O. Box 2539, Cleveland, GA 30528-0045. GrannyMooney@alltel.net.*

707. Jethro Jones

James Jethro Peter Jones was born June 18, 1837, in Coweta County, Georgia. He was the fifth of nine sons born to Thomas B. and Celia S. Velvin Jones. This family moved to Carroll County in 1838 and made their home in the 3rd District.

Jethro married Mary Francis Holland November 20, 1856, in Carroll County. She was the daughter of James Hudson and Mary Smith Holland. Two children were born to this union — James Henry who married Minnie B. Armour, and Mary Francis who married John William Johnson.

During the War Between the States, Jethro joined Company E, 1st Georgia Calvary. This unit served in Iverson's Brigade, Wheeler's Calvary. Jethro was captured July 22, 1864, at the Battle of Atlanta. They imprisoned him at Louisville, Kentucky, and Camp Chase, Ohio. He was exchanged in March of 1865 and was sick in a Richmond, Virginia, hospital on March 13, 1865. At the end of the war, he returned home to Carroll County. His wife, Mary Francis, died in 1865, leaving him with two motherless children. She is buried in Holland Meeting House Cemetery.

Jethro married Selina H. (Celia) Watson in Carroll County on December 13, 1866. She was the daughter of Tyre Watson. Jethro bought Tyre's estate in 1868. This farm was just south of Byers Crossroads in the 3rd District of Carroll County. This was his home for the rest of his life.

Jethro and Celia had seven children. (1) William Tyre who married Florence Harris; (2) Joseph Antsey; (3) Martha Watson (Mattie); (4) Sarah Anna who married Oscer Aderhold; (5) twins Thomas Jackson and (6) Robert E. Lee Jones; and (7) John B. Gordon Jones. Celia Watson Jones died November 24, 1889, and is buried in Jones-Watson Cemetery.

James Jethro Peter Jones. 1837-1907

Over the years, Jethro prospered. He owned large farms on both sides of the Chattahoochee River in Coweta and Carroll Counties. By 1900 he was one of the wealthiest planters in the area. It was said that every time one of his sons married, he was given a 250-acre farm.

Jethro married again to Emma Tolitha Hendly on May 4, 1890. There were no children by this marriage.

Jethro was murdered on November 29, 1907, and is buried in Jones-Watson Cemetery. He had caught six black men stealing a bale of cotton from his gin house and was shot in the face and hand with a shotgun and killed. Four of the men were sent to prison for theft. Two were tried and found guilty of murder and were hanged on the gallows in the Carrollton jail on February 14, 1908. This was the last execution in Carroll County.

Jethro Jones came home from the War Between the States penniless, but was a wealthy man at his death. He is a tribute to the perseverance of the Confederate veterans who rebuilt their lives, homes, and country during the turbulent reconstruction years. *Submitted by: Sam Pyle, 1471 Mandeville Road, Carrollton, GA 30117*
Sources: Georgia Department of Archives and History, Carroll County Cemetery book, Carroll County marriage and court records, and personal family knowledge.

708. Joseph Tyre Jones

Joseph Tyre Jones was born September 14, 1878, near Whitesburg in Carroll County, Georgia. His parents purchased a farm in the Miller Academy area of north Carroll County in 1890. This is currently part of the land owned by Raiford M. and Mildred Jones Taylor, son-in-law and daughter of Joseph Tyre Jones. In 1896 he married Veleta Ruth Cole and their union was blessed with fifteen children: James Selvy Jones, Maulsie Sylvester Jones Simpson, Henry Jackson Jones, Hoke Smith Jones, Daniel Webster Jones, infant Clarice Jones (lived five weeks), Ezra Almon Jones, Thomas Hamilton Jones, Joseph Tyre Jones Jr., Sara Mozelle Jones Daniell, Ruby Florence Jones Lanier, Mildred Evelyn Jones Taylor, William Clarence Jones, Hazel Rebecca Jones Edwards, Elsie Ruth Jones Williamson.

Joseph Tyre Jones Sr. was a hard-working husband, a devoted father, an accomplished musician, and a good friend and neighbor to the members of the community. This remarkable man provided for his family by farming his land as well as working as a carpenter, working in a sawmill, making syrup, and operating a cotton gin.

Friends and neighbors came to a seriously ill man's assistance when Mr. Jones was bedridden with a fever of unknown origin. With their help, his crops were worked and harvested that year. While recovering from this illness, Mr, Jones continued his lifelong quest for knowledge. He was a self-educated man who taught himself to read and write and became a very proficient mathematician. He was very proud of his children and their personal, educational, and career accomplishments.

Mr. Jones was also a Bible scholar who encouraged his children to read the Word and learn God's plan for their lives. He took every opportunity to study and read God's word. When Mr. Jones came in from the fields to rest, he would regularly pick up his Bible to read. The Word was also read at the dinner hour with the family. He was very dedicated to his church — Concord Primitive Baptist — where he served as a deacon for many years.

Mr. Jones passed away on February 8, 1958, during Sunday morning services at Concord Primitive Baptist Church. He opened the church services for the day, reading the 17th chapter of John.

> "These words spake Jesus, and lifted up his eyes to heaven and said, 'Father, the hour is come, glorify thy Son, that thy son may glorify thee.' "

He commented on his love for his family and what they meant to him. As he attempted to lay the Bible down, his soul departed his earthly body. Mr. Jones was an example to his children, grandchildren, and members of community. *Submitted by: Mildred Jones Taylor, 150 Cottage Lane Road, Apt. 2-12, Carrollton, GA 30117 and Written by: Sarah Daniell (daughter of Joseph Tyre Jones), 1315 Miller Academy Road, Carrollton, GA 30117*

709. Jones

Keeping up with some of the Jones of Carroll County, Georgia

Aaron Jones 2nd, and his wife Cynthia Ann Eliza Jane Holcombe Jones, left the home of her father, Jonathan Holcombe, in South Carolina in 1821 or 1822 and moved first to DeKalb County, Georgia, and within a year or two moved to the western portion of Georgia and settled in what was to become the Kansas (459th Georgia Militia) District of Carroll County. They had eight sons and three daughters.

Their eighth child was the writer's great-grandfather, Daniel Jones. In 1836 Daniel Jones married Luduska Cole and in the census of 1850 they were listed as residents of Chanceville, Carroll County, Georgia, along with their seven children. In the book by Pvt. Joe Cobb, it is mentioned that Daniel Jones had a mill on Buck Creek, a short distance below McPherson's, and that Hiram Spence, Justice of the Peace, held court at Jones Mill. A house with two large fireplaces on Spence Road near the intersection of Center Point Road near the original location of Concord Primitive Baptist Church and cemetery was their home.

My grandfather, John Wesley Jones, was born in 1855. It was told in the family that as a child he would carry a lunch pail to the mill for his father, with his mother's urging to run so it would not get cold.

Two of the older boys, Thomas Jasper Jones and William Henry Jones, enlisted in Company H, 56th Regiment, Georgia Infantry, on May 13, 1862, and fought from Vicksburg, Chattanooga, and through the Atlanta Campaign. The cannon fire during the Battle of Atlanta was heard by those here in Carroll County who were too old or too young to fight.

The present Jones property was purchased in 1856 by Daniel Jones for the sum of four hundred dollars for the land lot which was 202 1/2 acres. In 1882 Daniel Jones sold the south half of this land lot to John Wesley Jones.

After returning from the War Between the States, several of the Jones kinsfolk moved to Craighead County, Arkansas — about eight miles north of Jonesboro, Arkansas.

George and Ione Jones, 1925 wedding picture.

In 1878 John Wesley Jones paid $1 for state and county tax to Carroll County tax collector J.M. Hamrick. A long series of handwritten receipts and documents, dating from 1882 thru the 1940s, record the advances given in the spring for seed and fertilizer and the meager returns after the crops were sold. They show people who married into the family pitching in to raise and gather the crops. They also show farmers who were aware of the markets for various new crop and their willingness to try planting corn, peas, watermelons, and other crops for livestock food. Several receipts are made out to John Wesley Jones and one of his brothers, or a brother-in-law, as well as other parties who may have been tenants nearby.

On May 13, 1880, John Wesley Jones married Mary Emaline Stewart, daughter of William J. and Sarah Elizabeth Stewart who was born in Alabama but moved at an early age to Douglas County near Dog River, ten miles south of Douglasville, Georgia. This marriage produced six girls and one boy — my father George D. Jones who was born on August 16, 1893. During the late 1890s, John Wesley Jones had severe arthritis which required him to walk with two walking sticks the remaining years of his life. A handwritten document by Dr. W.L. Hitchcock states

> "This is to certify that J.W. Jones is physically unable to perform manual labor. He is laboring under nervous dyspepsia, torpid liver and indigestion and has been for years. He also has Bright's Disease of the kidneys. I recommend that he be excused from road duty."

The present house on the property was thought to have been started in 1913 and completed in 1914, but last summer as the sun reached its northern angle, I noticed a scratched "1911" in a brick next to the steps near the kitchen, so the foundations could have been laid out and started earlier. Floyd Lovell, the brother of Olin Lovell, who married Ora Jones, was a local carpenter who worked on the house along with George and the other young men who were available and willing. In 1917 Floyd Lovell was the carpenter who built the round barn at Hickory Level.

John W. Jones Family, 1935

The lumber — heart longleaf pine — was cut on the property and swapped out with the sawmill folks for the material for the house. John Wesley Jones would stand at the sawmill with his walking sticks and point which pile the board was to go on — the house pile or the sawmill's pile. The framing is all rough sawed two bys and all lumber was sixteen feet long. It was also cut to specified thickness according to its required use. The floor boards were finished to 1 1/8 inch thick, the wall and ceiling boards to 3/4 inch and the exterior siding to 5/8 inch thickness. They wanted higher ceilings in the first floor so the ceilings upstairs are lower, so the sixteen foot lumber was made to work. The rooms are also sixteen feet square.

George D. Jones remembered that the mason who built the two chimneys was paid $25. He also remembered that it was so cold when the chimneys were built that the bricks were heated on tin over a fire before they were laid, to keep the mortar from freezing.

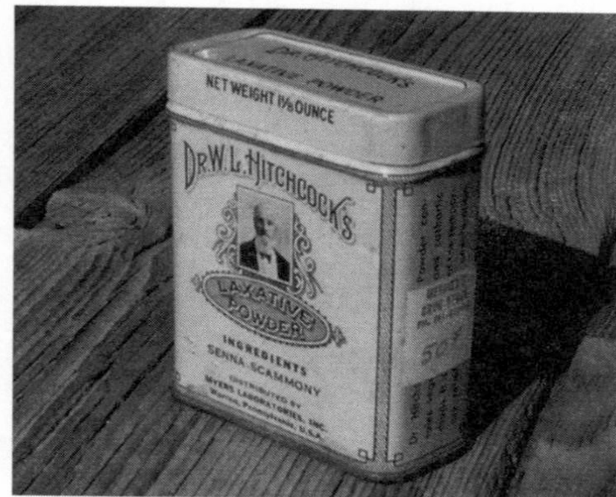

Dr. W.L. Hitchcock's Laxative Powder

As George D. Jones grew up, he joined in the farm work with his parents and sisters. He also started teaching school at Center Point School in the summer term of July 16, 1917, through September 7, 1917, and taught there through 1918. He taught at Bold Springs in 1919 through 1922, then at Pine Grove in 1923, and at Sangamo in 1924 and 1925.

On several calendars from 1923, 1924 and 1925, George D. Jones recorded short notes on the weather, all important to a farmer; the daily activities, such as taught school, whipped 4; cut wood all day, or went to town. At the end of the month he would give the number of chapters he read in the Bible that month. On Sundays they would attend whichever church was having meeting or a singing. He also noted many times, "Saw Ione in P.M." or at the singing.

The entry for November 15, 1925, was: "Sunday, rain all day, Got Married."

George D. Jones married Mamie Ione Kierbow, daughter of Rev. Milton Right Kierbow and Lilla Conna Garner. Their children are Mary Helen Jones, John Milton Jones and Sarah Ellen Jones.

Included in the John W. Jones family picture are Lula, Ora, Lottie, George, Lillie, Minnie, Molene.

The third picture shows a drug store item, Dr. W.L. Hitchcock's Laxative Powder, complete with these directions: "Put a large tea spoonful of the powder into half pint of boiling water, add a tea spoonful of sugar stir it well & let it settle then take three or four table spoonful of it every one or two hours [?]. W.L. Hitchcock, M.D." *Submitted by: John M. Jones, 91 John Jones Road, Carrollton, GA*

710. Lindsey Jackson Jones

Mr. Jones was born in Carroll County at Chanceville, a community near Whitesburg, the son of Thomas B. and Celia S. Velvin Jones, on October 18, 1850. He married Elizabeth Clarice Hogan, daughter of Hamilton and Jane Watson Hogan of Carroll County. Mr. Jones was a farmer and in 1890 he moved from south Carroll County to north Carroll County to a farm in the Miller Academy community. The farm of Joseph Tyre Jones, his son, is just south of the home place. Lindsey Jackson Jones, being the youngest of nine sons, was not old enough to serve in the War Between the States but seven of his eight brothers, excluding Robert Benjamin, served with the Confederate Army, and one brother James was killed in the war.

Lindsey Jackson Jones, October 18, 1850-October 13, 1906

Until recently, part of Mr. Jones' farm was owned by his granddaughter and her husband, Mildred and Raiford Taylor.

He and Jennie had eleven children: (1) John Hamilton who married Marie Elizabeth Reid and Arizona Rowell, (2) Mary Narcissus who married George Henry Cole, (3) Seley who married John Raburn, (4) William Smith who married Jessie Lee Henry, (5) Joseph Tyre who married Veleta Cole (a sister to George Henry), (6) Algin who died at age three, (7) Maude Fenella who married Franklin Joseph Cole (a sister to George Henry and Veleta Cole), (8) Temperance Cleveland who married John Robert Aldridge, (9) Ben Hill who died at age twelve, (10) Lloyd Camp who married Anna Estelle Lott, and (11) Elizabeth Mae who married first Robert Wiley Tillman, and second H.T. Wesley.

They were all raised in north Carroll County and all except Temperance and Elizabeth remained in the area after they married. John Hamilton, William Smith, and Lloyd Camp moved to Bremen and became active in the business community. They lived in Bremen until their death and are buried in area cemeteries. Mary Narcissus, Joseph Tyre, and Maude remained in Carroll County and raised their families. They are buried in area cemeteries of Carroll County. Temperance and family moved to East Point, Georgia, and Elizabeth and family moved to Cullman, Alabama.

All the children had large families except William Smith, who had one daughter. Many descendants still live in the Carroll County and Bremen, Haralson County area.

Lindsey Jackson died October 13, 1906, and his wife Elizabeth Clarice died March 27, 1926. Both are buried alongside each other and with children Celey and Ben Hill at Holly Springs Primitive Baptist Church Cemetery in north Carroll County.

Lindsey Jackson and his wife Elizabeth Clarice are native Carroll Countians and their parents were pioneer families, moving into Carroll County just after its formation when Chief McIntosh ceded Creek Indian lands to the State of Georgia in 1826. *Submitted by: Bill Jones, 703 Laurel Street, Bremen, GA 30110*

711. Lloyd Camp "Kemp" Jones

Mr. Jones, better known as "Kemp" by his wife and friends, was born in Carroll County, Georgia, February 26, 1889, the son of Lindsey Jackson Jones and Elizabeth Clarice Hogan. Mr. Jones moved to Bremen, Haralson County, Georgia in 1910 where he farmed for two years. In 1912 he was appointed agent for the Standard Oil Company and remained agent until his death.

Mr. Jones, who was the first distributor of Petroleum Products in Haralson County, started out driving a two horse wagon with a divided tank of 150 gallon capacity which carried both gasoline and kerosene. As the demand for gasoline increased, his tank wagons grew larger. In the winter months his team of mules increased to five — two pairs and a lead mule. The work required that he arise about 4:30 a.m. to go to the Oil Station to feed his mules and fill his tank wagon; then home for breakfast, then return to the station where he would hitch his team and be on the road by daybreak. His day was not completed until sundown or later. His territory covered Bremen, Waco, Tallapoosa, Muscadine (Alabama), Buchanan, Felton, Draketown, Temple, Jake, and several county stores in the area. The Model "T" truck made his life a little easier.

Some years later, Standard Oil Company began furnishing a larger White Motor Company truck which carried five or six hundred gallons of their products. In the later years when he entered the building material business he employed other men to drive the oil truck and devoted most of his time to developing and operating the City Lumber Company. He loved to saw mill and run his planer. One day while sharpening a blade on the planer mill, he cut his finger. This set up blood poisoning which led to his painful death.

Lloyd Camp "Kemp" Jones, February 26, 1889-April 22, 1945

In addition to being a successful businessman, Mr. Jones served on the Draft Board during World War II. He also was mayor and served on the city council of Bremen for several terms. Together with his son, Buell Jones, they established Jones Motor Company (Chevrolet dealer) in 1927.

Mr. Jones married Anna Estelle Lott in 1905 and fathered twelve children: Ezra Buell, Hamilton Chalmers, Cecile Baltimore, Jessie Mae, Ophal Clarice, Mable Pauline, Lloyd Camp Jr., Martin Jackson, Dixie Ruth, Hamlin Hogan, William Smith and Violet Peggy. Anna was the daughter of Martin Thomas and Sarah "Sally" Cole Lott of the Smyrna Church community in Carroll County. She was born February 21, 1889.

Mr. Jones died on April 22, 1945. His wife Anna died on July 22 1972. Both are buried in Bremen City Cemetery, Bremen, Georgia. They were members of Trinity Primitive Baptist Church in Bremen. Mrs. Jones later transferred her membership to Concord Primitive Baptist Church in Carroll County. Many of their children and grandchildren still remain in the Haralson and Carroll County area. *Submitted by: Hogan H. Jones, 617 Smith Street, Bremen, GA 30110*

712. Robert Allen Jones Family

Robert Allen Jones was born in Carroll County May 3, 1868, to Robert Benjamin Jones and the former Frances Jane Christian. Robert Allen was the grandson of Carroll County pioneers Thomas B. Jones and Celia Velvin. Robert married Jennie Lee Hughens, daughter of Joseph Alexander Hughens and the former Susan Calista Smith, on December 23, 1888, in Coweta County, Georgia. Jennie Lee was born December 23, 1872 in Coweta County.

Robert Allen was a railroad employee until he lost his arm in a railway accident. He then became a representative for the Watkins Company. The family lived on Cedar Street in Carrollton until the house was purchased to be used as a hospital. Then the family bought a house on Dixie Street. The house on Dixie Streert still stands today where Robert and Jennie raised their children.

The children of Robert Allen and Jennie Lee were: (1) Naomi Doris, born December 19, 1890. She married Raymond Harris Wolf from Savannah on June 29, 1922. Naomi had no children and Raymond had one child, Emilie, from a previous marriage. Naomi died February 1957 in Atlanta and is buried at Westview Cemetery.

(2) Daughter Gertrude was born in 1896. She married James Hodnett. Gertrude and James had three daughters: Phronsie, Mary Jo, and Jane Frances. They lived in Fairburn.

(3) Son Robert Alexander was born in 1899. He married Annie Bell Buckner. They had five children: Mildred, Virgil, Louie, James and Dorothy.

(4) Son James Plennie was born in 1900 and died in 1946. He had no children.

(5) Daughter Miriam Margurite was born October 21, 1904. She married William LaFayette Thompson. They had one son, William Alan. They lived in Douglasville. Margurite died December 1982 and is buried in Westview Cemetery in Atlanta.

(6) Inez Cardelia was born June 27, 1906. She married Edgar Ansley on June 15, 1924. They had two sons, Harold and Edgar Jr., and lived in Newnan. Inez died December 1981 in Coweta County.

(7) Lois Carlynne was born March 22, 1909. She married James Carroll Grant from South Carolina on September 2, 1934. They resided most of their lives in Covington, Georgia. They had five children: James Harris, who died in infancy and is buried next to his grandparents at St. Paul's Church; Joseph Allen; Frederick Jackson; Barbara Ann; and Harriette Carlynne.

L to R. Naomi, Robert A., Frances Jane, Jennie, Gertrude, and infant Robert. Circa 1899

Robert Allen died September 12, 1930, and Jennie Lee died June 24, 1949, in Atlanta while residing with her daughter Naomi. Both Robert and Jennie are buried at St. Paul's Church in Carrollton. *Submitted by: Daughter, Carlynne Jones Grant, and great-granddaughters Barbara Grant Engelhardt and Harriette Grant Moss.*

713. Family of Robert Benjamin Jones

Robert Benjamin Jones was the child of Carroll County pioneers, Thomas B. Jones and the former Celia Velvin, daughter of Robert Velvin and the former Frances Kilgore. Robert was born on May 24, 1830. He married Frances Jane Christian on December 20, 1853. Frances Jane was born January 24, 1839. All of the children of Robert Benjamin and Frances Jane were born in Carroll County and several are buried near their parents in St. Paul's Church Cemetery. Robert Benjamin died on April 19, 1892. Frances Jane lived with their son, Robert Allen, until her death on February 13, 1903. Both are buried at St. Paul's Church.

Sons of Robert B. Jones

Daughters of Robert B. Jones

The sons of Robert Benjamin and Frances Jane, as shown in the photo, are as follows: Seated: Robert Allen, who was born May 3, 1868. Robert married Jennie Lee Hughens from Coweta County on December 23, 1888. He died September 12, 1930, and is buried at St. Paul's Church; and Joseph Filmore, who was born March 4, 1866, married Susannah Smith. He died September 4, 1900. Standing are William T.J. who was born in 1869, and Benjamin (no information).

The daughters are, seated on front row, Julia F. who was born in 1863 and married her deceased sister's widower, John W. Huffmaster on October 7, 1887; Lucy was born April 18, 1861. She married Millard F. Cook on October 23, 1877. She died February 23, 1911, and is buried at the Jones Family Cemetery; Amanda Jane was born January 16, 1859. She married John C. Attaway on December 3, 1878. Amanda died July 7, 1934; Cecelia S., who was born October 7, 1856, married Robert Washington Richards on October 7, 1874. Cecelia died December 20, 1927 and is buried at St. Paul's Church.

Standing on back row are Emma, who was married to James Reneau; Josephene Victoria who was born in 1878. She married B.M. Gore; Elizabeth was born June 30, 1875. She married Emmett Hanson. She died January 1, 1923; Henrietta married Mr. Upchurch and after his death married W.R. Reaves.

Not pictured: Mary A. was born in 1855. She married John W. Huffmaster on November 28, 1872. After Mary's death, John married Julia F. Jones on October 7, 1887; Martha A. was born in 1873. *Submitted by: Granddaughter Carlynne Jones Grant, and great-granddaughter Harriette Grant Moss of Covington, GA.*

714. Thomas B. Jones

Thomas B. Jones was born November 8, 1806, in Jackson County, Georgia, the son of Benjamin Jones and Tabitha Fowler. Willis Dallas Jones family Bible, now in the possession of Weems Jones, who lives in Norcross, Georgia, lists Thomas B. as being born in Gwinette County, Georgia, but Gwinette was not founded until 1818. Gwinette was formed from Jackson County which is where Thomas B. was born. It lists Benjamin and Tabitha as being buried in Gwinette County. Tabitha had a sister, Mary E., who married a Jones and had several children. Mary died shortly after her last child was born. Some believe that Tabitha raised Mary's children. None of this has been proven nor marriage records found.

Thomas B. married Celia S. Velvin (born June 8, 1809) in Clark County, Georgia, about 1826. They are then found in Coweta County, Georgia, in the 1840 census with six sons. In 1840 they moved to Carroll County, Georgia, near Whitesburg where their last three sons were born. This union produced nine sons: Henry S. Jones, Robert Benjamin Jones, Nathan Cornelius Jones, William Moses Jones, Jethro Peter Jones, John Thomas Jones, James F. Jones, Willis Dallas Jones and Lindsey Jackson Jones.

Thomas B. and his family were farmers, and after coming to Carroll County they lived in the 4th District. By 1849 they were in the 3rd District where they built a log cabin, dug a well, and cleared their land to farm. The home place still stands near the Douglas County line and is occupied and in good condition.

Mr. Jones was of the Primitive Baptist faith and he raised his family in the Christian faith. He was an Elder in the Primitive Baptist Church and records indicate that he pastored several churches in Carroll County and preached at many others, including some in Coweta County. Some of the churches were Mt. Pearon Primitive Baptist Church, Concord Primitive Baptist Church, and Antioch Primitive Baptist Church.

Thomas B. Jones, November 8, 1806-June 13, 1880

All of the sons of Thomas B. and Celia S. Jones served in the Confederate Army except Robert Benjamin and their youngest son Lindsey Jackson. Their seventh son, James F. Jones, died in the war at Lauderdale, Mississippi, after fighting in the battle of Champion Hill which was a flanking action just south of Vicksburg, Mississippi. The other sons served with distinction and most returned home safely except Nathan C. was injured at New Hope Church and Willis Dallas who was injured while lifting baggage from a train in Quitman, Georgia. Both remained crippled for the rest of their lives.

Thomas B. died June 13, 1880, and is buried in the Jones Family cemetery across the road and just south of his home place. Celia S. died March 14, 1890, and is buried alongside her husband. They were a pioneer family of Carroll County and leave a great heritage and many descendants, some nearby and many in distant places. *Submitted by: William S. Jones, 703 Laurel Street, Bremen, GA 30110*

715. Descendants of Thomas B. Jones

Information we have been able to discover regarding the forebears of Elder Thomas B. Jones, born 8 November 1806 in Jackson County, Georgia, was that they all originated in Scotland and migrated to Virginia; Bute County, North Carolina; Wilkes County, North Carolina; Warren County, Georgia; and Jackson and Carroll Counties, Georgia.

Elder Thomas B. Jones lived in Jackson, Coweta, and Carroll counties. He was married to Celia S. Velvin, who was born on 8 June 1808 in Clarke County. Thomas B. Jones was listed in the 1850 census of Carroll County. Thomas B. died on 13 June 1880 and Celia died on 4 March 1880. Both are buried in the Jones-Cook-Hanson cemetery in Whitesburg, Carroll County. To this union, nine sons were born, six of whom served in the Civil War as follows: Pvt. Henry S. Jones, 8th Georgia Volunteer Infantry, Company I. Pvt. John Thomas Jones, 1st Georgia Regulars Infantry, Company I. Pvt. Jethro Peter Jones, 2nd Georgia Militia, Company D. Pvt. Nathan Cornelius Jones, 1st Georgia Cavalry. Pvt. Willis Dallas Jones, 27th Georgia Volunteer Infantry, Company. Pvt. William T. Jones, 56th Georgia Volunteer Infantry, Company.

Reuben and Julia Stitcher and grandson, Homer Hewett Jones

Nathan Cornelius Jones, the fourth son of Thomas B. Jones, married Julia Ann Watkins. They had two children: Robert Benjamin Jones (25 December 1848-10 April 1925) married Etta Iris Casey (30 May 1869-22 September 1938). This union produced nine children as listed below with their children: (1) Homer Hewitt Jones (11 December 1886-7 October 1977) married Margaret McGavity. They had four children: Roy

Robert Benjamin Jones, Etta Iris, James Albert, Iris, and Nora

Meda, Mabel McKensie, Georgetta Dukes, and Robert Jones; (2) Ella Nora Jones (30 September 1888-10 November 1984); (3) Myrtie Jane Jones (7 December 1890-16 August 1927) married James Duncan. They had one child, Margaret Agnes Duncan (14 August 1922-13 August 1993); (4) Reuben Edward Jones (20 November 1893-18 March 1950); (5) Nathan Reese Jones (26 June 1896-25 January 1985) married Inez Boyd (1 July 1898-6 September 1982). They had four children: Pauline Lumpkin, Grace, Jerrell, Libbie Moss, and Joan Haden; (6) Welcome Pascal Jones married Sophie Jones. They had one child: Patricia Ann Jones Camp; (7) Annie Lou Jones (28 November 1902-13 November 1999); (8) Bennie Iris, born 6 March 1910; (9) James Albert, born 17 February 1912, married Martha Roberts Harrison.

The second son born to Nathan Cornelius and Julia Watkins was Thomas Robert Jones (1860-1902). He married Sarah Barron. Both are buried in Carrollton City Cemetery. From this union, Jeff Jones was born in 1887 and died in 1981. He married Linda, born 1 June 1897 in Wigton, England, and died in 1996. Two children resulted from this union: William Thomas Jones (17 October 1913-April 1984 in Huntsville, Texas) married Edna Earl, born 13 September 1917; and E.J. Jones, born 3 December 1921, married Bonnie, born 23 May 1925.

After the death of Julia, Nathan Cornelius married Nancy Jane Pope Cansler. From this union, eight children resulted. *Submitted by: Libbie Jones Moss, 5440 E. Highway 166, Winston, GA*

716. William Moses Jones

William Moses Jones was born July 20, 1834. He was the fourth of nine sons born to Thomas B. and Celia Velvin Jones. Besides serving in the Confederate States Army, William was elected and served as constable in the 714th and 729th districts. He also held the position of Notary Public and Ex. Off. Justice of the Peace.

Henry Cheadle and Mary Ann Jane Banks Jones

William married Eustacia Lassetter who died at the age of twenty on March 8, 1864. According to an article in *The Carroll Free Press* dated December 20, 1917, there were four children born from this marriage. Since the names of only three of these children have been identified, it is possible that one of these children died at a very young age. Those children whom they identified were Henry Cheadle Jones, Sara Frances Jones, and Celia Parthenia Jones. After Eustacia's death, William Moses married Harlor Boon(e) in 1867. She helped raise William's three children.

William died December 13, 1917, and Harlor died January 6, 1936. Both are buried in the Carrollton City Cemetery. The grave of his first wife, Eustacia Lassetter Jones, has not been found.

They said that when William died, there was snow on the ground. His son, Chead, drove nails in the bottom of his shoes so he could walk to Clem and catch a train to attend the funeral.

The home of William and Harlor is still standing and located on Newnan Street. Hazel Jones Hopson, age seventy-eight, and a great-granddaughter of William, says the only visual difference in the house now is that it has been painted.

Mrs. Alice Fuller, age ninety-five, and a descendant of William Moses Jones, relayed a story about how Chead Jones had saved his family during the Civil War. Chead's mother, Eustacia, had died and his father William Moses was in the war. He and his siblings lived with his grandparents, William and Parthenia Lassetter. Yankees had come into their home and Chead, who was four or five years old at the time, cried and begged them not to take their food because they would starve to death. He also told them his mother was dead and to please not kill his daddy. The Yankee soldiers had compassion on him and left without incident.

Although remodeled, the home of Chead and Mary Ann Jane Banks Jones is still standing on Military Road. Chead and Mary Ann raised nine children. Their names were William Jacob, Henry Luther, Mary Louvella, Ella Mae, Margaret Georgia, Annie Belle, Ofelia Fannie, Harlon Eustacia, and Arthur Hutcheson Jones. *Submitted by: Denise Jones Turner, 192 Hendrix Road, Newnan, GA 30263*

717. Willis Dallas Jones

Willis Dallas Jones was born March 25, 1845, in Carroll County. He was the eighth of nine sons of Thomas B. Jones and Celia S. Velvin. He enlisted in the Confederate Army February 16, 1864, and was assigned to Company B, 27th Georgia Infantry. He injured his back unloading a train in Quitman, Georgia, in April 1864. He became cripple as a result of the injury and was cripple the rest of his life. He still managed to farm, preach, and raise a family. He became a Primitive Baptist Elder (preacher) as was his father. He married Margaret Jane (Maggie) Hanson. She was the daughter of Reuben Crawford Hanson Jr. and Caldonia Bearden. Margaret was born February 12, 1857. Willis Dallas and Margaret were married on September 9, 1875, at his father's house by Lindsey J. Holland. They had nine children. Alphie C. married F. Thomas Connell; William Thomas married Ada Belle Williams; George Washington married Roxie Ann Lumsden; Eula died at the age of one; Jethro Franklin did not marry; Joseph Thurman married Matt Sue Gladney; Maggie Mae died at the age of one; Arthur Hutchinson married Nora Sue Crook; Roy Calvin married Pearl Duncan. Willis Dallas Jones wrote poems to his two deceased daughters and had some of them printed in the Carroll County newspapers. Maggie Jones ran a store and the post office in Emily, which was a small community north of Whitesburg on Jones Mill Road. Willis Dallas Jones died April 17, 1921, and Maggie Jones died May 22, 1944. They are buried at Consolation Baptist Church.

This picture shows Willis Dallas Jones, the older man seated in the middle on front row. On his left is Margaret Jane Hanson Jones. *Submitted by: Jimmy R. Jones, 13 Velma Drive, Newnan, GA 30263-1525*

Sources: Family Bible, census records, Carroll County marriage records, Confederate records, and Carrollton newspapers.

Willis Dallas Jones and Family

718. The Jordan Family History

Johnson Pate Jordan was born to William Tedford (1810-1884) and Agnes Blair Jordan on February 21, 1852, in Coweta County and died April 27, 1928, in Carroll County from injuries received in an automobile accident. He married Celia Alice McKenzie (1859-1932), daughter of John P. McKenzie (born about 1810) and Mary Boatright (born about 1815). John P. and Mary Boatright McKenzie were married in Carroll County on July 24, 1856. Johnson Pate is buried at the Jordan Family Cemetery, just south of Bethany Christian Church on Highway 61 in Carroll County.

Johnson Pate Jordan, Nat Baxter, and Joe McKenzie were big mule traders. When cotton was "King" and everybody needed a mule to farm, they would go to Tennessee to buy mules. The mules would be shipped by rail back to Carrollton to a big holding pen. They would sell or trade the mules there or hold them until the first Tuesday of each month. All the people interested in buying, selling or swapping mules would come from all around. This was held near downtown Carrollton. There were truckloads of mules coming from Atlanta to trade. In those days this was a good business, if you knew what you were doing. If you didn't, you got "Skint."

Johnson Pate and Celia Alice McKenzie Jordan's children were Elizabeth Eugenia (July 12, 1881-January 13, 1961) who married Leon Davis Morgan (February 9, 1878-May 13, 1961); Emerson Grow (July 13, 1893-April 1, 1959) who married Alice Zelma Harris (October 7, 1893-February 13, 1964); Emily (July 13, 1893-) who married Lee Rigsby; Leona who married Luther Smith; Mary Agnes Almedia who married Jefferson Adkin Upshaw; Roy who married Gertrude McCoy; Joe who married Alzenia Horton; Annie who married Otis Hammond; and Sarah Ola (September 1879-) who married Andrew M. Duncan.

Alice Zelma Harris Jordan's parents were David Harris (1857-1925) and Nancy Alice Smith Harris (1858-1930). They are all buried in the Shady Grove Cemetery in Carroll County. Alice Zelma's grandparents were Colonel August and Sarah Smith.

David Harris gave the land for the Shady Grove Baptist Church and Cemetery. If one takes the Shady Grove Road east off Georgia Highway 27 the old school house stood on the right, and up the road stands Shady Grove Baptist Church. The old Harris Plantation was on the right. General Sherman burned the plantation house during his march through Georgia. The house was later rebuilt.

Johnson Pate and Celia Alice McKenzie Jordan's descendants are as follows: (1) Elizabeth Eugenia and Leon Davis Morgan had Duvall who married Beulah Harmon, and had Elizabeth who married Kenneth McLeroy; Dumah married Doyle; Dula Mae who married Clarence B. Sprewell; Gerallah who married Seaborn J. Jackson and had two daughters: Reba Jean who married Gene Gillespie, and Dacy who married Cecil Shealy; Dalton (died December 19, 1919); Raymon (1910-1998) who married Laura (1912-1988) and had a son, Charles Lee; Frances (September 10, 1912-December 7, 1894) who married Coyaban M. Holcomb (July 7, 1914-April 5, 1977) and had a daughter, Bivien; John D. who married Margaret and adopted a son, Ned; and Zellie who married Madeline;

(2) Emerson Grow and Alice Zelma Harris Jordan had Herbert Franklin Jordan, Elsie Adrian and Delphia Evelyn. Herbert Franklin married Syble Mote and had Judith Gayle, who married Lew Sayre; Jennifer Elaine; Donald Franklin who married Cathy Carlton and Rhonda King; Ronald Herbert who married Rhonda King and Michelle Hubbard; and Joni Alice who married Alfred Flores Sandoval and Faheik Fahim. Herbert Franklin also married Dorothy. Judith Gayle and Lew Saye had Richard and Dawn. Jennifer Elaine had Gary and Melissa Jordan, Michael Kinney, and Kimberly Elizabeth and James Taylor. Donald Franklin and Cathy had Robert and Shannon. Ronald Herbert and Rhonda had Duane and Veronica. Ronald Herbert and Michelle had Joshua. Joni Alice and Alfredo Flores had Rosa Maria. Elsie Adrian married Claude W. Perry and had Alice Marie. Alice Marie married Pat Wilkinson and had Butch, Rick, and Becky. She later married (2) Thomas Burk. Claude W. Jr. who married Loisa Jendersee and had Craig. Delphia Evelyn and Ray Bonner (1913-1996) had Jerry, Jimmy, and Joe.

(3) Emily (1893-?) and Lee Rigsby had Lavie and Franklin.

(4) Leona and Luther Smith had Hubert, Lola, Lois, and Alice.

(5) Mary Agnes Almedia and Jefferson Adkin Upshaw had Haskell Olin and Harvey Valentine.

(6) Roy and Gertrude McCoy had Azalea, who married Harvey Roberts.

(7) Joe and Alzenia Horton had Christine, Pauline, and Bernie.

(8) Annie and Otis Hammond had Aubry, Dewey, and Ruth.

(9) Sarah Ola and Andrew M. Duncan had Lamar.

The Johnson Pate Jordan family photograph was made in Carroll County about 1907 or 1908. On the front row, left to right, are Duval Morgan, Dumah Morgan, Dula Mae Morgan, Christine Jordan, Alice Smith, Ruth Hammond, Lamar Duncan, Harvey Valentine Upshaw, Haskell Olin Upshaw, Dewey Hammond, and Aubrey Hammond. Second row: Leon Morgan (standing), Gerallah Morgan (held by Leon Morgan), Elizabeth Eugenia Jordan, Emerson Grow Jordan, Emily Jordan, Roy Jordan, Joe Jordan, Alzenia Jordan, Leona Jordan, Luther F. Jordan, Otis L. Hammond (standing), Annie Jordan. Back row: Andrew Duncan, Sarah Ola Jordan, Johnson Pate Jordan, Celia Alice McKenzie, Jefferson Adkin Upshaw, and Mary Agnes Almedia Jordan. *Submitted by: Herbert Frankin Jordan, toto200@att.net, and Written by: Cecilia Wood Church, 128 Brock Street, Carrollton, GA 30117, cechurch@charter.net.*

The Johnson Pate Jordan Family, about 1907-1908.

719. Thelma Ricks Jordan

Thelma Ricks Jordan, born October 21, 1905, in Douglas County, is a self-educated woman who has lived most of her life in Carroll County. Her parents were Alfred and Emma White Ricks. Thelma, the oldest of nine children, speaks fondly of her parents, "Alf" and Emma, and siblings, Raymond, Esker, Esma, Ernest, Leona, Vera "Beedie," Tasker, and John "Moon" Ricks.

Her father Alfred Ricks was described by Thelma as a hardworking, honest man who was devoted to his family. She reported that he loved to entertain the children by playing his fiddle. She said that he was firm with discipline, but protective, by never allowing alcohol in his home. Thelma felt that he just didn't want his children exposed to this element of life. She also spoke with great affection about her grandparents, William and Ellen Brown White and Jack and Sarah "Linnia" Hunter Ricks.

Thelma described the time when her Grandpa Ricks died. She said she was about five years old and her Grandpa was away working in Lindale, Georgia. When word came that Grandpa was gone, she rode on her Popa's lap in the wagon to Carrollton, where they expected to catch the train bound for Floyd County. She said she remembers that Grandpa White drove them on that day. Grandma Ricks and Aunt Bessie were with them. Thelma described the day from her memory of ninety years with large tears in her eyes. She said that she could still remember her Popa's deep sorrow that day, especially when they all realized they had missed the train. Thelma related that Grandma and Aunt Bessie knew someone with a jitney for hire who took them to the next train stop. She said that after Grandpa died, Grandma eventually moved in with her family. Grandma was so good to the children, Thelma felt it was almost like having two mothers. Thelma said that Grandma smoked coffee in her clay pipe. She still remembers the wonderful fragrance.

The nine children of Alfred and Emma White Ricks

On November 10, 1928, Thelma married Carl C. Jordan in Carroll County. Thelma never had children of her own, but bestowed her love on family, friends, neighbors, and church members. Carl's family donated the land for Bethany Christian Church. Carl and Thelma donated the lot for the church parsonage in 1955.

Carl died on October 26, 1968. Thelma spends her days writing and keeping records on births, deaths and marriages, and other important events. History, especially about Carroll County, is important to Thelma. She still drives her old blue Chevy pickup truck from home to church across her property, without getting on the highway. The church even made a special parking place just for Thelma, so she would always have her own spot close to the front door. Thelma enjoys visits from her family and friends, especially sisters, Leona and "Beedie," and loves her plants, and pets — a dog, a cat, and a goat she named Jenny. *Submitted by: James and Andrea Ricks, 95 Gammon Road, Carrollton, GA 30117 and Compiled by: Bonnie Ricks.* Sources: Thelma Ricks Jordan and *Carroll County Times*, 1935.

720. Thomas Allen Jordan

Thomas Allen Jordan (12/26/1836-10/10/1920) was my great-grandfather and my great-great grandfather was William Tedford Jordan (1810-1884). William married Agnes Blair and they had nine children. Their children were Thomas Allen (12/26/1836-10/10/1920), Martin Van Buren Jordan (6/22/1841-2/1/1895), Jerry D., Dempsey J., Sarah Ann, William T., Emily E., Joseph T. and Johnson P. Jordan.

Thomas Allen Jordan married Sara Elin Dyer (6/13/1841-6/8/1913). Their children were Wiley, Clifton, James, Ella, Alonzo, Leonidas, Parks, Eva and Ida Jordan. Thomas had over 2,000 acres of land and gave his children 200 acres each.

My grandfather was Alonzo Mayfield Jordan (12/17/1871-5/27/1956). He and my grandmother, Fannie Williams (5/19/1880-10/8/1946), had three children: Clestell, (12/4/1904-3/24/1991), Bryce (1/20/1907-6/2/1998), and Mary (7/19/1910-3/18/1997). Clestell and Mary went to the Agricultural and Mechanical School which later became West Georgia College.

Thomas Allen Jordan

Mary graduated in 1928 and recalled traveling to classes on unpaved roads, often making the two and one-half mile trip "in the mud." Her memories of A&M included helping in the school kitchen and being in the senior class play.

Clestell married Freeman Brooks and had one daughter, Charlotte. Bryce married Myrtle Whaley and had two children, B.L. Jr. and Joy; Mary married Ralph Latimer and had four children, Sue, Jerry, David and Judy.

Jerry and Joyce Latimer live on 18 acres of the original 200 acres which was given to Alonzo. Their sons, John, Gary, and Jerry Jr. (J.J.) grew up on that land. John married Judith Alaine Cooley and they have two daughters, Sarah Elizabeth and Mary Grace. J.J. married Tina Annette Jackson and they have one daughter, Mikayla Jordan Latimer. *Submitted by: Jerry J. Latimer Sr., 2907 E. Highway 166, Carrollton, GA*

721. Thomas Allen Jordan Family

The first Jordan in the family record is William Tedford Jordan, born April 27, 1810, and he died September 26, 1884. He married Agnes Blair and they are buried in the Jordan Cemetery. Their children were: Thomas Allen, Martin Van Buren, Johnson, Joseph, Dempsey, Durah, Emily, and William.

Thomas Allen Jordan (b. 12-26-1836 d. 10-10-1920) married Sarah Elizabeth Dyer on December 30, 1858, in Carroll County, Georgia. They had five boys and five girls. Their names were Mary Elizabeth, Wiley Ann, Clifton Eldridge, James Nathan, Ella S., Alonzo Mayfield, Leonders K., Parks R., Ida B. and Eva R. Jordan. Thomas Allen Jordan owned 1800 acres in the Bethany Church area and he gave about 200 acres to each married child. James Nathan Jordan only lived to be 18 years and he never married.

The Jordan Cemetery was started when a family was passing through the area and their child fell off the wagon and died. They needed a place to bury the child and Thomas Allen Jordan give them a place which became the Jordan Cemetery. It is located on Highway 61, east of Carrollton and south of Sand Hill. The first marked grave was in 1862; however, there are numerous unmarked graves.

Clifton Eldridge, the third child of Thomas and Sarah, was born December 4, 1864, and he married Mary Etta Smith on April 8, 1888. Mary Etta was the daughter of Jasper and Louisa Hyde Smith. She lived in Fayette, Alabama, near the Mississippi line. Etta met Cliff in August 1887 when she came to visit her Uncle "Doc" and Aunt Mary Elizabeth Hyde and to attend the revival meeting at the Old Black Gum Church (now it is the Bethany Christian Church). Cliff was a young school teacher and they agreed to write each other. It took six to ten days for their letters to be delivered. Then in April 1888, Etta came by train to the Villa Rica Depot where Cliff met her and they were married. During the first years of their marriage, they lived in an old log cabin which was built by Mr. William Birdsong's great-grandfather about 1800. It was a homestead cabin. There was no wood flooring - just a load of white sand, a big wooden door and a window made of wood. There was no glass anywhere. But with the spring came daffodils, yellow bells, lilacs and lots of farm work.

Clifton and Mary Etta had a son, Carlos "Carl," and a daughter Jessie Irene. Jessie was born March 31, 1897, and she died December 8, 1898. Clifton gave one acre of land for the new Bethany Christian Church building and one acre for a church cemetery in 1927. The new church was dedicated November 3, 1928. In 1931 Guy Richardson was the first to be buried at Bethany.

Carl (b. 12-7-1893; d. 10-26-1968) married Evie Mae Baxley on November 30, 1914. Carl's second marriage was to Thelma Mae Ricks on November 10, 1928. Carl and Thelma lived in the old log cabin their first year of married life. Thelma says "we were happy." In 2001 the cabin is still someone's home. Even though Carl and Thelma have no children, they have been blessed with many other family members and friends. They gave land to the Bethany Christian Church for a parsonage and later Thelma gave land for the "Bethany Barn," as she called it (family center).

In January 1953 Hiram Bray interviewed Thelma in her home for his 15 minute radio program, Inspiration Chapel WLBB, about being a good neighbor. Thelma said, "I expressed my love for Bethany Church, my husband, family, and neighbors for helping me to be a good neighbor ... "

On June 1, 1986, Home Coming Day at Bethany Christian Church, the day was called "Thelma Jordan Appreciation Day" for what Thelma has done for Bethany and the community by the life she lives and her good example.

Ella, Mary, Ida, Wiley, Eva, Park, Leon, Alonzo, and Cliff Jordan.

A Centennial Quilt Program was held on November 9, 1995, by friends at the Neva Lomason Memorial Library to feature Thelma and her quilt collection. Many of her quilts are over 100 years old and were made by members of her family as well as her husband's family.

The Bethany Christian Church invited friends and family to a celebration of Thelma's 90th birthday on Sunday, October 22, 1995. During this year 2001, Thelma is still enjoying her family and friends. Even though she is not as strong physically as she once was, her faith is stronger than ever.

Ella S. Jordan (Thomas Allen and Sarah Dyer Jordan's fifth child) married Tommy M. Hamrick. Ella and Tommy had five children: Mayfield, Velma, Correne, Annie Mae, and Wilma.

The sixth child of Thomas Allen and Sarah Dyer Jordan was Alonzo Mayfield and he married Fannie Williams January 29, 1904, in Carroll County. Their children were Clestelle, Bryce Lee, and Mary Elizabeth.

The second son of William Tedford and Agnes Blair Jordan was Martin Van Buren Jordan (b. 6-22-1841, d. 2-1-1895 in Carroll County) and he married Elizabeth Ann Kelly, daughter of Thomas and Susan Harris Kelly. Martin Van Buren served in the Civil War. Their twelve children were: Madora Idella, Susan Agnes, Joseph Leonard, Ulysses Walker, Lucy Mae, Emily Louise, Maggie Abigail, Charles Edwin, Thomas Walter, Bertie Eugene "Bert," Ezra Curtis, and Beulah Gertrude.

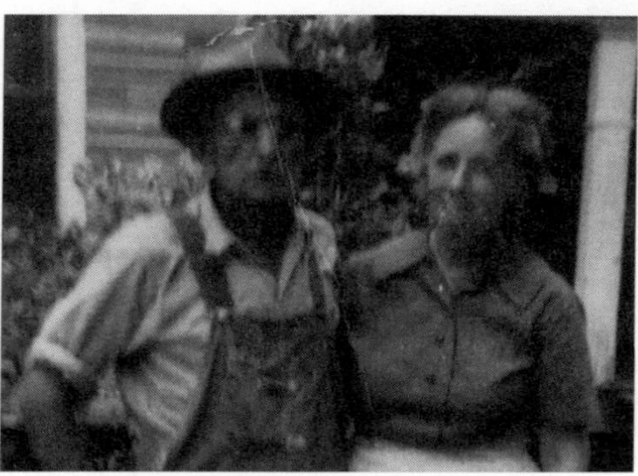

Carl and Thelma Jordan - dinner time in the country!

Ulysses Walker Jordan, the fourth child of Martin Van Buren and Elizabeth Ann Kelly Jordan, was born December 23, 1870, and died on November 18, 1965. He married Bertha Reese in about 1895 and they had the following five children: Reese, Weems, Blanche, Harvey, and Harold. Bertha Reese died in 1916 and in about 1921 Ulysses married Ammie Reese (Bertha and Ammie were first cousins). Ulysses and Ammie had one daughter, Mary Elizabeth, born May 27, 1923. Mary Elizabeth married Alvin Vernice Hardeman on September 16, 1946.

Charles Edwin Jordan (eighth child of Martin Van Buren and Elizabeth Ann Jordan) was born July 9, 1879, and he died March 31, 1885 after a dog with rabies bit him. *Submitted by: Thelma Ricks Jordan, 42 Carl Jordan Place, Carrollton, GA 30116*
Source: Researched and written by Violette Harris Denney.

722. Ulysses Walker Jordan Family

Ulysses Walker (U.W.) Jordan was born December 23, 1870, to Martin Van Buren Jordan and Elizabeth Ann Kelley Jordan. Most of his life he lived in the Sand Hill area. He attended school near his home. At one time, U.W. was asked to teach school at Temple. Because a stroke had disabled his father, he had to decline the job and remain home to tend the farm. In 1896 he married Bertha Reese. Five children were born to this union, Reese, Weems, Blanche, Harvey, and Harold. During these years he maintained a large farm located East of Carrollton. Reese married Clyde Johnson, Weems married Rose Smith, Harvey married Ila Braswell, Blanche married Herbert Brasher, and Harold married Claire Duffey. All the children lived and raised families here. The men were successful in their jobs and Blanche was a talented homemaker. Bertha died of cancer in November 1916.

Six years later in May 1922, he married Ammie Reese, who was first cousin to his first wife Bertha. One daughter, Mary Elizabeth, was born to them in May 1923. Mary Jordan married Alvin Vernice Hardeman from Ailey, Georgia, on September 16, 1946. They moved to Carrollton and had five children: Walter Vernice, Barbara Marie, Martha Louise, Frances Elizabeth and Lucy Ann. Mary is the only living child of U.W. and she continues to live on the original

U.W., Bertha, Harold, Harvey, Blanche, Weems, and Reese Jordan

Jordan farm. Two grandchildren also have homes on this farm.

U.W. was a very dedicated Christian husband and father. He was a member of Bethany Christian Church since its beginning. He remained an Elder-emeritus at the time of his death. He was a Mason at Sand Hill Masonic Lodge for more than 70 years, a member of the Sand Hill Ruritan Club and an original director of the Peoples Bank. Probably his greatest love was that of farming the land. As a well-known Carroll County farmer, he encouraged his family and friends to love the land also.

U.W., Mary, and Ammie Jordan. 1943

Many sharecroppers assisted on his farm and became lifelong friends. Helpers came from miles away, shared his table and slept at his home until the crops were harvested. There were many lean years when the family had to struggle to keep the farm going. He also helped his brothers financially to keep their homes.

U.W. Jordan was affectionately known as "Uncle Ule." Many will remember the often "stinging" pinch on the arm that he gave as a sign of affection. Bethany Church members will remember the "white haired gentleman," who after Communion service, would move a chair very close to the pulpit, cup one ear with his hand so that he would not miss one word of the sermon. This was my daddy!

He was loved by many, including a multitude of grandchildren and great-grandchildren. Today even great, great-grandchildren honor his memory. Ulysses Walker Jordan died on Thursday, November 18, 1965. Ammie Reese Jordan suffered declining health for many years. She died on Wednesday, July 15, 1968. U.W. is buried in the Jordan Cemetery beside his two wives. *Submitted by: His daughter: Mary Jordan Hardeman, 185 Holley Tree Rd., Carrollton, GA 30116*

723. Weems Jordan Family

My father, Weems Jordan, was born on July 24, 1899. He was the second oldest child born to Ulysses Walker Jordan and Bertha Reese Jordan. His siblings were Reese, Blanche, Harvey, Harold, and Mary. The original Jordan home was his birth place and it still stands on Pleasant Hill Road. He attended school at Oak Ridge, located very close to his home.

Rose Smith, my mother, was born to Harvey Lewis Smith and Leander Henslee Smith on August 21, 1901. She had ten siblings: Herman, Reese, Harvey, Homer, Hulett, Hub, Wilborn, Ella Mae, Dewey and Ione. Herman and Reese were half brothers. My mother was born and lived her earlier life in a home owned by her parents. It still stands on Highway 61 in the Five Points area.

Weems and Rose Jordan

My parents, Weems and Rose, married on December 10, 1927. He worked with Western Union for a few years. His job caused them to move to several areas of Georgia and Alabama. On July 6, 1930, Walker Lee Jordan was born. Walker attended Elizabeth Harris High, Sand Hill, and graduated from Villa Rica High School. He married Mary Lee Turner on November 10, 1950. A son, Gregory Walker, was born to them on July 7, 1961. Greg's marriage to Angela Hoomes on September 14, 1985, gave Walker and Mary two grandchildren, Victoria Rose (born December 28, 1993) and Benjamin Walker (born February 24, 1998). Walker is a veteran of the Korean War. Also, he worked for Georgia Power for thirty-five years and retired in 1989. Mary was a beautician for many years.

My name is Edna Juanita and I was born next on August 17, 1936. I attended Sand Hill and Villa Rich High School, graduating in 1954. On August 3, 1957, I married William E. Morrow at Bethany Christian Church with Minister George Boswell officiating. Two children, William Jefferson born June 20, 1961, and Jana Rose born March 11, 1970, completed our family.

Jana married Christopher Brian Green on October 1, 1994. One son Christopher Logan Green was born to them on April 18, 1996. Chris brought two daughters to this family from a previous marriage, Ashley and Jessica. Jeff has a stepdaughter, April Black Hile.

After a few years with Western Union, my father moved back to the farm with his wife and two children. Both my parents, Weems and Rose, worked in the field. Mother took care of us, made all our clothes and kept food prepared for the family and farm hands. For a few years, Daddy worked at Bell Aircraft but after a lay off he returned to the farm.

Times were severely hard. Chicken feed sack clothes and sausage biscuits for lunch (if we were lucky!) did not embarrass us at school. We had such love, that it's hard to remember just how tough times were. We were members of Bethany Christian Church. Daddy was a deacon for many years. For a period of time, Daddy, Walker, and Greg (father, son and grandson) served as deacons at Bethany.

Daddy worked for Carroll Electric Membership Corporation for a few years. Times became much easier. He retired this job in 1961 after suffering a heart attack. After recuperation, he worked for Garvie and Sarah Marks in their grocery store for a few years. Mother continued to be the best homemaker, wife, mother and grandmother. In 1980, after Daddy's health deteriorated so severely, we found it necessary to admit him to Pine Knoll Nursing Home. After fifty-five years of marriage, Mother voluntarily admitted herself to the nursing home where they shared a room once again. Daddy died very suddenly on August 21, 1985. Mother lived a few more years and died on February 13, 1994. They are both buried at Bethany Christian Church Cemetery. *Submitted by: Juanita J. Morrow, 2305 Pleasant Hill Road, Carrollton, GA 30116*

724. Stonewall Jackson Karr Family

On December 18, 1865, the thirteenth amendment to the United States Constitution was ratified abolishing slavery throughout the United States. Seven days later, Christmas 1865, Stonewall Jackson Karr was born to George W. and Catherine Karr in Fulton County, Georgia. A brother, Sherman, was born in 1867.

Jack Karr was a fourth generation Georgian. His great-grandfather, Samuel Karr, was in Wilkes County, Georgia, prior to 1780. He married Charity Bowers, the widower of Job Bowers. Grandfather John Karr was born in 1789 in Wilkes County, Georgia. On January 23, 1812, in Elbert County, Georgia, he married Polly Blair, born 1795 in North Carolina. Polly was the daughter of Thomas Blair and Letty Fanning who came from Caswell County, North Carolina, to Elbert County, Georgia. His father George was born in 1816 in Elbert County. The Karrs moved to Coweta County, Georgia about 1835. Samuel, Charity, and Polly died prior to 1850. John died in 1868.

Displeased with life in Atlanta, Jack moved to Villa Rica, Georgia, about 1877. Settling earlier in the area were half-siblings, William P. and Emily Karr, and Callie Karr and William Harper. Siblings of father were Sarah Karr and William Blair, Green B.W. and Sarah Karr, and in Douglas County, Rachel Karr and Jasper Williams.

Life in Carroll County pleased Jack, and in 1885 he married Hannah Della Ayers. Hannah was born January 22, 1866, to John P. Ayers and Susan Houseworth of Banning, Georgia. Hannah was named for her great-grandmother

Hannah Hollingsworth, wife of Phillip Housworth. Jack and Hannah had six children: George Washington, Della, Florence, Mitchell, Stephen, and Rachel.

Steve served in World War I and on his way home from Argentina contracted pneumonia and died January 28, 1919. He was twenty-six. Being a compassionate and loving father, Granny Jack often took his grandson, Glenn Karr, to visit the unmarked grave site of little Della in Banning.

Jack's one great pleasure in life was his pipe. He grew and cured his own tobacco. Tobacco harvested from his field and worn pipes are in possession of his great-granddaughter.

Jack and Hannah relocated north of Villa Rica to Paulding/Carroll County line. Jack operated a country store prior to his death on July 11, 1945. Due to heavy rains, the creek between Villa Rica and the Karr residence had risen over the bridge, making it difficult to cross. Relatives and friends would meet at the creek and friends pulled the cars across the creek. Jack and Hannah are buried at Concord Baptist Church in Paulding County. Hannah died April 4, 1949.

Son, George Karr, born October 5, 1886, moved to Carrollton and worked for Mandeville Mills, farmed land on Mt. Zion Road, and operated a grocery store on Maple Street. George and Ida Shockley Karr raised two children: Glenn Olin Karr who married Myrtle Hannah and Grace Opal Karr who married Claude Pyron. George and Ida are buried at Beulah Baptist Church.

Stonewall Jackson Karr Family

Shown in this family photograph are left to right, Steve, Rachel, Stonewall Jackson, George, Hannah, and Florence. *Submitted by: Shirley Karr McKinney, 1064 Pauline Street, Cantonment, FL 32533*

725. James Levi Kaylor

James Levi (J.L.) Kaylor was born in Randolph County, Alabama, on March 9, 1859. His wife, Sarah Jane Truit Kaylor, was born in Randolph County on August 25, 1862. They were married in Randolph County on December 9, 1880. Mr. and Mrs. Kaylor had seven children.

In the late 1800s the family moved to Carroll County. J.L. Kaylor became a prominent local businessman. Some of his pursuits included farming, horse trading, a cotton gin, a mercantile store and a combination lumber and trucking business. He also acquired a number of properties in Carroll County and Carrollton, including several in the downtown area. A seven-acre tract he purchased at the intersection of Maple Street and South Park Street (Highway 27) would become the site of the Kaylor family home.

Mr. Kaylor was also involved in community and church activities. He was one of the four members of the building committee for the original Tabernacle Baptist Church on Bradley Street in Carrollton. This was quite an undertaking for the time. When the church first opened in 1913 a local newspaper article stated that it probably had the largest auditorium of any church in the state. The following year it was used for hosting the annual Georgia Baptist Convention. Mr. Kaylor remained an active member of the church throughout his life.

The family in front of the Kaylor building, about 1915.

In 1920, J.L. Kaylor and several other local citizens embarked on a venture to organize what would become Carrollton's first major medical establishment — The Carroll County Memorial Hospital. A very large three story brick building that had been constructed on Mr. Kaylor's property on Maple Street would house this facility. Although it only operated for a limited time, this hospital was a significant step forward for the local medical community. Several local newspaper articles at the time praised the undertaking for providing a much needed service for Carroll County.

The swimming pool on the rear side of the Kaylor building.

After the hospital closed, Mr. Kaylor renovated the big brick building for use as his family home. He later converted it to serve as a combination family home and an inn. A full size concrete swimming pool at the rear of the building was probably one of the first of its type in Carroll County. This became a popular site for local residents and out-of-town visitors. The building was torn down in the early 1960s.

On April 20, 1932, J.L. Kaylor died at his home. His wife Sarah died on March 11, 1941. Mr. and Mrs. Kaylor are buried together in their family burial plot in the old Carrollton City Cemetery. It is interesting to note that their burial plot actually borders on the back side of what used to be the Kaylor home property on Maple Street. *Submitted by: Michael Moon, 276 Buckhorn Drive, Temple, GA 30179*

Sources: Carroll County deed books, *Carroll Free Press, Carroll County Times,* Cornerstone of original Tabernacle Baptist Church, information from friends and older family members.

726. Kelley Family

Robert W. Kelley was born between 1837 and 1843. He was a Private in Company C, 14th Alabama Regiment of Alabama in the Confederate States Army (CSA). The 1850 Chambers County, Alabama, census lists his father as born in North Carolina and his mother born in Georgia. Nothing else is known of his family.

Robert married Salina A. Rutland in 1864, the daughter of James and Susan Williamson Bonner Rutland. Robert and Salina had Watson R. who married Lavonia Gunn, James Monroe "Roe" who married Ella Victoria Bolan, Thomas who married Beulah Phillips, Charles W. who married Myrtle Buchanan, Anna who married Dr. J.L. Vinyard, and Sarah who married Boyd Buchanan.

James Monroe and Ella moved to Heard County and on to Carroll County. He and Ella had four children: Lloyd Gaines, born 1902, married Geneva Cammon; John Blake, born 1904, married (1) Irene Jackson (divorced), (2) Edna Turner; Claucie, born 1906, married David Cammon; Adele, born 1915, married (1) Barney Robinson (divorced), (2) ? Collier.

James "Roe" was a farmer, but he and Ella operated a boarding home on Hay's Mill Road for a number of years.

Ella died 7 July 1940 at 145 Dixie Street, present site of Tanner Medical Center. After Ella died, James "Roe" lived with Blake and Edna. "Roe" died 27 June 1946. He, Ella, and Claucie (daughter) are buried at Ranburne Baptist Church. Blake and Edna moved to Oxford, Alabama, where they worked in the textile industry and raised four children. *Submitted by: Alton Kelley, 921 Chesterfield Drive, Marietta, GA 30066*

Sources: Alabama and Georgia census records, Carroll County marriage records, cemetery markers, family and personal knowledge.

727. Kessler Family

Marion E. Kessler was born October 10, 1893, in Cleburne County, Alabama, and died February 21, 1978, in Carroll County, Georgia. He was married to Mary Leona Newbom Kessler, born April 14, 1900, in Cleburne County, Alabama, died August 21, 1970, in Carroll County at the old Watts Hospital in Bowdon.

They had seven children, six grandchildren, eight great-grandchildren, and one great-grandchild. Most reside in Carroll County.

When we moved to Bowdon from Alabama, Daddy went to work for Mr. Eunice Cox at the fertilizer warehouse and raising peppers. We had big fields of peppers.

The funniest thing I remember was I had to stay out of school a lot to help my mother. One day Mr. Wilson came by to see why I was not in school. Daddy had some Big Blue Velvet beans in a basket sitting out in the sun. One of them popped open. Mr. Wilson left and didn't come back any more asking questions.

Back then we didn't have grass in our yards. When I was home we had to sweep yards with a brush broom. On Fridays that was my sister and my job to sweep those yards clean, pick up any sticks or whatever. We didn't want anyone walking on them leaving tracks.

Marion E. and Mary Leona Newborn Kessler

One of my brothers, Ezra, cut hair on Dixie Street. For years he just had one hand. He cut hair for years for 50 cents a head. One brother, Harvey, worked for H.W. Richards Lumber Company for several years.

There's just two left now — Irene and me. Irene lives in Carrollton and I live in Bowdon. I have one son and daughter-in-law, Terry and Patricia.

It has been a pretty good life for us all. We had a good Christian home. *Submitted by: Bobbie Bradley, 5580 Smithfield Road, Bowdon, GA 30108*

728. Key Family 1870-2001 Part 1

George Zackary Key (11-14-1904 - 5-17-1958), son of George Edward Key (6-6-1870 - 10-3-1919) and Susanna Hutchie Gladney Key (3-4-1875 - 10-25-1949), and Annie Fay Latimer (7-28-1911 - 7-27-1998), daughter of George Earnest Latimer (11-19-1871 - 6-11-1927) and Mary Beulah Boatwright Latimer (2-20-1878 - 7-23-1945) were married on 12-5-1926 bearing three children, George Junior (9-24-1930), Milton Zackary (5-20-1933 - 8-18-2000) and Sandra Fay (1-2-1944).

George Zackary Key's family lived in Carroll County all their lives as farmers, blacksmiths, sawmillers, barber, homemaker and lunch room worker. They were hard workers and good neighbors. They were charter members of Cross Plains Christian Church. The Key family had lots to do with building the original church. George served as deacon, elder, secretary and house cleaner of the church.

Annie Fay and George Zackary Key in 1954

George Zackary's home

George Zackary's home never had any paint inside or outside, no wallpaper, no closets, carpet, or running water. The house still stands.

George Junior Key married Edna Julia Taylor (2-8-1929), daughter of Willie Lee (7-9-1898 - 3-27-1978) and Mary Lillian Cowart Taylor (1-18-1901 - 3-21-1973), on 12-25-1951. George Junior Key's family lived in Carroll County most of their lives. George served in the United States Air Force and worked for Eastern Air Lines until 1989 when Eastern went out of business. He continues growing chickens for Strain and Gold Kist. He now has five chicken houses. Edna taught school until 1981 when she became disabled due to health problems. George is an elder at Cross Plains Christian Church. *Submitted by: Edna Key, 2451 Cross Plains-Hulett Road, Carrollton, GA 30116*

729. Key Family 1870 to 2001 Part 2 George and Edna Key

George and Edna Key have three children. Alicia Karen Key (10-23-1957) married James Timothy Brannon on 6-21-1980, son of Boyd and Carolyn Cooley Brannon, having one daughter Casey LeAnn Brannon (1-14-1987). Alicia and Thomas Authur Wester (2-8-1947) were married on 8-1-1998. Tommy is the son of Thomas Ralph Wester (8-24-1905 - 11-29-1994) and Mary Bana Copeland Wester (7-13-1905 - 5-4-1983). Alicia taught school at Carrollton High School for nineteen years. She still lives in Carroll County but is now teaching home economics in Heard County.

George Junior Key Family

Theresa Yvonne Key (1-29-1961) married Bobby Alan Hubbard (9-6-1960) on 7-30-1988. Alan is the son of Bobby Hubbard (11-19-1937) and LaRue Sticher Hubbard (5-31-1940). Alan has one daughter, Kristen LeAnn (1-28-1984). Theresa is employed by George and Edna Key, doing all kinds of farm labor, and is a certified aerobics instructor and personal fitness trainer.

Joey Lee Key (8-20-1962) and Rita Sue Duke (11-8-1957) daughter of Jerry Rudolph Duke (8-2-1933) and Mary Jo Wallace Duke (11-11-1937) were married on 10-8-1994. Joey is a Farm Bureau Insurance agent in Carroll County.

Included in the picture of George Junior's family is: center front Casey Brannon and Kristen Hubbard; far left Joe and Rita; right George and Edna; back Tommy, Alicia, Theresa and Alan. *Submitted by: Joey Key, 850 Old Four Notch Road, Whitesburg, GA 30185*

730. Burrell J. and Samantha E. Farmer Key

Burrell was the grandson of Mary Elizabeth (Betsy) Jordan and Stephen Center Key. Betsy and Stephen had nine children, the third oldest being George Washington.

George W. was born in Georgia and married Unity Millie (aka) Unetta Leftridge in Newton, County on December 20, 1838. George and Unity were both born in 1816. Shortly after their first child Burrell J. was born, they moved to Randolph County, Alabama, near his parents. He later moved the family to the Tyus area of Carroll County where he continued his blacksmith business. He and Unity had several more children: Rebecca F., Louise C., Martha Jane, Lettie, Sitha A., Joel W., John M., Wiley Martin, Vergen Mary (Mollie), Eliza, Cynthia and Robert.

George W. died December 10, 1897, and Unity died November 19, 1885. Both are buried at Pleasant Grove Baptist Church Cemetery near Tyus, along with several of their children.

Burrell John Key was born July 19, 1841. He helped his father farm and worked with him in his blacksmith business. At the age of twenty-one on May 14, 1862, he enlisted in the Confederate Army in Wedowee, Alabama, and was assigned to the 47th Alabama Infantry Regiment, Company G. Three days earlier, his uncle Joseph Frances Marion Key had enlisted and was assigned to the same regiment and company. The 47th Alabama fought with Jackson, Law, Bugler, Longstreet, and Hood and fought in many battles including Gettysburg and Chickamauga. According to Civil War records, he was taken prisoner of war, was released, and surrendered with General Lee at Appomattox Courthouse in Virginia on April 9, 1865.

Wayne Parrish of Carthage, Mississippi, recalls his grandmother telling the following story many times: Burl didn't return home for a very long time after the war. The family had not heard from him and was getting worried he might not be coming home. His sister Becky had a dream where she and her sister Lizzie were picking Indigo when she looked up and saw Burl coming down the road. She told her mother about the dream. A few days later Becky's mother told her and Lizzie they needed to go pick Indigo. After they finished for the day and returned to the house, Burl was there. Burl had come home and a dream had come true.

Samantha Nancy E. Farmer and Burrell were married about 1867. Samantha was born in 1842 to parents Josiah and Elizabeth White Farmer who had resided in Carroll County for several years. The couple continued to reside in the Tyus area where Burl did farming and for several years served as Justice of the Peace of the 713th District south and a member of the Goshen Lodge No. 71 F. & A.M.

Their daughter Arizona Samantha Unetta was born 1869 and married John Benjamin Davis. Roxie Ann was born 1874 and married Rufus Robinson; Robert Lee was born 1877; and George Washington was born 1879 and married first to Buchanan and second to Viola Belle Chevas. All children remained in the county except George Washington who moved to Tampa, Florida, and had several orange groves.

Samantha preceded Burl in death, passing away in 1886. Burl passed away on March 30, 1895, and was buried with Masonic honors at the Pleasant Grove Baptist Church. Samantha and Burl were our great-great-grandparents. *Submitted by: Lessa Lester, Carrollton, GA. Researched by: June Brown Hayes, 6955 Lockridge Drive, Doraville, GA 30360*
Sources: CSA records, family stories and knowledge.

731. Sara Stipe and Hal Kidd

Sara Stipe, born 08 September 1938, married Hal Kidd (Harold L. Kidd Jr.) 19 July 1958. Sara was born in Carroll County and Hal, born 02 June 1938, was born and reared in Coweta County in and around Newnan, Georgia. Sara was a pharmacist and Hal an accountant.

Sara and Hal have three children, Patricia Lynn Kidd (Patti), born 26 August 1960, Julie Marie Kidd Mohs, born 28 April 1963, and John Christopher Kidd born 13 January 1967. Patti has two children, H. Dean Phillips Jr. and Jennifer Caroline Phillips.

Sara's parents are Clara Mae Martin born 25 October 1910, died 26 April 2001, and Sterling Henry Stipe Sr., born 05 August 1904, died 26 February 1966. Sterling and Clara are buried in the Stripling Chapel Methodist Church Cemetery.

Hal's father is Harold L. Kidd Sr., born 14 February 1913, and mother Eunice Newman Kidd, born 23 November 1915 of Coweta County. His grandparents are Grover Cleveland Kidd and Lena Kate Forbus Newman of Coweta County and William Stallings Kidd and Fannie Sue Wiggins Kidd of Coweta County.

Hal and Sara Stipe Kidd

Sara's paternal grandparents are Alvin Olenza Stipe born 04 September 1870, died 02 July 1926 and Annie Glenn Vineyard, born 12 February 1882, died 03 Mar 1967. They were married 14 October 1903. His parents are Henry Nelson Stipe and Mary Emmaline Steed of Carroll County, formerly of Old Campbell County near Fairburn. Henry, Emmaline and young family moved to Carroll County around 1875. Annie Glenn's parents are Judith Elizabeth Bailey Vineyard and William Glenn Vineyard of Sharpsburg in Coweta County, Georgia. William Glenn died of typhoid 28 September 1882. Sara knew her Grandmother Stipe and Great-grandmother Vineyard very well, having lived next to them most of her life.

Sara's father and uncle, Dr. Harvie Jordan Stipe, rode a horse or mule from their cotton farm to Carrollton High School going by way of Hay's Mill Road and leaving the horse at a mule barn near Adamson Square. Sterling made his home in Carroll County as a dairy farmer, and Harvie made his home in Fort Myers, Florida, as a physician.

Sara's maternal grandparents are Willie Watson Martin born 23 March 1881, died 26 February 1967, and Amy Pearl Jones born 22 March 1884, died 08 April 1966. His parents are James Edward (Ned) Martin and Martha Anne Rebecca Shadinger Martin of Carroll County. Willie married Amy Pearl Jones 28 November 1907. Her parents are William Orin Jones and Mary Jane Crider of Carroll County. Willie and Pearl had three children: Edna Pearl Martin Walker; Milton Jones Martin, and Clara Mae Martin Stipe.

Sara remembered life on the dairy farm and took part in many farm duties, one of which was delivering milk bottled on the farm. They bottled the cold milk with a manual stainless steel bottling machine in glass pints and quarts early each morning and delivered to households and stores around town under the name of Stipe's Dairy Grade A Raw Milk. Pasteurization requirements forced retirement of the bottling machine and selling the milk to a cooperative.

Submitted by: Sara S. Kidd

732. Solomon Perry Kierbow

and Descendants 1830

Solomon Perry Kierbow was born on February 26, 1830. Few details are recorded concerning his early life. In his obituary at his death on April 6, 1907, it states that his first wife died some fifty years before his death. In 1858, he married Mary Ann Pritchett who was born February 10, 1834. On August 13, 1862, Solomon P. Kierbow enlisted for three years or the duration of the war as a private in Company E, 44th Georgia Volunteer Infantry, C.S.A., Army of Northern Virginia, Freeman's Rangers.

Others of the Kierbow Family were in this unit. William N. Kierbow enlisted the same day and was appointed first corporal and was wounded at Wilderness, Virginia, on May 5, 1864, and was shown on roll for August 31, 1864, in hospital, wounded.

Daniel Kierbow enlisted in Company I, 13th Georgia Infantry on July 8, 1861, then enlisted in Company E, 44th Georgia Infantry May 4, 1862, and discharged, disability on October 4, 1862.

Elijah G. Kierbow enlisted March 4, 1862, and was wounded at Ellison's Mill, Virginia, on June 25, 1862, and died as the result of amputation of a hand in General Hospital #8, St. Charles Hospital, Richmond, Virginia, on August 7, 1862.

The 44th Georgia was heavily involved in the battles in Maryland and Virginia. At Antietam, Maryland, September of 1862, they suffered heavy losses south of Dunkard Church in the sunken road, later known as Bloody Lane. In December of 1862 they were at Fredericksburg, Virginia, when Union forces under General Burnside crossed the Rappahannock River and occupied the city. On May 2, 1863, the 44th Georgia was a part of the 26,000 Confederates with Lt. General Thomas J. (Stonewall) Jackson, who circled west and north to attack the Union Forces west of Chancellorsville, Virginia. Later that evening, General Jackson was out checking on troop dispositions when he was fired on by Confederate pickets and was severely wounded.

Solomon P. and Mary Ann Kierbow

On the next day, May 3, 1863, Private Solomon P. Kierbow was captured during the fighting and was taken to Fredericksburg, Virginia. On May 4, 1863, his name appears on a roll of prisoners forwarded to Old Capitol Prison, Washington, D.C. on May 10, 1863, Private Solomon P. Kierbow was sent to City Point, Virginia, for exchange. That same day, General Stonewall Jackson died at Guiney's Station. On May 13, Private Solomon P. Kierbow was one of 800 Confederate prisoners of war paroled for exchange. At this writing, Joy Lynn Jones Hurst, the great-great-granddaughter of Solomon Perry Kierbow, teaches at Turning Point School at Hopewell, Virginia, formerly known as City Point, Virginia.

The 44th Georgia occupied Hagerstown and Sharpsburg, Maryland and on July 1 through July 4, 1863, were part of Doles' Brigade and had many killed and wounded. They wintered near Mine Run Creek, and Solomon Perry Kierbow was shown as being paid by Capt. Neary on December 31, 1863.

On May 5, 6, and 7, 1864, the 44th Georgia fought in the Battle of the Wilderness. On May 8 they were part of Ewell's Corps posted in a salient called The Mule Shoe enclosing the McCool House. On May 10, they were fiercely attacked and swept out of the works with a loss of about one thousand prisoners and many dead and wounded. The Mule Shoe was later called The Bloody Angle.

Milton and Lilla Kierbow

In June of 1864, the 44th Georgia was entrenched at Cold Harbor and were attacked by General U.S. Grant's forces. The Union forces suffered approximately seven thousand casualties.

After the Battle of Cold Harbor, General Lee ordered General Early's Corps to the Shenandoah Valley. This led to engagements at Lynchburg and Staunton, Virginia. Private Solomon P. Kierbow appears on the muster roll for July and August 1864 as absent, wounded, in hospital. On September 19, 1864, during the Battle of Winchester, Virginia, General Rodes, the Division Commander was killed. On October 19, his replacement, General Ramseur, was critically wounded near New Market, Virginia. The 44th Georgia then became a part of General John B. Gordon's Corps during the siege of Petersburg, Virginia. Following the fall of Petersburg, the corps was covering the retreat of the wagon trains and at Sailor's Creek about eight thousand men were taken prisoners and most of the wagons captured by Union forces.

On April 9, 1865, at Appomattox Court House, Virginia, General Lee surrendered and 27,805 Confederate troops were released on parole.

After returning to Carroll County, Solomon P. Kierbow joined Waco Masonic Lodge and was a loyal member the remainder of his life. Four sons and three daughters were born to Solomon and Mary Ann Kierbow. Milton Right Kierbow was born on November 1, 1871. Mary Ann Pritchett Kierbow died on April 27, 1906 and Solomon P. Kierbow died on April 7, 1907. They were buried at Pleasant View Baptist Church Cemetery.

Milton Right Kierbow married Lilla Cona Garner on December 27, 1896. He was baptized and they joined Pleasant View Baptist Church in August 1898. He farmed their property between Miller Academy Road and Creel's Mill. Their two daughters were Myrtie Estill Kierbow born on July 26, 1901, and Mamie Ione Kierbow born on October 10, 1904. Myrtie and Ione attended school at Walnut Hill School where

Ione was allowed to start at the age of five to help secure enough students to be able to pay the teacher. Milton Kierbow was a Mason and was ordained to preach on October 16, 1926. He was pastor at Pleasant Ridge Baptist Church for several years. As young ladies, Myrtie and Ione later taught at several schools in the Carroll County area. Myrtie married Hershel T. Parrish on July 29, 1923, and Ione married George D. Jones on November 15, 1925. Several of their descendants are Carroll County residents today. *Submitted by: Mary Helen Jones Parker, 108 Fountain Head, Peachtree City, GA 30269*

733. James Kight

James Kight, a veteran of World War II, was born 31 March 1915 to Rev. Walter and Mary Wyatt Kight. He died 17 February 1985. He married Ocie Mae Brown 3 November 1933 the daughter of Lillie and George Brown. She was born 11 April 1914. They are buried in marked graves at Westside Memorial Gardens, all in Carroll County.

James was ordained a deacon at Pinetuckey Baptist Church in Carroll County. He served as chairman of the Deacon Board for a number of years. In January of 1974 he was called by God into the ministry of the gospel. He was later ordained and pastored Mt. Sinai Baptist, Mt. Lowell Baptist Church and Mt. Pleasant Baptist church, all in Carroll County.

James and Ocie Mae Kight

James and Ocie Mae had six children, all born in Carroll County. They were Frances Kight Beedles, Walter James Kight, Mary Jean Kight Tyler, Aron Kight, Linda Diane Kight Houston, and Annette Kight. Their fifth child, daughter Linda, was blessed with a gift to play piano. She started playing at age ten and is Minister of Music at the Westside Full Gospel Baptist Church. Their second child, son Walter, was called into the ministry in August of 1993. He was ordained May 1994 and called to pastor the Westside Full Gospel Baptist. He was elected Overseer of the Northwest District of the Full Gospel Baptist Church Fellowship under National Presiding Bishop Paul S. Morton Sr. and State Bishop Sherman L. Young in March 2000.

Overseer Walter James Kight currently serves and has completed seven years of pastoring at Westside Full Gospel Baptist Church May 2001. *Submitted by: Frances Kight Beedles, 532 Central High Road, Carrollton, GA 30116*

734. Benjamin King Family

Benjamin King was born in Abbeville, South Carolina in 1808 or 1809. He married Mary Ann Burson (daughter of Joseph, and granddaughter of Isaac Burson) in 1828, probably in Franklin County, Georgia. They were in Carroll County, Georgia, for the 1850 census and in the Bowdon District of Carroll County in 1860. Benjamin and Mary Ann had nine children.

1. Joseph G. King was born 18 November 1829 in Gwinnett County, Georgia. He married Indiana Langston (daughter of Ase Langston and Sarah Clementine Dodd) 31 January 1849 in Campbell County, Georgia. After Indiana died 25 August 1896, Joseph married Mary Frances Hayes (daughter of Beriah Hayes) on 6 December 1898. Joseph died 6 April 1925. All three are buried at Poplar Springs Primitive Baptist Church Cemetery. Joseph and Indiana had four children, all born in Carroll County: Sara Ann Elizabeth, William Carter, Benjamin Asa, and Hiram Mark.

2. Elizabeth A. King born 25 August 1831 in Gwinnett County, Georgia, married Aaron Styles 18 September 1845. Elizabeth's second marriage was to William Keaton. Elizabeth died 5 February 1880 and is buried in Keaton Cemetery, Douglas County, Georgia.

3. Thomas Hiram King born 15 July 1833 in Gwinnett County, Georgia, married Charity Matilda Chandler (daughter of Ambrose Chandler and Jerusha White) 29 December 1854 in Carroll County. They had George Washington M., Mary J., Joseph B., Eliza J., Martin Ambrose, Hiram B., John W., James D., Robert S., and Thomas C. Thomas Hiram was a farmer and a private in Company H, 41st Regiment, Georgia C.S.A. He died 1 February 1904, and Charity died 18 August 1905. They are buried in Poplar Springs Primitive Baptist Church Cemetery.

4. Frances Jane King born 5 August 1835 in Georgia, married Rowland Bryant Cooke 9 October 1851 in Carroll County. They had Benjamin David, Mary Antionette, Roland B., James J., Leamon, Monroe, George W.L., and Ross L. Frances Jane died 22 April 1887 and is buried in Temperance Congregational Methodist Cemetery, Carroll County, Georgia.

5. Nancy Caroline King, born 7 June 1837 in Georgia, married Ransom E. Smith (son of Gabriel Smith Jr.) on 13 July 1853. They had Ben J., Joseph G., Thomas A., James, John H., Hiram Carter, William C., Aaron F., Broton L., Mary E., and Martha Ann. Nancy died 13 February 1917, and Ransom died 11 August 1905. They are buried in Poplar Springs Primitive Baptist Church Cemetery.

6. Julia Ann America King was born 19 March 1837 and married Joseph Marion McClain. They had James Benjamin, Joseph, Mary J., and John H. Julia died in Cleburne County, Alabama.

7. Martha Emmaline King born 21 August 1841, married Henry Gaines Smith in Carroll County on 28 December 1865. They had Joseph E., Benjamin Aaron, Hiram Shaw, William R., John D., James H., and Carrie. Martha died 26 April 1900 and is buried in Poplar Springs Primitive Baptist Church Cemetery.

8. Mary Jane King was born 13 March 1846, died 9 December 1856, and is buried in Poplar Springs Primitive Baptist Church Cemetery.

9. Eliza Margaret King was born 22 July 1849, married 28 December 1865 to James Bryant "Polk" Smith. They had James Benjamin. Eliza died 6 December 1866 and is buried in Poplar Springs Primitive Baptist Church Cemetery.

Benjamin King was a farmer. In 1859 he owned fifty acres of land and paid a tax of $1.22. He was five feet, ten inches tall, with fair complexion and gray eyes. He and Mary were members of Poplar Springs Primitive Baptist Church, having donated land on which to build the church. He was a private in Company H, 41st Regiment Georgia C.S.A., became ill with pneumonia during the siege of Vicksburg, Mississippi, died in Mobile, Alabama, on his way home, and is buried there. Mary Ann died 6 September 1884 and is buried in Poplar Springs Primitive Baptist Church Cemetery. *Submitted by: Mary E. Byam, 3342 Tuxedo Avenue, Flint, MI 48507*

Sources: Census records, marriage records, marriage and death certificates, pension papers.

735. Joseph G. King and Indiana Langston King

Joseph G. King was the first of nine children born to Benjamin King and Mary Ann Burson. He was born on November 19, 1829, in either Gwinnett or Jackson County and his parents moved to Carroll County shortly after 1840. Although married and having four small children, Joseph entered the Civil War in October 1861. He was captured at Vicksburg, Mississippi, in 1863 along with his father and brother. Illness suffered during the war resulted in both severe and permanent health degradation. Although he lived to be 95, he was never able to do normal labor after being discharged from the military in 1865.

Indiana Margaret Langston was born in Georgia on June 22, 1820. She was the youngest of twelve children born to Asa Langston and Sarah C. Dodd. Based on available information on Indiana's parents and siblings, Asa and Sarah married in South Carolina. Shortly after that, they probably moved to Jackson County as this is where their first child was born. Sarah Dodd Langston died in Franklin County, Georgia.

Joseph and Indiana were married on January 31, 1848, in Campbell County, Georgia. All four of their children — Sarah Ann Elizabeth, William Carter, Ben Asa, and Hiram Mark — were born in Carroll County.

Sarah Ann Elizabeth was born October 7, 1851, and was married to Jefferson McGee McBurnett. Sarah and Jefferson moved to Texas and remained there until their deaths. They are buried in Sharp, Texas. (See related McBurnett article.)

William Carter was born July 24, 1853, and married to Lucinda Frances Burt. William and Lucinda moved to Cullman County, Alabama and are buried there.

Ben was born in April 1856 and married "Shug" Warren. Ben and Shug lived in both Carroll and Heard counties. They are buried at Poplar Springs Primitive Baptist Church Cemetery near Smithfield. Although generally this man is listed as Ben Asa King, he himself signed letters to his sister as A.B. King.

Hiram Mark was born circa 1859 and was married to Selah Laura king.

A few of the letters written by Indiana to her daughter Sarah McBurnett are with members of the McBurnett family. Contents of these letters reveal many interesting topics, but in a very consistent manner Indiana always gave a run down on the "local community news" plus a health status report on Joseph and herself. In a letter written just weeks before she died, Indiana wrote of all the church meeting "Pap" has attended and will attend — Shiloh, Cold Springs, Douglas, and Poplar Springs. So, age and poor health were no excuse for them to miss the church meetings.

Joseph and Indiana were active members at the Poplar Spring Primitive Baptist Church, Bowdon, Georgia. Indiana died in 1896 and is buried at Poplar Springs. Joseph then married Mary Frances Hayes, a daughter of Beriah and Mary Hayes, who were also active members at Poplar Springs. Joseph died in 1925 and Frances died two years later. Both were buried in Poplar Springs with Joseph between his two wives.

Submitted by: Charles Barrett Carroll Jr., Carrollton, GA

Source: Researched by: Betty Jo Carroll Parsons, Bowdon, GA

736. William and Gilly King

William King, my great-great-grandfather and farmer, was born about 1816 in Georgia. Gilly, my great-great-grandmother and housewife, was born about 1824 in North Carolina or Georgia. They were living in Randolph County, Alabama, in 1850 with their daughter, Mary E. King, my great-grandmother, born about 1842 in Georgia or Alabama. According to family, the Kings came from one of the counties in Georgia adjacent to Randolph County, Alabama.

Mary E. King was married first to James Asbury Hicks and had two children: Mary E. "Nettie" Hicks, born September 1862 and James William Asbury Hicks, my grandfather, born March 25, 1864, in or around the Rockdale/Wedowee, Randolph County, Alabama, area. James Asbury Hicks died a week before James William was born. We have not located his grave.

The Kings and the Hicks are found in the census for Randolph County, Alabama, in 1860 and 1866. On October 27, 1867, Mary E. Hicks married second to J.P. Jacob Smith in Cleburne County, Alabama, at the home of her father by Marell Collier, J.P. They lived with the Kings where Wehaga was the post office and are found there in the 1870 Cleburne County, Alabama, census. I lost the Kings after that census. The Smiths' children were Missouri "Cent," Solomon "Sol," William N., and Thomas Jefferson "Jeff." In 1880, they are found in White Plains, Calhoun County, Alabama. I lost the Smiths after that census. It has been told that Mary E. and Jacob are buried in unmarked graves at Mt. Zion/White Plains Cemetery near White Plains High School, White Plains, Alabama.

Solomon married Mrs. Ellen Smith in Calhoun County, Alabama. They are found in the 1900 census in Oxford, Alabama. Jeff and Sarah "Sally" Jane Singleton married and lived in Anniston, Calhoun County, Alabama. Their children were Norris, Cecil, Lee, Bennie, Varnie, Pearlie, and Trudie. Thomas died in Anniston in 1940. His obituary shows that Solomon was living in Sylacauga, Alabama. Thomas and Sarah are buried at Pleasant Ridge, Calhoun County, Alabama.

Nettie married James Denny on August 26, 1884 in Anniston, Alabama. They made their home around Lloyd's Hill. Their children were Julia, Willie and Frank. Nettie 51, and Frank 17, are found in the 1910 Anniston, Calhoun County, Alabama census. I cannot find them after that census.

James William Asbury Hicks married Safronia Adella Snider on May 2, 1885, in Calhoun County, Alabama. She is the daughter of William James and Nancy Owens Snider. The Hicks farmed and lived in Choccoloco Valley and had twelve children: William Jackson married Mallie Phillips, Abbie married Bertha Moore, Nancy married James Turner, Grover married Gussie Faulkner, Sella Mae married Jesse Turner, Lucille married Jay Dee Faulkner, Clayton Dewey "Jack," (my father) married first Mable Texas Brown and second Maggie Hogue Morgan (my mother), Charley married Era Jane Brown Faulkner, Nixie, Robert, Margaret, and James Kilby, who died at eleven months.

I married Conner W. Crumley in Oxford, Alabama. We have two children, Meghan Renay and Michael Christopher. Meghan married Chris Bunt from Oxford, Alabama. They live in Munford along with their children, Caleb age 7, Kimberly age 4, and Myles age 2½. *Submitted by: Jackie Elaine Hicks Crumley, 709 Beck Drive, Oxford, AL 36203, Jcrumley@aol.com.*

Sources: Census and marriage records, Mrs. Lucille H. Faulkner, Miss Margaret Hicks, Mr. Robert L. Hicks, Mr. Nix E. Hicks (all deceased) of Choccolocco, AL, and life experiences.

737. King - McBurnett - Carroll

Family Picture November 1917

This five-generation family picture was taken in November of 1917 when Sarah Anne Elizabeth King McBurnett of Texas was visiting her father Joseph G. King of Carroll County, and her daughter Minnie Lee McBurnett Carroll of Haralson County.

The King, McBurnett, and Carroll Families. 1917

On the front row are Mary Free and her sister. They were orphans and one of them was reared by Eliza King Wright. The other six on the front row were children of James Moses Blackburn Carroll and Minnie Lee McBurnett Carroll. They are Johnnie Beatrice, Irwin Jefferson, Thomas Marion (forefront), Henry Lawton, Charles Barrett (forefront), and Eucleod McAllister Carroll.

The second row from left is Eliza King Wright, a niece to Joseph G. King. Sitting next to Eliza is Sarah Anne Elizabeth McBurnett King, daughter of Joseph G. The two young boys in front of Sarah Anne are Brunice and Carnice Brown, sons of Willie Bell Carroll and Marvin Brown. Next is Joseph G. King and his second wife, Frances Hayes King. The last lady on this row is Martha Smith Barrow, grandmother of Lee Otis Barrow.

On the back row from left (and almost out of the picture) is Thomas Oree Carroll, brother to James Moses Blackburn Carroll. Lee Otis Barrow and wife Lillie Gayce Carroll Barrow are the next couple with Marvin M. and Willie Belle Carroll Brown standing next to them. The next two couples are William Ambrose Cooke and Cecil Fern Carroll Cooke, and Jimmie Lou Carroll and Eldridge Love. This is the only known picture of Jimmie. The last couple on the right side is Minnie Lee McBurnett Carroll and James Moses Blackburn Carroll.

Sarah Anne Elizabeth King McBurnett was my great-grandmother. The name on my own birth certificate reads Sarah Elizabeth Kite. Sometime before I started school, the "h" was dropped from Sarah, and later the "Elizabeth" was dropped. I became Sara Ann all the way through school. *Submitted by: Sara Ann Kite Pelot, Mount Pleasant, SC*

738. Kingsbery - Lassetter

Sanford S. Kingsbery (1805-1869) who had moved to Carrollton from Derby, Vermont, in 1830 seeking his fortune, purchased the first lots sold around the newly cleared Town Square of Carrollton on 2 May 1831 on the exact spot of the now-defunct Peoples Bank. On that corner, he became Carrollton's very first merchant. Kingsbery returned to Vermont in 1834 to marry Mary Ann Grow (1814-1874) on 23 September 1834 in Morgan, Vermont, and to bring his bride to Carrollton.

In 1847, Kingsbery bought "Oak Lawn," a Greek Revival style home on Rome Street in Carrollton, and the surrounding 400 acres of land. Kingsbery raised some of Georgia's finest livestock, including "Black Hawk" racehorses. Kingsbery also built and operated a corn and wheat grinding mill widely patronized by farmers from the surrounding countryside.

Mary "Mamie" Kingsbery and Cheadle Bartow "C.B." Lassetter. 1901

Kingsbery's daughters married Redwine, Nicholas Fain, and Wesley Stripling. Their sons married Smith, LaRoche, Bowie, Cleveland, and Juhan.

Kingsbery's son Paschal Paoli Kingsbery (1854-1913) married Alice B. Juhan (1856-1917) on 16 May 1876. Paschal and Alice had two sons, Juhan (1878-1878) and Harry Lee (1889-1960), and one daughter, Mary "Mamie" (1879-1964) who married Cheadle Bartow Lassetter (1861-1945). Benjamin Lassetter (1778-1869) born in North Carolina, married Elizabeth Hill (1785-1852) 5 May 1801, and was living in Carroll County in 1828 with grown and married children and grandchildren. Their daughters married Bassett Northern (schoolmaster), Wesley Camp (statesman), William Hendon, Benjamin Watkins, Jesse and William Boone (brothers who were related to Daniel Boone) and Lindsey Holland. Their sons married Browns, Ghoolsby, and Mullins girls. From an ancestor, Benjamin had a strain of Cherokee blood from possibly the Notaway Cherokee tribe in North Carolina that is Rutherford County.

Benjamin's son William Cheadle Lassetter (1819-1888) married Mary Parthenia Brown (1821-1883) on 22 December 1839. Their daughters married Borders, Abraham Houseworth, Joe

Sparks, Edmond Thomas Camp, John Williams, James Henry Baron, and Newton Allen Horton. Their sons married Barnett, Green, and Kingsbery.

William's son Cheadle Bartow (CB) Lassetter (1861-1945) married Mary "Mamie" Kingsbery (1879-1964) on 18 December 1901. This marriage joined the lineage between the Kingsbery and Lassetter pioneer families of Carroll County.

CB's two sons married Harman and Newton. Their only daughter, my mother, Mary Alice Lassetter, 28 August 1912, married John Frank Wilson (1908-2000) on 11 September 1932 and she currently lives in Birmingham, Alabama. Their daughter, Mary Katharine (1937), married George Hanlin (1930-1974. I, their only son, John Frank Wilson Jr. (18 June 1938) married Clara Maxine Bowen (25 June 1940) on 29 August 1959. Our marriage had two daughters — Clara Lynne Wilson (16 May 1961-28 May 1961), and Jill Frances Wilson (29 September 1970) married Lyman Hope Hines (1966) 11 April 1992 and has a son Ryan Carter (14 September 1998). Our two sons: John Frank Wilson III (27 October 1962) married Jennifer (1962) on 13 July 1985, has two daughters Sarah Elizabeth (1986) and Mary Caroline (1988); and James Frederick Wilson (29 December 1964) married Angela (1967) on 1 September 1989 has a son, Joshua Kyle (1992), and daughter Kayla Morgan (1994). *Submitted by: John Frank Wilson Jr., 1918 Vestavia Court, Arlington, TX 76018-2579*

739. Kinney

Family Letters

The following letters were written by Susannah Ward Kinney and her son William Kinney Jr., to their brother and uncle, Hiram M. Ward. The original letters are in the possession of Judge Hiram H. Ward, Denton, North Carolina. Judge Ward is the great-great-grandson of Hiram M. Ward. Permission to reprint from Judge Ward and the Genealogical Society of Davidson County (North Carolina) where they were previously published.

May 27th 1850

State Georgia
Carroll County
Dear Brother,

I do at this time take this opportunity of writing to you to inform you that your letter has come to hand, which was a great satisfaction to me to hear from you once more. We are all well at this time, hoping these lines may find you all in the Land of the Living and enjoying health and all the blessings and comforts of life. As regards myself, I can inform you that I am feeble and feel the decline of life very much. All my children have married and left me but three, two girls and one boy. Those that are married are William, Isaac, Jesse, Jeremiah and Sally. William has 5 children, Isaac has 4 children, Jesse 4 children, Jeremiah 3 children and Sally one child. Those that are living with me are Elizabeth, Anna and Jefferson. All of them live close to me except Jeremiah. He lives some distance from me. Myself, Elizabeth, Anna, Isaac and Sally are members of the Baptist Church. It would be a satisfaction to me to hear from you as regards your state in reference to Eternity, and if you are a member of any church or any of my relations.

If there is anything coming to me from the estate of Uncle Stephen I should like to get it. William talks like coming to attend to the matter but I think that he will not undertake the journey as the distance is considerable and he old and the amount so small, if any, that it would not be worth coming after. As to impowering you to attend to it for me I would be very willing myself, but Husband seems to defer doing anything in the matter. If there is anything coming I need it very much.

I want you to write us again. I want to know where Jonathan lives and William, Stephen, Sarah and Naomi, and Anthony. Inform the the state, county and post office if you know so that I can write to them.

In the conclusion I can say that I should be glad to see you once more in Life but this I never expect will be afforded me. But I hope we shall meet in Heaven where parting shall never be. So I close by subscribing myself your affectionate sister till Death.

Susannah Kinney

To Hiram Ward
Dear Uncle,

I cannot do justice to my feelings without sending you some additional lines along with Mother's from myself hoping it will be somewhat interesting to you.

The times in this country are only tolerable. The general health is good; we have no disease among us of a dangerous nature. Breadstuff is scarce; it is worth 75 cents per bushel. Bacon is plenty at 7 cents per pound, coffee from 5 to 6 pounds to the dollar: This article has advanced from 10 pound to the dollar to 5 and 6. Cotton thread and cotton fabricks all have advanced in price here, this I suppose as the result of the advance in the raw materials. Our crops of wheat look tolerable though somewhat later than usual. The crops of corn and cotton look small for the time of year. We have a very wet and cool spring; so far the cotton crops are badly injured thereby. There cannot be a good crop made in this country let the fall be ever so favorable, for the cotton is not on the ground [handwriting difficult to transcribe] and is still dying [handwriting difficult to transcribe]. There is I think ten times as much cotton planted here than any former year. All hands have planted cotton and lessened their corn crops. I think corn next summer will be very high.

Our state is advancing in improvements of all kinds, in building rail and plank roads for the transportation of goods from the seaboard to the interior of the state. Also we have the magnetic telegraph in operation in this state whose speed is as the lightning flash. And lastly this state has made liberal provision for the education for the poor and indigent. This I think is the best of all improvements and one that is calculated to perpetuate our liberties to unborn millions. The Free Soil question has been considerably discussed by our Legislature. Many hostile resolutions were passed and many inflammatory speeches made against the north and this state united with others to meet in convention in June next to consult on the dissolution of the union. This I think should be the last resort with both sections. Such an event I think would be disastrous to our liberties and free institutions. California, that Land of Gold, has aroused this dangerous question again to life. But I hope before this time the matter is settled by compromise, and that forever.

For myself, I am a tiller of ground. I cannot boast of wealth; I am poor and needy. Of children I can boast; I have property and make a plenty to sustain life and live comfortably and pay my debts. This should satisfy me but it does not. Such is the thirst of man for wealth.

I must close hoping that you will write to me or Mother. It's my desire to keep up an occasional correspondence by letter with all my relations. No more at present.

Respectfully yours,
William Kinney

To Hiram Ward, Esq.

Submitted by: Rev. Willard L. Moore Jr., 1912 Joslin, Cleburne, TX 76031

740. William and Lucinda Haynes Kinney

William Kinney Jr. married Lucinda Haynes December 17, 1839, in Carroll County, Georgia. She was the daughter of Jonathan Haynes and Cynthia McDowell. They lived on land lot 39 just north of Sand Hill and south of Villa Rica. (See related McDowell story.)

In the 1850 census, William is identified as a planter with property valued at $1000. He was Justice of the Peace from 1852-1854.

In 1862, William mustered with the Georgia State Guards, 4th Battalion Infantry, Company C. He died of measles in camp in 1863. It is unknown where he is buried. Lucinda Kinney not only lost her husband during the Civil War, but she lost her oldest son, Benjamin Franklin Kinney, also. After the Civil War, Lucinda moved her children to Polk County, Georgia. Her father, Jonathan, and her brother, James Monroe, also moved.

The children of William and Lucinda were: (1) Benjamin Franklin born 1840 in Georgia. He married Sophronia Elizabeth Turner Harper on April 25, 1863. He joined Cobb's Legion, Company F, in Petersburg, Virginia, during the Civil War. He died June 20, 1864, at the Battle of Chickamauga. They had one daughter, Virginia Magnolia Kinney, born June 8, 1864, and died October 7, 1894. (2) Susannah Kinney, born 1842 in Georgia. (3) Lucinda Adeline Kinney born 1844 in Carroll County; died 1916 in Alabama. She married James Thomas Scott in 1868 in Polk County, Georgia. (4) Nancy Jane, born 1846 in Georgia. She married Thomas Waters. (5) Mary E. Kinney, born 1848. Died in childhood. (6) Cicero Harrison, born 1850 in Carroll County. Died 1926 in Polk County, Georgia. He married Florence T. Bishop in 1876. (7) Joseph Lee Kinney, born 1851 in Carroll County. Died 1919 in Alabama. He married Ciddy F. Scott 1873 in Polk County, Georgia. (8) Elmira Josephine Kinney, born 1853 in Carroll County. Died 1912 in Polk County. Married Jackson Moore in 1871. He was the son of John Jackson Moore and Hannah Ewing. (9) Sarah M., born November 1855 in Polk County. She married William R. Ferguson in 1878. (10) Julia Ann, born 1857 in Carroll County. She married George W. Owens in 1885 in Polk County, Georgia. (11) William Riley born 1859 in Carroll County. He married Nety Emma Farmer in 1881 in Polk County, Georgia. He died in 1902 in Polk County. (12) Isaac Monroe born 1860 in Carroll County. Died in 1944 in Polk County. He married Mattie Louisa Hulsey in 1891 in Polk County.

In 1870, Lucinda was on the census in Polk County as the owner of $200 in property. In 1880, she was head of household with her daughter Julia, her sons William Riley and Isaac Monroe, and her father Jonathan Haynes. In 1900, she was living with her son Isaac in Polk County, Georgia. It is believed that she is buried at Stilesboro in McGregor Cemetery. *Submitted by: Mrs. Jane Patton, 1415 Bellevue Drive, Gadsden, AL 35904 and Written by: Cathy Moore Casper, 5335 Carbonton Road, Sanford, NC 27330*

741. William Kinney Sr. and Susanna Ward

The Kinneys go to Georgia

In 1827, William Kinney Sr. is a lucky drawer in the land lottery and earns land in Carroll County, Georgia. He had migrated to Habersham County, Georgia, in the early 1820s from Rowan County, North Carolina. He is on the first census of Carroll County, 1830. He becomes Justice of the Peace from 1843-1852. He lives out his life as a "gentleman farmer."

William Kinney was born in Rowan County, North Carolina, in 1783 and married Susanna Ward around 1809 in Rowan County. He was the son of a William and Sallie Parks Kinney of Rowan County, North Carolina. She was the daughter of William and Lydia Chamness Ward, also of Cabbin Creek in Rowan County.

Kinney Brothers. Jesse, William, Isaac, and Jefferson

William Kinney is last seen on the 1860 census for Carroll County. His estate is administered in August 1866 by his son, Jesse Kinney. His wife, Susannah is still alive and is a widow in the 1870 census for Carroll County. She is not seen again on census and is presumed to have died in that ten-year period.

William and Susannah Ward Kinney have the following children in North Carolina and Georgia: (1) Elizabeth Kinney, born 1809 and died 1866. She never married. (2) Anna, born 1812 in North Carolina; died 1898 in Carroll County, Georgia. She married Henry Pope in 1854. (3) William Lee Kinney Jr., born 1817 in North Carolina and died 1863, Civil War. He married Lucinda Haynes 1839 in Carroll County, Georgia. (4) Isaac Kinney, born 1818 in North Carolina and died 1899 in Carroll County. He married first Lureany Turner in 1842 in Carroll County. She was the daughter of Larkin Turner and Eleanor Driscoll. They had six children before she died. He then married second Martha Garst in 1858 in Carroll County, daughter of Christopher Garst and Sarah Coltharp. They had three children together. (5) Jesse Kinney, born 1822 in Habersham County, Georgia, and died 1912 in Carroll County. He married first Sarah Turner in 1844 in Carroll County, daughter of Larkin Turner and Eleanor Driscoll. He married second Mary Larkin Ward in 1891. (6) Jeremiah Kinney, born 1824 in Habersham County, Georgia; died 1864 in the Civil War. He married Nancy Jane McAllister in 1844 in Carroll County. Nancy Jane received a widow's pension from the Confederate Army. (7) Jefferson Kinney, born 1828 in Habersham County. Never married. Blacksmith by trade. (8) Sarah Kinney born 1831 in Carroll County. Died 1915. She married Moses A. McWhorter November 20, 1848. They had thirteen children (triplets Pollie, Mollie and Dollie born 1869).

There were many losses to this family in the Civil War. Susannah Kinney lost two sons: William Jr. to measles and Jeremiah died in battle at Resaca, Georgia. After the Civil War, William Jr.'s family migrates to Polk County, Georgia. Jefferson, Isaac, and Jesse stay in Carroll County. There is a tin photograph of brothers William, Isaac, Jesse, and Jefferson Kinney in the Civil War. *Submitted by: Cathy Moore Casper, 5335 Carbonton Road, Sanford, NC 27330*

742. Ellis Grover Kirby, M.D.

1885-1941

Ellis Grover Kirby was born and reared in Randolph County, Alabama. After graduating from Roanoke Academy, he farmed and taught school. He married Lena Pearl Tomlinson (1890-1939) and they had seven children: (1) Berma, born 1908, married L.D. Hamil; two children, Kirby Dow and Mary Ann. (2) Viola, born 1910, married Alvin O. Hallman; two children, Robert and William. (3) Horace, born 1911, married Etha Hanson; two children, Edwin and Donald. (4) Wilma, born 1915, married Howard Pringle; two children, Diane and Linda Sue. (5) Robert Ellis, 1917-1970, married Mary Francis Loftis; three children, Kay, Roberta, and Suzanne. (6) Harold Grant, born 1922, married Evelyn Norton; two children, Teresa and Ellis. (7) Kathleen "Kitty," born 1924, married Aubrey Kaylor.

Dr. and Mrs. Ellis Grover Kirby

Ellis Kirby and family located in Tyus, Georgia, after graduating in 1914 from Atlanta Medical College, later becoming part of Emory University. He practiced medicine nine years in Tyus and moved to Burwell for a year and then to Bowdon in 1923, where he practiced until his death in 1941. His practice started out in the horse and buggy era, making house calls all over Carroll County, Georgia, Randolph and Cleburne Counties, Alabama. He was extremely busy during the 1919 flu epidemic, working day and night. He and his daughter Viola (R.N.) went to Gainesville, Georgia, after the cyclone in 1936 to aid the injured people.

Children of Dr. and Mrs. Ellis Kirby

Dr. and Mrs. Kirby were active for many years in various organizations in the community. He was a member of the Carroll County Board of Education and served as chairman for fourteen years. During this time, consolidation of the many one and two teacher schools in the county occurred. Dr. Kirby was president of the Rural Superintendents and Board Members Association of Georgia during this time when the state had to pay the teachers in script because of lack of funds. He and other educational leaders made several trips to Washington, D.C. seeking additional funds for Georgia education.

Mrs. Kirby passed away in 1939, and Dr. Kirby passed away in 1941. They are buried in the Bowdon City Cemetery. *Submitted by: Kirby D. Hamil, 1289 N Highway 27, Roopville, GA 30170*

743. Lt. Col. Robert Ellis Kirby

1917-1970

Robert E. Kirby was reared in Bowdon, Georgia. He was the fifth child of Dr. and Mrs. E.G. Kirby. He attended West Georgia College and Aeronautical School in Jackson, Mississippi. He entered the Army Air Corp during World War II. He went to Sumter, South Carolina, for flight training and was trained as a B-24 pilot, later he was sent to Decatur, Alabama, for B-29 training. He was pilot of B-29 and was on his way to the Pacific when the war ended.

Lt. Col. Robert Ellis Kirby

One of his missions was to escort President Truman on his trip to meet with General MacArthur in the Pacific during the Korean Conflict. Later he was a pilot of B-36s in the Strategic Air Command and became a flight commander. He retired and lived in Mobile, Alabama, with his wife Mary Frances Loftis, and daughters Kay, Roberta, and Suzanne. He passed away in 1970 and is buried in Fort Barancus National Cemetery, Pensacola, Florida. *Submitted by: Kathleen Taylor, Carrollton, GA*

744. Ryan Philip Knott

My name is Ryan Philip Knott. I was born in Carrollton on January 27, 2000. I guess that makes me a new millennium child! I want to tell you a little bit about my family history. My dad, Philip Wilson Knott, was born October 31, 1969, in Carrollton to Wilson and Myra Knott. He attended Whitesburg School through the eighth grade and graduated from Central High School in 1987. He works at Georgia Power, Plant Wansley. My mom, Brynda Kay Clark Knott, was born April 39, 1971, in El Paso, Texas, to Ron and Caralyn Clark. She grew up in Florida, which was where she and daddy first met. She graduated from Milligan College in Johnson City, Tennessee, in 1992. My parents were married February 17, 1996, at First Christian Church in Carrollton. My mom worked there as office manager from December 1996 until I was born. She currently works part-time as marketing coordinator at The Stewart House Retirement Living. We live in Whitesburg and are members of First Christian Church in Carrollton.

Dad has one brother, David Joel, who was born July 30, 1971. Uncle David married Dana Denny on July 22, 1995. Their son, Kyle David, was born March 5, 1999. He is my only cousin. Mom has one brother, Ronald "Ronny" Paul Clark II, who was born January 6, 1974. He is married to Sharon and they live in Hampton, Georgia. She has one sister, Rochelle, who was born May 29, 1975. She is married to Joel Gibbons and they live in Indianapolis, Indiana.

The Knott and Weathington Families - April 30, 2000

My paternal grandfather, Wilson David Knott, was born June 13, 1941, in Whitesburg to Leonard David Knott (6/3/15-9/9/94) and Thelma Bishop Knott (7/4/19-2/2/94). He has an older brother, Donald. My great-grandfather was a textile worker and my great-grandmother was the manager of the Whitesburg School lunchroom until she retired. My great-great-grandfather, Henry Jackson Knott (2/12/1878-8/15/46) was the Chief of Police in Whitesburg. Most of the Knott descendants are buried in the cemetery at Ephesus Christian Church in Whitesburg. My paternal grandmother, Myra Diane Weathington Knott, was born July 1, 1943, in Columbus, Georgia, to Clifford L. Weathington (5/23/16-12/31/79) and Louise Carter Weathington (5/1/20). She has a younger brother, Danny. My grandfather was a member of the first graduating class from Central High School in 1960 and my grandmother graduated from Carrollton High School in 1961. They met in 1957 and were married July 2, 1961, at First Christian Church in Carrollton. My grandmother worked for C&S Bank in Newnan for sixteen years and is currently a travel agent for West Georgia Travel. My grandfather served in the Vietnam War from 1967-1968 as a sergeant in the U.S. Army. He retired from Georgia Power in 1999 after working there for thirty-six years. My uncle David and great-uncle Danny both work for Georgia Power also. Maybe I'll follow in their footsteps too.

My maternal grandfather, Ronald Paul Clark, was born March 8, 1946, in St. Louis Missouri to Ralph Clark (5/18/16-5/30/01) and Matty Williford Clark (12/18/16-2/6/98). He was the oldest of eight boys born to them in seven years. My maternal grandmother, Caralyn Bosworth Clark, was born July 14, 1947, in Webster City, Iowa, to Clair (4/24/08-11/6/71) and Cleo Pletcher Bosworth (12/28/13). She had two brothers and three sisters and they loved growing up on the farm.

Well that's about all the family history I know for now. I'm sure I'll learn more as I get older. Until then, I'll just spend my days being a little boy and making my own history! Pictured in the photograph (left to right) - Back row: Phil Knott, Danny Weathington, David Knott, Wilson Knott. Front row: Brynda Knott (holding Ryan), Myra Knott, Louise Weathington Phillips, Dana Knott (holding Kyle), Vicki Weathington. *Submitted by: Brynda Knott, 99 E. McIntosh Circle, Whitesburg, GA 30185*

745. Kytle History

The earliest Kytle history known to me is Singleton Kytle (1825-1888) who married Sallie Nearwood (1825-1904). They were both born in Habersham County of German ancestry who had possibly migrated from Savannah. One son, Singleton Calvin (1864-1922), married Annie Lee Perdue (1886-1944). They had Rayford Perdue (1892-1974), Emma Lee (1894-1984), and Laura (1900-) when they moved from a small house on Tanner Street to 309 Dixie Street. The third daughter, Annecal (1909-) was born there. This home still stands and is known as the Kytle-Aycock House.

Singleton Kytle was the proprietor of a furniture and undertaking business located on Adamson Square. The fine black gilt-trimmed hearse had full plate glassed sides in ornate molded frames and was pulled by a pair of horses blanketed in purple with gold fringe, an elegant last ride for many Carrolltonians.

In 1940 the funeral business was moved to 548 Newnan Street where it became Carrollton's first funeral home, Kytle-Aycock Funeral Home. Later, it was bought and still stands as Almon Funeral Home. Emma Lee Kytle had married Jack Aycock who then worked with his father-in-law in the furniture/undertaking business.

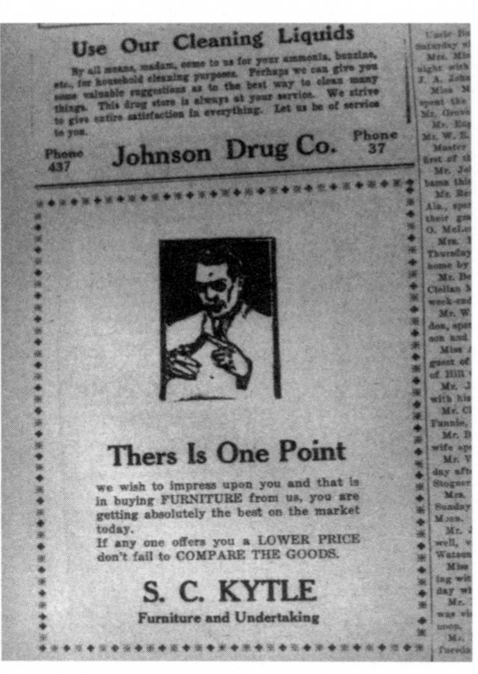

Advertisement from local newspaper, Carrollton, Georgia.

At Singleton's death, Jack continued in the business. The house on Dixie Street was transferred to Emma Lee Kytle Aycock and became a social center for music lovers. Emma Lee played her concert piano at home and taught many students there and at College Street School. She was the organist for several decades at Carrollton Presbyterian Church. The Jack Aycocks had three sons: Jack Jr., Edward, and Joseph. Rayford Perdue married Julia Sox, also of Carrollton, in 1913. Her parents were David Adam Sox and Arabella Bangle Sox. David Sox was a Lutheran minister and an inventor. He developed a folding ironing board as well as other useful articles. They had two sons: Rayford Perdue Jr. and Calvin. Laura Kytle married first Eric Folds of Carrollton, and second Homer Clyde Chestnutt, all of whom have lived away from Carrollton for years.

Of Jack and Emma Lee's children, Jack Jr., died in 1986 of illnesses contracted during World War II. Edward married twice, has four children, and eleven grandchildren. He now lives in Jefferson, North Carolina. Joseph married Mae Johnson and they have three children and live at Stone Mountain.

Rayford Perdue Jr. married twice and had two sons, Rayford III and James W. His second marriage was to Jean Harter Merkel who had two children, Dr. R. Lawrence Merkel Jr. and Kimberly M. Chen, and together they have six grandchildren. Ray and Jean returned to Carrollton after Ray's retirement from Reynolds Metals where he had been associated for forty-one years. Both were very active in local organizations and their church. In 1999 they returned to Richmond, Virginia, after fourteen years in Carrollton. Ray died in Richmond of a sudden heart attack on January 5, 2001. (Note: This article was submitted by Jean Kytle, shortly before her unexpected death in May of 2001.) *Submitted by: Jean Kytle, and edited from research done by Edward Aycock.*

746. Lambert Family

Martha Maude Chappell Robinson was always close to her Lambert cousins. The mother of Maude was Eldorado Chambers (2 March 1874-23 August 1914) who married Allen Dawson Chappell (25 December 1890-August 1924). (See the heading Martha Maude Chappell Robinson for more information on Chambers family tree.) Eldorado had brothers and sisters named Fannie E., William Elbert, Thomas Jordan, Benjamin Samuel, and Sallie Ruth. Sallie Ruth Chambers was born 3 May 1877 and died 13 May 1928. On 18 February 1895, she married Pleasant Eugene Lambert who was born 16 November 1875 and died 21 March 1926.

Their children were: (1) Harry Martin Lambert born 29 November 1895 at Grantville, Georgia, married Geneva Bass who was born 29 November 1895. (2) Samuel Chambers Lambert born 3 September 1897 married Lillian Hood born 1 January ?. (3) Frances Lucille Lambert born 6 September 1899 in Grantville married 15 August 1920 to Robert Oscar Ross Jr. born 13 February 1898 in Atlanta, died 13 April 1956 in Jacksonville, Florida. Lucille Lambert and Oscar Ross had five children: Frances Beulah born 12 September 1921 married Thomas Connell Curran in 1946 Jacksonville, Florida; Bobbie Lambert Ross born 15 November 1923 Winder, Georgia, married 7 February 1943 William Osborne Mims in Jacksonville; Patsy Lucille Ross born 27 December 1928 in Ft. Lauderdale, Florida, married 31 July 1948 Everett Bruce Wilsie born 29 May 1925; Betsy Lou Ross born 3 November 1926 died 2 April 1930 Ft. Lauderdale; and Rosemary Ross born 12 July 1930 in Ft. Lauderdale, married 21 December 1950 in Jacksonville, Frederick Myers Perkins Jr. born 7 October 1928 Tallahassee, Florida. (4) Ben Glenn Lambert born 14 June 1904 died 11 February 1959 married Gladys Benton born 16 October 1904 and died 4 May 1972. Ben and Gladys had one son Wallace Glenn Lambert born 26 July 1931 Newnan,

Lucille Lambert Ross

Georgia, married Katie Heck born 18 August 1938 in Miami, Florida. (5) Tommie Eugene Lambert born 9 March 1902 at Grantville married Ike Marvin Hudson born 2 October 1900 at Macon, Georgia. Tommie and Ike had one son Marvin Eugene Hudson born 5 August 1926 at Grantville and married Sue. (6) Pleas Eugene Lambert born 3 June 1906 in Moreland, Georgia, married Mary Eugenia Blalock born 15 November 1909 at Carrollton. (7) Jim Allen Lambert born ?, married Ruth Justice died 27 May 1945, killed in World War II and buried at Normandy, France. (8) Mattie Ruth Lambert born 6 December 1908 married Wilbur Thomas Jeter born 28 March 1908 and who died 25 May 1953; married second to J.B. Smith.

The children of Mattie Ruth Lambert and Dick Jeter are: (Note: two sets of twins) Lillian Ruth Jeter born 29 June 1930 died 3 June 1945 in Grantville; Mary Alice Jeter born 7 July 1933 La Grange, Georgia, married 19 May 1950 College Park, Georgia, to Francis Alvin Stallings; Martha Jean Jeter born 7 July 1933 in La Grange, married in Fair Oaks, California, to Albert B. Price; George Thomas Jeter born 5 January 1935 in La Grange, married Lila Karen Shuford; Wilbur Richard Jeter (called Dickey) born 22 July 1941 married Louise Childs in La Grange. He had a twin sister Sandra Sue Jeter born 22 July 1941 married in La Grange to Emmett L. Adams. (9) Sid Eugene Lambert born Grantville, Georgia, and married Bernice Alexander. Their children were Eugene and Ann. (10) Eleanor Maurice Lambert born 16 December 1917 Turin, Georgia, married Allen Thomas Newby born 8 October 1815 died April 1968 in Newnan. Their daughter Carolyn Elaine Newby born 9 June 1945 in Hattiesburg, Mississippi, married a Keeble. *Submitted by: Robin Calhoun, 515 Starpoint Road, Carrollton, GA 30116* and Research by: Lucille Lambert Ross.

747. George Risdem and Martha Arnold Lambert

George Risdem Lambert and his wife, Martha Arnold Lambert, moved their family to Carroll County before the 1850 census. George was born in 1820 in Putnam County, Georgia. Martha was born in 1819 in South Carolina. They lived in a log cabin just east of Holly Springs and south of Reid's Mountain.

George's parents, William Lambert and Mary (Polly) Parker Lambert, moved to Carroll County before the 1850 census as well, and they lived near Banning. William died in 1858. Listed in his assets were some oxen, a horse, and some personal items. He served in the Putnam County Militia during the War of 1812; subsequently, he petitioned and received eighty acres in Carroll County. Polly received eight dollars a month beginning in September 1872 under Widow's Pension number 6418.

George Risdem Lambert's family history parallels the family histories of many other Georgia families who migrated into the state from North Carolina. An article in the state archives suggests two Lambert men, John and James, were the two family heads from whence all the other Lamberts in the state derived. Beginning with just a few Lamberts, mostly relatives, moving into Wilkes County, Georgia, after the Revolutionary War, their number increased exponentially as they moved across the piedmont of the state during the 1800s. After Wilkes, Putnam, and a few other counties, William and Polly showed up on the 1840 Henry County census. Then, Carroll County seems to be the end of the westward migration for some of them, and today, many of their descendants still live in West Georgia and East Alabama.

Martha Arnold Lambert died around 1860 and George Risdem Lambert remarried in October of 1862. Rhoda Akin Reaves, his new wife, had recently lost her husband, Asa, who died in the Confederate Army in Mississippi. He served in Company H of the 41st Georgia Regiment of Carroll County. Similarly, George and Martha's son, William Spurlock Lambert, served in the same regiment, but he was in Company G.

George and Rhoda's marriage joined her two children with George's nine, but all of George's may not have still been alive. With close to a dozen children, George and Rhoda produced six boys of their own. George fathered children for almost forty years. His last one, Harrison, was born in 1878, about the time George died.

Maggie, age 16 and Harrison Lambert, age 21. Carrallton 11-18-1899.

One of George and Martha's sons mentioned earlier, William Spurlock Lambert, had an interesting life from a genealogist's point of view. He served in the Confederate Army in Mississippi, Tennessee, Kentucky, and Georgia (the Battle of Atlanta). After the war he lived for some indeterminate length of time, then he was buried in a little family graveyard, but it's not his family. The cemetery is unmarked and by the size of the trees around the tombstones, it hasn't been tended for some while. The Daughters of the Confederacy found it at some point because he has a veteran's marker. He is buried off Highway 166 near Vine Church south of Interstate 20 in Douglas County.

His burial away from other family members could be unimportant. He returned home from the Civil War and his world had certainly changed. Whether it impacted him much or not, his mother was dead and his father had remarried and started producing children again.

George, like his father, is buried somewhere nearby off Post Road between I-20 and Fairplay. One account of George states he and Mr. Reid of Reid's Mountain severely beat one of the outlaw "Pony Boys."

The "Pony Boys," also called the "Pony Club," was a gang on the frontier who harassed and robbed Cherokees, Creeks, and whites. Their hangout was the original settlement of Sandtown where the Fulton Industrial Complex is today near Atlanta, according to Marion Hemperly in his 1991 article in *The North Georgia Journal*. Later, the Pony Boys probably moved their base of operation to Carroll County.

Another account of George, he is reported to have traded land he owned near today's Lenox Square and Peachtree Creek in Atlanta for the property near Holly Springs. *Submitted by: Peggy Lambert Moody, 201 Stoney Point Cove, Carrollton, GA 30116 and Written by: Clint Lambert.*

Sources: Census records, Lambert Family files at Georgia State Archives, bounty land grant records, pension records, probate records.

748. George Risdon Lambert

George Risdon Lambert was born in Putnam County in 1820 the son of William Earnest Lambert and Mary Parker. In 1840 he married Martha Arnold who was born in 1819 in South Carolina. By 1850 they had moved to Carroll County just outside what was later Banning Mills. Their children were Susan (buried at New Hope Church in Villa Rica), Mary (Polly) A., William Sperlock, Jeanimia Abigail (buried at Macedonia Church in Sand Hill), Isaac M. (died before 1860), George H. (died before 1860), Sarah G.H., Randolph Arnold (married Melinda Phillips in 1872 in Carroll County), and Caleb Buchanan (married Thersay Jane Williams in 1875 in Douglas County that was part of Carroll County at that time).

George R. Lambert owned land between Peachtree Creek and Peachtree Road and land near Fairburn in Fulton County. He also owned land in Coweta County near Sardis Church. He traded the land near Sardis Church to a Methodist preacher for land near Holly Springs Church and by 1860 the family had moved into a log house on land that during the 1930s and 1940s was called Lovvorn's Farm.

William S. Lambert joined the 41st Georgia Infantry Regiment along with his cousins Seth Lambert and William P. Lambert. William S. Lambert is buried in Douglas County (that was Carroll County) near Little Vine Church in the Reynolds-Robinson family cemetery.

Randolph Arnold Lambert and Melinda C. Phillips Lambert's children were Enoch P., Martha E., Charles E., Effie L., and Myrtle. Randolph was the only known red headed member of the family.

Caleb and Thersay Lambert lived in the Villa Rica and Fairplay area except for a time when they lived in Alabama in about 1881. Their children were Lester Shields, Leo Meredith, Minnie Ola (born in Alabama 1881 and married John Craton), Philip Arnold (married Lucy Merrell), Claudia Oxana (married William Boyd), Maude Octavia (buried at New Hope Church), Albert Valentine (married Minnie Hembree), Reubin

Caleb and Thersay Jane Lambert's family and helpers chopping cotton.

Lester Lambert (son of Caleb) lying down in cane.

Oscar (married Minnie Lee), and Henry Stephen (married Era E. Crawford and is buried at New Hope Church).

Henry Stephen and Era E. Lambert are the parents of Carl D. Lambert who now lives across the road from Abilene Baptist Church. Minnie Walls, the daughter of Philip Arnold Lambert has a collection of family pictures including the one of the Caleb Lambert family chopping cotton.

By 1862 Martha Arnold Lambert had died and George R. Lambert married Rhoda E. Akin Reeves. Rhoda's husband Asa Reeves had died in 1862 in Mississippi in the Confederate Army. Rhoda had two children, John W. Reeves and Elizabeth P. Jane Reeves. George R. and Rhoda Lambert had the following children (all boys): Joseph Henry T. (married Amanda Dingler), Isham James (married Amanda Dingler Lambert, Henry's widow), Ezikiel Thomas (wife Nancy), Jasper U.G. (wife Nanny), Oscar Franklin (married Elizabeth Jane Pritchard), and Harrison N. (wife Maggie H.).

Isham died in 1894 and his brother Henry married his widow Amanda. Henry was the tax collector for Haralson County. Oscar operated a general store (Presnell-Lambert) with his brother-in-law, Napoleon Presnell, and was the tax collector for Carroll County about 1900. Also he was a Baptist minister and was the postmaster of Bowdon Junction until his death in 1929. Tom was a jeweler and along with Henry and Oscar had arthritis (called rheumatism). Harrison was a farmer and lived near Talapoosa.

See related article William Earnest Lambert.

Submitted by: Carl Lambert

Sources: Carl Lambert, Wallace T. Lambert, and Minnie Walls

749. Rev. Lester Phillip Lambert

Lester Phillip Lambert was the son of Oscar Franklin Lambert and Elizabeth Jane Pritchard. He was born in 1902 in the John Stephen Earnest log house located in what is now Bowdon Junction. The log house is now owned by his son Wallace. Lester had sisters Ruth, Stella, Bertha and Betsie, and brothers Hershell and Lewin. Lester attended school at Bowdon Junction and high school at Mt. Zion. In 1910 the Bowdon Railroad was completed and Bowdon Junction was founded. His father, Oscar Lambert, became postmaster and ran a general store Presnell-Lambert. Oscar and Elizabeth built the house where Mrs. Carl Albright now lives. While they were building the house, they moved back into the log house where Lester was born.

Lester married Verdie Wallace and he became an ordained minister, farmed, and carried mail on a rural route in a mule and buggy. Their house burned and they lost everything and moved into the Earnest log house. Lester and Verdie had married very young and they were determined to show friends and neighbors they could make it on their own and even though Lester's father owned a general store they had never taken any store-bought food without paying. At one point they were without any food and had decided that they had to ask Oscar and Elizabeth for some flour and salt. While walking up the railroad from the log house to the general store, Verdie found 25 cents on the railroad tracks and that was enough to buy the food they needed.

Rev. Lester Phillip Lambert (1902-1979)

In 1929 Oscar died and Lester and Verdie moved into the back of the general store and Lester took the test to become postmaster and made the highest score. He was postmaster for forty-seven years.

When he became a minister it was during a time when a preacher was judged by the volume of his voice. Lester had a soft voice and practiced preaching by standing on a tree stump in the middle of the woods preaching to the trees. He developed a voice that could be heard in the parking lot of the church. It was also a time that preachers were expected to preach as if their words came directly from God and therefore no preparation or notes. Lester, however, spent all week preparing for his Sunday sermon. He had a loose leaf Bible and he would place his sermon outline in the Bible at the appropriate place and the congregation could think he was reading from the Bible.

Lester and Verdie, along with Oscar and Elizabeth and others from Pleasant View Church, formed Harmony Church. Lester pastored several churches including Pleasant Grove (twice), Pleasant View, Abilene Shady Grove, Providence and Whitesburg in Carroll County along with Franklin, Hogansville, Grantville, and Riverdale. Once he pastored five churches at the same time. One each Sunday and one that had services on Sunday afternoon.

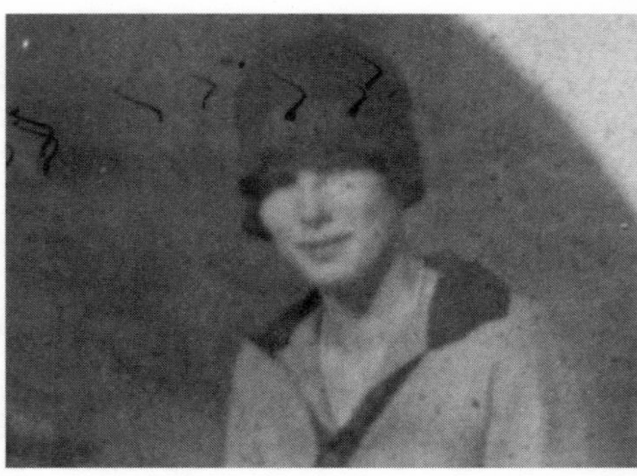

Verdie Wallace Lambert (1901-1987)

Lester married couples from all over West Georgia. Verdie kept the living room ready and people showed up at all hours to get married. Lester had only one rule, that he would not marry anyone who had been drinking. He helped people write letters and fill out forms and became an income tax return preparer.

When the telephone came to Bowdon Junction, not all people could get one. When anyone needed to be contacted, they called Lester during the day or in the middle of the night and he went to carry the message without pay. He considered it part of his responsibility as postmaster.

Lester founded a Boy Scout troop in Bowdon Junction and Mt. Zion. He organized baseball teams and with the help of Troy Holcombe, the County Agent, formed a 4-H boys rifle team.

Submitted by: Lynn Greene, Mink Hollow Drive, Carrollton, GA

Sources: Wallace T. Lambert

750. William E. Lambert in Carroll County

William Earnest Lambert was the son of George Lambert (a Revolutionary War veteran). William was a veteran of the War of 1812. William married Mary (Polly) Parker in 1812 in Putnam County, Georgia. After a couple of moves and as many as twelve children, William and Mary were in Carroll County by 1850. They were living in the same area of the county as some of their children near Whitesburg. One of their sons, George R., was one of the first farmers listed in the census of 1850 after the listing of the textile employees of the mill later named Banning Mills.

William died in 1858 without having a will. In court records the family contended that the court-appointed administrator had taken money due Mary, his widow. His assets were listed as a set of oxen, a horse, two milk cows, a wagon, a dressing table, one lot of land valued at $750 and a lot of books valued at $5.

Some of the children of William and Mary Lambert are Seth Harris, George Risdon, Jacob Parker, James M., Joseph E., and Elisha T. Seth Harris Lambert (named for Mary's twin sister's husband Seth Hearn), lived in the Cross Plains area. His son Seth Hampton Lambert served in the 41st Georgia Regiment, and married the girl next door to James M. Lambert; then moved to Center, Alabama, after the Civil War.

George R. Lambert moved to what is now Bowdon Junction. He and his wife Martha Arnold Lambert in 1850 had Susan, Mary Abigail, William Spurlock, J.M. and George H. By 1860, J.M. and George H. had apparently died and they had Sarah, Randolph and Caleb Buchanan (Buck). In 1861 Martha died.

William S. joined the 41st Georgia Infantry Regiment. In that regiment was Asa Reeves. Asa died and his widow Rhoda Akin Reeves came to live with her brother's wife, Sarah Akin. Isom Akin was away in the Confederate Army. George R. Lambert and Rhoda Akin Reeves were married and had Thomas, Henry, Harrison, Jasper and Oscar.

Sons of George R. Lambert and Rhoda Akin Reeves Lambert

Oscar Franklin Lambert married Elizabeth Jane Pritchard and was the Carroll County tax collector around 1900 and was postmaster at Bowdon Junction until his death in 1929. His son Lester was a Baptist minister who served several churches in the county and was postmaster for forty-seven years at Bowdon Junction.

William Spurlock Lambert (named after his great-grandmother who was always listed as Widow Spurlock) the son of George R. Lambert was in the 41st Georgia Regiment. He fought during the entire war and was so disappointed at the South losing that he became a hermit and never married. He is buried in a private cemetery near Little Vine Church at the Carroll County and Douglas County line.

Jacob Parker Lambert left for Texas in a dispute with the rest of the family over the direction the church which they were attending (probably Consolation) should take. His descendants moved to California and one (Randy Lambert) writes a Lambert family newsletter.

James M. Lambert lived along Snake Creek near Cross Plains. During the Civil War his son William P. Lambert was killed. Correspondence about his death was mailed to James M. Lambert at Chanceville post office in Carroll County.

Elisha T. Lambert lived near Bowdon and was in Company F of Cobb's Legion. He died in Yorktown, Virginia, in 1861. He was the great-grandfather of Hugh Lee Lambert, sheriff of Carroll County for several years.

Joseph E. Lambert married Jane Swann (who lived next door to James M. Lambert) in Carroll County in 1850. Both Joseph E. Lambert and James M. Lambert were in the 10th Georgia Calvary Regiment of Georgia State Guards during the Civil War. *Submitted by: Wallace T. Lambert*

751. Lambert – Douglas Family

Curtis Newton Lambert, son of John G. Lambert (1885-1962) and Willie Ophelia Robinson Lambert (1887-1964) was born 7-11-1911 and died 3-22-1957. He married Sarah Josephine Douglas, daughter of Charles Morrow Douglas (1886-1954) and Clara Irene Jennings Douglas (1894-1932). They were married 6-27-1936 at the home of Rev. Charles L. Matthews of Clem with Rev. Matthews performing the ceremony. Sarah was born 4-9-1914 and died 12-22-1990. Curtis and Sarah had three children: Douglas Newton Lambert died during childbirth on 12-28-1937, Martha Sue Lambert born 9-17-1938, and Sarah Jane Lambert born 7-13-1942.

Curtis attended Maple Street School until his parents moved to Whooping Creek Road, Carrollton. As a young man he became an automobile mechanic and body repairman. He was employed by Drake Motor Company (Ford) on Alabama Street and Morrow Motor Company (Buick) on Rome Street. At the time of his death he was self-employed at Lambert-Bagwell Garage on South Cliff Street, Carrollton. He received much pleasure in fishing and obtaining a wrecked vehicle and restoring it to like-new condition.

Sarah attended Harris High (near the current Carroll County Sales Barn) in Carrollton. Her mother died after giving birth to a daughter, Wyolene Douglas, 9-1-1932. As the oldest daughter in her family, she quit school to help her father care for a new baby and the other six children until she and Curtis married.

Curtis and Sarah resided with his parents until 1943 when they purchased a home on Reese Street, Carrollton. They joined Tabernacle Baptist Church and were baptized by Rev. John Tippett. They are buried in the Carrollton City Cemetery.

In 1961 Sarah opened Toddler's Corner Nursery in a building behind her Reese Street home. Because of her love for children, her business quickly grew and she had to add onto her building twice. She added a five year old kindergarten in 1970. At the time of her retirement in 1974, 125 children were enrolled in her facility.

Sarah purchased a home at 404 Stewart Street in Carrollton in 1971. She spent many enjoyable hours working in her garden and flowerbeds. Sarah truly had a "green thumb" as evidenced by the beauty she created in her yard for others to enjoy.

Curtis, Sarah, Martha Sue and Jane Lambert

On May 10, 1979, Sarah Lambert married Maurice Foster Burns, a former classmate who had lost his wife. Foster died 5-2-1989 and is buried beside Sarah in the Carrollton City Cemetery. Foster was a loving husband and grandpa to the family. Sarah and Foster enjoyed spending time with their friends playing card games such as Rook and Uno, having "get togethers," and taking long rides together to see the countryside.

Martha Sue Lambert married Bobby Lee Smith 6-4-1961. They have two children Beverly Jane Smith (9-27-1966) and Laura Lee Smith (10-6-1972). Sarah Jane Lambert married Mack Raymond Johnson 11-19-1961. They have two children Mark Newton Johnson (10-16-1962) and Todd Raymond Johnson (4-6-1968). Martha Sue and Jane feel blessed to have had such loving, caring parents and grandparents who lived and taught them Christian values. *Submitted by: Beverly J. Webb, 445 Ingram Road, Carrollton, GA 30117*

752. Lambert – Robinson Family

John G. Lambert, son of William Blakely Lambert (1846-1924) and Lucy Ann Jones Lambert (1848-1905), was born 2-20-1885 in Carrollton and died 2-25-1962. He was married to Willie Ophelia Robinson 6-8-1903 in Carrollton by Squire Norman. She was the daughter of Judge William Robinson (3-31-1860/4-22-1926) and Mary Scroggins Robinson (2-24-1866/11-17-1959). Willie Ophelia Robinson was born in Waco, Haralson County, Georgia 5-1-1887 and died 1-3-1964.

John Lambert joined West View Baptist Church, Carrollton, in 1917 and was baptized by Brother Hiram Boatright. He was a member of Mt. Pleasant Baptist Church, Clem, Georgia at the time of his death. Ophelia Lambert joined Mt. Pleasant Baptist Church in 1912 and was baptized by Brother John Stallings. Judge William Robinson, Mary S. Robinson, and John and Ophelia Lambert are buried in the Mt. Pleasant Baptist Church Cemetery.

John Lambert's siblings were Emma D. Lambert (married James L. Spence), William Blakely Lambert II (married Emma Jones), Lula M. Lambert (married Leon Stamps), Sally C. Lambert (married W.D. Pike), Jennie Lambert (married Tom Hendrix), Major W. Lambert (married Nannie Nicholson) and Annie E. Lambert.

Curtis, Sarah, Martha Sue, John, Jane, and Ophelia Lambert

Ophelia Robinson Lambert's siblings were Maud Robinson (married Tom Phillips), Henry Robinson (married Essie Hull), Eula Robinson (married William Edmondson), Eva Robinson (married Earl Helton and later Roy Haygood), Britt Robinson (married Myrtie Burnett), Jack Robinson (married Ruth Mote), Hoke Robinson (married Eva Taylor), Cora Robinson (married Jimmie Lee Shadinger), Annie Shadinger (married Erma Shadinger).

John and Ophelia Lambert had two children. Curtis Newton Lambert was born 7-11-1911 and died 3-22-1957 due to a cerebral hemorrhage. Henry Hamilton Lambert was born 12-23-1914 and died 11-13-1917 due to scarlet fever. John and Ophelia Lambert lived on Foster Street, Carrollton, and worked at Mandeville Mills. In 1925 they moved to the "country" when they purchased a farm on Whooping Creek Road, Carrollton. They grew cotton and later beef cattle. Every summer they had a large garden and enjoyed sharing their vegetables and fruits with their families, neighbors, and friends. They were faithful Christians who shared their faith and beliefs with all.

Upon reaching adulthood, Curtis Lambert became an automobile mechanic and automobile body repairman. He and Sarah J. Douglas were united in marriage on 6-27-1936 by Rev. Charles L. Matthews in Clem.

Sarah, daughter of Charles Morrow Douglas and Clara Irene Jennings Douglas, was born 4-9-1914 and died in her sleep 12-22-90. She was a homemaker while her children were young. She enjoyed making all their clothes, preserving the many vegetables grown in their garden, and growing beautiful flowers.

They had three children Douglas Newton Lambert who died during childbirth on 12-28-1937, Martha Sue Lambert born 9-17-1938 (married Bobby Lee Smith), and Sarah Jane Lambert born 7-13-1942 (married Mack Raymond Johnson). *Submitted by: Martha Sue Smith, 368 New Hope Church Road, Carrollton, GA 30117.*

753. The E.B. Lane Family

In Toccoa, Georgia, on March 8, 1917, Everage Brawner (E.B.) Lane entered this world, the eldest of two sons born to William Charles and Maude Ellen Segers Lane . His younger brother was Charles Earnest. Everage enjoyed normal boyhood activities and academics until his eighth grade school year. It was at this time that his father passed away. Being the oldest son, the responsibility of providing for his mother and younger brother became his, a task he admirably shouldered.

In nearby Bowman, Georgia, lived a striking young lady named Morris Evelyn Bryant, the daughter of Morrison and Essie Seigler Floyd Bryant. Everage and Evelyn met and were married March 8, 1941. On December 21, 1942, this union was blessed with the birth of a son, Mahlon Brawner. Almost two years later, on October 24, 1944, the family was again blessed with the arrival of a beautiful baby daughter, Linda Gayle.

After serving his country as part of the naval operations in the Pacific during World War II, Everage returned to his family in Bowman. At this time, he became affiliated with the J.R. Watkins Company. He was assigned a route in the West Georgia area and moved his family to Carroll County, never to leave. He and Evelyn purchased a small farm north of Bowdon on Highway 100, at the Turkey Creek Bridge. They participated in community activities and worshipped at Indian Creek Baptist Church. The years rapidly passed, the children grew, and Evelyn became employed by LaMar Manufacturing Company. Everage found employment with Standard Oil of Bremen until retirement. Everage went home to be with our Lord on October 22, 1977. Evelyn joined him October 13, 1999. Both are buried at Indian Creek Baptist Church.

Everage and Evelyn Lane

In 1960, upon graduation from Bowdon High School, Mahlon married Letha Oleria Acree, daughter of Henry Delvous and Eunice Merrell Acree of the Clem community, east of Carrollton. Now residing in Carrollton, they have one son Mahlon Anthony (Tony) and two daughters Sandra Merrell (Sandy) and Marnie Ann.

In 1980 Tony married Mary Ellen Cantrell. To this union was born one son, Kevin Chason, and one daughter, Kristy Suellyn. In 1991 Tony married Lanita Javon Gilman of Roopville. Sandra married Fredrick Pulse Rodes of Screven County in 1991. They have been blessed with two daughters, Sarah Elizabeth and Laura Ashton. Marnie and Shanon Dwayne Stephens of Heard County were united in marriage in 1993. Their special blessing has been a daughter, Savannah Shea.

Upon graduating from Bowdon High School, Gayle completed her education at Berry College, where she met and in March 1966 married Alex Durham Comegys of Fort Meade, Florida. Residing in Vidalia, Georgia, they have one daughter, Kimberly Robyn and one son, Russell Durham.

In 1994 Robyn married Frankie Parson of Vidalia. They were especially blessed with twin daughters, Kailee Alexis and Cassidy Lane. After graduating from the University of Georgia, Russ, an inspiring actor, makes his home in Atlanta. We've only shared in the last fifty years of Carroll County's history but we've made lots of good friends and memories. *Submitted by: Mahlon B. Lane, 655 Hilltop Road, Roopville, GA 30170*

754. Langston

Dilmus Belton Langston was born April 24, 1865, in Banks County, Georgia, and died February 13, 1948, in Carroll County, Georgia. He was the son of James A. Langston and Jane A. Ragsdale of Banks County. On December 8, 1889, in Gwinnett County, Georiga, he married Nancy M. Forrester who was the daughter of Thomas A. Forrester and Rebecca Wilson. Nancy was born December 11, 1870, in Gwinnett County and died May 12, 1943, in Carroll County. Dilmus and Nancy are both buried in the Powell Chapel United Methodist Church Cemetery in Carroll County.

Their children were all born in Carroll County, and are buried in the Powell Chapel Church Cemetery. Their names were:

Lula Mae Langston, born May 13, 1893, died October 23, 1980, was married to Arthur E. Gilland on November 8, 1919. Their children were Robert Sharon Gilland who married Maizie Veretha Sauls, Nan Gilland who married Carl Fields, and Frances Belle Gilland who married William Floyd Harper.

Charles W. Langston, born in July 1895, died November 30, 1930, in an automobile accident. He and his wife, Thelma Kate, had one daughter, Lavenda, who was born in 1919.

Myrtie L. Langston, born November 26, 1897, died September 11, 1968, and married Homer Candler Hembree on August 25, 1918. Their children were Jesse Astor Hembree who was declared missing in action on December 22, 1943, during World War II, Vivian Louise Hembree who married Warren K. Cruse, and Ernest Edwin Hembree who married Barbara Close.

Mary Flurnoy Langston, born November 6, 1899, died May 3, 1983, and married to Elbert Clinton Boyd on October 26, 1919. Their children were Virlyn Alexander Boyd who married Janette Virginia Lyle, Henry Grady Boyd who married Gladys Ruth Aderhold, and Charles Clarence Boyd who married Georgie Mae Holloman.

Velma Vidue Langston, born November 18, 1901, died January 3, 1989, and married Charles Lewis Williams on December 22, 1923. Their children were Charles Merritt Williams who married Madeline Saylors and James Neal Williams who married Sarah Doris Bivins.

Clara Belle Langston, born October 20, 1903, died October 29, 1968, and married to Levin Arthur Richardson on February 28, 1926. Their children were James Lamar Richardson who married Bertha Allene Hunton and Manuel Erwin Richardson who married Ruth Yvonne Fernander.

The Langston family had a very nice home in the Flat Rock Community and were very active in the Powell Chapel United Methodist Church. *Submitted by: Georgie Holloman Boyd, 93 Flat Rock Road, Villa Rica, GA 30180*

Sources: Research of census, marriage and cemetery records by Erlene C. Boyd

755. Lassetter

John Lassetter was born in 1694 and died in 1759. He married Rebecca in 1719 in Virginia. He had five children. His fifth son was Tobias, born in 1728, died in 1804, married Pleasent Sally. He was born in Nash County, North Carolina. They had six children. He was a Revolutionary War soldier, so he received a bounty grant of 287½ acres in Georgia for his service. He moved to Georgia some time after 1790 and died in Green County in 1801. His oldest son was Benjamin.

Benjamin was born in North Carolina in 1778. We don't know the exact date he came to Georgia. He married Elizabeth Hill in 1801 in Green County, Georgia. He was listed in the 1820 census in Gwinnett County. We do not know when he came to Campbell County (now Carroll County) but he was here in the 1830 census.

Benjamin and Elizabeth had twelve children. He built a large log house overlooking the Chattahoochee River. The family cemetery is near the house. Benjamin was a veteran of the War of 1812. He died August 23, 1869. He is not buried in the family cemetery with his wife. He died at his son William's home (with his second wife Duiene Embry) in 1854. So far as we know, he was buried at St. Paul's Methodist Church nearby. His first wife died in 1852. Benjamin's second child was Mariah, born 1805 and died 1893. She married Wesley Camp in 1823. He had settled land just up the river from Benjamin. Wesley came and settled this land with his father, Andrew, before Benjamin came here. Wesley and Mariah had several children. Their youngest was Walter who married Mary Jane Barron, daughter of Oliver Gaines and Clementine Brown Barron.

The rest of this history is in the article I wrote about the Camps. (See related Camp Family article.) *Submitted by: Thelma Pate, 199 Old Five Notch Road, Whitesburg, GA 30185*

756. Lassetter Family 1815-1914

Part 1

Henry Z. Lassetter was born in 1815 and died in 1856. The Family Bible lists Henry Z. Lassetter 1815-1856. His second wife was Margaret Stephens, June 26, 1848. Their children were Benjamin F., William Jackson (See below), Martha A., and Margaret S. Lassetter who married Cordial Z. Wellborn in 1867, buried at Mt. Zion Baptist Church Cemetery, Highway 5, Douglas County, Georgia.

In the Douglas County, Georgia, genealogy records we found this in *The Unrelated Lassetters,* Appendix A, page 15:

> Henry Z. Lassetter, born 1815-1856 is #196 on the 1850 Census of Carroll County: Henry Z. aged 35; Margaret 22; John H. 14; James 11; Mary I. 15; Elizabeth 7; Nancy 4. Henry married Margaret Stephens, June 26, 1848, Carroll County, apparently his 2nd wife. In 1850 Henry is shown living adjacent to James H. Lassetter, son of Benjamin, and nearby Benjamin's son William C.
>
> The 1860 census of Carroll, 5th district, shows Henry's widow as #33: M.S. (Margaret Stephens) Lassetter aged 33, weaver and spinner; Benjamin F. 9; William J. 6; Martha A. 4; again, Benjamin's son William lived nearby.
>
> In 1867 in Campbell County, widow Margaret Lassetter married C.Z. Wellborn. In 1880 she lived in the Fairplay district of Douglas County, adjacent to her son William J. Lassetter. Margaret S. Wellborn, 31 August 1824-8 February 1901 is buried at Mt. Zion Church, Douglas County, adjacent daughter Mattie L., born 27 April 1856, and her husband James S. Brown and Margaret's son William J. Lassetter, 1853-1914, wife Nancy J. 1853-1920."

There is some confusion (understandably so), regarding the two sets of Lassetters. I hope I can explain it. James H. Holland had a son, Lindsey Holland. Lindsey married an Elizabeth Laciter or Lasiter. They had a daughter, Nancy Jerusha Holland. Nancy married William J. Lassetter.

This name Lassetter is always spelled the same — double s, and double t — in his genealogy. Neither William J. Lassetter nor his father Henry Z. is found in names descended from the other Lasiter family. (See Tobias, Benjamin and Elizabeth Laciter/Lasiter in another article.) So, they are called "unrelated Lassetters." We have documented some interesting history from both sides. The Carden and Lassetter families are kin to both sides, because of Nancy Jerusha. Again, her mother was a Lasiter/Laciter and then she married a Lassetter, but there are two sets of families here. (See Holland/Lassetter Carden series in this book.)

William Jackson Lassetter and Nancy Jerusha Holland's Family

William J. Lassetter was born March 2, 1853, and died April 11, 1914 in Carroll County. He married Nancy Jerusha Holland on November 13, 1873. Nancy J. was born to Lindsey and Elizabeth Laciter Holland in 1853, and she died in 1920 in Carroll County. They are both buried in the Mt. Zion Baptist Church Cemetery, Highway 5, Douglas County, Georgia. (See related article on The Holland Family, James, and Lindsey Holland.)

William J. Lassetter and Nancy Jerusha Holland Lassetter

Mrs. Lillie Hilley, who knew this family, said, "William J. and Nancy J. were nicknamed Billy and Nannie." From what I can find, they lived in and around the Whitesburg community most, if not all, of their married lives. They had a wonderful family of nine children; my grandmother, Mollie Lassetter Carden, was one of their five daughters.

We Carden cousins (Sam and Mollie's grandchildren) knew most of these great-aunts and uncles and enjoyed being with them at our family reunions. Each exhibited a strong faith in and love for God. They produced two ministers, Wesley and Burnett, and all seemed poetic. William J. "Billy" and Nancy Jerusha "Nannie" Lassetter's children were: (1) Lindsey Lassetter married Lillie Todd October 14, 1906, (six children). (2) Joseph Lassetter married Hattie Carter December 16, 1906, (four children). (See article on Joe's family by Carole A. Lassetter Harper, granddaughter.) (3) Wesley Lassetter married Eula Norred, (five children). (4) Burnett Lassetter married Lillie Miller, (five children). (See Burnett Lassetter article.) (5) Lizzie Lassetter first marriage (Tucker Brooks, ten children), second marriage (Will Treadwell, one son). (6) Mary E. "Mollie" Lassetter, (Sam Carden, nine children). (See Carden Family Parts 1-14). (7) Mattie Lassetter (Carl Hilley, one son, Frank Hilley) Anniston, Alabama. (8) Hattie Lassetter (Perry Richards, twelve children; three died young; one killed in World War II, his body never found; and another son died in his forties with heart attack. Lived in Whitesburg.) (9) Rebecca "Becky" Lassetter (Grady Kite, four children).

William J. and Nancy J. Lassetter's children

The family photograph of William J. and Nancy J. Lassetter's children shows (standing) Lindsey, Joe, Wesley and Burnett. Seated are Lizzie, Mollie, Mattie, Hattie and Becky.

Their ninth and last child, Mollie Lassetter Carden, who died in 1926 at age forty-seven, left her little daughter Dorothy (my mother) a poem written in a very shaky hand. Mother would take it out lovingly through the years, read it, wipe a few tears, read it to us, and place it back in its keeping place. It is yellow with age and fragile now, but I think it is worth preserving in this history. It has a clear meaning — we need to be prepared and watchful for the coming of our Lord. His coming for us can be when we are young, in the prime of life, or in our golden years.

Poetry left to Daughter Dorothy Carden, age 11
By her mother
Mary E. "Mollie" Lassetter Carden

When the morn of life is beaming
And our hearts are full of joy
And we long for some endeavor
Which shall all our powers employ
When tis sweet to live with Dear Ones
Round about us in our homes
We shall watch as He commanded
For perhaps our Lord will come.

When our sun has reached the zenith
Of its glory and its power
And the fruits of toil are ripening
From the early bud and flower
When we stand at life's bright noon tide
Ere decline has begun
We should watch as He commanded
For perhaps our Lord will come.

If we watch for His appearing
We shall never watch in vain
For He promised His Disciples
He would surely come again
Though our eyes may not behold Him
Coming with the Angels throng
In our hearts He is begotten
While we watch in Prayer and Song.

If His coming be at morning, at the
Noon tide or at night,
May He find His children watching
In the thickest of the fight
With our faces toward Zion
Let us watch and labor on
Never doubting or discouraged
Knowing that our Lord will come.

Submitted by: Hugh and Jeff Boyd, Douglasville, GA, and Written by: Nancy Anne Willis Howell, 9049 Allison Court, Douglasville, GA 30134

757. Lassetter Family
Part 2
Burnett Lassetter and Lillie Miller

Burnett S. Lassetter was born November 9, 1890, and died July 4, 1972. He married Lillie Miller on November 19, 1911. Lillie was born on September 4, 1892, and died September 13, 1951. Their children were Millard, Clarence Jackson, Mattie Lee, Willie Mae, and James Albert who lived only three days.

Uncle Burnett, Aunt Lillie and their children (when young) always came to our Carden reunions. When I think of him, I still remember how he and mother loved looking at the scriptures. He knew the Bible! He also repaired our old "striking clock," many times.

The *Douglas County Sentinel* did a great story on Uncle Burnett. The headline reads:

'Preacher' Lassetter, Carroll's Bible Quoting Expert on Clocks.
By Hanna Ledford.

A retired farmer, Mr. Lassetter is a native of Douglas County but has lived in Carrollton since 1914. He recalls that his clock repairing developed after he purchased a new clock that stopped every night around midnight. Securing pliers and a screwdriver, he took the clock apart and carefully studied every tiny mechanism ... the inquisitive preacher thus became exposed to his only lesson in clock repair. He had that peculiar clock running "like nobody's business" and "was soon recognized as the only repairer of old clocks in the area." Many jewelers, who utilized his work, said the preacher knows more about clocks than they learned in college.

Remembers Scripture - Mr. Lassetter's clock skill isn't the only attribute for which he is appreciated. The resourceful preacher can be counted on to instantly locate scripture. Many ministers, Sunday School teachers, and lay readers are grateful to the preacher for his immediate and accurate response.

This dedicated layman acquired his Biblical knowledge through study and reading. He claims he never actually sat down and memorized the Bible or read it through in entirety, but on many occasions, in the middle of a sleepless night, he would light the kerosene lamp and read his text. Then the next day, while plowing the fields, Mr. Lassetter would meditate on what he had read.

An ordained deacon, Mr. Lassetter was baptized August 15, 1915 in Dog River. He was, at that time, a candidate for membership in the Prays Mill Baptist Church, Douglas County. Shortly after becoming affiliated with this church he became an Adult Sunday School teacher.

Having been encouraged to be ordained into the ministry, Mr. Lassetter refused to take this step saying, "I don't feel smart enough, or big enough for the job." However, he says he does "a right smart of preaching every time I'm called on."

Burnett and Lillie Lassetter

Most of Uncle Burnett's work on clocks was done at night after he had worked a full day in the fields. One story was told of a complicated repair job and "the owners of the 100-year-old-clock were so delighted with his work they offered him five dollars instead of the three he charged."

The Lassetter family has produced several more preachers. I am sure Uncle Burnett had a great influence on his descendants. *Submitted by: Angie Burks, Carrollton, GA, great-great-niece of Burnett Lassetter. Compiled by: Nancy A. Willis Howell, 9049 Allison Court, Douglasville, GA 30134*
Source: *Douglas County Sentinel,* August 25, 1966

758. Benjamin Lassetter Family

Benjamin Lassetter was born December 12, 1778, in North Carolina, the son of Tobias and Sally Lassetter. His grandparents were John and Rebecca Lassetter of Chowan County in North Carolina. Benjamin settled in Carroll County in the early 1820s on a 202-acre track

The ruins of the Benjamin and Elizabeth Lassetter's log house

of land that overlooked the Chattahoochee River. He married Elizabeth Hill in 1801. Benjamin, along with his in-laws, Cheadle and Mary Hill Cochran, came to this area at the same time. The two families lived in Jasper, Newton, Gwinnett and Henry Counties. When they arrived in Carroll County they already had grown children and grandchildren.

Benjamin and Elizabeth raised twelve children and he outlived several of them. (1) Sally born August 9, 1803, died January 4, 1856, married Bassett Northern. (2) Maria born June 30, 1805, died May 5, 1893, married Wesley Camp. (3) Pherabee born February 3, 1807, died May 4, 1889, married William Boone. (4) Hannah born March 10, 1809, died December 2, 1851, married Benjamin Templeton Watkins. (5) Mary (Polly) born February 9, 1811, died 1885, married William Hendon. (6) Nancy born February 4, 1813, married Jesse Boone. (7) John H. born May 10, 1815, died September 17, 1836. (8) James H. born October 11, 1817, married Amanda Laster. (9) William Cheadle born March 6, 1820, died February 15, 1888, married Parthena Brown. (10) Benjamin Hill born August 1, 1822, died February 15, 1888, married Ceclia Goolsby. (11) Elizabeth born November 16, 1824, died November 2, 1855, married Lindsey Holland. (12) Charles Cheadle born November 14, 1826, married Martha Mullins.

Mariah Lassetter Camp, daughter of Benjamin and Elizabeth Lassetter

A well known fact that Benjamin was raised as a Cherokee Indian was told by his son-in-law, Lindsey Holland. In a sworn affidavit before Notary M.D. Watkins on October 9, 1907, he tells his remembrances of father in-law.

> "When I first knew him he was rather tall and erect, straight as an arrow, before age let its mark on him. He wore his hair long, sometimes nearly to his waist. His hair was black, straight and glossy like an Indian's. His nose was straight, long and had the peculiar shape common to that tribe. He had high cheek bones. He loved the solitude of the woods and was an ardent and successful gunner and trapper and fisherman.

Mary (Polly) Lassetter Hendon, daughter of Benjamin and Elizabeth Lassetter

> Honesty was a prominent virtue in his make up. He was faithful to his friends, his promises, and the truth. Although he didn't know a letter, he was asked to serve on the Grand Jury in Henry County, Georgia. A law had been passed making it a crime to shoot deer by firelight. Not knowing this was against the law, Mr. Lassetter had been out "shining" several nights and always got the right game. It was always a deer.
>
> The judge charged the jury to fine any violators $5, as the cattle and stock were being killed nightly. Upon hearing the judge's charge he immediately insisted upon paying the $5 fine. The judge was so astonished and carried away with his frank, honest statement that he took his money."
>
> The spring after Lindsey and his wife Elizabeth married, they visited Benjamin. Two well-dressed young men passed on horseback and Benjamin exclaimed, "Law, Law, Law. How different! Look at them boys, Lindsey. I never had a hat nor shoes, nor pants till I was over eighteen years old." Asked how he got along in the winter, he replied, "I wore moccasins made of buckskins and an Indian bonnet instead of a hat. For pants I wore a slip or robe that had a hole for a neck, and was all in one. It came below my knee and had a band round it. I plowed many a day in one, and barefooted. I was raised by Indians and among them and this was the way they dressed. I never went to school a day and don't know one letter from another, but I know how to be honest and tell the truth."

The Lassetter home was a two-over-one log cabin with a dog trot through the middle and a sleeping loft over head. The family cemetery is near the site of the cabin and approximately 120 graves are there. Among those known to be buried there are Elizabeth and her sister Mary and Cheadle Cochran.

Benjamin died August 23, 1869, and is buried at St. Paul's Methodist Cemetery in Whitesburg, Georgia, and Elizabeth died July 14, 1852.

Their youngest daughter, Elizabeth, who married Lindsey Holland (son of James Holland) had a daughter Nancy Jehrusa, born November 11, 1853, died July 10, 1920, married William Jackson Lassetter, born March 2, 1853, died April 11, 1914, of Randolph County, Alabama.

William and Nancy lived in the Carroll County area and attended Mt. Zion Baptist Church. They raised nine children. They were Lindsey, Joseph, Wesley, Burnett, Lizzie, Molly, Mattie, Hattie, and Rebecca.

Joseph Benjamin Lassetter, son of William and Nancy, was born September 1, 1880, in Douglas County, Georgia. He married Hattie Mae Carter December 16, 1906. Their children were Benjamin Ray, Lillian, James Wililam, and Oscar Rainey. Joe and Hattie farmed his father's land in Douglas County for a few years and in 1918 they settled in Palmetto in Campbell County. Joseph died August 26, 1928, after an accident that caused the loss of a leg. Hattie died October 31, 1960. They were members of Ramah First Baptist Church, where he served as deacon and she taught Sunday School classes for many years.

Benjamin Ray Lassetter was born in Douglas County on August 30, 1908. He married Mary Jo Rodgers, born October 6, 1912, of Palmetto on April 15, 1933. Ray and Mary Jo worked in the Palmetto Cotton Mill most of their adult life. He retired from Dixie Lime and Stone as the purchasing agent. He was very civic minded and served as Master of Palmetto Lodge No. 74. He was active in the Better Home Town Club, was scoutmaster for a number of years and also a member of the Eastern Star. They were both members of Ramah First Baptist Church and he taught Sunday School there for many years. He died November 29, 1980, and she died January 3, 1993. They are buried in Holly Hill Cemetery in Fairburn, Georgia.

James Lassetter, son of Benjamin and Elizabeth Lassetter

Their children are Kenneth Ray Lassetter born October 2, 1934, and Carole Ann Lassetter Harper born July 26, 1937.

Kenneth married Marian Hammett on January 7, 1955. They have two daughters: Catherine Ann born March 19, 1958, and Susan Lynne born October 30, 1962. Kenneth married Ina Marie Clifton Reid on July 29, 1995.

Carole married Thomas Woodie Harper Sr. on July 15, 1955. They have two children: Thomas W. Harper Jr. born July 17, 1956, and Lisa Anne Hartzler born October 3, 1958.

Benjamin and Elizabeth Hill Lassetter are my great-great-great-grandparents. *Submitted by: Carole Ann Lassetter Harper, 9890 Hutcheson Ferry Road, Palmetto, GA 30268*

759. John George Washington Lassetter

John George Washington Lassetter was born July 2, 1858, in Carroll County, Georgia, the eleventh child of William Lassetter and Parthenia Brown Lassetter. He used to say there were four boys in his family and they had ten sisters apiece! When he set out to make his own way, he had the choice of two tracts of land. One had been cleared and farmed for a while, the other had never been cleared. He talked to his daddy who told him to buy the one that needed clearing, the land would last longer. That is how we ended up on Bankhead Highway west of Villa Rica. Grandpa used to tell of finding a wild turkey trap when he cleared the land. In the center of the pen was an intact arrow but it crumbled when he picked it up.

I know he did not marry for the first time until he was twenty-seven, so I figure he cleared the farm before 1883 when he married Mary E. Barnett. They had two children, one of whom died at age four, the other of whom grew up to be "Bill Casper" on the editorial page of the *Progressive Farmer* magazine, and incidentally my Uncle Casper (William Casper Lassetter, born August 31, 1887). Mary (Mollie) died August 14, 1909.

Grandpa married Granny (Addie Mae Green) January 1, 1913, and my daddy (Jack Lassetter named for his father and considered a Junior, since everybody called grandpa "Uncle Jack") was born November 6, 1913. James Green Lassetter was born September 16, 1916, and Marian Annette Lassetter (Wilkinson) was born April 19, 1919. So when Grandpa was sixty-five, he had three children under age ten to support. I have always found it interesting that he sent all of his children to college, considering that he was a farmer and that he himself was hard of hearing and had only finished third grade. I had figured Granny for the intellect, since she was a school teacher before she married and she was the one who sat in the glider on the front porch after dinner and read or worked the *Journal* crossword puzzle. Only after I passed the age of fifty did it occur to me that Grandpa stopping school after third grade might have had something to do with what was going on in the world when he was nine (1867). Recently, I realized he sent Casper off on the train (to return home only after his first year) to the University of Wisconsin before he married Granny.

Granny and Grandpa were members of Pleasant Grove Baptist Church. Grandpa's name is on the marble plaque embedded in the current church wall commemorating the rebuilding after the tornado of 1913. *Submitted by: Janice L. Kitchens, 124 Tall Pine Trail, Greenwood, SC 29646*

760. The Thomas Jackson Lawler Family

Thomas Jackson Lawler was the son of John Levi Lawler and Sarah Jane Croker Lawler. He was born September 14, 1893, at Constitution, Georgia, and died November 13, 1970, in Carroll County. His father died when he was five years old. At the age of ten, in order to support his mother and four sisters, Tom went to work at the Dallas Hosiery Mill. He was paid $6 per week for 60 hours of labor. In 1919 he was married to Mary Watson Nalley, descendant of early settlers around Villa Rica. She was born in 1894 and died in 1987.

Tom Lawler at Dallas Hosiery Mill in 1910

Tom Lawler served in Company I, 140th Infantry AEF in France during World War I. This was the company commanded by future president Harry Truman. After military service he returned to Fuller Mills in Villa Rica. He remained there until starting Lawler Mills with several other businessmen in Carrollton in

The Lawler Family

1926. As he said, there were "up years" and "down years." On the whole, the business was successful, selling children's anklets to stores such as K-Mart and Sears. "Mr. Tom" knew each of his employees and was loved and respected by them. His endless repertoire of humorous country stories endeared him to everyone he met.

He was the founder and first president of the Carroll Creamery Co-op; a founder and director of Carroll County Livestock Sales Barn; chairman of the board of directors of Carrollton Federal Savings and Loan Association; on the Hospital Authority of Tanner Memorial Hospital since it was established; one of the founders and first vice president of West Georgia National Bank.

Mr. Lawler was a founder, and for several years an officer of the *Carroll County Georgian* newspaper; was a charter member of the Rotary Club and was a recipient of the Founders Award of the State University of West Georgia.

Thomas Jackson Lawler

He was a life-time member of First Baptist Church and served as a deacon for thirty-five years. He served two terms as city councilman and two terms as mayor of Carrollton and judge of the City Court.

Tom and Mary had seven children: (1) Mary Ceylene born September 26, 1920, in Villa Rica. Married William Sparks McGinnis and had two children: Mary Joyce McGinnis, MD, and William S. McGinnis Jr. (2) Edna born July 1, 1922, in Villa Rica. Married William E. Harris (8-5-1915 to 4-24-1974) and had two children: Julia Beth and William Stephen. (3) James Thomas born October 11, 1925, in Villa Rica. Married Sarmita Runka and had two children: Mary Edith and James T. (4) Joyce born September 25, 1926, in Carrollton. (5) Rebecca Jane born February 20, 1929, in Carrollton. Married Aubrey W. Gilbert and had five children: Howard Wilson, Aubrey Warden Jr., John (Jack) Thomas, Marine Lt. Col. Retired, Carl Franklin and Mary Claire. (6) Jack Lawler born July 23, 1930, in Carrollton. Married Sheridan Boykin Leeburn and had one child: Sheridan. (7) Carol Anne Lawler born February 17, 1935, in Carrollton. Married Jimmy T. West and had two children: Thomas Cleveland and Timothy Victor.

Shown in the family photograph on back row are Joyce, Rebecca, Edna, Carol Ann, and Ceylene. On the front row are Jack, Mary, Tom, and James. *Submitted by: Ceylene L. McGinnis, 656 N. Superior, Decatur, GA 30033*

761. Johnny Ray League Family

Johnny Ray League was born 20 June 1941, the son of John Wesley League and Georgia Odessa Petty who married in Carroll County, Georgia, on 16 December 1939. Johnny Ray's brothers and sisters were: James Ralph, Linda Lou, Glenda Sue, Larry Lesley (1949-1969), Debra Jean, Melba Dean "Deannie," and Janice Rudene who died as an infant and is buried in an unmarked grave at Stripling Chapel Cemetery.

George Washington and Ida Mae Hight Petty, with baby James.

John Wesley League was born 2 June 1918 and died 2 September 1979 in Carroll County. Georgia Odessa Petty was born 31 October 1922 and died 7 February 1995. Both are buried at Carroll Memory Gardens. The father of Georgia Odessa Petty was George Washington Petty who was married twice. George Petty's first wife was Ida Mae Hight. With her he had a son named James, shown in the family picture. Georgia Petty was a daughter by George Petty's second wife, Minnie Peppers Petty.

John Wesley League was the son of George "Martin" League and Elzan Phillips who married in Carroll County on 29 January 1906. Martin League was born 9 March 1888 and died 31 March 1934. Mary Elzan Phillips was born 2 December 1881 and died 11 February 1953. Both are buried at Mt. Zion United Methodist Church Cemetery in Carroll County.

On 26 May 1963, Johnny Ray League married Linda Earline Taylor who was born 15 December 1945 in Carroll County, Georgia. Linda was the daughter of Mary Elizabeth Morgan (born 26 May 1907, died 1 April 1997) and Hulett Dorsey Taylor (born 9 March 1918, died 31 July 1980) who married in Carroll County on 22 November 1943. Mary Morgan was the daughter of James Robert "Bob" Morgan and Derah Idella Burnham. Hulett Taylor worked many years for the City of Carrollton. Both Mary and Hulett Taylor are buried at Antioch Baptist Church in Carroll County.

Hulett Dorsey Taylor was born 9 March 1918 in Meriwether County, Georgia, the son of Charlie Alban Taylor who was born 17 March 1879 in

Hulett Dorsey Taylor and Mary Elizabeth Morgan Taylor

Linda and Johnny Ray League

Carroll County. Charlie A. Taylor was the son of LeRoy Taylor and Martha Ann Anthony who married on 2 June 1861 in Carroll County. The Taylors were early pioneers of Carroll County arriving here as early as 1853 when LeRoy Taylor purchased Lot 89 in District 4 on 24 February 1853. Prior to coming to Carroll County, the Taylors had lived in Edgefield and Abbeville Districts of South Carolina. LeRoy Taylor was the son of John LeRoy Taylor born 1795 and wife Jane of Edgefield District, South Carolina. The next generation further back of ancestors is LeRoy and Jamima Taylor born about the time of the American Revolution. This family has been extensively researched by David Hay and privately published in *The Taylor Family.*

LeRoy Taylor was born 4 May 1821 in Edgefield District, South Carolina. On 3 March 1844 in Carroll County, he married first Catherine Dorris born 1818 in South Carolina, the daughter of John Dorris and Lucinda Williamson. Catherine died about 1856 and LeRoy then married a second time to Carolina Gibson. After her death, LeRoy married a third time to Martha Ann Anthony. In all, LeRoy Taylor had seventeen children by the three wives. By the first wife, he had: (1) Lucinda E., born 1845 in Carroll County, married 3 May 1861 Francis M. George; (2) John Martin, born 28 March 1847, married Sarah Elizabeth Cavender Roberts 18 August 1865, buried at Lowell; (3) William Taylor born 11 April 1849 in Carroll County, died before 1870, buried in Dorris Cemetery in Whitesburg; (4) Lee Roy Jr., born 10 April 1852 at Lowell, married 1869 in Heard County, died 14 February 1934. Four wives: Mary A. Clark, Nancy J. Jones, Susan Royster, and Lucy A. Smith. With the second wife, LeRoy Taylor had (5) Martha E. "Mattie" born 6 August 1858, married 2 March 1876 in Carroll to Joseph Pinson Webb, died 24 July 1892 (6) Elizabeth C. born 19 July 1860. With the third wife, Martha Ann Anthony, LeRoy had (7) Ivey Solomon born 28 March 1862, married Mary P; (8) Amanda Jane born 15 July 1864, married Leigray "Gus" Lambert 5 October 1890, buried Bonner Cemetery, Carroll County; (9) Joseph Washington "Joe" born 23 September 1866 in Carroll County, married 25 August 1912 Francis R. "Fannie" Balkman and second Lula Veatrice Smith, died 14 June 1936, buried at Mt. Zion; (10) George Franklin born 9 December 1868, married 4 September 1897 in Bivens, Texas, to Sarah Webb and second to Lea Nora McDonald, died 6 September 1945 and buried Bronson, Texas; (11) Corrie Emma born 7 November 1871 in Carroll County, married 27 July 1905 R.H. Gray, and second Elmer Mitchell; (12) Ellen born 1873, died 1884; (13) Della Estella born 22 March 1874, married 12 January 1896 George W. Jacobs, buried Roopville; (14) Alice Conoler born 26 September 1876, married 5 May 1895 in Carroll County to Henry H. Huckeba, buried New Lebanon Cemetery; (15) Charlie Alban born 17 March 1879, married 9 September 1906 in Heard County first to Mattie Huckeba and second to Ellen Bond, died May 1940, buried at Antioch Church Cemetery; (16) Clifford Raiford born 23 April 1883, died 17 February 1935; (17) Roxanna "Roxie" May born 7 November 1884, married 4 August 1907 Wayne Wesley Spruell, died 27 September 1935, buried Carrollton City Cemetery.

LeRoy Taylor and his son John M. Taylor served in the Civil War in 26th Battalion, Company C, Georgia Volunteers, C.S.A. Both were wounded in battle. John M. Taylor's brother-in-law, Cavender, served as 5th sergeant in Company F, Phillips Legion, Cavalry, C.S.A. LeRoy Taylor died 14 January 1900 and is buried in Dorris family Cemetery in Whitesburg.

Jeff and Anissa League, Justin and Donovan Jordan. August 14, 1999.

Courting Days — Johnny Ray League and Linda Taylor

Johnny Ray, Jr. and Angela Marie Cook League, with Hannah Marie and Katherine Hope.

Three children were born to Johnny Ray and Linda League. The first child was Johnny Ray League Jr. born 17 August 1964 in Carroll County. Johnny League Jr. graduated from Bowdon High School in 1982 and attended West Georgia College 1983-1984. He graduated with an A.S. degree in computer science in 1984. On 3 June 1989 Johnny League married Angela Marie Cook who was born 1 May 1966 in Carroll County, the daughter of Sondril Dwight Cook and Glenda Jeannette West Cook. Johnny Ray League Jr. is one of the founders of Retail Vending Software in Bremen, Georgia, where he works as the director of Product Electronic Commerce Systems. He also serves as pastor of Westview Baptist Church in Douglasville and is presently attending seminary classes at Rome, Georgia. Johnny is well known locally for his wonderful singing voice and is often called upon to sing at the weddings of family and friends.

Angela Cook League is a graduate of West Georgia College with a B.S. in early childhood education. Angela taught at Buchanan Primary School for three years before her marriage. She is one of the founders of Central Christian School which is sponsored by Central Baptist Church. Angela and Johnny League have two daughters — Hannah Marie League who was born 24

Bethany Olivia League

December 1993 and Katherine Hope League who was born 28 April 1997. Both girls attend Central Christian School. The Johnny League family lives on Clem Lowell Road in Carrollton.

The second child of Linda and Johnny Ray League Sr. is Jeffrey Scott League born 27 February 1968 in Carroll County. Jeff League graduated from Bowdon High School in 1986. He was married first to Lisa Newman on 19 June 1993, later divorced, and had one daughter, Bethany Olivia League born 21 January 1994. Jeff League married second to Anissa Smith Jordan, the daughter of Ernest Roy "Roscoe" Smith and Betty Darlene Layton Smith. Jeff and Anissa were married on 14 August 1999 in Haralson County at Salem Baptist Church. Anissa has two sons by a previous marriage — Austin Ryan Jordan born 26 March 1993 and Donovan Wade Jordan born 29 October 1990. Anissa's family is originally from Marietta, Georgia, but they have lived in Tallapoosa for the past twenty years. Anissa works as the manager of the bakery at Ingle's in Bremen. Jeff League works as a team leader in the receiving department at Mark Lynn, the condiment packaging firm located at Bremen. Jeff and Anissa League make their home at Waco, Georgia, and are members of Salem Baptist Church.

Valerie Renee League

The third child of Linda and Johnny Ray League is Valerie Renee League born 12 March 1970 in Carroll County. Valerie was a 1988 graduate of Bowdon High School. Valerie worked for about fifteen years at Robinson Drug Company in Carrollton, becoming an experienced pharmacy technician. Mrs. Melba Morgan Robinson of Robinson Drug Company was Valerie's "Aunt Melba" since Melba's father, J. Horry Morgan, was a brother to Valerie's grandmother, Mary Morgan Taylor. Valerie also became a certified travel agent but she discovered a natural talent for working with computers. Valerie went on to become certified in computer programming and is employed by the State University of West Georgia as an EPD-Technical Support Specialist II.

Johnny Ray League Sr. attended Carroll Tech 1969-1970 and became certified in all areas of welding. He worked for thirty years for Trent Tube Company, retiring in 1992. Retirement didn't last for long, though, and the Leagues moved to Blountville, Tennessee, where Johnny worked for Bristol Metals as a welding engineer for five years. Linda League worked as a sales clerk for Leggs-Hanes-Bali during those years. She also worked for the Homeless Mission during the time they lived in Tennessee.

Linda's first work experience after high school was as a clerk at "Uncle John and Aunt Melba's store" which is Robinson Drug Company. She went on to have many years experience as a clerk in Carrollton at a variety of the stores we remember as Robbins' The Leader, and Buttons n' Bows. She has also had long experience in working with children or caring for the elderly in their homes.

Linda is much loved and appreciated in her extended family as "the one who always cares and remembers you." She never forgets to visit friends and family in the hospital or in the nursing home. She will bring you some homemade soup or a bunch of jonquils picked from her yard. Just like her own mother, Mary Morgan Taylor, Linda has a heart of gold. Linda and Johnny Ray League are of the Baptist faith and reside on Antioch Church Road in Carrollton, Georgia. *Submitted by: Valerie League, 278 Harlan Lane Road, Villa Rica, GA*

762. Leathers Family

My maternal grandfather's father was Abney Monroe Leathers. He worked for the U.S. Postal Service for thirty-nine years. He began with a horse and buggy and got a car in 1920. Matilda Watkins was his wife's name, and they had six children: Cecil, Felix, Leroy, Lewis, Gladys, and Mary.

Felix was my grandfather, and he married Dorothy Pounds, daughter of Etta Bagwell. My grandmother doesn't remember her daddy because he drowned when she was six weeks old. Dorothy married Frank Kinney and had a daughter Patricia, and divorced shortly after that. Later, she met Felix and had two more children, Frances and Dianne. Felix and Dorothy opened a store in the Fullerville community in Villa Rica (known now as Open Pantry). They lived in a two-story house beside the store for years. Later, they opened a store near Temple that they called the Riverview Market. It was near what is now the Montessori School. I remember as a child the luxury of asking for whatever candy or soft drink I wanted, and they always gave it to me.

Patricia Kinney married Fred Pope and had two girls, Karen and Carol. Frances married Donald Willis (my dad) and had Don Jr., Felicia and Connie (me). Dianne married Lee DeVault and had two girls, Tanya and Tisha. Karen Pope married Rodney Gibbs and had two girls, Allison and Hannah. Carol married Greg White

Dorothy and Felix Leathers

and had one daughter, Andrea. Don Willis, my brother, never married or had children. He was killed in a car crash in Bowdon on September 18, 1999. My sister Felicia married Danny Higdon and had two girls, Michal and Kendall. I married Joe Nalley and we have a boy Joey, and a girl Nancy. Tanya DeVault married Steve Costello and had a girl Caitlyn, and then later married Scott Cohran and had a son Tyler, and two stepchildren, Lacy and Sierra.

Tisha DeVault married Tim Howell and had a son Lee Thomas, who died shortly after birth. Tisha and Tim divorced and Tisha later had a daughter Chloe, whose father Paul is from South Africa.

The Leathers family is a very industrious one that puts tremendous emphasis on work. All my life, I have seen my grandparents, aunts, and mother continually work and prosper. My grandfather Felix is the strongest person I know. They told him that he would never walk after having a case of polio as a child. He taught himself to walk (at excruciating personal cost), only to be injured again and told again that he would not walk. He is now almost ninety years old and walks unassisted. I admire him for his persistence and determination, and I hope I have inherited some of that. *Submitted by: Connie S. Willis Nalley, Sand Hill-Hulett Road, Villa Rica, GA 30180*

763. Leathers Family

The picture is of Alonzo Riley and Georgia Amanda McGuire with children Katie, Nellie, and George in 1884.

Nellie B. McGuire married William L. Leathers of Atlanta in 1912. They lived in Paulding County until 1934 then moved to Carroll County. Their children, Harold, Helen, Georgia, Eva Mae, Claude, Winnie, and Hugh were all raised in Carroll County.

Alonzo Riley and Georgia Amanda McGuire with children Katie, Nellie and George.

Harold married Evelyn Defoor in 1939. They had one daughter Jackie who married Franklin Richardson. Harold was owner of Leathers Truck Stop on Interstate-20. He was killed by a train in Villa Rica in 1970. Jackie and Franklin continued to run the Truck Stop until they sold it in 2001. Jackie and Franklin have two sons, Tant and Toby, both of Villa Rica.

Helen married J. Gid Robison in 1941. They had three children, Sandra, Sue and Ricky. Helen worked as a dietitian at Carrollton High School. At Gid's death she was appointed to his position as Ordinary of Carroll County. She later ran for office and remained in office until she retired in 1988.

Georgia married Q.P. Skinner in 1942. They had three children, Kenneth, Mack and Kay. Q.P. started Skinner's Poultry and it was a thriving business for years. Kenneth is Clerk of Court of Carroll County, Mack works with Primerica Financial Services, and Kay teaches school in Newnan.

Claude married Ann Shead. They had three children, Gail, Brad and David. Gail died at age two and one-half years, Brad and David both work for power companies. Claude retired from Ft. Gilliam and died in 1997.

Eva Mae married Henry Dyer in 1948. They have one daughter Linda. They live in Forest Park.

Winnie married Johnnie Dyer in 1950. They had one daughter, Marion Ann. Johnnie was killed in the gas explosion in Villa Rica in 1957. Winnie is now married to Thomas Baxter of Marietta and they reside on Highway 113 in Carrollton. Winnie has worked at West Georgia College and Westside Pharmacy. She was managing an Antique Mall when she had to retire due to cancer surgery in 1996. She is doing well now. Marion Ann married Danny Odom in 1971. They have one son Clayton.

Hugh Leathers was killed in an auto accident in 1954 at the age of twenty. *Submitted by: Winnie Baxter, 125 Highway 113 North, Carrollton, GA 30117*

764. Family of Samuel Solomon Lee and Rebecca Gainus Lee

Samuel Solomon Lee was born 16 October 1824 in York District, South Carolina. He moved with his parents and siblings to the vicinity of Hapeville, Georgia, when he was about nine years old. His parents are buried on the site of the family farm on Washington Road in College Park, Georgia.

Samuel Solomon married Rebecca Gainus on 30 October 1853 in DeKalb now Fulton County. Rebecca was the daughter of James and Betsy Gainus and was born in 1836. Samuel and Rebecca moved with their two daughters and five sons to Carroll County in 1886.

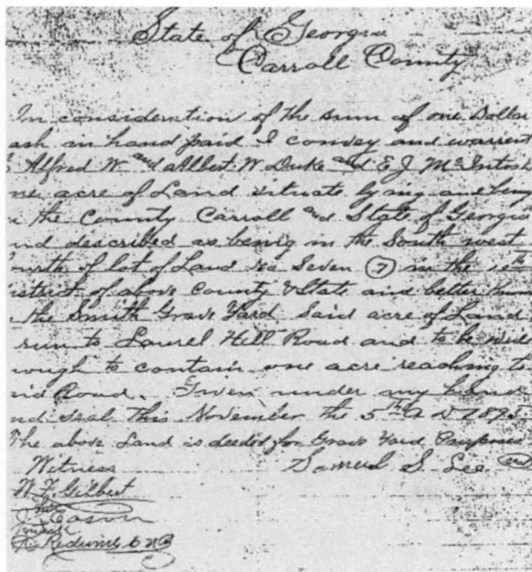

State of Georgia
Carroll County

In consideration of the sum of one Dollar [illegible] in hand paid I convey and warrant [illegible] Alfred W. [illegible] Albert W. Duke [illegible] E J McIntosh [illegible] acre of Land situate lying and being [illegible] the County Carroll and State of Georgia [illegible] described as being in the South west [illegible] of lot of Land No Seven (7) in the [illegible] [illegible] of above County & State and better known [illegible] the Smith Grave Yard. Said acre of Land [illegible] to Laurel Hill Road and to be wide [illegible] to contain one acre reaching to [illegible] Road. Given under my hand [illegible] seal This November the 5th A D 1895
The above Land is deeded for Grave Yard Purposes
Witness Samuel S. Lee (seal)
W. F. Gilbert
[illegible]
[illegible]

Deed for land given for grave yard.

Samuel Solomon Lee and his sons were active members of the Tallapoosa Farmers Alliance which met monthly in Carroll County in the 1800s. Samuel donated an acre of land in 1895 to neighbors for use as a graveyard which is now where Lee's Chapel Congregational Methodist Church is located on Bethesda Church Road.

Samuel Solomon Lee served in the Confederate Army in Company C, 63rd Infantry Regiment which was assigned to the Coastal Artillery to help protect the coast of Savannah. They sent his company to Fort Wagner in Charleston, South Carolina. One-half of his regiment was present when one of the Black Union regiments attacked the fort as portrayed in the movie. "Old Glory." Samuel was with the other half of his regiment in another location at the time of the attack. After William T. Sherman attacked Atlanta, they sent Samuel Solomon's regiment to Kennesaw to help defend Atlanta.

Rebecca Gainus Lee died on 10 October 1889. Samuel Solomon Lee died on 16 October 1900.

Both are buried at Tallapoosa Primitive Baptist Church on the Carrollton-Tyus Road.

Family of Samuel Solomon and Rebecca Gainus Lee

Left to right in family photo: Samuel Solomon Lee, 1824-1900; Rebecca Gaines Lee, 1836-1889; Roena J. Lee, 1854-1909; Aunt; Emma E. Lee, 1870-1888; John Franklin Lee, 1857-1945; Mary Creel Lee, 1861-1954; (baby) Eva Lee, 1881-1887; James Marshall Lee, 1859-1925; Alice Suttles Lee, 1862-1939; William Thomas Lee, 1861-1925; Charles Mentor Lee, 1865-1925; Tobeus A. Lee, 1868-1895. *Submitted by: Margie Nell Lee Dietz, 1917 Chamdun Way, Atlanta, GA 30341-1770*
Sources: Family histories by family members

765. William Thomas Lee's Descendants and Ancestry

In the summer of 1886, William Thomas Lee moved with his father and mother, four brothers, and two sisters to the southern part of Carroll County between Owensby Settlement and Buffalo Creek. They traveled from their old home in Fulton County, Georgia, near the Newnan Buggy Road, with their families in a number of wagons and camped along the way. When his father Samuel divided his farm acreage among his sons in 1895, he gave the home place to William Thomas for caring for him in retirement. William Thomas Lee and his brothers and sisters have a large number of descendants in every part of Carroll County.

William Thomas Lee (17 October 1861-9 April 1925) was born in Fulton County, Georgia, near Red Oak, the son of Samuel Soloman Lee and Rebecca Ganus. William Thomas was a farmer and store owner. He married Alice Rebecca Rowan (13 October 1866, Clayton County-31 August 1903, Carroll County), the first of his three wives, on 14 January 1886 in Clayton County, Georgia. Rebecca was the daughter of James Milton Rowan.

After Rebecca's death, Wililam Thomas Lee was married for the second time to Mary E Duke and last to Camilla Johnson. There were twelve children, ten of whom survived to adulthood and produced families. The ten surviving children raised thirty-five children of their own. William Thomas and Rebecca are buried at Tallapoosa Primitive Baptist Church near his father and mother.

Children of William Thomas and Rebecca include Emma Lura, Pearl, Hettie G., Leon Franklin Zachariah, Clara, and Clarence James. Children of William Thomas and Mary E. Duke (married 2 February 1905, born circa 1885 died circa 1910) include Charlie Eulas, Mollie Lee, and Willie Mae.

Samuel Soloman Lee. 1824-1900

William Thomas married Camilla Johnson (11 September 1881-October 1968) on 3 November 1910. Children include Susie Beatrice, Mary Delia, and Howard Thomas.

William Thomas Lee was the son of Samuel Soloman Lee, a Confederate soldier. He also was the grandson of John Lee, who served in the South Carolina militia in the War of 1812 from York

William Thomas Lee and Mary E. Duke. Children are unidentified.

County. William Thomas was the great-grandson of Henry Lee, originally of Maryland, later York County, South Carolina, and Butts County, Georgia, a soldier of the American Revolution. William Thomas Lee's great-great-grandfather was Edward Lee of Maryland.

William Thomas Lee's father, Samuel Soloman Lee (16 October 1824-16 October 1900), was an infantry private from Fulton County, serving in Company C, 63rd Georgia Infantry, Confederate States Army, serving near Savannah, Charleston, and the coast, and in the battles around Atlanta. When he moved to Carroll County, he gave acreage and timber for Lee School and for what became Lee's Chapel Church. Samuel had married Rebecca Ganus (1833-10 October 1889) on 30 October 1853 in Fulton County. Their children included Roena J., Ann T., Leonidas, Jane, John Franklin, James Marshall, William Thomas, Charles Mentor, Tobias A., and Emma E. *Submitted by: Dr. William R. Lee, 6303 Tudor Lane, Hixson, TN 37343*
Sources: *The Lees of Carroll County,* an unpublished manuscript by William R. Lee

766. Lenderman Family

Henry M. Lenderman, a third generation American who could trace his German ancestry to the arrival in America of his great-grandfather in 1740, was born in Greenville County, South Carolina, in 1815. When Henry was only twenty-six years old, his wife Ann (Hiott) died after giving birth to their second daughter. Sometime the following year Henry married his second wife, Polly (Mary A.Nelson). Within five years Henry and Polly had a daughter and two sons, and they decided to move their family to Coweta County, Georgia, where they had two more daughters and a son. Henry and two of his sons, William and Moses, served in the Confederate army. In 1872, the entire family moved to Carroll County, Georgia. One of the first things Henry did was to help organize the Church of Christ on August 3, 1872. It was referred to as the New Bethel Church, but was commonly called Lenderman Chapel. Henry was active in community affairs and was affectionately known as "Uncle Henry." Henry died in 1890. His obituary in the *Carroll County Times,* July 4, 1890, reads in part:

> "Old Uncle Henry Lenderman, a well known citizen of this county, living two miles east of town died on last Saturday. The deceased was a most excellent citizen and held in high esteem by his many friends in this section..."

William, the oldest son of Henry and Polly, served in the Georgia Infantry during the Civil War. Jacob Moses, the second son of Henry and Polly, was too young to be conscripted during the war, but served for a two-month period of time for his father while Henry was in the hospital in Newnan. After the war, Moses learned to read and write and eventually educated himself to become a teacher. When the family moved to

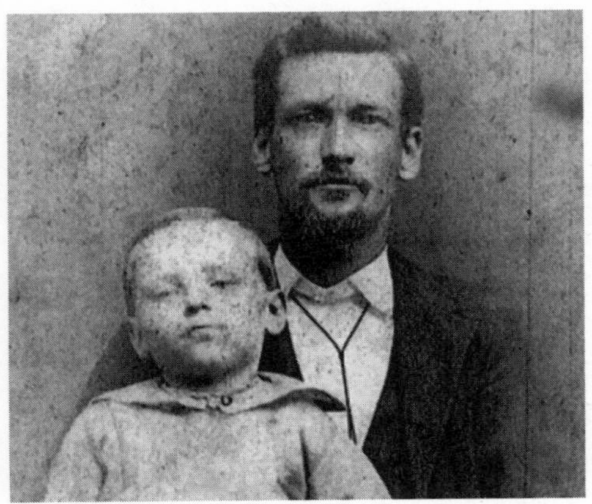

Jacob Moses and Henry Ottis Lenderman.

Carrollton, Moses obtained a teaching position at a small school just east of Carrollton. At the age of thirty-one, Moses married Lydia Jane "Janie" Reid. Their son Henry Ottis was born in 1879. Janie never recovered from giving birth and died when Ottis was only six months old. Moses lovingly built a wooden shelter to protect the grave of his lovely young wife. Moses became active in Saturday night debates that provided lively entertainment for the community. He served as the secretary, and later as president, of the Carroll County Farmers Alliance. In 1884 Moses married his second wife, Mary A. Giles. Moses and Mary had eight children, three of whom were born in Georgia.

Shelter built by Jacob Lenderman over the grave of his wife Lydia Jane Reid.

Sometime during the 1880s, Henry's married daughters (Cardis Holland, Sarah Frances Giles, Celia Garner), and his son William moved their families to Hulaco, a small community in Morgan County, Alabama. After the death of his father in 1890, Moses also took his family to Hulaco, where he held a teaching position and was active in farming. Benjamin, Henry and Polly's youngest son, died in Georgia in 1881 while still a young man. Five of Henry's children and their spouses continued throughout their lives to be active in church work and are buried in the Hebron Church of Christ Cemetery at Hulaco, Alabama. *Submitted by: Elaine L. Murphree, 7763 Wildcreek Trail, Huntsville, Al 35802*

767. Lepard Family

The earliest record of the Lepard family was found in the Coweta County, Georgia, census of 1850. Lewis Lepard was age 52, occupation potter, born in Alabama. His wife was Elizabeth, age 39, born in Alabama. Their children were Emily 17, Jane 12, James 8, all born in Alabama, Thomas 6, and Willis 3, place of birth not stated. In the 1860 Chambers County, Alabama, census, Willis was listed as a jug maker, with wife Elizabeth and Willis 12, the only child at home.

Listed in the 1880 Carroll County census, James Lepard was living with a Holland family. Willis R. Lepard was living in the home of Moses N. Almon and wife Mary and their three children. The ages from the 1850-60 census match, except Willis should be 34, not 24.

In the September 5, 1879, issue of *Carroll County Times,* Willis Lepard purchased Will O'Rear's store. On September 17, 1880, *Carroll County Times* reported "Squire W.W. Ragan was now with Pearce and Lepard." In the same year on July 2, *Carroll County Times* reported that Mr. Willis R. Lepard married Miss Laura Peace on the morning of June 27 at the home of the bride. Ceremony performed by J.J. Gaston, Esquire.

Willis R. Lepard operated a store and restaurant on the southeast corner of public square. An ad appeared in the paper on August 12, 1881, that lunch was 10¢ and a square meal was 25¢, with a full line of confections.

Willis and Laura Peace Lepard had four children: Emory born May 1882, married Henretta Bishop; James "Jim" born January 1884, married (1) Effie Peace, (2) Myrtle Senft; Henry Harmon born June 1886, married Dovie Iona "Onie" Posey; and Odessa born April 1888, married Luther "Bud" Herrin.

Willis Lepard died before the 1900 census was taken. Laura is listed as head of household with all four children at home. No information is available on any other ancestors of Willis. *Submitted by: Linda Patterson, Footpath, Powder Springs, GA*
Sources: Alabama and Georgia census records, Carroll County marriage records, *Carroll County Times,* and family knowledge.

768. Elijah H. Lewis

One early settler in western Carroll County was Elijah H. Lewis (1823-1864). Elijah was born in the north but settled in Carroll County and married Hariett M. Veasey (1834-??). We know of at least three children: Sarah J. Lewis (1857); Mary C.R. Lewis (1859); Araminta Lucretia "Minta" Lewis (1865-1930).

When the Civil War started, Elijah went back north to fight in the Union Army. In May of 1864, family tradition says that Elijah came home to check on the welfare of his family. It appears from historical events of that time that he must have been part of the Federal Army that was pushing through Northwest Georgia toward Atlanta.

Family tradition reflects that Elijah was seen by members of the Home Guard. Of that organization we find considerable reference in historical data. They were called "The Tallapoosa Rangers." We also know that Colonel John B. Beall was the commanding officer of the Rangers. Colonel Beall, who was severely wounded in the thigh at the Battle at Mechanicsville, had returned to Carroll County to convalesce. He helped to organize and train the Rangers and eventually assumed command.

Elijah H. Lewis and Harriett M. Veasey Lewis

Dovie Phillips Gray's old family Bible confirms that, "Elijah H. Lewis was shot dead May 12, 1864." That date caused my Uncle Rodric M. Phillips of Edmond Oklahama, some alarm as he entered genealogy data for my great-grandmother Minta since she was not born until 1865. Uncle Rod did a hasty calculation that revealed Minta was born nine months after her father was "shot dead."

Minta married A.B. Phillips and had eight children: Mary Ella (1879) who married Bob Hicks; Minnie Lee (1881) who married George Brock; Dovie Mae (1884) who married George Gray; Vannie Maud (1887); Roy (1891); Joseph Ernest (1896); Raymond Lewis (1899) who married Myrtle Pauline Carroll; and Thelma Alice (1905) who married Jack Conway.

Mary Ella and Bob Hicks had at least one child, Chris. Minnie Lee and George Brock had six girls: Angie, Mary Nell, Margie, Mozelle, Sara, and Ruby. Dovie Mae and George Gray had three children: William, George, and Mary. Raymond Lewis Phillips and Myrtle had four children, all boys: Raymond, Joseph Lewis, Rodric Morris, and George Steven. Thelma Alice and Jack Conway had two children: Bob, and Minta Van. While we won't begin to name or count grand and great-grandchildren, suffice it to say - there are many.

Think about that for a moment... About what might have been the result had great-great-great-grandfather Elijah H. Lewis been killed before he returned home to check on his family? Araminta would not have been conceived and born. Where would that leave the rest of us?

Submitted by: Amy Louise Phillips Riley, 146 Ardenlee, Peachtree City, GA 30269

Sources: [i]Dovie Phillips Gray Family Bible, in possession of Mary Gray Searcy, lifetime resident of Carrollton. [ii]*Georgia's Last Frontier: The Development Of Carroll County*, James C. Bonner, 82.

769. Charles Merrill Lipham 1880-1964

Excerpt from *Wesleyan Christian Advocate,* Thursday, July 22, 1965
By Edgar A. Pagett

"When Brother Charles M. Lipham died August 11, 1964, a stalwart leader in Georgia Methodism went on ahead of us to the Father's house. He had been in failing health many months, and had often expressed his readiness: 'I've got a good place to go to, and I'd like to go and get moved.'

"He was born in Haralson County, Georgia, on February 25, 1880, the son of William and Charlotte Merrill Lipham and half-brother of Hettie Lipham Downs. Raised in Carroll County, to the end of his days he spoke with fond appreciation of his parents, and frequently made references to expressions and witticisms of 'my sainted Irish Mother.'

"Charles Lipham and Annie Lois Longino were married December 20, 1905 in Fairburn, his first appointment. Before he left Fairburn, he built a parsonage and the church at Antioch.

"An 1898 graduate of Bowdon College, Charlie began his ministry in 1904 while a student at Emory at Oxford University. After graduation, his service then includes Epworth, Atlanta; Elizabeth Church, Marietta; Rockmart for two years where he remodeled the church, suffering a back injury from falling timber. During his next pastorate, at Calhoun, he built another church, and at Calvary, Atlanta, he bought a parsonage. Next, Milledgeville where he built a parsonage and finished the church basement and kitchen. At Dalton, he built a parsonage. In Newnan, he built the church and remodeled the parsonage. After St. James, Augusta, one year, he had four years of strong ministry in Inman Park Church, Atlanta, and two years at Rome First Church. From there to West Point where he built a parsonage. In Monroe, he remodeled the church.

"As superintendent of Dalton District for six years, he lifted morale, stimulated new growth, and helped plan many new buildings in his darling 'Glamour District,' as he called it. His last appointment was Elberton First Church where he helped complete a parsonage already begun. After two years because of ill health, he retired to Dalton to live in a home he built, and where he was associated with First Methodist Church and was loved and honored by all.

Charles Merrill Lipham, 1904, Emory at Oxford University.

"Mrs. Lipham and the two children, Elizabeth and Charles, survive him:... The funeral service was held in First Methodist Church, and interment was in West Hill Cemetery, Dalton.

"Brother Lipham loved people-rich and poor. Even on trips, he talked to everyone he met, and enjoyed the company of all. He had a marvelous vocabulary and preached 'the unsearchable riches of Christ' in language rich and beautiful.

"Brother Lipham believed God's church and His pastors should be housed in adequate, attractive buildings. He devoted his strength to improving properties in every place he lived. Few, if any, men have compiled such a record for building churches and parsonages, and North Georgia Methodism is stronger today for his labor as 'a wise master builder.'"

Submitted by: Eleanor Johnson Eldredge, 12124 North Oak Hills Parkway, Baton Rouge, LA 70810

770. John Monroe Lipham and Saphronia Davis Lipham

"Born in Troup County, Georgia, in 1830, John Monroe Lipham moved his family to Heard County, Georgia sometime before 1850. Here he married Sarah Saphronia Davis (1830-1904) in 1854, the youngest daughter of Joshua and Martha (Patsy) Trammel Davis, who had moved to Heard County from Wilkes County before 1830.

"John Monroe and Fronie, as she was called, lived in Heard County for several years after their marriage. According to census records, their first four children were born there. During the war years of 1863-64 they moved over into Randolph County, Alabama, where the remainder of their children were born. Sometime between 1875 and 1880, they moved to a farm on the Big Tallapoosa River, a few miles north of Tallapoosa, Georgia.

"John Monroe was a prosperous farmer and businessman. At one time he hired a tutor to come from Atlanta, live with the family and tutor his twin daughters, Ada and Ida. His youngest, Belle, graduated from the good graded school in Tallapoosa before 1900.

"Saphronia Lipham was hard-working, having inherited some of her 'get up and go' from her mother Patsy Trammell Davis, who was said to be very industrious. Fronie had a loom house where she spun and wove many things necessary for the family such as jeans (a wool material) from which the men's and boys' pants were made, as well as skirts for the womenfolk. She also spun and wove cloth for other clothing and quilts. As her children married, they were given woolen coverlets (tradition says twelve each), plus several cotton counterpanes, all of which she made. Some of these 'masterpieces' are still in the family today and are treasured by her descendants. [One of the coverlets is in the permanent collection of the Atlanta History Center, donated in 2000 by great-great-granddaughter Isabelle Johnson Whatley.]

"In 1887, John Monroe and Fronie lost their home by fire and were able to save only some of their household goods. A new house was soon erected at about the same place. My mother recalled that this was very pretty, with bannistered porches and gingerbread trim, furnished with nice furniture-velvet platform rockers and sofa in the parlor.

John Monroe and Sarah Saphronia Davis LIpham c. 1895.

"Fronie loved flowers and her yard was attractive and filled with boxwoods and a variety of shrubs. About 1900, at age seventy, farm live became too much for her and she and John Monroe moved to Tallapoosa, for by this time he had an established mercantile business and held quite a bit of property. They were strong supporters of Bethany Baptist Church, which is near their farm.

"Saphronia Davis Lipham died at her home in Tallapoosa May 12, 1904, after a long illness and was interred in the cemetery at Bethany. John M. Lipham died in his sleep at his home January 19, 1908. He also sleeps in the cemetery at Bethany, beside his beloved Fronie."

Submitted by: Ben Cox, 5330 Forest Brook Parkway, Marietta, GA 30016

Source:Excerpt from *Liphams-Old, Young And In Between,* by Clarice Cox, 1987, pp. 27-28, used by permission.

771. Samuel Boyd Little

The son of Frances Little and Mary Ann Boyd, Samuel was probably born in the Spartanburg District of South Carolina on November 23, 1819. Samuel moved to Campbell County, Georgia, with his father in 1836, then moved to Paulding and Carroll County. The exact date he moved to Carroll County is unknown to me.

In his youth he drove a stage coach carrying gold from Villa Rica to Mobile, Alabama. Samuel was born into a Methodist family, but became a Baptist minister in 1844. In 1850 he was living in the 11th District of Carroll County. However, he lived in Bowdon, Carrollton, and Waco.

Samuel married Anne Judson Reeves, daughter of Rev. James Reeves and Nancy Harper, on June 29, 1846. Anne was the granddaughter of Jeremiah and Jane Brazil. She was born in Villa Rica on September 16, 1828.

Samuel and Anne had nine children: (1) Antoninine F. born 1847, died after 1850. This child probably died in infancy; we have no other information on her. (2) Mary E. was born December 10, 1849, died April 7, 1871. She did not marry. (3) Francis Adrian born December 20, 1851, died October 3, 1921, married on November 12, 1872, to Minnie Strong and they had one son. Adrian owned a mercantile store in Waco. He is buried in the church yard of Waco Baptist Church. (4) Nannie Madora born January 21, 1855, died in Carrollton on August 8, 1877. She married Mr. McElreath and they had no children. (5) Joseph Posey was born November 20, 1858, died June 28, 1934. He is buried in church yard of Bowdon Baptist Church. Joseph married Georgia Savannah Colquitt, the daughter of William Terry Colquitt, on December 24, 1878. Joseph and Savannah had five children: (a) Boyd William married Pearl Bell Pritchard. They had one son Joseph Pritchard. Joseph married Peggy Anne Biggers and had no children. (b) Thomas Leman did not marry. He went west to Houston or San Antonio, Texas, early in life. (c) Mary Ann died in infancy at the age of one and one-half years. (d) George Mell married Lotte Hansell Trussell. They had two children, George Linsey and Charlotte Hill. George married first to Suzanne Donaldson and had one son, George Michael. George married second to Louise Boles Thornberry and had no children of their own. Charlotte married Jack R. Walker and had two children, John Mell and Cathryn Leigh. John married Sarah Ritchey and had two children. Cathryn married Cary Arthur Miller. (e) Jimsie Savannah married William Latimore Mosley and they had two children: Mary Neysa Mosley (married Virgil H. Coker and had two sons, Virgil H. Coker Jr. and Joe Little Coker). Neysa died in the polio epidemic in Anniston, Alabama, in 1952 at the age of twenty-seven; and Joseph Calvin Mosley (married Constance Elliott and they had one son Matthew Elliott Mosley). Joseph Posey was married second to Mrs. Mattie Chaney on March 14, 1895, and they had no children. (6) Milton Russell was born August 13, 1861, died September 19, 1832. He married Julia Joiner on December 20, 1888, and they had two children. He was a Baptist minister. (7) James Reeves was born July 30, 1864, died September 11, 1944, and was married to Roberta Perryman. They had two children. (8) George William was born August 4, 1866, died about 1955. He married Janie May Clements on February 7, 1900, and they had four children. (9) Samuel Boyd was born June 11, 1868, died January 10, 1919. He married LaRue Thompson on May 5, 1900, and they had no children. Samuel Boyd, a physician, was a resident of Athens, Georgia.

Anne Reeves Little died on April 25, 1873, and Samuel then married the widow of J.L. Latimer, on January 6, 1876. There were no children by this second marriage. Samuel died May 18, 1894. Samuel, Anne and her parents (James and Nancy Harper Reeves), and Samuel's second wife are all buried in the church yard of the Bowdon Baptist Church. *Submitted by: Matthew Mosley (currently serving in Bosnia), 328 Fern Street, Bremen, GA 30110*

772. Long Family

Part 1

The Longs who settled Carroll County were all descendants of John Long of Tennessee, who was born in or near Londonderry, Northern Ireland, in 1737. His parents were Ann and Joseph Long, thought to be supporters of Bonnie Prince Charlie, who emigrated to Northern Ireland and then to Rockingham (Augusta) County, Virginia, around 1754. John Long was a member of Shelby's regiment that fought in the Battle of King's Mountain.

Benjamin McFarland Long

In 1763, John Long married near Staunton, Virginia, a widow named Jane Young (Henry) with whom he had seven children: Joseph, James, Nancy, Robert (1770-1857), Ruth, Jan, and John Jr. John Long served as a soldier in Shelby's regiment at the Battle of King's Mountain. After the death of his wife, Jane Young, John moved in with his son Robert, a widower. Here the two men raised Robert's children. It is thought that he died in 1826 and was buried in McAnaly's Cemetery near Morristown, Tennessee. When the cemetery was flooded by Lake Cherokee, his body was moved to Bethesda Cemetery, just east of Morristown. His grave is marked with the original natural stone and a later marker.

John Long's son, Robert Long, married Isabella Leeper (1773-1813) in 1793. Their son John was born in 1797 and lived in Morristown, Tennessee, until around 1826 when he moved his family to Carroll County, Georgia, which had just been opened to settlement by a treaty negotiated in 1825. In 1827, John Long purchased Harttown, a house located on U.S. Highway 78 just west of Villa Rica. It was in this house that his son Benjamin McFarland Long was born on November 5, 1827. Given that the territory was still occupied by Native Americans, Benjamin long has the distinction of being the first white child born in the county.

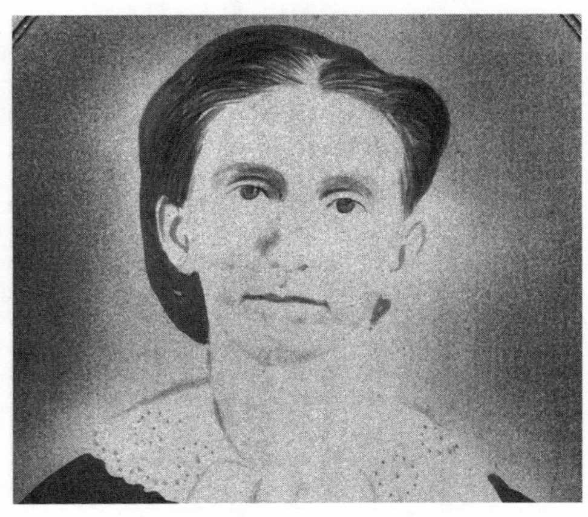

Caroline Amanda Long

John Long served as a justice of the Carroll County Inferior Court in 1827 to 1828; and also served as Clerk of the Court for many years. In addition, he served as a representative to the Georgia House of Representatives in 1868. In addition to Benjamin Long, John Long and his second wife, Nancy Davis Long, had seven children: John Orville (1829-1848) as a result of abuses as a prisoner during the Mexican War), Isabella Jane (1832-1906), Looney James (1835-1839 as a result of a fall from a wagon), Louisa Susan (1838-1848), William Leeper (1840-1865) who died as a result of a train accident on his return from Appomattox), and Caroline Eliza (1845-1933). John Long died in 1870 and is buried in the old Carrollton Cemetery along with his wife who died in 1880.

John Long and his first wife, Charity Taylor May, had a son, Robert Leeper Long, who was born in 1818. As a young child, he moved to Carroll County with his father. After his mother's death, a trusted family servant, Mammy Betty, took care of the young man. In 1836, he enlisted in Captain W.S. Parris' Company for the Creek Indian War, and in 1837 he went to the Seminole War as captain of the Carroll Rangers Cavalry. After leaving the army in 1838, he began the study of medicine at the Medical College at Charleston, South Carolina, and Tulane. He began the practice of medicine in Newnan in 1942. In 1949, he married Martha Ann Powell, the daughter of James Powell and Sara Summerlin. Robert Long served as a captain in the Confederate Army in Company D, Phillips' Legion Cavalry, and fought at Spotsylvania Courthouse, Gettysburg, The Wilderness, and Willamsburg. Their children were: Edgar H., John D., James J., Eugene, Charles Dana, Helen M., Robert Jr., and Mary Ida. Edgar married Eugenia Mandeville of Carrollton in 1878. *Submitted by: Dorothy Pittman, 302 Dixie Street, Carrollton, GA 30117*

773. Long Family

Part 2

Benjamin McFarland Long married Caroline Amanda Wootten, daughter of Pope Wootten and Melissa Caroline Hinton in the old Wootten house which at that time stood on the site of the present day Maple Street School. (The house is presently located on Lovvorn Road.) He was one of the first volunteers in the Mexican War, serving under the command of Robert E. Lee. After the Mexican War, Benjamin Long entered the mercantile business. In 1861, he organized the first company from Walker County, Alabama, and entered the Confederate Army as captain of Company G, Colonial Looney's Regiment, Hindman's Division. After the war, he lived in Jasper, Alabama until he moved to the town of Cordova, Alabama which he founded, naming it after a town he had visited in Mexico. He briefly returned to Carrollton where he served in the legislature in 1872 to 1874. When he died in 1903, he left quite a fortune to twelve children: Henry Whitfield (1855-), John Benjamin (1857-1907), Nancy Caroline (1858-1925), Thomas Leeper (1860-1931), Looney Jesse (1862-1863), Robert Wootten (1864-1910), Ida Jane (1866-1915), Effie Lou (1868-1937), Ada Sophie (1870-1940), Pope McFarland (1872-1956), Jesse Orville (1874-1937), and Edgar William (1876-1947). Of these children, all but two were born in Carrollton.

Henry Whitfield Long, born in 1855, married Lula Mandeville in 1881. During the latter part of the nineteenth century, Henry was a partner in his father's mercantile business in Alabama. He then returned to Carrollton where he was mayor in 1910. His home was a large Queen Ann style on "the hill" of Maple Street across from the Mandevilles. HIs business was later operated by his brothers Jess and Edgar. Henry and Lula had five children: Lula (1883-

1962), Benjamin Mandeville (Man) (1881-1973), Ida Stella (1885-), Mary (1889-), and Helen (1894-1986).

Lula and her husband Charles Roop who built a house on the corner of Dixie and Center Streets had one child, Mary Helen (1914-) who married Hugh W. Hosch of Gainesville, Georgia in 1938.

Mandeville Long married Helen West (died 1938) of Carrollton in 1909. From 1917 until his retirement in the 1960s, Man operated the Long Insurance Agency in Carrollton. Man and Helen had two daughters: Helen Celeste (1912-1986) and Frances Marion (1914-2000). Helen Celeste married William Aubrey Jones in 1944. Frances Marion married James F. McNamara in 1941. Their daughter, Marion Frances (1942-) married Nelson Barrett Dobbs in 1964.

Ida Stella married Frances Long, the son of John Benjamin Long and Missouri Musgrove, in 1903. They made their home in Jasper, Alabama.

Mary married Jesse Travis of Carrollton, and had one son, Jesse Travis Jr. (1917-1925) who died as a result of a traffic accident in Rome, Georgia.

Helen married Shirley Caffee Boykin (1889-1963) on December 18, 1913, in a wedding dress scorched from the devastating fire which destroyed her family home the day before. It seems that her sister Lula, decided to tidy up the room where wedding presents were stored. In the process, she moved the excelsior packing material too close to the furnace exhaust chimney which ignited the fire. Helen managed to save only her wedding dress by throwing it out of the second floor window.

John Benjamin married Missouri Musgrove of Walker County, Alabama. Their son Francis married Ida Stella Long in 1903.

Nancy Caroline married Newton Camak of Walker County, Alabama in 1878. The family made their home in Alabama.

Thomas Leeper married Augusta Sprott, daughter of Judge Samuel Henry Sprott and Lenora Brockway of Livingston, Alabama. He lived at various times in Jacksonville, Florida, Sanford, Florida, and Montgomery, Alabama.

Holderness Home place, 302 Dixie Street, Carrollton. About 1935.

Looney Jesse was born on 2 February 1862 in Carrollton and died on 26 November 1863. He is buried in Carrollton.

Robert Wootten married Kathrine McQueen and had one child. He settled in Cordova, Alabama and died there in 1910.

Ida Jane married John Miller of Jefferson County, Alabama, died in 1915, and is buried in Cordova, Alabama.

Effie Lou Long married Charles Horace Stewart of Carrollton in 1890. They had four children: John Wiley, Caroline (1897-1919), Horace Jr. (1899-), and Benjamin (1901-1902). John Wiley married Brooks Lovvorn and had two children who died as infants, and a daughter Caroline, and an adopted child Clare. Caroline married Claude Griffin in 1917 and had one son, Claude Griffin Jr. Family legend says that she died of tetanus when a cut on her finger became infected.

Horace Stewart Jr. attended Georgia Military Academy, the University of Georgia, and graduated from Oglethorpe University in 1922. In 1922 he married Lucile Long, daughter of Robert Leeper Young Long Jr. of Jasper, Alabama. Horace Jr. joined his father in the operation of his business, City Supply Company. As president of the Bank of Carrollton until its failure during the depression he was able to return to the depositors a large percentage of their money. Horace Jr. and Lucile had two sons: Robert Long (1924-) and Charles Horace III (1936-).

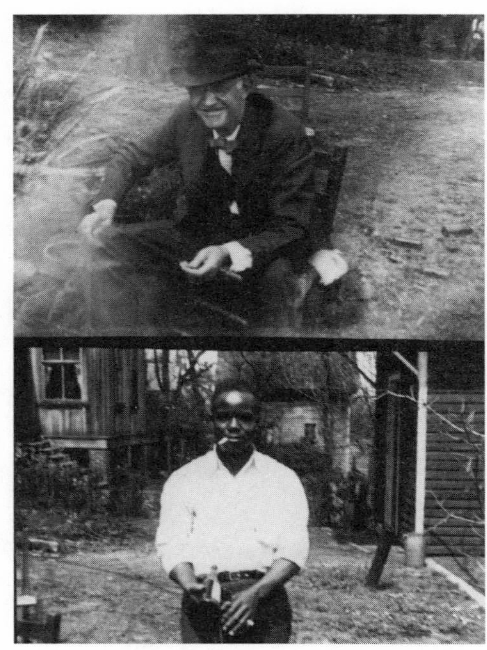

Sidney Holderness gardening in Carrollton. About 1935

Robert Long attended the University of Alabama (1941-1943) and West Georgia College (1947-1948). During World War II, he served as a sergeant in the U.S. Army in the South Pacific. He also joined his father in the family business (City Supply Company) and later operated his own business, Stewart Sales Company. He is a member of the Carrollton Presbyterian Church and was active in the Lions Club. Robert and his wife, Jean Penfield, whom he married in 1950, have three children: Robert Long Jr. (1952-), James Penfield (1955-), and Elizabeth Jane (1956-).

Charles Horace III graduated from the University of Alabama in 1950 with a degree in business administration. During World War II he served in the U.S. Navy as a petty officer. In 1945, he married Miriam Meeks of Carrollton. Horace was a member of the Carrollton Presbyterian Church and the Rotary Club. Their two children are Barbara Miriam (1951-), and Susan Lucile (1955-) *Submitted by: Mrs. S. Sprott Long, 3349 Donovan Place, Charlotte, NC 25215, and Written by: Dorothy Pittman*

774. Long Family

Part 3

Ada Sophie married Sidney Holderness of Carrollton in 1892. They had three children: Benjamin Scott (1895-1896) who died as the result of drowning in a shallow bath tub, Annie Clare (1897-1943), and Sidney Jr. (1899-1974).

Sidney Holderness Jr. attended Oglethorpe University, Atlanta, from 1916-1920, graduating with AB and MA degrees. He attended Law School at Harvard University and received his degree from the University of Virginia in 1924. In 1941 he married Elizabeth Werner, also a graduate of Oglethorpe in 1929. Their son Sidney Holderness III was born on May 8, 1947. Sidney Jr. practiced law for many years in Carrollton. He was also a Mason, a Shriner, Recorder for Hebron Commandery, Knights Templar and an elder in the Carrollton Presbyterian Church. Sidney and his family lived on Griffin Drive in Carrollton until his death.

Annie Clare graduated from Converse College in Spartanburg, South Carolina, and in 1933 married Brooks Oliver Pittman of Commerce, Georgia. Clare died of tuberculosis in 1943 and is buried in Carrollton.

Pope McFarland married Birda Ellis in Cordova, Alabama, and lived in Jasper, Alabama, until his death in 1956.

Jesse Orville received his education at Southern College (Birmingham Southern College) Greensboro, Alabama, and Howard College, Birmingham, and was a member of the Sigma Alpha Epsilon fraternity. In 1903, he married Nonie Belle Sprott (died 1959) who was the sister of Augusta Sprott, wife of Thomas Leeper Long. Jess Long engaged in various activities in Jasper, Alabama, including the operation of an early garage and the holding of public office until 1920 when he moved with the family in 1920. He was employed by the Atlantic Coast Railroad until his death in 1937. Jess and Nonie Belle had four children: Jesse Orville Long Jr. (1904-1975), Stewart Holderness (1908-1981), Margaret Sprott (1911-1996), and Samuel Sprott (1916-2000).

Jesse Orville Long was educated at Tennessee Military Institute, Sweetwater, Tennessee, and the University of Alabama, receiving a degree in electrical engineering. In 1936 he married Dixie McConnell. He served in the Navy during World War II, rising to the grade of captain in the Naval Reserves. Jess and Dixie had two children: Carol McConnell (1940-), and Jess Lawrence (1945-).

Jesse Orville Long Family reunion, Carrollton, Georgia, 1950.

Stewart Holderness Long graduated from Davidson College and Columbia Theoogical Seminary, Decatur, Georgia, in 1932. In 1934 he married Esther Margaret Hansen (died 2000) and had two sons: Stewart Hansen (1936-) and David Edwin (1937-). After serving for many years as a Presbyterian minister in North Carolina, Georgia, and Oklahoma, Stewart and his family served several churches in the Tampa, Florida, area until his death.

Margaret Sprott graduated from the University of Alabama in 1933 with a degree in education with a minor in library science. After serving as a librarian at Seminole High School in Sanford, Florida, Margaret moved to Birmingham, Alabama. During the summer after her first year as a librarian in Birmingham, Margaret suffered a detached retina in both of her eyes and was hospitalized at Emory University Hospital in Atlanta for eighteen months. In April 1944 she married Brooks Oliver Pittman whose wife, Annie Clare Holderness had died in 1943. After the end of World War II, Margaret and Brooks returned to Carrollton to live in the old Holderness home place on Dixie Street. They had two children: Margaret Brooks Pittman (1945-) and Dorothy Eugenia (1948-). In 1952 Brooks Pittman tragically died of a severe heart attack, leaving Margaret to raise their two young children. From 1954 until her retirement in 1972, Margaret worked as a librarian at Bowdon High School and Bremen High School. After her retirement, she was active in the Arts Study Club of Carrollton and the Women of the Church of the Carrollton Presbyterian Church, receiving a life membership.

Margaret (Peggy) Brooks graduated from Central High School in 1965 and married Richard G. Miller in 1972. Peggy and Richard had two children: Dorothy Ann Miller (1973-) and William Pittman Miller (1976-).

Margaret Sprott Long Pittman and Brooks Oliver Pittman. 1951.

Dorothy Eugenia graduated from Valdosta State College in 1969 with a BA in history, Florida State University with a MS in library science, and from the University of Edinburgh (U.K.) with a M.Litt. in medieval history. In 1975 she married Dr. David Hugh Adams of Rushmoor U.K., a fellow graduate of the University of Edinburgh. Dorothy and David had two children: Margaret Bain Pittman Adams (1982-) and Kenneth Brooks Pittman Adams (1986-). For many years, Dorothy worked as a librarian at the Cobb County (Georgia) Public Library, the Seminole County (Florida) Public Library, and the Harford (Maryland) County Library. In 1997, Dorothy purchased Horton's Books & Gifts, the oldest bookstore in Georgia and the oldest business in Carrollton. After her mother's death, Dorothy and her family moved into the family home (the Holderness home place) on Dixie Street.

Edgar William married Catherine Pheifer (died 1906) and Ruth Lacy in 1916. He died in 1947 and is buried in Jasper, Alabama. *Submitted by: Margaret Pittman Miller, 1267 Briarcliff Road NE, Atlanta GA 30306, and Written by: Dorothy Pittman.*

775. James W. Long

James W. Long was born 23 September 1854 in Georgia and married Phoebe Jane Katherine Holcombe 20 December 1877 in Haralson County, daughter of James Madison Holcombe and Jane Katherine Reid. Phoebe was born 27 September 1857 and died 20 May 1899, both Haralson County. James died less than a month later on 13 June 1899 from a brain tumor and both are buried in Little Vine Cemetery, Haralson County. Their children lived with James' sister, Martha, after their deaths.

James W. Long was the son of Thomas J. Long, born 1830, in Georgia. Thomas enlisted in the Civil War in Company G, 41st Regiment of Georgia and was captured at Perryville, Kentucky, in March of 1863. On 20 March 1863 Thomas was sent to Camp Butler with a leg wound that later resulted in amputation of the leg. His death resulted from complications of this amputation. James' mother was Susan A. Bradley, born 24 March 1833 in Fayette County, Georgia, and died 5 July 1891, Haralson County. Susan and Thomas were married 10 January 1852, Fayette County. Susan is buried Little Vine Cemetery and a Civil War Memorial marker was placed there in honor of Thomas. James W. had one brother and three sisters: Mary A., born 24 November 1852, married William J. Lewis, 3 February 1872, Haralson County; Martha T., born 14 October 1856 and died 5 March 1903, in Haralson County, never married; Joseph Brown, born 22 September 1859, married Sarah Indiana Holcombe 23 September 1884, married second Ada Butler 4 February 1912, Haralson County; Lula, may have died an infant. Mollie and William, Martha T., Joseph Brown and two wives are buried Little Vine Cemetery. Lula's burial unknown.

James W. and Phoebe farmed and had ten known children: Emma Clara Taullah, born 7 February 1879, married Kim Estes, 29 March 1900, Haralson County. Children: Grady, Ora, Alton, Myrtle, Alma, Cordie, Bertie, Lurline, Troy, Lessie, Ray, and Florie: Lowell Thomas, born 27 January 1881, married Margaret Jane Bell, 19 November 1905, Haralson County. Children: Charles, Flora, Eunice, Murdock, Quinton, Tommie Mae, and Amilee; Susan Katherine Long, born 8 January 1883, married James Reuben Frank Lewis, 8 July 1900, Haralson County. Children: Eula, Lola, Homer, Eva, and Carl; Delia 1884-1901; Abigale 1887-1887; Joseph Martin Dawson, born 9 October 1888, married Memory Ethel Westbrooks, 15 October 1911, Haralson County. Children: Fred, Hazel, and Clyde. Dawson was the postmaster in Bremen; Jane 1901, lived two days; William Leonard Franklin, born 16 January 1892, married Cordie Merrell, 14 October 1914, Haralson County. Children: Celeste, Jane and Leonard Jr.; Charles 1897-1897; Henry 1898-1898. Emma, Lowell, Kate, and Dawson lived in Haralson County and Leonard lived in Decatur, Georgia. Emma and Kim, Lowell and Margaret, Kate and Frank, Delia, Abigale, Jane, Charles, and Henry are all buried Little Vine Cemetery with their parents. Many descendants of this family now live in Haralson and Carroll Counties. *Submitted by: Jill Allen, 597 W. Hickory Level Rd., Temple, GA 30179 sloua@aol.com*

776. Thomas Lott

Thomas Lott was born October 4, 1826, in Benton County, Alabama, to Ellis Lott and Abigale Carpenter. Thomas and his bride, Mary Ann "Polly" Unknown, moved to Georgia shortly afterward to Carroll County. They and one other resident were the only ones living between Waco, Georgia, and Pleasant View Baptist Church. They built a log cabin of two rooms, one where the family slept and another where they spent most of the daylight hours which was heated and with a "fresh air breeze way" between.

Mr. Lott was a bad diabetic and died of this disease when he was only forty-six years of age. He died December 10, 1856. His widow raised the family which consisted of six children: (1) William Ellis, who died serving in the Confederate Army in the War Between the States in Kentucky, (2) John D., who moved to Cass County, Texas, after being discharged from the Confederate Army, (3) Martin Thomas, (4) Elmira, (5) Drady who married William Joseph Entrekin, and (6) Jose who died at an early age and is probably buried with her father in an unmarked grave on their farm just south of I-20 between Bremen and Waco, Georgia.

Mr. Lott's widow, Polly, and his daughter Elmira are buried in Pleasant View Cemetery in Carroll County. Martin Thomas, the third son, married Sara Elizabeth Cole and this union produced twelve children: Thomas Avian, Mattie Mae, Albert Warner "Bud," Claude B., Jimmie, Lula, Ovie Belle, Anna Estelle, Dollie, Cora, Minnie Kate, and Robert Lee.

Martin Thomas raised his family in the Smyrna Church community of Carroll County and several of his family remain in the area and have descendants living nearby today. Martin Thomas farmed and dealt in real estate. He died December 21, 1921, and is buried at Smyrna Church Cemetery in Carroll County. His wife, Sarah Elizabeth, died December 18, 1925, and is buried alongside her husband.

They enjoyed a long life and left a great heritage for their many descendants to enjoy. *Submitted by: Hogan H. Jones, 617 Smith Street, Bremen, GA 30110*

777. Andrew Jackson Lovvorn and John James Lovvorn

Andrew Jackson was born August 13, 1855, and married October 22, 1876, Haralson County, Martha Ellen Brice, born October 20, 1856. He had nine children with Martha: (1) John J. died as infant. (2) Elizabeth Jane, born June 26, 1877, married George L. Haas. (3) Sally Catherine, born March 1881, married Averett C. Hall. (4) Andy Frank, born April 15, 1883, in Bremen, married Mary Bessie Morrison. (5) Robert Leonard, born May 10, 1885, married Ada Pearl Barrentine. (6) Lee Augustus, born July 1889, married Missouri Dupree. (7) Henry Grady, born April 1890, married Lue Venice Burrell. (8) James Riley, born October 1893, married Sula Watson. (9) Infant born and died March 10, 1895.

John James Lovvorn Family

Martha died March 11, 1895. Andrew married second Estelle Wooten on March 28, 1897, in DeKalb County, Alabama. He and Estelle had one son, Joseph Louis Lovvorn Sr., born 1903 and married Rosa Turner. Andrew and his family migrated first to Jackson County, Alabama, and later to Alabama City in Etowah County, Alabama where he owned a store. Andrew died September 17, 1914. Andrew and Martha are buried at Pleasant View Cemetery in Jackson County. Estelle died January 14, 1930, and is buried in Forrest Cemetery, Gadsden.

The photograph of Andrew Jackson Lovvorn's family shows Andrew Jackson Lovvorn on the far right, with moustache; Andrew's wife Estelle holding Joseph Louis Lovvorn; holding bicycle is Andy Frank Lovvorn with wife Bessie; going left next to Andy is Robert L. Lovvorn; seated is Lee Augustus Lovvorn; behind Lee is Grady Lovvorn; Riley Lovvorn holding cat; in front of him Sally Hall wearing black and holding son, Andrew Hall; the young girl to the far left is Ellis Haas, daughter of Lizzie Haas who is wearing a white blouse and holding her son, Elbert Haas; with son Columbus Haas standing in front of Sally; boy in front of bicycle is not identified.

John James was born November 1857. He married first Elvira Alles (Alice) McGraw October 30, 1879, Carroll County, and second Lizzie Mosely on October 4, 1903, Etowah County, Alabama. He and Elvira had eight children: (1) Eva, born August 1880. (2) Ida, born February 1882, married Reuben Cary Busbin. (3) Ephriam Riley, born April 1884, married first to Cora Small and second to Lillie Alice Whitten. (4) Mealey, born January 1886. (5) Jethro Jackson, born November 1891, married Ethel Mattie Awalt. (6) Odesta, born April 1895, married

Andrew Jackson Lovvorn Family

McPherson. (7) William Jenous, born July 1897, married Mildred Sawyer. (8) Elniba, born November 25, 1900.

John James and his family migrated first to Jackson County, Alabama, then to Etowah County where he worked at Dwight Textile Mill. He died May 4, 1920, and Elvira died May 16, 1903. They are buried in Pleasant View Cemetery, Jackson County. The photograph of John James Lovvorn's family shows front row seated, John J. Lovvorn, wife Alice holding baby (probably Odesta), Jethro Jackson, John James' mother, Nancy Malinda Holland Lovvorn; second row standing, probably Eva, then Ida, Bud? (probably Ephriam Riley), and Mealy. *Submitted by: John C. Awbrey, great-great-grandson of Andrew Jackson Lovvorn.*

778. James Talton and Nora Folds Lovvorn

James Talton Lovvorn was born on December 31, 1879, near Bremen to Talton Washington Lovvorn and Nancy Catherine Shelnutt. He married Nora Folds on September 18, 1897, in Carroll County. Nora was born October 15, 1881. Jim died September 23, 1949, and Nora died November 11, 1969. They are both buried at Pleasant View Cemetery in Carroll County. They had five children: Bertha, Loyce V., Ralph, Dollie, and Milton Talton Lovvorn.

Jim and Nora Lovvorn

(I) Bertha Lovvorn married Millard Parker. They lived near Bowdon Junction. She died August 1967. They had one daughter, Anne Parker, who married first Sammy White. Anne and Sammy had three children: Connie, Robin, and Mindy White. Anne married second Tommy Baxter.

(II) Loyce V. Lovvorn (died 1978) married Mamie Reid. They had five children: (A) Mildred Lovvorn married J. Clark Gary. They had three children: (1) Richard Gary married Connie Gwenn and had two children: Jan and Chip; (2) Barbara Jean Gary married first Sammy Robinson and had one daughter, Angie Robinson. Barbara Jean Gary married second Clinton Watkins; and (3) Cheyenne Gary, who married Gerald Workman and had two children: Shane and Wendy Workman; (B) Loyce Lovvorn Jr. (born 1925) married Mae Williams. They had two children: Carole and Michael. Carole Lovvorn married Donald Wright and had two children: Donald Wright Jr. and Kristi Suzanne Wright. Michael Lovvorn (born 1951) married first Cathy Sawyer and had one son, Christopher M. Lovvorn (born 1977). Michael married second Kim Barrow; (C) Betty Jean Lovvorn married Gilbert Boone and had two daughters: Diane and Denise. Diane married Tommy Benefield and had two daughters: Tammy and Lisa. Denise married Michael Grubbs; (D) June Lovvorn married William Bishop and had one daughter, Linda. Linda married Jerry Walton and had one daughter Traci Walton, and one son Scott Bishop; and (E) Robert J. Lovvorn.

(III) James and Nora's third child, Ralph Lovvorn, married Jennie Belle Nichols. They had no children.

(IV) James and Nora's fourth child, Dollie Lovvorn, married first Curtis Baker and had one son, Billy Wayne Baker, who died in World War II. Dollie married second Bud Morris. She died about 1983.

(V) James and Nora's fifth child, Milton Talton Lovvorn, called Punk, married Flacey Smith. They had two children, Brenda Lovvorn and Dondra Lovvorn. *Submitted by: Loyce Lovvorn Jr.*

779. John Lovvorn and Della Cassel

John William Lovvorn was born February 29, 1884, and was the youngest child of Talton Washington (Wash) and Nancy Shelnutt Lovvorn. By the time he was eight, his parents were both dead. HIs older sister, Victoria (Vick) had married Frank Adams and was living at Mt. Zion. All three of Vick's brothers — Joseph Edgar, James Talton and John — lived with their sister and her husband but John being the youngest lived there the longest.

One day John stopped on the road to help Alfred Cassel who was in an ox-drawn wagon stuck in deep mud. Traveling with Alfred that day was Della, his pretty and petite daughter. After John pulled the wagon out of the mire, Alfred asked how he could repay John for his time and trouble. John responded "Well, Mr. Cassel, I'll just take little Della when she grows up." Several years later, John did just that! John and Della were married in Tallapoosa, Georgia, on May 1, 1904.

By this time, Victoria Lovvorn Adams and her family were living on the Georgia-Alabama state line near Macedonia Baptist Church. John and Della lived just on the Georgia side of the line on property adjoining the Adams land. John operated a sawmill, was a successful farmer, enjoyed hunting and kept hunting dogs. His old hunting gun, and a hunting horn he made, and on which he carved his name and the date, hangs now in the home of his grandson, Johnny Lovvorn.

John and Della's children were Eula, Herman, Frank, Eunice, Spencer, Bernice, and William Bernard. They were raising these seven children when John and their baby, Bernard, died during the influenza epidemic in 1918. John and Della's three young sons, Herman, Spencer and Frank, went to live nearby with their Aunt Vick as their father had done about thirty years earlier.

In later years, Della Cassel Lovvorn married Joseph Emory Jackson in Carroll County, Georgia. They had one daughter, Cliffie (1923-1996), who married William Wall and had one son, William Jr.

Lovvorn Family Reunion

(1) Eula (1905-2000) married Otis Balenger. Their children were Ralph Balenger who married Billie Jo Gulledge (three children, Belinda, Danny, Maurice); Roy Balenger who married first Elizabeth Stafford (two children, Eddie and Tammy), and second to Pauline White; (2) Herman (1907-1982) remained a bachelor; (3) Frank (1909-1948) married Hilda Cushing and their daughter Kathryn married Henry Butler (children were Stephen, Randall, Donna, and Nina); (4) Eunice (1911-) married Hugh McCollum and their children were Faye, June, Bobby. Faye married first Leo Browne (one daughter Gail), and second to Charles Ragland (one son Charles), and third to Bob Bettag. Bobby married Mildred Mosley (three sons, Joe, Mike, Mark) and second to Beverly Thomas. June married first Benjamin Williams (two children Barbara and Ben), second to Ronald Hiltner; (5) Spencer (1914-1980) married Eva Richardson and their children were LaRealia who married Ellis Camp (three sons, Ellis Jr., John, Bob); Johnny married Joyce Hendrix (two sons Johnny Spencer and Douglas); (6) Bernice (1916-) married Paul W. Roberts and their children were Shirley who married Bobby Hutcheson (two sons, David and Richard); Imajean (1937-2000) married Jep Daniel (five children, Ricky,

John Lovvorn and Della Cassel Lovvorn

Guerry "Pepper," Diana, Teresa and Vicky (1958-1965); Eleanor married first Roscoe Elner Stewart Jr., (two children, Scott and Cynthia), and second to George Travis Davis (1937-1994); Johnny married first to Diane Lipham (one son John) and second to Nancy Jiles.

Della Lovvorn Jackson died in Gadsden, Alabama, in 1978 at the age of ninety-one.

Note: Other variations of the Cassels surname used by family members include Cassell, Cassels and Castle.

The family photograph shows Spencer and Herman Lovvorn, and Eula Lovvorn Ballenger on the back row. On the front row are Bernice Lovvorn Roberts, Eunice Lovvorn McCollum, and Frank Lovvorn. Seated in front is Cliffie Jackson. *Submitted by: Eleanor Roberts Davis, 2535 Cardinal Lake Circle, Duluth, GA 30096*

780. Joseph Edgar and Roxie (McMullen) Lovvorn

Joseph Edgar Lovvorn was born January 27, 1876, near Bremen. He was the son of Talton Washington Lovvorn and Nancy Catherine Shelnutt. Joseph married November 8, 1896, in Carroll County, Roxie Jane McMullen, born March 6, 1879, in Carroll County. Roxie was the daughter of Mary Emily Tillman (March 25, 1842-August 16, 1920) and Arthur McMullen who was born in Carroll County, and died before June 1882 in Carroll County.

Joseph Edgar and Roxie (McMullen) Lovvorn

Joe and Roxie had three children who lived. All were born near Bremen. The children were Joseph Edgar Jr., (1899-1972), Winona Beryl Lovvorn (1901-1998), and Charles Jason Lovvorn (1904-1967).

In his early years Joseph was a school teacher, then he was a school superintendent in Polk County 1904-1908. He did not attend college but studied law, the term they used then was "read the law" under other attorneys and was admitted to the Georgia bar. The family went to Milledgeville, Georgia, where Joseph was superintendent of the State Reform School for Boys (1912-1916). In 1917 Joseph decided they should go to Okeechobee, Florida, which was just opening up for settlement. Joseph bought a two-story frame hotel where the family lived until Joseph's death in 1956. They operated it as a hotel and a rooming house. Later Joseph was a judge in Okeechobee. He was a Mason, a Scottish Rite degree, and a Shriner.

Joseph died in 1956 in Ft. Pierce, Florida, and Roxie died October 9, 1965 in Ft. Myers, Florida. They are buried with their son, Joseph Edgar Jr., in Okeechobee Cemetery. Joseph Edgar Lovvorn Jr. worked for the National Safety Commission in Chicago. He never married. Charles Jason Lovvorn (1904-1967), son of Joseph and Roxie Lovvorn, married Mary Evelyn Davis and had no children. They owned and operated a florist in South Florida and are both buried in Clewiston, Florida.

Beryl married September 12, 1925, Keathley "Kit" Bowden, born February 7, 1898 in Hammond County, Florida. They operated newspapers in several South Florida towns. Beryl and Kit had two children: Charles K. Bowden and Paul Bowden.

Charles K. Bowden, called K, is a retired USAF colonel. He married Patricia L. Williams and had five children: (1) Jan Lovvorn Bowden married first to Bryan Ashley Donahue, second to James Westley Coker; (2) Patricia Kelly Bowden married first to Michael Louis Jones, second to Lawrence Proctor; (3) Charles K. Bowden married Ande Marie Ackersley, (4) Florence E. Bowden, and (5) William Mathew Bowden (adopted). Beryl and Kit's second son, Paul, has married several times and has several children.

Kit died February 16, 1959, in Thomasville, Georgia, and is buried in Monticello, Florida. Beryl died June 2, 1998 in Lakeland Florida. Beryl's ashes were scattered and a marker for her was placed beside Kit's. *Submitted by: Charles K. Bowden, Wetumpka, AL*

Sources: Family Bible records, letters from Beryl Bowden

781. William Daniel Lovvorn

An active citizen of Bowdon and Carroll County, Georgia, William Daniel Lovvorn (sometimes called W.D.) was born in Henry County, Georgia, in 1831. With his parents, James M. Lovvorn Jr. and Bathsheba Traylor Lovvorn, he moved to Lamar, Randolph County, Alabama, in 1838.

William Daniel married Sarah Delila Burden in January of 1852. The couple lived and farmed in Lamar and attended the Missionary Baptist Church.

In 1859, William bought a new three-story wooden framed grist mill and 450 acres of timber and farming land at Newell, Alabama, in the red hills of Randolph County. During the Civil War, times were very lean and W.D. was ever-busy keeping the grinder and the thrasher going to feed the hungry and depressed civilians of Randolph County. He was a member of the Home Guard but he was against secession and owned no slaves.

While living in Newell, he became a justice of the peace for the county (similar responsibility of present-day judges) and in 1872 was elected Randolph County's representative to Alabama State Legislature.

In 1877, W.D. asked his oldest son, Thomas Jefferson Lovvorn, a math teach at "The Arithmetic School" at Poplar Springs, Alabama, to take over the mill so that he and Sarah could move to Bowdon, Georgia. He was concerned about the education of their younger children. They moved to Bowdon where he bought and ran the Lovvorn Mill on Indian Creek. He had one hundred acres of land and, in time, added a store, a sawmill, wool plant, a tannery, and a cotton gin.

Colonel W.D. Lovvorn was financially and constructively active in the erection of a new and much needed building for Bowdon College in the last quarter of the century. He served as chairman of the Board of Trustees for Bowdon College for over twenty years until his death in 1900.

William Daniel and Sarah's eleven children were born from 1853 to 1875 in Randolph County, Alabama. They were Thomas Jefferson (Tom) who was an educator and miller; Nancy Evelynn who married William Smith; Mary Elizabeth (Bob) who married Wesley Whitfield Johnson; Gaines Washington who was a miller; William Jeptha (Jep) who was a Baptist minister; Sarah Rebecca who married Columbus Morris; Robert Monroe (Dr. Bob) who was a medical doctor, a minister, and an educator; Martha Ellen (Ellen) married John William Barrow; Emma Cindonia (Donnie) married W.J. Whatley; Samuel Alex died when he was two years old; and Henry Oliver, who was a manufacturer in Carrollton.

My direct line of descent comes from Thomas Jefferson Lovvorn. Tom outlived his five wives. His last wife, Polly Ridley Owensby, was my grandmother. Polly Ridley and Tom Lovvorn had a son named Ales Ridley Lovvorn, my father. *Submitted by: Phyllis Lovvorn Hubbard, Dixie Avenue South, Bremen, GA 30110*

782. William Marion Lovvorn

William Marion Lovvorn was born April 20, 1851 probably in Fayette County. He was the son of William Riley Lovvorn and Nancy Malinda Holland. He married February 23, 1871, Virginia Caroline Awtrey who was born November 24, 1847. Virginia was the daughter of Eldridge Awtrey (born March 20, 1805, Georgia, died about 1865 in Haralson County) and Margaret George (born about 1813 in South Carolina, died after 1871 Haralson County). William Marion was a miller and called "Miller Will." Will died October 25, 1920, and Virginia died July 21, 1924, in Bowdon. Will and Virginia are buried at Indian Creek Cemetery. They had ten children, all born near Bremen in Haralson County. Their children were William Eldridge, Nancy Jane Rebecca (Nannie), Margaret Elizabeth, Zelphia Leola (Ola), John Wade Elijah, Marion Washington (M.W.), Frances Darthulia Eleanor (Darthulia), Martha Angeline (Mattie), Emma Irene, Elzie Phillip (E.P.).

William Marion Lovvorn Family

(1) William Eldridge was born February 18, 1872, and married Carrie Kuglar March 24, 1895. (2) Nancy Jane Rebecca was born January 17, 1874, and married William Holloway in 1893. (3) Margaret Elizabeth was born December 20, 1875. (4) Zelphia Leola was born November 18, 1877, and married John Styles. She died October 27, 1932. (5) John Wade Elijah was born October 8, 1879, and married Louise Hornsby. (6) Marion Washington was born September 7, 1881, and died in 1983. He married first Mattie Warren, second Laura Morgan, third Lila Lovvorn Gladney. (7) Frances Darthulia Eleanor was born December 20, 1884, and married Homer Burnham. At one time their address was 2817 Mt. Olive Street, Decatur, Georgia. (8) Martha Angeline was born February 21, 1887, and married Robert Powell. (9) Emma Irene was born July 1, 1888, died July 6, 1889. She is buried at the Holland Cemetery in Haralson County. (10) Elzie Phillip was born May 1, 1890, and married Effie Eason. At one time their address was Marietta, Georgia. The Family Bible record shows a Lizzie Lovvorn died May 19, 1889. This could possibly be the Margaret Elizabeth who has nothing further recorded.

Submitted by: Douglas Lovvorn

Sources: William Marion Lovvorn Family Bible record and family information told to James Lecil Lovvorn by Marion Washington Lovvorn; Miss Mildred Lovvorn, Mrs. Eunice Holloway.

783. William Riley Lovvorn Family

William Riley Lovvorn and his wife, Nancy Malinda Holland, migrated from Fayette County to Bremen between 1850 and 1867. The Holland family were among the founders of the Bethlehem Methodist Church in 1854 where William and Nancy's family and their descendants attended. However, William and Nancy were listed on the church membership rolls of the Bethel Baptist Church at one time where William was a deacon. They had ten children: Margaret E., Rebecca, Parmelia, Sarah, Mary Evaline, Talton Washington, William Marion, Hulda Jane, Andrew Jackson, and John James.

Nancy Malinda (Holland) Lovvorn

(I) Margaret E. was born about 1838. (II) Rebecca was born about 1839. They were both on membership roll of Bethel Baptist Church. (III) Parmelia Angeline, called "Meelie," was born about 1843. She married James Hudson in Haralson County December 23, 1868. They had at least two daughters, (1) Dora born about 1883 and (2) Lula (1900 census) or Leola (1910 census) born about 1876. She was head of household in 1900, listed as a widow in 1910, and also on the 1920 census with her daughter Dora Hudson. Meelie died October 9, 1922. She is buried at the Holland family cemetery on the "Old Shelnutt Farm" between Waco and Bremen. Also listed with her family is a nephew, J.E. Awtrey (written "Joseph" on 1900 census and "James" on the 1910 census), born about 1895. They lived in Waco. (IV) Sarah "Sack" was born about 1845. She married Lafayette Hazel (Fayette) in Haralson County, January 5, 1868. They had one child, John William Hazel. They apparently divorced as Lafayette Hazel married again in 1871. Sarah married J.E. Whitaker in Haralson County on November 5, 1902. John William Hazel married first Martha Frances McGraw in Haralson County, second Ollie Pounds Monroe, third Emma ____. He died March 5, 1936 in Hamilton County, Tennessee. Sarah is pictured with Frank Adams family. (V) Mary Evaline, born about 1847, married William E. Wray, January 18, 1871, Haralson County. They migrated to Crockett County, Tennessee, where they were listed on the 1880 census with son James, age nine. With family photographs is one marked James W.H. Wray, Humboldt, Tennessee. William E. Wray served in the Confederate Army. He was a private in Company A, 35th Georgia Infantry and applied for a pension from Crockett County in 1891. (VI) Talton Washington*, (VII) William Marion*, (VIII) Hulda Jane was born about 1853. She married January 11, 1874 in Haralson County, Millard Awtrey, brother of Virginia Awtrey who married William Marion Lovvorn. Jane and Millard's children, all born in Haralson County, were (1) Sarah A. born 1879, (2) George W., born April 1881, (3) Odessa born December 1885, (4) Samuel H. born December 1889, and (5) William L. born November 1891. The James or Joseph E. Awtrey born 1895 who was living with Jane's sister, Parmelia (Lovvorn) Hudson, in 1900 and 1910 may be their son also. Hulda Jane died January 29, 1895 and is buried at the Holland family cemetery. (IX) Andrew Jackson*, (X) John James*

*sons covered separately *Submitted by: Johnny Spencer Lovvorn, Newnan, GA, great-great-great-grandson of William Riley Lovvorn.*

Sources: Marriage Records, census records, information on John William Hazel from Charlotte Hazel, Awtrey Family Research by John Chambers.

784. Elijah Lovvorn / Loving

Elijah Lovvorn/Loving was born 1793 South Carolina. He served in the War of 1812. He married Elizabeth Robertson on April 7, 1814 in Clarke County, Georgia and they had two children, Thomas R. (probably died young) and William Riley. In Campbell County Elijah married Jinsey Shoemaker in 1839. They had three children, Adeline, Joseph, and Elijah W. In the Bible record, National Archives pension file, the name was written as Lovvorn for Elizabeth's children. This spelling has been used by the descendants of William Riley Lovvorn. The name was written Loving to record Jinsey's children. Elijah was a miller and there is evidence that occupation had been passed down through generations. In Elijah's pension file he is described as being five feet eight inches tall, black hair, black eyes, and dark complexion. Elijah was in Carroll County in 1870 near the present site of Cold Spring Church and at the same location (which had become Douglas County) when he died September 5, 1875.

Talton Washington Lovvorn

Elijah was the son of Thomas Loving/Lovvorn (born ca 1750 Virginia), who served in the Revolution, and Thomas' second wife Rosamond. Thomas is located in Pittsylvania County, Virginia, then North Carolina, South Carolina, Georgia, and by 1820 he went to St. Clair County, Alabama, which had just opened for settlers, everything between the Chattahoochee and St. Clair County being Indian lands. He died in St. Clair County before 1829. His will recorded in St. Clair County lists his children: James, Judy, Mary Ann, Edmond, Gabriel, John, Sally, Elijah, and Richard.

William Riley Lovvorn was born 1817. He married August 16, 1836, Fayette County, Georgia, Nancy Malinda Holland born 1818 in Georgia. They lived near Fairburn in Fayette County and in the same location in Campbell County when that county was formed. By 1870 they were living near Bremen and attended the Bethlehem Methodist Church. William was a miller and farmer. Their children were: Talton Washington, John James, Andrew Jackson, William Marion, Margaret E., Rebecca, Permelia Angeline, Sarah, Hulda Jane, and Mary Evaline. In the 1890s William and Nancy went to Jackson County, Alabama, with at least two of their children, John James and A.J. and families. They died in Jackson County, Alabama, and were buried at Pleasant View Cemetery in marked graves.

Talton Washington Lovvorn (Wash) was born in 1848. He married December 25, 1870, in Bremen, Nancy Catherine Shelnutt (born ca 1850) at the home of Catherine's grandfather, John Shelnutt. She was the daughter of Joseph David Shelnutt and first wife, Mary P. Jones. Joseph David was the son of John Shelnutt and Elizabeth White. John was the son of Andrew Shelnutt and Elizabeth Gentry. Wash was a farmer and worked in a gristmill. They had children: Mary Malinda (died age nineteen), Queen Victoria, Joseph Edgar, James Talton, and John William. Wash died in 1886. Catherine died 1892. Wash and Catherine were buried in the Holland family cemetery on the "Old Shelnutt Farm" between Waco and Bremen in marked graves. After Catherine's death, the sons went to live with their sister, Victoria, who was married to Frank Adams. *Submitted by: Larealia Lovvorn Camp, 547 Highway 16 W, Newnan, GA 30263*

Sources: National Archives Pension file; Clarke County, Ga. marriage records; North Carolina State Archives payment voucher; Oglethorpe County, Ga. deeds; St. Clair County, Ala. wills; Fayette County, Ga. marriage records; Haralson County, Ga. marriage and year's support records.

785. The Lovvorn of Bowdon

My paternal grandmother was Alice Lorene Lovvorn and she had the best report card I've ever seen. Her 1902 report card from Bowdon College was for two semesters. Some subjects were for one semester, some for two. In Latin, her grades were 99 and 100; in psychology, 100; in history of English literature, 91 and 98; in ancient history, 98 and 99+; in drawing, 95 and 96; in geology, 100; in trigonometry, 98 and 98; in astronomy, 100; in deportment, 100 and 100. Her average scholarship was 96 5/6 and 98 7/8. I am in awe of her scholarship. She became a school teacher and vice-chairman of the Carroll County Farm Bureau. Each succeeding generation included at least one Lovvorn who became a teacher.

Her parents were Gaines Washington Lovvorn and Virena Frances Johnson. They had children Alice Lorene, Emma Cindonia, Luney Albert, Bertha Ellen, William Oliver, and Thomas Roswell.

Gaines married second, Lillian Othello Coley and they had Robert Lynn, Gaines Stewart, Henry Garland, and Aletha Delilah, then Barney Edward and a daughter, who died infants. Then, Ruby Nell. Three more children died infants, a daughter, Theodore Franklin, and Lunie Lucile. The last two children were Ina Belle and James Ernest.

Her paternal grandparents were William Daniel Lovvorn and Sarah Delilah Burden. Her maternal grandparents were William F. Johnson and Martha Ann Wall.

Georgia's Last Frontier, states that Col. William D. Lovvorn gave $100,000.00 to Bowdon College. Col. Lovvorn was born in Henry County, Georgia and came to Bowdon in 1868 from Randolph County, Alabama. His children were Thomas Jefferson, Nancy Evelyn, Mary Elizabeth, Gaines Washington, William Jeptha, Sarah Rebecca, Robert Monroe, Martha Ellen, Samuel Alex, and Henry Oliver.

Alice Lovvorn married Thomas Simpson McLendon Sr. and had five sons: Gaines Preston McLendon, who was in the clothing industry, retired as head designer of MALE, a men's wear manufacturer in Atlanta. He is a Primitive Baptist and is still active in Sacred Harp music. He will celebrate his 97th birthday October 25, 2001. He married Mattie Novella Turner and had Gaines Earl McLendon who retired from RCA and GE after forty years; and Marganelle McLendon, an artist specializing in tole painting.

The Lovvorn Family

Gaines Earl McLendon married Janet Bryan. Their children are Douglas Alexander, David William and Mary Margaret. David married Carol Ross and had son, Jeffrey David. Mary married Tommy Walter Victor and had sons Emery Alexander and Bryan Martin.

Tom and Alice's second son, Paul, died young. Third son, Thomas Simpson McLendon Jr., married Mary Lou Crews and had Marian Louise and Brenda Gail. T.S. was a merchant and is living in LaGrange. Fourth son, Reece Olliver McLendon, married Irma Eugenia Godbee and had Betty and Joyce. Reece was employed by Western Auto.

Fifth son, William Lovvorn McLendon married Margaret Stephens and had Karen and Elaine and Dennis and Jeff. Lovvorn retired from GE in Huntsville, Alabama, where he worked on NASA projects, including moon shots. He recently moved to Chattanooga. *Submitted by: G.E. McLendon, 2545 Browns Mill Road, Atlanta, GA 30354*

786. George Ewell Lowry / Lowery

George Ewell Lowry came to Carroll County as a sharecropper and made his home in this area. He was born 17 June 1903 in Cleburne County, Alabama, the son of Abbey Anderson Lowry (1884) and Susan Alice Durrett (1883) and is also the grandson of William Harrison Lowry (1846) who served during the Civil War as a private from Heard County, and Serena Elizabeth Nesbitt (1849). William and Serena Lowry and Abbey and Alice Lowry are buried at the Ranburne First Baptist Church Cemetery.

George's siblings are Royce (1904) married Bessie Lee Stapler; Claud (1907) married Verta Hansen; Carl (1909) married Annie Bell Stapler; Charlie Mayfield (1910) married Mary Francis Teague; John Henry (1913) married Vertie Lee Williams; Viola Lurline (1918) married Herbert Townsby; Lila May (1919) married J.T. Duncan; Curtis Ray (1920) married Nora Noles; Katherine Elizabeth (1922) married Oscar David Caldwell. Many of these relatives live in this area and Alabama.

George married Delia Vanny Singleton 18 October 1925 in Carroll County. George was a very hard-working person, who provided for his family by toiling very long days farming. They had five children: Billy Thomas Lowry (1926) married Dola Imogene Eason (1931); Robert (1928-1928) James (1932-1933); Mary Ruth (1936-1936); and Rachel (1938) first married Burl Day and second Lee Borders. George died 28 April 1970 and he is buried at the Bowdon First Methodist Church Cemetery.

Delia Singleton Lowery was born 15 April 1906 in Cleburne County, Alabama, the daughter of Rufus Alvis and Sarah Beulah (Fletcher) Singleton. She worked in the Bowdon High School Cafeteria as a lunchroom worker for many years until she retired. She died 10 January 1978 after a short illness. She was laid to rest beside George in the Bowdon First Methodist Church Cemetery.

Billy T. Lowry, my father, served in the World War II when he was eighteen years of age. After the war, he met and married Dola Imogene (Jean) Eason on 19 March 1948. He worked for Roop Wholesale Company in Bowdon from 1947 until he went to work as a shipping clerk at Southwire Company in 1976. He retired from Southwire after fourteen years of service. Billy T. and Jean have five children: Thomas Matthew (1949) married first to Dixie Norrell and second to Carolyn Coggins; Vicky Dianne (1950) married Steve H. Sheffield; Steve Roger (1952) married Judy Gibbs; Bradley Ewell (1962); and Anthony Wayne (1964-1990) married Christine Thornton. *Submitted by: Bradley Lowery, 914 Sandy Flat Road, Bowdon, GA 30108*

787. Thomas Rice Luck

Thomas Rice Luck Sr. (1891-1963) and Jessie Hobgood Luck (1890-1986) moved to Carrollton from Atlanta in 1917. He and J. Kenneth Richards were partners in Carrollton Drug Company which was in the First National Bank Building, a four story building on Adamson Square. He soon became sole owner. When Mrs. Luck first came to Carrollton by train with her six-week old baby, Betty Jane, the road from the depot to the square was unpaved.

Jessie H. and Thomas R. Luck Sr.

Mr. Luck was born in old Campbell County (now Fulton), the son of Rosa Golightly and Lewis Simeon Luck. He grew up in Fairburn and attended the public schools there. He graduated with honors with a degree in pharmacy from Mercer University and was president of his class. Before coming to Carrollton, he practiced pharmacy in Fort Pierce, Florida; Oxford, Alabama; and at old Jacobs Pharmacy in Atlanta, Georgia. In Carrollton he was actively involved in community affairs. He was mayor from 1929-1939. In this capacity he presented the local proposal to the Georgia Board of Regents for the Fourth District A. & M. school to become West Georgia College. Other activities include: Masonic Lodge; Carroll Service Council; president of the Georgia Municipal Association (1936-1937); a founder and vice-president of Carrollton Federal Savings and Loan Association; director of People's Bank; charter member and president of Rotary Club; member and chairman of Deacons of the First Baptist Church. He received the Founders Day Award from West Georgia College and in 1960 the Outstanding Citizen Award from the Chamber of Commerce.

Mrs. Luck was the daughter of Dr. Lewis Martin Hobgood and Lula Palmer Hobgood of Fairburn. She attended LaGrange College and G.N.I.C. (now Georgia College). She was a devoted member of the First United Methodist, superintendent of the Primary Department and member of W.S.C.S. She was a member of the Abraham Baldwin Chapter, D.A.R.; life member of P.T.A.; and a charter member and president of the Carrollton Garden Club. In 1936 she was a delegate to the Democratic National Convention in Philadelphia.

They had three children: Jane (Mrs. Robert P.) Jenkins (1917-2000); Thomas Rice Luck, Jr. (1921-1997); and Mary Angie Luck Cook (Mrs. William Frank Cook Jr.) *Submitted by: Angie Luck Cook, 422 Oak Avenue, Carrollton, GA 30117*

Sources: Family records: Articles from *Atlanta Journal* and *Carroll County Times; Georgia Municipal Association Magazine*

788. Luther - Tolbert - Willis

Twin brothers Isaac and Frederick Luther came to Carroll County, Georgia, around 1840 with their families. Their father, Solomon Luther, born 1793 in North Carolina, was in the War of 1812. He was a cobbler (shoemaker) by trade. Solomon married Sarah Elizabeth Winston, born 1791 in North Carolina. Their children were (1) Frederick, born 1816, married Jane Bell, born 1814, on October 27, 1836, in Randolph County, North Carolina; (2) Isaac (1816 in North Carolina-November 18, 1882) married Sarah Loflin, born 1813, on August 8, 1833, in Davidson County, North Carolina. Isaac is buried in Old Town Cemetery in Villa Rica; (3) Sidney S., born 1825 in North Carolina, married Farlaney Hurley, born 1827, on May 14, 1846, in Randolph County; (4) Betsy, born 1829 in North Carolina, married Thomas Ledwell, born 1814; and (5) Barnaby, born 1836 in North Carolina.

Solomon Luther's father was George Luther, born in Strasbourg, France, on March 1, 1754. He came to America about 1759 and was in the Revolutionary War from 1776-1781. He was a cobbler and tanner by trade. George Luther's brothers moved to Indiana with their families. A sister, Barbara Luther, married Andrew Auman. George Luther married Elizabeth Auman, born 1763 in Maryland, on June 15, 1779 in Frederick, Maryland. Elizabeth and Andrew were siblings.

Frederick Luther and Jane Bell's children are Flora, born 1838; Alexander, born 1839; Emanuel, born 1843; Elizabeth, born 1844; Josephus, born 1846; and Sarah, born 1848.

John Thomas Harrison Tolbert

Isaac Luther and Sarah F. Loflin had three sets of twins along with six single births. Their children were Elizabeth, born 1834; Emily E., born 1834; Flarius, born 1836; Josephine Bonner, born 1838; Elizabeth, born 1838; Harris C., born 1840; Mary Maria L., born 1840; Frances M., born 1842; John H., born 1844; Georgia T. (1847-1926) married Mary A.C. Mitler on October 31, 1865, in Carroll County; Abraham J., born 1852, married Martha L.; and Martin A., born 1854, married Magdeline Roberts on August 12, 1877 in Carroll County.

Emily E. Luther, born on June 23, 1834 in North Carolina, married Roland Harrison Tolbert (February 28, 1833-July 8, 1862 in Atlanta, Georgia, during Civil War) on October 26, 1854, in Carroll County. Emily married again to Mr. Willis.

There are a number of Willis families in Carroll County. The 1900 census shows that Emily had four children: John Thomas Harrison Tolbert (1860-1947) married Nancy Susan Elizabeth Elliott (1859-1914), Mary Jane Mollie Tolbert (1858-1937) married Edwin Jackson Elliott (1856-1907), and Julia H. Willis, born about 1864. There was another child, but no one knows the name or any other information about him/her.

John Thomas Harrison Tolbert and Nancy Susan Elizabeth Elliott's children were Jesse Herd (1882-1960) married Eliza Waldrop (1886-1978); Elizabeth Lizzie (1884-1958) married Thomas Taft, died 1961; John Eual Harrison, born 1886, married Emma Waldrop (1891-1974); Edker Eugen (1889-1949) married Sophia Noland (1896-1973); and Maude Odessa (1892-1983) married Edgar Brackett (1884-1936).

Mary Jane Mollie Tolbert (1858-1937) married Edwin Jackson Elliott (1856-1907). Their children are Roland Harrison, born 1878, married Annie; John Wilborne, born 1885; and Bertha, born 1881, married Tolbert Baswell. *Submitted by: Juanita Cox, 1281 Little Deer Run, Canton, GA 30114*
Source: Patricia Nelson, 1789 Kellogg Creek Road, Acworth, GA 30102

789. Enoch Silas Lyle

Enoch Silas Lyle was born 19 July 1866 in Coweta County, Georgia. He died 10 October 1951 in Carroll County Georgia. He married Sarah Zipporah Powledge, known as "Sallie," the daughter of Robert Powledge and Nancy White. She was born 19 July 1869 in Lone Oak (Meriwether County), Georgia. She died 13 December 1935 in Carroll County. They were married at the home of Enoch S. Lyle, 1306 Dixie Street, Carrollton, Georgia. Both are buried in Stripling Chapel Cemetery in Carroll County.

Enoch, Sarah and Ralph Lyle

Enoch Silas Lyle was the son of Richard Calvin Lyle and Mary Ann Wood. Richard was a veteran of the Civil War, serving in Company C, 34 Georgia Infantry, until his capture at Vicksburg. Afterwards, he returned to Carrollton and began acquiring farmland. At one time he owned about 1,000 acres just south of town. Richard and Mary Ann had three sons: Enoch Silas, Earnest Wood and Norman Powledge. All are buried at Stripling Chapel Cemetery.

Enoch and Sallie lived in a large house directly across the road from Richard and Mary Ann. They made a living farming cotton and raising livestock. There were a couple of tenant houses on the farm where the sharecroppers lived. Later, Enoch gave up farming and opened Lyle's Country Store, a small building near the road in front of the main house. There was a small apartment in the back of the store where his brother "Earn" lived. He rented the farmland to a neighbor to raise crops to feed his dairy herd.

Enoch and Sallie had three children: Ralph Powledge, Lena Virginia, and Florence Caroline. Ralph died 3 July 1936. Florence was born 5 January 1897. She married Benjamin Franklin McPherson, known as Frank to all who knew him. They were married 11 June 1916 in Carroll County at her parents home on Dixie Street. Florence died 5 February 1979 in Carrollton and is buried at Stripling Chapel Cemetery. Frank and Florence had two daughters, Sara Nell and Mary Ann. Mary Ann was born 29 September 1922 and died 23 January 1971. Sara Nell was born 7 October 1917 and is still living in Carrollton in the Lake Carroll area. Sara Nell was married to Robert James "Rip" Bonner on 23 February 1936, in Heflin, Alabama.

Rip moved to Carrollton from Standing Rock, Alabama, as a teen-ager. In 1942, Sara Nell's grandfather, Enoch Lyle, gave her two acres of land on the southwest corner of the home place for the purpose of building a home. They lived there together until Rip's death in 1971.

The Old Lyle Homeplace can hardly be recognized today due to the growth in the area. But, thanks to the memories, old photographs, stories and books being written about Carroll County and its history, I know it will not be forgotten. *Submitted by: Sara Nell Bonner, 101 Lake Skiff Court, Carrollton, GA 30117*

790. Hinchia Parham Mabry

He was born on April 30, 1784, in Warren County, North Carolina, and died on August 19, 1841, in Carroll County, Georgia.

Hinchia was one of the first settlers in Carroll County, actually arriving before it officially became a county, and settled just west of what is now Roopville in an area that later became Laural Hill. He became the first postmaster July 31, 1833. Hinchia was a fifth generation American, being a descendent of Francis Maybury who arrived in Virginia in 1679.

The Mabrys of Carroll County were part of a long line of American military men. Hinchia's father served in the Revolutionary War. Hinchia himself fought in the War of 1812 and two of his sons fought for the Confederacy.

Hinchia was married on October 22, 1818 to Lynnea Stallings in Greene County, Georgia. They had eight children. (1) Charles W. Mabry (attorney), born August 22, 1819 in Greene County and died April 9, 1886, married Sarah B. Springer; (2) Francis Mabry, born about 1826, married Rhoda in Berrian County, Georgia; (3) Martha E. Mabry, born between 1820 and 1830 in Greene or Carroll County, married Redmond B. Young who died in Ellis County, Texas; (4) Lydia Mabry, born between 1820 and 1830 in Greene or Carroll County, married Dr. W.S. Tanner; (5) Woodford J. Mabry, born in 1828 in Carroll County, married Mariann L. Bird on December 27, 1843. She died after 1880; (6) Hinchia P. Mabry, born October 27, 1829, in Carroll County, married Sarah Abigail Haywood, daughter of William H. Haywood, in 1854. She died on March 21, 1884, in Sherman, Texas. He served in the Confederate Army, attaining the rank of brigadier general. He was an attorney in Jefferson, Texas, and served in the Constitutional Convention in 1866; (7) Phoebe G. Mabry, born in 1838 in Carroll County; (8) Sarah E. Mabry, born in 1840 in Carroll County. *Submitted by: Doug Mabry, Bethel Church Road, Carrollton, GA 30117*

791. The Arthur Cary Maddox Family

Arthur Cary Maddox and Alice Teresa Orzechowski were married July 27, 1945, in Philadelphia, Pennsylvania. They moved to Carrollton, Georgia, in February 1946. Cary was born July 20, 1909, in Hazelhurst, Georgia. Alice was born December 25, 1915, in Plains, Pennsylvania. Twin boys, William Cary and Willie Clifford, were born August 6, 1946, at the Carrollton Clinic. Willie died within twenty-four hours after birth. A daughter, Barbara Ann, was born September 6, 1948, at Tanner Hospital.

Cary had moved to Villa Rica, Georgia in 1931 as manager of the Hub Department Store. Then he moved to Carrollton in 1933 as manager of the Leader Department Store, a position he held, with the exception of the years he served with the United States Army during the mid-1940s, until his death. Alice was a homemaker and actively involved with her children's school, church, civic, and sports activities.

Both children attended Carrollton City Schools. Bill graduated in 1964 and Barbara Ann in 1966 from Carrollton High School. Bill attended Georgia Tech for a year and a half before transferring to West Georgia College (WGC). He graduated in 1969 with a bachelors degree in business administration. He then spent four years in the United States Air Force. He came back to Carrollton in 1973, where he returned to work at Southwire Company. He had first become employed there in June 1964. He met Wanda Ann Titshaw from Suwanee, Georgia, on New Years Eve 1973. They were married September 28, 1974, in Suwanee, Georgia. Their children are Meredith (born 1978), Elizabeth (born 1981), and Drew (born 1983). Bill returned to WGC and obtained his master's in business administration in 1980. He is employed at Southwire, having just completed thirty-seven years (the last twenty-five in the area of purchasing).

Wanda attended Gainesville Junior College and graduated from North Georgia College in 1973 with a B.S. degree in education. She obtained her master's in education from WGC in 1977. She is currently employed by West Central Technical College. The Bill Maddox family resides in Carrollton, Georgia.

Barbara Ann graduated from WGC in 1969 with a B.A. degree in French. She returned to WGC and obtained a master's in elementary education in 1974. She married Jerry Britt December 12, 1969, in Carrollton. Jerry graduated from WGC with a B.A. in sociology in 1967. They have sons: Doug (born 1979), Russell (born 1981), and Charlie (born 1983). Jerry is self-employed and Barbara Ann is in the teaching profession. They currently reside in Dunwoody, Georgia.

Alice Maddox passed away on December 29, 1977. Cary Maddox passed away on August 9, 1986. Both are buried, along with Willie Clifford, in Our Lady of Perpetual Help Catholic Church Cemetery in Carrollton. Cary had married again, after the death of Alice, to Mae Brown Smith of Bremen, Georgia. She currently resides in Bremen. *Submitted by: Bill Maddox, 74 Hampton Way, Carrollton, GA 30116*

792. Appleton Mandeville Family

Appleton Mandeville, son of Benoni and Dolly Waite Mandeville, was born February 26, 1802, in Delaware County, New York. In spring 1823, at age 21, he left his father's home in Monroeton, Pennsylvania, to go as a pioneer to the Creek Indian lands of Georgia. Suffering from consumption, he hoped to find a healthful climate. He not only found health there, but also prosperity, honor, and long life.

After living in several other Georgia counties, Appleton was urged by his friend Sanford Kingsbery to come to Carrollton in 1833. The two men operated a general store under the name Mandeville & Kingsbery.

In 1835 Appleton and Sanford traveled north together: Mandeville first visiting relatives in "York

State" and then joining Kingsbery at Derby Line, Vermont, in order to meet Kingsbery's eighteen year old cousin, Mary Ann Stewart. Mary Ann, born October 10, 1816, was the daughter of John and Mary Wilson Stewart. Appleton and Mary Ann met on Thursday and were married three days later on Sunday, August 23, 1835, in Derby Line. On Tuesday, they started for Georgia. Mr. and Mrs. Mandeville were twelve days sailing from New York to Charleston, then rode a stage to Augusta and on to Carrollton.

Appleton, and other Carroll County men concerned about the safety of their homes and families, marched off to stop an uprising of the Creek Indians in 1836. His name is engraved as third lieutenant on a marble block, 4½ miles east of Carrollton, marking where this company camped their first night. The Camp Odum marker, as it is called, was erected as a memorial on June 6, 1906, the 70th anniversary of the encampment.

In 1840, the Mandevilles and their two small children, Selina Francis and Patrick J., traveled to Vermont. By the time they returned home in 1841, they had added a third child, Mary "Mollie" Stewart, born in Vermont. (Selina married Eli H. Colclough; Molly married first, John W. Stansell; second, David G. Wilson.)

Appleton bought all the land from Alabama Street to South Street beginning at the Carrollton Square, thus becoming the largest landowner in Carroll County at that time. He paid $600 for this area. He built a two-story saltbox home on Bowdon Street. Mary Ann, however, pined for her native Vermont, so Appleton had maple trees brought down from New England to line their street. The name of the street was soon changed. Though their house no longer exists, the name Maple Street remains. (The house was located next to present-day Maple Street Mansion, originally the home of Appleton and Mary Ann's son Leroy Clifton Mandeville.)

Appleton Mandeville, 1885, age 83.

The slaves of the Mandevilles, Grace and faithful old Enoch among others, were always treated with kindness. In addition, Mary Ann taught them from the Bible and other books in the big kitchen or under the trees in the backyard.

In 1845 Appleton formed a partnership with his brother-in-law John W. Stewart, who had recently come from Vermont. The firm of Mandeville & Stewart prospered many years.

By 1859, seven more children had been born to the Mandevilles: Ellen "Nellie" Lou (married Ernest G. Kramer); Stella Maria; Leon Percival (married Esther Robinson); Leroy Clifton, (see separate article) (married Carrie Richardson); Mary Eugenia "Tott" (married Edgar H. Long); William Chester; and Tallulah "Lula" Emma (married Henry Whitfield Long). Mr. and Mrs. Mandeville loved books and reading and provided these for their children.

The War Between the States necessitated conserving and protecting food as well as household items. The Mandevilles built closets in the two upstairs rooms, filled them with grain, and then papered the entire room. Once, as northern soldiers raided Carrollton, Mary Ann walked to the front gate and talked with the army captain, who then stationed a guard at the gate until the entire force had passed, leaving the home unharmed. It was the year 1861, however, that brought the most grief to the Mandevilles. Their daughter Stella died of typhoid fever September 20, shortly before her sixteenth birthday. Less than one month later, on October 15, their oldest son Patrick, who had enlisted in the Carroll Guards, died in Lynchburg, Virginia. He was twenty one.

Mary Ann Stewart Mandeville, 1885, age 68.

Appleton was a Presbyterian, and for many years taught a Sunday School class. He also served as treasurer of the county 1875-1883. Though successful in business and blessed with an abundance of material goods, Appleton was quiet, modest, and reserved. He was also prudent, wise, and of unimpeachable integrity, making him a much-sought advisor.

On August 23, 1885, the Mandevilles celebrated their 50th wedding anniversary. Of their ten children, seven were living and present, along with eleven grandchildren and many friends. In a letter written for the occasion, Appleton stated,

> "... through the goodness of God, here I am with the partner of all my joys and sorrows ... to celebrate the 50th anniversary of our marriage." And "... we are blessed with sufficient measure of health and strength and mental vigor to enable us to enjoy the occasion. Truly God has been good unto us!" He continued, requesting that no gifts be brought, and that, instead, he would give a $20 gold piece to each of his living children and a $5 piece for each grandchild "... as a testimony of my love and affection."

Appleton died June 17, 1892, at age ninety. Mary Ann was eighty-three when she died July 30, 1900. They, along with nine of their children and numerous grandchildren, are buried in the Carrollton Cemetery. *Submitted by: Mrs. Susan Patton Hamersky, 23330 Calvert Street, Woodland Hills, CA 91367*

Sources: *Carroll County Times* October 13, 1927. Family papers. *Carroll County and Her People* by Pvt. Joe Cobb; *At Home in Carrollton* by Dr. Ben Griffith.

793. The Leroy Clifton Mandeville Family

Leroy Clifton Mandeville, son of Appleton and Mary Ann Stewart Mandeville, was born September 25, 1851, in their home on Maple Street. He was the seventh of ten children. First schooled at home under his mother and his oldest sister Selina, he later attended the Carrollton Masonic Institute. In 1872, at age twenty-one, L.C. opened a general store on the public square, corner of Rome Street. He had only $200 but obtained credit from a wholesale firm in Atlanta. Through his astute business sense and his honesty in all dealings, his store prospered from the beginning, soon allowing him to buy the building, and later, the whole block.

December 16, 1876, he married Caroline "Carrie" Louise Richardson (born April 3, 1857), the daughter of Major John M. Richardson, cofounder of Bowdon College. The Mandevilles had five children: Eugenia (1878-1915) married Homer Watkins; Nell (1880-1956) married Charles Kennon Henderson Jr., (see separate article), Appleton (1882-1941) married Lula Calloway; Clifton Jr. (1887-1949); and Camilla (1889-1972) married John Oliver Newell. The Mandevilles saw that their children had a college education and enjoyed extensive travel.

In 1888, along with other Carrollton businessmen, L.C. organized the Merchants and Planters Bank, which later became the First National Bank, then People's Bank, and is presently Nations Bank. He served first as vice-president, then twenty-eight years as president, retiring just months before his death.

The Mandevilles began construction on a three-story Victorian home in 1889 on Maple Street. The home, which used heart pine, was built at a cost of about $8000. Completed in 1894, the home still stands on its original location and is currently the Maple Street Mansion restaurant. The Mandeville home was the first in Carrollton to have running water through the use of storage tanks in the third-story walls, electricity, and a telephone.

Behind the home was a rather expansive area of groves and a fish pond. It was here, for many summers, that the Mandevilles set up camp using large tents with wood flooring. The kitchen and dining hall were permanent structures. Some of their children and grandchildren would spend the entire summer there. In addition to entertaining his many friends, L.C. delighted in hosting a variety of groups at the camp: teachers, church leaders, boy scouts, to name a few. Meals were cooked and dinners eaten in the kitchen/dining hall, which was a permanent structure. Often the general public was invited to dine at the Mandeville camp.

Leroy Clifton Mandeville, circa early 1900s.

L.C. was twice elected mayor of Carrollton, 1895 and 1896, without running a race. He contributed the salary he received from this office to the churches of the town.

Mandeville Cotton Mills was organized in 1900 and became Mandeville Mills, Inc. in 1902. Principal founders were L.C. Mandeville and J.A. Aycock. Operation began with 150 employees. The company grew steadily until it consisted of two large cotton mills in Carrollton, a cotton-seed oil mill, a fertilizer factory and several ginneries in different parts of the county, also a cotton mill and ginnery in Bremen, and a cotton mill in North Carolina. Even at the beginning of the Great Depression, the annual report on June 20, 1930, announced a net profit of approximately $757,000. In June, 1952, Mandeville Mills celebrated its fiftieth year of continuous operation. At that time, it was the county's largest industry, employing about 625 people, with an annual payroll of $1,200,000. The yarns sold from Mandeville Mills were used in a wide variety of products from household

L-R. Nell, Carrie, Gabriel Richardson, Camilla, Eugenia, Clifton, L.C., Appleton.

textiles to wire insulation to casket decorations. When L.C. Mandeville died in 1926, his son J.A. Mandeville was named president of the mills, followed by F.M. Kimble in 1941, and J.R. Newell (the son of L.C. Mandeville's daughter Camilla) in 1946. In 1953, the mills were sold after eighteen months of continued losses due to a downturn in the yarn industry.

In 1906, Mandeville and J.A. Aycock again teamed up to secure for Carrollton the Fourth District A. & M. School, which later became West Georgia College, and is now the State University of West Georgia. L.C. served till his death as treasurer of the A. & M. and gave to it land, money, time, and influence. One of the buildings still bears the name Mandeville Hall. Always interested in young people and education, he was a trustee of Agnes Scott College and Oglethorpe University, a benefactor of both, as well as of numerous other schools and institutions throughout Georgia and North Carolina. For many years, he served on the city school board.

Carrie Richardson Mandeville, circa early 1900s.

In 1911, L.C. built the four-story Clifton Hotel, later renamed Carrollton Inn, and now the home office of SMI. He was also vice-president of Gainesboro Telephone and Telegraph Company.

L.C. was active in Carrollton Presbyterian Church, having joined in 1875, he served as deacon from 1876-1915, after which he was an elder until his death. In addition, he also served for many years as both a teacher and Sunday School superintendent.

For several years before his death, September 7, 1926 at age 74, he had spent summers in North Carolina and winters in Florida. In May, 1926, he went to Nova Scotia for the summer, accompanied by his eldest grandson Mandeville Henderson. He was feeling much improved in health, and on his way home in September stopped in Asheville, North Carolina for a few days. One afternoon, in the lobby of his hotel, he collapsed from a stroke, never regaining consciousness, and died a few hours later. His son J.A. Mandeville and son-in-law C.K. Henderson Jr. left Carrollton immediately to accompany his body home. L.C.'s wife Carrie Richardson Mandeville died March 17, 1941 at age eighty-three. They, along with all five of their children, are buried in the Carrollton Cemetery. *Submitted by: Mrs. Kennon Henderson Patton, 244 Glenbrooke Way, Greenville, SC 29615*

Sources: *Carroll County Times* October 13, 1927. Family papers. My own personal recollections of my grandparents, L.C. and Carrie Mandeville.

794. Mapp Family

It is amazing when you start to research your family roots that you find a whole branch of your family lived in another county. That was the case for us. We found that many members of our Mapp family lived in Carroll County.

Otha B. Mapp was born on August 6, 1856 and lived in Campbell County where many of his children were born. He died at his daughter's house in Coweta County on May 25, 1938. He married Addie Bozeman born July 29, 1865, died May 17, 1933, in Carroll County, Georgia. Both are buried at Pleasant Hill Baptist Church Cemetery, Carrollton.

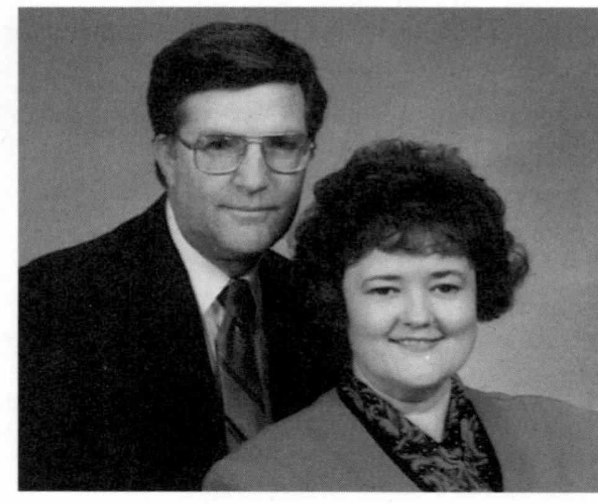

Charles and Debbie Mapp

Their children, with spouse in parentheses, are: Sidney (Margaret Cash); William M. (first Ida Bell Brown, and second Imogene Perry); Vassie (John William McElroy); Carrie (Henry Jackson McElroy) (sisters married brothers); Effie (John Burgess Eskew); Nellie (found in the 1900 Campbell County census); Bessie Mae (David Samuel Harmon); Florence (Harvey M. Costley); Earnest (Ida Stitcher); Hughie; Homer (Mamie Louise Pike); Bertha (William E. Cobb); Erma (George Monroe Walker); and our grandfather, Alfred Starling Mapp, born July 5, 1880, Campbell County, Georgia, died December 11, 1954, Coweta County, Georgia. He married Isabell A. Thomaston July 20, 1902, in Carroll County. She was born June 8, 1885, and died February 25, 1949, in Coweta County. Starling was a deeply religious man and any time that the church doors were open, he was there.

Their children are: Alfred James (Mildred Mary Martin); Brice (Sudie); Lumas Watson (Mamie Glennis Adams); Emmie Sue (first to Reese Alford Newell, and second to Melvin T. Melear); Della Irene (Avery B. Shellnutt); Gordon (first to Carrie Hughs, and second to Grace Elizabeth Wiggins); and our father, Alvin Ace Mapp, born January 29, 1905, Douglas County, died October 3, 1984, Coweta County. He married first Annie Ruth Lewis April 28, 1924, in Coweta County, daughter of Eugene Edward Lewis and Missouri Virginia Cato. She was born October 28, 1907, in Meriwether County, Georgia, lived in Coweta County most of her life, and died January 7, 1986, in Thomaston, Georgia. They had eight children (one son was stillborn). He was married second to Judy McMichael Scoggin March 30, 1958, in Coweta County.

Children of Alvin Mapp and Ruth Lewis are: Frances Belle (John Alton Callaway); Aubrey Eugene (Geneva Ruth Horton), born March 29, 1927, died February 8, 1972, Coweta County; Lunelle (Samuel Leroy Robertson Jr.) born May 21, 1932, Coweta County, died October 21, 1995; William Howard "Boots" (Edna Elizabeth Jones); Alvin Harris (Nancy Coffey), born May 21, 1934, Newnan, died May 3, 1997, Newnan; James Thomas (Joanne Barnes), born August 23, 1936, Fulton County, Georgia; died April 7, 1984, Coweta County; and Charles Raymond Mapp (Deborah Lynne Meade, married September 30, 1977. See Josiah Robert Stallings for details on this line.) *Submitted by: Charles and Debbie Mapp, 674 Welcome Road, Newnan, GA 30263. DeyubRoots@aol.com*

795. Marlow

Marlow, England, on the Thames River, is a busy riverside town with a wide and attractive Main Street, High Street, and West Street. There are still many Georgian houses and glorious views.

One of the first Marlows found in records is Sir Christopher Marlow. He was sheriff of London in 1402 and twice Lord Mayor (1407 and 1409). Another Christopher Marlow was a noted dramatic author in the 1500s. William Marlow was a landscape painter and engraver from 1750-1800.

Virginia records show Thomas Marlow living in James City County, Virginia, in 1623. In the period from 1657-1663, six others with the spelling Marlow and Marlowe arrived in America. William Marlow was among these, and his descendants came to South Carolina. Our William was born in South Carolina in 1775 and his wife Elizabeth was born there in 1777. This union lived and raised a family in Edgefield County and they continued to live there until their deaths in 1838. They had two sons, Wiley and John A. Marlow. I have a deed showing where William, Wiley's father, sold land to Joseph Rutherford on January 3, 1829, recorded in Edgefield County. I also have William's will dated May 16, 1838, where he named Wiley in his will.

Wiley Marlow was born April 4, 1804, in Edgefield County, South Carolina. He married Mary Elizabeth Trotter. The Trotters were early settlers in the same part of Edgefield County that borders the Big Saluda River and Persimmon

Creek. Wiley Marlow sold land to William Connally July 20, 1848, Edgefield County. In 1860 Wiley and his wife and children are included in census records of Coweta County, Georgia. In 1863 Wiley bought 100 acres of land in Carroll County — land lot 162, 11th District. They are also on the 1880 Carroll County census.

Wiley died June 1, 1887, in Carroll County, and his wife, Mary Trotter Marlow, died May 26, 1871. They are buried on this home place in the garden behind the house. Wiley's son, James Riley Marlow, placed marble markers on their graves. They are still there. Miss Bernina Rooks, who taught at Carrollton High School, lived there with her father who had bought the property. They carefully attended the graves with loving care as long as they lived.

Wiley and Mary E. Trotter Marlow had four daughters and two sons. John was born January 1827 and James Riley was born July 1833. Both sons were born in South Carolina and have descendants in Carroll County. Both John and James fought in the Civil War. James Riley lost a leg while fighting. He was captured at Perryville, Kentucky, and exchanged at City Point, Virginia. He was in the 41st Georgia Regiment, Company D. John and James Riley gave land and money to build churches in Carroll County. John gave money and land to build Salem Baptist Church on Salem Church Road. James Riley gave money and land to build Beulah Baptist Church in Carroll County on Beulah Church Road.

James Riley and wife, Mary Elizabeth Carter, had five sons and lived in the Beulah area until 1892. One of their sons was Reuben Richard Sawyer Marlow. James Riley bought the home at 309 Stewart Street. Mary Elizabeth Carter Marlow died April 19, 1903, and is buried in Carrollton City Cemetery. James Riley Marlow remarried later, but moved from Stewart Street. C.A. Walker bought his home and later sold it to Reuben R.S. Marlow in 1904.

Reuben Richard Sawyer Marlow married Bera Morris in 1908, daughter of N.B. Morris of Coweta County. Ruben R.S. Marlow died August 13, 1943, and Bera Morris Marlow died January 20, 1985. They are both buried in the same lot in Carrollton City Cemetery as James Riley and Mary Elizabeth. Reuben Richard and Bera Marlow had two children, Sawyer V.O. Marlow and Ruby Elizabeth Marlow.

Ruby Marlow Perry in front of the home she gave to the City for the Historical Society to use.

Ruby Elizabeth Marlow married Robert Lester Perry April 1937. Robert Lester died April 10, 1972, and is buried in Carroll Memory Garden. They had a son, Robert David Perry, born May 18, 1940. Ruby E. Marlow Perry and Robert David were both born in the family home on Stewart Street. After Bera died, Ruby Marlow Perry gave this house on Stewart Street to the City of Carrollton for the Historical Society's use. It was moved to West Avenue in Carrollton. (The accompanying picture shows Ruby Perry standing in front of this house.)

Robert David Perry and Mary Ann Jeter were married and lived in Carrollton. Their three children all live in Carrollton. (1) Judy Perry and husband Christopher Hicks have one son Christopher David Hicks born September 8, 1994. (2) James Robert and wife Laurie Brown Perry have one daughter, Katlin Elizabeth born May 21, 2000. (3) Mary Virginia Perry married Martin Harper. The Harpers and Martins are old settlers in Carroll County. *Submitted by: Ruby Marlow Perry, 305 Stewart Street, Carrollton, GA 30117*

796. Martin Family

John Christian and Emily Bates Martin moved to this area, which is now Oak Grove Church Road, from Edgefield County, South Carolina, to Luthersville, Georgia, then to Carrollton when their son Ben was four years old. Mr. Martin died June 1, 1925. Mrs. Martin died the following day. They were laid to rest in the same grave in the Stripling Chapel Cemetery. Their son Joseph "Joe" married Zema Barker in 1921. They had two daughters, Jessie Mable Craven and Homa Jeanette Archer. Homa still lives on the original home place with her husband, Roy Archer. They had three children: Alice Jeannette, James Archer, and John Benjamin. Alice Jeanette, and her husband, Warren Henson, also reside on part of the home place. John Benjamin died when he was eight-days-old in 1958.

Ben Martin Family. 1893

A grandson, Jay and Amy Denney and their daughters, Jessica and Allison, and James and Kathy Denney all still reside on the Martin home place. This makes a total of seven generations that have lived on this land.

The photograph shows Ben Hill, Vollie, and Delia Martin Hill on top row. Front row, Carrie is in Ben's lap, Alice, Jessie is in Delia's lap, and Joseph standing in front. *Submitted by: Homa Martin Archer*

797. Family of James Edward Martin

James Edward, born 27 November 1851 in Coweta County, Georgia, married Martha Anne Rebecca Shadinger 21 January 1877 and died 2 February 1914 in Carroll County, Georgia. He was the fifth child of John Christian III and Emily Bates Martin. John Christian born 10 March 1820 married 27 December 1843, died 11 May 1908, was married first to Emily Bates. They had nine children. Later he married Elizabeth Piper, then Margaret A.E. Jones. John and Emily moved to Carroll County from Coweta County around 1853.

James Edward Martin and Rebecca Martin had ten children: Looney Edward, John Marvin, Will Watson, Georgie, Maude, Jennie Lee, Florence, James Cliff, Mattie and Seaborn Glenn.

Looney was born 11 November 1877, married Emma Stipe 2 October 1901 and died 1 January 1971. They had nine children: Mary Rebecca, Hugh Hamil, Henry Felton, Lois Christine, John Wiley Aubrey Looney, Nina Mae, Everett Stipe, and Thyra Frances.

John Marvin born 6 March 1879, married Alice Chappell (sister to Will Chappell who married Georgie Martin) on 10 January 1901 and died 1981. They had eight children: Eddie, Dura, Zora, Eva, Margaret, James, Joe, and Walker Martin.

Willis and Pearl Martin, 50th Wedding Anniversary, November 1957.

Will Watson Martin, born 23 March 1881, married Pearl Jones 28 November 1907 and died 26 February 1967. They had three children: Edna Pearl, born 17 October 1908, married Carl Walker 10 November 1935; Clara Mae, born 25 October 1910, married Sterling Henry Stipe, 13 November 1927, died 26 April 2001, and Milton Jones Martin born 26 January 1913, married Hazel Mashburn 19 July 1936, died 34 January 1995.

Georgie was born 25 December 1882, married Will Dawson Chappell 26 December 1900 and died in 1980. They had eleven children: William Thelma, Martin Rufus, Reba, Bernie, James Franklin, Jewell, Reuben Spencer, Winfred, Lester, Talmadge, and Virginia Marlene Chappell.

Maude was born 3 April 1885 married Henry Almon 9 July 1905 and died 5 October 1974. They had six children: Samuel Wilbur, Mattie Beatrice, Evelyn Maude, Ima Lee, Charles (Chick) Henry and Verna Martin (PeeWee) Almon.

Jennie Lee was born 1887 and died 1888.

Florence, born 29 January 1889, married Charlie S. Boyd on 9 September 1906 and died in 29 November 1964. They had two children: Millican and C. Weems Boyd.

James Cliff was born 12 March 1891, married Eula Wiggins 22 September 1912 and died in 1974. They had two children: James Stewart Martin and George Marvin.

Mattie was born 14 March 1894, married Carl Nix 16 November 1914, lived in Canton, Georgia, and died 17 June 1993. They had seven children: Mattie Ethel, Myrtle, Mabel, Clinton, Victor, Goodwin, and Goss Nix.

Seaborn Glenn was born 1896, never married and died in 1968.

Most of his family is buried in Stripling Chapel Church Cemetery in Carroll County. The Rebecca Martin Home Demonstration Club was named for Mrs. James Edward Martin (Martha Anne Rebecca). Rebecca was born 30 August 1855, the fourth child of John C. Shadinger and Ellen Frances Jones Shadinger. She had four brothers and four sisters. The families of James Edward Martin and John C. Shadinger lived in the Stripling Chapel Community moving to Carroll County from Coweta County around the same time, circa 1847. *Submitted by: Edna Martin Walker*

798. John Christian Martin of Carroll County, Georgia

John Christian Martin came to Coweta County, Georgia in 1830 with his father who was also named John Christian. He married first Emily Bates in Coweta. John Christian and Emily, with their children, moved to Carroll County in 1860. John Christian Martin (the third with this name) was the great-grandson of the immigrant John Nicholas Martin who arrived at Philadelphia on the ship Barclay in 1754.

John and Emily had nine children. They were (1) John A.; (2) David Reuben who married Mary Ann Martin (maiden name Martin); (3) Rhoda Ann who married R.C. McDaniel; (4) Francis Albert who married Margaret Hamrick; (5) James Edward who married Martha Ann Rebecca Shadinger; (6) William Damascus who married Sarah A. Powell; (7) Susan E. who married John McGukin; (8) Ben Hill who married Delia Ann Colley; (9) Ann E.

John Christian's occupation is given as blacksmith on the 1860 Carroll County census. He is buried in the cemetery at Stripling Chapel. Delia Ann is buried in the Lambert Cemetery. John Christian's second wife was Elizabeth Piper and the third was Margaret A.E. Jones. *Submitted by: Mr. Crowder*

799. Looney Edward Martin and Emma Stipe Martin

Looney Edward Martin, son of James Edward and Rebecca Shadinger Martin, and Emma Stipe, daughter of Henry Nelson and Mary Emmaline Steed Stipe, were married 1 October 1901. Looney was born 15 November 1877 and died 10 January 1971. He attended Emory at Oxford and began teaching at an early age. His first position was teaching at a one-room schoolhouse located on the Stipe Plantation. The school was known to some as The Ant Hill School. Looney taught for thirty-six years at a number of schools throughout Carroll County. He taught most of his children and Emma's brothers and sisters, including his brother-in-law, John Gordon Stipe, vice president of Emory University at the time of his death in 1953. Emma Stipe, born 31 August 1881 and died 8 July 1962, was youngest of five children and Looney was oldest of ten children.

Looney E. Martin

Their nine children are Mary Rebecca, Hugh Hamil, Henry Felton, Lois Christine, John Wiley, Aubrey Looney, Nina Mae, Everett Stipe, and Thyra Frances.

Mary Rebecca, born 14 October 1902, married Jack Oliver Padgett 7 July 1931. She died in August 2000 at the age of ninety-eight. She taught school for a time with her father, Looney, at Sand Hill, Georgia. She was employed at Rich's Department Store in Atlanta for twenty-eight years. Mary and Jack had one child, Edward Padgett.

Hugh Hamil, born 26 June 1905, married Flora Nixon 4 January 1931. He died September 1991. He was a farmer in Carroll County. Their two children were Martha Rebecca and Carolyn.

Henry Felton was born 31 March 1907 and died in 1990. He married Mildred Bynum on 26 December 1931. He was employed at the Goodyear Tire and Rubber Plant in Akron Ohio. Felton's two children were Robert Macon and James Felton.

Lois Christine, born 20 November 1909, married James Frank Holland 7 February 1942. She worked in Rich's Department Store as head of the alterations department. She retired after twenty-six years. She had been employed as a teacher for a number of years at the old Tallapoosa School on Tyus Road in Carrollton, Georgia.

John Wiley, born 2 April 1912, married Mary Jane Withrow 4 February 1945. Wiley is a Carroll County farmer and retired employee of Lockheed in Marietta, Georgia, formerly known as Bell Bomber Plant. Their children are Ruth Emaline and Charles Edward.

Looney Edward Martin and Emma Stipe Martin, 1901

Aubrey Looney, born 25 November 1914, married Mary Frances Burnham 25 December 1935. He died 19 May 1998 and is buried in Peachtree Memorial Park, Norcross, Georgia. He was employed by Pfizer and Johnson & Johnson pharmaceutical companies. Their two children are Aubrey Steven and John Anthony.

Nina Mae, born 23 August 1916, married J. Lewis Miller Jr. of Dalton, circa 1947. Nina is a retired school teacher. Their children are John Martin Miller and Mary Jane Miller.

Everett Stipe, born 27 April 1920, married Clara Marlin Martin 20 April 1942. He is retired from Ohio Edison in Akron, Ohio. Their children are James Everett and Jalaine Karen.

Thyra Frances, born 8 July 1923, married Robert Jack Alexander 1 January 1942. Thyra is retired from Fulton County Board of Education and Jack from Nabisco Company. Their children are Jacquelyn, Marvin Dale, and Barbara Jean Alexander. *Submitted by: Thyra Martin Alexander, 115 Martin Sheffield Drive, Carrollton, GA 30116*

800. The Marvin Martin Family

George Marvin Martin was born 28 May 1921, the son of Cliff Martin and Eula Wiggins Martin. Marvin Martin grew up in Carroll County, Georgia, and graduated from Carrollton High School in 1938. He served in the Army Air Corps during World War II and during the Korean War.

Marvin Martin married Edna Lola Chance on 24 October 1943. Edna Chance was born 20 September 1923 and died 22 January 1981. Marvin and Edna Martin had three children. A son, Gregory Steve Martin, was born 6 September 1946 and married Donna Elizabeth Smith on 30 April 1977. Donna was adopted by a great uncle and grew up in his family. Greg and Donna Martin have two children: Matthew Scott Martin born 12 December 1977, who is graduating this year from West Georgia College; and Mary Elizabeth Martin who was born 30 March 1982 and is presently a freshman at West Georgia College. Greg Martin received his degrees in business and accounting from West Georgia College and from Georgia State University. He has been employed by Southwire for over thirty-five years.

Marvin and Edna Martin had a daughter, Constance Lynda Martin, born 27 August 1948 and she attended West Georgia College. Connie married Mike Weathers on 17 December 1967. They are parents of two children — Michael Martin Weathers born 28 January 1971 who now has his own landscaping business in Loganville, Georgia, and who is married with three children, Michael, Shannan, and Alexander. Connie and Mike Weathers have a daughter Wendy Michelle who was born 20 February 1974. She is working toward a master's of education degree at the University of Georgia. Connie Martin Weathers is employed by Georgia First, a network for hospitals and doctors. Mike Weathers (born 18 October 1946) is employed by Tatum CFO Partners.

Martha Ann Martin was born 18 March 1959 and was named for Martha Anne Robinson, who was the daughter of one of Marvin and Edna's best friends, John Robinson, the pharmacist. Martha graduated in 1983 with a degree in art and worked seven years for the *Times-Georgian* newspaper in Carrollton. She then did some freelance writing for the *Carroll Star News.* Martha has done research for movies like "Fried Green Tomatoes" and "Bagger Vance." She has also worked in wardrobe for the movies such as "Andersonville." Martha has long been a lover of animals and she co-founded the Humane Society in Carrollton over twenty years ago. Martha is presently living in Atlanta, Georgia.

Marvin Martin married second to Avery Shaw and they now make their home in Panama City, Florida. Marvin Martin is a freelance writer. *Submitted by: Greg and Donna Martin, 511 Ringer Road, Carrollton, GA and Written by: Jan R. Bell*

801. The Stewart Martin Family

Rebecca Martin was born 13 May 1942 in Carroll County, Georgia, the daughter of Stewart Martin and Agnes Scott who married in Carroll County on 24 December 1940. Agnes Scott was the daughter of Otis Tom Scott Sr. and Bessie Smith Scott. Stewart Martin was the son of James Clifton "Cliff" Martin and Eula Wiggins. Stewart Martin was the grandson of William Jasper Wiggins (25 March 1855-23 May 1916) and Amanda Melvina Stewart (25 October 1858-25 September 1904). Also, Stewart Martin was the grandson of James Edward Martin (27 November 1851-2 February 1914) and Martha Ann Rebecca Shadinger (30 August 1855 born in Carroll County-27 August 1936).

Stewart Martin is best remembered for his many years of serving as director of Martin-Hightower Funeral Home on Center Street in Carrollton. Agnes Martin was a beautician for Griffin's Department Store for many years. Stewart Martin was born 13 August 1913 and died 16 January 1993. Agnes Scott Martin was born 17 October 1913 and died 21 September 1998. Both were lifelong members of the Tabernacle Baptist Church. Stewart and Agnes Martin are buried in Carroll Memory Gardens. Rebecca Martin was their only child.

Rebecca Martin was a 1960 graduate of Carrollton High School and she attended West Georgia College. While there, she met her future husband, Doyle Ray Akins, also a student at West Georgia. Doyle was born 22 August 1941, the son of Albert William Akins and Alma Warmack Akins of Dalton, Whitfield County, Georgia. Doyle graduated from West Georgia College with an A.B. degree in biology. He went on to earn his MS.Ed. in education from the University of Georgia in 1966. He then taught biology at Bowdon High School from 1962-1967. Doyle has been employed by Community First Bank for the past twenty-eight years. The Akins have one daughter, Andri Anna Akins who is married to Gerald Pilgrim, the present mayor of Carrollton. The Pilgrims have one son, John Martin Pilgrim who is now three years old. (See Andri and Gerald Pilgrim story.)

Stewart and Agnes Martin with daughter Rebecca

James Stewart Martin grew up in Carroll County and graduated from Carrollton High School in 1930. He also attended Bowdon College and was a member of the first graduating class of West Georgia College in 1933. Stewart Martin graduated from Emory University in 1935 and returned to teach in the Farmer's High community at Tyus. After a while, Stewart decided to learn the family business which was then called Martin-Almon Funeral Home. Cliff Martin had first worked for Jack Aycock at his funeral home in Carrollton. This used to be located on the square where Green Lantern Frame Shop is today. Stewart also went to Gupton Jones College in Nashville, Tennessee. Later, Cliff Martin and his brother-in-law, Henry Almon, went into business for themselves. Henry was married to Cliff's sister, Maude Martin. About 1932, Stewart and Henry established Martin-Almon Funeral Home and Stewart became the director.

By the time that World War II came along, Stewart was appointed to serve as head of the Draft Board in Carroll County. Stewart Martin also has the distinction of being Carrollton's youngest mayor. He was elected at the age of twenty-six and served quite capably. Now, Stewart Martin's granddaughter, Andri Anna Akins Pilgrim is married to the second youngest mayor ever to serve in Carrollton. Gerald Pilgrim became the second youngest mayor when he was elected in 1999.

James Clifton Martin was born 12 March 1891 in Carroll County, the son of James Edward Martin and Martha Ann Rebecca Shadinger. Rebecca Shadinger was born 30 August 1855 and was the daughter of John Shadinger (6 July 1826-14 March 1915) and Frances Ellena "Ellen" Jones (30 November 1828-31 May 1909) who married in Coweta County, Georgia, on 17 December 1846. John Shadinger was the son of Andrew Shadinger (1804-10 November 1831) and Elizabeth Mitchell (1809-1871) who lived in Fayette County, Georgia. Andrew Shadinger died as a young man while cutting wood and the wind blew a tree over onto him and killed him. Elizabeth Mitchell was the daughter of Henry Mitchell of South Carolina who was born about 1775.

James Edward "Ed" Martin was born 27 November 1851 in Carroll County, and was married on 21 January 1877 to Martha Ann Rebecca Shadinger Martin in Carroll County. They were the parents of (1) Looney Edward Martin born 15 November 1877 died 10 January 1971 married Emma Stipe 2 October 1901; (2) John Marvin Martin 1879-1981, married 10 January 1901 to Alice Chappell (3) Will Watson Martin, 1881-1967, married Pearl Jones 28 November 1907; (4) James Clifton Martin born 12 March 1891, married Eula Wiggins 22 September 1912, died December 1974; (5) Georgia Martin married Will Dawson Chappell 26 December 1900; (6) Maude Martin 1885-1974 married Henry Martin Almon 9 July 1905 (7) Jennie Lee Martin 1887-1888; (8) Florence Martin 1889-1964, married Charles S. Boyd 9 September 1906; (9) Mattie Martin born 14 March 1894, died 1993 married Carl A. Nix who was born 10 January 1891, died 24 June 1971; (10) Seaborn Glenn Martin 27 July 1896-28 May 1967.

Rebecca Shadinger Martin was a founding member of what is still known today as the Rebecca Martin Club and the oldest club in Carrollton. This club was founded in 1874 and since the first meeting was held in the home of Rebecca Martin, the club has always kept that name in honor of her. The Rebecca Martin Club is a club for promoting friends and fellowship among the homemakers, especially around the community of Stripling Chapel Church. The club has participated in county fairs, barbecue suppers, recipe swaps, quilting bees, and all kinds of service projects over the years. During the Vietnam war, the club sent packages to servicemen. The club invites many outstanding speakers to lecture on topics of interest to homemakers. After a few years of meeting in members' homes, these ladies began to hope for a place to call their own and a real clubhouse was their dream. Finally, in 1940 they had saved enough and their clubhouse became a reality. It was built behind Stripling Chapel Methodist Church.

Andri, Rebecca, and Doyle Akins

J. Cliff Martin and Eula Wiggins Martin had three children. Stewart was the oldest son born in 1913. Another son, William C. Martin was born 15 October 1916 and died 8 June 1919. A third son was George Marvin Martin born 28 May 1921.

James Edward Martin died 2 February 1914 and the *Carroll County Times* of 5 February 1914 carried his obituary reading "Death of a Good Citizen." It refers to his home as "two miles south of Carrollton" and that he had lived in Carroll County since his early boyhood. Martha Ann Rebecca Shadinger Martin died 27 August 1936. The Martins are buried at Stripling Chapel Church Cemetery. *Submitted by: Rebecca and Doyle Akins, Oak Avenue, Carrollton, GA*

802. James and Elizabeth Mathews

The Mathews family, James and Elizabeth and their two daughters, Jeanne and Marianna, settled in Carrollton in 1960, when Dr. Mathews (Jim) accepted a position at West Georgia College as professor of English and chair of the Division of Humanities. From 1973 until his retirement in 1992 he served as chair of the Department of English. Elizabeth (Liz) was at one time librarian at Villa Rica High school and later at Arnco-Sargent School in Coweta County.

Both daughters graduated from Carrollton High School and then from different colleges, Jeanne from the University of Tennessee in Knoxville and Marianna from Queens College in Charlotte, North Carolina. Jeanne, who now lives in Brentwood, Tennessee, has two children, Raleigh and Andrew Mecklin, and Marianna, who lives in Trophy Club, Texas, has two daughters, Lindsey and Claire Folger.

Over the years the Mathews have been active in community affairs. Liz has served as president of the Arts Study Club and Jim as president of the Rotary Club. They are both charter members of the Little Tallapoosa Botanical Society and longtime communicants of St. Margaret's Episcopal Church, where they are members of the choir. *Submitted by: James and Elizabeth Mathews, 27 Lynda Circle, Carrollton, GA 30117*

803. Ezekiel Matthews Family

Ezekiel Matthews was the son of Thomas Matthews and his wife (unknown). He was born in 1775 in North Carolina. He married Rebecca Jones about 1791. Ezekiel died 7 October 1839 in Gwinnett County and is buried in Liberty Church Cemetery.

Their children were: (1) Rebecca Matthews, died 27 June 1839; (2) Abel Matthews, born 1792 in Laurens County. He married Nancy. He died about July 1875 in Carroll County. The will of Abel Matthews is found in the Carroll County probate records and reads as follows:

> In the name of God, Amen. I, Abel Matthews, of the county of Carroll and state of Georgia being of sound and disposing mind and memory do make and publish this my last will and testament hereby revoking all wills heretofore made by me. And First I commit my Soul to God who gave it. My worldly estate I dispose of as follows:
>
> Item 1 - I bequeath to my daughter Rhoda D. Weir my bed and bedding.
>
> Item 2 - I bequeath to all of my lawful heirs the remainder of my estate as follows - That all my land, stock, household and kitchen furniture be sold and an equal division of the proceeds hereof be made with each of them.
>
> Item 3 - I hereby appoint B.M. Long of the county and state aforesaid as my executor on this my last will.
>
> In witness whereof I the said Abel Matthews to this my will consisting of the foregoing two sheets of papers have set my hand and seal this ninth day of July 1872.

Children of Abel and Nancy Matthews were: (i) Rhoda born about 1822 in Gwinnett County, married Hugh N. Weir. Children of Rhoda and Hugh N. Weir were John B. Weir born 1846, and Levi H.S. Weir born 1848. (ii) Benjamin Ezekiel born in Gwinnett County, married Mahala Beasley. The children of Benjamin E. and Mahala Matthews were Mary E. born 1853; George A. born 1856; John H. born 1841; Nancy J. born 1846; Julia H. born 1847; and Rhoda C. born 1849. (iii) James C. born 1825 in Gwinnett County, died before 1875, married Rebecca about 1842 in Carroll County. Their children were Belinda born 1843; Saphronia born 1855, Albert? born 1847; and William born 1849. (iv) Elizabeth born about 1826 in Gwinnett County. (v) Julia Elitha born about 1830 in Georgia and died before 1870 in Carroll County, married Linsey Matthew Warnick (see Warnick Family). (vi) Nancy J. born 1832, married A.G. Williams. (vii) Sarah born 1834. (3) Julia Ather Matthews, born 29 July 1799 in Laurens County, South Carolina, died 8 May 1848, married Thomas Matthews III on 14 January 1821, born 30 April 1803, died 8 May 1878; (4) William Matthews; (5) Samuel Matthews; (6) Daniel Matthews married Amy Hood on 23 July 1849 in Union County, South Carolina. *Submitted by: Charles Harvell, 63 Mallard Drive, Guntersville, AL 35976*

804. Matthews - Mathews - Mathis

Abel and Benjamin Ezekiel Matthews

January 26, 1840, Carroll County court records state that $300 was paid to Abraham Miles of Harris County by Abel Matthews of Carroll County for land in the 5th District of Carroll County, Lot 216 containing 202 1/2 acres. Part of this land is now Lake Carroll.

Carroll County census lists Abel as head of household in 1840, 1850, 1860 and 1870. Abel was a landowner and farmer. His wife, Nancy, was a homemaker and the 1860 United States census of Agriculture L-Z of Carroll County Georgia lists and describes Abel's farm.

Abel Matthews (1794-1872) married Nancy (1800-?) (suspected maiden name Couch). They were both born in South Carolina. Burial site is not known. Children were: (1) Benjamin Ezekiel (South Carolina, 1816); (2) Rhoda (Georgia, 1822) married January 7, 1845 Carroll County Georgia Hugh H. Wier; (3) Elizabeth (Georgia, 1826); (4) Julia (Georgia, 1830); (5) Sarah (Georgia, 1834).

July 9, 1872 a petition to settle Abel Matthews' estate was filed in the Court of the Ordinary, Carroll County, Georgia, naming his son Benjamin Ezekiel as the administrator.

Carroll County census records show Benjamin Ezekiel as head of the household in 1840, 1850, 1860, 1870, and 1880. His occupations included instructor, farmer, and landowner. His wife, Mahala, was a homemaker.

1860 United States Census of Agriculture L-Z of Carroll County, Georgia, lists and describes Benjamin Ezekiel's farm.

Benjamin Ezekiel (ca. 1816 South Carolina-?) married (October 27, 1839, Carroll County) Mahala Beasley (1821 Georgia-?). Their children were: (1) John Henley (Georgia, May 23, 1841-March 5, 1925) wife Amanda M. Hicks (Henry County Georgia, April 13, 1836-April 28, 1919); (2) Nancy J. (1845) husband G. Williams; (3) Julia H. (1849-May 20, 1914) who married Tandy W. Fitts, and later Charles Alexander Heard; (4) Rhode C. (1850) husband James A. Nelson; (5) Mary E. (1853) who never married; and (6) George A. (October 5, 1856-November 12, 1914) wife Frances (August 17, 1856-March 22, 1918).

The parents and some of the children are buried at Liberty Christian Church, Liberty Church Road near Temple, Georgia.

Other related family articles: John Henley, Matthews, Hattie Matthews, and Orrill Morris. *Submitted by: N. Ted Westbrook, 6681 Pleasant Drive, Winston, GA 30187, twest5@aol.com*

Sources: Court, census, and marriage records of Carroll County. Tomb Stones at Liberty Christian Church

805. Matthews - Mathews - Mathis / Westbrook

Hattrice (Hattie) Beatrice

Hattrice (Hattie) Beatrice Matthews (December 19, 1874 - May 29, 1957) was surviving twin daughter of John Henley and Amanda M. (Hicks) of Carroll and Haralson Counties, Georgia.

Hattie Matthews married (Haralson County, 1892) Charles (Charley) Sterling Westbrook (April 20, 1866 - September 21, 1911) son of John Calhoun Westbrook of Haralson County, Georgia. Both are buried at Liberty Christian Church, Temple, Georgia.

Haralson County census records list Charley Westbrook as head of household in 1900. Hattie was a homemaker. Charlie was a farmer and machinist for the railroad. The family lived in Fulton and Haralson counties, Georgia as well as Selma, Alabama. After Charley's death, Hattie lived with either her son or daughter.

Hattie and Charley had two children who lived, Memory Ethel (November 4, 1894-September 28, 1967) and Noble Theodore Westbrook Sr. (May 16, 1909 - August 7, 1994).

Daughter, Ethel, worked at the Bremen Post Office. Ethel married (November 15, 1911) Joseph Dawson Long (October 8, 1888 - September 8, 1959) of Haralson County, Georgia. They are buried at Westview Cemetery, Atlanta, Georgia.

Haralson County census will list Joseph Dawson Long as head of the household: 1920, 1930, 1940, 1950 and Ethel 1960.

Hattrice (Hattie) Beatrice Matthews Westbrook

Ethel's and Dawson's children: (1) James Clyde, deceased, (Jo Overstreet of Plant City, Florida) daughter Jody Karen (Mrs. Scott Fidler); (2) Fred Sterling (1921-1957), (Billie McCain of Comfort, Texas) children Ethel Ann (Mrs. Dwain Smith), Dwight Dawson, James Sterling, (second wife Johnnie King of Chesterfield, South Carolina) children Mary Susan (Mrs. Terry L. Julian), Marsha Nelle (Mrs. Michael Randall), and John Sterling; (3) Hazel Amanda (1912-1978) (Ernest Goldin of Haralson County, Georgia), children: Brenda Jan (deceased) and Donna Lynn (Bill West, Joe Johnson).

Their son, Noble, married (February 4, 1938 Roopville, Carroll, Georgia) Lovie (Love) Mae Eaves (April 15, 1910 - August 20, 1986) daughter of James Lovelace Eaves of Buchanan, Haralson, Georgia. Love was trained as a beautician and teacher (State Normal and West Georgia College). She taught in Haralson County, majority in Bremen City School System. Both are buried at Forest Lawn, Bremen, Georgia. Noble married Joyce Braswell (August 1987, Haralson County, Georgia).

Haralson County census will list Noble head of household: 1940, 1950, 1960, 1970, 1980, and 1990.

Noble studied linotype operation in New Orleans, Louisiana, and worked on newspapers in Louisville and Bremen, Georgia. Most of his working life was spent at Bremen Post Office, retiring as postmaster. He enjoyed golf. He never met a stranger and loved new things and experiences.

Noble and Love's children are Noble Theodore (Ted) Jr. (February 20, 1943-) and Betty Louise (April 23, 1941-) (See Morris-Westbrook article.)

Their son Ted married (July 11, 1970, DeKalb County, Georgia) Carolyn Patricia Workman (August 4, 1945-) daughter of L.E. and Millie Mitchell Workman of DeKalb County, Georgia.

Douglas County, Georgia census will list Ted as head of household: 1980, 1990, 2000. Residences also included DeKalb County, Georgia.

Ted graduated from Auburn University (1965). Work life included BP Oil, Glidden Paint, and AOL Time Warner. Carolyn's work life included: BP Oil, Linen for You, Douglas County.

They have one daughter Mellisa Love (December 6, 1971-) a graduate from Georgia Southern University (1993). Her residences include Waycross, Statesboro and Peachtree City, Georgia.

See articles: Abel and John Henley Matthews, Orrill Morris. *Submitted by: N. Ted Westbrook, 6681 Pleasant Drive, Winston, GA 30187. twest5@aol.com*

Sources: Census, marriage, burial site records; Certificates of birth and death from Georgia Department of Public Health; university and college records; and retirement records.

806. Matthews, Mathews, Mathis

John Henley Matthews

John Henley Matthews (May 23, 1841-March 5, 1925) was the son of Benjamin Ezekiel and Mahala (Beasley) of Carroll County, Georgia. John's war records describe him as five feet six inches tall, having a dark complexion, brown hair, and gray eyes.

Georgia census records list John Henley as head of household in 1870 Carroll and 1900 Haralson Counties. John Henley was a farmer and his wife, Amanda M., was a homemaker.

John Henley married (Carroll County, December 23, 1869) Amanda M. Hicks (April 13, 1836 - April 28, 1919) daughter of Isham Hicks of Carroll and Henry Counties, Georgia. John Henley's immediate family is buried at Liberty Christian Church on Liberty Church Road near Temple, Georgia. Their children were: (1) George Emmitt (January 20, 1871 to February 21, 1939), wife Vassie (Redwine); children were Florie and Lunnie. (2) John Dewitt (1878 to after 1970), wife Effie (Baskin); children were James Dewitt (J.D.), Charles, Marilyn, Reba, and Ruth. (3) Philip (May 20, 1873 to November 11, 1928), wife Ida (Westbrook, daughter of William Augustus Westbrook); children were Annie Ruth, Hattie, Carl, and Errett.

John and Amanda Matthews with children and grandchildren.

(4) Hattrice (Hattie) (December 19, 1874 to May 29, 1957), husband Charles Sterling Westbrook (April 20, 1866 to September 21, 1911) son of John Calhoun of Haralson County, Georgia; their children were Ethel and Noble.

The Matthews family has had a strong alliance with Liberty Christian Church (established 1870). John Henley and his father-in-law, Isham Hicks, were two of the first preachers of the church. These men were considered "pine knot" preachers. This meant that they prepared themselves by their own initiative by the light of a pine knot (nor formal training). Their main income was from farming. Church membership still includes this family.

John Henley served as a private in Company H of the 56th Regiment of Georgia Volunteers of the Confederate Army. His war papers state that in 1863 he was a prisoner of war in Vicksburg, Mississippi, and again on August 20, 1864, in Chattanooga, Tennessee. He added his name to "the roll of Rebel deserters who took the oath of amnesty" and swore his allegiance to the United States. It is suspected that there was pressure from his father-in-law, Isham Hicks, who moved to Indiana to avoid taking sides.

John Henley's wife, Amanda, had a stepmother Eleanor Hicks. Eleanor inherited land from her husband Isham Hicks on August 30, 1872 (Land Lot 171 in the 5th District of Carroll County). Martha Jackson and M.T. Brady, the only children of Eleanor Hicks, issued a land deed on May 12, 1889, to John Henley Matthews of Carroll County giving him this land in return for the care of their mother for as long as she lived. Today, the property is near the intersection of Highway 61 and Old Airport Road where the Moose Club is located.

Also see related family articles, Abel and Benjamin Matthews, Hattie Matthews, and Orrill Morris. *Submitted by: Betty W. Morris, 184 Gina Drive, Carrollton, GA 30116 bettywmorris@cs.com*

Sources: Carroll County court, census, and marriage records. Tomb Stones Liberty Christian Church, Liberty Christian Church history, and Confederate Service Records.

807. Matthews - Tolbert

John Walker Matthews was born July 22, 1822, in Henry County, Georgia, and died January 22, 1892, in Paulding County. He married Lucy Tolbert who was born January 30, 1831, and died December 28, 1917.

Lucy's parents were Roland A. Tolbert, a miner, who was born July 3, 1799, and died July 1, 1896, and Elizabeth Tolbert who was born January 30, 1795, and died in March 1872. They were married September 19, 1819, in Montgomery County, North Carolina, and came to Carroll County, Georgia, in 1832 for him to work in the gold mines, until 1853 when he engaged in farming.

John Walker and Lucy Tolbert Matthews' children were James Roland, Gilbert, Mary Isola, John Thomas, Lucy Oriziba, William Glenn, Robert Burrell and Lillie Alice.

James Roland Matthews, was born December 2, 1849, in Carroll County and died January 24, 1927. On January 31, 1870, in Carroll County, he married Nancy Ann White, the daughter of Sidney White and Frances Hewett. Nancy Ann was born April 9, 1852, and died September 9, 1927. James Roland was a farmer and a Justice of the Peace. They are buried in Hillcrest Cemetery in Villa Rica, Georgia.

Their children, all born in Carroll County, were: 1. Fannie Alice Matthews was born February 3, 1871, and died April 27, 1937. She married William Sherman McCurdy who was born December 12, 1865, and died June 28, 1938. Both are buried in Hillcrest Cemetery. 2. John Sidney Matthews was born December 3, 1874, and died in 1957. He married Naomi Alice Leatherwood on June 7, 1896. She was born April 18, 1879, and died November 21, 1950. Both are buried in Hillcrest Cemetery. 3. Seaborn R. Matthews was born March 14, 1876, and died September 7, 1957. He married Adeline Odessa Furr who was born December 16, 1882, and died May 6, 1959. Both are buried in Hillcrest Cemetery. 4. Bersha Minerva Matthews was born September 28, 1880, and died July 11, 1978. She married J. Harris Davis who was born April 2, 1876, and died November 9, 1860. Both are buried in Hillcrest Cemetery. 5. Thomas Polk Matthews was born March 14, 1884, and died August 6, 1968. He married Ida Lorene Noles on December 26, 1911. She was born December 31, 1891, and died April 13, 1982. Both are buried in Hillcrest Cemetery. 6. Asa A. Matthews was born April 6, 1887, and died July 4, 1955. He married Pearl Furr who was born March 1, 1893 and died February 1, 1955. Both are buried in Hillcrest Cemetery. 7. Sam Matthews was born November 27, 1889, and died April 25, 1951. He married (first) Jessie Harper and (second) Vera Austin. He is buried in Carrollton City Cemetery. 8. Eugenia Watson Matthews was born in 1893 and died January 19, 1972. She married Wilson Furr who was born in 1888 and died in 1958. Both are buried in Hillcrest Cemetery. *Submitted by: Jack Donald Matthews, 2358 Carrollton-Villa Rica Hwy., Villa Rica, GA 30180*

Source: Personal knowledge and research of Helen Matthews

808. Mayfield - Duncan Family

William Asbury Mayfield was born May 1, 1847, died October 7, 1923, the son of Valentine Richard Smith Mayfield and Frances Bond. On May 11, 1871, he married Emily Elizabeth Duncan, the daughter of Samuel Wesley Duncan and Fairby Caroline Brock. She was born October 15, 1848, and died July 21, 1945.

They moved to Carroll County, Georgia, around 1890. Their children were Robert Wesley Mayfield, born April 28, 1872, died March 8, 1962, who married Mattie Caroline Sewell; Viola Elizabeth Mayfield, born September 29, 1873, died March 28, 1969, who married Richmond Burk Sewell; Ed Smith Mayfield, born August 21, 1876, died January 8, 1977, who married (first) Melvinie M. Harper, and (second) Martha Frances Kettle; Julie E. Mayfield, born April 3, 1879, died April 28, 1899, who married William Andrew Williams; Sarah Frances Mayfield, born October 11, 1881, died February 8, 1907, who also married William Andrew Williams; and John Wilburn Mayfield, born August 16, 1884, died January 14, 1970, who married (first) Maggie Lee Brock and (second) Inez Terry.

Robert Wesley lived in Atlanta, and Viola Elizabeth moved to Arkansas.

Ed Smith Mayfield remained in Carroll County. By his first married to Melvinie Harper, his children were Clifford, Leonard Oscar who married (first) Hattie Mae Swafford and (second) Hattie Belle Daniel, Roy, Carl Rader who married Ruby Fortner, Vera who married Clifford Fair, Eddie Estelle who married Terrell Reynolds, Bobbie Edmondson who married Ruth Wynn, Darce Pauline, and Frank Smith who married Mildred Gilland.

By his marriage to Martha Frances Kettle, his children were Kathryn who married (first) J.E. Van Landingham and (second) Gary Gentry, Envard who married Nancy Hembree, Herman Ed, Alice May, and William Smith who married Dale Dobbs. All but one child by the first marriage are deceased and are buried in the Powell Chapel Cemetery, Carroll County, Georgia.

Julie E. and William Andrew Williams had two children, Homer and Henry who died young. Julie and the children are buried in Powell Chapel Cemetery.

The children of Sarah Frances and William Andrew Williams were William Horace who married Marville Mildred Whitmire, Hattie Mae who married Robert Grady Anderson, Lillie Fae who married Jarvis Parker, and James Candler who married Linnie White. Sarah Frances is buried in Powell Chapel Cemetery.

John Wilburn and Maggie Lee Mayfield had one child, Maggie Lee, who married Willard Wilson. John Wilburn and Inez Mayfield's children were William Homer who married Leota Hamby, Lennie Fae who married Hugh Dorsey Hembree, Mary Frances who married Buford Camp, John Wesley who married Camely Aderhold, Bradford Watson who married Ezell Cole, Grady Lewis who married Ruth Thurmond, Allen Wilson who married Betty Jo Cole, Edna Louise who married (first) J.T. Shead and (second) Bob Adair, Betty Jean, Miriam Dallas who married Carolyn Boyd, and Esther Joan who married William Capes. John Wilburn, Inez, William Homer, Lennie Fae and Mary Frances are buried in the Glenn Memorial Cemetery in Carroll County, Georgia. *Submitted by: Joan Capes, 20 Horseshoe Bend, Carrollton, GA 30116. Researched by Erlene Boyd.*

Sources: Family Bible and personal knowledge.

809. McAllister and Chance

We could write volumes about the legacy of Malcom McRae McAlister, son of James Blanton McAllister and Margaret McRae McAllister. Today, that legacy speaks through the lives of his descendants who are spread over the country. His strong Methodist Episcopal upbringing is threaded through the lives of the McAllister family that continues to build a strong nation. Malcom was born April 3, 1831, in Blount County, Tennesee, but his family moved to Carroll County when he was only eighteen-months old. They made their home in the Hickory Level community and farmed the land. The study of medicine was Malcom's interest in life. He attended the Reform Medical College in Macon, Georgia, and graduated in 1860. Classes were suspended during the Civil War and resumed in 1867. Malcom commenced his practice in Benton County, now Calhoun, Alabama, but was back in Carroll County when he enlisted in the Civil War.

Malcom McRae McAllister and Nancy Jane Chance

Malcom enlisted in the Confederate Cavalry on August 1, 1862. He was a private in Company B, 7th Confederate Partisan Rangers, also known as Claiborn's Regiment Partisan Rangers. He supplied his own horse. The last company muster roll for him was dated August 31, 1864. He was thirty-one years old at the time of enlistment, blue eyes, dark hair, dark complexion, and 6'1" tall.

Malcom had married a neighbor girl, Nancy Jane Chance, on May 5, 1853. Her parents were Henry Smith Chance and Sarah (Clayton) Chance of Hickory Level. Henry Chance was born November 30, 1796, in Georgia. He was the postmaster of Chanceville (near Hickory Level) July 16, 1867, to September 28, 1866. He was a justice of the peace as early as 1854. He died January 1870. Sarah Chance was born September 5, 1799, and died after 1880.

Malcolm and Nancy had a son born March 11, 1854, but he died October 9, 1855. Martha Henrietta was born January 4, 1856. James David was born on May 28, 1862. After the war, Mary Ann "Millie" was born June 13, 1865. Another daughter and son were born, but they died in infancy. The family was in Hunt County, Texas, when their seventh child, Charles Wesley, was born on May 16, 1869. He died in Arkansas on November 12, 1874. The family moved to Polk County, Arkansas, on the head of Mountain Fork, and then moved to Scott County, Arkansas. Sarah Alice was born in Boles, Scott County, on June 27, 1872. The family moved back to Polk County by 1875 to Old Potter Township where William Wesley "Willie" was born June 27, 1875. The tenth and last child born was "Patty," born July 18, 1880. When Patty grew older, he gave himself the name "Charles Wesley" after his brother who had died in 1874.

Graduation Card, Reform Medical College, Macon, Georgia, Session 1859-1860.

Malcom was entitled to bounty for his service in the Civil War. They granted him a patent dated January 15, 1885, for one hundred sixty-two acres in the Gann Community, Polk County, Arkansas. Here is where he lived out the reminder of his life. He built a spilt rail log home in the style of the day with a breeze way. A back room was a "store." When he took goods to town, he didn't want to travel back empty, so he brought back supplies for the store. He continued his practice of medicine until his health began to fail. He would order some medicine from back East but made many simple remedies from leaves, roots, bark, etc.

Nancy Jane McAllister sang Christian songs as she went about her housework. She died December 14, 1884, at the age of forty-eight, leaving four-year-old Patty, nine-year-old Willie, and twelve-year-old Sarah Alice. The other children had homes of their own. Malcom then married Mrs. Sarah Catherine (Horton) Tyus.

His granddaughter, Alice (McAllister) Posey (born 1906) remembers seeing him sick in bed. He put his hand on her head and blessed her. Malcom died February 5, 1908. He is buried beside Nancy in the Rocky Cemetery located eight miles west of Mena, Polk County, Arkansas. *Submitted by: Goldie (Shook) Posey, Route 1 Box 48A, Wayne, OK 73095*

Sources: U.S. census records, cemetery records, death certificates, and personal knowledge.

810. The McAllisters and the McRaes

The McRaes

The progenitor of many of the Carroll County McRaes is Hugh Bain McRae from Scotland. Several researchers now believe that Hugh's parents were Malcomb M. McRae and Isabel Bain. Sufficient proof already exists that show Malcolm and Isabel were the parents of Alexander Bain McRae, who settled in Telfair County, Georgia. A complete proof has not been finalized showing Hugh and Alexander to be brothers.

Hugh Bain McRae married Nancy McDuffey sometime around the early to mid 1790s in South Carolina. They had five known children. Four were born in South Carolina and the other one in North Carolina. They were Daniel born in 1802, Margaret born in 1804, William J. born in 1808 in North Carolina, Malcolm Alexander born in 1810, and Hugh John born in 1813.

Around 1820 the McRae family left the Carolinas and moved to the newly acquired Hiawassee Purchase (Tennessee). They were known to be in Carroll County by early 1831. Three of the sons, Daniel, Malcolm, and Hugh, left Carroll County in the 1840s and went west. Daniel and Hugh went to Missouri. Malcolm, along with many from the Whisenhunt families, went to Pike County, Arkansas. Malcom lived there for a few years, then moved near Elwood in Fannin County, Texas.

Hugh Bain McRae died about 1853 reputedly around Rockmart or Cedartown, Georgia. The son William J. died in 1875 near Villa Rica. We do not know what happened to Nancy McDuffey or if she ever went to Carroll County.

The McAllisters

James Blanton McAllister was born in Tennessee around 1805. We do not know who his parents were. It is unclear just how or why the McRaes and the McAllisters ended up in East Tennessee, but we believe the McAllister family arrived in that area of Tennessee some time before 1823, as Margaret McRae and James Blanton McAllister were married in Tennessee about 1823. Their first five children, all born in Tennessee, were Nancy Jane (1824), William (1826), Alexander (1829), Mary (1830), and Malcom (1831). No evidence exists as to where in Tennessee the first four children were born; however, James first appears on the census records of Monroe County in 1830 with a wife and 4 children. We do know that Malcom McRae McAllister was born in Blount County, Tennessee on April 3, 1831.

James B. and Margaret McRae McAllister

James and Margaret came to Georgia in the fall of 1832 with their five children and settled near the Hickory Level community. Six more daughters were born to James and Margaret after moving to Georgia. They were Isabella Anne (1833), Barbara C. (1834), Mahaley (1837), Elizabeth J. (1839), Sarah Penelope (1843), and Martha M. (1847). Because no records have been found to show James lived anywhere in Georgia other than the Hickory Level area, we assume that the last six children were born in that community.

Family records passed down from Malcom M. McAllister show that James B. and his wife Margaret were active members in the Methodist Episcopal Church. James served as "exhorter," class leader, and Sunday School superintendent. Based on locality and other factors, we believe they attended the Concord Methodist Church. The "other factors" are centered on the man James Baskin, the first minister at Concord Methodist and the person probably most responsible for starting the church.

Some degree of friendship must have existed between James McAllister and James Baskin as Carroll County marriage records show Rev. Baskin conducted the marriage ceremonies for six of the McAllister children, and he was one of the three witnesses to James' last will and testament.

One of the daughters, Mahaley, died in 1859 at the age of twenty-two. James B. McAllister died in April 1860 at the age of fifty-five. Margaret died in 1870 and we assume she died in the Hickory Level community. No burial site has been found for Mahaley, James B., Margaret, Hugh Bain McRae, or William J. McRae.

Following is a brief summary on the children of James Blanton McAllister and Margaret McRae McAllister, their spouses, and their migration paths.

(1) Nancy Jane married Jeremiah Kinney in July 1844 and they moved to Calhoun County, Alabama, around mid-1850. Nancy and Jeremiah had six children.

(2) William married Elizabeth Cartwright in November 1846. They moved to Upshur County, Texas, and remained there until their deaths. They, too, had six children.

(3) Alexander married Adaline Garrison probably around 1852. It is thought that Adaline was the daughter of Thomas Galespa Garrison and Frances Hanks. No evidence has been found that Alexander and Adaline left Carroll County; however, documentation does show that many of the nine children went to Upshur and Wood Counties in Texas. Some family researchers believe all nine children went to Texas.

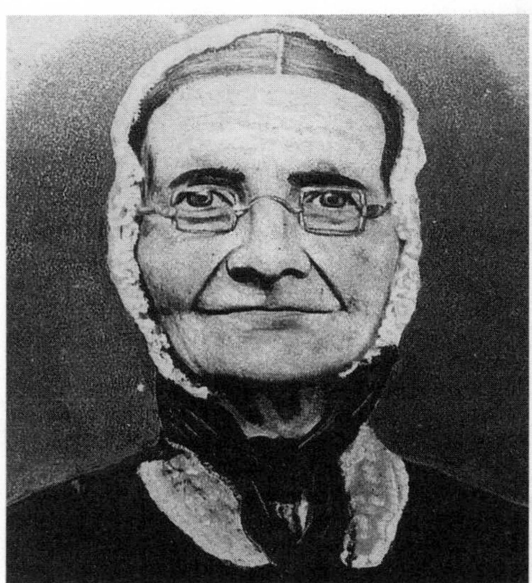

Margaret McRae McAllister

(4) Mary McAllister married James C. Howard in March 1854. They had five children, based on 1870 census records.

(5) Malcom McRae married Nancy Jane Chance, the daughter of Henry Chance and Sarah Clayton. Malcolm and Nancy had a total of ten children, born in Georgia, Arkansas, and Texas. They left Georgia and went to Arkansas, then on to Texas, and back to Arkansas where they remained until their deaths.

(6) Next was Isabella Anne who married Thomas Marion Carroll in October 1857. These were my great-grandparents and Rev. James Baskin married them. Thomas and Isabella lived most of their lives in Haralson County. Six children were born to this couple. Isabella died in 1906 and Thomas died in 1908. Both are buried in the Waco City Cemetery.

(7) Barbara C. McAllister was married to Jesse L.N. Fielder in Carroll County on September 15, 1859.

(8) Mahaley never married. She died December 1859 at the age of twenty-two.

(9) We have no information on the daughter Elizabeth.

(10) Sarah Penelope married Henry Clay Brown in September 1865 in Carroll County. They lived in Cedartown for several years and then moved to Birmingham, Alabama. Both died there and are buried in the Elmwood Cemetery.

(11) The youngest daughter Martha M. McAllister married Milligan Upshaw in 1866. Martha died in September 1916 and is buried at Concord Methodist Church Cemetery. *Submitted by: Great-great-grandson Stanley N. Carroll, 2109 Hansel Avenue, Huntsville, AL 35802*

Sources: Family records, U.S. census records, and research by other McRae and McAllister descendants.

811. The McBurnetts

My fourth great-grandfather was Daniel McBurnett, a soldier of the American Revolution. Daniel, born about 1755-1761, (place of birth unknown to me) was the progenitor of the McBurnetts who came to Carroll County between 1830 and 1840. He married Esther Wadsworth, daughter of Thomas Wadsworth, and they remained in the Wilkes, Franklin and Lincoln county areas until the death of Daniel in 1793. According to the Indian Depredation papers, Daniel was killed in an Indian ambush while driving a wagon for a Green family to the Providence of Florida. It was a few years later that the McBurnett family started their slow migration westward and eventually settled in Carroll and Haralson counties, with some members of the family settling in eastern Alabama.

It is believed that Daniel and Esther had at least three sons — James, Thomas, and William.

James McBurnett, probably the oldest son of Daniel and Esther, was born about 1776. He married Nancy Pate in Lincoln County, Georgia, about 1796. James served in the War of 1812 as a private in Captain James Meriwether's Company of Volunteer Riflemen attached to 2nd Regiment of the Georgia Militia. James died in October 1813. In 1820, Nancy lived with her six young sons in Walton County, Georgia.

Thomas McBurnett was born about 1780-1786. He married Sarah Smith in Clarke County, Georgia, on July 12, 1806, and they had five known children. Thomas is listed in the 1830 Georgia census records as a resident of Meriwether County, along with a 40-50 year-old female. I believe this is his mother, Esther Wadsworth McBurnett.

William McBurnett, born about 1793, was also in the War of 1812 as was his brother James. William and Mary Awtry were married February 19, 1813, in Morgan County, Georgia. He probably died before May of 1815, as Mary applied for Letters of Administration against his estate then. Later in 1827, Mary married Moses Ware of Morgan County.

Most of the McBurnett descendants in Carroll County come from the James McBurnett and Nancy Pate McBurnett line. They had six known sons: Daniel, Thomas, Nicholas, Albert, Joshua, and probably William (though I am not sure of this name). Nicholas is my direct line and the one featured in this history.

Nicholas McBurnett, the third son of James and Nancy Pate McBurnett, was born in Georgia about 1809. He married Lucinda G. Adams January 1, 1829 in Newton County, Georgia. By 1840 Nicholas and Lucinda, along with his widowed mother Nancy, were permanently settled in Carroll County, where they remained the rest of their lives. However, some records show that he was a resident of Randolph County, Alabama, for a short time. The mother, Nancy, continued to live by herself but close by other family members until age 91 when she declared herself retired and lived with Nicholas and Lucinda.

Eleven children were born to Nicholas and Lucinda McBurnett: (1) James was born about 1832, married Permelia Thompson December 15, 1856, died May 23, 1894, and is buried at Union Camp Ground Cemetery, Carroll County. (2) Mary was born December 25, 1833, married Isaac N. Ingram February 10, 1854, died November 2, 1890, and is buried at New Hope United Methodist Cemetery, Carroll County. (3) Nancy was born October 20, 1835, married James Seigler July 21, 1860, died July 13, 1916, and is buried at New Hope United Methodist Cemetery, Carroll County. (4) Iba Louisa was born April 6, 1837, married Shadrack Thompson on February 9, 1854, died November 5, 1907, and is buried at Union Camp Ground Cemetery, Carroll County. (5) Thomas was born about 1841, was a private in Company B of Cobb's Legion, died in Richmond, Virginia, on or about August 6, 1862. Probably wounded at Malvern Hill. (6) Joshua was born about 1843, also a private in Company B of Cobb's Legion, and died in Richmond, Virginia, hospital #27, July 30, 1863. Probably wounded at Chancellorsville. (7) John Nicholas was born about 1845, married Sophia Matilda Brown on December 14, 1869, probably died in Texas. (8) Daniel M. was born May 26, 1847, married Mary S. Price on December 24, 1868, died February 16, 1905 in Texas, and was buried at Mount Zion United Methodist Cemetery, Carroll County. (9) William A. was born about 1849, married Sara Elizabeth Jones on January 19, 1871, died in 1913, and was buried at Union Camp Ground Cemetery, Carroll County. (10) Jefferson McGee was born December 29, 1850, married Sarah Anne Elizabeth King on December 26, 1871, died April 15, 1915, in Sharp, Texas, and is buried in Sharp Cemetery. (11) Harrison Wardlow was born July 29, 1855, married Margaret C. Brown on December 2, 1875, died May 14, 1919, and was buried in McAlister Cemetery, Carter County, Oklahoma. Margaret and one son, Wesley, are also buried in this cemetery.

Nicholas McBurnett died in 1880 at age 71. He had been a resident of Carroll County for forty years. After his death, Lucinda made her home with her youngest son, Harrison Wardlow. It is believed that Lucinda died about 1885.

The McBurnett Cemetery

The McBurnett Cemetery is located off Harper Lane in Carroll County. As far as we know, only McBurnetts and Thompsons are buried there. There are nine headstones for the McBurnetts and three other markers for members of the Thompson family, and as many as fifteen unmarked graves. The McBurnett markers only show initials and the surname, so knowing exactly who these people are is difficult. It is possible that "N.I. McBurnett" is Nicholas; "N.A. McBurnett" could be the elder Nancy McBurnett, and "L.C. McBurnett" could be Lucinda, wife of Nicholas. *Submitted by: Betty Jo Carroll Parsons, 2085 Bowdon-Tyus Road, Bowdon, GA 30108*

812. Jefferson McGee McBurnett and Sarah Anne Elizabeth King

Jefferson McGee McBurnett, born December 29, 1850, in Carroll County, Georgia, was the tenth child of Nicholas and Lucinda Adams McBurnett. He married Sarah Anne Elizabeth King on December 26, 1871. Sarah Anne was the daughter of Joseph G. King and Indiana Langston King. As were most rural people, Jefferson was a farmer. It appears that he began to broaden his horizons in support of his young family, as he stated in the 1880 census records that he worked in a sawmill. He also served for a few years as postmaster in the Kansas Community of Carroll County beginning in 1876.

Jefferson and Sarah Anne were the parents of 13 children. (1) Minnie Lucinda Indiana McBurnett born October 29, 1872, married James Moses Blackburn Carroll June 6, 1890, and died September 7, 1950, in Atlanta, Georgia. She is buried in Waco Baptist Church Cemetery, Waco, Georgia. She was called "Minnie Lee." (2) Mary Fannie McBurnett born February 22, 1874, married Oscar Bruce Carroll on May 11, 1890, died January 24, 1960, in Texas and is buried in Rockdale, Texas. Oscar Bruce and the above James M.B. Carroll were brothers. (3) Joseph Wardlow McBurnett was born August 9, 1875, married Margaret Lillian Stone on September 11, 1898, died February 1, 1949, and is buried in Montevallo Cemetery, Shelby County, Alabama. (4) Laura Victoria Adalee McBurnett was born April 4, 1878, married first to Tom Edelmon and second to Ben Massey, died September 15, 1960 in Texas. (5) Benjamin Nicholas McBurnett was born April 8, 1880, married Ethel Davis on August 24, 1902, died November 19, 1959, and is buried in the IOOF Cemetery, Rockdale, Texas. (6) William Barto McBurnett was born September 16, 1881, married first to Della Kolb and second to Frances Davis in Texas. Bart's first wife and daughter were killed in the hurricane that hit the Corpus Christi area in 1919. Bart was also trapped in this hurricane but survived. He died March 6, 1939, and is buried in Rose Hill Cemetery, Corpus Christi, Texas. (7) Mark Corneilus McBurnett was born April 13, 1883, married Lillie Edna Davis on November 13, 1910, died January 25, 1951, and is buried in Miles, Texas. (8) Henry Cleveland McBurnett was born July 23, 1885, married Tommie Jones on June 10, 1923, died March 14, 1959, and is buried in Robstown, Texas. (9) Beatrice Ada McBurnett was born July 23, 1887, married Charles L. Britton on October 30, 1904, and is buried in Robstown, Texas. (10) Dovey Lois McBurnett was born May 6, 1889, married Felix Frierson, died May 19, 1952 and is buried in Haskell, Texas. (11) Dwynell McGee McBurnett was born May 24, 1891, married first to Blanche Homeyer and second to Clarabel Russell, died October 3, 1959, and is buried Seaside Cemetery, Corpus Christi, Texas. (12) Walter Lee McBurnett was born May 10, 1893, in Mary Lee, Alabama, married Marian Elva Lee on December 14, 1920, died March 24, 1907, and is buried in Robstown Memorial Cemetery, Robstown, Texas. (13) Buna Myrtle McBurnett was born August 10, 1897, in Sharp, Texas, married William Cullen Rutland on September 26, 1922, died September 18, 1959, and is buried in Corpus Christi, Texas.

All these McBurnett children were born in Haralson County with the exception of the last two. The first child born to this family, Minnie Indiana Lucinda McBurnett, is the line from which I am descended.

The first three children, Minnie Lee, Fannie, and Joseph Wardlow married while still living in Georgia. The other children married after the family moved to Texas.

After living in Carroll and Haralson counties for many years, Jefferson and Sarah Anne McBurnett, along with their large family, started their migration westward sometime around 1892. It is not known exactly how long this trip took, but apparently they were settled there around 1895 or 1896. Of the 13 children, my grandmother Minnie Lee was the only one who made Georgia her permanent home. The second daughter, Mary Fannie, who married Oscar Bruce Carroll, stayed in the Waco area until about 1906, when they also moved to Texas.

Perhaps in the beginning, life was not as comfortable in Texas as this young family thought it might be. In letters written in 1896 by Indiana Langston King to her daughter Sarah Anne, she expressed regret over their crops in Texas "being so sorry ... " while Carroll and Heard counties "had the best crops" she had ever seen! Whatever the conditions, Jefferson and Sarah Anne remained in Texas and continued farming, in addition to breeding and selling horses.

Jefferson McGee McBurnett died in Sharp, Milam County, Texas on April 15, 1915. Sarah Anne Elizabeth King McBurnett died in Robstown, Texas, April 15, 1942. Both are buried in the community of Sharp, Texas, near Rockdale.

Submitted by: Harlan L. Carroll, Carrollton, GA

Source: Researched by Betty Jo Carroll Parsons, Bowdon, GA

813. McCain Family

William Baskin McCain was born on November 27, 1794, in Lancaster County, South Carolina, the fifth of eight children born to Hugh McCain Junior and his wife, Isabella Baskin McCain. William's father had been in the Revolutionary War as an orderly sergeant in Captains Davis and John Foster's Companies of Light Dragoons under General Sumter's Command at the Battles of Hanging Rock and Camden. Hugh

Junior and several of his brothers were captured by the British at Camden. William's grandfather, Hugh McCain Senior, was hung by his neck by Tories fighting for British General Cornwallis at this time in an attempt to make him reveal where his money was hidden. Hugh Senior refused to talk but was saved from a slow death by one of his female slaves, Tenor, and her sons who ran the Tories away. Hugh Senior is believed to have come to Cane Creek in 1753, which was originally located in Anson County, North Carolina. In November 1753 John McCain, who appears to have been Hugh Senior's father, and Hugh's father-in-law, William Nutt, came from Beverly Manor, Augusta County, Virginia, after having lived there for ten years. They were given land grants in Anson County by the Colony of North Carolina. Before this time, the McCain family lived from 1725 to 1743 with other Scotch-Irish families in Marsh Creek Settlement, later to become Gettysburg, in Lancaster County, Pennsylvania. Both Hugh McCain Senior and Junior are buried at Tirzah Presbyterian Church, Waxhaw, North Carolina.

William B. McCain served as a private in the Seminole War of 1817-18 in Little's 2nd Regiment of Georgia Militia. He married his cousin, Margaret Nesbet McCain, the daughter of Joseph McCain, on December 13, 1821. They moved to Georgia in 1841, first settling in Troup County where he became a prominent planter and operated two grain mills. They had twelve children: Joseph Read, Hugh Palmer, Jane Moore, Isabella B., John Newton, James Alexander, Margaret Elizabeth, Thomas Jefferson, William Wilborn, Robert Harrison, Andrew Hamilton, and Benjamin Jasper. In October 1850 the family moved to Hickory Level in Carroll County where a related family, the Baskins, lived and established a farm on 800 acres where Buck Horn Lake is now located. The family prospered at this time. Jane married Alcimus H. Allen, the son of Harris and Cynthia Allen. Isabella married Jackson L. Hill. John, the oldest living son at the time, born November 16, 1829, married Margarett E. Miles, the daughter of William and Jane Miles, on November 7, 1850, in Harris County.

In 1859 John moved his family to Scott County, Mississippi, and lived next to his in-laws. John and Margarett's children were Mary Jane (Mollie), Martha Ann (Mattie), William Alcimus (Billy), Francis N. (Frannie), and Josephine Alcinath (Phenie). When the War Between the States began, John joined Company C., 39th Mississippi Infantry Regiment. After exhaustive marching following the Battle of Corinth, John died of exposure with Margarett at his side in a Confederate hospital at Brandon, Mississippi on December 7, 1862. Because of the fighting in Mississippi, Margarett brought the children back to live with the McCain family in the safety of Carroll County. By war's end, all of William B. McCain's sons, except Benjamin, were dead and his daughters had lost their husbands, except Alcimus Allen who was later killed in a hunting accident in 1868. William B. McCain died on July 24, 1865. His wife, Margaret, died six months later. Both are buried at Bethel Baptist Church. Most of the family's acreage was sold for a fraction of the original cost to pay taxes in 1867.

William A. McCain was born September 17, 1855. At age ten in 1865, Billy went from being a planter's son to a field hand. He had to take care of his mother, Margarett, and four sisters. Billy suffered from illnesses early in life which affected his ability to work later in life. Billy's first wife was Jasmine Brock. They were wed on March 18, 1881. They had no children and she died early in life. Billy later married Mary "Mollie" Narcissus Merrell, the oldest daughter of Judge George W. Merrell, on March 30, 1888. Billy's sisters all married eventually and he took care of his mother. Mary married Alexander H. Riggs. Mattie married James S. Tidwell and moved to California. Frannie married Price Browning. Phenie married Joseph D. Brock and moved to Cullman, Alabama. Billy and Mollie had six children: William Henry, George Newton, Eugene S., Percy Alonzo, Harry Carlton, and Sallie Lou (Sarah). Billy ran a small farm and moved to Atlanta in 1891 where the family sold produce. Billy moved the family back to Carroll County in 1903 saying that Atlanta was a bad place to raise children. Billy died on March 3, 1925, and Mollie passed away in 1932. Both are buried at Concord Primitive Baptist Church.

William Henry McCain was born August 28, 1889. He married Elsie Mae Marchman on December 4, 1920. Henry managed a large farm in South Georgia. They had no children. He died in 1949 and was buried at Concord Primitive Baptist Church.

Eugene S. McCain was born September 15, 1893. Gene worked as a farmer and grocer. His first marriage was to Elizabeth Huggins. His second marriage was to Elizabeth. There were not children by either marriage.

Percy Alonzo McCain was born June 8, 1896. Alonzo was a farmer. He married Drucilla Johnson. They had three children: Mollie Beatrice, Mattie Ezell, and Alonzo. Percy Alonzo died November 15, 1927, and is buried at Concord Primitive Baptist Church.

Harry Carlton McCain was born October 4, 1899. Harry was a mill worker. He married Ethel Huggins on July 27, 1918. They had five children: Margaret, Catherine, Reese, William, and an unnamed child who died in infancy.

Sallie Lou "Sarah" was born January 8, 1902. She married Frank Bell and lived on a farm near Red Oak, Georgia, selling produce and dairy products. They had four children: Sara Frances, Harold, Brewer, and Charlotte.

George N. McCain was born August 28, 1891, and had eight years of education when he became a teacher in a one-room school house near the Tallapoosa River. He taught eight grades at one time. He later went to work delivering mail on the Railway Mail Service. George married Mary Faye Reid, daughter of James H. and Laura A. Cole Reid, on June 10, 1916. They moved to Atlanta where he had a career with the Post Office. They had two children: George Carlton, born May 18, 1918, and Laura Jean, born September 18, 1921. George retired in 1954 and moved to Lake Jodeco, south of Jonesboro, where he enjoyed hunting quail and fishing. George died December 1, 1981, and Faye passed away in January 1985. Both are buried in Westview Cemetery in Atlanta.

Carlton McCain attended Georgia Tech and was an officer in the Third Armored Division. He fought in the European Theater in World War II. He married Frances "Frankie" Fitzgerald on April 25, 1942, the daughter of Grover and Onice Fitzgerald. Carlton retired from American Telephone and Telegraph. Frankie retired from the Bureau of Alcohol, Tobacco, and Firearms. They had two sons: Bruce Carlton, born February 25, 1948, and David Robert, born May 30, 1949. After retirement they spent many years enjoying the beauty of living on Lake Burton in Rabun County, Georgia.

Bruce McCain graduated from the University of Georgia in 1970 and began a twenty-two year career as a Regular Army officer, retiring in 1992 as a lieutenant colonel. He married Vicki R. Turnmire on October 18, 1975. They had three children: Travis Morgan, Laurie Elizabeth, and Amy Kathleen. Bruce's overseas assignments were in Korea and Germany. Since 1997, he has been manager for Chicopee Woods Nature Preserve in Gainesville, Georgia.

David McCain served in the Georgia Army National Guard and the Air Force Reserves in the late 1960s and early 1970s. David was the founder of Atlanta Textile Graphics and later a partner in the home remodeling firm of Russell & McCain. His wife is Lori Ford to whom he has been married since February 23, 1991, and resides in Marietta, Georgia. *Submitted by: Bruce C. McCain, LTC, USA (Ret), 5981 Pocahontas Drive, Flowery Branch, GA 30542-3147.*

Sources: McCain Family Bible records; U.S. Census records; Confederate Widow's Pension 1891; Letter of Guardianship, Carroll County, GA; County records from Pennsylvania, Virginia, North Carolina, South Carolina, and Georgia.

814. The McCain Family's Political History

Mr. Doyle F. McCain was the first Black to serve on the Villa Rica City Council. He was also one of the recipients of the 1984-85 Black Citizens of the Year award from the Neva Lomason Library.

He served on the council for seven years. He was a member of the public safety, streets, recreation, and housing committees, and served on the board of directors of the Chattahoochee-Flint Area Planning and Development Committee.

Doyle F. McCain

He served in the United States Army during World War II, and received a Victory medal, a good conduct medal, and an honorable discharge.

He devoted much of his time to working for Black causes, particularly working with young people. He was a scoutmaster, and one of the organizers of the Carroll County National Association for the Advancement of Colored People (N.A.A.C.P.) His greatest love was his church, Mt. Prospect Baptist Church. There he served as Sunday School superintendent, deacon, choir member, and church treasurer. He was married to Ellena Knight McCain. He was the father of Frances Bailey, Mayor Pro-Tem Shirley Marchman, Donald, and Michael. Mr. McCain died February 25, 1985. There is a street named for him in Villa Rica.

Five years later, his daughter Shirley followed in his footsteps. In January 1990, she started her journey into politics. She also serves on the housing authority, streets, and public safety committees. She was appointed mayor pro-tem and police commissioner in 1995. She serves on the board of directors of the Flint Regional Development committee as secretary, Community Action for Improvement (C.A.F.I.) Board, Democratic Party committee, received the outstanding Christian Women Award in 1995, president of the board of directors of the Thomas A. Dorsey Birthplace Gospel and Heritage Festival Inc., and president of the Thomas Dorsey Birthplace Choir. She is a member of the Mt. Prospect Baptist Church, where she serves as Sunday School teacher, member of the sanctuary choir, member of the missionary society, nurses guild, and volunteers for the community food bank. She is a lifetime member of the Carroll County N.A.A.C.P. where she served as secretary for twenty-eight years.

Shirley McCain Marchman

She is married to Willie F. Marchman and has two sons, Jerome and Deron, and three grandchildren, JeLinda, Christian, and Courtney. *Submitted by: Shirley Marchman, 224 Sunset Drive, Villa Rica, GA 30180*

815. The Alcimus Allen McCain Family

Alcimus Allen McCain was b. 5 June 1874 to Joseph Reid McCain and Cynthia Ann Eliza Jones McCain. He m. 31 Dec 1896 to Elizabeth Teresa Chance b. 2 July 1874, daughter of James. W. Chance and Martha Cochran Chance.

The A.A. McCain family lived on the 50 acres he was buying from his father-in-law, James W. Chance. He was able to add to it and had quite a large farm on the Center Point Road from Temple. The farm had a large orchard remembered by the children and grandchildren. A.A. McCain was a kind and gentle man who loved children and was very affectionate to all. He attended the Temple School Halloween Carnival even after his children were grown and enjoyed the children. He and "Lizzie" were able to celebrate their 50th wedding anniversary, although she became ill soon after. She was lovingly attended by her children and died at home in 1957.

Alcimus McCain and Elizabeth Chance McCain

A.A. McCain was very alert, even into his 90s and helped June Wester compile the McCain history. He died 26 Jan 1966. They are buried in Asbury Cemetery, Temple. They were longtime members at Bethel Baptist Church.

Children: 1. Ernest Washington McCain b. 25 Nov 1897 d. 3 Oct 1969 m. 25 Nov 1922 Thelma Caroline Keller b. 16 June 1901 d. 1990; one daughter, Joyce. 2. Dewey Earl McCain b. 6 Sept 1899 d. 27 Feb 1992 m. Nancy Manley, no issue. 3. Lois Pauline McCain b. 23 Dec. 1901 m. Eugene McGee June 1920, two sons: Edward and Melvin. 4. Ruby B. McCain b. 1 Dec 1903, living 2001 m. 24 Apr 1924 Reuben Loyd Wester b. 14 Nov 1895 d. 30 June 1974; 2 children: Bill and Linda. 5. William B. McCain moved to Akron and married there; no issue. 6. Mattie Lou McCain m. Harvey Oldham, 2 children: Jackie and Julian. 7. Ovie Teresa McCain b. 7 July 1910 m. Huell Hamil, 3 sons: Bob, Ned and Mac. 8. Mae, died age 3. *Submitted by: Jackie Oldham, Brunswick, GA; Written by: June Hart Wester, 133 Mountain Crest Drive, Canton, GA 30114*
Sources: Family reminiscences; *Hugh McCain of the Waxhaws and His Descendants* by Lawrence W. Maynard, and others, 1993.

816. The Alexander M. McCain Family

Alexander Moore McCain born circa 1806 and family did not appear on the Carroll County census until 1860, although he appears in the county record as administrator of the estate of Moses Williams with P.G. Garrison as his bond. This estate was between 1834-1845.

At that time he was living in Coweta on Cedar Creek among Garrison relatives. He had married Nancy Hall Garrison. By 1860 they had several children and his son, Joseph Reid McCain, was the overseer of the plantation of "Aunt Peggy" Garrison.

Alexander was the administrator of William P. McCain Sept. 1862. This was probably the estate of his son, William, who was twenty-one in 1860 census. William McCain is listed on the muster roll of Company E, 1st Georgia Regiment Calvary. Joseph R., brother, is listed as 4th corporal in the same unit. Joseph received a pension for his service.

Alexander M. McCain lived in the G.M.D. 1152 or Kansas near Buck Creek area, lot #253 in 7th land district. In 1874, tax list shows him as too old for the poll tax. That year he gave to his daughter and son-in-law, William and Mary Jane Campbell, for $5 and "natural love and affection," lot #282 7th district.

The father of Alexander M. McCain was Joseph McCain born 1777, living 1840 census of Chattooga County near another son, Robert McCain. These relatives moved to Calhoun County, Alabama, near Jacksonville. He died there and is buried there with wife Jennett Moore McCain. Around 1880 Alexander M. McCain and daughter and son-in-law left Carroll and went to Cullman, Alabama. No burial places have been found for him. *Submitted by: Ruby McCain Wester; Written by: June Hart Wester, 133 Mountain Crest Drive, Canton, GA 30114*
Sources: Court records, census records, family, *Hugh McCain of the Waxhaws and His Descendants* by Lawrence W. Maynard, and others, 1993.

817. The Joseph Reid McCain Family

Joseph Reid McCain born 12 January 1837 to Alexander M. McCain and Nancy Garrison McCain moved from Coweta County to Carroll County after the 1860 census. He married Cynthia Ann Eliza Jane Jones, daughter of Daniel Jones, called "Fanny!" She had been named for her grandmother Holcombe.

Children: 1. John D. McCain b. 10 May 1866 m. Elizabeth Hardaman. He had descendants in Cullman County, AL. 2. William T. McCain b. 18 Mar 1868 d. 1921 m. Lura Weathers. Worked on the railroad. They are buried Asbury Cemetery, Temple, GA. 3. George Washington McCain b. 8 Mar 1870 m. Myrtie Reid. He was a traveling salesman, m. age 50. Anna L. McCain b. 12 Aug 1872, died young. 5. Alcimus Allen McCain b. 5 June 1874 d 26 Jan 1966 m. Elizabeth Teresa Chance 31 Dec 1896. She b. 2 July 1874 d. 1957, buried Asbury Cemetery, Temple, GA. 6. Joseph L. McCain b. 18 Oct 1876 m. Janie McCalmon, bur. Bremen City Cemetery. 7. Wiley McCain b. 19 Mar 1879 m. Mamie Chance, bur. Asbury Cemetery. 8. Lula Idella McCain b. 7 May 1881 m. Alcemus Wren, bur. Bethel Baptist Cemetery, Hwy. 113. 9. Ida Louella McCain b. 12 Mar 1885 m. Benton Rowe, bur. Spence Cemetery behind George Spence's home.

Joseph Reid and Fanny Jones McCain

Joseph Reid McCain was listed as 4th Corporal in the Company E, 1st Georgia Cavalry along with his brother, William McCain. He received a pension. A powder burn on his face wa a wonder to grandchildren. He bought lot #253 of district 7 in Kansas G.M.D. on 10 Oct 1865. They lived in this area for years. They are buried in Asbury Cemetery, Temple, GA. *Submitted by: Mike McGee, Carrollton, GA; Written by: June Hart Wester, 133 Mountain Crest Drive, Canton, GA 30114*
Sources: Court records of Carroll County, census records, Bible, conversation with Ruby McCain Wester 2001.

818. The George Madison McCarty Family

George Madison McCarty was born in 1847, likely in Burke County, Georgia. He was the third child to Sampson McCarty and Elizabeth Byrd. George Madison McCarty's nickname was Matt. During 1850s, he moved with his parents to Carroll County, Georgia, and lived on the farm land granted to the orphans of Michael J. McCarty in the 1827 Georgia Land Lottery. This is near the town of Whitesburg and located just off present day Little New York Road. We know little of Matt's life as a youngster.

George Washington and Rhoda (Thompson) McCarty

While living in Carroll County, George Madison McCarty met a young lady by the name of Martha Ann Driver. Martha was a year younger than Matt, being born on June 14, 1848, to John M. Driver and Melissa Stranger. At the age of twenty-one, George Madison McCarty married Martha Ann Driver on April 16, 1868. While living in Carroll County, it is likely that they lived near his father, Sampson McCarty.

George Madison and Martha Ann (Driver) McCarty farmed for a living. At some point during the 1870s, they moved to Alabama and lived in Calhoun County near the community of Ohatchee. During the year of 1877, he and J.W. Abernathy farmed together. In order to plant and get through the season, they borrowed the sum of $43.11 from Rowan Dean & Company. The Calhoun County courthouse records this transaction in a lien on their season's crop. The debt was to be paid by November 1, 1877, or their crop would be seized and sold at private sale or public outcry to the highest bidder.

In the year following their marriage in 1868, George Madison and Martha Ann (Driver) McCarty became parents when Elizabeth Malissa McCarty was born on June 19, 1869. They lived in Carroll County, Georgia, at the time. Elizabeth married Sobaskia Sticher on May 20, 1884 in Carroll County.

The second child of George Madison and Martha Ann (Driver) McCarty was William Sampson McCarty, being born on April 16, 1871, in Carroll County. His nickname was Bud. Bud married Annie Elizabeth Helton on December 2, 1894, in Carroll County.

On the original homestead property of Sampson McCarty in Carroll County, the third child of George Madison and Martha Ann (Driver) McCarty is buried. Mary Francis McCarty was born on September 4, 1873, and lived almost five months. She died of unknown causes on January 30, 1874.

Fifteen months after the death of their baby daughter, another son was born. George Washington McCarty was born in Carroll County on April 27, 1875. He married Rhoda Josephine Thompson on August 13, 1893.

George Madison and Martha Ann (Driver) McCarty moved to Alabama between April of 1875 and December of 1876. While in Alabama, they gave birth to their fourth child, John Jackson McCarty on August 2, 1878. John married Mary Etta Taylor on September 6, 1895, in Carroll County.

George Madison McCarty borrowed $200 with his father, Sampson McCarty, for sharecropping during 1881. At that time, both Sampson's and George Madison's families were living near each other again in the community of Ohatchee in Calhoun County, Alabama. While we do not know the outcome of the 1881-cropping season, we know that George Madison and Martha Ann (Driver) McCarty had their sixth and last child. On August 25, 1881, Minner Ann McCarty was born. While census records indicate that she was born in Georgia, it is very possible that she was born in Alabama.

Unfortunately, George Madison McCarty died of unknown causes later the next year in 1882. He was thirty-five years old. He was buried in an unmarked, but identified grave located in the Gilley Cemetery in Carroll County, Georgia. While we don't know if he and his wife, Martha Ann (Driver) McCarty, had moved back to Carroll County prior to his death, it is interesting to see him buried in Carroll County. Following George Madison McCarty's death, Martha Ann did live in Carroll County. After all, her parents lived in Carroll County.

At the age of thirty-four, Martha Ann (Driver) McCarty became a widow with five living children. For the next two years, she remained unmarried. Then, on October 13, 1884, the wife of James W. Webb passes away. Reported in the *Carroll Free Press* newspaper in the Whitesburg community column dated October 17, 1884, Mrs. Webb's passing is indicated by the notation,

> "Mrs. J.W. Webb died Monday night Oct 13 Th 1884, after a long and severe sickness. The bereaved husband and children have our sympathy."

Far Right: Martha Ann Driver, seated, George Madison McCarty, standing

Sons of George Washington and Rhoda Josephine (Thompson) McCarty

Evidently, Martha Ann (Driver) McCarty and James W. Webb found themselves in similar situations. Both had children to raise and were widowed. On December 1, 1884, Martha Ann (Driver) McCarty married James W. Webb. They moved to a house in town immediately afterwards. Another notation in the Whitesburg community column appeared in the *Carroll Free Press* newspaper dated December 12, 1884, stating,

> "James W. Webb has rented land from L. Kendrick and is moving down to town into the W.M. Craig house."

James W. Webb has been described as a good father to Martha Ann's children. While James and Martha Ann never had any children together, their combined family continued to live in Carroll County. At the age of seventy-two years old, James W. Webb died on September 18, 1899. He is buried in a remote private family plot located near the Clem community in Carroll County. Traveling 2.3 miles down Happy Hill Road, off Georgia Route 16, then turning left and traveling 1.5 miles down Cook-Driver Road you can locate the cemetery. The grave is in a wooded area on the left about 200 feet off the road.

George Washington McCarty Family, Seated L: Martha Ann Driver Webb

George Madison McCarty's Bible has recorded the marriage, births and deaths of this family. It is one of the most remarkable documents to survive within the family. The Bible was published in 1827 and is in fair condition. *Submitted by: Donald Henry McCarty Jr., 3648 Grahams Ridge Court, Snellville, GA 30039-4115.*

819. The Michael J. McCarty Family

The orphans of Michael J. McCarty drew land in Carroll County during the 1827 Georgia Land Lottery on Land Lot 11, Fourth District of Section 5. These orphans were Sampson, Elizabeth, and George McCarty. Sampson McCarty and his wife Elizabeth Byrd moved from Burke County,Georgia, in 1858 to homestead the drawn land lot. Sampson McCarty was born to Michael J. McCarty and Margaret Byrd about 1814 in Edgefield County, South Carolina. After his father died in 1825, Sampson moved to Georgia with his mother and his siblings. They lived in Ross District of Jefferson County, Georgia, and then made their home in the First Ward of Augusta, Georgia. Sampson McCarty ran a beef market while living in Augusta.

It was during the second uprising of the Creek Indians in Georgia that Sampson saw military service. Since the federal forces were fully engaged in the Seminole Indian War in Florida, the States of Georgia and Alabama were told by the federal government that they would have to organize their own forces and fight this second Creek Indian War by themselves. During 1836, Sampson McCarty fought in the Second Creek Indian War, serving in the Major John H. Howard's Battalion under Captain Isaac McCray's command in the Georgia Mounted Volunteers of the Georgia Militia. He served three months, from March 10, 1836 to June 10, 1836, at Fort Twiggs in Columbus, Georgia. His military records show that he was given "62 rations of subsistence & 62 rations of forage in kind." A week prior to Sampson McCarty mustering out of service, a small well-documented skirmish occurred at Boykin's Ferry near Boykin's Plantation on June 3, 1836. This location is twenty-five miles below Columbus on the Chattahoochee River in Georgia. While we do not have an account of Sampson McCarty's action in this incident, it is clear that Captain Isaac McCrary's Company was involved.

Following the Indian War, Sampson McCarty married Elizabeth Byrd on December 20, 1837, in Richmond County, Georgia. Elizabeth was the daughter of William Byrd. William Byrd was Margaret Byrd's brother. Thus, Sampson McCarty married his first cousin.

During December of 1837, Sampson McCarty signed a Richmond County marriage bond for Madison M. McCarty to marry Henrietta Florence. While no record has been found to establish the exact relationship of Sampson McCarty to Madison McCarty, they were evidently very close in their relationship. Madison M. McCarty in turn signed the marriage bond for Sampson McCarty during the same month in Richmond County for his marriage to Elizabeth Byrd.

After Sampson and Madison McCarty married their respective wives in December of 1837, they moved to Burke County, Georgia. It is not clear when Sampson McCarty came to live in Burke County. In the 1850 census for Burke County, Sampson McCarty is shown as an overseer of a plantation. Madison M. McCarty is shown as a tavern keeper in downtown Waynesboro, Georgia. Burke County deed records reflect Madison beginning to purchase property in Waynesboro in 1848, with subsequent purchases in 1849 and 1850. Madison M. McCarty is shown to sell land to Sampson McCarty on July 8, 1851. Madison's wife Henrietta is known to have died in childbirth about 1846. After that tragedy, Madison M. McCarty came to Waynesboro where he married Georgia V. Wiggins. When Madison M. McCarty sold his Burke County property on July 8, 1851, to Sampson McCarty, Madison M. McCarty moved to Tuscaloosa County, Georgia.

Following Sampson and Elizabeth (Byrd) McCarty's move to Carroll County in 1858, they owned and farmed Land Lot 11 and 12 of the Fourth District. The 1860 census for Carroll County indicates Sampson McCarty was a slaveholder.

Sampson McCarty, son of Michael J. McCarty and Margaret Byrd.

At the point of the Civil War, Sampson McCarty was already a veteran soldier, having fought in the Indian Wars with the Georgia Mounted Militia. At the age of fifty-one, Sampson enlisted in the Georgia Militia as a reserve. Records reflect Sampson McCarty was a farmer living in the 26th Senatorial District and the 682nd Georgia Militia District.

During 1869, Sampson McCarty sold Land Lot No. 12 to John T. Goodman of Monroe County, Georgia and continued to live next door and farm on Land Lot No 11.

Isabella Tolbert McCarty at Blount County, Alabama, home about 1900.

Sampson McCarty and Elizabeth Byrd had five children. These children were Sarah A.M., born about 1840; John T., born about 1844; George Madison, born 1847; Alfred Morris, born November 1849; and Margaret M., born about 1852. All of their children were born in Georgia. While we don't know the circumstances of her death, Sampson McCarty's wife, Elizabeth (Byrd) McCarty, died on Easter Sunday, April 13, 1873.

Living in the neighborhood of Sampson McCarty, age fifty-nine in Carroll County was Isabella Tolbert, age thirty-three. Records indicate that she was an Indian. The family oral tradition states that she was a half-breed born in a cave near Gadsden, Alabama. She was soon Sampson's second wife following the death of Elizabeth Byrd. On November 11, 1873, Sampson and Isabella were married in Carroll County by Reverend J.S.N. Lewis.

Within three weeks following their marriage, Sampson and Isabella McCarty filed for homestead tax exemption in Carroll County on December 1, 1873. As this record indicated, they declared all of their personal property values and were living on Sampson's property located on Land Lot Number 11.

Phebe Ann McCarty Grigsby, Sampson and Isabella McCarty's daughter.

During the 1860s, Carroll County's agriculture and economy in general suffered a serious decline as a result of the Civil War. The economy did not improve until railroad connections were completed in the 1870s. Sampson McCarty and his new wife Isabella (Tolbert) McCarty sold a strip of land through Land Lot No. 11 for this first railroad constructed through Carroll County. They received $400 from the Savannah, Griffin, and North Alabama Railroad Company on December 10, 1873. The amount of property sold was a 100 foot wide strip described in the deed as "fifty feet from the center line of the railroad tract of the said corporation on either side of said track ... ." While the train traveled by their farm and home, Sampson and Isabella McCarty began to raise a family. Their first born was Francis Marion McCarty. Marion, as he was called, was born on March 3, 1875. Later, Arabella Mosley McCarty was born on April 3, 1877.

Although the train helped the economy of Carroll County, finances got tougher for Sampson and Isabella McCarty. The result was their loss of the remainder of their property on Lot No. 11 in District 4, Section 5 in Carroll County. A house painter by the name of William Amis painted the home of Sampson and Isabella McCarty in 1874. William Amis placed a lien on Sampson and Isabella (Tolbert) McCarty's property due to their inability to pay William Amis the agreed price of $44.40 for materials and labor. Therefore, a recorded deed dated December 4, 1877, transferred this property in a sheriff's sale to William Amis and his attorney, R.L. Richard.

The now homeless Sampson and Isabella McCarty moved out of the state of Georgia to Scottsboro, Jackson County, Alabama. Isabella McCarty was pregnant when they were forced to move. She gave birth to their third child, Phebe Ann McCarty, on February 10, 1878, in Alabama. While they continued to live in Scottsboro through 1880, they eventually moved to the small community of Ohatchee in Calhoun County, Alabama. Sampson and Isabella McCarty sharecropped with George Madison McCarty, Sampson's third child by his first wife, Elizabeth (Byrd) McCarty.

Phebe Ann McCarty Grigsby with children, Ethel, Carl, Cory, Clifton.

While sharecropping, both Sampson and his son George Madison McCarty borrowed money from a company by the name of Linder & Montgomery. As a result of the loan, a lien was placed on their crop and property. This lien is recorded in the Calhoun County, Alabama, courthouse. The outcome of George Madison McCarty's and Sampson McCarty's crop for 1881 is unknown. It certainly would have been a sad Christmas day if Linder & Montgomery acted on December 25, 1881, to seize the McCarty's entire crop and horses due to their failure to pay back the two hundred-dollar debt, as the lien allowed. What the McCarty family did not know in 1881 was the life was about to change. Sampson's son George Madison McCarty died in 1882 at the age of about thirty-five.

Sampson and Isabella McCarty continued to live in Alabama. Most of their belongings and records were destroyed in a house fire. It is not known exactly where they were living at the time. Family oral history indicates that after Sampson McCarty died in January of 1886, Isabella's house burned again. It has been suggested that the last fire was due to arson.

Francis Marion McCarty, Sampson and Isabella McCarty's son.

Based on a pension application by Isabella (Tolbert) McCarty in 1895, we have a very good glimpse about Sampson McCarty and his family relationships. Since Sampson McCarty was a veteran of the Indian War by serving during the 1836 in the Georgia Militia, Isabella was entitled to certain benefits as his widow. She was granted a land warrant of about eighty-one acres of land located in Cleveland, Blount County, Alabama.

The pension application file mentioned that Sampson McCarty died in Langston, Marshall County, Alabama, on January 18, 1886. The cause of his death is listed as "chills & piles & fever." Isabella (Tolbert) McCarty homesteaded the eighty-one acres of land in Blount County given to her by the United States government. While two of her children, Francis Marion McCarty and Phebe Ann McCarty married and started families, her second child's life, Arabella Mosley McCarty, ended in tragedy. During her wedding, both Arabella Mosley McCarty and her husband were poisoned. Both died on their wedding day.

Frances Marion McCarty.

Pension records indicate Isabella (Tolbert) McCarty continued to live alone at her Cleveland home until she became ill with tuberculosis on April 28, 1908. During her period of sickness, she moved in with her son-in-law and daughter, W. Sylvester and Phebe (McCarty) Grigsby, at their home in Blountsville, Blount County, Alabama. Isabella (Tolbert) McCarty remained under their care until her death on August 1, 1908. She is buried in the Austin Creek Cemetery in Cleveland, Blount County, Alabama. *Submitted by: Robert Alvin Scott Jr., 1609 April Drive, Warrior, AL 35180*

820. Jefferson M. McCollough Families

Jeff was born in Edgefield County, South Carolina, on February 19, 1834, to William Culpepper McCollough and Rebecca Bradfield McCollough. He was living with his parents in Chambers County, Alabama, at the time of the 1840 census, and in Coweta County, Georgia, at the time of the 1850 census. By December 16, 1858, he was living in Carroll County where he married Elizabeth Ann Hood at her parent's home on that date.

Except for the time he was a member of the Confederate Army, from June 16, 1862 to April 9, 1865, during the Civil War and some time when he was a bailiff in the county court of Carroll County, Jeff was a farmer all of his life. He initially enlisted in Captain L.J. Smith's Cavalry, and was transferred to Company F, 7th Georgia

Jeff and Elizabeth Hood McCollough Family

Regiment on August 17, 1864. He left a two-year old son, Newt, with his wife at the time he enlisted. Laura was born a short time later on October 20, 1862.

Elizabeth did not have an easy life during the time Jeff served in the Confederate Army. When Union troops visited her farm shortly before the Union Army burned Atlanta in September 1864, they took all the food and animals that she had on the farm. She and her two young children survived on some turnips, which the soldiers missed, and tree bark until the next spring. She was able to plant sweet potatoes in early 1865. The family survived mostly on those sweet potatoes during the winter of 1865 after Jeff got back to Carroll County.

In the accompanying photograph, on the first row are Minnie McCollough Traylor and Willie McCollough. On the second row are Laura McCollough Lester, Jeff McCollough, Elizabeth Hood McCollough, and Newton McCollough. The back row has Sussie McCollough Thomas, John B. McCollough, Emma McCollough Irwin, Mary McCollough Irwin, and Fannie McCollough Dingler.

Upon conclusion of the War in 1865, Jeff returned to Carroll County where he lived until he moved to Heard County in the late 1890s. Jeff and Elizabeth's marriage produced three sons and six daughters as shown in the picture. Jeff died on September 22, 1912, near Waresville, and was buried at the Bethel Christian Church in Heard County. Elizabeth Ann Hood passed away on August 19, 1931. She was buried next to Jeff. *Submitted by: Samuel J. McCollough, 4912 Behrens Road, Colleyville, TX 76034*

821. The McDaniel Family

The McDaniel Family was one of the pioneer families of Bowdon. Three brothers — John Baldwin, George Ambrose, and Charles Addison - helped turn this frontier settlement into a thriving little town. They were sons of John and Sara Ira Terry McDaniel of Henry. (now DeKalb) County, Georgia. Their paternal ancestors were of Scot-Irish descent. The name was first given the Scottish spelling "McDonald," and later the Irish spelling "McDaniel." Through marriage, this family included Baldwins, Terrys, Bibbs, Wyatts, and Goffs. Two daughters also settled in Bowdon. Mary Ann married John Adamson. Their son W.C. Adamson became a U.S. Representative who helped pass the eight-hour work week law. Martha Ann married John Thurman who preached at both the Bowdon College campus church and Smith's Chapel Methodist Protestant Church at Burwell.

John Baldwin McDaniel was a pioneer in moral reforms, leader in temperance and educational enterprises. He owned land in the Bowdon area as early as 1853 and was a charter member of the board of trustees of Bowdon College. John was elected state representative from Carroll County and senator of the 37th District between 1863 and 1866. He served the United States in various Indian Wars and the State and Confederacy as quartermaster of the garrison at Savannah. Nena Word now lives in the old John McDaniel house at Bowdon. Many of the outbuildings are still there.

George Ambrose McDaniel came to Bowdon in 1854 where he farmed until the War Between the States began. Then he engaged in merchandising and continued it for twenty years. Then George, his brother Henry Wyatt McDaniel, and Victoria McDaniel (widow of their brother Charles who was killed in the Civil War) bought land on the Little Tallapoosa River several miles east of Bowdon. By naming their lovely village for Victoria, it became known as Victory Mills. In 1897 George's son Henry built Victory Methodist Protestant Church overlooking his mill community. This church lasted 102 years until it was struck by lightning and burned on August 12, 1999. The Joiner family from the Tyus community rebuilt the church.

George married Martha Jane Lavendar in 1850. They had ten children: Sarah Adeline, Mary Melinda, Eliza A., Ella, Dr. John Lavendar, Martha Frances, Ida Bibb, James Henry, Lula, and Emma Blanche.

Sarah was a teacher and a very devout Christian who was licensed to preach. Mary Melinda also became a teacher. She graduated from Bowdon College as the first coed to graduate from a college in Georgia. Eliza married Ben F. Tisinger and moved to Texas. Dr. John L. McDaniel became a doctor in California. There are many McDaniel descendants in this family in California. Martha Frances "Fannie" married Rev. Wm. Jasper Causey, first pastor of Victory Methodist Church. (see W.J. Causey family). Her sister Blanche married William R. Causey, son of W.J. Causey. (see W.R. Causey family). Ida B. married George Tisinger (see George Tisinger family), and Henry married Martha "Mattie" Stephenson (see The Stephenson family), and Lula married Thomas A. Word.

Charles Addison McDaniel came to Bowdon to teach at the Bowdon Seminary on request of his older brother George. Charles earned a

Helen W., George Alexander, George Ambrose, and Martha Lavendar McDaniel.

degree from Emory at Oxford to preach and teach. After teaching in Perry, Georgia, for a year, he and his friend John M. Richardson founded Bowdon College. It was their dream to start an institution of learning for worthy, struggling young men of limited means. Charles was the first president. The students eagerly volunteered their services to the South when the Civil War started, and elected Charles Addison as their captain. They joined the Confederacy as Company B of Cobb's Legion. Charles was promoted to colonel of the 41st Regiment. On October 8th 1862, he was mortally wounded at the Battle of Perryville, Kentucky. His body was interred at Harrodsburg until 1871 when George McDaniel had the remains of his brother brought to Bowdon. This event was one of the largest public gatherings in Bowdon history.

There are still Tisinger, Causey, and Chambers descendants from his family in the Victory Community. These McDaniels were cousins to Governor Henry D. McDaniel who served as a major of the 11th Regiment, Georgia Infantry in the Civil War. The present Georgia State Capitol building was built during his term as governor with a surplus of $118.43 out of a one-million appropriation when it was completed. *Submitted by: John Carter Clay, 179 Cottage Hill Road, Carrollton, GA 30117*

John Alexander and Adelia Clementine McDonald and their children.

822. John Alexander McDonald

1847-1924

I never knew my great grandfather, John Alexander McDonald, but from reading his personal letters and listening to comments of family and friends, he has a special place in my heart. He moved his family to Bowdon, Georgia, Carroll County about 1892 when he accepted a position as principal of the Primary and Intermediate Departments of Bowdon College.

His father, John McDonald, born May 10, 1814, in South Carolina, married Sarah Ann Hollingsworth in Griffin, Georgia, July 24, 1845. There young John Alexander was born March 12, 1847. A month later John Sr. died, leaving Sarah to care for their infant. Sarah and young John lived with Grandmother Elizabeth Hollingsworth until Sarah married Dr. Joshua Cherry of Macon in 1851. Sarah died in Macon, Bibb County, April 10, 1852. The five-year-old orphan then went to live with his Hollingsworth grandparents, Elizabeth and Joseph A., in Heard County, Georgia.

May 13, 1862, fifteen-year-old John became a private in Company K, 34 Georgia Volunteers. His uncle, J.A. Hollingsworth, was a first lieutenant in the company. According to Union records, John was captured at Nashville, Tennessee, on December 16, 1864, and released at Camp Chase, Ohio, May 2, 1865. In a 1913 letter to his daughter "Edney," he describes a "very pleasant trip to RR" to a reunion of Confederate veterans in Chattanooga, "the city of all brands of Sorry Whiskey." He enjoyed the "grandest scenery of my life," but not the lodging: "My first night was spent with an old Irish woman who furnished me with one of the roughest beds I have slept on since the war."

By 1870, John lived with his Uncle Levi Hollingsworth, working on the farm. He met, fell in love, and married Adelia Clementine Pearce, daughter of Matilda J. Darden and Micajah Pearce. They exchanged vows January 3, 1873, at Yellow Dirt in Heard County, Georgia. In August 1875, they joined the Yellow Dirt Church. The couple had eleven children: J. Oscar, Clara, William H., Sarah Elizabeth, Cora Edney (Edna), Effie E., Ola I., Emma G., M. Jenny, Jonnie A., and F. Pearce.

When John Alexander McDonald moved to Carroll County, he purchased thirty-five acres near Bowdon and built a house on Rome Street. In this home, local young people were often entertained by "Squire and Misses McDonald." The family was active in Bowdon Baptist Church where he served as Church Clerk for many years. In 1893, he was commissioned as a Justice of the Peace in Carroll County. He was also a member of Bowdon Lodge No. 206 F. & A.M.

John Alexander McDonald: Orphaned at five! A soldier at fifteen! Many men would become bitter. Instead, he chose to live his life to the fullest. He died April 23, 1924, at his home in Bowdon and was buried beside his beloved wife in the Bowdon City Cemetery. *Submitted by: Janice Adelia Duncan, 420 East College Street, Bowdon, GA 30108*
Sources: Census records, McDonald family Bible, Confederate and Union war records, cemetery records, marriage and death certificates, Carroll County land deeds, church records, *Bowdon Bulletin, Carroll Free Press,* personal letters and will of John A. McDonald.

823. McDowell

Thomas Morgan McDowell (born 1871) married Lula Blair (born 1885) in Coweta County. Thomas' parents died young and he was taken in by the Hogan family. His brothers Dan McDowell was taken in by another family. Thomas and Dan did not see each other until they were in their twenties although they knew they had a brother. Both lived in Coweta County near Arnco and Sargent.

Thomas and Lula McDowell, with children John Daniel, Albert, Ila

Dan's son was Ollie McDowell and his wife is Bertha. Ollie and Bertha's children are Dennis, Loretta, Jimmy, and Dorothy. Dennis and Jimmy are in the residential home building business. They have built houses in Carroll and Coweta Counties. Loretta is a chiropractor in Carrollton and Dorothy is a school teacher.

Thomas and Lula lived in Carroll County off Mote Road and Center Point Road. Their children were John Daniel (Dan), Albert, Ila, and Ruby. Ruby married Lee Wessinger. Ila married George Durrough. Albert married Susie Crumbly. Dan married Ruth McKenzie. See related articles on McKenzies and Crutchfields. *Submitted by: Sarah McDowell Goldin*

824. Daniel McDowell

1774-after 1843

In 1827, the following were lucky drawers: Daniel McDowell from Habersham County for Carroll County, Georgia; Jonathan Haynes from Habersham County for Carroll County; William Kinney from Habersham County for Carroll County. About 1823, Daniel McDowell migrated to Habersham County, Georgia, from Buncombe County, North Carolina, Jonathan and Synthey McDowell Haynes, George and Catherine Owens Palmer, William and Susannah Ward Kinney, Jesse and Sarah Cox Kinney, Benjamin Merrill, and Daniel McDowell Owens migrated with him.

Suspected children of Daniel McDowell are: (1) Synthey/Cynthia, born between 1798 and 1802 in Haywood County, North Carolina. Married Jonathan Haynes in 1818. Daniel McDowell is listed as her father on her marriage bond. Migrated with farther from North Carolina to Georgia. (See related William and Lucinda Haynes Kinney story.) (2) Daniel McDowell born between 1795-1800 in Buncombe County, North Carolina. (3) Lucinda McDowell born December 25, 1818. Married William Watson in Haywood County, North Carolina, in 1835. (4) Alford McDowell (seen on land deals in Carroll County). (5) James V. McDowell, married Frances Bell on January 7, 1841, in Carroll County, Georgia. (6) Elnathan T. McDowell. Migrated to Alabama and is also known as Nathan. He is mentioned in 1850s in land deals concerning Daniel McDowell's land in Carroll County. He is also on census in 1850 for Carroll County. (7) Margaret McDowell, married Zachariah Butler June 29, 1831 in Carroll County, North Carolina. (8) Clansida McDowell, married James T. Wood in Carroll County, Georgia, on November 13, 1850.

Daniel is the only McDowell on 1830 census in Carroll County. Any Carroll County McDowells are likely connected to him in some way.

According to census records, Daniel was born sometime around 1774, probably in Rowan County, North Carolina. His parents, William McDowell and Elizabeth Templeton, were married there on February 27, 1772.

Daniel was a resident of Buncombe County, North Carolina, on census records of 1800. He was 20-29 years of age and had four children.

Haywood County was formed from Buncombe County in 1807 and Daniel became sheriff in 1808 until 1817 when he became a North Carolina state representative. In 1810, he was on Haywood County's census and had nine children.

Daniel was listed on the 1820 Haywood County, North Carolina census. He was on the 1830 Carroll County, Georgia, census. He was between 50-60 years of age. His wife was 40-50 years of age. There were two males under 5, one male 5-10, two males 10-15 and one female 15-20 years of age.

Daniel on the 1840 Carroll County census: He was over 60. His wife was 50-60. There was one male 5-10 years of age, two males 10-15 years of age, one male 15-20 years of age, one daughter 5-10 years of age.

He as not on the 1850 census of Carroll County, but he was on the 1843 tax lists "by representative." He was still mentioned on land deals as late as 1849 and 1854. The exact time and place of his death is unknown. It is believed to have been between 1843 and 1850. *Submitted by: Sylvia Mitchell, 2802 Vista Drive, Huntsville, AL 35803. Written by: Cathy Moore Casper, 5335 Carbonton Road, Sanford, NC 27330*

825. McGraw

Ephrain McGraw Sr. was born 1791 in South Carolina. His wife Nancy was born 1787 in South Carolina. They married in 1817. They had eight children: Lethia (1820), Stephen (1826), and Catherine (1828) were born in South Carolina; Mary Ann (1830), Nancy (1832), Ephrain (1833), Martha (1836), and Cornelius were born in Meriwether County, Georgia. Ephrain and Nancy are buried in Meriwether County.

James Asbury Howell, about 1910

Ephrain Wesley McGraw Jr. married Jamima Ann Kilgore. They had five children: (1) Roland Jackson (1859-1910) born in Coweta County, Georgia, and buried in Anderson, Alabama; (2) Elvira (1860); (3) William Alexander (1862); (4) Mary (1863) born in Georgia; and (5) Martha Frances (1868) born in Georgia. Ephrain Jr. served in the Civil War (1861-1865) Company K, 30th Georgia Volunteer Infantry, Conederate States Army. He died September 2, 1904. Jamima died in 1913. They are buried at Brice Cemetery in Bremen, Georgia.

William Alexander was born in 1862. Edna S. Miller was born in 1866. They were both born in Haralson County, Georgia. They married in 1883 and had six children. William was a track foreman for the railroad leaving Atlanta and continuing to Birmingham, Alabama. His main station was at Waco, Georgia. That is where the children were born: Mamie (1884), John Wesley (1890), Nora Elle (1894), Mallie (1895), Flora (1901), and Willie (1904). William and Edna both died in 1930 and are buried at Brice Cemetery in Bremen.

Nora McGraw and Mamie McGraw Howell, 1930s

Lillie McGraw, Mallie Autrey, Willie Cook, Flora Jackson, and Nora McGraw 1950s.

The family lived in Villa Rica around 1894 while William did his work. Mamie and Jim made attachments in Villa Rica. The family moved and lived near Anniston, Alabama, where Mamie met and married James Asbury Howell, a barber. All of her children were born in Ranburne, Alabama. In 1921, James died. The widow and her children moved to Waco to be near her family. In 1927, Mamie and her girls moved to Fullerville/Villa Rica. Forest (1905), her son, joined the Marines. At one time or another, the girls worked in the Villa Rica hosiery mill. Else, Anna Lois,and Edythe attended Villa Rica Elementary School. They went to work at age fourteen to help family finances.

Edna (1908), Elizabeth (1912); and Edythe (1919) married and moved away, living many places until the 1950's. Edna and Grady Bell lived in the Lithia Springs area, Elizabeth and J.R. Thompson lived in rural Coweta County, and Edythe and Ralph Sewell lived in Paulding Company beginning in the 1970s.

Louise (1910) married Lewis Carden a cattle dealer. They had four children: Betty Boyd, Frances Banks, Johnnie Sue Sticher, and Randy Lewis Carden, also a cattle dealer. They all attended Villa Rica Schools, Johnnie Sue and Randy's children attended Villa Rica schools. (See Wildcats).

Some of the McGraw descendants in the 1980's.

Elsie (1915) married Sam Spake from Temple.They had four children. Elsie was a practical nurse at the Villa Rica Hospital on Carroll Road and the newer hospital on Dallas Road. The children, Hazel Roberts, Anne Walker, Sue Ward, and Monroe Spake, all attended Villa Rica Schools. Hazel, Sue, Monroe's children, and Sue's grandchildren also attended Villa Rica Schools. (See Wildcats and Spake stories.)

Anna Lois (1917) married Rush Scroggins. They had one child to live, Charlotte Barber. In 1945, Ann a became a full time beautician. Rush was a barber. Charlotte and her husband, Ray Barber, had five children and ten grandchildren. (See Barber, and Wildcats.)

John Wesley McGraw, (1890-1948) married Lillie Mae Ashley, who was born in Villa Rica (1896). John and Lillie are buried at New Hope Church Cemetery, Villa Rica, Georgia, with three of their young children. They had one child to grow to maturity, Hugh Winfred McGraw (1931). Hugh graduated from Bremen High School in 1947. He lives in Bremen and leads Sacred Harp singings all around the West Georgia area. Hugh is married to Donnie Todd from Carrollton. They have two daughters, Ressa graduated Bremen High School in 1967, and Paula graduated Bremen High School in 1981. *Submitted by Hugh Winfred McGraw, Bremen, GA*

826. Robert and Jewel McGuire

I wish that I knew more about my grandparents, but I only knew my Grandmother McGuire and my Granddaddy Nixon. I knew Granddaddy Nixon better than Grannie McGuire because she died when I was almost five years of age. Granddaddy lived to be 91, so we were able to see him when we were younger.

My parents are Robert Lee McGuire and Jewel Agnes Nixon McGuire. They grew up in the Little Tallapoosa community. Robert's family lived several places, but ended up at the home place on the Tyus-Carrollton Road, where Robert and Jean Harman live now. Jewel's home was on the Salem Church Road, where Gilbert and Joy Sprewell presently live. Both families loved their children and taught them how to work and the importance of family. They attended Little Tallapoosa School and Jewel went on to A&M (which is now State University of West Georgia). She taught school at Reavesville before their marriage.

Robert Lee and Jewel Nixon McGuire, 1966

Robert's parents were E. Thompson McGuire and Pearl Mae Hammons McGuire. Thompson was born on October 12, 1879, and died on January 23, 1936. Pearl was born on May 31, 1879, and died on June 27, 1947. They are buried at Tallapoosa Primitive Baptist Church. Jewel's parents were W.A. Nixon and Lucy Vise Nixon. W.A. was born on March 18, 1870, and died on February 6, 1961. Lucy was born on September 16, 1872, and died on March 31, 1940. They are buried at Salem Baptist Church.

Robert was born on September 3, 1903, and Jewel was born on May 7, 1903. They grew up in the same area, dated for about three years and married on December 25, 1924. Their first home was behind Robert's home place, in a house built by Robert and farm help. They purchased land from his mother in 1935-36, and moved to what is now 792 Bonner Road. In the Hammons estate, each of his three daughters received 100 acres.

There was only a tenant house on the property, but Robert added on to the house over the years. Jewel has told many times that the prettiest thing on the place when they moved there was the water oak in the back yard, and thus the farm came to be named Treasure Oak Farm. Treasure Oak Farm has been a treasure to me.

When Robert and Jewel moved to Treasure Oak they had three children, Frances, Bobby and Betty. After their move, God blessed them with twin girls, Jerry and Jean, another daughter, Jo-Sybil and then a son, Steve. All grew up on Treasure Oak and have since brought their children and grandchildren back for visits on the farm.

Robert and Jewel were hard workers, teaching their children and grandchildren the importance of work. Robert farmed raising corn, hay, cotton, cattle and Jewel kept the home fires burning with a beautiful home, always having a garden, canning, freezing, sewing for her family, having flowers all around the house. Robert ran the canning plant at Little Tallapoosa Community Center and then later the one in town which was on South Cliff Street. He also worked with his team of horses dragging power poles when electricity was coming to Carroll County. After Southwire Company was opened, Roy Richards came and asked Robert to come to work for him. Robert thought about it for a while and did go to work, retiring on August 31, 1967. Even though he worked a full-time job, he continued to farm.

Jewel was active in the Home Demonstration Clubs, served as a 4-H Club advisor and in 1955 was voted Homemaker of Georgia (a well deserved honor). She went to New York was on TV, and enjoyed every minute of this adventure. Life was grand to Jewel and she believed in seeing and enjoying all that she was given an opportunity to experience.

Treasure Oak Farm has been the home for a large variety of farm animals, pets and otherwise. Many of the kindergarten children in the area have visited the farm and ridden in the pony cart with "Mr. Robert." Then they were served refreshments by "Miss Jewel," or ate their sack lunches under the giant water oaks there on the farm.

In 1955, Robert purchased his first Santa Gertrudis bull from J.W. Morris,whose farm was on the Mt. Zion Road. He loved to tell that Robert was the hardest sell he ever had to make. Robert and Jewel enjoyed the red cattle and after several years, had a purebred herd of Santa Gertrudis cattle. In 1976, Robert talked with Nora Goodman, another Santa Gertrudis breeder in the Temple area, and they contacted other breeders in the state, a meeting was set-up and in January 1978, the Georgia Santa Gertrudis Cattle Association was formed. Sales, shows, meetings and field days were enjoyed by the McGuire's many times. Robert served on the first board of directors for a number of years.

One of my favorite stories about Robert and Jewel is prior to their marriage. With Jewel teaching at Reavesville, she would be gone all week. On Friday when Robert had time, he would ride his horse, lead another and go down to Reavesville to pick her up. The school children all loved it when Miss Nixon's boyfriend was coming, as he could make his horse do tricks, like bow down, rear up, he could jump from side-to-side, run and jump on the horse from the back, giving the children a Wild West show - free for the asking. Robert always gave Jewel a box of candy at Christmas and our family annually shared with them their anniversary candy after the big Christmas dinner, which sometimes made it hard to eat, because we were already so full. The year Jewel passed away, Robert purchased yet another box of anniversary candy, to have his family enjoy this special treat.

The following is about the McGuire children and their families. Frances McGuire Graves, raised one son, Douglas Graves. She retired from Gold Kist and has moved from the farm now, living in Carrollton. Her son, Douglas and his family live in Elberton. Bobby Lee McGuire worked at Lockheed for many years, then a painter, living in the Atlanta area, and later moving to Carrollton. He passed away on September 22, 1984. Betty Ethyl McGuire Branson, worked for the *Times Georgian* for many years, but retired from Carrollton Federal, lives on the family farm close to her son, Tommy Branson, and his family. The twins, Jerry Nickey McGuire Eady, runs Jerry's Country Kitchen, lives in Carrollton with husband, Sammy Eady, their children are Renee Eady and Brock Eady; Lucy Jean McGuire Laney lives on the farm with husband Charlie "Chuck" Laney, their children are Lee Laney, Steven Laney, Faye Laney Gentry. Jo-Sybil McGuire, lives at the home place. Steve Rodney McGuire lived on the farm until 1996 when he passed away. His daughter, LeAnne McGuire Reese and her family live in his home.

Proud to be Americans was something that Robert and Jewel instilled in their children. It is with much pride that some of their children served in the armed forces. Bobby served in the Navy, Betty in the Navy, and Steve in the Marines.

As many contributors can relate, death takes its toll, and our family lost our precious mother, on September 17, 1981, with congestive heart disease. Daddy never got over missing his wife of almost 57 years and in 1985, he was diagnosed with lung cancer. He took treatment, but it did not help much and on February 13, 1986, he passed away. With his death so close to Valentine's Day, someone remarked "What a wonderful time for two lovers to be joined together again." They were laid to rest at Tallapoosa Primitive Baptist Church on the Tyus-Carrollton Road. Both had fought a hard battle, but death won out.

Many stories and much more could be told about the lives of Robert and Jewel McGuire. They are truly missed and were loved by many. *Submitted by: Jo-Sybil McGuire, 792 Bonner Road, Carrollton, GA 30117*

827. John McGukin
Farm Home Place

In 1869, John McGukin departed the home of his parents, located in the Townland of Ballyalbanagh, District of Ballyclare, Ireland, and made his way through New York to the Center Point Community of Carroll County, Georgia, where he and his new wife, Susan Martin McGukin, purchased five-hundred acres of farm land in the early 1870s. John McGukin became a successful farmer. He and Susan raised thirteen children. The last two were Russell and Arthur.

John McGukin Farm Home Place

Russell became the successor to the home place, having accepted his father's offer to remain on the farm as a partner. After John's death in 1931, four of his adult children — Nell, Arthur, Sam, and William — received one-hundred acres each. Russell received the home place and one-hundred acres. Russell married Clara Hurst in September 1921. In 1930, they razed the home place and built a six-room cottage where they nurtured five children to adulthood. Farming was difficult, so Clara began a career with Sewell Manufacturing Company in 1939 to help the family financially while Russell struggled with non-mechanical farming and a transition to a small dairy operation.

Clara and Russell's oldest son, Andrew, spent a significant portion of World War II in England. Their only daughter, Ruth, came home to live while her first husband fought in Europe during that war. John, Lester, and Eugene were the last three children who grew up in the friendly house, which was, in part, materials from the original home place of John and Susan. The five adult children gave Clara and Russell sixteen grandchildren. They spent many holiday and family celebrations in the little cottage. It is now the third generation "home place" All the grandchildren came to their grandparents for guidance and support. One grandson, Richard, built a home within a few hundred feet of his grandparent's house. Ruth and her husband, Bill built their home within sight of the cottage. Eugene and his wife, Ivee, constructed a home on the northeast side of the home place. Lester and his wife, Lois, moved and remodeled an old house from Atlantic avenue in Bremen to the southeast side of the home place.

The home place and eight acres are now owned and loved by grandson Douglas and his wife, Jennifer. They proudly nurture the memories of the past 130 years of history in the little cottage on McGukin Road, Center Point community, Carroll County, Georgia. Jennifer and Douglas have hosted one family reunion and plan another in the summer of 2001. *Submitted by: Eugene A. and Lester A. McGukin*

828. McKenzie

John P. and Mary McKenzie were in Carroll County in the 1850 census. Their children were Delia, Elizabeth, Kenneth, Emilne (Emily), Hiram, Lucinda, and William. John is shown as being born in South Carolina and Mary and all the children in Georgia. In the 1860 census, Lucinda is shown as Ella D. and there were additions of Mary J., James A. (Joseph), and Celia. In 1870 James A. is not listed but Joseph Alvin and Alice are added. Elizabeth, along with Prestily (age 8), was at the house of Hiram Sharp Sr.

Joseph Alvin McKenzie and Nancy Jane Shell McKenzie

Joseph Alvin Mckenzie (born 1857) married Nancy Jane Shell (born 1860). Their children were Beulah, Nora, Maggie, Eladee, Agnes, Mamie, Leon, Carrie, Lucy, and Wilburn Jackson. Joseph A. died in 1930 and Nancy Jane in 1927.

Joseph operated a mule barn off Rome Street at the square in Carrollton. He was a farmer and traded mules and horses. He would go to Atlanta to acquire mules and horses and bring them back to Carrollton to sell. It would take a week to make the trip and he and his family would camp along the way. Joseph acquired enough land and houses that he gave each of his children one hundred acres or fifty acres with a house. Joseph A. and Nancy's home is located on McKenzie Bridge Road and their great-great-great-grandson (Joey Sharp) now lives in the house.

Wilburn Jackson McKenzie (born 1888) married Florence Genava Crutchfield (born 1889) in 1906. Their children were Gladys Modell, Ruth

Mozell, Iva Novell, Jackson Oswell, Willard Oliver, and Joseph Alvin.

Wilburn farmed and continued the operation of the mule barn in Carrollton. They lived on the road now named McKenzie Bridge Road. The Little Tallapoosa river runs through the property. The McKenzies built a bridge across the river and allowed public access. Wilburn (died 1955) and Florence (died 1980) are buried at the Concord Primitive Baptist CHurch on Highway 113.

Jackson Oswell (J.O.) married Jannette Gordon and they operated a dairy farm. Joseph Alvin married Lorene Sullivan and their son Larry McKenzie lives in Carroll County. Ruth Mozell married John Daniel (Dan) McDowell in 1931. Dan and Ruth lived on McKenzie Bridge Road and later moved to Bowdon Junction. Dan farmed and then worked at Richard's Lumber Company during World War II. He and Ruth worked at Hubbard Pants Company and continued to farm.

Dan and Ruth's children are Kathryn Lillian McDowell and Sarah Jane McDowell. Kathryn married James Russell Hughes Sr. (Russell) and their son is James Russell Jr., (Jim). He married Tammy Faulkner and their sons are James Russell III (James) Hughes and Jonathan Faulkner Hughes. Jim Hughes owns Hughes Custom Homes Inc. and is part owner in Latimer-Hughes Construction Company Inc.

Sarah married Michael V. Goldin and their daughter is Sheila Ann who married Randy Lee Foster. Randy and Sheila's children are Michael James Foster, Leeann Renee Foster and Mark Alan Foster. Leeann and Mark are twins. *Submitted by: Ruth McKenzie McDowell*

829. McLendon

From the British Isles to Barbados to North Carolina to Carroll County, Georgia

According to Barbados records, Dennis McLendon, son of Bryan McLendon of Barbados, was in Virginia by 1687. Bryan's origins are believed to be in the British Isles. The first appearance of Dennis in American records is in 1696 in Perquimans County, North Carolina. Dennis served as juror, as road overseer, appraiser, and from 1704 until his death in 1706, as judge. Dennis had a son Thomas, and Thomas' son Jacob McLendon Sr. moved from Cumberland County, North Carolina, to Wilkes County, Georgia, which had recently been purchased from Indian lands. In 1774 "Jacob McLendon - North Carolina, a wife, 4 sons and 4 daughters from 8 to 1 year old. XXX acres of Fishing Creek." Two other sons, Jacob Jr. and Isaac came in 1775. Jacob Sr. and four sons fought at the Battle of Kettle Creek in Wilkes County, in 1783. There are headstones for Jacob Sr. and son Travis at Kettle Creek Battlefield. The first court held in Georgia after the Revolution was held in Jacob's home. Nine Tories were tried, found guilty and hanged ten days later. (Further information states they were not hanged, just brought to the gallows in fear of their lives, then released). There is a historical marker commemorating the event.

Jacob's son Isaac McLendon Sr. married Elizabeth Stribling. Isaac's son Lewis married Cynthia Powell Holderness and had nine children. Born in 1809, his son Willis McLendon, in 1828 married Martha 'Patsy' Hay and by 1831, moved to Meriwether County with son Isaac Newton McLendon Sr. Willis' son Isaac Newton McLendon, Sr. married Mary Ann Eliza Rowe in 1855 and moved to Carroll County. They had twelve children: Frances Olivia, who married James Franklin Morris; Augustus Jackson, who married first Eugenia Pentecost, second Minnie Lee Beavers, and third Ida Viola Laminack; Mary Elizabeth Turner remained a spinster, Martha Ella, who married William Thomas Newton Walker; William Beauregard, who married Lou Ross Martin; Sonora Alice, who married William Arthur Hubbard; Clifton Warner, who married Ora Byrd North; Willis Allen, who married Edna Lois Stipe; Isaac Newton Jr., who married Mary Susan Jones; Custis Lee, who married Annie Lavonia Shackleford; Virginia Emma, who married James M. Hendrix; and Thomas Simpson Sr., who married Alice Lorene Lovvorn.

Willis came to live with son Isaac Newton after the death of wife Martha is Meriwether. In 1885, he was walking to the home of another of his children when his deteriorating eyesight caused him to walk into Holland's Millpond where he was discovered days later. He is buried at Emmaus Primitive Baptist Church Cemetery, near son Isaac and Isaac's wife Mary Ann.

Many Youngs, Hubbards, Hendrixs, Denneys, Fullers, Kilgos, Martins, McWhorters, Muses, Shadingers, Snows, Walkers, Words, and numerous others Carroll County families, have this McLendon heritage.

At the first McLendon reunion in Carrollton since the 1930s, several young people were astonished to find that they were close cousins to some of their schoolmates. *Submitted by: Janet McLendon, 2545 Brown's Mill Road, Atlanta, GA 30354*

830. Elizabeth McLendon

Elizabeth was the daughter of Willis McLendon and Martha Patsy Hay McLendon. She was born in 1834 in Wilkes County, Georgia. She is a sister to Isaac and ten other children. Willis died in a strange way in May 1885. He fell in a pond and drowned. It seems he was on his way to visit one of his children.

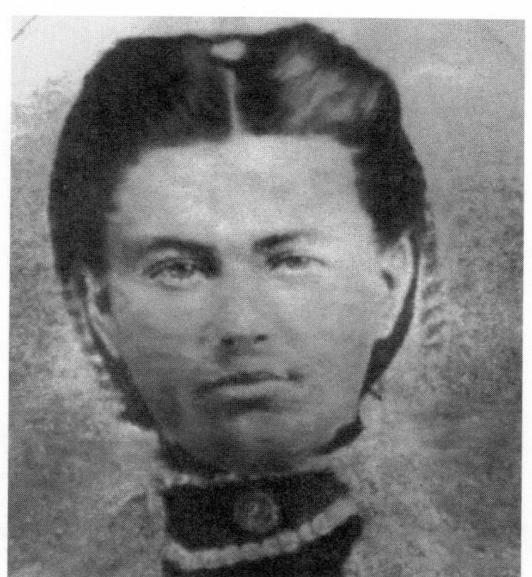

Elizabeth McLendon

Elizabeth married William Avis Cole, son of Jeremiah Cole and Charlotte Martin Cole, in 1854 in Carroll County. They had four daughters, Isabelle, Sarah, Synthia, and Frances. William was a Civil War soldier. He was killed in Lauderdale, Mississippi, on May 18, 1862. Elizabeth never remarried. She raised her four daughters and, at times, lived with some of them. She is buried at New Smyrna Church in Carroll County with one of her daughters under the name of Lott.

Frances Cole married Thomas Cole, son of Seaborn V. Cole, a cousin. They had seven children. Tom and Lula (Frances) moved to Arkansas in a covered wagon, but did not stay there. They came back to Carrollton and had a store on Mount Zion Road for years. They are buried at Pleasant View Church.

My great-grandfather was their son, Joe Cole. He married Nanny Kate Williamson, daughter of Georgia and Sarah Williamson. Today, my mother and I live on the land on which Joe and Kate Cole lived. *Submitted by: Julie Jarrell, 1001 Beulah Church Road, Carrollton, GA*

831. The McLendons

The MacLennan clan is an ancient Celtic clan descended from the royal family of Ireland. Their motto is "Dum Spiro Spero," meaning "While I Breathe, I Hope." During the reign of Charles II there was much political and religious unrest. Many Scots and Irish fled to the U.S. seeking freedom in the new land. Tradition has it that three MacLennan (McLendon) brothers sailed to America from Ireland. The MacLennan name has been spelled many different ways in Colonial records. Eventually MacLennan became known as McLendon.

It is thought that the McLendons first settled in Virginia, then made their way down through North Carolina and finally to Georgia. It was in Georgia in the year 1831 that Isaac Newton McLendon as born to Willis McLendon and Patsy Hay McLendon. He was the second of twelve children, and the eldest son. In 1855, he married Mary Anne Eliza Rowe and moved to Carroll County where they lived with his sister, Sophronia McLendon Almon. Later, Isaac and Mary built their first home, a log cabin located south of Carrollton. In the 1870s they built a large frame house on what was later known as Oak Grove Road.

The McLendons had a strong belief in God and family. Isaac did not believe in slavery and would buy Negroes and give them their freedom. In the 1860 census, Isaac owned one mulatto boy whom he raised and gave him his freedom. Isaac and Mary raised grapes which they used to make jelly, juice, and Isaac's peppermint cough syrup. Music was a big part of the McLendon family's daily lives. Sacred Harp singing was a favorite. The McLendons helped promote the continuance of Sacred Harp singing in the Carroll County area. Isaac helped found Emmaus Primitive Baptist Church located on Oak Grove Church Road and was the church clerk for many years. The graves of Isaac and Mary are both located there. Isaac and Mary Anne McLendon were survived by twelve children. Among those was Willis "Allen" McLendon born October 10, 1867, who married sixteen year old Edna "Lois" Stipe in October of 1888. They had eleven children.

Allen and Lois built a home near Allen's parents' farm on what was later known as McLendon Circle. Allen McLendon moved his family to Veal, Georgia, before 1900 to help his brothers, Lee and Billie, in a sawmill operation. Later Allen moved his family to Bowdon where he built a beautiful home for them. While Lois stayed in Bowdon with the younger children, Allen took one of his older daughters, Amma Josephine, to work with him at the sawmill and syrup mill. Amma worked keeping the books for the businesses as well as chauffeuring her father around.

When Willis Allen McLendon died of appendicitis at age fifty-five, the rest of the family moved back to McLendon circle into a house built by two of their sons, Henry Newton, (H.N.) and Byron. The school age children attended Rocky Mount Academy adjacent to Emmaus Primitive Baptist Church.

Amma McLendon married at age twenty-five, later than many women of the day. She married Lee Roscoe McWhorter and they had four children. Some years after their last child was born, Roscoe left Amma. Since he did not offer money to help support the family, Amma went to work. Her experience working with her father served her well. She was able to secure a position as a clerk in a dry goods store, and

Isaac Newton McLendon Family, circa 1900.

worked in one of Roosevelt's social programs (designed to give jobs to poor women) where she held a supervisory position. She later worked at Hubbard's in Bremen and Belk Rhodes in Carrollton. Their four children were Mary Josephine, Edna Lee, Malcolm, and Sherrod Stipe McLendon.

The oldest daughter, Mary Josephine McWhorter, married Thomas Felton Denney, son of Newman Edgar Denney and Wille Myrt Shadinger. Josephine is known as "Mama Jo" in the Oak Grove community where they reside. Felton and Josephine, along with several of their children, helped in founding the Rocky Mount Baptist Church on Roy North Road. Their entire family, including five children and their spouses, fourteen grandchildren and several of their spouses, and even some of their thirteen great-grandchildren, get together regularly to sing the old Sacred Harp music which is dear to both sides of the family. Felton was commissioned to the Georgia Forestry Board by Gov. Jimmy Carter. He also served on the Georgia Farm Bureau and National Farm Bureau Boards. Felton and Josephine farmed for many years in the Oak Grove area. Felton also bought many tracts of land in the Oak Grove area over the years as well as other areas.

The first of their five children was Mary Amma, who married Larry Charles Simpkins in 1964. They had three children: Mary Renita, Randy Charles, and Rebekah Jo. They have seven grandchildren: Jessica Elaine Folds, Elizabeth Jeanette Folds, Ria Alysse Kirk, Caroline Grace Folds, Zachary Charles Simpkins, Steve Tucker and Joseph Taylor Simpkins.

Second born was John Felton Denney who married Carole Vansant. They had two children: Leah Carole and John Seth. John is currently married to Tammy Stovall Denney. They don't have any grandchildren.

Philip Denney was their third child who married Frances Gayle Mashburn Denney at age seventeen. They had four children: Julie Ann, Kacey Gayle, Kelly Jo, and Philip Lee. Philip and Gayle have five grandchildren: Grady Waid Burgess, Jessy Lee Brown, Karis Quinn Askin, Eva Grace Horsley, and Skyler Lee Denney.

William Allen, known as Bill, was their fourth child. Bill married Priscilla Simpkins from Lowell. They had two children: Amanda Leigh and Dylan Thomas. They have one grandson, Samuel Hunter Johnsen.

Their fifth child and second daughter was Sarah Josephine who married James Edward Duffey Jr. They have three children: Lauren Alysse, Edward Parker, and Marshall Tyler.

This is one line of the many descendants of the McLendons that are scattered throughout the Carroll County area. *Submitted by: Renita S. Folds and Josephine Denney*

Sources: *The McLendons of Carroll County, Georgia, and Related Families* by Lois Clouse McLendon.

832. Elijah Daniel McPherson

Elijah Daniel McPherson was born in Rhea County, Tennessee, July 13, 1789, the son of Irish immigrants Daniel McPherson and Susannah Kincheloe. He married Sarah Small on October 15 1826. He died on December 9, 1875. Both are buried at Old Concord Primitive Baptist Church Cemetery on Spence Road, five miles north of Carrollton.

Elijah and Sarah had twelve children: John Howell, Emily, William Barton, Amanda, William Nelson, Louise, Mary Ann, Charles Lafette, Elijah Houston, Charles Lewin, Henry Livingston, and Delphia.

When Elijah was about ten years old, he ran away from home, then on or near the French Broad River, Roane County, Tennessee. He traveled by river boat along the Tennessee, Ohio, and Mississippi Rivers to New Orleans. He worked around the ports at New Orleans and Mobile and served as a sailor on ocean-going sail boats from 1806-1810. He then returned to his parent's home in Tennessee and attended some college. He was naturally gifted with mechanical and instrumental music skills.

When the War of 1812 broke out, he volunteered in Kingston for three month's service in Capt. White's Company, Cocke's Division, for service in the war with the Creek Indians. Another record shows him serving in Gen. Glascock's command, then transferred to Col. Samuel Birch's Regiment, and in Capt. William White's Military Regiment of Mounted Riflemen's Company, then discharged December 29, 1813, for which he received two bounty land grants of forty acres each and a pension which he received until his death December 9, 1875. His widow Sarah continued receiving his pension until her death April 23, 1897.

After the War of 1812, he returned to New Orleans and worked constructing levees and field surveys of land of the Louisiana Purchase. Around 1826, he returned to the family farm in Roane County, Tennessee. Soon after, he was attracted by reports of new country being opened in the state of Georgia including Carroll County. By December 11, 1826, settlers were pouring in and among them came Elijah Daniel McPherson. He found these new lands infested by mounted bands of organized thieves who came to be known as "Pony Clubs," principally for their horse stealing. Elijah and friends, recruited from East Tennessee, banded together with other pioneer citizens to establish a vigilante organization which became known as the "Slicks." War to the hilt broke out between the Slicks and the Pony Clubs. After several years the Slicks rid the county of the Pony Clubs and established law and order.

Elijah soon had a good farm, including two grain mills and a lumber mill, all water-powered. His saw mill was among the first in Carroll County, operating as early as 1840.

When past the age of 72, he traveled some 500 miles by ox wagon from his Carroll County home to the Confederate battlefields in North Carolina or Virginia to visit and carry clothing to his sons, Elijah Houston and Charles Lewing, serving in 7th Georgia Confederate Regiment. *Submitted by: Robert F. Bonner, 330 Linda Lane, Carrollton, GA 30117*

833. Malcolm Alexander McRae

Margaret and Malcolm McRae were born in South Carolina of Scottish parents, Hugh Bain McRae and Nancy McDuffy, who migrated to Carroll County. Hugh and Nancy McRae are buried somewhere in Carroll County. Following the natural westward migration, Malcolm eventually migrated to Texas. He is said to have walked into the general store in Elwood, Texas, a gun over his shoulder and $20,000 worth of gold in his knapsack. He retired in 1880, at the age of 70, giving each of his children 100 acres of land. On April 2, 1886, he wrote to a Bonham newspaper and told his own story. Eight months later he died at the age of eighty-six and was buried in the cemetery he had given to the community of Elwood, Texas.

Elwood, Fannin Co., Texas
April 2, 1896

Editor journal:

It is said multiply and replenish the earth. I was born on the 15th day of May, 1810. I was at one dance at about 17 years of age - my first and last. I have never gambled in my life. I commenced farming in the year 1830 and quit when I was three score and ten. I am now living a retired life, except working my garden.

I was married on the 22nd day of February, 1832. I have raised four sons and five daughters, all living to the age of maturity, and all learning to read and write. No free schools then. I have 44 grandchildren, 75 great-grandchildren and one great-great-grandchild. In the time of raising my family I made three long moves, first from Georgia to Southern Missouri. I made one crop and after gathering it I started to Texas on the 18th day of November, 1843. I came on foot and was gone 70 days with my gun and knapsack. I was in Dallas during my first trip to Texas. There was but one house between Bonham and Dallas.

When I got back to Missouri, I rested two weeks and found and I weighed 212 pounds. While I stayed in Newton County, Mo., I found 25 bee trees, killed 60 deer and 69 turkeys, made rails and fenced 40 acres of land and made two crops. On

Nov. 12, 1844, I started back to Georgia, arriving at my old home on the 8th of January, 1845, having been gone three years and one month.

It is strange to say, the number of years I have been a farmer, and the long moves that I have made. I have never put gears and harness on a pair of horses or mules and hitched them to a wagon and drove them in this fashion.

On the 4th of October, 1849, I started to Texas from Georgia in company with 97 persons, but on account of sickness was compelled to stop in Pike County, Arkansas. In 1851, I bought a farm on the main road leading from Little Rock, Ark., to Texas. After remaining until 1856, I resumed my trip to Texas and stopped in Fannin County, Tex., where I have made my home until the present.

In my travel since coming to Texas, I have visited Ft. Smith, Ark., Ft. Townsend, near the Red River in Choctaw Nation, Ft. Graham on the Brazos River, within a few miles of Ft. Arbuckle in Chickasaw Nation, Ft. Riley in the north part of Kansas, Ft. McCullough, Ft. Washita, Ft. McDonald in Kansas. I have crossed the northwest plains in two places; one at the mouth of the A. and R. Ry. tunnel at the timber line on the Rocky Mountains in a snow storm. I was in St. Louis on the 18th of December and found snow about six inches deep. After returning home I traveled but little. I will be glad to hear from anyone who can beat my record.

Malcolm A. McRae

The Carroll County Deed Book F, p 305, October 4, 1849, heirs of Adam Whisenhunt Sr. to John F. Tomlinson, deed for fraction parcels of lots 107 and 86 in 6th district of Carroll County, records *Malcolm A. McRae* as a witness.

Margaret McRae McAllister and her brother Malcolm Alexander McRae

Malcolm's sister, Margaret, married James Blanton McAllister. Margaret's daughter, Isabella Anne, married Dr. Thomas M. Carroll, in Carroll County, on October 29, 1857. Among other children of Thomas and Isabella were Roderick Wallace Carroll, who married Josephine Rebecca Hamrick on November 25, 1891, in Carroll County. One of Roderick's grandchildren, Rodric M. Phillips, son of Myrtle Carroll Phillips, was sent to Oklahoma City by the U.S. Air Force in 1956, where he met and married Dicki Joy Dunn. It turned out that Dicki is a great-great-great-granddaughter of Malcolm A. McRae, and Rodric is a great-great-grandson of Margaret McRae, Malcolm's sister. It is a small world, after all. Our McRae ancestors settled in Carroll County, then scattered through Texas and Oklahoma, only to reunite in the marriage of Rodric and Dicki. Eulalie McRae Burkes, Dicki's grandmother, traveled with her husband Andrew and two children from Elwood, Texas, into Broken Arrow, Indian Territory via a wagon train made up of other family members. Dicki's mother, Hazel Adeline Burkess Dunn was born in Indian Territory, before it became part of the new State of Oklahoma. Eulalie was the daughter of Alexander Franklin McRae and Texas Adeline Wyatt; granddaughter of Hugh James McRae and Cynthia Charlotte Holliday; great-granddaughter of Malcolm A. McRae and Mary Magdalene Whisenhunt, both of Carroll County; and great-great-grandfather of Hugh Bain McRae of Scotland and Nancy McDuffey. Judging from family reunions held in Oklahoma and Texas, this line of the McRaes believed as did Malcolm Alexander, "multiply and replenish the earth."

My mother, Alma Eula Burkes Grissom, born April 20, 1913, is another of Eulalie McRae Burkes' children, and another in the line of McRae descendants. I have recorded other McRae genealogies in the pages of two of the books I have authored: *Southern By The Grace Of God*; and *When The South Was Southern.*

Submitted by: Michael A. Grissom, 306 E. Seminole, Wynnewood, OK 73098

834. McWhorter Family

Part I

Allen Marlin McWhorter settled with his wife, Elizabeth Ann Baker, and their children in Carroll County, Georgia, about 1828. He was one of the first Justices of the Inferior Court. He is named in several interesting court cases and county proceedings. According to the minutes of Inferior Court dated March 16, 1829, an order was passed to purchase a lot of land for a new county site. Carroll County's boundaries were changing so the original site was no longer in a central location. Allen was the justice chosen to go and purchase land from Jesse Tollison - land that Jesse had won in Carroll County in the land lottery of 1827. McWhorter arrived at the Tollison house in Monroe County and was told Mr. Jesse Tollison was away for several days. Recorded in the Inferior Court minutes, November 9, 1829, McWhorter and the other justices decided to purchase lot number #128 in the Tenth District instead. This is the historic center of Carrollton today. Allen McWhorter would never have imagined that 146 years later his great-great-great-grandson, Don McWhorter, would marry Mr. Jesse Tollison's great-great-great-great-granddaughter, Carol Barnes.

Allen McWhorter's ancestors were from Ayrshire Scotland in 1600. After 1618 many Scottish Presbyterians including McWhorters left Scotland for Ulster in Northeast Ireland. Scot-Irish means Scots living in Ireland. An Irish Rebellion began October 3, 1641. Scots perished by the thousands, the McWhorter name was almost wiped out. Allen's ancestors, Alexander McWhorter and his wife, were massacred in 1641.

Their son, Reverend Alexander McWhorter, survived the rebellion that ended in 1649. He was a Presbyterian minister of Edinburgh Scotland. He lived in Ulster Ireland when his son, Hugh, was born about 1690-92.

Hugh McWhorter was married to Jean, pronounced "Jane" and listed as Jane in many accounts. She was also a descendant of McWhorters and lost her maternal grandparents with nine of their ten children in the same massacre of 1641. Her mother, an infant, was saved by a nurse. Hugh and Jean had eleven children. Their eldest son, Alexander, studied two years at the University of Edinburgh in Scotland and came to America to study for the ministry at Princeton. Alexander urged his father, Hugh, to give up his "position of standing" as a linen merchant in the county of Armagh in Northern Ireland to become a farmer in the New World. They came to America with three generations of McWhorters and landed at New Castle County, Delaware, in 1730. Hugh was a devout elder of the Presbyterian church. One of their daughters stayed in Ireland. Their other children were: Alexander, George, Thomas, John, Agnes, Jean, Jacob, Hugh, William, and Alexander.

Hugh's oldest son, Alexander, died at age twenty-two in 1734. One month later, on July 26, Hugh and Jean had their eleventh child and named him Alexander in love and memory. He became a graduate of Princeton and was awarded a doctorate of divinity degree from Harvard. He served in the Revolutionary War as chaplain and was in George Washington's camp on December 26th when American troops crossed the Delaware. In 1779 he was a minister in Charlotte, Mecklenburg County, North Carolina, and president of Charlotte Academy (now Queen's College). His sermons were published and are a great source of family information.

Hugh died in 1748 in Pencader Hundred, New Castle County. his will was probated in Wilmington March 6, 1749. His wife moved to North Carolina where her three oldest surviving children were. Jean lived with a daughter and died in 1757 in Mecklenburg County.

When George McWhorter, son of Hugh, came to America with his parents, he was already married and had children. George was born in Ireland. He had a land grant of 100 acres in Lancaster county, Pennsylvania, in 1737. He was still there on the tax list in 1739. George's children were: William, Henry, George, Aaron and Moses. His sons Henry and Moses were in the French and Indian War in 1760 in the Militia Company of Lancaster county. Moses died in this war.

Henry McWhorter, son of George, born about 1730 in Ireland, was a baby when he came to America. He lived in Lancaster County from 1750 to 1770. Henry married Mary (Marge) Beall. He was a tailor in 1756 in Colerain Township, Lancaster County. He was in the French and Indian War. In 1770-1771 they lived in Chancelford Township, York County, Pennsylvania, then Rutherford County, North Carolina, in 1771. During the Revolutionary War they lived in Mecklenburg County, North Carolina. About 1785 he and his sons moved to Abbeville District, South Carolina. He was still there in 1790. His children were Moses, Jeremiah, Aaron, James, Hugh, George, Henry and Sarah. Jeremiah, born 1755 and Aaron, born 1761 fought in the Revolutionary War. Aaron was with Captain John Foster and Lieutenant Leather in Colonel Hampton's Dragoons.

Moses McWhorter, son of Henry, was born in 1750, he died in 1797. His will is recorded in Edgefield County, South Carolina. Sons John, Landon and Moses Allen were by his first wife, a Burnett. Moses married second wife, Elizabeth Ann Puckett, August 26, 1793, and had five children: George Allen, Daniel Puckett, Sarah (Sally) Douglas McWhorter, Jane Allen McWhorter and Allen Marlin McWhorter.

Allen Marlin McWhorter, born May 16, 1795, in the Abbeville District of South Carolina, married Elizabeth Ann Baker, January 17, 1819, in the same district. They moved to Augusta, Georgia, Walton County, and then to Carroll County. He was a drawer in the 1827 land lottery of Georgia. There are several Carroll County tax and deed recordings of hundreds of acres bought and sold by Allen McWhorter. He was also a drawer in Georgia's Gold Lottery of 1832. His wife, Elizabeth (called Betty Ann), was born February 14, 1798, in South Carolina. Her parents were Thomas (Elijah) Baker and Beersheba Caudle Cain of Abbeville District. Beershaba Cain was the widow of William S. Cain who died in the Revolutionary War. Allen Marlin and Betty Ann McWhorter's children were: Elijah Harvey, born 1820; Beersheba Elizabeth, 1822; James Alcorn, 1824; Egbert Beall, 1826; Abbott Milton, 1828; and Dionishus Wesley born 1830 in Carroll County. Their oldest son, Elijah, was a Methodist Minister at Flint

Myrtle and Frank McWhorter Sr. and Family - 1921

Hill Church when it was a log cabin in McWhorter, Georgia. He served as Chaplin during the Civil War and was a blacksmith. On the 1850 census Allen and Betty Ann were no longer together. She was raising granddaughters, Drucilla and Callisti McWhorter. Betty Ann died in Carroll County 1863.

Allen McWhorter is on the 1850 census in Summerville, Morgan County, Alabama, with second wife Martina Vasti Roberts Martin. They had two sons Archibald Douglas McWhorter in 1852 and Allen Marlin McWhorter Jr. in 1854. Allen Sr. died about 1856. In 1860 Martina and children are in Mount Alvis, Winston County, Alabama.

Allen and his first wife Betty Ann have hundreds of descendants in Carroll County. (See related McWhorter story Part II). *Submitted by: Carol Barnes McWhorter, 126 Wilson Circle, Carrollton, GA 30117*

835. McWhorter Family

Part II

Egbert Beall McWhorter (son of Betty Ann and Allen Marlin McWhorter), born on May 28, 1826, was a baby when he came to Carroll County in 1828 with his parents. His wife was Lida or Lydia M. Tanner, born about 1829 in North Carolina. They were married October 19, 1847, in Carroll County. The 1850 census lists Egbert as a wagon maker in the Carrollton district. Their children were: Paul, Nathaniel, Egbert, Ebenezer, Clark, Leander, Augustus, Elizabeth Ann and Jane. Egbert Beall McWhorter died February 14, 1869, in Carroll County; he was forty-three.

Ethanel (Nathaniel) McWhorter, born June 9, 1848, in Carroll County, married Susana M. Chasteen (Chastain) on November 25, 1866, in Carroll County. She was born January 25, 1846. In the 1870 census, Ethanel is in Cleburne County, Alabama, with Susana and daughter Betty, age two. He was a farmer. Later they moved just west of Bowdon. Ethanel was a landlord and owned several farms. Tenant farmers worked the property he lived on. He had a blacksmith shop and was a member of the Masons. His tombstone bears the Masonic emblem.

Ethanel and Susana's children were: Frank, Tink, Julia, Lou, Clem, Bosh, and Allice. Most of them are named in Ethanel's will dated August 7, 1918. Benjamin Franklin born August 22, 1872, Tinker (Tink) born November 30, 1876, Julia born December 22, 1881, Lou Jackson, Clem Durrett, Vesper Bashaba (Bosh) Williams, and Homer and Hettie Hendrix. These last two were grandchildren in Cullman, Alabama, children of Allice McWhorter Hendrix who was deceased. Betty's name is not in the will but it could be the first or middle name of one of the girls. The will also names nieces Effie and Nettie McWhorter. Bosh lived in Decatur, Alabama. The others were living in Bowdon. Susana died March 29, 1896, she was fifty. She is buried at Macedonia with her husband, three grandchildren and two of her children, Tink who died May 17, 1953, and Julia who died September 3, 1952.

Ethanel married his second wife, Lucy O. Downs, September 19, 1899, in Carroll County. He owned the downtown Bowdon Inn at one time. He died July 29, 1918, and is buried with his first wife.

Benjamin Franklin McWhorter I (son of Ethanel and Susana) was born August 22, 1872. He married Myrtle DeWitt Hobgood on September 26, 1897, in Carroll County. She was born September 17, 1877. She was the daughter of Dr. Sherrod Pierce Hobgood born 1829 and Myrtice Victoria Hobgood born 1837. Dr. Hobgood was a doctor during the Civil War. They are buried in the Bowdon City Cemetery. Frank Sr. was a landlord over several farms he inherited from his father. He also had is father's blacksmith shop. Frank and Myrtle had thirteen children; Billy, Flora, Ray, Roscoe, Ben, Fred, Sherrod, Ruth, Lena, Hamp, unnamed Infant, Mattie, and Frank Jr. Myrtle was a homemaker and a loving, wonderful mother according to her children. She died accidentally February 5, 1946, Frank died August 27, 1951. They are buried in the Bowdon City cemetery.

William Ethaniel McWhorter (Billy), born 1898, died November 22, 1900, and is buried at Macedonia.

Flora M. McWhorter, born 1900, died May 4, 1901, is buried at Macedonia.

Myrtus (Ray) McWhorter married Aurelia Knight and they have one son, Tommy. Ray and Aurelia died in Columbus, Georgia. Tommy married Sue Attaway and their children are: Ray, Thomas (Trey), Sherrod, and Ellis Ann.

Lee (Roscoe) McWhorter was born September 12, 1903. He married Amma McLendon, born 1899. Their children are: Josephine, Edna, Malcolm and Stipe. Roscoe died July 4, 1983. Mary (Josephine) McWhorter married Felton-Denney, their children are: Mary Amma Simpkins, John Felton Denney, Phillip Denney, William Allen (Bill) Denney, and Sarah Jo Duffey. Edna Lee McWhorter married James Anderson Keel, their children are: Nathaniel Keel, Samuel Keel, and Dr. Edwin Keel. Malcolm McWhorter first married Lydia Trammell, their children are: Linda Kemp, Ann Linares and Malcolm Dwayne McWhorter. Malcolm's second wife was Joanne Huff Bell, their daughter is Dawn. Stipe McWhorter married Faye Carter, their children are: Beth Smith and Sherrod McWhorter.

Benjamin David McWhorter (Ben) married Katherine Grigorasi and their children are: Jimmy and Nancy. Ben and Katherine died in Detroit. James (Jimmy) McWhorter married Virginia and their children are: Cheryl, Lozon, Linda Maldaver, and Faith Quintana. Nancy McWhorter married Bob Wednieski, their children are: David, Lori Huelke and Billy.

Frederick McWhorter (Fred) married Kathryn. He died young in a car accident in Texas.

Sherrod Hobgood McWhorter married Ruth and moved from Bowdon to Michigan and then Dallas, Texas, where he died.

Selena Allice McWhorter (Lena), born 1910, married Clavin J. Rooks in Carroll County. Their children are: Tom, Ruth and Howard. Tom S. Rooks married Kathleen (Ginger) Gianola, their children are: David, Greg, Andrea and Kathryn. Ruth Rooks married David Sutton, their daughter is Susan. Howard McWhorter Rooks married Jackie Lovvorn, their children are: Lynn and Ed.

Ruth Jeanette McWhorter married Clyde Jackson. She died in childbirth in her early twenties and is buried at Sandy Flat Baptist Church near the Alabama-Georgia line.

Mattie L. McWhorter, born 1914, married Bernard UpChurch, born 1908. They have one daughter, Sherrod. Bernard died, Mattie married Henry Patton and they live in Carrollton. Sherrod UpChurch was married to Darrell Teal, their children are Scott and Connie. Sherrod is now married to Ed Federer, and she has two step-children, Robby and Heidi.

The tenth child, an infant, was born and died May 15, 1916, and is buried at Macedonia.

John Hampton McWhorter (Hamp) married Dickie Snoddy. Hamp has one son, Jerry Mack and three step-daughters, Billie, Phyllis and Patsy. Jerry Mack McWhorter married Nancy Ashley, they have two daughters, Tamara Bass and Molly.

Benjamin Franklin McWhorter Jr. (Frank), born October 15, 1919, in Carroll County, married Mildred Dorothy Ayers, born November 26, 1926. Mildred is the daughter of Jim and Lily Belle Ayers of Bowdon. Frank died October 3, 1993, he is buried in the Bowdon City Cemetery. Their children are: Tereasa, Mike, Ricky, Don and Tim.

McWhorter Cousins Family Reunion 2000

Tereasa DeWitt McWhorter, born August 10, 1946, married Robert (Wendell) Lynch. Their children are: Robert Franklin Lynch, Lynda DaGayle Lynch, and Kathryn DeWitt Lynch married to Anthony Hall, their son is Bailey Anthony Hall.

Michael Adrian (Mike), born September 27, 1947, was married to Denise Schoerner. Their daughter is Adrienne Marie McWhorter.

Richard Francis (Ricky), born May 10, 1949, is married to Judy Lenora McLeod. Their three children are: Ashley Lenora McWhorter, Richard Francis (Rance) McWhorter married to Kayla Paige Harrod and Cadian Ayers McWhorter married to John West Harrod, their son is Turner West Harrod and one child is on the way (Mattie Grace).

Donald Calvin (Don), born October 25, 1952, is married to Ellen (Carol) Barnes and their children are Arielle Autumn McWhorter and Alex Hayden McWhorter.

Timothy James (Tim), born February 14, 1955, is married to Kathryn Mount and their children are Ivan Hampton McWhorter and Timothy James (T.J.) McWhorter.

Five generations of McWhorters are still in Carroll County, too many to list them all. *Submitted by: Rance McWhorter, 728 Antioch Church Road, Carrollton, GA 30117 and Researched and Written by: Carol Barnes McWhorter*

836. George Washington and Nancy A. McWhorter

My great grandparents were George Washington and Nancy A. McWhorter who were both born in Carrollton, Georgia, in 1844. George W. was born in July 1844 and Nancy in February 1844. They had seven children but I only have the names of four: Monroe who was called Robbie, Marietta, Josephine, and Leila.

From left, Alma New and Leila McWhorter

Leila is my grandmother and she was born in October 1890. She married Arthur Morris around 1909 and they had two daughters — Annie Mae and Dellie Bell. When my grandfather died, my grandmother moved to Atlanta to find work. She worked in cotton mills, then she met and married J.P. Simpson. She lived in Mableton, Georgia and died there in 1981. She was ninety-one years old.

There were three uncles that I believe were McWhorters. Their names were Monroe, Lone, and Emory; and there were also two cousins named George and Clark.

My grandmother told me her sisters died in the early 1900s within a year of each other and that her brother was killed during a thunderstorm when he was crushed between a buggy and a tree. *Submitted by: Mrs. Bobbie Ann Pendlebury, 4852 Peachtree Drive, Buford, GA 30518.*

837. John Allen McWhorter and Sarah Jane Payne

John Allen McWhorter was born December 23, 1882, in Carroll County, a fourth generation Carroll County McWhorter. His great-grandfather, Rev. Leroy McWhorter, came from South Carolina to Carroll County and settled near Villa Rica with his wife and children. Leroy, a Baptist minister, was one of the founders, and the first pastor of Macedonia Baptist Church in 1847.

John Allen was the grandson of Moses McWhorter (1820-1902) and Sarah Kinney (1830-1915) and the son of William Leroy McWhorter (1857-1900) and Eliza J. Wren (1859-1894?).

William and Eliza had eight children: Eliza Della, born 1880; John Allen, born 1882; William Oliver, born 1883; Ida Jane, born 1885; Emma Angeline, born 1886; Alice Pearl, born 1888; Grover Emerson, born 1889; and Benjamin Franklin, born 1891. Eliza died about 1894. Afterward, William moved with the younger children to Cullman, Alabama, where he married Mrs. Selie Bentley in 1897. William died October 12, 1900, and is buried in Cullman.

John Allen McWhorter and Sarah Jane Payne

Dedicated to education and following in the footsteps of his uncle, Thomas Newton McWhorter, John headed for Athens, Georgia, where he attended college and became a school teacher. Both John and his Uncle Tom returned to Carroll County to teach. John fell in love with one of his students, Sarah Jane Payne, daughter of Joseph Joshua Payne and Louisa Elizabeth Boyd. John and Sarah were married August 19, 1906. They moved to Shellman, Georgia, where John had a teaching position. In 1908, their first child Ruby Faye (1908-1996) was born.

John and Sarah next moved to Turin, Coweta County, Georgia, where once again John taught school and Sarah gave birth to another daughter, Gladys Mae (1910-1995). Gladys became a musical child prodigy and by the age of five was amazing the neighbors with her classical piano skills.

With a growing family to support, John took a job as a mail clerk with the railroad and moved to Atlanta. There, in 1917, the couple's third daughter, Marian Payne, was born.

John and Sarah eventually settled permanently in East Point. Sarah's mother, Louisa, whom John called "Miss Lou," lived with them and helped with the child rearing. All the girls graduated from Russell High and Marian attended business college.

Faye married Leonard Barron, son of Raymond Barron and Carrie Myrtice Gill. They had two children: George Leonard Jr., and Beryl Leah.

Gladys married Frank McDuffie, son of Rodie McDuffie and Lillie Maude Coppedge. They had four children: Marjorie Faye, Francis Dennard Jr., John Rodie, and Laura Lizbeth.

William Leroy McWhorter, Eliza J. Wren, and family

Marian married William J. (Dub) Fowler, son of Luther Fowler and Lula Blake. They had three children: Judith Jane, Lula Kay, and William Jethroe Jr.

In 1938, John suffered a heart attack and after several days in the hospital died on July 26. Sarah lived in East Point until her death from a stroke in 1952. Both she and John are buried in College Park Cemetery. *Submitted by: Marian Payne McWhorter Fowler, 180 LaGrange Court, Fayetteville, GA 30214*

838. McWhorter - Couch - Otwell

LeRoy McWhorter was born on October 18, 1797, in Greenville County, South Carolina, and his death is unknown. He is probably buried in Carroll County, Georegia. LeRoy was the son of Moses McWhorter and Agnes Jeness of Greenville County, South Carolina.

Reverend McWhorter was Midway Macedonia Baptist Church's first minister, and he ministered at this church from 1847 through 1850.

One of LeRoy McWhorter's children was Moses Allen McWhorter who was born on November 25, 1820, in Greenville, County, South Carolina, and his death is unknown. Moses married Sara McKinney on November 10, 1848, in Carroll County. Sara was born in 1830 in Carroll County and her death is unknown. Moses McWhorter was a farmer and his farm was located in the Five Points community on Highway 61 in Carroll County. Part of the farm now owned by Donald Matthews was the Moses McWhorter farm at that time.

McWhorter Triplets - Dollie, Pollie and Mollie in 1887.

Moses and Sara were blessed with the McWhorter triplets, Dollie Ann, Pollie Ann, and Mollie Ann who were born on April 29, 1869 in Carroll County. Dollie Ann married a Couch; Pollie Ann married a Noles; and Mollie Ann married a Samples. Dollie Ann Couch died on March 31, 1955; Pollie Ann Noles died on April 18, 1957; and Mollie Ann Samples died on March 2, 1908. The triplets resided in Carroll County. According to a label on the triplets' picture, their father, Moses Allen McWhorter, was also a minister.

It was told that Moses was plowing in the field when the triplets were born. When the first triplet was born, one of the older girls went to the field and said, "Daddy, mama just had a little girl." His reply was, "That's good!" and he kept plowing. A little later, the little girl came out and said, "Daddy, mama has just had another little girl." He replied, "Good!" and he went back to plowing. A little later, the little girl came out again and said, "Daddy, mama has just had another little girl." Moses' reply this time was, "Whoa, mule!" "It's time that I go to the house and stop this foolishness."

One of Dollie Ann and George Harrison Couch's children was Sarah Alma (Sally) Couch. Sally was born on September 11, 1907, in Douglas County, Georgia, and died on April 11, 2000, in Carroll County. Sally married Albert Wilton Otwell on January 26, 1926, in Douglas County. Sally is buried at Midway Macedonia Cemetery in Carroll County.

Sally Otwell's paternal grandparents were Louisa and W.F. Couch who owned a store, a grist mill, and a cotton gin which were located on Flat Rock Road and Bay Springs Creek in Carroll County.

Wilton Otwell was the son of Albert Lonzo Otwell and Eula Haskins of Carroll County is and the grandson of Fletcher Otwell and Julia Crawford of Haralson County. Wilton Otwell was a farmer until 1949 when he took employment with Delmar Cabinet Company in Atlanta. He was employed at Delmar until he retired at age sixty-five. Sally was a homemaker. Wilton and Sally Otwell's children are Harold Wilton and Sara Ann.

Sallie and Wilton Otwell, 1990.

Harold Wilton Otwell was born on May 28, 1930, in Carroll County and married Martha Long on August 1, 1953. Martha was born on January 30, 1933, in Douglas County and she was the daughter of Emma Merrell who married Gaines Lovorn Long on August 18, 1930, in Heard County. Harold worked on the farm until 1949 when he took employment with Adams & Gates Realty in the Hurt Building in Atlanta. He was employed with this company until he was drafted into the Army on March 21, 1951, and he was discharged on March 7, 1953. Harold served in Korea during this time. After he was discharged from the Army, he was employed at Ft. McPherson and Ft. Gillem in Atlanta as an office appliance repairman where he repaired office equipment such as typewriters and adding machines. Later, he owned and operated Otwell Business Machines from 1964 until the present time. Martha was employed at Villa Rica Hospital for a time, and she is presently a homemaker. Harold and Martha Otwell's children are Harold Mitchell, Victor Keith, and Angela Joy.

Harold Mitchell Otwell was born on October 11, 1954, in Douglas County and he married Debbie Lee Cook who was born on April l4, 1955, in Haralson County. Mitchell and Debbie Otwell were married on November 1, 1974. Mitchell Otwell is a sergeant in the Office of Permits and Enforcement with the Georgia Department of Transportation. Mitchell and Debbie Otwell's children are James Mitchell, Crystal and Brandon Lee.

James Mitchell Otwell was born December 31, 1978, in Carroll County and married Shelly Beecham who was born on December 17, 1973, in Camp LeJuene, North Carolina. James and Shelly Otwell's child is Aubrey Noelle who was born on September 10, 1999 in Carroll County.

Crystal Otwell was born on July 10, 1980, in Tulsa, Oklahoma, and married Donald Lee Lathery who was born on November 30, 1978, in Frankfurt, Germany. Brandon Lee Otwell was born on June 10, 1982, in Carroll County.

Victor Keith Otwell was born on July 23, 1958, in Douglas County. Victor is employed as a Highway Emergency Response Operator for the Georgia Department of Transportation.

Angela Joy Otwell was born on March 30, 1963, and married on October 25, 1987, to Tony Grady Crawford who was born on November 1, 1957, in Carroll County. Angela was a Villa Rica (Georgia) High School honor graduate in 1981, and she is an office employee for a dentist in Carrollton. Tony is a landscaper for Fletcher Landscape Service.

Sara Ann Otwell was born on February 14, 1938, in Carroll County and died on June 5, 1964, in Carroll County. Sara Ann married Oscar Williams who was born on March 11, 1933, in Carroll County. Sara Ann died of cancer and she is buried at Midway Macedonia Cemetery in Carroll County. Sara Ann and Oscar Williams' children are Susan Janice and Sandra Kay.

Susan Janice Williams was born on April 22, 1957, in Douglas County and she married Ted Christopher Carden who was born On February 15, 1961, the son of Ted Carden and Annette Land of Carroll County. They were married on April 19, 1980. Janice was a Villa Rica (Georgia) High School honor graduate in 1975 and she is presently employed as an office employee at Tanner Medical Center Hospital in Villa Rica. Chris is employed as an office employee at Tanner Medical Center Hospital in Villa Rica. Chris is employed as superintendent for Aubrey Silvey Enterprises and they build power company sub-stations. Janice and Chris Carden's children are Christina Susanne and William Christopher. Christina Susanne Carden was born on October 6, 1986, in Carroll County. William Christopher Carden was born on October 20, 1989, in Carroll County.

Sandra Kay Williams was born on May 25, 1959, in Douglas County and married on August 19, 1978, to John William Holland who was born on December 29, 1957. Kay is employed at Publix and John is employed at Southwire in Carrollton. Kay and John Holland's children are Michael Jason, Kevin Matthew, and Steven Gregory. Michael Jason Holland was born on May 31, 1979, in Carroll County. Kevin Matthew Holland was born on October 28, 1982, in Carroll County. Steven Gregory Holland was born on February 23, 1985, in Carroll County. *Submitted by: Harold Otwell, 102 Goldmine Road, Villa Rica, GA 30180 and Written by: Pauline C. Roberts, P.O. Box 461, Villa Rica, GA 30180*

839. Meadows

In the 1820 Georgia census records, Daniel Meadows, his wife Anna Thompson Meadows, and their family are listed in Green County. In 1827 they are listed in Taliaferro County. This, however, does not mean that they had moved, for Taliaferro County was created in 1825 from portions of Green, Hancock, Oglethorpe, Warren, and Wilkes Counties. By 1840, the family had moved to Coweta County and was living near Grantville.

Warren M. and Mollie Meadows

The children of Daniel Meadows and Anna Thompson Meadows were: Vincent Meadows born June 2, 1804; Simeon Whatley Meadows born January 16, 1807; John Coggin Meadows born November 11, 1810; Mary Meadows born March 10, 1812; James Marion Meadows born December 23, 1813; a twin of James Marion died as a small child; and Samuel Meadows born July 20, 1816.

On November 7, 1839, James Marion Meadows married Clarisse Hannah Alexander, the daughter of William Alexander of Roopville, Georgia. Her birth date was September 20, 1823. They had two daughters, Ann and Florida; and six sons, William, Tolbert, Felix, Warren, Courtney, and Julius.

Mary Ann Emeline (Ann) Meadows, born May 28, 1842, married David Meriwether on December 12, 1865, in Coweta County. David was born in 1836 in Clark County near Athens, Georgia. They had seven sons. After they both died, her parents, James Marion and Clarisse, helped to rear the children.

About 1880, James Marion and Clarisse moved to Carrollton and bought a house on South Street next door to the Kramer home. One day a ladder was leaning against the house and a little goat belonging to Mr. Meadows climbed the ladder and walked over the roof all night.

Florida Jane Meadows was born November 6, 1847. She married Andrew Fowler. They had a large family and moved to Louisiana. In 1895 James Marion and Clarisse moved to Louisiana to live with them.

William and Tolbert Meadows answered the call often heard in those days, "Go west, young man, go west." They went to Louisiana where they met and married sisters, Lucy and Elizabeth Duke. Both raised large families.

Felix Meadows married Emma Richardson. They moved to Oklahoma. Their children were Manley, Cleg, Hugh, Olmey, Clara, Eugenia, and Louise. After Felix died, his wife brought the family back to Carrollton, where she taught school.

Courtney Meadows died as a young man and is buried in Carrollton.

Julius Meadows moved to Alabama and married Miss Leila Borders.

Warren Marion Meadows remained in Carrollton. He married Mary Caroline "Mollie" Blalock on May 8, 1889. Warren was a handsome man about 5'10" tall. He was a hard worker and had a wonderful disposition — even tempered, patient, kind, and gentle. He and Newt Benson once owned a dry good store called Meadows & Benson on the Square. He was Express Agent in Carrollton for thirty years. Warren and Mollie had one daughter, Nell Katherine Meadows, born February 17, 1899. She is still living in the house in which she was born.

Nell Meadows graduated from Carrollton High School, the State Normal School in Athens, Georgia, and the University of Georgia. She taught for thirty-five years in several places: Fayetteville, Tallapoosa, Valley Point School in Whitfield County near Dalton, LaFayette, Winder, and Maple Street School in Carrollton. She also taught in the Methodist Sunday School.

These family records are written in disobedience to the Bible, which says, "Neither give heed to fables and endless genealogies." Timothy 1:4. *Submitted by: Nell Meadows, 327 Maple Street, Carrollton, GA 30117*

840. Meeks Family History

Columbus Allen (C.A.) Meeks (1865-1956) in 1914 at the age of fifty purchased *The Carroll Free Press* and moved his family to Carrollton from Banks County, Georgia, where he had been publisher/editor of *The Banks County Journal* and a five term Clerk of the Superior Court. He was born in Banks County, son of William Harrison Meeks (1838-1915) and Sara Ann Hardy (1840-1891). W.H. Meeks had lost an arm in 1863 in the Battle of Chickamauga during the War Between the States. C.A. Meeks and his wife had been school teachers in Banks County when they were young.

C.A. Meeks circa 1910

He was married to Alice Agnes Mason Meeks (1869-1928) who was born near Fair Play, South Carolina (daughter of John Clark Mason and Mary Frances Maret Meeks). There were six children, all born in Banks County and of whom four would have careers in journalism.

C.A. Meeks knew that the newspaper was perhaps the only reading material in many of the homes in the county, except for the Bible. During the Great Depression, subscribers to *The Carroll Free Press* paid when they were able (a nominal fee of one or later two dollars a year) and were assured that their subscriptions would not be terminated.

In 1951 he was presented the West Georgia College Founder's Day Award for his long personal and newspaper support of the college. He was a member of the Georgia Press Association.

Alice Meeks was the first woman in Carroll County to register and vote. The Meeks family held strong political opinions and enjoyed the antics of the politicians.

Left, Lois Meeks; right, Mrs. Ralph Meeks circa 1935

William Allen Meeks, circa 1942

C.A. Meeks was Methodist while Alice Meeks and the six children were Baptist. Ralph (1891-1943), the oldest, had graduated from Mercer University where his classmate was William Raymond Robinson (1891-1941) of Carrollton. Ralph served as a second Lieutenant in World War I and married Lucille Withers of Atlanta who had studied elocution at Emerson College in Boston and then taught elocution in the Carrollton public schools from 1930-1935. Ralph worked in advertising with the Atlanta First National Bank, then with *The Carroll Free Press* before joining the Atlanta advertising firm of Liller, Neal & Battle.

Ralph Meeks Jr. (1925-1950), a graduate of Emory University and employed by the Associated Press, died in a naval reserve training flight accident from Chicago to Atlanta.

Alice Meeks assisted in publishing *The Free Press* as did Lester (1893-1980), the second son, who had attended Locust Grove Institute. Lester, the two daughters, Lois and Lucile, and the youngest child, Mason, never married. Mason (1910-1942), an information correspondent in the U.S. Army, died in the Philippines following the Death March on Bataan.

Lois (1903-1993) attended Bessie Tift College and the Normal School for Teachers before becoming society editor for *The Free Press*. She was a founding member of the Carrollton Business and Professional Women's Club. In 1945 she joined the staff of the West Georgia College library. Lois was a violinist and Lucile (1901-1993) was a pianist.

Roger Bradford Meeks (1895-1986), the third son, met his wife Ruby Robinson (1894-1922) through her brother Raymond, Ralph's friend. Their two children were William Allen (1916-1988) and Ruth Maret (1920-). Allen attended Georgia Tech and was a Naval officer in World War II. Ruth received the AB degree in journalism from the University of Georgia. Ruth was a founding member of the Carrollton Arts-Study Club. In 1927 Roger married Sylvia Brown and their two children were Miriam (1928-1988) and Donald (1929-1997). Roger was the Carrollton representative for the Harry Sommers Chryslter-Plymouth Agency in Atlanta.

C.A. Meeks was an enthusiastic vegetable gardener but his most consuming hobby was genealogy. He had traced his ancestors back to Littleton Meeks who lived in Virginia in the 18th century. The inscription C.A. Meeks placed on his wife's grave in the old Carrollton Cemetery is considered an example for all to follow. He listed her name, the names of her parents, birth date and place, date of marriage and to whom, and place and date of death. *Submitted by: Ruth Meeks Griffin, 360 West Club Drive, Carrollton, GA 30117*

841. L.W. Melear Family

According to Carroll County records, L.W. and Essephi Melear came to Carroll County in 1852 from Randolph County, Alabama. L.W. purchased the eastern half of Land Lot 82, Distirct 9 on August 16, 1852. In today's terms, this is approximately where Frost Road slants off Lovvorn Mill Road north of Bowdon. L.W. and Essephi's family had been in the Butts County, Georgia, 1850 census, so they weren't long in Randolph County, Alabama.

The family is in the 1860 census of Carroll County, but the oldest daughter, Mary, had married William McMichael in 1858 and is not in L.W.'s household in 1860. Two other daughters, Margaret and Susan, apparently never married. They are in the 1880 Carroll County census as a separate household.

L.W. and Essephi's other children were Andrew Jackson Sr. and his younger brother, George Washington. A.J. married Charity Anne Barnes/Arthur on January 3, 1867. Her first husband had been killed in the Civil War. She had two daughters, Mary and Elmira, by the previous marriage. A.J. himself was in Beall's Battalion during the War. George Washington Melear married Octavia Land on September 4, 1873. He lived in Cleburne County, Alabama in the 1880s and apparently moved to Texas after that.

L.W. and Essephi lived very near both Poplar Springs Primitive Baptist Church and Indian Creek Missionary Baptist Church. It is not known which, if either, of these churches they attended, but many of their descendants were members of Indian Creek and several are buried there. George Washington Melear was involved in starting the Old Hopewell Baptist Church in Cleburne County, Alabama, in the 1880s. No record of his Civil War service has been found. He was born in 1850, supposedly, so he would have been a borderline candidate.

John, Will, Drew, and Dud Melear

At least four generations of people with the Melear surname have lived in Carroll County in a span of more than 100 years. In the early 1900s, some of the Melears moved across Georgia Highway 100 to what is now Melear Road. On September 4, 1904, A.J. Melear Jr. (Drew), married Martha Eason, and on December 19, 1904, A.J. Melear bought 83 acres of Land Lot 57 on (now) Melear Road. So this move is thought to be connected with marrying into the Eason family as several Easons lived on what is now Melear Road. Melears actually lived at several different locations on the road. James Dudley Melear (Dud), youngest brother of Drew, married Geneva Eason. They last lived at Luckie Cross Roads and were apparently the last people with the Melear surname to live in Carroll County. Will Melear, also a brother of Drew, lived on the next road over (east of Melear Road).

Martha Eason Melear, A.J. Melear Jr.'s first wife, was the daughter of James Eason. She died in 1912, and Drew remarried and had children by both marriages. Ironically, James, Martha's father, married Drew's sister, Ella, in 1894. To some of Drew's children Jim Eason was

Grandpa, and to some he was actually Uncle Jim Eason, but they all called him "Grandpa."

John W. Melear, the oldest of the third generation Carroll County Melear boys, was born in 1869. Two of his wives (sisters Nancy and Julia Smith) are buried at Poplar Springs, and a third, Sug Phillips, with him at Indian Creek. He was also married to Rena Craven in 1947. He had a varied career of store owner, Notary Public/Justice of the Peace, and traveling shoe salesman. He is also credited with being the first of several Melear restaurant owners and professional barbecue cookers.

Will Melear married Annie Thompson in 1907. He is buried in Draketown, Haralson County, Georgia.

This third generation of Carroll County Melear men were mostly farmers, although John's varied interests were as noted above. A.J. Melear Jr. moved to Newnan in 1926. Although he lived in the city, he continued to farm and was a livestock trader of considerable note across several counties.

Sisters of the third generation Carroll County Melear boys were as follows: Ella married Uncle Jim Eason (above) and is buried with him at Indian Creek. Georgia married J.W. Whatley but died in 1914 and is buried at Indian Creek. Meda (Meade) married George Washington (Wash) Cooke, brother of A.J. Melear Jr.'s second wife, Eunice Mae Cooke. Meade was not his first wife. They moved to Cullman, Alabama. Fannie married W.G. Smith in 1889. He died in 1901. She later married John Browning, and they lived in Haralson County.

Like so many other families, the Melears moved across Georgia, looking for a better life. They moved with relatives, friends and maybe even in-laws. In tracing that journey, close to sixty possible spellings of Melear have been found. How "Melear" was the predominant survivor is not known.

Now they are all apparently gone from Carroll County - gone to Haralson County, Coweta County, the Atlanta area, Alabama, Texas, and other places. But Carroll County is still a special place — a place for returning to roots — to many of the descendants of those who moved on. *Submitted by: Jerrell D. Melear, 6970 Oak Leaf Drive, Fairburn, GA 30213-2646*

Sources: Carroll County probate and Superior Court records, Carroll County Genealogical Society Collections, Family history and tradition.

842. The Merrells Family of Carroll County

The deMerels were first known in France in the early 1500s. They were Huguenots and in 1572 were forced out of France. They migrated to England and changed the spelling of their name to Merrill.

In 1665 Richard and his wife, Sarah Wells, from Warwickshire, England, migrated to the New World. Richard's children split to New Jersey, Washington, and west.

Richard's son Captain Benjamin Merrell and his wife Jemima Smith landed in North Carolina. He was among the first North Carolinians to give his life for liberty, being hanged in Hillsboro on June 19, 1771.

The Merrells of Georgia descended from Captain Benjamin Merrell through his son John and his wife Mary Wiseman. Their son Benjamin Smith Merrell was born in Hancock County Georgia. Upon reaching manhood, he moved to Franklin County and married Patsy Chandler. In 1832, he moved his family, wife and ten children, to the wilds of Carroll County. He had not been here long until he was elected as Justice of the Peace, holding this office until his death in 1853. We know nothing of his children except Andrew Jackson, Henry Farmer and William Washington.

Home built by William Washington Merrell, late 1800s.

Andrew Jackson married the daughter of Frank Ward. He migrated to Lawrence County Arkansas, with about thirty other Carrolltonians, in 1842.

Henry Farmer married Clarissa Durham, making their home on Dixie Street. The site now occupied by Worthy Park, where the Sons of the Confederacy have placed a plaque commemorating his gallantry. The property at the corner of Dixie and Newnan Streets was acquired by the First Baptist Church from Henry Farmer. Some of Henry Farmer's descendants are Majorie Templemen, Celeste Tigner, Maida Rose Webb and Buddy Thomasson.

William Washington Merrell had five sons and two daughters by his first wife Mary Durham. His first son lived only six weeks. His other sons were George W., William Perry, Grisham D. and Charles H. His daughters were Mary J. who married John B. Beall, and Sarah Rebecca who married J.C. Carlton.

After the death of Mary in January of 1854, William Washington married Lucy Autrey in September of 1856. They had nine children. One daughter Emily C. who married J.W. Holmes, (a relative of Buford Holmes, Charlcie Stevens and Bobby Holmes) and eight sons, Ben J., Joe L., Ed A., Thomas H., Henry F., Hugh L., Felix, and Jesse M.

His son, Thomas H. was the father of Lolly Sponscler, Sadie Moncrief, T.H. Merrell, Wyolene Warren and Miriam Merrell. Another son, Jesse, was the father of J.M. Merrell, Horace Merrell and Lucy Merrell.

William Washington and Henry Farmer are buried with other relatives at the Merrell Plantation off Temple Road.

There are fourteen known generations of Merrells and many still live in Carroll County. *Submitted by: Eloise Merrell, 106 Ole Hickory Trail, Carrollton, GA 30117*

843. James (Jim) Benjamin Merrell and Lilla Alexander Merrell

Jim Merrell was born 1876, died 1944. He was the second son of William Perry Merrell and Susan Stephenson Merrell. His wife, Lilla Alexander Merrell was born 1878, died 1963. She was the daughter of W.S. and Mary Ann Frances Aiken Alexander.

Jim was a Mason, a member and a deacon of Roopville Baptist Church, and a trustee of the Roopville School. He was a farmer, owning land in both Roopville and in Heard County, and a mail carrier. Jim was very involved in the activities of his community and church.

Lilla was a beautiful young lady. As most ladies of that era, she spent her time caring for her husband, home, and children. Jim and Lilla had three children. First a daughter named Nell Ione, born November 6, 1903, died April 3, 1992, married Joe Oslcar Reagan of Cartersville. They had one son, Jimmy Reagan, he and Mary Nell had a son, Matthew and daughter Kristin. Robbie Alexander, born September 5, 1905, died June 5, 1970, married Marie Pettey of Hawkinsville, Georgia. They had two sons, Robbie A. (Bob) Jr. and Charles R. Bob and wife Rebecca had two daughters, Susan and Nancy. Charles and wife Linda had two sons, Scott and Chris.

The youngest child, Lucy was born 1909 and died July 8, 2000, married Charlie Woodbury of Tampa, Florida. They had one daughter, Carol who had one son and two daughters, Paul, Laura, and Lucy.

Jim and Lilla's (Nanna or Nan to the grandchildren) home, located on Old Franklin Street just north of and adjoining property of his parents Perry and Susan Merrell, is still standing. It has large rooms and very high ceilings and was a cool house in the hot summers, especially the porches, one on each side. The wrap around porch on the north and east side was a favorite place for the grandchildren to play and spend time on the big swing hanging from the ceiling. Sons-in-law, Charlie Woodbury and Joe Reagan, were great story tellers and each enjoyed trying to tell the funniest story. Jimmy Reagan fondly remembers sitting on the porch in the evening and falling asleep as the adults sat and visited. He and cousin Carol also recalled swimming in the swimming hole their grandfather built on the creek below the home and walking with Bobby and Charles to Terrell Huff's store to buy NuGrape sodas.

James Benjamin, Lilla Alexander and daughter Nell Iona

Lilla lived nineteen years in the family home after Mr. Jim's death. She always enjoyed the visits of family, especially the grandchildren. Bobby and Charles were next door and saw her often. Carol and Jimmy would visit on holidays and during the summer. Lilla was very excited when each of the great-grandchildren were born. When Bobby moved his family to Atlanta she cautioned the young parents, "Don't you leave that beautiful baby outside the store when you go shopping, someone would like to take her!" That baby was Susan M. Cantrell. *Submitted by: Charles Merrell, 70 Rock Cliff Road, Canon, GA 30114, Research by: Rebecca Merrell*

844. Joseph James Merrell

Joseph James Merrell (January 7, 1914-May 14, 1989) was one of four sons of George Washington Merrell, who lived from 1880 to 1962. George's father was William Perry Merrell (1842-1922) and his father before him was William Washington Merrell (1815-1900). William's father was Benjamin Smith Merrell (1792-1853), who came to Carroll County about five years after it was established.

Joseph was born in Heard County, but around 1930 moved with his family to Carroll County. He met and married Lucy Inez Phillips on August 25, 1933. She was born December 29, 1914, to Monroe Phillips of the Hulett Community. She died March 27, 1987. She was known for her quilt-making, along with other things. She made a lot of quilts by hand. They are being used in some homes around Carroll County.

Joseph and Inez Merrell

They raised their family on a farm in the Clem community. They raised cotton, corn, and syrup cane. They also had a syrup mill on the creek that crosses what is now Mt. Pleasant Church Road. They made syrup for their own use and for many others around the area. He drove a school bus for years for the Central and Whitesburg districts.

They were both good Christian people and belonged to the Primitive Baptist Church. When they joined the church in 1936, they belonged to Antioch Church in Whitesburg. They were baptized in Snake Creek in the Banning community. Around 1980 or 1983, they moved their letters to Whooping Creek Primitive Baptist Church — the same church where his grandfather, William Perry Merrell, was moderator for years. He still belonged there when he died.

Joseph was always into music and played in many square dances around the area. My husband, James Benjamin Merrell, remembers calling the dance for his dad when he was young. In later years, he got into bluegrass music and played at many festivals all over the area. They still have a festival in his honor once a year at the West Georgia Fairgrounds. His son, Billy Merrell, and wife Linda played with him. They still play.

Joseph and Inez had four boys and three girls. Their first child, Ada Merrell, was married to Bruce Slone. They had a boy and a girl, Terry and Dale Slone Elliott. Their second child, James Benjamin Merrell, married twice. By his first wife, he had four sons: Randy, Danny, Stanley, and Roger Merrell. By his second wife, Joyce (Justice) Rogers, he had two sons: Jasper and Byron Merrell. Joyce had two sons from her first marriage, Joseph and Michael Rogers. Benjamin Merrell is a deacon at Whooping Creek Primitive Baptist Church. His son Jasper is a minister of the Holiness faith.

The third child, William Perry Merrell, married twice; first to Dorothy Boyter and second to Linda Lane. He adopted two boys, Joseph and Scott Merrell, when living with his first wife.

The fourth child, Billy George Merrell, married Linda Stapler. They had three sons and one daughter, Michael, Wayne, Van, and Teresa Merrell. Their fifth child, Drucilla Merrell, died in early childhood. The sixth child, Dorothy Beatrice Merrell, married Ridley Gene Foster. They had three girls, Susanne, Kelly, and Janet Foster. The seventh child, Harold Ralph Merrell, married Betty Thomas. They had one son and one daughter, Jamie and Jessica Merrell.

Most of these still live around the Carroll County area. *Submitted by: Joyce Merrell, 293 Merrell Road, Carrollton, GA 30116*

845. Robbie Alexander Merrell Sr. and Marie Pettey Merrell Family

Robbie Alexander Merrell Sr. was born September 5, 1905, died June 5, 1970. Robbie was the middle child and only son of James Benjamin Merrell and Lilla Alexander Merrell. The family home was located at 108 Old Franklin Street.

Marie Pettey, one of nine children, was the oldest daughter of Samuel Burnette Pettey Sr. and Laura Ard Pettey. Marie was born April 17, 1905. At the age of eighteen, Marie moved from her family home in Cochran, Georgia, and came to Roopville to teach at Grady Academy, the Roopville public school. While teaching, she boarded with Nona Steed. Before long she caught the attention of Robbie and they were married April 1928. The young couple lived for a while in the Baptist church pastorium. After a few years, they built a new home next door to Jim and Lilla. The three bedroom house would be home for them and their two sons. Their first son, Robbie A. Jr. (Bobby) was born at home with Dr. Fitts attending.

Robbie A. Merrell and Marie P. Merrell

Robbie owned a partnership in the Texaco Distribution located in Carrollton and Marie continued to teach. The grandparents were next door and happy to have Bobby every day while his parents worked. Charles Ronald was born at home with Dr. Fitts attending, October 19th, 1940.

Marie, who had begun to teach after finishing high school in 1923, earned a college degree by taking correspondence classes and attending college during the summer school recess. She attended Auburn University, and received a degree in education from Oglethorpe University in Atlanta.

Many good times were enjoyed when Robbie's sisters, Lucy Merrell Woodbury and Nell Merrell Reagan and families would come home to visit their parents. Marie had six brothers and two sisters who came to visit from their homes in Cochran and Hawkinsville. Her sister, Alice Petty moved to Roopville to teach after finishing high school and met and married William H. (Pete) Alexander. Louise Pettey came to join her sisters after finishing nursing training at Plains, Georgia, and Grady Hospital in Atlanta. Louise worked several years at the clinic in Carrollton. During this time she met Bill Gray and they soon married.

Bobby attended Carrollton High School, West Georgia College, and worked at Folds Motor Company after school. He served three years in the Army, working for the National Security Agency. When he returned home he graduated from the University of Georgia. Bobby married Rebecca Dean June 26, 1959. Bobby and Rebecca have two daughters, Susan and Nancy.

Charles attended Carrollton High School and West Georgia College, then finished his veterinary degree at the University of Georgia. Charles married Linda Fuller in December 28, 1962. They reside in Canton, and have two sons, Scott and Chris, and they have three grandchildren. *Submitted by: Susan Cantrell, 54 Old Franklin Street, Roopville, GA 30170. Research by: Rebecca Merrell*
Sources: family interviews.

846. William Perry Merrell Family

William Perry born March 11, 1846, was the youngest son of William Washington and Mary Durham Merrell.

When he returned home after being wounded in the Civil War in 1862, he met and married Susan Ellender Stephenson Spruill. Susan was the widow of Zach M. Spruill, who was killed in the war. She had one son, John Thomas, whom Perry loved and raised with the rest of their children. W.P. and Susan had nine children. Ada born in 1869, died in 1952, married George Bell. Dora born in 1871, died in 1913, married Arthur W. Gentry. They also had two daughters who died in infancy, Mary and Ella. William Franklin (Frank) born November 15, 1876, died August 11, 1947, married Martha Caroline Morris. James Benjamin (Jim) born in 1876, died 1944, married Lilla Alexander. Rufus Cohen born May 3, 1878, died October 21, 1945, married Letha LeeDora Holloway. Twin sons, Charles Henry (Charlie) born February 20, 1880, died in 1955, married Laura Christine King and George Washington also born February 20, 1880, died in March 12, 1962, married Drucilla Clemintine Smith. Very little is known of their youngest son Homer who moved to Atlanta.

William Perry and Susan Merrell

Living in Roopville, W.P. farmed, and as a Primitive Baptist preacher, he served Enos, Tallapoosa, Concord, and Whooping Creek churches. As a poet, he wrote the words to many hymns, including *Rise Up, Oh Men of God.*

April 23, 1932, William Perry, at the age of eighty-six went to be with the Lord he loved so much. His body is buried by his wife at Tallapoosa Primitive Baptist Church on Tyus Road.

Home place of Cohen Merrell, corner Maple and Hay's Mill Road.

There are many third, fourth and fifth generation descendants of William Perry Merrell in Carroll County and surrounding area. Some of these known descendants include Sarah Ragland Tuggle and the Mark Tuggle Family. Jerry and Sammy Thomas families, all descendants of Frank Merrell. Marie Merrell, widow of Robbie Merrell, Bob and Rebecca Merrell, Susan and Phil Cantrell, Charles Merrell Family, all descendants of Jim Merrell. Part time residents of Roopville include Jerry and Marie Merrell and Virginia Kirkpatrick, descendants of Charlie Merrell. Cohen Merrell leaves one son, Ellis Merrell and wife Eloise, the families of Marilyn and Charles Hubbard, Alice and Jerry Teal, Oleria and Mahlon Lane and Johnny Acree, a stepgrandson and his wife Helen. Cohen Merrell moved to Carrollton in 1920 and purchased a house on corner of Maple Street and Hays Mill Road where he and his wife raised four children. The house remains in the Merrell Family today.

George Merrell leaves the most descendants still living in the area, including Bobby Merrell family, Alice Barfield family, families of Dusty and A.J. Merrell. Families of Benjamin and Joyce Merrell, Billy and Linda Merrell, Harold Merrell, Francis Long, Martha and Harold Otwell, Alan and Lorene Cook, Pearl Driver, Katherine Driver and families of William and Jean Driver, David and Louise Driver, Eleanor and Joseph Huckeba.

There are many other descendants living throughout the south and all across the country.

Throughout the generations the two most prominently noted characteristics of the clan are their religious trends and the spirit of adventure. The spirit of adventure brought them to Carroll County and their faith has produced preachers, deacons and worthy layworkers. Truly a family of character. *Submitted by: Oleria Lane, 655 Hilltop Road, Roopville, GA 30170*

847. The William Washington Merrell Family

William Washington Merrell is one of Carroll County's first historians who kept a personal journal from the time of 1839-1885, a time that spanned almost fifty years of our county's earliest development. He wrote about the people, places and events that prove to be of interest to so many people with families who were early pioneers. There are many descendants of W.W. Merrell in Carroll County today.

W.W. Merrell was one of the Carroll County men who went to Florida to fight in the Seminole Indian wars of 1836, and his account of those times is thrilling. A copy of *The Personal Notes of William Washington Merrell* can be seen in the Neva Lomason Library Special Collections. Much of the genealogical data about the Merrell, Chandler, and Durham families that appears here is abstracted from these notes. William Washington Merrell was born in the Gum Log District of Franklin County, Georgia, on 16 September 1815. This part of Franklin County was about one and a half miles from the South Carolina line on the Tugaloo River.

The first generation of Merrells known to us is Richard Merrell, the immigrant, who was born in 1642 in Wells, England, and died 12 May 1727. Richard was married to Sarah Wells born 1649, died 21 October 1722. The son of Richard and Sarah Merrell was William Merrell born 1678-80, died 23 February 1724. William's wife was Grace. William and Grace Merrell had a son named William Merrell Jr. born ca. 1700. He married Mrs. Penelope Von Princess Stout Jewell who was of Dutch ancestry. William and Penelope Merrell had a son named Benjamine Merrell born about 1731 who married Jemima Smith, a relative of the famous John Smith — of Pocohontas fame — of Virginia.

Benjamine Merrell was the first of the family to settle in the province of North Carolina. Benjamine Merrell was executed by Tories and they confiscated his large estate. He left seven sons, all of whom served in the American Revolution. Benjamine Merrell had a son named John Merrell born 11 December 1750 and died after 1832. John Merrell married Mary Wiseman on 20 January 1773. Mary Wiseman's father was English and Scotch and her mother was French. John Merrell was of English, Scotch, and Welch descent. He was called to war in 1774 and served in the American Revolution as a private soldier for three years, then re-enlisted for five years. He was promoted to "Captain of the Light Horse." Mary died after 1856.

John and Mary Wiseman Merrell were the parents of Benjamin Smith Merrell born 18 April 1792 died 25 September 1853. After the war and his honorable discharge, John Merrell moved to Sparta in Hancock County, Georgia, where he lived for several years. He apprenticed under his brother-in-law named Mershon to learn the blacksmith trade. John Merrell then moved from Sparta to Washington in Wilkes County, Georgia. Later, John moved to Franklin County, Georgia, and it was here that his son Benjamin Merrell — in his twenty first year — on 28 February 1813 married Martha "Patsy" Chandler, the eldest daughter of Joseph and Sarah Chandler. Martha was born 14 January 1795 and died 11 September 1879. Benjamin and Patsy Chandler moved to Carroll County in 1828.

William Washington Merrell

Joseph Chandler was a native Virginian who emigrated to Franklin County, Georgia, in 1797. Before he left Virginia in 1793, he married Sarah Farmer, daughter of John Farmer of Irish descent. John Farmer whose wife's maiden name was Newton came from Ireland with her parents when a child. "Grandfather Joseph Chandler was full Anglo-Saxon, large, fair complexioned with auburn hair and blue eyes. Grandmother Chandler was of dark complexion with black hair and eyes. He lived to be eighty — and she lived to be eighty one years of age."

Benjamine Smith Merrell was one of four sons: John, James, Benjamine S., and George. John went to Kentucky in 1810 taking his large family of children. John was twenty-five years older than his brother Benjamine S. James also went to Kentucky. George was stricken by lightning as an infant and "his senses were never right after that." He died unmarried at age twenty-five. There were several daughters older than Benjamine: One who married John Lyner and went to Tennessee; Rachel married a Rodgers and went to the West; Jemima married a Mershon and moved to Sparta, Hancock County, Georgia. Her daughter married B.F. Dense and kept a hotel at Milledgeville until 1864. There may have been other daughters.

The mother of W.W. Merrell — Martha "Patsy" Chandler — had three brothers: Henry Farmer Chandler, Thomas Chandler, and Asa Chandler. Thomas Chandler lived in Carroll County, Georgia, and was Carrollton's first attorney. His children married — Thomas moved to Texas in 1866; sister Martha married a Matthews in Texas; Marion went to Mississippi, Dorothy married a Wright and moved to Dougherty County, Georgia; Newton J. died in Bowdon; Mary Ann married a Thrower; Rhoda married first Bledsoe and then Baskin; and Harriet married a Baskin — all in Carroll County, Georgia. Thomas Chandler served in the Georgia Legislature and became good friends with General Robert Toombs. Thomas died at the age of 86 years. His wife Mary "Polly" Jackson Chandler lived to be over 70 years old. The Chandler home was there where the park on West Chandler Street is now located. A spring used to run through the park and was called Chandler's Spring.

William Washington Merrell was born 15 September 1815 and died 21 May 1900. He moved with his family of eight brothers and sisters from Franklin County, Georgia to Carroll County in 1830. The brother of W.W. Merrell was Henry Farmer Merrell and he, too, was quite prominent in Carroll County as one of the first attorneys. Mrs. Roy (Marjorie) Templeman is a present day descendant of Henry Farmer Merrell.

W.W. Merrell married first to Mary Durham. Mary was the 2nd daughter of Grisham Durham and Katy his wife. The Durhams had five sons: Kinerd, Isaiah, Dennis, George, and John, and four daughters — Elizabeth who married James A. Ward, Mary who married W.W. Merrell, Clarissa who married Henry F. Merrell, and Rebecca who married John Mullens. Katy Durham died in 1840.

Grisham Durham was one of the early teachers at the Carrollton Academy which was built in 1829. His future son-in-law, William Washington Merrell, was one of his students there in 1836. W.W. Merrell studied arithmetic, spelling, writing, and geography. Unfortunately, the Indian uprisings of that time interrupted W.W. Merrell's education and he had to go off to the Indian wars later in 1836. But later on W.W. Merrell returned to the Carrollton Academy where he taught school himself for a few months. W.W. Merrell came to revere three volumes that he said would teach the best lessons of life — the Bible, Blackstone's law book, and Shakespeare. He was known to quote from any of these frequently.

Grisham Durham moved with all his children except Mary and Clarissa to the West in 1842. All except Kinard Durham went to Lawrence County, Arkansas. Kinard went to west Tennessee with Samuel Rose whose daughter he married. Mr. & Mrs. Durham were born and raised in Spartanburg, S.C. They had married there and then moved to DeKalb County, Georgia, and then to Carroll County about 1830. Katy Durham was nee Westmoreland and a relative of the Drs. Westmoreland of Atlanta. Much of their family settled in Cobb and DeKalb Counties. They were also related to the Fowlers.

W.W. Merrell volunteered in Capt. William L. Parr's Company of Carroll Volunteers as first sergeant about 1 June 1836 to serve in the regiment of Georgia Militia Volunteers commanded by Col. Calhoun. The battalion commander was Major John T. Chambers. In 1837 W.W. Merrell worked on the farm of Isaac E. Cobb who lived at Carrollton right where the First Baptist Church now stands. Isaac E. Cobb was his uncle, having married "Aunt Frances C." and they raised a large family of children. The brothers-in-law were all quite prominent in Carroll County — who all married sisters of Thomas Chandler — General William Beall, Benjamin Merrell, Isaac E. Cobb.

W.W. Merrell was in the Seminole War — he joined up for active service on the 5th of October 1837. He volunteered as private at Carrollton, Georgia in the company of Georgia Mounted Volunteers commanded by Capt. Robert L.Y. Long, being in the 5th Battalion commanded by Wilson in the Brigade of Georgia Mounted Volunteers commanded by General Charles H. Nelson. They marched all the way to Tallahassee, Florida ... Fort Micanca, Dade's Massacree ... Fort Dade to Tampa ... came back to Columbus, Georgia on a steamer *Ezzard* and from Columbus walked to Carrollton. Merrell was honorably discharged May 1838. W.W. Merrell was admitted to the bar 1845.

W.W. Merrell had the following children with his first wife Mary Durham: A first child, a boy, lived only six weeks. Four boys grew to adulthood: George W., William Perry, Grisham D.,

Old Carroll County Courthouse

and Charles H. Merrell. Two daughters: Mary J. Merrell who married John B. Beall and Sarah Rebecca who married J.C. Carlton. Mary Durham Merrell died 15 January 1854. Ellis Merrell is the grandson of William Perry Merrell and is one of our present-day descendants of W.W. Merrell. Ellis and his wife Eloise are the parents of Marilyn Merrell who is married to Dr. Charles Hubbard, a native of Newnan, but a physician who has had his orthopedic practice here in Carrollton many years.

W.W. Merrell married 2nd to Lucy Awtrey on 12 September 1856 and had the following children: one daughter — Emily C. who married J.W. Holmes; then eight sons: Ben J., Joe L., Ed A., Thomas H., Henry F., Hugh L., Felix, and Jesse M. All married except Ben J. who went to Spokane Falls, Washington Territory 1885. W.W. Merrell's second wife, Lucy Naomi Awtry, was born 19 September 1836 and died 18 January 1918.

The son of W.W. Merrell and Lucy Awtry was Thomas Homer Merrell born 25 October 1867 and died 20 August 1929. T.H. Merrell married Phena Clark Robinson born 20 February 1872 died 12 May 1960. T.H. and Phena Robinson Merrell were the parents of four daughters and a son. (1) The oldest child was Sadye Cecil Merrell born 22 October 1894. Sadye married Frank Moncrieff of Newnan who later became president of a large Texas corporation. (2) Laulie Sims Merrell was born 5 June 1896. Laulie married Hugh Sponsler of Newnan on 6 October 1919 (3) Thomnas Henry Merrell was born 13 September 1904, married Velda Goldammer, lived and died in Houston, Texas (4) Wyolene Augusta Merrell born 26 July 1912, married John Beverly Warren 2 July 1933, lived in Carrollton (5) Miriam Clark Merrell was born 21 September 1914, lived nearly all her life in Carrollton.

Miriam wrote this of her father, T.H. Merrell: "My father chose the mercantile field when he was only seventeen years of age. At that time, he went to work for the J.A. Rhudy Company which was located in the corner now known as the Arcade. When he attained his majority, he traveled for a short time for the Just Right Shoe Company. He returned to Carrollton and opened a shoe store on the south side of Alabama Street. In 1901, he formed a partnership known as Merrell Brothers and opened for business at what is now the J.B. Warren location. The business moved to the square in 1922 and was known as "T.H. Merrel, Co, Inc." — "The Store of Service." After T.H. Merrell's death in 1929, the men's furnishings department was discontinued and Mrs. J.R. (Ammye) Sewell assumed the management calling it "Merrell & Company." "Miss Ammye" — as she was affectionately known — was T.H. Merrell's wife's sister.

Miriam Clark Merrell grew up in Carrollton and from an early age began to learn her family's business. Since the time that T.H. Merrell had established his store in 1901, the name of Merrell had become associated with "a place to buy anything you needed — especially if it was a pretty dress" for the next seventy five years.

Phena Robinson Merrell had another sister named Lora who married Ed Cheney. A younger brother of Phena, Howard, had died at age 32 as a result of a car running over him. It happened to be a doctor on his way to an emergency who hit him. The doctor stopped and gave emergency care to Howard but to no avail. There was one other brother named Ed Robinson.

"Miss Ammye" operated Merrell's Store for many years, and Miriam was a natural born saleslady. Miriam loved to whistle while she worked — and customers were often treated to one of Miriam's pretty tunes. Over the years, the store underwent many transformations to keep up with the times and the front of the store was changed to big glass display windows filled with mannequins dressed in the latest fashions of the 1950s and 1960s — and all the accessories, too — hats, scarves, jewelry.

Miriam Merrell moved the business in her later years from the square to the house on the corner of Robinson Avenue and College Street which was quite historic to Carrollton. This was the site where Miriam's ancestors — John T. "Jack" Robinson and his wife Nancy Caroline Aycock Robinson had bought the home that had once been the first log house in Carrollton built by Giles S. Boggess.

Over the years, the home had been renovated many times over and didn't look like a log cabin anymore. But the home still sits in the same place — on the corner of College Street and Robinson Avenue, a street which was named for Miriam's ancestors. So, the home took on a new look for awhile as "Merrell's Dress Shoppe" in the late 1960s. Later in 1971, Miriam sold the business to her cousin, Alice Ridley Teal, who then owned and managed the dress shop for several years. (Alice's mother was Leona Merrell who had married H.C. Ridley 14 October 1938.)

The people of Carrollton were in for a real big treat when the summer of 1965 rolled around — we just didn't know how big! That summer Miriam had decided to take a trip to Europe — and she was taking along two young ladies of Carrollton with her. The lucky two were Patti Parkman and Miriam's young cousin — Marilyn Merrell. Marilyn was the daughter of Ellis and Eloise Merrell — and was going to be a senior at Carrollton High School the next year.

Patti Parkman was the daughter of Stanley and Frances Parkman — Stanley was the publisher of Carrollton's newspapers. Patti had gotten to know Miriam quite well during her own high school years as she had done a lot of modeling for Miriam's fashions shows. A memorable "Sidewalk Fashion Show" by Merrell & Company was held in Carrollton on Wednesday, September 19, 1962. Some of the lovely ladies who modeled the latest fashions of 1962 on that date were: Grace Fitzgerald, Patti Parkman, Carroll Parkman, Glenda Ricks, Toye Lumsden, Sue Anne Shaw, Sue Scott, Sallie Harris, Susan Holmes, Susan Denney, Georgeanne Rose,

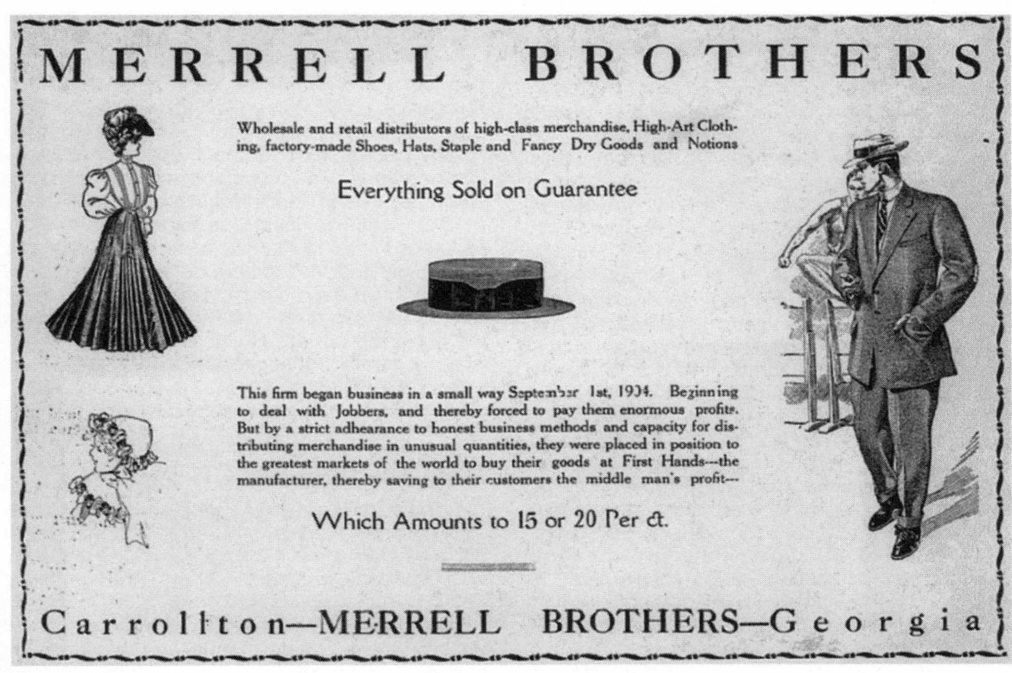
MERRELL BROTHERS
Wholesale and retail distributors of high-class merchandise, High-Art Clothing, factory-made Shoes, Hats, Staple and Fancy Dry Goods and Notions
Everything Sold on Guarantee
This firm began business in a small way September 1st, 1934. Beginning to deal with Jobbers, and thereby forced to pay them enormous profits. But by a strict adhearance to honest business methods and capacity for distributing merchandise in unusual quantities, they were placed in position to the greatest markets of the world to buy their goods at First Hands---the manufacturer, thereby saving to their customers the middle man's profit---
Which Amounts to 15 or 20 Per ct.
Carrollton—MERRELL BROTHERS—Georgia

Old ad for Merrell Brothers

Merrell's Fashion Show at Sunset Hills Country Club, 1949

Sally Ann Richards, Nancy Munn, Sandra Neill, Jan Lambert, Shelma Beam, Alice Ridley, Tresha Bonner, Suzanne Chrisman, Rossie Anderson, Fran Jordan, Marilyn Merrell, Nancy Patrick, Martha Jean Lumpkin, Bekka Anderson, Mildred Maddox, Carol Cole, Elaine Atkins, Gayle Toney, Laddie Smith, and Beth Parkman.

The picture of the "little beauties" in the Fashion Show of 1949 shows that many of the above young ladies modeled for Miriam for quite a long time: We believe we see from L-R back Sally Ann Ricahrds, Tamara ____, Bekka Anderson, Patti Parkman, ____, Jessica Jenkins, Georganne Rose, Sally Spangler and Laddie Smith. L-R front ____, Patricia Stephens, Celeste Tigner, Celeta Estes, Jo Johnson; Babies in front: Susan Holmes, ____, ____ and Marilyn Merrell.

Patti Parkman had graduated in December and had just begun her teaching career. But she was out for the summer and ready for the European tour Miriam was planning. Miriam was going to write columns for the Carrollton newspaper all summer long to keep the folks back home up to date on what the vacation was like.

It was so exciting to travel in this vicarious way with "The Three Graces" as they dubbed themselves — Miriam, Patti, and Marilyn. This vacation was to be "budgeted on a shoestring" and the plan was to spend some time staying with Miriam's brother's daughter, Catherine, who was married to Captain Cliff Polk who was stationed in the Air Force in Toulaire, France. The Polks had four children, but their country home in France was spacious enough to allow for the three guests for the summer. The Polk children were David, Nancy, Elizabeth, and Susan.

Things at home had to be completed first — Marilyn was a bridesmaid in Laddie and Bill Carter's wedding, and then the threesome left from Atlanta on a Pan Am jet. They arrived in London just in time for the celebration of Queen Elizabeth's birthday. Immediately, Miriam began sending back her articles for the local Carrollton newspaper and she walked us through every step of the adventure.

"When I was seven years old I moved from my birth home on Rome Street to live with my grandmother on College Street and I remember the large mahagony wardrobes that were in each room. They were like the ones that we see in our hotel rooms here in Europe ... Bedrooms didn't used to have closets like they do today, you know ... Patti loved Brussels, Belgium — the heart of the lace market — and is thinking that her sister Carroll may be wanting a bridal veil soon ... " (Carroll Parkman and Claude Wills did announce their engagement while Patti was on her tour ...)

Once they reached France, they found the talisman roses that grew all around the Polks' home to be breathtakingly beautiful and they became accustomed to having fresh cut flowers in the home everyday. They sent back reports of French chateaus like Fountainbleau and the vineyards of the Loire Valley. "We drank in the beauty of France," Miriam would say. And she would tell us of the stained glass windows, the beautiful stairs of Chambourd, tapestries in old monasteries, formal gardens with lighted statues and parks.

Once Miriam reported she could even "smell the huckleberries" and described a picnic they had in Spain with more friends in the Air Force — Ray and Shirley Nybros and their four little girls — and "it was just like being at Lake Carroll on the 4th of July." Other times, they were guests of the Officer's Clubs of the Air Force and "the Three Graces" enjoyed golf dates with the officers, too. They attended a real Italian opera and we could almost taste the real Italian spaghetti and meatballs! Miriam had taken along a lot of Kennedy half dollars which they used for tips as people in Europe were anxious to get these coins.

There was the humorous side of the adventure, too, especially when Miriam would report how everywhere they went Marilyn would try to order a chocolate sundae, but — because of language barriers — no one could follow her directions on how to make one. "We never knew what would be served," Miriam laughed. Imagine trying to communicate in English with a Southern accent, too! And how a large part of their baggage was hair rollers (remember this was 1965!) Finally, they purchased a car — a 1963 Peugot 404 so they could tour more of Europe on their own.

Back home in Carrollton, we read in our newspaper of their drive to Spain and we vicariously visited glove markets in Madrid and saw the bullfights. Their driving escapades and interpretation of international road signs was hilarious. Once Patti even had to park the car going down a 20-foot dropoff straight down! Then we visited art galleries and Miriam beautifully described the "Valley of the Fallen" the "beautiful shrine built into the mountainside by Franco in memory of the Spanish Civil War. The columns were shaped in the form of soldiers ... " Patti purchased a sword in Toledo and then had the burden of carrying it throughout the rest of the tour. She wore it everywhere!

So, the threesome even had a weapon if they needed one!

They wrote of the beauty of Lake Lucerne in Switzerland, the artists in Paris, the Sorbonne, the Louvre, and in Paris they saw the actual sword of Charlemange that had 135 carat diamonds on it. In Florence, they saw the church were Robert and Elizabeth Barrett Browning had married and described violins in Venice, and Roman ruins. They saw marionette shows in Germany, danced to the Beer Barrel Polka, and visited Adolph Hitler's retreat the "Eagles Nest". This was a dream of a vacation ...

Throughout the whole trip Miriam described their horsing around and singing "We ain't got a barrel of money ... " as they drove down the road. After two months of a summertime fun-filled adventure, they ended their trip in Austria — where filming had just completed for that classic "The Sound of Music." A tour of Shannon, Ireland followed and then they flew back to New York. There, Marilyn caught up with the Ebb Duncan family who were just returning from Bobby's wedding in London — and she made the journey back home with them.

Miriam and Patti did their tour of what people in her business in the dress world called the "Rag Market" which was 7th Avenue in New York City. This was such a memorable trip — and not only for Miriam, Patti, and Marilyn — but for all the rest of us in the community who "took the tour with them" by way of their fun-filled articles for the *Times Free Press*.

The Merrells have always been one of the most public-spirited families of our community — and patriotic, too. Miriam was always an integral part of the city government during her lifetime here in Carrollton. Miriam served as a Carrollton City Councilwoman for ten years. She served on the Board of Health and also on the board of the Neva Lomason Library. When the first D.A.R. was organized in Carrollton in 1953, Miriam was a part of that organization as an officer from the beginning — as she has always had an interest in preserving the history of her ancestors and of the community, too.

It was hard for Miriam to part with the community she had loved so much, but as she became older, she needed to move to Galveston, Texas, where her niece lived — and who was anxious to help care for her. Before Miriam left Carrollton she donated all her many years collection of genealogical books pertaining to Georgia — to the Special Collections at Neva Lomason. Miriam's great-grandfather — John T. Robinson — was born 31 May 1817 and grew up in the area of Newton County known as Rocky Plains, Georgia. He married Nancy Caroline Aycock in Newton County in 1846. Nancy Caroline Aycock was born 1826 and died 1901 in Carrollton. Their son, Henry Richards Robinson b. 24 January 1848 married Emily Caroline "Emma" Sims on 17 December 1868. Henry Richards Robinson was a physician in Carrollton for many years. Henry R. and Emma Robinson had several children — Phena, Lora, Ammye, Ed and Harold. Their daughter, Phena Clark Robinson, was Miriam's mother. Miriam's Robinsons had moved to Carrollton between 1870-1880 some years after my own family had moved here in 1859 — and they always called each other cousin. John T. "Uncle Jack" Robinson died in 1896. We hope through the publication of this Heritage book that we will find our family connection at last! *Submitted by: Miriam Clark Merrell, 2228 Seawall Boulevard, Galveston, TX 77550 and Written by: Jan Robinson Bell*

848. MICHAEL FAMILY

Barnabas "Barney" Michael, according to the 1850 census records of Carroll County, Georgia, was born circa 1769 in North Carolina. His wife Catherine was born in North Carolina, circa 1770. In Jefferson County, Tennessee, January 1800 Barney was appointed a road overseer of the road from Sevier County to the works on Dumplin Creek. Barnabas purchased estate property in 1801.

Barnabas Michael was on the 1805 tax list in Grainger County, Tennessee, with 150 acres of land. He and his son, William Michael, were on the 1814 tax list of Grainger County.

William Michael and Hannah Sellers were married in Jefferson County, Tennessee, May 5, 1815.

The families of Barnabas and William Michael moved to the Hiwassee District in Monroe County, Tennessee, in the 1820s, along with Peter Michael, soon after the former Indian land was settled. (See related Peter Michael story.) They purchased land in the Lakeside community on Bat Creek near Vonore and were there in the 1830 census. Peter Michael was one of several Lutheran church members who signed and submitted a petition to the Governor of Tennessee requesting a German-speaking minister for their congregation.

In 1831, Barnabas and William sold their land and moved to Carroll County, Georgia. Barnabas and Catherine Michael were parents of Barnabas B., James, William, Peter, Katherine and Sarah. Barnabas and Catherine Michael were received as members of the New Hope Primitive Baptist Church on October 21, 1846. Membership was transferred from Little Tallapoosa Church.

In the Carroll County census of 1850, Barney, age eighty-one, and Catherine, age eighty, lived in the house with their son William and Hannah Michael. Barney did not appear in the 1860 census. In the 1850 census, the children of William and Hannah were William Russell age twenty-one, Sarah age sixteen, Emanuel age twelve and James age nine. William Russell Michael later married Louisa Jane Bevan.

The 1860 census of Carroll County listed William R. Michael, age thirty, farmer, with his wife Louisa J., age twenty-seven. Children were John M. age five, William Lumpkin age four, Hannah M. age two, and Samuel age one.

William Russell Michael joined Company I, 56th Georgia Regiment of the Confederate forces on May 10, 1862, at Villa Rica, Georgia. He died of disease in Atlanta July 23, 1862. His son, William Lumpkin Michael, married Louisa Morris circa 1873 in Carroll County. They later moved to Cullman County, Alabama. Louisa Michael was in the 1900 census of Cullman County with children Joseph O., Walter, Lillia C. and Claude.

Claude Acoy Jerome Michael was married to Annie Mamie East in Madison County, Alabama, on December 12, 1909. They had four sons, Coy W., Elmer E., Audie L., Howard, and one daughter, Cleovia. Elmer married Mary W. Jones from Princeton, Alabama. They had two children, Coy E. and Rebecca J. Elmer Michael resides in Berry, Fayette County, Alabama. Coy E. Michael was born March 2, 1934, in Huntsville. Rebecca J. Michael Plemons was born September 7, 1939, in Huntsville, Alabama, and now resides in Rock Island, Illinois. *Submitted by: Coy E. Michael, 8908 Willow Hills Drive, Huntsville, AL 35802*

Sources: Family Bible and U.S. census records

849. Peter Michael

Peter Michael, son of Barnabas, was born September 24, 1814, in Tennessee. He lived in Monroe County, Tennessee, before moving with his father to Carroll County in 1831. He was age 15-20 in the home of his father, Barney, in the 1830 census of Monroe County, Tennessee. Peter married Rebecca Martin April 24, 1832, in Carroll County. Rebecca was born January 6, 1817 in South Carolina. Peter and Rebecca had a farm in Carroll County. The 1850 census of Carroll County reported Peter, age 37, as a blacksmith and owning $300 of real estate. Children in the household and their ages were: Rebecca, 33; Charlotte, 14, Mary 15; James W., 11; Sarah, 9; Louisa, 7; Rebecca, 5, and Carolyn, 3. All children were born in Georgia except Charlotte was born in Alabama.

The 1860 census read that Peter Michael and family were living in Villa Rica on a farm valued at $300. By 1870 Peter was living in the Carrollton District of Carroll County. He was fifty-two years old.

On December 27, 1873, Peter was baptized and he joined the Tallapoosa Primitive Baptist Church. Rebecca was baptized and joined the same church September 23, 1876. Peter died May 30, 1889, and Rebecca died July 30, 1905. Both are buried in the church cemetery.

When Barney and family moved to Carroll County in 1831, they were looking for land to purchase. On May 7, 1832, Barnabas Michael purchased Land Lot #115, 5th District, Carroll County, 202 ½ acres for $190 from Joseph T. Hawkins. An interesting story about this land purchase involves the first jail in the county. The Inferior Court minutes of the January term, 1828 reads:

> "Ordered that the town and country site be laid off according to the plan hereunto annexed" and "Ordered that the letting of the jail to be made of hewn timber be let to the lowest bidder."

Smith Bonner was a low bidder at $97. It was built on Lot #115 in the 5th District but very near the north line. By 1829, the jail was not in a convenient location and plans were made to build a new jail in Carrollton. While the county had agreed to the purchase of Lot #115 from Mr. Hawkins for the sum of $208, the county never discharged the obligation, never had title to it, and added further insult to injury by moving off and taking the jail with them. Poor old Mr. Hawkins finally unloaded #115 on Barnabus Michael Sr. in 1832, but not until he had lowered the price to $190. Barney later deeded three acres of the northeast corner to the Hopewell Church. *Submitted by: Coy E. Michael, 8908 Willow Hills Drive, Huntsville, AL 35802-3730*

Sources: Census records and records from Carroll County courthouse.

850. Ross Walter Miller Family

Ross first came to Carrollton in 1946 to attend West Georgia College. He was born February 13, 1929, in Woodland, Georgia, to Walter Glenn Miller, a native of Talbot County, and Mary Anne Ross, a native of Monroe County. He graduated from Woodland High School. His first student job at West Georgia College was with Mr. J.B. Stallings in expanding classroom space and converting shops to dormitory space in preparation for the influx of veterans for Fall Quarter 1946. He completed student teaching at Sand Hill School in the classroom of Mary White Davidson and served as teaching principal at Oak Mountain School with Effie Duffey McGuire. His classroom was the south room that is the location for Norman Rockwell's "The Country School."

Later, he taught at Talbot County High School, Woodland School, West Point Elementary School, and West Georgia College. He earned a bachelor's degree at the University of Georgia, a master's degree at Alabama Polytechnic Institute, and a Doctorate in education at the University of New Mexico. He held various church offices and was lay member of both the South Georgia and North Georgia Annual Conferences of the United Methodist Church. He also served as president of the West Point Jaycees.

Ross Walter Miller and Annie Laura Falls (see at Robert Edward Falls) were married June 17, 1962. Their first residence was on Longview Street in Carrollton. They later lived in West Point, Georgia, and Albuquerque, New Mexico. After several other residences in Carrollton they settled at 155 Greenwood Lane in Carrollton. To this marriage were born Robert Walter Miller and Eliza Anne Miller.

Robert Walter Miller was born in Carrollton June 27, 1964. He graduated from Central High School and attended Southern Technical Institute. Among his business pursuits was Westside Skates on Rome Street in Carrollton. He resides on Happy Hill Road in the Clem community.

Eliza Anne Miller was born in Albuquerque, New Mexico, on September 11, 1965. She graduated from Carroll Technical Institute and works in engineering design. She relocated to Houston, Texas. *Submitted by: Ross Miller, Carrollton, GA 30117*

851. Jessica Hall Mitchell

Jessica Hall Mitchell was born in Carroll County to Jackson Allen and Elizabeth Ruskell Mitchell, formerly of Bowdon, July 10, 1981. Paternal great-grandparents are Ben and Nancey Fields Mitchell and grandfather Billy Bob Mitchell. Jesse Edgar and Essie Mae Wysner were the parents of her grandmother, Betty Wysner Mitchell of Bowdon. Uncles and Aunts are: Sammy and Peggy Mitchell Pollard of Carrollton, Billy Mac and Jan Mitchell of Veal, and Penny Lee Mitchell of Bowdon. Maternal great-grandparents are George Channing Jr. and Madeleine Gertrude Calahan Ruskell, are the parents of her grand father George Channing Ruskell III. Dr. James Abston and Annie Hall Acuff McFerrin were the parents of her grandmother Douglass McFerrin Ruskell, formerly of Mount Pleasant, Tennessee. Uncles and Aunts are Virginia "Jan" Ann Ruskell of Carrollton, Julia Channing Ruskell of Carrollton, George Channing IIII and Rebecca Doss Ruskell of Canton, Georgia. She has two half-sisters: Joni Leigh Mitchell of Carrollton and Keira Leigh Ann Summers of Rhode Island.

Jessica H. Mitchell, Easter Sunday April 15, 2001

The name Jessica comes from the Hebrew origin, it means one with wealth; gift. She grew up in Canton, Georgia, where she attended Hickory Flat Elementary and Dean Rusk Middle Schools. She played basketball and softball. During many childhood summers she visited her Aunt "Jan" in Carrollton and attended Dott McNabb Day Camp at The University of West Georgia. She also attended Camp McIntosh, which is a boarding camp in Carroll County. When she was thirteen she moved to LaGrange, Georgia, where she attended Gardner Newman Middle and LaGrange High Schools. She graduated in 1999. She also attended West Georgia Technical College.

Jessica and Elvin Sysvester Gray Jr. (her husband to be) bought their first house in LaGrange. She was a substitute teacher for the Troup County Board of Education. *Submitted by: Jessica H. Mitchell, 102 Baugh St., LaGrange, GA 30241*

852. The Mobley Family

Marida (or Meridy per his grave marker) Mobley was born November 9, 1812. He was living in Paulding County in 1850 with his wife Rebecça when the federal census was taken. Marida and Rebecca S. Mobley had six children: Susan

Family of Jesse and Nancy Mobley, near Mt. Zion, Georgia

born 1841; Jesse M. born April 4, 1843; Matthew born May 26, 1845; Newton B. born 1847; Marida "Gus" born 1857; and Allen A. born October 2, 1857.

Susan married George W. Cason on September 6, 1863, in Paulding County, Georgia.

Jesse married Nancy Harriet Cason on January 17, 1864, in Haralson County. She was the daughter of John and Elizabeth Cason and the sister of George W. who married Susan. Jesse and Nancy were the parents of ten children: Susan J. born 1861, who married William James Reeves; Martha Lee "Mattie" born September 3, 1866, wife of William Samuel Harris; Missouri Ann born 1867, wife of (1) R.A. Hayes and (2) J.D. Brazil; A. Gertrude born June 16, 1870, who married W.M. Crumbley; Georgia born February 13, 1873, wife of Walter L. Nix; Emma born October 11, 1873, married (1) W.E. Merrell and (2) Hezekiah Ashmore; Luna V.D. married Charles Stevens; Josie who married Lewis Johnson; Wade and Otha A. Mobley.

Jesse M. Mobley died January 28, 1923. J.W. Bolton, minister of the Christian Church, had charge of his funeral and the Masons conducted a service at the grave. He included remarks about him being a soldier in the War Between the States and that he served in the Georgia Regiment, Company A. He also said Jesse became a member of the Bethany Christian Church, Paulding County, in about 1870, then was a member at Bethel near Carrollton and finally with the church in Carrollton. The Carrollton First Christian Church membership list at the beginning of 1912 included Jesse and Nancy Mobley and two of their children, Missouri and Gertrude.

Matthew Mobley married Rebecca and they had two children, William and John. Matthew and Rebecca are buried at the Mt. Zion Baptist Church Cemetery, Dallas, Georgia.

Newton B. (1847-1915) married Sarah Posey April 15, 1866, in Haralson County. Their three children are Jonah, Morgan, and Newton B. (1876-1934). Newton and Sarah are buried in the Union Hill First Congregational Methodist Church Cemetery, Bremen.

Marida "Gus" married Martha J. Pace on December 10, 1874, in Paulding County.

Allen A. and Mary Lou Mobley were married and had two children: Mayor Dennis born May 2, 1899, and Henry G. born November 1922. Dennis graduated from Dallas High School and in 1923 from the University of Georgia. He was State Director of Vocational Education, then moved from Dallas, Georgia, to Washington, D.C. with his wife, Ethyleen Hartley, and daughter Mary in 1951 to serve on the National Advisory Committee of Rural Areas Development and the President's Committee on Employment of the Handicapped. He was consultant to the War Department on Vocational Education in Germany and was involved as advisor to all congressional committees concerned with vocational education. He died April 7, 1967, and is buried with his wife and parents in the Mt. Zion Baptist Church Cemetery, Dallas, Georgia.

Mattie was the second child of Jesse and Nancy Mobley and on August 15, 1886, she married W.S. Harris. Eight children were born to this marriage and they were: Myrtie Lee, Lula Velmar, Lena Ethel, Lilly May, Earnest Marvin, Melvin Bee, Harvey Floyd, and Jesse Terrell. One day Melvin told his niece about staying with his grandparents and going to school in a covered wagon. He said that they lived on Mt. Zion Road between Carrollton and Mt. Zion, in the area near where Tanner Park is located.

The fifth child of Jesse and Nancy Mobley was Georgia and she married Walter L. Nix on November 29, 1891. There were four children born to this union: Grady Woodfin, James Lloyd, Cecil, and Ernest David. Grady married Hattie Duncan on December 25, 1913, and they had three children: Mary Marguerite, Sara Evelyn, and Harold Grady. Mary Marguerite married Newton Jackson White on September 28, 1936, and they had one son, Jack Newton born July 29, 1943. One January 14, 1966, Jack had been playing basketball at West Georgia College where he was a senior, had an aneurysm and died. He is buried with his father in the Carrollton City Cemetery.

I am the second child of Grady and Hattie Nix and my name is Sara. I married Jesse Louie "Buck" Street on April 2, 1942, in Carroll County. We had two sons, Joseph "Joe" Nix and James Louie. "Buck" was born August 17, 1911 and he died October 19, 1982.

The Mobley Family picture made in about 1895 shows the following seated in front from left to right: Walter with Grady, Georgia with Lloyd, Emma with Jesse, Jesse with (unidentified), Nancy, Susie with (unidentified), Mattie with Lilly and W.S. Harris behind her. *Submitted by: Mrs. Sara Street, 623 N. Cliff Ext., Carrollton, GA 30117. Research and written by: Violette H. Denney*

853. L.S. Molette
1895-1983

L.S. Molette, principal of the defunct Carver High School and pastor of the St. Paul A.M.E. Church for a number of years, was an outstanding leader in the Carrollton community for many years. After retirement from the public school system, Molette was elected to the Carrollton Board of Education where he served for almost two terms. He received the Silver Beaver Award in Scouting, having served as chairman of the West Georgia Division for many years, bringing scouting to hundreds of Black boys.

Molette became principal of the Carroll County Training School, located in Carrollton, in 1944, coming to Carrollton from Spalding County where he served as principal of one of the high schools for African Americans. Before coming to Spalding County, he worked in the agriculture department at Fort Valley State College.

Molette led the local Black school to accreditation by the Southern Association of Schools and Colleges and added the twelfth grade. Carroll County Training School housed both the high school and the elementary school. When the enrollment became too large for the existing building, Molette purchased old army barracks at Ft. Oglethorpe and, with the help of his high school boys, hauled the barracks back to the school site and constructed additional classrooms.

L.S. Molette

He introduced football to the students and served as their first coach, organized the school's first marching band, provided courses in woodwork and industrial arts, provided for business courses including typing, revived the school newspaper, produced the first school year book, and the list could go on.

L.S. Molette was born in Yazoo County, Mississippi, September 11, 1895, where he received his early schooling. He graduated from Hampton Institute in Virginia and earned a master's degree from Atlanta University.

He married the former Ida Pearl Cato. Together they raised an adopted son, Morris Kelly. L.S. Molette died Janaury 23, 1983. *Submitted by: C.B. Ward, Spring Street, Carrollton, GA 30117*

854. William Pleasant Moon
of Bowdon

William Pleasant Moon was born April 6, 1876, in Carroll County near Bowdon. He died January 20, 1961, in Bell County, Texas. His parents were Alphesus E. and Mary Elizabeth (Bridges) Moon of Bowdon.

Will married Rebecca Minnie Bell Craft, daughter of William Allen and Cloia Emeline (Hayes) Craft, and granddaughter of William L. and Martha (Turner) Hayes, all of Bowdon. Rebecca Minnie was christened in the Midway United Methodist Church near Bowdon in August 1889 along with her two brothers, William Jeptha and John Robert Craft. Nine children were born to this union.

Will's sister, Mattie (1872), married W.S. Arthur of Bowdon. Carrie was born in 1874. Jerdon J. (1875) married Nannie Harriet (Hanson). John Rufus (1886) married Pearl. All of William's brothers and sisters were believed to have been born and raised around Bowdon.

Alphesus, Will's father, was the son of Raleigh Moon. He raised a family of eighteen children in Heard County, Georgia. Raleigh Moon's parents were Thomas and Sarah (Brooks) from Columbia County, Georgia. Will's mother, Mary Elizabeth, was a Bridges. Her family was from Jerdon Bridges and Nancy (Suptrine) Bridges. There were ten children in the Bridges family, all of Bowdon.

Will and Minnie Moon

Will and Minnie (as they were known) had eleven children: Mary Virda (December 6, 1900 near Stateline); William Price (February 27, 1904); Lewis Jerdon (June 3, 1906); Effie Mae (April 8, 1907); Edna Bell (June 27, 1910); Cloia Etta (July 12, 1912); Jessie and Lessie (August 17, 1914); Jewell Melessie (February 13, 1919); Era Frances (September 1, 1921); and Lillie Marie (February 29, 1924). The first six children were born and raised around the Bowdon area going back and forth crossing the Georgia/Alabama stateline. Will and Minnie had eleven children, fifty-five grandchildren, ninety-five great-grandchildren, and one-hundred-fifteen great-great-grandchildren.

Records of all the above families of Moons, Bridges, Crafts, and Hayes place these families in Carroll County in the area of Bowdon, Georgia in the late 1800s and early 1900s. The Midway United Methodist Church has many of these families listed. Thomas and Raleigh Moon were very prominent plantation owners in the early history of Georgia. Thomas Moon's father, John Moon, was said to have been the progenitor of the Moons in Georgia as far back as the mid-1700s. *Submitted by: Michelle Cabaniss (granddaughter of William Pleasant Moon), P.O. Box 1663, Frazier Park, CA 93225*

855. The Moore Family

David Joseph Moore was born on November 3, 1825, in North Carolina and died on December 29, 1890, in Carroll County, Georgia. He is buried at New Hope Methodist Church. He married Nancy L. Wilson in Mecklenburg County, North Carolina, on October 8, 1845. Nancy was born on August 2, 1820, in North Carolina and died of fever on October 22, 1887. She is buried in Beal Cemetery, Carroll County.

David and Nancy were in Georgia by 1848. The 1850 Carroll County census listed them in the 10th District, 714 GMD, with daughter Nancy, age two. This census showed David's father as being born in Pennsylvania and his mother in North Carolina. Nancy's parents were born in North Carolina. David was a constable, a notary public and president of the Agricultural Association. He was a member of Carroll Lodge No. 68, F & AM and was a Mason for over thirty years. In 1860 he had 100 acres of land with a cash value of $1000 and no slaves. In 1887, New Hope Methodist Sunday School was reorganized with David as superintendent and Joseph as secretary.

The J.B. Moore Family around 1920.

David and Nancy had five children: Nancy (born 1848, died young); John William, "Billy," (born 1852, married Emeline Jane Crawford); Sarah Frances, "Fanny," (born 1854, married Elisha Ragan); David (born 1856, died young); and Joseph Brown (born April 14, 1861). After Nancy died in 1887, David married Mrs. M. Eliza Gable in 1889.

The youngest child of David and Nancy Moore was Joseph Brown Moore. He married Leonora (Lena) Buckelew on November 17, 1887, at the home of her parents, James L. and Carrie Proctor Buckelew. Lena was born on October 10, 1868, in Pike County, Georgia, and moved to Carroll County with her parents around 1887. Joseph Brown Moore and Lena had one son, Olin Garland Moore (born January 23, 1889). Lena contracted fever and died on September 2, 1889. She is buried at New Hope Methodist Church Cemetery. Olin married Lovie Beck and had four children, Mary Lee, Joe Beck, Rebecca Ann, and Emily Sue.

After Lena's death, J.B. married Georgia Ann Smith on January 26, 1890. She was the daughter of J.W. Smith and Margaret Mahala Creel. J.B. and Georgia had three children, Minnie Lee (born January 25, 1891, married Homer Yeats, died March 18, 1938), James Austin (born April 14, 1893, married Essie Dye, died December 30, 1966) and Nancy Leila (born January 25, 1891, married Fonzy Edward Arrington, son of Ambrose Jackson Arrington and Mary Ann Young Arrington, on December 24, 1923, died January 7, 1996). J.B. was a farmer, taught school at New Hope and had a store in the Plowshare community. In 1906, they moved to Bowdon, Georgia, where he opened a general merchandise store. His sons joined him in business and changed the name to J.B. Moore and Sons. Olin and James operated the store after J.B.'s death on January 7, 1934. Georgia Moore died on July 23, 1942. They are buried at Bowdon City Cemetery.

James Austin Moore and Essie Dye Moore had two sons, James (married Edna "Toby" Moody) and Bobby (married Sarah Williams). Leila Moore Arrington and Fonzy Arrington had three children: Mary Jo (born Februry 2, 1925, married Roy Edward Dobson on December 23, 1945); Wallace Jackson (born October 3, 1930, married Nova Dean Smith) and Fonzy Edwin (born January 22, 1933, married Darlene Wise). *Submitted by: Deborah Dobson Ivey, PO Box 704, Bowdon, GA 30108*

856. Moore Family

George Franklin (Pete) and Lois Irene Moore have been well-known and respected citizens of Carroll County all their lives. George, born and reared in Temple, Georgia, on September 9, 1909, the son of George T. (born April 13, 1877 - deceased July 27, 1944) and Annie Muse Moore (born April 11, 1877 - deceased December 25, 1961). Lois Timmons was born in Villa Rica, Georgia, on March 4, 1911, and reared in Carroll County.

The couple met at New Hope Church in Villa Rica and married on March 8, 1930. George worked as a farmer for several years. He then worked at Plywood Case Company in Carrollton in the lumber business and finished his career at Lockheed Aircraft Corporation in Marietta. Lois worked at Arrow Shirt Copmany in Bremen, Georgia, for many years and then became a homemaker.

The Moores moved to the City of Temple in 1945 and built a home on Sage Street. They became active members of the First Baptist Church of Temple and George served on the Board of Deacons and as chairman several times during his lifetime.

Moore family. Bill, Shirley, George, Lois, Linda

The couple had three children. (1) Billy F. Moore was born July 9, 1931, (2) Shirley Ann Moore born July 19, 1935 and (3) Linda Faye Moore born May 1, 1945. Billy worked in the building supply business his entire life and was owner of Temple Builders Supply. Shirley worked at The Citizens & Southern Bank in Atlanta and Crawford Door Company of Atlanta before starting her own family and becoming a homemaker. Linda has been working in the banking profession for thirty-eight years and is currently employed at Citizens Bank & Trust, Temple.

George passed away May 20,1986. Lois continues to live in the home they built in 1945 in Temple. Billy passed away October 7, 1998. Shirley (Padgett) is retired and lives in Roswell, Georgia. Linda (Willams) continues to reside in Temple. *Submitted by: Linda M. Williams, 255 Katie Street, Temple, GA 30179*

Sources: Personal knowledge and family members.

857. Moore Family of Carroll County

There have been Moores, Huddlestons and Cavenders living in Carroll County since the early 1830s. Visiting there to do family research is like coming home, it's almost déjà vu. I feel like I'm related to most of the people I meet; they are so kind and generous with their time and friendship.

Isaac Moore was born 1786 in Kent County, Delaware, the son of Isaac Moore (a Revolutionary War soldier) and Frankey whose last name is unknown. Isaac moved to Georgia before 1807 when he married Nancy Wyatt in Greene County. Nancy died in 1850 and Isaac in 1854 in Fayette County, Georgia. Their children were Mahaly, Sanford, Hilliard Judge, Elizabeth S., Hamilton K., Augustus, Norman, Cynthia, Jane, James, Amanda and Clara.

Hamilton K. was born 22 December 1821 in Greene County and was married first to Eliza A. Belcher 24 February 1842 in Fayette County. Their children were Augustus, Archibald, Mary Elizabeth, Rosie Jane, W.H., William, and Daniel, some of whom were born in Carroll County. Hamilton's second wife was Katherine L. Huddleston, no children. He died 22 September 1909 in Randolph County, Alabama.

Mary Elizabeth was born 8 December 1846 in Carroll County and married there 14 September 1870 to John Cimsey Huddleston. Both died in Fayette County, Georgia. Their children were Susan, Martha, John Calvin, Joseph S., Frances Missouri, Modest, Lorenzo Dow, Emily, James, Robert Hamilton, and T. Hugh. They are all buried in Fayette County.

Frances Missouri born 23 November 1876 in Randolph County, Alabama, and married 9 December 1894 to John Henry Nichols who was born 23 December 1874 and died 28 July 1924. Frances died 26 January 1938. Both died in Spalding County, Georgia, but are buried in Fayette County in the Brown Cemetery. Their children were Wade, Mose, Emily, Lorenza, Annie Lee, John Henry, Vera, Nettie Sue, Sara Inez, Mary Velma, Ruthie May, Carl, Thomas Watson. Ruth and Watson still live in Griffin, Spalding County.

Mary Velma was born 29 November 1912 and died August 1986. She was married first in 1930 to Charlie Thomas Browning who was born 1896 and died 1959 in Alamance County, North Carolina. They had two daughters, Betty Joyce and Barbara Jean. Mary Velma was married second to Louis Gregory Caron of Salaparuta, Italy. They had two children, Mary Velma and Louis Gregory.

Barbara Jean married in Arlington, Virginia, to Richard Lee Schulz of Sioux City, Iowa, and they had one daughter Vicki Lee who married David Facemire of Sutton, West Virginia. They live in Springfield, Virginia, with their three children Phillip David, Krista Lee, and Kathryn Lynn. *Submitted by: Barbara Schulz, PO Box 1502, Oneco, FL 34264*

858. D.J. Moore Family

Joseph B. Moore Family at home in Plowshare, 1904

David Joseph Moore was born November 3, 1825, in North Carolina, died December 29, 1890, in Carroll County and buried at New Hope Methodist Church Cemetery. He married Nancy L. Wilson in Mecklenburg County, North Carolina, October 8, 1845. Nancy was born August 2, 1820 in North Carolina. She died October 22, 1887. She is buried in Beal Cemetery, Carroll County, Georgia. After Nancy's death, David married Mrs. M. Eliza Gable in 1889.

David and Nancy were in Georgia by 1848. From the 1850 U.S. census, Carroll County, David and Nancy and a daughter Nancy, age two years, were living in 10th District, 714 GMD. David was a farmer, a constable, a notary public, and was president of Carroll County Agricultural Association. He was a member of Carroll Lodge No. 68 F&AM. In 1860, he had 100 acres of land valued at $1000. Thirty-five acres were improved land. He had asses and mules, milk cows, working oxen, other cattle, swine and sheep. The farm produced Irish potatoes, sweet potatoes, wool, cotton, corn, wheat, oats, honey and molasses. In 1883, among those living on lower Jacksonville road were David and J.W. Moore. New Hope Methodist Protestant Church was on the same land lot.

In 1887, the New Hope Methodist Church Sunday School was reorganized with David as superintendent and Joseph as secretary.

Nancy and David J. Moore were the parents of three sons and two daughters. Nancy born 1848, John William (Billy) born 1852, Sara Frances (Fanny) born 1854, David born 1856, and Joseph Brown born April 14, 1861. Nancy and David died young and are not found in 1880 censuses. Fanny married Elisha A. Ragan. Billy married first to Sarah E. and second Emeline Jane Crawford. Joseph Brown Moore married Leonora (Lens) Buckelew on November 17, 1887, at the home of her parents, James L. and Carne Proctor Buckelew. Lena was born October 10, 1868, in Pike County, Georgia, and moved with her parents to Carroll County about 1887. They had one son, Olin Garland Moore, born January 23, 1889. When he was still a baby, Lena contracted a fever and died on September 2, 1889. She is buried at New Hope Methodist Church Cemetery. Olin married Lovie Beck and had four children, Mary Lee, Joe Beck, Rebecca Ann and Emily Sue.

J.B. married Georgia Ann Smith on January 26, 1890. Three children were born to this union, Minnie Lee, James Austin, and Nancy Leila. Joseph was a farmer, taught school at New Hope and had a store in the Plowshare community. In 1906 the family moved to Bowdon, Georgia, where there was an opportunity for the children to obtain a higher education. He opened a general merchandise store. His sons later joined him in business and they changed the name to J.B. Moore & Sons. Olin and James operated the store after Joseph's death. Joseph died January 7, 1934, at Bowdon. Georgia died July 23, 1942, in Atlanta. They are buried in the City Cemetery in Bowdon.

Minnie (1891-1938) married Homer Yeats and had one son, J. Hugh. Jim (1893-1966) married Essie Dye and had two sons, James and Bobby. Leila (1902-1996) married Fonzy Arrington and had three children, Mary Jo, Wallace and Edwin. Leila was a pianist, organist and music teacher in Bowdon. *Submitted by: Rebecca Moore Singletary, 1771 Pack Creek Road, Blue Ridge, GA 30513*

Sources: Marriage records from Mecklenburg County, North Carolina and Carroll County, Georgia; J.B. Moore Bible and family records; U.S. population and agricultural census; *Carroll Free Press.*

859. The William Kirkpatrick Moore Family

William Kirkpatrick Moore was the son of Thomas Moore (1843-1898). He married Hannah Davis (1841-1913), daughter of Johnathan (1802-1887) and Mary Davis (1814-1889). They had eight children: John Thomas, James Edward, Burma Alberta, Mildred Lavada, William Crawford, Martha Ann, Valentine Brittian, and Sally Fannie Moore.

William K. Moore enlisted as private in Company I, 41st Regiment, Georgia Infantry, March 4, 1862. Transferred to Company K, 56th Regiment, Georgia Infantry, May 12, 1862. Captured at Baker's Creek, Mississippi, on May 13, 1863. He was paroled at Fort Delaware, Delaware, on July 3, 1863; then received at City Point, Virginia, on July 6, 1863. Pension records show he was on post at Abbeville, South Carolina, at the close of the war.

William Kirkpatrick Moore

Hannah Davis Moore

William Crawford Moore (1874-1950) married Adna Eugenia Wootson Richards (1881-1920), daughter of Charles Thomas Richards (1842-1930) and Sara Elizabeth Tally (1843-1922). Charles fought and was wounded in the Battle of Resaca (May 14, 1864).

"Croff" and Adna had six children: Lawton (1901-1902), Alma Kate (1902-1971), Charlie Clarence (1904-1971), Earl Walter (1908-1968), Thelma Irene (1910-), and James (1920-1920). Alma never married and resided in Carroll County her entire life. Charlie married Ruth Crawford from Stephens County. They had one daughter, Marcia Ruth Moore (1938-1995). Earl married Ethel Zorn from Upson County. Thelma married Theron Edwin Hubbard (1912-1991) from Carroll County. They had three daughters: Martha Ann (1937-), Ethel Carole (1939-), and Saundra Rebecca (1942-).

Adna died in 1922, leaving Croff with four children. Croff's sister, Fannie Mae Copeland, lived next door to him with her three children. Fannie's husband had died and so they raised their children together with neither remarrying. They told of picnics on the creek bank, Fa-So-La singings, and dinner on the ground. Charlie and Earl took Manor Copeland, Fannie's son, to these events on their backs because Manor had trouble walking (polio). They worked hard and told of chopping cotton and planting crops. Later, Croff had tenants to help with the farming while he served as constable of Carroll County. I remember my sister Carole and I standing in front of the Carroll County Coruthouse for his reelection. This was in the 1940s. He carried a gun wrapped in a white handkerchief in his back pocket — I'm sure to fulfill his duties on his job. He and our Aunt Alma would come to town and take us for a ride on Sunday afternoon.

Charles Thomas and Sara Elizabeth Tally Richards

Thelma and Theron Hubbard have three children. Martha Ann married Henry C. Haley (1935). They have three children. Christine (1961) married first Waymon Everett Ragan (1961). They have two children: Waymon Corey (1984) and Bennett Keith (1988). Her second marriages was to David Joel Fisher (1962). They have two children: David Joel (1995) and Haley Joy (1997). Second child, Nathaniel Jay (1964) is unmarried, and Matthew Calvin (1966) is married to Elizabeth Hunt (1973). They have one son, Matthew Jacob (1999).

Ethel Carole married Reese Denney Reeves (1938). They have three sons. Tony Reese Reeves (1958) married Sara Joyce Entrekin (1959). He served as sheriff of Carroll County from 1996-2001. They have two sons: Justin Tyler (1988) and Jacob Carson (1995). Second son, Timothy Scott (1960) married Lisa Gurley (1963). They later divorced. They have one son, Brandon Scott (1990). Their third son, Russell Edwin (1964) is unmarried.

William Crawford "Croff" and Adna Eugenia Wootson Richards Moore

Sandra Rebecca married Johnathan Andrew Harper (1942). They have three children. Steven Andrew (1964) married Rita Cook. Their children are: Lisa May (1984) and Shane Allen (1986). Second child, Rebecca Lynn (1966), married Curtis Wayne Swindle (1965). They have three boys: Benjamin Curtis (1993), Andrew Garrett (1996), and Zachary Wayne (2001). Third child, Patricia Ann (1968) married Jed Hughes (1968). They have two daughters: Sidney Ann (1998) and Meagan Lynn (2000). Saundra's second marriage was to Phil Nichols (1945). They have one son, David Phil (1985). *Submitted by: Martha Ann Hubbard Haley, (granddaughter), 1455 Boone Ford Road, Calhoun, GA 30701.*

Sources: Family Bible, *Shadinger Family* book, 1999 edition.

860. Moore - Beck Family

The Olin Garland Moore Family began March 11, 1920, the day he married Lovie Vesmal Beck in Bowdon, Georgia. They bought the Masonic Property at 311 Weedowee Street across from the Methodist Church, built a house and lived there until their deaths, Olin, August 11, 1945 and Lovie, March 12, 1996. They had four children: Mary Lee (first to Oley N. Smith, second Sylvan Edwards), Joe Beck (Evelyn Cowart), Rebecca Ann (Willie T. Singletary), and Emily Sue (Alfred G. Smith).

Olin, son of Joseph Brown and Lena Buckelew Moore, was born January 23, 1889 in Plowshare, four miles west of Carrollton. Lena died when Olin was seven months old. Joseph married Georgia Ann Smith on January 26, 1890. Olin joined Beulah Baptist Church at age fifteen and moved to Bowdon with his family in 1906. He was one of seventeen who graduated from Bowdon College, May 26, 1910. Olin was a member of the Bowdon Band, Bowdon Masonic Lodge, Yaarab Temple of Atlanta, American Legion and served on the Bowdon School Board. He was a sergeant in the United States Army during World War I. He was involved in the mercantile business practically all of his life with his father and half-brother, James A. Moore.

After Joseph's death, the business name was changed to J.B. Moore Sons. They continued to provide the needs of the community — overalls, shoes, coffee, flour, sugar, nails, furniture, rugs, ice cold drinks or cold water and a friendly atmosphere. The potbellied stove in the back was a gathering place. On Saturday nights they often stayed open until after the last picture show for customers to pick up their purchases.

Wednesday afternoons in the summer were special to Olin. The stores were closed and usually that meant making homemade banana ice cream, his favorite, and then pineapple, because that was Lovie's favorite. Those at the family gatherings enjoyed both.

Lovie was born January 23, 1895, in Carroll County to Isaiah Houston Price Beck and Mary Ida Jeter Beck. Her early school years were in a one-room schoolhouse with her father as the teacher. She told of riding to school in the buggy with him. One time she fell from the buggy as they crossed a flooded bridge. She was saved from drowning by her coat catching on a nail. She later attended school in Burwell and Bowdon. She became a member of Bowdon Methodist Church in 1905 and was active in all areas of the church. Lovie became a member of Order of Eastern Star, Bowdon Chapter 239 in 1925; she was an emeritus member of Bowdon Chapter 468. During World War II she was a Red Cross volunteer, rolling bandages and working at the blood bank. "Miss Lovie," as she was affectionately known, still found time to be a homemaker, PTA member and giving a helping hand to any one who needed it. After Olin's death, she and her son, Joe, continued to run J.B. Moore Sons.

Olin and Lovie Moore about 1940

She touched the lives of many in and around the Bowdon area. After retiring from the store, she continued to be interested and active in the church. In later years, she would spend her time working with flowers, reading, or rocking on her front porch and visiting with friends at her home. And she still loved to eat pineapple ice cream. *Submitted by: Emily Moore Smith, 2007 Bertie St., Greensboro, NC 27403*

Sources: *"The March of Time"* by V.D. Whatley, Beck Family Bible, Moore Family Bible, and Army Discharge Paper

861. Morgan Family

Alford "Alfie" Isaac Morgan spent several of his boyhood years in Carroll County, Georgia. He was born in the Acworth, Georgia area. In 1890 when he was two years old, his mother, Viney Armindy Elliott Morgan, died. He and his baby sister were taken by their father to live in the home of their Morgan grandparents. His grandparents, Isaac A. and Mouurning Huey Morgan, were living in Coweta County, Georgia, at that time.

In 1891, "Alfie's" father, Columbus "Lum" Morgan, married Etta Tinny of Coweta County. Before 1900, "Lum" moved his family to the Lowell District of Carroll County. The grandfather, Isaac, also moved to Lowell.

"Alfie" Morgan operated a water mill to grind corn and wheat in the Lowell District in the 1920s. He married Victoria "Vickie" Walker and

Mill operated by Alford Isaac Morgan

they had four boys, Lewie, Charlie, Hulet, and Marvin, and one girl Mendie Morgan White. His oldest sons, Lewie Morgan, was mayor of Whitesburg at one time.

Descendants of "Alfie" and "Vickie" Morgan are currently living in Carroll County, grandchildren, great-grandchildren, and their daughter Mendie. *Submitted by: Nalda Weaver, 31 Spruill Creek Lane, Temple, GA 30179*

862. Morgan Family of Shady Grove in Carroll County

My dad was Charlie Clifton Morgan, born July 12, 1886, near Shady Grove Baptist Church. His parents were William R. (Billy) Morgan and Martha James (Jimmie) Carter Morgan. Granddad was born February 20, 1861, and Grandmother was born February 19, 1863. Their birthdays were only one day apart. I never knew my grandmother. She died about six months before I was born. Granddad died when I was twelve years old. Their picture is beside the old car in the photo. Notice both of their hats on the hood of the car.

William R. and Martha James Carter Morgan

My grandparents had six children, three of whom died very young. The three who grew to adulthood were Jesse H. Morgan; Charlie Clifton Morgan (my dad); and Robert Lewellyn Morgan. I remember all three of them very well. We never called Jesse "Uncle"; we called him "Big Jesse." He was a country gentleman, if I ever met one. I loved to hear him talk at get-togethers with family. Uncle Robert was a very distinguished person and very articulate in his speech. He lived on Bethany Road and at the time was a farmer. He also ran a grocery story and gas pump next to his house. They did not attend the store, but when someone wanted to make a purchase, they rang the bell and one of them would come out and help them. What I can pass along to my children and grandchildren is that my dad was the finest Christian man I ever met. My granddad was a part-time minister at the now defunct Black Gum Christian Church, near Sand Hill, later to become Bethany Christian Church on Highway 61, near the triangle.

My grandparents are buried at Jordan Cemetery along with Big Jesse and his two wives. Uncle Robert is buried at Bethany Church Cemetery. My dad and mother are buried in the Masonic section of Westview Cemetery in Atlanta, Georgia.

After World War I, in the early 1920s, Mother and Dad came to Atlanta to live. Daddy was in the poultry and egg business for most of his active life in Atlanta. My brother Charles was born in 1924 and I was born in 1931, in the heart of the great depression.

My brother and I are both natives of Atlanta. You don't meet too many of them nowadays. Today, I live less than twenty miles from where I was born and about thirty miles from where my parents were born.

My grandmother was Martha James (Jimmie) Carter Morgan, her granddad was Thomas Carter. Thomas also had three brothers, Richard, Dan, and Charles. All of the Carter brothers were first cousins to the mother of Gen. Robert E. Lee, Ann Hill Carter Lee, of Shirley Plantation in Virginia. *Submitted by: Bob Morgan, 4005 Pittman Road, College Park, GA 30349-1438*

863. The Morgan Sisters

Susan and Charlotte, daughters of Lewie and Mabel Rooks Morgan, were born in Carroll County, Georgia. They attended and graduated from Whitesburg High School, Susan in 1952 and Charlotte in 1957. Their father Lewie Morgan was a trustee of Whitesburg High School in the late 1940s and early 1950s. He was a deacon at Whitesburg Christian Church,a councilman for several years, and mayor for one year.

Susan and Charlotte's Morgan family line was in Carroll County before 1900, through their great-great-grandfather Isaac A. Morgan. Their great-grandfather Columbus "Lum" Morgan and their grandfather Alford "Alfie" Isaac Morgan all lived for many years in Carroll County. The grandfather "Alfie" Morgan operated a water mill in the Lowell District of Carroll County in the 1920s.

Susan and Charlotte's Rooks family line, through their mother, was in Carroll County before 1830, dating back to William Rooks Sr., who drew in the land Lottery of 1827. His son, William Rooks Jr. served as a road commissioner and Justice of the Peace in Carroll County. Susan and Charlotte's great-great-grandfather was James Madison Rooks. He raised a large family in Carroll County. One of his sons was George Washington Rooks, the great-grandfather of Susan and Charlotte. He was better known as "Uncle Bob." One of Uncle Bob's sons, William Eugene "Gene" Rooks, was the grandfather of Susan and Charlotte.

Susan Morgan attended West Georgia College for a year after graduating from high school. She then moved to Atlanta, Georgia, and was employed in the statistician's office of Southern Bell. She married James Knight from Randolph County, Alabama. She had three children, James Jr., Barbara, and Pamela. James Jr. was born in Atlanta. Barbara and Pamela were both born in Carrollton. Susan's three children were all raised in Carroll County. She has five grandchildren, Jason, Larissa, and Jessica Davis, Caan and Anna McGuire.

Susan married Clarence E. "Gene" Gatlin in 1974, and in the 1980s moved to Cobb county, Georgia. She has served as pianist and treasurer of the Leland Christian Church for several years.

Susan Morgan and Charlotte Morgan

Charlotte Morgan has lived all of her life, except two years during World War II, in Carroll County. She married J.H. Horsley. She has three children, Jay, Sheila, and Matthew "Matt" Horsley. She has two grandchildren, Samuel and Sarah Horsley. A third grandchild is due to arrive in the year 2001.

Charlotte married Wayne Posey in 1992. They live in Whitesburg. Wayne is a councilman in Whitesburg. She attended Mrs. Ike's Business School and was a Sunday School teacher at the Whitesburg Christian Chruch for several years. *Submitted by: Susan M. Gatlin, 132 Leland Drive, Mableton, GA 30126*

864. Bob and Derah Morgan Family and the Descendants of James Morgan, the Ironmaster

The name Morgan is an ancient one that appears as early as the 4th century in the country of Wales. The legends of King Arthur are based in Wales and tell of a time when after a defeat with a local chieftain, Arthur removed his Queen to a place of safety on the coast of Wales, a place called Glamorganshire. The Queen's child, Arthur's youngest son, was born there and named Morgan, meaning "born by the sea."

Shown in the family picture are Bob and Derah Morgan and their young family. From left, Roger Morgan, Bob Morgan with Cleo, and Derah Morgan, James Horry Morgan (1900-1942). The baby is the grandfather of James Patrick "Jimmy" Morgan, who is the son of Bobby Morgan (1923-1996), who was the fourth generation of this Morgan family to live in Carroll County, Georgia.

The story of our Morgan ancestors begins in 1660 in Radnor, Wales, just north of Glamorganshire, with James and Jane Morgan who were staunch Quakers. The Morgans were suffering the penalties of double taxes and other types of persecution for their religion. James and Jame Morgan had several children, Thomas, Margaret, Evan, James, John, and David. James, who was born circa 1640, was our ancestor. James Morgan had a son named Cadwalader Morgan who married Jane Gryffth-Rhys. Cadwalader and Jane Morgan made their home in Penlyn Parish, Pennellyn, Wales.

Cadwalader Morgan decided to accept William Penn's offer of a safe haven for Quakers in the new world of America. So in 1683 Cadwalader and his wife and several children sailed on the *Morning Star* to America. Cadwalader had his certificate of removal, the papers required by the Quakers when removing from one place to another. They traveled with the Hugh Roberts Party.

Cadwalader made a new home for his family in the province west of the Delaware River called Pennsylvania. After his home was established, Cadwalader wrote to his family in Wales that

Roger Jackson Morgan, Bob Morgan with Cleo, Derah Morgan holding baby.

they should come to America, too. In 1691, Cadwalader's father and grandparents made this journey. However, James and Jane Morgan were quite old by this time. They journey was too hard for them and both died before the ship reached America. James and Jane were buried at sea at the head of the Bay of Bohemia off the western shore of Maryland. Cadwalader's father, who had also traveled on this journey with his parents, prayed for their souls at their burial at sea. James himself was a clergyman. After arriving in America, James Morgan purchased 450 acres of good land in Delaware County, Pennsylvania. James Morgan, Cadwalader's father, died 8 June 1751.

Cadwalader Morgan had three sons — James, Morgan, and John Morgan. John Morgan was born in Radnor Township in Bucks County, Pennsylvania. He married Sarah Evans who was the daughter of Evan Evans. They lived in Richland Township in Bucks County, Pennsylvania. This family would have a number of children who would make their mark in history in a variety of interesting ways.

First was Thomas Morgan, who was born about 1680 and died 1778 in Savannah, Georgia. Thomas married Rebecca Alexander, the daughter of Martin and Susan Alexander of Maryland. Thomas and Rebecca were the parents of the famous American Revolutionary War heroine Nancy Hart who was born as Ann Nancy Morgan circa 1744. Nancy Morgan married Benjamin Hart, a Revolutionary War soldier, and they would have six sons and two daughters.

Nancy Hart is remembered for her zealous love of liberty and how she would do anything to help "the Liberty Boys." On one hand, she might be seating them at her dinner table feeding them venison, hoecakes, and honeycombs she's gathered from the woods. Or Nancy might be sending out her daughter to blow the conch shell like a trumpet to warn of Tories approaching. Nancy was a sharpshooter, but was just as likely to fling ladles full of boiling soap into the faces of Tories. It is said that she fought alongside her husband in the Battle of Kettle Creek.

When Nancy and her husband received bounty land after the Revolutionary War in Elbert County, Georgia, the place they settled was given the name of War Woman' Creek in her honor. White's *Historical Collections of Georgia* (1854) has preserved many wonderful tales of Nancy Hart. A Nancy Hart State Park was established in Georgia in 1931.

Nancy Morgan Hart's sister, Sarah Morgan, also took her place in history by marrying Squire Boone in 1720 and becoming the mother of Daniel Boone. George Boone had come from Exeter, England, in 1717 with eleven children, Squire Boone being one of the grown children. Daniel Boone was born 28 October 1734. When Daniel Boone was about sixteen years old, the family moved form Pennsylvania to North Carolina. Daniel Boone became one of America's most famous frontiersmen and trailblazers into the wilderness.

The second son of John Morgan and Sarah Evans Morgan was our ancestor, James Morgan, who became known as "The Ironmaster of Durham Furnace." James Morgan settled in Durham Township on Plat #30 in Bucks County, Pennsylvania, in 1727. James Morgan married Eleanor Pawling, the daughter of Henry Pawling, who was of Dutch ancestry. James Morgan started out in Durham the year that the famous Durham Furnace began its operation.

Bob and Derah Morgan home place on Whooping Creek Church Road.

He would be a part of the history of Durham Furnace over the next half century. Eleanor Morgan died 12 December 1764.

James Morgan began as a charcoal burner but later became the superintendent and the owner of Durham Furnace. There were three furnaces at Durham and another across the Delaware River. The Durham Furance was a manufacturer of cast iron stoves and was especially known for their stove plates with artistic embellishments. One of their most popular stove plates was the Adam and Eve. This stove plate had the serpent and the apple tree along with Adam and Eve in the scroll work design of the door to the stove.

Cast iron stoves were once an important feature,and often the central focus, in the home. So, it became important for the stoves to have some kind of decorative theme about them. There was also a famous 1774 Durham Furnace stove door pattern which depicted "The Liberty Boys." James Morgan had become a co-owner with George Taylor and James Logan in 1741, and by 1772 he owned Plat #26 and 191 acres of the Durham Furnace. James Morgan gained his fame as the Ironmaster of Durham Furnace.

Bobby Morgan at little log cabin playhouse.

James Morgan and his wife Eleanor Pawling had six children. Their two daughters were Olivia and Sarah, and four sons who would distinguish themselves during the time of the American Revolution. One of these sons was General Daniel Morgan (1736-1802) who was born on Plat #30 Durham Township (*History of Bucks County, Pennsylvania* by Davis Vol. 11, page 153). Daniel Morgan was made a brigadier general and won a brilliant victory in the American Revolution against Cornwallis at Tarleton at Cowpens. He was married to Abigail Bailey.

Another son of James and Eleanor was Abel Morgan, who was a surgeon in the Pennsylvania Militia during the American Revolution. During a great epidemic in Philadelphia after the war, he removed his family to safety outside the city, but he returned to try to help stamp out the epidemic. Unfortunately, Dr. Abel Morgan fell ill himself and died.

Brothers to Daniel and Abel were Mordecai Morgan, James Morgan and Samuel Morgan who were lumbermen in Pennsylvania. They bought land for timber rights and operated sawmills in Wayne and Susquehanna counties in northeastern Pennsylvania. Samuel Morgan born circa 1740 is the brother who is our ancestor.

Samuel served in the America Revolution in Captain Benjamin Weatherby's Company under the regimental command of Col. Oliver Spencer. He served three years and eight months, according to the payroll accounts. Samuel served as a quartermaster and was in charge of wagon teams delivering supplies to the troops. He was present at the battles of Valley Forge, Kings' Ferry, Hackensack, and Camp Croton River, among others.

Samuel Morgan married Charity Van Sant on 20 May 1762 in Bucks County, Pennsylvania, and they had ten children. They moved to York County, South Carolina, for a few years and appear in the 1790 census there. They later migrated into Georgia where Samuel's first recorded deed is in Elbert County in 1793. At that time, the Morgans had nine children. By 1800, they were in Franklin County, Georgia. Samuel Morgan Sr.'s will is recorded in Habersham County, Georgia, 8 February 1833.

Cleopatra Morgan

Samuel and Charity Van Sant Morgan had three sons: Samuel Jr. was born 1779; John born 1784; and Thomas born 1787. Samuel had another son with a second wife, Nancy Hill, and his name was Jonathan, born 1801. In 1834 Samuel Morgan Jr. moved his family to Benton (now Calhoun) County, Alabama and became one of the first families of the Piedmont area. Samuel Jr. married Eleanor Garrison, and this would be only one of many marriages between Morgans and Garrisons. Thomas Morgan had a son named William who was born in 1822, not to be confused with our William born in 1819. Thomas died in Chatooga, Georgia, in 1852. Jonathan Morgan had five wives and fifteen children, but only one child — John Hill Morgan — lived to adulthood.

It is wise to note that there are no less than twenty-five men named William H. Morgan in the same time period and place as our own ancestor, William H. Morgan. This has required a lot of untangling. The research has gone on for almost forty years. For more on these twenty-five William H. Morgans, refer to the definitive work on *Morgans* by Cunyus at the Georgia Archives.

The Daniel Morgan who appears in Franklin County, Georgia, may be connected to Samuel Morgan and his sons, John and Thomas. It is our belief that this Daniel is either the grandson or a nephew to our Samuel. We do not know if Samuel's brother Daniel (the brigadier general) had a son by this name. Or, it is possible that one of the other Morgan brothers may have named a son for their brother, Daniel.

Caroline Hollingsworth

Daniel Morgan Jr. and wife Deborah pay 650 pounds for 300 acres on Eastonolle Creek on 8 August 1787. Daniel Morgan is on the muser roll of the Georgia Militia Dragoons in Greene County, Georgia, from 1 December to 31 December of 1794. John Morgan and wife Betsy (Stiles) pay 60 pounds for 287 1/2 acres on Eastonolle Creek 4 August 1789. Both parcels of land were purchased from John Smith. Daniel Morgan Sr. and wife Patience deed land to Daniel Morgan Jr. and wife Deborah in 1811. Daniel Morgan Sr. and wife Patience deed land to Zebulon Garrison and wife Rebeckah in 1803. John Morgan leaves a will in Oglethorpe County, Georgia, mentioning wife Elizabeth (Betsy Stiles), daughter Jincy, brother Thomas. Mentions his worthy friend Thomas Lumpkin, William Morgan, Samuel Tate, and Jesse Morgan. The will is probated 18 May 1797.

Our ancestor is William H. Morgan who was born in 1819 and is believed to be the son of Daniel Morgan Jr. and his wife Deborah, and possibly the grandson of John Morgan and his wife Betsy Stiles. In the Oglethorpe County, Georgia, census of 1820, the only Morgan family is Daniel Morgan. He shows three males under ten, one male 26-45, two females 10-16, and one female 26-45. Daniel appears again in the 1830 census of Oglethorpe County, Georgia. He shows one male under five, two males 10-15, one male 15-20, one male 40-50, one female 5-10, two females 20-30, one female 40-50, three slaves (two males, one female). Daniel disappears from the census by 1840. Our William H. Morgan is living in Greene County, Georgia, by 1850 census and by 1852, he has purchased Land Lot #50 in the 6th District from Ambrose Green in Carroll County, Georgia. The deed states he is of Oglethorpe County, Georgia.

We have never found the marriage record of our William H. Morgan. However, according to the 1860 census his wife's name is Susan. We believe she might be Susan Garrison since a Garrison family is living next door to them in Carroll County in 1860. The census shows household #137 as William Garrison age 75, born in South Carolina, wife Mary age 68, born in Delaware, Prudence age 35 born Delaware, John G., age 24 born Delaware. These could be Susan's parents. Household #138 is William Garrison, age 30 male, Charlotte age 22, Martha J. age 2, and James H., age 1 month. This could be the household of Susan's brother. This certainly points to the same route that the Samuel Morgan family took in their migration southward. Many of the Morgan brothers and sisters did marry Garrisons. To see how many, refer to *Morgans* by Cunyus.

William H. Morgan was the father of John Thomas Morgan and we believe it is significant that this child could be named for his grandfather and his uncle. John Thomas Morgan's interesting story is told under the heading of William H. Morgan. John Thomas Morgan was the father of James Robert "Bob" Morgan who was born 27 March 1873 in Carroll County, Georgia. Bob Morgan's mother was Mary Elizabeth (surname unknown).

Mary Elizabeth Morgan remains another family mystery. John Thomas apparently married her away from Carroll County, possibly even very far away. The only clue to her surname is that one of her sons was named Paul Askew Morgan. We cannot account for this name on the Morgan side of the family. Perhaps Paul Askew was Mary Elizabeth's father's name. Bob Morgan named a daughter after his mother, Mary Elizabeth Morgan.

John Thomas Morgan had a home place which was in the deep woods off Lowell Road and across the road from the Fred Hollingsworth property. Fred Hollingsworth (who married Mary Elizabeth's granddaughter, Cleo Morgan, in 1919) used to say that John Thomas Morgan's wife in her younger years had been an actress on the stage. She was very petite and quite pretty. Unfortunately, she was involved in a horse and buggy accident which crippled her later in life. We believe Mary Elizabeth Morgan was buried on the old Morgan home place, through her grave has never been found. We believe that she died about 1890.

Where the Lowell Road dead-ends into the Roopville Road, there sits an old home place facing the Lowell Road which was built shortly after the Civil War. This is the home place of Rev. Joel Colley Burnham. This is where young

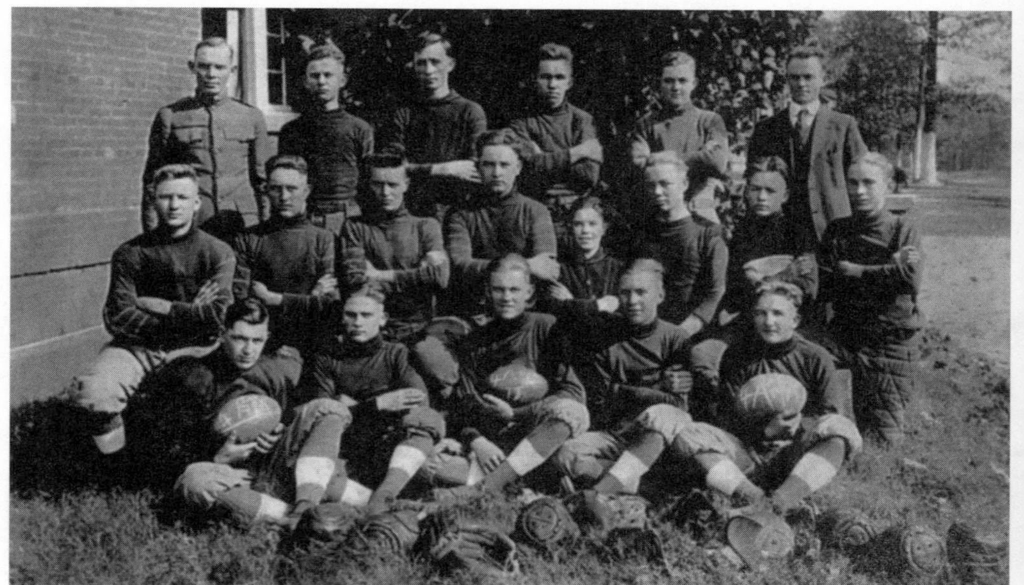

A & M football team, about 1917

Paul Askew Morgan

Bob Morgan would go a courtin' in the late 1890's to call on a pretty brunette with sky blue eyes named Derah Idella Burnham.

Rev. J.C. Burnham had three pretty daughters, Viola, Derah, and Winnie. But it was Derah that caught young Bob Morgan's fancy. And it didn't take Derah Burnham long to know that Bob Morgan was going to be the great love of her life. Anytime Bob was around, Derah used to say she would wear a bachelor's button (wildflower) on her collar, which was the custom then of how to let a boy know that you liked him.

Bob Morgan loved Derah, too, but in the 1890s, young men of Carroll County were all headed out to Texas. Bob Morgan wanted to visit Texas to see if this were a place where he would want to take a young wife and rear a family. So many people were leaving Carroll County for Texas that weekly reports were sent back to Carroll County of everything going on out there. The newspaper even gave reports on what the water tasted like.

Bob Morgan left for Texas, but with the promise to Derah that he would be back to marry her. He told her to brush her hair a hundred strokes every night for he loved her beautiful shining brunette hair. He said that before she reached about 50,000 strokes, he'd be back. And then he said they would decide if they wanted to make their home in Carroll County or out West. So Bob left on horseback, headed west for Texas.

Time went by and there was no word from Bob Morgan. Derah waited faithfully. But Derah's father was getting rather impatient over this situation. Derah was one of the prettiest girls in the county and many young men were wanting to call on her. Still, Derah would not hear of it! She was keeping her hopes high and waiting for Bob Morgan to return. She brushed her hair a hundred strokes every night at bedtime and would cry softly into her pillow, hoping for Bob Morgan to return.

Derah's family was not so sure if Bob were ever coming back, and they tried to persuade her to give up her foolish notion of waiting for him. They would tell her that Bob was a wild-blue-yonder kind of boy, and they would not likely see him again. Derah knew he had the "wild blue yonder in him" and in fact, that's exactly why she loved him. And Derah would not give up.

Sure enough, one fine day about two years after he'd left, Bob Morgan came riding back up the road to Derah's house. He had come back to marry her after all. When Bob returned, he told Derah that she'd never have to brush her hair the hundred strokes at bedtime again because from now on, he was going to brush that beautiful hair for her. It was a loving bedtime ritual they kept for the rest of their married life.

Bob and Derah Morgan married on 12 August 1895. Bob was skilled as a carpenter and his specialty was building bridges. He built many of the old wooden bridges in Carroll County. But he also could build houses. So he put his carpentry talents to work and built Derah a beautiful home place in the style popular in the late nineteenth century. The old farmhouse has seen the turn of two centuries and it stands today in 2001 as beautiful as it did in 1895.

The house was a white frame with wide porches about halfway around the house. It was built high on the hill on the Whooping Creek Church Road in front of the Lowell Road which it faced across a green pasture. For many years, the house has been the home of Coach Howard and Mrs. (Carol) Cleveland.

The old cotton storehouse still stands in the barnyard though the huge barn has been gone many years. There also used to be a smokehouse, chicken coop, hog pen, and a little log cabin playhouse. The same oak trees shade the front of the house as they did in generations past. It was just a little walking distance from the Morgan home place to the Burnham home place down the hill. Derah would walk that little distance a million times in the next sixty years of her life. Bob Morgan would come to know that Derah loved this little patch of earth in Carroll County, and she was never going to leave it.

Mary Elizabeth Morgan Taylor

Derah had about a million different kinds of flowers planted. How could she ever leave and not see her flowers bloom? Morning glories in the morning, four-o'clock's in the afternoon, moonflower vines in the evening. There were pansies that she called "kiss-me-over-the-graden-gate," Angel's trumpets, petunias and sweetpeas. This love of flowers and landscaping would pass down to Derah's grandson, Bobby Morgan, and to her great-grandson, James Patrick "Jim" Morgan. Derah was as devoted to her parents as she was to her flowers, and she never wanted to be too far away from them.

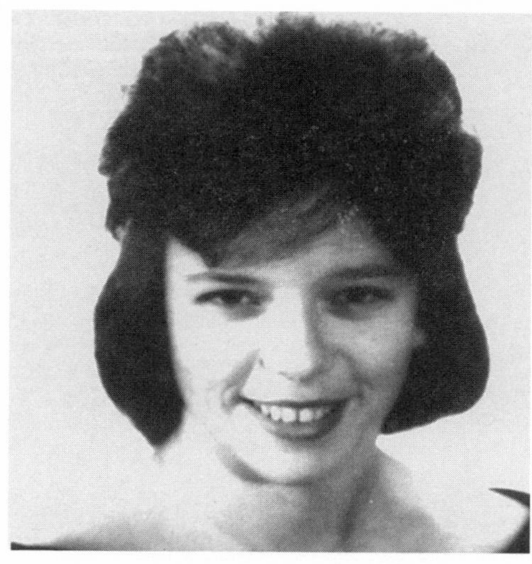

Linda Taylor League

Beginnig about 1890, there was a mass migration of people from Carroll County, not only to Texas but also to Cullman, Alabama. Deeds show that Bob Morgan purchased some land in Cullman County, but Bob and Derah never moved out there. Bob's father, John Thomas, with his second wife Sallie Shadinger Burden, moved to Cullman. They had married 28 February 1892. All of Bob's brothers and sisters (John, Billie, Ella, Emma, Anna, and Mattie) except Charlie went to Cullman; Charlie went to Oklahoma. But Bob never talked Derah into leaving home. They stayed in Carroll County.

Bob and Derah Morgan had six children. Roger Jackson Morgan was the oldest child. He would grow up, a handsome young man, but tragically died in his early twenties when a typhoid epidemic swept over the county. He had married Elizabeth Huggins 19 November 1913 and died 12 July 1914. So, this was the first son that Derah lost.

The next child born to Bob and Derah Morgan was a daughter, Cleopatra, born 28 November 1898. She would grow up to be quite a beautiful young lady, tiny and petite. Cleo joined the Oak Grove Baptist Churh 4 August 1914. She married James Frederick "Fred" Hollingsworth on 14 December 1919. Fred Hollingsworth was born 27 February 1896 and was a descendant of Levi Hollingsworth of Hollingsworth's Ferry fame.

The Hollingsworths built a home on the Lowell Road and their property became known as Holly Hill Farms. Fred and Cleo Hollingsworth had a son born 29 January 1922 who died as an infant. They then had one daughter, Sarah Caroline, who was born 31 March 1926. Fred Hollingsworth died on 10 July 1980 and was buried at New Lebanon Church Cemetery. Cleo Hollingsworth died 17 August 1981 and was buried beside him.

The next child born to Bob and Derah Morgan was James Horry born on 17 May 1901 and died 2 October 1942. Horry Morgan grew up on the farm on Whooping Creek Church Road and attended the 4th Distict A&M School. He played on the A&M football team of about 1915-17. The young men as pictured left to right are: Causey, center; Chambers, left guard; Combs, left tackle; Brown, right guard; Ware, right tackle; Pritchett, end; Horry Morgan, half back; Davis, quarterback; Barr, fullback; Holloway; Harris; Patridge; Harman; Causey; White.

But Horry's greatest passion was baseball. It was baseball that led him to meeting the young lady he would marry in 1921 — Trixie Patrick of Cullman, Alabama. Trixie and Horry Morgan would have two children: Melba Angeline Morgan born 28 May 1922, married John T. Robinson, died 23 January 1996; and James Robert Morgan born 14 April 1923, married Elizabeth "Betty" Louise Smith, died 25 March 1996.

Valerie League

The fourth child of Bob and Derah Morgan was Paul Askew Morgan born 22 November 1903 and died 3 November 1912. Little Paul's death was so tragic and Derah would say in later years it was the hardest loss of all. Some older boys from down the road had come up to play with the Morgan boys. They took the shotgun from where it hung over the mantle. Not knowing it was loaded, they fired at little Paul, killing him instantly there in the house. He was almost eight years old when he died, and he was buried at Emmaus Church. Derah kept his portrait, as you see here, in her bedroom.

The fifth child born to Bob and Derah Morgan was Mary Elizabeth Morgan, born 26 May 1907 and died 1 April 1997. Mary Morgan married on 29 November 1943 to Hulett D. Taylor. They lived in Carroll County and Hulett Taylor worked for the City of Carrollton. The Taylors also had a farm on Hays Mill Road located where the newspaper office now stands. Maude and Talmadge Robinson were neighbors to the Taylors for many years. Mary and Hulett Taylor are both buried a Antioch Church Cemetery. Hulett Taylor was a veteran of World War II. There are three generations of their family pictured here: Mary Elizabeth Morgan Taylor and her daughter Linda Taylor League and Linda's daughter, Valerie Renee League.

The sixth child of Bob and Derah Morgan was Johnnie Thelma Morgan born 22 June 1909 and died 15 January 1974. Johnnie Morgan lived in Walterboro, South Carolina, most of her married life. Her mother, Derah Morgan, lived with her during her last years from about 1954 until 1958. Johnnie's husband, Bob Housworth, worked for many years as a projectionist in the movie theater of Walterboro. The Housworths were living in Fayetteville, North Carolina, at the time of Johnnie's death. Johnnie was buried in Live Oak Memorial Gardens in Charleston, South Carolina.

Johnnie had married Robert W. "Bob" Housworth on 8 January 1933. Bob was a veteran of World War II who flew "the Hump" over Burma. He survived two disastrous airplane crashes during the war. Bob is pictured in the background photo in his uniform in the picture of Johnnie Housworth holding their newborn daughter, Betty.

Bob was a Carroll County boy and had a brother named Tyler Housworth who also lived in Carrollton. Tyler's wife was Marcelle Toney. Johnnie and Bob Housworth's only child was Derah Elizabeth Housworth, who was born in 1943 and who married Oscar Levi Myers in South Carolina. Betty and Levi Myers had one daughter named Virginia Dean "Deannie" Myers. They later divorced, and Levi Myers died not long afterwards. Betty and Deannie Myers moved to Nashville, Tenenssee, and in 1988 Betty was working on her Ph.D. in English at Vanderbilt University.

When the dreaded Spanish flu epidemic swept over Carroll County in 1919, it took a heavy toll on the Morgan family. Bob Morgan died on January 14, 1919. The front page of the *Carrol County Times* reported that

> "a genuine wave of sorrow swept over this community when it was learned that genial Bob Morgan had succumbed to the flu."

He was laid to rest at Emmaus Church beside his sons. Derah would live until the ripe old age of eighty-five. Derah was a quilter and she would leave her family a legacy of many beautiful quilts that kept the memories of her lifetime in the materials worn by her family. "This star quilt has the shirt of Little Paul." Or "The Bear Claw quilt is made from Bob's coat that he wore when we married." Derah died on March 25, 1958, and was laid to rest beside her husband at Emmaus, the Church her father had founded.

Johnnie Morgan Housworth

There is no sweeter story than that of the great friendship that flourished between Derah Morgan and her daughter-in-law Trixie. Derah had a fear of the "magnetic pull of Cullman, Alabama" for that was where all the Morgans had migrated to in earlier years. There had been so many letters and visits from Bob's sisters and brothers asking him to join them there. And then, of all things in the world to happen, Derah's son, Horry, fell in love with a girl from Cullman, Alabama!

Derah knew that this would make the magnetic pull even greater. Now Trixie's family would want the young couple to settle in Cullman This turned out to be true. Trixie's family put on quite a campaign to get the young couple to move there. But Horry was the only son that Derah had left to manage the Morgan farm. What if Horry's wife pitched a fit to move to Cullman? But Trixie didn't and Trixie and Horry stayed in Carroll County so that Derah would continue to enjoy her home place.

At first Derah Morgan treated Trixie like royalty had come to visit, but Trixie wanted none of that. She loved living on the Morgan farm in Carroll County, and she wanted to do her share of the work. Trixie and Derah were the perfect complements to each other — Derah liked to churn the buttermilk and Trixie liked to milk to cow. Derah liked to hoe the garden and Trixie liked to cook the turnip greens. Trixie was an excellent cook having learned all the skills of her mama, Angie Patrick, and from cooking at Angie's boarding house dining room in Cullman for many years. Trixie liked to be in the kitchen and Derah liked to be out in the daylight. Both liked to put up the bounty of the harvest, and the shelves of the cellar were always gleaming gold, green, and red.

Trixie and Derah were like the old legend of the bivalve seashells "split aparts" perfectly matched. They would remain so throughout their lifetime. Even after Horry Morgan died, Trixie remained on the farm with Derah. They were really more like sisters than mother-and daughter-in-law. Derah's birthday was April 10th and Trixie's was April 11th. These have been terribly confused over the years in each other's obituaries and other papers, but these are the correct dates for each.

Horry Morgan had gone on a visit in 1919 to see his Burnham cousins in Cullman, Alabama, and they had gotten up a baseball game. The Patrick sisters, Trixie and Fanny, came out to watch the Hanceville boys play the Cullman boys. Trixie was always the world's greatest baseball fan. Trixie used to tell us about the way love struck her — it happened as she watched Horry slide into second base. "It was just something about that slide ... " she said, and he simply stole her heart away.

Years later, Trixie's granddaughter, Jan Robinson Bell, would write a fifty-page poem called *"Baseball Fever"* about Trixie and Horry's love story and their lifelong love of baseball: "Please pass the chicken and dumplings was really all the young man said/ Then it caught them by surprise/ When he met Trixie's eyes/ And he didn't really care she'd passed the bread."

Trixie Patrick was born 11 April 1902 in Morgan County, Alabama, the daughter of George Lonzo Patrick (1874-1935) and Mary Angeline Ryan Patrick (1876-1953). The Ryans and Patricks lived at a place called Ryan's Crossroads, and it so happened they were the only two families who did live there. So, naturally, the Ryan brothers and sisters married the Patrick brothers and sisters, and they had more double first cousins that we can calculate.

The Ryans were pure Irish, and Irish customs abounded in that family. The Patricks traced their ancestry back to the Scottish Highlands and the Lamont Clan. Whole books of genealogy have been published on both our Patrick and Ryan family trees. Our Ryan ancestry is published in *More Ryan Roots* by Mildred B. Stout (1994) and our Patrick genealogy is recorded in *Patrick in Retrospect* by Dr. Lee Wellington Patrick. Since our Cherokee Indian side of the family has not been published before, we present it here for this book.

Johnnie Morgan Housworth and Derah Elizabeth "Betty"

The Ryans migrated from Kentucky into northern Alabama with General Andrew Jackson when they went with him to fight the Creek Indians in 1814. They thought the land was so beautiful and vowed to return there after the Indian wars were over. The Ryans did return. John Ryan (1806-1885) was the first to settle in Morgan County, Alabama.

John's son, Cephas Monroe Ryan (1854-1938) married Sarah Elizabeth Brown (1855-1927) who was one-fourth Cherokee Indian. She was a member of the influential Brown family of Cherokees who were related to John Brown whose Cherokee name was Yau-mi-gung-ski or "Drowned by a Bear." We believe John and Sarah's father (James) were brothers. John Brown was one of three Cherokees in 1827 of the Chattanooga District to be elected to attend a constitutional convention of the Cherokee nation at New Echota in northwest Georgia. He was a signer of the constitution which was adopted the next year.

Derah Elizabeth "Betty" Housworth Myers

Cherokee Indians had first moved into Marshall County, Alabama, about 1785 and were hostile to whites then. The first white settler in Marshall County was John Gunter, for whom Guntersville, Alabama, is named. He was a Scotsman who came to the site of the bend in the Tennessee River near present day George Houston Bridge.

Here John Gunter found salt deposits. He established a trading post and most of his customers were Cherokee Indians. A Cherokee who was Chief of the Paint Clan brought his beautiful fifteen-year-old daughter to trade her for salt. Her Indian name was Geh-go-he-h but John Gunter changed her name to Katherine and married her. Katherine's father and John Gunter signed a treaty saying "As long as the grass grows and the waters flow, the Indians can have salt." Gunter enjoyed such good friendship with the Cherokees that soon more white men moved in to the area and intermarried with the Cherokees.

John Brown had come from Will's Path and moved his family into the area known as Creek Path, later called Brown's Valley, named after him. John's father was white and his mother was Cherokee. John had three different wives — Tsu-luh, Sarah Webber, and Wat-tee or Betsy.

John Brown's daughter Catherine was baptized 18 January 1818, and she devoted her life to Christian service. She was educated at the Indian mission at Brainerd, Tennessee. Catherine returned to Creek Path and served as a teacher and a missionary. General Andrew Jackson met Catherine on his trip through the area on his way to the Horsehoe and wrote in his journal that she was "a woman of Roman virtue." Catherine Brown gave up her missionary work at the age of twenty-three because of tuberculosis. She died 18 July 1823.

Virginia Dean "Deannie" Myers

Catherine's brother, Richard Brown, was another member of the family well acquainted with General Andrew Jackson. Richard Brown was a noted Cherokee warrior, gaining his fame by fighting Creek Indians and not white settlers. Richard was the one who went with General Jackson to fight the Creeks at Horsehoe Bend in 1814. Brown was made a captain of the Cherokees and then received the rank of colonel because of his superb fighting and leadership at the Battle of Horseshoe Bend.

General Jackson wrote glowing reports of Richard Brown to Governor William Blount of Tennessee. Col. Richard Brown was severely wounded at the Horseshoe, but did recover to return to his home at Creek Path. He died 3 February 1818. Many other members of the Brown family, including James Brown, fought with General Jackson at the great Battle of Horseshoe Bend and in New Orleans, too.

David Brown, another son of John Brown, was the scholar of the Brown family. In the early 1820s, David was one of six Indians from the Cherokee nation who was selected to study in a New England Seminary. He furthered his education in Andover, Massachusetts, where he studied Hebrew, Greek, and Divinity. David Brown married Rachel Lowery whose mother, Lucy Benge, was a half-sister to Sequoyah. Sequoyah's wife was Sally Benge.

James Horry and Trixie Morgan with Bobby and Melba, about 1928.

Sequoyah had been crippled early in life because of a hunting accident, and this had led to his being a silversmith and a deep thinker. Sequoyah happened to be visiting his relatives, the Browns, when he was working on his famous alphabet for the Cherokees. David Brown assisted him with his alphabet, and when it was completed, David Brown sent a copy of it to the Bureau of Indian Affairs in Washington, D.C. Consequently, Sequoyah gained international fame for his Cherokee Alphabet.

Chief George Lowery, Rachel's father, and David Brown were among the very first to master the new 86-syllable alphabet, and they translated the New Testament directly from the Greek to the Cherokee language. The Bible manuscript was completed on 27 September 1872, and was widely circulated among the Cherokees at Creek Path. David Brown died at Creek Path on 15 September 1829. Sequoyah never learned to read or to speak English.

James Horry "Shine" Morgan

About 1830, many of these Cherokees moved out of Brown's Valley to north Georgia in the area around Rome and Cedartown. This is also when our Brown family relocated there, and explains why Sarah Elizabeth Brown was born near Cedartown on 7 November 1855. She was one-fourth Cherokee Indian, the daughter of James and Frances Oden Brown. Sarah's sister, Polly Ann, married William Thomas Ryan, who was known as "Tinker Tom." He was a gunsmith and clock repair man.

So Sarah grew up near Cedartown, but by the time of her marriage, her family had moved back to Brown's Valley in Marshall County, Alabama. Sarah Elizabeth Brown married Cephas Monroe Ryan on 18 September 1873 at the home of Hezekiah Oden, who gave consent for the marriage. Sarah Elizabeth and Polly Ann Brown were descendants of Armocette and Angeline Brown.

The name Angeline has appeared every other generation in our family for over a hundred years. Our present generation has Angeline Mariam Ansari who was named for her grandmother, Melba Angeline Morgan Robinson, the daughter of Trixie Patrick and Horry Morgan. Melba was named for her grandmother, Mary Angeline Ryan Patrick. Sarah Elizabeth Brown Ryan died 8 March 1927 and is buried at Center Grove, Alabama. Her husband, Cephas Monroe Ryan, died in 1938.

The Cherokee chief George Lowery has a large grave monument at the Tahlequah Cemetery in Cherokee County, Oklahoma. He was born on the Tennesse River in 1770 and died 20 October 1852 in Oklahoma. Reading the history of this family is not complete without seeing the fantastic pictures of these Cherokee Indians — and the reader should look for these in books of Cherokee Indian history. The Browns and Lowerys were so influential among the Cherokees that there are many pictures of them in history books.

J. Horry Morgan was a prominent businessman who had many irons in the fire. Of course, there was the Morgan farm which he owned, and the farm was capably managed by Willie Son Carter from the 1920s on. Horry Morgan also owned a sawmill and bought up many timber rights. Again, Son Carter was his right-hand man. Then, there were just all kinds of wheeling and dealing that went on every day at the Crepe Myrtle Hotel, which used to be where CFB stands now across from the Court House. The businessmen of Carrollton gathered almost daily for lunch at the Crepe Myrtel Hotel, and this is where many important business transactions took place.

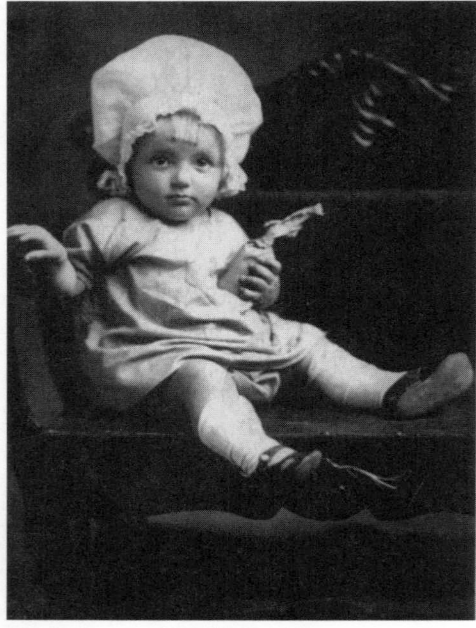

Melba Angeline Morgan

We suppose that now — nearly a hundred years later — it's time to confess that our grandfather, J. Horry Morgan, was the country's most famous moonshiner during the years of Prohibition. Yes, that's where he go this nickname of Shine Morgan. Everybody knew Shine Morgan, and he was quite a colorful character especially during the years of the Great Depression. There was a huge grand piano in the living room of the Morgan home place — that never played a note. Instead, it concealed a lot of mason jars full of moonshine. We now confess that nobody in the Morgan household even knew how to play the piano!

Trixie and Horry Morgan had two children, Melba and Bobby. Shine used to take them to town for ice cream in the 1930's, and Melba said that once the children of the town spotted Shine Morgan's car, they all squealed and ran after the car until it reached the ice cream shop on the square. He was liked the Pied Piper. The children knew that if they were standing outside the ice cream store Shine Morgan would buy ice cream for everybody. And he always did. It was a great treat for these children in the Great Depression. Shine Morgan had a heart as big as a Georgia watermelon on the Fourth of July and has been remembered for his generosity. He was always dressed smartly in the neatest of business suits and a hat of 1930s style as you see in the picture here.

When Horry Morgan's grandson, Jimmy Morgan, decided to build some new electronic carwashes in Carrollton in 1999, he was trying to come up with the perfect name for these businesses and asked for suggestions from his cousin, Jan Bell. Of all things, they came up with the name of "Shine" for the carwash, named after their grandfather, Shine Morgan. "Shine" car wash has been so successful that now there is a second carwash by Lake Carroll, and it even has an electronic light show at nighttime! Now you can see a picture of who the carwashes are named for — Shine Morgan.

Jimmy and his sister Pam Morgan Dematteis own and manage the many Amoco stations that dot Carroll and Douglas counties today. Betty Morgan has only recently retired from Morgan Oil and will probably tan our hides for bringing this family skeleton out of the closet. (It was in the closet with the secret stairway that led up to the storage room for all the mason jars!).

We have a funny story in our family of how Joe Dudley Patrick of Cullman, Trixie's brother's son, came to visit his cousin Bobby Morgan in the 1930's. As young boys he, Bobby, and Frank Searcy had gone out in the woods hunting somewhere around Ringer's Store. The boys had gotten separated, and Joe Patrick got lost and could not find his way back. Finally, he made it to some farmhouses where he told them he was staying with Horry Morgan. It was incredible that nobody knew who this was. Joe knew he couldn't be that far from Horry's home place. Many neighbors were asked, and no one had a clue who this was. Finally, Joe mentioned that Horry was also known as Shine Morgan. Suddenly, everybody knew exactly where to take this little lost boy! And Joe Patrick was safely returned to the Morgan home. Everybody knew Shine Morgan.

Melba and Bobby Morgan had a wonderful childhood growing up on the Morgan home place, and Bobby especially loved exploring the woods behind the home. Bobby discovered an old Indian village deep in those woods, and it was the remnants of what had been left behind of an old Creek Indian village when the Creeks had been removed from Georgia after Chief William McIntosh had sold the Creek lands. Throughout his boyhood, Bobby and his friends explored and excavated the village. They found a treasure trove of old arrowheads, clay pots, spears, beads, all kinds of Indian artifacts. In fact, it was such a fabulous collection that word of it spread far and wide.

One day a man appeared from The University of Florida asking to buy Bobby's collection to add to an Indian collection they were working on at the university. A deal was struck with the young boy and the man left with it, telling Bobby that someday he could view his collection as a part of a much bigger collection at The University of Florida. Our family has always meant to make a trip to see this Indian collection, but somehow time got away and we have never been there. Perhaps Jimmy's sons, Patrick and Michael Morgan, may get to make the trip someday and view their grandfather's wonderful boyhood collection of Creek Indian relics. Melba used to say it was utterly fantastic. She always regretted that Bobby had parted with it, but during the Great Depression, fifty dollars had sounded like a fortune to young Bobby. And that is now much Bobby had sold it for.

Melba and Bobby Morgan, about 1925

One of the things that Trixie and Horry Morgan are most remembered for in Carroll County is their fish camp on the Chattahoochee River. Though it was nothing fancy, it was a wonderful place that people enjoyed for recreation in the 1930s. People could fish on the Chattahoochee and then bring their catch of the day to the fish

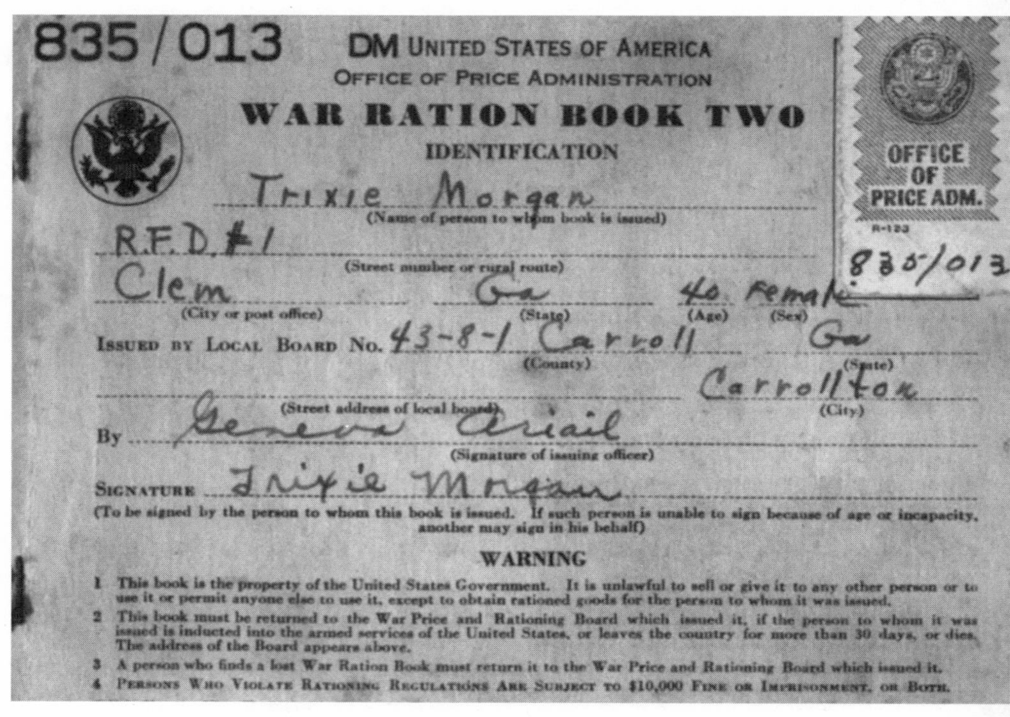

835/013 DM UNITED STATES OF AMERICA
OFFICE OF PRICE ADMINISTRATION

WAR RATION BOOK TWO

IDENTIFICATION

OFFICE OF PRICE ADM.

R-123

Trixie Morgan
(Name of person to whom book is issued)

R.F.D. #1
(Street number or rural route)

830/013

Clem ... Ga ... 40 ... Female
(City or post office) (State) (Age) (Sex)

ISSUED BY LOCAL BOARD No. 43-8-1 Carroll ... Ga
(County) (State)

... Carrollton
(Street address of local board) (City)

By Geneva Ariail
(Signature of issuing officer)

SIGNATURE Trixie Morgan
(To be signed by the person to whom this book is issued. If such person is unable to sign because of age or incapacity, another may sign in his behalf)

WARNING

1 This book is the property of the United States Government. It is unlawful to sell or give it to any other person or to use it or permit anyone else to use it, except to obtain rationed goods for the person to whom it was issued.

2 This book must be returned to the War Price and Rationing Board which issued it, if the person to whom it was issued is inducted into the armed services of the United States, or leaves the country for more than 30 days, or dies. The address of the Board appears above.

3 A person who finds a lost War Ration Book must return it to the War Price and Rationing Board which issued it.

4 PERSONS WHO VIOLATE RATIONING REGULATIONS ARE SUBJECT TO $10,000 FINE OR IMPRISONMENT, OR BOTH.

War Ration Book

George Harris, John Robinson, Bobby Morgan, PeeWee Lang, Frank Searcy.

camp. While they waited on the screened porch and listened to the honky-tonk music, the fish were cleaned and fried to golden perfection.

Miss Trixie ran the kitchen at the fish camp and became quite famous for her hush puppies. Jimmy Morgan has inherited the huge cast iron skillet and the secret Morgan hush puppy recipe that was once used at the fish camp. Both Melba and Bobby Morgan worked at the fish camp as teenagers. This was one of the first places that Melba Morgan got to know John Robinson, whom she would later marry. John was friends with Bobby before he had known Melba.

In the picture, you see some boys headed for the fish camp about 1938: from left to right are George Harris, John Robinson, Bobby Morgan, Pee Wee Lang (killed in World War II), and Frank Searcy. Another picture shows the fish camp in the background while Bobby Morgan shimmies up a tree with the help of John Robinson.

Bobby Morgan, U.S. Navy, World War II.

Trixie and Horry Morgan had been married for twenty-one years when Horry died of cancer. Trixie died at age ninety-three, outliving all her people. Trixie was an invalid with her heart for many years and lived with her daughter and son-in-law, Melba and John Robinson. Back in the 1950s, heart patients were put to bed and had to stay there — nothing like the cardiac rehabilitation programs of today. But Trixie still enjoyed her baseball games by way of the radio and television. Trixie was like a baseball encyclopedia and could remember everybody's batting average. All her grandsons enjoyed this!

Since Trixie was a shut-in for many years, she did enjoy friends and neighbors who came to visit her. She had lovely neighbors on Kramer Street in Carrollton, Libby Thomasson, Ellen Rose, Jinny Seaton, Miss Bert Cole, Bonnie Rose. Over the years a favorite visitor was Mrs. Hugh (Sallie Gladney) Johnson who was the visitor assigned to Trixie through the Tabernacle Baptist Church — Trixie adored her and so looked forward to her visits. Sally Gladney was "the prettiest girl in Carrollton" in her young days and she is still quite a beauty to us. Orea Lee Mays gave excellent companionship and care to Trixie and they enjoyed "their stories" together in the afternoon soap operas. "Like sands through her hour glass, So are the Days of Our Lives ... "

Dr. E.V. Patrick took care of Trixie for about half a century. We always wondered exactly how Dr. Pat and Trixie might be kin; he was the son of John Henry (was Willard but he changed it) Patrick of Butts County, Georgia. Dr. Pat and his wife Lucy were so good to Trixie, as were Frank and Mary Searcy. Betty and Bobby Morgan checked on her needs every day. Trixie spent her last years in the nursing home in Franklin where she was given such excellent care and she as adored by all the staff there. Trixie Morgan died on March 1, 1995, and was laid to rest beside her husband at Stripling Chapel Church Cemetery. *Submitted by: Jimmy and Michelle Flake Morgan, Wynwood Drive, Carrollton, GA 30117*

865. The Derah Burnham Morgan Genealogy

The old Roopville road where the Burnhams lived used to be called the Dry Pond Road because folks thought there weren't enough watering places for the mules coming on that road into town. But fresh water was not a problem at the Burnham home place, for they lived directly in front of the old Hubbard's Springs, some of he freshest and purest water in the county.

Rev. Joel Colley Burnham (9 December 1828 - 4 April 1907) was born in Walton County, Georgia, the son of Thomas Burnham and Mary Frances Manning. After Thomas died in 1835, the Burnhams moved to Redbone in Heard County for a number of years. J.C. Burnham had brothers James Early 1823-1910, William W. 1821-1863, Thomas Jefferson 1825-1890, David born 1830, and Benjamin born 1834. A sister's name is unknown.

J.C. Burnham served as a Confederate soldier during the Civil War for Carroll County Company D, 9th Georgia Infantry. He signed up with the CSA in Bowdon in July of 1861 and was with General Robert E. Lee when he surrendered at Appomattox Couthouse on April 9, 1865. As Regimental Chaplain, he was the first to offer a prayer to heal the wounds between the North and the South. After the war, Rev. Burnham returned home to Carroll County and continued in his calling to serve the Lord. He served as pastor of Centralhatchee Baptist Church and Enon Grove Baptist Church in the 1860s. He helped to establish the Emmaus Church in 1871 and his name appears on the cornerstone at Emmaus as first pastor there.

Rev. J.C. Burnham fell in love with Mary Caroline "Mollie" Jackson, daughter of Reuben and Elizabeth M. Jackson of Heard County, Georgia. Reuben Jackson was the son of Joseph Jackson and Elizabeth Booker who had moved to Heard County from Greene County, Georgia.

The Jacksons were Quakers who had first lived in England. Anthony Jackson moved to Ireland in 1649 due to religious persecution of the Quakers. Anthony had a son named Thomas Jackson who bought land in 1715 in Pennsylvania, and Thomas came to America in 1717. Thomas Jackson died in East Marlborough, Pennsylvania, in 1727. Thomas was the father of several children including Benjamin Jackson who had been born in County Antrim, Ireland.

Benjamin Jackson had come as a child with his father to America in 1717. Benjamin had brothers Samuel and Isaac. Benjamin Jackson and his wife Elizabeth Clark, and his brother Isaac, moved to Orange County, North Carolina and then to the Quaker settlement at Wrightsboro in Columbia County, Georgia. Benjamin died circa 1782 there. All these records can be found in Hinshaw's *Quaker Genealogy.* Isaac Jackson served in the American Revolution under the command of General Washington. Isaac received a land grant of 1200 acres in Hancock County, Georgia, for his service.

Benjamin was the ancestor of our Joseph Jackson who was born in Greene County, Georgia, in 1792 and who later moved to Heard County, Georgia. Joseph Jackson married Elizabeth Booker in Putnam County Georgia, on 15 July 1813. The Jacksons were devout Quakers until the American Revolution came along, and this had forced the Jacksons to choose between religion and duty to country. The Quakers did not believe in war and fighting, so the Jacksons had parted with the Quaker community in order to help win American independence.

The next generation of Jackson men would fight for the Confederacy. Joseph's son, Reuben Jackson (born 1822), served as a Confederate soldier and he died far away from home, of measles, during the Civil War. His burial place is not known. Reuben's wife was Elizabeth M. (surname unknown). Reuben Jackson had been a most popular blacksmith in Heard County.

Another son of Joseph Jackson who served in the Confederacy was Joseph J. Jackson, the ancestor of our well-loved Superior Court Judge Jospeh C. Jackson who died April 1, 1992, at age seventy. Judge Jackson was very interested in genealogy and helped to search much of this Jackson history. He was a Superior Court judge in the Coweta Judicial Circuit, which includes Carroll County, from 1974-1986.

The Burnham Brothers

Joseph C. Jackson was born in 1921, the son of Benjamin Reuben Jackson of Heard County. His ancestor, Joseph J. Jackson had made boots and shoes for the Confederate Army. His wife, Mary F. Jones Jackson, was a seamstress who made the Confederate uniforms. Both Joseph J. and Mary Jackson wisely insisted on being paid in gold (instead of Confederate money) and it is said that when Jopseph J. Jackson died he left each one of his seventeen children $1000 in gold.

Both the brothers Reuben Jackson and Joseph J. Jackson had daughters they named Cumilla — and called "Que" as the nickname. Cumilla, our Molly Jackson Burnham's sister, married James Andrew Shadinger 6 December 1875 in Carroll County, Georgia. Many of the Jacksons of this family married people of Carroll County. For this reason, we felt the Jackson genealogy would be of interest for this book.

Judge Joseph C. Jackson often said that he hoped a book such as this one would be published one day, and he hoped to stamp out an erroneous tale that had been "put out" on his family. He extracted a promise from this writer many years ago that if he did not live to see such a book — and I did — that I would make this correction on his behalf.

In the course of his many years of research, Judge Jackson discovered that someone had "put out" the story that when the recruiters came to sign up men fro the Confederate Army that his ancestor (Joseph J. Jackson) had "hidden in a stoned up well." This was *not* true. Judge Jackson tracked down this story as relentlessly as a Scotland Yard detective and did discover who had actually hidden in the well. However, it was not a member of the Jackson family, nor was it Joseph J. Jackson who served the Confederacy in the honorable capacity as previously described. Thus, we can put that rumor to rest. As for the true culprit who hid in the well — my lips are sealed. There, I have honored my long-ago promise to Judge Jackson who is fondly remembered as cousin and as a judge in Carroll County.

The Burnhams trace their ancestry to Robert Burnham and Mary Andrews of Norfolk, England whose three sons — John, Robert, and Thomas — came to America on the ship *"Angel Gabriel"* in the year 1635. The young boys were actually on a pleasure trip just to vacation in America with their uncle who was the captain of the ship. Unfortunately, the ship went down in a terrible storm on August 15, 1635, just off the coast of Maine and many perished. But Captain Andrews helped the young boys, who were then but seventeen, twelve, and eleven to safety on shore.

Our family is descended from the son John who was born in 1618 and who married Elizabeth Manning. John Burnham's descendants lived in Bertie County, North Carolina, at the time of the American Revolution. Thomas Burnham married Mary Frances Manning who was born in 1792 in North Carolina. However, they married in Pulaski County, Georgia, in 1818 and later moved to Walton County, Georgia, where Thomas was one of the first road commissioners.

Joseph C. Jackson

One of the earliest Burnhams to come to Carroll County was a cousin of Rev. J.C. Burnham. His name was Elisha Burnham and he was born in Connecticut. He was forty-nine years old in the 1850 Carroll County census and his wife Mary was forty-two. A son Wareham was twenty and Needham was seventeen. The other children were Julia 16, Kyle W. 14, Amy 12, Martha 11, Andrew 9, Rachel 7, and Elisha 3.

Rev. Joel Colley Burnham married Mollie Jackson in 1868 and they resided in Coweta County, Georgia, for a few years. Mollie was born 10 March 1849 so there was more than twenty years difference in their ages. Nine children were born to them: (1) Viola Frances Burnham b. 9 Jan 1869, m. William Barto North s/o Marcus Bowlin North and Lucendia Ellis Vinyard on 4 November 1886, d. 9 April 1931; William North b. 20 August 1861 d. 21 February 1902, buried Old Camp Church (2) Thomas Robert Lee Burnham b. 24 November 1870, m. Ida May Lyle d/o Joseph Algernon Lyle and Julia Ann Ragland on 23 January 1891, d. 10 Jan 1834; Ida Lyle b. 22 February 1875 d. 16 December 1959 buried Carrollton City Cemetery (3) Derah Idella Burnham b. 10 April 1873, m. James Robert "Bob" Morgan d. 25 March 1958 (4) Reuben Jackson Burnham b. 9 March 1875, m. Martha A. "Mattie" Moore on 28 December 1897, d. 20 April 1955 buried at Hopewell in Cullman, Alabama, Mattie Moore b. 10 November 1896 d. 30 November 1958 (5). Joel Rufus Burnham b. 1 July 1878, m. Bana Almon 17 August 1913 d. 10 August 1933; Bana Almon b. 2 January 1879 d. 1 September 1948 buried Carrollton City Cemetery (6) Sampson Burnham b. 1 Dec 1883, never married, d. 17 Oct 1948 buried Emmaus (7) Walter Leonard Burnham b. 3 Dec 1886, m. Callie Braselle Hancock, d. 27 June 1958; Callie Hancock d/0 John Thomas Hancock and Emma Frances Braswell, born 29 December 1888 in Pike County, Georgia, d. 31 October 1974 buried Mt. Pleasant Baptist Cemetery; — sons Denzel and Walter Burnham, daughter, Mrs. Aubrey L. Martin (8) Jospeh Claudius Burnham b. 31 August 1888, m. Minnie Alma Moore on 22 November 1914, d. 20 April 1964; Minnie Moore d/o Thomas Moore and Georgia Shadinger b. 16 September 1895 d. 22 June 1998, buried Oak Grove Church — daughters: Reba, Rudene (Mrs. Glenn Hollingsworth), and Louise (Mrs. E.H. Hearn) (9) Winnie Mae Burnham b. 23 Jan 1890, m. William Edward Crews of LaGrange b. 21 June 1909 d. 26 April 1975; Ed Crews b. 3 January 1886 d. 9 December 1956 buried Stripling Chapel Methodist Church, Carroll County.

Rev. Joel Colley Burnham was a prominent Baptist minister throughout his life and performed many of the early marriages of Carroll County. He died 4 April 1907 at his homeplace in Carroll County. His wife, Mollie, died during the Spanish influenza epidemic on 26 January 1919. Both Rev. J.C. Burnham and Mary Caroline Jackson Burnham are buried in the cemetery at Emmaus Church. Mary Frances Manning Burnham who lived to be over 100 years old is also buried in the old cemetery at Emmaus Church.

The Burnham brothers are as pictured in the old photo: L-R seated Joel Burnham, Reuben Burnham, Robert Burnham, Sampson Burnham. Standing L-R Claude Burnham, Walter Burnham. *Submitted by: Linda Taylor League, Antioch Church Road, Carrollton, GA 30117 and Written by: Jan Robinson Bell*

866. Leon Davis "Lee" Morgan

Lee Morgan (1878-1961), son of John David and Lucy Kelly Morgan, married Eugenia "Genie" Elizabeth Jordan (1881-1961), daughter of Johnson P. and Celia Alice McKenzie Jordan. Lee and Genie are buried in Shady Grove Baptist Cemetery, Carroll County, Georgia. They had eleven children: George Lee (1898-1899), Dalton (1919), Osborne (1925), Duvall (1900-1996, cremated), Dumah (1901-1987), Dula Mae (1904-2000), Gerallah (1908-), Raymon (1910-1998), Frances (1912-1984), John D. (1915), and Zellie (1922).

Duvall, Dumah, Dula Mae, Gerallah, Raymon, Frances, John D., and Zellie Morgan

Duvall married Beulah Harmon. They had three children: William Lee and Helen, deceased, and Elizabeth McLeroy lives in Carroll County. Duvall moved to California in 1924. He married Marie Eckerle and they had two daughters: Mary Ann Bottini lives in California, and Carol Lee Davidson, deceased. Duvall married Emma Plattner. They had no children. Dumah married Doyle Savage. They are buried in Salem Baptist Cemetery, Carroll County. They spent four years in South America with their children. Harold lives in South Carolina and Suzanne Dilthey in North Carolina. He retired from the textile business.

Dula Mae married Clarence Sprewell. They are buried in Carroll Memory Gardens, Carroll County. Their children: Bamah Wood, Fred, Gilbert and Bobby, deceased, live in Carroll County, Evelyn Williams in Tennessee. Dula Mae retired from Sewell Manufacturing and is known for her tatted crosses.

Gerallah married Seaborn Jasper (SJ) Jackson, son of Seaborn Joseph and Minnie Burham Jackson. SJ is buried in Shady Grove Baptist Cemetery. Gerallah lives with daughters Reba Jean Gillespie, Bremen, Georgia, and Dacy Shealy, Carroll County. She is known for her beautiful handmade quilts and tells numerous stories of her childhood.

Lee and Genie Morgan, 1957, on their 60th Anniversary.

Raymon married Laura Lee, daughter of Ovid and Mildred Jackson Lee. Raymon and Laura are buried in Salem Baptist Cemetery. Raymon was an expert mechanic and mayor of Bowdon, Georgia where son, Charles Lee, lives.

Frances married Coyban Holcomb, son of William and Mamie Rigsby Holcomb. They are buried in Salem Baptist Cemetery. Frances retired from Sewell Manufacturing. Their daughter Bivian Stephens lives in Atlanta.

John D. lives in Douglas County, Georgia. His son Ned is buried beside his mother Margaret Roberson Morgan at Abilene Baptist Cemetery, Carroll County. John D. worked at Sewell Manufacturing and Douglas-Lomason.

Zellie married Madelyn Shackelford, daughter of Benjamin Frank and Dora Isabel Blandenburg Shackelford. Zellie was in the Navy during World War II, retired from Lockheed and enjoys flying. Their children: Karen Little and Davis live in Bremen, Barry in Connecticut.

Lee Morgan was a farmer and cow trader. He operated a mule-drawn syrup mill, was one of the first directors of Carroll EMC, a founding trustee of Farmer's High School, and ordained a deacon at Salem Baptist Church. He attended the funeral of President Woodrow Wilson's wife in Rome, Georgia.

Genie Morgan was a joy. She never tired of playing games with grandchildren and carrying them fishing, telling them the fish wouldn't bite if they talked! She will always be remembered for her beautiful delicate needlework and flower gardens. She was never seen without a hat or "breast pin" and proudly wore the "wings" given her by Zellie. She taught her girls the art of quilting, tatting, crocheting, sewing, cooking and preserving.

In 1908 Lee built their home at Farmer's High, which was destroyed by fire in 1943. There is one barn and corn crib still standing. Lee and Genie moved to the Jordan home place in 1932 and lived there until 1945. They lived with Gerallah and Frances during 1945 until they built a house in 1946 on the original site, where they lived until their deaths. Parcels of the land are owned by grandchildren Reba Jean, Dacy, Bivian, and Bobby; great-grandsons Walter Shealy and Gordon Sprewell.

Lee and Genie celebrated their 63rd anniversary in 1960. Five of their children — Dumah, Dula Mae, Gerallah, Raymon and Zellie — and three grandchildren have celebrated fifty or more years of marriage. Three of the grandchildren have enjoyed being a part of both sets of grandparents' golden wedding anniversary and many of the grandchildren attended the Morgan's 60th wedding anniversary. *Submitted by: Dacy Shealy, 151 Lee Morgan Road, Carrollton, GA 30117*

Sources: Family records, *David Morgan and His Descendants*, Second edition, 1983, by Jackson K. Morgan.

867. William H. Morgan, Sr.

Our Morgan family first came to Carroll County, Georgia, in the year 1852 and after seven generations there are still many descendants living here today. William H. Morgan Sr. (born 1819 in Georgia) was listed in the 1850 census living with his family in Greene County, Georgia — William H. age 31, farmer, wife Susan M. age 29, daughter Mary Elizabeth age 10, daughter Samantha J. age 8, son John Thomas age 5 (born 14 June 1846), son William H. Jr. age 4 months. In 1852 when William H. Morgan Sr. purchased Land Lot #50 in the 6th District of Carroll County, Georgia, he was listed as a resident of Oglethorpe County, Georgia. The land was purchased from Ambrose C. Green who was headed west to join others seeking their fortune in the Gold Rush of California.

By 1860, the William H. Morgan Sr. family appears in the Carroll County census, but Samantha J. who would have been eighteen years old by that time does not appear. It is possible that she may have married. Another son, born in 1856, Richard R. Morgan does appear with this family. However, tragic events were to occur in this family soon after the 1860 census had been taken on the 19th of October that year.

A band of gypsies passing through the county asked permission to make camp in the Morgans' pasture for the night. Permission was given, but by the next dawn the gypsies were gone. They had taken with them the Morgans' young son, John Thomas. Perhaps from the grief over her kidnapped child, Susan Morgan became devastated and lost her health. She died sometime before 1862. A search for many years turned up no trace of the lost boy. On October 14, 1862, William H. Morgan Sr. married a second wife, Mary Jane Jennings (born in Tennessee) in Carroll County. By May 6, 1868, William H. Morgan had died and his will was probated. It had no mention of John Thomas Morgan in it, as the family believed he was probably dead. The burial place of William H. Morgan Sr. and his first wife Susan is not known.

The Morgan children grew up and married in Carroll County. Mary Elizabeth Morgan married Jackson Cagle on October 13, 1862. William H. Morgan Jr. married Sarah L. Adams (1854-1931) on December 8, 1870. In the 1870 census, Mary Cagle is shown living in the household with her brother William's family. Perhaps her husband died in the Civil War. There are no known records of Richard R. Morgan beyond 1868 when he was mentioned in his father's will as a minor.

Leonard Taylor, Linda Taylor League, and Brenda Taylor

In years to come, a miraculous event was to occur in this family. One day while walking down the street in Newnan, Georgia. William H. Morgan Jr. accidentally bumped into his long lost brother, John Thomas Morgan. The brothers immediately recognized each other and were happily reunited. John Thomas Morgan still had the scars of the rope burns on his neck from when the gypsies had stolen him away as a boy. By 1880, John Thomas Morgan had moved his family from Alabama to the Lowell District of Carroll County. With his wife, Mary, he already had eight known children.

The oldest son of John Thomas Morgan was William H. Morgan, always called "Billie" born 12 August 1870, married Margaret Cochran 27 December 1896, died 4 December 1932. My ancestor, James Robert "Bob" Morgan born 27 March 1873, married Derah Idella Burnham 12 August 1895, died 14 January 1919, buried at Emmaus Church Cemetery. Mattie Morgan was born 1877 and died 1947, married Ernest

Adams. John Mogan was born 30 October 1879, married Nellie V., died 19 February 1951. Anna O. Morgan was born 2 January 1882, married Thomas Ed Tolbert, died 20 June 1948. Ella B. Morgan was born 9 May 1884, married Elbert Arthur Chandler in 1913, died 15 May 1972. Emma Morgan was born ca. 1886, married Tom Norris. Charlie Morgan — no dates known — but this son moved away to Oklahoma sometime after 1919. All of the other children moved away to Cullman, Alabama, in the early 1900s except for Bob and Derah Morgan who remained on their farm at Clem in Carroll County. Mary Morgan, John Thomas' first wife, died sometime around 1890. A family tradition says that she was in a wheelchair after a horse and buggy accident in her later years. Her burial place is not known.

William H. Morgan Jr. and his wife Sarah L. Adams Morgan had the following known children: Susan I. born 1872, Sarah F. born 1875, William born 1877, Edmond A. born 1880, Samantha J. born 1881, Ula I. born 1884, James D. born 1886, and Louise L. born 1898. The last child was born in Alabama, so it is known that William H. Jr. had moved his family to Cullman County by that year. There was a great migration of people from Carroll County to Cullman in the early 1900s because of the rich black dirt there. Soon, William H. Morgan Jr. had persuaded his older brother to also move to Alabama. By 1902, John Thomas Morgan had moved to Cullman and most of his children followed.

John Thomas Morgan had married a second wife, Sarah Jane, "Sally," Shadinger Burden, the widow of David Burden. With David Burden, Sally had the following children: Katie Frances born 1 Dec 1880, married William Wesley Gray, died 22 Nov 1948. W.W. Gray and a grandson Ben Roper died when struck by lightning 21 June 1948; Stella R. Burden born 28 Oct 1883 died 11 Dec 1955; Donnie Calamar Burden born 30 Nov 1885 married Sparks, died 14 Sept 1933; Archie Burden — died 1932, buried at Emmaus Church. David Burden was buried on Shadinger's Ridge. Sally Shadinger was the daughter of John Shadinger and Ellen Jones, also early pioneers of Carroll County and Emmaus Church.

With his second wife, Sally whom he married on 28 February 1892 in Carroll County, John Thomas Morgan had two children: Maude Morgan born 15 Dec 1892, married James Reese, died 15 July 1915; Albert Walter Morgan born 28 July 1895, married Emma Mae Cochran 1914, died ? After this family moved to Cullman, Alabama, in 1902, they remained there for the rest of their lives. Sally Shadinger Burden Morgan died 4 May 1923. John Thomas Morgan died 18 February, 1935. Both are buried in Fellowship Cemetery in Cullman.

I am a fourth generation descendant of this Morgan family of Carroll County. My Mother was Mary Elizabeth Morgan born 26 May 1907, the daughter of James Robert Morgan and Derah Burnham Morgan. Mary Elizabeth Morgan married 22 November 1943 to Hulett Dorsey Taylor who was born 9 March 1918 in Meriwether County, Georgia, the son of Charlie A. Taylor and Ellen Bond. Mary and Hulett D. Taylor had three children: Linda Earline Taylor born 15 December 1945 married 26 May 1943 to Johnny Ray League; Brenda Louise Taylor born 26 October 1948 married first Charles Wayne Meeks, second Jerry Agan. Brenda and Wayne Meeks had one son, Chadwick Wayne Meeks who was later adopted by Jerry Agan. Chad Agan is married to Erica Musick and they have two daughters: Addison Brook Musick born 17 September 1996 and Emma Kate Agan born 22 March 2001. Leonard Dorsey Taylor was born 16 April 1952 in Carroll County. Leonard D. Taylor attended Central High School and worked as a John Deere mechanic and later for Temple Wood Products. He is now a resident of Mt. Zion. *Submitted by: Leonard D. Taylor, Mt. Zion, GA, and Written by: Jan R. Bell.*

868. Morris Family

George Lyon was born in 1732 in the British Isles and wed Elizabeth, born November 13, 1734. Their two daughters were lace makers while their son, Joseph Emmanuel Lyon who had been well educated, became a jeweler by trade. When the American colonies rebelled against England, Joseph came with the British Expeditionary Army to America. He fought under the British Generals, Sir William Howe and the Earl of Cornwallis. On October 4, 1777, at the Battle of Germantown, Pennsylvania, Joseph was captured by the American Continental Troops. Shortly thereafter he took oath of allegiance to the struggling United States of America and joined the Americans in their fight for independence. In the fighting, Joseph Emmanuel Lyon was seriously injured and lost an arm as the result of his wounds. Upon recovering, he settled in South Carolina where he taught school and wed Mary Ann Marshbank of Lancaster, South Carolina. They became the parents of five children. For his faithful services in our war of independence, our federal government gave Joseph a bounty grant of 100 acres of land on the South River in the state of Georgia. As of 1973, the 100 acres is and has been continuously owned and occupied by the Lyon descendants. His sons bought more land until at one time the plantation ran two miles on the north bank of the South River from Little Stone Mountain to Flat Shoals. DeKalb County was named for Baron DeKalb, the brilliant general from Germany, who gave his help to the Americans in their struggle for independence.

Mr. and Mrs. Napoleon Bonapart Morris

George Lyon, born December 1, 1787, one of Mary Ann Marshbank and Joseph Emmanuel Lyon's children, married Elizabeth Howard on October 9, 1806. They had thirteen children, one of whom was Lavinia Offer Lyon, born March 7, 1829. She married John Headspeth Morris on May 1, 1845. They had eight children, one of whom was Napolean Bonapart Morris, born January 14, 1848, in Henry County, Georgia. He married Martha Jane Jackson November 25, 1865, in Carroll County, Georgia. They had nine children: Venie, Marcus, Tollie, Mary Elizabeth,Willis, Walter, Frank, Bera, and Annie.

Willis, born October 14, 1876, married Beulah Gordon. They had nine children, one of whom is Margie Morris Sanders, who still lives in Carroll County.

Bera, born March 6, 1884, married Ruben Marlowe. They had two children, Ruby Marlowe Perry and Sawyer Marlowe. Ruby and Sawyer still live in Carrollton, Georgia.

Marcus, born December 14, 1868, married Ella Hartley on December 2, 1888. They had twelve children, one of whom is Inez, born February 22, 1911. She married Joe Banks and they had four children: Mary Jo, Sara, Alan, and Gloria. Inez, Alan, and Gloria still live in Carroll County.

Another one of Marcus and Ella's children was Lola Almeda, born January 28, 1904, in Carroll County. She married Clarence Clayton Chance Sr., a blacksmith, on December 4, 1921, in Carrollton. They had five children: Edna, Betty Jean, James Eddie, Clay, and Steve.

Betty Jean still lives in Carrollton. She married Bobby Hendon on June 16, 1946. They had one child, Carol, born March 18, 1947. Carol married Rance Cain on October 30, 1971. They have three children, Jennifer, Melissa, and Betsy. Bobby was killed in an automobile accident in 1966. Betty Jean worked and retired from Southern Bell Telephone and Telegraph Company. For many years, the office — including the switchboard and operators — was located upstairs above the Groover-Smith Furniture Company on Adamson Square. Betty Jean later married J.H. Mullins, Jr. *Submitted by: Betty Jean Mullins, 116 Pinecrest Place, Carrollton, GA 30117*

Sources: Lyon family history and Lyon genealogy, Morris family Bible, filed at Georgia Department of Archives and History.

869. Caroline Elizabeth Ward Morris

Elizabeth, born in Carroll County, Georgia, on July 12, 1907, and died September 19, 2000, was the only daughter of Hulty Ann Elizabeth Waddell (December 29, 1872 to July 11, 1957) and Asa Franklin Ward (February 10, 1842 to September 5, 1916), son of John Ward, born 1785. Asa volunteered in the Confederate States Army (CSA) (1861-1864). He became a prisoner of war and incurred various wounds.

With her three brothers, Dwight (1901-1954), Rube (1903-1963), and Hershel (1915-1984), Elizabeth walked through creek and woods to attend Wesley Chapel School in Villa Rica until the sixth grade. Three siblings died in infancy.

As a young woman, at Grandma Mary Frances Reeves Waddell's request before her death, Elizabeth created a beautiful burial gown with tatting, hand embroidered daisies, and embellished with French knots at the yoke. This was characteristic of the pride in her every endeavor throughout her life.

A black iron cat bank from Pa Asa, a boot latch hook of Ma Hulty, and many household items are still with Elizabeth's family.

In 1933, Elizabeth's spirited, high-principled Ma requested Pa Asa's C.S.A. pension, sixty-nine years after his retirement. She never applied for social security.

Elizabeth Ward Morris, 1921

Hubert, Richard, Ruth, Lois, Helen, Carl, Katherine, Marie, Henry, and Elizabeth Morris

They met when she was eleven and he was thirteen. She won his nickel playing checkers. The Sunday afternoon social was watching the train come through town. The year was 1922, September 17, when Elizabeth married Henry Allen Pendleton Morris (February 23, 1905 to August 12, 1998). Justice of the Peace Ed Allgood performed the ceremony on a "fine weather" afternoon in Paulding County. An uneventful honeymoon was picking cotton.

Henry was the firstborn of Sarah Camp Morris (1880-1914) and the ninth of seventeen children of Joseph Andrew Morris, whose ancestors arrived in Georgia from Edinburgh, Scotland, before 1830.

After a brief adventure to Newport News, Virginia, in a 1928 rumble-seat, Model-A Roadster, they returned to Georgia.

Elizabeth and Henry reared a resilient family who sharecropped, producing twenty-five prime cotton bales one year, only to be plagued by boll weevils another. Henry supplemented the family income with carpentry.

Their eight children are: Richard (born February 14, 1925) married Mildred Brown (born November 30, 1924); Lois (born October 10, 1926) married Harvie Brown (July 19, 1924 to September 19, 2000); Hubert (born August 19, 1929) married Martha Phillips (born October 8, 1939); Katherine (born March 13, 1931) married Guy Brown (born December 3, 1926); Helen (born April 21, 1933) married Hugh Shepard (born January 16, 1921); Carl (born September 15, 1935) married Judith Wright (born August 21, 1946); Ruth (born September 9, 1939) married Jerry Goldin (born August 30, 1939); and Marie (born February 3, 1942) married George Barnett (born May 26, 1935).

Together the family confronted many hardships — a son in World War II, food tokens, the Great Depression, and being under quarantine when one child was afflicted with infantile paralysis (polio). Clothes and sunbonnets sewn from guano or flour sacks, hand knitting, tatting, and quilting were commonplace for this resourceful group.

This was the wonderful era of visiting peddlers, ice men, aromatic iron pots of food on the open fire with corn pone, poke salad, and home-grown meats, vegetables, and fruits. There were delightful family games, music generated with guitars, harmonicas, spoons, and combs. The beauty of Elizabeth's flowers always surrounded the family.

Celebrating Henry and Elizabeth's seventy-fifth year of marriage was a lovingly orchestrated event by all eight children and their families. They were inundated with warm greetings to mark this exciting milestone from five generations, friends, and President Clinton. Three children have celebrated their fiftieth wedding anniversaries.

Elizabeth's loving interest and active involvement with her extended family of ninety-nine was intense all during her ninety-three years. Henry and Elizabeth are buried at Yorkville Baptist Church, Paulding County, where they were members many, many years. *Submitted by: Ruth Goldin, 2865 Eldorado Place, Snellville, GA 30078*
Sources: Family records, and International Headquarters, Sons of Confederate Veterans.

870. Descendants of James Morris and Elzador Morris

James Alvin Morris was born February 5, 1920, in Newnan, Georgia, located in Coweta County. He married Elizabeth Elzador Chambers September 28, 1940, in Carroll County. James sold potato chips thirty-three years, then changed careers. Presently he works as a bailiff at the Carroll County courthouse. He has served as a deacon in the Tabernacle Baptist Church where he has been a member for forty-five years. James and Elzador celebrated 60 years of marriage in September 2000.

Elizabeth Elzador Chambers Morris was born May 31, 1920, in the Tyus community of Carroll County. She is a homemaker and a water color artist. Elzador has been a member of the Tabernacle Baptist Church for forty-five years and has been a greeter at the door for many years.

James and Elzador have three children, two grandchildren and one great grandchild. Bruce Wayne Morris, son of James and Elzador Morris, was born November 11, 1941, and died November 14, 1941. Bruce Wayne was buried at Pleasant Grove in Tyus, Georgia.

James Richard Morris, son of James and Elzador Morris, was born January 29, 1948, in the Carrollton Clinic in Carrollton, Georgia. Richard is a pharmacist and resides in Marietta, Georgia. He married Rebekah Lynn Andrews April 21, 1973. Richard and Becky celebrated 28 years of marriage in 2001.

Rebekah Lynn Andrews was born December 2, 1948, in Newberry, South Carolina. She is a former schoolteacher and a fashion model coordinator. Richard and Becky have two children, and one grandchild.

Jonathan Justin Morris, son of Richard and Becky Morris, was born October 9, 1975 in Marietta, Georgia. When Jonathan was about six years old, the family was having lunch and Jonathan would not eat his vegetables. His mother said, "Jon, there are lots of hungry children in this world who would love to have your food." He picked up his plate and said, "Well give it to them." He is a sales executive with Dodge in Canton, Georgia. He married Jennifer Grant in 1997. They have one child, Carley Michelle Morris. Jennifer Grant Morris was born September 22, 1975 in Cobb County. She works in Cobb County as a doctor's assistance.

Carley Michelle Morris, daughter of Jonathan and Jennifer Morris, was born May 6, 1997, in Marietta, Georgia. Jessica Leah Morris, daughter of Richard and Becky Morris, born June 15, 1981, in Marietta. She is a student at Kennasaw College in Kennasaw, Georgia. Jessica also models part-time and has been featured in the *I DO* magazine.

Vicki Lynn Morris, daughter of James and Elzador Morris, was born April 20, 1953, in Carrollton at the Tanner Medical Center. She taught elementary school for four years and presently has been working for MCIWORLDCOM for twenty years. She resides in Atlanta, Georgia. *Submitted by: Vicki L. Morris, 2582 Drew Valley Road, Atlanta, GA 30319*

871. Morris
Orrill Hayes, Betty Louise Westbrook, and Kathryn Love

Betty Louise Westbrook, daughter of Noble Theodore and (Love) Lovie Mae Eaves Westbrook of Haralson County, Georgia, married (August 7, 1965, Haralson County) Orrill Hayes

Children and grandchildren of John Pinkney and Martha Chambers.

Morris Jr. (August 6, 1936-) son of Orrill Hayes Sr. and Maurine Cornelia Owen Morris of Atlanta, Fulton, Georgia.

United States census will list Orrill Hayes Morris as head of household in Georgia; Carroll County 2000, DeKalb County 1990 and 1970, as well as 1980 South Carolina census.

The family residences include Newton County, Georgia, 1965-66; Philadelphia, Pennsylvania, 1966-68; DeKalb County, Georgia (1968-72), (1973-78), (1984-98); West Dulwich (London), England 1972-3; Searcy, Arkansas (1978-80; Columbia, South Carolina 1980-83; Cobb County, Georgia 1983-84; and Carroll County, Georgia 1998.

Betty, Orrill, and Kathryn Morris

Betty earned a B.S. degree in home economics from Jacksonville State College (University) Alabama in 1963. She was selected to be included in Who's Who in American Colleges and Universities (1963). She taught in DeKalb County, Georgia, co-owned and worked in TransAmerica Printing, and is a homemaker. Orrill earned B.S. in industrial engineering 1958, and M.S. in industrial management 1960, degrees from Georgia Tech. His career included positions in engineering, manufacturing, sales, management and consulting. He was employed by Firmbuy, CMAC, Utilities Analyses, TransAmerican Printing, Moore Lambert Industries, Communications Technology, ABB Brown Boveri, McGraw Edison, Coopers & Lybrand, Brunswick, and Westinghouse Electric.

Betty and Orrill have one daughter, Kathryn Love (August 14, 1968-) who earned her B.S. in history from Brenau Women's College (Gainesville, Georgia) in 1991, and her master's degree in special education from the State University of West Georgia (Carrollton, Georgia) in 1999. Residences include Dunwoody and Carrollton, Georgia.

See other family articles, John Henley Matthews, Abel Matthews, and Hattie Matthews. *Submitted by: Betty W. Morris, 184 Gina Drive, Carrollton, GA 30116. bettywmoris@cs.com*

Sources: Certificates of birth, marriage records Haralson County, college and university records, work records.

872. Morrow

I, Sadie Morrow Hughes, am writing this as the oldest living member of the Morrows descending from the Robert Morrow line from North Carolina.

William Hurley (Robert's son), born 1755, died 1810, moved to Jonesboro, Georgia, in the early 1800s. Eventually, along with other members of the family, he helped establish the town of Morrow, Georgia.

His son James Hodge was the father of Bannister, who moved with his wife Victoria Floyd Morrow to Tallapoosa, Georgia, a boom town around 1870.

Shortly thereafter they moved to Carrollton. To this union a son John Wesley was born in

James Hodge Morrow, father of Bannister Morrow

1875, also a daughter Willy Morrow Lucas. Two more children died in infancy. John Wesley was my father and he resided in Carrollton until his death in 1931.

I am the youngest daughter of John and Lela Ethel McWhorter Morrow. The oldest child was Mable Morrow Kent, born 1905, died 1955; Janette Morrow Lamb born 1907, died 2000; James William Morrow born 1912, died 1993; Sadie Morrow Hughes born 1915, and resides in Carrollton.

Bannister R. Morrow, father of John Wesley Morrow.

The living descendants of John Morrow residing nearby are: James W. Morrow Jr. married to Deanna Duffy Morrow, and their children; Mrs. John Harris (Lori) and children in Carrollton; Jon Morrow and children living in Dalton, Georgia; Robert Gregory and children living in Rome, Georgia; Ellen Morrow Turner and children living in Louisville, Kentucky; Mrs. Mark Street (Robin) and children in Carrollton; Mrs. Billy Ayers (Susan) and children living in La Grange; Mr. C.E. Lamb Jr. and children of Charlotte, North Carolina is the son of Janette Morrow Lamb (deceased); James Danny Hughes and children of Carrollton; Mrs. J.S. McEachern Jr. (Nancy Morrow Hughes) and

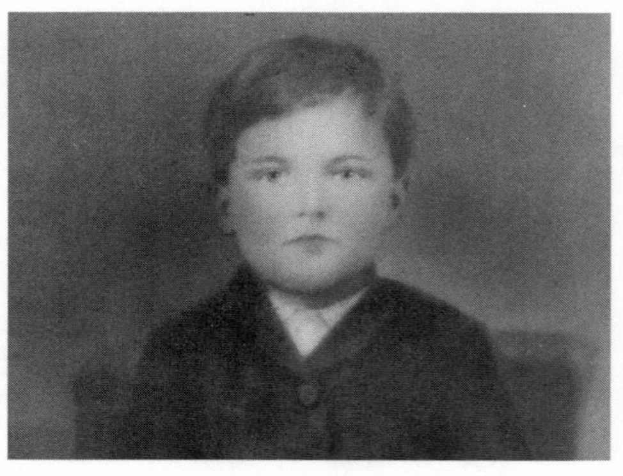

John Wesley Morrow, age six.

children of Bremen; Clifton Eugene Hughes Jr. and children of Tyler, Texas. James Danny, Nancy, and Clifton are the children of Mrs. Sadie Morrow Hughes.

It is interesting to me that my father John Wesley Morrow spent his entire life in Carrollton. His son James William (Billy) also resided in Carrollton all his life, except his college years. His son James Jr. has lived and raised his family in Carrollton, except his college years. I, Mrs. Sadie Morrow Hughes, have returned to Carrollton after living elsewhere for nearly sixty years. I feel certain my son and nephew, along with his children, will continue to be good and productive citizens of the community. *Submitted by: Sadie Morrow Hughes, 530 Northside Drive, Apartment C215, Carrollton, GA 30117.*

873. Peter Mosteller Jr.

In 1826, a Dutch millwright named Peter Mosteller Jr. came to what was to become Carroll County, Georgia. He worked a three-year circuit. He would contract to build a mill with a customer. He would then cut and rack the timber and build the mill dam. Three years later he would return and do the final trim on the dam. By this time the lumber would be well seasoned. He would then build the mill building and teach the owner how to operate the machinery.

At the time he was fifty-four years old — too old to continue this traveling lifestyle — he built his own mill on Crawfish Creek, between Flat Rock Road and Fairfield Plantation. This mill was later known as Allen's Mill, and around 1900 it was known as Harper's Mills.

After the mill was finished, he returned to Lincoln County, North Carolina, and returned with his wife Mary Dillinger Mosteller, his son Jonathon, daughter Elizabeth and her husband Henry Earney (Arney). The Earneys were married on April 12, 1821, and had three children: Ephram, who never married; a daughter who married Eldoradus Robards; and Mary Magdalena, who married another Carroll County pioneer, Larkin A. Allen. He had purchased three land lots (606 acres) near double bridges and Georgia Highway 113. Larkin and Mary had twelve children.

In 1909 a family reunion was held at the old home place. *Submitted by: Monroe Spake, Villa Rica, GA*

874. Martha Lewis Munro - Ingram

On November 9, 1955, the Regents of the University System of Georgia named the Martha Munro Building at West Georgia College in the memory of Martha Lewis Munro-Ingram, daughter of Anna Merritt-Munro and George Pierce Munro. Anna Merritt was a graduate of Wesleyan College, Macon, Georgia, and a member of the Adelphian Sorority, which later became Alpha Delta Pi. George Pierce Munro was the first chairman of the board of trustees of the Fourth District Agricultural and Mechanical School, and in this capacity he assisted in selecting the original site of the A & M School, which became West Georgia College in 1933.

Martha Munro joined the faculty of the A & M School as a teacher of English and dramatic arts. She was there a year before Irvine Sullivan Ingram was employed as principal of the school. She married Irvine Sullivan Ingram in 1921, and in 1924 Anne Gayle Ingram was born in the house that was known as the "Old President's Home" and was later renamed the Alumni House.

Martha Munro-Ingram was acting principal from 1932 to 1933 while her husband was completing his education. She was an expert gardener who planted many of the flowering shrubs on the campus. Mr. Troy Holcombe, the college's landscaping director in later years, told the newspaper in an interview that every effort was made to keep the beautiful design she had created, as there was no way they could improve it. "There's no doubt about it, she did it for love," Mr. Holcombe said, speaking of the forty-acre garden campus single handedly cultivated in the college's early days. Even today, the front campus retains the same design, as planted and nurtured by WGC's first landscape gardener.

She did beautiful handcrafts — four crocheted bed spreads, an afghan, crocheted place mats, and beautiful tatting or lace. Another hobby of hers was collecting fine china. She read extensively and quoted numerous poems from memory. She was a member of Lit-Mu Club of Carrollton for many years.

Martha Lewis Munro-Ingram

She loved cats. The family had a white Persian cat for sixteen years that they named Georgie Porgy. She did her own housework and was an excellent cook. A unique factor in her character was that she trusted all people equally and was oblivious to social position or race.

Her adult life was spent on the campus in the interest of her family and the institution. Her creative vision and dedication to students in the interest of developing their intellect and appreciation for beauty and respect for the truth left an indelible imprint on those who knew her.

She died of cancer when she was fifty-nine years old, after fighting a courageous battle to live. She died on April 19, 1955, and is buried in the Carrollton City Cemetery in Carrollton, Georgia. *Submitted by: Rose Munro Bagshaw, Lynchburg, VA and Written by: Anne Gayle Ingram, Carrollton, GA.*

875. The John B. and Nancy Murchison Family

The name in Scotland was MacMurchadaidh, Murquhsoun, Murchieson, and Murchison, and various other spellings. The 1790 census records list twelve families by the name of Murchison living in North Carolina. The ancestors of John B. and Nancy Murchison emigrated from Scotland and settled in North Carolina.

John B. Murchison was born January 12, 1774, in Cumberland County, North Carolina, and died August 26, 1847, in Coosa County, Alabama. He married Nancy Murchison, believed to be the daughter of Kenneth Murchison and his first wife Katherine McIver Murchison. Kenneth Murchison was born in 1753 in Scotland, came to this country at an early age and settled in Moore County, North Carolina. He died July 7, 1834. Katherine McIver was born in 1759, Isle of Skye, Scotland, and died August 17, 1800, in Moore County. Her parents were Roderick and Nancy McIver.

John B. and Nancy Murchison had eleven children: Alexander, Kenneth, John, Katherine, William E., Duncan, Mary Phoebee, Rora McIver, Margaret, Jane Isabella, and Nancy Elizabeth. The family moved to Washington County, Georgia, in 1818, then to Carroll County in 1827. They were listed in the 1830 census with three sons and five daughters.

Kenneth and Rora McIver Murchison served in the Carroll County Rangers, guarding against Indian hostilities.

Alexander Murchison married Flora Isabella McKay on December 29, 1836, in Cumberland County, North Carolina. He died in 1888. Both are buried in the Summerville Presbyterian Cemetery, Harnett County, North Carolina.

Kenneth Murchison, born August 18, 1806, married Flora Gillis on November 4, 1830. They had ten children. He died February 8, 1892, in Collin County, Texas.

John Murchison married Sarah Ann Robinson in 1830 and went to Texas.

Katherine Murchison married Neil Gillis in January 1834 in Carroll County.

Duncan Murchison married Elizabeth Moore Snow in Georgia on April 8, 1834.

John B. and Nancy Murchison, along with the remaining children, went to Coosa County, Alabama, in August 1836. They bought land from the Creek Indians and settled among the Indians. The family is listed in the 1840 census of Coosa County, Alabama, with two sons and three daughters.

Rora McIver, born March 27, 1816 in Cumberland County, North Carolina, and died September 7, 1875, in Coosa County, Alabama, was my great-grandfather. Many descendants of this family continue to live in Alabama, Georgia, Texas, and other states. *Submitted by: Nellie Kate Murchison Morris, 20631 U.S. Highway 231, Titus, AL 36080.*

Sources: Deed records, 1840 census, and marriage records from Coosa County, Alabama; marriage records from Carroll County, Georgia, and Cumberland County, North Carolina.

876. Muse Family

George Muse, born in 1768 in Prince William County, Virginia, married Elizabeth Jackson (1769 - 1845), and they are listed in Wilkes County, Georgia. George and Elizabeth had four children: William P., Drury Jackson, Elizabeth, and Mary A. Muse. William P. Muse (born 30 December 1801 - died 13 June 1872) married Mary A. Williams (born 25 December 1810 - died 29 October 1895). George died in 1809 and is buried on a farm in Tignal, Georgia.

William and Mary's children are: George W. (1828), John H. (1831), Jesse William (1833), Joseph M. (1836), Elizabeth (1842), Zachariah W. (1843), Thomas P. (1847), and Jackson P. Muse (1851). Jesse William Muse (4 December 1833 - 9 August 1887) married Eliza Ann Threadgill (19 October 1836 - 3 December 1881) on 19 October 1854, in Carroll County.

Jesse William and Eliza Ann Threadgill Muse had thirteen children; (1) Henry Pope born 28 September 1855 - died 24 January 1933; (2) Sara born 10 July 1857; (3) Alice J. born 1859; (4) Jefferson Davis born 15 May 1860, died 12 April 1930; (5) Harriet E. born 1866; (6) William A. born 13 May 1865; (7) Benjamin Sylvanis born Mar. 1867; (8) Zachariah born 1871; (9) Mary Jane born 1871; (10) John M. born 1873, died 1939; (11) Elam born 20 Feb 1875; (12) Jesse N. born 30 July 1878; and (13) Reese A. born 1881. All the children were born in Carroll County.

William P. with wife, Mary Williams Muse, and Jesse William with wife, Eliza Ann Threadgill Muse, are buried at Bethel Baptist Church Cemetery, Temple, Georgia.

Many descendants of these families are still in Carroll County, Georgia. The fourth child of Jesse William and Eliza Ann was Jefferson Davis, and he married Martha Evaline Parrish (1856-1946). Jefferson Davis and Martha had two sons, Warner Leon and Newt, and two daughters, Lela and Nora. Warner Leon Muse (born 1 May 1890 - died 11 June 1969) married Zela Morris (born 11 July 1890 - died 6 Oct 1969) on 1 May 1912, and they had seven children: Joseph Buford (1914), Mildred Nora (1916), James Clifton (1918), Frances Myrl (1920), Mable Martha (1924), Jesse Leon (1926), and Jackson Davis "J.D." (1928).

Warner Leon and Zela's son named Jesse married Mary Allen on 21 February 1947, and they have two daughters, Mary Josephine "Mary Jo" and Sally. Their youngest son, J.D. (3 July 1928 - 30 April 2000) married Eris Denney on 21 March 1947 and they had three daughters: Susan, Phyllis, and Cynthia. J.D. and Eris celebrated their 50th wedding anniversary in 1997.

Jesse remembers going to town with his dad to sell bales of cotton and to trade mules when he was about twelve years old (about 1938). His great uncle Jesse ran the "Mule Barn" behind the offices on Newnan Street. He furnished the working stock for the farmers. The story goes that he traveled to Tennessee and would walk horses back to Georgia to sell. He also sold Owensboro Wagons, both the one-horse and the two-horse kinds. These were made in Owensboro, Kentucky. Jesse remembers one day when they didn't finish their business in town that his dad put the mules in the barn to be fed, and they slept in the wagon and finished taking care of business the next morning. This would have probably have been Jesse N. Muse born in 1878 and the one from whom Jesse Leon was named.

The seventh child of Jesse William and Eliza Ann Threadgill Muse was Benjamin Sylvanis (b. 20 March 1867 d. 2 February 1936), and he married Elmira Elizabeth Hamrick (born 1866 died 1954). They were married on 30 December 1890 in Carroll County. They had eight children: Arlena Mae (30 May 1892), James Clifton (5 June 1893), Annie Tolulah (5 Oct 1894), Warner Sylvanis (26 August 1896 - 24 December 1966), Irene Rebecca (21 August 1899 - 8 December 1899), William Roy (30 December 1900), Infant boy (born dead on Friday 15 February 1907), and Raymond Benjamin (3 September 1908 - 11 June 1970). Benjamin and Elmira are buried at Abilene Baptist Church Cemetery on Highway 113.

James Clifton was the second child of Benjamin and Elmira Muse and on 6 August 1919, he married Ruby Oelia Kilgore (4 August 1900). James Clifton and Ruby Oelia Kilgore Muse had nine children: Marilyn Virginia (1920), James Clifton Jr. (1922 - May 1997), Daniel Davis (1923), Bruce Auther (1925), Elizabeth "Betty" (1927 - 1929), Peddy Ann (1929 Infant death), Susan "Sue" Priscilla (1930), Zelda Juanita (1938), and Teresa Diane (1944).

I am Marilyn, and I am the first child of James Clifton and Ruby Oelia Kilgore Muse. On August 4, 1954, I was married in Aiken, South Carolina, to John Robert "J.R." Lynch (born 3 August 1927 in Griffin - died about 1997), and we had one son named John Benjamin Lynch, born in Chicago, Illinois, on 2 June 1955. John Benjamin married Vickie Braswell, and they have two children, Hailey Victoria and John Tyler Lynch.

As far back as I can remember we had family reunions at my Grandma and Grandpa Ben Muses' house in the summer with over 100 people there. The family names I remember being there were the Muses, Hamricks, Threadgills, Gordons, Baxters, Perdues, and Huffmans. In addition there were the friends and neighbors who came, like the Browns, Brocks, Huggins, Brigmans, Rogers, Robinsons, etc. After Grandma Elmira died in 1954, the reunions stopped. I really miss these get-togethers because that was our way to keep in touch and share our favorite dishes and stories. *Submitted by: Marilyn Lynch, 325 West College Street, Bowdon, GA 30108*

877. The Thomas P. Muse Family

Thomas P. Muse was born May 15, 1847, in Wilkes County, Georgia. He was the youngest of seven children born to William P. Muse and Mary Williams Muse. He was the grandson of George Muse and Elizabeth Jackson Muse. His father brought the family to Carroll County, Georgia, in the mid 1850's. William was a farmer, and he bought land in the Hickory Level area and continued farming. He bought other lands in the Abilene Community.

Thomas' older brother, Zachariah, volunteered for service in the Civil War. He enlisted as a private in Co. F., 3rd Regt., Georgia State Troops on October 13, 1861. He was appointed 4th Sgt. December 14, 1861, and was mustered out April 1862. He enlisted again May 13, 1862, and was appointed 4th Sgt. of Co. H 56th Regt. Georgia Infantry. He was captured at Vicksburg, Mississippi, July 4, 1863, and paroled the same day. He was home on furlough at the close of the war. Thomas P. Muse enlisted as a private in June 1864. He was with Co. H 56th Regt., Georgia Vol. Infantry, Army of Tennessee, C.S.A., Carroll County, Georgia, Carroll Invincibles. He surrendered at Greensboro, North Carolina, April 26, 1865.

Thomas P. Muse Family

Thomas P. Muse married Louisa N. Hawkins July 19, 1866. After the death of his father in 1872, the lands in the Abilene Community were divided among his heirs. Thomas received farmland and a house in the area now known as the Fred Colwell property.

On May 12, 1881, J.M. Muse and Thomas P. Muse petitioned the county for a grant or pass to make a public road starting at J.B. Lovins and going westward over the new bridge across the Tallapoosa River, then to run along the lines of the 6th and 10th Districts intersecting Cedartown Road, now known as Highway 113 near Abilene Baptist Church.

Thomas lived in this area until his death on September 28, 1921. He is buried along with his wife Louisa in the Abilene Church Cemetery. His parents are buried in Bethel Church Cemetery on Highway 113, Temple, Georgia. Several of his descendants still live in the area of what is now known as Old Muse Road and Muse Bridge Road in the Abilene Community. *Submitted by: John C. Muse, 474 Old Muse Road, Carrollton, GA 30116 and Written by: Louise M. Petty, P.O. Box 305, Carrollton, GA 30117*

878. Musick Family

John C. and Curmilla Musick were born in 1876. They lived in the Lowell community of Carroll County. Five children were born to them: three sons Alton, Buford, Colbert, and two daughters, Mae and Alma. They were farmers and attended Liberty Methodist Church.

Colbert Musick was born in 1899. He married Ida G. Cowart. Six children were born to them: two sons, Edmond and Harold, and four daughters, Vautell, Dorothy, Verna, and Jewell. He was a farmer, also. He rented the land for many years. In the early 1900s, he purchased the property from Lee Jackson and lived there until his death in 1970.

Edmond Musick, son of Colbert and Ida Musick, married Earlene Wilson in 1941. They have four children, one son Michael, and three daughters Martha, Marie, and Marsha. He was a farmer in the Lowell community. He attended school at Lowell. That building is now occupied by Fashion Star.

Edmond Musick

This picture is Edmond Musick preparing the land for planting.

Descendants of John and Curmilla Musick live in Carroll County today. *Submitted by: Granddaughter Jewell Mashburn, and great-granddaughter McIlwain, of Carrollton, GA*

879. George Musick

George Musick was born August 6, 1795 in Rutherford County, North Carolina. He died October 27, 1871, in Carroll County, Georgia. He married Mary Gray December 23, 1817, in North Carolina. She was born April 23, 1802, in North Carolina. She died July 25, 1879, in Carroll County, Georgia. Their burial places are not known.

They had the following children: Elizabeth L., Samuel D., Frances M., James W., George W., Rebecca H., David M., Eli J., Martha Elvira, Jonathan Colbert, Joseph Marion and Elasia P.

George left North Carolina between 1824 and 1826 along with several of his brothers and his father, Austin. They went to Chambers County, Alabama, but by 1830 George and Mary were living in Carroll County. He was sworn in as a constable in 1846. They lived mainly in the Lowell Community. Six of their sons served in the Civil War with Joseph and George W. giving their lives for the cause.

Benjamin Franklin and Drusilla Cavender Musick.

Jonathan Colbert Musick Sr. was born March 10, 1839, to George and Mary in Carroll County. He died in 1912 and is buried at Liberty Church in Lowell. He married Sarah C. Roberson August 18, 1859. She was born in 1839 and died December 11, 1882, in Carroll. Her burial place is unknown. John served in Company B, Glenn's Cavalry.

John and Sarah's son, Benjamin Franklin Musick, is my great-grandfather. He was born March 12, 1870, died May 2, 1946. He married Roland Drusilla Cavender on December 23, 1891, in Carroll. They are both buried at Liberty Church. Drusilla was the daughter of James Washington Cavender and Sarah L. Roberts. (The Cavender's were also a pioneer family of Carroll County.)

Benjamin and Drusilla had nine children, one of whom was my grandmother, Olive Mae (Dolly) born May 18, 1900, died May 28, 1971 in Newnan, Georgia. Dolly was known as a very good alto singer. She frequently sang at church and at fairs. The day she married Grady Ward, October 13, 1915, she and the group she sang with had won a first prize blue ribbon. She had it on her lapel in her wedding picture. She and Grady built their first home place next door to Grady's parent's home on Liberty Church Road. His parents were Andrew Jackson Ward and Emily Fleming both of whom are buried in Carroll. Emily's parents, George Fleming and Sarah Johnson, are buried at the Concord Methodist Church Cemetery in Hickory Level. Grady was born September 5, 1894, in Carroll, died January 30, 1974 in Newnan, Georgia.

Grady and Dolly had nine children: Clide, Mildred, Henry Grady "H.G.," Harold, Frances, Dorothy, Virginia, Sarah Nell and Bobby Wayne. My mother was Virginia, born June 11, 1927, died November 8, 1996, married Albert Faulkner September 19, 1942. Although Dolly and Grady left Lowell when their youngest child, Bobby, was a few months old, my mother still had many memories and ties to Carroll County.

My heritage in Carroll is rich. We have so many family connections to the county that even though I wasn't born there, I feel so much a part of this county. *Submitted by: Carolyn Evans, 225 Inland Circle, Newnan, GA 30263.*

880. James Press Neely

James Pressly/Preston Neely was born 13 August 1848 in Georgia. James P. — known as Press — was one of nine children born to Benjamin and Elizabeth Neely. Benjamin was born about 1800 in Kentucky and Elizabeth was born 16 January 1821 in Tennessee. Benjamin listed his occupation as a bridgeminder on the census. Benjamin is believed to have died between 1860 and 1870 as Elizabeth and three boys are found living in the household of William Hatchell. At this time the relationship to William Hatchell is unknown. In 1880 Elizabeth is residing with her son Nicholas Jackson Neely in Douglas County, and she joined the Winston Methodist Church in Douglas County in 1881. From Elizabeth's tombstone in Bethany Christian Cemetery in Paulding County, we find her death 30 November 1899. Benjamin and Elizabeth's nine known children are: Benjamin F. born about 1841 (Eliza); Terrisa Jane born about 1842 (Henry Truett); Nancy Caroline born about 1843; Mary born about 1844; William B. born 27 April 1845 (Eveline Annie Matthew); James Pressly/Preston born 1848 (Sarah Elizabeth Truett); John T. born about 1850; Robert born 1852; Nicholas Jackson born about 1856 (Margaret Viana Polk).

In May 1863 at Wedowee, Alabama, Press joined Company E, 17th Alabama Infantry and he stated in his pension that he was discharged around May 1864 for being under age. Press rejoined 1 July 1864 in Company E, 41st Georgia Infantry, and was present with his company at the surrender in Hillsboro, North Carolina, on 26 April 1865.

On 18 December 1867 Press married Sarah Elizabeth Truett in Harris County, Georgia. Sarah Elizabeth was born 4 December 1852, one of seven known children born to Walter Frank and Sarah Elizabeth Wilkins Truett. Sarah's siblings are Samuel H.; Mary Jane

(Newton Shell); David Morris (Vesta Johnson); Martha J.; Frances Ada (William F. Brown); and Walter Frank (Rhoda Adams).

Press and Sarah were blessed with six known children: John W. born 31 January 1870 (Mattie Robinson) and their children were Homer James, Maggie B., Ambros Aubrey, and Moses J.; Janie Elizabeth born 31 August 1875 (George W. Williamson) and their children were Effie J., George Asbury, James Thomas, Nellie Kate, Robert L., Annie Ruth, Martha Ellen (twin), and John Willie (twin); Rena Linnie born 18 February 1879 (Phillip L. Robinson and J. Rufus Hammonds), and their child was Arthur Shelton Robinson; Sam P. born about 1881 (Acilla Leola Groover) and their children were Lloyd, Fred, William K., and an infant; Hattie born 10 May 1887 (James Groover) and their children were Mildred, Claude J., Lillian, Bessie Janette, and Ella: Maggie Luella born about 1890 (James Powell) and their children were Wilma and Lona.

On 19 December 1892 we find Press issuing a mortgage deed to Hesta C. Gravitt for land lot 117 in the 9th District of Carroll County.

Sarah Elizabeth died 6 December 1925 and is laid to rest in the Indian Creek Cemetery near Bowdon. Press died 21 January 1929 and was buried beside his wife. Kytle-Aycock was paid $100 for his funeral expense listed in his pension. Many descendants of this family live in Georgia and Alabama. *Submitted by: April Harris, 708 Twin Brook Court, Marietta, GA 30060, sloua@aol.com*

881. Neill Family

Samuel Neill was born about 1760 and died about 1825. He is buried in Laurens County, South Carolina. He married Eleanor Cannon, who was born about 1763 and died November 23, 1847, in Coweta County, Georgia.

One of their sons was Josiah, born about 1793 in South Carolina and died August 20, 1839, in Coweta County, Georgia, married Respah Couch in about 1820. She died July 18, 1887, in Coweta County. Respah was the daughter of James Couch and Mary Henderson Couch. Both Josiah and Respah Neill are buried at Bethel Methodist Church in Coweta County. Josiah held church meetings at his home, which was the beginning of the Bethel Methodist Church.

Josiah and Respah's son, Green Berry Neill, was born October 10, 1822, in South Carolina and died December 23, 1907, in Carroll County. He is buried at Bethel Methodist Church in Coweta County. He married Sara (Sally) A. Bailey in Coweta County on December 12, 1843. Sally was born May 17, 1828, in South Carolina to William and Mary Bailey. Sally died October 10, 1908, in Carroll County, and is buried at Bethel Methodist Church.

Green Berry and Sally's daughter, Martha Jane Neill, was born September 15, 1846, in Coweta County and died March 5, 1926, in Carroll County. She is buried at Bethel Methodist Church. Martha Jane was married to Malvin Texas Neill on December 8, 1868. He was born September 6, 1848, and died June 6, 1944, in Carroll County. He is buried at Bethel Methodist Church. Malvin Texas was the son of Respah Lockey Pennington and her first husband.

The parents of Respah were William Henry Pennington and Mary Elizabeth Coggin of Pike County, Georgia. Respah married James A. Neill on February 8, 1855. He was the brother of Green Berry Neill. Both James A. Neill and Green Berry Neill were sons of Josiah Neill. James A. Neill adopted Malvin Texas as his son.

Martha Jane and Malvin Texas had three sons. Green Berry Neill II was born October 12, 1873, in Coweta County and died December 31, 1970 in Carrollton. He is buried in Carrollton City Cemetery. Green Berry married Ala Belle McKnight in Coweta County on April 23, 1899. Ala Belle was born October 17, 1882, in Coweta County and died April 1, 1972. She is buried in Carrollton City Cemetery. The parents of Ala Belle McKnight were Charles Richard McKnight and Mattie Rebecca Stewart of Coweta County. Green Berry and Ala Belle Neill's children were Ethel, Charlie, Pauline, J.B. and Wynnelle. *Submitted by: Wynnelle N. Rumble, 631 Longview Street, Carrollton, GA 30117*

882. Noel Nelson

Noel Nelson was born on July 11, 1832, in Walton County, Georgia. He is believed to be the son of Moses Nelson and Sarah Malcom. Noel married Martha Jane Williams in Pike County, Georgia, on January 3, 1850. Martha Jane was born in April 1832 in Georgia. Moss Nelson was the son of Noel Nelson and Carrie Melton Nelson of Morgan County. Sarah Malcolm was the daughter of John Malcom of Walton County.

Noel appears in Carroll County on the 1852 Tax Digest and is found listed in the Carroll County Inferior Court records as a juror for the January term in 1852. He lived in Carroll County until 1867. He owned and farmed land in lot number 184 in the 10th District along with his brother, Ashley. This land was located northwest of present day Carrollton.

On April 19, 1862, Noel enlisted as a volunteer for service in the Confederate Cavalry at Tallapoosa, Georgia. He was a private in Company H, 1st Regiment Georgia Cavalry. His pension papers indicate that after the battle of Chickamauga, he was discharged because he was physically unfit for service.

In 1868, Noel and family migrated to Cleburne County, Alabama, where he purchased land and lived until his death. Noel and Martha Jane Nelson were members of the Primitive Baptist Church of Christ at Mars Hill and are buried in the cemetery there. Noel died November 23, 1890. Martha Jane Nelson died January 18, 1919.

Noel and Martha raised five children, the oldest four having been born in Carroll County, Georgia: Moses, Sarah Ann, John Barnett, Julia, and Joanna Elizabeth. Moses Nelson was born on November 25, 1852 and died September 15, 1901. He never married. He is buried at Mars Hill Cemetery. Sarah Ann Nelson was born in January 1856 and died on May 10, 1904. She married on December 25, 1873, to Levi Simpson Brooks, the son of John Henry and Nancy Couch Brooks. It is believed Levi and Sarah are buried in Union Grove Cemetery in the Golden Springs area of Calhoun County, Alabama, in unmarked graves. John married Penina Emma Brooks, daughter of John Henry and Nancy Couch Brooks, on December 31, 1885. John and Emma raised seven children: Julia, Bertha, Martha, John Noel, Moses, Lethelda and Ettie Mae. John and Penina were also members of Mars Hill Primitive Baptist Church, and are buried there. John was born June 11, 1858, and died November 27, 1935. Julia was born in approximately 1867 and probably died in childhood. Johanna Elizabeth married Newton N. Waddle on December 25, 1891. Jodie, as she was affectionately known, was born in May 1872 and died December 24, 1841, in Okfuskee County, Oklahoma, where the family relocated in 1905. Newt and Johanna had nine children: Ellen, Robert, Luther, Elmer, Herbert, Hazel, Jewell, Acie and Marie.

Levi and Sarah were my great-grandparents. They raised nine children: James Otis, William Amos, Nancy Jane, Rufus Noel, Elizabeth, Annie Lee, Mollie, Jethro, and Freddie. My grandfather, Levi Jethro Brooks, was born in Ingram Wells, Calhoun County in 1895. Jethro married Maude Esther Lyle of Cedartown, Georgia. They raised four boys and two girls in Wellington and Alexandria, Alabama. *Submitted by: Babs Robinson, 3450 NE 187th Ct., Williston, FL 32696.*

Sources: Federal census records, tax digests, court records, land deeds and family recollections.

883. David Nix

David Nix, who was born December 12, 1822, in Union County, South Carolina, moved to Coweta County in 1847. There he met Emily Lenderman (August 15, 1826-August 17, 1867) whom he married on May 9, 1847. David and Emily moved to their home located one mile east of Sargent, Georgia. The father of eight children, David joined Company I, 37th Infantry of the Georgia Militia (C.S.A.) and was captured by Union forces at the Battle of Utoy Creek during the Battle of Atlanta on August 7, 1864. Sent as a prisoner of war to Camp Chase in Columbus, Ohio, he died of pneumonia on December 12, 1864. He is buried in the Camp Chase Cemetery in Grave 605.

James N. Nix 1850-1917, great-grandfather of Sara Nix Street.

The children of David and Emily Nix included Arminita, James Nathan, John, William, Columbus Alonzo, Julius Allen, Augustus Edgar and Hasmard Clementine.

Augustus Edgar Nix (1861-1940) was editor and publisher of the *Carroll County Time* newspaper, as well as newspapers in Waco and Buchanan. He served two terms as tax collector 1908-1914. He married Flora Swan in 1886 and they had eleven children.

James Nathan Nix, son of David and Emily Nix, married Martha Callister Pitts (1854-1941). James Nathan was born on August 16, 1850, and died in Lowell in Carroll County on April 10, 1917. James N. Nix's eulogy was delivered by his brother, Augustus Edgar Nix, who said of him,

> "Well and truly do those who knew my brother speak when saying 'he was a good man.' And many could go further by saying he was not only a good man, but also a Christian, having made the good confession while quite young and living a life of righteousness." He went on to say, "it fell to my brother's misfortune, but to my good providence, to have him not only as a brother, but to act as a father to me on account of having lost my father in the Civil War, and very soon thereafter Mother, too, was taken away. Being the oldest child, he took charge of the home affairs while yet in his early boyhood where three younger brothers and one sister had to be taken care of."

James N. Nix was instrumental in beginning the Christian Churches in Lowell and Carrollton.

James and Martha Nix had eight children including Walter, David R., Oscar, Paul, Francis, Beulah, Fannie, Pearl and Allie Ruth.

Walter Nix was born on October 7, 1874. He married Georgia Mobley (1873-1901). Together they had four children: Grady Woodfin, James Lloyd, Cecil and Ernest David. Following the death of Georgia Mobley, he married Judson Aldridge (1878-1921). Together they had seven children: Charley W., Lawrence Aldridge, Erline, Cliff, Jefferson Davis, Frank and I.V. (born 1914). Walter died October 19, 1963.

Many of the descendants of David Nix still live in the Carroll County area and have distinguished themselves both in the home as well as in the community as civic leaders, educators, business people and leaders in the church. *Submitted by: James L. Street, 4845 Glen White Drive, Duluth, GA 30096*

884. Abner Nixon Family

Abner Nixon was born March 14, 1821. The place of his birth and the name of his parents are unknown. The first we know of Abner is that he marries Eliza Matilda McSwain who was born February 29, 1842. Eliza was the daughter of Alfred and Lucenda Evans McSwain. They were married in Randolph County near Goldridge. It was there that the first six children were born. They were Emily Jane, Amanda Armentia, Henry Madison, Mary Frances, Perry Decatur, and Silas Dean. Abner was a farmer.

On August 12, 1861, he volunteered to serve in the Confederate Army during the War Between the States. He volunteered from Randolph County, Alabama, and was assigned to the Alabama 13th Regiment at Richmond, Virgiia. In August 1862, he was in the 41st Georgia Regiment near Chattanooga, Tennessee.At the battle at Perryville, Kentucky, on October 8, 1862, he was wounded in the foot. He returned home for a while but returned to serve on guard duty. The family has several interesting letters written by Abner to his wife and children during his time in service.

When he returned home, he continued to farm and to teach in nearby schools. Two other sons, Robert Paron and Wilson Asbury, were born.

In the early 1870s, Abner moved his family to Carroll County to a place just east of the Tallapoosa River at Simonton's Mill on what is now Highway 166. All the children moved with the family except Mary Frances, who had married William E. Mathews and remained in Alabama, and Henry Madison who married Eliot Prichard and moved to Texas. Armentia had married Levi Loveless who died. She and her son, William, moved with the family to Georgia.

On February 3, 1878, Eliza died and was buried at Old Camp Methodist Church near where they lived. A few years later, Abner and his family moved to a farm just west of the Tallapoosa River on what is now Salem Road.

Abner and others around him became interested in a new church. In 1883 they organized a Salem Baptist Church. Abner was clerk of the new church. His name is on the marker there.

Abner died November 18, 1886, at his home. He was buried by the side of his beloved wife Eliza at Old Camp Methodist Church. Emily Jane lived with her father until his death. After her father's death, she married four widowers and cared for them until their deaths. They were John Weir, Marion Bonner, Robert Bishop, and William McElroy. Amanda Nixon Loveless married Parks Chandler. She later moved to North Alabama with her son. Perry Decatur married Tabitha Brown and moved to Bowdon. Silas Dean married Margaret Fletcher. They reared their large family near Salem Church. Robert Paran married Annie Bohannon. They moved to Bowdon in 1907 so that their children could go to school there. William Asbury married Lucy Vise and they reared their family in the Salem community.

There were thirty-six grandchildren, many of whom reared their families in Carroll County. There are many descendants in the area who have contributed to the development of Carroll County. They have been interested in education, government, county development, and the religious life of the county.

The accompanying photograph ws taken at the Nixon reunion in October of 1905 at the home of Robert P. Nixon. On the front row are George Nixon, Ethyl Nixon, Eliza Nixon, Thomas Boyd, Beulah Price, Alma Price, Myrtle Nixon, Albert Nixon, Maude Nixon, Abner Nixon, Olivia Nixon. Second row, Emily Nixon Wier, Perry D. Nixon, Tabitha Nixon, Lucy Nixon with Dura, Georgia Boyd, Eula Price, Annie Nixon, Sally Nixon, and Lee Nixon. Third row, John Wier, Laura Mathis, Fanny Nixon Mathis, Willson A. Nixon with Jewell, Ida Nixon with Oscar, Armentia Nixon Chandler, Parks Chandler, Robert P. Nixon, Margaret Nixon, Alice Nixon. Top row, Asbury Nixon, Joseph Abner Mathis with Owen, Brown Nixon, Mr. Boyd, Sam Nixon, Silas Dean Nixon. *Submitted by: Mildred Nixon and Mabel Nixon Walls, Grand Court, Carrollton, GA*

885. Abner Nixon

Abner Nixon was born 14 March 1821, probably in Georgia. He married Eliza Matilda McSwain, daughter of Alfred McSwain and Lucinda Rebecca Evans on 24 December 1846. Abner and family are found in the 1850 and 1860 Randolph County, Alabama, census and then in the 1870 Cleburne County, Alabama, census. They are then found in the 10th District of Carroll County, Georgia, for the 1880 census. Abner died at his home in Carroll County on November 18, 1886. He and Eliza are buried at Old Camp United Methodist Church, Carroll County.

Children of Abner and Eliza are: Emily Jane, 31 October 1847-13 January 1941; Manda Arnimenta, 31 January 1850-9 July 1920; Henry Madison, 8 January 1852-January 1928; Mary "Fannie" Frances, 30 January 1854-24 May 1926; Perry Decatur, 8 October 1856-20 January 1940; Silas Dean, 8 April 1859-29 April 1941; "the babe" born and died 11 July 1864; Robert Paran, 9 October 1867-10 June 1939; Wilson "Bud" Asbury 13 March 1870-6 February 1961.

Abner Nixon wrote of Robert's name in the family Bible:

"I name this child in honor of Dr. Robert Steele of Pinkingville, Illinois, a Federal Surgeon, and Mr. Paran; a Confederate Soldier. Dr. Steele amputated my wounded foot March 24, 1863 and treated me kindly while I was prisoner of war. Mr. Paran was from Texas. He nursed me while confined after my foot was amputated. To the kindness of these two men and the helping of God, I owe my life. I do not name this child in honor of the Federal cause. I am, was, and will be a States Rights Democrat."

In 1861, Abner enlisted with the 13th Alabama Regiment. Then on 4 August 1862,he reenlisted as a private with Company H, 41st Regiment of the Georgia Volunteer Infantry (known as the Wool Hat Boys) from Carroll County. During his service, his right foot was wounded, requiring amputation at Perryville, Kentucky.

Little is known about Abner's siblings and parents. We know he had a sister, Sarah, born 9 December 1816. She was married to Harvey Hicks in Franklin County, Georgia, on 5 January 1835. Children of Sarah and Harvey were: Washington Richy Hicks, born 30 January 1836 in Georgia; James Asbury Hicks, 17 June 1837 in Georgia-17 March 1864 Randolph County, Alabama; Isaiah Williams Hicks, 25 December 1838, Georgia-5 February 1860 Randolph County, Alabama; William Abner Hicks, born 27 February 1841.

Sarah married second to William Williamson.

We believe Millington Asbury Nixon was Abner and Sarah's brother. Millington was born about 1818-1820 in Georgia. His wife was Tabitha. They had at least seven children, including Charlotte born 1843 in Georgia; Martha born 1844-45 in Alabama; William A. born 1847 in Alabama; and Francis M. born 1849 in Alabama. Millington is living next to Abner in the 1850 Randolph County Alabama census. He is then found in Calhoun County, Alabama in 1860.

Millington and Abner are listed as Patentees for three land lot transactions in Range #12 E, Section #17S of Alabama on March 1, 1850.

For the 1880 census, Abner states his father was born in South Carolina and his mother in Virginia. Family legend has it that his mother was Indian and that his father was hung after he killed man who had slurred his wife's heritage. Abner writes of a peer in a letter home during the war, "He knows all my folks at Powder Springs." Powder Springs is in Cobb County, Georgia, which was formed in 1831 from Indian lands.

Abner Nixon, along with J.A. Marlow and F. Stamps, donated the land on which Salem Baptist Church was built. The church is located between Carrollton and Bowdon in Carroll County off Highway 166.

It appears Abner married a second time. Carroll County marriage records show a marriage on 25 August 1878 for Abner Nixon and (Mrs.) Martha E. Walker. Martha Nixon and her daughters, with the last name of Walker, are living next to Abner and his children in the 1880 census. On the other side of Mrs. Martha Nixon is Abner's son, Perry Nixon.

Submitted by: Valerie Freeman, Tustin, CA and Written by: Helen Foster, Bowdon, GA

The Nixon Family 1905

886. Wiley Nixon

Wiley Nixon was a farmer in the Mandeville community of Carroll County, Georgia. He was born in Oglethorpe County, Georgia, on September 15, 1816.

The Memoirs of Georgia published in 1895, Volume 1, reports:

> Wiley was the son of Joseph and Martha Ward Nixon. Joseph (Joe) was born in what is now Wilkes County, Georgia about 1775. Joe was bound out as a boy and learned the carpenter's trade. When older, he engaged in farming and was a soldier in the War of 1812. Joe moved to Coweta County in 1830 and settled in the woods where he lived in a dirt floor cabin. Martha died in July 1860 in Coweta County from typhoid. Joseph died between 1833 and 1840. This is based on the fact that their youngest child Joseph Jr. was born in 1833 and Martha is listed as "head of household" in the 1840 census. Martha and Joseph Sr. are buried in an old family cemetery (off Gordon Road between Luther Bailey Road and the access road for Mt. Pilgrim Cemetery near Haralson, Coweta County).
>
> Wiley Nixon came to Coweta County with his father. Wiley was a member of Mt. Pilgrim Evangelical Lutheran Church; church records indicate he was admitted by baptism on August 25, 1871. He lived in Coweta County until 1874, when he moved and settled on a partly-cleared farm in Carroll County. He cleared the remainder of the land and eventually owned 600 acres of good land in Carroll County.
>
> *Memoirs of Georgia* also said:
>
> "He (Wiley Nixon) began life very poor, has worked hard on the farm all his life, and although not rich, he has a competency and is rich in the possession of sincere friends, and the consciousness of a well-spent life. He owns 600 acres of good land, a farm well improved and a good home in which to spend his declining years. Mr. Nixon has been a member of the Masonic fraternity more than 40 years and is regarded as one of the most substantial, and is among the most respected of the county's citizens."

He was married on July 20, 1852, to Elizabeth Fullilove, born in Coweta County on February 18, 1838. Wiley died in 1903. Elizabeth died in Carroll County on December 25, 1927. She and Wiley are buried together at the former Smyrna United Methodist Church, Highway 27 North, Carrollton. Elizabeth's parents were Lud and Alsa (Freeman) Fullilove.

Children of Wiley and Elizabeth Fullilove Nixon: (1) William Weldon, one source says he was born July 31, 1854, but tomb reads 1856; (2) George Page, born February 6, 1858; (3) Fannie M., born April 5,1862; (4) Elsie Rebecca, born August 2, 1865; (5) Martha D., born May 14, 1868; (6) Almadia R., born May 4, 1870; (7) Ludwell, born March 22, 1874; (8) Nannie P., born September 22, 1876, (9) Wiley J., born July 27, 1881; (10) Bessie Ada, born June 14, 1883. *Submitted by: Sam Gentry, 167 Little River Road, Carrollton, GA 30117*

Sources: *The Memoirs of Georgia*, Vol. 1, 1895; church records and tombstones, U.S. census records.

887. Henry Curtis Norris

Henry Curtis Norris was born 25 March 1866 in Upson County, Georgia. His parents were Amos P. and Mattie Norris. He died August 1959 in Fulton County. Henry married Carrie Cleo Tyson. She was born 27 February 1870 in Meriwether County, Georgia, and died 19 December 1923 in Carroll County, Georgia. They are buried at Stripling Chapel Church, Carrollton, Georgia. They had eleven children, some of whom died in infancy. Included are Infant, Bessie Norris Folds, Sallie Norris, Lillie Norris, Jimmy Norris, Infant, Hallie Norris, Virgie Norris Robertson, Ester Norris Key, Delia Norris Skeen, William Thomas Norris.

Henry Curtis Norris Home

Delia Skeen is still living in Atlanta, Georgia, at age ninety-five.

The home place was 124 Dixie Street just past the railroad track where Robinson Drug Store stands today. Deed records from the Carroll County courthouse revealed that Henry owned approximately 2,000 acres of land on Dixie Street where Tanner Medical Center stands today. He also owned property on West Center, South Park, Stewart and Maple Street. He sold most of it in lots for as little as $75 each.

At some point, Henry moved to West Center Street. It was told that he built the sidewalks on that street, but did not put one in front of his house. It remains that way today.

He had a cement company and did lots of pavements and sidewalks all over Carrollton. He built the first paved square, pavements down the streets off the square, around the courthouse, the brick parking area behind the old post office, which is still there. The cemeteries are full of his work, walks and tombstones.

Records found showed that the street, which went past the old ice plant, was once named Norris Street.

Henry's son, William (Bill) Norris spent his lifetime in Carrollton and was also a very good mason. He helped build the original building of the State University of West Georgia, the old city gymnasium and others.

He and his wife, Lora (Hightower) Norris are buried at the Carrollton City Cemetery.

Henry Norris still has grandchildren, great-grandchildren and great-great grandchildren living in Carrollton. *Submitted by: Helen Marie (Norris) Horton, Bonnie (Norris) Powers, Curtis Edward Norris, and Lisa Susanne (Powers) Harper*

888. Ogletree

James M. Ogletree purchased a quarter section of land in the 5th District of Carroll County from Eli Benson in November 1880. At the time, he and his wife Cordelia Williams Ogletree were living in Butts County with their four children. His brother, William T. Ogletree, bought land in Carroll County at the same time.

James and William were two of nine children of Absalom and Matilda Stewart Ogletree from Monroe County. Absalom was a minister and one of the founding fathers of the Congregational Methodist Church. Absalom's father, William, had received land lottery grants in Monroe County as a Revolutionary War veteran and had moved there in 1835 from Wilkes County.

James M. Ogletree grew up in Monroe County but attended school before the Civil War in Bowdon. After returning from the war, he married his sweetheart Cordelia Williams on January 11, 1866.

In 1881, due to a malaria epidemic, they decided to move and chose Carroll County for its

(L to R) Howell C., James M., James T., Cordelia W., and Elena W. Ogletree. 1913.

"cooler climate." James M. and his two oldest sons, Augustus and Early, drove a wagon with the household goods and livestock from their Butts County home to Carroll County. Cordelia, along with the youngest son, Howell Clark (my grandfather) who was seven at the time, rode the train to Clem. Another son, Philemon H., was born after the family had moved to Carroll County in 1882 but only lived to be four years old.

In 1887, James M. bought an adjoining quarter section from James H. Archer with a dogtrot style house that featured a detached kitchen (see photo). At one point the house caught on fire from a kerosene lamp and the family put it out with buckets of well water. My grandfather was young at the time and said he tried to take out something of value to save from burning and all he could think of to save was his father's Sunday hat.

In 1893 a tornado hit and the family gathered in the detached kitchen and prayed for their lives. The tornado lifted the roof off the main house and deposited it in the front field but did not touch the kitchen.

James M.'s brother, William T., settled with his wife (also named Cordelia) and son Wilbur on a farm behind where First Tuesday Mall is today. My father told of the time in 1910 when he visited them after their house had burned. He arrived to find them living in their chicken house. William had died by this time and his son sold out and moved to Oklahoma.

My father used to love to listen to his grandpa James M. tell his Civil War stories. As he would listen, my father would rub the bullets still lodged in his grandpa's leg and arm. My father also told how he and his grandpa would walk to the fields together following the wagon roads. My father being very young and his grandfather being very old traveled at the same speed and both enjoyed the walk. James M. never took his clay pipe to the fields with him, so at exactly 10:00 a.m. and 3:00 p.m. (quartering time) they would head back to the house so that James M. could get his pipe (always kept over the fireplace) and have a break and a smoke.

Going to the back field of the present farm, there are still-used rutted wagon roads. As you travel those roads, you can see the rock piles along the property lines that my forefathers put there.

Around 1911, James M.'s oldest sons had married and moved to farms of their own. He told my grandfather Howell C. that if he would assume the mortgage notes, provide for him and his wife and allow them to live out their lives on the farm, he would sign it over to him. At that point, he had only been able to pay the interest on the farm. Howell did take over the farm and paid off the mortgage by raising cotton using a mule to plow the ground.

My father James Thomas (JT) Ogletree, was born in 1907 and had two other siblings who died soon after birth. However, he did get to grow up in the house with his grandparents until their deaths in 1920. They died seven months apart. *Submitted by: Robert H. Ogletree, 1091 Old Newnan Road, Carrollton, GA 30116*

Sources: *John Ogletree Sr. 1740-1822 Two Hundred Twenty Five Years of Descendants*, by Kyser Cowart Ptomey, 1986. Carroll County deed records.

889. Albert Lonzo Otwell Family

Albert Lonzo Otwell was born on January 14, 1880, in Haralson County, Georgia, and died September 15, 1958, in Carroll County. Albert married Ernestine Eula Haskins of Campbell County, Georgia, who was born July 13, 1878, in Campbell County, and died March 15, 1971, in Carroll County. They are buried at Midway Macedonia Church Cemetery in Carroll County.

Albert Otwell was the son of Fletcher Otwell and Julia Crawford whose farm was located at County Line in Haralson County. Albert's farm was located on Mooyn Road in Carroll County, and he was a farmer and a grist mill and gin employee.

Otwell - Albert and Eula, Circa 1948

Eula Haskins was the daughter of Mary Brock and Tom Haskins of Campbell County. Eula was a homemaker.

Albert and Eula Otwell's children were: Floye Corine, Marjorie Claire, Cuma Beatrice, Elsie Miriam, Albert Wilton, Charlie Wayne and Bernice Estelle.

Floye Corine Otwell was born on November 24, 1900, in Haralson County, and died on November 12, 1991, in Douglas County. Floye married James Riley Lewis who was born on April 6, 1893, in Fayette County, Georgia, and died on June 10, 1983, in Fulton County, Georgia. They are buried at Holly Hill Cemetery in Fairburn, Georgia.

Floye and Riley owned a feed store in Fairburn, Georgia. Floye was employed at a sewing plant during World War II, and later she was employed at a grocery and a feed and appliance store for ten years. Riley was a carpenter before they bought the store.

Floye and Riley Lewis' children were: James Riley Jr., Ronald Otwell, Vespa Arnold, Emily Frances, William Thomas, Murray Denver, and Helen Beatrice.

Marjorie Claire Otwell was born on September 14, 1902, in Haralson County, died January 27, 1992, in Carroll County and married on September 20, 1925, Samuel Watson Roberts who was born on April 22, 1894, in Carroll County and died August 2, 1981, in Carroll County. Sam and Claire are buried at Midway Macedonia Church Cemetery in Carroll County.

Albert Otwell family reunion, Circa 1948.

Claire was a school teacher in the Hulett school, a seamstress, and a substitute teacher at New Georgia School in Paulding County for a short time.

Sam Roberts was the son of Richard Polk Roberts and Mary Lou Sewell of Carroll County and the grandson of Reverend James Rainwater who was one of three ministers who ministered at Pleasant Grove Baptist Church in Carroll County from 1850 to 1860, and he was also the minister of the First Baptist Church in Carrollton in 1858 and 1859. Sam was a school teacher at Hulett, Clem, Walnut Hill and Flat Rock schools in Carroll County for ten years, and he was a Soil Conservation Supervisor in Carroll County for forty years. Later, he was employed at Cannon Casket and also dealt in real estate for many years.

Sam and Claire Roberts' children were: Robert Glenn, Eva Ruth, and Samuel Watson Jr.

Cuma Beatrice Otwell was born on September 16, 1904 in Haralson County and died on February 19, 1991, in Carroll County. Beatrice is buried at Midway Macedonia Cemetery in Carroll County. Beatrice never married and she kept children for working mothers in her home.

Elsie Miriam Otwell was born on January 31, 1907, in Haralson County, and died on October 14, 1991, in Carroll County. Miriam married Ezra Floyd Moore who was born on November 9, 1897, in Carroll County and died March 31, 1964, in Carroll County. They are buried at Bethany Christian Church Cemetery in Carroll County.

Miriam was employed in a pants factory for ten years and Ezra was a carpenter and a farmer.

Miriam and Ezra Moore's children were: Harvey, Clarence Dale, Billy Floyd, Donald Hugh, Frances Annette, Evelyn Wynelle.

Albert Wilton Otwell was born March 19, 1909, in Haralson County and married Sara Alma Couch who was born on September 11, 1907, in Douglas County, and died April 11, 2000, in Carroll County. Sally is buried at Midway Macedonia Cemetery in Carroll County. Wilton was a farmer and a cabinet maker, and he was employed at Delmar Cabinet Company in Altanta until he retired at age sixty-five. Sally was a homemaker. Wilton and Sally Otwell's children were: Harold Wilton and Sara Ann.

Charlie Wayne Otwell was born August 9, 1911, in Haralson County and died September 19, 1999. Wayne married Lois Jane Boatright who was born September 29, 1905, in Carroll County and died August 17, 1995, in Carroll County. Lois was the daughter of Hiram Woody Boatright of Carroll County who was a Baptist minister. Lois and Wayne are buried at Meadowbrook Gardens in Carroll County.

Wayne owned a store at Sand Hill for many years and later he was employed and retired from Delmar Cabinet Company in Atlanta. Lois helped in the store and was a homemaker. Wayne and Lois Otwell's child was: Marjorie Imogene.

Bernice Estelle Otwell was born on August 13, 1913, in Haralson County and died on April 1, 1995, in Haralson County. Bernice married Carl Couch who was born on April 26, 1909, in Carroll County and died April 4, 1992, in Carroll County. Bernice and Carl divorced. Bernice was a seamstress and she was also employed at Villa Rica Hospital in food services and laundry for seven years. She is buried at Melrose Gardens in Paulding County and Carl is buried at Midway Macedonia Cemetery in Carroll County. Bernice and Carl Couch's children were: James Hugh and Cecil Otwell. *Submitted by: Scott Holder, Apartment B, Atlanta, GA 30307 and Written by: Pauline C. Roberts, P.O. Box 461, Villa Rica, GA 30180*

Sources: Family records and family knowledge.

890. Robert Fletcher Otwell Family

Robert Fletcher Otwell was born in Cleburne County, Alabama, on August 17, 1850, and died in Haralson County, Georgia, on March 9, 1930. Fletcher married on May 19, 1870, Julia Crawford who was born on September 20, 1854, and died on July 19, 1930 in Haralson County.

Fletcher Otwell's parents were William N. Otwell and Malinda Teague. Julia Crawford's parents were Garland Gallant Crawford and Carion Riland. Garland Crawford was a veteran of the Indian Wars. They are all buried in the County Line Cemetery, west of Center Point community in Carroll County.

*Fletcher and Julia Otwell's children were: William G., Jefferson James Robert, Henry Wyatt, Cornelia C., John Fletcher, Albert Lonzo,

Fletcher Otwell family, County Line North of Center Point, Circa 1901.

Arthur Airy, Naomi, Walter D., Alice, Marshall Luther, Beulah, and Emmitt Teague.

*William G. Otwell was born on November 17, 1871, in Haralson County, and died on July 31, 1929. William G. married Martha Mattie McDaniel. William and Martha Mattie Otwell's children were: William F., and Rowena.

Rowena taught music in Villa Rica, Georgia, which was noted in the *Carroll County Times* in 1926.

*Jefferson James Robert Otwell was born on August 12, 1873, in Harlason County, and died on March 11, 1964, married Lillie Keneley. Jefferson and Lillie Otwell's children were: Ethel, Annie Saluda, Wyatt Paul, Floyd, Ruth, Avis, Myrl, and Lena.

*Henry Wyatt Otwell was born on June 6, 1875, in Harlason County, and his death is unknown. Wyatt married Janie Doster. Wyatt and Janie Otwell's children were: Lonnie, Lois, Louise and Clyde.

Robert Fletcher and Julia A. Crawford Otwell, Circa 1901.

*Cornelia C. Otwell was born on December 10, 1876, in Haralson County, and died August 28, 1877. She is buried in County Line Cemetery in Carroll County.

*John Fletcher Otwell was born on February 9, 1878, in Haralson County, and his death is unknown. John married Ethel Hartley. John and Ethel Otwell's children were: Thomas Jackson, Hobart Deforest, Frances Bell, James Robert, John Fletcher Jr., William Eugene (Billy), Kathrin Shell and Jerry Verna.

*Albert Lonzo Otwell was born January 14, 1880, in Haralson County and died on September 15, 1958, in Carroll County. Albert married Eula Haskins who was born on July 13, 1878, in Campbell County and died on March 15, 1971, in Carroll County. They are buried at Midway Macedonia Cemetery in Carroll County. Albert and Eula Otwell's children were: Floye Corine, Marjorie Claire, Cuma Beatrice, Elsie Miriam, Albert Wilton, Charlie Wayne and Bernice Estelle.

*Arthur Airy Otwell was born on February 12, 1882, in Haralson County and his death is unknown. Arthur married Vella Estella Lovern. Arthur and Vella Otwell's children were: Sarah, Raymond and Ralph.

*Naomi Otwell was born on November 27, 1885, in Haralson County and her death is unknown. Naomi married Samuel Andrew Buttrill Sr. Naomi and Samuel Buttrill's children were: Zuma, Marcus, Dupree, Brown Otwell, Samuel Andrew Jr., Florence.

*Walter D. Otwell was born on June 12, 1886, in Haralson County and his death is unknown. Walter married Lily Hamrick. Walter and Lily Otwell's children were: Cecil, Ray, Pauline, and Jean.

*Alice Otwell was born on December 21, 1888, in Haralson County and her death is unknown. Alice married Erby Hughes. Alice and Erby Hughes' child was: Erby B. Jr.

*Marshall Luther Otwell was born on September 23, 1890, in Haralson County and died on September 16, 1977. Marshal Luther married Mary Ezzie Camp. Marshall and Mary Ezzie Otwell's children were: Julia Freece, Edna Iris and Reba Louise.

*Beulah Otwell was born on November 21, 1891, in Haralson County, and her death is unknown. Beulah married William L. Spake. Beulah and William L. Spake's children were: Arthur, Frances, Alice, Inez and Fred.

*Emmitt Teague Otwell was born on August 10, 1898, in Haralson County, and died on August 18, 1967. Emmitt Teague married Lela Ann McConnell. Emmitt Teague and Lela Ann Otwell's child was: Robert Earl. *Submitted by: Mark Holder, 815 Ponce De Leon Terrace N.E., Atlanta, GA 30306 and Written by: Pauline C. Roberts, P.O. Box 461, Villa Rica, GA 30180*
Sources: Cemetery records, family records, and personal knowledge.

891. Owens - Robinson - Hammond

On August 19, 1837, William Owens purchased Land Lot #134 in the 8th District, Fifth Section, of Carroll County from Thomas J. Stephens of Oglethorpe County, Georgia. Stephens had drawn the lot in the Creek Lottery, known as the 1827 Land Lottery of Georgia, on July 17, 1833.

While washing a pan of potatoes, taken from a patch near the present stamp mill, bright specks of gold were noticed in the dirt. Investigation of the potato field substantiated the hope thus raised and resulted in the discovery of a rich surface deposit. Owens soon began mining operations, which he successfully continued for several years.

During this time he erected a twelve-stamp mill on Walker Creek and did considerable vein mining as well as surface work. William Owens sold the mine to Edmond W. Holland about 1847 when he moved to Arkansas.

His daughter, Jane Ann Owens, was born July 3, 1828, and died May 5, 1899. On April 11, 1847, she married John Lavender Robinson. He was born September 19, 1828, and died March 21, 1860, of pneumonia. Their children were born in the part of Carroll County that is now part of Haralson County, Georgia. Their names were:

1. John William Robinson, born January 25, 1849, died January 7, 1926, who married Louisa Patience Powell who was born July 24, 1854, and died February 18, 1925. Both are buried in Carrollton City Cemetery.
2. Thomas Jefferson Robinson was born February 19, 1851, and died in 1911. He married Ella Cassandra Cousins, born 1857 and died 1937 in Meriwether County, Georgia.
3. Madison Edward Robinson was born August 20, 1853, and died 1922. He is buried in Brown's Cemetery at Temperance Methodist Church at Sand Hill, Carroll County, Georgia.
4. Willis M. Robinson was born November 27, 1855, and died in Florida about 1893. He married Ruth Toole and is probably buried in Troup County, Georgia.
5. Charles H. Robinson was born November 3, 1858, and died in Atlanta. He married Mary Brown, born 1863 and died 1905.

Jane Ann Owens Robinson married Elisha Quincy Hammond on January 19, 1869, in Coweta, County, Georgia. He was born March 25, 1825, and died on March 17, 1883, and was buried in Coweta County. They had one daughter, Helen May Hammond, who was born December 10, 1871. She married Charles Forest Richards on December 28, 1892, in Carroll County. He was the son of William Thomas Richards and and Nancy Elizabeth Boyd. He was born August 16, 1867, in Carroll County and died on February 18, 1966, in Carroll County. They are both buried in Brown's Cemetery at Temperance Methodist Church Cemetery on Highway 61 near Sand Hill Community, Carroll County. *Submitted by: Roger A. Matthews, 342 Thomas Dorsey Drive, Villa Rica, GA 30180*
Sources: Personal knowledge, Bible records and research of Helen Matthews

892. Ann Aaron and Thomas C. Padgett Jr. Family

Thomas Clinton Padgett Jr. was born 8 October 1964 in Columbus, Mississippi, during his father's Air Force years. He grew up all over the United States since his father was in the service. He graduated from high school in Burke, Virginia. Tom Padgett Jr. is the son of Thomas Clinton Padgett Sr. and Joy Hilliard Padgett of Carrollton. On 5 September 1987, Tom Padgett Jr. married Angel (Ann) Aaron. She was born in Edinburg, Texas, on 6 June 1962, the daughter of Hollis Aaron and Iren Johnson Aaron. The Aarons live in San Antonio, Texas.

Tom Padgett Jr. received his B.B.A. with a major in finance from West Georgia College in 1986 and took flying lessons from Johnny Fletcher. Tom later became an Air Force pilot, flying B52s.

Tom Padgett Jr., received the Airman's Medal for an act of heroism on Veteran's Day 1991. On that day, Capt. Padgett and his family had been driving along Highway 82 near Reform, Alabama, when they suddenly witnessed a pickup truck flying through the air and landing upside down in a ditch. A nineteen-year-old college student had tried to make a blind pass on a hill and there had been a collision with the truck at the top of the hill. A seventy-nine-year-old man who'd been driving the pickup truck was trapped in the flaming vehicle and was difficult to extract from the truck, but Padgett and another man on the scene were finally able to remove him. Capt. Padgett then turned his attention toward the young college girl who was seriously injured. He gave emergency care until paramedics arrived.

Unfortunately, the nineteen-year-old was pronounced dead at the scene. The elderly man survived a few weeks but then contracted pneumonia, and died. They awarded Capt. Padgett the Airman's Medal for Heroisim. "Tom's act of complete selflessness exemplifies the high quality of people we have in the Air Force," said Maj. Mike Hainsey, chief of wing safety. "I'm really glad to have someone of his caliber representing the safety office and what it stands for." Tom Padgett Jr. later said, "This shows how important it is to wear a seatbelt no matter how easy it is to drive a car, you can never let down your guard."

1976 Mess Dress. Capt. Thomas C. Padgett Jr. and Ann Aarons Padgett

During their years in the Air Force, Tom Padgett Jr. and his family made their home in Michigan, Mississippi, and Texas. They were living in Oklahoma City at the time of the bombing of the federal building there. They lived eight miles away but felt the house shake as if it were an earthquake. Tom Padgett Jr. left the Air Force in December 1998 and is now employed as a pilot for American Airlines. He and his wife Ann and family make their home in Dallas, Texas.

The children of Tom Padgett Jr. and Ann Aaron Padgett are (1) Joy born 6 September 1981 (2) John Clayton Padgett born 17 October 1985 (3) Lindsay Padgett born 3 August 1988 and (4) Thomas Clinton "Chipper" Padgett III born 15 September 1997. *Submitted by: Ann and Thomas C. Padgett Jr., Dallas, TX, and Written by: Jan Robinson Bell.*

893. The Dr. Thomas C. and Joy Hilliard Padgett Family

Being a college town has always been a bonus to our community in that it draws many people to Carrollton who like it so much here that they decide to stay. The Padgett family first came to Carrollton in 1982 when Dr. Tom Padgett had just retired from the Air Force after twenty years. Several other friends of theirs who had retired from the Air Force — Jay and Margo Inman, Frank and Jo Hunsicker, and Gene and first wife, Barbara Poindexter, encouraged the Padgetts to come join them here — and they did.

Dr. Thomas C. Padgett and Joy Hilliard Padgett

Both Dr. Tom Padgett and his wife, Joy, have taught at West Georgia College — and have been a part of the transition of West Georgia College to the now State University of West Georgia. Dr. Tom Padgett is now the chairman of the Department of West Georgia's Management and Business Systems. Joy Padgett no longer teaches but writes occasional columns for the *Carroll Star News.* She is also editing books, has co-authored one book with a friend, and is nearing completion of her memoirs. Joy has won several awards for her writing talents. Joy is the president of the West Georgia Writer's Guild, Inc. Many people in Carrollton remember Joy for her wonderful store 1987-1992 called The Balloon Factory.

Tom Padgett and Joy Hilliard, Valentine's Day 1956

Thomas Clinton Padgett was born 18 December 1940 in Tattnall Co., Georgia, the son of Mary Gillingham and Jewette Mercedes Padgett. Tom grew up in Glennville, Georgia, and Joy Hilliard was his high school sweetheart. They are pictured here at Joy's fourteenth birthday party, which was a Valentine's Dance in 1956. They had just finished dancing to the music of "Twilight Time." Both Tom and Joy graduated from Glennville High School.

Tom Padgett received his bachelor of music education degree from the University of Georgia in 1962. While at the University of Georgia, he and Don Hall were members of the Dixie Redcoat Band. Later on, Don Hall became well known in Carrollton as the director of the Carrollton High School Band.

Shortly after graduation, Tom joined the Air Force. After 20 years in the Air Force, he retired in 1982 as a Lt. Colonel. During his years in the Air Force, Tom completed his master's of science in industrial management at the University of North Dakota. He also completed his Ph.D. in business administration and management at Florida State University in 1975. After his retirement from the Air Force in 1982, he became a professor of business management at West Georgia College.

Dr. Padgett is an accomplished pianist and often entertains his family with original musical scores that he has written. He also plays the guitar and sings — and has quite a wonderful sense of humor. He likes to cook and his barbecued ribs are the best in the South. All these talents come together to make family gatherings at the Padgett home a lot of fun! The grandchildren call Joy and Tom — Gamma and Pop. Jan Robinson Bell would like to take this opportunity to say that she thinks her son, John, is the luckiest one in the world to have married into such a special family.

Mary Gillingham Padgett, 1938

Dr. Tom Padgett is a descendant of the Gillingham family through his mother Mary Gillingham. The first of the Gillinghams in America was Yeamans Gillingham who came from the south of England about 1685. He purchased land in Philadelphia in 1691. Yeamans was a Quaker and his wife was Mary Taylor who left a will in 1727 in Philadelphia. Yeamans' will was probated in Philadelphia on 21 July 1722. The line coming down seven generations from Yeamans Gillingham is as follows:

Yeamans > James > John > Samuel > Jonathan > John Ware > Jonathan Gillingham.

John Gillingham was born in Bucks County, Pennsylvania, 6 September 1847. He married Henrietta "Nettie" Smith, the daughter of Henry Smith, who was born in Easton, Pennsylvania, 20 October 1847. Christi Padgett Bell inherited the beautiful amethyst engagement ring that Jonathan gave to Nettie. It is inscribed with her name and their wedding date on the inside — September 14,

Jewette Padgett, 1938

Dr. Clinton H. Gillingham

1873. Jonathan Gillingham was a newspaperman who wrote under the pseudonym of "Sculls" and was well known in boating circles. He was also warden of the Port of Philadelphia. Both Jonathan and Nettie are buried in the old cemetery at Easton, Pennsylvania.

The son of Jonathan and Nettie was Clinton Hancock Gillingham who was born at Philadelphia 29 September 1877. He died at Maryville, Tennessee, 18 July 1955 at the age of 77. Dr. Clinton H. Gillingham was for 22 years a professor of Bible and Religion at Maryville College in Maryville, Tennessee. In 1929, Rev. Gillingham moved to Philadelphia to become the president of Tennent College of Christian Education. In 1943, this school was merged into the Princeton Seminary.

Thomas Harold Hilliard and Georgia Lee Wilkes

Dr. Gillingham spent a year of study in the Holy Land — and after his return from this trip, the *Knoxville Journal and Tribune* published a series of articles he'd written about this trip between 21 July 1923 and 12 January 1924. Dr. Gillingham also gave many lectures on his experiences in the Holy Land.

Clinton H. Gillingham married Nancy Virginia Gardner 2 November 1903 at Hyden, Kentucky. Nancy Gardner was born in Salyersville, Kentucky, on 27 January 1882, the daughter of

Georgia Lee Wilkes Hilliard and Joy Hilliard

Tom Padgett Sr. and Tom Padgett Jr.

Joseph Gardner and Nancy Jane Williams. Joseph Gardner was well known throughout Kentucky and at the time of his death in 1887, he was the candidate on the Democratic Party ticket for Lt. Gov. of Kentucky. Nancy Jane Williams was the daughter of Dial David Williams and Mary Ann McCormick. Nancy Jane was the granddaughter of Mason Williams and Sarah Cope — pioneer settlers of Kentucky.

Maryville College had been established in 1819 by the Presbyterian Synod. It had to close 1861-1865 while General W.T. Sherman used the campus as a camp for his troops. The school reopened in 1865. Nancy Gardner entered Maryville College in 1898 where she excelled at Latin, Greek, mathematics, French and German. She was always an outstanding leader holding numerous offices in the Bainonian Literary Society, was president of the junior class 1901-1902, and president of her graduating class 1902-1903. She was captain of a basketball team that was never defeated. She won an oratorical medal contest in 1903 — her reading of the "Chariot Race" from *Ben-Hur* being noteworthy. Of her short readings a favorite was "When Grandma Danced the Minuet. Nancy graduated with an A.B. degree in 1903 at the age of 21.

Candi Padgett Wages, Steve and Madison Wages

After her graduation, Nancy accepted an appointment with the Board of Missions of the Presbyterian Church as a mission teacher at Hyden, Kentucky — at that time, 60 miles from the nearest railroad. Nancy contracted typhoid fever and everyone feared that she lay on her deathbed. Her brother John telegraphed Clinton Gillingham at Maryville College to "come quickly

John and Christi Padgett Bell (used with permission of Glenn Holmes Photography)

lest it be too late." Clinton did rush to her and he married Nancy on 2 November 1903 as she lay in her sickbed. He stayed and helped nurse her back to health. Then he returned to Maryville. A few months later, her strength regained, Nancy rode 100 miles on horseback across the Kentucky mountains and joined Clinton at Maryville.

Clinton H. Gillingham graduated from Maryville College in 1905 with an A.B. degree. He then attended Princeton Theological Seminary 1905-1906. He received his master of arts from Maryville College in 1907. He received his bachelor of divinity degree in 1908 from the Theological Seminary of Kentucky at Louisville. Maryland College conferred on Clinton H. Gillingham the degree of doctor of divinity in 1919. During World War I, Professor Gillingham was commissioned in December of 1917 a major commanding the 2nd Battalion of the 5th Tennessee Infantry of the National Guard.

Joy Hilliard was born 12 February 1942 in Toombs County, GA the daughter of Harold and Georgia Wilkes Hilliard. Joy received her B.S. in English from Georgia Southern in 1965. Joy Hilliard and Thomas C. Padgett were married on 1 June 1963 in Glennville, Georgia.

Thomas Harold Hilliard on Hilliard Home Place

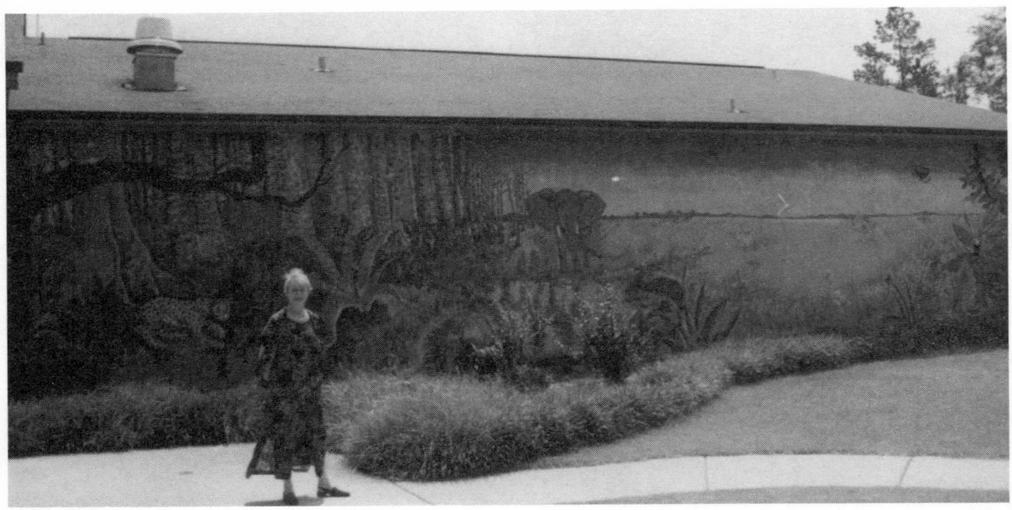

Joy Padgett in front of mural at Carrollton Manor

Three children were born to the Padgetts: Thomas Clinton Padgett Jr. born 8 October 1964 in Columbus, Mississippi. Tom Jr. is married to Angel "Ann" Aarons of San Antonio, Texas. Tom Padgett Jr. received the Airman's Medal for an act of heroism on Veteran's Day 1991. (See the separate write-up on this family.).

Robert Quitman Wilkes "Pop"

The second child of Joy Hilliard and Dr. Tom Padgett Sr. is Candace Lee Padgett born 13 November 1966 on Grand Forks Air Force Base in North Dakota. Candi received her degree in marketing from West Georgia College and is married to Steve Wages, who is self-employed in Snellville. Steve is an engineer noted for his design of adhesive applying equipment used in packaging. Steve is the son of Ray Wages, now deceased, and Robbie Jackson Wages. Robbie Wages was employed for many years as the director of Human Resources of Northlake Regional Medical Center. Candi works as an office manager for a general contractor in Duluth and enjoys being stepmom to Steve's daughter, Julia Madison Wages.

The third child of Dr. Tom and Joy Hilliard Padgett is Mary Christian "Christi" Padgett b. 21 May 1970 at Vandenberg AFB in Santa Barbara County, California during her parents' years in the Air Force. Christi is married to John Robinson Bell. (See the separate heading for this family).

Joy Padgett continued her education with completion of her master's at Troy State University in Montgomery in 1978. She taught as an adjunct professor at West Georgia College from 1982-1984. Then, she taught English at Carrollton High School from 1985-1989. She again taught as an adjunct instructor and tutored the athletes at West Georgia College from 1992-1998.

Joy also loves to paint and she and Susan Muse are the artists who donated their time and talent to paint the 600 sq. ft. African mural on the walls of the Carrollton Manor nursing home. Joy is active in two local water color classes and also enjoys working in oils and acrylics. Joy has a knack for interior decorating which involves her in many wallpapering and painting projects, etc.

The Hilliards date their genealogy back to William Hilliard who in the spring of 1635, at the age of 21, came to this country from London on the ship *Elizabeth and Ann*. In 1637, William became a part of the Plymouth Colony and in 1639, he was given the right to erect the first grist mill there. After King Phillip's War, William and his wife Esther moved their family — William, Esther, and Mary — to Little Compton, Rhode Island. The Hilliards eventually migrated southward and after several generations they had settled in the Carolinas and then later in Bowersville, Hart County, Georgia. A famous Hilliard cousin from Bowersville is Dr. Sam Hilliard, now retired, the cartographer, who taught at Louisiana State University. He has made many maps of interest for genealogists who research the Hart County, Georgia area.

Ruby Wilkes "Gamma"

Joy Hilliard Padgett is the daughter of Georgia Lee Wilkes (born 12 June 1919 died 1963) and Thomas Harold Hilliard (born 13 November 1917 died 1967). Harold Hilliard was a veteran of World War II and during the war the family lived in Texas and Florida — but home was Lyons, Toombs County, Georgia. Harold Hilliard is pictured here in his uniform with his wife, Georgia. Another favorite photo of Joy's is the one with her father posing with his gun on the Hilliard home place. After the war, Harold Hilliard went into Soil Conservation and lived in Screven County for awhile, finally setting in Glennville, Georgia.

The parents of Georgia Lee Wilkes were: Ruby Wilkes and Robert Quitman Wilkes — both of whom died in 1962 only three weeks apart. The Wilkes were Presbyterians and Quitman Wilkes was a Mason. The Wilkes made their home in Toombs County, Georgia and were the original "Gamma and Pop" to Joy Hilliard. The parents of Ruby Wilkes were William Wilkes and Josephine Ryals McLeod Wilkes of Montgomery County, Georgia. Georgia Lee Wilkes parents' were distant cousins to one another — so the Wilkes family tree is an extensive one.

Missouri Williamson Wilkes, 96 years old

The mother of Quitman Wilkes was Missouri Williamson Wilkes "Vidalia's most venerable lady" who has an interesting family story. After the Civil War, Missouri traveled by foot with her brother — all the way from Jacksonville, Florida to Vidalia, Georgia. Since she was born in 1856, this trip was when she was a little girl. Missouri's husband died as a young man, and she inherited enough money to build a boarding house. It was built in Vidalia and this is how she supported herself and her children. Missouri is pictured here on her 96th birthday on Thanksgiving Day in 1952.

The newspaper write-up mentions that Missouri is "the widow of a prominent Vidalian, John A. Wilkes." Her children mentioned are: "Quitman Wilkes of Lyons, Mrs. L.S. Mosley and Mrs. G.F. London of Greenville, S.C., and Mrs. Emma Wardlaw of Lincolnton, N.C." A daughter-in-law, Mrs. Emmett Wilkes is also mentioned. The old fading newspaper article mentions that Mrs. Wilkes has been "a resident of Vidalia for 52 years, is a staunch Democrat, and is upset over the landslide election of Eisenhower."

The parents of Thomas Harold Hilliard were Tom Hilliard of Bowersville, Georgia (d. 1969) and Lura "Lurrie" Ashford Hilliard (d. 1984). The Hilliards were farmers all their lives in Hart County, Georgia. They are pictured on their 50th wedding anniversary. Harold's younger brother, Horace, and his wife Catherine, still live

Tom Hilliard and Lurrie Ashford Hilliard

Padgett Family Reunion

with their children Judy and Bill on the Hilliard home place in Bowersville. Horace and Catherine were most helpful in putting together the Hilliard family history.

In the Padgett family group picture, left to right are Candi Padgett Wages, Joy Padgett, Dr. Tom Padgett, his mother, Mary Padgett, Raymond Padgett and "Boo" Padgett (Tom's brother and his wife), then Raymond and Boo's children, Joel Padgett and his wife, Laura, and Joel's sister, Jennifer Padgett.

Rev. James Stripling

Joy Hilliard Padgett has one brother, Thomas Harold Hilliard Jr. who was born 15 September 1947 in Lyons, Georgia. Tommy Hilliard and his wife, Lynna, and sons, Clayton and Ben, reside in Glennville, Georgia. Their home in Glennville, built in 1923, was the first home built in Glennville using blueprints — and they have enjoyed renovating this old home over the years. Tommy is a former smoke jumper with the U.S. Forest Service and Bureau of Land Management. Although he no longer jumps, Tommy Hilliard has led crews in the Florida wildlife disaster in 1998 and during the fires in the western USA during the summer of 2000. He is currently the Chief Forester at Ft. Stewart, Georgia.

Dr. Tom and Joy Padgett are active members of Stripling Chapel United Methodist Church where they both sing in the choir. They are proud to have called Carroll County, Georgia "home" for the past twenty years — and look forward to the next twenty! *Submitted by: Dr. Thomas C. and Joy Hilliard Padgett, 104 Hampton Way, Carrollton, GA 30116 and Written by: Jan Robinson Bell.*

894. Ellen Nooe Rose Pafford

and Early History of St. Margaret's Episcopal Church

The first building in Carrollton that would be called St. Margaret's Episcopal Church is the very same building that today is known as The Kennedy Interdenominational Chapel on the campus of the State University of West Georgia. This building originally stood on the corner of White Street and West Avenue and the very first service conducted there was on July 15, 1893. It was in 1892 that Almarine Cowdry Slade had sold a piece of property to J.H. Phinazy for $300 and this money was donated towards buying a lot and building Carrollton's first Episcopal church.

The Slade family was an early one to Carroll County the first Slade making his appearance here when the county was only a few years old. This was Thomas Bog Slade of Jones County, Georgia, who witnessed a deed in Carroll County on 28 November 1829. Later on, in 1839, David Slade of Putnam County, Georgia, purchased Land Lot #145 in the 10th District of Carroll County, this being located on the Tallapoosa River. Then, on 24 April 1854, Daniel Slade of Putnam County sold this same property to Elihu Stidham. Thomas Bog Slade the son of the above mentioned Thomas Bog Slade was born in December 1834 in Clinton, Georgia.

Thomas Bog Slade married Miss Almarine Cowdry probably in Muscogee County, Georgia, prior to 1872. Four known children were born to this family: (1) John Henry Slade born 22 November 1872 in Muskogee County, died 27 October 1949; (2) Almarine Slade born 1878 in Muskogee County, died 17 April 1980; (3) Anne Evelyn Slade born 15 November 1879 in Lee County, Alabama, died 13 January 1966 Carroll County. She was an 1898 graduate of Carrollton High School; (4) Kate de Roulchac Slade born 26 December 1884 in Muskogee County, Columbus, m died 8 September 1957. Miss Kate Slade taught school at College Street for many years. All this family is buried in Section C of the Carrollton City Cemetery.

Thomas B. Slade came with his wife Almarine and family to Carrollton in 1882 from Columbus, Georgia. Almarine's sister, Kate Cowdry, also accompanied them. This was a family of educators who had come to teach at Reese's Academy. Mrs. Slade became the head of the Academy in 1884 teaching the standard subjects. Her sister, Kate, taught elocution and calisthenics. The daughter of the Academy's founder, Minnie Reese, taught music. Old records tell us that it was through the efforts of Mr. and Mrs. Thomas B. Slade that the tiny Episcopal Church was built in Carrollton.

In those first days, the church was actually a tiny mission church without a regular schedule of worship services. The church depended on the goodness of a missionary, the Reverend William M. Walton, who had founded the Episcopal Church in Carrollton in 1887. Rev. Walton, along with about ten other missionaries supported by the Episcopal Diocese of Georgia, would visit Carrollton to provide morning prayer services and evening prayer services. The Episcopal Bishop from Atlanta would visit every few months in order to take care of any new confirmations in the church.

Some of the very earliest members of the Episcopal Church in Carrollton were Mrs. T.B. Slade and her daughters, Annie, Almarine, and Kate. Also, the Broadnaxes, the Phinizys and Dr. and Mrs. Charles C. Fitts were early members. From the old A&M School came Miss Martha Munro, one of the teachers at the school, who later married Dr. Irvine S. Ingram who became the president of West Georgia College. The Episcopal Church has always had many members from the college. Though Miss Munro never actually joined St. Margaret's, she worked and worshipped with the many faithful women who kept the church alive. By 1993, the George C. Adams family, Miss Marie Campbell, and Mrs. M.E. Howell had also joined St. Margaret's Church.

Ellen Rose

In 1942, St. Margaret's became an organized mission. The Rev. J.B. Hunt Jr. of the Cedartown Parish began to hold services every other Sunday afternoon. By this time, Carrollton was beginning to grow and St. Margaret's Parish was beginning to grow along with it. New industries were bringing more Episcopalians into town. Increased attendance and regular worship services brought many improvements to the tiny church - electricity was installed and an organ was purchased. A small parish hall had been built due to the generous donations of Ned and Louise Blackman who had moved to Carrollton.

In 1948, Mr. D. William Durden was appointed Lay Reader for St. Margaret's. By 1952, the members began to talk about needing a larger building. By this time, St. Margaret's had welcomed many more new families into its fold. Among these were the Frank Watson Rose Jr. family who had moved to Carrollton from Cohutta, Georgia.

Frank Watson Rose Jr. was the son of Frank Watson Rose Sr. and Bonnie Lee Rollins Rose (born 28 January 1897). Frank Rose Sr. and Bonnie Rose were natives of Cohutta and were buried there at the Hopewell Baptist Church. Frank W. Rose Jr. was born 3 September 1917 in Whitfield County, Georgia. Ellen Nooe was born 5 November 1921, the daughter of Louis Albert Nooe and Myrtle Hill Pilkington Nooe of Ridgeway, South Carolina. Myrtsie, as she was called, was born 27 January 1898. In later years, Louis and Myrtsie Nooe would be buried at St. Bartholomew's Episcopal church in Pittsboro, North Carolina.

Frank Rose Jr. was a graduate of Georgia Tech who had a degree in civil engineering. He had served in the U.S. Army during World War II with Roy Richards, who was to become Carrollton's most famous industrialist with the establishment of his Southwire Company after the war. After the war had ended, Roy Richards, also a Georgia Tech graduate, had asked two of his lieutenants – Frank Rose Jr. and Jim Feagle – to come to work for him at his Richards & Associates firm in Carrollton.

Roy Richards and his wife, the former Alice Huffard of Bluefield, Virginia, both were Episcopalians as well. Alice Richards was a graduate of the University of North Carolina at Chapel Hill and had met Roy Richards when she came to Atlanta to work after finishing college. The Richards became members of St. Margaret's after their marriage in 1958. In the coming years, the Richards' seven children would fill the front pew – Roy Jr., Jim, Nancy, Lee, Robin, Beth, and Laura.

Frank Watson Rose Jr.

Once they'd arrived in Carrollton, the Roses would begin a lifetime of service for St. Margaret's Church. Over the years, Ellen would serve on the Vestry, on the Altar Guild, as Senior Warden, as chair of the Episcopal Churchwomen, and also she would sing in the choir. The Roses had four children who would grow up in Carrollton – Georganne Radcliffe Rose born April 11, 1946, Frank Watson Rose III born December 29, 1949, Margaret Rollins Rose born January 4, 1954, and Richard Nooe Rose born July 21, 1955.

Margaret Rollins Rose would become one of the first females to become an Episcopal priest. She was ordained in Massachusetts in 1981. She married Rev. Mark James Baker, also an Episcopal priest, and they moved to Atlanta in 1992. Rev. Margaret Rose Baker has her own church in St. Dunstan's in Atlanta. Rev. Mark James Baker has his own church in Church of the Holy Comforter in Atlanta. Margaret and Mark have two daughters, Hannah Rose Pilkington Baker and Miriam Ellen Rose Baker.

Georganne Rose married Charles Baker Cunningham III, a native of St. Louis, Missouri, and the Cunninghams make their home there. Baker Cunningham is the CEO of Belden, Inc. Georganne received her Ph.D. in education from St. Louis University and now is in private practice in St. Louis as an education consultant. Georganne also teaches at the University of St. Louis in Missouri. Georganne and Baker Cunningham have two children, Margaret Barclay Cunningham and Charles Baker Cunningham IV.

Frank W. Rose III is now a resident of Denali Bluffs, Alaska, where he owns and manages two popular hotels there. You can see Frank's hotels on www.denalibluffs.com. The hotels adjoin a national park there. Frank's two sons are: With first wife Connie, Frank Watson Rose IV of Houston, Texas and with second wife Carolyn, Christopher Rollins Rose of Fairbanks, Alaska. Many Carrollton residents have enjoyed Frank's hospitality in his hotels and the sons of Dr. and Mrs. Charles Hubbard of Carrollton have worked there for summertime jobs. Mrs. Hubbard is the former Marilyn Merrell who grew up as a neighborhood friend of the Roses.

Ellen and Ward Pafford at home.

Richard Rose graduated from The Asheville School in North Carolina. Richard Rose married an Agnes Scott graduate, Catherine Brown, the daughter of Dr. and Mrs. William Morris Brown of Macon, Georgia. Richard and Catherine Rose are the parents of three sons, Richard Nooe Rose Jr., William Turner Rose and Davis McCord Rose, all of Fairfax, Virginia.

Ellen Rose was a dedicated Godmother for 50 years to all the John T. Robinson children who were members of St. Margaret's Church. Ellen Rose would call her next door neighbor, Melba Robinson, "the sister I never had," and they would be dearest of friends at home and at church. Melba Robinson taught Sunday School at the Episcopal Church for many years. And John T. Robinson would serve several terms as Church Warden.

Ellen Rose was a great supporter of Camp Mikell, the Episcopal church camp, and often encouraged all the children of her neighborhood to ride the train from Atlanta to Toccoa to spend some weeks of their summer at Camp Mikell. Jimmy and Frankie Pierce and their three daughters – Virginia, Jane, and Ann – often helped to transport all the children to and from camp in the North Georgia mountains.

One of Ellen Rose's favorite church traditions was "the flowering of the cross" at Eastertime at St. Margaret's. All the children in the church would come forward on Easter morning to add their tiny bundle of flowers to the wooden cross at the front of the church. Ellen would round up her neighborhood of children to make sure that none missed this most special occasion. Some of her frequent visitors to such special events were her neighbors Bill and Ann Seaton, and Tommy, Beth and Amy Thomasson.

The Stanley Rodwell family moved to Carrollton from England and became lifetime members of St. Margaret's as well. Their children, David and Pauline, grew up in the church. Dr. and Mrs. Irving deGaris were early members. Dr. de Garis was a popular Carrollton dentist who had seen much action as an aviator during World War II. The de Garis children were Irving, Ben, and Rebecca. Mrs. de Garis was the former Reba Hollingsworth, a family with deep roots in Carroll County's history.

Mr. and Mrs. Vernon Folds became active members of St. Margaret's as well. (Their home would later become the first Oak Mountain Academy). Mr. and Mrs. Chester A. Roush would become devoted members who would add their special talents to St. Margaret's in many ways. Mrs. Roush was a talented artist. She would so generously donate many of her prized paintings to the annual Christmas bazaar at St. Margaret's, an event in which all the churchwomen would donate their special handicrafts to sell for the funding of special church events. Chester Roush was an early sales manager of Southwire and later owner of Roush Oil. The Roush children were Jan and Alex.

In 1952, the Rev. Martin Dewey Gable would become the first vicar of St. Margaret's. He was St. Margaret's very first resident priest. Under his leadership, the expansion of the membership and influence of the church expanded greatly so much so that by 1953 St. Margaret's had outgrown the tiny church on the corner of White Street and West Avenue. A building committee was formed and plans were made to purchase property on Newnan Street to build a new church.

Vernon Folds was the director of the building committee, but two of the best "movers and shakers" in the construction of the new church building were Frank W. Rose Jr., and Chester A. Roush. The present church was designed by the late Atlanta architect, Francis P. Smith who also designed the Cathedral of St. Phillip in Atlanta. St. Margaret's Episcopal Church to this day is admired for its beautiful design and structure, every detail lovingly attended to by those early members. The present church on Newnan Street was dedicated on All Saint's Day on July 26, 1953.

In 1954, St. Margaret's Church advanced to the status of an aided parish. Sunday school classes, youth groups, and women's groups were organized. Mr. Harold Valerius, a Bremen resident, was an operatic tenor and contributed much to the leadership of the choir. The Rev. Edgar Stewart Wood became the vicar of St. Margaret's in 1956. He organized the first meeting of Alcoholics Anonymous to be held at the church. Rev. Wood built up quite a following of college students from West Georgia. This was called The Canterbury Club.

A home was later purchased near the church for meetings of college students and Sunday School classes and it was named The Canterbury House. It was also used for women's clubs, youth groups, church bazaars, church suppers, and many other events. One favorite annual event is the Patronal Festival of St. Margaret of Scotland, the patron saint of St. Margaret's. Years later, the first Head Start classes would be held in The Canterbury House. Also, a clothing bank for needy school children was begun here and this later developed into St. Margaret's Thrift Shop. St. Margaret's gained

Dedication of Kennedy Chapel, 1964

full parish status in 1965. St. Margaret's has known many talented organists, soloists, and choir directors. Mary Lou Munn was one of the first organists at St. Margaret's and many young people of Carrollton took their piano lessons from her in her home. Mary Lou Munn is also responsible for preserving much of the early church's history through her writings. Much of the church history here is abstracted from her collection. Danny Hagan was also a talented organist of the 1960s. Dr. Robert W. Coe was a favorite choir director and his wife Katherine Coe would sing lovely soprano solos.

Rev. Donald Harrison was rector from 1960 until 1965. After Rev. Harrison left the church, it was almost a year before another new rector was selected. During that time, Dr. Robert K. Lampton, a West Georgia College professor of biology carried on with services as Perpetual Deacon. Dr. Lampton and his wife, Kay, were both devoted to St. Margaret's and Kay embroidered the beautiful prayer cushions that are still used for kneeling at the altar.

A new parish hall for St. Margaret's was planned in the late 1960s with Frank Rose Jr. as finance chairman and Chester A. Roush as building chairman. This new addition, dedicated in 1970 by Bishop Milton I. Wood, added an assembly hall, church school rooms, nursery, rector's office, choir room, church office, kitchen, storage rooms and rest rooms – badly needed rooms and space by the ever growing church. Unfortunately, Frank Rose Jr. would not live to see the completion of this project. In 1969 he died of a heart attack. The whole community genuinely mourned his loss – a finer fellow we had never known. His family remained in Carrollton, still active members of church and community, and Ellen Rose remained a devoted Episcopalian. When the parish hall was completed, it was dedicated "to the Glory of God and in memory of Frank Watson Rose Jr., Senior Warden 1917-1969."

On May 28, 1986, Ellen Rose married Dr. Ward B. Pafford, who was the fourth president of West Georgia College. Both Ellen and Ward Pafford remained active at St. Margaret's for many years. Ellen Rose Pafford died on 19 November 1999 and was laid to rest beside Frank W. Rose Jr. at Carroll Memory Gardens.

Ward Bascom Pafford first came to reside in Carrollton in July 1971 to serve as the fourth President of West Georgia College. He and his wife, Sally Jones Pafford lived in the college president's home on Maple Street for four years until 1975. At that time, the Paffords retired and returned to their home in Valdosta, Georgia. Later in 1983, they returned to live in Carrollton. The Ward B. Pafford Building on the campus of The State University of West Georgia is named in honor of Dr. Pafford. The Pafford Building houses Departments of Sociology, Anthropology, Criminology, History, Psychology, and Political Science.

Ward Bascom Pafford was born October 25, 1911 in Jesup, Wayne County, Georgia, as the son of Bascom Anthony Pafford and Jeanette Dukes Pafford. Bascom Anthony Pafford was born October 2, 1886, in Coffee County, Georgia, as the son of Elias Moore Pafford and Ellevyanne Brown Pafford. Jeannette Dukes Pafford was born in Bryan County, Georgia, as the daughter of Norman L. Dukes and Susan Denmark Dukes.

Sally Jones Pafford was born October 8, 1912, in Columbus, Muscogee County, Georgia as the daughter of Louie Chester Jones and Connie Wheelis Jones. Sarah "Sally" Jones Pafford died in June 1984 in Carrollton. Ward Pafford continues to live in retirement at Cottage Lane in Carrollton. By his first wife, Sarah Jones Pafford, Dr. Pafford has two daughters, Martha Pafford Schindelm of Bridgewater, Connecticut, and Connie Pafford Broom of Decatur, Georgia.

As for the tiny church that has served as the Episcopal Church on the corner of White Street and West Avenue, an interesting future was in store for it, too. It was deconsecrated in 1953 when the Episcopalians had moved out and into their new church building on Newnan Street. Then, it became the Our Lady of Perpetual Help Catholic Church with Monsiengnor Regan as priest. Then, in 1962, the Catholics moved into their new church building, so generously donated by the movie actress Susan Hayward and her Carrollton husband, Eaton Chalkley. The new Catholic church property was located on the Center Point Road near where the Chalkleys made their home.

For the first time in sixty-nine years, the tiny church that had been Episcopal, then Catholic, stood vacant. Still mounted on the back wall of the chapel was a plaque that reads:

> "Pray for the souls of Mathew and Catherine O'Donell and family in whose memory a generous generous donation was made to this church ..."

The Carroll-Haralson Ministerial Association rallied to attempt to preserve this old church and with the support of the Catholic community, an idea was born to move the church to the campus of West Georgia College. It was decided that once on the college campus that the old church would become an interfaith chapel.

Because of the recent assassination of President John Fitzgerald Kennedy on November 22, 1963, many in the community wanted to do something to honor his name. A ground breaking ceremony was held on the West Georgia College Campus on May 27, 1964, to dedicate the newly arrived chapel in honor of the 36th President of the United States. Attorney General Robert Kennedy was the featured speaker at the dedication.

Robert Kennedy said in his speech that his brother's presidency had "exemplified tolerance" and that it was good that this interfaith chapel would be "an expression of the same spirit of tolerance." Since that day, the church has served all denominations of students on the campus of West Georgia and several couples have married in the quaint old chapel.

In the picture with Robert Kennedy, which was taken at the dedication of the Kennedy Chapel in May 1964, the little girl looking up at Kennedy is Margaret Rose. The young lady with the smile is Robin Reeve, because Robert Kennedy held her hand all during the prayer. In front of Robin is Denise Young. Far right is Glenn Holmes. The photograph was taken by Dr. Tom Reeve Jr. *Submitted by: Dr. Ward B. Pafford, 152 Cottage Lane, Carrollton, GA 30117*

St. Margaret's Episcopal Church, Carrollton, GA

895. Enoch Parker

Enoch Parker was born circa 1760 in Lincoln County, North Carolina. Enoch married Catherine Eaker prior to 1794 in Lincoln County. Catherine, born about 1764 in Lincoln County, was the daughter of Christian Eaker and Eve Catherine Whisenhunt of Lincoln County. Enoch and Catherine came from Lincoln County to Georgia about 1824, presumably to Lincoln County. They were living in Carroll County, Georgia, by 1830 and had at least six children. Enoch and Catherine's oldest son (1) John was born 1800 in Lincoln County, North Carolina. He went from Carroll County to Pike County, Georgia. He lived there and farmed. John married Margaret Byrum on January 13, 1833, in Pike County. Margaret was born 1808 in Mecklenburg County, North Carolina, to Beverly Byrum and Sally Williamson. Beverly and Mary came to Pike County, from Mecklenburg County, North Carolina, by 1830. John died about 1860 in Pike County. Margaret died after 1860 in Pike County; (2) James was born 1812 in Lincoln County, North Carolina. He married Mary Hammock April 6, 1834 in Pike County, Georgia. James died after 1862 in Carroll County. Mary was born 1816 and died in Carroll County; (3) Susan Ann was born December 30, 1815, in Lincoln County, North Carolina. Susan married Green Berry Hammock March 20, 1834, in Pike County, Georgia. Susan died January 4, 1884 in Carroll County. Both are buried at First Methodist Church Cemetery in Carrollton.

Henry G. Parker was the fifth child born to John Parker and Margaret Byrum Parker. Henry was born December 10, 1842, in Pike County, Georgia. He enlisted in Company H, 44th Regiment, Georgia Volunteer Infantry, Army of Northern Virginia, Pike County, on March 4, 1862, in Zebulon, Georgia. The 44th was in the battles of Seven Days Battles, Beaver Dam Creek, Gaines' Mill, Malvern Hill, South Mountain, Antietam, and Chancellorsville. He was wounded in the right leg at the Battle of Chancellorsville, Virginia, on May 2, 1863. The ball entered the middle third of his leg causing compound fractures. His leg was amputated by circular operation below the right knee on May 3, 1863. He entered General Hospital #2 in Richmond, Virginia, on May 12, 1863. On May 25, 1863, he was going about on crutches. On May 26, 1863, he was transferred. Since he was disabled from further service, he came home. Henry went to Coweta County, Georgia, and lived there and farmed. He married Sarah Cannon on February 6, 1868, in Coweta County. Sarah was the daughter of George Washington Cannon and Mary A. Elliott, who were among the early settlers of Pike County, Georgia. Henry and Sarah came to Carroll County in 1875. They settled in Harmony, later named Bowdon Junction, where he bought a three-hundred-acre farm, which he paid for and improved to make him and his family a comfortable home. Henry came out of the war a very poor and disabled man, yet secured a good home by his own industry and economy. The community in which he lived held Henry in worthy esteem. Sarah was a member of the Bowdon Junction Methodist Church. Henry died July 22, 1913, and Sarah died about 1925. Both are buried at Pleasant View Missionary Baptist Church Cemetery in Carroll County.

Henry and Sarah had nine children: (1) James Aaron was born December 1869 in Coweta County, Georgia. He married Florence E. Murphy May 5, 1901, in Carroll County. James died in Cleburne County, Alabama, and is buried at Oak Level United Methodist Church in Cleburne County. Florence was born in 1872 and died in Cleburne County; (2) Henry Steve was born June 1871 in Coweta County. He married Emma Kathy (Kate) Casey January 14, 1894, in Carroll County. Steve died in 1943. Kate was born in 1875 and died in 1953. Both are buried at Mt. Zion Methodist Church in Carroll County; (3) Mary J. was born December 12, 1871, in Coweta County. She married James Henry Johnson August 9, 1888, in Carroll County. She died September 23, 1944. James Henry was born July 24, 1872, and died October 31, 1947. Both are buried at Pleasant View Missionary Baptist Church in Carroll County; (4) George Washington was born March 1, 1873, in Coweta County. He married Frances Ellen (Fanny) Barlow September 13, 1892, in Carroll County. He died December 18, 1957, in Cleburne County, Alabama. He is buried at Fruithurst Missionary Baptist Church in Cleburne County. Fanny was born July 6, 1871, in Carroll County to Virgil Barlow and Susan Burrows. She died November 8, 1928, and is buried at Oak Level United Methodist Church in Cleburne County; (5) Sarah E. was born July 7, 1876, in Carroll County. She married William Larkin Evans December 19, 1895, in Carroll County. She died August 29, 1938. Larkin was born March 9, 1874, and died October 26, 1930. Both are buried at Pleasant View Missionary Baptist Church in Carroll County; (6) Ella Cornelia was born January 3, 1878, in Carroll County. She married William Jasper Duke May 28, 1899, in Haralson County. She died February 26, 1965. William was born October 26, 1841 in Newton County, Georgia, and died November 27, 1920. Both are buried at Bremen City Cemetery, Haralson County; (7) Harriet Henrietta was born September 14, 1880, in Carroll County. She married Wilbur Edward Wallace November 15, 1896, in Carroll County. She died December 15, 1904, and is buried at Pleasant View Missionary Baptist Church in Carroll County. Wilbur was born January 1877 in Spalding County, Georgia, and died 1950 in Cullman County, Alabama; (8) Martha Jane was born June 22, 1883, in Carroll County and died January 15, 1885. She is buried at Pleasant View Missionary Baptist Church in Carroll County; (9) Leila Frances was born 1886 in Carroll County. She married Van Kierbow October 23, 1910, in Carroll County. She died March 2, 1963. Van was born October 8, 1891, in Haralson County and died February 17, 1919. Both are buried at Pleasant View Missionary Baptist Church in Carroll County. *Submitted by: Kathy P. Hanson, 514 Browns Creek Road, Guntersville, AL 35976*

Sources: Census records, Confederate Civil War records, Coweta County marriage records, *Medical and Surgical History of the War of the Rebellion, Part III, Vol. II.,* and *German Speaking People West of the Catawba River in North Carolina River,* Lorene Shell Eaker.

896. George Washington Parker

George Washington Parker, born March 1, 1873, Carroll County, Georgia, died December 18, 1957, Cleburne County, Alabama. George was the fourth child born to Henry G. Parker and Sarah Cannon Parker of Carroll County. George was a great-grandson to Enoch and Catherine Parker who were among the early settlers of Carroll County. George came from a family of six children. He married Frances Ellen (Fanny) Barlow September 13, 1892, Carroll County. Frances Ellen, born July 6, 1871, in Carroll County, died November 8, 1928, buried Oak Level United Methodist Church, Cleburne County, Alabama. Fanny was the daughter of Virgil Barlow and Susan Burrows of Carroll County.

George and Fanny had the following children: (1) Minnie Susan born September 30, 1893, Carroll County, married Paul Ferguson December 21, 1913, Cleburne County, Alabama. Paul born October 6, 1896, Cleburne County to John David Ferguson and Sarah Ann Barton. Minnie died May 28, 1880, Paul died December 19, 1933, both buried at New Hope Baptist Church, Marshall County, Alabama. (2) Idis Verna born April 12, 1895, in Carroll County, married Lela Ann Rayburn March 13, 1916, Carroll County. Lela born August 31, 1900, Carroll County to John and Annie Rayburn. Verna died July 1966, Lela died February 1951, both buried at Pleasant View Missionary Baptist Church, Carroll County. (3) George Searcy born January 22, 1896, in Carroll County, married Willie Lavana Land July 2, 1917, Carroll County. Willie born March 3, 1903, Carroll County to Andrew Berry Land and Ann Elizabeth Rayburn. George died March 1, 1974, Willie died October 14, 1995, both buried at Concord Baptist Church, Cullman County, Alabama. (4) Loney Dell born October 2, 1898, Carroll County, married Henry Franklin Speights January 12, 1919, Cleburne County, Alabama. Henry born September 28, 1896. Loney died July 26, 1985, Henry died December 31, 1979, both buried at Forrest Hill Cemetery, Birmingham, Alabama. (5) Milburn Lloyd born 1902, Carroll County, died 1928, buried Oak Level United Methodist Church, Cleburne County, Alabama. (6) Enice Wiley born December 5, 1905, Carroll County, married Lillian Pilgrim April 6, 1942, Carroll County. Lillian born September 5, 1922, in Jefferson County, Alabama, to Jesse Green Pilgrim and Era Beatrice Collier. Wiley died April 4, 1975, in Boaz, Alabama, buried at Mt. Paran Baptist Church, Cleburne County. Lillian died April 7, 1996, buried New Canaan Baptist Church, Marshall County, Alabama. (6) Sarah Florence born September 1909, Carroll County, married Frank Benjamin Murray in Cleburne County. Frank was born July 30, 1901, Calhoun County, Alabama to Joel Murray and Ida Beecham, died January 27, 1929, Cleburne County. Sarah married 2nd: Buford Phillips, he was born in Cleburne County, died Dade County, Florida. Sarah died August 1943 in Cleburne County. *Submitted by: Bessie Mae Garner, 830 Candy Lane NE, Birmingham, AL 35215*

Sources: Georgia and Alabama census records, Carroll County Marriage Index, Book H, p. 21

897. Henry G. Parker Family

Henry G. Parker, a Civil War veteran born in Coweta County, Georgia, in 1842, was married to Sarah Cannon. After suffering from a leg wound during the war and later amputation, Henry G. had a "peg leg" but that did not keep him from plowing his own fields, even in the rain. With their three small children, George, Jim and Steve, they left Coweta County about 1875 and settled in Harmony, now known as Bowdon Junction. Two more children were born there, Lela in 1876, and Ella Cornelia in 1878. Lela married Van Kierbow in 1910, and Ella married William Jasper Duke in 1899.

Henry G. had little use for banks and he kept his own gold in a chest in the "front room." One night in 1900 while the family was in the kitchen, someone came into the house and took the chest which contained $300 to $400 in gold coins, a fortune in those days. The chest was found on the trail the next day, minus the gold. Henry acquired lots of land, and at one time was one of the richest men in Carroll County. He gave each of his children a sixty-acre farm. He died in 1913 and is buried in Pleasant View Cemetery at Bowdon Junction, along with his wife Sarah and other members of the Parker family.

George Parker, my grandfather, was born March 1, 1873. He died December 18, 1957, and is buried in Fruithurst, Alabama. He was married to Frances Ellen Barlow in Carroll County in September of 1892. She died November 8, 1929, and is buried in the United Methodist Church Cemetery in Oak Level, Cleburne County, Alabama. They had seven children: Verna born April 1895; George Searcy born February

1896; Milburn Loyd born in 1902; Ennice Wylie born in 1905; Minnie (Furguson) born August 1893; Lonnie Dell (Speights) born October 1898; and Sara Florence (Phillips) born in 1909. After Frances Ellen's death, George married Daisy Porter on June 23, 1932, died in October 2000 and is buried at Mount Creek Baptist Church in Cleburne County, Alabama. They had two children: Ruth born and died in 1934, and Marvin born in 1936 and died in 1937.

Verna Parker was my father. He married Lela Ann Rayburn in Mandeville community near Bowdon Junction in March of 1916. They moved to Bowdon, Georgia, where he farmed. They had eight children: Myrtle, Earl (who died from polio at age eight), Hoyt, Myrleen, Sara, Lorine, Jean and Franklin (who died at age ten months).

Myrtle married A.F. Turner and had a daughter Rachel who died in infancy, and a son Billy who married Sheila Hames. Their daughter Gayla married Tracy Roberts, whose children were Heather and Jacob; Billy's son was Michael whose children were Michael Wayne Jr., and Amanda Blair.

Jean Pruitt, Lorine Butler, Sara McLain, Myrleen Porter, Hoyt Parker, Myrtle Turner.

Hoyt married Jessie Mae Richardson and had five children: James (born June 4, 1945, died August 15, 1959), Ann, Linda, Martha June, and Charles Phil. Ann married Harold Thompson and had two daughters, Vanessa and Lucretia. Vanessa married Gary Thomas. They have a son Nathan, and two daughters Marrisa and Kadian. Lucretia married Doug Gibbs. They have two daughters Whitney and Toni, and a son Bradley. Ann is now married to Ken Ezzell. Linda married Randy Harris and they have two children, Candy and Chad. Candy married Travis Thomas, and Chad married Teleah Dearman. They have a daughter, Kelsey. Martha June married Ricky Holmes and they had a daughter Holly, who is married to Steve Daniel. They have two daughters, Kimberly and Stevie. Martha June later married Mike Bailey with whom she had a son, Berkett, who married Hermanda Benefield. Hoyt's son, Charles Phil, has a daughter Pamela.

Myrleen Parker married Kenneth Farlow and had two sons, Charles and Bobby. Bobby died August 26, 1977. He had a son, Bobby Leon Jr., born March 26, 1978, and died June 25, 2001. Charles has a daughter, Lindsey. Myrleen is presently married to Gordon Porter.

Sara Parker married Curtis McLain. They have a son Jerry and he married Gloria Johnson. They have one son, Brandon. Jerry is now married to Pattie Oliphant.

Lorine Parker married Morgan Butler. They had six children: Sandra, Sue, Sally, DeDe, Steve, and Ginger. Sandra married Earl Kelley Jr. They had two children Sandy and Scottie. Sandy married Scott Loughridge and they have three children, Mason, Merrick and Sheridan. Scottie married Lori Allen and they have a daughter, Divan. Sandra is now married to James Spivey and they have a daughter Ashton. Sue married Wallace Walton and they have three daughters, Susie Pollock, Christie Taylor, and J.J. Humphries. Christie has two sons, Neil and Parker. J.J. has a son, Hunter. Sally married Richard Schiener and their children are Whitney and Evan. DeDe married Jim Dominey and their children are Abby and Rick. Steve has a daughter Mandy who married Stephen Dick, and a son Patrick. Ginger married Jeffrey Harper and they have a daughter Ragan and a son Garrett.

Jean Parker married James W. Ashmore in November 1947. He died April 12, 1977. They had four children: Michael (1951), Anthony David (1954), Medra Jewell (1955) and Gregory Scott (1962). Michael died March 10, 1998, at the age of forty-six. Anthony married Patricia Autherholtz and they had one son, Chris. Anthony later married Margaret Alleman and they have two children, Christopher and Samantha. Jean married Robert W. Pruitt in September 1996.

The railroad came through Harmony community but was later named Bowdon Junction when a short line was built in 1910 to serve the Bowdon area. When I was a little girl, my family often visited Aunt Leila Kierbow at her home near the railroad in Bowdon Junction. The ugly train, called "the Bowdon Duggan," would come down the tracks, which were lined with trees on both sides, while I was out playing in the yard, nearly scaring me to death! Wheeler Barker was the engineer.

When I was young, my father killed hogs after it had turned cold in the fall. He salted them down in the smoke house to keep all winter. One year, our meat was stolen. My dad went to a very famous fortune teller, Mayhaley Lancaster, over in Heard County, and asked her who had taken our meat, hoping that he might be able to get it back. She told him the name of the person who took it, said they lived across the creek. We recognized the name, but — like my great-grandfather and his gold — we never got it back. We lost a lot of good eating that winter! *Submitted by: Jean Parker Pruitt, 45 West Honeysuckle Lane, Carrollton, GA 30116*

898. James Parker and Henry Parker

James Parker (born in 1812) was the son of John Parker Sr. and in 1834 married Mary Hammock in Pike County. They moved to Carroll County with other Parkers, Hammocks, and Burrows. Their children were Elizabeth (married Eason Stamps), James C., Sarah A., and Mary (Polly) (married William Green Austin), Mary (Polly) and William Green Austin had six children, Jimmy, Charlie (son Leo), Elmus (son Rayford who is the father of Lanett Austin Horton), Jossie, Luster (US Navy WWI), and Dora who married Marshall Putnam (daughter Mary Ellen). Mary and William Green Austin are both buried at Union Camp Ground Cemetery near Mt. Zion. The accompanying picture of Mary Parker Austin is a copy of a damaged tintype.

Henry Parker 1842-1913

James Parker's brother, John Parker Jr., married Martha Bryan. James and Mary moved to Carroll County but John and Martha remained in Pike County. John and Martha's son Henry Parker joined the Confederate Army and was in the 44th Georgia Infantry Regiment along with his brother-in-law Anderson Prince. In the battle at Chancellorsville, Virginia, Henry was wounded in his leg which required amputation. It was fifteen days after that before he reached a hospital. Anderson Prince brought Henry home to Pike County near Zebulon, Georgia, and his wife (Henry's sister) nursed him back to health.

Mary (Polly) Parker, daughter of James and Mary Hammock Parker

As soon as he could stand on crutches, Henry Parker married Sarah Cannon and they moved to Carroll County to be out of the path of Sherman's army. They lived in a house located where their grandson Carlos Kierbow now lives near Holly Springs Church. Henry, with Sally's help, is said to have plowed the fields with a peg leg. He acquired quite a bit of farm land and had his gold money in a trunk in the house. One night while everyone was in the front of the house, someone came in the back and took the trunk with the money. Henry became a minister and was called "Peg Legged Parker." His grandson Milard Parker was the railroad depot agent at Bowdon Junction for several years. A granddaughter Verdie Wallace married Lester Lambert. Another granddaughter Avis Parker married Grady Brock and lived at Mt. Zion. Another grandson was Homer Wallace who started Wallace Builders Supply located in Bowdon Junction. Henry is buried at Pleasant View Church cemetery.

When Henry and Sarah came to Carroll County, Sarah's sister Harriett Cannon Entrekin and her husband Thomas Entrekin also moved to Mt. Zion and were the grandparents of Plez Entrekin. Wawena, his daughter, lives at the Entrekin home place.

Anderson Prince and his family moved to Carroll County. His daughter Molly married Wilbur Wallace after his first wife Harriett (daughter of Henry Parker) died. Another relative was Quinton Prince who was principal at Mt. Zion High School and was Carroll County School superintendent. *Submitted by: Donna Wallace Strickland.*
Source: Information furnished by Wallace T. Lambert

899. Parkman Family

David Stanley Parkman Jr. was born in Chattahoochee County, Georgia, July 17, 1915, the oldest son of D.S. Parkman Sr. and Alice Crawford. Another son, Nathaniel Toliver Parkman was born in 1918. Mother Alice died in 1920 and in 1924 D.S. Parkman Sr. married Frances Johnson of Cusseta, Georgia, and the family moved to Gadsden County, Florida.

David Stanley Parkman Jr. (Stanley) graduated from high school in Chattahoochee, Florida, and worked on weekly newspapers in Chattahoochee, Marianna, and Quincy, Florida.

Stanley married Frances Middlebrooke in Marianna in 1937 and they had two sons born there: David Stanley Parkman III, and Ralph Melvin Parkman. A daughter, Patricia Ann, was born in Quincy in 1942.

The family moved to Carrollton in 1944 when Stanley went to work with the *Carroll County Times* and the *Carrollton Free Press*. The two weekly newspapers had been consolidated during World War II.

Stanley had decided to leave Carrollton and accept a newspaper job in Tennessee, but before leaving a group of business and professional leaders persuaded him to remain in Carrollton and lead in the establishment of a new newspaper. The new newspaper, named *Carroll County Georgian,* published its first issue November 8, 1945, with Stanley as editor and publisher.

A daughter, Carroll, was the only one of the Parkman children born in Carrollton and was given the name Carroll Lynn in honor of Carroll County. She has retired from banking and real estate and lives with her husband Claude Wills in Cobb County. A son, Preston Parkman Wills, died in 2000.

All of the Parkman children attended Carrollton schools and graduated from Carrollton High School. All of them also attended West Georgia College.

David Stanley Parkman III received a degree in journalism at the University of Georgia, a U.S. Marine Corps commission, and was publisher/editor of newspapers in Bremen and Douglasville before joining the staff of West Georgia College where he is now vice president of the Alumni and Advancement Department. David is married to Beverly F. Parkman and they have a son Mark Parkman, and a daughter Julie Ivey.

Ralph Melvin Parkman attended Florida State University and graduated from WGC. After a newspaper career in Carrollton, Oxford, Alabama, and Georgetown, South Carolina, he now lives with his wife JoAnn at Panama City Beach, Florida. He has one son, Ralph Melvin Parkman Jr.

Patricia (Patti) Burlage received a degree in education from WGC, has taught school in Atlanta, Los Angeles, Phoenix, Arizona, and St. Petersburg, Florida, where she now lives with her husband Ted.

Frances Parkman died in 1971 at Tanner Medical Center and is buried in Carroll Memory Gardens. She had been a faithful member of First Baptist Church since the family moved to Carrollton.

Stanley Parkman and Mary Pritchard Pass married in 1973. Mary and her husband Floyd moved to Carrollton from Griffin, Georgia, in 1949. At the time they moved to Carrollton they had a son, Jerry, who was eighteen months old. Floyd Pass was a veteran of WWII and served in North Africa and Italy. They were in the plumbing business here until he died of cancer September 4, 1967. He was a member of the First Christian Church and is buried in Carroll Memory Gardens.

Jerry Pass graduated from Carrollton High School, West Georgia College, OCS school and served a tour of Army duty in Vietnam. His career has been with Equitable Insurance in Atlanta, Columbia, South Carolina, and now in Marietta. He is married to Lynn M. Pass. They have a son Wes, who is in his fourth year at the U.S. Naval Academy.

A daughter, Milah Pass, was born in Carrollton, graduated from Carrollton High School, attended West Georgia College and graduated with a degree in nursing from the Medical University in Augusta. She now lives with her husband, Steve Lynn, and their two children, Whitney and Josh, in Nashville, Tennessee.

Stanley and Mary Parkman together have six children, six grandchildren and three great-grandchildren. *Submitted by: Stanley Parkman, 999 N. Highway 113, Carrollton, GA 30117*

900. Parr - Brown

Matthias Parr was the father of John Parr who married Mary Currin. They were the parents of Matthias, John and Benjamin Parr. Benjamin was born 1 September 1760 in Roxbury Township, Morris County, New Jersey. He married Martha "Patsy" Duncley McKinney on 25 September 1790 (who was age twelve) in Wilkes County, North Carolina. Benjamin died in Carroll County, Georgia, on 22 December 1842.

Benjamin was a Revolutionary War soldier, serving from the state of New Jersey. After the war he moved with his two brothers to Wilkes County, North Carolina. In 1794, they moved to Georgia and lived at Barnett's Fort (present day Barnett's Shoals) of Clarke County. The early records of Mars Hill Baptist Church of Oconee County, Georgia, show they were members there.

Benjamin and Patsy had eleven children and nine lived to adulthood: Mary Currien; William Lenoire Sr. married first to Ann Weir and second to Jane Bell Weir, daughters of John Weir and Isabel Black; Martha "Patsy" Duncley married Edward Robertson Akin; John Currien married first to Margaret Bolton and second to Martha Lattimore; Rebecca Carlton; Charles Daughtery married Mary Phillip White Earnest; Elizabeth Easley married first to Rodman Sisson and second to Anderson Smith; Daniel Weldon Easley McKinney married Nancy Allums; Benjamin James married first to Maria Wilson and second to Sarah Catherine Sisson; Samuel Jackson married Lucasa Humphree; and Babe (sex unknown) Parr.

Benjamin was appointed as a constable for Jackson County, Georgia, in 1796 or 1797. He ran a store and mill in Clarke/Oconee County in 1810. He drew Carroll County land granted on 3 February 1829. He later followed some of his children to the Carroll County area. According to an obituary in *The Banner* newspaper of Athens, Georgia, dated 20 January 1843,

> "Another Revolutionary Soldier Gone, Mr. Benjamin Parr, the subject of this notice, died at the residence of his son in Carrollton, Carroll County, Georgia, on the 22nd day of December last ..."

William Lenoire Parr Sr. was clerk of the Inferior Court of Carroll County during the 1830s and 1840s. He was a soldier in the War of 1812 and in the Creek and Seminole Indian Wars. His name appears as captain on the monument at Camp Odum located in Carroll County. He and Jane Bell Weir had the following children: Unnamed male; John Benjamin; William Lenoire Parr Jr., Confederate soldier, died at Fairgrounds Hospital in Atlanta, Georgia; Samuel Howard; Isabella Jane married Thomas Beard; Francis Marion, Confederate soldier, killed in Mississippi during the war, married Mary A. Rebecca Beard; Melinda Martha; Mary Ann Elizabeth married William Chambers; Isaac James, a Confederate soldier; Nancy Carlton; Susan Allevia "Mattie" married John S. Long, a Confederate soldier; and Robert J. Parr married first to Victoria J.L.A.M. Long and second to Mary E. Edmonson.

Monuments have been placed at New Hope Methodist Cemetery in Carroll County in memory of Benjamin, William Sr., and Francis Marion Parr. A monument has been ordered for Isaac James Parr.

Susan Allevia "Mattie" and John S. Long were married in Carroll County on 25 December 1870. John is buried at Pleasant Hill Cemetery in the Horsley Mill community of Carroll County. Children to this union were Laura B. married W.W. Hyde; Ida L. married A. Lee Williams; Estella married Hutson W. Cavender; Walter married Hallie Pearl Burks; and Lena Mae Long married James "Jim" Blalock Crawford.

Lena Mae Long and James "Jim" Blalock Crawford lived at Route 8, Carrollton, Georgia, until their deaths. They are buried at Cross Plains Christian Cemetery. Their children were Lora Mattie Lee; Pauline "Polly;" James Dewey Crawford Sr. married first to Phillips and second to Effie Mae Hennings; Ruby married Price Ford; infant son #1; Wyley Burford; Leona G. married John T. Eason; Homer Lyle married Eunice Lee Johnson; infant son #2; and Clara Bell Crawford married Jack Thomas Chandler.

Homer Lyle Crawford, Eunice Lee Johnson, and a daughter Peggy Lee are buried at Carroll Memory Gardens, Carrollton. Other children to them are Jo Ann married Garry L. Baughtman and B. Kay married Ray Elliott Brown.

Ray Elliott Brown and B. Kay Crawford reside in Carrollton. Their children are Jennifer Rebecca; Jonathan Marc married Christina Michele Randles; Joshua Aric; Jasper Kohlby; Jordan Christia deceased; and Jared Paul Brown.

Jonathan Marc Brown and Christina Michele Randles are the parents of Jacob Marc Brown. *Submitted by: Marc Brown, 112 Terry Terrace, Carrollton, GA 30117, Researched and Written by: Ray Elliott Brown, Patriot Treasures.*

901. Parrish Family

Isaac Martin Parrish came to Georgia from North Carolina with his friend, Newt Pierce, in the late 1820s. He married Mary Eskew in 1830 with whom he had four known children. Isaac served with Company H, 56th Regiment, Georgia Infantry, in the War Between the States and was elected captain by the members of his company. During a lull in the battle, he lay down in a trench to read his orders with his knee propped. A sniper shot him in the kneecap. Having nothing to keep infection down, we assume he died of blood poisoning a few days later. His name is listed in the registry book at the Vicksburg National Military Park.

After the war, Mary Eskew Parrish lived in Carroll County and reared her children there: Mattie Parrish Muse, Liza Parrish Rainwater, Lou Parrish Fields, Mary Jane Parrish Hunter, John Wiley Parrish, Willie Parrish McKenzie, and James Newton Parrish.

John Wiley Parrish married Florence Baxter. They lived in the vicinity of the Oak Grove community. One of their ten children was my grandfather, Oscar Daniel Parrish. Oscar married Harriett Elizabeth Threadgill in 1905. They were blessed with two daughters, Margaret Pauline Parrish (Truitt), and Florence Pearl Parrish (Otwell), and one son, Claude Alcimus Parrish. John Parrish died in 1919 and is buried at the Concord Methodist Church Cemetery alongside his wife who died in 1914.

Pauline married Clyde Arzroe Truitt. They had one son, Clyde Arzroe Jr. He was the only grandchild for a number of years and was much beloved. He graduated from the Georgia Institute of Technology and married Betty Jo Carroll of Bremen. Only a few months after the wedding, he died of leukemia in 1954. Pauline died in 1985.

Pearl married Raymond Otwell of Bremen at the age of sixty. Pearl had a long and successful career with Sewell Manufacturing Company in Bremen.

Claude was born May 3, 1915. He and Alice Faye Mathews eloped on Sunday evening, November 6, 1938. They went to the Temple Methodist Parsonage and the pastor who was serving the church married them with the pastor's wife as the only witness. There was a rumor that a close friend of the pastor's was hiding in a back room and also witnessed the ceremony.

Claude served in the Army during World War II and was sent to Germany. He returned home in early 1945 and began his family. Daniel Claude Parrish was born in 1947, Dale Reid in 1949, and Claudia Faye in 1952. Dan married Vickie Jo Payne in 1970. He has three children. Dale married Sheila Nolin in 1971 and they had one son. In 1996, Dale married Lynn Lee and adopted her daughter. Claudia married Robert Patrick Waldrop and they have two children.

Claude died of lung cancer in November of 1989. Faye died in January of 1998. Dan lives in Natchitoches, Louisiana, Dale in Temple next door to the Parrish home, and Claudia and her family live in Carrollton.

The John Parrish Family. 1914

The family photograph was taken in 1914 and shows John Wiley Parrish, his wife Florence Baxter Parrish, and their ten children. Seated in front are John Wiley and Florence. Second row from left are Jim, Robert, Oscar, Marvin, and Wiley. On the back row standing are Lula, Lelia, Mollie, Bessie, Omie. *Submitted by: Claudia Parrish Waldrop, 257 Mink Hollow Drive, Carrollton, GA 30116-6406*

902. Julius Grady Parrish (Parish)

Julius Grady Parrish was born 26 May 1921 in Carroll County, Georgia, son of Augustus Franklin (Gus) Parrish and Mary Lee Clark. His paternal grandparents were John Parrish and Almeda Roseanna Summerville. His maternal grandparents were James Clark and Tempie Adeline Pirkle.

Gus and Mary came to Temple, Georgia, before 1921. All four of their children were born in Temple between 1921-1930: Julius Grady married Dorothy E. Allen; Rosa Lee married Harold Kiser; Earl Franklin; and Ruby Parrish. They farmed in the Temple area in their early years. Gus later was employed by Dave Williams Cabinet Shop, then Bell Aircraft Corporation in Marietta. He was a Mason and attended Lodge in Temple.

Grady and Dorothy were married 21 February 1942 at the home of Rev. E. Baskin in Temple. Dorothy's parents were George Parker and Elfie Chance Allen.

Grady registered for and was called up for service in World War II in November 1942. He applied for and was accepted in the USAAF, receiving training in Miami Beach, Florida; Amarillo, Texas; Las Vegas, Nevada; Walla Walla and Spokane, Washington. He also took some training maneuvers at Camp Pendleton, Oregon.

On 18 January 1943, Dorothy and Grady's son was born, being delivered by Dr. T.M. Spruill of Temple. His name is Julius Allen Parrish. Grady received furlough 30 August 1943 for ten days; He spent six days traveling and three days at home. Dorothy and Julius returned with him and spent five weeks before he left for overseas.

S/Sgt. Julius Grady Parrish, May 26, 1921 - Feb. 22, 1944.

His crew was stationed near Bedford, England, at Thurleigh AFB. They were returning to base on 22 February 1944 from a raid over Bernberg, Germany, when they were attacked by enemy aircraft. Their plane — Big Time Operator Wolf — was demolished. Five crew members bailed out or were blown out and survived in German prison camps until the war was over. Five were killed instantly as the plane exploded. Grady, as Ball Turrett Gunner, was killed. His body was returned in 1950 and interred in Bethel Baptist Church Cemetery (Highway 113, between Temple and Carrollton) where his father and mother are buried beside him.

Julius Allen Parrish has two sons and two daughters: Todd Allen, Derek, Ginger, and Mary Parrish. He has two grandchildren, Autumn and Austin Parrish. Julius is married to Judy Bryant, daughter of Wallace and Reba N. Tyson Bryant. They live in Villa Rica, Georgia. Julius is employed by McNeilus Company. Judy is employed by M.D. Hodges Company. Ginger is attending State University of West Georgia in Carrollton. Mary is in eighth grade at Bay Springs Middle School in Villa Rica.

Julius and Dorothy, his mother, were privileged to travel to England in 1992 at the Eight Air Force celebration of the 50th year commemorative of their "First Over Germany" event. They surveyed what remained of Bedford Air Force Base (Thurleigh) and met some of the survivors. *Submitted by: Julius Allen Parrish, Villa Rica, GA 30180*

903. Parsons - Carroll

John Rudolph (Rudy) Parsons, son of William David and Bela Hubbard Parsons, and his twin Richard Asbury were born October 21, 1931, in Gadsden, Alabama. Two other children were born to the Parsons — Jackson Hubbard Parsons who died at birth on September 24, 1915, and William David Parsons Jr. born March 6, 1917, in Leeds, Alabama. William David Parsons Sr. died on January 21, 1932, shortly after the twins were born; Richard Asbury died December 21, 1932; and Bela Parsons died the following year on December 22, 1933. John Rudolph Parsons made his home with an aunt and uncle, Fred and Erdele Hubbard Munroe, and William Jr. made his home with an uncle and his grandmother, Mary C. Parsons Williamson.

Rudy is the grandson of John F. Parsons and Mary Cornelia Abercrombie of Leeds, Alabama, and William Asbury Hubbard and Martha Emma Striplin.

Betty Jo Carroll, born September 22, 1933, in Haralson County, Georgia, is the daughter of Ollie Melvina Warren and Eucleod McAllister Carroll. (See related Warren and Carroll stories.) She graduated from Bremen High School as valedictorian of her 1950 class, and was a graduate of West Georgia College in 1952. She has six brothers and one sister: Warren Opal (deceased); Kenneth L., living in Huntsville, Alabama; James Quinton (deceased); Hilda Melvina (deceased); Victor Lee (deceased); Charles Eucleod, living in Bremen; and Stanley N. Carroll living in Huntsville, Alabama.

Rudy and Betty Jo were married on July 23, 1959, in Bremen, Georgia. They have two children, both born in Oconomowoc, Wisconsin. Carolyn Kay was born February 14, 1961, and William David was born June 18, 1963. Both graduated from Hope College in Holland, Michigan, and followed their parents south after graduation. After living in Wisconsin for twenty-three years where Rudy was a sales representative for Hubbard Pants Company, they moved to Knoxville, Tennessee, in 1982, just in time for the World's Fair! Upon their retirements in 1994 and 1997, they moved to Bowdon, a few miles from where Betty Jo's parents grew up.

With no grandchildren to lavish their attention on, they have chosen to raise dogs. At present, they have seven Tibetan Mastiffs. Their other main interest centers around family research and history, having completed a history last year of our Parsons line. *Submitted by: William David Parsons, Chattanooga, TN*

904. Paschal

Part 1

Samuel Joel Paschal and Mary Michele Burns

Samuel Joe Paschal was born August 22, 1960, at Tanner Medical Center in Carrollton, Georgia. He was the third son of George William Fred Paschal and Reba Crawford Paschal. He attended the Central Primary and High Schools in Carroll County and was a member of the FCA, French and Science Clubs.

During his childhood, he had many hobbies, including collecting rocks and fossils, coins, and stamps. He graduated with honors from Central High School in 1977. He was also nominated by his teachers for Who's Who in American High School Students. He worked several jobs after high school, including machine operations.

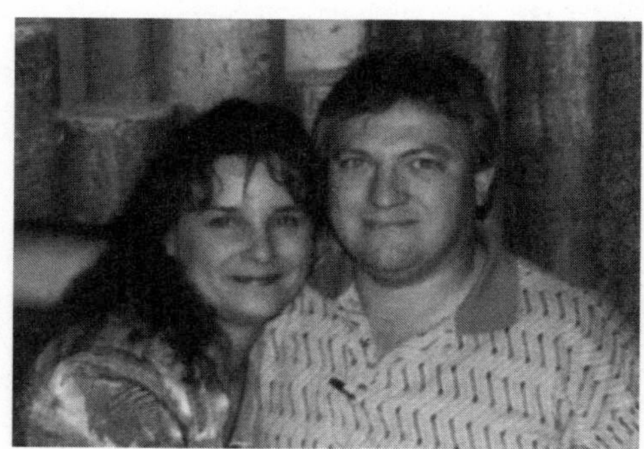

Joel and Michele Paschal

Mary Michele Burns was born October 27, 1962, at Palomar Hospital in Escodido, California, where her father, Donald T. Burns Sr. was stationed at Miramar Naval Base in San Diego, California. She is the youngest of two children born to Donald T. Burns Sr. and Joyce Laverne McCosh Burns, who were married April 21, 1959, at Woodward Church of God in their hometown of Athens, Tennessee. Their son Donald Taylor Burns Sr. married Sandra Regina Rogers, of Moreland, Georgia. "Tate" and Regina now reside in Tampa, Florida.

Michele's father was in the U.S. Air Force, so they moved several times during Michele's childhood. They lived in North Dakota, Montana, and North Carolina and other areas. They moved to Carrollton in 1971 from Andrews, North Carolina. He worked at Southwire Company and was in the reserves at Dobbins Air Force Base in Marietta, Georgia. Joyce owned and operated Busy B's Catering and Cake Decorating Center in Carrollton, where many women from the Carroll County area enjoyed her cake decorating classes given at her shop and at the Carroll Tech adult classes. Michele has acquired her mother's culinary skills and love of entertaining. Joyce McCosh Burns has a brother and sister-in-law, Douglas and Nancy McCosh, who still live in the Carroll County area. Their grown children also live in Carroll County.

Her parents moved to Whittier, North Carolina in 1981, where Don currently designs and builds porch rockers and swings. Joyce works at Birdland Enterprises in Cherokee, North Carolina.

Michele attended Carrollton Junior High School. She attended Carrollton High until the eleventh grade, where she was in FBLA, FHA and Octagon Clubs. She then moved to Central High School, where she graduated in 1980.

In 1979 Joel and Michele met at a gospel singing in Carrollton, where Joel sang with brothers Stanley and Mark, and Mark's wife Connie, in a gospel band. They were married August 9, 1980, at the Congregational Holiness Church in Carrollton. Joel's father, Rev. G.W. Fred Paschal, performed the ceremony.

Joel and Michele Paschal have owned and operated Paschal Recreation Solutions since 1989, where they design and sell commercial park and playground equipment throughout the southeast. They have attended Christ Fellowship Church since 1988. They are active in foreign mission programs. They support missionaries and children's feeding programs in Guatemala. They have been on short-term mission trips to Jamaica. *Submitted by: Nancy McCosh*
Source: Researched by: Joyce McCosh Burns

905. Paschal
Part 2
George William Fred Paschal and Reba Myrl Crawford Paschal

George William Fred Paschal was born on July 2, 1916, in the Simpson community, Heard County, Georgia. He was the third son of Arthur Jefferson Paschal Sr. and Nancy Lancaster Paschal. Their family moved to Carrollton in 1922. Fred Paschal was a man of integrity and held strong religious convictions.

Reba Paschal and Rev. Fred Paschal

Reba Myrl Crawford, born December 9, 1924, was the only child of Abbie Crawford and Alline Griffin Crawford. She was a sweet Christian lady, devoted to serving the Lord and her family. The Crawford family moved into the Clem community in the early 1800s. They were some of the earlier farming settlers.

Fred Paschal and Reba Crawford met while working together at local cotton mills. They married on December 19, 1943, and a short time later, Fred was inducted into the army.

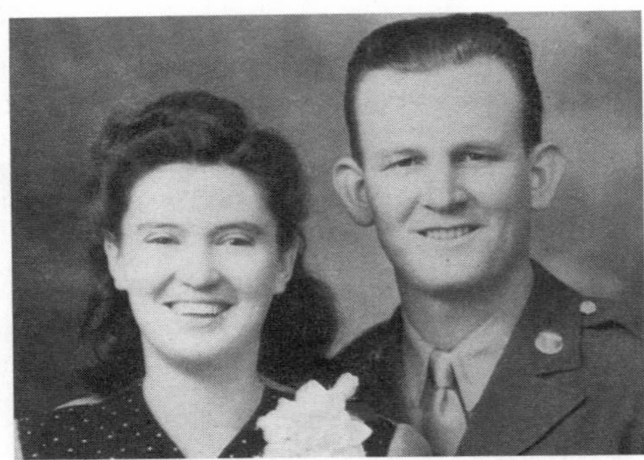

Reba Crawford Paschal and Rev. G.W. Fred Paschal, 1943

William Meredith Paschal was born in Carrollton on October 9, 1944. He married Gwendolyn Faye Bryant, of Griffin, Georgia, on March 14, 1970. Faye was born June 13, 1947. They have one daughter, Amy Millicent Paschal, born December 15, 1972. She married Evon Turner Middleton, of Parrott, Georgia, on May 14, 1994. Turner was born May 14, 1972. Both couples currently reside in Griffin.

Stanley Lee Paschal was born October 2, 1954 in Carrollton. He married Vickie Rene Sullivan (daughter of Julius and Winnie Sullivan) of Carrollton on October 31, 1970. Vickie was born in Carrollton on July 3, 1956. They have one daughter, Emily Renee Paschal, born in Atlanta, Georgia, on August 18, 1976. Michael Andrew Paschal was born September 13, 1986 in Newnan, Georgia.

Mark Eugene Paschal was born August 27, 1959, in Carrollton. He married Connie Francis Morgan (daughter of J.D. and Ellna Morgan) of Carrollton on June 9, 1979. Connie was born in Tennessee on April 3, 1962. They have four children. Christina Marie Paschal was born in Carrollton on July 31, 1980. She married Robert Clifford Thacker, from Griffin, Georgia, on December 24, 1999. Rob was born August 10, 1974, in Griffin. Joshua David Mark Paschal was born in Carrollton on September 15, 1982. Matthew Joel Paschal was born in Carrollton on December 19, 1984. He died on May 30, 2000, from severe head injuries in a jet ski accident on Lake Buckhorn, near Temple, Georgia. Carla Bethany Paschal was born on July 2, 1986, in Carrollton.

Samuel Joel Paschal was born August 22, 1960 in Carrollton. He married Mary Michele Burns, of Carrollton on August 9, 1980. Michele was born October 27, 1962, at the Palomar Hospital in Escondido, California, where her father was stationed at the Miramar Naval Base, San Diego, California. Michele's family moved into Carroll County about 1971. Her parents, Donald Taylor Burns Sr. and Joyce McCosh Burns lived in the Lowell community for a few years before moving into Carrollton. They moved to Whittier, North Carolina in 1981, where they currently reside. *Submitted by: Amy Paschal Middleton, 305 Sunset Drive, Griffin, GA 30223*

906. Paschal
Part 3
Arthur Jefferson Paschal Sr. and Nancy Camilla Lancaster

Arthur Jefferson Paschal Sr. was born in Heard County, Georgia, on April 7, 1882, and died in Carrollton, Georgia, on September 18, 1972. Nancy Camilla Lancaster Paschal was born in Heard County on June 6, 1890, and died in Carrollton on March 27, 1973. Arthur was a son of George William Paschal, born December 15, 1857, in Heard County, and Annie Cook. Nancy was a daughter to John B. Lancaster and Eliza Hertt Lancaster. The family of Arthur Jefferson Paschal Sr. and Nancy Camilla Lancaster Paschal moved to Carrollton in 1922. Their home place is located at the corner of Old Newnan Road and Burns Roads and included lands on both sides of Newnan Highway.

Families in those days were primarily farming families with little wealth. Farming families generally had many children out of necessity, due to the manual labor required to operate farms. The Paschal family included eight children.

Arthur Jefferson Paschal Sr., Nancy Camilla Lancaster Paschal, and children.

Charles Green Paschal, born about February 1911, died August 27, 1981. He married Lorene Smith. Sallie Kate Paschal, born in 1912, (never married) died May 4, 1996. Arthur Jefferson Paschal Jr., born June 22, 1914, died June 26, 1987. He married Emogene Ashmore. George William Fred Paschal, born July 2, 1916, married Reba Myrl Crawford (See George William Fred Paschal and Reba Myrl Crawford Paschal story) and died in the V.A. Medical Center, Decatur, Georgia, on November 17, 1988. Jimmie Lee Paschal, born in 1918 currently resides in Lilburn, Georgia with his wife Mildred and family. Annie Harriett Petty Paschal, born January 1, 1922, currently lives in Carrollton near her family.

Paschal Family Reunion

She was married to Bernice Cleven Petty. B.C. Petty died in 1988. Mary Alice Paschal, born August 22, 1925, (never married) died June 12, 1990, in Carrollton. Harvey Albert Paschal, born November 5, 1927, died in Carrollton in October 5, 1929, of pneumonia at two years of age.

Most of the children of Arthur Jefferson Paschal Sr. and Nancy Lancaster Paschal grew up in the Carroll County area. Their grandchildren and great-grandchildren also continue to call Carroll County home. The families of Charles Green Paschal and Jimmie Lee Paschal, with their wives and families, moved into Gwinnett County and DeKalb County, Georgia, in the 1950s.

On an interesting side note, Nancy Lancaster Paschal had a sister named Mayhayley Lancaster. Mayhayley lived in Heard County, Georgia, and was a well-known fortune teller in the area. In the 1980s, a made-for-television movie was produced called "Murder in Coweta County" which included actors Andy Griffith and Johnny Cash. Mayhayley was the fortune teller in a true life story about a murder investigation, trial and conviction, where she helped the Coweta County sheriff find the burned bone fragments of a murdered sharecropper of a powerful landowner. These bone fragments provided evidence vital to the prosecution's case. *Submitted by: Annie Paschal Petty, 208 Old Newnan Road, Carrollton, GA 30117*

907. Paschal
Part 4
George William Fred Paschal

George William Fred Paschal (See George William Fred and Reba Myrl Crawford Paschal story) was shipped overseas near the end of World War II. His ship was en route to the Philippines from Pearl Harbor when the war ended. He served in the Philippines as an Army medic. Also, during his carrier trips overseas, he served as a barber. After his return to the United States, he continued his work as a barber in Carrollton. His first shop was on Maple Street next to the railroad tracks.

Fred was a friend to many people. He enjoyed the fellowship tremendously, so he made barbering his vocation for life. During the 1960s, haircuts were in less demand, so he sought other employment. He lubricated machinery at the Southwire Company for eleven years, still operating his barber shop which he had moved to his home on Horsley Mill Road. Often he cut hair for patients in local hospitals and nursing homes. He served for several years as chaplain of the local American Legion chapter.

He was also called to preach as an ordained lay minister, preaching in area churches. He preached Sunday morning sermons on radio station WLBB-AM in Carrollton. He witnessed of his personal faith to fellow workers and led many people to accept Jesus Christ. Gardening was one of his favorites. Fred and Reba raised crops and cattle, always sharing with family and people in need. He occasionally sold crops to pay expenses. He loved seeing things grow.

Reba Crawford Paschal helped move her parents in 1963. They were better able to take care of her parents (see Abbie and Alline Griffin Crawford story) after moving them to a home next door. Fred and Reba Paschal also reared four sons. Reba was a great homemaker, mother and daughter. She "loved the Lord and her family" as she put it. Rearing four sons, she also attended to elderly parents. She also battled physical ailments herself. She enjoyed flowers, quilting, cooking and reading the Bible. Fred and Reba were members of the Congregational Holiness Church on South Street. *Submitted by: Meredith Paschal (formerly of Carrollton), 822 Ashton Place, Griffin, GA 30223*

908. Paschal
Part 5
Abbie Crawford and Alline Griffin

Abbie Crawford was born October 24, 1900, in Clem, Georgia. He was a son of William Henry Crawford and Laura Godbee Crawford. Alline Grifin was born January 14, 1903, in Clem. She was a daughter of Rev. Thomas Anderson Griffin and Dolly Elizabeth Little. They married on December 26, 1923. Both the Crawford and Griffin families were early settlers in the Clem community area of Carroll County. Both families moved into Carroll County in the early 1800s.

They had one daughter, Reba Myrl Crawford. Reba was born December 9, 1924. Reba attended Oak Mountain School in Carrollton. She married George William Fred Paschal in 1943 (see George William Fred Paschal and Reba Myrl Crawford Paschal story).

Alline Griffin and Abbie Crawford

Abbie served in the U.S. Army for about one year after World War I, from 1921 until 1922. He was a private on the 13th Ammunition Division. Abbie Crawford worked in the Mandeville cotton mills in Carrollton for a number of years. Later, he worked on machinery at Southwire Company before bad health forced him to retire. Abbie Crawford served as a caretaker at Mt. Pleasant Baptist Church in Clem. Abbie Crawford died March 19, 1979.

Alline Griffin Crawford was a fine Christian lady, known for her good works and Christian friendship. Early in life, she was a member of Mt. Pleasant Baptist Church in Clem. Later, they transferred their membership to New Hope Baptist Church near the Horsley Mill community. She suffered with a number of physical ailments most of her adult life, requiring much attention. Alline died on October 22, 1970. Abbie and Alline Crawford are buried at Oak Grove Baptist Church Cemetery. *Submitted by: Stanley L. Paschal, 1305 Old Newnan Road, Carrollton, GA 30116*

909. Paschal
Part 6
Early Paschal Family History

The Paschal family (*see Arthur Jefferson and Nancy Lancaster Paschal story*) has its roots as a farming family. We can trace the Paschal family in the United States back directly to Thomas Paschal, who was born about 1523 in Bristol, England. Family lineage has its earliest documented roots in Auvergne, France, where John Paschal was born in 1475. The French Paschals were Protestants who were severely persecuted, so they left for England during the late 1400s or early 1500s. The first family members moved to Essex, then later to Bristol, where Thomas Paschal was born. His son Andrew Paschal was the first to leave England for the New World in the late 1500s or early 1600s.

Upon entering the United States, Andrew Paschal and his descendants lived in the Middlesex County, New Jersey, area. A few generations later, William Paschal was born in Philadelphia, Pennsylvania, on July 22, 1693. He married Phereba Ward. In the mid 1700s, when the United States government began the North Carolina Land Grants, William Paschal and family moved south into Warrenton County, North Carolina, just south of the Virginia border. They farmed and lived in this area. They had several children. The present-day Paschals here in Carroll County descend from a son, Samuel Paschal. William and Phereba Paschal had another son, Isaiah. He had a grandson, George Washington Paschal Sr., who married Sarah Ridge. George Washington Paschal Sr. was born in Greene County, Georgia, November 23, 1812.

Sarah Ridge, a Cherokee Indian princess, was the daughter of the second highest chief of the Cherokee Nation. Major Ridge, chief of the Chickamauga tribe, married Susannah Wickett. Major Ridge and his family made their home in what is today known as Rome, Georgia. Major Ridge was one of the three Cherokee leaders who signed the treaty at New Echota (present day Calhoun, Georgia) with the U.S. government, which led to the relocation of the Cherokees to Oklahoma, in exchange for $5,000,000 and lands out west. His conviction was that after much fighting and bloodshed, leaving peacefully for Oklahoma was the only way for the Cherokee to survive as a nation and culture. He believed that education and peaceful civilization would better the lives of the Cherokee.

George Washington Paschal Sr. and wife Sarah Ridge Paschal moved to Arkansas in 1837. George was appointed the chief justice of the Arkansas Supreme Court by the state legislature. In 1847, they moved to Austin, Texas. He was a friend and advisor to Sam Houston. He defended Indian claims against the United States government.

In the early 1800s, descendants of Samuel Paschal continued their migration into South Carolina. From Abbeville County, South Carolina, family members moved into Carroll and Heard County, Georgia. Several generations lived on farms in these two counties. Most settled here in Carroll County or still live nearby. Arthur Jefferson Paschal Sr. and Nancy Lancaster Paschal and all of their children moved to Carrollton from Heard County. Most of their children reared their families in Carroll County and continue to live here. *Submitted by: Joel Paschal, Carrollton, GA 30116*

910. Pate

This is a partial history of the Pate family. We can't go any further back than Fayette County, Georgia. We found where Wyley A. Pate went to the Civil War from Fayette County. He was in Company C, 53rd Regiment in Georgia. He was killed in the Battle of the Wilderness in Virginia, May 6, 1864. His wife's name was Margaret. His children were Catherine, Lucinda, Caroline, Jim, Mary, and Wyley.

Jim Pate married Minnie Jones. We don't know what year they came to Carroll County, but it was some time in the late 1800s. Their children were Caldonia, Fannie, Tommy Willie, Annie, Lela, Arthur, Clifford, Grady, Paul, and Mary.

Tommy, born 1884, married Viola Clark, born 1895. They married July 14, 1917. Their children were John Thomas (Jack), Juanita, Marvin, and Mary Jean.

Juanita, born 1930 in Carrollton, married Billy Marshall Roberts June 11, 1955, in Coweta County. Bill was born November 22, 1931, in Alabama. They have two children: Pam, born October 20, 1956, and Tommy, born October 6,

1958. She has five grandchildren and two great-grandchildren. She and Bill have lived in Florida since they married. Bill was in the Navy. Her two brothers, Jack and Marvin, and her sister, Mary Jean, live in Georgia. Her oldest brother, Jack, has lived in Carroll County for eighty-two years. *Submitted by: Mrs. Juanita Pate Roberts, 214 Soter Street NW, Fort Walton Beach, FL 32548*

911. Pate Family

We know very little about the Pate history. We only know that Wiley A. Pate, age 23, joined the Confederate Army in Fayette County, Georgia, on May 1, 1862. He was in Company C, 53rd Georgia Infantry. He was killed in the battle of the Wilderness in Virginia on May 6, 1864. His wife was Peggy Pate. She was found in the 1880 census of Coweta County, Georgia. She was 45 years old then. She had four daughters and two sons. The two sons later came to Carroll County, but we don't know what year. We do know that in the 1880 census James Pate, age 21, and his wife Minnie, age 21, lived in Coweta County. He is our ancestor. He had no children then, but sometime in the late 1800s or early 1900s, he came to Carroll County and raised his family here. He died in 1931, his wife died in 1947. Both are buried at St. Paul Methodist Church in Carroll County. They raised nine children. His wife was an orphan, so we know nothing about her family.

Tommy Willie (Will) Pate, born in August 1884, died in 1959, was the son of James and Minnie Pate. He married Viola Clark (born 1895) in 1917. She died in 1979. Both are buried in Oak Hill Cemetery in Newnan, Georgia. They lived in Carroll County.

John Thomas (Jack), son of Will and Viola, was born November 10, 1918, in Carroll County. He married Thelma Rooks, daughter of Ernie and Eunice Rooks. She was born June 24, 1913, in Campbell County. Their children are (1) William Jackson Pate, born December 1943, married Jean Smith on December 15, 1968. She is the daughter of John and Kathleen Smith. They have two daughters, Jodi Pate Foster and Brooke Pate; (2) John Daniell Pate, born January 2, 1946, married Judy Holloway Moore on December 11, 1982. They have one son, John Pate, born September 11, 1985; and (3) Larry Marvin Pate, born July 29, 1951, married Jackie Sue Bagwell on December 19, 1969. They all live in Carroll County. *Submitted by: William Jackson Pate, 2728 E. Highway 5, Whitesburg, GA 30185*

912. Patterson Family

William Tryon Patterson Sr., born about 1785 probably in Franklin County, Georgia, married Elizabeth Moore and they had several children including sons William (b. 1805) and Tryon Jr., (b. abt. 1814). William married Sydney Viccary and one of their children was Tryon (b. 11-8-1832) whose second wife was Lucinda Smith. Tryon and Lucinda's first child James Marion (b. 11-23-1866) was my great-grandfather. James Marion married Deliah Huckeby and their first son was John Marion Washington "Johnny" (b. 4-29-1885). Johnny married Julia Henrietta Patterson (b. 2-17-1884) and their second child was Elma Janette (my mother).

Tryon Jr., married Eliza Prewett and their fourth child was Henry J. (b. 2-23-1845) who married Emma Chane O'Neal (b. 7-12-1850). Henry and Emma's fifth child was Julia Henrietta Patterson and she married Johnny Patterson on September 13, 1903 in Carroll County. (Julia married her second cousin once removed - Johnny.)

Johnny and Julia had eight children: Ruby, Elma, Emanuel, Newton, Kermit, Lanoy, Everlena, and Robert. Johnny was a carpenter and brick mason. He even made most of their furniture. Julia was a homemaker and fine seamstress. Ruby and Elma were born in Heard County and the others were born in Carroll County.

Patterson brothers in 1913: Johnny, Will, Rob, Oscar, and Ezra.

Elma Janette Patterson, my mother, married Jesse Terrell Harris in 1925, Carroll County. He was the son of William Samuel (W.S.) Harris, born 1866, and Martha Lee (Mattie) Mobley. W.S. was the son of William Washington (W.W.) Harris, born 1847, and Elizabeth Tyson.

W.W. and Elizabeth Harris had eleven children: William Samuel, Charles, Louisa, Alexander Cliff, John Horatio, Annie Elizabeth, Myrtice Leona, Virgil, Ella Janie Camilla, Ollie Bernard, and Lilly Pearlie Viola. W.W. Harris was born in Coweta County and Elizabeth Dixon Tyson was born in Meriwether County. All their children were born in Carroll County. Elizabeth Tyson Harris is the descendant of two Revolutionary War soldiers, Jehu Tyson and John Beverly.

Johnny, Newton, Emanuel, Julia with Kermit, and Elma Patterson 1913.

W.S. and Mattie Harris had eight children: Myrtie Lee, Lula Velmar, Lena Ethel, Lilly May, Earnest Marvin, Melvin B., Harvey Floyd, and Jesse Terrell, my father.

Terrell and Elma Harris had ten children: Wynona, J.T. Jr., June, Violette, Dennis, Glenda, Conner, Francine, Johnnie, and Julia. They were all born in Carroll County.

Violette Harris married James Donald Denney on February 24, 1951, Bethany Christian Church, Carroll County. Their two children, Anthony Donald and Jeffery Alan, are both married. Donald is retired from General Motors and Violette is retired from the U.S. Treasury Department. Their home place has been in the Harris family since January 1, 1894.

The Elizabeth Harris School was named for my great-grandmother, Elizabeth Harris, and W.W. Harris, my great-grandfather, gave the land for the school in 1917, just after she died. The school was located east of Carrollton on Highway 166. The cement foundation is still there.

Several Patterson men served in the Confederate Army. Tryon Patterson, born in 1832, was a private in the Georgia Infantry, Confederate States of America, and was captured in Vicksburg and later again in Nashville and forwarded to Louisville, Kentucky. Tryon's brother, Henry Francis Patterson, born 1829, died during the Civil War on May 11, 1862, in Lauderdale, Mississippi. Cousin Henry J. Patterson was also a Confederate soldier. He enlisted in 1864 in Atlanta and was in the Georgia Militia.

Tryon Patterson's wife Lucinda Caroline Smith, born 1838, was the daughter of Gabriel D. Smith, Jr., born 1798 in Elbert County, and granddaughter of Gabriel D. Smith, born 1764 in Anson County, North Carolina. Gabriel D. Smith served in the Revolutionary War in Montgomery County, North Carolina. *Submitted by: Violette Harris Denney, 135 Maple Hill Road, Carrollton, GA 30116-7014*
Source: Family and research.

913. Millard Kermit Patterson

My first recollection is of living in a small, frame farmhouse on a dirt road three miles north of Carrollton. The house had no ceiling and you could see the sturdy, wooden shingles overlapped on the top. Thank goodness it didn't leak, but it was mighty cold in the wintertime. You would have to break the ice in the water bucket in the morning before you could wash the sleep from your eyes.

I was born on September 12, 1912, the fourth child of John W. and Julia P. Patterson. Eventually there were three other children.

When I was about six, I started school in a one room schoolhouse which still stands (barely) on Shady Grove Road. We didn't have enough money for me to buy a book, so I had to look on with a classmate to do my lessons. I remember Mr. Robert Green was my first teacher. The next school I attended was Shady Grove, which was next to Shady Grove Church. We had to walk about three miles one way to get there everyday. I had to drop out of school in the eighth grade to help my brothers plant the fields and cut wood for the cook stove.

Boxing was a big sport in those days and I really admired the stories of the professional boxers and dreamed of being one myself. Finally, I saved enough money for two sets of boxing gloves and challenged everyone I could to a match. I was pretty good, too, and I could whip all of the local school boys. Soon, older boys from Carrollton started coming out to fight me too, and I would whip them as well. One day they decided to play a trick on me and brought in a stranger I did not know. A stranger that boxed for a living professionally in Atlanta. Needless to say, I didn't whip that one.

My Dad had been taking note of my boxing. One day he told me that he could whip me and challenged me to a match. We put on the gloves and went at it. I managed to duck his punches and tried to hold back my own. I didn't want to hurt my dad or make him mad at me. After we traded a few punches he decided he didn't have much for boxing. After my bout with the stranger, I decided I didn't either.

My Dad had a modest, two-horse farm which we rented from Mr. Gene Richards. Our crops were corn and cotton and later we added wheat. There was always a big vegetable garden and many fruit trees. A large wooden barrel held the best of the Yates apples. They lasted well into the fall, sometimes until Christmas. Well, they would last that long if we boys wouldn't slip and get more than our share of them.

After we boys had gotten old enough to do most of the farm work, Dad had bought a home place for us and had himself hired out as a carpenter to supplement our income. The depression was nearing and times were hard. Sometimes we would get caught up with our farm work and hire out to pick cotton on neighboring farms so that we would have spending money.

Soon the older boys married and left home. I was left to do all of the farming, with the help of my sisters, and I had to cut all of the stove wood.

Kermit and Cloteal Patterson, 50th Wedding Anniversary Celebration

I met Maggie Cloteal Peek (born 5-1-1913, died 11-18-1986) while attending a singing school at Shady Grove Church. I was seventeen years old and she was sixteen when we began courting. We became engaged on August 2, 1928, and I continued to work on my father's farm until it was fully paid off. On December 23, 1931, Cloteal and I were married. After staying with my family for a short time, we moved into the tenant house of Willy Smith and farmed on halves. Mr. Smith furnished the land, horses, seed and fertilizer, and Cloteal and I did the labor.

The days of the depression were especially hard. I remember sitting in the woods, many times, looking for a squirrel or rabbit to shoot for our supper. Rabbits were really good with biscuits and gravy. To make ends meet, I would cut hair for ten cents a head on Sunday mornings. We didn't have a car to ride to church then, so sometimes we would ride with the Smiths in their horse drawn buggy.

On January 30, 1934, our first daughter was born. We named her Joyce Annette. Years later she married Edwin Russell Smith and they had one son, Millard Clark. After Edwin's death, Joyce married Charles Oly Duncan. They have three grandsons: Edwin Drake, Sean Luc and Taylor Clark Duncan.

I began working part-time at Mandeville Mills. I made repairs and laid brick for additions to the mill. I finally decided to give up farming because the boll weevils had gotten so bad. I became a brick layer full time.

Our second daughter was born August 29, 1941. She is Janis Elaine Patterson Black. She gave us two granddaughters: Vonya Joy, who married Wayne Bartlette and they have one daughter, Ashley Teal, and one son, John Carey. Janis' second daughter, Sharon Donnay married Phillip Spann and they have one son, Andrew Paul.

Our family was bigger, so we needed a larger house. I took out a loan and bought 50 acres of land nearby, and then built our house upon it.

Building is in the Patterson's blood I was always told, so I decided to become a builder and let someone else lay the brick. Maynard Thompson and I formed a partnership and began to build houses. After a few years, we split up and built houses separately.

Clark Duncan with children Luc, Taylor and Drake.

During this time, I had a tenant farmer who lived in our tenant house and farmed our land. I will never forget one of the horses I bought for him to plow the land. The horse was a beautiful, reddish brown with a white streak running down its nose. The horse's name was Simon and he was very temperamental. Simon was very good at plowing, even without a plow line. The horse would even turn on its own accord at the end of each row without any direction at all.

It was around this time that the first airport was built in Carrollton on the land adjoining mine. The pilots soon learned that if they buzzed their planes low enough, it would spook the plow horses and they would run like blue blazes. I came home from work one day and found out this had been going on, and that the field hands had to stop plowing because of the commotion. I remember I was really angry. If I had been there I probably would have shot at the planes, so I guess the Lord knew best.

Carole, our third daughter was born on March 1, 1951. She married Barry Williamson and they have a daughter, Brooke Lauren.

Building was a joy to me. I have built more houses than I can remember. I continued to build houses until I was 80 years old. There are two houses that stand out in my mind the most. The large, brick and rock house I built for the family of Roy Richards, and the one I built for Eaton and Susan Hayward Chalkley. I have been blessed and made many dear friends in my life as a carpenter.

I have been a Christian for many years, and the work that gave me the most pleasure was the building of many Christian churches in the West Georgia area. I built or remodeled the following Christian Churches: First Christian of Carrollton, Whitesburg, Douglasville, Villa Rica, Kings Street, Bremen, Union Grove and Bethany of Carrollton. I have also built several parsonages for the pastors and their families. While building many of the churches, I would also attend as a member and serve however needed. I was a Sunday School teacher, elder, deacon, Boy Scout leader, and served however I could.

I am 88 years old now and only have one regret — that I didn't finish my schooling. Having an education is very important.

My ambition now is to outlive my oldest ancestor. My great-grandmother O'neal lived to be 99 years old, so I want to live to be 100! *Submitted by: Joyce P. Duncan, 468 Maple Hill Road, Carrollton, GA 30116.*

914. William Joseph Tryon Patterson

William Joseph Tryon Patterson was born 11 March 1833 in Gwinnett County, Georgia, to William Tryon Patterson and Sidney Jane Vickers. The Pattersons had moved to Georgia sometime after the 1830 Carroll County Land Lottery. Tryon Patterson served in Company B, 56th Regular Georgia Volunteer Infantry, C.S.A.

Prior to 1852, he married Dorcas Holder and had seven children born in Carroll County: William, Richard, Ben, Millie, Sidney, John, and Thomas.

He married Lucinda Caroline Smith, daughter of Gabriel Smith Jr. on 11 March 1866. Their children were Sarah, Martha, Robert, and Joseph Tryon.

Joseph Tryon Patterson (Joe) was born on 17 March 1876. He married Martha Elizabeth (Betty) Robinson around 1895. She was the daughter of William Robinson and Nancy Mayfield. Together they had twelve children: Annie, Henry, Arvella, Buford, Marion, Grady, Laura, Lucinda, Emmett, Levi, Delbert, and Rogers (Doc). They moved to Haralson County in 1906 from the Burwell community. In 1920, Joe purchased the farm on Highway 100, just south of what is now Interstate-20, from a Col. Wright. Joe was a successful farmer and syrup maker.

Betty died in 1928 and Joe married Lizzie Barrow. Joe died 16 September 1949. He and Betty are buried in Poplar Springs Cemetery, Carroll County. *Submitted by: Brenda Sammie Robinson (great-granddaughter of Joe Patterson), 226 W. Lake Circle, Madison, AL 35758*

Joe and Betty Patterson with ten of their children.

915. James C. Payne Family

James C. Payne, the son of William Jasper and Mary "Polly Ann" Woods Payne, was born June 20, 1858, and died July 23, 1897, in Carroll County. James was a very young child when his father went off to war and he never saw him again. His father took the measles while on retreat from Yorktown to Richmond, Virginia, and died late May 1862. He is buried in the Hollywood Cemetery at Richmond, Virginia. James married Mary Elizabeth Pope on October 30, 1877, in Carroll County. She was born May 31, 1857, and died July 9, 1930, in Carroll County. They are buried at Midway Macedonia Baptist Church in the Sand Hill community. After the death of James, Mary married H.W. "Bud" Richardson on July 31, 1903, in Carroll County. Mary is the daughter of John R. and Mary Emily Boyd Pope of Carroll County. She was loved by everyone who knew her.

James and Mary Elizabeth Pope Payne had eight children. (1) Thomas Oscar born April 22, 1879, married Myrtis Roberts. (2) Luna L. born February 21, 1881, married John Wesley Duncan. (3) Emily O. Payne born October 3, 1884, died September 18, 1897. (4) Mamie E. Payne born April 8, 1886, died September 21, 1897. (5) Frank born February 10, 1888, died June 4, 1945, married Ola Mae Daniel. (6) William Claude born January 7, 1892, died unknown, married Effie unknown. (7) Lois Irene born February 16, 1896, died November 24, 1972, married John Howard Powell. (8) Jimmie born April 4, 1898, died July 31, 1973, married Earl Mann.

James C. and Mary Elizabeth Pope Payne

Lois Irene Payne and John Howard Powell were my parents. They had six children, Mary Ellen married Clarence Turner; Annie Grace married Earl Eugene Dial; Virginia Ruth married Delcer Floyd Agan; John Howard Jr. married Reva Louise Dillard; James Roy married first to Dorothy Mull (deceased) and second to Lilly Brooks; Peggy Nell married Vernon Carpenter.

I married Earl Eugene Dial on July 21, 1934, in Haralson County. He died October 6, 1989, in Carroll County. We had five children. Charles Eugene married Jeanette Jiles, William Ray married Elizabeth Ann Gore, Glenda Sue married first Larry Miller and second Vernon Roberson, Donald Norton (deceased) married Merle Thomas, Jerry Wayne married first Lavangie Wilkey and second Glenda Faye Moss.

We had fifteen grandchildren, sixteen great-grandchildren, and one great-great-grandchild. I will be eighty-five years old come July 25, 2001. *Submitted by: Annie Grace Powell Dial, 1008 Old Draketown Trail, Temple, GA 30179*

Sources: Census records, war records, Carroll County marriage records, and personal knowledge.

916. Joseph Joshua Payne and Louisa Elizabeth Boyd

Joseph Joshua Payne was born January 20, 1854, in Georgia. His parents, William Jasper and Mary (Polly) Ann Wood(s) Payne, came to Carroll County from Tennessee sometime after their marriage in 1852 and settled near Villa Rica. They had six children, all raised in Carroll County: Elizabeth, Joseph Joshua and Fleming Caleb (twins), Rachel, Hannah Jane, and James C. When the Civil War broke out, Jasper enlisted on June 22, 1861, and served with the Villa Rica Gold Diggers. Jasper died in Richmond, Virginia, and is buried there. Polly was left to raise her children alone. There is some indication that the boys may have been "farmed out" to relatives and friends to raise, but the girls remained at home with their mother.

In 1877 Joseph Joshua Payne married Louisa Elizabeth Boyd (1858-1950), daughter of Robert B. Boyd and Sarah Ann LeGuin.

Joseph and Louisa set up housekeeping on a farm near Villa Rica and Joseph became a circuit riding Methodist preacher, although he was never ordained. Joseph and Louisa had five children: Coie Lonzo, born 1878, died 1962; Robert Stephen, born 1882; Milie Ann, born 1885; Sarah Jane, born 1888, died 1952; and Gooly Ross, born and died in 1891. Gooly died with typhoid fever when the was only five months old and three months later at the young age of thirty-seven, Joseph succumbed to the same disease. They are both buried in Powell's Chapel Cemetery. Their gravestones are marked simply, "JJP" and "GRP."

Louisa tried to keep the farm going with the help of her sons, but it was an impossible task and she was forced to sell. After her children married, she lived with first one and then another, helping to raise her grandchildren, always with a firm but loving, devoutly Methodist hand. No card-playing or dancing was allowed.

Coie Payne married Annie Belle Hyde, daughter of William Hyde and Laura Beula Long, and lived in Newnan and Carrollton. They had three children: Ralph Woodrow, born 1912, died 1982, married first to Frances Foster and second to Lucille Honea; Kathleen Fern, born 1919, died 1994, married Henley Logan; and Celeste, who died at age three.

Robert (Bob) Payne married Delia McPherson and moved to East Point. They had one son, Bruce.

Milie Ann Payne married William J. (Will) White, a carpenter who moved around as jobs were available. They eventually settled on Highway 78 just west of Austell and had three children: Louise, married Joe Wingo; Guy, married Opal; and Christine, married Otis Creel.

Sarah Jane Payne married John Allen McWhorter, a schoolteacher from Carroll County. They settled in East Point with their three daughters, Ruby Faye (Baryon), Gladys Mae (McDuffie), and Marian Payne (Fowler).

Louisa lived with Sarah and John well into the 1930s, then moved in permanently with her daughter Milie Ann. Louisa died at age ninety-two and is buried in Powell's Chapel beside Joseph. Her gravestone is marked as simply as his, "LEP." *Submitted by: Jean Payne Byrd, 720 Reed Road, Smyrna, GA 30082, and Judy Fowler Kilgore, 2197 Highway 154, Newnan, GA 30264*

917. Perry - Copeland

One of the most beautiful homes in Carrollton today is what we now call the Ed Copeland home place at 530 Newnan Street. Mr. Ed Copeland is 91 years young and truly you can hardly believe his age, or that the home itself is almost 100 years old. "My grandfather, Mr. W.O. Perry built this home just after the turn of the century. He first came to Carrollton in 1866, but this home was not built until 1909," says Ed Copeland. The home has stayed in the family ever since and has recently undergone some remodeling and refurbishing under the guidance of Ed's creative wife, Edna Reams Copeland. All the furniture is antique in keeping with the period of the house itself and you feel as if you just stepped back in time — to about 1850 — to visit Twelve Oaks or Tara.

William Owen Perry

Although the Perry family did not come to Carrollton until after the Civil War, the Copeland family had arrived here much earlier, making them true pioneers of Carroll County. Jonathan Copeland was fifteen years old when he traveled in the wagons with his father's family as they migrated from the eastern part of Georgia to Carroll County. They settled at Bowdon, Georgia and the Copeland family put down deep roots there for many generations. Jonathan Copeland was born 14 November 1836 and it was 1851 when his family made their journey across the state of Georgia.

On 5 April 1864, Jonathan Copeland married Julia Ann Rebecca Jeter in Carroll County. This wedding took place during the Civil War and Jonathan was a Confederate soldier. His bride was the daughter of William W. Jeter who had moved to Carroll County in 1853 when he had purchased Land Lot #133 in the 11th District for $1200 from Edmund Duke. The Jeter family had been living in DeKalb County, Georgia, during the 1850 census.

The Jeters had migrated to Georgia from North Carolina, but William Jeter's wife, Sarah, indicated on census that she had been born in South Carolina. The 1860 Carroll County census shows William W. Jeter age 52; his wife Sarah, age 46; Nancy A., 23; Sidney W., 21; Dudley, 19; Robert H., 16; Julia A., 13; Sarah C., 10; James W., 9; and John, 5. Julia Ann Rebecca Jeter was born 29 August 1846.

Jonathan and Julia Ann Copeland had eight children. There were five sons: Charles Copeland (of Bremen), John Copeland (moved to Cornelia, Georgia), Newt Copeland (Ocala and Miami, Florida), George Thomas Copeland of Carrollton, and Whit Copeland of Bowdon. The daughters were Annie Copeland (Mrs. Harman) Wicks, Katheryne Copeland (Mrs. Garland) Lovvorn, and Lockie Flo Copeland (Mrs. Earnest) Fleming. Jonathan Copeland died 28 January 1922 and was buried at Bowdon City Cemetery. His obituary was printed on the front page of the *Carroll Free Press* of 2 February 1922 and said

> "He was a good man and a good citizen and Carroll County and Bowdon has lost one of her best men."

Jonathan had lived to be 85 years 2 months and 14 days. His wife had preceded him in death by nine years. Julia Ann Copeland had died 28 July 1909.

George Thomas Copeland was born 28 November 1873 in Carroll County and grew up in Carrollton. He married on 26 November 1902 to

Mary Elizabeth Perry, the daughter of William Owen Perry and Martha Linch. G.T. Copeland would become a prominent businessman in Carrollton in the wholesale grocery business. At first, he was in partnership with Newman N. Johnson. Later on, G.T. Copeland bought an interest in the C.M. Tanner Grocery Company and became a vice president in that corporation for many years.

Crossing over the Chattahoochee River into Coweta County, the Perry and Linch families were some of the earliest pioneers there. Mr. William Owen Perry was born 27 March 1845 in Coweta County, Georgia, the son of King William Perry. King William Perry's ancestors lived in Prince George County, Maryland, during the 1650-1750 time period and they married into the Washington, Dawson, Davis and Williams families. About 1789, the Perrys began to migrate into Newberry, South Carolina. King William Perry is believed to be descended from Nathan Washington Perry born 9 April 1735 in Charles County, Maryland, and who died 6 September 1800 in Newberry, South Carolina.

King W. Perry began as a merchant in the community of Line Creek in Coweta County, but by 1831 he had established a store in Newnan about where the old Woolworth's used to be. On 15 April 1834, King William Perry married Rhoda E. Owen in Coweta County. When the Civil War began, though W.O. Perry, who was called Owen, had barely reached the age of sixteen, he joined up with the Confederacy. He served honorably with Phillip's legion throughout the war. Though he was captured twice during the war, he always managed to escape and always said he never missed a roll call.

After the war had ended, William Owen Perry married Martha E. "Mattie" Linch in Coweta County on 13 November 1866. The Linch family was also one of Coweta's earliest pioneers. They had arrived with a large number of families from Newberry, South Carolina, who had migrated together about 1829 to Georgia. The Linches had a family heritage that went all the way back into Colonial times of America. The name had originally been spelled Lynch in the beginning but a surveyor had misspelled the name as "Linch" on some deeds he drew up. In order for the property to remain in the family, they changed the spelling of their name to Linch.

The Lynches had lived in Derry, Ireland for about 200 years prior to coming to America. The immigrant ancestor of the family was a Captain Johnson Lynch who was a ship's captain sailing in and out of Charleston Harbor in the early 1700s. His wife was Susannah Schulf. Johnson Lynch died 22 August 1712. Johnson's son was John Lynch and John's son was David Lynch born 1747 in Newberry, South Carolina.

David Lynch married Esther Embry born ca. 1751 in Newberry. David and Esther were the parents of Rev. Elijah Linch who was a well-known Universalist minister in South Carolina. Elijah was born 28 June 1773 in South Carolina and died 10 August 1842 in Prosperity, South Carolina. Elijah had four brothers who served in the American Revolution and they were of the same family as Thomas Lynch (1749-1779) who signed the Declaration of Independence.

Thomas Lynch was born in Winyaw, South Carolina, and was graduated from Cambridge University in England. He became a planter in South Carolina and was a major landholder. His plantation was called Hopsewee Plantation. He served in the 1st South Carolina Regiment in the American Revolution and in 1776 he was elected to the Second Continental Congress.

According to family tradition, it was Thomas Lynch III who actually signed the Declaration of Independence. His father, Thomas Lynch Jr. was supposed to sign, but he suffered a stroke just prior to time for the signing. So, Thomas III was elected to sign in his place. This Thomas Lynch III was married to Betsy Shubrick on 14 May 1772. Unfortunately, Thomas III and his wife perished at sea when they were on a voyage to France in 1779. Thomas Lynch III had been the son of Thomas Lynch Jr. who was married to Elizabeth Alston on 5 September 1745. The Alstons have an extensive family tree that is traceable all the way back to King Alfred the Great. The Lynch family tree is extensively covered in *Coweta Chronicles* compiled by Mary G. Jones and Lily Reynolds, DAR, Newnan, Georgia, 1928.

Rev. Elijah Linch married Elizabeth Chapman on 27 October 1792 and they had a son named David Linch born 14 February 1805 in Newberry, South Carolina. In December of 1832, David Linch married Mary Beam of Fairfield, South Carolina. This young lady had exactly the same birthday as his, 14 February 1805. It was said that they "spent their honeymoon blazing a trail through the wilderness" to their new home in Coweta County, Georgia. They enjoyed watching the "wild turkeys and the deer come night and morning to refresh themselves" at the little stream in front of their new home. David and Mary Linch were staunch Universalists and they founded the Harmony Universalist Church near Senoia.

David Linch and Mary Beam Linch were the parents of Elijah Oliver, William David, Mary Elizabeth, James Andrew, and Martha Linch. Martha Linch who was born 12 December 1842 married William Owen Perry, the Confederate soldier but she also had a brother who valiantly served the Confederacy.

Martha's brother, William D. Linch, was born 19 February 1840 in Coweta County. He had barely reached his twenty-first birthday when he answered the call to war. In May 1861, he enlisted in Company A, 7th Georgia Volunteers under Captain S.W. Lee. He was quickly promoted to second lieutenant and then was promoted again, serving as captain until the end of the war.

Captain Linch had a long and honorable record. He took part in both battles at Manassas, the seven day's fight at Richmond, Malvern Hill, Cold Harbor, Knoxville, Wilderness, Fair Oaks, Sharpsburg, Gettysburg, and many more engagements. He was wounded three times — in the arm at Loudon, Tennessee, in the shoulder at the Wilderness, and received a bullet in the neck at Fort Harrison. Captain Linch was with General Lee when he surrendered at Appomattox.

An interesting story was told by the Banks brothers of Coweta County who had served under Capt. Linch's command and were with him at Appomattox. Ira Bentley Banks later said, "Lee surrendered standing under a little apple tree. Within a short time, the tree had been cut to pieces and even the roots dug out of the ground and carried off as souvenirs by the soldiers." Ira Bentley Banks and his brother William Hubbard Banks stacked their guns with Captain Linch after the surrender and then they "walked all the way home from Appomattox to Elder's Mill area south of Turin." (From *The History of Coweta County,* compiled by The Newnan-Coweta Historical Society, 1988).

William Owen Perry and Martha Linch were the parents of the following children: (1) Walter Lee Perry born 29 May 1868 and died 14 July 1915, died unmarried (2) Mary Elizabeth born 26 June 1871 and died 12 September 1959 married George Thomas Copeland (3) Sarah Rebecca "Sallie" Perry born 10 November 1872 died 26 January 1930 married William Isaac "Will" Cobb; their son William Owen Cobb married Louise Steed - had sons Will Owen Steed, Eugene Steed, James Steed (4) Willie J. Perry born 30 November 1874, married Belle Brown. Children were Colquitt Perry and Hugh David Perry. Willie died and was buried in Newnan (5) William Owen Perry, Jr. born 20 April 1883, married Ella Clair Cutts, one child Owen Cutts, W.O. is buried in Atlanta.

Mary Elizabeth Perry and George Thomas Copeland were the parents of three children. Elizabeth was born 16 November 1903 and graduated from Wesleyan College in Macon. Elizabeth became a schoolteacher and later married George Hudson Tumlin of Gainesville, Georgia. The Tumlins owned a large farm there. They were parents of three children: The oldest son was Hubert Edwin Tumlin who was the namesake of J. Edwin Copeland. The twins, George Hudson Tumlin and Guy Perry Tumlin were born in 1941, but George Hudson died shortly after birth. Elizabeth lived in Gainesville, Georgia, until her death on 9 February 1989. She is buried at Cumming, Georgia.

The second child was George Perry Copeland, born 9 February 1906 and died 25 February 1978. Perry Copeland distinguished himself as quite an athlete during his years at Carrollton High School. He excelled at football, baseball, and track. He held the CHS pole vaulting records for many years. In 1954, Perry Copeland and his brother Ed Copeland went into partnership together with the opening of Copeland's Supermarket which was a favorite place for Carrollton shoppers to buy their groceries for the next twenty years. Perry Copeland married Helen Hall (born 28 March 1912) of Albany, Georgia. They were the parents of two daughters, Helen and Susan. After five years in business in Copeland's Supermarket, ill health forced Perry to quit work. At that time, he sold his interest in the business to his brother Ed, and a few years later Ed Copeland formed a corporation with the business as it remained until 1975. George Perry Copeland died 25 February 1978.

The youngest child of G.T. Copeland and Mary Elizabeth Perry is Joseph Edwin Copeland born 13 May 1910. Ed Copeland always rose to leadership positions in all his endeavors. See the biographical sketch of him preceding his feature article on *History of the Grocery Business in Carroll County, Georgia.* Ed Copeland married Louise Williamson and they were parents of two daughters, Carole and Caren. Louise Williamson Copeland died on 20 May 1993 and was buried in the Carrollton City Cemetery. Ed's parents, George T. Copeland died 19 June 1951 and Mary Elizabeth Perry Copeland died 12 September 1959. Both are buried in the family plot at Carrollton City Cemetery.

Carole Copeland was born 28 August 1937 and grew up in Carrollton, graduating from Carrollton High School. She married Joseph Bertrand McGinnis who was born 18 August 1936. Their three sons are: Joseph Bertrand McGinnis Jr. born 27 April 1960; Gilbert Copeland McGinnis born 31 August 1965; and Glenn Fowler McGinnis born 18 August 1972. Carole has always had a love of antiques and for many years had her own shop on City Hall Avenue in Carrollton. Now, Carole has a booth in the Antique Mall at Groover-Smith's in Carrollton. Joe McGinnis has served two terms as a popular mayor of Carrollton in addition to being an independent businessman here. Joe received his degree from Georgia State University in business administration in 1963.

Caren Copeland was born 26 September 1947. She graduated from Carrollton High School and later married William Wayne Entrekin who was born 10 December 1946. Two sons were born to the Entrekins: William Wayne Entrekin born 29 November 1966 and Walter Copeland Entrekin born 26 April 1974. Caren and Wayne Entrekin later divorced. Caren has worked for twenty-five years in the Medical Records department at Tanner Medical Center. She furthered her studies at West Georgia College with many courses in psychology. Caren has given many volunteer hours to the Mental Health Center as a counselor.

Ed Copeland loves to talk about his heritage and the history of Carrollton, too. He has given many taped interviews to the West Georgia students who participate in the history preservation project. Ed has written many articles of historical interest for the Carrollton newspapers, some of which are reprinted here in this book.

"When my Grandfather, W.O. Perry first came to Carrollton he purchased a 50-acre farm which was located about where Hugh Richards' lumber company is now. He opened up a mercantile store called Farmers' Alliance which sold farming equipment and supplies. W.O. Perry was awarded the Cross of Honor for his service in the Confederacy and for twenty years he served as a delegate of Phillips' Legion of Carroll County to all Confederate veteran conventions. W.O. Perry was on the Mandeville Mills board of directors and also on the board of directors of the First National Bank. He was on the Board of Stewards of the First United Methodist Church in Carrollton. W.O. Perry was healthy and active up to the end of his life on 9 March 1932. He died when he was 86 years old sitting in a chair listening to the radio."

W.O. Perry died on 9 March 1932 and his wife Martha Linch Perry died 12 October 1913. Both are buried at Carrollton City Cemetery.

The great-grandchildren of J. Edwin Copeland who will carry on this proud heritage are: Stephen Andrew Entrekin, Benjamin Wayne Entrekin, and Erin Ashley McGinnis. *Submitted by: J. Edwin Copeland, 530 Newnan Street, Carrollton, GA 30117 and Written by: Jan Robinson Bell, Carrollton, GA.*

918. The George Washington Petty Family

George Washington Petty was born in Campbell County on September 22, 1882. His father was James Anderson Petty and his mother was Sarah Jennings Petty. He came to Carroll County in the late 1800s, and was married to Ida May Hight on September 18, 1904. Their children were James W., Laura M., Mary E., and Lora, who died in infancy. James lived most of his life in Cobb County and worked as a mechanic in the hosiery industry. Laura lived most of her life in Fulton County and was a housewife. Mary was employed at Lawler Hosiery Mills in Carrollton for a time, and lived most of her life in Carroll County.

George Washington Petty and wife, Minnie Peppers Petty

After the death of Ida May, George was married a second time to Minnie O. Peppers on May 28, 1916. Their children were Ethel C., Georgia O., B.C., Lillian, and Harold. B.C. was manager of the A&P Food Store in Carrollton for several years. Ethel was employed at Lawler Hosiery Mills in Carrollton for a number of years. Lillian and Georgia were housewives. Harold was employed at The Georgia Department of Labor in Carrollton and Atlanta from 1960 to 1987.

George was employed by the railroad for a number of years, and later was employed by Burns' Gin on Dixie Street in Carrollton. Burns' Gin was located in the area where Whitman's Glass is now located. George was a member of the Rock Springs Methodist Church in Whitesburg. He and Minnie are buried at Stripling Chapel Methodist Church on Highway 27 South in Carroll County. George died on February 7, 1953. Minnie died on January 20, 1981.

James Anderson and Sarah Jennings Petty are buried at the Providence Baptist Church Cemetery in the Rico community in Fulton County. Other Petty Family members are also buried there. Many descendents of George and Minnie Petty still reside in Carroll County. *Submitted by: Harold Petty, Post Office Box 305, Carrollton, GA 30117*

919. James Alexander Phillips and Sarah Angeline Smith

James Alexander Phillips was born in Georgia on October 3, 1851. He was probably the first son of Enoch Phillips and Susan Bean.

Sarah Angeline and her twin sister, Anne Avaline, were born in Carroll County on February 10, 1846. They were the second set of twins born to Gabriel D. Smith Jr. and Nancy Cain.

James Alexander and Sarah Angeline Smith were married in Carroll County on September 17, 1867. They are recorded on the 1880 Haralson census records where James is shown as a farmer. Their four children were all born in Georgia: (1) Ranson M. (? Mulberry) born 1871; (2) Elvira Elizabeth, born about 1872; (3) William F. (? Franklin) born about 1875, and (4) Jordan Oscar born about 1876.

It is not known what year James and his family moved to Texas, nor to where in Texas they went. However, in the late 1920s and early 1930s they were in Tioga in Grayson County. This is the town where Henry Newton Phillips and his wife Martha Ann Warren Phillips are buried. James and Henry were brothers and their wives were aunt and niece.

James and Sarah's daughter Elvira was married to Jesse Napolian Silvey, a brother to Drury Melvina Silvey Warren who was my grandmother (see Warren history). We do not know just how much Elvira and Melvina corresponded with one another, but several of Elvira's letters to Melvina and one to Martha Mae Warren were found after the death of Mae Warren in 2000. All of these letters appear to be written around 1932. Only one envelope survived and it has a postal stamp showing 1932, but all letters seem somewhat continuous in time.

In her letters, Elvira always refers to the oldest brother as Mulberry and to the youngest as Jordan. In one letter Elvira states that her parents are buried in the Tioga Cemetery and that Jesse (her husband) has been taking care of the cemetery grounds until he can find a job. Often Elvira wrote of money worries and expressed concern as to what people would do until the depression was over. Elvira was still in Tioga when Jesse died, as she wrote about his death in another letter. There is no grave marker in this cemetery for James, Sarah, Jesse, or Elvira. Lack of money is the probable explanation why there are not visible tombstones for these people.

Elvira had deep roots back to Carroll County. In each letter she always asked about her relatives and friends of Carroll County, and wanted to know how the membership of Poplar Springs Primitive Baptist Church was doing. She often gave the status of her own church in Tioga and asked Melvina to please keep her posted about her church in Bowdon. *Submitted by: Silvey Warren Patterson, Bowdon, GA*
Source: Researched by: Stanley N. Carroll, 2109 Hansel Avenue, Huntsville, AL 35802

920. Joseph Ernest Phillips

Joseph Ernest Phillips was born August 29, 1896, the sixth of eight children of A.B. Phillips and Lucretia Araminta "Minta" Lewis, of Carrollton, Georgia. During the depression era, Ernest served in the Civilian Conservation Corps (CCC) as a prerequisite for enlisting in the United States Navy.

Ernest had completed his Navy training and was serving aboard the aircraft carrier *U.S.S. Yorktown (CV-5)* when the Japanese attacked Pearl Harbor. The *Yorktown (The Fighting Lady)* was deployed to the Pacific after Pearl Harbor to play a gallant role in the Pacific Campaign of World War II. Ernest remained on board until the *Yorktown* was sunk during the Battle of Midway. While it was severely damaged during the Battle of the Coral Sea, it was repaired and returned to service for the Battle of Midway. The accompanying photo is an official USN photo taken as the *Yorktown* was being abandoned June 4, 1942.

Ernest was severely wounded during the *Yorktown's* Midway battle, but was evacuated along with other wounded before the *Yorktown* sank. Uncle Rod recalled the grief in the family as early reports of the sinking listed Ernest as missing-in-action, and my father's efforts to determine his brother's fate via the Red Cross in Atlanta. They ultimately learned that Ernest had been unconscious for a lengthy period after his rescue, so the hospital staff in Hawaii where the was taken did not know who he was until he regained consciousness. His dog-tags were not on him when he arrived at Hawaii medical facilities.

Joseph Ernest Phillips, and U.S.S. Yorktown sinking, June 4, 1942.

Ernest lived in Carrollton with his sister, Dovie Gray, at her Sims Street home for a number of years after World War II. He worked at the Carrollton Water Works during most of that time. During one summer, my dad spent several weeks with his Aunt Dovie Gray while Ernest was living with her. At that time, Frank and Mary (Gray) Searcy were also living with Aunt Dovie (before Sue and Alice were born.) Dad spent a night or two with his Uncle Ernest at the Water Works and he and Dad fished all night on the creek. Dad said he was a great fishing buddy, but he forgot to tell Dad all about poison ivy. Dad must have gotten it on his hands and then rubbed his eyes, because a few days later his eyes swelled shut. Poor Frank, he had to take Dad to the doctor every day for about a week for shots. Afterwards, dad's Aunt Dovie patiently bathed Dad's eyes open with cool water each morning so he could see.

Ernest later moved to Orlando, Florida, to be near his nephews Buster and Bill Gray. Dad did not learn until years after Ernest's death that he had been married, and that his wife Katherine had died during childbirth. Ernest died on December 4, 1961. *Submitted by: Lori Shannon Philips Mayberry, 1204 N.W. 141st, Edmond, OK 73013*

921. Rodric Morris "Rod" Phillips

My dad, Rodric Morris Phillips Sr., was born August 12, 1937, in Carrollton, the third child of Myrtle Pauline Carroll (1905-1964) and Raymond Lewis "Dutch" Phillips (1899-1957). Dad's oldest brother was Raymond Lewis Jr., but he died at birth in 1926. Uncle Lewis (Joseph) was seven years older than Dad (1930-1994), and Uncle Steve (George Steven) was two years younger (1940).

Dunn-Phillips Wedding in 1957

Dad's family moved from Carrollton to Atlanta in about 1941, some time prior to the Japanese attack on Pearl Harbor. He attended school in Atlanta and later attended and graduated from Hapeville High School in Hapeville, Georgia. Dad and his best friend, Tracy Tolar, enlisted in the U.S. Air Force together in September 1955. Dad and Tracy attended boot camp at Lackland, A.F.B. in San Antonio, Texas. After technical training, Dad was stationed in Oklahoma City, Oklahoma, and Tracy at Ardmore, Oklahoma.

Dad met and married my mom, Dicki Joy Dunn (1939), while stationed in Oklahoma City. Tracy was able to come up from Ardmore to serve as best man. Mom was the daughter of Roy Charles Dunn (1909-1991) and Hazel Adeline Burkes Dunn (1907). It should be noted here that Grandma Hazel was born in Broken Arrow, Indian Territory. Grandma McRae's ancestors migrated from Carroll County to Fannin County, Texas. While doing genealogy research on my mom's McRae heritage, Dad discovered that he shared that same McRae lineage — Dad through Margaret McRae McAllister (1804-1870) and James Blanton McAllister (1805-1860), and Mom through Margaret's brother, Malcom Alexander McRae (1810-1896) and Mary Magdalene Whisenhunt (1809-1878). Both Margaret and Malcom were children of Hugh Bain McRae (1757-1856) and Nancy McDuffey (1764-??). (See related McRae-McAllister article.)

Mom and Dad have three children: Diane Hope Phillips (1958); Lori Shannon Phillips Mayberry (1960); and me, Rodric M. Phillips Jr., M.D. (1961). Lori and her husband Rob Mayberry have three children: Shannon Joy (1982); Eric Blake (1987); and Robyn Diane (1989). My wife Susie Lynn Kurtz (1963) and I have four boys: Joshua Rodric (1989), Jordan Dean (1992); Andrew Roy (1995); and Jackson Luke (1997). Mom and Dad will celebrate forty-four years of marriage on November 28, 2001.

Dad spent the first three-plus years of his life in Carrollton, but spent countless summers with his Aunt Dovie Phillips Gray at her Sims Street home in Carrollton. Dad remembers the ice wagon coming to deliver blocks of ice for the icebox and lying under the wagon on a hot summer day letting the cold water from the melting ice in the wagon drip into his mouth, or feeding fresh apples to the horse. And, oh, how he talks about those days of riding shotgun on the Coca Cola truck with cousin Buster Gray, delivering Cokes all over the county, and drinking twenty-one Cokes in one day and not wanting any supper that night. *Submitted by: Dr. Rod Phillips, 1649 Saratoga Way, Edmond, OK 73003*

922. William David Phillips

William David Phillips was born 22 September 1861 in Campbell County, Georgia, and died 4 December 1934 in Carroll County, Georgia. On 9 December 1883 in Douglas County, Georgia, he married Ellen Virginia Wright, born 12 August 1861 and died 11 January 1938. She was the daughter of Isaac C. Wright (veteran of War Between the States) and Martha Freeman. They are buried in St. Paul's Methodist Church, Carroll County. They were the parents of: Robert Clifford Phillips married Louvella Josephine Young; Mirtle Irene Phillips married Stephen Ephriam Wilson; Charles Wesley Phillips married Nora Pearl Duke; Isaac Raymond Phillips married Nettie Alma Boatright; Thomas Monroe Phillips (more later); Rachel Gordie Phillips married Cellie Croft Duke: Clark Phillips married Aileen Baritone; Sylvia Gladys Phillips married Thomas Grady Crews.

In the 1890s William David and Ellen Virginia moved to Limestone County, Texas. They returned to Carroll County after the 1900 census and in 1902 bought the family home on Jones Mill Road. The home is still occupied by William David's grandson, Audrey Ralph Phillips.

William David Phillips was the son of Robert Crowley Phillips and Lucy Ann Neill, daughter of William Neill, a veteran of the War of 1812, and Eleanor Endsley. Robert Crowley and Lucy Ann were married 4 December 1860 in Coweta County, Georgia. They were the parents of William David, Lula, Edgar Monroe, Lucy Ann. Robert Crowley married second Louisa Antoinette McEwen and they were the parents of Lavinia, Emma and Annie. William David's grandparents were Henry Phillips and Lavinia Atkinson, daughter of Thomas Atkinson, a veteran of the War of 1812, and Rhoda Ivey. Lavinia's grandfather Thomas Atkinson was a veteran of the American Revolution, serving on the Georgia line. Henry and Lavinia were the parents of eleven sons: Whitmill A., Thomas Henry, Zachariah, Columbus Hiram, Arrington, Benjamin Franklin, Elijah Madison, Martin Van Buren, Warren Hull, Armistead, and one daughter, Martha Catherine. All eleven sons served in the War Between the States.

William David's son, Thomas Monroe Phillips, born 14 February 1894, died 30 March 1977. On 15 February 1914, Thomas Monroe married Jennie Beatrice Tate, (died 28 January 1929). She was the daughter of William Samuel Tate and Lucy Ann Cole, daughter of William Robert Cole and Octavia Massey. They were the parents of: Lucy Inez Phillips married Joseph James Merrell; Thomas Wesley Phillips (more later); Dorothy Christine Phillips married first Roy Bates, second McGuffin; Ralph Audrey Phillips never married, Isaac Curtis Phillips married Arlette Hautmont; Gordon Osborne Phillips married Edna Irene Storm; William David Phillips never married, died in Korea.

Thomas Wesley Phillips, born 16 May 1917, died 18 July 1976, and Ruth Williams, born 11 November 1922, died 12 March 1979, were the parents of Tommie Anne, Billy Wesley, Jackson Monroe, Bobby Ray, Constance Jean, Cynthia Lynne. Tommie Anne Phillips married Anthony Joseph LaCavera Sr., and they are the parents of Tara Lynn, Tracy Marie and Anthony Joseph LaCavera Jr. *Submitted by: Tara L. LaCavera, 606 Lake Avenue, Pascagoula, MS 39567*
Source: Research done by: Tommie Phillips LaCavera

923. Raymond Lewis "Dutch" Phillips and Mrytle Pauline Carroll

Raymond Lewis "Dutch" Phillips was born in Carrollton on July 19, 1899, the son of A.B. Phillips (1855-1918) and Araminta Lucretia "Minta" Lewis (1861-1930). Myrtle Pauline Carroll was born July 30, 1905, the daughter of Roderick Wallace Carroll (1869-1956) and Josephine Rebecca Hamrick (1872-1919). Dutch and Myrtle, were married in Carrollton on October 18, 1925, and had four boys: Raymond Lewis Jr., died shortly after his birth in 1926; Joseph Lewis (March 12, 1930); Rodric Morris (August 12, 1937); and George Steven (March 16, 1940).

Dutch worked for some time as a route salesman for the Coca-Cola Bottling Company. During his employment at Coca-Cola, Dutch was involved in a serious on-the-job vehicle accident that left him with two broken legs. I have vague memories of two of Dad's friends (one of whom I suspect was Bay Hay) carrying him into the house, setting him in a chair, and pulling up an ottoman under his feet to elevate both legs.

In 1940-41, after a brief time with the Carrollton Fire Department, Dutch had the opportunity to take a job as a firefighter at Lawson General Hospital, a large Veterans Administration Hospital facility near Chamblee. As a young boy, I visited Dad's workplace, and walked the hospital wards with Dad as he performed fire-safety inspections. I recall the shock of seeing so many mangled young men returning from World War II for medical care and therapy.

Dutch worked for Pinkerton after retiring from Lawson General. He died on Good Friday 1957. Myrtle worked as a seamstress following Dutch's death. Son Steven was still in high school at the time and at home until his graduation and marriage. Rodric married Dicki Joy Dunn in Dell City, Oklahoma, on November 28, 1957. Steve married Mary Louise Hargett in August of 1960. Myrtle died of cancer on February 5, 1964. Lewis married Madeline Nix shortly after Myrtle's death.

Myrtle Pauline Carroll and Raymond Lewis Phillips

Mom (Myrtle) told a funny story about when she was growing up in Tallapoosa. Mom and her sisters, Belle and Rachel, decide they couldn't wait all year for another watermelon, so they saved the watermelon juice from that last melon in a Bell jar. They hid the juice under their house. The plan was to retrieve the juice about mid-winter. What a great day that would be! They waited as long as they could, and decided one day that the day had arrived. They retrieved the juice but remained under the house for fear they would have to share their treasure if they were seen. Mom said it didn't smell like watermelon juice and didn't taste all that great — but they drank it anyway — then were all sick. It sounded like it may have been a case of "watermelon wine." They were probably just a little intoxicated, because Mom mentioned being dizzy. I think the juice may have just naturally fermented. *Submitted by: G. Steve Phillips, 495 Crabapple Rd., Fayetteville, GA 30214*

924. Gerald and Andri Akins Pilgrim

Andri Anna Akins was born on 13 December 1968 in Carrollton, Georgia. She is a descendant of some of Carroll County's oldest pioneer families — the Martins, the Shadingers, the Stewarts, the Becks, the Wiggins. Andri is the daughter of Rebecca Ann Martin and Doyle Ray Akins. Andri grew up in Carrollton and graduated from Carrollton High School in 1986.

She went on to earn her B.A. degree in psychology from Agnes Scott College in 1990 and her M.S. Ed. from West Georgia College in 1992. She completed her six-year certificate in education from West Georgia College in 1994.

In her first year of teaching, Andri received the national "Sallie Mae Foundation Teacher of the Year" award. She later became one of the first "Board Certified" teachers in Georgia. Andri teaches at H.A. Jones Elementary School in Bremen, Georgia. On 22 June 1992, Andri Anna Akins married Gerald Arthur Pilgirm at Tabernacle Baptist Church in Carrollton.

Gerald Pilgrim was born on 31 January 1969, the son of Raymond Dobbins Pilgrim (born 7 November 1937) and Peggy Marie Edmondson (born 29 July 1938). Peggy's family was originally from Cornersville, Tennessee, which is near Nashville. Raymond's family was from Marietta, Georgia, and he is related to the family for whom Dobbins Air Force Base is named.

Raymond Dobbins Pilgrim was the son of Rev. Dr. William Arthur Pilgrim who was the Methodist minister over the North Georgia and South Georgia United Methodist Conferences. Dr. Pilgrim lived at Summerville, Georgia, and is buried at Marietta. Dr. Pilgrim was married to Miss Hattie Dobbins of Marietta.

Hattie Dobbins was the daughter of Albert Dobbins who established the Albert Dobbins Furniture Store and Funeral Home in Marietta. This is the way that funeral homes were traditionally managed back in the early 1900s. Just about all of them began as a combination furniture store in the front and funeral home in the back parlor. The Martin-Almon Funeral Home of Carrollton (established by Andri's great-grandfather, Cliff Martin) was also a combination furniture store and funeral parlor in the early 1900s.

Gerald's mother, Peggy Edmondson Pilgrim, was the daughter of Robert Clark Edmondson and Margaret Shelton who both grew up and married in Cornersville, Tennessee. Today, Gerald's parents enjoy restoring old Victorian homes in Tallapoosa, Georgia. Peggy Pilgrim has beautifully restored one such Victorian home next to the library and has opened it up as the Pierce-Pilgrim House, a place for ladies to enjoy a Victorian style luncheon.

Gerald Pilgrim graduated from Joseph T. Walker High School in Marietta in 1988. He then attended Kennesaw State College and went on to earn his degree in mortuary science from Gupton Jones in Atlanta. He is employed by Martin-Hightower Funeral Home in Carrollton. In 1999, Gerald Pilgrim was elected as the second youngest mayor of Carrollton. The first youngest mayor was his wife's grandfather, Stewart Martin, who was elected in 1939 at the age of twenty-six. At that time the statue read that the mayor had to be at least twenty-five years old. Later, they changed the requirement that the mayor be at least thirty years old. When Gerald Pilgrim was elected, he was thirty years old. Already, we are seeing some fruits of Gerald's term as mayor of Carrollton — the completion of our new gymnasium and ground will be broken soon for the new Fine Arts Center.

Andri's great-grandparents were Eula and J. Cliff Martin who married in 1912. Eula Wiggins Martin was called Grandma Wiggy by her Martin grandchildren. Eula Wiggins was the daughter of William Jasper Wiggins and Amanda Stewart. Amanda Stewart Wiggins lived to see nine grandchildren and one great-grandchild, but her life came to an end due to an automobile accident.

Her obituary in the *Carroll Free Press* read:

> "Mrs. W.J. (Amanda) Wiggins for thirty years a beloved resident of Carrollton, died Thursday night at the Carrollton Clinic as a result of fatal injuries received from an automobile accident on the preceding Sunday. Having been a devout member of the Baptist Tabernacle and a faithful attendant of all services, the final rites for Mrs. Wiggins were conducted from the church at the time for the eleven o'clock service ... " The obituary continued, "When the accident occurred in which she sustained fatal injuries, Mrs. Wiggins with a son and friends was returning home after attending services at Ephesus where she first professed the Christian faith and united with the church at the age of twelve ... Member of a family long prominent in western Carroll County where she was born on 25 October 1858, Mrs. Wiggins was the daughter of the late William Stewart and Mary 'Polly' Beck Stewart, pioneer settlers of this section. On 1 November 1874, Amanda Stewart was married to William Jasper Wiggins and they lived in the Tyus community until 1906 when they moved to Carrollton;"

William Stewart was born in South Carolina and moved to Carroll County before 1830. Isaiah and Elizabeth Beck, the parents of Mary "Polly" Beck, were natives of North Carolina. Isaac Beck Jr. had married in Campbell County, Georgia, to Elizabeth Tanner. They moved to Carroll about the same time as William Stewart did.

Andri Akins, John Martin, and Gerald Pilgrim

The known brothers and sisters of Polly Beck as they appear in the census are: Myriam M., Priscilla E. and Drucilla B. (twins), Elizabeth D., Mary A., Thomas D., Marilla J., Martha A., Susannah, Joseph D., Whit H., and Delanianna. Also, there is a brother, Isaac Beck Jr. Pvt. Joe Cobb wrote in his 1906 book, *Carroll County and Her People,* that Isaac Beck was an old pioneer citizen who had "numerous sons." Older sons may have remained behind in North Carolina.

In the 1830 census of Carroll County, Isaiah Beck Sr. is age 50-60 and his wife is 40-50. Living next door, Isaiah Beck Jr. has two sons under age five, he is age 20-30 and his wife is 15-20. William Stewart is living next door and is age 20-30 and his wife is age 15-20. They have one daughter under age five. By the 1840 census, Isaiah Beck Jr. has one son under five, two sons 5-10, one son 10-15, and he is 30-40. There are four daughters under five, one daughter 5-10, and the wife is 20-30. Isaiah Beck Sr. has two sons 10-15, he is 60-70, and his wife is 50-60. In 1840, William Stewart has one son under five, two sons 5-10, he is 20-30, one daughter under five, one daughter 10-15, and wife 20-30.

Andri and Gerald Pilgrim have one son, John Martin Pilgrim, who was born 10 April 1998. The Pilgrims reside on Kramer Street in Carrollton and are members of the First United Methodist Church. *Submitted by: Gerald and Andri Pilgrim, Kramer Street, Carrollton, GA 30117 and Written by: Jan Robinson Bell.*

925. Pirch

The Story of the Pirches

In 1981, the Pirch family moved from Indiana to Carrollton, Georgia. Michael would be entering sixth grade and Stefanie had just finished kindergarten. James was four years old and David had recently turned two. Throughout the next twenty years, the composition of the family changed as the members moved in a variety of directions.

All four children attended the Central schools and their individual talents and abilities took them on stage and behind the scenes with the Carrollton Parks, Recreation and Cultural Arts Department's Children's and Community Theatre. Mike, James and David played football at Central High School, with Mike having the privilege of being on both the 1986 and 1987 State Championship teams. He served as president of the Fellowship of Christian Athletes, was named to *Who's Who Among American High School Students* and was recognized as one of 1988's Outstanding Catholic Youth in the Atlanta Archdiocese. Stefanie devoted her extra curricular time to Color Guard and Performing Arts Group at Central and was Governor's Honors alternate for theatre. She was a charter member of Central's chapter of the National Thespian Society, and participated in One Act Play Competitions. Listed in *Who's Who,* Stefanie was an honor graduate and recipient of the Hope Scholarship. James was selected as a delegate for Boy's State and as an alternate for Governor's Honors in Art. He upheld the family tradition of inclusion in *Who's Who,* and received recognition for several individual works of art as well as a Fine Arts award for artistic contributions to the school and the community. David served as a class officer and was honored as Homecoming King his senior year, as well as being named an Outstanding Senior. In addition to playing football, David played on the Central High School tennis team.

After graduation in 1988, Mike attended West Georgia College where he was a brother of the TKE fraternity, then served in the United States Navy for four years. Completing his service, he settled in Jacksonville, Florida, where he is employed as a shipping and receiving manager for Sports Authority. Softball is his passion and he plays on several teams there.

Stefanie was a member of the first class to graduate from the State University of West Georgia following its name change and earned her master of fine arts degree in technical theatre design from the University of North Carolina at Greensboro. While studying at UNCG, she earned Kennedy Center for the Performing Arts American College Theatre Festival awards for set design, costuming, and lighting design. She is employed by Flat Rock Playhouse, the State Theatre of North Carolina, as a set designer.

James married Cindy Jackson of Villa Rica and is the father of one daughter, Leigh. He holds a bachelor of arts degree from the State University of West Georgia and is an art teacher and coach at East Coweta High School in Sharpsburg, Georgia, where he also works as a commission artist.

David attends the State University of West Georgia and is employed by United Parcel Service in Atlanta. He intends to study education and follow in the family footsteps as a teacher and coach.

Mom, Terry Hingerton Pirch, decided to complete her degree at West Georgia College, receiving both bachelor's and master's degrees in education. She taught for ten years in the Central schools, then left to develop a Cultural Arts Division for the Villa Rica Recreation Department. She has been involved in theatre productions for eighteen years as costumer, publicist, makeup designer, and director, and is a cofounder of the Carroll County Teen Theatre program which has drawn young people to summer productions for seventeen years.

The Pirches have created a lifetime of memories in this area. Each has friends held dear and the recollection of experiences and events which helped shape the family and its members. Terry Pirch and her children, Mike, Stefanie, James and David, are glad to have had the opportunity to come to Carroll County — it's been a great place to live! *Submitted by: Terry Pirch, 541 North White Street, #12, Carrollton, GA 30117*

926. Anderson J. Pope and Elizabeth Ann Carroll

Anderson J. Pope (Andrew) born 1826, died December 30, 1864, in Rock Island, Illinois, military hospital and prison camp. He married Elizabeth Ann Carroll on October 5, 1848, in Dallas, Paulding County, Georgia. I have no knowledge of their family before this time. The censuses show other Pope, Brooks, Wilson, and Carrolls living in the area.

After living in Villa Rica, Georgia, they moved to Gadsden, Alabama. Andrew is listed as a mechanic. They are listed in the 1860 Cherokee County, Alabama census.

Anderson J. Pope's military record is as follows: joined August 13, 1863, Hale's Infantry private, Company A, 31st Regiment. Hale's Infantry became the 31st, then became the 49th. Andrew was captured near Big Shanty, Georgia.

Elizabeth was born about 1829, died 1907 in DeKalb County, Alabama. It is believed that all their children were born in Carroll County, Georgia.

Ruby and George Pope, grandson of Anderson and Elizabeth Pope. 1950

Children of Anderson J. Pope and Elizabeth Ann Carroll are William C. born 1849, married Mollie; John W. born 1854, married Savannah C.; Mary Jane born 1856, married Goders; Joshua Smith Pope born January 26, 1859, died February 4, 1930, married first about 1880 to Janie Brooks, born December 1, 1859, died January 20, 1917, and second on July 28, 1917, to Nancy Ollie Mae Wright, born 1874, died 1949; Francis William born 1861, died 1935, married Mary M. Brooks, born 1864, died 1939, buried at Concord Cemetery, Henagar, Alabama.

After Andrew's death, Elizabeth moved back to Villa Rica. She is listed in the 1870 census, Villa Rica, with all her children living with her. In the 1880 census, Sixth District, Joshua S. Pope is listed with wife Janie Brooks and first child, William J. Joshua (spelled different ways) who was born in 1859. After Janie's death in 1917, Joshua married a former sister-in-law, Nancy Ollie Wright Brooks. She was married to Mary and Janie's brother, Dock R. Brooks who died 1915. Joshua's occupations were farmer, blacksmith and preacher. He had eleven children.

One son, George Washington Pope, married first to Inda Bell Sparks, born between 1894 and 1918. Their children were Vinie May, Joshah F., died as infants, and Fred Henry (1913-1985), married second to Ruby Bell Twilley. They had eight children, born in DeKalb County, Alabama: Joseph (1920-1920), Nellie Irene (1921-1996), Florence AnneBelle (1924-), Nancy Larue (1926-1984), Auburn Calvin (1927-1991), John William (1929-1982), Gordon (1931-1966), and George Washington Pope Jr. (1932-died in infancy). John married Vena Lou Stephens in 1953 (my parents). As children, they remember visiting relatives in Carroll County but weren't sure how they were related. Frank, born 1861, was the youngest son. He married Mary Brooks in 1884, sister of Janie Brooks.

By 1900 Elizabeth had moved to DeKalb County, Alabama, near some of her children. The census shows her living alone. Elizabeth was eighty-two years old at her death. She is buried at Sylvania, Alabama, beside her son Joshua and his wife Janie. There are two unmarked graves beside them. Frank and his family are buried at a church nearby. *Submitted by: Teresa J. (Pope) Faloon, Rome, GA 30165. TJFaloon@bellsouth.net.*

927. Henry Pope Family

Henry Pope was a pioneer of Carroll County, Georgia, coming about 1849. He was the son of John and Susannah Hewell (Morris) Pope. He was born November 25, 1810, in North Carolina and died April 1868 in Carroll County. He was buried in the family burial grounds not far from the old home place, about four miles southwest of Villa Rica on Highway 61. He was married once and maybe twice before he came into Carroll County. He had nine children when he settled in the Bay Springs area. A farmer and land owner, he owned Lot 94, south Lot 93, and 50 acres (more or less) on north part of Lot 68 — totaling about 351 acres. Bay Springs Creek runs through the land.

His children were (1) Charity Ann Pope born September 5, 1831, married Andrew J. Williams. (2) Wiley Pope born March 25, 1833, married Martha Isabelle Greene. (3) Micajah J. Pope born January 1, 1836, married Rhoda Gross. (4) Thomas Pope born March 3, 1838, married Nancy Jane Causler. (5) John R. Pope born February 28, 1840, married Mary Emily Boyd. (6) Mary E. Pope born June 16, 1842, married first to Leroy J. Williams and second to George White Boyd. (7) William Henry Pope born August 27, 1844, married Susan F. Hamrick. (8) James F. Pope born June 1, 1847, married Mary Ella Juhan. (9) Jasper N. Pope born March 1, 1849, married Mallisa Catherine Kinney.

After settling in Carroll County, Henry married Anna Kinney who was born September 14, 1812. She was the daughter of William Kinney II and Susanna Ward Kinney. They had two sons: Francis M. Pope born March 14, 1853, married Mary E. Pirkle; and Jefferson A. "Jeff" Pope born March 26, 1856, married Emma E. Wilson.

Henry was my third great-grandfather and I descend through his son John R. and Mary Emily Boyd Pope. Mary's parents were Joseph and Jane McMillian Boyd. John and Mary had nine children: (1) Mary Elizabeth born May 31, 1857, married first to James C. Payne and second to H.W. "Bud" Richardson. (2) Austin born January 11, 1859, married Ida Tyson. (3) James C. Pope born 1862. (4) John H. born September 5, 1863, married first to Josie L. unknown and second to Millie Ann Yates. (5) Rufus Lon Pope born 1866, married Tippi Couch. (6) William Charlie born 1867. (7) Occia C. Pope born 1872, married first to Florence McPherson and second to Nora Griffis. (8) Rilla A. born July 26, 1873, married Charles E. Smith. (9) Nancy Ruth "Nannie" born July 16, 1877, married Ryburn Harrison Chambers.

Mary Elizabeth and James C. Payne's daughter Lois Irene married John Howard Powell. Their daughter Annie Grace Powell married Earl Eugene Dial and they are my parents. *Submitted by: William Ray Dial, 1062 Old Draketown Trail, Temple, GA 30179*

Sources: Carroll County census and marriage records, Ed Pope of Oklahoma, Kathryn Cook of North Carolina, family knowledge and personal research.

928. David A. Posey

David A. "Dave" Posey was born about 1840. He came to live with the Posey family at the age of seven. In the 1870 Carroll County, Georgia census, Dave is listed as age 30.

When the Emancipation Proclamation was signed, the Poseys informed Dave he was free to go. Dave stated he had no where to go or knew none of his family or their location. He was allowed to remain with the Poseys as a family member.

Dave was a normal child. Grandpa Posey found Dave urging the cat up the Martin (bird) pole, he asked Dave, "Don't put the cat up the Martin Pole." When Grandpa Posey came from the barn, Dave continued urging the cat up the pole. Grandpa Posey spanked Dave. From family stories, this was the only spanking Dave ever received.

As the older generation died, a will was made in 1889 leaving Dave fifteen acres of land. Tax records of Carroll County in 1899 and 1905 show Dave as a colored taxpayer on eighteen acres of land. In the 1910 Georgia census, Dave is age 70 living with Uel Posey, head of the family, age 56.

Neighbors began reporting seeing Dave without clothes in the community. As a family member emerged from the barn after milking the cow, there stood Dave without clothes. They said, "Dave, aren't you ashamed, go home and put on some clothes." One morning as this family member looked out to check on her five-year-old son, Dave had attached a rope to a tree limb and tied a noose in the other end. He had the five-year-old standing on a chair. The mother said, "Dave, don't put that rope around his neck."

After this incident, the family had a legal guardian appointed on 25 March 1912. On 4 April 1912, the court declared Dave a lunatic. He was transported to Milledgeville State Hospital. Dave died shortly thereafter. He was buried in Milledgeville, Georgia.

Dave was past age 70, had a long white beard. He left the land to a family member. *Submitted by: L. Kelley, 485 Buncombe-Waco Road, Waco, GA 30132.*

Sources: Haralson and Carroll County census, Probate and Court records and family knowledge.

929. Powell

This photo **(top of page 412)** was made on October 27, 1940 at the home of Dr. and Mrs. B.C. Powell, Colonial Manor in Villa Rica. The occasion was their Golden Wedding Anniversary. The Carroll County Medical Society presented a gold loving cup and Dr. H.L. Barker served as master of ceremonies and delivered a touching speech. The members then sang, "When You and I Were Young, Mamie." Left to right, first row, Dr. F.S. Scales, Mrs. J.E. Powell, Dr. J.E. Powell, Mrs. B.C. Powell, Dr. B.C. Powell, Miss Eleanor Berry, Dr. R.L. Berry and Dr. H.J. Goodwyn, Back row: Dr. W.L. Hogue, Dr. W.B. Brock, Mrs. F.S. Scales, Mrs. W.B. Brock, Mrs. D.S. Reese, Dr. D.S. Reese, Dr. O.R. Styles, Dr. T.M. Spruell, Dr. W.P. Smith, Mrs. W.P. Smith, Dr. H.L. Barker, Mrs. H.L. Barker and Mrs. H.J. Goodwyn. *Submitted by: Leslie Carter, Carrollton, GA*

930. John William Powell

John William Powell b. 3 Sept 1852 in Coweta County to Levi Thomas Gardner Powell and Nancy Selena Redwine Powell m. (1) Frances Louellin Green b. 30 Jan. 1860 to Joseph Reuben Green and Panola Shipp, daughter of Mark Shipp of Acworth.

The wife and two children of Joseph Reuben Green died on the way home from Alabama in the winter after the Civil War when many families refugeed away from the fighting in Cobb County. "Lou" was the only child to survive; her mother and siblings were buried alongside the road somewhere in Alabama. Her father would never talk about the tragedy.

50th Wedding Anniversary – Dr. and Mrs. B.C. Powell

In the Hickory Level community, the family of J.W. Powell lived near other Powell families and attended the Concord Methodist Church. Two children were born, Bertha Lee Powell 12 Feb 1881 and William Buna Powell 12 Dec 1883. Then their mother died 28 June 1886 (stone). J.W. Powell married (2) 22 Dec 1887 Ellen Hill and had two other children (no children named in his obit).

John William Powell and Frances Louellin Green Powell

After the death of John William Powell 12 April 1895, since there were no blood relatives in the household, the Powell brothers and sister took the first two children into their homes to live with them. Uncle Buna Columbus Powell became their legal guardian. The administrator of the estate was John W. Baskins. He was granted letters after giving bond and taking the oath 9 May 1895.

The Powell brothers bought the farm of John William Powell from the widow Ellen Powell. This was 1/3 of the west 1/2 of land lot #90 in district 6. This gave Ellen and her children monies to buy other land nearer her family. This land had been deeded to J.W. Powell from his father, L.T.G. Powell 10 Dec 1889. *Submitted by: Sidney Elliott, Washington, DC and Written by: June Hart Wester, 133 Mountain Crest Drive, Canton, GA 30114*
Sources: Court records of Carroll and Coweta counties, cemetery records of Carroll County, CCGS, and recollections of Bertha Lee Powell Hart

931. The Levi Thomas Gardner Powell Family

After the death of his father, John Powell, in Coweta County, L.T.G. Powell bought lot #90 6th district of Carroll County and moved there with his wife, Nancy Selena Redwine Powell, daughter of Lewis Redwine and Mary Merritt Redwine. She died 5 May 1886.

They soon became members of the Concord Methodist Church, and he preached, as did his brother, William Francis Spaight Powell. Together, they founded the Powell's Chapel in Carroll County. He d. 2 May 1897, bur. Concord Methodist Church Cemetery.

Children: 1. Michael Powell m. Thomas J. Moore, Carroll County 1869. She d. 1882. 2. Mary Merritt Powell m. Thomas Wynn 1867. She d. 1881. 3. John William Powell m. (1) Nov. 1881 Frances Louellin Green, who died 28 June 1886 leaving two children, Bertha and William Buna Powell. He m. (2) Ellen Hill and had two children, Howard and Myrtle. He d. 1895. 4. Sarah Cowart Powell m. John W. Baskins 1875. 5. Lewis Redwine "Lew Red" Powell m. Nannie Mae Hancock 1883. He died 1923. 6. Francis Park Powell m. Luradine Allen "Frank" 1881. He d. 1933. 7. Elizabeth D. Powell "Lizzie" m. John W. Davis 1879. She d. 1899. 8. Thomas Gardner Powell m. Frances Yates "Tom" 1886. He d. 1933 or 37. 9. Buna Columbus Powell, "Dr. B.C.," m. May Estelle Wheeler 1890 d. 1961.

Powells — B.C., John W., Frank, Tom, Lizzie Davis, Lew Red

This family is first listed in the 1860 census Hickory Level Post Office, with six slaves. Two were the property of the wife, who received them from her father. The 1873 tax list gives him owning 202 1/2 acres of #90 and Nancy S. as owning 150 acres of #71/6. This was a homestead which was tax exempt for her. She sold 50 acres of this lot in 1871 to R.L. Turner for benefit of herself.

This family produced many upstanding citizens in the medical, educational and religious areas, who have proven to be a blessing to Carroll County. Present day descendants continue to be serving citizens, and it is a pleasure to be descended from such fine ancestors. *Submitted by: Sara Powell Duncanson, New Orleans, LA; Written by: June Hart Wester, 133 Mountain Crest Drive, Canton, GA 30114*
Sources: Patterson, *History of the Redwine Powell Families;* Anderson, *The History of Villa Rica;* Family reminiscences, court records, census tracts, and tax lists.

932. Levi Thomas Gardner Powell Family

Rev. Levi Thomas Gardner Powell, the son of John Stephen and Sarah E. Cowart Powell was born April 2, 1826, in Coweta County, Georgia, and died May 2, 1897, in Carroll County. He married Nancy Selina Redwine on February 1, 1848, in Coweta County. She was born December 20, 1825, in Franklin County and died May 5, 1886, in Carroll County. She was the daughter of Lewis Parks and Mary Merritt Redwine of Coweta County. Levi and Nancy Powell are buried at Concord Methodist Church in the Hickory Level community. The inscription on his tombstone reads

"Our Father has gone to a mansion of rest,
to the glorious land by the deity blest."

Rev. Levi Thomas and Nancy Selina Redwine Powell had nine children. (1) Michael Florence married Thomas Moore. (2) Mary Merritt married W. Thomas Wynn. (3) John William married Ellen Pamelia Hill. (4) Sarah Cowart married John Baskin. (5) Lewis Redwine married Patience Lee Rhyne. (6) Francis Parks married M. Luradine Allen. (7) Thomas Gardner married Frances I. Yates. (8) Dr. Buena Columbus married Mary Estelle Wheeler.

Ellen Pamelia Hill and John William Powell with children John Howard and Myrtle Bell.

Rev. Levi Thomas Powell was a property owner, a Methodist minister, a schoolmaster, and an early settler of the Hickory Level community. Rev. Levi Thomas Powell and his brother Rev. William Speight Powell were instrumental in founding Powell's Methodist Church on Flat Rock Road in Carroll County.

Rev. Levi Thomas and Nancy Selina Powell's son John William was my great-grandfather. John was born September 3, 1852, in Coweta County and died April 12, 1895, in Carroll County. He married Ellen Pamelia Hill on March 3, 1881, in Carroll County. Ellen Pamelia was born March 8, 1858, in Carroll County, Temple, Georgia and died November 17, 1941, in Carroll County. John William Powell is buried at Concord Methodist Church in the Hickory Level community beside his first wife Frances Green and Ellen Pamelia Powell is buried at Bethel Baptist Church in Temple. John William was also a Methodist minister.

John William and Ellen Pamelia Powell had three children: a son John Howard (my grandfather) born December 21, 1891, in Carroll County and died October 9, 1963, in Floyd County, Georgia; a daughter Myrtle Bell born July 1894 in Carroll County, died October 17, 1936, in Carroll County, married Lowell A. Muse November 17, 1913, in Carroll County; and an unnamed infant.

John Howard Powell married Lois Irene Payne March 21, 1913, in Carroll County. They had six children all born in Carroll County, Mary Ellen, Annie Grace, Virginia Ruth, John Howard Jr., James Roy and Peggy Nell.

Annie Grace Powell married Earl Eugene Dial on July 21, 1934 (my parents). They had five children: Charles Eugene, William Ray, Glenda Sue, Donald Norton and Jerry Wayne. I am the second son and I married Elizabeth Ann Gore on July 27, 1956. We have three children living and two died at birth.

Cheryl Lynn married Douglas Merlin Braswell, Donna Jean married Samuel P. George, and Melissa Ann married Perry Vance Hardegree. We have seven grandchildren, Jason and Jennifer Braswell, Brandon, Brent and Bryan George, and Casey and Cary Hardegree. *Submitted by: William R. and Elizabeth Gore Dial, 1062 Old Draketown Trail, Temple, GA 30179*

Sources: Census and marriage records, family and personal knowledge.

933. The Powers Family

The Potato Famine and the Revolution of 1848 in Ireland influenced brothers John, James, and Michael Powers to move to America. They departed Liverpool, England, June 26, 1848. Their parents James and Madge Coley Powers and several other children remained in West Meath County, Ireland, with hopes of coming to America later. A sister Ettie came in 1870; she settled in Connecticut and married a Welch.

It is thought they came to a port in New York. They settled in the North for the first year. It is uncertain whether they came to the West Georgia area once they left the North. They probably stopped in North Carolina. According to a newspaper article of March 18, 1911, they were living in Coweta County, Georgia, in 1855. John Powers left his brothers in Georgia in 1855 and departed for Evanston, Illinois.

James of Coweta County served in the Confederate Army; Michael of Carroll County did too. John hired someone in Evanston for $300 to serve in the Union Army because he didn't want to fight against his brothers. They had a reunion in Newnan in March 1911, after not knowing the whereabouts of each other for fifty-six years.

Michael Powers, a ditcher born in Ireland, was living in the home of W.G. and Martha Huckeba June 15, 1860. On November 27, 1860, Michael married Nancy Louisa Michael. They had nine children: John P. "Pete" Powers, Marcie Powers Dyer, Mary Powers Duke Lee, G.W. "Grimpz" Powers, Loretta "Etta" Powers McIntosh, Pat C. Powers, Michael Sylvester Powers, Joe L. Powers, and Sally Lee Powers Horton.

Michael Sylvester married Alma Jordon, October 1, 1903. They had seven children: Mary Lou Powers Grainger, Harvey Oliver Powers, Irene Powers, Letha Powers Patterson Johnson Merrill, Chalmer S. Powers, Dallas Powers Holcomb, and Bonnie Powers Wilson.

Harvey Oliver married Ilver Gladys Hightower on April 3, 1927, and they had three sons, Merlin Oliver, Kermet Jasper, and Jerry Byron. Harvey, like his grandfather Michael and father Michael Sylvester, was a Carroll County farmer until 1951. Harvey and family moved to Atlanta in 1952 where he worked as a carpenter's helper.

My parents, Merlin Oliver and Earline Johnson Powers were married June 4, 1952, at Pleasant View Baptist Church, the first wedding held in the present sanctuary. They attended Georgia Southern in Statesboro, Georgia, during the summer of 1952. Then, Villa Rica was their home for the next ten years.

The Powers Family

I, Timothy E. Powers, was born January 2 1956, and my brother Gregory Kenneth was born May 14, 1960, at Tanner Memorial Hospital.

Merlin was a school administrator. We moved to Buena Vista, Georgia, in August of 1962 and my father served as principal of Marion County High School. Later we lived in Toccoa, Lithonia, and Fayetteville, Georgia. Merlin served as school superintendent of Fayette County for eight years.

In 1981, my parents returned to Villa Rica after living elsewhere for nineteen years. Merlin was principal of Paulding County High School at the time of his sudden heart attack death on July 6, 1983.

Earline was a business education teacher. She started teaching at Roopville High School at age nineteen. Later she taught at Villa Rica High School, Stephens County High School, Stone Mountain High School, and the last twenty-one years of her career were spent at Campbell High School in Fairburn, Georgia. She still lives in Villa Rica. She enjoys my children Cherri and Michael, and Greg's children Molly and Rebecca. Also, she attends church, Elderhostal programs, researches genealogy, and travels. She is currently serving as president of Carroll/Heard Retired Educators.

During 2000, Mom and I traveled to Ireland searching our family roots.

The Powers family is shown in the accompanying picture. Seated left to right are Mary, Pete, Michael, Louisa, and Marcie. Standing are Sally Lee, Joe, Michael Sylvester, Pat, Jim, and Etta. *Submitted by: Tom Powers, 258 Matthews Road, Fayetteville, GA 30215*

934. Prickett Family

of Burwell

George Prickett was born about 1735 and came to Franklin County, Georgia, from Randolph County, Virginia. George Prickett's first son was Israel Prickett who was born 26 June 1763 in Virginia and died 2 September 1837 in Franklin County. Israel married Sarah Hargrove on 10 October 1783. Israel Prickett served in the Revolutionary War. Their tenth son was Jacob Prickett who was born 15 December 1803 in Franklin County and died about 1850. Jacob Prickett married Nancy Sewell on 8 February 1827 in Morgan County, Georgia. Their fourth child was Pierce Sanford Prickett born about 1832.

Pierce Sanford Prickett married Rebecca Ann Griffin on 26 November 1857 in Carroll County, Georgia. Rebecca Prickett was born 4 June 1841 and died 19 August 1914. Pierce served in the Civil War as a private in Company B, 56th Regiment, Georgia Volunteers, and died of wounds and pneumonia in an Atlanta hospital in 1864. He is buried near Roopville in Carroll County. Rebecca Prickett later married Samuel Craven and had six or more children from that marriage.

John Sanford Prickett was born in Carroll County on 20 June 1861 and died in 1945. Sanford was the second child of Pierce Sanford and Rebecca Prickett. He married Lula Permelia "Minnie" Hearn on 19 February 1889. Minnie Hearn was born 8 June 1871 and died 25 January 1953. Sanford Prickett always lived near the community of Burwell, Georgia, and farmed cotton, corn, and other crops. Minnie Prickett was a teacher and taught Sunday School at Shiloh Methodist Church all her life. They are buried at Shiloh Methodist Cemetery in Burwell. They had six sons and one daughter: Charles, Dewey, Parks, Forrest, Nannie, Griffin, and John S. Jr.

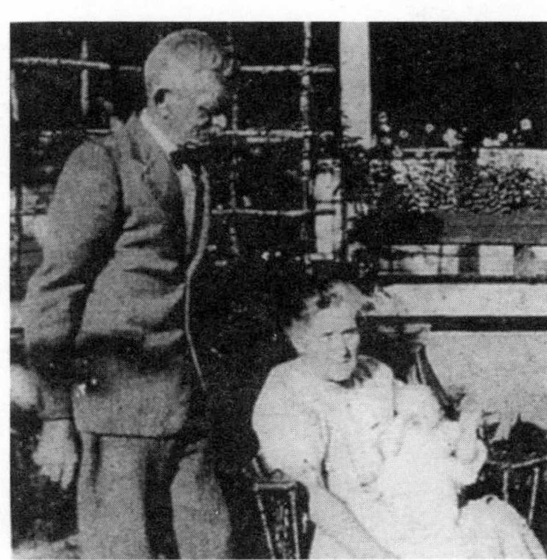

Sanford and Minnie Prickett with grandson Sanford III

Six children were teachers/educators and one a farmer. Several sons served in either World War I or World War II.

Their youngest son, John S. Prickett Jr. was born 26 January 1910 in Burwell and died 13 September 1993. He married Burnell Wright of Bowdon, Georgia, on 20 June 1931. Burnell Wright was born 28 January 1912 near Burwell and died 19 May 1987 in Atlanta. John and Burnell attended Bowdon College. Both are buried, along with their son Lanny, at Shiloh Cemetery at Burwell. John worked many jobs — including surveying, teaching, farming — to pay for his education. He eventually graduated from the University of Georgia with a master's degree in education. John Prickett became the director of the Georgia Division of Vocational Rehabilitation, served on several president's committees and was elected president of the National Rehabilitation Association in 1973. They had four children: Sanford, Betty, Lanny, and Rebecca.

John Sanford Prickett III presently lives on the old Prickett homestead outside Burwell on Davenport Mill Road at Turkey Creek. *Submitted by: John Sanford Prickett III, PO Box 664, Bowdon, GA 30108*

935. Phillip T.C. Pritchard

Philip T.C. Pritchard was born in 1836. He married Mary Ann Turner in 1858 in Fulton County. Philip and both his parents were born in Georgia. In 1860 Philip and Mary Ann lived in West End in Atlanta. Philip worked for the Atlanta and West Point Railroad. In 1870 he was a conductor on the railroad. Their children were Sarah Frances, Joseph L., Mary Ellen, Elizabeth Jane, William W., and Ann Lee. Mary Ann, wife of Philip, died and he married Emily Dean in 1877 in Haralson County. Their children were Palenam, and Louvale.

Sarah Frances Pritchard married William Hesterly in Haralson County in 1879. Joseph L. Pritchard married Harriett Posey in Haralson County in 1885.

Louvale married Napoleon J. Presnell and their children were Austin, Lester, and Valnma. Elizabeth Jane (Lizzie) married Oscar Franklin Lambert in Haralson County in 1890. Their children were Lester Philip, Hershell, Lewin, Ruth, Stella, Bertha, Betsy, and Harvey Lee.

Philip Pritchard

Napoleon and Oscar operated a store in Bowdon Junction named Presnell-Lambert General Store. The post office was in the store and Oscar Lambert was the postmaster from 1910 until his death in 1929. Between the world wars, Hershell (son of Elizabeth and Oscar) joined the Army but he wanted to get out before his enlistment was up. He could get out if he paid the Army an amount to reimburse them for his room and board for the time he was there. Elizabeth used her savings to pay for him to come home. Although Hershell had only limited service time he obtained experience that was needed in World War II and although he was over the draft age he was drafted back into the service and made a master sergeant at the hospital at Camp Wheeler in Macon.

Harvey Lee had died as a baby. Stella, her baby, and Betsy all died in 1914. Lester, Elizabeth's son, became the postmaster and he paid her for the post offices boxes and the window front used in the post office. The postmaster had to furnish the facilities for the post office. The front and boxes have been installed in the log house owned by Wallace T. Lambert, her grandson. After Oscar's death, Elizabeth lived with her daughters Ruth and Bertha. Both Elizabeth and Ruth died in 1936.

Lester married Verdie Wallace, Lewin married Lovella Entrekin, Herschel married Clyde Prentice, Bertha married Arthur Stamps, Stella married R.H. Evans, and Ruth married Manuel Wallace. *Submitted by: Lovella Lambert*

Source: Information furnished by Wallace T. Lambert

936. William H. Pyron 1802-1872 and Mary Elizabeth LeMaster 1802-1860

William Pyron and Elizabeth LeMaster were married in the mountains of East Tennessee. They later migrated down to Atlanta, Georgia, to the area now known as Stone Mountain where they lived in a log cabin on several hundred acres at the mountain side.

During the War Between the States, his daughters and grandchildren came to live with him. Yankees came through, marauding homes and civilians. William grabbed his gun and tried to defend his home and family, but the Yankees tied him to a horse that dragged him down the road. He lived through the ordeal, but was forever scarred. Being totally disillusioned with the area, William moved his family to Carroll County, where he took up residence in the Laurel Hill community. He lived there until his later years when he moved in with his daughter and family. The obituary states that he died of the fever at the home of his son-in-law, Judge Juhan. His burial place is unknown. The children were: Mary E. (1828-1892) who married D.B. Juhan, Elizabeth Ann (1830-unknown), James A. (1832-1860s-died in the war), Joseph L. (1835-unknown), Frances (1837-unknown) who married John Andrew Kelley, Rachel Emmeline (1840-unknown) who married James Wilbur Mitchell, and William James (1843-1914).

William James married Julia B. Morris (1849-1897) in 1866. He served in the War Between the States in the Volunteer Infantry, Company B, 56th Regiment. He was wounded in the lungs and captured at Baker's Creek, Mississippi on May 16, 1863, later being paroled on the battlefield. On July 22, 1864, he sustained a neck wound in Atlanta. He drew a veterans pension. William and Julia are buried in unmarked graves in the Laurel Hill Cemetery. Their only child was James William (1867-1958) who married Leonora Elizabeth Duffey (1867-1950), daughter of Samuel S. Duffey (1845-1913) and Mahulda Jane Maxwell (1851-1933).

James William and Leonora Elizabeth, known as Jim and Onie, lived in both the Laurel Hill and Lowell communities. They are buried at Stripling Chapel. Their nine children include: James Azzie (1888-1956) who married Essie Cottle, Sarah Alvada (1889-1987) who married James Franklin Stewart (1884-1960), son of Isaiah F. Stewart and Josephine Hill, Etta A. (Lena) (1892-1968), Nettie May (1894-1975) who married Mr. Wheelis, then Kelbey Taylor, Julia L. (1898-1920), Gertrude Annie (1900-1992) who married Fred Phillips, Grady Monroe (1901-1985) who married Vera Mabel Cowart, Lois Geneva (1905-1994) who married Clarence C. Brittain, and Claud Lee (1906-1984) who married Grace Opal Karr.

Sarah Alvada, known to all as Vada and J. Frank Stewart made their home in the Lowell community. They also are buried at Stripling Chapel. Their children are Dora, Carmon Inez, and Norman E.

Norman married Mary Beverlyn Stewart and settled in Atlanta, with their five children: Norma Elizabeth, Ronald Stephen, Dean Allan, James Keith and Timothy Arden. *Submitted by: James Keith Stewart, 2440 Temple Johnson Road, Snellville, GA 30278*

Pyron Family Reunion Circa 1929

937. Thomas Rabun Family

Thomas Rabun, son of Hodge and Amanda Watkins, was born about 1779 in North Carolina. His father was a state senator from Burke, Haywood, and Buncombe Counties, North Carolina. His cousin, William Rabun, was governor of Georgia for five years.

Thomas was married first to Sara Curtis and had one daughter, Constance. He was married second to Mary Stroud, and they were the parents of seventeen children: Elizabeth, John, Hodge, Thomas Jr., Nancy, James Matason, Martha Jane, Unknown, Amanda, Melvina, Willis Monteville, Joannah, Mary, Sarah, Susannah Margaret, Aramintha, and Emily.

Thomas and brother Hodge came to Carroll County about 1832. They lived in or around Villa Rica. Thomas was a road commissioner for Carroll County in 1835 for the Sixth District. He was a trustee of the New Hope Meeting House. After the Civil War, Thomas, Mary, and daughter Mary went to Bell County, Texas. Their daughter Sarah, who married Robert Leonard Moore of Paulding County, Georgia, also went to Texas. Thomas was eighty years old when they made the move. He died about 1870 in Van Zandt County, Texas.

Thomas had two sons and one son-in-law who served in the Civil War. James M. served in Company H. 2nd Battalion, 1st Confederate Regiment Infantry. Willis served in 40th Regiment, Georgia Volunteers (Haralson Defenders). He was captured at Missionary Ridge, Tennessee, and sent to Rock Island where he died 1 March 1864. Robert Leonard served in Company G, 7th Georgia Infantry, and was wounded. *Submitted by: Mrs. Harley Humphrey, 218 Marigold Street, Lake Jackson, TX 77566-3156*

Sources: Census records, Rabun Family Bible, Civil War records, *Annals of Haywood County, North Carolina,* by W.C. Allen 1808.

938. Ragland History

Early records show that the Raglands originated from England and Wales, the name originally being "Raglan." They migrated to America with Stanover Company of Virginia about 1720 (Mechamps Creek near Pamunkey River, Virginia). From there some members went to Tennessee, South Carolina, Georgia, Alabama, and Texas.

The name Raglan became anglicized; a "d" added accent on the first syllable and Welsh pronunciation was "Roglon." The welsh for "rag" — old piece of clothes — is an entirely different word.

The coat of arms consisted of three lion's heads on field argent. Raglan Castle in Manmouthshire, Wales gave name to the family through John Raglan, son of Robert Herbert. Raglan Castle is in the Raglan-Somerset family.

Henry Thomas E. Ragland was born February 1, 1866, and died July 23, 1899. He married Elizabeth (Lizzie) Jones at Stripling Church in Carroll County, Georgia, on December 25, 1890. Nuptials were presided over by Reverend Reese. Henry and Lizzie had two sons and one daughter: Cliff was born in 1892 and died 1947; Lynn was born in 1896 and died in 1964; and Evelyn.

Cliff married Lavora Gray and they had five children: Ilaree, Myrtle, Herbert, Henry, and Clara. Lynn married Bessie Merrell on November 9, 1919, at Roopville (Georgia) Methodist parsonage. They had five children: Jennie, Ason Clyde, Jean, Sara, and Carol. Evelyn married Lyle Mullenix and they had one daughter who died at birth. *Submitted by: Sarah Ragland Tuggle, 195 Dowdy Road, Roopville, GA 30170*

939. Davis Stephens Reese

In 1906, after graduating from The Atlanta School of Medicine and Surgery, which became Emory Medical School in 1907, Davis Stephens Reese came to Lowell for five years before moving to Carrollton in 1911. While in Lowell, his practice moved from horseback to buggy to automobile. He spent the rest of his life dedicated to medicine, his family, and serving the community, his church and the Baptist denomination. In 1929, he, Dr. Hulett Askew, and Dr. Charles Fitts opened the Carrollton Clinic on College Street to provide hospital facilities for the area. From the mid-thirties, he maintained the clinic alone until Tanner Hospital opened in 1949. Because of his desire for an accredited hospital facility which he and several local citizens had worked for after 1945, it was fitting that he should be named the first chief-of-staff in 1949. The clinic was also a consideration for locating West Georgia College in Carrollton for student medical treatment. During this period, he organized the Carrollton Health Department and later the county department.

In addition to his civic duties, Dr. Reese was a Trustee for Georgia Baptist Hospital for over 20 years and on the President's Board for Tift College for many years. In the First Baptist Church, he served as deacon for over fifty years and contributed to the two annexes added to the building. Seeing a need, he began a Sunday program at the county prison, which culminated with a chapel dedicated in May 1967, two months before his death 9 August 1967.

Scouting was a lifelong interest and he supported Boy Scout activities for many years. For his long dedication, he received the Silver Beaver Award, their highest award.

Other honors given him were the West Georgia Founder's Award in 1956 and the Carrollton Chamber of Commerce Man of the Year Award in 1966.

These activities did not prevent him from time with his immediate and extended family. His wife was Eva Tommie Philips whom he married in 1911. She was the daughter of Abram Charles Philips and Zillah Ann Garrard of Putnam County, Georgia. After her death in April 1925, he married her niece, Zillah (Catherine) Kathryn Roquemore, on 8 May 1926 and had two children from this marriage, Davis Roquemore Reese and Betty Ann (Reese) deVane.

Dr. D.S. Reese

Dr. Reese was born in Coweta County, Georgia, on 23 February 1881, the tenth of their eleven children. His parents were William Irvin Reese and Temperance Elizabeth Davis. Educated at home by his mother, a teacher, and at Handy High School, he went on to North Georgia College and medical school, working his way through both schools. Irvin Reese was born 7 April 1847, served in the Confederate Army as a teenager, and moved to Carrollton about 1910. Both parents died in Carrollton. Irvin's parents were T.X. Reese and Ann Cordelia (Davis) Jordan. Through his mother and grandmother he was descended from different William Davis' in Wilkes County, Georgia. Elizabeth Davis was born 25 May 1841 to Jephta Vining Davis and Temperance Daniel, his first wife. William Davis and Nancy Eastin were her grandparents. They had been born in Orange County, Virginia, in 1765 and moved to Georgia in the 1790s where Jeptha was born. Temperance Daniel's parents were Henning Daniel and Hannah Asbury of Greene County. Other earlier family lines were Bankston, Henderson, Irvin, Lanier, Tempte, Thornton, and Tucker. *Submitted by: Betty R. de Vane, 1121 Rome Street, Carrollton, GA 30117*

940. Thomas Ellis Reeve Jr. Family

Thomas Ellis Reeve Jr., son of Methodist missionaries to Africa, was born in 1920. He finished Emory Medical School and a surgery internship and was commissioned lieutenant junior grade in the Navy where he was stationed at the U.S. Naval Hospital in Dublin, Georgia, in 1944. In 1945 he married Ruth Hadley of Statesville, North Carolina. She was born in 1922, graduated from Greensboro College, North Carolina, and then trained at American University, Washington, D.C. to be a Red Cross Recreation worker. She was stationed at the Dublin, Georgia, Naval Hospital.

Three months after meeting, the couple married in North Carolina in 1945. After World War II, they "shopped around" for a small town near Atlanta, discovered Carrollton in 1949 because of its new hospital, good public school system, West Georgia College, and the First Methodist Church which had sponsored T.E. Reeve Sr. while serving as missionary in Africa from 1916-1929.

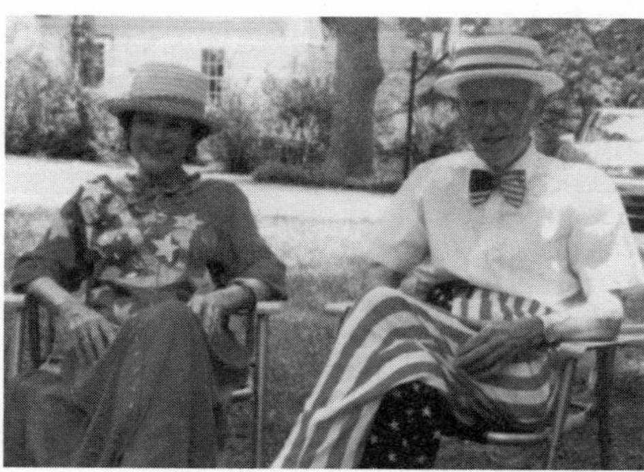

Ruth and Tom Reeve, July 4, 2000

Dr. Reeve was the first board-certified surgeon in Carrollton and served in many capacities on the hospital staff and board, the American College of Surgeons, and as past president of the Georgia Surgical Society. Although involved in his profession, he found time for civic duties and was named Man of the Year by the Chamber of Commerce in 1986. For twenty-five years he served on the City of Carrollton Board of Education during which time he played a major part in the smooth, successful integration of the city schools.

Though not involved professionally, Dr. and Mrs. Reeve were ardent supporters of music and the arts; they were members of the First Methodist Choir for over fifty years and participated in other programs of the church.

Dr. and Mrs. Reeve have four children: Susan Reeve Ingle (wife of Dr. Richard Ingle), Robin Reeve Allen (wife of Richard W. Allen), Thomas Ellis Reeve III (husband of Dana Walton) and Timothy Hadley Reeve (husband of Wendy Weber).

In his retirement, Dr. Reeve pursued his many hobbies of photography, traveling, reading, and spending time with his fifteen grandchildren and three great-grandchildren. *Submitted by: Ruth Hadley Reeve, 146 Griffin Drive, Carrollton, GA 30117*

941. The Hiram Alexander Reeves Family

Hiram Alexander Reeves was born March 16, 1884, in Sand Mountain, Alabama. He was the fourth child of Charles Henry and Emeline Rebecca (Evans) Reeves. Brothers and sisters of Alex were: Clida Eujenior, Meinty Ann Elizabeth, William Joseph, George Washington, Phoebe Selone, Emma Estell, Susan Adda Bell, Myrtie Vivion, Charly, Leornia Pertunia, and Jessie Madison. The youngest, Jessie, is still living and resides at Autumn Square on Oak Grove Church Road. As told by Jessie in the 1990s, Charles and Rebecca moved from Jackson, Mississippi, to Sand Mountain, Alabama, and then to the Mandeville Community near Bowdon Junction around 1887.

Hiram Alexander and Lena Griffin Reeves

Alex's first marriage was to Lena Evan Griffin on September 16, 1906. Five children were born to this union: Harold, Oliven, Olen, Florene, and Hiram. Lena was born on September 21, 1889, to Manuel and Lou (Lyle) Griffin. She passed away on August 22, 1929.

Alex's second marriage was to Annie Bell Denney on December 6, 1935. To this union was born one son, Reese Denney Reeves, born on March 18, 1938. Annie was born on October 3, 1900, to Cullie and Mollie (Yates) Denney. She was a member of Emmaus Primitive Baptist Church. She had a great love for Sacred Harp singing. She was an accomplished stitcher and left many handmade pieces that are now family treasures.

Annie Bell Denney Reeves

Alex was a farmer during most of his lifetime. In his earlier years, he worked on the railroad. It was remembered that he helped furnish lumber for the Rockridge School located just south of Carrollton.

Alex passed away on September 5, 1965, and was buried beside his first wife, Lena, in the Oak Grove Baptist Cemetery. Annie died on October 16, 1960 and is buried at Emmaus Primitive Baptist Church.

Alex and Annie's oldest grandson, Tony Reese Reeves, served as sheriff of Carroll County from 1996 until 2000. *Submitted by: Carole Hubbard Reeves, 25 Carole Drive, Carrollton, GA*

942. Monsignor Michael J. Regan

Msgr. Michael Joseph Regan was one of Carroll County's most well-known and beloved Catholics. He was born in Philadelphia, Pennsylvania, November 22, 1921, the son of Michael and Nora Regan. On May 30, 1946, he was ordained a priest of the diocese of Philadelphia. In 1950 they sent him to Georgia for a six-month assignment, and he remained in the state until his death nearly fifty years later.

In Georgia, Msgr. Regan served first in the diocese of Savannah. He accompanied Bishop Hyland when he established the new diocese of Atlanta in 1956. He served at St. Thomas Aquinas Mission in Roswell, Georgia, from 1957 to 1961; at Immaculate Heart of Mary in Atlanta from 1961 to 1972. In 1972, Msgr. Regan became pastor of Our Lady of Perpetual Help Church in Carrollton. He served as pastor for twenty-four years and remained active in parish life as pastor emeritus until his death August 8, 1999.

Msgr. Regan loved animals and began collecting "pets" when he moved to the rural setting of Our Lady of Perpetual Help. He soon acquired a menagerie of animals which served almost as a petting zoo for local children. Because of his love of animals, they often called him the Saint Francis of Carroll County.

Monsignor Michael J. Regan

Msgr. Regan also showed a generous charity to all persons with whom he came in contact. He ministered to Catholics, Protestants, and people of all faiths. One of his favorite ministries was visiting the sick and hospitalized.

He was also active in the issues of his time. During the 1960s while living in Atlanta, he marched with Dr. Martin Luther King Jr. In the 1980s, he participated in Operation Rescue, a pro-life organization and was arrested and jailed for his defense of the unborn.

He was a priest who was dedicated to loving and serving all, and is fondly remembered by his parish and the community at large. *Submitted by: Carol C. Nelson, Carrollton, GA*

943. Davis Reid Family

Davis Reid was born in 1806 in Gwinnett County, Georgia, and died after 1860 in Carroll County. He is buried in Old Concord Baptist Cemetery, Carroll County. Davis was the son of Henry Martin Reid who was born on 3 February 1773 and died after 1853 in Carroll County, and Edith Harrison born about 1781. Davis was married first to name unknown, and second to Jane Warnett (born about 1816) about 1831 in Georgia. He lived many years prior to his death in the community of Old Concord Primitive Baptist Church, which is about four miles north of Carrollton on the Temple road. Old Concord is now a pasture.

Front, Henry Martin and Mary Elizabeth Reid. Back, Ella Ayers and Henry Martin Reid.

The children of Davis Reid were: (1) Andrew Reid, born about 1828, died 23 December 1910 in Carroll County; (2) Henry Martin Reid, born 12 June 1831 in Gwinnett or Carroll County, died 17 June 1912 in Bowdon; (3) Elisha Marian Reid, born about 1837; (4) Newton D. Reid, born about 1838; (5) Francis Nicie Reid, born 1839; (6) Reuben D. Reid, born 2 December 1840, died 10 April 1912 in Carroll County; (7) George Reid, born 4 June 1844 in Georgia, died 12 November 1924; (8) Alexander Reid, born between 1845 and 1846 in Carroll County; (9) James P. Reid, born 20 December 1849, died 1 November 1920.

Henry married Mary Elizabeth Williams on 20 September 1855. She was the daughter of Stephen Rowlings and Rebecca Embry Williams. She was born 1 May 1836 in Pike County and died 5 September 1899. Both are buried in Bethlehem Primitive Baptist Church Cemetery. H.M. Reid was a private in the Civil War, Company F., 19th Georgia Infantry. He received a pension for wounds received in this war. Children of Henry Martin and Marty E. Reid were Martha Lester born 21 August 1857, died 26 June 1873; Cynthia Ann born 11 September 1859, died 15 February 1940, buried in family cemetery in Carroll County, married J.B. Owensby; Lydia Jane born 26 July 1861, died 4 November 1879, married Jacob Moses Lenderman (see Lenderman Family); Elmira Catherine born 13 February 1866, died 2 Febraury 1910, married George W. Kemp; Mary L. "Mollie" born 23 February 1868; Lazora Elizabeth born 22 February 1871, died 1949, married E.C. Simpson, born 1868, died 1934; Nicey Rebecca born 3 October 1873; and Henry Martin born 2 March 1877, married Ella Ayers.

Following the death of Lydia Jane Lenderman, her sisters helped to care for her son, Henry Ottis, until he and his father moved to Alabama. Ottis used to tell that his grandfather Reid would disappear into the woods for a while and when he came back he would have small bag of gold. One day Ottis and a friend decided to follow him to see where he was finding this gold. They went around and around in the woods, but what they didn't know was that the old man was smarter than they thought. He led them on a wild goose chase and ended back at the house without ever disclosing the whereabouts of his stash. *Submitted by: Margene Hemrick Black, 2201 Loveless Street, Guntersville, AL 35976*

944. Gus Reid 1908-1993

Gus Reid dwelt in or around Roopville for the better part of his eighty-six years of living. Gus was the second of eleven children. He was born February 8, 1908, in Heard County, Georgia, to Pless W. Reid (born September 7, 1895) and Lilla Riddley Reid (born January 1887). Gus married Lucille Brooks of Lafayette, Alabama, on November 18, 1947. They have four children; Margaret Reid, Roger Lee Reid, Gus Albert Reid (died in infancy) and Emanuel Lenard Reid. Gus was a man blessed with many talents and abilities. He was best known for his carpentry. Of the homes he built, seven are in Roopville and are still occupied to this day. He was also an accomplished plumber, farmer, electrician, mechanic, barber and a fair block and brick layer. Oh, and I must not forget he loved to play checkers. Gus was a member of Pleasant Grove Baptist Church in Roopville where he served as the cemetery clerk. He served in the army during World War II as a fleet mechanic and driver stationed in Boca Raton, Florida.

Gus and his family lived in Heard County up until he was about fifteen years old. Then they moved to Lowell onto the Jim Hollingsworth place around 1923, and eventually moved to the Roopville area where Gus's father Pless died January 4, 1950. Gus's family consisted of his father and mother, one older sister Charligene born May 13, 1907, died December 12, 1982. He had seven younger brothers: Quillion born November 1908 and is deceased; Garnett born in 1911 and died December 19, 1984; Roy born around 1912 and died February 19, 1986; Howard born April 16, 1915, died May 21, 1976; Taylor born December 1919 and yet lives in Columbus, Ohio. There were two other brothers who died in infancy while the family was living in Lowell. Gus's grandfather on his father's side was Henry Reid, born August

1844. Henry was married to Mary Reid. Gus's wife Lucille continues to reside in Roopville among her three children, seven grandchildren and three great-grandchildren. Gus Reid died December 9, 1993.

The Reid Family

The family photograph shows on the back row Gus Reid, Quillion Reid, a cousin, and Howard Reid. On the front row are Pless Reid, Lula Lynch Reid (second wife), a cousin, and Garnett Reid. *Submitted by: Emanuel Reid, P.O. Box 21, Roopville, GA 30170*

945. Fred L. and Anne C. Richards

Fred (Luther) and Anne (Cohen) Richards moved to Carrollton in 1975 from Greeley, Colorado, to share a teaching position in the Psychology Department at the State University of West Georgia (then West Georgia College). Fred established a private practice in 1978 at 309 Tanner Street, became a Licensed Professional Counselor, and in 1998 was chosen Georgia Counselor of the Year by the Licensed Professional Counselors Association of Georgia. Anne, who studied with such well-known psychologists as Arthur W. Combs, Sidney M. Jourard and Abraham H. Maslow, remained on the faculty of the university for twenty-six years, retiring in May, 2001. The Richards had no children of their own, but involved themselves in numerous activities and projects contributing to the growth and development of many in the college/university and Carrollton communities.

The Long/Richards home during an infrequent winter snow.

Anne was active in the American Association of University Professors (AAUP), served on numerous faculty committees, authored or co-authored several books and articles on psychology and education, and was recognized for her teaching excellence. Fred, active in the Carrollton Kiwanis Club since 1978, was twice chosen Outstanding Kiwanian of the Year and was honored as a George E. Hixon Fellow of Kiwanis International, the Kiwanis Club's most distinguished award. As Club Herald of the Kiwanis Club, Fred has roasted/introduced guests to the club since 1980.

Fred and Anne Richards circa 1985.

Considered something of a local character, Fred was involved in community theatre, was a founding board member of the Community Children's Home (Alice's House), and over the years has been seen dressed as a clown, Santa, a rabbit or Charles Dickens' Spirit of Christmas Present while driving his 72 Dodge pick-up covered with bumper stickers.

Fred Richards and his bumper-sticker truck (circa 1995)

In 1979, the Richards bought the property at 301 Dixie Street, becoming the second family to live in the home built in 1914 (at a reported cost of $14,000) by Benjamin M. Long and Helen Long. The house is a classic example of the Craftsman style popular in Carrollton in the 1910s, a style emphasizing simplicity, craftsmanship and heavy, solid construction. A couple of years before her death, Mrs. Long told the Richards that as a teenager she was taken to Atlanta by an aunt and told to pick out lighting fixtures. She chose four matching brass chandeliers which were put away by her family until several years later when she and her husband built their "honeymoon house on Dixie Street." The chandeliers remain to this day, lighting the three front rooms and downstairs hall of the house.

In 1999, both Fred and Anne were named Paul Harris Fellows by the Carrollton Rotary Club in recognition of their community service. *Submitted by: Fred and Anne Richards, 301 Dixie Street, Carrollton, GA 30117*
Sources: Fred and Anne Richards

946. Grace Talley Richards

Grace Talley Richards was born May 18, 1918 in Villa Rica, Georgia. Grace's parents were Walter Monroe Talley and Mary Lenora Roberds, both natives of Georgia. Mr. Talley was born in Powder Springs and Miss Roberds was born in Villa Rica. Walter and Mary Roberds were also the parents of Cecil Fae, George Earnest, Mary Rebekah, William Edgar, Walter Lewis, and Sara Roberds.

Grace Richards' maternal grandparents were Leonidas Roberds who was born in Carroll County August 22, 1847, and was a physician/surgeon and the son of Thomas Howard Roberds who was also a physician who practiced in Carroll County for forty-six years; and Martha Emiline Cheeves. Grace Richards' paternal grandparents were Alonza Henry Talley born in Newton County on February 21, 1847, and Eugenia Ann Green born in Paulding County August 04, 1845.

Grace Talley graduated from Villa Rica High School in 1934. She graduated from Georgia State College for Women with a B.F.A. degree in music and a minor in education in 1938. After teaching music for one year in south Georgia she married Hugh W. Richards, a Carroll County native, on June 10, 1939. They moved to Carrollton where Hugh was in business with his brother, Roy Richards, constructing power lines.

Grace and Hugh had two children. Thomas Talley Richards, born October 18, 1940. Tom Richards graduated from Georgia Tech in 1962 and received his MBA from Harvard Business School in 1964. On October 15, 1966, Tom married Cornelia Kingman Storey who was born September 24, 1942, the daughter of Frederick George Storey Jr. of Columbus, Georgia and Jean Kingman Lucas of Berwyn, Maryland. Cornelia received her bachelor's degree in fine arts from the Atlanta College of Art. Tom and Cornelia have two daughters: (1) Margaret Cunningham "Puddin" Richards born September 29, 1969; married Patrick Earl Bass of Leslie, Georgia; their daughter, Grace Talley Bass was born October 10, 1998. (2) Cornelia Lucas "Nelia" Richards born May 21, 1973 and now lives in New York.

Grace Talley Richards

The daughter of Hugh and Grace Richards is Sally Ann Richards born January 28, 1947. Sally Anne was a popular cheerleader at Carrollton High School and after her graduation attended Converse College in South Carolina. Sally Anne married John Patrick Malloy and together they had two children: (1) John Patrick Malloy Jr. born June 6, 1967; married Carol Ann Carter, daughter of William Preston Carter and Patricia Ann Chappell Carter, who was born October 7, 1967; one daughter Zoe Frances Malloy born June 26, 1999. (2) Mary Amanda "Mandy" Malloy born March 9, 1972; married Peter Maierhofer on March 22, 1997, at Callaway Gardens, Peter the son of Mrs. Sandy Stephens and Dr. Richard Maierhofer; Mandy earned her BA degree in art education in 1996 and is an art teacher; one daughter, Madison Grace born September 8, 2000. Sally Anne is currently married to Bruce Bobick who is the head of the art department at the State University of West Georgia.

Grace Richards was a member of the First Baptist Church of Carrollton for over forty years and was organist for approximately thirty-five years. She was a member of the Arts Study Club and Lit-Mu. She served as a trustee of the West Georgia College Foundation. She was a charter member of the Trinity Baptist Church.

Grace Talley Richards died January 27, 1999, at her home in Carrollton. She was predeceased by her husband and six siblings. She is buried at Carroll Memory Gardens. *Submitted by: Tom Richards, Carrollton, GA*

947. Hugh Willie Richards

Hugh Richards was born April 8, 1914, in Carroll County, Georgia, to Thomas Wiley Richards born May 21, 1870, and Ida Myrtle Stovall born October 30, 1888, both of Carroll County. Hugh Richards' paternal grandparents were William Thomas Richards born September 7, 1838, in Randolph County, Georgia and Nancy Elizabeth Boyd born July 15, 1834, in Meriwether County, Georgia. Hugh Richards' maternal grandparents were Elishia Thomas Stovall born August 31, 1849, in Douglas County, Georgia and Armanda Elizabeth Ayres born July 2, 1866, in Carroll County.

Hugh Willie Richards

Hugh Richards graduated from the 4th District A&M School in 1931 and then attended Georgia Tech where he remained until 1935. In that year, Hugh and his father, Wiley Richards, established the company of T.W. Richards and Son, a lumber and construction business. Hugh also joined his brother Roy in 1937 to form Richards Brothers, the company that would erect the first rural electric lines in Carroll County. After the death of his father in 1943, Hugh Richards established the H.W. Richards Lumber Company and expanded his retail business supply stores to Carrollton, Douglasville, and Tallapoosa. Hugh's principal business was the construction of homes, which he did continuously, except during World War II, from 1939 until his death.

During the war years of 1942-1945, his company's entire efforts were devoted to building ammunition boxes and crates for the government. During World War II, due to the shortage of local lumber, German prisoners of war at Ft. McPherson were transferred to Carrollton daily to help with the production of these ammunition boxes and crates. During the Korean and Vietnam wars, Hugh also produced similar wooden boxes for shipping ammunition.

Hugh Richards served for ten years as a member of the Carrollton City Council. He was a deacon in the First Baptist Church, a Mason, and a Shriner, a member of Carrollton Lions Club, and served as president of the Carrollton Junior Chamber of Commerce. He was one of the founders of the West Georgia College Foundation and the first chairman of A-Day, an annual fund raising effort for the college. In 1963, Hugh Richards was presented the Founders Day Award at West Georgia College for "Outstanding Service to Education".

Hugh Richards was also one of the founders and directors of the American Heritage Life Insurance Company of Jacksonville, Florida; a founder and director of Haralson Federal Savings and Loan of Bremen; and a director of the West Georgia National Bank.

Hugh married Grace Annette Talley on June 10, 1939. Grace was the daughter of Mary Leonora Roberds and Walter Monroe Talley of Villa Rica, Georgia. They were prominent people in church, civic and business affairs of that town. Together Hugh and Grace Richards had two children. Thomas Talley Richards, born October 18, 1940. Tom Richards graduated from Georgia Tech in 1962 and received his MBA from Harvard Business School in 1964. On October 15, 1966, Tom married Cornelia Kingman Storey who was born September 24, 1942, the daughter of Frederick George Storey Jr. of Columbus, Georgia and Jean Kingman Lucas of Berwyn, Maryland. Cornelia received her Bachlor's degree in fine arts from the Atlanta College of Art. Tom and Cornelia have two daughters: (1) Margaret Cunningham "Puddin" Richards born September 29, 1969; married Patrick Earl Bass of Leslie, Georgia; their daughter, Grace Talley Bass was born October 10, 1998. (2) Cornelia Lucas "Nelia" Richards born May 21, 1973 and now lives in New York.

The daughter of Hugh and Grace Richards is Sally Anne Richards born January 28, 1947. Sally Anne was a popular cheerleader at Carrollton High School and after her graduation attended Converse College in South Carolina. Sally Anne married John Patrick Malloy and together they had two children: (1) John Patrick Malloy Jr. born June 6, 1967; married Carol Ann Carter, daughter of William Preston Carter and Patricia Ann Chappell Carter, who was born October 7, 1967; one daughter Zoe Frances Malloy born June 26, 1999. (2) Mary Amanda "Mandy" Malloy born March 9, 1972; married Peter Maierhofer on March 22, 1997, at Callaway Gardens, Peter the son of Mrs. Sandy Stephens and Dr. Richard Maierhofer; Mandy earned her BA degree in art education in 1996 and is an art teacher; one daughter, Madison Grace born September 8, 2000. Sally Anne is currently married to Bruce Bobick who is the head of the art department at the State University of West Georgia.

Hugh Richards died December 1, 1983, and is buried at Carroll Memory Gardens. *Submitted by: Sally Bobick, Carrollton, GA*

948. Jethro Gordon Richards Sr. Family

Our Richards family was among the earliest settlers of Carroll County. Tom Richards (my great-great-grandfather born circa 1799) was the founder of this Richards family in Carroll County. He married Mary Lee (Polly) Tate in 1818. They moved here from Morgan County, settled a forest home on the southeastern side of the county in the community of Lick Skillet, a famous Justice Court ground about two miles from where Mt. Zion Church in Douglas County now stands. We know that the fourth of their eleven children, John Perry (my great-grandfather), was born in Carroll County in 1825.

John Perry married Nancy Elizabeth Camp in 1848. He was a Civil War soldier in Company K 30th Georgia Infantry. The company, comprising local men, was called the Chattahoochee Volunteers. His brother, William B. Richards, was their Captain. John Perry and Elizabeth had twelve children.

Their third child, Robert Washington Richards (my grandfather, 1853-1920), was regarded as a very smart man. He was well-read in matters of law and could quickly "figure a bale of cotton in his head." He and his wife Cecelia (Celie) Jones (married 1874) raised their ten children near Whitesburg.

My father, Jethro Gordon Richards Sr. (1886-1962), was the seventh child of Robert Washington and Celie Richards. Gordon's first wife Mattie Copeland, infant daughter Mildred, and second wife Ethel Jones, all died during or shortly after childbirth. Jethro Gordon Richards Jr., born May 6, 1914, to Ethel, lived with his mother's sister, Miss Edna Jones.

Gordon was working in Akron, Ohio, in October 1917 when they inducted him into the army, the only one of six brothers inducted. He was a sergeant in Company C, 21st Bn., US Guards, Army, World War I when discharged in January of 1919 by reason of "demobilization of organization." After his discharge, he returned to Whitesburg and married Annie Eva (Johnnie) Phillips in 1921 and farmed the rest of his life doing the work he loved. Primary crops were cotton and corn. After he became partly disabled, he raised cattle. Fortunately, this enabled him to qualify for Social Security benefits when farmers became eligible. I, Imogene Richards Frazier, was born May 4, 1925.

J.G. Richards weighing cotton

My father was an exceptional farmer. Plowing, planting and tending crops was done solely with mule-drawn equipment. Roosevelt Robinson (see picture) and family lived on the farm as hired help. Roosevelt was furnished a house, land to use for gardening, and paid 75 cents a day in the 1930s. Junior got 50 cents. Geannie helped at the house.

To provide food and recreation, Gordon fished the Chattahoochee and hunted wild game. He often trained bird dogs for other people. He also killed hogs, ground corn meal, made sorghum syrup, and had fresh milk, butter and vegetables. He grew such productive vegetable gardens that I mused he could have made a fortune if he'd had an available market.

After the demise of his Model T Ford in the early 1930s, we walked or rode the wagon for transportation. Neighbors took us to Carrollton occasionally. Atlanta was a distant place. Hard times, also happy times for my parents. I was blessed with doting parents and a host of dear relatives.

My brother Jethro G. Richards Jr. (1914-1966) was a skilled automotive mechanic. He married Ethelene Milam, a beautiful local girl. They had two children, Delano (1936), and Anthony (1944). Their mother, Ethelene, provided most of the following information.

Delano married Grace Chappel and they had two daughters, Lynn and Ginger. Ginger has one daughter, Alexandria. Ginger, Lynn and Alexandria live in Peachtree City. Delano is a retired State of Georgia employee and lives in Griffin, Georgia.

Anthony married Vickie Lyle, lives in Fayetteville, and they have two grown children, David and Dawn; no grandchildren. Tony retired from Delta Airlines and is now in business for himself.

I, Imogene Richards Frazier, (Gordon's daughter) married Kenneth Frazier, had three children, six grandchildren, and five great-grandchildren.

My son, Clay Richards Frazier, was born November 1950 and died November 1992. Clay was a member of the Army Band when he and wife Cheryl Hunt Frazier had their daughter Sera in 1970. Sera (now thirty) lives in Woodstock, Georgia, with husband Dale Jones and children Amberleigh (age eleven) and Nicholas (age three).

My daughter, Marsha Frazier Harpe Robinson, was born September 1953 and died October 2000. She and husband Reginald Harpe Jr. had two sons: Reginald born 1979, and Jesse Burson Harpe born 1971. Reginald (Rusty) has one son Tiler Blake Harpe (1998).

My one surviving child, Kenneth Gregory Frazier, was born November 1946. He and his wife Tresea Loveday Frazier live on the family farm my parents bought in 1942. Gordon and Johnnie would be so pleased. Greg retired from TVA, Knoxville, Tennessee.

Gregory Frazier has three daughters — Lisa, Bethany, and Stacie — born in 1971, 1974, and 1978 to Greg and Diane King Frazier. Lisa Rosemary lives in Knoxville, Tennessee, with husband Todd Koob and infant son Nicholas. Bethany lives in Florida and has one son Daniel, age seven. Stacie is a college senior in Murfreesboro, Tennessee.

I hope that my children and grandchildren will keep and continue to expand this record for their children. *Submitted by: Imogene Richards Frazier, P.O. Box 124, Whitesburg, GA 30184*

949. Robert Washington and Ceclia Jones Richards Family

This is the Robert Washington Richards and Ceclia Jones Richards family. Robert was a son of John Perry and Nancy Elizabeth Camp Richards and a grandson of Thomas and Polly (Mary) Tate Richards, who were some of the earlier settlers in the County Line District of Carroll County.

The children of Robert and Ceclia were Benjamine, Eugene, Frances, John Perry, Cicero C., Gordon, Mattie, Bertha, Reuben, and Dora Lee. There are still many direct descendants of this family living in Carroll County today.

Bertha married Thomas Wesley Music in 1913. Their children were Doris, Mattie, Ceclia, Mable, Weselyn, and Robert.

Doris married Sherman Boyd, son of Oscar and Lelah Crawford Boyd. Their children were Janice, Reuben, Carolyn, Thomas, and Delano.

In 1964, Thomas married Ressie G. Boatright, daughter of Cecil A. Boatright and Ressie McElwaney Boatright. Their children are Steven and Kevin. Members of these families still live in the County Line District of Carroll County today. *Submitted by: Ressie G. Boyd, 242 Old Five Notch Road, Whitesburg, GA 30185*

Family of Robert Washington and Ceclia Jones Richards. Early 1900s.

950. Roy and Alice Richards Family

The Richards family of Carroll County, Georgia, are descendants of the immigrant George Richards Sr. who was born in England in 1727 and who served in the British Royal Navy. Thus, it was as a naval officer that George Richards Sr. first came to the shores of America. He liked it so much here that he settled in Virginia. He married Tabitha Hudson, the daughter of Robert Hudson II and Martha Hancock, in Nansemond County, Virginia, before 1765. Together they had six sons. George Richard Sr. served in the French and Indian wars, and he also served under General George Washington during the American Revolution. He was with Washington in Maryland at Braddock's defeat in 1755. All of the six sons of George Richards Sr. served in the American Revolution from North Carolina.

Roy Richards, founder of Southwire in Carrollton, Georgia

In December of 1760, George Richards received from the Earl of Granville a Royal Land Grant in Granville County of the Royal Province of North Carolina. This grant consisted of 430 acres on both sides of Fox Swamp. In 1761 George Richards Sr. appears in records in Granville, and this larger county gave land to Bute County in 1764. Bute was dissolved in 1769 and then Franklin County was formed from lands of Bute in 1779.

One of the sons of George Richards Sr. was named Thomas Cupples Richards. We know of one other son, George Richards Jr., who was born in 1758 in North Carolina. George Richards Sr. died on 27 July 1818 in Franklin County, North Carolina. His obituary appeared in a Raleigh, North Carolina, newspaper on 31 July 1818.

William Thomas Richards, 1838-1917

There was another by the name of George Richards who served in the American Revolution though it is not a proven fact that he was related to our George Richards Sr. This other George Richards was born in 1759 in Virginia and has been recognized by the Daughters of the American Revolution (DAR) for his service as an American spy against the British during the war for independence. This George married Catherine Bush and died after 1833. He is mentioned in order to prevent any confusion between the two George Richards since they were both contemporaries, and at times appear in records together.

George Richards Jr. married Lydia "Liddy" Vinson who was the daughter of Frances and David Vinson Jr. (died in 1810 in Franklin County, North Carolina).

Nancy Elizabeth Boyd Richards, 1834-1891

Many of the Revolutionary war soldiers were given land grants in Washington County, Georgia, and George Richards Jr. and his wife, Lydia, were among them. After the American Revolution the Richards settled near the historic site where the Treaty of Shoulderbone Creek had been negotiated with the hostile Creek Indians in 1786. The land along this creek was highly prized for its rich dirt for farming. Records show that George Richards Jr. was also given a land grant for his service in the American Revolution, but the deed was not recorded until 1807. In 1786, Greene County was formed from parts of Washington, Oglethorpe, and Wilkes Counties. So the Richards family, though they had not moved, found themselves living in the newly-formed Greene County.

George Richards Jr. and Lydia were the parents of a large family. They gave many of their sons Old Testament names. The following children were born to them: (1) Jedidiah born circa 1790 married Nancy and died 9 June 1847, leaving a will in Greene County, Georgia; (2) Tabitha born 27 September 1791 and married John H. Puckett; (3) Azariah born circa 1795 married Leila Wood 30 October 1820; (4) Terah E. born circa 1798 married Lucy Bates 17 December 1818; (5) Uriah born 1813 married Martha Wheeler; (6) Matilda married James Harden 27 March 1821; (7) Della married James Bruce 2 May 1816; (8) Priscilla born 1805 married Ephraim Bruce 21 November 1822; (9) Martha married Coalson Copeland; (10) Jane died 1814; (11) a daughter, name unknown, who married an O'Rear; (12) possibly a son named John. All marriages took place in Greene County, Georgia. The names are derived from the will of George Richards Jr., and his death occurred sometime prior to 1823. The daughters, Jane and Martha, were minors at the time of his death. In 1828, the heirs signed a deed to their mother, Lydia, which represented her widow's dowry for land on Shoulderbone Creek.

Terah Richards is a rather colorful ancestor in that he had three different wives, twenty-two children, and seemed to have moved to whichever area was the newest frontier to tame. He married Lucy Bates in Greene County, Georgia, in 1818 and by 1827 was living in Monroe County, Georgia. It was from there that Terah Richards participated in the 1827 Land Lottery. This was the lottery that divided the lands into Carroll, Troup, Coweta, Lee and Muscogee Counties. These were the old Creek Indian lands, their treasured hunting grounds for many generations.

Thomas Wylie Richards and Mary Housworth

Terah Richards drew Land Lot #215 in District #28 in Lee County. His mother, Lydia, as the widow of a Revolutionary War soldier, also drew land in Lee County. Sumter County was created out of Lee County, and it was here that the first son, Obadiah Richards, was born 10 August 1819.

Joshua D. Richards was born 27 March 1821, and Lucy died shortly after his birth. Joshua Richards would grow up and eventually migrate to Florida where he died in Lake City, Florida, on 18 November 1894. The names of any other brothers and sisters of Obediah Richards are not known.

About a year after Lucy died, Terah Richards married a second time. This wife's name is not known, but it is believed they married in Monroe County, Georgia. They had the following children: a daughter name unknown, James, Jehu, Joseph, William, Nancy, David, Elizabeth, Sarah, George, and Pamela Hudson Richards (born 1847). It is believed that Terah's second wife died before 1850. Terah then married a third wife, Naomi, who was born in South Carolina. With Naomi, Terah had the following children: Naomi Hudson, Sally, Tabitha, Fairaby, Drucilla, Uriah, Perry, Susan, Rebecca, and Wiley and John (twins).

By 1850, Terah had acquired 500 acres of land, and his grown children lived all around his property. The family tradition is that Terah Richards was a prosperous man and proof of this was that he owned the only crosscut saw in the community. A crosscut saw was considered a luxury item in 1850, and it also shows that Terah had an inclination towards mechanics and having the proper tools for accomplishing any job, a trait that would certainly carry forth in the future generations of Richards men.

Thomas Wiley Richards in his first auto, a 1907 Brush

Sometime after 1850, Terah sold his land in Sumter County, Georgia, and moved to Coffee County, Alabama. After residing on his land for six years, he learned that his deed was false. The property had been previously granted to a school. Terah then moved to Pike County, Alabama, where he died. Terah Richards was buried at Mt. Zion Church in Coffee County, Alabama. Terah's oldest son, Obediah Richards, had left home as a young man "to go west" and had ended up living in Randolph County, Georgia, which was still inhabited by Creek Indians. In 1825, the Treaty of Indian Springs had ceded these lands to the state of Georgia. Lee County had been created in 1826, a very large county. The following year, Lee had given up land for the creation of Randolph County. The territory was declared open to settlers and hundreds came. There was a log fort, a double log house with just one room created for the safety of women and children during Indian raids. A great battle was fought by the Georgia militia on Echowanochaway Creek on July 27, 1836, and the Creek Indians were defeated.

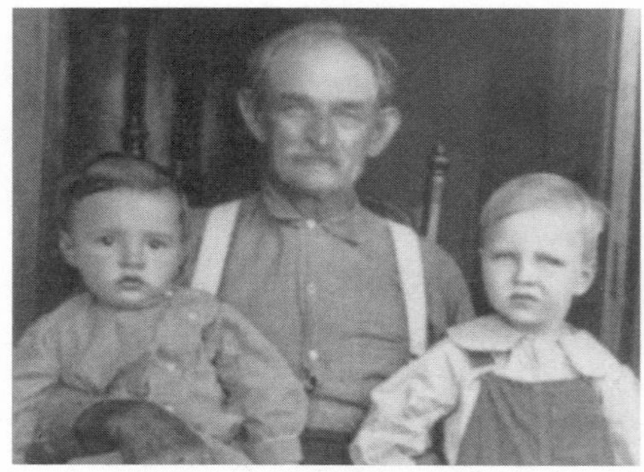

Roy Richards sitting on lap of George Crook who ran the planing mill.

It was in this time period in Randolph County, Georgia, that Obediah Richards married Sarah Caroline Lambert, daughter of William and Mary Lambert, on 15 June 1835. Sarah was born on 24 January 1818. The newlyweds lived for several years in the home of the bride's parents. Later, Obediah moved his family to McDonough in Henry County, and by 1850 he appeared in the DeKalb County, Georgia, census. The Obediah Richards family lived near Buckhead when Atlanta was a small village known as Marthasville.

Sometime before 1850, Obediah's father-in-law, William Lambert, had bought a tract of land in Carroll County, Georgia. In 1851, William Lambert sold to Edward R. Burns of Henry County for $500 Land Lot #39 in the 5th District. Lindsey Holland and E.T. Lambert witnessed the deed. Some of William Lambert's land was deeded to William's own son, George R. Lambert. Later, George Lambert sold this property to Obediah Richards on 26 August 1854. Obediah and Sarah probably moved to Carroll County so that they could be closer to his wife's parents. The property to which they moved is the farm now known as the Tyre Holland farm near Hulett. In 1858, William Lambert died and his widow continued to live at the Lambert home place.

Obediah Richards died on 18 May 1874 and was buried in the Lambert Family Cemetery in Carroll County. Obediah's wife, Sarah Lambert Richards, died in 1892 as a result of burns she received when her long skirt caught fire. Sarah Lambert Richards was buried at Powell's Chapel in Carroll County. The reason Sarah was not buried beside her husband was because the Lambert property by this time had changed hands, and the new owner would not allow any more burials to take place in the Lambert Family cemetery.

Together Obediah and Sarah Lambert Richards had six children: William Thomas born 7 September 1838; Sarah born 1844 and married Richard Henderson; George W. born 1846 (all children were born in Randolph County, Georgia); Tompkins; John F. (1849) (both born in Henry County, Georgia); and James K.P. Richards. George W. Richards was a Confederate soldier who was captured in Pennsylvania and settled there when he was released after the war.

William Thomas Richards, like his father before him, was a farmer. He owned several hundred acres of land, but the harsh conditions of Reconstruction forced him to sell almost all of it. However, in 1884, he was able to buy a farm in Hulett on the east side of the county, and there he settled. William married Nancy Elizabeth Boyd on 11 July 1861 in Carroll County. Nancy was born 15 September 1834, the daughter of Joseph Boyd and Jennie McGinnis Boyd of Meriwether County, Georgia. The Boyds gave the newlyweds fifty acres of land on which they built a large log home. This was located in the Powell's Chapel-Flat Rock community in Carroll County.

Together William Thomas Richards and Nancy Elizabeth Boyd had two sons and two daughters: (1) Josephine Elizabeth born 19 August 1864 and married Joseph Peek on 29 July 1888, died 29 March 1948; (2) Charles Forest born 16 August 1867 and married first Helen May Hammond 28 December 1892, married second to Ella Foy in 1940; (3) Thomas Wiley born 21 May 1870 (more on his family to follow); (4) Ella Jane born 4 April 1873 and married George Chance on 7 September 1891. Nancy Boyd Richards died 26 March 1891 and was buried at Powell's Chapel in Carroll County.

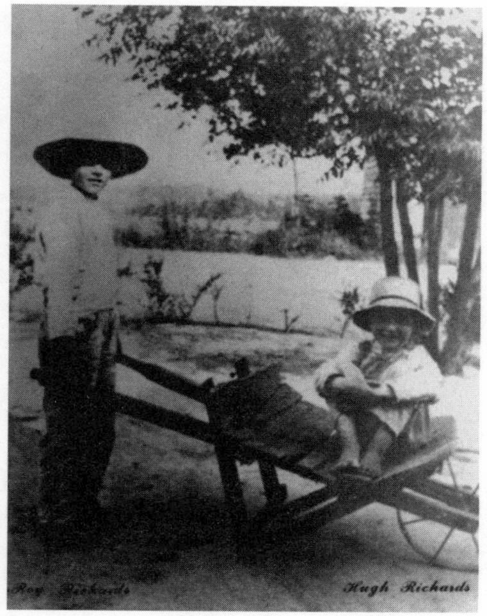

Roy pushing brother Hugh in wheelbarrow

William Thomas Richards had married a second time by 1893 in Carroll County. His second wife was Dollie Millians, daughter of William and Harriett Millians of Newnan. Children with the second wife, Dollie, were Hulette Hall Richards born 18 August 1894 and Ruby Richards born 3 July 1898. Hulette Hall Richards married Ethel Smith. Ruby Richards married Irby W. Keaton on 18 June 1922 and they were the parents of Hoyt W. Keaton and Hyatt A. Keaton (twins) born 31 March 1924.

William Thomas Richards was exempt from service as a soldier in the Confederate Army because he performed a much needed service in his blacksmithy shop. Blacksmiths repaired wheels for wagons and shoed horses which were the main mode of transportation. Blacksmiths also forged Confederate swords in their shops and repaired the much needed weaponry, such as guns and cannon, used in the Confederacy.

After the Civil War in 1873, the Richards family moved to South Street in Carrollton, purchasing a home from Eli Benson, who was Carrollton's first Mayor. William Thomas Richards liked to say that his family and the railroad had both arrived in Carrollton at the same time. The Savannah, Griffin, and North Alabama line had just been completed to Carrollton. The back lot of the Richards home adjoined the S.G. & N.A. railroad tracks.

Charles Forest Richards would later say that "it was while living in this home that my brother Wiley first displayed his remarkable mechanical genius." Wiley Richards built what is today called a model railroad complete with switches and turntable. Like Richards men before him, he obviously had an aptitude for engineering. During this time, Wiley's father opened a mercantile store facing the old brick courthouse in the center of the square.

The days of Reconstruction proved to be hard times for everyone, and William Thomas Richards had allowed many farmers to buy on credit. When they were unable to pay, W.T. Richards sold his store and moved to a farm north of town where he operated a wheat threshing machine. His son, Wiley, loved working with anything mechanical so he enjoyed traveling about the countryside with the threshing machine. His neighbors treated him to the "best of fare" for threshing their wheat. It was customary for the neighbors to feed the wheat threshers two meals a day.

Wiley's brother, Charles Forest Richards, studied medicine under Dr. Smith for two years. Later he decided that he preferred the field of education, and he became a teacher. He taught school at Bay Springs, Cross Plains, and Sand Hill. In 1918, C.F. Richards initiated first adult classes in agriculture in Georgia. He later moved to Mitchell County, Georgia, where he continued to teach until his retirement.

As a young man, Wiley Richards left the family farm to seek work in Newnan. By happenstance, he met a Mr. Dresser who was in the process of installing the first private electrical plant in Newnan. Mr. Dresser was impressed by Wiley's inquisitive mind and eagerness to work. He hired Wiley and put him to the task of setting electrical poles and stringing wire. After this job was completed, Wiley became involved in designing, building, and operating the first power plant in Newnan. Wiley invited his brother C.F. to come over to watch him flip the switch "the first time the lights were turned on in Newnan, Georgia." Wiley Richards worked for Mr. Dresser for eight years as manager and operations engineer. After his employer's death, Wiley went into business for himself and became a pioneer in the electrification of western Georgia.

Wiley Richards married Mary Housworth in 1896. She was the daughter of Abraham Housworth and Celathia Lassetter. Wiley and Mary Richards had the following children: (1) Wellborn born 11 October 1898, died 11 December 1898; (2) Barton born 17 July 1901, died 30 December 1902; (3) Dora Elizabeth born 21 October 1902, died 2 January 1924; (4) Frank Cole born 2 October 1904 married Katherine Milligan; (5) Harry Thomas born 18 September 1908. Mary Housworth Richards died in childbirth on 1 October 1909 at the age of thirty-two and was buried alongside her infant sons at St. Paul's Church Cemetery. Both Frank and Harry later moved to California.

The next year on 28 August 1910, Wiley Richards married Ida Myrtice Stovall, the daughter of Elisha Tom Stovall and Armendie Elizabeth Ayers Stovall. Together Wiley and Myrtice had two sons, Roy Richards and Hugh W. Richards. Roy Richards was born 11 April 1912 and Hugh Willie Richards was born 8 April 1914.

Both Richards boys attended the public schools of Carroll and Douglas counties. Also, both boys went to work at the family sawmill on the Dog River. It was Roy's job at age ten to fire the boiler. Then, when Roy was fourteen years old, his father put him in charge of the whole sawmill. Wiley went off to see about other business pursuits, so young Roy was left in charge of hiring and firing the work crews. He also had to meet the payroll, so his business judgment of men and events was sharpened at an early age.

It was not all work and no play for the Richards boys in growing up. They loved to swim in the nearby swimming hole. Roy's mechanical genius was displayed early on according to Addie Ault, one of his neighbors from down the road. Miss Addie said "Roy always had some idea rolling around in his head." When the boys were learning to swim — and there was no such thing as water wings back in those days — Roy came up with the idea to tie gourds to their arms to keep them afloat, and it worked!

Another time, Miss Addie said that Roy and Hugh as little boys had decided to build an airplane. No one much believed their efforts could produce from an old Model-T engine a machine that would really fly. But sure enough, the boys managed to get the plane cranked. It went bolting across a field, almost lifted into the air, and then wrecked into a tree. Miss Addie continued, "No one was hurt, at least not until Miss Myrtle, their mother, found out. She fanned their tails with a peach branch!"

Roy took a year off from school when he was fourteen to manage the sawmill, but he would later say that this experience was invaluable to him. In the fall of 1928, when he was fifteen, Roy attended the Martha Berry School in Rome, Georgia. This was a school established for the children of Georgia who could not afford to further their education. At this school, they could work on the farm or perform other chores to earn their education. While at Berry, Roy was put in charge of the sawmill, something he was expert with by now. This is how Roy Richards worked his way through school at Berry.

The next year when he was sixteen, Roy attended the 4th District A&M School and completed his high school work there in 1931. While at the A&M School in Carrollton, he was greatly influenced by his teacher, Dr. Irvine S. Ingram, who was also principal. Dr. Ingram felt that Roy was the kind of student who could go to great heights if given the opportunity to further his education. He encouraged Roy to go to Georgia Tech and helped him apply for a scholarship there. Roy would say in later years that he was indebted to Dr. Ingram for encouraging him to go to Georgia Tech, "for I never would have gone without his insisting."

Hugh, Miss Myrtie, Wylie, and Roy at home place in Hulett

Roy Richards entered Georgia Tech in the fall of 1931. Here he further proved what a clear and disciplined mind he had. He was totally focused on getting the best education he could, and he wanted to find some way "to put all the skills he was learning into practical everyday use and to make things better for everyone." While Roy was at Tech, he worked his way through school by waiting on tables in the dining hall. Roy graduated from Tech with honors in 1935 with a B.S. degree in mechanical engineering. Roy was a member of Pi Tau Sigma, an honorary society for mechanical engineers. He maintained a high scholastic record at Tech and participated in many campus activities. He was inducted into Omicron Delta Kappa, a national leadership society for college men.

Roy Richards, age 14, manager of his father's sawmill

Roy stayed very busy in his early years. First, he established Richards Brothers with his brother Hugh, a company that could bid on the many electrical projects about to come into being with the Rural Electrification Administration (REA). Roy's company won the bid to build the first power lines in Carroll County. The first power was turned on in Carroll County on 31 July 1937. However, Roy's important job was suddenly interrupted with the advent of World War II. Roy was advanced to captain in the U.S. Army, and he was a professor of military science at Georgia Tech. He trained the Coastal Artillery Guards until the end of the war in 1945.

After the war, Roy returned to Carrollton and immediately became involved in the community project of building a modern hospital, one adequate for the 40,000 people in Carroll County. The doors to Tanner Memorial Hospital were opened on 30 October 1949. The next day, the doors were opened to the wire manufacturing company Roy had been building at the same time that the hospital was being built. This was Southwire.

After the war, Roy wanted to return to setting power poles and stringing wire to bring more electricity to people of the South, but there was a shortage of wire. Roy had been told that it might be four years before he could get any more wire. Roy and the people of the South did not want to be this long without power. So Roy established Southwire, the first wire manufacturing company in the South. Roy quickly became a young executive at the head of a million dollar company. He stayed busy with the Young Presidents Organization and attended many business seminars at Harvard to keep up to date on how to deal with the management and finances of big business.

Roy Richards reached the age of forty and still had not married. People were beginning to wonder if he ever would marry. In the late 1950's, the ladies' clubs of Carrollton seemed to think it was their job to try to get Roy married. "He was smart, good-looking, and charming, and every single woman around wanted to go out with him," Judge Bob Tisinger said. But there was only one who ever captured the heart of Roy Richards, and that was the lovely, dark-haired Alice Huffard of Bluefield, Virginia.

Roy met Alice in Atlanta where she was working after her graduation in 1952 from the University of North Carolina at Chapel Hill. Alice attended Stephens College and earned her degree in communications and journalism from Chapel Hill. She was sharing an apartment with several other recent female grads. Their apartment was behind the governor's mansion and was called "The House of Flowers" in reference to a play that was very popular and currently running on Broadway. Joe Cumming wrote in his booklet *Roy Richards, the Legend, the Legacy,* that during these days, Alice Huffard was in the happy go-working girl-social whirl of Atlanta.

A mutual friend, Lib Hunt, decided that Alice and Roy had a lot in common and might enjoy meeting each other. Finally, Roy and Alice had arranged to have a blind date, which turned out to be quite a story. Roy was on the way to Atlanta to pick up Alice when his car broke down. He had to send back to Carrollton and ask someone to bring him a car that could get him there. He tried to phone Alice but her phone was out of order. When he finally arrived at Alice's apartment three hours late, she had already prepared for bed and had retired. Roy had certainly learned much about the art of diplomacy with the business of his wire manufacturing mill, and he perfected the art on this date! Roy finally explained to Alice exactly what happened, and that he really did want her to get dressed and still go out on a date with him. And so, Alice did.

Roy was just beginning his plant in Brazil at this time, and he was frequently gone on business to South America, even for a month at a time. So it was often a "long-distance romance" but it was the beginning of a beautiful romance that would last a lifetime. Roy was forty-five years old and Alice was twenty-six, but the age difference never mattered — not in the beginning, nor throughout their lives together. Alice was a vibrant and beautiful person, inside and out, and a sweetness of nature was a hallmark of her character. Alice was the very sunlight of the morning to Roy Richards, and he had found real love, the one ingredient that had been missing from his otherwise full life. Chester Roush, who was Roy's friend and early sales manager at Southwire said, "Roy was brighter and more enthusiastic than I have ever seen him when he told me that he and Alice were to be married."

Like Roy, Alice had a strong sense of self — who she was, her own code of honor, what she wanted for goals in her life. Although this was before women had equal rights, Alice Huffard was a young lady who was intelligent and very much a person of her own mind and ready to stand up and be counted for any cause she believed in. It is no wonder that Roy Richards was smitten with Alice and saw in her the perfect helpmate of his life.

The Huffards were a prominent old family from Bluefield, Virginia. James Hudson Huffard was born 3 September 1899 in Tazewell County, Bluefield, Virginia. In November of 1929, James Hudson Huffard married Frances Elizabeth Coyner of Marion, Virginia. Frances was born 2 December 1905. Three children were born to James Hudson Huffard Sr. and Frances Elizabeth Coyner: (1) Alice Coyner born 19 June 1931 and married Roy Richards; (2) Nancy Valentine born 30 July 1934 and married Edgar Gentry Barton; (3) James Hudson Jr. born 24 February 1938 and married Judy Krupis. James Hudson Huffard Jr. was the third generation of his family to run the family furniture business, the Chicago House Furnishing Company of Bluefield, Virginia. James H. Huffard Sr. was very active in civic affairs and served as mayor of Bluefield for thirty years. His son, James H. Huffard Jr., also served as mayor of Bluefield for five years.

James Hudson Huffard Sr. was the son of Samuel Nye Huffard and Alice Elizabeth Yost who was born 1882 and was the daughter of Henry Yost of Tazewell County, Virginia. The S.N. Huffards were prominent in business and had established the Chicago House Furnishing Company about 1900. Frances Elizabeth Coyner was the daughter of Elliott Kemper Coyner and Jamie Valentine. Frances Coyner married James Hudson Huffard Sr. in November 1929. Frances Coyner Huffard died May 1951 in Chattanooga, Tennessee, and was buried in Marion, Smythe County, Virginia. James Hudson Huffard Sr. died in November of 1971, and he was buried in Bluefield, Virginia.

Roy Richards, U.S. Army, World War II

Roy Richards married Alice Coyner Huffard 25 January 1958 at St. Luke's Episcopal Church in Atlanta, Georgia. Roy and Alice had seven children with an interesting assortment of personalities. All the children grew up taking job responsibilities at home and all worked in some capacity at their father's business, Southwire. Roy would also take the children along with him on business trips to visit other plants in other parts of the world. Ever the mind of an engineer at how to solve a problem, Roy would take a length of cord and knot it at intervals. Then he would have each child hold onto a knot so that nobody would get lost as they made their way through busy airports.

Alice Richards was born to be a mother, and she made motherhood to her brood of seven a wonderful adventure for her whole family. She allowed each child to find his or her own natural abilities and special niche in the world. Her children have said of her that her philosophy with children is "First give them roots, and then give them wings!" A defining characteristic of Alice Richards has always been that she nurtures. "Honor and love" was the family motto on the old crest of the Richards family in England, and these are certainly two qualities that Alice Richards has nurtured in her own children, as is evidenced by the fine quality of adults they are today.

Roy Richards was very much a family man, and it was a tradition that the family would be seated together around the dining table for supper. Roy always said the blessing and ended with " ... and make us grateful for the good things of life." Togetherness was the hallmark of the Richards' family. They attended St. Margaret's Episcopal Church and the rule was "If you're home, and you're healthy, and it's Sunday, then you're going to church!" It took a full pew to seat the Richards family in tiny St. Margaret's.

Rev. James Callahan once said, "I've never known any man in whom the Kingdom of God and the Christian faith have come into focus the way it has in the Richards family." Roy also became a personal friend of Rev. Norman Vincent Peale. Roy was especially inspired by Dr. Peale's sermon on "Thinking Big," and he made sure every employee of Southwire received a subscription to Dr. Peale's magazine, *Guideposts*.

Though Roy and Alice Richards attained great wealth in their lives, they never indulged their children. Roy stated once that he never spent more than a tenth of his income. The children earned their own allowances and each worked at one time or another at Southwire to learn the family business. Their family motto was "There will be no handouts around here!" Roy used to say that he really did not work for the money itself, that was just a byproduct. He was in business to find a better way of doing things and to meet new and interesting people. Joe Cummings wrote of Roy Richards, "He delighted in hard work. It was his choice and his joy to use himself to the full limit of his strength and wit. Yet, the very center of who he was always belonged to his wife, Alice, and his seven children."

The people of Carrollton and colleagues of the wire industry have grown to love the tradition of the Richards' family Christmas cards over the past forty years. Each year, the family would be pictured together, often in a vacation setting such as the one shown with them rafting down the Dog River. Robin is in front; next row shows Elizabeth, Alice, Laura, Nancy, Roy; and in the back are Lee, Roy, Jim. The next year they might be on horseback or in bathing suits. In 1983, the family was pictured dressed in formal attire to celebrate Roy and Alice's 25th wedding anniversary. Roy and Alice renewed their wedding vows at St. Margaret's Episcopal Church with close friends and family attending.

On 24 February 2001 the family gathered at St. Simon's Island for the wedding of Laura Richards and James Matthew Naughton. The family is pictured (on page 424) left to right: Lee, Loren, Chris and Robin, Bob and Nancy (behind), Elizabeth (in front) with Lee F. and Grace, Laura and Jim Naughton, Behind: Alice, Jim Richards, Virginia and Roy Jr. The boys in front are Evan, Conor Chase, Phillip, Nicholas, (not pictured are Carson and Raphaela.)

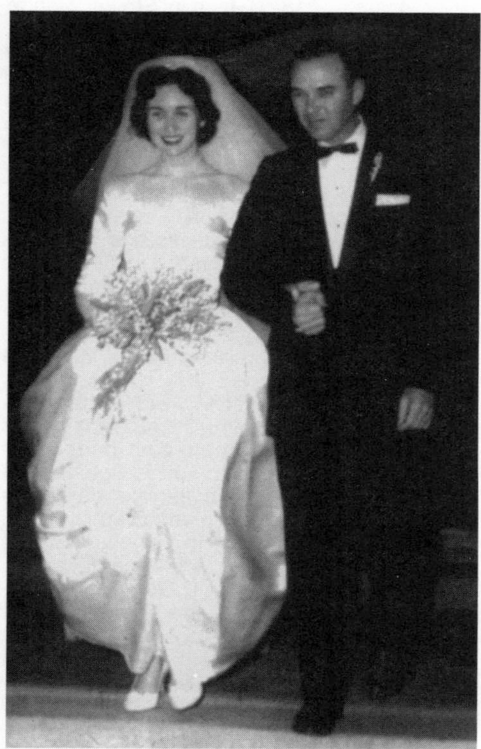

Roy and Alice Huffard Richards

The Richards family rafting the Dog River

The children of Roy and Alice Richards are:

(1) Roy Richards Jr. born 19 December 1958; Roy grew up in Carrollton and attended Oak Mountain Academy; he graduated from Woodward Academy. Roy studied mechanical engineering at the Georgia Institute of Technology where he received the Outstanding Engineering alumnus award. Roy was a member of Phi Delta Theta social fraternity. Roy also holds an honorary doctorate from the State University of West Georgia. He is CEO of Southwire Company in Carrollton. Roy serves on the Board of Trust for Public Land, the Carter Center, and the Georgia Lottery Corporation. He was elected CEO of the year for 1999. Roy married Virginia Cobb McGee on 11 September 1999. She is the daughter of Dr. and Mrs. John Asbury McGee Jr. of Charlotte, North Carolina. The wedding ceremony took place at The Cathedral Church of Saint John the Divine in New York City. Virginia is a graduate of Davidson College and the University of North Carolina School of Law. She is an attorney with the law firm of Jones, Day, Reavis & Pogue in New York City where she practices environmental law. Roy and Virginia have one daughter Ruth Carson Richards born 31 July 2000. They make their home in Carrollton.

(2) James Case Richards born 31 December 1959; Jim is named for Major A.A. Case who was his father's mentor and professor at Georgia Tech and who helped train the first employees of Southwire. Jim grew up in Carrollton and attended Oak Mountain Academy; graduated from McCallie Academy in Chattanooga, Tennessee; received his degree in economics from Georgia Institute of Technology where he was a member of Phi Delta Theta social fraternity; married Janet Chase, 13 June 1987, later divorced; three sons: (1) Chase Richards born 15 July 1990, (2) Nicolas Richards born 21 November 1991, and (3) Phillip Richards born 15 December 1993. Jim Richards established the Foxhall event which is a pre-Olympic test for horses. Jim has also maintained about thirty horses in training at his Foxhall Farm on the Chattahoochee River for pleasure horses or polo horses. Jim served as co-president of Southwire Company after his father's death, but is now the CEO of the Richards Capital Investment Company.

(3) Nancy Huffard Richards born 7 February 1961; Nancy grew up in Carrollton and attended Oak Mountain Academy, graduated from The Westminster School in Atlanta, Georgia. She received her B.A. degree in French and economics from Vanderbilt University in 1983 where she was a member of Delta Delta Delta social sorority. On 28 December 1983, Nancy married Robert V. Farese Jr. of Tampa, Florida. He is the son of Dr. and Mrs. Robert V. Farese Sr. also of Tampa. Bob Farese is the grandson of Mrs. Margaret Farese and the late Joseph Farese of St. Petersburg, Florida, and also of Mr. and Mrs. Frank P. Butler of Fort Lauderdale, Florida. Mr. Farese is a graduate of Plant High School in Tampa. He received his B.S. degree in chemistry from the University of Florida in 1981 where he was a member of the Phi Beta Kappa and Phi Kappa Pi honorary societies, and the Sigma Alpha Epsilon social fraternity. He graduated with his M.D. degree from Vanderbilt School of Medicine and went on to a Fellowship at Denver, Colorado. Dr. Farese is now an endocrinologist in research at the University of California in San Francisco; he is working on the mystery of "fat genes." The Fareses make their home in San Francisco. They are the parents of five children: (1) Loren Farese born September 1986; (2) Conor Farese born 1989; (3) Lee Farese born 3 May 1991; (4) Evan Farese born 11 November 1995 (twin); and (5) Grace Farese born 11 November 1995 (twin).

(4) Lee Wiley Richards born 27 May 1962; Lee grew up in Carrollton and attended Oak Mountain Academy; graduated from Woodward Academy in Atlanta, Georgia; attended Berry College for two years and graduated from Auburn University with a degree in business administration; was a member of Kappa Alpha social fraternity at Auburn. Lee is now the vice president in charge of strategic planning at Southwire and lives in Atlanta. Lee also attends Harvard University's Executive Management Program. Lee is active in the Young Presidents Organization (an international group), and is a board member of Oak Mountain Academy.

(5) Elizabeth Kemper Richards born 11 January 1964; Elizabeth grew up in Carrollton and attended Oak Mountain Academy; graduated from Salem Academy in Winston-Salem, North Carolina; graduated from the University of the South in Sewanee, Tennessee, with double majors in Spanish and philosophy. Elizabeth has done a variety of things in her career, such as teaching school and modeling. She travels extensively with Adventure Travel Trips and is currently preparing to tour Norway, France, Italy, Spain, and Switzerland. Elizabeth is a talented artist of the impressionistic style and works as an artist out of her home in Scottsdale, Arizona. Elizabeth has been quite successful in selling her artwork on the Internet. Since childhood, Elizabeth had been a great lover of horses and she keeps several horses now on her ranch near Prescott, Arizona.

(6) Robin Anne Richards born 11 November 1965; Robin grew up in Carrollton and attended Oak Mountain Academy; graduated from Woodward Academy; was a member of Delta Delta Delta social sorority at the University of North Carolina; graduated Phi Beta Kappa from The University of North Carolina at Chapel Hill with B.A. degree completed in 1987; received her graduate degree from the Stanford Graduate School of Business in 1994 and is a venture capitalist. Robin works with the new formed ".com" companies to help them go public. Robin married Christopher John Donohoe of Menlo Park, California, on 26 September 1998 at St. Margaret's Church in Carrollton. Chris Donohoe is the son of Yolanda Marie Ciotek and the late John Joseph Donohoe of Menlo Park. He is the grandson of Lillian Durazzo of Burlingame, California. Chris Donohoe graduated from the University of California at Davis in 1990 and is a television weather anchor. Robin is the family historian of the present generation of the Richards family. In 1985 she collected her father's memoirs and published them privately for her family in a book called *Memories of Roy Richards.* Robin and Chris have one daughter, Raphaela Donohoe, born in December of 2000.

(7) Laura Hudson Richards born 7 May 1972; Laura grew up in Carrollton and attended Oak Mountain Academy; graduated from Westminster School in Atlanta. She graduated as Phi Beta Kappa from University of North Carolina at Chapel Hill with a degree in business and international studies. She was a member of Delta Delta Delta social sorority. Laura has enjoyed participating in and leading many bike tours of Europe. Laura married James Matthew Naughton on 24 February 2001 at Christ Church, Frederica, on St. Simon's Island, Georgia. Laura is an editor of physicians' magazines for McMahon Publishing in New York. Jim Naughton is employed by Milliken & Company, a textiles and chemical concern, as the business manager of the elastic fabrics unit. He graduated from Manhattan College and received an M.B.A. from Fordham University. He is the son of Harriet and Brian Naughton of Bayside, Queens, New York.

One of the defining characteristics of Roy Richards was that whenever he was told "it can't be done," he would never give up. When faced with such "doubting Thomases" and negative reactions to his wild ideas, Roy wasted no time in debate over the issue. He simply went out and did it. It should be of no surprise to learn in climbing this family tree that his ancestors were always on the cutting edge of technology, even in the early 1800s. Some of Roy's mother's ancestors, the Stovalls, were responsible for bringing the railroad to Morgan County, Georgia, in 1841. The Georgia Railroad was the first railroad chartered in Georgia in December of 1833, and it was also one of the first in the country.

The railroad was desperately needed for the transport of cotton from middle Georgia to Augusta so that it could be shipped overseas. Even so, there were many negative remarks made towards the feasibility of building a railroad into Morgan County. The Stovall men, many of them cotton merchants, were in support of the railroad.

The pioneer determination that the Stovall men displayed in helping to achieve the coming of the railroad is the same kind of pioneer determination that their descendant, Roy Richards, would display a hundred years later in attempting to bring electricity to the rural South. He was willing to do whatever it took to get the job done. The Stovall men of the 1800s did the same, and they invested heavily in their belief in themselves that they could bring a railroad to Morgan County.

The Georgia Railroad stock the Stovalls purchased is evidenced in their wills as it passes to each succeeding generation. And, of course, the trains came steaming into Morgan County, Georgia, by 1841. By 1845, the railroad had reached the little village called Marthasville, which would later become Atlanta. This was the most wonderful progress! Newspapers advertised that a person could now travel from Augusta to Marthasville by train and it would only take ten hours.

The Richards family at Laura and Jim's wedding on St. Simon's Island – 24 February 2001

The mother of Roy and Hugh Richards was Ida Myrtice (Miss Myrtle) Stovall who was born 30 October 1888. Myrtle was the daughter of Elisha Tom Stovall (1849-1925) and Armendie Elizabeth Ayers Stovall (1866-1957). (See their picture under Thomasson-Denney story.) Myrtle's parents are buried at Little Vine Cemetery, which is south of Ayers Creek and near the Douglas County line. The Stovall family history on the maternal side of the family is as interesting as the Richards genealogy.

The first of the Stovalls to arrive in America was Bartholomew "Bart" Stovall who was born 24 August 1665 in Albury, Surry Shire, England. Bart Stovall was the son of George Stovall II and the grandson of George Stovall I, both of whom had deep roots in Surry Shire, England, dating back into the 16th century. Bartholomew Stovall came to America in 1684 and married Anne Burton in Old St. John's Church, Henrico County, Virginia, on 8 August 1693. They had three known sons: John Sr., George Sr., and Bartholomew Jr. John Stovall Sr. is the progenitor of Myrtice Stovall's family line.

Extensive records on Bartholomew Stovall in Goochland County, Virginia, show him to reside on the south side of the James River in 1732. See *Cavaliers and Pioneers 1695-1732* by Nell Marion Nugent. The largest number of descendants named Stovall in Georgia today descend from the six sons of John Stovall Sr. of Granville County, North Carolina, who was the son of Bartholomew Stovall, the immigrant.

John Stovall Sr. was born circa 1712 in Henrico County, Virginia, and died November 1781 in North Carolina. John Sr.'s wife was Dorcas Poole. In 1734, John sold 400 acres in Goochland County, Virginia, and Dorcas signed her dower rights. In 1750, John Stovall Sr. moved from Virginia to Grassy Creek in Granville County, North Carolina. He and two of his sons, John Jr. and Bartholomew, were members of the North Carolina militia in 1754. John Stovall Sr. was also recognized by the DAR for his patriotic service in the American Revolution.

The children of Dorcas and John Stovall Sr. were Delilah, Susannah, Bartholomew, Elizabeth, William, John, George, Josiah, Thomas, Anne, Drury, and Benjamin. Benjamin Stovall was born circa 1755 in Granville County, North Carolina. It is this Benjamin Stovall (1755-1828) who migrated to Oglethorpe County, Georgia. Benjamin's son, Samuel Stovall (1777-1848), moved to Morgan County, Georgia, and appeared there on the 1820 census. It is from this son, Samuel Stovall, that the Carroll County Stovalls are descended. The first time that Samuel Stovall appeared in Carroll County records was when "Edmund Duke, administrator of John S. Duke, deceased, wills to Samuel Stovall and Willie A.B. Maughan of Morgan County on 22 October 1835 security for Edmund Duke Land Lot #34 in 5th District," Deed Book B, page 440.

Benjamin Stovall (1755-1828) settled in Capt. Elsberry's district of Wilkes County, Georgia, by 1785. Benjamin's son, Samuel Stovall (1777-1848), married Sarah Arrington and they became the parents of a large family: Benjamin born circa 1802 in Lincoln County, Georgia; Lucy born circa 1805; Stephen Franklin born 7 October 1806; Richard D. born 23 March 1809; Mary born circa 1810; George W. born 1811; Elizabeth H. born 16 March 1813; Isham born 12 March 1814; Samuel born circa 1816; Ann born 6 March 1818; Benjamin Stovall died in Oglethorpe County, Georgia, in 1828.

The grandfather of Myrtice Stovall is Stephen Franklin Stovall who was born in Morgan County, Georgia, on 7 October 1806. Stephen Franklin Stovall married Frances Thomas in Morgan County 26 February 1829. By 1850, Stephen had moved his family to Campbell County, Georgia. The census for 1850 reads: Stephen Stovall age 42; Frances age 40; Jefferson C. age 17; Ann J. age 15; Nancy age 12; Frances age 10; Elizabeth age 7; Stephen E. age 5; Lucy K. age 3; and Elisha T. age 10 months. Stephen Stovall died on 6 February 1858 and was buried in the Stovall Cemetery in Carroll County.

Stephen's family continued to live in Carroll County after his death, and they appear there in the 1860 census. Jefferson C. Stovall had married Almetia Watkins on 16 December 1856. In 1860, Jefferson C. had his own household close to his mother. Jefferson is age 27, his wife Almetia is listed as 22, his daughter Frances E. is age 2, and a son Stephen is 11 months. This family lived in Fairplay district. Jefferson C. Stovall was a first lieutenant in Company G, 41st Regiment, Georgia Infantry, Army of Tennessee, C.S.A. He died in battle at Columbus, Mississippi, on 5 May 1862.

In the 1860 Carroll County census, Frances Stovall is listed at Fairplay-Sand Hill, age 51. Her daughter Ann is 24, Frances M. is 19, Elizabeth M. is 17, Stephen F. is 15, Lucy C. is 13, and Elisha Tom is 10. Tom Stovall is the father of Myrtice Stovall who was born in 1888.

The effects of all that Roy and Alice Richards have done for our community are still being felt into the new century. Roy played an important role in spearheading the community drive to fund building a new modern hospital here, and he remained the chairman of the Hospital Authority for thirty years. He stood by the hospital in the early years when there was no operating capital, and would send his engineers and secretaries from Southwire to "help get the job done." Our modern Tanner Medical Center continues to thrive.

Though Roy himself was a part of the bricks and mortar of the hospital, it was his wife, Alice, who was the heartbeat. Since about 1950, the hospital had Grey Ladies provided by the Red Cross, but after capably serving for many years, these ladies had grown too old for this duty. Hospital administrator, Bill Warren, had stated a need for a local hospital auxiliary to be established. In response to this need, Alice Richards was the founding president of the Pink Ladies in 1966.

From gray to pink was the first colorful change in the uniforms of the volunteers. Many younger people with fresh new ideas were brought in as volunteers. The nurses at the hospital noted that Alice "pinked up" a lot of other things. The Cheer Cart was a successful new idea. Volunteers would roll the cart to all patients of the hospital to offer newspapers, magazines, life-savers, and other items.

The Pink Ladies evolved into more responsible jobs at the hospital, such as managing the hospital gift shop, and helping with admissions and courier services. Many men joined the organization, wanting to be a part of the volunteer services, too. The Auxiliary has raised thousands of dollars for purchasing new equipment and funding new programs for the hospital. Alice Richards has been the inspiration for a long and distinguished history of the Tanner Medical Center Auxiliary helping the hospital in many ways. "My family feels strongly that we should give back to the community which has been good to us and to the people who have nurtured us through happy days and sadness."

Alice Richards' community service has not been limited to the hospital, however. She has served on the board of directors for the Georgia Council of the Arts, Southwire Company, Ossabaw Island Foundation, CB&T Bank, the High Museum of Art, and the Tanner Medical Foundation. She has served on the board of trustees for the State University of West Georgia Foundation as well as the board at Berry College. Alice has been a long time financial supporter of the West Georgia Foundation and has been recognized in the Senior President's Club for her philanthropy. Alice was awarded the State University of West Georgia's highest honor, the Founder's Award, in June of 2001.

In 1991, Tanner Medical Foundation held its first Magnolia Ball as a fund-raising event. It was meant to be a one-time event and was held in a cow pasture on the farm of Bill and Patsy Rucker. Tom Richards, Hugh's son, was in charge of the logistics of that gala evening and 500 people were expected. Then it rained, and it rained. It became a gully washer! Cars were getting stuck in the mud everywhere. But rather than being a dismal failure, the party was a huge success. "It sort of took on the tone of a hurricane party," Dr. Peter Worthy observed, "and we had as much fun as children splashing in mud puddles!" The Magnolia Ball was a great success, in spite of being a "frog-strangler" as Woodfin Cole called it, and $220,000 was raised for worthy projects for the hospital.

Since 1992, through Alice Richards hospitality and generosity, the Magnolia Ball has continued to be a successful fund-raiser for the Tanner Medical Center Foundation. The Magnolia Ball has also become the social scene of the year each May in Carrollton. Each year, more and more people in the community have become involved. The Richards home has proven to be the perfect spot for this event, as the cars are parked at Southwire and the guests are bused over by Steve Adams Transports to the tent set up at Richards Lake. The Richards have long been prepared for serving a crowd, serving as many as 7,000 at their famous Fourth of July Southwire picnic. In 1996, Alice Richards was the honorary chairman of the Magnolia Ball, and that year the proceeds went to the Tanner Cancer Center. The Tanner Medical Foundation has contributed millions of dollars for worthy causes at the hospital. The publicity of the Magnolia Ball has also helped to attract other donations, gifts, and grants.

In 1993, Evalyn Parrish and other concerned citizens in Carrollton began to make plans for a community home for troubled children of Carroll County. These were children from homes where family violence, drug addiction, and alcoholism were taking its toll. There were not enough foster homes to take care of these children locally, and social workers and judges had to find emergency shelter for them in other counties.

Ida Myrtice Stovall Richards, proudly displaying her collards.

On March 6, 1997, the doors opened to Alice's House — the Carroll County Community Children's Home. It is dedicated to the welfare of children who need a safe place to protect them from abuse or neglect. The home is named in honor of Alice Richards who has been a long time supporter of the needs of children and citizens of our community. Alice's House accepts children from the Department of Family and Children's Services, ages five through sixteen, and is licensed to keep ten children. Alice Richards' own children have been very supportive of this childrens' home. Local civic clubs have donated much in time and services. The quilting society made sure each room in the home had a quilt. A needs list is published twice a year, and those who wish can donate these items — anything from band-aids to school supplies.

On the day of the dedication of Alice's House, Judge Tommy Greer of Carrollton's Juvenile Court praised the community's response to the problem of finding a shelter for the abused children of the county. "I want to say thank you for all the children who will be coming through these doors in the next few years," Judge Greer said. Alice Richards was overwhelmed with joy as she was given the golden key to unlock the door to The Alice Huffard Richards Community Children's Home. Alice declared the whole place to be "A Wonderland" and said, "This is the most wonderful project I've ever been involved with." Alice Richards remains a lifetime charter member of the board of Alice's House.

Roy Richards died on 2 June 1985 at the age of seventy-two, and his body lay in state in the entrance to his Southwire Company where many thousands of people of Carroll County and from all over the South and the world came by to pay their respects. The funeral was held at his home outdoors in the riding ring where so many happy hours had been spent with his family. He was laid to rest in a grove of trees at his home, from which the view is Southwire across Richards Lake. The inscription on his monument reads "He dreamed a great dream ... lived it. He found a high road and walked it. He lived and loved and died in peace."

The Chinese have a proverb that says, "He who gives the gift of a good name gives a gift that lasts for a thousand years." Roy and Alice Richards have certainly made sure that their children and grandchildren — and generations to come — will share in this wonderful legacy. The Richards family is proud to have been a part of the heritage of Carroll County, Georgia. *Submitted by: Alice Richards, Blandenburg Road, Carrollton, GA 30117*

951. Thomas Richards Family

Thomas Richards, born 1794 in Georgia, married Mary Lee Tait, (daughter of Robert Lee and Martha Brewer Tait of Virginia) in 1818 in Madison County, Georgia. Thomas was enumerated in the 1830 census, in the 11th District of Carroll County, where he was a farmer. The will of Thomas Richards was probated in Carroll County in 1858. Mary died in 1876. They are buried in the Richards family cemetery along Highway 5 near the Douglas County line. The only marked grave in the large cemetery was that of Sarah H. Moseley, first wife of William B. Richards. The Sons of Confederate Veterans cleared and maintain the cemetery and placed a Confederate marker on the grave of William B. Richards, who served with Company K, 30th Georgia Regt. and died in 1892. All eight sons and son-in-law, William Vines, served the Confederacy in the War Between the States. Children of Thomas and Mary Richards were: Robert Lea born 1819, married Elizabeth Elrod, lived at County Line, was a farmer, blacksmith, Mason, lawyer, Ordinary of Carroll County and member of the Georgia Legislature. He died in 1888 and was buried in St. Paul Methodist Church cemetery. Their children were, Thomas, William, Andrew Jackson, Mary, Almeda, Tompkins, Smantha and James Richards; William B. born 1821, married Sarah H. Moseley, daughter of Elijah and Susannah Hubbard Moseley. Sarah died in 1872 leaving children Roxana, Marietta, Alabama Missouri and Sarah Florence Richards. William then married Mary Wilson, then Sarah Elizabeth Ballard Bryant and had daughter, Willie. William was a farmer, Mason and Justice of the Peace in Carroll County; Martha Kendall born 1823, married John Burns and moved to Arkansas; John Perry born 1825, married Nancy Elizabeth Camp, daughter of Wesley and Maria Lasseter Camp. John died in Whitesburg in 1880. Their children were Benjamin, Cicero, Mary Texas, Walter Jackson, Robert Washington, Sarah Kelly "Callie," Martha Mariah "Babe," Frances Amanda, Julius, and Lillian Elmra; Elizabeth Haskins "Betsy," born 1828, died 1904, married William E. Vines, lived

John Thomas and Sarah Florence Johnston

in the 3rd district of Carroll County, had Mary, Martha, Ann, Anna, Mille Ann, Roxanne, Thomas Jefferson and Edmund L. Vines; Edmund born 1829, married a Miss Hodge and moved to Arkansas; Nancy E. born 1832, died 1915 in Carroll County, married Jeff Barron, had Lou, Robert, Billy, and Benjamin. After Jeff's death Nancy married Frank F. Morris and had Tom, Joseph, and Susie "Sudie" Morris; James born 1834, married Elizabeth Storey, had Ella, John, Frank and Newt Richards; Andrew Jackson born 1836, married Martha Owens, had Lewis, Mary and William Richards. After Martha's death Andrew married Nancy Summerlin and then Ella R.L. Beall; Francis Marion born 1837, married Mary Benton, had Sally, who married first cousin James R. Richards, son of Robert Lea, Tom, Frank, Harvey, Ralph, Earl, Lela, Henry, Robert Jackson and William Nathan Richards; George Washington born 1840, died in 1862 of disease contracted while serving in the Confederate Army. *Submitted by: Laquita Vice, 477 Laurel Ridge Dr. #4203, Ellijay, GA 30540*
Sources: *Alvin Lee Richards Family Tree and Autobiography*, published privately; *Roster of the Confederate Soldiers of Georgia 1861-1865* by Lillian Henderson; descendants Patricia Yates and Lucy Moye.

952. Elias Richardson's Children

Elias and Lizzie (Anderson) Richardson have many descendants living in Carroll County today.

Their children were: (1) John Wesley died young. (2) James (November 22, 1872-August 19, 1951) married Annie Thompson (1877-1952). Their children were: Lola married Silas Smith; Oscar; Walker; Lilie Velma; Jeptha Edgar married Gwendolyn Skinner; Ruthie May; Idus married Mary Smith; Curt Oliver; Maron Jedith married Vera Allen; Imon; Ozell married ____ Brooks. (3) Frances Cynthia Ann Melissa (August 20, 1874-April 29, 1971) married Henry Clinton Deese. They had fifteen children: Arbie married Erastus Skinner; Luther married Bessie Jackson; Ophie married David Smith; Elisha; Alton married Belma Anderson; Estelle married Henry Brock; Millard married Carrie Armstrong; Henry Otis; Lindsey; Horace Buford; Roy; Ruby married Buford Marlow; Lloyd; Gratis married Newton Johnson; Othe married Alvin Preston. (4) William Jefferson (November 3, 1875-December 20, 1947) married Nancy Elizabeth White (March 26, 1878-November 24, 1938). Their children: Evie married Tom Farlow; Albert Johnny married Verta Traylor; Amos (1900-1937) married Inia Williamson; Omie Ophia married Sidney Gibbs; Hubert Edgar married Louise McLeod; Hattie married Carl Brock; Zeddie Arnold married Daisy Brand. (5) David Warner, died young. (6) Lilla Luella (1880-1977) married James Albie Langley (1874-1949). Their children were: Emory Leonard married Maude Nolen; Lem; Virgle married Ann Benefield; Dura married Nathaniel Smith; Vera married Hars Hewey; Lee married ____ Blair; Clifton married Maurice Blair. (7) Robert Solomon (October 3, 1882-April 9, 1963) married Cora Stamps (September 24, 1882-July 22, 1965. Their children: Doyal; Essie Mae married ____ Pollard; Walter; Lovie; Buren; R.G.; Hattie; Sybil; Cecil. (8) Joseph Arthur, (September 23, 1886-June 2, 1949) married Lena Farmer (December 15, 1886-February 1979). Their children: Lennie married Olin Rigsby; Letcher Elvin; Lettie married Newman Wiggins; A.G. married Melba Adamson; Lanetta married ____ Green; Robert married Elaine McGuire; Poolie Estelle married Irene Kesler; Venelene married Wayman Baker. (9) Jephtha Walter Richardson (April 23, 1884-December 1, 1962) married Esby Turner (1884-1948), daughter Mamie (1906-1907). (10) Lonnie is covered separately. (11) Liddmay (1891-1899). (12) Lunie Edgar (October 28, 1893-ca 1970) married Annie Nolen. Their children were: Ludie married Leonard Armstrong; Wordie Bell married Caylor Cooley; Addie married Paul Johnson; A.V.; Lewis Beason married Ruth Gay; O.C. married Lillian Gibbs; Gladys married Wilbur Swaford; Marie married Hoyt Gay; Charles married Edna Hornsby; Willis married Kathren Koone; Jewell married V.L. Mathis. (13) Lester Manly Richardson (June 12, 1896-July 30, 1935), married Ida Rooker (1898-1973). Their children were: infant 1914; Bertis married Eli Jenkins Gravitt; Versie married Wilbur Curtis Estes; Hubert Belton married Margaret Marie Bice; Evelyn married Carl Leon Pressley. (14) Zeddie Mathew (1898-1899). *Submitted by: Cory Camp, Grantville, GA and Written by: LaRelia Camp*
Sources: Richardson Family Bible and family members.

953. Elias and Lizzie Anderson Richardson

Elias Marion Richardson was born in 1842 in DeKalb County, Georgia. He was the son of John Wesley Richardson and wife Sarah Harbin. By 1850 they were living in Cherokee County, Alabama, where Elias enlisted in Capt. Kirkpatrick's Company of the 19th Alabama Regiment of the Confederate Army in 1861. He was captured at Missionary Ridge and taken to the Union prison at Rock Island, Illinois. The Union Army was not prepared for so many prisoners and had no place to house them all. He was there during a bitter winter with little food, heat, quilts, or clothing. Many prisoners were dying from starvation and smallpox. They gave Elias a choice of remaining there or joining the Union Army and being sent out west to guard the mail route from Indian attack. He joined Company D, 3rd Regiment, U.S. Infantry, October 1864 and was sent to Julesburg, Colorado, until the end of the Civil War. He was discharged November 1865. He is described in his pension application in 1901 as 5 feet 9 inches, 140 pounds, a dark complexion, blue eyes, gray hair. After the war, he went to Randolph County, Alabama, where he was living in the home of Robert McCarley in the 1870 census.

He was married on August 28, 1870, to Lucinda Elizabeth (Lizzie) Anderson, born 1854, Lamar, Randolph County, Alabama. She was the daughter of John Priar Anderson and Martha Fincher who are buried at Ranburne. John was the son of Wesley Anderson and Frances Harris, buried at High Pine Cemetery, Roanoke, Alabama. Martha was the daughter of Lucinda McClendon (Zion Cemetery, Woodland) and Thomas Fincher. In 1889 Elias and Lizzie moved to Carroll County near the state line at Ranburne.

They had fourteen children: John Wesley; James married Annie Thompson; Frances married Henry Deese; William married Nancy White; David Warner; Lilla married James Langley; Solomon married Cora Stamps; Walter married Esby Turner; Arthur married Lena Farmer; Lonnie married Ellen Whitley; Liddmay; Lunie married Annie Nolen; Lester married Ida Rooker; and Zeddie. Many of these children's descendants live in Carroll County today.

Lizzie made her thread with a spinning wheel and then made all her cloth with a loom. Elias was a farmer and a shoemaker. At Christmas it was the custom for their children's families to take cakes and gather at Elias and Lizzie's house to celebrate. About ninety grandchildren would be present. Lizzie always had a big tree and hung the grandchildren's gifts on it as the only decorations. One year hanging on the tree was a doll for each little girl and a bag of marbles for each little boy. She was Scot-Irish descent and when she got upset she spoke with a Scottish dialect. Lizzie would yell at the grandchildren, "doncha be akickin mi cat now."

Elias died in 1929, and Lizzie died in 1936. They are buried in marked graves at Ranburne.
Submitted by: Robert Camp
Sources: National Archives Pension file; Richardson Family Bible: Childhood memories from Eva Richardson Lovvorn

954. Lonnie and Ellen Whitley Richardson

Lonnie Richardson was born 1889. He was the son of Elias M. Richardson and Lucinda Elizabeth Anderson. He married September 2, 1906, Cleburne County, Alabama, Mary Ellen Whitley, the daughter of Robert Lee Whitley buried at Pine Hill Cemetery, Newell, Alabama, and Artilla (Teelie) Hanson buried at Ranburne Cemetery. Robert Whitley was the son of James Whitley and Susan Frances Lemond buried at Pine Hill Cemetery. Teelie was the daughter of Sanford Hanson and Nancy C. White buried at Ranburne Cemetery.

When anyone died in the area, someone would go to the church and start ringing the bell. The ringing could be heard for miles around. Men would stop whatever they were doing, get a shovel, and head for the church to start digging a grave, not knowing who the grave would be for until they got there. Lonnie used a lot of Scottish dialect all his life. For example he would say "wee bairn" meaning a little baby.

Lonnie and Ellen's children were Ivor, Arlen, Myrtle, Eva, Ezelle (died when a baby), and Belton. The children attended Chigger Ridge School and rode there on a school bus that was

Elias and Lizzie Richardson in their buggy

a long wagon with lots of seats and was pulled by mules. In the winter they took hot rocks or hot baked potatoes wrapped in cloth to warm their feet on the ride. They attended a one-room schoolhouse and took their lunches in lard buckets. They would float their lunch buckets in a branch to keep the food cool and tie the bucket to a limb to prevent it from floating downstream.

Lonnie and Ellen Richardson and family

(1) Ivor married Eslie Robinson and had four children: Buford married first Videra Otwell (two sons Jerry and Terry); and second Beverly (three children, Cheryl, Larry, and Eddie); Hazel married Bob Hosey (two daughters Judy and Kathy); Juanita married Alan Brown (two daughters, Debra and Lynn); Shelby married first Joe Partridge (one daughter Tina), and second Mack Whitley (one son Eric).

Lonnie and Ellen Richardson and baby Ivor

(2) Arlen married Mollie Lovvorn and had two children: Lenar Mae married Jimmy Pollard (four children, Sammy, Cheryl, Penny, and Jimmy); and Peggy married Donnie Jennings (two daughters, Tammy and Susie).

(3) Myrtle married Carl Eason and had three sons: Sylvan; Wilburn married Shirley Dean (two sons, Randy and Wayne); Styles Janver married Diane Gill (one daughter Jennifer).

(4) Eva married Spencer Lovvorn and had two children: LaRealia married Ellis Camp (three sons, Ellis Jr., John, and Robert); Johnny married Joyce Hendrix (two sons, Johnny Spencer and Douglas.

(5) Ezelle.

(6) Belton married Elsie Cook and had three children: Lucille married Jimmy Carter (two daughters, Leslie and Susan); Buel married Lynn Slaton (four children, Sheila, Brian, Cynthia, and Becky); and Willard married Debra.

Ellen died in 1965 and Lonnie died in 1978. They are buried in marked graves at Ranburne.

Submitted by: Ellis Camp Jr.

Sources: Richardson Bible, Family records, childhood memories of Eva Richardson Lovvorn.

955. The Alf and Dahlia Ricks Family

Jackson "Jack" Ricks (b. October, 1854, d. 1910 Floyd County, buried Lindale, Floyd Co., GA) was married on 03-11-1874 to Sarah Adeline "Linnia" Hunter (b. 07-07-1849, d. 02-20-1935 Carroll Co., buried Bethany Christian Church Cemetery, Carroll Co.). Jack and Linnia had 11 children and the 5 who lived beyond childhood were Alfred "Alf" Thomas Ricks (b. 10-16-1876, Campbell County, GA, d. 08-08-1935 Carroll Co., buried *Bethany Cemetery); William J. Ricks (b. 11-1881); Robert D. Ricks (b. 09-1884); James Allan Ricks (b. 08-25-1891, Douglas Co., GA, d. 12-12-1957, Rome, Floyd Co., GA, buried Floyd Co., GA) and Bessie Ricks Harper Shepherd, (b. 09-12-1895 Douglas Co., d. 09-07-1971 Carroll Co., buried Concord Methodist Church, Hickory Level).

On 01-01-1905 in Douglas Co., Alf Ricks married Emma Dahlia White (b. 05-11-1878, Douglas Co., d. 07-10-1966 Carroll Co., buried Bethany Cemetery). Dahlia White was the granddaughter of Nancy Jane Hilderbrand (b. 11-18-1838 near Villa Rica, d. 12-07-1924, Douglas Co.) and Samuel Jefferson White (b. 11-05-1836 near Powder Springs, d. 06-27-1884) who served in the Civil War. Jane H. and Samuel J. White were married on 08-02-1855. Jane Hilderbrand's siblings were Elizabeth H. McLarty, Minervia H. White, Mandy H. Hallman, Margaret H. Willoughby, Martha H. Leathers, William Hilderbrand, Josie H. Leathers and John Hilderbrand. The Hilderbrands lived near Villa Rica. Jane H. and Samuel J. White lived in Douglas County on a farm after Samuel came home from the Civil War and are buried at Ephesus Cemetery, Douglas Co. Their three children were John, William Causby Dawson and Margaret. Dahlia White was the daughter of William Causby Dawson White (b. 05-10-1856, d. 07-17-1949 Carroll Co., buried Ephesus Church Cemetery, Douglas Co.) and Ellen Brown White (b. 06-17-1856, married 1-06-1876, d. 05-22-1930, buried Ephesus Church Cemetery, Douglas Co.). Family lore is that Ellen White's family was separated in the Civil War. She was taken with Union prisoners to a prison camp called Sweetwater near Lithia Springs where, at about six years old, she stood in a chair and washed dishes for soldiers. After the war, Judge and Mrs. John Edwards from Buchanan took her from the camp and she lived with them until her marriage. Judge Edwards was also a pastor and he carried Ellen with him to Ephesus Church in Douglas Co. where she met Samuel J. White and later married him. The farm where Samuel and Ellen lived had a copper mine where the copper was dug and shipped by train from Atlanta. Samuel J. and Ellen Brown White's children were Dahlia, Minnie Virginia, William, Leonard and Nellie.

Alf and Dahlia Ricks moved to Carroll Co. in 1907. Their children were Thelma Mae (b. 10-21-1905, Douglas Co.); William Raymond (b. 04-11-1907, Carroll Co., d. 01-07-1990, Carroll Co., buried Bethany Cemetery); James Esker "Eck" (b. 06-22-1909, Carroll Co., d. 10-22-1994, Carroll Co., buried Bethany Cemetery); Susan Esma "Susie" (b. 09-12-1910, Carroll Co., d. 01-15-1982, Carroll Co., buried Bethany Cemetery); Alfred Ernest (b. 01-12-1913, Carroll Co., d. 07-03-1988 Muscogee, Co., buried Bethany Cemetery); Ruby Leona (b. 01-03-1915, Carroll Co.); Uvera "Beedie", (b. 04-12-1916, Carroll Co.); Alford Tasker "Porter" (b. 11-07-1917, Carroll Co., d. 02-05,1983, Fulton Co., buried Villa Rica City Cemetery); and John Wilbur "Moon" (b. 06-06-1919, Carroll Co., d. 02-14-1978, buried Bethany Cemetery).

On 11-10-1928, Thelma Mae Ricks (b. 10-21-1905, Douglas Co.) married Carlos "Carl" Jordan (b. 10-07-1893, d. 10-21-1966 Carroll Co., buried Bethany Cemetery). They had no children. Carl's family donated the land for the original Bethany Christian Church and Cemetery. Carl and Thelma donated land for a parsonage, and Thelma donated land for the Family Center.

On 12-10-1930, William Raymond Ricks (b. 04-11-1907, Carroll Co., d. 01-07-1990, Carroll Co., buried Bethany Cemetery) married Nannie Ione Smith (b. 06-16-1913, Carroll Co., d. 03-06-1995, Carroll Co., buried Bethany Cemetery). They had one daughter, Julia Frances (b. 01-01-1936 Carroll Co.). On 11-12-1954, Julia Ricks married Andrew "Andy" J. Carnes (b. 01-09-1934, Douglas Co., d. 04-20-1998, Douglas Co., buried Bethany Cemetery). They had one son Phillip Andrew "Phil" (b. 04-14-1956, Carroll Co.). Phil Carnes married Ann Marie Tumlin (b. 10-24-1958, Polk Co. on 05-26,1986 in St. Mary's, GA). They have no children.

Alf Ricks and Thelma Ricks Jordan standing. Dahlia Ricks, seated.

In Carroll Co. on 06-20-1931, James Esker "Eck" Ricks (b. 06-22-1909, Carroll Co., d. 10-22-1994, Carroll Co., buried Bethany Cemetery) married Ruby Mae White (b. 09-04,1913, Carroll Co., d. 10-07-1981, Carroll Co., buried Bethany Cemetery). Their first two children were boys who died shortly after birth. They were Jodie Willard (b. 07-29-1934, d. 07-30,1934, buried Bethany Cemetery) and Sammy Neil (b. and d. 08-01-1937, buried Bethany Cemetery). They then had Sandra Zann (b. 10-20-1938, Carroll Co.) and Sylvia Lou (b. 11-27-1945, Carroll Co.).

Sandra Zann Ricks married Gregg Byron Brown (b. 02-07-1938, Carroll Co.) on 12-22-1956 in Carroll Co. at the family home. Their children are Gregg Byron "Ron" Jr. (b. 01-01-1958, Carroll Co.), Zann Katrina (b. 05-07-1959, Carroll Co.) and Melissa Denise "Lisa" (b. 04-27-1961, Carroll Co.). Sandra and Gregg Brown live in a home they built in 1969 on the family home place on Sand Hill-Shady Grove Road, Carrollton, Ga.

Ron Brown married Debra Lynn Compton (b. 04-24-1958, Polk Co.) on 04-18-1989 in Las Vegas, NV. They have one son, Cody Compton Brown (b. 12-07-1990, Rome, Floyd Co.). They live in a home they built in 1992 on the Compton family farm in Rockmart, Paulding Co., GA.

Zann Katrina Brown married Larry Allen Hayes (b. 07-21-1949, Coweta Co.) on 08-09-1980 at First United Methodist Church in Villa Rica. They have one son, Cameron Allen Hayes (b. 07-25-1990, Newnan, Coweta Co.). They live in Newnan in a home they built in 1988. Zann raised three stepchildren: Tonya

Leigh Hayes (b. 07-14-1969, Dekalb Co.), Tracy Lynn Hayes (b. 12-08-1971, Dekalb Co.), and Jason Allen Hayes (b. 10-08-1975, Dekalb Co.). Tonya Hayes married Michael David "Mike" Bridges (b. 02-29-1968, Andrews, NC) on 04/30/1994 at Cumming United Methodist Church and they live in Cumming, GA. Tracy Hayes married William Christopher "Chris" Wakefield (b. 01-28-1971, Dothan, AL) on 05-16-1998 at Cumming United Methodist Church. They have one son, Tanner Hayes Wakefield (b. 07-17-1999, Northside Hospital. Atlanta) and they live in Cumming also.

Melissa Denise "Lisa" Brown married Dwight Leon "D.L." Moody Jr. (b. 06-08-1966, Anchorage, Alaska) on 12-14-1991 at Villa Rica First United Methodist Church. Their two sons are Zachary Benjamin "Zack" Moody (b. 10-05-1993, Newnan, Coweta Co.) and Tyler Jackson Moody (b. 09-25-1996, Newnan, Coweta, Co.). They live in Newnan, GA in a home they built in 1997.

Sylvia Ricks has one daughter, Kelli SuZanne (b. 09-13-1966, Carroll Co.). Sylvia was married to Johnny Phil Hembree on 09-13-1964 in Carroll County (div. 1977). Sylvia was married to Randy Lee Wallace (b. 05-12-1945 Carroll Co.) on 08-27-1993 in Carroll County. She has a stepson, David J. Parks (b. 11-18-1970, Fayette Co.) and a stepdaughter, Mary Elizabeth "Beth" Wallace Rutledge (b. 10-02-1969 Carroll Co.). Kelli SuZanne Hembree married Craig Todd Smallwood (b. 10-11-1965, Carroll Co.) at the family home on 02-27-1999. They have one son, Logan Philip Smallwood (b. 02-26-2000 Cobb Co.). David Parks married Elizabeth Ashley Dunnigan (b. 09-21-1970) in Lexington, KY on 07-12-1997. They have one son Graham William Parks (b. 12-18-1999, Lexington, Fayette Co., Kentucky). Beth Wallace married Randall Murdoc Rutledge, II on 06-28-1995 in Duck, N.C. They have one daughter Sydney Madison Rutledge born on 01-16-1999 in Cobb Co. Sylvia and Randy Wallace reside in the Eck and Ruby Ricks home place on Sand Hill-Shady Grove Road.

On 11-17-1934, Susan Esma "Susie" Ricks (b. 09-12-1910, Carroll Co., d. 01-15-1982, Carroll Co., buried Bethany Cemetery) married Samuel Ray Latimer (b. 12-23-1910, Carroll Co., d. 2-9-1985, Carroll Co., buried Bethany Cemetery). Their children are Janice Daphene (b. 09-20-1935, Carroll Co.) and Thomas Isaac (b. 02-19-1942, Carroll Co). Janice Latimer Astin's children are Beth, Susan and Randy. Thomas Latimer married Patricia Ann Gantt (b. 4-21-49) on 6-3-1968 in Carroll Co. Their children are Stephen Thomas (b. 6-7-1972); Christopher Ray (b. 8-26-1976) and Jeffery Allen (b. 8-27-1983).

On 04-18-1936, Alfred Ernest Ricks (b. 01-12-1913 Carroll Co., d. 07-03-1988, Muscogee Co., buried Bethany Cemetery) married Mary Inez Carter (b. 09-03-1912, d. 06-23-1993, Muscogee Co., buried Bethany Cemetery. Their son was Jimmy Alfred Ricks (b. 02-17-1938, d. 03-25,1939, buried Bethany Cemetery). Their girls are Shirley Ruth (b. 01-08-1940; Joyce Faye (b. 06-05-1945); and Donna Delora (b. 01-14-1951). Shirley Ricks married Tommy Barker on 06-27-1958. Joyce Ricks married Roger Elliott.

On 11-12-1960, Ruby Leona Ricks (b. 01-03-1915, Carroll Co.) married Earl Augusta James (b. 05-07-1904, Carroll Co., d. 01-12-1974, Carroll Co., buried Bethany Cemetery. Leona had one son, Larry Neil Ricks s(b. 04-04-1941, Carroll Co., d. 08-08-1965, Carroll Co., buried Bethany Cemetery).

On 12-24-1938 in Carroll Co., Uvera "Beedie" Ricks (b. 04-12-1916, Carroll Co.) married James Eugene Richards (b. 08-26-1919, Carroll Co., d. 05-24-2000, Carroll Co., buried Shady Grove Baptist Church Cemetery). Their children are Betty Jean (b. 08-10-1939); James Dawson (b. 11-11-1944) and Brenda Sue (b. 04-22-1949).

Betty Jean Richards married Melvin Harold Norton (b. 05-02-1938) in Carroll Co. on 03-16-1958. Their children are: Debra "Debbie" Lynn Norton (b. 04-11-1959, Bay County, FL); and Ronald Harold Norton (b. 03-12-1965, Clayton Co.). Debbie Norton Willard has one daughter, Cynthia Lauren Willard (b. 10-06-1981, Carroll Co.). Ronald Norton married Dana Cole (b. 06-29-1965) on 11-04-1989. Their children are Jared Cole Norton (b. 03-06-1993) and Amanda Nicole Norton (b. 12-08-1996) in Carroll Co.

Dawson Richards married Mary Anne Loftin (b. 02-27-1948) on 06-23-1968 in Carroll Co. Their children are Elizabeth Anne "Betsie" Richards (b. 10-30-1974, Carroll Co.) and Mary Susannah Richards (b. 11-13-1980, Carroll Co.).

Brenda Sue Muse married Tommy Carroll Muse (b. 10-06-1948) in Carroll Co. on 08-06-1967. They have one son, Tommy Carroll Muse Jr. (b. 12-08-1969, Carroll Co.).

Tommy Carroll Muse Jr. married Cynthia Lynn Musselwhite (b. 02-05-1971) on 06-17-1995 in Carroll Co. Their children are: Logan Thomas Muse (b. 06-06,1997, Carroll Co.) and Tyler David Muse (b. 02-25-1999, Carroll Co.).

On 10-15-1938 in Carroll Co., Alford Tasker "Porter" Ricks (b. 11-07-1917, Carroll Co., d. 02-05-1983, Fulton Co., buried Villa Rica City Cemetery), married Mary Cloteal Craig (b. 4-15-1922, Douglas Co., d. 12-16-1996, Carroll Co., buried Villa Rica City Cemetery). Their children are Albert "Buddy" Benjamin Franklin (b. 05-19-1939, Carroll Co.); Martha Paulette (b. 7-20-1946, Carroll Co.); Debra Ruth (b. 8-21-1959, Carroll Co.); and Terry Tasker (b. 10-10-1963, Haralson Co.).

In 1956, Albert married Willie Victoria "Vickie" Wallis (b. 07-09-1940) in Carroll Co. (div. 05-06-1969). Their adopted son was William Joseph "Joe" Ricks (b. 02-03-1963, Fulton Co., d. 12-04-1996 Carroll Co., Pleasant Grove Cemetery). Joe Ricks married Sherry Holder and their son is William Joseph Ricks Jr. (b. 06-19-1984, Carroll Co.). On 02-14-1970, Albert "Buddy" Ricks married Sonja Lay (b. 04-16-1939, Barrow Co.). The children of Albert and Sonja Ricks are Albert Benjamin Ricks Jr. (b. 11-24-1970, Cobb Co.) and Alford Neal Ricks (b. 09-21-1975, Carroll Co.). Albert's stepchildren are James N. Nixon (b. 09-30-1962, Cobb Co.); Kimberly Nixon Miller (b. 10-06-1962, Cobb Co.); and Jodi Nixon Mattox (b. 07-22-1965, Cobb Co.).

James H. Nixon married Judy Muse (b. 11-12-1959, Carroll Co.). Their children are Wanda L. Nixon (b. 12-12-1981, Carroll Co.) and Jessica Amanda Nixon (b. 03-27-1983, Carroll Co.). The child of Wanda Nixon is Dashea Brianna Coffey (b. 02-02-01, Cobb Co.). The child of Jessica Nixon is Elijah Dewayne Puckett (b. 01-06-01, Cobb Co.).

Kimberly Nixon married Wayne Miller (b. 08-10-1963, Polk Co., d. 11-29-1984, Carroll Co.) on 02-10-1979. Their children are Candi Miller (b. 09-15-1979, Carroll Co.) and Wayne Miller Jr. (b. 06-01-1984, Carroll Co.). Kimberly Nixon Miller married Marvin Head (b. 12-24-1947, Gwinnett Co.) on 11-17-1991. Their child is Caleb Head (b. 07-06-1993, Fulton Co.). Candi Miller married Uriah Hales (b. 11-01-1979, Carroll Co.) on 05-05-1996. Candi's children are Payton Brown (b. 12-17-1995, Cobb Co.) and Karley Hales (b. 12-22-1999, Cobb Co.).

Jodi Nixon married Timothy Ray Mattox (b. 07-15-1959, Carroll Co.) on 09-21-1991. Their son is Braydon McKain Mattox (b. 10-04-00, Cobb Co.).

Albert Benjamin Ricks Jr. married Tracy Halstead (b. 03-20-1972, W. VA) on 11-03-1989. Their children are Stephanie Ricks (b. 06-22-1990, Carroll Co.) and Tyler Ricks (b. 03-09-1995, Douglas Co.).

Alford Neal Ricks married Shea Davidson (b. 01-05-1977, Polk Co.) on 12-02-1994. Their child is Taylor LeeAnn Ricks, (b. 01-26-1995, Bartow Co.).

On 7-19-1966 (div. 4-18-1997), Paulette Ricks married Larry Neil Butler (b. 2-24-1946, Carroll Co.). Their children are Tanny Renee (b. 12-15-1966, Carroll Co.); Valarie Denise (b. 4-18-1968 Carroll Co.); and Cecelia Beth (b. 11-17-1976, Carroll Co.). Tanny Butler married Richard Gary Seals (b. 6-19-1966, Carroll Co.) on 01-17-1987. Their children are Lauren Renee (b. 03-28-1990, Carroll Co.) and Hannah Leigh (b. 08-15-1992, Carroll Co.). Valarie's two adopted children are Penny Elizabeth Butler (b. 09-11-1985, Fulton Co. and Timothy Brian Butler (b. 12-14-1990, Douglas Co.). On 06-12-1999, Cecelia Butler married Sonny Tyson Brown (b. 02-29-1976, Bay Co., FL).

On 12-07-1984, Terry Ricks married Donna Lynn Elsberry (b. 05-25-1958, Carroll Co.). Stepdaughter Misty Wade Chandler was born 11-14-1978, Carroll Co. children are Tamra Annie (b. 02-09-1983, Carroll Co.); Terri Lynn (b. 06-18-1985, Carroll Co.); Jessi Mary-Ellen (b. 8-28-1994, Cobb Co.); and Zeke Porter (b. 09-22-1996, Cobb Co.). On 11-13-1999, Misty Chandler married Robert Adam Watts (b. 11-14-1978, Douglas Co.). On 06-23-2001, Tamra Ricks married Adam Clinton Easterwood (b. 12-03-1981, Carroll Co.).

On December 13, 1942 in Carroll Co., Jonn Wilbur "Moon" Ricks (b. 06-06-1919, Carroll Co., d. 02-14-1978, buried Bethany Cemetery), married Annie Belle Todd (b. 05-14-1911, Carroll Co.). Their daughter is Glenda Jean (b. 05-18-1945, Carroll Co.). She married Thomas Lynn Parker Jr. (b. 06-18-1944, Carroll Co.) on 08-18-1963 in Carroll Co., (div. 1970). Their children are Christi Anne (b. 06-16-1964, Carroll Co.) and Sally Suzanne (b. 10-14-1969, Carroll Co.). On 11-18-1995 in Rockdale Co., Christi Parker married Ronald Craig Goddard (b. 03-10-1968, Dekalb Co.). Their children are Tyler Daniel (b. 05-05-1998, Cobb Co.) and Benjamin Todd (b. 05-16-2000, Cobb Co.). On 03-04-2000 in Carroll Co., Sally Parker married Robert Russell Cadenhead (b. 11-04-1968, Fulton Co.). On 09-22-1977 in Carroll Co., Glenda married Robert Arthur Perdue III Jr. (b. 11-15-1948, Polk Co.). Robert's son, Robert Arthur Perdue III (b. 07-24-1971, Bullock Co.) married Susan Gilbert (b. 10-22-1971) on 02-07-1995 in Greenwood, IN.

*Bethany Christian Church Cemetery is located on Highway #61, Carrollton, GA. *Submitted by: Sylvia Ricks Wallace, 802 Sand Hill-Shady Grove Road, Carrollton, GA 30116*

Sources: Information furnished by family members.

956. James Allen Ricks

The Ricks family line runs from Norfolk County, England, through Colonial America to Carroll County, Georgia. Allen Ricks, son of Jackson "Jack" Ricks, was born August 25, 1891, in Villa Rica, and spent his childhood as a farmer's son in Carroll County.

Allen's ancestor, Isaac Ricks, was born at Brancaster in 1638. Isaac left during England's Civil War, arriving in Jamestown, Virginia, around 1645. Isaac, his wife Kathren, and eleven children became Quakers and lived near Isle of Wight County, Virginia.

Isaac Jr. (born 1669) relocated after 1722 to Chowan County, North Carolina, with wife Sarah McKinnie and ten children. Around 1752, Isaac III (born 1702, his wife Sarah Burke and four children moved to Tar River in Edgecombe County, North Carolina. Their son John (born about 1732) was a Revolutionary Patriot who rendered material aid during the war. He married Mary Holton, became a Quaker, and fathered thirteen children. Two sons, Redmond and Lary, moved to Georgia.

Lary Ricks married Eleanor Mayse on July 19, 1810, in old Randolph County. Of their four children, son Andrew Mayse Ricks moved to West Georgia when Indian lands opened. He married Temperance Cook and had nine children. At least one son was born in Carroll County. In 1860 they lived at Campbellton on the Chattahoochee River. On September 17, 1861, Andrew and sons, John H., Charles W., Jesse B., and William J., joined Company C, 35th Georgia Infantry, C.S.A. Jesse and William were wounded at Spotsylvania Courthouse, Virginia, on May 20, 1864. William's wounds proved fatal. He was buried at Spotsylvania Confederate Cemetery. His widow Lucinda raised their four children — Martha, Sarah, Thomas, and Jack.

Allen's mother was Sarah Adelaine "Linnia" Hunter (born 1849), daughter of Jackson W. and Mary Ann Hunter. Jackson was born about 1825 in Tennessee and farmed in Douglas County's Fairplay District by 1880.

Jack Ricks and Linnia Hunter were married March 11, 1874, in Douglas County by Reverend Elijah H. McWhorter. They moved to Carroll County, had eleven children, and were farmers in West Hulett's District by 1900. Only Alfred, William, Robert, Allen, and Bessie lived beyond childhood. Thelma Ricks Jordan of Carrollton, daughter of Alfred, said their other children were buried in unmarked graves in Prays Mill Cemetery at Bill Arp. Jack died in 1910, and Linnia resided with Alfred until her death on February 20, 1935. She was buried at Bethany Christian Church Cemetery in Carrollton. Many Ricks descendants still reside in Carroll County.

James Allen Ricks and Jessie Lee Brock Ricks

After his father's death, Allen moved to Rome, Georgia, worked for Fox Manufacturing Company, farmed, and made boats. On June 22, 1911, he married Jessie Brock, daughter of O.C. Brock and Annie Reeves of Floyd County. Their children were Raymond (married Viola MeDermett), Roy (married Jessie Davis), Edna (married Wilson Heath), Ruby (died young), Opal (married William Cowan), Doyle (married Evelyn Walker), and Glenn (married Glenna Jean Denton). They also had twelve grandchildren, twenty-two great-grandchildren, and many great-great-grandchildren. Allen died in 1957 and Jessie in 1964. Both are buried in Floyd County. *Submitted by: James Timothy and Bonnie White Ricks, 5121 Oakdale Drive, Douglasville, GA 30135-5240.*

Sources: *History and Genealogy of the Ricks Family of America, DAR Patriot Index, Carroll County Times, Consolidated Muster Roll Confederate Soldiers from Campbell Co. GA.*, marriage records, probate records, census records, Bible records.

957. H.C. Ridley

Henry Columbus Ridley, born September 23, 1913, Whitfield County, Georgia, came to Carrollton in 1938 when he married Leona Merrell, whom he had met when she was serving as a home demonstration agent for Murray County, Georgia. They lived with her father, Rufus Cohen Merrell, and H.C. helped Mr. Merrell run his dairy while Leona taught sewing for the Youth Works Administration at West Georgia College. The dairy farm included the house at the corner of Maple Street and Hays Mill Road. The Ridleys enjoyed the fact that at one time the city limits ran through the center of the house so that the family slept in the town but ate in the county.

Years later H.C. bought the Texaco full-service station at the corner of Newnan and Tanner Streets, where the County Court House Annex now stands. He was a charter member of Sunset Hills Country Club and attended the First Baptist Church of Carrollton. In the Carrollton Association of Gasoline Retailers he held numerous offices including the presidency; and he also served as delegate for the Georgia Association of Petroleum Retailers to numerous national association conventions. In 1958 his peers at the state organization named him Mr. GAPR.

H.C. and Leona Ridley

H.C. wanted a playground for the children on the west side of town because, as he explained, the city playground was located "all the way across town." Thus he became the driving force behind the Oil Industries Playground project, sharing his dream with fellow service station dealers and talking with the people who owned the plots of land he wanted for the playground. He visited one elderly man who was known for his thriftiness, told his story to the man — who was an invalid — and the man rather than selling his land to the project donated it to H.C. with the stipulation that H.C. take him to the first baseball game at the new field. These oil men developed a nonprofit group in 1958 that secured a loan and held barbecue suppers to raise the funds for both the land and later for the park pavilion, playground equipment, and ball field. He contacted the owner of the Dairy Queen-Brazier franchise in another town and persuaded him to open a similar store in Carrollton, on the front of the playground property, so that the rent from the retail eatery would provide for the balance owed on the land and maintain the entire project for the families of Carrollton in the future. "He put his heart and soul into it" according to Ned Gable, who worked with Ridley on the project. The Oilfield Industries Park was given to the city in 1973 with H.C.'s stipulation that it must always remain a park.

Two streets in Carrollton are named for H.C. and Leona Ridley's only child, Alice Lane and Ridley Drive. Alice married Jerry E. Teal, and they had two sons, Jerry Jr. (Jay) and Jonathan Andrew (Andy) Teal. *Submitted by: Alice Ridley Teal*

958. Dr. Thomas Howard Roberds

As a pioneer doctor in Villa Rica, Dr. Thomas Howard Roberds practiced medicine from 1839 until his death in 1885. He was born February 23, 1814 in Savannah, Georgia. His father was from Limerick, Ireland. His mother was from Devon, England. His mother apprenticed him in Columbia County, Georgia, when he was two years old to John and Rebecca Melton. At the

Dr. Thomas Howard Roberds

age of 17 he drew land lot 61, District 3 in southwest Carroll County near the Chattahoochee. He moved there along with the Meltons in 1831. He "read medicine" in Newnan, Georgia, under Dr. Joel Terrell, attended and took the first course of lectures in Augusta, Georgia, and graduated and received a diploma in Philadelphia. He married Sarah Mosteller in 1838. They moved to Villa Rica in 1839 to a land lot purchased by Sarah's father, Peter Mosteller (land lot 192, District 6). Tanner Medical Center-Villa Rica is located on this property near the house Dr. Roberds built on Old Town Road.

Mary Talley Anderson, author of *The History of Villa Rica,* and the great-granddaughter of Dr. Roberds, said that he kept a stable full of horses which he drove in pairs to see his patients who resided in a fifteen mile radius. She recalled family stories of his high beaver hat, tailed coat, white vest, Buster Brown tie, and high boots.

Dr. Roberds was survived by two sons and six daughters. The cemetery at Concord Methodist Church in Hickory Level is the burial cite for Thomas Howard Roberds and Sarah Mosteller Roberds. *Submitted by: Elmo M. Roberds Jr., 103 S. Nixon Street, Carrollton, GA*

Sources: Columbia County, Georgia, Early Court Records, 1827 Land Lottery of Georgia, U.S. 1880 Carroll County census, *The History of Villa Rica,* letter to Mrs. Elmo M. Roberds Sr. in 1976, *Carroll County Times* April 17, 1885.

959. John and Martha Roberson

John Newton Roberson was born February 17, 1843 in DeKalb Co. GA to Wiles Goram Roberson and Elizabeth Thurman. When he was 17 the family moved to nearby Carroll Co. GA. They attended the Shiloh Methodist Episcopal Church when it was still a fledgling congregation. His father was a Unionist, but after the Civil War began, young John N. joined with the Confederate troops of Carroll County as a private in Company C, 56th Regiment, Georgia Infantry. They were in a skirmish at Cumberland Gap in Kentucky where he was captured on September 8, 1862, and released September 16-17, 1862. In 1863, he (with his regiment) was caught in the siege of Vicksburg, Mississippi, by General Grant's Union forces. He witnessed the starvation of man and beast as the weeks passed and they had barely food to eat. Their commander finally surrendered, rather than see all his soldiers die by starvation. Their release came on July 8, 1863. When food arrived to feed the starving soldiers, some ate so much they died. After the others recovered, they went back to battle.

On Lookout Mountain on November 23-25, John was wounded in the knee and was separated from his company. Using a rifle for a crutch, he found his way to a farmhouse, where he was nursed back to health. At this point he lost the desire to fight and saw no more glory in it. He just wanted to go home and marry his sweetheart Martha Ann Davenport, born March 3, 1843, the daughter of James Gillam Davenport and Rachel

Cicely Hammock. Rev. Greenberry Jenkins married them on September 22, 1864, at Haralson, Coweta County, GA. Martha's wedding shoes were heavy men's work shoes, as she had no others. They suffered through the hard times the war left them and were very poor, like everyone else. Their children were Robert Franklin b. 1866, William Edgar born 1868, Sarah Elizabeth born 1870, John James born 1871, Persia Viola born 1773, Charles Aquilla, born 1876, Marcus Andrew born 1880, and Martha May born 1887.

John N. and Martha D. Roberson

In September 1878 John and Martha were baptized by missionaries of the Church of Jesus Christ of Latter Day Saints, and when their parents found out, both of them were disowned. They left Georgia on the train with others of their new faith, and went to San Luis Valley, Colorado, to begin a new life in the West. John worked on the railroad, which he did for some time then moved his family to Moab, Grand County, Utah, and started a shoe shop there. Later, John and Martha took separate residences.

In 1913 John went back south to attend the Civil War reunion in Chattanooga, and stayed to visit with family and old friends. He had a recurrence of yellow jaundice, from which he died on July 26, 1915 in Anniston, Alabama. The funeral and burial took place at Seddon, Alabama. Martha waited for him to return, and when he did not, she moved to Maeser, Uintah County, Utah, to live with her daughter, May Bingham. She died March 12, 1931 and was buried there. *Submitted by: Maxim W. Derhak, 7499 South Spring Dr., West Jordan, UT 84084 and Written by: Pauline McConkie Derhak*

960. Robert Glenn Roberts

Robert Glenn Roberts, born July 2, 1926, Carroll County, GA; married June 19, 1948, Pauline Carden, born on February 27, 1930, Haralson County, GA, daughter of Clifford and Nettie Hicks Carden of Carroll County.

Robert's parents were Samuel Watson Roberts and Marjorie Clarie Otwell of Carroll County.

Robert served during World War II in Germany with the 10th Armored "Tiger" Division from Trier to Garmisch, Germany. He was on a half-track that hit a mine and he was blown through an apple tree; a wrist watch was pulled off his arm and he did not miss it until later. Another time, while his squad was scouting a small town, he was cut off behind German lines and considered missing in action. While hiding in the woods, buried in leaves, he was almost stepped on by German troops. On Easter Sunday in 1945, a P-47 plane was hit and went into the ground 50 feet from his foxhole. A piece of the pilot's jawbone with two teeth was found on the hood of the half-track. Another time, while riding the rear of a column at night, a German tank joined the column, thinking they were with Germans. Radio contact was made with the lead tank and it pulled off and ambushed the German tank.

After the war ended in Europe, Robert returned to the U.S. and he was assigned to the Finance Department at Ft. Dix, NJ. In order to get an assignment closer to home, he reenlisted and spent the rest of his duty at Ft. Jackson, SC, where he was in charge of the Automotive Parts Department for the V Corps Headquarters.

Shortly after he returned from the Army, Robert married Pauline Carden who was employed with Southern Bell Telephone Company in Atlanta at the time. Robert took employment with the Army General Depot in Conley, GA, and in July of 1953, he went to Lockheed Aircraft in Marietta. While there, he was employed in supervision over a number of manufacturing shops for many years, and later he was leadman over the propeller shop. He was also a member of the Lockheed Management Club while in supervision.

Pauline was also employed at Lockheed in July 1953, and she was a secretary in the Engineering Test Pilots' Organization, in manufacturing engineering and in engineering program management at the time of her retirement. She and Robert retired the same day on February 29, 1989, each having almost 36 years service time. Pauline graduated from two business schools and she attended West Georgia College for two years. She was also a member of the Professional Secretaries International, Atlanta Chapter, for twelve years.

Robert and Pauline Roberts' child is David Paul.

David Paul Roberts was born on August 6, 1949; married April 28, 1972, to Sherry Roberta Norvell who was born on July 21, 1953, in Fort Worth, TX.

Sherry's parents are Robert D. and Joyce Norvell of Ft. Walton Beach Fl. Robert Norvell was born June 15, 1921, at Lee's Summit, Missouri; Joyce was born April 10, 1921, in Rock Island, Illinois. Robert Norvell was a flight test engineer with General Dynamics at Eglin AFB, FL when he retired. He presently owns an automotive shop in Ft. Walton Beach, FL. In the early years, Joyce Norvell was a chiropractor.

R.G. Roberts in Garmisch, Germany, June 1945.

David was in the Air Force in electronics-navigation systems for four years during the Vietnam War. He met Sherry while he was stationed at Hulbert Field, FL.

David and Sherry Roberts' children are: Brian David Roberts born August 13, 1983; and Jennifer Sherry Roberts born June 29, 1988. Brian will graduate from Woodstock High School with honors on May 26, 2001, and he has been accepted at Georgia Tech. Jennifer will be in the eighth grade at Woodstock Middle School, fall of 2001.

David attended West Georgia College and Southern Tech. Later, he returned to Southern Tech and audited college-level technical writing courses. He holds a certificate in technical writing from Southern Tech; and a B.S. in business administration from Shorter College. David is a technical writer for ADP in Alpharetta, GA.

Sherry Roberts holds an A.S. Degree from Oklaloosa-Walton College, Ft. Walton Beach, FL; and a bachelor's in business administration from Georgia State University. Sherry is a management analyst for the U.S. Department of Agriculture, Food and Nutrition Service, in Atlanta.

Robert and Pauline enjoy researching family genealogy, traveling with their grandchildren in the U.S. and abroad, and also cruising. They have lived in Villa Rica most of their lives, and they have been members of the Villa Rica First Baptist Church for 25 years as of June, 2001. *Submitted by: David P. Roberts, 279 Sabrina Court, Woodstock, GA 30188, based on research by Pauline C. Roberts.*
Sources: Family knowledge.

961. Samuel Watson Roberts Family

Samuel Watson Roberts' roots have been traced to Thomas Roberts Sr. who was born about 1760, the place of birth is unknown. He died August 1818 in Rockingham County, NC. He married Sarah Joyce, date and place of birth are unknown, but it was probably in Rockingham County.

One of Thomas Roberts Sr.'s children was Thomas Roberts Jr. who was born January 19, 1810, in Rockingham County, and died August 11, 1865 in Rockingham County. He married Arena Wortha Hopper who was born March 10, 1817 in Rockingham County, and she died February 28, 1889 in Rockingham County. They are buried in the Roberts Cemetery in the Price Community on Price Road in Rockingham County, near Reidsville, NC.

One of Thomas Roberts Jr.'s children was Richard Polk Roberts who was born April 12, 1846, in Rockingham County, and died April 1, 1926, in Carroll County, GA. He married Mary Lou Sewell who was born May 27, 1859 at Roscoe, GA, Coweta County, and died December 16, 1934, Carroll County, GA.

Richard Polk Roberts served with the 10th VA Cavalry in the Civil War. After 1870, he came to Georgia on a wagon loaded with home-processed tobacco products. He sold out in west Alabama, and on his way back, he met Mary Lou Sewell in Roscoe, GA.

Mary Lou's parents were Pierce Sewell who was born December 29, 1824, in Franklin County, GA, and died March 18, 1883, in Coweta County, GA; and Elizabeth Rainwater who was born June 16, 1829, in South Carolina, and died April 9, 1871, in Coweta County. Elizabeth Rainwater's father was the Reverend James Rainwater who married Polly Mason. Reverend Rainwater founded the Ramah Baptist Church in Palmetto, GA, and he ministered there for twenty-six years. He also ministered in churches in Carrollton, GA, and Pleasant Grove Church in Carroll County. Pierce Sewell, Elizabeth Rainwater Sewell, Reverend James Rainwater, and Polly Mason Rainwater are all buried at Ramah Baptist Church Cemetery in Palmetto.

Richard Roberts was a carpenter with Pierce Sewell in the construction of Sewell's Mill. While working there, he met and married Mary Lou Sewell on December 23, 1877. Before 1890, they settled in the New Brooklyn Community, east of Temple, GA. In the 1890s they owned a farm near Wesley Chapel, north of Villa Rica, GA.

Richard Roberts was a farmer, a community dentist, a veterinarian, a cobbler, and a carpenter. He built many water wheels for grist mills in this area, and he also built houses. In fact, one house is still standing and is inhabited. In 1890, Richard owned 76 acres of land in District 6, Land Lot 229 in Carroll County. It is located near Villa Rica on Highway 101.

Richard and Mary Roberts' children were: Thomas Alton, Hansel Earley, William Ernest, Myrtie Ellen, Richard Polk Jr., Lena May, Paul William, Samuel Watson, and John Barnes.

Thomas Alton Roberts was born in 1878, and there is no information on his death date and place of burial.

Hansel Earley Roberts was born in 1880, and there is no information on his death date and place of burial.

William Earnest Roberts was born in 1882, and there is no information on his death date and place of burial.

Myrtie Ellen Roberts was born July 3, 1884, in Carroll County; and died January 3, 1954, in Carroll County, married Oscar Payne. Myrtie and Oscar Payne are buried at Hill Crest Cemetery, Villa Rica, GA. Oscar Payne was a Villa Rica mail carrier. Myrtie and Oscar Payne's children were Frank, Thomas, and Claude.

Richard Polk Roberts Jr. was born in 1887, and there is no information on his death and place of burial.

Lena May Roberts was born May 30, 1889, in Carroll County, died September 8, 1966 in Carroll County. Lena never married, and she is buried at Hill Crest Cemetery in Villa Rica.

Paul William Roberts was born January 18, 1892, in Carroll County, died June 24, 1970; married Ruth (Unknown). Paul is buried in Miller Cemetery in Gary, Indiana. Paul was a metalurgist with U.S. Steel in Gary, Indiana, until he died. Paul and Ruth Roberts' children were Paul Jr., Georgia Lee, and Richard.

Samuel Watson Roberts was born April 22, 1894, in Carroll County, died August 2, 1981, in Carroll County; married Marjorie Claire Otwell who was born September 14, 1902, in Haralson County, GA; died January 27, 1992, Carroll County. They are buried at Midway Macedonia Baptist Church, Carroll County. They are buried at Midway Macedonia Baptist Church, Carroll County.

John Barnes was born June 15, 1896, in Carroll County and died May 11, 1957 in Paulding County, GA; married Bernice Hicks, John is buried at High Shoals Baptist Church Cemetery, Paulding County. John was a school teacher, and he farmed and lived in the New Brooklyn community. John and Bernice Roberts' children were Jewel and Lois.

Samuel Watson Roberts married Marjorie Claire Otwell on August 20, 1925, in Carroll County. She was the daughter of Albert Lonzo Otwell who was born January 14, 1880, and died September 15, 1958; and Earnestine Eula Haskins, born June 18, 1878, and died July 13, 1971, in Carroll County. Albert Otwell was the son of Robert Fletcher Otwell and Julia Crawford. Their farm was in Haralson County, west of Center Point community.

Eula Hoskins' parents were Thomas Haskins and Mary Brock who lived in Old Campbell County, just south of Campbellton, GA.

In 1916 Samuel Watson Roberts successfully complete a law course from the LaSalle University in Chicago, Illinois.

Samuel Watson Roberts graduated in the Class of 1924 at the old A&M College in Carrollton (presently known as the State University of West Georgia), and he was a member of the West Georgia College Alumni Association.

He was a school teacher and taught at Clem School, Flat Rock School, Hulett School, and Walnut Hill School in Carroll County in the 1920s and 1930s. A record shows that Sam Roberts taught the fourth through the eighth grades at Flat Rock School in Carroll County in 1924. He was paid $60 for the period beginning November 17 through December 12, 1924.

In the mid-1930s, he was instrumental in obtaining the Civilian Conservation Camp, known as the CCC Camp, which was located on the Felix Williams Farm south of Villa Rica. He was also one of the directors of the camp.

Durig World War II, Sam was the Carroll County U.S. Department of Agriculture War Board chairman. He was also vice chairman of all the West Georgia District at that time. He was featured frequently on radio farm programs on WSB Radio during World War II, as noted in a script dated, Friday, July 3, 1942, with announcer Bill Prance, WSB Farm Director. Sam's topic for this program was, "Farm Goals and the War."

Samuel Roberts was employed with AAA Farm Program from 1933 to 1938 when AAA Farm Program's name was changed to Soil Conservation Service.

Samuel Roberts was Soil Conservation supervisor for many years. He was honored in December of 1965 in Macon, GA at the 22nd Annual Convention of the Georgia Association of Soil and Water Conservation District Supervisors. He was presented a Certificate of Appreciation for Distinguished Service as Supervisor from 1938-1968 by the West Georgia Soil and Water Conservation District.

During the 1960s and 1970s, he was contracting officer over the Watershed Lakes for the West Georgia District. Later in life, he was employed at Cannon Casket Company, and he also dealt in Real Estate during that time.

During 1928 and 1929, Claire Roberts taught school at the Hulett School in Carroll County.

Sam and Claire Roberts on Sam's 75th birthday in April of 1975.

Claire was a homemaker and a seamstress. She was also involved in the Georgia State College of Agriculture Home Demonstration Club, as noted in a certificate where she completed the requirements of a nutrition program at the Georgia State College of Agriculture, Athens, GA, dated January 21, 1932.

From the early 1930s to the mid-1940s, Claire made clothes for people in the community, and as far away as New York City, NY and Los Angeles, CA. The lady that she sewed for in Los Angeles was a librarian who sent boxes of books to the children for many years which stimulated their interest in reading.

In the 1950s, she took the job as substitute teacher at the New Georgia School in Paulding County, GA, while her daughter, Ruth Holder, took a leave from teaching to take classes at the University of Georgia.

Sam Roberts was a farmer and all of his children were born and reared on his 250-acre farm which was located on Bay Springs Road in Carroll County. They grew cotton, corn, peanuts, pimento peppers, and vegetables on this farm. They also grew fruits, such as apples, peaches, pears, plums, grapes, strawberries, and figs. Their fig orchard consisted of approximately twenty-five trees around the house. Claire canned and dried fruits and vegetables, and she also canned sausage for family use every year. Their cash crops were cotton, peanuts, pimento peppers, and butter and eggs.

Sam and Claire Roberts children were Robert Glenn, Eva Ruth, and Samuel Watson Jr.

Robert Glenn Roberts' was born July 2, 1926, in Carroll County; married on June 19, 1948, Pauline Carden who was born on February 27, 1930, in Haralson County, GA. Her parents were Clifford Anderson and Janette (Nettie) Hicks Carden of Carroll County.

Robert served in the Army in Germany during World War II, and after his tour of duty, he was employed at the General Depot in Conley, GA. Later, he was employed at Lockheed Aircraft and worked as a leadman over the propeller shop and supervisor over several manufacturing shops for many years. Robert was a member of the Lockhead Management Club while in supervision.

Pauline graduated from two business schools and attended West Georgia College. She also was a member of the Professional Secretaries International, Atlanta Chapter, for twelve years. She was also employed at Lockheed, and she worked in Engineering Program Management as a secretary at the time of her retirement. She and Robert both retired on February 29, 1989 from Lockhed with each having almost 36 years service.

Robert and Pauline Robert's child is David Paul Roberts.

David Paul Roberts was born August 6, 1949, in Carroll County, and married Sherry Roberta Norvell, born July 21, 1953. Sherry is the daughter of Robert and Joyce Norvell of Ft. Walton Beach, FL.

David served in the Air Force in electronics-navigational systems for four years during the Vietnam War. He attended West Georgia College in Carrollton and Southern Tech in Marietta, GA. Later, he returned to Southern Tech and audited college-level technical writing courses. He holds a certificate in technical writing from Southern Tech; and a B.S. in business administration from Shorter College, Rome, GA. David is a technical writer for ADP in Alpharetta, GA.

Sherry holds an A.S. degree in data processing from Oklaloosa-Walton College, Ft. Walton Beach, FL; and a bachelor of business administration degree from Georgia State University in Atlanta. She is a management analyst with the U.S. Department of Agriculture, Food and Nutrition Service in Atlanta.

David and Sherry Roberts' children are: Brian David Roberts, born August 13, 1983; and Jennifer Sherry Roberts, born June 19, 1988.

Brian will graduate May 2001 and he has been accepted at Georgia Tech; Jennifer will be in the eighth grade at Woodstock Middle School, Woodstock, GA, fall of 2001.

Eva Ruth Roberts was born January 23, 1932 in Carroll County; married on August 22, 1952, to Burrell Williams Holder, born February 24, 1927, DeKalb County, GA; died February 27, 1984, Carroll County. Burrell's parents were Isaac Jasper and Marie Carnes Holder of Carroll County. Burrell is buried at Meadowbrook Memory Gardens, Villa Rica, GA.

Ruth holds a B.S. in education; a master's in education; and a specialist in education from the University of Georgia. She was a school teacher and taught in Paulding and Carroll Counties. At the time of her retirement, she was a media specialist at Temple, GA High School. Ruth retired in 1993 with forty years service time.

Burell Holder held a B.S. in education; a master's in education; and a specialist in education from the University of Georgia.

He also served as a pharmacist's mate third class in the Navy in World War II.

Burell was a school teacher and he taught school in Temple and Roopville; he was the Federal Funds Coordinator of Carroll County Schools; he was chairman of the Temple, Centennial Committee; and he was named Temple Citizen of the Year in 1984.

Ruth and Burrell Holder were the authors of the books *A Historical Sketch of Temple,* published in 1976; and *A History of Temple, Georgia,* published in 1982.

Ruth and Burell Holder's children are: Kerry Mark Holder, born August 27, 1954 in Carroll County; and Scott Roberts Holder, born September 9, 1958 in Carroll County.

Mark holds a B.S. in pharmacy from the University of Georgia, and he graduated magna cum laude. He is a pharmacist at a CVS store in DeKalb County, GA.

Scott holds an A.B. in geology and a master's in business administration from West Georgia College; and a master's in library science from Clark Atlanta University. He is self-employed as a securities trader.

Samuel Watson Roberts Jr. was born July 20, 1933, in Carroll County, first married Betty Farr of Carroll County. His second marriage was to Annette Vaughn on March 3, 1962. Annette Vaughn was born in August 3, 1939, in Douglas County, GA. Her parents were Jesse Paul and Louella Hall Vaughn of Douglas, County.

S.W. attended West Georgia College and Georgia Tech, and later he served in the Army. He was employed at Lockheed Aircraft as a communications and electronic instruments repairman; he retired with almost forty-three years service time. Annette is a part-time clerk at the Carroll County livestock barn.

S.W. and Annette Roberts' children are Debbie Lynn, Barry Lee, Dana Kay, and Andrea Brooke.

Debbie Lynn Roberts, born October 9, 1963, in Carroll County; married on May 16, 1987, Philip G. Lazarra, born February 26, 1956, from New York. Phil's parents are Epiphanio and Betty Dupont Lazarra from New York.

Debbie holds a B.S. in computation math from Brigham Young University, Provo, Utah; and a master's in computer science from Johns Hopkins University, Baltimore, Maryland.

Phil holds a B.S. in math from Oneonta State University in New York; a master's in math from Michigan State University; and a master's in computer science from Johns Hopkins University.

They are both employed with the National Security Agency at Ft. Meade, Maryland; Debbie is a computer science researcher; and Phil is a computer science technical leader.

Barry Lee Roberts, born December 9, 1966, in Carroll County, married on May 6, 1995; Martha Palmer, born March 24, 1966, in Utah. Martha's parents are Paul and June Dillistone Palmer of Provo, Utah.

Barry holds a B.S. in computer science from Brigham Young University, and he is employed as a senior systems analyst with Xactware in Orem, Utah.

Martha holds a B.S. in zoology from Brigham Young University, and she also holds a teacher's certificate.

Barry and Martha Roberts' children are Sadie Magdalene, Avonelle (Nellie) June, Jesse Paul Vaughn, and Havalah Zoe.

Sadie Roberts was born July 10, 1996, in Salt Lake City, Utah.

Avonelle (Nellie) Roberts was born July 10, 1996 in Salt Lake City.

Jesse Paul Vaughn Roberts was born October 29, 1999 in Orem, Utah.

Havalah Zoe Roberts was born March 1, 2001 in Orem.

Dana Kay Roberts, born November 22, 1970 in Carroll County; married on February 18, 1995, Justin James Matekovik, born February 15, 1972, from Denver, Colorado. Justin's adoptive mother is Gloria Anderson of Denver.

Dana holds a B.S. in statistics from Brigham Young University, and Justin an arson investigator in Denver.

Dana and Justin Matekovik's children are Chais Elizabeth and Cody James.

Chais Elizabeth Matekovik was born November 3, 1997, in Denver; Cody James Matekovik was born June 24, 1999, in Denver.

Andrea Brooke Roberts, born September 22, 1975, in Carroll County; married on August 19, 1995, Aaron Robert Blum, born on September 11, 1973 in the state of Washington. Aaron's parents are Robert and Sylvia Anderson Blum of Washington.

Andrea holds a B.S. in early childhood development from Brigham Young University; and Aaron holds a B.S. in physics from Brigham Young University. He is an A-10 Warthog pilot with the U.S. Air Force.

Andrea and Aaron Blum's child is Audrey Claire Blum, who was born February 18, 2001, in Fayetteville, North Carolina. *Submitted by: Robert G. Roberts, P.O. Box 461, Villa Rica, GA 30180 and Written by: Pauline C. Roberts*

Sources: Census, Court Records, Personal Records, Family Relatives.

962. John Robertson

John Robertson, born 1634 in Scotland. King James conferred Coat of Arms on him for saving him from a would-be assassin.

John Robertson, born 1675, migrated to Ireland and married Elizabeth Randolph of Belfast.

John Randolph Robertson, born Ireland, married Mary Gower whose parents were Abel Gower, sea captain, born 1718, and Mary Gower, born 27 January 1716 Brunswick County, Virginia. The Laurens County, South Carolina, Robertsons were descended from four known Robertson brothers who took oaths in Virginia in 1832. These four brothers, born 1705 to 1713, were Charles, William, James, and John Randolph.

Manoah Dixon Robertson was born Brunswick County, Virginia, circa 1743. His mother was probably Amelia Elizabeth Owings. This family moved to Orange County, Virginia, then to Burke County, North Carolina, when it was cut from Rowan County in 1779. This section later fell in Buncombe County, North Carolina. His brothers and sisters were: John Jr. born 1772, Elizabeth born 1774, William born 1778, Rebecca born 1780, Barnett born 1782, Polly (Mary) born 1784, Sara Frances born 1786, Margaret (Peggy) born 1788, Reuben born 14 February 1794, Amelia (Milley) born 1797, Toliver born 13 July 1800.

Old John Robertson had been widowed while in North Carolina and remarried Susan Couch. He died in 1802 in Laurens County, South Carolina. He left a will and four unmarried daughters. He is believed to have been buried at Shuffletown but I have been unable to learn where that is located.

Manoah married Mary Caroline Sammons in Richmond County, Georgia, in 1828. After they left South Carolina they changed the spelling of their name to Robison. They were in Heard County, Georgia, in 1840, and in Randolph County, Alabama, with a large plantation and sixty slaves when the Civil War broke out. Manoah organized a company at Graham, Alabama, which became Company E, 13th Alabama Regiment. He was a captain of this unit. His son, John Dixon Howell, was first lieutenant. They were stationed at Yorktown and fought through the bloody battles of Bull Run, Seven Pines, Fair Oaks Station, Seven Days Battle, Battle of Cedar Mountain, Second Battle of Bull Run, Antietam, and Harper's Ferry. Captain Monoah Robison was severely wounded at Antietam (Sharpsburg) and was captured by the Federal Army. He was paroled 29 October 1862. He returned home and did recruitment duties until the end of the war. He served as the moderator of the Bethlehem Primitive Baptist church in Carroll County, Georgia. He died in 1868 and is buried at Pleasant Grove Baptist Church, Route #5, Carroll County.

John Dixon Howell Robison, the eldest son also became a preacher in Alabama and Georgia. He married Catherine Jane Johnson (said to be a Cherokee Indian), the daughter of Alexander Johnson and Sarah Morgan, who was the daughter of David Morgan and Elizabeth Rylee. She married Alexander Johnson in Madison County, Georgia, 27 March 1817.

In the 1870 Georgia census, we find John Dixon Howell and Catherine Jane living in Carroll County with three daughters, two sons, two Ponder orphans, Mary Caroline Robison, and Rebecca Johnson all living in the same household. Times were hard and I would imagine that they banded together in order to survive.

Jefferson Davis Robison was their youngest son, born in Alabama in 1861, the year after his father left to fight in the War of Northern Aggression. He was also my father's father and my paternal grandfather. *Submitted by: Robert Howell Robison, Villa Rica, GA and Written by: Helen Foster, 1924 Victory Church Road, Bowdon, GA 30108*

963. "Miss Sallie" Robinson

Mary Josephine Robinson was born 7 October 1853 in Worthville, Butts County, Georgia, the oldest daughter of William Osmus Robinson and Rosannah Helen Sinah Lofton Robinson. She came with her family to Carroll County in the Fall of 1859 as a little girl. Sallie is the nickname that she was called her whole life long and she became Miss Sallie to the hundreds of school children that she taught in Carroll County. Miss Sallie never married — her sweetheart had died young, the family always said — but Sally enjoyed a lifelong career as a teacher. She taught at Hickory Level, Shady Grove, Pleasant Hill, Buffalo and taught for twenty years at Oakridge School. In her later years, she took care of her aged father. Sallie was also the family historian and because of her writings for the *Carroll Free Press* in 1930, we know the stories of our ancestors. She wrote *A Sketch of My Life* and *Just Some Memories of Carrollton As A Village Long Ago.*

"Miss Sallie" Robinson

According to Sallie Robinson's own records, she began her schooling in 1869 at the old Carrollton Seminary on College Street. Her teacher was Miss Mollie Thomasson. Then, in 1871-1872, she attended the school of that "master teacher" Professor A.C. Reese. At that time, he was teaching at the Old Academy located where the Carrollton Train Depot is today. In 1874 Prof. Reese began teaching in the New Academy where Sallie attended 1874-75.

Augustus C. Reese is a part of Carrollton's great early history. He was a native New Yorker who had earned his master of arts degree in New York and moved to Carrollton after the Civil War. He erected a school at his own expense on the west side of the train depot, large enough to accommodate 200 students. This was dedicated on 14 November 1872 as Reese's Polytechnic High School, generally known as The New Academy. This later became the local school for girls and the Masonic Institute became the school for boys. The tuition charged was $2 to $3.50 per month. The school terms ran year round with accommodations made for planting and harvest times. The fall term began on the third Monday in July and ran until December. The spring term began the third week in January and ended in July. Sallie Robinson received her teaching certificate from Reese's Polytechnic High in 1876. In her writings, Sallie mentioned that the spinster sisters Abbie and Cynthia Wier were the organizers of Carrollton's first kindergarten. During her teaching days at Oakridge School, Miss Sallie lived in the homes of Mrs. James Story and Mrs. James Hogan, and she loved living with these families.

Sallie wrote about a serious illness that befell her in 1917 and that for three months she was a helpless invalid. She praised Dr. W.L. Fitts and Dr. Charles Fitts who treated her "every day — early or late — they came to my bedside

"Miss Sallie" Robinson and students at Oakridge School, 1905

doing all they could do to relieve my suffering." Sallie brothers hired "an Antebellum nurse, Callie Benson" to care for Sallie during her long illness. The name of Fitts was long associated with medical practices in Carrollton.

Dr. William Washington Fitts was born in Elbert County, Georgia, 3 November 1833 and his father moved to Pike County. In 1855, the young W.W. Fitts became the medical pupil of Dr. Westbrook and Dr. Shackleford at Bowdon, Carroll County, Georgia. He also attended Atlanta Medical College and graduated from there in 1860. W.W. Fitts was married at Bowdon in 1855 to Miss Augie Brown and they were the parents of ten children — five boys and five girls. After receiving his medical degree, Dr. Fitts resided in Calhoun County, Alabama, until the Civil War. He entered the Confederate Army as a major and surgeon of the 44th Alabama Regiment.

Dr. William Washington Fitts

After the Civil War, Dr. Fitts became a resident of Carroll County again in 1863. He became one of the energetic personalities that surely left its mark on our county. He worked long and hard with B.M. Long, Patrick Garrison, and John W. Stewart to help prevent the railroad route from going to Lowell instead of Carrollton. For his efforts, he was made a director of the railroad. But the crowning work of his long career was in helping establish a splendid public school system. He served as president of the Carrollton School Board for twenty-five years. He also was influential in building the waterworks and sewerage system to help promote public health. He actively practiced medicine in Carroll County for fifty years.

In her old age, Miss Sallie Robinson lived out her days at the family home place. Her brothers, W.O. Robinson Jr. and John Henry Robinson were devoted to her, stopping by every week to bring her groceries and medicine.

Sallie Robinson died on 19 January 1934 and was laid to rest alongside her parents and sister, Sinah Robinson Horton, at Old Concord Methodist Church at Hickory Level. *Submitted by: Sue Robinson Bonner, Horsley Mill Road, Carrollton, GA*

964. Catherine Sanders Robinson

We believe we have a picture of Catherine Sanders Robinson, as it was the very first tintype in the old velvet photo album belonging to William Osmus Robinson, and Catherine bears a striking resemblance to all our family. Catherine Sanders married Joseph Robinson in Putnam County, Georgia, in 1810. I have found others of Dutch ancestry who migrated from the area of Sullivan County, Tennessee, to middle Georgia in the early 1800s. Catherine Sanders was the mother of William Osmus Robinson born in 1825 in Morgan County, Georgia.

Catherine Sanders was born in Sullivan County, Tennessee, on 8 September 1783, the daughter of John Sanders (Xanders — Dutch spelling) and Elbertine Tenbroeck of Albany, New York, and eastern Tennessee. Catherine had a brother John born 5 July 1785 and a sister named Sarah. John's Sanders — the father — was born 2 October 1757 and died 30 March 1834. John was the son of Johannes Sanders and Deborah Glen of Beverwyck settlement, New Netherland, later Albany, New York. Elbertine Tenbroeck was born 23 November 1760 and the daughter of Dirck Wesselse Tenbroeck and Catheryn Conyn (born circa 1724) who married 28 June 1743 according to Albany, New York, Dutch records.

Dirck Wessele Tenbroeck was the son of Samuel Tenbroeck who married 7 November 1712 to Maria Hendricksen VanRensselaur (born 1682 and died 4 April 1756 Greenbush, New York). Samuel Tenbroeck was the son of Dirck Wessels Tenbroeck born Kingston, New York, 18 December 1638 and died 18 September 1717, married Christina Van Buren who was born 1644 and died 26 November 1729. Maria Van Rensselaur was the daughter of Hendrick Van Rensselaur and Catherine Van Brugge. Christina Van Buren was born 1644 and died age 85 was the daughter of Cornelius Maas Van Buren and Cathalina Martens. Both of these parents died on the same day in 1648.

Catherine Conyn or Conine was the daughter of Leendert Philpse Conyn born 9 September 1683 and married 28 June 1713 to Jannetje Emmitie Van Alen born 1686 and died March 1758. Jannetje was the daughter of Stephanus Van Alen and Maria Cornelise Mulder. Leendert Philipse Conyn was the son of Philip Leendertse Conyn born 1662 in Albany, New York and Wyntje Dirkse Van Vechten born 17 January 1662. Philip Leendertse Conyn was the son of Leendert Philipse Conyn and Agnietje Casperse. Wyntje Dirkse Van Vechten was the daughter of Dirk Tuinesin Van Vechten born 1632 in Vechten, Utrecht, Netherlands, and died 27 November 1702 in Albany, New York. Tuinesin (or Jeunisen) was the son of Teunis Dirkse Van Vechten born 1612 died 1687. Wyntje Dirke Van Vechten's mother was Jannetje Michelrelse Vreelant born 1637 in Bergen City, New Jersey and died 25 November 1702. Jannetje was the daughter of Michiel Jansen Vreelant and Fytje Hartman.

Going back to Stephanus Van Alen, he was the son of Laurens Van Alen who was descended from King James I of Scotland. Laurens Van Alen was the son of Johannes Van Alen who emigrated from Oldenzall, Holland, to Kinderhook, New York. Johannes VanAlen married Catherine Von Mierborch. The mother of Stephanus Van Alen was Elberte Evertsz Backer who was born in 1656 and married on 13 January 1669 when she was twelve years old. She was orphaned on the ship *de Bruyvis* that was bringing her family to America. Her father was Evart Lucayse Backer and her mother was Jannetje Emmitse Volkerts. Both parents died on the voyage to America and Elberte married Laurens Van Alen on the ship after her parents died. All these families seemed to migrate to the area of New York that was then called New Netherland, near Beverwyck, which was later called Albany. They are all found in the old Dutch records of that area. The area called Kinderhook, New York was in Columbia County, New York. *Submitted by: Nassim Ansari, Duluth, GA*

965. Dr. Jerry Charles Robinson Family

Jerry Charles Robinson was born 30 June 1940 in Carroll County, the son of Henry Grady Robinson and Lona Jerusha Gray. Jerry attended the public schools of Carrollton and was valedictorian of his Carrollton High School Class of 1958. After high school, he attended the University of Georgia, graduating with a degree in mathematics in 1965. Jerry Robinson and Mary Alice Clayton were married on 3 June 1967. Jerry continued his education at The Medical College of Georgia in Augusta, receiving his doctor of medicine degree in 1969.

Mary Alice Clayton was the daughter of Charles Allen Clayton Jr. (29 December 1898-3 May 1999) and Rena Burke Witt (2 May 1904-10 February 1983). Born in Copperhill, Tennessee, on 26 August 1945, Mary Alice attended school in Copperhill. She graduated from Copper Basin High School in 1963. After high school, Alice attended Brenau College in Gainesville, Georgia. She graduated from Brenau with an A.B. degree in biology in 1967. Alice began her teaching career by teaching seventh and eighth grade science at Akin Junior High School at Akin, South Carolina. Then, while Jerry was in his internship at Spartanburg General Hospital in Spartanburg, South Carolina, she taught fifth grade at Pine Street Elementary School in Spartanburg. In 1970-71 while Jerry was in his residency in Charleston, she taught biology at James Island High School there. Alice took time off when her sons were born, but after they had finished school, she earned her master's degree in education in 1996 from West Georgia College in Carrollton. Since that time, she has taught second grade at Oak Mountain Academy.

Robinson Family (from back L): Joe, Jason, Jerry, Alice

Alice's father was a railroad engineer for the Louisville & Nashville Railroad for fifty years. Charlie Clayton had met Rena Witt in the train station and often said that the first time he laid eyes on her that she was "as pretty as an armful of roses." Rena was a principal and teacher who began her career in education in a one-room school in Delano, Tennessee. She worked in the schools until she was in her sixties. Charlie and Rena Clayton would move to Carrollton, Georgia in later years to live close to their daughter, Mary Alice.

Rena died in 1983 but Charlie lived to the ripe old age of 100. Charlie was so happy to be able to maintain living independently until the end of his life. Charlie lived on Cedar Street which was close to the old post office in Carrollton. Even in his 90s, Charlie enjoyed taking a daily walk to the post office where he could see and visit with all the people of Carrollton coming in and out. He had many friends in Carrollton and was a member of the First Baptist Church in Carrollton. Charlie died in 1999 and is buried next to his wife, Rena, and other family members at Benton Cemetery in Polk County, Tennessee.

The Claytons and Witts have a long history in the state of Tennessee — Rena Witt's father was Benjamin Bouger Carroll Witt, a lawyer who practiced in Benton, Tennessee. He died at the age of eighty-three, the oldest living lawyer in Polk County, Tennessee. Charles Clayton Sr. was an agent for the Louisville and Nashville Railroad as well as president of the Etowah Bank.

Dr. Jerry Robinson completed his residency in radiology at the Medical University of South Carolina at Charleston in 1973. Dr. Robinson was then employed at Tanner Memorial Hospital from 1973-1993. Since 1993, he has been employed by Haralson Radiological Group, P.C. at Higgins General Hospital in Bremen, Georgia. Dr. and Mrs. Robinson attend both the Tabernacle Baptist Church and St. Margaret's Episcopal Church in Carrollton. Alice serves on the Altar Guild at St. Margaret's.

Dr. Jerry C. and Mary Alice Clayton Robinson are the parents of two sons. Jason Charles Robinson was born 12 April 1974 in Carroll County. Jason attended the Carroll County school system and graduated from Central High School in 1992 as valedictorian of his class. After high school, Jason attended the University of Georgia where he was a member of Sigma Chi fraternity, Delta Chapter. Jason was a member of Golden Key National Honor Society at the University of Georgia. Also, he was a member of Psi Chi National Honor Society. Jason received the Outstanding Senior Award from Delta Epsilon Iota being recognized for his academic excellence and leadership abilities.

When Jason graduated from Georgia in 1997 he was awarded An American Chemical Society approved B.S. Chem in chemistry and a B.S. in psychology. In his chemistry degree, he graduated cum laude, with high honors. At the present time, Jason is pursuing a doctorate in physical chemistry at the University of California at Berkeley. Jason is a pioneer in his field called Molecular Beam Reactive Scattering and Photodissociation. Jason has received invitations on the international circuit to lecture on this topic. Jason will receive his Ph.D. upon graduation in May of 2002.

The second son, Joseph Clayton Robinson, was born 28 June 1977. Joe attended Central High School and was a member of Who's Who in America High Schools. Joe graduated from Central High School in 1995. He attended West Georgia College and graduated from the School of Fitness and Nutrition in Atlanta, Georgia in 1998. Joe is interested in health and fitness and can often be seen pumping the irons at Gold's Gym in Carrollton. He has established his own business in Carrollton which is called Joe's Landscaping. Joe enjoys working in the outdoors and has many fine customers who look to him for the care of their lawns, shrubberies, and flowers. He also is self-employed in the construction business here in Carroll County. Joe now lives in the home that had once belonged to his grandparents, Charles and Rena Clayton, on Cedar Street. *Submitted by: Dr. and Mrs. Jerry C. Robinson, Horsley Mill Road, Carrollton, GA.*

966. Florence Robinson

Florence Robinson was born 2 October 1898, the daughter of John Henry Robinson and Margaret Josephine Green. Florence grew up in the Pleasant Hill community and married Cecil Earle Bryant, the son of Alexander H. Bryant and Florence Swann Baker. Florence and Earle Bryant had one daughter who was Nell Bryant born 13 August 1924.

Nell Bryant married on 12 September 1941 Dr. John Ernest Powell Jr. (7 May 1921-16 February 1978). He was the son of John Ernest Powell Sr. and Pauline Pope of Villa Rica. Pauline Pope was born 1894 the daughter of Wiley Oscar Pope and Kate Perkerson. Pauline

Dr. and Mrs. John Ernest Powell Sr. with Ernest Jr. and Kathryn.

was the granddaughter of William Henry Pope and Susan Hamrick and of Thomas Jefferson Perkerson and Sophia McLarty.

Dr. John Ernest Powell Sr. (1892-1964) was the son of Lewis Redwine Powell and Nannie Hancock. Nannie Hancock was the daughter of Gallanus Wynn Hancock and Sara Frances Hancock. Dr. Powell Sr. was the grandson of Rev. Levi Thomas Gardner Powell who was pastor of Old Concord Methodist Church at Hickory Level. Rev. Powell was married to Nancy Selina Redwine. Nancy Redwine was the daughter of Lewis Redwine who died 17 April 1867 leaving a will in Coweta Co., Georgia naming sons: William M., John M., and Columbus D. Redwine.

Sanford Kingsberry

John M. Redwine married Georgia Persis Jerusha Kingsberry. She was the daughter of Sanford Kingsberry (24 June 1805-28 December 1866), an early Carroll County pioneer. Jerusha Kingsberry's brothers and sisters were: Sanford Theodore b. 1837, Joseph b. 1840, Charlels Samuel b. 1842, Amelia b. 1845, Edwin b. 1847, Mary Ann b. 1850 m. Lt. Nicholas Fain, C.S.A., Katie m. Capus Stripling, and Paschal. Jerusha was the mother of John Kingsberry Redwine born 27 June 1865 and he

Wiley Oscar and Kate Perkerson Pope

Seated, Elizabeth and Lewis Redwine Powell. Standing, Buna Columbus, John William, Francis Parks, and Thomas Gardner Powell

married 1st Lizzie Roop, 2nd Ida Evelyn Johnson, and 3rd Mattie D. Moore. John Kingsberery Redwine was a prominent citizen who lived in Carrollton all his life.

The first lots being sold in Carroll County, GA were advertised in May of 1831 in *Columbus Enquirer* which was the nearest newspaper of that time. Sanford Kingsberry was born 24 June 1805 in Derby, Vermont. He married Mary Ann Grow in Orleans County, Vermont on 23 September 1834 and shortly afterwards moved to Henry County, GA. Mary Ann Grow was born in Orleans Co., VT on 17 April 1814. In 1843, Sanford and Mary Ann Kingsberry purchased 360 acres one mile north of the center of Carrollton and built a beautiful white columned home that they named "Oak Lawn."

Homer Hesterlee, Leon Powell, Addie Hesterlee, Annie Powell, and Ernest Powell.

There is an interesting tale told about how Sanford Kingsberry acquired the property known as Oak Lawn — told by his son in the *Carroll County Times* for the centennial celebration in 1927. Sanford Kingsberry was a famous breeder of Black Hawk horses known for their speed and their excellence. The property known as Oak Lawn in Carroll County consisted of 400 acres owned by an individual who lived 300 miles away. The property was "entailed and could not be bought until the death of a certain party" and there were many people who were anxious to buy the property when it became available.

At the death of that person, "several men started out on a race for Springfield — the only place the trade could be consummated." Mr. Kingsberry was absent from home and did not receive the word that the property was now available until the other men had had a day's start. Even so, Kingsberry hitched up his Black Hawk horses and started out on the journey. "He drove 50 miles per day for three days, bought the land, and met his competitors forty miles back this way," according to his son.

Sanford Kingsberry was one of Carrollton's earliest merchants — and could even claim that some of his best customers were Creek Indians. Other early merchants were Thomas McGuire, Y.J. and John Long, General William Beall, and Isaac E. Cobb. The Kingsberry home on Rome Street was built in 1835 and had four rooms — two above and two below. Later the verandas and ells were added. This home later became the home of the William Osmus Robinson family. Sanford Kingsberry d. 28 December 1869. Mary Ann Kingsberry d. April 1874.

The Kingsberry Family was prominent in England and even claimed William Shakespeare as a descendant. The first of the family to come to America were two brothers, Joseph and Henry Kingsberry, who came with Gov. Winthrop of Massachusetts on the ship "Tolbot" in 1630. Henry was the progenitor of the southern branch of the family — Sanford and three brothers settled in Carroll County — Henry, Charles and George Kingsberry.

Pauline Pope graduated from Georgia Normal Industrial College.

Paschal P. Grow, brother of Mary Ann Grow Kingsberry, also moved to Carroll County. He was born in Vermont 27 April 1811. He married Elmyra Walcot on 3 December 1835. The great-grandfather of Paschal P. Grow was John Grow an early settler of Vermont. Paschal's grandparents were Samuel and Jerushia Stowell Grow. Paschal's parents were Joseph and Tirzah Sangor Grow — all of Vermont. Both Joseph and Samuel Grow were soldiers in the Patriot Army in the American Revolution.

Dr. John Ernest Powell Sr., 1915

In 1840 the Grow family traveled for eight weeks over several hundred miles in a Jersey wagon to settle in Carroll County. Mr. Grow was a farmer and a merchant. He died in 1861 leaving Elmyra with five children. Elmyra Grow b. 11 August 1812 in Barnett, Vermont was one of the first women to establish a school in Carroll County and was a much loved schoolteacher. The Grow children were: Paschal, Jacob C., Lewis R., Emerson, and Augusta (who married Pvt. Joe Lafayette Cobb — Carroll County's first genealogist and historian, author of *Carroll County and Her People (1906)*.

Three of the Grow sons served in the Confederacy — Paschal P. died at Manassas, Lewis K. was killed at Petersburg, and Jacob C. became a Presbyterian minister in Texas. Elmyra Grow died 8 December 1893. The son of Paschal P. Grow was Samuel Emerson Grow who became a prominent attorney in Carrollton. In 1882, he was Mayor of Carrollton. S.E. Grow married in 1877 to Lenora McDaniel, daughter of Col. Charles A. and Victoria Hines McDaniel. Col. McDaniel was a founder and President of Bowdon College until the war began and was Col. of the 41st Regiment, and killed at the battle of Perryville, Kentucky. By and large, the Grow family was always a family of educators and other members of this family have carried on this tradition.

Dr. John Ernest Powell Sr. graduated with honors from Emory Medical School in 1915, the youngest in his class. He practiced medicine in Villa Rica GA for fifty years and was one of the

T.J. Perkerson Family, 1899

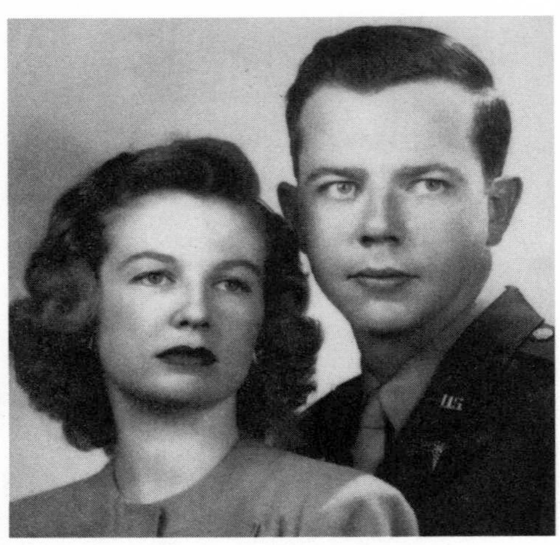

Nell Bryant and Ernest Powell Jr.

founders of the first Villa Rica Hospital where he served as medical director. His brothers were: Leon G. Powell m. Genevieve Shackleford, Lewis R. Powell m. Urabell Turner; Sisters: Annie Powell m. Robert L. Berry, Mary Ellen Powell m. Alvin Baxley.

The children of Dr. Powell Sr. and Pauline Pope are: (1) Dr. John Ernest Powell Jr. (2)Kathryn Ann 1924-1926 (3)Carolyn Pope m. David C. Paris. Dr. Powell, Jr. graduated from Emory University School of Medicine, served in U.S. Army and then practiced medicine in Villa Rica for 31 years. In the 1950s, Dr. John Earnest Powell Jr. donated property to the City of Villa Rica for the development of a Recreational Center. A large recreation building, swimming pool, and lighted tennis courts were erected.

Florence Robinson Bryant

Dr. John Earnest Powell Jr. and Nell Bryant were the parents of (1) Leslie Elaine Powell b. 2 September 1945 in Atlanta, attended Emory at Oxford and later graduated with B.S., M.Ed. and Ed.S. degrees from West Georgia College in Carrollton; m. Phillip Terry Carter (b. 22 January 1948); received B.A. from West Georgia College and M.Ed and Ed.S. from Georgia State University; vice president of Economic Development of West Central Technical College. Leslie is a teacher at H.A. Jones Elementary School at Bremen. Phil and Leslie Carter's children are Susan Powell Carter b. 4 October 1978 and Samuel Phillip Carter born 28 March 1981. (2) John Earnest Powell III b. 15 January 1951, received MBA from West Georgia College married Janet Caylor daughter of Rev. John Caylor and Katie Dorsey Caylor on 18 March 1978. Janet received her A.S. from West Georgia College and B.S. in nursing from University of South Carolina. Later, Janet earned a master's in nurse practitioner and works as a nurse practitioner on the Catawba Indian Reserve in Columbia, South Carolina. John and Janet have the following children: Jessica Courtney, Joshua Ryan and Adam Walker Powell. They reside in Columbia, S.C. *Submitted by: Leslie Powell Carter, West Allison Circle, Carrollton, GA 30117*

967. Henry Grady Robinson Family

Henry Grady Robinson was born 11 November 1892, the son of John Henry Robinson and Margaret Josephine Green, of the Shady Grove community of Carroll County. The Robinsons later became major landholders on the Horsley Mill Road in the Pleasant Hill community when six adjoining farms were merged together to create the Robinson farm. Much of this property remains in the Robinson family today-representing the homes of Grady and Lona's children-Dr. Louis Robinson, Dr. Jerry Robinson, Sue Carol Robinson Bonner, and a grandson, Henry Michael Robinson.

Grady Robinson was educated in the early public schools of Carroll County and became a farmer with many interests in managing his father's properties. Grady entered World War I in 1917 and was transported with his unit to Europe where he fought in The Battle of the Argonne Forrest and other major battles in France and Belgium. After World War I had ended, Grady returned to his native Carroll County and on 4 October 1924, he married Lona Jerusha Gray, daughter of Willie Gerald Gray and Lura Roena Broom. Lona Gray was born 22 July 1906 in Carroll County and was affectionately called Miss Lona by everyone during her many years as a nurse in Carroll and Heard Counties. Miss Lona was an important influence in the lives of her children-and inspired two sons to become medical doctors.

Grady Robinson and his brother Talmadge Robinson were engaged in many farming ventures together in Carroll County. Grady was especially known for his luscious grape vines and created his own original recipe for homemade wine. Everyone among his friends and neighbors and relatives would say "All we want for Christmas is some of Uncle Grady's homemade wine." And it was a treasured gift.

Grady Robinson was for many years associated with the Anderson Clayton Company, the foremost buyers of Carroll County cotton. Grady, like his father John Henry Robinson, was considered to be a most excellent judge when it came to grading the post harvest cotton. Grady Robinson was later associated with Alton Lane, his cousin by marriage, in the farm supply and farming equipment business. In 1925, Alton Lane married Jewel Robinson who was the daughter of William Osmus Robinson Jr.-a brother to John Henry Robinson. Robinson & Lane also owned a large cotton warehouse. Their business was located at the present site of Burson's Feed and Seed in Carrollton.

Grady Robinson and Lona Gray Robinson were the parents of four children. Henry Donald Robinson was born 15 August 1928. He was educated in Carrollton public schools, graduating from Carrollton High School in 1946. Donald attended Clemson University before being called into active service during World War II. He served in the 508 Red Devils Airborne Unit. Donald was recalled into active service again during the Korean War. He served as first lieutenant in U.S. Air Force from 1959-1963. Later he went into business as a Certified Public Accountant. Donald was married four times: first, Louise Mae Longest, two daughters-Carole and Dale Robinson. His second marriage was to Teresa Rowe-one child: Rhoda Alyssandra Robinson who was born 19 March 1969 in Carroll County, married Wayne Albonie Skerrett, a native of New Zealand. The Skerretts have two daughters, Albonie and Annaleise and all live in New Zealand. Donald's third marriage was to Wilhelmenia, no children. Donald's fourth wife was Shirley-no children.

The second son of Grady and Lona Robinson was James Louis Robinson born 22 April 1931 in Carroll County. Louis attended Carrollton High School where he was a member of the Beta Club. He graduated from Carrollton High School in 1948 and was honored with the Appleton Mandeville Citizenship Award for his academic achievements. Louis' name is inscribed on the marble tablet at the Old CHS along with other recipients of this award in years past. Louis served in the U.S. Army during the Korean War as Corporal in the 24th Infantry Division. After the war, he completed his undergraduate work at West Georgia College. Louis then entered Auburn University where he received his B.S. degree in pharmacy.

Henry Grady Robinson entering World War I

Louis Robinson worked for several years for Robinson Drug Company as a pharmacist. Later on, Louis attended The Medical College of Georgia at Augusta where he received his doctor of medicine in general practice. His medical internship was spent at The Medical Center in Columbus, Georgia. Dr. Robinson entered into private practice in Woodbury, Georgia, and was for many years a most loved physician of that community. Dr. Robinson was one of the founders of The Flint River Academy, a private college preparatory school there in Woodbury. For several years, Dr. Robinson served as consultant in Public Health for District 4 of Georgia. He later opened a private practice in Heard County, Georgia, operating a clinic in Franklin. He also worked for Palmetto Health Services in Franklin during these years. In 1997, he sold his clinic to Tanner Medical Center and he worked as a physician for TMC until his retirement.

On 10 June 1956, Dr. Louis Robinson married first Shirley Anne Wilson, daughter of Zealous Francis Wilson and Mary Lou Etta Gosdin of Heard County, Georgia. Shirley was born 6 August 1936. She graduated from Heard County High School. Shirley was a sister to Curtis

Robinson Family: Grady (with grandsons Jason and Joe), Lona. Standing L to R: Jerry, Louis, Donald, and Sue Carol

Wilson, a popular teacher and basketball coach at Carrollton High School for many years. Shirley attended West Georgia College to study broadcasting. She obtained her second class broadcasting license and hosted an interview/talk show on WWGC/FM. She later worked for the Carrollton radio stations WBTR FM & WLBB AM. Shirley also worked for many years as office manager for Dr. Robinson's clinic in Franklin, Georgia. Shirley is presently employed at Belk's Department Store in Carrollton. Dr. Louis and Shirley Robinson had one son, Henry Michael Robinson.

Henry Michael Robinson was born 8 March 1958 in Carroll County, and married Pamela Elaine Lasster on 16 August 1981. Pamela Elaine Laster was born 10 August 1962 in Bowdon, Georgia, the daughter of Render Terrell Laster and Myrtice Virginia Kent of Heard County, Georgia. Michael graduated from Carrollton High School in 1976 and attended West Georgia College. He received his degree in radiologic technology from Emory/Crawford Long Hospital in 1985 where he received the Outstanding Student Award. Mike was employed by Tanner Medical Center for twelve years serving as technical director of the Ultrasound Laboratory until November 1995. Mike is now employed by the PAPP Clinic of Newnan as the technical director of Ultrasound Imaging and Hemodynamics Laboratory. Elaine graduated from Heard County High School in 1980. In 1983, she graduated from West Georgia College with an A.S. degree in nursing. She has been employed by Tanner Medical Center for twenty years, working as Intensive Care Unit nurse and as Overhouse supervisor. Elaine is presently pursuing her B.S. degree in nursing.

The Robinsons love outdoor camping and Mike is a skilled craftsman in woodworking. He has built many beautiful cabinets and bookcases. Mike is also an accomplished writer who was the first of the family to research all of W.O. Robinson's descendants down to present day. His book on our genealogy is in Special Collections at Neva Lomason Library in Carrollton.

Mike and Elaine Robinson have three daughters. The oldest daughter is Leslie Allison who was born 12 March 1983. She is presently a senior at Central High School and has received the National Merit Award and is in Who's Who in American High Schools. Leslie plans for a career either in nursing or dental hygiene. Rachel Anne Robinson was born 6 May 1986 and is presently a ninth grade student at Central High School. She is a cheerleader for football and other competitions. Kendall Elizabeth was born 12 May 1993 and is in the second grade at Central Elementary School. She enjoys performing gymnastics at Kids Kountry in Carrollton. Kendall's special talent is doing back hand springs. The Robinsons attend Oak Grove Baptist Church.

After forty years of marriage, Dr. Louis and Shirley Robinson were divorced. On 4 July 1992, Dr. Robinson married second to Gail Chatman who was born 23 May 1955 in Carroll County.

The third child of Grady and Lona Robinson was Jerry Charles Robinson. (See separate heading for this family).

The fourth child is Sue Carol Robinson born 26 August 1942 in Carroll County. Sue graduated from Carrollton High School in 1960. She married Robert Bonner 5 June 1960 in Carroll County. He was born 26 February 1937 in Carroll County. Robert was the son of Robert James "Rip" Bonner who died 1971 and Sarah Nell McPherson of Carroll County. Rip Bonner is buried at Stripling Chapel Church Cemetery.

The Bonner and the McPherson families were early pioneer families in Carroll County. Elijah McPherson was one of the first residents of Center Point community in Carroll County. According to Pvt. Joe Cobb in his book, *Carroll County and Her People,* Elijah McPherson lived near the headwaters of Buck Creek where he built a sawmill and operated it off the water power from the creek. Lumber would be carried by wagons from as far as 25 miles away. The forests were full of pine and blackjack oak trees. The mill could cut 200-300 feet of lumber a day. A very interesting eye-witness account of this sawmill in operation is written by George Martin Holcombe in the *Cullman Tribune* newspaper 28 January 1915.

G.M. Holcombe was born in Carroll County, Georgia in 1843 and later served as pastor of Little Vine Church. In 1888 he moved to Cullman, Alabama, and in 1914-1915, Rev. Holcombe wrote a series of articles about his recollections of early Carroll County (1850-1870) and also about his service as a Confederate soldier during the siege of Vicksburg. He was a member of Company G, 40th Regiment of Georgia Volunteer Infantry, C.S.A. which included many of the boys who enlisted from Carroll and Haralson Counties. This is a very descriptive account of those times and a fascinating read. There is a reprint of Holcombe's "Reminiscences of an Old Man" in Special Collections, Neva Lomason Library in Carrollton.

Elijah McPherson's oldest son was killed during the Civil War. His next oldest son, Hute, lived at Temple. Elijah McPherson had a grandson named Col. L.D. McPherson who practiced law in Carrollton. Uncle Elijah, as he was affectionately called, was a cousin of the Union General McPherson who was killed at the Battle of Atlanta on 22 July 1864. According to Cobb's writing of 1906—

> "There is a magnificent monument on the spot where he fell...Fort McPherson barracks was named for him."

Sue and Robert Bonner had the following children: Richard Jeffrey Bonner born 5 March 1963. Jeff graduated from Central High School. Jennifer Carolyn Bonner and Judith Elaine Bonner were twins born on 1 March 1969. Both Jenny and Judy Bonner graduated from Carrollton High School in 1981. Sue Robinson is now employed at the Carroll County Public Health Department.

Grady Robinson died 30 May 1981 and is buried at the Robinson Family Cemetery on Horsley Mill Road in Carrollton. Lona Gray Robinson died 1 March 1988 and is buried at Temperance Methodist Church Cemetery at Sand Hill in Carroll County. *Submitted by: Dr. Louis Robinson, 304 Horsley Mill Road, Carrollton, GA 30116*

968. J.D. Robinson and Helen S. Maier

John David (J.D.) Robinson was the eldest son of Walter Hill Robinson and Jacqueline Zora Harris. He was born in Carroll County and raised in Carroll County and Atlanta. His parents divorced sometime after 1926 and remarried 28 years later. J.D. left school in the eighth grade to help support the family through the depression. He was in the Navy during World War II and met the son of Thomas Watson, the founder of IBM. J.D. worked on one of the first Navy computer systems in the Navy to handle payroll and inventory systems. After leaving the Navy, he worked for IBM as a systems analyst. He later graduated from Woodrow Wilson College of Law School on May 23, 1949, and passed the Georiga bar. He worked at Gulf Oil Corporation as an attorney. However, he soon returned to IBM as he loved systems analyst work. He then worked for Lockheed as a systems analyst. He retired in the early 1960s, planning to open a nursery in Snellville, but he died before fulfilling his dream.

On April 1, 1934, J.D. married Helen Standridge Maier (born Jan. 14, 1915 in Brooklyn Queens County, New York, and died July 26, 1998) and raised an adopted daughter, Joanne Robinson Mason (born Dec. 11, 1944) who now lives in Snellville.

Both J.D. and Helen are buried at Rest Haven Memorial Gardens in Decatur, Georgia. *Submitted by: Joanne Robinson Mason, 3494 W. Elmwood Circle, Snellville, GA 30278*

969. Joanne Robinson and Perry Reid Mason

Joanne was the daughter of John David Robinson, son of Jacqueline Zora Harris and Walter Hill Robinson of Carroll County.

Joanne was born in Ventura, California, on December 11, 1944, and was adopted shortly thereafter by John David and Helen Standridge Maier. She was raised in Eastlake, Georgia. She has an associates degree from Dekalb College. She married Perry Reid Mason (born May 9, 1943, in Montgomery, Alabama) on January 12, 1961, Joanne has been a long time member of White Oak Baptist church in Gwinnett County. She has worked for BAPCO (the Yellow pages division of BellSouth) for many years and plans to retire in 2004.

They settled in Snellville, Georgia. They had two children. The first was Russell Troy Mason, born January 10, 1966. Troy graduated from Brookwood High School in Gwinnett County, Georgia. He married Robin Renea Ringler on February 14, 1989. They had a daughter, Charli Ann Mason, on August 8, 1989, and were later divorced. Troy still lives in the Gwinnett County area.

The second child of Joanne and Perry was Leigh Anne Mason, born December 12, 1976, at DeKalb General Hospital. She is a graduate of Young Harris College in the North Georgia mountains and will graduate from Georgia State in December 2001. She is a talented artist and plans to make her career in the arts.

Submitted by: Mike Harrelson, 12207 Dorwayne Court, Houston, TX 77015-6113

970. John and Melba Robinson

Melba Angeline Morgan was born 28 May 1922 in Carroll County, Georgia, the daughter of James Horry Morgan of Carroll County and Trixie Patrick, a native of Cullman, Alabama. Melba grew up on the Morgan home place on Whooping Creek Church Road and attended Roopville High School. Melba was valedictorian of her 1939 graduating class. She attended West Georgia College in Carrollton for two years and then spent her junior and senior years at the University of Alabama.

John Talmadge Robinson and Melba Angeline Morgan, wedding day 1944

When Melba's father was diagnosed with cancer in 1942, Melba cut her education short to come home and help care for him. J. Horry Morgan died in October 1942 which was during World War II and Melba's only brother, Bobby Morgan, had just left to go into the Navy. Melba stayed home to help her mother, Trixie Morgan, and her grandmother, Derah Morgan, get situated. People in Carroll County had loved Horry Morgan and Melba would later say that when harvest time for the cotton came, people who were friends and neighbors just appeared one day and they picked all the cotton for Horry's widow. They did it just out of the goodness of their hearts and would accept no pay for their hard work.

From 1942-1944, Melba taught school at Whitesburg, Georgia, and then did some secretarial work for Georgia Power Company. Melba had taken some business courses at Cullman, Alabama, and these courses she would prize all her life. Melba could type like a whiz and quickly mastered all the business machines of that era. She would often say that these skills carried her through life.

Melba Morgan married John Talmadge Robinson on 14 April, 1944 in Carroll County, Georgia. They then moved to Miami, Florida, to live where John was a Marine Flight Instructor at Masters Field. He was training the many pilots who would be sent into the Pacific theatre of war. That was also where Bobby Morgan was stationed — in the middle of the worst of the fighting in the South Pacific.

John T. Robinson, USMC, World War II

Melba worked at Pan American Airways during that time — again using those treasured secretarial skills. After World War II had ended, John and Melba went to Athens, Georgia, to live while John pursued his degree in pharmacy from the University of Georgia. Melba also worked towards completing her education at the University of Georgia and received her B.S. in home economics in 1949. She would return to Roopville to teach home economics at her old alma mater in the early 1950s. The Robinsons lived with Melba's family on the old Morgan home place.

When John Robinson established his Robinson Drug Company in 1952 in Carrollton, Melba gave up her teaching career to become the general manager and vice president of Robinson Drug. She did all the bookkeeping, secretarial work, clerked as needed, and also managed the hospital equipment rentals that later came into being as an important part of the business. Melba was never too busy to not take the time to talk to the customers who came into the store. She and John created an atmosphere of friendliness in their business that kept people coming back for years and years.

Melba would become active in civic affairs — always working hard for the P.T.A. in the local schools and she also was leader for Girl Scouts. Melba and John joined St. Margaret's Episcopal Church and became active members there. Both Melba and John were later recognized by the Rotary Club for their outstanding work in promoting education in the community. Both were named Paul Harris Fellows by Rotary International.

No biography of Melba Robinson would be complete without mention of her wonderful skills as a cook. Her grandchildren loved to eat a meal at Grandmama Robinson's house — they knew it would be specially cooked with all their favorites. We had a funny experience when Ben Bell was a student at Maple Street Elementary School in second grade. The school was only a few blocks from the Robinson home and well within walking distance. The Robinson girls had always walked to school at Maple Street when they were little girls.

One day about lunchtime, Ben Bell suddenly appeared in the kitchen at Grandmama Robinson's house. When Melba inquired as to why was he not in school, Ben had replied, "I'm hungry." Melba asked him, "But aren't they serving lunch at Maple Street?" Ben had replied, "Yeah, but that food is artificial. I came to get some Real food." Melba and Trixie thought that was the best compliment they'd ever had about their cooking. Of course, Ben was then served up a meal fit for a King — and promptly returned to Maple Street School.

When Melba's grandson, Joe Bell, was away at college at Georgia Southern in 1987, he wrote his Grandmama how he truly missed the delicious beef roasts that she had always served for Sunday dinner. Melba devised a way to try to give Joe one of those home cooked roasts by way of the U.S. mail. Melba cooked the roast, froze it, and then rushed the frozen roast to the Post Office just in time for the 5 p.m. mail. She mailed the roast special delivery — and Joe received the roast the very next day

Joe and his roommates eagerly heated up the roast and were relishing every bite. The roast was tender, but one of the roommates bit down on something hard — and spit out a bullet. After that, Joe teased his Grandmama that when he had written her how much he longed for a taste of her roast that he hadn't known she would go out and shoot the cow!

John Talmadge Robinson was born 1 November 1921 in Carroll County, Georgia, the son of Talmadge Whitfield Robinson and Martha Maude Chappell Robinson. John's early years were spent at Hapeville, Georgia, where the Robinsons had a home on Springdale Road there. By a stroke of fate perhaps, the home was located just next to the old Candler airfield. Here the barnstormer pilots would do their loops and stunts up above in the old biplanes of World War I — and young John found these daredevil aviators — such as Doug Davis and Beeler Blevins — to be his early heroes.

In 1927 just after Charles Lindbergh had made his solo flight across the Atlantic Ocean, he made a victory journey around the USA and one of his stops was at Candler Field. Young John was able to watch the whole ceremony from his upstairs bedroom window.

John Robinson, USMC, World War II, dive bomber pilot

Later on during the Great Depression, John's father rejoined the Army — due to lack of jobs — and John's mother went into nurse's training. So, John went to live with his grandparents, John and Maggie Robinson on Horsley Mill Road in Carroll County. John also spent time with his mother's aunt and uncle, Ben and Gena Chambers, whom he adored. And as he grew older, John would also board in the homes of some of his boyhood friends — such as Marvin Martin and Harold Dunaway.

John also became friends with boys who lived in the country like Bobby Morgan and Frank Searcy — which was a stroke of luck — for this is how John met Melba Morgan. John had gone frog-gigging with Bobby Morgan and

John Robinson and Julian Brock beside a Meyers trainer

Frank Searcy in the 1930s — and then they'd gone home with Bobby to spend the night. The sack with the frogs was not tied tightly enough and in the middle of the night all the frogs escaped. The frogs woke everybody up — and Derah Morgan got up to see what was going on and stepped barefoot on a cold bullfrog right beside her bed. What a screech! Years later, people used to say to Derah: "Miz Morgan, you sure have a lively household." She used to reply, "Yes, it's just jumping with frogs!"

John was a 1938 graduate of Carrollton High School and he also completed two years at West Georgia College, which was at that time a junior college. In 1941, since jobs were scarce, John had gone to live with an uncle, Hoke Chappell, in California where Hoke could help him get a job with Douglas Aircraft building airplanes.

John was living in California with his Uncle Hoke and Aunt Lily Ponza Chappell, and working at the Douglas Aircraft Plant at the time that Pearl Harbor was bombed on December 7, 1941. Of course, President Franklin Delano Roosevelt declared that America was now in a state of war with Japan. John immediately signed up for the draft there in California — even though he was told that he would probably be exempt from the draft since he was working in a job classified as defense. Soon, John decided to come home to Carroll County so that he could join up in the same units as his other boyhood friends from Carrollton.

Once back in Carroll County, John Robinson and Marvin Martin traveled to Atlanta together to sign up in the Army Air Corps. Marvin was accepted, but the recruiter told John that he could not accept him into the Air Corps since he'd signed up for the draft in California. That night, John and Marvin went to their local hangout — which was at that time, McGee's Bakery on the square in Carrollton. Gene McGee was always there late into the night baking cakes and doughnuts. The local boys would drop by the bakery to talk to Gene and his son, Ed McGee — and they'd always get samples of whatever he was baking.

John explained his plight to Gene McGee and how that if he was going to fight in the war — he wanted to be in air warfare. John wanted to be an aviator, but now he had been rejected by the Army Air Corps. Gene gave him the sage advice, "Why not join the Navy? They have an air corps, too."

Max Ohlinger, World War II, beside a Stearman Millington Messerschmidt

The very next day, John visited the Navy recruiter in Atlanta and explained his story to him. The Navy recruiter advised John to "come back tomorrow but don't tell anyone what you've just told me — just sign up." John asked him if the Army would try to get him back from the Navy if the draft letter had already been sent. The recruiter laughed and said, "Son, nobody from the Army has gotten anybody back from the Navy yet!" By 4 p.m. the following day, John was standing in a lineup of new recruits taking their oath as Naval Aviator Cadets.

Shortly after that, John was sent to Austin Peay College in Clarksville, Tennessee, where he received his very first training — and this was where John would first fly a plane solo. Unfortunately, the United States had been caught off guard by the strike at Pearl Harbor, and the country was poorly prepared to launch a full scale military retaliation at the beginning of World War II. John saw that the government even found it necessary to ask private citizens who were pilots to donate their planes for wartime service. This resulted in there being just about every kind of plane that there was at Outlaw Field. The private citizens who could fly also came along with their planes to help train men how to fly.

There were many men who did not survive even their first flight training. In the accompanying picture, John Robinson is standing next to Julian Brock of Greenville, Tennessee, another naval aviator at Outlaw Field. On the last day of his solo flying course, the plane stalled and Julian bailed out — but his chute caught in the plane itself — and he crashed to his death only a few days after this picture was made. The plane in the picture is called a Myers Trainer, and old biplane.

Next, the Naval Aviator Cadets were transferred to the University of South Carolina where they would receive many college courses of importance to them as flyers. Mathematics was greatly stressed. Back in those days, there was no gasoline gauge on the airplanes and the flyer had to keep track of how many miles he'd flown and how much gasoline he had left. To make an error in calculation here could be fatal. Other courses in the sciences were taught as well — and navigation was stressed. The cadets spent a few months here, but as of yet had still not had what was real military training. Up to now, they had had college type courses preparing them for what was to come later.

The Naval Aviator Cadets met with their first real experiences of boot camp when they were transferred to The University of Georgia at Athens, Georgia. This is where they were under the command of a Lt j.g. who would completely indoctrinate them into the "Navy way." Here, they would learn military discipline, uniforms of the day, naval history, how to salute, and how to "be Navy." There were a lot of Marine drill instructors brought in expressly for the purpose of helping to break these green cadets into shape.

Daily drills were performed on the football field at Sanford Stadium. Of course, there were no airplanes here and the cadets were eager to get on toward more flight training.

After about three months of boot camp at the University of Georgia, the naval cadets were finally transferred to Memphis where they would get to fly Stearmans (Millington-Messerschmidts). These were biplane trainers and the cadets would learn spins, stalls, loops, lazy 8's, snap rolls, all kinds of acrobatic flying. Some real military primary flight training took place at Memphis, Tennessee. Pictured is John's roommate, Max Ohlinger, climbing into a Millington-Messerschmidt.

The Naval cadets were next transferred to Pensacola Naval Air Station at Pensacola, Florida. It would be here that the cadets would learn "dog fight" training and many mock air battles took places in the sunny skies over Pensacola. And as John would say later on, "And the sun would shine every day." At this particular time in the war, there had just been a victory at Guadalcanal and many of the Marine pilots were being flown back from there to help train more pilots in the States. Just about all the flight instructors at Pensacola had seen the action with the Marines in the South Pacific. John recalls when his helmet blew off in one of these mock "dog fights" one day over Pensacola and he had to pay $35 to replace it. John still has the old goggles that he wore from these flight days in World War II. John earned his gold wings as a Naval Aviator Cadet at Pensacola in 1944 and was commissioned as a second lieutenant.

Almost immediately, John was instructed to report to the Marines for additional flight instructor's training. The Marines had picked up on John's natural abilities for teaching and writing flight instruction manuals. And the Marines needed not only pilots — but men who could teach others to become pilots. So, John became a U.S. Marine and was told to report to Deland, Florida, for dive bomber training.

John Robinson in the early days of Robinson Drug Company

John was stationed at Miami, Florida, throughout the rest of World War II training young aviators in instrument flight training. John took his job seriously because he knew that these men's very lives would depend upon what they learned from his instruction. Most of these young Marines were transported directly to the South Pacific to take part in some of the fiercest battles of World War II. Some of the flyers never made it into the war — they were training in the very area off Florida known as The Bermuda Triangle.

Some of these flyers took off and were never heard from again.

After World War II had ended, John worked for a brief time for the Morgan sawmill with his brother-in-law Bobby Morgan, who had safely made it home from the South Pacific. John would later take advantage of the GI Bill and return to complete his education at the University of Georgia. John earned his B.S. degree in pharmacy in 1949. For two years after his graduation, John worked at Carrollton Drug Company for Dr. Thomas R. Luck, who became John's good friend and mentor. Dr. Luck had always been very active in the civic affairs of Carrollton and John shared this mutual interest. In 1952, John T. Robinson opened up his own drug store in Carrollton which was Robinson Drug Company on Dixie Street.

This business would prosper and grow and become one of Carrollton's most successful retail and independent drug stores in the era before the large corporate pharmacies. John would operate the pharmacy end of the business and his wife, Melba, managed the retail business. John was actually following in a family tradition since his own great-grandfather, William Osmus Robinson, had in the 1860s opened up an early kind of drug store that sold the popular liniments and salves, horse pills and panaceas of his own era. W.O. Robinson's store was located on the west side of the square in Carrollton.

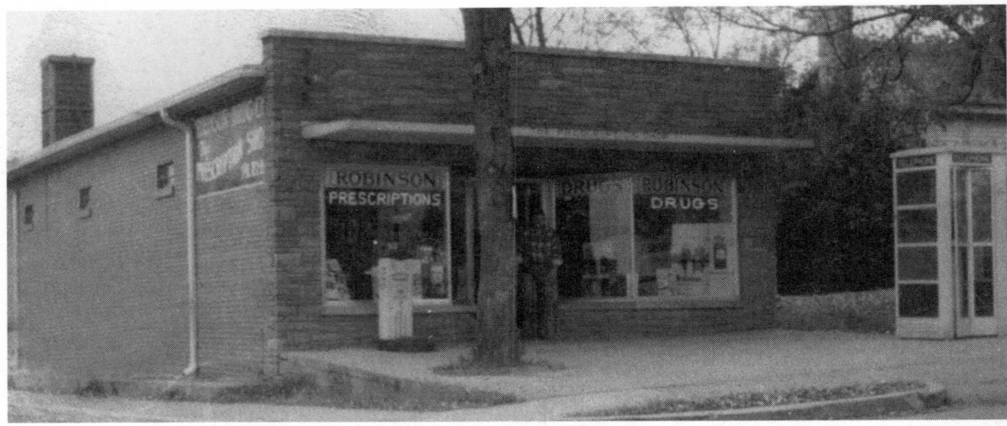

First Robinson Drug Company, 1952

In 1954, John and Melba Robinson built a new home in Carrollton on Kramer Drive and moved their family there. They now had two daughters — Janice Trixie Robinson born 8 June 1947 and Martha Anne Robinson born 18 November 1954. When the Robinsons moved to Carrollton, Melba's mother, Trixie Morgan, also came to live with them. Derah Morgan — with whom the Robinsons had lived up until then — moved to Walterboro, South Carolina to live with her daughter, Johnnie Morgan Housworth. In the following years, two more children would be born to John and Melba Robinson. Susan Elaine Morgan Robinson was born 29 February 1956 and a son, James Morgan Robinson was born 5 June 1959. This only son died at birth and was buried at Carroll Memory Gardens.

John Robinson became very active in civic affairs and served as a member of the city council in the late 1950s during the time that Henry Lumpkin was mayor of Carrollton. Then, in 1965, John Robinson was elected the mayor of Carrollton — a job in which he would serve with great pride. John served three terms as mayor of Carrollton during the 1960s and 1970s.

One of John's proudest accomplishments as mayor was the construction of the new library in Carrollton, the Neva Lomason Library. Mayor Robinson had worked diligently with Edith Foster director of the library, and Mrs. Wyche T. (Louise) Green, who was president of the board of the library — in order to obtain the grants and donations needed in order to bring this new library to Carrollton. William "Bill" Wiggins, who was our 4th District Representative, and his wife Mary were also very influential in helping to obtain the funds needed for the construction of a new library. Bill Lomason of Douglas and Lomason was the library's great benefactor and the library was named in memory of his late wife who had loved reading and books.

The Neva Lomason Library remains to this day as one of the finest libraries anywhere — and has a wonderful Special Collections room for genealogists. Another important accomplishment during John's mayor years was the building of the West Georgia Regional Airport. John also credits his good friend and city manager, Dudley Crosson, with this accomplishment. Dudley's wife, Betty, had a family with deep roots in Carroll County — the Upshaws, the Brocks, and the Cheneys.

Melba certainly played an important role during the mayor years as she acted many times as hostess for the City of Carrollton as the mayor's wife. Melba's knowledge of how to cook for a crowd certainly came in handy! She was a graceful hostess and knew how to show Southern hospitality at its finest. And many times, too, Melba had to take on full responsibility of managing the drug store when John had to be away for his mayor's duties.

In 1967, John Robinson, Dr. E.V. Patrick, and Frank Green of Carroll County took part in a People to People Tour around the world. This tour was sponsored by the University of Georgia — and agriculture educators there were the leaders of the tour. This was a goodwill tour of businessmen, doctors, cattlemen, agriculturalists, etc. from America to the governments of many foreign lands. John Robinson was the only pharmacist on the tour. Frank Green of Villa Rica- who was, incidentally, John's cousin on the Green side of the family — and who lived in the beautiful old home called Sugar Hill written about in the Green genealogy in this book — represented the cattlemen of Georgia.

Jan, Martha Anne, and Susan Robinson

Dr. E.V. Patrick was one of several physicians on the tour. Dr. Patrick's wife, Lucy, also joined them for part of this tour. In India, they toured medical facilities and it was quite a learning experience. They toured many industries and Frank Green's nephew was an official of the IBM plant they toured in Japan. The purpose of the tour was to help to interpret to people abroad the American traditions and ways — while at the same time helping Americans to appreciate the culture and traditions of other lands.

Melba Robinson and Frances Plunkett, Mayor's Day

Governor Carl Sanders said the purpose was also to portray to citizens of other countries the concepts and principles of the Democratic system. General Dwight D. Eisenhower, who was the chairman of the board of the People to People Tours, said:

> "Given a chance, people will make friends across, around, over and under all the natural man-made barriers that separate them.
>
> Understanding peoples is the passport to peace. If people get together, so eventually will governments."

The People to People Tour left Atlanta on May 4, 1967 and visited Belgium, France, Italy, Greece, Lebanon, Jordan, India, Thailand, China, and Japan. While in Japan, the Tour were guests of Governor Katsushi Terazono who gave them a special tour of this "sister state" to Georgia as set up by Governor Carl Sanders. The tour also visited Nagasaki the site of the atomic bomb and Tokyo which was then the world's largest city. The tour concluded with Hawaii and Alaska.

Senator Richard B. Russell and Senator Herman Talmadge arranged for many special events for the tour through the embassy officials in many of these countries. The trip lasted 32 days and was one of the highlights of John Robinson's life. He brought many learning

Dr. and Mrs. E.V. Patrick, Magnolia Ball, 1994

Roopville High School

experiences from this tour into his work for the city of Carrollton as mayor. In 1969, John Robinson was honored by the Chamber of Commerce as Carrollton's Man of the Year.

John and Melba Robinson had been good friends of Jimmy and Rosalyn Carter during the years that Jimmy Carter served as governor of Georgia. Rosalyn had even visited in the Robinson home and spent the night there during one of her campaign tours to Carrollton. She is a very lovely and down-to-earth person. Both Melba and John worked very hard in the presidential campaign to help get Jimmy Carter elected president. Later on, after Carter was elected president, Melba and John Robinson made the trip to Washington, D.C. to participate in the inaugural festivities and they danced at the Inaugural Ball. This, too, was a highlight of the lives of John and Melba Robinson.

Standing, Melba Robinson, Frances Plunkett, and Betty Sanders, wife of Gov. Carl Sanders.

John and Melba Robinson continued to run their business as an independent drug store even though the competition became quite stiff in the years when the large corporate pharmacies began buying out all the "Mom and Pop" stores in the community. But they worked hard through the years and kept their business a success. They would take time off to travel with their good friends, Dr. and Mrs. E.V. (Lucy Minter) Partick to the Kentucky Derby each year in May. Also, for many years from 1950-1962 the Robinsons and the Patricks had always vacationed together in the summertime at Daytona Beach, Florida. The Robinson children — Jan, Martha Anne, and Susan — and the Patrick children — Carol, Nancy, and Danny — were best of friends and Daytona Beach was one of the highlights of their childhood together.

John Robinson loved automobile racing and he started a tradition of going to the Daytona 500 every year. He started up a club of his good friends in Carrollton called The Daytona Racing Club. Each February they'd head out for the Daytona 500 — and over forty years, this included, Gene Beckham, Roy Denney Jr., Howard Martin, Cliff Barnes, Aubrey Gilbert, Dudley Crosson, Norman Banks, Pat deHaven, and Mitt Connerly.

John Robinson kept up his interest in aviation over the years and when he was 48 years old, he watched on TV as the first man walked on the moon in 1969. That was the same year when his namesake, his grandson John Robinson Bell, was born. John Robinson had watched aviation go from the old biplanes of World War II into the Space Age. John enjoyed taking his grandsons, Joe, John, and Ben Bell to watch the lift-offs of the Apollo spacecrafts from old Cape Canaveral in Florida. They also watched the liftoff of Apollo 13 — and later were all glued to the TV set's when Apollo 13 sent back the message to Earth, "Houston, we have a problem..."

The new Robinson Drug Company on Dixie Street

Both John and Melba Robinson worked together at Robinson Drug Company for over forty years until 1993 when Melba suffered a stroke. Melba remained hopeful that she would get to return to work — and she saved her "high heel shoes" so popular in the era when she had been a professional businesswoman. Melba had never been but 4'10" tall and those high heel shoes had always been her trademark. Melba died on 23 January 1996. She was laid to rest at Carroll Memory Gardens alongside her infant son who had died at birth.

John Robinson is now approaching 80 years old, but he still maintains his same schedule of working as a pharmacist at Robinson Drug Company. Next year, he will celebrate fifty years of his business being open on Dixie Street in Carrollton. He was recently recognized by the Georgia Pharmacy Association, for having worked as a pharmacist in the state of Georgia for 50 years 1949-1999. He still lives in the family home on Kramer Street that was built in 1954. He has seven grandchildren and three great-grandchildren. John's oldest daughter, Jan Bell, lives with him and one of the hobbies they enjoy together is genealogy. *Submitted by: John T. Robinson, 315 Kramer Street, Carrollton, GA 30117 and Written by: Jan Robinson Bell.*

971. John Henry Robinson Family

John Henry Robinson was born 12 April 1867 on the Robinson farm at Shady Grove in Carroll County, Georgia. He was the son of William Osmus Robinson and Rosannah Helen Sinah Lofton Robinson who had first come to Carroll County in 1859. John Henry received his education in the early schools of Carroll County and became a merchant, farmer, and cotton buyer for the Anderson Clayton Company.

He was known as one of the best for grading the post harvest cotton in the county. About 1908, John Henry Robinson purchased six adjoining farms on Horsley Mill Road in the Pleasant Hill community. He married and reared a large family there and resided in the home place he built for thirty-eight years before his death on 2 May 1946.

On 22 August 1886, John Henry Robinson married Margaret Josephine Green who was the daughter of Doctor Franklin Green and Eliza Jane Jones. The Jones genealogy is an extensive one dating back to Col. John Jones the regicide. The Jones family had to migrate to America because of the part that Col. John Jones played in the beheading of King Charles I. There were forty men who signed the King's death warrant, thus they became known as regicides. It is an interesting history but that is another story! Eliza Jane Jones was the daughter of James Jones and Lucinda Black. Lucinda Black was the daughter of Paul Black and Elizabeth Abney of Edgefield District, South Carolina. There were many Revolutionary war veterans in her family tree. The Blacks were from Newberry, South Carolina, in a previous generation, but the Abneys had a long history in Edgefield, South Carolina.

John Henry Robinson Family, 1905

John Robinson, about 1883

Doctor Franklin Green was a Confederate soldier who fought at the siege of Vicksburg. He came by his unusual name in that he was named for the doctor who delivered him. Though he never received any formal training as a doctor himself, he had a natural ability for doctoring farm animals. Any farmer in Carroll County whose livestock became ill quickly consulted "Doc" Green for what remedy to administer.

D.F. Green was the son of Ambrose Green and Mariah Frances Russell Green who were some early Carroll County pioneers. Ambrose Green was the son of William Mercer Green and Nancy Porter Green. Ambrose Green left for California to participate in the "gold rush" of 1852 and was never heard from again. His wife, Mariah stayed on in Carroll County living close to her grown children. The children of Mariah and Ambrose Green were: William, Doctor Franklin, Alfred C., Eugenia Anne, Thomas, John R., James M., and Margaret Josephine (b. 1855) who was the sister that D.F. Green named his own daughter for later on. When D.F. Green's daughter, Margaret Josephine was born on 9 June 1870, she was the newest little leaf on a family tree that extended all the way back to her immigrant ancestor.

The first of the Green ancestors to come to America is believed to be Thomas "the Seagull" Green who was born in 1636 on the ship bringing him to America. The tradition is that Thomas was given this name since at his birth the seagulls were sighted and it meant that the long ocean voyage to America had ended. Several generations later in our family, William Green, "the Patriot," as he would become known for his service in the American Revolution, was born in Prince Edward County, Virginia on 6 February 1762. William Green married Kezziah Stroud (b. 1763 in N.C.) on 9 February 1781 at Hillsborough in Orange County, N.C. From an old family diary, we know that it was snowing on their wedding day. Kezziah's younger sister, Susannah Stroud Mashburn, was a bridesmaid at the wedding. Kizziah Stroud was a daughter of Peter and Naomi Stroud of Orange County, N.C. Peter Stroud was the son of William Stroud and Margaret Rose.

William Green was living in Orange County, N.C. when he was drafted into the military service of the Colonial Army as a private in February of 1780. He served two tours of duty fighting with the N.C. troops against the British. On the first tour, he was captured while fighting the British at Charleston, S.C. — being released after 8 days on 19 of May 1780. In his second tour of duty, William Green was in engagements at Cox's on the Deep River and at Hillsborough. Green was honorably discharged shortly after the surrender of Cornwallis. Those who are interested can read more of this family in the book called *William Green The Patriot* by Lawrence Maynard. There is a copy of this book in Special Collections at Neva Lomason Library in Carrollton, Georgia.

It was after the American Revolution that William Green and his wife Kezziah moved to Burke County, N.C. They remained there through the 1790 and 1810 census. In 1819, William Green purchased 130 acres of land located on the east side of Pigeon River in Haywood County, N.C. It was while William Green was living in Haywood County that he made application for his pension as a Revolutionary war soldier in 1832. The following year, 1833, William and Kezziah were divorced in Haywood County. William died a few years later on 2 March 1837. Though William did not name all is children in his will, all of their names do appear on a deed of Haywood County, N.C. when William Green divided his property.

Kezziah Green moved with her son Anderson Green to Carroll County, Georgia in the early 1830s. When Kezziah filed for her pension as a widow of a Revolutionary war soldier in 1846, her son Anderson Green was the one who witnessed her application. Kezziah Green died on 1 August 1849 and is buried in Old Bethel Cemetery located between Carrollton and Villa Rica. Many of the other descendants of William Green who came to Carroll County in 1830 are also buried there.

The children of William Green "the Patriot" and Kezziah Stroud are: Thomas S. b. 24 October 1781; John b. ca. 1784; William Mercer Green b. 1786 and m. Nancy Porter on 29 March 1811, moved to Haywood County, N.C. by 1818 and to Carroll County, Georgia in the early 1830s; Sarah b. ca. 1790, Silas M. b. ca. 1796, a schoolteacher in Madison Co., AL in 1850 who m. Sarah W. Horton in Franklin Co., TN on 10 June 1848; Martha b. ca. 1801 m. 1st Austin Pack by 1823 and 2nd Charles Justice 5 April 1832 in Haywood County, N.C.; Elizabeth b. ca. 1803 m. an Allen, had a son named James A. Allen; Anderson b. ca. 1806, Tillman b. ca. 1810 m. Mary Daniell in Stewart Co., TN in 1838.

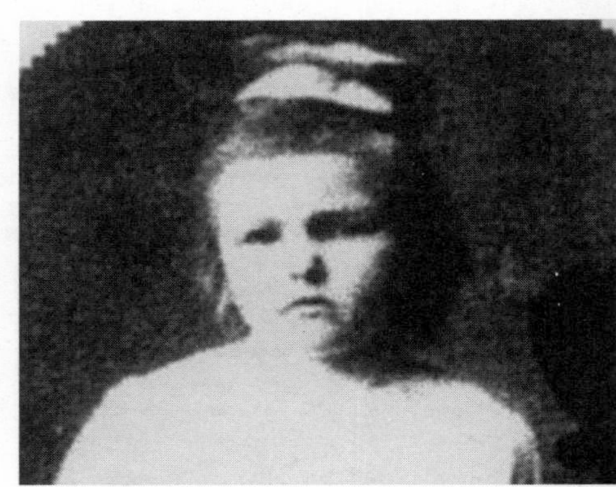

Nellie Mae Robinson

In 1830, the brothers Anderson Green and William Mercer Green bought land adjoining each other on the Little Tallapoosa River a few miles west of Villa Rica in Carroll County. William bought 202 acres Lot 137 District 6 from John Brooks for $1200 on 24 July 1830. This deed was witnessed by William Porter who was possibly William M. Green's father-in-law. Even though the land was purchased in 1830, the family did not move from N.C. until the home was built and crops planted in 1832. William Mercer Green built his log home called Sugar Hill on a high hill overlooking the Little Tallapoosa River which ran near the road from Villa Rica to Temple. It is possible the home was named in honor of Sugar Jones one of the ancestors of the

John Henry Robinson home place in Pleasant Hill community.

Adjoining drug store is Robinson and Benson

A favorite view of Carrollton City Cemetery

Green, Porter, Russell and Jones families who were Quakers that migrated together and intermarried for generations. The name "Sugar" came from the name of Abigail Shugan, a French Hugenot who married Edward Jones in 1733. She was known in her lifetime as the "first white woman to cross the Great Shocco Creek" (in Granville County, North Carolina). This is how our set of Jones came to be known as The Shocco Joneses — and it helps to sort us out from all the rest. Sugar Hill grew into a beautiful antebellum home and remained in the Green family for generations.

Nancy Porter Green died 6 March 1847. William Porter Green died 24 March 1847. We know from an old Bible that both Nancy and William's funerals were preached the same day. Both are buried at Old Bethel Church Cemetery.

The children of William Mercer Green and Nancy Porter Green were: Ambrose C. Green born 1813 in Burke County, N.C., Rebecca, Alexander Porter, Mary E., Nancy, Robert Albert, Thomas Walter, William Mercer Jr. (b. 1829) John Young, a daughter name not known, Martha Isabella, and Martin Lafayette.

The children of Doctor Franklin Green and his first wife Eliza Jane Jones were: Charlie b. 8 January 1867; Robert Monroe "Bob" b. 6 September 1869; Margaret Josephine "Maggie" born 9 June 1870 d. September 1962, LouElla Frances b. 27 February 1872; James b. 6 November 1874; Thomas Jasper b. 23 April 1876; Annie Earnest (twin) b. 13 May 1878; William Earl (twin) b. 13 May 1878; Lula Florence b. 21 May 1880; Beatrice b. 10 March 1882; Jessie Maud b. 20 January 1884 d. 19 October 1884. Eliza Jane Jones Green died 4 October 1884 about two weeks before the death of her last baby. Eliza Jane was buried at Pleasant Grove Church Cemetery near Villa Rica.

Doctor Franklin Green's second wife was Avalona Edwards b. 7 July 1866. Doc and Avalona married on 4 November 1886 in Douglas County, Georgia. With Avalona, D.F. Green had the following children: Henry Sterling b. 19 February 1890; Hattie Pearl b. 7 December 1891; Edgar Paul b. 17 February 1894; Lillian May b. 25 February 1896; John Hoyt b. 7 July 1898; Joseph Edward b. 19 September 1903; Gertrude Edwin Julia b. 29 October 1905, and Eva Deborah b. 14 July 1908. D.F. Green farmed in Carroll County until 1890 when he moved to Powder Springs in Cobb County, Georgia. He moved to Atlanta about 1908 and lived there until the ripe old age of 91. He was one of the last living Confederate soldiers and was quite impressive with his long white beard. Many great-grandchildren were brought to see him and sit on his lap. D.F. Green died on 15 November 1932. Avalona Edwards died 18 December 1950. Both are buried at Westview Cemetery in Atlanta, Georgia.

Margaret Josephine Green was a tiny lady who never stood five feet tall in her stocking feet. In her later years, she was affectionately called Little Grandma. She was the best of cooks and our mouths still water for one of her delicious sweet potato pies. Maggie Robinson is also remembered for her crocheting talents and the items she crocheted can only be described as exquisite works of art. She made the most beautiful crocheted counterpanes and tablecloths for her family. Even in her old age — after her eyesight was gone completely, she could still crochet beautifully, never having to look at the crochet hook one time. There is a good picture of Maggie Robinson under the heading of Martha Maude Chappell Robinson — when all Jan's living grandmothers and great-grandmothers attended her 3rd birthday in 1950.

Together, John Henry Robinson and Margaret Josephine Green had the following children together: (1) Walter Hill Robinson born 30 September 1888 died 6 September 1975, see separate heading; (2) Talmadge de Whitfield

Robinson born 20 May 1890 died 10 May 1972, see separate heading (3) William Paul Robinson born 27 May 1891 died 13 October 1891 buried at Shady Grove (4) Lou Ella Robinson born 8 April 1893 died 11 March 1918, see separate heading; (5) Henry Grady Robinson born 11 November 1894 died 30 May 1981, see separate heading for this family (6) Celeste Maude Robinson born September 1896 died 1898 buried at Shady Grove (7) Florence Robinson born 2 October 1898 died 8 December 1981, see separate heading (8) Annie Belle Robinson born 12 July 1901 died 23 July 1973, married Lawrence Smith and lived in Griffin, Georgia, buried at Oak Hill Cemetery there (9) Nellie Mae Robinson born 29 December 1905 died 12 January 1988, see her family under heading of Rosannah Helen Sinah Lofton Robinson," Note in the family photo that Maggie Robinson was pregnant with her ninth child, Nelle, so the photo was made in 1905. Margaret Josephine Green died 2 September 1962 and was buried alongside her husband, John Henry Robinson, in the Carrollton City Cemetery. *Submitted by: Michael Robinson, Horsley Mill Road, Carrollton, GA 30117 and Written by: Jan Robinson Bell.*

972. John Winslow Robinson

John Winslow Robinson was a native of Virginia but removed to North Carolina where his son John Winslow II was born in 1797. He was married to Margaret Elizabeth Horsley, a native of South Carolina. They were the parents of John Winslow Robinson III who was born in 1827. He married Mary Mann Burrow. Her parents were Eliza Bradbury Burrow and William Bradbury, who were among the earliest settlers of Georgia. The family established a large farm, home and several businesses in Shiloh and Burwell in Carroll County, Georgia. They were the parents of a large family, including Margaret Louisa, born 16 August 1859, who became the wife of Jefferson Davis Robison, second son of John Dixon Howell Robison. They became the parents of George Howell Robison who married Mary Ethyl Nixon. They became my parents as well as those of my two brothers — Robert Howell and Ray Lowery. I, Helen Nixon Robison, married William Green Foster III. We have four daughters, four grandchildren, and three great-grandchildren. *Submitted by: Helen Foster, 1924 Victory Church Road, Bowdon, GA 30108*
Sources: Census records, family records, *Memories of Georgia*.

973. Lou Ella Robinson

Lou Ella Robinson was born 8 April 1893 in the Shady Grove community to John Henry Robinson and Margaret Josephine Green. Lou Ella married Landis Aquillian "Quill" Eidson (24 August 1881-14 December 1962). He was the son of Landis and Sarah Jane Eidson.

LouElla and Quill Eidson married on 15 December 1906 when LouElla was fifteen and Landis was seventeen, but they received parental permission by promising that they would not have a baby for five years-and they did keep that promise! And that baby-Annie Ruth Eidson-their only child-was born 16 January 1914. When LouElla became pregnant with her second child, the great flu epidemic was sweeping the county. LouElla caught the flu, lost her baby prematurely, and then she, too, tragically died on 11 March 1919.

After Lou Ella had died, Ruth went to live with her grandparents, John Henry and Maggie Robinson. They owned a large farm in the Pleasant Hill community on Horsley Mill Road. Both of Ruth's parents-LouElla and Quill Eidson are buried at Pleasant Hill Baptist Church Cemetery in Carroll County.

Ruth Eidson married Euell Williams on 25 December 1931 at Cross Plains in Carroll County. Euell Williams was born 26 December 1914 in Carroll County. Euell Williams is remembered as one of Carroll County's most respected and most skillful carpenters. Hammer and nail, saw and level were his tools- and he used them like an artist in his trade. Euell—like the old saying goes-always "measured twice and sawed once." The homes and businesses that he built were uniquely crafted-and they were not only beautiful to see but had so many useful elements that they were a joy to live in and work in as well. Ruth became a seamstress and was quite skillful with the needle and sewing machine. She did alteration sewing for J. Carl Dry Cleaners in Carrollton for many years.

Ruth and Euell Williams had two daughters-the first was Margaret born 24 November 1932 at Cross Plains in Carroll County. Margaret was educated in the public schools of Carrollton. She then attended West Georgia College where she received her B.S. in business education in 1968. Margaret continued her education at Mercer University where she earned her master's in guidance counseling in 1969. Then, in 1972, she received her education specialist degree.

Margaret taught in the Business Department of Carroll Technical Institute from 1968-1972. She was then promoted to vice president of Student Services, being the first woman vice president in Technical Education in Georgia. She continued her administrative duties at Carroll Tech for some twenty years, retiring in July of 1988. Margaret first married Wyman A. "Sonny" Matthews 2 October 1954 in Carroll County. Sonny Matthews was born 10 August 1931 in Upson County, Georgia. He received his degree in pharmacy from Mercer University. Children born to Margaret and Sonny Matthews were:

(1) Cindy b. 13 March 1956 in Petersburg, VA, graduated from Bowdon High School, received a B.S. in early childhood education and later a master's degree in education, m. Allen Lawler Jr. b. 14 December 1974 in Bowdon, GA; his occupation is in Food Services at Carroll Vocational School. He has a degree in food service education. Their children are Jennifer Anne and twins Joshua Matthew and Jason Allen.

(2) Jeff Matthews b. 26 January 1957 in Broward County, FL, graduated from Bowdon High School, attended West Georgia College and Mercer University where he received his B.S. in pharmacy. Married Renee Smith 1 October 1983 in Carroll County, GA; Their children: William Austin Matthews and Jon Alex Matthews. Jeff is employed as a pharmacist at Eckerd Drugs in Carrollton.

(3) Susan Matthews b. 22 April 1961 in Carrollton, attended Bowdon High School and received B.S. in education (middle grades) and B.S. in accounting in 1988. She received her master's degree in 1996. Susan was "Miss Carrollton" in 1982; also in the "Miss Georgia" contest in 1983 and was in the top ten finalists. She later became a member of the Super Stars (a dance and baton twirling team) touring the Southeast. She taught dance and baton from 1982-1988 and was owner of Studio One. She has also done modeling for Chez Agency in Atlanta. She is currently teaching at Bremen High School in Bremen, GA. Susan m. Bryan Garrett, son of Roy and Lumas Garrett on 12 October 1985. Bryan was b. 8 August 1962 in Carrollton; His occupation is in agribusiness equipment and construction. His degree is from Carroll Vocational Tech in this field. Their children are: Ty Solomon Garrett and Elijah Garrett.

Margaret married a second time on 3 December 1988 to Copeland Ozier of Bowdon, Carroll County. Cope Ozier was born 1 November 1917 in Fort Gaines, Georgia. He was a graduate of Montezuma High School in Macon County, Georgia. He attended Mercer University and Georgia Southern where he was awarded a B.S. in education. He served in the U.S. Air Force during World War II as a pilot. He has had a successful farming business all of his life and is now retired.

Patricia Jane "Pat" Williams was born 7 October 1943 in Carrollton, the second daughter of Ruth and Euell Williams. Margaret had been named for her Grandmother Robinson and Pat was named Jane after her Grandmother Eidson. Pat graduated from Carrollton High School and continued her education at West Georgia College. She worked at the People's Bank for many years. She now works for Bank America.

Pat married Jerry Donald Strickland 18 December 1962 in Carroll County. They have one daughter, Kelly Elaine Strickland who was born 17 December 1963. Jerry is employed by Carrollton Office Equipment for many years. Kelly was educated in the Carrollton City Schools and is a graduate of Carrollton High School and also of Carroll Area Vocational Technical School. She received her degree in data processing. Kelly married James Donald "Jim" Marks 18 May 1983. Jim was b. 14 December 1962 in Haralson County, GA. Kelly and Jim have one son William Marshall Marks. *Submitted by: Pat and Jerry Strickland, and Written by: Jan Robinson Bell*

974. Mildred Inez Robinson

The Robinsons are believed to have come to Carroll County from South Carolina.

Albert Matthew Robinson (10/1856 - 5/1/1897) married Mary Ellen Arthur (1/5/1859 - 4/4/1928) and ran a store near the old city gym; they later moved to Burwell (children: Emory, William, Luther, Buford, Zella, Lizzie, Estelle and Minnie).

William Matthew Robinson (8/16/1881 - 1/23/1933) ran a store in Burwell with brother Luther across from Shiloh Campground/Burwell Methodist Church and married Annie Mae McGarity (7/11/1884 - 9/19/1973), daughter of Seaborn McGarity (1852 - 1942) and Sarah Frances Barnes (1855 - 11/22/1936). Annie would say later that during the depression Mr. Robinson let so many people have needed supplies to keep their families fed that he lost the store and everything they owned. He was commissioner of Roads and Revenue in Carroll County and also appointed associate member of State Council on Food Production and Conservation during World War I. He and Annie are buried at Bethesda Baptist Church.

William Matthew Robinson, Annie McGarity Robinson, Gladys, Abe and Jewel

Together they had five children: Gladys (1/29/1902 - 3/2/1971) married Roy Williams and lived in Chattanooga (children: Ethel and Mary Anne).

Joseph Earl "Abe" (5/29/1903 - 7/19/1994) played football on a scholarship at Auburn and married Mary Tom Russell (7/13/1906 - 1979). After ten years of coaching and teaching he worked 35 years for the Department of Agriculture. They then operated a wholesale nursery and tree farm in Irvington, Alabama.

Jewel Myrtle (9/24/1907 - 6/10/1990) married/divorced Gordon Nalley. During World War II they worked at Bell Aircraft in Marietta (children: Winton, Warner, Betty and William, all of Carroll County).

Mildred Inez (12/1/1911 - 7/15/1975) married Edgar Henry Garrett (8/18/1905 - 1/1/93) (children: Bobby William (8/10/1928 - 3/6/1960) married Tommie Lee Bandy (5/3/1931); Juliette (8/19/1931) married Joe C. Rainwater (1/29/1927) and lives in Goodman, Missouri (children: Cathy, Ellen, Jearan); Earl Holmes (9/30/1936) married Margie Nell Daniell (2/5/1936) (children: Lance, Joey and Sheila (twins) and Nancy); and Joan Elaine (7/11/1949) married/divorced Robert Herrin (1/26/1947 - 6/15/99) (children: Kelly and Adam).

Ima (Laura) (4/15/1917 - 7/24/1992) met and married James William Hoback while she and her mother lived with her sister Gladys in Chattanooga. Bill was associated with *Chattanooga News Free Press*. Their only son Jim is now a cardiac surgeon there.

In 1928 Mildred and Edgar Garrett were at the Robinson's home on Mandeville Avenue in Carrollton when Mildred gave birth to Bobby. He was five years old when his parents bought the farm on what is now Pleasant Hill Road in Carrollton. Edgar and Mildred grew cotton, and corn, and were some of the first chicken farmers in Carroll County. They worked hard on the farm and also worked at the Bell Bomber plant in Marietta during World War II. They sold the home farm to Bobby and Tommie in 1955. The farm is still maintained by Tommie and their children: Vesta married Ralph Ayers (children: Ryan (married Andrea Wilson) and Russ); Lyle who lives in New York City; and Celia married/divorced Dwayne Leatherwood (children: Katie (married Brandon Fehring; children: Layne and Haley) and Chad. Celia subsequently married Ken Miller.

Although the Robinson name changed through marriage and is not reflected here, Carroll County still has many residents who are descendants of William and Annie Robinson. *Submitted by: Celia Miller, 1631 Pleasant Hill Road, Carrollton, GA 30116*

975. Nathan and Mae Robinson's Family

My parents, Nathan Robinson and Mae Huddleston Robinson, married in 1919 when Daddy was nineteen and Mama was fifteen. My birthday is January 25, 1929, the fifth of eleven children: Iva Benefield, Denney, Wayman, Frank, Inonch (died as a toddler), Myrtle Hearn, Walter, Joyce Garrett Hope, Henton, Helon Johnston, Hinston, and Charles.

Our parents instilled a good work ethic in their children from an early age. Daddy managed the farm, built homes and other buildings in the community, and also stayed politically active. He was a member of the Democratic Party of Georgia. In the election year of 1952 he changed his loyalties to support Dwight Eisenhower and remained a lifelong supporter of the Republican candidates. He was also a justice of the peace and a notary public. He was an active member of the original group that chartered The Cotton Producers Association, which evolved into Gold Kist, Inc., one of the largest corporations in America. Mama managed the home, large garden, milked the cows, and made all of our dresses, canned vegetables and fruit to last until the next season. Flour, salt, baking powder, and soda were the only groceries bought. Mama always had something for us to eat after school, but I especially enjoyed the baked sweet potatoes and hot chili and biscuits.

One day while on the way to the creek to do the laundry, Mama, with two toddlers and another due soon, learned that Daddy had hired field hands. She immediately returned to the house to cook dinner (the large meal of the day) from scratch for the family and Daddy's hired hands.

Nathan and Mae Robinson with their oldest children, Iva, Frank, and Wayman

We always served up a mid-day meal for hired help, based on a strong community tradition. We called our evening meal supper.

Sometimes relatives helped when a new child was born, but if not Daddy hired help to stay for two weeks following the birth. Hired help was impossible to find during World War II, so that year Daddy paid us for our work. I stayed with Mama when a new baby was born, even though I didn't know how to cook or keep house. Most of the housework and cooking was always done by Mama, since she felt we had enough work to do in the fields. I took the large bread tray to the side of the bed and she made the biscuits. I earned $20 to help pay for college, but felt I was overpaid. In those days women stayed in bed for a long time after birth. It was a good thing, so Mama got some needed rest. She never sat down from the time she got up until she went to bed. The only other hired help for Mama was on laundry days after the last two children were born.

We never missed school to work on the farm; however, work was always ready for us after school. Daddy installed a pump after I left home, but until then I filled the huge reservoir on the side of the stove each day. Each child had a daily chore and other chores were assigned as needed.

Basketball really made school enjoyable for me. Nell Garrett Smith, my beloved coach, also taught many of my brothers and sisters. We played on a dirt court but Miss Nell took us to Carrollton to practice on an indoor court before our tournaments. We won several county tournaments, even though one year we had only six players and no substitutes. No one dared to foul out, for fear of forfeiting the game.

Daddy offered to loan the funds for each child to attend college. Walter went to Berry College. I went to West Georgia. I owed $500 after one year and it seemed like a fortune. I decided to go to Atlanta, get a job and attend Georgia Evening (Georgia State University) at night. Bob and I were engaged but I felt that I could not marry until I repaid Daddy and a large dental bill. After I saved enough to repay Daddy, we agreed to marry and repay the dental bill later.

I am fortunate to have Nathan and Mae Robinson for parents and continue to receive their blessings each day. *Submitted by: Myrtle Hearn, 228 Palo Verde Dr., Leesburg, FL 34748*
Sources: Hinston Robinson and Joyce Robinson

976. Rosannah Helen Sinah Lofton Robinson

In our family, we like to say that we had a great-grandmother who had a very big name, but an even bigger family tree. This is the ancestry of Rosannah Helen Sinah Lofton Robinson, wife of William Osmus Robinson. Rosannah is the ancestor of Taylor, Jack, and Cooper Bell.

Leonard Loftin born 1616 in London, England, first came to America on the ship *West* on 12 July 1636 settling at Philadelphia, Pennsylvania. He was the son of an English tailor who reportedly invented the thimble. Leonard Loftin would become the progenitor of the Loftin families in America through his three sons: Leonard Jr. (1654-1720) of NC; Cornelius (1657-1736) of VA; and William (1658-1678) of MD. Leonard Loftin Jr. moved to NC in 1654. He was a member of the General Assembly in 1711-1712. He first lived in Chowan County but later moved to Craven County, NC. Leonard's wife, Elizabeth, died about 1716 and Leonard died in 1720. Both were buried at their estate at Edenton. Leonard had been a member and warden of St. Paul's Parish Vestry.

Our Lofton family is descended through Leonard Jr. who had three sons; Cornelius born 1695, Leonard born 1697, Benoni born 16 January 1705, and three daughters Jane, Joyce, and Dorcellay. President Jimmy Carter is a descendant of Cornelius Loftin through his daughter Elizabeth Loftin who married William Nunn of Craven County, NC. Our ancestor is Benoni Loftin who appears in the Colonial militia records of NC. He appears as a private in Col. Thomas Graves' Company on 17 October 1754 in Craven County, NC. For his service, his female descendants have the honor and privilege of becoming a member of The Colonial Dames of America. The name of Benoni's first wife is nee Lovick, and by her he had Thomas and Elkannah. He married second to Susannah Burtonshall, daughter of Richard Burtonshall (died 1740) and Margaret Jones. Richard was the son of Richard and Priscilla Burtonshall who came to America in 1701 and settled in Tyrrell, NC.

John Lofton

Benoni Loftin and his second wife, Susannah Burtonshall, lived on the family estate called Jericho in Craven County, NC. This home was built in 1750 near Winston-Salem. Benoni and his first wife had two children, Thomas and Elkannah. Elkannah (1726-1792) married Rachel Herring (the ancestors of many Heard County, GA, Loftins). Benoni and Susannah Burtonshall Lofton's children were Elizabeth (married John Torrance); John Loftin, our ancestor; Leonard; Frederick; Francis (1753-1810) married Lovissa; Samuel; Ezekiel married first Charlotte and second Jennie Linder. Our ancestor, John Loftin, born ca. 1749 died 3 September 1814, would marry Mary Elizabeth Blocker about 1740 in Craven County. Mary Elizabeth was a descendant of Michael Blucher of Prussian descent who settled at Edgefield. The name was Americanized to Blocker later on. (Note: Loftin descendants of the above mentioned families were some of the first settlers to arrive in Carroll County. John Henry Loftin was born in 1827 in Carroll County to Eli Loftin).

John Loftin born 1740 would be the father of two sons, Robert (born 1768) and Zachariah who married a Herring. Land records show that John Loftin moved from NC to Berkeley County, SC, about 1773. By the time of the American Revolution, this family had moved into Edgefield District, SC. Zachariah served as a soldier in the American Revolution, but Robert was not old enough.

Later, when President James Madison called for people to help spark enthusiasm for the War of 1812, Robert Loftin became one of the first newspaper editors in SC. His newspaper was called *The South Carolina Republican.* It was published at Pottersville, SC and was a means to keep people up to date on political issues and news of the war.

Robert Loftin had a son named John Loftin born 13 December 1791 in Edgefield, SC. John grew up working at the newspaper office setting the block letters in the old style printing press. Each letter had to be set by hand. It seemed that when it came time to place the editor's name in the corner of the paper, John would run out of I's but he had plenty of O's, and that is how the spelling of the name Loftin was changed to Lofton.

Robert Lofton was married to Sinah Harden, daughter of William Harden of Edgefield. William Harden died in 1813 leaving a widow and seven surviving children. William had been an extensive landholder in Edgefield, including land on Stephens Creek and Horn's Creek. At the final settlement of his estate, his children named were William C. Harden, the younger; Henry G. Harden, a minor under twenty-one; Priscilla, wife of Marshall Pittman; Rachel, wife of Jefferson Pittman; Elizabeth, wife of Daniel Marshall; Sinah, wife of Robert Lofton; and Mary, wife of John McDaniel.

Rosannah Helen Sinah Lofton Robinson

The wife of William Hardin at time of his death was not the mother of his children, as the first wife had died some years earlier. Margaret Ryan was also a wife who had died. The widow was Sarah Marsh, sister of Rev. Samuel Marsh. William Hardin was descended from another William Harden, a French Huguenot from Rouen, France, brother of Mark Hardin (1660-1734) who had settled in Prince William, later Faquier County, VA.

The Loftons were charter members of Horn's Creek Baptist Church in Edgefield. Their newspaper was sold to Abner Landrum in 1824 and the name of the paper was then changed to *The Edgefield Advertiser.* On 9 April 1856, this obituary appeared in the paper:

> "Died at his residence in Edgefield district in January 1856, Robert Lofton in the 88th year of his age ... He left an aged widow and three surviving children."

Sarah Jester

In the same year that the newspaper was sold – 1824 – John Lofton decided to move his own family to GA. The Indian lands were opening and John saw many opportunities there. He was one of the very first to move into this new frontier that would later be called Butts County, GA. He established a general store and trading post on the Key's Ferry Road which led to the ferry to take people across the Ocmulgee River. His business soon became a beehive of activity, and his store became the post office and a stopping point for the stagecoach. The whole community took on the name of Lofton's Store. Years later, the name would be changed to Worthville, but the name is only found now on early maps of that era. It was described in 1882 as "8 miles northeast of Jackson and 18 miles from Covington, population 75, steam sawmill and cotton gin, one school, mail four times a week on horseback."

In those days, there was a stagecoach that ran between Covington and Macon via Indian Springs, where Chief William McIntosh had a home. Chief McIntosh also had a home in Carroll County on the Chattahoochee River near Whitesburg. The old Indian path that led from McIntosh's home in Indian Springs to his home in Carroll County was known as McIntosh Trail and would later be an important route for travelers making their way to Carroll County.

On the Key's Ferry Road, as the stage coach approached the community of Lofton's Store, the driver would give the number of toots on his horn to indicate the number of passengers he had in his coach. That way the innkeeper would know just how many places to set at the dinner table. At the store, John Lofton would keep everything in stock that anybody needed - this ranged from kettles to plows to tonic for mule colic to satin slippers for dancing at the old Indian Springs Hotel, which was just up the road.

John Lofton had married Sarah Jester (b. 1793) in Edgefield District on 22 January 1815. Bible records show the following children born to them: Mary Ann Catherine, b. 26 November 1815, married John Hill McDonald 1830; Jane Deanna, b. 18 February 1817, married Leonard Mason 1833; Justina Adalina, b. 24 July 1818, married William F. Stodghill 1837; Jesse Blocker, b. 31 December 1821, d. 20 October 1863; Lucretia, b. 20 November 1819, died at birth; Benjamin Franklin, b. 2 July 1822, d. 1846; Narcissa, b. 15 May 1825, d. 23 May 1825; Francis Ann, b. 8 May 1825, married John McBride 1842; John Hardin, b. 8 February 1827, married Ann Gunn 1847; William James, b. 24 October 1829, d. 1865; Rosannah Helen Sinah, b. 8 September 1833, married William Osmus Robinson 25 December 1851; Robert Levi Henry, b. 30 July 1835; Georgia Ann Elizabeth, b. 8 October 1837, died at birth; LaFayette b. 8 April 1838, died at birth.

Rosannah Helen Sinah Lofton was named for both of her mother's grandmothers, Rosannah Helen Frazier Jester and Sinah Harden Lofton. (The name of Sinah would carry on down in our family for generations. In deciphering the old handwriting, the name is often mistaken for Sarah but it is definitely Sinah.) The *Federal Union* newspaper of 29 July 1851 reported,

> "Died of dropsy of the chest at Worthville, Butts County, GA, on Sunday the 13th of July 1851, John Lofton, Esq. in the 61st year of his age. He was for many years a respectable merchant at this place ..."

The Jesters were Scottish Highlanders who came to America in 1746 after the Scots were defeated on Culloden Moor near Iverness on 16 April 1746. Many Scots remained loyal to the son of the king who had been forced out in 1688 and believed that James Stuart was the rightful heir to the throne of England. In 1715 the Scots had attempted to place James on the English throne but failed. The attempt in 1746 was to place the son of James, who was known as Bonny Prince Charlie, on the English throne, and this was a terrible defeat which destroyed the hopes of the House of Stuart forever. The Scots who were loyal to the Stuarts were called Jacobites, Jacobus being the Latin name for James. They would cut sprigs of yew from the great yew tree that grew close to their home castle, Castle Dounie, and wear these in their caps and bonnets to display their loyalty to James.

The English took swift revenge against the Jacobites who had opposed them in battle. Many of the Scottish chieftains were executed outright. The Scots had lost about 1000 men in battle, another 1000 were taken prisoner and many were shipped to Barbados to work as slaves on the sugar plantations there. The Scots were no longer allowed to wear their kilts and the bagpipes were also banned. Property was seized and no Scot was allowed to hold office or speak in Gaelic. In short, the whole Scottish way of life and all their traditions, of which they had always honored with fierce pride, were abolished. The Scots migrated to America in droves.

There were three brothers who came together to America in 1746 after their defeat on Culloden Moor. The three brothers were William (b. 1728 in Scotland), Maxwell, and Jacob (b. 1732). The Highlanders settled in the mountains of the Carolinas which reminded them of the Scotland they had left behind. William Jester served as Patriot to the Army of the American Revolution, NC. He had two known sons, Levi and Thomas.

Levi Jester was b. in 1760 in Edgefield District, SC. Levi Jester was also a Revolutionary war soldier, enlisting when he was only sixteen years old. He received a land grant in 1838 in Georgia as payment for his service. Levi Jester had moved his family to Butts County, GA in 1826, not long after his daughter Sarah Jester Lofton had moved there. The D.A.R. would later erect a monument in Levi's honor in Butts County in 1925. A front page article about this occasion was printed in *The Atlanta Journal* newspaper of 22 June 1925.

The D.A.R. regent, Mrs. J.B. Settle of Jackson, gave an eloquent history of Levi Jester and his role in the American Revolution. She said,

> "When only sixteen years old, in the green days of his unripened manhood, Levi Jester joined the Colonists in their immortal and marvelous struggle to unfetter themselves from British rule and keep forever burning the light of human liberty on these shores. He played an important part in vindicating the rights of humanity and helping to lay the foundation of a great republic on the pillars of national independence."

The marker was erected in the old Jester family burial ground, located halfway between Jackson and Griffin, and was still standing in 1998. After a friendship of more than fifty years, Carrollton residents John T. Robinson and Dr. E.V. Patrick discovered that they were not only friends, but cousins, both of them descendants of the same Revolutionary War hero from Butts County. Dr. Patrick descended from Rosa

Jester and John Robinson descended from Sarah Jester. William Jester is also buried in this family cemetery. He was about one hundred years old when he migrated with his son's family from SC to GA.

Levi Jester married Rosannah Helen Frazier in 1787 in Edgefield District, SC. Rosannah was the daughter of John Frazier (b. 1730 Inverness, Scotland) and Lydia Riddle, also of Scottish ancestry. John Frazier and Lydia Riddle married in Chatham County, NC, in 1754. Their children were Ann Nancy, b. 1762, m. John Oliphant 1818; Rosannah Helen, b. 1765, m. Levi Jester 1787; James, b. 10 April 1767, m. Charity Wright Cotton; William, b. 1768; Jesse, b. 9 March 1772, m. Nancy Norris 1796; Margaret, b. 1774, m. Andrew Gomillion 1817; Col. Benjamin, b. 1779. He had five wives — Patsy, Rebecca, Emeline, Susan, and Sarah; Mary, b. 1780, m. Henry Livingstone 1798; John Jr., b. 1784, m. Nancy; Elizabeth, b. 1786, m. Daniel Gunnels. (From Frazier Bible records.) It was about 1800 when the Fraziers moved to Edgefield District, South Carolina, and established a large plantation there. The name of Riddle derives from the occupation called "riddler." The riddler was the man who kept turning the wine bottles during the fermentation process. John Frazier was also a Patriot of the American Revolution and had helped to supply the troops during the war for independence. Many descendants have joined the D.A.R. on his record.

In Scotland, the Fraziers had traditionally been in the business of salmon fishing. They exported smoked or dried salmon to the Continent. John Frazier had come to America with four brothers, all of them forced to flee into political exile after the defeat at Culloden Moor in 1746. The Fraziers and Jesters had been friends in Scotland prior to the migration to America. One old tradition in the family indicates that the name of Jester actually derived from "jouster" and that they were the jousters who belonged to the Frazier Clan in medieval times. The Fraziers truly had to flee for their lives in 1736 since their Frazier Clan had been first on the field to support Bonny Prince Charlie.

Nelle Robinson Long

The Fraziers had fought, too, with William Wallace Braveheart who was one of the first Scottish heroes to fight for Scottish independence from the British in the 14th century. The Fraziers belonged to the Noble House of Lovat in Scotland and it was Simon Lord Lovat himself who was the last Scottish nobleman to be beheaded in 1747 at the Tower of London in retaliation for the Scottish uprisings. All these events were told over and over again in the Frazier family after their exile to America and they remained true to their convictions and fiercely proud of their Scottish heritage.

The children of Levi Jester and Rosannah Frazier were John Glenn, b. 26 May 1788; William, b. 22 February 1790; James, b. 20 April 1792; Sarah Jester, b. 17 December 1793 in Edgefield District, South Carolina, and died 14 December 1850, m. John Lofton; Nancy Ann, b. 2 February 1798, m. Charles Hammond 1815; Mary, b. 20 January 1800, m. William Foster; Benjamin, b. 23 March 1804 (twin); Henry, (twin) b. 23 March 1804, m. 1842 Mary Ann Lindsey; Abner, b. 22 February 1806, m. Angeline Foster; and Rozanna, b. 1808. The Jesters made their home at Beaver Dam Creek in Edgefield District and moved to Butts County, GA in 1826. Levi Jester died 17 June 1851 and his wife Rosannah died 14 January 1851. Both are buried in the old Jester burying ground which is now in some deep woods but was once located behind their home place. It is found on the Colwell Road about halfway between Jackson and Griffin, GA. Our family visited the old cemetery in 1998, and the monument to Levi Jester was still standing.

Benjamin McFarland Long

The origin of the Frazier name is an interesting one. The story is told that the King of France was once passing by a castle located in Anjou. There were beautiful fields of strawberries ripe for the picking that surrounded the castle. The owner of the castle sent out a pretty young maiden with a basket filled with fresh strawberries for the King. The King was so delighted with this gift that he bestowed the name of Frazier upon the owner of the castle. The word "frasier" in French means strawberry grower. The King also commanded that from henceforth the bearers of Frazier arms would have a family crest decorated with strawberry flowers. The Frazier arms to this day bear silver strawberries on a field of blue. The Fraziers were of Norman descent and they first went to England with William the Conqueror in 1066. They were awarded many lands in the north of Scotland as payment for their loyalty.

I am a great-granddaughter of Rosannah Helen Sinah Lofton and William Osmus Robinson. My mother, Nelle Robinson, was a daughter of John Henry Robinson and Margaret Josephine Green. Nelle Robinson married Selma Long, son of Walter L. Long and Hallie Pearl Burks, on 17 August 1929. My father worked for the City of Carrollton Fire Department for many years. My mother was a well known and excellent seamstress. Nelle Long was proud to be the seamstress to Academy Award winning movie actress of 1958, Susan Hayward. During the time that Susan Hayward Chalkley lived in Carrollton (1957-1966), she could often be seen rushing in and out of the Long home on Sims Street as she came and went for her many fittings. Susan kept her weight at 114 pounds and was very petite. She often brought my mother souvenir dresses that she had worn as costumes in her movies. One of my favorites was the antebellum dress she wore when she played the wife of President Andrew Jackson in "The President's Lady." When Susan completed her movie called "Where Love Has Gone," she asked J. Ebb Duncan, who owned the local Carroll Theater, to have a private screening of this movie just for Nelle and any friends or relatives that she would like to invite. This was a most memorable occasion in 1964. Susan Hayward sat right there with us — seeing the movie for the first time herself — in living Technicolor!

There had been a dispute between the two actresses in the movie — Susan Hayward and Bette Davis — over which actress would die at the end. Susan had said the director filmed the ending both ways and she would be finding out for the first time which actress would die in the end - it turned out to be Susan. There was no love lost between these two actresses and Susan could turn into a real spitfire of a redhead whenever Bette Davis' name was mentioned!

Susan Hayward loved Carrollton and called it her hometown. She was buried alongside her husband, Eaton Chalkley, in the Catholic cemetery here. Susan Hayward is most fondly remembered by our family.

The Long family has been with Carroll County from its earliest beginnings. John Long, b. 20 November 1798, left his ancestral home at Marshall's Ferry, Grainger County, Tennessee, to come to Carroll County in 1826. His son, Benjamin McFarland Long, was renowned as the first white child to be born in Carroll County on 27 November 1827 at Harttown, three miles from Villa Rica. B.M. Long was the father of H. Whit Long who served several terms as mayor of Carrollton. A list has been preserved of the earliest mayors of Carrollton. The first mayor was Eli Benson in 1872; E.W. Wells, 1873-1875; L.G. Pirkle, 1876-1877; E.W. Wells 1878-1880; W.P. Cole, 1881; S.E. Grow, 1882; J.J. Gaston, 1883; T.L. Long 1884; O.L. Reese 1885; B.F. Burns 1886; O.L. Reese 1887-1899; B.F. Burns 1890; B.F. Bass 1891; G.H. West 1892-1893; J.R. Brown 1894; L.C. Mandeville 1895-1896; W.A. Coleman 1897; W.D. Hamrick 1898-1899; H. Whit Long 1900-1901; T.C. Bledsoe 1902-1903; H. Whit Long 1904-1908; J.M. Burns 1908-1909; H. Whit Long 1909-1910; Shaw 1911-1913; Spence 1914-1916.

Barbara Long Huffman

John Long served as Carroll County's Clerk of Superior Court for more than forty years and ran a successful mercantile business. Ben Long married Amanda Wooten of Carroll County and was elected to the state legislature in 1872 as a Republican. While Ben Long was serving in the state legislature, the question of reapportioning the number of representatives from each county in Georgia was brought before the House. Long made a successful effort for Carroll County by carrying the bill, giving Carroll two representatives instead of one. Because Long was a Republican in a Democrat-dominated House, it has been called one of the most remarkable victories ever won in the Georgia Legislature.

Ben Long moved later to Walker County, Alabama, where he became one of the pioneers there of Cordova. Twelve children were born to

B.W. and Amanda Long, and Whit Long was one son very prominent in affairs of Carroll County for many years. Ben Long was also well known for gathering a group of men from Carroll County to go off and fight in the Mexican War. These men were named in B.M. Long's obituary of 24 June 1903 — William T. Woffard, captain, Hugh N. Weir, Abner E. Upchurch, Collins Easterwood, J.C. Ashley, J.C. Benson, J.W. Benson, Joseph Cates, W.E. Curbs, Vincent Holly, and John O. Long. John Long, the progenitor of the family, died on 17 October 1870.

Nelle Robinson and Selma Long had only one child, Barbara Long who was born 25 April 1937 in Carroll County. The Longs were members of Tabernacle Baptist Church. Nelle R. Long was born 29 December 1905 and died 12 January 1988. Selma Long was born 28 September 1903 and died 20 September 1976. Both are buried at Carroll Memory Gardens. Barbara worked until her retirement from West Georgia College in Carrollton. On 23 July 1988, Barbara married Monroe Huffman, born 18 March 1928. Monroe Huffman is now retired from Delta Airlines. The Huffmans make their home in East Point, GA. *Submitted by: Barbara Long Huffman, 853 Glenway Drive, East Point, GA and Written by: Jan R. Bell*

977. Sinah Justine Robinson

Sinah Justine Robinson was born 25 March 1857 in Worthville, Butts County, Georgia. She was the daughter of William Osmus Robinson and Rosannah Helen Sinah Lofton. Sinah was named for her mother's maternal grandmother, Sinah Hardin, of Edgefield District, South Carolina. She was also the namesake of her mother's sister who was Justina Adalina Loftin who married William R. Stoghill. Aunt Justina saved the old photographs of her parents, Sarah Jester and John Lofton, as you see them pictured here. The story goes that Sarah Jester Lofton got herself into a snit one day and intentionally cut her hair quite short. Since the hairstyles then were much longer, we think she was just a liberated woman.

Shown in the family picture are Joseph W. Horton and Sinah Robinson Horton on the first row, with Alzena standing between them. The three girls in back are Willie Josephine Horton, Lee Arlena Horton, and Sallie Robinson.

When Sinah was about two years old, her family packed up everything into a covered wagon and moved from Butts County to Carroll County. Many people of this era were heading farther west. People back then did not know about crop rotation and fertilizers, and since everyone lived off the land they had to keep moving westward where the land would produce crops.

Sinah's mother inherited the Lofton family home place in 1851 when her father, John Lofton, died. The Lofton plantation in Henry County had been sold and the profits divided among all the Lofton children. W.O. and Rosannah Robinson had also inherited a number of slaves and a prosperous business. This was the general store-stagecoach stop-post office that John Lofton had established about 1826 near the Key's Ferry on the Ocmulgee River in Butts County. W.O. Robinson continued to manage the store until his move to Carroll County in 1859. This experience is what led him to go into this type of business later in Carrollton.

Sinah Robinson and Joseph W. Horton Family

Sinah Justine Robinson married Joseph Wesley Horton 12 January 1882 at the Robinson home place at Shady Grove in Carroll County. Joseph Wesley Horton as born 13 December 1860 in Carroll County. He died 17 April 1912 and was buried at Concord Methodist Church at Hickory Level where the rest of his family would also be buried. He was a farmer. The following verse appears on his monument at Hickory Level:

> "Dearest husband, we must lay thee in the peaceful grave's embrace: But thy memory will be cherished till we see thy heavenly face."

Written by Sinah his loving wife.

The Hortons had four daughters. The first was Willie Josephine Horton born 21 December 1882 in Carroll County. She died 11 October 1924 from complications of childbirth. She married James Lamar Jackson on 1 November 1903 at her home place at Shady Grove. James Lamar Jackson was the son of James Henderson Jackson and Celestial Marlowe. James L. Jackson was born 10 January 1883 and died 14 January 1956, buried at Beulah Baptist Church Cemetery. Willie Horton and James L. Jackson had four children: Sina Jewell Jackson, Grace Eugenia Jackson, Willie Irene Jackson, and James Milford Jackson.

Wedding day, Horton home place, November 1, 1903

Willie's wedding day picture is shown here. From left to right are Mary Alzena Horton, "Miss Sallie" Robinson, Lee Arlena Horton, Joseph Wesley Horton, Sinah Justine Horton Robinson, James Lamar Jackson, the groom, and Willie Josephine Horton Jackson, the bride. Notice the cat on the roof.

The second daughter of Sinah and Joseph Horton was Jackie Pauline Horton who was born 4 November 1888 and died 16 July 1889.

The third daughter of Sinah and Joseph Horton was Lee Arlena Horton born 5 September 1891 in Carroll County. Arlena first married Oscar James Morgan on 25 July 1907. He died 24 November 1930. Legend has it that while plowing the fields one day, Oscar Morgan found a substantial amount of gold hidden by Creek or Cherokee Indians living in that area before they were removed from Georgia to the west.

Seven children were born to the Morgans: (1) James Earl Morgan; (2) Gladys Arlena Morgan born 17 September 1910, taught school for thirty years, married James Mann Norris 9 June 1938 in Carrollton. James was born 25 January 1903 in Meriwether County, Georgia. He died 15 October 1985 in Atlanta. They had one child, James Morgan Norris; (3) Grace Morgan; (4) Ruby Anne Morgan; (5) Mary Nell; (6) Thomas; (7) Joseph Wesley. Arlena Horton Morgan married second to Van Watkins Sr. on 27 September 1950 in Carroll County. Arlena is buried next to her first husband at Old Concord Methodist Church at Hickory Level. Arlena preserved the old portrait of her grandfather, William Osmus Robinson, for us.

Oscar James Morgan was the oldest son of James Thomas Morgan who was born 5 June 1869 and died 31 July 1932, and who married on 4 October 1888 to Mary Elizabeth Hamrick (23 October 1868-13 April 1924). This Morgan family has been extensively documented in the book *David Morgan & his Descendants* by James Kindred Morgan. Oscar Morgan's brothers and sisters were Virgil Davis born 30 March 1892, Izora Florance born 27 October 1893, Lucy Alzoda born 26 January 1897, Susan Estell born 17 April 1899, Pearl Amanda born 20 February 1901, Ollie Floyd born 24 October 1903.

The fourth daughter of Sinah and Joseph Wesley Horton was Mary Alzena Horton who was born 9 September 1894 in Carrollton. She married Joseph Johnson William Jordan on 17 July 1910. He was born 31 January 1891 in Carrollton and died 14 August 1972. This family is buried in the Carrollton City Cemetery. They had the following children: Flossie Christine Jordan, Addie Pauline Jordan, and Sina Bernie Jordan. *Submitted by: Gladys Norris, Rhudy Street, Carrollton, GA 30117 and Written by: Jan Robinson Bell.*

978. Susan Morgan Robinson

Susan Morgan Robinson was born on leap year day, 1956 to Mayor and Mrs. John Talmadge Robinson, in Carrollton, Georgia, into a family of Scottish and Irish ancestry. She was raised in a learned atmosphere of free thinking tolerance and remembers among her most influence mentors in her early childhood education as Miss Wawena Hughes, Mrs. Hugh Brock, Mrs. Mary Smith, and Mrs. Charlotte Hinesley at the Maple Street School. She was an avid reader and by the age of six had read every book in the Carrollton Public Library. At the age of twelve, she won the state essay contest from the Daughters of the American Revolution for her essay entitled "Sidney Lanier, Georgia's Sweetest Singer of Songs." Among her most cherished early childhood memories of Carrollton are her personal interactions with Susan Hayward.

> "Susan Hayward would come over to my Aunt Nell's for fittings for her gowns. Sometimes I'd be there, just hanging around as

Susan Morgan Robinson, Atlanta, May 2001.

Mother always hoped and prayed I'd learn to sew. I never did. But Susan Hayward would load me up in her pickup casually dressed as she always was in her tight fighting jeans with a rope tied around her waist for a belt and we'd ride up to the Jitney Jungle to shop for her groceries, me in my pigtails riding in the front seat of her grocery cart, and we'd talk about how much she loved Carrollton or how much I wanted to go away to some faraway land and she'd tell me how boring movie stars were and she'd tell me how much nicer Carrollton folks were. She would make time for me and was always so kind to me and would tell me what a smart and pretty little girl I was before we would go back to my Aunt Nell's." And to this day that's still how I relate to all famous people whether it's a president, movie star or a prince, just the way I did to Susan Hayward."

Then there was that first Kennedy Kiss.

"Robert F. Kennedy came to town to dedicate a chapel to his brother, John, and he stopped by the Maple Street school and he picked me out of all the other kids and lifted me up in his arms and hugged me real tight and kissed me right on the cheek right in front of everyone. It made me feel so special and all the teachers said to never wash my face again and I remember really worrying for a long time if they were serious."

Susan entered the Oak Mountain Academy in the seventh grade and distinguished herself under the tutelage of Professor Karen Rollins as an excellent debater winning the State Championship Title for the academy as Top Team and Top Speaker for the consecutive years 1972 and 1973. She also excelled in drama and music and had the starring role in the critically acclaimed production of the Oak Mountain Academy's *The Curious Savage* with Susan starring as Mrs. Savage and won the OMA Drama Award. Susan also was the editor of the first high school annual published by the academy. At the academy she also was a well rounded student and was elected to the student council, the Bell Choir, the soccer team, the volleyball team, French and geometry awards, and attended the Presidential Classroom for Young Americans in Washington, D.C. She was, and struggles to remain, an avid tennis player, equestrian, cliff diver and snorkler. She also participated in the weekly-required assembly musical or skit presentations in the OMA drawing room by singing, acting, or playing her guitar.

Beginning in the summer at the age of thirteen, she was treated to a transatlantic education and attended during the summers a number of university and college programs and was tutored in Bruges, Belgium, Paris, France, Florence and Rome, Italy, London, England, and Lucerne, Switzerland in various subjects including applied art, art history, international politics, history, literature and applied music (piano and guitar) and music history. Today her music compositions and recordings reflect her exposure to these cultures. She also worked and traveled extensively throughout the Caribbean, especially Jamaica. She graduated from the Oak Mountain Academy in 1973 as valedictorian and was named Carrollton's Junior Citizen of the Year. She attended a number of experimental acting and political programs in London involving drama and politics and was awarded a debating scholarship to the Colombian College of Arts and Sciences of the George Washington University in Washington, D.C.

While attending college, she studied international politics, presidential speech writing and decided to pursue a career in law. In 1978, she earned her bachelor of arts in communication with high distinction in speech communications and broadcasting in 1978. She worked at the Senate for U.S. Senator Sam Nunn and befriended Senator Herman Talmadge. Later, she worked for President Jimmy Carter writing position papers for his presidential campaign and began writing speeches for the former first lady Rosalyn Carter under the direction of Mary King, the wife of Peter Bourne, the psychiatrist who is credited with having talked Carter into running for president and the inventor of methadone.

James Patrick Morgan, Jeremy Andersson, Susan Morgan Robinson, the Hon. John T. Robinson

While at the George Washington University, Susan was awarded the prestigious and coveted Isaac Davis Cup for Public Speaking, for a speech entitled *The Paranoid Style of American Politics.* It is a highly competitive Annual Silver Cup given to one George Washington senior per year for the Best Oration. She was the first and only woman and only Georgian to ever win the award. For this, first lady Rosalyn Carter sent her a warm letter from the White House congratulating her on behalf of all Georgians.

After graduation from college, Susan attended the Gambrell School of Law at the Emory Law School. Her advocacy skills were recognized by her immediate election to the highly competitive Emory Moot Court Society and her Freshman Brief was selected for permanent placement in the files of the Emory Law Library for Excellence in Brief Writing. She is a gifted writer for the *Emory Law Times* and two of her articles, *A Case of MultiNational MalPractice* on the Dalkon Shield and *Judicial Homicide of Children* were front-page feature stories. Morgan, as she was now called after her beloved little brother, James Morgan Robinson who died shortly after he was born, also performed in the Law School Follies, with her own band as the featured performer in the Law School Blues Band, performing original compositions, the most popular of which was *Dragonlady Blues* a parody about Nancy Reagan.

In 1982, Morgan Robinson earned her Juris Doctor from the Emory Law School in Atlanta, Georgia. She entered the private practice of law in Atlanta, Georgia, and been a member of the State Bar of Georgia since that time. Upon graduation, she primarily counseled clients in the field of entertainment law and criminal and civil litigation. She was for many years the attorney for the Grammy Awards and was awarded the President's Award by the National Academy of Recording Arts and Sciences for her many years of service. Through her law practice, she has met and counseled numerous celebrities, and been fortunate to counsel, work with or meet many presidents and first ladies and even members of various royal families, including the late H.R.H. Princess Diana during the Olympic negotiations. She was the chairwoman for the State Bar of Georgia's Entertainment and Sport Law Section Luncheon Lecture Series for five years and has served on the Senate Music Industry Committee for the State of Georgia. Robinson has made numerous radio and television appearance over her twenty-year career in the entertainment industry. Her appearances have included locally *The Layman's Lawyer, Savannah, West Coast Jazz, The Buckhead Weekly, and PowerLunch.* She is well known in the entertainment litigation field for securing the rights of visual artists and for continuing to expand the area of premise liability law for artists while they are on tour. She has been featured in a number of publications including *The Atlanta Journal and Constitution, The Atlanta Business Chronicle, The Times Georgian,* and numerous other national and international publications. She has served as an adjunct professor of law at the Georgia State University and as a visiting professor to numerous other colleges and universities. Morgan Robinson is the president of her own firm Morgan Robinson, P.C. located in the Buckhead district of Atlanta, Georgia.

In 2000, she founded a production company (Goddess Records) and began recording original compositions. Her debut CD is scheduled for release this fall. Robinson has studied drama with Betty Roberts Motes (the mother of Julia Roberts and founder of the Actors Workshop) and voice with Jan Smith, the former executive director for the Grammys. She was married to Ralph Arthur Andersson from May 7, 1982 until April 1, 1992. She has one son Jeremy Randolph Andersson born on February 20, 1984. She is currently single, practicing law, transcribing her journals and living in the Woods of Briarlake, Atlanta, Georgia with her collies and Maine Coons.

The Subpoena

By Robert Morris, writer and Press Representative for Governor Roy Barnes; Written and Read for Susan Morgan's Robinson birthday celebration at the Piedmont Driving Club hosted by Mrs. Bruce F. Woodfruff Jr.

Great is Morgan; She has conquered
Seven Kingdoms
First was the kingdom of Radical Ideas:
Then it was Senator Sam, really, women,
get thee to the mail room or kitchen?
But instead of yessiring and pushing that
honorable's stamp of approval,
She used inflexion and accent to question
old order.

Great is Morgan; She has conquered
Seven Kingdoms.
Second is the Kingdom of Law and Order:
Paper chasers and the all night revue
busters on caffeine and status,
She asked nightowls to chase more than
their own tails,
But cause and conviction, in a law can be
harsh

Jeremy Randolph Andersson

Without public sacrifice, efficient but equitable.
Great is Morgan; She has conquered Seven Kingdoms.
The Third is the Kingdom of the Closed Door:
Music was great liberator, frequencies that set free
Were almost recorded symbols of value
Where contracts are cut in the man's world,
Until she kicked in the door and demanded her twirl.
Great is Morgan; She has Conquered Seven Kingdoms.
The fourth was the Kingdom of Motherhood;
In this World of immovable shields and sheltering Barbarians
That brandish the irresistible sword
And lead back to broken palaces, she was made
Constant negotiator and shape changer to raise this brilliant boy.
Great is Morgan; She has conquered Seven Kingdoms.
The fifth is the Kingdom of Friendship.
When the call won't come in, she makes it,
When we dislike a thing, she'll change it.
When we want to go nowhere, she comes with us,
And when the barbarians invades us, she chortles with it.
Her friendship is freedom of mind.
Great is Morgan. She has conquered Seven Kingdoms.
The sixth is the kingdom of Comedic Presence.
Last night it was woo-woo and oooh-ooh,
They did what and yes without what and way layed
Past that which accosts and offends into the realm
Of divine humor that saves us from embracement —
Some lions she lions
A stallion of wit.
Great is Morgan; She has conquered Seven Kingdoms.
The seventh is the Kingdom of the Old Soul;
One of the Shakespeare's actors with sword or chicken leg and baud,
Or yet again a Duchess whose court yields
Great Renaissance wonders, defeat without danger,
The epochs of transient are not her matter,
No, Morgan lives for the fullness or time.

Robinson ties to Carrollton and her father, former Mayor John Talmadge Robinson, remain strong. "My favorite things in the world to do is to drive to Carrollton and eat a homemade sandwich with my son and my father in Carrollton on a quiet Saturday afternoon. Just the three of us eating a turkey and Swiss sandwich on whole wheat bread talking about how folks and things in Carrollton are the best there are. I treasure those moments in time more than any in the whole wide world."

Jeremy Randolph Andersson

Jeremy Randolph Andersson was born February 20, 1984, in Atlanta, Georgia to Susan Morgan Robinson and Ralph Arthur Andersson. Jeremy earned his first title of Little Mister Dogwood from the Atlanta Playhouse Theater Guild at the tender age of four when he excelled in the field of oral interpretation of literature and drama by reciting poetry, *I've Gone to London* to a crowd of journalist and drama critics at Georgia Tech in Atlanta, Georgia, in May 1988. He is a stellar athlete in the sports of baseball and football and a gifted thespian.

Jeremy Randolph Andersson and Katherine Houston Pope

He currently attends The Asheville School in Asheville, North Carolina. He lettered in junior varsity and varsity football and baseball and has held starring roles in *Twelfth Night, Once Upon A Mattress,* and *Godspell.* He was elected cast captain for his excellence in drama during his Fifth Form year for his performance in *Once Upon a Mattress.* He is the vice president of the senior class at the Asheville School and shows great promise in the field of leadership and politics. *Submitted by: Susan Morgan Robinson, Atlanta, GA*

979. The Talmadge and Maude Chappell Robinson Family

This is the story of my grandparents, Martha Maude Chappell Robinson and Talmadge Robinson, who were born in Carroll County, Georgia, and lived here nearly all their lives. My sister, Jan Robinson Bell, has spent a lifetime in climbing up the family trees of both Maude and Talmadge — and we now share her research with you. Martha Maude Chappell Robinson was the daughter of Allen Dawson Chappell (11 December 1870-13 October 1893) and Eldorado "Rada" Chambers (2 March 1874-23 August 1914) of Carroll County.

The Chambers family traces its roots back to early Lunenberg County, Virginia, where Edward Chambers was a judge in Colonial days. He had a son named Thomas Chambers Jr. who married Millicent Hurt. It would be their son, Thomas Chambers Jr., who would eventually migrate to Elbert County, Georgia, and become the progenitor of a large Chambers family there.

Thomas Chambers Jr. married Sarah "Sally" Alston and had the following children: Edward M., Charity Alston, Thomas J. b. ca. 1800, George Alston b. 15 September 1807 in Elbert County, GA (our ancestor), Mary A.R. b. 1809, James Alston b. ca. 1815. It is no wonder that almost all the Chambers children were given a middle name of Alston — for the Alston family was such a respected one. Their extensive family tree can be documented all the way back to King Alfred the Great of England. In *History of Alstons of North and South Carolina* by J.A. Groves, M.D. the lineage is traced back for centuries. A copy of this book can be seen at the Georgia State Archives.

Sarah "Sally" Alston's parents, Charity and William Alston, were cousins. Charity was the daughter of James Alston b. 1710 and Christian Lillington of New Bern, N.C. Christian's father, George Lillington, was a soldier in the American Revolution from Orange County, N.C. William Alston was the son of Solomon Alston born 1701 and Nancy Ann Hinton b. 1712 in Nansemond County, Virginia. (The Hintons descend from a Royal family tree, so their line is also extensively documented.) The Alstons were descended from John Alston, a revenue collector for the King of England, who was the son of John Alston (1652-1704) who married Anne Wallis, daughter of the famous mathematician, John Wallis b. 1616 in Kent, England.

William Alston was a Lt. Colonel for Halifax County, NC that met 27 December 1774. Afterwards, he was a member of the Provincial Congress from Lincoln County that met at Hillsboro in 1775. At that time, William Alston was appointed Lt. Col. Of the 3rd Regiment of Continental Troops. He served under Col. Jethro Summer and Major Samuel Lockhart. William Alston's service is documented in the D.A.R. through #49019. After the American Revolution, William Alston moved his family to Elbert County, GA and he died there in 1810.

The children of Lt. Col. William Alston and Charity Alston are: (1) James m. Catherine Hamilton (2) William Hinton m. Elizabeth Rucker (3) Philip Henry m. Mrs. Winn Woolfolk (4) Solomon (5) George died early in life (6) Mary m. Lt. James Clark of VA (7) Elizabeth m. Thompson (8) Christian died unmarried (9) Nancy m. J. Minor Tate of GA (10) Sarah or "Sallie" m. Thomas Chambers Jr. According to an old Bible record in our family, Thomas Chambers Jr. graduated from Yale.

Martha Maude Chappell Robinson

George Alston Chambers was born 15 August 1802 in Elbert County, GA. In young manhood he graduated from the University of South Carolina. George then entered the teaching profession and taught first in Coweta County, then in Talledega County, Alabama, and later in Carroll County. About 1826, George A. Chambers married Jane D. Caldwell daughter of Col. William Harris Caldwell (4 May 1774-29 October 1885 buried Talledega, AL) and Elsy Jane Davis (1765-d. 8 December 1829 buried Abbeville, SC) of Abbeville, South Carolina. Col. William Harris Caldwell gained his title from the SC Militia. W.H. Caldwell was the son of James

Caldwell b. ca. 1738 in Anson, NC. James Caldwell was a Revolutionary Soldier who married about 1757 to Elizabeth Harris and died in Abbeville County, SC. James Caldwell was the son of David Caldwell of County Donegal, Ireland, b. ca. 1705 who married Ann Harriss b. 1715 in County Donegal, Ireland, the daughter of James Harriss and Mary Simpson. Elsy Davis b. ca. 1765 SC was the daughter of Moses Davis who died in 1804 leaving a will in Abbeville County, SC. The derivation of the Caldwell name comes from earlier ancestors who actually owned "cold wells" in France where people came to obtain their fresh drinking water. The Caldwells later migrated from France to Scotland and from there migrated to America.

Children born to George A. Chambers and Jane D. Caldwell are: (1) Sarah C. b. 29 May 1827 in SC m. Thomas M. Banks 4 April 1850 d. 26 July 1900 buried Centralhatchee Baptist Church Heard County (2) William Harris b. 15 February 1829 in SC m. Sarah Houston 9 April 1852 (3) Francis E. b. 28 April 1831 in SC m. Samuel Herring 3 March 1860 (4) Irena Elvira b. 13 October 1833 in SC m. Abraham J. Ayers 14 March 1867 d. 16 October 1908 buried Little Vine Cemetery Carroll County (5) James Alston Chambers b. 3 November 1835 in Talledega County, AL m. Martha Anne Fowler 31 March 1856 d. 5 July 1912 buried Stripling Chapel Church Carroll County (6) Jefferson L. b. 1 May 1838 d. before 1850 (7) George W. b. 18 February 1841 in Coweta Co., m. first Catherine Phipps 7 April 1867 Bartholomew County, Indiana — children by this marriage stayed in Indiana, second m. Nancy Emaline Barr 2 September 1883 buried Waco Baptist Church Haralson County, GA (8) Joseph A. b. 29 January 1844 m. Martha Ann Barr 2 February 1869, buried Goshen Church Heard County (9) Benjamin F. b. 12 October 1847 m. Louisa Jane Barr (b. 24 June 1849 — d. 27 November 1930) married on 16 January 1870, d. 10 September 1900 buried Mt. Zion Methodist Church (10) Robert D. b. 1847 m. Lucinda Cash 26 May 1868 d. 19 September 1919 buried Whooping Creek Church Carroll County.

The three Chambers brothers married three Barr sisters. The sisters — Nancy E., Louisa Jane, and Martha Ann — were daughters of Josiah Kanady Barr b. 14 March 1817 and m. on 21 December 1834 to Jane O. Griffith b. 4 April 1818. Josiah Barr was the son of Joseph Barr b. 29 September 1787 and Eliza Barr b. 14 January 1788. Jane O. Griffith was the daughter of Davied Griffith b. 1775 in Wales and d. age 104 in 1879 at Lowell, GA. Written in the Family Bible is a story that Grandpa Griffith had left behind a fortune in Wales that was worth millions of dollars. About 1861 Grandpa Griffith had asked his son-in-law, J.K. Barr, to travel to Wales to collect the fortune for him. J.K. Barr started out on horseback but soon the Civil War broke out. J.K. Barr's son George was killed in the war — after that no one attempted to go to Wales. This is as it was written in their family Bible. George A. Chambers died 15 May 1883 and was buried in the old Walker Family Cemetery on the Dairy Road near Goshen Church in Heard County. Jane D. Caldwell died 8 April 1890 and was buried alongside her husband. A descendant, Hugh Martin Chambers has placed new markers on these graves.

On 31 March 1856, James A. Chambers m. Martha Anne Fowler the daughter of Elbert Fowler (b. 1808) and Nancy Treadwell (b. 1808). Nancy Treadwell is related to the many Treadwell families of early Carroll County and is believed to be descended from the Treadwells of Clarke County, GA who migrated to Coweta County. (See the postings to "Biography" of U.S. GenWeb for Clarke County, Georgia.) Nancy Tredwell and Elbert Fowler m. in Fayette County, GA on 6 February 1825. Together Elbert and Nancy Fowler had the following known children: William H. b. 1829; two sons names unknown; Jerusha b. 1832 and m. Jordan Holland; Nathaniel H. b. 1836; Martha Anne b. 1838; Andrew C. b. 1840 m. Florida J. Meadows 24 December 1868. Nancy died sometime before 1869 because Elbert Fowler married second Angeline Knight Gladney of Carroll County on 30 July 1869. Angeline had two children by her first marriage: Berry H. and Elisabeth Gladney. Angeline may have had a sister, Francis C. Knight who m. Samuel M.C. Gladney on 5 January 1860 in Carroll County, GA. Elbert and Angeline Fowler are believed to be buried in Carroll County.

Talmadge Whitfield Robinson, World War I

James Alston Chambers (b. 3 November 1835) m. Martha Anne Fowler (b. 27 March 1837) on 31 July 1856 in Coweta County and settled down in Carroll County, Georgia. James A. Chambers enlisted at Newnan, GA during the Civil War and was a Pvt. in Co. F. Philip's Legion of GA Cavalry, CSA. On 26 June 1864, he was recorded as being injured and held at Wayside Hospital in Richmond, VA. James A. Chambers was discharged at Greensboro, NC in 1865. He received his Confederate pension in 1903. James A. Chambers died 5 July 1912. His wife, Martha Anne, preceded him in death — she died on 29 March 1901. Her tombstone reads:

"A tender mother and a faithful friend."

Both James A. and Martha Anne Chambers are buried at Stripling Chapel Methodist Church in Carroll County.

Children of James A. Chambers and Martha Anne Fowler were: (1) Fannie E. b. 4 April 1858 m. David W. Walker 27 June 1890 — had sons Jim and Calhoun Walker (2) William Elbert b. 2 June 1860, died young (3) Jordan Thomas b. 7 May 1864 m. Maggie Burns 28 February 1887 d. 20 November 1893 — three daughters; according to newspaper Jordan Chambers was murdered — see *Carroll Free Press* issue of 24 November 1893 (4) Benjamin Samuel b. 20 May 1870 m. Eugenia Wootson "Wootsie" Huckeba, (b. 11 December 1870) on 30 October 1890. Ben d. 12 October 1948; Gena d. 3 October 1948, buried Carrollton City Cemetery. (5) Eldorado "Rada" b. 2 March 1874 m. Allen Dawson Chappell 25 December 1890 d. 23 August 1914 buried Stripling Chapel Church alongside her parents (marked with fieldstones) (6) Sallie Jerusha or "Sallie Ruth" b. 3 May 1877 m. Pleasant Eugene Lambert 18 February 1895 d. 13 May 1928; — See a separate heading for Sallie Ruth Chambers and the Lamberts.

Our Chappell line begins with Allen Chappell b. 1798 in NC who marries Martha "Patsy" Purviance on 11 January 1820 in Cabarrus County, NC. Allen is the brother of Jesse F. Chappell who was born 16 March 1789 and married on 19 September 1813 in Cabarrus County to Sally Purvians (b. 26 November 1791 — buried at Concord Methodist Church, Hickory Level). Martha was the daughter of James Purviance by his third wife Deborah Sherrill. Sally was the daughter of James Purviance by either his first or second wife.

The Purviance family history begins in the Scottish Highlands in the area now identified as County Perth. In the 13th century there were many attendants of the King of Scotland — who were called pursuivants. About the time of the reign of King Alexander II of Scotland, one of the pursuivants was given the job of Purveyor. He was an officer of the court who provided "Purveyance" or the supplies and services required by the Crown. So, this occupation became the basis for the surname of Purviance. Naturally, having so much experience from this type of occupation, it is no wonder than many of the descendants decided to enter into the mercantile business. And over the generations, the family became quite successful.

By the mid 1750s, the Purviance family had established quite a fleet of ships to participate in international commerce. By this time, many of the Purviance family had settled in America as well. Some of the ships they owned were named *Sloop General Gates, Brigatine Hibernia, Ship Experiment, Ship Marquis de la Follette, Ship Buckskin, Sloop Richmond, Sloop Abingdon, Schooner Swallow, and Schooner Savage* — in all there were more than 50 ships in the Purviance fleet. The family were involved in the manufacture of sail, rope and tar.

The Purviance family took an active part in the cause of the American Revolution. For some 300 years they had fought their foe — the British — on the Battlefields of Scotland. Hue Purviance of Lanark was executed after the Battle of Bothwell Bridge in 1683 for refusing to swear allegiance to the King. The Purviance family were well acquainted with all the major figures of the Revolutionary period — they corresponded with them and entertained them in their homes. Samuel Purviance and his brothers William and John all served as chairmen of the Committee of Safety in Baltimore, Maryland and Mecklenberg, N.C. The Financial House of Robert and Samuel Purviance served as the Financial Agents for the Continental Congress during the years of Revolution and they became known as the major contributors to the cause of the American Revolution. All their ships and their entire fortune were eventually donated to this cause.

Dr. Steve Worthy receives award from Dr. Irvine S. Ingram

David Purviance II was the first of our line to come to America — he was the son of David I and the grandson of John b. at Castle Finn in Ireland ca. 1708. David Purviance I b. ca 1738 m. 1 May 1758 in Lancaster County, PA to Margaretha S. McEntyre. They had ten children — some born in Pennsylvania and others in North Carolina where they moved in 1760. They settled about three miles from Concord, NC. The family used spellings of Purvians, Purviance, and Purvines — and later Vines. The family lived in Cabarrus County, NC and attended Poplar Tent Presbyterian Church. David's children were John b. 1760, James b. 1758, Joseph b. 1764, David b. 1769, Robert b. 1772 Martha, and Margaret, Mary, others unknown.

Jan Robinson's third birthday party with all her grandmothers.

Our Martha was born 1798 (d/o James Purviance) who married Allen Chappell in Cabarrus County, NC in 1820.

Even before the land lotteries began Allen and his brother Jesse F. had migrated down into Georgia purchasing land first in the area of Greene County. They both appear there in the Headright Land Grants. There is also a John Chappell in Greene County but we do not know if he is related to Allen and Jesse. When John Chappell died in Monroe County GA in 1828 he mentions in his will: wife, Sarah P. (Could he too have married a Purviance?), Nancy Bonner, Martha Heath, Eliza Douglas, Abraham H., George A., Sarah H., John D., and Joseph T. Chappell. In 1827 Allen won a parcel of land in Troup County in the lottery but sold this land by 1828. In 1830 Allen and his family appear in the census records of Upson County, GA. By 1840, Allen and Martha had moved to Heard County, GA. The children of Allen and Martha Chappell were: Crosby Dawson b. 1826; Martha b. 1832; Vina b. 1837; Allen H. b. 1838; and a daughter born before 1840.

By 1850, Allen Chappell had moved his family to Tallapoosa County, Alabama. By 1860, Jesse F. Chappell had moved next door to Allen's family. By this time, Jesse F.'s first wife had died and was buried at Concord Church at Hickory Level. (On her tombstone her name appears as "Vines" instead of Purvians.") Jesse F. Chappell had married Melinda Wise in Carroll County on 7 September 1848. By 1870, Allen Chappell had moved his family back to Heard County and it is here that he lived for the remainder of his life. Allen appeared in the 1870 census as 73 years old. Martha appeared as 76 years old in 1870. Both are believed to be buried in the old Walker Cemetery near Goshen Church.

Jesse F. Chappell had children who remained in Carroll County. One of these was G.D. Henderson Chappell, b. 1815 in NC, living in Carroll County in 1850 m. 1844; Matilda Chappell b. 16 November 1816; Mahalia Chappell b. 1818; Malina Chappell b. 8 July 1822; Eliza Ann Chappell b. 26 November 1824 who later married Alexander Porter Green 23 November 1843 James Lawrence G. Chappell b. 6 January 1827 d. 23 December 1866; Sandy Allen Chappell b. 11 December 1830 m. Emily Reynolds 27 October 1857 d. 1862 as a soldier in the Civil War. There is a deed recorded in Carroll County dated 14 October 1840 when a deed of gift "for love and affection" from Jesse F. Chappell named his three sons — Henderson D., Sandy A. and James L. H.D. and J.L. Chappell continue to appear in records of Carroll County through 1880.

Our family is descended from Allen Chappell through his son Crosby Dawson Chappell born in 1826. In the 1850 census, Crosby Chappell was living in Coweta County. The census showed that Crosby was 24 years old and his wife, Martha E. Jones Chappell was also age 24. By 1860, Crosby had moved his family to Tallapoosa County, Alabama, living near his parents. But by 1870, Crosby had moved his family to Villa Rica, Georgia. In May 1870, Crosby's last child, a son, Allen Dawson Chappell was born. The children of Crosby Dawson Chappell and Martha E. Jones are: James M. b. ca 1845 in Carroll County, GA m. Martha Elizabeth Walker ca 1865, died 16 October 1868 — buried Walker Cemetery, near Goshen Church; Sarah; Mary b. 1852; John b. 1859; Thomas b. 1860; June b. 1862; Dora b. 1864; Ella b. 1866; Allen Dawson Chappell age 1 month at time of census on 1 June 1870.

Allen Dawson Chappell was born May 1870, the youngest son of Crosby Dawson Chappell and Martha E. Jones. Allen was a carpenter by profession and worked on many building projects around Carrollton and Atlanta, Georgia. Allen Chappell m. Eldorado "Rada" Chambers (b. 25 December 1874) on 25 December 1890 in Carroll County. The following children were born to them: (1) Martha Maude Chappell b. 25 November 1891 who m. Talmadge Whitfield Robinson (2) Byrd Morton b. 23 November 1893 d. 20 January 1920 (3) Carl Benjamin b. 15 July 1897 d. 1 September 1923, never married (4) Alma Pauline b. 5 July 1900 m. Joe Stephens on 21 March 1920 in Atlanta (5) Smith Eugene Chappell (twin) b. 16 April 1907 d. 10 December 1924, never married (6) Hoke Chappell (twin) b. 16 April 1907 — m. Lily Ponza — 2 children: Alice Joyce b. 1 October 1930, Carl Allen Chappell b. 17 October 1931 (7) Mary Louise b. 4 May 1909 married twice: first Joseph Walter Cooper — two children — Joseph Walter Cooper b. 15 January 1927 and Rosemary b. 20 November 1928; second husband, Joe Copeland.

When the youngest child, Mary, was only five years old, her mother Rada Chambers Chappell died in 1914 during a typhoid epidemic. Not long after that, Allen Chappell suffered a stroke and was left debilitated. My grandmother, Maude Chappell, was then 23 years old and the oldest child of the family. She took on the responsibility of being the caretaker for her father and younger brothers and sisters. The twins — Hoke and Smith were only seven years old and her sister Pauline was fourteen at the time.

Mary Chappell went to live with her Aunt Gena and Uncle Ben Chambers who lived on the Chambers home place located on Gray Road in Carroll County. Aunt Gena and Uncle Ben had not been able to have children of their own, but they took into their home many orphans — or children who just needed a home that could give them special attention.

Aunt Gena loved to play the piano and have everyone sing the popular tunes of the day. She taught my grandmother how to play the piano, although Maude never learned to read music. Maude had a special talent of listening to a song and then being able to play it by ear alone — and to perfection. Aunt Gena had a "Lincoln Library" and loved to encourage the children to read. She also had beautiful china and taught the children how to set the tables properly — and she taught them exquisite table manners, too. All her nieces and nephews adored Aunt Gena and the twins Hoke and Smith gave her their tiny silver baby cups engraved with their names — presented to them by Governor Hoke Smith of Georgia for whom they were named. These were placed carefully in Aunt Gena's china cabinet where all the special treasures of the children could be displayed. Aunt Gena kept all the family pictures and kept the Family Bible up to date — she also would include the names of any black children born on their farm. (These Bible records have been placed on the Internet on the Carroll County, Georgia site of U.S. GenWeb under "Bible Records.")

Uncle Ben had one of the finest farms in the county — the original property that was James A. Chambers' land — but he also had another job that kept him busy. He was the mule buyer for Carroll County in the early 1900s. Mules were of great importance in that era for they were the real workhorses of the farm — and everybody had a farm. Uncle Ben would ride the train to St. Louis, Missouri which was the main market for mule auctions. Ben Chambers knew everything there was to know about a mule. For instance, he could tell if a mule would work better on a farm or in a mine, if he would pull a load with a team or was he a loner? Was he the kind of mule who would walk in a circle all day to turn the syrup mill or was he the kind who wouldn't walk in a circle? Uncle Ben had a special talent in choosing exactly the kind of mule that the farmer wanted. It was said that Uncle Ben could pick you out a mule that could make "15 cents cotton". There were many post cards sent back and forth in this family because of Uncle Ben's many trips to St. Louis — and the old post card collection certainly demonstrates the close ties of this family over a lifetime.

Martha Anne Robinson Ansari, January 15, 1977

After her younger brothers and sisters were grown, Maude Chappell could finally begin with her own life pursuits. She and her sister Pauline found work at the Georgia Baptist Orphans Home in Hapeville, GA. It was while living there in Hapeville that Maude met a young man from back home in Carroll County, Talmadge Robinson, who had just returned from World War I. Talmadge was working in Atlanta in charge of the U.S. Mail for the Southern Railway. A romance blossomed and they were married in Atlanta, Georgia on 20 March 1921.

Talmadge Robinson had quite a military history to tell about. He had first joined the U.S. Army as a young man and was stationed in the American

Martha Anne and Ali's wedding day

west under General John J. "Blackjack" Pershing. Mostly, they were dealing with renegade Indians in the early 1900's. But in 1916 civil war had begun in Mexico and this led to many problems on the southern border of the U.S. A Mexican outlaw named Pancho Villa had ridden into Columbus, New Mexico with 1000 of his bandits — and they'd pulled American citizens off a train and shot them. Then, they had burned the town.

This was not to be tolerated and President Woodrow Wilson had sent the American troops under General Pershing into Mexico to "chase Villa." Those were the orders — "to chase Villa" not capture or kill him as Wilson feared starting a war with Mexico. So, as Talmadge would tell it in later years, the soldiers under Pershing chased Pancho Villa all over the badlands of Mexico. One of the other soldiers in Pershing's unit who would later gain fame was George S. Patton — later World War II's General Patton. As a result of this warfare with Pancho Villa, it just happened that General Pershing's unit was the only one of the U.S. Army that was getting any "active duty." So, when President Wilson decided that America would join World War I that was raging in Europe, General Pershing's unit was the only one considered "fit and ready to fight." General Pershing's unit was given the nickname of "Pershing's Darlings" and they were immediately transported "Over There." Talmadge Robinson would always say he was on the "first boatload to go over" and the "last boatload to come back." General Pershing's troops participated in the major battles of World War I in France and Belgium.

The Robinsons lived on Springdale Road in Hapeville after their marriage, but Maude later wanted their first child to be born in Carroll County since that was always called "home." Maude and Talmadge's only child, John Talmadge Robinson, was born 1 November 1921 on his grandfather's farm on Horsely Mill Road.

During the years of the Great Depression, Talmadge Robinson rejoined the U.S. Army and was stationed in the Panama Canal Zone while the Panama Canal was being built. When he retired from the Army, Maude and Talmadge settled down on a farm in Tryon, N.C. for a while. Later, they moved to a farm on the Hays Mill Road in Carrollton. They built a lake across from their home and Talmadge could often be seen on a summer's day fishing there. When World War II came along, Talmadge did his part for the war effort by working at the old Bell Bomber Plant in Marietta, Georgia. This later became Lockheed.

While Talmadge had been away in South America, Maude had entered into nurse's training at the old Battle Hill Sanitorium in Atlanta which specialized in treating tuberculosis patients. She worked there from 1931-1937. Since her work hours were long, Maude sent John to live with his Robinson grandparents back home in Carroll County. Maude instilled in John a great love of family, history, and civic pride. These qualities would carry him far in life and he would grow up to become one of Carrollton's finest citizens and mayors.

Maude Robinson continued with her nursing career many years and served as nurse-nanny to the Dr. Steve Worthy family in the 1950s when Dr. Worthy took his family to Boston while he pursued his specialty in OB/GYN. Maude and Dr. Worthy were cousins on the Chambers side of the family. Maude lived with the Worthy family — Dr. Steve and his wife, Imogene (nee Shore), children Emily (b. 22 July 1942), Ben (b. 4 July 1946), Ellen (b. 30 March 1948) and Peter (b. 6 February 1951).

After Dr. Worthy completed his degree, they all returned to Carrollton to live and Dr. Worthy became one of Carrollton's most loved and respected OB/GYN physicians. Dr. Steve Worthy had many honors bestowed upon him during his lifetime — and Maude enjoyed being able to always "clip out his picture from the newspaper" for her many scrapbooks. Dr. Worthy is pictured here receiving the Founder's Day Award, the highest honor, from Dr. Irvine S. Ingram of West Georgia College in 1972. Maude Robinson was always very proud of her cousin "Dr. Steve."

In their retirement years, Talmadge and Maude Robinson enjoyed sweet potato farming on Hays Mill Road. Maude tended her many flower gardens and also she was a talented seamstress. She loved to design patterns, and make dresses for her three granddaughters — and would also make dolls with doll dresses to match.

Maude decorated her home with a beautiful collection of fans which friends and family brought her from all over the world. Even in her old age, Maude kept a beautiful complexion which is that pale skin treasured by Southern women — "like moonlight on magnolias." She said her secret was never letting the sun shine on her face — and patting buttermilk on her cheeks every night before retiring to her old four poster bed. Maude's trademark was always wearing a big beautiful hat — preferably decorated with flowers on top — and a string of pearls. Maude died on 18 November 1973 and was buried alongside her husband at Carroll Memory Gardens. Talmadge Robinson had died 10 May 1972.

The second daughter of John T. and Melba Robinson was Martha Anne born on 18 November 1956 — and named for her paternal grandmother, Martha Maude Chappell Robinson. Martha Anne attended school at Maple Street, and later at Oak Mountain Academy for several years before transferring to Ashley Hall in Charleston, S.C. She graduated from Ashley Hall in 1972. Martha Anne then began her college studies in Europe, first attending Schiller College in London, England, from 1972-1974. There, she met her future husband, Ali Morad Massoud Ansari, who was the son of Abdoul Hossein Massoud Ansari (1890-1983) and Fatima Massoud Ansari (1912-1998). Both Martha Anne and Ali's parents are seen pictured here at the time of the wedding in 1977.

Ali's father had a long and distinguished career serving at different times as the Iranian Ambassador for the Soviet Union, India, The Hague, Holland and was also appointed by the King to be Governor of three states in Iran. Ali's grandfather, Ali Gholi Massoud Ansari, for whom he was named, was the Minister of Foreign Affairs for Iran in his lifetime and he signed for Iran at the Treaty of Versailles, the treaty that ended World War I. Ali's mother was a descendant of the Quajar Dynasty which ruled Iran for over 400 years until the Shah of Iran came into power in 1930. The Massoud Ansari family can trace their family back 1200 years into ancient Persian history.

Martha Anne and Ali transferred to Heidelberg, Germany campus of Schiller College and both graduated from there in 1976. Martha Anne received her B.A. in European studies and minored in art history. Ali received his B.S. in business administration. After graduation, Martha Anne Robinson and Ali Masaud Ansari were married at Heidelberg Castle on 15 January 1977. They moved to Teheran, Iran, to live near Ali's parents for several years. Their first child, a daughter, Nassim (which means "breeze" in Persian) was born there on 16

Amir Ansari, Angeline Ansari, Nassim Ansari

December 1979. They lived through the Iranian Revolution when the Shah was deposed — and escaped to America just before the bombing of the airport of Teheran. Ali became an American citizen in 1983.

Martha Anne and Ali lived in Denver, Colorado, for several years during which time they both continued their education at the University of Denver. Ali received his master's degree in public administration in 1978. Martha Anne received her master's degree in art history in 1982. By this time, they had added a son to their family, Amir "Brad" Ansari b. 16 July 1981. The Ansaris moved back to Georgia for a few years and Ali earned a second master's degree in decision sciences at Georgia State University in 1983. In 1985, a daughter was born, Angeline Mariam Ansari, on 18 July 1985. Angeline has the distinction of carrying a traditional name of Angeline that has been in the family over a hundred years. Angeline was named for her maternal grandmother, Melba Angeline Morgan Robinson (1922-1996) who was in turn named for her maternal grandmother Mary Angeline Ryan Patrick (1876-1953). Angeline Patrick was named for her maternal grandmother, Angeline Brown (b. ca. 1820) wife of Armocette Brown.

The Ansari family has lived in Lawrenceville, GA since 1990. Martha Anne has attended the University of Georgia and served as vice president of the Association of Graduate Art Students there. Martha Anne is very active in her church, St. Mary and St. Martha of Bethany of Buford, GA. She serves on the board of Outreach for the Needy and is directress of the Altar Guild. Martha Anne inherited her grandmother's love of flowers. Martha Anne also carries on the tradition of the name of Martha which her own grandmother, Martha Maude Chappell, received from her grandmothers — Martha E. Jones Chappell (b. 1826) and Martha Anne Fowler Chambers (1837-1901) both of Carroll County. Martha Anne has been busy pursuing her master's degree in social work which will be awarded in May of 2002.

Ali is employed by SunMicrosystems. He also has taught many classes in computer science at Gwinnett Technical Institute. In 1995, Ali was recognized with an award as Outstanding Teacher at Gwinnett Tech. Nassim Ansari is now 21 years old and works as a travel consultant for American Express in Atlanta. Brad Ansari attended Colorado Mountain College and is now serving in the U.S. Army in Columbia, S.C. Angeline Ansari is a tenth grade student at Collins Hill High School in Suwanee, GA. Angeline is planning to attend the State University of West Georgia after her graduation from high school in 2003. *Submitted by: Martha Anne Robinson Ansari, 2535 Lockmeade Way, Lawrenceville, GA*

980. Walter Robinson

Walter Ernest Robinson is the second and middle child of Walter Hill Robinson Jr. and Mercedes del Socorro Figueroa Robinson, and the grandson of Walter Hill Robinson Sr. and Jacqueline Zora Harris of Carrollton, Georgia. He was born September 18, 1950 at French Hospital in San Francisco, California.

In 1952 the family moved to Palo Alto, California, where Walter attended school, graduating from Cubberley High School in 1968. As a child, Walter spent many hours learning from and helping his father in their home wood shop, building functional and decorative things for the home and even a small sailboat. As a child, Walter had an aptitude in the visual arts, which he was encouraged to pursue. He inherited his father's abilities to draw, design, and build, as well as his mother's intuitive creativity.

After high school he attended California College of Arts and Crafts and San Francisco Academy of Art, where he received his master of fine arts degree in 1978, majoring in sculpture. When his parents moved to Carroll County in 1980, Walter spent four months there helping them set up the infrastructure on their property on Jones Mill Road. While attending college, he worked as a carpenter, remodeling Victorian homes in San Francisco. In 1982, he became a licensed general contractor and a member of the California Builders Association. He continues to work part-time on residential and commercial projects.

Marty Sohl, Walter Robinson, Mercedes Robinson, Carmen Robinson, Justin Walter.

Walter also continues to pursue a career as an artist. He is represented by galleries in San Francisco and New York, and shows and sells his sculptural work and drawings nationally and internationally.

Walter has lived in San Francisco with his common-law wife Martha Jane Sohl since 1991. They have no children. Born on December 26, 1947, in Bloomington, Illinois, Martha is the daughter of Roberta Jean Gordon and Jerry Sohl. A former ballerina, she has worked as photographer for San Francisco Ballet and San Francisco Opera since 1982. Her father Jerry is a writer known for his science fiction novels and his T.V. scripts for Star Trek, Twilight Zone and Alfred Hitchcock. *Submitted by: Walter Robinson, 1347 14th Avenue, San Francisco, CA 94122*

981. Walter Hill Robinson and Jacqueline Zora Robinson

Walter Hill Robinson (born 9 September 1888 and died 6 September 1975) was the son of John David Robinson and Margaret Josephine Green of Carroll County. He is buried at Shady Grove Cemetery in Carroll County with his wife Jacqueline Zora Harris. Walter was one of several children. He worked for the Southern Railroad Company sorting mail on the train cars. He married Jacqueline Zora Harris around 1908-1910. They had three children, John David Robinson (born September 13, 1910, died September 3, 1962), Christine Vivian (born September 20, 1912, died October 1944) and Walter Hill Robinson Jr. There was a fourth child who died in infancy and is also buried at Shady Grove, Allie Inez Robinson (born October 2, 1909, died November 11, 1909).

Walter and Jacqueline were divorced in about 1927. Jacqueline married a farmer (whose last name was Jones) in Carroll County. He became ill and passed away. At one point Jacqueline ran a small restaurant on the square in Carrollton. She remarried again to a widower whose last name was Johnson. He shot himself over his first wife's grave two weeks after marrying Jacqueline. After divorcing Jacqueline, Walter married again and raised two stepdaughters, Thelma and Katherine. He divorced his second wife. Sometime in the 1950s, Jacqueline and Walter remarried. They lived in Melrose, Florida, tending their garden and worm bed. They often walked to Santa Fe Lake to fish. They moved to Snellville, Georgia, in the early 1960s, living on the same property with their oldest son, John David, until Jacqueline's death. Walter then moved to a retirement home. At the time of Walter's death, his only living child, Walter Hill Robinson Jr., was working in Indonesia for two years. Walter Jr.'s oldest daughter, Nancy Kathleen, attended the funeral. It was the first time she had met the Carrollton Robinsons and remembers fondly what a warm welcome she was given by John and Melba Robinson, and how exciting it was to know that her family had roots. She was given a portrait of W.O. Robinson in a frame with handmade nails, which is still in the family. *Submitted by: Justin Walter, 770 Walker Avenue, Ashland, OR 9752*

982. Walter Hill Robinson Jr. and Mercedes Del Socorro Figueroa Robinson

Walter was born in Atlanta on January 19, 1923. His parents were Walter Hill Robinson and Jacqueline Zora Harris. Walter Hill Robinson Sr. (born September 30, 1888, died September 6, 1975) was born in Carroll County. Jacqueline Zora Harris, of Carroll County, was born January 10, 1892, and died July 19, 1969.

Walter Hill Robinson Jr. was raised in Atlanta and Carroll County. He attended the Boys Technical School in Atlanta and Georgia Institute of Technology. His studies were cut short by World War II. He served as a seaman's mate in the Pacific, as a Navy weatherman. After the war, Walter settled in San Francisco, California, where he met Mercedes del Socorro Figueroa in November of 1947, marrying three weeks later on Christmas Eve 1947. Their offspring are Nancy Kathleen Robinson born November 17, 1948, Walter Ernest Robinson born September 18, 1950, and Jacqueline Carmen Robinson born January 20, 1952.

Walter H. Robinson Jr. and Mercedes del Socorro Figueroa

Walter moved his family to Palo Alto in 1951. He worked as a draftsman for CecoSteel and in 1959 returned to school, San Jose State College, for three years, graduating as a civil engineer. The family car was destroyed during this time in an accident. The family used bicycles or walked for over a year. At Christmas, Walter grabbed one end of the Christmas tree and his daughter, Nancy Kathleen, the other and they rode their bicycles home carrying the tree between them.

After earning his degree, he spent the rest of his career at Bechtel Corporation, designing oil refineries. He retired in 1978 and returned to Carrollton to forty-four acres on Jones Mill Road. Walter was always a studious person, interested in foreign languages, astronomy and meteorology and gardening. After retiring, he earned his Georgia Master Gardener Certificate and was the editor for the American Cryptography Association for the cryptograms in foreign languages.

Mercedes was born in Metapan, El Salvador, on September 21, 1914. She was raised in the city of San Salvador by her mother's brother, Ernesto Figueroa, and his wife, after her mother died during a typhoid epidemic in 1920. Her adoptive parents owned a grocery store and later a coffee roasting plant. When her adoptive parents passed away, Mercedes took a bus to the United States with the idea of working in cities for a few months and then moving to another city so that she could see the United States. She settled first in San Francisco, sewing wedding gowns, and married Walter five months later.

Mercedes was challenged when her husband retired to the middle of forty-four acres in Carrollton. She had always lived in the city with friends and neighbors nearby. She continued to engage in her love of growing flowers and learning new arts and crafts after moving to Carrollton. When Walter passed away in 1996, she lived in Lilbum, Georgia, with her oldest daughter, Nancy Kathleen, and then moved to Longview, Washington.

Submitted by: Mercedes Robinson, 2025 Tibbetts, Room 214, Longview, WA 98632

983. The William Osmus Robinson Family

Oh, those Robinsons and their tangled roots! Robinson researchers who have turned to look at this page know the agony and the ecstasy that we speak of! There were many Robinson families who migrated from the Carolinas and eastern Tennessee into middle Georgia in the 1790-1805 time period — even before the Indian lands had opened up — and this is about the time that our Robinsons came as well. They settled first in Putnam County, then Morgan, and later Newton County, Georgia.

William Osmus Robinson

William Osmus Robinson was born 20 September 1825 in Morgan County, Georgia, the son of Joseph Robinson and Catherine Sanders who had married in Putnam County, Georgia in 1810. Joseph and Catherine Robinson sold their Putnam County land in 1811 to Benjamin Whitfield. No relationship to the Whitfields has ever been determined but the name Whitfield came down in our family for several generations. We have never found the names of W.O. Robinson's brothers or sisters — though we know there must be some. W.O. Robinson possibly had one brother named John T. Robinson — a name which has also come down into our present generation — and many know John T. Robinson of Carroll County, Georgia of today who has been a well known pharmacist here at his Robinson Drug Company on Dixie Street for over fifty years.

By tradition, our family has always known that we are Dutch-Irish. Joseph Robinson was descended from Irish Quakers (George Robinson Sr. and Valentine Hollingsworth) who first came to America in 1682 from County Armagh, Ireland, and settled in New Castle County, which was then Pennsylvania — and later became Delaware. They were some of the first Quakers invited by William Penn to settle in his new Province and they sailed there from Belfast on the ship *The Antelope*, one of Penn's fleet bringing Quakers to America. Both the Robinsons and the Hollingsworths were instrumental in helping William Penn establish his "safe haven for Quakers" in the New World.

George Robinson Jr. married Catherine Hollingsworth on 2 November 1688 in New Castle County, Delaware. It is interesting to note that the Hollingsworths of Carroll County are descended from Valentine Hollingsworth through his son Thomas. The Robinsons of Carroll County are descended from Valentine Hollingsworth through his daughter Catherine. The descendants of George and Catherine Robinson later moved into Frederick County, Virginia, during the French and Indian war. Later on, before the American Revolution, they moved into the newly established Wautauga settlement which was then in "North Carolina beyond the mountains." This area later became known as eastern Tennessee and it was here where the Robinsons intermarried with the Dutch.

The Dutch families were the descendants of the founding fathers of the old Beverwyck settlement of New Netherland along the Hudson River which later became Albany, New York. The Dutch name of Sanders is sometimes spelled Xanders.

Catherine Sanders was born in 1783 in Sullivan County, Tennessee, of pure Dutch ancestry on both sides of her family going back about seven generations. Catherine was the daughter of John Sanders (born 2 October 1757 died 30 March 1834) and Elbertine Tenbroeck (born 23 November 1760 died 23 July 1840). Catherine's family tree alone would fill many volumes, but certainly one of her most colorful ancestors was Dirck Wesslese Tenbroeck.

Dirck Wesselese Tenbroeck was born in Europe in 1638 and came to New Netherland with his father who worked for the Dutch West India Company. Dirck worked for the fur trader, Pieter Van Allen, during his youth and before long, Dirck was shipping out 5,000 furs a year on his own behalf. By 1660, this young man was considered the principal fur trader of his community. In 1663, he married Christina Van Buren who had been raised on Papskanee Island. Thirteen children were born to them and they established a beautiful home on State Street. They also had a country estate on the Roeloff Jansen Kill.

In 1676, Dirck became a court magistrate and over the years he would hold almost every elective and appointive office on the local level. He became a major landholder in the upriver region of New York. He served as mayor of Albany, New York, and also as Indian commissioner. He had always had a good rapport with the Indians from his many fur dealings with them over the years. He became the representative of Albany County when New York was made a Royal Province. Dirck Wesselse Tenbroeck died on 18 September 1717 at the age of 80 years. He left a will that detailed the disposition of his estate to his wife and eleven surviving children. Dirck Tenbroeck is considered to be a major figure in the early history of New York and is only one of Catherine Sander's many interesting Dutch ancestors. The other surnames of ancestors of Catherine Sanders are: Xanders, Conyn, Glenn, Van Brugh, Van Buren, Van Rensselaer, Van Vechten, Maas, Martens, Vreelandt. The Conyn family also moved into Putnam County, Georgia — and Richard H. Conine who married Martha Patsy Boon was the brother of Catherine's grandmother, Catherine Conyn. Conyns also intermarried with Robinsons in middle Georgia.

W.O. Robinson named his first son Obadiah Levi Sanders Robinson — and the name of Sanders was repeated in later generations as well. We would love to find a Bible record for the Joseph Robinson and Catherine Sanders Robinson family. Hopefully, through this publication, we will find other descendants and the names of all their other children.

William Osmus "Ossie" Robinson Jr.

The only Robinson family of Carroll County that has ever claimed any kin to us is that of John T. "Jack" Robinson (born 1817) who married Nancy Caroline Aycock in Newton County, Georgia, on 6 January 1846. This family lived at Rocky Plains in Newton County and later moved to Carroll County after W.O. Robinson had moved his family here. Uncle Jack Robinson's children always called W.O.'s children cousin. The children of John T. and Nancy Robinson were: Henry Richards born 24 January 1848 m. Emily Caroline Sims 17 December 1868; Orrie F. (female) born 12 October 1849; William T. born 28 May 1857; Whitfield F. born 12 April 1862, moved to Birmingham; Jackie b. 20 January 1868 m. 24 February 1889 I.A. "Zake" Almand; Carrie May b. 4 September 1871 d. 2 October 1931 m. J. Lee Vaughn. One of the well known descendants of this line is Miss Miriam Merrell, now of Galveston, Texas, who owned Merrell's Dress Shoppe here in Carrollton for many years. Miriam's mother was Phena Clark Robinson, the daughter of Dr. Henry Richards Robinson and Emily Caroline "Emma" Sims Robinson, lifelong residents of Carroll County. We all still call each other cousin but we still have never proven the exact relationship. But it is perhaps significant that this set of Robinsons and ours, too, came from the area of Newton County, Georgia.

In our family the story is told that W.O. Robinson's father was only a young boy at the time of his family's migration to Georgia — but even so, he was given the big responsibility of managing the reins of one of the wagons all by himself. The name of Ausmus is the footprint name that tells us from which way our ancestors came. The Ausmuses never came to Georgia, but they lived in eastern Tennessee in the time when our Robinsons were there. (And

King Cotton comes to town. Adamson Square, Carrollton

remember, it was called North Carolina when they lived there — only after the Robinsons had left was it named Tennessee. If you research Robinsons, you have to learn to re-invent the wheel every single day!)

Johann Peter Ausmus was born in 1711 in Mecklenburg, Germany, and migrated to Rotterdam, Holland, as a part of the great Palatine migration from Rhineland. There, Johann married Catharina who was Dutch. Years later they sailed on the ship *Neptune* — with grown children — to America, landing in Philadelphia on 4 October 1752. Catharina had died on the ocean voyage and was buried at sea. Johann's son, Phillip Ausmus — who was a surveyor — later migrated into eastern Tennessee. Phillip Ausmus' brother, Benjamin, remained in Virginia and was the physician to a young surveyor there named George Washington. Washington's name appears on many of the early deeds of this family. Benjamin Ausmus died an old bachelor — so Phillip was the progenitor of the family. The Ausmus family was German-Dutch — and they intermarried with other German, Dutch, and Swiss (Beeler, Bollinger) families that were a part of the Pennsylvania Dutch community. The Ausmus name is sometimes spelled "Osmus" — and this is where our ancestor, William Osmus Robinson, came by his unusual name.

In 1830 in Cocke County, Tennessee, there are Jesters living next door to Robinsons — and we believe this is the area of Tennessee where our Robinsons came from in an earlier time. Our W.O. Robinson would marry on Christmas Day of 1851 in Butts County, Georgia, to Miss Rosannah Helen Sinah Lofton. She was the daughter of Sarah Jester and John Lofton. The Loftons and Jesters were originally from Edgefield District, S.C. and many people in the Cocke County, Tennessee, area migrated from Edgefield. Levi Jester, the Revolutionary War soldier later honored with a monument in Butts County, Georgia, was the progenitor of a large Jester family that would eventually fan out in all directions in the south.

John Lofton, Rosannah's father, had been a successful merchant in Butts County of the community known as Lofton's Store on Key's Ferry Road. W.O. Robinson was already managing Lofton's Store before the death of John Lofton and W.O. Robinson was one of the witnesses to John Lofton's will. After John Lofton died, W.O. Robinson married Rosannah and became a partner in the store with his brother-in-law, William Francis Stoghill. Stoghill had married Rosannah's older sister, Justina Adalina. The store became known as Robinson & Stoghill for several years afterwards. W.O. Robinson and his wife Rosannah lived in the Lofton home place that she had inherited and several children were born to them.

The first child born was Obadiah "Obe" Levi Sanders Robinson on 20 December 1852. Obe married first Mary Ann Baker — had sons Frederick Sanders, Cole Lee, Hugh Melvin, and married second, Mary Elizabeth Vaughn — and had children Carrie Love, Lee Gay Nell, and William Thomas Robinson. Obe died 10 September 1933, buried Macedonia Church, Coweta County, GA.

Two years after Obe was born, his sister Mary Josephine — always called Sallie — was born on 7 October 1854. (See separate heading.) Another sister, named Sinah Justine was born 25 March 1857 (See separate heading). During these years, the family was growing and the business prospered. In those days, it seemed that everyone was excited with the news of new areas opening up farther west.

A story in our family tells that the Robinsons decided to move west and they settled in the "cotton belt Delta of Mississippi" possibly near Tunica County, Mississippi. We believe that this family who migrated west may have been Joseph and Catherine Sanders Robinson for we lose them in the records in Georgia about the time of this migration. There is still a Robinsonville in Tunica County, Mississippi today. We have never found W.O. Robinson in the 1850 census anywhere and it is possible that he first went west with his family and later on returned to Georgia.

In the Fall of 1859, W.O. Robinson did load up his wagons with children, lock, stock, and barrel and headed west himself. Even Rosannah's brother William James Lofton, made the trip with them. It is not known if the Robinsons set out with intentions to go to Mississippi, but Carroll County is where they stopped. They had probably followed the old McIntosh Trail that led from Indian Springs to Carroll County — to near where Chief William McIntosh had once had his home near Whitesburg. There were wonderful lands for farming there — rich with Georgia red dirt and so many beautiful trees - oak, hickory, chestnut, sweet gum, cedars and pine. It is no wonder that five generations of their descendants have remained here.

The Robinsons first settled on a farm that was known as the old Head Place. This was in the Chanceville Community about twelve miles from Carrollton. They had not been on the new farm very long when on January 19, 1861, Georgia seceded from the Union. The Civil War had begun and the South would never be the same again. On February 16, 1861, the Ready Rifle Company was organized and met at the County Line Church not far from the Robinson home. On September 25, 1861, Rosannah's brother, William James, went to Campbell County to enlist in Company K 30th Regiment of Georgia Volunteers, Infantry Army of Tennessee, C.S.A.

During these turbulent war years, more children were born to the Robinsons — Laura Jane was born 27 April 1862. On 7 April 1863, W.O. Robinson sold 202½ acres of land to G.W. Camp. On 13 April 1863, W.O. Robinson paid $4600 for a 355 acre farm located in the Shady Grove community of Carroll County. This was located near Hickory Level between Carrollton and Villa Rica. Then, by the first of August, W.O. Robinson at the age of 38 enlisted in the Confederate Army. He was made sergeant of Company I in the 10th Regiment, Calvary of Georgia State Guard. The old musket that he carried with "I" carved on it for his Company is a treasured heirloom in the Robinson family to this day.

On 14 July 1864, Rosannah and W.O. lost their two year old daughter, Laura Jane to dysentery. She was buried in the cemetery behind old Concord Methodist Church at Hickory Level. Six months later, on 17 December 1864, Rosannah gave birth to a son named William Oscar "Ossie" Robinson Jr. We believe the name was changed from Osmus to Oscar because there was so much misunderstanding about the Osmus name. "People were always trying to make it Oscar anyway," my grandfather Talmadge Robinson had said in later years.

John T. Robinson

Shortly after the baby Laura had died, Rosannah had received the sad news that her brother, William Jones Lofton, had been captured by Union soldiers in Alabama and he had been placed in a prisoner of war camp in Camp Chase, Ohio. On 24 February 1865, William James Lofton died and was buried in a Confederate cemetery there. It was only two months later that General Robert E. Lee surrendered on April 9, 1865 at Appomattox Courthouse.

Carrollton Night at the old Atlanta Stadium

Even though the war was over, families still faced all kinds of hardships. It was in 1866 that the Holland daughters came to live with the Robinsons. Rev. James H. Holland (of County Line Church in Whitesburg) had made a train trip in the wintertime to bring home a son, Lindsey, who was a wounded Confederate soldier. Rev. Holland caught pneumonia from the damp of the train trip and died on 4 March 1862. He had two young daughters by a second wife (Mary A. Christian) whom he married 15 November 1855 in Carrollton. These daughters were Martha Ann b. 12 November 1856 and Lucy Holland b. 29 January 1860. The Robinsons became the guardians of these little girls and they would rear these little girls with their own children. Martha married 4 December 1873 to Worth Morris. Lucy married Jesse Carroll Hilley 20 October 1879. Whether there was real kinship there, we have never known. But the Holland family always seemed to be closely associated with the Robinsons and they often migrated from one place to another together — from Tennessee to Georgia, and then from Morgan County to Carroll County.

The family of Rev. James Hodson Holland Sr. was as follows: James Hodson Holland was born 21 October 1801 in Greenville, S.C. He married on 1 February 1821 to Mary Frances "Polly" Smith in Madison County, Georgia. James H. Holland died 4 March 1862. "Polly" Holland died 9 September 1855 and was buried in Holland Cemetery, Whitesburg, Georgia. James H. and Polly Holland had the following children: (1) Lindsey A. born 28 July 1824 m. Elizabeth Lasseter, daughter of Benjamin Lasseter; Lindsey in CSA Company F. 7th GA Infantry; (2) Harriet Ann born 15 March 1827 m. Andrew J. Shelnutt (3) Letty Ann born 15 January 1829 m. Joshua Lang (4) Jordan William b. 7 September 1832 m. Jerusha Fowler (5) James H., Jr. born 2 March 1835 m. Sarah Frances Stovall; James in Co. B Cutts Battalion (6) Tyre Watson born 18 July 1837 m. Martha Stovall; guardians of Elizabeth and Rebecca after their father died; Tyre was in CSA (7) Mary born 29 December 1840 m. Jethro Jones (8) Elizabeth born 16 November 1842 (9) Valentine born 7 April 1845 (10) Rebecca born 2 January 1848. Rev. James H. Holland's mother was named Rebecca Shumake. Rev. Holland established Holland's Meeting House which later became St. Paul's Methodist Church. According to census, Polly Holland was born in Kentucky.

On 12 April 1867, John Henry Robinson was born on the Robinson farm at Shady Grove. By the fall of that year, W.O. Robinson had decided to give up his farm and focus more on the business that he now owned in town. This was a store much like Lofton's Store had been — except it did have a slant towards selling the medicines and panaceas of that era. On the 1870 census, W.O. Robinson listed his occupation as "Druggist." It would be three generations later that his great-grandson, John T. Robinson, would follow in his footsteps and become a pharmacist — and establish a successful drug store in Carrollton — Robinson Drug Company on Dixie Street. According to the 1868 Tax Digest, W.O. Robinson still owned the 355 acres of land in 6th District Section 5 and his town property as well.

On 9 June 1869 James de Whitfield Robinson was born — and this son was called "deWhit." This little boy would only live to be three years old — and he died 8 June 1872. He was laid to rest alongside his little sister Laura Jane at the cemetery at old Concord Church at Hickory Level. Many of the oldest pioneers of Carroll County are buried in the cemetery at this old church. It is very unfortunate that the old records of this church have never been made available for genealogical research. Michael Robinson put a new tombstone for the Robinsons at Hickory Level in 1998 in honor of our first ancestors to migrate to Carroll County.

In 1870 W.O. Robinson began to play an important role in the development of Carrollton. He was instrumental in building many of the structures of the town square — one of them a cotton warehouse where Cole's Jewelry now stands. W.O. and his partner Eli Benson built two buildings — later W.O. and L.J. Smith built a grocery store and mercantile business. W.O. Robinson along with Z.P. Worthy, J.M. Blalock, W.C. New, and L.P. Mandeville were elected Carroll County's commissioners. The commissioners ran the city before there was a mayor. The newspaper reported

> "These are all solid and substantial citizens of our town and thoroughly identified with and deeply interested in our future welfare — we have no doubt they will give us a good town government."

(15 March 1872 *Carroll County Times*. W.O. Robinson's great-grandson, John T. Robinson, would again follow in his footsteps — and would serve three terms as mayor of Carrollton.

In mayor days of John Robinson, Dr. Jimmy Morrow gained funding from the state and Gov. Lester Maddox for a track at Carrollton High School. Left to right are Coach Charlie Grisham, H.M. Fulbright, Dr. Jack Birge, Red Lambert, Gov. Lester Maddox, Coach Jimmy Bonner in front of Maddox, Dr. Jimmy Morrow, Elmer Bohannon, Coach Vernon Wilkes, Ronnie Young, and Mayor John Robinson.

One of the important issues of this era involved the railroad. In 1871, the Savannah, Griffin, and North Alabama Railroad was completed to Newnan. There was much debate over which route this railroad would follow next. Of course, the city fathers knew that it would be a real boost to the economy after the war if the railroad came to Carrollton. Finally by 1872 the site was chosen and the depot was built on what was then called South Street between the homes of John Stewart and W.O. Robinson. The Robinson home of 1872 now stands across the street (now Bradley Street) from the beautiful old Bradley home with white columns which is now the home of our Representative of the 4th District, Tracy Stallings. It was 1874 when the first train engine came steaming into town and the depot was a busy spot for many years. Passenger trains came into Carrollton until 1950.

W.O. Robinson was one of the founders of The Industrial, Scientific, and General Improvement Society of Carroll County. In the August 16, 1872 issue of the *Carroll County Times* the stated purpose of this society was: (1) To develop the mineral resources of the county (2) To improve agriculture (3) To cultivate art, science, and letters (4) To collect and preserve the legends, traditions, and historical incidents of the past (5) to foster an honest and manly pride in growth and prosperity of the entire county and (6) to elevate all physically, socially, intellectually, and morally. These goals sound pretty good

Carrollton Parks and Recreation Department

even for our new century in Carroll County! W.O. Robinson was a lifelong Democrat and he served as a delegate to the Democratic convention held in September of 1872.

W.O. Robinson and his wife Rosannah lived to see many of the fine accomplishments of their own children. O.S. "Obe" Robinson moved to Coweta County where he established a successful farm and reared a large family there. Many of his descendants live in Coweta County today. William "Ossie" Robinson Jr. married first Sarah Frances Morgan, daughter of John D. Morgan on 18 April 1886 — and their children were: William Raymond, Ina Ruby, and Jewel. Ossie Robinson married second Mattie Walker 3 May 1923.

Ossie Robinson worked for Johnson, Fleming & Copeland in 1900 and later bought an interest in that business. This firm was succeeded by Robinson & Walker. From early 1900s advertisements we know they sold dry goods, hats, shoes, general farm supplies, fertilizers, men and boy's clothing. Later the business was called Robinson & Harman and they sold more of the same with additional items like Queensware and crockery.

Robinson & Harman also purchased poultry, butter and eggs from local farmers and sold those at the store, too. One of Ossie's best suppliers of butter and eggs was his own sister-in-law, Maggie Robinson, wife of John Henry Robinson. Maggie was fastidious in the cleanliness of her kitchen and was notorious for scalding her butter churns. People were good customers of Maggie Robinson's butter and eggs and John Henry was often seen carrying the goods to town to be sold. Maggie Robinson was a tiny thing, never even five feet tall in her stocking feet. Later, she would be called Little Grandma.

John T. Robinson

One of the descendants of W.O. Robinson Jr. in Carrollton today is Ruth Maret Meeks Griffin, wife of James Griffin, one of Southwire's early executives. Ruth has a treasured painting of the old Sanford Kingsberry home of Carrollton her ancestor W.O. Robinson Jr. bought for his own home.

Rosannah Helen Sinah Lofton Robinson died at age 55 at her home place at Shady Grove on 23 April 1889 and was laid to rest at Concord Church at Hickory Level. W.O. "Buck" Robinson lived to see eight grandsons and six granddaughters born before he died on 17 September 1898. He also is buried at Hickory Level. For the names of descendants up to the present day, see *William Osmus Robinson — Forward* by Henry Michael Robinson (1998) in Special Collections at Neva Lomason Library in Carrollton, Georgia.

Since we've spent half a century untangling these Robinson roots in Carroll County, here's some information that may help others. One other identifiable set of Robinsons in this county is that of "Sir John" Robinson of Tallapoosa, Georgia. These are probably our cousins from way back in Scotland, for that is where our own ancestors were found before they lived in Northern Ireland. The Robinsons were Scottish Highlanders and members of the Gunn Clan. Their ancestral castle was called Dunrobin, which meant "Fort of Robin." Our Robinsons intermarried with the Dutch, but this set of Tallapoosa Robinsons is of Scottish extraction.

James Griffin

Sir John Robinson of Tallapoosa was descended from Jeffrey Robinson (sometimes spelled Robertson) born 1654 in Edinburgh, Scotland, and who first came to America in 1703. Jeffrey died in Henrico County, Virginia, in 1734. Jeffrey Robertson I married Elizabeth Bowman, daughter of John and Eller Elam Bowman. Jeffrey Robertson II born 1709 in Henrico County, Virginia, married Mrs. Judith Tanner Mills born 1710. Jeffrey Robertson III born 15 January 1737, married Sarah Norvell. Jeffrey Robertson III born circa 1738 in Chesterfield County, Virginia, and died 23 February 1815 in Rhea County, Tennessee, was the father of Tyre Robinson. Tyre Robinson married circa 1770 in North Carolina to Mary "Polly" Adams who was born circa 1740 in Virginia. The children of Tyre Robinson and Polly Adams were Tyree, Jeffrey, Mills, Mary, Elizabeth, John Mills "Sir John," Nancy, Jane, and Nathan. These children were born in Anson and Montgomery Counties, North Carolina. Polly Robinson died 17 October 1823 near Tallapoosa and was buried there.

Sir John Robinson was born 27 July 1787 in Anson County, North Carolina, the son of Tyre Robinson and Polly Adams. He died 12 July 1879. Sir John moved to Carroll County, the part that is now Haralson County. He became friends with the Lavender family, who were Welsh extraction. Their name was originally Laubinger. George M. Lavender appears in the 1830 Carroll County census. The Robinsons and Lavenders opened a trading post for the Indians which was about seven miles northwest of Rome in a place called Lavenderville. The Lavenders had migrated from Virginia to Knoxville to Lavenderville. Sir John Robinson married Polly Gilliam Lavender on 27 January 1822 in Rhea County, Tennessee. Polly was born 3 May 1805 and died 12 July 1846. Polly and Sir John Robinson had three children: (1) Saphronia North Carolina Robinson who married Simon B. Stope in 1841; (2) Adeline Eliza born 1824, married Dennis Hammond of Newnan and of Atlanta since he served as mayor of Atlanta; (3) Norval M. Robinson born 1826, died 1890, buried Oakland Cemetery in Atlanta; (4) John Lavender Robinson born 1828 married Jane Ann Owens and had a son named John; (5) Bethenia born 1832; (6) George Michael born 1834; (7) Susan Edelia born 1836, married Thomas Sanford Garner, born buried Oakland Cemetery in Atlanta; (8) Barbara born 1838; (9) Polly born 1840; (1) Nancy born 1842; two children unidentified. Polly Lavender Robinson died 12 July 1846 and was buried on private land lot #174, 8th District, Tallapoosa.

Second wife of Sir John Robinson was Martha Augeline Fain, daughter of Joel Fain and Nancy Lay. She was a descendant of Revolutionary war soldier, William Fain 1757-1837, and Sallie Juda McMahan, who is buried near Cassville, Georgia.

Sir John was sixty-one years old and Martha was sixteen when they married. These are the children of Sir John and Martha: Frances Caroline, Thomas Adams, Eugenia Frances, Joel Fletcher, William Fain Robinson. Martha's obit of 8 August 1925 lists another son, J.A. Robinson of Rabun County, Georgia. Sir John died 12 July 1879. Many of his descendants moved from Carroll to Coweta County. Of course, once you get into research over there, you get all tangled up with the descendants of Randal Robinson, the Revolutionary war soldier who also settled there. He was of "high born Scots ancestry" too. It is neverending!

In our family we have a theory about Sir John. Suppose he liked to wear a black top hat, so fashionable in England in that era? The Indians at the trading post might have given him a nickname of "Sir John!" *Submitted by: Jason Robinson, San Francisco, CA*

984. Rogers

Daniel Lafayette Rogers was the first of the local line of the Rogers family born in Georgia. He was born in 1827 in Meriwether County, shortly after his parents moved to Georgia. He was the son of Frances and Sutley Rogers, who migrated from South Carolina.

Daniel Lafayette married on February 2, 1848, Martha C. Hamrick, daughter of Rebecca and Harrison Hamrick. They had seven children: Sarah F. born 1849 and married William Redwine Williams; Emily Virginia born 1850 and married Singleton Walker; James Harrison born 1852; Elnora Elizabeth (Ella) born 1854 and married John Hardegree; William Benjamin Franklin born 1856 and married Mary Catherine Smith; Daniel Lafayette Jr. born 1858 and married first to unknown, and second to Beatrice Brook; Thomas Edgar born 1860, and married first to Rena Beatrice Entrekin and second to Elizabeth Jeanette Bearden.

Daniel Lafayette served in the Civil War after he enlisted in Carroll County under Capt. J.C. Bonner in Company L, 7th Confederate Cavalry. He was at home on leave when the war ended and was discharged from North Carolina as a sergeant.

During the war Daniel Lafayette's wife and children had a difficult time even having enough to eat. A story has been handed down through the family showing how desperate Martha was for food supplies for her children. Once she hitched the mule to the wagon, put her children in, took a loaded shotgun and drove to a neighbor's house. When the neighbor refused her request for food, she reached for her shotgun and said "My younguns are starving, and I don't have anything to feed them. I am going to back my wagon up to your crib and load it with corn and syrup!" The neighbor relented and had his slaves load her wagon with supplies. Whether this is truth or fiction, one has to admire the spirit of that mother. Her hardships continued as her husband died at age forty-two shortly after the war ended, and left her with seven children. Her father, Harrison Hamrick gave her fifty acres of land in 1862. Her oldest son, James Harrison, tried to eke out a living by farming the land. Mrs. Hamrick's brother, a physician, encouraged the other boys to become doctors. William Benjamin migrated to Mississippi where he practiced medicine. Daniel Lafayette practiced in Waco with his brother, Dr. Thomas Edgar Rogers, but after a brief time he moved to Texas. He died at an early age from an injury when his horse kicked him.

Edd, as Thomas Edgar was known, practiced medicine in Waco and Bremen throughout his life. He was loved by everyone in the community and was the father of eleven children.

Daniel Lafayette resided just north of Stripling Chapel Church on U.S. Highway 27, south of Carrollton, and he and his wife are buried in the cemetery at Stripling Chapel Church.

James Harrison Rogers, the oldest son of Martha C. Daniel Lafayette Rogers was born on November 18, 1852. He married on January 6, 1878, Margaret Elizabeth Copeland, daughter of Lula Palmer and George Copeland. The marriage took place in Carroll County, Georgia. Harrison and Martha lived for several years near the Sardis community. They had several children before relocating to Heard County in 1889 to the Loftin community where he had purchased land.

Harrison and Martha were active members of Emmaus Primitive Baptist Church in Carroll County, and later in Hopewell Primitive Baptist Church in Heard County. Harrison was active in the community. Harrison and Martha had thirteen children: David Harrison who married Sephronia Denney; Beulah who married Green Kelly; William Lee who married Fannie Holsombeck; Charlie Fletcher who married Lena Cater; George Franklin who married Tessie Lenora Word; Emmie Ivee who married William Thomas Brazeal; Otha Lee who married Minnie Davis; Minnie, who married Walter Traylor; Thomas Edgar who married Ethia Jane Bentley; Annie Elizabeth who married John Columbus Bentley; Walter Harvey who married Eva Estelle Gentry; Looney Monroe who married Vertie Medlock; and Reuben Whitton who married Emily Mae Upchurch.

Several of this family raised large families in Carroll County and Heard County. A large number of descendants of James Harrison and Martha Hamrick Rogers still reside in Carroll County. James Harrison died on October 1, 1919, and Martha died on December 27, 1943. Both are buried in the cemetery at Hopewell Primitive Baptist Church, a place that was dear to them. Many of the descendants gather at this church in June each year for singing and fellowship.

Many families have connections with descendants of Daniel Lafayette Rogers, including the Walkers, Hardegrees, Copelands, Kelleys, Chambers, and others. A large number of descendants reside in Carroll County. *Submitted by: Opal Rogers Cannon, P.O. Box 206, Leesburg, GA 31763*

985. Reverend Luther Guy Rogers

Reverend Luther Guy Rogers, born on December 1, 1906, was a Baptist minister, serving churches in Carroll and Heard Counties and in Alabama for forty-seven years. He and his wife, Vesta Leona Kent Rogers, were married on March 28, 1928. They were residents of Carroll County most of their married life.

Guy was the second oldest child of George Franklin Rogers and Tessie Lenora Word Rogers of Heard County. He was one of fourteen children. His wife, Vesta, was the second oldest child of Edward (Eddie) Kent and Rebecca Hamm Kent of Heard County. She was one of six children. Both Guy and Vesta were teachers in their early married life. However, Vesta became a full-time homemaker when their second child was two years old. They reared four children: Charlotte Ann Rogers Hester, Dr. Luther Rayford Rogers, Sara Mae Rogers Cutler and Raymon Edward Rogers. Three of the children followed in their parents' footsteps and became educators. The other chose the field of cosmetology.

Guy and Vesta Rogers

As a minister, teacher, school principal, and later the supervisor of the transportation and maintenance department of the Carroll County Schools, Guy touched many lives in a very positive manner. He was known as a man with strong convictions and a staunch, abiding faith in God, who lived his religion every day. He dedicated his life to serving God and his fellow man. During his ministry, he performed numerous religious services, including 1130 funerals, an average of two each month. He wanted all to know that the Bible was a lamp to his feet and a light to his pathway. When he died on January 30, 1987, he was buried in Carroll Memory Gardens with a smile on his face and his Bible in his hand! His wife, Vesta, is presently a resident of Pine Knoll Nursing Home. One of his favorite childhood stories was about his first encounter with electricity. His family went to visit his Grandfather Word just over the state line in Alabama. He and three of his brothers shared the same bedroom for the night. When they were ready to go to sleep, they tried to blow out the electric light, then tried to fan it out with their shirts. Finally, they had to call their grandfather for help.

Guy was a great storyteller, as was his own father. As a school principal, he often entertained the whole school on rainy days at "recess" time with a continued story. It was hard to wait until another rainy day for another episode. *Submitted by: Charlotte R. Hester*

986. Rooks

William H. Rooks, father of James Madison (Matt) Rooks, came to Carroll County in 1828 from Jackson County, Georgia. James Madison Rooks, born in 1917 in Jackson County, Georgia, would have been eleven years old when they came to Carroll County. I don't know what his mother's name was. William died on the land he had settled.

Matt married Sussanah Dover (born 1823) in 1840 in Carroll County by William Springer. In his younger days, Matt accumulated about 1,500 acres of land on which he reared twelve boys and six girls, most of whom settled on the parental estate. That is why the area was called Rookstown. My great-grandfather, Allen G. Jackson Rooks, was one of the twelve boys. He was born November 26, 1851, and died in 1913. He married Ellen Kaziah Edgeworth, born 1855. She was the daughter of Richard Edgeworth.

His oldest son, Ernie Jackson Rooks, was my grandfather. He was born in 1878 and died in August 1943. He married Eunice Camp, daughter of Walter and Molly Camp. She was born in 1883 and died in August 1946. They are both buried at Mt. Zion Baptist Church in Douglas County. They had only one child, Thelma Jackson Rooks, who was born in 1913. She married John Thomas (Jack) Pate in 1940. He was born in 1918. They have three sons: (1) William Jackson Pate born 1943, married Mary Jean Smith in 1968. They have two children: Jodi Pate Foster born in 1971, married Shane Foster; and Brook Jackson Pate born in 1980. (2) John Daniell (Dan) Pate born in 1946, married Judy Holloway (born 1951) in 1982. They have one son, John Daniell Pate, born in 1985. (3) Larry Marvin Pate born 1951, married Jackie Sue Bagwell (born 1951) in 1969. All three boys have built a home on land given to them by their father. *Submitted by: Jodi Foster, 603 Lovinggood Tr., Woodstock, GA 30179 and Written by: Thelma Pate*

987. Rooks Family

William Rooks Sr. was a Revolutionary War Veteran. He moved from North Carolina to Gwinnett County, Georgia. He drew in the Land Lottery of 1827 Carroll County, Georgia. Land granted on December 20, 1830, in Land District No. 4 and Land Lot No. 55. This was later known as the Whitesburg District No. 682.

William Rooks Jr. was born 1795 in North Carolina. He married Sarah Cook. William and Sarah were the parents of nine children, four boys and five girls. He was listed in the 1830, 1840, and 1850 censuses of Carroll County in the Whitesburg District No. 682, Land District 4, Land Lot No. 55. For years, this was known as Rooks Hill and was located on the Old Stagecoach Route through Carroll County. William was appointed Justice of the Peace January 14, 1841, in Carroll County. He was appointed a Road Commissioner for the 682nd District on January 21, 1846.

George W. Rooks (born 1850), Susan Alice Walker Rooks

James Madison Rooks was born October 19, 1818. He was a son of William Rooks Jr. He married Susannah Dover March 22, 1840, in Carroll County. James was known as "Matt." He was a member of the Carroll Rangers. James M. Rooks acquired an estate of sixteen hundred acres of land in one body, located about 4-1/3 miles below Clem. Here he reared a family of twelve boys and six girls, all of whom grew to manhood and womanhood. Many of them settled on the parental estate. That area was known as "Rookstown." He was instrumental in the establishment of Ephesus Christian Church.

George Washington Rooks was a son of James Madison Rooks. He married Susan Alice Walker December 24, 1871. George and Susan were the parents of eleven children who survived to adulthood, eight sons and three daughters. George and Susan were known as "Uncle Bob and Aunt Alice." He was a rural mail carrier on Whitesburg Route 2 for many years. He was instrumental in the establishment of Whitesburg Christian Church. One of his sons, Oliver, settled in Whitesburg. His son William Eugene "Gene" Rooks settled a very short distance from the former home of Matt Rooks.

Descendants of this Rooks family spread from Georgia to California. There are numerous descendants living in Carroll County at the present time. *Submitted by: Susan M. Gatlin, 132 Leland Drive, SW, Mableton, GA 30126-1839*

988. Martin Roop Family

Martin Roop was born in South Carolina, the son of John and Phoebe Roop. In 1845 he migrated to Georgia with his wife, the former Elizabeth King, to whom he was married in 1839. They settled first in Jackson County, later in Coweta, and in 1855 moved to the vicinity of Roopville. To this family were born ten children: John K., William W., Robert H., Benjamin J., Thomas M., Henry O., James G., Sarah Elizabeth, Savannah, and George W.

When the Roops settled, the area was very much undeveloped. Native timber had not been cut. Surrounding the rocky ridge were rich uplands and well-watered bottomlands. Before the area was further settled, the Roops had to be self-sufficient. Mrs. Roop carded, spun, and wove all their clothing. She also made clothes for the soldiers in the Civil War. The Roops ate from pewter dishes.

Martin Roop was one of the most important figures in the development and prosperity of the entire region. He was a Mason and an influential and respected man. Mr. Roop's eldest son, John K., became the dominant figure during the early years of the settlement. John K. was born in 1839 before his parents left South Carolina. In 1861 he enlisted in the Confederate Army and served in both Company D of the First Regiment of Georgia Infantry and in the Phillips Legion Cavalry. In 1872 he was married to Eliza Moore of Henry County, Georgia. To this union were born five children: Nora L. (wife of Dr. Benjamin J. Veal and later wife of L.A. Ware), Henry A., Judge Charles E., Bessie (wife of Dr. H.J. Goodman) and Fanny (wife of W.C. Veal).

Upon returning to civilian life, John resumed farming. He became the owner of over 2000 acres of land, much of which he donated to enhance the growth of the area. He would often establish a business or build a residence and sell it to new people coming into the area. He built a gin near Theo Bell's spring, hired a Negro to run it, and later sold it to Charlie Wood. He established a blacksmith shop where Mr. Jim Merrell's home is located and sold it to Jordan A. Wood. In 1882, Thomas M. Roop became postmaster and at that time the city was officially named Roopville.

Mr. Frank Roop, son of Mr. Thomas M. Roop and Mrs. Florida Alexander Roop Brock was the last of the Roop family to live in Roopville. He served in the Roopville Baptist Church for many years holding many positions including deacon, teacher and clerk. Frank never married and had no heirs. His picture can be found in both the archive and the Frank Rook Brotherhood Hall at the Baptist Church.

There are no Roops in Roopville today but many people still have fond memories of the Roops and an appreciation of their contributions. Decendants frequently come to Roopville searching for information on their ancestors. *Submitted by: Rebecca Merrell, 124 Old Franklin Street, Roopville, GA 30170.*

Sources: *Roopville Baptist Church History*, 1983; *The Carroll County Story as told by Her People, 1976.*

989. Quannah Parker Roop Family

Martin and Elizabeth Roop are the parents of George W. Roop. George W. was born in 1858 on a farm in what is now Roopville in Carroll County, Georgia. He invested a gift of $200 from his father to start a successful retail grocery business.

In 1880, George W. married Eliza Almon. They had five children: M.C., Q.P., Addie Lou, Will C. and Mildred.

Marvin Cleveland (M.C.) became a successful businessman in Carroll County. He was president of West Georgia (National) Bank and owner of Southeastern Motor Lines, a bus company. He married Alma Barfield of Lineville, Alabama. They had no children.

Will C. Roop married Mable Lovvom. In addition to being a partner in Roop Wholesale Company, Will was to become president of the Commercial Bank of Bowdon. They had one daughter Billie Ann, who married C. Copeland Ozier. They had four grandchildren.

Addie Lou Roop married J. D. Bartlett. Mr. Bartlett was a salesman for Roop Wholesale Company and, along with his wife, they operated the Bowdon Inn which stands today in the center of Bowdon. They had two daughters, Helen Wiggly and Betty Davis. They had one grandchild.

Mildred Roop married George W. Burson. Mildred was in business with her niece, Doris (Dot) Steed, operating a clothing store The Hi-Lo Shop, which was a fixture in downtown Bowdon for many years. The Bursons had no children.

Quannah Parker Roop

Quannah Parker (Q.P.) is the only child to produce a son to continue the Roop family name. He married Winnie David of Lineville Alabama. This union produced three children: Mary Nell (Mrs. E.H. Rainwater Jr.); Billy David (married to Jessie Barnes); and Doris Glen (married to Robert P. Steed). Q.P. and Winnie had six grandchildren and many great-grandchildren.

Mary Nell Roop Rainwater, who died in 1939, had one daughter, Ann Rainwater Sanders (Gerald) and two grandchildren.

Billy David had three children: George David (married to Nelva Garrett), Peggy Roop Crawford (Keith), and Patti Roop. He had five grandchildren.

Doris (Dot) Roop Steed had two sons: Robert Lee Steed (married to Linda McElroy), and Michael Parker Steed (married to Cheryl Johnson). She had six grandchildren.

Quannah Parker was initially in the grocery business with his father when the store moved to Bowdon. It was located in town next door to a store owned by William J. Barnes. Later, with his younger brother Will, Q.P. opened a wholesale grocery company serving clients from LaGrange in Troup County up to Rome in Floyd County. The growth of the wholesale business was steady and in 1948 the company built a large office and warehouse facility adjoining the Bowdon Railway tracks. Much of their merchandise was brought in by rail until sometime in the late 1950s when the Bowdon Railway Company ceased operations. In the 1950s, Will Roop began to split his time between the grocery company and the Commercial Bank of Bowdon. Q.P.'s son Bill had been with the company since 1940 and assumed the role of general manager. Years later, Bill's son G. David took over the management of the company until it closed in 1983 due to consolidation of the wholesale grocery industry. Several of Q.P. Roop's great-grandchildren spent time working at the company, thus there were at least five generations of Roops affiliated during the company's lifetime.

Many of the descendants of Q.P. and Winnie Roop continue to live in Carroll county and surrounding areas. They have been active in business and other professions and remember Q.P. for his many years of hard work and Winnie for her sparkling sense of humor, a trait that persists with their offspring. *Submitted by: Mike Steed, P.O. Box 769, Bowdon, GA 30108, and Nelva Roop, 400 Ellenwood Drive, Bowdon, GA 30108*

990. Rowe Family

John Rowe was born before 1758 in Virginia and died December 23, 1812, in Edgefield, South Carolina. He was a Revolutionary War veteran. He married Elizabeth Thornton in Virginia. Both John and Elizabeth are buried in Edgefield County. Their son William Rowe was born April 30, 1768, in Virginia and died May 15, 1843, in Monroe County, Alabama. He married Ann O'Neal November 8, 1791, in South Carolina. She was born November 11, 1772, in Laurens District, South Carolina, and she died October 9, 1845, in Monroe County, Alabama. Her parents were Hugh O'Neal and Mary Parkins. William and Ann had nine children, one of whom was named Allen Rowe. He was born in Edgefield County, South Carolina, on October 7, 1799, and died in Carroll County, Georgia, August 7, 1885.

Allen had two wives. First was Mary Lewis who was born January 1, 1805, in South Carolina. They were married in South Carolina on November 24, 1824. Mary was the daughter of Richard and Mary Lewis. Allen and Mary went to Meriwether County, Georgia, shortly before it became a county. While living there, Allen served two terms as a state representative. Allen and Mary had six children. Mary died in Meriwether County on December 14, 1850. Allen married Huldah Rebecca Hay in Meriwether County on July 27, 1851. Huldah was the daughter of William Howell Hay and Nancy Wooten. Huldah was born December 3, 1825, in Wilkes County, Georgia, and died in Carroll County on December 11, 1908. Allen and Huldah, along with the Hay family, moved to Carroll County in 1851. Allen bought land lot 243 in the 10th District. Allen deeded three and one-half acres of his land to Concord Primitive Baptist Church where he and his brother-in-law, David Hay, were deacons.

Allen was one of three men who represented Carroll County when Georgia withdrew from the Union. They voted to stay in the Union. Allen and Huldah are both buried in Concord Primitive Baptist Church Cemetery off Spence Road in Carroll County.

My ancestor was William Howell Rowe, one of their six children. William was born March 7, 1854, in Carroll County and died June 12, 1902. He was married August 3, 1876, to Phedora Spence. Phedora was born March 18, 1855, in Carroll County and died April 27, 1924. She and William are buried in the Spence-Rowe Cemetery in Carroll County. Phedora was the daughter of Hiram Spence and Angeline Caroline Cheney. My grandfather was Walter Hampton Rowe, one of William and Phedora's seven children. He was born July 10, 1877, died September 6, 1926. He married Susan Ida Bonner on March 26, 1899. Susan was born in Carroll County on December 13, 1880, and died June 4, 1958. She was the daughter of Thomas Jefferson Bonner (born March 12, 1855, in Carroll County and died June 24, 1951, in Cullman County, Alabama) and Susan Emma Treadwell. The father of Thomas Jefferson Bonner was John Bonner who was born February 17, 1817, and he died August 25, 1893. John Bonner married Martha M. Gillespie on November 13, 1835. Martha was born November 15, 1815, and died March 9, 1857. The maternal grandfather of Susan Ida Bonner Rowe was Stephen Thomas Treadwell born November 19, 1825, and died April 19, 1896. His parents were Stephen D. Treadwell who married Sara Bonner, sister to John, Abigail, Thomas, and

Zadock Bonner. Stephen Thomas married Ruth Sara Daniel McIntosh in 1849. She was born April 23, 1834, and died April 12, 1896. Her parents were Jessie Daniel McIntosh and Margaret Ann Lucinda Head. Walter Rowe and Susan Ida Bonner are both buried in the Spence-Rowe Cemetery in Carroll County. They had six children one of whom was my father, Jewell Prince Rowe Sr. who was born December 24, 1899, and died August 7, 1925. He was a school teacher and a Baptist minister. He is also buried in the Spence-Rowe Cemetery. He was married August 7, 1920, to Ethel Neill born September 16, 1900, in Coweta County, Georgia, and died April 5, 1987, in Carroll County. Ethel's parents were Green Berry Neill and Ala Belle McKnight Neill. My mother, Ethel, is buried in Burwell, Georgia, in the Methodist Church Cemetery with her second husband, Joe Hearn McGiboney. *Submitted by: J.P. Rowe, 207 Plantation Walk, Carrollton, GA 30117*

991. Jim and Mary Rowell

James Lovvorn Rowell (Jim) was born on July 5, 1916, in Bowdon. He was the youngest of eight children born to William Bryor Rowell and Victoria Lee Rowell. He was named for Dr. James Lovvorn, the delivering doctor.

Mary Elizabeth Dobson was born in Bowdon on March 4, 1914, the first child of George Washington Dobson and Adren Delaney Saxon Dobson. She was named for her maternal grandmother, Mary Elizabeth Saxon.

Jim and Mary grew up in Bowdon and attended Bowdon schools and Bowdon Normal and Industrial College where Jim played football and Mary studied to be a teacher.

On June 12, 1936, they drove to a local minister's house. Finding him visiting with relatives on the porch, they called him to the car where he performed a "curb service" ceremony with the bride and groom remaining in the car while he stood outside. Since neither of their parents knew of the wedding plans, they returned to their respective homes and kept the wedding a secret for several weeks.

Jim and Mary Rowell

Jim worked for a number of years for Lockheed Corporation and during his tenure there, he helped to develop the prototype of the C-130 plane, followed the first model through assembly and accompanied it to California for testings. He later owned and operated several businesses including Dobson-Rowell Drug Company. At the time of his retirement he was the tax assessor for Carroll County.

Mary rarely worked outside the home except the years when the family owned Dobson-Rowell Drug and later when she and Jimmy owned J and M Gift Shop in Bowdon. She is a charter member of the Bowdon Area Historical Society. For many years, she collected historical Bowdon memorabilia, and in 1990 she co-edited *Bowdon The First Hundred Years: 1853-1953,* a pictorial history of Bowdon.

On April 20, 1943, their first son, James Lovvorn Rowell Jr. (Jimmy) was born. He married Judy Copeland on June 12, 1966 (Jim and Mary's 30th wedding anniversary). Jimmy and Judy had two children. Julie Carol Rowell was born on October 1, 1971, and on August 1, 1998, she married Derick Nelson Steed. Mattie Celestial Steed was born on October 31, 2001. Copeland James Rowell was born on May 19, 1980.

On December 20, 1949, their second son, George Edward Rowell (Eddie), was born. He married Jennifer Mount on August 28, 1971. Eddie and Jennifer had two children. Tracy Edward Rowell was born on July 16, 1976. He died in an accident on August 20, 2000, and is buried in Bowdon City Cemetery. Spencer Mount Rowell was born on January 27, 1982.

Jim and Mary celebrated their 50th wedding anniversary in 1986. Jim Rowell died on March 7, 1997, and is buried in the Bowdon City Cemetery. Mary Rowell died on December 15, 2001, and is buried in Bowdon City Cemetery. *Submitted by: Mary D. Rowell, 222 Mill Street, Bowdon, GA 30108*

992. W.B. Rowell Family

William Bryor Rowell was born on June 12, 1867, in Haralson County, Georgia, the son of William D. Rowell and Arminda A. Smith Rowell. Early in his life he moved to the Indian Creek community near Bowdon where he joined Indian Creek Baptist Church at the age of twenty. He was a rural mail carrier from the Bowdon Post Office for twenty-nine years. He was a church deacon and a Mason.

William Bryor and Victoria Lee Rowell

At the age of nineteen, on December 18, 1887, he married Miss Victoria Lee. She was born on February 4, 1870, the daughter of John Lee and Louisa Elizabeth Widner. The wedding was performed by the groom's uncle, Squire Ransom Smith, at ten o'clock in the morning at the home of the bride. They had eight children — four daughters and five sons (one of whom died as an infant).

Victoria Lee Rowell, whom they characterized in her obituary in the *Bowdon Bulletin* as one whose life was filled with humor and who could see that which was pleasant and good in living, died on June 11, 1940. William Bryor Rowell died on February 5, 1956. Both are buried at Indian Creek Baptist Church Cemetery. Their grave site is partially covered by a bed of thrift which was moved from Victoria's garden at the time of her death.

Children of William Bryor and Victoria Lee Rowell were: Grover, Mag, Leonard, Hershel (Hut), Minnie, Eva, Lloyd, Mable, and James (Jim). *Submitted by: Eddie Rowell, 349 Tarpley Street, Bowdon, GA 30108*

993. Clyde and Nell Rowland

Samuel Clyde Rowland was born in Bowdon, Georgia, December 30, 1905, the eldest child of Wiley Wash Rowland and the former Alberta Ruth Walker. On August 7, 1930, he married Eula Nell Spence born December 5, 1908, the daughter of John Robert Spence and the former Eula Beatrice Foster of Lowell, Georgia. Four children were born to this union, two of whom survived to adulthood, Kay Nell and Alice Jan.

Nell attended school in Lowell and was a member of the Lowell Methodist Church which her mother helped found. She came to Bowdon in 1926 to finish high school and attend Bowdon College. Nell and Clyde met while both were students at Bowdon College. Nell played basketball, and Clyde played football, baseball, basketball, and even summer semi-pro baseball.

Clyde, Jan, Kay, and Nell Rowland in the Smoky Mountains

After graduation from Bowdon College in 1929, Nell worked for thirteen years in Whitesburg, Bowdon, Tyus, and Burwell teaching everything from third grade to high school French. Though serving briefly as principal, her favorite position was seventh grade English teacher. In 1934 Clyde purchased the Ford dealership in Bowdon. In 1935 he purchased the Chevrolet dealership. His business, the West Georgia Motor Company, anchored the west end of Bowdon's business district for twenty years. He also owned a 500 acre cattle farm near Bowdon.

Clyde served in the third army 163rd combat engineers during World War II. Nell resigned her teaching position to follow him to Camp Van Dorn in McComb, Mississippi, where he was stationed for basic training. After the war, Clyde and ten friends built a lake on twenty-nine acres of his land for recreational fishing and swimming. Originally called Riverside Lake Club, the name was later changed to Lake Clyde after his death.

Both Nell and Clyde were active members of Bowdon Baptist Church. Clyde joined the congregation of his parents and grandparents in August 1921, and Nell joined in 1953. Nell taught Sunday School in the children's department for years, and Clyde was ordained a deacon in 1954.

Clyde served three terms on the Bowdon City Council, helping bring the Textile Rubber Company to Bowdon. In February 1945 Clyde made a motion that Dr. James Watts be granted a permit to build a sixteen room hospital in Bowdon. The motion carried. Clyde also served on the original Tanner Hospital Authority.

In June 1946 Clyde was named to the Carroll County Board of Education. Elected chairman in 1951, Clyde spearheaded the building program and bond issue proposals that resulted in the facilities which currently house Bowdon, Central, and Villa Rica High Schools. The last summer of Clyde's life in 1955 was spent helping build Ava Sewell Hall after Bowdon's wooden gymnasium burned. He attended his last school board meeting in November 1955 before leaving for Atlanta with Nell for a checkup. He died December 9, 1955.

The board paid tribute saying, "We owe and shall always owe much to Clyde's leadership and sincere interest in the welfare of the county, even beyond his line of duty." *Submitted by: Jan Rowland Johnson, 442 E. College St., Bowdon, GA 30108*

994. Victoria McClain Rowland

Widowed at 41 with six children ages seven to twenty, Victoria McClain Rowland had lost her own father, Samuel J. McClain, when she was fifteen. Samuel McClain was born in 1820 and married Adaline Landrum April 1841 in Greene County, Georgia. He was mustered into service a corporal in Company F., 21st Regiment, Georgia Volunteer Infantry, Army of Northern Virginia on July 9, 1861. He was promoted to sergeant December 5, 1861. He died at Liberty, Virginia, June 1862. During the war, Victoria remembered helping herd the family's cattle into the marsh to avoid confiscation by soldiers.

Victoria McClain Rowland

Born in LaGrange, Georgia, November 28, 1847, Victoria McClain was nineteen when she married Wiley B. Rowland on June 9, 1867. They were married by Justice of the Peace Walton Whatley in Troup County. Wiley B. Rowland was born February 21, 1834, in Troup County, the son of Wiley and Elizabeth Akers Rowland. Born in 1799, Wiley Rowland was an early settler of Troup County and a large land owner in the Antioch community, His son Wiley B. served in Company B. Fourth Regiment, Georgia Volunteer Infantry, Army of Northern Virginia, LaGrange Light Guards, having been mustered into service April 26, 1861. They were mobilized in Augusta May 3, 1861, and arrived at Camp Jackson, Virginia, May 30. After almost a year of training, the fourth regiment advanced to the front and saw action at numerous battles including Malvern Hill, Sharpsburg, Fredericksburg, Chancellorsville, Gettysburg and Spottsylvania. The fourth regiment advanced on Washington July 11, 1864, and was present at Appomattox. Three of Wiley B's brothers, Littleberry B., William H., and Samuel J. also served in the Army of Northern Virginia.

The nine children of Victoria McClain and Wiley B. Rowland were Frank A., born in 1868, Sterling Turner born 1869, William Henry born 1871, Little B. born 1872, Mary Emma born 1874, Sammie T. in 1876, Elizabeth Lou in 1878, Annie Irene in 1880, and Wiley Wash in 1881. Three of the children, William, Little B., and Annie did not survive infancy.

When Wiley died March 19, 1888, in Troup County, his widow Victoria sold their farm and moved in 1889 to Bowdon near the college. Vachael D. Whatley, a Troup County neighbor, made his first visit to Bowdon to see the Rowlands in 1889, resulting in his entering Bowdon College where he later served as president.

Victoria and her children were members of Bowdon Baptist Church. She spent her later years in the home of her youngest son Wiley Wash and his wife the former Alberta Ruth Walker and their children Samuel Clyde born 1905, Walker Wayne born 1907, Claude Roop, born 1910, Dorothy Naomi born 1913, Jo Nell born 1916, Alice Louise born 1921, Carl Julian born 1924, and Floy Marie born 1927. Alberta "Berta" Rowland often remarked that she didn't know how she could have cared for her eight children if Victoria had not lived with them. The death of the valiant Victoria November 29, 1934, saddened all who admired her cheerful personality and indomitable spirit. *Submitted by: Jan Rowland Johnson, 442 East College Street, Bowdon, GA 30108*

995. Richard V.C. Ruffin

Richard Veale Carney Ruffin was the son of James and Margaret Veal Ruffin. He was probably named for his mother's side of the family. Margaret was the daughter of Thomas and Elizabeth Carney Veale and had a brother named Richard. Both the Veale and Ruffin families lived in Bertie County, North Carolina, and (based on census records) we estimate that Richard was born around 1800.

James, the father, was one of nine children born of a tobacco planter. We think that he and Margaret decided to leave Bertie County because of the worn out condition of the land from all the tobacco, and take up a new life in Georgia around the spring of 1818 by raising cotton. His sons were old enough to help by this time, and the opening up of the Indian lands in Georgia probably drew them.

Unfortunately, the financial situation in America was not good, and we know that James lost to a sheriff's sale (January and February 1819-Jones County) several Negro slaves, as well as some land that he had purchased in Jones County, Georgia. James died around 1821, leaving his orphaned sons to draw in the land lotteries.

R.V.C. was married to Elizabeth P. Harrell on November 9, 1823, in Jones County. In October of 1829 he was a justice of peace in Houston County, but by the 1840 census he had moved his family to Carroll County near Villa Rica. On September 15, 1835, he signed a petition about a road in Villa Rica.

The known children are: James (1828-died before his father); Samuel S. (1830) married Elizabeth Hunt June 24, 1868; Margaret Anna (1833); Sarah E. (1838); and Charles J. (1843).

R.V.C. was Justice of the Peace in Villa Rica for many years. He was a member of the New Hope Baptist Church and, according to his will, was buried in the New Hope Cemetery although no tombstone remains. His will was probated April 1861. Elizabeth was living with her son Samuel in the 1870 Carroll County Census. *Submitted by: Virginia Crilley, 4500 Kenny Lane, Waco, TX 76710-2058*

996. Warner Franklin Rush Sr. and Bessie Stone Rush

Warner Franklin Rush was born August 14, 1902, in Haralson County, son of William C. Rush (January 9, 1850-January 10, 1916) and Nettie Frances Roberson Rush (January 12, 1861-1938). Both are buried at Piney Woods Church Cemetery, Haralson County.

Bessie Mae Stone was born July 14, 1901, in Haralson County, daughter of Sarah Ellen Vaughn Stone (July 20, 1878-August 4, 1963) and John Allen Stone (September 18, 1876-January 16, 1962). Both are buried at Pleasant Grove Primitive Baptist Church Cemetery.

Bessie and Warner were married on February 12, 1920, in Haralson County. Bessie was a homemaker with a special love for sewing. She had a great sense of humor. Warner was a farmer. They moved several times to different rental farms until 1945 when he bought a tract of timber land. He sold enough timber to pay for a farm. The remaining timber was milled for a house and barn. He went to work for Bell Bomber (now known as Lockheed) and later at Del-Mar Cabinet Company. Bessie died in their home of cancer on July 2, 1957. Warner died of an accidental gunshot wound on October 26, 1957, on his farm. Both are buried at Asbury Cemetery.

Bessie and Warner Rush Sr.

They had eight children: Cecil Allen was born April 25, 1921, in Haralson County and died January 20, 1996, at Tanner Medical Center; Gertrude was born March 17, 1923, in Turner County where the family lived for only one growing season; Otho Andrew was born August 27, 1925, in Carroll County and died December 23, 1987, at Tanner Medical Center; Warner Franklin Jr., was born February 4, 1930, in Carroll County and died June 24, 1978, in Louisiana; Lee Roy was born January 11, 1935, in Carroll County and died October 16, 1994, at Villa Rica Hospital; Ollie Mae was born November 24, 1936, in Carroll County; James Fred was born August 24, 1940, in Carroll County and died March 25, 1990, at his home; and Robert Levi was born September 19, 1946. Cecil, Otho, Warner Jr., Lee Roy, and Fred are buried at Asbury Cemetery in Temple, Georgia.

Four of the eight children served in the U.S. Military: Cecil Allen in the Army, W.F. Jr. in the Air Force, James Fred in the Marines, and Robert Levi in the Army.

Cecil married Mary Stephens on August 7, 1946. They had five children: William Allen, May 11, 1947; Evelyn Annette born June 1, 1948, and died June 2, 1948; Judy Ann, February 14, 1950; Janice Annette, February 21, 1953; and Cynthia Diane, May 9, 1954.

The Rush Family

Gertrude married Roy F. Yearty Sr. on May 20, 1939. They had five children: Cora Mae November 9, 1940; Sandra Louise January 28, 1943; Roy Franklin Jr., October 6, 1945; Sara Frances July 9, 1950; and Debra Ann born November 4, 1955 and died March 7, 1994. All were born in Carroll County.

Otho married Inez Terrell on June 17, 1944. They had five children: Jerry Kenneth born June 22, 1945, and died 1993; Barbara Jean October 19, 1947; Frances Louise September 26, 1949; Donna Sue August 1, 1954; and Ronnie Edward February 22, 1960.

Warner F. married Betty Davenport. They had two sons: Frankie and Larry Wayne on May 30, 1957. They divorced and the children were adopted. Lee Roy never married.

Ollie married Marvin Sudduth on December 13, 1952. They had five children: June Alice born August 19, 1953; Debra Ann born 1955 and died 1955; Shirelene born March 27, 1959; Pamela Ann born August 24, 1961; and Janice Marlene September 10, 1965. They divorced. She is now married to Eck Carroll.

Fred married Rachel Stitcher on May 29, 1964. They had two children: Kimberly Lynn June 23, 1969, and Kamron Lane November 2, 1974.

Robert married Glenda Upchurch in September 1964. They had one daughter: Rhonda Renee August 6, 1967. They divorced. He married Frances Weaver Lee on May 5, 1979. They have one son: Robert Deric April 7, 1980.

The photo of the Rush family includes back row: Robert, Fred, and Lee Roy Rush, and front row: O.A. Squeeky Rush, Gertrude Rush Yearty, Ollie Rush Carroll, and Cecil Rush. *Submitted by: Gertrude Yearty, P.O. Box 173, Temple, GA 30179*

997. Jan Ruskell

I am descended from John Alston who settled in Chowan County, North Carolina, on the northwest side of Bennett's Creek in 1711. He came to America from England. He was active in the local government serving as juror, justice of the peace, revenue collector and sheriff. He also served as vestryman of St. Paul's Parish in Chowan County. He married Mary Clark. He had several children, but I am descended from his daughter Charity who married John Dawson. Their son John Dawson born about 1759 married Elizabeth Dorothy Atherton. John represented Northhampton County in the North Carolina legislature in 1780-82. He moved to Halifax and represented the legislature form 1787-90. Their son John married Martha Green Hunter daughter of Jacob Hunter and Patience Williamson. Jacob Hunter was descended from Solomon Alston on his mother's side. Jacob's uncle Jesse moved with his family to Georgia. Jacob and several collateral relatives moved to Tennessee.

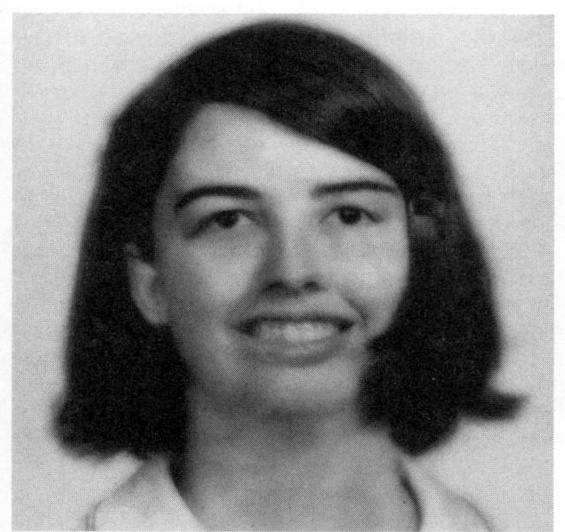

Jan Ruskell

The Hunters moved to Tennessee about 1822. They settled in Maury County where Jacob died in 1843. The family continued to live in Maury County. Their daughter Charity Alston Hunter married a Kittrell whose family also came from North Carolina. They had several children. Charity's brother Jacob had settled in Forest City, Arkansas. Charity stayed with him during the Civil War as several of the children were born in Arkansas. One of the daughters always hated Abraham Lincoln because of the hardships of the Civil War.

One of Charity's daughters married an Acuff. Their daughter Annie Hall married James Abston McFerrin October 11, 1911. He was a doctor and raised thoroughbred trotters. Their daughter Virginia Douglass married George Channing Ruskell III. They had four children Virginia Ann (Jan), Julia, George Channing, and Elizabeth McFerrin.

I was born in Nashville, Tennessee. My family moved to Georgia when I was ready to go to college. I graduated from Reinhardt College and Emory University. I attended George Peabody College and earned an M.L.S. Robert Simmons, the director of the library at West Georgie College taught in summer school at Peabody. I interviewed for a job and moved to Carrollton. I immediately loved the beauty of the campus. I always felt like moving to Carrollton was going home. Only later did I realize that the early settlers of Carroll County were from eastern North Carolina. The people that settled Carrollton have the same background and values that I have. That is why I have worked so hard to preserve the history of the county and make the current residents appreciate their past. *Submitted by: Jan Ruskell, Box 844, Carrollton, GA 30117*
Sources:The Alstons and Allstons of North and South Carolina, Joseph A. Groves

998. Harris Russell and Leah Steed

In the 1830s, Harris and Leah Steed Russell migrated from North Carolina to Coweta County, Georgia. Harris, 1799-1873, was a son of Gabriel Russell and his wife Candis. Leah, 1800-1885, was a daughter of Hilkiah Steed and Sarah (Sally) Hearn.

A story has come down in the Steed line about a caravan of fourteen covered wagons which left North Carolina in the mid-1830s, bound for new lands in Georgia. The journey lasted over three months. Harris and Leah brought seven children from North Carolina to Georgia and settled in Coweta County, living in a dirt-floor cabin.

By 1870, after living in Talladega County, Alabama, for a time, Harris and Leah had returned to Georgia, settling in Carroll County. Of their surviving children, all except Moses moved on to Texas. Descendants in Texas today have been told the story of the Russell wagon train which traveled from Georgia and Alabama to East Texas.

Harris Russell is buried at Old Camp Methodist Church in Carroll County. Leah Steed Russell went to Texas in 1877 to live with her daughter Martha Ann. Leah's burial place in Texas is unknown.

Children: Calvin Augustus, 1822-1856, married Emeline Elizabeth Wilkerson. Their children: Susan Ann, Sarah Frances, infant daughter, Marshall Emsley, Wiley Harris, Calvin Augustus (female).

Martha Jane, 1824-1884, married her cousin, Emlay K. Russell, settled in Texas. Children: Gabriel H., Margaret A.N., Aby, Sarah Emiline, Leah Leola. Nancy Ann, 1826-1907, married Wesley M. Ballard. Settled in Texas. Their known children: William, Ellen, Francis (Fannie), Emily, Ollie. Melvina, 1828-1863, married first a Ballard. Married second James Butler Madison Landers. Children: Allison W. (son); Wiley Harris, Mary Elizabeth, James Butler Madison Jr., Sarah Catherine, Frances Julia, Roxie Susan, Robert Houston, William, and one other who died in 1855. Wiley Washington, 1830-1856, married Levonia Carlton. Their children: John Harris, Wiley Abner. Louisa, 1832-1854, married Walter K. Franklin. No known children. William Nelson, 1833-1854, never married. Moses Richard, 1835-1922. See the article on his family. Gabriel Jackson, 1837-1857. Sarah Elizabeth, 1839-1860, married Dr. B.S. Smoot. One child died in infancy.

James Harris, 1844-1931. He was a dentist and a prominent citizen of Texas. Married first his first cousin, Lucy Caroline Steed, daughter of Agrippa Steed. Married second Josephine Adaline Steadham. Children: Cora, Emma, John Earl, Malcolm Musick, Josephine Maud, James Claude, Blanche, Opal, Willie Mae, Katie, Loreign. *Submitted by: Jennifer Gilmer, 1583 McLendon Ave., Atlanta, GA 30307*

999. Moses Richard Russell

Moses Richard Russell (1835-1922) was the son of Harris Russell and Leah Steed who migrated from North Carolina to Coweta County, Georgia, where Moses attended school in a dirt-floor log cabin which had a big fireplace, a dirt and stick chimney, and square holes cut through the logs for light.

Moses served the Confederacy and settled in Carroll County where he served on the Board of Education, as superintendent of schools, and as a county commissioner.

Moses married first Frances Lumpkin (Fannie) Bell (1841-1873), the daughter of Sylvanus Bell and Elizabeth Mary Stipe. Moses married second Fannie's first cousin, Elizabeth Lucie (Betty) Brown (1847-1909), the daughter of Franklin Brown and Agnes Stipe. Moses, Fannie, and Betty are buried at Old Camp Methodist in Carroll.

Russell Family

Children by Frances Lumpkin Bell: Elizabeth Lumpkin (Wrennie), (1859-1941), married D. Ezra Martin. Children: Ruthie, 1885-1886; Rufus Russell; Hal C.; Fannie Kate. George Bell, born 1861, married Florence (Turner?). Settled in Texas. Children: Seth; Fannie; Leta; Gladys; Ernest. Joseph Irene, 1864-1938, married Green Washington Davenport. They settled in Texas. Children: Charles Russell; Walter Grover; Bessie Mae; Comer C.; Maud R.; Alsie Lee; Beula Floy; Marvin Edward; Wiley Ripley. Robert Lee, born 1867. He married his first cousin, Emma Russell. Emma and their four children were killed in a tornado in Texas in 1906. Marvin Edgar, 1869-1951, married Mollie Handley. They settled in Arkansas. Children: Maudie Belle; Moses R.; Charles A.; Retha L.; Wiley S.; Flora May; Elsie R.; William E.; Arthur P.; Bertie C.; Gilbert L.; Comer Glenn; Velma; Vera. Rush Limbaugh is a great-grandson of Marvin Edgar Russell. Kate, 1870-1949, married Oscar Perry Baskin. Children: Lois; Sidney Roy; Russell; Paul Callaway; Irene Yvonne; Earl.

Children by Elizabeth Lucie Brown: James Harris, 1874-1945, married Ida Bell (daughter of William Pittman Bell and granddaughter of Sylvanus Bell and Frances Lumpkin). Children: Willie; Moses Richard; Samuel Sullavan Cox; Ida Sue. Lula, 1875-1959, married W. Oscar Ashmore. Children: Mabel Gladys; Mary Ruth; Bessie Mildred; Glynn Russell; Edgar Parks; James Fred; Paul Augustus; Homer Carl. Annie Agnes, 1876-1969, married Robert Lee Smith. Children: John R.; Robert Lee, Jr.; Bessie. Buena Vista, 1878-1958, married William Franklin Hinesley. Children: Willie Ernest; Guy Russell; Pierce Franklin; Annie Mae; Hugh; Florence Ezelle; Alton Jesse. Frances Lillian (Frank), 1880-1954, married Thomas Otho Hamrick. She was the organist at Old Camp

Methodist Church and is buried there. Tom was the sheriff. Children: Ray; Alton P.; Agnes; Richard; Jim; Robert Whitten; Russell; Mary; Julian; Frances Anne. Hugh Buchanan, 1882-1922, married Mattie Lou Holmes. He is buried at Mt. Zion Methodist, Carroll. Children: Annie Ruth; Margaret; Charles; Hoke S. Grover Cleveland, 1884-1929, married Nancy Louthella Florence Davis. Children: Henry Moses, born 1908; Frances Willard, 1910-1998; Annie Belle, 1912-1980; Mignon, 1915-1997; Edwin, 1923-1926.

Photograph identities: Seated: Moses, Betty, James. Standing: Buena, Grover, Hugh, Frances. *Submitted by: Joel L. Gilmer, 648 Pine Tree Dr., Marietta, GA 30067*

1000. Samples - Jordan

John Bunyan Samples was born November 3, 1844, in Newton County, Georgia, and died November 23, 1897. He was the son of Jacob M. Samples and Mary Rice who lived in Heard County, Georgia. On June 26, 1861, in Heard County, he volunteered for Company E, 19th Regiment, Georgia Voluntary Infantry, Army of Tennessee, CSA. He was captured and paroled at Warrenton, Virginia, on September 29, 1862. On December 13, 1862, he was captured at Fredericksburg, Virginia, then admitted to 9th Ft. Ascension USA General Hospital at Washington D.C. on December 18, 1862, with a wound in left side. On release from the hospital, he was returned to Old Capitol Prison on February 27, 1863, and exchanged at City Point, Virginia, on March 29, 1863. On February 20, 1864, at Ocean Pond, Florida, in the Battle of Olustee, he was wounded in his right leg, requiring amputation. He was retired to Invalid Corps on August 25, 1864.

Sarah Ann Jordan and John Bunyan Samples

On August 4, 1864, he married Sarah Ann Jordan, daughter of William Tadford Jordan and Agnes Blair. She was born January 22, 1845, in Coweta County, Georgia, and died November 14, 1926. John, Sarah Ann, and three infant children are buried in the Jordan Cemetery, Carroll County. Their living children were:

1. William Martin Samples, born April 9, 1865, in Carroll County, and died March 10, 1933, in Coweta County. He was a Baptist preacher. On August 27, 1885, in Carroll County, he was married to Molly Ann McWhorter, daughter of Moses Allen McWhorter and Sarah Kinney. She was born April 29, 1869, in Carroll County, and died March 16, 1908, in Douglas County. Both are buried in Powell Chapel United Methodist Church Cemetery, Carroll County. Their children were: John Milton Samples who married Mamie Sears; Moses Monroe Samples who married Ethel Florence Boyd; Henry Grady Samples who married Ruby Bearden; Joseph J. Samples who married Queenie Bell Tyson; Franklin Roger Samples who married Ritha Miller; Thomas Jefferson Samples who married Eva Christine Steed; Ernest Willis Samples who married Bernice Stella Smallwood; Martin Samples who died as a child; Sarah Annie Belle Samples who married William Harvey Payton; Lemuel Samples who died as a child; Mary E. Samples who married Rufus Milam; and Mattie Lou Samples who married Thomas Clewey Hembree.

William Martin's second marriage was to Wynola Entrekin on August 29, 1910, and there were no children. His third marriage was to Alzie Mitchell on February 19, 1914, and there was one child, Martin VanBuren Samples who married Bertha Claris Parrish. According to family legend, Alzie Mitchell was of Indian blood.

2. John Thomas Samples, born November 7, 1874, and died March 21, 1953. He married first Idemma Burnett. Their children were Homer Judson Samples, Wesley Hugh Samples who married Mattie Lee Fordham, and Ruby Mae Samples who married Wyley Reynolds. He then married second Lena McHam and they had two children, Bertie F. Samples, and George Washington Samples who married Effie Akers. His third marriage was to Martha Frances Adams and there were no children.

3. Birdie Iva Nona Samples was born September 20, 1879, in Carroll County and died February 7, 1969, in Fulton County. She married first Wesley Benjamin Burnett Jr., and they had two children, John Allen Burnett who married Climmie Pearl O'Kelley, and James Oliver Burnett who died as an infant. She married second Robert Clark and had two children, Ida May Clark who married Jody Lambert Garner, and Molly Ann Clark who married Cloise Taft Bowen. The second marriage ended in divorce. She married third John T. Fountain, and there were no children.

4. Frank S. Samples was born October 1881 in Carroll County. He married Mary Polk and had three children, Lavela Samples, Jewell Samples, and Mary L. Samples. He was a lawyer, and he moved his family to Texas.

After John Bunyan Samples died, Sarah Ann married a second time to Green Sanders Fountain on October 14, 1900, in Carroll County. *Submitted by: Lowell H. Boyd, 1539 Flat Rock Road, Villa Rica, GA 30180*

Sources: Personal knowledge, Confederate records, census, marriage, and cemetery records researched by Erlene Boyd. Picture courtesy of Pat Pittman, 172 Pat Mell Road, Marietta, GA 30060

1001. Scroggins

Part 1

William Marshall Scroggins Sr. and his two sons were living in Carroll County when the Kansas Territory was opened to white settlers (1854). They went to Kansas but the mosquitoes were so bad that William Sr. and William Jr. decided to come back to Georgia. They settled in the Sand Hill area. William Marshall Scroggins Jr. married Mattie Nelson. They had two children, Ethel and William Marshall Scroggins III. When William III was very young, his mother died. William Jr. married again. They had three children. When William Marshall III was five years old, he changed his name to Grover Cleveland, the president's name at that time. He was known as Grover Scroggins the remainder of his life.

When Grover was twelve years old, his family moved from Sand Hill to Hannah Swamp in Paulding County. When he was seventeen, he went to work on the farm of Richard Hannah.

Isaac Hannah and his family moved from North Carolina before 1850. He and his family were charter members of Wesley Chapel which is just over the Paulding County line into Carroll County (1854). Isaac and Jane had seven children. Their son Richard was a twin to Jesse Hannah. Allen died in 1865 during the Civil War, part of the Army of Tennessee in North Carolina. Richard was with General Robert E. Lee at Appomattox when he surrendered the Confederate Army in April 1865. Before the war Richard was married to a Tennessee girl, Elizabeth Shores. She stayed at the cabin with Isaac and Jane during Richard's absence. Isaac died in 1871, but he lived to see his first two grandchildren, Lucinda Jane (1867) and Robert Lee (1869). There were three more children born to Richard and Eliza: Fannie Ivy, Reuben, and Richard (Bud) Hannah Jr. *Submitted by: Phyllis Sheppard*

1002. Grover Scroggins

Part 2

Grover Scroggins married Lucinda Jane Hannah in 1904. They had three children: Essie, Rush and Celia. Essie and Celia married and moved away from Paulding County. Rush stayed with his parents until he was nearly twenty-one. He began to work in Villa Rica with "Big Boy" Cliff Richards at his barber shop on the weekends. When Mr. Taft died, Rush bought his barber shop. Over the years, he worked with Bud Heath, Carl Townsend, and Lemuel Gladney. Later, after living in Florida for two years, Rush worked with T.C. Daniell in T.C.'s shop. Rush Scroggins cut hair for sixty years in Villa Rica. He died in 1991 at the age of eighty-four. He married Anna Lois Howell in 1934. Anna Lois was a hairdresser for fifty years. Rush and Anna Lois had one child to live, Charlotte S. Barber. She married Ray Barber in 1953 and they had five daughters: Beverly Swafford, Phyllis Sheppard, Jane Jackson, Elizabeth Rainwater, and Amie Williams. Charlotte and Ray Barber have ten grandchildren: Anna and Beau Swafford; Meg and Lauren Sheppard; Joel and Sara Jackson; Andrew, Hannah and Daniel Rainwater; and Riley Williams. They all live in Carroll County. Ray was the mayor of Villa Rica from January 1986 through December 1991. Charlotte Scroggins Barber taught school in Paulding County for five years and taught fifteen years in Carroll County.

Celia divorced Mr. Williams, father of Max. She married Dan Spinks in 1935. They had Jo Spinks Irish and Danny. Celia moved to Maple Street in Villa Rica in 1942. After World War II, Dan came home. They lived there until their deaths, Celia in 1970, and Dan in 1984 (?).

Mattie Nelson Scroggins is buried in the grave yard at the Temperance Church in Sand Hill. A great number of Hannahs are buried at Wesley Chapel in Carroll County. Grover Scroggins is buried between his two wives in Paulding County at Concord Baptist Church. Rush and Anna Lois are buried at Hill Crest Cemetery in Villa Rica.

The Hannahs and the Scroggins were baptized in the Methodist or the Baptist faith. Grover Scroggins' half-brother, Emmett Scroggins, raised his family in Douglasville. Many of his descendants live there now. Ethel raised her family in Coweta County. Her daughter was Nan Williams. *Submitted by: Charlotte S. Barber, 524 North Avenue, Villa Rica, GA 30180*

1003. Beheruz Nariman Sethna

The Sethna family was the last "first family" to live in the President's House at West Georgia. They moved into the house on August 26, 1994, and lived there until October of 1995 when they moved into their own private residence. Dr. Sethna designated the house as the Alumni House at that time, in recognition of the importance of alumni to the institution.

Dr. Beheruz N. Sethna, the sixth president of West Georgia College and the first president of the University, his wife Madhavi, and children Anita and Shaun, arrived in Carrollton, Georgia, having driven from Texas in the preceding twenty-four hours. However, the journey of 660 miles to Carrollton was just the most recent phase of a journey that had started many decades earlier and many thousands of miles away.

Beheruz Sethna was born on July 31, 1948, in Bombay, India, to Nariman and Mithu Sethna. He was the only child of his parents and grew up under what, in the United States, would be considered very straightened means. Nariman was a young officer in the Royal Air Force and later the Indian Air Force, and Mithu did not work outside the home. After he left the Air Force, Nariman joined a private import-export firm where he worked for approximately forty-five years until he passed away in 1999, having gone to work as recently as his 87th birthday. Mithu lives in Bombay and has visited Carrollton several times.

Anita, Madhavi, Beheruz and Shaun Sethna

Dr. Sethna recollects having no discretionary money in his youth because his parents insisted on saving every spare amount for his education. His father's income (the only income in the family) was Rs. 500 a month (which, in today's terms, is $11 a month). Although the conversion rate was more favorable then and the money went further than it does today, it was still a very modest income. He wore hand-me-down school uniforms in middle school, and learned to do without the discretionary expenditures that many of his friends could afford. He credits his parents with raising him with solid values of hard work, frugality, and a love of higher education.

Dr. Sethna's father wanted him to go to a very competitive engineering school called the Indian Institute of Technology, which he did essentially to please him. He credits his father for pushing him to achieve those credentials that he received at the end of his seven-year undergraduate program (which included the foundation of an arts & sciences degree). He earned his bachelor of technology degree with honors in 1971, and then earned an M.B.A. at the Indian Institute of Management, the premier Management School in Asia, in 1973. After working briefly for an advertising agency, he came to America in 1973 to do his Ph.D. at Columbia University in New York.

Dr. Sethna's early months in America were not much easier than his life in India. Because of a bureaucratic glitch, it was several months before he could draw his scholarship check; for many months, he had to budget eating expenses to be one dollar a day. After several months, the scholarship came through and life improved a little, particularly after he got a part-time job at Lever Brothers in New York, where he worked until 1976. He completed his master's degree in philosophy at Columbia in 1975, and his Ph.D. in 1976.

Beheruz met Madhavi while in graduate school and they were married on May 25, 1974. After her M.B.A., Madhavi also joined Columbia and earned her master's degree in special education there.

After Madhavi completed her degree, they moved to Clarkson University in Potsdam, New York. They lived in Potsdam for thirteen years. Dr. Sethna was promoted and tenured, and served as Department Chair and Director of Graduate Programs. Madhavi earned her third master's degree there in MIS, and worked in the school system and at Clarkson. Anita was born in Potsdam in 1978, and Shaun was born in Bombay (while the family was on sabbatical) in 1980.

After thirteen years at Clarkson, the family moved to Beaumont, Texas, for five years, where Dr. Sethna served as Dean of the College of Business at Lamar University and later Interim Executive Vice President. Madhavi worked as an assistant professor at Lamar. Then, the family moved to Carrollton, Georgia, after a journey from Bombay via New York and Texas, which had spanned forty-six years. *Submitted by: Dr. Beheruz Sethna President, University of West Georgia, 1600 Maple Street, Carrollton, GA 30118*

1004. Sewll - Watson - Bryce - Medders

Greenberry Sewell died before January 20, 1846, in Carroll County, Georgia. His son Alexander Sewell and Seletha Baker were married in Carroll County, Georgia, on February 17, 1846. Their son James W. Sewell was born in Haralson County April 15, 1847, died August 22, 1926, in Weaver, Alabama. James married Harriett Alevier Watson on December 30, 1869, in Haralson County. She was born in Haralson County on December 8, 1850, died May 11, 1918, in Weaver, Alabama. Both are buried at Four Mile Cemetery just off Highway 21 between Jacksonville and Anniston, Alabama.

James William Sewell, Harriett Alevier Watson Sewell, Jessie Alevier Medders Clark, Katie Ellen Sewell Medders

Their children were: (1) Marion Willis born November 10, 1872, died April 21, 1941, married Ettie Viola Hall on December 2, 1896. (2) Mary Anna Sewell, born November 17, 1874, died November 13, 1955, married Wyatt Mattison Brown November 6, 1892. (3) John William born January 1, 1877, died January 16, 1959, married Bertie Call. (4) James Arthur Alexander born January 8, 1880, died December 3, 1954, married Zora Call. (5) Thomas Luther Sewell, born June 12, 1881, died July 12, 1942, married Mattie Kilgore. (6) Katie Ellen, born September 7, 1888, died August 28, 1978, married Robert Sidney Medders September 5, 1905. Sidney was born in Haralson County December 25, 1880, and died in Whittier, California, in 1940. His parents were Bailey Sylvester Medders and Perlonia Daniel. Bailey's father was William Enoch Medders. Katie and Sidney had one child together, Jessie Alevier born June 23, 1906, died April 8, 1998, Calhoun County, Alabama. Jessie married James Jackson Clark born March 19, 1905, died January 5, 1994. Jack and Jessie had three children, all born in Etowah County, Alabama. (A) James Frederick Clark born November 8, 1931, died February 1, 1999, married Peggy Getts. (B) Kenneth Jackson Clark born June 16, 1939, married Brenda Lowry. They had two girls, Lee Ellen (Drew Simpson), Candice Beth (John Lee), grandson John Lee IV. (C) Linda Gail Clark born June 17, 1941, married Phillip W. Fields. They had two girls, Rita Kay (Edward R. Wright), Duska Deanne (Scott P. Fields), grandchildren Jessica Wright, Whitney Wright, Hunter Fields, Clark Fields. (7) Harriett Josie born February 9, 1892, died October 14, 1893.

Harriett Alevier Watson was the daughter of Burton Watson born about 1820 in Virginia, and Ellen Bryce (Brice) born about 1821 in South Carolina. Burton is listed in the 1840 Carroll County Census and Burton and Ellen are listed in the Haralson County censuses of 1860, 1870 and 1880. My grandmother (Katie Ellen Sewell Medders) said they called him Captain Watson. He was the treasurer of Haralson County Masonic Lodge 113 in 1866. Grandmother also said his son George and another man were sitting up with a corpse at a neighbor's house. George went outside to the bathroom and was never seen again. One of Burtons daughters, Annie, corresponded with Harriet and wrote all her letters in prose. Ellen Bryce was the daughter of William Bryce born December 12, 1773, Irvine, Ayr County Scotland, died 1840-1850 Carroll County, Georgia, and Mary Bryce born May 29, 1774, Ayre, Scotland. They were living in Carroll County by 1827 and could be buried in the Brice Family Cemetery in Bremen. William was appointed as a commissioner for the town of Carrollton in 1829. My grandmother said Ellen related stories about her or her parents fighting Indians. One of the Indians picked up a small child by the heels and slammed his head against a tree. Ellen also related that her mother Mary nearly starved when they first came to this country because she was use to eating rye bread and all they had here was cornbread. Ellen had a brother who was a ship-builder and named a ship after her. Grandmother said her grandparents, Burton and Ellen, lived to be ninety-one and ninety, respectively. *Submitted by: Linda Clark Fields, 816 Pine Ridge Road, Wellington, AL 36279, L4Fields@aol.com*

1005. Shackleford History

in Carroll County

Francis Shackleford and his wife Anna Davis Shackleford settled in the southeast portion of Carroll County in the 1830s. Francis had previously settled in Gwinnett County and while there he had drawn land in Coweta County in the state lottery of 1827. He sold that land and bought land and settled in Carroll County.

Francis and Anna were born in Virginia, he in 1787 and she in 1793. Their children were Richard Nunn, Elvina and Melissa. We have no record of Anna's death, however Francis died intestate around 1855 while visiting relatives in Gwinnett County.

Since Francis died without a will, his son Richard was appointed by the court as his administrator to settle any debts, and distribute the property.

Richard Nunn Shackleford (in Confederate uniform)

By 1860 Richard Nunn Shackleford had become a teacher and had married Elizabeth Jones of Morgan County, Georgia. On March 4, 1862, Richard, then age thirty-five, enlisted in Company G, 41st Infantry Regiment of the Confederate Army (Army of Tennessee). At that time he and Elizabeth had four children: Melissa, Francis Robert, William and Thomas. A fifth child Richard Jones Shackleford was born on October 5, 1862, just nine months before his father's death. Richard Nunn Shackleford became ill and died in a Vicksburg, Mississippi, hospital on July 5, 1863.

Elizabeth Jones Shackleford

Elizabeth was left with five children and no means of support. She and her children were destitute. The railroad gave passes to Confederate widows so that they might ride the trains free. Elizabeth would board the train at Whitesburg and ride down to Griffin to the textile mills. The mills would also give remnants and scraps of fabric to widows. In this way she was able to sew for her family. Relatives and friends living nearby contributed what food they could spare; however, she had an extremely difficult time. As they grew older, the four boys did farm work for others to provide income for the family. Elizabeth died around 1885 and is buried in an unmarked grave at Friendship Baptist Church in southwest Douglas County.

As far as we know, Richard Jones Shackleford was the only one of this family to stay in Carroll County. He became a farmer and a merchant. About 1886, he married Sallie Jones, also a native of Carroll County and the daughter of Nathan C. and Nancy J. Jones.

Richard and Sallie had seven children who lived to adulthood. They are Bernard Leonidas, Nathan Cicero, Finella Jane, Alma Ursula, Bennie Frank, Tommie Lester and Cassie Jeanette. None of these children are living today.

Richard Jones Shackleford died in December of 1952, Sallie had predeceased him in 1949. Both are buried at Stripling Chapel Methodist Church. Several of their children are also buried there.

Grandchildren of Richard and Sallie who live in Carroll County today are Nat Shackleford, Madelyn S. Morgan and Florrie C. Spivey.

Submitted by: Betty A. Shackleford, 2441 Nancy Lane NE, Atlanta, GA 30345

1006. Shadinger Family

In about 1856 John Shadinger and his mother, Elizabeth Mitchell Shadinger Jones (born about 1809), bought 202½ acres on what is now Highway 27 South. Elizabeth had married Willis Jones after Andrew Shadinger's death and Jones probably was already dead before they came to Carroll County. Andrew (1802-1831) died as a young man, according to family stories; while cutting wood the wind blew a tree over on him. When Elizabeth died (about 1871), apparently her other children were already dead because John inherited all 202½ acres.

John Shadinger (born in Fayette County, 1826-1915) married Frances Elenna (Ellen) Jones (1828-1909) in Coweta County, Georgia, on December 17, 1846. Their children were James Andrew, Mary Elizabeth, Sara Jane (Sallie), Martha Ann Rebecca, William Carroll (Billy), John Henry, Thomas Bureguard (Tommy), Ella, and Georgia Ann. John gave all his children 75 acres of land when they married.

In 1863, when John learned that his sickly sixteen year old son was to be inducted into the Confederate Army, he took his place even though he was thirty-six years old at the time. He served until the end of the war in Company I, Storey's Regiment, of the Georgia State Troops. He was awarded the Confederate Cross of Honor by the United Daughters of the Confederacy in 1904.

John Shadinger helped to organize and build the Emmaus Church. His interest and influence in the schools were far reaching. But he was probably best known as the builder of the rock fence along Shadinger Ridge. It was built without mortar, and was about eight feet high, two feet wide and extended several hundred yards. The wall was torn down during the paving and widening of Highway 27 South in 1934. The fence was mentioned in Dr. J.C. Bonner's book *Georgia's Last Frontier*. Bonner also wrote about a fox hunt along Shadinger's Ridge in which thirty-nine men and as many dogs participated.

His family and friends gathered at Emmaus Primitive Baptist Church, Carroll County, to pay tribute to him as a Veteran of the Civil War and placed a marker on his grave, May 19, 1985.

Billy Shadinger was born in 1857 in Cobb County, and he married Massuria Phillips (1861-1890) in 1885 in Carroll County. Ella Elizabeth and Joseph Ceaph were their children. Billy married again in 1892, Carroll County, to Burma Alberta Moore (1869-1948). Billy and Burma had the following children: Eva Alice, Susie Mae, Alberta Missouri, Willie Myrt, Fannie Lois, Eunice Velma, Mary Louise, Nellie Ruth, Georgia Watson, and James Shadinger. Billy told his wife when they were married that all the girls were his and she could have all the boys.

Billy and Burma's second child, Susie Mae, was born 1895 in Carroll County, and this is where she died in 1929. She married Lewis Garvey Denney (1890-1973) in 1914 and their children were Lewis Everette, born 1915; Merlin, born 1917; Bernard Awtry, born 1918; Annie Maureen, born 1920; Garvey Melvin, born 1923; Allene, born 1925; James Donald, born 1927, and Millard Fillmore, born 1929.

Susie Mae died when some of her children were very young and they cannot remember much about her, but the older children remember her to be a devoted mother to her children and a devoted wife to their father. They will never forget the way she let them know she would not be with them much longer. Just before she passed away she called the children to her bedside one by one. She asked them to be a good boy or good girl and kissed each one goodbye. The longer they live, the taller she gets for the heroic way she faced her death. She not only showed them how to live but also how to die.

John (75) and Ellen Jones (73) Shadinger in about 1901.

Several years after Susie Mae S. Denney died in 1929, Lewis Garvey Denney married Kathleen Wilson in 1935. She was a good homemaker and cared for the children as if they were her own. The grandchildren visited for a week at a time and had many happy times with Mama Denney, as they called her. They especially remember the delicious, little hot biscuits she baked for breakfast.

Everette joined the U.S. Navy and entered the service on October 27, 1941. He was assigned to the *USS Hughes* in the Pacific. He was a fire controlman first class and was discharged on October 15, 1945. Everette married Moena Lane in 1946 at Moena's aunt's house, Mrs. Alton Lane.

Merlin was born in 1917 and died in 1919. He went to the spring to get a drink of water for his mother and fell in and drowned. He had heard her say that she wanted a fresh drink of water.

Billy and Burma Shadinger in 1914 with their children.

Bernard married Alene Smith on December 20, 1942 in Heard County, Georgia, by Bernard's Uncle Alvin Gore. Alene is the daughter of Clark Smith (born 7-1-1891 in Carroll County and died 5-16-1972) and Minerva (Nervie) Herron (born 8-28-1895 in Heard County and died 12-31-1972). Bernard and Alene have three children: Peter Michael, born 12-29-1943 in Toccoa, Stevens County, Georgia; Cheryl Lynn, born 1-26-1948 in Toccoa, Stevens County; and Trudy Lori, born 2-1-1961 in Atlanta, Fulton County.

Bernard entered the Navy on June 20, 1944, and went to Camp Perry, Virginia, for basic training. He was stationed in New Orleans, Louisiana for a while. He was assigned to the *USSLST (United States Ship-Landing Ship Tank)* in the Pacific including Japan. Bernard returned to the States on the *USSLST 1068* and was discharged January 27, 1946.

Maureen Denney married Willard Quinton Jones (1920-1992) on September 16, 1992 in Atlanta, Georgia.

Melvin married Doris Truitt (1926-1991) on 1-6-1951 in Bowdon Junction, Carroll County. Melvin married Iva Robinson Benefield on 3-5-1993.

Allene married Charles Howell Vaughn Jr. (1925-1995) on June 6, 1947 in Atlanta.

Donald married Violette Harris on February 24, 1951, Carroll County.

Millard Fillmore was born April 29, 1929 and died June 29, 1929 in Carroll County. He only lived five days after his mother died.

Pictured left to right: Ruth, Mary, Susie Mae, Alberta, Willie Myrt, Lois, Eunice, (front) Billy, Norman, Burma, and Georgia. *Submitted by: Bernard Denney, 420 Denney Road, Carrollton, GA 30117 and Researched and written by Donald and Violette Denney*
Sources: Family and family records

1007. Shadrix - Hendrix

Thomas W. Shadrix was born in Coweta County, Georgia, in March 1854. He was the son of Marion R. Shadrix and Sarah Elizabeth Bryant. On October 4, 1874, in Coweta County, he married Elizabeth Jane Hendrix, the daughter of George W. Hendrix and Nancy Isabella McAlister. Elizabeth was born September 23, 1855, in Georgia, and died July 14, 1898, in Carroll County, and is buried in Shady Grove Baptist Church Cemetery.

George W. Shadrix, born June 29, 1875, in Coweta County, died May 7, 1927, Carroll County, who married Ola Matilda Rigsby on September 15, 1895, in Carroll County.

Robert Marion Shadrix, born June 11, 1879, in Coweta County, died February 8, 1945, in Carroll County, who married Ila Lenora Baxter on March 16, 1899. She was born May 24, 1881, in Carroll County, and died March 23, 1935. Both are buried in Shady Grove Baptist Church Cemetery. Their children were: Nellie Shadrix who married Grover C. Bradley; Dura Shadrix who married (1) Wade Cartwright and (2) David Hess; Haskell Newton Shadrix who married Luvie Jenette Griffis; Vester Washington Shadrix who married Ruby Carden; Annie Lee Shadrix who married Durell E. Rogers; Ollie Marion Shadrix who married Lois Margie Keaton; Selma James Shadrix who married Mary Estavanko; and Hattie Pearl Shadrix who married John Kocsis.

John Henry Shadrix, born January 31, 1881, in Coweta County, died December 11, 1968, in Carroll County, who married Ella Spence on September 13, 1908. She was born August 8, 1886, and died March 21, 1941. Both are buried in Abilene Baptist Church Cemetery.

Alton G. Shadrix, born February 23, 1884, in Carroll County, died December 4, 1961, in Carroll County, who married Mary Agnes McKensie. She was born February 7, 1885, and died May 25, 1971. They are buried in the Shady Grove Baptist Church Cemetery.

Lillie Belle Shadrix, born September 1887, in Carroll County. She married Walter N. Carter, on May 3, 1907, in Carroll County.

Thomas W. Shadrix second marriage was to Lela E. Camp on May 6, 1894, in Carroll County. She was born about 1860. They had one son, Samuel K. Shadrix, who was born June 10, 1902, and died December 1, 1968, who married Vera Parrish on August 11, 1926, in Carroll County.

Thomas W. Shadrix third marriage was to Nannie Bevins on August 1, 1906, in Carroll County. No children were born.

Thomas died before 1920 and is probably buried in Shady Grove Baptist Church Cemetery in an unmarked grave. *Submitted by: Gerald Shadrix, 80 Bivins Road, Villa Rica, GA 30180*
Sources: Research of Census, Marriage and Cemetery Records by Erlene Boyd

1008. Hiram Sharp

One of the early settlers of Carroll County (before the county was organized in 1826) was Hiram Sharp. He accumulated and owned a large tract of land. He lived well as a farmer. He was the father of George S. and Hiram Sharp Jr. He homesteaded three thousand acres of land and as times got "hard," he would sell some land.

In the 1800s, there was a school on the Sharp property near where the present school is located near Sharp's Creek. This land was formerly occupied by the Cherokee Indians.

Franklin Jackson Sharp was born on June 25, 1863. He married Ida Spence, who was born on November 11, 1874. They had ten children. The house where they lived still remains on the south side of Sharp's Creek.

There is a Sharp burial ground located on the property overlooking the Sharp Creek Lake. *Submitted by: Lynette Sharp Gibson, 165 Ho-Lynn Trail, Carrollton, GA 30117*

1009. Sharp - Williams - Brown - Lassetter

People to whom I am related started coming to Carroll County even before the county was organized. One of the first was Hiram Sharp, born in Maryland 18 November 1787. Hiram was brought to Augusta by his mother and her two brothers while he was still a baby. He later married Sarah Anne Owen who was born in Maryland in 1786.

They lived in Morgan County for a time, then moved to a location south of what is now Temple and took up land in 1825. He was fondly known as Uncle Hiram in those parts. The Sharp Middle School now stands on their land. Their daughter, Elizabeth Sharp, married my great grandfather, William Williams, who owned land near Bay Springs Creek south of Villa Rica. They are buried one half mile east of Highway 61 on Bay Springs Road.

William's father, Leroy Williams, was born in Rutherford County, North Carolina, in 1791. He was the son of Revolutionary War soldier William Williams and William's wife Nancy Middleton. Leroy came to Georgia by way of Jasper County where he married LuDicey Kelly. The couple moved to Carroll County in the 1830s. Leroy owned land near his son and he and LuDicey are buried in the Williams Cemetery on the Bay Springs Road.

William and Elizabeth's son, John Worth Williams, born 27 October 1847, married a lady from Whitesburg. She was Martha Caldonia (Lasseter) Williams, born 22 December 1852, my grandmother. Martha's father was William Lassetter, born 6 March 1814, a farmer near Whitesburg. Her mother was Parthenia Brown, born 8 June 1821. William's father was Benjamin Cheadle Lassetter born in North Carolina 10 December 1778, and his mother was Elizabeth Hill born 17 February 1788. Benjamin served in the War of 1812. Benjamin's father was Tobias Lasseter, born 1738 in Chowan County, North Carolina. Tobias is listed as a Patriot in the Daughters of the Revolution Patriot's Handbook. Tobias' wife was Sarah B. Northern, reported to have been an Indian.

As mentioned above, William Lassetter's wife was Parthenia Brown, daughter of John George Washington Brown, who was born in Kershaw County, South Carolina, on 21 March 1784. He married Sara Carruthers, born 18 May 1790. This couple came to Carroll County early in the 1800s. They settled near the Chattahoochee and are buried in the old Lassetter Cemetery near the river. *Submitted by: Dr. William G. Mitchell, 55 Goldworth Road, Villa Rica, GA 30180*

1010. Sheffield Sweep

Anyone traveling down Shady Grove road in rural Carroll County will be impressed by the number of mailbox stands of all shapes and sizes that can be seen, but the old mule drawn cultivator holding the Sheffield's mailbox probably has more history behind it than any other in the county — not everyone has a Sheffield Sweep holding their mailbox. Marvin Sheffield (10/08/1910-2/9/1980) did not invent the attachment for holding mailboxes, he invented it to help farmers who had to work rough, rocky land. In Marvin Sheffield's words, he used the sweep "on the roughest farms in Carroll County for three years." From its humble beginnings in a small blacksmith shop to its use even today, the Sheffield Sweep has left its mark in Georgia agriculture history with a production of around forty years.

Sheffield Sweep

Marvin Sheffield's invention did not come to him in a dream, but instead through hours of hard work plowing his father's (W.J. Sheffield) fields in 1934. Cotton was still a major crop in the South at this time so it was grown along with a small amount of corn. While the cotton plants were young, weeds and grass in the middles between the rows had to be cleared away. This was usually done with a cultivator, a multi-toothed mule drawn plow.

When the cultivator was pulled through the rows by the mule it would bump along through the rocks where it would either drag rocks up on the plants damaging them, or else it would drag on top of rocks leaving grass and weeds still in the ground. Marvin needed some way to clear the rocks away from the plants in order to have a smooth area to drag the cultivator on. Someone has said that inventions are born of necessity, and for Marvin this was a time of necessity.

Marvin and his wife, Myrtle Houston Sheffield moved to a farm of their own and there he built his own blacksmith shop. Work on the attachment was trial and error, working the fields with it, making changes on it in the shop, and then back to the fields again. When the sweep was finally perfected to Marvin's satisfaction, he called it the Sheffield Sweep because it would sweep rocks and chunks of dirt out of the way of the cultivator teeth where the teeth could then do their job of digging up grass and weeds. After using his invention in his own fields, Marvin decided he might have a product that other farmers might like to buy. Farming was a common occupation during the 1930s, and rough, rocky fields were just as common for most farmers.

A patent was finally obtained on March 16, 1937. Blanton Plow Company in Rome, Georgia, agreed to manufacture the Sheffield Sweep and market it, paying Marvin fifty cents commission for each one sold.

As tractors became more readily available to farmers, Marvin perfected a tractor drawn sweep and a patent was finally received on February 7, 1956. *Submitted by: Marvin Sheffield's grandson, John M. Latimer, 1356 Oak Grove Rd., Temple, GA 30179*
Source: This is an excerpt from a Georgia History assignment which John researched and wrote as an assignment at West Georgia College.

1011. Myrtle Houston Sheffield

Myrtle Sheffield was correspondent to the *Times-Georgian* for Shady Grove Baptist Church for many years from the 1960s to the 1990s.

Annie Myrtle Houston was born 10/10/09, the first child of Tom and Sallie Fannie Gladney Houston. Other children were Charles (7/12/1912-1991), Opal (4/27/1918-3/17/1985), Frank (4/4/1924-12/12/1977), Hazel (10/02/1920).

Myrtle married Marvin Jacob Sheffield 3/19/1933. Charles married Doris Duncan, Hazel married George Adel Beard, Opal married Henry Dooley (Shep) Sheffield, Frank married Myra Prince.

Charles Thomas (Tom) Houston's (3/19/1885-5/10/1957) parents were Thomas Oliver (11/19/1857-5/17/1901) and Martha Anna Arrington Houston (10/21/1864-5/7/1922). They married 12/06/1908. Thomas and Martha's children were Charles Thomas, William Rufus, Matilda Kate, Annie Lee, Mary Valentine, Tempie Oliver, Lucy Russell, Emily Kansas, and Louise Gertrude. Thomas Oliver's parents were William and Mahala Catherine Pearson Houston.

Charles Thomas and Fannie Houston with Annie Myrtle

Sallie Fannie Gladney Houston was the daughter of Leila Rhodes and John Anderson Gladney. John's parents were Limael M. and Francis C. Knight Gladney. John and Leila's children were Sallie Fannie, Maude, Minnie, Callie, Berta, Robert, Roy, Johnny B., and Willie.

My grandmother, Myrtle Houston Sheffield (10/10/1909-6/7/1997) wrote to my brother, John Latimer, when he was in elementary school at Sand Hill when he had an assignment to find out how schools were in his grandparents' day.

> "I'll try to tell you some things about my early school. In my first school we had four grades in the same room. When we had our classes we had long benches at the front of the room and that is where we came to read or have math (arithmetic then) We always stood in a line for our spelling class and spelled aloud telling the meanings.
>
> We had one big heater to heat the large room. We burned wood and sometimes coal. We had no water coolers. The larger children would bring two buckets and sit them in the room. All of us had an individual drinking cup and if you were lucky you'd get a drink at recess or lunch.
>
> We carried our lunch in a small basket with two handles.
>
> My first year Uncle Bob Gladney stayed with us because we lived about three miles from school and I was afraid to walk alone. We walked through the woods part of the way.
>
> At school we made little play houses and the boys would run through them and tear them down.
>
> When I was older, we would play on bales of cotton near the school yard. By this time we lived about 2½ miles from school. The ground would be frozen and we would walk on the frozen banks. When it rained sometimes we would wade in the ditches on side of road. When it sleeted as it did often our clothes would be frozen when we arrived at our destination.
>
> Our teacher's punishment was using a switch of a hickory tree, sometimes writing words missed in spelling 100 times or more."

Submitted by: Gary M. Latimer, 47 Jennifer Lane, Carrollton, GA

1012. William Joseph Sheffield

William Joseph "Joe" Sheffield was born in Douglas County, Georgia, on 19 June 1870, the son of John Brantley (1844-1904) and Ritha (Carnes Polk) (1837-1919) Sheffield. The part of Douglas County where they lived was once a part of Carroll County.

On 6 January 1890 in Douglas County, William Joseph married Lula Jane Keaton, daughter of Henry Hendon Keaton (1845) and Margaret Cansler (1841). In 1904, William Joseph, Lula Jane and their eleven children traveled by wagon from Douglas County to the Shady Grove area of Carroll County. They had several more children to make a total of fourteen.

William Joseph always told that he would never own any slave, he would raise his own and he did. He farmed for a living by raising crops. He was a carpenter in the off-season. It is told that he helped to build the round barn at Hickory Level. His children by Lula were Effie Leola (1890), Homer Jackson (1891), Johnnie B. (1892), Cora Ann (1893), Myrtie Elizazbeth (1895), Addie Lenora (1896), Rilla Mae (1897), Henry Dooley (1899), Dana Zelma (1901), Maydell Hester (1902), Raymond Joseph (1904), Jennie Florence (1906), Lois Madgelene (1909), and Marvin Jacob (1910). After his wife's death on 20 September 1938, Joe married a much younger lady, Bonzie Presnal on 25 December 1938 in Carroll County. This union produced three children, Rayford Allen (1939), Lavy Joe (1941), and Olin Dale (1945).

Joe and Bonzie live on Stewart Street in Carrollton. On his eighty-first birthday, Joe celebrated this occasion with fifteen living children. These children ranged in age from five to sixty-one. Joe was especially proud of the achievement of his son Marvin who invented the "Sheffield Sweep" to go on a cultivator. Marvin made a model of his sweep out of tobacco cans and sent it to Washington for a patent.

Marvin married Annie Myrtle Houston on 20 March 1933 in Carroll County. She was the daughter of Thomas Oliver Houston and Sallie Fannie Gladney. Marvin and Myrtle lived for a short time in Rome. However, they returned here to live out the rest of their lives. They reared three children: Annie Joyce (1940), Steve Houston (1948), and Janet Annice (1954) in the Shady Grove community.

William Joseph Sheffield Family

The photograph shows Effie, Homer, Cora, Myrtie, Addie, and Rilla on the back row. Hester, William Joseph, Lula holding Raymond, Henry, and Zelma are on the front row.

Joe died 22 July 1953 and is buried beside Lula at the Shady Grove Baptist Church Cemetery. *Submitted by: Chris Sheffield, 80 Martin Sheffield Drive, Carrollton, GA 30116*

1013. The John Shelnut Family

The history of the early Shelnut family was written by Nathaniel (Nat) Shelnut, a judge and one of the founders of Bowdon, Georgia. His grandfather, John Shelnut, came to America from Germany. It is thought that John's wife's name was Catherine. John had five sons and two daughters. They were George, Thomas, Henry, William, Andrew, Barbara, and Katie. George and Thomas fought in the Revolutionary War. Thomas died as a soldier, and George was taken prisoner by the British forces and taken to Nova Scotia. He was later discharged from the army in South Carolina but returned to Nova Scotia to live. Henry married Mary Bell and settled in Edgefield County, South Carolina. William married Rachel Ferguson and settled in Walton County, Georgia. They had seven sons and two daughters.

Andrew, the fifth son of John Shelnut, married Elizabeth Gentry about 1797 in Franklin County, Georgia. They lived in Franklin County, Georgia; Edgefield District, South Carolina; Abbeville District, South Carolina; Elbert County, Georgia; and finally settled in Fayette County, Georgia, about two miles west of the present city of Fairburn. Andrew was born April 15, 1772, in Ninety-Six District, South Carolina, and died October 15, 1825 in Fayette County, Georgia. Elizabeth Gentry Shelnut was born March 11, 1775, in South Carolina and died March 16, 1854, in Carroll County, Georgia. She was living with her son, Andrew J. Shelnut, in Carroll County in the 1850 census.

Andrew and Elizabeth had thirteen children. They were John, Rebecca, William, Lavina, David, Thomas, Polly D., Susannah (Susan), (see related Lindsey Holland family story.) Laura, Elizabeth, Andrew Joseph, Henry, and Nathaniel (Nat), author of the history of the early Shelnut family in America. John, Susan, and Andrew Joseph all moved to Carroll County.

John, the oldest son of Andrew and Elizabeth, was married for about a year to a woman whose name was unknown. He moved to North Carolina and married Elizabeth White about 1821. Elizabeth was born January 21, 1797, in North Carolina. John and Elizabeth had eleven children. They were Thomas Pink born June 15, 1822; Eatha

Malinda born February 17, 1824; Harriet; Joseph David born August 21, 1826; Mariah born October 2, 1828; John Jr. born September 1, 1830; William born September 1, 1832; Amanda C. born September 23, 1835; Lavina born September 23, 1835; Susan E. born July 14, 1838; and Nancy Jane born March 23, 1840. Elizabeth died October 4, 1840, in Campbell County, Georgia. John then married Edna (unknown) Cochran Miller January 10, 1841, in Campbell County, Georgia. Edna was born about 1810 in South Carolina. John and Edna had three children. They were James Henry born January 4, 1842; Mary H. born July 18, 1843; and Rebecca Saphronia born December 4, 1844.

Edna had a son, John William Miller, born December 4, 1827, and a daughter Carolina Cochran, born October 22, 1832, by her previous marriages.

John Shelnut died July 8, 1879, and Edna died May 18, 1883, near Waco, Georgia. *Submitted by: Larry W. Holland, 222 County Road 383, Dutton, AL 35744*
Sources: Census, land, marriage, cemetery, and court records in Fayette, Carroll, and Haralson County, Georgia; *Histories of the Holland and Shelnut Families* by Fred Simpson; *The Shelnutt Book of Records* by Jane (Cobb) Shelnutt; and *The Miller Family Tree* by Brett L. Whiteside.

1014. Nancy Catherine Shelnutt

Nancy Catherine Shelnutt was the grandniece of Judge Nathaniel Shelnutt who founded the town of Bowdon, Georgia. Nancy Catherine's great-grandfather, John Shelnutt, and Nathaniel Shelnutt were brothers. John was the oldest child of Andrew J. Shelnutt and Elizabeth Gentry and Nathaniel was the youngest.

Andrew J. Shelnutt was born 15 April 1772 in South Carolina and died 15 October 1825 in Fayette County, Georgia. He married Elizabeth Gentry about 1797 in Franklin County, Georgia. Elizabeth was born 11 March 1775 in South Carolina and died 16 March 1854 in Carroll County, Georgia. The children of Andrew and Elizabeth are John, Rebecca, William, Lavina, David, Thomas, Polly, Susannah, Laura, Elizabeth, Andrew Joseph, Henry and Nathaniel.

Nancy Catherine Shelnutt 1851-1892

John Shelnutt Sr., grandfather of Nancy Catherine Shelnutt, was born 02 November 1798 in Franklin County, Georgia and died 08 July 1879 near Waco, Haralson County Georgia. He married Elizabeth White 25 December 1819 in North Carolina. Their children, Thomas, Etta, Harriett, Joseph David, John Jr. and Mariah were born there. They moved to Georgia where Amanda, Lavina, Susan and Nancy Jane were born. Elizabeth died 04 October 1840 in Campbell County, Georgia and John married Edna Miller Cochran, a widow. By her first marriage Edna had a son, John Miller, born about 1829 and by her second marriage she had a daughter, Carolina Cochran, born 22 October 1832. Edna and John Shelnutt Sr. had three children, James H., Rebecca S., and Mary.

Nancy Catherine Shelnutt's father, Joseph David Shelnutt, was born 21 April 1826 in North Carolina, he married Mary P. Jones 29 September 1847 in Fayette County, Georgia. They had five children, Susanne, Nancy Catherine, Mary, John Henry and Joseph Andrew. The last child was born July 1858. Mary must have died during or shortly after the birth of the last child. All of Joseph David's children were under the age of ten when he married Elizabeth Ann Thompson on August 31, 1859. Joseph David died in 1887.

Nancy Catherine, the second child of Joseph David Shelnutt and Mary P. Jones, was born in June of 1851 in Campbell County, Georgia. She was married to Talton Washington Lovvorn 25 December 1870 in Haralson County, Georgia. Nancy Catherine and Wash, as he was called, were married at the home of Nancy's grandfather, John Shelnutt, by the Rev. L.N. Holland who was a cousin to Wash. They attended Bethlehem Methodist Church about four miles north of Waco. Nancy Catherine and Talton Washington Lovvorn had seven children, two of whom died as infants. The other children were Mary Malinda, Queen Victoria, Joseph Edgar, James Talton, and John William. Joseph Edgar Lovvorn married in Carroll County to Roxie Jane McMullen, James Talton Lovvorn and his family lived in Carroll County and he is buried there. John William Lovvorn died in Carroll County and is buried in Cleburne County, Alabama. *Submitted by: Kathryn Lovvorn Butler, P.O. Box 867, Guin, AL 35563*

1015. Amos Shepard Family

Amos Shepard was born in 1813 in South Carolina, and he died in 1870 in Gilmer County, Georgia. His wife's name was Elizabeth, and she was born in 1813 in Georgia and died after 1870. Nine children were born to this union: John W. Shepard was born in 1832 in North Carolina and died after 1907. He married Mary Stancel on January 18, 1854. Elizabeth C. Shepard, who married Tom Ellison, was born about 1837 in North Carolina and died after 1870. Alford W. Shepard was born August 1, 1838, in Georgia and died on May 3, 1918. He married Sarah T. Bramlett on March 24, 1859. She was born September 27, 1844, and died December, 1926. William L. Shepard was born about 1841 in Georgia and died in 1880. He married Margaret Cloninger who was born about 1838 and died after 1880. Charles A. Shepard was born about 1843 in Georgia and he died after 1880. His wife's name was Louisa. Zemicah "Zemery" Shepard was born June 5, 1845 in Georgia and died September 16, 1920. He married Mary Alice Reese on November 19, 1871. She was born January 30, 1844, and died February 16, 1916. Memory Shepard (twin to Zemery) was born June 5, 1845, in Georgia and died in the Civil War. Benjamin Shepard was born in August, 1848, in Georgia and he died in 1901. He married Malinda J. Sutton on August 17, 1879. She was born in 1850 and died in 1936. Thomas W. Shepard was born in Georgia in 1850 and died after 1880. He married Mary J. Wright on January 30, 1872. She was born about 1853 and died in 1902. Anna M. Shepard, who married John Reece, was born about 1852 in Georgia and died in 1870.

Most all of Amos Shepard's children are buried in Gilmer County, Georgia, in the Mt. Vernon Church Cemetery. Amos was the great-great grandfather of William Hugh Shepard, a former resident of Temple, Georgia, for forty years. He was also the great-great-great grandfather of Gail (Mrs. Dennis) Shepard Conner of Temple, Georgia. *Submitted by: Gail Connor, P.O. Box 185, Temple, GA 30179*
Source: Census records of Gilmer County, Georgia

1016. Zemery Shepard and Mary Alice Reece

Zemery Shepard, son of Amos and Elizabeth Shepard, was born June 5, 1845, in Georgia and died September 16, 1920. Zemery married Mary Alice Reece on November 19, 1871. She was born January 30, 1844, and died February 16, 1916. They are buried in Freindship Baptist Church Cemetery, Braswell Mt. Road, Paulding County, Georgia. Zemery and Mary had seven children. The first five were born in Gilmer County, Georgia.

Hulda was born September 10, 1872, and died September 14, 1877. She is buried in Gilmer County.

John William Shepard was born May 17, 1874, and died May 27, 1954. He married Lorrinda Elsberry on May 23, 1897. She died in 1898. John then married Nancy Hicks on August 27, 1899. She was born February 4, 1877 and died September 24, 1941. They had eight children.

Sarah Jane Shepard was born January 2, 1876, and died January 25, 1945. She married Joseph Raliegh Camp on November 27, 1898. He was born July 3, 1876, and died January 25, 1965. They had eleven children.

Zemery and Mary Alice Reece Shepard

James Alford Shepard was born December 15, 1877, and died April 29, 1953. He married Margret Hicks on December 19, 1898, and they had one daughter. Margret died in January of 1903. He then married Vida Tant on July 12, 1908. She was born July 28, 1891, and died September 15, 1987. They had nine children.

Rufus Quiler Shepard was born March 7, 1880, and died April 3, 1961. He married Loudie Frances Hicks on February 4, 1906. She was born April 14, 1887, and died October 23, 1975. They had eleven children.

Mary Alice Shepard was born April 3, 1882, and died June 4, 1962. She married John Blalock who was born May 30, 1881, and died June 4, 1965. They had eleven children.

Savannah E. Shepard was born September 23, 1884, and died October 6, 1966. She married Minor F. Meadows on April 10, 1910. He was born December 24, 1874, and died October 9, 1940. They had six children.

In the fall of 1880, Zemery and Mary loaded all their belongings, themselves, and four children on a one-horse covered wagon and a two-wheeled cart pulled by little steer and headed south from Gilmer County to Paulding County, Georgia, and settled in the Braswell Mountains. They hired to pick cotton on their way down. John William Shepard, who was six years old at the time, remembered having to drive the cart. *Submitted by: William Hugh Shepard, 1429 Crossroads Church Road, Rockmart, GA 30153*
Sources: Family records, Gilmer County census, Grave markers, and talking with many cousins.

1017. Sherrill Family

Adam Sherrill forded the Catawba River into North Carolina from Virginia in 1747 into Indian territory. He was the first white settler of the Catawba River. This site was named Sherrill's

Ford. Adam had eight children, with the last child named Moses Sherrill. Moses had four children, with the last child called Michael Sherrill. Michael Sherrill is the father of Henry William Sherrill.

Henry William Sherrill moved from Sherrill's Ford to Forsyth County, Georgia. Henry was captured during the Battle of Gettysburg on Culp's Hill in the 2nd North Carolina Infantry Battalon. Later, he escaped, but was recaptured in an area sixty miles from Gettysburg. Then he was sent to prison in Delaware, probably where he died since his family never heard from him again.

Henry's son, Joseph, and wife, Sophronia, moved to Bowdon in 1893, leaving their widowed mothers, who had lost their husbands in the Civil War, to live in a tenant house on the Lipham farm. They had six children: Robert, Wilbur, Bright, Joe, Elie, and Ivey. These sons were the children of a tenant farmer, but each of them eventually had their own farms. On their farms, they had twenty-six children.

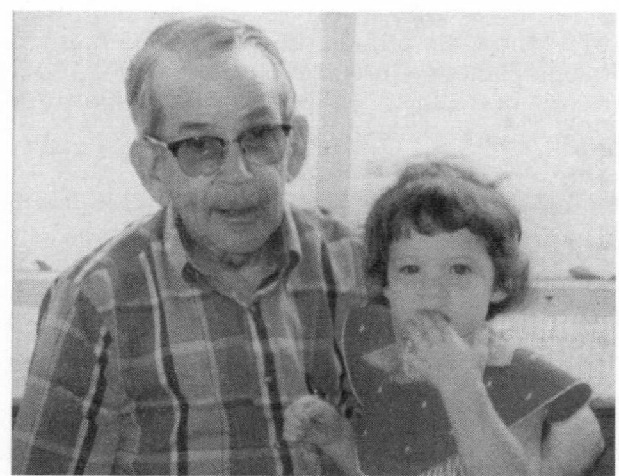

Lewis Sherrill and granddaughter, Alexandria Garrard, at 1992 Sherrill Reunion

My grandfather Joe, (Joseph Julius), reared the largest family on his Reavesville Road farm. He and my grandmother had nine children: Wayne, Mary, Martha, Joe Max, Shirley, Marion, Reuben, Lewis, and Billy. My grandmother was Florence Thornton. My father, Lewis Sherrill, and mother, Eva Whitman Sherrill, live in my grandparents' home where I was reared, along with my sisters, Mary Ann and Lucy. My daughter Alex (Alexandria Thornton Garrard) is the fifth generation to live in the Bowdon area.

This summer in August (2001) the Sherrills will gather at Shiloh Campground in the Burwell community for the seventy-second reunion of Joseph and Sophronia Sherrill's children. The first reunion was in 1929 to celebrate my grandfather's birthday. We decided at the party to have an annual reunion, which continues today.

Joseph and Sophronia Sherrill and Joseph (Joe) and Florence Sherrill are buried at First United Methodist Church Cemetery in Bowdon. *Submitted by: Penelope Sherrill Garrard, 173 North Carroll Street, Bowdon, GA 30108, with a debt of gratitude to our family historian, Uncle Shirley Sherrill, of Santa Barbara, California.*

1018. Henry Lewis Shiflett

Henry Lewis Shiflett was born on June 7, 1842, in Elbert County Georgia. Shortly before the Civil War began, the family relocated to Gordon County. In October of 1880, Lewis purchased 202 ½ acres in land lot 250 of the 9th district of Carroll County, from S.B. Seay of Bartow County. This land was in the area known today as Blackjack Mountain.

From his home in Gordon County, Lewis loaded a wagon with his wife, children, and all their possessions and headed south. His father's family had been devastated by Sherman's union troops as they engaged the Confederate Army in battle upon his own farm. Throughout the next three decades, Lewis would struggle to raise and care for his five sons and two daughters. The years of reconstruction after the war were very hard on families as they pulled together all of their resources just to survive. Many companies gained advantage over families by loaning money against their property of which many were unable to pay back, therefore forcing a foreclosure against them. Lewis was one of many to lose their farms to The New England Mortgage and Security Company of Suffolk County, Massachusetts. By the late 1800s, two of Lewis's sons, Edgar L. and George E. Shiflett, had purchased farms of their own and the family continued. But in 1902 Lewis's marriage to Marrietta L. Clemmons was over. Lewis left Georgia for Alabama and re-married Monte (Mott) Calhoun Dourough. (Mrs. Dourough's granddaughter, Mrs. Margaret Entrekin and her family have been lifelong residents of Carroll County) This marriage union produced two more sons, Marion Bass and Melvin Shiflett. Lewis died on December 31, 1913, leaving behind two families — one in Georgia and one in Alabama. He is buried with a good many friends and kinfolk at Pleasant Grove Baptist Church on Highway 5.

In April of 1910, Lewis's son (my grandfather) William Augusuts (Gus) Shiflett, died leaving a freshly planted crop to be tended by his widow and children. In the early 1920s, after my grandmother Mary Etta re-married a Mr. McClendon, the family relocated to a ninety acre farm in Tift County. All of my father's (Newton Milton Shiflett) family except his oldest sister, Millie Orie Shiflett, would leave Carroll County. Aunt Orie married John Willis Kelley and remained in Carroll County all of her life. Their daughter-in-law, Rena Day Kelley, her youngest daughter Pam Fuller and her family still reside here.

Lewis's youngest daughter, Emily Elizabeth married James Jethro Owensby in the early 1900s. Great-aunt "Ema's" youngest daughter, Mrs. Allie Myrtella Owensby Robison, her husband Mr. William Jefferson (Roy) Robison and their beautiful family are also still residing in Carroll County.

The Shiflett family spent only a few years here and their name is now gone. However, their roots took and have grown deep into the soil of this beautiful county. The memories I have as a child from my visits here are locked away inside me in a special place that I visit often. Every Mother's Day was a long awaited event. Our family would come together again as we did each year and meet for "Decoration Day" at Pleasant Grove Church, where we would place flowers on family graves, listen to "Ole fashion preachin," and you know, I believe I can still smell that dinner on the ground! *Submitted by: K. Michael Shiflett, P.O. Box 1431, Carrollton, GA 30117*

1019. Jesse Bryan Silvey Family

Jesse Bryan Silvey was born about 1815 in Jackson County, Georgia, and died in 1886 in Carroll County, Georgia. He married Jane B. Hanson, born 18 August 1820 in Morgan County, Georgia, died 1888 in Carroll County. Both are buried in marked graves in Indian Creek Cemetery in Bowdon, Georgia. Jane was the daughter of Reuben Crawford Hanson, born 1790-1800 in Fauquier County, Virginia, and Margaret "Peggy" Jones.

Jesse Bryan Silvey was the son of Drewry Silvey, born 1780 in South Carolina, and is first found in Georgia in the 1805 Tax List of Greene County. Drewry Silvey's spouse was Margaret "Mary" Ann Womack born 12 July 1793 in Georgia and died 1864. They were married in Oglethorpe County, Georgia, on 16 February 1805. Drewry won land in the 1805 Land Lottery in Jackson County where the family moved. In 1818, the area they were living in became Gwinnett County. The Silveys then moved to Campbell County around 1828 and remained there until their death. Drewry died in 1860. Both he and Mary are buried in the Silvey Family Cemetery located between Fairburn and Campbellton just off Hall Road. Their graves have markers placed there by granddaughter Katie Silvey Speer.

Jesse Bryan had the following brothers and sisters: 1. George Washington Silvey born 1809 and died 3 July 1861; married first to Mary Davis; married second to Sarah Bachellor on 28 November 1836. 2. Milly Silvey born 1811; married John Prichard. 3. Elizabeth Charlotte "Charity" born 1813 and died 1862; married James Jones. 4. John Silvey, born 21 December 1817 and died 3 March 1897; married Nancy Adeline Dougherty. 5. Mary Caroline Eleanor "Ellie" born 1819 and died May 1884; married first to William Wells, married second to E.W. Munday. 6. Emily born 1820 and died 1894; married Eli Tillinger Hunnicutt. 7. Joseph C. Silvey born 1824. 8. Martin Drewry born 1828; married Lucinda Cates.

Jane's parents came to Campbell County, Georgia, from Morgan County, Georgia. Reuben's father, Jesse, came to Georgia sometime in the late 1795 from Fauquier County, Virginia. Reuben's grandfather was Robert Hanson (sometimes spelled Henson) who died in 1802 in Fauquier County, leaving a will naming all his living children. Jane had the following sisters and brothers: 1. Nancy born 29 November 1818 and died before 1870; married Richard Bearden. 2. Sally born 3 April 1822 and died 4 November 1822. 3. Elizabeth born 17 October 1823 and died 16 October 1827. 4. Mahala born 6 January 1826 and died after 1880; married Lewis Odom about 1843. 5. Henry Butler born 20 February 1828 and died 5 August 1897; married Sarah H. Stewart, born 26 March 1828. 6. Mary born 30 March 1830; married Martin R. Boon, born 1830. 7. Margaret born 3 June 1832; married E.Z. Lambert (Lamberth). 8. Reuben Crawford Jr. born 15 May 1834 and died 11 September 1909; married Caldonia "Donia" Bearden about 1852. 9. William W. Hanson born 14 March 1836. 10. John Jesse Hanson born 14 March 1840 and died 19 May 1914; married Sara Arkansas Vines, 11 March 1869. 11. James Frances Marion born 1 January 1848 and died 28 August 1945; married Almodia "Mede" Childress in 1869.

Reuben Crawford Hanson was born about 1793 and died 20 November 1848. Margaret "Peggy" Jones Hanson was born about 1797 and died about 1870. They are buried in the Jones Family Cemetery on the right side of the road just into Douglas County on the southern boundary of Consolation Baptist Church and Dingles Crossroads. Their graves are unmarked. Reuben C. Hanson (listed as Henson) served two tours of duty in the 2nd Regiment (Jenkins) Georgia Volunteers and Militia.

Jesse and Jane Silvey had the following children: 1. William Drewry born 1837 and died from disease during Civil War; married Mary Holland Pitts. 2. Mary Jane born 1836 and died 1854; married Edward Bearden. 3. Reuben born about 1841 and died at a young age being killed accidentally by a mill gate. 4. John Henry born 28 November 1844 and died 16 October 1919; married Caroline "Carrie" Rebecca Pesnell on 4 November 1869. 5. Francis Napoleon "Polie" born 1853; married Julie E. Tyler in 1880.

Following William Drewry's death, Jesse and Jane opened their home to their son's children. Mary Silvey, being a very young widow, married again and had other children. William Drury's children remained with their grandparents who unselfishly accepted the responsibility of their training and care. The 1860 census reveals that

Josephine Bearden, age six, was also in the Silvey household and may have lived with them a while following the death of her mother, Mary.

We have no record of just when Jesse and Jane arrived in Carroll County but it is believed that it was probably sometime in 1856. Jesse was a farmer but he evidently had other talents as records in 1863 and 1864 Carroll County give his occupation as a shoemaker. This skill may have been born out of necessity during the war years when goods were in short supply and shoes had to be repaired instead of being replaced.

Though Jesse never realized any financial gain from any of his inventions, he enjoyed spending time in the pursuit of creating a useful discovery that might or might not be commercially profitable. Jesse was found dead in the stables where he had been caring for the horses reportedly belonging to his brother, John Silvey, who owned a well-known dry good business in Atlanta.

One of the family legends about Jane is that she enjoyed dipping snuff. This was not an uncommon practice in years past and was even considered fashionable during one period in America. This habit probably contributed to Jane's death which resulted from cancer of the mouth.

Both Jesse and Jane demonstrated their love and giving-spirit to both their children and grandchildren. Before they died in the 1880s, they deeded their property to be equally divided among their children and grandchildren. *Submitted by: Barbara Barton, 102 Ridgewood Road, Conroe, TX 77304-1729*

Sources: Family records, census records, tax records, land records, probate records. War of 1812 Service records. *Carroll County Genealogical Quarterly,* Hanson Family Bible, *Westbrook and Allied Families,* research of Margaret Hanson Hill of Fairburn, Georgia, and Barbara Barton's personal research.

1020. George and Doris Jackson Simpkins

George David Simpkins was born and grew up in the big community of Clem, Georgia. He is the son of David Appleton and Mary Ethel (Key) Simpkins. George has two sisters, Clara Banks and Margaret Dickens, and one brother, Carl Appleton Simpkins. His father was a farmer and a carpenter.

As a young boy George and his family traveled in a horse and wagon to attend Mt. Pleasant Baptist Church. Of course, the roads were not paved then, so that made for a bumpy ride. They had to walk to school back then, and George recalls how he would bribe his sisters all the way home from school not to tell his parents he got a spanking at school. Teachers were allowed to spank pupils who misbehaved back in those days.

George graduated from Whitesburg High School in 1942. He joined the navy, serving on the aircraft carrier *USS Bennington* as a radar operator. After the war he studied electronics and became a radio repairman with Mac's Radio Shop on the square in Carrollton. In about two years when television came out, they started installing and repairing them. In 1949 George married Doris Kathleen Jackson and they moved to Bremen to start his own business which lasted about forty years; he retired in 1988.

George and Doris attended the First Baptist Church, Bremen, where George is an ordained deacon.

Doris is the daughter of Robert Loyd and Alice Mae Rooks Jackson. "Pop Loyd" and "Mama Mae" as they were called by all who knew them, lived in the Shady Grove area of Carroll County, attending Shady Grove Baptist Church. Pop was one of the oldest deacons there when he passed away at age eighty-five. After he retired from Jackson Brother's Garage, he began restoring old model cars in a garage next to his home. This was his life. He told about several famous race car drivers who came to see him. Mama Mae sold Avon for fifteen years in the country area where they lived.

George and Doris had two children. Robert David Simpkins is married to Mary Ann Whitton, with one son, Robert Aaron who is married to Jane Deetanna. George and Doris's daughter Velecia (Lecia) Ann is married to Garven Daryl Sellers. They have four children: (1) Justin Eric is married to Kerry Marriott. They live in Carroll County and are expecting their first child in November. (2) Wendy Alison is married to Chris Bennett; they live in Bremen. (3) Courtney Elizabeth Sellers is attending Carroll Tech and studying nursing. (4) Mary Kathleen Sellers will start Chattahoochee Tech taking graphic design in the fall.

I guess this covers the Simpkins, Key, Jackson, and Rooks families that grew up in the great Carroll County. *Submitted by: Doris Jackson Simpkins, 330 Lakeview Drive, Bremen, GA 30110.*

1021. Rufus Alvis Singleton

Rufus Alvis Singleton was born 20 February 1873 in Alabama, son of Webster A. (1841) and Mary Elizabeth Roberson (1853) Singleton. In Alabama, he met and married Beulah Sarah Fletcher on 20 June 1897. After the birth of their first four children, they moved to Carroll County to live out the rest of their lives. Rufus Singleton worked for the railroad that traveled through Bowdon until he retired. During retirement, he took up farming for making a living until his death on 10 May 1935. He is buried at the Bowdon Methodist Church Cemetery.

Rufus and Beulah Singleton

Better known as "Big Mama," Beulah Sarah Fletcher Singleton (1878-1972) was the daughter of Robert Monroe Fletcher (1850-1893) and Mary Elizabeth Brown (1849-1921), granddaughter of James Monroe Fletcher (1816-1904) and Sarah Roundtree Hanes (1822-1895). Beulah died at the age of ninety-four on 28 September 1972 and is buried at the Bowdon Methodist Church Cemetery.

Rufus and Beulah had nine daughters: (1) Minnie Lee married Robert King Robertson, (2) Willie Mae married Lake M. Tarpley, (3) Myrtle Eunice married Fred Musick, (4) Delia Vanny married George W. Lowry, (5) Alice Mae (twin) married Ben Smith and Fleet Hester, (6) Eula Alma (twin) married Bert Calhoun, (7) Nell Margaret married Charlie Calhoun, (8) Nannie Elizabeth married Lloyd Smith and Jess Jackson, and (9) Angie married Jeff Calhoun. *Submitted by: Vicky Sheffield, 1276 Sand Hill-Shady Grove Road, Carrollton, GA 30116*

1022. Skinner Family

Part 1

Isaac H. Skinner and Mary Ann Harley

Isaac H. Skinner, born 1800, died circa 1887 in Carroll County, married Mary Ann Harley (1806-1870) on September 30, 1824, in Newton County, Georgia. Isaac is probably buried in the old Skinner Cemetery near Hopewell, Alabama. He was the son of John H. and Susannah Coaker Skinner and grandson of Revolutionary War Captain Isaac Skinner and Jane Jackson Skinner.

Isaac H. Skinner lived in Jackson, Newton, Henry, Coweta and Carroll Counties. He stopped long enough in Newton County to marry Mary Ann Harley on September 30, 1824. Mary Ann was the daughter of Captain William Joseph Harley who married Elizabeth Pryor in 1808 in Columbia County, Georgia, and the granddaughter of Revolutionary War Lt. Joseph Harley (1720-1807).

This couple had at least twelve known children and lost two of their sons in the Civil War. Their children were: (1) Francis Marion born December 10, 1825, in Jackson County, Georgia, died May 12, 1904, married first to Alsa, second to Elizabeth, and third to Mary Ann Hatfield. He married Mary Ann Hatfield on January 3, 1875, in Carroll County. He is buried at Indian Creek in Carroll County. He served in the CSA Army of Tennessee, Company I, Second Regiment, Georgia Stateline Troops. (2) William Jasper born August 31, 1827, died June 7, 1862, in Lauderdale Springs, Mississippi, married Mary Arthur on July 23, 1848, in Coweta County, Georgia. He died while serving in Company H, 41st Georgia Infantry, CSA Army of Tennessee. This company was known as, the Wool Hat Boys of Carroll County (See Civil War Letters from William Jasper Skinner.) Mary Arthur born between 1825-1828, died in 1897, was left in Carroll County with five little children to raise. The Reconstruction period was hard and she was a long way from her early roots in Bedford County, Virginia, the home of the Arthur family. She was descended from Barnabas Arthur (born 1735 in Brunswick County, Virginia, died November 4, 1799, in Campbell County, Virginia, and lived in Bedford County, Virginia) and his wife Martha Talbot, born August 25, 1740, in Bedford County, Virginia, died after 1808 in Wilkes County, Georgia. Martha Talbot came to Georgia with her sons after the death of Barnabas Arthur and settled in Wilkes and Oglethorpe Counties, Georgia. She was the sister of John Talbot and aunt of Matthew Talbot, an early Governor of Georgia. Her son William Arthur was married first to Sally Calloway and second to Jane McDowell. William Arthur's son Barnabus Arthur married Martha "Polly" Burditt about 1790 in Pittyslvania County, Virginia. They were the parents of John Arthur, born 1796 in Virginia, who married Matilda Gibson in 1817 in Oglethorpe County, Georgia. Matilda was the daughter of James Hugh Gibson, an early pioneer of Coweta County, and his wife Sarah Foster. (3) Susan Elizabeth born December 19, 1828, married John Hyde about 1854 in Coweta County. They lived in the Panther Creek District and had at least three sons. (4) Lucy Ann born October 11, 1831, died September 28, 1833 (from Bible records). (5) John Newton born February 20, 1834, died April 10, 1862 in Lauderdale Springs, Mississippi, married Carolyn Hyde on February 24, 1856, in Carroll County. He died while in Civil War service. He was probably buried close to his brother William Jasper. They were in the same company, the Wool Hat Boys (see Civil War letters). (6) Nancy Rine, born January 24, 1837, died November 1848. (7) Leweasy Emily Vashty born August 18, 1839, married J.T. (Y) Smith, July 13, 1885, in Coweta County (8) Wylie W. born February 9, 1842, died August 15, 1921, married Mary E. Hatfield November 10, 1867. He was buried at Macedonia Baptist Church, Hopewell, Alabama. He served in the Army of Tennessee, CSA Company A, 4th Regiment, Georgia State Troops and Company C, 56th Regiment Infantry. He was captured at Vicksburg. (9) Samuel P. born October 25, 1844, died March 4, 1894, in Cleburne County, Alabama, married Martha L. Gentry on March 17, 1867, in Carroll County. He served in the Army of Tennessee, CSA Company A, 4th Regiment, Georgia State Troops, and Company C, 56th Regiment, Georgia Infantry. (10) James Thomas Jefferson born December 28, 1846, in Coweta County, died February 7, 1932, in Cleburne County, Alabama, married Mrs. Martha Gay Stamps on January 5, 1868, in Carroll County. He was buried at Macedonia Baptist Church, Hopewell, Alabama. This couple had seven children and two stepsons. There is a possible Civil War record. (11) Isaac H. born January 29,1849 in Coweta County, married first to Nancy Banks on November 27, 1870, in Coweta County and second to M.J. Strickland on September 27, 1898, in Cullman County, Alabama. In the 1880 census, he and Nancy Banks had three little girls. (12) Andrew Jackson born June 7, 1851, Coweta County, died 1908, married first to Allora in 1870 and second to Rebecca A. McElroy Phillips in 1872, and third to Ora White in 1903. A.J. is buried at Pleasant Grove Church cemetery in Cleburne County, Alabama. *Submitted by: Kimberly Beavers Grisham, 578 Carrollton-Tyus Road, Carrollton, GA 30117 and Written by: Peggy Jackson Hughes.*

Sources: Bible records and Civil War records.

1023. Skinner Family
Part 2
William Jasper Skinner and Mary Arthur

William Jasper Skinner, born August 31, 1827, married Mary Arthur on July 23, 1848, in Coweta County, Georgia. He died June 7, 1862, during the Civil War. He is buried in Lauderdale Springs Civil War Cemetery in Mississippi with his brother John Newton Skinner who also died in 1862 (See Civil War Letters). His parents were Isaac H. Skinner (1800-1887) and Mary Ann Harley Skinner (1806-1870) of Carroll County. This couple had deep roots in early Georgia history (see Isaac Skinner Family) and they were descended from Revolutionary soldiers Capt. Isaac H. Skinner and Capt. William Joseph Harley, early Indian fighters and pioneers of early Georgia.

Mary Arthur, born between 1825 and 1830, died 1897, married William Jasper Skinner in Coweta County, Georgia, on July 23, 1848. She was left with five little children to raise all by herself when her husband died in the Civil War (See Isaac Skinner Family History). Mary Arthur Skinner was a daughter of John Arthur, born 1796 in Virginia, and Matilda Gibson Arthur, born 1803 in Oglethorpe County, Georgia. She was the granddaughter of James Hugh Gibson, early pioneer of Coweta County, Georgia, and Sarah Foster Gibson. The Gibson and Arthur families came from Oglethorpe to Greene, to Henry, to Coweta, and finally helped settle Newnan, Georgia. The Skinner family moved on over into Carroll County, Georgia, but most of the Gibson family remained in Coweta in the Newnan area. John Arthur was listed in the Carroll County census of 1850 in the Bowdon area with the Skinners, but had moved to Marion County, Alabama, by the 1860 census. His sons returned to Carroll County to fight in the Civil War, but John Arthur, his wife Matilda Gibson, and youngest daughter are lost from sight by 1870. His sons remained in Carroll County. Most Arthurs from Carroll County today are descended from them. John Arthur was descended from Barnabas Arthur (1736-1789) and Martha Talbot (1740-1802) (died in Wilkes County, Georgia), from Bedford County, Virginia. This family was descended from Charles Talbot and Walter Talbot, the Tenth Earl of Shrewsbury.

The children of William Jasper Skinner and Mary Arthur Skinner are: (1) William Marcus Skinner, born 1849, married Sarah Ann Couch, daughter of John Couch and Nancy, on August 13, 1868. He is buried at Macedonia Baptist Church, Hopewell, Alabama. (2) John Gibson Skinner, born 1851, married Susan E. Gay on September 16, 1868. (3) Lucy Ann Skinner, born 1854, married William R. Langley. (4) Alexander Calhoun "Coon" Skinner, born January 4, 1858, married Edna Mae Langley (1857-1926), August 19, 1875, in Carroll County, Georgia. (5) Edney Ugeney "Edna" Skinner, born February 21, 1860, married Joseph Elbert "Joe Turk" Smith July 29, 1875 (See Joseph Elbert "Joe Turk" Smith Family History). Edna Skinner Smith died of typhoid fever August 10, 1904 and is buried beside her husband in the Macedonia Baptist Church Cemetery. Her mother, Mary Arthur Skinner, long a Civil War widow of William Jasper Skinner, is buried nearby. *Submitted by: Kay Beavers Stone, 530 Carrollton Tyus Road, Carrollton, GA and Written by: Peggy Jackson Hughes.*

1024. Skinner Family
Part 3
Letters written by William Jasper Skinner during the Civil War

Dear wife,

I take my pen in hand to let you know that I am well at this time and i hop when thes few lins come to you thay will find you all well. Mary I have a heep to tell you when i com home. I cant rite well enough to giv you the particulurs of my trip i have been cut off from home three times sense i left home but now i have got back to my ridgment safe sound. Thay was twenty captin ross [1] company with me and thirty of captin lesters company and a bout fifteen hundred of cavalry and several of artilre.

Mary John m burt ses howd'a he ses tel you he sleaps with me and he thinks you ought to rite a few lines to him mary doant be uneasy about me far i beleave that god will restore me to you want farwell

Dear Friend I seat myself to drop you a few lins to you. Know that I am well and I hope thes few lins will come hand and find you and family in God's blessing. I have not seen SL Jackson [2] in about three weak but I heard from him today he is well he is wating on the sick at lauderdale Springs. We are a bout two hundred miles apart I want you wright to me as often as you can and write me all the news you have. So I will come to a close for this time only I remaind your friend until death.
W I Skinner
Ira Jackson [3]

Dear wife there is non of my mess with me but Wm Meniekal (?) And Marion Sims Babe is sick he left Bethel Springs last Saturday he was real bad off when he had to go to the hospittle I have bin cut of from the Redgment a bout three weeks but I fared fine our men was taking prisners every day. Dear wife there is a great deal of sickness in our company and a heep of death I am sorry to inform you that Brother John [4] is dead and Francis Paterson is dead and John Alen Reeves and RH Gamble Thomas Entrican There is seventeen of the company dead

Mary tell Farthers folks that I would rit to them but I bin cut of so that I had no __? and no paper to wright on paper is very high here and everything else. tabaco is two dollars per pound Me and Brother John was about two hundred miles a part when he died Mary I want you to wright to me how the wheat crop in Carroll and how you are getting long a farming and how your corn looks.

Direct your letters to Corrinth Mississippi I will come to a close for this time only I remaind your husband untill death.
WI Skinner
to Mary Skinner

Submitted by: Suzanne Osborn, 1355 Tyus Carrollton Road, Carrollton, GA 30117 and Written by: Peggy Jackson Hughes.

Sources: [1]Capt. Newton J. Ross, Company H, 41st Georgia Infantry, William Jasper Skinner died June 7, 1862 from measles. He is buried in Lauderdale Springs, Mississippi. He was in Company H, 41st Georgia Infantry Regiment. He married Mary Arthur, daughter of John Arthur and Matilda Gibson in Coweta County, Georgia on July 23, 1848. [2]S.L. Jackson was Samuel Lawson Jackson who came home from the Civil War and later had a large family. William Jasper Skinner and Enoh H. Smith both died in the Civil War. [3]Ira Jackson was the great-grandfather of Woodrow Jackson who married Sybil Smith; also great-great-grandfather of P. Hughes. [4]Brother John was William Jasper's younger brother. Both were sons of Isaac Skinner.

1025. Smith Family

William Jackson Smith was born in Coweta County, Georgia, on December 2, 1858. He was the only child of Marcus De Lafayette Smith and Mary A. Puckett-Smith. His grandfather was William "Hell-Nation" Smith of Virginia, a Revolutionary War veteran. His father died in 1862 while serving in the Confederate Army, and his mother later remarried. His stepfather was William L. Hogan, a Confederate veteran himself, who raised William along with several half brothers and sisters, in Douglas County, Georgia.

William Jackson Smith married Mollie Chandler in Carroll County, May 14, 1881. They had born to them a daughter, Missouri, June 17, 1887 (married Luther Marks), but wife Mollie died soon after. William then married Mary Caroline Smith, July 6, 1889. Mary was the daughter of Samuel L. Smith of Calhoun County Alabama, and Mary C. Blair-Smith from Carroll County. Her father had been wounded in the Ciivl War at the Battle of New Hope Church. In a 1929 Carroll County newspaper, a front page article proclaimed her parents as the oldest (in longevity), married couple in the county. Later that same year, they both died, barely two weeks apart.

William Jackson Smith Family, circa 1916.

William Jackson Smith and Mary Caroline Smith settled in the Sand Hill area of Carroll County where they purchased sixty-seven acres of land. The first of five children, Tilero was born in 1891. He later married Jennie Harper, and started Smith's Grocery on Stewart Street in Carrollton. Tilero died April 11, 1950. John W.D. "Demps" Smith, their second son, born in 1893, never married. He was struck and killed by lightning May 27, 1915. A third son Phillip M. Smith was born May 29, 1896, married Marvie Lee Hesterlee. He died November 29, 1965. A daughter Mary A. Smith was born May 2, 1902, married Mayfield Driver. She died

February 18, 1941. The youngest a son, Ira B. Smith was born March 13, 1909. He married Iva Dell Harper, March 24, 1929; after her death he married Lovella Williams, November 27, 1968. Along with factory work and farming, he was also a minister of the gospel and pastor of several Methodist churches in the county. People well remember his love and knowledge of animals, from the common barnyard variety to the more exotic hamsters and dwarf-rabbits. He died February 19, 1984.

William Jackson Smith died June 21, 1939, his wife Mary died May 25, 1949 and they are buried together at Bethany Christian Church near Sand Hill. The old homestead no longer exists, but once stood near the present day intersection of Highway 61 and Ira Smith Road near Sand Hill. Pictured are left to right, Phillip M. Smith, William Jackson Smith, Harvey Marks, Mary A. Smith, Ira B. Smith, Garvey Marks and Mary C. Smith. *Submitted by: Garry B. Smith, 631 Tom French Rd., Eva, AL 35621*

1026. The Smith Family

Reaching back to North Carolina in the mid 1700s, we find Hiram Lester who is probably the most "famous" ancestor in our line. Because he was supposed to have lived to be 129 years old, he was somewhat of a legend. In fact, his age was such a curiosity that he was said to have been on exhibit at the Cotton States Exposition held in Atlanta in 1891 as the world's oldest person. (1) The story goes that he married his third wife, Mary Mosley, during the Exposition and this was billed as quite an event witnessed by a host of people who paid the admission price. The bride was reported to be 70 and the groom 124. (There is some confusion about Hiram's exact age because Sherman's troops destroyed all of the family papers.)

Elisha W. and Ellen Lester Smith

Since his life spanned more than a century, he told many things about the earlier years. Among the things he claimed to know was that in England one of the ancestors was a vice-regent of the crown. He also claimed to have spent three nights at Mt. Vernon with General and Mrs. Washington.

Hiram died in 1896 in Henry County, Georgia, and is buried near Flippen.

Hiram's second wife was Suzanne Atkinson, who it has been determined, is the mother of the line of Smith's in and around Bowdon and about whom this article is written. Hiram and Suzanne, then living in Monroe County, Georgia, produced a daughter named Ellen (Ellender or Elenor), born August 22, 1828.

At about this time, Archibald Smith, who was born in 1791 and his wife Sarah (Tolleson) Smith, who was born in 1796 or 1797, were raising a family in what was then Randolph or Clay County, Alabama. To this union was born a son, Elisha W. Smith, on July 18, 1815.

On June 9, 1840, Elisha and Ellen were married in Monroe County, Georgia, and from there they moved to Carroll County. To this union were born eight children: Hiram Jackson Smith, Susan L. Smith, Nancy J. Smith, Archibald Jefferson Smith, Stephen Lee Smith, Andrew Smith, James Smith and Sarah Smith.

In his later years, Elisha and his son, A.J. Smith, operated a blacksmith shop in the Victory/Farmer's High community near Bowdon. The ledger from this shop shows their transactions in the last half of the 1800s. Elisha died on March 22, 1899, and Ellen on April 23, 1897. They are buried in Bethesda Baptist Church cemetery near Carrollton. *Submitted by: Stanley M. (Pat) Smith, 1518 Victory Church Road, Bowdon, GA 30108*

Source: (1) *The Atlanta Constitution,* October 1891

1027. "Hominy" John Smith

John Smith was born April 19, 1809. He died on September 6, 1884, and is buried in the Smith/Upshaw Cemetery in Hickory Level, Carroll County, Georgia. He married Sarah (Sallie) Watson in 1834 in Elbert County, Georgia. Sarah was born July 19, 1815, and died September 6, 1884. She is also buried at the Smith/Upshaw Cemetery in Hickory Level.

According to family history, Hominy Creek is named for John Smith because he grew so much corn on his farm. This is why any time his name was mentioned he was called "Hominy John." John Smith had many acres in Hickory Level. As is stated in the book *Carroll Co. and Her People* by Pvt. Joe Cobb, John Smith, of Hominy Creek, was a successful farmer and businessman. Several of his sons were in the Confederate Army and were always as "true as the needle to the pole." The two sons who were in the Confederate Army were Labon Jackson Smith and Christopher Columbus (Lum) Smith.

Children of John and Sallie are: Labon Jackson Smith married Drucilla Linn; Henry Smith married Elizabeth Hambrick; Christopher Columbus Smith married Martha Stripling; (Elizabeth (Betsy) A. Smith married John F. Bryce; Martha M. Smith married John Upshaw; Eldridge W. Smith married Julia Jones; Mary Leticia Smith married William Monroe Allen; Charles B. Smith; Sarah M. Smith married Joseph Meigs; Celia E. Smith; and Nancy H. Smith married David Harris.

Many of John and Sallie's descendants still live in Carroll County and some in Hickory Level. Lynn Smith, Dianne Smith and Beverly Smith Lang live in Hickory Level. *Submitted by: Peggy Ethridge Nix*

1028. The A.J. Smith Family

Archibald Jefferson Smith was born February 18, 1848, the son of Elisha W. Smith and Ellen (Eleanor) Lester Smith. Marih Walden was born on May 24, 1848, the daughter of Jessie Walden and Sarah Pace Walden.

The Arch and Marih Smith's home place was located on what is now Garrett Creek Road, near Bowdon. The family relocated from the current Barnes Mill Road area to this property, thought to be that of the original Victory Church. The land is still in possession of family descendants and the home place still stands. Arch and Marih had three sons — Tom, Murray, and Fornie — and three daughters — Adella, Minnie, and Myrtie.

Tom married Lela Peacock and their children were Luna, Derotha, Ivella, Tommie Lee, Hoke, Milford, and Dorsey. Tom was a carpenter, perhaps learning those skills from his grandfather, Elisha, who was a carpenter and blacksmith.

Murray married Mamie Causey and they farmed next to his parents' home place.

Fornie married Ada Muse. After living near Salem Church, they settled near the home place on Victory Church Road. Children of this marriage were Loice, Kate, Reba, Stella, Archie Christine, Fornie Lee "Sol," and Stanley Murray "Pat."

Arch and Marih Smith and granddaughters Loice and Luna

Adella was the second wife of John Copeland. They had two children, Elwyn and Myrta Lou. Their home was near the present Bowdon City limits on the same road as her home place. Minnie married Gaines Wilson. The children of this marriage were Cecil, Curtis, Nettie, Mable, Christine, Vivian, and Selby. They reared their family in several homes in the Victory area.

Myrtie married Albert Traylor. Before Albert's death at age twenty-nine, Lerlie and Louise were born. Myrtie returned to the family home and raised her girls, caring for her parents until their death in the 1930s.

Arch and Marih are buried in the Victory Methodist Church cemetery near Bowdon. *Submitted by: Julie Rowell Steed, 4517 Parkwood Lane, Niceville, FL 32578*

1029. Charles Smith 1833-1907

Many residents in Carroll County trade their ancestry through a Smith line. I am no exception. My great-great-grandfather was Charles Smith, born August 19, 1833, in Franklin County, Georgia. In late 1836 when he was three, his father Gabriel D. Smith Jr., his grandfather Gabriel Smith Sr., and other family members and neighbors moved to Carroll County.

In Montgomery County, North Carolina, Charles' grandfather Gabriel Smith Sr. (born December 12, 1764, Anson County, North Carolina) entered the Revolutionary militia under Capt. Thomas Childs in 1780. His regiment joined Gen. Gates at Camden, participated in the march to Mars Ferry and the skirmish at Bettises Bridge on Downing Creek, and was taken prisoner. In the fall of 1781 after three weeks in captivity, he escaped. Determined to support the fight for freedom, he volunteered again in October 1781.

In 1785 Gabriel Sr. married Sarah. Records indicate Sarah's surname may have been Downs or Dobbs. In 1816 Richard Downs deeded 94.5 acres to Gabriel Smith Sr. "For affection and past services rendered." The family migrated to Georgia after Gabriel Sr. applied for and received Wilkes County, Georgia, land grants totaling 200 acres in 1787 and 1791. Gabriel D. Smith Jr. was born there in 1798. In 1802, Gabriel Sr. was granted 200 acres in Franklin County, Georgia. Families and neighbors migrated with him. His son, Gabriel D. Smith Jr., married Nancy E. Cain and had thirteen children. One of those children was my great-great-grandfather, Charles Smith. (Also, see related Lizzie and Emory Smith article.)

The Smith's next migration was to Carroll County in 1836. They settled in what is now the Smithfield community where young Charles grew up. His grandfather, Gabriel Sr., died in 1841 and was buried in the Old Poplar Springs Primitive Baptist Church Cemetery. Charles' father and mother are buried in the newer Poplar Springs Cemetery.

After Charles married Sarah Jane Barrow (born October 29, 1828) on November 14, 1852, they lived in the Bowdon area until his death. They had eight children: Nancy C., William Wesley, John Turner, James David, Lucinda E. (Cindy), Emory Eli, Elvira S., and Cintilla.

October 13, 1861, Charles enlisted as a private in the Confederate Army, Company D, 3rd Regiment, Georgia State Troops, and mustered out at Savannah, Georgia, on April 20, 1862, with an honorable discharge. He was then appointed fourth sergeant of Company B, 56th Regiment Georgia Infantry, on May 5, 1862, captured at Vicksburg, Mississippi, on July 4, 1863, and paroled July 8, 1863. Near New Hope Church, Georgia, on June 27, 1864, he was wounded in the right leg, necessitating amputation above the knee.

Charles and Sarah Jane Barrow Smith, and daughter Cindy (Lucinda)

After the war, Charles returned to his residence in Bowdon. His property included land where the present Community First Bank (CFB) is located. Charles was an active member at Indian Creek Baptist Church and later a charter member of Kansas Baptist Church. His nephew Archie Smith said "If Uncle Charles' lost, the world's a goner." In his later years, Kansas was too far so he attended Bowdon Baptist Church. Charles Smith died November 12, 1907, and is buried at Indian Creek Baptist Church Cemetery beside his beloved Sarah Jane. His tombstone inscription reads,

"A sinner saved by grace."

Submitted by: Janet Vernelle Warren Cooke, 896 Jefferson Drive, Conyers, GA 30094

Sources: *Book of Confederate Soldiers' Roster,* military records, Carroll County newspapers, church records, Smith Family Bible, family letters and stories, cemetery records, marriage records, land records, *Carroll County Stroy as Told by Her People, Ancestors and Descendants of Smiths* by Linda G. Cheek, Easley, SC, *"A Brief History of Gabriel Smith and Some of His Descendants"* by S.H. Adamson of Signal Mountain, TN, and *Our Smith-King Families* by Marie McBride.

1030. Edward and Marie Smith Family

George Edward Smith was born in a house on the corner of Burson Avenue and Aycock Street in Carrollton, Georgia on Nov. 27, 1919, to Sam and Lula Turner Smith. He began first grade at the Tallapoosa School on the Tyus Road. He attended Old Camp Methodist Church as a youngster. The family later moved to the Beulah community, where he went to Beulah School, and they attended New Hope Methodist Church. Edward had five brothers: Otha, Pearce, William, Bobby, and Charles. The Smiths grew up during the Great Depression. Their father was a farmer and worked at the Mandeville Cotton Mill, and their mother was a homemaker. On Jan. 7, 1941, Edward went into the U.S. Army, hoping to serve for one year. In his eleventh month of service, while stationed at Ft. Jackson, Pearl Harbor was bombed and he was thrust into World War

Edward and Marie Smith Family in 1999

II for five years. His company maneuvered in the Yuma, Arizona, desert for six months, and then was sent to Camp Forest, Tennessee. He left on Thanksgiving Day, 1943 to go overseas. First, they went to Northern Ireland and then landed on Normandy Beach on July 4, 1944. They were in combat in France, Luxembourg, Belgium, and Germany. The combat lasted until they met the Russians on the Elbe River on May 8, 1945, when the war ended.

When he returned, he met a beautiful woman he had met before as a child. Margaret Marie Bartlett had been born just over the Heard County line on Nov. 17, 1927 to John Henry Bartlett and Lucy Viola Holmes Bartlett. She was one of eight children. Her brothers and sisters include: Newt, Lewis, and Ed Bartlett, Vassie Crutchfield, Mary Steed, Elizabeth Bartlett, and Sarah Daniell. They had lived in the New Hope community, had attended Mt. Zion School, and New Hope Church.

Edward and Marie were married on Nov. 22, 1947, by Rev. Alton Smith at the preacher's home. During the war, Marie had worked at Bell Bomber (Lockheed), but after their marriage worked for Southern Bell Telephone Company. She and Edward began farming shortly after their wedding. While he was overseas, Edward had sent his paycheck to his father to make payments on a farm. That farm was to be their home and livelihood for over fifty years. They began by raising chickens and also dairy farming. They have two children: Peggy Joy Smith (born Feb. 16, 1958) and Kenneth Edward Smith (born April 29, 1961). Both children attended Mt. Zion Schools and then West Georgia College. Joy married Rev. Wes Griffin, who is a Methodist pastor. They have served churches in Georgia and also as missionaries to the country of Estonia after the Soviet Union collapsed. Joy and Wes have two children, Hannah Marie (born Sept. 4, 1989), and Caleb Edward (born Oct. 23, 1991). Kenneth works with electrical substations, and has three children: Matthew Clifton (born July 21, 1987), Michael George (born Feb. 24, 1989), and David Kenneth (born Sept. 5, 1990).

Edward and Marie have lived in the New Hope/Eureka Church community throughout their marriage. They have wonderful neighbors who have always been good friends. They are members of the New Hope United Methodist Church, and are also active participants in the Bethel Campmeeting, which is over 100 years old. *Submitted by: William Smith, 320 Almon Rd., Carrollton, GA 30117*

1031. Emory and Lizzie Smith

My great-grandparents, Sarah Elizabeth McDonald (born December 28, 1878, in Heard County, Georgia) and Emory Eli Smith (born March 16, 1874, Bowdon) were married in Bowdon, Carroll County, Georgia, at the home of the bride's father on October 26, 1902. She was the fourth child of Adelia Clementine Pearce and John Alexander McDonald. His parents were Sarah Jane Barrow and Charles Smith. In this small western Georgia town, they raised their four children: Mozelle, Blanche, Roy, and Iris.

Religion played an important role in their home. Emory was the first member to join "by experience" the newly organized Kansas Baptist Church (1897) north of Bowdon, later transferring to Bowdon Baptist Church. He attended Bowdon College as a young man. By profession, he was a farmer and carpenter. He was a member of the Bowdon Masonic Lodge.

After retirement, he and Lizzie lived with their daughter Blanche. He advised students in the woodworking shop at Bowdon High School, managed the Bowdon Canning Plant, and spent his time maintaining the home. He always planted a huge garden that not only provided fresh vegetables for the family but enough for friends and neighbors. In 1938 he used his carpenter skills to help Blanche's husband build the family home in Bowdon. His granddaughter, Janice, lives there today.

Until the mid-fifties, he kept a cow and chickens — a small farm in the "city." My mother, Janice, has fond memories of time spent with him: watermelon cuttings each summer afternoon; evening family talks on the porch listening to his tales of the past; carrying his lunch to the canning plant and tasting food being prepared, especially hot sausage; trimming his hair between cuttings so he could save his money; emptying pockets of money so she could be "Queen of the Carnival." His nickname for Janice was "Baby," even when she was in her teens. To her he was a second "Daddy." His nephew Archie Smith said, "My mother said he (Uncle Emory) was the finest man she ever knowed." This seems to be the consensus of all who knew him.

Emory and Lizzie Smith

Lizzie and her siblings attended Bowdon College where their father was in charge of the intermediate and primary departments. She taught with her father before marrying Emory. After marriage, her time was devoted to raising their children and keeping the household in order. My mom has cherished memories of her grandmother. Janice was no "latch key" child because Grandma Lizzie was home serving as second mother while Blanche taught at the local high school. Mom recalls hurrying home from school to see what Grandma had saved in the warmer of the old wood stove (bread pudding, custard, especially); having her grandmother act as "Grade Mother" at school; getting homework help with spelling; her grandmother offering her a dollar each time she brought a report home without "Whispers too much." Grandmother Lizzie was always available. The love and attention she had showered on her own children, she also gave to her granddaughter.

Together Lizzie and Emory reached out to others their entire lives, sharing and helping as a team and bringing joy to others. Emory died September 6, 1961, and is buried in the Bowdon City Cemetery. Lizzie died three years later October 6, 1964, and is buried beside her beloved husband. My mom says, "I never once heard them argue. They never raised their voices. Theirs was a quiet way, touching others with love." *Submitted by: Jan Cooke, 896 Jefferson Dr., Conyers, GA 30994*

1032. Emory Eli Smith

Granddaddy

Neither rich nor famous,
He squeezed and stretched his pension check
to bring me joy.
Beside his mantle clock
(That did stop when he died)
Candy chocolate drops beckoned.
The only time I wore a crown,
He measured out his meager earnings,
Assuring me the top spot.
I was his companion,
helping him roll cigarettes
(which he smoked 'til he got mouth cancer,
then he chewed, convinced the tobacco healed);
playing nurse to his sliced hand
but fainting at the sight of his blood;
holding the lantern so he could
capture the culprit in the chicken house.
Summer evenings the family retreated
to the porch to escape the Georgia heat.
Mama and Grandma shelled peas and snapped beans.
I listened to him recount the old days,
making pine boxes for private departures.
He talked of algebra and math,
How he dreamed solutions to unsolvable problems.
That was his life.
That was my granddaddy!
An achiever of the unachievable!

Granddaddy (Emory Eli Smith)

This poem was written by my grandmother, my Gran, Janice Adelia Duncan. In it she recalls memories of her grandfather, the father figure in the home where she grew up. When she talks of her fond memories of him, I regret that I never knew personally my great great grandfather, Emory Eli Smith. *Submitted by: Matthew Warren Cooke, PO Box 1121, Bowdon, GA 30108*

1033. Gabriel D. Smith Jr. Family

Gabriel was born on June 18, 1798, in Elbert County, Georgia. He came from a family of twelve children, he being the ninth child born to Gabriel D. Smith Sr. and Sarah Downs. His father was a Revolutionary War veteran from North Carolina and had received a land grant in Georgia. Between 1834 and 1836, there were several families who moved from Franklin County to Carroll County. This included young Gabriel and his wife, his mother and father, and several other siblings and their spouses. Several from the Smith families became early members of the Tallapoosa Primitive Baptist Church. Later, most of the Smiths moved into the 9th District and their church letters transferred to the Poplar Springs Primitive Baptist Church where most of them remained until their deaths.

Nancy E. Cain was born in Georgia on January 21, 1802. Names of her parents are unknown, although an older letter dated 1854 shows she had a brother named Abel living in Monroe County, Mississippi. Research shows that Abel Cain had brothers named William and Thomas who lived in Monroe County. These two names are mentioned in the said letter where Abel tells of their respective family health status. Also, there was either a brother or nephew named John. When Abel wrote the aforementioned letter, their mother was living with John but the location was not indicated. Persons researching the Cain line show Nancy also had a brother named Ransom.

Tombstone for Gabriel D. Smith, Poplar Springs Primitive Baptist Church

Nancy Cain and Gabriel Smith were married in Franklin County, Georgia, around 1820. Thirteen children were born to this union, which included two sets of twins. The first seven were born in Franklin County and the last six were born in Carroll County. Names, birthdays, and marriage information for the children are (1) Diademmy Indianna born March 1, 1822, and married James H. Hendon, (2) Permelia born March 6, 1824, and married Calvin H. Powell, (3) Gideon born February 25, 1826, and married Emily Mildred Barrow, (4) Mary Elizabeth born July 3, 1829, and married Walter T. Warren (these are my great-grandparents; see related Walter T. Warren article), (5) Ransom born October 4, 1831, and married Nancy Caroline King, (6) Charles born August 19, 1833, and married Sarah Jane Barrow, (7) Mary Martha born September 15, 1835, and married John Turner Barrow, (8) Lucinda Caroline born August 24, 1838, and married first to James M. Wright and second to William Tryon Patterson, (9) Arminda Adaline born August 24, 1838, and married William D. Rowell, (10) J. Darius born January 28, 1841, and married Emily Caroline Michael, (11) James "Polk" Bryant born March 14, 1843, and married first to Elizabeth Margaret King and second to Nancy Ann Nichols. (12) Sarah Angeline born February 10, 1846, and married James Alexander Phillips (see related James Alexander Phillips article), (13) Anne Avaline born February 10, 1846, and married Henry D. Brock.

Three of the Smith children — Gideon, Charles, and Martha — married children of Rev. James and Lucinda Barrow. Ransom and Polk Smith married daughters of Ben and Mary King, Gabriel and Nancy had five sons and two sons-in-law to serve in the Civil War. Regarding their sons, only Charles suffered major injury; however, sons-in-law James M. Wright and John T. Barrow lost their lives. Census records from 1830 through 1870 show that Gabriel's only occupation was farming.

Tombstone for Nancy Smith, Poplar Springs Primitive Baptist Church

Gabriel died on October 3, 1880, and Nancy died on September 27, 1885. Both are buried in the Poplar Springs Primitive Baptist Church Cemetery on Smithfield Road near Bowdon. There are seventy-seven known graves in this cemetery for direct descendants and spouses of Gabriel and Nancy Smith. Counting both the old and new cemetery burials, there are about 121 known graves for direct descendants of Gabriel's parents. *Submitted by: Frances D. Crow (g-g-granddaughter), 577 Richeytown Road, Eastaboga, AL 36260-7215*

Sources: Family records, U.S. census records research by Girlilee D. Thomason.

1034. Gabriel Smith Family

Gabriel Smith, 1764-1841, a Revolutionary War militiaman from Montgomery County, North Carolina. He served from August 1780 until Cornwallis was taken at Yorktown, October 1781, and until peace was declared (about eighteen months). He was born in Montgomery County, North Carolina, on December 12, 1764, and he moved to Wilkes County, Georgia, where he was given a land grant in 1784, and to Franklin County in 1802. Gabriel married Sarah Downs (born 1767 died about 1835) about 1785 and they had the following children: Ezekiel, Gideon, William B., Richard W., Mary (Polly), Morning, Grace, James C., Gabriel D. Jr., Mark, Sarah, and Hugh. In the 1830s, he and several of his twelve children moved into Carroll County and settled the area around Poplar Springs Church. On September 30, 1837, Gabriel was married to his second wife, Matilda Chandler Carter, in Carroll County.

Gabriel Smith joined the Tallapoosa Primitive Baptist Church by letter on June 10, 1837. In August 1840 he is listed on the new member list at Poplar Springs Primitive Baptist Church (this information was taken from the Church Conference Records (1840-1872, while Donnie Robinson was church clerk at Poplar Springs).

The ninth child of Gabriel D. and Sarah Downs Smith was Gabriel D. Smith Jr. (born 4-6-1798, died 10-3-1880) and he married Nancy Cain (born 1-21-1802, died 9-27-1885) in 1821, Franklin County, Georgia. The children of Gabriel D. Jr. and Nancy Cain are as follows: Diademmy Indianna, Pamelia Amelia, Gideon, Mary Elizabeth, Ransom E., Charles, Mary Martha, Arminda Adaline, Lucinda Caroline, J. Darius, James Bryant (Polk), Anna Avaline, and Sarah Angeline.

Mary Elizabeth Smith was the fourth child of Gabriel and Nancy Cain Smith, and she was born July 3, 1829, and died October 20, 1910. Mary Elizabeth married Walter Tilman Warren on August 14, 1853. (See the Walter Tilman Warren story.)

The fifth child of Gabriel and Nancy Smith was Ransom E. Smith (born 10-4-1832, died 8-11-1905) and he married Nancy Caroline King on July 18, 1852. They are buried at the Poplar Springs Primitive Baptist Church Cemetery, Bowdon, Georgia. Ransom Smith served as church clerk from January 26, 1867, until June 1905 just before he died. The children of Ransom and Nancy were Ben G., J.G., T.A., James Darius, John H., Hiram Carter, William C., Aaron Flemon, Braten Levi, Mary Elizabeth, and Martha Ann.

Braten Levi Smith (born 2-26-1874, died 6-17-1954) who married Clara Moon on August 27, 1899, was one of their eleven children. Braten and Clara Smith were parents of eleven children also and they were named: Herschel Braten, Annie Elizabeth, Parry Navada, Mamie Elizabeth, Mary L., Newton Rance, Adell, Arty J. (Artie), Sarah Lee, and two infants who died. Artie (born 3-21-1915, died 10-23-1999) was their ninth child and he married Essie Pollard in Heflin, Alabama, on February 21, 1942. Artie was retired from the Bremen-Bowdon Investment Company, an Army veteran of World War II, and a member of Mt. View Baptist Church. Essie shared this poem written to a family member named Molly by her sweetheart July 14, 1880, Carroll County.

> Won't you tell me Molly Darling that you love non else but me
> for I love you Molly Darling, you are all the world to me.
> O tell me Molly that you love me, put your little hand in mine,
> take my heart sweet Molly Darling, say that you will give me thine.
>
> Stars are shining Molly Darling through the mist vale of the night.
> They seem lonely Molly Darling when fair lilacs hide her sight.
> Oh none are like unto the flower when they bow their heads with shame.
> My modest Molly Darling when they hear me call your name.
>
> Molly dearest, fairest, sweetest look up darling tell me this,
> do you love me Molly Darling, let your answer be a kiss.
>
> I must leave you Molly Darling, though the parting gives me pain
> when the stars shine Molly Darling I will meet you here again.
> Oh good-bye Molly, good-bye loved one, happy may you ever be.
> When you are dreaming Molly Darling don't forget to dream of me.

On August 24, 1838, Lucinda Caroline was born to Gabriel and Nancy Cain Smith. She was their ninth child and on December 30, 1859, she married James M. Wright. James joined Company H, 41st Regiment, Georgia Vol. Infantry, CSA (Wool Hat Boys), as a private on March 4, 1862, and he died May 2, 1863, at Columbus, Mississippi (from the *Roster of the Confederate Soldiers of Georgia,* Vol. 4, Page 489).

Lucinda's second marriage was to Tryon Patterson on March 11, 1866. Tryon served in the CSA from May 5, 1862, until June 12, 1865. He was captured in 1863 in Vicksburg, Mississippi, and again on December 16, 1864, near Nashville, Tennessee. He was transferred on January 2, 1865, to Camp Chase, Ohio, where he took the oath of allegiance. Lucinda and Tryon had five children: James Marion (1866-1936), Sarah E. (born 1868), Martha E. (born 1872), Robert Newton (1874-1943), and Joseph (Joe) Tryon (1876-1949).

The first child, James Marion, married Deliah Huckeby on November 6, 1883. Sarah E. married William E. Abercrombie on November 17, 1887. No record was found of Martha E. marrying. Robert Newton married Mary Elizabeth McGuire on June 6, 1943. Joseph married Martha Elizabeth "Betty" Robinson and later married Lizzie Farrow on March 12, 1930.

James Marion and Deliah Huckeby Patterson had seven children: John Marion Washington "Johnny," Wilburn Lonzo "Will," Lucinda Ardella "Della," Robert M. "Rob," Jordan Oscar, Joseph Ezra, and Gertrude Lillian.

Robert Newton was the fourth child of Tryon and Lucinda Patterson. He and his wife Mary Elizabeth McGuire had thirteen children: Claybourn, John Flemming, Minnie, Pearlie Gertrude, Earl Hugh, Sarah Olivia, Charlie Clifford, Albert Tryon, Theodore Herbert, Rosa Inez, Elzie Oland, Robert Marion, and Ella Marcelle. The next child of Tryon and Lucinda was Joseph Tryon and he and wife, Martha Robinson had twelve children: Annie, Robert Henry, Arvella, Buford Edgar, Marion Rufus, Grady George, Laura Ophelia, Nancy Lou Cindia, Joseph Emmett, Levi, Thomas A., and Roger.

As you can see I, Jeffery Alan Denney, have many ancestors — like Abraham, so many you can't count them! John Marion Washington Patterson was my great-grandfather. Actually I am a member of the eighth generation after Gabriel Smith, the Revolutionary War veteran. *Submitted by: Jeffery Alan Denney, 2735 Wyndham Place Drive, Lawrenceville, GA 30044, based on research by Donald and Violette Denney.*

1035. JOHN G. SMITH

The first known record of either John G. or Matilda Smith in Carroll County was the 1850 purchase by Matilda from George Creel of 100 acres of land lot 196 in the area then known as Laurel Hill. Matilda appears in the 1850 census living with five children. She paid taxes on this tract until she sold it to John G. Smith in 1850. The first known record of John G. Smith in Carroll County was the January 1855 purchase from Mathilda Smith of the same 100-acre tract. The birthplace of John G. Smith is unknown. The 1860 census gives his birthplace as South Carolina, and the 1870 census gives it as North Carolina. John G. and Matilda Smith lived on the Laurel Hill property until their deaths. He died January 7, 1877, in Carroll County. She died January 8, 1902, in Carroll County. John G. Smith's family consisted of:

(1) Caroline A. "Carrie" Smith, born October 11, 1834, died May 1909. She married William D. Bloodworth on October 11, 1857. They lived in Carroll County until 1868 when they moved to Wilkinson County, Georgia. They had four children: Jerusha Matilda Jane, born about 1858, married Samuel Lauson Harrington; Minnie Lee "Cinda" born September 1859, married Abram Moore on February 14, 1882; Amanda born about 1861; Joanna, born about 1863; married John Milton Harrington on December 13, 1881.

(2) Lucinda Angeline Smith was born about 1836. She married James W. Farmer on March 20, 1873. He was born about 1837. They had three known children: James H. born about 1875; Matilda A. born about 1877; Jeperson T. born about 1879.

(3) Martin Van Buren Smith was born October 23, 1838, and died March 23, 1899. He married Sarah Jane Nixon in 1860. She was born October 7, 1840, and died January 29, 1919. They had seven children: Frances A. "Fannie" born May 12, 1861, died March 16, 1937, married Isham Freman "Ice" Hightower. He was born December 9, 1851 and died March 23, 1917; John Morgan (twin of Frances A.) born May 12, 1861, died April 6, 1949. He married Ellen Rebecca Rowe, born March 6, 1863, died December 16, 1944. Both are buried at Pleasant Grove Baptist Church in Carroll County; Zilla Elizabeth "Betty" born August 15, 1864, died November 1, 1935. She married first James Benjamin Franklin Hightower, brother of Isham Freman Hightower, born June 2, 1857, died June 14, 1932. She married second Judson Cook Barr in 1894. He was born February 19, 1852, died February 6, 1948. Betty and Judson Cook Barr are buried in the Roopville Cemetery; Ella Matilda born June 7, 1867, died May 6, 1931, married Joseph B. "Joe" Yates born February 3, 1862, died January 14, 1944. Both are buried at Bethlehem Primitive Baptist Church in Carroll County; Laura Isabel born July 18, 1868, died October 31, 1925, married James Thomas "Jim" Denney, born November 23, 1863, died March 26, 1938; Roxie Ann Smith born January 2, 1872, died June 20, 1948, married Robert Lee "Bob" Williams on September 25, 1897. He was born February 14, 1866, died June 30, 1945; Thomas Newton "Tom" born December 16, 1873, died November 30, 1932, married Susan Temperance "Tempie" Jackson on March 2, 1898. She was born March 28, 1870, died October 17, 1947. When they were married, he worked as a carpenter for Judson Cook Barr in Tyus, and she was a schoolteacher in Roopville.

(4) Mary Catherine "Mollie" Smith was born about 1842. She married John Dickerson Hightower on April 29, 1883. He was born in 1825, died October 11, 1899.

(5) Joseph M. "Joel" Smith was born in 1844.

(6) Nancy J. Smith was born in April 1845. *Submitted by: Jack Upchurch, 5000 San Pedro Court, Milton, Fl 32583*

1036. LABON JACKSON SMITH

Labon Jackson Smith was born on August 28, 1835, in Carroll County, Georgia and died February 24, 1876. He is buried in the Jordan Cemetery in Carroll County. "L.J." is the son of "Hominy" John Smith, born April 19, 1809, died September 6, 1884, and Sara (Sallie) Watson born July 19, 1815, and died December 2, 1896. Labon J. married Drucilla Linn, born October 7, 1838, in Warren County, Georgia. Drucilla was the daughter of John Linn and Mildred (Milly) Wood. Milly's second husband was Joseph Broom.

L.J. enlisted in the Confederate Army on May 10, 1861, at Carrollton, Georgia, in Company F., 7th Georgia Volunteer Infantry. This was the first company to leave Carroll County for the war. He was promoted to first lieutenant on January 9, 1862. On June 16, 1862, he was promoted to captain of Company B, 7th Regiment Confederate Cavalry. He transferred to Company B, 10th Regiment Georgia Cavalry on July 11, 1864. He surrendered at Greensboro, North Carolina, on April 26, 1865.

He came back to Carroll County to start a business on the square in Carrollton. Family history as told by Hance Williamson, a grandson of Labon, was that the house of the L.J. Smith family was on the site of what is now the courthouse. He would tell of the dispensary on the square and about the solid steel safe that was the largest in town at that time. People would come to town to sell their cotton and would keep their money in the safe as they went about other business.

Hance would also tell about the bear caught in the woods. He was given the name Harvey. He got out of his collar and followed the children right up to the door. The children were taken inside and Harvey proceeded to get on top of the house. The Smith children had an interesting childhood. How did they ever get that bear down? Labon was also active in politics as he was appointed as a delegate to the Democrat Convention of 1872.

Children of Labon Jackson Smith and Drucilla Linn Smith are: Lucius J. Smith married Missouri Bentley, Marion Jackson Smith married Darthula Almyra (Myra) Brown, Sarah M.A. Smith married William Barnabus Williamson, Anna Lee Smith married Leroy Floyd Broome and Charles H. Smith married Cora E. Parker. *Submitted by: William L. (Billy) Ethridge*

1037. Marion Jackson Smith

Marion Jackson Smith born February 4, 1866, in Carroll County and died June 30, 1928, in Carroll County. He is buried in the Pleasant Grove Baptist Church Cemetery in Villa Rica, Georgia. He married Almyra Darthula (Myra) Brown born October 23, 1877, in Coweta County, Georgia, and died August 28, 1972, in Carroll County. She is buried in the Pleasant Grove Baptist Church Cemetery in Villa Rica. Marion J. and Myra were married on December 5, 1895, in Carroll County.

This union was blessed with eleven children. The children of Marion and Myra were: Charlie Robert Smith, Lee Jackson Smith, Mary Elizabeth Smith married Henry Clifford Birdsong, Buna Christopher Smith, Samuel William Smith married Lola Lazell Reynolds, Melvin Otis Smith and his twin (not given a name), Joe Brown Smith married Eleanor Jane Hewitt, Lynn Tolbert Smith married Lottie Doris Dyer, and Eugene Marion Smith married first Mary Broom and second Rebecca Evans Stallings.

Myra Brown Smith and grandchildren.

The grandchildren and many of the great-grandchildren spent many a happy day visiting Granny at her home in Sand Hill — fishing in the two lakes, playing in the front yard around the huge tree with big rocks around it, turning out the lights and telling "ghost stories" (it sure did get dark in the country), taking walks down the little dirt road and going to Uncle Gene's house, bringing in wood for the wood stove and those wonderful smells that would come from the kitchen (like homemade biscuits, fresh corn, green beans, squash, and fried chicken), just sitting and talking with grandmother about the "good ole days" and the family that we wanted to know about. She could remember names and dates. Granny could tell the most interesting stories about our family. We had a wonderful grandmother. Our family also was blessed with our Aunt Mary. Aunt Mary was a special person and she was so dear to our family. Our Uncle Lee Smith had for many years a store in Sand Hill.

The grandchildren of Marion and Myra were Peggy Smith Catchings, Myra Smith Kremin, Carolyn Birdsong Worley, Rachel Jones Perrin, Jack Smith, Linda Smith Ethridge, Eleanor Jones Bostwick, Carole Smith Reed, Brenda Smith Edwards, Betty Smith Morgan, Laura Smith Warren, Dianne Smith, Donna Smith Camp, Beverly Smith Lang, Joe Smith, Jane Smith Leslie, David Smith and Anna Smith Holeman. *Submitted by: Linda Smith Ethridge, 1169 Pine Knoll Lane, Conyers, GA 30013*

1038. Martin Van Buren Smith

Martin Van Buren Smith was born October 23, 1838 in Alabama. He was the son of John G. Smith. In about 1850 he moved with his family to Carroll County, Georgia. In 1860, he married Sarah Jane Nixon, daughter of Charles W. Nixon and Jane Adams of Carroll and Heard Counties. He and Sarah Jane lived in Carroll County until after the Civil War when they moved to northern Heard County. He died March 23, 1899, at the home of his daughter, Zilla Elizabeth "Betty" Barr, in Roopville. Sarah Jane died January 29, 1919. Both are buried in an unnamed cemetery at the intersection of Georgia Route 5 and Bethesda Road in Carroll County.

On May 10, 1862, in Bowdon, Georgia, Martin Van Buren Smith enlisted in Company C, 56th Regiment, Georgia Volunteers, Confederate States Army. He fought in the Battle of Vicksburg, Mississippi, and was captured at the time of surrender of the city. He was paroled July 8, 1863. He returned to the army and was present at the surrender in Greensboro, North Carolina, on April 26, 1865.

Martin Van Buren and Sarah Jane Nixon Smith had seven children: Frances A., born May 12, 1861, died March 16, 1937, married Isham Freman "Ice" Hightower, born December 9, 1851, died March 23, 1917. They had six children: 1. Pallie Alto born October 13, 1876, died May 22, 1939, married William H. Barker, born June 25, 1869, died February 13, 1929. 2. Charles Arneld born February 12, 1878, died July 10, 1919, married on July 28, 1901, to Lena Bonner, born November 1883, died December 1953. 3. Exa A. born May 22, 1881, died October 14, 1970, married on June 2, 1898, to John Thomas Cook, born February 11, 1871, died April 7, 1934. 4. James Luther M. was born December 23, 1883, and died May 19, 1901. 5. Cara Tivole born May 1887, married J.C. Smith on September 15, 1901. They moved to Cullman County, Alabama. 6. J.D. "Jay" born November 21, 1890, died August 28, 1937, married on December 24, 1911, to Beulah E. Denney, born 1894, died January 9, 1967.

John Morgan (twin to Frances A.), born May 12, 1861, died April 6, 1949, married Ellen Rebecca Rowe on December 5, 1881. She was born March 6, 1863, and died December 16, 1944. They had nine children: 1. Lula Bell born October 2, 1882, died October 17, 1933, married on August 28, 1898, to Rolf B. Beck, born May 6, 1878, died July 26, 1956. They moved to Lawrenceburg, Tennessee. 2. James D. "Jimmie" born September 28, 1885, died February 8, 1956, married first Beulah Prince on October 8, 1905, and second on February 15, 1914, to Mattie Lena Brown, born February 26, 1894, died January 16, 1944, and third on November 18, 1944, to Mollie S. Taylor, born 1885, died 1969. 3. Florence born May 1887, died April 7, 1958, married on August 24, 1902, to William L. Harper, born March 10, 1875, died December 9, 1962. 4. Willie Alto born March 16, 1891, died January 13, 1980, married in June 1907 to Charles Bunion "Bun" Word, born October 24, 1888, died April 13, 1961. They moved to Coweta County. Willie Alto Smith Word was the grandmother of the noted writer and humorist Lewis M. Grizzard Jr. She was the "Mama Willie" he often wrote about. 5. Oscar Lee born March 3, 1893, died April 11, 1915, married Euna Oxford on November 15, 1914. 6. Thomas B. born August 7, 1895, died June 1, 1978, married first to Cleo M. Wessinger on August 29, 1914, born March 4, 1899, died January 7, 1974, and second to Ethel Thompson on October 6, 1975. 7. Lena Pearl born December 7, 1897, died March 24, 1973, married on December 28, 1916, to Joseph Clark Mosley, born December 9, 1895, died November 18, 1972. 8. Johnnie Rhea born November 20, 1899, died October 9, 1964, married on December 9, 1917, to Ernest Kramer Jackson, born January 2, 1897, died July 25, 1954. 9. Bonnie Irene born August 10, 1901, died July 19, 1935, married on May 22, 1931, to William Ralph Shirah, born September 20, 1902, died July 31, 1983.

Zilla Elizabeth "Betty" born August 15, 1864, died November 1, 1935, married first to James Benjamin Franklin Hightower (brother of Isham Freman Hightower), born June 2, 1857, died June 14, 1932. They had four children. She married second in 1894 to Judson Cook Barr born February 19, 1852, died February 6, 1948. Zilla Elizabeth Smith and Benjamin Franklin Hightower had three children: 1. Henry C. "Dovie" born January 8, 1880, died July 31, 1952, married first on February 24, 1903, to Georgia E. Wood, born November 21, 1883, died September 17, 1932, and second on January 3, 1934, to Lulu Estelle Chance, born August 13, 1900, died December 3, 1948. 2. John Newton born August 25, 1881, died October 3, 1971, married on February 5, 1908, to Annie Zetha Huffman, born February 8, 1891, died August 7, 1973. 3. Ambus A. born June 29, 1884, died February 18, 1962, married first on July 5, 1905, to Myrtle Lee Wood, born December 4, 1889, died January 20, 1931, and second to Verna M. Tuggle, born April 8, 1897, died June 10, 1980.

Ella Mathilda, born June 7, 1867, died May 6, 1931, married on October 27, 1897, to Joseph B. Yates, born February 3, 1862, died January 14, 1944. They had twelve children: 1. Amer Alice born December 1, 1883, died September 29, 1975, married on October 27, 1897, to Thomas J. Miles born March 1879, died September 10, 1947. 2. James Milton born August 31, 1888, died November 10, 1968, married October 3, 1909, to Flonnie M. Lott, born May 8, 1893, died October 8, 1967. 3. Georgie Garland born September 23, 1890, died July 27, 1972, married first to John Warren Willingham on August 10, 1906, and they had four children; and second to James Franklin Maxwell on August 19, 1925. 4. Henry Grady born October 10, 1892, died November 23, 1965, married on September 19, 1915, to Bessie J. Wiggins, born February 18, 1894, died January 28, 1985. 4. Burns Buren born February 1895, died January 27, 1969, married on June 22, 1919, to Claire Hay, born February 5, 1899, died November 24, 1979. 6. Thomas Ervin born January 20, 1897, died November 19, 1971, married on July 22, 1917, to Cora Hardegree born October 16, 1899, died August 9, 1984. 7. Jeffie D. born March 1899, died young. 8. Janie B. born March 1899, died young. 9. Infant born about 1901. 10. Lawrence born 1902, married Clara Jackson. 11. Eunice Geneva born March 6, 1904, died June 16, 1941, married on October 31, 1926, to Steve C. Payne, born November 19, 1896, died December 5, 1969. 12. Vannie Alby born June 22, 1905, died September 16, 1973, married on November 19, 1922, to George Dewey Pritchett, born August 24, 1899, died March 19, 1965.

Laura Isabel, born July 18, 1868, died October 31, 1925, married James Thomas Denney, born November 23, 1863, died March 26, 1938. They had thirteen children: 1. Newman Edgar born November 13, 1885, died April 16, 1976, married on October 8, 1916, to Willie Myrte Shadinger, born May 8, 1899, died February 13, 1984. 2. Jeames Anna born January 21, 1887, died July 15, 1975, married on February 17, 1907, to Walter Lee Bonner, born August 6, 1885, died May 9, 1966. 3. Lonza Wilburn born September 23, 1888, died November 23, 1968, married first on January 7, 1912, to Lula Mae Stephens, born May 14, 1894, died November 14, 1974, and second on November 3, 1951, to Tokay Jeannette Bivins, born October 4, 1931. 4. Ima Reatha born April 30, 1890, died December 9, 1972, married Joseph Franklin Chambers, born February 16, 1888, died May 11, 1943. 5. Charles Thomas born February 24, 1892, died January 14, 1893. 6. Eula Cleantine born February 21, 1894, died January 15, 1895. 7. Homer Uclet born December 3, 1895, died October 3, 1966, married on December 25,

1927, to Leone Little, born January 28, 1900, died November 22, 1974. 8. Hampton Enoch born March 18, 1898, died June 26, 1991, married on December 25, 1926, to Sarah V. Crow, born October 3, 1906, died April 14, 1994. 9. Harvey Bagwell born July 28, 1900, died September 3, 1989, married on October 14, 1928, to Alma Mae Striplin, born December 5, 1905, died March, 1993. 10. Octavia J. born April 12, 1902, died August 11, 1979, married on August 24, 1919, to Henry Benford Bell, born December 25, 1898, died October 2, 1963. 11. Paul Olin born December 4, 1905, died November 28, 1971, married on June 14, 1931, to Velma Ruth Striplin, born January 11, 1911, died May 20, 1998. 12. Parrie Gerila born May 12, 1909, died November 6, 1998, married on June 17, 1928, to William Clyde Atkinson, born October 8, 1902, died May 16, 1998. 13. James Fred born August 4, 1911, died September 15, 1966, married on July 22, 1939, to Anna Maude Quarles, born December 17, 1918.

Roxie Ann, born January 2, 1872, died June 20, 1948, married on September 25, 1887, to Robert Lee Williams, born February 14, 1866, died June 30, 1945. They had four children: 1. Alice Sonobra born June 25, 1888, died September 21, 1909, married on December 25, 1904, to James Rufus Williams, born March 3, 1881, died May 18, 1965. 2. Cora Lee born August 7, 1890, died May 14, 1972, married on December 24, 1914, to Melbourn Rush Robinson, born September 9, 1893, died July 28, 1938. 3. Virgil Buren born September 7, 1897, died July 15, 1959, married on December 23, 1917, to Willie Mae McIntosh, born September 17, 1901, died March 22, 1972. 4. Sarah Henrietta born December 10, 1902, died August 19, 1998, married on December 24, 1919, to Minnie Neal Stephens, born August 20, 1899, died September 11, 1982.

Thomas Newton, born December 16, 1873, died November 30, 1932, married Susan Temperance "Tempie" Jackson, born March 28, 1870, died October 17, 1947. At the time of their marriage, she was a school teacher in Roopville and he was a carpenter in Tyus. They had eight children: 1. Buren Jackson born May 27, 1899, died March 15, 1988, married first to Benita Emma Grote in 1929; second on December 26, 1940, to Frances Emmylyn Popino, born April 6, 1900, died June 9, 1967; third to Lili Layai; and fourth to Isabel Arburola de Ramirez. 2. William Thomas born November 20, 1901, died March 9, 1953, married first to Dora Wortham on October 26, 1919, and second to Lonnie Irene Edins. 3. Frank Amis born December 2, 1903, died June 17, 1904. 4. Theodore Atkinson (twin to Frank Amis) born December 2, 1903, April 16, 1918. 5. James Van born April 6, 1905, died August 19, 1993, married first on March 1, 1925, to Eula Mae Kidd, born March 23, 1907, died December 9, 1984; second to Sarah Denney; and third on August 9, 1980, to Clyde Heard Welborn, born November 18, 1919. 6. Susan Temperance born June 4, 1908, died December 10, 1993, married on December 24, 1932, to John Benjamin Edmondson, born March 30, 1906, died April 27, 1985. 7. Infant son born and died May 30, 1911. 8. Sarah Elizabeth born August 13, 1914, died May 10, 1915. *Submitted by: Ronald S. Edmondson, 201 Concord Road SE, Smyrna, GA 30082-3701*

1039. Sam and Lula Smith Family

Samuel Russell Smith was born November 11, 1892, just a few miles past Roopville in Heard County, Ga. He had four brothers, John and Henry who raised their children here, and William who was thrown from a mule and died as a boy, and Enoch who was killed by a car in 1930. Sam moved to Carroll County and worked in the Mandeville Cotton Mill for years. He married Emma Lula Turner, who was originally from Alabama, born on April 29, 1888. She was one of four sisters, Minnie, Mary and Dussy and had one brother, John, whose descendants are scattered over Carroll County.

Together, Lula and Sam raised six sons: Otha Lanier Brightwell, born in 1911; James Pearce Smith, born in 1916; George Edward Smith, born in 1919; William Curtis Smith, born in 1924; Bobby Lee Smith, born in 1930, and Charles Kenneth Smith, born in 1933. The Smiths lived in the Old Camp community in the 1920s and attended Old Camp Methodist Church. The boys attended Tallapoosa School on the Tyus road. In the 1930s the family moved to the Beulah community. During those years the children attended Beulah School. Then in the 1940s the Smiths moved nearby to the New Hope community, where they lived the rest of their lives. Sam farmed, and Lula was a homemaker. The family was active in New Hope Methodist Church, and the boys attended Mt. Zion School.

The sons married, and most of them raised their own children in Carroll County. Otha married Sally Rayvee Brown. Pearce married Mary Jane Stewart. Edward married Margaret Marie Bartlett. William married Shirley Kathleen Goldin. Bobby married Martha Sue Lambert. Charles married Julia Diane Bell. The sons and wives gave Sam and Lula nine grandchildren and eighteen great-grandchildren. Lula died on May 15, 1974. Sam died on April 11, 1976. Pearce died in 1983. They are all buried in the New Hope Methodist Church cemetery, off the Mt. Zion Road. Otha died in 1997, and is buried in the Carrollton City Cemetery on Alabama Street.

Sam and Lula Smith Family in 1959

Most of the descendants still live in Carroll County at this writing. Grandchildren who make their home here with their families are: Kathy Smith, Joy Smith Griffin, Kenneth Smith, Susan Smith Horsley, Beverly Smith Webb, and Laura Smith Jacobiak. Melissa Smith Farmer, Malinda Smith Bennett, and Margie Smith all live in the Atlanta area. The Smith Family lived through many changes in Carroll County. They lived through two World Wars, the Great Depression, years with and without modern conveniences, such as indoor plumbing, radio, television, telephone, and electricity. They tell many stories of studying their school lessons by candle and kerosene lamp light. Though all worked hard in the fields, they enjoyed visiting on neighbors' front porches after a long day's work. They mostly walked or traveled by wagon in the early decades of the century. By the 1930s and 1940s, automobiles began to be on the scene. Carroll County has changed much in the 100+ years that this family has lived here, but it is still Home, and the Smiths are happy to live here with the friends and neighbors they grew up with and love. *Submitted by: Joy Smith Griffin, 26 Brandy Chase, Carrollton, GA 30117*

1040. The Thomas Jefferson Smith Family

Thomas (Tom) Smith, son of Archibald Jefferson Smith and Mariah Walden Smith, was born in Carroll County, Georgia on September 13, 1873. He married Lela Peacock in 1902. Lela, daughter of Robert Fleming Peacock and Josephine Fincher Peacock, was born in Clay County, Alabama, on March 4, 1886. Tom operated a water grist mill on the Little Tallapoosa River in the Farmer's High Community; he was also a carpenter and farmer.

The Thomas Jefferson and Lela Peacock Smith Family

Tom and Lela had seven children: four daughters, Luna, Derotha, Ivella, and Tommie Lee, and three sons, Hoke, Milford, and Dorsey. Hoke died of pneumonia at age eighteen in LaGrange, Georgia, while the family was living there temporarily. After leaving LaGrange, the family moved to Sand Mountain, Alabama.

Luna married J.B. Harris and they had no children.

Derotha married James (Jim) Henry Fletcher, also a Carroll Countian, and they had one daughter, Martha Ann.

Ivella married Thara Jolley. The children of this marriage were four daughters, Bonita, Peggy, JoAnn, and Bobbie.

Tommie Lee married Durward Stephenson and they had two sons, Billy and Gerald.

Milford married Opal Jolley and their two sons are Owen and David.

Dorsey married Marjorie Elrod and they had twin daughters, Paula and Paulette (Paulette died in infancy).

Tom died on March 23, 1943 in Wilsonville, Alabama, and Lela died on April 8, 1974 in Gadsden, Alabama. Both are buried in the Salem Baptist Church Cemetery, Bowdon, Carroll County, Georgia.

As one of their grandchildren, I, too, was born in Carroll County (Jonesville Community) on February 23, 1933. My family moved to Riverdale, Georgia in 1934. My husband, John Holt, and I have three sons: Fletcher, Ferrell, and Stacey. *Submitted by: Martha Ann Fletcher, 4685 Highway 92 N., Fairburn, GA 30213*

1041. W.M. Smith Family

Walter Melvin Smith was born 17 October 1888, the son of G.L. Smith (15 October 1858-11 February 1927) and Dora Smith (30 March 1867-30 January 1867-30 January 1897) of Carroll County. W.M. Smith had brothers Charlie L. born 17 January 1886 and Edgar L. Smith. Charlie's children were R.F. Smith of Cedartown, G.L. Smith, and Dewey Smith of Carrollton. There was one known half-sister, Mrs. John Tillman of Cullman, Alabama. Many of the Smiths are buried at Shady Grove Cemetery in Carroll County.

W.M. Smith grew up in Carroll County and was a resident of Carrollton for thirty-eight years. On 11 November 1923, he married Flonnie Agnes Denman of Tallapoosa, Georgia.

Flonnie was born 9 January 1904, the daughter of John Wiley Denman and Elizabeth Mercer. The Denmans had ten children and the known names are Flonnie, John, Ernest, Allen, Maude Vester and Claude Chester (twins), Edna, Pearl, and Ruth. The Denmans were early pioneers of Carroll County as they appear on the 1830 and 1840 census records of Carroll County.

John Wiley Denman was born 12 August 1856 and died 20 November 1928. He was the son of John Denman, a Confederate soldier serving in Texas who died during the Civil War. John W. Denman was married to Elizabeth Jerome Mercer who was born 1 January 1866 and died 19 February 1948. Elizabeth Mercer was the daughter of Jake Mercer and Agnes Pate. Agnes was born 31 May 1842 and died 3 March 1914. The Mercers were residents of Newnan, Georgia. Jake Mercer was also a Confederate soldier killed during the Civil War. According to family tradition, Jake Mercer was related to the Mercer who was the founder of Mercer University.

The Denmans were early pioneers to Carroll County who were in Habersham County, Georgia, first. According to a deed of 14 November 1836 in Carroll County for Land Lot #140 in the 7th District (now Haralson County), the heirs of James Denman and his wife Sarah were James R. Denman, Absolum Denman, and Delilah Denman who inherited the property mentioned. There were numerous deeds between 1843-1855 for Absolum Denman and James Denman.

Mr. and Mrs. W.M. Smith, 1950s

John Wiley Denman appears in the 1850 census of Carroll County as age 43, with wife Elizabeth age 18, Claranna age 3, and Hepshiba age 8 months, all born in Georgia. There is also an A.W. Denman age 28, with wife Martha age 22, James age 2 and Caroline age 1, all born in Georgia. Madison Hardeman, age 22 male, also lives in the household with the young A.W. Denman family.

Both W.M. Smith and his wife Flonnie were active in civic affairs. Flonnie served as one of the first presidents of the Business & Professional Women's Club which was organized in 1935. Flonnie was active in the Garden Club and a member of the Georgia Chrysanthemum Society. She had many prize winning mums over the years. Both W.M. Smith and Flonnie were active in the Tabernacle Baptist Church where W.M. served as a deacon.

W.M. Smith was one of Carrollton's most enterprising businessmen during his lifetime and was a charter member of the Kiwanis Club in Carrollton. He established the Smith Oil Company in 1935. During the years of World War II, he was responsible for keeping the county supplied with gas, which was rationed in those years. When the gas was delivered in the nighttime, the driver would toot his horn in front of the Smith home on Dixie Street and young Betty Morgan would run in her pajamas and turn on the porch light to signal that Mr. Smith had heard the signal and would go to the Smith Oil Company to let the truck in to make his delivery. Smith Oil used to be where Southwire is today. Now the company called Morgan Oil is located just across the street on Fertilla Street.

The company grew under Smith's direction and he was later rejoined in the business by his son-in-law, Bobby Morgan. The business became associated with American Oil in 1956. The name of the business became known as Morgan Oil when Bobby Morgan took over after the death of W.M. Smith. Today, Morgan Oil is owned and operated by W.M. Smith's grandson, Jimmy Morgan.

W.M. and Flonnie Smith were the parents of three children: W.M. Smith Jr., born 25 March 1931, died at birth; Elizabeth Louise "Betty" Smith was born 1 December 1927; and Patrick Ann "Patsy" Smith who was born 27 March 1933. Betty graduated from Carrollton High School in 1945 and Patsy graduated in 1950.

Betty Smith graduated from West Georgia College in 1959 with a major in elementary education. She taught at Rockridge, Centralhatchee, and Mt. Zion grammar schools. In later years, Betty served as a substitute teacher at Carrollton High School. After her husband, Bobby Morgan, took over the gasoline business, Betty became involved in the duties of the corporation. Since her retirement in 1999, Betty has enjoyed traveling with tour groups to New England, Alaska, American West, Mexico and abroad.

Bobby Morgan was famous as a track star at Carrollton High School. He ran the 100-yard dash in 9.8 seconds in 1941 and this record stood at Carrollton High for forty years. They called him "greased lightning." He was the first inductee into the Trojan Hall of Fame when they established it in 1976.

After high school, Bobby Morgan was quickly called into service in World War II. He joined the Navy after high school and served as a radio operator on ships in the South Pacific where he was in the middle of many of the historic naval battles fought there. After his return from the war, he worked for a while with his father, J. Horry Morgan, in operating his sawmill. After Bobby married Betty Smith, he became a part of her father's business, Smith Oil.

Betty Smith married James Robert "Bobby" Morgan on 24 January 1947. They had three children: Walter David Morgan was the oldest child born on 4 September 1956; Pamela Louise Morgan born 7 December 1958; and James Patrick Morgan born 27 August 1964.

Bobby and Betty Morgan were active in civic affairs. Bobby belonged to the Kiwanis Club and Betty was elected "Woman of the Year" in her sorority Beta Sigma Phi. Betty Morgan has also served on the Auxiliary of Tanner Medical Center for many years. Bobby Morgan died on 25 March 1996, a short time after his sister Melba had died in January. He was laid to rest in Carroll Memory Gardens.

Both Betty and Bobby enjoyed landscaping and flowers. Bobby experimented with cross pollination of flowers and created many new varieties never seen before. He was also an avid hunter and fisherman. "Bobby could catch 'em and Betty could cook 'em." Betty is remembered for the delicious hush-puppies that she served up with the many fish-frys that she and Bobby hosted over the years. Bobby and Betty always loved to entertain and entertained we were whenever we were guests under the spell of their hospitality. Betty is still an excellent cook and a family favorite is her stuffed celery. We like the apron that Betty's daughter-in-law Michelle made for her that is embroidered with "Queen Bee."

Bobby and Betty Morgan were devoted to the care of Bobby's mother, Trixie Morgan, who was widowed at an early age. Trixie often said that Betty was more like a daughter than a daughter-in-law to her. In more than fifty years together, they were friends and never a cross word was spoken between them.

Betty has also enjoyed a special relationship with her niece, Jan Robinson Bell, as Jan was born the year that Betty and Bobby married. Since Jan's father was an only child, and Melba had only the one brother, Betty Morgan is the only aunt that Jan had. Betty was the only one who had the patience to stand in line so Jan could sit on Santa's lap and tell him her Christmas wish list!

Pam Morgan graduated from Carrollton High School in 1976 and later that year married Michael Alan DeMatteis on 28 December 1976. They had two children: Ashley Michele DeMatteis was born 26 July 1982, and Michael Morgan DeMatteis was born 7 June 1985. Ashley is a student at Carson Newman College in Jefferson City, Tennessee, pursuing a double major in Spanish and religion. She is working as a missionary in Tennessee this summer along with other college students. Mike is a student at Carrollton High School where he is on the football team. Both Ashley and Mike enjoyed their trips to the ski slopes where their Uncle Jimmy treats them to an annual vacation. Pam and Michael Dematteis later divorced. Pam works as secretary-treasurer for Morgan Oil in Carrollton.

Betty and Bobby Morgan

Jimmy Morgan grew up in Southgate subdivision around the corner from the Joe Bell Jr. family. Jimmy's cousins, Joe, John, and Ben Bell, were just a few stair steps in years younger then he, so all the boys grew up together in the same neighborhood and enjoyed being more like brothers than cousins. Jimmy Morgan graduated from Carrollton High School where he had been a part of a remarkable CHS band during his high school years. Jimmy received his degree in marketing from West Georgia College in 1986. After a brief stint of working in Washington, D.C. in the office of Congressman Newt Gingrich, Jimmy returned to Carrollton to work for the family business, Morgan Oil.

Michelle Leigh Flake also graduated from West Georgia College in 1986 with a degree in business administration. Michelle was a member of Alpha Gamma Delta social sorority at West Georgia. The next year, Michelle received her master's degree in business administration. Michelle was the co-owner of the bookstore. A Likely Story, for many years but has since sold her part of the business. Michelle loves to sew and has made many of her own clothes and home furnishings. She also plays tennis and belongs to the Atlanta Lawn and Tennis Association. She regularly travels with them to play in tournaments and chairs many benefits in the community, as well.

Jimmy Morgan and Michelle Leigh Flake married on 22 December 1992. Theirs was a beautiful wedding in which Michelle wore the very same wedding dress that her own mother, Mary Kay Flake, had worn at her own wedding. Since it was a Christmas wedding, instead of playing "Here Comes the Bride" as Michelle came down the aisle, the organist played "Hark the Herald Angels Sing" and it was simply beautiful. Also, the new Tabernacle Baptist Church had never looked prettier than for this occasion and it was one of the very first weddings held in the new church.

Michelle Morgan is a native of Stone Mountain, Georgia. She is the daughter of Maury Leo "Skip" and Mary Kay Flake. Michelle has two brothers, Steve and Mike Flake. Jimmy and Michelle Morgan have two sons: James Patrick Morgan Jr. born 15 April 1998, and Michael DePorter Morgan, who is named for Michelle's mother's maiden name, who was born 2 December 1999.

The second daughter of W.M. and Flonnie Smith is Patsy Smith who married Larry Wingo Hollingsworth. (See the Larry Hollingsworth story.) *Submitted by: Pam DeMatteis, Mountain Oaks Drive, Carrollton, GA 30117*

1042. Walter and Mary Jim Smith

Mary Jim Gilreath Smith was born September 11, 1912, in Jersey, Walton County Georgia. Always known by her nickname, "Jack," she eventually became so revered in the Bowdon community that everyone simply called her "Miss Jack." She was the second of Henry and Essie Mae Gilreath's seven daughters. One of the daughters died in infancy, and the eldest, Nannie Mae, died in 1992.

In 1927, at age fifteen, Miss Jack met her future husband, John Walter Smith (born 3-5-1905), at his father's Bowdon grocery store. Walter was the son of Minor C. Smith and Mattie Coker Smith. Walter and Miss Jack were married December 16, 1928, in Tyus Georgia, by a justice of the peace. They had four sons: John Walter Smith Jr. (12-23-29), Claude Edward (12-11-32), and twins, Gene Timothy and Jerry Thomas (8-29-41).

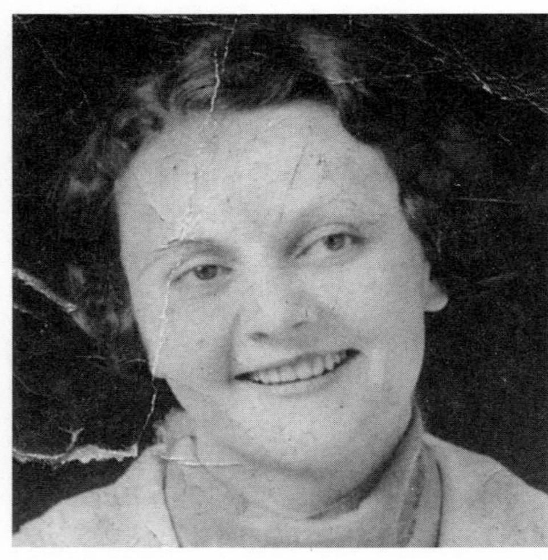

Mary Jim Smith, 1935

In 1944 at the age of thirty-nine, Walter was diagnosed with bone cancer. Years later in a rare admission of fear and uncertainty, Miss Jack recalled feeling as if her entire world had collapsed. Her youngest sons were only three years old at the time. Though given only a short time to live when the diagnosis was made, Walter lived thirteen more years. Much of that time he was confined in body casts and bed, enduring tremendous pain and debilitation. Miss Jack tended to all his needs, the needs of her sons, her grandsons, and her neighbors while working at Sewell Manufacturing Company to support her family. Because she could not drive and she had no car, she walked everywhere she had to go. But she was never one to be discouraged or deterred. When she was about fifty years old she learned to drive, and true to her indomitable spirit, she taught herself.

She never remarried after Walter's death in 1957. Her priorities were always her faith and her family. Her home was a haven for neighborhood children because of her generous nature, her immeasurable knowledge of plants and animals, and her delicious cooking. She worked for the Sewell company thirty-eight years, continuing on after retirement as a part-time employee until she was eighty-two. She was conscientious and loyal in her work and she worked in several departments over the years: sewing, repairs, inspection, and quality control. She taught many young people the value of work through her example.

John Walter Smith Sr., 1928

She is a member of Bowdon First United Methodist Church, where she has served on the official board, taught Sunday School, and tirelessly volunteered her time. Always eager to learn, she's also enjoyed other activities such as sewing, macrame, art classes, ceramics, cake decorating and garden club. In May 1996, she suffered a stroke that took away her physical strength. However, she still has the powerful faith and independent spirit that enabled her to prevail over many of life's trials. Even now she attends to others through daily prayers on their behalf. Miss Jack Smith has influenced so many people in the Bowdon community, and she remains an inspiration to all who know her. Romans 8:28 *Submitted by: John Smith, 214 East College Street, Bowdon, GA 30108*

1043. William Smith

Smith's Studio

In March 1946, William "Bill" Smith came home from World War II seeking a job. He met Emory Tate, a photographer from Chattanooga, who had purchased W.M. Boyton Studio in downtown Carrollton. Bill worked for a year as an unpaid apprentice for Tate, and a year later purchased the studio for $300. Later he graduated from the New York Institute of Photography where he attended double sessions to make the most of his time. He married Kathleen Goldin of Bremen in 1950. They had two daughters, Kathy Smith born 1957, and Susan Smith born 1961. Kathy has a son Ross Crawford born 1979, and Carrie Smith was born in 1987.

Bill Smith and his daughter, Susan Smith Horsley

His career spanned more than fifty-one years without interruption. He photographed thousands of weddings, and perhaps the most famous picture of Carrollton's Adamson Square ever taken. Bill remembers the photo very well. Although Smith's Studio has been located at the corner of West Center Street and Highway 27 for thirty-two years, he spent his first fourteen years in business operating from a shop on Adamson Square. The picture was taken in 1954, but he has rarely been acknowledged as the photographer. Overwhelmingly romantic, this picture has hung in restaurants and shops for decades, but few know who owns the negative and who, leaning out of the upstairs window of his shop one afternoon, snapped the original photograph.

It was through his training in New York and elsewhere that Bill Smith the artist emerged. Over the years, he has developed a philosophy and vision toward photography that he has imparted to the people, like his daughter Susan Smith Horsley, whom he trained in the business. In 1997 Bill finally decided to retire and turned the studio over to Susan who has been there full-time since June 1979. Susan married Jay M. Horsley of Carrollton in 1987. They have two children, Samuel born in 1989, and Sarah born in 1992.

Adamson Square taken in 1954 by Bill Smith

Smith's Studio has always specialized in weddings and portraits. Smith's Studio has withstood the test of time and after fifty-five years of operation Susan plans to possibly turn the business over to yet a third generation. Smith's Studio is more than just a job, it's tradition. *Submitted by: Susan Smith Horsley, 208 West Center Street, Carrollton, GA 30117*

1044. Smith - Lambert Family

Bobby Lee Smith, son of Samuel Russell Smith (1892-1976) and Lula Turner Smith (1888-1974), was born in Carrollton June 27, 1930. He and Martha Sue Lambert were married June 4, 1961, at the home of her family by Rev. Lewis H. Brazell. She was born in Carrollton September 17, 1938, the daughter of Curtis Newton Lambert (1911-1957) and Sarah Douglas Lambert (1914-1990).

Bobby attended Mt. Zion High School and served two years in the U.S. Army during the Korean conflict. He worked at Carrollton Coca-Cola Bottling Company in Carrollton (1948-1968) in various positions. Bobby retired from West Georgia College Plant Operations in 1994.

Martha Sue attended College Street School and graduated from Carrollton High School in 1956. She was employed by Carroll Publishing Company (*Times Free Press-Carroll County Georgian*) (1957-1972), Carroll Realty & Insurance Company (1974-1984), and West Georgia College, now State University of West Georgia (1984-retiring 2000).

Bobby and Martha Sue have resided on New Hope Church Road, Carrollton, since 1962 and are members of New Hope United Methodist Church. They have two children: Beverly Jane Smith, born September 17, 1966, and Laura Lee Smith, born October 6, 1972.

Beverly graduated from Carrollton High School in 1984. She married Corey Earl Webb on December 27, 1986. Corey Webb, son of Ellis Webb and Alice Carter Webb, was born January 3, 1967. He graduated from Mt. Zion High School in 1985. Beverly has been employed by J. Smith Lanier Insurance Company, Carrollton, since 1984 as an agent and customer service representative. Corey has been employed by Carroll Electric Membership Corporation, Carrollton, since 1987 as a journeyman lineman. Beverly and Corey's children are Kirstin Laci Webb, born June 12, 1991; Kobie Judson Webb, born May 15, 1993; and Kace Ellis Webb born April 3, 1995. They are students at Mt. Zion Elementary School. They have resided on Ingram Road, Carrollton since 1990 and are members of New Hope United Methodist Church.

Laura graduated from Mt. Zion High School in 1991 as valedictorian of her class. She graduated from the State University of West Georgia in 1998 with a B.B.A. majoring in administrative systems. She is employed by Tanner Medical Center's Management Service Organization. She is a member of New Hope United Methodist Church. On November 21, 2000, Laura married Craig Ronald Jakubiak (born June 23, 1965) in Fredonia, New York. Craig has a son, Conner Joseph Jakubiak (born May 24, 1993). Craig is the son of Walter and Darlene Doyle of Fredonia, New York. He is employed by PrintPack Inc. as a machine operator. Conner is a student at Carrollton Elementary School. They reside on New Hope Church Road.

On Bobby and Martha Sue's second date, August 16, 1957, they attended services at Bethel Camp Meeting. Since then, they have been very active at Bethel Camp Ground with Bobby currently serving as chairman and Martha Sue as secretary-treasurer. Bobby enjoys gardening and having vegetables to share with their family. Bobby and Martha Sue enjoy preserving vegetables and fruits to share with family and friends. They value being a close-knit family and enjoy spending time with their children and grandchildren. *Submitted by: Laura Jakubiak, 442 New Hope Church Road, Carrollton, GA 30117*

1045. Smith - Skinner Family

Part 1

Joseph Elbert "Joe Turk" Smith and Edney Urgeney Skinner

Joseph Elbert "Joe Turk" Smith was born July 5, 1855, probably in Randolph (later Cleburne) County, Alabama, on the Stateline farm which was half in Carroll County, Georgia, and half in Alabama. He was the son of William Enoch H. Smith and Sarah Couch. He was the grandson of Robert H. Smith and Sarah Crumpton, and William "Billy" Joseph Couch.

Joe Turk Smith was only seven years old when his father, William Enoch H. Smith, died in Tennessee in the Civil War. This left Sarah Couch a very young widow with five little children to raise. Sarah Couch, born 1832 in Coweta County, Georgia, was the daughter of Billy Couch and belonged to the large Couch family of Coweta County. She died in 1924 in Winston, Alabama, is buried at Littleville Methodist Church beside her daughter Lucinda who married Val Crumpton.

Joseph Elbert "Joe Turk" Smith married Edna Skinner on February 29, 1875, the daughter of William Jasper Skinner (1827-1862) and Mary Arthur (1825-1887). Joe Turk and Edney must have had many sad memories of the Civil War because Edna (1860-1904), too, had lost her father, William Jasper Skinner (1827-1862) in the Civil War. He died in Mississippi after the Battle of Shiloh from illness and exhaustion. Edney was only two years old when her mother Mary Arthur, a very young widow also, was left with five children to raise. Mary Arthur Skinner (1825-1887) was born in Coweta County, Georgia, to John Arthur, born 1796 in Bedford County, Virginia, and his wife Matilda Gibson, born 1803 in Oglethorpe County, Georgia. Matilda Gibson was the daughter of James Hugh Gibson (of Oglethorpe, Greene, and later Coweta County) and his wife Sarah Foster, who died in 1815 in Oglethorpe County. Sarah Foster was the daughter of John Hardin Foster and Martha "Patsy" Wingfield, the daughter of John Wingfield (1723-1793) who came to Wilkes County, Georgia, from Virginia. These families were early settlers of Georgia in Wilkes and Oglethorpe Counties. Mary Arthur Skinner was a long way from her "roots" in Carroll County during the years following the Civil War. Life must have been very hard for her. Mary Arthur Skinner was also descended from Barnabas Arthur (1736-1799) and his wife Martha Talbot (1740-1802) from Bedford County, Virginia. The Arthur and Talbot families received land grants in Wilkes and Oglethorpe Counties, Georgia, for their services in the Revolutionary War. Matthew Talbot, a cousin, was an early Governor of Georgia.

Joseph Elbert "Joe Turk" Smith Family

William Jasper Skinner was the son of Isaac H. Skinner (1800-circa 1887), an early pioneer of Carroll County, and his wife, Mary Ann Harley (1808-1870). He was the grandson of John H. Skinner and Susannah Coaker and Capt. William Joseph Harley and Elizabeth Pryor, all early settlers of Georgia. Capt. William Joseph Harley was the son of Revolutionary War soldier, Lt. Joseph Harley (1720-1807) and his wife Elizabeth Jackson. John H. Skinner was the son of a Revolutionary soldier, Capt. Isaac Skinner and his wife Jane Jackson.

Joseph Elbert "Joe Turk" Smith owned and operated large amounts of farmland in Carroll County and Cleburne County, Alabama. He married twice and was the father of fourteen children. His first wife, Edna Skinner, died of typhoid fever in August 1904, leaving Joe Turk with eleven children to raise. Children of Joseph Elbert "Joe Turk" Smith and Edney Ugeney "Edna" Skinner were: (1) "Lucy" Ann Malinda Frances Smith, born August 24, 1876, died September 2, 1961, married S.E. "Ed" Deese. (2) Mary Etta Smith, born December 4, 1878, died February 4, 1956, married John Baker on September 4, 1900. (3) William Enoch Gibson Calhoun "Buck" Smith, born March 2, 1881, died August 22, 1898 of typhoid fever, married Marshy "Pat" Hardigree on November 22, 1897. (4) Warner Nathaniel Smith, born August 5, 1883, married first to Sally Glass, and second to Emmie Buchanan. (5) Loveler Victory "Lovella" Smith, born February 12, 1886, married Bob Glass. (6) Cora Elizabeth Smith, born July 4, 1888, died April 27, 1958. Cora was injured in a buggy accident when she was young. She lived with her sister Lucy Deese and her family. (7) Seaborn Rufus Smith, born July 10, 1891, died June 4, 1940, married Lillie Ethel Hill (1894-1964) on May 19, 1912, daughter of James Martin "Jim" Hill and Susannah Durrett Hill. (8) Dussie Othellar Smith, born May 6, 1894, married William "Bill" Buchanan. (9) Emory Huel Smith, born March 6, 1896, died March 28, 1933, married Ora Burson (1894-1939). (10) Newman Hershal Smith, born June 9, 1898, married Lou Etta Handley, January 28, 1916. (11) Anderson Jethroe "Sam" Smith, born November 12, 1900, married Bessie Walker, May 22, 1932.

Five Sons of Joseph Elbert "Joe Turk" Smith and Edna Skinner

Joseph Elbert "Joe Turk" Smith was married second to Mattie Estella Buchanan on February 28, 1905. She was born November 11, 1880. Their children were: (1) Myrtle Smith, born July 6, 1906, married Riley Parker September 25, 1921. (2) Mackie Smith, born May 15, 1908, married Henry Hale December 24, 1934. (3) Etta G. Smith, born November 1, 1909, married Emmett Thomas Pollard.

The family group picture taken about 1903 shows the Joseph Elbert "Joe Turk" Smith family at the Georgia/Alabama Stateline Road home. Seated are daughter Mary Etta Smith Baker and her three children, "Joe Turk" Smith holding young son Sam, Edna Skinner Smith, and Newman. Standing on back row are Cora, Dussie, Huel, and Seaborn Rufus Smith.

The second picture, made about 1930, shows the five sons of Joseph Elbert "Joe Turk" Smith and Edna Skinner. Seated in front are Warner and Seaborn Rufus "Rufe" Smith. Standing on back row are Sam, Newman, and Huel. *Submitted by: Jo Ann Hancock, 8th Street, Chamblee, GA and Written by: Peggy Jackson Hughes*

1046. Smith - Skinner Family

Part 2

Seaborn Rufus Smith and Lillie Ethel Hill

Seaborn Rufus Smith, born July 10, 1891 on the Joseph Elbert "Joe Turk" Smith farm which straddled Carroll County, Georgia and Cleburne County, Alabama, married Lillie Ethel Hill on May 19, 1912. Ethel Hill was the daughter of James Martin "Jim" Hill and Suzannah Durret Hill. She was the granddaughter of the Rev. Martin Hill and Sarah Ann Tumlin, and the great-granddaughter of Greenberry Hill (War of 1812) and his wife Martha Ivey.

The Smith and Hill families lived in the Sandy Flat community between Bowdon, Georgia, and Ranburne, Alabama. They were farmers, blacksmiths, and owned large amounts of land in both Carroll County and Cleburne County.

Seaborn Rufus Smith was the son of Joseph Elbert "Joe Turk" Smith and his first wife Edna Ugeney Skinner. Joe Turk was a large man with a large family and owned several farms in the area of Bowdon, Georgia, and Macedonia, Hopewell and Ranburne in Alabama. He also owned and operated mule barns in the Stateline area and stores in Ranburne.

Rufe Smith and Ethel Hill on their wedding day in 1912.

Seaborn Rufus Smith and Ethel Hill lived in Carroll County on the John Wesley Jackson home place at the time of his death on June 4, 1940, leaving her as a very young widow with several children to raise and several farms in Carroll County and Cleburne County, Alabama, area to look after. Ethel Hill Smith was a strong Christian woman and sold all of her farms except the one in Hopewell, Alabama. She moved and raised her children there. The children of Seaborn Rufus Smith and Lillie Ethel Hill were: (1) Q.P. Smith, born 1914, died 1986, buried at Sandy Flat Church, married Ora Belle Williams, December 28, 1940; two children, Diane and Dawn. (2) Lewis Clyde Smith, born March 22, 1916, died February 1993, married Edith Sellars; three children, Johnny, Jimmy, and Betty. (3) Sybil Verlie Smith, born April 11, 1918, married Woodrow Wilson Jackson, May 1933; three children, Peggy, Sandra, and Ernie. (4) Mable Helen Smith, born February 19, 1920, married Heaton Turner, February 11, 1939; four children, Randal, Cathy, Steve, and Hal. (5) Archie Ernest Smith, born February 11, 1922, died April 1993, buried at Macedonia, married Vernell Williams, Novemer 23, 1946; two children, Tim and Rhonda. (6) Dorothy Joanne "Joe Ann" Smith, born July 29, 1924, married Oscar E. Hancock, December 4, 1947; four children, Suzanne, Eddie, Becky, and Trez. (7) Doris Jean Smith, born November 15, 1926, married first to Lanford Freeman in 1943, one son David; and married second to Hugh Granger. (8) Jimmy Hill Smith, born 1929, died March 18, 1937, buried at Sandy Flat Church. (9) Bruce Hampton Smith, born 1933, died June 16, 1934, buried at Sandy Flat Church. (10) Seaborn Rodney Smith, born 1935, married first to Louise Oatswell in 1967, two children, Tiffany and Jenny; and married second to Alice Deese Warren. (11) Kay Ella Smith, born March 21, 1937, married James Cosper, May 2, 1953; four sons, infant son, Phillip, Michael, and Marty.

Ethel Hill Smith lost her mother, Susannah Durrett Hill, daughter of James Durrett and Matha Ross in 1938. She lost her little son Jimmy Hill Smith on March 18, 1937, and three days later gave birth to her youngest child Kay on March 21, 1937. She had lost her baby son Bruce Hampton Smith in 1934. It must have been the lowest point in her life when she lost her husband, Seaborn Rufus "Rufe" Smith, on June 4, 1940. Rufe Smith left her with several farms to manage and her youngest child was only three years old. She sold all of her farms, paid off all her debts, moved to the Macedonia community and gathered her family together. Her daughter, Sybil Smith Jackson and son-in-law Woodrow Jackson got the big old John Wesley Jackson home in the corner of Carroll County at the crossroads between Bowdon, Georgia, and Ranburne, Alabama, where they lived for several years. Her sons, Lewis Clyde Smith and Archie Ernest Smith, were off fighting for America in World War II, and Q.P. Smith, his wife Ora Belle Williams, and Ethel Smith moved the remaining children to Macedonia. Mable Smith had married Heaton Turner and they were already in Ranburne, Alabama.

Ethel Hill Smith died in January 1964. She was buried beside her husband who had died so many years before and her two little sons at Sandy Flat Church which was very near the home she had lived in when she had lost so many of her loved ones. *Submitted by: Sybil Smith Jackson, 445 Ayers Road, Bowdon, GA 30108 and Written by: Peggy Jackson Hughes.*

1047. R.B. Sparks Family

The Sparks families originally came to the America from England. Joseph M. Sparks came from Clay County, Alabama to Carroll County, Georgia, and married DeLorria Lassetter. They built a pretty house and raised a family in the Cross Plains community. Their children were Lora, Lilla, Eugene, Ida, Bartow, and Guy.

The Bartow Sparks Family

The picture taken by my neighbor, William Birdsong, was made at Christmastime one year. Seated are Bartow and Vivian Sparks. Standing are Melba Sparks (right), and her brother Alton (left). (See related Crews-Sparks-Richards-Horsley Family picture.) *Submitted by: Melba Sparks Leggett, Villa Rica, GA*

1048. Robert Toombs and Camilla Brown Spearman

Toombs Spearman was born June 23, 1889, to Robert Arnold and Lucendia C. "Lizzie" Spearman, who farmed south of Lowell. On April 14, 1914, he married Camilla Brown born December 17, 1895, to Retha Jackson and Miles Avender Brown of Heard County. She was the third girl born in the family of six siblings. Toombs and Camilla's wedding was performed by the Glenloch Baptist minister at the home of her parents.

Robert, Toombs' father, who could not hear well, was run over by an automobile near A&M School in Carrollton. His untimely death in 1913 left Toombs' mother and Etta, his younger sister born 1892, under his care. As a young school boy, Toombs had admired a home built by Walter Nix and in 1917 he achieved his childhood dream and moved his wife and young son, Robert Arnold born March 14, 1915, to the heart of the Lowell community where he lived until his death January 18, 1979. One other son, Jim Selby born August 31, 1918, and three daughters, Thelma Louise born December 31, 1921, Marie Ruth born August 2, 1926, and Wyolene born July 26, 1929, completed the family. Robert was deceased October 4, 1997.

Toombs farmed his place in Lowell as well as the home place south of Lowell and operated a sawmill. As a charter member of the newly established Methodist Church in 1919, he served on the building committee and sawed the lumber for the church. Etta and his mother were also charter members of the church. Camilla was also a faithful member of the church until her death November 2, 1980,

Two farm helpers, Camilla, Toombs, Robert, Etta and Lizzie at Spearman home place. 1913

Ernest Strickland and his family were dependable workers who helped Toombs farm and operate the sawmill. Earnest sharpened his carpenter skills by building a playhouse for the girls, Ruth and Wyolene, which still stands and was the envy of little girls in the community. Toombs leased land near his sawmill for a cotton gin to be built around 1925. For many years the Scantlin family also helped in the farming operation, which included crops of corn, cotton, sorghum, and raising pigs and cattle. The farm supplied most of their food needs. The family had a milk cow which Louise remembers milking before going to school each morning. *Submitted by: Louise Spearman Blackwelder, 393 Blackwelder Road, Carrollton, GA 30116*

1049. Hiram and Angelina Cheney Spence

Two years after their marriage December 5, 1844, in Morgan County Georgia, Hiram S. and Angelina Cheney Spence and their young son William Martin, born December 1, 1845, moved to Carroll County. Hiram's parents, George born March 25, 1797, and Mary Knight born November 19, 1801, settled on 400 acres in Morgan County, Georgia, where Hiram was born February 24, 1821, the oldest of ten children. Hiram's grandfather, John Spence was born September 7, 1772, and came to Georgia by ox cart about 1795 from Maryland.

Angelina, born August 3, 1824, was the daughter of Thomas Benson Cheney, born in Maryland January 25, 1788, and moved to Wilkes County Georgia with his father in 1800. Angelina's mother was Lucy Middlebrooks Cheney, whose father Issac Middlebrooks served in the Revolutionary War, was present in 1779 at the Battle of the Savannah River and assisted in carrying the body of Count Casimir Pulaski from the battlefield after the British mortally wounded him.

In 1847 Carroll County was so unsettled when Hiram and his family arrived that they cut the road as they traveled to the area they settled about six miles north of Carrollton. Part of the way they traveled over a road cut by his relative George Sharp who had moved to the county in 1829. The present Pole Branch was so named because they had to cut poles and lay across it before proceeding.

Hiram built a log house, which had the distinction of having a board floor. The family lived in the log house for eight years before moving to a house. Beginning in 1849 Hiram bought four tracts of land in Districts 5 and 6 consisting of over six hundred acres between Carrollton and Temple. For many years there were only three houses between his home and Temple and only five between his home and Carrollton.

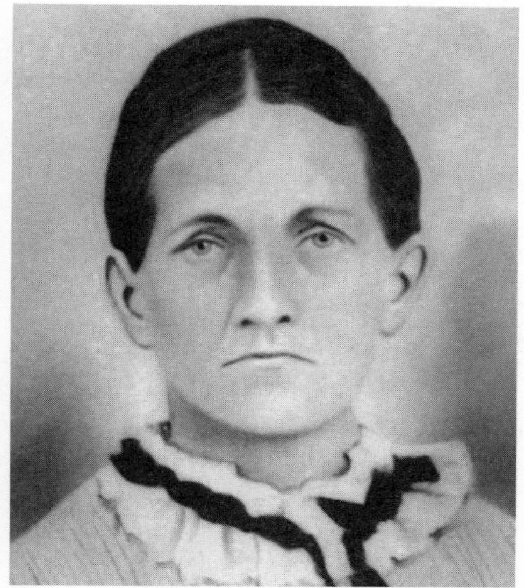

Angelina Cheney Spence, wife of Hiram Spence

Hiram's father, George, served as one of three delegates from Walton County to the Secession Convention in Milledgeville in 1861 and voted to stay with the Union, but ultimately voted to withdraw in order to present a united stand. At the age of forty Hiram volunteered to serve in the Confederate Army, Company K, 2nd Georgia Regiment, and served for three years under Generals Joseph E. Johnston and John B. Hood. On March 4, 1864, at Camp Rough, his eighteen-year-old son William M. "Billy" Spence joined Hiram and both fought in the Atlanta Campaign. Billy later wrote that his regiment "was almost destroyed on April 16, 1865, at Columbus, Georgia ... when Wilson's raid killed, imprisoned and scattered our command." Billy told of his long barefooted walk back to his home in Carroll County.

Other children of Hiram and Angelina were Isaac Newton Benton born April 10, 1850, became a medical doctor and practiced in Social Circle, Georgia; George Marion Lee born November 22, 1851, remained in Carroll County and farmed near his home place; Columbus Washington Spence born July 4, 1855, moved to Florida and owned an orange grove near Kissimmee; Thedora Octavius born March 18, 1857, married William Howell Rowe; Liberia Philadelphia Neptune, born February 26, 1859, married Robert W. West; Thomas Spence born December 10, 1891, died in infancy; Ella Esterilla born December 25, 1862, married James Ephram Bartlett and moved to Florida; John Robert Spake Spence born February 9, 1866, taught school and farmed in the Lowell community; Moses Enoch Virgil, born October 2, 1869, taught school and farmed in the Center Point community.

Hiram, who died July 9, 1889, and Angelina, who died October 8, 1908, were both buried near the site of their homestead in the Spence-Rowe Cemetery with several of their children and other family members. Both were members of the Concord Primitive Baptist Church. *Submitted by: Kay Rowland Whatley, 383 Plainville Road, Rome, GA 30181*

Sources: Family documents, *Memoirs of Georgia* and personal notes.

1050. John Robert Spake and Eula Foster Spence

John Robert Spake Spence born February 9, 1866, was the eighth child of Hiram and Angelina Carolina Cheney. He was reared north of Carrollton in the Center Point area on his father's farm. Their mother taught John and his siblings their ABCs using the family Bible. They attended school in a log cabin in the woods with a dirt floor, seats made of slabs, chimney made with mud and rocks, and square holes cut through the sides for windows. A regular job for the children at night was to separate the lint from the cottonseed. Each had to work until his shoes were filled with seed.

When John was about fourteen years old he began to attend the Masonic Academy for Boys in Carrollton, walking or riding his horse each day the distance of six miles. He told of reading his books as he walked. He graduated in 1884 being recognized as a boy of honor, and standing at the head of his class. In the fall of 1884, he entered Bowdon College as a freshman. While in college he was a leader in many activities, serving as senior class president, president of the Clay Calhoun Society, and member of the debating club. In 1888 he represented his society in debating at the annual commencement and received his A.B. degree, cum laude. From 1888 to 1890 he served as a professor at his alma mater and in 1891 Bowdon College conferred on him an honorary A.M. degree. He lived at Horace, northeast of Bowdon, during this time. John felt that his real calling was to teach the boys and girls in the rural communities and from 1890 to 1892 he taught at Temple in Carroll County. In 1893 he moved to Lowell to be the sole teacher in the one-room school and remained there throughout his life teaching for twenty five years and farming. He was a Mason and served his lodge as Worshipful Master for several years.

John R. and Eula Foster Spence

In 1894 he ran for state representative and served in the Georgia House of Representatives 1894-1895, and two other terms 1911 to 1914 and 1923 to 1924. While in the legislature he always worked for passage of laws that would help in educating the boys and girls of the state. He was always very concerned about the future of youth. In an address he gave August 1936 he said "... to the youth of our community, be industrious, be sober, be gentle, be kind, be loyal to principle and when your sun of life shall like ours, be setting behind the horizon of time, may it send back its rays in beams of soft and mellow splendor, painting your virtues upon the hilltops, the mountains and the skies and departing, hand on the record to future generations, bright with new names that shall live after you."

During his initial tenure as representative, he met Eula Beatrice Foster, born October 11, 1874, daughter of James M. Foster and Rebecca Ann Raven of McDonough, Georgia. Eula was a teacher in the Mt. Carmel area of Henry County, Georgia. After corresponding for several years, they were married November 17, 1897, at residence of Mr. and Mrs. J.B. Dickson in McDonough. They took the train that afternoon for their future home in Lowell. They built a home on land purchased from L.C. Mandeville, and John R. continued to teach and farm. Their first son Leo Virgil, born February 9, 1899, taught school and farmed, dying at the home place February 9, 1968. Five more sons: Hope died in infancy in 1900; Lewis Adel born November 16, 1901, also taught school and farmed in the area and died April 12, 1983; John Render born March 7, 1904, was a merchant and farmer and died November 17, 1988; Woodrow Wilson born July 1, 1910, and died August 12, 1986; and Marshall Ney born August 14, 1913, moved to Bowdon, worked as a businessman and died April 2, 1968; two daughters Angeline born July 21, 1906, and died August 31, 1984; and Eula Nell born December 5, 1908, also a teacher, completed the family. Most are buried in the Lowell Community Cemetery where their mother Eula was the first to be buried there August 14, 1920. Her funeral was the first in the uncompleted Lowell Methodist church that she had helped to organize in 1919.

John reared the children with the help of the dear cook and housekeeper, Sally Mae. He disposed of his land holdings by giving each of his children seventy-five acres of land. At the age of eighty he suffered strokes and was in declining health for three years until his death September 19, 1949.

Judge Henry H. Revill, of the Coweta Judicial District said of him "He has been one of the most useful and independent forces for Carroll's welfare. Always fearless in his convictions, he never hesitated to express his opinion on all matters affecting the interests of his county. He has been a valuable asset to Carroll County and to the state of Georgia." *Submitted by: Angie Hollingsworth Stober, 1071 Lowell Road, Carrollton, GA 30116*

Sources: Personal records, *The History of Bowdon College* and *Carroll Free Press*

1051. Lewis Adel and Leila Rivers Spence

Eight children were born to John Robert Spake Spence and Eula Beatrice Foster Spence. The third child was a son, Lewis Adel, born on November 16, 1901. Adel was an active, healthy child, and an avid learner. He excelled in the Lowell community school. To pursue his higher education, he enrolled in Bowdon High School in 1922. Upon graduation, he entered Bowdon College where he received a normal degree in teaching in 1926 and a bachelor of science degree in 1928. Adel not only excelled in academics, but also sports. Work on the family farm had made him very physically fit and had created an agile athlete. He participated in baseball, football, and basketball. He was captain of his college basketball team in 1926.

After graduation, Adel returned to the Lowell community where he would spend over two decades as teacher and principal. Only twice did he teach outside of Lowell and that was at Ephesus and Roopville. He would be known as a strict — yet fair — disciplinarian, intelligent educator, and an inspiring mentor. Students would, in later years, return to be tutored and to tell how he had influenced their lives and instilled the value of education.

His career, and the fact that he had entered it somewhat late, had occupied so much of Adel's time that at forty-two he was still a bachelor. He had courted many of the local ladies, but at a church picnic some fifteen years earlier, a lovely red-head had caught his eye. Leila Rivers had moved with her parents, Jewel and Will, along with five siblings, from the Clem community in the late 1920s. Adel and Leila, ten years his junior, would marry on November 24, 1943, Thanksgiving Day, at the home of Preacher Mathis. For his new bride, Adel had purchased and begun renovations of the Holder home on the old McIntosh Trail Road.

Leila and Adel would have a daughter, Ladel, four years later. Then in two years, a second daughter would be born. She would be named for Leila's sister, Jane Marie, who had died at an early age. Adel would convey his love of books and learning on a nightly basis as he read with the girls. Leila would maintain the home and continue her talent and love of sewing. She would boast that she had "made clothing for half of the population of Lowell."

Adel would continue to teach and become an industrious farmer on the land that he loved. Adel, his pickup truck, and old black dog would be seen traveling throughout the county. As he worked with sharecroppers, they would find him to be "a gentleman and man of his word." Taking an active role in community affairs in his later years, he would also dabble in county politics and teach an adult Sunday School class at Lowell Methodist Church, the church which his mother, Eula, had founded.

Leila and Adel Spence

During the eight years before his retirement from the Carroll County Schools in 1968, Adel pursued a different component of education as Visiting Teacher. Recognizing the connection between attendance and academic success, he would solicit the help of Carrollton merchants and citizens to provide clothing for needy children. He remained an advocate for the child and education until his death on April 12, 1983, at Emory University Hospital in Atlanta.

Celebrating her ninetieth birthday on June 10, 2001, Leila continues to reside in the home that she and Adel shared for forty years. She enjoys her community, daughters, four grandchildren, and new great-grandson. She remains the same gentle, kind, Southern lady that Adel met at that church picnic years over seven decades ago. *Submitted by: Ladel Spence Griffin, 473 Emily Drive, Lilburn, GA 30047*

1052. William Eloscar Spence

After the Civil War ended, William Martin Spence met and married Delphia McPherson on November 5, 1868. They raised nine children. The fifth was William Eloscar Spence, born September 20, 1880, who married Margie Lee Shackelford on August 17, 1904. Their only place of residence was a house built in 1885. The house still remains in an upgraded and remodeled condition on the Carrollton-Temple Road near the intersection with Center Point Road.

Will and Margie were married for sixty-seven years before Will's death May 23, 1971. They had five children: Monzua Eugenia born June 1905, Delphia Thelma born October 1907, William Albert born January 1911 and served in the US Navy 1942-44, Ernest Ervin born May

William Eloscar Spence, 86th birthday at his home.

1914, and Wilton Billy born April 1916. CDR-USNR. Ret. World War II.

It is on this original home site that the Spence swimming pool was built in 1935. Albert Spence, the oldest son of William Eloscar Spence, designed and constructed the pool. The pool was on the farm land at a relative level area located at the end of a sloping ground around which the essential fresh water creek could be channeled by a trench from a dam below where the double bridges creeks merged to form one creek. The trench was about 1500 feet long and was contoured to give the proper flow rate to the pool, and was protected against rainwater run-off.

All of the excavation and building of the surrounding walls to be collapse-proof was done by Albert alone with a mule drawn double-handed dirt scoop. Albert did the surveying and sloping of the fresh water channel from the creek dam to the pool. The sides of the pool and the 12-foot high diving tower were wood construction. He built the dressing room, and dance hall was built with some carpentry help.

Spence's swimming pool was a very popular meeting place for young people in Carroll County since there was no other public swimming pool of this type and size in existence. It was closed in 1949 for public use. However, at the time of my last visit to the old homestead in April 1995, the pool was still in good condition with fresh water flowing through to keep plenty of fish alive. *Submitted by: CDR Wilton B. Spence USNR, 456 Pine Villa Drive, Atlantis, FL 33462*

1053. Clarence B. and Dula Mae Morgan Sprewell

Clarence B. Sprewell, born April 24, 1902, died January 15, 1978, and Dula Mae Morgan, born June 6, 1905, died August 18, 2000, were married February 6, 1921, in Carroll County. They lived in the Farmer's High Community all their lives.

When Dula Mae cooked a meal, it was fit for a king. When we lived in Tennessee, Kentucky, or Atlanta, we would come visit. During the late afternoon before we arrived, Dula Mae would kill a frying chicken. Can you believe that she would get up the next morning and fry that chicken for breakfast, along with biscuits, gravy, and eggs? Of course, there was always a pitcher of sorghum syrup and a plate of butter on the table. In the summer, she would slice a big juicy muskmelon (cantaloupe). Dula Mae's tea cakes and fried pies were the best in the county.

Cooking was not Dula Mae's entire life. She was also a master seamstress. She sewed for the public and her family, made quilts, crocheted doilies, and later afghans. When she was about seventy-five years old, she decided to learn to tat (make lace). She was fantastic at that also. I do not know how many tatted crosses she made, but every member of the family has at least one. Many people outside the family also have one.

Dula Mae was a girl at heart all her life. I remember her coming out and playing baseball with the children and grandchildren. She loved to play. When Bamah was very young, either Dula Mae or Clarence was chasing the other one with a dipper full of water. They were having so much fun that they didn't hear someone knock at the door. Bamah answered the door. When the person asked for her mother or daddy, Bamah told him that they were in the kitchen "fighting."

She lived at her home on Salem Church Road until she was about ninety-five years old. Her sons, Gilbert and Bobby, checked on her regularly and brought food so she wouldn't have to cook. Dula Mae was the hub around which our family rotated. I think we all feel disconnected and lost without her.

Clarence carried a pocket watch, the only person in the family who had a pocket watch. Since all the grandchildren loved that pocket watch, he would use it to entice the grandchildren to sit on his lap and listen to the watch. When the children were very little, he would put the watch to their ear. These little ones would get wide-eyed when they heard the ticking. Every one of the grandchildren loved to climb up into Granddaddy's lap to listen to his watch.

Dula Mae Morgan and Clarence B. Sprewell

He and Uncle Charley (Charles Spurgeon) were twins. They had a language of their own. They would sit, knee to knee, under a big shade tree and talk and talk. Of course, no one else could understand a word they were saying. Occassionally, one of them would look up to someone who was in their vicinity and ask, "Ain't that right?" I don't think anyone ever told them that they didn't understand them. They would just nod and go on their way.

Clarence had debilitating arthritis. But, on occasion, he would join the baseball game out in the pasture. He was so much fun when he was playing baseball.

Many of Clarence and Dula Mae's grandchildren also have children. See "The Lineage of the Carroll County Spruells/Sprewells," included herein, for the details of their descendants.

This family group and each of its members are people of whom we are proud. *Submitted by: Bamah Sprewell Wood, 360 Hopewell Road, Roopville, GA 30170*

1054. Spruell - Sprewells

Lineage of the Carroll County

Dr. Godfrey Spruill was born about 1650 possibly in Scotland, and died August 15, 1718, in North Carolina. He arrived in Virginia before 1684. Godfrey received a patent of land (No. 399) of 340 acres on October 31, 1684, in James City County, Virginia.

Godfrey married Joannah (1654-1718). Samuel William Sr. (circa 1688-circa 1760), the eighth of at least nine children, married Elizabeth

Swaine (1692-before 1760) in 1713. They had John Read (1721-1760), the third of twelve children, who married Mary in 1760. John Read's son John (1748-1808), the first of five children, married Mary Swain (circa 1728-1765) in 1774. William was the first-born. Gabriel (before 1830-1883), the youngest of William's children, married Susan Mann (1811-before 1867) in 1814.

Gabriel moved with his family to Carroll County in 1844. John F. Spruiell (1837-1883), Gabriel's second child, enlisted in the Confederate Army on May 10, 1862, and served in Company B, 56th Georgia Regiment. He was the only son to survive the war. When he returned to Carroll County, he married Martha Frances Veazey (1843-1927) in 1865. They lived with Martha's mother, Catherine Anderson Veazy, until her death in 1872. The Veazey's land was purchased by John F. Spruiell and Thomas B. Carden, another son-in-law.

John F. Spruiell built a rather large house on this land and lived there until his death. He left his property to his widow by a verbal will made on his death bed.

John and Martha Spruiell's son, Caleb Marshall Spruell, reared a large family on the farm land he inherited from his parents. Caleb's son, Charles Spurgeon, reared a family on this same farm land. Today, Roy Edwin Sprewell's family lives on the land.

Caleb Marshall Spruell (1866-1928) married Sarah Amanda "Sally" Walker (1870-1931) in 1889 in Cleburne County. Their descendants are as follows:

Caleb Norman Spruell (1891-1942) married Mary Belle Treadaway (1892-1969) in 1911. They had Mary Clarice, who married Kermit Basil Cox (1913-1993) in 1934. Clarice and Kermit had Mary Carol, who married John Richard Beall in 1961. Carol and John had Elizabeth Paige, who married David Gedeon, and had Luke, Regan, and Grey; and Jon David, who married Tammy Bryant, and had Cathlyn and Bryant. In 1973, Carol married Thomas Worley Mock and had Kirby Rudolph. Clarice and Kermit had Benjamin Norman, who married Clara Frances Hinesley in 1968, and had Benjamin Norman Jr. and Christopher Alan. Christopher Alan married Joanna. Larry Kermit, the third-born of Clarice and Kermit, married Mary Joni Fitzgerald in 1976.

Norman and Mary Belle had Doris Nelle, who married Zack Davis (1914-1990) in 1940. Doris and Zach had Evelyn Louise, who married John McMurray Carpenter III in 1963. Julie Margaret, John McMurray IV, and Claire Davis were born to the Carpenters. Doris and Zach had Martha Susan, who married Frank Chastain Jr., and had Samuel Trey, who was later adopted by Sam Weatherman. In 1974, Martha Susan married Sam Weatherman. They had Samuel Trey and Matthew Scott. The next child of Doris and Zach was Nancy Margaret, who married Eugene Griffith in 1973, and had Dax, Zachary Andrew, and Meredith Davis. Norma Louise was the third child of Doris and Zach. She married Lon Harvey Wessinger Jr. (1914-1990) in 1937. They had Lon Harvey III (1939-1976), who married Rosalind Carder in 1963, and had Patricia Suzanne and April Dawn. Louise and Lon had Linda Louise, who married Duell Harvey Robinson in 1965, and had Brian Scott and Amy Ellen. Next, Kathy Joan was born. She married Paul Anthony Gibbs in 1975. They had Joel Wesley and Laura Louise. Louise and Lon's fourth child is Robert Lynn, who married Charlene Davis in 1971 and had Lynn Marie. Norman and Mary Bell's fourth child was Doyce Frank (1922-1944).

Rilla Frances Sprewell (1893-1952) married M. Luther Foster (1893-1960) in 1913. Rilla and Luther had Eunice Viola (1916-1969), who married Carl Hightower (1906-1970) in 1933, and adopted a son, David. Their second child is Opal Mae who married Lee Gower.

Caleb and Sally's third child was Sarah Alice Elizabeth Sprewell (1895-1986), who married Howell S. Word (1894-1964) in 1913. They had Sarah Etheleen who married Joe Broome (1916-1971) in 1943.

John Bryan Spruell (1897-1943), Caleb and Sally's fourth child, married Lela Harmon (1901-1984) in 1918. Their children were John Melvin (1919-1973) who married Linda Annolia Pirkle (1916-1987) in 1940, and had Terry Logan who married Laura Reynolds in 1976; Michael Joe, who married Nancy Sue Rindt in 1967 and had Russell David and Chistina Marie, and Betty Lee, who married Robert Lee Tucker in 1969; Herbert Bryan married Mozelle Denson in 1944 and had Susan Darlene, who married Roberts, and had Todd. Sandra Gayle married Albert Wayne East in 1970, and had Andrea Lowery and Duane Bryant. Howard Stanley married Sarah Stallings in 1954 and had Mark Anthony, who married Kay Spruell in 1982, and Bradford Neal.

Martha Eula Sprewell (1899-1987) married Zack H. Barnes (1889-1965) in 1916 and had Sarah Mildred, who married Luther B. Wooley Jr. (1912-1973) in 1937, and had Danny Braden, Monty Barnes, and Sonny Sprewell, who married Eva Jane Fincher in 1975. Their second child was Mary Lillian (1920-1924).

Caleb M. Sprewell Family, circa 1906-1907

Charles Spurgeon Sprewell (1902-1959) married Nelle Brock (1902-1959) in 1921. They had three children. (1) Spurgeon Charles (1923-1992) who married Catherine Robison (1925-1990) in 1942. They had John Spurgeon (1946-1970); Charles Dale who married Janis Tucker in 1974, and had Matthew Ryan; and William Don who married Vickie Mitchell in 1982. (2) Joyce married Melvin B. Lane Jr. in 1949. They had five children: Larry Melvin; Charles Steve, who married Kathy Thomasson, had Stephen Brittian; Charles Steve married Patty Benney; Ricky Joe who married Cindy Coyer in 1981, and had Julie Ann, Jennifer Marie, and Jessica; Tim, who married Tamara Pearce in 1980 and had Tara Denise, Maghan, and Sawyer; and Rhonda Nell, who married Eddie Duncan in 1993, and had Benjamin Lee and Jacob Lane. (3) Jane married Willie Brown Dukes (1929-1998) in 1963. They had Billie Jane who married Russell Gossage, and had Mallory Skye, and Mary Jean who married Perry Milliken. Jane married William Ray Chandler in 2001. Charles Spurgeon married Vera Gillespie (1904-1981) in 1962. Clarence B. Sprewell (1902-1978) married Dula Mae Morgan (1904-2000) in 1921. They had five children.

(1) Bamah Lanette married Clifton Q.P. Wood (1921-1990) in 1941 and had Cecilia and Dr. Morgan Clifton. Cecilia married Leo Gene Church (1925-2000) in 1963 and had Robin Gayle, who has a son Kyle Thomas, and Michael Leo. Morgan Clifton married Lisa Kay Lambert in 1988 and had Morgan Clifton II. In 1999 Morgan married Sarah Elizabeth "Beth" Blalock.

(2) Zellie Fred married Bonnell Gentry (1928-1992) in 1944. Denis Jasper, their first-born, met Laura and had Michael. Denis married Barbara Kilgore in 1965. They had Branna Lynette who married Dwayne Harris and had Anna Lynn, Mary Catherine, and Zachary Clinton; Beverly Danette who married Vince Bivens and had Britni Nichole. Beverly later married Gene Arrington and had Dillon; Nisha Marie married Kevin Martin; and Sharla Nichole married Miles. Denis married Cindy-Ann Mullinix in 1989 and had Abigail. Kanea Sue, Fred and Bonnell's second child, married Jim Collier Ward in 1967 and had Kevan Eulis, David Collier, Jamie Edgar, and Jeremy Fred. Wyvonne Nelle, Fred and Bonnell's third child, married Johnnie M. Hobbs in 1972. They had Sean Alan who married Lori Moone in 1997 and had Caleb John; and Traci Leigh who married Bryan Hostager in 1996 and had Cameron Scott-Conley. The fourth child, Harry Caleb, married Elizabeth Ledbetter in 1970. They had four children: Christy Elizabeth who married David Madden and had Charity Faith and Mathew David; Cindy Pauline who married Jeff Stovall and had Jeffery Logan; Chad Caleb who married Tina Ivey in 1995 and had Cody Caleb and Dylan James; and Cherie who married J.D. Fortson and had Lacon Cherie. In 1991 Harry married Linda Brown. The fifth child is Roy Edwin, who married Debra Elizabeth Watson in 1974, and had Brian and Brandon Fraser. Now, Roy is married to Dana Nixon. The sixth child is Mark Maron who married Freida Ann Davis in 1976. They had Mark Maron Jr. who married Amanda Richards in 1999. The youngest child is Evan Morgan who married Judy Bearden in 1977. They had two children: Brandy Delaine who married Keven Prater and had Rachel Lynn, and Angela.

(3) Harold Gilbert married Joy Bryant in 1951. Gilbert and Joy had Samuel Kirby who married Jennifer Carol Johnson in 1979. Amy, their child, married Ken Gossett and had Harrison. Their second child is Sidney Harold who married Charlsie Walker Freeman in 1981. Their children are Charles Wesley and Kirby Ann. The third-born is Stuart Nathan who married Angelia Dukes in 1985. Their children are Joshua Stuart, Matthew Bryant, Lindsay Suzanne, and Emily Michelle. The fourth child is Susan Anna who married Brook McDaniel in 1991. They have Samantha Brooke.

(4) Evelyn Dacy married Harold Caswell Williams (1927-1969) in 1947. Evelyn and Harold had Paula Mae who married Samuel Larkin. Paula and Sam had Harold Raymond; Aaron Dwayne who married Renee; Tiffany Diane who married Tim Roach-Larkin and had Dekota; and Jan. Their second child, Thomas Harold, married Dianna Hazel Sprewell. Tommy and Diana had Amelia Clarisse who married Brandon Steed, and Jonathan Thomas. Later, Tommy married Linda, and had Nathan and Lisa. Evelyn and Harold's third child is Allan, who married Brenda Oakley (-1998) and had Ginger.

(5) Leldon Bobby married Hazel Grimes Guilford in 1954. Their eldest child, Dianna Hazel, married Thomas Harold Williams and had Amelia Clarisse who married Brandon Steed, and Jonathan Thomas. Bobby and Hazel's second child is Leldon Mark. The youngest is Gordon Maris who married Toni Hansen in 1986. Their children are Jonathan Anthony, Jessica Ashley, and Kelsey Lynne.

Lena Grace Sprewell (1905-1984) married L.J. McKinley Barnes (1902-?) on August 31, 1929. Their children are John Tyler who married Joyce Hendrix in 1953 and had Sherrie. John Tyler married Diane Murphy in 1978 and had Kellie Annette. The second child, Nona Jeanette (1935-1979), married Salvador Ficcarrotta, and had Paul, Joe Salvador, Nina (1968-1979) and Eldred McKinley. The youngest child is Sarah Jean who married Grady Adair (1910-1978). They had Erich, who married Sabrina Ware in 1981, Sarah Diane, Dawn, and Leah.

Most were married and reared their families in Carroll County.

Our ancestry has not been traced into Europe. Although many genealogists believe that Dr. Godfrey came from Scotland, no one has ever found proof.

This family photograph, made about 1906 or 1907, shows the Caleb M. Sprewell Family. Front row, left to right, are Caleb Norman Spruell, Clarence B. Sprewell, Caleb M. Sprewell, Charles Spurgeon Sprewell, Sarah Amanda Walker, Lena Grace Sprewell (on Sarah's lap, and Rilla Frances Sprewell. On the back row are John Bryan Spruell, Sarah Alice Elizabeth Sprewell, and Martha Eula Sprewell. *Submitted by: Cecilia Wood Church, 128 Brock Street, Carrollton, GA 30117, E-mail: cechurch@charter.net.*

Sources: Research done by Clarice Cox, compiler of *Gabriel Spruill of Carroll County: Descendants and Allied Families,* and Cecilia Wood Church. *William and Mary Quarterly* Vol. 12, Series 1, page 106.

1055. The Sprewells Who served our Country in the Armed Forces

This family has fought in nearly every war since our arrival on American shores. James Veazey, father of John F. Spruiell's wife, Martha Frances, fought in the Revolutionary War.

The Spruells provided a large force during the Civil War. John F. Spruiell served in Company B, 56th Georgia Regiment, Confederate States of America (CSA). He moved with his family to Carroll County in November 1844. John F. was the only son of Gabriel and Susan Mann Spruiell to survive the Civil War. Their other sons were (1) William Jonathan Mitchell Spruill born circa 1835 in Fayette County, Georgia, and died November 24, 1862. Before 1860 he moved his family to Carroll County. He was married to Jalocca Jane Mabry, born about 1830 and died circa 1898 in Carroll County. He served in the CSA, Company C, 56th Regiment Volunteer Infantry Company, Georgia Volunteers: (2) James M. Sprewell was born in 1839 probably in Alabama and died May 14, 1863. He served in the 63rd Regiment, Georgia Volunteer Infantry Company C; (3) Pvt. Zachariah M. Spruill born September 1, 1841, in Carroll County. He volunteered for the CSA on May 10, 1862. He served in Company C, 56th Georgia Infantry and was captured May 16, 1863, at Champion Hill. He first appeared on the Roll of Prisoners of War at Camp Morton, Indiana. According to his sketchy war record, he died of chronic diarrhea at the Confederate States Hospital in Petersburg, Virginia on July 29, 1863. (4) Caleb M. Veazey was born about 1845 in Carroll County and died about 1863 in the CSA. Many other Spruells served in the Civil War. All are related to the Carroll County Spruells, but have no roots in this county.

World War I was not so severe to the Carroll County Spruells. One served in the U.S. Army, First Trench Artillery Battalion, Coast Artillery Corps. He was Sgt. Maj. Marvin L. Spruill, born September 1890 in Cleburne County, Alabama, and died February 12, 1919. He was waiting to return home from France after World War I. Marvin is buried at Plot D Row 20 Grave 27, Oise-Aisne American Cemetery, Fere-en-Tardenois, France. His father, L.W. Fletcher Spruill (LWF), was born in Carroll County in 1851, but soon after LWF's marriage to Jerusha Carline Robinson in November 1872, in Carroll County, they moved to Cleburne County, Alabama.

Some of our men involved in World War II were (1) Spurgeon Charles Sprewell, born December 3, 1923, and died September 26, 1992, and (2) Leo Gene Church, born July 3, 1925, in Wichita Falls, Texas, and died May 4, 2000, in Carroll County. He enlisted in the U.S. Navy on March 09, 1943, for the duration. He obtained the rank of gunner's mate and was discharged in 1945. He was one of only a few survivors from the battleship *USS Toucient L'Overture.* The medics picked him up from the beach at Guadalcanal. He was decorated with the Bronze Star, two Purple Hearts, and many other medals; and (3) Pfc. Doyce Frank Spruell, born September 15, 1922, in Carroll County and died June 6, 1944, in France during the invasion of Normandy on D-Day. He served in the U.S. Parachute Infantry.

Harold Gilbert Sprewell, served during the Korean War. He was born October 24, 1927, in Carroll County.

The Sprewells Who Served in our Armed Forces

Vietnam claimed so many of our nation's men. Capt. John Spurgeon Sprewell gave the supreme sacrifice. He was born December 20, 1946, and died May 19, 1970. He was killed by hostile fire that shot down his helicopter at Dinh Tuong, South Vietnam. His tour of duty began on July 17, 1969. Maj. Lon Harvey Wessinger Jr. was killed when the plane he was piloting crashed into the Atlantic Ocean off Jacksonville, Florida, on February 6, 1976. His body was never recovered. He was serving with the Florida National Guard. Lt. j.g. Benjamin Norman Cox, born February 2, 1944, served in the U.S. Navy.

We, as a proud Carroll County family, have fought bravely for our country. Lest we forget the sacrifice these men and their families made, we honor all those who are no longer with us, and salute every person who has served in our Armed Forces to keep the United States of America free.

This picture shows the Sprewells who have served in our Armed Forces. Top row, left to right, Harold Gilbert Sprewell (U.S. Army, Korea); Major Lon H. Wessinger Jr. (Florida National Guard); M.Sgt. Leo Gene Church (U.S. Navy, WWII and U.S. Army); PFC Doyce F. Spruell (U.S. Army, WWII); Capt. John S. Sprewell (U.S. Army, Vietnam); and Sgt. Maj. Marvin L. Spruill (U.S. Army, W.W.I). *Submitted by: Michael Leo Church, 130 Brock Street, Carrollton, GA 30117*

Sources: Researched by: Mary Clarice Spruell, *Gabriel Spruill of Carroll County: Descendants and Allied Families,* 1984, and Cecilia Wood Church, 128 Brock Street, Carrollton, GA 30117.

1056. William Green Springer

William Green Springer was born in 1790, the son of the Reverend John Springer, a Presbyterian minister of Wilkes County, Georgia, and his wife, Anne Green. He married Mary Baxter, who was born in 1794, the daughter of Andrew Baxter and Elizabeth Harris. By the time Carroll County was opening up for settlement, William Green Springer had become a contractor and owned and operated a hotel in Sparta, the county seat of Hancock County. His hotel and tavern, called the Old Eagle, was a stagecoach stop on the Augusta to Macon line.

About 1828 Springer, his wife, and his sister-in-law, Eliza Baxter, decided to sell out in Sparta and move to new land along the Chattahoochee River in Carroll County. It was agreed that William would build a plantation home and that all three would own it. Their land was just to the north of the McIntosh Reserve in the Fourth District. The place became known as Rotherwood, a name said to have been given to the Springer home by an English lady who, on an early visit to the Springers, noted the similarity of the Carroll countryside to that described in Scott's novels. On February 27, 1829, a post office was established at Rotherwood with Springer as postmaster. Rotherwood remained a post office until 1868, when it was discontinued for a few years and then reopened under the name Ratherwood. It was closed permanently in 1897.

Springer was prominent in early county affairs and was at one time a justice of the Inferior Court. In 1832 he was foreman of the grand jury that exonerated and complimented the Slicks for suppressing the Pony Club. At the same time this grand jury submitted a report supporting Governor Lumpkin's opposition to South Carolina's nullification stance. Judge Colquitt, after hearing the grand jury report read in open court, refused to allow it to be recorded in the minutes of the court. Springer openly defied the judge, calling the grand jury the most independent body of men on earth with the unquestioned right to express their views on any subject of a public nature. Springer had his way. The report was recorded.

Physically, Springer was a very large man, said to weigh over 400 pounds. He was also an intellectual heavyweight. He is supposed to have originated the idea for the state railroad, his idea being to secure a charter for a railroad from Augusta to Carrollton and one from Macon to Carrollton where they would unite and continue together to Chattanooga. In 1837 he ran for the state Senate with this plan as the main plank in his platform. Jonathan Haynes opposed and defeated him. Haynes had the backing of those who earned a livelihood hauling freight to county merchants. In 1838 Haynes again defeated Springer, this time by only thirty-one votes. In 1839 Springer defeated Haynes by thirteen votes. However, he failed to secure passage of his plan and died the following year. Had he been successful, Carrollton and not Atlanta would have been the hub of Georgia's railroads.

The children of William Green and Mary Baxter Springer were: 1. Elizabeth, born in 1809, married first to Dr. Fitzgerald Bird and second to Thomas Napier. She died in 1848 and is buried at Rotherwood. 2. John, born in 1811 and died in 1815. 3. Andrew Baxter, born in 1813 and died in 1825. 4. Ann, born in 1815, married Thomas S. Martin in 1831 and died the same year. 5. Mary, born in 1817, married Thomas S. Martin in 1832 and died in 1855 at Rotherwood. 6. Catherine, born in 1819, married James H. Rodgers. 7. William, born in 1821 and died in 1823. 8. John, born in 1823 and died in 1848. 9. Lucinda, born in 1827, married Nicholas Tompkins in 1845. 10. Georgia, born in 1827, married C.C. Shumaker, died in Texas in 1863. 11. Sarah, born in 1827, married Dr. Hugh Ector in 1848 and later married Charles W. Mabry. 12. Robert Henry, born in 1830. 13. Thomas Baxter, born in 1832 and died in 1833. *Submitted by: Myron Wade House*

Sources: J.C. Bonner's *Georgia's Last Frontier, Carroll County Georgia, Souvenir-Historical Edition,* and William J. O'Donnell, Jr., *The Springer Ancestry, Carroll County Genealogical Quarterly,* Fall 1993, 87-91.

1057. The Family of John F. Spruiell

John F. Spruiell, the second child of Gabriel and Susan Mann Spruiell, was born in Fayette County, Georgia, in 1837. He moved to Carroll County with his parents circa 1844-45. Tradition is that he was married to a Miss Evans in Louisiana who died of brain fever a few weeks after their marriage. He later married Martha Frances "Matt" Veazey, daughter of Caleb and Catherine Griffin Veazey, on 10 December 1865 in Carroll County. John F. and "Matt" lived at the Veazey home place with her mother until she died in 1872. John F. then bought part of the Veazey property and lived there until his death 3 May 1882. He left his wife and six children, age ten months to fifteen years. Martha died 5 August 1927, and is buried beside her husband at the First Methodist Church in Bowdon, Georgia. Their children were Caleb Marshall Sprewell born 1 October 1866, Amanda Susan Spruiell born 5 April 1869, M.F. Spruiell (daughter) John William Spruill born April 1873, Leonidas G. Spruell born 17 June 1876, Rufus Marion Spruiell born 16 February 1878, and Mary Beettus Spruill born 13 July 1881.

Caleb Sprewell married Sarah Amanda Walker in Hightower Alabama in December 1889. They reared a large family in the Salem Church community of Carroll County on farm land that was a part of the estate left by John F. Spruiell. Caleb M. Sprewell was an ordained Baptist minister. Caleb died 10 February 1928, and Sarah died 5 February 1931. Both are buried in the Salem Baptist Church Cemetery. Their eight children were: Caleb Norman, Rilla Frances, Sarah Alice, John Bryan Spruell, Martha Eula, Charles Spurgeon, Clarence Broadus, and Lena Grace Sprewell.

Caleb Norman Sprewell was born 18 September 1891 and married Mary Belle Treadaway 24 December 1911. He was killed in a highway accident 20 March 1942. She was born 1892, and died 20 October 1969. Both are buried at Salem Baptist Church. Their children were Clarice born 14 February 1915, Doris Nelle born 30 April 1917, Norma Louise born 21 March 1920 and Doyce Frank Spruell born 15 September 1922.

Clarice married Kermit Basil Cox 29 November 1934. They lived in the Farmer's High community of Carroll County. Kermit was a farmer and retired sawmiller. He died July 24, 1993, and is buried at Salem Baptist Church. Their children are Mary Carol born 5 January 1941, Benjamin Norman born 2 February 1944, and Larry Kermit Cox born 16 September 1950. Carol married Jon Richard Beall. Their children are Elizabeth Paige and Jon David Beall. Paige married David Michael Gedeon and their children are Luke, Regan and Grey Gedeon. Jon married Tammy Bryant. Their children are Kathlyn and Bryant. Carol later married Thomas Whaley Mock. She is a registered medical technologist. Ben Cox married Clara Frances Hinesley on 22 June 1968 in Carroll County. Their children are Benjamin Norman married Elizabeth Paige Davenport and Christopher Alan Cox who married Joanna Federico of Syracuse, New York. Larry Kermit Cox works as a mechanic, and lives on the family home place at Farmer's High.

The Caleb Sprewell Family

Doris Nelle Spruell married Zach Davis on 25 December 1940. He died January 1990; and Norma Louise Spruell married Lon Harvey Wessinger on 24 December 1937, died in 1990. Both are buried in Carroll Memory Garden. Their son Lon Wessinger Jr. (B.S. Georgia Tech) was killed when the plane he was piloting crashed into the Atlantic Ocean off Jacksonville, Florida, February 1976. His body was not recovered. He was serving with the Florida National Guard with the rank of major. He was married to Mary Rosalind Carder. Their children are Patricia Suzanne and April Dawn. Other children of Norma Louise and Lon Wessinger were Linda Louise, Kathy Joan and Robert Lynn Wessinger. The fourth child of Norman Sprewell was Doyce Frank Spruell, born 15 September 1922 in Carroll County. He was killed in action in France 6 June 1944 while serving with the U.S. Parachute Infantry in France, World War II. His remains are buried at Salem Baptist Church. *Submitted by: Clarice Spruell Cox, 102 South St., Carrollton, GA 30117*

Sources: *Gabriel Spruill of Carroll County Georgia*

1058. Spruill Family

The family name of Spruill was found to be spelled several ways. Among them are Spruill, Spruell, Sprewell, and Spruiell. In this article I will spell it the way found in research.

Godfrey Spruill: Godfrey Spruill was born about 1650, possibly in Scotland and died August 15, 1718, in Tyrrell County, North Carolina. He married Joannah (unknown). They had nine children. Hezekiah Spruell, Joshua Spruell, Godfrey Spruell Jr., Henrietta Spruill, Anna Margaritta Spruill, Mary Spruill, Susannah Spruill, Samuel William Spruill Sr. and Joseph Spruill Sr.

Samuel William Spruill Sr.: Samuel William Spruill Sr. was born about 1688 and died in Tyrrell County, North Carolina. Samuel married Elizabeth Swaine, born 1692 in Nantucket County, Massachusetts. Other spouses were Jamina Long and Mary Spruill. Samuel had eleven children. They were Ann Elizabeth, Samuel William Jr., Godfrey, John Read Sr., Nehemiah, Joanna, Zelpha, Jemima, Joseph, Jeremiah and Lillian.

John Read Spruill Sr.: John Read Spruill Sr. was born 1721 and died in 1760 in Tyrrell County, North Carolina. He married Mary Swain. They had five children, John Read Jr., Even, Jemima, Deborah and Elizabeth.

John Read Spruill Jr.: John Read Spruill Jr. was born in 1748 in Tyrrell County, North Carolina. He died January 1808 in Abbeville County, South Carolina. John married Ruth Mitchell Nash in 1774. His children were Samuel, Sally, William, George C., Nancy, Gabriel, Simon, Luke, John, Simeon Jeptha, Thomas Wesley, Peggy. (I believe he was married before Ruth because of birth years of some of the children.)

William Spruill Sr.: William Spruill Sr. was born about 1767 in Abbeville, South Carolina. He died in DeKalb County, Georgia. His wife's name is unknown. His children were William Spruiell Jr., Stephen Thomas Spruiell, John and Gabriel Spruiell.

Gabriel Spruiell: Gabriel Spruiell was born before 1830 in South Carolina and died April 23, 1883, in Cleburne County, Alabama. Gabriel married Susan Mann on November 20, 1834, in Fayette County, Georgia. Other spouses were Charity J. Evans and Isabelle Beard. His children were William Jonathan Mitchell Spruill, John F. Spruiell, James M. Sprewell, Zachariah M. Spruill, Milton Spruill, Martha F. Spruiell, L.W. Fletcher Spruill and Susan E. Spruiell. This family moved to Carroll County before 1840.

John F. Spruiell: John F. Spruiell was born in 1837 in Fayette County, Georgia. He died May 3, 1883. John F. married Martha Frances "Matt" Veazey on December 10, 1865, in Carroll County, Georgia. She was born December 25, 1843, in Carroll County, and died August 5, 1927, in Douglas County, Georgia. Their children were Caleb Marshall Spruell, Susan Amanda (Sudie) Spruell, M.F. Spruell, John William Spruell, Leonidas G. Spruell, Rufus Marion Speuiell, and Mary Beettus (spelled Beattrice on death certificate) Spruell.

Mary Beetus (Beattrice) Spruell: Mary Beettus (Beattrice) Spruell was born July 13, 1881, and died December 4, 1921, in Carroll County, Georgia. Mary married Joseph L. (Joe) Crumbley on November 24, 1895, in Carroll County. Joseph Crumbley was born March 29, 1872, and died February 6, 1946, in Carroll County. They had twelve children. See Crumbley Family article for picture and more information on this family. *Submitted by: Clarence Crumbley*

Sources: Research by Clarice Cox. More information on this family in her book on the Spruell's in the Carrollton Library. New and corrected information on the Mary Beettus (Beattrice) Spruell family by Jerry Crumbley.

1059. John Marvin Spruill

The name Spruill and its variations of spelling was a name of long-standing in Scotland as early as 1294 AD.

One of the first Spruills of record to come to America was Godfrey Spruill who received a patent of 341 acres in James City County, Virginia, in October 1864. He also received a grant of 640 acres on Scuppernong River in Tyrrell

County, North Carolina on 6/25/1704. He was one of the earliest physicians in North Carolina.

Gabriel Spruill is thought to be the earliest Spruill living in Carroll County. He was born around 1808 in Abbeville, South Carolina, and married Susan Mann on 11/20/1834. They came to Carroll County in 1844-45.

Several Spruills fought in the Revolutionary and Civil Wars. Gabriel had five sons who fought for the Confederacy. Only one survived. Zachariah, third son of Gabriel, served in Company C, 56th Georgia Infantry, was wounded, captured at Champion Hill, exchanged and died in a Petersburg, Virginia, hospital on 7/29/1863. He married Susan Stephenson, born 1/2/1844. The only child of Zach and Susan was John Thomas Spruill, born on 8/3/1861, and married Martha "Mattie" Worley, born 12/14/1864. She was the daughter of Captain Columbus "Lum" Worley, born 8/21/1840 in Dahlonega, Georgia, and "Lizzie" Barnes born 8/27/1844. Captain "Lum" served in Company D, 52nd Georgia Infantry.

John Marvin Spruill U.S. Marine Corps, World War I

John Marvin Spruill was the fifth child of John Thomas and Mattie. He was born in Carroll County near Roopville 2/1/1891 and married Ruth Huddleston, born 7/11/1907, in Carroll County on 3/30/1924 in Carroll County.

They had three children, Evelyn Azilee (Polly), Bonnie Jeanne and Dudley Darrow. Marvin, died 7/27/72 and Ruth 6/27/1966 both buried in Arlington Memorial in Atlanta.

Marvin served with the Marine Corps during World War I, attended Rhinehart College and Emory at Oxford, was employed by the civil engineering firm, Swift & Company in Atlanta for several years before purchasing land in the Smithfield community adjacent to his father's. He became a farmer and leader of the community.

He was an early believer in education and was active in the promotion of school consolidation in Carroll County with Smithfield School being consolidated from Hill Crest and High Point Schools. He was in charge of construction of the rock building known as Smithfield School completed in 1939. He was the first person, in conjunction with the Carroll County Board of Education, to purchase and own a school bus, affording students a ride to school for the first time.

Next to education, he loved music. He was well known for leading gospel songs at "All Day Singings" and attended these at churches for miles around where people also enjoyed delicious "dinners on the ground."

He engineered the building of the dam at Tanner's Lake and many other lakes in the area. He believed that everyone should leave a monument when they were gone and one of his greatest was the bags of food he gave to people less fortunate than he during the depression. Many of those gave tribute to this at his passing.

His daughter Bonnie Jeanne married Hugh W. (Bill) Barrow the son of Hugh Witt and Virginia Trammell on 7/31/1946 in Bowdon. Their children are: Hugh Jr., a medical doctor of Spartanburg South Carolina; Lew Spruill, a lawyer in Columbus; Ann Barrow Harris, director of Medical Science for U.C.B. Pharmacals in Atlanta and Martha Rebecca, an anesthetist at the University of Texas Hospital in Galveston.

Submitted by: Bonnie S. Barrow, 1511 Thornebrooke Circle, Dalton, GA 30720, bonniebill@alltel.net

1060. Stallings in Carroll County

Moses Stallings and his brother Wilson Stallings lived in Carroll County by 1840. They had moved from Green County. Another brother, Josiah Stallings, lived in Heard County. All were the sons of Elias Jr. and Elizabeth Roundtree Stallings. Moses had married Nancy White in Carroll County in 1847. Moses is shown as being born in Georgia while Wilson and Josiah are both shown as being born in North Carolina. Other brothers and sisters were still living in Newton County with their parents. These were Mary, John, Palasiah, Sarah, William and Frances.

In 1862 John Martin Daniel (always shown as JMD) Stallings, son of Josiah Stallings and Duke Stallings, son of Moses Stallings, enlisted in the 56th Georgia Infantry Regiment at Bowdon. JMD was in battles at Vicksburg, Missionary Ridge, Dalton, Peachtree Creek, Jonesboro and the battle of Atlanta. For a while his regiment was assigned as guards at Andersonville prison. He was among the twelve surviving members of his company who surrendered at Greensboro, North Carolina at the end of the war.

JMD Stallings returned to Carroll County and married Mary Elizabeth (Molly) Moore. JMD Stallings was a farmer and a Baptist Minister. He pastored and/or started many of the Baptist churches in Carroll and Heard Counties. In Carroll County these included: Abilene, Bethel, Bethesda, Beulah, Harmony (first pastor), Macedonia, Mt. Pleasant (first pastor), New Lebanon (several times and is buried there), Oak Grove (first pastor), Pleasant Grove, Pleasant View (first pastor), Providence, Salem, Shady Grove, Tabernacle of Carrollton (one of the founders) and Temple (first pastor.)

J.M.D. Stallings and his sons

JMD and Molly had twelve children including twins. Their son, James Thomas Stallings, was the father of Lucille Stallings Maxwell. Lucille and Rudy Maxwell had twins, Billy and Bobby Maxwell, and Patsy (Pat) Maxwell.

One of JMD's sons, Lewis Whitaker Stallings, married Maggie Brannon and was a farmer and Baptist minister. They had ten children. Some of their children lived in Carroll County. His daughter Sadie married J.C. Tuggle Jr. and one of their sons, Jimmy Tuggle, is a Carrollton attorney. Mary Stallings worked at Bell Bomber (Lockheed) and after retirement moved back to Carroll County.

One of Lewis and Maggie's sons, Horace Stallings, was a farmer and contractor. He married Mary Ellen Putnam and their children are Tracy Putnam Stallings and Charlcie Jane Stallings. Charlcie married Wallace Lambert. They have three children. Their youngest daughter, Lynn Lambert Greene, is a CPA and employed by the Carrollton City Schools. Tracy married Shirley Crawford and they have four children. Tracy was the mayor of Carrollton for fourteen years and is now in his fourth term as a state representative from Carroll County. Tracy and Shirley's children are Scott, Beverley, Pamela, and Shannon. Shannon and her husband, Dr. Luke Lipham, own the All About Animals Veterinarian Clinic in Carrollton. Pam married Randy Almon, who is employed at Southwire.

Another of JMD Stallings' sons was John William Benson Stallings and one of his sons was J.B. Stallings. His sons Elwyn and Winton Stallings live in Carrollton. John William Benson Stallings' son, Charles M. Stallings, was a Baptist minister. *Submitted by: Tracy Stallings, Bradley Street, Carrollton, GA*
Source: Wallace T. Lambert

1061. John Martin Daniel Stallings

Josiah Stallings, son of Palasiah Stallings and Mary Edwards (*Morgan County, Georgia Heritage 1807-1997,* page 235) was born 20 February 1800 in Morgan County and died 01 March 1857 in Carroll County. He married Johanna Whitaker and they were parents of nine children, including John Martin Daniel Stallings who was born 20 February 1842.

John Martin Daniel Stallings

JMD Stallings was a Civil War veteran. He enlisted at Bowdon, Georgia, on 05 May 1862 and served in the 56th Georgia Infantry. His regiment was among those taken prisoner at Vicksburg, Mississippi, on 04 July 1863. In recounting the experiences of Carroll County Confederate soldiers during the Vicksburg siege, Private Joe Cobb in a Memorial Day address to the Annie Wheeler Chapter of the United Daughters of the Confederacy on 26 April 1906, stated "...the companies subsisted for a long time at Vicksburg on roots, herbs, mule beef and wharf rats..."

JMD was paroled and exchanged on 08 July 1863. On 23 July 1863, he was given a furlough at Enterprise, Mississippi, and returned home.

He later returned to the war effort and was serving with Company C of the 39th Georgia Infantry at Greensboro, North Carolina, at the close of the war. He was paroled at Greensboro on 01 May 1865 in accordance with the terms of a military convention between General Joseph E. Johnston and Major General William T. Sherman. For his service in the war, he later received a Cross of Honor from the United Daughters of the Confederacy. He is listed among the members of Confederate Veterans Camp McDaniel-Curtis No. 487 in Carroll County.

Stallings siblings, c. 1918 Sereptha Jane (Talley), Lucinda (Burnham), Susan (Kidd), JMD, Martha (Huckeba)

In his application for a Civil War soldier's pension dated 29 September 1916, he states his military record and describes his personal property and possessions. His response to the inquiry of annual income was "I receive from churches that I serve, net $100. Rents $36.00 making a total of $136.00 annually." His service in the church began at the Yellow Dirt Baptist Church of Heard County where he was baptized in 1866 by Reverend Trusten Phillips. He entered the ministry in 1871 and on 14 November 1874 was ordained to the full work of the ministry, a calling he pursued with vigor for the next forty-seven years. During this period he was instrumental in the formation of numerous area churches and also served many as pastor. The *History of the Carrollton Baptist Association 1873-1973 Centennial Edition* is replete with the fruits of his ministry. Among the Baptist churches he organized or served as pastor were Abilene, Bethel, Bethesda, Harmony, Macedonia, Mount Pleasant, New Lebanon, Oak Grove, Pleasant Grove, Pleasant View, Providence, Salem, Shady Grove, Tabernacle, and Temple. A column in the *Carroll Free Press* entitled "To the Memory of Rev. J.M.D. Stallings" records the following:

> "Hundreds of persons were converted under his preaching and hundreds of couples were made man and wife under his ceremonies. As a gospel preacher none were more careful to observe the injunction. 'preach the word.' His sermons, as a rule, were short and concise expositions of the scripture text with but little or no room or time for effort at illustrations such as are frequently repulsive rather than helpful to interested hearers; his one object being to present Jesus as the world's only hope."

JMD Stallings was married twice. First, he married Mary Elizabeth (Mollie) Moore, a daughter of Robert and Sara Moore of Newberry, South Carolina; then, following Mollie's death in 1895, he married Emily Huckeba in 1897. The children of JMD and Mollie were Sarah Joanna who married James Leroy Bartlett; Josiah Robert who married Lucy Wren; John William who married Mildred Aline Lavador; Idella Wootson who married John Williamson Washington Webb; Mary Alberta Calista who died at age two; Cora Gertrude who married Charles C. Williams; James Thomas who married Minnie Lou Copeland; Palasiah Franklin who married Fannie Nestlehutt; twins Luther who died in infancy and Lucius Monroe who married Myrtie Akin; and Louis Whitaker who married Maggie Brannon.

Descendants recalling humorous incidents involving pranks by JMD's sons related the occasion his wife Mollie had laid out his clothes as he bathed and prepared to attend a church foot-washing service. The boys, perhaps thinking to enliven the service, secretly sprinkled a little chimney soot into the socks. Imagine the surprise when JMD removed his socks to participate in the foot washing! Another incident recalled was the time the boys slipped a few playing cards into JMD's folded handkerchief. When, during his sermon, he flung open the handkerchief to wipe away perspiration, the cards were strewn across the platform to the astonishment of the congregation and to the delight of the perpetrators. It was said that he kept his composure through it all and only commented "those devilish boys have been at it again."

His obituary printed in the *Carroll Free Press* on 15 March 1921 concluded as follows:

> "Mr. Stallings was a man of stern honesty, and duty was never shirked by him. His influence was always for the best in life, and if his crown of glory is to have a star for every noble deed there will not be room enough to contain his stars. In his walk on earth he sought to place his feet as nearly as possible in the steps made by the lowly Nazarene. Few men on bended knee have lifted their voice to God more than he. The undertaker who prepared his body for burial stated that there was a corn about the size of a half dollar on one knee caused by the regular and constant kneeling in prayer. A useful life has ended and a soul has gone to claim the wealth it has sealed in the vaults of Heaven. Wrapped in the embrace of the sod he loved so well, he waits the sound of the last trump."

John Martin Daniel Stallings was laid to rest on 15 March 1921 at New Lebanon Baptist Church in the Lowell Community. His descendants continue to honor his legacy at family reunions held in Carroll County each Labor Day weekend. *Submitted by: great-great grandson, Willis Milton Stallings, 814 Providence Church, Newnan, GA 30163*

1062. Josiah Robert Stallings

My great-grandfather, Josiah Robert "Bob" Stallings, was born November 13, 1868, and died October 19, 1960, in Wellington, Alabama. He was the son of Mary Elizabeth Moore and John Martin Daniel Stallings, a well-known Baptist minister and pastor of many churches in Carroll County.

Josiah Robert married Elula H. "Lucy" Wren on October 27, 1885, in Temple, Georgia. She was the daughter of William Wren and Martha Wilson. She was born February 02, 1866, in Heard County, Georgia, and died September 18, 1938, in Carroll County, Georgia. At time of his death he had thirty-three grandchildren, seventy-six great grandchildren and nineteen great-great-grandchildren.

My sister remembers him living in Whitesburg and that he ate peas with a knife! He always wore a hat and suspenders and had a white mustache. My mom said he walked round-trip from Whitesburg to Newnan to a dentist to get a tooth pulled and was charged $5. He said, "I tell you right now, I won't go back to that dentist. I'll pull them myself!"

Children of Josiah Stallings and Elula Wren are William Martin, Annie M., Lula Pearl, Cora I., Susan C., R. Benson, Emma V., Joseph Lee, Madge D., John Daniel, and Charlie Frank Stallings.

My grandmother was Lula "Pearl" Stallings born April 29, 1890, in Carroll County. She married Byron Clifford Stone on December 31, 1906. He was also born in Carroll County on January 9, 1889, son of George Tarpley Stone and Ellenda "Ellie" Williamson Stone. They had twelve children: (1) Lela Bertha born October 31, 1904, died November 05, 1978, Villa Rica, Georgia; married Cleve Carlton Cruse. (2) Raymond Clifford born January 17, 1910, died May 04, 1990, Coweta County, Georgia; married Sarah "Vera" Gladney. (3) Leonard David born August 09, 1911, died March 25, 1976, Coweta County, married Annie Lou Hanson, then Thelma Paris. (4) Lloyd Taplin born 1912, died in infancy. (5) Lula Mae born December 23, 1914, died March 02, 1995, Newnan, Georgia; never married. (6) Velma Evangeline born abut 1916, died in infancy. (7) Lois Idomia born December 01, 1917, died April 18, 1969, Coweta County, married Willie W. Freeman. (8) Dana Lavonia married Thomas Vernon Meade. (9) Hiram Chester born August 11, 1922, died March 09, 1977, Gadsden, Alabama; married Doris Ruth Haun.

Josiah Robert Stallings

All of the above children were born in Carroll County, Georgia. After moving to Coweta County, the following children were born: (10) Gleama Ruth born March 31, 1914, died July 31, 1980, Miami, Florida; married Noel Douglas Harris. (11) J.P. born May 19, 1926, died May 25, 1998; married Mildred Gertrude Walker. (12) Mildred Lucille born January 11, 1928, died August 05, 1934, Coweta County. She was the baby of the family and died at the age of six years from strep throat.

My parents are Dana Lavonia Stone and Thomas Vernon Meade (died April 23, 1991) who married January 6, 1951, and had two children — Deborah Lynne, married to Charles Raymond Mapp (the Mapp family has roots in Carroll County, too), and Mary Elizabeth, married Robert Harris Dean. They have one child, Kathryn Elizabeth Dean. *Submitted by: Mary Meade Dean, 47 Nanette Drive, Newnan, GA 30265.* and Compiled by: Debbie M. Mapp, 674 Welcome Road, Newnan, GA 30163. DeyubRoots@aol.com

1063. Steadham

William Laburn Steadham Sr. was a Temple merchant until his death in 1938. He had tenant farmers, sold caskets, wagons, and mules. In the spring the wagons were delivered by train.

As the wagons were unloaded onto the railroad siding, Mr. Steadham sold them to the farmers from north Carroll County. Mr. Steadham and an employee would go to Atlanta on the train to buy mules. The employee would walk the mules to Temple while Mr. Steadham rode back on the train. Sometimes the mules would become frightened when they came to a bridge and break free from their lead. Then the chase would begin. It would usually take two days to walk the mules from Atlanta to Temple. He owned and operated two cotton gins. He also owned a fertilizer plant and an oil mill which extracted the oil from cotton seed. Mr. Steadham purchased an electric generator which provided electricity for Temple Baptist Church, his home, and several businesses. First Baptist was the first church in the area to have electric lights. He provided land for his church to grow and sell cotton. It was called God's Acres.

At age fifty, Mr. Steadham married Era Hixon, age thirty, from Villa Rica, Georgia. Era Hixon Steadham graduated from Draketown College and taught school in the Pleasant Grove community. Their house, next door to the First Baptist Church, was built in 1920 for the new bride. For many years, she was president of the E.L. Connell Sunday School class.

They had one child, William L. (Bill) Steadham Jr. He was a Temple Merchant and a cattle farmer. He was a World War II veteran of the South Pacific. Bill became mayor of Temple at age twenty-one and served on the city council for twenty years. Later he served as the Temple representative on the Carroll County Board of Education and also served as vice chairman of the board. He married Helen Shadrix from the Abilene community near Carrollton. Her parents were John Henry and Ella Spence Shadrix, who raised cotton on abut 500 acres north of Carrollton. Today part of that acreage is Sharp Creek Reservoir which is part of Carrollton's water supply. Several subdivisions have been developed around the lake.

Bill and Helen have two sons and daughters-in-law, two grandchildren, and two great-grandchildren. The oldest son is Doug Steadham and his wife is Rhonda. He is a graduate of West Georgia College and a local builder and horse breeder. John Steadham, the second son, has a BBA and MED from West Georgia College and teaches fourth grade at Mount Carmel Elementary School in Douglas County. John and his wife, Zan, have restored the old Steadham home on Carrollton Street in Temple. Doug's sons are Ron and Trey. Ron lives in Carroll County with his wife, Amy, and their two children, Megan and Cameron. Trey and his wife, Tina, live near Nashville, Tennessee. *Submitted by: W.L. (Bill) Steadham Jr., 51 Carrollton St., Temple, GA 30179*

1064. The Courtship of Mildred Downs and Warren Steele

In August, 1931, a group of young men sharing expenses going north to Pennsylvania and New York stopped by the G.L. Downs home in Bowdon, Georgia, to have dinner. They were students at the University of Alabama and had become friends of Bowdon girls, Mary Downs and Blanche Smith, while the girls were in summer school there. Mary's younger sister Mildred stayed in the kitchen to help her mother, but after dinner Mildred's mother insisted that she join the young people on the front porch. At first Mildred declined, saying they were older and wouldn't be interested in being with her. But finally she joined the group. By this time everyone had decided to walk up town to the drug store. Warren Steele asked Mildred if he could walk with her, and they went to the drug store and had a dish of ice cream.

On the way back they stopped by to see the new Baptist Church that was under construction, and Warren asked her for a date if the young men stayed overnight.

However, when they returned to the Downs home, everyone was waiting for Warren to continue their trip north. He gave Mildred his address in Pennsylvania and told her he would write. Happily, Mildred told this to her mother who said, "Yes. That is the way the Yankees do the Southern girls, and they never hear from them again." This upset Mildred. However, in a short time she received a letter from Warren telling her that his father had become ill with pneumonia and had died. She wrote a sympathy note. Their correspondence had begun as letters followed.

Mildred and Warren Steele, Genesee, PA 1933

Warren planned to return to Alabama in the summer and complete his master's degree, for he wanted the southern viewpoint on history. He planned to bring his mother and rent an apartment for them in Tuscaloosa. Sadly, she also became ill with pneumonia and died a short time later, so Mildred never met either of his parents.

Warren continued with his plans to attend Alabama and arranged for Mildred to keep his Boston Bulldog, Arrow, while he was in school. They had a few dates that summer, but Mildred's family told her he wanted to see Arrow, and of course he would see her then, too. At the end of the term, Warren proved them wrong by proposing. But before he could present her an engagement ring, he had to hurry back to Genesee, Pennsylvania where he was principal of a high school there.

One day Mildred came home from school (Bowdon College) and saw a small package addressed to her hanging on a light string. She opened it. Warren had sent her engagement ring by mail. Excitedly, she ran to show it to her mother Hettie and brother Olin. Olin teased, "It looks pretty good to have come out of popcorn." Of course, Hettie scolded Olin.

Mildred Helen Downs (born January 23, 1912) and Warren Hugh Steele (born April 17, 1909) were married in Bowdon, Georgia, on December 26, 1932, at the home of her parents, George Luna and Hettie Lipham Downs. Her mother was very sick at the time and did not get to attend the ceremony, but most of her immediate family members were there. The newlyweds spent nights in Spartanburg, South Carolina, Washington, D.C., and Harrisburg, Pennsylvania before arriving at their first home in Genesee, Pennsylvania. After only a month, Mildred was called home due to the illness of her mother. She helped with the nursing for about a month. When Hettie got better, Warren came for Mildred and they returned home via Washington, D.C. and saw Franklin Roosevelt's first inauguration on March 4, 1933. Mildred still had the official inaugural program at her death in 1998.

On February 4, 1934, fraternal twin boys were born to Mildred and Warren Steele: Ulysses Moody and Novice Richard. In adulthood, both boys became paratroopers but did not make the military a career.

Although Warren was a teacher when they married, he later became interested in the Episcopal Church and decided to become a priest of that church. While he was in seminary (1945-46) at the University of the South, Sewanee, Tennessee, Mildred and the boys lived with her mother and sister in Bowdon, Georgia. Mildred taught the third grade that year.

During his ministerial career, Warren had parishes in Hammondsport, New York; Bath, New York; Greenville, Tennessee; and Memphis, Tennessee. After a third coronary in 1968, Warren retired, and he and Mildred moved to their home in Seagrove Beach, Florida. They spent many happy years there and on December 26, 1982, celebrated their 50th Wedding Anniversary. They were planning a tour of England, but, unfortunately, Warren died of an aneurysm about a month later on February 4, 1983. Mildred continued to live at Seagrove until her own death on May 7, 1998.

Mildred said, "Being a teacher's wife and a priest's wife: life is very much alike. Of course, the road was bumpy at times, but our love was there to smooth the bumps." *Submitted by: Carolyn Wilson Bolan (Niece of Mildred Downs Steele), 2056 Darrell Drive, Marietta, GA 30066*

Sources: Personal knowledge and article written by Mildred Downs Steele, November 26, 1996

1065. The Mel Steely Family

Mel Steely, born in 1939 in Atlanta, brought his family to Carroll County in 1964. After growing up in Cedartown, Georgia, and graduating from Carson-Newman College and Vanderbilt University, Mel taught for a year at Lambuth College (Tennessee). He and his wife Judy and their one-year-old daughter Bonnie moved to Carrollton. Hired by Dr. John Martin as an assistant professor of history at West Georgia College, he began teaching in the old administration building on front campus. Judy taught school in Mt. Zion and Sand Hill. They lived on Cunningham Drive and Alice Lane. In 1965 a second daughter, Karen, was born at the old Tanner Hospital.

Mel Steely Family, Christmas 1999

The Steely family belonged to the First Baptist Church. They enjoyed trips to Tanner Beach, occasional trips to Atlanta, and shopping on the town square. They liked looking for toys at the old Empire Store on Alabama Street and in the loft of the old Carrollton Hardware store on the east side of the square. Cunningham Drive was close enough to the school that Mel could walk through the woods to work, accompanied by his black German Shepard who would wait by the steps of his building while he was at work. In 1966, Mel returned to Vanderbilt to finish his doctorate and do research in Germany. They returned in 1968 and lived for two years in Chapel Heights before moving to 60 South Greenwood Drive, where the Steely family would remain for more than thirty years. Judy worked for the city schools and they joined the First United Methodist Church where Dr. Larry Bauman was pastor. They found much to occupy their time. The city and church youth programs were excellent and the church outreach program kept them busy as did the children's school band activities. There were also special events, such as the moon landing, the Bicentennial activities in 1976, and the people's parade.

After a divorce in 1982, Judy moved to Franklin, Georgia, and married Thomas Miller. Mel remained at the house on South Greenwood and in 1987 married Nancy K. Boozer. She worked as a probation officer and ran the battered women's shelter. She also worked as office manager and tax preparer for Frank Boozer, CPA. Mel was active in politics working for local and state candidates. He served as an aide to United States Representative Newt Gingrich (1979-1993) and as an AAUP lobbyist. He was involved in numerous civic groups, such as the Kiwanis.

Bonnie married Ken Vernon from Kentucky in 1984. They have two children and live in Franklin where she is a teacher. Karen married Vance Campbell from Waco, Georgia, in 1994. They have three children and live in Bremen, Georgia. *Submitted by: Mrs. Mel Steely, 60 South Greenwood Drive, Carrollton, GA 30117*

1066. The Stephenson Family

John Stephenson, born in 1732, his wife Hannah and five children, Thomas, William, Joseph, Mary and Elizabeth, were Scot-Irish Presbyterians. They made their home twenty miles north of Belfast. In 1768, they sailed to America to enjoy religious freedom and flee high taxation. He died in Greene County, Georgia, in 1794. Their son Thomas, 1755-1799, married Mary Waddell in 1781. Their children were: John Stephenson born November 1786 in Wilkes County, died January 20, 1871, in DeKalb County, and married Susan Ann Peeler in 1812. Thomas Stephenson lived and died in Clark County, Georgia. Sarah (Sally) Stephenson married William Anderson in Greene County February 2, 1819. Polly Stephenson married Edward Callahan and moved to Mississippi. Mary Stephenson married Josephus Shaw and moved to "upper Georgia," and William Stephenson moved to Mississippi.

The children of John and Susan Ann Peeler Stephenson were: Thomas U., James Peeler, Susan, John Elbert, Anthony Franklin, Joseph, Moses Randall, William, Elizabeth Ann, Mary, John Alexander and Jacob Henry Stephenson.

Anthony Franklin Stephenson born August 1, 1820, died July 31, 1893, and married twice. His first wife, Jane Gardner, died May 14, 1856. Their three children were John Wilburn born May 23, 1840, married Saphronia Pitts and had two children, Roy and Annie Stephenson. James Madison Stephenson born October 29, 1841, and married Eudora Virginia Weaver. Franklin Thompson Stephenson, born October 31, 1842, died September 17, 1918, married Dora Ann Gaston.

A.F. Stephenson married a second time to Louisa Smith Black. She had one daughter Thompsie Black. Then they had one child, Martha Susan, born May 7, 1866, in Carroll County, died March 1958, who married James Henry McDaniel. Henry and Martha "Mattie" had four children: "Jessie" Frances McDaniel who married Franklin David "Frank" Hamrick and had one son, Radford Hamrick (1913-1972). Radford married Ruth Williams and they had one son Terry. Terry married Melba Adams and they had Ellen, Frank, and Michael. Ellen married Geoffrey Ammann. They have two children, Madalyn and Copeland.

Jessie Hamrick

Jessie Hamrick and her son Radford were considered the historians of Carroll County for many years. She described her grandfather's settling in Carroll County where the land was virgin forest with many cold water springs flowing through. He paid fifty cents per acre and fifty dollars for a place to make a home. He brought his wife Jane and three sons from DeKalb County. On the day after they arrived, other settlers invited to their "house raising" gathered wood, cut logs, and built a one room cabin for them on Land lot #44, 10th District. They brought what possessions they could on a one-horse wagon — bedding, clothes, garden tools, dried vegetables and fruit, meat from their hog killing and especially seed for spring planting. They also drove their cow all the way from Dekalb County.

James Peeler "Happy Jim" Stephenson, second son of John was born December 31, 1814, married Betsy Stancil. Their children were Frank, Edward, Frances, Ann, Susan, Laura, Mandy, Sally and Emma. He moved his family from DeKalb to Carroll County sometime between 1850-1860, and settled on Land Lot #21, 10th District where the home of Clarice Cox now stands.

Frances and Ann lived together in a log house on the property of their father while their husbands served in the Civil War. His property was located where Farmer's High School was built in 1917. In order to have a livelihood, Ann plowed a crop with the family milk cow while Frances kept the house and the children. Another daughter, Susan, married Zachariah Spruill and Emma married Jim Copeland. Emma's children were Robert, John and J.B. "B" Copeland. *Submitted by: Terry Hamrick, 135 Cimarron Court, Gray, GA 31032*
Sources: *Gabriel Spruill of Carroll County Georgia* by Clarice Cox, personal knowledge

1067. The Stephenson Family History

Among the Scot-Irish-Presbyterian immigrants were John Stephenson, born 1732 in Ireland, his wife Hannah, and their five children, Thomas, William, Joseph, Mary and Elizabeth. In 1768 they sailed to America (fifty-six days at sea). Their son Thomas was thirteen years old at the time. The Waddell family came on the same ship. Years later, Mary Waddell, who was twelve years old, would become Thomas' wife.

Upon their arrival in America, John Stephenson and his family settled in Iredell County, North Carolina. Soon after serving in the Revolutionary War, Thomas, John's son, moved to Georgia. John Stephenson also moved to Georgia. Records show that he died in Greene County. John Stephenson's will, written November 11, 1793, and probated June 30, 1794, mentions his wife Hannah; their sons, Thomas and William as executors; and their daughters, Mary and Elizabeth and her son Joseph.

In 1781 Thomas Stephenson married Mary Waddell and six children were born to them: John, Thomas, Sarah, Polly, Mary, and William. Thomas died in Greene County in 1799. Mary Waddell Stephenson died in DeKalb County, January 1840.

In 1812 John, born November 12, 1786, in Wilkes County, married Susan Ann Peeler in Greene County. They moved to DeKalb County in 1825 where they settled with their family of twelve children: Thomas U., James Peeler, Susan, John Elbert, Anthony Franklin, Joseph, Moses Randall, William, Elizabeth Ann, Mary, John Alexander, and Jacob Henry. John Stephenson died January 20, 1871 and his wife, Susan Ann Peeler Stephenson, died August 10, 1860 in DeKalb County. James Peeler Stephenson moved his family to Carroll County between 1850-1860 and settled on Land Lot twenty-one in the Tenth District, where he built a nice house. His wife, Betsy Stancil Stephenson, died of typhoid here. Their children were: Frank married Mary Jane Gillispie, Edward died young, Frances married (1) Unknown (2) William Gay, Ann married Gillispie, Susan married Zachariah Spruill, Laura, Mandy married John Brown, Sally married Harrison Hanes, and Emma married Jim Copeland.

James Peeler later married to Elizabeth "Betsy" Gay. Tradition is that his second wife became fearful that the first wife's children would demand the Stephenson home be sold in order for them to share their inheritance from their mother, since it was her money that bought the farm when they moved to Carroll County. The second Betsy influenced James Peeler to sell the farm and move to Marshall County, Alabama, where they lived the remainder of their lives. The Carroll County farm was later the home place of W.I. "Buck" Harmon. The home place of Kermit and Clarice Spruell Cox now stands on this spot.

The John Thomas Spruill Family

Susan Stephenson and Zachariah Spruill's only son, John Thomas (August 3, 1861-September 1, 1928) married Martha Frances Worley (December 14, 1864-November 04, 1907) in December 1882. Their children were Susan Elizabeth, Ollie, Zachariah Columbus, Lida Lenora, Vann Linley, John Marvin, Mittie Irene, Robert Marvin, Eva, Myrtie Lee, William Cohen, Cora Novana, and Alma. All their children were born in Carroll County except Vann Linley and Robert Marvin were born in St. Clair County, Alabama, and Eva was born in Randloph County, Alabama.

The photo shows the John Thomas Spruill Family. Front row, left to right, are Elizabeth, William, John Thomas, Novana, Mattie F. (Stephenson), Myrtie, and Zach. On the back row are Rena, Ollie, Marvin, Nora, and Eva. The doll in the small chair in the front row represents the unborn child that Mattie F. Spruill was carrying when this picture was taken. This was Alma Spruill, born 3 July 1905. *Submitted by: Clarice Spruell Cox, and Written by: Cecilia Wood Church, 128 Brock Street, Carrollton, GA 30117-8911*
Source: From information compiled and written by Clarice Cox in *Gabriel Spruell of Carroll County: Descendants and Allied Families.*

1068. Stevens Family

Old English records indicate the Stevens family was originally located in Gloucester and are listed in the Hundred Rolls of 1273. Early American historical records indicate settlers bearing this name settled in Boston, Massachusetts during 1638.

Louallen Edward Camp Stevens, known to his family and friends as Allen, was born in Moreland, Georgia, located in Coweta County, April 19, 1894. He was the fourth child of L.A. Stevens and Sallie Scoggins Stevens, who were married in 1889. His brothers and sisters in birth order were: Millington Stevens, Vivian Stevens Parrish, Kathleen Stevens Pope, Lawrence Stevens, Thelma Stevens Baxter, Ethel Stevens Baxter, and Loranzer Stevens.

Allen and Grace Stevens

L.A. Stevens was a tenant farmer. It has been said the family moved frequently to break new ground. During his later years, L.A. Stevens was a Temple, Georgia, merchant and part owner of Stevens Manufacturing Company. This wood products factory was founded in 1926 with his sons Millington, Allen, and Lawrence Stevens.

Sallie Stevens died in 1931, and L.A. Stevens died in 1957. They are buried in the Abilene Baptist Church cemetery with their infant son, Loranzer.

Allen Stevens married Adra Grace Brown December 18, 1920. She was born September 1, 1899 in Temple, Georgia. She was the first of three daughters born to Joe T. Brown and Lenona Kinney Brown. The other two daughters born were Bernice Brown Robinson and Dortha Brown Wynn.

Joe Brown was a Temple cotton gin manager and a former mayor of the town. Also, Grace Stevens' great-grandfather, Jesse Kinney, was the first mayor of Temple when it was incorporated in 1883.

The children of Allen and Grace Stevens in birth order, including their spouses, are: Agnes Stevens, Mary Joe Stevens, Brown Stevens married to Myrtle Eubanks in 1946, Richard Camp Stevens, Jane Stevens married to John McGukin in 1947, Clair Stevens married William (Bill) Cash in 1950, Max Stevens, and Burt Stevens married to Emma Bell in 1960. All of their children were born at home in Temple, Georgia, except Agnes, who was born in Union City, Georgia. Mary Joe and Richard died in infancy. All of the other children presently live in Carroll County except John and Jane McGukin who live in Andalusia, Alabama.

Allen Stevens was a World War I U.S. Navy veteran. Having little formal education, he was a self educated man. After acquiring his father's and brothers' interests in Stevens Manufacturing Company, he and his wife Grace managed the company until 1962 except during World War II, when the factory was leased. The wood furniture factory was sold to Parrish Cabinet Company of Center Point in 1965. He also was a farm owner, carpenter, and architect. He designed the Asbury cemetery chapel in Temple, the Temple United Methodist Church annex, and drafted numerous house construction plans in the Temple area. He donated land to Sewell Manufacturing Company of Bremen when they built a clothing plant in Temple.

Allen and Grace Stevens were members of the Temple United Methodist Church. Today the church has members from the fourth, fifth, and sixth generations of the Jesse Kinney family.

After almost fifty years of marriage, Grace Stevens died October 7, 1970, and Allen Stevens died September 17, 1973. They are buried in the Temple Asbury Cemetery.

Today, many of the grandchildren, great-grandchildren, and great-great-grandchildren of Allen and Grace Stevens live in the Temple and Carroll County area. *Submitted by: Max E. Stevens, 598-5 South Park Apartments, Carrollton, GA 30117*

Sources: Family Coat of Arms History; *A History of Temple, Georgia* by: B.W. and Ruth Holder published in 1982

1069. Stevens Family

John W. Stevens was born 22 December 1861 in Coweta County, Georgia, son of John W. and Sara Frances Almon Stevens. John married Mary Frances Foster in 1882 in Carroll County, daughter of William Sims Foster. They had four sons to live to be grown: John Thomas born 17 August 1885, married Selina Dunlap; William Russell born 20 December 1882, married Maude Stella Carreker; Otis born 1891, married Sallie Cheney; and Lee Alexander born 3 September 1887, married Carrie Hyde. All were born in Carroll County, Georgia.

John and Mary Frances (Molly) moved to Cook Springs, Alabama, in 1891. John operated a livery stable and farmed. William Russell died in 1922 in a train accident. Molly died May 1910 in Cook Springs, Alabama.

John W. Stevens

John remarried approximately two months later to a niece of Molly's. John married Lula Jane Foster 21 June 1910 in Carroll County, Georgia, daughter of George W. Foster. They lived in Cook Springs, Alabama, and had Lillie Mae who was born 16 November 1911 and Byrom J. before moving to Florida. George H. and E. Elisha were born after John and Lula moved to Florida.

John and Lula moved back to Carroll County in the early 1920s and were members of Tallapoosa Primitive Baptist Church. John was buried in the church cemetery.

John Stevens had three siblings: Elisha, Nancy Louise II, and Louellen A. who married Sallie Almeia Scoggins. They had John M., Leola V., Kathleen, Louallen E., Lorance T., Rose Thelma, Sarah E., and Earnest L. All were Carroll County residents during their formative years.

John and Lula moved to Flint Corner area of Carroll County where they farmed and ran a store. John died in this area on 27 March 1934. Lula lived with her children after his death. *Submitted by: Clarice Nixon, Prater Road, Waco, GA*

Sources: Some Early Families of Moreland, Georgia, 1910 St. Clair County, Alabama census, Carroll and Haralson County marriage records, church and Bible records, cemetery headstones, Coweta County, Georgia 1870 census.

1070. Isaiah Franklin Stewart 1853-1936 and Josephine Hill 1860-1892

Isaiah Franklin (Dudley) Stewart was born in Carroll County to William Stewart and Mary "Polly" Beck, daughter of Isaiah Beck Sr. and Dorcas York. The Becks and Stewarts were Carroll County pioneer families, winning land in the 1827 land lottery. They settled in the New Mexico district. Isaiah's siblings include: Martha Jane who married Joel Pinkney Yates, George W. who married Virginia C., F.M., Hiram Warner who married Eliza C. Bridges, John B. who married Rhoda Jones, Andrew Jackson who married Martha Ann Elizabeth Bishop, Anna A. who married James K.P. Craven, Nancy H. who married George W. Adams, then J.H. Jackson, Amanda Melvina who married William Jasper Wiggins, and Mary An Elizabeth who may have died in infancy.

James Franklin Stewart and Sarah Alvada Pyron with Dora c. 1907

About 1879, Dudley married Josephine Hill, known as Josie, daughter of James Harvey Hill and Atha Aimee Barker of Heard County. Josie's siblings include: William L. (Bud) Flourney who married Martha L. Mosely, Thomas M. who married Ann Thomas Daniel, James Manley who married Sarah Luella Brown, and Sarah Jane, her twin sister, who married William Valentine Brazeal. Before Josie died in childbirth in 1892, four children were born: Ola, Lula Mary, James Franklin, and Fannie. Isaiah then married Josephine Edwards Roberson, who was a widow. They had one son, William Burl. Dudley and Josie are buried at Pleasant Grove Baptist Church along with his parents.

Ola (1880-Unknown) married James (Smiley) Duffey. Lula (1882-1962) married Homer Bussey. Fannie (1887-Unknown) married William Frank Davis. Burl (1894-1972) married Katie Odessa Lewis, and moved to Cedartown where he lived and died. James "Frank" (1884-1960) married Sarah Alvada Pyron (1889-1987), daughter of James William Pyron and Lenora Elizabeth Duffey, on March 5, 1905.

Frank and "Vada" made their home in the Lowell Community, right beyond Lowell United Methodist Church. Frank was a quiet man who farmed and later worked in construction/carpentry. Vada was known throughout the community for her beautiful flowers and to her family for her sweet potato pie. Two sons died at birth. Other children are Dora (born 1906), who married Alexander Shay Portwood. Their children include: Stewart, Donald and Phyllis. Carmon Inez (1909-1994), who married James W.S. Hollingsworth remained childless, and Norman (1912-1999). Frank and Vada are buried at

Stripling Chapel Cemetery in the community where they lived in later years.

Norman, known as Stewart to his friends, moved to Atlanta and worked in the grocery business where he met and married Mary Beverlyn Harris of Pike County in 1947. In 1949 they purchased a grocery store in Smyrna. Stewart's Supermarket was his livelihood until they sold it in 1963. They lived in Southwest Atlanta and had five children: Norma Elizabeth, Ronald Stephen, Dean Allan, James Keith and Timothy Arden. Stewart worked at the Atlanta Farmers Market in the produce business until retiring. Inheriting his mother's green thumb, he grew beautiful and luscious vegetables in his rather large garden, which he liked to admire from his favorite swing. He delighted in giving away his garden's bounty to friends, family and neighbors, until his death in Piedmont Hospital from emphysema.

Norma married Jerry Lawrence Ford. They live in Tyrone with their son, Tyler Seth. Ronnie married Sandra Ann Carden and lives in Jonesboro. They have a son, Matthew Franklin and a daughter, Christina Ellen. Christy is married to Daniel Matthew Palmer and resides with their daughter Rileigh in McDonough. Dean is working on assignment in Basel, Switzerland. James is married to Rhonda Jean Miller, daughter of Donald Eugene Miller and Rachel Arlene Loftin of Heard County, and live in Snellville with two sons, James Cullen and Chase Sterling. Tim resides in Rico, Georgia *Submitted by: Norma Stewart Ford, 163 Jenkins Road, Tyrone, GA 30290 larryford@mindspring.com*

1071. Noah Solomon Sticher

According to census records, Noah Solomon Sticher was born in Maryland in 1793. Family legend says he emigrated at the age of eighteen from Germany as a stowaway on a ship landing in South Carolina. His reason for leaving his homeland was to see the "new world." The 1820 census for Frederick County, Maryland, lists Solomon Stickle, and by 1830 he had moved to Campbell County, Georgia, where he purchased property in 1832 along with two of his wife's brothers. This property became part of Carroll County.

The remainder of Solomon's life was spent in the Cross Plains section of Carroll County. At one time he was a Justice of the Peace and he also served as a road commissioner.

The 1840 census for Solomon shows a male 30-40 years old in his household who undoubtedly was George Sticher, born 1810, and who was either a son or a brother. Assuming George was a son would mean Solomon had married at a very young age and lost his first wife.

On June 18, 1822, in Greene County, Georgia, Solomon married Mary Bays. Mary was born abut 1794 in Greene County and died before 1840 in Carroll County where she is buried in the Sparks Cemetery. Mary was the daughter of Zachariah Bays and Mary Woodall of Greene County. Solomon and Mary had six children:

Amanda A. was born September 15, 1823, in Campbell County and died August 1898, in Haralson County. She married James R. Head on February 24, 1842, in Carroll County.

Joseph was born October 1, 1827, in Campbell County, died February 28, 1891, in Carroll County. He married Sarah Elmira Morgan on March 2, 1854, in Carroll County. They are buried in the Cross Plains Baptist Church Cemetery, Carroll County.

Artalissa was born February 27, 1830, in Campbell County, died about 1914 in Douglas County. She married Charles Winston Angle on February 21, 1858, in Campbell County. It is believed they are buried in the Flint Hill Methodist Church Cemetery in Douglas County.

Moses was born May 18, 1832, in Campbell County and died July 2, 1921, in Cullman County, Alabama. He married Mary Malissa Morris on August 12, 1858, in Campbell County. Both are buried in the Holly Pond Cemetery, Cullman County, Alabama.

Solomon Pulaski was born in June 1834, and he died November 16, 1902, in Carroll County. He married first Nancy Ann Hannah on April 12, 1866, in Carroll County and second Georgia Ann Peek on April 14, 1881, in Carroll County. He is buried in the Antioch Primitive Baptist Church Cemetery at Whitesburg in Carroll County.

Elias L. was born January 13, 1835, in Carroll County, and died October 25, 1896, in Cullman County, Alabama. He married Matilda M. Mullins on October 19, 1865, in Carroll County. Both are buried in the Holly Pond Cemetery, Cullman County.

Solomon's last marriage was to Emaline Wilkins on April 1, 1841, in Carroll County. Emaline was born about 1823 and died before 1900 in Carroll County. She is buried in the Sparks Cemetery in Carroll County. Solomon and Emaline had ten children:

Aaron was born April 10, 1842, and died August 12, 1904, in Carroll County. He married Susan Caroline Kiser on August 31, 1871, in Carroll County. Both are buried in the Kiser Cemetery, Carroll County.

Sophronia Zippora was born about 1844 and died after 1920 in Carroll County. She never married.

Marlin George was born about 1845 and died before 1910 in Carroll County. He married Susan Jossie Young on March 10, 1870, in Haralson County.

Sarah was born in September 1848 and died after 1910 in Carroll County. She never married.

Enoch was born in April 1852 and died after 1920 in Troup County. He married Sarah J. Winkles about 1872.

Sebasko was born July 20, 1853, and died in May 1935 in Carroll County. He married Melissa Elizabeth McCarty on May 20, 1884, in Carroll County. Both are buried in the Cross Plains Baptist Church Cemetery, Carroll County.

Elizabeth was born about 1854 and died before 1920 in Carroll County. She never married.

Mary A. was born about 1858 and died after 1920 in Carroll County. She never married.

Orpha was born March 15, 1860, and died January 19, 1926, in Carroll County. She married James L. Williams on December 11, 1879, in Carroll County. Both are buried in the Cross Plains Baptist Church Cemetery, Carroll County.

Martha was born in 1863 and died after 1920 in Carroll County. She never married.

On May 31, 1861, in Carrollton, Georgia, Solomon, age sixty-nine, enlisted in the Confederate Army in Company F, 7th Regiment, Georgia Volunteer Infantry. On September 9, 1861, he was discharged because of inability due to age. According to CSA Records, he was blond (gray), had deep blue eyes and a fair complexion.

According to family hearsay, Solomon may have worked in the circus as a young man, but it has not been proven.

No religious records have been found, but Solomon, Mary and Emiline appear to have been temperate people who used Biblical names for several of their children. Three of the children gave property for churches.

Solomon died before 1880 and is buried in the Sparks Cemetery in Carroll County. He did not wish to be buried underground, so his remains were placed on top of the ground and rock walls built around him with a slab on top.

Solomon was the father of seventeen children and grandfather of eighty-five. Many of his descendants still live in the Carroll County area. *Submitted by: Erlene Camp Boyd, 1539 Flat Rock Road, Villa Rica, GA 30180*

Sources: Census, court, marriage and cemetery records; Verma Garner, Newnan, Georgia; Doug Hall, San Antonio, Texas; Donald R. Sticher, Rancho P.V., California; Christopher Tanner, Waynesville, North Carolina; Gary Cassells, Titusville, Florida

1072. Sticher and Kiser Families of Cross Plains

Solomon Sticher, born in 1793, in Frederick County, Maryland, is believed to be from the Sticher family of Baden, Germany. He came to Georgia and married Mary Bays in 1822 in Greene County. They lived in Campbell County around 1830, and then set up residence in Carroll County near Cross Plains. They had several children until Mary died before 1841. Solomon married Emmaline Wilkins (born 1823) in 1841. The following year they had their first child, Aaron. There are several stories that have been passed down about Solomon. He once drove a team of horses across the Potomac River, while it was frozen. Also, Aaron told of his father taking him, as a small boy, to the circus in Carrollton to meet and talk with some of the circus people. Solomon was a five-feet, eight-inch tall farmer who served as justice of the peace in Carroll County around 1841. He joined the Confederate Army in 1861 along with three of his sons. He was discharged after four months due to his old age of around sixty-eight years. He died in 1880 and is buried in Sparks Cemetery between his two wives. His sons carried his granite grave marker to his resting place near his homestead.

Aaron and Susan Kiser Sticher Family

Aaron Sticher (1842-1904) married Susan Caroline Kiser (1844-1927) in Carroll County in 1871. Susan's parents were George Kiser (born 1797) and Rebekah Catherine Wilson (born 1798) of Lincoln County, North Carolina. The Kisers, of German ancestry, were among a group of eight families that came to Carroll County before 1839. They traveled from North Carolina by covered wagons pulled by oxen. They stopped at a town with one blacksmith shop and one mercantile store to ask about land with abundant springs. Eventually, they settled at Cross Plains, Georgia, and built the Kiser homestead. George and Rebekah lived there until their deaths. They thrived on the nearby spring water for many years before the two wells were built. Among the families with them were Rebekah's parents, Moses Wilson (1766-1843) and Mary Barbara Costner (1767-1846), and Rebekah's grandmother, Mary M. Costner (1748-1839). They are all buried at the Kiser Cemetery, at the homestead, along with others, including some Stichers. Since George had no living sons, he purchased a slave named Allen (1816-1890) to help with the farm. Allen continued to live and work for the Kisers after he was freed. He was treated as one of the family, initially living in the main house. George later gave Allen five acres of prime bottom land, as recorded at the Carrollton courthouse. Allen remained there until his death. He is buried at the Kiser family cemetery. Aaron named one of his sons after Allen.

Around 1880, after George and Rebekah's death, Susan and Aaron inherited the farm and home where they had been living with the Kisers. Among their many children were Allen, Peter, Gus, and Ben. Gus (born 1883) married Vennie Melinda "Bea" Cole in 1905 in Carroll County. Bea's parents were James Henry Buchanan Cole and Vennie Melinda Trapp. Both had ties to Carroll County and died here in the early 1900s. Gus and Bea started their family in 1905, and had many children, including Bryce, Myrl, Byrl, Gladys, Buford, Ila, Verma, George, and Clarice. He was a farmer who moved several times before he settled in Coweta County. At one time the family lived in Hulett in Carroll County.

One of Gus' daughters, Verma, recalls memories of the family. Her grandmother Susan wore long dresses and high-top shoes. She told Verma about the Civil War and how they had to hide their livestock and bury their valuables underground. Also, Verma remembers the old spinning wheel her grandmother used, and fondly recalls that she "taught me the art of sewing with a needle when I was six years old." Verma still follows the patterns her grandmother taught her. Susan also made pen and ink drawings with intricate borders.

Gus Sticher (center) at Kiser-Sticher home where he was born.

Verma spent time at the Sticher home with her Uncle Ben. He took her to the little creek nearby to play in the cold water and showed her a rock with "indentions." It is believed that the Creek Indians had cracked hickory nuts and walnuts on the rock. Ben was a farmer who resided with his mother until his untimely death. Ben was musically inclined. In a letter to his mother from Morven, Georgia, he writes. "There are a heap of pretty girls here. They were here last night to hear me play the fiddle." When he lived in Carrollton, Ben received a postcard from his cousin Ann from LaGrange, Georgia. It was dated May 1916 with a picture of movie star Norma Talmadge.

Gus Sticher's family, among others, would gather at his brother Pete's in Carroll County, where they made syrup at the mule-drawn mill. The families would bring their own cane. Also, when the corn crop was ripe, they would take it to the Horsley family gristmill, who were relatives of Pete Sticher by marriage.

Through the years, the families from the area have gathered at the Cross Plains Baptist Church for "Decoration Day" to remember those who have passed. Some of the Sticher family are buried in the cemetery behind the church. The community families built the old schoolhouse across the street in 1876. Several generations of the Sticher family attended the school. The school has applied for historical recognition. In 2001, a group of Kiser descendants began restoring some of the markers at the Kiser Cemetery. Supposedly, a professor from West Georgia College acquired some of the chimney rocks from the Kiser home for preservation. Julie Clarke, Verma's granddaughter, graduated from West Georgia College in 1983.

In writing this family history, the information and resources obtained from other family members is very much appreciated. *Submitted by: Julie Garner Clarke*
Source: Verma Sticher Garner

1073. James Howard Stidham Sr.

James Howard Stidham Sr. was born in 1790 in what is now Lexington County, South Carolina. He married Rachael Steedman in 1816 in Lexington County. Rachael Steedman was born on 10 March 1796 in Lexington County, the daughter of George Steedman Sr. and Mary Barton. George Steedman Sr. was in the South Carolina State Troops during the Revolutionary War, and was a descendant of Sir Andrew Barton, an Admiral of the Scottish navy who was knighted by King of Scots, James IV. The family name was changed from Barton to Stedman in 1565 by an edict from Mary, Queen of Scots, to enforce inheritance laws. The spelling was later changed to Steedman and Steadman.

James Howard Stidham Sr. was the son of Zachariah Stidham Jr. and Mary Howard. Zachariah Stidham Jr. was a private in the South Carolina State Troops during the Revolutionary War and lost an eye at the battle at Eutaw Springs, South Carolina, in 1781. He was a descendant of Timon Stidden who settled in the Swedish colony of Fort Christina, now Wilmington, Delaware, in 1654. The name was later anglicized to Stidham with variant spellings. Zachariah "Stedham" was enumerated in the 1840 census of Carroll County, Georgia, as a pensioner living in the household of James H. "Stedham." Zacharah lived in Carroll County for several years before returning to South Carolina.

James Howard Stidham moved his family to Georgia before 1829 and was in Walton County before coming to Carroll County in 1831. He purchased the southern half of Lot 111, 5th District in the Sand Hill community and built a home on the property. He purchased other adjoining parcels in 1841 upon which he grew farm produce and livestock.

James and Rachael Stidham had eight known children. John Adam, born 1822, was married to Sarah Vines in 1844. He was a Confederate soldier in the 26th Georgia Infantry Battalion. James Howard Jr., born 1826, was married to Sarilda Jordon in 1848. He was a Confederate soldier in Cobb's Georgia Legion. Rachel, born 1829, was married to John W. Carroll in 1847. (See related John Workman Carroll article) Elizabeth, born 1836, was married to Joseph Chavers in 1876. Zachariah George, born 1838, was married to Sophronia A. Burke in 1858. He was a Confederate soldier in the 56th Georgia Infantry Regiment. Mary Ellen, born 1840, was married to Abraham H. Pollard in 1873. Martha A., born 1841, was married to Reubin F. Stidham in 1874. The last child was Minerva, born in 1842. All of these marriages occurred in Carroll County.

In 1857 James Howard Stidham Sr. sold his land in Sand Hill and moved to the northern half of Lot 256, 7th District of Carroll County which, in 1875, became part of Haralson County. His sons also purchased land nearby in western Carroll County. Rachael Steedman Stidham died about 1872, and James Howard Stidham Sr. died in 1877. Their place of burial has not been located *Submitted by: Tim Turner, 4430 Eastern Pines Road, Greenville, NC 27858*
Source: Researched by: A.E. Turner

1074. Henry Nelson Stipe

Henry Nelson Stipe (12 January 1847-August 1929) married Mary Emmaline Steed (26 January 1848-22 February 1911) on 29 October 1869. They moved to Carroll County around 1875 to live on a farm on Hay's Mill Road. Their children were Alvin Olenza, Edna Lois, Mattie May, Emma, and John Gordon. Henry married again in 1916 to Miss Fannie Sewell. They moved to Houston County, Georgia. He is buried in Stripling Chapel Church Cemetery.

Henry Nelson's parents were John Wesley Stipe (1804, North Carolina-1890) and Emily Smith (1815-1909). They lived in the vicinity of Fairburn, Georgia, in Old Campbell County, now included in Douglas County. John Wesley and Emily are buried at Antioch Methodist Church in Fairburn. Emily lived with Henry Nelson in Carroll County until her death. He hired a horse drawn hearse to carry her to Fairburn for burial.

Henry Nelson and Mary Emmaline Stipe with son Gordon Stipe, early 1900s

Henry Nelson's grandparents were Henry (Steibe) Stipe (1775-1850) and Elizabeth Lampkin (1750-?). They had ten children and lived in the area of Fairburn. Henrich Steibe (1741-?) was Henry's great-grandfather.

Henry Nelson had seven brothers and sisters: John Wesley (1841-1917); Martha (1845-1888); William Talley (1850-1908); Lewis (1852-1895); Richard (died in childhood); Mary married Frank Parker; and Everett (1859-1925).

Alvin (4 September 1870-2 July 1926) married Annie Glenn Vineyard (12 February 1882-3) March 1967), from Sharpsburg, Georgia, on 14 October 1903. They had two sons: Sterling Henry (5 August 1904-26 February 1966); and Harvie Jordan (19 October 1905-12 July 1983). Three more children died in infancy: Sterling, Alvin, and Annie Glenn. The three babies are buried in Stripling Chapel Church Cemetery, Carroll County.

Henry Nelson around 1910

Edna Lois Stipe (15 July 1872-2 December 1932) married Willis Allen McLendon (10 October 1867-11 November 1922) on 06 October 1888. She was sixteen years of age. Both are buried in Stripling Chapel Church Cemetery. Their children are Edna Ola, Lester Allen, Addie Merl, May Jewel, Amma Josephine, Tristan, William Bond, Henry Newton, Byron Gordon, Mary Emmaline, and Willis Stipe McLendon.

Mattie May Stipe (31 May 1876-13 December 1929) married Thomas Wilburn Moore (8 January 1866-22 February 1914). They are buried at First Methodist Church Cemetery,

Bowdon, Georgia. Their children are Mary Grace, Wilburn Herschel, Thomas Herman, Glenn Stipe, Lois Evelyn, Henry Olenzo, Lyman, and Ralph Nelson Moore.

Emma Stipe (31 August 1881-8 July 1962) married Looney Edward Martin (15 November 1877-10 January 1971) on 2 October 1901. Both are buried at Stripling Chapel Church Cemetery. Their nine children are Mary Rebecca, Hugh Hamil, Henry Felton, Lois Christine, John Wiley, Aubrey Looney, Nina Mae, Everett Stipe, and Thyra Frances.

John Gordon (26 September 1885-8 June 1953) married Annie Dillard on 11 June, 1911. Their children are Lelita, John Gordon Jr., and Mary Steed Stipe. On 19 September 1941, he married his second wife, Miss Nell Burruss Parker. He was vice president of Emory University at the time of his death in 1953. *Submitted by: Clara Martin Stipe, 638 Bonner Road, Carrollton, GA 30117*

1075. Stone Family

Neal Stone, born 1800 in North Carolina, was the son of Daniel Stone. Neal married Lavinia Turner, born 1805 in Georgia and was living in Carroll County around 1828. Neal purchased land near what is now Lithia Springs. They and their seven children are listed in the 1850 census book of Carroll County.

Carroll County originally encompassed Douglas, Paulding, Haralson, Heard, Carroll, and part of Campbell counties. Neal served as the first sheriff of this area.

Neal's third son, William Prentice (born 4-8-1840 in Campbell County, died 4-11-1916), married Josephine Elizabeth Embry (born 3-3-1845 in Carroll County, died 2-10-1893). They first lived in Old Town; then, Villa Rica; and finally on 500 acres at the corner of the Bowdon Highway and the Tyus Road. There were eleven children from this marriage. After Josephine's death, William married Minnie Dolly Poor (born 1-17-1860 in Kentucky, died 9-11-1936). They had one son. William and Josephine are buried at Pleasant Grove; Minnie, in Atlanta.

William, a farmer, was also an architect and builder. He designed and built each of his homes with each becoming larger and more complex. The Old Town community called upon him to design and build a non-denominational church. When he moved to Villa Rica, he was asked to design and build both the Methodist Church and the school. After moving to the Bowdon and Tyus Roads corner, he designed and built a church for the Old Campgrounds. This church became known as Old Camp Church and still stands today. For this church he served as lay preacher and as Sunday School superintendent.

William's oldest son, Edwin Prentice (born 2-6-1870 in Villa Rica; died 10-1-1927) married Martha Alice Estep (born 10-26-1870, died 11-21-1920) on 1-10-1894. They had six daughters. Prentice farmed an area which is now Greenwood Estates and, until it burned, owned the Stone Hotel which stood on the spot of today's Carrollton City Hall. He and his wife are buried in the Carrollton City cemetery.

Prentice's fourth daughter, Miriam (born 7-8-1903, died 12-21-1993) married Samuel Jefferson Boykin Jr. (born 5-10-1901, died 9-26-1972) on 4-27-1922. They are buried in the Carrollton City cemetery.

Samuel was the judge of the Coweta Judicial Circuit from 1941-1961. While on the bench he presided over a trial which was of historic importance. In this case for the first time in jurisprudence a corpus delicti did not have to be found to prove murder and for the first time in the South a black man's word was taken over that of a white man.

Miriam's daughter, granddaughter and great-granddaughter still reside in Carroll County. *Submitted by: Alice Boykin Robertson, 120 Fairlawn Drive, Carrollton, GA 30117*

Sources: Research done by Bess Stone McRae, Martha Stone Gosweiler, and my own personal knowledge.

1076. Stone Family

Jeremiah Stone was born around 1790 in Spartanburg, South Carolina, and died August 07, 1868, in Randolph County, Alabama. He married Sarah Johnson on February 17, 1833, in Pendleton, South Carolina, daughter of Reuben Johnson and Nancy Greenlee. She was born around 1790 in North Carolina, and died around 1873 in Randolph County, Alabama.

I know they had at least one son, Caleb Stone, who was my great-grandfather, born December 1835 in Randolph County, Alabama; died May 15, 1903, Carroll County Georgia. He married Martha A. Ledbetter March 29, 1853, in Heard County, Georgia. She was born May 1831 in Heard County, and died about 1907 in Carroll County. It is said that the Stones had come on hard times; apparently, something to do with the railroad that caused Caleb to lose his land and his money. Prior to that and the war, they had been fairly well off — not rich, but solid.

Byron Clifford Stone

The children of Caleb Stone and Martha Ledbetter are: James William (Mary Richard Williamson) eventually moved his family to Troup County, Georgia; Hiram L.; Matilda E. Stone settled in Troup County; Emily J.; Harriet Mahala (Benjamin Seaborn Williamson) settled in Troup County; Martha Ada (H.L. Adair) moved to Troup County; Visa E. (Thomas Mermon Hanvey) moved to Alabama; and George Tarpley Stone.

George Tarpley Stone, my grandfather, was born October 18, 1858, in Randolph County, Alabama, and died May 22, 1943, in Carroll County, Georgia. He married Ellenda Ann "Ellie" Williamson January 17, 1887, in Carroll County, daughter of William Zachariah Williamson and Frances Rasco. She was born June 16, 1864, in Carroll County, and died December 10, 1945, in Carroll County. Zachariah Williamson has the distinction of being the first white child born in Coweta County.

George was a farmer in Alabama, Coweta County and Carroll County, Georgia. I think all of the children of George and Ellie are buried in Carroll County except for my father, Byron C. Stone, who was buried in Coweta County after living there for a little over twenty years.

The children of George Stone and Ellie Williamson are: Martha Frances (first to ? Billingsley; second to S.F. Clay; third to ? Ballenger); Byron Clifford (Lula Pearl Stallings); Exer Ashley (Uriah George Warren); James Albert (never married); Hiram Benjamin (never married); Tempie Lavonia (Ben F. Barnes); Isabel (Terrell C. Smith); George Roland (Erma Lee Warren); and Posey Davis (Bootsie Strickland).

Byron Clifford Stone (born January 9, 1889, in Carroll County) and Pearl Stallings Stone (born April 29, 1890, in Carroll County) were my (Dana Meade's) parents. They were married on December 31, 1906, and had twelve children. Their lineage is listed in the Josiah Robert Stallings article. *Submitted by: Dana Stone Meade, 18 Carmichael Street, Newnan, GA 30263.*

Source: Complied by: Debbie M. Mapp, 674 Welcome Road, Newnan, GA 30263. DeyubRoots@aol.com

1077. Storey - Herston - Gentry - Robertson - Warren

John S. Storey, the son of John (Revolutionary War veteran) and Nancy McIlwain Storey, and the grandson of George and Nancy Cantor Storey, was born 15 September 1797 in Spartanburg County, South Carolina. He married Melinda Herston. He died 15 April 1875 in Summerville, Georgia. Melinda died 1898 at age 83 in Lindale, Georgia.

John S. moved from South Carolina to Coweta County, Georgia, with his brother William M. about 1830. They were blacksmiths.

John S., Melinda, and five children moved to Carroll County, Georgia about 1840. Their twin sons, Jasper Lafayette and Newton, were born 20 November 1841 in Carroll County. The other five children were Martha Lucinda who married Charles Carter; Harriett Marie who married Jimmy Rush; Pickney Means, born 8 November 1832 in Coweta County, Georgia, died 20 December 1911 in Floyd County, Georgia, married first to Martha Hully Thomas, second to Etta Hair; Melinda Henderson who married Sandy Stewart; Rhoda Ann who married? Griffin; Newton died in the War between the States.

Jasper Lafayette married Nancy Susan Gentry, daughter of William and Sarah Ann Robertson Gentry, on 11 January 1866 in Coweta County. Nancy Susan was born 29 June 1841 in Coweta County and died 4 April 1924 in Floyd County, Georgia. Jasper Lafayette died 14 March 1920 in Floyd County. Jasper Lafayette and Nancy had five children: Carrie who married John H. Price on 16 January 1912 in Floyd County; Newton A. who married Carrie Barnette; John William, born 10 May 1874 in Dirt Town, Chattooga County, Georgia, died 3 August 1937 in Tuscaloosa, Alabama, buried in Oak Hill Cemetery in Attalla, Alabama, married Eula Levada Warren on 2 December 1894 in Floyd County — she was born 2 September 1876 in Floyd County, died 30 October 1943 in Attalla, Etowah County, Alabama, daughter of Benjamin Franklin B.P. and Sarah Parizade Ware Warren; Irene; Susan, born 1879, died 4 August 1970 in Florida, married James A. Jones on 9 October 1902 in Floyd County.

John William and Eula Levada had four children and adopted Myrtis Warren after the death of her parents, Charley Franklin and Bertha Mae McGuillian Warren. Eula Levada and Charley Franklin were siblings. Will and Eula's four children were Grace Elizabeth born 9 October 1895 in Floyd County, died 31 March 1985 in Gadsden, Etowah County, Alabama, married Clyde Almuth Curry on 27 January 1917 in Alabama City, Etowah County, Alabama-he was born 28 June 1892, died 8 May 1973; William Ivey born 30 October 1897, died 12 October 1969, married Edith Velma Stanley on 8 November 1933 in Cleveland, Boliver County, Mississippi-she was born 7 August 1908, died 31 May 1979; Robert Clifton born 28 December 1900, died 10 March 1960 in Olean, New York, married Mattie Clarice Stapleton born 17 December 1902, died 16 November 1979; Lollie Juanita born 14 November 1905, died 28 April 1993 in Colorado, married (1) Spencer Westinghouse Allen on 19 October 1926-he died 12 July 1946 in Jefferson County, Alabama, (2) John Lawrence Armbrust on 17 October 1950-he was born in 1890, died 14 September 1975 in St. Petersburg, Florida. *Submitted by: June Curry Maddox, 6301 Third Street, Gadsden, AL*

Sources: John William Storey Family Bible, Oak Hill Cemetery, Attalla, AL, Bethel Cemetery, Summerville, GA, *The Family Storey,* Georgia Archives, Atlanta, GA, family knowledge.

1078. Strickland and Horton

I, Elizabeth Anne Eanes Richardson, was born on 8 March 1945 in the old Carrollton Clinic in Carrollton, Georgia. My cousin, Charles Johnson, was born 2 August 1940. Charles' family lived on Oak Mountain at the time of his birth. His grandfather owns a lot of land there. I would like to share the credit with him. His mother was Ara Strickland Johnson, one of Uncle Bud's daughters.

My parents were Frances M. Horton Eanes, born 7 September 1916 at the same clinic in Carrollton, and William Joseph Eanes, born 7 September 1906. He was from Spray, North Carolina. He came to work in the mill at Sergent-Arcno as a foreman. My parents were married on 21 September 1943 while Dad was in the Navy at Ft. Meyers, Florida, and all her family were born in Carroll County.

Thomas L. Horton brought his family from Alabama. One of his sons, Alner Morris "Al" Horton (born 6 August 1876), stayed in Alabama with his family until his wife died. He then moved to Georgia. Alner came with two little girls, Mollie and Myrtie. He had a brother, Robert "Bob," and sisters, Emma Lou and Annie. When they were grown, Bob married Lorna Dale. They are buried in Coweta County. Emma Lou married Aroan Borders. Annie married Roy Books and moved to Alabama.

My Papa was Alner (he was called Al). He married Annie Elizabeth Strickland Horton on 13 May 1908. She was born 18 June 1877 and died 3 June 1959. Papa passed away on 17 June 1945, not too long after I was born. From that second marriage came my mother, her sister Elizabeth, and a brother Burnett Horton. Burnett served in World War II. I'm not sure about their births or deaths.

Annie, her brothers and sisters number eleven children, the youngest died as an infant. There was Charles who married Fannie Lou Scroggins, W.T. "Bud" married Evie Whitehead on 9 September 1900, Walter married Marinda Farmer on 4 December 1904, Carrie married George Caldwell on 29 December 1889, Fannie Bell married Bob Bearden on 26 March 1893, Matilda married Jim Walker, Rosie married Frank Stephens, Ector M. married Leola Dyer on 25 October 1906, and Lee married Betsy Sewell on 1 January 1908. Their parents were William Warren Strickland, born 6 November 1843 in Spalding Count, died 28 March 1919, married Elizabeth Marrow on 10 October 1865. She was born 11 September 1845 and died 8 May 1929. Both are buried in Carroll County, 5th District, Mt. Pleasant Baptist Church Cemetery.

W.W. Strickland is a descendant of Matthew Strickland, who was born in England and moved to Virginia where he died in 1698 at Isle of Wight, Virginia. W.W. Strickland also served in the War Between the States in the Army of Northern Virginia, Confederate States Army (CSA), Ringgold Rangers.

Some of the things I can remember about Carrollton are from the 1950s, when the square was a park with a CSA soldier in it, instead of red lights.

When we lived on College Street, I went to a little white schoolhouse; the last time I went by there it was still standing. My father worked at the fire station that is not too far from the library today. To me, that was a long time ago and look how Carrollton has grown. *Submitted by: Elizabeth Richardson, 39 Turkey Creek Drive, Newnan, GA 30263*

Strickland Family Reunion 1920 or 1903.

1079. The Stripling Family

Mary Stripling with her sons David, James, and Robert and other family members moved to Carroll County before 1830 from Jones County, Georgia, where they were living in 1820. She was the widow of Robert Stripling by 1813 and the mother of several children. Mary was born in 1776 in South Carolina and died in Carroll County June 12, 1857. Her obituary stated that she was a member of the M.E. Church some fifty-two years at the time of her death. She was a widow of forty-five years and raised eight children. Three of her sons were ministers of the gospel, one other a useful "exhorter."

David Stripling was born September 6, 1806. He married Ann Mason Butler Dane November 23, 1828, in Butts County. She was a widow with two young daughters, Anne Butler Dane and Eliza Hope Dane. She was born May 11, 1802, in London, England.

David Stripling became a well-respected, beloved Methodist minister in Carroll County. He was the founder of Smyrna Methodist Chapel in 1853. Stripling's Chapel founded in 1857 was named for him.

David and Ann Stripling were the parents of seven children. Henry Marcus Stripling born May 1830, who married Sara Jane Norman July 3, 1856, in Carroll County. (See related Henry Marcus Stripling article.)

Francis B. Stripling born January 8, 1832, who married James Joseph Whisenhunt in Carroll County January 8, 1848 (a son Marcus Whisenhunt was born 1849 in Carroll County). Francis died in February 1899 in Parks, Arkansas.

Catherine H. Stripling was born April 21, 1834, died unmarried July 17, 1877, and was buried in Smyrna Churchyard Cemetery.

Mary T. Stripling born September 13, 1836, married John H. Bevins August 16, 1859, in Carroll County, died October 1, 1916. She was buried in Smyrna Churchyard Cemetery.

Robert Stripling born 1838, married Jane Maddox September 11, 1859, in Carroll County.

James W.G. Stripling was born April 4, 1841, married Susanna Avery Peacock. He later lived in Scott County, Arkansas, and died January 21, 1925, in Heavener, Leflore County, Oklahoma.

Martha Jane Stripling born 1844 married Simeon Hartley. David Stripling was a member of the Home Guard during the Civil War. His sons Henry Marcus and James W.G. Stripling served together in Company F. Cobb's Legion, to the end of the war.

David was a member of the Masonic order. He was a member of the Villa Rica Lodge No. 72 from 1849 to 1864 and on the Carrollton Lodge No. 69 rolls 1864 until his death in 1882.

David's ministry is documented in Harold Lawrence's book. *Methodist Preachers of Georgia 1783-1900*. He often said he wanted to die in service to his Lord. His ministry in the Methodist faith continued until his death. On August 13, 1882, after closing services at Shiloh Camp Ground he became ill and died. He was buried in Smyrna Churchyard Cemetery beside his wife Ann who died June 11, 1876. *Submitted by: Bettye J. Payne, 11208 Cinderella Lane, Dallas, TX 75229*

Sources: Census, deed, land lottery, marriage and cemetery records form Carroll, Jones, and Butts counties; guardianship records Stripling-Dane; *Southern Christian Advocate* obituary for Mary Stripling; *Carroll County Times* obituary for David Stripling.

1080. Henry Marcus Stripling

Henry Marcus Stripling, by family tradition, was the son of David and Ann Stripling. (See related Stripling family article.) He was born in Carroll County about May 1830. He was a farmer by occupation in Carroll County most of his life. He was of the Methodist faith.

He married Mary Margaret Vaughn. They were the parents of Sadie, Josephine, George Alexander and Mary Elizabeth (Lizzie). After the death of his wife, Sadie and Josephine were taken to Lafayette County, Mississippi, by their mother's family. George and Mary Elizabeth remained with their father in Carroll County where they were in 1860. George Alexander Stripling married Callie Auston Sartor on December 11, 1873, in Lafayette County, Mississippi. Sarah Ann (Sadie) Stripling married Joseph B. Vaughn December 26, 1869, in Lafayette County, Mississippi. Josephine Stripling married James Leemore Moorman. Mary Elizabeth Stripling born June 1853 married Henry A. Kilgore (Kilgoe) December 25, 1875, in Carroll County. They later moved to Floyd County.

Henry Marcus Stripling married his second wife, Sara Jane Norman, July 3, 1856, in Carroll County. She was the daughter of Benjamin and Catherine Arnold Norman who moved to Carroll County from Laurens County, South Carolina, in January 1848. Sara Jane was born October 1833 in South Carolina.

The children born to Henry and Sara Jane Stripling were Malinda Catherine born September 1857, married John Robert Williams August 14, 1872. John H.W. Stripling born 1861, married Delia Brooks December 25, 1884. Lula born 1863, married Lee Lumpkin November 19, 1894, in Floyd County. Maude Jane born September 1867, married Thomas Mansfield Priest. Ann born May 6, 1870, married Joe Lanham. David Stripling born November 1875 married Rose Collins.

Henry Marcus Stripling served as a Confederate soldier during the Civil War. He was a private in Cobb's Legion of the Georgia Volunteers. He served honorably and was present with his unit when the surrender was announced. He walked home from Virginia with his scanty belongings tied to a walking stick. (This walking stick was in possession of his daughter, Maude Jane Priest of Sapulpa, Oklahoma, in 1938).

Malinda Catherine Stripling Williams told her children of climbing up on the looms stored at the side of their house to watch her father leave to join his unit. She watched until he was out of sight.

Henry Marcus Stripling was a small man about five feet five inches in height. He had dark hair and small piercing brown eyes. He wore his hair shoulder length and had a beard. In later years, failing health forced the move to Floyd County to be with their daughters. They lived near their son-in-law and daughter in Lindale. He died March 24, 1894, and was buried in a cemetery near Rome.

Sara Jane Norman Stripling died in October 7, 1908. She was buried next to her husband in a family plot where their sons John and David were later buried. Their graves are not marked. *Submitted by: P.A. Payne, 3308 Sungate, Killeen, TX and Researched by: Bettye J. Payne, 11208 Cinderella Lane, Dallas, TX 75229*

Sources: Census Records Carroll County, Floyd County; Marriage Records Carroll County, Floyd County; Widows Pension Georgia Archives; Confederate Records National Archives; Carroll County Deeds; Memories: Ida Catherine (Zeida) Williams Pritchett 1879-1975; Bible 1867 belonged to Sara Jane Norman Stripling in possession of Ida C. Pritchett in 1967, resident of Hawaii Gardens, Calif.; Letters: Oxford, Mississippi 1980s from R.E. Stripling Owens

1081. Swanson

Robert John Swanson was born 3 March 1942 in Middletown, Connecticut, to John and Martha Bahr Swanson.

Robert married Karen Mae Vanderburgh, born 30 April 1943 in Poughkeepsie, New York, to John and Bessie Likley Vanderburgh, on 11 January 1964 in Poughkeepsie. Bob and Karen had three children: Robert John Jr. 12 November 1966, Eric Jeffrey 21 July 1970, Debra Elizabeth 7 June 1974.

Bob and Karen Swanson

Moving from Lee, Massachusetts, the family arrived in Carrollton in July 1977. They built their home at 427 North Lakeshore Drive and raised their family there. All three children attended and graduated from the Carrollton City Schools.

Bob, a manufacturing engineer, worked for several years at Haralson Metals in Bremen and the Hon Company in Cedartown. He also worked for an Ohio company, TIPCO, as a sales engineer in the Southeast. Karen, a dental hygienist, was a full-time mother for many years but returned to her profession when Bob Jr. was ready for college. All three children graduated from college — Bob Jr. from Oglethorpe University in Atlanta, Georgia, Eric and Debbie from the University of Georgia in Athens.

The family are members of St. Margarets Episcopal Church in Carrollton. Bob was an assistant Boy Scout leader for a while. Karen volunteered in the schools and was a member of and treasurer and president of the Carrollton Junior Womans Club.

Eventually their parents moved to Carrollton to spend their remaining years with their children and grandchildren. Both sets of parents are buried at Carroll Memory Gardens.

Bob and Karen look forward to living in Carrollton for many more years and enjoying their children and grandchildren. *Submitted by: Karen Swanson, 427 North Lakeshore Drive, Carrollton, GA 30117*

1082. Swearingen - Earnest

Jimmie Lee Swearingen (May 4, 1913-December 3, 1998) was born in Dodge County, Georgia, the third child of James Council Swearingen (1861-1922) and Minnie Davidson Swearingen (1874-1936). Jimmie grew up and attended school in Dodge, Laurens, and Pulaski Counties. She attended business school in Eastman, Georgia, and became a bookkeeper. She moved to Jacksonville, Florida, in 1940 and went to work for Western Auto, where she met Hugh Boyd Earnest (October 13, 1913-July 10, 1965). They were married in 1941 in McClenny, Florida. Soon afterwards, they were transferred to Macon, Georgia where he became a manager and she worked in a government fuse plant. After World War II, they moved to New Orleans, Jacksonville, Atlanta, and Birmingham. They left Western Auto and began to raise broilers and beef cattle and Jimmie worked as a bookkeeper for a number of companies in Carroll and Haralson counties. Both were Methodists, Democrats, active church members, and community activists.

Hugh B. Earnest was the son of A.A. Earnest (1877-1955) and Nan Nixon Earnest (1876-1976). He graduated from Mt. Zion Seminary in 1934. His ancestor, George Earnest (Revolutionary soldier) left Virginia and settled in Burke County, Georgia, in the 1780s. Later they moved to Jackson County (now Clark) where one of George's grandsons (Thomas Richard Earnest) was married. Their next move was to Meriwether County where George (R.S.) is buried in a cemetery near Luthersville. His grave is marked.

In the early 1850s, the Earnest family moved to Carroll County settling near Holly Springs Primitive Baptist Church. After the Civil War, they moved to Mt. Zion where Thomas Richard Earnest built a two-story log house (site is occupied by Lewis Earnest's Tool Shop in 2001). His children began to settle all over Bowdon Junction and Mt. Zion. Thomas Richard's grandson was A.A. Earnest, the father of Hugh Boyd Earnest. *Submitted by: Jonathan Dorsey (grand nephew), 59 Boulder Drive, Carrollton, GA 30117*

1083. Walter Monroe Talley

As a member of an old and distinguished Georgia family, Walter Monroe Talley upheld the illustrious traditions of his forebears by occupying a place of outstanding prominence in the social, civic and business life of Villa Rica, where he was recognized as one of the most successful cotton merchants and financiers for over forty years. Not only did he contribute substantially to the commercial progress of his surroundings but he also was a leader in supporting all movements and organizations designed to better the general welfare.

Walter Monroe Talley was born in Powder Springs, April 15, 1872, the son of Alonzo Henry and Eugenia Ann (Green) Talley, both natives of this state, the former from Newton County, and the latter from Paulding County. They were also the parents of the following children: (1) William Edgar, who married Alline Nichols. (2) Louella Eugenia, who married R.E. Guffin. (3) Rosilee Ann, married Arthur A. Floyd. (4) Margaret Josephine, married Thomas V. Henderson (5) Henry Alonzo, married Wilhemina Osborn. (6) Theophilus Pound, a physician, who married Rose Bishop. (7) Leila Mae, married J.M. Phagan, (8) Clarence Newton.

Walter Monroe Talley

Mr. Talley's father, who was born February 21, 1847, was a teacher by profession and engaged in farming. He received his education at Oxford Academy at Covington, Georgia, and during the War Between the States served with the Confederate forces. The Talley family trace their Georgia ancestry to Henry Talley, a planter, who was born in Cumberland County, Virginia, in 1760, served during the Revolutionary War, was registered from Hanover County, Virginia, and married Edith Hubbard in York District, South Carolina, December 1, 1795. He moved to Newton County, Georgia, where he died on June 4, 1836. He was the father of eight children: (1) Lucy, married Alex McWaters of Newton County. (2) Henry Hubbard. (3) William, (4) Nathan. (5) Sallie. (6) Louisa, married Joab Hinton. (7) Betsy Crumpton, married Alex Farmer. (8) George W., grandfather of Walter Monroe Talley. He was born in Newton County, September 27, 1822, attended Oxford Academy and married Louisa Anderson of Newton. She was the daughter of Thomas Anderson and was born in Union District, South Carolina. The couple settled in Cobb County where George Talley was a planter. During the War Between the States he served with the Confederate forces. George W. and Louisa Anderson Talley were the parents of three children: (1) Monroe Newton, who died on his way home from the War Between the States. (2) Alonzo Henry, father of Mr. Talley. (3) Elizabeth, who married S.J. Scott.

Mr. Talley secured a general education in the public schools of Cobb County and later completed his studies at the Villa Rica High School. He embarked on his business career in 1893, establishing himself as a merchant and becoming associated in his activities with the Villa Rica Cooperative Store. He continued in this work until 1897 and then formed a partnership in the cotton business with G.B. Malone, which was continued until 1899, when he became associated with E.J. Cheves under a similar arrangement. Nine years later, in 1908, he withdrew from this firm and established himself in the cotton fertilizer business, which he maintained until his death, under the name of W.M. Talley. Throughout his long and distinguished career he was ranked among the leading business executives of this section, and in this connection came to play a vital and important part in a number of the most important enterprises in this vicinity. From 1907 to 1930 he held a partnership in the Villa Rica Mercantile Company and for a number of years was a member of the board of directors of the Merchants and Planters Bank.

His business success was matched by his civic accomplishments. He was clerk of the city council for four years and served with that body for a number of terms. He also was a member and served as president of the local school board on numerous occasions and was a member of the Carroll County Board of Education, to which he was elected in 1934. He also served with this body from 1928 to 1931. Socially he was a member of the Villa Rica Civitan Club and fraternized with the Knights of Pythias, where he was a keeper of records and seal. In his religious convictions he worshiped at the Baptist Church, an institution in which he served as treasurer for many years. Mr. Talley has been characterized by his daughter, Mary Talley Anderson, in the following terms:

> Honesty has been his greatest asset. No fight has ever been too difficult for him when he has convinced himself of the justice of his course. His progressiveness and charitableness have been invaluable. He has been a civic and religious promoter of the highest type.

On June 28, 1894, Mr. Talley married Mary Lenora Roberds, daughter of Leonidas and Martha (Cheves) Roberds. Her father was a physician. Mr. and Mrs. Talley are the parents of seven children: (1) Cecil Fae, born November 27, 1895, (2) George Earnest, born August 6, 1900. (3) Mary Rebekah, born July 15, 1903. (4) William Edgar, born December 3, 1907. (5) Walter Lewis, born November 30, 1910. (6) Sarah Roberds, born June 18, 1914. (7) Grace Annette, born May 18, 1918. *Submitted by: Mary Anderson, Villa Rica, GA*

Source: *"The Story of Georgia"* Cooper; 1935

1084. The Charles Mabry Tanner Family

The history of the Tanner family and the history of Carrollton, Georgia, have intertwined over the years like the ivy that climbs the columns of the old Tanner home place on Dixie Street. It has become almost impossible to think of one name without calling to mind the other.

Charles Mabry Tanner was known as "Carrollton's First Citizen" and its greatest benefactor during his lifetime. He was a man of great vision and later said that it was "the dream of his life" to see Tanner Memorial Hospital become a reality in 1949. The building of the hospital would not have been possible without C.M. Tanner's most generous donation at a time when the Great Depression was just ending. It was C.M. Tanner's enthusiasm that initiated the community drive to raise other funds towards building the hospital, which has grown into our modern facility of today known as Tanner Medical Center since 1985. Over the last fifty years, the hospital has not only survived but thrived.

The history of the Tanner family in Carrollton begins with the arrival of a doctor's horse and buggy in 1850 carrying Dr. William S. Tanner and his young family to town. Dr. Tanner was born William S. Tanner on 5 August 1813 in Georgia. By young manhood, he was a physician practicing in the Roscoe community of Coweta County until 1850 and had delivered just about every baby in that community, but now he had decided to move his practice into Carrollton.

He left Coweta County with the greatest respect of his patients there who would later say of him, "There was never weather too cold nor a night too dark for him to attend to the sick." Dr. Tanner was one of the last country doctors to make house calls in his horse and buggy in the Roscoe area. Dr. C.C. Elliot replaced him in that community after his move to Carrollton.

We believe that Dr. Tanner may have been doing some courting in Carroll County prior to his move here because it was in Carroll County that he married on 20 November 1844. There were several Mabry families in Carroll County in the 1840 census and one family — that of Branch M. Mabry — had a daughter the right age to be Dr. Tanner's "sweetheart," Lydia Mabry. Also, not long after the Tanner family moved to Carrollton, the Seth Mabry family moved right next door to them. Seth Mabry was 47 years old in the 1850 census with wife Nancy age 30, children: Charles age 9, Martha, age 7, Jonathan M. age 5, and Susan A., age two. All in this family were born in North Carolina.

In 1850 Dr. Tanner was 37 years old, his wife Lydia E. Mabry Tanner was age 25 on their arrival to Carrollton. They had three children accompanying them, Jerusha J. who was five years old, James G. age three, and a bouncing seven month old baby named Margaret L. They had arrived in time for the 1850 census which was taken on the 19th day of August. So, Dr. Tanner had hung out his shingle in Carrollton and had begun his medical practice there.

The C.M. Tanner family

Several more children would be born to the Tanner family over the years. William S. Tanner Jr. was born in 1856, Katie was born in 1863, then Charles Mabry Tanner was born in 1867. The older Tanner children had been born during the antebellum years of the South, just prior to the Civil War, and would witness that era that would later be "gone with the wind that swept over Georgia." The younger children would be born during that conflagration of war between North and the South.

During the Civil War, Company F of the regiment known as the Heard County Volunteers was under Captain Charles W. Mabry who lived at Laurel Hill near Bowdon, and who later was promoted to major. His brother, Henche Parham Mabry, was at the same time a colonel in a Texas cavalry regiment. These may have been Lydia Tanner's brothers.

An older man by the time of the war, Dr. William S. Tanner stayed on in Carrollton during the war years to continue to serve the needs of the people in the community at home. Dr. Tanner died on 7 January 1868 and was buried in Carrollton City Cemetery. His marker indicates he was a Mason. In later years, the rest of his family would be buried in the family plot beside Dr. Tanner. Tombstones there read: Lydia E. Tanner born 12 August 1825 died 7 June 1908; Jarusha J. Tanner born 30 September 1845 died 15 October 1865. An infant Tanner with no dates; Katie A. Tanner born 1 April 1863 died 20 May 1888.

After Dr. Tanner's death, his wife Lydia continued to live in Carrollton with her children nearby. All the Tanner children would grow up to lead productive lives in Carrollton, but it was the youngest son, C.M. Tanner, who would distinguish himself the most.

Charles Mabry Tanner was born 4 August 1867 and grew up in the Reconstruction years after the Civil War. He was not even a year old when his father had died. On 7 July 1892, when he was 25 years old, he married Miss Mamie Rhudy who was 18 years old at the time. Mamie was born 13 July 1874. Together C.M. and Mamie Tanner would have seven children: Charles M. Tanner Jr. was born 18 January 1895 (died 1982); Sue Tanner (McKenzie) was born 4 April 1897 (died 1961); Lydia Tanner (Weaver) was born 8 November 1900 died (1961); John Wesley Tanner was born 5 November 1902 (d. 12 December 1981); Mary Tanner (Patillo) was born 24 August 1904 (died 1989); Katherine Tanner (Gilreath) was born 5 January 1911; James Rhudy Tanner was born 17 September 1913 (d. 2000).

The young C.M. Tanner Family is shown in the family picture. Front row L-R, Mamie Rhudy Tanner, James Rhudy Tanner, Katherine Tanner (Gilreath), C.M. Tanner, Back row L-R, John W. Tanner Sr., Sue Tanner (McKenzie), Charles Mabry Tanner Jr., Lydia Tanner (Weaver), Mary Tanner (Patillo).

About 1893, C.M. Tanner had become a salesman for a branch of the Iron Belt Mercantile Company of Anniston, Alabama. They were the wholesale grocers of this area and J.S. Stokley was the manager. Within two years, in 1895, C.M. Tanner and J.S. Stokely had bought the business and named it The Carrollton Grocery Company.

In 1898, C.M. Tanner bought the business and renamed it the C.M. Tanner Grocery Company as it remains today. Under his leadership the business would grow into the largest grocery wholesaler in the state. C.M. Tanner was a true philanthropist at heart and would donate his money generously towards every worthy community project of the next half century.

C.M. Tanner had joined the Methodist Church early in his manhood and was the first one to note that the Sunday School rooms were no longer of adequate size to meet the needs of a growing membership. He was the one who launched the building program to construct the

Charles Mabry Tanner

large addition that remains on the city block behind the First Methodist Church in Carrollton today. C.M. Tanner was a lifetime honorary member of the Board of Stewards.

C.M. Tanner would serve as a director of Mandeville Mills for 25 years, as a director of Carrollton's first telephone exchange, and as a president of the Carrollton Hardware Company. Also, he was a member of the board of directors of the First National Bank, which was one of the four main banks in Carrollton before the depression. He always was on the cutting edge of technology and was noted to be the "first person to drive a Model-T to Florida." He had a second home in Daytona Beach and loved to vacation there.

In 1913, C.M. Tanner bought the Georgia Provision Company which was another wholesale company that had opened in Carrollton owned by Newman N. Johnson and George Thomas Copeland. These men, in turn, bought interest in C.M. Tanner Grocery Company which greatly increased Tanner's stock of goods. C.M. Tanner was the president, N.N. Johnson, the first vice president, G.T. Copeland, the second vice president, and C.M. Tanner Jr. was the secretary. By 1913, ten people were employed and three trucks were used for deliveries. So business was booming and C.M. Tanner had made his dream for a successful business come true. Then he began to have an even bigger dream.

For many years, C.M. Tanner had been noting the need for a modern hospital that would be adequate to serve the needs of Carroll County. Just after World War II, it was not uncommon for people to undergo "kitchen table surgery" by the light of kerosene lamps. There was no ambulance service — only the local funeral homes provided a hearse to pick up accident victims — and the driver of the hearse had no training in how to treat an accident victim. About all he could do was "haul them," as author Ben Moon would later note.

There were several clinics around Carrollton but none of them were equipped to handle serious cases. Critical patients had to be transported to Atlanta or Birmingham. Bed space was limited at the clinics and sometimes the clinics were open or closed as funds allowed. The three tiny clinics located in Carrollton, Villa Rica, and Bowdon could barely handle the county's needs of 40,000 people.

On May 11, 1943, *The Carroll Free Press* announced C.M. Tanner's plan for a new hospital in Carrollton. He would donate $75,000 to the building fund if the people of Carrollton would add $25,000 to that. A week later, a community-wide fundraising group was organized and goals were set. A hospital corporation was formed naming C.M. Tanner the general chairman emeritus of the board of directors and they unanimously agreed upon his request to name the hospital "The Lydia and Mary Tanner Memorial Hospital" in honor of his mother and his wife. The community drive met the goal of $25,000 but construction had to be delayed because of World War II and shortages of materials during wartime. By 1946, the war was over and luckily Congress passed the Hill-Burton Act which provided federal matching funds for hospital construction. R.D. Tisinger, a local attorney, donated his time into working out the details of how Carrollton could become eligible for these federal funds. On January 22, 1948, Tanner Memorial Hospital was the first hospital in Georgia to get state approval and thus qualify for the new federal program.

C.M. Tanner had in mind one up-and-coming young man in Carroll County whom he believed was the right man to serve as the pioneer chairman of the Hospital Authority. He handpicked a young businessman — Roy Richards — who was in the beginning stages of establishing his Southwire Company in Carrollton. Roy Richards would later describe C.M. Tanner as "a man of character who would look you straight in the eye." Richards accepted Tanner's invitation to take a businesslike approach towards the hospital project and "get things done."

Construction began in spring of 1948 and on October 30, 1949, C.M. Tanner himself cut the ceremonial ribbon and turned the key in the lock to the front door to officially open Tanner Memorial Hospital. And through all the years since, the C.M. Tanner family has continued to give generously and establish charitable foundations and trusts that amount to a multimillion dollar gift that is used to provide new services and new technology for the hospital.

At the Tanner Family Reunion in 1994, appropriately held at John Tanner State Park, there were 123 family members attending. The year before in 1993, the C.M. Tanner Grocery Company had celebrated its 100th anniversary, having opened in 1893 as the first wholesale grocer in Georgia. The business is now in its fourth generation of the Tanner family. John Wesley Tanner III is the president and CEO of Tanner Grocery Company today. Tanner Grocery remains the oldest firm in the West Georgia area. Mamie Tanner died 20 July 1949. C.M. Tanner died 12 December 1953 and was buried in the Sunset Section of the Carrollton City Cemetery alongside his wife and family.

In 1990 the administrator of Tanner Medical Center, Jim Giffin, made a special request of his employees at the hospital. He asked them to take a few moments to write down just what it meant to them to have a hospital like TMC in the middle of our community. One of the Critical Care R.N.'s, Jan Bell, wrote a letter to Mr. Giffin that touched him deeply and he asked her if he could take her letter to read to the various civic clubs in town as he made his yearly round of speeches. In part, the letter said:

> "Whenever I pass by the portrait of Mr. C.M. Tanner that hangs in the hallway of the hospital, I whisper a little thank you to him for giving each and everyone of us in this community the 'gift of the golden hour'. Any doctor will tell you that the first hour of a medical emergency is the most crucial. And if you can reach medical help within that 'golden hour' it can truly mean the difference between life and death."
>
> "We now have a modern hospital that is equipped to handle any emergency, and for anyone who calls 911 in our community an ambulance can reach them within minutes and deliver them to expert medical hands within minutes. We do not have to travel to Atlanta or Birmingham as they did in the olden days. In those days, many people lost their 'golden hour' as it was spent entirely in travel time, with no emergency treatment given. Many lives were lost. Some said the death rate was as much as ten times greater than it should have been. When Mr. C.M. Tanner gave his generous donation that spearheaded the building of our hospital here in the middle of our community, he gave us each a gift that is truly priceless — he gave us each our 'golden hour.'
>
> "To me, the 'golden hour' is a rather unique gift in that it is something that you

cannot see, you cannot touch. The only way to even define 'the golden hour' is to say that it is a kind of golden clock that begins ticking the moment that you find yourself in a medical crisis, whether it is a baby that has stopped breathing or a child who is bleeding from an injury, or a grandmother who is having severe chest pains. Suddenly, when this is your baby, your child, or your grandmother, the golden clock becomes very real and you are painfully aware of every minute that passes by. Each minute that you have to wait to receive help for your emergency seems like an eternity."

"For those of us who live in Carrollton and Carroll County, we do not have to lose our 'golden hour' because of lengthy transport time to some faraway hospital equipped to handle the emergency. We have that hospital right here in our midst, only a few minutes away really when you call 911. So, to me, this is the greatest gift — the 'gift of the golden hour' — that Mr. C.M. Tanner gave to each and every one of us. And it is a gift that is eternal, it keeps on giving the golden hour to generation after generation in our community. Mr. C.M. Tanner was a very wise man and truly a great philanthropist down into the deepest recesses of his heart."

Submitted by: Sally Tanner Macauley and Written by: Jan Robinson Bell

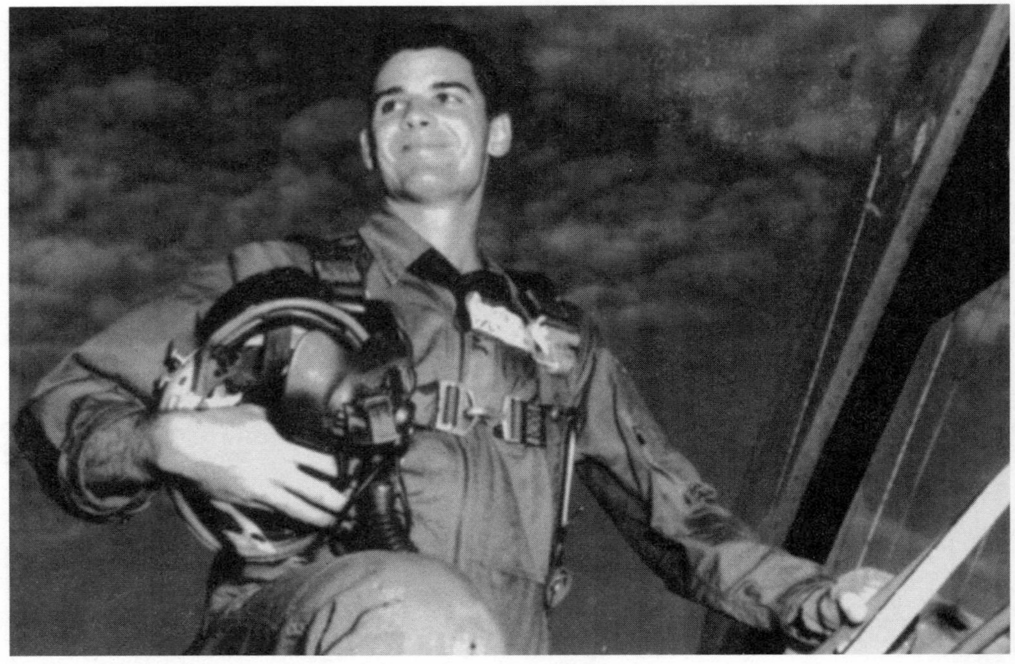

John Wesley Tanner Jr., about 1955,

1085. The John Wesley Tanner, Jr. Family

John Wesley Tanner Jr. was born 27 May 1933, the son of John Wesley Tanner Sr. and Frances Elizabeth Williams Tanner. John had one sister, Sally Tanner. John Jr. grew up in Carrollton, Georgia, and during his teenage years, he worked in the family business which was C.M. Tanner Grocery Company. He worked in the warehouse, loaded trucks and delivered orders — and he became familiar with the layout of the business and the stock. The business was at that time largely under the management of Julian Freel since John Tanner Sr. was spending a good portion of his time in managing Tanner's Beach. Later on, when John Tanner Jr. would take over the business, Julian Freel would remain his right-hand man for many years.

John Tanner Jr. attended Darlington Prep School and graduated from the University of Georgia with a B.S. in business administration in 1955. While at Georgia, John was a member of Phi Delta Theta fraternity and also Phi Kappa Phi, the honors fraternity. Barbara Reed was also a member of Phi Kappa Phi. John W. Tanner Jr. married on 18 March 1955 Barbara Joyce Reed, who had been his high school sweetheart — and she was also named the Sweetheart of John's fraternity, Phi Delta Theta, while they were both at the University of Georgia. Barbara was the daughter of Clarence Moses Reed and Rosa Lee Steed Reed who had moved to Carrollton in 1941 from Hartwell, Georgia.

John Tanner Jr. had been in ROTC during his college years and after his graduation in 1955, he had joined the Air Force with the rank of first lieutenant. John is pictured climbing aboard one of his jets during the time he trained as an Air Force pilot in Texas. Two children were born to John and Barbara Tanner during the Air Force years: Barbara Lynn Tanner was born 16 June 1956 in Laredo, Texas, and Mary Sally Tanner was born 2 May 1958 in Eau Gallie, Florida. In 1959, John Tanner Jr. completed his tour of duty and he and his family returned to Carrollton where he went to work for C.M. Tanner Grocery Company.

John Tanner Jr. was active in the Kiwanis Club for many years and used to say that he "introduced every visitor there until Fred Richards came to town." John was proud to wear his 30-year pin for Kiwanis. John Tanner Jr. taught Sunday School for 25 years at the Methodist Church and now an award is presented in his name each year. The John Tanner Jr. Plaque is presented in appreciation to those who have long and dedicated service to the Methodist Sunday School. Mrs. F.M. (Loraine) Chalker was the first recipient.

Three more children were born to Barbara and John Tanner Jr. Their third child was a son, John Wesley Tanner III, born 8 February 1961. Another son, Reed Tracy Tanner — named for John's good friend Tracy Stallings who is our 4th District Representative — was born 4 December 1962. Then, the youngest child was Elizabeth Lee "Leesa" Tanner born 16 December 1971.

In 1978, John Jr. had lost his good friend and manager Julian Freel when he had died of a heart attack. Then, another manager, Lee Cook, had suffered a stroke. John Jr. had continued to run the business for several years with no manager — until his son Johnny came on board in 1986. This was a tremendous help to John Jr. and relieved him of many responsibilities. It also gave Johnny Tanner the opportunity to learn the ropes of the business. Reed Tanner also joined the business after finishing his degree at Georgia State University.

In 1988 tragedy struck the Tanner family when John Tanner Jr. was struck by lightning and killed instantly while on a fishing trip to West Point Lake. John and his good friend, Carrollton attorney Henry Head, had been fishing on the lake when a storm came up. They realized they needed to go in — and had begun walking up a path through the woods when lightning struck, knocking both John and Henry several feet into the air. Henry survived this terrible accident, but John did not. John Tanner Jr. died on 25 June 1988 and he was buried on Barbara's birthday — the 27th of June. They had been happily married for 33 years. John was only fifty five years old at his death.

Barbara Joyce Reed was born 27 June 1933 in Hart County, Georgia. She was the daughter of Clarence Moses Reed who was born in Lincoln County, Georgia, on 27 February 1900 and died 10 November 1970. C.M. Reed was a teacher of agriculture and principal of Sardis County School. Later on, he became the Assistant Georgia State Superintendent of Vocational Education.

C.M. Reed married Rosa Lee Steed who was born in 1896 in Wilkes County, Georgia. Her home town was Metasville, which was near Washington in Wilkes. Rosa Lee Steed was the daughter of Emma Virginia Candler and William Thomas Steed. W.T. Steed was born in 1864 and died in 1935. W.T. Steed was the son of Jane Elizabeth Ware and Adoniram Judson Steed who was a Confederate soldier who left an interesting account of his war years. See the heading of Tanner-Reed-Candler-Steed for more about Barbara Reed Tanner's family.

Barbara Reed attended Carrollton High School and during those years, she was in many of the local beauty pageants and was one of the lovely girls who rode the float through Carrollton in the Pimento Festival of 1948. In 1949, Barbara won the Maid of Cotton beauty pageant. Barbara graduated from Carrollton High School in 1950 and then attended West Georgia College. Barbara was elected the Homecoming Queen at West Georgia College in 1952 by the student body. She was also winner of the Gordon Watson Leadership Award while at West Georgia. She went on to earn her degree in recreational education from the University of Georgia. While a student there, Barbara was on Pandora's Beauty Court. Barbara worked for Callaway Mills in the Recreation Department after graduation and before her marriage to John W. Tanner Jr. in 1955.

The children of John Wesley Tanner Jr. and Barbara Joyce Reed Tanner are:

(1) Barbara Lynn Tanner was born on 16 June 1956 in Laredo, Texas, while her father, John W. Tanner Jr. was stationed in the Air Force there. Lynn moved with her family back to Carrollton when she was four years old and she grew up in Carrollton. Lynn graduated from Carrollton High School in 1974. She then attended Emory at Oxford and graduated from the Medical College of Georgia with a degree in physical therapy. She is a registered physical therapist in Augusta and works with handicapped children. On 11 August 1979. Lynn Tanner married Dr. Scott Alan Riley. Scott is the son of Vance Buran Riley of Houston, Texas, Retired Air Force and Eastern Air Lines pilot. Scott's mother is Ruth S. Riley Kessler of Tampa, Florida. Scott is a graduate of Emory University with a B.S. in chemistry, honored as Phi Beta Kappa. He is also a graduate of the Medical College of Georgia as an anesthesiologist. Dr. Scott Riley is the head of the Anesthesia Department of St.

Joseph's Hospital in Augusta. The children of Lynn Tanner Riley and Dr. Scott Riley are: Jennifer Lynn Riley born 3 August 1983 and Richard Stephen Riley born 24 August 1986. Both are students at Lakeside High School in Evans, Georgia. Both Jennifer and Richard were dedicated gymnasts until injuries forced them to give it up. Lynn is an experienced rider and enjoys foxhunting in and around Thompson, Georgia. The Rileys attend the Lakemont Presbyterian Church in Augusta.

(2) The second child is Mary Sally Tanner who was born 2 May 1958 in Eau Gallie, Florida, during her father's Air Force years at the Cape. Sally moved with her family back to Carrollton in 1959 and graduated from Carrollton High School in 1976. From an early age, Sally knew that she wanted to do something involving sales — she was a natural born saleslady! Sally graduated from Florida State University with a degree in fashion merchandising in 1981. She took a job after graduation with Moss Brothers of Tampa, Florida. Later, her friend, Jay Whorton, who used to work for the newspaper in Carrollton, helped Sally to get a job working for the Marietta Daily Journal. Sally went on to work in sales for The Atlanta Business Chronicle winning Regional and National Salesperson of the Year 1988. She was next regional sales manager of Hotel-Motel Management Magazine and national sales manager of Hotel Business Magazine. Now, Sally is employed by Docupak, a national fulfillment company. On 21 November 1992, Sally Tanner married Hugh Angus Macaulay III. He is a native of Waynesboro, Georgia, the son of Hugh Angus Macaulay Jr. of Waynesboro and Dorothy Belle Gracy Macaulay of Murfreesboro, Tennessee. Hugh Macaulay III was born 2 March 1957. He graduated from Athens Academy in Athens, Georgia, and the University of Georgia where he earned a BBA in management in 1980. Hugh Macaulay III works in sales and marketing. Sally Tanner Macaulay and Hugh Macaulay III are the parents of: Katherine Rachel "Katie" Macaulay who was born 22 December 1993; Elizabeth Claire Macaulay born 23 June 1995; and Hugh Angus Macaulay IV born 14 May 1998. The Macaulays reside in Kenesaw, Georgia, and attend the First United Methodist Church in Marietta.

(3) The third child is John Wesley Tanner III who was born on 8 February 1961 in Carrollton, Georgia. Johnny Tanner grew up in Carrollton and graduated from Carrollton High School in 1979. In 1984, he graduated from West Georgia College with a degree in marketing. He was a member of Sigma Nu fraternity while in college. Johnny Tanner married Alison Dawn Williams on 26 June 1993. Alison's family is originally from Billings, Montana, and they are all quite proud of their Sioux Indian heritage. Alison is the ggg-granddaughter of the famous Sioux Chief American Horse who led a delegation to Washington, D.C. in 1891 to ask for better treatment of his people. This visit brought about many improvements for the Sioux and he is revered in the Sioux nation. Alison is the daughter of Bill and Nancy Lee Williams who now live in Woodstock, Georgia. Alison's father worked for the Pangburne Candy Company. Alison graduated from West Georgia College with a degree in early childhood education and master's and specialist degrees also in this field. Johnny Tanner is the president and CEO of C.M. Tanner Grocery Company of Carrollton. He has been working for about three years in the company before his father was killed by lightning in 1988. Since that time, Johnny Tanner has served capably as the fourth generation of his family to take on the management of the wholesale grocery company that has been in Carrollton over one hundred years. Johnny and Alison Tanner have two children: A son, John Wesley Tanner IV was born 13 July 1996. One

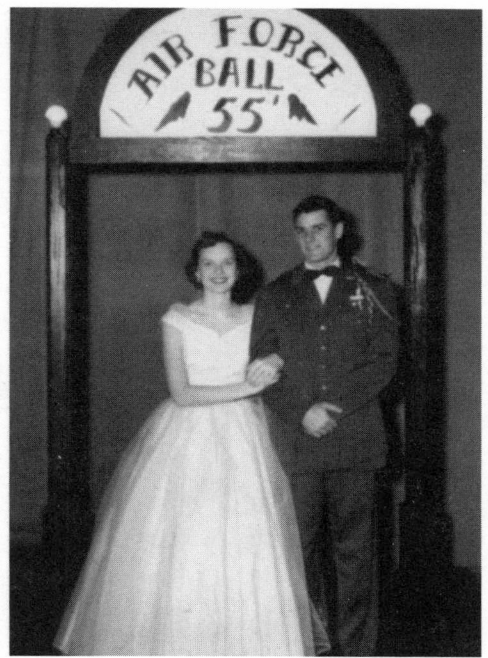

Barbara Reed and John W. Tanner Jr. 1955.

infant son, James William Tanner, died at birth on 25 October 1998 and is buried at Carroll Memory Gardens. Their daughter Catherine Mabry Tanner is proud to share the same initials "C.M." as her famous ancestor, C.M. Tanner Sr. who was the founder of Tanner Grocery Company in 1893 and the benefactor of Tanner Memorial Hospital in 1943. Catherine was born 22 October 1999. The Tanners attend the First United Methodist Church in Carrollton. They live in the home that previously belonged to John W. Tanner Sr. and Frances "Lady" Tanner on South Lakeshore Drive. Johnny is an avid hunter and fisherman.

(4) The fourth child is Reed Tracy Tanner who was born on 4 December 1962 in Carrollton. He was named for his father's good friend, Tracy Stallings, who is the representative of our 4th District. Reed Tanner grew up in Carrollton and graduated from Carrollton High School in 1981. He attended West Georgia College and was a member of Sigma Nu fraternity. Reed has always been musically inclined, a talent he inherited from his grandfather, John Wesley Tanner Sr. Reed first studied at the Shenandoah Music Conservatory in Virginia. Later, he transferred to Georgia State University where he earned a B.S. degree in business music in 1988. On 22 February 1992, Reed Tanner married Jennifer Joy "Jenny" Baker, the daughter of Olin and Shirley Baker of Carrollton. Olin Baker has been retired from Carrollton Federal since 1991. Jenny Baker graduated from Central High School and from West Georgia College where she received her degree in Spanish with a master's in education. Reed and Jenny Tanner lived in Nashville, Tennessee, for awhile — Reed is a writer of country music and also teaches piano. While living in Nashville, their son, Reed Tracy Tanner Jr. was born on 17 December 1997. Since that time, Reed and Jenny Tanner have moved back to Carrollton and Reed is pursuing a degree in electronics from Carroll Tech. He is planning to go into business repairing electrical equipment and keyboards. Reed also is a member of the popular Back Street Band that plays locally. He also continues to teach piano and write country music. The Tanners live on the Clem-Lowell Road and attend the Oak Grove Baptist Church.

(5) The fifth child is Elizabeth Lee "Leesa" Tanner who was born 16 December 1971 in Carrollton. Leesa Tanner grew up in Carrollton and many will remember the rave revues she received when she performed on stage in the starring role of "Annie" for the Carrollton Children's Theater when she was eight years old. Leesa has continued her love of drama and has had many starring roles since then. She now performs at the old Springer Opera House, which is the oldest opera house in Georgia — it is The State Theater of Georgia. Leesa Tanner graduated from Carrollton High School and then attended Auburn University where she was a member of the Auburn University Singers. She graduated summa cum laude with a degree in speech pathology from Auburn University. Then, she earned her master's in speech pathology from the University of Georgia. Leesa now works at the Columbus Speech and Hearing Center in Columbus, Georgia. On 23 July 1994, Leesa Tanner married William Scott Barber, a native of Carrollton also. He is the son of William C. Barber. His mother, Scottie Barber Jennings owns The Furniture House in Carrollton. Scott Barber was born 1 October 1970 and graduated magna cum laude from Samford University in Birmingham with a degree in public

The Tanner Family Christmas, 2000

administration in 1993. Scott next earned his law degree from the University of Georgia in 1996. Scott Barber works as an attorney with Tisinger Law Firm in Columbus, Georgia. Leesa and Scott Barber attend the St. Andrew's Presbyterian Church in Columbus, Georgia.

The Tanner family Christmas 2000 picture shows from left to right on the front row: Jenny Tanner, Reed Tanner holding Reed Jr., Alison Tanner holding Catherine Tanner, John Tanner III holding John Tanner IV, Barbara Tanner, Leesa Barber holding Claire Macaulay, Scott Barber holding Katie Macaulay. Back row: Dr. Scott Riley, Jennifer Riley, Lynn Riley, Richard Riley, Sally Macaulay holding Hugh Macaulay IV, and Hugh Macaulay III. In the background is the Tanner home place on Dixie Street in Carrollton. *Submitted by: Barbara Reed Tanner, 119 Dixie Street, Carrollton, GA 30117 and Written by: Jan Robinson Bell.*

1086. The John Wesley Tanner, Sr. Family and Tanner's Beach

John Wesley Tanner Sr. was born 5 November 1902 the second son of Charles Mabry Tanner and Mamie Rhudy Tanner. John Tanner Sr. grew up in Carrollton, Georgia, and then attended the University of Georgia where he played the trombone in The Dixie Redcoat Band. He graduated in 1929 with a degree in business administration.

John Tanner Sr. and Lady Tanner in front of their home.

In his early manhood, John Tanner Sr. went to Florida where he went into the real estate business. While in Florida, he met his future bride to be who was Frances Elizabeth Williams of Palatka, Florida. Her father had helped to build the railroads in Florida — and her mother had the unforgettable name of Sally Marie Oglerita Williams. John and Frances Williams Tanner moved to Atlanta, Georgia, early in their marriage. They were living there in the early 1930s when their son, John Wesley Tanner Jr. was born on 27 May 1933. A daughter, Sally, was born 19 October 1936 after the family had moved to Carrollton, Georgia.

Sally Tanner graduated from Carrollton High School in 1953 and attended Wesleyan College in Macon. She married James "Jim" Hubert Farmer Jr. of Dothan, Alabama, in October

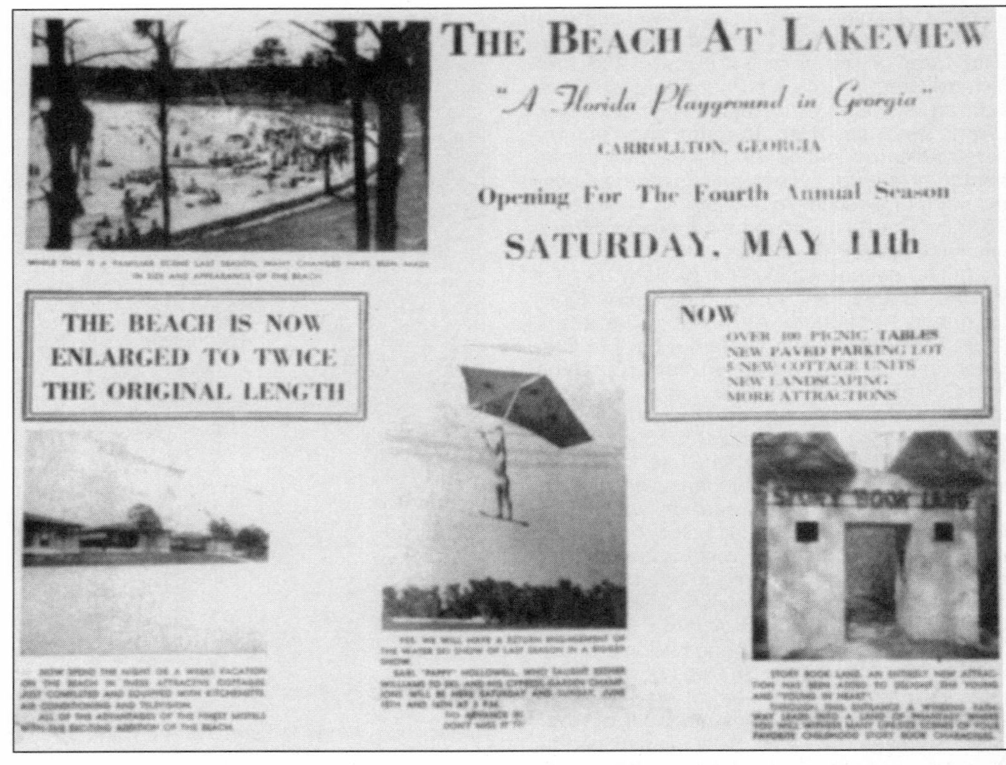

THE BEACH AT LAKEVIEW

"A Florida Playground in Georgia"

CARROLLTON, GEORGIA

Opening For The Fourth Annual Season

SATURDAY, MAY 11th

THE BEACH IS NOW ENLARGED TO TWICE THE ORIGINAL LENGTH

NOW

OVER 100 PICNIC TABLES
NEW PAVED PARKING LOT
NEW COTTAGE UNITS
NEW LANDSCAPING
MORE ATTRACTIONS

The Beach at Lakeview. Newspaper proclaims opening of the fourth season of "A Florida Playground in Georgia."

1956. Jim Farmer was an attorney in Dothan with Farmer & Farmer Law Firm. He and Sally had three children together: Frances Laney Farmer of Atlanta, Sally Katherine Creel of Dothan, Alabama, and James Hubert Farmer III of Nashville, Tennessee. There are two grandchildren: Katherine Elizabeth Lester and Steven Trent Lester Jr. of Dothan, Alabama. Jim Farmer died 28 May 1999.

John Tanner Sr. joined his father's business in Carrollton in 1933 and remained an important part of Tanner Grocery Company for almost thirty years. After C.M. Tanner went into semi-retirement, he spent most of his time at his home in Florida. The business was left in his son John's capable hands — and it grew and prospered. Like his father, C.W. Tanner, John Tanner Sr. also was a dreamer — only his dream was of a different kind for Carroll County. His dream was for a beautiful recreation center that would provide something for fun for the whole family. Perhaps inspired by his years spent in Florida, he had a dream of bringing a "little bit of tropical paradise" right here to our community.

In 1953, John Tanner Sr. began hauling 22 box car loads of Florida sand to construct a beach that was 500 feet long and 175 feet wide — with sand 6-10 inches deep — on the site of a beautiful lake surrounded by woods off Mt. Zion Road. The grand opening was held 1st of May 1954 and hundreds of people came from miles around to see the beach at Lakeview as it was originally called.

John's wife, Frances Tanner, put her writing talents toward writing articles for the newspaper about what the beach had to offer. In 1956, she wrote about "Little Charlie's Day at the Beach" and these were some of the highlights that she mentioned:

> "Children love to come to spend their Annual End of the School Year Picnic at the Beach at Lakeview — first you go into the "bath house" filled with beautiful tropical flowers and plants — change into bathing suits — and you get a key to keep your clothes in a locker. Next you get a float and head for the beach! Beautiful white sands to sink your toes into — and then splash into the water! A lifeguard on his stand watches out and blows his whistle if anyone goes too far out in the water "past the rope." Safety is always a first at the beach. Out in the deeper part of the

Bathing beauties at the Beach at Lakeview. 1956.

John and Lady Tanner with Susan Hayward and Eaton Chalkley.

Tanner Family Reunion at Tanner's Beach. July 1963.

lake are the kids pedaling the Love Buggies like bicycles.

You hear the little train — "The Beach Express" — ringing its bell — and it's time to climb aboard and make a trip to Story Book Land. The little train takes you over a bridge made of seashells, and cypress knees. You travel through a forest where Spanish moss (imported from Florida) hangs from the trees. You enter Story Book Land where there are little houses you peer into — and see Goldilocks and the Three Bears — all your favorite storybook characters are here!

You pass by orange and lemon trees on your way to the animal zoo — and there are even real live alligators! Then, back to the Snack Bar for a Sno-Cone made of shaved ice — grape is the best! Also, if you're hungry — have a hot dog with mustard, relish, and ketchup. You can sit on the picnic tables in the cool shade of the pine trees while you enjoy your meal. There is a second lake which is for fishing — and fathers like that! There is something for everyone!"

This beach was built in an era long before any other type amusement parks were anywhere near Carrollton, and it became the greatest recreation area in this part of the state. It became the place for family reunions and annual picnics for schools and businesses. Beauty pageants were held here and in 1959 the beautiful movie actress Susan Hayward participated as one of the judges for the contest. In 1960, John Tanner Sr. decided to expand the beach and brought in 40 more box car loads of white sands from Florida and enlarged the beach by 1000 feet. The name was then changed to Tanner's Beach and a putt-putt golf course was added. A dance hall for teenagers was also a popular addition. A giant slide was added in the 1960s.

Soon after Tanner's Beach became a full-time job in itself, John Tanner Sr. left Tanner Grocery in the capable hands of his manager, Julian Freel, so that he could devote full time towards managing the beach. Then, in 1959, after his son John W. Tanner Jr. came home from the Air Force and brought his family to Carrollton — John Jr. became the third generation of his family to take over the C.M. Tanner Grocery Company as president and CEO.

John Tanner Sr. managed Tanner's Beach for many years until 1971 when he sold Tanner's Beach to the state of Georgia to be made into a state park. It was appropriately given the name John Tanner State Park and continues to provide the greatest quality of fun and recreation that John Tanner had dreamed about for this area. John Wesley Tanner Sr. died 12 December 1981 and Frances Williams Tanner died on 23 September 1991. Both are buried at the Carrollton City Cemetery next to John's father and mother. *Submitted by: Reed Tracy Tanner, Carrollton, GA and Written by: Jan Robinson Bell.*

1087. Tanner - Reed - Candler - Steed

Lynn Tanner Riley has quite an interesting family tree on the maternal side. Her mother, Barbara Reed Tanner, is the daughter of Clarence Moses Reed who was born in Lincoln County, Georgia on 27 February 1900 and died 10 November 1970. C.M. Reed married Rosa Lee Steed who was born in 1896 in Wilkes County, Georgia. Rosa Lee Steed was the daughter of Emma Virginia Candler and William Thomas Steed. W.T. Steed was born 1864, the son of Confederate soldier, Adoniram Judson Steed. A.J. Steed left an interesting account of his Civil War years.

A.J. Steed wrote:

"I was born and raised in Columbia County, Georgia. I moved to Wilkes County in September 1860 where I went to war. I joined the Lamar Confederates from Lincoln County, 15th GA Regt. Co.G. Benning's Brigade, Fields Division, Longstreet Corps, Army of the Potomac. In September 1863, we went to the western Army. I was in on the fight at Chickamauga September 19, 1863. I was shot before I had a chance to shoot. I was wounded in my right breast, coming out at my right side. On 12th of May 1864, at the (Battle of) Wilderness, I was shot in the cartridge box. In a few steps, I was shot in my right arm, a flesh wound. On September 25th at Fort Harrison, I was shot through my left hand as I was raising up to shoot. The ball went through all of my clothes, knocking me double for a awhile. I was with Lee when he surrendered at Appamattox Courthouse. My name is A.J. Steed and I was born April 7th, 1837 and if I live to see April, I will be 74 years old."

A.J. Steed is pictured wearing his Cross of Honor, C.S.A.

Clarence Reed and Rosa Lee Steed were the parents of four children. Mary Agnes Reed (m. William Arnold Knapp Jr.) was born 16 January 1928 in Hart County, Georgia; graduated from the University of Georgia with a degree in home economics, taught at Lindale High School near Rome, Georgia. Arnold Knapp Jr. also graduated from University of Georgia with degree in veterinary medicine and went into research. Their children were Mary Ellen Knapp Word, Sharon Ann Knapp Lambreth, and Barbara Carol Knapp Coley.

Adoniram Judson Steed, Confederate Soldier wearing his Cross of Honor, C.S.A.

The second child of Clarence and Rosa Lee Reed was William Clarence "Bill" Reed born February 14, 1929; Bill married first to Dorothy Holmes of Bowdon, Georgia. Dorothy died and is buried at Augusta, Georgia, where they had

The Pierce Ann Hardy Candler Family

lived. Bill Reed is an attorney who graduated from University of Georgia. His law firm is Fulcher, Fulcher, Hagler, Harper & Reed in Augusta, Georgia. Bill is now retired. His two sons by his first wife are Dr. William Thomas Reed who is an internist at Northside Hospital in Atlanta; and David Candler Reed who is a financial counselor for Archibald Medical Center in Thomasville, Georgia. Bill's second wife is Elizabeth Anne Floyd whom he married in Augusta, Georgia on 22 June 1991. Anne is a native of Wilmington, Ohio.

Donald Lee "Don" Reed was the third child born on March 17, 1931. Don married Frances Ray from Burlington, North Carolina. Don graduated with a degree in industrial engineering from Georgia Tech. He worked as an engineer until his retirement from Western Electric. Don and Frances live in Burlington, N.C. They have two daughters: Suzanne Reed Smith and Catherine Reed Stewart.

The fourth child was Barbara Joyce Reed, my mother, who was born 27 June 1933 and who moved from Hartwell to Carrollton in 1941. (See The John W. Tanner Jr. Family for more on Barbara Reed Tanner.)

The Reed family tree is an interesting one that dates back to George Reed born 1795 and Emelia Reed born 1799. In our direct line, we are descended from their son Moses Thomas Reed (1833-1896) who married Mary Elizabeth Prewitt (1837-1896). The Reeds lived in Hart County, Georgia. In turn, they were the parents of Thomas Henry Reed (1865-1931) who married Lucy Fleming (1874-1956). Thomas and Lucy Reed were the parents of Clarence Moses Reed (1900-1970) who was Barbara Reed Tanner's father.

Another interesting branch of our family tree is that of the Candler family. Though our Candlers lived in other counties of Georgia, the Carroll County Candlers are her cousins. Barbara's great-grandmother was Pierce Ann Hardy who married Cornelius Capers Candler in Lincoln County, Georgia. Cornelius Candler was the son of Mark Anthony Candler and his second wife, Lucy White of Wrightsboro, Georgia — the old Quaker settlement. Mark Anthony Candler was the brother to Daniel Candler who was the ancestor of the Carroll County Candlers. Both Mark Anthony Candler and Daniel were sons of William Candler who first came to Georgia with his wife, Elizabeth Anthony in 1769.

Mark Anthony Candler and his wife lived in the old Revolutionary Fort in Wrightsboro, Georgia. They were parents of nine children-William Henry and Julia were twins, Mary, Lucy, Albert, Thomas, Susan, Mark and Cornelius. Mark Anthony Candler died in 1828. Twins would run in the Candler family — and Cornelius Candler and Pierce Ann Hardy Candler would also have a set of twins — George and Emma Virginia Candler. George would die in childhood, but Emma Virginia Candler would marry W.T. Steed and become Lynn's mother's grandmother.

Mark Anthony Candler was the son of William Candler who served as a Col. of the Upper Regiment from Richmond County, Georgia in the American Revolution. William Candler owned 6000 acres, 27 slaves, and owned the first brick house in Augusta. Daniel and his wife Elizabeth Anthony had eleven children — Mary (m. Ignatious Few, their son was the founder of Emory at Oxford College), Henry (a major in the American Revolution), William (never married), Charles (died young), Falby, Elizabeth, John K. (never married), Amelia, Joseph (died childless), Mark Anthony (m. first a Young and second Lucy White), and Daniel (who m. Sarah Slaughter.

Emma Virginia Candler and William Thomas Steed in a loving pose together, about 1932.

Elizabeth Anthony was a descendant of an Italian family of Genoa with an interesting family history. Elizabeth's Grandfather Anthony as a young boy had decided to "run away to go to sea." But he was captured by Algerian pirates who kept him a "bound boy" on a ship for three years before he could escape. When he did escape, he settled in Bedford County, Virginia and became a wealthy miller.

William Candler's ancestors also had a colorful history. His grandfather — also named William Candler — was from Northampton County, England, and married Ann Villiers, a widow of Capt. John Villiers and they settled in Callan Castle in Ireland in 1653. (The famous Callanwolde of Atlanta — the old Candler family home there — was named for this castle in Ireland.) The castle had been awarded to Lt. Col. William Candler in 1650 as a bounty of war when the English forces of Parliament under the command of Oliver Cromwell had ridden to subjugate the Irish. Though much property was confiscated from the Irish and awarded to the English, the Candlers were unique in the way they managed their lands. They did not try to "rule from afar in London" but rather, they moved to Ireland themselves. They became involved with the Irish people and became "a part of the soil" there.

Lt. Col. William Candler and Ann Villiers had three children — Thomas, John, and Mary. Our family descends from Thomas who married first Elizabeth Burrell and second to Jane Tuite (our ancestor.) Jane Tuite was the daughter of Sir Henry Tuite and Diana Mabot, the niece of Edward Hyde who was Prime Minister to King Charles II. Edward Hyde was the father of the Duchess of York, the first wife of King James II. This Duchess of York — first cousin to Diana Mabot — was the mother of Queen Mary and Queen Anne.

Thomas and Ann Candler were the parents of four known children — Rev. Henry Candler DD, Rev. William Candler DD, Thomas Candler of Dublin, and our ancestor who was Daniel Candler who married an Irish girl named Anna. By the time that Daniel married Anna, it was no longer punishable by death for an Englishman to marry an Irish girl, but they were still socially ostracized severely. After several years of marriage, Daniel and Anna Candler had decided to make a new beginning for themselves in America. They landed in Charleston port in 1735. They moved northward where Daniel's uncle, Edward Hyde, had been granted the Royal Charter for the Province of North Carolina. But Daniel and Anna eventually settled permanently farther north in Bedford County, Virginia, near the present day city of Lynchburg. The Candlers, Moormans, Clarkes, and Anthonys were Quaker families that intermarried for generations there. The book called *Lynchburg's Pioneer Quakers and Their Meetinghouse* gives an interesting account of these Quaker families in this era.

Daniel Candler served in the French and Indian War and was also distinguished throughout Western Virginia as a surveyor. The state line between North Carolina and Virginia was surveyed by Daniel Candler and until the 20th century you could still see the markers "DC" all along the line. Daniel and Anna Candler had seven known children — John Candler (Maryland and Virginia Candlers), Zedekiah Candler (North Carolina Candlers), William Candler (Georgia Candlers), Elizabeth, Eleanor, Thomas and Henry (both died before 1765).

William Candler was born 21 April 1736 in Virginia. There is an old letter in the family that describes him as a surveyor

> "lining up a Royal Charter for a family named Anthony."

In 1760, William married Elizabeth Anthony who was ten years younger than he. Her family disapproved of the marriage and disinherited Elizabeth. By 1767, William and Elizabeth Candler had moved to the Quaker settlement at Wrightsboro, St. Paul's Parish in Georgia. William received a land grant of 250 acres on the Little River which is now in Columbia County. Later William acquired another land grant of 500 acres when he established a mill on German Creek. William Candler was one of the best educated men of the settlement at Wrightsboro and quickly rose to a position of leadership.

When it became apparent that Georgia was going to side with the other twelve colonies in fighting for American independence, William Candler resigned his commission in the English militia and joined with the rebel forces. He was made a major and advanced to the rank of colonel. He participated in many of the southern battles.

As the English forces advanced closer to Georgia — and defeat seemed imminent — William Candler and Elijah Clarke took their families and those of their fighting men to a place of safety in the wilds of Tennessee. Of this remarkable trek, little is known except that it was a journey of extreme hardship. The trip was across 200 miles of wild and mountainous terrain with 400 women and children to be transported and protected. Finally, after eleven days, they settled their families between the French Broad and Holston Rivers and then these men returned to the fighting. William Candler was one of the heroes of the Battle of King's Mountain and his name is inscribed on the monument there.

After the war, William Candler went to work to help rebuild the state of Georgia and he became a member of the legislature there. In 1785, he became a full-fledged justice of Richmond County, Georgia. Willam Candler died 1 November 1784. His widow, Elizabeth, later remarried to Capt. Cornelius Dysart of Baldwin County, Georgia.

The Daniel Candler born in 1779 who was the ancestor of the Carroll County Candlers was one of the babies carried in his mother's arms on that trek to the wilds of Tennessee during the American Revolution. In 1799 this Daniel Candler married Sarah Slaughter, the daughter of Samuel Slaughter and Fanny Gill who had moved to Georgia from Virginia. This Daniel and Sarah Candler were the parents of Samuel Charles Candler who would become one of Carroll County's pioneers.

Samuel C. Candler was born 6 December 1809 on the original land grant of his grandfather, William Candler. Samuel's father, Daniel, died when he was 32 and left him fatherless at a very young age. Samuel actually spent many years in the home of his cousin, Ignatius Few, the educator and received an excellent education from him. Few later became a Methodist minister.

In 1830, Samuel Candler moved to the area known as Villa Rica, the City of Gold. He was a representative of a British mining company interested in gold mining in the area. About 1832, Samuel moved to Cherokee County, another gold mining area of Georgia. There, he married Martha Bernetta Beall, a descendant of that illustrious Scotsman, Ninian Beall, who first came to America in 1652. The Beall and Candler lineages are extensively covered in *The Carroll County Genealogical Quarterly,* Fall and Winter 1981.

Samuel Candler and his bride settled down in Carroll County and reared an outstanding family there. Samuel Candler became a state representative and a senator from Carroll County. He was a large land owner, farmer, merchant, land developer, gold miner, and statesman. He built up a considerable fortune before the Civil War.

It has been written by many that the family produced in Carroll County by Samuel and Bernetta Beall Candler has been one of the most outstanding families ever produced by the state. Their children were: (1) Milton Anthony, an Atlanta attorney 1837-1909 (2) Ezekiel S., a Mississippi attorney 1838-1915 (3) Noble David, an invalid 1838-1913 (4) Florence Julia 1842-1946 (5) Sarah Justina 1845-1921 (6) William Beall, a large planter and merchant 1847-1928 (7) Elizabeth Francis 1849-1922 (8) Asa Griggs, the Atlanta industrialist who was the founder of Coca-Cola 1851-1929 (9) Samuel C. Jr. 1855-1911 (10) Warren Akin, a Methodist Bishop, founder of Emory University 1857-1941 and (11) John Slaughter, a judge of the Georgia Supreme Court 1861-1941.

Cornelius Capers Candler and Pheribe Pierce Ann Hardy of Lincoln County, Georgia were the parents of fourteen children, some of whom died in infancy. Our ancestor is the twin, Emma Virginia Candler who married W.T. Steed. The accompanying picture shows Pierce Ann Hardy Candler with some of her children and grandchildren around her. First row left to right, Bessie Mae Albea, Bertha Louella Albea, Albert Albea (a baby) on lap of Sally Candler Albea, Pierce Ann Hardy Candler, Lewyn Steed, Harry Steed, Sally Agnes "Allie" Steed (baby) on lap of Emma Virginia Candler Steed (who is pregnant with Rosa Lee Steed, who would be Lynn Tanner's grandmother), and William Thomas Steed. On the back row left to right: Charles Albea, Roy Albea, Clarence Albea, Maggie Mae Candler Dyer, Walter Candler, Bessie Candler Strickland, and Susan Pheribe Candler. *Submitted by: Lynn Tanner Riley, Augusta, GA and Written by: Jan Robinson Bell*

1088. Tant Family

Kinyard (Kinion) Tant was listed in the 1860 census of Carroll County, Georgia. An early deed shows that he bought land in the 4th District of Carroll County from Eli Benson on January 20, 1863. As a farmer, he married Josephine Jarrett. Kinyard was born March 15, 1822, in Georgia and died January 26, 1903, in Carroll County, Georgia. Josephine was born July 17, 1832, in Belmill, Alabama. The date of her death is unknown. They are buried at Mt. Pleasant Baptist Church Cemetery in Carroll County. Their known children were:

Kinyard (Kinion) Tant, during Civil War

(1) Mary Elizabeth (Betty) Tant born May 17, 1851, in Georgia and died March 16, 1901, in Carroll County from smallpox. She married Samuel M. Davis on August 12, 1869. He was the son of Enoch and Sarah Davis.

(2) Catherine M. (Katie) Tant born July 17, 1853, and died September 7, 1928, in Carroll County. On November 2, 1871, she married Allen J. Driver. He was born February 18, 1848, and died March 5, 1926, in Carroll County. They are buried at the Clem Methodist Church Cemetery in Carroll County. Allen J. Driver was a Civil War veteran.

Kinion and Josephine Tant

(3) John Tant was born around 1865 in Georgia. His date of death is unknown.

Kinyard served in the Civil War. He was in Company I, 2nd Georgia. According to pension records, he drew a pension from 1890 to 1903. He had body wounds from the battle at Fort Boggs, Georgia, on February 1863. At the time of his death he was a member of Mt. Pleasant Baptist Church. Josephine was a member of Mt. Pleasant also. *Submitted by: Gabby Duncan, 1115 Davis Road, Carrollton, GA 30116*
Source: Research by Judy Duncan.

1089. Taylor Family

The family records on our line of the Taylors indicate that they migrated to this country from England. I know that my ancestors were in Edgefield County, South Carolina. Much of the information I am providing is credited to my cousin, David W. Hayes. He has been wonderful to share his many hours of research with the family. David also organizes the huge Taylor reunions each October.

The Taylors served in the Revolutionary War for the Patriots in South Carolina. It is believed that my family is descended from Joseph Taylor. Joseph, born in North Carolina in approximately 1761, married Anna. He was given a land grant for service during the Revolutionary War.

Dora (Dorey) Taylor, the son of Joseph Taylor, married Mary in Edgefield, South Carolina. Family members have told us that they are the parents of my ancestor, Leroy Taylor. Dora moved to Georgia (I believe, after Mary's death) and married Matilda Jinks on October 21, 1821. Matilda was born in 1793 to Burwell and Elizabeth Jinks. The children of Dora and Matilda were Nancy, Robert, Elizabeth, Moses, I.N., Anne, Mary Angeline, Dora Franklin, and Matilda. Dora was listed on the 1840 census of Carroll County, living in the 653rd GMD. They were early members of the Bethany Baptist Church. Dora died on May 13, 1854, and Matilda died in 1888. They are buried in the Pinetucky Baptist Church cemetery in Micaville, Alabama.

My great-great-great-grandfather, Leroy Taylor, was born May 4, 1821, in Edgefield County, South Carolina. He married my great-great-great-grandmother, Catharine Dorris, on March 3, 1844.

Catharine, daughter of John Dorris and Lucinda Langley, was born in 1818 in Carroll County. Their children were Lucinda, John M., Lee Roy, and William. After Catharine's death in 1856, Leroy married Carolina Gibson on March 26, 1857. Their children were Martha C. and Elizabeth. Carolina died in early 1861. His third wife was Martha Ann Anthony. Their eleven children were Ivey, Amanda, Joseph, George, Corrie, Ellen, Della, Alice, Charlie, Clifford, and Roxie. Martha Ann died in 1913. Leroy was a farmer and landowner in the Roopville area. He and his son, John M. Taylor, served in the Civil War with the 26th Battalion, Company C, Georgia Volunteers, Confederate States Army. Both were wounded in battle. Catharine and Carolina are buried in Dorris Cemetery. Leroy and Martha Ann are buried in the Roopville City Cemetery. Leroy died January 14, 1900, in Carroll County.

My great-great-grandfather, Lee Roy Taylor, was born April 10, 1852 in Carroll County. He married my great-great-grandmother, Lucy A. Smith, in January 1869. Lucy, daughter of John D. and Eliza Smith, was born on May 30, 1853, in Carroll County. Their children were John W., Frances L., Levi, Martha M., Mary Etta, Nora, Annie Lee, Walter, and Samuel. Lucy died on July 7, 1886, and is buried in Lowell cemetery. Lee married Mary Ann Clark on September 5, 1886. Their children were James, Elizabeth, Lucy, Thomas, Kelly, Leroy, Henry, Katie, Harvey, William, Andrew, and Allie Mae. Mary died July 3, 1910, and is buried in Lowell cemetery.

He married his third wife, Nancy Jones, in 1910 and had two children, Leon and Lillie. Nancy died January 17, 1912, and is buried in the Dorris Cemetery. Lee married Susan Royster in 1916 and their child was Lee (Buddy). Susan died in 1919 in Guntersville, Alabama. Lee died on February 14, 1934, in Carroll County and is buried in the Lowell cemetery. He was a farmer and landowner in the Roopville area.

Levi and Minner Ann Taylor

My great-grandfather, Levi Taylor, was born August 15, 1873, in Carroll County. He married Minner Ann McCarty on August 1, 1897. Minner Ann, daughter of George Madison McCarty and Martha Driver, was born on August 25, 1881. Their children were Emmett, Eva, Grady, Lela May, Pearlie, Willie Lee, Homer, Olen, Amos, Etta, Eula, and Hoyt. Levi was a farmer and landowner. Levi died November 12, 1939, and Minner Ann died June 6, 1945, in Carroll County. Levi and Minner Ann are buried in the Ephesus Christian Church Cemetery.

Willie Lee and Lillian Taylor

My grandfather, Willie Lee Taylor, was born July 9, 1898, in Carroll County. He married Mary Lillian Cowart in November 1915. Lillian, daughter of Joe and Amanda Julia Catherine Smith, was born January 18, 1901. Willie Lee and Lillian were on their way to get married when they met a preacher they knew in another buggy. The preacher stopped and married them in the road. Their children were Clera, Reba, Ray, Lilli, Willie, Edna, Milford, Betty, Jackie, Calvin, and Judy. There were two infant sons who died at birth. Lillian died March 21, 1973, and Willie Lee died March 27, 1978, in Carroll County. He was a farmer and landowner in the Whitesburg-Lowell area. Before the depression, Willie Lee had tenant farmers and a store on his land. He lost the store and crops during the depression. Willie Lee and Lillian are buried in the Ephesus Christian Church Cemetery.

My father, Milford Earl Taylor, was born July 5, 1931, in Carroll County. He married Vivian Irene Bradford on April 17, 1950. Vivian, daughter of James Thomas Bradford and Meda Momie Owens, was born April 19, 1931. Their children are Sherryll, Kathy, and Deborah. Milford retired from Georgia Power and lives with Vivian in the Whitesburg area.

Sherryll Taylor married Stephen Hight in 1971. They have one daughter, Casey. Casey Hight graduated from the University of Georgia and is attending Law School at Loyola University in New Orleans, Louisiana. Sherryll married Fred Miles in 1983, and lives in the Whitesburg area.

Kathy Taylor married Tony Yates in 1973. They have two daughters, Meagen and Emily. Meagen attends the State University of West Georgia. Emily attends Central High School. Tony and Kathy live in the Carrollton area.

Deborah (Debbie) Taylor married Dr. Steven Powell in 1983. They have two sons, Robert and Bradford. Robby attends Greenbrier High and Brad attends Augusta Prep. They currently live in Evans, Georgia. *Submitted by: Sherryll Taylor Miles, 2554 West Highway 5, Whitesburg, GA 30185*

1090. Taylor - Dorough - Hall

The William H. and Eliza H. Taylor family lived in Carroll County at the time of the 1850 census. They lived in the Hickory Level community, District Six, on land lot number seventy-two. William H. was born June 10, 1793, and Eliza H. was born January 18, 1805. They both were born in North Carolina as were their three oldest sons, James, Robert, and Charles B. Their other five children, John, William P., twins Rebecca and Dorcus, and Eliza, were all born in Georgia. William P. died March 4, 1865, at the age of twenty-two and is buried at Concord United Methodist Church Cemetery.

John W. Taylor was born July 25, 1840. He married Theodocia C. McEachern, daughter of D.N. and M.A. McEachern of Cobb County on October 29, 1868. John W. purchased the family farm from his brother Robert F. in 1886. Robert F. was living in Texas after the death of their parents. William H. died July 25, 1873, and Eliza H. died on October 9, 1884. Both are buried at Concord Church Cemetery.

John W. and Theodocia lived in Hickory Level. They had one daughter, Florence, born March 13, 1885. John W. passed away on July 11, 1900, and Theodocia on May 8, 1934. Both are buried at Concord.

Edmond Walter Dorough was born March 12, 1882, in Heard County. He was the son of George W. and a Lucindia Spearman Dorough. Walter married Florence E. Taylor on Sunday, December 1, 1991, at the home of Mrs. T.C. Taylor.

Florence (Taylor) and Walter Dorough, November 12, 1944

Walter and Florence lived in the Hickory Level community and were members of Concord Methodist Church. They had eight children: Florine C., who was born October 29, 1903; John Wesley, who was born May 15, 1907; Edmond Herschel, who was born May 5, 1909; George Preston, who was born November 15, 1911; Carrie Lualla, who was born January 2, 1914; Robert Merle, who was born October 30, 1917; Maggie Lee Francis, who was born November 27, 1919; and Charles Grady, who was born January 23, 1928.

Walter was a farmer and the builder of the famous round barn in the Hickory Level community. Walter and Florence both passed away in 1957: Walter on May 21 and Florence on November 4. Both are buried at Concord United Methodist Church Cemetery.

Herschel Dorough and Willie Elsie Henry were married on August 24, 1929. They purchased the Dorough farm at the death of Herschel's parents. Elsie was born March 19, 1913, daughter of O. Preston and Annie Lou Allen Henry. They had two sons: Lemyoul Joe and Herschel Allen. Joe was born on September 27, 1933, and Allen on October 26, 1937.

Allen married Marianne McWhorter. They had one daughter, Kathy. They lived in Austell until Allen passed away on September 7, 1979. He is buried at Concord United Methodist Church.

Brenda and Ronnie Hall and daughters, Adecia, Whitney, and Breanna

Joe married Georgia Elizabeth Smallwood on December 19, 1954. Elizabeth is the daughter of Titus and Ada Morrow Smallwood. She was born on July 5, 1935. They had one daughter, Brenda Jo, born on March 29, 1958. They lived on part of the family farm. Joe was a carpenter and gifted wood crafter. He passed away on May 6, 1988, after a lengthy illness. He is buried at Concord United Methodist Church Cemetery. Elizabeth lives in Hickory Level with her husband, Wayne Bivins.

Herschel passed away on February 7, 1982 and Elsie on November 23, 1987. Both are buried at Concord, where they both faithfully worshiped until their health declined.

Brenda Jo Dorough grew up in the Hickory Level community. She graduated from Villa Rica High School in 1976 as valedictorian. She attended West Georgia College and graduated magna cum laude from the Medical College of Georgia in Augusta in June 1980. She received her B.S. in medical technology and is employed as laboratory manager for West Georgia Family Medicine. She married her high school sweetheart, Charles Ronald Hall, on December 20, 1980. Ronnie is the son of Lee Roy and Opal Griffis Hall. He was born January 2, 1958, and grew up in the Hulett community. Ronnie was a 1976 honor graduate of Villa Rica High and received his B.S. in physics from West Georgia College in 1984.

Ronnie and Brenda have three lovely and talented daughters: Adecia Beth, who was born October 8, 1984; Whitney Joelle, who was born August 26, 1989; and Breanna Lee, who was born August 3, 1994. Ronnie, Brenda, and their daughters live in the Hickory Level community on the Dorough family farm in the home they built in 1986. They worship at Concord United Methodist Church. *Submitted by: Brenda D. Hall, 3006 NE Hickory Level Road, Temple, GA 30179*

1091. The Lunie Everette Teal Family

Mr. and Mrs. Lunie Everette Teal reared their family in the very same house in which Mrs. Lunie Teal was born and reared. Mrs. Lunie Teal's father, James Asbury Windom, (1860-1905) purchased the land from the original owner who received it in the lottery which was conducted when the land was received from the Indians. The land is located on Mt. Zion road near Eureka Baptist Church. The house that was built on the property was constructed in the traditional architecture of the era. There were rooms to the right and left of a foyer. Additionally, there were four rooms upstairs. At some point in time, Mr. James Windom used one or more of the upstairs rooms to construct trunks. He sold these to supplement his farming income. Some of his creations are now prized possessions of relatives.

The original house was completely destroyed by fire in 1975 when it was struck by lightning. Soon thereafter, a similar house was moved onto the original foundation. The replacement house looks very much like the first house. The main difference is that there is no second story on the second home. That second house is still on the site of the Teal farm.

Mr. and Mrs. Teal had ten children, three boys and seven girls. All of the children were educated beyond high school. Some graduated from business school, others from college and some received advanced degrees. There are presently eighteen grandchildren, nine great-grandchildren and one great, great grandchild.

Mrs. Lunie Everette Teal or Jimmie Lee Windom Teal (1904-1980) told her children and grandchildren stories of attending the school sponsored by the Seminary at Mount Zion and sharing a double desk with Edith Shaw Wright.

Mr. and Mrs. L.E. Teal

Additionally, she recalled Indians who rode bareback to and from a reservation near Bunkham. She said that her mother always had the children come inside when Indians were seen.

Her sister, Nell Windom Cosby, told a cute story from their childhood. It seems that Nell, who was older, wanted to visit neighbors. Jimmie Lee, the youngest in the family, wanted to go along. Her mother said, "Okay, you may go, but you must hold your tongue. You talk too much!" Well Nell observed her little sister with her hand over her mouth, she asked why and was told, "My mama said I had to hold my tongue."

Jimmie Lee Windom Teal's mother was Emma Bearden Windom (1862-1936). Her family had moved to Carroll County from Campbell County, a county now incorporated into south Fulton County.

Mrs. Emma Bearden Windom was the last generation to wear floor length skirts and high top shoes. Her family reports that she was an early rural health nurse assisting families in her area who were in need of her care. Mrs. Teal's father, mother and a sister, Esther, who died at age sixteen, are all buried at Mount Zion Methodist Church Cemetery.

As an adult, Mrs. Jimmie Lee Windom Teal was active in the local school, community, and her church. She taught the Matron's Class at Eureka Baptist Church for many years. She and Mr. Teal are buried in the Carrollton City Cemetery.

Mr. Lunie Everette Teal (1896-1966) was born to William Thomas Teal (1874-1908) and Lillian Duffey Teal (1875-1952). Lillian Duffey was the daughter of Mr. Samuel "Smiley" Duffey (1845-1913) and Mahulda Jane Maxwell Duffey (1851-1933) of the Stripling Chapel area of the county. William Thomas, nicknamed "Lawyer" because of his self-acquired knowledge in the area of law, was the son of Thomas Littleton Teal (1852-1899) and Marguerite Gosdin Teal (1849-1904) of the Caney Head community in Heard County. When Lillian and Lawyer married they settled in the Tyus community where they farmed for many years. Lillian and Lawyer had two sons, Lunie Everette and Dewey Aaron. When the boys were still very young their father developed a goiter. He went by train to Rome, Georgia, to have it removed. Sadly, the surgeon severed the jugular vein and he died on the operating table. Lillian was forced to run the farm when her husband died. Later both the boys registered for World War I, but only Lunie was called for service.

Lillian enjoyed Sacred Harp singing, in which she sang the high treble part. She was also an astute business woman. One preacher commented at her funeral that she has loaned more money in the area than the bank. She was instrumental in the establishment of West Carrollton Baptist Church.

Later in her life, she married Mr. Francis Marion Brock. She and her son, Dewey, are buried at Stripling Chapel Methodist Church Cemetery. Lawyer's father, Thomas Littleton Teal was the son of William R. Teal (1829-1876), moved to the Caney Head community from Alabama. His father, Joshua Teal (1790-1870) came with his father, William Teal Jr. from Anson County, North Carolina. His father, William Teal Sr. came to this country with his father, Wilhem Teale from the Black Forest region of southwest Germany.

These pioneers to the western part of central Georgia from whom Mr. and Mrs. Teal are descended came to an area where they believed they could find a better life for their families. Hopefully, they realized some of their dreams. They were hard working people who toiled during the week and worshipped on Saturday and Sunday. Although their descendants toil at different kinds of work, they often have get-togethers in the house that is located on the farm. All the land is still owned by family members. *Submitted by: Ramona Teal*

1092. George Robert Teel

George Robert Teel was born April 8, 1891, in Sand Mountain, Alabama, the son of James Robert Teel and Lula Ann Cooper Teel. He was the oldest of four boys in the family of sixteen children, twelve of whom reached adulthood.

Upon completion of regular school, his father offered him a choice: mule and plow for farming or another year of education. He continued his education at Draketown Academy in Draketown, Georgia. This is where he met his wife. On December 21, 1913, he married Bertha Geneva Stephens, daughter of John Young Stephens and Martha Elizabeth Brooks Stephens.

He tried farming for a few years in Draketown. During this time, two children were born: Martha Elizabeth on December 13, 1914, and Robert Eugene on November 15, 1917. Elizabeth married John Clyde Estes. Gene married Annie Mae Howard.

Just after World War I, Robert Teel started his selling career. He bought army surplus socks and shoe strings, dyed them black and began traveling and selling. After moving to Temple, he traveled to retail stores, selling furniture for factories in Temple, Tallapoosa, and Atlanta.

Two more children were born in Temple: Raymond Daniel on June 26, 1924, and Willa Jane on July 22, 1932. Raymond married Rachel Ballenger. Willa married James Dalton Carter.

In the early 1940s, Robert Teel was ordained as a deacon in Temple Baptist Church, now First Baptist Church of Temple. He served several years on the Temple School Board of Education.

Sixty-fifth Wedding Anniversary of Robert and Geneva Teel

During the World War II years, gas and tires were rationed, so he couldn't travel. He worked at Stevens Manufacturing Company for a short time. He also served as mayor of Temple. He returned to traveling, selling furniture in Georgia, Alabama, and Tennessee. He retired at the age of eighty-five.

George Robert Teel died in March 1979 and Bertha Geneva Teel died in May 1982.

Their grandchildren are Clyde Graden Estes, Robert Joseph Estes, Sylvia Jean Teel, Terry Ray Teel, Phyllis Teel, Danny Teel, James Dalton Carter Jr., and Karen Elizabeth Carter.

Their great-grandchildren are James Clyde Estes, Robert Joel Estes, Sharon Renee Estes, Robert Joseph Estes Jr., Michael Allen Estes, Camilla Lewis, Gene Lewis, Laurie Lewis, Scott Lewis, Jason Teel, Amber Hicks, Crystal Hicks, Mandy Wade, Ciara Crystal Carter, Lindsey Nicole Carter, Stacy McClendon, Kelly Leigh McClendon, Tiffany J. McClendon, and Christopher Thomas Carroll.

Their great-great-grandchildren are Shanna Estes, Kimberly Estes, Joey Estes, Cory Estes, Brandon Estes, Ryan Estes, Garrett Summerville, Elizabeth Lewis, Jessica Lewis, Dylan Lewis, Rehannon Hobey, Logan Hechley, Luke Hechley, Avery Wade, Haleigh Elizabeth Johnson, Michael Damion Brown, Devin Allen Brown, Taylor Leigh Walker, and John Austin Robinson. *Submitted by: Willa Carter, P.O. Box 327, Temple, GA 30179*

1093. William Martin Thomas

William Martin Thomas born March 1, 1867, died November 19, 1951. He married Martha Elizabeth "Mattie" Adams on November 1, 1891. She was born August 19, 1870, in Arkansas, daughter of Mr. and Mrs. William Adams. She died September 16, 1940. They are both buried at Old Camp Methodist Church in Carrollton.

Will Thomas spent his entire life in Carroll County as a farmer and also worked at sawmills. Mrs. Thomas was a housewife.

They had ten children, two died in infancy. Daughters were Arrilia Thomas, Celesta Thomas Whitehead, and Altoona Thomas Thompson. Sons were William Martin Thomas, Robert Morris Thomas, Ezra Alexander Thomas, Troy Thomas, and Claude Thomas.

(1) Arrilia Thomas born October 4, 1893, and died December 17, 1893.

(2) Celesta Thomas married Barton Whitehead and they are both buried at Bethesda

Baptist Church. Their children are Nellie Robinson, R.J. Whitehead, Viola Brown, Velma Rabun, and Estelle Brown.

(3) Altoona Thomas married Willie Thompson. They lived around Hogansville and they are both buried at Franklin Methodist Church in Heard County. Their children are Willie J., Myrtle Thompson Siggers, Norman "Pete" Thompson, Albia Thompson Dollar, Curtis Thompson, Wortham Thompson, Grace Thompson, H.C. Thompson, O.W. Thompson, and Charles Thompson. One daughter died in infancy.

(4) William Martin Thomas (son) married Beulah Jo Neighbors. They lived around Carrollton and are both buried at Beulah Baptist Church in Carrollton. Their children are Gerald Pete Thomas, James Earnest Thomas, William Martin "W.M." Thomas, Clarence Bell Thomas, Alton "Sam" Thomas, Beulah Altoona Thomas Parks, Stanley Leon Thomas, and Martha Jo Thomas Smith.

(5) Robert Morris Thomas married Tessie Hewitt and they lived around Carrollton. They are both buried at Pleasant View Baptist Church. Their children are Robert Henry Thomas, William Lee Thomas, Mary Magalene Thomas Tuggle, Martha Elizabeth "Mattie" Thomas Hutcheson, Clennie Rachel Thomas Cole, Autry Marie Thomas Brock, Jerry Morris Thomas, and Joyce Louise Thomas Norton.

William Martin "Will" Thomas

(6) Ezra Alexander Thomas married Thelma Folds. They lived around LaGrange and are both buried at Goshen Cemetery, Roopville, Georgia. Their children are Horace Wortham Thomas, Merlin West Thomas, James Grover Thomas, Nellie Faye Thomas Meadows, Argel Richard Thomas, Helen Marie Thomas, and Charles Harold "Pete" Thomas.

(7) Troy Thomas married Nell Steed and lived around Carrollton. They are both buried at Bethesda Baptist Church. Their children are Russell Thomas, T.L. Thomas, Hildred Sue Thomas Williamson, and Eva Mae Thomas Craft.

(8) Claude Thomas married Idella Dukes. They lived several years on Sand Mountain but moved back to Carrollton. They are both buried at Old Camp Methodist Church. Their children are Bonnell Thomas Vickery, W.L. Thomas, Buford Thomas, Dorthy Thomas Walker, and a son died in infancy.

William Martin Thomas had a brother named Dave. He had a son named Wilburn and his wife Elsie F. They had three boys — Grady, Merlin, and Paul. He had a sister listed in his obituary in 1951 as Chettie Cosper of Americus, Georgia. *Submitted by: Clarence B. Thomas, 1065 Beulah Church Road, Carrollton, GA 30117*

1094. Thomassons

A Carroll County Family

The origins of the Carroll County Thomasson family are the British Isles. Several members of the family's earliest relatives were born in Louisa County, Virginia, in the early 1700s. George Thomasson, born 11/10/1703 married Mary Pollard, born 11/6/1706, had eleven children, and George died 8/22/1783 in Louisa. His son, Thomas, born 2/25/1737, married Anne Garland, and he died about 1820 in Granville County, North Carolina. They had eight children. William Pollard Thomasson, born 2/4/1763, married Mary Reeves, and he died in the York District of South Carolina, 1/31/1818. They had nine children. James Thomasson, born 1/9/1800, married Jane Barron (6/30/1823), and he died about 1860 in Heard County, Georgia. Beverley Daniel Thomasson, born 11/18/1805, was the youngest child of William Pollard and Mary Reeves Thomasson.

Thomas Jefferson, son of James and Jane Barron Thomasson, and Sarah Ann Tomlinson married about 1850 in Heard County and their only son, James Jefferson was born April 27, 1851, "At Liberty Hill in Heard County, Georgia ... His paternal grandmother was the daughter of a very wealthy planter of York District South Carolina and his maternal grandmother was a half sister to General Robert Toombs. His grandfather James Thomasson was a pioneer of Carroll County coming here from York, South Carolina, shortly after the county was organized, and [grandfather] John Fleming Tomlinson, also a pioneer of Carroll, [was] one of the early early Clerks of Carroll Superior Court."

"His father was a very successful merchant both at Carrollton and at Liberty Hill, who died early from an accident ... a great uncle Judge B.D. Thomasson and his wife reared him as one of their own children." His mother died the August following his birth, and his father died within two years. He came to Carrollton to be "reared by a great uncle, Judge Beverly D. Thomasson." These are the words of James Jefferson Thomasson in the *Carroll County Times* April 21, 1938.

> "The family were pioneers, coming to Carroll County within a few years after the Creek Indians were removed ... William [Pollard Thomasson] enlisted in the Colonial Army, first as a substitute for his father, but later in his own stead and fought through the Revolutionary War in the ranks of the colonies." At some time after William Pollard Thomasson died, " ... when the Creek Indians exchanged their lands, and Carroll County was formed she [Mary Reeves Thomasson] and several of her sons and daughters moved to this county ... She was born in North Carolina on December 31st, 1764. If she died in 1851 her age and that of her great grandson, J.J. Thomasson, born that year, 1851, combined reaches back ... a period of 174 years and ante dates this government nearly a quarter of a century — just two lives and one of them is still going. (1938)"

Mr. J.J. Thomasson might have been an orphan, but his great-uncle made a home for him and no doubt laid the basis for a life of intellect and service. But at the end of the "war of the sixties," both uncle and nephew were penniless. J.J. Thomasson was schooled at the Carroll Masonic Institute. "He paid his way in college the first year by acting as janitor, sweeping the house, building fires, etc. and the second year by acting as tutor and teaching several periods each day, indeed he was either writing or teaching every period during the day except one, doing all of [his] studying at night." He surveyed what became the Central Railroad and mineral lands around the present site of Birmingham, Alabama. "In November 1872 he cast his first vote, under protest and against his wishes he voted for Horace Greeley for president, he having the endorsement of the Democratic party. Later in the same month, together with [his] father's only brother Capt. Wm. B. [William Barron] Thomasson, he moved to Arkansas." He taught school in Vienna, Louisiana. He read law in Chattanooga, Tennessee. He returned to Carrollton in 1874. He married Amanda Frances Blalock on September 28, 1874. Their children include: Eva Thomasson (Mrs. William Scott) Campbell (1875), Katie Lu Thomasson (Mrs. Joseph M.) Harris (1878), Sada Thomasson (Mrs. John Clifton) Thomas (1880), Beverly Blalock Thomasson (1883), William Edward Thomasson (1885), Jesse Lee Thomasson (1888), Evan Wirt Thomasson (1888), James Toombs Thomasson (1890), Frank Tomlinson Thomasson (1893), and Mary (died in infancy). His early benefactor, great uncle Beverly Thomasson died in Arkansas in 1885 during a period when J.J. Thomasson was teaching school.

Mr. J.J. Thomasson

In 1880 "he returned to Arkansas, settling in Clark County where for 16 years he taught school and in the fall having broken his health teaching in a private school 10 months a year and 8 hours a day, he embarked in the newspaper business and the practice of law." He became a journalist and practiced law in Okolona; a decade later he wrote for the *Prescott Democrat.* "At that time Populism was in flower around Nevada County, and Prescott was its strong hold in Arkansas. Indeed that was what induced him to locate there. The democrats wanted his services to fight that political party. During the two campaigns, 1890 and 1892, but particularly in that of 1892, very exacting campaigns were waged. The latter campaign, that of 1892 culminated in the election of Grover Cleveland to his second term as president.

> "On the advice of friends, so bitter was the campaign that year, that he kept a double barrel shotgun loaded with buck shot sitting at his desk all the time. He was threatened with cow-hiding and bodily harm by both men and women, but only once was he attacked and that to the discomfort of his antagonist ... The election that fall resulted in a complete rout and overthrow of the Populist party, not only in Nevada County, [but] throughout Arkansas."

President Cleveland appointed him to a claims adjustment board in the Cherokee Strip. Of more than 2000 cases that needed his direct attention, being the only lawyer on the board, he was required to adjudicate all contested claims, "only four appeals were taken from his decisions and each of these involved a new and unadjudicated principle of law. Each of these decisions were confirmed and made the law."

In 1894 he bought half interest in the paper, but the paper was burned out by enemies. Once again he was penniless, but somehow he "bought out his partners" interest in the ashes of the dead paper and never missed an issue ... a new outfit was bought in St. Louis, Mo. And the paper went right on until December 1899."

In 1899 he returned to Carrollton and purchased the *Carroll County Times,* "a paper that as a school boy in 1871 he had seen established." For more than forty years after returning to Carrollton, J.J. Thomasson provided journalistic and public service to Carroll County.

Dr. Will Thomasson

Journalistically, J.J. Thomasson was the editor and owner of the *Carroll County Times* from 1899 until he sold it in 1941, and edited the *Bowdon Bulletin.* He was active in the Georgia Press Association, an affiliate of the National Editorial Association, serving as vice president, and he was a member of the World Press Congress. Locally, he had various leadership roles in the development of Carroll County's public schools, the establishment of what is now West Georgia University (1906), and the public utilities of water and sewage (1905). He demonstrated his love of history by serving as official historian for the Coweta Circuit Bar and Carroll County. He traveled extensively in 42 of the then 48 states and most of the states of Mexico.

In *The Atlanta Constitution,* published on his 90th birthday, "He arose at 5 o'clock after an Edisonian sleep of six hours, and he needed no alarm clock. He has instinctively come within five minutes of that mark for years.

> "He fed and milked his cow, attended his chickens, donned his long-cuffed canvas gloves and tied up the lot, ate breakfast and reached the office by 8 o'clock ...
>
> "As the hour hand edges toward 5 in the afternoon, Editor Thomasson will arise and pronounce whimsically:
>
> "'Well, if there is nothing else for me to do around here, I think I'll go home.'
>
> "About an hour later, clad in overalls and gloves, his face ruddy from barnyard chores, he will reappear to hand a quart of milk through the door to his son, Frank Thomasson, tireless publisher of the *Times.*
>
> "His pecan grove then will get his attention. He is rated a topflight pecan grower and markets a considerable quantity each year. Or, there will be work in the garden.
>
> "After the dinner hour, it will be a review of the Atlanta papers and magazines, and articles on pecan culture, horticulture or agriculture. In any event it will be culture, for that is a fetish with him."

The home at 16 Maple Street (now 124 Maple St.) was called "Magnolia Terrace." A city street, later abandoned for driveways, separated the home from the Presbyterian Church (thus the view of the house pictured was the front of the home.) It must have been a full house with parents and eight children, ranging in age from 25 down to about 7 years. The house and pecan grove were purchased by the Presbyterian Church in 1985 after the death of Howard Thomasson; the pecan grove was given to the city and has become a lovely and well-kept city park.

In his farewell editorial, J.J. Thomasson wrote

> "It is with feelings of profound sadness that I lay down this work, a work that has been a great pleasure ... But soon I must take my place among my kin in the old cemetery and when I do I will be the fifth generation of the Thomasson clan that sleeps there."

He was preceded in death by his two wives: Amanda Blalock in 1919 and Saphronia Hopkins Trawick Blalock in 1935.

One of his sons, Will, was a country doctor to Carroll County. The following is his obituary or eulogy, probably written by his sister Eva Campbell:

> "William Edward Thomasson, second son of James Jefferson and Amanda Frances Blalock Thomasson was born October 10th 1885 at Amity Arkansas, where his father was Superintendent of schools.
>
> "At an early age, only two or three years old, he evidenced a deep seated desire to become a doctor, and with his doctor satchel would toddle around, or ride on his make believe horse, and administer his 'medicine' to his patients, his mother and other members of the family, being known as 'Dr. Jones', the name of a doctor neighbor and friend of the family.
>
> "Later his parents moved to Prescott Arkansas, where his father embarked in the newspaper business. There he attended Tom Allen High School.
>
> "In 1899 his family moved to Carrollton, Ga., his parents native home. Perhaps a few of our oldest residents may remember, or at least have heard of his mother's honored father, Judge J.M. Blalock, the first and for many years Ordinary of Carroll County.
>
> "In Carrollton, Will, as he was known to his many friends, continued his studies in the public schools, also carrying on especially, with the assistance of a private tutor, such studies as would be helpful in his preparation to become a doctor, which aim was the mainspring of his life. After satisfactorily completing his work in the Carrollton schools, he entered Atlanta medical Schools, which later merged with and is now Emory University. In 1911 he graduated from that institution. In the fall he located at Andersonville, a suburb of Americus, where he spent about 16 years, enjoying a splendid practice of his profession and a wonderful fellowship among a host of friends.
>
> "In 1916 he was happily married to Miss Howard Bradshaw of Roanoke [actually Bacon Level], Alabama. Shortly after their marriage they went to Augusta, where he did special work in Augusta Medical School. Later they went to New York City where he interned in New York Lying in Hospital for three months, also doing special work in Willard Parker Hospital. Later he attended Tulane University at three different times, six weeks each. He attended the Baby Clinic, at Seluda, N.C. each summer for a number of years. After moving to Carrollton he with his wife, went to New York City again, where he took a course at New York Post Graduate School.
>
> "Truly dedicated to his work as a physician, he was anxious to perfect himself in his knowledge in order that he might be truly useful to his people, his state and his nation. Had he thought that, by going to one of our larger cities he might have had a broader field and made a greater name, but his desire was to be of service to the common man, the people, and in that he succeeded admirably, he is enshrined in the hearts of many. His work was well done. He still lives.
>
> "He was a steward in the First Methodist Church, an Elk, a Shriner and Mason, a member of the Rotary Club and Sunset Hills Country Club, taking an active part in all civic work, a man of few words, but deep sincerity — and loyalty in all things that make life worth living.
>
> "Still interested in his work and his patients, tho' at an Atlanta Hospital where he had gone for personal surgical work a few days before, on the last day of June, 1958, in its closing hours he answered the Call of His Maker ... "

His only daughter Sara Elizabeth Thomasson married her high school sweetheart from Americus, Luther O'Hern. She studied medical technology at Georgia State College for Women at Milledgeville and took her degree in chemistry. She and Luther were married in Miami; and he, as an Army Air Corps pilot, was stationed in Cuba and the Caribbeans during most of World War II. He advanced in rank until he retired on Pentagon assignment as colonel.

Magnolia Terrace about 1935

Soon after Dr. Will Thomasson died, his granddaughter Sara Candace O'Hern moved to Carrollton to stay with "Mama" Howard Thomasson and complete her high school years. She still enjoys, not only the memory of her Carrollton years — Girl Scouting with Mrs. Celeste Tigner, Swing Band, girl friends (Celeta Estes, Kitty Griffin, Francisca Jordan, Mildred Huff, June Wirsing, Susan Stephens, Charlotte Channell), but the rich life of a small town. From earlier times she remembers a knock at the back door in the middle of the night when "Doc" might bring the injured into the kitchen and do a quick stitch job, or set an arm. Then, a week or two later, answering another knock, someone would be there with a live chicken, a ham, a mess of greens, a chess pie — the gratitude of the patient for the country doctor. Candy married John Childrey in the First Methodist Church in Carrollton after they met during college years. They have two children, Amy Thomasson Childrey (Mrs. Robert) Nast and Sean O'Hern Childrey who married Donna Kramer. Joshua James Nast is the grandson and great grandchild in this branch of the family, at least as of 2001.

Billie Ann O'Hern (Mrs. Pete) Lehr, the second daughter to Sara and Luther O'Hern, practices law in St. Petersburg, Florida. She has two daughters, Laura Caroline Wiest (Mrs. Aaron) Hull and Courtney Elizabeth Wiest; they both live in Florida. *Submitted by: John Childrey, 11055 NW 38th St., Coral Springs, FL 33065*

Sources: Holograph notes of J.J. Thomasson, no date; holograph eulogy of Will Thomasson, 1958; *The Thomasson Family* compiled by Evan W., James Jefferson and William Warren Thomasson, co-publishers of the *Newnan Times-Herald,* June, 1976.

1095. The James Jefferson Thomasson Family

James Jefferson Thomasson was born 27 April 1851, in Heard County, Georgia. He was the son of Thomas J. Thomasson who had

James Jefferson Thomasson

come to Carroll County, Georgia, as early as 1848. Thomas J. Thomasson appears on early deeds of Carroll County along with his brother who was Beverly D. Thomasson. On 26 October 1849 Thomas J. Thomasson sold to John Wood and A.J. Boggess for $165 a town lot #1 "except for the northwest corner where B.C. Thomasson law office stands, town of Carrollton." He also sold town lot #22. Witnesses were William Washington Merrell and John W. Palmer, J.P. (Carroll County Deed Book F, p. 333.) Beverly D. Thomasson was a prominent attorney who practiced law in Carroll County and adjoining counties for many years. He was once Solicitor General according to Pvt. Joe Cobb's *Carroll County and Her People.* Cobb described Beverly D. Thomasson as "An able and profound lawyer and judge — he was a Democrat and a strong and influential man in elections."

Both Thomas J. Thomasson and Beverly D. Thomasson were charter members of Carrollton Masonic Lodge #69 which was first organized in 1848. Thomas J. Thomasson was elected as the first secretary. The Masonic Lodge was the first two-story building to ever be built in Carrollton. It was located on the southwest corner of the public square. The first floor was a store, but the top floor was used as a lodge room. This building was used until after the Civil War when it was destroyed by fire.

We do not know what tragedy befell the Thomas J. Thomasson family in the mid 1850s — we only know that a few years after James Jefferson Thomasson was born in 1851, both Thomas J. Thomasson and his wife died leaving J.J. Thomasson an orphan. The name of Thomas J. Thomasson's wife is not known, but she was possibly the sister of George W. Brittain of Heard County. James Jefferson Thomasson is believed to have been an only child because he alone inherited the Thomasson farm in Heard County along with 13 slaves.

J.J. Thomasson lived on the farm during the Civil War with an uncle and his family. Many years later, J.J. Thomasson would tell his grandchildren stories of the Civil War and how he climbed tall trees on the farm to hear the guns firing during the Battle of Atlanta. When the Civil War ended, the Thomasson farm and all their property was confiscated by the Union Army. So, J.J. packed up and moved to Arkansas to live with some other family members. It is possible that the uncle he had lived with was Beverly D. Thomasson since he, too, moved to Arkansas after the Civil War.

J.J. Thomasson enjoyed careers as a teacher, a surveyor, an engineer, and a lawyer before deciding to become a newspaper publisher in Prescott, Arkansas. There he established *The Prescott Democrat.* About 1897, J.J. Thomasson returned to Georgia and purchased *The Carroll County Times* from the Sharp family. As editor, J.J. Thomasson wrote a regular column for the paper — "Reminiscing" — and these articles are a treasure trove of historical information about Carrollton and its people. In one article, J.J. Thomasson even mentions that "while in Shreveport, Louisiana, I visited with my mother's mother," so genealogical clues abound. J.J. Thomasson was the one who was given the credit for the foresight in organizing and the preparations made for the highly successful Centennial Celebration of Carrollton in 1927.

About 1941, J.J. Thomasson sold his newspaper business to the Meeks family and he began doing commercial job printing exclusively. That was the beginning of Thomasson Printing Company in Carrollton. And this was to become a family business that would remain in the Thomasson family for the next four generations.

J.J. Thomasson continued to edit *The Newnan Times* and *The Bowdon Bulletin* until his death in 1946. J.J. Thomasson's son, Evan Wirt Thomasson, had moved to Newnan, Georgia in 1935 and had started *The Newnan Times* in 1936. Ten years later, E.W. Thomasson and his son, James Jefferson Thomasson, bought *The Newnan Herald.* In 1947, the two papers combined into *The Newnan Times-Herald.* And that newspaper remains in the William Warren Thomasson family today.

A few other highlights of J.J. Thomasson's life would be that he surveyed a good portion of the Central of Georgia Railway between Newnan and Carrollton. He taught the Young Men's Bible Class of the First Methodist Church for many years in the early 1900s. In 1933, J.J. Thomasson was invited by President Franklin D. Roosevelt to visit him at Warm Springs, Georgia, and to discuss the Rural Electrification needs and other issues important to rural Georgia. Kathleen Thomasson (Malone) who was age six at the time was invited to go along with her mother — Kathleen McLean Thomasson — and her grandfather on this trip to Warm Springs. She recalls the warm greeting from the President and Mrs. Roosevelt and that the President asked her to sit on his lap saying that he had a little granddaughter just about her age.

James Jefferson Thomasson was born 27 April 1851 and died 28 December 1946. He was married to Amanda Francis Blalock on 28 September 1874 in Carroll County, Georgia. Amanda Blalock was the daughter of Captain James M. Blalock who was one of Carroll County's early pioneers. Capt. Blalock was the Ordinary before, during, and after the Civil War until 1868 when he decided to go into the mercantile business. In 1862, Capt. James Blalock organized and carried off to the Civil War the first regiment of Confederate soldiers from Carroll County.

The 1850 census of Carroll County listed the Blalock household as: James M. Blalock age 45, his wife Mary Ann, age 44, Jesse Y. Blalock age 21, a teacher at Carroll Masonic Institute; Margaret E. age 20; Emma L. age 17; James E., age 16; Amanda F. age 14; Samuel A. age 12; Katie age 8; Mary age 6; Robert L. age 4. Also living in the household with them was Edward Gresham, age 72, who was Mary Ann's father. There is an early deed of Carroll County dated 20 December 1854 of Harrison Crow of Randolph County, Alabama to Edward Gresham, Carroll County, $200 for Land Lot #195 in 7th District of Carroll (now Haralson) County.

Pvt. Joe Cobb wrote the Blalocks in his *Carroll County and Her People* — referring to J.Y. Blalock as "a splendid businessman, a good calculator and far seeing". The daughters were Maggie E. Blalock who married James G. Tanner 24 May 1871, Emma L. Blalock who married Benjamin F. Brown 23 July 1872, Amanda Francis who married James Jefferson Thomasson on 24 September 1874 and Mollie C. who married W.M. Meadows 8 May 1889. All marriages took place in Carroll County. James Marion Blalock born 30 March 1825 and died 18 June 1872 is buried in the Carrollton City Cemetery. His wife, Mary Graham Gresham born 10 May 1826 and died 4 October 1872 is buried beside him. Amanda Blalock Thomasson was born 1855 and died 1919. Her baby daughter Mary Estelle 1895-1897 lies next to her in the Carrollton City Cemetery.

J.J. Thomasson and Amanda Francis Blalock were the parents of ten children. The oldest child was Eva Thomasson b. 24 July 1875, m. William Scott Campbell who was b. 23 September 1869 and died 12 February 1949; Eva & William Campbell had three children: (1) Sara Katherine Campbell b. 12 July 1912 and m. Manlove Earle Davis on 21 October 1945, one daughter Sally Campbell Davis b. 11 February 1950; (2) William Beverly Campbell Sr. b. 21 May 1916 d. 31 October 1989 who m. Naomi Blanche Evans on 19 June 1940, their children were William Beverly Campbell Jr. b. 8 September 1942 m. Dawn Cheryle English on 8 April 1967 (their children: William Beverly Campbell III b. 18 August 1968 and Heather Dawn Campbell b. 14 August 1979); James Evan Campbell b. 2 July 1947 m. Diana Marie Kuhfal (b. 8 May 1957) 29 December 1979 (their children: James Evans Campbell Jr. b. 7 February 1982 and Kristy Ann Campbell b. 23 August 1983);

Sons of James Jefferson and Amanda Thomasson. Front: Will, Beverly, and Jesse. Back: Toombs, Evan, and Frank.

Robert Scott Campbell b. 8 June 1955 m. Bettina Ann Fowler (b. 31 October 1956) on 16 December 1977 (their son Robert Scott Campbell b. 22 June 1991.)

Continuing with the third child of Eva Thomasson and William Campbell, Frances Blalock Campbell b. 31 July 1920 m. Thomas Walter Reeves Jr. (b. 14 August 1920) on 9 October 1946 (their children: Thomas Walter Reeves III b. 19 July 1949 m. Gloria Hendley on 29 November 1969 — one daughter Amanda Elizabeth Reeves b. 29 June 1971; Nancy Nelle Reeves b. 14 July 1952 m. Chester N. Childers on 29 June 1974 — children Walter Lee Childers b. 3 March 1978, Douglas Cambell Childers b. 4 October 1980, Patrick Thomas Childers b. 12 September 1982; Scott Campbell Reeves b. 20 August 1956.

The second child of James Jefferson Thomasson and Amanda Frances Blalock was Katie Lu Thomasson b. 8 March 1878 m. Joseph M. Harris 23 October 1932 and d. 1 March 1979. The third child of J.J. and Amanda Thomasson was Sada Thomasson b. 23 August 1880 m. John Clifton Thomas (11 April 1885-3 September 1969), Sada died 2 December 1963.

The fourth child of J.J. and Amanda Thomasson was James Toombs Thomasson Sr. b. 29 October 1880 m. Clair Downs (b. 31 August 1899) on 15 December 1919. Their son was James Toombs Thomasson, Jr. b. 1 March 1922 m. 7 June 1947 to Josephine Moncrief (22 July 1924-8 January 1969). After the death of his first wife, James Toombs Thomasson Jr. m. Romanzia Hurley (b. 6 November 1934). The son of James Toombs Thomasson Jr. was James Toombs Thomasson III b. 23 August 1953.

The fifth child of J.J. and Amanda Thomasson was Beverly Blalock Thomasson born 13 February 1883 and died 12 June 1911. This son was named for his uncle who was Beverly D. Thomasson.

The sixth child of J.J. and Amanda Thomasson was William Edward Thomasson, M.D. b. 10 October 1885 in Amity, Oklahoma m. Annie Howard Bradshaw (20 April 1892-3 December 1884) on 1 October 1916. Dr. William E. Thomasson was a prominent physician of Carrollton for many years and was one of the founders of Tanner Memorial Hospital here. Dr. Thomasson was a member of Men's Bible Study at First United Methodist Church in Carrollton, a Shriner, a Rotarian, an Elk, and a member of the Georgia Medical Association. Dr. W.E. Thomasson and Annie Howard Bradshaw had a daughter, Sara Elizabeth Thomasson b. 11 May 1918 who m. George Luther O'Hern on 8 November 1941. They had two daughters: (1) Sara Candice O'Hern b. 15 March 1943 m. 19 June 1965 John Albert Childrey Jr. - their children Amy Thomasson Childrey b. 16 December 1968 and Sean O'Hern Childrey b. 1 May 1972. (2) Billie Ann O'Hern b. 30 November 1947 m. John Andrew Wiest (b. 13 April 1946) later divorced; their children were: Laura Caroline Wiest b. 21 August 1969 m. Aaron Lee Hull (b. 27 February) on 14 February 1991; and Courtney Elizabeth Wiest b. 3 March 1978.

The seventh child of J.J. and Amanda Thomasson was Jesse Lee Thomasson (b. 7 May 1888-26 September 1976) who m. Florence Estelle Harris (13 September 1888-6 February 1953) on 2 October 1912. Their first daughter Beverly Thomasson b. 7 May 1917 m. Edward William Gnehm, Sr. (13 June 1918-28 August 1981) on 3 May 1943. The son of Beverly and Edward Gnehm Sr. is Edward William Gnehm Jr. b. 10 November 1944 and m. Margaret Scott (b. 4 August 1946). Edward Gnehm Jr. served as Ambassador to Kuwait during the Gulf War and after America was victorious in Desert Storm, he rode in on one of the victory tanks. Edward Gnehm Jr. is presently the ambassador to Australia from the United

50th Wedding Anniversary of Frank Tomlinson Thomasson Jr. and Libby Folsom Thomasson.

States. Margaret and Edward Gnehm Jr. are the parents of Cheryl Lynn Gnehm b. 29 September 1971 and Edward William Gnehm III b. 30 October 1974.

The first daughter of Edward William Gnehm Sr. and Beverly Thomasson is Barbara Gnehm b. 19 October 1946 who m. Albert Johnson 23 December 1983, later divorced — their children were Laurel Louise Johnson and Albert Edward Johnson. Laurel Louise m. David Rozar 24 October 1992 and had children: Michael Allen Rozar b. 25 September 1986, Brittany Nichole Rozar b. 31 January 1990. Albert Edward Johnson m. Diane Fincher in December 1991 and had a son Eddie Lee Johnson b. 25 July 1990.

The second daughter of Edward William Gnehm Sr. and Beverly Thomasson is Jane Ellen Gnehm b. 7 June 1948 m. Fred O'Donnell b. 19 January 1947, later divorced, and their children are: Deanna Renee O'Donnell b. 27 February 1970 m. Matthew Hednicki; Celena Jo O'Donnell b. 11 June 1972; and Robert Lake O'Donnell b. 1 September 1978.

Jesse Lee Thomasson and Florence Estelle Harris had a daughter, Lula Watters Thomasson, b. 18 July 1921 who married David C. Garrett Jr. (b. 6 July 1922) on 11 September 1947. David C. Garrett was later the president of Delta Airlines. The children of Lula Thomasson and David C. Garrett were: (1) David C. Garrett III b. 20 July 1948 who m. Vickie Krantz on 13 September 1969 - their children: Angela Dawn Garrett b. 11 April 1971 and Courtney Elizabeth Garrett b. 17 November 1981. (2) Virginia Carlyn Garrett, M.D. b. 20 May 1952 married on 12 July 1975 Michael R. Mork (b. 30 March 1948, later divorced, their daughter Jennifer Carlyn Mork b. 20 August 1978. Virginia Carlyn Garrett, M.D. m. second to Lance Scott Galvin (b. 30 January 1948) on 10 June 1989 and had one daughter, Elizabeth Lula Galvin b. 4 April 1990. (3) Charles Thomasson Garrett b. 8 September 1954 m. Andrea Johnson (14 July 1950) on 3 October 1986. Jessie Lee Thomasson married a second time on 15 September 1955 to Marian R. Andrews b. 14 July 1901.

Jesse Lee Thomasson and Evan Wirt Thomason were twins. The eighth child of J.J. and Amanda Blalock Thomasson was Evan Wirt Thomasson (b. 7 May 1888-24 September 1983) m. in 1908 to Betty May Clay (14 March 1891-4 January 1957). Evan Wirt Thomasson and Betty May Clay were the parents of one son James Jefferson Thomasson, Sr. (18 December 1909-14 July 1979) who married Emeline Caroline Cheney (4 August 1908-1 January 1936) and had two children with her: (1) Emily Caroline Thomasson (1 October 1932-21 October 1989) who m. on 27 May 1956 to Albert Lanier Sealy b. 29 January 1927. (2) James Jefferson Thomasson Jr., M.D. b. 22 August 1934 m. Susie Arnall Mann (b. 11 November 1934) on 30 June 1956.

Dr. J.J. Thomasson, Jr. has been a prominent physician in Newnan, Georgia for many years. Dr. J.J. Thomasson and Susie Mann Thomasson are the parents of four children. First, Myrtle Mildred Thomasson b. 30 September 1958 m. on 24 March 1990 to Carlton Estes Pender (b. 18 November 1951) later divorced; Myrtle Mildred Thomasson m. second Ronald Steven Sale b. 4 May 1954 — their children were Katie Arnall Sale b. 30 January 1984 and Ronald Steven Sale, Jr. b. 3 April 1987. Second child of Dr. J.J. Thomasson is Emeline Mann Thomasson b. 15 January 1960 m. on 2 July 1988 to Edward Christopher Forbes Loughlin b. 6 April 1960 — their son is Edward Christopher Forbes Loughlin, Jr. b. 17 February 1991. Third child of Dr. J.J. Thomasson is James Jefferson Thomasson III b. 25 March 1962 m. on 12 November 1988 to Jennfier Ann Jennings b. 11 April 1963 — their children are James Jefferson Thomasson IV b. 3 September 1993. The fourth child of Dr. J.J. Thomasson is Alton Arnall Thomasson born 1 February 1972.

James Jefferson Thomasson Sr., the son of E.W. and Betty Clay Thomasson, married second to Ida Askew (19 December 1916-17 June 1981) on 15 September 1938. They had one son: William Warren Thomasson b. 8 September 1941 who m. on 30 March 1973 to Frances Marianne Carlisle (b. 3 July 1949). One daughter was born to them: Elizabeth Carlisle Thomasson b. 15 August 1980.

The ninth child of J.J. and Amanda Blalock Thomasson was Frank Tomlinson Thomasson (16 April 1893-11 March 1956) who married on 3 February 1922 to Kathleen McLean (9 November 1903-22 November 1979). Frank Tomlinson Thomasson acquired Thomasson Printing Company in Carrollton when his father died in 1946. For the next 10 years, he operated this business which became Carrollton's foremost commercial printer.

The son of Frank Tomlinson Thomasson Sr. and Kathleen McLean was Frank Tomlinson Thomasson Jr. b. 13 December 1924 in Carroll County. On 17 January 1947, Frank Thomasson Jr. married Libby Jo Folsom (b. 28 May 1928). Libby Folsom was the daughter of Joseph Royal Folsom Jr. and Elizabeth Swearingin. Libby's paternal grandparents were Joseph Royal Folsom Sr. and Alma Smith of Dublin, Georgia. Her maternal grandparents were John Tracy Swearingin and Carrie Murray of Fernandina, Florida. Libby's father died when she was six years old and her mother, along with her grandparents, J.R. Folsom Jr. and Alma Smith Folsom, established Folsom's Dress Shoppe in Carrollton in 1935. For many years this was a favorite store to visit in Carrollton for the finest in ladies' fashions.

Frank Thomasson Jr. became the third generation of his family to go into the printing business and he became president and CEO of Thomasson Printing in 1956. In 1972, Frank Thomasson Jr. served as the president of the Georgia Printing Association. He also was active in civic affairs and served as president of the Carrollton Kiwanis Club.

In 1948 Libby and Frank Thomasson Jr. were the first to build a home on the newly established Kramer Drive in Carrollton. Three children were born to Libby and Frank Thomasson Jr. — first was a son Frank Tomlinson Thomasson III born 14 August 1950 and married on 15 June 1974 to Barbara Anne Denney. See the separate heading for this family.

In 1997, Thomasson Printing Company celebrated its 100th Anniversary and four generations of Thomassons at the helm of this successful business. Although the business is now a part of a larger conglomerate that includes nineteen different printing firms, the business still maintains the name of Thomasson Printing and Tommy Thomasson still is the CEO and president.

The second child of Libby and Frank Thomasson Jr. is Elizabeth Ashley Thomasson born 5 January 1953. She was named Elizabeth for her maternal grandmother, Elizabeth Swearingen, and Ashley for her maternal step-grandfather who was Ashley Thomas Wigelsworth. Beth Thomasson married on 26 August 1971 to Charles Daniel Procter, M.D., who is a vascular surgeon practicing in Gainesville, Georgia. Dan is the son of Charles Walter Procter (born 13 June 1929) and Emma Lou Smith Procter (born 25 April 1929) both of Ada, Oklahoma. Both Beth and Dan graduated from Carrollton High School. Dan graduated from West Georgia College and then from the Medical College of Georgia. He performed his medical residency in Lexington, Kentucky. Dan then served in the U.S. Air Force. The children of Beth and Dan Procter, M.D. are Charles Daniel Procter Jr. born 10 January 1972 and Zachary Walter Procter born 27 December 1978.

The third child of Libby and Frank Thomasson Jr. is Susan Amanda Thomasson born 2 May 1954. Amy was named Susan for her mother's aunt, Susan Folsom, who is remembered for her many years with Folsom's Dress Shoppe in Carrollton. The Amanda part of her name is for her great-grandmother Amanda Francis Blalock Thomasson. Amy Thomasson grew up in Carrollton and graduated from Carrollton High School. Amy received her A.B. degree from Queen's College in North Carolina. On 3 June 1978, Amy Thomasson married William Crowell Little. Bill Little is the son of Ralph Augustus Little (born 31 March 1913 in Newton, North Carolina) and Mary Ellen McCaffrey (born 25 December 1918 in Peru, Indiana). Bill Little is the grandson of Kate Cole McCaffrey of Asheville, North Carolina. Bill Little earned his degree in biology from the University of North Carolina in Charlotte and is now affiliated with Burlington Industries. Bill Little served in the U.S. Army from 1961-1964. The Littles have two children: William Cole Little born 24 January 1981 and Elizabeth McLean Little born 22 October 1982. The Littles reside in Troutville, Virginia.

The daughter of Frank Tomlinson Thomasson and Kathleen McLean was Mary Kathleen Thomasson b. 22 February 1927. Kathleen Thomasson m. William Wesley Mayfield (26 July 1924-21 April 1968) on 7 July 1948. Two children were born to them: (1) Kathleen Thomasson Mayfield b. 8 February 1952 m. 15 March to Ronald H. Scherdin b. 14 April 1952. Their children were: Lisa Dawn Scherdin b. 26 March 1977 and Kathleen Lucille "Katie Lu" Scherdin b. 17 August 1981. (2) William Wesley Mayfield III b. 25 December 1954 m. on 7 April 1990 to Jacqueline Eugenia "Genia" Minor b. 15 August 1959. After the death of her first husband, William Wesley Mayfield, Mary Kathleen Thomasson m. Thomas Steele Malone Jr. (b. 5 July 1924) on 14 February 1970 and they make their home in Bainbridge, Georgia.

The tenth child of J.J. and Amanda Thomasson was a daughter named Mary Estelle who died in infancy (1895-1897). J.J. and Amanda Thomasson, as well as many other family members, are buried in the Carrollton City Cemetery.

Frank Tomlinson Thomasson Jr. and Libby Folsom Thomasson celebrated their 50th Wedding Anniversary at the home of Dr. and Mrs. (Beth) Dan Procter in Gainesville, Georgia. The family picture shows, front row seated left to right, Cole Little, Amelia Thomasson, Elizabeth Little, Frank Tomlinson "Tee" Thomasson IV, kneeling is Beth Thomasson Procter. Standing on second row is Anne Denney Thomasson, Kathleen Thomasson Malone, Libby and Frank Thomasson Jr., Amanda Thomasson Little, Alma Folsom Perkerson (Libby's aunt), Thomas Steele Malone, Nancy Cabe Folsom. Third row, Frank Tomlinson "Tommy" Thomasson III, Zachary Procter, Charles Daniel Procter Jr., William Little, Dr. Dan Procter Sr., and Libby's only brother Joseph Royal Folsom III.

The Thomasson family is proud to have been a part of the heritage of Carroll County, Georgia, for the past five generations. *Submitted by: Frank and Libby Thomasson, 309 Kramer Drive, Carrollton, GA 30117 and Written by: Jan Robinson Bell, Carrollton, GA*

1096. Thomasson - Denney

Frank Tomlinson Thomasson III was born on 14 August 1950, the son of Frank Tomlinson Thomasson Jr. and Libby Folsom Thomasson. The Tomlinson name is a family name that has been passed down for generations. Tommy Thomasson, as he is known in Carrollton, Georgia, is the fourth generation of his family to serve as president and CEO of Thomasson Printing Company. Tommy Thomasson is married to Barbara Anne Denney who is a descendant of many of the well-known pioneer names of the Hulett community in Carroll County.

Barbara Anne Denney was born 26 December 1950 and grew up in Atlanta, Georgia. She graduated with a B.S. in elementary education from West Georgia College in 1972 and in 1978 she received her M.S.Ed. She also has earned a B.S. degree in art design. Anne taught school for nine years at Central Primary School. She is very artistically inclined and interior design is one of her favorites. She enjoys painting murals and textured walls.

Barbara Anne Denney is the daughter of William Franklin Denney who was born 9 October 1922 in Athens, Clarke County, Georgia. William Franklin Denney was the son of Willie Jones Denney and Fannie Frances Stevens of Athens. W.J. Denney was a veteran of World War I and in spite of a serious wound he received in France, he lived to the age of 88 years. Though long native to Clarke County, the Denney family later moved to Atlanta about 1923. In July of 1947, William Franklin Denney married Wyolene Elva Holland who was the daughter of Raymond Roy Holland of the Hulett-Villa Rica community. Her mother was Annie Ruth Stovall. Raymond Roy Holland and Annie Ruth Stovall had married on 1 January 1922 in Carroll County.

Wyolene Holland Denney was born 28 September 1923 and died 4 December 1975. She was buried in Westview Cemetery in Fulton County, Georgia. Wyolene Holland Denney had one sister who was Clarice E. Holland who married Harold M. Wilson. William Franklin Denney married a second time after the death of his first wife and still lives in Carrollton.

William Franklin Denney and Wyolene Holland Denney were the parents of three daughters, including one set of twins. Barbara Anne Denney and Frances Marie Denney were born on 26 December 1950. Frances Marie Denney died on 14 February 1975. Another daughter was Rosemary Denney who was named by her twin sisters. Sadly, this infant died at birth. She is buried next to her mother at Westview Cemetery in Fulton County, Georgia.

The Hollands and Stovalls were farmers in Carroll County when "Cotton Was King" and they were "good salt of the earth" people who made their home in the Hulett community. The Stovalls were related to many of the old pioneer families around Hulett — Boatrights, Ayers or Ayres, Crews, McClendons, Richards, Wards, Fountains, Gillands — to name but a few. The progenitor of many of these families was Abraham Ayres born in 1795.

Armendie Ayers and Tom E. Stovall

Anne Denney Thomasson is a descendant of Abraham Ayres through his son Dr. William B. Ayres, who married Sarah Parker in Carroll County on 26 March 1851. Dr. William B. Ayres and Sarah Parker Ayres were the parents of the following children. (1) David A. Ayres who married Mary A. Baggett (2) James C. Ayres who married Louise Hembree 24 February 1872 in Carroll County (3) Nancy M. Ayres who married Willie K. Barton 12 December 1878 in Carroll County (4) Alonzo Ayres who married Milaam Hembree and second to Nola Morris (5) Inez Ayres who married Buford C. Boggs (6) Sarah J. Ayres who married Reese W. Neal (7) Julia Ayers who married J. Henry Chastain (8) Armendie E. Ayres who married E. Tom Stovall on 30 October 1884 in Carroll County (9) Rev. W.L. Ayres who married Anna Robinson (10) Jabus A. Ayres who married Lora Stovall and second to Ethel Howsworth and (11) Elsie Ayres who married a Horton. This information is taken from a very intricate family tree beautifully drawn and constructed some years ago that does not follow the usual format of a family tree. Instead, it resembles a drawing by an engineer. We do not know for sure who drew this beautiful family tree, but we believe it may have been drawn by Roy Richards in his early years, perhaps when an engineering student at Georgia Tech, as a gift for his grandparents,

The Denney Family, about 1950.

Armendie and Tom Stovall. He was always deeply interested in his family.

Armendie E. Ayres and E. Tom Stovall would become the parents of first a daughter, Viola Stovall, who married William R. Ward. Second, another daughter, Ida Myrtice "Myrtie" Stovall who married Wylie T. Richards.

Myrtie and Wylie T. Richards were the parents of Carrollton's most famous industrialist, Roy Richards, who was the founder of Southwire in 1949. Roy Richards married Alice Huffard of Bluefield, Virginia, in 1957 and brought his bride to Carrollton to live. They became the parents of seven children together — Roy Jr., Jim, Nancy, Lee, Robin, Beth and Laura. Roy Richard's brother, Hugh Richards, married Grace Talley and they had two children, Tommy T. Richards and Sally Ann Richards. Even though they rose to the top in the world of business, the Richards brothers never forgot their roots in the Hulett community of Carroll County.

Later on, after the Richards had moved into Carrollton to be closer to the business, they gave the Richards home place to their grandparents — Armendie Ayres and Tom Stovall — to live in for the rest of their lives. Roy remembered to come back to "give all the family a ride" when he bought his first convertible. Thomas Wiley Richards (1870-1943) and Ida Myrtice Stovall (1888-1967) are buried next to E. Tom Stovall (1849-1925) and Armanda Stovall (1866-1957) at Little Vine Church which is south of Ayres Creek and near the Douglas County line in Land District 2 Land Lot 236, GMD 1542.

The third child of Armendie E. Ayres and E. Tom Stovall was S. Francis Stovall who married Joseph M. Wallis. Earnest Stovall was the fourth child who married first to Cleo Watkins. His second wife was Beulah Crews. "Miss Beulah" is fondly remembered as the dental hygienist in Dr. Selby Cramer's dental office of the 1950-1960 era. Earnest and Bernice Stovall were twins. The fifth child of Armendie and Tom Stovall was M. Bernice Stovall who married Homer L. Campbell. The sixth child was Annie Ruth Stovall who married Raymond Roy Holland on 1 January 1922.

Annie Ruth Stovall Holland died in 1988 and her husband Raymond Roy Holland died in 1975. Both are buried at Mars Hill Baptist Church in Carroll County.

Raymond Roy Holland is remembered in the family for his jet black hair which has passed on down in the family for many generations. Annie Ruth Stovall Holland was a talented seamstress who loved to make quilts. Quilting bees were a part of community life back in her days and she left more than 30 beautiful hand made quilts for the family to enjoy. These have many old patterns such as Bear Claw, Wedding Ring, Trip Around the World, etc. One of the beautiful heirloom quilts has the name of each person who worked on the quilt embroidered there.

Frank Tomlinson Thomasson III and Barbara Anne Denney have two children. Amelia Kathleen Thomasson was born 16 February 1982 and is presently a student pursuing a degree in business administration at the State University of West Georgia in Carrollton. Her goal for after graduation is to go into the family business and become the manager of the Thomasson printing plant located in Atlanta. She would love to live in Buckhead.

A son, Frank Tomlinson "Tee" Thomasson IV was born 20 October 1986. He is presently age fourteen and attends Carrollton Junior High School where he plays the trumpet in the band. He is following in the footsteps of his Grandfather William Franklin Denney who won a scholarship in his younger days to Georgia Military Academy for playing the silver trumpet. Tee is musically inclined and loves to play the guitar. He has also inherited his other's creative talents.

In 1997 Thomasson Printing Company celebrated its 100th Anniversary and four generations of Thomassons as CEO and president. Tommy Thomasson has served as president of the Georgia Printing Association, as a trustee of the First Methodist Church, as chairman of the Housing Authority, and is on the board of directors of the West Georgia National Bank. He is also an active member of the Carrollton Rotary Club. Tommy and Anne Denney Thomasson make their home in Heritage Hills in Carrollton.

The group picture shows the Denney family about 1950. From left to right are William Franklin Denney, Bernice Stovall Campbell (twin), Armendie Ayers Stovall, Ernest Stovall (twin), Wyolene Holland Denney, and in front are the Denney twin girls, Barbara Anne (named for her maternal grandmother) and Frances Marie (named for her paternal grandmother). *Submitted by: Tommy and Anne Denney Thomasson, Stonewall Drive, Carrollton, GA, and Written by: Jan Robinson Bell, Carrollton, GA.*

1097. The Thompson Family

The Thompsons moved from Virginia to Carroll County in the late 1700s or early 1800s. They settled in the Jake community. This was Shade Thompson who married Louisa McBurnett. Shade was a soldier in the War Between the States.

Shade and Louisa had two sons who lived in the same community. They were Isaac and Nicholas Thompson. Isaac married Eva Byrd and they had ten children: Henry, Monroe, Wordlaw, Marvin, Judge, Lunier, Louise, Mae, Bell, and Ruby. Mae died May 4, 2001. She was 104 years old. Bell is still living and she is 98 years old.

Ruby married Dick Hightower and they moved from Tennessee to Bremen in 1945 and started Hightower Funeral Home, which their son and grandsons still run today.

Some of the Thompsons moved from this area to south Georgia and some to Alabama.

Nicholas had six children: Luther, Charlie, Joe, Hattie, Louisa, and Will. Luther has a son, J.L. Thompson, who lives in Sylvester, Georgia. Charlie has a grandson, Charles Thompson, who lives in Tallapoosa.

Shade Thompson was involved in the start of Union Church. The recorded records state the Union Church land was donated by W.A. McBurnett, Shade Thompson, and Nick McBurnett in 1884. Today, the name of the church is Union United Methodist Church. On October 4, 1889, almost ten acres of land was bought and deeded to the trustees of Union Methodist Campground for the sum of $45. The trustees were George McDaniel, R.H. Parker, John Garrett, Benjamim McGariety, and R.C. McDaniel. The first tents were built and occupied by the families of McDaniel, Garrett, W.C. Adamson (who was a U.S. Senator), Charles Copeland, J.W. Morrison, and Dr. H.M. Henderson who was a professor at the old A. & M. School in Carrollton. He was also a Methodist preacher.

In October of 1948, Rev. C.L. Harris, a well-known minister in Carroll County, was elected president of the Board of Trustees. Rev. Harris, a minister in the North Georgia Conference of the Methodist Church and a native of West Georgia, had a special interest in the camp. Under his leadership as president, much progress, both materially and spiritually, was made. He was the longest-serving president so far for the campground.

In the early years of the encampment, they had no electric lights and no running water, but today they have modern conveniences. It was told that one weekend fifty-two people slept in the T.M. Carroll tent. Most had to sleep on pallets on the floor.

Frances Lively (now Frances Evans) served many years in Africa as a missionary.

The Union Church caught on fire in the early 1900s and Marvin Thompson climbed up in the attic and kicked the shingles off the roof that was on fire and put out the fire!

We are thankful for the small part the Thompsons have played in Carroll County and for the church and campground. *Submitted by: Wayne Thompson (great-grandson of Shade Thompson), 6147 Mt. Zion Road, Waco, GA 30182.*

1098. Ransom T. Thompson

Ransom T. Thompson was born in Pendleton District, South Carolina, in 1778. His father was Joseph Thompson Sr. (1747-1810) and his mother was Mary Jolly (1747-1849). On 23 May 1801 he married Ann Dalrymple (born 22 December 1785, died 1874) in South Carolina. Ann's parents were Samuel and Sarah (Pollock) Dalrymple. Ransom and Ann had twelve children born in South Carolina before the family moved to Carroll County, Georgia, to be listed in the 1830 federal census records.

(1) James Dalrymple Thompson, born 7 October 1802, died 4 November 1877 in Cleburne County, Alabama. He married Mary S. (Polly) White, born 8 October 1822 in South Carolina. She died in 23 November 1863. They had ten children. They died in Cleburne County, Alabama, and are buried in the Cole Cemetery in Cleburne County, Alabama. More information on this line is published in *The Heritage of Cleburne County, Alabama.*

(2) Elizabeth Thompson was born on 11 July 1804.

(3) Joseph C. Thompson born 1 August 1806, died in 1880. He married Emily Orr (born 1815) on 29 August 1833 in Carroll County, Georgia. Emily died in 1910. Joseph and Emily had ten children, all born in Georgia and Alabama. They were: (1a) Rev. James L. Thompson, born 1835, married Louisa J. Hunnicutt 13 December 1857 and they had eight children. Louisa was born 01 May 1836, died 06 Jun 1927 and was the daughter of John L. Hunnicutt and Rebecca Jane Thompson. (2a) Lavania (Vinnie) Thompson, (3a) William Tyler Thompson married Willie Elkins, (4a) Caroline E. Thompson married Thomas M. Baker in Cleburne County, Alabama, (5a) Lawrence Thompson married Rhonda Coats. (6a) Ransom Asbury Thompson married Mary J. Katherine Powell, 13 August 1865 in Haralson County, Georgia, they had eight children. (7a) John Thompson married Mollie Wiggins, 18 January 1870 in Cleburne County, Alabama, they had five children. (8a) Jessie Travis Thompson married Nancy E. Sides, 24 January 1867 and they had seven children. (9a) Julia Ann Thompson married George Washington Little 1 December 1878 and they had three children before she died in 1948. (10a) George Francis (Frank) Thompson born 15 January 1851 in Birmingham, Alabama, married Mary Ellen Bentley. They lived in Cleburne County, Alabama, and raised six children until Mary Ellen died in 1896. Their children were George Henry Thompson born 12 January 1884, Rose Ellen Thompson born 16 May 1886, Thomas Luther Thompson born 12 April 1888, Effie Mae Thompson born 2 June 1890, Martha Jane Thompson (my grandmother) born 14 June 1892 and Mary Estella Thompson born 28 September 1894. Frank died 1929 and is buried in Birmingham, Alabama. Martha Jane married Josephus Able Stephen Clotfelter, 13 November 1912 in Alabama. Joseph was born 24 December 1880 in Rockdale County, Georgia, died 20 November 1950 in California. Martha died 12 February 1984 in California. Both are buried at Rose Hills, Whittier, California. They had six children all born in Alabama. Millard Thomas was my father, born 10 October 1919, died 11 September 1996 in Paulsbo, Washington.

(4) John William D.F. Thompson was born 8 March 1808. He married Elizabeth Beeson and they had ten children.

(5) Samuel D. Thompson was born 17 February 1810. He married Elizabeth Barnwell 7 September 1830 in Carroll County, Georgia.

(6) William S. Thompson was born 11 November 1811.

(7) Dudley H. Thompson was born 15 September 1813. He married Margaret Huey.

(8) Rebecca Thompson was born 30 May 1816.

(9) Robert King Thompson was born 23 August 1818.

(10) Zacheriah Talifero Thompson born 27 July 1820, died 19 May 1902. He married Mary Jane Malone 9 January 1844 in Carroll County, Georgia.

(11) Mary Ann (Polly) Thompson was born 4 April 1822.

(12) Sally Ann (Sarah) Thompson was born 22 February 1824. *Submitted by: Linda Waldron, 3851 Nations Drive, Douglasville, GA 30135*

Sources: Census records and Carroll County estate records of March 28, 1846.

1099. The Threadgill Patriarch

Tragedy brought the Threadgill family to Carroll County in 1853. The family - descendants of an orphan boy - has been in the county ever since.

The story of the Threadgills in the 19th century is intertwined with the Allen family. The Threadgills and Allens both were in Anson County, North Carolina in the late 18th and early 19th centuries and likely knew each other in that rural county. By the 1830s, both families were headed south into Georgia. Many of the Threadgills would end up in Alabama, which was opening up for settlement. On February 19, 1835, Henry Ledbetter Threadgill married Mary Frances Frederick Allen in Houston County, Georgia. By 1850, the couple was in Chambers County, Alabama, with five children ranging in age from six months to 14. A sixth child was born in 1851.

Typhoid fever struck the Threadgill household in the summer of 1853. Mary, 35, died of the fever on July 7. Henry, 43, died the next day. Their two youngest children - Thomas, 3, and Mortha, 2 - also died then from the fever.

Mary's brother, Alcimus Allen, was a recent arrival in Carroll County with a young family of his own. Alcimus became guardian of his sister's children on November 7, 1853. At the time, Alcimus was 29 and his wife Jane almost 27 with three young children (ages 2 to 6) of their own. They took in and brought to Carroll County the Threadgill orphans - Eliza Ann, 17; Harriett Virginia, 10; Eugenia, 8; and Alcimus, 5. Alcimus Threadgill would become the patriarch of all the Threadgills now in Carroll County.

Harris Threadgill, taken in 1948 with Newt Spence on left.

The Allen family lived in the Hickory Level community, and the Allens were charter members of Concord Methodist Church. Eliza was the first of the Threadgill children to leave the household, marrying Jesse Muse in October 1854. Her sister, Eugenia, married Walker Gray in August 1863. Harriett Threadgill died of pneumonia in 1862, leaving only 15 year old Alcimus remaining in the care of his aunt and uncle ten years after his parents' deaths.

Alcimus Allen reportedly served during all four years of the Civil War, leaving his nephew Alcimus with a lot of responsibility on the farm during the war years. Tragedy struck the family again in 1868. Alcimus Allen, 43, was accidentally killed by his nephew, Walker Gray, while they were deer hunting. Alcimus Threadgill was still living with his aunt, uncle and cousins at the time.

In 1874, Alcimus Threadgill married Margaret Hamrick and began a family of their own with three sons - Harris, Walter and Glenn and a daughter, Elizabeth (Lizzie). Each one sought out their opportunities in face of the changes in farming and the depression that came about in the 1920s and 1930s. Glenn left Carroll County to work for the Railway Mail Service in Macon and retired in 1953 in Washington, D.C. The other children continued to live and work in the same area they grew up in and raised their families. Alcimus died in 1913 and his wife, Margaret, died in 1936. Her obituary noted they had seventeen grandchildren and eleven great-grandchildren at that time. To date, there have been five generations of the Threadgill family in Carroll County which began in 1853. *Submitted by: Jack E. Threadgill Sr. and Jack E. Threadgill Jr., 119 Lakepoint Drive, Carrollton, GA 30117*

1100. Thurman Pioneers

John Thurman and Anne (Morecraft) Thurman, along with their three children Elizabeth, Joan, and John Jr., came to America from England in 1636. They settled in James County, Virginia, and from there their descendants spread throughout the country. They fought in all the wars from the Revolutionary to the Gulf War. They also fought on both sides of the Civil War.

Two of John Jr. and Mary Thurman's sons, John and Benjamin, moved their families from Virginia to North Carolina in 1775. It was thought that they moved to South Carolina after the Revolutionary War, but what happened was the border between North and South Carolina was moved. This moved them to South Carolina.

Benjamin Thurman and four of his sons, Benjamin Franklin, David, Richard, and William, moved their families from South Carolina to DeKalb County, Georgia, and Atlanta in 1826. When the railroad came in the neighborhood, Rev. John Thurman (son of Richard and Nancy Little Thurman) said it was time to move.

Richard Thurman, his wife Nancy (Little) Thurman, their eight children, their spouses and their children moved to Carroll County, Georgia, in 1851. They settled near Bowdon where Smith's Chapel is now located. The first six children were born in Chesterfield, South Carolina. Rev. John was born 28 November 1810; Mary was born 1804; Martha born 1812; Nancy born 1822; Sarah born 1825 and buried at Smith's Chapel; Julia Ann born 1827 in DeKalb County, married Samuel Nichols 12 August 1847 and both buried at Smith's Chapel; and Richard Enoch Thurman born 8 June 1830 in DeKalb County.

The Rev. John Thurman, with the help of John McDaniel and George and some of the neighbors, cleared a place on his land large enough to build a church. It was a modest log structure with two doors and a large fireplace. The roof was made with boards hewed from large hardwood trees; some were more than four feet wide. With his church complete, the Rev. Thurman asked all the people in the community to come for the service. The first sermon was preached from fourteenth chapter of St. John. The church was named Mount Pleasant. A short time later, the church was admitted to the Methodist Conference.

Lieutenant Richard E. Thurman

Twenty eight years later a new church was built using sawn lumber, nails and windows. This was after the Civil War. The new church was also used for a school. The first school teacher was Miss Nannie Thurman, daughter of Rev. Thurman. The Methodist Conference replaced Rev. Thurman as pastor. The conference sent The Rev. Seaborn Smith. The people of the new church decided to name it Smith's Chapel in honor of their new pastor, Rev. Seaborn C. Smith. Rev. John Thurman sold the church and the cemetery to the trustees of Smith's Chapel for $5.00 on 10 September 1892. Rev. John Thurman died 7 November 1894 and was buried at Smith's Chapel. There are approximately forty-seven Thurmans and their descendants buried at Smith's Chapel.

My great-grandfather Richard Enoch Thurman, son of Richard and Nancy (Little) Thurman, was born 8 June 1830 in DeKalb County and died 15 July 1917 in Whitesburg. He married Emily Nichols 28 February 1850. His brother, the Rev. John Thurman, performed the ceremony. Richard joined Company C, 56th Regiment Volunteer Army, 25 October 1861. He was appointed second lieutenant on 2 July 1862. Richard and Emily had the following children; Mary Augusta born 1852, Sarah born 1854, George Washington Thurman born 11 January 1857, Charles Merrill born 11 August 1859, Tildy married Boss Burdette, Mattie married Jesse Carr, Emma married Dock Barnwell, Carrie married W.W. Barker.

Richard married second Ada Moore 2 September 1899. Their children were twins Sebie and Rebie born 5 February 1901. Sebie married Joe Gaines; Tyre born 1903, W.J. born 15 January 1910.

George Washington Thurman married Georgia Martha (Musick) Thurman. They had the following children: Charles Brown Thurman (my father) born 26 October 1887, died 11 September 1957, married Ludell Clark 28 July 1928; William Howard born 8 January 1890; Annie Emma born 11 September 1892, married Jim Legg; Harry A. born 25 October 1898, married Emma Davison; Lillie Mae born 19 March 1903, married Bob Brown; Mary Pauline, born 20 December 1906, married first to Louie Sanders and married second to Leo Musick. Charles Thurman was one of the founding deacons of Happy Hill Baptist Church in Carroll County.

Submitted by: George Brown Thurman, 150 Railroad Street, Whitesburg, GA

Sources: *Thurman Family History* by William Taylor Thurman Jr., *Smith's Chapel History* by Rev. Seaborn C. Campbell

The G.W. Tisinger Family of Victory

1101. The Tisinger Family of Victory

David Franklin Tisinger married Sarah Rebecca Freeman on November 25, 1854, in Talbot County, Georgia. He served during the Civil War, in Company C, 3rd Georgia Calvary; and the 20th Alabama Light Artillery, before being ordered to the Quartermaster Corp. and Government Shop in Columbus to help repair wagons for the Confederate wagon trains. After the Civil War, David was a wheelwright who made carriages and buggies. He moved to Bowdon with his family in 1874 to be near Bowdon College. Just before they moved, their eight-year-old son Robert died in Talbot County; and soon after they got to Bowdon, their son Thomas, age fifteen, died. He is buried at Bowdon Methodist Church Cemetery. Their other children were Benjamin Franklin who lived in Texas, Edna Eloise who married Sidney Brown, George Washington, Annie Davie who married James Lavendar Thurman, and Lizzie Amanda who married Robert Morris.

David's parents, George W. Tisinger and Malinda Smoot Matteauer came from North Carolina, to Upson County, Georgia, after receiving land in the 1827 Land Lottery. Their children were Robert Smoot, James Stinson, David Franklin, Edward Tamplin and Caroline Elizabeth.

David's son, George W. Tisinger, was born November 25, 1860, in Talbot County, and died January 29, 1926, in Carroll County of complications from having several teeth pulled. At that time, all of the family gathered in a circle at their house and vowed to support and take care of their mother and each other. His wife, Ida Bibb McDaniel was born in Bowdon on January 1, 1862, and died October 2, 1943. She moved with her family to Victory the Christmas of 1878. She was the daughter of George A. and Martha Lavendar McDaniel.

The G.W. Tisinger Family has been a vital part of the Victory community since he married Ida McDaniel in October 26, 1887. Around 1920, as the family grew bigger, George built a large stately two-story home over four years as the crops came in. A lovely pecan grove stands across the road from their home today. Their nine children as shown in the photo are George Elmer, Harvey, Bob, Nell, mother Ida, Mary, Pansy, Tom, Lavendar and Julian.

Mary was an assistant principal at the 5th District A & M school in Monroe, Georgia. She was an artist, and enjoyed growing flowers. She married George King. Nell was a schoolteacher at Sackville and Farmer's High in Carroll County. She married George Chambers. Their children are George, Eugene, and Ethan Alvin. Alvin and his son George manage a large cattle farm in the Victory community.

Thomas was a captain in the Army during World War I, and was a realtor in Atlanta. Dr. Emmett L. was head surgeon in San Bernardino, California, Julian was a farm manager in Carroll County, George Elmer was a tariff rate clerk for Southern Railway, and Harvey was an attorney in Carrollton. Harvey was only four feet five inches tall, but was very tough in the courtroom. For many years, he served as a District attorney in Atlanta.

Pansy graduated in 1926 with the first nursing class at Emory University (where she nursed Asa G. Candler). Upon graduation, she went to California to work at Hollywood Hospital. She nursed cowboy movie star, Tom Mix, when his horse kicked him. She was superintendent of the Carrollton Clinic, and the first nurse at Southwire. She married Herman F. Brown. They operated the Cottage Hill Farms and later Cottage Hill Greenhouses. Their children are David Robert and Gwyn. (See Daniel Brown family).

Robert David was a lawyer and judge and established the distinguished law firm of Tisinger, Tisinger, Vance & Greer in Carrollton. He was a pioneer in rural electrification, farmed and served in many organizations for improvement in the community. (See Judge Robert David Tisinger) He married Naomi Evans. Their sons are David Harvey and Richard (Dick) Gardner Tisinger. David's sons are John David and Joel. Dick's sons are Richard and Russell (Russ). Richard married Susan Del Mastro, June 20, 1992. Their children are Katie and Andrew (twins) and Sophie. *Submitted by: Dick Tisinger, 208 Old Hickory Trail, Carrollton, GA 30117*

Source: Family

1102. Tolbert

Jesse Herd Tolbert great-grandson to Roland A. Tolbert who came to Villa Rica to mine for gold around 1828.

Jess Herd Tolbert was born in Villa Rica, Georgia, on May 15, 1882 to John Thomas Harrison Tolbert 1860-1947 and Nancy Susan Elizabeth Elliott 1859-1914. Jesse died May 5, 1960. He married Eliza Jane Waldrop on December 1, 1907, in Villa Rica and she was born August 18, 1886, to William Henry Waldrop 1858-1932 and Marther Elizabeth Woods 1862-1932. Eliza died December 26, 1978. Jesse and Eliza are both buried in Hillcrest Cemetery in Villa Rica.

Eliza and Jesse Tolbert and granddaughter Patricia Tolbert Nelson. 1948

Jesse farmed in the Flat Rock area till about 1927. When they moved from Flat Rock area they loaded up the farm wagons and put two year old Oscar on the back of the hog so he would not get lost or hurt. Trying to keep all the livestock together, it took them all day to go about ten miles. They farmed 1927 till around 1945 close to the Callie Harbin Missionary Baptist Church area. Jesse and sons farmed with seven mules and plows. Most of the seven sons were not tall enough to plow till their father modified some of the plows shorter for them. The rest of the children, who were not plowing, had to hoe the field. They grew cotton, corn, and grain. Then in 1945, they moved to town on Candler Street in Villa Rica.

Bill, John, Paul, Edgar, Oscar served in World War II. All five sons came home.

Jesse still had a large garden in town and worked in the sulfur mines on Highway 61 and worked as a night watchman at the mills in Villa Rica.

Jesse and Eliza's children and grandchildren are: (1) William Jack 1909-1927, spouse, Corine Harbine, children Jack, Tommy, and Tony. (2) Mary Elizabeth 1910-1954, spouse James Clyde Furr, children Jean, Mary Nell, Betty, Billy 1935-1987, Wendell, and Larry. (3) Thomas Wiburn (Bill) 1912-2000. (4) Abraham Harry 1914-1918. (5) Robert Herd 1815, spouse Virginia Bell Braswell 1923-1988, children Sandra and Richard. (6) Sarah Betty 1917-1995, spouse Lewis Jackson Brown, children Shirley 1937-1995, Marion 1940-1974, Edward, Jane, Bobby, and Wayne. Second spouse John William Capes 1933-1991, their child Ray. (7) John Frank 1919-1998. (8) Paul Leonard 1920, spouse Margaret Maxine Massengill 1925-1987, children Patricia, Ilene, Annette, Diane, and Charlene. Second spouse Glennie Watkins 1929. (9) Edgar Ray 1922, spouse Elouise Lovell, children Judy and Terry 1949-1973. (10) Oscar James 1925-2000, spouse Betty Turner.

Paul Leonard Tolbert worked at the Roberts Lumber Company from 1935 to 1942. On January 5, 1942, Paul enlisted into the army and came out October 8, 1945, as a sergeant of the 1928th Quartermasters Truck Company. He was in the battles and campaigns, Algeria - French, Moroccan, Tunisia and Sicilian.

Paul married Margaret Maxine Massengill December 23, 1945, in Villa Rica. Their children are: (1) Patricia 1947, married David Arthur Nelson, their children are David A. Nelson Jr. and Juanita Evonne. (2) Ilene 1948, married Bennie Nelson, their children are Edwain 1965-1966, Bonnie, and Terry. Second spouse of Ilene is Gene Bowman (3) Annette 1952, married Wayne Coleman, children are Samantha, Wanda, and Elizabeth. Second spouse of Annette is Gray Castile. (4) Diane 1953, married Eugene Fain, children are Gregory, David, LaGina. Diane's second spouse is Tim Wilkerson. (5) Charlene 1957, married Tony Wasno, her child is Tracy.

Paul Leonard Tolbert. 1942

Patricia Elaine Tolbert married David Arthur Nelson on August 18, 1963. He was born November 20, 1942. Their children are: (1) David Arthur Nelson Jr. born November 17, 1964, in Villa Rica. (2) Juanita Evonne Nelson born November 24, 1966 in Villa Rica. She married David Arthur Cox August 27, 1989, and their children are Patricia Ann Patty Cox and Lee Benjamin Cox both born January 29, 1991.

Submitted by: Patricia Tolbert Nelson, 2789 Kellogg Creek Road, Acworth, GA 30102

1103. Tolbert
1828 to 2001

Thomas Tolbert, born in Ireland, came to America around 1750. He married Judia Reeves. One of their children was Thomas Tolbert who was born 1780 in Montgomery County, North Carolina, and died after 1860 in Carroll County.

Thomas married Lucy Andrews (born 1773, Mecklenburg, Virginia, died after 1850, Carroll County) in 1798 in Randolph County, North Carolina. Her parents were Roland Andrews, who died 1786 in Randolph County, and Henrietter. Thomas and Lucy had a son Hezekiah Andrews (born January 19, 1793, died December 25, 1864, Randolph County), who was in the War of 1812. On September 18, 1818, he married Delancy D. Jordan in Randolph County. In 1860, at the age of eighty, Thomas, a farmer, had Leaner 35, Netta 19, Noah 7, Uriah 5, and a six-month-old female in his household.

Roland A. Tolbert, 1799-1896

Thomas and Lucy Tolbert's children were:

(1) Roland Rowland A. (born July 3, 1799, in Randolph County, North Carolina, and died July 1, 1896, Villa Rica), who married Elizabeth Tolbert (born January 30, 1795, Randolph County, died March 25, 1872), daughter of Josiah Tolbert (1770-1855 Randolph County) and Bersheba Cranford (born 1770 in North Carolina, died after 1850 in Randolph County). Both are buried in Hillcrest Cemetery, Villa Rica. Roland was a private in the Georgia militia, Captain Jiles S. Boggess's "Turks." He helped to remove the Indians to Oklahoma on the Trail of Tears. On the trip back home to Villa Rica, winter set in and food was scarce. He and others traveling with him were so hungry that they ate their mules to survive. Roland A. served as a constable in 642nd GM district for more than fifty years. He was a Democrat from the beginning of the party. He had no patience with carpetbaggers. Roland was a member of the Methodist Church. He came to Georgia around 1827 and arrived in Villa Rica about 1828 to work in the gold mines. He worked the mines until 1850. Afterward, he farmed until 1870. He lived with his son Josiah Thomas Tolbert until he died;

(2) Osborn (born 1804, died February 13, 1880, in Pickens County, Georgia), who married Martha Lucinda Wiley (born 1803, died March 9, 1882);

(3) Harmon (born November 10, 1806, in Randolph County, North Carolina, and died September 21, 1892, in Madison County, Georgia), who married Permelia Williams;

(4) Female, born 1800;

(5) Thomas M. (born 1813 in Randolph County) who married first Martha Lamb, born 1814 in North Carolina, and second Elizabeth;

(6) Richard (born August 23, 1815, Randolph County and died 1888), who married Mary E. Ledbetter, born March 2, 1830. He is buried at Wesley Chapel, Carroll County.

Roland A. and Elizabeth Tolbert's children were:

(1) Clark (born July 11, 1820, in North Carolina, and died July 11, 1869), who married Elizabeth Taylor born (1824) on November 20, 1842, in Carroll County. Their children were Elisha, born 1853; Henry, born 1845; Syrus, born 1847; David, born 1849; and Amanda, born 1850;

(2) William H., born 1823 in North Carolina, who married Milly (born 1822). Their children were Elizabeth, born 1843; Josephine, born 1845; Mary, born 1847; and unnamed child, born 1850;

(3) Mary Ann, born 1829, who married James R. Mathews (born 1827) on January 1, 1850, in Carroll County;

(4) Lucy, born January 30, 1831, in Villa Rica and died December 28, 1917, Paulding County, Georgia, married John Walker Mathews (1822-1892). Their children were James Rowland (1849-1927), who married Nancy White; Gilbert Smith (1851-1929), who married Augusta McCurdy; Mary Isola (1853-1922), who married Jack Eubanks; Lucy Oriziba (1855-1856); John Thomas (1858-1931), who married Emma Hargroves; William Glenn (1860-1950); Robert Burrell (1867-1957), who married Sallie S. Driskell; Lillie Allice (1871-1943), who married Joseph Marion Fuller;

(5) Roland Harris (born February 28, 1833, in Villa Rica, died July 8, 1862, (Atlanta Hospital during Civil War), who married Emily Luther (June 23, 1834, in North Carolina, died March 11, 1910) on October 26, 1854, in Carroll County. Both are buried in Hillcrest Cemetery, Villa Rica. Emily was the daughter of Isaac Luther and Sarah F. Loflin. Roland and Emily's children were (1) John Thomas Harrison (1860-1947), who married Nancy Susan Elizabeth Elliott (1859-1914); (2) Mary Jane "Mollie" (1858-1937), who married Edwin Jackson Elliott (1856-1907). Their children were Roland Harrison, born 1878, who married Annie; John Wilborne, born 1885; and Bertha M., born 1881, who married Tolbert Baswell; and (6) Josiah Thomas, born 1836 in Villa Rica, who married Elizabeth on December 19, 1866. Their children were Thomas W., born 1868, who married Julia Stone; Elizabeth, born 1870; Lyman; Minnie; Elba; Abby; and Montra.

John Thomas Harrison Tolbert, 1860-1947

John Thomas Harrison Tolbert (December 7, 1860-February 8, 1947) married Nancy Susan Elizabeth Elliott (September 18, 1859-1914), daughter of Doctor Ewell Elliott and Rose Eiseman. Their children were (1) Jesse Herd (1882, Villa Rica-1960), who married Eliza Jane Waldrop (1886-1978). Their children were William Jack (1909-1972), who married Corine Harbine; Mary Elizabeth (1910-1954), who married James Furr; Thomas Wilburn "Bill" (1912-2000); Abraham Harry (1914-1918); Robert Herd, born 1915, who married Virginia Braswell (1923-1988); Sarah Betty (1917-1995), who married first Lewis Brown and second John Capes (1933-1991); John Frank (1919-1998); Paul Leonard, born 1920, who married first Margaret Maxine Massengill (1925-1987) and second Glennie Watkins, born 1929; Edgar Ray, born

1922, who married Elouise Lovell; and Oscar James (1925-2000), who married Betty Turner; (2) Elizabeth Lizzie (1884-1958), who married Thomas Taft, died 1961; (3) John Eual Harrison, born 1886, who married Emma Lou Waldrop (1891-1974). Their children are John Harold, born 1915, who married Annie Spain (1916-1988) and Bertha Louise, born 1917, who married Terrell Towns, born 1912; (4) Edker Eugene (1889-1949), who married Sophia Noland (1896-1973). Their children are Frank Eugene (1913-1992), who married Charlotte Ragsdale; Ellie Doris, born 1916, who married Charles Hallman; James Roland, born 1919; Donald Albert, born 1924, who married Tibbie Gibbs, born 1925; William Gordon, born 1927, who married Carolyn Barker, born 1930; Shuley (1932-1980), who married Eugene Chapman; and Louis Marie, born 1935, who married William Willis; (5) Maude Odessa (1892-1983), who married Ester Brackett (1884-1936). Their children are Edith Eugene, born 1923, who married Howard Wagon; and Mildred Ruth (1927-1983), who married Warren Webb, died 1987. *Submitted by: Diane Wilkerson, 6 Cardinal Drive, Austell, GA 30168*
Source: Patricia Tolbert Nelson, 2789 Kellogg Creek Road, Acworth, GA 30120

1104. Tolbert - Matthews

Roland Tolbert was born in North Carolina in July 1799. He came to the area of Carroll County now known as Villa Rica by the late 1820s. It was first called Hix Town. The area was originally Creek Indian land. He worked in the gold mines and was one of the early constables. The name Villa Rica means City of Gold. He was married to Mary Elizabeth Andrews. Census records show she also was born in North Carolina. They had several children. I'm not sure how many. After the death of Elizabeth, Roland lived with their son, Josiah. Roland died in 1896.

Roland and Elizabeth had a daughter, Lucy born in 1831. She married John Matthews who was born in July 1822 in Henry County. John and Lucy had eight children. John served in the Confederate Army, 43rd Infantry Division, organized at Big Shanty, Georgia, in April 1862. The division consisted of men from several counties including Cherokee, Pickens, Cobb and Forsyth. The unit moved to Tennessee, then Mississippi, under the command of General Barton. It was involved in the conflicts at Chickasaw Bayou and Champion's Hill, and was captured when Vicksburg fell. After being exchanged, the 43rd was assigned to General Stovall's Brigade, Army of Tennessee.

Robert Burl Matthews, 1867-1957

They were in numerous campaigns of the Army from Missionary Ridge to Nashville, and ended the war in North Carolina. In December 1863, it totaled 283 men and in November 1864 there were only 130 fit for duty. On April 26, 1865, the unit surrendered. Some commanding officers were Colonels Bell, Harris, and Kellogg.

Roland, Bill, Gilbert, and Ivan Matthews. Early 1940s.

Fortunately John made it home safely because his two youngest children were born after the war.

One was my grandfather, Robert, born in December 1867. When Rob, as he was called, was nineteen and already engaged to be married, he met a pretty fifteen-year-old girl with long auburn hair. He broke his engagement that same day. The girl, Sallie Driskell, was an orphan whose father, Dr. William Driskell, had also served in the Confederate Army. Rob and Sallie Matthews were married in 1887. They had fifteen children, fourteen lived to grow up. My father, Roland Matthews, was their eleventh child. He was a namesake of his great-grandfather, born April 20, 1908. He would laugh and say April 20th was a holiday. To me, it was.

In the 1940s when I was a little girl, we lived out on what is now Highway 61 in the same direction where Roland Tolbert had worked in the gold mines a hundred years before. *Submitted by: N.M. Bryan, 3183 Country Club Court, Kennesaw, GA 30144*
Sources: Family history, census records, and Georgia Confederate records.

1105. George James Towns and Maiden Lou Stallings Towns Family

George James Towns, born November 29, 1882, died May 3, 1949. His parents, Reason Augustus Towns, born in Dooley County, July 22, 1840, died May 4, 1904; Mary Annie White Towns, born September 23, 1844, died May 21, 1911, on November 12, 1905, he married Maiden Lou Stallings, born January 15, 1887, died December 9, 1990. Her parents, Madison Augustus Stallings, born September 26, 1857, died January 3, 1925 and Dora Zene Wood. Madison's parents were Duke W. Stallings, born 1834, died 1922, and Martha Fields White, born February 18, 1825, died December 4, 1905, married 1849.

George and Maiden married November 4, 1883. They had eight children; Vernon Lyndell (Big Brother) born September 23, 1906, died June 10, 1990, married Lucille Williams; Velma Rosell (Sister) born January 24, 1909, married Loonie G. Johnson December 30, 1928; Robert Daniel (Bob) born December 19, 1912, died April 9, 1989, married Onie Ruth Buchanan June 10, 1933, and Sara Dadisman May 23, 1953; Terrell Augustis, born December 19, 1912, married Louise Tolbert, May 14, 1938; Ollie Mae born October 11, 1914; Dora Ethel Towns born December 29, 1916, died February 12, 1995, married Hubert Arlin (Bud) Dean, November 7, 1937; Dorothy Jean (Dot) born March 29, 1919, died August 24, 1999, married Charles B. Conant April 25, 1938; George James Jr. born August 26, 1923, died March 5, 1999, married Juanita (Nita) Jackson, Christine Caldwell, and Dorothy Williams.

George's family came to Carroll County from South Georgia where the family owned a plantation, losing much of the family holdings during Civil War. His mother, Mary Annie White, attended the first class at Tift College at a time when many young ladies were not fortunate enough to further their education. Some members of the family moved to the western states.

Most of George's adult life was spent as a farmer, carpenter, and baliff. One interesting building project George is credited with is the old Roopville jail, presently owned by Judson Bell. It was built with the 1 X 4 planks stacked onto one another, the ceiling was filled with stones to make escaping more difficult. The jail had one small window and door. Many of the local prisoners were kept for a short time until they could be transported to Carrollton. Several carpentry and farming tools which George used, and later his son Vernon, have been donated to the Roopville Archive.

Maiden (Madie) stayed busy with the responsibilities of wife and mother to her large family. She was frequently called upon by neighbors and friends to minister first aid. Madie enjoyed helping others and later in life was among the first group of ladies to do volunteer work at Tanner Memorial Hospital, known as Gray Ladies. Madie was a faithful and loyal member of Roopville Baptist Church. Her parents, Dora and Madison Stallings, were founding members of the church.

Madie and George loved their grandchildren. When George knew the little ones were coming to visit, he would be sure to have candy hidden. If they came unannounced, he was up early the next morning, walking or riding a mule to town to get the candy. He was affectionately called "Big Daddy" by all of the eleven grandchildren. Big Daddy had a large pocket watch which he would proudly show to the little ones, letting them hear its tick tock.

George, who had been a share cropper during the time he was raising his family, built a new house on Highway 5, in Roopville in the 1940s. He was able to complete the house working when he could although he was not in good health. He wanted to provide a good home for Madie to spend the rest of her life. Her life extended far beyond the average. She lived to be 105 years young. Though her last fifteen years were spent living with others or in a nursing home, she had many good years in Roopville.

George James Towns and Maiden Lou Stallings Towns

Vernon remained on the family farm for several years assisting his father and later found work in the Atlanta area. He was called into service during World War II. He and his wife first lived in Atlanta, later purchasing a farm in Winston. They had no children.

Velma and Loonie lived in the Roopville area a few years; their first child, Wylene, was born there, later moving to Atlanta where daughter Eleanor was born. Velma now resides at Meadow Brooks Nursing Home.

Bob left for Atlanta after finishing school, working most of his years at Nabisco Company, he and Onie had one daughter, Patsy. Bob and Sara had no children.

Ted went to Atlanta and worked at Nabisco Company. He and Louise had one son, Terrell T. (Buddy) and daughter, Donna. Ted and Louise reside in Conyers.

Ollie went to Atlanta and trained to be a beautician. She owned a shop with eleven employees, retired in 1979, worked part-time till she was eighty years old. Ollie did not marry but claimed all of her nieces and nephews as "her children." She is loved by them all.

Dora and Bud remained in Roopville, had three daughters, Rebecca, Linda, and Beverly and one son, Steven. (See the article on H.A. and Dora Dean)

Dorothy and Charles met in school, married, and moved to Florida. Charles worked at a hospital, served in the Army, and later employed by NASA. They had two daughters, Carolyn and Cynthia.

James finished school, worked in Atlanta, served in the Army, then returned to the Atlanta area. James had no children. *Submitted by: Ollie M. Towns, 503 Highland Avenue, Palmetto, GA and Researched by: Rebecca D. Merrell*
Sources: Family Bible and relatives

1106. Family of William Traylor

William Traylor was born March 29, 1891, in Randolph County, Alabama. He married Emma Cosper November 11, 1916. He moved to Carrollton in 1919 to manage The Farmers Store located on City Hall Avenue. He managed the store for almost forty years. He was a leader in The First Christian Church until his death January 7, 1970. He was one of the organizers of Carrollton Federal S & L, was on the board of the Peoples Bank, and was an active member of the Lions Club. He served on the Carrollton School Board and served one term as mayor of Carrollton.

The Traylor family first lived on Tanner Street, then on Cedar Street. They rebuilt the Dr. Hitchcock house on Stewart Street in 1936 and lived there until their death in 1973.

Mrs. Traylor was very active as a homemaker. She was also very active in the PTA, the Garden Club and the First Methodist Church. She was very talented as a gardener and was proud of the gardens around her home.

The Traylors had two children, Hilma born July 7, 1921, and William Jr. born November 3, 1929.

Hilma attended West Georgia College and graduated from the University of Georgia. She married John E. Freeman of Millegeville. They had two daughters and now live in the Atlanta area.

William Jr. attended West Georgia College and graduated from the University of Georgia. She married John E. Freeman of Millegeville. They had two daughters and now live in the Atlanta area.

William Jr. attended West Georgia College and graduated from Emory University. He married Betty Plexico of Lancaster South Carolina, June 3, 1950. They have four children, Terri born October 15, 1954, William P. III born November 18, 1955, Sloane born November 22, 1957, and Susan born March 6, 1962.

William Jr. served in U.S. Army 1952-1954 during the Korean Conflict.

He operated Traylor's Feed Mill from 1955 to 1965. He built and operated the first fast food drive in restaurant in Carrollton called the T Burger from 1962 until he was hired as city manager for Carrollton in 1973. He served the City of Carrollton for the next twenty-five years as Community Development director and the last thirteen years as executive director of the Housing Authority and Community Development director.

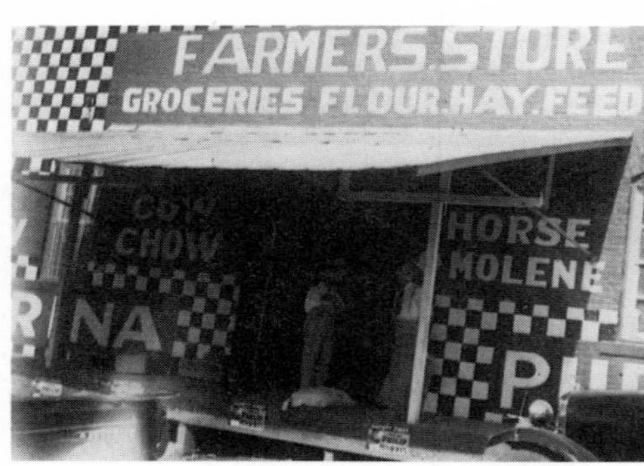

Farmers Store, City Hall Avenue, J.L. Talley center William Traylor right.

He has been a lifelong active member of the First United Methodist Church. He served eight years as a city councilmen, was active in the Jaycees, was an Eagle Scout and served as Cub master and scoutmaster.

Mrs. Traylor was a homemaker for her children until she went to work as an accountant in the business office of West Georgia College until she retired in 1992. *Submitted by: William Traylor Jr., 321 Almon Road, Carrollton, GA 30117*

1107. Coleman Clay Turner

Coleman Clay Turner was born on 25 July 1898 on Oak Mountain in Carroll County, the eldest son of Edmund Lee Turner and Idella Chastain Turner. Known as "Coley," he grew up on the family farm at Oak Mountain and attended the nearby Pleasant Hill school. On 17 March 1918 he married Nettie Roena James, the daughter of Jerusha Elizabeth Broom and Samuel Reese James of Sand Hill. Nettie Roena was born in Sand Hill on 1 July 1897.

The Turners began married life as farmers near Pleasant Hill, but in early 1920 Coley accepted a position as postal clerk in Atlanta. In November 1920 they returned to Carroll County, moving from Atlanta to Whitesburg, and Coley served as the Banning postal carrier from 1921 to 1928. He and Nettie joined the Whitesburg Christian Church in 1921 and he began studying for the ministry. In 1925 he was ordained as a minister in the Christian Church, in 1926 founded the Cross Plains Christian Church and was pastor there from 1926 to 1931. He was pastor of the Ephesus Christian Church in 1932 and 1933, the Whitesburg Christian Church from 1934 until 1937, and the Banning community church from 1938 to 1941.

In 1929 Coley was licensed by the state of Georgia as a school teacher and taught in the Carroll County school system at Whooping Creek, Clem, Rotherwood, and Cross Plains until 1933. In 1934 he took a position at the Banning mill, moving to Banning from Whitesburg in 1938. At the beginning of the war in 1941, Coley accepted a position with the government at the Atlanta Quartermaster Depot and the family moved from Banning to East Point, Georgia, where Nettie and Coley lived until he retired in 1963. During this period he was pastor of several Atlanta area churches. In 1963 he and Nettie moved to Pantego in Beaufort County, North Carolina, at the urging of two sons who lived in that state. He served a number of churches in eastern North Carolina over the next decade.

Coleman Clay Turner

Nettie and Coley Turner were the parents of five children. Ruth, born at Sand Hill in 1919, married Ira Dorsey Knott in Whitesburg in 1936. Carl, died in infancy in 1920 at Atlanta, is buried at the Temperance Methodist Church Cemetery in Sand Hill. Harold Clay, born at Whitesburg in 1922, married Dorothy Pece in East Point in 1942, and died in North Carolina in 1985. Coleman Reese, born at Whitesburg in 1925, married Jane Hughes in 1948 in Mississippi, and died in North Carolina in 1999. Alfred, born at Clem in 1929, married Betty Anne Cartee in 1956 in Atlanta.

Nettie Roena Turner died on 7 February 1975 in Washington County, North Carolina, and is buried at the Davis Cemetery, Pantego, North Carolina. In 1987 Coleman Clay Turner returned to Georgia to live with his daughter, Ruth, and died in Carrollton on 25 August 1988. He is buried in the Davis Cemetery, Pantego, North Carolina. *Submitted by: Anne Childs, 12451 N. Shawdee Drive, Huntsville, AL 35803*

1108. Edmund Lee Turner

Edmund Lee Turner was born on 14 September 1870 in Washington County, Texas to Irvin Scott and Mary Cooper Turner. His father was a native of Carroll County, Georgia, and a former Confederate soldier who had gone to Texas following the War. (See related Irvin Scott Turner article) Edmund was eight years old when his father brought the family to Carroll County in 1878, purchasing farmland in the Hickory Level community where Edmund and his siblings attended school. About 1886, the family moved a few miles south to a farm near Sand Hill.

Edmund worked on his father's farm until the summer of 1892. On 30 August 1892 he married Idella Chastain at Powell's Chapel Methodist Church in Carroll County, near the old Campbell County line and about two miles from his home. Idella Chastain was born on 6 July 1876 in Carroll County to James Henry and Julia Ann Ayers Chastain.

Edmund and Idella Turner first lived near Villa Rica and became members of the New Hope Primitive Baptist Church in old Campbell County. About 1897 they moved to Oak Mountain near Carrollton. Edmund farmed on about forty acres of land near the intersection of what are now Oak Mountain Road and Truitt Road and supplemented the family income by doing carpentry work. In 1907 Edmund and Idella moved their membership from the New Hope Primitive Church to the Hopewell (Old Carrollton) Primitive Baptist Church near Sand Hill. Edmund served as church clerk there for about twelve years.

Ed and 'Della Turner

Edmund and Idella were the parents of nine children and seven were born on Oak Mountain. The first two were Lavonia Naomi, born and died in 1893 and Ola, born and died in 1897. The first child born on Oak Mountain was Coleman Clay, born in 1897, married to Nettie James in 1917, and died in 1988. Alta Maud was born in 1900 and died in 1933. Joyce Lougenia was born in 1904, married James Duncan in 1929, and died in 1989. Mattie Novella was born in 1906, married Gaines Preston McLendon in 1923, and died in Fulton County in 1995. Henry Scott was born in 1908, married Eubie Word in 1940, and died in Clayton County in 1974. Julia Edna was born in 1911, married (1) Seaborn Roddy in 1931 and (2) Marion Ozburn about 1970, and died in Gwinnett County in 1990. Hugh Lee was born in 1916, married Irene Wilson in 1939, and died in Clayton County in 1985.

In 1929 Edmund Turner sold his property on Oak Mountain, having been in poor health for several years and unable to continue farming, and moved to Longview Street in Carrollton. He died there on 26 August 1935 and was buried in the Hopewell Primitive Baptist Church cemetery. Idella Turner moved to East Center Street in Carrollton where she supported herself and the family as a seamstress. She died there on 8 January 1942 and was buried beside her husband in the Hopewell cemetery. *Submitted by: David Turner, P.O. Box 221532, Chantilly, VA 20153*

1109. Hiram Turner

Hiram Turner was born on 22 August 1811 in Jasper County, Georgia, the son of Larkin and Eleanor Leah Driskill Turner. When the family came to the Hickory Level community of Carroll County in early 1828, he helped his father construct a log cabin for the family and clear land for planting crops, and for the next four years helped tend the farm.

On 3 January 1833 he married Arminda Louisa Caroline Williamson in Carroll County with the Reverend James Baskin officiating. Arminda Louisa Caroline Williamson, known as Caroline, was born on 11 November 1816 in Jackson County, Georgia, the daughter of John and Sarah Braswell Williamson who came to Carroll County in 1831. In February 1837 Hiram Turner purchased the land adjacent to his father's property in Hickory Level and here grew a variety of crops and livestock.

There were thirteen children born to Caroline and Hiram Turner in Carroll County. Frances Minerva Sophrona Allethia was born in 1834 and married William Bryce in Carroll County in 1851. They moved to Texas and then to the Oklahoma Territory where she died before 1900. Levi John Wooten was born in 1835, married Sarah Pollard about 1865 and moved to Rusk County, Texas, where he died in 1915. Larkin James Allen was born in 1837, married Julia Embry in 1871 in Carroll County, and died there in 1916. Irvin Scott Turner was born in 1839, married Mary Cooper in Washington County, Texas, in 1869, and died in Carroll County in 1900. (See related Irvin Scott Turner article). Sarah Arminda Leah was born in 1841, married Joseph Eaton in Carroll County in 1860, and died in Cobb County in 1920. William Hiram was born in 1843 and died in 1862 in Virginia. Mary Caroline was born in 1845, married Alexander Broom in 1866 in Carroll County, and died in Etowah County, Alabama, after 1900. Riley Fletcher was born in 1847, married Elizabeth Hesterly in 1866 in Carroll County and died there in 1930. Daniel Lee was born in 1849 and died in 1855. Alfred Dorman was born in 1851, married Mary Baskin in Carroll County in 1875 and died there in 1912. Sarah Laura Ann was born in 1853, married first Millard Filmore Sims in 1871 in Carroll County and second Charles Bird in 1896 in Rusk County, Texas. She died in Rusk County in 1928. Martin Grey was born in 1857 and died in 1858. Martha T.L. was born in 1860, married Jones Cooper in Carroll County in 1882 where she died in 1908. Five of Hiram's sons were Confederate soldiers in Georgia units: Levi in Cobb's Legion; Larkin in the 56th Infantry; Irvin in the 13th Infantry; William in Cobb's Legion; and Riley in the 56th Infantry. Of the five, only William did not survive the war.

Hiram Turner died 30 December 1864 and Caroline Turner died on 6 May 1877, both in Carroll County. They are buried in the Concord Methodist Church cemetery in Hickory Level. *Submitted by: Becky West, 401 Northwood Road, Washington, NC 27889; and Researched by: Anne Childs*

1110. Irvin Scott Turner

Irvin Scott Turner was born on 18 March 1839 in Carroll County, Georgia, to Hiram and Caroline Williamson Turner who lived in the Hickory Level community of Carroll County. He attended school in Hickory Level and was a member of the Concord Methodist Church. Scott, as he preferred to be called, was employed on the plantation of his uncle, Riley Turner, in Meriwether County in 1861 when he was called into the service of the Confederacy.

Irvin Scott Turner

On 8 July 1861 he enlisted as a private in Company B, 13th Regiment, Georgia Volunteer Infantry at Greenville, Georgia. The company was mustered in at Griffin in Spalding County, Georgia, on 13 July 1861, then went to DeKalb County, Georgia, for indoctrination after which they were sent to Henrico County, Virginia, for training. The regiment was assigned to western Virginia but in December 1861 they were transferred south after a report by the Inspector General, which said in part "the severe winter of western Virginia will be fatal to these southern men." They spent the winter and the spring on the Georgia coast near Savannah. Scott Turner was assigned duties as a teamster in May 1862 at Camp Causton's Bluff, in Chatham County, Georgia. The regiment returned to Virginia on 7 June 1862, saw action at Gaine's Mill on 27 June 1862 and at Malvern Hill on 1 July 1862, suffered casualties in the battles at Bristol Station, Crampton's Gap, Sharpsburg, and Fredricksburg in 1862 and at Gettysburg in July 1863. In September 1863, Scott Turner was assigned duties as an ambulance driver. The regiment had more casualties in 1864 at Wilderness, Spotsylvania, Cold Harbor, and Cedar Creek, Virginia, and surrendered at Appomatox Courthouse, Virginia on 9 April 1865.

Scott Turner returned to Carroll County but went to Texas before 1867, settling in Washington County, and started a business building wagons. He married Mary Louginia Cooper in Washington County on 17 January 1869. She was the daughter of James Cooper and Amelia Bobo Cooper who had come to Texas from Union County, South Carolina in 1865. Scott Turner's father died in 1864 and his mother died in 1877 in Carroll County, leaving a sizable estate to be divided among the children, so he returned to Carroll County by 1878 and purchased farm land in Hickory Level. By 1886 he had sold this land and purchased property east of Sand Hill near the northern shore of Treasure Lake.

The first six children of Irvin Scott Turner and Mary Cooper were born in Washington County, Texas, and the rest were born in Carroll County, Georgia. They were James Hiram, Edmund Lee, Hardy Smith, Mamie C., Eula Eugenia, Martha Jones, Georgia Laura Ann, Buren Robert, Bert Scott, Jeanette Beatrice, Nora Estelle, Raymond Hill, and Earl Victor. (See related Edmund Lee Turner article).

Irving Scott Turner died on 25 June 1900 in Carroll County and Mary Cooper Turner died on 7 January 1920 in Carroll County. Both are buried in the Concord Methodist Church Cemetery at Hickory Level. *Submitted by: Mike Turner, 750 Ashfield Dr., Fayetteville, NC 28311*

1111. Larkin Turner

Larkin Turner was born on 15 April 1770 in Virginia. In 1798 he married Eleanor Leah Driskill in Hancock County, Georgia. She was born in 1778 in Maryland. Larkin Turner was in Hancock County as early as 1795, moved to Jasper County about 1808, and to Butts County in 1826. He and Eleanor came to Carroll County in early 1828 with nine of their eleven children and built a home in the Hickory Level community about one mile east of the Concord Methodist Church. Larkin was a farmer, growing cotton, corn, oats, and wheat and he also raised cattle, sheep, and swine. He was a Justice of the Peace in Carroll County in 1831.

The children of Larkin and Eleanor were born in Hancock and Jasper counties. Tabitha, born 1801, married James Herrin about 1823. Tabitha and James Herrin came to Carroll County with Larkin Turner but moved to Tallapoosa County, Alabama, in 1836. Tabitha died there in 1838. Lavinia, born 1805, married Neill Stone about 1820. Neill Stone became the first sheriff of Carroll County, sworn into office 17 March 1828. The Stones had moved to Cobb County by 1840 and then to Campbell County about 1850. Riley was born in 1807. He did not come to Carroll County with his parents, going instead to Meriwether County with his sister, Allethia, who was born in 1809. Her husband was Levi M. Adams, a founding father of

Greenville, which became the county seat of Meriwether County. He was clerk of the Ordinary and Superior courts in Meriwether County for many years.

The sixth child was Emily, born in 1810. She married Thomas Cartwright in 1845 in Carroll County. She died in 1845 and is buried in the Concord Methodist Church Cemetery. Hiram, born in 1811, married Arminda Caroline Williamson in 1833 in Carroll County. He died in 1864 and is buried at Concord. Elizabeth, born 1813, married Alexander Eaton in 1833 in Carroll County. She died in 1904 and is buried in Cobb County. Larkin Lee was born in 1816 and died in 1851. Lurene or Louranie, born 1816, married Isaac Kinney in 1842 in Carroll County. She died in 1857 and is buried at the Concord Cemetery. Leah Eleanor, born 1820, married William Henry in 1841 in Carroll County. She died in 1855 and is believed buried in the Concord Cemetery. Sarah, born in 1824, married Jesse Kinney in 1844 in Carroll County. She died in 1889 and is buried in Asbury Cemetery in Temple.

Eleanor Leah Turner died 18 February 1857 and is buried in an unmarked grave at the Concord Methodist Church Cemetery. In 1863, Larkin disposed of his property and moved into the nearby home of his son Hiram. After Hiram's death in 1864, Larkin moved to Meriwether County to the home of elder son, Riley, where he died on 23 February 1878. He is buried in the family cemetery adjacent to the old Riley Turner home in Oak Ridge, Meriwether County. *Submitted by: David Turner, P.O. Box 221532, Chantilly, VA 20153*

Tallapoosa Community School, John Henry Knight, teacher

1112. Turner - Harman

Thelma Harman was born April 19, 1909, in the Farmers High Community of Carroll County, Georgia, the daughter of William Virgil Harman and Kate Strickland. Whispering Pines, the Strickland home place, was located on Old Camp Church Road. Her mother "Mama Kate" wrote the Tallapoosa Community news for the local paper for sixty years. Thelma Harman Turner has three sisters, Clara Harman Stewart, Ethel Harman Manley, Florence Harman Ford and one brother, now deceased, William Marion Harman.

Mary Elizabeth Strickland, W.V. and Kate Harman, Thelma, Clara and Marion.

On December 25, 1928, Thelma married Charles McNiel Turner, son of Charlie Patillo Turner. Three children were born to Thelma and Niel: Charles Harman Turner, a dentist in Maitland, Florida; William Robert Turner, an executive with Shell Oil who lives in Kingwood, Texas; and Ann Turner Wolf, who lives in Riverdale, Georgia. All three of the children were born in Rome, Georgia, where Thelma and Niel lived for forty-five years. Mrs. Turner has ten grandchildren and eighteen great grandchildren.

Thelma Harman Turner is the great-granddaughter of George Washington Camp who moved to Carroll County from Coweta County in the late 1850s. He had five children, four boys and a girl. He first bought land in the Whitesburg area where he built a mill and a beautiful home. He later purchased about 1500 acres of land in Carrollton. His plantation included what is now the State University of West Georgia. It extended from the present day Highway 27 and Maple St. to the Little Tallapoosa River. In 1875, George Washington Camp was the largest tax payer in Carroll County. He owned a successful mercantile business on the square in Carrollton. His building began at the Rome Street corner of the square and extended to the Johnson Drug Company corner.

Her grandmother, Mary Elizabeth Camp, married Henry Harrison Strickland on December 21, 1871. The wedding took place at the Camp family home, known locally as the Bonner House. The home was located on what became the front campus of West Georgia College. George Washington Camp, along with other community leaders attempted to finance a rail line into Carrollton. A large deposit of granite was found along the proposed line in the Whitesburg area. This delayed the progress and cost the investors so much extra money that Mr. Camp was forced to mortgage his land. His uncle, Hiram Camp, purchased the land and parts of it remained in the Camp family until the 1980s.

Mrs. Turner remembers her grandmother telling that in the summer all the land owners in the surrounding area would hire a preacher and get together at what is now Old Camp Church. There was a large spring there. They would take their children and servants, their cow, and trunks of food that would keep. They spent three days socializing and attending religious services. *Submitted by: Thelma Harman Turner, 102 South St., Carrollton, GA*

1113. Tyson Family

John Henry (Jehu) Tyson (1828-1899) arrived in Carroll County in the 1850s with his mother Penelope and brothers Josiah, Clement, and Alexander. Jehu settled south of Villa Rica near the current Douglas County line on what is now Tyson Road. For Jehu's family, Carroll County was the end of a 200-year journey that included migration from Europe to Virginia in the mid-1600s, with stops in Pitt and Anson Counties in North Carolina, and Meriwether County, Georgia.

The Tysons were farmers and were also active in the community. For example, Josiah was a justice of the peace, and Alexander donated land for the Powell Chapel Methodist Church and cemetery located on Flat Rock Road.

Jehu and his wife Mary Elizabeth Pattillo (1830-1897) raised seven children: Horatio (Rache), William (Willie), Nancy, Joseph, Alice, Ida, and Soloman. In early 1863, Jehu enlisted in the Confederate Army as a private (Captain D.C. Smith's Company, Evans' Regiment, Georgia Infantry). Clement and Alexander also served during the war, and Clement died of pneumonia in a Union prison at Camp Chase, Ohio.

Jehu and Mary Elizabeth are buried at Powell Chapel Cemetery. A freed slave - Aunt Molly Youngblood - continued to live with the family and took care of Mary Elizabeth in her later years. After Mary Elizabeth's death, Molly lived with Mary's youngest son Soloman. She is buried beside Jehu and Mary Elizabeth.

Flat Rock Community Band, early 1900s.

Jehu's grandsons William David (Will D) and Tom inherited portions of the original home place in the 1920s. Will D's children — Wayne, Edna, Mary, Ronald, and Donald — and Tom's children — Doris, Frances, and Bill — recall life on the farm in the 1920s, 30s, and 40s. Some of their fondest memories are of making sorghum syrup at the family's syrup mill.

Area farmers brought their cane to be processed into syrup (on shares) at the mill located in the hollow between the families' home. The mill consisted of two large rollers that were originally powered by mules walking in a circle. In later years, a tractor replaced the mules. The cane was pressed through the rollers and juice ran down a long wooden trough into a shallow metal-lined vat. A very hot fire cooked the juice as it flowed through various sections of the vat. The skim that formed as the liquid boiled was removed with a handmade scoop on a long handle. When fully cooked, the syrup ran out a spout into jars.

Syrup was cooked according to the directions of the person who brought the cane — sometimes thin syrup and other times very

Syrup Mill, early 1900s.

thick. Someone once asked that his syrup be thick enough to hang on a nail in the winter!

Most of the Tyson share of the syrup was sold to supplement their farming income. No one remembers ever getting more than $1.00 a gallon, and the Tysons provided the jars!

Several Tyson families currently live near the original settlement. If you are ever in the area, stop by to discuss the "good old days."

Shown in the Flat Rock Community Band photograph is Will D. Tyson, B. Harper, Tom Tyson, Gene Williams, Sam Edge. Shown at the syrup mill are Will D. Tyson at the pan, and Willie Tyson seated. *Submitted by: Ronald Tyson, 635 Tyson Road, Villa Rica, GA 30180*

1114. Henry Doris Tyson

Henry Doris Tyson was born November 4, 1922, in Carroll County, Georgia. He was the son of John Thomas Tyson and Nora Helen Henslee Tyson. His paternal grandparents were Willie Tyson and Lenora Hay Tyson. His maternal grandparents were Rudolph Sonny Henslee and Laura Ayers Henslee, all of Carroll County. On August 26, 1941, he married Wilma Annette Brasher who was born on July 26, 1924, the daughter of J. Herbert Brasher and Gertrude Blanche Jordan Brasher, all of Carroll County. She is the granddaughter of Uyllus W. Jordan and Bertha Reese Jordan and Thomas W. Brasher and Jessie DeAlva Eady Brasher; great-granddaughter of John T. Eady and Frances E. Dixon Eady.

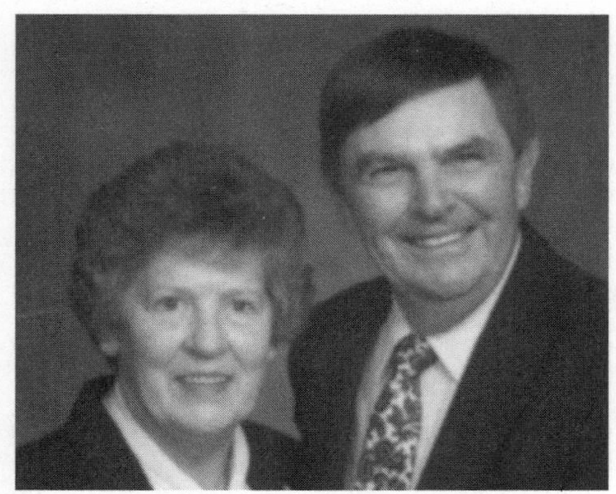

H.D. and Annette Tyson, Sr.

Henry Doris Tyson spent his boyhood years on his father's farm in the Flat Rock community of Carroll County. He is the oldest of three children: sister Frances Tyson Hembree, and brother Wilton B. Tyson. After graduation from Villa Rica High School, he was employed with Roy Richard's Construction Company, Carrollton. He was inducted into the U.S. Army July 17, 1943, serving as first sergeant Battery A 276th Armored Field Artillery Battalion European Theater, World War II. Upon being discharged November 8, 1945, Doris and Annette returned to Carroll County and purchased a farm near Villa Rica. Five children were born and educated in Carroll County: Henry Doris Jr., October 28, 1946, married to Brenda Gail Stegall, Cartersville; Helen Marcella, November 5, 1948, married Lee Thomas Brown Jr., Panama City, Florida; Phyllis Elaine, January 13, 1950, married Phillip Matson Miller Jr., Villa Rica; John Marshall, January 14, 1954, married Julia Bagwell, Augusta; Janie Blanche, September 17, 1960, married Otis Michael Redding, Douglas County. Thirteen grandchildren and two great-grandchildren reside in Georgia.

Henry Doris, Annette and children were members of Flat Rock Baptist Church, Villa Rica. Doris was ordained deacon October 27, 1946, and was church music director and taught Sunday School, always a progressive leader with a vision for his church and community. Doris, Annette, daughters and their families are active members of First Baptist Church, Villa Rica, all active in the music ministries of the church. Doris served on the school board, hospital authority and is a member of the chamber of commerce. He was a home builder/contractor in the Atlanta Metro area until his retirement. His interests are his cattle farm, gardening, flying and traveling with his family. He owns the farm where he was raised in Flat Rock community. His daughter and family reside in the restored home place and share in his cattle farming. The Tyson Reunion is held annually in "The Grove" shared by his brother. Music is a part of the family heritage, passed down to each generation, and enjoyed when family members are together. Doris and Annette celebrated their 60th Wedding Anniversary on August 26, 2001, and still reside on their farm near Villa Rica, Highway 61, in Carroll County, Georgia. *Submitted by: Henry Doris Tyson, 2011 Carrollton Highway, Villa Rica, GA*

1115. Tyson

Ray Tyson, a Wildcat (1938), was a survivor of the December 6, 1957, gas explosion and burning of Berry's Pharmacy. He was married to Freddie Mae Cole. They had six children, all of whom were Villa Rica Wildcats: Jerry, born 1962; Wilma, born 1963; Gail, born 1965; Kathy, born 1968; Robert, born 1973; and Nancy, born 1983. Robert and Nancy were members of the Beta Club and the student council. Robert was the salutatorian of his class.

Jewel Cole Barber, Esma Cole Sauls, and Freddie Cole Tyson.

Wilma married Billy Fountain, also a Wildcat. Their children, Kim and Billy Jr., were Wildcats. Billy Jr. is a teacher at Central High School. Kim moved to Daytona, Florida.

Gail raised her children, David and Kay, with Ray and Freddie. They were Wildcats. David played Football with the 1986 State Champion team. Today, David is a coach in Statesboro. Kay moved to Carrollton after marrying Mike Willingham. Nancy married Frank Boyette. They have two children, Tyson and Jessica, who are Wildcats.

Ray and his children enjoyed horses as a sport. The children still enjoy the Villa Rica Saddle Club on Pleasant Grove Road in Villa Rica. Ray died in 1981. *Submitted by: Freddie Mae Cole, Villa Rica, GA*

1116. James Upton

James Upton moved to Carroll County from McMinn County, Tennessee, before the 1830 census. He was there for the 1840 census, but by 1850 had either died or moved to another county. Records indicate he had siblings including Winney who married Martin Mahaffey (they were briefly in Carroll County); Elizabeth married Samuel Ford; Thomas married Emmey Wilson; and Nancy married Charles O'Neal. The family came from Kentucky.

Children of James and Anna Upton:

(1) Susannah Upton born circa 1800, married first to Wright Majors and they had four children: Calvin, Caroline, Willian W. and James Minor; married second on 25 August 1843 in Carroll County to William Ray and had two more children, Mary and Benjamin.

(2) Elizabeth Ann Upton born circa 1803, died 3 October 1873, married John D. Wright.

(3) Anna Upton born circa 1805, died 1878, married Alexander Hogan (see related Alexander Hogan article) and they had eight children: William married first to Sarah Franklin, married second to Mary Margaret Green; James married Elizabeth Nixon Porter; Sarah Elizabeth married Irwin W. Ayres; Thomas L. married Lavonia Villers Elizabeth Rosser; Bennett married Elizabeth V. McWaters; Emily married John Corly Porter; and two other children who died as infants.

(4) James M. Upton born 23 June 1809, died 11 April 1880, married first to "S." and married second to Elizabeth Jane (Porter) Doss and had six children: Essa C., Nancy J. married J.S. Baxter, Seaborn A., James H., Felix, and Henry.

(5) Asa Upton, no information.

(6) Monroe Upton, born 9 October 1818, died 22 March 1891, married first to Eleanor Catherine McWilliams and they had six children: Anna married Thomas Henry Ragsdale; Eliza E. married John D. Williams; James Newton married Elizabeth C. Rabb; Amy Jane married John T. Rabb; Mary Frances married Alger Washington Hyatt; Julia Isabella married Charles Ragsdale. Monroe Upton married second to Alminta Brown and they had ten children. Martha Adeline married first to John Kelly and second to Melrose Jack Killinger; Irvin Ayres married Martha Arabella Patton; Lydia Irene married John Ford; Belton; Walter married Ollie Dean Ford; Asa Henry; Alice Eugenia married William Henry Patton; Florence married Robert Harper; Monroe married Ida Cox; Claudia Alminty married Robert Styler.

(7) Mahala Utpon born 1826, died after 1880, married Green Hicks and they had seven children: James P., William F., Martha E., Missouri A., George W., Archie A., and Mary C. *Submitted by: Carol A. Hogan, 440 NW 23rd Street, Grand Prairie, TX 75050*

Sources: Census records, probate records, tax and land records, family records, and *The Pioneers Were Our Ancestors* by Irwin A. Watson, privately published.

1117. William J. Vaughan Family

In the mid-1880s, William J. Vaughan was born in Carroll County to early pioneer parents. His father was of Welsh ancestry and his mother was Native American. He was one of several children whose mother died when they were very young. His father, unable to care for the little ones, placed them in various homes where they could be cared for. Little is known about his childhood, parents, or siblings.

In the late 1880s William married Annie Bell from the Villa Rica area. They had ten children — my mother, Mellie V. Foster was the eldest, born in October 1892. The Vaughans were tenant farmers, living on Old Bowdon road (now Highway 166) when picture #1 was made. Three of the sisters — Mellie, Addie, and

William J. Vaughan family, about 1919

William J. Vaughan with extended family. About 1929

Bessie — eventually married three brothers, Ramah, Lumie and Jimmie Lee Foster. They all attended Old Tallapoosa School on Tyus Road, where they met and got to know each other.

Mother and her sisters loved music and learned Sacred Harp singing. Momma sang treble harmonizing beautifully with sisters Addie, Della, Bessie, and Nora. Aunt Minnie played piano. Also while in school, Mother won first place in many spelling bees. As a child, we always had her help us with spelling in all English and literature compositions — and she was always right. During the Great Depression, the work was hard and money scarce on the local farms but we always knew we were loved and we were never hungry.

In picture #1, made circa 1919, the individuals are as follows: first row left to right is Nora, Minnie, William J., Drew, Annie Bell and Homer Vaughan, Loyce and Herschel Foster; second row left to right is Hubert, Della, and Dewey Vaughan; Ramah, Mellie (holding Ray), Lunie, Addie (holding Emogene), Jimmie Lee, and Bessie Foster.

Picture #2, circa 1929, shows William J. and Annie Bell Vaughan (grandma and grandpa) while they lived near Center Point. They're pictured with their children, their children's spouses and grandchildren. In the mid to late 1920s, Aunt Nora married Gabe Daniel; Aunt Della married Raymond Sheffield; Uncle Hubert married Elma Threadgill and Uncle Dewey married Emma Brannon. Uncles Drew and Homer married in the early 1930s, after this photo was taken. Drew married Connie Ivey; Homer married Martha Pope.

Two final notes of interest: my Uncles Hubert and Dewey Vaughan were barbers in the early 1930s with shops in Austell, Clarksdale, Powder Springs, and Lithia Springs. They both retired in the early 1970s. Also, my grandparents William J. and Annie Bell Vaughan are laid to rest at Shady Grove Baptist Church on Sand Hill-Shady Grove Road. *Submitted by: Sarah Foster Spruell, 645 Lovvorn Mill Road, Bowdon, GA 30108*

1118. Caleb Veazey Family

Caleb Veazey was a native of Greene County, Georgia, having been born in the area about 1788. He was the son of William and Annie Umstead Veazey and grandson of James Veazey (Revolutionary Soldier) and Elizabeth Hollingsworth Veazey who were natives of Cecil County, Maryland.

Caleb Veazey was first married to Mary Ann "Molsie" Tippett and they had seven children as follows: Sallie Ann Veazey who married Matthew Downing in Greene County before moving to Heard County and on to Randolph County, Alabama, by 1850; Rebecca L. Veazey; William Veazey who moved to Carroll County and on to Macon County, Alabama; Winneford Marian Veazey; Rutha Veazey; Wesley Veazey, born October 2, 1825, married Anne Warren in Carroll County before moving to St. Clair County, Alabama. And Virginia Veazey, who came to Carroll County as a girl, married 25 September 1847 to Joseph B. Huckeba. It is believed that Mary Ann died before the family came to Carroll County.

Around 1840, Caleb married a widow, Catherine Griffin. Her children were James Robert, Thomas A., Jane, and Catherine Griffin. John Robert Griffin married Sarah E. Martin in Carroll County and reared a large family here. Catherine Griffin married James Roberts on 22 July 1852, and reared a family here.

Caleb and Catherine settled on Land Lot #41, Tenth District, Carroll County, about 1840. Caleb owned several hundred acres of land and was active in community affairs. They were members of Eden Baptist Church near Bowdon. Their children were: (1) Harriett Veazey, born ca. 1842, married Thomas Carden, 22 October 1857. Their child, William A. (Billy) Carden married Miss Oria Downs. (2) Martha Frances Veazey, born 25 December 1843 married John F. Spruill on 10 December 1865, the son of Gabriel and Susan Mann Spruill. Their children were Caleb M., Susan A. Velvin, John William, Leonidas, Rufus, and Beettus Crumbley. John F. Spruill died in 1882 and Martha F. Veazey Spruill died 5 August 1927. They are buried in First Methodist Church Cemetery, Bowdon, Georgia. They have many descendants living in Carroll County. (3) Caleb M. Veazey born ca. 1845 was killed or died while serving in the Confederate Army.

Caleb died in 1862 and Catherine Veazey died 13 June 1871. They were buried on the family home place on Land Lot #41, Tenth District on Salem Road in a pasture on land that was owned by Claude Rigsby. *Submitted by: Ben Cox, 5330 Forest Brook Parkway, Marietta, GA 30068*

1119. Waldrup - Waldrop

Abraham James Waldrop came to Carroll County sometime after 1850 with his widowed mother, Gracie Richardson Waldrup, born in 1819 in South Carolina, died sometime after 1900. Gracie is buried at the Ephesus Baptist Church in Winston, Douglas County, Georgia, where she was a member. Gracie's husband, Allen Christian Waldrup was born about 1810 in South Carolina and died around 1850. Allen's parents were Harmon Waldrup, born about 1761 and died after 1850, and Nancy Hallman, born about 1769 and died after 1850 in Newton County, Georgia. Some of their children were Allen Christian (1810-1840), Milton, and Abraham, who married Susan Lecoy.

Allen and Gracie's children were Mary F. (1835-1855), Abraham James (1836-1923), Hiram Harmon (1840-1924), Nancy E. (1842-?) married Miles D. Carnes, and William A. (1847-1918).

Abraham James Waldrop was born January 18, 1836, in DeKalb County, Georgia, and died November 18, 1923. He is buried at Ephesus Baptist Church, Winston, Georgia. Abraham married Eliza Hallman (born September 18, 1833, in South Carolina and died November 18, 1930) on July 22, 1857, in Carroll County. Abraham gave the land where the Ephesus Baptist Church is in Winston, Georgia.

Eliza Hallman Waldrop's parents were Christian Hallman Holman (born 1802 in Lexington, South Carolina, and died 1860) and Rebecca Taylor, born 1807. They were married on May 27, 1828 in Lexington.

Abraham and Eliza's children were William Henry (1858-1932) married Marther Elizabeth Woods (1862-1932); John Washington (1859-?) married Sudie Aclin; Mary Ellen (1861-1891) married H.C. Bell; Joseph Abraham (1863-1912) married unknown (1862-1942); Margaret

William Henry Waldrop, 1858-1932

Anne (1867-1896) married Eli T. Grubbs; Allen Christian (1872-1934) married Odessa Entrekin (1876-1959); Milton Thomas (1877-1958) married Dula Chrestine Willoughby (1880-1968); and Louise (1882-1960) married O.O. Morris.

William Henry and Marther Woods Waldrop's children were James Abraham (1879-1948) married Beulah Gunter (1889-1986); Mary Ann (1880-?); W. Arch 1882-1944) married Stella Bentley (1889-1987); Eliza Jane (1886-1978) married Jesse Herd Tolbert (1882-1960); Emma Lou (1891-1974) married John Euel Harrison Tolbert (1886-?); John Lester (1893-1969); Mault (1896-1970) married Minnie T. (1902-1980); Roy (1898-1966) married Nellie Carr (1899-1986); Charlie Prude (1900-1980); Opel C. (1901-1976); Joe Julian (1903-1986) married Josie Mae Partain (1904-1989). The parents of Marther Woods Waldrop were William Woods and Elizabeth Grubbs. Marther Elizabeth Woods Waldrop's father was killed in the Civil War near Marietta, Georgia. When he was given leave to go home for his daughter's birth, he was killed as he left the trenches. *Submitted by: Paul Tolbert, 7511 Banksmill Road, Douglasville, GA 30135 and Researched by: Patricia Tolbert Nelson, 1789 Kellogg Creek Road, Acworth, GA*

1120. Josiah James Walker

Josiah James Walker, Confederate soldier and Bowdon postmaster, was born in South Carolina March 31, 1842, to William J. Walker and Lucinda McCain born 1799 and 1809 respectively. After his family moved to Heard County, Georgia, Josiah joined the Goshen Congregational Methodist Church as a child. After moving to Bowdon in 1884, he attended the Methodist Episcopal Church near his home, but he later joined Bowdon Baptist Church with his wife Amanda.

Josiah Walker was a member of Company A, 9th Battalion, Georgia Volunteer Infantry, Army of Tennessee. In May, 1863, he was transferred to Company D, 37th Regiment which was formed from remnants of the 3rd and 9th Regiments of the Georgia Infantry. He was wounded in 1863, taken prisoner at the fall of Vicksburg July 4, 1863, and paroled four days later. The Army of Tennessee was virtually destroyed at the Battles of Spring Hill, Franklin, and Nashville, and Josiah Walker was captured at the Battle of Nashville December 16, 1864. He was held prisoner at Kentucky Military Prison in Louisville and was finally released at Camp Chase, Ohio, June 1865.

Josiah Walker married Louisa Durrough February 1866. They had five children: Emelia born 1867, John William born 1868, Martha Elizabeth born 1871, Charles Milton born 1873, and Ellah Naomi born 1875. After the death of Louisa January 1877, Josiah married Amanda Missouri Jackson born July 5, 1854. Their children were James Edmond born 1878, married Ruth Whatley; Lucy Idellah born 1880; Joseph Arthur born 1882 married Mertie Pentecost; Alberta Ruth born 1883 married Wiley Wash Rowland; Ada Mae born 1886 married James Will Word; Susan Alice born 1888 married Otis Barrow; Myrtis Annabelle born 1892 married Roy Alexander; Earl Franklin born 1895 married Mildred Barrow.

Josiah Walker served as postmaster at Bowdon for thirteen years from 1900-1913 under appointments by Presidents McKinley, Roosevelt, and Taft. His daughter Alberta often helped him post the mail after school. In 1890 Josiah served on the Bowdon City Council.

Joe and Amanda Walker

Josiah Walker owned 315 acres of land in Heard County four miles west of Hollingsworth ferry on Wedowee Road. On November 30, 1883, he purchased the former Charles A. McDaniel house adjacent to Bowdon College. He acquired the property from George R. Adamson for $983. The house became home to the growing Walker family for a quarter of a century. Being convenient to the academy and Bowdon College was advantageous for the Walker children. Alberta remembered hurrying across the school yard for lunch at home, and friends frequently followed her. Edmond and Ada Walker graduated from Bowdon College. the former Bowdon College president's home provided the setting for the weddings of two of Joe Walker's daughters, Alberta and Ada, who descended the central stairway to meet their grooms.

The house was sold in 1909 and Josiah and Amanda moved to a house they owned on Mill Street. They later moved to a farm in the Sandy Flat area. After Amanda died November 8, 1923, Josiah lived with his children until his death September 1, 1927. Engraved on his tombstone is "Deo Vindice 1861-1865." *Submitted by: Jan Rowland Johnson*

1121. Rogers R. Walker Family

Rogers and Gladys Walker moved to their farm in Carroll County, three miles northwest of Roopville, in 1942. Rogers established one of the first dairy farms in Carroll County. He and his sons, Cecil and Ray, designed and built the dairy barn and milk house. In the beginning, cows were milked by hand; later, milking machines were used. During World War II when Cecil served as a paratrooper in the 82nd Airborne Division and Ray served in the Naval Air Corps, the daughters, Betty and Mary Ruth, assisted with the dairy.

For twenty-three years, Gladys was manager and buyer for the boy's department at Belk-Rhodes in Carrollton. After retirement, she worked at the polls, delivered Meals on Wheels, and visited shut-ins for the First United Methodist Church in Carrollton where she and Rogers were active members. She was a member of the Carrollton Civic Woman's Club and was selected as Mother-of-the-Year in 1983. Gladys crocheted and knitted afghans, made crewel and cross-stitch pictures and pillows, and completed numerous other craft items for family and friends.

Gladys and Rogers Walker

Rogers served as chairman of the board of the Federal Land Bank, director of Farmer's Mutual Exchange, chairman of the board of Carroll Creamery Co-op, and chairman of the board of Carroll County Family and Children's Services.

Rogers, born in Carroll County in 1903, was the second of eleven children of Will and Fannie Walker. Gladys, born in Carroll County in 1905, was the third of five children of Wilson and Cora Kemp. They were married in 1923 and lived in Atlanta where Rogers owned and managed a meat market in a neighborhood grocery store. Rogers selected beef for his market from refrigerated rail cars that came from the Midwest to the rail yards in what is now Underground Atlanta. Soon, Gladys was taking grocery orders over the telephone, selecting and bagging groceries, and checking the delivery boys (on bicycles) in and out. Rogers moved his family to Carroll County and established the diary when meat was rationed during World War II.

Rogers R. Walker Family. L-R: Ray, Jerry, Cecil, Rayann, Mary Ruth, Betty, Clemmie

When Rogers retired from the dairy business, the barn was converted to a modern cabin. It is here, next to his eighteen-acre lake, that one hundred fifty to two hundred descendants of Rogers' parents, Will and Fannie Walker, gather annually to reminisce and share good food and fellowship. Will and Fannie reared a closely knit family, continuing a great heritage from their parents — the Walkers and the Lyles — faith in God, commitment to family, and loyalty to country. Rogers and Gladys have forty-five descendants. After Rogers' death in 1993, Gladys maintained her home until 1999 when she moved to Stewart House Retirement Home.

Cecil and Ray graduated from Georgia Tech in 1950. Cecil (married to Clemmie Dilworth) retired as chairman of the board and chief

executive officer of Heyward Incorporated, Charlotte, North Carolina. He presently serves as chairman of the board of trustees at Oak Mountain Academy. Ray (married to Rayann Wallace) retired as assistant regional manager of Insurance Services Office in Atlanta. Betty (Gray) is a graduate of the University of North Carolina with a master's degree from Georgia State University. She established Montessori School of the Foothills in central, South Carolina. She retired as adult education instructor at Carroll Technical Institute. Mary Ruth is a graduate of West Georgia College and currently works as secretary-treasurer of Kitchens International, Inc. which she owns with her husband Jerry Chambers and son David Chambers. *Submitted by: Cecil and Clemmie Walker, Carrollton, GA*
Sources: Family records and interviews with the family.

1122. Thomas Alexander Walker

Thomas Alexander Walker was born in the vicinity of Big Lick, Virginia, November 28, 1846. Big Lick is in the eastern part of Virginia near Roanoke and in Botetourt County. He moved with his mother to Athens, McMinn County, Tennessee, at an early age. The first known record we have of Thomas Alexander Walker is in the 1860 census. He was listed in the Seventh Civil District of McMinn County, Tennessee. Walker was living with Joseph S. Yoder, age 31, a millwright. Thomas A. Walker was listed as 14 years old. His mother, Sarah Walker, was listed as age 40 years and was born in Virginia. Thomas A. Walker may have been serving an apprenticeship to become a millwright for in later years he did run a mill.

Thomas Alexander Walker – 1846-1927

Joseph S. Yoder sold a house and one acre track of land to Sarah Walker May 26, 1860, recorded in Deed Book M McMinn County, Tennessee. The land was on the road leading from Athens, Tennessee, to Fite's Bridge adjoining the Hamilton land. Thomas A. Walker was reared by his mother, Sarah or Sallie, and there is no proof whom her husband could have been. There is no indication that he had any brothers or sisters.

Sarah Walker was the daughter of Jesse and Susannah Walker. Jesse Walker was born 1777 and died 1850. He married Susannah Clegg July 17, 1800 in Botetourt County, Virginia. She was born 1776 and died 1868 in Newport, Missouri. She was the daughter of Alexander Clegg, born 1743, near Belfast, Ireland, and died 1822 in Botetourt County, Virginia. He married Susannah Marion, who was born 1746 and died 1823 in Botetourt County, Virginia.

Jesse and Susannah Walker had thirteen children, the oldest was James. Sarah was perhaps the tenth child and was born in 1814 and died 1897. Jesse and Susannah lived in Botetourt County, Virginia, and are listed on the 1810 to 1840 census in that County. They moved to McMinn County, Tennessee, and are listed on the 1850 Tennessee census. After Jesse died, Susannah moved to Missouri with one of her children, Minna Walker Foster, who married a William Foster.

On November 12, 1867, Thomas A. Walker married Texie E. Wells born 1852. Texie was the daughter of Benjamin J. Wells and Fatama Prather Wells. Texie E. Wells lived next to the Walker land, and they had a large farm. Benjamin J. Wells and Fatama Prather had seven children - Texie E. Wells being the fifth child. Thomas A. Walker and Texie Wells had five children: Benjamin (Wallace) Walker born July 1871; Mattie and Minne Walker born May 16, 1873 (twins); Sallie Walker born 1876; infant born 1884, died July 10, 1884; Adeline Henderson Walker born Decemberr 27, 1878. All were born in McMinn County, Tennessee. On August 5, 1890, Texie E. Wells died in child birth. There is no record of the child. She was 38 years old at the time. This information has been passed down in the family.

On December 16, 1894, Thomas A. Walker married Laura Ann Shelton. She lived with her parents William (Bill) C. Shelton and Dorcas Milinda Paris Shelton on the Shelton farm several miles from the mill and farm Thomas A. Walker was running. Thomas A. Walker was 29 years older than Laura and had daughters as old as she.

From this marriage, a second family of Walkers was born. Felix Jackson (Jack) Walker born Nov. 14, 1895; James Nathaniel (Nat) Walker born April 8, 1897; Nell Eulah Walker born Aug. 14, 1899; Thomas Alexander Walker Jr. born June 3, 1902; Shelton Reid Walker born July 23, 1905; and Mary Dorcas Walker born March 26, 1911. About 1906, the family moved to the Shelton farm for Bill Shelton (Laura's father) had died July 17, 1904, and Dorcas Shelton died on February 13, 1906. The farm was later sold to W.C. Lewis on March 10, 1910. W.C. was married to Callie Shelton, one of Laura's sisters. Thomas Walker stayed and worked the farm until around 1916, then moved to Etowah, Tennessee. Thomas A. Walker spent his last years in Etowah, Tennessee, and died at 2:10 P.M. on January 31, 1927, at his home. His funeral services were conducted from the M.E. Church South, and he was buried at the City Cemetery of Etowah.

Thomas Alexander Walker Jr., son of above, married Clifford Cecelia Withers May 22, 1936, in Athens, Tennessee. They moved to Chattanooga, Tennessee, and had two sons. Thomas Alexander Walker III and Reid Withers Walker.

Reid Withers Walker married Carolyn (Gail) McBride August 10, 1964, and moved to Carroll County in 1979 due to a job change with Plantation Pipe Line. They have three daughters: Deda Carol Walker married William (Bill) Frederick Band IV 5 September 1998 and lives in Raleigh, North Carolina; Tracey Ann Walker married Robert (Wayne) Aiken February 3, 2001 and lives in Charleston, South Carolina; and Karen Beth Walker married Daron Thomas Young November 6, 1999 and lives in Carroll County.

Bill and Deda Band have one daughter Adalena Gail Band (Addie) born 17 April 2001. *Submitted by: Reid W. Walker 5196 Fern Ct., Villa Rica, GA 30180*

1123. Walker

William Eldred (Willie) Walker and Ora Lee Hightower were married in Carrollton, Carroll County, Georgia on December 27, 1934.

Willie was the seventh child of eleven born to William Singleton (Will) Walker and Francis Jane (Fannie) Lyle Walker. He graduated from Tyus School where he was a member of the basketball team. He was a member of Bethesda Baptist Church. He died on April 23, 1991, at the age of 78 and is buried in Carroll Memory Garden.

Ora Lee Hightower was the fourth child of seven born to Robert Willis Hightower and Nina Estelle Arrington Hightower. She attended school at Tyus which was in the community where she lived. She is a member of Bethesda Baptist Church.

Willie and Ora Lee raised seven children. They were farmers and in the early years of their marriage; they farmed with mules. They grew cotton, corn and a big garden. In later years, they bought a tractor to replace the mules. They expanded their farming operation to include cattle and poultry. Their four sons and three daughters also worked on the farm.

The four older children attended the Tallapoosa Elementary School in the community where they lived and Bowdon High School. The three younger children attended Central Elementary and High School. Willie and Ora Lee always kept their children in school even during the busy seasons because it was very important to them that their children get an education.

Family of Willie and Ora Lee Walker

Their examples of honesty, fairness and compassion for others has been passed on through their children and grandchildren. Their family has now grown to include sixteen grandchildren and twenty great-grandchildren, plus thirty step-grandchildren and step-great-grandchildren. The family meets once a month for a covered dish meal at the home place where "Mama Walker" always has a welcome hug for everyone.

The family photograph shows Willie and Ora Lee Walker seated on the front row. Their children are Donald Singleton (front left), Linda Joyce Walker Doss, William Eldred Walker Jr., Nina Joan Walker Cole, Jimmy Lee Walker, Nancy Jane Walker Rigsby, and Robert Arnold Walker seated on right. *Submitted by: Jane Walker Rigsby, 1490 Tyus Carrollton Road, Carrollton, GA 30117*

1124. William Singleton Walker

Singleton Walker was born May 15, 1848, in Troup County. Emily Virginia Rogers was born June 8, 1850. They were married in Carroll County on February 27, 1873. William Singleton (Will) Walker was born in Carroll County on August 1, 1877, the third of eleven children of Singleton and Emily.

Will Walker married Frances Jane "Fannie" Lyle in Carroll County on January 31, 1901. Fannie Lyle was born on May 23, 1882, in Harris County, the ninth of thirteen children of James Davis Lyle and Nancy Mary Ann Champion. James Davis Lyle was born in Coweta County on March 22, 1844. Nancy Mary Ann was born in Muscogee County on March 15, 1851. They came to Carroll County in 1877 and lived on Oak Mountain during Fannie's childhood. James Davis and Nancy Mary Ann are buried at Oak Grove Baptist Church Cemetery.

Will and Fannie were farmers and grew cotton as their main source of income. He was an active deacon at Oak Grove Baptist Church and at his death was memorialized with an article praising his life.

The children remember Will's positive outlook on life and his high morals. He was never known to utter a curse word. He was a man of few words who meant what he said when he did speak. His word was his bond. He did not speak unkindly about others, nor did he let his family do so. Although his children respected his authority and discipline, they always felt free to sit on his lap. Even in difficult times, Will brought the children a sack of stick candy whenever he went to town.

William Singleton and Frances Jane Lyle Walker, wedding day 1901.

Fannie often assisted families in the community when a baby was born or when there was an illness in a family. She would help nurse and cook, treating everyone kindly. Fannie loved animals, especially horses, and was a great story teller. She sang ballads to her grandchildren and told riddles.

Fannie was a good cook. She served buttered biscuits and sorghum syrup every morning for breakfast. She prepared a large dinner, then served cornbread with leftovers for supper. Her grandchildren fondly remember her tea cakes.

Fannie Walker and her eleven children.

Will Walker died in Carroll County in 1935, and Fannie in 1974. Both are buried in Stripling Chapel Cemetery. They left the same great heritage to their descendants which they had received from the Walker and Lyle families — faithfulness to God, commitment to family, and loyalty to country.

The family photograph shows the eleven children of Will and Fannie Walker. Standing, left to right, are Mildred Virginia Merrell (1910), Thomas Edgar (1918), William Eldred (1912), Roy Goodwyn (1922), Jesse Larkin (1908), Dumah Adrian (1924), Mary Eskalona "Essie" McLendon (1904), James Rayford (1915), Davis Singleton (1906), Rogers Raymond (1903). Seated are Reuel Clyde (1901), and Frances Jane "Fannie" Lyle Walker (1882).

Submitted by: Betty Walker Gray, 761 Old Airport Road, Carrollton, GA 30116

1125. Barney Lee Wallace Family

The great-grandfather of Barney Lee Wallace (born 10-19-1901, died 7-6-1972) was Benjamin Wallace born in 1801. His grandparents were William Henry Harrison Wallace (born circa 1843, died after 1920) and Eliza Ann Cramer (born 1838, died before 1920). Barney's parents were Walter Wilson Wallace (born 9-29-1874, died 12-14-1949) and Georgia Josephine Smith (born 2-19-1878, died 7-23-1970). They moved from Douglas County to Carroll County in 1910. Barney, his parents and grandparents are buried in the Powell Chapel Methodist Church Cemetery, Flat Rock Community, Villa Rica.

Barney had five sisters: his twin Margie Lou Wallace Worthington (born 10-18-1901), Mable C. Wallace Hembree (born 1906), Irma M. Wallace Saback (born 1911), Lela Nell Wallace Newell (born 1916), and Montez M. Wallace Graben (born 1918).

The minister of the Methodist Church in Villa Rica Georgia married Barney Lee Wallace and Erma Otelle Steed (born 10-21-1904) on April 26, 1925. They took up residence in the Flat Rock community of Carroll County at that time and have since remained.

Their children are Barney Eugene (born 1-17-1926), Jacqueline Elizabeth W. Seagraves (born 7-18-1929), Jimmie Ernest (born 8-19-1932), Martha Joann W. Herrell (born 2-14-1936), Linda Sue W. Shadrix (born 7-6-1938), Max Erwin (born 1-15-1942), Randy Lee (born 5-12-1945), Dwight Ellis (born 4-5-1947) and Teresa Karen W. Williams (born 2-1-1950).

Barney Wallace moved to the Flat Rock community of Carroll County with his parents at the age of ten from White City in Douglas County. In those days the mode of transportation was horses, horse drawn wagons or buggies. Lighting was by kerosene lamps and candles.

Barney was a "Jack of all trades." He was a farmer, raising row crops, cattle and hogs. He was a retail grocery peddler. He had a regular route of farm product customers in the West End area of Atlanta. He would gather the farm products that he and his family grew and that of many of the neighbors on Friday afternoon and carry them to Atlanta early Saturday morning. His basic sales were eggs, fresh farm butter and buttermilk. To this he would add seasonal items of fresh garden vegetables, fresh pork, sugar cured hams and other farm products. He would take special orders from his "city" customers. Some of the more unusual orders would be dogwood trees, woods dirt, stable manure, wild rabbits, and snapping turtles. He had a knack for being able to find a way to fill most of these special requests.

He worked with the railroad for a while. He was employed as night watchman at the Villa Rica Oil Mill for a period of time. He said that a trick he would use to stay awake during the long nights was to hold a large metal pipe in his hand so if he nodded off the noise from the falling pipe would awaken him.

At one time he operated a new and used furniture store, Barney's Swap and Shop, located in Villa Rica where Twelve Oaks Farm Supplies is presently located.

He continued to work into his late sixties and early seventies with the Carroll County school system in building maintenance and as a school bus driver.

Barney died at the age of seventy-two from lung cancer, likely as a result of decades of cigarette smoking. His twin sister lived to age ninety-two. Don't smoke!

Erma Steed's parents were John Henry Steed (born 4-3-1882, died 12-15-1924) and Belzora Eugena Hembree (born 9-7-1885, died 12-1-1982). Erma had one sister, Eva Christine Steed Samples (born 12-24-1906, died 7-20-2000). Erma and Eva were true soul mates for over ninety-four years.

Erma Steed lived in Dark Corner located in Douglas County until she was twelve years of age. She moved to the Flat Rock community in 1916. However, that part of Flat Rock community was located in Douglas County.

Erma (Steed) Wallace was the inspiration and guiding hand of raising a family of nine children. She cooked all the meals, did all the laundry (before and after the advent of the washing machine), worked in the fields, canned vegetables, cured meat and a multitude of other jobs to keep her family healthy. She prepared all summer for the coming winter.

Erma was for many years known as the local barber of the Flat Rock community. For a dime you could get a hair cut. With five boys of her own, her hair cutting skills were developed as a necessity.

Erma was a schoolteacher. She taught the combined grades of first through fourth at Flat Rock School in 1928. The Flat Rock School closed in 1951 with students being relocated to the Villa Rica schools.

In addition to her family duties, Erma has been a matriarch in the Powell's Chapel Methodist Church for over fifty years. Her dedication to the church and the people of the Flat Rock community, where she presently lives, has never wavered during her life of ninety-six years.

Erma's community service has always been recognized as outstanding. In 1992, at the age of 88, she was selected as the American Heart

Barney and Erma Wallace family.

Association's Volunteer of the Year for her many years of work with that activity.

The Barney and Erma Wallace family have lived in Carroll County since 1925. A large number of their sixty-nine descendants remain in Carroll County. All nine children graduated from Villa Rica High School. All five of their sons served in the armed forces, three in the Army and two in the Air Force. All four daughters were star basketball players for Villa Rica High School. All nine children have enjoyed successful lives in a variety of occupations — owners of retail stores and shops, residential developers and builders, teachers, engineer, insurance agent, and real estate brokers.

Barney and Enna Wallace are a tribute to Carroll County and exemplify the stock of what Carroll County is made of. *Submitted by: Randy Wallace, 803 Sand Hill-Shady Grove Road, Carrollton, GA 30116*

1126. The Wallis - Wallace Families

Simpson Franklin Wallis was in the Walton County in 1839 where he married Sarah A. (Sallie) Smith, daughter of Britain Smith and Christian Duckworth (who had been married in Hancock County in 1813). Simpson is listed as being an ensign in the Walton Volunteer Rifle (militia) unit in 1848. He was probably named for his aunt's husband William Simpson. Simpson Wallis' brother Mitchell Colen Wallis was probably named for their other aunt's husband, William Mitchell.

Manuel Wallace 1892-1969

In 1850 Simpson and Sallie moved to Gwinnett County. By 1860 Sallie had died and Simpson remarried to Sarah (Sallie) Moran and they were living in Spalding County with their children Christian, Thomas William (T.W.), Susan, Samuel, Daniel, Matilda, Francis, John F., and Martha Tabatha.

On April 23, 1864, Simpson went to Barnesville, Georgia, and enlisted in Company K of the 3rd Georgia Reserves for 30-day period. He then went to Macon on May 4, 1864, and enlisted again. He was sent to Andersonville Prison Camp (Camp Sumter) as a guard. He was forty-nine years old. His son Thomas William (T.W.) joined the same regiment Company G at Jackson, Georgia, in August 1864. Simpson became sick with the fever and went home on August 20 and died September 20. His son Samuel Marion (S.M.) went to Andersonville and enlisted in the 3rd Georgia Reserves in August and died there in September 1864. A nephew of Simpson, John Thomas, also in the 3rd Georgia Reserves appears to have also died about the same time.

After the close of the Andersonville Prison, T.W., his cousin Edward T. Wallis, and the rest of the Regiment were assigned to General Wheeler. They numbered 387 men on December 26, 1864, and were at Coosawhatchie, South Carolina.

Mitchell Colin Wallis had moved to Campbell County with his family and was in the 10th Cavalry Regiment of Georgia State Guards (militia). He caught pneumonia and died in December 1864.

The family of Mitchell Colin Wallis moved to Fulton County and then to Sand Hill in Carroll County. The family of Simpson Wallis stayed for a while in Spalding County, then moved by 1900 to Carroll County, and with T.W. and his wife Phereba Caroline Evans Wallis lived in the area that is now Bowdon Junction. Caroline's father, Benjamin Franklin Evans, and two uncles had been killed during the war.

Homer Wallace 1898-1968

T.W. and Caroline's children were Wilbur, Walter, Manuel, and Viola. Wilbur married Harriett Parker and had Homer and Verdie. After Harriett's death he married Molly Prince and they had Bertha. Manuel married Ruth Lambert and had Zelma and Florence. Viola married Natham Lambert and had Lela Mae Lambert (married M.E. White). Walter married Maude Holcombe. Walter's daughter, Charlene, still lives at their home site at Mt. Zion. The Wallace family were very active members of Holly Springs Church and involved in keeping Sacred Harp singing alive.

Somewhere along the way, Homer and Walter changed the spelling of their name to Wallace. Verdie married Lester Lambert and their son is Wallace Lambert. Homer Wallace married Mamae Johnson and their son W. J. runs Wallace Builders Supply in Bowdon Junction. Another son Reese runs Wallace Farm Supply. Tabitha Wallis married Newton Columbus Hutson and moved to Carroll County. Their son Jim married Minnie Folds and they are the grandparents of Floyd Hutson. Earnest Leo Hutson married Mary Elizabeth Akin and their daughter Helen married Jewell Prince Rowe. Rev. W.O. Wallis is one of the descendants of Mitchell Colen Wallis in Carroll County. *Submitted by: W.J. Wallace, Bowdon Junction*
Source: Wallace T. Lambert

1127. Wallis - Childress - Abercrombie

Jesse Mitchel Wallis was born July 29, 1852, in Georgia, and died November 10, 1923, in Carroll County, Georgia. Jesse was the son of Mitchel Colin Wallis, born November 10, 1813, and died December 10, 1864. His mother was Sarahan Griffin who was born September 19, 1821, and died April 11, 1908. She is buried at Old Carrollton Primitive Baptist Church Cemetery, Carroll County.

Jesse first married Harriet Hepsie Childress on February 14, 1875. She was born February 24, 1858, and died August 19, 1886.

Their children were: 1. Oscar Luther Wallis, born January 11, 1876, died January 16, 1942, who married Anna Latimer on January 6, 1907. Both are buried in the Carrollton City Cemetery. 2. Jesse Mitchel Barnet Wallis, born July 31, 1878, died May 7, 1950, who married first Eula E. Barnett on November 18, 1900, second to Mary Heath on May 18, 1904, and third to Mattie Bell Holland on November 24, 1927. He and his first wife are buried at Old Carrollton Primitive Baptist Church. 3. John William Edwin Wallis, born July 9, 1881, died December 23, 1953, who married O'Rilla Josephine Ward on December 24, 1908. Both are buried in the Carrollton City Cemetery. 4. Stephen Columbus Wallis, born June 17, 1883, died November 6, 1955, who married Velma E. Holland on December 4, 1910. Both are buried in the Carrollton City Cemetery. 5. Joseph Montgomery Wallis, born March 31, 1886, died July 29, 1953, who married Frances Stovall on August 30, 1908. Both are buried in the Old Carrollton Primitive Baptist Church Cemetery.

Jesse's second marriage was to Susannah Abercrombie on January 17, 1887, in Douglas County. Susannah was born December 3, 1858, in Campbell County and died August 4, 1938, in Carroll County. She was the daughter of James R. Abercrombie and Jane Dunlap.

Jesse and Susannah's children were: 1. Thomas Sanford Wallis, born May 7, 1888, died April 15, 1976, who married Nettie Victoria Kilgore on September 11, 1913. Both are buried in Carrollton City Cemetery. 2. James Smith Wallis, born December 21, 1889, died December 5, 1972, who married Margaret Peek on December 19, 1915. Both are buried in the Carrollton City Cemetery. 3. Evie Estell Wallis, born January 19, 1892, died August 6, 1953, in Oxford, Alabama, who married Ernest T. Grizzard on February 7, 1909. 4. Homer Wilson Wallis, born August 4, 1894, died September 6, 1985. 5. Rellie Ezekiel Wallis, born September 9, 1896, died October 28, 1984, who married first Pearl Brooks on January 15, 1922, and second Mary Grace Nally Bozeman on November 25, 1953. He is buried at Midway Macedonia Baptist Church. 6. Henry Childress Wallis, born May 27, 1899, died January 4, 1991, who married Lois Helena Richards on September 12, 1920. They are buried in the Brown Cemetery next to the Temperance Methodist Church at Sand Hill. 7. Horace Jefferson Wallis, born August 16, 1902, died May 8, 1996, who married first Lucy Jewell Dyer on September 16, 1923, and second Lucille Rooks Moody on October 27, 1979. He is buried in the Jordan Cemetery.

Jesse and his two wives are buried at Old Carrollton Primitive Baptist Church Cemetery. *Submitted by: Helen Matthews, 2358 Carrollton-Villa Rica Hwy., Villa Rica, GA 30180*
Sources: Personal Knowledge, Family Bible

1128. Asa Franklin Ward

Asa Franklin "Acy" Ward, son of John Ward (1785 in North Carolina), was born in Carroll County, Georgia, on February 10, 1842. The family relocated to Carroll County according to the 1850 census.

Acy enlisted on May 15, 1861, in Company F, Infantry Battalion, Cobb Legion, Georgia Volunteers, Confederate States Army Corps, as a private under Captain McDaniels. He served under Captains Robinson, Crane, and Powell in Carrollton. Later he fought in Newnan, Georgia, Guilford County, North Carolina, and on to Richmond and Lynchburg, Virginia. He was compensated $11 monthly. During 1862, Asa was taken prisoner of war at Ft. McHenry, Maryland. Company muster rolls indicate that he was hospitalized several times as a result of wounds to his right thumb, right leg (musket ball remained), side, and one eye. His Certificate of Retirement was dated November 19, 1864. He returned to Carroll County to farm.

Tales were passed through generations as evidence of his frugalness. It was told how a tiny gourd sufficed to measure muzzle-loader gun powder, while a long-handled, quart-size gourd hung on the wall functioned as a dipper.

Asa's first marriage was to Margaret Marinda Winkles (July 7, 1846-August 17, 1902) on August 25, 1863, and they had eleven children: Sarah Elizabeth (March 21, 1862) married Ernest Keith Sr.; William (January 5, 1864); Mandy Ann (November 25, 1865-October 6, 1949) married Agustia Williams; Orena (June 25, 1868) married John Butler; Edker (June 10, 1871-November 14, 1954) married Catherine Spence (April 30, 1860-August 29, 1948) on December 31, 1893; Little Elijah (born and died on April 12, 1872); Elijah Frederick (September 20, 1873-November 2, 1946); George Hamilton (September 9, 1879-April 12, 1958) married Lela Mae Long (July 1, 1885-October 10, 1935) on November 17, 1901; John (January 7, 1880); Della (October 8, 1882); and Fannie (March 16, 1887-August 23, 1939) married Joe Capes (1881-1945). Many are buried at Abilene and Cross Plains Baptist Churches.

Asa Franklin Ward

On March 16, 1904, at the court house in Buchanan, Georgia, Asa married Hulty Ann Elizabeth Waddell (December 28, 1872-June 11, 1957). She was the daughter of Mary Frances Reeves (1854-1937) of Cherokee Indian heritage, and John William Waddell Sr. (1852-1893), a descendant of David Waddle (1735-1800) of Wilmington, Delaware. The seven children from this union were Dwight John William (June 1, 1901-November 1, 1954) married Willie Etta Wallace (September 16, 1895-April 9, 1982); Ruben Jonas James Washington (August 23, 1903-March 10, 1963) married Eula Morris (March 31, 1911-March 13, 1998); twins Judius and James (born and died on December 9, 1904); Caroline Elizabeth (July 12, 1907-September 19, 2000) married Henry Allen Pendleton Morris (February 23, 1905-August 12, 1998); Joseph (born and died on October 18, 1911); and Hershel Franklin Murdock (May 26, 1915-September 29, 1984) married Dura Lee Pollard (February 6, 1929) on December 20, 1958.

Many of their household items remain as special possessions with family — a peddle sewing machine, trunk, grind graphophone, five-leg solid wood dining table, quilts, washstand, rocker and dresser.

Medications most often utilized during this time were a poultice of sassafras, asafetida, and digitalis. Family members have collected their boxes and bottles.

Death befalls Asa on a sultry September day in 1916, immediately after drinking a large quantity of fresh-drawn well water at Gould Pope's home. He was in the midst of a long brisk walk. Asa is buried at Cross Plains Baptist Church in Carroll County alongside siblings and other family members. *Submitted by: Helen Morris Shepard, 1429 Crossroad Church Road, Rockmart, GA 30153*

Sources: Family records, and International Headquarters of Sons of Confederate Veterans.

1129. Linsey Matthew Warnick and Julia Elitha Matthews

Linsey Matthew Warnick, son of Matthew and Elizabeth Warnick, was born in 1832 in DeKalb County, Georgia. He married Julia Elitha Matthews on 15 August 1853 in Carroll County. She was born in 1830 in South Carolina and died before 1870 in Carroll County. She was the daughter of Abel and Nancy Matthews. Linsey served in the Georgia Volunteer Infantry, Army of Tennessee, Company H, 56th Regiment. Records say he was killed at Vicksburg, Mississippi, on 4 July 1862 but his military records state that he took the oath of allegiance to the United States 26 September 1864.

Robert Matthew Able and Tempie J. Giles

The children of Linsey and Julia Warnick were: (1) Lucinda Jane born 11 June 1854 in Carroll County, died 13 July 1904 in Indian Territory, Oklahoma, married John Newton Collier on 19 March 1871 in Cleburne County, Alabama. Their children were Lindsey Marell, James Tomas, Robert Berton, John W., Amanda, Francis Jane, William Albert, Alice Vennie, Henry Davis, Lillie Idabelle, Nancy Loucille Ada, and John Wilburn. (2) Nancy born about 1856 in Carroll County, married James A. McGrant on 2 March 1874 in Carroll County. (3) Elizabeth born about 1858 in Carroll County. (4) Robert Matthew Able born 20 January 1860 in Carroll County, died 16 November 1933, married first to Tempie Janie (see Giles Family) on 22 January 1878 in Carroll County. She was the daughter of John Griffin Giles and Elizabeth Ann Proctor. Their children were Cora Lavonia, born 13 January 1879 in Carroll County, died 29 May 1958 (see Lenderman Family); Atha born 17 February 1881 in Carroll County, died 11 April 1906, married Ed L. Martin on 9 September 1900 in Marshall County, Alabama; Dona Ola born 12 March 1884 in Carroll County, died 11 July 1898; Lillie L. born 11 July 1886 in Carroll County, died 29 August 1906; Homer L. born 20 December 1889 in Carroll County, died 25 January 1894; Velmer E. born 2 April 1897 in Marshall County, died 28 October 1901; Leonard McClarty born 3 June 1895 in Marshall County, died 10 July 1953, married Persis Holland. Matthew Able married second to Etta Jeffers Green, born 28 August 1873, died 23 March 1963. All of the above are buried at the Hebron Church of Christ Cemetery, Hulaco, Morgan County, Alabama. Matthew Able and Etta had one daughter, Verna, who married Tyrus "Tat" C. Bailey. Their children were Joan, Linda and Robert; (5) Patrick George Linsey born 7 February 1862 in Carroll County, died 27 October 1923, buried in Old Arab Cemetery, Marshall County, Alabama. He was married first to Sarah S. Harper on 7 January 1882 in Cleburne County, Alabama. She was born 25 December 1867 in Georgia and died 6 April 1901 in Alabama. Their children were Sarah (1882-1884); Joseph born and died in 1885; John Robert (1889-1898); Amos Wesley 1893-1968, married Lillie Bell Hughes on 25 August 1912 in Marshall County; Minner Lee born 1896, married Silas Paul Chambers. Pat married second to Lydia Ann Dunkin on 17 July 1902 in Marshall County. Their children were Lindsey Austin 1909-1935; Willie Norene born 1914, married Hosimer Turner; Lillie Lorene, twin to Norene, married Cleston Smith; James Afton born 20 August 1918 in Marshall County, Alabama. *Submitted by: Robert Lenderman, 119 Norwood Drive, Rainbow City, AL 35906*

1130. Charles Marion Warren 1862-1940

My mother's interest in genealogy has piqued my curiosity of family history. Ties between the early Carroll County residents intrigue me. In my own family, I have discovered that the Warren name I received at birth is only one way I am related to the Warrens. Another link is found in the lineage of my great-grandmother Arabelle Warren Duncan, daughter of Charles Marion Warren. The following Warren story is recorded as it was told to me by my mother, Janice Adelia Duncan:

"Charles Marion Warren was born March 31, 1862, in Carroll County, Georgia, to Elizabeth Smith and Walter T. Warren. Elizabeth was a descendant of the Gabriel Smith Sr. who moved with his family to Carroll County from Franklin County, Georgia, sometime in 1836. Walter T. was a descendant of John O. Warren.

"Charles (or Charlie as he came to be called) had nine living siblings plus two siblings who died as infants: William Gabriel 'Gabe' (born 1854) married Drury Melvina Silvey in 1879; Mary Elizabeth 'Shug' (born 1857) married Asa Benjamin King; James Walter (born 1860) married Rebecca Adeline Turner; Peter Columbus (born 1866) married Mary Adele 'Mollie' Silvey; Martha Ann (born 1867) married Henry Newton Phillips; Joseph Abel (born 1870) married Cora C. Stogner; David Solomon (born 1871) married Rosa Ada Kuglar; and Ida Lelia (born 1873) who married Asa Taylor Wright Jr."

[As a point of interest, David Solomon is my father James Vernon Warren's grandfather and, therefore, my great grandfather. David Solomon was a brother to my great-great-grandfather Charles Marion, the focus of this story. Another Warren link is through my great-great-great-grandmother Elizabeth Smith Warren who was a sister to Charles Smith, my great-great-maternal grandfather. These examples depict the intertwining of families mentioned earlier.]

"October 19, 1882, Charles Marion married Josephine Robinson (born 1862-died 1951). The couple built their log home in the Indian Creek community on Highway 100 north of Bowdon. There they raised their eleven children: Effie A. (born 1884) married John T. King; Arabelle (born

1886) married S.B. Duncan; Dora B. (born 1887) married Thomas C. King; Gordan Henry (born 1889) married Donie Lee; Albert H. (born 1892) married Vassie Eason; Robert L. (born 1894) married Frances May Ragan; Marion F. (born 1897) married Minnie Brock; Annie Rhoda (born 1900) married George Rudy Batchelor; Alma (born 1903) married Alvin S. Batchelor; and Gladis Irene (born 1908) married Ray F. Cook. Two had died in infancy.

"My grandmother, Arabelle, told of helping her dad gather honey from the bees. Ringing a dinner bell caused the bees to settle on a tree limb. They could then be moved into the beehive. Arabelle's daughter Florice remembers her grandfather Charlie as a quiet, humble man who talked little but worked hard. She loved visiting him. Florice remembered the long table in the dining room where the family gathered. The July 4 Warren reunions were filled with love and caring where cousins kept in touch. 'As a child,' Florice said, 'I thought Grandpa's seemed a long way off,' a distance that took hours traveling from Bowdon Junction via Jake to the home place! Summers, her brother, Eugene, and sister, Alera, hooked up the wagon and went to help Grandpa on the farm."

Charles Marion Warren with wife, Josiphine Robinson Warren

I wish I could have known my great-great-grandfather "Charlie" and experienced first-hand the closeness of my Warren family. I know he made Carroll County a better place. *Submitted by: Nanette Warren Trout, 2714 Placid Ave., Ft. Pierce, FL 34982*

Sources: U.S. Censuses, Interview with Florice Duncan Akin, Family histories and lore

1131. James Walter Warren Family

James Walter Warren was born on May 31, 1860, and his wife, Rebecca Turner Warren, was born on September 4, 1862. They lived in the Jake community six miles north of Bowdon.

James was a farmer and very interested in politics. Many in the community depended on his judgment in political affairs.

James and Rebecca had two sons: John Warren and Newton Warren. They also had six daughters: Lillie Warren Digby, Olivia Warren Alexander, Parrie Warren Wright, Mattie Warren Lovvorn, Thelma Warren Garrett and Carrie Lee Warren.

Rebecca died on November 30, 1905, leaving her husband to live as a widower until his death on November 11, 1928. Both James and Rebecca are buried in the Indian Creek Baptist Church Cemetery north of Bowdon.

The photograph shows James Walter and Rebecca Turner Warren and their family early in 1905. From left to right are John Warren, James Walter Warren, Rebecca Turner Warren, Thelma

James Walter and Rebecca Turner Warren family, 1905.

Warren Garrett, Lillie Warren Digby, Marion Lovvorn, Lester Lovvorn, Parrie Warren Wright, Mattie Warren Lovvorn, Olivia Warren Alexander, Newton Warren, and Carrie Lee Warren. *Submitted by: Mildred Lovvorn, granddaughter, 244 South Lakeshore Drive, Carrollton, GA 30117 and Written by: Paula Wilson Steed, great-granddaughter.*

1132. Joseph Marion Warren and Othella Thomas

Joseph Marion Warren, son of William Gabriel and Melvina Silvey Warren, was born November 2, 1894, in Carroll County, Georgia. At the age of twenty-two, Joe married Othella Thomas, daughter of Frank and Ida Darnell Thomas. Othella was born February 22, 1897, also in Carroll County.

To this union were born nine children: Silvey (1918), Winton L. (1920), Corine W. (1922), Hinton Perry (1925-1929), Edsel (1928), Neal (1932-1977), Jerry Max (1934-1990), Eugene Talmadge (1936), and Norman (1939).

Joe attended A. & M. School, which later became State University of West Georgia. Othella was a school teacher before she became a housewife. Joe worked for several years as an automobile mechanic, but when they organized REA, he began wiring homes in the rural areas. As World War II broke out, Joe was working with the International Brotherhood of Electrical Workers (IBEW) where he remained until retirement.

Joseph Marion and Othella Thomas Warren

The couple lived in Alabama briefly, and for a short time in Charleston, South Carolina, where Joe worked at the "dry docks," but mostly their home was in Georgia and Carroll County.

Joe and Othella had a full life. They enjoyed lots of friends and truly enjoyed their church. Joe was quiet and as honest as the days are long. At times, he could be mischievous but he was thrilled with company of any age. In his younger days, Joe enjoyed riding his motorcycle — which was unusual in those days. One day, after rounding a sharp curve on a dirt road, he crashed into a Caterpillar tractor left in the middle of the road by a county work crew. He gave up his motorcycle then.

Joe enjoyed Sacred Harp singing while Othella loved the "New Book" singing. Joe was known to travel many miles and maybe even spend the weekend in Florida to attend Sacred Harp singings.

Joe was an ardent Talmadge (Eugene) supporter in the political arena and he worked tirelessly to support the governor. One year he was chosen as a delegate to the Georgia Democratic Convention held in McRae, Georgia. So much was his enthusiasm for both Gene and Herman Talmadge, Joe named one of his younger sons after this family.

In later years, Joe built two fish ponds, an octagon-shaped pavilion under which chairs and benches were placed for seating, and a large circular concrete table upon which meals could be spread out and enjoyed. He also constructed a cover over a well curb into which flowed sparkling clear spring water. Joe grew his own gourds, dried them, and then designed them into dippers. He hung them around the spring so visitors could enjoy a drink of fresh spring water.

They beautifully landscaped the grounds surrounding the lakes, the spring, pavilion and table with flowers of various colors. Joe lovingly did all of this for the enjoyment of neighbors and friends, who were given special invitations to attend the yearly Sacred Harp singing and fish fry at "Little Joe's Lakes." Most guests arrived at the break of day to begin fishing. The catch was later cleaned and cooked to perfection in a special stainless steel vat. This was the main course of the meal.

Joe made sure there was an abundance of food for everyone. On the very first occasion of his fish fry, he reported that 768 pounds of fish were caught, cleaned, and cooked. Barely a scrap was left at the end of the day! He allowed no one to leave hungry. They served fried chicken, fish, hush puppies, cole slaw, baked beans, potato salad, rolls, home-baked cakes and pies, soft drinks, tea, and of course Aunt Mae's famous freshly squeezed lemonade. For a very nominal fee of $1.00 you could have "all you can eat." They later raised this fee to $1.50.

During the afternoon at these fish fries, people gathered under the pavilion for singing. Some played horse shoes, croquet, or perhaps a game of checkers. A select few played Tennessee Marbles. Joe had one strict rule for playing marbles, however. You were required to attain the minimum age of 65 before being allowed to participate. It was a truly enjoyable day for all ages.

At their deaths — Joe in 1977 and Othella in 1983 — they were buried at Poplar Springs Primitive Baptist Church Cemetery, surrounded by a host of relatives. *Submitted by: Corine Warren Adams, 68 Drue's Road, Bowdon, GA 30108*

1133. Ollie Melvina Warren and Eucleod McAllister Carroll

Ollie Melvina Warren, the daughter of William Gabriel Warren and Drewry Melvina Silvey, was born in Carroll County on 21 January 1899. Eucleod McAllister Carroll, son of James Moses Blackburn Carroll and Minnie Indiana Lucinda McBurnett, was born 23 June 1893 in Waco, Haralson County, Georgia.

The young Mr. Carroll from the Buncombe area, and the young Miss Warren from the Indian Creek area near Bowdon, first met at a Union Camp Ground meeting one Sunday afternoon. Our father did not relate to us if he felt love at first sight but he did admit to taking immediate steps to make the acquaintance of the pretty young lady. Thereafter, he made frequent visits to the Warren home on Sunday afternoons, driving his buggy and white horse. They were married January 13, 1918.

During the next eighteen years, eight children were born to this couple. In the course of their lifetime they would move at least six times, survive a depression, see a war take four sons and then return each of them. In the later years when the responsibility of rearing a large family was over, they continued to be a stronghold, not only to their children and grandchildren, but to parents, brothers and sisters, and friends.

After the early years when they lived in a small house near Grandpa (James Moses Blackburn) Carroll in Buncombe, they moved to Newnan, Georgia, where our father worked in the cotton mill repairing machines. The next move was back to Haralson County — this time to Tallapoosa where they remained until about 1934, at which time they moved their large family to an equally large old house situated on the site where the Bremen Recreation Center and tennis courts are now located. Two or three years later, within sight of the public school and the future Methodist Church, they built what was to become their permanent home at 329 Georgia Avenue. They resided there for the remainder of their lives with the influence of school and church etched deeply into each of their children.

Eucleod McAllister Carroll and Ollie Melvina Warren Carroll. 1965

Our father was an automobile mechanic by trade. Sometimes it was hard to tell his vocation from his avocation. Two other things he enjoyed throughout his long life were baseball and hunting. Our mother was primarily a homemaker. She worked at Hubbard Pants Company during World War II, and then again at the Bremen school cafeteria in the early 1960s. She surely is well remembered for the beautiful irises that she grew.

Each child carries his or her own memories, but probably none are more poignant than opening day of baseball season or the beginning of a World Series, or the cool crisp days of fall when the woods seem to be calling the hunters, or an early morning spring walk through the dew-laden iris garden.

The eight children in this family were: 1. Warren Opal Carroll, born 27 December 1918, died 24 March 1990, buried Mt. Harmony Memory Gardens, Mableton, Georgia; married Margaret Graham Stallings 22 December 1951. 2. Kenneth Lamar Carroll, born 30 July 1920, (now residing in Huntsville, Alabama); married Stella Ruth Plant 20 July 1957. 3. James Quinton Carroll, born 03 September 1923, died 09 December 1987, buried Bremen City Cemetery; married Madell Gwendolyn Bagwell, 14 February 1948. 4. Hilda Melvina Carroll, born 07 August 1925, died 27 April 1999, buried Woodlawn Cemetery, Knoxville, Tennessee; married first to Walter H. Phillips Jr. 05 April 1943, and second to William W. Luttrell 24 March 1974. 5. Victor Lee Carroll, born 18 July 1927, died 14 April 1982, buried Bremen City Cemetery; married first to Annie Lee Stogner 23 November 1947, and second to Elizabeth Jones 30 July 1957. 6. Charles Eucleod Carroll, born 03 June 1931 (now residing in Bremen, Georgia); married Betty Jean Whatley 08 June 1957. 7. Betty Jo Carroll, born 22 September 1933 (now residing in Bowdon, Georgia); married first to C.A. Truitt Jr. on 17 January 1954 (born 1931, died November 1954), and second to John Rudolph Parsons 23 July 1959. 8. Stanley Neal Carroll, born 31 August 1935 (now residing in Huntsville, Alabama); married Betty Joyce Cole 27 December 1957. *Submitted by: Kenneth L. Carroll, Huntsville, AL*

1134. Wallis Warren Family

Wallis Warren and wife, Mary, from South Carolina were in Carroll County, Georgia, by 1829. They remained there until they moved to Rome, Floyd County, Georgia, in 1840.

Their children were John K.A. who married Sallie J. White on 4 November 1862 in Floyd County; George W., born 5 February 1843, died 1 July 1919, married Mary A. Camp on 17 February 1870 in Floyd County; Mary A.; Georgia born 6 July 1849 in Floyd County, died 4 August 1925 in Attalla, Etowah County, Alabama; Alford; Benjamin Franklin Prisco Pierce born 23 May 1853, died 5 January 1904, married Sarah Parizade Ware on 10 January 1875. She died 12 January 1896; Jerusha; William; Matt married Mr. Glenn.

Three of the sons served in the War Between the States. John K.A. and George W. survived. William did not.

Benjamin and Sarah Warren had nine children. All were born in Floyd County, Georgia. They were Mary Ethel born 25 August 1875, died October 1875; Eula Levada born 2 September 1876, died 30 October 1943 in Attalla, Etowah County, Alabama, married John William Storey on 2 December 1894 in Rome, Floyd County, Georgia. He was born 10 May 1874 in Dirt Town, Chattooga County, Georgia, died 3 August 1937 in Tuscaloosa, Alabama, buried in Oak Hill Cemetery, Attalla, Alabama; William Isom born 26 April 1879, died 18 December 1943 in Attalla, Etowah County, Alabama, married Annie A'Dair; Alva Ora born 16 September 1881, died 5 March 1932 in Floyd County, married George Pierce Pass on 6 December 1901; Charley Franklin born 5 February 1884, died 12 March 1929 in Attalla, Etowah County, Alabama, married Bertha Mae McGullian; Dollie Mae born 3 August 1886, died 12 July 1968 in Chattanooga, Tennessee, married Solon Eucklett Collett; Isabelle Inez born 10 October 1884, died 11 June 1890; Charlcie Irene born 9 May 1891, died in Munford, Alabama, married Hudson Allen Gray on 11 August 1911; Rubye Leigh born 5 May 1893, died 16 September 1974 at Avondale Estates, Atlanta, Georgia, married (1) Aubrey R. Tarpley on 2 April 1914 in Etowah County, Alabama and (2) Zeke Sibley.

John William Storey, the husband of Eula Levada Warren, was a blacksmith. He made the andirons for Martha Berry's first one-room school.

The following Warren children moved from Rome, Floyd County, Georgia to Attalla, Etowah County, Alabama about 1904: Eula Levada, William Isom, Charlie Franklin, Dollie Mae, Charlcie Irene, and Rubye Leigh.

Please read "Storey, Herston, Gentry, Robertson, Warren" for additional information. *Submitted by: June Curry Maddox, 6301 Third Street, Gadsden, AL 35903*

Sources: Carroll County, Georgia Court House, Floyd County, Georgia Court House, Rome-Floyd County Library, Oak Hill Cemetery in Attalla, Alabama, and family knowledge.

1135. Walter Tilman Warren and Mary Elizabeth Smith

Walter Tilman Warren was born March 5, 1830, in Henry County, Georgia. He was the second of thirteen children born to John O. Warren and Serena Stewart. John O. Warren and two of his brothers, Thomas and Peter, first appeared on the Carroll County census records in 1840. Mary Elizabeth Smith was the daughter of another long-time Carroll County family — Gabriel D. Smith Jr. and Nancy E. Cain. Mary Elizabeth was born July 3, 1829. Walter Tilman Warren and Mary Elizabeth Smith were married on August 14, 1853, in Carroll County, Georgia. They lived in the Smithfield community and were farmers. They had nine children to reach adulthood and close to one hundred grandchildren.

Their children were (1) William Gabriel Warren born in 1854, and married to Drewry Melvina Silvey (see Warren history). (2) Mary Elizabeth "Shug" was born 1857, died about 1940, and was married to Ben Asa King. Mary and Ben are buried at Poplar Springs. (3) James Walter was born 1860, died in 1928, and was married to Rebecca A. Turner. James and Rebecca are buried at the Indian Creek Baptist Church Cemetery. (4) Charles Marion Warren was born in 1862, died in 1940, and was married to Josephine Robinson. They also are buried at Poplar Springs Primitive Baptist Church Cemetery. (5) Peter Columbus was born 1866, died in 1940, and was married to Mary Adele Silvey, a first cousin to our grandmother Melvina. (6) Martha Ann Warren was born 1867, died in 1959, and was married to Henry Newton Phillips. (7) Joseph Abel Warren was born 1870, died in 1933, and was married to Cora Cornelia Stogner. Joseph, Cora, and their eleven children are all buried at Indian Creek Baptist Church Cemetery. (8) David Solomon was born in 1871, died in 1959, and was married to Rosa Ada Kuglar. Both are buried at Indian Creek Baptist Church Cemetery. (9) The last child was a daughter Ida Lelia born in 1873, died in 1956, and was married to Asa Taylor Wright Jr. They are buried at Mt. Zion United Methodist Church Cemetery.

Walter Tilman Warren had an older brother named Peter Columbus who died in the Civil War in 1863, and it is believed that Walter and Mary Elizabeth named their fifth child born in 1866 after this brother. Except for Peter Columbus and Martha Ann, all of the children remained in or nearby the Smithfield area. Peter and his wife went to Rusk County, Texas, after a short stay in Louisiana. Martha and Henry's first five children were born in Georgia, then they moved to Texas about 1894.

Many of the grandchildren of Walter T. and Mary E. Warren attended Liberty Hill School which was located near the intersection of Smithfield and Lovvorn Roads in Carroll County. (See related article and picture.) The 1911 school picture of Liberty Hill shows a total of seventeen Warren children. These children belonged to the families of William Gabriel, Charles Marion, and David Solomon. An original of this picture belonged to Mae Warren (one of the seventeen) who had thoughtfully recorded the names of all fifty-six students plus the teacher, Mr. Aubrey Barrett, on the back of the picture.

Walter Tilman died in May 1915 and Mary Elizabeth died in October 1910. Both are buried in Poplar Springs Primitive Baptist Church Cemetery in Carroll County. *Submitted by: Edsel Warren, Waco, GA*

Sources: Stanley N. Carroll, 2109 Hansel Avenue, Huntsville, AL 35802, and Betty Jo Carroll Parsons, 2085 Bowdon-Tyus Road, Bowdon, GA 30108

1136. William Gabriel Warren and Drewry Melvina Silvey

William Gabriel Warren, born August 10, 1854, in Lowell, Georgia, was the son of Walter Tilman Warren and Mary Elizabeth Smith. Drewry Melvina Silvey, born April 28, 1864, was the daughter of William Drewry Silvey and Mary Hollan Pitts.

William Gabriel Warren Family

According to Bible records, *(Hitchcock's New and Complete Analysis of the Holy Bible)* William Gabriel Warren and Melvina Silvey were married August 19, 1879. However, the marriage license shows August 17th. The marriage ceremony was performed by Ranson E. Smith, JP, an uncle to William Gabriel. This Concordance, believed to have been purchased about 1888, was originally owned by William Gabriel and Melvina Warren. After the death of Melvina Warren on April 17, 1950, it was passed to the youngest daughter, Mae Warren of Bowdon, Georgia. It is now in the possession of one of Melvina's granddaughters.

Friends and family of this young couple called them "Gabe" and "Melvina."

Melvina's father, William Drewry Silvey, died near the end of the Civil War in Virginia. She and her brother and sister, Jessie Napolian and Virginia Missouri, were raised by their grandparents Jessie Bryan and Jane Hanson Silvey. After the death of her father, Melvina inherited sixty acres of land. Gabe had inherited about ten acres from his father, Walter T. Warren, and then continued to buy more acreage from his brothers and sisters and friends whose property adjoined theirs.

Gabe and Melvina first lived in a one-room house on Smithfield Road, after which they built a two-room house across the road. As the family grew, the Warrens continued to add more rooms to their original house. They farmed the accumulated 160 acres in spite of his poor health. Grandfather Warren was a semi-invalid after about age twenty-five; he suffered from a severe case of what was known then as catarrh. Because of his poor health, all the children in this family learned to work at an early age. We do not know much about our grandfather since he died rather young, but one personal characteristic he had was very small feet for a man — he wore a size five shoe.

Gabe and Melvina were members of Poplar Springs Primitive Baptist Church in Carroll County and both are buried there. Although our grandfather died well before we were born, we remember attending the Annual Communion Service with our grandmother and observing the ritual of washing feet. As young children, we did not understand the meaning of the ritual but we remember the solemnity of the service and how humble our grandmother was. Another family story relates the deep religious faith Melvina had. Her fervent prayer was that Gabe would live to see his ten children grown. He died when the youngest child was twenty-one years old.

Many of the Warren grandchildren remember their grandmother's strict dinnertime rules — no talking and no laughing at the table. And they didn't.

Twelve children were born to Gabriel and Melvina Warren, with ten of them living to adulthood. The first was a stillbirth about 1881. Mary Elizabeth (called Lizzie) was born April 7, 1883, and married William Oscar Davis on November 2, 1901. Ella was born April 1, 1886, and married Gerome Horsley on May 12, 1907. Drucilla was born May 31, 1888, and married James Leon Davis on March 10, 1907. William Jesse was born September 27, 1890, and never married. Annie Virginia (called Verd) was born December 4, 1892, and married Leonard Warner Arthur on December 4, 1910. Joseph Marion Warren was born November 2, 1894, and married Othella Thomas on August 19, 1917. Minnie Leola (called Lee) was born January 6, 1897, and married Marlin Augustus McKibben on December 25, 1921. Ollie Melvina was born January 21, 1899, and married Eucleod McAllister Carroll on January 13, 1918. Martha Mae was born April 17, 1901, and never married. Arvella was born April 11, 1903 and only lived three months. Boyce Newton was born December 21, 1905, and married Kathleen Duffy on February 4, 1934.

The two children in this family who remained single, William Jesse and Martha Mae, were the ones who primarily took responsibility for their mother Melvina after the death of Gabe. Jesse, the oldest son in the family, served in World War I. Mae said she remembered Jesse walking to town (probably Bowdon) to enlist in the army. He told no one of his plans until he returned home that day. Jesse talked very little about those war years, but he did relate a story of a woman he met in France who reminded him of his own mother. She was especially kind to him and on occasion provided him with extra food. After the war, Jesse worked for the U.S. Postal Service. He first worked in Atlanta and later was a rural mail carrier out of the Bowdon post office.

Mae's first job after completing some classes at a business school in Birmingham, Alabama, was with Alabama Mills in Birmingham. Several years later (World War II years) she took the civil service examination, passed it, and accepted a position with the Navy Department in Washington, D.C. She later returned to Bowdon to help care for her ailing mother and remained there until her brother Jesse was transferred to Bowdon. This left Mae free to return to her old job at Alabama Mills in Birmingham. After Alabama Mills was bought out by Dan River Textiles, Mae was transferred to the office headquarters in Montgomery, Alabama, where she remained until her retirement in 1966.

After her retirement, she returned to the Smithfield community and bought her brother's (Boyce) house located on the same property where her parent's home once stood. She and Jesse only had about a year to enjoy living close to each other again, as he died in March of 1967.

Mae had many unforgettable attributes — her laughter; her love of family, and it was hard to tell but she may have loved her dogs even more so; she despised housework and didn't like cooking, but loved digging in her garden and growing flowers; she adopted a various assortment of dogs and each one was greater than the previous one.

Unlike her sisters, Mae did not learn the art of quilting from her mother. But when she was about eighty years old, she decided it was time to tackle the job. A nephew built and installed a quilting frame for her, nieces took her shopping for fabric, she ordered books, and she was well on her way. After about six years and 45 beautiful quilts later, she called it quits. Most of her quilts were given to family members.

Although Mae never married, she claimed all generation levels of nieces and nephews as her own children and would often boast that no sister had more than she! A great-niece once asked her why she never married and she replied: I guess I was just lucky.

The old idiom — What goes around comes around — certainly holds true with this Warren family. No children could have done more for their mother than was done for Melvina Silvey Warren.

When Mae Warren died in August of 2000, she had been surrounded for years by nieces and nephews who bestowed this same care on her. She was just six months short of being one hundred years old. Because she outlived all her siblings, she was like a mother to many of us. But more importantly, she inspired many in the family to expect and achieve a higher standard for themselves.

Both William Jesse Warren and Martha Mae Warren are buried at Poplar Springs Primitive Baptist Church Cemetery, Bowdon, Georgia. The family photograph made 1905 shows seated from left: William Gabriel Warren, Drewry Melvina Silvey Warren, Martha Mae, Mary Elizabeth Warren Davis, William Oscar Davis. Standing, from left: Minnie Leola, Ella, Joseph Marion, Ollie Melvina, Annie Virginia, Drucilla, and William Jesse.

Submitted by: Carolyn Parsons Mendrek (great-granddaughter of William Gabriel and Melvina), Huntsville, AL

Sources: Stanley N. Carroll and Betty Jo Carroll Parsons

1137. Moses Denman Watkins Family

William Word, Moses Denman Watkins' father-in-law, was born 15 March 1813 in Franklin County, Georgia, died 26 November 1881 in Carroll County, married 20 March 1836 to Elizabeth Merrill Embry who was born 29 November 1816 and died 6 June 1889 Carroll County. William was the son of Joshua Word and Amelia H. Hooper of Franklin County, Georgia. He was the grandson of Charles Word Jr., a Revolutionary soldier, born 9 July 1740 in New Kent County, Virginia, died in the Battle of Kings Mountain 7 October 1780.

William and Elizabeth lived on the same piece of property through three county boundary changes. First Campbell County, second Douglas County, and now Carroll County. They are buried in marked graves in the family cemetery on the Word place at Five Notch Road, Carroll County.

They had four children: Thomas Jefferson, Mary Jane, Amelia Frances and Divine Howard in the birth order.

Thomas Jefferson Word born 1857 and married Martha Wooten. Mary Jane Word was born 1838 and married James C. Attaway. Amelia Frances was born 1840 and married Benjamin Watkins. Divine Howard Word married Moses Denman, a younger brother of Benjamin. Benjamin and Moses Denman are sons of Reece and Elenor Watkins.

Moses Denman Watkins was born 8 March 1845 and died 8 August 1916 Carroll County, married 23 October 1866 Carroll County. Divine Howard was born 23 June 1843 and died 23 November 1923 Carroll County Georgia.

Divine and Moses had four sons and three daughters all born in Carroll County. Only three sons had children, the daughters had no children. Edgar Watkins, the oldest had four sons; Homer Watkins, World War I Veteran, decorated war hero, had one daughter and one son; Howard Watkins, the youngest, had one son and one daughter.

Moses Denman ("M.D." as he was known) was mayor of Whitesburg for twenty years and was a state legislator from Carroll County from 1908 to 1912. In this time frame, Georgia had only twenty-seven representatives in the lower house. Some became governors, U.S. senators, and representatives. The record shows that M.D. presented bills for establishing the Whtiesburg School System and the Commission of Roads and Revenue for Carroll County that passed 27-0 and were sent on to the governor to sign.

Moses D. Watkins

The Whitesburg Cemetery holds Moses Denman and Divine Howard Watkins, with their children, Hershall Reese and Elizabeth. The Carrollton City Cemetery is the resting place for Moses Denman's youngest son, Howard Denman, and his wife Margaret Simonton Watkins. *Submitted by: Robert C. Watkins Jr. (great-grandson), 140 High Point Walk, Atlanta, GA 30342*

1138. Ida Mavis Coley Watts

Ida Mavis Coley Watts, daughter of Joel Judson Coley and Myrtle Ruth Pirkle Coley, was born in Ranburne, Alabama, on January 11, 1915. Mavis grew up in the Gold Ridge-Ranburne area. She finished nurse's training in Birmingham, Alabama. As a registered nurse, she traveled to New Orleans, Louisiana, and began work at Charity Hospital. There she met an intern, Dr. James W. Watts. Their first date was to a flower show. The tickets were given to Dr. Watts by a patient. A year later they were married and the following year their daughter Susan was born.

The family moved to Thomasville, Georgia, where Dr. Watts completed a surgical residency and in 1942 to Bowdon, Georgia, to begin his private practice. Mavis served as her husband's right hand as his office nurse and made house calls with him. Mavis served many capacities when the Watts Hospital opened. In addition to recruitment of additional nurses to work in the hospital, the shortage of registered nurses put many other jobs under her leadership. She worked side by side with her husband in the operating room giving the anesthetic to patients undergoing surgery. She continued this until her husband's death in 1964 and never went

Mavis Coley Watts

into the operating room again. The hospital continued serving the community under her leadership until 1972. She donated land to the City of Bowdon for construction of the Bowdon Area Hospital. The Jubal Watts Memorial Hospital closed the day the new hospital opened.

Mavis had two children after she and James moved to Bowdon. James Wyly Watts Jr. was born March 14, 1945, and Jubal Robert Watts was born July 17, 1947.

Mavis made national news in 1947. According to the *Washington Post,* July 5, 1947, she saved a man who had been bitten by a rattlesnake. Dr. Watts, who had his own airplane, was on a pleasure flight around the area. When Mavis saw his plane, she used a pocket mirror to flash morse code to him. He landed, treated the man and the man fully recovered.

Mavis became the first woman in the history of Bowdon to run for mayor. In 1950, she had two opponents, James Moore and Lloyd Holloway. She lost the election by only twelve votes, 132 to 144.

Mrs. Watts moved to Carrollton, Georgia, in the early 1970s where she was active in St. Margaret's Episcopal Church and served on the Vestry. She loved to play bridge, golf and fish, but the flowers in her garden were her preference. She shared her flowers with anyone who asked and her flowers were used for numerous occasions.

A mother of three, grandmother of nine and the great-grandmother of two, Mavis continues to give encouragement and leadership as the matriarch of the Watts family. *Submitted by: Coley Alison Watts, Athens, GA*

1139. James W. Watts

James W. Watts, M.D., son of Joel Forrester Watts and Annie Hicks Davis Watts, was born March 20, 1912, in Vernon Parish, Louisiana. Dr. Watts worked his way through Louisiana State University and Louisiana State University Medical school. He served his medical internship at Charity Hospital in New Orleans, Louisiana, where he met Mavis Coley. Mavis, a registered nurse, came to New Orleans to work at Charity after finishing her training in Birmingham, Alabama.

Nurses at Charity were to show respect for all doctors by standing when a doctor entered a room. Mavis always stood when James entered the room even though he was only an intern. This gesture must have gotten his attention. They were married a year later and on April 2, 1941, the following year their daughter Susan was born.

After completing his internship, Dr. Watts, his wife and daughter moved to Thomasville, Georgia, for his surgical residency. In early 1942, Bowdon citizens asked Dr. Downs, a pharmacist, and Lee Otis Wiggins, barber and brother-in-law of Mavis Watts, to go to Thomasville and offer Dr. Watts assistance to come to Bowdon, Georgia, where there was a need for a young doctor. Mavis had been raised in nearby Ranburne, Alabama, which increased the likelihood of their relocating to Bowdon.

Dr. Watts moved to Bowdon and set up an office in the Johnson house, located downtown on the corner of Johnson Avenue and Main Street. Here Dr. Watts and Mavis worked as a team treating people from the area, delivering babies, and making house calls. House calls were usually on muddy dirt roads to homes with no running water or electricity. Babies were delivered in bedrooms at home and overnight care meant the doctor stayed all night. Payment for services was often a "mess" of beans, a chicken or two, or whatever the people could pay. On one call, a patient asked Dr. Watts how much he owed and Dr. Watts replied, "That bird dog with the broken leg out in the yard." Although the dog's leg had to be amputated, it became a three legged fixture around the office for years.

James W. Watts, M.D.

The only available surgical facility was the Carrollton Clinic. The operating room was located on the second floor and patients were carried by stretcher up and down stairs because there was no elevator. Dr. Watts' saw the need for a hospital and in 1945 the first hospital in Carroll County was built in Bowdon, Georgia. At the time, it was the most up to date hospital between Atlanta and Birmingham. Jubal Watts Memorial was named for Dr. Watts' grandfather who was a doctor during and after the Civil War.

A son, James Wyly Watts Jr. was born March 14, 1945, and another son, Jubal Robert Watts was born in 1947.

Dr. Watts served his community in other areas. He was an active member of civic clubs, served on the city council and was mayor 1949-50, 1952-53, 1960-61, and 1963 until his death March 2, 1964. *Submitted by: James W. Watts Jr., Bowdon, GA*

1140. The Wells Family

The Wells family originated in Basel, Switzerland, which is located on the river Rhine in the Jura Mountains and bordered by France and Germany. The family migrated to Normandy, France, eventually settling in County Essex, England. Among the earliest settlers in New England was Thomas Wells, who became a member of the Virginia Company in 1620. The family traveled from Mulberry Island in Warwick County, Virginia, to New Bern, North Carolina, settled in Georgia in 1827 and in Carroll County in 1860. My paternal grandfather, James Charles Wells, who was born in 1868, was the son of James Henry Wells and Nancy Almeida Chapman. My grandfather, who was known in the community as "Mr. Charlie," was a cotton farmer in the Temple area of the county and in

1891 married Susan Blanche McPherson, also of Carroll County. They had five children: Guy Herbert, Otis Lafayette, Charlie Clifford, Claudie Eugine, and Zelma Ruth. After Blanche's death, "Mr. Charlie" married my grandmother, Martha Emily Sims in 1911. "Miss Mattie," as my grandmother was known, was born in 1876 at Sugar Hill on the Little Tallapoosa River. She was the daughter of Robert Toombs Sims and Josephine Wynn. My grandparents had four children: James Lewis (my father), Robert Thomas, Roy Sims, and Nancy Josephine.

James Charles and Martha Sims Wells

It has been said that the Wells family had a very strong love for both liberty and education. Several members took part in the American Revolution, the Civil War, and both World Wars. Other Wells family members have included poets, journalists, political economists, and numerous writers and authors. The late Dr. Guy H. Wells, my uncle and a Temple resident for many years, was a Georgia educator for over fifty-five years. He served as president of both Georgia Southern College and later Georgia State College for Women. He served as a Peace Corps consultant in the Kennedy administration and served on the United States Civil Rights Commission in the 1960s. His daughter, the late Dr. Anne Wells Branscomb, was a researcher, author, and Harvard professor.

Temple home of "Mr. Charlie" and "Miss Mattie" Wells

In the early 1950s, it was my pleasure to spend much time with my paternal grandparents, "Mr. Charlie" and "Miss Mattie." They lived in a huge white house on Carrollton Street in Temple, which everyone in the family referred to as "the big house." Life in this house revolved around the kitchen. It was the center of everything. Some of my fondest memories are of Granny Wells in her kitchen. It was a rare occasion to see her without her apron. During this time, she cooked on a "newfangled" electric stove, which had replaced the massive wood-burning stove she had used for years. For a family of four children, five stepchildren, and assorted grandchildren, nieces, and nephews, she produced, among many other things, wonderful cobblers, tea cakes, and a chocolate bread pudding that I have tried for years to duplicate. She used no recipes. Even now, I can almost smell the huge pots of bubbling preserves which became a part of each summer's day. Meals were "events," always beginning with an enormous breakfast, followed by dinner (there was no such thing as lunch), then supper. No sooner had the breakfast dishes been cleared away than dinner plans would be underway. Supper preparations would closely follow the midday meal. My grandparents never heard of cholesterol and, indeed, they both lived to ripe old ages.

Granny Wells no longer washed and boiled clothes in a big, black pot. That gave way to the modern washing machine and wringer-type dryer.

Although my grandparents once managed a working farm, gone were the days when they milked cows, churned their own butter, kept assorted farm animals, and plowed gardens in the spring. Even though they both conceded to various modern conveniences, they still preferred the old-fashioned ways of doing most things. Granny made her own clothes and was a wonderful and talented quilter. She tried in vain to teach me the fine art of crochet. She also managed to grow, without much effort at all, the most amazing spider plants I've ever seen.

Summers were a lazy time spent on the back porch, in the woods behind the house picking blackberries, or listening to my grandparents talk of the old days. There was a special room in the back of the house which Granny referred to as "the plunder." Inside this fascinating room were all manner of discarded memorabilia. These were treasures to a small child like me: boxes of old clothes from which quilting scraps would be gleaned, knickknacks, broken furniture, books. One might stumble across almost anything in "the plunder." Other special memories are of a red, silk-covered sofa and love seat, gingham sunbonnets, the tortoise shell combs my grandmother used in her red hair, and a wonderful white porch swing that was my special place to be in the summertime.

Granddaddy Wells died at age ninety-three in 1961 and Granny followed at age ninety-four in 1970. At the present time my mother, Lois Ezelle Dean Wells, remains the only surviving Wells family member still residing in Temple. My remembrances are of a much simpler time when people actually paused along their way to smell the flowers and enjoy life. *Submitted by: Dinah Wells Taylor, 4867 Judith Avenue SE, Acworth, GA 30102-2865*
Sources: *The Wells and Allied Families,* 1938, Guy Herbert Wells, Milledgeville, GA

1141. Edgar Johnson and Mary Viola Wessinger

Edgar Johnson "Ed" Wessinger Sr., born 9-23-1881, and Mary Viola King, born 8-29-1881, were married 1-27-1901. His parents were James W. Wessinger (1840-1893) and Neaty Ann Johnson Wessinger (1847-1924). Her parents were Ben Asa King (1856-1917) and Mary Elizabeth Warren King (1856-1940).

Ed and Viola Wessinger were married for fifty-seven years until Ed's death 11-5-58. Viola died 11-26-71. They were the parents of ten children, all of whom lived to adulthood: Villa Gladys (1903-1966), Stella Mae (1905-1994), Clifford Travis (1908-1987), Lilly Clara (1911-1994), Lucius Clyde (1911-1960), Leonard Leon (1914-1974), Harvey Lon (1914-1990), Eunice Ethel (4-25-17), Edgar Johnson "E.J." Jr. (1920-1990), and S.J. "Skeets" (1923-1983).

The family moved to the Tyus community in 1923. The move was made in part so the children could have better educational opportunities. Travis, Clara, and Clyde attended Bowdon College. Clyde graduated from the University of Georgia. Eunice and E.J. attended West Georgia College. Ed was a resourceful man who enjoyed buying, selling, and trading. One trade in particular, a "Delco Plant" battery system, afforded the family the first electricity, running water, and indoor plumbing in Tyus.

Ed learned brickmasonry from his father, but he also was a farmer. In addition to farming, he opened a store in Tyus in 1930. The stock included groceries, gas, oil, school supplies and other basic necessities. Soon he extended the store business with a peddling truck that delivered door to door. The truck operated five routes five days per week. The first driver was Claude Thigpen. However, Ed's son, Lon, took on responsibility for the peddling routes after he graduated from high school.

Wessinger 50th Wedding Anniversary with all ten offspring, 1951

Viola was a gentle, sweet-natured person who only saw the best in others. Once when a friend commented that one of her grandsons was "worst in the bunch" of otherwise very fine youngsters, she responded "I hope so, because he's such a good boy." Her belief in his goodness encouraged him throughout his lifetime. Viola was a person of deep faith, who believed that everything is a gift from God. Her faith supported her when two of her children preceded her in death.

World War II brought changes for many families, and the Wessingers' two youngest sons, E.J. and Skeets, were both drafted. Ed and Viola prayed every day for their safe return and considered it a great blessing that their prayers were answered. Ed suspected that the day of the small country store was over, so the family moved to the city of Bowdon in 1941. Even though he was over sixty, Ed wanted to contribute to the war effort so he took a job in a defense plant at Anniston, Alabama, for the duration of the war. The Wessingers were members of Tyus Baptist Church, and later Bowdon Baptist Church. When his defense plant work prevented him from attending revival one year, he gave his entire week's salary.

Ed and Viola Wessinger were good parents, good citizens, and good people. *Submitted by: Eunice Wessinger Holloway, 140 Frances Street, Bowdon, GA 30108*

1142. Edgar Johnson Wessinger Jr.

Edgar Johnson Wessinger Jr., known as "E.J.," was the son of Edgar Johnson Wessinger Sr. and Mary Viola King Wessinger. He was born in Heard Coutny, Georgia, on his father's birthday, September 23, in 1920, the ninth of ten children. Mary Ruth Douglas was the daughter of Charles Morrow Douglas and Clara Jennings Douglas. She was born March 28, 1919, in Carroll County, the fourth of six children who lived to maturity.

Mary's father, Charlie Douglas, was orphaned at a very young age, and his wife Clara died in childbirth. Mary was thirteen at the time, and the loss of her mother was pivotal in her life. Mary and her older siblings assumed considerable adult responsibilities in order to keep the family together. After she completed high school, she worked at General Shoe Company and later at Dandee Company. This was at a time when working outside the home was uncommon for young women. Her intelligence, honesty, and assertiveness earned her supervisor positions.

E.J. grew up in a family which, like Mary's, was familiar with hard work. Most of his childhood years were spent in Tyus, Georgia, and Tyus remained dear to him throughout his lifetime. He graduated from Bowdon High School in 1939 and had entered West Georgia College when he was drafted into the Army Medic Corps. The Tyus farm boy traveled to England, France, the Philippines, and Japan. When he returned, he vowed to stay home, and he mostly made good on his promise except when recalled to active duty during the Korean conflict. At the end of World War II, he began working with his older brother, Lon, who owned a grocery store in Carrollton. It was there E.J. met his best friend and life partner, Mary Douglas.

E.J. and Mary Wessinger, 1947

Years later, Mary told the story of their first meeting. Lon's store was near her job, so she would go there on occasion. She noticed the young clerk would save candy and other treats for her. "I think he liked me," she said, and indeed he did. She was talented, quick-witted, and somewhat fiery, while he was gentle, unassuming, and charming. Both had strong family values. They were married in 1947 and their union lasted until E.J.'s death on August 28, 1990, forty-three years later.

Soon they became parents of two children, Mary Mignon and Douglas Edwin. They built a modest home in Bowdon adjacent to E.J.'s parents. E.J. started his own business as a Gulf dealer and Mary became a fulltime mother. They were loving, devoted parents. Mignon was a sickly infant and at times money was tight. Once they needed money for medicine and all they had was one silver dollar. They spent their last dollar for medicine and considered themselves fortunate to put it to that use.

E.J.'s generosity in his business was renowned in the Bowdon Community and many wondered how he prospered at all. But he counted meeting others' needs as a test of his Christian faith, and their actions thereafter as a matter of individual conscience. Eventually, he made investments that became quite lucrative, an occurrence that amazed and amused him.

E.J.'s health forced his retirement in 1982. However, the remaining years of his life were among his happiest because he and Mary had time to enjoy being together. After his death she lived five years, the last proving beyond doubt her courageous nature as she battled a debilitating stroke. She joined E.J. in death on February 27, 1995.

E.J. and Mary Wessinger were genuinely good and principled people. They left the world a better place because of the lives they lived. *Submitted by: Mignon Wessinger, P.O. Box 25, Bowdon, GA 30108*

1143. James W. Wessinger

James W. "J.W." Wessinger was born 1-9-1840 in Richland County, South Carolina. 1850 census records for Richland County indicate that Jacob (born 1798) and Celia (born 1808) Wessinger had four children: Catherine (born 1829), Sarah (born 1831), James (born 1840), and Ellen (born 1844). J.W.'s great-grandfather, Mathias Wessinger, arrived in Charleston in 1752 with his family aboard the ship *Snow Rowand.* It's likely they emigrated from Ulm, Germany near Munich. Mathias Wessinger was born in Damsbach, Baden, Germany. He appears on South Carolina militia rolls 1759-60, and he served under Col. Chevilette and Capt. Morrison.

J.W. Wessinger married Neaty Ann Johnson who was born 2-26-1847 in Georgia. After J.W.'s death, Neaty Ann married W.F. McElroy 11-30-1902. Neaty Ann's mother, Lucinda, was born 2-4-1826 in Georgia and she died 11-21-1903. Little else is known of her though she's buried in Bowdon Baptist Church cemetery beside J.W. and Neaty Ann. Her headstone is inscribed Lucinda Couch, so it's likely she had a second marriage.

It's unclear exactly when J.W. Wessinger came to Carroll County, but family lore has it that he left South Carolina around the age of fifteen. Bowdon founder Nathaniel Shelnutt notes in the 1859 Articles of Incorporation that J.W. Wessinger was then living in the home originally occupied by the Shelnutts in 1849. He enlisted 8-27-1861 in Bowdon Volunteers, Company B, Cobb's Legion and was discharged July 25, 1862 because of illness.

J.W. had a brickyard as well as a store in Bowdon. He was a brickmason and a carpenter. In 1887 his store was one of five destroyed in a fire that engulfed an entire block. However, he reestablished the business and his wife continued to operate it after his death 1-19-1893. On the store ledger and in personal correspondence, she always signed her name N.A. Wessinger. She's said to have been a lively, petite woman who loved music and loved to dance. She even enjoyed an occasional toddy, somewhat shocking to her teetotaling relatives. Neaty Ann Johnson Wessinger McElroy died 3-22-1924.

James W. and Neaty Ann Johnson Wessinger

J.W. and Neaty Ann Wessinger had eleven children: Charley Thomas (11-26-1863), Alice Margaret (8-11-1865), James Franklin (11-2-1867), Walter Wills (10-31-1870), Alonzo Woodrow (4-15-1873), Lydia Ada (4-14-1875), Samuel Jacob (8-7-1877), Leonora Annie "Doll" (9-25-1879), Edgar Johnson (9-23-1881), Lucinda Gertrude (12-17-1883), and Sara Ellen Kate (3-31-1886).

A receipt remaining in the family shows that on 1-8-1890, J.W. Wessinger paid the $6.75 Bowdon College spring term matriculation fee for his son Lon. *Submitted by: Mignon Wessinger, P.O. Box 25, Bowdon, GA 30108*

1144. Lon and Louise Wessinger

Lon Harvey "Rip" Wessinger, born January 8, 1914 in Tyus, Georgia, and Norma Louise Spruell, born March 21, 1920, in Farmer's High, Georgia, were married December 24, 1937. His parents were Edgar Johnson Wessinger (1881-1959) and Mary Viola King (1881-1971). Her parents were Caleb Norman Spruell (1891-1942) and Mary Belle Treadaway (1892-1969). Both lived their lifetime in Carroll County where they raised four children, Lon Harvey Jr. "Lonnie" (1939-1977), Linda Louise (1943), Kathy Joan (1951) and Robert Lynn "Bob" (1952). Lon and Louise were married for fifty-two years until Lon's death on August 29, 1990. Louise passed away four years later on June 3, 1994.

Lon and Louise Wessinger

Lon graduated from Tyus High School in 1933 and began working in his father's grocery store in Tyus. Louise graduated from Bowdon High School in 1937. Later that year they married. Louise ran the store while Lon ran the peddling truck that delivered door to door. In 1945 Lon and Louise moved to Carrollton and started Wessinger's Grocery Store on Maple Street. The family lived in three rooms in the back of the store. They made many friends especially the children at Maple Street School who bought candy and school supplies. Lon worked long hours six days a week, but still found time for his family. Louise helped at the store, kept house and raised the children. Lon would extend credit to his customers when they were unable to pay. He was a quiet unassuming man who was always willing to help families that "traded" with him. I was recently acquainted with a girlhood friend who shared her feelings that "her family might not have had food on the table many times if it weren't for Mr. Rip."

Lon and Louise built their first home on Longview Street and lived there from 1949 until 1971. Lon's family helped build the house and he paid for it in cash. In fact, Lon never carried a loan in his lifetime, believing that you should not buy anything unless you could pay for it. Louise found time even with four children to visit and help her neighbors, sew clothes, garden and help at the store.

They were members of Tyus Baptist Church, then Tabernacle Baptist Church, and later joined Antioch Baptist Church.

They helped send all four children to college to receive their degrees. Lon Jr. entered the Air Force as a pilot after graduating from Georgia Tech. His jet crashed at sea in 1977. Linda received a biology degree from West Georgia College and became a medical technologist. Kathy received her pharmacy degree from the University of Georgia. Bob received his degree from West Georgia College and is a retired Naval officer.

In 1970 Lon sold the store. They bought land, built a home and moved to Lovvorn Road in 1971. Lon built a small lake and raised cattle. Louise worked on a rural mail route. They spent many happy years there especially enjoying time spent with their family fishing, playing cards, and pool. They were good friends and neighbors to many but most of all wonderful, loving parents. *Submitted by: Kathy Wessinger Gibbs, 3886 Willow Ridge Court, Douglasville, GA 30135*

1145. West Orphans Move to Carroll County

When the widow Margaret Athaline Pence West was ill with influenza, five of her six children were almost as critically ill as she was. Eight-year-old Emmett tried as best he could to care for his family. But Maggie died on March 10, 1920. The six orphaned West siblings then came to Carroll County, Georgia, from Bradley County, Tennessee. Their uncles, Dr. Grover West and James Benjamin West, lived in Carroll County. Also, their paternal grandmother, Martha Lucinda Spriggs West spent part of each year with those sons in Carroll County. These children needed some adults to help look after them if they were to continue living together.

The West orphans were James Spurgeon (born May 27, 1903), Martha Jewell (born January 5, 1905), Jonathan Royal (born April 9, 1907), Wilma Ruth (born July 19, 1909), Grover Emmett (born November 29, 1911) and William Willie Gilbert (born March 17, 1914). My father Royal (second oldest boy) along with the oldest sibling Spurgeon, drove a contrived covered wagon pulled by two mules. With their household possessions in this wagon and leading their cow, Spurgeon and Royal traveled through the Cohutta Mountains of North Georgia, camping out at dark.

Spurgeon, Wilma, Bill, Emmett, Jewel, and Royal West (c. 1936)

Meantime, Martha Jewel, the oldest girl, brought the "little ones" on the train from Cleveland, Tennessee, to Carrollton, Georgia.

Daddy told tales of camping along the way, especially in the mountains. They would keep a fire burning each night because of the wild animals and because of the fire, only one of them could sleep at a time. When they came into Gordon County, they had friends where they could stay to rest a few days, having lived in Gordon County some years when their father was pastoring a church at Ramhurst when he died in 1915. In later years, when Daddy and Uncle Spurgeon talked about their great adventure, neither could remember the exact number of days the journey took, but they agree that it was close to two weeks.

Aunt Jewel never talked much about the train journey. However, Aunt Wilma's children recall that their mother always became very sad each time she heard a train whistle, that she hated trains.

The children were met at the Carrollton depot by the uncles and taken home with them to await the arrival of the boys. When Spurgeon and Royal arrived, they moved into a sharecropper house in the Tyus-Veal community. There, they raised crops and survived as best they could together for the next five or six years, attending school at Veal when they could.

While the six young people were eking out a living, they were also becoming a part of the community, meeting and socializing and worshipping. In August of 1925, the first to leave the farm was Jewel who married Homer Mize and moved to a house on the Mize home place which is where Lake Clyde is now.

Apparently, the crop of 1926 was so poor that they could not longer afford to continue to keep house, because in the fall of that year, the youngest, Willie, went to live with an uncle, Jonathan Roscoe West, in Dawsonville, and the West orphans scattered to various locations and lifework. *Submitted by: Barbara West Billert, 95 East Barbara Lane, Carrollton, GA 30117*

1146. West Siblings

My sister related the story of how our father, J. Royal West, and his five siblings came to live in Carroll County as orphans in the early 1920s. This essay relates their later lives. The children lived and farmed as sharecroppers in the Tyus-Veal area until 1926. That year's crop was so poor, the siblings had to find other ways to get on with their lives. It was such a devastating year that 57 years later, Uncle Bill wrote a rhyme and mailed it to Daddy in 1983:

SHARE CROPPER, 1926

We turned the soil
And sowed the seeds;
Then prayed for rain
While chopping weeds.

From early spring
Till late July
We tended crops
Then "laid them by."

And waited for
The summer sun
To finish what
We had begun.

When crops were gathered
In the fall
We'd little cash
Or none at all.

But once
With all the cotton sold
We had some change
And were so bold

To fling caution
To the breeze
And blow our earnings for the year
On crackers and a pound of cheese!

Among other family stories is one which occurred in the mid 1960s when Emmett Harrod went to meet his fiance's maternal grandparents: When the Dennys learned that Emmett was the son of Wilma West Harrod, one of the West orphans, they told Emmett that Spurgeon and Royal stopped at their house with their wagon filled with their possessions and asked directions to Dr. Grover West's.

Sometime during the 1920s Spurgeon West graduated from A. & M. We do know that 1926 was the last year the West orphans were together. At this time, Bill went to Dawsonville; Wilma, Emmett and Royal probably entered Berry School where they all three graduated high school, with Emmett, Royal and Bill completing college there. Wilma attended Bowdon College and probably West Georgia College.

These orphaned youngsters all went on to contribute to their various communities in many ways: Spurgeon worked in Atlanta, Chattanooga and at the Oak Ridge plant during World War II, before moving back to Carroll County where his two sons graduated from Bowdon and Central Highs. Jewel, after her marriage to Homer Mize, taught school in Carroll County, worked at Sewell's and raised three daughters who graduated from Bowdon High. Royal went to work for the New Deal's Farm Security Administration (after a six-week stint teaching at Tyus School), married Lucille Boyd of DeKalb County, lived in Chatsworth and Cedartown before being assigned to the Carrollton office of the re-named Farmer's Home Administration. One of his daughter graduated from Cedartown High, one from Carrollton High. Royal also bought an old farm that later became Linda Lane, Barbara Lane, etc., named for his two daughters. Wilma married Olin K. Harrod, raising four Bowdon High graduates, teaching all around western Carroll County. Emmett married Mary Harrod of Bowdon, raised two Bowdon High graduates, retiring from the U. S. Postal Service as a rural mail carrier, ultimately donating the land on which the Bowdon Public Library stands. After Berry, Bill entered the Marines, serving in the South Pacific in World War II. He married a Californian, Freida Trink, and settled in California where they had three children. With graduate degrees, he retired as an elementary school principal in Corcoran, California.

seated: Jewel, Emmett, Wilma; standing: Bill, Royal, Spurgeon (1972)

Grover Emmett West died in 1972, Jewel West Mize in 1975, James Spurgeon West in 1986 and Jonathan Royal West in 1989. All are buried in Carroll County. Wilma West Harrod is ill, living in the Harrod home place on Highway 100 in Bowdon. William Gilbert (Bill) West lives in an assisted living apartment in Sonoma, California. *Submitted by: Linda West Plunk, 55 Mary Lane, Carrollton, GA 30117*

1147. William and Winnefred West

William West was born about 1788 in North Carolina. His only known wife, Winnefred, was born about 1786 in South Carolina. This couple was in Greenville District of South Carolina in 1820 and 1830. In Carroll County by 1833, this family was the first to occupy Buck Horn, which later became the Buck Horn Tavern. William and Winnefred probably died sometime between 1870 and 1880. Their burial places are unknown.

Their nine known children, all born in South Carolina, are: (1) George W. born about 1820, married Clara Ann Hay on April 9, 1854, in Carroll County. They had no children. (2) Mary Ann born about 1822, died after November 18, 1899, apparently never married. She was also called Polly Ann. (3) Edna Hampton West (see separate article about Allen Hill Eady). (4) Sophronia born about 1824, married David Bryant on August 11, 1842, in Carroll County. Their children were Thomas S. born about 1843; William P. was born about 1845; Mary M. was born about 1846; Edna M. was born about 1848; James Whitley born 1850, married Sarah A. Chance; Edley H. born about 1853, married Martha A. Rains; Marcus L. was born about 1855; Belsora P. was born about 1857; Elizabeth W. born about 1859, married George I. Forbes; Robert E. was born about 1860; and Sarah C. was born about 1869. (5) William S. West (1826-1897), married Mahala J. Adams on March 23, 1856, in Carroll County. He served in Company B, Capt. Benson's, Glenn's Squad, Mounted State Troops, Cavalry. He is buried at Concord Methodist Church in Carroll County. Their known children are Robert W. (1858-1937), married Liberia F. Spence; Gilbert T. (1864-1907); Thomas S. (1867-1952) married Sara Emma Henry; Allen A. born about 1871, married Sara A. Pitts; Talullah J. born about 1873, married Z.W. Muse on December 15, 1892, in Carroll County; Anatha (1879-1900); and two others whose names are unknown. (6) Thomas H. West (1828-1892) married Frances Lenora Hay on December 23, 1856, in Carroll County. Both are buried at Carrollton City Cemetery. Their known children are George H. (1857-1911); Talullah born about 1862; and Charles M. (1867-1875). Charles M. is the little boy buried in the Upshaw-Routon Cemetery in Carroll County. He is shown on the 1875 records of deaths in Carroll County as dying of typhoid fever. (7) Robert was born about 1831. (8) Eliza Jane born about 1832 and died after November 18, 1899, never married. (9) A son is indicated on 1830 and 1840 censuses but is not on the 1850 Carroll County census. *Submitted by: Max Dyer Harper, 60 West Ridge Drive, Temple, GA 30179*

1148. William Wister West Family

Seven generations of the West family have lived in Carroll County within five miles of their first home place at Buckhorn Tavern at Temple, Georgia.

William Wister West, great-great-grandfather of William T. (Bill) West, came to Georgia from South Carolina with his wife, Winnefred (Winney), and six children: George W., Mary, Edna, William Smith, Thomas H., and Robert; then Eliza was born in Georgia. He was the grandfather of G.H. West of Carrollton and the great-great-grandfather of Mrs. B.M. (Man) Long of Carrollton. He bought six hundred thirteen and one-half acres (land lots 169, most of 170, 184, and part of 151 in district six) east of Ringers Cross Roads (now Temple, Georgia). In 1833 he built what is now known as Buckhorn Tavern. He ran this stagecoach stop as an inn and a tavern until it was purchased by Isaac Cobb.

William Smith West and Mahala Adams West

William Smith West (1826-1897), son of William and Winney West, married Mahala Adams (1834-1919). She was the daughter of Absalom Adams (1810-1875), who came from Tennessee and settled at Ringer's Cross Roads. William was a carpenter, a doctor, and a farmer. They lived between Center Point and Carrollton at the Loyd Wester home place. William and Mahala had six children: Gilbert, Thomas Smith, Allen A., Talulae, Arthur William, and Robert W. West.

Gilbert West was in the Civil War and is buried at Concord Methodist Church Cemetery.

Allen A. West married Anna Lovell, moved to Birminigham, and they had three children: Belle, Lillian and Ophie. Belle married P.E. Martin; Lillian married R.F. Craig and they had two children, Robert and Betty; and Ophie married Russell Pruitt.

Talulae West better known as Leola, (or Lula) married Zach Muse. Their children were Vernon, Ruie, Jerome, and Gladys (Billie). Ruie married Emmett Wester. They ran a shoe store in Carrollton for a number of years. They were killed in an automobile accident at the intersection of Highway 166 and 61. Jerome, who married Bertha Taylor, once had a paper business in Carrollton. Vernon married Ray Sharp and their children were Frances, Jack, and Milford. Gladys married Olin Boynton.

Thomas Smith West (1867-1952) married Sarah Emma Henry (1875-April 16, 1935), daughter of James Greer Henry and Mary Kirk. Tom was Past Master of Temple Lodge #322 and a Mason for sixty years. They had six children: Elena, Euell, Edith, James Harold, Pearl, and Mary Ella.

Thomas and Emma West

Elena (Lena) was born in March 1890 and died in 1968. She taught school at Center Point for awhile and also made hats and ran a millinery in Temple. She once painted a stage curtain for Temple High School with different colors of mud. She married Irvin Thompson and moved to Old Campbell County near Fairburn, Georgia, where she also taught school. They had two sons: Hoyt and Jim. Hoyt traveled in Florida for a cosmetic company, and while in his forties he had a heart attack and died while crossing the street in Fort Myers, Florida. Jim married Emily Woodall from Fairburn, Georgia. They had three daughters: Sallie, Martha, and Patricia Ann. Sallie, born in 1945, has one daughter, Amanda, and one granddaughter, Shayla Beth. Patricia Ann (Pattie) married Roy Richardson. They had three daughters: Jessica Ann, Laura Emily, and Rachel Elise.

Mary Ella married Bernard Hamrick of Cullman, Alabama. After her divorce, she came back to Temple to live where she taught music, and she also had several songs published in the Stamps-Baxter song books. She had no children.

Euell Smith West (April 1, 1895-November 4, 1950) married Jane McBrayer (September 12, 1895-February 22, 1986). They lived at the West home place off Center Point Road out of Temple the first year they were married. They then moved to Fairburn, Georgia, Union City, Georgia, and back to Temple where they bought the Joe Griffin home place on Montgomery Street and lived there until their death. From 1943 until 1967, Jane ran West's 5 & 10 Cent Store in Temple. They had one son, William T. West, born January 16, 1928. He married Catherine Yates of Villa Rica, Georgia, and later he married Mary Frances Freeman of Cedartown, Georgia. He and Catherine had four children: Gregg, Andrea, Keith, and Alan. Gregg married Lynn Myers from Fort Myers, Florida. They had two daughters: Kari and Jami. Kari married Michael Richards. They have one daughter, Emma Lee. Jami married Michael Bartlett. Gregg later married Dolly Burns. Andrea married Ridley Hubbard of Bremen, Georgia. They have two children, West and Janie Hubbard. West married Amanda Brooke Hollingsworth. They have two children, Julia Ridley and Andrew Chase. Keith married Melissa Gibbs from Bowdon, Georgia. Alan married Susan Berry. They have two children, Kristen Taylor and Zackery. Taylor and Zackery are the seventh generation of Wests to live in Carroll County within five miles of the first home place, Buckhorn Tavern at Temple, Georgia.

Edith West married Guy Jacobs. They were both active in the Eastern Star Chapter in Temple. They had two daughters, Lois and Margaret. Lois married A.G. Ashworth, and they had two sons, Greg and Jarrett. Jarrett had two sons. Greg had one son, Richard Allen Ashworth. Margaret married John Jones. They had two children, Mike and Margaret Ann. Mike has three children: James Michael, Amanda Mechelle, and Matthew Britt. Margaret Ann married Shannon Dempsey. They have two children.

James Harold West, who was born August 21, 1911, married Estell Tillman from Bremen, Georgia. They lived in Atlanta, Hapeville, College Park, East Point, Temple, and Douglas County. They had two children, Max and Joyce. Max married Edna Swinson. They had two children, Eddie and Laura. Joyce married William P. McGloin, and they had two children, Kathleen and William P. McGloin Jr. She later married Mike Gibson.

Pearl West, who was born August 31, 1913, married Eston Hunter. They had two children, Robert Eston and Thomas West Hunter. Robert Eston married Barbara Tillman. They have one daughter, Elizabeth. Thomas West married Dee McCoy, and they have one child, Frances Leigh Hunter.

Robert William West, son of William Smith and Mahala (or Mahalia) Adams West, was born September 22, 1858, and died October 8, 1937. He married Libera (or Liberia or Libira) Spence (1860-1924), who was the daughter of Hiram and Angeline (Cheney or Chaney) Spence. Their children were: William Hiram (August 1, 1880-date of death unknown); Annie Phedora, (June 13, 1889-March 24, 1974) who was born in Carroll County and died in Douglasville, Georgia; Ada, Wilburn Wester, Robert Newton, Emmitt Moses, and Mamie whose birth and death dates are unknown. (It looks like there was one named George who died in infancy?)

Euell and Jane West

Ada West married Harry Crockett. Their children were Clarence, Buford, Ray, who died in infancy, Mozelle, and Raymond, who also died in infancy. Clarence Crockett married Era Wren. They had one daughter, Shelby Jean. Mozelle Crockett married William Stallings. They had one daughter, Gloria Sue.

Wilbur Wister West married Katherine Boatright, and they had one daughter, Dorris Isabelle.

Robert Newton West married Lillian Sewell. Their children are Robert, Lucy Goldsmith, and Elizabeth.

Emmett West married Novelle Threadgill. They had one son, Robert.

Annie Phedora married James Gilbert Parrish. Their children were James Grady, Annie Ruth, Emmett Lester, Frances Libira, and Iva Mae.

Annie Ruth Parrish married Jesse Dangar. They had two children, Roderick and Gail. Gail married Datha Bell and they had one daughter, Deena.

Iva Mae Parrish (May 13, 1909-June 24, 1984) married Cecil Luther Levans (who was born April 5, 1903.) Their children are Donald, Jerry, and Judy. Iva was a homemaker and worked at Sewell Manufacturing Company. Her interests were painting, family, and travel. Donald Levans was born February 21, 1931, Carroll County, Georgia. He married Betty Ruth Sims, daughter of William Sims and Winnie Redding. Their children are Michael Luther who married Jane Letcher Waller, and Melanie Lynn who married Robert Bryan Olson. Jerry Zack Levans married Julia Ann Allgood. Their children are Johnny Zack, Janet Ann who married Randy Carver, Joyce Rebecca who married Chris Beauchamp, and Linda Jo who married Chris Bell. Judy Levans married Gerald Allgood, and they had one son, Jody Allgood. She later married Wendell Furr, and they had one daughter, Stacy Gail who married Bo Martin.

Grady Parrish married Ida Bell Eargle. Their children are James (Jimmy) and Joan. James married Martha and they had one son, Andrew James. He then married Paula, and their daughter was named Paula.

Emmett Lester Parrish married May Young. Their children are Emmett Jr. and Diane.

Frances Liberia Parrish married Albert Cosby. Their children are Kathy who married Greg Barnes, Iva Joyce, Allen, and Linda. Allen's wife's name was Peroska, and their child is Albert II. Linda married Tom Carpenter and their children are Callie and Stewart. *Submitted by: William T. West, P.O. Box 157, Cave Spring, GA 30124*
Sources: Family records

1149. William L. Westbrook

William L. Westbrook was born in 1808 in Sampson County, North Carolina, and died 2 July 1893. Buried at Emmaus Primitive Baptist Church Carrollton, Georgia. First married Mariah Vaughn in 1834 in Franklin County, Georgia, and the 1840 census from Franklin County show them with one son and two daughters.

James Grady Westbrook and Velma Phillps

He married second Lavinia "Viney" Crider (born January 1836 in Georgia) 25 December 1866 in Carroll County. On the 1880 Carroll County census he is with children (1) Lucila "Ella" born about May 1866; (2) John Pendleton born 12 September 1870 in Georgia; (3) Ida born about 1873; (4) James Lewis born May 1876; (5) William R. "Will" born April 1879; (6) Jackson born about 1882 in Georgia; (7) Mary Jane.

William L. Westbrook's parents were William and Elizabeth Dougherty Westbrook of Sampson, North Carolina. Lavinia "Viney" Crider's parents were John Crider of North Carolina and Martha Vines of Georgia. Lavinia died 10 September 1915 in Carrollton and is buried beside William L. Westbrook at Emmaus Primitive Baptist Church, Carrollton. The 1900 Carroll census show her living with son James. Lavinia married third, W.A.J. Jarrett on 21 December 1902 in Carroll County.

William L. Westbrook was a member of the 36th District 757th Georgia Militia in the War Between the States. Carroll County voter registration, 1867-68, shows him registered in the 729th election district called Lick Skillet.

James Lewis Westbrook, born May 1876, was a blacksmith. He married first Mary Lynch (born 1879 in Georgia, daughter of Elija O. and Jenett H. Lynch of Coweta County, Georgia) 14 February 1900 in Carroll County. He had the following children: Lois Lillian, born 30 May 1905, died 23 March 1928, married Nathan L. Johnson born 16 July 1902 died 10 June 1989; James Grady Westbrook, born 6 March 1908, died 27 April 1979, married Velma Phillps born 30 March 1911, died 11 September 1996; Gladys, born 24 August 1909, died 2 May 1964, married Nathan L. Johnson (same as above).

Lois Lillian Westbrook and Nathan Johnson

Lois Lillian, born 30 May 1905, died of tuberculosis at age thirty-two. At the time, she and Nathan lived at 39 1/2 Whipple Avenue, Egan (East Point), Georgia. She is believed to be buried in Flat Rock Cemetery at College Park, Georgia. They had one daughter, Ruby Virginia, who married James C. Corley. Their children were Kenneth, David, Roger, and Charlotte.

David E. Corley, born 1944, retired from Atlanta Fire Department, married Sherry Sue Gentry, daughter of J.P. and Tula Blackmon Gentry from Haralson County. Children were Joe Aaron who married Paula M. Eversole, daughter of Paul and Rosemary Eversole of Coweta County. They were graduates of State University of West Georgia; and Justin Daniel Corley, presently a student of State University of West Georgia.

James Grady Westbrook, born 6 Mar 1908, married Velma Phillps. He was retired industrial supervisor with the U.S. Penal System, seaman first class aboard *USS La-Prade De409,* U.S. Navy in World War II, and textile supervisor at Arnall Mills in Sargent for thirty years. Their children were Frank, Joe, Terry.

Gladys Westbrook and Nathan Johnson lived in High Point, North Carolina. They worked in the textile mills and farmed. Nathan became a preacher and built a church where he served as pastor. They had no children, but adopted a girl named Sue.

James married second Velma Maude Pitt. He died 10 December 1930 in Arizona. He is said to be buried in Boot Hill, Phoenix Arizona. *Submitted by: David E. Corley, 5 East First Avenue, Newnan, GA 30265*
Sources: Carroll County Genealogical Library, Westbrook Family Bible

1150. The James Daniel Wester Family

James Daniel Wester b. 22 Mar 1866 in old Henry County, twin to William Benjamin Wester, came to Carroll County with their father, James Madison Wester and mother, Melissa Ann Hendon, from Campbell County after the Civil War. With them came James Madison's brother W.A. J. Wester and sister, who had married a Harper.

James Daniel Wester m. 21 Dec. 1890 to Lucy Armeda Bartlett b. 30 Nov. 1869, daughter of Reuben S. Bartlett and Mary Pennington Bartlett. The family lived in the Kansas G.M.D. of the county near Center Point community during most of their life. For a few years they lived on Coleman Street in Carrollton, while J.D. "Bud" Wester was a guard at the county prison camp.

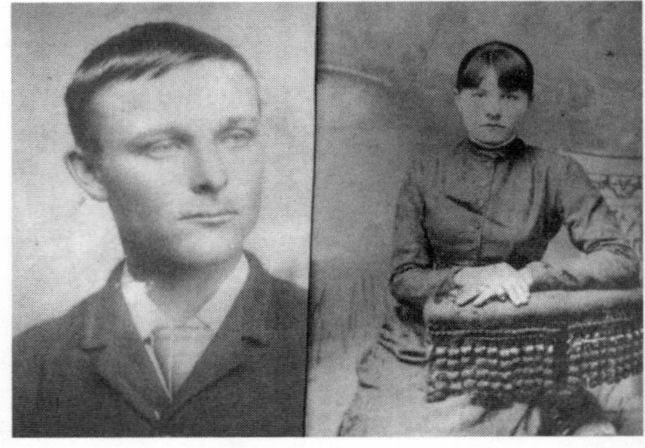

James Daniel Wester and Lucy Bartlett Wester

Children: 1. James Marvin Wester b. 5 Nov 1891 m. May 1913 to Bessie P. Parrish, one child, James Daniel II. 2. William Olin Wester b. 26 Nov 1892 m first Ella Hamrick, mother of his children, m. second Odessa McEachern, two daughters Mary and Mildred and one son Alton. 3. R. Loyd Wester b. 14 Nov 1895 m. 24 April 1924 Ruby McCain, son William Loyd Wester and daughter Linda Sue Wester. 4. John Emmett Wester b. 24 May 1898 m. 9 Mar 1921 to Rhue Mae Muse. No children. 5. Thomas Ralph Wester b. 24 Aug 1903 m. 1 June 1929 to Bana Copeland, one son, Thomas.

The James Daniel Westers were founding members of the Center Point Methodist Church after it was founded from the County Line Church. Their picture appears at the first quarterly meeting. Lucy Bartlett was the granddaughter of Rev. Ephraim Pennington, and was honored by the church with the naming of her circle (missionary society members) in her later years.

The couple in their last years lived in an apartment at the home of son, Ralph Wester, in Carrollton. He died 5 Dec 1948 and she died Jan. 1958. *Submitted by: J.D. Wester, Carrollton, GA and Written by: June Hart Wester, 133 Mountain Crest Drive, Canton, GA 30114*

1151. The James Madison Wester Family

James Madison Wester b. 7 Oct 1825 d. 16 May 1899 bur. County Line Cemetery near Center Point Community, Carroll County. He served in Company B. Georgia Reserves Confederates at age 45. His father, Daniel Wester, died in Campbell County. The estate was administered by Samuel Paschall, brother of the widow, Fereba Paschall Wester.

James Madison was accompanied to Carroll by brother, W.A.J. Wester and sister, Mary Virginia and husband, Thomas Benjamin Harper. Together they owned and operated a mill on Buck Creek. Later the others left Carroll and went to Cherokee County, Alabama, where descendants live today.

Melissa Hendon Wester and James Madison Wester

The wife of J.M. Wester was Melissa Hendon b. 23 Dec 1836 d. 9 Sept 1881, daughter of William A. Hendon and Mary "Polly" Lasseter Hendon. The nine children are by Melissa. After her death, J.M. married second Mary Stovall.

Children: 1. Mary Elizabeth Wester b. 1 April 1855 m. John (James) W. Stovall 4 Dec. 1873, ten children. 2 Feriby Ann Wester b. 18 Sept 1857 m. Wyatt "Jeff" Crawford, five children. She d., bur. County Line Cemetery, Center Point. 3. Sarah Jane "Sally" b. 9 Mar 1860 m. James Crockett and the family moved to Montana, four children. 4. Idella Jackson Wester b. 25 Aug 1862 m. first Ezra McCalmon, one child, m. second John B. Bartlett, two children. Bur. Mt. Zion Cemetery. 5 & 6: Twins: James Daniel "Bud" Wester b. 22 Mar 1866 d. 5 Dec 1948, m. 21 Dec 1890 Lucy Armeda Bartlett, five boys. William Benjamin Wester "Will" b. 22 Mar 1866 m. Ella Spence 20 Dec 1891 d. 10 Nov 1931, four girls and one boy. 7. George Madison Wester b. 26 Mar 1869 m. Pearl Chance 11 Jan. 1903, three daughters. 8. Samuel Oscar Wester b. 23 Jan 1875 d. 7 Aug 1896. 9. John Edward Wester b. 27 Sept 1877 d. June 1914 unm. *Submitted by: Mary McCalmon, Carrollton, GA and Written by: June Hart Wester, 133 Mountain Crest Drive, Canton, GA 30114*
Source: Ruby Wester Middlebrooks research

1152. The R. Loyd Wester Family

R. Loyd Wester, son of James Daniel and Lucy Bartlett Wester b. 14 Nov 1895, was a World War I veteran. He was born in Carroll County and lived there all his life except for service in combat duty at Dijon and Lemans, France in a motor repair unit. He had trained at Georgia Tech and Camp Johnson, Jacksonville, Florida.

He met Ruby McCain and they married in 1924. She was the daughter of Alcimus Allen McCain and Elizabeth Chance McCain of the Temple area. Their first home was in Bremen, and they suffered through the drought after the birth of their first child, William Loyd Wester.

Loyd and Ruby Wester

After moving to Carrollton, where he worked for the Folds Motor Company, they lived on Tanner Street next door to the Henry Worthy family. Steve Worthy was a fine playmate for the tot, and the families were good neighbors.

Later they lived on Rome Street when Bill attended College Street School. Next door neighbors were the G.M. Westers family with whom they were good friends. Loyd Wester owned half of a farm with his brother Emmett. After Bill graduated from College Street School they exchanged their new home on Rome Street for the farm.

A young sister had joined the family, Linda Sue Wester, b. 15 Feb. 1939. The move to the farm was hard, as they, along with many others, suffered as the country lived through the beginning of World War II, and Bill was subject to the draft. After he graduated from Temple High School he joined the Air Force Reserve. He entered the war with the 15th Air Force and was wounded over Italy. During the war, Loyd taught the NYA (National Youth Administration) school in the mechanics division. He also worked at various wartime posts doing motor repair, at which he was a master mechanic.

When son "Bill" married June Hart from Temple they had two children, Julie and Charles William. Sister Linda married George Willis Crusselle and had four children, G.W. Crusselle Jr., Caroline, Benjamin, and Matthew. The farm today is a retreat for the entire family. One of the Crusselle sons has built a home on the acreage. Loyd Wester d. 30 June 1974. His widow, Ruby McCain Wester, has a clear memory of all the family treasurers at age ninety-seven. *Submitted by: Linda Wester Crusselle, Powder Springs, GA and Written by: June Hart Wester, 133 Mountain Crest Drive, Canton, GA 30114*
Sources: Personal memories and family collections

1153. The W.L. "Bill" Wester Family

When Bill Wester and June Hart met at Temple High School in 1940, none of us knew that World War II was just around the corner. Bill was waiting notice from the Air Force when June went to West Georgia College as a freshman. Later, she went to the University of Georgia. Bill was inducted into the Air Force. After his overseas transportation was delayed they bought the engagement ring in Athens. Then Bill went back and was sent overseas to the 15th Air Force in Italy. On a raid over Vienna, the B-24 was shot up and limped home to Italy, where the crew ejected. Bill was wounded and word came to Carroll County he was in the hospital after surgery.

Bill, June, Julie, and Charlie Wester. 1954

The wedding took place in August 1945 as soon as Bill could walk without a cane and the lilies were blooming! After his release, the couple lived in Carrollton. He started work for the Georgia Power Company, a career which lasted for forty-three years. Although materials were scarce, they built a small home on Penn Avenue near other Wester kin. Two children were born, Julie in 1950 and Charles William in 1952. After living there for nine years they built a home on Ridley Drive. The children attended Maple Street School and Carrollton Junior High.

The family was active in the First Baptist Church, Jaycees, Brownies, Cub Scouts, the VFW, Lion's Club, Spade and Trowel Garden Club, and Beta Sigma Phi.

June worked at the West Georgia Regional Library as reference librarian until 1964 when they moved to Rome, Georgia, where Bill became district appliance superintendent, Georgia Power Company. *Submitted by: Julie Wester Teague, Sacramento, CA and Written by: June Hart Wester, 133 Mountain Crest Drive, Canton, GA 30114*
Source: Personal knowledge

1154. Samuel Dorsey and Isabelle Johnson Whatley

Charlsie Isabelle Johnson Whatley was born in Bowdon, Georgia on October 25, 1917, to William T. Johnson Jr. and Evie Lee Downs Johnson, both of Bowdon and later residents of Atlanta. By age ten, Isabelle had decided to be a nurse and in 1938 received her R.N. degree from Georgia Baptist Hospital, Atlanta. That same year she married her high school sweetheart, Sam Whatley, who was born January 30, 1915, in Hapeville, Georgia, son of Vachel D. and Lizzie Ola Lowe Whatley.

Isabelle Whatley 1938 graduation, Georgia Baptist Hospital Nursing School

Sam began to build a career in the railroad industry, and their first child Eleanor Jeanne was born in 1939. World War II intervened, and although he had deferment, Sam volunteered for the U.S. Navy. He was immediately assigned to Ship's Company at Camp Peary near Williamsburg, Virginia, where Isabelle and daughter joined him for fourteen months, and Isabelle worked as a nurse in the only hospital. Then Sam was transferred to a Pennsylvania billet, necessitating Isabelle's return to Atlanta with Jeanne. Shortly afterward, their son Sam Jr. was born. It was not an easy time, as with thousands of other families during the war. In 1946 Sam was honorably discharged from the Navy and returned to work at the railroad; the family circle was rejoined, all thankful and happy.

His executive abilities earned Sam continued promotion within Southern Pacific RR, first to Louisville, Kentucky in 1959, then to Washington, D.C. in 1964, and finally as district manager, Cincinnati, Ohio, in 1972. In each city, Isabelle graciously created homes for Sam Sr. and son Sam Jr. as well as doing private duty, doctors' office and hospital nursing, earning a special place in her patients' hearts. Daughter Jeanne was attending University of Georgia, Athens, and later married.

Sam D. Whatley, Yeoman 2nd Class, US Navy Reserve, 1944-1946

In 1970 Isabelle and Sam tragically lost their beloved son. Only twenty-five, Sammy was a fine young man who had enlisted in the Marine Corps and who had been voted outstanding recruit in his graduating class at Parris Island boot camp. He had wed Esther Dianne Burger in 1965.

Upon retirement in 1980, Sam and Isabelle came to live in Marietta where they had many friends and became active in Marietta First Baptist Church. Jeanne and her husband Douglas G. Baldwin moved near them, and they saw their granddaughter Shelley often.

Mr. and Mrs. Sam D. Whatley, 1998, 60th Wedding Anniversary

Sam's most ardent interest was tennis, and he was known as a fierce and competitive player, not giving up the game until late 1999 when he was sidelined by recurrent Lymphoma. Sam died on March 18, 2000, at Tranquility Hospice in Cobb County, Georgia. Isabelle carried on gallantly, but finally her heart simply broke and on February 4, 2001, she passed away at her home - oldest daughter, first grandchild, her memory cherished by family and friends. The devoted couple are buried next to Sam Jr. at Westview Cemetery, Atlanta, Georgia. *Submitted by: Shelley Scott Garrett, 1050 Ponce de Leon Ave., Apt. 417, Atlanta, GA 30306*

1155. Family of Vachel Davis Whatley

Vachel Davis Whatley (April 1868 in Antioch, Georgia-September 11, 1946) married Alberta Fields. He graduated from Bowdon College in 1898. He served as head of Rock Mills and Roopville High School, was principal of Villa Rica High School and Tallapoosa Public Schools, and was president of Lineville (Alabama) College, Hutcheson Collegiate Institute, and Bowdon (Georgia) College. Mr. Whatley taught several years in the Fourth District A&M School and was superintendent of Carroll County Public Schools. He was editor of Lineville, Alabama *Headlight Newspaper,* part owner in Roop-Whatley Hardware Store in Carrollton, organized and owned the Whatley Drug & Grocery Store in Bowdon, and was one of the organizers/stockholders of the Villa Rica Light and Power Company. He is buried in City Cemetery, Carrollton.

Lizzie Alberta (Berta) Fields (December 1877 near Roopville, Georgia-March 27, 1932) married Vachel Davis Whatley. Mrs. Whatley taught in the Carroll County Public School system and became the first home demonstration agent in Carroll County from 1917 until her death. She was a member of the Daughters of the Confederacy. She is buried in City Cemetery, Carrollton.

Front row left to right: Vachel Davis, Lizzie Alberta, George Fields. Back row: John Walton, Annice Lucille, Vachel Davis Jr., Render Lee.

Vachel Davis and Lizzie Alberta Fields Whatley had the following children: John, Annice Lucille, John, Vachel Davis Jr., Render Lee, and George Fields.

Annice Lucille Whatley (August 1900 in Bowdon, Georgia-April 2, 1975 in West Palm Beach, Florida) married Henry Cameron. She graduated from Carrollton High School and Georgia State Normal School in Athens. She taught school in Newport News, Virginia, and Deland, Lakeland, and West Palm Beach, Florida. She is buried in Palm Memorial Gardens.

Vachel Davis Whatley Jr. (November 1903 in Villa Rica, Georgia-November 1996 in Raleigh, North Carolina) married Margaret Virginia Lampke. He attended Carrollton High School, Mercer University in Georgia, and graduated from West Point Military Academy. He served in the U.S. Army and was stationed in many areas including Hawaii and the Philippine Islands (commanded by General Douglas MacArthur and Lt. Col. Dwight Eisenhower). In 1942 he was ordered to the War Department in Washington. He was decorated with many medals and reached the rank of colonel. He is buried at Arlington National Cemetery, Virginia.

John Whatley (December 1905 in Whitesburg, Georgia-December 21, 1987) attended Carrollton High School, Mercer University, and University of Georgia. He is buried in the Bowdon Baptist Cemetery.

Render Lee Whatley (November 1907 in Lineville, Alabama-April 4, 1999, in Seminole, Florida) married Mary Beck Tatham. He graduated from Carrollton High School and received a degree in electronics from Georgia Technical Institute in Atlanta. He worked at General Electric, RCA, and Naval Avionics in Indiana.

George Fields Whatley (September 1911 in Bowdon, Georgia- October 17, 2000) married Helen Terretha Hunt, and later married Arta Mae Johnston. George attended Carrollton High School, Bowdon Georgia State N & I College, Berry College in Rome, Georgia, and University of Georgia. He served in the U.S. Army. He was principal of Clem (Georgia) Junior High School, worked at Palm Beach, Florida, Post and Post Office, was editor of the *Polk County, Georgia Times,* was manager of Georgia State Department of Veterans Service, was the postmaster of Polk County, was Polk County Commissioner Administrator, and worked with the Georgia Department of Labor. He is buried in Pensacola, Florida. *Submitted by: Eugenia Whatley Googe*

1156. Wayne Arthur and Debra Swanson Wheeler

Debra Elizabeth Swanson and Wayne Arthur Wheeler were married at St. Margaret's Episcopal Church on Newnan Street on June 29, 1996. Bridesmaids were Bryna Bobick of Carrollton, Jennifer Hall Hermann of Carrollton, and Heather Harper of Carrollton and Nashville. Groomsmen were Albert Wheeler Jr. of Waco. Billy Joel Lockhart Jr. of Tallapoosa, and Kolt Bell of Anchorage, Alaska. The Wheeler's first home together was at 42 Terry Terrace, Carrollton. They moved to Allison Circle in Carrollton in 1998.

Debbie's first job after graduating from the University of Georgia in 1996 was division safety coordinator at Gold Kist in Carrollton. She then worked as the Environmental, Health and Safety Coordinator at the State University of West Georgia and as an Environmental, Health and Safety Coordinator at Fitel-Lucent Technologies in Carrollton. As of May 2001, she is pursuing a master of biology degree at SUWG. Wayne was one of the first officers hired at the West Georgia Boot Camp in Bremen, Georgia. He was stationed at the Olympic Games in Atlanta in 1996, and he met several well-known athletes. In 1999 he graduated from SUWG and after graduation, he worked for E*Trade, the internet investment company, as a broker. In 2000 he bought Pizza K on Maple Street, but he sold the restaurant in 2001.

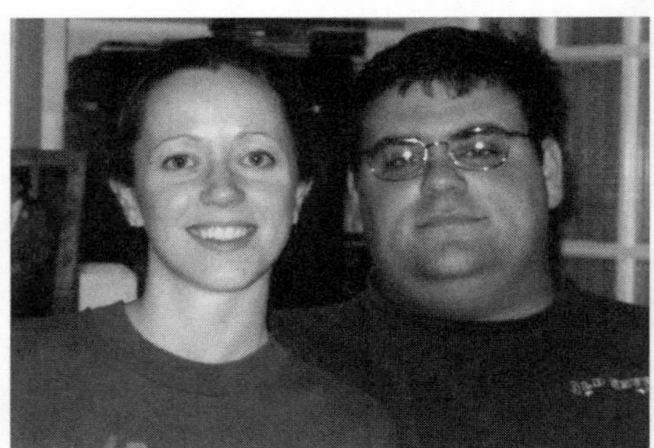

Debbie and Wayne Wheeler

As of May 2001 Debbie and Wayne did not have any children, but they were the proud parents of two cats, Hercules and Guinness, and two dogs, Snickers the chocolate lab and Zeus the all American. *Submitted by: Debbie Swanson, 133 East Allison Circle, Carrollton, GA 30117*

1157. White Family

Our Carroll County family lineage began in the winter of 1866 when Abda White and Mary Bradbury White left Henry County, Georgia, coming here with nine of their twelve children. The names of their twelve children were Anderson, Robert, Sarah, Marjorie, Emily, Cornelius, Americus, Nicholas, Mary Ann E., Nancy, Abda Reece, and John. Anderson, Sarah, and Emily remained in Henry County.

The Civil War brought strife and destruction to many Georgia families including the Whites. The Confederate Army had defended these families in numerous battles during Sherman's march to the sea, such as the conflict that nearly destroyed the White farm in the Mount

Mt. Carmel School 1904 with four of the White children.

Carmel community of Henry County. The cold Georgia winter nights caught the Union soldiers by surprise and by the time the battle had moved on, even the vital fence posts had been used as firewood.

A Carroll County war widow also had family in Henry County and longed to return to her former home. Abda and Mary White were anxious to start over and a deal was struck to exchange farms with this woman. The White family settled in Carroll County along with Mary's parents, Robert and Sarah Bradbury. They named the area Mount Carmel after their home in Henry County.

During the 1870s, Robert Bradbury was the first person buried in the White family cemetery. There are a number of unmarked graves there today, including Mr. Bradbury's. The family later donated this cemetery to the Mt. Carmel Church. The church was also the community's only school until 1938 when it was consolidated with the Temple school.

Mount Carmel was a very remote community preceding Temple by sixteen years. They had to travel three miles to their nearest neighbor and there were only two houses between them and the closest town, Villa Rica. The closest gristmill was on Sweetwater Creek in what is now Douglas County and they had to travel to Atlanta to trade at the market.

Most of the White children stayed in the area farming and raising their own families. In 1906 Cornelius White moved his family to Cullman County, Alabama. His daughter, Mary Mallory married Will Massey and remained in Georgia. Their daughter Velma married Cliff Hudsputh. They later had a son Hugh and daughter Cecile. Ruby Carmichael, also the daughter of Will and Mary Massey, is the last living granddaughter of Cornelius White. Mrs. Carmichael is in her mid to late 90s and lives in Decatur, Georgia, with her son.

William Anderson White, son of Cornelius White, and his wife Georgia Ann Dobbs White also moved to Cullman, Alabama, in 1906. Their children Laura, Olin, Luther, Payton, and Ervin were born in Georgia. Trudy was born in Alabama. Payton White married Bessie Boone in 1920. They had ten children. Aaron, Leon, Buel, Erlene, Helen and Betty were born in Alabama. In 1936 they returned to Georgia and completed their family with Shirley, Joice, Buddy, and Eddie. Two of Payton's sons have three sons that carry on the White family name. *Submitted by: Shirley White Smallwood, 338 Bolijeri Boulevard, Villa Rica, GA 30180*

1158. Abda and Mary Ann Bradbury White

Abda White was born on May 4, 1809, in Georgia. He was the son of Anderson and Margary Pullium White who came to Georgia from Virginia. Mary Ann Bradbury, daughter of Robert and Sarah Bradbury, was born on July 24, 1814, in Georgia. Abda and Mary Ann were married on April 4, 1830, and lived at Jonesboro in Henry County, south of Atlanta, Georgia.

During the Civil War, the Union and Confederate armies burned all of Abda's rail fences and he could not buy any timber to rebuild his fences. One of his neighbors had a daughter who was married to a McVickers, a soldier in the Confederate Army. Mr. McVickers was killed in the war, leaving his wife with a lot of land in Carroll County. Abda traded for the land and he moved his family to Carroll County in the winter of 1866 and 1867. Abda and Mary Ann had twelve children: Anderson, James Robert, Sarah M., Marjorie T., Cornelius, Mary Emily, Americus, Nicolas, Nancy Jane, Mary Ann Elizabeth, Abda Reese, and John Thomas.

When they came to Carroll County, there were only two home places between their farm and Villa Rica — the old Shedd home place about three miles from Mount Carmel Church, and the old Bagwell home place about three miles north of Villa Rica. Mount Carmel Church was used as a church and school for a long time. It was originally a Methodist Church. In 1909 the New Hope Baptist Church was permitted to organize there and it has been a Baptist Church since then.

The gristmill for grinding corn into meal was on Sweetwater Creek, about fifteen miles from their home. Atlanta was the only market. Several men would go together and take their cotton and buy provisions for their families. It would take them a week or ten days to make the trip and they would go once or twice a year.

Mary Ann's parents, Robert and Sarah Bradbury, also moved to Carroll County. Mr. Bradbury was the first person buried in the Mount Carmel Cemetery. A Captain Long donated the land where Mount Carmel Church stands but no provisions were made for a cemetery. Abda White had land that he had planned to use as a family burial ground and he donated it for the church cemetery. Abda and Mary Ann were also buried there. Abda died March 12, 1891, and Mary Ann died December 15, 1900. *Submitted by: Nancy White, 3060 Friendship Road, Arab, AL 35016. jnwhite@mindspring.com*

Sources: Abda White Family Records (original author unknown), census, and cemetery records.

1159. Daughters of Abda White

When Abda and Mary Ann White came to Carroll County in the winter of 1866 and 1867, they were the parents of twelve children. Their daughters were:

Sarah M. was born March 8, 1836. She married Nicholas Pritchett on October 5, 1862. Nicholas had served in the Creek Indian Wars of the 1830s as a private in Dodson's Company, 2nd Georgia Volunteers. His first wife, the former Mary Ann White (a cousin of Sarah) had died, along with a newborn infant daughter, on May 7, 1862, leaving him with two children: James Nicholas and Elizabeth Jane. Children born to Sarah and Nicholas were Mary Ann, Martha Ella, George Washington, and William Henry. Nicholas and Sarah reared their family on the property presently known as Lake Erma in the Sixth District of Henry County. Sarah and Nicholas are buried in the Conkle Family Cemetery in Henry County.

Marjorie T. was born April 22, 1838. She married Payton S. Turner. He was a soldier in the Confederate Army, and was killed in Virginia on May 23, 1865. Payton S. Turner Jr. was born on May 2, 1865. Marjorie did not remarry. She lived to be ninety or older, outliving her son by ten or fifteen years.

Mary Emily was born May 16, 1842. On April 26, 1859, she married William A. Mitchell, who was born April 14, 1832. (William's brother was grandfather of Margaret Munnerlyn Mitchell, author of *Gone with the Wind.*) Their children were Mary Elender, James Franklin, John Henry, Americus Randolph, Nancy Dora, William Isaac, Charlie Oscar, Wesley Crofford, Sarah Ofelia Gurtrude Alice, and Thomas Abda White.

Nancy Jane was born May 20, 1849. Her first husband, Andrew A. Brown, was killed by Crate Hicks and two other men at Pace's Cross Roads, just south of County Line between Carroll and Paulding counties. Hicks was taken to the Newnan Coweta County jail to await trial. He escaped with two other prisoners, but was caught and returned to jail. He then escaped by himself, went to Texas, and was never caught and punished for his crime. On August 14, 1877, Nancy married George A. Alls from Henry County near Hampton in the Mount Carmel Community where she was born. George's first wife, the former Kitty Hamilton, had died leaving him with two daughters, Dicey and Hoppy, and a son, George W. George and Nancy had two children: Tennessee Frances and Mary Rosa Lee. Nancy Jane died on April 2, 1935, and is buried in the Mount Carmel Cemetery in Henry County, next to her second husband.

Mary Ann Elizabeth was born April 12, 1851. Her husband was Thomas R. "Bud" Rutledge. He operated the post office at Berlin above Mount Carmel. Their children were James A., Benjamin A., Mary Jane, and Thomas R. Bud and Mary Ann are buried in the Mount Carmel Cemetery in Temple, Georgia. *Submitted by: Roger L. White, 1032 Thornwood Drive, North Augusta, SC 29860 rwhite5440@aol.com*

Sources: Abda White Family Record; Georgia census and cemetery records; Belle Pritchett Polk (descendant of Sarah M. White); Sally Alls (Alls researcher)

1160. Sons of Abda White

Abda and Mary Ann White, who moved to Carroll County after the Civil War, had seven sons and five daughters. Their sons:

Anderson was born February 28, 1831. He married Rebecca Conkle.

James Robert (Bob) was born November 28, 1832. His first wife was Melinda Avery, and they had a son, James Anderson. He later married Margaret Ross, and their children were

Mary L., Martha, Abda Reece, John, and Sarah. James Robert served in Company F, 53rd Georgia, during the Civil War. He died in 1904, and is buried at Mount Carmel.

Cornelius (Neil) was born April 23, 1840. He married Sarah Agnes Poe in Calhoun County, Alabama. Neil served in Company C, 30th Alabama Infantry, during the Civil War. Children born to Neil and Sarah were Abda Reese, Sarah Jane, Mary Malry, Starling Mitchell, Jonathan Zimmer, William Anderson, Martha Ida, and Lieu Deller. Sarah died in 1894. In 1896, Neil married Edna Bryant. The family moved to Cullman County, Alabama, in 1906. Neil died in 1920 in Alabama, and was buried with his first wife in the Mount Carmel Cemetery, Temple, Georgia.

Americus (Mack) was born December 20, 1844. He married Nancy Parham in Henry County. Their children were Sallie Ann Ophelia, William Anderson, John Robert, Mary Jane, Charles Americus, James Abda, Lillie Frances, and Harvey. Mack served in Company C, 3rd Alabama, in the Civil War. He died in 1925 and is buried at Mount Carmel.

Nicholas (Nick) was born March 19, 1846. He married Louisianna Cathryn Maner from Paulding County. Their children were Sarah Emily, Marion Joseph and Mary Ellen (twins), Margie, Thomas Abda, Nicholas, Harris, Ollie, Claude, and Olen. Nick died in 1898, and is buried at Mount Carmel.

Abda Reese (Dock) was born September 7, 1853. One leg was about six inches shorter than the other and he walked with a cane. He did not marry until he was fifty years of age or older. After the death of his mother, Dock moved to Atlanta and went into the mercantile business with his nephew, Payton Turner Jr. Dock married a widow Evans, but they were divorced after a few years. He later married a widow Lyons who was a dressmaker in his dry goods store. (Widow Lyons had a daughter who became a famous actress. Her stage name was Gertrude McCoy; a theater was named for her in Baltimore, Maryland). Dock died in 1938 in Atlanta.

John Thomas was born May 22, 1856. He married Arciney Chance, and their children were Andrew and Mary. When he was very young, John Thomas had a severe illness with an extremely high fever. He never completely recovered and could not accept responsibility. Abda gave him fifty acres of land, and other family members made sure that he and his family had food and clothing. John Thomas died when he was about fifty years old.

Descendants of Abda and Mary Ann Bradbury White remain in the Carroll County area to this day. *Submitted by: James L. White, 3060 Friendship Road, Arab, AL 35016 jnwhite@mindspring.com*

Sources: Abda White Family Record; Georgia census, marriage, and cemetery records; Ted and Frances Waddell Randles (descendant of James Robert White); Michael E. Massey (descendant of Cornelius White); Sonja Bailey and Danielle Balint (descendants of Americus White); Zelda White (descendant of Americus White); Roger L. White (descendant of Nicholas White)

1161. Jonathan Payton White Sr.

Our branch of the White family tree began when Jonathan Payton White Sr., born July 16, 1901, in the Mount Carmel Community of Carroll County, Georgia, married Bessie Alta Boone, born March 16, 1904. They were married on September 26, 1920, in her birthplace of Cullman County, Alabama. In April 1936, Payton returned to Mount Carmel with his wife and six children: James Aaron, May 3, 1922; Jonathan Leon, January 29, 1925; Herbert Buel, November 23, 1926; Edna Erlene, May 16, 1929; Helen Martha Ann, February 17, 1933; and Betty Faye, December 8, 1934.

Payton was a farmer who grew mainly cotton and corn. Soon, he had established a means for the family to scratch out a living while trying to overcome the effects of the Great Depression. Bessie and the children had to spend every spare minute working alongside Payton in the fields. The crops would bring them dinner and a little extra money for necessities.

Payton and Bessie White, 1920

Four other children were born in the Georgia home. On June 27, 1937, Shirley Ann was born, followed by Barbara Joice on March 31, 1940. Jonathan Payton Jr. (Buddy) was born on March 3, 1943, and Eddie Marcus, the tenth child, was stillborn on September 17, 1945.

Until 1938, the children were taught in the Mount Carmel Community Church that also served as the one-room schoolhouse. That was the year when the new school was built in nearby Temple and the Mount Carmel children began attending there.

In 1940, the family moved west of Temple near the Haralson County line where they continued to farm until World War II began. Payton left farming to begin work at the Bell Bomber Plant. Aaron followed his father to the plant. They both worked there until it closed at the end of the war. Payton returned when the plant reopened as Lockheed. Bessie worked at Sewell Manufacturing in Bremen from 1946 until 1966.

When they were old enough, Aaron and Leon received draft notices. Aaron was deferred, but Leon served from April 1943 to December 1945 as a private first class in the Fourth Infantry. He was in an engineering company that saw action all over Europe. He was wounded during the breakthrough at St. Lo in France.

White Family, 1968

Buel served with the U.S. Navy from March 1945 until his release in May 1946. He reached the rank of seaman first class. He was stationed in Great Lakes, Illinois, and Norfolk, Virginia.

Jonathan Payton White Sr. died July 30, 1972, at the age of seventy-one. Bessie Boone White lived well into her ninety-second year, passing away on February 18, 1997. Bessie lived to see her family flourish. She helped to raise all of the twenty-four grandchildren, most of the forty-five great-grandchildren, and several of the five great-great-grandchildren.

All of Payton and Bessie's nine children are still living. Aaron, Helen, Shirley, and Joice have remained in Carroll County or have returned to make their homes here. Buddy plans to return after his retirement. Leon lives in Smyrna, Buel in Dunwoody, Erlene in Bremen, and Betty in Canton. *Submitted by: Craig Smallwood, 1412 Northgate Drive, Villa Rica, GA 30180*

1162. White - Durrett - Hanson - Whitley

Matthew Jackson White was born on January 30, 1815. He was the son of William White Jr. born in 1776 in Virginia, and Nancy Hooper born in 1783 in North Carolina. William White Jr. was the son of William White Sr. (ca. 1743-1818). Matthew Jackson White married Agnes Durrett, daughter of Joseph Francis Durrett (1777-1848) and Penelope Cocks, on December 14, 1836, in Carroll County, Georgia.

Jack and Aggey, as they were called, had one daughter Nancy C. White. Aggey probably died during childbirth since Jack married Martha Whatley shortly after Nancy's birth. Jack and Martha had several children. Nancy White married Sanford Harold Hanson (August 26, 1823 in Morgan County, Georgia-May 15, 1892 in Cleburne County, Alabama). Sanford was the son of Armstead Hanson and Jane Petty. Sanford served in the Confederate Army as a private in Captain O.W. Shepherd's Company. He was described in his pension application as born in Georgia, a farmer, with a dark complexion, and six-feet tall.

Sanford Hanson and Nancy White

Sanford and Nancy's children were Margaret who married David Harper; Mary E. who married James Beam; Nancy who married John Ballenger; Felon who married Margaret Armstrong; Artelia who married Robert Lee Whitley; Emma who married Joseph Wade; Milly who married John Green; Julie who married William Cavender; Ada who married Stephen Cavender; and Ida who married several times.

Artelia Hanson and Robert Lee Whitley were called "Teelie" and "Good." He is the son of James Whitley and Susan Frances Lemond, both buried in Pine Hill, Newell, Alabama. Susan Frances is the daughter of Elizabeth Tomlin and Robert L. Lemond. James Whitley was born in North Carolina and lived in Roopville before living at Newell. James' death certificate lists his father as Tommie Whitley. Some of James and Susan's children, in addition to Robert Lee, was Benjamin Green Whitley, Bill Whitley, and Delia, who married a Cofield.

Ada, Emma, Ida, Felon, Julie, Teelie Hanson

Teelie and Good's children were Mary Ellen who married Lonnie Richardson; Sanford; Jack who married Jennie; Frazier who married Jack Cofield (son of Delia Whitley); Robert; Hugh who married Dovie; Jodie who married a Biggers; Sam who married Rebecca Daniel; and baby Anna who died. Teelie is buried at Ranburne beside Anna (marker is engraved "R.T. Whitley"). Robert Lee is buried at Pine Hill in Newell.

Teelie Hanson and Robert Lee Whitley Family

Around 1905, Felon and Margaret Hanson's son, Jim Hanson and Laura, the girl he married, went on an outing with Jim's cousin, Mary Ellen Whitley and Lonnie Richardson, the man she would marry. They all packed a picnic basket, caught the train, and went to LaGrange. They ate their lunch, took in the sights of LaGrange, then rode the train back home. Mrs. Laura Hanson told this story as she looked at old pictures in 1960. Her eyes lit up at the memory.

The picture of Robert Lee and Teelie Hanson Whitley's family shows in the back row: Jack, Sanford, Ellen, and Frazier. Front row, Robert Lee, and Teelie with Joe, Robert, and Hugh. I don't know the individual identities of each young boy. *Submitted by: LaRealia Lovvorn Camp, Highway 16 West, Newnan, GA 30263*

Sources: Mrs. Laura Hanson, Hanson family; Mr. Meynard Traylor, Lemond family; and Mr. Ed Whitley, Whitley family information; Confederate Pension Record-Sanford Hanson; Durrett family information from Peggy Hughes as published in *Cleburne County Heritage Book*

1163. White - Hooper Family

William White and Nancy Hooper

William White, born December 9, 1776, in Fluvanna County, Virginia, married Nancy Hooper around 1800 in Pendleton, South Carolina. She was born in 1783 and died before 1837. She was the daughter of Capt. Richard Brooks Hooper and Elizabeth Adams Word Hooper. William White died June 15, 1875, in the home of his son Matthew Jackson White on the Georgia/Alabama Stateline Road. This family came into Carroll County, Georgia, as early as 1827. William and Nancy, with several members of their family, are listed on the church rolls of Tallapoosa Primitive Baptist Church on Tyus Road. They came with the Word and Hooper families and began buying land lots all over Carroll County. At one time, William owned much of the land lots around the square in Carrollton, Georgia. (He owned land lots #18, #19, #20, #45, #46, #47.)

William White was the son of William White Sr. (1740-1818) and Mary Hooper (1745-1839). His grandparents were John White and Phoebe Carter, and Obediah Hooper (1720-1803) and Maslavia Brooks.

Nancy Hooper (1783-before 1837, Carroll County) was the daughter of Capt. Richard Brooks Hooper (1756-after 1840) and Elizabeth Adams Word, widow of Charles Word who died in the Battle of King's Mountain. She was the granddaughter

Amanda White Jackson

of John Adams (1706-1769) and Eleanor Powell (1707-after 1769) from Halifax County, Virginia.

William and Nancy Hooper White had eleven sons. The names and dates are taken from their Bible records. (1) Carter White, born December 1, 1801, married Martha Speed Dorch. (2) Obediah White, born May 20, 1803, died 1878, married Jemimah Sparks. (3) David White, born September 17, 1805, married Mary H. Word Jones. (4) John Adams White, born May 19, 1807, married first to Mary, and second to Nancy. (5) Richard White, born June 4, 1811, died 1885, married first to Mary Phillips, and second to Charity Tolliver.

Roma, Andrew, Leo, Van, Celia, and Woodrow Jackson, about 1918.

(6) William White III, born February 18, 1812, married Mary Armstrong. (7) James Francis White, born July 18, 1813, died 1885, married Sarah Elizabeth "Sally" Durrett, daughter of Joseph Francis Durrett and Penelope Cocks Durrrett. James Francis White was a colorful figure in and around his home district of the Georgia/Alabama Stateline area. He owned land in both Georgia and Alabama from Bowdon, Georgia, to Ranburne, Macedonia, and Hopewell, Alabama. He was a school teacher, notary public, justice of the peace, tax collector in 1843, and commissioner of Randolph (now Cleburne County), Alabama, from 1857-1867, before, during, and following the Civil War. He served in the Creek Indian Wars alongside his father and his brothers. He and Sally Durrett White had five children: Ellen Jane, Peyton, William Jasper, Nancy Penelope, and Amanda White who married John Wesley Jackson (see Jackson History-John Wesley). (8) Matthew Jackson White, born January 30, 1815, died April 21, 1902, married first to Agnes Durrett, and second to Martha Whatley. (9) Benjamin Perry White, born January 1817, married first to Ann Whatley, and second to Louisa (Elizabeth). (10) Joshua Word White, born July 18, 1819, died 1901, married Mary Whatley. (11) Clark Terrell White, born January 1, 1823, died 1872, married Frances Whatley.

Note: Two of the sons married Durrett sisters, and three of the sons married the daughters of Archie Whatley (1769-1847). Martha Whatley who became the second wife of Matthew Jackson White was their niece. *Submitted by: Woodrow Jackson, Carrollton, GA and Written by: Peggy Jackson Hughes*

1164. The Whitman Family

Whitmans in Carroll County today descend from Revolutionary War patriot Christopher Wedeman/Weideman/Whitman who came with colonists from Bavaria, Germany, 1700s to Dutch Fork, Newberry County, South Carolina. These Protestant followers of Martin Luther sought asylum from European Catholicism and from the Hundred Years War which had devastated their country land.

Descendent Christopher Whitman, c. 1795-c1855 married 1824 Elisabeth Smith in Jasper County, Georgia; Elisabeth is buried Ranburne, Alabama. Their son Hiram Strong Whitman 1826-1884 married 1846 in Fayette County, Georgia, Elizabeth Alewine daughter of Reuben and Priscilla Buchanan Alewine; buried Ranburne, Alabama.

Whitmans, 1939: Orin, Mary, Curtis, Izora, Flora, Ervin, John, Fannie

Lt. Hiram Strong Whitman served in the Civil War: Company E, 13 Regiment, Alabama Infantry. The Hiram Strong Whitman family (and the Alewine family) joined Bethany Baptist Church, Tallapoosa, April 26, 1867. Hiram was appointed church clerk the very same day, writing that day's minutes. Later he served as deacon and church treasurer.

Hiram and Elisabeth Whitman's son Hiram Jackson Whitman 1851-1924 married 1872 in Cleburne County, Alabama, Sarah Ham daughter of John and Elizabeth Ham; buried Cleburne. Their son John Edward Whitman 1877-1966 married 1901 in Heard County, Fannie Jones daughter of William and Louisa Langley Jones; buried Cleburne, Alabama. Their children are: John Ervin 1905-1977 (married Myrtle Langley: children Dennis, Pierce); Flora Leona 1908 (married Milton Ewell Skinner son of Charlie and Laura Hardigree Skinner: children James, Reid, David); Izora Desta 1911 (married James Alton Pollard son of Lee and Louisa Pollard: children Wayne, Frances); William Curtis 5/10/1916-7/5/1996 (married in Cleburne County 1938 Hazel Otwell 12/30/1921 daughter of Silas DeWitt and Emma Jane Pollard Otwell: children June, Larry); Mary Lee 1918-2000 (married 1936 in Carroll County Van Jackson son of Andrew and Clelia White Jackson: children Carolyn, Janice, Johnny); Orin Sylvester 1922 (married 1947 Carroll County Edna Ruth Pullen daughter of Robert and Emily Eliza Hyatt Pullen: children Jack, Nancy). The youngest three children of John and Fannie - Curtis, Mary (see Jackson article), and Orin - moved to Carroll in the 1930s and 1940s.

Curtis and Hazel Whitman had two children: (1) Virginia June 7/28/1939 married 1961 William Lee Garrett II 2/24/1939 son of William Lee and Antoinette (Pearce) Garrett. They live in Opelika, Alabama. Three children: Virginia Lynn 11/29/1963 (married Jonathan Floyd Fravel, children: Khani Lee and Zachary Pearce.) Gayle Elizabeth 7/17/65 (married Otis Fleming Jones III, children: Garrett Fleming and William Cole.) William Lee Garrett III (married Jann Foushee.) (2) Larry Curtis married first Nancy Jones and had Jefferson Grady

Whitman; married second Linda Clifton and had Kristen Lee (married Bryan Agan) and Susan Elizabeth.

Curtis and Hazel enjoyed gardening at their home on Blandenburg Road. Blessed with a clear tenor voice, Curtis enjoyed blue grass music. Hazel has worked with flowers almost fifty years.

Orin and Edna Ruth Whitman had two children: (1) Jack Edward 12/20/1948 married Bonnie Olivia Brooks, child: Andrew Brooks 8/25/1984. (2) Nancy Ruth 4/20/1951 married Larry "Hut" Hutcheson, children: Daniel Whitman 1974 and Matthew Robert 1978. Dan married Lara Walston, child: Madison Leigh, 12/24/1997.

Mary and Orin Whitman, 1923

Orin is a veteran of World War II. With the 81st Infantry Division, US Army, he fought on Peleliu Island, and was also in Hawaii, Anguar, Guadalcanal, and Japan. In 1946 he began Whitman's Glass Shop on Dixie Street and continues working today in the family business with Jack and Hut. *Submitted by: Nancy Whitman Hutcheson, 1501 Tyus Road, Carrollton, GA 30117.*

1165. David and Sara Wiggins

Dr. David Wiggins, born in 1952, came to Carrollton in 1970 to attend West Georgia College. He is the son of Findley and Merle Wiggins of Rockmart, Georgia. Although a native of Polk County, he has strong roots to the area. He is the great-great-grandson of Jesse Wiggins who in the 1850s lived in an area just beyond Bowdon in Randolph County that became Cleburne County after the War Between the States. David's great grandfather, McAllen Batts Wiggins, was the only one of six brothers to survive the war. He and four brothers were members of Company K 13th Alabama. James K. Wiggins, a brother and a brother-in-law, Robert Sloman, died while in the service of the Bowdon Volunteers, Company B Cobb's Legion.

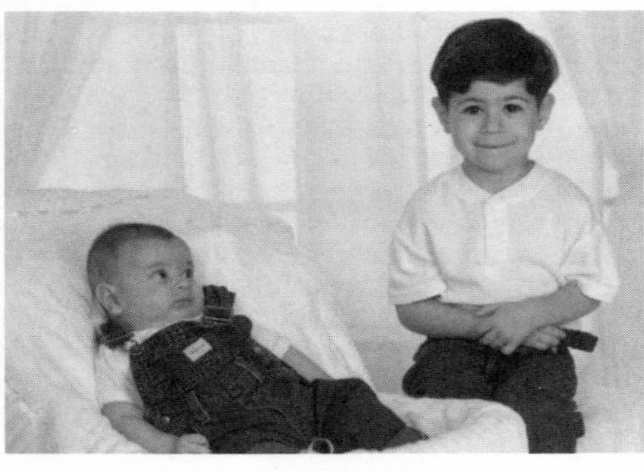

Asher and John Knight Pate

On David's mother's side, his great-great-grandfather was Rufus Weaver who married Kesiah Jordan in Carroll County on August 26, 1851. Kesiah was the daughter of Benjamin Jordan and Martha Smith Jordan. Benjamin died in Carroll County on December 28, 1848. Through the Weaver line, David is a descendent of Revolutionary soldier David Weaver Sr. and is related to President Thomas Jefferson. Through the Stackhouse family line on his father's side he is related to both Presidents Bush.

Denise, Asher, Jayson, John, Sara, Errol, Kacey, Karis, and David

After arriving in Carrollton in 1970 to attend West Georgia College, David Wiggins graduated in 1974 with a B.A. in biology. He minored in education and did his student teaching at Central High School in the spring of 1974 and was hired as a full time teacher in the fall. He served the school in different roles: teacher, coach, assistant principal and athletic director. He served the school for fifteen years. In 1989 he was asked to create a school to help the Carroll County School system with a high dropout rate, thus the creation of the Open Campus Night High School. He served as principal for the school for ten years until being asked to move to Mt. Zion High School in 1999 as principal. In the spring of 2001, he was asked to return to the Open Campus Night High School, which had been moved to Bowdon.

David received a M. Ed. in science education from West Georgia College in 1976, an administrative add-on in 1980, and a doctorate of education from Nova Southeastern University in 1994. He has been honored as a Who's Who in Georgia 1988, West Georgia recipient of the Phi Kappa Phi Administrator of the Year in 1992, State Officer in the Georgia Association for Alternative Education 1995-1998, and named Educator of the Year by the Carroll County Association of Educators in 1999.

Sara Magriso, born June 17, 1945, is the daughter of Menahem and Ester Magriso. She was born and raised in Istanbul, Turkey. While in Turkey, she attended the Nisantasi Kiz Enstitusu, a home economics school for girls. She came to Carrollton in 1971, by way of Auburn University with her first husband, Kerim Askin. Kerim and Sara Askin moved to Carrollton as he took a job with Southwire as an engineer. They have two children, Denise born June 26, 1971, and Errol born July 20, 1972. Sara Askin was known locally as an outstanding tennis and bridge player and owned and operated Sara's for several years in Carrollton. The store specialized in fine women's clothing.

In 1989, David and Sara started dating and on June 27, 1992 they were married in Carrollton at the United Methodist Church. Sara Wiggins has worked as a secretary at Central Elementary School for ten years.

On November 12, 1994, Denise Askin married Jayson Knight Pate. Jayson is the son of Brenda and Wilson Knight Pate of Whitesburg, Jayson and Denise both graduated from Central High School in June of 1989. Jayson graduated with cum laude honors from Jacksonville State University in Jacksonville, Alabama, in May 1993. He earned a degree in law enforcement and has a minor in forensic investigation. Denise graduated with magna cum laude honors from the State University of West Georgia with a BBA degree in finance. They have two children: John Knight Pate, born June 12, 1998 and Asher Knight Pate born March 6, 2001.

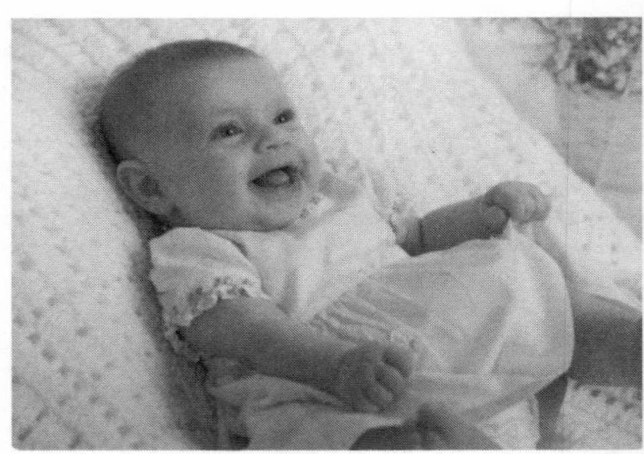

Karis Quinn Askin

Errol Askin married Kacey Denney on September 16, 1995. Kacey is the daughter of Philip and Gayle Denney of Carrollton. Errol graduated from Central High School in 1990. Kacey graduated from the Georgia Country Day School in 1994 after being jointly enrolled with the Georgia School and Agnes Scott College in Decatur. Kacey received a B.F.A. in art education from the State University of West Georgia. Kacey is an art teacher at Central Elementary School. They have one child, Karis Quinn Askin, born February 4, 2001.

David and Sara are looking forward to retirement, traveling, and playing with the grandchildren. David also plans to continue work in family genealogy and on several historical books. *Submitted by: Dr. David Wiggins, 1093 Oak Grove Rd., Carrollton, GA 30117; Denise Pate, Whitesburg; Kacey Denney, Carrollton*

1166. The Thomas Camp Wiggins Family

Pictured here are April Dawn Young and Donald Scott Young, children of Don and Pam Walker Young. They are the great-grandchildren of Thomas Camp Wiggins and Sarah

Percy Fleming Wiggins. Thomas Camp Wiggins was born in 1889, the son of William Jasper Wiggins and Amanda Melvina Stewart. William Jasper Wiggins was born 25 March 1855 and died 23 May 1916. Amanda Melvina Stewart was born 25 October 1858 and died 25 September 1904. Amanda Stewart was the daughter of William Stewart and Polly Beck, some of Carroll County's earliest pioneers who arrived here in time for the 1830 Carroll County census.

Seven children were born to Jasper and Amanda Wiggins. The oldest was a son named W.N. Wiggins who moved to Holly Pond, Alabama, and died there unmarried. The second son was G.L. Wiggins who moved to Cullman, Alabama, and also died unmarried. Both these brothers were cotton farmers. The third son was J. Hubert Wiggins who married and lived in Carrollton all his life. He had a daughter named Paloma Wiggins who married James H. Blanchard of Columbus, Georgia. One son was born to them — James H. Blanchard Jr. and he became quite well known in the world of banking.

The fourth child of Jasper and Amanda Wiggins was Addie Lee who was born 13 November 1883 and died at age 20 on 25 September 1904. Addie is buried at Pleasant Grove Church at Tyus. The fifth child of Jasper and Amanda Wiggins was Berlie who married J.A. Burnett and had a daughter named Sarah. Sarah Burnett worked at the People's Bank in Carrollton for many years. The seventh child of Jasper and Amanda Wiggins was Eula who was born on 13 June 1894. Eula Wiggins married J. Clifton Martin on 22 September 1912 and resided in Carrollton all her life. Eula and Cliff Martin were the parents of Stewart, William, and Marvin Martin. The Martins were well known for The Martin-Almon Funeral Home.

The sixth child of Jasper and Amanda Wiggins was Thomas Camp Wiggins. Thomas Camp Wiggins married on 25 March 1914 to Sarah Percy Fleming, daughter of George Washington Fleming (8 September 1862–27 September 1939) and Alice Amanda Morgan (18 October 1865–18 November 1921). Sarah Percy Fleming was born 27 November 1887 in Carroll County. Her father, G.W. Fleming was an early president of the People's Bank of Carrollton.

The People's Bank was chartered on 10 November 1909 with authorized capital of $60,000. It opened for business on 1 December 1909. The original directors of the People's Bank were: J.R. Adamson, G.C. Cook, J.M. Jackson, W.S. Campbell, Joe H. Harris, W.O. Robinson, Jr., E.A. Merrell, Dr. H.J. Goodwin, W.G. Johnson, R.H. McClung, W.J. Perdue, U.W. Jordan, and A.J. Baskin. J.R. Adamson served as the first president of the Bank but because of failing health, he had to resign on 1 December 1912. George W. Fleming then was elected president in January of 1913 and he served in the capacity until 6 January 1931.

The Flemings came first to Carroll County when Isaac N. Fleming of Hall County, Georgia had a fortunate draw in the Land Lottery of 1827 — his land was awarded 2 March 1836 in the 10th District, 5th Section. Robert Fleming was a Revolutionary War soldier who drew Lot #45 and #206 in 2nd District (now Haralson County) on 2 July 1831. John Robert Fleming was born 15 October 1853 and on 17 February 1876 married Mollie E. Pentecost (20 December 1856–10 January 1917). Mollie Pentecost was the daughter of Joseph S. Pentecost who married Frances C. Barnett in Carroll County on 15 January 1847. The children of Joseph S. Pentecost were Valentine, Martha "Mollie," Mary, and John W. Pentecost.

Joseph S. Pentecost was one of Carroll County's Confederate soldiers who lost his life on the battlefield during the Civil War. On May 10, 1862, he left his home at Lowell and joined Company C, 56th Georgia Volunteer Infantry. His unit was assigned to the Army of Tennessee and spent the winter of 1862 near Chattanooga. In Spring of 1863, the Army was sent to defend Mississippi from the invading Union Army. While advancing on an enemy position, Pentecost met his fate — struck by an enemy bullet, he fell mortally wounded. Pvt. John M.D. Stallings and C.T. Richards, also from Lowell, buried their comrade there in the Mississippi soil. Frances never remarried and is buried at New Lebanon Church.

The children of George W. Fleming and Alice Amanda Morgan were: (1) Oscar David Fleming born 2 September 1883 m. 5 September Bertha Ellen Lovvorn (2) Abner Earnest Fleming m. 15 December 1907 to Lockie Copeland (3) Cordova Lenora Fleming b. 14 May 1886 m. 15 December 1901 George W. Adams (4) Sarah Percy Fleming b. 27 November 1887 m. 25 March 1914 Thomas Camp Wiggins (5) Henry Parks Fleming b. 26 September 1892 m. November 1916 Adel Johnson (6) George Bernard Fleming b. 15 January 1897 m. 25 November 1920 Mary Jo Moss.

April Dawn Young and Donald Scott Young

George W. Fleming's wife, Alice Amanda Morgan, was the daughter of John David Morgan (3 August 1833–4 February 1891) and Lucy D. Kelly (17 January 1841–20 October 1898) who married in Coweta County, Georgia, on 15 January 1856. John David Morgan was the son of James M. Morgan (1804-1876) and Mary Burgess (1803-1845). John D. and Lucy Kelly Morgan lived in Carroll County all their lives and are buried in the old Jordan Cemetery on the Villa Rica Highway. David Morgan sold Land Lot #104 in 7th District to John K. Holcombe in 1844, property he had purchased 1 December 1840.

The children of Thomas Camp Wiggins and Sarah Percy Fleming are: (1) Doris Amanda Wiggins b. 13 December 1914 m. on 11 August 1936 to Hoyt Bradley Young. Bradley Young was born in 1909 and is buried at Rocky Branch Church in Newell, Alabama. Doris Young was the first employee of Robinson Drug Company which opened for business in 1952. She worked as a pharmacy technician there for over twenty years and later worked for Tommy Haney in his pharmacy. Doris has enjoyed playing the piano and organ for many church events over the years and is an active member of Tabernacle Baptist Church (2) George Fleming Wiggins b. 19 March 1917 m. Ellie Harwell (3) Thomas Camp Wiggins Jr. b. September 1918 m. Mary Ellen Mullins (4) Sarah Alice Wiggins born 13 December 1921 and never married. (5) William Jasper Wiggins b. 18 March 1925 m. Mary Brinkley who is a native of Sparta, Georgia, and a talented artist. William Wiggins received his degree from University of Georgia in law and came back to his hometown to practice law. He has served as the city attorney of Carrollton for many years.

The oldest child of Doris Amanda Wiggins and Hoyt Bradley Young is Bradley William Young born August 1936 in Carrollton. Bradley Young married Betty Ralston of Gainesville, Georgia. Their children are Rebecca Yvonne and William Bradley Young Jr. Rebecca married Robert Finkel of Pittsburg, Pennsylvania and had three sons: Daniel, James and Joseph. Bradley Young was an American Express investment counselor for years in Carrollton, then retired after many years with General Motors. The Youngs live in Marion, North Carolina.

The second child is Jane Young, born 30 October 1940. She graduated from Carrollton High School and received her B.S. in education from West Georgia College. She earned her M.Ed. from the University of Tennessee. Jane married Dr. James Chester Coomer who was a professor of political science at Mercer University (now retired). Jane Young Coomer is principal of Chattahoochee School in Gwinnett County, Georgia. The Coomers have one daughter, Alice Amanda.

The third child of Doris and Bradley Young was Donald Young born 15 April 1947. Don graduated from Carrollton High School and served in the U.S. Army in Vietnam. Don Young is remembered as one of the most genial fellows in Carrollton, and as someone who from a very early age knew that his love was automobiles, engines, and racing. Don became a successful businessman in Carrollton, the owner of West Georgia Engines, where he could take apart and put together car motors to his heart's content. And when he wasn't doing that — Don was racing professionally. In 1984 Don won his first World Championship of the International Hot Rod Association.

Don Young always responded when the schools asked him to come give a talk to the children about race car driving. He loved to see their eyes light up when he talked about his own love of racing — and he'd let them sit behind the wheel of his hot rod. He'd give them a full demonstration and let them watch as his braking parachute opened behind his dragster. He was a popular speaker for school children and he always focused on safety. Don was in the lead on September 22, 1985 — the day he was competing for the 1985 Fall National (IHRA) Championship at Bristol, Tennessee. Tragically his car hit the guard rail, and Don died instantly from the crash.

Don Young had been married for thirteen years to Pamela Dawn Walker and they had two children — a daughter, April Dawn Young who was four, and a son, Donald Scott Young who was two years old when Don died. April graduated from Central High School in 1999 and now works as a receptionist for Specialty Printing in Carrollton. Donald Scott Young is now a seventeen year old student at Central High School. After Don's death, Pam Young married again to Mike Eady and then a few years later Pam died of cancer. Doris Young praised Mike Eady for always being such a good stepfather to April and Scott and especially after they had lost both their parents. Pam Young Eady was born 1953 and died 1994. Both she and Don are buried at Carroll Memory Gardens.

The fourth child of Doris Wiggins and Hoyt Bradley Young is Joyce Young who was born 9 December 1948 in Carrollton, Georgia and graduated from Carrollton High School in 1966. Joyce has always had a natural talent for cooking and catering. She is now a professional caterer for a private country club locally.

Thomas Camp Wiggins died in 1951 and Percy Fleming Wiggins died in 1973. Both are buried in the Carrollton City Cemetery. *Submitted by: Mrs. Doris Young, 412 West White Street, Carrollton, GA 30117 and Written by: Jan Robinson Bell*

1167. Anson J. Williams

Anson J. Williams was born circa 1830 in Georgia and died 11 October 1862 in Perryville, Kentucky, during the War Between the States. The first record found of him is on the 1850 census for Meriwether County, Georgia, where he is living in the household of John C. (80 years old) and Elizabeth (68 years old) Adcock.

In Meriwether County on 19 December 1850 Anson married Mary Young Miller, born 24 August 1834, died 27 November 1916. Barby Miller is listed on the 1850 Meriwether County census with her three daughters: Mary, Melvina and Permelia. She was born in South Carolina, the girls in Georgia.

By 1860 Anson and Mary were living in Carroll County. They were the parents of seven children: Silas married Sarah F. Burnett; Barbara Ann married William T. Coggins; John Robert (more later); William Jackson married Rebecca Holbrook; James Augustus married Nancy A. Ward; Sarah married Ben Lassiter; and Permelia married G.W. Blair.

Anson's son John Robert Williams, was born 10 November 1856, died 7 October 1907. He was burned to death when his house was destroyed by fire. John Robert married Malinda Catherine Stripling, born 13 September 1857 and died 7 July 1900. She was the daughter of Henry Marcus Stripling and Sarah Jane Norman. Henry Marcus was a veteran of the War Between the States.

John Robert and Malinda Catherine Williams were the parents of: Missouri (more later); Henry Marcus married Emma Fortner: Deloniga married M.J. Dingler; Zelda Catherine married J.T. Pritchett; Franklin Virginia married Bill Whitfield; Benjamin Franklin died infancy. After the War Between the States, the family lived in Cleburne and Cullman County, Alabama, for a while before moving back to Carroll County.

John Roberts' daughter Missouri Ann was born 24 February 1873. In 1892 she married Earnest Hancock in Alabama and they had one child, Ernest Jackson. Missouri and Earnest were divorced after the birth of her son and she left him with her parents to raise. She later married Bob Daniel in Alabama and they had a daughter named Pearl.

In 1900 John Robert was living in Polk County, Georgia. Living with him was his grandson Earnest Jackson Hancock, born 16 July 1893, died 25 August, 1983. John Robert listed his grandson as Ernest Jackson Williams on the census record. No further record was found on Missouri Ann.

On 31 December 1921, Ernest Jackson Williams married Tressie Ann Ball, born 16 July 1897, died 3 December 1976. She was the daughter of Daniel Benjamin Ball and Ada Spencer Jinks. Two children were born to this marriage: Ruth Mildred Agnes (more later) and Hoyte Junior Williams who married Mary Jim Adams. By previous marriages, Ernest Jackson had Opal who married James Oliver Hampton; John who married Katherine Robinson and Betty.

Ruth Mildred Agnes Williams married Thomas Wesley Phillips 13 June 1937 in Carroll County. (For more on Thomas Wesley Phillips see family of William David Phillips). *Submitted by: Tommie Phillips LaCavera, 419 Boulevard, Athens, GA 30601-1964*

Sources: National Department of Archives and History; American Revolution Records and Pensions; War Between the States Records and Pensions; War of 1812 Records and Pensions; Bible, census, cemetery and marriage records

1168. Charles Benjamin Williams Family

Charles Benjamin Williams (1856-1909) was a son of Henry Roland Williams and Elizabeth "Betsy" Osborn (see article about that family). The accompanying photo was made at the family home on West Wayside Road, owned today by a descendant of Charles' uncle, Joel Casper Williams. Near the home, at the intersection of Hodge Road and West Wayside, is the location of the store which Charles operated for a time. Charles married Susan Ella Haynes in 1872.

Susan Ella "Susie" Haynes (1854-1918) was a daughter of James H. Haynes and Cassie Ann Threlkeld, who married in Elbert County, Georgia. James H. Haynes was a son of James G. Haynes and Rebecca Rainwater, who came to Georgia from Spartanburg District, South Carolina. Brothers and sisters of Susan Ella Haynes were Thomas J. Haynes, who married Sophia A. Williams; Eliza Ann Haynes, who married John F. Powell; William Henry Harrison Haynes, who married Sarah J. Stephenson; Cynthia Rebecca Haynes, who married James Thomas Hamrick; and Amanda Caroline Haynes, who married James F. Brock. Charles and Susie, both buried at Jordan Cemetery, were the parents of nine children. Laura A. Williams married Leonders K. Jordan. Lula E. Williams married Enoch M. Davis and had children, Clifford and Margaret. She later married George B. Spangler. Edward Foster Williams married Ila I. Alexander and had children: Edward Foster Jr. and Robert. Fannie Williams married Alonzo Mayfield Jordan and had children, Alpha Clestelle, Brice, and Mary. William Samuel Williams (1882-1931) married Willie Patience Eady (see article about her family). Their children were Clara Elizabeth Williams, William Harold Williams, and Dickson Williams. Henry Lee Williams married Emma Moffitt. Ohma Hamilton Williams married Pauline Speck. Newton Sebron Williams married Ethel Williams, and later Jewel Leonard. Iula Ethel Williams married Charles DuPont Screven and had children: Frances Elizabeth and Mary Ella.

Charles Benjamin Willaims Family

Identities of the people in the photo are, back row, left to right, Henry Lee Williams, Fannie Williams, Lula Williams, William Samuel Williams, Ohma Hamilton Williams; front row, left to right, Edward Foster Williams, Newton Sebron Williams, Charles Benjamin Williams, Iula Ethel Williams, Ella Susan Haynes Williams, son of Laura Williams Jordan, Laura Williams Jordan. *Submitted by: JoAnne Williams Moore, 3875 Pittman Road, College Park, GA 30049*

1169. Henry Roland Williams Family

Henry Roland Williams was a son of Thomas Barnes Williams and Hannah Pinson (see article about that family). He was born in Laurens District, South Carolina, in 1825 and came with his family to Carroll County in the early 1830s. He had a home on what is today's West Wayside Road. He married Elizabeth (Betsy) Osborn in 1848. Betsy Osborn was a daughter of Langston Osborn and wife Mary, also from Laurens District. Langston was a son of Daniel Osborn and Elizabeth Drew. Brothers and sisters of Betsy Osborn were Daniel; William Riley, who married Susan Holcomb and settled in Mississippi; Cynthia, who married Abner Lee; Mary, who married James Spradlin; John D., who married Sarah Jones; Samuel T., who married Serena Wright; and Langston Y., who married Tabitha J. Neely.

Henry Roland Williams Family

Henry and Betsy were parents of five known children: John T. Williams (1849-1865), who died when a tree he was cutting fell on him; Charles Benjamin Williams (1851-1909) (see the article about his family); George L. Williams (1853-1875), who married Amanda R. Boatright. Both are buried at Jordan Cemetery; Henry W. Williams (1854-1855); and Joel Hood Williams (1857-1938), who married Mary Luradene Swords. Henry and Betsy are buried at Jordan Cemetery.

Indentities for photograph are as follows: standing, left to right, Charles Benjamin Williams, Joel Hood Williams; seated, left to right, George L. Williams, Betsy Osborn Williams, Henry Roland Williams. *Submitted by: JoAnne Williams Moore, 3875 Pittman Road, College Park, GA 30049*

1170. James Henry and Sarah Davidson Williams

James Henry was born to Thomas Barnes (Barney) and Hannah Pinson Williams on April 2, 1814 in Laurens County, South Carolina. He was the first-born of thirteen known children. In 1832 this family, some extended family, and some neighbors left South Carolina and traveled by wagon to settle in what has become Carroll County, Georgia.

On December 19, 1835 James married Sarah Davidson. Some researchers feel that Sarah might have been the daughter of John Davidson and the sibling or cousin of Martha Davidson Baugh, Mary Davidson Adams, and Washington Davidson.

Thomas Barnes Williams died intestate sometime in 1856, and James H. and his brother-in-law John J. Hinesley (husband of Nancy Williams) administered the estate. Family stories claim that James' mother Hannah died in 1868.

Meanwhile in about 1858, something (perhaps the lure of cheap land) drew James and Sarah to Winston County, Alabama. They were accompanied by their two youngest children Hannah Elisabeth (who married James Wood McCullar), and Jasper Jackson (who married Eliza Jane Wooley). Their daughter Lucinda and her new husband William J. Davidson also moved with them. Their two oldest children John and Joel Williams stayed in Carroll County and then disappeared. We suspect that they died during the Civil War.

Shortly after the Williams arrived in Alabama, Alabama seceded from the Union. The pro-Union inhabitants of Winston County tried declaring Winston County to be the Free State of Winston, in protest over Alabama's secession. Though unsuccessful, this act caused considerable tension between the state of Alabama and the people of Winston County.

On January 18, 1864 the probate judge for Winston County, Thomas P. Curtis a Union sympathizer, was taken prisoner by the Confederate Cavalry. He was found five days later, frozen, with the shreds of his commission papers for probate judge scattered on the ground around him. In this strained and politically charged environment, James Henry Williams was appointed to take his place.

James served as probate judge of Winston County from June 14, 1864 till August 29, 1865, the last year of the Civil War. James lived close to the old courthouse and walked through a field and across a creek to work. In the 1920s James' grandson Charlie Williams pointed out to his son Earl the exact high point where the homesite had once been. This property now lies along a deserted spur of Highway 278. All signs of anyone having lived there are now gone and the paper companies are in the process of completely stripping the land.

It's been said through the generations that James knew he was dying and picked the spot under a big Oak tree where he wanted to be buried. He died on April 29, 1867, leaving wife Sarah and son Jasper still at home. This spot is now known as the Williams Family Cemetery and James, Sarah, Jasper and other family members are buried there. It is 500 yards northeast of the Houston Church of God in Houston, Alabama. *Submitted by: Thomas Earl and Nancy DeVore Williams, 1301 Howell Drive, Fort Payne, AL 35967. just-cuz@mindspring.com*

Sources: Gravestones, Carroll County deed books and marriage records, census records, Winston County, Alabama death certificates, oral family history. *Annals of Northwest Alabama* by Donald B. Dodd.

1171. The Orea Lee Mays Williams Family

Orea Lee Herring was born 28 March 1931 in Carroll County, Georgia, the daughter of Carrie Crowder Herring and Lewis Herring. Carrie Crowder was the daughter of Mattie Horton Crowder and Wyatt Crowder. The Crowders were originally from Coweta County and had Cherokee Indians in their ancestry. There is a beautiful picture of a great-aunt — Carrie Crowder — who was part Cherokee and she was the sister of Wyatt Crowder, Orea Lee's grandfather. Wyatt Crowder grew up in Coweta and Heard Counties and later owned a grocery store on High Street in Carrollton.

Carrie Crowder

Lewis Herring was the son of Lela Terrell Herring and Claude Herring of Carroll County. Lela is buried at an old Methodist Church in Roopville, Georgia, which has been torn down in later years. Lewis Herring is also buried close to his mother in this same cemetery. Claude Herring is buried somewhere in Ohio. The Crowders are buried at Piney Grove Baptist Church Cemetery in Carroll County.

Orea Lee Herring had a twin brother named Fred Lee Herring. She had another brother born 28 October 1933 who was Robert Lee "Bob" Herring. Bob's daughter is Kim Herring who lives in New York and is a paralegal. Orea Lee's sister was Tommie Lou Herring who was born 25 March 1935. The Herring children attended Carver High School in Carrollton. On 27 December 1947, Orea Lee married James Henry Mays who was born 8 September 1927. Together, they had eight children all born in Carroll County.

The oldest child was (1) James Lee Mays born 23 October 1948, he later divorced his wife Angeline, they had two children Elonda and James Jr. Next, was (2) Martha Mays, born 28 November 1949 who is not married. (3) Wynelle Mays was born 20 January 1951 and married Johnny Trammell. (4) Al Joseph Mays was born 19 May 1952 and has four children: Daniel, Al Joseph Jr., Donald, and Maria. This family lives in Arizona. (5) Michael "BoBo" Mays was born 1 September 1953 and married Gale. (6) Cherry Mays was born 13 November 1954 and is not married. (7) Yvette Mays was born 10 May 1956 and married Norman Thomaston who was born 13 June 1955. Yvette and Norman Thomaston have two sons, Shon Thomaston, born 1 November 1972; a 1991 graduate of Carrollton High School and who graduated from Brewster-Park College in South Georgia. Shon teaches at Carrollton Junior High School and also coaches Carrollton High basketball. Another son is Travis Thomaston born 31 May 1979 who will graduate from State University of West Georgia in December 2001 and he also plans to teach. Travis works now with disabled children at Oak Grove. Yvette Mays Thomaston works for Bluewater Rope Company in Carrollton.

Orea Lee Herring Mays Williams and Yvette Mays Thomaston

The youngest son of Orea Lee and James Mays is (8) Steven Patrick "Kimbo" Mays who was born 13 November 1960 and was named for Dr. Steve Worthy and Dr. E.V. Patrick. Patrick Mays is married to Evelyn Nunn and has one child with Evelyn, Marcus "Magic" Mays. Kimbo Mays has four stepchildren: Tabitha Nunn, Maurice Nunn, Al Nunn, and Jerome Shepard. Orea Lee and James H. Mays later divorced.

On 3 September 1985, Orea Lee married Willie "Sonny" Williams in Carroll County, Georgia. Orea Lee and Sonny Williams did not have any children together, but they have loved and given a home to so many children! Orea Lee has loved children all her life and she has taken in many babies from birth and brought them up as her very own. One of these is Gwendolyn Demetrica Boling. Later on, Orea Lee took in Gwen's daughter, Demetrica Deon Boling, who was born 25 November 1984. DeDe as she is called, will be a junior at Carrollton High School

Shon and Travis Thomaston

next year 2002. DeDe's sister is DeAshley Shanta Boling. A special goddaughter to Orea Lee is Deidra Parks Wilson.

Orea Lee is loved by a lot of children — black and white — and she has worked in the homes of many families in Carrollton. She has been a part of the John T. Robinson family for over twenty-five years. She has worked for St. Margaret's Episcopal Church, the Roy Denney Jr. family and the Roger Schoerner family to name but a few. There is not a word to describe the job Orea Lee has performed for all these families. "Domestic engineer" comes close but does not quite encompass it all! It is too harsh a word somehow, and leaves out the "sky-high, mile-high lemon pies" that she used to serve to us and the love that she tendered upon us through the years.

Patrick Steven "Kimbo" Mays

Orea Lee has adored children and they have adored her back. She has become quite a legend in her own time since Jan Robinson Bell immortalized her in that novella called *The Kramer Street Kids* written in 1999. This novella was written by Jan Bell for Johnny and Ann Seaton Fletcher's daughter, Maggie Fletcher, for the occasion of Maggie's tenth birthday. It was a novella written about all the children, Ann Seaton included, who grew up on Kramer Street together and some of their mischief in the 1950-1960s era. These "chillun" will never forget those famous words of Orea Lee:

> "You're going to learn how to act right on Kramer Street NOW because if you don't, you won't ever act right on anybody's street!"

Orea Lee liked to deliver her sermons from her "pulpit," which was the ironing board set up in the den so she could watch her stories (soap operas on TV) while she ironed. That's why so many of the Kramer Street kids now associate the love they felt in childhood with the Psssssshhhhhhhhh of the steam iron. *Submitted by: Yvette and Norman Thomaston, 141 Fawn Circle, Deer Run Subdivision, Carrollton, GA 30117 and Written by: Jan Robinson Bell*

1172. Thomas Barnes Williams and Hannah Pinson

Thomas Barnes Williams and his wife Hannah Pinson, daughter of Isaac Pinson of Laurens, South Carolina, were one of Carroll County's early pioneer couples, migrating from Laurens District, South Carolina, by 1832. Barney and Hannah were staunch Primitive Baptists, with Barney being a leader in the Concord Church until they left to become founding members of Hopewell Primitive Baptist Church (later called Old Carrollton), located on what is now Highway 61 at Sand Hill. This church remained active until 2000, when it disbanded following the death of Elder James Embry, a great-great-grandson of Barney and Hannah.

Barney was born about 1790 in South Carolina and died in late 1855. Hannah was born about 1795 and died before 1870. Both are thought to be buried in the Williams Cemetery in a field near Pleasant Hill Road.

Their children, all of whom grew up in Carroll, were:

James H. Williams, 1814-1867, married Sarah Davidson. Both are buried in Winston County, Alabama. Children: John, Joel, Lucinda, Hannah Elizabeth, and Jasper Jackson.

Moses Williams about 1815-1843, married Mary Adams. See the article about this family.

A son who was born after 1830 and died young.

Sally Williams, 1818-1937, buried in Old Concord Cemetery. Her gravestone is homemade, with someone taking care to carve fancy letters on it.

Joel Casper Williams, 1821-1872, married Mary Barbara Kiser. Both are buried in the Kiser Cemetery in Carroll. Children: Rebecca Catherine, married Leonidas J. Reese; Amanda Elizabeth, married Jasper Green McKee; Mary Ann Hannah, married Robert Independent Reese; George Thomas, married Margaret Ann Ayers; Moses, married Mary Lizabeth Ayers and Mary Norton; Sarah Manassas; Martha Susann, married Joseph Benjamin Boatright; Joseph Johnson, married Bessie Davis.

A daughter, born about 1823, who married Vincent Holly. Their daughter, Sarah Jane, was in Barney's household in 1850 and received a share of his estate.

Henry Roland Williams. See the article on this son.

Nancy Catherine Williams, married John Jefferson Hinesley. See a Hinesley article for more information on this daughter.

Elihu M. Williams, married Mary Ann Hinesley. Children: Octavia, James, Robert.

Mary Ann A. Williams, married Duke Nail. Children: Davis, Joel, and Enoch.

Lucinda F. Williams, married first William J. Patterson, one son John J. Patterson. Married second William M. Hendrix. One known child, Columbus Newton Hendrix who married Nancy Arrie Reid.

Hannah Melissa Williams, married Timothy D. Edwards. Children: Mary A.H., John Jeff. Hannah Melissa died before 1870.

Barbara Martha Jane Williams, married William Cook.

About the photograph: Fewer than ten people in this gathering of descendants of Thomas Barnes Williams and Hannah Pinson have been identified. *Submitted by: Nancy E. Wiliams, 701 Wind Grove Rd., Marietta, GA 30067. nelizw@aol.com*

Williams Family Reunion, early 1870s.

1173. Tom Williams

Thomas (Tom) Benjamin Williams was born February 26, 1870, four and a half months before Georgia was readmitted to the union (July 15, 1870). Living in Carroll County all of his life, he married Martha (Mattie) Pierce on December 18, 1895, and had two sons, Homer Lee Williams (January 14, 1897) and Guy Thomas Williams (May 7, 1903).

Mattie and Tom Williams May 9, 1948 at their Temple home.

Working as a farmer, Tom grew cotton and corn, and on December 1, 1919, he bought a five-room, frame house on eight acres in Temple (now known as Rome Street). With no electricity or city water in Temple at the time, Tom and Mattie pulled their water from a well. Outhouses were also common throughout the city. Tom and Mattie raised chickens, and Tom shod horses at his blacksmith shop beside the house.

Mattie and Tom's first son, Homer, died at the age of thirty, leaving a wife, Dessa Ragan Williams and three children, Jewell, Mae and Charlie. Homer Jr. was born posthumously on October 18, 1927.

Homer Williams Jr. lives on East Johnson Street in Temple with his wife, Gwen. Elected as mayor of Temple from 1968 through 1972, he also was a partner in Temple Manufacturing Company, building kitchen cabinets and furniture until his retirement in 1983.

The second son, Guy, married Gaudie Mae Cooke on October 17, 1926. Following in his father's footsteps, Guy was also a farmer. He later worked as a policeman for Villa Rica and Temple. Guy is most remembered, however, for Williams Service Station, the Standard Oil gas station and garage he owned and operated for eighteen years on the corner of Highway 78 and Center Point Road in Temple.

Guy and Gaudie had two children, Reba Nadine Williams (July 11, 1931) and Guy Thomas (Tommy) Williams Jr. (July 25, 1938).

When his parents became elderly, Guy moved his family into Tom and Mattie's house to look after his parents. Tom died on October 15, 1952 and Mattie on March 14, 1969.

Guy and Gaudie deeded land to their daughter, Nadine, where she built a five-room house in 1970. Riding a Greyhound bus and carpooling for forty years, Nadine worked as an accountant and auditor at Fulton National Bank (later Bank South), Atlanta. She married and divorced Doy Cole with whom she had two children, Anthony Doy Cole (January 3, 1951) and Melissa Nadine Cole (June 17, 1952).

Anthony lives on Lake Buckhorn in Temple and has one child, Emily Marie Cole (August 6, 1981). Melissa lives on Fortenberry Road, Temple, with her husband, Michael Moore, and their two children, Nicholas Charles Moore (December 13, 1977) and Meghan Melissa Moore (June 12, 1983).

Guy died September 1, 1980 followed by Gaudie on April 8, 1996. Their son, Tommy, remodeled the Rome Street house in 1991 and moved there with his wife, Jerri. Tommy has one child, Teresa (Terri) Aileen Williams, and she has one daughter, Kristen. Tommy worked for more than twenty-seven years with Bell South. *Submitted by: Tom Williams' granddaughter, Nadine Williams Cole, 60 Rome Street, Temple, GA 30179.*

1174. Willie "Sonny" Williams

Willie Robert "Sonny" Williams was born 2 October 1937 in Chattanooga, Tennessee, while his family was visiting some relatives there. Since his Grandfather, Levi Wimberly, worked for the Central Railway, Sonny's family often made trips by train. The Williams family actually called Coweta County, Georgia, "home." Levi Wimberly had lived around Gadsden, Alabama, before moving to Coweta.

Leola Meadows Wimberly

Sonny Williams spent his first few years living in the home of his maternal grandmother who was Leola Meadows Wimberly. Leola was the daughter of Robert Meadows and the granddaughter of Willie Robert Meadows. Leola Meadows married Levi Wimberly in Coweta County, Georgia, and they were the parents of two girls.

The first daughter was Lillie Mae Wimberly who was born 1918 and died February 1979. Lillie Mae was married three times: first to a Bolton, second to Ernest Williams. 1918-1969 — and third to a Koger. Lillie Mae separated from Sonny's father a few years after Sonny was born and she moved to Washington, D.C. Sonny was left in the care of his grandmother, Leola, and he adored her. Also living in Leola's household was his first cousin, Minnie Louise Dodds. She was the daughter of Minnie Beatrice Wimberly Dodds

Sonny Williams and Minnie Louise Dodds

who was Lillie Mae's sister. Sonny later said that he and Minnie Dodds grew up just like brother and sister.

Sonny Williams attended Pinson Street Elementary School in Newnan and later on went to seventh grade at Warner High School on Savannah Street. In the eighth grade, he left Newnan to live in Washington, D.C. for awhile with his mother. There he entered Garnett Patterson Junior High School. But after a year there, he decided to come back to school in Newnan and once again lived with his grandmother, Leola. Education was always important to Leola — her father had been an academic teacher in one of the early black schools in the Arnco-Sargent community of Coweta County.

Sonny Williams (far left) during his tour of duty in Vietman

After graduation from Warner High School in 1955, Sonny decided to join the military. He joined the Air Force but was on special assignment as a technical administrative supervisor under U.S. Army jurisdiction. Sonny served in the Air Force for twenty-one years as a non-commissioned officer. In 1968, Sonny Williams was sent to Vietnam where the war was raging. He was stationed at Binh Thuy Air Base and was involved in surveillance. During this time, Sonny Williams was wounded but when offered the Purple Heart, he refused it since he felt that his wound was not that significant and did not merit that great honor. He saw many men losing limbs or getting killed in battle every day.

After returning from his tour of duty in Vietnam, Sonny Williams worked at the Pentagon for the Department of Defense for over ten years. At age 38, he decided to retire from the service but he remained in the Washington, D.C. area. He attended the University of the District of Columbia where he studied psychology and applied sciences, including mortuary science. He received his degree in applied sciences in 1982. He was only lacking three credits in order to have a double major in psychology — which has always been a field of interest to him.

Demetrica Deon "De De" Boling

Sonny Williams moved back to Georgia after 1982 and settled down in Coweta County once again. This time he took a job at Douglas & Lomason in Carrollton. Later, he went to work at West Georgia College as a custodian. On 3 September 1985, Sonny Williams married Orea Lee Mays, a widow with eight children. Sonny is retired now and he and Orea Lee Williams and family make their home on Woodland Drive in Carrollton. Though they never had any children of their own, Sonny and Orea Lee Williams have opened their hearts and their home to many babies and children they have reared like their own. One of these was Gwendolyn Boling, who now works at Southwire, and another is Demetrica Deon Bolling. "De De" Boling will be a junior at Carrollton High School in 2002. *Submitted by: Sonny Williams, 110 Woodland Drive, Carrollton, GA 30117 and Written by: Jan Robinson Bell*

1175. Williams - Hendrix

William Wesley Williams and Sarah Elizabeth Hendrix, both from the Fifth Land District of Carroll County, Georgia, were united in marriage on June 19, 1865, in Carroll County by a local Methodist minister, William Francis Spaight (W.F.S.) Powell. The Rev. Powell had just completed his tour of duty as a captain of Company F, Cobb's Legion, Georgia Volunteers. Rev. Powell was a founding member of Concord Methodist Church at Hickory Level, Temperance Methodist Church at Sand Hill, and Powell's Chapel on Flat Rock Road (now Douglas County).

William Wesley Williams, born in Carroll County, Georgia, on May 21, 1840, was the son of Moses Williams and Mary Adams, grandson of Thomas Barnes Williams and Hannah Pinson. William had one sister, Phebe A.H. Williams. William's father, Moses, died young and he and Phebe chose Moses' older brother, James Williams, as their legal guardian. At the age of twenty-one on March 21, 1862, William Wesley Williams joined the Confederate Army at Carrollton, Company E, First Regiment, Georgia Cavalry. William was paid forty cents per day for his horse and arms. According to a grandson, William was wounded in the leg and walked with a limp. His white horse, Old Dan, was also reported to have been wounded in battle.

Sarah Elizabeth Hendrix, born in Carroll County on August 8, 1842, was the daughter of James Hendrix and Letta Unknown Hendrix of the Fifth District of Carroll County.

William Wesley Williams and Sarah Hendrix had the following nine children: (1) James Marvin Williams married first to E.L. (Ann) McWilliams, and second to Maggie P. Lusk. (2) Amanda Elizabeth (Mandy) Williams married Joseph Hillsman West. (3) John Wesley Williams married Amanda Jeffers. (4) Andrew Martin (Dude) Williams married Mamie Hester Gwin. (5) David Benjamin (Ben) Williams married Lenora Ann (Nora) Richards. (6) Ollie Lettie Williams married Thomas Monroe Putnam. (7) Annie Idella Williams married Julius Kirk Hall. (8) Mary Etta Williams married George Henry Richards. (9) Effie Williams married Benjamin Ephraim Goodwin. *Submitted by: Felicia D. Williams, 268 Villa Rosa Way, Temple, GA 30179*

1176. Williams - Jeffers - Hendrix

John Wesley B. Williams was born in Carroll County Georgia, 23 March 1869. He was the son of William Wesley Williams and Sarah Elizabeth Hendrix, the grandson of Moses Williams and Mary Adams and the great-grandson of Thomas Barnes Williams and Hannah Pinson. He was married in Haralson County 11 December 1890 to Amanda F. Jeffers. They lived on Beech Creek in Haralson County, part of which was formerly Carroll County. John died in Cullman County, Alabama, on 29 October 1922 and is buried at Welti Cumberland Presbyterian Church in Cullman County.

John Wesley Williams. 1869-1922

Amanda F. Jeffers Williams was born 11 September 1873 in Georgia, the daughter of Louis Sanford (L.S.) Jeffers and Mary Fuller, granddaughter of Lewis Jeffers and Rhoda (Ruddie) Dabbins/Dobbins, great-granddaughter of John Jeffers and Frances Unknown Jeffers from the Brownsville Community in Paulding County, Georgia. Amanda died 3 January 1916 and is buried at Macedonia Primitive Baptist Church in Buchanan, Georgia, near Beech Creek with a host of other Jeffers and Williams buried there. James Hendrix, the grandfather of John Wesley Williams, donated the land for Macedonia Church.

James Hendrix had considerable land holding in Carroll and Haralson counties. A granddaughter of James tells a story of the missing copper box. James farmed and raised cotton in Carroll and Haralson Counties and kept his money hidden in a copper box. James had a stroke and was never able to tell the family where the box was hidden. According to the granddaughter, all James could say was "the barn," but the box was never found in or around the barn. She said they found his glasses on a rock on Kiser Creek sometime later. She said that her mother and a doctor friend had planned to come back from Alabama with a metal detector to see if the box could be found, but her mother never lived to return to Georgia.

John Wesley Williams and Amanda Jeffers had the following six children: (1) Willie John

Addrine Williams married first to Mattie Maudell Hayes and second to Lizzie Parl Hayes, all buried at Pleasant View Cemetery in Bowdon Junction, Georgia. (2) Grover Cleveland Williams, married first to Lottie V. Bachelor and second to Vassie Jeffers, buried at Buchanan City Cemetery. (3) Homer Williams died at one year of age and is buried at Macedonia. (4) Lewis Wesley Williams married Grace Estelle Phillips of the 5th District of Carroll County. Lewis is buried at Buchanan City Cemetery and Grace is buried at Center Hill Baptist in Cullman County, Alabama, with a host of other Phillips family members .(5) Molly Bell Williams married Harrison Newt Worthy Jr., and they are buried at Buchanan City Cemetery. (6) James Marvin Williams married Rilla Lovella Swann and they are buried at Fellowship Baptist in Haralson County. *Submitted by: Debra White, P.O. Box 193, Buchanan, GA 30113*

1177. Williams - Phillips

The families of my grandparents, Lewis Wesley Williams (1897-1957) and Grace Estelle Phillips (1895-1929), came out of the Fifth Land District of Carroll County, Georgia, and from the waters of Snake Creek. The Williams were a founding family of Concord Primitive Baptist Church (1834) on Highway 113 and charter members of Old Carrollton Primitive Baptist (formerly Hopewell) on Highway 61 at Sand Hill. The early descendants of the Williams families were members of Cross Plains Baptist Church and New Hope Baptist Church in the Fifth Land District. My Phillips families were members of Mt. Carmel Methodist Church in the Fifth Land District.

Lewis is the son of John Wesley Williams and Amanda Jeffers, grandson of William Wesley Williams and Sarah Elizabeth Hendrix, great-grandson of Moses Williams and Mary Adams, and the great-great-grandson of Thomas Barnes Williams and Hannah Pinson.

Grace Estelle Phillips and Lewis Wesley Williams.

Grace Estelle Phillips is the daughter of Joseph F. Phillips and Nancy M. Roundtree, granddaughter of Jessie Richard (J.R.) Phillips and Rebecca F. Norman, and great-granddaughter of Robert Phillips and Mary (Polly) Beck.

Lewis and Grace Williams had four children. (1) Odell died at birth (1922). (2) Viola Williams (1923-) married Conrade Howse. They had one daughter, Betty Jean Howse. Viola's second marriage was to Dan Carden. (3) Willie Wesley Williams, my father, (1925-1969) married Dora Rilla Carroll (1923-1969). They had three children, Dondra, Dennis, and Debra Williams. (4) John Lewis Williams (1928-1978) married Ruby Sandlin (1930-1999). They had three daughters, Pat, Barbara, and Sandra Williams.

I have been doing genealogy research, part-time for about fifteen years. I have about three-thousand relatives on-line at Roots Web, World Connect Project, listed as "Williams and Allied Family Files." My current email address is DenniWGA@Juno.com. *Submitted by: Dennis W. Williams, 326 Rockmart Road, Villa Rica, GA 30180*

1178. Benjamin Williamson of Carroll County

Benjamin Williamson was born in 1792. He married Susannah Miller on October 4, 1824. Susannah was born about 1809 and the daughter of Andrew Miller of Jasper County. They lived in Carroll County in the 1840s. On the census of 1840, Carroll, he is listed as the head of household. Then on the census of 1850, Heard, he is listed as a farmer by trade and his net worth $1,400. Other records show they were in Carroll the rest of their lives. They had ten children: Andrew Miller, John Clarke, Benjamin P., Rueben, Elizabeth A., Emily E., Jonathan Capps, William T., George Wesley, and Thomas L. Williamson. Susannah died in the 1860s and Benjamin later in 1881.

The descendants of George Wesley Williamson are many. He was born on December 26, 1845, and died November 24, 1936. He married Nancy Johnson on January 7, 1872. She was born in 1824 and died in 1927. Both are buried together in the Old Johnson Family Cemetery, west of McIntosh Reserve, Carroll County. George and Nancy had five children: Mack Duffie, Seaborn Thomas, James Franklin, Bill, and Thomas Williamson. They lived most of their lives in Carroll County.

James Franklin (Jim Frank) Williamson was born on November 13, 1872. He married Julia Voranna Hubbard on October 5, 1895. She was born on August 1, 1869, the daughter of Francis and Albert Hubbard. Jim Frank and Julia had seven children: Lillie Bell, James Rufus, Arthur George, Leon, Horry, Emma Francis, and Alfred Williamson. After Julia's death on June 27, 1927, Jim Frank married Minnie Crutchfield. They had no children. Jim died on February 12, 1959, and Minnie on April 18, 1967.

Walking up in the yard, seeing folks gathered in the shade, peeling apples is what you may have seen when you visited Alfred, Lois, and Ida's home in Carrollton some few years ago. A warm welcome is what you received when you went there. Just peaceful folks living peaceful lives. Alfred Williamson was born on March 1, 1910. He married Lois Ruth Farmer. A quote from the family Bible "Alfred and Lois married on a rainy Sunday afternoon December 11, 1932. I had borrowed brother Rufus' 1926 Chevrolet and the road was muddy" (Alfred). Lois was born on April 4, 1917, and was the daughter of Newton and Ida Lee Traylor Farmer. Alfred and Lois had four children: Bobby Lee, Franklin Ray, Martha Ann, and Linda Ruth Williamson. Lois passed away on April 17, 1996, and Alfred on May 17, 1998.

Bobby Lee Williamson, first son of Alfred, married Barbara Jean Herrin. They have three children, Debra Kaye, Michael Wayne, and Joseph Allen Williamson. Debra married Rickey Thomas and they have one son named Jeffery Adam Thomas. Jeff married Alison Barr. Michael married Wanda Gail Vise. Joseph married Tina Louis and they have two children, Brian Allen and Ashley Nicole Williamson.

Bobby's second marriage was to Martha Timms and their three children are Jeremy, Matthew Scott, and Amanda Victoria Williams. Jeremy married Rebekah Madden and has a daughter Alyssa Ann Williamson.

Franklin Ray, second son of Alfred, married Gwendolyn Weir. They have three children, Brian Ray, Sandra Lynn, and Wesley Alan Williamson. Brian married Sonia Robinson and they have two children, Breanna Marie and Matthew Eric Williamson. Lynn married Robert Jerald Rooks III and they have two children, Lindsey Elaine and Robert Jerald Jr. Williamson.

Martha Ann Williamson, third child of Alfred, married William J. Dean Jr. They have two children, Rebecca Ann and William Steve Dean.

Linda Ruth Williamson, fourth child of Alfred, married Windle Walker. They have three children, Kimberly Ann, Krista Ruth, and Lori Kay Walker. Kimberly married James Ozier and their children are Walker James, Marianna Rose, and Laurel Kelly Ozier. Krista married David Arthur and their children are Cole and Mason Arthur. Kay married Chris Benton and their children are Joshua and Jarod Benton. In searching the Williamsons of Carroll County, I found there are many lines that go back to Benjamin and Susannah. Some moved to Texas, some to Alabama, even as far as Hawaii. Some of the Williamsons still live within a few miles of the early settlers, a community we call Lowell. The most asked question that I hear is "Where is Ole Benjamin and Susannah buried?" Maybe one day, we'll find out ... *Submitted by: Mike Williamson, 186 County Road 604, Ranburne, AL*

1179. John Williamson

John Williamson was born on 17 February 1767 in Virginia. He died 3 April 1843 in Carroll County, Georgia. He married Sarah Braswell on 12 December 1811 in Franklin County, Georgia. Sarah Braswell was born in 1784 in South Carolina and died in 1856 in Carroll County. She was the daughter of Elizabeth Doughtery and Frederick Braswell, a Revolutionary soldier who served in the 1st Battalion of Minute Men of the Georgia State Line.

John Williamson settled in Carroll County in 1831, coming from Jackson County, Georgia. According to tax digests of Carroll County, his land holdings in Lowndes, Appling, Early, Lee, Irwin, Dooley, and Wilkinson counties totaled over two thousand acres. Except for the Appling County property that came from the estate of Frederick Braswell, the land was purchased from fortunate drawers in various Georgia land lotteries. He also owned six hundred acres in Carroll County. Most of the property was leased to tenant farmers or for harvesting of timber. He evidently did not believe in recording deeds because the transactions were either recorded by a purchaser, described in tax digests and in his last will and testament, or recorded after his death.

In 1832 he was living on Lot 79, owned Lot 80 and one-half of Lot 111, all in the 5th District of Carroll County, which made up a sizable portion of the Sand Hill community. In 1837 he bought Lot 82 and thus owned most of what was to become the business section of Sand Hill. How much of this land was under cultivation is not known but he might be seen inspecting the fields riding a bay horse with the unusual name of "Tantribogess." The land was willed to his wife and children upon his death with each receiving a specified tract.

John and Sarah Williamson were the parents of seven children. Julia Ann was born in 1815 in Franklin County. She married Stukly S.C. Parker in 1830 in Jackson County and they came to Carroll County with her parents and left the county before 1867. Armanda Louisa Caroline was born in Jackson County in 1816 and married Hiram Turner in 1833 in Carroll County, and died there in 1877 (See related Hiram Turner article). John B. was born in 1818 in Jackson County and married Catherine Hopper in 1839 in Carroll County. He died in Carroll County in 1898. James Smith Alexander was born about 1820 in Jackson County and married Susan Boatwright in 1842 in Carroll County and moved to Coosa County, Alabama, about 1856. Narcissa was born about 1823 in Jackson County and married Elijah H. McWhorter in Campbell County in 1839. She died in Carroll County in 1843. Andrew Scott was born in Jackson County about 1824, married Rebecca Jackson in 1844 in Carroll County. He died about 1868 in Crenshaw County, Alabama. Sophrona Catherine was born about 1828 in

Jackson County and married Charles Duke in 1844 in Carroll County. She died after 1880 in Cleburne County, Alabama. *Submitted by: W.F. Cartee, 198 Cloud Street, Jonesboro, GA 30236 and Researched by: A.E. Turner.*

1180. Joseph Charles Williamson

Joseph Charles (J.C.) Williamson spent many years in Carroll County. He was born in 1928 in the Glenloch community in adjoining Heard County. He died in 1976 while living in Villa Rica.

After graduation from Centralhatchee High School in Heard County, he attended West Georgia College in Carrollton, earning a junior college certificate in 1946. He also received a degree in physics with a minor in education from the University of Georgia. To complete his formal education, he earned his doctorate in administration and supervision from Auburn University in Alabama.

J.C. Williamson Family, 1973

In 1948, J.C. Williamson married Inez Jackson. She was the daughter of R.C. (Buster) and Lucille Shumake Jackson. Inez, a graduate of West Georgia in Carrollton and Tift College in Forsyth, was also a teacher. They had three sons Gregory, Michael, Teddy, and one daughter Susan Williamson Gordy. All four children continue to live in Carroll County with their families. Four grandchildren, Crystal, Heath, and Brittany Williamson, and Will Gordy, live in Carrollton and Villa Rica.

For a number of years J.C. taught physics and chemistry in Heard, Butts, and Taylor counties. In 1958, he came to Villa Rica High School where he taught and was assistant principal. In 1964, he became principal at Villa Rica. At the time of his death in 1976, he was an assistant superintendent for the Carroll County School System having served as Title I Coordinator and later director of physical facilities including the building programs going on in the county at the time.

J.C. Williamson was ordained as a deacon at the First Baptist Church in Villa Rica in Carroll County. He was a teacher for an adult men's Sunday school class. He served as president of the Villa Rica Lion's Club. He was also a member of several professional education organizations where he served the cause of education throughout Carroll County, the state of Georgia, and Alabama.

J.C. Williamson was a devoted husband, father, and educator who spent time with his family in work and play. He is buried at Hillcrest Cemetery in Villa, Rica, Georgia. *Submitted by: Mrs. Inez Jackson Williamson, 635 Rocky Branch Rd., Villa Rica, GA 30180*

1181. Reuben Williamson

Reuben Williamson was born 16 March 1836 in Georgia. Reuben married Emily Wilson Todd 22 August 1865 in Carroll County. Emily was born about 1832 in Georgia, one of seven children born to George Asbury Wilson and Absilla Newsome. Her siblings were: John Hinnard, Rhoda Spence, Elizabeth, Appleton White Newsome, Cincinatus and Susan J. Wilson. Emily died about 1897 in Cleburne County, Alabama, and has an unmarked grave in Old Harmony Primitive Baptist Cemetery, Cleburne County. When Reuben died some sixteen years later, 15 December 1916, in Carroll County, family legend says it was bitterly cold, in fact too cold for the wagon trip from Bowdon to Cleburne County. Reuben rests in Bethlehem Primitive Baptist Cemetery south of Bowdon.

Reuben was the son of Benjamin Williamson born circa 1792 in Georgia and died Carroll County sometime after 1880. His mother was Susannah Miller, daughter of Andrew Miller, born about 1809 in Georgia and died between 1860 and 1870 in Carroll County. Their burial is unknown. Benjamin was in the 1840 census of Carroll County in the Whitesburg district, 1850 in Heard County, 1860 back in Carroll County owning two slaves. Reuben had eight brothers and two sisters: Andrew M., married Sarah Davidson 1856 in Alabama; John Clarke, married Louisa D. and lived in Carroll County; James F., married Vestie and Mary Noel, lived in Carroll County; Benjamin P., married Martha Johnson lived in Carroll County; Jonathan C., married Mary Johnson, lived in Carroll County; William T., married Harriett Jones, residence unknown; George Wesley, married Nancy Jane Johnson, lived in Carroll County; Thomas L., married Nancy, residence unknown; Emily (twin) and Elizabeth (twin).

Reuben enlisted 1861 in the Civil War in Company F, 19th Regiment Volunteers in Carrollton and when the war ended, was at home sick on furlough. Shortly after the war, he married Emily Wilson Todd, who lost her husband James M. Todd in battle. Family legend has it that Reuben and James were together when James was injured and James asked that Reuben return and tell Emily what happened to him and they later married. Reuben and Emily, with her three small children moved to Cleburne County and lived there till Emily died. Her Todd children were: Oscar, married Georgia Cavandar 1875, moved to Atlanta; Louisa, married Meredith Lokey 1876, lived in Cleburne County, Alabama; and George Asbury married Elizabeth Groover, 1885 and lived in Anniston, Alabama. Reuben and Emily had three children: Susan, born circa 1867, no other information; George Washington born 4 January 1870, married Janie Elizabeth Neely, 24 April 1892 and lived in Carroll County. Children: Effie 1893 (Joe Head), George Asbury 1895-died at three years; James 1897 (Myrtle Kemp), Kate 1899 (Shell Traylor), Robert 1901 (Gladys Cullpepper), Annie 1903 (Jim Johnson), Ellen a twin 1906 (Curt Allen), children: Charles, Wilbur, Ray, Elizabeth and Ruth; and Bill a twin 1906 (Thelma Phillips). Thomas Clarke, born 14 March 1873, married Emma Carpenter, lived in Alabama. Children: Reuben R., Martha E., George T. and Jessie Marlow. Many descendants of this family now reside in Georgia and Alabama. *Submitted by: Jill Allen, 579 W. Hickory Level Rd., Temple, GA 30179 sloua@aol.com*

1182. Robert Williamson

Robert Williamson and Matilda Goggans Williamson lived and farmed acreage valued at $1000 in Edgefield District, South Carolina, prior to their migration to Carroll County in 1854. They carried their children (John, Elizabeth, Robert, Frederick, Jasper, Balsora, James and George Washington) and their possessions on a four-horse wagon and a one-horse cart to their new homestead. Robert was born on 4 January 1791 to Joseph (died 16 October 1797, Newberry, South Carolina) and Elizabeth (died 31 August 1840, Newberry). Matilda was the daughter of Daniel Goggans (died 5 September 1803) and Naomi Peterson (died 30 November 1840). Robert served in the War of 1812 in Tucker's Regiment of the South Carolina Militia. Robert died 7 February 1869 in Carroll County, having farmed land valued at $1800. There is some evidence that Matilda Coggans died in 1843 and that Robert married a second Matilda (Carter) in May 1844. The second Matilda is the daughter of Charles and Lydia (Scurry) Carter. In that case, Balsora, James and George would be the children of the second marriage.

George W. Williamson in buggy

George Washington Williamson was born in Edgefield District/Newberry on 14 January 1849. He married Sarah Emma Ferrell on 20 February 1881 in Carroll County. Samuel and Elizabeth Crumbley Ferrell gave birth to her and her twin, Nanny Kate, on 30 September 1854 (see Ferrell entry). George W. and Emma had four children: (1) Henry Clifton born 15 July 1882, died 9 April 1957; (2) Robert Samuel born 16 December 1885, died 31 May 1954; (3) Matilda Elizabeth born 19 June 1889; and (4) Nanny Kate born 3 September 1891. George W. died in January of 1921. Emma passed on 18 January 1939. Both are buried in Carrollton City Cemetery.

Henry Clifton Williamson met Fannie Odessa Meigs (born 22 October 1878) and they married on 1 May 1904. She was the daughter of James Alexander Meigs and Francis Ann Elizabeth Rush. Robert Samuel Williamson married Annie Crockett on 1 July 1906. Nanny Kate married Joseph Clayton Cole on 10 January 1912. All married in Carroll County. The children of Henry C. and Fannie were: Landis Meigs born 13 May 1908, died 3 June 1990; Blaine born 17 May 1911, died 3 December 1977; and Catherine.

Blaine Williamson's favorite cousin was J. Carl Williamson, son of Robert Samuel. He told many stories of their growing up in Carrollton. Henry eventually moved his family to Birmingham with his work in the railroad industry. Blaine met and married Myrtle Marie Busby (born August 1910, died July 1971) in Birmingham, daughter of John Lee and Vanna Franklin Busby. During World War II, Blaine supervised blueprint layouts in the shipyards of Mobile. After the war, the family relocated and settled in West Palm Beach, Florida, where they are both buried. There are two surviving children, AnnMarie Ballard Williamson and Robert Blaine Williamson, and three grandchildren.

The picture shows George W. Williamson seated second in the buggy. Standing is Rip Crockett. *Submitted by: Robert B. Williamson, 6714 Stonecutter Drive, Burke, VA 22015*

1183. Willis Family

Charles Hampton Willis and Rebeckah Lucinda Caroline Bates

Charles Hampton Willis was the seventh child of Thomas and Susan Willis. He was born on March 9, 1867, and died December 28, 1920, in Carroll

County, Georgia. He married Rebeckah Lucinda Caroline Bates in July 1893. She was the daughter of Eliphus and Sarah Bates (see Bates family). Rebeckah was born July 9, 1874, and died January 13, 1962, at the home of her daughter, Mrs. Bernie Cleveland in Mableton, Cobb County, Georgia. Both Charley and Becky are buried in the Macedonia Baptist Church Cemetery.

Children of Charles H. Willis and Rebeckah Bates are: (1) Lela Ann Elizabeth Willis was born August 6, 1894. She died December 12, 1982. (2) Ada Susan Willis was born August 11, 1896. She died March 1, 1986. (3) John Hampton Willis was born January 6, 1899. He died August 19, 1973. (4) Eula Mae Willis was born November 5, 1901. She died February 10, 1915, at the age of fourteen from pneumonia. (5) Thomas Milton Willis was born November 5, 1903. He died October 14, 1986. (6) Robert E. "Lee" Willis was born January 29, 1906. He died May 31, 1984. (7) Harvey Charlie Willis was born May 10, 1908. He died May 25, 1981. (8) Ira Horace "Sharpey" Willis was born July 22, 1910. He died July 28, 1985. (9) Lurlie Willis was born July 22, 1913. (10) Bernie Beatrice Willis was born February 22, 1918. She died June 2, 1999. More information on these children in the following articles.

Charles H. Willis Family

The people in the family picture are (front row) Charles, Rebeckah holding Lurlie, Harvey, Lee, Ira, Eula (standing). Back row: Ada, Oscar Lenton McGuire, Lela, John, Tom. This picture was taken approximately 1913.

My mother, Jerry Cleveland Crumbley, and her mother, Bernie Willis Cleveland, were both born at the Willis home place on Highway 61 in Carrollton. The house is still standing to date.

My mother told me the earliest memory of her Grandmother Willis was when they went to visit. Grandmother would sit on the steps and tell the small children "Soap Sally would get them if they went up the stairs."

Grandmother sold the farm when my mother was small and she would go from one child to another every Sunday unless someone was sick or had a baby. Then she would stay until they were well. No matter where Grandmother Willis was in July of every year, they had a family reunion to celebrate Grandmother's birthday.
Submitted by: Cynthia Davis
Sources: Bible, census, land, marriage records and personal information researched by Jerry Crumbley.

1184. Willis Family

Part 1

Lela Ann Elizabeth Willis

Lela Ann Elizabeth Willis was born August 6, 1894, and died December 12, 1982, in Carroll County, Georgia. She married Oscar Lenton McGuire on July 27, 1913, in Carroll County. He was born July 27, 1889, and died May 27, 1948. Both are buried at Macedonia Baptist Church Cemetery. They had two sons.

(1) Harold D. McGuire was born October 20, 1914, and died December 1, 1996. He is buried

Lela Willis and Oscar Lenton McGuire

in the Macedonia Baptist Church Cemetery. He married Evelyn Louise Maroney. They did not have children. Louise and Harold donated land to Midway Macedonia Baptist Church in the 1990s. The new church was built on this land. Harold served in the military during World War II and received the Silver Star.

(2) Clarence E. McGuire was born May 12, 1917, and died April 12, 1974. He is buried in the Macedonia Baptist Church Cemetery. He married Sarah Louise Campbell. They did not have children. He served in the military during World War II.

The picture of Lela Willis and Oscar Lenton McGuire was made on their wedding day.
Submitted by: Mrs. H.D. McGuire
Sources: Census, land, marriage records and personal information researched by Jerry Crumbley.

1185. Willis Family

Part 2

Ada Susan Willis

Ada Susan Willis was born August 11, 1896, in Carroll County, Georgia, and died March 1, 1986. She married John Henry Broome in Carroll County on October 17, 1915. John was born February 28, 1891, and died Dec. 23, 1959, in Carroll County, Georgia. Both are buried at Macedonia Baptist Church Cemetery.

Ada and John Broome

They had seven children. (1) Ralph Henry Broome was born November 11, 1916, in Carroll County and died November 4, 1994. He married Willene Brasseale on April 23, 1938, in Carroll County. Ralph was a Methodist minister. (2) Wilbur Charles Broome was born March 1, 1919, in Carroll County and died January 21, 1998. He married Myrle Lee on June 7, 1941, in Carroll County. (3) Sarah Frances Broome was born August 9, 1921, in Carroll County and died December 29, 1993. She married W. Paul Camp. (4) Mary Catherine Broome was born April 30, 1924, in Carroll County and died April 7, 1987. She married Eugene M. Smith. (5) Annie Rebecca Broome was born June 28, 1928, in Carroll County and died November 29, 1990. She married Ronald Williams. (6) Norma Ruth Broome was born February 2, 1932, in Carroll County and died July 21, 1997. She married B.L. Crowe. (7) Myrtie Lee Broome was born March 14, 1938, in Carroll County. She married Farris Richardson. *Submitted by: Joy Williams*
Sources: Census, land, marriage records and personal information researched by Jerry Crumbley.

1186. Willis Family

Part 3

John Hampton Willis

John Hampton Willis was born January 6, 1899, and died August 19, 1973. He married Hepsie Melissa Wallis on December 5, 1920, in Carroll County. Hepsi was born July 8, 1903, and died September 11, 1981, in Carroll County, Georgia. Both are buried at Macedonia Baptist Church Cemetery. They had four children.

Hepsie and John H. Willis

(1) Marie Willis was born November 6, 1922. She married Aaron Moses Matthews. (2) Charles Edwin Willis was born July 10, 1927. He married Doris Yarbrough. (3) Wallis Barnett Willis was born July 7, 1934. He married Dorothy Smallwood and Melba Luke. (4) Carolyn Jean Willis was born January 22, 1937, and died June 10, 1938, of pneumonia. She was buried at Macedonia Baptist Church Cemetery. *Submitted by: Mrs. Marie Matthews*
Sources: Census, land, marriage records and personal information researched by Jerry Crumbley

1187. Willis Family

Part 4

Thomas Milton Willis

Tom was born to Charles Hampton Willis and Rebecca (Rebeckah) Lucinda Caroline Bates on November 5, 1903. He died October 14, 1982, in Douglasville. He married Clarice Dorothy Carden on September 25, 1932, at the home of Sidney and Annie Carden Camp, Whitesburg, Georgia. (See memorial page for Tom Willis family.) Dorothy, a twin, was born May 8, 1914, to Solomon D. "Sam" and Mary E. "Mollie" Lassetter Carden and she died December 9, 1984, in Douglasville, Georgia. They had 3 children: (1) Nancy Rebecca Anne Willis, born January 4, 1934, married Walter Asbury (W.A.) Howell at Midway Macedonia Baptist Church on July 20, 1952. Their children were Walter David and Valerie Ellen Howell. (2) Donald Milton Willis, born November 8, 1936, died July 31, 1989. He married Frances Lois Leathers in January 1960. Their children were Donald Milton Willis Jr., born October 26, 1960, died September 18, 1999; Dorothy Felicia Willis (Higdon); and Connie Sue Willis (Nalley). The four great-grandchildren are Michal and Kendall Higdon, and Joey Willis Nalley and Nancy Elizabeth Nalley. (3) Thomas David "Tommy" Willis, born June 3, 1944, died January 3, 1982. Tommy married Nancy Joanne Arnold December 23, 1972, in Albany, Georgia. Their children are Brett Matthew Willis and Trent Ashley Willis.

Mother and Dad lived in and around Villa Rica most of their lives, except for two years in Temple and one in Douglasville during World War II. They moved back to Carroll County and lived one year near The Flying S Ranch, after which Dad purchased the old Johnson home place on Moss Ferry Road off Highway 61. He built several lakes behind and to the side of their home, which were opened several years for fishing.

During World War II, Dad was one of many men to be drafted but a bad leg caused him to be turned down. Leaving farming, he learned to weld and worked all during the war welding jack clamps for big ships. I can remember how proud I felt that his job was helping America win a horrible war.

When the war was over, a man he worked with, Buddy Stockmar, started a welding business and hired my dad, Tom Willis, and Marchman Boyd. When Stockmar retired, Tom and Marchman bought the equipment and started their own business, Villa Rica Metal Manufacturing Company, which was located behind the grist mill. They developed (patented) and built stalk cutters, selling them to farmers in Georgia and Alabama.

Mother did her share helping with chores — milking cows, washing and ironing clothes, and cooking good meals. The larger meals were prepared at noon, since Dad came home to lunch every day. Dad plowed and planted large gardens that usually produced well, necessitating several trips to the Villa Rica High School canning plant, as well as many hours in our own kitchen preserving the good vegetables Mother and Daddy grew.

Tom and Dorothy Willis on their wedding day, September 25, 1932

My mother and dad celebrated their 50th wedding anniversary on September 25, 1982, at Douglas General Hospital where Dad was in the last stages of his battle with cancer. *The Douglas County Sentinel* did a nice article with pictures and the hospital nutritionist planned a special 50th celebration with cake and trimmings. When the *Sentinel* asked my parents for their advice to couples entering marriage bonds, Dad, who was very weak, said "Work together and figure together. Try to work your plans out." Mother said, "Just stick in there through thick and thin, whatever comes and goes. There are good times, and bad and sad times." They had lost their youngest son Tommy from a sudden heart attack just eight months before.

They were and are right! Fifty years had issued them some hard and sad times, but thanks be to God, they did endure.

When you and I in this generation consider how our families and ancestors endured through the Great Depression years, hard labor in fields of cotton, the big war, plus the untimely deaths of their loved ones, could we have done as well? They were a great generation!

With so much for which to be thankful, I offer these words as a tribute to my parents. *Submitted by: Felicia Willis Higdon, granddaughter, Franklin, TN and Written by: daughter Nancy Anne Willis Howell, Douglasville, GA.*

1188. Willis Family
Part 5
Robert E. Lee Willis

Robert E. Lee Willis was born January 29, 1906, in Carroll County, Georgia, and died May 31, 1984. He married Jewell Boatwright in Carroll County. Jewel was born March 2, 1912. Lee is buried at Macedonia Baptist Church Cemetery. They had seven children. (1) Billy Gene Willis was born August 20, 1930, and died November 13, 2000. He married Alice Idella Strickland. (2) Bobbie Joe Willis was born June 20, 1932. She married William Samuel (Jack) Raven. (3) Winford Lee Willis was born January 18, 1934, and died October 10, 1979. He married Geraldine New. (4) Willard James Willis was born September 7, 1935, and died May 17, 1979. He married Polly Easterwood. (5) Betty Virginia Willis was born January 15, 1937, and died September 18, 1998. She married Dalton Powers. (6) Max Wyndal Willis was born July 21, 1938. He married Dorene Jones. (7) Larry Benny Willis was born January 22, 1941. He married Brenda Ponder. The people in the family picture are: Betty, Bobbie Jo, Lee, Jewel, Billy, Larry and Max Willis. *Submitted by: Mrs. Jewel Willis*
Sources: Bible, census, land, marriage records and personal information researched by Jerry Crumbley

Robert E. Lee Willis Family

1189. Willis Family
Part 6
Harvey Charlie Willis

Harvey Charlie Willis was born May 10, 1908, and died May 25, 1981. He married Elsie Elizabeth Maroney. She was born July 4, 1914, and died December 3, 1973. Both are buried at Macedonia Baptist Church Cemetery. They did not have children.

Harvey and Elsie Willis

Harvey served in the Navy during World War II.

Harvey married Lois Morrow Simpkins on June 20, 1975. Lois is buried in Carrollton, Georgia. *Submitted by: Timothy S. Crumbley.*
Sources: Bible, census, land, marriage records and personal information researched by Jerry Crumbley

1190. Willis Family
Part 7
Ira Horace Willis

Ira Horace "Sharpey" Willis was born July 22, 1910, and died July 28, 1985, in Carroll County, Georgia. He married Jewel "Judy" Wren. She was born July 28, 1914, and died July 28, 1985. Ira and Judy were killed in an auto accident in Carroll County. They were active members at Macedonia Baptist Church where they are buried.

Ira and Judy Willis

They had three sons. (1) A son that was born stillborn. (2) Charles Marvin Willis was born January 1938. He married Phyllis D. Fennel. (3) Kenneth Willis was born June 21, 1942. He married Kay. *Submitted by: Kenneth Willis*
Sources: Bible, census, land, marriage records and personal information researched by Jerry Crumbley

1191. Willis Family
Part 8
Lurlie Willis

Lurlie Willis was born July 22, 1913, and married George Furr. He was born September 1, 1910, and died in 1979. They were married November 13, 1937.

Lurlie and George Furr

They had two children. (1) Linda June Furr Brown was born October 6, 1938. (2) Howard Lamar (Sonny) Furr was born November 9, 1940. *Submitted by: Mrs. Lurlie Furr*
Sources: Bible, census, land, marriage records and personal information researched by Jerry Crumbley.

1192. Willis Family
Part 9
Bernie Beatrice Willis

Bernie Beatrice Willis was born February 22, 1918, and died June 2, 1999. She married Garnett William Cleveland, born January 18, 1910, and died December 2, 1992. They were married on June 11, 1938, in Heflin, Alabama. Both are buried at Westview Cemetery, Atlanta, Georgia.

Bernie and Garnett W. Cleveland

They had six children: (1) Jerry Willis Cleveland was born March 29, 1939, in Carroll County, Georgia. She married Robert Daniel Crumbley in Fulton County, Georgia. They have three children. (2) Roger Dean Cleveland was born February 12, 1941, in Cobb County, Georgia. He married Phyllis A. Deeter. They had two children. (3) Sheila Ann Cleveland was born August 17, 1944, in Carroll County. (4) Rebecca Star Cleveland was born July 2, 1947, in Cobb County and died March 10, 1949, of pneumonia. She was buried at Westview Cemetery, Atlanta. (5) Phyllis Dianne Cleveland was born August 21, 1951, in Cobb County. She married Robert Hall. (6) Garnett Phillip Cleveland was born November 4, 1957, in Cobb County. He married Carolyn Schulner.

Garnett W. Cleveland was a builder/contractor in Cobb and Fulton counties. He built most of the subdivisions in west Cobb County between 1950 and 1980. Bernie was a seamstress. She could sew anything that the public would bring to her. Sometimes people would bring her a picture of a dress and she would make it for them. In her late fifties she started painting. She enjoyed painting old barns. She sold some, but gave a lot more away to friends and family. *Submitted by: Stephanie Crumbley*

Sources: Bible, census, land, marriage records and personal information researched by Jerry Crumbley.

1193. Willis Family

Thomas Henry Willis and Susan Idelia Richards

Thomas Henry Willis was born September 15, 1815, in North Carolina and died July 21, 1880, in Carroll County, Sand Hill community, Villa Rica, Georgia, He married Susan Idelia Richards in 1850. Susan was the daughter of Francis Marion Richards and Angeline (last name unknown). She was born in May 1831 in Georgia and died in 1910. They are buried at Macedonia Baptist Church Cemetery across the road from the church.

Thomas H. Willis and Susan Richards Willis

Their children were: (1) Monroe Ferrell Willis was born January 21, 1851, died September 18, 1880. He married Sarah J. Helton. (2) John Willis was born in 1853. He married Janie (unknown). (3) Marietta (Sis) Willis was born in 1854. She married Bill Jordan. (4) King Henry Willis was born May 16, 1857, and died February 16, 1881. He married Essobell (Isobelle) Jacobs. (5) Thomas Watson Willis was born July 14, 1859, and died June 6, 1938. He married Susan (Sudie) Della Pearson McAdams. (6) Joseph Denmon (Den) Willis was born June 14, 1861, and died October 5, 1934. He married Lou Ella Helton. (7) Julia V. Willis was born in 1865. She married John Newton (Newt) Hays. (8) Charles (Charley) Hampton Willis was born March 9, 1837, and died December 28, 1920. He married Rebeckah Lucinda Caroline Bates. (9) Amelia (Millie) Ann Willis married John S. Blair.

Information found on Thomas Henry Willis: He came to Carroll County in the late 1830s from North Carolina, settled in the Sand Hill community. He was a farmer and millwright. Tax information found in 1852: Thomas Willis found in Carroll County, District 6. Census in 1860 shows Thomas and Susan with five children in Fairplay community, Carroll County, Georgia. Thomas Henry Willis gave nine acres of land where the Macedonia Baptist Church was built in 1858. Note: On June 27, 1988, Macedonia Baptist Church name was changed to Midway Macedonia Baptist Church. *Submitted by: Jerry Crumbley, P.O. Box 1635, Carrollton, GA 30117*

Sources: Census, land, marriage records researched by Jerry Crumbley

1194. Thomas R. Willoughby

Around 1852, Thomas Willoughby and his brother John came to Villa Rica, Georgia, from Cornwall, England. They were miners, looking for gold and better opportunities. Deciding to stay, Thomas sent for his wife Christiana and their children, Thomas Jr., William James, John, Oliver, Louisa, Charlie, Liggas, and Emeline, who arrived in Villa Rica in the late 1850s. John, brother of Thomas, migrated to the mines at Pittsburgh, Pennsylvania, where he raised his family. Thomas settled near Pine Mountain, then Carroll, now Douglas County. In 1859 Christiana and Thomas had son Joseph, their only child born in America. An 1888 deed shows Thomas was a deacon of Pine Mountain Baptist Church.

When the War for Southern Independence began, Thomas, with four sons, volunteered. Thomas Sr. joined Company I, 56th Georgia Regiment where he became fourth corporal. On July 4, 1863, when the Army of Tennessee, including 56th Georgia, surrendered at Vicksburg, Thomas Sr. went home! Family stories say that he went looking for his other sons, Thomas Jr. and John. The 1864 Georgia census shows him, age fifty, at home. William James, also in Company I, 56th Georgia Infantry, was captured at Vicksburg, paroled there on July 8, 1863, rejoined and was captured again at Missionary Ridge. He took the United States oath of allegiance at Military Prison, Louisville, Kentucky, and was released north of Ohio River July 31, 1864. Thomas Jr. joined Company A, 10th Regiment, Georgia Volunteer Army, Muscogee County, and was captured near Knoxville, Tennessee, December 1863. He is listed as dying at Camp Nelson, Kentucky, on December 28, 1863. John (born 1844) joined the Villa Rica Golddiggers, Company I, 19th Regiment, was wounded and died at Chimborazo Hospital #4, Richmond, Virginia, August 27, 1862. Oliver joined Company G, 1st Georgia Militia, was sent home due to sickness where he died in 1862 at age of sixteen. Christiana died August 1868, Thomas Sr. died 1893. They are buried with son Oliver at Hillcrest Cemetery, Villa Rica.

Thomas Jr. had married Amanda Kennedy October 1861 in Carroll County. Before 1870, he took his wife, two small children, sister Liggas and moved to Texas. William married Margaret Hilderbrand in December of 1864. Many descendants of this family live in Carroll, Douglas, and nearby counties today. Louisa married William Nalley who helped establish New Hope Baptist Church now in Douglas County. Emeline married Ambrose Nalley, William's brother. They lived in Carroll County and raised a family of eleven children, where many Nalley descendants still live. Charlie and Joseph moved to Alabama and both raised large families there.

By 1870 censuses, Thomas Sr. had married Amanda Ragan. Thomas bought property near the Douglas/Carroll County line on Dallas Highway, and about 1874 he built a two-room house, later sold to his grandson William Robert after his death. William Robert's additions made it a beautiful farmhouse. In 1935 he gave the house and acreage to William Robert Jr. who had married Mary Spinks. It now belongs to their estates. Thomas' third great-grandson Wesley Willoughby and wife Melissa live in the original Willoughby house today. *Submitted by: Linda Willoughby Leatherman, 355 Horseshoe Bend Road, Carrollton, GA 30116*

Sources: *The Willoughbys*, by Cleo Twilley Willoughby, Deacons of Pine Mountain Baptist Church, *Roster of Confederate Soldiers of Georgia, 1861-1865*, by Lillian Henderson, census, deed, and marriage records of Carroll County.

1195. William Robert Willoughby Sr.

William Robert Willoughby Sr. was born 10/5/1872, the son of William James Willoughby and Margaret Catherine Hilderbrand. His early years were spent in Douglas County where his parents lived. His grandfather, Thomas Willoughby, along with his father, came from England to the Villa Rica area in the 1850s. They were miners by trade, working the gold mines around the Pine Mountain area. Later they also acquired land and became farmers. William Robert, called Bob, had four brothers and two sisters. Upon the death of his grandfather, he purchased the Willoughby home place on Dallas Highway north of Villa Rica, at the Douglas/Carroll County line.

On 12/27/1896, he married Mary Elizabeth McBrayer, daughter of Peter Paul and Mary Frances Cooper McBrayer. To them were born seven children. Paul Cooper and Kate Pearl, twins, were born on 8/30/1897. Paul died 6/5/1898. Kate married Frank Ragan and settled below Pine Mountain on what is now Ragan Road. Maino was born in 5/31/1899, married Glenn Dailey and lived in Cobb County. Audrey, born 8/13/1901, married Frank Steve Herrell and lived on what is now Herrell Road. Audrey taught school for many years at Villa Rica Grammar School. Iva married Thomas Stuart and lived mostly in Florida and Seattle, Washington. Frances, born 10/6/1907, married Dewren Chastain and lived in the old Wicks Tavern house in Old Town Villa Rica. William Robert Willoughby Jr., born 2/23/1916, married Mary Spinks and moved back to the Willoughby home place in the 1930s. There he raised a family of ten children and lived until his death in 1996, except for five years in Dawson County.

Bob was elected to the Georgia House of Representatives from Douglas County and served two years, 1919-1920. Not liking politics, he refused to run again and returned to farming. In October 1924, he moved "to the old Baptist Church - or the Bud Haynes place" (his words) in Old Town Villa Rica. He served in many capacities, salesman, school teacher, farmer, land owner and banker. When many banks failed due to the depression, Merchants and Planters Bank was able to repay all their customers. Bob, as liquidator for the Merchants and Planters Bank, served diligently in this endeavor.

Bob died 3/18/1936. Mary continued to live in their home place in Old Town, now the site of the Medical Center and Clinic, until ill health compelled her to live with her children. She died 8/30/1967 at age ninety-one and is buried, as is Bob, at Friendship Baptist Church in Paulding County. Their last living child, Frances Chastain, died January 2001 at age ninety-three. Frances' son Alfred and wife Jane donated the old Wicks Tavern to the Sons of Confederate Veterans, which they moved to Villa Rica and have rebuilt in the original style of the old tavern. *Submitted by: Chuck Willoughby, 2156 Dallas Highway, Villa Rica, GA 30180 and Written by: Linda Leatherman.*

Sources: *The Willoughbys* by Cleo Twilley Willoughby, *Douglas County, Georgia, from Indian Trail to Interstate 20* by Fannie Mae Davis, undelivered letter to Wm. E. Defoor written by W.R. Willoughby Sr., personal knowledge

1196. Wilson

All my ancestors have been in Carroll County since the middle or early 1800s. At least one line came in the early 1830s. The Mostellers came from Amsterdam, Holland, on the ship *Townsend* to York County, Pennsylvania, to North Carolina in 1770, and then to Carroll County, Georgia, in 1832 near Hickory Level. Peter Mosteller is buried at Concord Methodist Church. Peter's daughter, Margaret Mosteller, married Moses Wilson Jr. and came to Carroll County in the early 1830s.

Peter S. and Nancy Amy Wilson with sons William O. and Herculese Lee Wilson.

Moses had two brothers who came from North Carolina about the same time. One settled near Cross Plains and the other settled in Villa Rica.

Moses Wilson and his wife Margaret are buried in the Wilson Cemetery on land lot 63 in District 1297 just south of Old County Line Primitive Baptist Church near the Chattahoochee River. Moses and Margaret Wilson's son, Peter S. Wilson, owned land lot 63. Peter fought in the Civil War. Peter S. Wilson married Nancy C. Avery, daughter of William and Marinda Nash Avery. The Averys owned the land lot down the river from the Wilsons, with only the Joe Hutchinson farm between them. The Averys were buried on the sight of their home place. Peter and Nancy are buried at St. Paul Methodist Church on Jones Mill Road. Peter and Nancy had only two sons, William O. and Herculese (Herck) Lee Wilson. Land lot 63 was divided between the two sons.

My father, W. Buren Vines, and my mother, Verna Wilson Vines, bought half of the land that my grandfather Herck Wilson owned. They lived there the rest of their lives. Herck Wilson married Pearl Hilley, daughter of Robert Hilley and Almeda Richards Hilley on May 19, 1907. Herck and Pearl are buried at Mt. Zion Baptist Church just on the Carroll County line in Douglas County on Highway 5. Herck and Pearl had three daughters: Verna, Sybil, and Ruth.

Verna married W. Buren Vines in October 1927. They had one son and three daughters. My mother Verna graduated from Whitesburg High School in 1927. I graduated from the same school in 1949. My daddy was the son of James (Jim) Vines and Katie Jones Vines. They had six boys and three girls. Katie's family lived around Abilene. Jim and Kate are buried in Whitesburg Cemetery.

All my grandparents were farmers. Herck did work in Banning Mill before he married. I was born in the house my mother was living in when she died on October 11, 1999, at the age of ninety-one. My father died November 28, 1970. They are buried at Mt. Zion Baptist Church on Highway 5, just across the Carroll County line in Douglas County.

I was born September 2, 1931. I live in the house that my grandfather Herck Wilson built about 1915. I bought it from my grandmother after Herck died in 1949. *Submitted by: Lawrence Vines, 485 Wilson Road, Whitesburg, GA 30185*

1197. The Descendants of Lizzie Bell Wilson

The Wilson family is now the Bailey, Lovett, William, Wilson family. This family group all started when Govern Wilson (playfully called Governor) and wife, Lizzie Bell, moved to Carroll County. They had four daughters; Louize, Mary, Eleanor, and Ollie. These ladies grew up and started their own families. Louize married John Lovett and had four girls. Mary had five boys and one girl. Eleanor married Willis Bailey and had five boys and two girls. In Ollie's first marriage to Henry Evans, she had two boys. In her second marriage (after her first husband died) to Robert William, she had three boys and two girls. Every year, the Baileys, the Lovetts, the Williams, the Wilsons have a reunion to commemorate the impact Lizzie Bell Wilson had on Carroll County.

Lizzie Bell Ward was born on December 3, 1878, in Milltown, Alabama. After growing up and getting married, she moved to Georgia. It was not long after moving to Carroll County that her lifelong career began. This is how she described the beginning of being a midwife.

> "I was at the home of a white family, and I couldn't leave because of rain, and the doctor couldn't get to the house because of the flooded creek. The mother asked me if I could help and I replied 'I'll do the best I can'."

The rest is history. It was a routine birth. When Dr. B.C. Powell could get to the home to examine the mother and child, he responded that he could not have done a better job himself. After a whole lifetime in the Baptist Church — New Hope in Milltown, 48th Baptist in Temple, and lastly Mt. Prospect in Villa Rica, she finally felt she had found her calling. She became a midwife.

Midwife Bell Wilson rendered her services whether the people were able to pay immediately or even not at all. There were times it was snowing so bad people had to carry her to and from the car. She would go where the doctors could not or would not go. Her faith in the Lord helped her through the difficult deliveries she had sometimes, and always guided her as each blessing was born. She always said, "I just talked to the Lord and He helped me."

In the fall of 1963, at age eighty-five, Bell Wilson retired from being a midwife. She was presented a retirement award and a letter of commendation from the Department of Public Health. It is estimated that Bell Wilson delivered nearly two thousand babies. On November 6, 1964, almost a year after retiring from midwifery, Bell Wilson retired from this life. On the day of her passing there were twenty-one grandchildren, seventy-one great-grandchildren, and eight great-great-grandchildren.

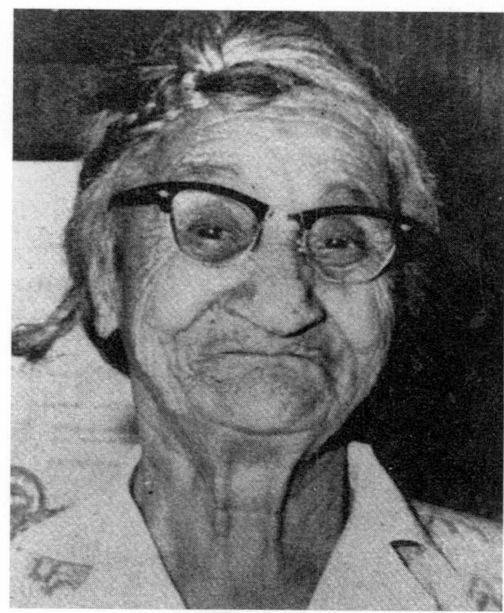

Lizzie Bell Wilson

Today the descendants of Bell Wilson total nearly three hundred. The majority still stay in Carroll County. And many of the people who live in Carroll County are descendants of people she delivered. Thank you, Lizzie Bell Wilson. *Submitted by: Sallie Bell Hudson, 340 S. Wilson, Villa Rica, GA 30180 and Written by: Charles Hudson, 945 S. Lassetter Circle, Villa Rica, GA 30180*

1198. James Jefferson Wilson Family

James Jefferson Wilson was born October 30, 1876, the son of Edward M. and Amanda M. Wilson. His wife, Edna Estelle Jackson Wilson, was born September 27, 1878, the daughter of Jimmie and Amanda Gillespie Jackson.

Edna Estelle Jackson Wilson around 1950

In 1917 they purchased a home at 305 Tarpley Street in Bowdon and farmed the surrounding land. The home place still remains in the family, belonging to their granddaughter, Glenda Wilson Richardson.

Jim, as he was called, and Edna had six children: Hoyt Wilson, Eunice Wilson Kaylor Thompson, Joel "Dick" Wilson, Leta Gene Wilson Strickland, Lloyd "Pete" Wilson, and Irene Wilson Turner.

Jim died in 1937 and Edna died in 1954. They are buried at the First United Methodist Church Cemetery in Bowdon. *Submitted by: granddaughter, Paula Wilson Steed, 41 Pine Court, Carrollton, GA 30117*

1199. Lloyd Maxwell "Pete" Wilson Family

Lloyd Maxwell "Pete" Wilson was born on Tarpley Street in Bowdon, Georgia, on November 23, 1914, the son of James Jefferson Wilson and Edna Estelle Jackson Wilson. His wife, Pauline Wright Wilson, was born in Carroll County on September 12, 1914, the daughter of Asa Asbury Wright, and Parrie Warren Wright.

Pete and Pauline Wilson on their 50th wedding anniversary in 1985.

Both Pete and Pauline went through the Bowdon schools and were married on August 24, 1935. During the very early years of their marriage, Pete farmed, but later he moved his family to Atlanta and Marietta where he was a Greyhound bus driver.

After the death of Pete's mother in 1954, he moved his family back to his home place at 305 Tarpley Street in Bowdon where he remained the rest of his life, working as a long haul truck driver.

Pete and Pauline had three children: James Asbury Wilson, Glenda Wilson Richardson and Paula Wilson Steed. They were loving parents and devoted grandparents to their eight grandchildren: Billy McGuire, Michael Wilson, Stephen Wilson, Elizabeth Ann Wilson Baker, Mark Wilson, Angela McGuire Cambas, Lorrie Steed Pate and Derick Steed.

Only two weeks after celebrating their fiftieth wedding anniversary, Pauline unexpectedly died on September 7, 1985. Pete lived three more years, dying on September 24, 1988, following a brief illness. Both Pete and Pauline are buried at Bowdon First United Methodist Church Cemetery in Bowdon, Georgia. *Submitted by: Granddaughter, Lorrie Steed Pate, 203 Valleyview Drive, Ozark, AL 36360 and Written by: Paula Wilson Steed*

1200. Mrs. Mary T. Wilson

On May 29, 1969, Mrs. Mary T. Wilson was honored with a tea at Bowdon Primary School celebrating her retirement after twenty years of teaching.

Mrs. Mary Wilson and parents at retirement reception, 1969

Mothers of her current classmates served as hostesses. They were Mrs. Bobby Word, Mrs. Frank Lane, Mrs. Amon Daniel, Mrs. Travis Loftin, Mrs. Wallace Arrington and others.

Her first graders presented her with a pin with her initials.

The following poem was written by Miss Peggy Robinson in honor of Mrs. Wilson:

The Retiring Teacher

You can take her out of the classroom
You can send her home to stay.
But you really can't retire her,
She'll still be there each day.
In her mind she'll see the children
Who've all come under her care
And she can tell you exactly
How well they'll be doing next year.
Even though she's there at home,
Somehow she'll hear each day,
Every bell that rings to signal
Time for lunch and work and play.
She's taught too long to change now
Her life is conditioned that way.
You really can't retire her
She'll still be there each day.

Submitted by: Penny Akins, 4590 State Line Rd., Bowdon, GA 30108

1201. Edward Alton and Dora Ellen Windom

Edward Alton Windom was born in Carroll County on March 18, 1885. His parents were William Jefferson "Bill" Windom and Mary Jane Elizabeth "Bettie" Bearden. Bill was born in Coweta County, Georgia. Bettie was born in Fayette County, Georgia. After Bill and Bettie married, they moved to Carroll County.

Dora Ellen Cantrell was born December 12, 1886, at Burwell, Georgia. Her parents were Ira "Frank" Cantrell and Emmaline "Emma" Crumbley. Frank was born in Cleburne County, Alabama, and Emma was born in Henry County, Georgia. Her parents moved to the Burwell community and that is where she and Frank met.

Alton and Dora Windom

Alton met Dora at a Bethel Camp Meeting and decided right then this was the girl for him. They were married March 1, 1908, at her parents' home. Alton was a farmer. After his and Dora's first two children were born, they sold their farm on what is now Craven Road and purchased a farm one mile from Burwell on the Carrollton-Burwell Road. Here they raised their four children — Roy, Christine, Emily, and Betty. Emily and Betty were born there. After purchasing the farm, Alton began to clear the forest of trees and stumps and prepared the land for planting cotton and corn. These were his main crops. They built a large barn, chicken houses, and other necessary outbuildings. They always had a big garden and raised almost all their food. Summer was for canning, fall for harvesting, winter for killing and preserving their meats, and spring was for all the hard work involved in planting their fields and garden. Dora and the children canned shelves of food. She dried fruits to make those delicious fried pies. She also used her feed, flour and sugar sacks to make dresses, Alton's shirts, and most of their undergarments. She was an excellent quilter and recycled clothing for quilt pieces along with her sacks. They both were Christian people who loved their family. They went through the depression with food to eat and were able to keep their farm. Later they were able to buy "ready made" clothing and purchase fabric for dresses.

Roy married Doris Turner and had two sons, Rev. Frank Windom and Michael Windom. Frank lives in Atlanta and has one daughter, Hannah. Mike lives in Tampa, Florida, with his wife Deb.

Christine married Harold Upchurch, also reared at Burwell. They lived in Chattanooga where Harold had a shoe shop. After Harold died, Christine moved to Carrollton. They had no children.

Emily married Curtis Daniel and has one son, Dr. Douglas Daniel. Douglas and wife Marsha have two sons, Will and Blain.

Betty married Jesse Hendrix and they have four daughters — Glenda Sue, Linda, Barbara, and Deborah. They have six grandchildren: Steve and Kelly are Linda's sons; Matthew and Michele are Barbara's children; Richie and Christina are Deborah and husband Joe's children. They also have three great-grandchildren, Nicholas, Michael and Dedra.

Alton and Dora are buried in their beloved Eureka Church Cemetery. *Submitted by: their daughter Christine Windom Upchurch, 544 North White Street, Carrollton, GA 30117.*
Sources: Family history and personal knowledge.

1202. The Wingo Family

In the early 1920s, a young man with horse and buggy drove his preacher, Mr. Oliver Moore, from Heard County to the old Blackgum Church (now Bethany Christian Church) for a revival meeting. The young man, Paul Wingo, was about twenty-two years old.

The young lady playing the old pump organ at Blackgum was Nellie Richardson, daughter of Thomas Peek and Minnie Butler Richardson, residents of the community. Nellie and Paul met, enjoyed each other's company, and were married on December 3, 1922. After their wedding, they lived in the Waresville-Glenn community of Heard County for about a year before coming back to Carroll County, settling in the Wayside-Pleasant Hill community.

In 1926, their son Charles Reese (named for Dr. D.S. Reese, the family physician) was born. Nine years later, in 1935, Ruth came along; then, in 1937, Edna was born.

In the meantime, Paul and Nellie bought the Cheney home place with seventy-five acres of land. This is now the home of the Jim Lasseter family on Pleasant Hill Road near the intersection of Maple Hill.

Farming was the meager livelihood of the Wingos until Paul took a job with Alton Lane's store (now occupied by Burson Seed and Feed). The family sold the farm and moved into Carrollton in the summer of 1947. Charles had already married (in 1944), Ruth began eighth grade at Carrollton High School, and Edna enrolled at College Street School in fifth grade.

Paul's work continued with now Lane Truck and Tractor (the building now occupied as part of Tanner Medical Center on Dixie Street); Nellie worked at various stores around the square. She will be remembered for her work at McConnell's, Empire, the Leader, and mostly at Belk-Rhodes.

Charles married Louise Land on May 20, 1944. Louise was a student at West Georgia College and also a full-time teacher at Sand Hill School. Later, Charles entered college to become a minister, and the couple moved from Carroll County. They currently live in Naples,

Wingo Family c. 1940 Back — Charles, Nellie, Paul. Front — Edna, Ruth

Florida, after ministries in several states. They have four children and seven grandchildren in Florida and Tennessee.

Ruth is married to Lester McLain and still lives in Carroll County following retirement from a successful career in management with Kraft Foods. Her two daughters, Dr. Ronee Griffith and Sheryl Crawford, along with their families, are successful business persons and residents of Carroll County.

Edna married Charles Herndon (also a minister). After being away from Carroll for twenty-five years, they settled in the Sand Hill community in 1979. Edna, recently retired from twenty-eight years in education (mostly in Carroll as teacher and principal). After Charles' death in 1995, Edna still lives at Sand Hill. The Herndons' two children, Paula Rabun and Jeff Herndon, along with their families, are all Carroll County residents.

Paul and Nellie were strong leaders at Bethany Christian Church. Nellie played the piano for about seventy years and taught Sunday School. Paul was an elder, Bible School superintendent, Sunday School teacher, and mentor for those who followed. Paul died on April 19, 1956, in an accident while loading a tractor for delivery. Nellie died on February 11, 1991.

From Paul and Nellie have come forty-two descendants (including children, in-laws, grandchildren and in-laws, great grandchildren and in-laws, and four great, great grandchildren). Paul and Nellie Wingo made many contributions to the area; but they also received many benefits from being Carroll Countians. *Submitted by: Edna Herndon, 1878 Four Notch Rd., Carrollton, GA 30116*

1203. Wood Family

James P. Wood was born 7 September 1824 near Greenville, Spartanburg County, South Carolina. He married Rebecca P. Jones in 1845. The 1850 and 1860 census records list them as residents of Hall County, Georgia. The 1870 census shows them living in Haralson County.

James P. Wood enlisted in Company H, 35th Georgia Infantry, County Line Invincibles, at Hog Mountain, Georgia, on 24 September 1861. He fought in battles at Seven Pines, Mechanicsville, and Cold Harbor. He was captured at Gettysburg on 1 July 1863 and sent to prison at Ft. Delaware. He was paroled in February 1865 and was part of a prisoner exchange at James River, Virginia, on 10 March 1865.

James was a farmer after the war and for a while was one-half owner of a grist mill. According to Wood family legend, he was an expert whiskey maker and made some for the government.

James and Rebecca had eight children. One of the children was my grandpa, Willis B. Wood, born 13 June 1859. He married Mattie E. Deering on 10 March 1889. Mattie died 14 September 1939 and Willis died 14 December 1945. Both are buried in the Kansas Baptist Church Cemetery.

One of the six children of Willis and Mattie was my daddy, John William Wood Sr., born 24 January 1895. Mother was Effie Estelle Maxwell born 5 April 1898. They were married 5 August 1914. They had eleven children including me. It's a little unusual the way it worked out. I had five brothers and five sisters, and five were older and five younger.

John Wood was a farmer and worked for a time at Arnco Mill. When I was born, we lived in the area of what is now Oak Grove Road. The family later moved to what is now Hays Mill Road. Mother died 8 April 1974 and Daddy died 2 July 1979. Both are buried in Carroll Memory Gardens.

I am Myrtle Margaret Wood Cook, born 23 October 1929. I married Harold Aubrey Cook on 2 June 1951. We had four children, Alfred Wayne, Patricia Diane, Millard Glenn, and Clifford Henry "C.H." Cook. Wayne and Millard reside in Carroll County and Patricia lives in West Virginia. C.H. died on 23 January 1990 and is buried in the Ephesus Christian Church Cemetery.

The Wood Family about 1903

The family photograph was taken at Willis B. and Mattie Wood's house about 1903. Pictured left to right are Ernest Wood, Tom Wood, Willis B. Wood holding Gus Wood, Eva Wood Moore, Mattie Deering Wood, John W. Wood Sr. *Submitted by: Myrtle Cook, 73 Davis Road, Carrollton, GA 30116*

1204. John William Wood Family

John William Wood Sr. (1895-1979) was the son of Willis Benson Wood (1859-1945) and Mary Elizabeth "Mattie" Deering (1864-1939). Willis Benson was the son of James P. Wood (1823-1911) and Rebecca Jones (1823-1908), who arrived in the Tallapoosa area of Haralson County soon after their marriage in 1845. John William married Effie Estelle Maxwell (1898-1974) in 1914 in Carroll County. They lived in the southern part of Carroll County, near Roopville. Their children are:

(I) Dura Virginia, who married Roy Alton North (1900-1966) in 1933 in Carroll County, and had (1) Carl William (1934-1988), who married Montene Cowart in 1951, Mary Anise Burnes in 1982, and Betty Jean Scott in 1962; (2) Bettie Marie, who married Kenneth Lucian Newman in 1954; (3) Burnette, who married Howard Pat Tarpley in 1955, Tony Michael Pitts, and Carlton Grady Turner; (4) Herman Barto, who married Laura Ann Gosden in 1963; (5) Roger Alton, who married Barbara Ann Marks in 1960 and Verna Rue Hutchison Cline in 1976; (6) Donald Earl who married Joyce Marie Hines in 1964, (7) Ray Dillard married Sonja Jeane Flemming in 1963 and, again, in 1972, Gloria Jenkins Lane in 1978, and Lynda Spurlin in 1996; (8) Hershel Delmer (1946-1985), who married Retha Sue Cook in 1967; (9) Nellie Elaine, who married Ray Henson and David White; and (10) Patsy Ann, who married Anthony Ivan Hall in 1974. Dura later married Travis Spruill.

(II) Elbert Newton, who married Mary Nett Lyle in 1946, and had Mary Marie, who married Richard Charles Sparks in 1966; David Lyle who married Patricia Ann Swafford in 1970; and Michael Alan (1953-1996) who married Sheryl Diane Barger in 1974.

(III) Oscar Lee, who married Jean Telva Cook in 1945, and had Jerry, who married Gail Lambert and Laura Anderson Cutten; Larry Lester (1948-1969) who married Patricia Akin in 1969. Larry died from hostile fire in Binh Duong, South Vietnam; and Barry O., (1949-1968).

(IV) Nora Louise.

(V) Clara Pearl, who married Cyril Sticher in 1950, and had Peggy Ann, who married Freddy Woodard, Jonny Williamson, and Maron Tomell Rogers in 1987; Randy Allen, who married Rebecca Jean Baity in 1974; Randall Doyle, who married Pamela Ann Lewis in 1988; Annette, who married Brian Swain and Steve Myron Bates in 1983; and Robbie Kay, who married James Harvey Smith in 1976.

(VI) Myrtle Margaret, who married Harold Aubrey Cook in 1951, and had Alfred Wayne who married Janice Marie Watson in 1972; Patricia Dianne; and Millard Glenn.

(VII) John William Jr., who married Helen Christine Weathington in 1959, and had Lisa Christine, who married Jeffery T. Jackson (1967-1998) in 1979; Dale Nan, who married Dennis Littleton, Joel Chambers, and Tony McElwaney; Gale Nan, who married John Asa Haney in 1983; and John William III, who married Jane A. Kavanagh in 1989.

(VIII) Reece Albert (1934-1992), who married Joan McCarty in 1961, and had Mark Albert, who married Cynthia Fulton in 1986; and Melissa Joan, who married William Charles Willoughby in 1987.

(IX) Jesse who married Mary Ann Hammond in 1955, and had Tony James, who married Mary Ann Hammond in 1976; Delores Diane who married Anthony Alan Bell in 1988; Rickey Lee who married Faye Elizabeth Ann France in 1981 and Jenita Lynn Carroll in 1986; and Timothy Mark, who married Cynthia Denise Ivie in 1985.

(X) Nellie Jean, who married Terry Olin Smith in 1959, and had Hal Gregory, who married Tonya Gunn.

(XI) Geneva, who married Harry Hamil Bradley in 1963, and had Tammy Denise (1966-1966); Harry Neil, who married Vickie McGuire in 1985, Julie Denney in 1989, and Tayna Todd.

Carl and Montene had Vickie Jane, who married Mitchell Clyde Robinson in 1968, and had Matthew Darrell, Benjamin Andrew, and Carl Mitchell; Ricky Carl, who married Deborah Mae Brock in 1973, and had Shara Sunshine, Richard Eugene (1974-1974), and Joshua Blake; Wendell Euell, who married Judy Dawn Sutton in 1976 and Mary Anise Burnes in 1982. Wendell and Mary Anise had John McKenzie; Deborah Francene, who married Timothy Ray Jones in 1977, and had Misty Amber and Eric Ray. Carl and Betty had Becarla Jean, who married Keith Treadwell in 1980, and had Thomas Joshua, Brian Keith, and Glynn Bailey.

Bettie and Kenneth had James Alton, who married Kimberly Lynn Glass in 1987; Marie Annette who married Shell Elmer Prossner in 1982; and Mary Lynn.

Burnette and Howard had Bobby Harold; David Howard, who married Denise Drew in 1982, and had Patrick Shane, Kayla, and Shannon; Sonja Jane who married Phillip Clinton Voyles in 1979, and had Lora. Sonja Jane and Tony Michael had Andrew Jesse.

Herman and Laura had Amanda Ann, who married Craig Allen Crews in 1987, and had Tyler; and Randy Joel, who married Sherry Wynette Muse in 1988, and had Christopher and Jonathan.

The Willis B. Wood Family, about 1903.

Roger married and Barbara had Michelle, who had Angela, Whitney, and Luke; Greg; and Kevin Scott.

Donald and Joyce had Tammy Marie, who married Donnie Newt Muse in 1985, and had Sadie Marie, Mollie Elizabeth, Allie Beth, and James Conner; Connie Elaine, who married Rodger Miles, Jr. in 1990, and had Michael Coby; and Christy Dianne, who married Roy Brock in 1998, and had Carley Elizabeth.

Ray Dillard and Sonja had Paul, who married Tammy Wright in 1987, and had John Jeremiah and Elijah; Jody who married Sharron Austin in 1987, and had Nicholas. Jody married Molly Folk in 1995 and had Madison Leigh. Ray and Gloria had Kelly Lynn who married Brian Freeman in 1995, and had Brian Hunter and Mallory Alyssa.

Hershel and Retha had Roy Alton, who married Lisa McGuire in 1987, and had Pamela Diane, who married Robert Wade Norton in 1987, and had Jeffery Ross. Pamela Diane married Carmon Keith Sheppard in 1994, and had Camron Brady.

Patsy and Anthony had Christopher Matthew and Jeremiah McIvan.

Mary and Richard had Sean Allen and Cheryl Lynn.

David and Patricia had Brenda Lorraine, who married Matthew House in 1991.

Jerry and Gail had Jerry Benjamin, who married Amy Duke in 1971, and had a child; and Connie Loraine, who married Ron S. Jordan in 1996, and had Libby Ann.

Clara and Cyril had Peggy Ann, who married Freddy Woodard, and had Lee Ann; and Tracy, who married Kidder in 1970, and had Amber. Peggy and Jonny had Jennifer. Peggy and Maron Tomell Rogers had Megan and Monica.

Randall and Pamela had Chris and Lori.

Annette and Brian had Daniel. Annette and Steve had Jeremiah and Tyler.

Robbie and James had Patty

Alfred and Janice had Melanie Gail, Emily Kathleen, and Rachel Elizabeth.

Lisa and Jeffery had Jennifer Lynn and Laura Leigh.

Dale and Dennis had Megan. Dale and Joel had Lucy.

Gale and John had Elizabeth Ann and Matthew Tyler.

John, III and Jane had John William, IV and Hunter Montana.

Mark and Cynthia had Taylor Albert and Steven Allan.

Melissa and William had William Reece and Amy Elizabeth.

Tony and Mary had Crystal Marie.

Delores and Anthony had Troy Jesse and Zachery Buchanan.

Rickey and Faye had Casey Lee. Rickey and Jenita had Andrew James and Ashley Lynn.

Hal and Tonya had Dana.

Harry and Vickie had Zachery. Harry and Julie had Grady Waid. Harry and Tayna had Thadeau Dylan.

This photograph shows the Willis B. Wood family about 1903. Seated, left to right, are Willis B. Wood, Augustus Edward Wood (on Willis' lap), Martha Elizabeth Deering. Standing are Ernest L., James Thomas, Eva Pearl, and John William Wood. *Submitted by: David Lyle Wood, padawood@bellsouth.net, and Written by: Cecilia Wood Church, 128 Brock Street, Carrollton, GA 30117 cechurch@charter.net Research by: Kenneth L. Newman, 906 Second Street, NE, Jacksonville, AL 36265-2602*

1205. Spencer Paul Wood Jr. Family

The life of Spencer Paul Wood Jr. began on September 5, 1913, in Heard County, Georgia, as the son of Spencer Paul and Idella Dunson Wood. Although Spencer was a native of Heard County, he spent the majority of his life in Carroll County, Georgia.

On April 17, 1935, Spencer was united in marriage with Emma L. Henderson. Emma was born September 5, 1921, and departed life on September 20, 1945. Marriage came again to Spencer; on July 27, 1946, he was wed to Elnorah W. Dukes. Elnorah was born May 21, 1915, and passed away August 4, 1997.

Spencer Paul Wood Jr. 1993 Submitted by: Alma W. Satterwhite

The Woods had a total of seventeen children: Eljean, Grover, Charlie Willis (CW), Hazel, Margie, Jessie, Alton, Charles Felton, Alma, Johnny B., Annie Lizzie, Martha, Spencell, Wynell, Nolen, Mary Lois, and Clovell.

During the early 1950s Spencer, along with his wife Elnorah, founded the first African-American nursery and landscaping business in Carroll County, Many family members labored to make Wood's Nursery a successful business and it flourished for many years.

Spencer was an ordained Baptist deacon, Sunday school teacher, member of the Layman Brotherhood, singer in the Wood's Gospel Singers (which consisted of his brothers and sisters), guitar and harmonica player, blacksmith, and farmer. Also, he managed the Mountain Wildcats Baseball Team from the Clem area (a local Negro League team).

On February 3, 1995, at the age of eighty-one he died from injuries sustained in a house fire. He loved life, he loved his family, but most of all he loved God.

Spencer and Elnorah Wood. Submitted by: Wynell W. Pugh

There are descendants of Spencer Paul Wood Jr., living in Carroll County, various other counties in Georgia, as well as other states. *Submitted by: Alma Wood Satterwhite, 614 Aycock Street, Carrollton, GA 30117.*

1206. Charles Mabry Word

Charles Mabry Word was born 15 June 1858 in Carroll County, Georgia. He died 30 April 1934 in Carroll County. Both he and his wife, the former Nida Fowler, are buried at Pleasant Grove Baptist Church.

Charles was one of five children of Thomas Anderson Word and Susan Catherine Mabry, the daughter of Branch Mabry and Catherine Langford. Thomas died in Chattanooga, Tennessee, 27 November 1862 while serving in the Confederate Army. Susan died 3 September 1890, and is said to have been buried on part of the old Mabry land between Bowdon and Tyus, Georgia.

Susan Catherine did not remarry. She was left to raise five children, John Branch, Amelia Catherine, James Madison, Charles Mabry and Elizabeth Judith. Their ages ranged from eleven to one year. She farmed the land that Thomas had purchased and left to his "beloved wife Susan" in the 11th district of Carroll county. The land adjoined the land of John B. Word, father of Thomas Anderson Word.

We know nothing of the early life of Charles, but after his marriage to Nida, said to have been one-quarter Creek Indian, he farmed the land left to him by his mother and also "doctored cows." He traveled the southwestern part of the county in his buggy, answering calls to doctor a sick cow or to attend the birthing of a calf. His grandson, Reuben, remembers him getting his hard case satchel, hitching up "Kate" to the buggy and taking off. His grandson also remembers walking with him to Bowdon.

The home of Charles was on Old Word Road. It was a two story structure, unpainted, sitting on a hillside. The barnyard was across the road. Nine children were raised on that farm, Alver, Charles, Emma Bell, Mittie, Essie, Ura, James Brysom, Felton and Thelma.

James Brysom Word was born 8 May 1900, he died 10 Oct 1972. After his marriage to Alma Hightower he moved from the farm to Carrollton. He was a mechanic, and in his latter years managed the International Harvester dealership. His children were Reuben Mabry, Garvie

Willis, Ruthie Mae and James Brysom Jr. After the death of Alma in 1959 he married Mary Bartlett.

Reuben Mabry Word was born 31 May 1922 in Carroll County, Georgia. He served in World War II as a pilot. He completed his legal education and returned to the Air Force for a tour of duty during the Korean War. After returning to Carrollton, he accepted the position as pilot and attorney for Southwire in Carrollton. In 1962 he opened his office in downtown Carrollton for the practice of general law. Reuben married Mary Florence Arthur in 1944. They have three children, David Arthur, Gerald Patrick and Susan Gayle Word Kypreos. Grandchildren Patrick, Stephen and Abigail Word and Nicholas Kypreos.

Charles Mabry Word and Nida Fowler Word

The Word family emigrated to the colonies about 1652. Among the descendants of the original John Word can be found lawyers, doctors and writers including William Faulkner and Lewis Grizzard. *Submitted by: Mary Florence Word, 805 Rome Street, Carrollton, GA 30117*

1207. James Brysom Word Jr.

World War II gave the J.B. Word family of Carrollton, Georgia, an opportunity to show their love for their country. Reuben, the oldest of three boys enlisted in the Army Air Corps. The next oldest, Garvie, went into the U.S. Army and saw service in Europe in the tank corps.

J.B. Jr., the youngest of the four children was too young to join the service. He found a way to do his part by the sale of U.S. War Bonds and Savings Stamps. As a carrier for the Atlanta Journal, he led all the carriers in sales of bonds and stamps.

J.B. Jr. was recognized at a Fourth of July celebration on the square in Carrollton in 1943. The program featured others for their patriotism. The ceremony was broadcast on radio station WSB out of Atlanta. *Submitted by: James Brysom Word Jr., Corpus Christi, TX.*

1208. James Madison Word

These are some things I remember about my grandfather James Madison Word.

We lived in one of his houses around 1924 or 1925 near his home place. I know he was a Christian and was a member of Pleasant Grove Baptist Church near Tyus, Georgia. I remember hearing him sing "I Love to Tell the Story" as he was walking past our house on the little dirt road.

He loved his grandchildren and often gave us advice. He said "Don't ever say 'I don't care.'"

My sister Norma and I would sit on the porch steps and he would peel fruit and give to us.

James Madison Word was born May 28, 1855, and died July 30, 1927. The day he died he was quoting Scripture from the Bible. *Submitted by: Eubie Word Turner, age 82; daughter of Rufus and Viola Word.*

James Madison Word and Hannah Cathrine Yates

James Madison Word, Cynthia Ann Caledonia, James Horrie and Leathia

1209. Family of James Madison (Jim Matt) Word

James Madison Word was born May 28, 1855. He was the son of Thomas A. and Susan Word. Jim Matt was a farmer, as was his father, and spent his life in the communities of Tyus, Veal and New Mexico. On November 11, 1877, he was married to Hannah Catherine Yates. Hannah was born February 21, 1851. She was the daughter of Joel Pinckney Yates and Martha Jane Stewart Yates. Jim Matt and Hannah had five children: Martha Eugenia Word Eason, May 7, 1879; Susan Evelyn Word Barr, April 7, 1881; Rufus Anderson Word, December 14, 1882; Manuel Brown Word, July 26, 1884; and Charles Bunyan Word, October 24, 1888. Their life centered around the family, farming, and their church, Pleasant Grove Missionary Baptist Church, located in the New Mexico community. Their mode of transportation was a horse drawn wagon. There were, of course, fancy buggies in that time. Their life took a dramatic turn on September 10, 1900, as Hannah passed away. Jim Matt had five children to raise with the youngest being twelve. Jim Matt and Donnie Simpkins were married about a year later and that union produced five children: Letha Word Terrell, Ina Word, Eldred Word, Horrie Word, and Euwell Pete Word.

Manuel Brown and Fannie Mae Johnson Word

Jim Matt passed away on July 30, 1927. Donnie passed away June 23, 1950. Jim Matt's first born son passed away March 8, 1986, after his 103rd birthday, and that was Rufus Anderson Word. (See photo of James Madison, Jim Matt, in a short story by E. Word). The second son of James Madison and Hannah was Manuel Brown Word. He was called Man as an adult. He was married to Fannie Mae Johnson in 1907. Fannie was born in December 1892. Her parents died of tuberculosis when she was a young child. She was raised by an Uncle Will and Aunt Savannah Ayers who had no children of their own. The union of Man and Fannie produced four children: Homer Alvin, 1908; Dillard Lee, 1912; William Ellis, 1916; and Catherine Pearl, 1926. Like his father, Man was also a farmer in the same communities that he had been reared in. The main crops were cotton and corn. A common sight was a horse or mule drawn wagon loaded with cotton headed to the cotton gin. The children of Man and Fannie were not true farmers as were their ancestors. In their early adult years they were, but other means became available. Such as the textile industry, logging and eventually the chicken industry became a large business in the area and still is. Most people who farmed just eked out a living. A good sense of humor was a necessity and Man Word possessed just that. He loved picking and joking with his kids. Even he was amazed at the answers he got when he asked one of his favorite questions. "When was the last time your Mama and Daddy had a fight?" Man passed away in 1946 and Fannie

James Madison Word Family group. Early 1900s.

passed away in 1962. Man's brother Bunyan "Bun" had a grandson named Lewis Grizzard, a famous humorist, that made us all laugh. Homer Alvin married Rusha Gladys Rampy May 18, 1929, sitting in his 1929 Model A by Preacher Thornton. Their witnesses were his brother Dillard and Rusha's sister Erma Rampy. Their union produced four children: Bobby Dwight Word, Sarah Ellen Word Anderson, Betty Jean Word Parmer, and Judy Carol Word Cantrell. Alvin and Rusha were married more than fifty years. Alvin passed away in 1981 and Rusha passed away in 1987.

Dillard Lee and Erma Rampy were married in Alvin's Model A, sitting in the car by the same Preacher Thornton, in December 1932. They had two children: Martha Nell Word Brown, and Patsy Ann Word Stephens. Dillard passed away in 1983 and Erma passed away in 1978. William Ellis married Gladys Christine Holloway in a more traditional way at Sardis by Preacher Kent in December 1935 and their union produced one son: Dwain Ellis. Ellis passed away in 1973. Catherine Pearl married Allewis Gosdin in January 1946 and their union produced three children: Brenda Sue Gosdin Nelson, Barbara Ann Gosdin Wiggins, and Donnie Lee Gosdin. Allewis Gosdin passed away in 1996 and their daughter Barbara passed away in 2000.

The family church is still Pleasant Grove Missionary Baptist Church for the majority of this family of James Madison, Hannah and Donnie Word. You will find many grave markers with the names of Word, Yates, Simpkins, Stewart, Johnson, Eason, Lowry, Wright, and Rampy.

Submitted by: Grandchildren of Manuel Brown and Fannie Mae Johnson Word.

1210. John Bryson Word

John Bryson Word was born 1 January 1796 in Surry County, North Carolina. He died 6 February 1882 in Carroll County, Georgia. He married Amelia Sparks, the daughter of Elijah Sparks and Judith Humphries. She was born 15 June 1803 and died 26 July 1868. They were married 22 July 1819 in Franklin County, Georgia. They are buried in marked graves on the original Word home place in Carroll County. In 1871 John Bryson Word married Mrs. Ann Handley. They had no children. Her place of burial is unknown.

The Word Family

John Bryson Word was the son of William Word and Elizabeth Bryson. His grandfather, Charles Word, died during the Revolutionary War at the battle of Kings Mountain, North Carolina. His grandmother, the former Elizabeth Adams, married second Richard Hooper and moved with him to Franklin County, Georgia. William, one of the eight children of Charles and Elizabeth Adams Word also settled in Franklin County. In 1820 William and his wife moved to Hamilton, Monroe County, Mississippi, where his home served as a temporary courthouse until a permanent one could be built. William died in Monroe County in 1826. Tax lists in Monroe County, Mississippi, indicate that John Bryson Word lived there in 1821, 1822 and 1823.

John Bryson Word was ordained a deacon at the Eastenaller Baptist Church in Franklin County, Georgia, in 1830. He served as justice of peace in Franklin County from 1833 to February 1836. In January 1836 he purchased land lot number 194 in the eleventh district of Carroll County. From his diary we learn that he "landed in Carroll County 18 February 1836." Just ten days after his arrival he and his wife were received into the Tallapoosa Primitive Baptist Church. He was clerk of the church for four years. In 1840 he joined Eden Baptist Church. He served as a justice of the Carroll County Inferior Court, first appointed in 1837.

John Bryson Word built a two story frame house overlooking the Little Tallapoosa River. According to a story told by Dr. J.T. Tisinger, whose family lived close by, Indian assassins of Chief William McIntosh (1825) camped near the future site of the home after they fled from the McIntosh Plantation. The Word house has been renovated and is still occupied. John Bryson Word farmed about a hundred improved acres of the over four hundred that he owned. He grew cotton, corn and wheat plus sheep, cows, and swine.

John B. Word had eleven children, eight of whom were born before he came to Carroll County. Harriet Perry, James O.R., Elijah Sparks, Martha Humphrey, William Adams, Thomas Anderson, Benjamin Cleveland, Amelia Elizabeth, John Humphries, born about six months after their arrival in Carroll, Sarah Ann and Mary Francis.

James O.R. Word, Benjamin Cleveland Word, John Humphries Word and Thomas Anderson Word served as Confederate soldiers in the Civil War. Thomas Anderson Word died in an army hospital in Chattanooga, John Humphries Word lost a leg at South Mountain.

Submitted by: Mary Florence Arthur Word, 805 Rome Street, Carrollton, GA 30117

1211. John Humphrey and Virginia Colquitt Word

"John H. Word was born in Carroll County in 1836, son of John Bryson and Amelia Sparks Word. He was reared on his father's farm in Carroll County, along with ten siblings, and made this his home until he married in 1866.

"In 1861 Word enlisted with the other Bowdon College boys in the Bowdon volunteers, Company B, Cobb's Legion, and participated in many hard-fought battles, among them being Dam No. 1, Yorktown, Seven Days' fight around Richmond, and Malvern Hill. He received a severe leg wound at South Mountain, Crampton's Gap, Maryland, September 14, 1862, and was taken prisoner. A month elapsed before the limb was amputated. After this, he contracted smallpox, was struck by lightning, and then had to submit to a second amputation, and that without anesthesia. Only four of his company escaped death or wounds.

"In 1863 he returned home, opened a general merchandise store at Bowdon, and did all he could to keep the 'home fires burning.' He was beginning to succeed in his new business before the war ended, but in spring 1865 some Federal troops, passing that way, robbed him of everything he had. Also in 1863 he was elected Clerk of the Superior Court, serving two years, and was Bowdon's notary public for six years. In 1884 he was elected to represent Carroll County in the General Assembly of Georgia. In 1893 he was elected county commissioner of Carroll County and took an active part in the building of the new courthouse."(1)

"In 1866 he married Miss Virginia Colquitt (1845-1908), daughter of William Terry and Ann Stringer Colquitt. Due to the war, when they began keeping house they were destitute, but by hard work, honest living and good management, they became prosperous. In the early 1900s, John H. Wood donated to Bowdon a triangle of land for a city park. When ladies first started to come to town there was no restroom facility. Members of the Woman's Federation of Clubs, realizing this lack, suggested that a clubhouse be constructed in the park which could also serve as a meeting place. In 1922, the log clubhouse was constructed with donations, providing the first public restroom in Bowdon, also a kitchen and meeting area.

"John H. Word was a trustee of Bowdon College for more than 30 years and treasurer of the board for ten years. Like his in-laws, the Colquitts, he was a liberal contributor to all worthy causes but more especially when the needs of Bowdon College were concerned. He never turned a deaf ear to its needs. He lived to a ripe old age and is buried beside his wife in the Bowdon Cemetery."(2)

John H. and Virginia Colquitt Word, c. 1885.

Submitted by: Philip Thomas Johnson, 2972 Cheshire Drive, Marietta, GA 30062

Sources: (1) Quoted from *Memoirs of Georgia,* Vol. 1, pages 448-449, Atlanta, Georgia, The Southern Historical Society, 1895. (2) Quoted from *The History of Bowdon College,* by Render R. Caswell, 1978, pages 37-38.

1212. Rufus A. Word

My father, Rufus A. Word, was born the 14th of December in 1882 at the Word settlement near Victory, Georgia. He grew up in a time when they didn't have modern conveniences. He cut hair for about twenty years at Tyus for 25 and 50 cents. He learned to swim in the old Tallapoosa River down at the Victory Mill. He finished the tenth grade at Fairview School near Tyus. As a young boy, he played baseball at Shiloh, Roopville near Carroll County. Baseball was his favorite pastime.

He married his first wife Lena Blackwelder on August 23, 1904. They had four children: Lois, Eunice, Amon, and Barney. Lena passed away April 24, 1917. He later married Viola Farmer on February 8, 1918. Together they had ten

Rufus A. Word and Mary Lena Blackwelder Word

children: Eubie, Norma, Doc, Curl, Thomas, Wilma, Bonnie Rea, Maureen, Frank, and Robby.

My father was a very smart and hard-working man. He would get up every morning about five o'clock. We would be on the farm working at six o'clock. We grew up in Tyus where we had no electricity or running water. We would put water in a washtub outside in the sun so that we could take a hot bath. We had an outhouse out back and a Sears catalog we used for toilet paper. We did all of our cooking on a wood stove. Our only transportation was a wagon and mule. We would pick cotton for other people so we could buy clothes.

Rufus A. Word and Viola Farmer Word

On March 8, 1986, while Rufus Word was sleeping, the Lord called him home to be with his family — all of whom are walking on the streets of gold. He was the oldest member at Pleasant Grove Church near Tyus where he was laid to rest. He had thirty-eight grandchildren and fifty-four great-grandchildren. My father was a well-respected man who will never be forgotten. (Also see John Madison Word and Thomas A. Word.) *Submitted by: Thomas M. Word, 6691 Songwood Drive, Austell, GA 30168*

1213. Columbus W. Worley

Everybody here knew the frank, genial, and honest face of Captain Lum Worley. "None knew him but to love him." There was no trace of sham in his makeup. His life was an open book "known and read by all men," who were so fortunate as to share his acquaintance.

Captain Worley was born in Dahlonega, Georgia. He was married to Miss Lizzie Barnes in Carroll County in April 1862.

He first enlisted as a private in Company H, 1st Georgia Infantry, March 18, 1861, for twelve months. He was one of the very first volunteers of the war.

When the twelve months expired, he reenlisted in the same company and regiment and was appointed adjutant of his regiment — a post of honor — and so acted until his company called him back by voluntarily and unanimously electing him first lieutenant of the company.

When his captain retired from being severely wounded at New Hope, he was promoted to the captaincy. He filled the office with marked distinction to the final surrender. After the surrender, he, with 100 others, undertook to go to the Confederate forces in the West but never quite reached them.

Captain Worley took part in many memorable engagements, among which were Laurel Hill and Caror Ford; Cheat Mountain; Green Briar; Reidville; Cumberland Gap; Perryville, Kentucky; Franklin, Tennessee; Lookout Mountain; Missionary Ridge; Vicksburg; New Hope, Atlanta, Resacca; and others.

He was wounded — three ribs fractured — by a piece of bombshell at the Battle of Atlanta July 22, 1864. He was wounded by a minnie-ball below the right knee in the leg.

He was a pensioner and was awarded the Cross of Honor.

I gathered these facts from his written statements furnished to me prior to his death and I knew the man and am satisfied of the truth of them. Under the heading "Special Remarks," Captain Worley says,

> "Well, there's so many just like my experience, that I don't know that it would do any good.
>
> "After my captain was disabled, I was captain and it looked like they always detailed my company when they wanted a bad job done.
>
> "I have often responded when they called for companies to volunteer to dislodge the enemy at some special point, and I am proud to say we generally succeeded, and that I always did my best."

Captain Worley, surrounded by weeping friends and relatives, "crossed over the river to rest under the shade of the trees," June 29, 1913. Peace to his ashes, honor to his name! *Submitted by: Watson Worley, 225 Plantation Walk, Carrollton, GA 30117*
Source: *Carroll Soldier Boys* originally written and published by G.W. Merrell, March 5, 1914.

1214. Worthy Family of Carroll County

The first Worthy to move to Carroll County was Zachariah P. Worthy. Zachariah moved to Carrollton from Chambers County, Alabama, in 1868 after the Civil War. He opened a dry goods shop on the town square. Zachariah's son, William Harrison Worthy, also stayed in Carrollton. He was a tailor, later taking over his father's dry goods store. William Harrison Worthy married Sarah A. Worthy. He died on August 16, 1909, and is buried, along with Sarah, in the Worthy plot of the Carrollton City Cemetery.

Henry J. Worthy, William Harrison's son, was born on December 29, 1875. He married Emily C. Worthy. Henry grew up to become a druggist. He owned and operated Worthy's Drug Store, located on the square in the present Relic's Antique building. Henry and Emily had two sons: Ed, who moved to Washington, D.C., and Steve. Henry, who died on July 3, 1963, and Emily, who died on June 11, 1967, are also buried in the Worthy plot of the City Cemetery.

William Steve was educated in the Carrollton City School System, and went on to attend the Fourth District A&M School, which is now the State University of West Georgia. He graduated from Emory University in Atlanta and attended the Emory University School of Medicine. He completed his internship in New York and his residency in obstetrics and gynecology at Massachusetts General Hospital.

Upon the completion of his education, the United States was on the brink of World War II. Steve was drafted for the Medical Corps of the United States Army and served as a surgeon in Africa, Italy, and France. He was awarded the Bronze Star for combat surgery. He returned to Carrollton where he was the area's first OB/GYN. Not only was he the first specialist to practice west of Atlanta, he was a founding member of the Tanner Memorial Hospital.

Steve married Imogene Shore Worthy of Habersham County, Georgia in 1940. They had four children. (1) Emily Worthy Nisbet, born on July 22, 1942, now resides in Fernley, Nevada with her husband, Jerry. They have four children: Jerri, Kelli, Alec, and Mendi, and seven grandchildren. (2) Ben Worthy, the second child, was born on July 4, 1946. He married Mary Bell of Bremen, Georgia. They have two children. Molly Worthy is a teacher in Cobb County. Gretchen Worthy is employed by Deutche Bank in Atlanta. Both Ben and Mary reside in Carrollton next to Worthy Park, a park where the Worthy family home once stood. (3) The third child of Steve and Imogene Worthy was Ellen Worthy Stokes. Ellen was born on March 30, 1948 and now resides in Fredericksburg, Virginia with her husband Jerry. They have three children: Worth, Kirk, and Shore. (4) The fourth child of Steve and Imogene Worthy was Thomas Peter Worthy, born on February 6, 1951. Peter attended Baylor Military Academy, Oxford College at Emory University, Emory University, and Emory University School of Dentistry. He has been a practicing dentist in Carrollton for twenty-six years. He is a member of the Rotary Club, American College of Dentists, the Georgia Dental Association, the Gridiron Secret Society of the University of Georgia, and is past president of the State University of West Georgia Foundation Board of Trustees.

Peter married Joan Dunlap Worthy of Hopkinsville, Kentucky, on October 15, 1977. Joan later became the business manager of Peter's dental practice, where she still works. She is a member of the Lit-Mu Club of Carrollton. She was co-chairman of the First Annual Magnolia Ball (1991), benefitting Tanner Medical Center.

Joan and Peter have two children. William Thomas Worthy was born on April 17, 1983, at Tanner Medical Center in Carrollton. He is a 2001 graduate of Oak Mountain Academy in Carrollton. He will attend Washington and Lee University in Lexington, Virginia, in the fall of 2001. Sarah Elizabeth Worthy was born on January 20, 1987, at Tanner Medical Center. She will be a freshman at Oak Mountain Academy in the fall of 2001.

The entire Worthy family still living in Carrollton attends the First United Methodist Church, as did Zachariah P. Worthy over 130 years ago. *Submitted by: William Thomas Worthy*

1215. Wren - Wilson

William M. Wren was born April 20, 1835, in North Carolina. According to CSA pension papers, he married Martha A. Wilson in August 1854, in Heard County, Georgia. Martha was born May 13, 1837, in Randolph County, Alabama, died September 12, 1923, in Carroll County, and was buried in the Bethel Baptist Church Cemetery at Temple, Georgia. She was the daughter of James Wilson and Elizabeth Toler. William and Martha lived in Heard County, Carroll County and Cullman County, Alabama, where he died on April 13, 1898, and was buried at Emeus Baptist Church Cemetery in Cullman. Martha returned to Carroll County after 1900. Their children were:

Alice Ann Adaline Wren was born in June 1857 in Heard County, and died May 20, 1931 in Cullman County, Alabama. She was married to Andrew Jackson Gilland on December 25, 1877, in Carroll County, Georgia.

John C. Wren was born February 8, 1858, in Heard County. His wife's name was Emily and they married in 1875. He died on June 16, 1903, in Cullman and is buried in the Emeus Baptist Church Cemetery.

Eliza J. Wren was born September 17, 1859, in Heard County and died before 1897 in Cullman

County. She was married to Leroy William McWhorter on November 28, 1878, in Carroll County.

Mary A. Elizabeth Wren was born in 1863 in Heard County.

James William Wren was born in 1864 in Heard County and died in 1939 in Carroll County. He married Alice Ida Muse on January 1, 1882, in Carroll County. They are buried in the Bethel Baptist Church Cemetery in Temple, Georgia.

Lucy H. Wren was born February 2, 1866, in Heard County and died September 18, 1938, in Coweta County, Georgia. She married Josiah R. Stallings on October 27, 1885 in Carroll County. Both are buried in the New Lebanon Baptist Church Cemetery at Whitesburg in Carroll County.

Simeon M. Wren was born in March 1868, in Heard County and died April 14, 1953, in Fulton County, Georgia. He married Sarah Adline Justus on February 19, 1893, in Cullman County, Alabama. Sarah was born in May 1876 in Cullman County and died December 30, 1947, in Carroll County. Both are buried in the Bethel Baptist Church Cemetery. Their children were Lela who married Wilmer E. Maroney, James Omar who married Tommie Chambless, Ethel, Evie, Hattie Mae who married Homer Brinkley Capes, Lonie, Charlie who married Euna Couch, Dewey who married Ruby Phillips, Roy, Jewell, and Inez.

Emma Temperance Wren was born December 16, 1869, in Heard County and died February 4, 1947, in Carroll County. She married G. Brittain Thompson on December 25, 1890, in Carroll County. Both are buried in Midway Macedonia Baptist Church Cemetery in Carroll County.

Robert L. Wren was born May 11, 1872, in Georgia and died March 31, 1955, in Cullman County. He married Eliza J. Cochran on December 24, 1893 in Cullman. They are buried in Emeus Baptist Church Cemetery.

Charles J. Wren was born March 5, 1875, probably in Carroll County, and died March 23, 1964 in Cullman County. He married Mahala Humphrey on September 23, 1894, in Cullman. Both are buried in Emeus Baptist Church Cemetery.

Walter Wren was born March 9, 1878, in Carroll County, and died April 22, 1958, in Cullman County. He married Nancy A. King on February 28, 1897, in Cullman County. Both are buried in Emeus Baptist Church Cemetery in Cullman. *Submitted by: Sherri Capes Shellnutt, 68 River Ridge, Carrollton, GA 30117*

Sources: Census, marriage, and cemetery records researched by Erlene Boyd.

1216. Wright Family

John C. Wright was born in 1812 in Georgia. He was married April 1, 1835, in Coweta County, Georgia, to Elizabeth Kelly born in 1822 in South Carolina. She was the daughter of Moses Kelly born about 1797, and Elizabeth Dyer born 1801. James Marion Wright — one of John C.'s seven children — was married to Lucinda Carolina Smith on December 30, 1859. James Marion was born 1839 and died May 2, 1863, in Columbus, Mississippi, while in the Civil War. His sons were John T., (born 1860, died October 1942) and Thomas Wright.

At age eighteen, John T. married Eliza Jane King, age fifteen. She was the daughter of Hiram Thomas King (born August 1863, died August 29, 1932) and Charity Matilda Chandler King. To this union were born Joseph, John Willie, Jerusha, Mary Ann, Charity Lucinda, Martin Loyd, Robert, Ella, Shubert, George B., Lisha and Lige, and Hiram Thomas Wright. John T. farmed near Kansas, Georgia, and had a country store for several years. He also had a blacksmith shop, gin, and gristmill.

(1) Joseph M. married Minnie Shell and remained in Carroll County. (2) Willie married Mary Ann Teague and moved from Carroll County to a farm in Haralson County. (3) Jerusha married Jim Shell and moved from Carroll County to Albertville, Alabama, where most of their children were born. (4) Mary Ann Wright married John Clayton Teague and remained in Carroll County. (5) Lucinda married George Thompson. They moved to Iowa and then to Seattle, Washington, and later Wenatchee, Washington, where they were buried. (6) Martin Loyd lived until 1926 in Carroll County, then bought a farm in Haralson County where he lived the remainder of his life. (7) Robert Daniel "Bob" lived in Carroll County in his younger days. He married Janie Williams and moved to South Georgia where they spent the remainder of their lives. (8) Ella married Rufus Williams and lived at Mt. View in Carroll County, later moving to Bremen, Georgia, where they died. (9) Shubert married Mary Frances Free and moved from Carroll County to Haralson County where they remained. (10) George B. "Bud" married Ella Smith, lived in Carroll County in their early years but moved to Ocilla, Georgia, where both were buried. (11) Lisha and Lige were twins born in 1903 and died in infancy. (12) Hiram Thomas, the youngest son, married Annie Britt and remained in Carroll County until their deaths.

Martin Loyd Wright married Susie Ozella Phillips in 1914. They had three children — Dorothy Irene, Derah Odean, and Myron Edwin. Dorothy Irene resides at the family home at Buncombe, Haralson County.

Derah Odean married Rev. T.L. Stephens. He was pastor of churches in Carroll and Heard Counties for thirty-two of the thirty-four years he was ordained. He retired due to his health in July 2000. Their daughter Celeta Joy married James Author Page. They live in Carroll County with their only son Stephen Ray Page.

Myron Edwin married Emogene Pollard in 1956. Their daughter Terri Gail married Ricky Parmer and they have one son, Seth. Their son Dennis resides in Atlanta, Georgia. *Submitted by: Derah Wright Stephens, 52 Campground Road, Waco, GA 30182*

1217. Asa Asbury Wright Family

Asa Asbury Wright was born on February 4, 1888, the son of John and Dora Wright of the Smithfield community near Bowdon. His wife, Parrie Warren Wright, was born on March 19, 1887, the daughter of James Walter Warren and Rebecca Turner Warren. Asbury and Parrie were married in 1907.

Asa Asbury Wright and Parrie Warren Wright around 1906

Asbury Wright was a rural mail carrier and very active in the Burwell Lodge No. 546, serving as its Master for three years. He also served as Master of the Carroll County Masonic Convention. He died in 1930 at the young age of 42, leaving his wife and five children.

After Asbury's death, Parrie worked as a cook for the lunchroom in the Bowdon schools. In 1948 she broke up housekeeping and moved to the home of her daughter, Burnell Prickett, in Avondale Estates, Georgia.

Parrie and Asbury's five children were Clarence Wright, Burnell Wright Prickett, Pauline Wright Wilson, Sybil Wilson Scott, and Warren Wright.

Parrie died on January 18, 1964. Asbury and Parrie are buried at Indian Creek Baptist Church Cemetery north of Bowdon, Georgia. *Submitted by: Sybil Wright Scott, 269 Old Four Notch Road, Whitesburg, GA 30185 and Written by: Granddaughter Paula Wilson Steed, 41 Pine Court, Carrollton, GA 30117*

1218. George Benjamin Wright

Carroll County Transplants

In 1966 I married into a wonderful family that originated in Carroll County, Georgia. The George Benjamin (Bud) Wright and Josie Ella Smith family moved from there to Irwin County, Georgia, in the late 1930s seeking productive farmland. Bud and Ella loaded up their children — Talmadge, Dirl, Elbert, Lloyd, Joe and Betty — and followed Wilburn Smith, Ella's brother, to what they prayed would be a better life. Talmadge also brought along his new wife Edwina Brock. Soon the Wright clan added two more daughters and three grandchildren. Bud and Ella's last two daughters, Martha and Barbara, were born within months of Talmadge and Edwina's children, Dean, Joyce and Talmadge Jr. The Wrights worked hard and prospered in their new home, but their hearts would always be in North Georgia.

George Benjamin and Josie Ella Smith Wright

To understand the pull North Georgia holds on this family, one must first know their ancestry. Bud's parents were John Thomas Wright and Eliza King (see related Wright story) and his line goes as far back as John C. Wright, Benjamin King, Joseph Burson, Ambrose Chandler, Moses Kelly, Gabriel Smith, William White, and Thomas Dyer. Ella also had deep roots in Carroll with parents Benjamin Frank Smith (my genealogical "brick wall") and Ruth Ella Warren, descending from Thomas Warren and Peter Michael. Edwina's parents were Henry Y. Brock and Estelle Deese and their bloodlines reach back to Henry Brock, Jeremiah Cole, Joel A. Deese, Anthony F. Crumbley II, John Wesley Richardson, and John Priar Anderson. All the ancestors named above settled in and around Carroll County during the early 1800s. The cemeteries at Poplar Springs, Indian Creek, Kansas, Tallapoosa and Macedonia, just to name a few, are filled with their kin.

By the time I joined this family by marrying Talmadge (June) Wright Jr., it was already large and an important addition to Irwin County.

Bud and Ella's eight children have "gone forth and multiplied" and these descendants have made this couple proud. The closeness and love they display for each other always amazes me. Not only do I feel this love in our Irwin County family but the Carroll County kin as well. As June and I visit kinfolk and go "bone hunting" in Carroll County, I feel at peace. It's almost like all those forefathers and mothers are reaching out from their graves with comforting arms.

June and I added two sons to the clan. Our oldest, Andrew Paul, graduated from West Georgia College and now works with physically and mentally handicapped adults. Our youngest, Eric Todd, is a farmer with a deep love of the land like his forefathers before him. So you see, North Georgia will always hold a strong bond for the descendants of "Carroll County transplants" no matter the age. *Submitted by: Mary Clyde Wright, 175 Whitley Road, Ocilla, GA 31774. Camel@surfsouth.com*

1219. William Wright Family

William M. Wright, born in 1783, in Virginia, married Winifred Ann Jones 17 December 1805 in Oglethorpe County, Georgia. William and "Winnie" were living in the home of their son, Asa, in Carroll County, Georgia in 1860. William died in 1863, while "Winnie" continued to live with Asa until her death in 1875. Both are buried in Wright Family Cemetery in Bowdon, Carroll County on the land William acquired through a lottery. They had three children.

William Asa Wright and Louisa "Lucy" Smith

1. Mason J. Wright, born 12 March 1812, in Haralson County, Georgia, married Mehetabel Collins, 16 September 1845 in Carroll County. They had Asa Taylor Sr., born 27 June 1848, John, and Jack. Asa Taylor Sr. married Mary Murrah in Wedowee, Randolph County, Alabama, in 1866 and had Asa Taylor Jr., John William, and Caroline. Asa Taylor Jr. married Ida Lelia Warren (daughter of Walter T. Warren and Elizabeth Smith). They had nine children.

2. Mary Wright was born about 1814 in Haralson County.

3. William Asa Wright, born 27 February 1822, in Haralson County, married Louisa "Lucy" Smith (daughter of Richard, granddaughter of Gabriel Sr.), 24 December 1845 in Carroll County. Asa and Lucy had fifteen children. 1. & 2. The first two children were unnamed twins who died at birth about 1846 in Alabama. 3. James Ellis Wright, born 10 December 1848 in Alabama, married Mary Josephine Bearden 3 August 1871 in Carroll County. They had Mary Jane, Emily Virginia, William, Julia, and Lucy. 4. Martha Wright was born 1847 in Alabama and died June 1850 in Carroll County. 5. Nancy Wright, born 20 November 1850, in Carroll County, married Samuel Thomas Jones (son of Stephen Thomas Jones and Rebecca Davis), 7 August 1873 in Carroll County. They had Asa Andrew, Lucy, Melissa Elizabeth, William Stephen, Henry T., James Fletcher, Miles Ammon, Nancy Jane, Mary Virginia, and E. Luford. Nancy died 30 January 1925, and Samuel Thomas 27 December 1934. Both are buried in Fellowship Primitive Baptist Cemetery, Cullman County, Alabama. 6. Melissa Wright, born 18 September 1852, in Carroll County married Hiram S. Crawford 7 March 1877 in Carroll County. They had four daughters. Melissa died 13 November 1932 and is buried in Poplar Springs Primitive Baptist Cemetery, Carroll County. 7. Asa William Wright, born 1 July 1854, married Virginia Missouri Silvey (daughter of William Silvey and Mary Pitts), 5 December 1876 in Carroll County. They had Della, Lucy Melvina, Drewry, William Jessie, and Ossie Virginia. Asa William died 28 March 1945 and Missouri Virginia died 22 February 1934. They are buried in Haralson County. 8. Willis Williamson Wright, born 22 March 1856, married Marina K. in 1874. His second marriage was 12 December 1883 to Margarette M. Lee. Willis Williamson had eight children: William R., Willis Martin, Shelly, John A., Louisa Victoria, Eula M., Warner Earnest, and James Vester. Willis died in Alabama and is buried in Fellowship Primitive Baptist Cemetery, Cullman County, Alabama. 9. Lucy Wright, born 6 February 1857, in Carroll County, married John Riley McKibbin 31 October 1877 in Carroll County. They had Lucinda F., Thomas W., and Joseph David. Lucy died 30 May 1938 and John Riley on 4 January 1939. They are buried in Kansas Missionary Baptist Cemetery, Carroll County. 10. Henry Nolen Wright, born 13 October 1859, in Carroll County, married Mary Loucinda Farlow (daughter of Edward Farlow and Mary Jane Clark), 29 November 1882 in Carroll County. They had Lucy Jane, Dochia Ann, Henrietta, Nancy Dora, Asa Asbury, and William McKinley. Henry Nolen died 31 August 1919 and Mary Loucinda on 12 December 1936. They are buried in Chulafinnee Methodist Cemetery, Cleburne County, Alabama. 11. John Lewis Wright, born 24 May 1865, in Carroll County married Etta LaDora Farlow, 21 November 1886 in Carroll County. She and Mary Lou Farlow were sisters. They had Asa Asberry, Lucy Jane, Alice, Maude Esta, Arlin Lincoln, John Clifton, Mildred Lura, and Hoyt Clarkston. John Lewis died 25 February 1931 and Etta La Dora on 26 May 1934. They are buried in Indian Creek Missionary Baptist Cemetery, Carroll County. 12. Abraham Lincoln Wright, born 22 May 1867, in Carroll County married Julia Louise Morris (daughter of Homer Monroe Morris and Mary Clark), 22 January 1891 in Simsboro, Louisiana. They had Howard Nolan, Evvie, Dura, and Alton Lincoln. Abraham Lincoln died 22 December 1944, and Julia Louise 6 September 1966. They are buried in Pine Grove Cemetery, Alexandria, Louisiana. 13. Ulysses Grant Wright, born 1869, died young and is buried in Wright Cemetery. 14. Emily Virginia Wright, born about 1870, died young and is buried in Wright Cemetery. 15. Winifred Ann Wright, born about 1872, died young and is buried in Wright Cemetery.

Asa and Lucy were in Carroll County for the 1850 Census. In 1859 he paid tax on 350 acres of land, 90 of which were orchards. During the Civil War he was permitted to produce brandy for soldiers. One granddaughter remembered Asa boasting of his Irish ancestry. In their later years, son John Lewis and wife moved into the home to live with them. William Asa died 3 September 1903 and is buried in Wright Cemetery.

In *The Carroll County Story as Told by the People.* "Lucy" Wright is called

> "The 'Florence Nightingale' of this part of the county. Her little black satchel and her side saddle were kept ready for her 'errands of mercy'." She is reputed to have delivered hundreds of babies and "also ministered to the other sick, sometimes being gone for several days at a time."

John Clifton Wright (son of John Lewis and Etta LaDora) was born 17 November 1904. He knew his grandmother "Lucy" well, having grown up in the household while she was living. He said she was never any trouble, very gentle, kind and in fairly good health prior to her death. She talked about her early years and witnessing the last of the Indians leaving Carroll County. "Lucy" died 2 January 1921 and is buried in Wright Cemetery. *Submitted by: Karen Wright Casey, 1302 Somercotes Lane, Channelview, TX 77530-2228*

Sources: Carroll County and Randolph County (Alabama) census records, marriage records from Carroll County and Oglethorpe County, Georgia.

1220. Wynn(e)

At the Concord Methodist Church Cemetery in the Hickory Level community, Sloman and Mahaley Wynne (with an "e") are buried. No birth or death dates are noted on their monuments. He was my great-great-great grandfather.

S.R. (Richard) and Nancy C. Wynn. About 1895.

My father used to tell the story of how Sloman was the chorister at Concord Church and belonged to a group of men who drove out horse thieves from the community. I always thought this was an odd combination but when I read the book, *At Home in Carrollton 1827-1994,* it told of the group called the "Slicks." The Slicks drove out the horse thieves who were called the "Pony Club."

According to deed records at the Carroll County courthouse, Sloman Wynne purchased a land lot north of the Hickory Level community in 1832. He then bought two more land lots that adjoined the first one in 1837. This was a total of 606 acres. According to probate records, he died in February 1884.

Also buried at Concord Cemetery are Sloman Richard Wynn and wife Nancy C. Wynn. He was called Richard since his father was called Sloman. For some reason, he decided to drop the "e" at the end of the family name.

Richard Wynn was born in 1829 and died in 1897. Nancy was born in 1829 and lived to within three months of her 100th birthday. Together they had five sons and four daughters named John, Ezra, Bob, Tom (my great-grandfather), Billy, Mary W. Evans, Molly W. Gaddy, Tarsey W. Gray, and Lela W. Cartwright. Family stories were that Grandma Wynn used to say she did not lose any children in infancy and never used a doctor with any of them.

She spent the last eleven years of her life in a wheelchair because she had fallen and broken a hip. Of course, there was no such thing as hip surgery then. Lela cared for her mother during the last years of her life as well as caring for two of her brothers. Nursing homes were not available then.

Nancy Wynn had been a member of Concord Methodist Church for over seventy-six years. She had moved to Carroll County from Green County, Georgia. Her obituary notice in the county paper said, "She was the great-granddaughter of General Nathaniel Green of the Revolutionary War."

I vaguely remember Billy Wynn or "Uncle Billy" as he was called. He was my great-uncle.

In his later years he had been a "drummer" selling Watkins and McNess products. I remember his having paperback copies of the New Testament to give away to his customers along his routes. In his younger days, Uncle Billy was a teacher. I remember my father telling me that Uncle Billy always kept a "fining comb" on his desk to comb lice from the children's hair.

My great-grandfather Tom S. Wynn (May 7, 1857-July 11, 1944) married Sarah Lassetter (April 4, 1861-September 27, 1937) on November 16, 1884. They had one daughter Lena Wynn (April 11, 1886-February 26, 1940) who was my grandmother. She died sixteen years before I was born. *Submitted by: Robert H. Ogletree*
Sources: Carroll County deed records, and obituary from Carroll County newspaper 1928.

1221. Yates Family

Villa Rica

William W. Yates came from Virginia and settled in old Campbell County, Georgia, along with his wife Rebecca many years ago. Their son Elijah Matthew Yates married Martha Steed and they are interred at Pleasant Grove Cemetery, Villa Rica. This means the Yates moved westward to Carroll County.

Elijah and Martha had the following children: William, Robert, Berry, Ada, Eugenia, Addie and Fannie.

Robert Atticus Yates married Ada Ozella Hixon and they had four children — Myrtie, Minnie Kate, Raymond and Margaret. Robert and Ada, along with children Myrtie and Raymond, are interred at Pleasant Grove Cemetery.

Raymond married Mildred Wilson and they had six children. Robert was killed in World War II. The other children were Wilson, Frank, Cathryne, Frances and Malline. Wilson and Frank live in Villa Rica. *Submitted by: Frank Yates, Villa Rica, GA. Researched by Margaret Y. Durrett.*

1222. The Elisha Yeager Family

Elisha Yeager was born 1809 in South Carolina. He married Caroline Hester Ann Johnson December 17, 1845, and soon moved to Carroll County. They lived in the Starpoint community near Lowell where he owned many acres of land and served as the justice of peace. She died in 1882 and he died in 1891. They are buried at New Lebanon Baptist Church on Highway 5.

Elisha and Hester Ann Yeager

It is believed that this Yeager line begins back with Claus Yager in Germany, then Paul, Nicholas, Adam, Michael Yager, and John Yeager who was Elisha's grandfather, born November 28, 1750, in Culpeper County, Virginia, died January 31, 1831, and married Anna "Nancy" Render. Their children were John, Samuel, William, Ezekial, Reuben, Abijah, Ira, Mary "Polly," Abner, Lewis, Elizabeth, and Ruth. Many of these families lived in Bibb County, Alabama, or Lincoln County, Tennessee.

Elisha's father, William Yeager, was born about 1779 in Culpeper, Virginia, and died in Coweta County, Georgia, after 1830. His children were Jane born 1821; Nancy born 1823; Thomas Jacob born 1808 in Laurens, South Carolina, moved to Douglas County, Georgia; Elisha born 1809; William born 1817; Abner born 1819; and Peachy T. born 1828.

Elisha and Hester Ann's eight children were Henry Allen who married Susan E. Moore and moved to Lovelady, Texas; Henrietta Elizabeth who married Lewis Jefferson Mordaki Camp and lived at Starpoint; William Johnson who married Susan Elizabeth Jackson and lived at Starpoint; Thomas Jefferson and James M. who moved to Tennessee; Sara Ellen who married James Edward Moore and lived at Starpoint; Joseph D. who married Georgianna Brown and lived in Prairie Grove, Arkansas, and Tulsa, Oklahoma; and Georgia Texas who married James Robert Brown and lived in Carrollton.

The children of Ellen Yeager and James Moore were Daun, Landon, Kenny, Lee, and Dalton. Daun married Wiley Storey. Their children were Nellie Lee born January 6 1918; Rhoda Christine born May 26, 1920, died September 18, 1995; and James Clifford Storey who died December 8, 1943, while serving in the Navy in World War II. They enjoyed playing barn dance music. James Landon married Mary Lou Hogan and had a large family that mostly stayed in Coweta County. Kenneth married Nora Jackson and lived at Lowell. Their daughter was Sinah and her son, Hoke. Lee and Dalton were the other sons. Lee had Moore's Appliance Store in Carrollton. Dalton was born in 1905 and died in 1940 from a heart attack. He married Jewell Walker. Their son James still lives at Lowell and has two sons, Ronnie and Randy.

The youngest son of Elisha was Joe. His sons were Dalton, Spurgeon, Thurman, Lester, and Marvin, and daughters Roxie and Velma. The boys owned the Yeager Wholesale Grocery Company for many years in Tulsa. Elisha's youngest daughter, Georgia Texas, born October 3, 1869, and died March 20, 1958, married J.R. Brown on Ground Hog Day February 2, 1869. He traded mules and cows and she sold milk and eggs from their house. She suffered a stroke but lived to the age of eighty-nine; he lived to be ninety-six years old. (See Daniel Brown Family.) *Submitted by: Gwyn Chesnut, 185 Cottage Hill Road, Carrollton, GA 30117*
Sources: Personal knowledge and research from Marsha Brown records.

1223. The Frances Whisenhunt Yearty Family

Susan Hinson married Arthur Whisenhunt on December 29, 1848. They bought a 202½ acre farm off Rainey Road in Temple from her Uncle Iron Hinson for $50. In 1857, Susan donated one acre of land to build Temple's first church, Asbury Methodist Church. It was named for Francis Asbury, one of Methodism's early bishops. Mr. Whisenhunt died in the Civil War and is buried at Vicksburg. Susan died in 1899 and is buried in Asbury Cemetery, Temple, Georgia. The Whisenhunts had two daughters, Frances and Susan. They divided their land between the two girls: one hundred-one acres to each.

Susan married John Moore. They had five children: Walt, George, John Jr., a daughter, and Matt.

Frances married Jim Yearty, an Irishman. They had three children: Uly Arthur Yearty (May 31, 1879-October 3, 1960), Aron Lumpkin Yearty (February 16, 1884-December 3, 1963), and Margaret Yearty who died at age five from smoke inhalation when her clothing caught fire. Jim Yearty left the family when Uly was five years old.

Frances Whisenhunt Yearty

Frances had a hard time raising the children on her own. She sold milk, butter, and eggs. She grew most of the food they ate. She had to sell part of the land to make ends meet. When her two sons were grown, she divided the ninety-three remaining acres between them. Francis' home burned, so she lived with Uly and Cora until her death in 1927.

On October 7, 1900, Uly Arthur married Cora Jane Muse (September 26, 1883-December 4, 1978), daughter of Henry Pope "Bud" Muse and Martha Sharp Muse. Uly farmed and ran a sawmill. He powered the saw from an old truck motor that someone had trashed. It has been said that he could take an old piece of machinery that no one else could get to run and use it for twenty years. He milled the timber and built his home, barn, smokehouse, and corn crib. Cora was a homemaker and enjoyed visiting with friends and neighbors. They had seven children: James Robert (Jimmy) (August 29, 1901-December 3, 1964); infant daughter not named (November 22, 1903-January 12, 1904); Clifton Henry (Cliff) (April 28, 1907-November 29, 1986); infant son (April 28, 1907-April 28, 1907); Bertie Frances (March 28, 1912-September 23, 1974); Roy Franklin (April 12, 1919-February 2, 2001); and John Fletcher (August 3, 1927-).

Cora and Uly Yearty "Granny and Pa," August 1956

Jimmy married Eula Dobbs (September 9, 1901-October 10, 1999). They had three sons: James Robert Jr. (February 2, 1924-September 13, 1988); Samuel Joe (September 30, 1928-December 21, 1981); and Gene (1940-).

Clifton married Grace Timmons (February 5, 1906-December 12, 2000). They had one daughter, Dorothy (September 7, 1927-).

Bertie married Ralph J. Casey (May 24, 1907-September 9, 1971). They had no children.

Roy Franklin married Gertrude Rush (March 17, 1923-). They had five children: Cora, Sandra, Roy Jr., Sara, and Debra.

John Fletcher married Marilyn Matthews. They have no children. *Submitted by: Sara Y. Parrish, 540 Asbury Road, Temple, GA 30179*

1224. Yearty

Seven Generations on the same Farm

Roy F. Yearty Sr. was the third of seven generations on the same farm land in Temple. From his great-grandmother, Susan Whisenhunt, to his great-granddaughter, Ansley Powell, a member of the family has continuously lived on this land.

Roy was born April 12, 1919, in the home his father, Uly Yearty, built from timber he milled at his sawmill. Uly and Cora Muse Yearty raised five children: Jimmy, Cliff, Bertie, Roy, and Fletcher.

On May 21, 1939, Roy married Gertrude Rush. They bought the farm from his parents in 1949. Roy worked in the CC Camp until he went into the Army during World War II. He fought in Germany and France. While he was in the war, Gertrude worked hard keeping the farm and raising their children. After the war, Roy was chief of police in Temple and Villa Rica in the late 1950s. He retired from police work and started building custom cabinets. Gertrude worked at Sewell's. Together they farmed. They had five children: Cora, Sandra, Roy Jr., Sara, and Debra.

Cora married Gene Holloman. They have one daughter, Jan, married to Pat White with two children Daniel and Tonya. Sandra married Russell Cummings. They have two sons, Lance and Scott. Lance married Candy Walls and they have two sons, Alan and Chris. Scott married Hiromi and they have a daughter Sara Ann, and a son Jesse. Roy Jr. married Judy Keener. They have two children, Dulcie and Jim. Dulcie married Steve Powell and they have a daughter, Ansley. Jim married Mary Thomas. They have no children. Sarah married Gary Parrish. They have no children.

When Roy Jr. and Judy married, they moved into a farm house built by his grandfather. Dulcie and Steve have built a new home on some of the original farm property. Cora and Gene live on farm land that has been in the Holloman family for five generations. Sandra and John Stillwell, Sarah and Gary Parrish, and Jan and Pat White have homes built on farm land next to Roy Sr. that belonged to his sister, Bertie, and Ralph Casey. This makes four generations on that property.

The Yearty Family

Roy and Gertrude instilled in us love of family and the importance of the land. Keep your land, money slips through your fingers, but land is forever. On February 12, 2001, after battling cancer for ten years, Roy F. Yearty Sr. died in the same room where he was born eighty-one years and ten months earlier. He left behind Gertrude Rush Yearty, his wife of almost sixty-two years. She was the strength behind the man and capable of holding the family and the land together with love.

The photo included shows in the back row, Sandra Yearty Stillwell, Gertrude and Roy Yearty Sr., in the front row, Cora Yearty Holloman, Sara Yearty Parrish, Debra Yearty, and Roy Yearty Jr. *Submitted by: Sandra Yearty Stillwell, 620 Asbury Road, Temple, GA 30179*

1225. Young Family

Hugh Lee Young was born March 11, 1923 in Carroll County, Georgia. He was one of eight children born to Charlie B. Young and Parrie Potts Young. All of the eight children at one time were members of Roopville Baptist Church. Hugh Lee is the only one left at the church at this time. He grew up in Roopville, Georgia, where he attended school. There he met his wife, Mertha McLendon. Mertha is the daughter of Bessie Denney McLendon and Warner Cleveland McLendon. She married Hugh Lee Young on August 1, 1943. Hugh Lee Young volunteered for service in World War II at Ft. McPherson and entered service on October 20, 1942, at the age of nineteen. He was stationed in Africa, England and Italy. he was a member of the 376 BUMB Group, 514 Squad/15th Air Force. While on his 27th mission, his plane was shot down on December 28, 1943. He parachuted out of the aircraft over Northern Italy and was taken as a prisoner of war and was later sent to a German POW camp in Austria. He was held as a POW for eighteen months and was discharged from the service on October 6, 1945. He received the Purple Heart, POW medal, European African Middle Eastern Campaign and the World War II Victory Medal. He was honored as DAV Veteran of the Year on April 13, 1996.

When he returned home from the war, he bought a farm in Heard County, Georgia, and began farming. While there he and his wife had two children, Dennis Hugh Young and Donna Sue Young. In 1962 they moved to Carrollton where Hugh Lee worked at Southwire for twenty-six years. He retired in 1988. Dennis Young married Monica Lambert on July 5, 1980, and they had one son, Ian Isaac Young, born on May 13, 1990. Donna Young married Hubert Roy Dorrough on August 1, 1980, and had two daughters, Alaina Beth Dorrough, born March 24, 1985, and Amy Leigh Dorrough, born February 6, 1990. Monica Young died on December 1, 2000. *Submitted by: Mrs. H.L. Young, 3279 Shady Grove Road, Carrollton, GA 30117*

Harold Petty remembers his brother, B.C.

B.C. Petty
U.S. Army

B.C. Petty (b. 5-1-1926 d. 2-15-1988) was drafted into the United States Army October 5, 1944, shortly after his eighteenth birthday. He served with the 38th Infantry at Camp Swift, Texas, where he received promotion to Private First Class. He subsequently served in France and Germany. He was also stationed at Camp Carson, Colorado and Fort Benning, Georgia. He was discharged on November 27, 1946 with the rank of Technician Fifth Class.

Harold Petty was drafted into the US Army on Jan. 7, 1953. He was assigned to the 47th Infantry Division, Camp (now Fort) Rucker, Al., for basic training. Then he was assigned to the Far East Command and subsequently to the Seventh Division, 32nd. Infantry Regiment, Co. M., in South Korea. He served with the 7th Division until October, 1954. His last duty assignment was Platoon Sergeant, Heavy Machine Gun Platoon. He was then assigned to the 4th Infantry Division which was returning to the US from South Korea and was discharged December 3, 1954, at New Orleans, Louisiana.

Harold Petty
U.S. Army

Denneys' Tribute To WWII Veterans

The brothers shown below are the sons of the late Lewis Garvey and Susie Mae Shadinger Denney and they were all in the US Navy at the same time during World War II.

Lewis Everette Denney

Lewis Everette Denney

(born 11-1-1915)

He joined the U.S. Navy on 10-27-1941 and was assigned to the USS Hughes in the Pacific. Everette was a Fire Controlman First Class and was discharged October 15, 1945.

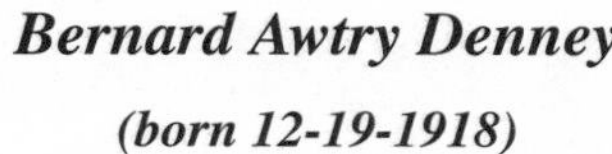

Bernard Awtry Denney

(born 12-19-1918)

On 6-20-1944 he reported to the Navy and was assigned to the USSLST 810 (United States Ship-Landing Ship Tank) in the Pacific including Japan. He was discharged January 27, 1946.

Bernard Awtry Denney

Garvey Melvin Denney

Garvey Melvin Denney

(born 11-3-1923)

He entered the Navy in April 1944 and was assigned to the Willis Destroyer Escort. He served in the N. Atlantic from Newfoundland and south to Cuba. He was in Pearl Harbor when the war ended. His ship sunk two submarines and received the President's Citation.

James Donald Denney

(born 4-6-1927)

He volunteered for the Navy for the duration plus six months in April 1945. Donald was shipped to the Philippines on the USS Henrico troop ship and was transferred to the USS Chaffee DE 230-Destroyer Escort. Discharged July 18, 1946.

James Donald Denney

God Bless America!

Emmaus Primitive Baptist Church

Oak Grove Church Road, Carrollton, Georgia 30117

On November 27, 1871 the organization meeting of Emmaus Primitive Baptist Church was held at the Rocky Mount School, in Carroll County. The school was located near where the Emmaus Church was later built. The male members listed at the organizational meeting were J.C. Burnham, C.D. Chappell, and E.L. Hand. The following month's conference was held on December 23, 1871 and this was copied from the Church record, "Georgia, Carroll County, The Baptist Church of Christ at Emmaus met at John Shadinger's, according to Adjournment and after Divine Services by Brethren E. Phillips and Burnham met in conference." Quoting again from the conference, "The Church went into choice of Supply and Clerk and chose J.C. Burnham, Moderator; E.S. Hand, Clerk. They promised to serve the Church with the best of their ability. No more business, Conference closed in order this December 23, 1871." (Enoch Phillips, Mod. Protem, E.S. Hand, Church Clerk)

Emmaus Church - 2001

The February 24, 1872 conference met at John Shadinger's home. At this conference the Church agreed to move the meeting place to the vacant house on John Shadinger's place on the Carrollton Road between Brother J.C. Burnham's and John Shadinger's homes. The date the first building was erected has not been established but the Church Conference minutes of April 26, 1873 states, "2nd opened door of church for reception of members and received Bro. I.N. McLendon and Sister Mary A.E. McLendon, his wife, by letter." Brethren I.N. McLendon and C.D. Chappell were appointed trustees to receive the deeds to the land donated to the Church at Emmaus on this same day.

In 1907 a church building was constructed and it served as the meeting place until 1987 when lightning caused a fire which burned it. The building committee members are listed as follows: I.N. McLendon, John Shadinger, C.D. Chappell, J.C. Burnham, Thomas Hamrick and James A. Fielder. The cornerstone shows "Emmaus Church, Constituted 1871, First Pastor Eld. J.C. Burnham, First Clerk I.N. McLendon, Pastor Eld. Frank L. Andrews, Present Clerk Newman E. Denney, Deacon L.G. Denney, and Contractor Howard Reid (1970)." In 1970 the bricks were added.

Brother Lewis Garvey Denney joined the Church in 1934 and was baptized in Buffalo Creek. He served as Deacon for many years continuing as long as he was able. Brother Newman Denney, served as Church Clerk for over fifty years.

In 1952 Sister Helen Reid joined her parents, Deacon R.N. and Sister Nellie Miles, who had previously moved their membership to Emmaus. At the time the Church burned on August 3, 1987, these were the only living members and Sister Reid was serving as Church Clerk. There was a tremendous outpouring of love and contributions came from near and far as plans started immediately to rebuild.

A groundbreaking ceremony for the rebuilding was held on September 12, 1987. Dedication services of the new Emmaus Church building were conducted on March 20, 1988. Sufficient funds with the volunteered hours of labor were received to completely pay for the Church building. It stands in the same place with services and reunion gatherings continuing as usual. The new cornerstone reads as follows: "Emmaus Church, Constituted 1871, First Pastor Eld. J.C. Burnham, First Clerk I.N. McLendon, Former Clerk N.E. Denney, Former Deacon L.G. Denney, Pastor Eld. Frank L. Andrews, Deacon R.N. Miles, Clerk Helen Reid, Contractor Howard Reid (1970). Church Burned 8-3-1987. Rebuilt with love offerings 1987-February 1988." To God be the glory, great things He has done!

Worship Services Every 2nd. Sunday, except August, 10:30 AM. Pastor: Elder Frank Andrews

Emmaus Church before it was bricked in 1970.

Submitted by: Mrs. Howard (Helen) Reid

First Christian Church

Carrollton, Georgia

The Church is an independent Congregation patterned after the New Testament Church, with no creed but Christ, and wearing only the name Christian (Acts 11:26).

According to information gathered by Miss Buvena Rooks for the Church Centennial History Book (1872-1972), the Church was organized and met first on August 1872. Andrew C. Borden placed a notice in the Friday, August 2, 1872 issue of the Carroll County Times: "I will organize a church in the Baptist Church House, by their consent, Saturday next at eleven o'clock." Then in the August 9, 1872 under the section entitled "Church Directory" was this announcement: "Christian Church ... Rev. A.C. Borden will preach at the Baptist Church on the first Sunday and Saturday before in each month, until changed, in which case, the public will be notified. The people will observe this announcement." (The Baptist Church stood across from the present depot on Bradley Street.)

In May 1873, the place was changed to the "Seminary" on College Street. The "Seminary" offered elementary, high school and even a college curriculum and hence the street name College Street. It was located where the "College Street School" was and where county offices are currently located.

In the 1880s the group met at Bethel Church and Borden's School house; then later at New Bethel on Neal's Ferry Road; First Christian at the corner of Newnan and White Streets and finally in 1947 First Christian at the corner of College and Ward Streets. In April 1898 a deed was granted to J.D. Perryman and R. Lee Sharpe, trustees of the First Christian Church of Carrollton, Georgia, to land on the corner of Newnan and White Streets. The congregation met there from 1898 to 1947. A deed dated March 29, 1946 was granted to W.J. Aldridge, Lester Reeves, and William Traylor, as trustees of First Christian Church, to a lot at the corner of Ward and College Streets. The congregation moved into this Gothic type architecture building with buff brick veneer in October 1947 and dedication day was November 2, 1947. Later an annex was added to provide Sunday School Rooms.

The old Post Office building on College Street was purchased, renovated, and "the Worship Center" was dedicated on January 29, 1995. The office building on Ward Street was acquired and "The Children's Center" was constructed and opened on April 12, 1998. And, the "Family Life Center" was dedicated on April 16, 2000. These additional facilities provided space for additional services and activities. Sunday School for all ages meets at 10 A.M. each Sunday. We have three Worship Services on Sunday A.M.: at 9 A.M. the "Plugged In" service meets in the Family Life Center, at 11 A.M. the "University Praise" service is held in the Chapel while the Traditional Worship service is underway in the Worship Center. Fred Skinner has been the Minister since November 1992. He delivers the same message to all three morning worship services. Since the additional services have been added the attendance has increased more than 75%. At 6 P.M. on Sunday and 7 P.M. on Wednesday there are study groups and activities for every particular age group. Bible Study, drama practice, choir for adults and children, prayer group, sports activities and several different ministries are available for those interested. On Wednesday morning at 9:30 A.M. there is a coffee fellowship with Bible Study at 10 A.M.

Some of the ministers serving were Zach Hardigree, 1890; Owen Still, 1921-1922 and 1925-1926; Oliver Moore, 1928-1931; M.B. Ingle 1932-1934; Ernest Miller, 1938-1940; George Bondurant, 1942-1944; Hugh D. Morgan, 1945-1952; Marvin Blackwell, 1952-1957; Clarence Shepard, 1958-1962; Robert Stewart, 1962-1967; T. Deering Manning, 1967-1973; Leo Beller, 1973-1982; Robert Shell, 1982-1992 and Fred Skinner, Jr., 1992 to present. Other part-time ministers were A.C. Borden, R.J. Miller, J.A. Perdue, Newton J. Tumlin, Ernest C. Mobley, J.F. Lambert, D.A. Brindle, Fred B. Powell, John Moore, Charles B. Holder, D.M. Joiner, Walter Willis, J.W. Bolton, Simon Peter Miller, and James Barfield.

The following were listed as charter members in 1898: J.D. Perryman, Allen Williams, J.M. Linderman, Jesse Mobley, Gus Nix, John Martin, and J.N. Nix.

There have been several ministers ordained at First Christian Church, Carrollton, and among these are L.A. Nix on June 6, 1926, H.D. Mann on January 23, 1958, Dale Lovelady on June 22, 1969, Marvin Horsley on January 8, 1961, and Garry Ned Gable on July 23, 1972.

Marjorie King Reeves was the first Youth Director (1946-47). The first paid song director was Louanne Stevens Hutcheson (1971-72). Deering Manning directed the first Vacation Bible School in 1953. The first annual picnic was on July 13, 1958 at the Boyce Warren farm and was suggested by Brother Shepard. Other picnics were held at Lake Carroll but the favorite place for many years is Woodland Christian Camp. The "First Christian Memorial Scholarship Fund" was established in 1962. The first annual Atlanta Christian College Choir concert and dinner hosted by FCC was the first Sunday in December 1949. All these continue to the present.

In 1972 these members were recognized for continuously being members since 1942: June Baker, Mrs. John Martin, Maurice Ingle, Mrs. Elbert Traylor, T.F. Rooks, Hazel Ingle, Maynard Thompson and Naomi Thompson. In 2000 we are blessed to still have Naomi Thompson and Maurice Ingle (Maurice has been Church Treasurer since 1961. He served as assistant treasurer and financial secretary from 1950 to 1961.).

The following were Elders in 1972: Harold Sullivan, Maurice Ingle, Lawrence Nix, Dewey Scott, Ned Gable, and Snead Johnson. And, the deacons were: Ed Brett, Jodie Parker, Chester Mitchell, Gary Aldridge, J.B. Branon, Jerry Latimer, Milford Weathington, Hamp Sullivan, Grady Baker, Herb Sullivan, Michael Musick, and William Arwood. The following were staff members in 1972: Minister Deering Manning, Youth Director Joe Street, Secretary Anne Jones, Custodian Richard Jones and Director of Music Louanne Hutcheson.

Serving for a decade or longer in the music department with Louanne Hutcheson are Susan Ingle, Dawn Broome, Martha Kay Williamson, Florence Treadwell, Flora Brett, James Hutcheson, Mike Broome, Richard Ingle, and Snead and Marie Johnson.

Long term teachers, for at least ten years, who are still teaching: Maurice Ingle, Marvin Horsley, Richard Ingle, Edith Baskin, James and Irene Duffey, Marie Johnson, Joey Westbrook, Neva Higgs, Jill Colwell, Donald and Violette Denney.

Missions have always been an important part of the Church and over 20% of the total budget is devoted to world-wide evangelism. We have had hands-on participation in training ministers and building church buildings in Sri Lanka and India.

The youth program has steadily grown over the last ten years under the leadership of Dwayne Hicks. A "Power House" was purchased for youth activities and Bible Study in 1991 and seven choir tours have resulted from the musical talent in this group. All youth are encouraged to attend conventions and Woodland Christian Camp with scholarships being provided as needed.

Elders for the year 2001 are: Mike Broome, Nathan Collins, Donald Denney, James Duffey, Keith Higgs, Richard Ingle, Dale Johnson, Larry King, Frank McMonigle, Sonny Reeves, Greg Shackelford, Herb Strobino, and Phillip Wynne. Elected to serve as Deacons: Mark Anderson, Morgan Brooks, Kevin Charest, Johnny Culwell, Mike Farr, Jack Harris, Scotty Hicks, Jay Horsley, Curtis North, Brad Tuggle, Tony Ward, and Danny Weathington. The Church Staff consist of the following personnel: Minister Fred Skinner, Youth Minister Dwayne Hicks, Children's Minister Skip Broome, Youth Intern Jordan Weldon, Secretary Kari Jarrett, Music Director Louanne Hutcheson, and Custodian Bud Streetman.

Serving as President (1947 to 2000) of the Women's Council: Christine Powell, Corrine Martin, Inez Presnal, Marietta Ingle, Marie Johnson, Irene Duffey, Montes Kenerly, Buvena Rooks, Marjorie Aldridge, Hilda Lambert, Martha Jackson, Martha Kay Williamson, Elizabeth Weathington, Terri Tucker, June Strobino, Betty Harris, Susan Ingle, Letha Chambers, Violette Denney, and serving again in 2000 is Irene Duffey who has served a total of five years.

Submitted by:
Violette H. Denney,
135 Maple Hill Road,
Carrollton, GA 30116-7014

Source: Church Records

First Christian Church, 306 College Street, Carrollton, Georgia, by Bill Anderson.

MIDWAY MACEDONIA BAPTIST CHURCH

Todd Wright, Pastor

"A Fellowship of Excitement"

2000-2001 New building on the hill!

1969 Church building completely remodeled.

1865-1876 Third building constructed.

1858 Erected a larger building across the road from the original log cabin.

The Baptist Church of Christ was established on July 15, 1847 with 11 members. Currently the facility has primary seating to accommodate over 1100 in one service.

Purpose Statement: Midway Macedonia exists to reach non-believers and equip believers to love and honor God through obedience and personal ministry throughout the world.

10 Core Values (1) We desire for MMBC to be more and more like Jesus. (2) We consider personal worship of God to be our number one ministry priority. (3) We are committed to reaching as many people for Christ as possible, locally and globally. (4) We believe preaching and teaching God's work is central to disciplining believers. (5) We believe in the unchanging message of the Gospel. (6) We are committed to having a "Kingdom Vision" for ministry. (7) We are committed to being faithful stewards. (8) We believe prayer is our power source. (9) We are committed to ministry with excellence. (10) We believe in "Extra Mile" servant ministry.

3915 Carrollton-Villa Rica Highway • 770-832-9605 • www.midwaymacedonia.com

ROOPVILLE BAPTIST CHURCH

Old Fashion Day - 1985

New Church Van

Old Fashion Day, 1985, Lunch at Church

Old Fashion Day
Audie Causey

1985 Children's Choir

1985 Adult Choir

Youth Valentine Party

Ruth Farr and Pearl Bell

Valentine Party, Terrell Bailey and Joan McWhorter

Lucy M. Woodbury, Nell M. Reagan, Walter Johnson and Barney Garrett

Jean Johnson Daniel and Emily Huckeba

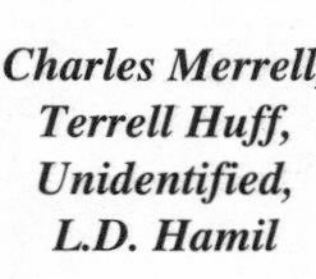

Charles Merrell, Terrell Huff, Unidentified, L.D. Hamil

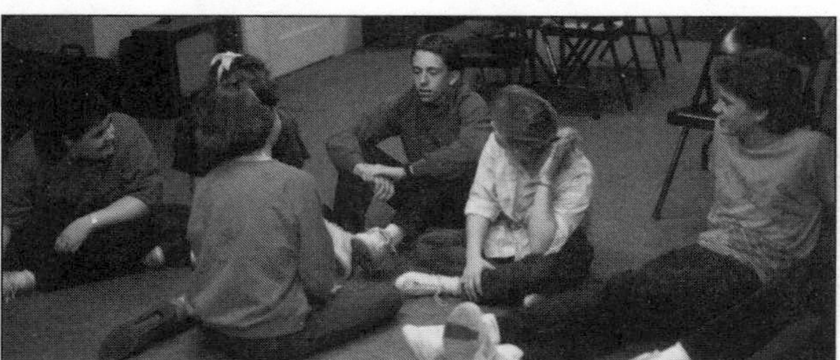

Youth Lock-In

Roopville Yesterday ...

Thomas W. Roop

James C. Story

Ed Pentecost

William Arthur Garrett

Jack and Genevia Towns at Roopville Baptist Church

Gus Reid

Rev. W.W. Roop

Florida Alexander Roop Brock

Ed and Annie Pentecost

Henry Brock

Henry Brock

Guthrie Hotel

Joseph G. Dean Family

Terrell Huff

Odus D. and Jenny M. Garrett

... and Roopville Today

Flag Bearers 1976 Parade

Parade 2000
Central High School Band

Bobby Holcombe

Roopville Elementary Cheerleaders
2000 Parade

Roopville Baptist Church

Ribbon Cutting at the Roopville By-pass

Festival 2000 Peggy's Dance School

New Park Picnic Tables, Judson Bell,
Curtis Spivey, Phil Cantrell, Bob Merrell

City Christmas Dinner, Rodney Farmer, Rebecca
Merrell, Amari Reid, Caleb and D.J. Johnson

1976 Baptist Church Parade, Children's Choir
and Mrs. Huckeba

1985 Parade, Steve and Barbara Dean,
Irene Teal

1997 Christmas Dinner, Senator Sam Roberts
and Family, Sheriff Tony Reeve

Renovation on Bank, Sherrell Fordice
and Bobby Holcombe

Santa and Mrs. Clause
Judson and Nancy Bell

Centennial Celebration
1885, Rebecca and
Bob Merrell, Judson Bell

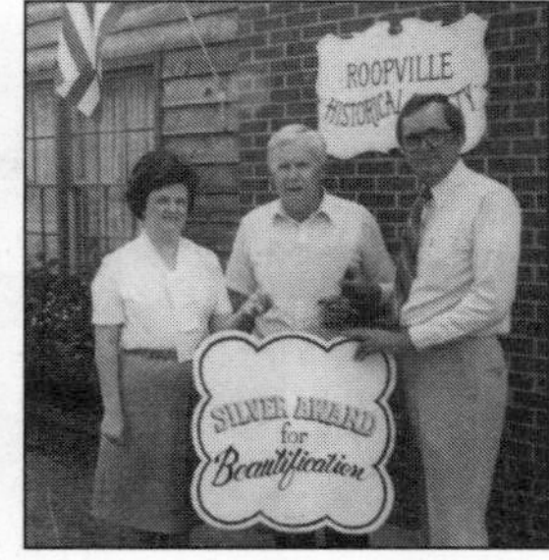

Emily Huckeba, J.L. Dean
and Mr. Nunis
Chamber of Commerce

Doris and Jesse Bell
on a bicycle built for two.

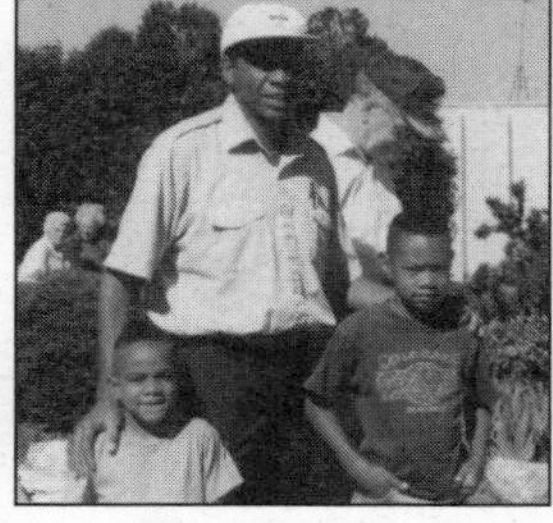
Enjoying the Parade
Emmanuel Reid, Bob
Merrell, Lenard and
Hyrum Reid

Villa Rica High School

— Class of 1950 —

Villa Rica High School - Class of 1950

We remember with fondness and love the members of our class that are deceased. The following have gone before us: Hubert Chandler, Joe Dorough, Frank Duncan, Wanna Formby Whitaker, Doris Graben, David Harris, Durwood Herrell, Tommy Hooten, E.L. Langley, Betty Lloyd, Ruby Dean Morrow, Hamey Pace Skinner, Edwin Smith, Jimmy Williams, and W.H. Ward.

Pictured at the 45th year reunion on October 7, 1995, front row beginning on the left: Bobbie Jo Willis Raven, Mary Nell Furr Pilgrim, Hazel Spake Roberts, Christine Walker Turner, Martha Sue Horsley Hesterlee, Louise Muse Petty and Joe Porter (teacher); second row: Albert Ariail (teacher), Eva Hamrick (teacher), Nell Phillips Waller, Violette Harris Denney, Harold Petty, Betty Brown Jeffers, Edith Howell Sauls, Carolyn Dodgen Watters, Jean Walton Craft and Nancy Willis Howell; third row: Jack Morris, Lester McLain, Bobby Broom, Ronald Tyson, S.W. Roberts, Jr., James Smith, Billy Smith, Richard Roberds, Clyde Golden, Kenneth Dobbins and W.H. Ward.

The Villa Rica Graduating Class of 1950 observed their 50th Year reunion on October 7, 2000. Pictured from left to right, back row: Ronald Tyson, Kenneth Dobbins, Bob Broom, Sam Roberts, Billy Smith, Lester McLain, Jack Morris, Bob Hamrick, Jimmy Wallace and James Smith; middle row: Christine Walker Turner, Hazel Spake Roberts, Edith Howell Sauls, Mary Nell Furr Pilgrim, Harold Petty, Louise Muse Petty, Nancy Willis Howell, Don Carroll and Clyde Golden; front row: Carolyn Dodgen Watters, Imogene Blair, Betty Brown Jeffers, Violette Harris Denney, Louise Gilley Estep, Martha Sue Horsley Hesterlee, Melba Stitcher Keaton, Jean Walton Craft, Wynelle Thompson Lewis and teacher, Joe Porter.

45th Year Class Reunion - 1995

50th Year Golden Reunion - 2000

Submitted by: Violette Harris Denney, and the VRHS Class of 1950, 135 Maple Hill Road, Carrollton, GA 30116-7014

VICTORY UNITED METHODIST CHURCH

What once was lost ...

Old Victory Church

On August 12, 1999, a fire caused by lightning destroyed the original Victory Church. We want to thank every one who contributed to the rebuilding of our new church which was dedicated on August 5, 2001.

... has now been rebuilt!

Victory United Methodist Church - 2001

VICTORY

Victory, Oh Victory, Again, how proud you stand,
On the hill o'er the green meadow,
Symbol of the goodness of man.
Oh yes, our church was lovely, It's members satisfied,
Till the thunder of that evening day,
Took away our complacent pride.
As we look at the burned-out building, And saw the task ahead,
We didn't have a plan in mind,
We stood by faith instead.
Both friends and strangers from afar, Answered "Let me be a part,"
And they gave in heaping measure,
To build this work of art.
The spirit of the workmen, Was something to behold,
A sermon from the pulpit,
Could not be better told.
We are so very grateful, For the work of many hands,
For all the contributions,
From throughout our nation's land.
This church is our testimony, A victory of God's love,
We want to return our blessings,
and find more ways to serve.
So as you travel down the road, Along life's busy pace,
Please stop and rest at Victory,
God's quiet holy place.

Gwyn Chesnut - August 5, 2001

Worship Service

11 A.M.
Every First Sunday

Tommy Greer, Pastor

1994 Victory Church Road
Bowdon, Georgia

City of Villa Rica

Villa Rica had its beginning in Philadelphia, Pennsylvania. This was in a tavern in 1823, when a group of men gathered to discuss the possibilities of mining gold southward through the Appalachian Mountains. These men were from Pennsylvania, New Jersey and Delaware. They loaded their wagons and started the journey south. This journey took three years. On April 18, 1826 following Sweetwater Creek, they arrived in what is now Villa Rica.

Approximately two miles northeast of Villa Rica, they discovered where Creek Indians had been mining gold. It was the richest vein of gold they had seen yet. Here they set up a mining camp and dubbed it Pine Town. So it was decided to make this area their home. From Pine Town they moved the settlement to what is now the old town area of Villa Rica. Log houses, taverns, stores and saloons sprang up along almost the exact same route as the present Dallas Highway. That settlement was known as Hixtown.

Early Settlers Working Gold Deposits

Most of the gold found was in the form of dust. The first method used in finding the gold was called panning. Using this method, the miners placed the dirt, gravel and gold rocks in a long handled skillet and covered with water. Then by rocking it from side to side with the debris sloshing over the side, the miner continuously replaced the water until only the gold dust remained. Quicksilver was used in collecting the gold around the edge of the skillet. After it dried, the gold was scooped up in a goose quill.

The placer or rocker method involved the splitting of a tree trunk, hollowing out the inside and lining it with metal sheeting containing tiny holes. Handles, placed on either end, were grasped by two men who rocked it gently as they would a cradle. Like panning, the sand and gravel settled to the bottom and gold would be removed.

In 1915-1917, T.H. Aldridge, Henry Adolphus Stockmar, a Mr. Pasley and a Mr. Treptor introduced the chemical method. Using this method, rocks were blasted and placed in huge concrete vats over which was placed a combination of water and chemicals. The gold was liquefied then returned to solid state and refined. The mines were worked again around 1925-26 but the mining expense was higher than the worth of gold found. Thus, the era of gold mining ended.

Ore Tanks each hold 350 tons of gold ore. There are two tanks still in existence at the Villa Rica mine.

Then in 1882 came the event that changed the history and direction of the town. A large tract of land that lay to the south of Villa Rica, extending from Hixon's Bridge on the west to New Hope Church on

FRIERSON & LEAK · · · · · · Auctioneers.

BIG SALE AND EXCURSION

VILLA — "VILLAGE OF GOLD." — RICA

THIRTY-EIGHT MILES ON G. P. R. R.

94 Beautiful Lots at Auction

TUESDAY, AUGUST 15th.

Delightful Ride Over the New G. P. R. R. Pleasant Recreation and Dinner in the Shady Grove.

1881 Notice of Land Auction "Thirty Eight Miles" west of Atlanta in Villa Rica which brought in people from everywhere.

Cotton Gin on Temple Street

the east, was owned by Allison Cheves and known as Chevestown. Through Chevestown came the Georgia-Pacific Railroad. Several buildings were moved from "Old Town" to the new location; this was accomplished by rolling the buildings down the road on logs. Crowds of people gathered from miles around to witness the arrival of the first train. The men were interested in the engine, while the ladies were in awe over the two small coaches, with gaslights and upholstered seats of red velvet. On August 15, 1881 an excursion was organized by the Georgia-Pacific Railroad to Villa Rica where an auction was held and the lots for the downtown area were sold.

Mrs. S.C. (Martha Beall) Chandler and Dr. Hodgson named the new town Villa Rica, which means "Rich Village" in Spanish. Villa Rica was incorporated on September 13, 1883 by the General Assembly of the State of Georgia; the corporate limits of the City extended one-half mile in every direction from the Depot Building on the Georgia Pacific Railroad. It was further "enacted that an election be held on the first Thursday in October of 1883 for a Mayor and five councilmen who shall serve for one year".

Growth continued and Villa Rica became well known as an important cotton center. In the 1940's boll weevils and armyworms took their toll on the cotton crops and destroyed the agricultural era. Industries such as the hosiery and cotton mills remained to rescue the economy.

Three major tragedies have struck the town; in 1908 fire destroyed a city block on Montgomery Street. Some years later a fire destroyed a business block on Main Street and in 1957 a gas explosion caused many injuries and deaths. This explosion completely destroyed four stores in downtown but typical of the Villa Rica citizens, each time they bounced back with renewed hope.

Today, Villa Rica is one of the largest towns in Carroll County with a population of over 5,000.

UNION CROSSROADS SCHOOL

Mrs. L.L. Brock furnished this picture which was made in 1909 or 1910 at Union Crossroads School which was located on the Miller Academy road. Members of the class were: back row, from left, Miss Mamie Blandenburg, teacher, Arthur Stamps, Bertha Lambert, Jewell Johnson, Beulah Bell, Lola Cole, Olin Stamps, George Bell and Homer Miller; second row from back, Emmett Miller, Frank Eidson, Delphia Weir, Mamae Johnson, Leon Stamps, Effie Maxwell, Lulah Bell, Vera Cole, and Mary Cole; third row from back, Grady Eidson, Harvey Cole, Lizzie Maxwell, Loyd Green, Roy Cole, William Eidson, Miller Ferrell Johnson, Lewis Weir, Percy Johnson, and Selvey Jones; fourth row from back, Ora Brock, Laura Stamps, Vera Brock, Myrtie Kierbow, Vesper Stamps, Lewis McKissick, Grady Bell, Loy McKissick, Aubrey Hammond, Hesper Miller, Felix Cole; front row from left, Henry Jones, Ralph Cole, Winnie Cole, Etta Brock, Alma Cole, Ione Kierbow, Eula Green, Lula Stamps, Lula Maxwell, Ruby Bell, Lavada Cole, Ruth Cole, Maulsie Jones, and Bertha Stamps. – Submitted by: Gradyne Bell Myers

In Memory of

Judie Seals Bailey

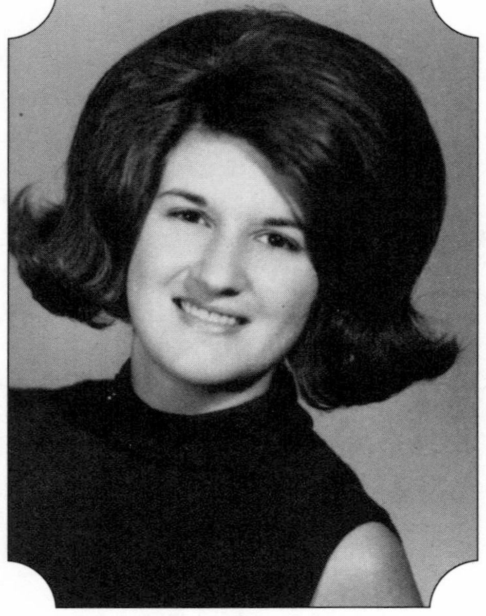

November 30, 1947 - October 30, 1969
Daughter of Max and Dorothy Allen Seals

In Memory of

James Fred and Cleo Patra Morgan Hollingsworth

James Fred Hollingsworth
b. February 27, 1896 d. July 9, 1980

Cleo Patra Morgan Hollingsworth
b. November 28, 1898 d. August 17, 1981

Submitted by: daughter Caroline Hollingsworth Chappell

City of Whitesburg

On March 2, 1874, an act of the General Assembly of Georgia was approved to incorporate the town of Whitesburg, in Carroll County, GA. It was enacted in this act that the corporate limits of the town should extend one half mile in every direction from the depot of the Savannah, Griffin, and North Alabama Railroad, and that John O'Rear, W.W. Boone, J.W.B. Kelley, J.A. McMullen and John S. Pentecost were appointed commissioners of the town.

Whitesburg had been settled as a town in 1872. The railroad crossed the Chattahoochee River and reached Whitesburg in 1873. Captain W.W. Harris was the first depot agent in town.

Whitesburg School, 1926-1960

Professor Henry Newton built a good one room school house about 1873. Wings and other additions were built onto the original one room from time to time. In October, 1929, a brick school house was completed. This school served Whitesburg and surrounding areas for many years. In 1976 a new school building was erected.

Captain L. Kendrick owned one of the first stores in Whitesburg. Captain Kendrick owned considerable land around Whitesburg, and it was he who donated the land for the City Cemetery.

March 1, 1874 saw the organization of Whitesburg M.E. Church. Many members came from New Hope Church and entered Whitesburg Church as charter members, helping to organize the new church. In 1895 they had 357 members. The trustees of the church operated a school for several years. Along about 1901 to 1903, only about ten years after the school had been placed in the hands of the local church trustees, it became difficult to find the money to keep the school running.

The Whitesburg Baptist Church began as the New Providence Baptist Church, which was organized and it's meetings held some miles west of Whitesburg. New Providence moved to town and sometime between 1874 and 1875, New Providence changed its name to Whitesburg Baptist Church, and built a new and substantial church house. Captain W.W. Harris owned land in Whitesburg, and donated the land on which the Baptist Church was built.

The Masonic Lodge was organized in Whitesburg in 1891.

J.W.B. Kelley edited a newspaper in Whitesburg for a while. Later Mr. Kelley was connected with the *Carroll County Times*.

F. Roy Almon came to Whitesburg in 1903. He perhaps more than any other, put Whitesburg upon the map of Georgia, with his breezy articles which appeared each week in the *Carroll County Times* signed R-O-Y.

Jeremiah A. McMullen is said to have been Whitesburg's first postmaster. In 1938 Mrs. Jewel Bailey became postmaster. Wilson Holder became postmaster in 1950. The current postmaster, Mrs. Imogene Richards Frazier, has held the position since 1978.

Rural free delivery of mail began from Whitesburg, with Route 1 being established February, 1903. Route 2 was established November, 1903. In 1916, Route 3 was established. Benjamin L. Camp was a rural mail carrier of Route 1. He was president of the Georgia Rural Letter Carriers Association in the 1920s. From the obituary of George W. Rooks, dated September 26, 1929, he was a rural mail carrier on Route 2 for many years. Hamilton Morris was a rural mail carrier for Routes 2 and 3 for 40 years.

Whitesburg's first bank was organized in 1907. The first president was the Hon. Jethro Jones, a planter who lived only a few miles from town. Mr. Jones was murdered in 1907 by a band of cotton thieves, whom he apprehended in the act of carrying off his cotton. After his death, his oldest son, William Tyre Jones, succeeded him as president of the bank. He died of pneumonia in January 1923, and was succeeded by Mr. T.W. Camp.

1937 Post Office in Whitesburg

In 1916, under the administration of T.J. Jones as mayor, Whitesburg installed an electric light system. With the advent of electricity the town soon had an electric corn mill. The mill was installed by T.J. Jones, William T., and R.E.L. Jones.

George W. Rooks wanted to see a Christian Church in Whitesburg. He contacted Preacher Dodson of Atlanta. Owen Still came to Whitesburg and ran a three week evangelistic meeting in October, 1920. The congregation met in the Whitesburg school building until they could find a desirable lot upon which to build the church. Land was donated by Mr. and Mrs. Harry Love. The first church was completed in October, 1921.

In 1925, C.D. Goodroe installed a mattress factory in the brick warehouse built by the Jones brothers. This business was known as the Lucile Manufacturing Company. There was a furniture shop added to this. In 1926, another mattress factory was installed by R.L. Huggins, a former employee of the Lucile Manufacturing Company.

The town well, which for perhaps forty years was in the center of the main street of the town, with watering troughs built around it, was filled in, in 1926. This was the year when State Highway No. 16 was being built. Another well was dug in a more out of the way place.

In the early summer of 1926, fire of unknown origin started in the night and destroyed seven of the old business houses of the town. No residences were burned. Had it not been for the cool determination of the people of Whitesburg, the entire town, residences, churches and all, would probably have been destroyed that night.

There was only one hotel ever built in the town. It was famous in the early history of the town and was kept by Captain W.W. Harris. It was torn down in 1927.

In 1928 there were five grocery stores, three general merchandise stores, one restaurant, one lunch house, two blacksmith shops, one automobile repair shop, one drug store, one barber shop, one soda fountain, and two or three homes that had meals and lodgings.

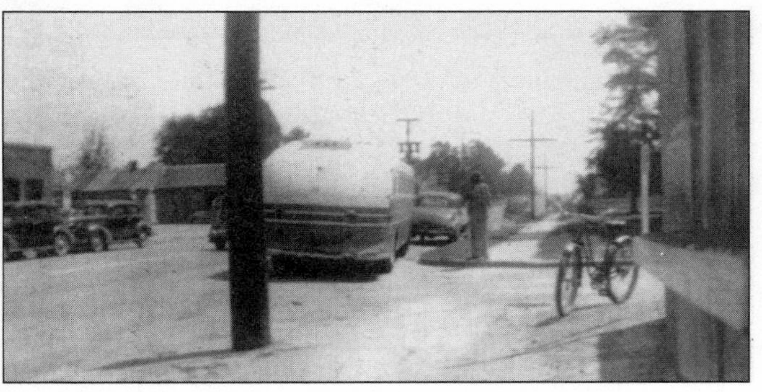

Southeastern Motor Lines Bus.
The transportation to Carrollton in 1940.

Virginia Manufacturing Company was established in Whitesburg in the late 1940s. Prior to this, Whitesburg had a cotton mill. In 1957, Virginia Manufacturing Company became West Georgia Mills. In the late 1960s the company became Wellington Georgia Mills.

In 1952, under the leadership of Douglas Holloway as mayor, Whitesburg gained a city water system.

Tradition says that Captain W.W. Harris was the first mayor of Whitesburg. Some of the early mayors were, Dr. W.F. Friddell, J.O. Almon, Welcome Parks, Dr. G.W. Burnett, W.S. Cruse, C.A. Duncan, T.R. Watkins, W.B. Kelley, Thomas J. Jones, H.R. Watkins, W.F. Lassetter, J.A. Sims, C.O. Jones, and W.T. Richards.

Some of the other mayors of Whitesburg have been, Lewie Morgan, Lewis Stevens, and Johnny Hight. The only woman to ever be mayor of Whitesburg was Rebecca Mayfield. Robert Gamble held the position of mayor for 13 years. The current mayor is Bud Hines.

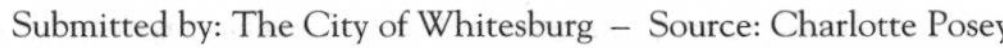

Submitted by: The City of Whitesburg – Source: Charlotte Posey

To honor and remember

Samuel Newton and Annie Ruth Martin Boggs

and the

Dimmock and Martin Families

This page is in honor of our parents, Samuel Newton and Annie Ruth Boggs. They were descendants of Irish-Scottish-English Ancestors. Also, honored with this memoriam are the families of Dimmock and Martin, of which our mother was a descendant. Our father came to Carroll County from Union County, North Carolina. He lived in the Hickory Level Community. Our mother was born in the Carrollton Area. They had six children that consisted of five males and one female. They lived primarily at Forty Stewart Street. Annie Ruth attended West Georgia College and was a music teacher. Samuel Newton was at one time a fireman but was basically a barber. He raised racehorses and won many trophies. All of their sons served in W.W.II. Malcolm, Jason, and James served their country not only in W.W.II but also in the Korean and Vietnam conflicts.

This picture, which was taken in 1931 at the corner of Stewart and Sims Streets, includes not only the Boggs Family but also the Dimmock and Martin Families. Pictured from the left in the back is John Martin, Ruff Martin, Sam Martin, Tom Martin, Earl Martin, Billy Boggs, Gerald Martin, Doris Dasher, and Louise Martin. In the next to the back row is Bob Martin, Mary Ella Martin, and James Boggs. Front row, Edna Earl Martin, Mary Frances Dimmock, Howard Martin, Corrine Martin, Helen Martin, Flonnie May Dasher Martin with Carolyn, Annie Ruth Martin Boggs with Wade, Thomas Earl Martin, Grandmother Molly (Mrs. Emmanuel Butler Martin), Mattie Dimmock, Minnie Martin, Edna Martin, and Sue Martin. Sitting on the ground in front is Malcolm Pierce Boggs, Bertha Dimmock, Molly Ann Boggs, Lillian Martin, and Ida Martin.

I am Malcolm Pierce Boggs, born July 2, 1926, and I married Juanita Jarrell on September 3, 1954. Our four children are Malcolm Pierce Jr., Patricia Ann, George Samuel and Jane Leigh. Juanita Jarrell Boggs was born September 3, 1931 and she died April 19, 1995. She is buried in the Greenville City Cemetery.

Submitted by: Malcolm Boggs, 1779 Clegs Ferry Road, Greenville, GA 30222

Joseph Warner Stone Memorial

October 28, 1874 - October 29, 1936

"The many friends of Mr. J. Warner Stone were inexpressibly shocked at the news of his sudden death on Thursday afternoon at 2:30 o'clock at his home on Center Street in this city. On that day he had been attending to his business affairs as usual, he having made a trip to the section around Hulett to show a prospective purchaser a farm, and in going over the property received a fall that was severe. But he did not think the injury he received of enough importance to consult a physician. On his return he went home for mid-day meal and retired for a rest when stricken. He was 62 years of age, having been born at Villa Rica in 1874 and spent all his entire life in Carroll County, and for the last thirty-one years made his home in Carrollton.

He was one of the most useful and outstanding citizens of Carrollton and Carroll County, and served the people in a number of public and private capacities. He was Clerk of the Superior and City Courts for eight years. He was a member of the Board of County Tax Assessors and was County Administrator at the time of his death. He served as member of Carroll County Draft Board during the late World War. He was a director of the Peoples Bank of Carrollton for a number of years up to the present. Was a member of the Methodist Church practically all his life, and served as a District Lay Leader for a number of years. He was a steward of the First Methodist Church at the time of his death.

He was married to Miss Ola Dorris of Douglasville some thirty-five years ago. He is survived by his wife, daughter, Miss Dorris; three brothers, A.E. Stone, of New Orleans, Dan Stone, of California and Howard Stone, of Atlanta; five sisters, Mrs. Thos. J. Powell and Mrs. O.F. McRae, of McRae, Ga., Mrs. A.S. Sands, of Sydney, Australia and Miss Bernice Stone, of Jacksonville, Ala. Also survived by a number of nephews and nieces, one of whom is Mrs. S.J. Boykin, of Carrollton. The late Mr. E.P. Stone, of Carrollton was a brother.

The most pleasing commentary that can be said of Mr. Stone was his tender devotion to his wife and daughter and his love of home life and that when he was not attending to his business, there you would find him at home, a home which he cherished so highly that he was outspoken about it in his contacts with his fellow men.

Funeral services for Mr. Stone were conducted at the First Methodist Church on Saturday morning at 10:30 o'clock by the pastor, Rev. H.C. Emory, assisted by Rev. E.A. Kilgore.

An interesting eulogy and tribute to the life's work of the deceased was delivered by Col. W.J. Millican. Appropriate musical selections were rendered by the church choir composed of Mr. D.L. Hearn, Mr. E.W. Johnson, Mrs. W.C. Cantrell and Mrs. Carl Carter assisted by Mrs. Louise Camp.

The pallbearers were the following: S.J. Boykin, J.G. Robertson, Dr. O.W. Roberts, M.E. Griffin, J.L. Veal, L.M. King, T.J.H. Robertson and H.J. Worthy. The members of the Board of Stewards of the First Methodist Church and the members of the Carrollton Bar Association composed the honorary escort.

The large number of floral offerings attested to the love and respect for Mr. Stone by his fellow citizens and friends."

Warner Stone was one of Carroll's most widely known citizens.

Submitted by: Mrs. Dorris S. Carel, c/o Mrs. Vivian C. Trammell, 803 Grindstone Place, Marietta, GA 30060

Source: Newspaper Obituary

In Loving Memory of

EDNA EARLE TEAL, R.N.

Submitted by:
Edna Teal Mission Group,
First Baptist Church, Villa Rica, Georgia

Born April 15, 1879, in the Villa Rica area, appointed by Southern Baptist Convention 1910 as a medical and evangelistic missionary to Yang Chow, China, Kiangsu Province. Retired 1943; returned to Villa Rica to live and minister until her Heavenly departure March 11, 1968.

This memorial page is dedicated by Denzel Burnham to

Joel and Mary Caroline Burnham, my grandparents; Walter and Callie Burnham, my parents; and Annelle Smith Burnham, my beloved wife.

Joel Colley Burnham, born in 1828, served as a private, second corporal, fifth sergeant, and regimental chaplain in the Confederate States Army. He surrendered with General Robert E. Lee on April 9, 1865, at Appomattox. After the war, the Reverend Burnham married his wife, who was 20 years younger, and moved to Carroll County. Blessed with nine children, the Burnham's seventh child, born on December 3, 1886, was Walter Leonard Burnham. On January 2, 1908, Walter married Callie Braselle Hancock. A farmer, policeman, saw miller, car salesman, and later the Superintendent of City Streets in Carrollton, he was honored by having a street named after him. Walter and Callie's eldest child was Denzel Fay Burnham, born September 8, 1910. On October 10, 1937, he married Annelle Francis Smith, daughter of William Eugene Smith, a school superintendent, and Mattie Griffin, homemaker and church pianist at Wesley Chapel Methodist Church. Denzel was employed from 1930-39 in the Carrollton water, fire, and streets department, then served three years as Superintendent of Works Projects Administration, and in 1943 was hired by the City of Dalton and later became Superintendent of Water, Gas, and Sewer services. It was here he earned the nickname of "Mr. Utility." He and Annelle celebrated 61 years of marriage and were members of the Dalton Methodist Church for 56 years before her death in 1998. Together they lived through 15 different Presidents, two world wars, the Korean and Viet Nam War. Dedicated to her job of mother and homemaker, Annelle raised their three children to serve others. Michael works with GMAAC, a resource for refugee and immigrant youth in Atlanta, David is a Christian songwriter and guitarist located in Greenville, and Linda is a freelance Christian writer who resides in Nashville, Georgia.

Joel Colley and Mary Caroline Burnham

Walter Leonard and Callie Hancock Burnham

Denzel Fay and Annelle Smith Burnham

Denzel Burnham (3rd from left) with children David Gene Burnham, Linda Burnham Yawn, and Michael Denzel Burnham

Submitted by: D.F. Burnham, 1008 W. Willow Park Dr., Dalton, GA 30720

In loving memory of our Parents

Claude "Lewis" and Louise Howell Carden

Lewis and Louise loved their family.
They enjoyed having a good time
with family and friends.
We all loved being with them at home!
And, we will again!

Bette and Carlton Boyd,
Hugh and Trudy Boyd,
Jeff and Melissa Boyd,
Frances, Robert and Reneé Banks,
Wendell and Sue Carden Sticher,
Buddy and Lisa Sticher Thompson,
John and Terry Sticher,
Jason and Kim Sticher,
Randy Carden, Bryan and Sally Carden,
Jackie Ray and Sylvia Carden Vietch,
And, all the Great Grandchildren.

Melissa Collins Memorial

"Her love and smile is shining down from Heaven upon all of us. She would want us to be strong and keep a smile on our faces until we meet again!"

-quote from a close friend.

We love you and miss you!
July 18, 1980 - November 2, 1998

"Growing Love"

Love is all around you.
As you sit and watch
Couples walking by holding hands ...
Friends chatting merrily ...
And children playing games ...
You realize that love is an evolving feeling.
Life without love would be hollow.

Spending your life
In love ... Together ...
Sharing everything ...
Has to be an earth-shattering experience.

Mourning the loss of a loved one is
A long, saddening process.
After you begin to heal the deep wounds of loss,
The memories allow you to still feel
As if the loved one is with you.
Although the love between the two-can
No longer be physically expressed,
The emotional love will never die.

As long as we never forget
Those who have gone before us ...
And always remember those to come ...
Love will never die.

-exert from essay written within the last month of Melissa's life.

In Loving Memory of

Charles Royce Conkle, Sr.

Born February 9, 1922 - Died September 13, 1998

Royce was a dedicated Christian and served his Lord faithfully as an ordained Deacon and in many other capacities.

This is in tribute to a kind, gentle, and loving husband and father, by his wife, Betty, and children, Charles Royce Conkle, Jr., Victor Lynn Conkle and Constance Conkle Jarrell.

He was proud of his grandchildren, Christi Conkle Sauls, Vickie Conkle Clark, John Conkle, Paul Jarrell and Emily Jarrell, and great-grandchildren, Katelyn Sauls, Trevor, Amber and Kaitlin Clark.

Royce served his country proudly in the U.S. Army, 1942-1945, in World War II, 84th Div. Co. B. Med. Bn. He fought in Germany in the Battle of Bulge, earned three battle stars and the Bronze Star Medal for meritorious service.

What can we say? We miss You!

In Honor and Memory of the

G.L. Downs Family of Bowdon, Georgia

George Luna Downs
1871-1940

George and Hettie Downs
1933

Hettie B. Lipham
Downs
1875-1952

Evie Downs Johnson
1894-1938

Ruth Downs Wilson
1897-1940

William Olin Downs
1899-1961

Charles Emory Downs
1901-1972

Mary Downs Smith
1906-1990

Mildred Downs Steele
1912-1997

Submitted by: Eloise Wilson Downey

Holly Elizabeth Harman

November 21, 1976 - January 19, 2000

Holly Elizabeth Harman was in a coma from October 1996 until her death in January 2000. Holly fell into a coma after being given a date rape drug called G.H.B. Holly was a beautiful young lady who loved life and had countless numbers of friends. She was such a loving, giving and active person. She was always busy and friendly - she never met a stranger. Holly played basketball, softball and ran track at Carrollton Schools, Recreation Department and Oak Mountain. Holly graduated from Carrollton High School and was attending West Georgia College at the time of her hospitalization. Holly was the daughter of Karen Marlow and Ned and Patty Harman. Holly's brother Luke preceded her in death. Holly's living sisters are Dawn Harman and Rachel Phillips Robinson. Her living brothers are Shane Harman and Josh Harman. Holly is loved and missed by all.

Submitted by: Ned Harman

A Memorial to my parents

Hillard C. Seaton & Virginia Cole Seaton

February 21, 1911 - October 1, 1993 **August 28, 1913 - April 11, 1999**

Hill Seaton came to Carrollton after W.W.II and became the Area Conservationist for The U.S. Soil and Water Conservation Service. He also served as Head of the Civil Defense Unit. Seaton was instrumental in the development of the watershed system and the building of Lake Carroll that both supply Carrollton's water today. Virginia "Miss Jinny" Seaton was well known for her canning and preserving of the bounty produced by Seaton's farm. She cultivated over 300 beautiful azaleas in her yard. The Seatons were lifelong members of the First United Methodist Church. They are buried at Carroll Memory Gardens. *Submitted by: Bill Seaton*

"Jinny" Virginia Seaton with Bill and Ann Seaton

Bill Seaton and Bob Newell

Ann Seaton and Margaret Rose Piano Recital

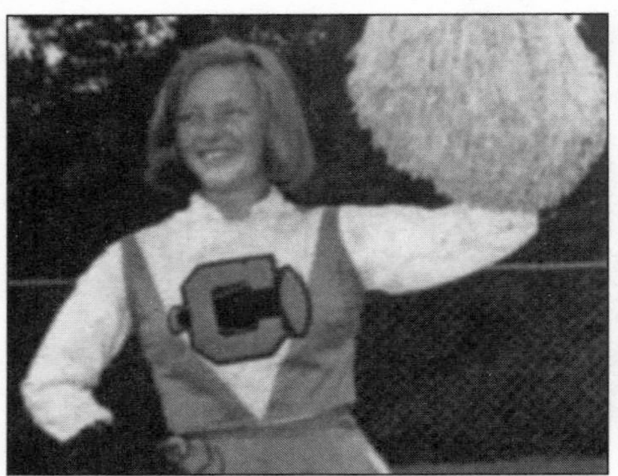

Ann Seaton - Carrollton High School Cheerleader

The Seaton Family

Hill Seaton

Jinny and Hill Seaton and Grandson

Both Hill and son Bill served as Presidents of Rotary

Bill with sons Michael and David and a friend

The Harris Family

David Terrell "Terry" Martin

Oct. 16, 1949 - Aug. 30, 1986
Son of Earl Martin & June H. Strobino
Brothers: Keith Martin & Jody Rollins
Married: Linda Akin, Dec. 7, 1969
Sons: Chris and David Martin
Served: US Navy, Nuclear Submarines
Jan. 7, 1969 to Nov. 12, 1972

Anthony Scott Denney

Apr. 3, 1975 - Aug. 29, 1976
"Heaven seems even sweeter now."
(Grandson of Violette)

With love and honor we remember our parents Jesse Terrell (1905-1985) and Elma Patterson Harris (1906-1982). They are pictured above on their Golden Wedding Anniversary, December 23, 1975, surrounded by their most prized possession, their children. Their sons from left to right are Owen Conner, J.T. Jr. (1929-1993), and Dennis Hoyt Harris. Their seven daughters are Wynona Payton, Johnnie Baldwin, Francine Bundrum, Violette Denney, Glenda Middleton, June Strobino, and Julia Swanner. We treasure the sweetness of our precious memories.

E.N. Keith Family Memorial

Bill Reynolds, Gov. George Busbee, Grace Keith, Mrs. Charles Walker and Mrs. Reuben Walker at the Cattlemen's Association.

"Father and Son"
E.N. Keith Sr. and Jr.

E.N. and Grace Luther Keith on their wedding day - June 8, 1940.

Grace Keith (2nd. from right).
"Pink Ladies"

Grace & E.N. Keith on their Honeymoon in 1940.

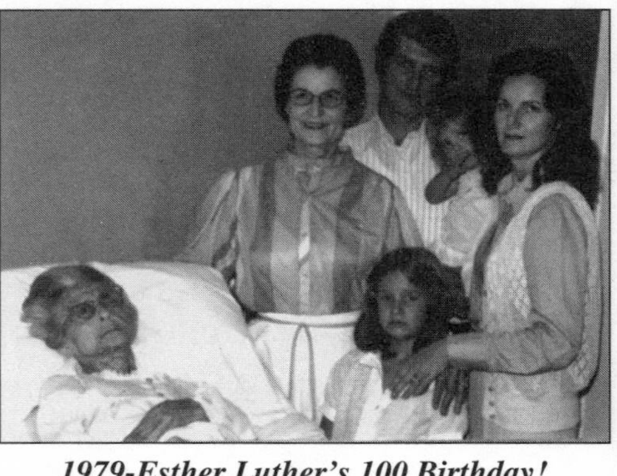

1979-Esther Luther's 100 Birthday! with Grace, Etheridge, Judy, Amanda & Ashley

Etheridge Keith
High School Years.

Judy and Etheridge Keith

Grace and E.N. Keith in front of their home and beautiful Azaleas.

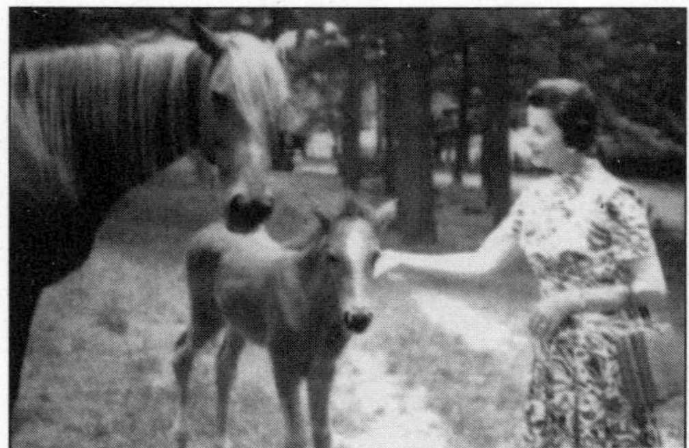

Grace Keith loved horses! After this picture was made, the horse ate Grace's straw purse ...

Grace & E.N. Keith

E.N. Keith Family Memorial

Miss Wawena Hughes' first grade class at Maple Street School in 1952.

E.N. and Grace Keith
Judy and Etheridge

E.N. Keith, R.W. Oertel and Judge
Robert D. Tisinger at Lions Club.

1935 Civil Conservation Corps at Villa Rica
E.N. Keith (far left).

Amanda Harrill,
Ashley Harrill Bedosky,
Grace Keith and
Judy Harrill

C.J. Lee, Horace Luther, Frank Green, Robert McDowell
of Villa Rica Masonic Lodge #72 F&AM receiving 50 year membership awards.

Piano Recital - Pupils of Mary Lou Munn

6-2-1959 - 7th Grade Graduation Dance
at Sunset Hills Country Club.

Contributed by Judy Keith Harrill

IN MEMORIAM

Etheridge Norton Keith, Jr.

Etheridge Norton Keith, Jr. was born 30 April 1943, the son of E.N. Keith, Sr. and Grace Luther Keith. Etheridge grew up in Carrollton, Georgia and attended Carrollton High School. Like his father, Etheridge had the love of the land from the beginning. He was a natural born farmer and spent much of his time on the Keith farm learning animal husbandry. He loved the 175 year old cabin that was built there by the original Carroll County settlers.

Etheridge followed in his father's footsteps and established his own farm close to Ranburne, Alabama. He owned 200 acres of rich farmland and the best of bulls and cattle. Etheridge was also a member of the Ranburne Fire and Rescue Squad for many years. Etheridge died tragically of a sudden heart attack in 1999 at the age of 56. His passing was mourned by both communities where he had lived, in Carroll County, Georgia and in Cleburne County, Alabama.

The name of Keith is one that dates back into greatest antiquity. It fills many volumes of the romantic tales and history of Scotland. In the times of the Roman conquest a people who called themselves Chatti lived in the area later called Germany. They were defeated by the Romans and forced to find a new country. A storm forced their ships into the north of Scotland and this is where they stayed. They were a separate people from the Scots, having their own chiefs and their own laws.

In the year 1010, the Scots won a great victory over the Danish invaders when Robert, a Prince of the Chatti, slew with his own hands Camus, the General of the Danes. King Malcom of Scotland, in whose cause Robert was fighting, came over and dipped his fingers in the blood of the slain general and then drew a red stripe across Robert's shield. This explains the significance of the red stripe on the Keith's coat of arms to this day. The King also knighted Robert and awarded him with many valuable lands in the Barony of Keith, from which Robert's descendants took their name. From this beginning came one of the most historic clans of the Scottish Highlands.

Robert Keith was appointed the hereditary Great Marshal of Scotland. This high office continued in this family for over seven hundred years. This was indicated on the Keith coat of arms by the thistles and crown, the badge of office of the Great Marshal. In 1715, the Keiths aligned themselves in the rebellion with other Highland clans on the side of James Stuart who laid claim to the English throne. Because this cause was defeated, these clans had to forfeit their lands. This began the large migration of so many Scots to America in 1715, including the Keiths.

Cornelius Keith I was born in Scotland in 1689 and married Elizabeth Johnson. They had six children together, one of whom was the son Cornelius Keith II. Cornelius Keith I was a stone cutter who made the grinding stones which were used in small grist mills. They were a necessity in that era. Cornelius Keith I was an educated man for he was a Lay Reader for the Anglican Church after he migrated to Virginia. Cornelius and Elizabeth Keith were held in high regard by their neighbors in Brunswick County, Virginia. This is evidenced by the great number of wills and deeds which they were asked to witness. Cornelius Keith I died about 1742.

Cornelius Keith II was born 2 May 1715 in Loch Lomond, Scotland. When but a small boy, he came with his family to America where they settled on the Roanoke River in Brunswick County, Virginia. Cornelius Keith II married first to Juda Thompson about 1741 and together they had 12 children. After Juda's death, Cornelius Keith II married Mary Bohannon and with her he had four more children. Their son, John Keith, is said to have "served up the British some tea" in that most famous "Boston Tea Party." John's brother, Cornelius Keith III, a son by the first wife, Juda, was also a soldier in the American Revolution. His wife, Mary Lafoon, was a heroine of the Revolution in her own right. Stories are preserved of how Mary rode her horse to warn the Americans of the advancing British. In the wild ride, her cloak was lost and captured by the British. Later on, the American soldiers returned the cloak to her. Scraps of it remain in the family to this day as treasured heirlooms.

Cornelius Keith II became the earliest pioneer of Pickens County, South Carolina, where he built a "log mansion in the wilderness." A monument has been erected to Cornelius Keith II in the Oolenoy settlement. It displays the Keith coat-of-arms with the three stag heads and the motto "Veritas Vincit - Truth Conquers." George Keith, son of Cornelius Keith III and Mary Lafoon, had a son named Cornelius after his father. This Cornelius IV married Huldah Anderson, daughter of Isaac Anderson.

As a young boy, Isaac Anderson hid in a hollow log from the Tories and lived to tell the tale. He later married Polly Lay and they "moved in a sled" to Pickens District, South Carolina when it was all grown up in cane break. Unfortunately, Indians were hostile to new settlers and five of the Anderson family were murdered in an Indian raid. Isaac and his wife Polly Lay Anderson were buried in what later became known as the Nimmons Cemetery. Cornelius IV and Huldah Anderson Keith had a son who was named Isaac Anderson Keith.

Isaac A. Keith was a Confederate soldier and he married Elizabeth McRenney. Isaac Keith served in Company B, 39th Regiment, Army of Tennessee and was captured at Vicksburg. He was later wounded at Missionary Ridge on 25 November 1863. Isaac and Elizabeth Keith were the parents of George McRenney Keith who married Amanda Adaline Donaldson. These were the parents of Etheridge Norton Keith, Sr.

Etheridge Norton Keith was born 7 July 1915 in Fulton County, Georgia, and had only one sister named Rachel. E.N. was always called "Keith" throughout his boyhood and adult life. Unfortunately, Keith lost his father in 1923 when he was only eight years old and then lost his mother in 1927 when he was only twelve. Rachel went to live with some aunts, but Keith went to live in the wonderful foster home of Clarence and Betty Peeler of Fulton County, Georgia.

The Peelers had one son, Clarence, who would grow up with Keith as if they were real brothers. The two have remained very close throughout the years and Judge Clarence Peeler now resides in Atlanta, Georgia. Clarence Peeler, Sr. worked for the railroad and Betty Peeler was the Secretary for the Office of Georgia County Commissioners.

Keith first came to Carroll County in 1935 as a member of the Civil Conservation Corps which was then based at Villa Rica. After World War II, E.N. Keith became the District Supervisor of Carroll and Haralson Counties for the U.S. Soil and Water Conservation Service. The love of the earth was in Keith's blood and he was a protector of the environment even before this became the trend. With true Scottish industriousness, Keith put his farming knowledge to work and our county was greatly enriched for his talents. Keith is pictured with the original men of the CCC in Villa Rica. Carroll County soon became home to Keith and on 8 June 1940, E.N. Keith married Grace Elizabeth Luther of Villa Rica, Georgia.

Etheridge Keith, Jr., was the firstborn child and he had only one sister, but with her he shared a special bond throughout his life. Judy Elizabeth Keith was born 11 February 1946 and from that time on, Etheridge was his sister's champion. Both Judy and Etheridge attended Maple Street School and Carrollton High School. Judy Keith graduated from CHS in 1964 and earned her Marketing degree from The University of Georgia in 1968. Judy's future husband, Steve Harrill, earned his degree in Marketing from Georgia State University in 1970. Steve Harrill was born in Augusta, Georgia on 26 June 1946, the son of Max Harrill, a native of Cleveland County, N.C. and Carolyn Mauldin Harrill, a native of Anderson County, South Carolina. Steve served in the U.S. Army in Vietnam in 1968-1969.

Judy and Steve had a Christmas wedding on 20 December 1969 at the First Methodist Church in Carrollton. Judy and Steve Harrill lived in Springfield, Missouri for many years but they returned to Carrollton in 1997 to be closer to Judy's family. Steve is the genealogist in the family who has spent 30 years climbing the family tree. Steve Harrill now works for the American Red Cross and the Harrills are members of the First United Methodist Church.

Etheridge Keith was always a special uncle and adored his two nieces, Ashley Elizabeth Harrill born 5 March 1972 and Amanda Leigh Harrill born 26 June 1977. Both girls grew up in Springfield, Missouri, and attended school there. Ashley graduated from The University of Missouri with a degree in Fashion Merchandising and Marketing. She worked as the Business Analyst for Victoria's Secret in Columbus, Ohio before her marriage on 4 February 1995 to Michael John Bedosky, Jr. Mike Bedosky is a former NFL player for the Atlanta Falcons and the Cleveland Browns. Mike now teaches history and coaches high school football at Chapel Hill High School in Douglas County. Ashley and Mike Bedosky, Jr. have two sons, Steven Michael Bedosky born 21 December 1997 and Michael John Bedosky III born 3 September 2000.

Amanda Leigh Harrill graduated from Southwest Missouri State University where she was a member of Alpha Delta Pi social sorority. Amanda majored in Business Administration and is now employed by Limited Corporation in Atlanta. She makes her home in Carrollton, Georgia. Judy and Steve Harrill have built a lovely home on Lake Carroll at the site which was the scene of many happy memories from Etheridge and Judy's childhood. In the breathtaking view from the back deck high above the lake, one can almost picture the two of them, Etheridge out in the motorboat pulling Judy behind on the water skis so much the way they did in happy years before.

Etheridge Keith died on 4 October 1999 and was laid to rest at the Carroll Memory Gardens. Etheridge is remembered with the greatest fondness by all who knew him.

Submitted by: Steve and Judy Harrill, 232 S. Lakeshore Dr., Carrollton, GA 30117 – Source: Steve Harrill

IN MEMORIAM

Grace Elizabeth Luther Keith

Grace Elizabeth Luther was born 4 October 1912, the daughter of Reuben Oscar Luther and Esther Clower Luther of Villa Rica, Georgia. The heritage of Grace's family is a rich one - German, Swiss, and French Hugenot. The Luthers trace their family tree to John George Luther II who was born 1 March 1754 in Strausbourg, Germany, at that time a part of the Rhineland that was called "Switzerland." This was information written in German in the old family Bible that traveled with the family from Switzerland to America. George Luther arrived in America just in time to jump into the fray of the American Revolution. There is a fascinating account of his service in the 4th Regiment of the Maryland Line.

In his pension application in Randolph County, N.C. in 1832, Luther stated that his company marched through York County, Pennsylvania, crossing the Susquehanna on the ice at Anderson's Ferry, to Philadelphia where they drew arms. Then, they marched to Trenton, New Jersey, on to Lord Sterling's Castle arriving in February of 1777. The British under Lord Cornwallis were stationed at Brunswick and engaged in fighting at Piscataway. Luther's company later joined with the army of General George Washington and remained with him until the Battle of Germantown on 4 October 1777. Luther was one of the guards who later conducted the prisoners of Cornwallis' army, which consisted of 2000 British, 600 Hessians, and 500 Tories.

John George Luther II was the son of John George Luther born 15 June 1714 and Maria Barbara Naegel born 1717 in Strausbourg, Germany. The Luthers of Villa Rica descend from John George Luther II and Elizabeth Auman through their son Solomon Luther (born 1793) and his wife Elizabeth Winston (born 1795). Their son Isaac Luther was born in 1816 in Randolph County, North Carolina and married Sarah Loflin born 1816 in Davidson, N.C. Isaac Luther was the father of George Taylor Luther who was born in Carroll County, Georgia in 1847. Reuben Oscar Luther was born 9 May 1879, the son of George T. and Mary Martha "Mollie" Miller. Esther Clower married Reuben Oscar Luther in Carroll County on 27 July 1902. The Luthers had two children, Grace Elizabeth and a son, Horace Oscar Luther, born 24 July 1903.

Horace Luther was the Engineer for the City of Villa Rica for 45 years. He is pictured with C.J. Lee, Frank Green, and Robert McDowell of Villa Rica, Masonic Lodge No. 72 F & AM, receiving awards for 50 years membership. Horace Luther married Claudia Mae Blair and had two sons: (1) James Lewis Luther born 7 July 1928 and (2) Lawrence O'Neal Luther born 10 May 1930, died 15 March 1990. Horace Luther died 1 April 1985. The Luther family appears in the wedding picture of E.N. Keith and Grace Luther. R.O. Luther died 21 June 1971 and his wife Esther lived to be more than 100 years old. Her family is pictured around her bed on her 100th birthday.

Esther Clower was born 24 June 1879 and could remember coming to Carroll County in a covered wagon with her family as a little girl. Esther was the daughter of John Wesley Clower, Jr. and his wife Vesta Alice Juhan. The Juhans were of Swiss descent, first migrating to Nova Scotia in the mid 1700s. They settled in Halifax, Nova Scotia and there John James Juhan married Marie Payzant, the daughter of French Hugenots, Louis Payzant (1740-1840) and Marie Anne Noget (1747-1804). The history of this family is chronicled in *The Payzant and Allied Jess and Juhan Families of North America* by Marion M. Payzant, 1970. The son of John James Juhan and Marie Payzant was Stephen Alexander Juhan who migrated into South Carolina.

On the 29th of February 1792, Stephen Alexander Juhan married Eliza Martha Bordeaux, the daughter of Pierre DuBordeaux. The DuBordeaux family had come to America from Bordeaux, France in 1690 to Charleston. The descendants of Stephen Juhan and Eliza Bordeaux later became pioneers of Gwinnett County, Georgia. The Juhans were the founders of the Zoar Methodist Church at Centerville in Gwinnett County, Georgia. Many of the Juhans and Clowers are buried at this old church cemetery.

The Klauers/Clowers had originally come from the area of Neuweid, Germany in the late 1600s, settling with other German speaking people called "The Pennsylvania Dutch." The Clowers intermarried with the Morgans who were of Welch ancestry. George Clower married Elizabeth Morgan, the daughter of James Morgan and Eleanor Pawling, daughter of Henry Pawling, a Dutchman. Elizabeth was a sister to General Daniel Morgan of Revolutionary War fame.

The son of George Clower and Elizabeth Morgan was Daniel Clower born 18 July 1762 in Pennsylvania. Daniel was a Pvt. in Mills Co., Lytes and Dixon Regt. of the North Carolina Line in the American Revolution. About 1785, Daniel Clower married Nancy Wilson (1766-1846). George Clower deeded 139 acres of land on the Little River of Orange County, N.C. to his eldest son William "for love and affection". Later on, William Clower deeded 269 acres of this same land to his brother Daniel. Daniel Clower died 30 September 1847 and was buried at Bethesda Methodist Church in Lawrenceville, Georgia.

Daniel and Nancy Wilson Clower had a son named John Clower (1794-1879) who married Nancy H. Winn (1797-1879. Nancy was the granddaughter of Philadelphia Wynne and Thomas Winn of Lunenberg County, Virginia and a daughter of Lemuel Winn (1770-1841) and Elizabeth Cofer, pioneers of Gwinnett. The Clowers appear in Georgia as early as 1805 when they participated in the Land Lottery.

John Clower and Nancy Winn Clower had a son named John Wesley Clower (1823-1906) who married Sarah Melvina Martin (1824-1905) the daughter of Samuel Martin and Frances Hall of Spartanburg, South Carolina. Samuel Martin was the son of Abraham Martin (1775-1852) and Betsie Harris (1780-1830) also of Spartanburg. John W. Clower, Sr. and Sarah Martin Clower were the parents of John Wesley Clower, Jr. (born about 1850-1927) who married Vesta Alice Juhan (1858-1939). These were the parents of Esther B. Clower. John W. Clower, Jr. died 10 March 1927 and is buried near Draketown.

The Luthers were early Carroll County pioneers appearing in the Carroll County census of 1850. Isaac Luther is head of household, age 34 born in N.C. His wife, Sarah, age 39, was born in S.C. Then, their children are listed: (twins) Elizabeth and Emily E. age 16, Florius J., age 14, (twins) Josephine and Elizabeth age 12, (twins) Harris C. and Mary, age 10, Frances M., age 8, John H. age 6, and George T., age 3. Three sets of twins!

In the 1860 census Isaac Luther is gold-mining in addition to his farming pursuits at Villa Rica. Villa Rica was known as "The City of Gold." In Isaac's household appear Sarah, his wife, Josephine (now Bonner), age 23, Maria L., age 19, Abraham, age 9, and Martin A., age 7. In 1870, Isaac and Sarah have only the two youngest sons living with them. George Taylor Luther appears in the 1880 Carroll County census with his family: George T. Luther age 32, farmer, wife, Mary A., age 35, Leonidas, age 12, Martha E., age 10, George O., age 8, John W., age 6, Etta L., age 4, and Reuben O. age 1.

George Taylor Luther was a Confederate soldier who went to war as a sixteen year old. He served with the Villa Rica "Golddiggers" and was captured at the Battle of Vicksburg. Another ancestor, George W. Clower, Jr. was in Co. B., 42nd GA Infantry, C.S.A. He was also captured at Vicksburg. Both Luther and Clower were later paroled and went on to fight for the Confederacy in the Battle of Chickamauga.

In 1956, Grace Keith became associated with the West Georgia National Bank as teller and she rose to a management position rapidly. Grace became the first manager of the "motor bank" and worked there many years until her retirement. Both Grace and E.N. Keith were active in community affairs. Keith was a member of the Carrollton Lions and often presented speakers on conservation issues. Grace volunteered many hours of service to the Tanner Medical Center Auxiliary as a "Pink Lady." Both Grace and E.N. were active in the Cattlemen's Association and they maintained a prize herd of cattle and one of the most beautiful farms in Carroll County. The Keiths still own 73 acres of the original farmland located at 361 Keith Road. Both farm and horses were enjoyed by the Keith children and all their friends as they were growing up in Carrollton. Grace is pictured with the horses on a humorous occasion - why humorous? Because after the picture was snapped, the horses proceeded to eat Grace's straw pocketbook that she was carrying!

The Keiths established a beautiful lot on Lake Carroll for their boat. Friends and neighbors enjoyed their hospitality for many Sunday picnics and water skiing for many years. The Keiths had two children: Etheridge born in 1943 and Judy born in 1946. In 1949, the Keiths purchased a beautiful wooded lot from Ruth Brock Kramer who was establishing a new street in Carrollton. The Frank Thomasson, Jr. family was first to build on the street, and the Keiths and Estes soon followed. These neighbors would be dear to each other over the next half century.

Grace's love of flowers filled her yard with camellias and azaleas in the Spring and this was a favorite scene for Sunday drivers enjoying the view. Also, Grace loved to do her own yard work and would often wave to passersby as she raked autumn leaves in the Fall. In 1960, when the Highway 27 Bypass was being constructed, Ruth Brock Kramer moved her old Southern mansion — white columns and all — from South Street to her lot next door to the Keiths. People came from far and wide to watch as the one hundred (100) year old mansion was moved on railroad tracks down the bypass to its new location. Grace Keith was a wonderful co-worker, neighbor, wife, mother, and grandmother. Grace never looked her age, so it is hard to believe she lived to be 88 years old. A tall, slender, dark-haired beauty who was proud to stand every inch of her height with her regal posture, Grace was the loveliest of Southern ladies. She will long be remembered in Carroll County, Georgia. Grace Keith died on 15 September 2000 and was laid to rest at Carroll Memory Gardens alongside her son, Etheridge.

Submitted by: Judy and Steve Harrill, 232 S. Lakeshore Dr., Carrollton, GA 30117 – Source: Steve Harrill

IN LOVING MEMORY OF

Tina Annette Jackson Latimer

August 21, 1971 — August 9, 2000

Beautiful wife to Jerry J. Latimer, Jr. (J.J.)
Loving mother to Mikayla Jordan Latimer
Loyal daughter to Martha Lambert Jackson and Stephen Jackson
Caring teacher of special needs children at East Coweta High School
We love you and will always miss you.

In Memory and Honor of

Jim Johnson Family - 1929

*Front row, left to right: James "Jim" Johnson, *W. Jay Wallace, Leon White, *Eric Duncan, * James Duncan, and Harriet "Hattie" Creel Johnson. Second row, left to right: Eskrine White holding *Howell White, *Clovis Duncan, Maurette Duncan Waters, and *Leroy White. Third row, left to right: Lucious White, W.D. Duncan, Homer Wallace holding Harriet Wallace, Gomer Johnson holding *Margaret Johnson Harruff, and Miller Ferrel Johnson. Fourth row, left to right: Percy Johnson, Avice Matthews Johnson, Era Johnson White, Jewell Johnson Duncan, Mamae Johnson Wallace, Genevieve Sylvester Johnson, Virgie Olgetree Johnson holding Creel Johnson, and Gladys Johnson Foster. * Still Living*

Sewell and Johnston Families

Sewell Family circa 1915, Hewlett, Georgia

Back row: Hiram Sewell, Nelle Doss Sewell, Fred Sewell, Annie Sewell, (baby) Thelma Sewell, Rhodes Sewell, Winnie Sewell. Front row (baby) Winston Sewell, Sarah Francinia (Fannie) Sewell Stipe, Green Berry Sewell, Frank Sewell, George Embry Sewell, Ota Kenney Sewell, (baby) Robert Sewell, John Newton Sewell, in front of parents: J.D. Sewell.

My father, George Embry Sewell, was descended from a long line of Sewells who first came to this Country in 1620. Englishman, Henry Sewell and his wife, Alice Willoughby made a home in the wilderness area of Virginia that came to be known as Sewell's Point, now the Norfolk Naval Base. They had seven sons. Milton Newton Sewell was my father's grandfather. Green Berry Sewell was my father's father. His mother was Sarah Henrietta McGarity Sewell. My father was born March 1, 1885. He was about five feet, eight inches tall. He had light brown hair and blue eyes.

He was always interested in building and cabinet making. He built many homes, schools, churches and other public buildings. He drew his own designs for many of the buildings he built.

Daddy and mother, Ona Gertrude Johnston were married January 12, 1916 in her home which was about half-way between Sand Hill and Hulett. The Fairfield Plantation is built where my mother's home once stood. My father's family lived in Hulett. They later moved to Elko in middle Georgia. Daddy always said that marriage was the way to double your joys and halve your troubles. I believe that too. My husband and I were married sixty-one happy years. He died at age 85.

My mother was a multi-talented woman. She was a good student and learned well. She went to Sand Hill and then to Villa Rica High School. She lived with a cousin in Villa Rica. She had to pay tuition and I have a receipt for $10.00 given to my grandfather Johnston. This was around 1900. She could still read Latin and work algebra problems when I was in high school taking those subjects in the mid 1930s. Grandpa wanted all of his children to develop any musical talent they might have, so he hired a music teacher, who boarded with them, to develop whatever potential they had. Mother played the piano and pump organ in her church that was Macedonia Baptist at Sand Hill. My brother, John Sewell, lives in Magalia, California near Chico. He inherited the musical talent. John plays the piano and the fiddle. Daddy played the fiddle. I'm thankful mother and daddy taught us many of the old hymns that tell us so clearly and beautifully about the love of Jesus who gave His life that we may have eternal life if we put our faith and trust in Him.

After graduating from Villa Rica High School I went to West Georgia College. I graduated in 1938. I was married to Henry Gheesling on September 10, 1938. He graduated from Berry College in 1937. He had a very successful career in the active Army and Army Reserves and retired as a Colonel. He was in WW II and overseas in England, Belgium, and France from September 1942 until September 1945. He came home in good health and our marriage continued to be a blessing until he died July 31, 1999. He also worked for the Civil Service Commission. He retired from the Veteran's Administration. Adjusting to life without him has been possible with the help of the Lord, my church, my family, and friends.

Henry and I have two children, a daughter, Nancy Ethiel born February 19, 1941 before WWII and Henry Patrick born March 22, 1950. We have three grandchildren. Nancy has two girls, Jessica and Justine. Pat has one son, Dominick.

Submitted by: Sarah Sewell Gheesling

Johnston Family circa 1893, Sand Hill-Villa Rica, Georgia

Back row: Ona Johnston Sewell, Ona's grandmother Johnston, Josephine (Aunt Jo) Johnston, Thomas Galloway Johnston, Cordova Dickson Johnston, Cora Johnston. Front row: Carlo (the dog), John C. Johnston, Bess Mae Johnston, Nancy Johnston.

Remembering our precious

Starla Jewell Wheeler

with the poem that she wrote just before she died suddenly.

Starla was born February 7, 1979 and she died April 4, 1995

"CHOICES"

by Starla Wheeler

Life is like the sands of time
never stopping not even in mind
Continuing on until that faithful day
When all around you shall fade away
Your body may die, but your soul isn't lost
It lives on eternally at all cost
When you reach those pearly gates
Then and there will decide your fate
God shall weigh your deeds on a scale
Good against evil, heaven against hell
If you receive hell you'll wish your soul was gone
But that's not your decision, it shall live on
If you earn heaven your soul will rest
Forever cradled in God's breast
The constant burn of hell's flames
Will make you regret all your earthly shames
Don't prolong your sin filled life
Come to God's grace and proclaim His might
Then you will live in Christian peace
Everyday paying your heavenly fees
Satan will knock loud at your door
God gives you strength to follow him no more
Befriend those who share His glory
For those who don't tell them His story
Go and spread the gospel around
To any person that can be found
The Bible would be a likely place
To look for answers to things you might face
In this statement I shall end
Come to God's glory and repent of your sins

Pansy Tisinger Brown

January 3, 1905 - January 10, 1994

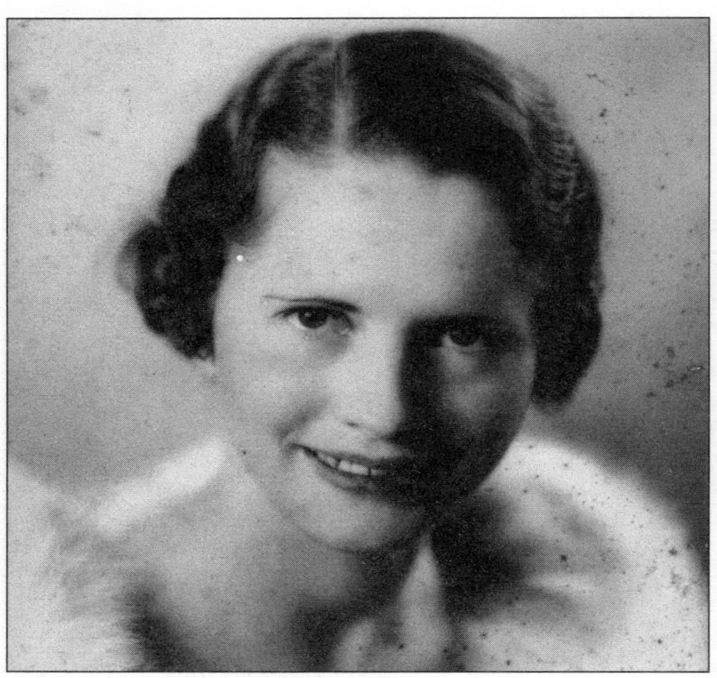

Beloved Nurse

* *Graduated in first nursing class at Emory University.*
* *First Superintendent of Carrollton Clinic on College Street.*
* *First Industrial Nurse at Southwire.*

Lover of Flowers

Pansy and Herman Brown owned and operated the Cottage Hill Greenhouses where they grew plants and arranged flowers for all occasions from 1945 to 1985.

By Gwyn Clay Chesnut

Naomi Evans Tisinger

February 14, 1908 - May 22, 2001

Naomi Evans Tisinger was born in Knoxville, Tennessee, on Valentine's Day, 1908. She moved to Atlanta in the 1920s where she worked as a sales representative for Stone Bakeries, sold cemetery lots and later was one of the first licensed dental hygienists in the State of Georgia.

During the Depression she met Robert D. "Bob" Tisinger in Sunday School at the Grace Methodist Church in Atlanta, Georgia. She married him on June 30, 1933, at the Tisinger Homeplace in the Victory Community where she lived for the remainder of her life. Without benefit of electricity, she became an accomplished homemaker and gardener.

She was mother of two sons, David, born in 1937; and Dick, born in 1941. She was a devoted and involved mother who devoted much of her time to parent-teacher organizations, the band program, and other school activities.

To those outside her family, she was known as a warm and welcoming person who always maintained a positive attitude and received her guests and friends with warmth and grace. She was also a giving person, quietly devoting herself to many church and community activities, as well as serving as benefactor to many individuals in need.

Naomi died on May 22, 2001, at the homeplace where she had lived for almost 67 years.

Naomi

Submitted by:* *David and Dick Tisinger

In Memory and In Honor of the late

Benjamin Aaron and Sarah Elizabeth Johnson Styles

and their Family

Benjamin A. and Elizabeth Styles' – Home and Family in 1911.

Samuel Styles (b. 1763, d. July 23, 1843) married Selah (Celia) Langston (born approximately 1771). They moved to Laurens County, South Carolina from Virginia. They had 11 children, six daughters and five sons. Their homeplace was still standing in 1965, and the town is named Stylesville.

One of Samuel and Celia's sons was Claiborne M. Styles (born July 11, 1800, died August 4, 1876), who married Nancy Kemp (born October 17, 1803, died approximately (1849). They moved to Georgia in 1824, settling in Gwinnett County. He owned land in Gwinnett, Coweta, Campbell and Carroll Counties. Their last home was in Campbell County. They are buried in Palmetto, Georgia. They had ten children, six sons and four daughters.

Claiborne and Nancy's first child, Aaron Styles, was born in Greenville, S.C. on March 20, 1822. He married Elizabeth (Betsy) Ann King (born August 23, 1831, died 1879) on September 18, 1843. She was the daughter of Benjamin and Mary Ann King. Aaron and Betsy had two sons, Benjamin Aaron (born February 5, 1849, died December 23, 1928) and Henry Claiborne Styles. Aaron Styles died in September, 1850, when Benjamin Aaron was just a few months old. Claiborne Styles became guardian of his grandsons, Benjamin Aaron and Henry Claiborne. He sent them to boarding schools and provided tutors, so they would receive a good education.

When Benjamin Aaron was a young man, he moved to Carroll County, the Kansas Community, in Georgia. He lived and worked with his mother's brother, Joseph King. There he met and married Sarah Elizabeth Johnson (born October 29, 1851, died May 22, 1929) on September 18, 1873. Sarah Elizabeth was the daughter of William David and Arminda Smith Johnson. Arminda Smith was the daughter of James C. and Sarah Burt Smith. James C. was the son of Gabriel Smith, the Revolutionary Soldier.

Sarah (Lizzabeth) was the oldest of nine daughters. With no boys, the girls had to help their father with the farm work, learning to plow cotton and corn, using steers to pull the plows. Both her paternal and maternal ancestors were pioneer settlers of Carroll County.

Sarah's father, William David A. Johnson, served in the Civil War. Her mother, Arminda Smith Johnson, experienced great hardships during the conflict, as well. One story recalls that she hid a ham under her skirt to prevent Union soldiers from taking it.

Sarah's grandfather, Gabriel Smith, Sr., entered the militia as a 15 year old in 1780. He was taken prisoner of war in 1781. He escaped three weeks later and continued to serve until Lord Cornwallis surrendered at Yorktown, Virginia in October, 1781. In 1784, he submitted his claim for service and was paid twenty pounds and five shillings.

Benjamin Aaron was a farmer and a good businessman, buying and selling many tracts of land in Carroll and Haralson Counties. Benjamin and Sarah owned a nice home in the Kansas Community and donated land for two Kansas School buildings and Kansas Baptist Church and Cemetery. His greatest ambitions were in education and politics. He nominated his good friend, the Honorable William C. Adamson, for the U.S. Congress from Georgia's 4th and 5th districts in Indian Springs, Georgia.

Benjamin and Sarah had nine children, seven sons and two daughters. He insisted that their children receive as much education as possible. Arminda Ann, twins Henry Claiborne and Benjamin David, Joseph Cornelius, John Carter, Aaron Gordon, James Tillman, Oscar Rance, and Lois Elizabeth.

Their first child was Arminda Ann Styles (born July 26, 1874, died January 30, 1937). She married Augustus Adair. They had four daughters: Gussie, Jessie, Jewel, and Gerelda.

Next, twins, Henry Claiborne (born February 24, 1876, died May 9, 1899) and Benjamin David (born February 24, 1876, died February 20, 1964) were born. Henry Claiborne married Nora Wilner. They had no children. Benjamin David married Etta Batchelor, and they had nine children: Reese, Otis, David, Olivia, Novie, Perry and Parrie (twins), Lilly and Nona. Etta Batchelor Styles died on January 28, 1917. Benjamin D. remarried, and he and his wife, Bertha Reagan Styles had six children: Marion, Milton, Irma, Ray, Reagan and Fred.

Joseph Cornelius Styles (born March 4, 1878; died February 8, 1946) married Laura McKibben. They had three children: Lillian, Lloyd and Eunice. Joseph was a merchant.

John Carter Styles (born October 29, 1881; died January 15, 1959) married Lee Ola Lovvorn. They had eight children: Roy, Elizabeth, Eva, Claiborne, Darthulia, Irene, Mattie Lois and Raymond. Lee Ola Lovvorn Styles died on October 27, 1932. John Carter married Elma Cagle on April 27, 1935, and they had six children: Hazel, Louise, Betty, Mary Julia, Sarah and Nelda.

Aaron Gordon Styles (born July 4, 1884, died August 17, 1962) married Sarah Fannie Horsley (born October 7, 1884, died September 4, 1940) on July 10, 1905. Aaron Gordon was an educator. He attended Bowdon College, Bagwell Business College in Atlanta and Locust Grove Bible School. He pastored many Baptist Churches. Sarah Fannie was a homemaker and a great singer. They had ten children: Mona, Zella, Mildred, Floyd, Goldie, Ernest, Pauline, Elizabeth, Louise and Jean.

James Tillman Styles (born May 24, 1886, died May 24, 1956) married Maud Carpenter. They had one son, Myrl. James Tillman was an Industrial Engineer.

Oscar Rance Styles (born September 8, 1888) married Annie Phillips on August 19, 1906. They had four children: Nellie Fay, Ima Mae, Oscar, Jr., and Charles. Oscar Rance was a Medical Doctor.

Lois Elizabeth Styles (born August 13, 1893, died December 18, 1926) married Walker Maxwell on August 13, 1911. They had no children. Lois Elizabeth was a sales clerk.

Many descendants of Benjamin A. and Elizabeth Johnson Styles have followed those we have named. They have pursued varied careers: medicine, law, farming, music, business, education, writing, art, etc. They have been dedicated to their Christian faith and served as church leaders. Many continue to have homes and businesses in Carroll County today.

Since 1955, the Benjamin A. and Elizabeth Johnson Styles Family has held a family reunion annually in mid-July. Every five years they have a big reunion called the "Super Styles Reunion."

Submitted by: Mildred Styles Johnson, Dr. Styles Johnson & Paula Teal Raymond

In Memory and In Honor of the late

Benjamin Aaron and Sarah Elizabeth Johnson Styles

and their Family

"Super Styles" Reunion, in 1995, at Stone Mountain, Georgia.

Benjamin Aaron and Sarah Elizabeth Styles and Annie

William David Johnson, Father of Sarah Elizabeth Styles

Part of James C. and Sarah Burt Smith's log home built in 1836

Sarah Burt Smith, Grandmother of Sarah Elizabeth

Dr. and Mrs. James Irvin Vansant

Remembering Dr. Vansant 1919-1972 and Honoring Mrs. Helen Lackner Vansant

Van and Helen Vansant, who were married July 10, 1943.

James Irvin Vansant, Jr. was born July 6, 1919 in Roopville, Georgia. He was the only child born to James Irvin Vansant, Sr. (from Douglas County) and Annie Louise Goodwin Vansant (from Coweta County). Annie Louise died in 1927, when James Irvin Vansant, Jr. was eight years old. He and his father remained in Carroll County most of his youth where he attended the local public schools, graduating from Centralhatchee High School. The elder Vansant died in 1937 when James Irvin Vansant, Jr. was eighteen years old. With the assistance of aunts and uncles he was able to continue his education at West Georgia College. He completed his Business degree from the University of Georgia.

When World War II broke out, he enlisted in the Navy as a cadet where he trained as a Naval Aviator. During this training period he was nicknamed "Van." He was stationed at Floyd Bennet Field in New York, where he met Helen Lackner. They were married on July 10, 1943. During the remainder of the war, he served as a dive-bomber and fighter pilot aboard the Bellow Wood Aircraft Carrier in the Pacific theater. After the war ended, Van returned to his native Georgia with his wife and daughter Sue Ann who was born in 1945.

He completed his lifetime dream of becoming a physician in 1950 graduating from Emory University School of Medicine. While attending medical school Van and Helen had two additional children, Patricia born in 1948 and Mary Elizabeth born in 1951. After interning at Crawford Long Hospital in Atlanta, the Vansant family moved to Villa Rica, Georgia, where the young Dr. Vansant joined the family medical practice of Powell-Berry-Powell.

Dr. and Mrs. Vansant had two more daughters Jamie born in 1954 and Laura born in 1958. Dr. Vansant enjoyed a successful medical practice for almost twenty years until his death on November 24, 1972. Mrs. Vansant continues to live in Villa Rica with her daughter Laura and her family. The daughters married and live in Georgia. They have given Mrs. Vansant twenty-one grandchildren and fourteen great-grandchildren.

Submitted by: Mrs. Mary Beth Day, 555 Tumlin Lake Road, Temple, GA 30179

— Walker Memorial —

Daniel "Danie" Lee Walker

B. July 9, 1875 D. Sept. 8, 1964

Maude Eugenia Kelly

B. Oct. 5, 1884 D. April 1, 1971

Married: January 29, 1902
Carroll County, Georgia

Children:	*Curtis*	*Kelly*
	Alen	*Velma*
	Preston	*Alma*
	Effie	*Eugene*
	Myrtie	*Inez*

Floyd Curtis Walker & *Mary Louise Shadinger*

B. June 21, 1904 D. Oct. 29, 1995 — B. July 19, 1904 D. Sept. 26, 1997

Married: April 25, 1926, Carroll County, Georgia

Children: *Melba Doris, Curtis Wendell, Burma Joyce and Nina Carol.*

Willis Family

In loving memory, we the Willis Family remember and honor these members of our family who have gone before us. The love of God that was in the hearts of Dorothy, Tom, Donald, Tommy and Don, Jr. lives on in us, their descendants. How grateful we are for the good examples they shared!

Dorothy and Tom Willis
Next to God's love comes a Mother and Father's love
(See the Willis Family Article)

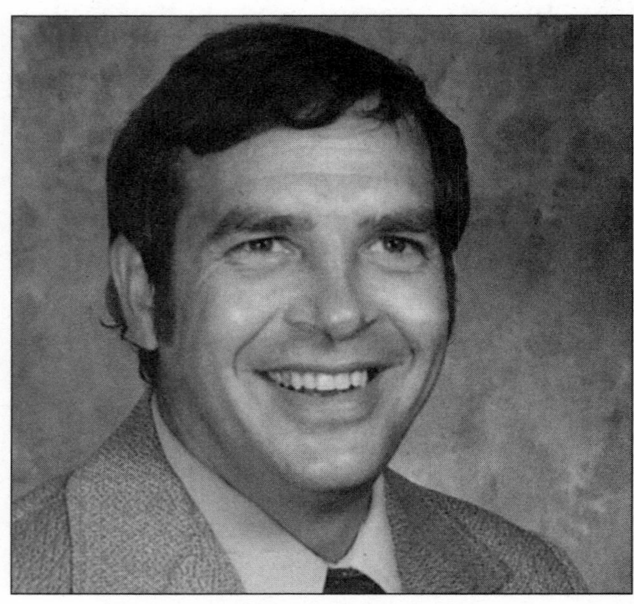

Donald Milton Willis, Sr.
November 8, 1936 - July 31, 1989
"The twinkle in his eyes will always be remembered."

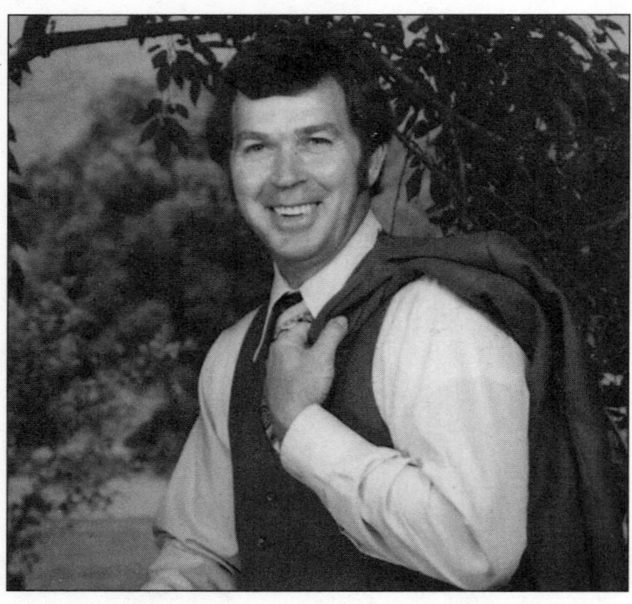

Thomas "Tommy" David Willis
June 3, 1944 - January 3, 1982
"He was the most unselfish person, I have ever known."
Joanne A. Willis Trammell

Donald Milton Willis, Jr.
October 26, 1960 - September 18, 1999
"A sweet, kind, and gentle spirit, not of this world."

Joanne A. Willis Trammell
Brett Matthew Willis
Trent Ashley Willis

W.A. and Nancy Willis Howell
David and Julie Howell
Valerie Ellen Howell

Frances C. Willis Newton
Danny & Felicia Willis Higdon
Joe and Connie Willis Nalley

Great Grandchildren: Kendall Paige and Michal Danielle Higdon
Joey Willis and Nancy E. Nalley

In Memory

Paul and Nellie Wingo

Paul	**Nellie**
June 10, 1898	***Feb. 6, 1901***
April 19, 1956	***Feb. 11, 1991***

Wonderful parents,
Workers,
Church and community
Examples

By the Wingo Children

In Memory

Charles J. Herndon, Sr.

August 23, 1933 - December 10, 1995

Wonderful Husband,
Father,
Minister,
Teacher,
and
Friend.

USAF 1951 - 1955
Korean War Veteran

By Edna Wingo Herndon

158 CLINIC AVENUE
CARROLLTON, GEORGIA 30117

770-834-1008 – 1-800-248-4657
Fax 836-8303

In July of 1976 John Ellington Godard, M.D., established the Carrollton Eye Clinic, P.C., in the now-demolished Groover Medical Building near the then Tanner Memorial Hospital, now Tanner Medical Center. At the same time, Roger Michael Rossomondo, M.D., established the West Georgia Eye Clinic, P.C., at 101 Clinic Avenue, the former office of Dr. Roy Denney. In 1978 local architect Alex Roush and Ra-Lin Construction, Co., built a new facility for the Carrollton Eye Clinic at 160 Clinic Avenue. In 1994 Drs. Godard and Rossomondo merged their practices. The new Carrollton Eye Clinic office (again designed by Roush and constructed by Ra-Lin) was located at 158 Clinic Avenue and included the area's first ASC (Ambulatory Surgery Center). Subsequently Drs. Godard and Rossomondo opened additional offices in nearby Bremen and Villa Rica.

Carrollton Eye Clinic, P.C., continues to serve the people of West Georgia and eastern Alabama with medical ophthalmology, cataract surgery, LASIK, pediatric ophthalmology, oculo-facial plastic surgery, and many procedures performed in their Aesthetics Center.

JOHN E. GODARD, M.D. **ROGER M. ROSSOMONDO, M.D.**

History of
CARROLLTON PARK, RECREATION, AND CULTURAL ARTS
Department

Organized recreation began in Carrollton in 1945 in response to the closing of three school-related playgrounds. The Carroll County Service Council's panel on Education and Recreation and the Carrollton Athletic Association added lighting to the Carrollton High School (currently the Carrollton Community Activities Center) athletic field thus bringing professional baseball to the area during the summers. The Service Council began sponsoring basketball and social activities in the City Gym. The Council took over the City Pool and the three playgrounds. In 1963, Mr. James Dean became the first full-time Recreation Director.

From these humble beginnings, the Carrollton, Parks, Recreation and Cultural Arts Department has grown into a program that services thousands of children and adults in the Carroll County area. CPRCAD oversees area parks, recreation facilities, the City Cemetery, Senior Activities, Cultural Arts, Athletics, Special Populations, The Carrollton Visitors Bureau, Aquatics, and Leisure Programs and Special Projects Division. In addition, the department provides meeting places for area residents and civic organizations to host special events and programs of their own.

The Athletics division provides sports activities for children as young as six through adult. Sports include football, basketball, softball, baseball, track, soccer and boxing for children. Adults participate in volleyball, basketball, softball and boxing.

The Seniors Division moved into a new facility behind the Carrollton Community Activities Center in January 2001. Seniors enjoy a wide variety of activities including quilting, arts and crafts, ceramics, field trips, billiards and many other special events. In addition to daily hot lunches for participants, the Senior Center oversees the Meals on Wheels program.

The Cultural Arts Division was formed in 1978 and, under direction from a 12 member advisory board, hosts an annual Arts Gala. The Cultural Arts Division holds over 25 art camps each summer, supports adult, primary, children, and teen theater groups, a growing Community Chorus, Art in Education programming, Gallery 118 for artists to promote their work, annual creative writing and juried art shows and many cultural special events throughout the year. Construction has begun on a new Cultural Arts Center that will be located on Alabama Street.

The Leisure Programs and Special Projects Division manages a diverse group of programs and facilities. They include therapeutic programs, special events, aquatics, leisure programs, Westside Center, and Lake Carroll. Special projects that serve thousands of participants each year include Daddy/Daughter and Mother/Son Dances, Special Olympics, swim lessons, summer day camps, gymnastics, tennis, aerobics, equestrian training, karate, cheerleading, the Fitness Center, twirling, and homework helper. Leisure programs are noncompetitive and of a learning, self-improvement or social nature. A new state of the art Aquatics Center, A Multi-purpose Gymnastics Center and renovation of Westside Center will all be a part of the 2001/2002 additions supported by the citizens of Carrollton.

Today, under the direction of a six member recreation commission, Director Ronnie Young, many part-time workers, volunteers and a full-time staff of 40 dedicated professionals, Carrollton Parks, Recreation and Cultural Arts Department continues to fulfill its mission of providing quality recreation to the citizens of Carrollton and surrounding areas.

Submitted by: Penny Lewis

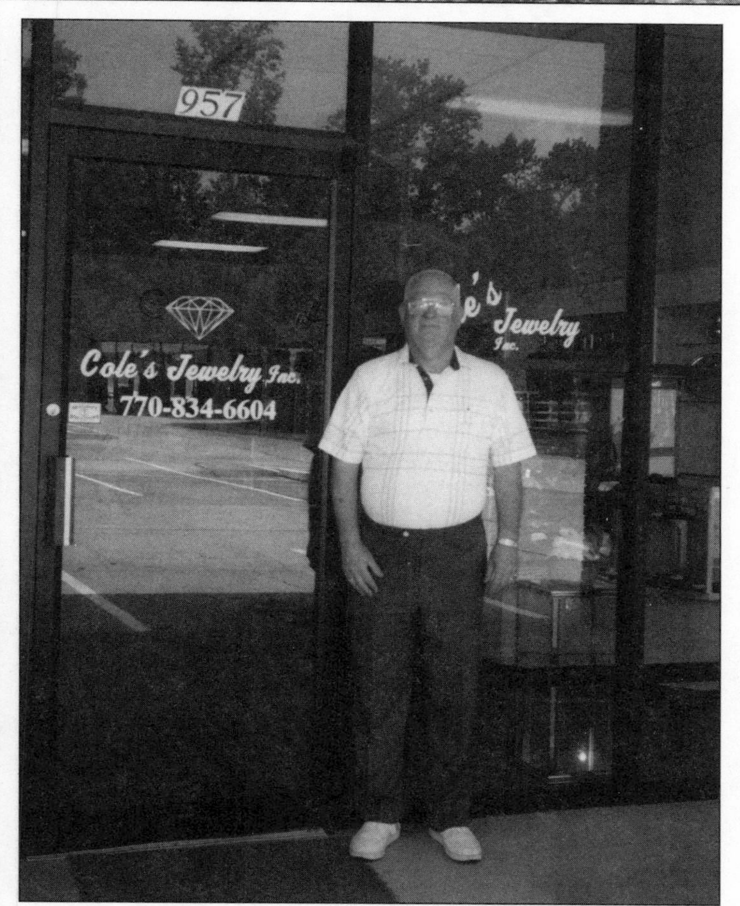

COLE'S JEWELRY, INC.

770-836-6604

Cole's Jewelry was started March 25, 1959. J. Reeves Cole bought Moore's Jewelry store at 113 Newnan Street. Reeves Cole also had a jewelry store in Monroe, Georgia for several years. His son Franklin Cole came from Monroe to run the Carrollton store. Reeves brother Robert Cole was the "watch repairman." Approximately two years later Robert retired and Reeves' son Joel came down to do the watch repair. Sometime later Lillian Bohannon joined Cole's as bridal consultant. After several years Cole's Jewelry moved to 104 Adamson Square which was formerly the Johnson Drug Store building.

When Reeves Cole retired Frank and Joel Cole bought the business. After being partners for several years, Joel had a serious stroke just after his fiftieth birthday. One and a half years later, Frank Cole bought out Joel and continued to have Cole's Jewelry on the downtown Square until April 1, 2001.

Frank Cole and his family now have Cole's Jewelry, Inc. at 957 Maple Street in Westover Square and continue to give top quality service and merchandise to our customers. We appreciate all our customers and future customers.

Thank you for forty-three years of service to Carrollton and Carroll County.

Frank

The Company with the Personal Touch ...

Duffey Realty

1441 North Park Street
Carrollton, GA 30117

(770) 836-1117
***Toll Free* 1-877-861-1117**

http://www.duffeyrealty.com

REALTOR® EQUAL HOUSING REALTOR® MLS

Sales • Leases
Farm Property • Self Storage

Groover-Smith Furniture Company, Inc.
and
Antique Mall

106 Adamson Square, Carrollton, Georgia 30117

Groover-Smith Furniture Company, Inc., as it is now known was founded by Walter Neal Groover in May 1932 as Mather-Groover Furniture Company. Mr. Groover went into business with Mr. Mather of the Mather Furniture Chain out of Atlanta. The store opened in the Holderness building on Adamson Square which it still occupies. The day the business opened, due to the state of the nation's economy, the Banks closed.

Soon after the business was established Mr. Groover rented the adjoining building then owned by The Southern Bell Telephone and Telegraph Company and bought out Mr. Mather, thus occupying all three buildings. Walter and his wife, Sallie, worked long and hard to make the business survive. Sallie kept the books and often helped customers in decorating their homes. Being a great seamstress she even made drapes for many customers.

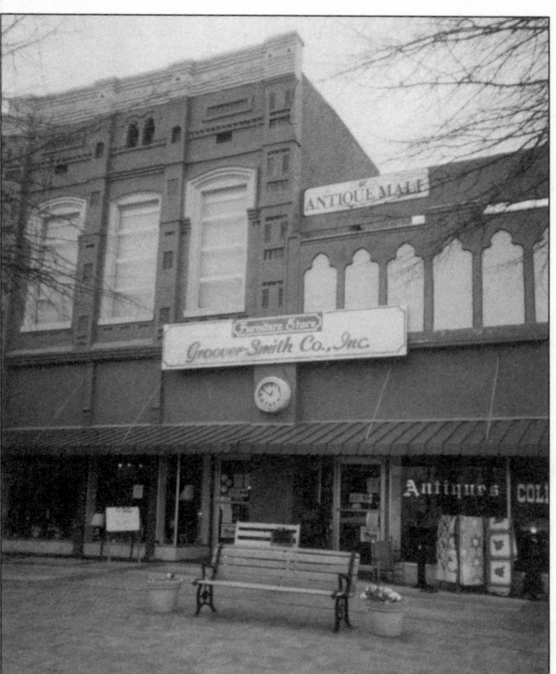

Groover-Smith Furniture Co. Inc. and Antique Mall, 2001.

In 1934 Walter and Sallie Groover's youngest daughter, Haysel Helen, married Ed M. Smith from Newnan and he went to work in the business. They opened a second store in Villa Rica. Later, Ed joined the business in Carrollton and it became known as Groover-Smith. Mr. Groover bought the building from Southern Bell about this time.

Like her mother Haysel also became active in the business helping with buying and decorating. Due to her influence the store pioneered in selling accessories for the home.

Having been in business for such a long time the company has seen many economic fluctuations. Mr. Groover would jokingly tell this story about the business.

> "During the war lumber was so scarce for making furniture that the companies used material so green that when they picked up a load of furniture in Atlanta and set it up on the showroom floor the next morning they would have to trim the twigs off the pieces before they could open."
>
> As stated, the business started in the Holderness building. This building was built by Sidney Holderness in the late 1800s. In 1920 Mr. Holderness did some remodeling to the building. An agreement was made with The Gainsboro Telephone and Telegraph Company, then owners of the Groover Building, that there always had to be a 24" air space between the two buildings. A number of businesses operated out of the basement of the then telephone building. On the basement door up in the 24" space spelled out in square-head nails is the name Hamrick Rides.

Records show some of the businesses that have occupied the three buildings that are now Groover-Smith Company and Antique Mall as the following. In 1895 it was a drug store and a restaurant. The Gainsboro Telephone and Telegraph Company bought the building and later they moved to one side renting part of the building to the People's Bank, and at some point another bank occupied the area. In 1930 The Southern Bell Telephone and Telegraph Company bought the telephone building. Mr. Groover purchased the building in the early 1940s and rented the upstairs to Southern Bell. At one time the Holderness Building was the Post Office (1903-1914), a dry goods store and a meat market. As stated Mr. Groover opened the furniture store in this building in 1932.

In 1947 the adjacent property owners decided to build a building facing Newnan Street which would close the alley way behind the Holderness building. There was a lawsuit and papers are available today testifying as to why the alley should remain open including some from postal workers stating that it was always open for loading mail in wagons. The suit was settled and the building was built. Ironically, this year, 2001, the building has been gutted leaving the original front facing Newnan Street and the alley opened back up as a foot passage way.

Groover-Smith Furniture Company is still located in the same location on Adamson Square and is owned by the third generation, Ed and Haysel Groover Smith's daughter, Laddie, and her husband, Bill Carter.

Bill and Laddie bought the business in 1990 and leased a portion to Rodger and Sally Miles, sister and brother-in-law to the Carter's for an antique store, Miles Haus Antiques. When the Miles' closed that business Bill and Laddie converted part of Groover-Smith into the Antique Mall. There have been several instances where the Antique Mall has sold merchandise that was originally bought from Groover's in the 1930s and 40s.

Today, Groover-Smith Furniture Company, Inc. and Antique Mall offers to the public a large selection of name brand furniture, accessories, gifts, and antiques with the same friendly service that was offered by Mr. Groover when he started the business in 1932. The owners attribute the business' longevity to a faith in God who has blessed them in many ways. Two being, loyal employees who have been like family, and dedicated customers whom they appreciate and enjoy serving.

Submitted by: Laddie Smith Carter

Ed Smith, Walter N. Groover (Picture), and Laddie Smith Carter – Three Generations!

R.D. Merrill Company and Merrill Gardens

Corporate History

R.D. Merrill Company is a private holding company formed in the early 1890s by timber pioneer R.D. Merrill. The Seattle, Washington, based company is still owned and directed by Merrill family descendants. Charles B. Wright, III, a fourth generation Merrill, is the current chairman.

Merrill Gardens, LLC was formed in 1993 to provide an alternative to traditional retirement housing. In eight years, the company has grown from eight employees to about 2,500. Merrill Gardens owns and operates 59 communities in 15 states. The communities are located in Alabama, Arizona, California, Colorado, Florida, Georgia, Indiana, Louisana, Nevada, New Mexico, North Carolina, Oklahoma, Tennessee, Texas and Washington.

Merrill Gardens purchased its first independent and assisted living community in Seattle eight years ago, gaining insight into the basic operating profile of the industry. The company then built a community from the ground up in Monroe, Washington, learning design and construction. Through new construction and acquisition of existing communities, Merrill Gardens is now the largest for-profit operator of retirement communities in Washington State and the second largest private operator in the United States.

Each Merrill Gardens community is different in physical structure, reflecting the characteristics of the area where it is located and the needs of residents. The management and resources of the R.D. Merrill Company ensure high standards of service and long-term commitment to quality, security, choice and privacy in all Merrill Gardens communities.

The mission of Merrill Gardens is focused on residents. The company provides the best in retirement Community living by:

* Supporting the independence, individuality, privacy and decision making abilities of each resident.
* Meeting the changing needs of residents with the best available assisted living, social and wellness services.
* Providing outstanding facilities and a vibrant community living environment for residents. Merrill Gardens provides housing in three areas: independent living, assisted living and Alzheimer's care.

Merrill Gardens is, above all, a company dedicated to quality and built on a strong foundation of family, community, long-term commitment and entrepreneurial spirit.

Tish Anderson Nix, General Manager

530 Northside Drive, Carrollton, Georgia 30117

770-214-1988 and Fax 770-214-1945

www.merrillgardens.com

Southwire
Southwire
Southwire
Southwire®
We Deliver Power...
...From Carrollton

We stand the test of time.

State University of West Georgia

Founded in 1906

Memories by David Wiggins

Jayson and Denise Pate, Kacey and Errol Askin, Sara Wiggins

Mr. and Mrs. F.A. Wiggins

John Knight Pate

Asher Knight Pate

Open Campus High Leadership Team

To my family, friends, and colleagues, and my extended families of Central, Mt. Zion, and Open Campus High Schools, thank you from the bottom of my heart, for a lifetime of wonderful memories.

Love, David.

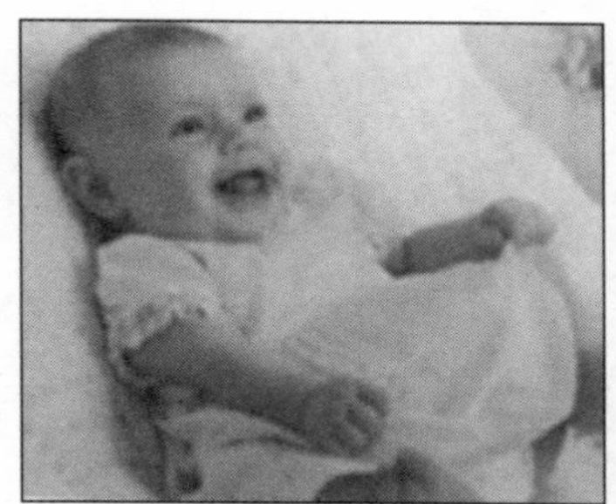

Karis Quinn Askin

1980 Central Lions 7AAS Champions

Best Men - Todd, Steve, Dad, David, Errol, Denzil, Alan

Central High Faculty 1974-1975

Mt. Zion Faculty and Staff 2000-2001

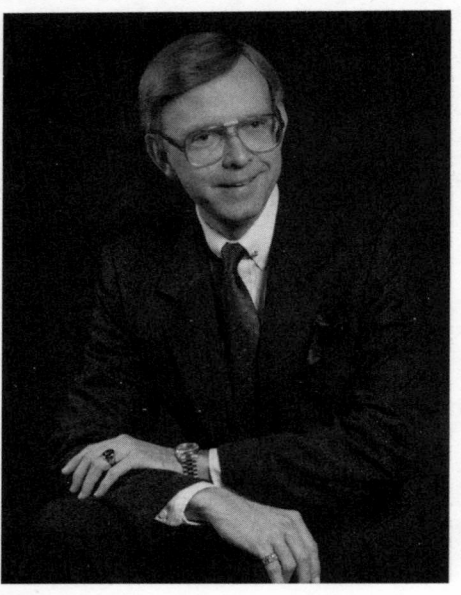

INDEX

Note: numbers refer to *ARTICLE NUMBERS*, and not page number

D

E

F

G

H

I

J

K

L

M

X

Y

Z

INDEX FOR TRIBUTES, MEMORIALS AND BUSINESSES

Note: numbers refer to *PAGE NUMBERS*, and not article number

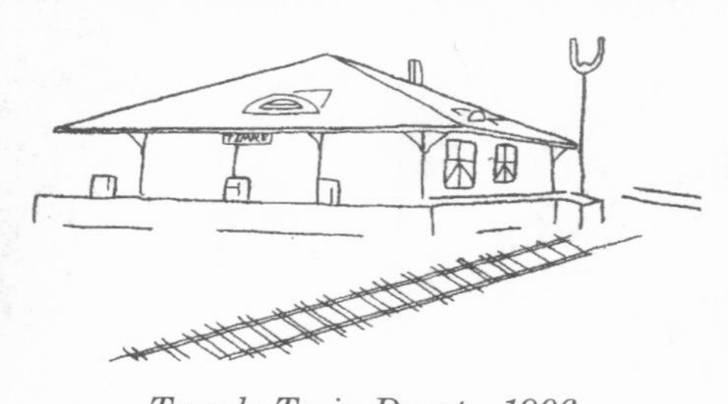
Temple Train Depot - 1906

Round Barn at Hickory Level - 1917

Cross Plains School

Stewart House

Tabernacle Baptist Church

Carroll County Courthouse

Abilene Baptist Church

Statue at Carrollton City Hall

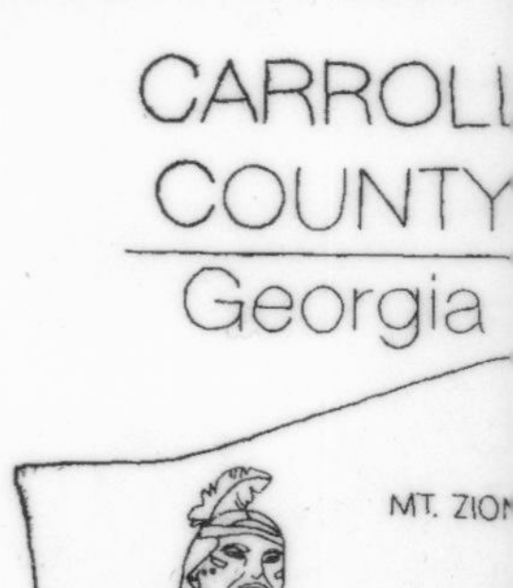

Shiloh United Methodist Church

Appleton Mandeville Home

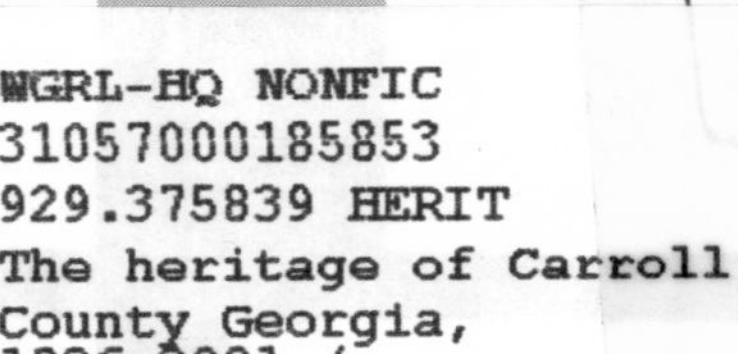

Aycock House

Carrollton First Christian Church

Green Front Restaurant

Bookmobile

Lovvorn Home - Bowdon

Bethesda Baptist Church

ANATOMICA

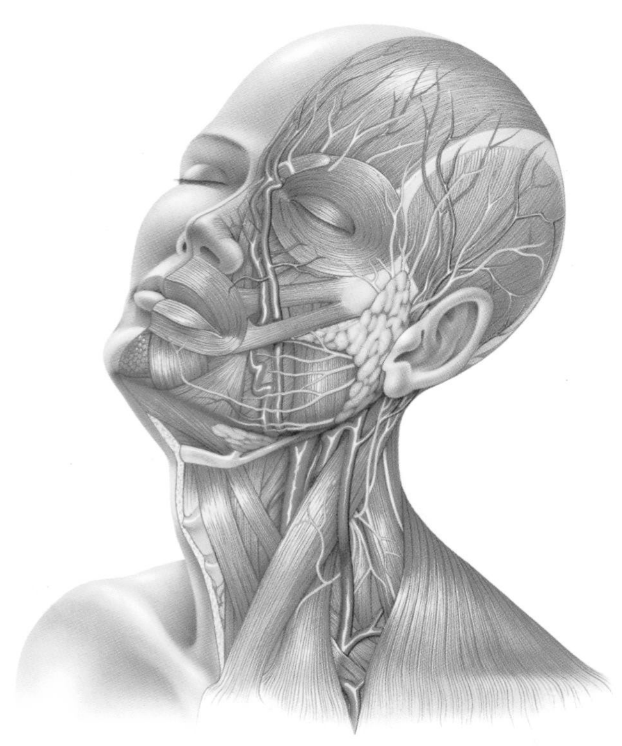

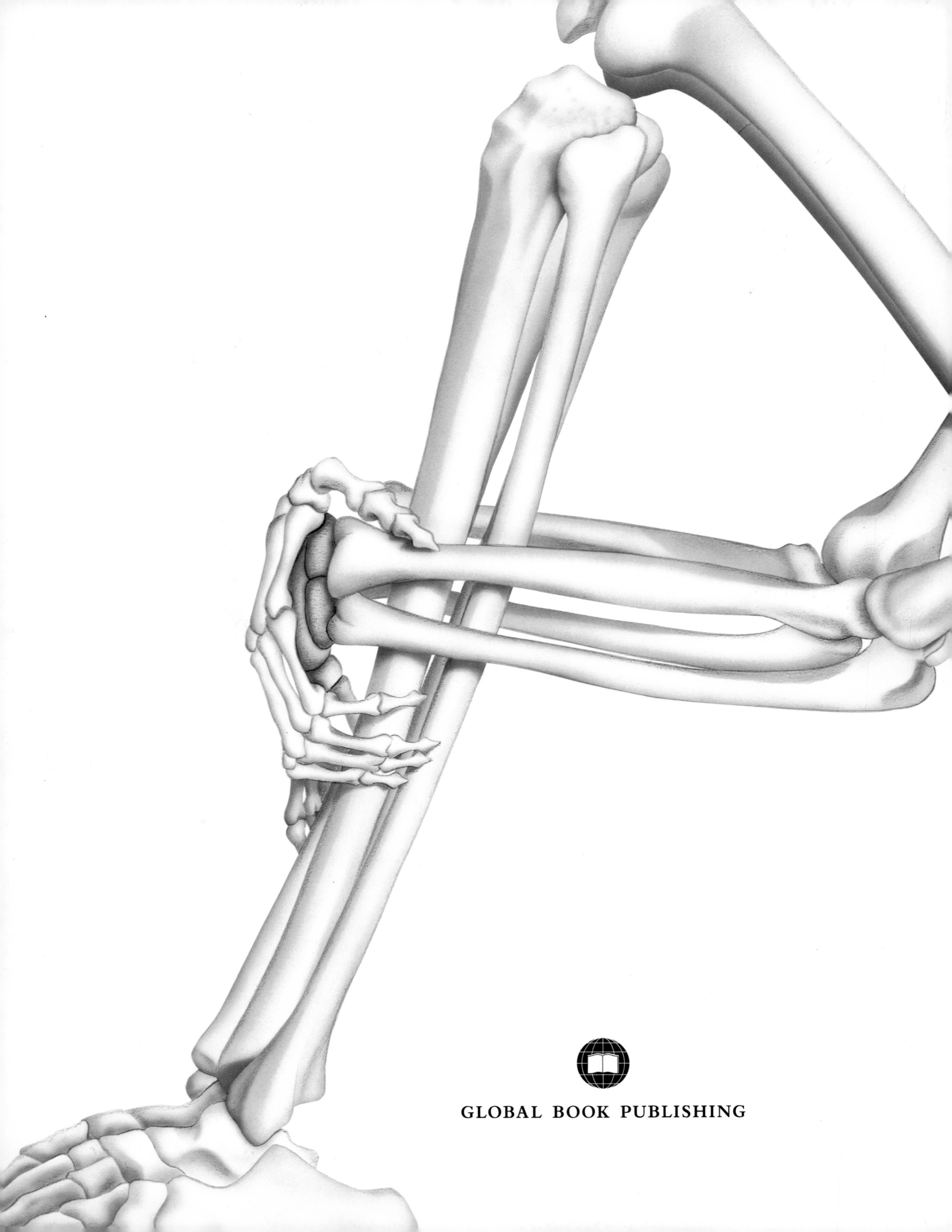
GLOBAL BOOK PUBLISHING

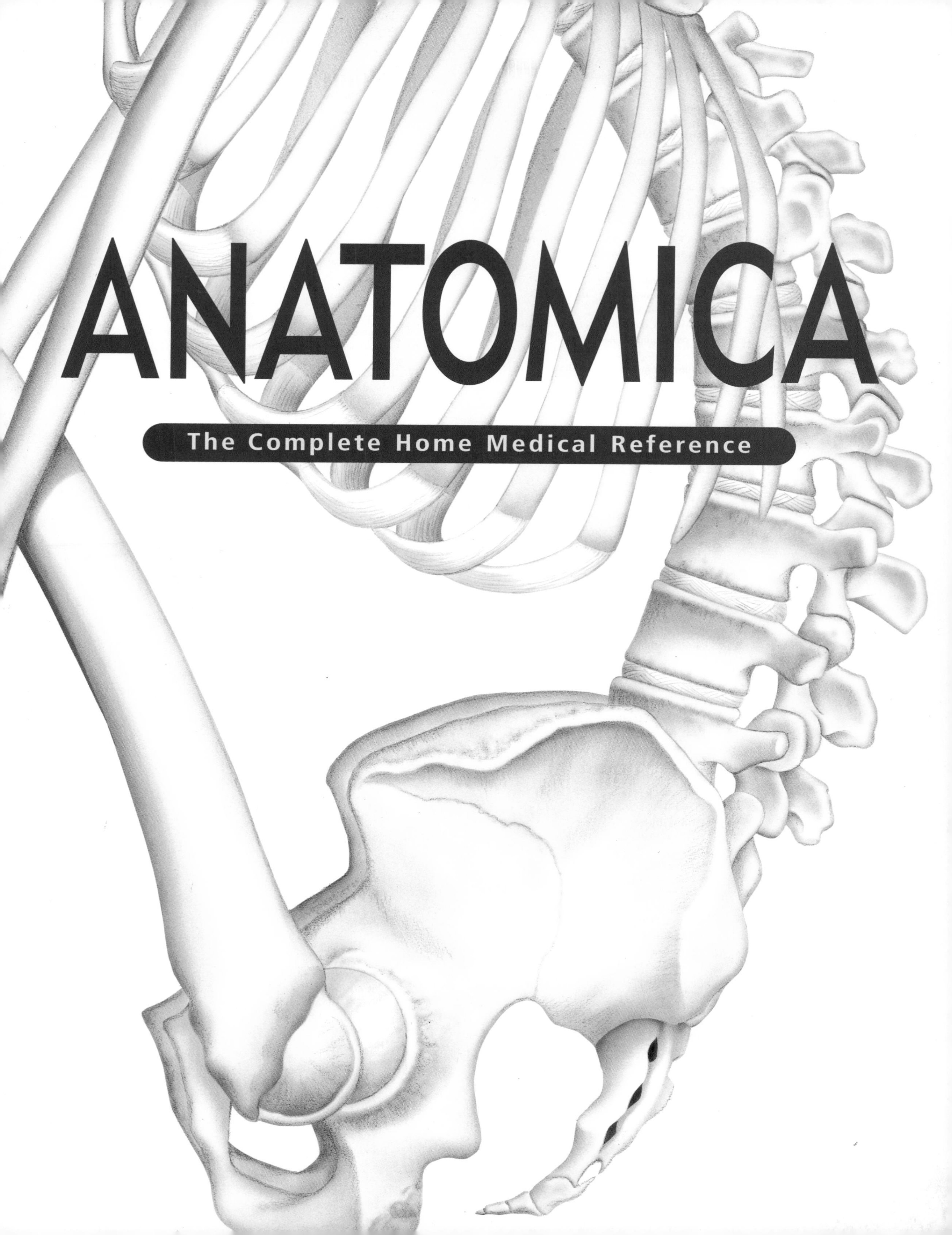

ANATOMICA
The Complete Home Medical Reference

Publisher **Gordon Cheers**

Associate publisher **Margaret Olds**

Text managing editor **Kate Etherington**

Illustration managing editor **Anna Cheifetz**

Chief illustration consultant **Dzung Vu** MD MBBS DipAnat CertHEd

Illustration consultants **John Frith** MBBS BSc(Med) DipEd MCH
David Jackson MBBS BSc (Med)

Symptoms table text **Jenni Harman**
Melanie George MBBS DipPaed
Annette Kifley MBBS
Robyn McCooey BAppSci (Speech & Hearing)
Sue Markham BAppSci (Phty)

First aid information provided by **St John Ambulance Australia**

Illustrators **David Carroll**
Peter Child
Deborah Clarke
Geoff Cook
Marcus Cremonese
Beth Croce
Wendy de Paauw
Levant Efe
Hans De Haas
Mike Golding
Jeff Lang
Alex Lavroff
Ulrich Lehmann
Ruth Lindsay
Annabel Milne
Tony Pyrzakowski
Oliver Rennert
Caroline Rodrigues
Otto Schmidinger
Bob Seal
Vicky Short
Graeme Tavendale
Jonathan Tidball
Paul Tresnan
Valentin Varetsa
Veronica Varetsa
Glen Vause
Spike Wademan
Trevor Weekes
Paul Williams
David Wood

Senior editor **Denise Imwold**

Text editors **Michael Wall**
Anne Savage
Heather Jackson
Margaret Malone
Diana Marks
Dannielle Doggett
Michael Roberts

Illustration editors **Janet Parker**
Heather McNamara
Alan Edwards
Jan Watson
Louise Buchanan
Kavita Enjeti
Barry Grossman
Bernard Roberts

Labels **Thao Vu**
Jin-Oh Ree

Art director **Stan Lamond**

Cover design **Stan Lamond**

Page layout **Paula Kelly**
Claire Edwards
Emma Seymour

Typesetting **Dee Rogers**
Deanne Lowe

Index **Michael Wall**

International rights **Sarah Sherlock**

Publishing assistant **Erin King**

Production assistant **Rosemary Barry**

First published in 2000 by
Global Book Publishing Pty Ltd
1/181 High Street
Willoughby, 2068
NSW, Australia
Phone 61 2 9967 3100 fax 61 2 9967 5891

ISBN 1 74048 0309

Illustrations from the Global Illustration Archives

For all sales, please contact Sarah Sherlock at
Global Book Publishing Pty Ltd
Phone 61 2 9967 3100 fax 61 2 9967 5891

Printed in Hong Kong by Sing Cheong Printing Co. Ltd
Film separation Pica Colour Overseas, Singapore

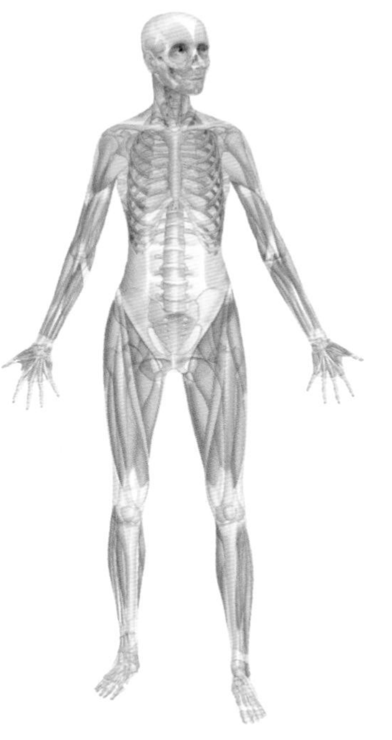

While every care has been taken in presenting this material, the medical information is not intended to replace professional medical advice; it should not be used as a guide for self-treatment or self-diagnosis. Neither the authors nor the publisher may be held responsible for any type of damage or harm caused by the use or misuse of information in this book.

CONSULTANTS

CHIEF CONSULTANTS

Kurt H. Albertine PhD is Professor of Pediatrics (Neonatology), as well as Adjunct Professor of Medicine (Pulmonary) and Neurobiology and Anatomy at the University of Utah School of Medicine in Salt Lake City, Utah, USA.

Dr Albertine received a bachelor's degree in biology from Lawrence University and a doctoral degree in human anatomy from the University of Chicago, Stritch School of Medicine. He received postdoctoral training at the University of California, San Francisco, Cardiovascular Research Institute. He has taught human gross anatomy for twenty-five years, and is currently the course director for gross anatomy at the University of Utah. One of his current scholarly projects is developing radiographic holograms for learning 3-dimensional human anatomy.

David Tracey BSc, PhD studied for his PhD in neuroscience at Stanford University and has worked as a neuroscientist in Munich, Paris, Melbourne and Canberra. In 1982 he joined the School of Anatomy at the University of New South Wales, where he teaches musculoskeletal anatomy.

He became Professor of Anatomy there in 1995 and is Head of Department. His research has included work on the anatomy and physiology of the spinal cord, and currently focuses on mechanisms of pain following nerve injury. He is a board member of the Federation of Australian Scientific and Technological Societies.

The Honorable Emeritus Professor Peter Baume AO, MD, BS (Syd), HonDLitt (USQ), FRACP, FRACGP, FAFPHM has been a professor since 1991. He was Head of the School of Community Medicine at the University of New South Wales until May 2000, and is currently with the Social Policy Research Centre within the University of New South Wales. He is Chancellor of the Australian National University.

He is a physician who holds a doctorate and several fellowships. He has been a consultant physician, a Senator for New South Wales (1974-91), Minister for Aboriginal Affairs, Minister for Health, Minister for Education and a Minister in Cabinet.

He is a Past President of the Public Health Association (New South Wales Branch), Chair of the Drug Offensive Council of New South Wales, a member of the Minister for Health Advisory Committee in New South Wales. He has published widely and was made an Officer in the Order of Australia in 1992. He is married with two children.

SENIOR CONSULTANT

John Frith, MB, BS, BSc(Med), GradDipEd, MCH, RFD is a general practitioner and lecturer in general practice at the School of Community Medicine, University of New South Wales, Sydney. He graduated from the University of New South Wales in 1973, 1976 and 1994, and Sydney College of Advanced Education in 1988. His experience is in clinical and academic general practice and community health. Professional memberships include Member of the Royal Australian College of General Practitioners and medical officer in the Royal Australian Naval Reserve. Other committee memberships include drug and alcohol education and prevention, health and safety in child care, and motor accidents compensation scheme. He lectures in undergraduate general practice and medical ethics and law, and postgraduate primary health care, public health, and environmental health.

Dr Frith has contributed to publications and books on general practice and on public health.

CONSULTANTS

Laurence Garey MA, DPhil, BM, BCh, recently the Professor of Anatomy at the University of London, in the Division of Neuroscience of Imperial College School of Medicine at Charing Cross Hospital, London, is now the Professor of Anatomy in the Faculty of Medicine and Health Sciences at the United Arab Emirates University, Al Ain.

He qualified in medicine at Worcester College, Oxford, and St Thomas' Hospital, London, and obtained a doctorate in Oxford, based on research on the mammalian visual system. He worked in neuroanatomical research in Oxford, Berkeley, Lausanne and Singapore, before returning to London in 1990.

His research interest is on the structure, development and pathology of the human brain, especially the cerebral cortex. For some years he has been active in research on the pathophysiological basis of schizophrenia.

He has contributed to the *Oxford Companion to the Body*, and translated a number of biomedical science books from French, including *Neuronal Man* by Jean-Pierre Changeux (1985), *The Population Alternative* by Jacques Ruffié (1986), and *The Paradox of Sleep* by Michel Jouvet (1999). He has also translated (1994) from the German the famous *Localisation in the Cerebral Cortex* by Korbinian Brodmann, written in 1909.

Dr R. William Currie BSA, MSc, PhD is Professor of Anatomy and Neurobiology in the Faculty of Medicine at Dalhousie University, Halifax, Nova Scotia, Canada. In his academic career, Dr Currie has taught all aspects of gross anatomy to medical, dental and health professional students. He is a pioneer and leader in his research on the protective role of heat shock proteins in the heart and the brain. He is a founding member of the editorial board of *Cell Stress and Chaperones*.

Gareth Jones BSc (Hons), MB, BS (Lond), DSc (Univ West Aust), CBiol, FIBiol is the Professor and Head of the Department of Anatomy and Structural Biology, University of Otago, Dunedin, New Zealand. His main specialties are neurobiology—the organization and plasticity of synaptic connections in the brain; bioethics—issues related to the human body and human tissue; and anatomical education. His recent book projects include *Medical Ethics*; *Speaking for the Dead*; *Universities as Critic and Conscience of Society*; and (forthcoming) *Synapses in the Central Nervous System*.

CONTRIBUTORS

Robin Arnold **MSc** is a lecturer in the Department of Anatomy at the University of Sydney. Her general professional interests include teaching gross anatomy, microscopy, medical history and dental histology. In the area of research her main interests lie in comparative mammalian female reproduction and atherosclerosis.

Ken Ashwell **BMedSc, MB, BS, PhD** graduated in medicine from the University of New South Wales in 1983. After a short time in clinical medicine he returned to research and teaching, undertaking a PhD studying processes in abnormal brain development and graduating from the University of Sydney in 1988. He has been teaching anatomy to medical, chiropractic and science students since 1984 and maintains an active involvement in research on brain development (both normal and abnormal) and brain evolution. He is the author of over fifty scientific papers, two books and two book chapters and is currently Associate Professor in Anatomy.

Deborah Bryce **BSc, MScQual, MChiro, GrCertHEd** is a lecturer in the Department of Anatomy at the University of Sydney. Her special interests lie in teaching and learning in higher education and she has completed studies in this area at the University of NSW and University of Technology, Sydney. She has been central in the development of online teaching resources at the University of Sydney, including an online anatomy museum and anatomy glossary. Her particular area of teaching interest is musculoskeletal anatomy and the vertebral column.

Carol Fallows **BA** and **Martin Fallows** are joint founders of several consumer magazines in the areas of health and parenting. Both began their writing careers in the magazine industry and they share a passion for providing consumers with accurate up-to-date information. Carol is the author of several books on parenting including *The Australian Baby & Child Care Handbook* and *Having a Baby*. Martin is a freelance editor and publishing consultant.

John Gallo **MB, BS (Hons), FRACP, FRCPA** is a Senior Staff Hematologist at South Western Area Pathology Service and Liverpool Hospital, Sydney, Australia. He graduated in medicine from the University of Sydney in 1976 and, as part of his post-graduate training, was a Research Fellow at the University of Maryland Cancer Center in Baltimore, USA, in 1982–1983. His research interests were in the fields of chromosomal abnormalities in leukemia, and the cell cycle. After completing his specialist training he was in private clinical hematology practice in Sydney for 10 years. His main clinical interests are in Hodgkin's lymphoma and bone marrow disorders of the elderly.

Brian Gaynor **MB, BS, FRACP, FRACGP, MRCGP (UK) DCH** is a retired general pediatrician who is currently enjoying life as a part-time family doctor and part-time columnist on the internet. His experience in pediatrics has covered many aspects including hospital consultant, staff specialist in community pediatrics, superintendent of a large home for intellectually handicapped children, plus stints in remote areas, including Fiji, Iraq and Papua New Guinea. His writing career began as part of a midlife crisis when he started as a columnist for a Sydney daily newspaper, then progressed to being a feature writer for different newspapers, magazines and other publications.

Sally Gillespie **BA, DipHerb** has been in private practice in Sydney since 1983, working as a natural therapist and a dream and sandplay therapist. She is the author of *Living the Dream* and *The Book of Dreaming* and the co-author of *The Knot of Time*. In her work as a freelance writer she has contributed articles to *New Woman, Family Circle* and *Nature and Health* magazines.

Jenni Harman **BVSc, BA (Hons I)** is a freelance medical writer specializing in medical education. She trained and worked as a veterinary surgeon before completing an arts degree and working as a research assistant in a university education faculty. As a medical writer, she has specialized in continuing medical education for primary care physicians and specialists, as well as newspaper journalism. Her recent projects include the development of small-group discussion-based educational programs for doctors on asthma, cardiovascular disease and psychiatry, teaching resources for specialists, and fact sheets for patients.

Rakesh Kumar **MB, BS, PhD** graduated in medicine from the All-India Institute of Medical Sciences, New Delhi, and took up an appointment at the University of New South Wales, Sydney in 1977. He subsequently completed a PhD at the University of New South Wales and is now Associate Professor of Pathology. He is an enthusiastic teacher and is involved in courses for both medical and science students. He has a long-standing interest in chronic lung disease and his research focuses on mechanisms of inflammation of the airways in asthma.

Peter Lavelle **MB, BS** graduated in medicine from Sydney University in 1983 and practiced as a primary care physician for several years before becoming a full-time medical writer. He contributes regularly to the *Age* and *Sydney Morning Herald* newspapers, the *Australian Doctor* and the *Medical Observer*.

Lesley Lopes **BA Communications (Journalism)** is a journalist and editor who began her career in publishing as a cadet newspaper reporter 15 years ago. She edited photographic and home entertainment magazines in Sydney for six years before working for a London publishing firm developing a range of children's and lifestyle publications. Lesley recently held the position of Features Editor of Australia's *Better Homes and Gardens* magazine.

Karen McGhee **BSc** is a Sydney-based freelance journalist. Her work has focused on the areas of science and the environment for more than a decade. She has written for newspapers (including the *Sydney Morning Herald*), magazines (ranging from *Time* to *Australian Geographic*), books and television documentaries for both Australian and overseas audiences.

Emeritus Professor Frederick Rost **BSc (Med), MB, BS, PhD, DCP (London), DipRMS** was born in London in 1934 and arrived in Australia in 1937. He was Professor of Anatomy at the University of New South Wales from 1974–95. Retired, Fred is now a freelance author, photographer and artist, and has honorary appointments at the University of New South Wales and Macquarie University. He is currently writing his fifth major book. His interests include cosmology.

Elizabeth Tancred **BSc, PhD** is a Senior Lecturer in Anatomy at the University of New South Wales, with more than 20 years experience in teaching anatomy. Following a BSc with honours in anatomy, she completed a PhD in neuroanatomy in 1983. Her early research was in the area of visual neuroscience but she is now focused on the role of information technology in medical education. She is the author of several software packages for teaching neuroanatomy and cross-sectional anatomy, most notably, "BrainStorm: Interactive Neuroanatomy" which is used widely in universities throughout the world.

Dzung Vu **MD, MB, BS, DipAnat., GradCertHEd** is an orthopedic surgeon and clinical anatomist. He teaches clinical anatomy to medical students and candidates of specialist degrees, and is the author of many teaching videotapes and computer-assisted learning programs in anatomy. He was the recipient of the Vice Chancellor's Award for Excellence in Teaching at the University of New South Wales in 1992 and is an examiner of the Royal Australian College of Ophthalmologists. He is also a gifted medical illustrator and belongs to the Australian Institute of Medical and Biological Illustration, among many other national and international professional associations.

Phil Waite **BSc (Hons), MBChB, CertHEd, PhD** obtained a BSc in physiology followed by a PhD in sensory neurophysiology at University College, London. After emigrating to Australia, she held teaching and research positions at Monash University, Melbourne, and then at the University of Otago in New Zealand. She later graduated in medicine at Otago University and is now a Professor of Anatomy at the University of New South Wales, working on brain development and the effects of injury.

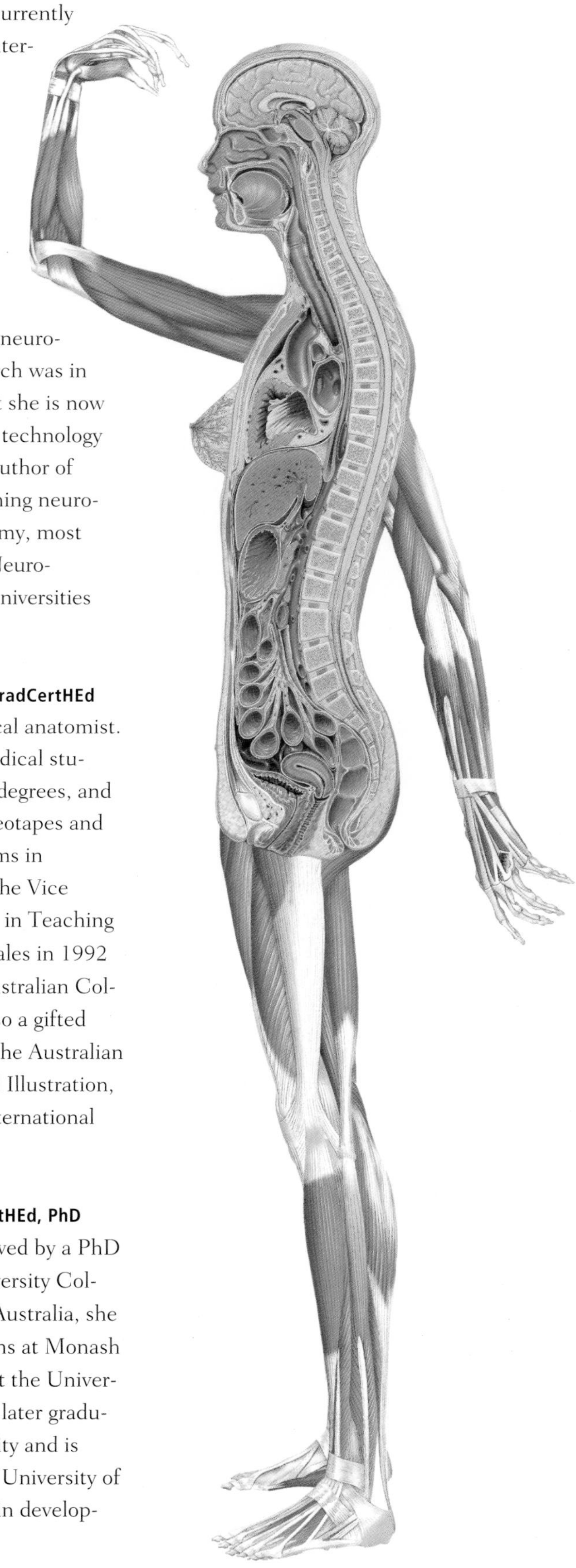

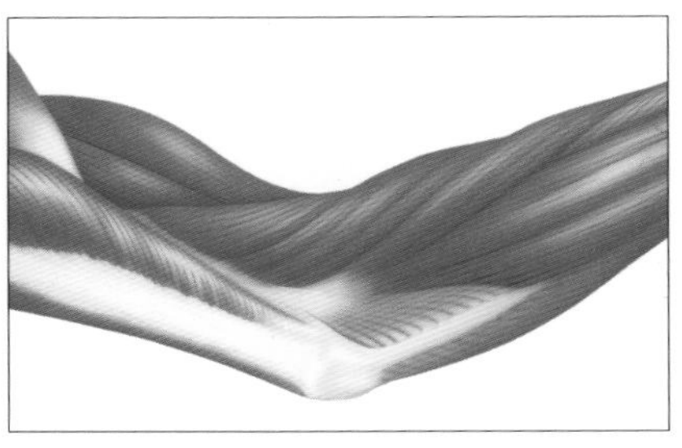

C O N T

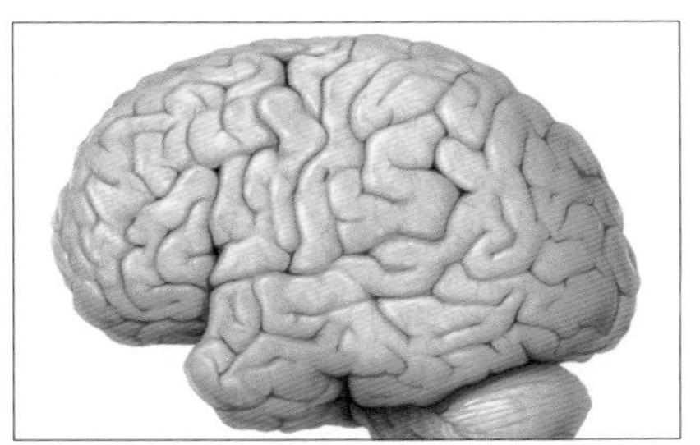

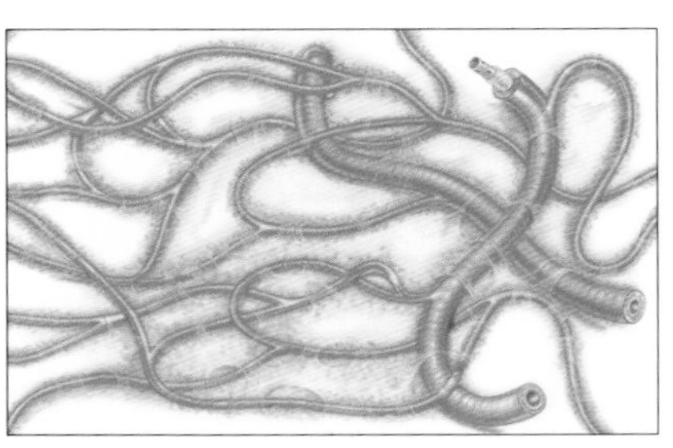

A to Z ENCYCLOPEDIA

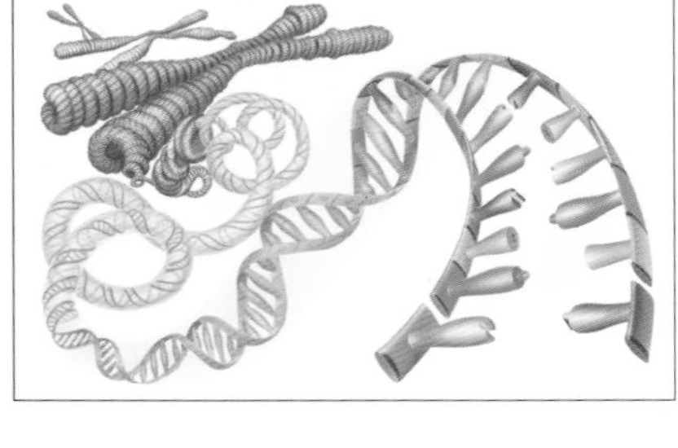

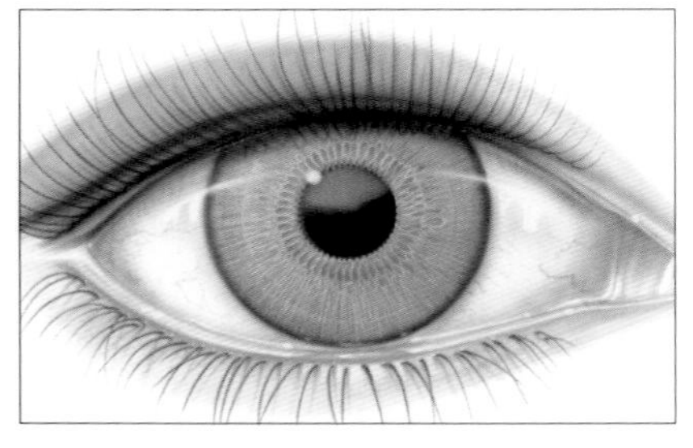

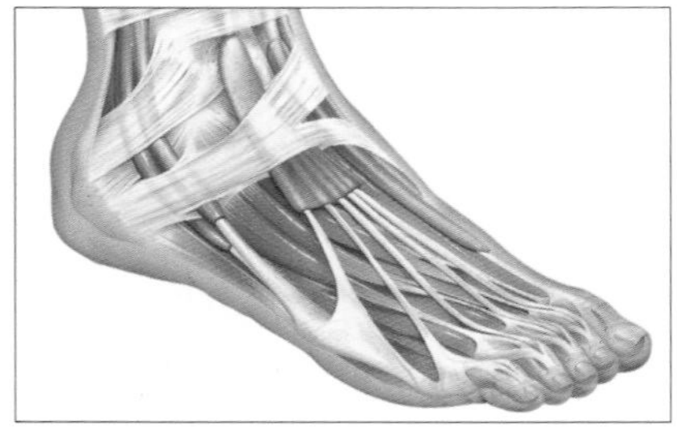

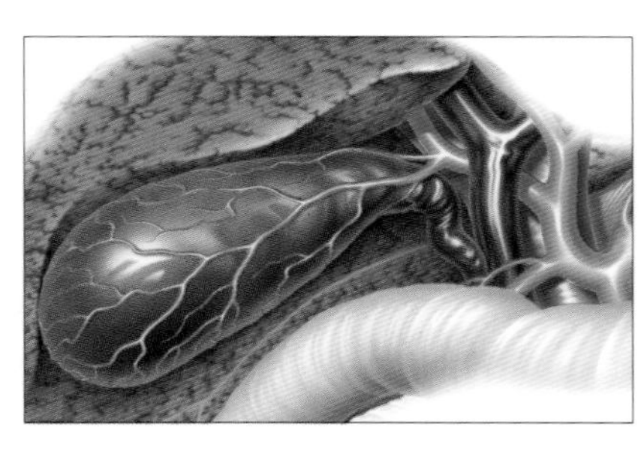

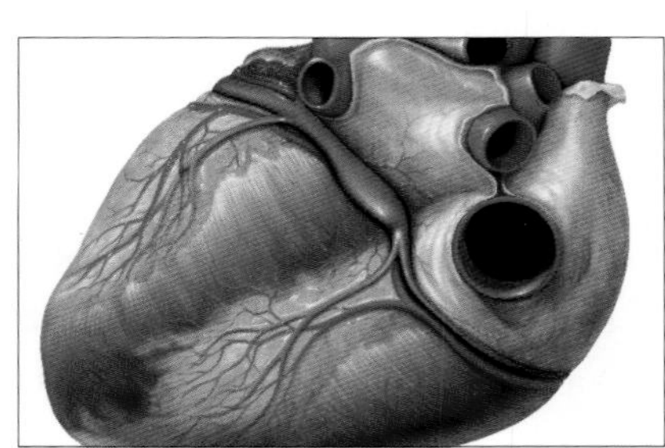

E N T S

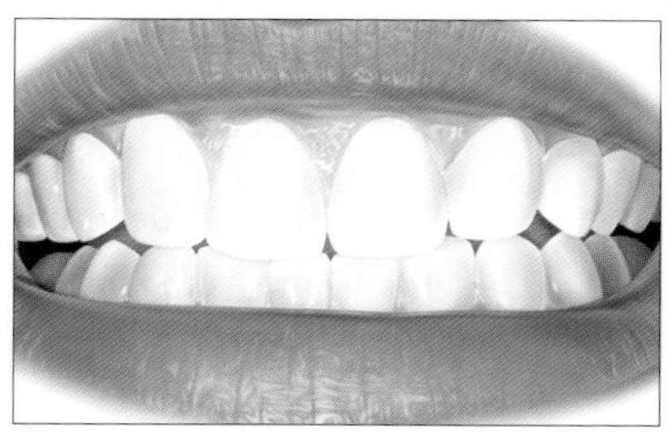

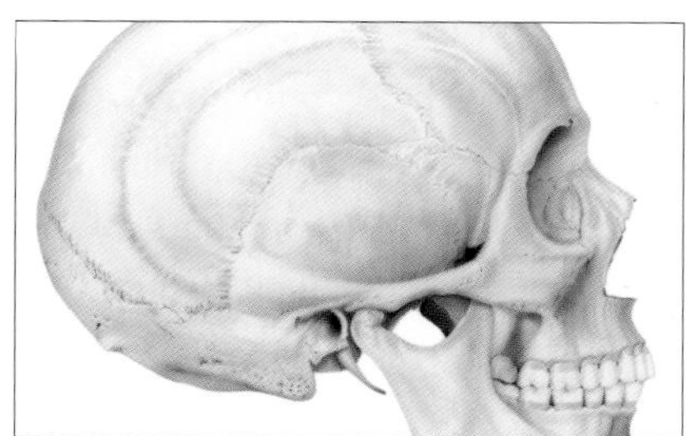

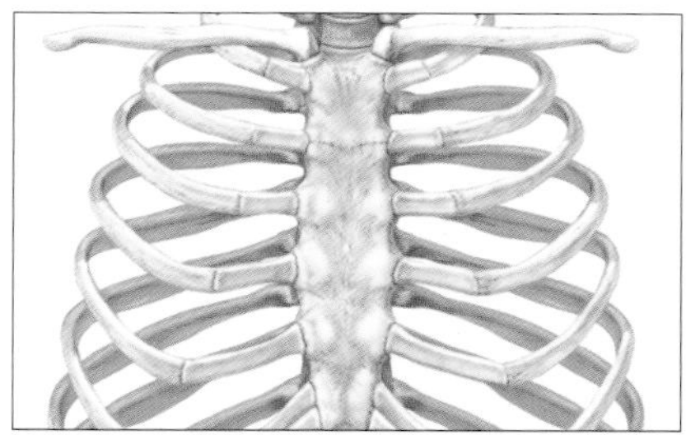

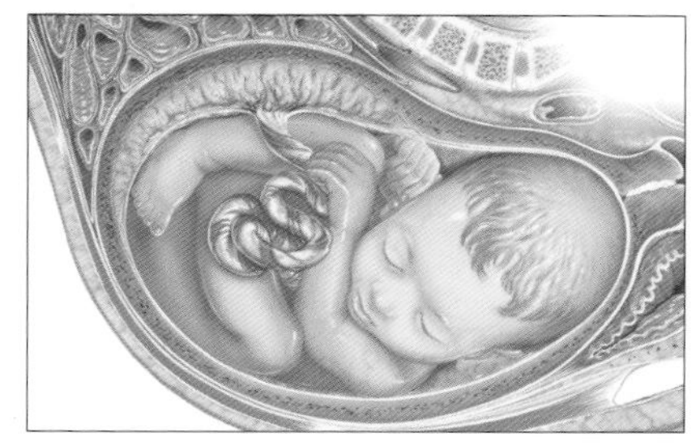

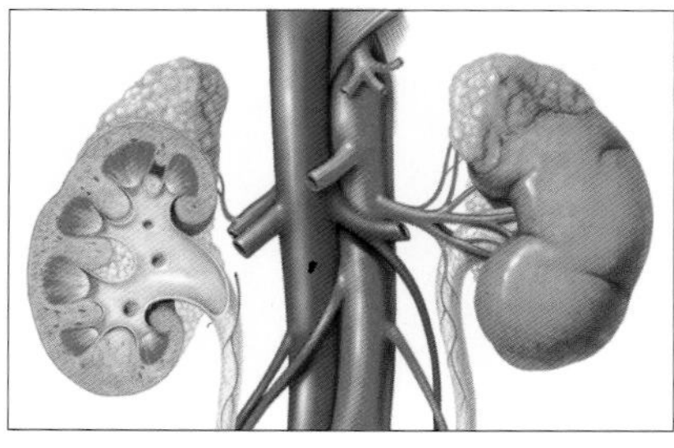

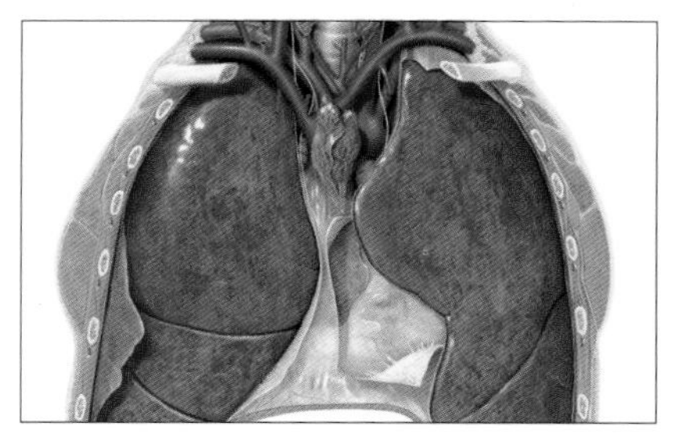

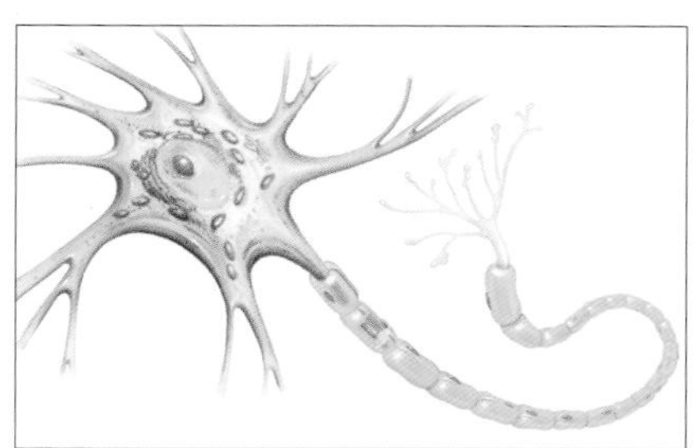

HOW THIS BOOK WORKS

Anatomica is a complete illustrated reference to the human body. However, it is not just a book on anatomy; *Anatomica* is also a comprehensive and authoritative family medical encyclopedia.

The book is divided into several sections. The first section contains the major body systems (Circulatory, Digestive, Endocrine, Lymphatic/Immune, Muscular, Nervous, Reproductive, Respiratory, Skeletal and Urinary) and provides a clear overview of the workings of the body.

The second, and largest section, is an alphabetical listing of entries. It includes descriptions of the various organs and parts of the body, such as the heart, lungs, head and spine. It also contains listings for a large variety of diseases, conditions and injuries—for example, measles, acne, asthma, fractures, hypertension and glaucoma. There are listings for procedures, techniques and diagnostic tests (biopsy, electrocardiograph and CAT scan, to name but a few), and entries for various types of medication, such as anticonvulsants, anti-inflammatory drugs and sedatives.

The A–Z section also contains entries dealing with every stage of life: pregnancy, infancy, childhood, adolescence, menopause, ageing, geriatric medicine and palliative care. There are articles pertaining to aspects of preventive medicine, such as nutrition, diet, exercise and immunization. *Anatomica* recognizes that a person is not simply a physical entity, but also a complex, mental, emotional and social being, and to that end, discusses such topics as alcoholism, domestic violence, grief, sexuality, stress and personality disorders. The book also includes a wide range of alternative therapies, from acupuncture to yoga.

The last part of the book has a chapter on First Aid, which covers every type of emergency. There is also an informative Symptoms Table, which looks at symptoms ranging from abdominal pain to rashes, and advises when to see a doctor. The final section, The Time of Your Life, highlights developmental milestones and preventive health issues for men and women. An extensive index completes the volume.

The detailed illustrations are a visual connection and complement to the text, facilitating understanding. The corresponding captions and labels are relevant and instructive. In some instances, the illustration has removed one part of the body so another may be viewed more clearly; for example, in some of the illustrations of the abdominal organs the liver has been peeled back to show the gallbladder. This is also true of some of the lung illustrations. Many illustrations are supplemented by a locator diagram, which indicates where the organ is in relation to the rest of the body. The appearance of an organ depends on the angle from which it is viewed, and for this reason some of the locators (for example, the uterus) may appear slightly different from the main illustration.

For each alphabetical entry there is a heading, and if there is an illustration, it will include a caption and labels. The SEE ALSOs refer the reader to other relevant A–Z entries; where the cross reference is to a body system, for example, Respiratory system, the reader will need to go to the appropriate section in the front of the book.

For ready reference, colored alphabetical tabs (margin markers) are printed on the margins of the A–Z section and move down the pages to help readers find the entry they are looking for.

Because of the nature of *Anatomica*, technical terms are unavoidable, but we have tried as much as possible to make the language and style interesting and accessible.

Illustrations

Illustrations show what is described in the text. They may show a whole body system, a single organ, microstructure, or the effects of damage or disease on a particular part of the body.

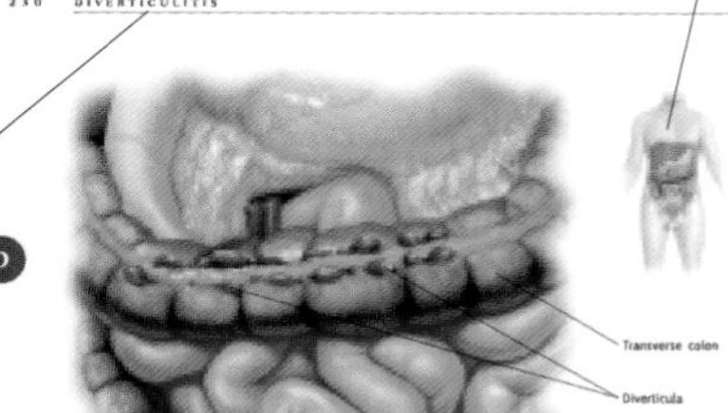

Locator diagrams

Locator diagrams are included to give an indication of where a body part is located in relation to the rest of the body.

Page headings

Page headings on each spread give the name of the first new entry on the left-hand page and the last entry on the right-hand page to make it easy to find the entry you are looking for in the A–Z section.

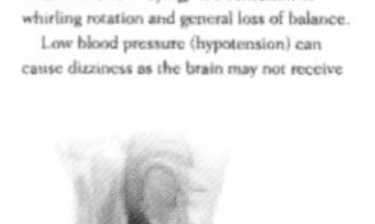

Margin markers

Colored tabs on the edges of the pages help you find your way to the section you want.

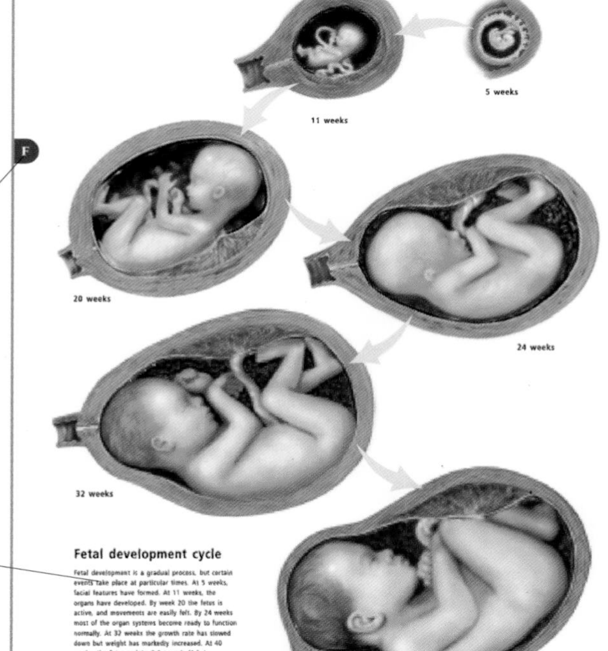

Headings

The entries run in alphabetical order, with a heading marking the beginning of the entry.

Captions

The captions to the illustrations make it easy to understand what the illustration is showing.

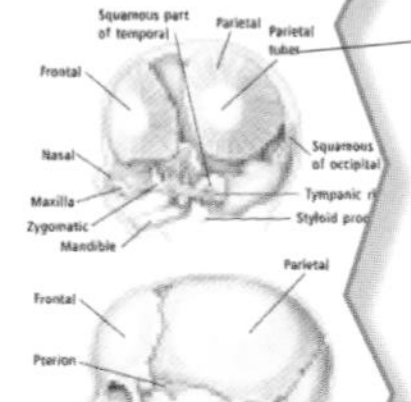

Labels

The labels on each illustration label particular elements that are relevant to the purpose of that illustration.

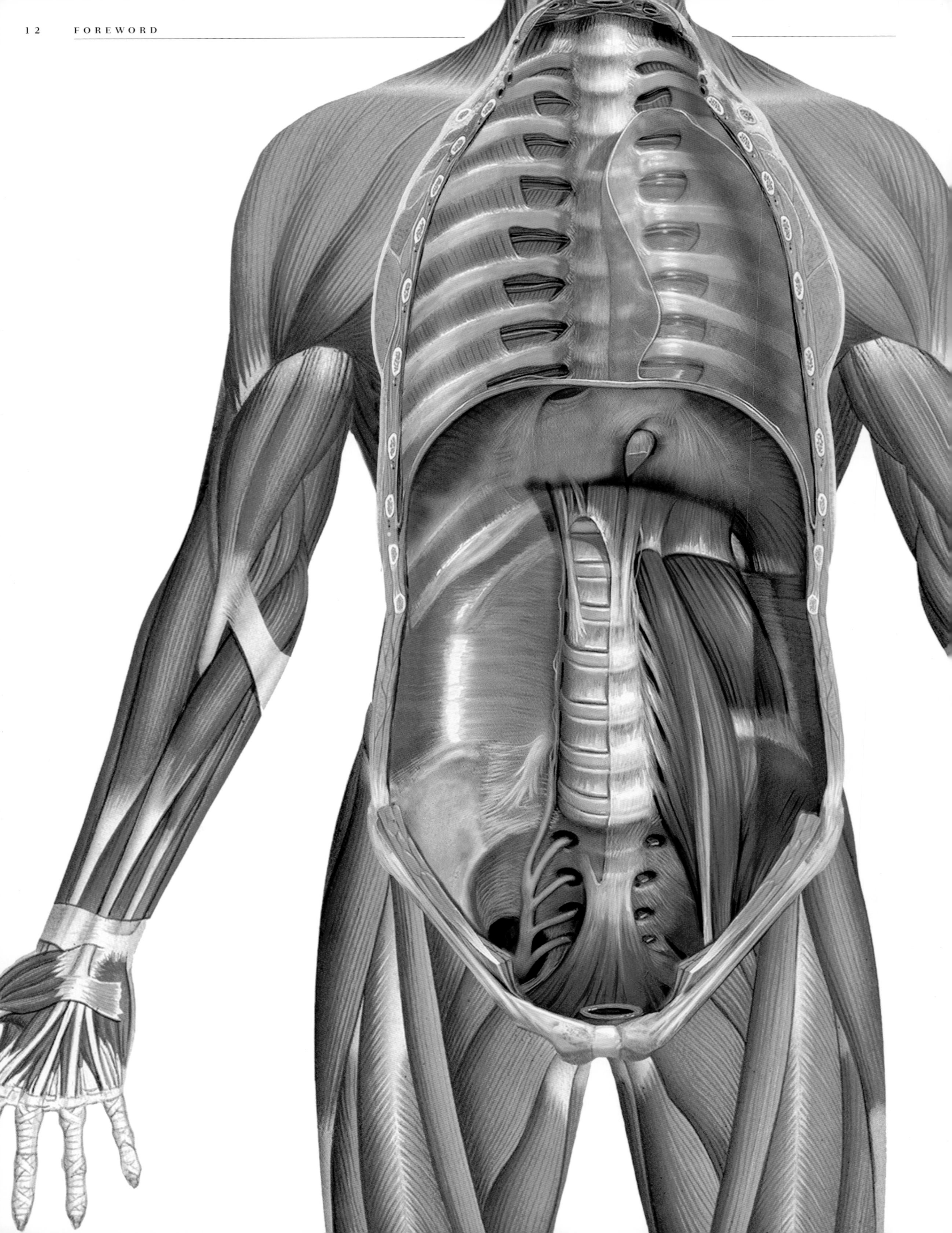

FOREWORD

The name *Anatomica* suggests that this is a book about, or at least very closely associated with anatomy—the structure of the human body. Many books have been written on anatomy, but the great majority of these have been textbooks, targeting medical students and health professionals. *Anatomica* is not a textbook, and is not aimed at health professionals. The concept is to present human anatomy in the context of medical knowledge, and to do so in a way which is accessible to everyone.

However *Anatomica* is not confined to anatomy in isolation. While the text and beautiful illustrations cover the human body and its structure and function, they also cover numerous medical conditions, showing both the normal and the damaged or diseased body.

An understanding of the structure of the body is fundamental to an understanding of how it works. It is therefore a vital part of medicine and an essential part of medical training, but this knowledge is not the exclusive preserve of the health professional. We may not be too concerned about the structure and function of our bodies while they are working perfectly, but as soon as something goes wrong most of us would like to understand what has gone wrong and how it can be treated. *Anatomica* provides a guide to normal structure at all levels, from the arrangement of bones and muscles which we can see with the naked eye, to the arrangement of cells and their components which can only be seen with the light microscope or the electron microscope.

Medical therapies are included, with specialist terms for treatments and medications clearly explained. Alternative therapies are also covered, showing how they may fit into the wide array of health care offerings available today. The important thing to remember is that no one form of therapy is a panacea.

Anatomica is not a medical dictionary, but it is a book that provides a great deal of information about our bodies in good health and in poor health. The broad subject matter is covered in an easy style. Accurate scientific detail has not been sacrificed, but the book will be accessible to a wide audience.

Anatomica is intended to help readers understand their bodies and to know what sorts of solutions are available for the body's ills. It is not intended as a "do-it-yourself" manual, or as a substitute for the advice and expertise of health professionals.

Doctor Kurt Albertine

PROFESSOR OF NEONATALOGY
DEPARTMENT OF PEDIATRICS
SCHOOL OF MEDICINE
UNIVERSITY OF UTAH
SALT LAKE CITY, UTAH

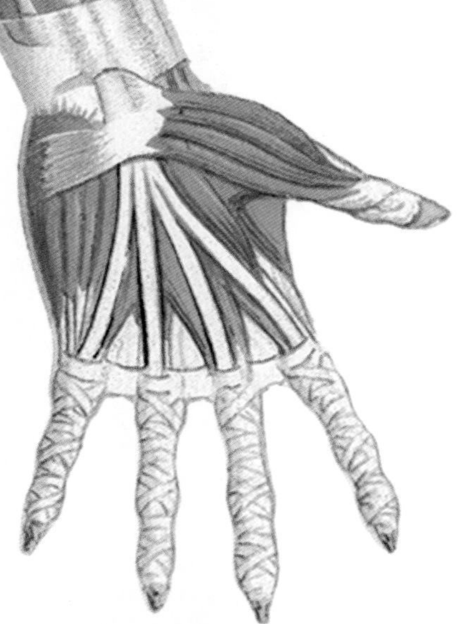

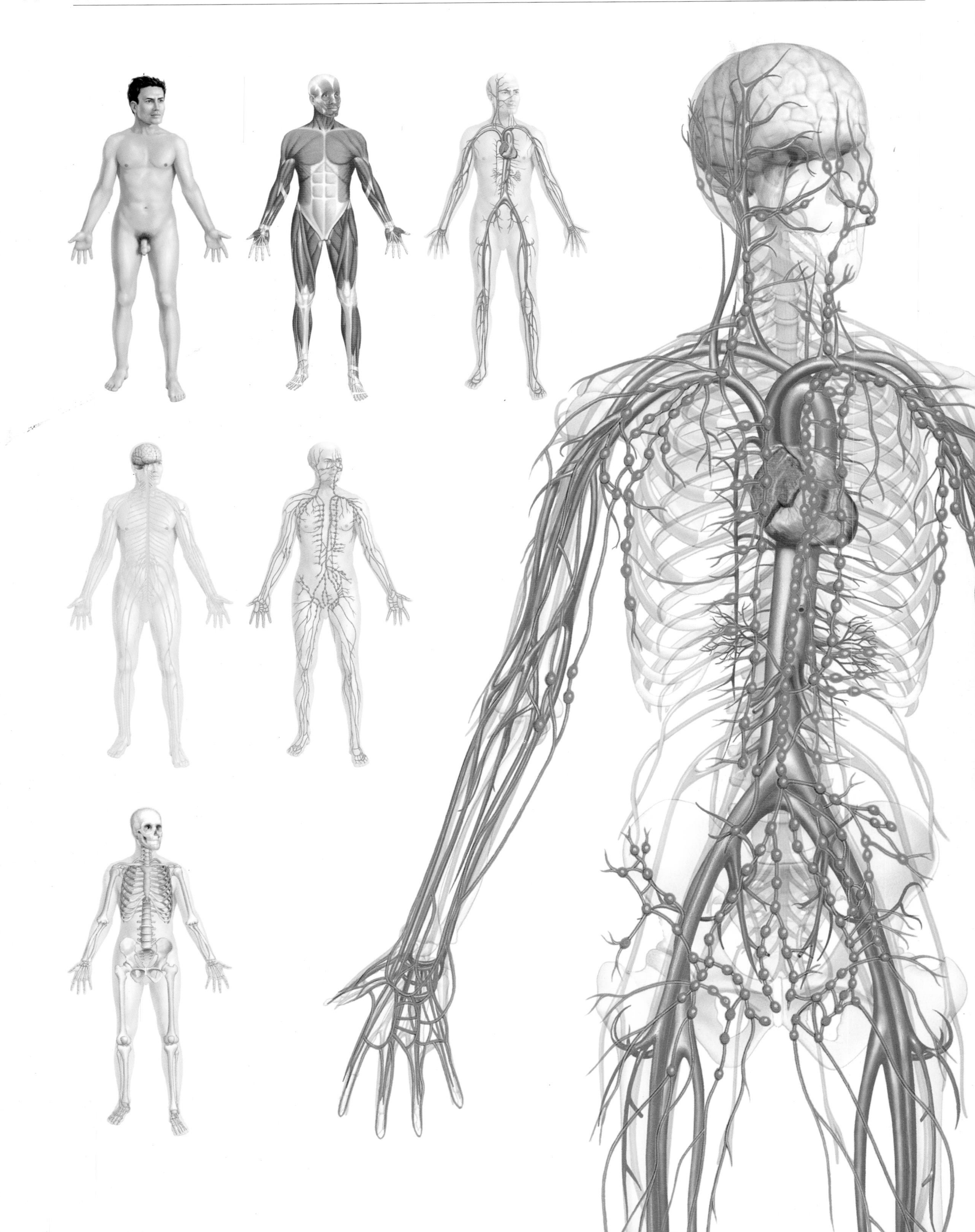

BODY SYSTEMS

When considering the structural and functional organization of the body, it is usual to divide the body into various systems. Actually, body systems collectively make up just one level of structural organization. The most basic structural unit of the body is the cell. Cells group together to make tissues, which in turn are grouped together to make organs. Organs work together to make body systems and these systems cooperate to form a complete human being.

The systems of the body are each concerned with a particular function or a group of related functions. To understand how they work together to produce a complete person, we need to briefly consider the function of each system. The skeletal system is composed of the bones, and the cartilage and ligamentous structures associated with them. It protects and supports soft tissues and provides scaffolding for muscle attachment. The muscular system produces movement and is composed of muscles, tendons and sheaths around muscles and lubricating sacs called bursae. The nervous system collects and analyzes information about the environment and internal body function and controls and coordinates body function. The nervous system consists of the central nervous system (brain and spinal cord); the peripheral nervous system, which includes all the nerves outside the brain and spinal cord; and the autonomic nervous system, which controls the automatic internal function of the body and partially overlaps with the peripheral and central nervous systems. Another system which is also concerned with control of the internal body function is the endocrine system, which uses circulating chemical messengers called hormones to exert its effects. The circulatory system consists of the heart and all the blood vessels (arteries, veins and capillaries) and is responsible for moving nutrients, waste and some special proteins (for example hormones) and cells around the body. The lymphatic system is also an important transport system for the body, moving excess tissue fluid back to the veins and transporting fat from the gut to the bloodstream. Its other important role is the defense of the body, and for this reason some elements of the lymphatic system are referred to as the immune system. The respiratory system is concerned with gas exchange and the intake of oxygen, needed by all the body's tissues and cells. The digestive system is concerned with the ingestion, processing and absorption of nutrients, as well as the elimination of some types of waste. The urinary system controls fluid and salt balance in the body and excretes nitrogen waste. The reproductive system is concerned with production of the next generation and is linked during fetal development with the developing urinary system.

Apart from responding to changes in the external environment, producing the activity which outside observers see as human behavior, the body must also act to produce a relatively constant internal environment. This process is called homeostasis and involves many facets of internal function, including maintaining constant body temperature, relatively constant blood sugar levels, blood pressure and blood calcium levels. Homeostasis is achieved by the coordinated action of the autonomic nervous and endocrine systems on the other systems in the body. The hormones produced by the glands of the endocrine system often stimulate the production of other hormones in the target organs. These secondary hormones act on the gland that produced the first hormone, thereby reducing its production. This type of negative feedback system brings about the constant balancing of internal body function.

SKELETAL SYSTEM

The skeleton is the framework of the body and is usually described in two parts, the axial skeleton and the appendicular skeleton.

The axial skeleton

The axis of the body is formed by the skull, the vertebral column (backbone) and the thoracic cage (chest).

The skull

The skull forms the skeleton of the head. It consists of the cranium, the mandible (lower jawbone) and the hyoid bone at the base of the tongue. The top part of the skull (the cranial cavity) houses and protects the brain and part of the brain stem. The facial skeleton is the lower part of the skull that underlies the face. The upper jaw is fixed and formed by two bones called the maxillae.

Where the cranial cavity meets the facial skeleton, there are two orbits, or sockets, for the eyes. Underlying the nose is the nasal aperture of the skull that leads to the nasal cavity.

The base of the skull articulates with the first bone of the spine: the atlas vertebra. This joint allows the head to flex and extend (as in nodding) and to move sideways.

Many bones of the skull are hollow. The cavities inside them are called sinuses. They lessen the weight of the bone and give resonance to the voice.

The vertebral column

The vertebral column (backbone or spine) is a stack of small bones known as vertebrae. There are 7 vertebrae in the neck, 12 in the thorax (the chest region), and 5 in the lumbar region (the small of the back, behind the abdomen). The last two bones of the vertebral column, the sacrum and the coccyx, are formed by vertebrae which fuse after puberty (5 in the sacrum, 4 in the coccyx).

Vertebrae articulate with one another on intervertebral disks. These are flexible pads of cartilage that separate one vertebra from another. Each vertebra can only move a few degrees at its intervertebral disk, but the sum of all these individual movements gives great mobility to the vertebral column.

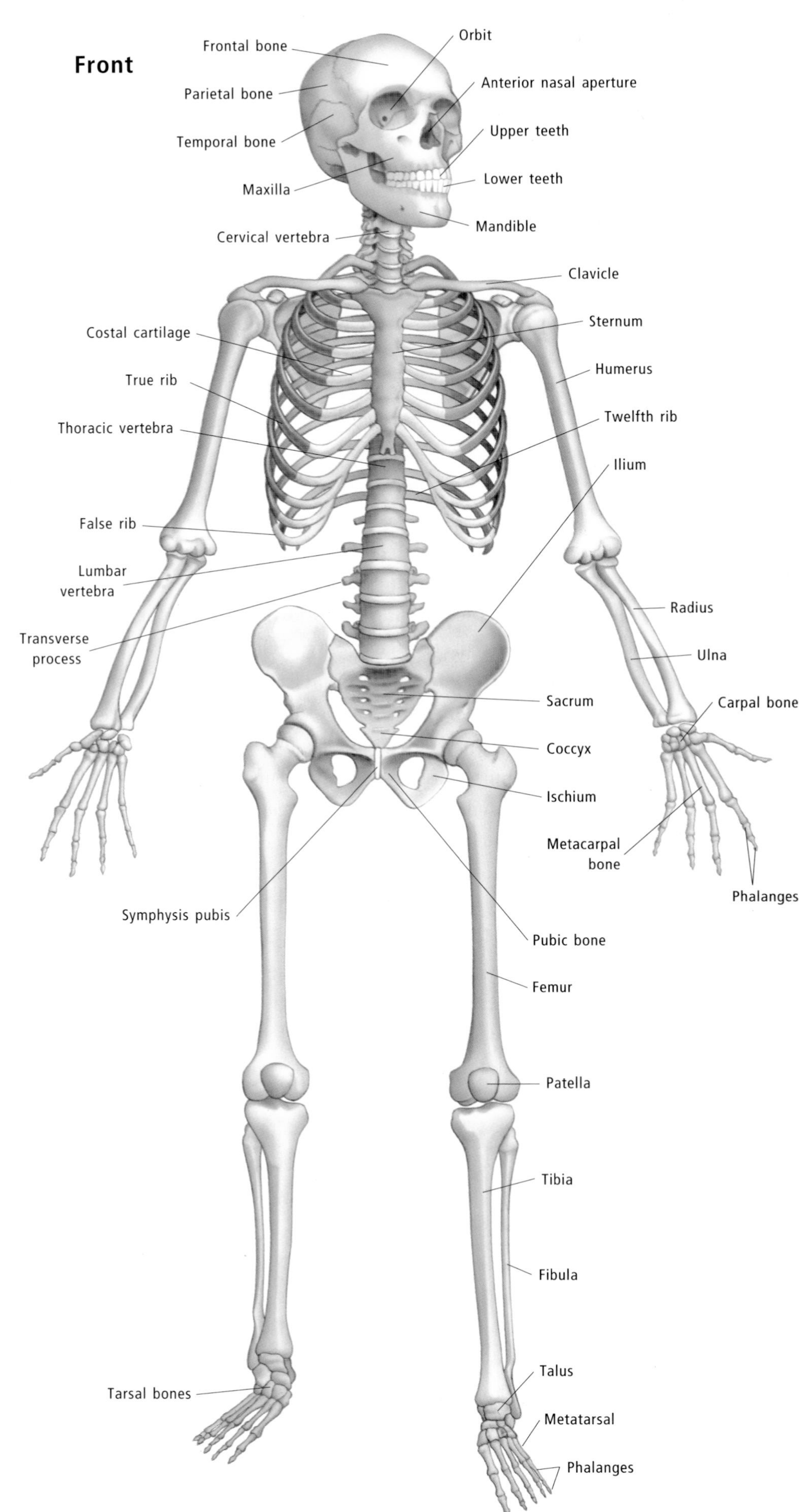

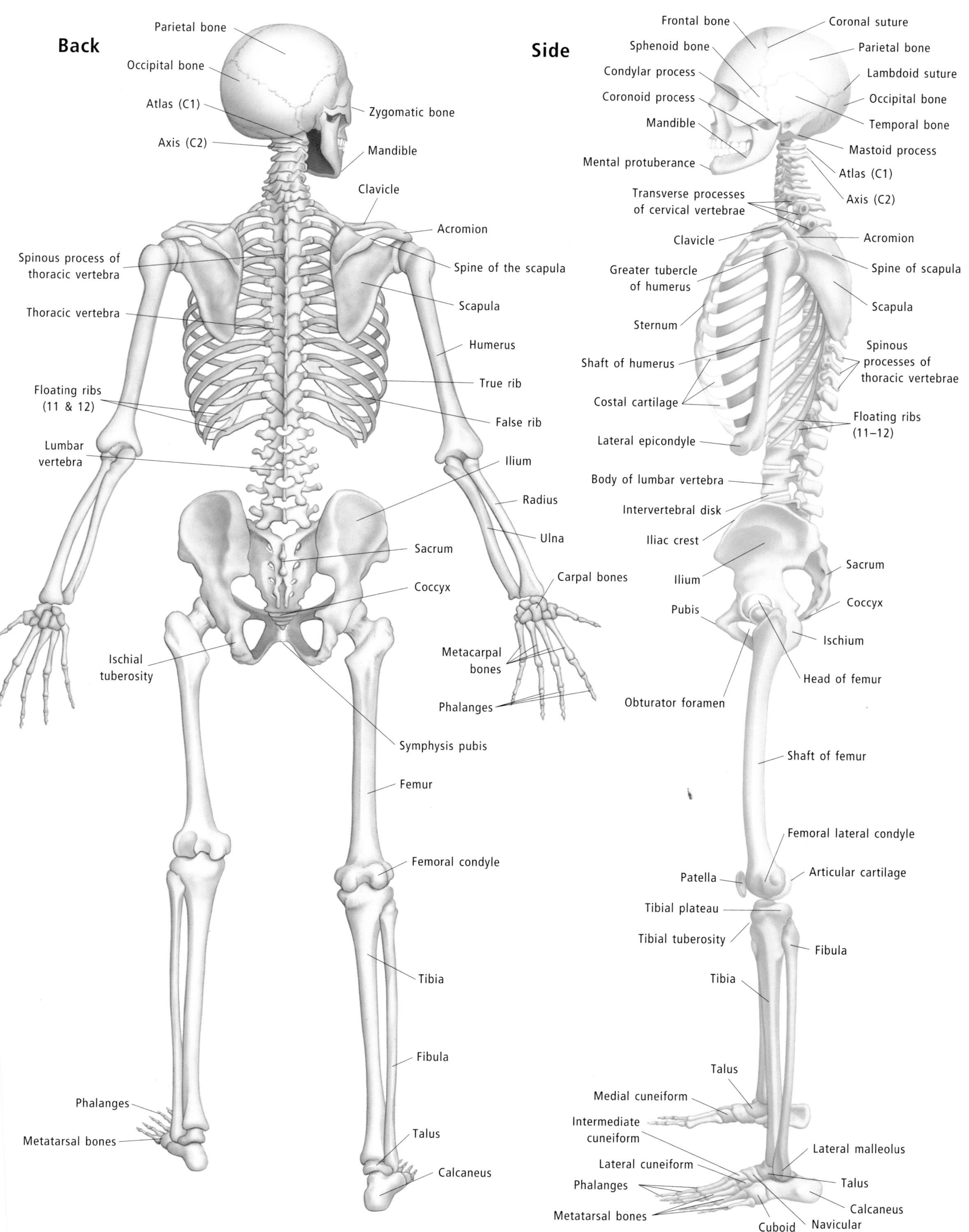
Back
Parietal bone
Occipital bone
Atlas (C1)
Axis (C2)
Zygomatic bone
Mandible
Clavicle
Acromion
Spinous process of thoracic vertebra
Spine of the scapula
Scapula
Thoracic vertebra
Humerus
True rib
Floating ribs (11 & 12)
False rib
Lumbar vertebra
Ilium
Radius
Ulna
Sacrum
Carpal bones
Coccyx
Ischial tuberosity
Metacarpal bones
Phalanges
Symphysis pubis
Femur
Femoral condyle
Tibia
Fibula
Phalanges
Metatarsal bones
Talus
Calcaneus
Side
Frontal bone
Coronal suture
Sphenoid bone
Parietal bone
Condylar process
Lambdoid suture
Coronoid process
Occipital bone
Mandible
Temporal bone
Mastoid process
Mental protuberance
Atlas (C1)
Transverse processes of cervical vertebrae
Axis (C2)
Clavicle
Acromion
Greater tubercle of humerus
Spine of scapula
Scapula
Sternum
Spinous processes of thoracic vertebrae
Shaft of humerus
Costal cartilage
Floating ribs (11–12)
Lateral epicondyle
Body of lumbar vertebra
Intervertebral disk
Iliac crest
Sacrum
Ilium
Coccyx
Pubis
Ischium
Head of femur
Obturator foramen
Shaft of femur
Femoral lateral condyle
Patella
Articular cartilage
Tibial plateau
Tibial tuberosity
Fibula
Tibia
Talus
Medial cuneiform
Intermediate cuneiform
Lateral malleolus
Lateral cuneiform
Talus
Phalanges
Calcaneus
Metatarsal bones
Cuboid
Navicular

When you carry a heavy weight, the vertebral column is turned into a rigid pillar by the contraction of muscles at the back of the column. When you bend forward to lift a load, the force applied to the intervertebral disk can be large enough to damage the disk.

The thoracic cage

The thoracic cage, or chest, is made up of the 12 thoracic vertebrae, the ribs and the sternum. The top 7 true ribs extend from the vertebrae at the back and curve around the front to the sternum and connect to it by extensions of cartilage, the costal cartilages. The next 3 ribs, the false ribs, do not extend all the way around—their costal cartilage fuses onto the cartilage of the last true rib. The final 2 ribs, the floating ribs, do not reach the front. The rib cage protects the heart and lungs. The ribs, moved by the intercostal muscles, are involved in breathing.

Appendicular skeleton

The appendicular skeleton consists of the bones of the limbs and the shoulder and pelvic girdles, the bones that support and attach the limbs to the axial skeleton. The upper and lower limbs are similar in their composition. The shoulder girdle of the upper limb corresponds to the hip or pelvic girdle in the lower limb. The long bone of the upper arm is the humerus; in the lower limb the long bone is known as the femur. The forearm and the lower leg both have 2 long bones; the wrist has 8 bones, the ankle has 7. There are 5 bones in both the palm of the hand and the sole of the foot, with 14 bones making up the digits of both the hand and the foot.

The lower limb has to support the body weight and therefore is less flexible than the upper limb. The scapula (shoulder blade) can slide freely on the rib cage because it is attached to it by muscles. It is only stabilized at the front, by a strut known as the clavicle (collar bone). By contrast, the pelvic girdle is fixed to the axial skeleton where the 2 hip bones articulate with the sacrum at the base of the vertebral column. In front, the 2 hip bones join at the symphysis pubis. Each hip has an acetabulum, a deep socket that accommodates the head of the femur.

Bone structure

The cylindrical shape and internal structure of bones provides maximum strength without being too heavy. Bones have several outer layers enclosing a central cavity which contains bone marrow.

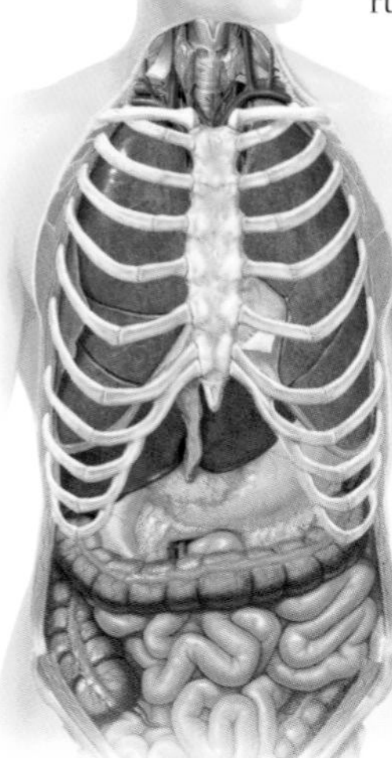

Protection for internal organs

The heart and the lungs are protected by the thoracic cage, a structure of bone comprising the ribs, sternum and the vertebral column.

Structure and function of bone

Bone tissue is formed by a matrix of connective tissue with a heavy deposition of calcium salts. In addition to its obvious functions such as the support and protection of vital organs, the skeleton is thus a reservoir of mineral salts, especially calcium, and plays an important role in calcium metabolism.

Although skeletons in museums give the impression that bones are brittle, living bones are much stronger than dry bones. Their structure is designed to best serve their mechanical functions and is continually remodeled throughout a lifetime.

The role of the bones in body movement is best seen in the limbs. The limb bones act as levers which are moved by the muscles attached to them in much the same way that the arms of a crane are activated by motors. The femur must be mechanically strong enough to bear the weight of a person's body but light enough to minimize the muscle force required to move that weight. A metal tube is much stronger against bending than a solid rod made out of the same amount of metal. Similarly, the shaft of a long bone, such as the femur, is made up of a cylinder of compact bone. In the center of the femur is spongy bone formed by bands of bone called trabeculae. The spaces between the trabeculae are filled up with bone marrow. This cylindrical arrangement is repeated within the compact bone, which is made up of tiny cylinders formed by concentric layers of bone surrounding blood vessels and nerves. The gaps between these microscopic cylinders are packed with thin plates of bone (laminae) running in all directions.

At the ends of the long bones, the trabeculae are aligned along the lines of stress applied to the bone. The body weight received by the head of each femur is transmitted down the neck of the bone to the shaft; the trabeculae there form arches along the lines of stress just like arches under a bridge.

The structure of a bone changes according to the stress applied to it. Exercise strengthens bones, while a prolonged state of inactivity weakens bone structure. When new bone is formed to bridge over a fracture, the trabeculae are rearranged along the line of stress. Weight bearing is therefore recommended during bone healing to promote the optimal development of new trabeculae.

The joints

Wherever two bones come into contact with each other, there is a joint: this is known as articulation. The bones may be separated by cartilage and often fluid. Not all joints are mobile. There is no perceptible movement at the sutures of the skull, for example, where the serrated edges of the skull bones interlock. There is only a small amount of movement at joints such as the symphysis pubis where the bones are connected to one another by cartilage. The most mobile joints are the synovial joints, found in the appendicular skeleton.

The articular surfaces of a joint never fit together perfectly. The better the bones fit together, the more stable the joint becomes. Looser joints are more mobile but less stable.

The hip joint must be stable to support the body weight, so the acetabulum is deep and fits snugly on the head of the femur. For the same reason the hip bones are fixed to the vertebral column, and the thigh has limited movement.

By contrast, the articular surface of the scapula is smaller and does not fit well with the head of the humerus. The shoulder joint is thus very mobile but not stable; it dislocates easily. Free sliding of the scapula on the rib cage further increases the range of movement of the arm.

Where there is a series of joints, the total range of movement is the sum of the movements of the individual joints. The vertebral column is one such example of a chain of joints. The 8 carpal bones of the wrist allow a wide range of movement of the hand. The 7 tarsal bones of the ankle allow the foot to be tilted in many directions to negotiate uneven ground.

Synovial joint

In a synovial joint, the ends of the bones are smooth, and covered by articular cartilage with an extremely low coefficient of friction.

The two bones are bound together by a capsule of fibrous tissue. The fibrous capsule is lined on the inside by a synovial membrane that secretes synovial fluid to lubricate the joint and nourish the cartilage.

The joint is reinforced by ligaments. Some ligaments are just thickened areas of the capsule itself, while others are attached to the bones. The cruciate ligaments of the knee joint, for example, are very strong fibrous cords that are separate from the capsule of the knee joint.

Capsules and ligaments are both made up of fibers of connective tissue. While the fibers in capsules are randomly arranged, those in ligaments are densely packed and run parallel in one direction. This arrangement gives ligaments a shiny appearance and great tensile strength in the direction of the fibers. In some injuries, bones break before ligaments rupture.

When a synovial joint is injured, it becomes swollen either because of bleeding into the joint or as a result of increased secretion of synovial fluid. Inflammation of the joint is called arthritis and can be caused by either infection or diseases of the synovial membrane or cartilage.

When a joint is sprained, the ligaments may be stretched or ruptured. When a joint is immobilized for a long period of time, such as in a cast, the capsule and ligaments contract and become stiff, reducing the range of movement of the joint when the cast is removed. Physical therapy and stretching exercises often help the joint regain its mobility.

SEE ALSO *Ankle, Arm, Arthritis, Back, Bones, Cartilage, Collar bone, Connective tissue, Disk, intervertebral, Femur, Hand, Hip, Humerus, Joints, Knee, Leg, Ligaments, Pelvis, Ribs, Shoulder, Skull, Spine, Sternum, Synovial fluid, Synovial membrane, Vertebrae, Wrist*

Tissue types in a synovial joint

In a synovial joint, cartilage acts as a cushion between the bones. Ligaments reinforce the joint. Spongy bone tissue, containing air pockets, forms most of the bone with compact bone underlying the cartilage. Hyaline cartilage is made up of connective tissue and is flexible and elastic. Ligaments also comprise connective tissue, but the tissue fibers are densely packed and run parallel in one direction to provide great tensile strength.

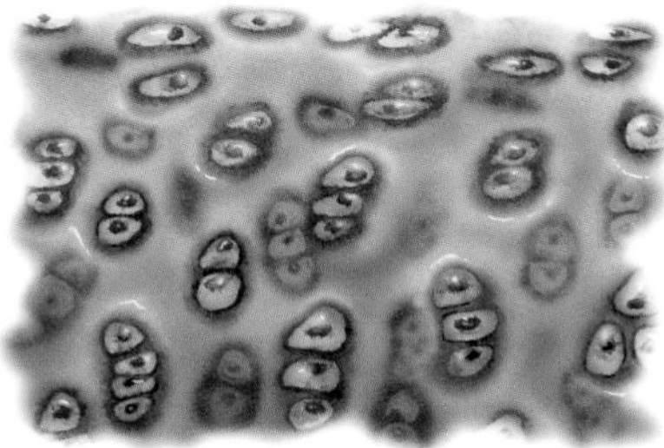

Hyaline cartilage

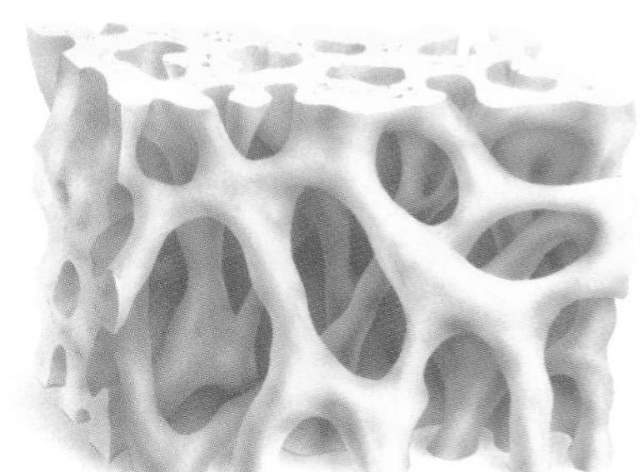

Spongy bone tissue

Ligament

Movement of joints

A joint is more mobile if the articular surfaces are not a perfect fit. The shoulder joint has the widest range of movement of all the joints, because the articular surface of the scapula does not fit exactly with the head of the humerus bone.

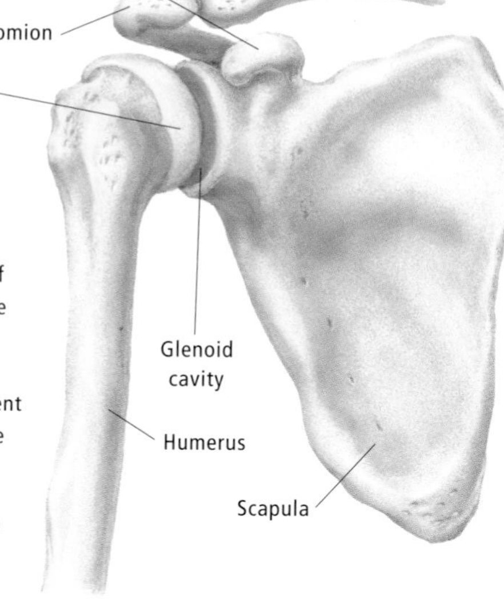

MUSCULAR SYSTEM

The muscular system which brings about bodily movement includes the voluntary muscles of the body. These muscles range in size from the tiny muscles that wrinkle the forehead to the large muscles of the thigh. The voluntary muscle system does not include muscles like the cardiac muscle of the heart or the smooth muscles in the walls of internal organs such as the stomach, which are classed as involuntary muscles (not under conscious control).

There are about 700 muscles in the human body. Most of them have Latin names which may describe their location (brachialis, muscle of the arm), beginning and end (brachioradialis, running from the arm to the radius), shape (trapezius, shaped like a trapezium), location and shape (orbicularis oris, circular muscle around the mouth), organization (quadriceps, muscle with four heads) or function (dilator naris, dilator of the nostril).

When a few muscles have the same name, qualifiers are added to distinguish between them. Of the two flexors of the thumb, the flexor pollicis longus is the long muscle running from the forearm to the thumb, while the flexor pollicis brevis begins in the wrist. The three muscles of the buttocks are named according to their size: gluteus maximus for the largest, gluteus medius and gluteus minimus for the medium and smallest. Some muscles have fancy names; the buccinator (trumpeter) in the cheek is so-called because it blows air out of the mouth. Interestingly, the very small muscle that raises the upper lip and the nostril has one of the longest names: levator labii superioris alaeque nasi.

Muscles vary greatly in size. The stapedius, which restricts movements of the eardrum, looks like a few millimeters of cotton thread. The gluteus maximus, on the other hand, forms the bulk of the buttock.

The organization of fibers also varies. In the common spindle-shaped muscles, all muscle fibers run from one tendon to another. In pennate (*penna*, meaning feather) muscles, fibers run obliquely down to the tendon, like a feather.

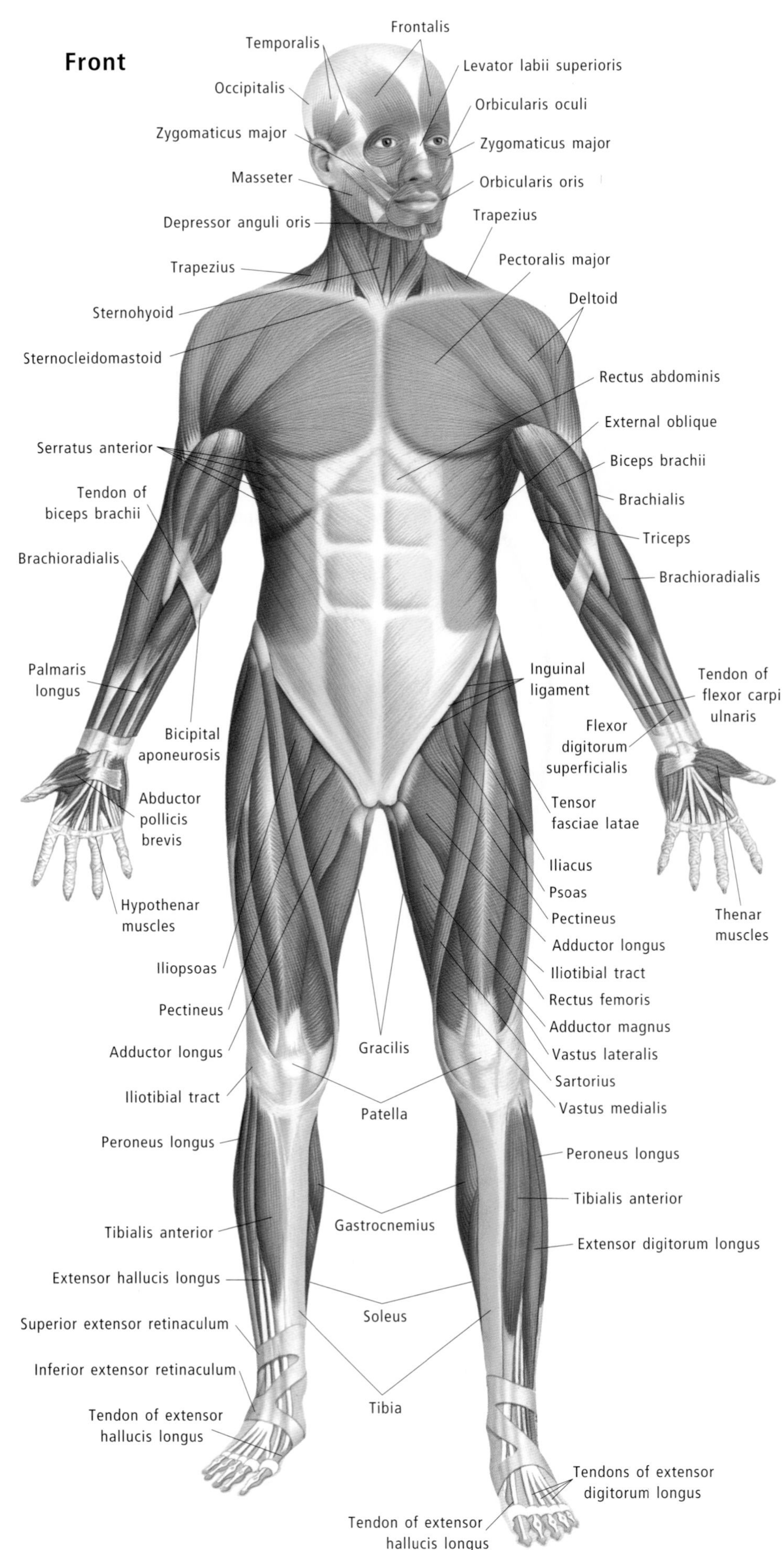

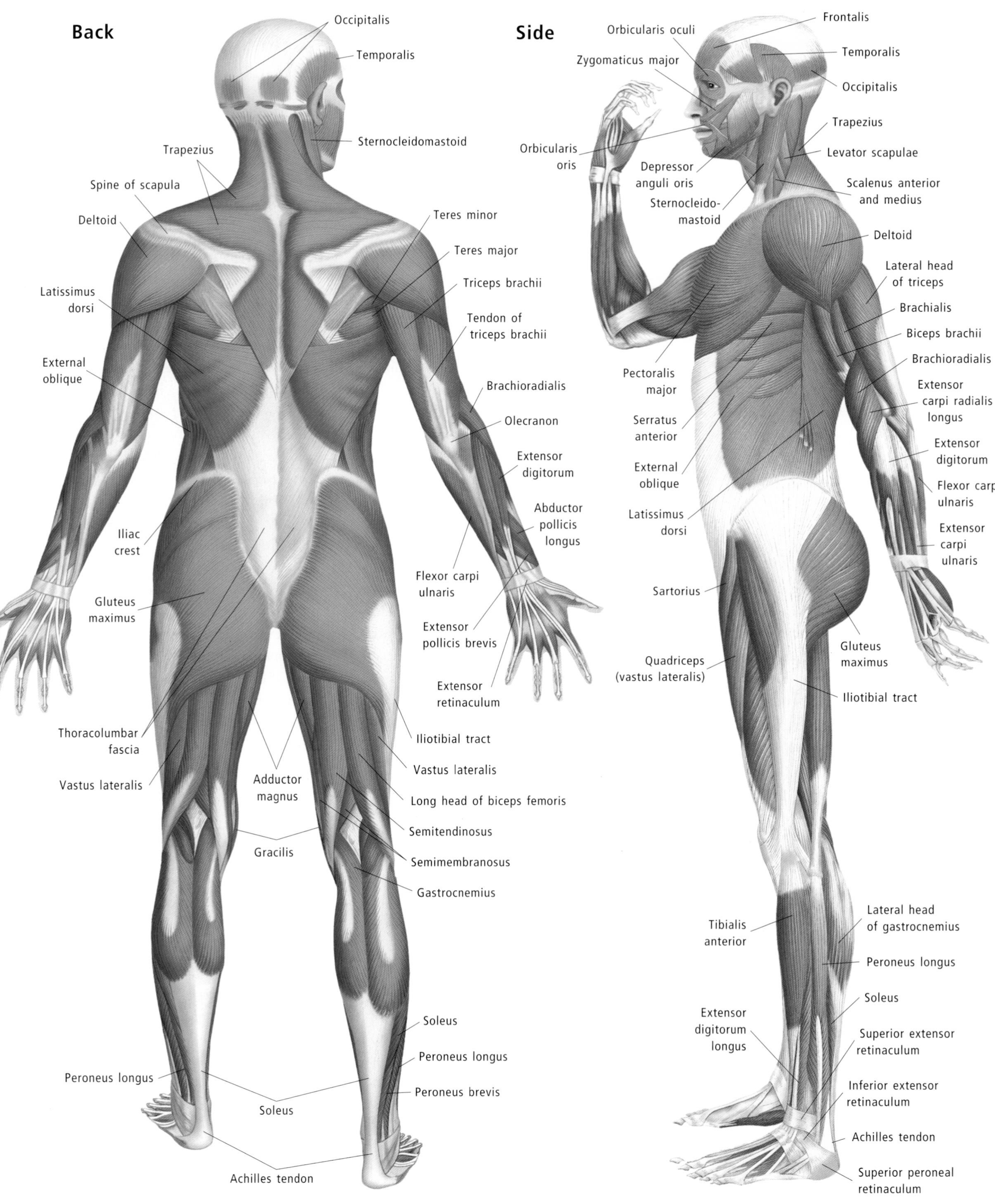
Back
Occipitalis
Temporalis
Sternocleidomastoid
Trapezius
Spine of scapula
Deltoid
Teres minor
Teres major
Triceps brachii
Latissimus dorsi
Tendon of triceps brachii
External oblique
Brachioradialis
Olecranon
Extensor digitorum
Abductor pollicis longus
Iliac crest
Flexor carpi ulnaris
Gluteus maximus
Extensor pollicis brevis
Extensor retinaculum
Thoracolumbar fascia
Iliotibial tract
Vastus lateralis
Adductor magnus
Vastus lateralis
Long head of biceps femoris
Semitendinosus
Gracilis
Semimembranosus
Gastrocnemius
Soleus
Peroneus longus
Peroneus longus
Soleus
Peroneus brevis
Achilles tendon
Side
Frontalis
Orbicularis oculi
Temporalis
Zygomaticus major
Occipitalis
Trapezius
Orbicularis oris
Levator scapulae
Depressor anguli oris
Scalenus anterior and medius
Sternocleido-mastoid
Deltoid
Lateral head of triceps
Brachialis
Biceps brachii
Brachioradialis
Pectoralis major
Extensor carpi radialis longus
Serratus anterior
Extensor digitorum
External oblique
Flexor carpi ulnaris
Latissimus dorsi
Extensor carpi ulnaris
Sartorius
Gluteus maximus
Quadriceps (vastus lateralis)
Iliotibial tract
Lateral head of gastrocnemius
Tibialis anterior
Peroneus longus
Soleus
Extensor digitorum longus
Superior extensor retinaculum
Inferior extensor retinaculum
Achilles tendon
Superior peroneal retinaculum

Some muscles have several tendons at one end—for example, two in the biceps, three in the triceps and four in the quadriceps.

Muscle fibers attach either directly to a bone, or to a tendon which is fixed to a bone. The force produced by the contraction of the muscle fibers is transmitted to the bone by the tendon. Tendons are made up mainly of strong collagen fibers that run parallel in one direction and are tightly packed together to give maximum strength in the line of force of the muscle.

Structure of muscles

The contracting part of a muscle consists of bundles of muscle fibers which themselves are made up of myofibrils.

Each myofibril is made up of thousands of thin actin filaments and thicker myosin filaments, which overlap. Where they overlap they are linked by connections (cross-bridges), which change shape to draw one set of fibers towards the other, thus shortening the muscle.

There are two main classes of muscle fibers, called fast twitch (F) and slow twitch (S) fibers. F fibers generate more power and contract faster, but fatigue more quickly than S fibers. The relative proportion of the two types of fiber varies in different individuals and in different muscles. People tend to excel in sports that are suited to their predominant fiber type. For example, 95 percent of fibers in the gastrocnemius muscles in the legs of marathon champions are S fibers, compared to only 25 percent in champion sprinters.

Muscle contraction

When a muscle contracts, it shortens and exerts a pull on the muscle attachment. The action of a muscle depends on its position in relation to the joint it works on. The tibialis anterior, for example, crosses in front of the ankle and moves the foot upwards.

Tibialis anterior

Tendon sheath

Movement and support

The muscles of the shoulder joint, known as the rotator cuff muscles, provide important support for the joint, while allowing a wide range of movement.

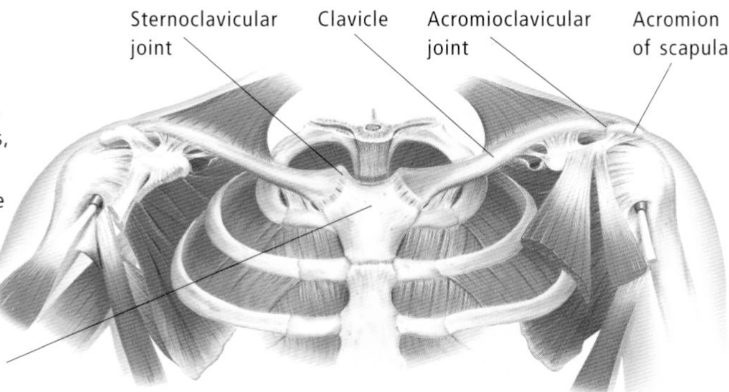

Actions of muscles

Usually a muscle shortens when it is activated (or "contracts"), but not always. When holding a camera up in front of the eyes, for example, the muscles of the arm generate force against gravity to prevent the camera from falling, but do not change length. This kind of "contraction" is called isometric (meaning "same length") contraction. In the action of putting the camera down on a desk, the muscles that bend the elbow generate a force which is smaller than the pull of gravity on the camera. In this case the muscles of the arm are lengthened by the force of gravity and work to slow down the fall of the camera. Sometimes "contraction" is a poor term to describe muscle action.

The action of a muscle depends on its position in relation to the joint it works on. The biceps, crossing in front of the elbow, flexes the elbow; the triceps tendon crossing the back of the elbow straightens it.

The deltoid on the outside of the shoulder brings the arm out, away from the body (abducts the arm). The pectoralis major, running from the upper part of the arm towards the breastbone (sternum) pulls the arm in (adducts the arm).

However, most muscle actions are not as simple as these examples. The upper part of the pectoralis major, which runs from the clavicle to the arm, tends to raise the arm from a position of rest at the side of the body. Its lower part, which runs downwards to the lower ribs, tends to pull the arm down when it is above the head. In muscles like this with different parts, the resulting movement depends on different levels of activity of different components.

Coordination of muscles

Each movement of a limb, however simple, is the result of a number of muscles working together. In kicking a football, the quadriceps is the prime mover, or agonist muscle. Its attachment on the femur is stabilized by muscles of the hip. The hamstring muscles, which have the opposite action to the quadriceps, begin to contract as the leg picks up momentum to control the force of the kick. The contraction of these muscles, which are called antagonist muscles, is maximal at the end of the kick to stop the movement.

The cooperation of the muscles in this example must be well orchestrated, each muscle having to contribute the right force at the right time. If the antagonist muscles contract too early, before the leg has gained enough momentum, the kick will be too weak. If they come in too late, the leg will extend too far and damage the knee joint.

The cerebellum of the brain is important in fine muscle (motor) control. Just watch a very young child attempting to throw a ball. The young cerebellum has not learned to program muscle actions. The arm flings out too far and the hand does not release the ball at the right time. Even movements that we take for granted, such as walking and running, are only possible after much training in the first years of life. More sophisticated muscle coordination, such as dancing, requires years of intensive training. When the cerebellum fails to work properly, either temporarily in a drunk person, or permanently in cerebellar diseases, even walking becomes difficult.

When a muscle is used repeatedly in lifting weight, it develops more strength and also enlarges because of the increase in diameter of individual muscle fibers. The best exercises to increase muscle bulk are those that make the muscles lengthen while they contract, such as slowing the fall of a weight.

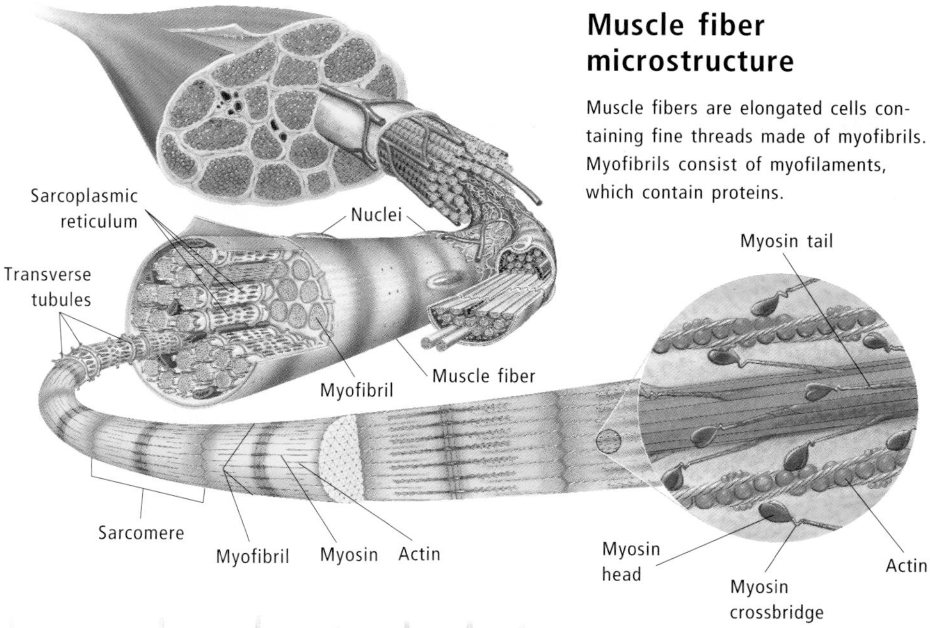

Sarcoplasmic reticulum
Nuclei
Transverse tubules
Muscle fiber
Myofibril
Sarcomere
Myofibril
Myosin
Actin
Myosin tail
Myosin head
Myosin crossbridge
Actin

Muscle fiber microstructure

Muscle fibers are elongated cells containing fine threads made of myofibrils. Myofibrils consist of myofilaments, which contain proteins.

Unipennate
Bipennate
Multipennate
Spiral
Spiral
Radial
Quadrate
Strap
Strap
Cruciate
Triangular
Multicaudal
Fusiform
Bicipital
Tricipital
Quadricipital
Digastric
Circular

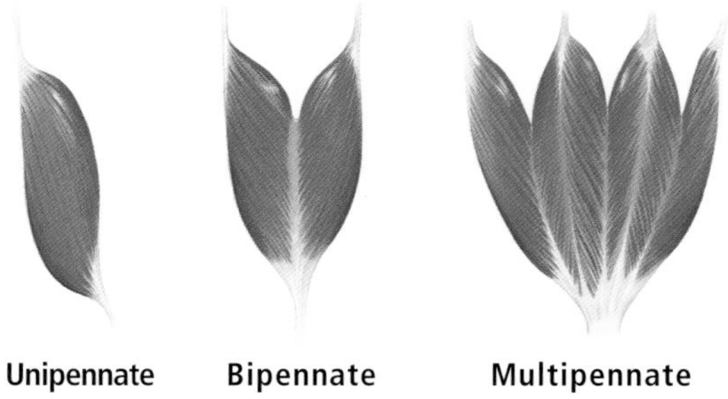

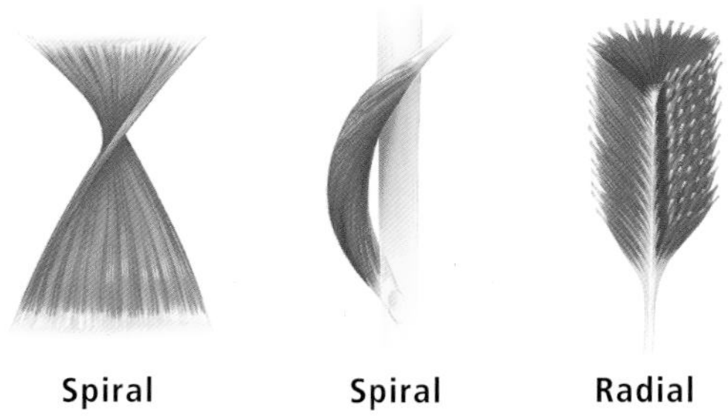

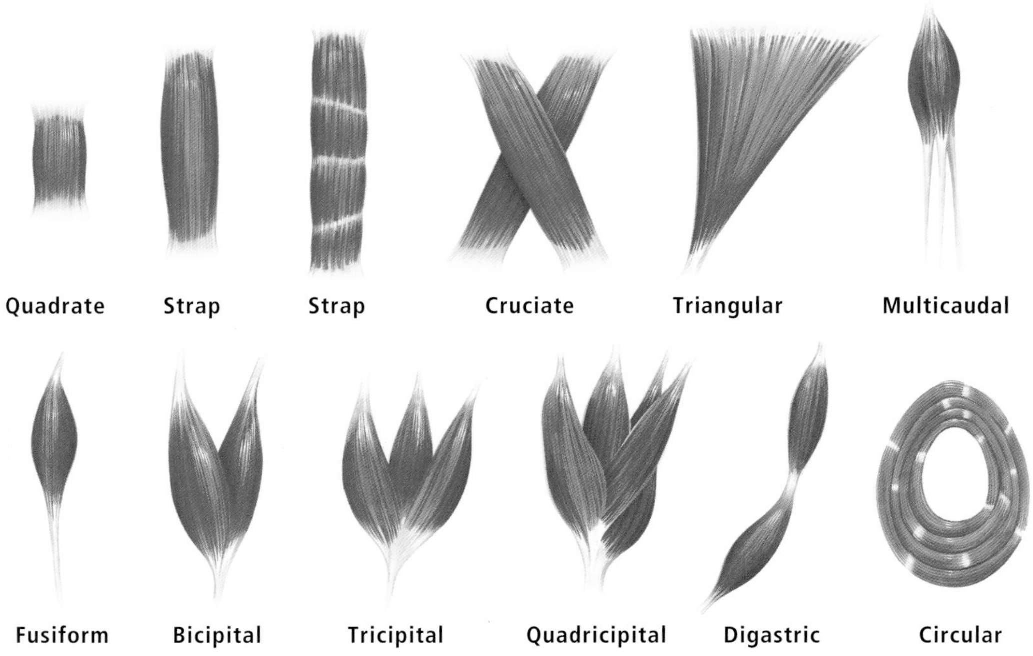

Muscle fibers

Muscles consist of bundles of fibers which can be organized in different ways according the function of the muscle. The force exerted by a muscle depends on its cross-sectional area.

When muscles are inactive, they decrease in both size and strength and their tendons become weaker. Muscle wasting (atrophy) is most obvious when the muscles are completely paralyzed by nerve injury; it is also seen in some congenital or metabolic diseases of muscle such as muscular dystrophy. Our knowledge of muscles and their actions has advanced tremendously as a result of recent physiological and biomechanical studies and has had far-reaching applications in many different fields, from sports medicine to engineering and robotics.

Involuntary muscles

Skeletal muscle is under conscious control and is therefore called voluntary muscle. In contrast, the cardiac muscle of the heart is controlled by nerve impulses produced by a natural pacemaker called the sinoatrial node, the rate of which is controlled by the autonomic nervous system. Smooth muscle is found in the digestive system, reproductive system, major blood vessels, the skin and internal organs, and is also controlled by the autonomic nervous system.

SEE ALSO *Hamstring muscles, Muscle, Muscular dystrophy, Quadriceps muscle, Tendons, Trapezius muscle*

Cardiac muscle tissue

Muscle in the heart (cardiac muscle) is similar to striated or voluntary muscle but its contractions are controlled by the heart's pacemaker.

Smooth muscle tissue

Smooth muscle is found in the skin, major blood vessels, and the reproductive and digestive systems. It is controlled by the autonomic nervous system.

NERVOUS SYSTEM

Along with the endocrine and the immune systems, the nervous system is one of three systems concerned with coordinating the activities of the body. The nervous system receives information about the outside world and internal organs, determines the appropriate response to changes in both domains and responds rapidly. Information is processed and transferred by means of nerve cells firing electrical signals called action potentials, which can move along nerve fibers at speeds of up to 320 feet (100 meters) per second. The endocrine and immune systems respond more slowly because they depend on chemicals or cells released into the blood to communicate responses.

Divisions of the nervous system

The nervous system is divided into a central nervous system (CNS) and a peripheral nervous system. The CNS is made up of the brain and spinal cord, while the peripheral nervous system consists of all the nerves distributed throughout the rest of the body. The parts of the peripheral nervous system concerned with controlling aspects of body function over which we have no voluntary control are called the autonomic nervous system. Although most of the constituent nerve cells of the autonomic nervous system are located peripherally, some are also located in the CNS. The autonomic nervous system is also under the control of parts of the brain such as the hypothalamus.

There are also many nerve cells located in the wall of the gastrointestinal tract (stomach and intestine) that coordinate and control the movement of the gut and the secretions of the gut glands, and also transport sensory information about conditions in the gut. Gut nerve cells may actually outnumber those in the spinal cord.

The brain and spinal cord consist of nerve cells and their processes, along with bundles of nerve fibers. Gray matter refers to the parts of the CNS where nerve cell bodies are concentrated; white matter refers to parts with very few cells and many nerve fibers.

A typical nerve cell has a cell body with a nucleus and a number of branching processes (dendrites), which receive incoming information, and an outgoing fiber (axon),

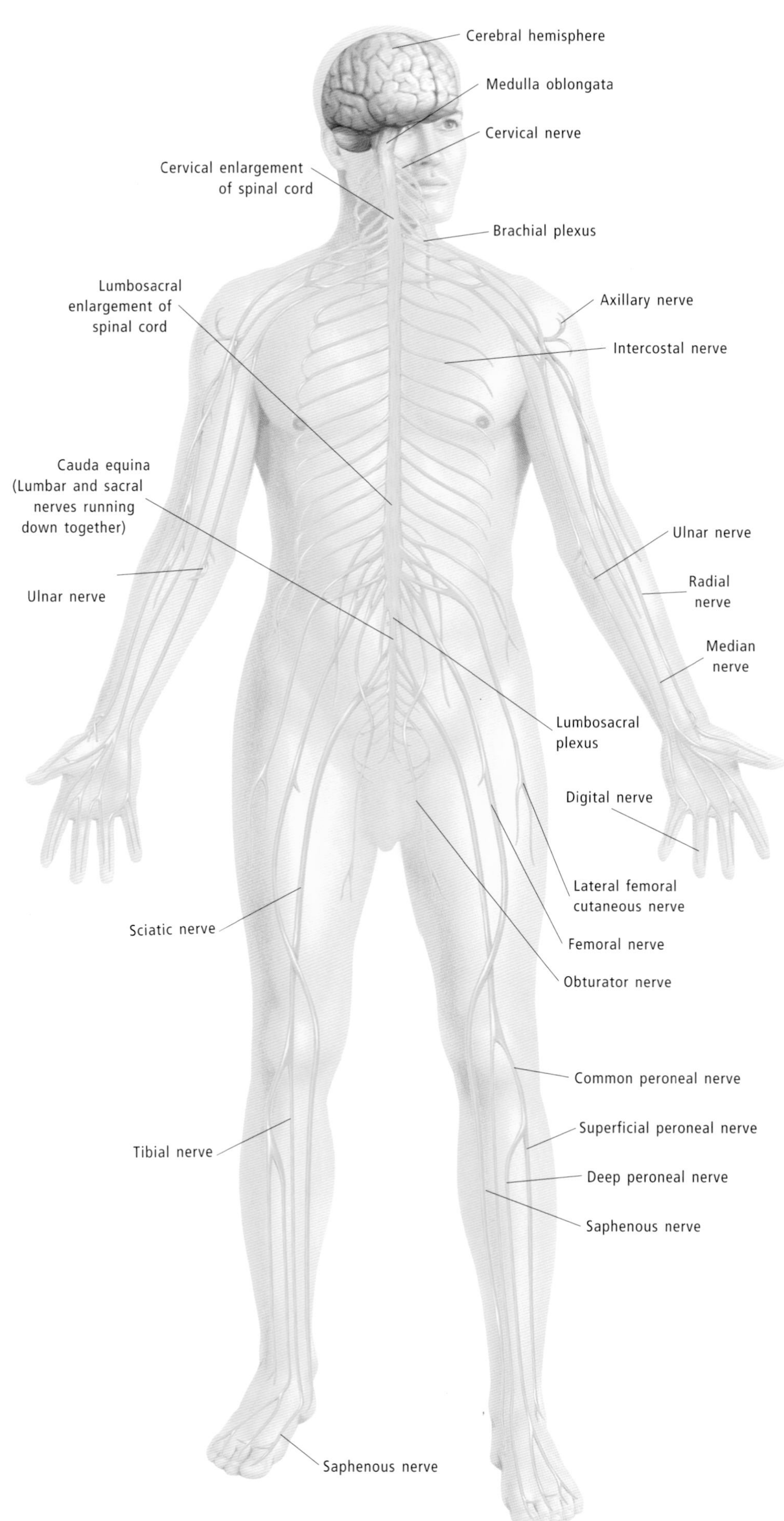

which carries information away from the nerve cell body. The dendrites are quite short, usually less than 1/16 inch (1–1.5 millimeters), while the axon may be very long, anywhere from 1/16–36 inches (1 millimeter to 1 meter). Many axons are coated in layers of a fatty material (myelin), essential for the rapid transmission of nerve impulses (action potentials) along the axon. In diseases such as multiple sclerosis, where the myelin sheath is damaged, the transmission of nerve impulses is severely impaired. Nerve cells communicate with each other by releasing chemicals (neurotransmitters) at sites where the processes of two or more cells meet (synapses).

The CNS also contains many cells called glia. These fulfill diverse roles such as the formation of myelin, maintaining the correct concentrations of salts and chemicals in the spaces between the nerve cells, and providing surveillance against invading microorganisms.

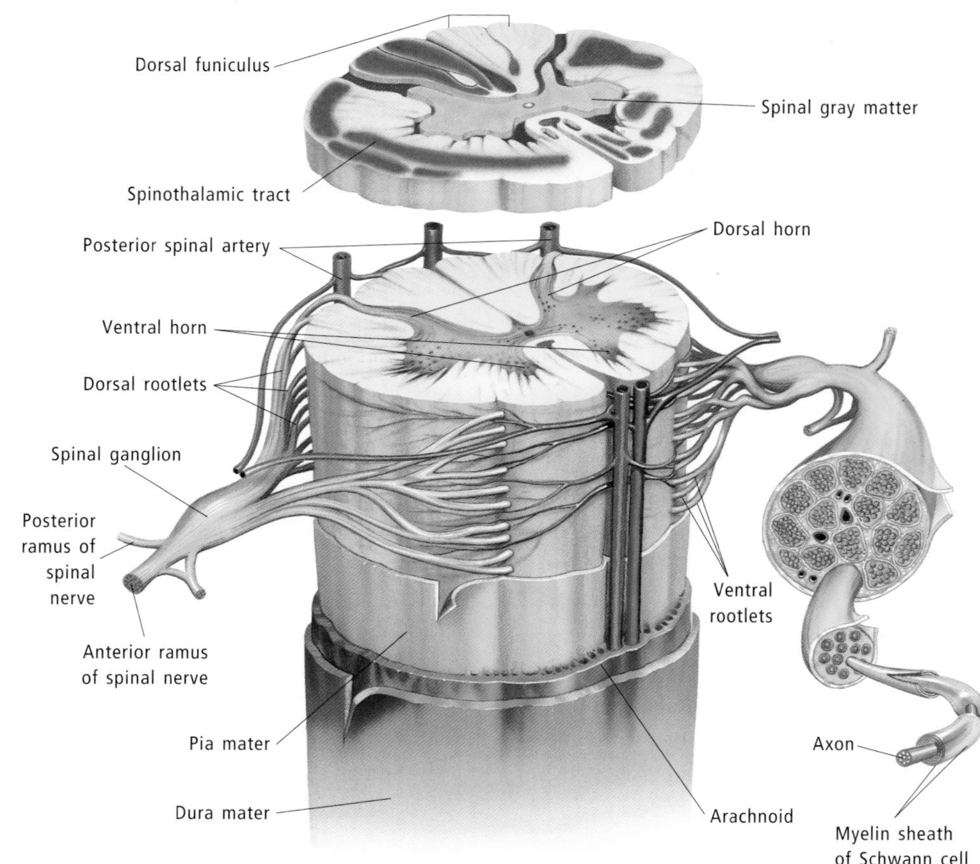

Spinal cord cross-section

The spinal cord is part of the central nervous system that runs down the vertebral canal. The central core of gray matter receives and processes sensory information, and sends signals to the muscles. The surrounding layer of white matter contains axons which communicate between the brain and spinal cord.

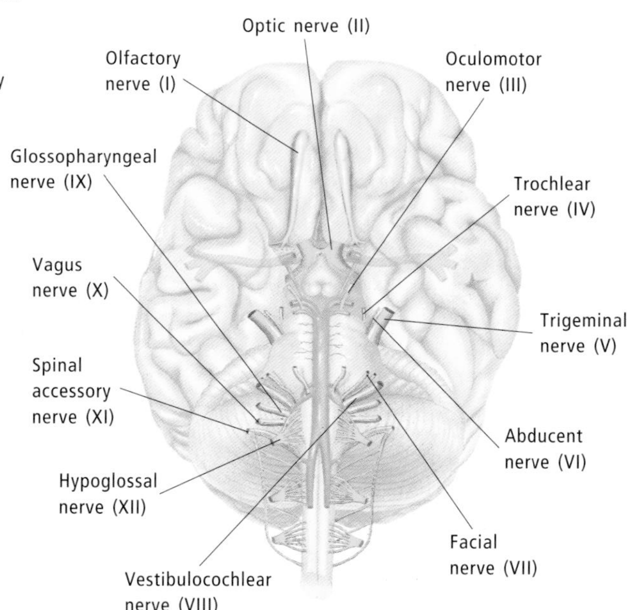

Nerves in the brain

There are 12 cranial nerves which are visible at the base of the brain. In addition to their motor and sensory functions, the cranial nerves serve the 5 systems for special senses.

Central nervous system

From a functional viewpoint the CNS can be divided into parts concerned with interpreting sensory information (sensory systems), with controlling the function of the body (motor systems), and with higher brain functions, such as memory, language and social behavior. In practice, a few brain regions may combine all three functions.

Sensory systems are concerned not just with the senses of vision, touch, hearing, smell and taste, but with many other senses of which we are not usually aware, such as the sense of up and down, feelings of rotation or acceleration, bladder fullness, stomach distension, joint position and blood pressure. Motor (effector) systems are concerned not just with controlling our muscles and movement, but also with controlling many automatic functions, including sweating, blood pressure and gut movements.

Anatomy of the brain

Anatomically, the brain is divided into three main regions—the forebrain, midbrain and hindbrain. The forebrain contains most of the brain substance and is capped by the highly folded cerebral cortex. The midbrain and hindbrain carry many fiber bundles that convey information to and from the upper parts of the brain. The hindbrain can be further divided into the pons, medulla and cerebellum. The midbrain, pons and medulla, collectively called the brain stem, contain many nerve cell groups that control the muscles of the face and head and process information about touch on the face, taste and hearing.

Other important functions of the brain stem are the control of breathing, blood pressure and heart function.

The forebrain is a very complex and important region. At its surface, the cerebral cortex is broadly organized into the frontal lobe, the occipital lobe at the back, the parietal lobe in the middle and the temporal lobe below. Each lobe contains many different areas concerned with particular functions.

At the very front of the frontal lobe, the prefrontal area is concerned with the control of social behavior, motivation and planning.

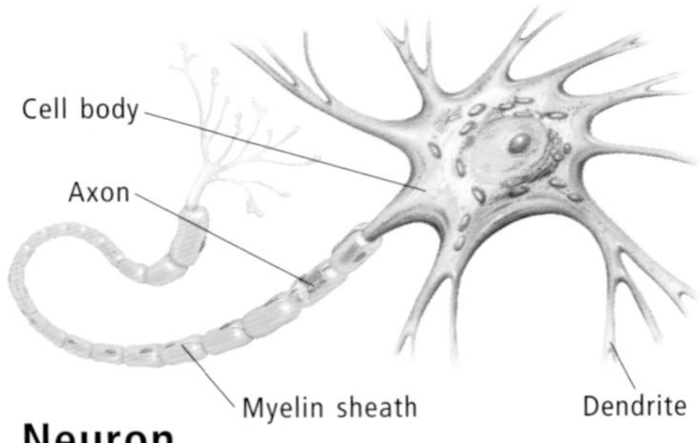

Neuron
Neurons are nerve cells that are specially designed to conduct nerve impulses to and from all parts of the body.

Behind the prefrontal area lie the premotor cortex, which plans motor actions, and the primary motor cortex, which sets those motor commands into action. The lower part of the left frontal lobe contains Broca's area, concerned with the expression of language. The occipital lobe contains a series of visual areas. The parietal lobe contains a primary somatosensory area, concerned with processing sensory information about touch, pain and joint position from the body and face. Further back in the parietal lobe lies a region that generates our sense of the spatial organization of the outside world. The temporal lobe contains areas concerned with hearing, smell and memory. At the junction of the temporal and parietal lobes lies Wernicke's area, concerned with understanding language. Deep inside the forebrain are groups of nerve cells called the basal ganglia, which are primarily concerned with motor control, but may also be involved in some higher functions like language and thought. The forebrain also contains the thalamus, which is primarily concerned with relaying sensory information to the cerebral cortex and controlling motor activity. Below the thalamus lies the hypothalamus, which serves as the interface between the brain and the autonomic nervous system and controls food and water intake, sexual function and body temperature, among other functions.

The spinal cord

The spinal cord acts as an intermediary between the peripheral nervous system and the brain. It extends from the base of the skull to a point about two-thirds of the way down the back, running through the vertebral canal. The spinal cord has many nerve fibers attached to it, arranged in sets and named according to their level on the cord. The cord itself has a central region of gray matter, which is divided into posterior (dorsal) and anterior (ventral) horns and an intermediate region. The gray matter is surrounded by white matter carrying ascending and descending fiber tracts.

At each level, the spinal cord receives sensory nerves, which convey information about touch, pain, temperature, muscle tension and joint position. This information may be used at the level at which it enters the spinal cord to control muscle tension or stimulate reflex responses, such as withdrawing a hand from a hot object, or it may be transmitted up the white matter of the cord to the brain for conscious appreciation of the information.

The spinal cord also gives rise to motor and autonomic nerve fibers, which control muscles and affect internal organs, respectively. The brain sends controlling signals down through the white matter of the spinal cord to spinal motor neurons, so that we can consciously control our muscles.

Peripheral nervous system

The peripheral nervous system consists of nerve fibers or axons that control muscle activity or carry sensory information back to the spinal cord or brain stem. The motor axons come from cell bodies located in the anterior horn of the spinal cord, while the sensory axons arise from cell bodies located in clumps or ganglia alongside the spinal cord. Many axons in the peripheral nervous system are coated with myelin (much like axons in the central nervous system) produced by Schwann cells.

An important difference between the peripheral and central nervous systems is that peripheral nerves have the ability to repair and regenerate, where central axons do not. This difference may be partly due to the behavior of Schwann cells after nerve injury.

Diseases of the nervous system can be considered by category. Probably the two most important types of central nervous system disease in Western society are trauma and vascular disease. Motor vehicle, diving and other accidents may cause injury to the spinal cord, resulting in either complete or partial separation of the fiber tracts joining the brain to the lower spinal cord. Depending on the level of the injury, the patient may be paralyzed in the lower limbs (paraplegia) or all four limbs (quadriplegia). Vascular diseases of the brain can involve bleeding into the brain from ruptured vessels or death of brain tissue due to the obstruction of brain arteries. Tumors may spread to the brain from tumors in other parts of the body or arise in the brain itself, usually from glial cells. Degenerative diseases of the brain include Alzheimer's disease and Huntington's disease.

SEE ALSO *Alzheimer's disease, Autonomic nervous system, Brain, Cerebellum, Endocrine system, Huntington's disease, Hypothalamus, Lymphatic/Immune system, Multiple sclerosis, Spinal cord*

Reflexes
A reflex is a response to a stimulus, in which sensory information triggers an automatic response in muscles or glands. The response usually involves nerve cells in the spinal cord and does not involve a conscious reaction.

A. Stimulus is registered by sensory receptors
B. Receptors send message along nerve fibers to spinal cord
C. Spinal cord (central nervous system) processes information
D. Spinal nerve sends signal along peripheral nerves to motor nerve cells
E. Muscle is activated by signal from motor nerve cells

AUTONOMIC NERVOUS SYSTEM

The autonomic nervous system is the part of the nervous system concerned with controlling relatively automatic bodily functions. The body's tendency to maintain a constant internal environment and a constant heart rate and blood pressure, is called homeo-0stasis. While many body systems contribute to homeostasis, the autonomic nervous system is probably the most important.

Most of the activities of the autonomic nervous system occur without our being aware of them, and so the system could also be called the involuntary nervous system. Nevertheless, some bodily functions can be influenced by conscious activity—the effect of relaxation therapy on blood pressure is an example of this.

While most of the activities of the autonomic nervous system are actions on body organs and tissues (for example, motor functions) there are also many sensory nerves accompanying the autonomic motor nerves. These sensory nerves relay information about internal organs (such as the tension in the wall of a full stomach or blood pressure in parts of the cardiovascular system) back to the central nervous system (CNS).

This information is important for keeping the brain and spinal cord informed about changes in the body, and allows appropriate control procedures to be carried out to keep conditions in the body's interior in a relatively constant state.

Structure

The autonomic nervous system consists of some nerve cells (neurons) in the brain and spinal cord, their fibers which leave the central nervous system, collections of nerve cells in the various body cavities, and nerve fibers which are distributed in the internal organs.

Collections of nerve cells in the body cavities are called ganglia. These ganglia are often embedded in networks of nerve fibers called plexuses, which are located near the heart and lungs, in front of the aorta in the abdomen, and in front of the sacral bone in the pelvis.

The autonomic nervous system differs in a number of ways from the somatic nervous system, which is concerned with voluntary control of the body's muscles. The autonomic nervous system has a series of two or more nerve cells between the CNS and the organ that is being controlled, while the somatic nervous system has only one nerve cell between the CNS and the muscle being controlled.

The somatic nervous system neurons have their cell bodies in the brain or spinal cord and axons or nerve fibers that run directly to the muscle being controlled. Those autonomic nervous system neurons whose cell bodies lie inside the spinal cord or brain stem are called preganglionic nerve cells, while those neurons whose cell bodies lie in ganglia are called postganglionic nerve cells.

While both the somatic and autonomic nervous systems may use acetylcholine as a neurotransmitter, the sympathetic part of the autonomic nervous system also uses the chemical norepinephrine (noradrenaline), which is released from the postganglionic nerve cells onto smooth muscle and other target tissues.

Another difference between the somatic and autonomic nervous systems is that all the nerve fibers controlling voluntary muscles in the somatic nervous system have thick myelin sheaths, while usually only the preganglionic nerve cells of the autonomic nervous system have myelin sheaths. Since myelin sheaths around nerve fibers contribute to the rapid conduction of nerve impulses, it follows that the somatic or voluntary nervous system usually acts on the muscles much more rapidly than the autonomic nervous system can influence the internal organs.

Divisions of the autonomic nervous system

Traditionally, the autonomic nervous system is divided into a sympathetic and a parasympathetic division. The two divisions are considered to be anatomically and functionally separate, but there are several places in the body (such as the nerve supply of the pelvic organs) where the two may overlap.

Sympathetic division

The sympathetic division is often referred to as the "fight-or-flight" system. It comes into play during emergency situations when our bodies need extra energy to avoid or overcome danger. During emergencies we experience a pounding heartbeat, cold sweaty skin, rapid breathing and enlarged pupils—all produced by activation of the sympathetic nervous system. In addition, the sympathetic nervous system can cause changes such as increased blood pressure, a dry mouth, increased blood sugar levels, and dilation of the small airways of the lung. The sympathetic nervous system also increases the flow of blood to muscles and diverts blood away from the gastrointestinal tract. All of these effects increase the individual's ability to cope with the emergency.

The sympathetic nervous system also has an important effect on the control of body temperature. Some sympathetic nerve cells stimulate the activity of sweat glands in the skin to increase sweat production and lower body temperature by the evaporation of perspiration. Other sympathetic nerve cells control tiny smooth muscles in the skin, which when stimulated pull on the hairs of the skin causing them to stand up. This change is commonly called "goose bumps" and keeps a layer of relatively still air close to the skin to minimize heat loss.

In the eye, the sympathetic nervous system causes enlargement of the pupil to increase the amount of light reaching the sensitive retina at the back of the eye.

Anatomically, the sympathetic nervous system consists of nerve cells in the thoracic and lumbar levels of the spinal cord as well as a long chain of nerve cells which lies alongside the backbone. This long chain is called the sympathetic trunk and gives off nerves to other plexuses and internal organs. Some sympathetic nerve fibers go to the adrenal medulla, which is part of the endocrine system.

These nerve fibers stimulate the adrenal medulla, which contains modified nerve cells, to release epinephrine (adrenaline) and norepinephrine (noradrenaline) into the bloodstream. These hormones are released in emergency situations where energy reserves need to be rapidly mobilized.

Parasympathetic division

The parasympathetic division is most active when the body is not under threat and when

Sympathetic and parasympathetic divisions of the autonomic nervous system

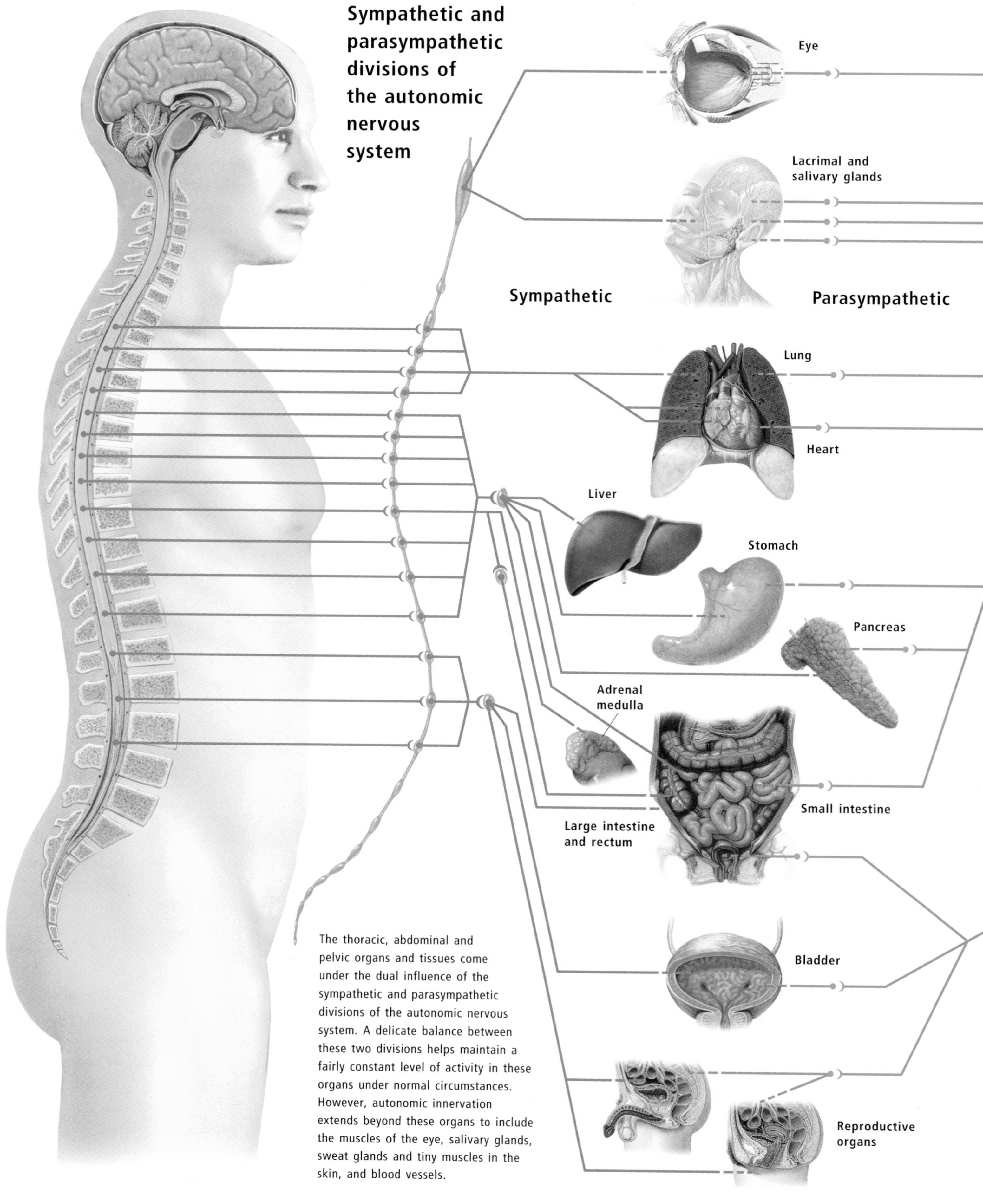

The thoracic, abdominal and pelvic organs and tissues come under the dual influence of the sympathetic and parasympathetic divisions of the autonomic nervous system. A delicate balance between these two divisions helps maintain a fairly constant level of activity in these organs under normal circumstances. However, autonomic innervation extends beyond these organs to include the muscles of the eye, salivary glands, sweat glands and tiny muscles in the skin, and blood vessels.

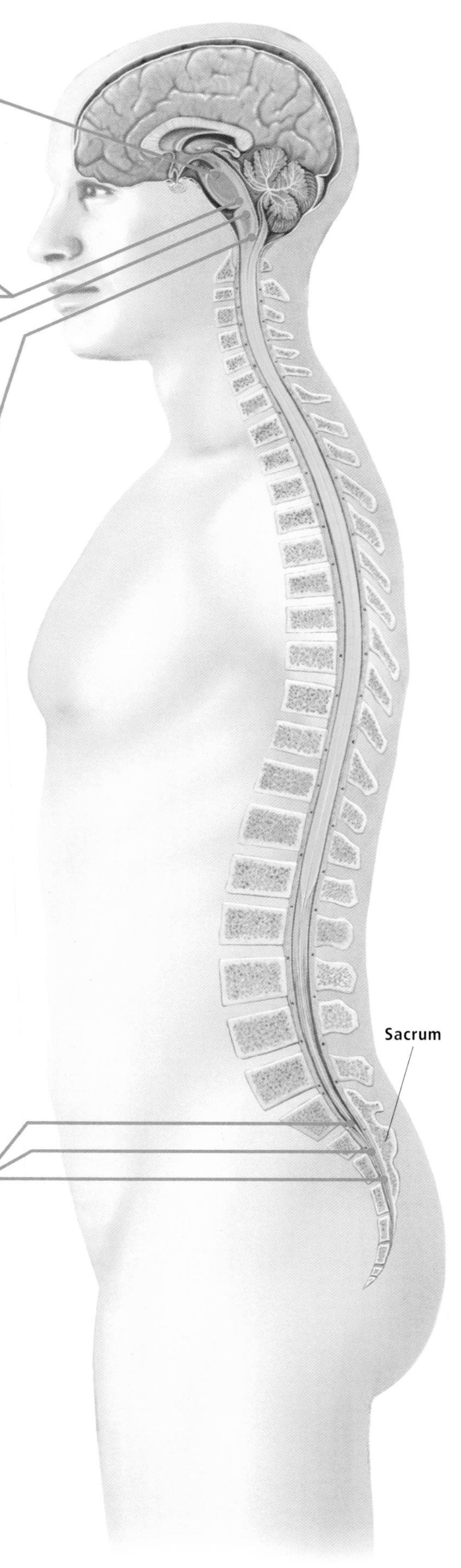

the person is largely at rest. Its main function is to conserve energy, restoring the internal body state to normal by promoting digestion and eliminating urine and feces from the body.

In the head, for example, the parasympathetic nervous system increases the production of saliva by the salivary glands, while in the stomach and intestines it increases the activity of the smooth muscle and glands. The increased activity of the smooth muscle in the gut increases the movement called peristalsis, which helps to move food along the gut and break it up into a more readily digestible consistency. The increased activity of glands in the gut will increase the production of digestive enzymes to break down food, and the production of mucus and other fluid to promote the absorption and movement of food along the gut.

In the cardiovascular system, the parasympathetic nervous system lowers the heart rate and blood pressure and diverts blood from muscles to the gut to assist with digestion.

In the lungs, it causes constriction of the small airways and increases the activity of the small glands in the airways, which will increase the amount of secretions.

In the eye, the parasympathetic nervous system closes down the pupil of the eye, decreasing the amount of light reaching the retina, and stimulates contraction of the ciliary muscle, which leads to bulging of the lens of the eye for close vision.

Involvement with the urinary and reproductive organs

The sympathetic and parasympathetic nervous systems have important complementary actions in the urinary and reproductive organs. The release of urine from the bladder is stimulated by the parasympathetic nervous system, which relaxes the sphincter muscle at the outlet from the urinary bladder and causes contraction of bladder wall muscle. Urination is inhibited by the sympathetic nervous system, which constricts the sphincter muscles around the outlet from the urinary bladder. In the male reproductive organs, the parasympathetic nervous system causes erection of the penis by increasing the flow of blood into the cavernous spaces of the penis.

The system is also involved in ejaculation, the process of expulsion of semen from the penis. If a man experiences anxiety about his ability to perform sexually, then the sympathetic nervous system will be more active. This may cause difficulty in obtaining and maintaining an erection—a problem called impotence or erectile difficulty—and/or a too-rapid progression from arousal to ejaculation, known as premature ejaculation. This type of sexual dysfunction is often responsible for sexual problems in younger men, but in older men impotence is more likely to be due to vascular problems and diabetic damage to pelvic nerves.

Diseases and disorders

The autonomic nervous system can be affected in a variety of diseases. In Raynaud's phenomenon, patients experience episodes of pallor and blue coloration of the ends of the fingers and toes. The phenomenon may occur in young women with no apparent cause (Raynaud's disease), or it may accompany connective tissue disease or occupations involving the use of vibrating tools. Patients with this problem may develop ulcers on their fingertips and, in severe cases, develop skin infections. Treatment consists of keeping the hands and feet warm, but if this is not effective, surgically cutting sympathetic nerves to the fingers may be of assistance.

Deliberate destruction of part of the sympathetic nervous system may also be helpful in some other conditions such as arterial obstruction due to atherosclerosis, excessive sweating, and frostbite.

Patients with diabetes mellitus may experience problems as a result of damage to the autonomic nervous system. Male patients may develop impotence, while both sexes may suffer from nocturnal diarrhea, problems maintaining adequate blood pressure when standing, and occasionally problems of retention of urine in the bladder with urine overflow.

SEE ALSO *Atherosclerosis, Brain, Diabetes, Endocrine system, Epinephrine, Eye, Ganglion, Nerves, Nervous system, Neurons, Peristalsis, Raynaud's disease, Reproductive systems, Retina, Sexual dysfunction, Spinal cord, Sympathetic nervous system, Urinary systems*

LYMPHATIC/ IMMUNE SYSTEM

The lymphatic system is a network of vessels, aggregates of lymphoid tissue (lymph nodes) and lymphoid organs, and has two main functions. Apart from bringing back to the heart much of the interstitial fluid which bathes all cells of the body, it is also loaded with specialized white blood cells (lymphocytes) and macrophages, which sweep up foreign bodies or invaders, such as bacteria, viruses, and cancer cells.

Lymph vessels

Unlike the complete circle of the circulatory system, the lymphatic system is a one-way system, which begins with a capillary network of blind-ended tubes. These capillaries absorb large molecules and particles (foreign bodies and nutritional elements), and converge to form gradually larger lymphatic vessels that carry the lymph towards the heart. Lymph vessels have valves to ensure one-way flow. Along the lymph vessels are found collections of lymphoid tissue or lymph nodes (frequently and colloquially called lymph glands).

Lymph nodes and lymphoid tissue

The lymph nodes are small pea-sized organs located in groups at the confluence of lymphatic vessels. Each node is connected to incoming and outgoing lymphatic vessels. Incoming lymph spreads throughout the node to pass through aggregations of lymphocytes and macrophages. Debris or foreign matter and cancer cells are engulfed by macrophages and specialized lymphocytes called killer cells. Invaders such as bacteria are also digested by the macrophages, which extract essential and unique parts of the bacteria (antigens) to present to nearby lymphocytes. Activated by the contact with the antigens, these lymphocytes produce antibodies (antidotes for particular antigens). This type of lymphocyte proliferates as necessary to step up the production of required antibodies. Thus lymph nodes not only filter out and destroy foreign bodies before they get into the circulation, they also activate the cloning of lymphocytes to produce specific antibodies, which is part of the immune response.

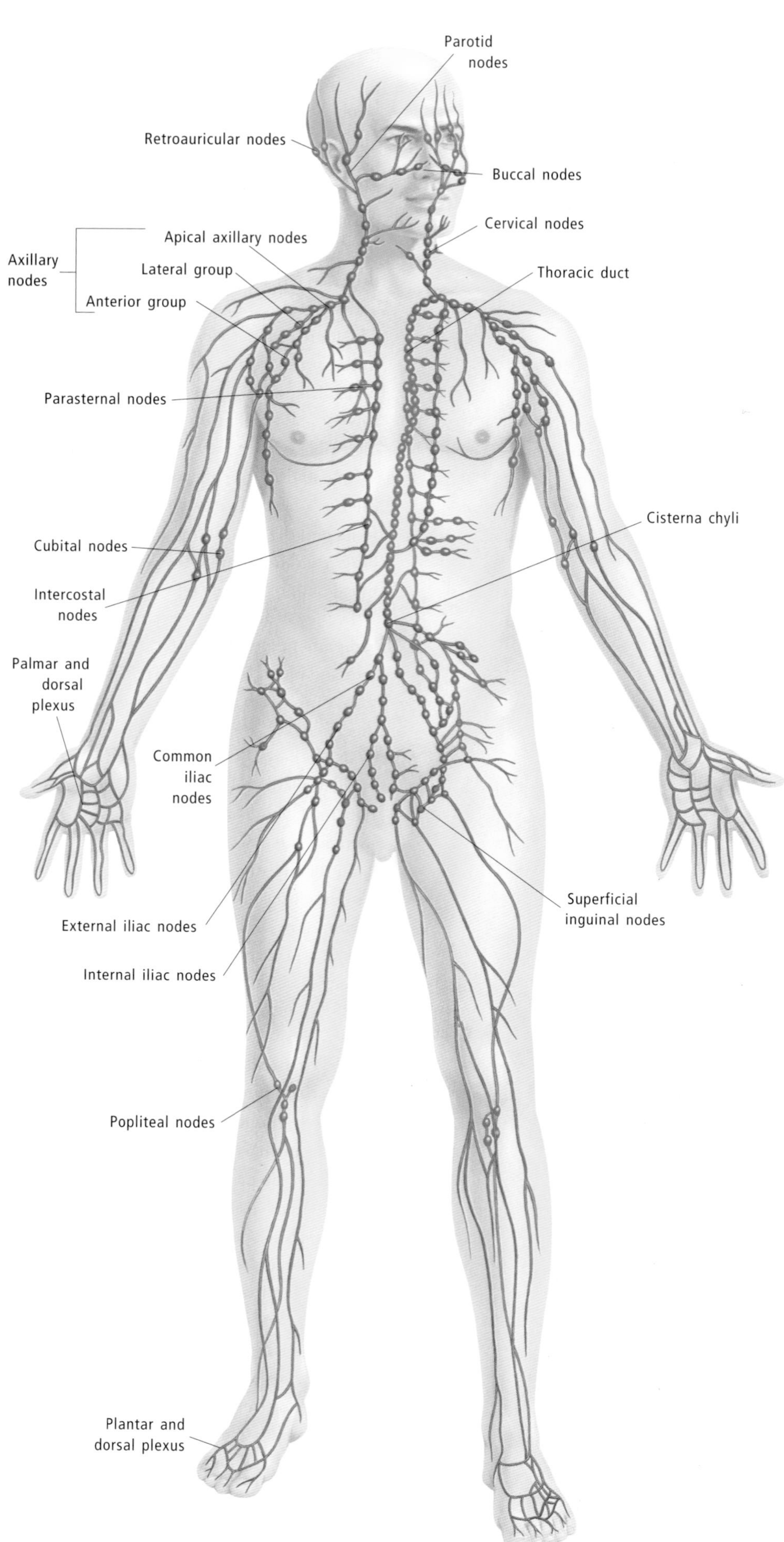

Lymph nodes can be compared to outlying fortresses along the main highway into a city. The battle against invaders begins in the outermost fortress. If the first fortress fails to contain the invasion, fighting will continue along the highway, fire and smoke progressing to fortresses closer in. In a similar fashion, inflammation traveling along major lymph vessels is sometimes visible as red streaks under the skin (lymphangitis). Inflammatory reaction to bacteria in lymph nodes results in swollen, red and painful nodes. When cancer cells colonize the nodes, they become swollen and hard, but not painful, because the enlargement is more gradual. The track of enlarged lymph nodes (lymphadenopathy) gives clues to the origin of infection or the progress of cancer cells.

The tonsils at the back of the oral cavity and the so-called adenoids at the roof of the throat are aggregates of lymphoid tissue.

How lymph returns to the general circulation

The peripheral lymph vessels converge into large lymphatic trunks, which link up in turn to the right lymphatic duct and the thoracic duct, which empty into the large veins at the base of the neck. An overwhelming infection can thus spread along lymph vessels into the general circulation causing "blood infection" (septicemia), which can be fatal.

Lacteals are lymphatic vessels in the walls of the digestive system, which collect large molecules and lipids (chyle) extracted from food. They play a major role in the absorption of fats. They engorge after a meal and become visible as fine whitish streaks in the mesentery. The lacteals empty into the cisterna chyli, a sac located below the diaphragm.

Lymphatic vessels from the head and neck pass through a collar of lymph nodes under the lower jaw, to end in chains of nodes along the internal jugular veins. Cancer of the tip of the tongue spreads first to the nodes under the chin, then to cervical nodes. Some lymph nodes in the lower part of the neck (jugulodigastric nodes) are called tonsillar nodes because they become enlarged in tonsillitis.

Lymphatic vessels of the upper limb ascend from the hand to the armpit (axilla). The nodes in the axilla, which can be felt along the upper arm and against the upper part of the rib cage, also receive lymph from the chest wall, back and the breast. They become enlarged in breast cancer.

Lymphatic vessels of the lower limb ascend from the foot to the inguinal lymph nodes in the groin. These nodes also drain the buttocks, the back and parts of the genitalia, and empty into the cisterna chyli.

Lymph from the internal organs of the thorax and abdomen drains into chains of lymph nodes along major arteries and the aorta. Lymph nodes draining the lungs are located around the bronchi and trachea. Enlargement of these nodes in lung cancer (bronchogenic carcinoma) can be seen on chest x-rays. Lymph from the abdominal and pelvic viscera drains into lymph nodes along the iliac arteries and the aorta, and eventually into the cisterna chyli. These deep nodes, when enlarged, are visible on CAT scans and magnetic resonance imaging (MRI) scans. They can be visualized through radiography after injecting radiopaque dye into the lymphatic vessels (lymphangiography).

The cisterna chyli empties into the thoracic duct, which ascends through the thorax into the neck and empties into the junction of the left internal jugular and subclavian veins. The thoracic duct also collects the lymph from the thoracic organs, from the left upper limb and left half of the head and neck.

Lymph from the right half of the head, neck, and thorax, and the right upper limb, converges in a short right lymphatic duct which empties into the junction of the right internal jugular and subclavian veins.

Lymphoid organs

The lymphoid organs include the thymus, the spleen, and mucosa-associated lymphoid tissue.

Lymph node

A lymph node consists of a mass of lymphatic tissue that is surrounded by a fibrous capsule. Each lymph node is connected to an incoming and outgoing lymph vessel.

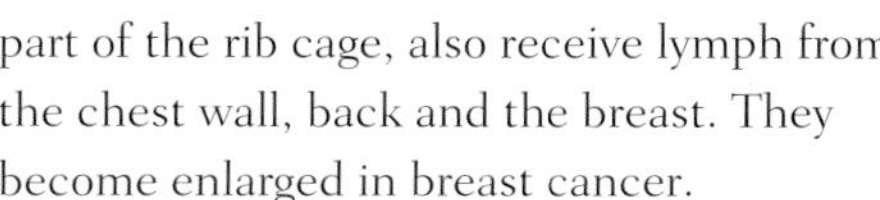

Lymph circulation

The lymph vessels contain numerous valves which prevent the backflow of lymph. The lymph is returned to the general circulation by two large lymphatic vessels which empty into the large veins at the base of the neck.

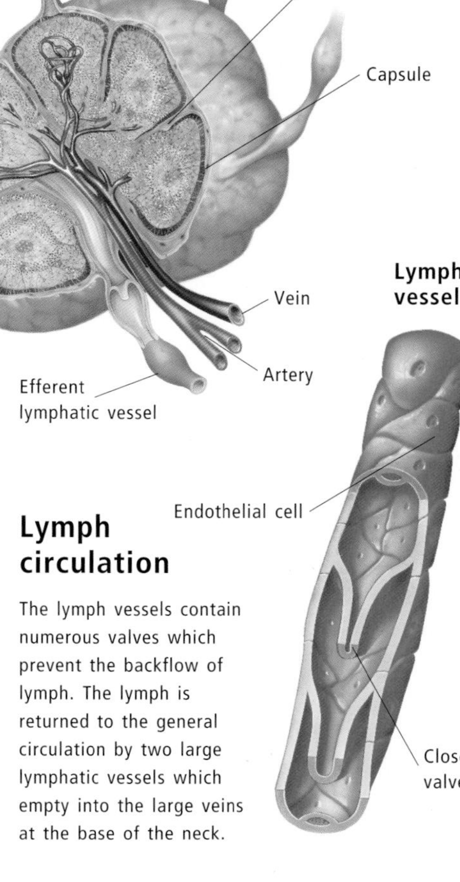

Thymus

The thymus lies in the upper part of the thorax, between the heart and the sternum. It is the first lymphoid organ to develop in the embryo, and reaches 1–1½ ounces (30–40 grams) at puberty. It is gradually replaced by fat and fibrous tissue to become unrecognizable in old age.

Lymphocytes, which are manufactured in the lymph nodes and bone marrow, mature as they are pushed from the outer cortex of the thymus into the central part (medulla), and from there enter the circulation. Most of the lymphocytes in the thymus are T lymphocytes, which are able to recognize foreign-body antigens. B lymphocytes recognize only the body's own cells and antigens. The thymus also secretes hormones that regulate T cell production and function. When the thymus regresses after puberty, T cells continue to proliferate, thus maintaining an adequate number throughout life.

Spleen

The spleen lies under the left ninth, tenth and eleventh ribs, near the end of the pan-

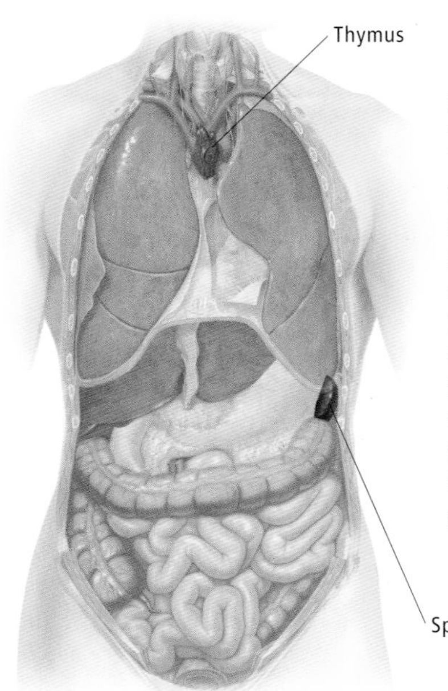

Organs of the lymph system

The thymus gland is an important lymphatic organ in infancy, but gradually regresses after puberty. The spleen is the largest concentration of lymphatic tissue in the body; other concentrations of lymphatic tissue are found in the lymphatic nodules of the gut, and in the tonsils.

Lymphatic tissue

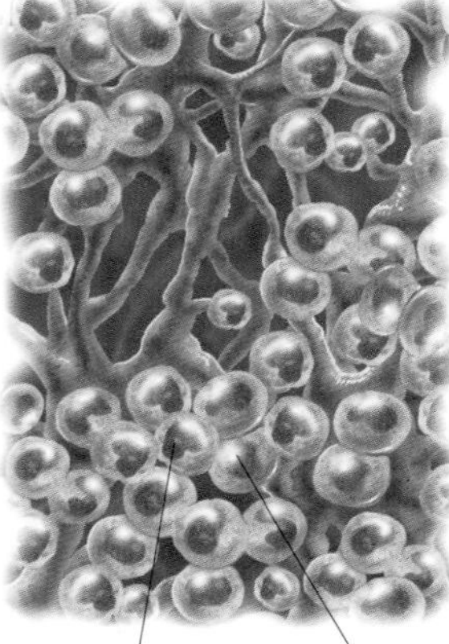

creas. It normally weighs about 5 ounces (150 grams) but can become extremely enlarged in conditions such as malaria and leukemia. It has a rich network of blood capillaries and sinusoids, called the red pulp, and aggregates of lymphocytes around branching arteries, called the white pulp.

The spleen removes particles and aged red blood cells from the circulation. Old red blood cells have rigid membranes and break when they squeeze through the narrow spaces between reticular cells of the spleen.

The spleen also plays an important role in building the immune response, functioning in a similar way to lymph nodes.

Mucosa-associated lymphoid tissue

Masses of lymphoid tissue are found in the linings (mucosa) of the respiratory system, urogenital tract and digestive tract. These mucosa-associated lymphoid tissues contain B and T lymphocytes and serve the same protective function as lymph nodes in the cavities of the body exposed to the external environment.

Lymphocytes and the immune response

Lymphocytes play a central role in the body's immune system. There are three major types of lymphocytes: natural killer cells (NK cells), B lymphocytes and T lymphocytes.

NK cells do not react to specific antigens like T lymphocytes, but kill a variety of target cells, including cancer cells.

T lymphocytes derived from the thymus can be either effector or regulator cells. Each effector T cell recognizes and is activated by one antigen. Activated T cells present antigen to antibody-producing cells to stimulate production of antibody to the particular antigen. Regulator T cells include T helper cells and T suppressor cells, which either facilitate or inhibit the immune response.

B lymphocytes, which come from bone marrow, produce specific antibodies. Each B cell is specialized in producing immunoglobulins or Ig (antibody) to a single antigen. There are five general classes of immunoglobulins: IgG, which is the most important serum globulin; IgM, which is the first antibody to appear in response to infection; IgA, which is found in secretions such as tears or saliva; IgE, which initiates allergic and hypersensitivity reaction; and IgD, which is found on the surface of B cells to help in binding antigens.

When a specific set of T and B cells are activated by an antigen, they multiply to increase production of the appropriate antibody as long as infection lasts. Some T and B cells, called memory cells, remain after the infection is over to ensure a quick response the next time the body is exposed to the same antigen.

Immune disorders

Allergy happens when a substance (allergen), which is not generally harmful to the body, triggers an inappropriate and exaggerated immune response. The immunoglobulin responsible is IgE. The binding of allergen with IgE on mast cells causes them to release histamine and other chemical mediators which initiate a series of reactions: red eyes, urticaria, constriction of the bronchi due to smooth muscle contraction, and mucus secretion in the nasal glands causing sneezing and runny nose. Antihistamine drugs such as phenergan can block these reactions. Common allergic conditions are asthma, allergic rhinitis, allergic conjunctivitis and dermatitis.

Anaphylaxis is an extremely quick overreaction to an antigen caused by widespread activation of mast cells in the body. Extreme cases lead to the potentially fatal anaphylactic shock, when there is a sudden drop in blood pressure. Anaphylactic reaction to penicillin is a well-known example.

Autoimmune disease results when the immune system reacts to the normal cells and antigens of the body, producing autoantibodies which damage or destroy normal tissues. Common examples are psoriasis, rheumatoid arthritis, thyroiditis and systemic lupus erythematosus.

Immunodeficiency diseases can be acquired when the production of immunoglobulin and/or T lymphocytes is inadequate to protect the body from even the most benign infections. Acquired immunodeficiency syndrome (AIDS) is caused by the human immunodeficiency virus (HIV), which binds to CD4 membrane proteins on the surface of T helper cells. When enough infected T helper cells are destroyed, the immune system collapses. Microorganisms that do not affect individuals with a normal immune system can cause lethal opportunistic infections in HIV-infected patients. A marker used to follow the progress of HIV infection is the number of CD4 helper cells in the blood. To date, all efforts to find a vaccine or cure for AIDS have been unsuccessful.

SEE ALSO *Adenoids, AIDS, Allergies, Autoimmune disease, Immunity, Immunodeficiency, Immunosuppression, Lymph, Lymph glands, Lymphatic vessels, Lymphocytes, Spleen, T cells, Thymus, Tonsils*

Lymphocytes

A lymphocyte is a type of white blood cell that plays an important role in the immune response. There are several types, including B cells, T cells and natural killer cells.

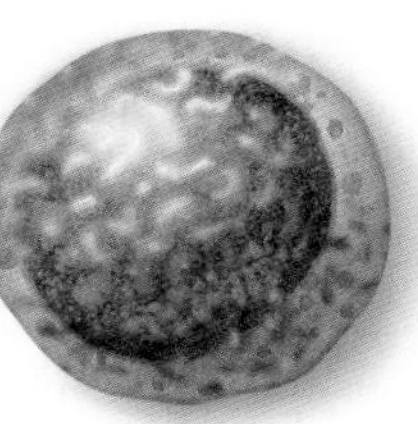

CIRCULATORY SYSTEM

The circulatory system includes the heart and blood vessels, which form a closed ring. The heart has four chambers. It pumps blood out from its two pumps—the left and right ventricles—and collects returned blood into its left and right atria. Blood is pumped out of the ventricles through arteries into a distribution network of tiny vessels, invisible to the naked eye, called the capillaries. After exchanging gases and nutrients with surrounding tissues, blood returns to the atria by the veins.

There are two separate circulations in the circulatory system, which are connected in series. Blood from the left ventricle is distributed to the capillaries throughout the body to deliver oxygen and nutrients to the entire body, and returns to the right atrium. This is the systemic circulation. Blood returning to the right atrium is depleted of oxygen and loaded with carbon dioxide. It then flows into the right ventricle where it is pumped into the capillary network in the lungs, from where, after exchanging carbon dioxide for new oxygen, blood returns to the left atrium. This is the pulmonary circulation. From the left atrium, blood flows to the left ventricle and the cycle continues.

The phase of the heart cycle when both ventricles contract is known as ventricular systole. The ventricles dilate during diastole to receive blood from the atria. In the last part of diastole, the atria contract to squeeze their contents into the ventricles.

Anatomy of the heart

The heart lies in the midline of the thorax, between the lung, surrounded by a double-layered membrane called the pericardium. The heart looks like a pyramid lying on one of its sides, with the apex pointing forward and to the left side. The right and left atria are located at the back, and the right and left ventricles at the front. A septum divides right and left atria, and right and left ventricles. Abnormal development of this septum in the embryo results in "holes in the heart", either between the atria (atrial septal defect), or between the ventricles (ventricular septal defect). Each atrium opens into a

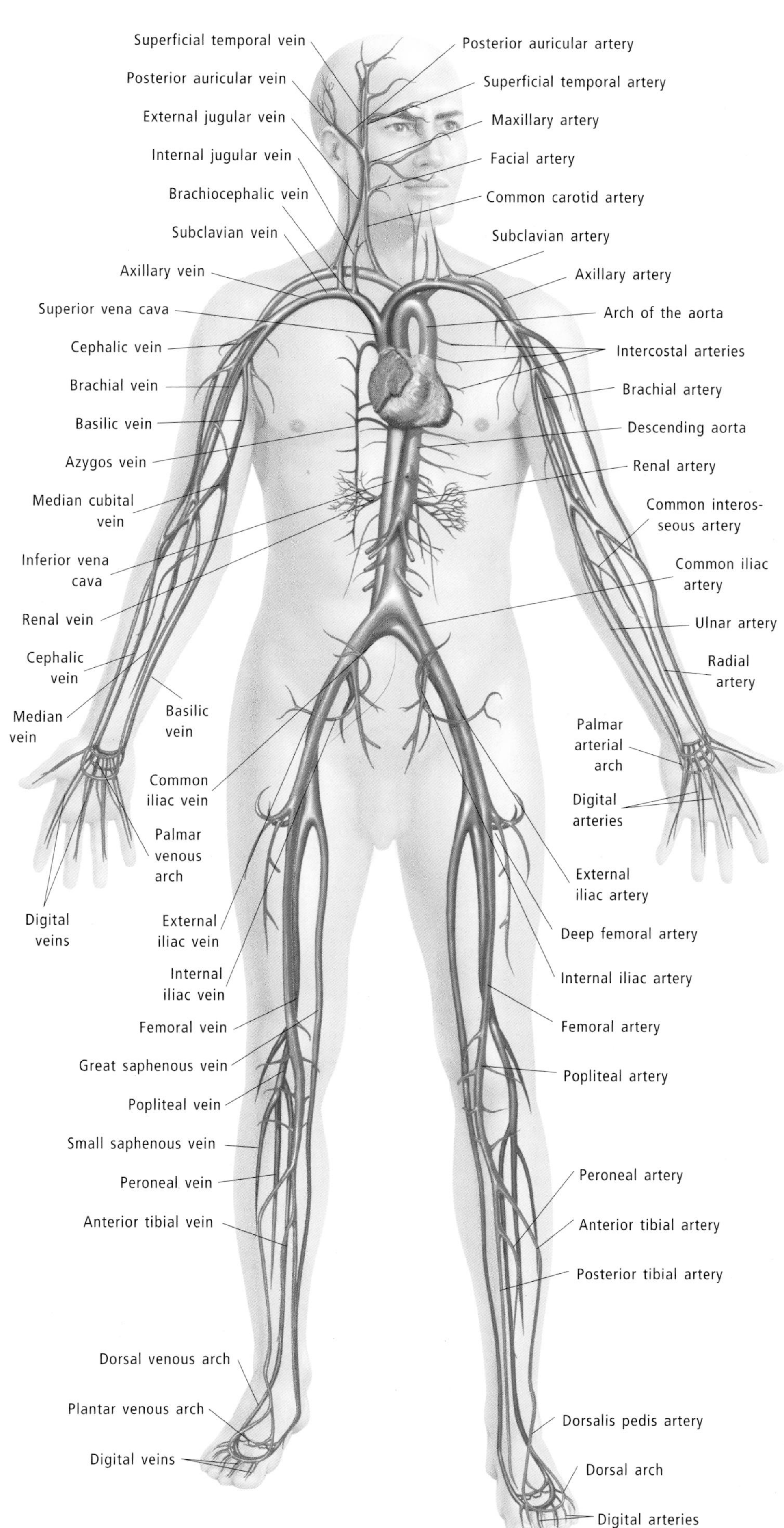

ventricle by an atrioventricular orifice, which is guarded by a valve to ensure that blood flows only in that direction. The valves consist of leaflets (cusps) located in the ventricles and attached to the rim of the orifice. Blood can flow unimpeded into the ventricle, but when it tries to run backwards into the atrium, it pushes the leaflets back towards the rim and closes down the orifice. The right atrioventricular valve has three cusps and is called the tricuspid valve. The left atrioventricular valve is called the mitral valve because its two leaflets look like the split top of a bishop's mitre.

The aortic and pulmonary valves, which prevent reflux of blood back into the ventricles, are formed by three pockets attached to the inside wall of the aortic and pulmonary arteries. They are squashed against the arterial wall by outgoing blood and present no resistance to blood flow, but blood trying to return to the heart will fill up the pockets and close down the opening.

When any of these valves fail to close completely, blood is forced back, causing damage to the heart chamber behind them. In mitral valve incompetence, for example, the left atrium and the pulmonary circulation become overloaded. When the cusps of a valve stick together, the opening is narrowed down (stenosed). In aortic stenosis, the left ventricle is enlarged (hypertrophied) because it has to pump blood against increased resistance. Valvular diseases can be treated by open heart surgery, which is now commonplace.

The end stage of most heart problems is cardiac failure, when the "pump" fails. The common causes are damage to the heart muscle due to a heart attack (myocardial infarction) or valve problems, or diseases of the heart muscle itself (cardiomyopathy).

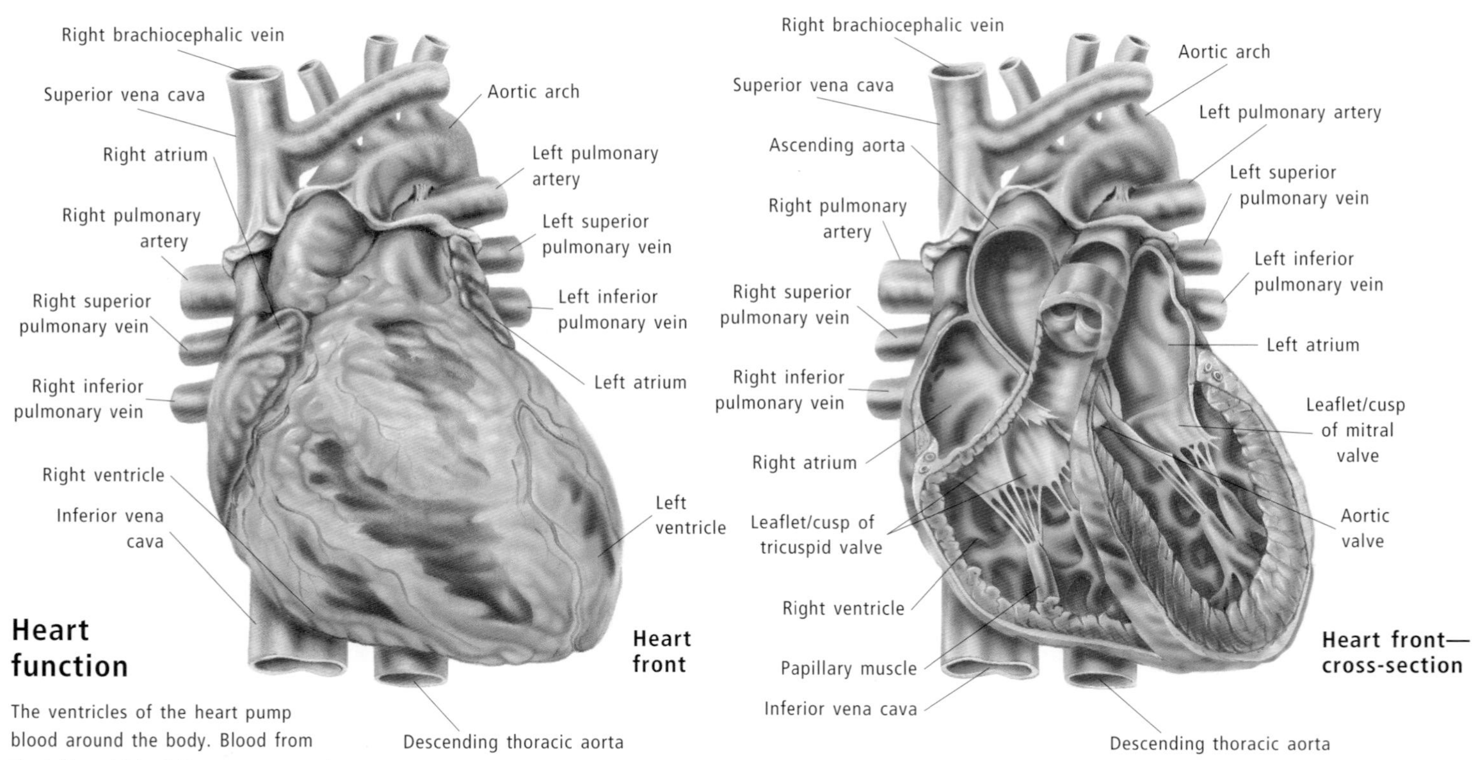

Heart front

Heart front—cross-section

Heart function

The ventricles of the heart pump blood around the body. Blood from the left ventricle delivers oxygen and nutrients to the whole body via the systemic circulation. Blood from the right ventricle collects oxygen from the lungs via the pulmonary circulation.

Heart valves

During ventricular systole (when the ventricles contract), the aortic and pulmonary valves open to allow blood to be pumped into the pulmonary and general circulatory system, while the mitral and tricuspid valves remain closed. During ventricular diastole (when the ventricles dilate), the aortic and pulmonary valves close while the tricuspid and mitral valves open to allow blood to pass from the atria into the ventricles.

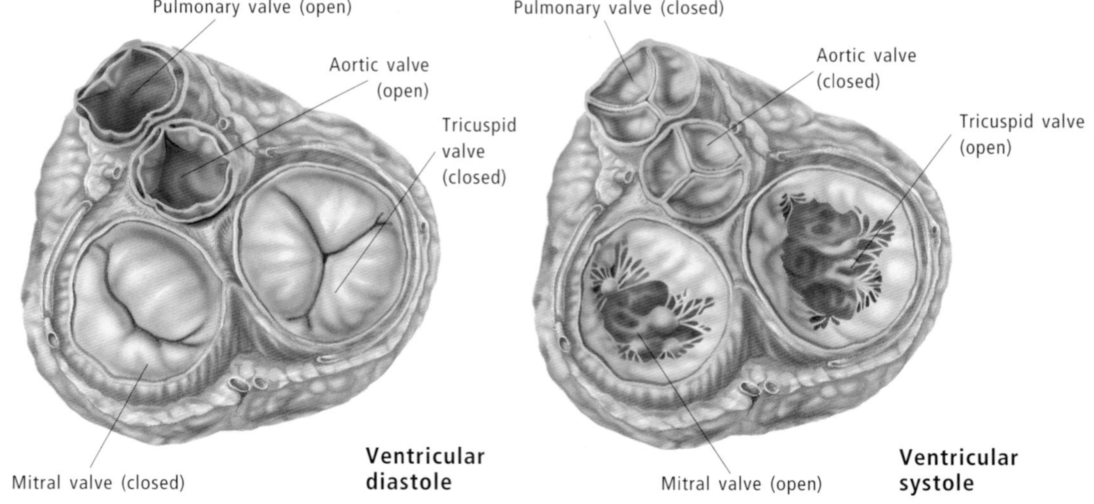

Ventricular diastole

Ventricular systole

Coronary arteries

The heart is only the size of the human fist, yet it is responsible for about 8 percent of the body's total oxygen consumption.

Blood supply to the heart comes from the right and left coronary arteries, so-called because they wrap around the heart like a crown.

The right coronary artery runs in the groove between the right atrium and the right ventricle to the back of the heart, where it turns 90 degrees to run in the groove corresponding to the interventricular septum. The left coronary artery divides shortly after its beginning into the anterior interventricular artery, which runs in the groove of the interventricular septum at the front of the heart, and the circumflex artery, which runs in the groove between the left atrium and left ventricle.

Deposits (plaques) inside the arteries can reduce blood flow. If this happens in a coronary artery, part of the heart will not receive adequate blood supply. With moderate blockage, blood supply becomes inadequate when the heart has to pump harder to cope with physical exertion or mental stress. This lack of blood supply, called ischemia, causes sensations of pain and pressure over the chest known as angina pectoris. When blockage is complete, an area of heart muscle dies, resulting in a heart attack.

Nerve supply

The heart can continue beating when taken out of the body because it has a built-in nerve supply. The sinoatrial node, located in the right atrium, is the pacemaker triggering the contraction of the right and left ventricles. The autonomic nervous system, by way of the cardiac plexus, modifies the intrinsic heart rhythm and adjusts heart rate and contraction power to the requirements of the body. In some cases, when the innervation of the heart malfunctions, an artificial pacemaker must be connected to drive the heart.

In the condition known as arrhythmia, the heart rhythm is disturbed: it may be too fast (tachycardia), too slow (bradycardia), or have added beats or skipped beats.

Blood vessels

The three types of blood vessels are arteries, veins and capillaries. The arteries carry the blood from the heart to the capillaries, where oxygen and other nutrients are exchanged with surrounding tissues. The veins then carry the blood from the capillaries back to the heart.

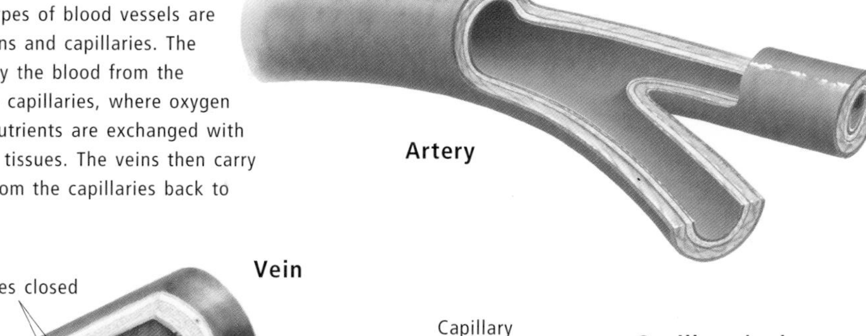

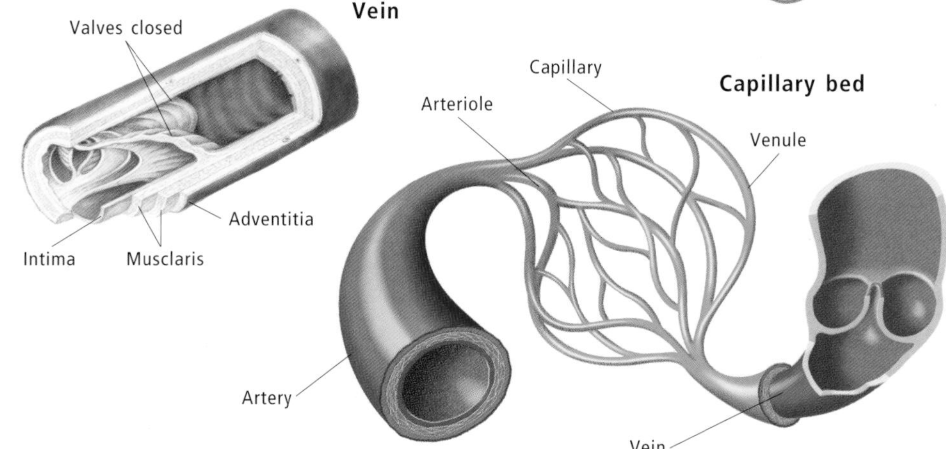

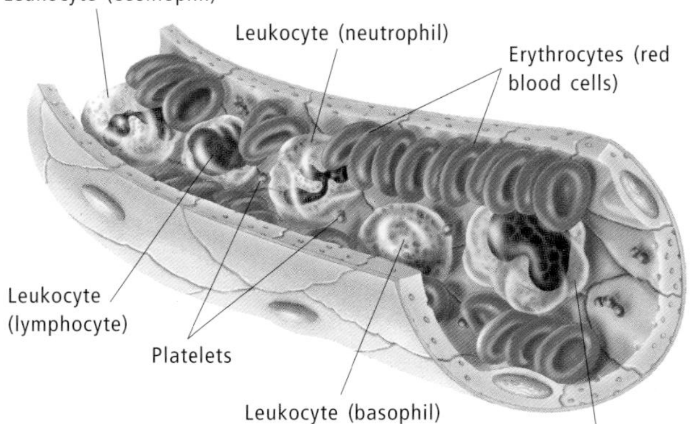

Blood composition

The blood is composed of red cells, white cells (leukocytes), platelets and plasma. Red blood cells carry oxygen to the tissues while plasma carries essential nutrients to the tissues. This illustration shows all the components of blood and is only representational in its proportions.

Blood vessels

The major arteries of the systemic circulation are derived from the aorta: these are the carotid arteries for the head and neck, the axillary arteries for the upper limbs, and the iliac arteries for the pelvis and lower limbs.

Arteries can be blocked by plaque deposits, or become stiff, resulting in raised blood pressure (hypertension). This is usually associated with a high cholesterol level in the blood (hypercholesterolemia).

There are two main systemic veins, the superior vena cava, which returns blood from the head and upper limbs, and the inferior vena cava, which returns blood from the lower limbs. The four pulmonary veins return oxygenated blood to the left atria. The systemic veins form a storage system for blood.

The deep veins of the legs are often the site of the formation of a blood clot, or deep vein thrombosis, when blood flow is sluggish due to prolonged immobilization. This condition can be fatal. Disorders of the superficial veins are not as serious. If veins are dilated, as in varicose veins, they can be removed by surgery.

Many diseases of the circulatory system are the result of smoking, poor eating habits and lack of exercise, and in many cases can be alleviated (or prevented) by adopting a healthier lifestyle. Heart disease is the greatest cause of death in Western countries.

SEE ALSO *Angina pectoris, Aorta, Arteries, Blood vessels, Cardiomyopathy, Coronary arteries, Heart, Hypertension, Ischemia, Mitral valve, Myocardial infarction, Pericardium, Stenosis, Thrombosis, Tricuspid valve, Veins, Ventricle*

RESPIRATORY SYSTEM

In the process of metabolism, the human body consumes oxygen and produces carbon dioxide as a waste product. The respiratory system is designed to exchange the carbon dioxide accumulated in the blood for oxygen in the airways, which enters the lungs as air from the surrounding atmosphere. This air is breathed into the airways via the nose, pharynx, larynx, trachea and bronchi.

Nose

The visible part of the nose is supported by cartilage and is only the front opening of the nasal cavity. The nasal septum divides the nasal cavity through the middle, and is formed by septal cartilage at the tip and by bone closer to the skull. When the septal cartilage is curved in septal deviation, half of the nasal cavity may be narrowed although the external nose still looks symmetrical.

The inner surface of the nostril is covered by skin with coarse hairs that trap dust from air that has been drawn in (inspired). The remainder of the nasal cavity is lined by mucous membrane with many blood vessels and mucus-secreting glands. Blood heat warms up inhaled air, while the moist sticky mucus traps more dust. Three curved structures known as conchae, jutting out from each side wall into the nasal cavity, increase the surface area for warming up inspired air. In the common cold, the nose is blocked by swollen mucous membrane and increased secretion of mucus.

A small area in the roof of the nasal cavity is supplied (innervated) by the olfactory nerve for smell.

Pharynx

The pharynx lies behind the nasal cavity, oral cavity and larynx and ends in the esophagus. Located in each side wall of the pharynx, just behind the nasal cavity, is the opening of the auditory tube, which connects the pharynx with the middle ear cavity. It equalizes pressure of the ear cavity with atmospheric pressure. When the pharynx is inflamed as the result of a common cold, the opening of the auditory tube is blocked, the eardrum cannot vibrate freely because of the pressure difference, and sounds are muffled.

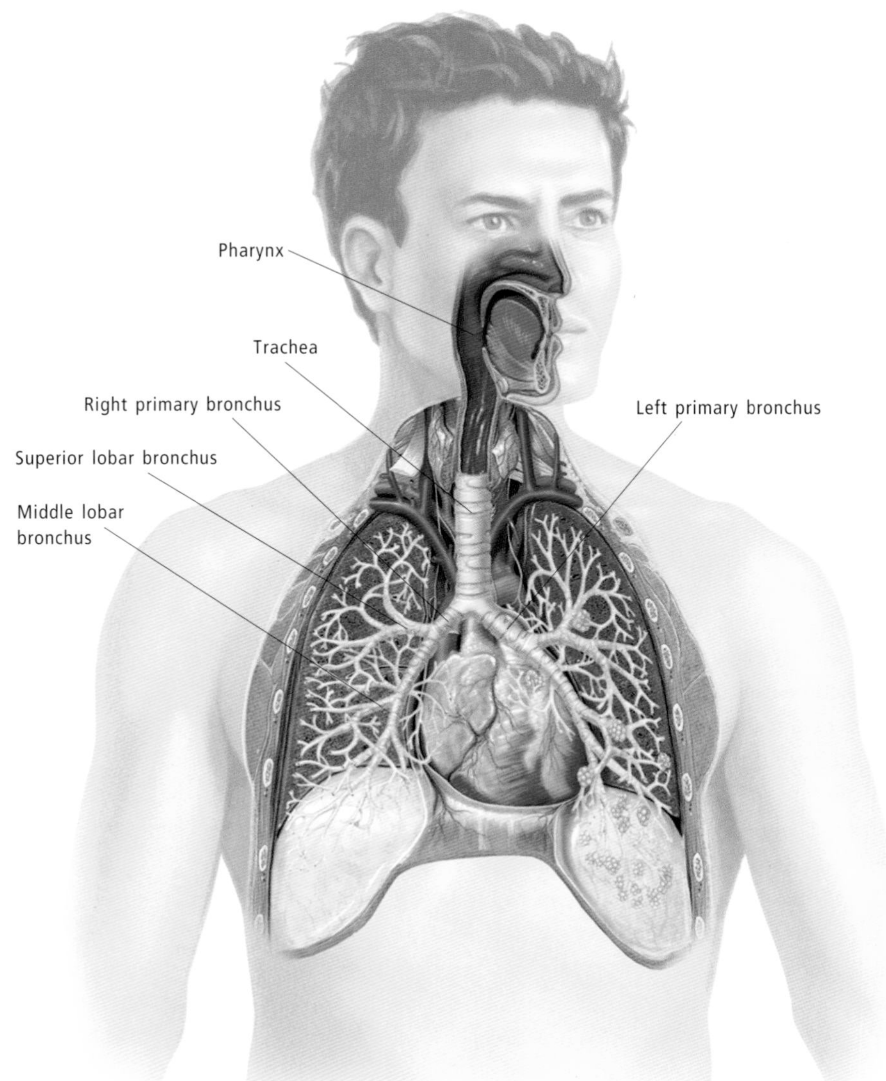

NB: The top two-thirds of the lungs have been removed to show the heart and bronchial tree.

The larynx and speech

The larynx is a tube located in front of the pharynx and made up of a membrane reinforced by muscles. It begins with a cartilage—the epiglottis—which closes the entry into the larynx when we swallow to prevent food from passing into the airway. This tube has two segments separated from each other by a small gap. The top segment begins at the upper edge of the epiglottis and ends below it at the vestibular folds or "false vocal cords". The lower segment begins at the vocal cords and ends where it is attached to the cricoid cartilage. The cricoid cartilage is attached to the trachea below. The vocal cords are attached to the thyroid cartilage at the front and to the arytenoid cartilage at the back of the larynx.

We speak by blowing air from the lungs into the larynx, which vibrates the vocal cords. The arytenoids spin around a vertical axis, bringing the vocal cords close together or further apart. The thyroid cartilage tilts on the cricoid to control the tension of the vocal cords and the frequency of the vibration. The vibrations of the cords are converted into the different sounds of speech by the position of the tongue and lips.

When the larynx is surgically removed due to cancer, a device similar to an electric razor held against the throat can be used to transmit a pure vibration to the column of air breathed out (expired). Movements of the tongue and lips turn the vibration into robot-like speech which is not as clear as normal speech and lacks inflection but is still intelligible.

The thyroid cartilage protects the front of the larynx. It has two plates (laminae) joined together at an angle, like the spine of an open book. The upper end of the angle is more prominent in males and known as the "Adam's apple". The thyroid cartilage is connected by membrane to the hyoid bone above and cricoid cartilage below. The larynx moves up and down when we swallow or when we want to sing with a vibrato effect.

Trachea, bronchi and lungs

The trachea is a stack of 15–20 C-shaped cartilages, connected to each other by fibrous tissue, forming a vertical gutter opening at the back. The trachealis muscle connects the ends of the Cs, closes up the gutter and turns it into a tube.

Food passing down the esophagus bulges into the trachea through the trachealis. A large mass of food (bolus) stuck in the esophagus can block the air passage and choke the victim to death. If the larynx is obstructed by edema (swelling), as in smoke inhalation, tracheostomy may save life by creating a temporary opening in the trachea at the root of the neck.

The trachea ends by dividing into the right and left main bronchi for the right and left lungs. The left lung is divided into upper and lower lobes by an oblique fissure. An additional horizontal fissure divides the right lung into three lobes, the upper, middle and lower lobes.

Inside each lung, the main bronchus divides first into lobar bronchi, then into smaller and smaller bronchi (bronchioles). The lining (epithelium) of the trachea and bronchi has hairlike structures known as cilia and contains many goblet cells and mucous glands that secrete mucus to trap dust. Dust trapped in mucus is moved upwards by the cilia. The bronchial epithelium also contains lymphoid tissue which secretes antibody IgA. The bronchioles are entirely muscular and have no cartilage in their walls. During asthma attacks, the channels of the bronchioles are narrowed by edema of the mucous membrane, by increased mucus secretion, and by spasm of the smooth muscle in their walls.

The bronchial tree ends in the air sacs, or alveoli, that branch out of the terminal bronchioles like bunches of grapes. Alveoli are separated from one another by interalveolar septa which greatly increase the surface area available for gas exchange.

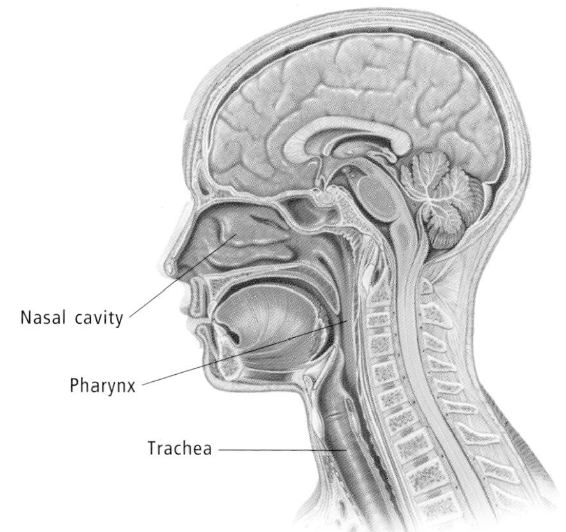

When interalveolar septa are destroyed in emphysema, the architecture of the alveoli is destroyed and gas exchange is compromised. The walls of the alveoli are thin and contain a network of capillaries. Blood coming from the pulmonary artery is depleted of oxygen and rich in carbon dioxide, while inspired air is full of oxygen and low in carbon dioxide. Gases move across the alveolar membrane: carbon dioxide passes into the alveolar air, and oxygen passes into the blood. The blood leaving the alveoli is again saturated with oxygen, and carbon dioxide in the alveoli is expelled into the atmosphere with expired air.

The alveolar walls also contain cells that secrete surfactant, a substance that reduces surface tension of the alveolar wall, enabling the alveoli to expand in inspiration and preventing alveolar collapse during expiration. In infantile respiratory distress syndrome, the alveoli collapse because they are deficient in surfactant. Lying on the inner surface of the alveolar wall are macrophages which engulf inhaled bacteria, dust or carbon particles.

Pleura

Each lung is surrounded by a double-layered membrane called the pleura. Just imagine a slightly inflated balloon containing a teaspoonful of oil. Wrap the balloon around the lung, stretching it until it reaches the entrance of blood vessels and bronchus, and you have an image of the pleura. The half of the balloon in contact with the lung corresponds to the "visceral layer" of the pleura, the other half visible from outside corresponds to the "parietal layer" of the pleura. The parietal layer is attached to the inside of the rib cage. The small amount of fluid in the pleura allows frictionless movements of the lung against the ribcage.

The common term "pleurisy" refers to accumulation of fluid in the pleura. A large collection of fluid in the pleura—such as serum in some cases of viral infection or blood caused by stab wounds to the chest—must be aspirated out. Expansion of the lung is also hampered by the presence of air in the pleural cavity (pneumothorax). Pneumothorax may be caused by a chest wound or it may be spontaneous in some young, tall and lean individuals. Exposure to asbestos is a common cause for mesothelioma, a cancer of the pleura.

Upper section of the respiratory system

The upper part of the respiratory system consists of the nose, the nasal cavity and the pharynx. The pharynx is shared by the respiratory and digestive systems.

Muscles used for breathing

The diaphragm and intercostal muscles are involved in breathing. During inspiration these muscles contract to increase the front to back, side to side, and vertical size of the rib cage. Expiration is a passive process involving the recoil of the ribs and the return of the diaphragm to its normal position.

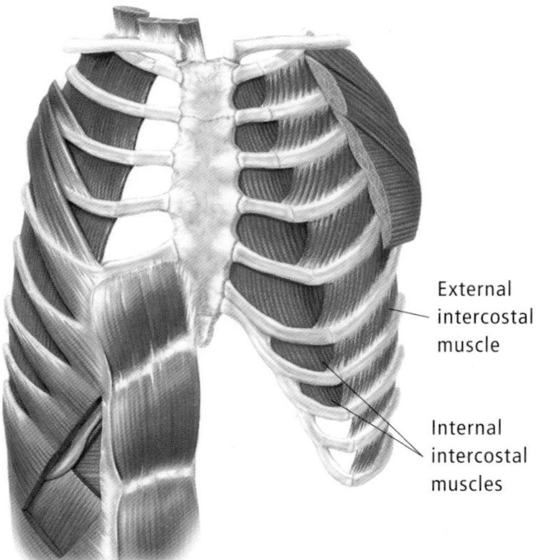

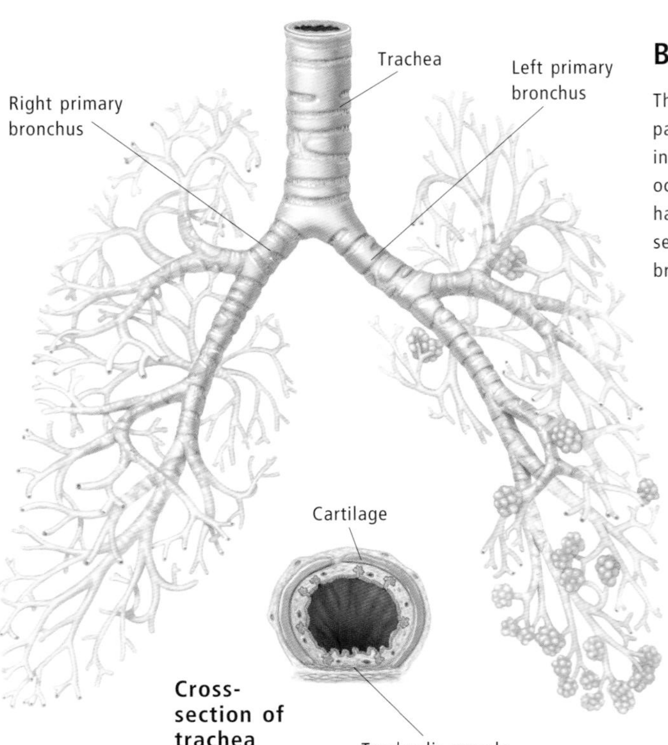

Cross-section of trachea

Bronchial tree

The bronchial tree provides a passageway for inspired air to pass into the alveoli where gas exchange occurs. Bronchi contain cilia (small hair-like structures) and mucus-secreting glands, which ensure the bronchial airways remain clear.

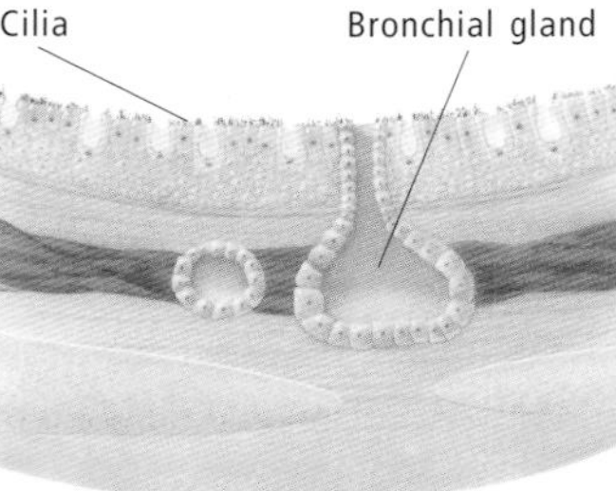

Cross-section of bronchi

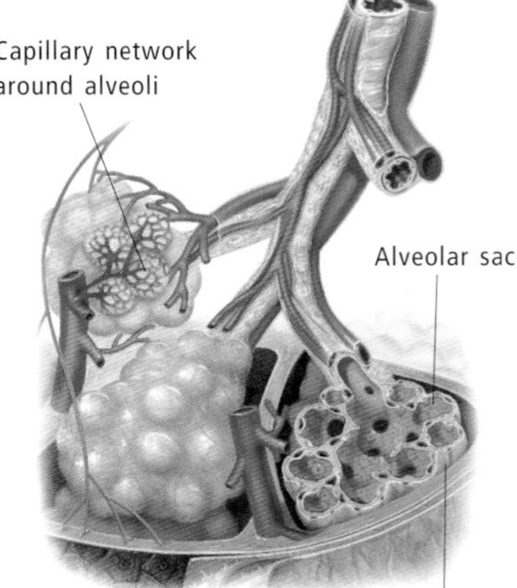

Gas exchange in the alveoli

The smallest bronchioles end in alveoli (air sacs). The sac walls are surrounded by small blood vessels which allow oxygen from the air to enter the bloodstream and carbon dioxide accumulated in the blood to pass into the alveoli to be breathed out.

Blood and nerve supply

Deoxygenated blood from the body is pumped by the right ventricle of the heart through the pulmonary arteries into the lungs. Branches of the pulmonary arteries follow the bronchial tree and end in the capillaries that surround the alveoli, where gas exchange occurs. Reoxygenated blood is collected by venules that converge into two pulmonary veins for each lung, and returns to the left atrium of the heart so that it can be pumped back around the body.

In mitral stenosis, the narrowed mitral valve increases resistance to bloodflow from the left atrium to the left ventricle. The increased pressure is transmitted back to the capillary system in the lungs, making the lungs stiffer and breathing difficult. If the pressure is high enough, serum leaks out of the capillaries causing pulmonary edema, capillaries burst into the alveoli and the patient coughs up blood—this is known as hemoptysis.

The airway and lungs receive oxygen and nutrients from the small bronchial arteries. Deoxygenated blood returns to the heart via the pulmonary veins.

Lymphatic vessels from the lungs eventually empty into the thoracic duct. The lymph nodes are located in the root of the lungs (where vessels and bronchi enter the lungs) and around the bronchi and trachea. When they are enlarged in lung cancer, they become visible even on standard chest x-rays.

How do we breathe?

The rib cage is an airtight cylinder, with the diaphragm as its base, and the root of the neck as its top lid. The wall is made up of the ribs running from the thoracic vertebrae to the sternum, and connected together by three layers of intercostal muscles. When we breathe in, the ribs rotate around their vertebral articulations, and the sternum at their front ends is raised, increasing the front-to-back as well as the side-to-side diameters of the rib cage. The diaphragm moves down, increasing the vertical size of the rib cage. The capacity of the thoracic cavity increases, resulting in a decrease in intrathoracic pressure to a value below atmospheric pressure. The air is sucked into the lungs through the airway. This mechanism fails if there is a large wound in the rib cage equalizing the intrathoracic pressure with atmospheric pressure.

Breathing out is a passive process—the recoil of the ribs and the lungs and the return of the diaphragm to a higher position squeeze the air out. In asthma attacks, resistance in the airway causes more trouble in the expiratory phase of breathing. Patients have to make an effort to squeeze air out of the body, and the wheezing noise of breathing is more prominent in expiration. To overcome the resistance, patients often have to sit up, grasp a fixed object like the bed post, and use "accessory respiratory muscles" in the neck to generate extra pull on the first rib and sternum. When airflow is severely reduced, for example when movements of the ribs are hindered in a bedridden patient, stagnation of air and secretion in the lungs increases the risk of respiratory infection (pneumonia). Physical therapy of the chest is vital for the prevention of pneumonia in bed-bound, chronically ill patients.

Lung cancer

Lung cancer is actually cancer of the airway and properly called "bronchogenic carcinoma". Smoking causes constant irritation and infection of the bronchi (chronic bronchitis), and is also a proven cause of lung cancer. Lung cancer can be more dangerous than other cancers because it is insidious, and unlike skin or breast tumors, it gives no external visible sign. Lung cancer is often already well developed by the time it is suspected or diagnosed.

See also Asthma, Breathing, Bronchus, Common cold, Epiglottis, Larynx, Lung cancer, Lungs, Mesothelioma, Metabolism, Mitral valve, Mucous membranes, Nose, Pharynx, Pleurisy, Pneumothorax, Pulmonary edema, Ribs, Speech, Trachea, Vocal cords

URINARY SYSTEM

The urinary system is essential to life. It excretes the waste products of metabolism and maintains the balance of water and electrolytes in the blood.

Blood and the internal environment

All cells and tissues of the body consume oxygen and nutrients and produce carbon dioxide and waste products. The respiratory system removes carbon dioxide from the body. Waste products are filtered out of the blood by the kidneys and excreted in the urine.

An inorganic compound such as salt (sodium chloride) breaks down into sodium and chloride ions when dissolved in water. These ions allow the solution to conduct electricity and so are called electrolytes.

The cells of the body contain intracellular fluid and are surrounded by extracellular fluid that includes serum from the blood. All chemical reactions in the body and the functions of the nervous system depend on a constant concentration of electrolytes inside the cells and in the extracellular fluid. Sodium is the main electrolyte in extracellular fluid; potassium is the main electrolyte in intracellular fluid.

Changes in the proportions of ions in intracellular and extracellular fluid can have serious consequences. A high concentration of potassium in extracellular fluid can cause cardiac arrest; a low concentration may result in muscle paralysis. Hydrogen ions and bicarbonate ions determine the acidity of the blood, which influences the conduction of impulses in the nervous system and metabolic reactions of the body. The kidney is one of the main regulators of the balance of electrolytes and acids.

Kidneys

The kidneys are located on the back wall of the abdomen on either side of the vertebrae, enveloped by a renal capsule and enclosed in perirenal fat. Their position, below the last rib, explains why some kidney diseases cause pain at the angle between the lumbar vertebrae and the twelfth rib.

The right kidney lies behind the duodenum and is slightly lower than the left, which lies behind the pancreas and the stomach. The ends of the transverse colon, where it joins the ascending and descending colon, are located in front of the two kidneys. The adrenal glands cap the upper tip of each kidney.

Internal structure of the kidney

Each kidney has an outer part (cortex) and an inner part (medulla). The cortex contains filtration units (glomeruli and tubules). The medulla is made up of about a dozen renal pyramids, so-called because of their shape. The major component of each pyramid is a bundle of collecting tubules which collect the urine produced by the filtration units in the cortex.

The tips of the pyramids project into the sinus as small papillae, each of which is capped by a small cup-like minor calyx. Minor calices join to form major calices which empty into the renal pelvis; this joins with the ureter.

Each renal artery branches off the aorta and divides into branches that enter the renal sinus to reach the medulla and cortex of the kidney. The veins accompany the arteries and end in the inferior vena cava.

The functions of the kidney

The kidney performs both excretory and endocrine functions.

Excretory function: the kidney filters the blood, removing metabolic waste products such as urea and any other unwanted substances. It maintains the balance of electrolytes in the blood and the water content of the body.

Diuretic drugs, which increase the excretion of water by the kidneys, are often prescribed in cases of mild hypertension to reduce the amount of water circulating in the body, and to treat mild heart failure by reducing the load on the heart.

Each kidney has about a million microscopic functional units called renal tubules or nephrons. Each nephron begins with a glomerulus that is made up of a tuft of capillaries surrounded by the Bowman's capsule (a filtration membrane that is tightly wrapped around the capillaries of the glomerulus). Filtrate from the blood leaves the capsule and passes through the proximal and distal convoluted tubules of the nephron, where vitamins and various electrolytes are reabsorbed.

A part of the nephron (the loop of Henle) dips into the medulla of the kidney, and plays an important role in the reabsorption of water, sodium and potassium ions. Reabsorbed water and electrolytes enter the networks formed by the capillaries that leave the Bowman's capsule. Waste products and toxic substances are either not reabsorbed or are actively secreted into the urine.

The last part of the nephron, the collecting duct, is also the site of the reabsorption of water and electrolytes and plays an important role in adjusting the concentration of urine. The collecting ducts are bundled in the pyramids and open at the papillae.

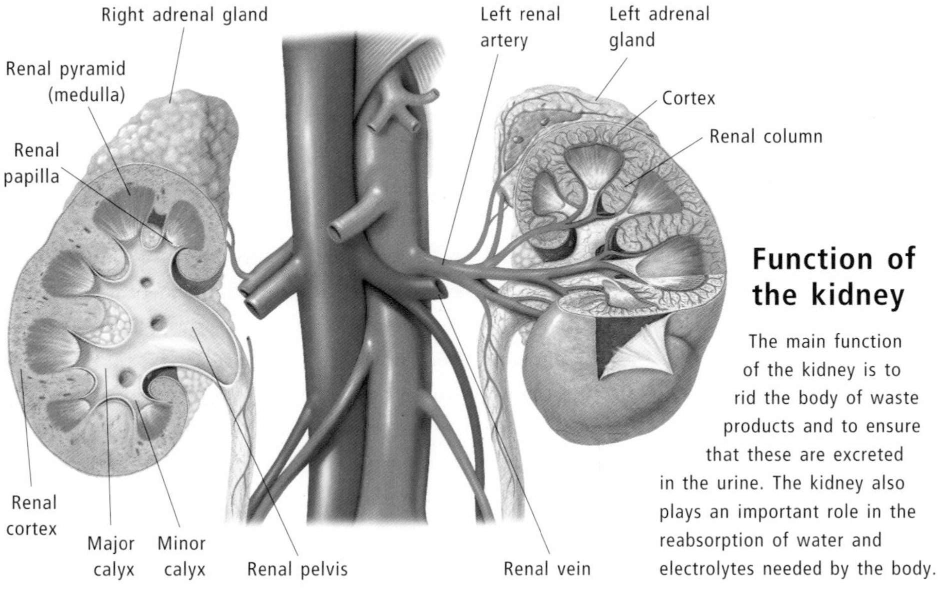

Function of the kidney

The main function of the kidney is to rid the body of waste products and to ensure that these are excreted in the urine. The kidney also plays an important role in the reabsorption of water and electrolytes needed by the body.

The average urine output in the adult is about 1–1½ quarts (1–1.5 liters) a day. The amount and concentration of urine varies according to fluid intake and fluid loss through respiration, perspiration and fecal elimination. When the body is dehydrated only a small amount of very concentrated urine is produced.

People prone to urinary tract infections or kidney stones should maintain an adequate urine output to avoid the recurrence of infection or stone formation.

The filtration membrane in the renal glomerulus is a complex structure that can be damaged by the body's own immune reaction in glomerulonephritis. This disorder often develops after streptococcal infections or in some autoimmune diseases. In diabetes mellitus, thickening of the basement membrane of capillaries in the glomeruli disturbs the function of the glomeruli and causes renal failure.

The abuse of painkillers (analgesics) may cause severe damage to renal tubules. The tubules can also be blocked by hemoglobin released from muscles that have been destroyed by massive crush injury or excessive overheating in marathon runners. Damage to the renal tubules results in drastic changes in the composition of extracellular fluid. Renal failure may be fatal because concentration of some ions, such as potassium, can rise to lethal levels.

In late-stage kidney disease, life may be sustained by dialysis or artificial kidneys, both requiring close monitoring and constant intervention by a renal physician.

The function of the kidney extends far beyond simple filtration of the blood. Infection of the kidney is a common complication which used to result in death for bedridden patients. Even with recent advances in medicine, kidney failure is still an end stage of many general medical conditions.

Endocrine function: the kidney's endocrine function involves the release of hormones into the blood: erythropoietin affects blood formation and hydroxycholecalciferol is involved in calcium metabolism.

Where the distal convoluted tubule joins the capillary in the glomerulus, specialized epithelium can sense blood concentration and endocrine secretion. This setup (the juxtaglomerular apparatus) also senses reductions in sodium concentration in the blood and responds by releasing renin, an enzyme that triggers a chain reaction to reestablish electrolyte balance.

Renin converts angiotensinogen in the blood into angiotensin I, which is converted into angiotensin II by the lungs. Angiotensin II stimulates the adrenal cortex to secrete aldosterone, which acts on the nephron to increase the reabsorption of salt. This increases the output of diluted urine, restores the concentration of salt in body fluids, and raises blood pressure.

Many antihypertensive drugs work by suppressing this renin-angiotensin-aldosterone system.

Ureter

The renal pelvis continues into the ureter, a muscular tube that carries urine to the bladder. Small kidney stones originating from the renal pelvis may become lodged in the ureter, especially where it is slightly constricted, such as at the junction with the renal pelvis. The smooth muscles above the blockage contract violently as they try to push the stone through the ureter, causing intense waves of pain (renal colic).

The first line of treatment is simply loading the body with water to increase urine flow, and using a muscle relaxant to relax the ureter and facilitate the passage of the stone. The stones can either be removed by surgery or destroyed by ultrasound.

The ureter descends almost vertically along the line of the tips of the transverse processes of the lumbar vertebrae. At the hip bone it turns backwards to enter the back of the bladder near the midline. The ureter is narrowest when it pierces the bladder wall. It runs obliquely for about ¾ inch (2 centimeters) in the bladder before opening to a slit-like aperture.

When the bladder is full, the increased pressure compresses the part of the ureter inside the bladder wall, preventing reflux of urine back to the renal pelvis. When there are bacteria in the bladder, reflux can spread infection to the kidney (pyelonephritis). If the ureter runs perpendicularly through the bladder wall because of defective development, this "flap-valve" mechanism does not operate and kidney infection by reflux occurs frequently.

The urinary bladder

Urine is continuously produced by the kidney and stored in the bladder, a muscular sac that resembles an inverted pyramid. The urethra emerges from the neck (apex) of the bladder, which is located just behind the symphysis pubis. The rear surface of the bladder is in front of the rectum and receives the ureters. The openings of the two ureters and the urethra form the three corners of the triangular trigone.

The bladder is behind the pubis when empty; when full, it rises above the symphysis pubis and can be ruptured by a direct blow above the pubis. In males, the bladder rests on the prostate and is anchored to the pubis and to the side walls of the pelvis by ligaments attached to its neck.

The male urethra

The prostate, located below the apex of the bladder, rests on the pelvic floor, which is reinforced by a layer of muscles—the urogenital diaphragm. The urethra leaves the neck of the bladder and passes through the prostate and the membrane formed by the muscle layers before reaching the penis; it is usually divided into prostatic, membranous and penile parts.

The male urethra is the common passage for sperm as well as urine and is closely related to the reproductive system.

The urethra is a muscular tube reinforced by muscle fibers that extend like slings from the bladder around the upper part of the prostatic urethra. An enlarged prostate distorts the geometry of this sphincter and interferes with the mechanism that closes the urethra after voiding (micturition). This sphincter is under autonomic control. Among the muscles of the urogenital diaphragm is another sphincter, which is under conscious control.

The full bladder sends a message to the reflex center in the sacral part of the spinal cord where it triggers a reflex contraction of the muscle of the bladder and causes the neck of the bladder to relax. This reflex is suppressed until there is an opportunity to relieve the bladder. Voluntary control is lost (incontinence) when the reflex center in the spinal cord is damaged and the bladder overflows when filled to capacity. Incontinence also occurs when the pathway for inhibition

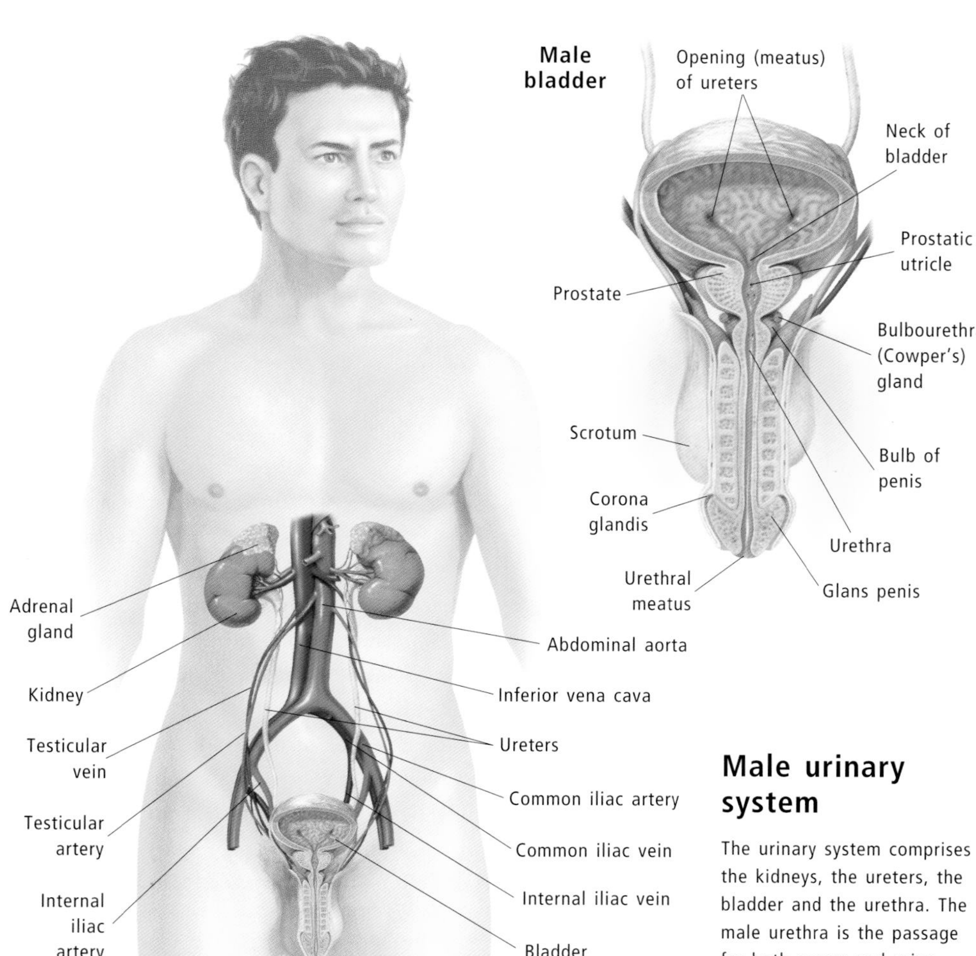

Male urinary system

The urinary system comprises the kidneys, the ureters, the bladder and the urethra. The male urethra is the passage for both sperm and urine.

Control of the closure of the urethra is less efficient in the female than in the male. Distortion of the muscle floor of the pelvis, or damage to the sphincters of the urethra by several pregnancies, often results in stress incontinence. Urine may leak with the slight raise in intra-abdominal pressure caused by a simple cough, for example.

The short urethra allows easy examination of the inside of the bladder using a cystoscope, but also provides an easy route of entry for bacteria. Thus infection of the lower portion of the urinary system (called urinary tract infection) is more common in females than in males, especially in young girls who have an even shorter and straighter urethra than adult women.

SEE ALSO *Adrenal glands, Bladder, Cystitis, Cystoscopy, Diuretics, Electrolytes, Glomerulonephritis, Hypertension, Kidney, Potassium, Reproductive systems, Sodium, Urethra, Urinary incontinence, Urinary tract*

from the brain is damaged by spinal injury and the bladder empties automatically.

Female urinary system

The structure and organization of the urinary system is similar in both sexes from the kidney down to the bladder. However, the position of the ureter within the pelvis is slightly different. One example is the close proximity of the female ureter to the artery that supplies the uterus. During removal of the uterus (hysterectomy), surgeons have to be careful not to accidentally damage the ureter when they clamp and cut the artery.

Female bladder and urethra

The vagina lies between the rectum and the rear surface of the bladder, with the uterus lying on the top of the bladder. The urethra passes directly through the pelvic floor. As the female urethra is not involved in the reproductive system, it is very short and opens out in front of the entrance of the vagina.

Female urinary system

The female urinary system is essentially the same as the male, except that the female urethra is much shorter. This provides bacteria with an easy route into the body, and is the reason why urinary tract infections are far more common in women than men.

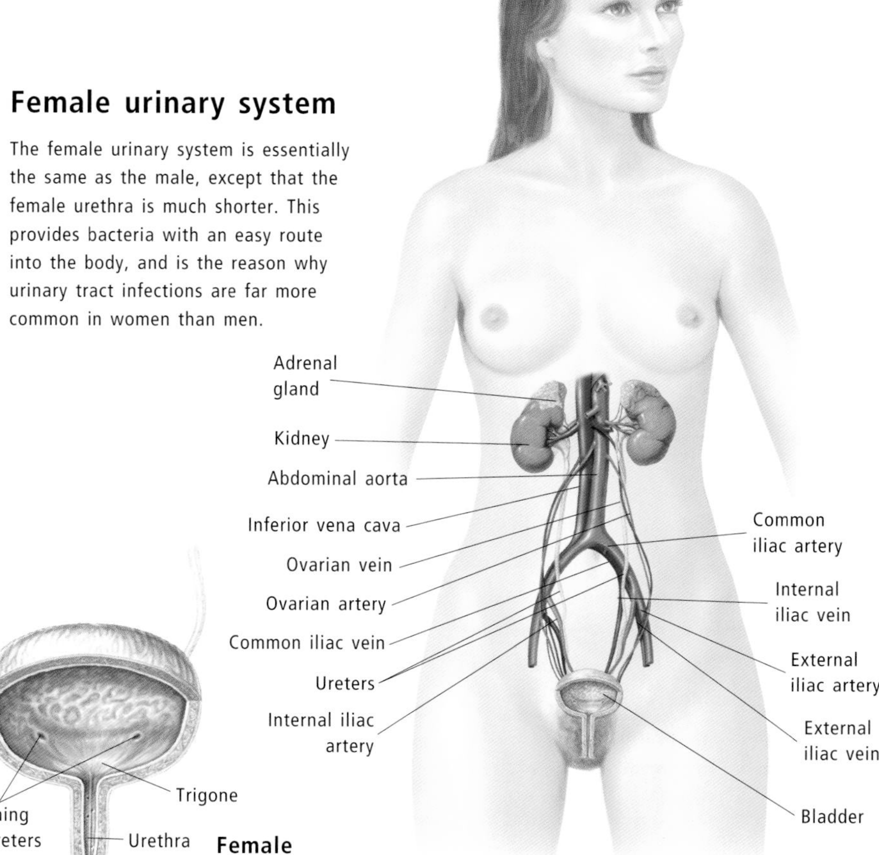

DIGESTIVE SYSTEM

The process of digestion breaks down foods into small, simple molecules for absorption and use as building blocks for human cells.

The design of the digestive system

The mechanical action of the digestive tract optimizes the chemical actions of enzymes. The entire tract is made up of smooth muscle fibers running in circular and longitudinal directions. In some places, the circular fibers are condensed into a thick ring (sphincter), which contracts to close down the cavity (lumen) within the tract. The circular fibers can contract sequentially along the tract (peristalsis) in order to knead the contents with digestive enzymes or to squeeze it along.

Digestive enzymes split the three main groups of food into their components: carbohydrates into glucose, proteins into amino acids, and lipids into glycerol and fatty acids. There are more than two dozen amino acids, most of which are common to all animal species. For example, human proteins are made up amino acids that are derived from meat proteins.

The digestive tract and glands

Food is bitten into mouthfuls by the incisor teeth, shredded by the canines, and ground by the premolars and molars. It is pushed around in the mouth and held between the molars by the tongue and the buccinator muscles in the cheeks. The top surface of the tongue is rough due to the presence of papillae which carry taste receptors.

Saliva in the mouth comes from three pairs of salivary glands. The largest, the parotid glands, are located just below the ears. The submandibular and sublingual glands are under the floor of the mouth. Saliva wets the food to facilitate chewing and swallowing. It also contains the enzyme amylase, which digests carbohydrates, and antibodies to help resist infection.

Inadequate production of saliva (as seen in Sjögren's syndrome) makes speaking and swallowing very difficult.

At the beginning of swallowing, food is rolled into a round mass (bolus) which is pushed to the back of the mouth by the tongue. Muscles of the pharynx then push the food bolus down the esophagus.

The esophagus runs vertically down behind the windpipe (trachea), passing through the diaphragm to end in the stomach. The opening of the stomach into the small intestine (the duodenum) is controlled by a thick bundle of circular muscle fibers, the pylorus. Food is retained in the stomach where proteins are digested by hydrochloric acid and pepsin secreted by gastric glands. At intervals, the pylorus relaxes to empty the gastric content, now a half-digested mix known as chyme, into the duodenum.

The small intestine has three parts: the duodenum, jejunum and ileum. The lining of the duodenum and jejunum has many transverse folds called plicae circulares (circular folds). On each fold are numerous tiny projections called intestinal villi, giving the lining a velvety appearance. The plicae and villi greatly increase the surface area available for the absorption of nutrients. Glands at the root of the villi and in the submucosal layer secrete intestinal juice that protects the lining against acidity and digestive enzymes.

Most of the digestive process occurs in the duodenum due to the action of pancreatic enzymes. The pancreas is an elongated gland lying behind the stomach. Its large head is framed by the C-shaped loop of the duodenum, while its tail ends near the spleen. Pancreatic secretions are collected by the main pancreatic duct which, together with the bile duct, enters the duodenum at a common opening, the duodenal ampulla.

The pancreatic juice contains inactive proenzymes that are converted by the duodenal hormone (enterokinase) into active enzymes that digest carbohydrates, proteins, nucleic acids, and lipids. In pancreatitis, the proenzymes are activated inside the pancreas and thus cause massive destruction of the gland.

One of the many functions of the liver is bile production. The bile duct passes through the head of the pancreas to open at the duodenal ampulla.

Cancer of the pancreas can constrict or block the bile duct. The resulting raised bile concentration in the blood is one cause of jaundice, in which the skin and the white of the eyes take on a yellow tinge.

The gallbladder is located under the liver and connected to the bile duct. It concentrates and stores bile to be discharged into the duodenum when chyme containing fat enters from the stomach. Bile emulsifies the fat to facilitate digestion by the pancreatic enzyme lipase. Gallstones are formed by the precipitation of components of bile in the gallbladder; these irritate the lining, causing inflammation (cholecystitis). Gallstones migrating down the bile duct can cause severe pain or block the duodenal ampulla.

As the chyme reaches the jejunum, the products of digestion are ready for absorption. Small molecules enter the blood capillaries of the villi. Larger molecules enter small lymphatic channels in the villi (lacteals), and flow along the mesenteric lymph vessels into the general circulation. Vitamin B_{12} is absorbed in the last portion of the ileum in the presence of intrinsic factor, a protein secreted by the stomach.

The ileum joins the large intestine, which consists of the cecum, colon, and rectum. The cecum—the blind-ended pouch of the colon—and the ileum meet at the ileocecal valve. Near the valve is the appendix which can become inflamed in the condition called appendicitis. The contents become feces as they move along the parts of the large intestine: the ascending, transverse, descending, and sigmoid colon. The colon absorbs water and bile salts, and contains bacteria that synthesize some vitamins such as vitamin K and biotin. The epithelium (the lining) of the colon here contains numerous goblet cells and mucus-secreting glands to facilitate the movement of the feces. When peristalsis of the colon is reduced in aged people, more water is absorbed and the feces become dry and impacted, causing severe constipation. When the balance between normal colonic flora and pathogenic bacteria is disturbed by some antibiotics, pathogenic bacteria may prevail causing diarrhea.

The last parts of the large intestine are the rectum and anal canal, situated just in front of the sacrum. The anus is closed by an involuntary and a voluntary sphincter, which open up during defecation. When the rectum is distended by feces, the defecation reflex is initiated if the voluntary anal sphincter is intentionally relaxed. Fecal incontinence results when the sphincters or

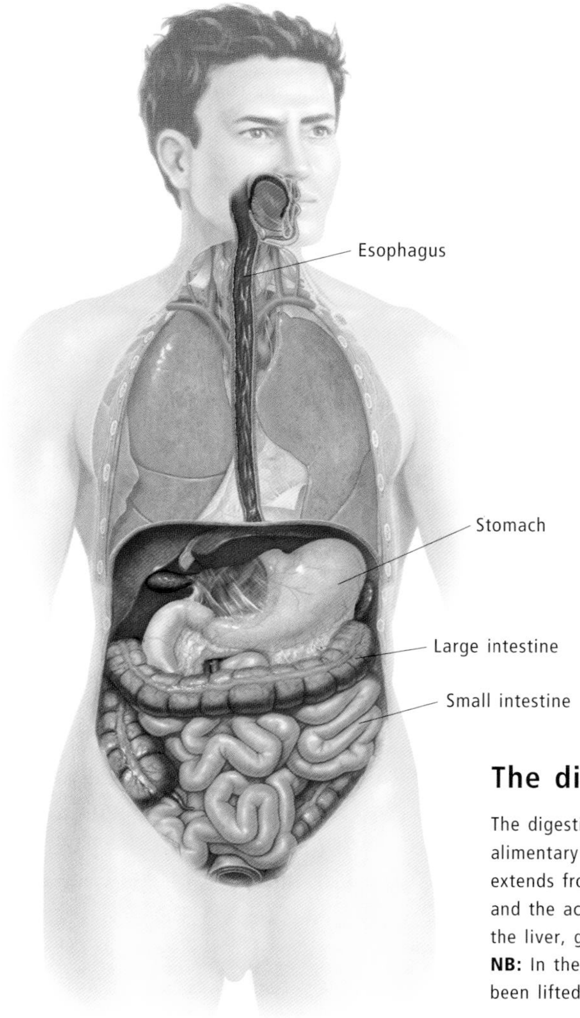

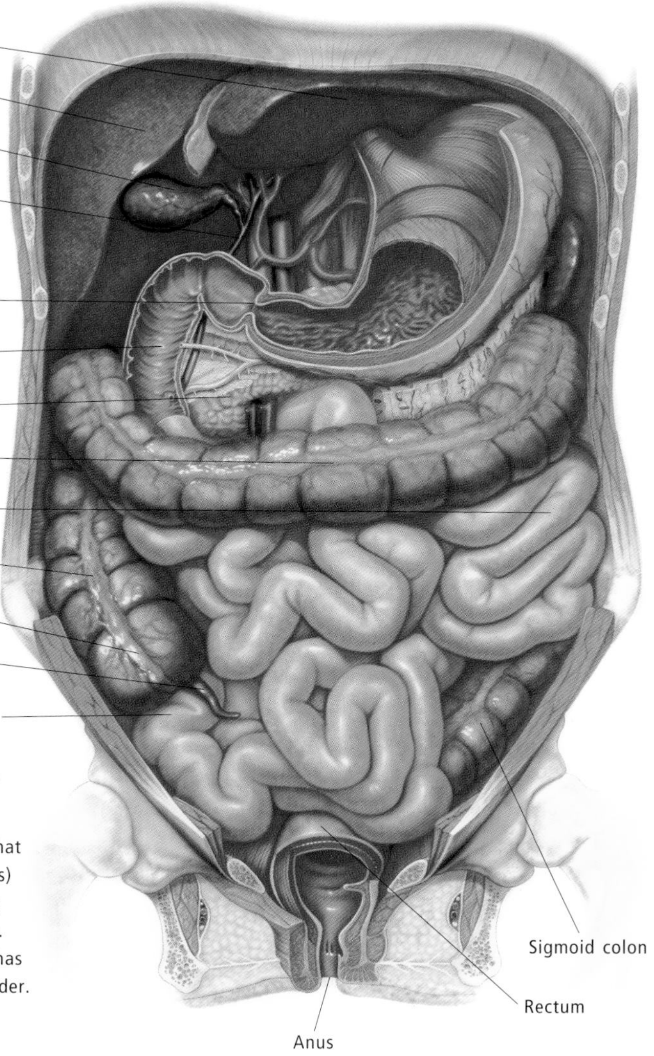

The digestive organs

The digestive organs consist of the alimentary tract (a muscular tube that extends from the mouth to the anus) and the accessory organs (including the liver, gallbladder and pancreas). **NB:** In these illustrations the liver has been lifted up to show the gallbladder.

the neural mechanism controlling them are defective. A network of veins in the lining of the rectum and anal canal facilitates the passage of feces. When these veins are dilated, they become hemorrhoids and may protrude from the anus during defecation, and may bleed. Cancer of the colon is common in Western countries, and involves the rectum in 50 percent of cases.

Control of the activities of the digestive system

The mechanical and secretory activities of the digestive tract and its glands are controlled by neural and hormonal mechanisms. The autonomic nervous system sets the general level of activity of the digestive system; the parasympathetic system increases the contraction of the gastrointestinal wall and the secretion of the digestive glands. There are networks (plexuses) of autonomic nerves in the intestinal wall which coordinate muscle contraction, and the secretion of gastric acid may be initiated by the central nervous system via the vagus nerve.

A system of "local" hormones ensures that secretions begin and end at the right time. When the stomach is distended by food, its lower part secretes more gastrin which increases the secretion of acid by gastric glands. The arrival of chyme in the duodenum initiates the release of hormones which inhibit gastric secretion and stimulate secretion of bile and pancreatic enzymes.

When treating stomach ulcers, the stimuli for acid secretion can be reduced by surgically resecting the endings of the vagus nerve on the stomach (vagotomy), or the gastrin-secreting portion of the stomach (gastrectomy).

SEE ALSO *Bowel cancer, Cholecystitis, Colon, Constipation, Duodenum, Gallbladder, Gastrectomy, Ileum, Intestines, Jejunum, Liver, Pancreas, Peristalsis, Rectum, Saliva, Stomach, Teeth*

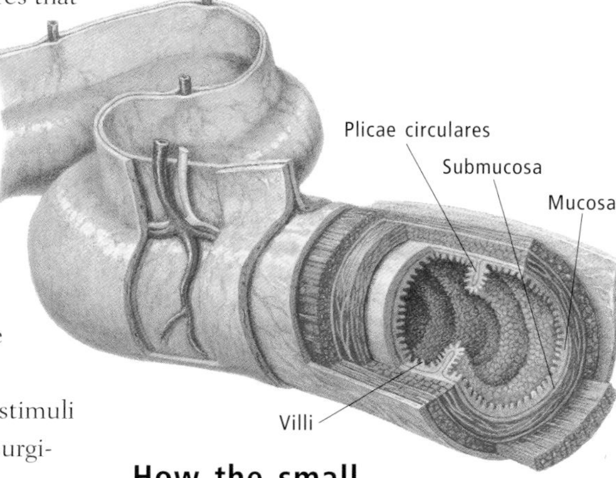

How the small intestines function

The vast majority of digestion and absorption takes place in the small intestine. The lining of the small intestine has many small transverse folds (plicae circulares) and numerous tiny finger-like projections called villi. The plicae and villi greatly increase the surface area available for the absorption of nutrients.

FEMALE REPRODUCTIVE SYSTEM

The reproductive system of the female includes two ovaries that produce ova (eggs) and female hormones, two fallopian (uterine) tubes that convey eggs to the uterus, the uterus itself, and the vagina, which is connected to the external genitalia.

Ovaries

The ovaries are almond-shaped organs in the side wall of the pelvis, situated just below the division of the common iliac artery. They are slightly flattened sideways, with a vertical axis measuring about $1^1/_2$ inches (3.5 centimeters). All the ovary's blood vessels and lymphatics enter its upper part. Its lower part is bound to the corner of the uterus by a band of connective tissue, the ligament of the ovary.

The ovary is enveloped by peritoneum, the membrane that surrounds all organs in the abdomen. Inside its covering epithelium is a shell of cortex which encloses the medulla at its core. The bulk of the ovary is the supporting structure called the stroma. The cortex contains ova at different stages of development.

Unlike the testis, which produces sperm continuously, the ovary is endowed in embryonic life with a fixed number of ova. By birth, each ovary has about a million ova; by puberty, the number has been reduced to about a quarter of a million.

The ova begin as primordial oocytes, surrounded by a layer of flat cells called granulosa cells. With the onset of puberty, hormones from the pituitary gland stimulate the development of more mature primary and secondary follicles. The granulosa cells multiply and form the multilayered theca interna that secretes estrogens; the surrounding stromal cells form the theca externa. A split appears in the theca interna and expands to form a fluid-filled cavity that pushes the oocyte to one side; the follicle is now a tertiary or Graafian follicle, which is visible as a small blister on the surface of the ovary. Ovulation takes place in the middle of each menstrual cycle—a Graafian follicle ruptures to release its ovum, which enters the fallopian tube.

The empty follicle fills with blood and regresses into a corpus luteum ("yellow body"); the yellow color is caused by the lipid-rich granulosa cells. If the ovum is fertilized, the corpus luteum will persist and continue secreting progesterone to maintain pregnancy. If not, it shrinks into a small mass of collagenous tissue (the corpus albicans).

Fallopian tubes

The fallopian tubes, or uterine tubes, are small tubes that begin as funnel-shaped passages with many finger-like projections called fimbriae. The ovum released from a burst Graafian follicle is "captured" by one of the fimbriae and moved along to the uterine cavity by the action of cilia of the epithelium and the contraction of the tube. Fertilization happens in the outer third of the fallopian tube if a sperm penetrates the ovum and its nuclear material fuses with that of the ovum. If the ovum is fertilized it will implant in the uterus and begin to develop into an embryo.

A constriction of the tube may block the progress of the fertilized ovum, resulting in an ectopic pregnancy in which the ovum implants and develops in the tube. As the tube can only be dilated to slightly more than an inch (a few centimeters) in diameter, it will burst after a few weeks of pregnancy, causing torrential bleeding which can only be controlled by emergency surgery.

Uterus

The uterus looks like a slightly flattened, upside-down pear, with a slight constriction dividing it into two parts. The upper two-thirds is the body, the lower third is the cervix. The body rests on the bladder and has a very thick wall of smooth muscle. The uterus is flattened from the front to the back. The uterine tubes open into the two top angles and the angle below opens into the lumen of the cervix.

The cervix is a cylindrical muscular tube that protrudes into the vagina. The lumen of the cervix is a spindle-shaped cervical canal.

The epithelium of the cervical canal secretes mucus that becomes thick, scanty and more acid after ovulation, a characteristic that can be used to determine the time of ovulation. The secretion is also thick during pregnancy, and forms the "mucus plug" which closes the cervical canal.

The epithelium at the vaginal end of the cervix is the most common site of cancer of the cervix, detectable by a Pap smear.

The inner lining of the uterus, the endometrium, is highly vascular and contains numerous tubular glands. It is shed at the end of each menstrual cycle. When the ovum is fertilized, the endometrium persists, and its glands secrete mucus rich in glycogen in preparation for implantation of the fertilized ovum. The part of the endometrium surrounding the developing embryo develops into the placenta.

Endometriosis is a condition in which islands of functioning endometrial tissue are found outside the uterine cavity, on the surface of abdominal or pelvic organs. They can cause bleeding or the formation of an abnormal mass.

During pregnancy, the uterus is distended to accommodate the developing fetus, extending beyond the umbilicus at full term. The muscular wall expels the fetus during labor and compresses the blood vessels to stop bleeding after expulsion of the placenta.

The uterus is fixed in place by connective tissue which runs inwards from the pelvic wall together with vessels and nerves destined for the vagina and uterus. Weakness of the pelvic floor may result in prolapse of the uterus. In extreme cases, the cervix protrudes from the vulva.

Vagina

The vagina is a fibromuscular tube that runs from the cervix to the vestibule of the vulva. Normally, its front and back walls lie close together, but it is capable of much distension and elongation. The epithelium of the vagina is thin before the menarche (onset of puberty), becoming thicker and undergoing cyclical changes during the menstrual cycle. With the cessation of hormonal stimulation after the menopause, it becomes thin and atrophic. This can be reversed by hormone replacement therapy (HRT) or by applying hormone cream directly to the vagina.

External genitalia

The external genitalia can also be called the pudendum or vulva. The lower end of the vagina continues into the labia minora. At their junction is a thin fibrous membrane called the hymen which, even when intact, allows the passage of menstrual blood. The labia minora may be pigmented and are devoid of hair. The space between them, the vestibule, receives the openings of the greater vestibular glands (Bartholin's glands).

The erectile bodies are comparable to those in the male genitalia. The equivalent of the corpus spongiosum is split into two masses flanking the vaginal opening. The corpora cavernosa occupy the same position as in the male. Corresponding to the penis is the clitoris, which also has a prepuce, a small hood formed by the junction of the labia minora.

The skin outside the vaginal opening is thickly padded with subcutaneous fat and forms the labia majora. They join and continue over the symphysis as the mons pubis (mons veneris), a small mound raised by a thick underlying pad of fat. The mons pubis and labia majora are covered by hair, the distribution of which is controlled by female hormones.

Menstrual cycle

After puberty, the endocrine system has reached maturity, and the menstrual cycle becomes regular.

The menstrual cycle begins from the first day of bleeding. Under the influence of follicle stimulating hormone (FSH) from the pituitary gland, one or more follicles in the ovary mature, releasing estrogen into the blood, and stimulating the proliferation of the endometrium and its glands. At midcycle, about day 14, the surge of luteinizing hormone (LH) from the pituitary gland triggers ovulation and initiates the development of the corpus luteum, which secretes progesterone, maintaining the proliferation of the endometrium in anticipation of implantation of the fertilized ovum. Without fertilization, LH and FSH secretion ceases, the corpus luteum breaks down, and the levels of estrogen and progesterone drop. The endometrium then degenerates, dies, and sloughs off, causing menstrual bleeding which usually lasts about four days.

The pituitary gland, the master gland controlling the menstrual cycle, is under the influence of the hypothalamus and the limbic system, the part of the brain that controls emotions. Menstrual cycles can be disturbed in times of emotional distress.

Irregularity and abnormality of the menstrual cycle are common problems, including absence of menstruation (amenorrhea), painful menstruation (dysmenorrhea), and excessive menstrual bleeding (menorrhagia). The cycle often becomes erratic near the menopause. It is important to seek medical advice for abnormal bleeding, as it may be an early warning sign of cancers of the reproductive system.

SEE ALSO *Cervix, Clitoris, Contraception, Endometriosis, Endometrium, Estrogens, Fallopian tubes, Graafian follicles, Hormones, Menopause, Menstruation, Ovaries, Ovulation, Ovum, Pap smear, Pituitary gland, Placenta, Pregnancy, Progesterone, Retroversion of uterus, Sexual intercourse, Urethra, Uterus, Vagina, Vulva*

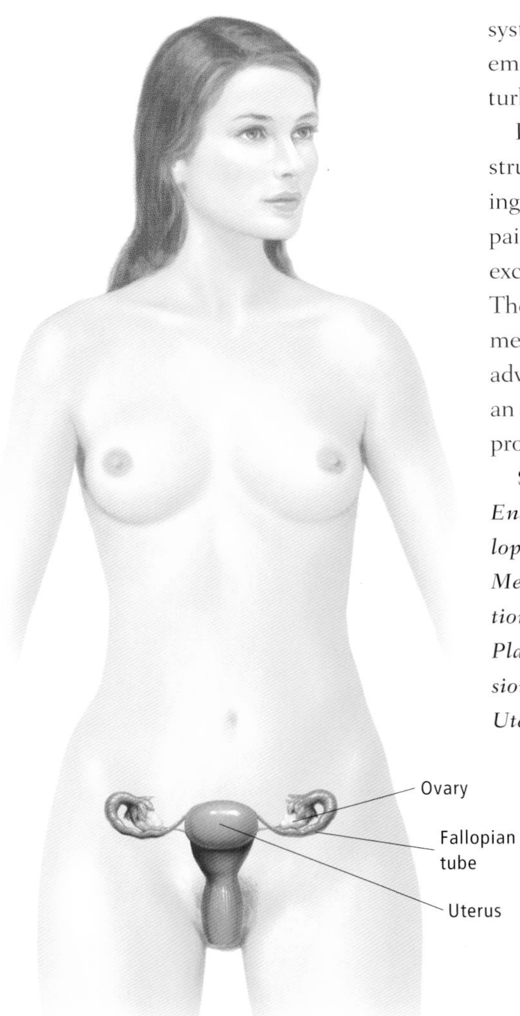

Female reproductive system—cross-section

The uterus is located behind the bladder and in front of the rectum. The upper two-thirds of the uterus is known as the body while the lower third is known as the cervix. The vagina is a long fibromuscular tube that extends from the cervix to the vulva.

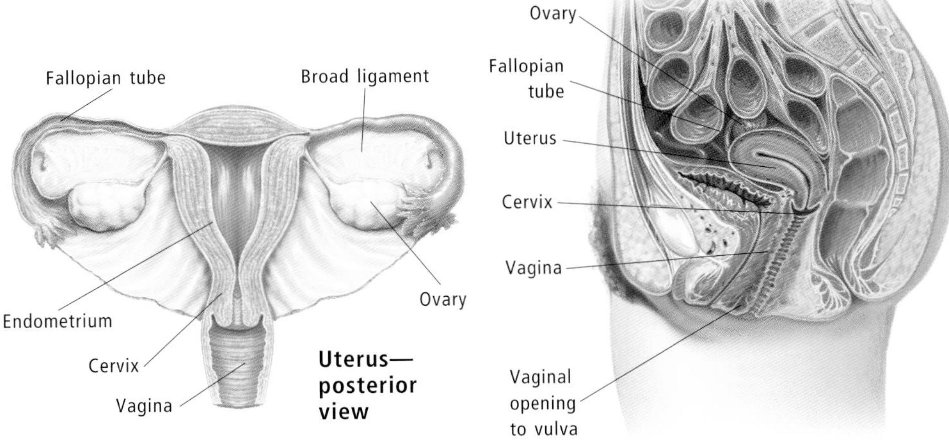

Female reproduction

During each menstrual cycle the ovary produces an oocyte (ovum) which enters the fallopian tube and travels towards the uterus. Fertilization (if it occurs) normally takes place in the outer third of the fallopian tube, and the fertilized ovum then implants into the inner lining of the uterus and develops into an embryo.

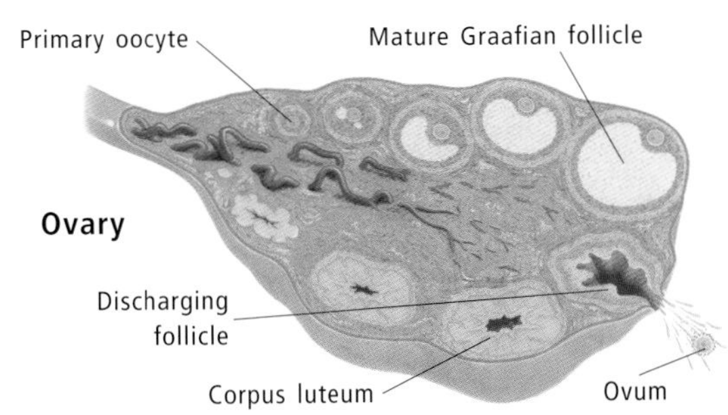

MALE REPRODUCTIVE SYSTEM

The reproductive system of the male includes two testes which produce spermatozoa (sperm) and male hormones, a system of ducts which convey sperm, glands which contribute secretions to semen, and the external genitalia, the scrotum and penis.

Testes

The testes are two oval organs contained in the scrotum, the right one usually higher than the left by nearly 1/2 inch (about 1 centimeter). At the back, the testis is capped by the epididymis. The epididymis has a large head at the top, tapers towards its lower end, then makes a sharp turn back to become the ductus deferens (or vas deferens, hence the term vasectomy).

The testes are separated by a central partition. Surrounding each testis is a double-layered membrane, the tunica vaginalis. Each testis has a tough inelastic fibrous wall called the tunica albuginea which sends partitions inwards to divide it into about 300 lobules. Each lobule contains coiled seminiferous tubules that produce sperm, and converge into a network which sends about 20 small ducts through the tunica albuginea into the epididymis. The ducts become larger and convoluted, forming the head of the epididymis, and gradually fuse into the ductus deferens, which runs back up towards the inguinal canal in the groin.

The tunica vaginalis is an extension of the peritoneal cavity in the embryo, and later separates. If the closure is not complete, a painless swelling known as a hydrocele develops, caused by a collection of fluid above the testis.

Squeezing the testes and epididymis causes a peculiar painful sensation. This tenderness not only makes the testes a vulnerable area to be protected in contact sports, but is also used to roughly assess the functional status of the testes. In old age or in severe liver failure, when the testes are no longer active, they are not tender to pressure. Because of the inelastic tunica albuginea, inflammation of the testes results in an increase in pressure and extreme pain.

The germ cells in the seminiferous tubules—the spermatogonia—undergo division (meiosis) to become spermatids. Spermatids mature into sperm that have a head and a long tail.

The head is capped by an acrosome which releases enzymes to help the sperm penetrate the ovum (egg). The tail propels the sperm like the tail of a tadpole. The spaces between the seminiferous tubules contain clumps of endocrine cells called interstitial cells or Leydig cells.

These interstitial cells synthesize the male hormone testosterone, responsible for the development of sexual characteristics in the adolescent male and the functioning of the reproductive system.

Ductus deferens

The ductus deferens (or vas deferens), is a thick-walled muscular tube, which can be felt above the testis through the loose part of the scrotum. This is where a vasectomy is performed. The ductus deferens is surrounded by the testicular artery, lymphatic vessels, autonomic nerve fibers and a plexus of veins called the pampiniform plexus. All these structures, enveloped by layers of connective tissue and muscle fibers, form the spermatic cord.

The spermatic cord runs upwards to the level of the pubic tubercle on the pubic bone, passes through the inguinal canal, then turns sharply to enter the pelvic cavity. The ductus deferens then heads towards the back of the prostate where it expands into an ampulla, and joins the duct of the seminal vesicle to form the ejaculatory duct.

The muscle fibers in the spermatic cord (cremasteric muscle) pull the testes up in cold weather to maintain an optimal temperature for sperm formation. The pampiniform plexus fuses into a testicular vein that empties into the inferior vena cava on the right side, and the renal vein on the left side. When the plexus is dilated, which more often happens on the left side, it is known as a varicocele.

In a condition called torsion of the testis, the testis can be twisted around the spermatic cord, causing severe pain. Torsion of the testis is a surgical emergency because the arteries become obstructed by the torsion, resulting in "death" of the testis.

Seminal vesicle

The seminal vesicle is a single tube coiled upon itself into a pyramidal organ. It lies on the outer side of the ductus deferens. The fusion of its duct with the ductus deferens forms the ejaculatory duct, which penetrates the prostate gland to open into the prostatic urethra.

Secretion from the seminal vesicle makes up about 60 percent of semen.

Prostate

The prostate is shaped like an inverted pyramid and lies under the bladder, with the apex pointing downwards. The urethra emerging from the neck of the bladder runs vertically through the prostate, leaving it just in front of its apex.

The prostate has two major groups of glands. The central zone surrounding the urethra contains periurethral glands and is the site of benign prostatic enlargement. The peripheral zone containing the main glands is usually the site of prostate cancer. All the glands open into the prostatic urethra and secrete the enzyme acid phosphatase, fibrinolysin, and some other proteins. Prostatic secretion makes up about 25 percent of semen.

The prostate is commonly enlarged in old age (a condition called benign prostatic hypertrophy) and blocks the urethra. It can be removed by inserting a cutting instrument through the urethra, in an operation known as transurethral resection of the prostate (TURP). Because the prostate lies just in front of the rectum, prostate cancer can easily be detected by a digital rectal examination.

After leaving the prostate, the urethra runs through the muscles of the urogenital diaphragm, and enters the penis. Here it receives the ducts of the paired bulbourethral glands. The secretion of these glands precedes the emission of semen and perhaps has a lubricating function.

Penis

The penis is the organ of copulation and is made up of three cylinders of erectile tissue. The midline cylinder is the corpus spongiosum (the spongy body) which contains the urethra. Its front end flares out into the bulbous glans penis, which has in its center the opening of the urethra. On each side of the corpus spongiosum runs a corpus cavernosum (the cavernous body). All three cylinders are enveloped in a thick cylinder of tough connective tissue. The glans is covered by a hood of loose skin called the prepuce, or foreskin. The foreskin can be retracted to the base of the glans. If the prepuce cannot be retracted past the glans, in a condition called phimosis, it can be removed by circumcision.

The three cylinders are structured like a sponge, the interconnecting spaces containing blood.

When the blood flows through them, they are flaccid. When the outflow of blood is prevented by closure of the veins, these cylinders become engorged with blood, thereby causing an erection. The connective tissue around the cylinders helps to build up pressure.

The mechanism of erection is controlled by the parasympathetic component of the autonomic nervous system and is the result of a very intricate interplay of many neurotransmitters. Thus erection is not under voluntary control, and can fail when the autonomic system is disturbed in psychological conditions such as depression or anxiety.

Erection can also fail when the arteries delivering blood to the penis are blocked by vascular diseases such as atherosclerosis or diabetes.

Implanted devices, including pump-up cylinders, can be inserted into the corpora cavernosa to give rigidity to the penis. Knowledge of the chemical mediators of the erection mechanism has led to the development of drugs that can induce or improve erection. The drugs can be mixtures to inject into the penis, pellets to insert into the urethra, or oral tablets.

Erection facilitates the entry of the penis into the vagina. When stimulation during intercourse reaches a threshold, the sympathetic system triggers a powerful emission of semen (this is known as ejaculation). The ejaculate, although it measures only about a teaspoon (5 milliliters), contains a few million sperm.

Fertility depends on the number of normal, healthy, motile sperm that is present in the ejaculate.

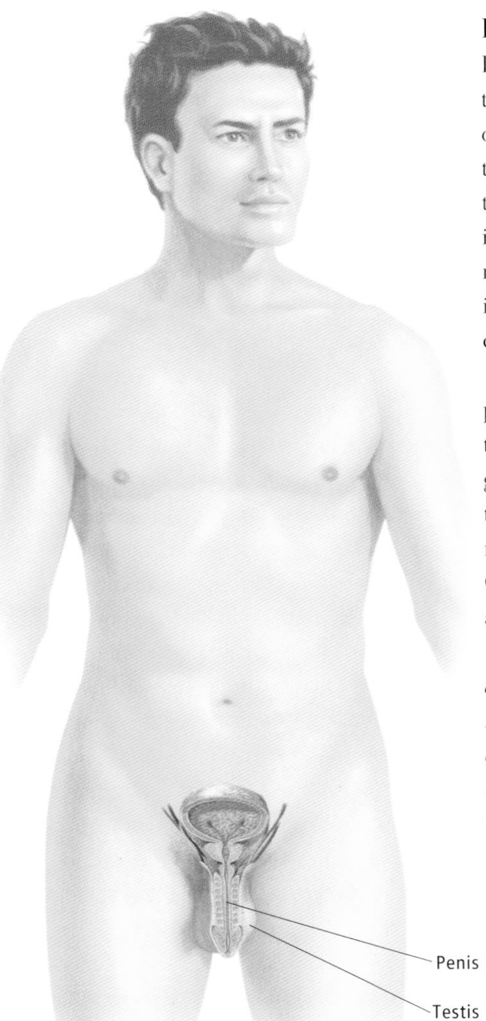

Organs of male reproduction

Sperm is formed in the testes, then passes along the ductus deferens which joins the duct of the seminal vesicle to form the ejaculatory duct. During ejaculation the sperm combine with secretions from the prostate and seminal vesicles to form the seminal fluid.

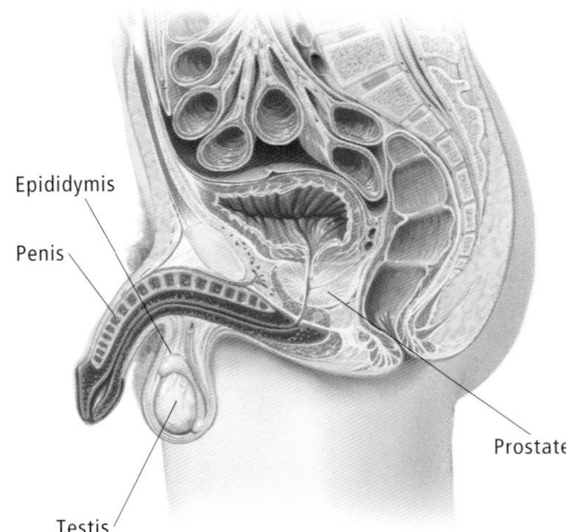

Descent of the testes

During the development of the fetus, the testis moves down from its original position on the side of the upper lumbar vertebrae to the scrotum, carrying with it an extension of the peritoneum which is later pinched off into the tunica vaginalis. If the descent is not complete, the testis may be stuck in the inguinal canal, hidden from sight (this condition is known as cryptorchidism).

If the body temperature is too high for production of sperm, the man with a cryptorchidism is usually infertile; he also has greater risk of developing cancer of the testis. The lymph nodes of the testis are next to the aorta in the lumbar region. Cancer of the testis spreads first to these aortic lymph nodes.

SEE ALSO *Bladder, Circumcision, Epididymis, Erection, Fertility, Glans, Hormones, Hydrocele, Impotence, Penis, Premature ejaculation, Prostate cancer, Prostate gland, Scrotum, Semen, Sexual intercourse, Sperm, Testes, Testosterone, Urethra, Variocele, Vasectomy*

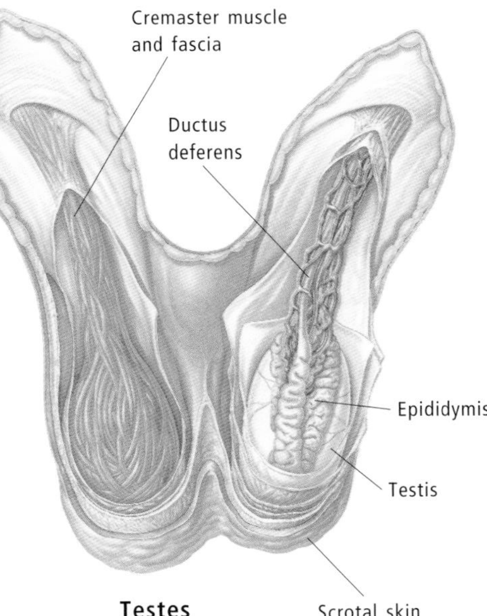

Testes

Male reproductive system—cross-section

The male reproductive system consists of the testes, the ductus deferens, the seminal vesicle, the prostate and the penis.

ENDOCRINE SYSTEM

The endocrine system, involved in coordinating the activities of tissues throughout the body, acts by means of organic chemicals called hormones. Hormones, made of amino acids or steroids, are released from endocrine cells at specific times and in precise amounts to act on target organs often at some distance from their site of release. Hormones usually act by combining with special receptor sites on or inside target cells.

Endocrine organs (often called endocrine glands), secrete only into the bloodstream or body cavities, unlike exocrine glands which usually secrete their products onto the skin surface or the linings of the digestive and respiratory systems.

Endocrine hormones affect the nervous system and many endocrine organs are stimulated or inhibited by nerve cells. The hypothalamus of the brain has an intimate connection with the chief organ of the endocrine system, the pituitary. This means that the endocrine and nervous systems share control of body functions: the nervous system usually controls activities occurring rapidly or in the short term, while the endocrine system controls slow or long-term changes.

The endocrine system (pineal, thymus, thyroid, parathyroids, adrenals, pancreatic islets, ovaries and testes) acts under the control of the pituitary gland. The ovaries and testes also function as endocrine glands, producing hormones which control sexual function and secondary sexual characteristics.

The pituitary, the central coordinator of the endocrine system, lies immediately below the hypothalamus of the brain and is closely controlled by it. The pituitary is divided into anterior and posterior lobes. The anterior lobe contains many different types of cells, which produce growth hormone, prolactin, follicle-stimulating hormone, luteinizing hormone, thyroid-stimulating hormone, adrenocorticotrophic hormone and melanocyte-stimulating hormone. The posterior lobe contains oxytocin and antidiuretic hormones, produced in the hypothalamus and transported to the pituitary within nerve fibers.

Growth hormone stimulates the growth of long bones, and is particularly important during childhood and early adolescence.

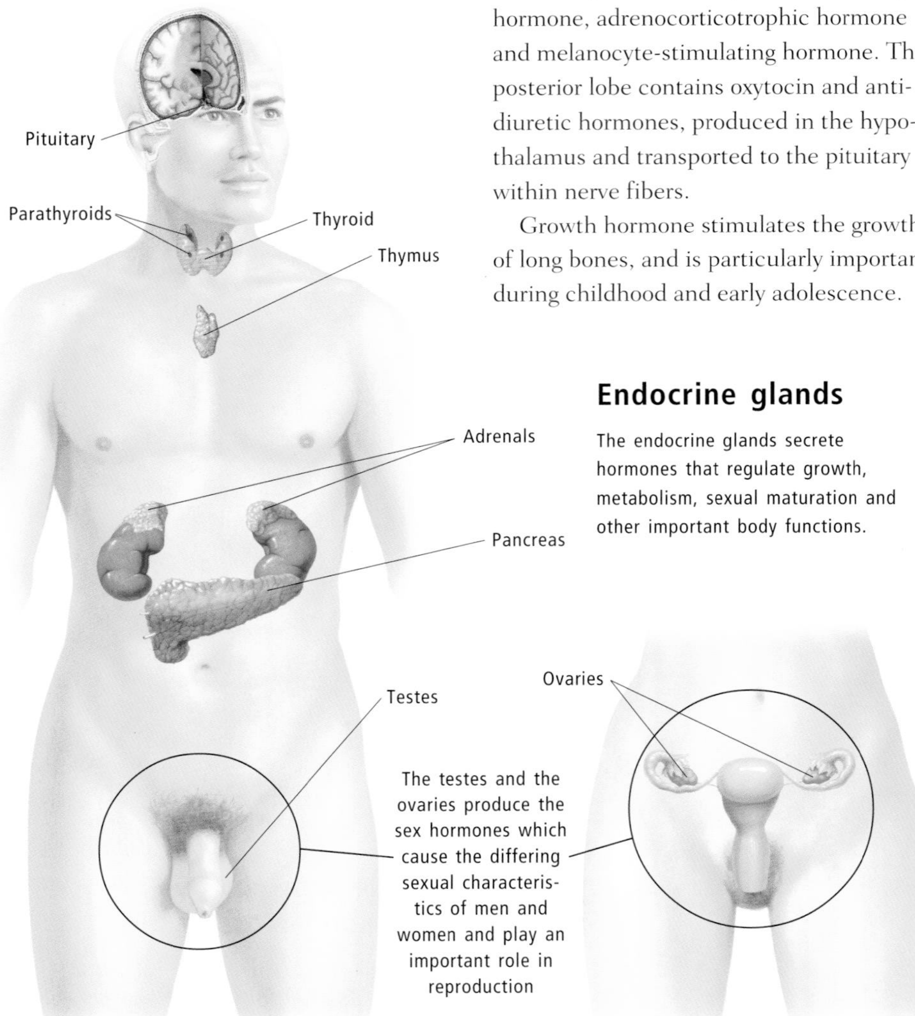
Pituitary
Parathyroids
Thyroid
Thymus
Adrenals
Pancreas
Testes
Ovaries
The testes and the ovaries produce the sex hormones which cause the differing sexual characteristics of men and women and play an important role in reproduction

Endocrine glands

The endocrine glands secrete hormones that regulate growth, metabolism, sexual maturation and other important body functions.

Prolactin or lactogenic hormone acts on the mammary glands of the breast to stimulate and maintain the production of milk. Follicle-stimulating hormone (FSH) stimulates the production of eggs in women and sperm in men. Luteinizing hormone stimulates the release of eggs and the production of the hormone progesterone in women, and the secretion of testosterone in men. Thyroid-stimulating hormone (TSH) stimulates the production of thyroid hormone and promotes its release into the bloodstream. Adrenocorticotrophic hormone stimulates the production of corticosteroid hormone by the adrenal gland. Oxytocin promotes contraction of the smooth muscle cells in the uterus and around the milk glands in the breasts. Antidiuretic hormone, or vasopressin, promotes the reabsorption of water from the urine in the kidney, thereby helping to control the concentration of salts in the blood.

The thyroid gland, under the influence of TSH from the pituitary, produces thyroxine and triiodothyronine, which act on cells throughout the body to increase energy production. Thyroid hormones also affect the developing brain; insufficient thyroid hormone during prenatal development can lead to mental deficiency (cretinism). Parafollicular cells or C cells, also found in the thyroid, produce calcitonin, responsible for reducing the concentration of calcium in the blood.

The parathyroid glands produce parathyroid hormone, which acts to raise the concentration of calcium in the blood and reduce the concentration of phosphate ions.

The adrenal glands lie on the upper end of each kidney. Each has an inner part (medulla) and an outer part (cortex). The adrenal medulla contains many modified nerve cells, which produce the hormones epinephrine and norepinephrine (adrenaline and noradrenaline). Epinephrine and norepinephrine are released in bursts during emergency situations or accompanying intense emotion (such as fright). These two hormones act to increase the strength and rate of heart contraction, raise the blood sugar level and elevate blood pressure.

The adrenal cortex produces three main types of hormone: glucocorticoids, mineralocorticoids and sex steroids. Glucocorticoids, produced and released under the control of adrenocorticotrophic hormone (ACTH)

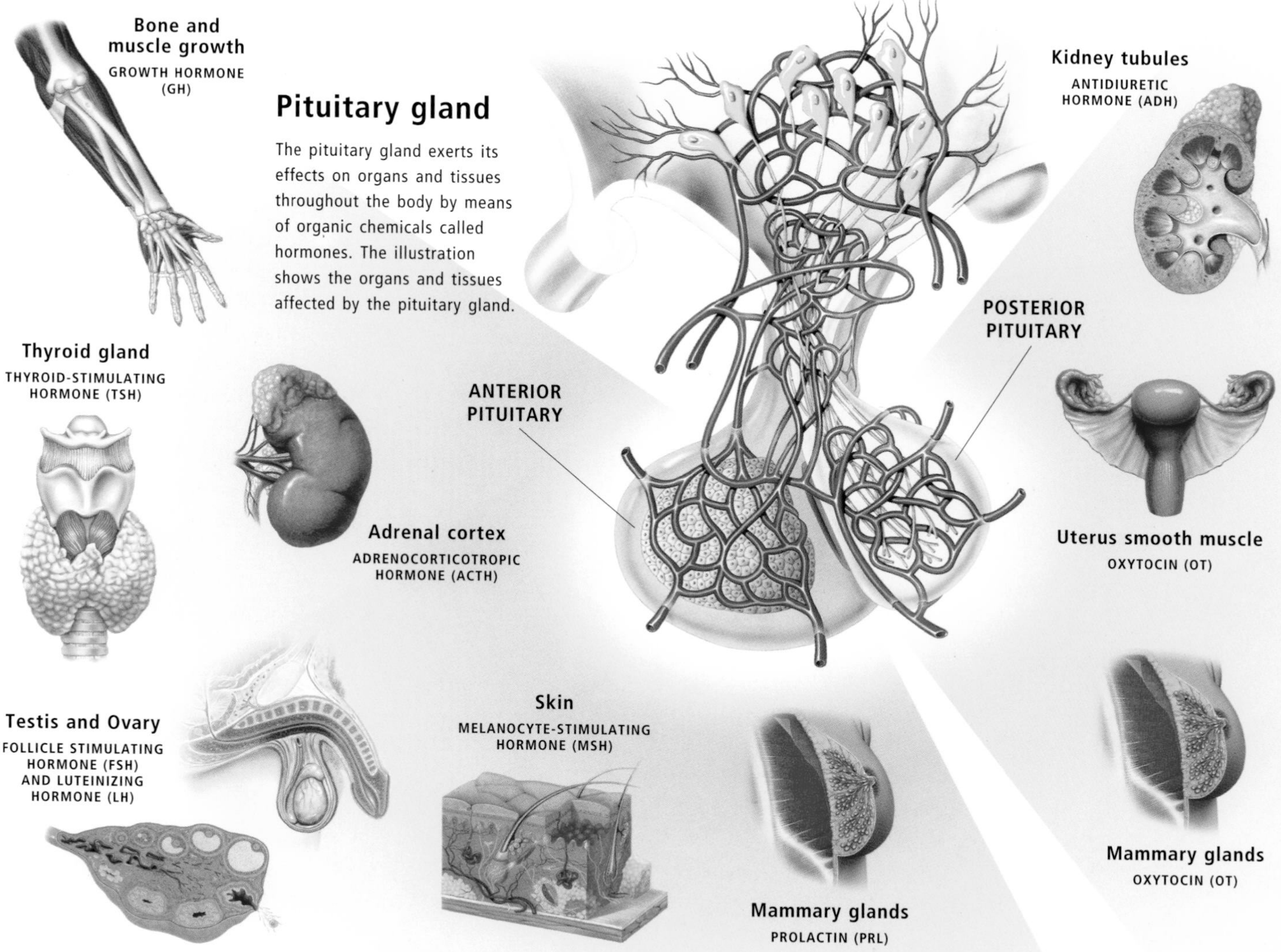

from the pituitary, influence the metabolism of fat, protein and carbohydrates, promoting the breakdown of protein and the release of fat and sugars into the blood stream. Mineralocorticoids, such as aldosterone, stimulate the absorption of sodium in the kidney. The sex steroid produced by the adrenal cortex, dehydroepiandrosterone, has masculinizing effects if secreted in large amounts. Excessive amounts of glucocorticoids in the blood, usually due to medical treatment with high doses of the hormone, causes a condition known as Cushing's syndrome, in which the patient develops a moon-shaped face and obesity around the trunk. Insufficient production of corticosteroids produces Addison's disease, a condition in which patients experience weight loss, dehydration and low blood pressure. Excessive production of dihydroepiandrosterone in boys results in early puberty, while girls may develop an enlarged clitoris, and may be mistakenly raised as boys if clitoral enlargement occurs before birth.

The pancreatic islets (the islets of Langerhans) are located within the pancreas, an abdominal organ mainly concerned with producing digestive enzymes for the gastrointestinal tract. The islets produce hormones responsible for controlling blood sugar level. Insulin acts to lower blood glucose concentration, while glucagon acts to raise it.

The small pineal body is located inside the skull cavity, surrounded by the brain. It produces melatonin, whose concentration varies in tune with the 24-hour cycle of the day (the circadian rhythm). The pineal gland probably has an effect on the ovaries and testes and may influence mood; its precise role is uncertain.

The ovaries produce estrogen and progesterone. Estrogen causes growth of the breasts and reproductive organs, among other functions; progesterone maintains the lining of the uterus in a state suitable to receive a fertilized ovum. Estrogen and progesterone undergo cyclical changes in level every 28 days under the influence of FSH and luteinizing hormone from the pituitary.

During pregnancy, the placenta acts as an endocrine organ, producing a hormone to sustain the pregnancy (human chorionic gonadotrophin). The placenta also produces estrogen, progesterone and relaxin (which relaxes the pelvic ligaments), along with human placental lactogen, which promotes milk production and fetal growth.

The production and release of hormones by glands such as the thyroid and adrenals is constantly regulated by a mechanism called feedback inhibition, in which high levels of the hormone suppress its further production. Other glands, such as the pancreatic islets and the C cells of the thyroid, detect changes in blood concentrations of sugars or calcium respectively, and modify their hormone production accordingly.

SEE ALSO *Adrenal glands, Ovaries, Pancreas, Parathyroid glands, Pituitary gland, Testes, Thymus gland, Thyroid gland*

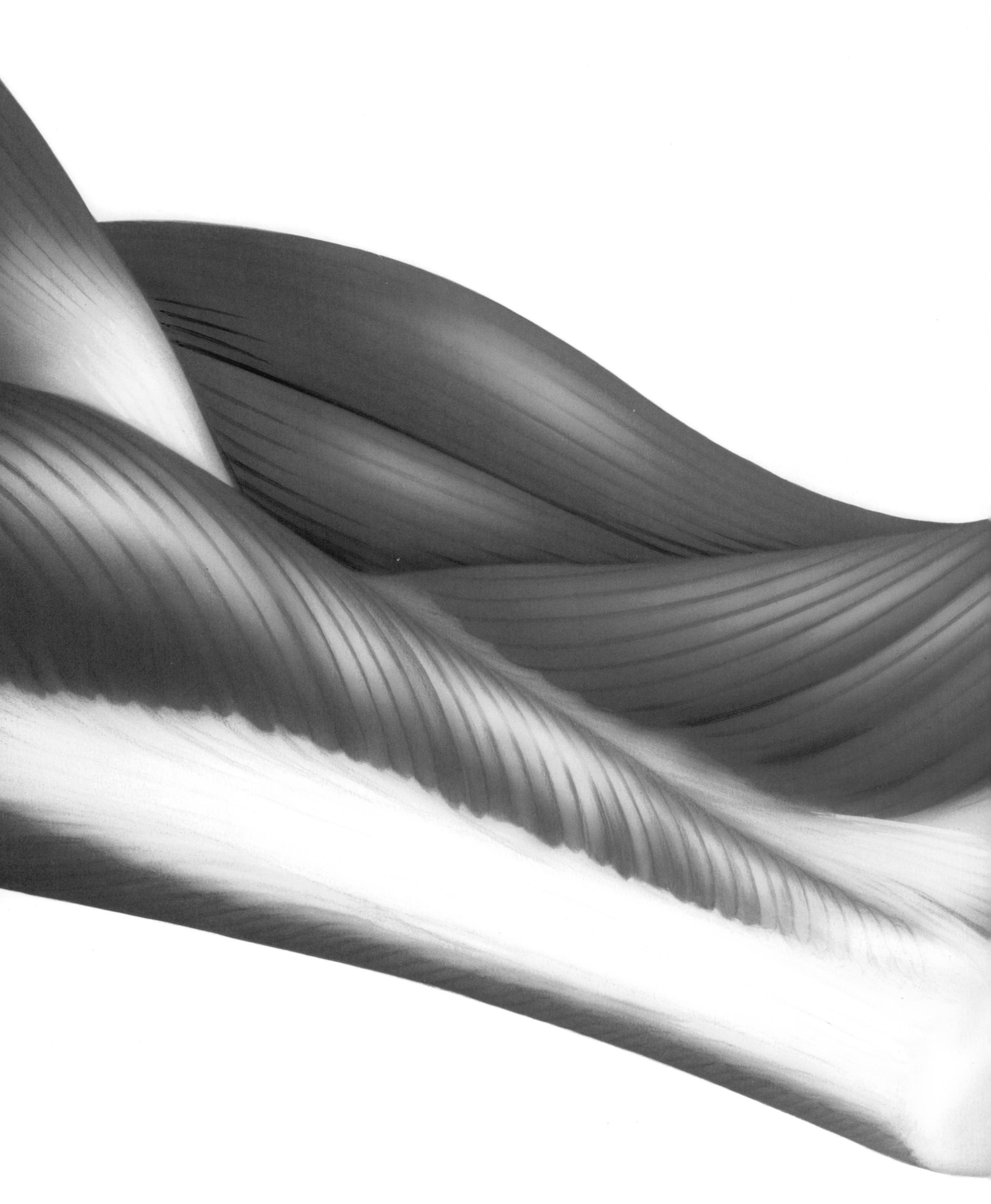

A

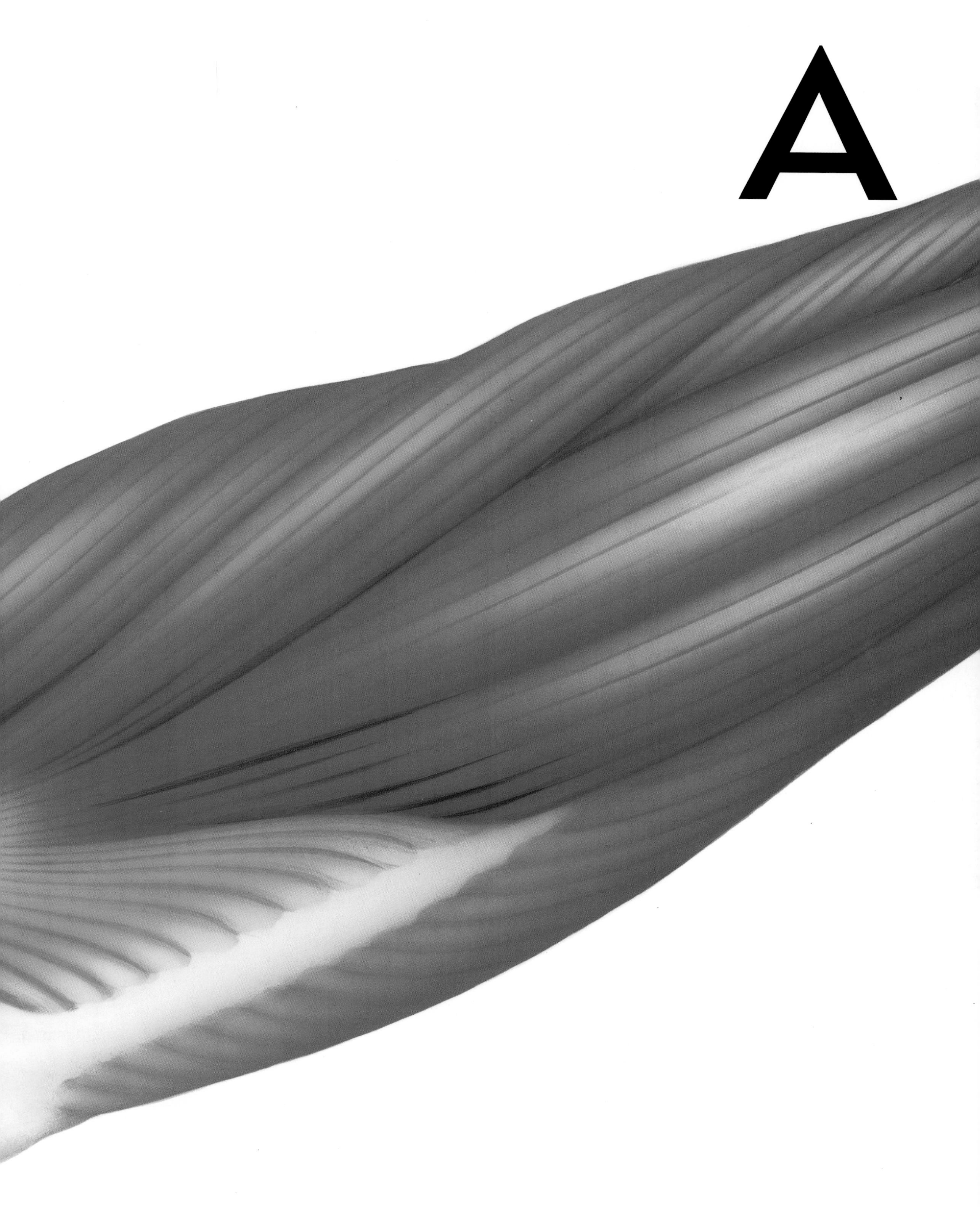

A

ABDOMEN

Situated between the thorax and the pelvis, the abdomen is the larger of the body's two major cavities (the other is the thorax, or chest). The abdomen contains some of the body's most important organs—those organs associated with digestion (the stomach, small and large intestine, liver, gallbladder and pancreas), elimination (kidneys, ureters and bladder) and, in females, reproduction (ovaries and uterus).

Parts of the abdomen

The sides (the lateral walls) and the front (the anterior wall) of the abdomen are made up of layers of muscle covered by fat and skin. When they contract, the muscles raise the pressure in the abdomen to aid breathing and passing of feces. The back (or posterior wall) of the abdominal cavity is formed by the vertebral bones of the spinal column and by the muscles that run up and down them. The roof of the abdominal cavity is formed by the diaphragm, a dome-shaped sheet of muscle separating the abdomen from the thorax. When the diaphragm contracts, it raises the pressure in the abdominal cavity and assists breathing.

The pelvic cavity is usually also considered to be part of the abdomen (though some consider it separately, while others refer to both the pelvic cavity and the abdominopelvic cavity). The pelvic cavity contains the bladder, rectum, and, in females, the uterus and the ovaries. The floor of the pelvic cavity is formed by muscles and bones.

Lining the abdominal cavity, and also extending out into the cavity to cover the organs within, is a thin lubricating membrane, the peritoneum. Folds of the peritoneum attach the organs to the back of the abdominal cavity, while allowing the intestines to move relatively freely, in order to aid movement of food down the alimentary canal. Other folds of the peritoneum, called mesenteries and omenta, supply the organs with nerves, blood vessels and lymph channels.

To make it easier to identify internal organs, and to help locate where abdominal pain is coming from, health professionals divide the abdomen into four quadrants: right upper, right lower, left upper and left lower.

Abdominal disorders

Because the abdomen contains a large number of important organs, it is not surprising that abdominal disorders are common. Symptoms of abdominal disease include heartburn, pain, cramps, constipation, diarrhea, vomiting and nausea. Indigestion (known as dyspepsia), food poisoning and gastroenteritis are common maladies that can be treated at home or by a primary care physician (general practitioner).

More serious conditions, which will require some sort of treatment by a specialist physician or surgeon, include a gastric or duodenal ulcer, hepatitis (inflammation of the liver), colitis (inflammation of the large bowel), as well as cancers of the stomach, liver and large bowel.

An abdominal illness can be an emergency. An acute abdominal infection such as peritonitis, appendicitis, cholecystitis (inflammation of the gallbladder) or salpingitis (inflammation of the fallopian tube) can be serious and life threatening. A perforated gastric or duodenal ulcer and injury from trauma are other common abdominal emergencies. "Acute abdomen" is the term health professionals use to refer to an abdominal emergency.

SEE ALSO *Bladder, Gallbladder, Intestines, Kidneys, Liver, Ovaries, Pancreas, Stomach, Ureter, Uterus*

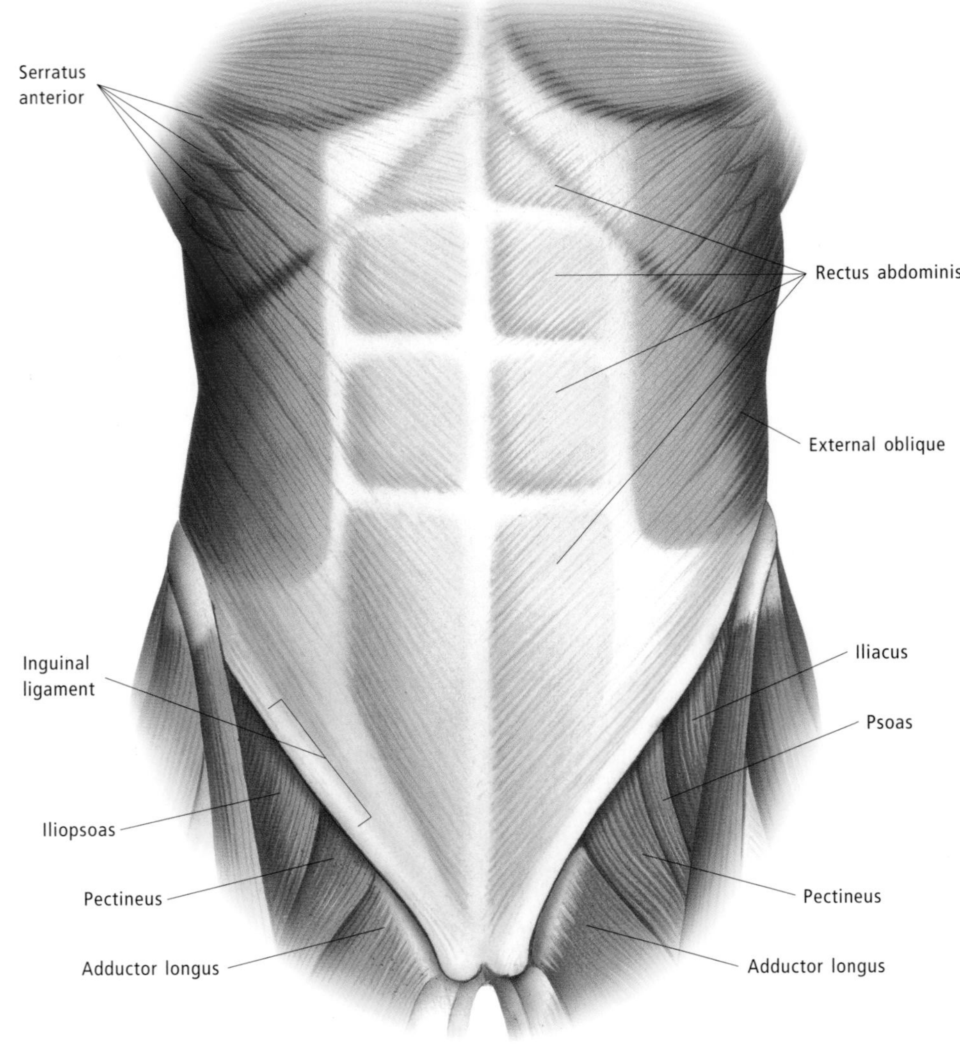

Muscles of the abdomen

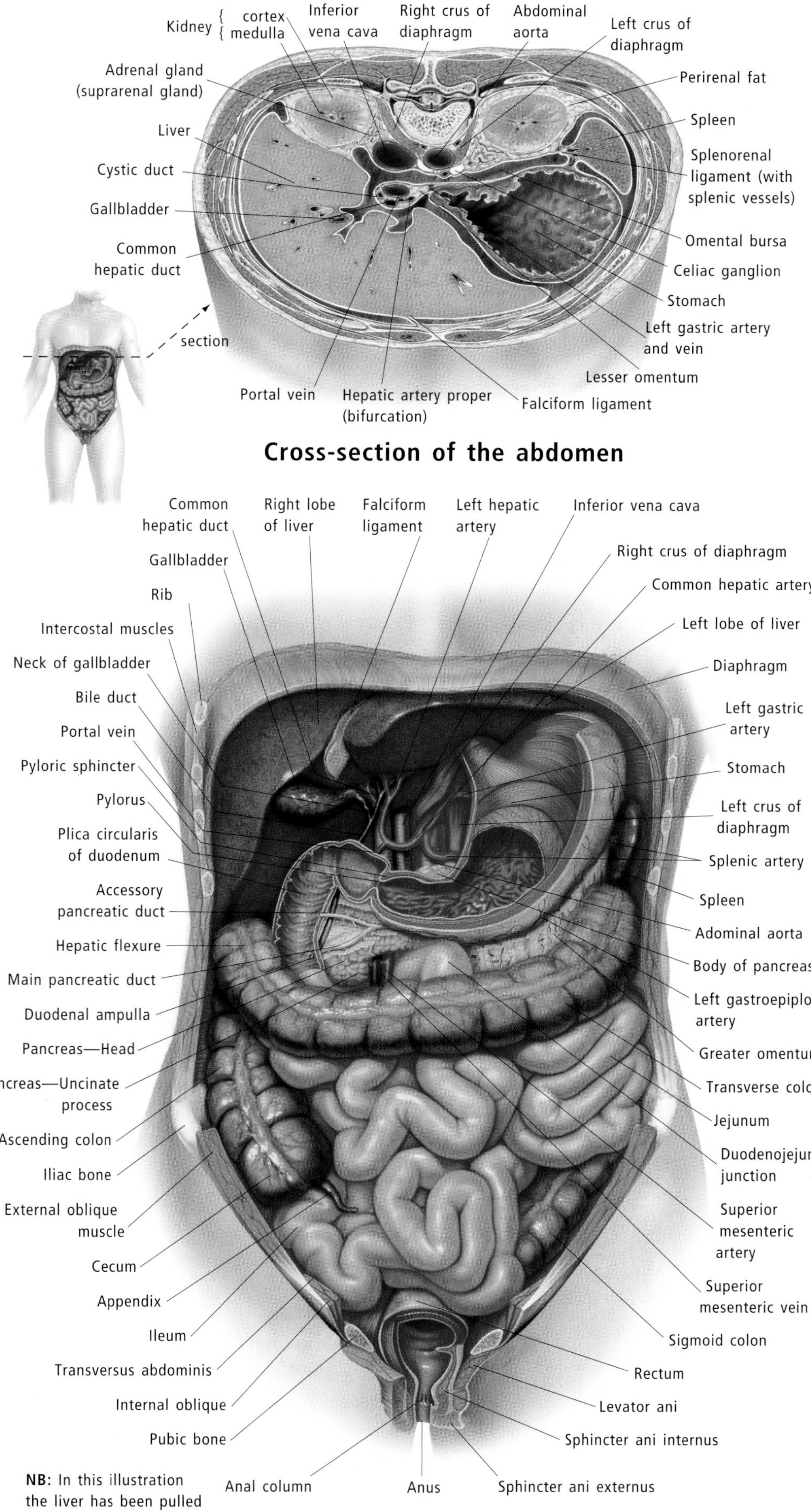

Cross-section of the abdomen

Organs of the abdomen

ABORTION

An abortion is a pregnancy that ends prematurely with the loss of the embryo or fetus, either spontaneously or by artificial induction. In common speech, the word "abortion" refers to artificial induction, while a spontaneous abortion is generally known as a miscarriage.

Abortion is an issue that raises strong passions. Those supporting abortion argue that it should be made legally available to women who choose to have it, and that refusing to do so often leads to women trying various unsafe ways of aborting the fetus themselves. Those against abortion argue that it as soon as an embryo is conceived it is a life, and that to abort it is to take this life.

The decision to have an abortion is never free of conflict, and counseling is very important. When antenatal testing reveals that the fetus has a lethal abnormality such as anencephaly, or a defect which can be a major disability such as spina bifida with hydrocephalus, termination is acceptable to many parents. Some women choose not to have an antenatal test if their beliefs would not allow them to have an abortion; or they may decide not to abort a fetus even if it has a high risk of a birth defect. In any situation, difficulties can arise and counseling is advisable, and imperative when defects with less predictable outcomes are detected.

History

It could be said that since the beginning of humanity people have tried to terminate unwanted pregnancies, using either external or internal methods. External methods included hot sitz baths, binding the abdomen, jumping from high places, punching or pummelling the abdomen, and abdominal massage. Of these, only the last one is thought to have been at all successful, and most were highly dangerous.

Internal methods included herbal concoctions which attempted to induce menstruation, strong purgatives (some containing lead and mercury compounds) and instruments such as knitting needles, bottles and syringes. Again, these methods had mixed results and were often dangerous.

Not until the nineteenth century were civil laws passed in most Western countries making abortion a criminal offence. It was in 1869 that Pope Pius IX decreed that abortion was murder. What followed was legislation against the procedure, which, it is frequently argued, led to a "back-street" abortion industry, the continued use of unsafe practices and considerable loss of life.

In the late 1960s and early 1970s Western countries began to pass more liberal legislation relating to abortion. Today abortion laws and their enforcement vary from country to country, and continue to generate passionate debate and even violent protests.

Types of abortions

There are several methods of performing an abortion. The method used generally depends on how far the pregnancy is advanced, with the duration of the pregnancy being calculated from the date of the woman's last menstrual period.

Surgical evacuation—removing the contents of the uterus through the vagina—is the method used in over 95 percent of abortions and almost always for pregnancies of less than 12 weeks. The technique is known as suction aspiration or suction curetting. The cervix is dilated and the lining of the uterus, containing the embryo, is drawn out by suction. A curette may also be used to scrape the uterine walls. This takes up to two minutes. If the cervix needs to be dilated more widely (this can be used for a pregnancy of seven weeks or more) then laminaria (strips of a special seaweed which expand as they absorb moisture) are inserted a few hours before the procedure, or even the night before.

For pregnancies over 12 weeks and under 20 weeks, dilation and evacuation (D&E) is used. When the cervix is dilated enough, forceps and a combination of suction and curettage remove the fetus. This can be done under general or local anesthetic.

A hysterotomy, the cutting open of the uterus to remove the embryo or fetus, is the same procedure as a cesarean delivery and is used only when the pregnancy must be terminated quickly in order to save the mother or when other methods are impossible.

Drugs such as mifepristone (RU-486) and prostaglandins are used in some cases, especially after 16 weeks of pregnancy, though mifepristone may be used shortly after conception. Taken as a tablet, it is followed 48 hours later with a prostaglandin and the abortion starts soon after this. In over 95 percent of cases it is completed quickly with minimal blood loss. If it is not successful, surgical termination is necessary.

High dose oral contraceptives (known as the "morning after pill") are sometimes prescribed to prevent conception after people have had unprotected intercourse.

Complications

Induced abortion before the twelfth week of the pregnancy and performed by a skilled doctor in a safe environment is a safe procedure. However, as with any surgical procedure, there are possible complications and some risks. The probability of complications increases with the duration of the pregnancy.

Complications include: infection (many clinics routinely prescribe antibiotics to reduce this risk and women are advised of the symptoms, as immediate medical attention is needed); incomplete abortion (this will require a further curettage); hemorrhage; perforation of the uterus (a rare complication when the operation is performed by a skilled doctor); and tearing of the cervix (which will require stitching). Occasionally, the abortion is unsuccessful and the pregnancy continues.

Bleeding, similar to a menstrual period, is normal within a few days of the abortion and a checkup is part of the normal procedure.

Many women find an abortion can have psychological repercussions. These are less common when counseling is part of the procedure. They are more likely to occur if the abortion was performed late in the pregnancy, the pregnancy was terminated for medical reasons, or there are psychiatric problems.

As well as psychological counseling, women often choose to seek advice about reliable forms of contraception, and find out which one may be most suitable for them.

SEE ALSO *Congenital abnormalities, Contraception, Dilation and evacuation, Pregnancy*

Decay
Root canal
Pus
Bone
Alveolar vein
Alveolar nerves
Alveolar artery

Tooth abscess (advanced)

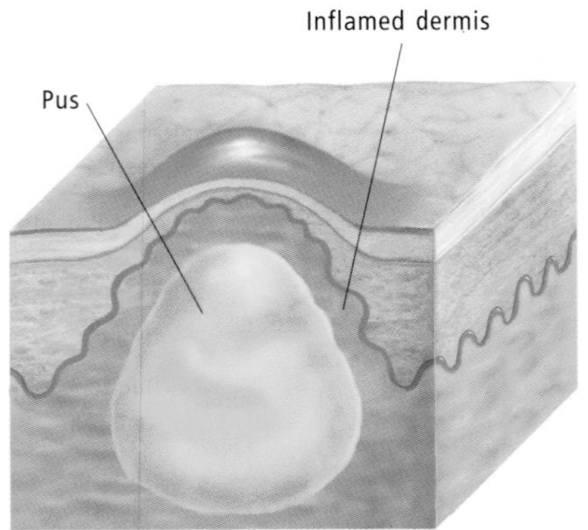

Skin abscess

Abscess

An abscess is an infection that contains pus and causes inflammation of the tissues. Abscesses are common on the skin and teeth but also occur on internal organs such as the liver, lung or brain. In teeth, the pulp and nerves break down in the root canal. Treatment involves antibiotics and proceeding with root canal therapy.

ABSCESS

An abscess is a collection of pus. The pus is made up of dead white blood cells, destroyed tissue and cells, and dead and live microorganisms (usually bacteria) which are all by-products of inflammation and infection. It can form in an internal organ such as the large intestine, lung, liver or brain, when it is often the result of another debilitating disease, for example AIDS. Most abscesses are bacterial or fungal in origin, although they are sometimes caused by ameba (especially in the liver) or by the tuberculosis bacillus. These are carried to the internal organs through the bloodstream and once there cause inflammation and infection.

In healthy people abscesses more often occur in the soft tissues beneath the skin. The invading organism finds its way through the skin via an infected wound or bite, or the abscess may begin in a hair follicle, when it is known as a boil. Boils are most common in hairy sites such as the nostrils, the armpits, the back of the neck and between the legs and buttocks. An abscess below the skin is usually very painful, looks swollen and red, and feels hot to the touch. An abscess may also cause fever, sweating, tachycardia (rapid pulse rate) and malaise.

Antibiotics are often given, usually intravenously, although their usefulness is limited, as drugs do not readily penetrate past the abscess lining into the abscess.

The mainstay of treatment is surgical drainage. This involves making a cut into the abscess and providing a drainage route either through a drainage tube or by leaving the abscess open to the skin (though an abscess will often burst through the skin by itself). A dressing is then applied daily until the wound and infection have healed.

SEE ALSO *Bacteria, Boil*

ACHALASIA

Achalasia is a disease of the esophagus and prevents normal swallowing (peristaltic action) that allows food to pass from the mouth to the stomach. The esophagus is a muscular tube connecting the throat (pharynx) to the stomach. It can expand and contract at its upper and lower ends using circular muscles called sphincters. The upper sphincter relaxes to accept food from the pharynx, and the food is moved by muscular contractions to the lower sphincter, which relaxes to let food enter the stomach. It then closes to prevent gastric reflux (return flow).

In achalasia, nerve damage prevents the lower sphincter from relaxing and food cannot pass. The cause is not known, although tension may be a contributing factor. Treatment involves muscle-relaxing drugs, or in more extreme cases, surgery may be used.

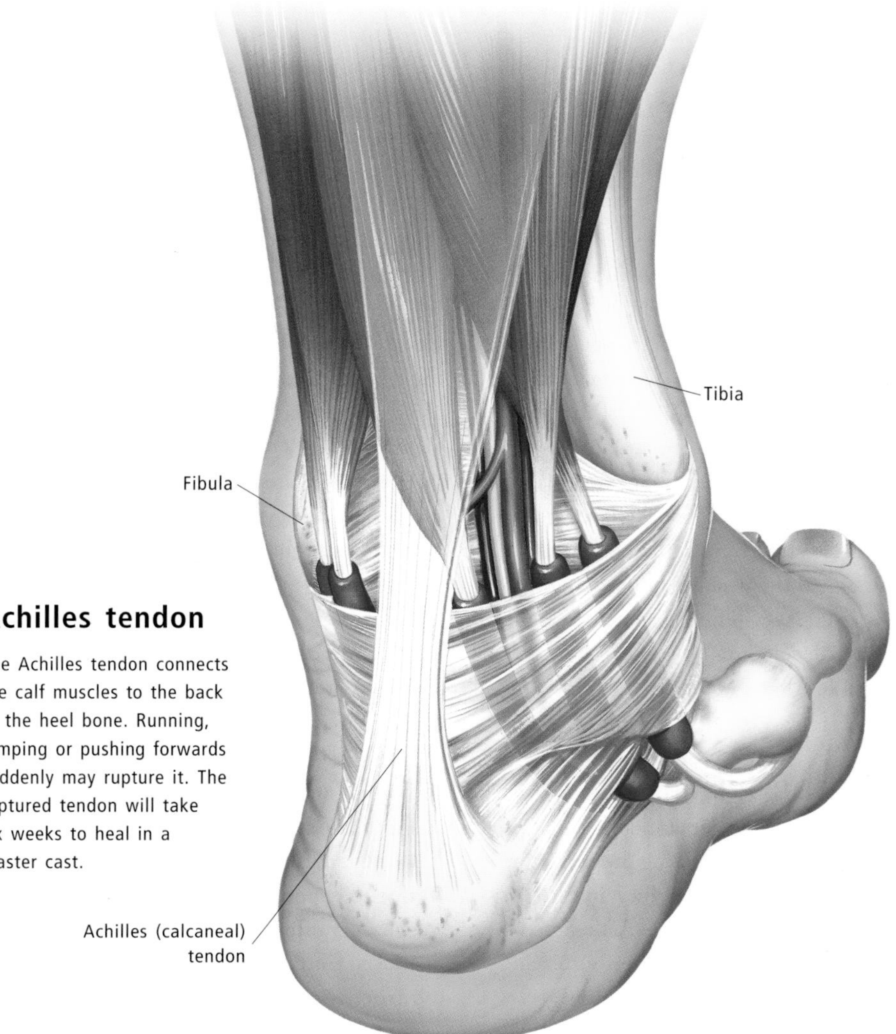

Achilles tendon

The Achilles tendon connects the calf muscles to the back of the heel bone. Running, jumping or pushing forwards suddenly may rupture it. The ruptured tendon will take six weeks to heal in a plaster cast.

ACHILLES TENDON

The Achilles tendon is a band of fibrous tissue that connects the calf muscles to the back of the heel bone. It is named after the legendary Greek hero of the Trojan Wars whose body was invincible except for the heels (he was beaten only after the tendons were cut). When you stand on tiptoes, your calf muscles contract, pulling the heel up via the Achilles tendon.

Rupture of the tendon

The Achilles tendon is a weak spot and if subjected to sudden stress—running, jumping, pushing forwards—it may snap. This most commonly occurs in sportspeople and middle-aged men. When it happens, there is a snapping sensation and immediate pain in the heel or the back of the leg. Flexing the foot downwards becomes difficult.

To treat an Achilles rupture, the doctor usually puts the back of the patient's foot, ankle and the lower part of the leg into a plaster cast, with the toes pointing downwards, so that the two ends of the tendon are close and can heal. The patient uses crutches, keeping weight off the foot, for six weeks. After removal of the plaster, physical therapy is needed to restore the function of the calf muscles and ankle joint. It usually takes about six months to return to normal.

Another option is surgery. Under general anesthetic, the two ends of the ruptured tendon are sewn together by a surgeon, and the foot goes into plaster for six weeks, followed by months of physical therapy.

Achilles tendinitis

Achilles tendinitis—inflammation of the Achilles tendon—can develop if the tendon suffers too much wear and tear. It happens most often after strenuous activity, especially by those not used to exercise. Wearing shoes with high heels or with worn heels, both of which place abnormal stresses on the tendon, may also cause inflammation.

A

Sufferers feel pain in the affected tendon, which gets worse with activity. The Achilles tendon may become thicker than it normally is and be painful or tender when it is touched. An inflamed Achilles tendon is susceptible to rupture.

The treatment for Achilles tendinitis is rest, analgesics and anti-inflammatory drugs, which relieve the symptoms but do not cure the condition, which tends to recur. In rare cases, the tendon can be removed under anesthetic by an orthopedic surgeon and replaced with artificial or natural tissues.

The best treatment, though, is prevention. Warming up before exercise, leg and calf muscle stretching before and after running, and the wearing of proper shoes during exercise will help prevent the condition from developing.

SEE ALSO *Ankle, Foot, Leg*

ACHONDROPLASIA

Achondroplasia is a genetic defect that prevents cartilage from forming properly during the body's development, which in turn prevents the formation of bones. The bones—especially the limbs—become shorter and thicker than in normal development.

The most common cause of dwarfism, achondroplasia occurs about once in every 10,000 births. The condition is a dominant genetic trait, which means that there is no such thing as a carrier—anyone carrying the genetic trait will show the symptoms. This also means a parent with the disorder has a 50 percent chance of passing it to a child. However, most sufferers do not inherit the condition; it develops as a genetic mutation in the uterus. It is diagnosed at birth from the characteristic appearance of the infant.

Persons with achondroplasia have abnormally short arms and legs. The trunk and head are normal-sized, but the head often appears large because of the smaller arms. The forehead is prominent; there is an exaggerated curvature in the lower back; and the bridge of the nose has a scooped-out appearance.

Unfortunately there is no treatment for achondroplasia. But many of the complications—which include bowed legs, nerve compression in the spine, hydrocephalus and, in children, middle ear infection, which can result in hearing loss—can be treated. Achondroplasia does not interfere with the capacity to reproduce nor does it affect mental capacity. Most people with achondroplasia can remain in good health and have a normal life span.

SEE ALSO *Growth disorders*

ACIDOSIS

Acidosis is an excess of acid in the body's fluids. Body metabolism works best in a narrow pH range—between 7.35 and 7.45 (pH is a measure of acidity). It is the job of the lungs, kidneys and chemical buffers in the blood (such as bicarbonate) to keep the pH at this level. But in illness, the pH can fall, causing acidosis. If uncorrected, it can lead to death.

There are two types of acidosis. Where the excess acid is produced by a metabolic process, it is known as metabolic acidosis. Diabetes, kidney failure, loss of bicarbonate from the body, diarrhea, drug overdose or abnormal metabolic states can cause this. If due to hypoventilation, or inadequate respiratory effort, it is known as respiratory acidosis. Cardiac arrest, asthma or other obstructive lung disease and drug overdose can cause respiratory acidosis.

In mild cases of acidosis the symptoms are agitation, headache and tachycardia (abnormally fast heartbeat). In more serious cases it causes lethargy, confusion, seizures, stupor and coma.

The treatment of acidosis is, if possible, to correct the underlying cause. If the acidosis is severe, the patient is given sodium bicarbonate intravenously.

SEE ALSO *Alkalosis, Metabolism*

ACNE

Acne (cystic acne, acne vulgaris) is a skin condition that commonly occurs in adolescence. It can start at puberty and continue as a problem into adulthood.

The hormones active at puberty stimulate the sebaceous (oil-producing) glands, and the excess oil produced makes a fertile breeding ground for bacteria. Bacterial infection creates debris and waste matter (pus) that blocks the gland. The area becomes red and inflamed and a whitehead appears, developing into a pimple—this may become a blackhead, or develop further into a painful cyst or boil. The most commonly affected areas are those that are naturally greasy, including the forehead, face, nose, chin, chest and back.

Acne affects adult men and women as well as adolescents. Polycystic ovaries can be a cause of continuing acne for women. An excess of the hormone androgen in adulthood can be another cause. Contrary to popular belief, the cause of acne is not poor hygiene and probably is little affected by particular foods. Acne is a skin disease, although it is not infectious, and taking good care of the skin can help to control the symptoms and lessen the chance of scarring.

Severe acne, acne vulgaris, will require medical treatment. Medication may be prescribed to fight the acne bacillus, usually antibiotics such as tetracycline or retinoic acid, which is derived from vitamin A.

Skin care routine

- Wash the face and other affected areas gently twice each day. Use a mild soap or special cleansing lotion, to degrease the skin and dissolve blackheads.
- Wash the hair each day and tie it back away from facial skin. Use only non-greasy hair gels.
- Do not squeeze pimples—this can lead to infection and scarring.
- Keep makeup away from pimples. Do not use any preparation that could block the oil glands.

There are several skin cleansers available that are recommended for acne. Some may contain benzoyl peroxide, which induces peeling in the skin's surface layer; they may also contain retinoic acid, which dissolves blackheads—but this is not to be used during pregnancy.

Medical treatments

See the doctor if acne persists, particularly if there is no improvement four to six weeks after onset, if there are cysts or boils, or if the condition is causing distress.

Antibiotics work but may not be a long-term cure. The most common prescription treatments are erythromycin applied in a lotion and tetracyclines taken in tablet form.

The absorption of tetracyclines can be reduced by milk in the diet. Minocycline is an alternative that has the advantage of not being affected by milk consumption, but which carries some risk of arthritis. Women may treat acne with a contraceptive pill that contains the sex hormone cyproterone. A moderate amount of sunlight (UV light) can aid treatment and reduce the occurrence of acne.

Isotretinoin is used to treat recurrent acne. It is similar in structure to vitamin A but acts differently, reducing the oil content of the skin. It also inhibits the growth of bacteria in the skin that are the cause of inflammation and the pus associated with acne. There are some significant side effects with this substance, including dry skin and possible liver upsets. Isotretinoin is harmful to a fetus so is not to be taken if you are pregnant, or for a certain time before conceiving a baby—seek the advice of your doctor.

Acne

Right: Acne affects the skin, with inflammation, pustules (pimples) and plugs (blackheads). Here some of the pustules have broken through the skin. Below: Overproduction of sebum may block the outlet of a sebaceous gland and its hair follicle, forming a blackhead. Later, the area becomes inflamed and pus may form under the skin, producing a pustule.

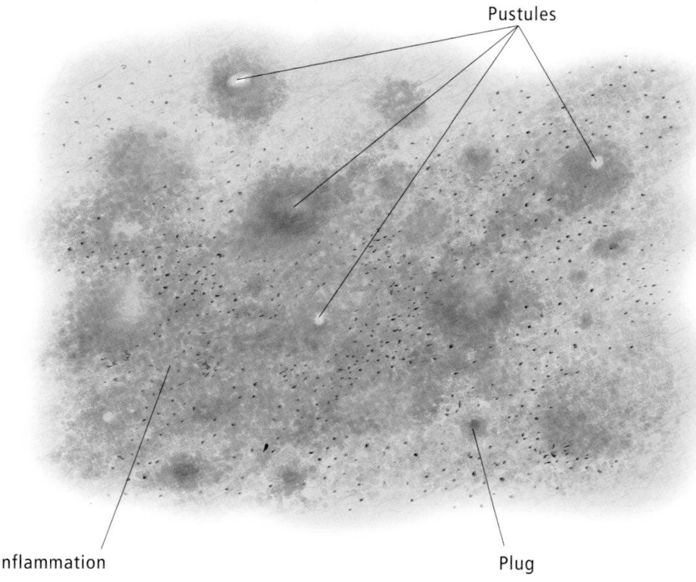

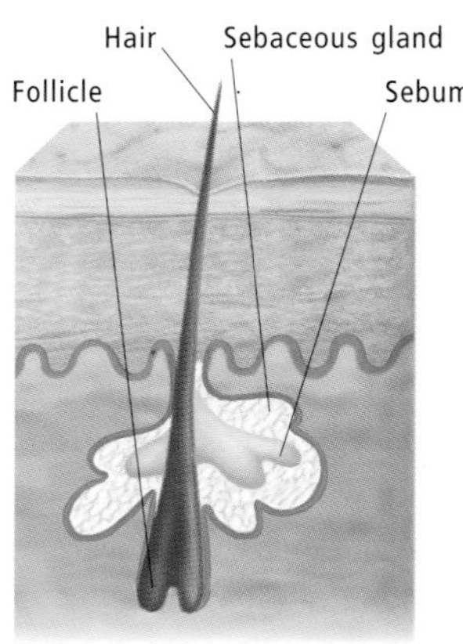

Clear skin

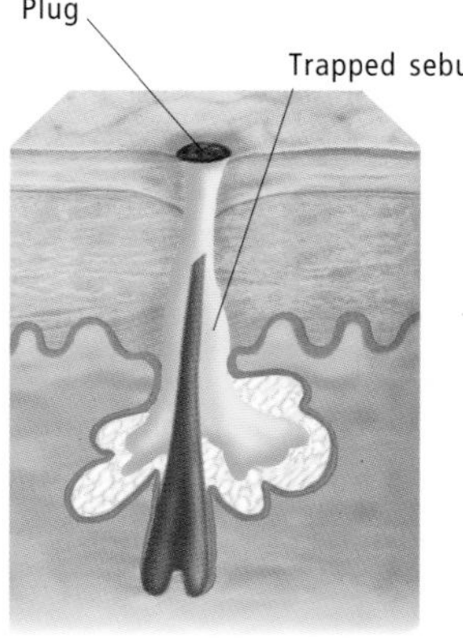

Blackhead

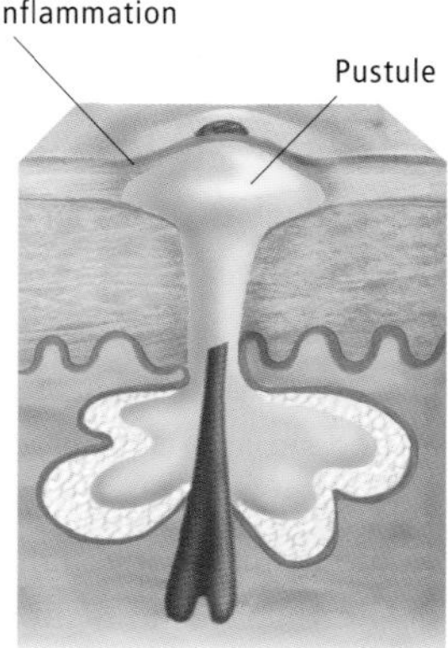

Infected follicle

ACNE ROSACEA

Acne rosacea, also called rosacea, is an inflammation of the skin of the face. It is more common in males, especially alcoholics.

Unsightly red, thickened excess skin tissue forms on the nose, cheeks and forehead, associated with changes in the hair follicles, sebaceous glands and surrounding connective tissue. The exact cause of acne rosacea is unknown, though it sometimes results from an overuse of steroid creams on the face.

Antibiotics are taken orally or applied in a cream or lotion on the affected area to treat this condition. The excess tissue may be removed with a scalpel or laser.

ACROCYANOSIS

This is a harmless, often painless, but annoying discoloration of the extremities, brought about usually by cold but sometimes by emotional states.

Mostly a disease of women, it starts sometime before the age of 30. The hands are most often affected, but the feet may be affected also. They turn blue, cold and sweaty. Warming the hands or feet restores their former pink color.

The cause is thought to be overreaction of the sympathetic nervous system, which controls nerves to the arterioles (small arteries) of the hands and feet. The arterioles contract, restricting the supply of oxygen to the hands and feet; enough oxygen gets through the constricted arteries to keep the tissues of the extremities alive, but not enough to give them their normal healthy pink color. Despite this, there is no permanent damage to the tissues or to the skin of the hands and feet.

Sufferers are advised to dress warmly and avoid exposure to the cold to keep the symptoms at bay. Gloves are a good idea. Rarely, in very troublesome cases, drug treatments are prescribed. Surgery, which consists of cutting the sympathetic nerve supply to the arterioles, is also an option.

SEE ALSO *Arteries*

ACROMEGALY

Affecting only about 1 in every 20,000 people, acromegaly is a rare hormonal disease that causes overgrowth of the body's bones, muscles and other tissues. It is caused by overproduction of an essential hormone called growth hormone (GH) by the pituitary gland.

In young children this can cause abnormal growth of long bones in the limbs. The condition is then called gigantism. If it happens in older children or in adulthood, the disorder is called acromegaly.

Acromegaly can cause the affected person's hands and feet to grow. The facial features coarsen; the jaw line, nose and forehead grow; the tongue grows larger and teeth get more widely spaced as the jaw grows larger. The voice gets deeper because of swelling of the larynx.

The cause of the overproduction of GH is usually a small benign tumor in the pituitary called a pituitary adenoma. As it grows, the tumor may also press on surrounding structures, especially the optic nerve nearby, so that vision may be affected. Changes to the menstrual cycle and abnormal production of breast milk are also common. Growth hormone can also have other unwanted metabolic effects, including diabetes, high blood pressure, gallstones and kidney stones.

Treatment is surgical removal of all or part of the pituitary adenoma. Drugs such as bromocriptine and octreotide, which suppress growth hormone production by the pituitary, are often used as well.

SEE ALSO *Gigantism, Growth disorders*

ACROPHOBIA

Acrophobia is a fear of heights. Acrophobics will feel anxiety or distress when in a high place or when just imagining themselves to be. This excessive fear is termed a phobia because it is an irrational and unrealistic perception of the danger of being in the imagined situation. Research has shown that acrophobics imagine that far greater injuries would result through falls from a given height than would really be the case.

Their level of fear is well above that of a normally cautious person; it can prevent them from climbing ladders or going up a flight of stairs, and can be associated with aerophobia, a fear of flying. Recent studies have questioned previous views that phobics know their fears are unreal. In many cases sufferers believe themselves to be in mortal danger, and, whether they are reacting to fear of the danger or are apprehensive about the possibility of a panic attack, their feelings are real and the effects are debilitating.

With treatment, many phobics can lead normal lives. Medications may help them control and manage their fears, and therapy (including self-help groups) can also be used; these are often used in combination.

SEE ALSO *Anxiety, Panic attacks, Phobias*

ACUPRESSURE

Acupressure, or *tui na*, is a form of traditional Chinese massage where pressure is applied to acupuncture points by the practitioner's fingers, and occasionally their elbows or feet. The depth and duration of pressure is an important aspect of the treatment.

The practitioner diagnoses which points to use by taking a case history and pulse readings (six in each wrist) and by physical examination. Acupressure can be practised on someone in a sitting or lying position and can be performed through clothing. It is also possible to do acupressure on oneself. Acupressure is used to strengthen overall health and to relieve pain and discomfort.

ACUPUNCTURE

Acupuncture is a major branch of traditional Chinese medicine, a healing system that dates back to about 1000 BC. Its earliest text is the *Huang Ti Nei-Ching* or the *Yellow Emperor's Manual of Internal Medicine*, thought to have been written about 200 BC. This text included a systematic approach to acupuncture treatment that provided a foundation for all later developments. By the time of the Tang dynasty (AD 618–907) the Imperial Medical College taught acupuncture and medical theory based on Taoist philosophies in which the notions of harmony, balance and energy flow were applied to the treatment of illnesses.

In modern China, acupuncture continues to be an essential part of the medical system alongside Western medical practices. Acupuncture in the West has spread rapidly in the twentieth century. It is practised by both traditional Chinese medicine practitioners and by medical doctors who are not necessarily trained in all aspects of traditional Chinese medicine.

Philosophy

Acupuncture, along with all other types of traditional Chinese medicine, is based upon the principle that optimum health is achieved and maintained by balancing the flow of life energy through the body. This life energy flow, which is known as *ch'i* or *qi*, is seen to be made up of two polarities: the *yin*, which is passive, internal, contracting and cold, and the *yang*, which is active, external, expanding and warm. For good health to be maintained, the theory is that *yin* and *yang* need to be in constant interplay —flowing, balancing and moving between each other. If either *yin* or *yang* energy becomes excessive in the body, it automatically creates a deficiency state in the other which, if not corrected, will lead to ill health. For example, an infectious disease where there is fever is seen as an excess *yang* condition while chronic fatigue syndrome, where there is pallor, is seen as an excess *yin* condition.

The theory is that *ch'i* travels through the body along twelve pathways known as meridians, each corresponding to a particular body organ or system. The twelve meridians are the gallbladder, liver, lung, large intestine, stomach, spleen/pancreas, heart, small

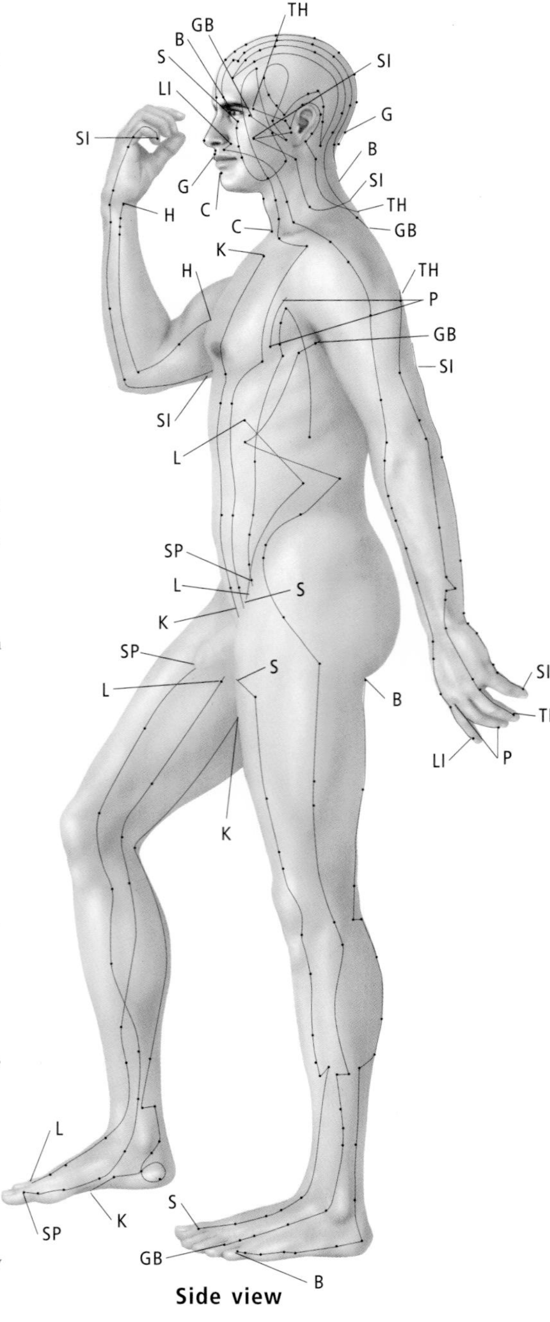

Side view

intestine, bladder, kidney, pericardium (which controls circulation and is important in sexual activity) and triple heater (which controls the endocrine system). Two extra meridians, the governor and the conception, run up the midline of the body. The meridians overlap with the circulatory and nervous systems but are separate to them. Some modern research supports the idea of meridians, suggesting their flows may relate to fluctuations in the body's electromagnetic field.

Acupuncture works through points, or gates, located along the meridians. Traditional acupuncture identifies 365 points; modern charts show up to 2,000 points. Each meridian has a point of entry and a point of exit. Diagnosis takes into account the way *ch'i* acts in relation to all the parts of the body. Treatment involves regulating *ch'i*, drawing it in or dispersing it.

To further understand the flow of energy through the body, traditional Chinese medicine aligns the body with the five elements of nature. Each of the five elements is associated with major organs of the body: fire (heart, small intestine); earth (stomach, spleen); metal (lungs, colon); water (kidneys, bladder); and wood (gallbladder, liver). The elements are seen to work cyclically through the body; an understanding of these cycles forms a vital part of acupuncture diagnosis and treatment.

Diagnosis

Traditional acupuncturists diagnose a patient's condition through observing their voice, tongue, eyes, complexion, hair texture, body language and physical symptoms. Lifestyle, sleep patterns and food preferences are also taken into account. The acupuncturist puts light pressure with the fingers on the patient's twelve pulses, six

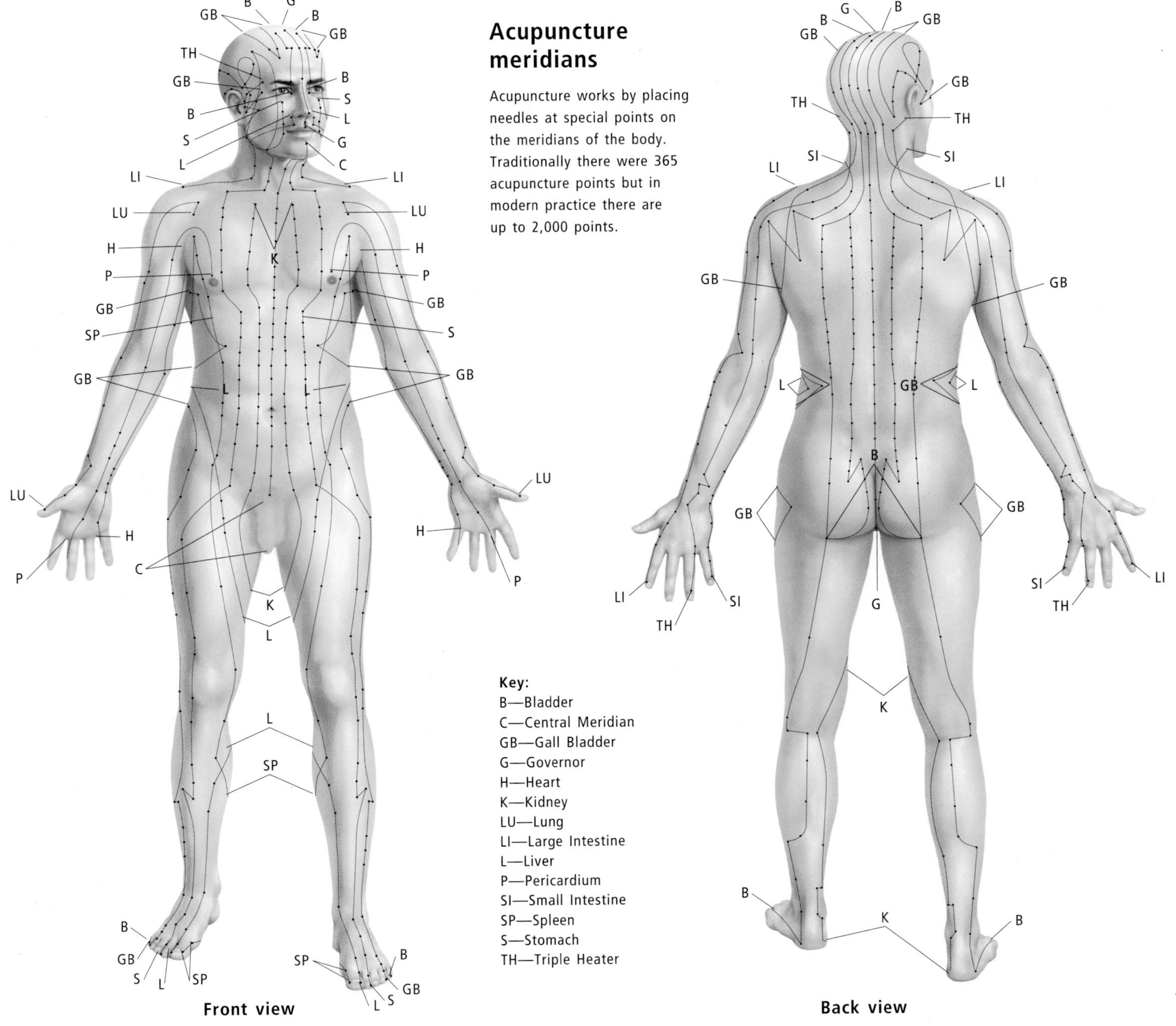

Acupuncture meridians

Acupuncture works by placing needles at special points on the meridians of the body. Traditionally there were 365 acupuncture points but in modern practice there are up to 2,000 points.

A

in each wrist, to measure the flow of *ch'i* through the organs. Diagnosis aims to understand the imbalances in the body which underlie the illness. This understanding forms the basis of an individualized treatment for the patient which goes beyond mere symptom relief.

Treatment

In the most common form of acupuncture treatment, the surface of the skin is pierced by very fine stainless steel needles on specific points. The depth to which the needle is inserted varies according to both the patient and the point used. The needles are left in for varying lengths of time up to about 45 minutes. The acupuncturist may briefly manipulate the needles with slight touches during this time. The number of needles used varies considerably, depending on the acupuncturist's technique and the patient's condition. Acupuncture treatment usually takes place at regular intervals over a few months, depending on the condition that is being treated.

Acupuncture should not be a painful procedure, as long as it is done with precision and expertise. Usually there is no more than an awareness of a pinprick when the needle is first inserted. This can be followed by a tingling sensation, a sensation of dull heaviness around the needle, or a warm spreading feeling. Often in the course of the session the patient becomes very relaxed.

Modern developments

There have been several modern developments in acupuncture treatment.

Ear acupuncture is a procedure in which needles are applied to points on the outer ear. Studs (small stainless steel plugs) are also inserted over the points and left in for some days. In the West, ear acupuncture has been used in drug and alcohol detoxification programs to help relieve anxiety.

In electro-acupuncture, electrical stimulators delivering small regular pulses are attached to the needles. The stronger stimulation of the needles means that fewer needles than normal are required.

Laser acupuncture utilizes laser-light emitted from a hand-held wand to stimulate the acupuncture points.

Uses of acupuncture

Acupuncture treatment based on the principles of traditional Chinese medicine is said to have a wide application, including boosting the immune function, normalizing circulation, assisting the female reproductive system, relieving headaches, migraines and musculoskeletal pain, and treating respiratory and digestive disorders. In China it is also used in conjunction with, or as a substitute for, surgical anesthesia.

ACUTE RESPIRATORY DISTRESS SYNDROME

Acute respiratory distress syndrome (ARDS), sometimes called adult respiratory distress syndrome, is a name given to several conditions in which fluid leaks out of the blood vessels and into the alveoli of the lung, causing pulmonary edema, respiratory failure, and in some cases death. The syndrome, also known as pump lung, stiff lung or white lung, may be caused by a number of conditions, including shock, fluid overload, narcotic overdose, disseminated intravascular coagulation and massive trauma or burns.

Clinical signs include breathlessness, rapid heartbeat, cyanosis (a bluish discoloration) and hypoxia (lack of oxygen). A lung x-ray shows evidence of interstitial and alveolar edema.

The condition is treated with mechanical ventilation. Diuretics such as frusemide may be used to decrease the amount of fluid in the lung, and antibiotics may be needed to combat lung infection. If the underlying condition is treatable the prognosis is good.

SEE ALSO *Blood vessels, Cyanosis, Lung, Pulmonary edema*

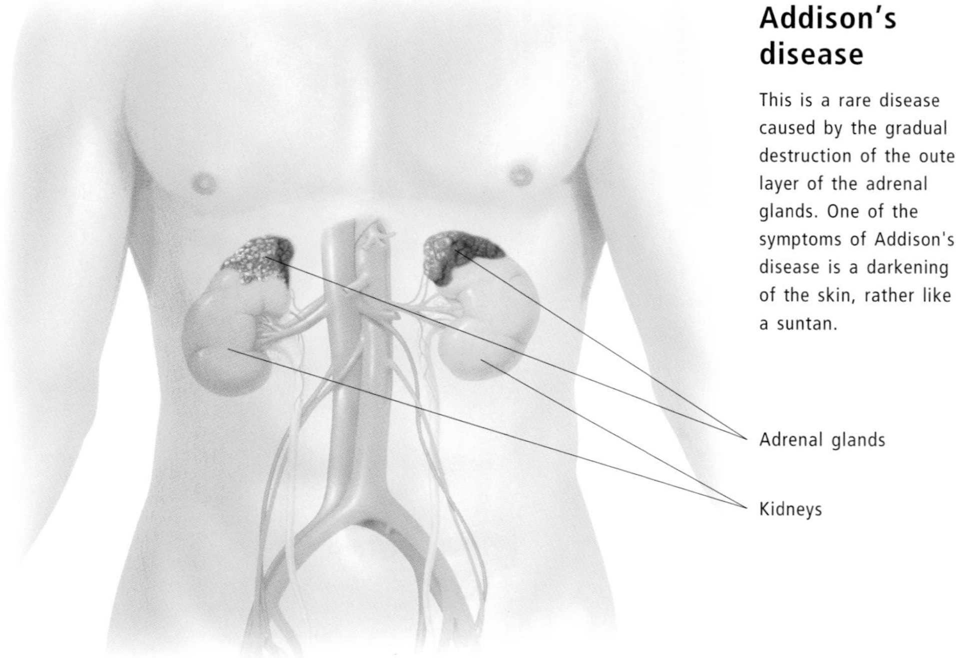

Addison's disease

This is a rare disease caused by the gradual destruction of the outer layer of the adrenal glands. One of the symptoms of Addison's disease is a darkening of the skin, rather like a suntan.

ADDISON'S DISEASE

This rare disease mainly affects people between 30 and 50 years of age. It is caused by the gradual destruction of parts of the adrenal glands. An adrenal gland is situated on the top of each kidney. The glands produce steroids such as hydrocortisone (cortisol) which are vital to the body's metabolism. In Addison's disease, the adrenal cortex, or outer layer, is destroyed and the adrenal glands can't produce enough hydrocortisone for the body's needs.

The usual cause of the destruction is an autoimmune process in which the body destroys its own cells. Diagnosis is made after a blood test shows low hydrocortisone levels.

The early symptoms are loss of appetite and weight, and a feeling of increased

A

tiredness and weakness. There may be abdominal symptoms, such as diarrhea or constipation, and mild indigestion with nausea and vomiting. Usually the skin becomes darker. If untreated, the condition leads to acute adrenal failure and coma, requiring emergency treatment in hospital.

The treatment of Addison's disease is replacement hydrocortisone hormones in the form of tablets which need to be taken daily and continued for life. Affected people who take their tablets regularly will lead a normal, healthy life.

SEE ALSO *Adrenal glands*

ADDUCTION AND ABDUCTION

Abduction is a movement in a direction away from the center line of the body. For example, if you are standing and then lift your right leg off the floor to the right side, you are abducting it.

Adduction is the movement in the opposite direction, back towards the center line of the body. For example, if you return your leg to the original standing position so that the foot once again rests on the floor, you are adducting it.

With the fingers, the midline of the middle digit serves as the reference point, with the palms facing forward; abduction is defined as movement away from this point and adduction movement towards it. In the case of the toes, the midline of the second toe represents the point of reference.

Some muscles in the body are named after their ability to abduct or adduct limbs or other parts of the body. For example, abductor pollicis longus is the long muscle that abducts the thumb.

SEE ALSO *Muscle, Muscular system*

ADENOIDS

The adenoids are two glandular swellings at the back of the throat, above the tonsils, usually present in children before the onset of adolescence. Composed of lymphatic tissue, the adenoids are thought to assist the body in fighting throat infections. They are one of the first barriers against microscopic invaders entering the body via the nose and mouth.

Enlargement

Normally, adenoids grow slowly in size from the age of three until the age of five, when they shrink again, disappearing around puberty. But in some children who suffer repeated throat infections, they keep growing, becoming swollen and painful. The tonsils often also become enlarged. Eventually the adenoids may block the space between the nasal passages and the throat. Inflammation of the mucous membrane of the nose (rhinitis) and of the air sinuses behind the nose (sinusitis) may follow.

The adenoids can also block the opening of the narrow eustachian tube that connects the middle ear to the throat. When this happens, bacteria grow inside the middle ear and infection (otitis media) can develop. Repeated infections in the ear can turn into a chronic (long-term) condition known as "glue ear" and can cause deafness.

A child with enlarged adenoids tends to breathe through the mouth, snores at night, and speaks with a nasal-sounding voice. The child suffers repeated blocked or runny nose, a cough (especially at night) and painful ear infections. The child may do poorly at school or show other signs of deafness.

The diagnosis is made by a pediatrician or primary care physician, who will examine the back of the child's throat, using a mirror with a light attached. Hearing should be tested and an x-ray of the sinuses may be required. Usually the adenoids themselves don't need to be treated, as they decrease in size around puberty. Any infections that arise must be treated with antibiotics.

If infections are very frequent or persist in spite of antibiotic treatment, then an operation to remove the adenoids may be necessary. This procedure is called an adenoidectomy and is performed by an ear, nose and throat or pediatric surgeon in hospital, under general anesthetic. Removal of the tonsils (tonsillectomy) is often performed at the same time. The child is in hospital for about three days and usually recovers rapidly.

SEE ALSO *Otitis media, Rhinitis, Sinusitis, Tonsils*

ADENOMA

An adenoma is a benign tumor of glandular tissue. Adenomas can occur in specialized glandular tissues such as the thyroid, pancreas or pituitary, or in organs and tissues that contain glandular tissue. They are common in the breast, ovaries and uterus, where glandular tissues are stimulated by hormones throughout a woman's reproductive life, and can also occur in the colon.

As long as it remains benign, an adenoma poses no problems and needs no treatment. Occasionally it may press on surrounding structures and cause pain or other symptoms. If this happens, or if it becomes unsightly, it may need to be removed by a surgeon under local or general anesthetic. In some cases an adenoma can become cancerous. It is then known as an adenocarcinoma, and surgical removal is advised.

Adenomas of endocrine glands (those which produce hormones, such as the pituitary gland, thyroid gland, adrenal glands and pancreas) can cause excessive hormone

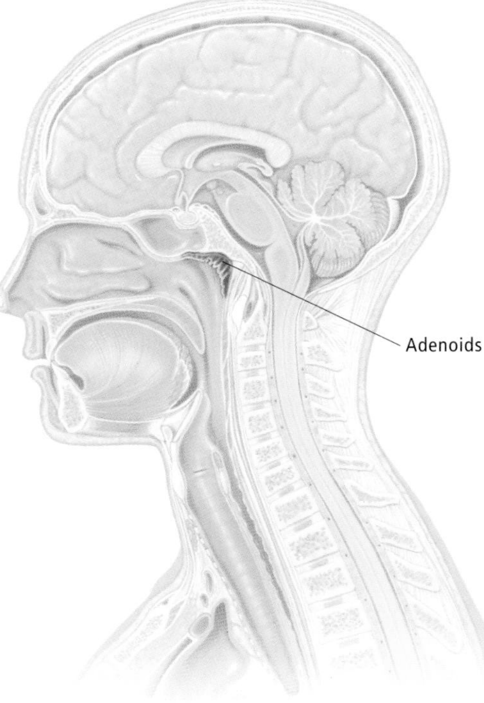

Adenoids

The adenoids are glands children have at the back of the throat, and which tend to disappear at puberty. It is thought they fight throat infections, but sometimes they can swell, which can lead to infection and difficulty with swallowing, breathing and hearing.

A

Adenoma

An adenoma is a benign (mild) tumor that can grow in the lining of the colon (as in this picture) or in other glandular tissue, such as the thyroid, pancreas or pituitary. In a woman, they can occur in the breast, ovaries or uterus throughout her reproductive life.

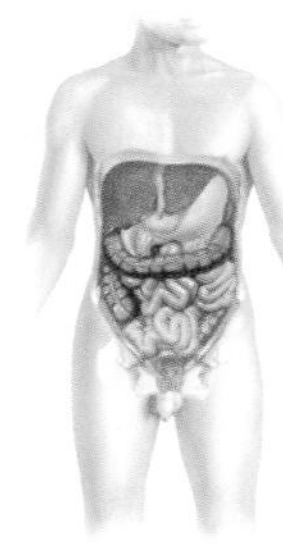

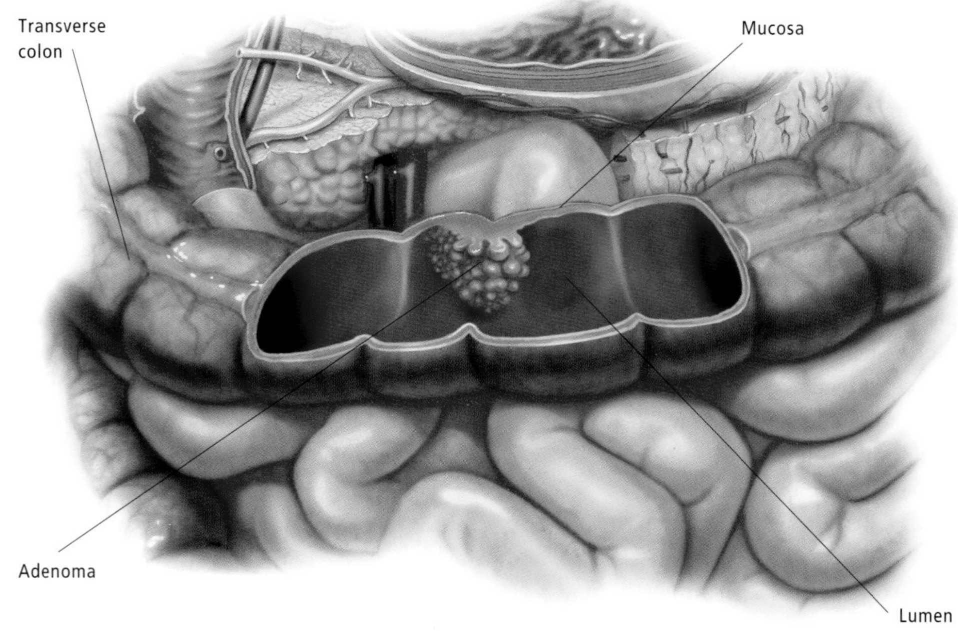

production, leading to disease. Pituitary adenomas, for example, can result in acromegaly or Cushing's syndrome. If two or more different endocrine glands are involved, the condition is called adenomatosis.

SEE ALSO *Acromegaly, Cushing's syndrome, Endocrine glands*

ADENOVIRUS

Adenoviruses are a group of DNA viruses that mainly cause diseases of the upper respiratory tract. They most commonly affect infants and children, particularly between autumn and spring, when they cause an acute upper respiratory tract infection, with sore throat, fever and swollen lymph glands in the neck, sometimes with bronchiolitis and pneumonia. They may also cause a condition called pharyngoconjunctivitis (sore throat and fever with inflammation of the conjunctiva) often seen in children on summer camps. Adenoviruses can cause an acute diarrheal illness in children, and in immunosuppressed people, such as those with AIDS, may cause severe pneumonia.

There are no effective treatments for adenoviruses. However the course of the infection is usually mild and the child makes a good recovery. Vaccines for some adenoviruses have been developed but their use is currently limited.

SEE ALSO *Conjunctivitis, DNA, Pneumonia, Viruses*

ADHESIONS

Adhesions are thin bands of scar tissue that form in a body cavity after an operation or a severe infection. They occur most commonly in the abdomen. Though adhesions are painless, they may restrict movement and function of surrounding organs. For example, the intestines may become pinched or entangled by them. When this happens, the normal movement of food material through the intestines may be prevented—abdominal obstruction, vomiting, abdominal swelling and pain can occur. If untreated a bowel obstruction can lead to death.

Treatment is by surgery. While the patient is under general anesthetic, the surgeon opens the abdomen, locates the adhesion(s) and cuts them, releasing the trapped bowel. Unfortunately they have a tendency to grow back after the operation. Some sufferers undergo multiple operations.

ADOLESCENCE

The period between childhood and adulthood, adolescence roughly corresponds to the teenage years. It coincides with and overlaps with puberty, when the secondary sexual characteristics appear, marking the onset of physical and sexual maturity. Adolescence begins with the onset of puberty and lasts until about 18 years of age.

Changes in personality

Adolescence is a time of great change, both for the individual and the family. Adolescents must control and direct sexual drives, begin an occupation and career orientation, develop a mature set of values with responsible self-direction, and learn to modify behavior in response to expectations from an adult world. And they must still rely on adults for emotional and financial support. It can be a confusing and disorienting time.

Particularly if the bonding in childhood has been poor, adolescents may rebel against parental standards and expectations. They frequently adopt outrageous modes of dress and behavior. They may not readily be able to control aggressive drives, which can end up in outbursts of temper or antisocial behavior. An adolescent may take persons outside the family as role models—often sports stars or pop stars. It could be argued that there is greater chance of psychological and behavioral problems if an adolescent comes from a disturbed or deprived home environment, but even in a relatively stable home environment most adolescents go through a stage of rebellion.

Physical and sexual changes

Adolescents must come to terms with changing body shape and self image. Between the ages of 12 and 18, muscle mass, strength, fat distribution and secondary sexual characteristics develop rapidly. In a girl, breasts develop and menstruation begins between 11 and 14, pubic hair from 10 to 14, and by 16 menstruation is usually occurring regularly. In boys, the testes and penis begin to enlarge from around the age of 12, body hair develops from around 13, and from 14 to 15 the voice deepens.

A

Accompanying these physical changes is anxiety about sexual attraction, and preoccupation with physical appearance, especially skin, hair and weight. Conditions such as acne and eating disorders are more prevalent in adolescence than at any other time of life.

Sexual experimentation inevitably takes place during adolescence. Many adolescents question their own gender; homosexual feelings are normal in this period, though they often do not last. Masturbation usually begins during this time.

If sexual intercourse takes place in adolescence, it tends to occur later rather than earlier. There are also the risks of sexually transmitted diseases and unwanted pregnancy. These can be avoided if the adolescent has access to helpful information, which can be provided by parents or carers only if the communication lines are open and the relationship is built on mutual trust.

Experimentation

The desire to experiment, and peer group pressure, among other factors, can lead to adolescents using drugs and alcohol for the first time. The use of "soft" drugs—cannabis, alcohol and tobacco—is common. Drugs and alcohol may also be a means to relieve anxiety and depression. A factor in managing drug and alcohol use is to make sure the adolescent fully understands the health problems and risks associated with drug and alcohol consumption. Parents can help by not smoking, and drinking in moderation.

Managing adolescence

Adolescents are often referred to doctors and psychologists because parents or teachers are worried about their behavior. But only a small percentage need psychiatric treatment. However, problems should be taken seriously and never dismissed.

Good communication remains the key to managing adolescence. It can encourage self-confidence and responsibility and so prepare an adolescent to cope with life. This may take some flexibility on the part of parents. Presenting a united front, parents should emphasize those issues which affect the adolescent's health and safety. Rules such as informing parents of their whereabouts, never driving a motor vehicle after drinking alcohol and so on may be considered important, whereas other issues such as dress may not be so important.

After the age of about 18, having left school, joined the workforce or gone to higher education, young people are more willing to compromise and accept advice, and tend to become more constructive and sensitive in dealings with others.

SEE ALSO *Acne, Eating disorders, Puberty*

Adolescence

Change, both physical and emotional, is the characteristic feature of adolescence, a period that begins with puberty and continues through the teenage years.

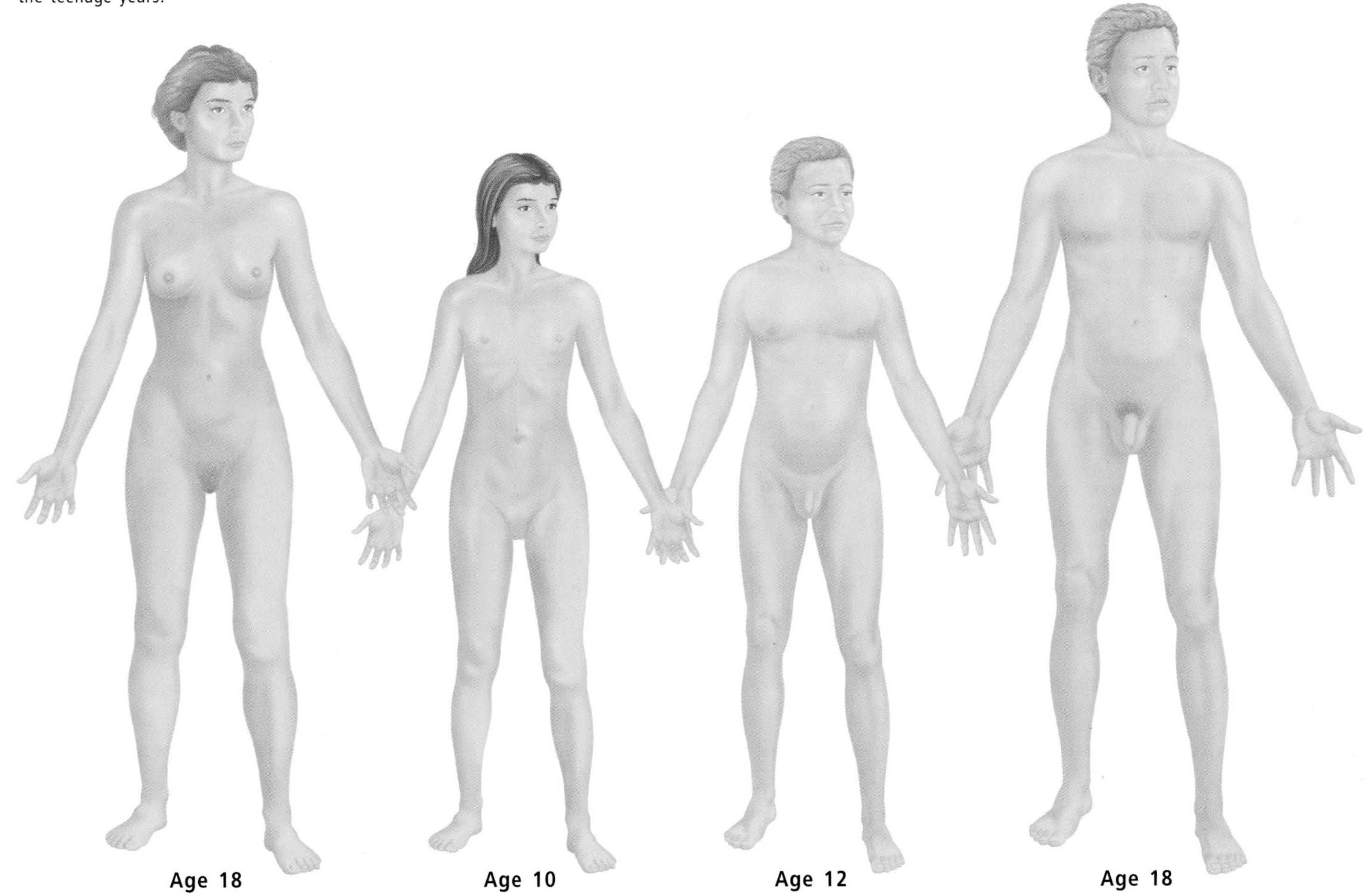

A

ADRENAL GLANDS

The two adrenal (or suprarenal) glands lie one on top of each kidney at the back of the abdomen. Each adrenal gland is 1–2 inches (3–5 centimeters) long, somewhat triangular in shape and yellowish brown in color. Each gland has two parts, an outer region, the adrenal cortex, and a core, the medulla. Both produce and secrete hormones but differ in structure, function and development.

Hormones

Hormones are chemicals produced by certain glands (called endocrine glands, which include the adrenals) and secreted into the tissues and blood vessels. They act by changing the activity of specific cells, which can be localized or widespread, and may be some distance from the endocrine gland. The adrenal glands release several hormones from both the cortex and medulla.

The adrenal cortical (cortex) hormones are produced from cholesterol and are called steroids. They are divided into glucocorticoids such as cortisol, mineralocorticoids such as aldosterone, and androgens, which are similar to sex hormones.

Glucocorticoids are involved in the metabolism of glucose and the response of the body to injury. One of the effects of glucocorticoids is to reduce the body's immune response. This has led to their use in treating tissue rejection after organ transplants, and in reducing allergic responses.

Aldosterone is the most important of the mineralocorticoids. It increases the retention of sodium in the kidneys and other tissues such as the sweat and salivary glands; it also causes secretion of potassium. The effect of aldosterone on sodium retention is important in controlling blood volume. If there is a decrease in blood flow or blood volume in the kidney, renin is released from the kidney and acts on a second hormone, angiotensin, to increase aldosterone levels. This helps conserve sodium and hence to restore blood volume.

Androgens contribute to the development of male sexual characteristics. Excess production in women causes masculinization.

The amount of glucocorticoids and androgens secreted by the adrenal glands is controlled by adrenocorticotropic hormone (ACTH). This is a hormone secreted by the front (anterior) lobe of the pituitary (the hypophysis). ACTH then travels via the bloodstream to the adrenal gland to stimulate the release of the glucocorticoids and sex steroids from the adrenal cortex. ACTH secretion is regulated by the hypothalamus, which secretes corticotrophin-releasing hormone (CRH), which stimulates ACTH secretion. Cortisol acts to control both CRH and ACTH, by a mechanism known as a negative feedback loop, in which an increase in cortisol leads to a decrease in CRH and ACTH and vice versa.

The adrenal medulla is derived from neural (nerve) tissue and is concerned with production and secretion of epinephrine (adrenaline) and norepinephrine (noradrenaline). These hormones can cause increased heart rate, widening of the airways, and breakdown of glycogen to glucose for energy. All of these make the body more equipped to handle emergency situations.

Adrenal disorders

If the levels of the hormones produced by the adrenal glands fall below or increase to above normal, various disorders will result.

Adrenal hyperplasia

Adrenal hyperplasia is an enlargement of the adrenal gland and affects the outer region, the cortex. It can be caused by overproduction of ACTH from the pituitary, such as can occur with pituitary tumors. The excess ACTH leads to excess stimulation of the adrenals, with enlargement (hyperplasia) and excess production of cortisol and androgens. The hyperplasia may also be caused by a defect in cortisol production. High ACTH leads to masculinization in women, including excess facial hair, deepening of the voice and loss of menstrual periods. If the cortisol defect is present in a fetus, the baby can be born with congenital adrenal hyperplasia (this is the condition known as adrenogenital syndrome).

Addison's disease

Addison's disease is caused by insufficient adrenal cortical hormones. Symptoms include tiredness, weakness, loss of appetite and vomiting, and a brownish pigmentation of the skin. Treatment involves lifelong steroid therapy.

Cushing's syndrome

Cushing's syndrome occurs when there is an excess, or prolonged use, of cortisol. Symptoms of Cushing's syndrome include weight gain, muscle weakness, high blood pressure, a "moon" face and facial hair. Diagnosis is based on symptoms, with blood and urine tests to confirm increased cortisol levels and magnetic resonance imaging (MRI) or CAT scan to reveal any tumors.

Pheochromocytoma

Pheochromocytoma is a tumor involving the medulla of the adrenal gland or associated tissues. It causes the excess production of epinephrine (adrenaline) and norepinephrine (noradrenaline). These tumors are most common in young and mid-adult life and are generally not malignant. Symptoms include severe headache, rapid heart rate and palpitations, sweating, abdominal pain, nervousness, irritability, increased appetite and loss of weight. Patients generally have high blood pressure, and diagnosis is based on raised hormone levels in the blood or urine. Treatment can be by medication to block the hormones, or may involve removal of the tumor.

SEE ALSO ***Addison's disease, Androgens, Cushing's syndrome, Endocrine glands, Hormones, Pituitary gland***

ADRENOGENITAL SYNDROME

Adrenogenital syndromes are an inherited group of disorders, present from birth, in which there are enzyme deficiencies. Depending on which enzyme is reduced, the effects can be masculinization of women, or more rarely feminization of men, or early sexual development of children. In some severe forms, metabolic changes due to the lack of a hormone called aldosterone can cause vomiting, dehydration, electrolyte changes and cardiac arrhythmias in the newborn, which can lead to death if untreated.

These conditions are caused by a lack of an enzyme needed by the adrenal gland to make the steroid cortisol. The pituitary gland secretes a hormone called adrenocorticotropic hormone (ACTH) that stimulates the adrenal gland, causing the overproduction of male hormones (androgens) but without causing any increase in cortisol. This causes females to be born with an enlarged clitoris and male-like genitalia, though the ovaries, uterus and fallopian tubes are normal. As a girl grows, masculine features (deepening of voice, facial hair) appear, and she fails to menstruate at puberty.

No obvious abnormality is present in the male newborn, but secondary sexual characteristics such as deepening of the voice, enlargement of the penis and appearance of pubic hair appear well before puberty. At puberty, the testes are small.

The condition can be diagnosed by blood and urine tests which show abnormally low levels of cortisol and aldosterone, and abnormally high levels of androgens. Treatment involves replacement therapy with steroid hormones. Medication must be given daily and continued for life. Reconstructive surgery is usually performed in the first few years of life in girls with masculine external genitalia. Prospective parents with a family history of adrenogenital syndrome should have genetic counseling.

SEE ALSO *Adrenal glands, Androgens, Congenital abnormalities, Feminization, Genetic counseling, Hormones, Pituitary gland, Steroids, Virilization*

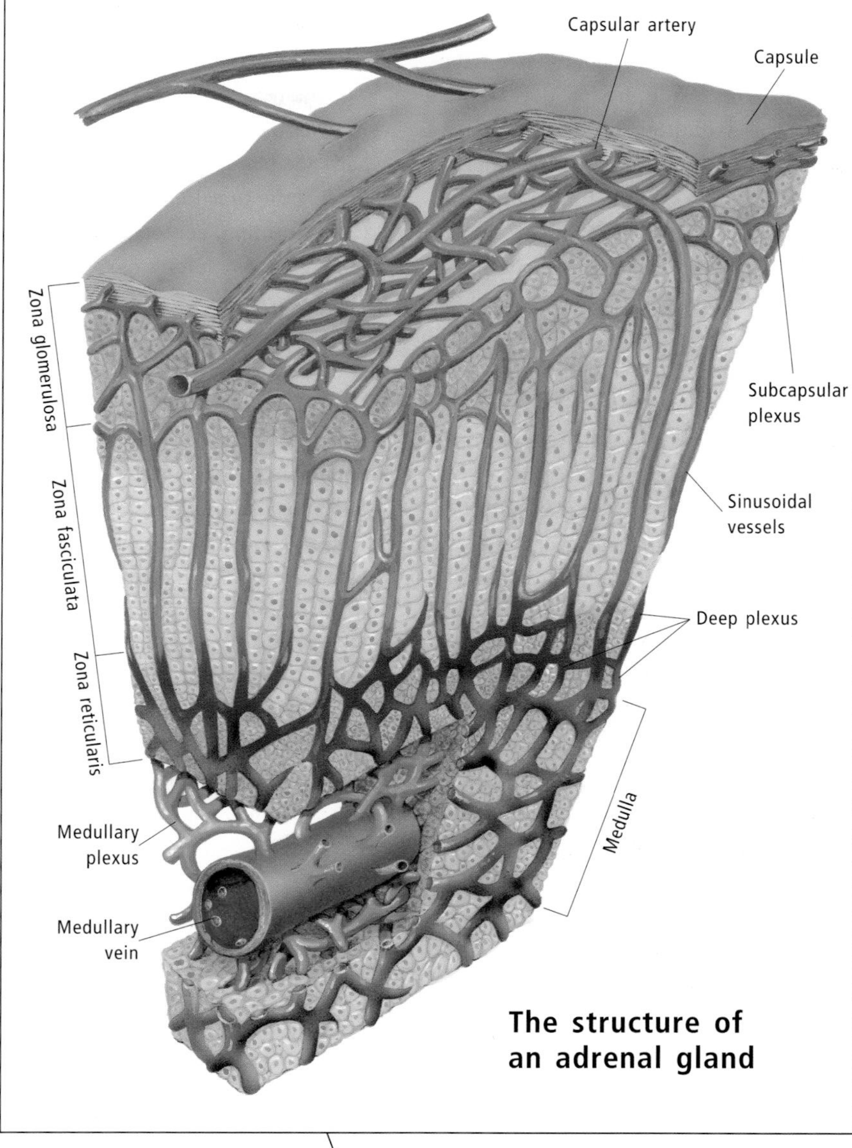

The structure of an adrenal gland

Adrenal glands

These tiny glands are just as essential to our health as the much larger organs all around them. They secrete steroids, which deal with glucose, help the body respond to injuries, keep the volume of blood at the right level, and, in males, contribute to the development of sexual characteristics.

Aorta

Adrenal gland

Kidney

Inferior vena cava

Right adrenal gland

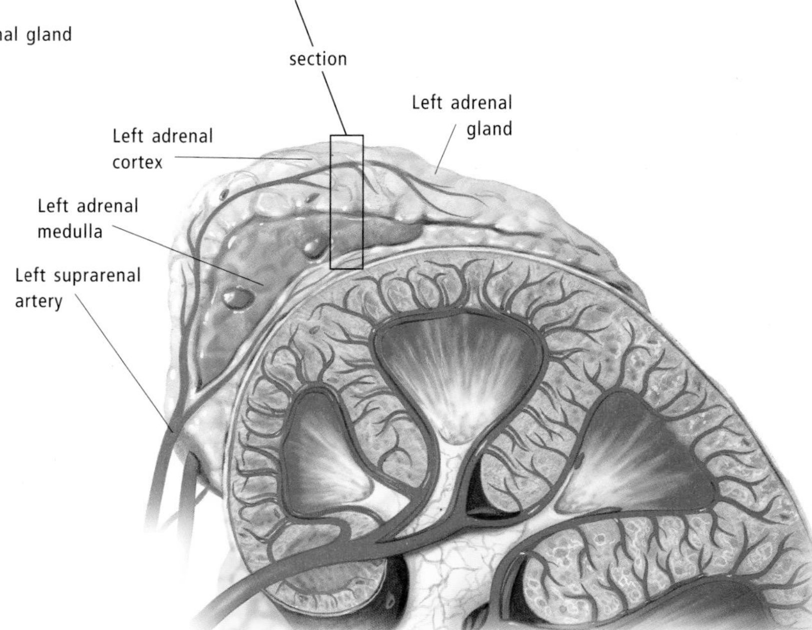

A

AGEING

A human develops through the stages of infancy, childhood and adolescence to become an adult. After physical development peaks by mid-adulthood, the ageing process begins and continues until death. There is no fixed or universal time frame, but the periods in the human life span are characterized by changes in outward structure and in the function of body systems.

Childhood

Childhood begins after the first year of infancy and ends with the changes of puberty. A child is not an adult in miniature. A baby's head at birth makes up about a quarter of the baby's total length; however the eyes are relatively large because they have almost reached their adult size. Fat cells increase in both size and number in the first two years of life, then change very little after that, except in severely obese children.

Children's bones of the arms and legs still have cartilage at the ends. Growth of the cartilage plates causes bone to lengthen. During the first 12 years of life, ossification (bone-forming) centers appear in the heads of long bones (epiphyses) and bone gradually replaces the cartilage.

The first set of teeth appears in the first two years, then from the sixth year they are shed and replaced by permanent teeth.

X-rays of the ossification centers and the appearance of teeth are used to assess age and physical maturity. The *Factory Act* in England, which was passed in the early nineteenth century with the aim of preventing exploitation of young children, only allowed children with second molar teeth to work in factories.

The brain grows rapidly in childhood: from half the adult size at two years of age to about 90 percent of adult size at age six. By a process called myelination, nerve fibers are progressively coated in myelin, a substance that improves conduction of nerve signals. The cortex of the brain is almost fully myelinated by age seven, when children can use language effectively and can think logically about concrete things that they experience in everyday life.

Adolescence

Adolescence is the stage characterized by structural, physiological and psychological changes that occur when a boy or girl undergoes puberty. The most noticeable structural change is the growth spurt that begins at about the age of 10 or 11 years in girls and about two years later in boys. Height typically increases by 3 inches (8 centimeters) or more each year, and the body proportion becomes more like an adult's. The growth spurt of muscles results in a dramatic increase in physical strength and endurance.

The appearance of pubic hair is followed by underarm hair one to two years later, and facial hair a year after that. However, growth of fat under the skin layer slows down and the lymphatic system, especially the thymus, even regresses. The sebaceous and sweat glands of the skin are more active, making acne a common problem of puberty.

The key event of puberty is the maturation of the reproductive system. In girls, the onset of menstruation (menarche) usually occurs somewhere between 11 and 14 years of age. The uterus develops its adult shape

How women grow and age

At about 10 years of age, girls have a growth spurt, and pubic hair and underarm hair start to grow a year or two later. Soon the reproductive system develops, with the first period arriving around the age of 13. By 18 the body is approaching maturity and from there it continues to change, but not grow. From 35 the production of eggs and sex hormones decreases, culminating in menopause. Without the hormonal effects, the breasts and skin lose firmness, fat distribution changes, bones thin and height decreases.

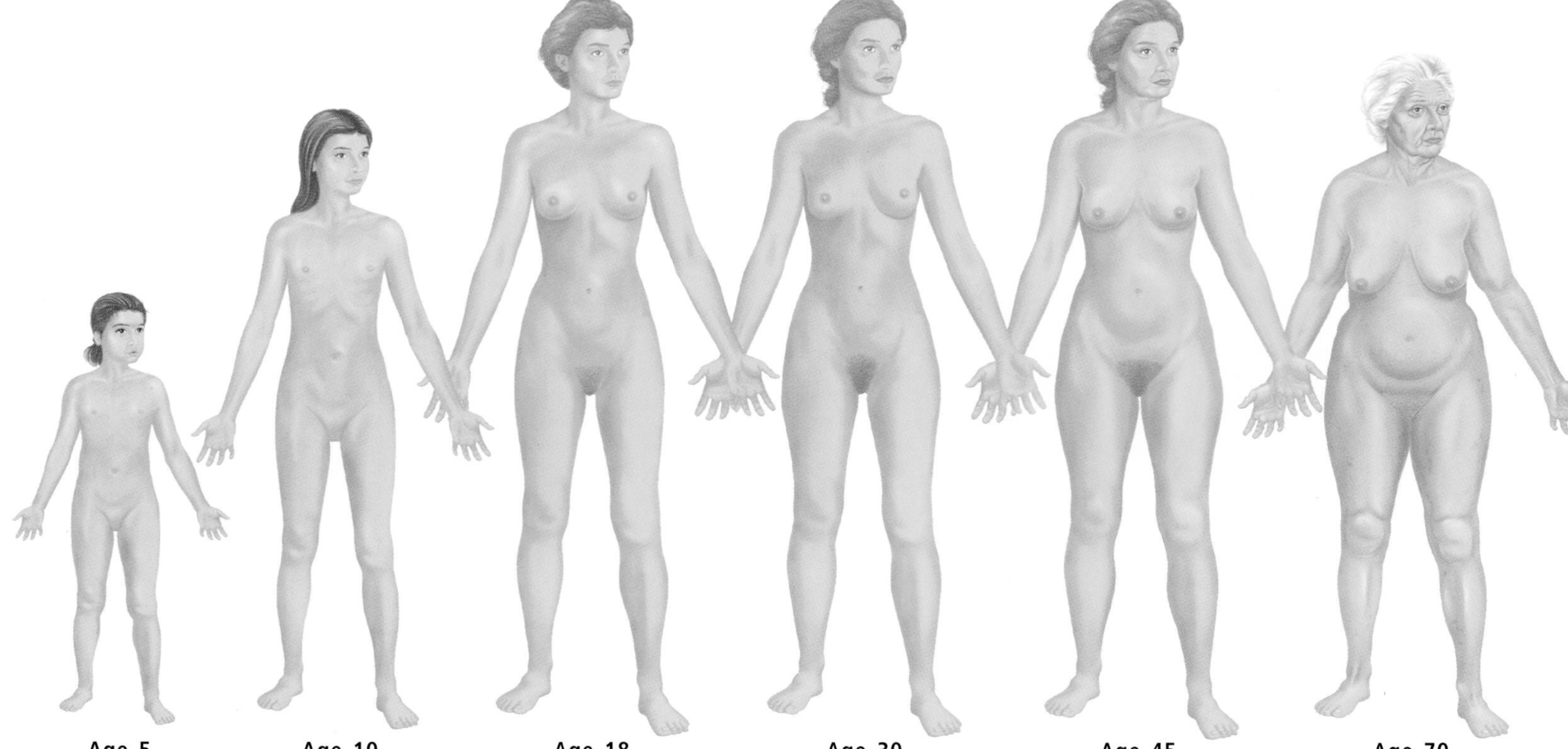

and the first period occurs. Increased secretion of sex hormones by the ovaries leads to development of breasts and female pattern of pubic hair. The external genitalia also mature, with a thickening of the fat pad over the pubic bone and enlargement of the labia majora and clitoris.

In boys, the testes grow rapidly and begin to secrete testosterone and produce sperm. The first ejaculation usually occurs around age 14 or 15 but may not contain sperm. Testosterone is responsible for secondary sex characteristics such as facial and pubic hair. The scrotum grows, and its skin becomes darker and wrinkled. The penis increases in length and girth, and develops a glans at its tip. Compared to girls, boys have broader shoulders, narrower hips and smaller buttocks; also the cartilage of the larynx (voice box) is more prominent (making what is known as the "Adam's apple") and the voice is deeper as the vocal cords are longer. The voice begins to break at about age 14 and this process is complete after about a year.

Puberty also brings about cognitive changes. Adolescents progress beyond the concrete thinking of childhood to develop more abstract and conceptual thinking. But they can often see only their own point of view, and have difficulty in appreciating views of others. This transition from childhood to adulthood is a critical time and carries with it risks of emotional problems, as adolescents have to develop a personal identity, of which sexual identity is an important part.

Adulthood and senescence

There is no definite age for the beginning of adulthood, although in most Western societies it is legally set at 18 or 21 years of age. Adulthood can be understood as the stage in which the individual has reached full anatomical, physiological and sexual maturity.

The bones have ceased to grow because the cartilage growth plates have been entirely replaced by bone. All the body systems are now fully functioning. However, the body continues to change in response to environmental changes, and to physical as well as emotional trauma. The bones, for example, heal after fractures and are continually remodeled to adapt to pressure applied to them. The processes of adaptation and repair are vital for survival of the individual. However, adaptation and repair are not always completely successful. The genetic coding which controls them is altered by external influences such as radiation, or by errors introduced by cell division over the years. This decline in function is called the ageing process. Although old age (senescence) is said to begin at age 65, the ageing process has already begun much earlier.

The structural changes of ageing are well known. The skin becomes thin, fragile and wrinkled. On the face, the skin sags and forms bags under the eyes and a double chin. Dark "age spots" become more and more numerous. Baldness begins as hair loss exceeds replacement rate. Poor function of melanocytes (cells which produce the dark pigment melanin) causes hair to go gray. Muscle mass is reduced and muscle tone declines. Bones become more porous and weak because of loss of bone substance and minerals, especially calcium, and osteoporosis may develop. Spongy bones such as vertebrae partially collapse, reducing height.

How men grow and age

Boys' growth spurt occurs at around 13 or 14 years of age. Muscles begin to bulk up and body hair grows. The testes grow and produce sperm, and the voice deepens. As men mature the body reaches full muscular development, then starts to decline. The production of male hormones and sperm reduces. The skin and muscles become softer, fat may increase, the prostate enlarges, production of male hormones and sperm reduces, and hair loss occurs.

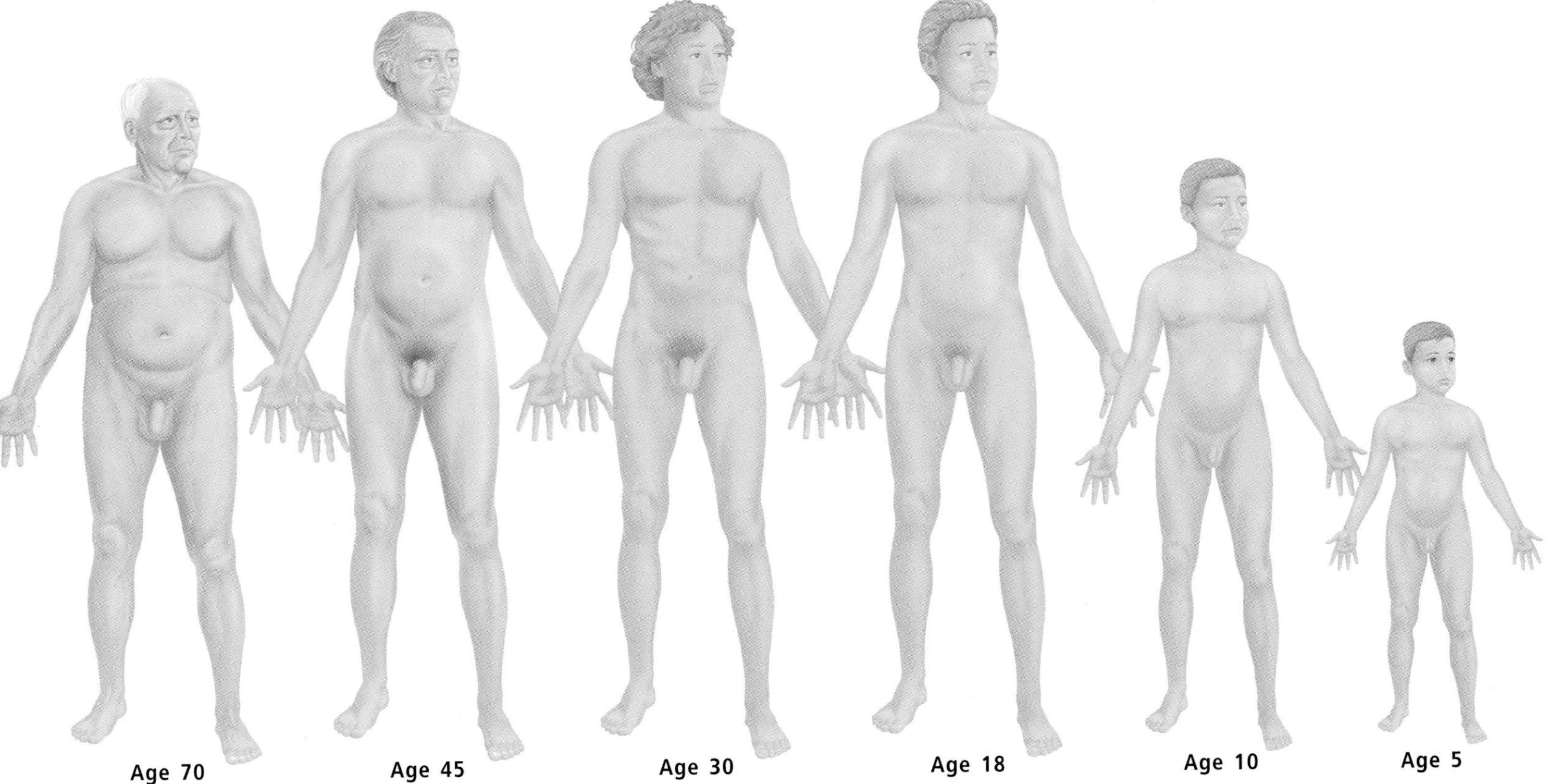

A

Hip and wrist fractures are common. Wear and tear of joints leads to osteoarthritis.

All body systems deteriorate. For many, by 50 years of age, hearing is reduced and the lens of the eye loses some elasticity, making small print difficult to read. For some the lens may also become clouded by a cataract. The immune response is reduced because of the decline in the activation of both T and B lymphocytes, which fight infection. Thus people over the age of 60 should be immunized against common infections such as influenza in winter. The arteries become thicker and less elastic, predisposing the elderly to hypertension. The heart is less efficient as a pump. The lungs begin to lose their elasticity, making breathing more laborious and oxygen exchange less efficient. Digestion becomes slightly less efficient because of reduced secretion of digestive enzymes. Absorption of some important molecules extracted from food, such as calcium and vitamin B_{12}, is impaired. Vitamin B_{12} deficiency leads to impaired nerve function and anemia.

The kidneys shrink and their filtering function declines, resulting in the build-up of waste products like urea. The bladder which collects urine from the kidney and contracts to empty its contents now does not expand and contract as effectively, resulting in more frequent trips to the bathroom. In males, the prostate, which is located under the neck of the bladder and encircles the urethra (the tube conducting the urine out from the bladder), frequently becomes enlarged, constricting the urethra.

The reproductive system undergoes dramatic changes. At the climacteric (the male equivalent of menopause), the production of testosterone and sperm in the testes are reduced. The sperm count may be low, but is still adequate in some instances to produce offspring until a very old age. Semen volume is also reduced. Erection is more difficult to obtain and to maintain, even in the absence of problems in the blood vessels of the penis. Research is progressing in this field.

In females, the production of eggs and sex hormones by the ovaries is reduced. From the mid-thirties, the risk of chromosomal abnormalities such as Down syndrome increases sharply because the eggs may be more genetically defective. The complex balance of sex hormones begins to be disturbed by the fourth or fifth decade, resulting in irregular menstruation, hot flashes and mood swings. Without the stimulation of the hormone estrogen, the breasts lose their firmness, distribution of fat in the body changes, and pubic hair becomes sparse. The external genitalia become wrinkled because of loss of pubic fat, the vagina is less elastic and its lining thins, making sexual intercourse potentially painful. Loss of the protective effects of estrogen results in a higher risk of cardiovascular diseases. Hormone replacement relieves many of these changes but, according to some authorities, may carry a small potential risk of breast cancer. Isoflavones extracted from plants such as soy beans may be a safer alternative.

As the nervous system ages, cognitive function begins to decline. The brain shows increasing atrophy with age, and loss of nerve cells is more localized in some special areas. Attention is not affected by age, but loss of neurons (nerve cells) in the hippocampus results in impaired memory function. Older people take longer to learn new information or a new skill, but can retain the knowledge for as long as younger people. The ability to form new concepts also declines with age, as does performance in intelligence tests, although this only drops significantly after 70 years of age. Dementia is also a problem in the ageing population; Alzheimer's disease and incidents causing lack of oxygen in the brain.

The cellular basis of ageing

Scientists have been studying bacteria and single human cells to find out the cellular basis of ageing, with a strong focus on proteins and genes. Proteins are important structural and functional molecules in cells. The synthesis of each protein is controlled by a gene, a segment of a DNA molecule of a chromosome. Each DNA molecule is a string of genes. Some genes control protein synthesis, some turn other genes on or off. Scientists are making progress in mapping all the genes of the human chromosomes and have formulated a number of hypotheses to explain how and why cells age.

We can think of chromosomes as the hard disk which contains all the programs that can run on a computer. A free demonstration program may have a code built into it so that it will be deactivated at the end of the 30-day trial period. The "programmed cell death" hypothesis holds that some genes will initiate cell death at the end of the cell's life span. These "suicide" genes have been isolated. Other genes have been discovered that can rescue the cell from the action of the death genes. Scientists have succeeded in using these rescue genes to extend the life span of cells.

Another hypothesis can also be explained using our computer analogy. Every now and then the computer crashes, either because of an error in reading the file from disk, or some instability of the power line. The computer can automatically search the corrupted file and repair the errors. DNA molecules can be damaged either by spontaneous changes (mutation), by environmental agents such as radiation, by accumulation of toxic waste products in the cell, or simply by errors introduced during copying of the genes. DNA can repair these damages, but when the repair is imperfect, abnormalities in DNA will accumulate and may contribute to the ageing process or lead to cancer. This is the "error accumulation" hypothesis.

One group of potentially damaging chemicals produced by cells is "free radicals". Normally oxygen molecules take up those free electrons which are products of chemical reaction in the cells, then combine with hydrogen atoms to form harmless water. When this process fails, excess electrons will join up with other molecules, forming free radicals, which can damage DNA molecules. (Fruit flies do not have enzymes which can destroy free radicals. When the genes for these enzymes were inserted into embryonic fruit flies, they could produce these enzymes and their life span was increased.) In addition to enzymes, cells also fight free radical damage with antioxidants.

Current research in cell and molecular biology has unlocked some of the secrets of ageing and even prolonged the life of some simple organisms. However, studies suggest that regular activity, a healthy diet and mental stimulation may help abate the deterioration of ageing.

SEE ALSO: *Adolescence, Childhood, DNA, Geriatric medicine, Menopause, Puberty, Reproductive systems*

AGORAPHOBIA

Agoraphobia (the word is derived from the Greek word for marketplace, *agora*) is a fear of being in open spaces or in crowded places. It can cause people to stay only within familiar surroundings, avoiding public places and gradually restricting themselves to areas closer to home. Symptoms may continue to increase in severity to the point where sufferers are unable to go out without experiencing symptoms of panic.

Associated with agoraphobia are feelings of helplessness, depression, fear of being alone, dependence on others, fear of losing control in public, and depersonalization or loss of identity. Women are more usually afflicted than men, and the disorder often has its root cause in a previous incident or a panic attack suffered in a public place. Agoraphobia may then be a way of attempting to prevent the embarrassment of that incident from recurring. When severely affected, people may be housebound for years and be quite cut off from normal relationships.

Specialist treatment is essential and is aimed at enabling the person to function normally. Prescribed medications can overcome anxiety and depression, but there is a risk that the person can become dependent on these if a cure is not achieved.

SEE ALSO *Anxiety, Panic attacks, Phobias*

AGRANULOCYTOSIS

This rare condition, occurring in one person in every 100,000, is a disorder of neutrophil production in the body's bone marrow. Neutrophils are a type of white blood cell whose purpose is to fight bacteria and other invading organisms. They are formed in the bone marrow and released into the blood to fight infection.

In agranulocytosis, production of neutrophils in the bone marrow slows or stops altogether, usually as a side effect of certain drugs. If the production of red blood cells and platelets is also affected, this is called pancytopenia. If there are not enough neutrophils circulating through the blood, the body becomes susceptible to opportunistic infections. These may range from mild illnesses, such as a sore throat or mouth ulcer, to serious and life-threatening illnesses, such as pneumonia.

The diagnosis is made by the primary care physician (general practitioner) after a physical examination and a blood test which shows a lower than normal neutrophil count. A specialist physician or hematologist will then do a bone marrow biopsy in order to confirm the diagnosis. It is generally recommended that the patient discontinue the drug that is causing the problems. The bone marrow should then recover naturally. Any infection should be treated with antibiotics. In rare cases where the bone marrow does not respond, drugs that stimulate the bone marrow may be given. The disease may recur in a mild form, but most people have no further problems.

SEE ALSO *Bone marrow biopsy, Opportunistic infections, White blood cells*

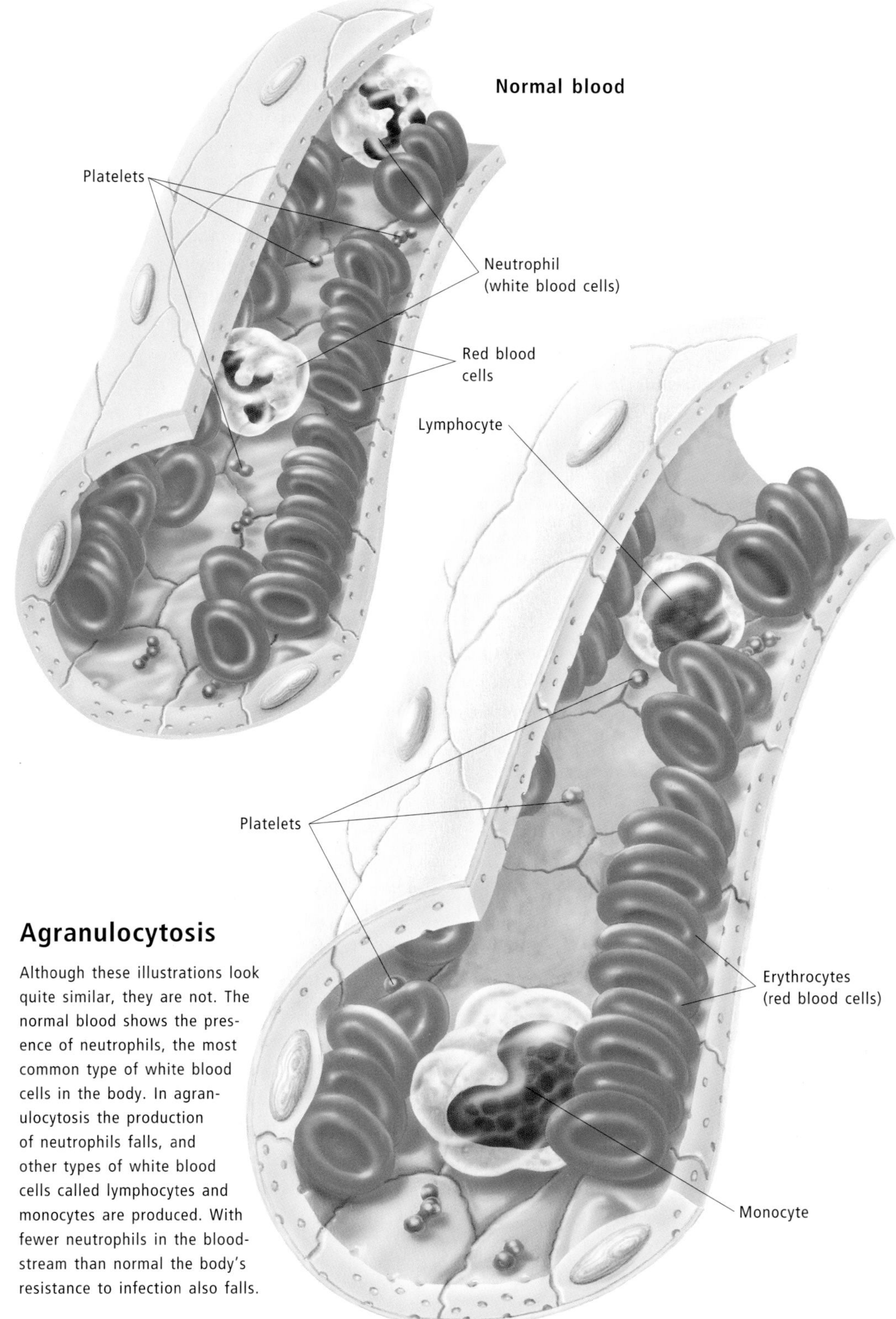

Agranulocytosis

Although these illustrations look quite similar, they are not. The normal blood shows the presence of neutrophils, the most common type of white blood cells in the body. In agranulocytosis the production of neutrophils falls, and other types of white blood cells called lymphocytes and monocytes are produced. With fewer neutrophils in the bloodstream than normal the body's resistance to infection also falls.

A

AIDS

AIDS stands for acquired immune deficiency syndrome. It is caused by the HIV (human immmunodeficiency virus). AIDS is the final and most serious stage of HIV disease. The illness is characterized by severe immune deficiency, leaving the body vulnerable to life-threatening illnesses.

The HIV attacks and destroys certain types of white blood cells called T4 lymphocytes (also known as CD4 or T helper lymphocytes), which are responsible for patrolling the body and destroying foreign invaders. Because the HIV destroys these cells, they are no longer available to fight common bacteria, yeast and viruses which normally would not cause disease. The body's lowered defenses, then, leave it susceptible to these invaders which cause opportunistic infections.

It is these infections, not the HIV, that eventually cause the death of AIDS sufferers. First recognized in the USA in 1981, the disease has grown rapidly to become one of the world's major health problems. The World Health Organization estimates there are more than 20 million cases of HIV infection worldwide and most of these are in the developing countries of Africa and Asia.

Transmission

The HIV virus is transmitted, among other ways, through sexual contact (including oral, vaginal and anal sex). It is also transmitted via blood through transfusions, needle sharing or accidental needlestick injury. It is possible for a pregnant woman to pass the virus to the fetus, and a nursing mother can infect her baby through her milk. The infection is not spread by touching and hugging, or by contact with inanimate objects.

High-risk behaviors include promiscuity, especially when involving anal intercourse, and intravenous drug use with shared needles. Others at high-risk include infants born to mothers with HIV, the sexual partners of those exhibiting high-risk behavior and people who received blood transfusions before screening for the virus was introduced (around the mid-1980s). Contrary to some popular perceptions, AIDS is not a "homosexual disease"; in Africa and other developing regions, in particular, transmission is predominantly through heterosexual contact.

Development of the illness

The initial illness resembles a mild flu, with fever, headache, fatigue, loss of appetite, swollen lymph nodes and skin rashes. The symptoms appear within two to four weeks of exposure. The illness can then lie dormant for as long as ten years. During this time there may be no symptoms at all.

Then the sufferer may develop low-grade fever, chronic tiredness and weakness, appetite loss and loss of weight, with swollen lymph nodes especially in the neck, jaw, groin and armpits. Diarrhea, malnutrition and minor infections such as oral thrush are common. This stage is sometimes known as AIDS-related complex, or ARC.

In a small percentage (between 1 and 10 percent) of those infected with HIV, the illness doesn't progress any further. But in the great majority, immunity levels eventually fall off to below critical levels and infections become more serious and life threatening. These include *Pneumocystis carinii* pneumonia, toxoplasmosis, tuberculosis and a range of viruses, including cytomegalovirus, herpes simplex virus, varicella zoster and Epstein-Barr viruses. This stage represents full-blown AIDS; people with full-blown AIDS may die within two years if not treated.

AIDS-related cancers

Lymphocytes play an important role in the body's fight against cancer. When T4 cell function is damaged, cancers may develop. Kaposi's sarcoma is the most common form of AIDS-related cancer. Lymphomas (tumors of the lymphatic system) are also frequent.

Diagnosis

HIV infection is confirmed by an HIV antibody test, which looks for HIV antibodies in the blood formed in response to infection with HIV. If the test is positive, a follow-up is always performed to confirm it. The test becomes positive within three months of exposure. Someone who has been recently exposed, yet has a negative result, should be tested again three months after exposure. Progress of the disease can be monitored by regularly measuring the T4 cell count in the blood. The lower the count, the further the disease has progressed. Serious infections are likely to develop at counts of below 200 cells per cubic millimeter.

Herpes simplex virus

Genital herpes, mouth ulcers and cold sores are caused by the herpes simplex virus which is common in AIDS patients with severely compromised immunity.

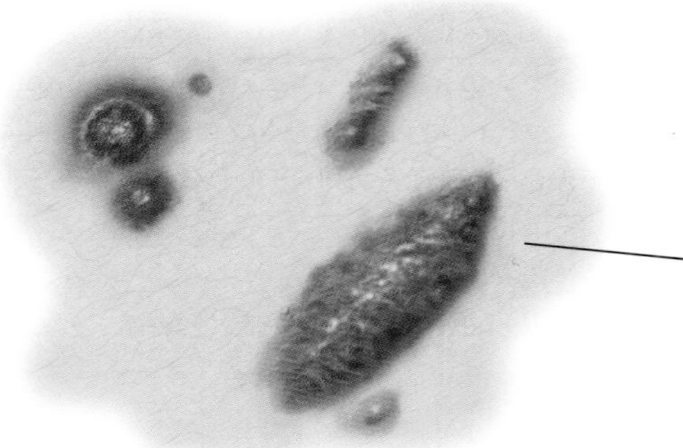

Kaposi's sarcoma

The most frequently occurring cancer in AIDS sufferers, Kaposi's sarcoma produces raised, purple-brown skin lesions. In late stage of the disease it may also affect the lungs and other internal organs.

Lymphoma

Low T4 cell counts in AIDS result in increased cancer incidence. Non-Hodgkins lymphoma, which spreads through the lymphatic system, may develop.

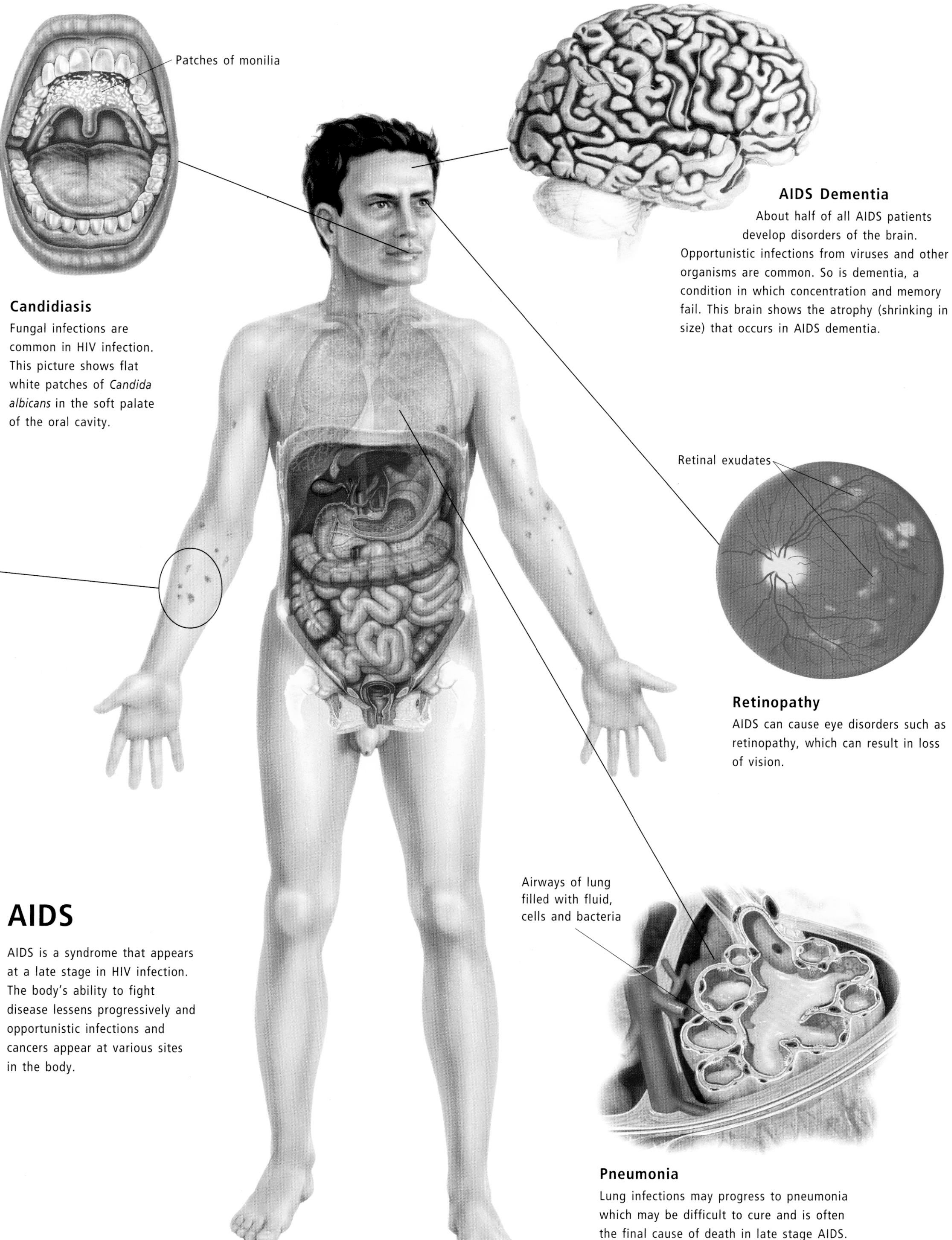

AIDS Dementia
About half of all AIDS patients develop disorders of the brain. Opportunistic infections from viruses and other organisms are common. So is dementia, a condition in which concentration and memory fail. This brain shows the atrophy (shrinking in size) that occurs in AIDS dementia.

Candidiasis
Fungal infections are common in HIV infection. This picture shows flat white patches of *Candida albicans* in the soft palate of the oral cavity.

Retinopathy
AIDS can cause eye disorders such as retinopathy, which can result in loss of vision.

AIDS

AIDS is a syndrome that appears at a late stage in HIV infection. The body's ability to fight disease lessens progressively and opportunistic infections and cancers appear at various sites in the body.

Pneumonia
Lung infections may progress to pneumonia which may be difficult to cure and is often the final cause of death in late stage AIDS.

Treatment

AIDS and HIV are treated by a primary care physician (general practitioner) or by a specialist physician in an outpatient department or hospital clinic. In the later stages of the illness, when serious infections develop, the condition must be treated in hospital.

No cure exists for HIV infection itself. Until recently, the only treatment for HIV was to treat the opportunistic infections with antibiotic and antiviral drugs. However, over the past few years, antiviral drugs such as AZT and acyclovir have been developed to try and slow down the body's loss of immune function and susceptibility to disease.

These drugs suppress the HIV virus replicating itself in the body and so effectively arrest the progress of the disease. They are often used in combination. They are expensive, and they may not be well tolerated by the sufferer. Nevertheless, when used with conventional treatment of opportunistic infections, it is thought they can prolong life indefinitely. Prior to combination antiviral therapy, the mortality from full-blown AIDS was generally thought to be 100 percent.

Still, prevention remains the major tool in combating HIV and AIDS. Practising safe sex and using condoms (which have the added advantage of protecting against other sexually transmitted diseases such as chlamydia and gonorrhea) are the most effective means of stopping HIV transmission. Intravenous drug users should never share needles. Before entering into a sexual relationship with anyone who is at risk of having or contracting HIV, it is wise to find out about their HIV status first.

Thanks to AIDS awareness and safe sex campaigns, rates of new HIV infections are falling, at least in the developed world. Unfortunately, however, because of the cost of combination therapy drugs, widespread use of them in developing countries is impractical. Management of AIDS and HIV in these countries depends on public awareness campaigns and on the hope of finding a cheap and effective method of immunization.

SEE ALSO *HIV, Kaposi's sarcoma, Opportunistic infections, T cells*

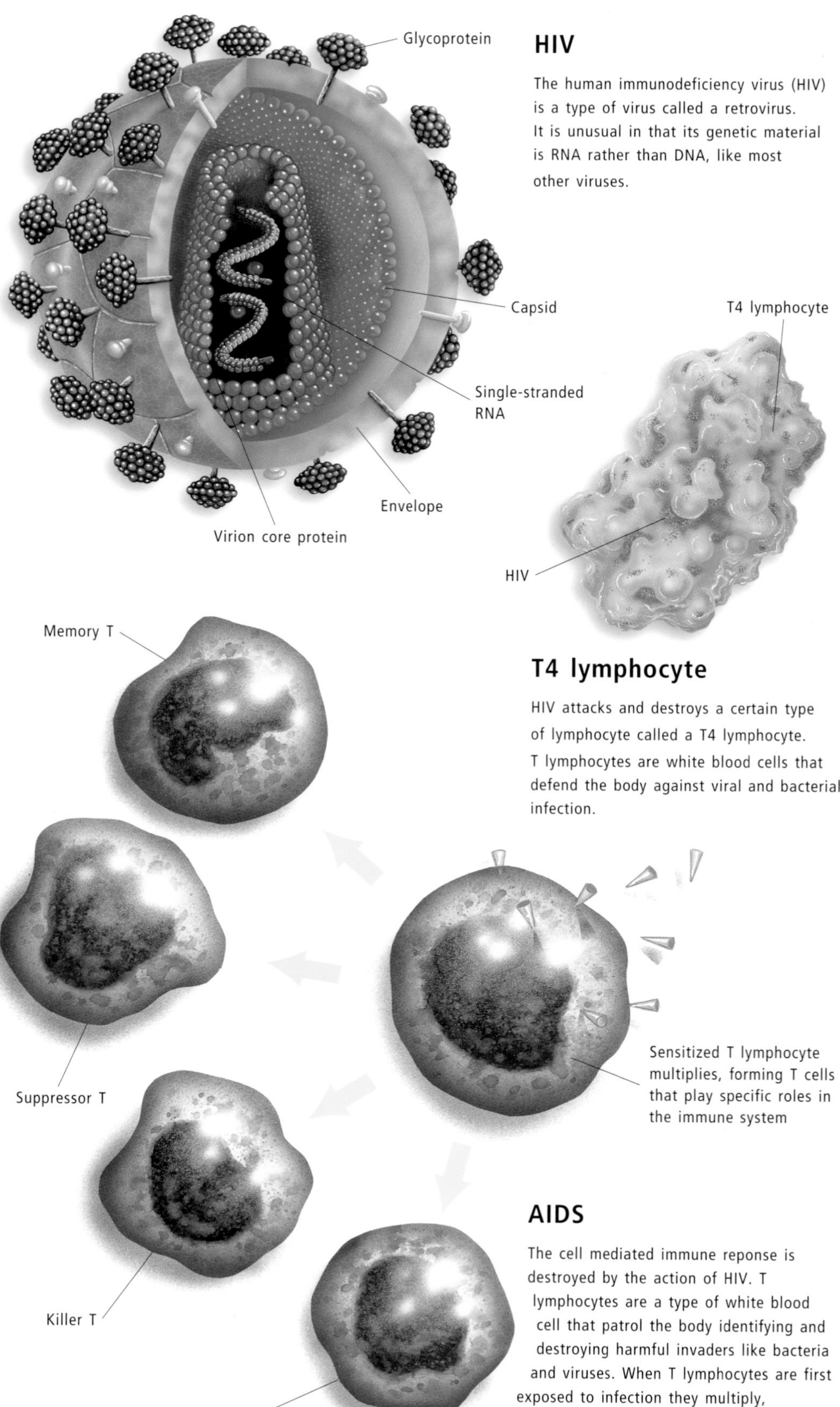

HIV

The human immunodeficiency virus (HIV) is a type of virus called a retrovirus. It is unusual in that its genetic material is RNA rather than DNA, like most other viruses.

T4 lymphocyte

HIV attacks and destroys a certain type of lymphocyte called a T4 lymphocyte. T lymphocytes are white blood cells that defend the body against viral and bacterial infection.

AIDS

The cell mediated immune reponse is destroyed by the action of HIV. T lymphocytes are a type of white blood cell that patrol the body identifying and destroying harmful invaders like bacteria and viruses. When T lymphocytes are first exposed to infection they multiply, producing four types of lymphocytes: memory cells, suppressor cells, killer cells and helper (T4) cells, each of which play an important role in the body's immune system. Helper (T4) lymphocytes direct our immune response by identifying foreign invaders and calling other lymphocytes to attack. These helper Ts are destroyed by HIV leaving the body with lowered immunity and vulnerable to opportunistic infections such as pneumonia.

ALCOHOLISM

Alcoholism is a progressive disease marked by a physical, mental and emotional dependence on alcohol. It affects all ethnic, socioeconomic and age groups. In recent years, the number of female and teenage alcoholics has markedly increased.

Alcohol and its effects

Alcohol (ethanol, ethyl alcohol) is present in beers, liqueurs, spirits and wines, and also in many common medications. Because alcohol is a potentially dangerous yet widely available drug, its use is restricted by law in certain situations. Health authorities generally recognize that men can safely consume up to two standard drinks per day, and women one standard drink (the specified quantity is lower for women because of their lower body weight). During pregnancy, abstinence is the wisest course. Abnormalities in the developing fetus have been linked with regular consumption of only two standard drinks per day.

Alcohol acts as a sedative on the brain. A small amount will slightly reduce a person's inhibitions, helping them to overcome shyness and relax in social situations.

Moderate social drinking is generally accepted in Western societies. Most adults can maintain their alcohol intake at an acceptable level. Greater amounts can suppress internal controls and lead to socially unacceptable behavior. Continued drinking may affect muscle control. People who have consumed a large amount of alcohol may slur their words, stagger, lose concentration and eventually lapse into unconsciousness. All heavy or persistent drinkers place their general health at risk. A single bout of alcohol abuse can severely damage health and even cause death. Inexperienced drinkers are very much at risk because they have no tolerance to alcohol and do not know their own limits or what is safe.

Who is an alcoholic?

Alcoholism may, like diabetes or asthma, have genetic causes. Social environment and peer group influences are also triggers in susceptible people. Alcoholics do not conform to just one type; rather, they seem to fall into several categories. Professor E. Jellinek, an American specialist, grouped alcoholics into five different types, according to their various drinking patterns. Some alcoholics may fit more than one category.

Type I alcoholics are depressed, anxious people who drink to elevate their mood and to feel "normal".

The Type II alcoholics do not suffer from the mental obsession with alcohol to the extent that the other types do, but their excessive drinking causes serious physical damage such as pancreatitis or cirrhosis.

Often known as "periodic", "bender" or "binge" drinkers, Type III alcoholics can go for days or weeks without drinking, but once they start they lose the power of choice over when to stop. As the disease progresses, the benders become closer and more severe.

Type IV alcoholics don't often get falling-down drunk, but are usually never sober either. They will "top up" with small portions of alcohol through the day and night.

Type V is similar to Type III, but the binges are more intense, yet further apart.

Behavior problems

Alcoholics can suffer from a wide range of physical and behavioral symptoms. They experience a physical craving for alcohol, usually combined with a mental obsession. When alcohol is not taken, withdrawal symptoms can include nausea, sweating, shakiness, distress and fits. Alcoholics often develop an increasing tolerance for drink, so that greater amounts are needed to get the desired effect. Conversely, as the disease progresses, tolerance may decrease, and one or two drinks will be enough to make the person drunk or sick.

Alcoholics may behave totally out of character when under the influence, and are described as having "Dr Jekyll and Mr Hyde" personalities. They become deceitful and secretive about their drinking, as well as feeling guilt, shame and remorse. Blackouts may occur—these are lapses of consciousness that can last for minutes or up to many hours, and afterwards the person cannot remember what happened during that period.

Needless to say, alcoholics have unmanageable and chaotic lives. They may become unable to fulfil work or school commitments, often losing jobs and failing courses. They may cause injury to themselves and others, becoming involved in dangerous situations such as driving or operating machinery when drunk, and continuing to drink despite a worsening effect on health, finances, and sexual and personal relationships. Alcohol is a common factor in traffic accidents and crimes of violence.

Health problems

Alcoholism can cause many serious disorders of the body and mind. Poor nutrition is commonly associated with long-term alcohol abuse, as consumption of alcohol reduces appetite. The alcohol replaces food but does not supply the protein, minerals and vitamins the body needs.

Alcohol can also cause pancreatitis, in which the pancreas becomes inflamed and results in abdominal pain. Chronic pancreatitis is due to the small ducts in the pancreas narrowing and becoming clogged. It may damage the cells which make insulin and so lead to diabetes. Acute pancreatitis follows when ducts are completely blocked, and this can result from an alcoholic binge. It causes severe persistent pain just below the breastbone, with accelerated heartbeat and shallow breathing. Blood pressure may fall and bring on shock. This is a life-threatening condition requiring emergency treatment.

Liver damage is common in the later stages of alcoholism. This can be an accumulation of fat, producing no symptoms or only mild tenderness and enlargement. Inflammation, also called alcoholic hepatitis, can produce greater enlargement, pain, fever and jaundice. Cirrhosis scars liver tissue, making it hard and inefficient. This damage is permanent, but can be stopped as long as drinking is halted.

Polyneuropathy (also known as peripheral neuritis or polyneuritis) is an inflammation of the peripheral nerves, producing muscle weakness and numbness, particularly in the hands and feet. Physical therapy and vitamin B_1 (thiamine) can relieve symptoms.

Dementia is an organic brain disease marked by loss of memory and reasoning power and can be a consequence of alcoholism. The symptoms are confusion, disorientation and apathy.

Delirium tremens causes confusion and mental disorder; it is induced by the withdrawal of alcohol after a period of severe intoxication. Symptoms include trembling, hallucinations, delusions, fever, dilated pupils, sweating and very rapid heartbeat.

Wernicke-Korsakoff syndrome is a brain disease caused by a deficiency in vitamin B_1 (thiamine); this can occur because alcoholics replace food with alcohol and become malnourished. Symptoms include confusion, memory loss, and lack of muscular coordination, which produces twitching and random movements, particularly of the eyes, and a staggering walk. Brain damage may be permanent with this disease.

Treatment

The first step in treatment is acceptance by the drinker that there is a problem, as alcoholism has been termed "the disease of denial". Medical treatment can include admission to a hospital detoxification unit. The alcoholic may be given drugs such as tranquilizers to aid withdrawal from alcohol, naltrexone to help with physical cravings, or disulfiram, which causes nausea when alcohol is taken. Vitamin B injections are also beneficial.

Once the alcoholic has physically detoxified, the next challenge is to learn how to live without drinking. Unfortunately, the percentage of alcoholics who stop drinking and then remain sober is very low. Some clinics offer controlled drinking programs, which aim to teach the alcoholic how to drink socially through behavior modification. However, many experts believe that no alcoholic is ever able to drink again with safety, and recommend total abstinence.

Alcoholics have a much greater chance of long-term recovery if they go to a treatment or rehabilitation center. These centers offer residential programs, usually lasting three to eight weeks, and provide psychological counseling, education, group therapy and nutritional guidance. Recovery is likely to be more successful if treatment is followed up by further counseling (particularly if there is an underlying depressive illness) and regular attendance at Alcoholics Anonymous (AA) meetings. AA is a self-help program founded in 1935 by two alcoholics: Bill Wilson, a New York stockbroker, and Dr Bob Smith from Akron, Ohio. They believed that no one can help or understand an alcoholic as well as a fellow sufferer can. AA now has a membership of hundreds of thousands of men and women around the world. In AA meetings, people share their stories and support each other in leading healthy and productive lives.

SEE ALSO *Cirrhosis of the liver, Delirium tremens, Detoxification, Drug dependence, Fetal alcohol syndrome, Pancreatitis, Wernicke-Korsakoff syndrome*

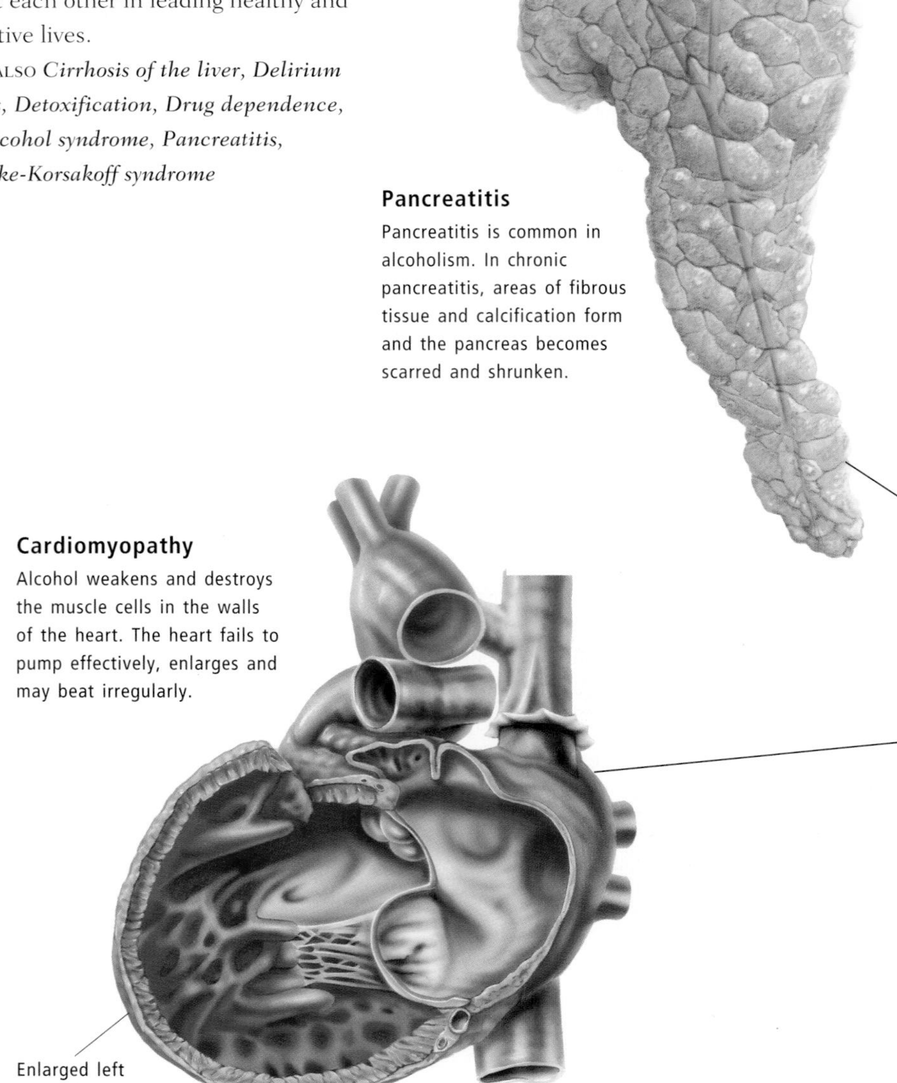

Pancreatitis
Pancreatitis is common in alcoholism. In chronic pancreatitis, areas of fibrous tissue and calcification form and the pancreas becomes scarred and shrunken.

Cardiomyopathy
Alcohol weakens and destroys the muscle cells in the walls of the heart. The heart fails to pump effectively, enlarges and may beat irregularly.

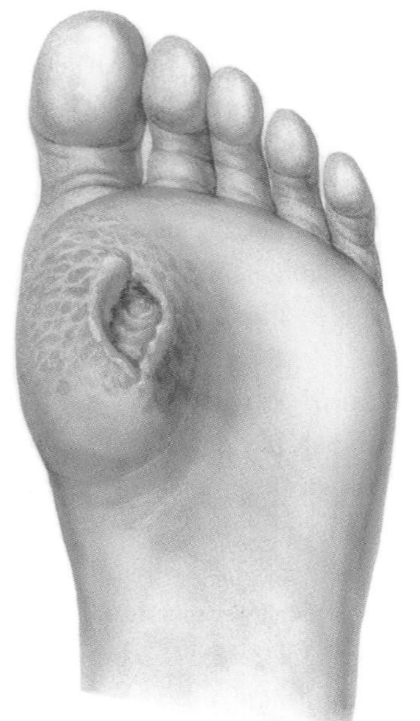

Neuritis
Alcoholism can cause damage to peripheral nerves (peripheral neuritis) which can lead to foot ulcers.

A

Esophageal disorders

Chronic alcoholism can cause disorders such as esophageal reflux, which produces irritation and heartburn. Cancer is a possible outcome of long-term damage.

Wernicke's encephalopathy

This is a brain syndrome suffered by chronic alcoholics. It is caused by a deficiency of thiamine (Vitamin B_1) in the diet. The lack of this vitamin causes damage to certain areas in the brain stem, resulting in confusion, drowsiness, an unsteady gait, and paralysis of the eye muscles.

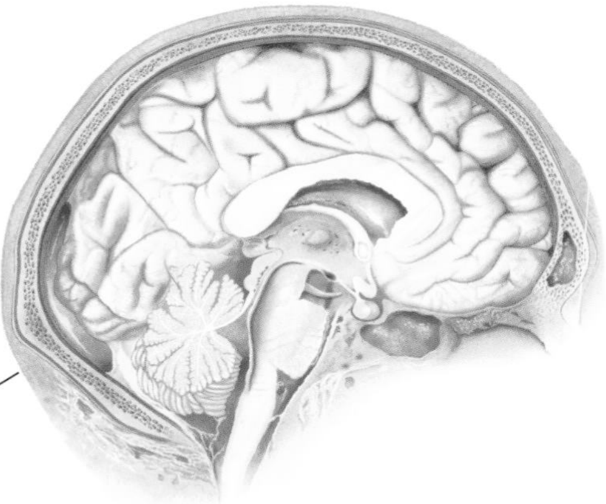

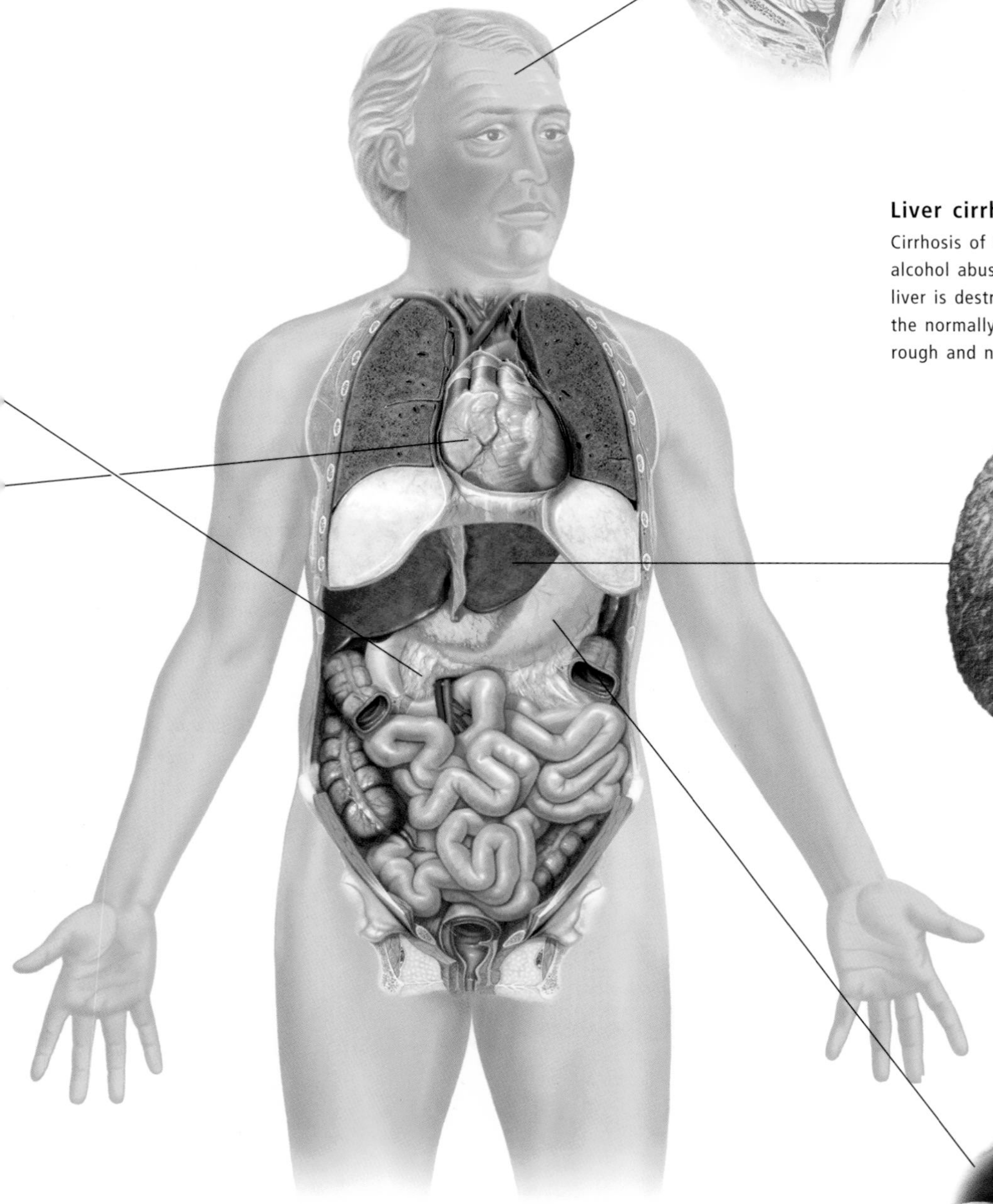

Liver cirrhosis

Cirrhosis of the liver occurs in longstanding alcohol abuse. The lobular architecture of the liver is destroyed by bands of fibrous tissue and the normally smooth surface of the liver appears rough and nodular.

Gastric ulcer

A gastric ulcer is a hole in the lining (mucosa) of the stomach. It is more common in alcoholics than in the general population.

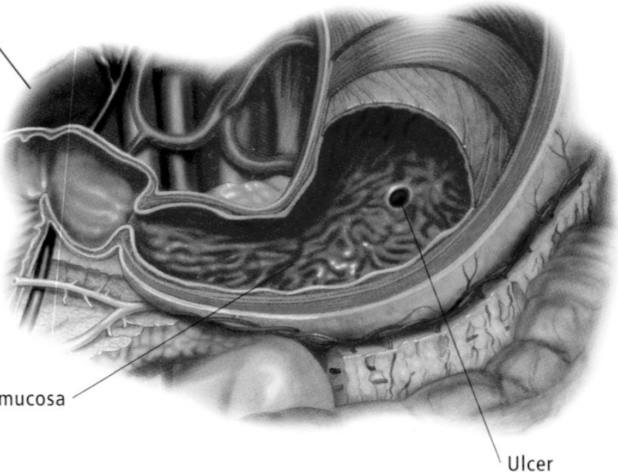

Normal mucosa

Ulcer

Alcoholism

In small or moderate amounts, alcohol does no permanent damage to the body. But if used in excessive amounts over a long period of time it can damage many organs. Chronic alcoholics suffer disorders of the heart, the muscles, the alimentary tract, brain, spinal cord and nerves.

A

ALEXANDER TECHNIQUE

The founder of the Alexander technique was the Australian-born actor Frederick Matthias Alexander (1869–1955). He developed his technique as a consequence of regularly losing his voice during his recitals. Finding no relief from medicine, Alexander began to study himself declaiming in front of carefully positioned mirrors. He observed that he was in the habit of pulling his head back and tightening the area around the larynx. Convinced that this was the cause of his problem, he painstakingly retrained himself to lift his head vertically and free his neck. Not only did he find that his voice problems disappeared, he also felt healthier and more self-confident.

This experiment inspired Alexander to make a lifelong study of posture and to devise his technique to retrain the muscle system, focusing particularly on the relationship between the head, neck and torso.

In 1904 Alexander traveled to England to teach his technique, and then to the USA, attracting a following among actors, writers and educators. His most famous book *The Use of Self* was published in 1932. Today the Alexander technique is claimed as having health benefits, particularly for those suffering from back pain, repetitive strain injury, breathing problems, high blood pressure and stress-related illnesses.

Learning the technique

Alexander believed that most adults needed to relearn the correct way to stand, sit, walk, lift objects and breathe. His technique is based upon posture, corrective exercise and balance, all combining to realign the body so that it can function more efficiently. Alexander's dictum is "let the neck be free to let the head be forward and up, and the back widen and lengthen". This fundamental realignment of the head and upper torso is known as the "primary control". One way to regain primary control is to visualize a cord coming out of the top of your head pulling you gently towards the sky, counterbalancing the effects of gravity.

The Alexander technique teaches you to observe and "unlearn" your habitual responses through focusing awareness on the body. The technique is learnt from a teacher in individual sessions or classes. The first step is for the teacher to observe how you habitually stand, sit, walk, move and breathe. From that point the teacher helps you to gain an experience of what it will mean to make these movements in a more natural way. You are asked to focus on the means of movement rather than on the end result. Using touch, the teacher guides your body into its correct balance as you sit, stand and lie down.

The experience of the benefits of a more coordinated body in a lesson becomes the incentive to develop a greater awareness of your body and its means in daily life. Practice and self-discipline are required to prevent the body falling back into its bad habits. The technique takes some time to establish itself in a person's mind and body and a series of lessons is required to support the change.

ALIMENTARY CANAL

The alimentary canal (otherwise known as the digestive tract) is a long muscular tube (about 30 feet, or 9 meters) extending from the mouth to the anus. It is made up of layers of circular muscles which contract and move the food in waves along the tract; this process is known as peristalsis. Its function

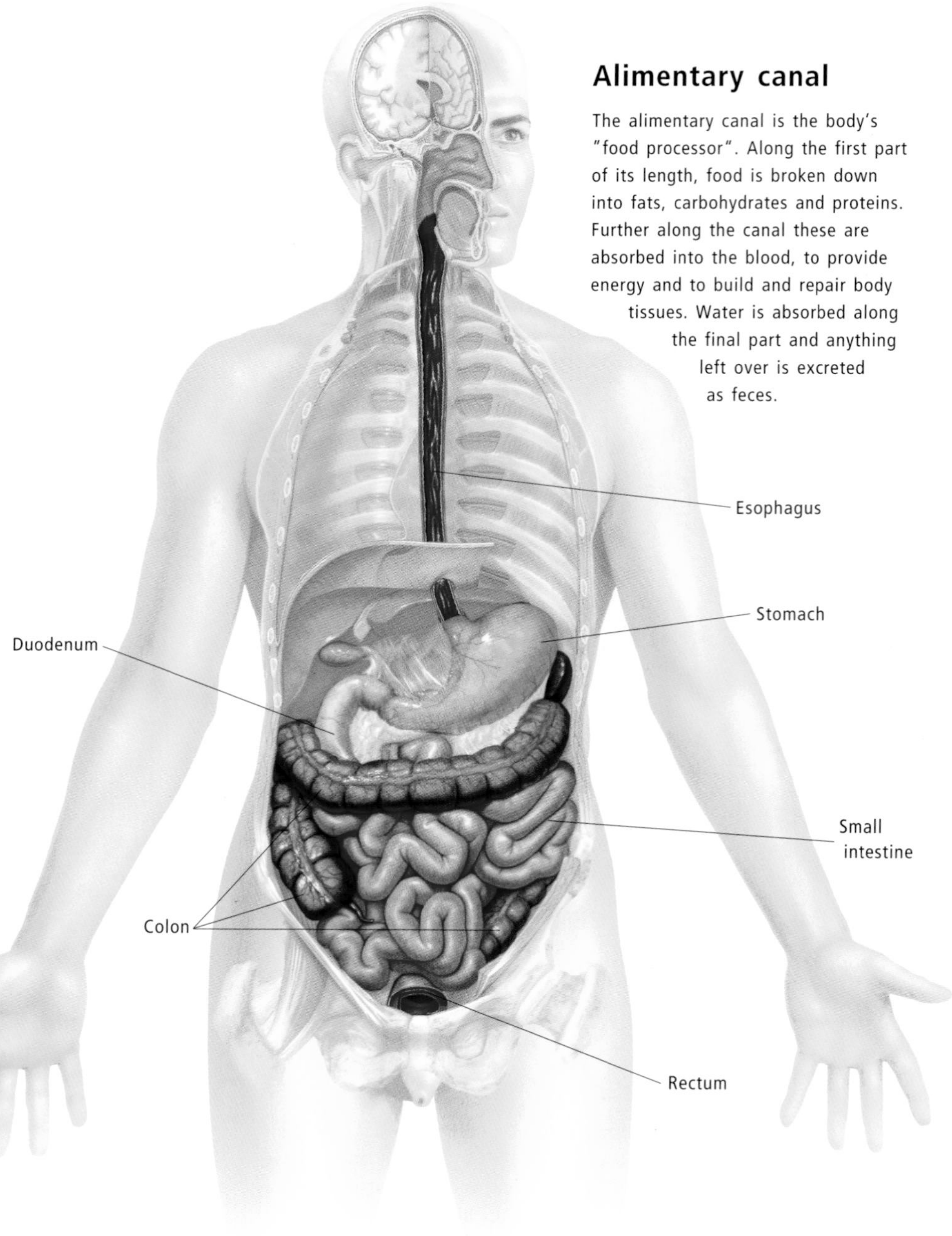

Alimentary canal

The alimentary canal is the body's "food processor". Along the first part of its length, food is broken down into fats, carbohydrates and proteins. Further along the canal these are absorbed into the blood, to provide energy and to build and repair body tissues. Water is absorbed along the final part and anything left over is excreted as feces.

is to break food down into smaller and smaller particles, absorb the nutrients along the way and expel the rest as waste. Different parts of the tract have different functions.

Food enters through the mouth, or oral cavity. Jaws, tongue and teeth work to mash and mix the food into smaller pieces. Saliva, secreted from the salivary glands placed around the oral cavity, moistens the food to make it easier to transport, and contains enzymes (digestive proteins) that begin the process of breaking down the food.

From the mouth, food passes down a muscular tube called the esophagus into an acid-rich pouch—the stomach. In the stomach, the food is gradually broken down by pepsin, an enzyme, into a semi-liquid stew of food, acid and digestive juices.

Next, the mixture passes into the duodenum, which is the first part of the small intestine. More digestive juices are added to the mix: bile from the liver and digestive enzymes from the pancreas. As the food particles move further down the intestine they are reduced to smaller and smaller constituents—carbohydrates, proteins, fats, vitamins and water. These are absorbed through the lining of the small intestine and pass into the bloodstream. They are stored in the liver to be used in the body's metabolic processes.

Two other organs are essential in this process. One is the liver, which, as well as storing nutrients, also produces bile. Via the gallbladder and bile ducts, bile travels into the small intestine where it aids in the absorption of fats and fat-soluble vitamins. Then there is the pancreas, which makes the amylase, protease and lipase enzymes needed to break down carbohydrates, proteins and fats in the small intestine.

Once food has reached the end of the small intestine, what's left is essentially waste material. The waste enters the large intestine, or colon—a tube that is wider but shorter than the small intestine. As it travels along the colon, water is reabsorbed, the waste hardens and becomes feces. The fecal material is then stored in the last part of the large intestine, the rectum, before being expelled through the anus.

As the digestive tract is located within the abdominal cavity, it can be difficult for medical professionals to visualize the tract. Gastroenterologists use methods such as ultrasound, x-ray and endoscopy to "see" various organs. Endoscopy is an examination using a flexible fiberoptic rod which is inserted through the mouth or via the anus. The endoscope has a lens and camera attached, allowing a detailed view of the interior of the alimentary canal. A separate attachment can be used to take a biopsy if necessary.

SEE ALSO *Colon, Digestive system, Endoscopy, Intestines, Liver, Pancreas, Peristalsis, Stomach*

ALKALOSIS

Alkalosis is an excess of alkali in the blood and other body fluids. Normally, the body's regulatory mechanisms keep the pH of the blood slightly alkaline, within the range of 7.35 and 7.45 (pH is a measure of acidity). But certain conditions cause it to rise above this level, causing alkalosis.

There are two types of alkalosis. Metabolic alkalosis occurs when there is a loss of acid from the body fluids. This can happen during kidney failure, vomiting and intestinal obstruction, or due to the effect of some drugs. Metabolic alkalosis can also occur if there is excess absorption of alkali, as occurs sometimes after a blood transfusion or excess ingestion of bicarbonate in drug preparations.

The other type is respiratory alkalosis. This is caused by hyperventilation (rapid breathing) that results in excessive loss of carbon dioxide. Respiratory alkalosis can also be caused by head injury, lung disease, liver failure and salicylate (aspirin) poisoning.

Symptoms of alkalosis include tingling skin, muscle weakness and muscle cramps. The condition is confirmed by a blood test which shows changes in blood pH, bicarbonate and oxygen and carbon dioxide levels.

Alkalosis is a serious condition. Hospitalization is necessary to correct the underlying cause and to facilitate replacement of lost body fluids. In some cases, intravenous administration of acidic compounds will be needed to restore the pH to normal levels.

SEE ALSO *Acidosis, Metabolism*

ALLERGIES

An allergy is a physical reaction to certain substances. In the allergic person, the immune system mistakenly identifies a substance as being harmful and mounts a defense against it. This unnecessary defense reaction is often excessively vigorous, and the antibodies manufactured to fight the substance have irritating or harmful effects, which constitute an allergic reaction.

Allergies tend to run in families but are also affected by environmental factors. They develop through exposure to substances, and a process called sensitization that can occur on first contact, or over a brief period or even through repeated exposure over several years. During this period, the immune system is activated to react against what is usually a relatively harmless substance.

Allergies can show up at any age but they often appear first in childhood, particularly contact allergies that are a reaction on first contact with the allergenic substance.

Asthma and hay fever, allergic rhinitis and sinusitis, cows' milk allergy and various other food allergies are well-known conditions. If you are a sufferer, contact with the offending substance will trigger a variety of unpleasant symptoms that could include skin rashes, itching or swellings, red and swollen eyes, runny nose, severe nasal inflammation, wheezing and shortness of breath. Sometimes a severe reaction can require immediate emergency treatment.

Allergens

Any substance that will produce an allergic reaction is an allergen. Contact with an allergen is the event that triggers the allergic reaction. The substance may be quite harmless to others, but to a person with a specific allergy it will be a substance to avoid.

Common respiratory allergens are grass pollen, mold spores, nettles (in Europe), poison ivy (in North America), the house dust mite and its droppings, dandruff and animal hairs and fur.

Pet allergy is a reaction to contact with animal fur or dander (minute particles of skin) and can build up over a period of regular contact. Cat hairs are a very common trigger for asthma as well as hay-fever-type allergic reactions and it is advisable to avoid potential problems in susceptible people rather than have to get rid of a loved pet.

Allergies to drugs can arise even after previous treatments with the same drug

A

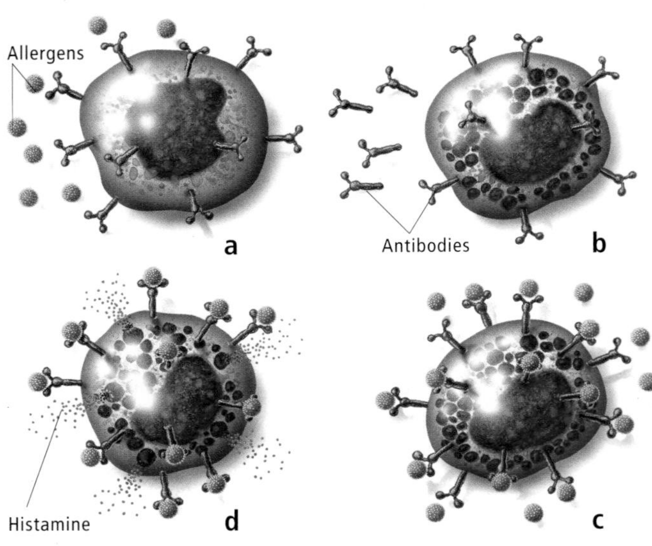

Allergic reaction

An allergic response is a reaction by the body to foreign irritants called allergens. The four-step process involves specialized cells and a chemical called histamine.

(a) Allergens enter the body and stimulate plasma cells to produce antibodies

(b) These antibodies attach to mast cells

(c) The next time allergens enter the body they bind to the antibodies on the surface of the mast cells

(d) Mast cells release histamine which produces the irritating effects of the allergy

Urticaria

When allergens enter the body they stimulate the release of histamine, which can produce itchy, slightly elevated skin wheals known as urticaria or hives.

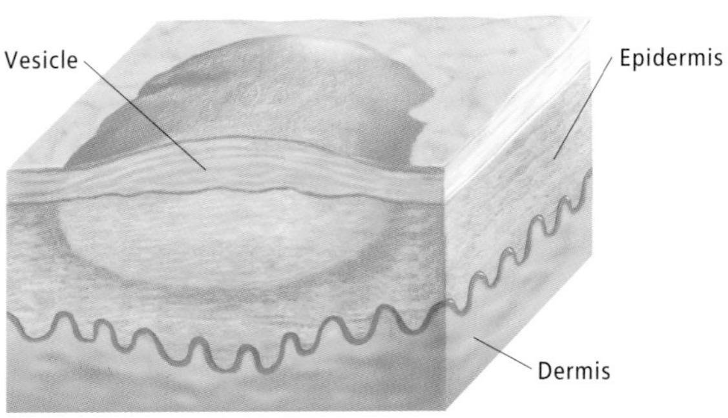

produced no adverse reaction, and can be triggered by very small amounts. Reactions can be mild or severe, even including anaphylactic shock, which is life-threatening, and people known to be at risk should wear medical bracelets or carry information cards.

Serum sickness is an allergic reaction that occurs eight to twelve days after a vaccination and may produce a skin rash or swellings, enlarged lymph glands and fever.

Foods can also be allergens, with cows' milk, eggs, peanuts, strawberries, wheat and wheat flour, shellfish and seafood all possibilities. Insect bites, chemicals, drugs and dyes can all cause allergy problems. Milk can cause allergies to milk proteins or drugs such as penicillin in the milk. However, lactose intolerance is not the result of an allergy; it occurs when the enzyme responsible for breaking down lactose is lacking.

Bee stings can produce a severe allergic reaction. Latex, a component of rubber, has caused allergies to develop through repeated exposure over time in many adults. Sunlight can also be responsible. Solar urticaria is a condition where exposure to ultraviolet light produces wheals on the skin.

The physical effect of exposure to an allergen is that the body will produce antibodies, normally manufactured in the body to fight invading germs. In an allergic reaction, allergens and antibodies act together to cause the release of histamine that then acts on capillaries, mucous glands and muscles of the stomach and internal organs, stimulating them into excessive, and often harmful, activity. Every time an allergic person is exposed to a particular allergen it is likely that the same response will result, and the reaction may become more severe over time. The level of exposure to the substance at which an allergic reaction will be triggered is the person's allergic threshold.

Allergic reactions

Allergic reactions can take many forms, from mild (involving minor discomfort such as a rash or indigestion) to severe (involving extreme irritation of skin or mucous membranes, respiratory distress or anaphylactic shock). In rare cases an allergic reaction may prove to be fatal.

Allergic reactions can be divided into four types: immediate, where the allergen is inhaled or ingested, as in most of the common allergies; reactions against foreign substances in the bloodstream, which occur for example in mismatched blood transfusions; autoimmune diseases, where the body's defenses attack its own tissue; and delayed reactions caused by repeated exposure, such as contact dermatitis produced by metals in jewelry.

It is not known to what extent allergic reactions are controlled by the nervous system; stress and emotional problems may increase their probability and severity.

Allergic reactions can appear on the skin as a rash. Respiratory allergens may affect breathing and the respiratory system, as in asthma, with a narrowing of the airways of the lungs and a feeling of tightness in the chest; or they may cause sneezing, as in hay fever; or even more severe irritation and inflammation of the mucus membranes of the nose as in chronic rhinitis. They also may cause skin rashes, dermatitis and swellings and nasal polyps (swollen tissue in the nose) that can obstruct the airway.

Food allergies and gastrointestinal allergies, thought to be caused by the protein component of certain foods, can also affect respiration but more usually symptoms include vomiting, diarrhea, skin rashes or swellings, swellings inside the mouth and, rarely, anaphylactic shock. Reaction follows swiftly after contact with (touching or eating) the food.

Sensitivity to certain foods may not necessarily be an allergy. Food intolerance is a term used to differentiate between suffering side effects from certain components or ingredients of foods and the more severe allergic reactions. Food intolerance is quite common and can produce a range of symptoms similar to those of allergies. And because food sensitivity—a term covering both allergy and intolerance—is a complex condition with many possible causes and symptoms, specialist diagnosis is essential.

Anaphylaxis, or anaphylactic shock, is an extreme allergic reaction where histamine and other chemicals are released within the body. This is a medical emergency.

Diagnosis and treatment

Diagnosis may be a lengthy process, unless the allergic reaction is immediate and the allergen can be identified beyond doubt. A medical examination may be done while the patient is suffering an allergic reaction and will take account of blood pressure, pulse rate, skin condition, breathing and general mental condition.

Antigen tests aim to find the substance (the antigen) in the blood of the allergic person that results from contact with the allergen—the food or chemical in the environment or diet. It is the allergen that starts the reaction, and the antigen that combines with antibodies in the blood to produce the physical effects of the allergic reaction.

A medical specialist will do antigen tests as part of a course of treatment. First, the presence of an allergy must be diagnosed to establish that what has happened before is not just an isolated reaction. Then tests are undertaken to find the allergens in the diet or environment of the allergic person so that contact with them can be avoided or completely eliminated. There may be skin or blood tests, or more long-term procedures where contact with all substances suspected of causing problems is eliminated. Controlled dieting is an elimination method used to detect digestive food allergies. Foods that commonly cause allergies are removed from the diet, then returned one at a time to see if the allergy also returns.

There is no complete cure for allergies: they can be identified and the causes revealed, but the allergy remains. The benefits of correct diagnosis and treatment are that the allergy can be managed, and life can go on as normally as possible in the circumstances. Untreated allergies tend to become worse. Treatment may mean strict avoidance of the allergens responsible or may require medication to control the allergic reaction. Antihistamines and steroids are the most commonly used medications in cases of respiratory allergies; for digestive allergies, other drugs (known as H2 antagonists) may be prescribed.

SEE ALSO *Anaphylaxis, Antibodies, Antigen tests, Antihistamines, Asthma, Autoimmune disease, Conjunctivitis, Dermatitis, Desensitization, Eczema, Hay fever, Lactose intolerance, Photosensitivity, Urticaria*

ALVEOLUS

An alveolus, also known as a pulmonary alveolus, is one of the tiny air spaces in the lung where blood exchanges carbon dioxide for oxygen. There are about 300 million alveoli in each human lung, grouped in grape-like clusters (alveolar sacs).

Inhaled air enters through the mouth or nose, travels through the throat, larynx and windpipe (trachea) and via the left and right bronchial tube to the lungs. The bronchial tubes (bronchioles) narrow and divide into alveolar ducts, ending in the alveolar sacs.

Alveoli give the lungs their huge surface area, estimated to be 1,000 square feet (93 square meters), and the thin-walled blood vessels in each provide the means for gases—carbon dioxide and oxygen—to be exchanged by diffusion.

ALZHEIMER'S DISEASE

Alzheimer's disease is a common brain disease which results in dementia (confusion and loss of intellectual function). It usually occurs in elderly people but may occasionally appear in middle age.

This is the most common (but not the only) cause of senile dementia. After a person reaches the age of 65, the risk of Alzheimer's disease doubles with each five years of age. As the average life expectancy of the world population continues to rise, the number of those affected will continue to increase.

The symptoms of Alzheimer's disease appear very gradually, followed by a progressive deterioration over a period of five to ten years. Its major feature is increasing forgetfulness—initially forgetfulness of the

Alveoli

The small air spaces at the end of the air passageways of the lungs are called alveoli. Each lung contains millions of these tiny sacs. In an alveolus, oxygen is absorbed into the blood and carbon dioxide passes from the blood into the alveolus, to be breathed out by the lungs.

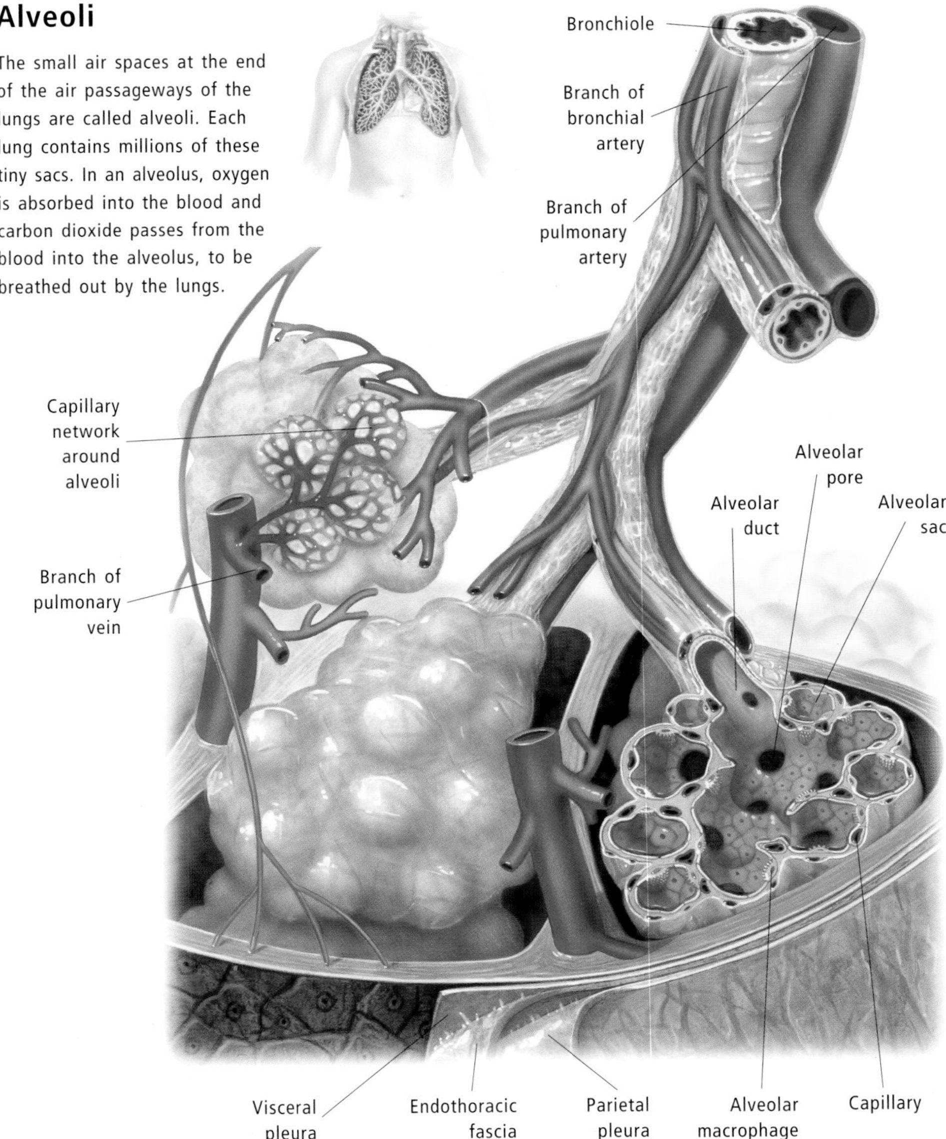

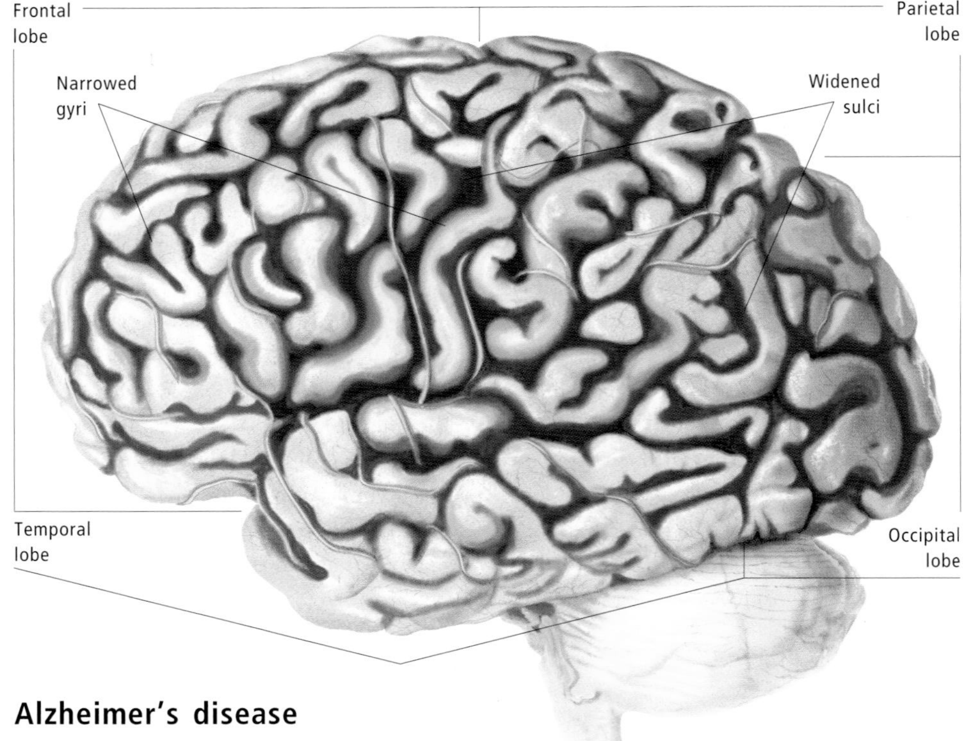

Alzheimer's disease

Alzheimer's disease is a common disease of old age, affecting the memory. In this brain of a sufferer, the brain has shrunken slightly and the gaps between brain matter have widened. Nobody knows exactly what causes the changes.

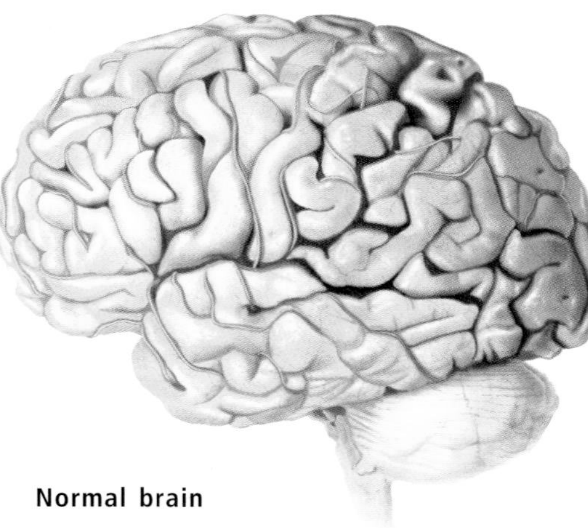

Normal brain

names of objects, people and places as well as day-to-day events. The person begins to miss appointments and lose possessions. One of the most striking features in the early stages of the disease is that, although sufferers can't remember recent events, they may be able to describe in great detail incidents or people from early in their life. Unfortunately the ability to recall even old memories fades as the disease progresses.

Affected people gradually become more and more disorientated and confused, frequently getting lost or forgetting how to do simple tasks such as getting dressed or setting the table. Their intellectual capacity diminishes—reading, writing, mathematical skills and decision-making are all affected. Eventually they undergo personality changes, neglecting personal hygiene and exhibiting uncharacteristic and sometimes bizarre patterns of behavior, such as paranoia or sexual indiscretions. They gradually become immobile, bedridden and susceptible to infections.

The development of Alzheimer's disease is not considered a normal consequence of ageing—it is a real disease in which there are characteristic changes in both the structure and chemistry of the brain.

Alzheimer's sufferers lose up to 20 percent of their normal brain volume, with the shrinkage (cell death) occurring mainly in parts of the temporal, frontal and parietal lobes of the brain. These are the areas which are responsible for creating and storing memory and for intellectual processing. Parts of the brain dealing with motor and sensory functions (vision, touch and hearing) seem relatively unaffected. Examination of affected tissue under a microscope shows three main characteristics: large spaces formed by dying cells; abnormal protein deposits, called senile plaques; and twisted, knotted bundles of fibers, known as tangles.

What causes these changes in the brain is not yet understood. Less than 5 percent of cases have a proven genetic basis and these are almost invariably cases which have an early age of onset. For the vast majority it appears likely that the disease results from long-term exposure of genetically susceptible individuals to a combination of (as yet unidentified) environmental factors.

At present there is no known cure for the disease. Several drugs are currently being trialed but at best they only slow down the intellectual decline—they cannot stop the progression of the disease.

SEE ALSO *Confusion, Dementia, Memory*

AMINO ACIDS

Amino acids are the building blocks of proteins. The body needs proteins in order to build cells and grow, and to maintain its metabolic functions. To make proteins, it needs amino acids.

There are two groups of amino acids: non-essential (if we don't include them in our diet the body itself can make them) and essential (they must be included in the diet if we are to stay healthy).

Lack of essential amino acids in the diet can lead to malnutrition and protein deficiency disorders such as kwashiorkor. These are common in the developing world where protein in the diet is scarce. Rich sources of amino acids include meat, fish, poultry, egg white, milk, cheese, peas and beans.

SEE ALSO *Kwashiorkor, Malnutrition*

AMNESIA

Amnesia is partial or complete loss of memory. It is usually caused by brain damage due to trauma or disease, though it can sometimes be caused by psychological trauma. Memory loss is usually temporary and selective, being confined to one part of the affected person's experience, such as memory of recent events.

Causes of amnesia include Alzheimer's disease, head trauma or injury, seizures, general anesthetics, alcoholism, stroke or transient ischemic attack (TIA), drugs such as barbiturates or benzodiazepines, electroconvulsive therapy (especially if prolonged) and brain surgery.

There are various types of amnesia. Anterograde amnesia involves the loss of one's ability to form new memories. The affected person has difficulty remembering ongoing day-to-day events following an injury to the head, although they remember events prior to this. It may also affect alcoholics and usually leads to dementia.

In retrograde amnesia, the affected person has difficulty recalling events prior to an episode of head injury. Part or all of the memory loss may return in the days, weeks or months following the trauma.

In a condition called transient global amnesia (TGA), the affected person, who is usually elderly, suddenly forgets how they came to be where they are. Their name and the names of family and friends can be recalled, but not the events leading up to the attack. The condition is thought to be caused by unusual electrical activity in the temporal lobe of the brain. Recovery usually takes place in four to six hours. The condition does not cause permanent damage and requires no medical treatment.

In Wernicke-Korsakoff syndrome, memory loss is caused by a thiamine deficiency due to alcohol abuse. The affected person will have normal short-term memory, but will have difficulty acquiring new information and in remembering events that happened before the illness. It is a progressive disorder, usually accompanied by neurological problems such as uncoordinated movements and loss of feeling in fingers and toes.

Hysterical amnesia (also known as fugue amnesia) is usually temporary and is triggered by a traumatic event that the mind of the affected person cannot cope with. Usually the memory returns after a few days, though the memory of the traumatic event may remain incomplete.

The treatment of amnesia is to reverse the underlying cause if possible. Support of the family is important. The family may need to orientate the affected person by providing familiar music, objects or photos, and relearning programs are also helpful. Medication schedules should be written down so they are not forgotten and lost. Nursing home and other extended care facilities may be needed if safety, nutrition or other basic needs are at risk.

SEE ALSO *Alcoholism, Alzheimer's disease, Convulsions, Dementia, Electroconvulsive therapy, Memory, Psychotropic drugs, Stroke, Trauma, Wernicke-Korsakoff syndrome*

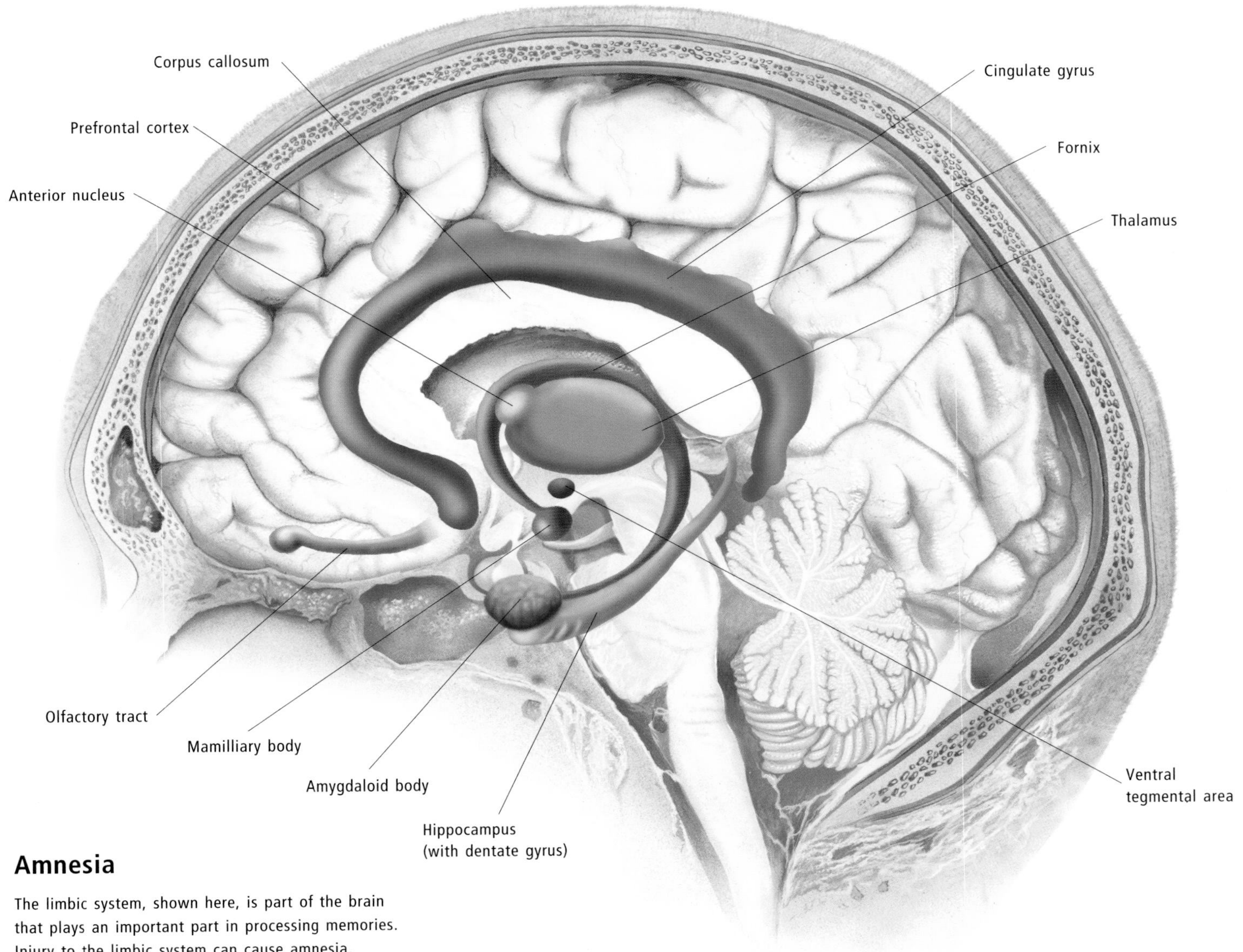

Amnesia

The limbic system, shown here, is part of the brain that plays an important part in processing memories. Injury to the limbic system can cause amnesia.

A

AMNIOCENTESIS

Amniocentesis involves a sample of amniotic fluid being taken from the amniotic sac. A hollow needle is inserted into the mother's uterus through the abdominal wall, using ultrasound to determine the needle's position. The fluid is cultured in a laboratory, a process that can take up to four weeks. Women found to be carrying a baby with an abnormality are usually offered an abortion.

Amniocentesis is performed between the 14th and 18th week of a pregnancy on women deemed to be at high risk of having a baby with physical defects of the central nervous system (such as spina bifida or anencephaly) or genetic abnormalities (such as Down syndrome). Those at greater risk are usually women whose family history indicates there may be a problem, or women over 35 years of age. Counseling should be offered to the woman and her partner before the procedure takes place, as well as after the procedure if an abnormality is detected.

Amniocentesis is sometimes performed late in the pregnancy where there is a risk of placenta previa (in which the placenta obstructs the birth) or premature birth.

There is a risk of miscarriage with amniocentesis of between 1 and 2 percent. There is also a 0.5 percent risk that the baby will be born with a very low birth weight.

SEE ALSO *Chromosomal abnormalities, Congenital abnormalities, Pregnancy*

AMPHETAMINES

Amphetamines are stimulants, and are used in the treatment of uncontrollable attacks of sleep or drowsiness (narcolepsy). In children over the age of three years, however, they are prescribed for hyperactivity disorders.

Side effects of taking amphetamines include restlessness, insomnia, dryness of the mouth, twitching and loss of appetite. Overdose may cause coma and death. Treatment for overdose is to induce vomiting (in order to prevent further absorption).

Amphetamines should be used only under medical supervision. There is a danger of dependency with long-term use. Use of amphetamines is prohibited in competitive sports.

SEE ALSO *Attention deficit hyperactivity disorder, Drug dependence, Stimulants*

AMYOTROPHIC LATERAL SCLEROSIS

Amyotrophic lateral sclerosis (ALS) is a progressive, fatal disorder resulting in the loss of the use and control of muscles. Also called Lou Gehrig's disease (after the American baseball hero who suffered from it), ALS is a member of the class of disorders known as motor neuron diseases.

The condition is caused by gradual degeneration of nerve cells in the brain and spinal cord that control voluntary movement. As neurons shrink and disappear, the muscles under their control weaken and waste away. Symptoms include poor coordination, paralysis of hands and arms, twitching and cramping of muscles, and difficulty in speaking, swallowing and breathing. Symptoms usually do not develop until well into adulthood, often not until after 50 years of age. Mental faculties remain unaffected.

The condition is confirmed by electromyography (EMG), which shows the nerve and muscle degeneration. There is no cure for ALS, although one drug, riluzole, has been shown to prolong the survival of people with the condition. Physical therapy, rehabilitation and use of appliances such as braces or a wheelchair will assist the affected person to stay mobile as long as possible.

ALS is usually fatal within five years after symptoms appear. The condition may run in families; if so, genetic counseling is advisable.

SEE ALSO *Muscles, Rehabilitation, Spinal cord*

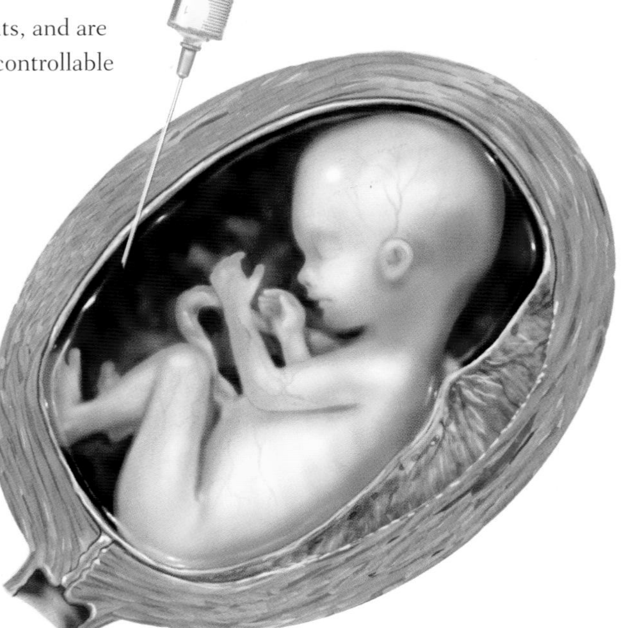

Amniocentesis

Amniocentesis can detect over 40 different types of inherited fetal disorders. The technique samples skin cells and biochemical substances in the amniotic fluid that have come from the fetus.

ANABOLIC STEROIDS

Some naturally occurring steroids produced by the body, for example testosterone, have anabolic (muscle-building) effects. Increasingly, and controversially, synthetic anabolic steroids are being used, especially by athletes, to enhance muscle strength and power. Similar to testosterone, these drugs have been shown to increase strength and muscle mass when combined with exercise.

But they can also be dangerous. To be effective they must be used in dosages that are 10 to 40 times greater than those normally found in the body. As well as being anabolic, they are androgenic (they enhance male sexual characteristics) which in females can result in masculinization. Anabolic steroids have also been known to cause liver failure, arteriosclerosis, acne, baldness and blood lipid disorders. Their use can also lead to increased aggression, known as "roid rage". Increasingly, their use is being banned from organized sport.

SEE ALSO *Testosterone*

ANALGESICS

An analgesic is a drug that reduces or eliminates pain without loss of consciousness. Aspirin (acetylsalicylic acid) is the oldest

A

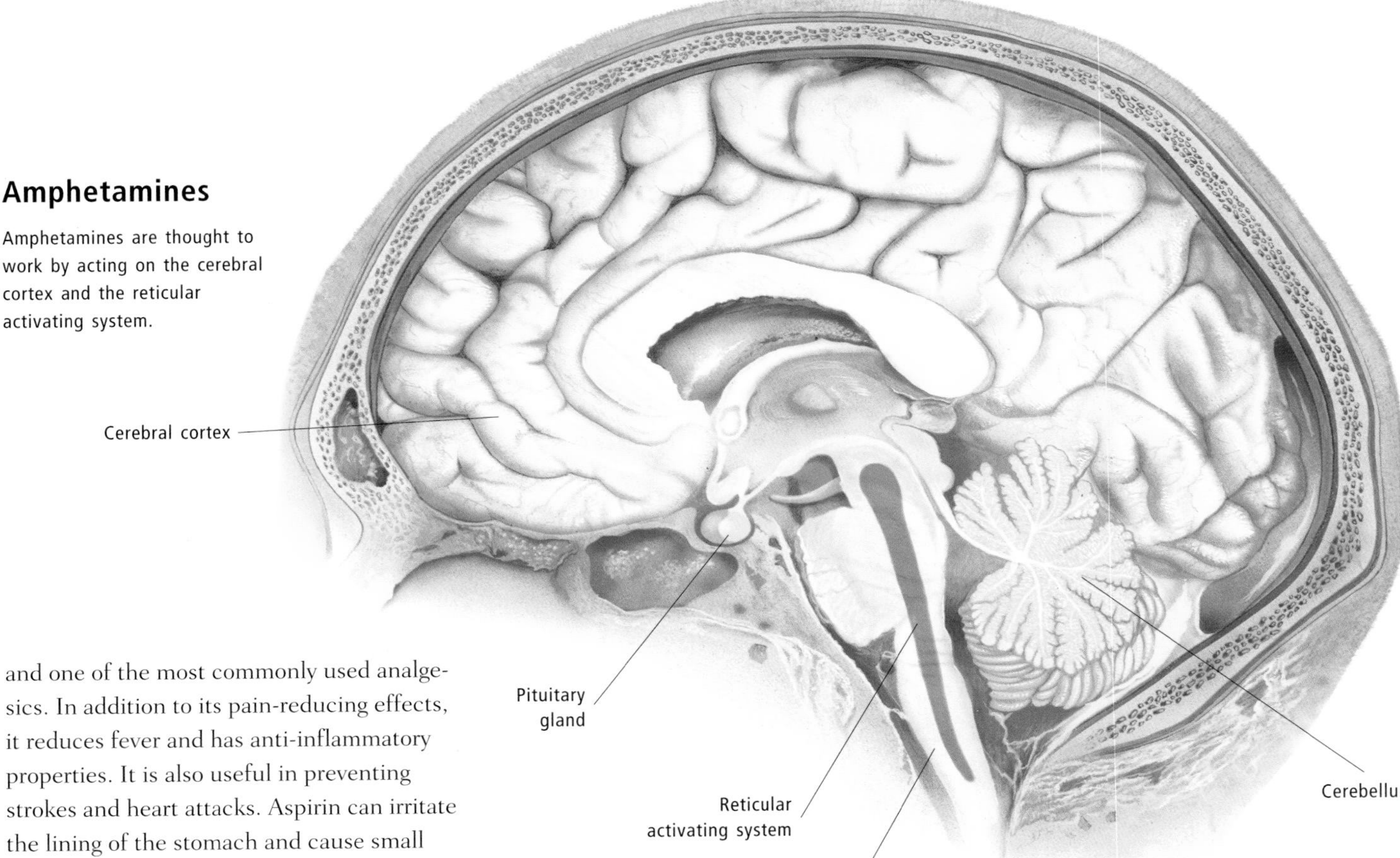

Amphetamines

Amphetamines are thought to work by acting on the cerebral cortex and the reticular activating system.

and one of the most commonly used analgesics. In addition to its pain-reducing effects, it reduces fever and has anti-inflammatory properties. It is also useful in preventing strokes and heart attacks. Aspirin can irritate the lining of the stomach and cause small amounts of stomach bleeding; anyone who has a peptic ulcer or indigestion, or who is taking anticoagulants, should use another analgesic such as acetaminophen (paracetamol). Aspirin should not be given to children, as it may cause Reye's syndrome.

Acetaminophen relieves pain and reduces fever. It is often used in its own right, or as a substitute for aspirin. It doesn't reduce inflammation, so it is not as useful as aspirin in treating inflammatory conditions such as arthritis. Side effects are not very common, but an overdose may cause liver or kidney damage.

Codeine is an opium derivative that is used for stronger pain. It is also used as a cough suppressant and a treatment for diarrhea. Prolonged use of large quantities of codeine may produce dependency. Codeine is often combined with aspirin or acetaminophen in analgesic preparation.

Other narcotic analgesics, such as morphine and its derivatives, are used for severe pain. They can also produce drowsiness, constipation and nausea. Prolonged use of these may be habit-forming, and an overdose can lead to death.

SEE ALSO *Morphine, Narcotics, Pain, Reye's syndrome*

ANAPHYLAXIS

Anaphylaxis is an immediate and violent reaction brought on by hypersensitivity to a particular substance. It is an extreme allergic response that occurs when a person comes into contact with a substance—an antigen—to which they are already allergic.

Antigens stimulate the body's immune system to fight them with specific antibodies and the release of histamine. The histamine within the body triggers the violent response known as anaphylactic shock. Capillaries enlarge and leak fluid into surrounding tissues; blood pressure collapses; the brain's oxygen supply is reduced; airways narrow and breathing is restricted; skin is pale and damp; there may be nausea and vomiting; there is a risk of heart failure and death. Anaphylaxis is often associated with insect bites or certain medications, such as penicillin.

Treatment often involves the injection of epinephrine (adrenaline) to restore blood pressure, and of other drugs such as steroids and antihistamines. People at risk often wear bracelets inscribed with their personal medical information and may even carry their own adrenaline injection kits. First aid is the same as required for a person who is in shock, and medical assistance is essential in all cases.

SEE ALSO *Allergies, Antihistamines, Epinephrine, Steroids*

ANDROGENS

Androgens are steroid hormones that produce male sex characteristics. The two main androgens are androsterone and testosterone. In men, they are secreted into the bloodstream by the testes (and to a lesser extent the adrenal glands) under stimulation from the pituitary gland. In women, smaller amounts are secreted by the ovaries and adrenals.

At the onset of puberty, production of testosterone in boys increases; facial and pubic hair develops, the larynx enlarges (so that the voice deepens), the penis and testes enlarge and there is an increase in body muscle strength. Virilism is the appearance of masculine characteristics in women or children, caused by excessive secretion of testosterone by the adrenal glands. In women, a male body hair pattern develops, the voice deepens, acne and baldness may develop, and menstrual periods may cease. In boys, it precipitates early puberty.

SEE ALSO *Pituitary gland, Puberty, Testes, Testosterone, Virilization*

ANEMIA

Anemia is a condition in which the red blood cells fail to provide sufficient oxygen supplies to the tissues of the body. It can be caused by decreased amounts of hemoglobin in red blood cells, or decreased numbers of red cells in the blood. Signs of anemia include tiredness and weakness, pallor (especially in the hands and eyelids), fainting, breathlessness and rapid heartbeat. To diagnose anemia, a physician takes a small sample of blood from the patient and counts the number of red blood cells and the concentration of hemoglobin in the sample. Normal levels of hemoglobin in the blood are approximately 14–17 grams per 100 milliliters (deciliter) for males and 12–15 grams per 100 milliliters for females.

The size and shape of the red blood cells can give a clue as to the cause of anemia. In pernicious anemia, for example, the red blood cells are larger than normal, whereas in iron deficiency anemia they are often smaller and paler than normal.

There are several causes of anemia. Iron deficiency anemia is caused by decreased absorption of iron, loss of iron from the body (usually from bleeding), or an increased need for iron. Malabsorption and/or poor nutrition may result in decreased absorption of iron and iron deficiency anemia. Premature babies often have low stores of iron at birth. Heavy menstrual bleeding or gastro-intestinal disease with bleeding (such as bowel cancer) may deplete the body's iron stores. Pregnancy or rapid growth may place too much demand on the body's iron reserves. Treatment is to maintain an adequate iron intake through a well-balanced diet or supplements, and to correct the underlying cause.

Pernicious anemia is the result of inadequate absorption of vitamin B_{12}, normally found in meat, fish and dairy products. It is

Androgens

The pituitary gland produces the hormones that trigger the release of androgens (androsterone and testosterone) by the adrenal glands and testes in men. These hormones are also produced in small amounts by the adrenals and ovaries in women. Androgens increase muscle mass and strength when combined with exercise. They are sometimes used by body builders to build muscle bulk.

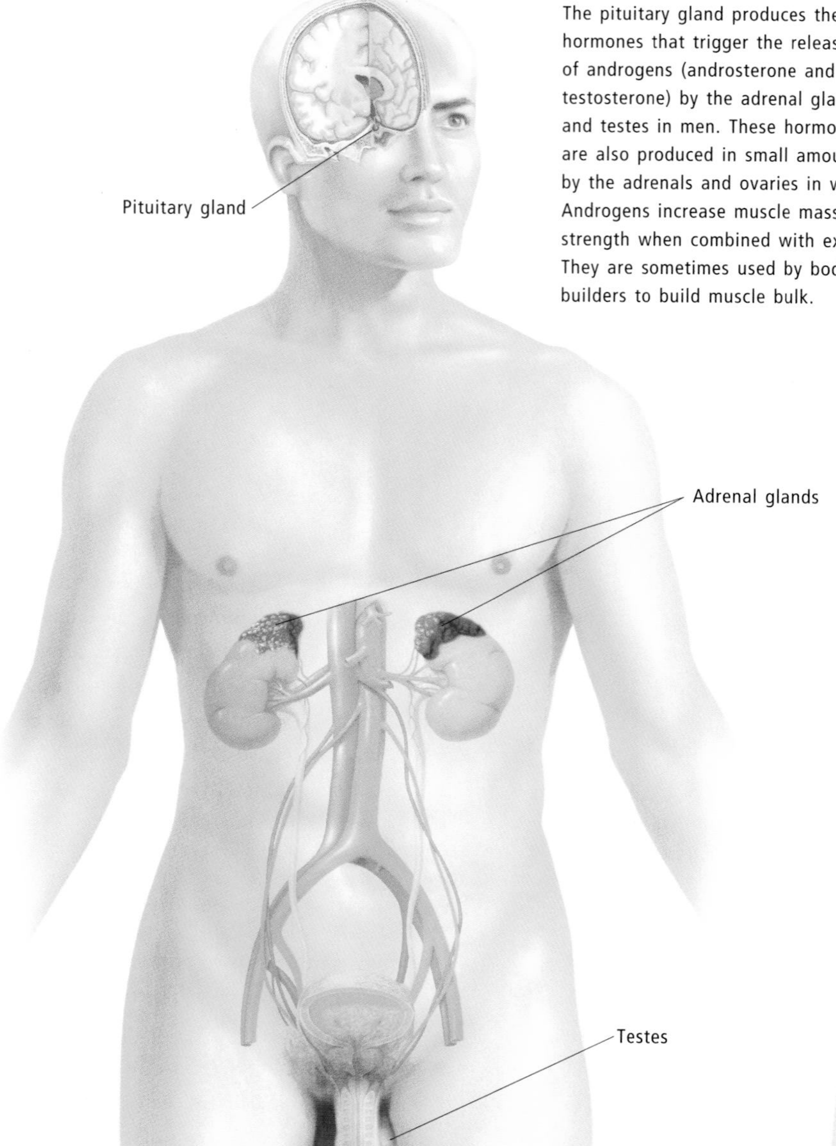

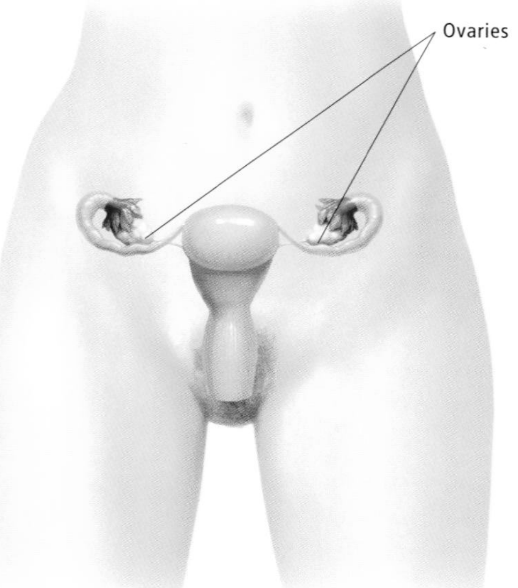

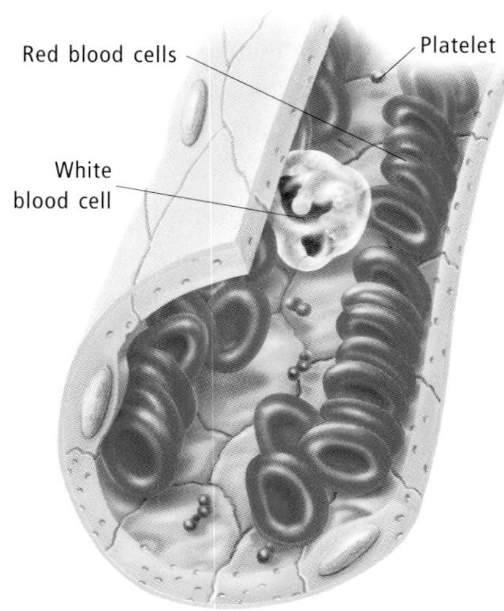

Normal blood

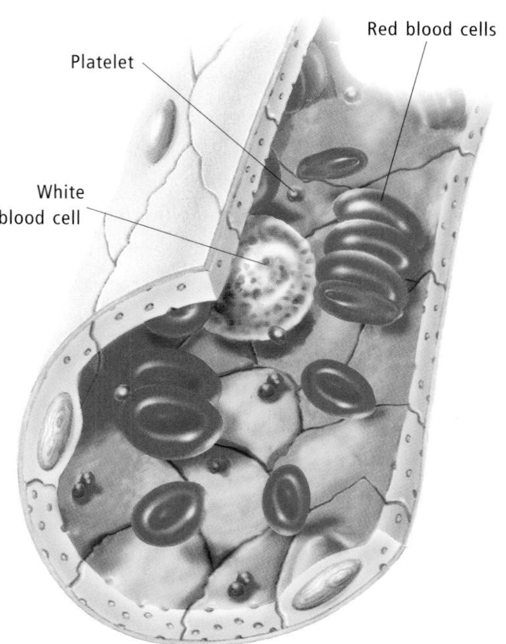

Iron deficiency anemia

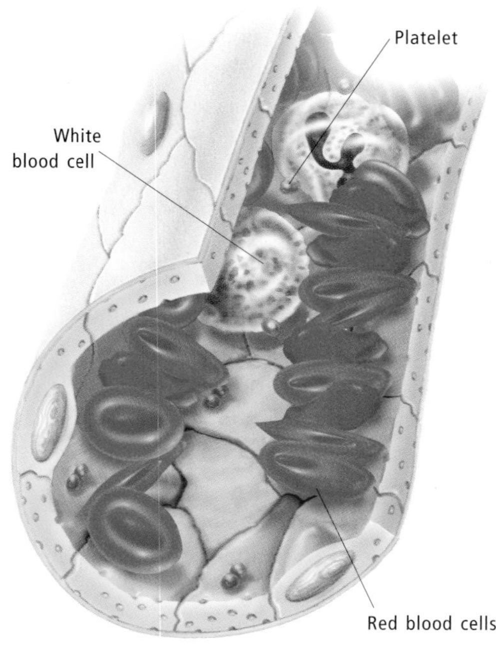

Sickle cell anemia

Anemia

In iron deficiency anemia the red blood cells (as shown here in a capillary) are smaller and paler than normal; in sickle cell anemia they are shaped liked a sickle.

caused by the absence of intrinsic factor, a chemical secreted by the stomach's lining which assists in the absorption of vitamin B_{12}. It may occur as an autoimmune disease or after stomach surgery. Pernicious anemia cannot be cured, but symptoms can be controlled with regular injections of vitamin B_{12}. Treatment needs to be continued for life.

Aplastic anemia is caused by decreased bone marrow production of red blood cells. Platelet and white blood cell production is also diminished so that, as well as anemia symptoms, the patient suffers abnormal bleeding and reduced resistance to infections. The condition is most often caused by drugs, especially immunosuppressant drugs, anti-cancer drugs, chloramphenicol or chemicals such as benzene. It may also be caused by immunodeficiency or severe illness. The patient should be isolated in hospital to avoid infection, and may receive blood transfusions and bone marrow transplantation.

Hemolytic anemia is caused by hemolysis, the premature destruction of red blood cells. The cells may be destroyed because they are abnormal or because of antibodies that attack them; bone marrow cannot produce red blood cells fast enough to compensate. Along with other symptoms, there may be jaundice (yellow skin and eyes, dark urine) and an enlarged spleen (splenomegaly).

The condition may be inherited (as in hereditary spherocytosis, sickle cell disease or thalassemia) or acquired, from blood transfusions or drugs. Acquired hemolytic anemia is treated by removing the cause. Immunosuppressant drugs may also be needed. Inherited forms of the condition are incurable, though symptoms can be controlled. Splenectomy (removal of the spleen) is sometimes needed.

SEE ALSO *Hemoglobin, Hemolytic anemia, Iron, Red blood cells, Sickle cell disease, Thalassemia*

ANESTHESIA

Anesthesia is loss of sensation, particularly to pain. Anesthetics are drugs which halt the sensation of pain through the body's nervous system. The nervous system is made up of neurons (nerve cells) which send information to the brain. The brain then processes this information and relays it to the muscles via motor neurons. Anesthetics act in various ways, such as affecting certain parts of nerves (called axons) and interfering with transmission between neurons.

History

Before anesthetics were available, surgery was a frighteningly painful ordeal. The practice of surgery was changed when in 1846, William Thomas Morton, in front of a group of physicians at Massachusetts General Hospital in Boston, demonstrated that ether could be used as a general anesthetic in an operation. Before that a British chemist had suggested that nitrous oxide (laughing gas) could be used but no-one tried this until an American dentist extracted his own tooth using it in 1844.

Four years later a Scottish physician, Sir James Simpson, gave chloroform to women in childbirth and Britain's Queen Victoria was among the first to promote it.

Both ether and chloroform had all kinds of ill effects, including death of the patient. As they were administered using simple devices made of glass or metal containing sponges soaked in the anesthetic, there was no control of the dosage given. Modern inhalation anesthetics such as trichlorethylene and halothane are administered by a machine which the anesthetist can control precisely.

Before today's extremely effective local anesthetics, many different substances were used to relieve the pain of surgery—cannabis, opium and rum being among the most common. Cocaine was the first generally used local anesthetic and since then it has become the convention to end the names given to local anesthetics with "caine", for example procaine, lidocaine, and tetracaine.

A

Types of anesthetics

There are three types of drug-induced anesthesia: local anesthesia, which involves the numbing of a local nerve and can be administered in the form of a cream, injection or eye drops; regional anesthesia, which is the numbing of larger areas, for example a limb, and is done by a series of local anesthetic injections around a nerve or number of nerves; and general anesthesia, which renders the person totally unconscious and involves the inhalation of gas, the injection of drugs into the bloodstream or a combination of both.

When local anesthetics are applied directly to mucous membranes they are known as topical anesthetics—teething gels being an example. When a local anesthetic is injected into the space just outside the membranous sheath of the lumbar spinal cord (dura), it removes sensation from the lower part of the body, either partially or completely. This form of regional anesthesia is known as a lumbar epidural injection or epidural anesthesia and is commonly used in childbirth. Spinal anesthesia, which is rarely used because of complications, is an injection into the cerebrospinal fluid in the lower spine.

Acupuncture, which uses fine needles inserted into key areas of the body to stimulate lines of energy, provides relief for many, though how it works is still poorly understood. Hypnosis can also be used to reduce the amount of pain a person is experiencing. Rather than actually anesthetizing, hypnosis is most useful in relaxing the patient prior to anesthesia and in improving the effect of the drugs, as well as reducing the dosage required. Both acupuncture and hypnosis have been found to reduce the need for other forms of analgesia in childbirth. In the treatment of intractable pain, hypnosis is a useful tool and it is also sometimes used in dental treatment.

TENS (transcutaneous electrical nerve stimulation) is a method which involves the application of a gentle current to the surface of the skin. It is a form of pain relief which is used for back, neck and joint pain, as well as arthritis, migraines and the pain of childbirth.

SEE ALSO *Acupuncture, Cocaine, Epidural anesthesia, Hypnotherapy, Pain, Synapses*

ANEURYSM

An aneurysm is an abnormal dilatation of a blood vessel, usually an artery, caused by weakness in the vessel's wall.

An aneurysm of the aorta, the major artery connecting the heart to other arteries of the body, typically occurs in an older person and is usually caused by arteriosclerosis. Often it has no symptoms for many years, then eventually ruptures, resulting in profuse bleeding into the chest or abdomen. Symptoms are searing chest pain, shortness of breath, collapse with low blood pressure (hypotension) and shock from blood loss.

A rapidly expanding or ruptured aortic aneurysm is a medical emergency requiring resuscitation, hospitalization and surgery. Death occurs in 50 percent of cases. However, if the aneurysm occurs in the abdominal aorta and is detected early, allowing surgery before rupture occurs, chances are better.

An aneurysm can also occur in the large arteries at the base of the brain (berry aneurysm). It is usually congenital and hereditary. Bleeding from the aneurysm into the subarachnoid space in the brain is known as subarachnoid hemorrhage; this causes severe headache and stroke with paralysis and coma. Emergency surgery may be life saving, but the mortality rate is high.

SEE ALSO *Aorta, Arteries, Arteriosclerosis, Blood vessels, Subarachnoid hemorrhage*

ANGINA PECTORIS

Angina pectoris is the name given to chest pain caused by lack of oxygen to the heart, due to arteriosclerosis in the coronary (heart) arteries. It is usually brought on by exercise. In severe arteriosclerosis, the pain may be felt at rest, when it is known as unstable angina. The pain is felt across the chest and may also be felt in the neck, between the shoulder blades and in the arms. In severe cases sufferers describe the pain as "crushing", and may also feel cold, sweaty and anxious, and have difficulty breathing.

Angina pectoris can be confirmed by an electrocardiogram (EKG), which shows certain changes while the pain is present. If pain is not present, changes can be demonstrated while the patient is undergoing exercise (stress test). Other tests include cardiac angiography and perfusion scanning.

The condition is commonly treated with drugs that dilate the coronary arteries and increase the blood flow to the heart muscle. These include nitroglycerin tablets, which can be taken under the tongue (they usually relieve pain within seconds and confirm the diagnosis of angina). Nitrates can also be given as tablets or skin patches. Beta-blockers and calcium antagonists (channel blockers) are also used to treat angina. Balloon angioplasty and bypass surgery are other options.

Angina can be treated at home if it responds to drug treatment. If not, or there is unstable angina (pain at rest), hospitalization may be necessary, as the angina may then be a sign of myocardial infarction (heart attack).

SEE ALSO *Arteriosclerosis, Beta-blockers, Coronary artery disease, Electrocardiogram, Heart*

ANGIOEDEMA

Angioedema is a severe allergic reaction, similar in many ways to urticaria. The chief difference is that urticaria affects the surface layers of the skin while angioedema affects the deeper layers. It may occur with or without urticaria. Like urticaria, angioedema is caused by an allergic trigger. This may be an insect bite or sting, food (shellfish, nuts, food additives or strawberries), exposure to animals or pollen, or a reaction to a drug such as penicillin.

While the hives and wheals of urticaria are annoying, they are not dangerous. In angioedema, however, the eyes, lips and skin around the eyes may swell markedly. If the swelling spreads to the throat, suffocation may occur. As with urticaria, mild cases of angioedema can be treated with antihistamine tablets. In more serious cases an intravenous injection of hydrocortisone or epinephrine (adrenaline) is given to reduce the swelling and remove the risk of suffocation. Any trigger factors known to bring on the condition should be avoided.

SEE ALSO *Allergies, Urticaria*

ANGIOGRAPHY

Angiography is an investigative x-ray technique that is used to show the nature and extent of disease in arteries, veins and lymph vessels. It involves insertion of a catheter,

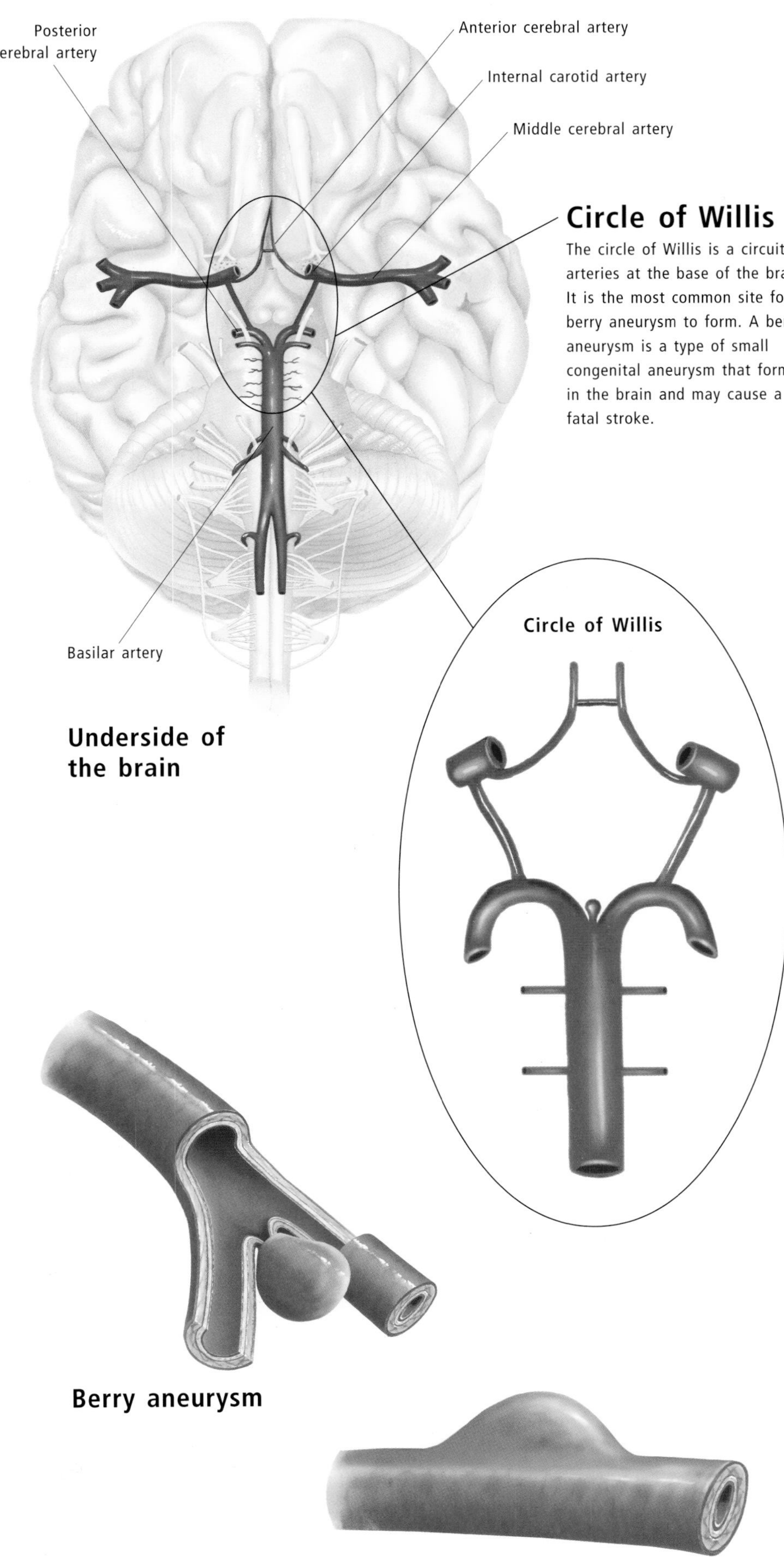

Underside of the brain

Berry aneurysm

Aneurysm

Circle of Willis

The circle of Willis is a circuit of arteries at the base of the brain. It is the most common site for a berry aneurysm to form. A berry aneurysm is a type of small congenital aneurysm that forms in the brain and may cause a fatal stroke.

followed by the injection into the artery of a dye that is opaque to x-rays. X-rays are taken, and any areas of abnormal blood flow or blockages of arteries are highlighted by the dye. Angiography is used by the physician or surgeon to decide if arterial disease is present, and, if so, which arteries to treat.

Arteries commonly examined this way include femoral (thigh) arteries and the coronary arteries of the heart. It is commonly used before heart surgery. In the great majority of cases, the procedure is very safe and is performed with the patient sedated but conscious. A few patients are allergic to the dye and may develop hives or, in more serious cases, anaphylactic shock. Hence, the procedure is carried out in hospital with resuscitation facilities nearby. Treatment of shock is with intravenous epinephrine (adrenaline). Allergic people are treated with steroids before the procedure to prevent an allergic reaction.

SEE ALSO *Angioplasty, Arteries, Arteriosclerosis*

ANGIOMA

An angioma is an abnormal, though benign (non-cancerous), growth of small blood vessels. It may occur internally, or as a soft, purplish or reddish mark on the skin. Cherry angioma, spider angioma and strawberry nevus are common examples.

Treatment may not be necessary if the disfigurement can be concealed by cosmetics. If treatment is required, a small angioma in the skin may be burned or cauterized, but larger ones need plastic surgery.

An angioma in the brain may bleed, causing subarachnoid hemorrhage or a stroke. An angioma that bleeds in the digestive tract may cause anemia, black stools (melena), or vomiting of blood.

SEE ALSO *Anemia, Blood vessels, Stroke, Subarachnoid hemorrhage*

Aneurysm

When an artery wall is weakened by a disease such as arteriosclerosis, blood pressure may force the walls of the artery out. This ballooning of an artery is called an aneurysm.

A

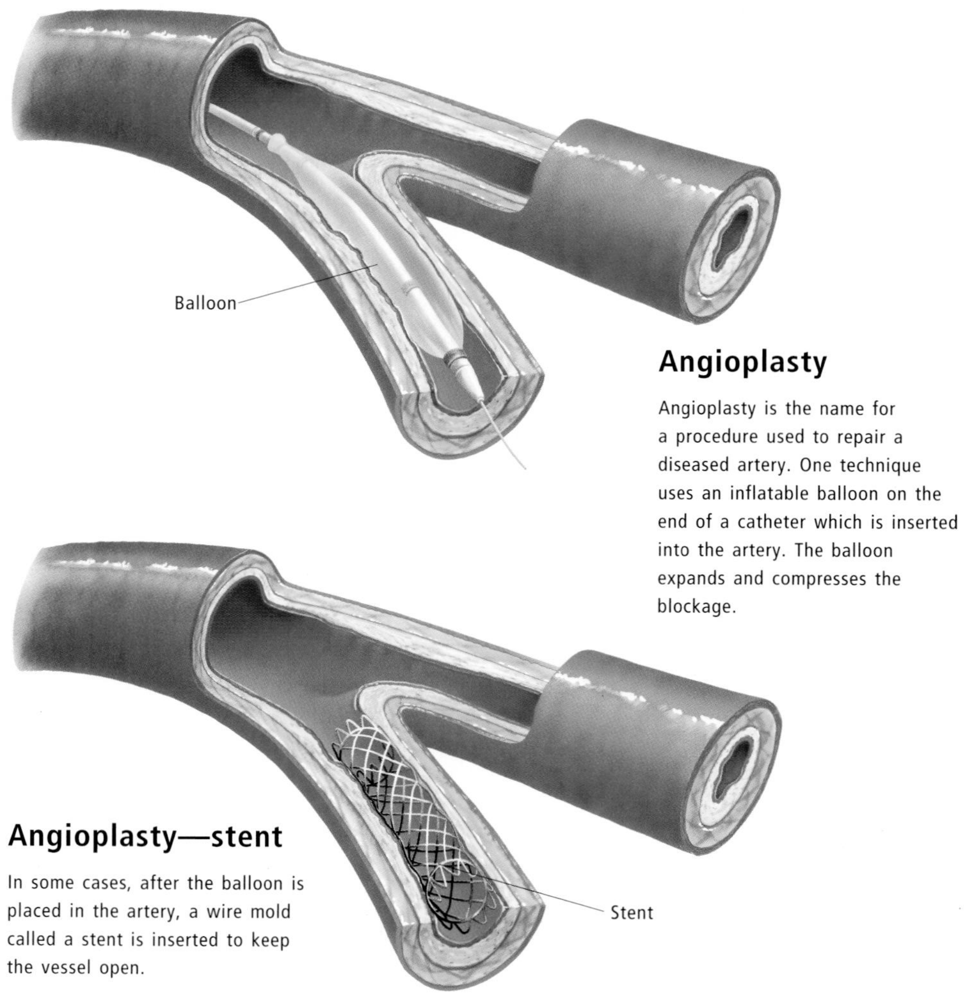

Angioplasty

Angioplasty is the name for a procedure used to repair a diseased artery. One technique uses an inflatable balloon on the end of a catheter which is inserted into the artery. The balloon expands and compresses the blockage.

Angioplasty—stent

In some cases, after the balloon is placed in the artery, a wire mold called a stent is inserted to keep the vessel open.

ANGIOPLASTY

Angioplasty is the repair of blood vessels affected by disease (usually atherosclerosis). It may be performed in the blood vessels supplying the heart or in the arteries of the limbs, brain or kidney.

Angioplasty may be surgical or non-surgical. In surgical angioplasty, segments of the affected artery are removed and replaced with tissue from a vein from elsewhere in the body, or synthetic tissue. This procedure provides an alternative to bypass surgery.

Balloon angioplasty is a non-surgical method of removing atherosclerotic plaque, the fibrous and fatty deposits on the walls of blocked arteries. A catheter with a balloon-like tip is threaded up from the arm or groin through the artery until it reaches the blocked area. The balloon is then inflated many times, flattening the plaque and widening the blood vessel; the balloon is then removed. Often a wire mold called a stent is then inserted into the vessel to keep the vessel open. This technique is especially suitable when only one vessel is blocked.

Laser angioplasty involves a similar technique, except that the catheter has a camera lens on its tip connected to a screen, allowing the physician to spot areas of plaque build-up. A laser fixed to the tip is used to destroy the plaque.

SEE ALSO *Arteries, Atherosclerosis, Blood vessels*

ANKLE

The ankle is the region where the lower leg joins the foot. The ankle attaches the bones of the lower leg, the tibia and fibula, to the talus, one of the bones of the foot. The ankle joint is what's known as a synovial hinge joint and is fairly stable. It allows the heel to be raised from the ground, as in pointing one's toes (plantarflexion) and for the upper surface of the foot to be brought closer to the front of the leg (dorsiflexion). Prominent features of the ankle joint include the medial malleolus, a bony protrusion on the end of the tibia and the lateral malleolus, a similar bony landmark at the lower end of the fibula. The two malleoli, together with a part of the tibia, form a socket in which the talus can move. Because the talus is wider at the front, the joint is most stable when the heel is raised, where the fit between the talus and socket is tightest.

Several ligaments help to make the ankle joint stronger and more stable. The deltoid or medial ligament is a broad, strong, triangular-shaped ligament which connects the medial malleolus to three of the tarsal bones (talus, navicular and calcaneus). On the outside of the ankle there are three cord-like ligaments that attach the lateral malleolus to the talus and calcaneus. These cords are not as strong as the deltoid ligament so they can be more easily damaged. Ligaments between the tibia and fibula also help ankle joint stability by strengthening the socket.

The main muscles producing dorsiflexion of the ankle lie at the front of the lower leg while the main muscles producing plantarflexion are at the back of the lower leg (calf muscles).

Sprain

A sprain is an over-stretching or tearing of ligaments; sprains are particularly common around the ankle joint. A frequent injury, referred to as "twisting the ankle", occurs when the foot is forcefully turned inward. This usually occurs as a result of a fall on an uneven surface and leads to tearing of the ligaments on the outside of the ankle. This will cause pain and swelling in front and below the lateral malleolus and can make the ankle joint quite unstable.

As for most sprain injuries, ice packs, rest and elevation will reduce swelling and aid healing. Injuries to the deltoid ligaments (when the sole of the foot is turned outwards) can also occur but are less common, because these ligaments are stronger.

Fractures

Fractures of the ankle are fairly common, and include breaking of the lateral malleolus and an injury known as Pott's fracture. Pott's fracture occurs when the foot is forcefully

Ankle fracture

The ankle bones are prone to fracture because the ankle is a weight-bearing joint and is easily put under stress. The ankle fracture shown here is called a Pott's fracture.

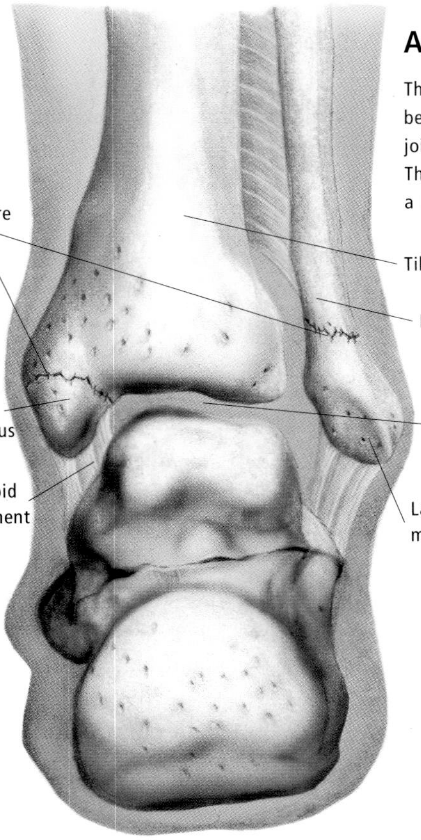

Pott's fracture
Tibia
Fibula
Medial malleolus
Talocrural joint
Deltoid ligament
Lateral malleolus

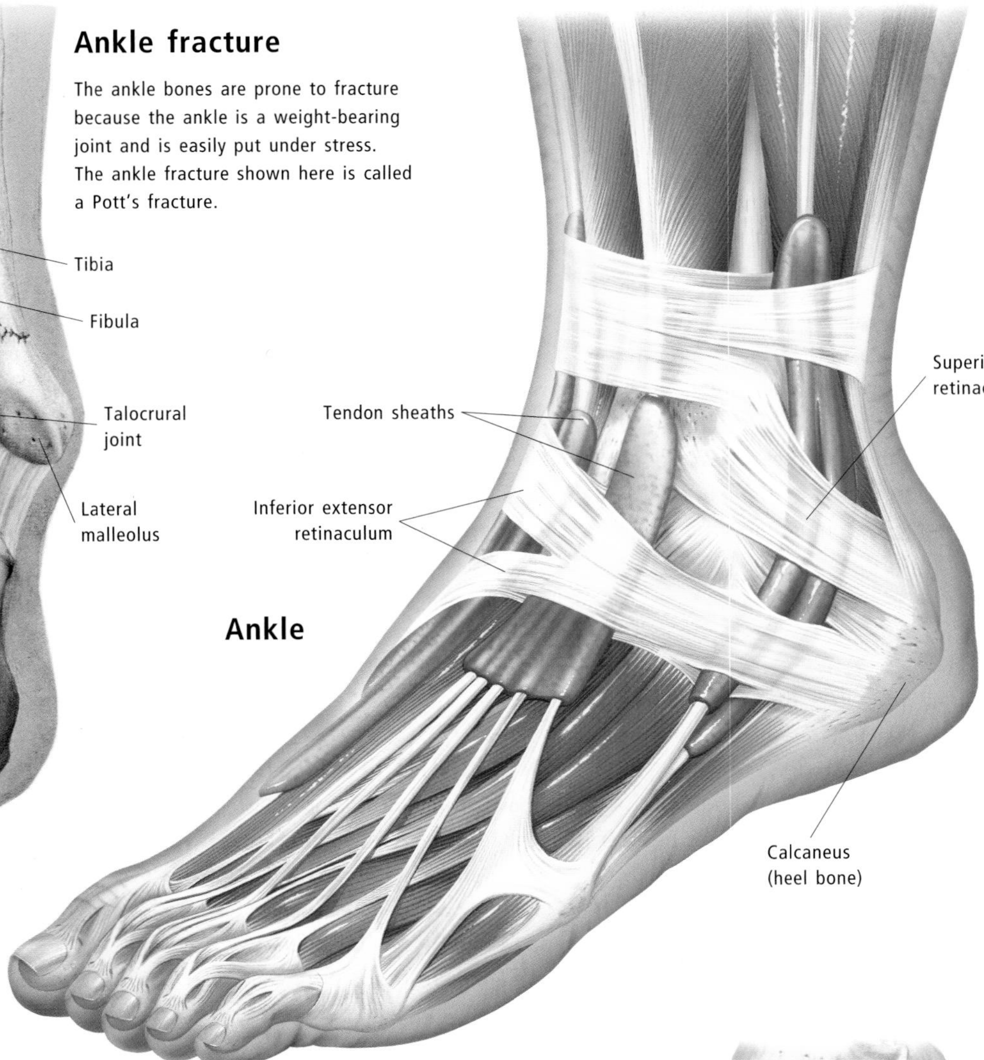

Superior peroneal retinaculum
Tendon sheaths
Inferior extensor retinaculum
Calcaneus (heel bone)

Ankle

turned outward. The medial malleolus is broken and there is also an associated fracture of the fibula, either at the lateral malleolus or higher, on the shaft of the bone.

SEE ALSO *Foot, Fractures, Leg, Sprain*

ANKYLOSING SPONDYLITIS

Ankylosing spondylitis is a form of arthritis affecting young men between 15 and 40 years of age. It involves the spine, the sacro-iliac joints in the pelvis, the hip and the shoulder. Over the years these joints gradually become inflamed and eventually stiff and immovable. The cause is unknown, though the disease tends to be inherited and to run in families.

The first sign of the illness is often low back pain and stiffness, which is worse in the morning, gets better during the day with exercise, but occurs again at night, often waking the sufferer from sleep. As the disease progresses, back pain and stiffness

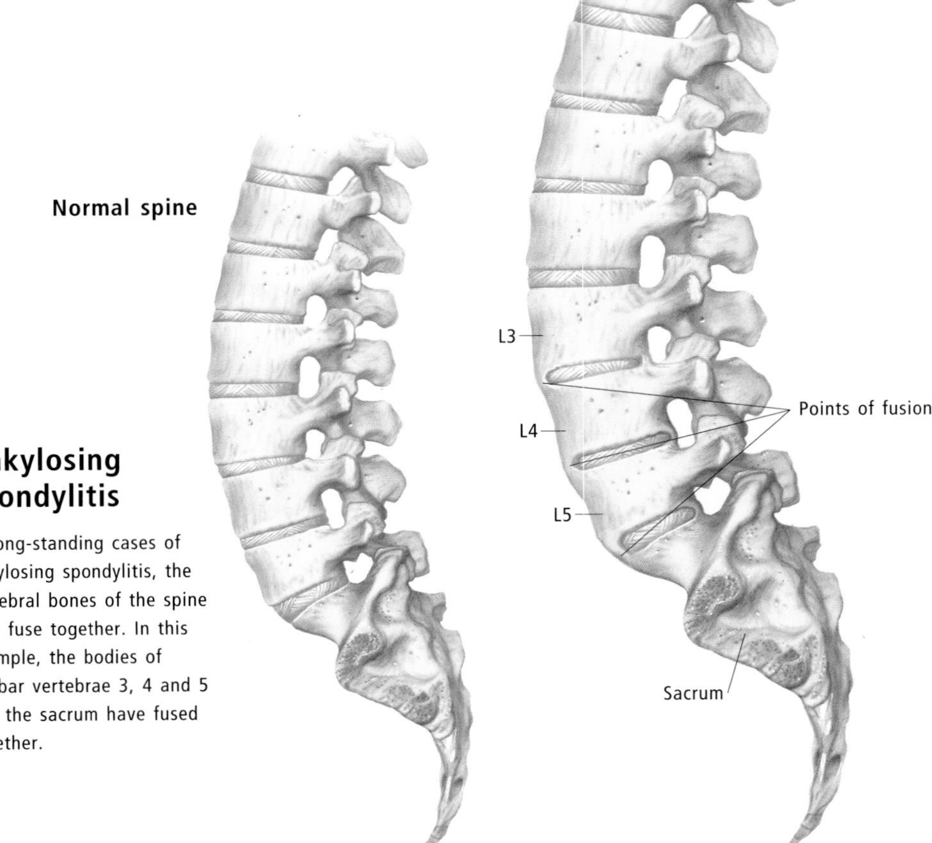

Normal spine

L3
L4
L5
Points of fusion
Sacrum

Ankylosing spondylitis

In long-standing cases of ankylosing spondylitis, the vertebral bones of the spine may fuse together. In this example, the bodies of lumbar vertebrae 3, 4 and 5 and the sacrum have fused together.

eventually affect the upper part of the spine and sometimes the neck. The vertebrae in the spine may become fused, creating an abnormal curve in the upper spine. Hips and shoulders are affected in a third of cases. A quarter of cases develop uveitis, or inflammation of the front part of the eye.

There is no cure for ankylosing spondylitis, but some measures can lessen the effects of the disease. Breathing exercises, and exercises to maintain posture, help with the curvature of the upper spine. Analgesics and anti-inflammatory drugs are commonly prescribed. Surgery, for example hip replacement, may be required in severe cases.

SEE ALSO *Arthritis*

ANTHRAX

Anthrax is an infectious disease caused by the bacterium *Bacillus anthracis*, rarely seen in the Western world today, but which still exists in Africa, Asia and the Middle East. The infection is transmitted to humans most commonly by farm animals such as sheep, cattle, horses, goats and swine, and is transmitted through a break in the skin.

Symptoms include nausea, fever and the occurrence of a skin boil that forms a dark scab. The boil forms slowly and may spread to form other boils.

In another (rarer) form, anthrax spores are inhaled and cause a rapidly fatal pneumonia —hence experimentation by some governments with anthrax as a biological weapon.

Immediate treatment with penicillin or tetracycline is usually effective in treating the skin form of anthrax. A vaccine is available for travelers at risk of exposure to animals or animal products in affected areas.

Anthrax

Anthrax is an infectious disease transmitted from farm animals. In this case it has caused an ulcer on the skin of a finger. The dark area is dead skin and tissue.

ANTHROPOSOPHICAL MEDICINE

Rudolf Steiner, the Austrian philosopher and scientist, pioneered anthroposophical medicine in the early twentieth century. At the heart of its approach is the belief that a person is more than just a body, and that medical treatment needs to integrate the physical and spiritual components of being.

Natural and creative therapies are favored, including herbal and homeopathic preparations, art therapy, music therapy and massage. Best known of the anthroposophical treatments is the mistletoe (*Viscum album*) remedy, given intravenously to cancer patients, and believed to have an anti-tumor action through its immune stimulating effects. Anthroposophical medicine is officially recognized throughout continental Europe.

ANTIARRHYTHMIC DRUGS

Antiarrhythmic drugs control irregularities of the heartbeat. The oldest antiarrhythmics are digitalis and quinidine, both of which were originally plant extracts. Modern antiarrhythmics include beta-blockers, calcium antagonists and disopyramide. Digitalis medications (digoxin and digitoxin) help control the rate of contractions and regulate the rhythm of the heart. If the dose is too high, digitalis toxicity can occur, producing unusual visual effects, nausea and vomiting; blood tests need to be done regularly to monitor blood levels. Beta-blockers such as propanalol, atenolol and pindolol decrease heart rate by affecting conduction in the heart. Beta-blockers can cause asthma attacks, so are not suitable for asthmatics.

SEE ALSO *Heartbeat*

ANTIBIOTICS

Antibiotics are drugs that fight bacterial infection. They work either by preventing an infection from growing (bacteriostatic antibiotics) or by destroying an existing infection (bactericidal antibiotics). Some are effective against a broad range of bacteria (broad-spectrum antibiotics), while others are only effective against certain types of bacteria.

Antibiotics are produced either from a mold or a fungus, or are produced synthetically. Common forms include aminoglycosides, macrolides, penicillins, tetracyclines and cephalosporins. They may be given orally, or via intravenous or intramuscular routes in more serious infections.

The modern trend is against using antibiotics indiscriminately or for the wrong reasons—for example, in treating viral illnesses (on which they have no effect).

A course of antibiotics must be finished to prevent bacteria re-establishing infection and developing immunity against the drug.

Side effects may include rashes, nausea, diarrhea and secondary infections such as thrush. In rare cases, anaphylaxis may occur. Tetracyclines should not be administered during pregnancy, or given to young children as they may discolor developing teeth. Aminoglycosides such as gentamicin, amikacin and tobramycin can cause damage to the auditory nerves and to the kidney.

SEE ALSO *Bacteria, Penicillins*

ANTIBODIES

An antibody forms part of the body's defense against infection. When an invader (antigen) such as a virus or bacterium enters the body during an infection, specialized white blood cells known as lymphocytes react by making proteins called antibodies. These combine with the invader and neutralize it. The presence of antibodies indicates past exposure to a disease. Many blood tests for diseases work by identifying antibodies in the blood.

Antibodies can be created artificially in the body by immunization. This involves exposing the body to a weakened or killed form of virus or other invader. It causes the body to manufacture antibodies, so that if later exposed to the real disease, it can launch a prompt and effective immune response.

SEE ALSO *Immunization*

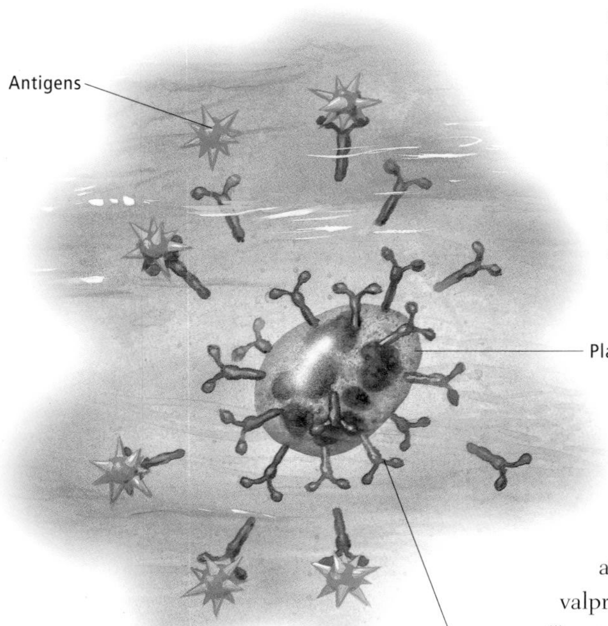
Antigens
Plasma cell
Antibodies

Antibodies

Once the body recognizes a foreign substance (antigen) has entered the body, B lymphocytes are activated, become plasma cells and begin producing antibodies. The antibodies attach to the antigens, which are eventually neutralized.

ANTICOAGULANTS

Anticoagulants are drugs that interfere with the normal clotting of blood. They are used in myocardial infarction (heart attack), strokes, embolism and during surgery in order to prevent blood clotting (thrombosis). Warfarin is an oral preparation suitable for long-term therapy. Heparin is a quick-acting intravenous or intramuscular preparation used over shorter periods, for example in a hospital setting. Low-dose aspirin is taken by many people as a low-grade anticoagulant.

As too much anticoagulant can cause bleeding, people taking them require regular blood tests to ensure correct dosage. They should also carry a card or wear a bracelet identifying the drug and dose in case of accident. Some medications affect the action of anticoagulants—check with your doctor.

SEE ALSO *Blood*

ANTICONVULSANTS

Anticonvulsant drugs prevent epileptic attacks by depressing the activity of the brain. Some are more suited to particular types of seizures and not to other types. They are often used in combination. Anticonvulsants need to be taken for the long term: years, or even for life. However, once the sufferer has been free of seizures for several years, the dose can be reduced or the drugs stopped. Commonly used anticonvulsants include carbamazepine, phenytoin, lamotrigine, gabapentin, topiramate and valproate for generalized ("grand mal") seizures; and valproate or ethosuximide for smaller ("petit mal") seizures. Possible side effects include drowsiness, rashes, dizziness, headache, nausea and indigestion.

SEE ALSO *Convulsions, Epilepsy*

ANTIDEPRESSANTS

Antidepressants are drugs that alleviate depression. They work by correcting the biochemical imbalance in the brain that is thought to be the cause of depression.

The oldest are the tricyclic antidepressants such as amitriptyline and imipramine, which elevate the levels of the neurotransmitters serotonin and norepinephrine (noradrenaline) in the brain. Side effects may include dry mouth, blurred vision, sweating, constipation, urinary problems and impotence (in males).

The monamine-oxidase (MAO) inhibitors are less popular as they interact dangerously with foods such as cheese, some meats, alcohol and yeast extracts. They are usually used only if other antidepressants fail.

The newest category of antidepressants are the serotonin-specific reuptake inhibitors (SSRI). As they work quickly and have few side effects, they are the most commonly prescribed nowadays. Examples include fluoxetine (Prozac) and paroxetine.

It takes from two to six weeks for an antidepressant to begin to work. The initial dose is usually kept low to minimize side effects and is increased over time until the desired result is reached. Most side effects disappear in a few days or weeks.

SEE ALSO *Depression, Psychotropic drugs*

Antidepressants

Serotonin is a neurotransmitter which activates nerve cells in the brain. Sending cells pass serotonin across the synapse to receiving cells but also reabsorb a certain amount. Depression may occur when too much serotonin is reabsorbed by the sending cells and does not reach the receiving cells. Antidepressant drugs called serotonin-specific reuptake inhibitors work by slowing down this reabsorption process, allowing more serotonin to reach receiving cells.

ANTIDIARRHEALS

Antidiarrheals are drugs used for the relief of symptoms of diarrhea. Some are simple absorbent substances such as kaolin, chalk or charcoal. They absorb water and help harden the feces. Others, such as diphenoxylate (often used in combination with atropine), slow down the contractions of the bowel muscle so that the contents are propelled more slowly and more water is

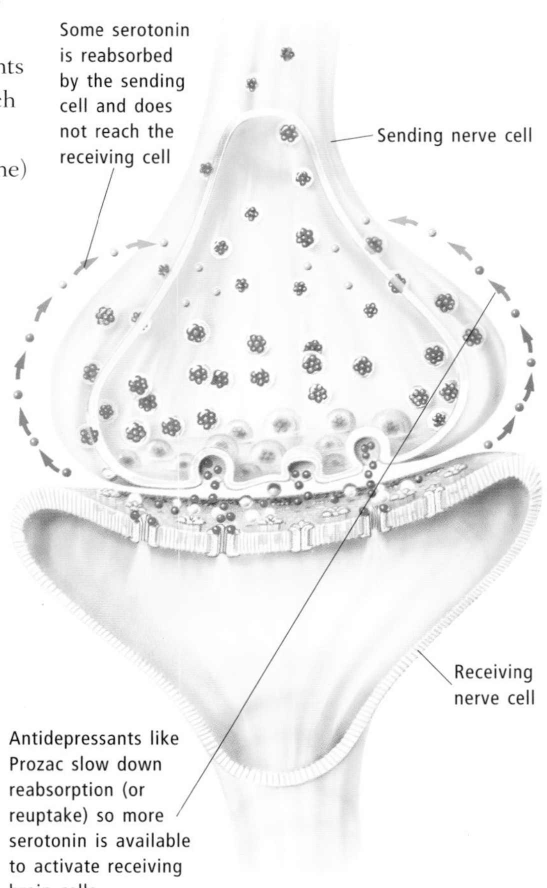
Some serotonin is reabsorbed by the sending cell and does not reach the receiving cell
Sending nerve cell
Receiving nerve cell
Antidepressants like Prozac slow down reabsorption (or reuptake) so more serotonin is available to activate receiving brain cells

A

absorbed by the bowel. Overtreatment with anti-diarrhea drugs can cause constipation and abdominal cramps, so excessive or extended use is not recommended. Codeine, an analgesic, also relieves diarrhea, though prolonged use may cause addiction.

SEE ALSO *Diarrhea*

ANTIEMETIC DRUGS

Antiemetic drugs are used to treat the symptoms of nausea and vomiting. Phenothiazines, a type of major tranquilizer, are the most potent antiemetics, but they also have the greatest number of side effects, including drowsiness, hypotension (low blood pressure) and movement disorders.

Antihistamines (usually used to treat allergies) are also useful in treating nausea, especially when it is associated with motion sickness. Antihistamines may produce drowsiness, so people who take them should not drink alcohol, drive automobiles or operate machinery.

Anticholinergics, which slow the actions of the smooth muscle in the bowel, are often used in the relief of nausea and vomiting associated with vertigo and motion sickness. Side effects of these drugs can include blurred vision, dry mouth and tachycardia (rapid heart rate). They should not be used for treatment of people with glaucoma and urinary retention as they worsen these conditions.

SEE ALSO *Antihistamines, Nausea, Vomiting*

ANTIFUNGALS

Antifungals are used to treat infections such as ringworm, candidiasis and athlete's foot (tinea pedis). Those commonly used include clotrimazole, miconazole and ketoconazole.

Since fungi tend to be more resistant to treatment than other microorganisms, a lengthy duration of treatment is usually required to cure a fungal infection.

Antifungals may be taken in tablet form or applied as creams, ointments or pessaries. Serious internal fungal infections such as actinomycosis, blastomycosis and histoplasmosis may be treated by antifungal injections.

SEE ALSO *Candidiasis, Ringworm, Tinea*

ANTIGEN TESTS

The immune system responds to molecules that are recognized as foreign: these are called antigens and are carried by bacteria (e.g. salmonella), viruses (e.g. hepatitis B), toxins and other substances such as allergens. Antigen tests are used to detect which foreign substance is causing illness or other reactions in the affected person.

It is possible to test for the development of different types of immune responses to an antigen in a number of ways, but an important group of antigen tests is that used to detect responses to allergens in the environment. These allergens include, for example, cat and dog fur; feathers; house dust mites; cockroaches; various molds; and pollens of grasses, weeds or trees. Testing for an allergic response involves introducing small amounts of antigen into the superficial layers of the skin by a prick or scratch, then measuring the resulting zone of redness and wheal formation 30 to 60 minutes later. Multiple antigens are usually tested at once. People predisposed to developing allergic responses often react to several antigens.

SEE ALSO *Allergies*

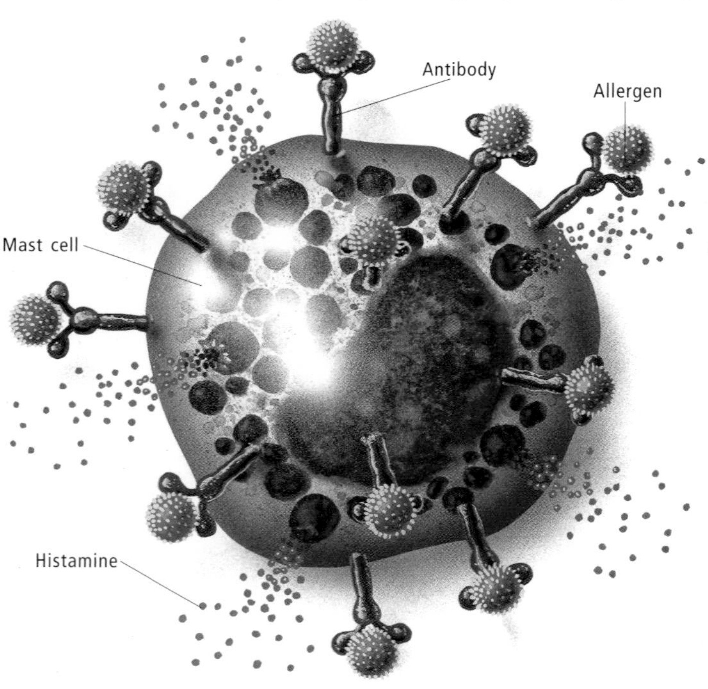

Antihistamines

When mast cells are activated by invading allergens they release a chemical called histamine. This is responsible for the unpleasant effects of allergies like hay fever or hives. Antihistamines block the release of histamine.

ANTIHISTAMINES

Antihistamines form the main group of medicines used in treatment and control of allergies. They work by blocking the action of histamine, a chemical produced in the body as part of an allergic reaction. They can also fight nausea and so can be used to counter travel sickness. The side effect of most antihistamines is drowsiness (though some newer types are less sedating), so they should not be taken before driving or operating machinery, and it is not safe to drink alcohol while on the medication. They are often used at night, and their sedative effect can be useful for treating insomnia.

SEE ALSO *Allergies*

ANTIHYPERTENSIVES

Antihypertensives are drugs used to treat high blood pressure (hypertension). They may be given orally or by injection for rapid effect, and may be used alone or in combination.

Beta-blockers decrease heart rate and cause relaxation of small peripheral blood vessels, lowering blood pressure. They are not suitable for asthmatics as they may cause an asthma attack. Thiazide diuretics relax small blood vessels and also cause the kidneys to increase the amount of salt and water eliminated in the urine. Potassium levels may drop, so doctors also commonly prescribe a potassium supplement.

Calcium channel blockers influence the movement of calcium ions into the cells of the heart and blood vessels, lowering blood pressure and decreasing the heart work load. Alpha-adrenergic blockers and angiotensin-converting enzyme (ACE) inhibitors act by dilating blood vessels. There is evidence that antihypertensive treatment reduces vascular and organ complications (such as to eyes and kidneys).

Because there are often no symptoms, people with high blood pressure may feel normal whether or not they take their medication. But medication should be taken according to the doctor's instructions; treatment may need to be continued for life. Since some medications have annoying side effects, non-compliance with treatment becomes an increasing problem over time.

SEE ALSO *Beta-blockers, Hypertension*

ANTI-INFLAMMATORY DRUGS

Anti-inflammatory drugs reduce inflammation, and are used in conditions such as rheumatoid arthritis, osteoarthritis and connective tissue disorders. They do not cure these disorders, just control the symptoms.

Aspirin is one of the most popular over-the-counter anti-inflammatory drugs. Side effects include irritation of, and bleeding from, the lining of the stomach. The drug should not be given to children, as it may cause Reye's syndrome.

Nonsteroidal anti-inflammatory drugs (NSAIDs) cause fewer digestive problems than aspirin and are often used to treat headache and menstrual cramps. Ibuprofen and naproxen are two common NSAIDs.

To control more serious inflammatory disorders, corticosteroids such as hydrocortisone (cortisol) are often used. However, because of potential side effects such as bruising, osteoporosis, infections, diabetes and high blood pressure, their use is limited to short courses when other therapies fail.

SEE ALSO *Arthritis, Corticosteroids, Nonsteroidal anti-inflammatory drugs, Reye's syndrome*

ANTIOXIDANTS

Antioxidants are substances that deactivate free radicals, protecting cells from damage. Free radicals are oxygen byproducts that are produced both in our bodies and in the environment by factors such as cigarette smoke. They can severely damage human cells, allowing diseases such as cancer to develop.

Vitamins C and E are the most important antioxidants. They appear to prevent carcinogenic (cancer producing) compounds from forming in the stomach, and help prevent atherosclerosis (hardening of arteries).

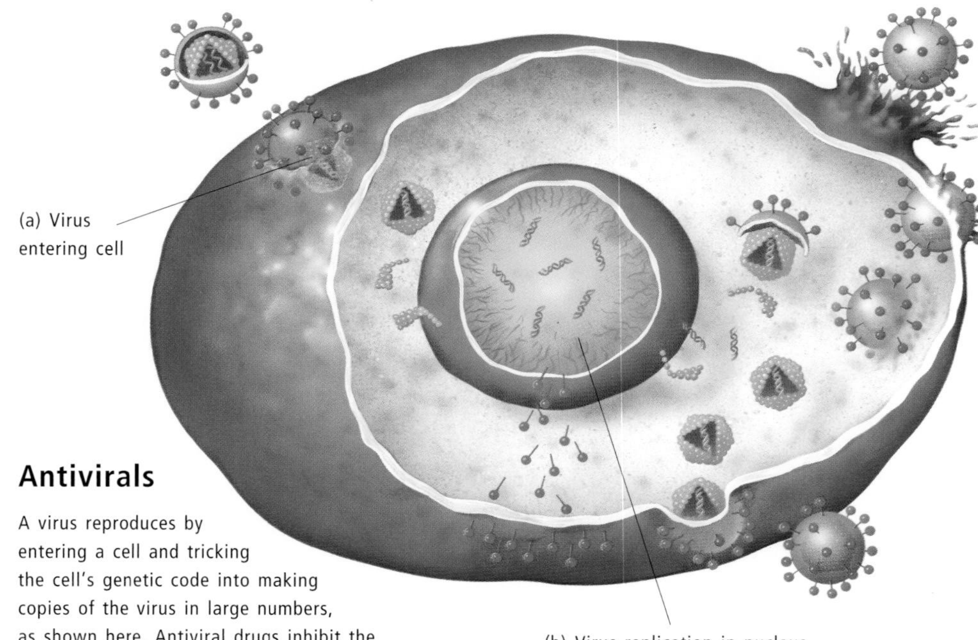

Antivirals

A virus reproduces by entering a cell and tricking the cell's genetic code into making copies of the virus in large numbers, as shown here. Antiviral drugs inhibit the process by preventing the virus from entering the cell; or preventing the cell from making new viruses.

Nutritionists recommend eating a balanced diet that includes at least five to six servings daily of fruits and vegetables, which are high in antioxidants.

SEE ALSO *Atherosclerosis, Nutrition, Vitamins*

ANTIPSYCHOTICS

Also known as "major tranquilizers", antipsychotic drugs (neuroleptics) reduce many of the symptoms of schizophrenia. They do not cure the disorder, but reduce such symptoms as agitation, confusion, hallucinations, distortions and delusions. They allow the sufferer to think more clearly and make better-informed decisions. Response to an antipsychotic can vary. Most schizophrenic patients show improvement, some will experience little or no effect, and others don't need them at all.

In most people, the side effects of antipsychotics are mild. These include drowsiness, rapid heartbeat, dizziness when changing position, weight gain, decrease in sexual ability or interest, menstrual problems, skin rashes or increased susceptibility to sunburn. More serious side effects include muscle spasms of the neck, eye or back, a slowing down of movement and speech, and a shuffling walk.

Tardive dyskinesia is a disorder characterized by involuntary movements affecting the mouth, lips and tongue. These symptoms are usually seen in long-term treatment with older antipsychotics such as haloperidol or chlorpromazine. Most of them can be controlled with an anticholinergic medication. Several new antipsychotic drugs have been introduced, including clozapine, risperidone and olanzapine. They are better tolerated and safer than the older drugs.

SEE ALSO *Schizophrenia, Tranquilizers*

ANTIVIRALS

Antivirals are drugs used to treat viral infections or to prevent them from developing. Usually they work for only one kind of virus infection. Many viruses, including the common cold, don't respond yet to antiviral drugs. Those that do include herpes simplex (cold sores) and herpes zoster (shingles). Treatment with antiviral drugs must be started early if they are to work.

Acyclovir is used to treat the symptoms of chickenpox, shingles and herpes virus infections of the genitals, skin, brain, lips and mouth. It is also used to prevent recurrent genital herpes infections. Although it doesn't cure herpes, it helps relieve pain and discomfort and promotes healing of the sores. Idoxuridine is an antiviral drug that is commonly used to treat viral infections of the eye.

SEE ALSO *Chickenpox, Genital herpes, Herpes simplex, Shingles, Viruses*

A

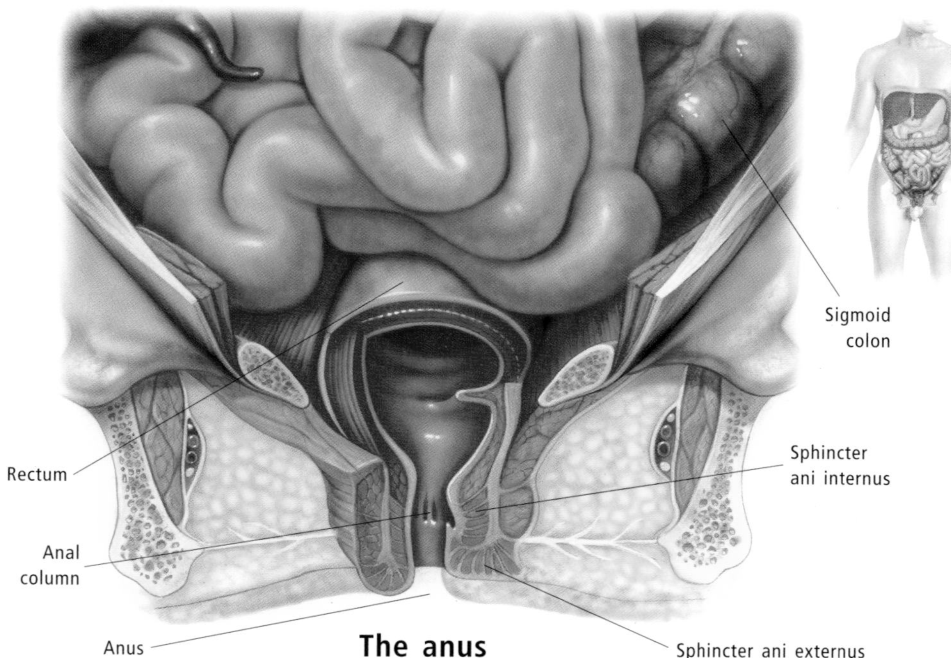

The anus

ANUS

The anus is a short tube about 1½ inches (3–4 centimeters) long leading from the rectum through the anal sphincter to the anal orifice, through which feces are expelled.

Anal fissure

An anal fissure is a slit or tear in the mucosa (or lining) of the anus that produces a tearing pain when feces are passed. Bright red bleeding from the fissure is common. The best treatment is a high-fiber diet and anti-inflammatory ointments. A chronic fissure may result in anal spasm or stenosis (narrowing), requiring minor surgery.

Anal itching (pruritus ani)

Anal itching is caused by irritation of the anal skin. It can be caused by diarrhea, infections (especially yeast infections), skin diseases, or other problems such as hemorrhoids or tearing of the anal skin. Treatment is to clean and dry the area thoroughly. Cortisone cream applied to the anal skin relieves the symptoms.

Hemorrhoids

Hemorrhoids are varicose veins in the lower portion of the rectum or anus. They are common in pregnancy. Symptoms include anal itching and pain during bowel movements. A high-fiber diet helps, and ointment can relieve pain. Ligation (tying off), surgery and injections can also be used.

SEE ALSO *Hemorrhoids*

ANXIETY

Anxiety is an emotional state characterized by feelings of tension, apprehension and uncertainty brought about by anticipation of a real or imagined threat. It is a basic emotion and can be experienced from early childhood.

Most people will experience feelings of anxiety from time to time, and in the mentally healthy these will be manageable. Some measure of anxiety is normal for anyone who has responsibilities or is under pressure. Tensions may even be constructive sometimes, stimulating action. But when fears and worries dominate daily life, particularly when there is no obvious cause and no apparent problem, then anxiety becomes a disorder and needs treatment.

Where anxiety becomes severe it can make normal life, work and relationships impossible. If fears are related to specific situations, such as high places (acrophobia) or spiders (arachnophobia), then the disorder is termed a phobia. When there is no such specific relationship, a generalized anxiety disorder or anxiety neurosis may exist. Anxiety neurosis is thought to arise through repression of emotional issues.

Withdrawal of antidepressants can cause anxiety with symptoms of agitation, irritability, vertigo, light-headedness and fever. These drugs should be started and discontinued only under medical supervision.

Anxiety disorders can be mild or severe, with excessive worry building insidiously to destroy relaxation and lower energy. Sufferers will feel edgy and may startle easily. They may be so obsessed with their worries they cannot wind down, and this may lead them to rely on drugs such as alcohol.

Despite constant anxiety, at this stage they may be coping and might not seek help.

A more severe level of anxiety may show up as an anxiety attack (panic attack). Anxiety attacks can occur without warning, even while relaxing in a seemingly friendly environment, and with no apparent reason. An anxiety attack consists of intense feelings of impending death or physical collapse, panic or crisis. The symptoms can be irregular heartbeat (tachycardia), palpitations, sweating, disturbed breathing, trembling, paralysis and mental confusion. Constant anxiety can be harmful, physically and mentally. Physical symptoms can include irritability, muscle tension and sleeplessness. Over a long period this may lead to depression.

Treatment of anxiety disorders can use a combination of medication and therapy. Various types of tranquilizers such as benzodiazepines and antidepressants can give short-term relief. Other treatments include relaxation techniques, psychotherapy and biofeedback. If there are lifestyle factors that can be changed for the better, this will help to achieve long-term success.

SEE ALSO *Agoraphobia, Biofeedback, Depression, Panic attacks, Phobias, Psychotherapy, Relaxation techniques, Tranquilizers*

ANXIOLYTICS

Anxiolytics (also known as mild tranquilizers) are drugs that reduce anxiety; they include barbiturates, benzodiazepines and buspirone hydrochloride. They provide relief from anxiety and muscle spasm and can be used in treatment of alcohol withdrawal and epileptic fits. Anxiolytics are sometimes given to patients prior to surgery.

People using these drugs will be drowsy and less alert than normal. More rare side effects can include trembling, lack of coordination, rash, low blood pressure, nausea, muscle weakness and jaundice. There is a danger of dependency with extended use, so supervision is needed.

SEE ALSO *Anxiety, Barbiturates, Drug dependence, Psychotropic drugs, Tranquilizers*

AORTA

The aorta, a thick elastic tube, is the largest artery in the body. It arises from the left ventricle of the heart, arches upward, backward and to the left, then down the back of the thorax through the diaphragm and into the abdomen. From the thoracic aorta, arteries arise that supply the heart, head, neck and arms. From the abdominal aorta, arteries supply the abdominal organs, pelvis and legs.

Aortic aneurysm is the abnormal stretching of the walls of the aorta. It is often caused by arteriosclerosis (hardening of the arteries), which usually occurs in older people. It can lead to symptoms such as chest pain and shortness of breath, and can worsen to be a medical emergency requiring hospitalization.

Aortic stenosis is narrowing of the aortic valve, caused by valvular heart disease such as rheumatic fever. The narrowing causes an additional strain on the heart that may lead to angina and heart failure. Surgical replacement with an artificial valve is usually the preferred treatment.

SEE ALSO *Aneurysm, Arteries, Heart*

Aorta

The aorta is the biggest artery in the body. It receives blood from the heart and channels it to the other major arteries of the body.

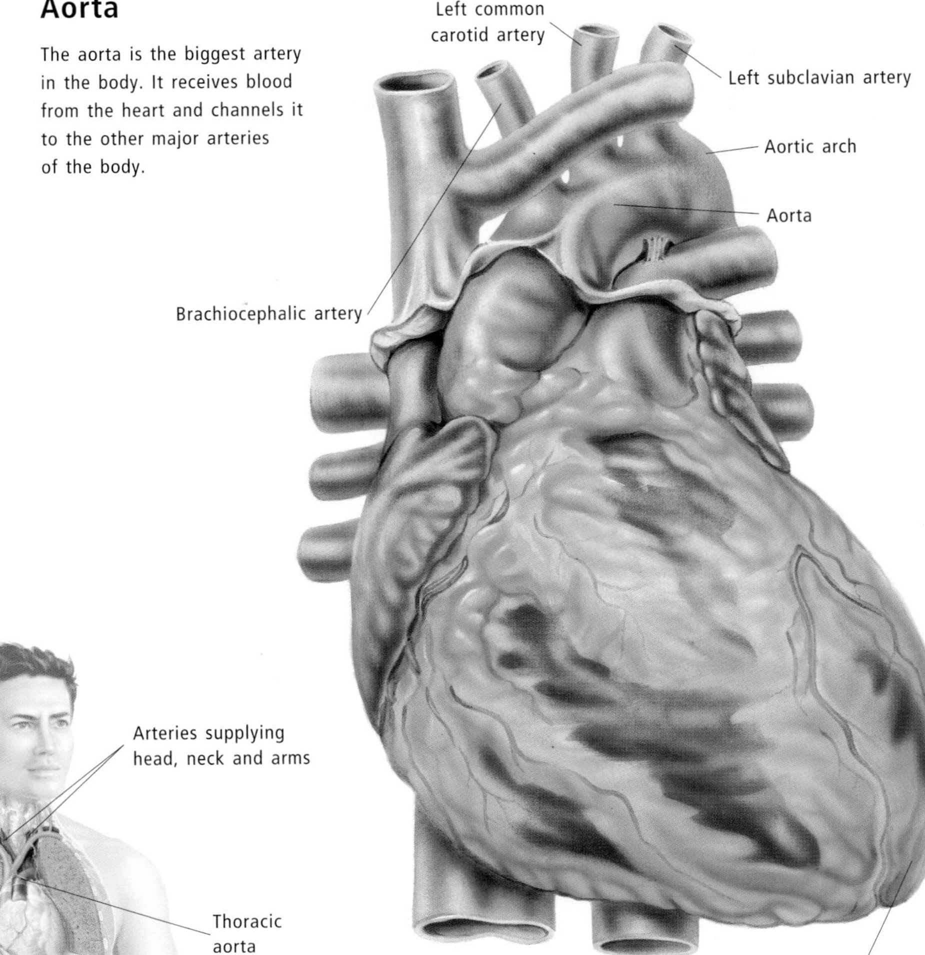

Arteries supplying head, neck and arms

Thoracic aorta

Location of the aorta

Disorders of the aortic valves

Normally the aortic and pulmonary valves open and close at the same time, allowing the heart to pump blood out into the large arteries. In a heart with an incompetent aortic valve, blood will leak back from the aorta into the heart after a pumping action. In a heart with a stenosed (narrowed) aortic valve, the heart will have trouble pumping blood through the valve into the aorta.

Incompetent valve

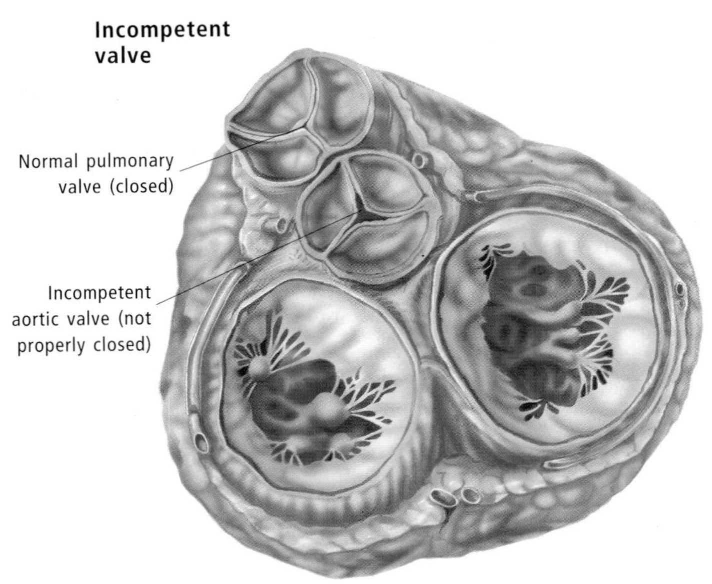

Stenosis of valve

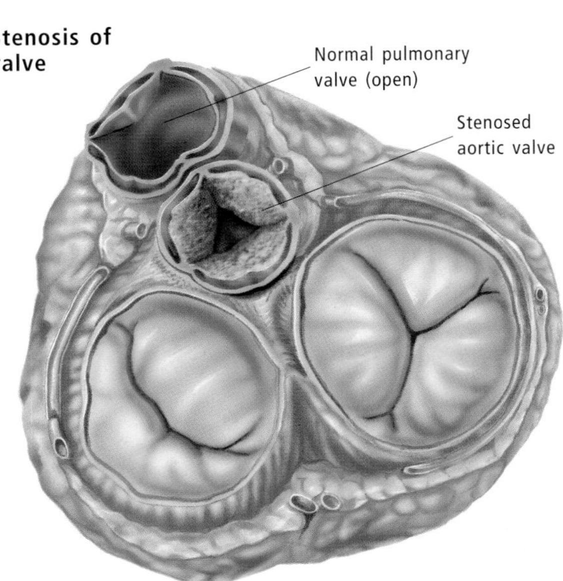

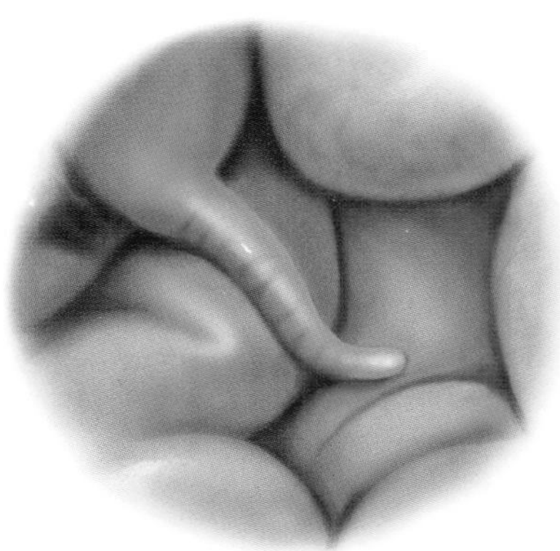

Normal appendix

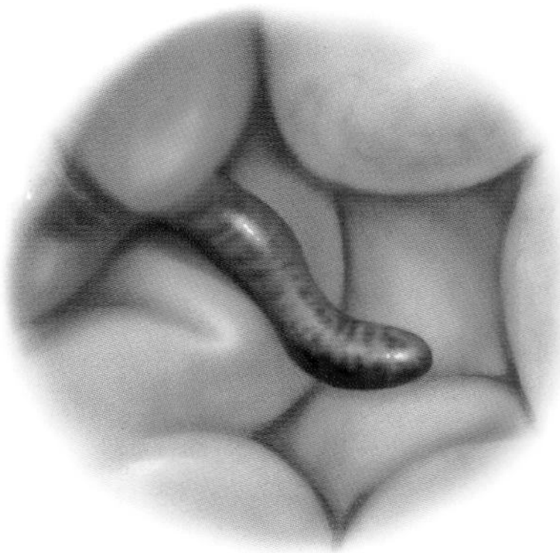

Inflamed appendix

Appendix

The appendix is a redundant organ which is attached to a part of the large bowel. In children especially, it may become inflamed and if so, will need to be surgically removed in hospital. The term for an inflamed appendix is appendicitis.

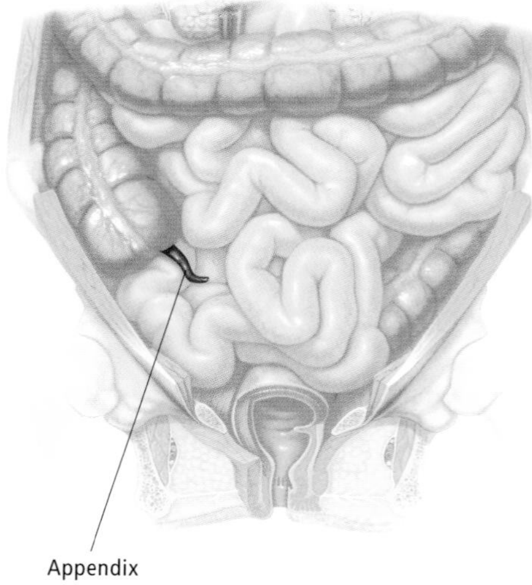

APHASIA

Aphasia is a brain disorder resulting in the loss of speech or ability to understand language, including the ability to read and write. It is usually caused by brain disease, stroke or injury affecting the speech areas of the cerebral cortex. An aphasic seizure is a brain disturbance causing temporary speech loss.

APPENDIX

A thin, worm-shaped pouch, $3\frac{1}{2}$ inches (9 centimeters) long, the appendix is attached to the first part of the colon (large intestine). It has no function and appears to be a relic of evolution. When it becomes inflamed, the condition is known as appendicitis.

Appendicitis

Appendicitis is thought to be caused by an obstruction of the opening into the appendix, possibly by feces or lymph tissue; inflammation of the appendix follows. Pain develops in the lower right side of the abdomen, which is spasmodic at first, but then becomes constant. Other symptoms include fever, nausea and vomiting. In some cases, the inflammation can turn into an abscess which can burst, causing peritonitis.

Appendicitis is treated by urgent surgery. The surgeon removes the appendix through an incision in the lower right side of the abdomen. Recovery from appendectomy takes about a week, and usually there are no further problems.

SEE ALSO *Peritonitis*

APPETITE

Appetite is a general term to express the body's desire for a substance or stimulus. Appetite is most often associated with the need for food or drink, but it can also express the need for sexual intercourse, or for other bodily cravings such as substances to which the body is addicted, including cigarettes, alcohol or drugs.

The need for food or drink is signalled by hunger, a strong and sometimes unpleasant sensation that may result in pain felt in the abdomen or stomach area. The normal response is to seek food or drink and to eat until a feeling of being full overcomes the hunger. The level of glucose in the blood rises as the food is digested and signals that further eating is unnecessary. An area in the hypothalamus of the brain can detect low levels of glucose in the blood and produces the sensation of hunger.

Appetite may disappear temporarily during illness but usually responds to the gradual reintroduction of foods. Anorexics will deliberately choose to ignore hunger pains to exert control over their appetite.

In societies where people generally have enough food to sustain healthy life, personal appetites may regulate dietary habits and people will eat what they like rather than what they actually need; the sensations of deprivation produced by true hunger will rarely be experienced. Research shows that high-fat foods may not generate a feeling of fullness that is the signal to stop eating.

Exercise lowers the blood sugar level and, when taken regularly, can help to regulate the appetite so that food intake matches the body's energy needs. Insulin, a hormone produced by the pancreas and missing in diabetics, lowers blood sugar levels and can stimulate appetite by inducing hunger.

When food intake is not properly regulated a person may easily eat more, or less, than is necessary for health. They become overweight or obese through overeating and suffer related physical problems. Undereating will cause weight loss plus a range of additional problems resulting from the lack of proper nutrients in the diet.

Appetites change when people from one culture go to live in another. Traditional foods may not be available, or new foods may be more attractive or be seen as more socially acceptable. Regulating the appetite may be difficult with new foods to choose from. This trend is seen in Japan where imported dairy foods and meat are widely eaten, replacing traditional foods which are relatively low in protein.

Appetite suppressants are drugs sometimes used to reduce hunger and make it easier to follow a weight reduction diet. Their effect is temporary and they carry a risk of dependency or addiction plus worrying side effects such as increased blood pressure, restlessness and insomnia.

SEE ALSO *Diet, Nutrition, Obesity*

ARM

The arm, or upper limb, extends from the shoulder, where it is attached to the trunk, to the wrist, where it joins the hand. It has two parts: the upper arm, the section between the shoulder and elbow, and the forearm which extends from the elbow to the wrist. The whole limb is designed for mobility. It gives the hand such a range of motion that it can reach most regions of the body and manipulate external objects.

The upper arm

The upper arm contains one bone, the humerus, which joins the shoulder blade (scapula) at the shoulder joint. This is a ball and socket joint, in which the head of the humerus engages with a shallow socket on the shoulder blade. The shape of the joint gives mobility to the upper arm.

The shoulder joint is strengthened by ligaments and by the long tendon of the biceps muscle, which passes through the joint cavity. Important muscles involved in shoulder movements include the deltoid, which makes the rounded contour over the upper surface of the arm and shoulder, and a group of four muscles known as the rotator cuff muscles. These help to raise and rotate the arm, and also contribute to

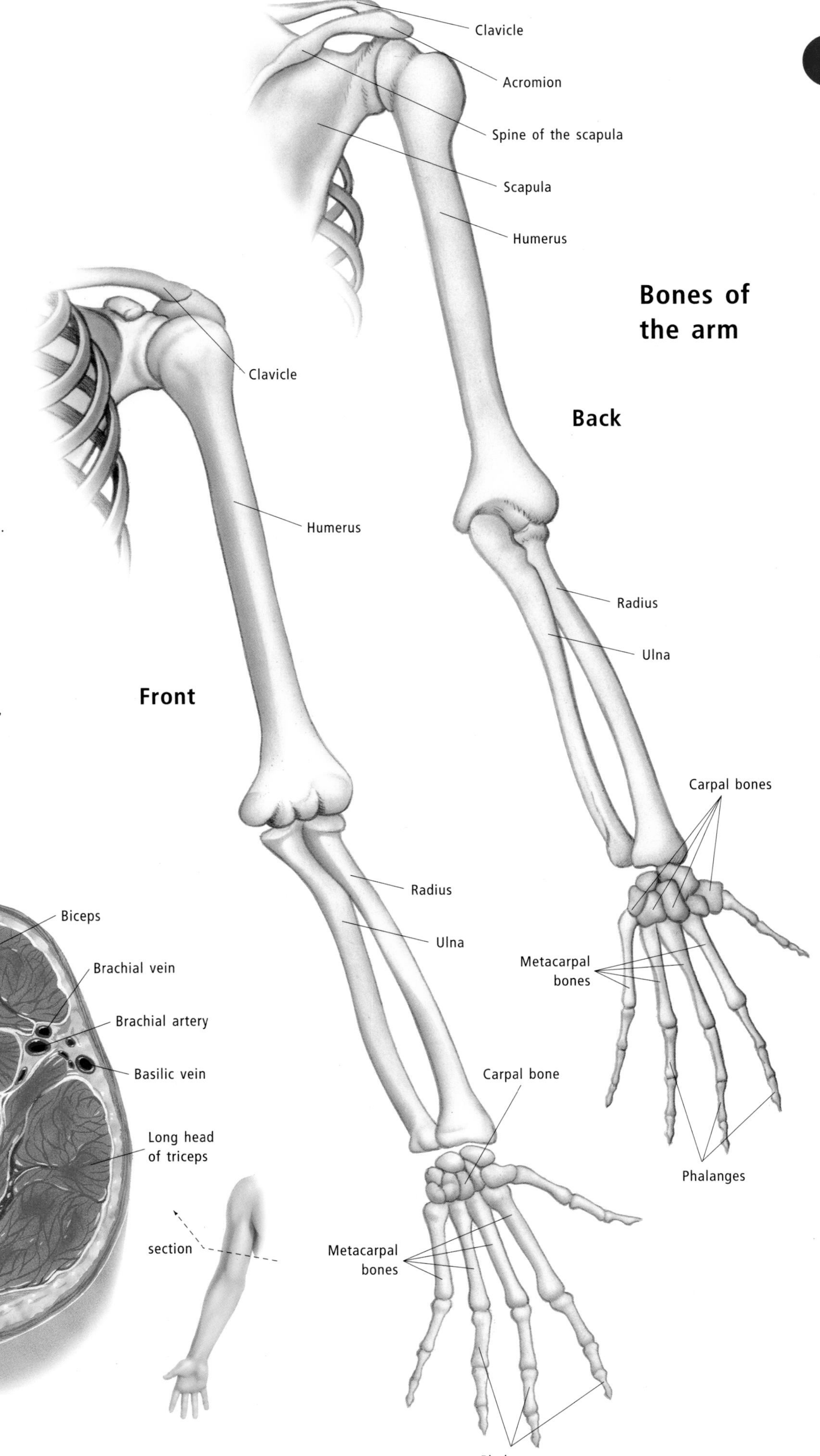

A

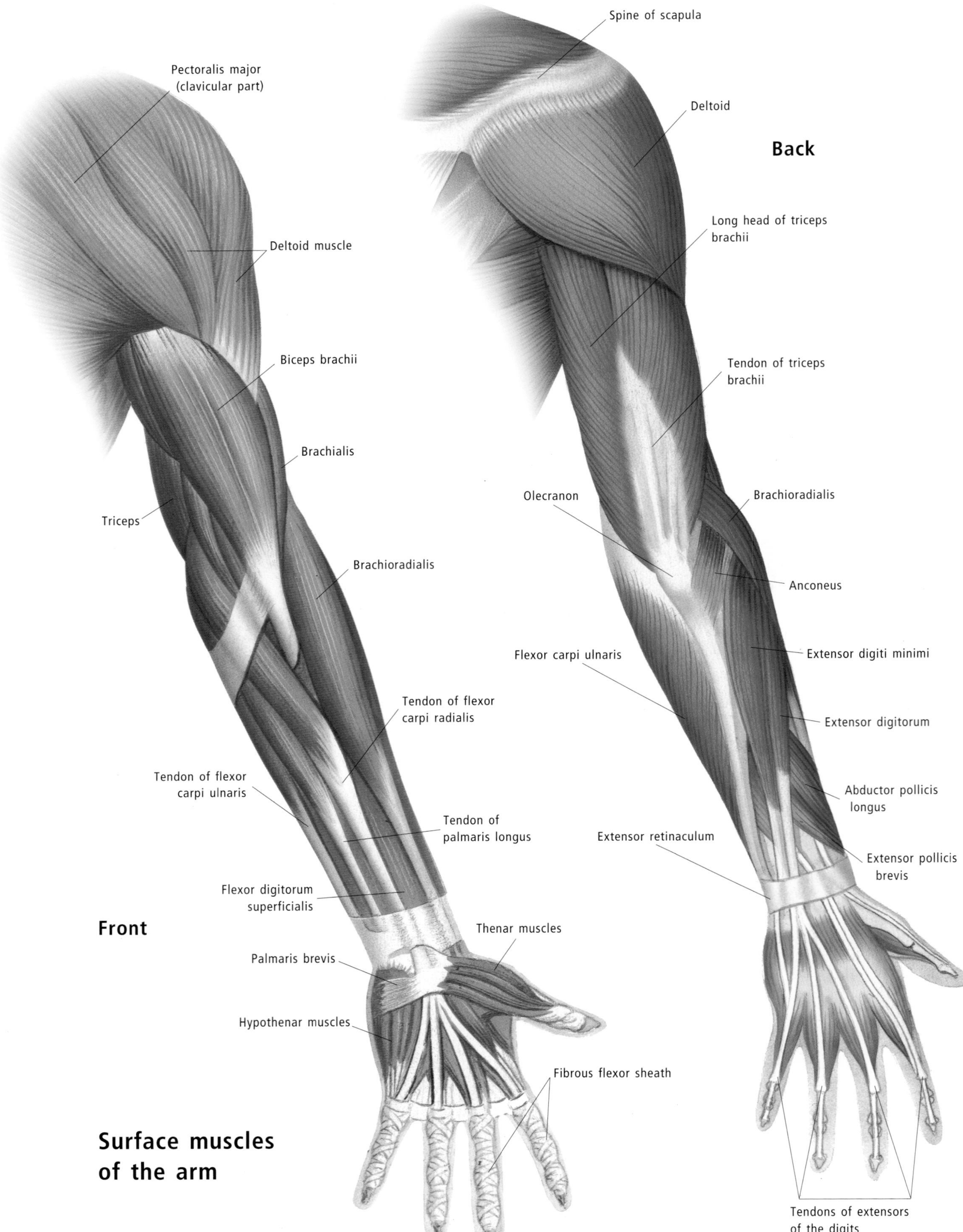
Pectoralis major
(clavicular part)
Deltoid muscle
Biceps brachii
Brachialis
Triceps
Brachioradialis
Tendon of flexor
carpi radialis
Tendon of flexor
carpi ulnaris
Tendon of
palmaris longus
Flexor digitorum
superficialis
Front
Thenar muscles
Palmaris brevis
Hypothenar muscles
Fibrous flexor sheath
Spine of scapula
Deltoid
Back
Long head of triceps
brachii
Tendon of triceps
brachii
Olecranon
Brachioradialis
Anconeus
Flexor carpi ulnaris
Extensor digiti minimi
Extensor digitorum
Abductor pollicis
longus
Extensor retinaculum
Extensor pollicis
brevis
Tendons of extensors
of the digits

Surface muscles of the arm

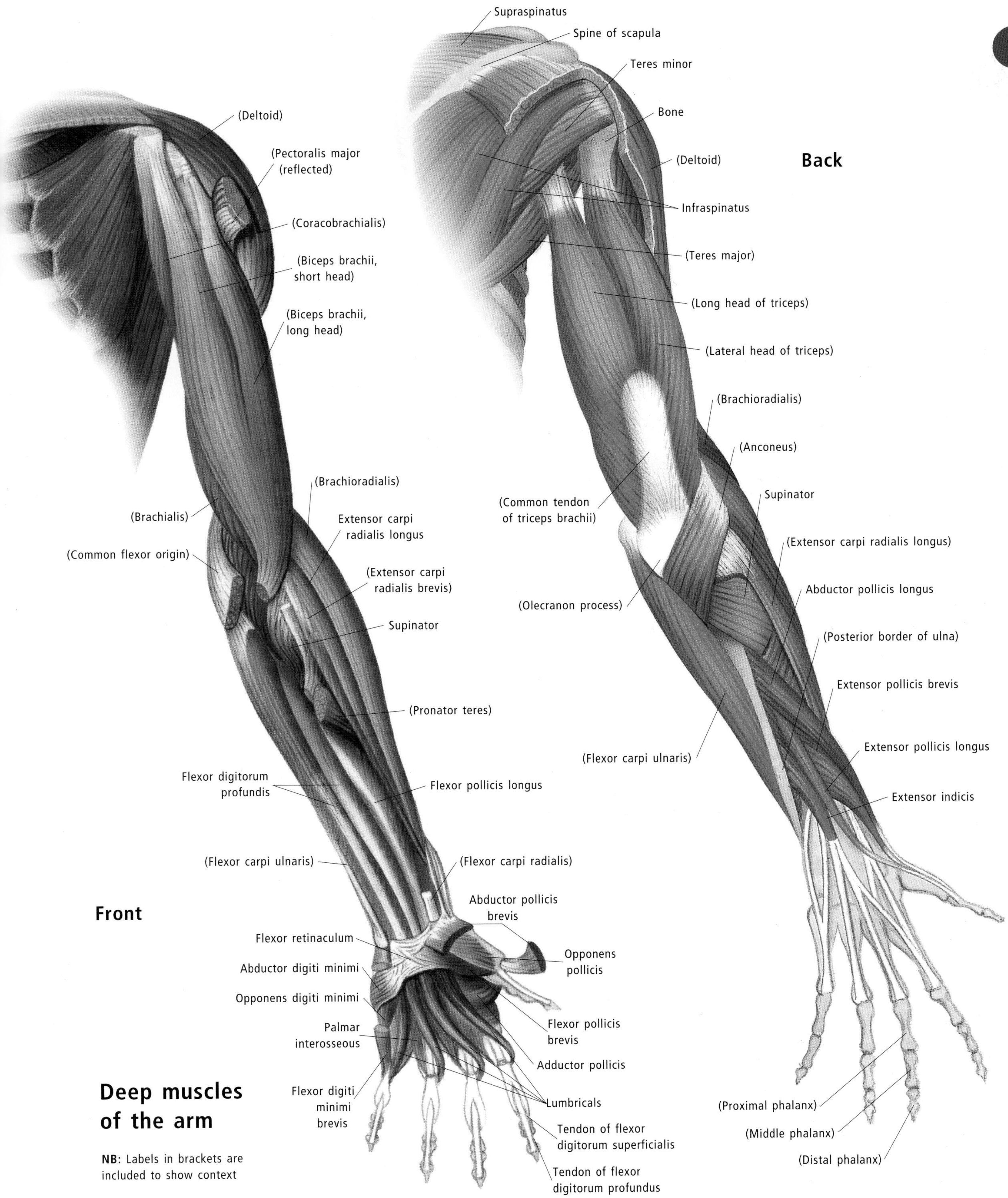

A

Front

(Deltoid)
(Pectoralis major (reflected))
(Coracobrachialis)
(Biceps brachii, short head)
(Biceps brachii, long head)
(Brachioradialis)
(Brachialis)
Extensor carpi radialis longus
(Common flexor origin)
(Extensor carpi radialis brevis)
Supinator
(Pronator teres)
Flexor digitorum profundis
Flexor pollicis longus
(Flexor carpi ulnaris)
(Flexor carpi radialis)
Abductor pollicis brevis
Flexor retinaculum
Opponens pollicis
Abductor digiti minimi
Opponens digiti minimi
Flexor pollicis brevis
Palmar interosseous
Adductor pollicis
Flexor digiti minimi brevis
Lumbricals
Tendon of flexor digitorum superficialis
Tendon of flexor digitorum profundus

Back

Supraspinatus
Spine of scapula
Teres minor
Bone
(Deltoid)
Infraspinatus
(Teres major)
(Long head of triceps)
(Lateral head of triceps)
(Brachioradialis)
(Anconeus)
Supinator
(Common tendon of triceps brachii)
(Extensor carpi radialis longus)
Abductor pollicis longus
(Olecranon process)
(Posterior border of ulna)
Extensor pollicis brevis
(Flexor carpi ulnaris)
Extensor pollicis longus
Extensor indicis
(Proximal phalanx)
(Middle phalanx)
(Distal phalanx)

Deep muscles of the arm

NB: Labels in brackets are included to show context

A

shoulder joint stability. The tendon of the supraspinatus, one of the rotator cuff muscles, can become inflamed as it passes under a bony projection of the shoulder blade. This can cause pain when the arm is raised to a certain position, a condition known as a painful arc. The shoulder joint is relatively unstable and can dislocate downward fairly easily, by a direct blow to the shoulder, for instance, as in sports injuries.

The region just below the shoulder, between the trunk and upper arm, is known as the armpit or axilla. Blood vessels and nerves supplying the arm travel through this region. The armpit also contains lymph nodes which drain the arm, hand and breast. These nodes can become swollen, as a result of an infection in the hand, for instance. They can also become sites of secondary growths in breast cancer. Their removal in a radical mastectomy can lead to a swollen arm.

The major artery of the arm, the brachial artery, starts at the top of the arm and passes down the inside of the arm to the front of the elbow. Fractures to the shaft of the humerus can damage the brachial artery, or the radial nerve, which winds around the back of the humerus.

The elbow

The elbow joint separates the humerus from the two forearm bones, the radius and the ulna. This is a synovial hinge joint, which is a relatively stable joint. It allows the arm to flex (bend) and extend. Important muscles for flexion include the biceps and brachialis, while the main extensor muscle is the triceps. The sharp point of the elbow is due to a projection of the ulnar bone called the olecranon. The olecranon is covered by a sac, or bursa, which can become swollen and inflamed, leading to a condition commonly known as bursitis.

At the elbow, the brachial artery divides into two branches, the radial and ulnar, and these arteries supply the forearm and hand. Veins lying close to the surface of the inside (front) of the elbow region are a common site for taking blood samples.

Three major nerves—the ulnar, median and radial—also pass through the elbow region. These three nerves control the feeling and movement of the forearm and hand. The ulnar nerve is particularly vulnerable where it passes behind the elbow joint, just under the skin. A sharp tap on the elbow in this region—hitting the "funny bone"—activates the ulnar nerve and sends a shooting pain down the side of the arm.

Colles' fracture

A Colles' fracture is often caused by a fall on the outstretched arm. The broken fragments must be realigned and held in place by a plaster cast covering the wrist and elbow until healed.

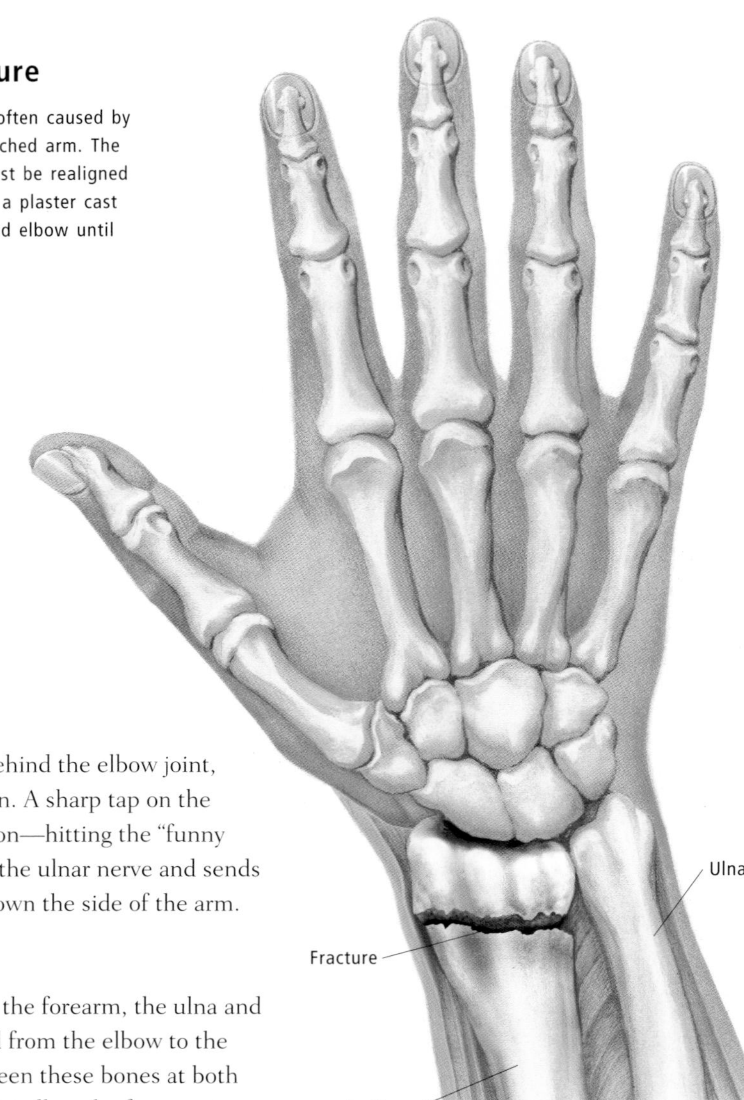

The forearm

The two bones of the forearm, the ulna and the radius, extend from the elbow to the wrist. Joints between these bones at both the elbow and wrist allow the forearm to be rotated, from the palm held upwards (supination) to the palm held downwards (pronation). These are the movements that are used when you are undoing a screw top bottle (supination) or tightening a screw (pronation). In these movement the radius pivots around the ulna. Occasionally in young children the joint between the radius and ulna closest to the elbow can dislocate when the child is forcefully lifted or pulled forward. This can normally be treated quite easily by a doctor.

The forearm contains many of the muscles involved in hand movements. Most of the powerful muscles for gripping an object or making a fist (the flexor muscles) lie in the inside (front) of the forearm. Similarly the extensor muscles which are used for straightening the fingers lie on the outside (back) of the forearm. Extensive use of these muscles can cause pain: pain in the extensors is known as "tennis elbow", while for the flexors it is "golfer's elbow". Both can be helped by rest and physical therapy. The long tendons of these finger flexors and extensors have to pass across the wrist joint and hand to reach the fingers. They can therefore be damaged by cuts or inflamed by overuse, as can occur with prolonged typing.

The forearm is supplied by two arteries, the ulnar and radial. The pulse can be felt easily in either of these vessels if they are pressed against the underlying bone at the end of the forearm, close to the wrist.

The forearm is the site of one of the commonest fractures, known as Colles' fracture. It usually occurs when someone falls and lands on an outstretched arm. The deformity is described as "dinner-fork", with the broken part of the radius closest to the wrist pushed behind the remaining part. Treatment includes repositioning the bone and immobilizing the wrist and elbow.

SEE ALSO *Elbow, Shoulder*

A

AROMATHERAPY

Aromatherapy is based on the principles of holistic health. It consists of the use of natural aromatic essences extracted from plants for therapeutic purposes. Aromatherapists believe that the actions of the oils maintain and restore the natural life force which supports the body's own healing mechanisms. The oils are said to have both physiological and psychological actions, the latter operating via the sense of smell. Physiologically the oils are believed to work by being absorbed in minute amounts through the skin and mucous membranes into the bloodstream, affecting the entire body's organs and systems.

Aromatherapists most frequently employ therapeutic massage to administer oils, using in addition a variety of techniques that may include shiatsu and reflexology. Individual blends of oils are made up for each patient, taking into account the volatility of the oils, the therapeutic effects of each oil and the patient's preferred smells. Aromatherapy has also become popular for home use, especially in baths and oil burners.

History

The history of aromatherapy dates back at least 4,000 years in the Middle East and in China. Scented oils were widely used as perfumes, bath and massage oils by ancient Greek and Roman physicians. The production of essential oils through distillation was mastered by the Arabian physician Avicenna in the late tenth century and their use was spread to Europe by the returning Crusaders.

By medieval times, these oils were an important part of the physician's dispensary. They were universally acknowledged for their antiseptic properties; it was believed that perfumers were rarely affected by cholera and other illnesses.

With the advent of modern medicine in the nineteenth century, the medical use of essential oils declined. However, in the early twentieth century, French and Italian physicians and biochemists, most notably Rene Gattefosse, utilized scientific research and advanced distillation techniques to build up a modern system of aromatherapy which these days is becoming increasingly popular worldwide.

Essential oils

Essential oils, also known as volatile oils, are the odorous extract of plants. They differ from fixed oils (e.g. olive, sunflower) in two ways: they can be distilled; and they do not leave a permanent grease mark on paper. Essential oils readily evaporate at room temperature when exposed to air and, like fixed oils, are not readily soluble in water.

Essential oils are compounds whose many constituents unite to produce their unique therapeutic and aromatic signature. The most common constituents belong to chemical families including alcohols, aldehydes, esters, phenols, nitrogen compounds and sulphur compounds. However it is not so much the individual constituents which are considered by aromatherapists to be therapeutic as the effect of their combined action. For this reason the oils are extracted from the whole plant (including bark, flowers, seeds, leaves or roots) with maximum preservation of all of their constituents.

The quality of essential oils varies considerably, depending on the time of day and year in which the plant was harvested and its soil conditions and climate. The amount of oil present in plants varies quite considerably, between approximately .01 percent and 10 percent.

There is a variety of methods for extracting essential oils. The main methods are distillation (open-fire, steam or vacuum), maceration (softening by soaking) in vegetable oils or fats, dissolving by volatile solvents, and pressing. The cost of oils varies enormously depending on their quality, availability and method of harvesting and extraction. Only essential oils that are 100 percent pure are considered suitable for therapeutic use.

Aromatherapists classify essential oils according to their various therapeutic properties. Many essential oils are antiseptic.

Aromatherapists also classify oils by their volatility, classifying them into one of the three following groups.

Top notes are fast-acting oils which are the most stimulating and uplifting to body and mind (e.g. bergamot, lemon and eucalyptus).

Middle notes are moderately volatile oils that work on the body's functions (e.g. chamomile, lavender and peppermint).

Base notes evaporate slowly, and have relaxing and sedating qualities (e.g. sandalwood, patchouli and ylang ylang).

Methods and uses

Aromatherapy utilizes the essential oils therapeutically through a number of different methods. These include the following.

Baths (full body, sitz, hand or feet) are considered useful for insomnia, muscular disorders, circulation problems, vaginal infections, rheumatism and arthritis. A few drops of oil are added to a full warm bath.

Burners and diffusers scent a room. The soothing vapors may help in respiratory disorders, anxiety and depression.

Compresses soaked in warm water with oils added may relieve bruises, muscular problems and headaches.

Inhalations are recommended by aromatherapists for respiratory disorders and skin conditions. A bowl of hot water with oil added or a handkerchief sprinkled with oil are the suggested methods of inhalation.

Internally, oils can be taken in very small doses added to sugar, honey and water, wine or tea (though see the warning following about ingestion of these oils). This method is used for digestive disorders, cystitis and dysmenorrhea.

Massage is recommended for muscular problems, rheumatism, arthritis, circulation problems, skin conditions, depression, anxiety and headaches. Essential oils are added to a fixed carrier oil such as cold-pressed apricot kernel, sweet almond or grape seed. Small amounts of wheatgerm oil or vitamin E oil are added to prevent oxidation.

The most commonly prescribed essential oils include the following.

Lavender is a versatile oil, used for treatment of insomnia, headaches, depression, anxiety, burns, wounds, heat exhaustion and insect stings.

Eucalyptus is used for treating respiratory infections, fevers, exhaustion, cramps, wounds and skin ulcers.

Rosemary is said to relieve poor circulation, headaches, general debility, poor memory, muscular aches and pains.

Tea tree can be used for respiratory infections, skin conditions, fungal conditions, wounds and insect bites.

A

Peppermint is often used for digestive disorders, headaches, influenza and colds.

Chamomile is used for digestive disorders, balancing the female reproductive system, headaches, muscular and rheumatic pain, nervous tension and insomnia.

Jasmine is used for the treatment of dysmenorrhea, nervous debility, depression, apathy and poor libido.

Sandalwood is used to treat urogenital infections, respiratory infections and skin inflammation.

Clary sage is used to balance the female reproductive system, and may help with debility, depression and nervous conditions.

Warning

Essential oils should be used with caution as some are highly toxic and irritating to the skin. For safe use, always observe the following guidelines:

- Do not take internally unless prescribed by a qualified practitioner.
- Use only under professional guidance if you are pregnant, suffering from blood pressure disorders or epilepsy.
- Before using any oil on the skin, patch test on the skin, using a diluted amount of the oil, to check for allergic reactions.
- Always use in dilution.
- Do not use for prolonged periods.
- If your symptoms are not relieved by aromatherapy, consult a primary health physician (general practitioner).

ARRHYTHMIA

An arrhythmia (also known as a dysrhythmia) is a variation in heartbeat from the normal rhythm. An arrhythmia may be a normal variation in the heartbeat, or it may be due to disease that has damaged the heart muscle and caused irregularities in nerve conduction and muscle contraction. Certain drugs, including caffeine, cocaine, psychotropics, and sympathomimetics, can also cause arrhythmias.

Not all arrhythmias are dangerous. In sinus arrhythmia, a normal occurrence in children, the pulse rate increases or decreases with breathing. Sinus arrhythmia usually does not require treatment.

Some other arrhythmias (varying in their degrees of danger) include atrial fibrillation, paroxysmal supraventricular tachycardia, sinus tachycardia, sinus bradycardia, bradycardia associated with heart block, sick sinus syndrome and ectopic heartbeat.

Certain types of arrythmia can be life-threatening. Ventricular fibrillation and ventricular tachycardia, for example, can cause cardiac arrest and severe decrease in blood flow to tissues and organs.

Symptoms of arrhythmia include noticeable changes to the rhythm or pattern of the pulse, a sensation of awareness of the heartbeat (palpitations), chest pain, shortness of breath, light-headedness, dizziness or unconsciousness. In ventricular fibrillation, the first symptom may be loss of heartbeat; sudden death can occur in this situation.

To confirm and diagnose an arrhythmia, tests such as an electrocardiogram (EKG) and 24-hour Holter monitoring are often performed. An echocardiogram and coronary angiography could show heart disease that may be producing an arrhythmia.

Arrhythmias are usually treated with drugs; either traditional antiarrhythmic drugs such as digitalis and quinidine, or more modern antiarrhythmics such as beta-blockers, calcium antagonists and disopyramide. Some arrhythmias are treated by electrical destruction of diseased tissue, and sometimes a surgical implant is inserted.

SEE ALSO ***Angiography, Antiarrhythmic drugs, Echocardiogram, Electrocardiogram, Fibrillation, Heart, Heartbeat, Holter monitor, Tachycardia***

ART THERAPY

Although artwork created by patients had been studied by psychiatrists such as Jung and Freud from around the turn of the twentieth century, it was not until after World War II that art therapy gained widespread acceptance in both the UK and the USA when it was used to treat traumatized veterans.

In art therapy, patients are encouraged to express themselves through drawing, painting, sculpting and other art media. The focus of the therapy is not on creating a masterpiece but on the actual process of art making, and the sharing with the therapist of the thoughts and feelings that arise out of this. Interpretations of the art come from the patient rather than the therapist.

Art therapy has been found to be valuable in its ability to provide a safe place for the release of painful and potentially destructive feelings. The patient is able to express unconscious concerns, thus helping resolve old issues that have been repressed or new issues that may be only just arising.

Art therapy is used in mental health programs with people of all ages, and in children's hospitals, rehabilitation centers and in private practice. Sessions can be undertaken individually or in couples, families or groups.

ARTERIES

Arteries are flexible, thick-walled, tube-shaped blood vessels that carry blood away from the heart to the rest of the body.

The largest artery is the aorta, which channels blood from the heart to other arteries, and to the body's organs and other structures. Two small branches of the aorta, the coronary arteries, supply the blood to the heart muscle itself. The right and left carotid arteries carry blood to the two sides of the neck and head. Blood flows to the shoulders and arms through the right and left subclavian arteries. In the abdomen, the aorta divides into two large branches, the left and right iliac, supplying blood to the pelvic region. The iliac arteries then continue into the legs, where they are called the femoral arteries.

From the arteries, blood passes into very small blood vessels called capillaries, and from there to veins and then back to the heart. The heart pumps the blood through the pulmonary artery to the lungs, where it becomes oxygenated. The blood is then returned to the heart, where it is once again pumped out through the aorta.

Arteriosclerosis

Arteriosclerosis is a disease in which the arteries thicken and lose their elasticity. It is often referred to as "hardening of the arteries". The most common cause of arteriosclerosis is a process called atherosclerosis (also known as atheroma) in which fatty deposits called plaques are deposited within the endothelium (the inner lining of the arteries). The plaques make the blood vessels narrower, restricting blood supply.

Angiography

Angiography is an investigative x-ray technique that is used to show the nature and extent of disease in arteries, veins and lymph vessels. It is often used prior to surgery. If angiography shows extensive disease, a vascular surgeon may perform endarterectomy (removal of the deposits in the arteries) or angioplasty (repair of the affected arteries) or may bypass the diseased section.

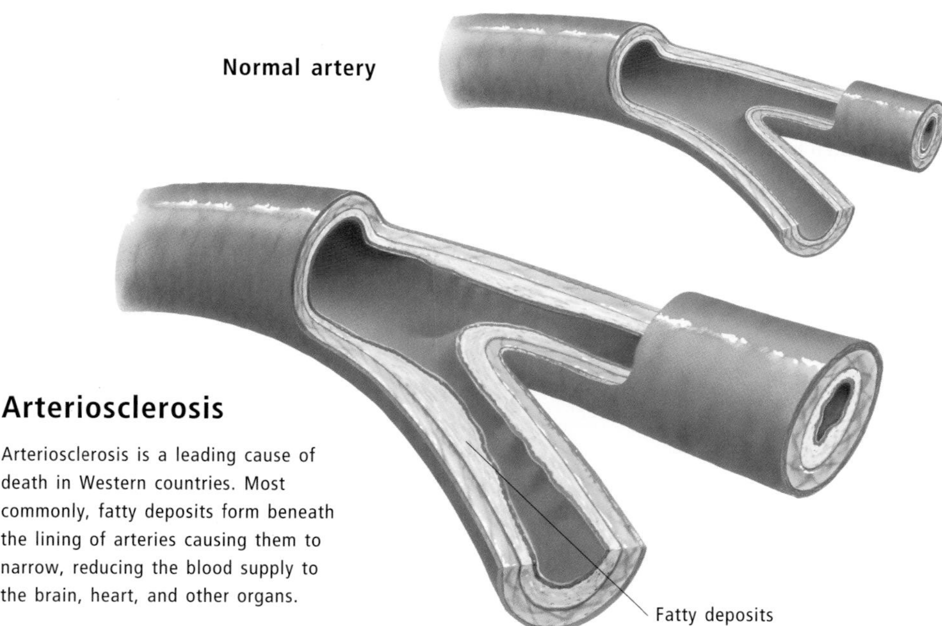

Arteriosclerosis

Arteriosclerosis is a leading cause of death in Western countries. Most commonly, fatty deposits form beneath the lining of arteries causing them to narrow, reducing the blood supply to the brain, heart, and other organs.

Vasculitis

Vasculitis (angiitis) is a general term for a group of autoimmune diseases which feature inflammation of the blood vessels. Polyarteritis nodosa, for example, affects arteries in the muscles, joints, intestines, nerves, kidneys and skin. Diagnosis of polyarteritis nodosa is confirmed by a biopsy of the relevant tissue. Other examples of vasculitis include Kawasaki disease, Behçet's disease, Wegener's granulomatosis, Churg-Strauss syndrome, Takayasu's arteritis, giant cell arteritis (temporal arteritis) and Henoch Schönlein purpura. Vasculitis is treated with corticosteroids and other immunosuppressant drugs.

Arteries

Heart

SEE ALSO *Angiography, Angioplasty, Aorta, Arteriosclerosis, Blood vessels, Hypertension, Ischemia, Raynaud's disease, Stroke, Vasculitis*

ARTERIOSCLEROSIS

The major cause of death in the developed world, arteriosclerosis is commonly referred to as "hardening of the arteries".

The most common cause is the formation of fatty deposits (plaques, also known as atheromas) within the inner lining of the arteries, a process called atherosclerosis. The plaques narrow the blood vessel and diminish the blood supply to the tissues. A clot, or embolism, may form at the plaque, then detach and lodge further downstream. Or the plaque may weaken the artery wall so that it balloons out, forming an aneurysm; this may burst and cause a hemorrhage. Other forms of arteriosclerosis are characterized by thickening of the walls of the arterioles (small arteries) or damage to the middle layer of the arteries.

When arteriosclerosis develops in the coronary arteries it can cause angina, cardiac ischemia or myocardial infarction (heart attack). In the cerebral arteries it can cause cerebrovascular accidents or strokes. In the arteries of the leg it can cause intermittent lameness, pain or gangrene. Arteriosclerosis can also cause kidney and eye damage.

The disease has no single known cause, but risk factors include high blood pressure (hypertension), cigarette smoking, obesity and elevated levels of cholesterol in the blood. Physical inactivity and a family predisposition are also risk factors. In advanced cases, surgery may be necessary, involving removal of the deposits in the arteries (endarterectomy) or replacement of the affected arteries (angioplasty).

SEE ALSO *Angioplasty, Arteries, Atherosclerosis, Cholesterol, Hypertension, Myocardial infarction, Stroke*

ARTHRITIS

Arthritis is inflammation of one or more joints, causing redness, swelling, pain and sometimes loss of joint mobility. There are many different kinds of arthritis. Arthritis may result from wear and tear on the joints (osteoarthritis) or from active joint diseases such as gout or rheumatoid arthritis. It may also be a symptom of a generalized disease, such as connective tissue disease. Symptoms of arthritis include joint pain

A

(arthralgia), joint swelling, early morning stiffness and reduced joint movement. There may be warmth and redness of the skin around a joint, and more general symptoms such as unexplained weight loss and fever. Swelling is often due to a fluid collection called an effusion. The joint may be tender, and painful when moved. Treatment depends on the underlying cause. Rest and exercise, physical therapy, drug treatments and surgery all play a role in managing it.

Osteoarthritis

Osteoarthritis is a chronic disease causing deterioration of the weight-bearing joints of the knees, hips and spine in older people. It may also affect the hands. The sufferer notices the gradual onset of aching joint pain, which becomes worse after exercise or weight bearing, and is often relieved by rest. The joint becomes stiff, and movement becomes painful and grating. X-rays of the joints in the affected areas will show degenerative changes.

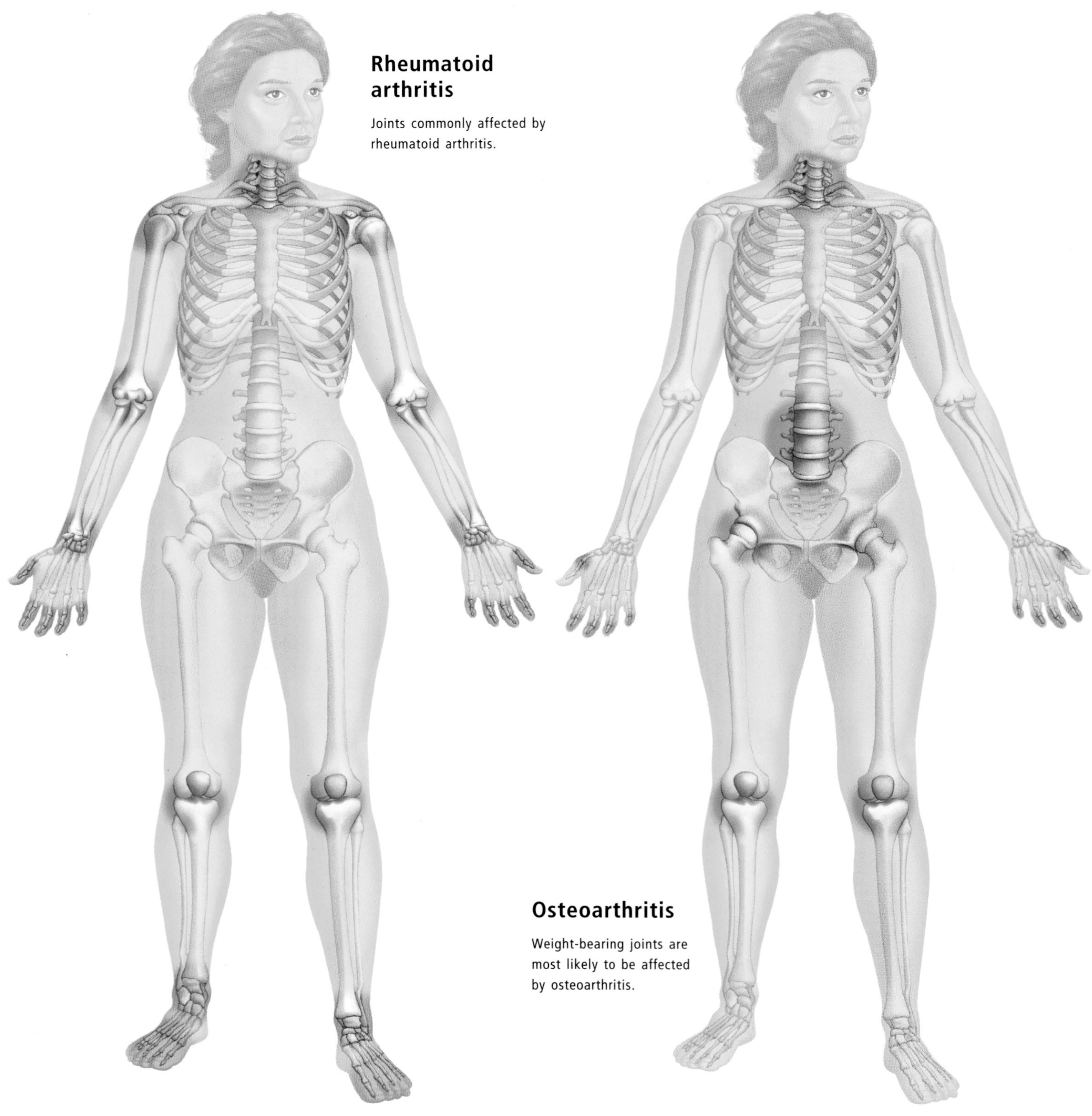

Rheumatoid arthritis

Joints commonly affected by rheumatoid arthritis.

Osteoarthritis

Weight-bearing joints are most likely to be affected by osteoarthritis.

Osteoarthritis cannot be reversed, but the symptoms can be relieved. Weight loss reduces the risk of developing knee osteoarthritis, especially in women. Treatment includes exercises, physical therapy and medications, which include a variety of nonsteroidal anti-inflammatory drugs (NSAIDs). Corticosteroids, which are injected directly into the joint, may also be used. Surgical treatment to replace or repair damaged joints may be needed in severe, debilitating disease. Surgery options include arthroplasty (total or partial replacement of the deteriorated joint with an artificial joint) and arthrodesis (surgical fusion of bones, usually in the spine).

Rheumatoid arthritis

A chronic inflammatory disease, rheumatoid arthritis affects the joints and surrounding tissues. Hands, wrists, elbows, shoulders, knees and ankles are the most frequently affected. In about a quarter of cases, painless hard round nodules called rheumatoid nodules appear under the skin, usually on pressure points such as the elbow or Achilles tendon. Unlike osteoarthritis, rheumatoid arthritis can cause damage throughout the body in the skin, muscles, blood vessels, eyes or lungs. The cause is unknown. It can occur at any age, but typically begins between 25 and 55 years of age. Women are affected three times more often than men.

Rheumatoid arthritis has no known cure. Treatment, which needs to be lifelong, can relieve many of the symptoms, however. Drug treatment will usually consist of aspirin or anti-inflammatory drugs such as naproxen or sulindac. Injections of gold salts, D-penicillamine and chloroquine are sometimes used. Use of corticosteroid drugs can dramatically improve symptoms, but side effects can be a problem. These include bruising, osteoporosis (thinning of the bones), cataracts, susceptibility to infections, diabetes and high blood pressure. Occasionally, surgery is needed for severely affected joints.

SEE ALSO *Anti-inflammatory drugs, Autoimmune disease, Connective tissue, Corticosteroids, Non-steroidal anti-inflammatory drugs, Osteoarthritis, Rheumatoid arthritis*

ARTHROSCOPY

Arthroscopy is a surgical procedure in which a small telescope known as an arthroscope is inserted into the cavity of a joint through a small incision to allow examination of joints for damage or disease. Surgical instruments have been devised for use in arthroscopy, and operations conducted in this way generally heal more quickly because of the small incision made.

ARTIFICIAL INSEMINATION

The introduction of semen into the vagina or cervix of a female by any method other than sexual intercourse is known as artificial insemination. It is a procedure used as a solution to infertility to impregnate women whose partners are sterile or impotent; it is also used in animal breeding.

Developed in the early part of the twentieth century in Russia for use in animals, its use spread internationally in the 1930s. In animals it has the advantage of passing on the desired characteristics of a bull or other male livestock animal to the offspring and producing more offspring than would be possible in the natural course of events. In humans, apart from sterility or impotence problems in the male, artificial insemination can also be an option when the female's cervical mucus is unreceptive, or when the infertility is unexplained.

Semen may be freshly obtained or it may be frozen. It may be from the partner (if he is not impotent) or from some other male donor (if the partner is sterile), in which case it may be described as donor insemination. If freshly obtained from the partner, he needs to masturbate and ejaculate in the hour before the insemination is scheduled to take place. If it is to be frozen then it is drawn into plastic straws before storing in liquid nitrogen. Frozen sperm can be kept for long periods and used, for example, if the partner is about to undergo medical treatment, often for cancer, which could render him infertile.

At around the time of ovulation, determined by checking her temperature or cervical mucus, the woman goes through a simple procedure in which the sperm is introduced by a syringe into her vagina or cervix. The technique has been reasonably successful, with 50 to 65 percent achieving conception and pregnancy. Where insemination is by donor the legal and emotional aspects are complex. Counseling is essential. Although the father is the social and birth father, he is not the genetic father. The mother is the genetic, birth and social parent.

Surrogate motherhood occurs when a woman (the surrogate mother) bears a child for a couple unable to produce children in the usual way, usually because the woman is infertile or unable to undertake a pregnancy for medical reasons. Surrogacy can take two forms: one in which the surrogate mother is impregnated using artificial insemination and the father's sperm; the other in which the woman's egg (ova) and the man's sperm are joined in the process of in vitro fertilization. When an embryo results it is implanted in the surrogate mother. Usually the surrogate mother gives up all legal rights, though this has been legally challenged.

SEE ALSO *Infertility*

ASBESTOSIS

Asbestosis is a disease in which the lungs become inflamed through the inhalation of asbestos particles. It can develop into asbestos cancer (mesothelioma), which is a malignant tumor of the lining of the lung, chest or abdominal cavity.

Asbestos is an extremely poor conductor of heat and so was used industrially as an insulating material for many years. It is fibrous, and the fibers are easily shed and inhaled with air. The fibers can then accumulate in tissues of the airways and lungs and inhibit the exchange of oxygen between inhaled air and blood. Asbestos is no longer used because of its harmful effects; removing it from old installations requires special breathing apparatus and protective suits.

SEE ALSO *Cancer, Mesothelioma*

ASCARIASIS

Ascariasis is an infection caused by the parasitic roundworm *Ascaris lumbricoides*. Inadequate sanitation and poor personal hygiene are major contributing factors behind the spread of ascariasis. The worm's microscopic eggs are spread in soil, water, on the hands, and on vegetables and fruit

A

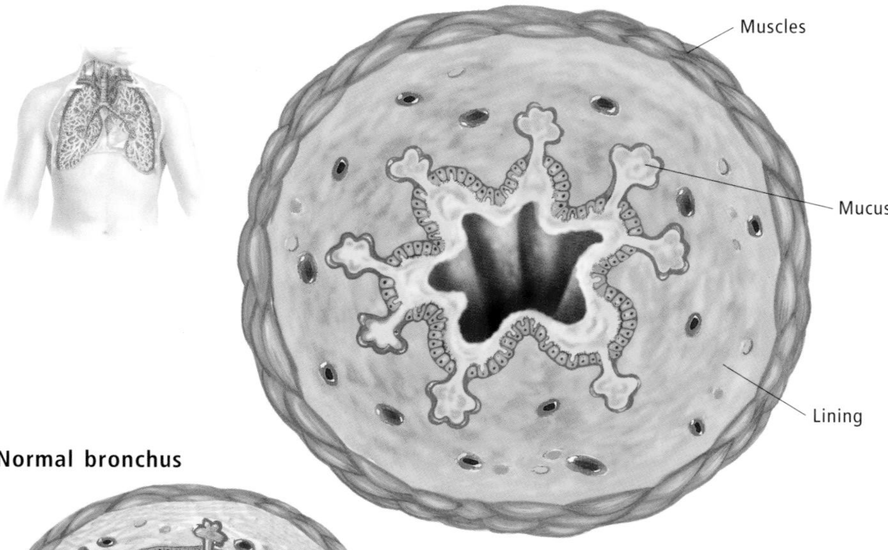

Normal bronchus

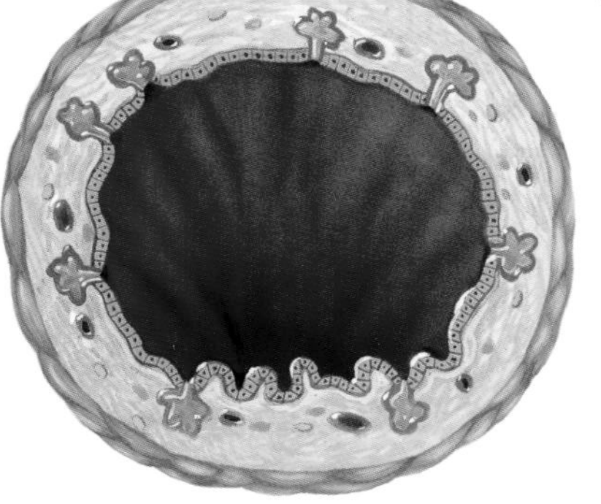

Asthma

In asthma, the lining of the bronchi become inflamed and swollen. The smooth muscles of the bronchial walls go into spasm, and the bronchi produce excessive mucus.

fertilized with untreated sewage. Early signs of infection include irritability, poor appetite, fatigue and weight fluctuations. Adult worms live in the intestine and, when infestations become heavy, can cause abdominal discomfort, obstructions and malnutrition. As part of their life-cycle, larval worms migrate through the lungs of the host, producing a cough and discomfort while breathing. Effective medications are available. Surgery is sometimes needed to clear internal blockages.

SEE ALSO *Roundworms*

ASCITES

Ascites is an abnormal accumulation of fluid around the tissues and organs of the abdominal cavity. It can indicate a range of disorders, but cirrhosis of the liver, cancer or heart failure are among the most common causes. If enough fluid is present, ascites can cause the abdomen to become distended and painful.

Ultrasonography is one of the best ways to confirm the condition, particularly in overweight patients. The cause of ascites is indicated by its appearance and chemical content. Collection of the fluid for analysis is done using a medical procedure called paracentesis. This may also be used to drain fluid to relieve discomfort. Treatment of ascites usually targets the underlying cause.

SEE ALSO *Paracentesis*

ASTHMA

Asthma is a disease of the bronchi (or air passages) of the lung, characterized by periodic attacks of wheezing alternating with periods of normal breathing. The muscles of the bronchi contract, reducing airflow and producing shortness of breath, coughing and wheezing. Mucus production increases and the lining of the bronchi becomes inflamed.

In industrial countries, asthma currently affects one in twenty people, and the number of sufferers is rising. Asthma is more prevalent in children than adults, affecting one in ten children; by adulthood, many children seem to have outgrown it. The disorder is more common if there is family history of asthma, eczema or allergies. In some cases asthma does not develop until adulthood. Commonly an adult asthmatic is short of breath early in the morning. Cough is less frequent than in childhood asthma. Adult asthma is often associated with cigarette smoking or chronic (long-term) lung diseases such as chronic bronchitis.

Asthma attacks typically come and go. There may be intervals of days, months or years between attacks, or there may be attacks every day. Symptoms can occur spontaneously or can be set off by trigger factors. The most common form of asthma (allergic bronchial asthma) is caused by an allergic reaction. Many pollens, molds, dusts (especially house dust and wood dust), cigarette smoke, feathers and animal hair can cause allergic-type asthma attacks. Asthma is sometimes associated with hay fever.

Respiratory infections, exposure to cold, industrial fumes and certain emotional and psychological states can trigger an asthma attack. Drugs such as aspirin, anti-inflammatory drugs and beta-blockers are other precipitating factors. Asthma from these causes may occur in people who have no history of allergic reactions, as well as in those who do. Exercise may trigger asthma; symptoms of exercise-induced asthma (coughing, wheezing, chest tightness lasting several minutes to an hour or more) are different from the deep and rapid breathing that quickly returns to normal after exercise.

In a mild attack, wheezing may be barely audible and the wheezing occurs only during exhalation. As the attack worsens, wheezing becomes louder and may also be present with inhalation; the sufferer breathes rapidly, gasps for breath, and becomes agitated. In a severe asthma attack, if the bronchioles become totally blocked, airflow may diminish and wheezing may stop. In children especially, this is a sign of serious trouble. An attack of asthma may be prolonged and may not respond to treatment. This condition is called status asthmaticus. An attack of status asthmaticus requires hospitalization and urgent treatment.

Diagnosis and tests

Usually it is not difficult for a physician to diagnose an asthma attack, especially if the sufferer is already known to be asthmatic. Wheezing sounds, audible through a stethoscope, and rapid improvement of symptoms after treatment confirm the diagnosis. Breathing tests such as spirometry show reduced airflow across the airways during attacks, which improves after treatment.

Chest x-rays are usually normal. In some asthmatic people, eosinophils (white cells associated with allergies) are found in the blood and sputum.

Other conditions that can cause shortness of breath or other lung problems may need to be ruled out with further tests. These conditions include blood clots in the lung, lung cancer, heart failure, cystic fibrosis, emphysema and chronic bronchitis.

Management of asthma

Unlike other lung diseases such as emphysema or chronic bronchitis, asthma is usually a reversible condition; the narrowing of the airways caused by bronchospasm improves spontaneously or in response to medications.

Several simple measures can reduce the risk of attack. Trigger factors such as pollens, animal furs and foods known to cause asthma should be avoided. A person with allergic asthma should sleep in a room without carpets or rugs. Blankets and pillows of synthetic fiber reduce the risk of house dust and mites. Asthmatics should not smoke, nor should others smoke in the same house. Asthma medication should be taken prior to events known to trigger an episode—before exercise, for example.

Several different medications are available for use in treating acute attacks, and for the long-term prevention of asthma. Often they are used in combination. Bronchodilators dilate the bronchial wall, allowing air through and relieving the symptoms of asthma. Some of these are "beta agonists", so called because they act on the beta adrenoreceptor of bronchial wall muscle, which results in bronchodilation. Others, known as anticholinergic agents, also act on the bronchi, though using a different mechanism to relax and open the airway passages. Both types of bronchodilator may be used together. Side effects of bronchodilators include nervousness, restlessness, insomnia and headache. Elderly patients and children may be more sensitive to the effects of bronchodilators.

When symptoms of asthma are frequent and difficult to control with bronchodilators, preventive medications are used. These medications do not cure an attack of asthma once it has begun. Instead, they prevent attacks from recurring. Physicians believe that long-term damage to the bronchi is minimized by using preventive medications.

Commonly, bronchodilators and preventive medications are used together—the bronchodilators to treat the symptoms of an attack and the preventive medication to stop attacks from occurring. Corticosteroids are the most commonly used preventive medications. They reduce bronchial inflammation and airway obstruction and improve lung function. Sodium cromoglycate is another preventive medication; it stops the release of chemicals such as histamine into the bronchi, which can cause asthma. Sodium cromoglycate is useful for asthma triggered by exercise, cold air and allergies, such as to cat fur.

In the treatment of asthma, inhaled medications are generally preferred over tablet or liquid medicines. Inhaled medications act directly on the surface of the airways; absorption into the rest of the body is minimal so side effects are fewer compared with oral medications. Inhaled medications include beta-agonists (metaproterenol, albuterol and terbutaline sulfate); anticholinergics (ipratropium bromide); corticosteroids (beclomethasone dipropionate, triamcinolone acetonide and flunisolide) and sodium cromoglycate.

Inhaled medications are administered via a metered dose inhaler, or a puffer. In children who have difficulty with inhalers or puffers, or in adults with a more severe attack, asthma medications can be given by nebulizer, which administers the medication in the form of a fine mist inhaled through a mouth mask. Some people may experience minor side effects of hoarseness and thrush (a fungal infection of the mouth and throat) from using corticosteroid inhalers. These and other problems can be minimized by rinsing the mouth and using a spacer device, which reduces the amount of medication residue left in the mouth and the throat.

Oral corticosteroids, such as prednisone, methylprednisone and hydrocortisone, may be used as preventive medications. However, they have more side effects than inhaled corticosteroids, so long-term use is not recommended, except when other treatments have failed to restore normal lung function and the risks of uncontrolled asthma are greater than the side effects of the steroids. Corticosteroids may also be given intravenously in severe attacks requiring hospitalization, for example in status asthmaticus. Intravenous epinephrine (adrenaline) and oxygen may also be needed during a life-threatening attack.

Asthma plan

As the severity of an asthma attack varies so much from person to person, it is helpful for an asthmatic to have an individual management plan in case of an attack. The plan should be made available to carers, teachers, nurses, parents and anyone else who has responsibility for that person.

In the event of an asthma attack, follow the asthma plan and help the sufferer to take the medication as directed in the plan. Get emergency help if the person fails to improve or if those symptoms listed on the plan as emergency indicators are present.

A simple device called a peak flow meter, which measures how well air moves out of the airways, can be used regularly at home to measure lung function. Monitoring peak flow helps an asthma sufferer monitor changes and to adjust the medication dosage up or down as needed. Each person has a personal-best peak flow reading, which should be noted in the asthma plan. A peak flow reading less than 80 percent of the personal best indicates the need for action.

An asthmatic patient should seek medical advice promptly when suffering from a respiratory infection. Generally, any infection producing green or yellow sputum should be treated with antibiotics quickly. Some asthmatics may benefit from breathing exercises. These help the lungs to function more effectively and give the sufferer a psychological boost during an attack. Asthmatics whose symptoms are triggered by allergies may benefit from a course of desensitizing allergy injections, though benefits are variable and may not last.

SEE ALSO *Allergies, Bronchitis, Bronchodilators, Corticosteroids, Emphysema, Lungs*

ASTIGMATISM

An astigmatism is a lack of symmetry in the curvature of the cornea of the eye (the cornea is the transparent wall in front of the pupil and iris). It can also be a lack of symmetry in the crystalline lens. The result is that the patient sees an image which is blurred or smeared in one direction, either vertically, horizontally or obliquely.

The cause is not known, though some types of astigmatism may run in families. Astigmatism is rarely serious, and corrective lenses can be used if necessary. Surgery and laser treatment are used in some cases. The first contact lens, developed by Adolf Fick in 1887, was made of glass and designed to correct astigmatism.

SEE ALSO *Cornea, Eye*

ATELECTASIS

A partial or complete collapse of a lung is know medically as atelectasis. It is most often caused by a blockage in a bronchus or bronchioles, the air tubes leading to the lungs. Obstructions can include tumors, inhaled objects, or thick mucus from infections or a disease such as cystic fibrosis. A form of atelectasis can also occur as a postoperative complication caused by the effects of surgery.

Acute atelectasis can lead to a sudden and major collapse accompanied by chest pain, rapid and uncomfortable breathing, dizziness and shock. Alternatively, the signs of atelectasis may include a less dramatic, more gradual collapse, cough, shortness of breath and a fever.

Atelectasis is not normally fatal and the affected lung usually reinflates once any obstruction has been extracted or dislodged. A procedure called a bronchoscopy may be required to remove a blockage. Pneumonia and permanent scarring of lung tissue are potential complications of atelectasis.

SEE ALSO *Bronchoscopy, Lungs, Pneumonia, Respiratory system*

ATHEROSCLEROSIS

Atherosclerosis is a disease of the major arteries in which fatty deposits called plaques collect on the interior walls, leading to narrowing and obstruction of blood flow. This build-up is a contributing factor in cardiovascular disease which causes heart attack. Calcium accumulates in the fatty material as part of a process known as arteriosclerosis, or "hardening of the arteries".

Severe heart attack and perhaps death can occur as a result of sudden arterial blockage. This may be due to plaques rupturing and releasing fatty deposits, or a blood clot attaching to the plaque. Smoking, obesity and high cholesterol may be contributing factors, along with high blood pressure, excess fat intake and a family history of heart disease.

Atherosclerosis can occur in the carotid and vertebral arteries leading to the head and brain, as well as in the coronary arteries. It generally has no symptoms until complications set in. When blood flow in the heart is severely restricted it may cause chest pain. Stroke and damage to the body's organs are also possible results of blockage.

Treatment includes the inflation of a balloon-tipped catheter in the artery to clear blockages, or surgical bypass of blockages in the heart using veins from the legs. A cold laser can destroy plaques with ultraviolet light, or a drill-tipped catheter may be used. Certain drugs can reduce cholesterol and fats in the blood, and anticoagulants such as aspirin reduce the chance of clotting.

SEE ALSO *Angioplasty, Arteries, Arteriosclerosis*

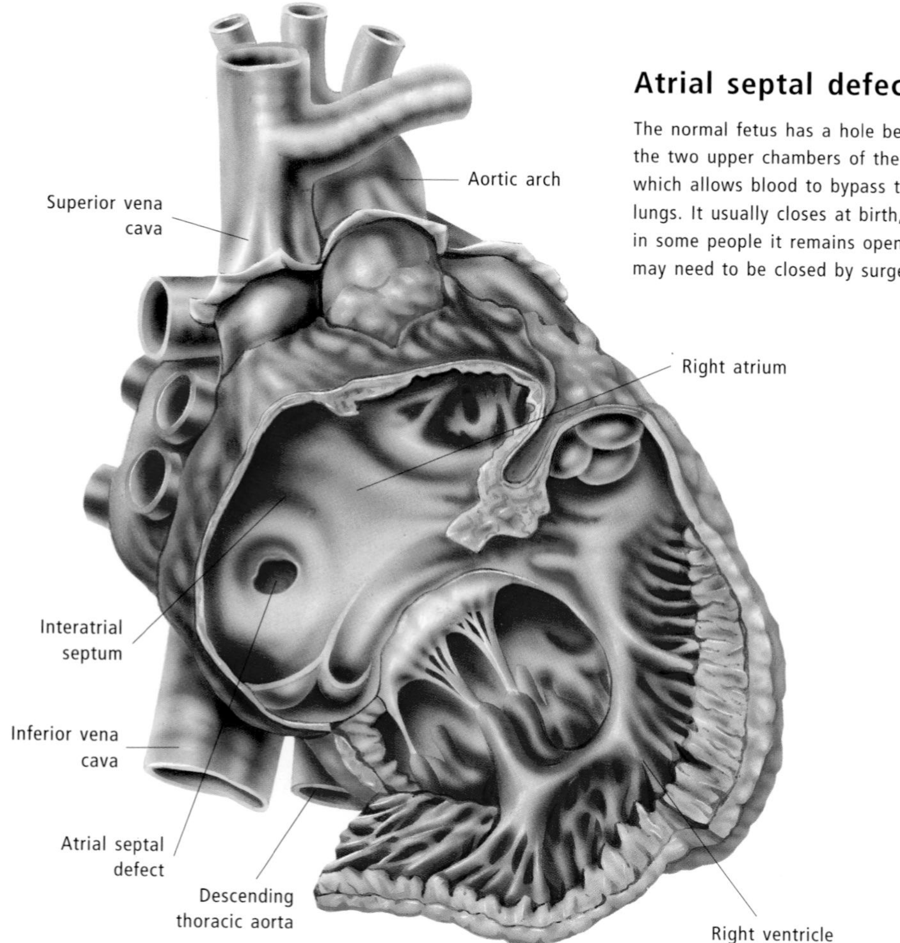

Atrial septal defect

The normal fetus has a hole between the two upper chambers of the heart, which allows blood to bypass the lungs. It usually closes at birth, but in some people it remains open and may need to be closed by surgery.

ATHETOSIS

Athetosis is involuntary slow and twisting movements of the head, limbs, trunk or neck, creating abnormal and often grotesque postures. The symptoms typically improve or disappear during sleep but worsen during exercise (such as walking) and emotional stress. Athetosis is caused by a disorder of certain nerve pathways in the brain, and is seen in a number of conditions, including cerebral palsy, encephalitis and Huntington's disease. It can be a side effect of certain drugs. Treatment (if any) depends on correcting the underlying cause.

ATRIAL SEPTAL DEFECT

Atrial septal defect (ASD) is a congenital "hole in the heart" between the two upper chambers of the heart (the atria). In the fetus, this opening is normal, and allows blood to bypass the lungs (which are not in use).

At birth, this opening usually closes to allow blood to be pumped into the lungs once breathing starts. In persons with ASD, the hole doesn't close. Most people with ASD don't have symptoms, but if the opening is large enough there may be symptoms of shortness of breath and irregular heartbeats (palpitations). These symptoms often don't develop until adulthood.

Through the stethoscope, a physician may hear abnormal heart sounds in a person with ASD. An ultrasound of the heart or an echocardiogram will show the hole. An EKG (electrocardiogram) may also be abnormal, as the hole interferes with the normal conduction of the heartbeat through the heart.

No treatment is necessary if there are no symptoms; if there are symptoms or the hole is large, surgical closure of the defect may be needed. People affected with ASD will need to take antibiotics during dental and surgical procedures, as they are at increased risk of developing bacterial endocarditis.

SEE ALSO *Endocarditis, Heart*

ATROPHIC VAGINITIS

Atrophic vaginitis is a skin condition of the vagina caused by a lack of estrogen in the body. It occurs most commonly in women after the menopause, or following surgical removal of the ovaries. The lining of the vagina becomes thin and easily damaged, giving rise to vaginal itching. Urinary symptoms such as burning and greater frequency and urgency are common.

Treatment is with estrogen replacement therapy. This is prescribed as a pill or skin patch, or as an estrogen cream or pessary which can be applied to the vagina.

SEE ALSO *Vaginitis, Vulvitis*

ATTENTION DEFICIT HYPERACTIVITY DISORDER

Attention deficit hyperactivity disorder (ADHD), formerly known as hyperactivity, is a behavioral disorder which shows itself in an inability to concentrate and in excessive restless, impulsive, destructive, disruptive behavior often coupled with irritability and aggression. Attention deficit disorder (ADD) is a similar condition without the hyperactivity and is less common. Children with either of these conditions find it difficult to make friends.

Statistics differ between countries; for example, in the USA between 10 and 15 percent of young males are diagnosed with ADHD or ADD, and in Australia the figure is between 2 and 6 percent. Boys are more likely to be affected and it usually manifests itself once school starts, though a very small number of children seem to be hyperactive from birth. These babies are often described as "high need" rather than as having ADHD. It is thought to be mainly a biological condition with family, environmental, genetic and social factors coming into the equation.

Diagnosis and misdiagnosis

ADHD can be incorrectly diagnosed, so a thorough, wide-ranging investigation is necessary. Criteria for the diagnosis of ADHD include fidgeting and squirming, difficulty staying seated, and difficulty in taking turns and following instructions. Also, the child is noisy and talks incessantly, does not seem to be listening, loses things, and gets involved in physically dangerous activities without considering consequences.

Parents, teachers, psychologists and doctors should be involved, and other possibilities such as learning difficulties investigated. Children who do not relate to their school curriculum or who have learning difficulties may be seen to have ADHD.

Some professionals doubt that it is a real condition and others believe that hyperactivity is a subjective assessment, as all adults perceive children's behavior differently. Between 12 and 20 percent of children suffer from a range of learning difficulties, with 2 to 4 percent suffering quite severely. If children are having difficulty with listening, speaking, reading, writing, mathematical or reasoning skills, they are seen as not being able to give proper attention to tasks at hand and may be misdiagnosed. Therefore assessment for learning difficulties should precede diagnosis of ADHD.

Depression can also be confused with ADHD as depressed children have low self-esteem. Between 1 and 3 percent of children suffer depression, and it is hard to detect. Sleep problems have also been suggested as causing ADHD. Early diagnosis is important in treating antisocial behavior.

Treatment

Treatment includes short-term medication together with behavioral and educational strategies and family counseling. Dietary restrictions or interventions have not been proven to work and are no longer considered appropriate. Adequate nutrition is important for growth and many diets intended to address the problem of hyperactivity were severely restrictive.

There are dangers with long-term use of brain stimulant drugs which are often used to treat the condition, as some research suggests it could lead later to cocaine addiction.

The management of ADHD is never simple. Many people need to be involved if treatment is to succeed. As children grow older some of the behaviors improve, but often many of their difficulties continue into adulthood. ADHD has been diagnosed in adults, though this is controversial.

SEE ALSO *Amphetamines, Behavioral problems, Learning disorders*

AUDIOMETRY

Audiometry is a very precise method of measuring a person's ability to hear. In normal hearing, sound reaches the eardrum and inner ear through the air and through the mastoid bone behind each ear. An instrument called an audiometer electronically produces pure tones at a specific pitch and volume; it is used to test each ear, with different tests for measuring air conduction and bone conduction hearing. In both tests the volume of each tone is reduced to the point at which the person can no longer hear it. These sound thresholds are charted or graphed to produce an audiogram.

Audiometry can also measure the speech threshold to show how words are heard and understood at specific volumes. This involves listening to a series of words and repeating each one as it is heard. A separate speech test measures the ability to discriminate between similar-sounding words.

Tympanometry is a test used to establish the cause of hearing loss, particularly in children. It can differentiate between problems caused by a blocked eustachian tube, fluid in the middle ear and malfunction of the bones of the middle ear.

SEE ALSO *Ear, Hearing*

A

AUTISM

Autism is part of the spectrum of conditions called pervasive developmental disorder (PDD). It involves problems with social interaction and communication. This developmental disorder usually becomes apparent by the time the child is three years old; signs include self-absorption, lack of reaction to other people, and a quite narrow range of activites and interests.

Evidence suggests autism is a problem of the nerve system that can be caused by genetic disorders, brain injury (either before or after birth), metabolic disorders, viral infections or diseases. Four times as many boys as girls suffer from this condition.

There are varying degrees of autism. Children with mild autism, also called high functioning autism, can be high achievers; children with the most severe form avoid eye contact as well as physical contact and show no understanding of other creatures, including people and their own family. Behavioral patterns, such as hand flapping, will be repetitive. Autism can be confused with intellectual disability.

Autistic children can be affectionate, though on their own terms. Routine is paramount and any changes can cause a major upset. Autism affects the capacity to make sense of the environment. For an autistic child the world is chaos. In autistic children language is either non-existent or very poorly developed. They do not attempt to communicate, make gestures or imitate sounds, or show other signs that are part of normal language development. Persistent, purposeless and seemingly involuntary repetition of certain sounds or phrases, known as echolalia, is also a symptom.

There is no cure or prevention for autism, but early intervention can have great benefits. The child needs to be assessed by an experienced child psychologist or psychiatrist. Treatment is very specialized and labor intensive. From about age three, children can be enrolled in programs that have the ultimate aim of integrating them into school and the community. No medications have been found to make a difference to autism.

AUTOIMMUNE DISEASE

Autoimmune diseases develop when the body's immune system fails to recognize normal body tissues and attacks and destroys them as if they were foreign. The cause isn't fully understood, but in some cases is thought to be triggered by exposure to microorganisms and drugs, especially in people with a genetic predisposition to the disorder. A single organ or multiple organs and tissues may be affected.

Examples of autoimmune diseases and the tissues they attack include: Hashimoto's thyroiditis (thyroid); pernicious anemia (blood); Addison's disease (adrenal cortex); diabetes mellitus (pancreas); rheumatoid arthritis (joints); systemic lupus erythematosus and dermatomyositis (connective tissues); and myasthenia gravis (muscles).

Symptoms of autoimmune disease are related to the lack of function of the organ or tissue involved. In addition, generalized symptoms common to all autoimmune disorders include tiredness and fatigue, dizziness, malaise and low-grade fever. The diagnosis is made from blood tests and other tests which indicate the degree of loss of function in the organ system involved. A blood cell count may show increased numbers of white blood cells. Levels of certain immuno-globulins and other proteins in the blood may be higher than normal.

There is no cure for an autoimmune disorder. Thyroid supplements, insulin injections or other supplements may be required to alleviate the symptoms, depending on the specific disease. Disorders that affect the blood components may require blood

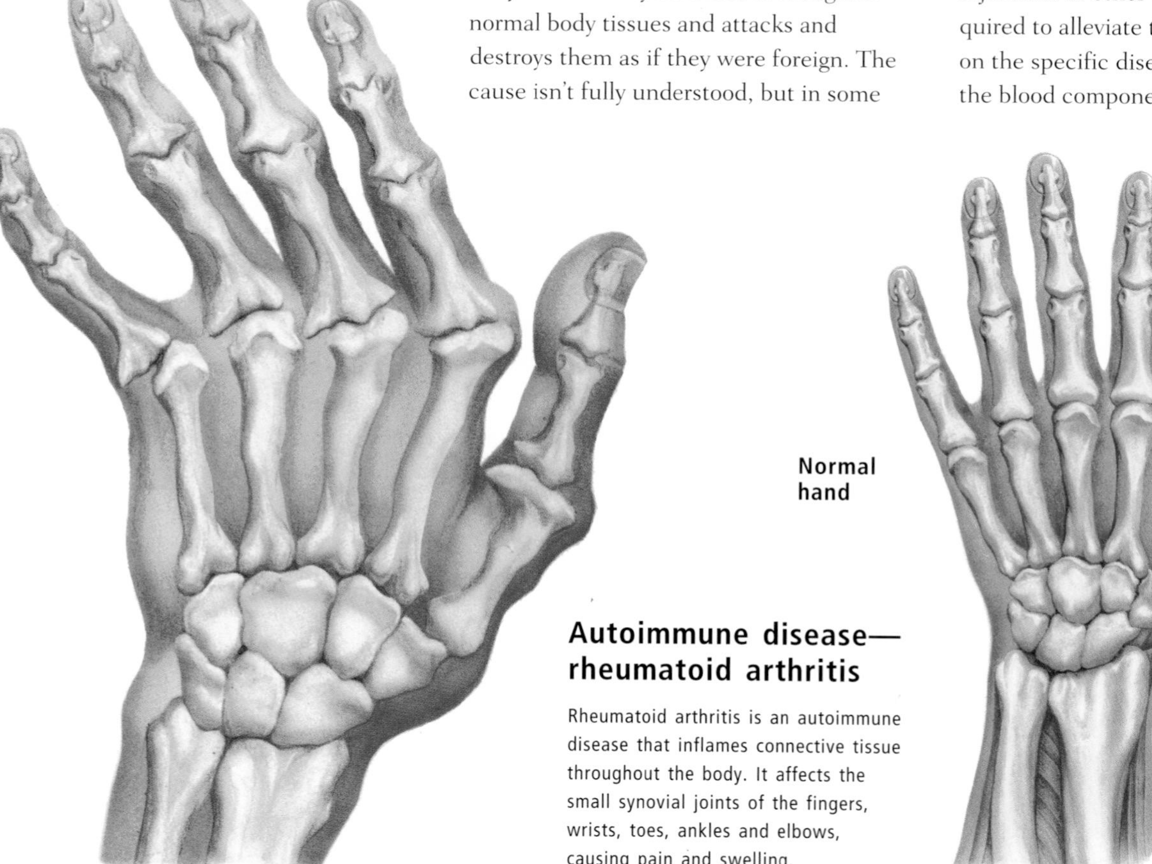

Autoimmune disease—rheumatoid arthritis

Rheumatoid arthritis is an autoimmune disease that inflames connective tissue throughout the body. It affects the small synovial joints of the fingers, wrists, toes, ankles and elbows, causing pain and swelling.

transfusions. Measures to assist mobility or other functions are sometimes needed for disorders that affect the bones, joints, or muscles. Symptoms can often be controlled by corticosteroids. However, side effects such as osteoporosis (thinning of the bones), bruising, susceptibility to infections, diabetes and high blood pressure are common. Immunosuppressants (drugs that suppress the immune system) such as cyclophosphamide or azathioprine may also be used.

Lupus erythematosus is an autoimmune disease that affects connective tissue. There are two forms of the disorder: discoid lupus erythematosus (DLE) and systemic lupus erythematosus (SLE). Both conditions affect the skin. SLE involves other tissues and organs as well.

Rheumatoid arthritis is one of the more common autoimmune diseases, affecting the joints; typically the hands, wrists, elbows, shoulders, knees and ankles. Skin, muscles, blood vessels, eyes and lungs can also be involved. There is no cure, but treatment, which usually needs to be lifelong, can relieve many of the symptoms. Drug treatment consists of anti-inflammatory drugs and injections of gold salts. Oral corticosteroid drugs are also used, but have side effects. Occasionally, surgery is needed for severely affected joints.

Vasculitis (angiitis) is a general term for a group of uncommon autoimmune diseases which cause inflammation of the blood vessels. Examples of vasculitis include Kawasaki disease, Behçet's disease, Takayasu's arteritis, Churg-Strauss syndrome, giant cell arteritis (temporal arteritis) and Henoch Schönlein purpura. Polyarteritis nodosa affects the arteries in muscles, joints, intestines, nerves, kidneys and skin. Diagnosis of polyarteritis nodosa is confirmed by a biopsy of the relevant tissue. Anti-inflammatory and immunosuppressant drugs are used in treatment.

SEE ALSO ***Addison's disease, Connective tissue, Dermatomyositis, Diabetes, Hashimoto's disease, Lupus erythematosus, Myasthenia gravis, Rheumatoid arthritis, Vasculitis***

AYURVEDIC MEDICINE

The term Ayurveda comes from the Sanskrit words *ayur* meaning life, and *veda*, meaning knowledge or science.

Ayurveda is the basis of the traditional health system in India, tracing its history back to the ancient Hindu texts of the *Rig Veda*. Within this system an individual is seen to be a microcosm of the larger macrocosm of the earth.

In Ayurveda everything in the universe is divided up into five elements: *prithvi* (earth), *ap* (water), *teja* (light, fire or heat), *vayu* (air) and *akasha* (space or ether). Food is composed of these elements and different foods are seen to work either with or against the elemental balance in the body. Ruling everything are the three basic forces, known as the *doshas*. *Vata* is equated with the wind and governs the central nervous system; *pitta* is like the sun and governs the digestive system and biochemical processes; and *kapha* is like the moon and governs cell growth and the fluid balance of the tissues.

In dealing with the body, the Ayurvedic practitioner is interested in the *dhatus*, or the seven basic constituents of the body: *rasa* (food), *rakta* (blood), *mamsa* (bone), *meda* (fat and perspiration), *asthi* (bone marrow), *majya* (viscidity) and *shukra* (satisfying movements).

In Ayurveda the health of an individual depends on the balance between the life-giving energies which flow through the various organs and systems of the body. Illnesses are seen as the result of imbalance, and are classified under four groupings: accidental, physical, natural and mental. The physician's task is to assess the balance of the various elements at play in the body and to prescribe treatment which will bring the body back into harmony. The primary emphasis is on prevention rather than cure. Where illness has already developed, the emphasis is on treating the source of the disease, not the symptoms.

The Ayurvedic practitioner aims to identify the innate disposition/constitution of each patient, which is believed to be determined at the time of conception. Personal lifestyle, diet, work and life stage are all taken into account, along with a physical examination of the urine, stools, sweat, skin, nails, eyes, tongue and voice.

Treatments prescribed can include dietary changes, fasts, exposure to the sun, massage, baths, inhalations, enemas and homeopathic and herbal medicines. Yoga and yogic breathing techniques are considered particularly important in their ability to control the mind through the physical discipline of the body, which in turn can strengthen the mind's ability to influence the overall health of the body. Meditation is also valued for its ability to reduce stress and tension.

Ayurvedic medicine is still widely practised and taught in India, often in conjunction with orthodox Western medicine. It was initially popularized in Western countries by the Maharishi Mahesh Yogi, and more recently through the work of Dr Deepak Chopra, whose work places a strong emphasis on the role of consciousness in medical therapy.

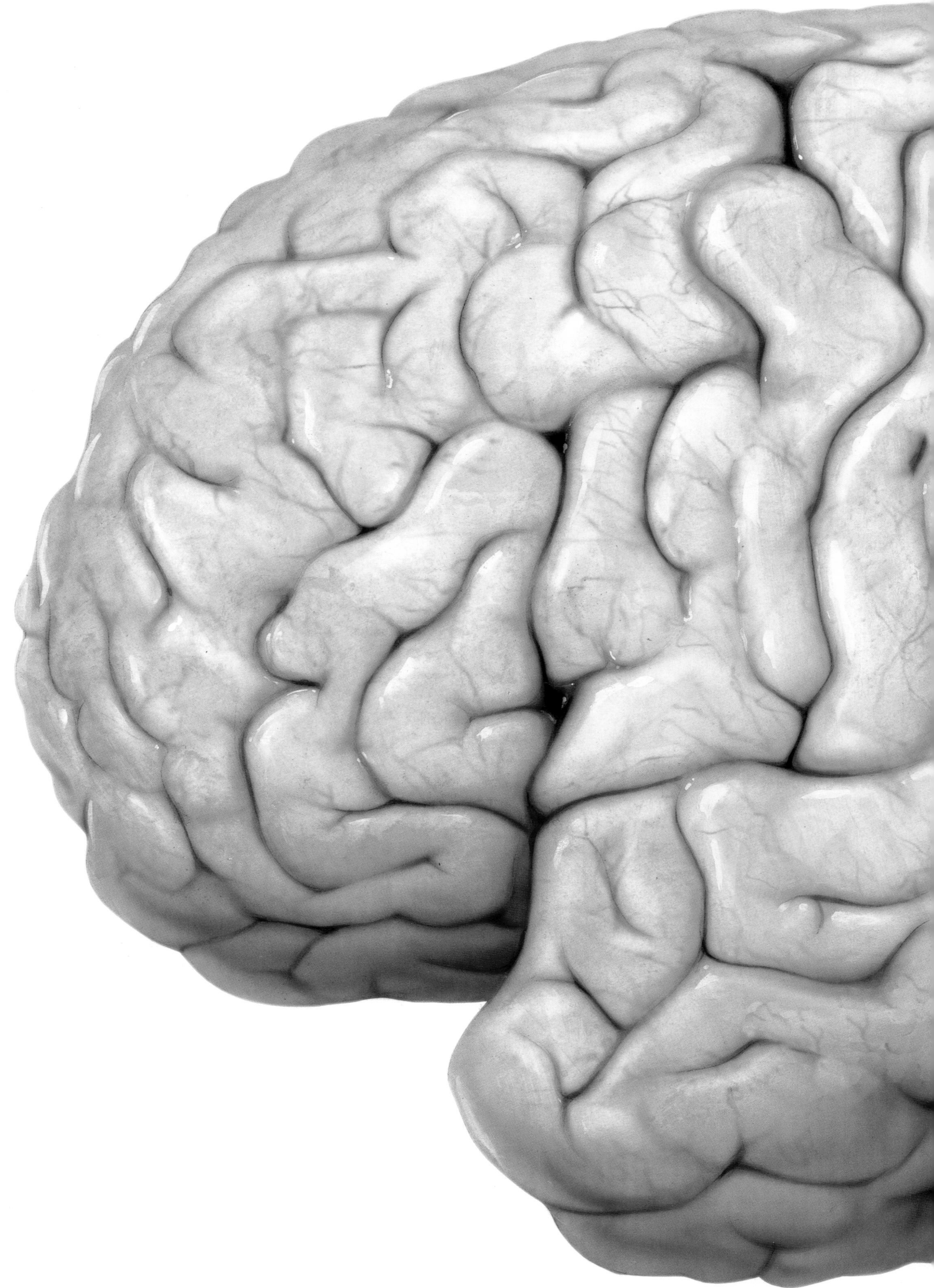

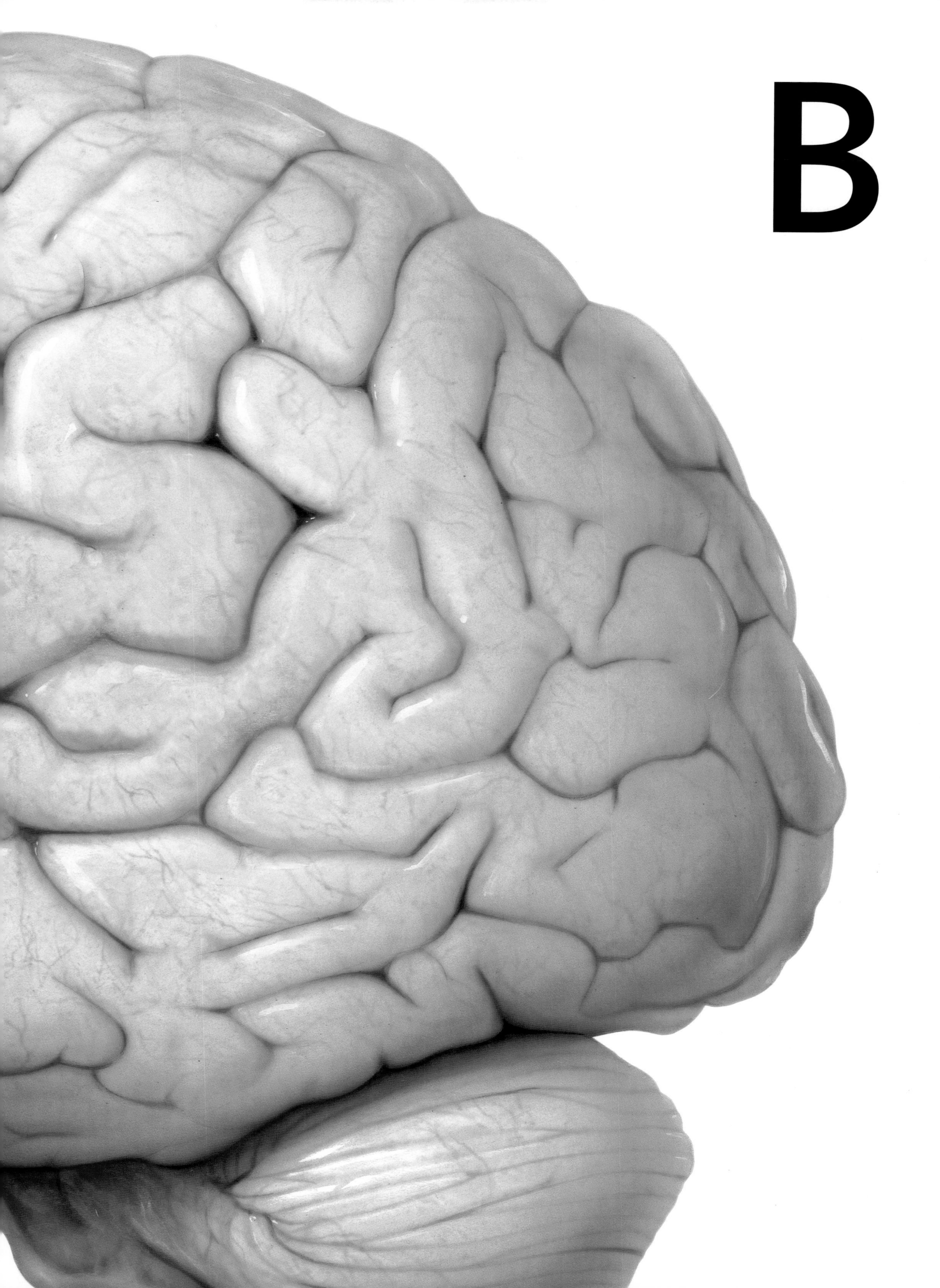
B

B

BACK

The back is the part of the human body from below the neck to the lower end of the spine, just above the buttocks. The bones of the spine are known as the vertebrae and are joined to each other by disks (invertebral disks) and joints (facet joints) to form the vertebral column; the spinal cord runs through a canal formed by the vertebrae. The spinal cord is composed of nerve tissue, and nerves branch off through spaces between vertebrae.

The vertebrae are separated from each other and cushioned by the invertebral disks, which are flexible. The disks are designed to bear weight and to cushion the surfaces of the vertebrae as the spine moves.

The vertebral column protects the spinal cord and spinal nerves, supports the weight of the body and head, and anchors the rib cage. It plays a major role in movement and posture, and provides an attachment point for muscles of the trunk, arms and legs.

Moving down from the head, there are 24 separate vertebrae: 7 cervical (C), 12 thoracic (T) and 5 lumbar (L). A further 5 are fused together and form the sacrum, then another 4, the smallest vertebrae, are fused to form the coccyx (the tail bone). The normal number of vertebrae is 33, but there may be one more (this most often occurs in males) or one less (mostly in females). The largest are the lumbar vertebrae, which bear the most weight. It is the fifth lumbar vertebra (L5) that carries the weight of the whole upper body and transfers it to the sacrum.

Paget's disease—in which bones enlarge and soften—can cause the spine to weaken and deform. Height is lost and the deformity may pinch nerves, causing pain or paralysis.

The arteries that supply blood to the brain stem travel up the cervical vertebrae. When bloodflow through them is reduced, as may happen when one has arteriosclerosis, turning the head can produce a feeling of dizziness.

Anesthetics are sometimes injected directly into the epidural space in the spinal column for operations on the lower trunk and legs, and during childbirth and delivery by cesarean section.

Injuries and diseases

The spine may be deformed by forward curvature or hunching (kyphosis), hollowed or sway back (lordosis), being curved to one side (scoliosis), or being both hunched and curved (kyphoscoliosis).

Abnormalities can be caused by injury or muscular weakness, habitually poor posture, deformities at birth, or inherited disease such as ankylosing spondylitis. This disease affects connective tissue, inflaming the spine and large joints such as hips, shoulders and knees, producing pain and stiffness and a tendency to stoop. Many back problems are correctable without surgery. Considerable improvements can be made by developing strong back and abdominal muscles to counter poor posture.

The disks can be damaged by violent movement (such as in accidents or sporting collisions), by lifting very heavy weights, or by poor posture. They may be squashed or deformed, causing one or more to protrude, the classic condition known as a slipped disk. This may cause back pain and often will occur at the fourth or fifth lumbar vertebra (L4 or L5).

This type of injury becomes more common with increasing age as the disks lose their water content and become less flexible. They also become thinner, which results in the loss of height seen in old age. Damaged disks may impinge on the spinal nerves which form the sciatic nerve, resulting in sciatica—pain down the back of the thigh and into the leg. There may also be muscular spasm (an involuntary contraction of a muscle group), which is a protective mechanism.The muscles in spasm act as a splint to prevent further damage, and they are associated with pain, distortion of normal movement and a twisted, unnatural posture.

Whiplash injury can damage the cervical vertebrae. It is often caused by accidents in motor vehicles and contact sports where the head moves backwards (hyperextension) and forwards (hyperflexion) violently and farther than normal. This movement can cause vertebrae to fracture or, more often, injure the ligaments which connect the vertebrae. Dislocated vertebrae can damage the spinal cord.

Falls on the head or sporting injuries involving head-on collisions can result in fractured vertebrae or ruptured disks. Fractured vertebrae can injure the spinal cord and cause paralysis or death. Disks that rupture will bulge out from between the vertebrae above and below, causing pain as they touch and compress the spinal nerves.

Strains and sprains are less severe injuries to muscles that result from extreme rotations or extensions of the spine. Adequate warm-up routines and stretches can help to prevent back strain injuries.

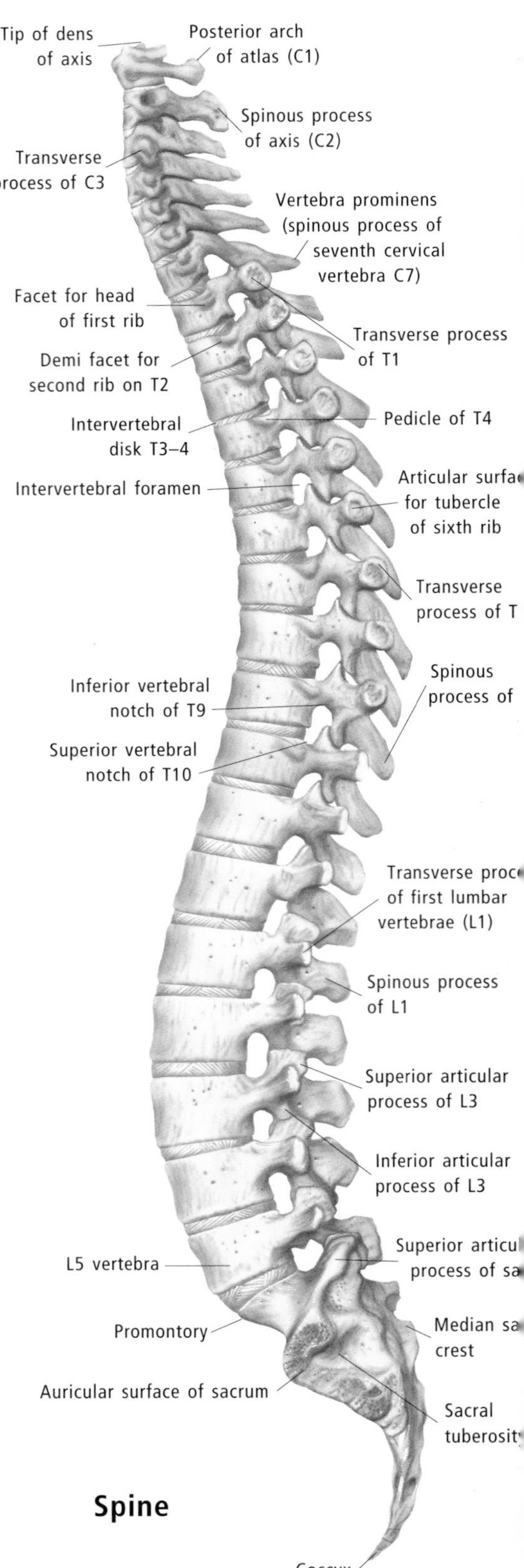

Spine

Spinal cord injuries may cause shock and paralysis below the injury site. This could result in paraplegia (paralysis in both legs and the lower body) if the injury is in the lumbar spine, and quadriplegia (paralysis in all four limbs) if the injury is above the fifth cervical vertebra. If spinal injury is suspected, the person should only be moved by trained paramedical workers. If inappropriate movements are made, this could result in further injury and even paralysis.

Osteoporosis, a degenerative bone disease, is especially disabling and painful when it affects the spine. Loss of minerals from bones causes them to become more porous, and therefore brittle, than normal. Vertebrae become weak and may collapse or fracture, causing pain and immobility or paralysis. Bone cancer can also be a cause of pain but symptoms are usually felt elsewhere in the body.

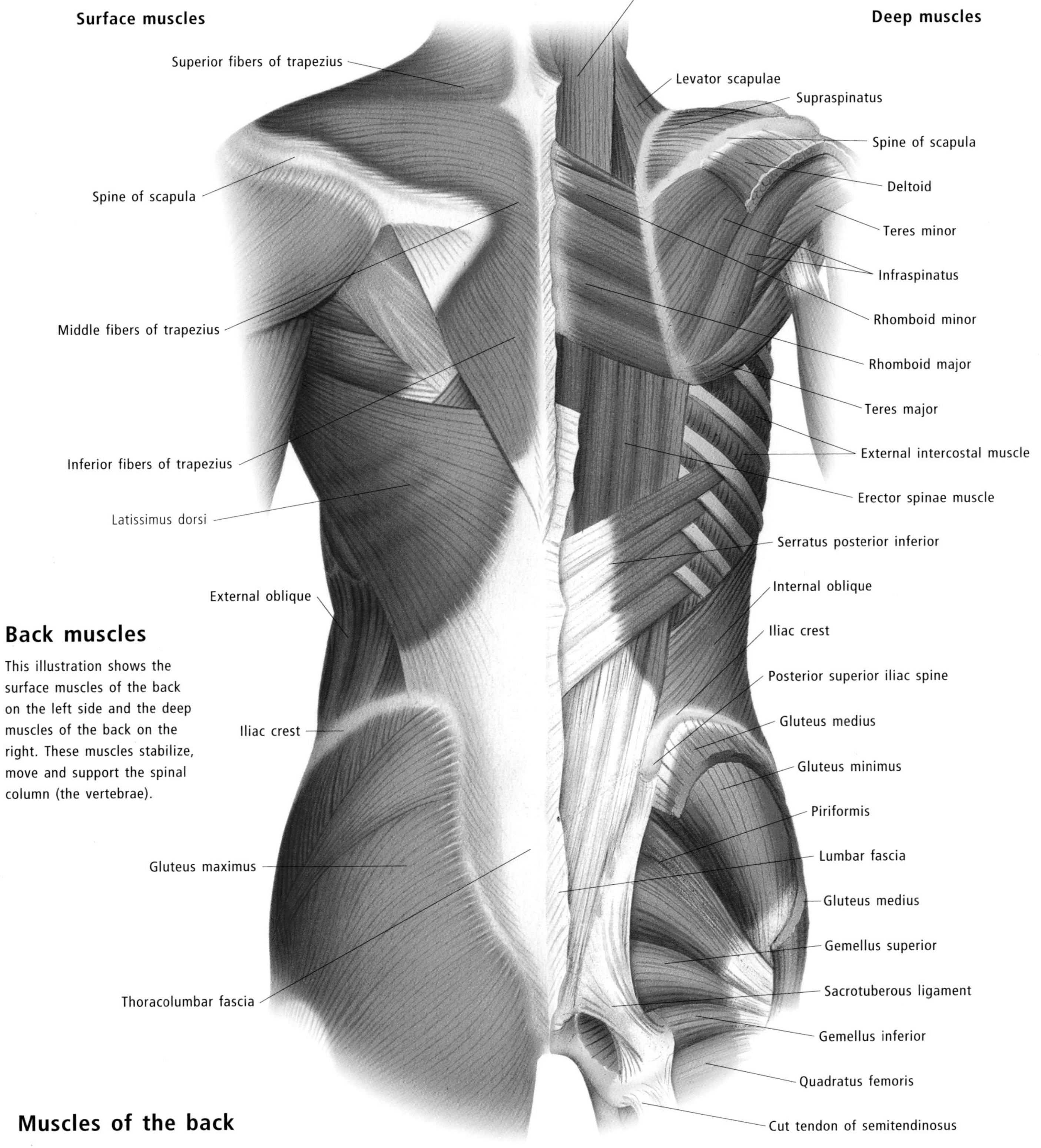

Back muscles

This illustration shows the surface muscles of the back on the left side and the deep muscles of the back on the right. These muscles stabilize, move and support the spinal column (the vertebrae).

Muscles of the back

Causes of back pain

Low back pain is a very common complaint in many societies because of the increasingly sedentary nature of daily work. Symptoms can be pain or numbness in the lower back and surrounding areas, commonly called lumbago. When pain extends down the buttocks and into the upper legs it is associated with pressure on spinal nerves which form the sciatic nerve and is known as sciatica. Factors which place people at risk of back strain injury and low back pain include the following.

Poor physical condition. Good muscle tone in the abdomen and deep muscles which support the spinal column is essential to allow the full range of movement without displacing the disks. Poor muscle tone does not of itself cause back pain, but it brings a greater risk of injury if you are lifting, bending or rotating when the spine is under load.

Loading unprepared muscles. Starting any sporting activity or lifting any significant weight without warming up is dangerous. It is important to prepare for such exertion with stretching, gentle flexing and extension of the muscle groups to be worked. This applies to manual work as well as to sports.

Poor posture. Forward bending of the back compresses the disks at their front edges, and they tend to bulge to the rear. This causes the disk protrusion known commonly as slipped disk and causes pain when the surrounding muscles go into spasm and the disk aggravates spinal nerve roots.

Lifting heavy weights. The knees should be bent when lifting weights from low places, and the back kept as straight as possible. The weight should be kept close to the body as reaching out or up high for a heavy load brings a greater risk of injury. Lifting should be a smooth action as jerking can strain the back. The load should not be too heavy for the lifter. Injuries are common when people do not respect their limitations. Back belts and trusses are poor insurance against injury compared to good muscle tone and common sense.

Care of the back

Back care starts with good posture, whether sitting, standing or working. Good muscle condition plays a very large part, as poor posture often results in muscle weakness. It is important to maintain muscular strength in both abdominal muscles and in the deep muscles that act directly on the spinal column. If working at a desk, it is important to be in a comfortable posture with the seat backrest supporting the back. Having frequent breaks is a good preventive measure.

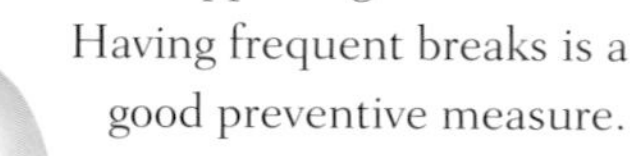

Good back care is essential in pregnancy when changes in weight affect posture and when tendons and ligaments are softer due to the action of the hormone progesterone. Low back pain can be due to poor posture, or the growing baby may cause the uterus to press on the sciatic nerve.

When pain or discomfort occur, good diagnosis is essential to establish whether muscular strain or spasm are responsible, or whether there is more serious injury involving the structure of the spinal column. X-rays may be taken, or a back specialist may make a diagnosis after extensive observation and examination of symptoms. Muscles may be in spasm if there is underlying damage to disks. Traction may be used to relieve the pressure on compressed disks and help them regain normal shape. Later treatment may involve exercise to strengthen underused muscles.

There are a number of alternative therapies that may help to alleviate the symptoms of back pain. Acupuncture may relieve acute spasm and muscle tension, easing back pain sufficiently for massage or manipulation to be given. Aromatherapy massage and baths with essential oils such as lavender, rosemary and peppermint are said to be useful in treating muscle spasm and tension. Massage eases chronic pain associated with postural imbalance, occupational strain or muscle fatigue. Chiropractic manipulation may relieve pain through restoring normal movement to the joints of the back. Osteopathy may provide relief from pain with gentle manipulation and massage of spine and surrounding soft tissue. Postural therapies such as Alexander technique, Feldenkrais method, Pilates, tai chi and yoga may correct postural imbalance and reduce stress.

Exercise can help prevent back problems by correcting poor posture and strengthening vital supporting muscles. However, some back conditions can be made worse by the wrong type of exercise. Specialist advice is essential if you have an injury or an existing back problem.

SEE ALSO *Ankylosing spondylitis, Coccyx, Epidural anesthesia, Exercise, Kyphosis, Lordosis, Lumbago, Osteoarthritis, Osteoporosis, Paget's disease of the bone, Sciatica, Scoliosis, Skeletal system, Spina bifida, Vertebrae, Whiplash injury*

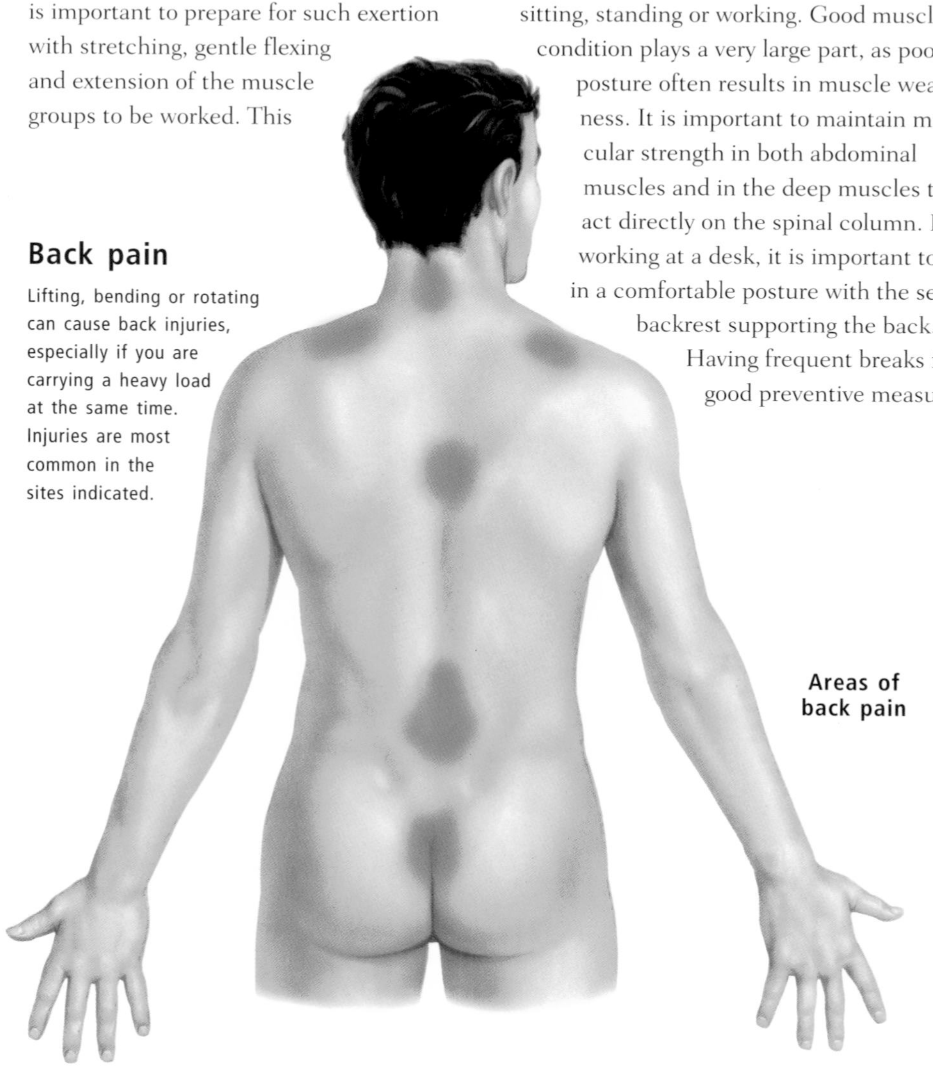

Back pain

Lifting, bending or rotating can cause back injuries, especially if you are carrying a heavy load at the same time. Injuries are most common in the sites indicated.

Bacteria

Streptococcus

Meningococcus

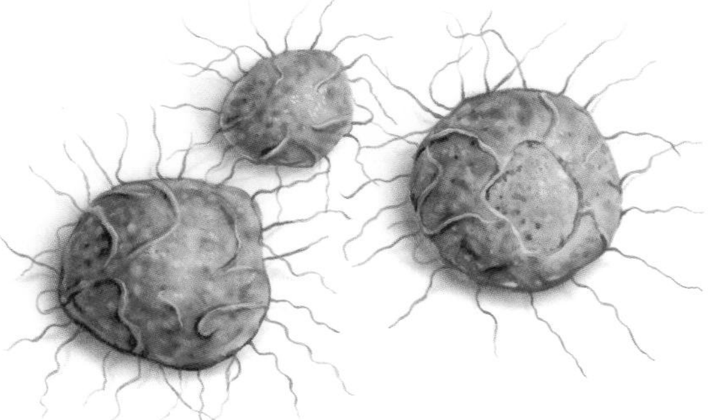

Gonococcus

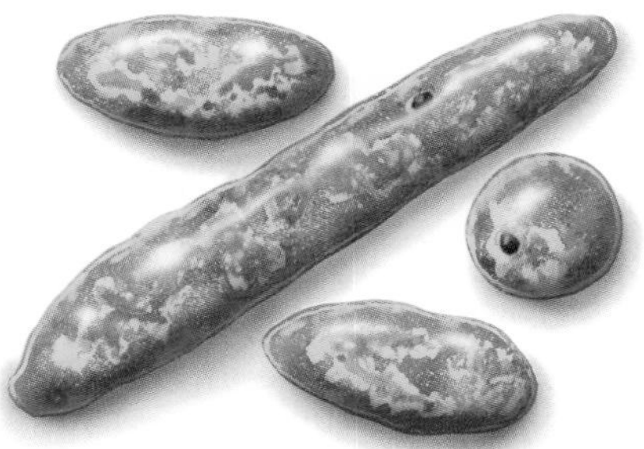

Legionella bacillus

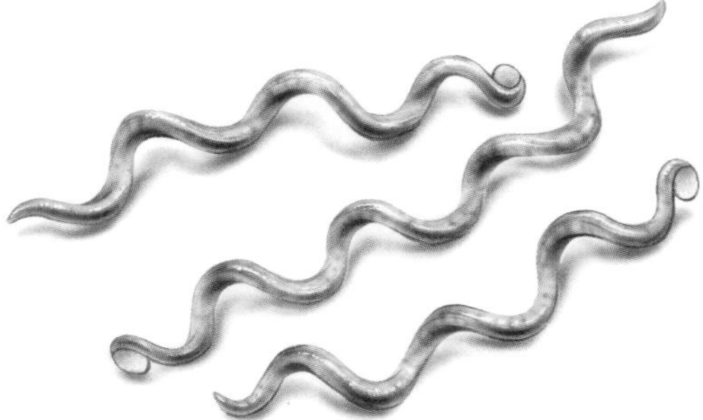

Syphilis spirochete

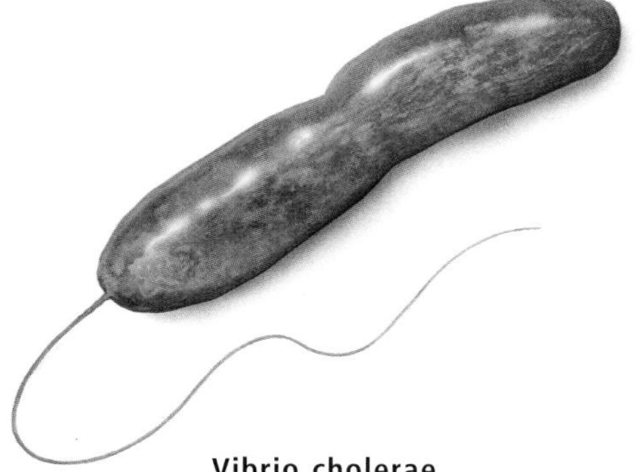

Vibrio cholerae

Bacteria
Bacteria are classified according to their shape; usually they are either spherical (coccus), rod-shaped (bacillus), coil-shaped (spirochete) or comma-shaped (vibrio).

BACTERIA

Bacteria are simple organisms of microscopic size and were one of the early forms of life to evolve. Many are beneficial and live in harmony with humans—in the digestive system aiding the breakdown and absorption of food, and in soil and water breaking down dead matter and animal wastes, a process which maintains conditions for life on our planet. Some are harmful and can cause and spread infections such as cholera, pneumonia, tuberculosis and whooping cough, or release deadly toxins that cause illness or death. Botulism, a serious type of food poisoning, results from bacterial growth in food stored without proper sterilization.

Immunization is a way of stimulating the body to make antibodies to a specific disease without first catching the infection. Public health authorities in most countries now recommend immunization for all citizens against the most common diseases of childhood. Widespread immunization has been very successful in preventing the spread of many once devastating bacterial (as well as viral) diseases. Antibiotics are drugs commonly prescribed to fight bacterial infections.

Immunization and the use of antibiotics have controlled many serious bacterial diseases within human society and eradicated smallpox. Unfortunately, antibiotics may eliminate beneficial as well as harmful bacteria; this can be a cause of digestive disorders and secondary infections. Overuse of antibiotics may be the reason that some bacteria, notably *Staphylococcus aureus,* are resisting treatment.

Shape is a major feature used in the classification of bacteria. There are four main forms: spheres (cocci), rods (bacilli), coils (spirochetes) and commas (vibrios). Within these groups, there is much variation. Rods, for example, can be thick or thin, long or short, and have pointed or rounded ends. Bacteria may also occur as single cells or in groups such as chains, pairs or clusters.

SEE ALSO *Antibiotics, Immunization*

BALANCE

Changes in body position are detected by different sensory receptors in the semicircular canals and otolith organs of the inner ear, the eyes, and the sensors in the joints and muscles that send messages to the brain. These organs, together with the nerves and muscles that control motor coordination and movement, maintain the body's balance.

Any disruption to these organs and pathways can lead to disturbances of balance. Inner ear infection (labyrinthitis) can affect the semicircular canals, causing disturbance of balance. Vertigo, in which balance is so severely affected that the room seems to be spinning around, may be a symptom of Menière's disease or some other ear disorder.

Lack of an adequate blood supply, and thus oxygen to the brain, may disrupt balance. Anemia, heart disease and circulatory disorders may cause dizziness, faintness and loss of balance.

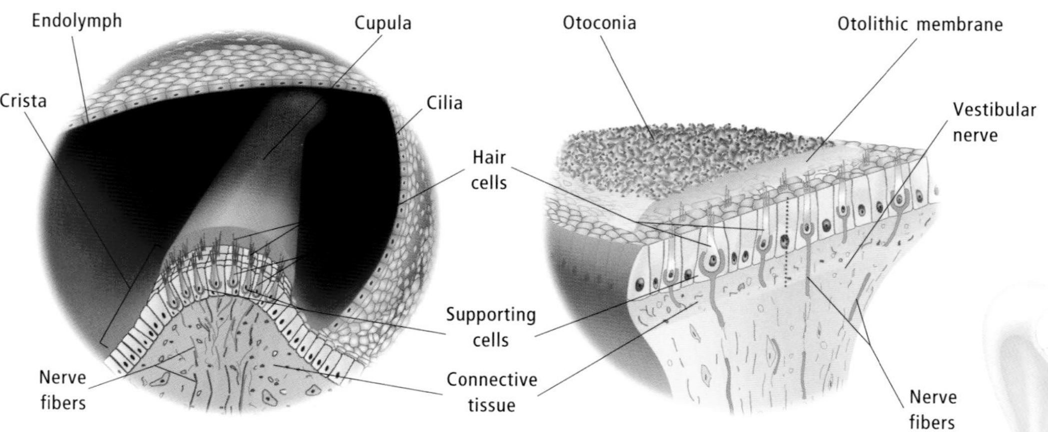

Ampulla of semicircular canal

Macula of otolith organ

Balance

Specialized organs in the inner ear known as the semicircular canals and the otolith organs contain tiny hairs that are sensitive to the body's position in space. Changes in position excite the hairs which send nerve signals via the vestibular nerve to the brain. The brain uses this information to help balance the body.

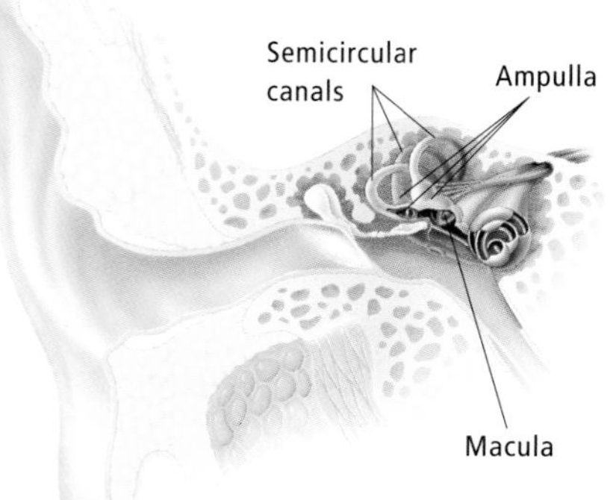

Balance mechanism in the ear

Motion sickness is discomfort caused by repeated movements in cars, boats, airplanes and amusement rides such as carousels and roller coasters. Symptoms include nausea and vomiting. More common in children, motion sickness often disappears with age as the semicircular canals in the ear become less sensitive to movement.

SEE ALSO *Ear, Menière's disease, Motion sickness, Otitis media, Semicircular canals, Vertigo*

BALDNESS

The most common cause of loss of hair (alopecia) is male hormones. Hair loss can take several forms, but the most common, androgenetic alopecia (male pattern baldness) occurs in both sexes and is an inherited condition associated with sexual development. It is characterized by a receding hairline, progressing to leave only a peripheral rim of hair. Another type is alopecia areata, a non-scarring, inflammatory hair loss disease which gives the hair a patchy, moth-eaten look, and is thought to be an autoimmune disorder that can affect men, women and children.

Common among people of the European and Australian races—in Australian Aborigines alopecia is often accompanied by balding of the calves of the legs—baldness is less common in native Americans, Africans and Asians. It affects between 50–80 percent of Caucasian men and between 20–40 percent of women. In men it is age related, affecting around 30 percent of men in their thirties, 40 percent in their forties, and so on; it is not age related in women.

Temporary hair loss can be caused by illnesses that are accompanied by high fever, but can also be caused by pregnancy, chemotherapy, x-rays, ingestion of metals, malnutrition, some skin diseases, endocrine disorders, chronic wasting diseases and trauma such as chemical damage to the hair.

Not all hair loss needs treatment. If it is caused by illness, trauma or pregnancy, regrowth will take place within three to four months. There are three treatments: hair transplantation from an area where hair is growing; the drug minoxidil, which stimulates regrowth and is applied to the scalp; and the drug finasteride, which may promote growth. If hair loss is not hereditary, tests for thyroid disease, autoimmune conditions and anemia should be done.

SEE ALSO *Androgens, Anemia, Autoimmune disease, Hair, Hormones, Thyroid gland*

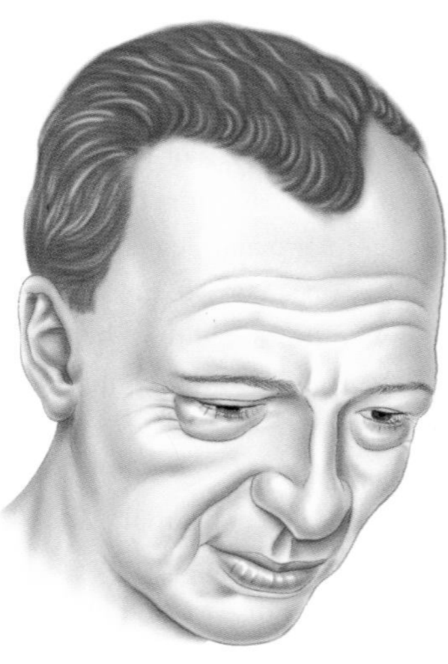

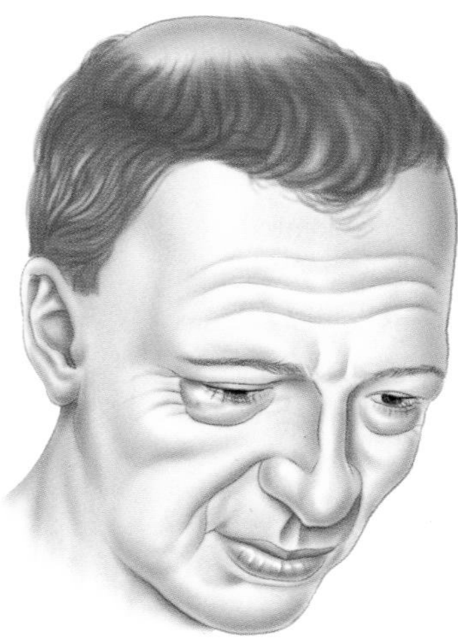

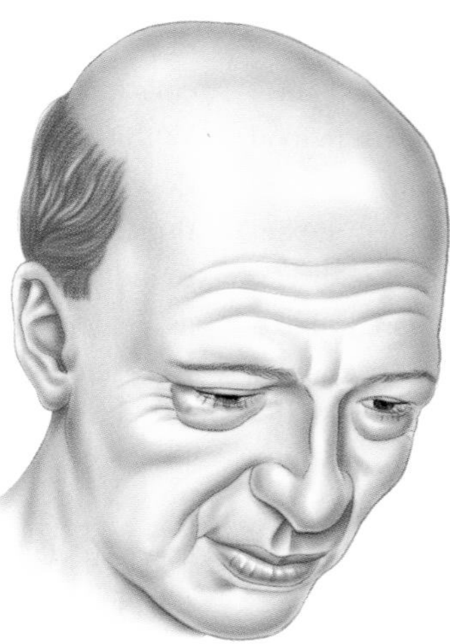

Male pattern baldness

Hair loss follows a typical sequence in male pattern baldness. It begins at the temples, continues at the top and back of the head until finally, in severe cases, hair grows only at the sides of the head.

B

BARBITURATES

Barbiturates are sedative and sleep-inducing drugs derived from barbituric acid. They act by depressing the central nervous system. In larger doses, they lower the blood pressure and slow down breathing. Once commonly prescribed for insomnia and anxiety, they have fallen from favor in recent years because they are habit-forming and, in larger doses, especially if taken with alcohol or other drugs, can result in a fatal overdose.

They have largely been superseded by safer, more modern drugs. However, barbiturates are still used in the treatment of epilepsy, and in intravenous form as anesthetics. Barbiturates commonly used as anticonvulsants for the treatment of epilepsy and seizures include mephobarbital, metharbital and pentobarbital. Those used as anesthetics include sodium pentothal.

SEE ALSO *Anticonvulsants, Anxiolytics, Drug dependence, Epilepsy, Psychotropic drugs*

Barium meal

Also called a barium swallow, a barium meal gives the doctor an idea of the condition of the esophagus and stomach (pictured), and how well foods and liquids travel through them.

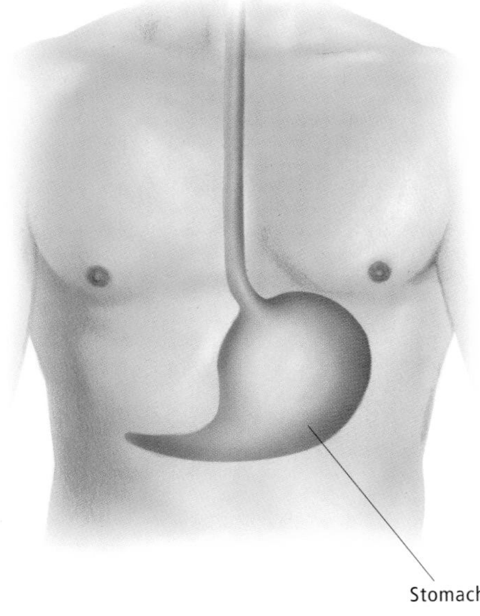

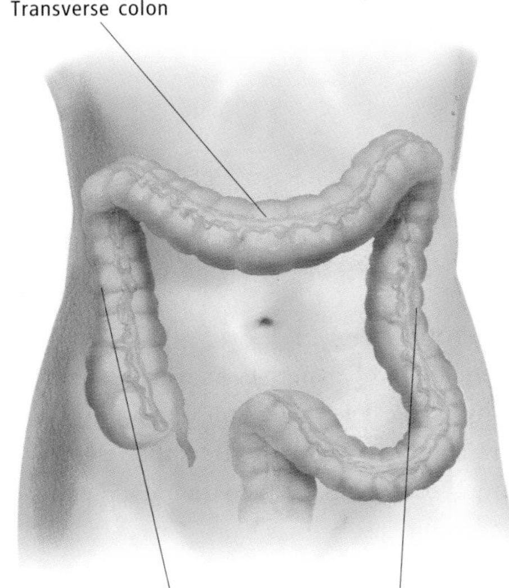

Barium enema

In a barium enema, a white-colored liquid called barium is introduced into the rectum and moved around the colon (shown at left) by a radiologist. Bowel movements may be white or lighter colored in the days following the test.

BARIUM ENEMA

Barium enema is a procedure used to examine the large intestine. The patient's bowel is emptied, and an enema tube containing a solution of barium sulfate is inserted through the anus and into the colon. Barium is opaque to x-rays and lines the bowel so that if polyps, cancers or other such features are present, they will show up.

Used in conjunction with sigmoidoscopy, barium enema is almost as effective as colonoscopy in detecting abnormalities.

SEE ALSO *Colon, Contrast x-ray, Intestines*

BARIUM MEAL

Barium meal is a procedure used to examine the upper gastrointestinal tract. The patient swallows a solution of barium sulfate, then its course is followed by x-ray down the esophagus (gullet) into the stomach.

Largely superseded by endoscopic direct viewing into the stomach, barium meal remains useful for diagnosing hiatus hernia when narrowing of the esophagus prevents endoscopy, and when checking the wave forms of the esophagus during swallowing.

SEE ALSO *Contrast x-ray, Endoscopy, Esophagus, Hiatus hernia*

BARTHOLIN'S GLAND

Bartholin's glands are lubricating glands located on either side of the vaginal opening at the innermost part of the labia.

Blockage of the opening of a Bartholin's gland may cause the gland to swell, forming a Bartholin's cyst. Symptoms include a feeling of vaginal stretching and discomfort, particularly during intercourse. The gland may become infected and form a painful abscess (Bartholin's abscess).

If treatment is considered necessary because of discomfort or infection, the gland can be surgically removed. The procedure can be done under local anesthesia in a doctor's office.

SEE ALSO *Vagina*

Bartholin's gland

Normally Bartholin's glands cannot be detected. But if one becomes blocked, a Bartholin's gland may form a cyst.

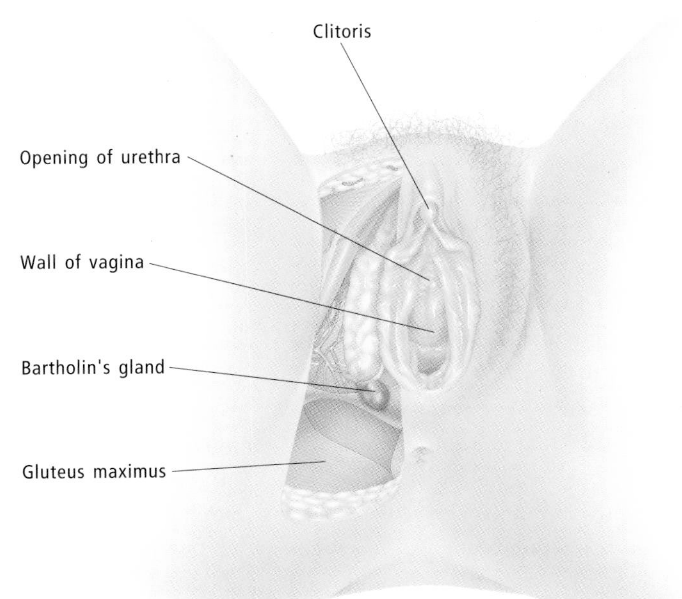

B

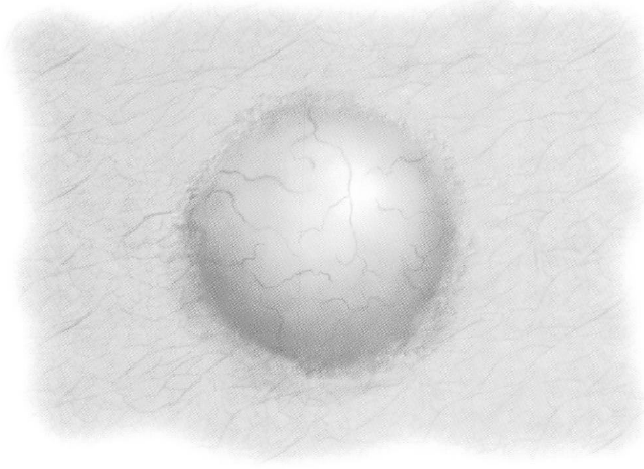

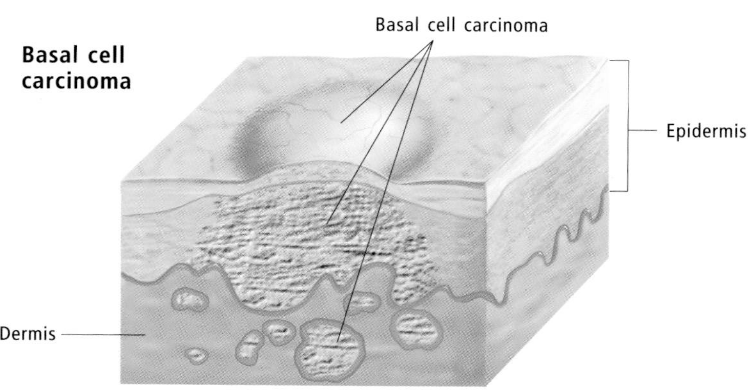

Basal cell carcinoma

A basal cell carcinoma, as it appears on the skin and in cross section. The best treatment is prevention; anyone who spends a lot of time outdoors, and in particular children, should wear sunscreen and a hat and avoid exposure to direct sunlight.

BASAL CELL CARCINOMA

Basal cell carcinoma (BCC) is a common form of skin cancer. It usually appears on the face, and is caused by excessive exposure to sunlight over the years. At first, the sore appears as a small, pear-like nodule, which slowly grows and ulcerates in the center to form a small scab. Basal cell carcinoma is treated with cautery (application of heat or electric current), liquid nitrogen, or low-dose radiation therapy. Larger tumors will need to be removed surgically. Early treatment achieves a cure rate of more than 95 percent. Ongoing checkups should be carried out, as once a basal cell carcinoma has occurred, the chance of getting further basal cell carcinomas is increased.

SEE ALSO *Skin cancer*

BED-WETTING

Also known as enuresis, bed-wetting commonly refers to involuntary discharge of urine, usually during sleep at night. Children can only be said to be bed-wetting if they are still unable to control urination during sleep at the age of five. Even at this age, however, it is still quite common. In extreme cases, enuresis can continue into adulthood unless treatment is sought.

Causes

There are three main factors which affect bed-wetting. The first factor is heredity—if both parents were bed-wetters then there is a three-out-of-four chance their child will experience similar problems. The second factor is the ability, or inability, of the bladder to send a signal to the brain strong enough to wake the sleeping person. The third is over-productive kidneys—in some cases the kidneys produce the same quantity of urine at night as they do during the day.

It is usually recommended that parents wait until a child is seven or eight years old before seeking assistance; however, if the problem is causing a great deal of distress to the child or family, or if the child suddenly starts to wet the bed after being dry, then help should be sought. The first step should be a medical checkup to make sure that the cause of the bed-wetting is not organic, such as developmental or physical problems or infections of the urinary tract.

Treatment

The usual forms of treatment are counseling with behavior therapy, use of alarms, and drug therapy. Counseling is usually the first course of action; it involves both parents and child and is best sought from a continence specialist. It will include behavioral modification programs. Bed-wetting alarms, used on the bed or the body, and under specialist supervision, are usually successful. Bladder training programs also have a good record of success. Medication is usually the last resort and needs to be prescribed by a specialist. Punishment for wetting, limiting the amount a child drinks, and waking the child to go to the toilet during the night are not helpful.

Bladder control

Bladder control develops in the following stages. When the child is up to one year old the bladder empties automatically when it is full. At one to two years of age an awareness of when the bladder is full develops. At three, the ability to hold urine grows as the bladder becomes able to contain larger quantities. At four, the ability to stop urine at will is fully developed. Most children are dry at night by this age. By the age of six, the ability to pass urine on command is possible.

SEE ALSO *Behavior therapy, Bladder, Kidney*

BEHAVIOR THERAPY

Behavior therapy is also known as behavior modification and it uses counseling, or group interaction and support, to change behavior that is unwanted, potentially harmful or unacceptable. It can also be used to treat habits such as cigarette smoking, overeating, alcoholism, stress-induced conditions, and stuttering and tantrums in children.

Developed in the 1950s and '60s, the techniques of behavior therapy are based on theories derived from the work of Ivan Pavlov, John Broadus Watson and B. F. Skinner. Watson, who started work in 1915 as an animal psychologist following in the footsteps of Pavlov, is credited as being the American psychologist who established behaviorism as a therapy. He believed that, if correctly conditioned, babies would grow up to be socially competent, emotionally healthy individuals. Skinner saw human behavior in terms of physiological responses to the environment.

Behavior therapy is based on the idea that human behavior is a result of a stimulus–response interaction and that observable behavior can be modified. The stimulus–response interaction says that all complex types of behavior, including reasoning, emotional reactions and habits, are made up of simple stimulus–response events, which can be measured. Once the stimulus and the response it elicits are identified, an individual's behavior can be predicted. Then, if the stimulus is controlled, the individual's behavior can be controlled.

There are two possible kinds of response: elicited—the response that occurred in the presence of the stimulus; and emitted—the response that occurred not in reaction to a stimulus but was emitted by the organism.

There are also two forms of conditioning: respondent or classical conditioning (the theory developed by Pavlov), which is a learned response that can be evoked by a new stimulus—for example, a kangaroo that flees as soon as it smells a dog; and operant or instrumental conditioning, in which a new response is learned as a result of satisfying a need, for example milking cows coming to the milking sheds at the same time each day because they have a need to be milked as well as fed.

With application, most people can use behavior modification to change their own behavior.The techniques they use include changing the stimuli in their environment, monitoring their behavior (keeping records), making commitments, and setting up consequences for their behavior.

The critics of behaviorism say that it oversimplifies human behavior and that the human being has a free will and is not an automaton. However, behaviorism can solve behavior-related problems and it has had, and will continue to have, an important role in learning.

SEE ALSO *Counseling, Psychotherapy*

BEHAVIORAL AND EMOTIONAL PROBLEMS

Adults, teenagers and children can suffer from disorders that affect their behavior and emotions. Some have a physical cause involving the chemistry of the brain; others are caused by an individual's response to stressful experiences or circumstances.

In most instances, professional help should be sought, initially from a primary care physician. A patient can then be advised of the different types of therapy availalable.

SEE ALSO ***Alcoholism, Anxiety, Bipolar disorder, Depression, Drug dependence, Eating disorders, Obsessive-compulsive disorder, Panic attacks, Personality disorders, Phobias, Posttraumatic stress disorder, Schizophrenia, Seasonal affective disorder, Smoking***

BELL'S PALSY

Bell's palsy is a paralysis caused by a swelling or cutting of the facial nerve; it affects one side of the face. The sufferer is unable to close the eye on that side, or to contract the muscles controlling the forehead, mouth or cheek. The mouth droops and the face is distorted. The unaffected side retains normal function. The disorder may appear after a short period of pain and there may be loss of the sense of taste on the tongue. Treatment is with steroids and antiviral drugs. Most sufferers will recover, but a few will remain permanently impaired.

SEE ALSO *Paralysis*

BETA-BLOCKERS

Beta-blockers are drugs that block the effects of epinephrine (adrenaline) in the heart cells and blood vessels. Beta-blockers slow the heart down and reduce the heart's need for oxygen. They are used to treat angina (chest pain), some arrhythmias (irregular heart rhythms) and hypertension (high blood pressure). They can also be used to treat migraine headaches, hyperthyroidism and glaucoma.

Beta-blockers are not suitable for asthmatics, as they tend to constrict breathing passages. They should not be used by people with heart failure, bradycardia (slow heart rate) or heart block. Patients with diabetes mellitus should take beta-blockers with caution. Side effects include drowsiness, sleep disturbances, weakness, dizziness and shortness of breath.

SEE ALSO ***Angina pectoris, Arrhythmia, Epinephrine, Glaucoma, Heart, Hypertension, Hyperthyroidism, Migraine***

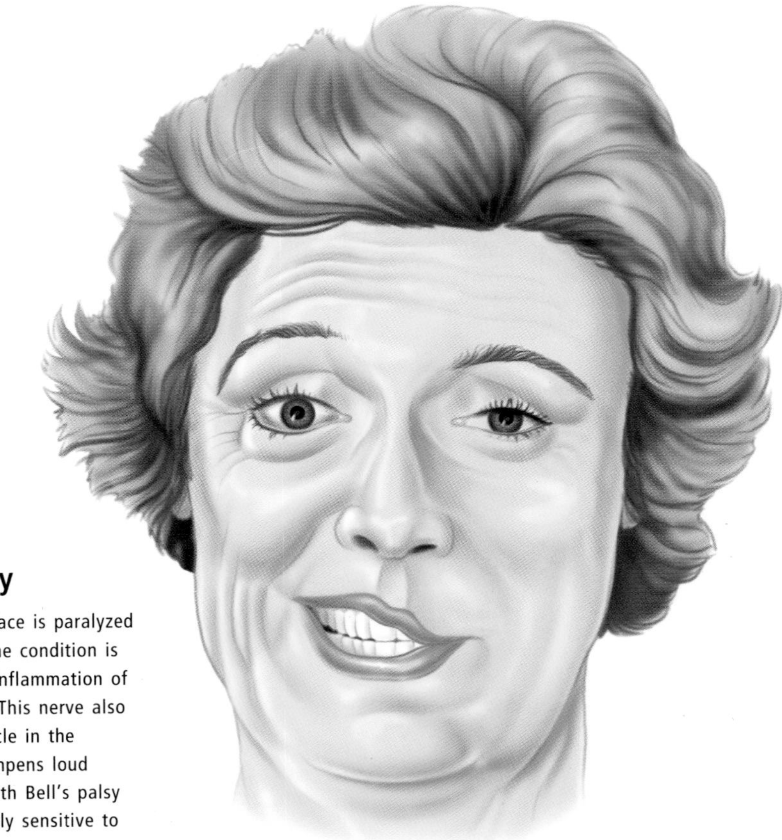

Bell's palsy

One side of the face is paralyzed in Bell's palsy. The condition is due to injury or inflammation of the facial nerve. This nerve also controls the muscle in the eardrum that dampens loud noises; people with Bell's palsy may be abnormally sensitive to loud sounds.

B

BILE DUCTS

The bile ducts (sometimes collectively called the biliary tree) are the narrow tubes through which bile flows in the liver. They are found in various parts of the body, but work together as a system. The hepatic ducts transport bile from the liver (where it is made) to the rest of the biliary system. The hepatic ducts join to form the common bile duct, which transports bile to the duodenum (the first part of the small intestine). The cystic duct transports bile from the gallbladder (where bile is stored) to the common bile duct.

Bile ducts can be blocked by gallstones or cancers, or may become inflamed. Endoscopic retrograde cholangio-pancreatography (ERCP) is an x-ray procedure in which a physician inserts an instrument called an endoscope into the duodenum and uses it to inject dye that is opaque to x-rays into the common bile duct in order to demonstrate any blockage of the hepatic, cystic, or common bile ducts.

SEE ALSO *Cholangitis, Duodenum, Gallbladder, Gallstones, Liver*

BIOCHEMIC TISSUE SALTS

Dr W. H. Schuessler, a nineteenth-century homeopath and chemist, maintained that there are twelve mineral salts vital for the healthy functioning of the cells in the body. He recorded the action of each salt and the symptoms caused by a lack of each. To remedy mineral salt deficiencies, he developed his twelve biochemic tissue salts, also known as cell salts, which he prepared in a homeopathic 6x potency for easy assimilation.

Schuessler did not regard his remedies as homeopathic because they do not follow the "like cures like" philosophy of homeopathy; his belief was that they cure symptoms that result from a deficiency.

SEE ALSO *Homeopathy*

BIOFEEDBACK

Biofeedback is the process of measuring body and mind activity using electronic machines and using these signals to modify behavior or body functions. The machines use detectors attached to the patient's skin which pick up changes that relate to the body's heart rate, skin temperature, muscle tension, brain waves, pulse rate and breathing. This feedback is relayed by the machine in the form of electronic beeps or flashing lights, which can then be interpreted.

With the use of biofeedback machines, researchers have discovered that it is possible for a person to train themselves to control their so-called "involuntary functions", such as their heart beat or pulse rate. Patients can learn to recognize the fluctuations in the body's responses/functions by following the flashes or beeps from the machine. They then learn how to positively affect their involuntary functions through the use of techniques such as concentration, meditation, visualization or breathing exercises.

The ability to recognize and alter body functions has been found to be particularly helpful for people suffering from chronic anxiety states, and related illnesses such as migraine and hypertension. Biofeedback machines have also been used to assist people with epilepsy and cerebral palsy.

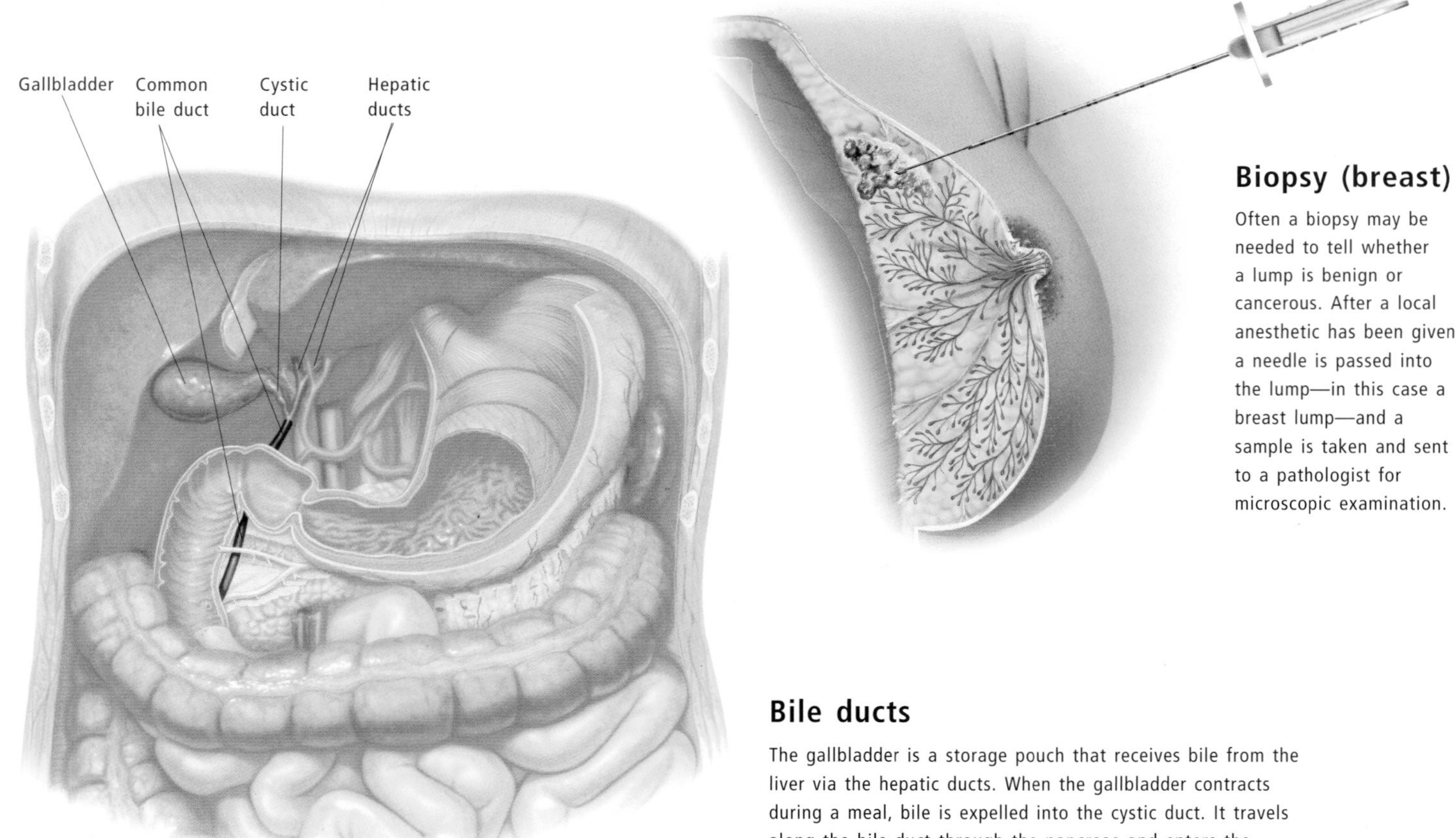

Biopsy (breast)

Often a biopsy may be needed to tell whether a lump is benign or cancerous. After a local anesthetic has been given, a needle is passed into the lump—in this case a breast lump—and a sample is taken and sent to a pathologist for microscopic examination.

Bile ducts

The gallbladder is a storage pouch that receives bile from the liver via the hepatic ducts. When the gallbladder contracts during a meal, bile is expelled into the cystic duct. It travels along the bile duct through the pancreas and enters the duodenum where it helps digest fats.

B

Bipolar disorder

The changes in mood that people with bipolar disorder experience are thought to be caused by biochemical changes in the limbic system of the brain, shown here.

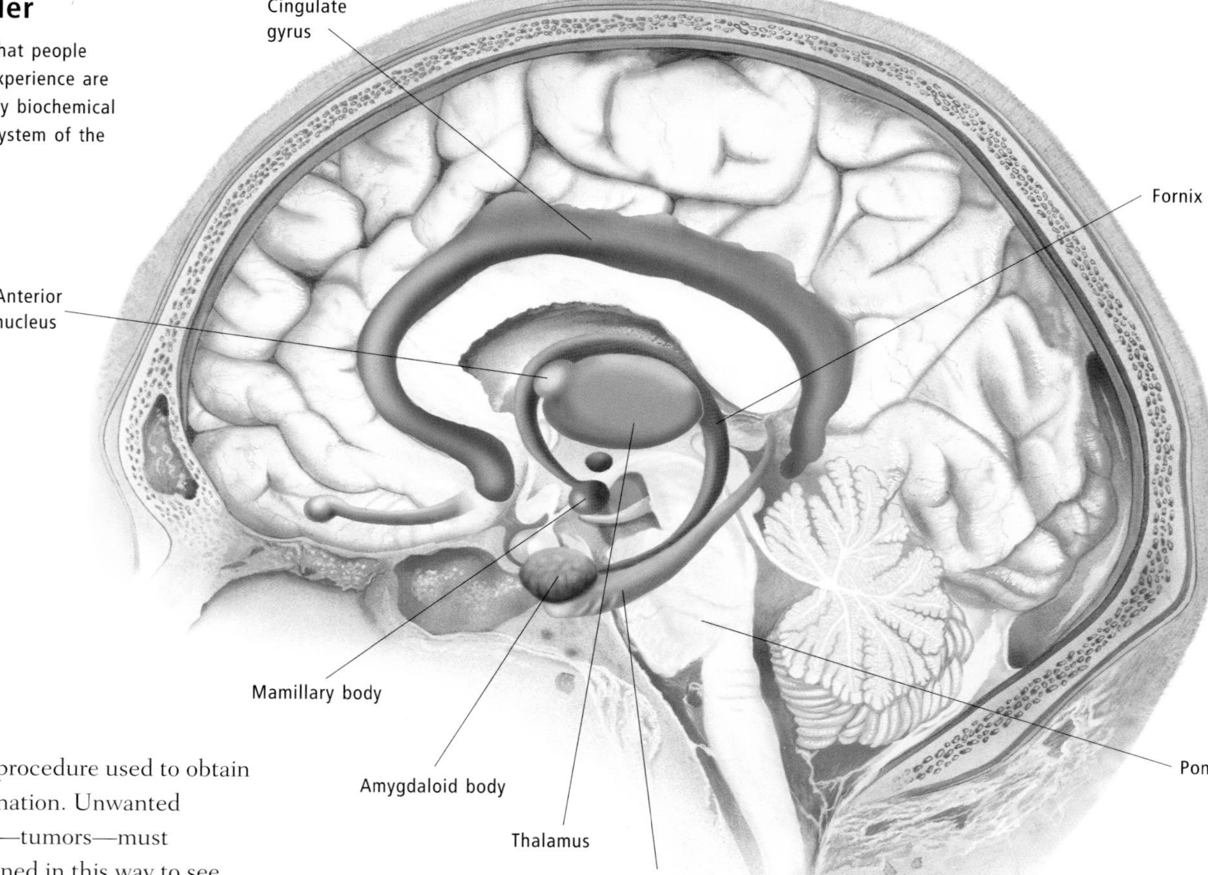

BIOPSY

Biopsy is a medical procedure used to obtain live tissue for examination. Unwanted growths in the body—tumors—must sometimes be examined in this way to see whether they are benign (harmless) or malignant (cancerous). Under anesthetic a small piece of tissue is surgically removed and sent to a laboratory for examination.

Biopsy can aid diagnosis of various diseases. A small sample of tissue or cells from lymph nodes, internal organs such as the liver, or from bones, can be obtained simply for intensive examination and the correct diagnosis made without unnecessary surgery.

SEE ALSO *Tumors*

BIORHYTHMS

Scientists in the early part of the twentieth century identified three energy cycles, or internal body clocks. The theory holds that a physical cycle of around 23 days governs resistance to disease, strength, vitality and sex drive; an emotional cycle of 28 days is linked to sensitivity, moods, perceptions and mental balance; and an intellectual cycle of around 33 days is linked to decision-making, memory and alertness. Because these cycles are of varying lengths, their "highs" and "lows" rarely coincide.

A computer can calculate individual biorhythm charts; these charts may be used by a natural health practitioner to detect swings in behavior and mood, and their effects on their patient's health.

BIPOLAR DISORDER

Bipolar disorder, also known as manic-depressive illness, is a mental illness which is characterized by episodes of mania ("highs"), followed by depression ("lows"). Moods swing from one extreme to the other, with relatively normal moods between.

In the manic phase, which may last from several days to months, the person feels elated and hyperactive, talks rapidly, has inflated self-esteem, is easily distracted and has no desire for sleep. Uncharacteristically poor judgment, increased sexual drive and intrusive or aggressive behavior are common.

Feelings of guilt, worthlessness, sadness and low self-esteem are symptoms of the depressive phase. The sufferer loses interest in ordinary activities, including sex, and may feel suicidal. In both high and low phases, dependence on alcohol and drugs such as cocaine or sleeping medications is common.

Bipolar disorder can have devastating consequences, including marital breakups, job loss, alcohol and drug abuse and suicide. Gambling, sexual promiscuity and poor decision-making are some of the behaviors that can affect the sufferer, spouse, friends, employers and family.

Symptoms of bipolar disorder begin between 15 and 25 years of age, affecting men and women equally. There is no known cause, although a chemical imbalance in the brain is thought to be involved. It also tends to run in families and may be inherited. The condition may occur in younger children, when it is often confused with attention deficit hyperactivity disorder (ADHD).

Treatment

In severe forms of the disorder, hospitalization is necessary, particularly during the depression that follows a manic phase, when the danger of suicide is high.

Lithium carbonate, a drug with complex effects on the nervous system, is generally effective in controlling the symptoms and preventing future episodes. Lithium's effects usually begin within one week of starting treatment, and the full effect is seen after two to three weeks.

However, side effects of lithium deter some sufferers from taking it. These include fine hand tremor, dry mouth, weight gain, increased thirst, increased frequency of urination, mild nausea or vomiting, impotence, decreased libido, diarrhea and kidney abnormalities, among other things. Non-compliance with a medication schedule can sometimes be a problem.

The anticonvulsants carbamazepine and valproate are also useful as mood stabilizers, and they are often combined with lithium. Antidepressants may also be used to treat the depression.

Psychotherapy is often helpful and sufferers may benefit from belonging to a support group. Children and adolescents with bipolar disorder are generally treated with lithium, but carbamazepine and valproate are also used. If severe bipolar disorder does not respond to drugs, electroconvulsive therapy (ECT) may be used.

Because manic-depressive illness is recurrent, treatment must be long term and, in some cases, permanent.

SEE ALSO *Anticonvulsants, Antidepressants, Depression, Electroconvulsive therapy, Mania, Psychotherapy*

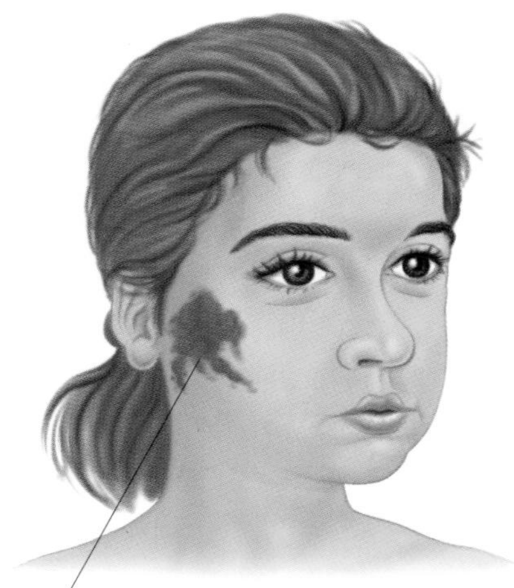

Port-wine stain

Congenital pigmented nevus

Birthmarks

Although most birthmarks are harmless, they may be regarded as a problem and some may be unsightly. They may be hidden by cosmetics or treated by plastic surgery, laser surgery, cautery (electric current) or cryosurgery (freezing). Some birthmarks disappear of their own accord. Their cause is unknown.

BIRTHMARKS

Babies are sometimes born with marks, spots or patches on their skin, known as birthmarks. These marks remain, unlike bruises that are caused by the trauma of birth. The most common birthmarks include the following.

Mongolian blue spots are blue-colored "bruises" or nevi. These are common on dark-skinned and Asian babies. These spots are harmless and they will disappear during childhood.

Salmon patches are red marks on the eyelids, nose or back of head. Formerly called "stork bites", they are very common and will usually disappear over time. They are a type of hemanigoma.

Port-wine stains are also a type of hemangioma. They are reddish purple-brown lesions that do not fade but can be treated with surgery.

Cafe au lait spots appear as coffee-colored patches on the skin. They are quite common and will not disappear.

Congenital pigmented nevi are moles which vary in color from light brown to black and which may have hairs. They are usually surgically removed.

SEE ALSO *Hemangioma*

BISEXUALITY

Bisexuality means being sexually attracted to both sexes. The development of sexuality is a complex process and often involves experimentation with members of the same sex, which doesn't necessarily indicate a preference for homosexuality. Similarly, a person may live as a heterosexual within a traditional family yet maintain their preference for sexual partners of the same sex. Bisexuals are physically normal and may give no outward sign of their bisexuality.

SEE ALSO *Homosexuality, Sexuality*

BLADDER

Found in the pelvic cavity, the bladder is the part of the urinary tract that collects and stores urine via the ureters from the kidneys. When the bladder is full it empties, expelling urine from the body through the urethra. In most adults, the bladder holds about one pint (475 milliliters) of urine when full. It passes from 24–68 fluid ounces (700–2000 milliliters) of urine a day.

There are several conditions affecting the bladder. Cystitis or inflammation of the bladder, usually from bacterial infection, is the most common. The symptoms are frequent, painful urination, and blood in the urine. Cystitis is confirmed by a urine test, which identifies the bacterium that is causing the infection. Treatment is with antibiotics and fluids by mouth. Drinking unsweetened cranberry juice may help to reduce the number and severity of bacterial infections, although the reason behind this is not clear.

Stones, or calculi, may form in the bladder. Composed mainly of salts, cholesterol and some protein, calculi may grow in the bladder slowly without causing symptoms. When they grow to a certain size, they may block the outlet to the urethra and cause urinary obstruction. Cystitis often accompanies calculi. Treatment is usually surgical. This may mean lithotomy—an operation to remove a stone through a surgical incision. Alternatively, the stone may be destroyed by lithotripsy, a procedure in which an instrument called a lithotrite is passed through the urethra into the bladder and used to crush the stone or shatter it with an electrical spark. Ultrasonic lithotripsy is similar except that high-frequency sound waves are used to destroy the stone without inserting any instruments into the body. The crushed fragments of the stone can then be passed out of the body.

Bladder cancers usually arise from cells lining the bladder. The most common form of bladder cancer is a papilloma—a slow-growing wart-like growth, or tumor, attached to a stalk. Tumors other than papillomas are less common but have a poorer prognosis, spreading by penetrating the bladder muscle, infiltrating surrounding fat and tissue, and eventually invading the bloodstream and lymphatic system. In its early stages, bladder cancer may not have obvious symptoms; later symptoms may include blood in the urine, frequent urinary tract infections, frequent and painful urination, abdominal or back pain, persistent low-grade fever and anemia.

Male bladder

Urine is stored in the bladder and expelled through the urethra, which passes through the prostate gland and travels the length of the penis. In old age an enlarged prostate can obstruct the flow of urine at the outlet of the bladder and surgery may be required.

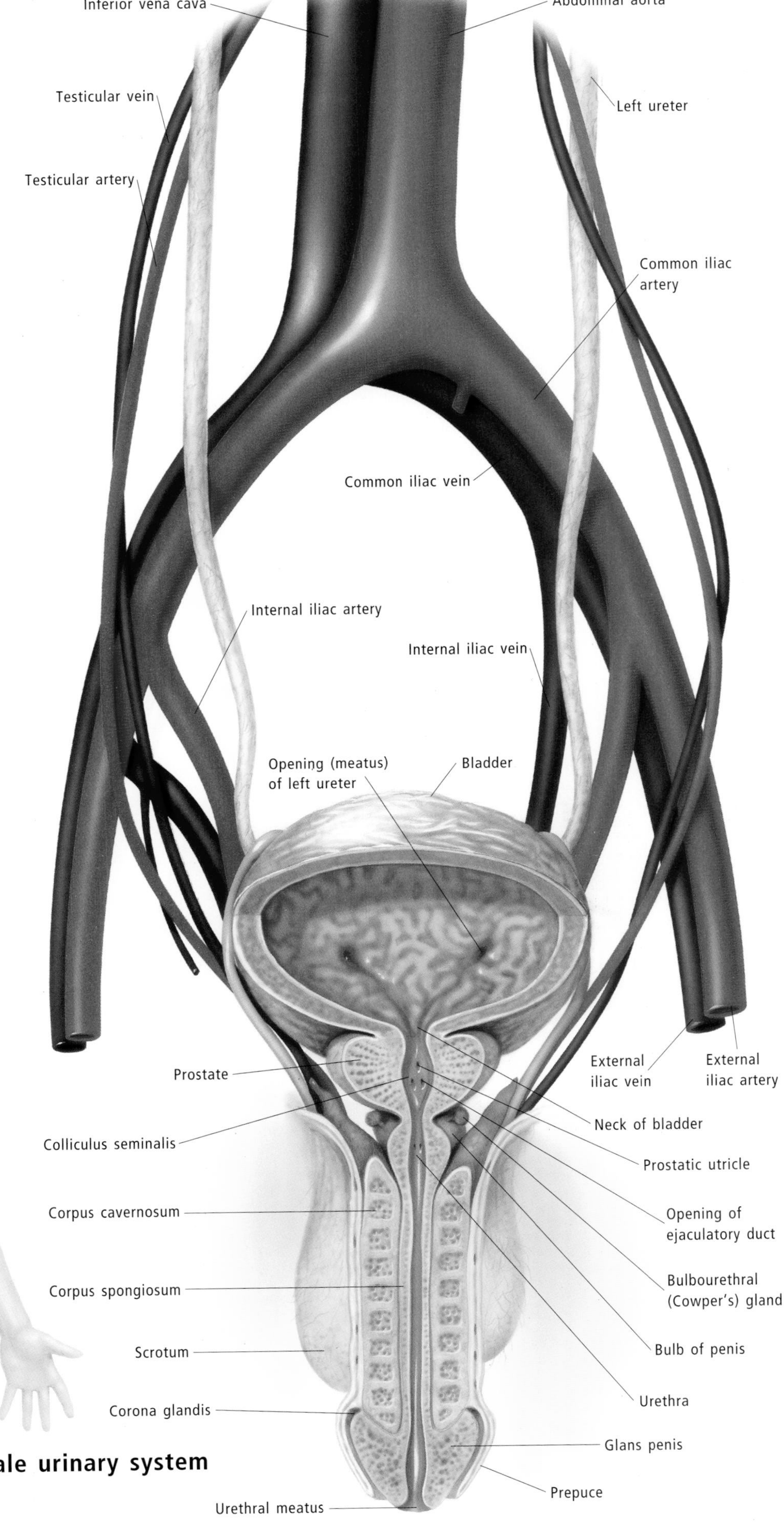

Male urinary system

B

Bladder cancer has no known cause. However, it has been firmly linked to exposure to cancer-promoting chemicals (carcinogens). Cigarette smokers, painters, truckers, leatherworkers, machinists and metalworkers, rubber and textile workers, and people exposed to industrial dyes are at increased risk. It is more common over the age of 40. If detected early, papillomas can usually be treated successfully by transurethral resection (TUR). In this procedure the urosurgeon inserts a small tube into the bladder and removes or cauterizes the tumor. It may be combined with chemotherapy or radiation therapy. Larger, more invasive cancers require radical cystectomy (bladder removal) and construction of an artificial storage organ.

Obstruction of the outlet of the bladder may cause urinary retention, particularly in older men, due to benign prostatic hypertrophy (enlargement of the prostate). TUR of a part of the prostate usually relieves the obstruction.

Calculi, cancers and other bladder disorders can be identified using x-ray, ultrasound, computerized axial tomography (CAT) scan or magnetic resonance imaging (MRI). The urologist can also view the bladder through a fiberoptic tube known as a cystoscope, which can also be used to take a biopsy. A cystogram is an x-ray taken of the bladder after dye that is opaque to x-rays is injected into a vein. Filtered out by the kidneys, the dye passes into the bladder, showing stones, papillomas, cancers and other conditions.

SEE ALSO *Biopsy, Cystitis, Cystogram, Cystoscopy, Kidney, Prostate gland, Urinary systems*

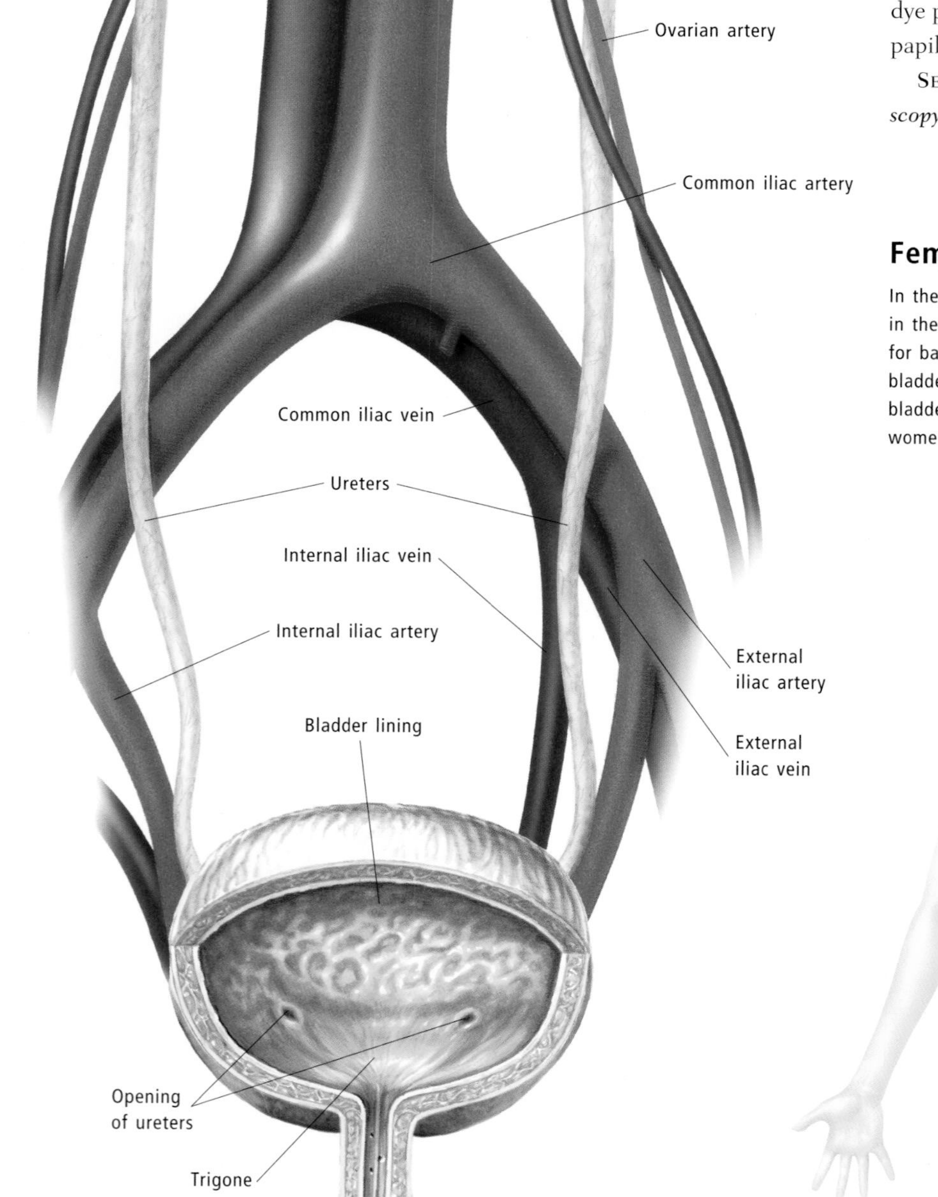

Female urinary system

Female bladder

In the female, the urethra is much shorter than in the male. The shorter urethra makes it easier for bacteria from outside the body to enter the bladder and cause cystitis (inflammation of the bladder). As a result, cystitis is more common in women than in men.

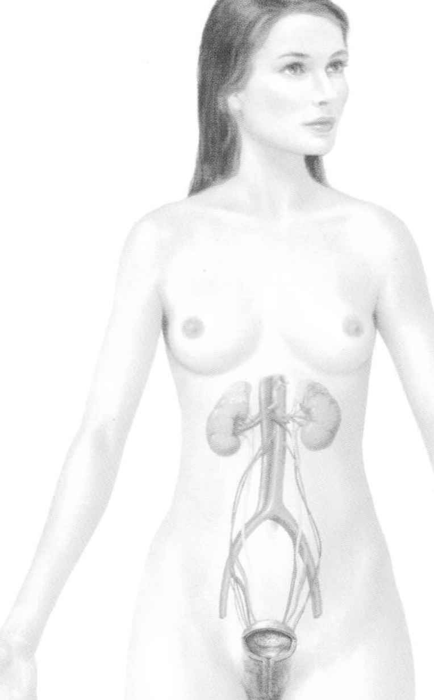

B

Bladder transitional cell carcinoma

Bladder cancers such as this one are often caused by cancer producing chemicals such as cigarette smoke, dyes, paint and rubber. Most can be easily cured by removal or cauterization (burning) with an instrument that is passed through the urethra and into the bladder.

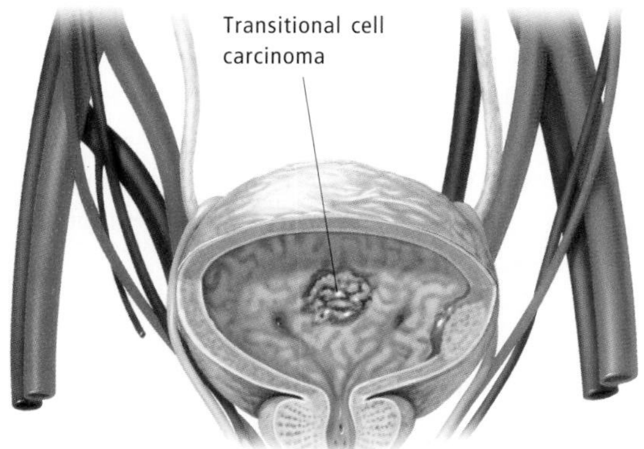

Bladder stones

Bladder stones grow slowly and often cause no symptoms until they are large. They may block the outlet of the bladder, or cause bladder infections. These (from left, mulberries, jackstones and gravel) are shown at their actual size.

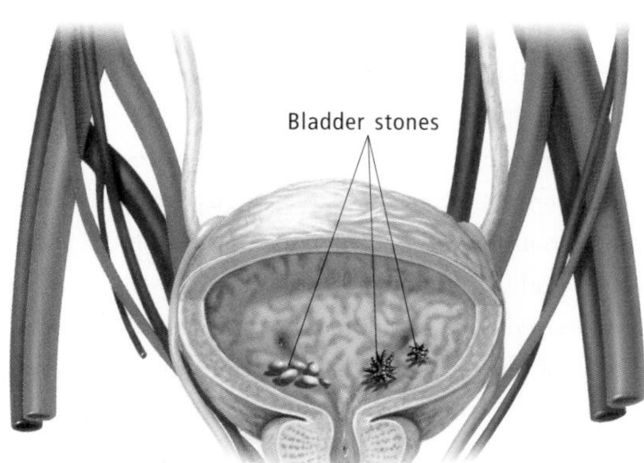

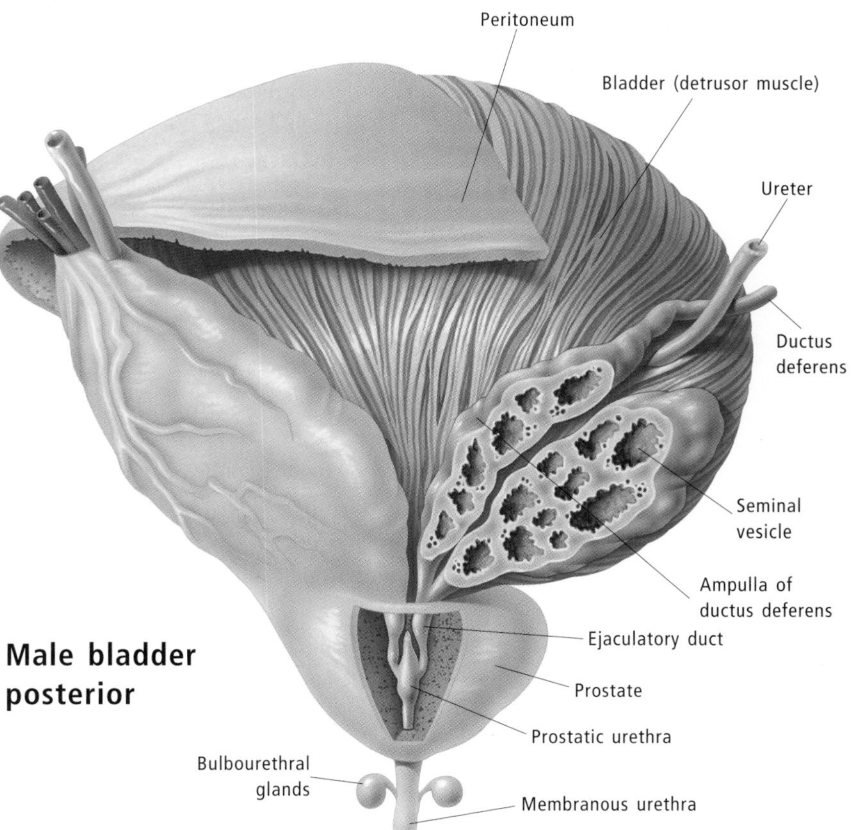

Male bladder posterior

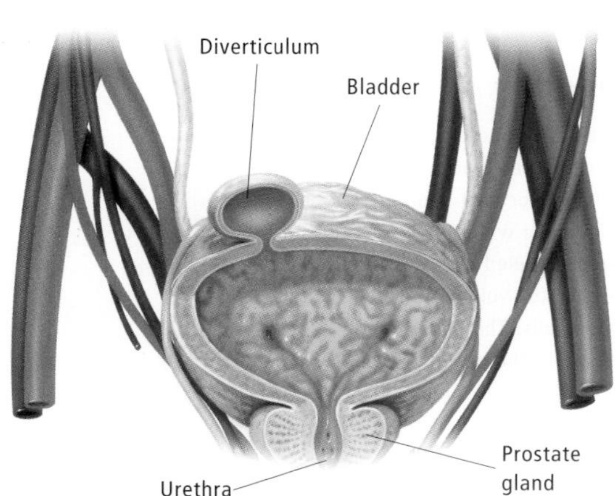

Bladder diverticulum

A bladder diverticulum is an abnormal pouch of the wall of the bladder, usually caused by a weakness in the wall. If untreated it may cause recurrent bouts of cystitis (inflammation of the bladder). It can be repaired by surgery.

BLINDNESS

Blindness can be a total or partial inability to see. Total blindness means the inability to distinguish darkness from light. Partial blindness means having some sight in one or both eyes. A person may have partial sight but still be declared blind—that is, blind according to a definition in law. This may be important in establishing a right to benefits, or training or employment allowances.

Blindness may be congenital, that is, present at birth, or may be acquired through illness or injury.

Industrial accidents are common causes of eye injury. Infections after injury can also cause permanent sight loss. A violent blow or accident can cause the retina to be detached from the inner layer of the eye called the choroid, with loss of sight. In snow blindness, vision is lost due to corneal damage caused by the sun's bright ultraviolet rays reflecting on the snow. Color blindness is the inability to see, or at least differentiate between, specific colors.

Complete or partial blindness may also be due to injury to the neural pathways from the retina to the visual cortex.

SEE ALSO *Cataracts, Color blindness, Diabetes, Macular degeneration, Night blindness*

B

BLOOD

Blood is a suspension of red and white blood cells, platelets, proteins and chemicals in a straw-colored fluid called plasma. It is the means by which oxygen and essential nutrients are transported from the lungs and digestive tract to other parts of the body.

Blood transfers waste products to organs such as the kidneys and lungs, which eliminate them. It transports antibodies and white blood cells to the sites where they are needed to fight infection. And it transports heat from inner parts of the body to the skin to keep body temperature body stable. A normal-sized adult has about 10 pints (nearly 5 liters) of blood. At rest, the heart pumps all of it around the body in about one minute.

The disk-shaped red blood cells (also called erythrocytes) are the body's means of transporting oxygen to the body's tissues. In a healthy person, each cubic millimeter (0.006 cubic inches) of blood contains between four and six million red blood cells. The oxygen is carried by an iron-containing compound in the red blood cells called hemoglobin. When oxygenated, hemoglobin appears red—hence the red appearance of blood in the arteries. Once the red blood cells reach the tissues, the oxygen is exchanged for carbon dioxide, which the hemoglobin then carries back to the lungs, where it is exhaled.

White blood cells (also known as leukocytes) are the agents of the body's immune system, traveling via the blood to sites of injury and infection. Some types of white cells, called neutrophils and monocytes, engulf invading bacteria and small particles. Others, called lymphocytes, produce antibodies which destroy foreign organisms and are responsible for establishing ongoing immunity. A healthy person has between 4,000 and 10,000 white blood cells per cubic millimeter (0.006 cubic inches) of blood.

Platelets (or thrombocytes) are small fragments of cells responsible for clotting. Clotting is the normal way the body stops bleeding and begins the healing process following injury. It involves complex chemical reactions between many substances that are present in the blood plasma.

In order to deliver oxygen and remove waste products, blood must reach the tissues. In the so-called systemic circulation, oxygenated blood is pumped from the heart through arteries to capillaries in tissues where the oxygen is removed, and then back to the heart via the veins. In the pulmonary circulation, deoxygenated blood flows from the heart to the lungs and then returns, oxygen-rich, to the heart.

Blood

Blood is composed of red blood cells, various types of white blood cells (leukocytes) and platelets in a solution of water, electrolytes, and proteins called plasma. About 40 percent (by volume) of blood is red blood cells. This illustration shows all the different types of blood cell—it does not accurately represent the proportions present in the blood.

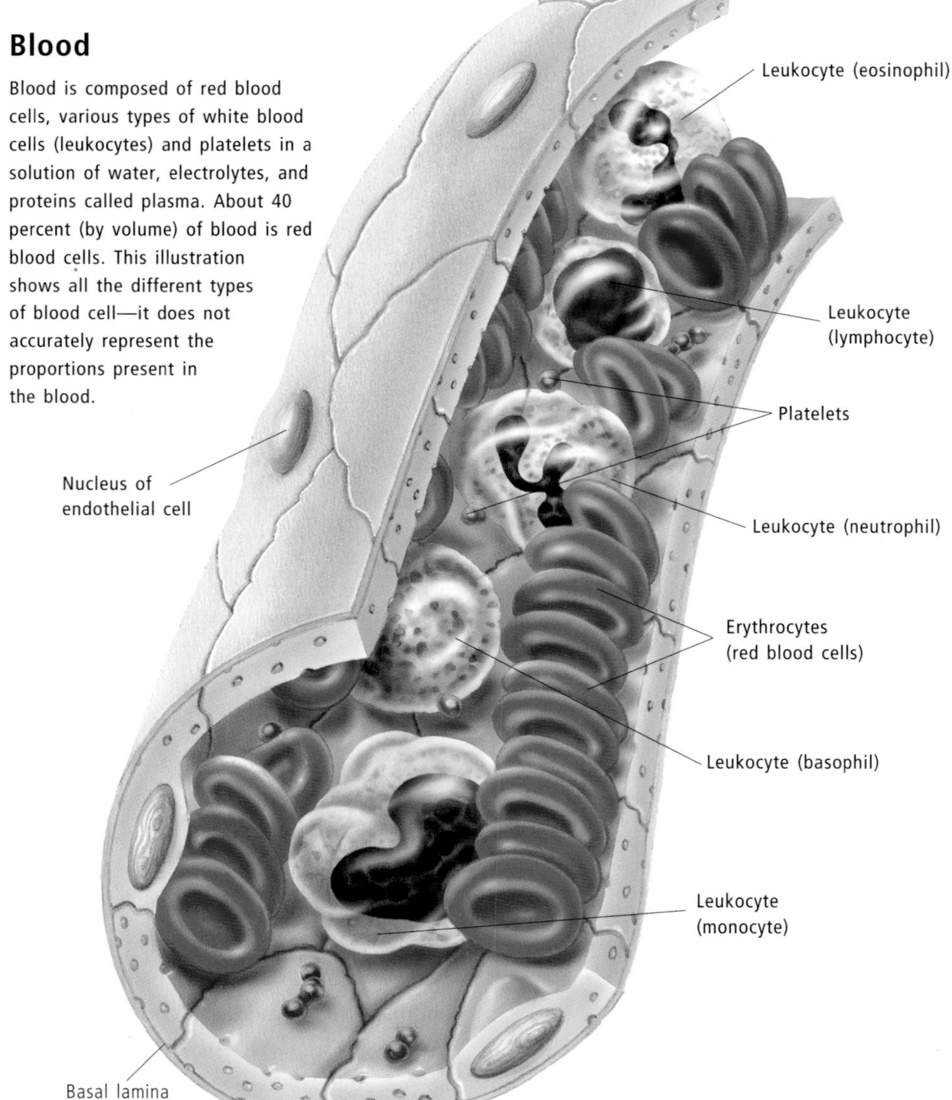

Anemia

Anemia is the failure of the red blood cells to provide enough oxygen to body tissues. It may be caused by a decreased number of red blood cells or a decreased amount of hemoglobin in red blood cells.

There are several causes of anemia. Blood cells may be too few in number because of blood loss or abnormally rapid destruction of circulating blood cells by the body. There may be inadequate amounts of hemoglobin in red blood cells because vital compounds needed to make hemoglobin are missing, as in iron deficiency and vitamin B_{12} deficiency anemias. Or hemoglobin levels in red blood cells may be normal but the hemoglobin may be defective, as in sickle cell disease and thalassemia.

Physicians diagnose anemia by taking a small sample of blood from the patient and counting the number of red blood cells, as well as measuring the concentration of hemoglobin, in the sample. Normal levels of hemoglobin in the blood are approximately 14–17 grams per 100 milliliters (deciliter) for males and 12–15 grams per 100 milliliters (deciliter) for females. In order to treat anemia, the cause must be reversed. Iron or B_{12} supplements, corticosteroid drugs, blood transfusions, or surgery to correct blood loss may be required, depending on the cause.

In some conditions there are too many red cells. This may occur as a compensatory mechanism in chronic lung disease. It may also occur because of an abnormal increase in red blood cell production by the bone marrow, such as in polycythemia vera.

Clotting

Normal blood clotting, or coagulation, is a complex process involving as many as 20 different plasma proteins known as coagulation factors. These factors interact to form a reaction that leads to the production of fibrin, a protein that stops bleeding. In bleeding disorders, certain coagulation factors are deficient or missing. Such a disorder may be hereditary, such as hemophilia. Abnormal bleeding may also be caused by vitamin K deficiency, severe liver disease or prolonged treatment with anticoagulants.

A clot within a blood vessel is called a thrombus. Thrombi can form on damaged blood vessel walls; hence they are more likely in people with arteriosclerosis. A slower than normal flow of blood through the veins can also cause clotting, for example in varicose veins and in people who require prolonged bed rest. Smoking and some birth control pills can also cause blood clots.

A thrombus can block an artery and cause tissues downstream to die from lack of oxygen; it can also block a vein. If it occurs in an artery to the brain, it can cause a stroke. The blood clot may dislodge and travel further upstream, causing ischemia (lack of blood) where it lodges. It is then an embolus. A thrombus can form in a leg or pelvic vein, then detach and lodge in the lung.

Blood clot

This picture of a blood clot as seen by an electron microscope shows red blood cells trapped in a network of fibrin fibers.

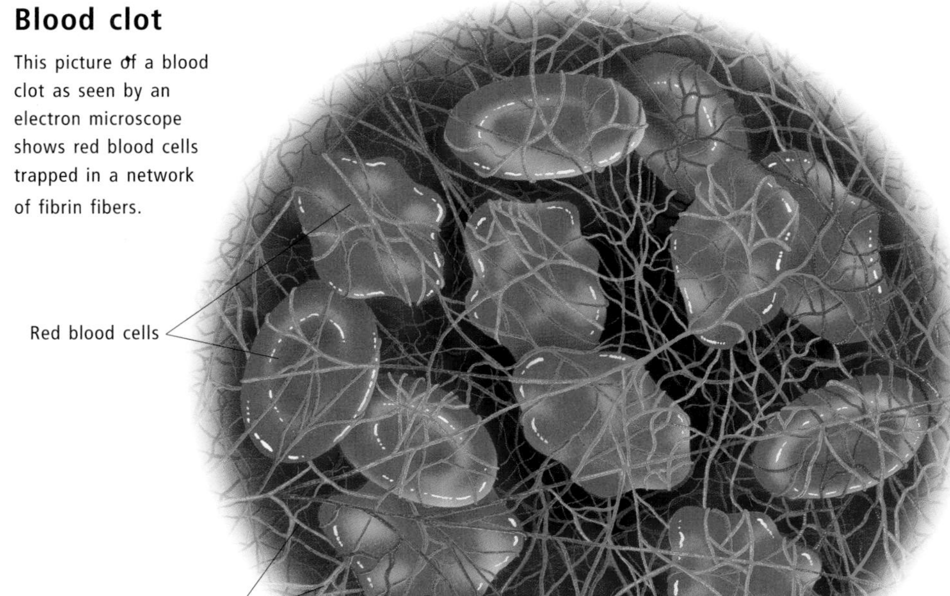

Bacteremia and septicemia

Bacteremia and septicemia (also called blood poisoning) occur when bacterial infection has entered the bloodstream. Once infection has spread to the blood, it may be carried to other parts of the body. Symptoms include high fever, sweating, malaise and chills.

The difference between bacteremia and septicemia is one of degree; septicemia is more serious and usually indicates that the bacteria are multiplying in the blood and causing serious illness. In extreme cases of septicemia, abscesses may form in internal organs such as the liver or brain. Severe blood poisoning may be fatal. The condition requires urgent treatment with intravenous antibiotics in hospital.

SEE ALSO *Anemia, Arteriosclerosis, Embolism, Hemoglobin, Ischemia, Plasma, Platelets, Red blood cells, Septicemia, White blood cells*

Blood clotting

Blood clots in three stages:

a. When a blood vessel is damaged, platelets and red blood cells spill into the damaged tissues.

b. Platelets increase in number and begin to attach to damaged surfaces. Strands of a protein called fibrin are formed.

c. Blood cells, platelets and strands of fibrin become enmeshed in a fibrous tangle called a clot.

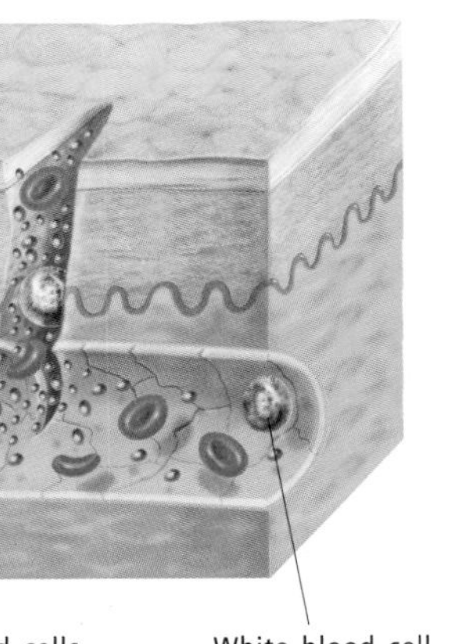

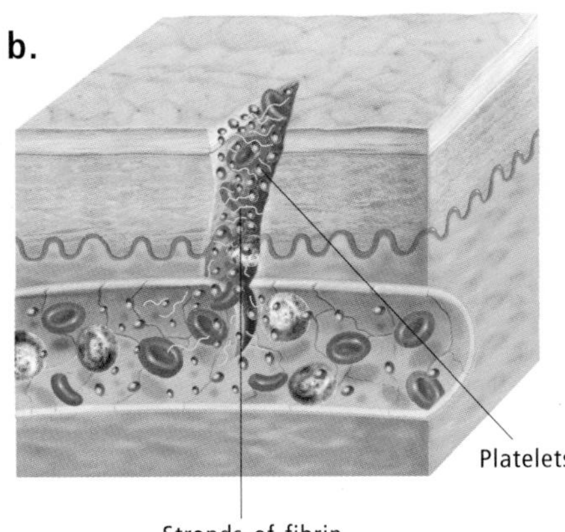

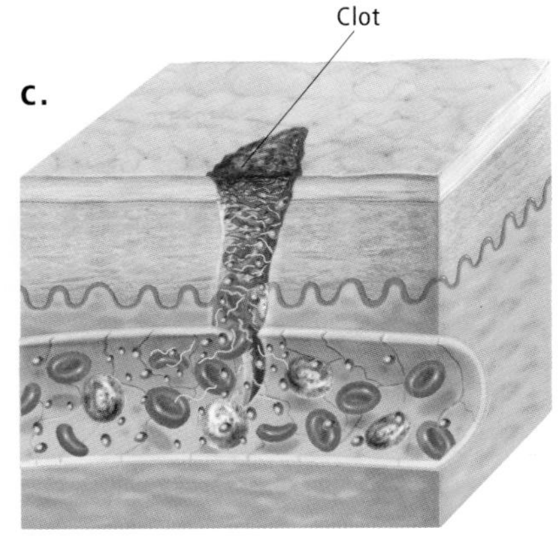

B

BLOOD COUNT

A blood count is a test to establish the number of red cells, white cells, platelets and hemoglobin in the blood. A blood sample is taken and then the number of blood cells counted electronically, or visually using a microscope.

Other laboratory tests determine the hemoglobin level and the percentage of red and white cells in the sample. Some infections can be suspected if the white cell count is too high, while too few white cells could indicate damage to bone marrow.

SEE ALSO *Blood, Hemoglobin, Platelets, Red blood cells, White blood cells*

BLOOD GAS ANALYSIS

Blood gas analysis is a test done on arterial and venous blood to measure oxygen and carbon dioxide levels and hydrogen ion concentration (pH).

The sample can be taken from an appropriate artery or vein. The levels will show how well carbon dioxide is being removed from the blood and how efficiently the lungs are working to re-oxygenate it. Gas analysis of arterial blood also gives a correct measure of the blood's acidity.

SEE ALSO *Acidosis, Alkalosis*

BLOOD GROUPS

Blood is classified into groups, or types, based on antigens (substances which produce immune responses) found on the red blood cells. The main blood groups are A, B, AB and O. In any of these groups individuals can be either Rh positive or, more rarely, Rh negative. In pregnancy, Rh incompatibility will cause the mother to generate antibodies against the fetus' red blood cells, and in later pregnancies a fetus may suffer anemia or jaundice, or not survive.

Blood typing is vital for safe blood transfusions. Mixing incompatible blood types will cause the red cells to clump together, blocking blood vessels and even causing death. Blood typing, as well as a test called cross-matching, performed prior to transfusion, ensures that blood of donor and host are compatible.

SEE ALSO *Blood transfusion, Rhesus (Rh) factor*

BLOOD PRESSURE

Blood pressure is the pressure blood exerts against the walls of the arteries. The amount of pressure depends upon the strength and the rate of the heart's contraction, the volume of blood in the circulatory system and the elasticity of the arteries.

Normal blood pressure varies from person to person, but usually normal blood pressure at rest is about 120/80 mm Hg. It is lower in children. Systolic blood pressure, the top number, represents the maximum pressure in the arteries as the heart contracts and ejects blood into the circulation. Diastolic pressure, the bottom number, represents the minimum blood pressure as the heart relaxes following a contraction.

Blood pressure is measured using an instrument called a sphygmomanometer. A single blood pressure reading, unless it is very high or very low, should not be considered abnormal. Usually, several readings are taken on different days and the results are then compared.

High blood pressure (hypertension) is a major disorder that requires treatment. Untreated, it can damage the heart, blood vessels and kidneys. Low blood pressure (hypotension) is often just normal for a particular person. It may, however, indicate disease such as vasovagal syncope or hypoaldosteronism. It is sometimes a side effect of drugs, particularly antidepressants.

SEE ALSO *Hypertension, Hypotension*

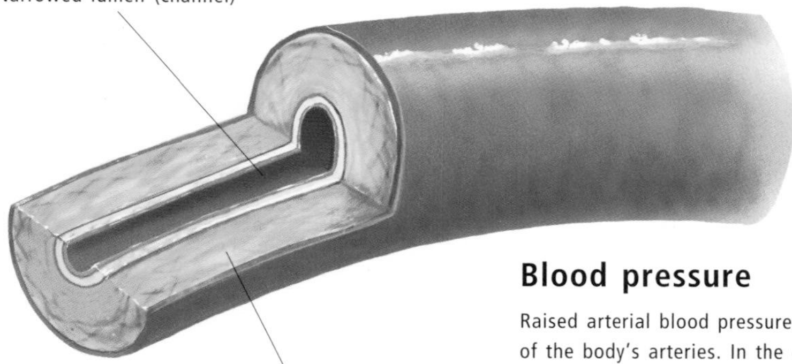

Blood pressure

Raised arterial blood pressure can damage the wall of the body's arteries. In the early stages, the artery wall becomes thickened, as shown here. Later, fatty patches known as atherosclerotic plaques form in the wall and further reduce the flow of blood through the artery.

BLOOD SUGAR TESTS

Blood sugar tests determine the level of glucose in the blood. Glucose is a simple sugar obtained from digesting carbohydrates in food, and is needed to nourish cells throughout the body. It circulates in the blood. If sugar is present in the urine this will indicate a high level in the blood, and a blood sugar test may then be done in order to confirm this.

A person with a low blood sugar level (hypoglycemia) will feel hungry, weak and tired, may have a headache, be sweating and feel faint, and may even lapse into a coma. A high blood sugar level (hyperglycemia) means the body is not properly controlling the absorption of glucose; this can be a symptom of diabetes.

SEE ALSO *Diabetes, Hyperglycemia, Hypoglycemia*

BLOOD TRANSFUSION

Blood transfusion is the transfer of blood from one person to another. A transfusion may be required in serious cases of anemia, either as a result of disease or from a loss of blood, or it may be part of the treatment of acute shock. Blood for transfusion usually comes from a donor and is stored in a blood bank (though the bank may store your own blood to be given back to you later for elective surgery). The donor's blood is screened for HIV and other viruses prior to the transfusion. Blood is cross-matched by the bank to prevent incompatibility between the donor's and the recipient's blood. Incompatibility can cause a transfusion reaction, which in severe cases can be fatal.

An exchange transfusion is the complete replacement of a person's blood. It is sometimes necessary in newborn babies or for people suffering severe poisoning.

SEE ALSO *Blood*

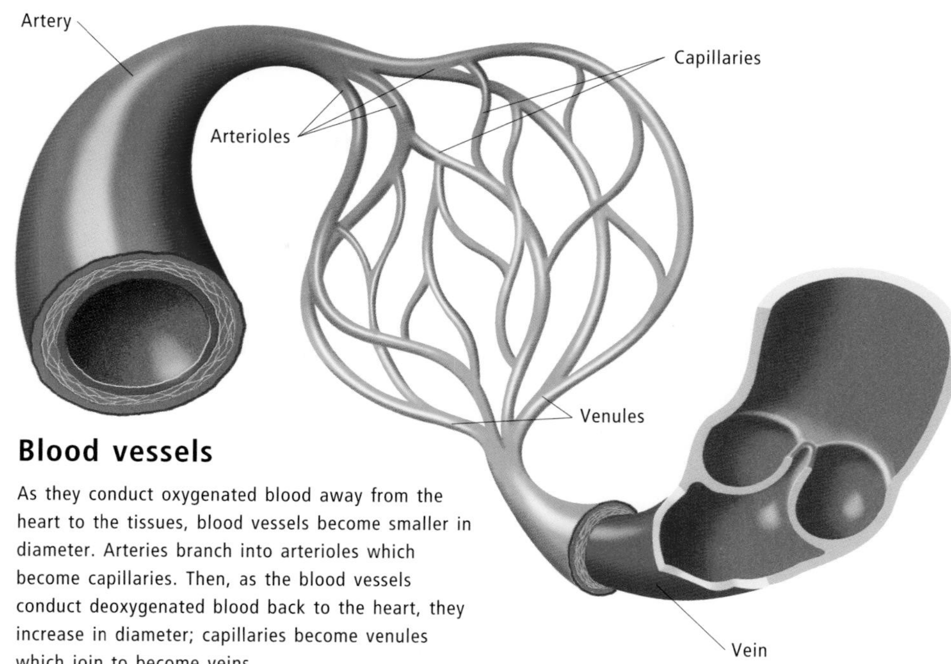

Blood vessels

As they conduct oxygenated blood away from the heart to the tissues, blood vessels become smaller in diameter. Arteries branch into arterioles which become capillaries. Then, as the blood vessels conduct deoxygenated blood back to the heart, they increase in diameter; capillaries become venules which join to become veins.

BLOOD VESSELS

Blood vessels form an intricate system through which the blood circulates in a continuous cycle. The heart pumps blood into the aorta, a large elastic artery, which sends off branches to supply the head and arms, the internal organs and the lower limbs. Repeated branchings form thin-walled capillaries, across which oxygen and nutrients are transferred to all body cells and through which carbon dioxide is transferred away from the same cells. Specialized capillaries in the kidneys, known as glomeruli, allow waste to leave the body as urine.

After leaving the limbs and organs, blood is channeled into veins of increasing size, returning eventually to the heart to repeat the cycle.

SEE ALSO *Aorta, Arteries, Blood, Capillaries, Heart, Kidney, Veins*

BODY LANGUAGE

The means by which humans exchange information can be categorized as verbal and non-verbal communication. When newborn babies gaze directly into their mothers' or carers' eyes, they are using the skills for non-verbal communication that humans possess at birth. From the very beginning, a baby must draw a loving response from a mother or carer that will ensure the baby is fed and cared for. Smiling develops within the first six weeks of a baby's life and is important in strengthening the bond between baby and carer. The ability to smile is shown by children born without sight.

The messages conveyed by body language in every face-to-face encounter between humans are estimated to convey more than half the communication—making the body language more important than what is actually said. Signals, signs and gestures are the components of non-verbal communication. Some are present at birth; some are cultural, that is, they are in common use and thus are learned from the family along with spoken language; and some may be genetic, innate to the species and sex.

Studying body language

Actors and dancers know that movement and gesture alone can be powerful tools for communication, and they use a rich vocabulary of body language for expression and communication in their art. The modern study of body language started in the 1950s when an American anthropologist analyzed the behavior of people during conversations recorded on film. To establish meaning, postures, eye movements, facial expressions and gestures with hands and arms were related to the context and the culture in which they occurred.

Cultural differences

Some deliberately used signs and gestures seem to be common to all human cultures. Smiling generally indicates friendliness or welcome. A snarl, or baring the teeth and flaring the nostrils, are strong signals of anger and hostility.

Other gestures may have one meaning in one culture and a completely different meaning in another. In the UK, the "V" sign, made by holding up the straightened index and second fingers in the shape of the letter V, means "victory" (palm facing out towards the recipient) or an obscene gesture of defiance (palm facing in), but in Europe generally both versions would mean either "victory" or simply the number "two", and a completely different gesture is used for the disdainful insult.

Personal space

The definition of personal space—the clear area needed around a person to make each individual feel comfortable—is a vital component of body language. Personal space requirements are dictated by relationship, status, intentions, the culture and the occasion, and will be different for each instance. Standing close during conversation may be normal for one person, but may invade the personal space of another and thus convey completely the wrong message. Depending on the sex of each person, this could merely cause discomfort or else it could wrongly signal either hostility or sexual attraction.

Using body language

Knowledge of everyday body language is particularly useful in situations of face-to-face communication such as interviews, introductions, personal relationships, sales meetings and negotiations.

Participants in a negotiation or business meeting can observe the body language of the other parties to read signs that may reinforce or run counter to what is being said. Posture is important: it can indicate openness and acceptance or the opposite, distrust or disbelief. Hand gestures and

B

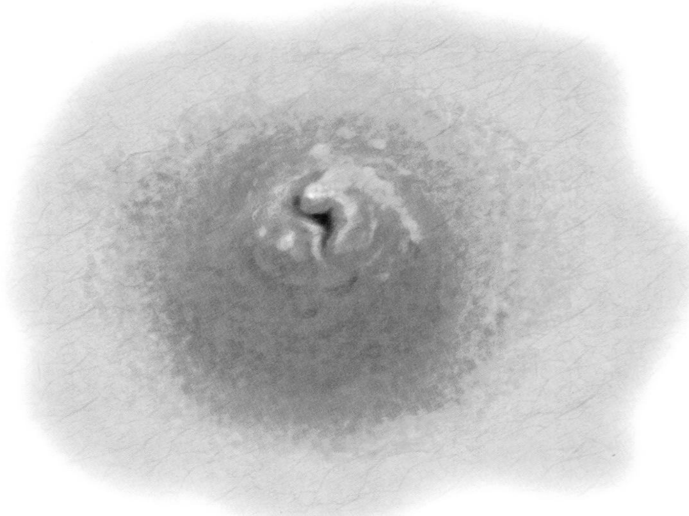

Boil

A boil is a bacterial infection of a hair follicle. This boil has burst through the skin and is discharging pus.

positions can reveal a state of mind or attitude which is unspoken: a hand on the chin may show thoughtful consideration, while a hand over the mouth may indicate disbelief or discomfort with what is being said. Posture can also have meaning. Crossing legs or ankles can convey a defensive attitude, while sitting with legs splayed could indicate boredom, or indifference, or a desire to dominate the proceedings.

BODY MASS INDEX

Body mass index (BMI) is a figure used to determine whether an individual is of healthy, normal weight in proportion to height. It is more useful than using a standard "weight for height" chart and more meaningful to the individual who wants to know whether they are overweight or underweight, and how far they are outside the range of what is considered healthy.

The BMI is calculated according to the following formula: BMI = weight (in kilograms) divided by height (in meters) squared. For example, a man weighing 220 pounds (100 kilograms) and measuring 6 feet (1.8 meters) in height would have a BMI of 30.9 (100 divided by 1.8^2).

A BMI of 20–24 is accepted as normal for men, while for women a range of 19–24 is accepted as normal. A figure higher than this suggests a person is a bit overweight, with the term obesity being used when the BMI is above 30.

Overweight people who wish to reduce their weight can use the BMI to set a target weight range. A person's target BMI will be a weight within the normal range where they feel comfortable, and may be at the higher or lower end of that range.

SEE ALSO *Nutrition, Obesity*

BODY SHAPE

Human bodies are categorized into three body shapes (somatotypes): endomorphic—soft, rounded body shape, and with a tendency to store fat; mesomorphic—strongly framed, muscular and evenly proportioned; and ectomorphic—lean, angular in shape, fragile in appearance and rather low in fat.

Neither overeating nor dieting will change a person's body type, but can change the shape superficially by altering the amount of fat stored. The majority of dieters are women, whose shape is affected by fat stores at hips, thighs, abdomen and breasts. When overweight, fat deposits at these places will be greatly increased.

Fluid retention, which may occur with menstruation in women, and in either sex as a result of illness, can affect body shape. Exercise can affect body shape when it tightens slack muscles, aids loss of excess weight by reducing fat stores, or improves posture. But it will not change a person's somatotype. Cosmetic surgery may offer a solution (rather drastic though it may be) for people who wish to change their body shape.

Body image is the individual's perception of their own shape. This may be distorted, as in sufferers from eating disorders who may see themselves as grossly overweight when they are emaciated and starving. Perceptions of body shape are, to a great extent, dictated by fashion. Adolescent girls often have a distorted body image, and they are the main group at risk of dieting to excess in an effort to conform to a certain standard.

SEE ALSO *Cosmetic surgery, Eating disorders, Obesity*

BODY TEMPERATURE

In adults the normal temperature, taken orally, is 98.6°F (37°C). When taken under the armpit, it is about 1°F (0.5°C) lower than the oral temperature. The rectal temperature is about 1°F (0.5°C) higher. In the elderly, the body temperature tends to be slightly lower. In a child, it varies more than in an adult, so a moderate temperature increase in a child is usually of less significance.

SEE ALSO *Fever, Heatstroke*

BOIL

A boil, also known as a furuncle or carbuncle, is a bacterial infection of a hair follicle. It appears as a painful, swollen red lump, most commonly on the face, neck, armpit, buttocks or thigh. A boil contains pus, a thick yellow fluid that is a byproduct of inflammation, made up of white blood cells, dead tissue matter and bacteria. Boils may heal spontaneously, or they may grow in size, burst, drain and then heal. Most boils must be drained surgically by a primary care physician (general practitioner).

BONE MARROW BIOPSY

This is a procedure in which a needle is inserted into a bone to obtain a sample of the cells of the bone marrow—a process known as aspiration. Bone marrow biopsy can also involve removing a piece of bone tissue, including the marrow; this is correctly termed biopsy. Bone marrow samples are usually taken from the sternum (breastbone) or iliac crest (hip bone), under local anesthetic.

Bone marrow biopsy is valuable for establishing a specific diagnosis for several groups of diseases of the blood and bone marrow such as anemia, leukemia and lymphoma.

SEE ALSO *Anemia, Biopsy, Leukemia*

B

Body shapes

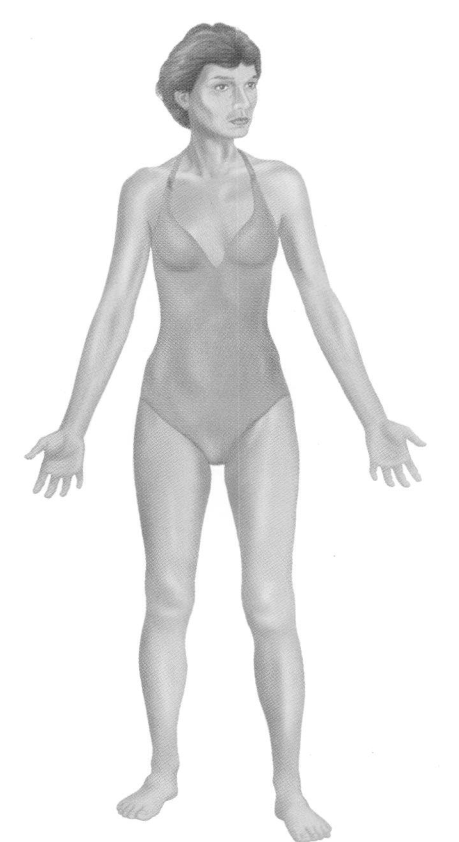
Ectomorph female

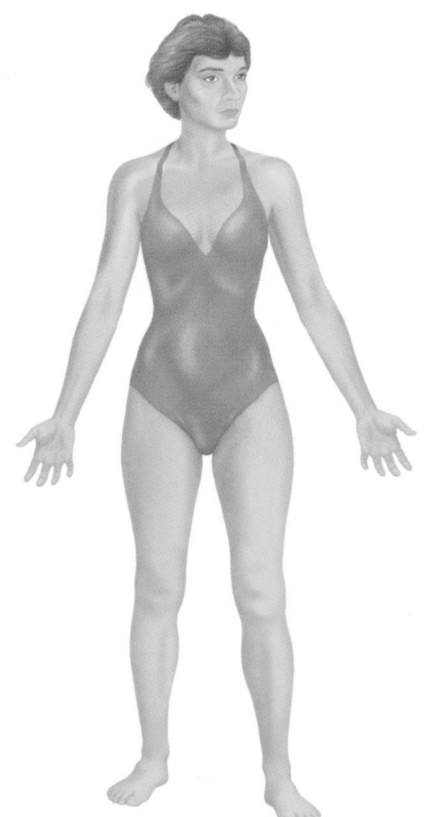
Mesomorph female

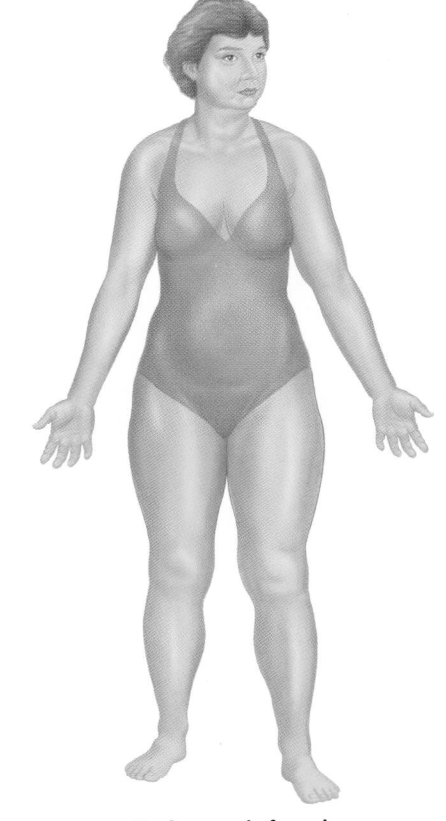
Endomorph female

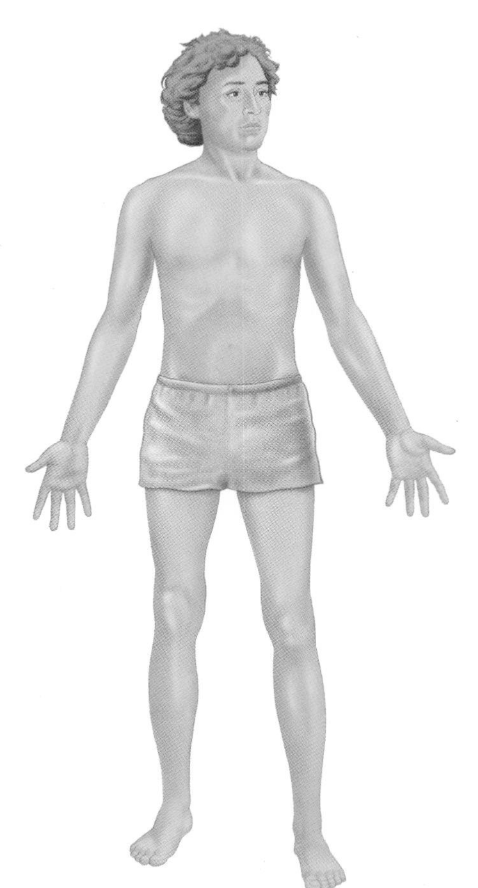
Ectomorph male

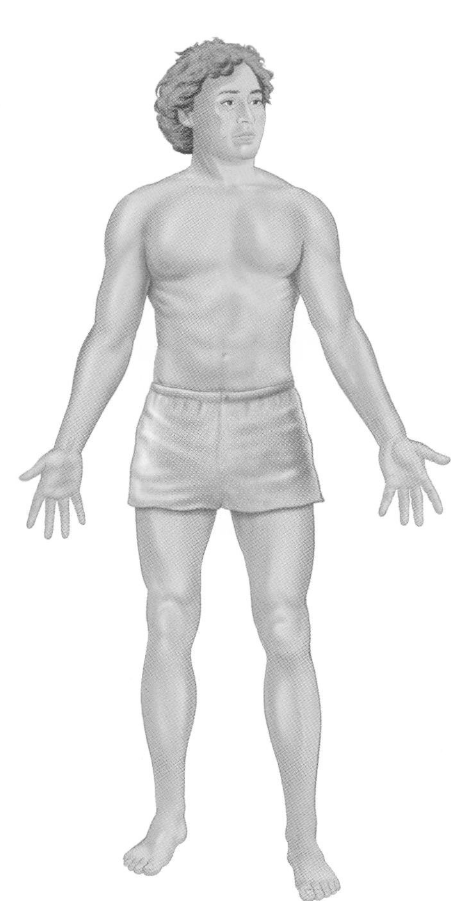
Mesomorph male

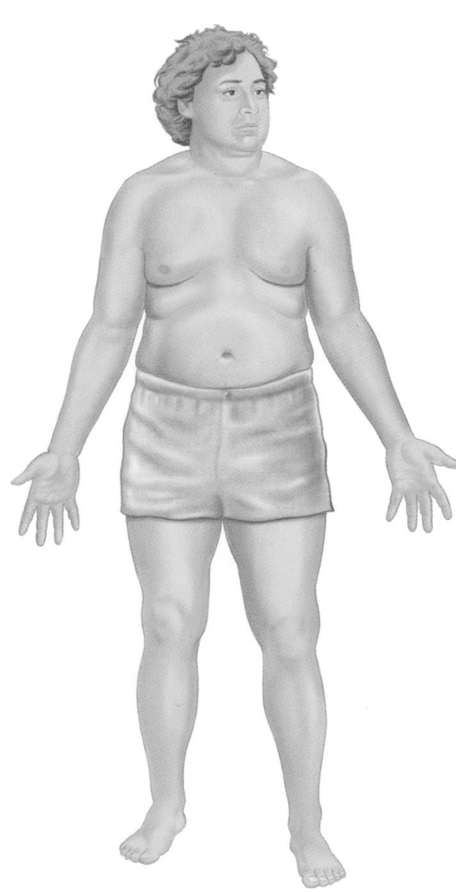
Endomorph male

Bone

Bone is made up of different layers, the outermost of which is the periosteum. Beneath this is the compact or cortical bone which surrounds the spongy or cancellous bone. At the core is the bone marrow.

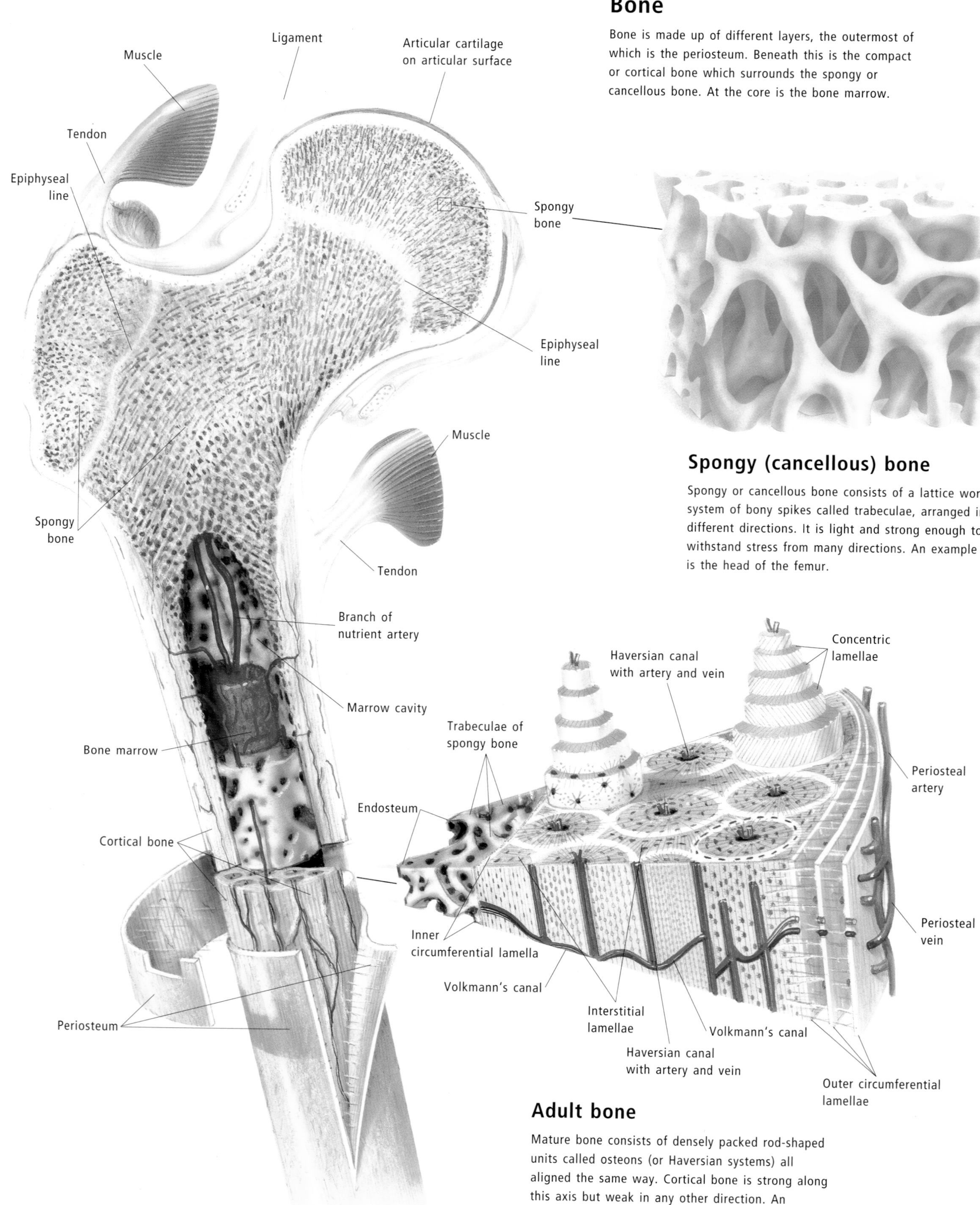

Spongy (cancellous) bone

Spongy or cancellous bone consists of a lattice work system of bony spikes called trabeculae, arranged in different directions. It is light and strong enough to withstand stress from many directions. An example is the head of the femur.

Adult bone

Mature bone consists of densely packed rod-shaped units called osteons (or Haversian systems) all aligned the same way. Cortical bone is strong along this axis but weak in any other direction. An example is the outer part of the shaft of the femur.

B

BONES

Bone is the rigid, calcified tissue that makes up the skeleton. It supports the body and surrounds and protects its internal structures. It acts as a store of calcium, and houses the bone marrow in which blood cells are manufactured. Bones provide an attachment for muscles, which contract, allowing the body to move. There are 206 bones in the body in all.

Being connective tissue, bone is composed of cells in a matrix. The major components of the matrix include mineral salts (mainly calcium phosphate), which provide hardness, and collagen fibers, which give strength.

Four types of cell are present: osteoprogenitor cells, osteoblasts, osteocytes and osteoclasts. Osteoprogenitor cells develop into osteoblasts, which form bone tissue. Osteoblasts mature into osteocytes, which maintain bone tissue. Osteoclasts, which occur on bone surfaces, are involved in the reabsorption of the matrix, required for bone development, growth and repair.

A typical mature long bone has a central shaft—the diaphysis—and ends known as epiphyses. Inside the diaphysis is the medulla, which contains yellow bone marrow, and is lined by the endosteum, a layer rich in osteoprogenitor cells and osteoclasts. The diaphysis meets the epiphysis at the metaphysis. This is the location, in an immature bone, of the cartilage layer from which length-wise growth occurs. Most of the bone is protected and nourished by the periosteum, a membrane served by nerves and blood vessels that enter the bone.

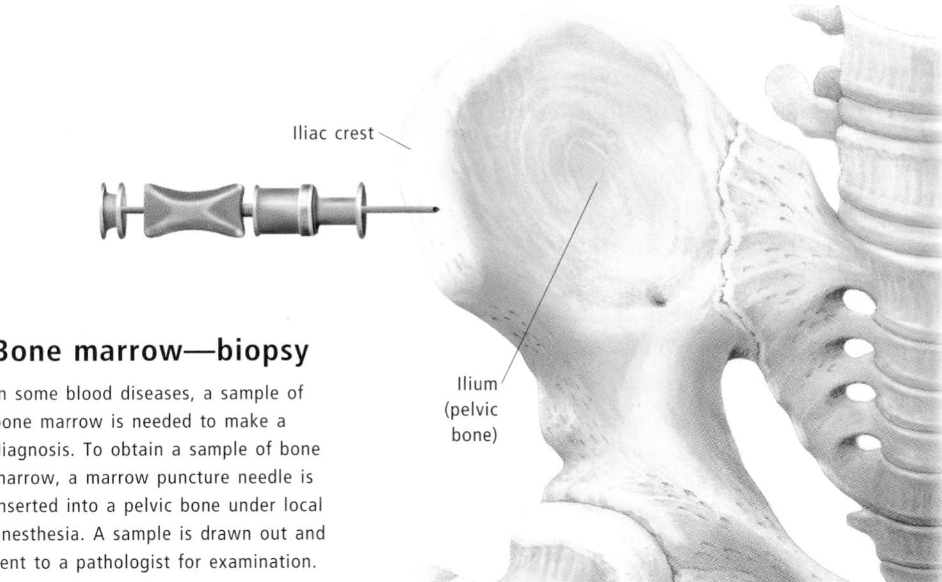

Bone marrow—biopsy

In some blood diseases, a sample of bone marrow is needed to make a diagnosis. To obtain a sample of bone marrow, a marrow puncture needle is inserted into a pelvic bone under local anesthesia. A sample is drawn out and sent to a pathologist for examination.

Bone fractures and diseases

A break in a bone is called a fracture. Any bone in the body can be fractured, but some bones, because of their vulnerable positions (for example, the long bones of the arms and legs), tend to fracture more often than others. Most fractures occur as the result of injury or accident. Sometimes, a bone breaks following repeated minor strains. Some bones have a tendency to fracture easily because they are weak from a disease, osteoporosis for example. Treatment for all fractures is to place the broken ends of the bone as close together as possible, in the original position, and to hold them there until new bone has had time to heal the break. This can be done with a plaster of Paris or fiberglass cast, or with screws, metal plates, thick pins or wires. Healing can take from three weeks to three months or more.

Osteomyelitis is an infection of the bone, usually caused by bacteria. The bacterial infection reaches the bone via the bloodstream from another area of infection—a septic tooth or a boil for example. Or it may reach the bone through an injury, such as an open fracture. Symptoms are pain, fever and tenderness at the site of infection. Swelling occurs and the skin becomes red. X-rays are normal at first, but a bone scan will reveal the infection. Large doses of antibiotics are given intravenously in hospital. If there is an abscess it is surgically drained.

Osteoporosis is a condition which is characterized by the progressive loss of bone density and thinning of bone tissue, resulting in brittle, fragile bones that are subject to fractures. It occurs in older age groups, especially women after the menopause. It can be prevented by exercise and maintaining a healthy diet which includes a sufficient

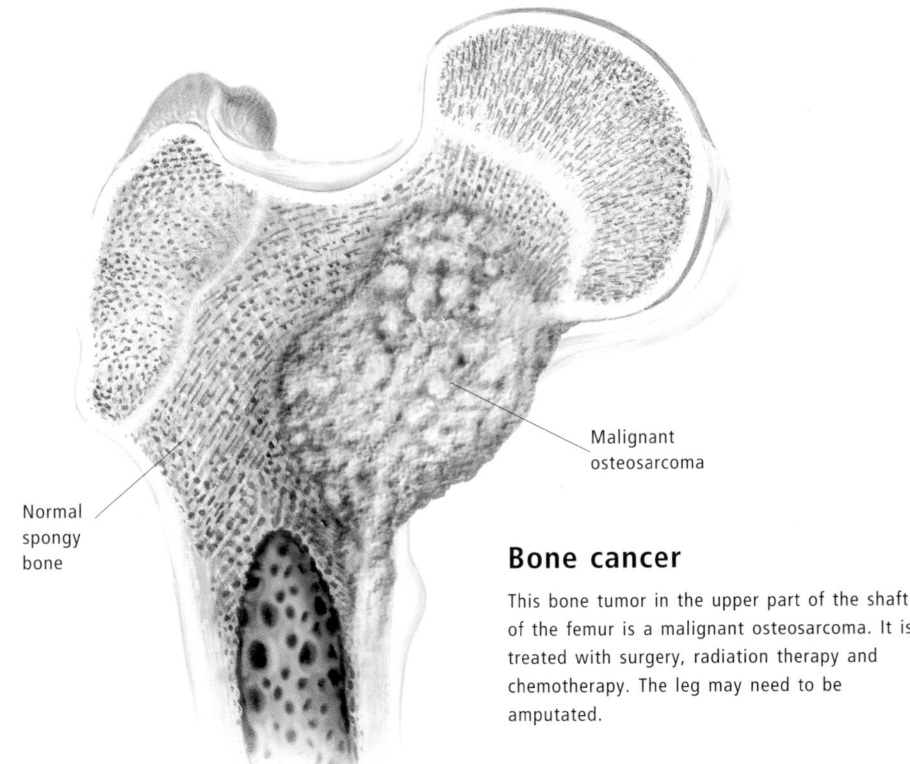

Bone cancer

This bone tumor in the upper part of the shaft of the femur is a malignant osteosarcoma. It is treated with surgery, radiation therapy and chemotherapy. The leg may need to be amputated.

amount of calcium, phosphorous and vitamin D. Postmenopausal women with osteoporosis may be treated with estrogen replacement therapy.

Bone tumors (cancers) may be benign or malignant. Benign tumors include osteochondromas (the most common) and osteomas. They usually do not require treatment but can be removed for cosmetic reasons. Malignant bone tumors usually arise from primary cancers of the breast, lung, prostate, kidney or thyroid. Primary malignant bone tumors are rare and are more common in young men. These include osteosarcomas, Ewing's sarcoma, fibrosarcoma and chondrosarcoma. They require surgical removal followed by radiation therapy and chemotherapy. Often, an affected limb may need to be amputated.

Tests

There are several tests for bone disease. Blood tests can show abnormally high or low levels of calcium, phosphorus and bone enzymes such as alkaline phosphatase. An x-ray can be used to detect fractures, tumors or degenerative conditions of the bone. A bone scan is a test that detects areas of increases or decreases in bone metabolism. This is done by determining how a radioactive isotope collects in the bone. It can be used to identify tumors or bone infection. Bone marrow biopsy uses a needle to extract bone marrow for examination. This test is used to diagnose leukemia, secondary bone tumors, anemia and infections.

SEE ALSO *Calcium, Ewing's sarcoma, Fractures, Muscle, Osteomyelitis, Osteoporosis, Skeletal system*

BOTTLE FEEDING

Breast milk is ideal food for babies, particularly in the first weeks of life. However, for some mothers, breast feeding can be physically and emotionally demanding, and they may choose not to breast feed. Others may have difficulties such as sore nipples which can make feeding painful. Occasionally babies do not thrive on breast milk alone.

Bottle feeding is the feeding of babies (human and animal) with a bottle containing artificial baby milk (for humans it is usually called infant formula) and a teat. Artificial baby milk consists of a powder which, when made according to directions, makes a liquid which resembles human milk; it is nutritionally complete but does not contain all the properties of breast milk.

Bottle feeding requires a number of sterile bottles and teats, infant formula and boiled water. It is essential that the formula is mixed accurately, according to directions given, and that the water in which it is mixed is sterile. It is also important that the equipment used to feed the baby is kept sterile. This can be done chemically with sterilizing solution, or by boiling. Diarrhea, dehydration and malnutrition can be caused by unsafe bottle feeding, but these problems rarely occur in societies with a good standard of hygiene. It is best to serve the milk at body temperature.

If correct methods are followed, bottle feeding can be a positive and rewarding experience. The mother needs to hold the baby close to her body, so they can both enjoy the warmth of physical contact. It is not safe to let babies feed themselves. Bottle feeding also gives other members of the family a chance to feed and bond with the baby.

SEE ALSO *Breast feeding, Infancy, Newborn*

BOWEL

The bowel consists of two parts: the small bowel (or small intestine) and the large bowel (or large intestine). The small bowel (containing the duodenum, jejunum and ileum) is mainly concerned with the final stages of digestion, and absorption of nutrients from food. The large bowel (colon and rectum) is concerned with absorption of water and salts. Generally speaking, the bowel occupies the lower two thirds of the abdominal cavity.

SEE ALSO *Colon, Duodenum, Ileum, Intestines, Jejunum, Rectum*

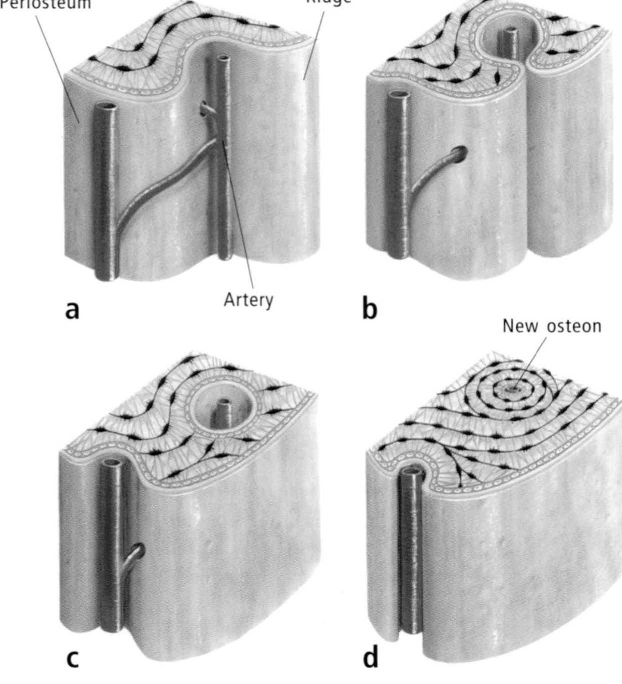

Bone formation

Bone grows in width as new bone is laid down in ridges (a) either side of a blood vessel. The ridges grow together and fuse, enclosing the vessel (b). More bone is laid down, diminishing the space around the vessel (c), and eventually an osteon is formed. The process continues, enclosing parallel blood vessels and causing the bone to become thicker (d).

BOWEL CANCER

Bowel cancer almost always arises from the layer of cells lining the inside of the large intestine (which includes the colon and rectum); it is also known as colorectal cancer. In the economically developed nations of the world, it is one of the three most common cancers (the others being lung cancer and either prostate cancer in men or breast cancer in women) and is a major cause of death from cancer.

Causes

Dietary factors appear to play an important role in the development of bowel cancer. In particular, diets low in fiber and high in fat are associated with an increased risk, though it is not known exactly why this is.

There is good evidence that for most bowel cancers a sequence of abnormal

Bowel cancer

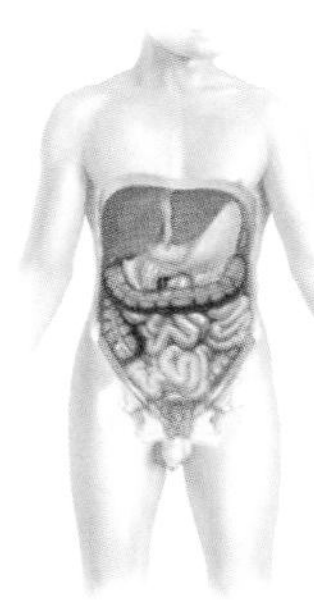

This bowel cancer is growing out from the wall of the transverse colon. It will need to be surgically removed, along with some surrounding bowel and nearby lymph nodes. If the cancer has not spread beyond the walls of the bowel, the prospects for long-term survival are very good.

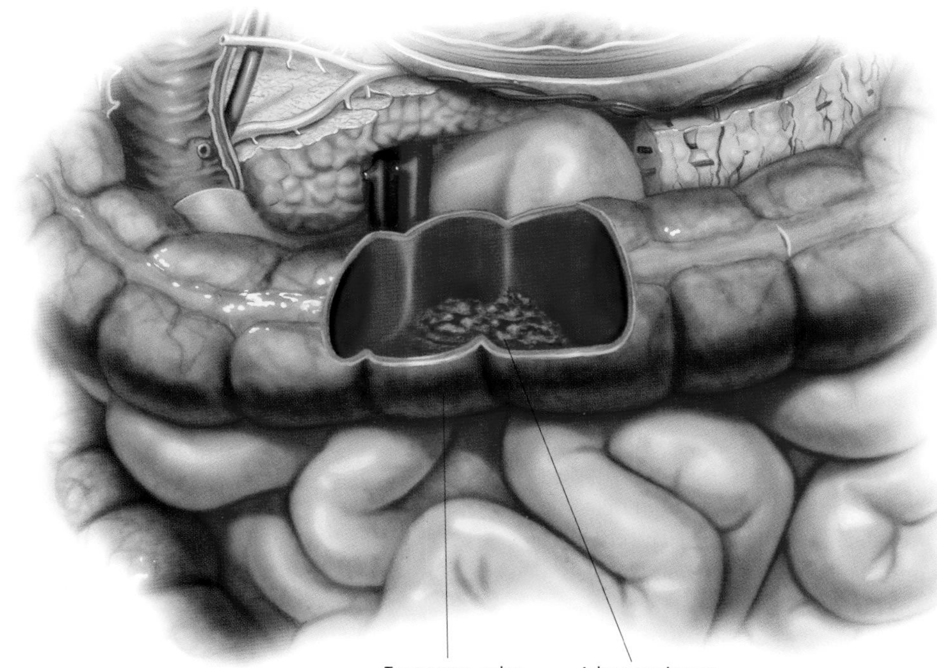

changes in the bowel wall precedes the emergence of a cancer. One of these is the development of pre-cancerous polyps (outgrowths of the lining of the bowel), although not all polyps are pre-cancerous. Several inherited disorders that lead to the formation of multiple colorectal polyps have been identified. There are other inherited conditions associated with bowel cancer but without polyp formation. Also, there is an increased risk of bowel cancer in patients with long-term inflammatory bowel diseases, such as ulcerative colitis or Crohn's disease.

Symptoms

Cancer of the large intestine usually develops in persons aged 50 or older. It is somewhat more common in men. The symptoms are variable and often vague. Pain is unusual at first. Cancers cause bleeding from the lining of the bowel, but in the upper part of the large bowel this blood is mixed with the liquid intestinal contents so that no blood is evident in the feces and may not be detected until the tumor is far advanced, when the patient becomes pale, weak and easily tired because of anemia.

About half of all large bowel cancers develop in the lower third of the colon or the rectum. Bleeding from these tumors may be visible, but often goes unnoticed. Such cancers may produce crampy abdominal pain, constipation, or alternating constipation and diarrhea.

How bowel cancer develops

Bowel cancers grow relatively slowly, so early recognition of symptoms by the patient and prompt diagnosis of the disease by the doctor has enormous potential to save lives. Blood screening of feces can also help recognize the disease early. Diagnosis is by barium enema (an x-ray investigation), colonoscopy (using a flexible fiberoptic instrument) and sampling of blood for a chemical released by cancer cells—the carcinoembryonic antigen (CEA). Many bowel cancers are, however, not diagnosed until the tumor has spread.

The spread of bowel cancer is initially through the wall of the bowel, then by lymphatics to the nearby draining lymph nodes and later via the blood to the bones, liver, lungs and other organs. As is true for many cancers, the extent of spread of the cancer at the time of diagnosis is the most important factor that determines the course of the disease and the patient's chances of survival.

Treatment

Treatment of bowel cancer is by surgery, removing the tumor and surrounding bowel and lymph nodes, and sometimes radiation therapy for those patients for whom major surgery may be too risky. If caught early, when the cancer is limited to the inner lining of the bowel, the likelihood of the patient surviving at least five years from the time of diagnosis is almost 100 percent. If it spreads through the wall and to nearby lymph nodes, this figure falls sharply.

As early diagnosis is the key to surgical cure, a screening procedure for bowel cancer would be extremely useful, but at present there is no inexpensive reliable test for the disease at an early stage. However, because bowel cancers usually bleed, testing for blood in the feces has some value. Colonoscopy with biopsy is the most effective method of early diagnosis currently available.

SEE ALSO *Anemia, Barium enema, Bowel, Cancer, Colon, Colonoscopy, Crohn's disease, Intestines, Rectum, Ulcerative colitis*

BRACES

Braces are orthodontic devices used in the correction of protruding or crooked teeth and misaligned jaws.

Designed to improve appearance, function and dental health, they usually consist of stainless steel or clear ceramic brackets that are fitted over each tooth or cemented to them. These are connected by wires which are adjusted at regular intervals over a period of up to three years to slowly change the position of the teeth. Springs, rubber bands or appliances which fit to the teeth may also be attached to the braces to generate the necessary tension and to speed the straightening process.

Braces are commonly worn in adolescence, when the teeth and jaw are easier to manipulate, but have become more popular with adults in recent years. They are fitted by an orthodontist, who assesses each dental problem with the help of x-rays and plaster molds of the teeth. Some teeth may need to be removed before braces are fitted.

B

BRAIN

The brain is the headquarters of the nervous system. As well as providing overall control of vital body functions, it enables us to perceive and respond to incoming sensory information, to think, speak and make decisions, and to carry out a whole range of purposeful, coordinated movements.

Its average weight is around 3 pounds (1.4 kilograms) and it lies mostly within the cranial cavity of the skull. It is made up of billions of nerve cells (neurons) and supporting cells (glia). Messages are transmitted from one part of the neuron to another electrically, and from one neuron to another by the release of chemicals. The complexity of the connections between different neurons in the brain is almost incomprehensible, with some neurons commonly making 10,000 or more connections with other neurons. In the nervous system, neuronal cell bodies group together as gray matter and their processes group together as white matter.

The human brain can be divided into four main parts: the cerebrum, diencephalon, brain stem and cerebellum.

The cerebrum

The largest part of the brain is the cerebrum. This is formed by the cerebral hemispheres that are joined together by a massive bundle of white matter called the corpus callosum and covered by the cerebral cortex. This is a sheet of gray matter (1.5–4 millimeters thick). The cerebral cortex is the site where the highest level of neural processing takes place, including language, memory and cognitive function.

The cortex makes up about 40 percent of the total brain mass, its surface area being so great in humans (just over 1 square yard, or approximately 1 square meter) that it is thrown into numerous folds in order to fit inside the cranial cavity. The basic pattern formed by these folds is similar in all humans, but the size and shape of some folds varies between individuals. The cortex covers the frontal, parietal, temporal and occipital lobes.

We know from studies on patients who have sustained damage to the cortex that the results of damage depend on which part of the cortex is affected. For example, the occipital lobe is involved in the perception of vision, the temporal lobe in memory, and the parietal lobe in the perception of touch and the comprehension of speech. The fron-

The limbic system

The components of the limbic system govern emotional states and behavioral drives. They are the link between the cerebral cortex and the unconscious functions of the brain stem. The limbic system also helps store and retrieve memories.

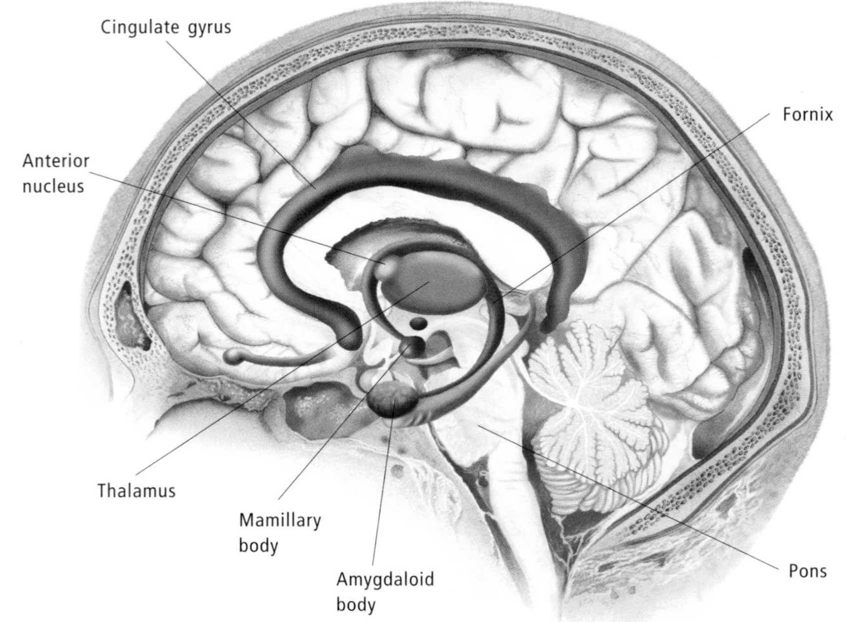

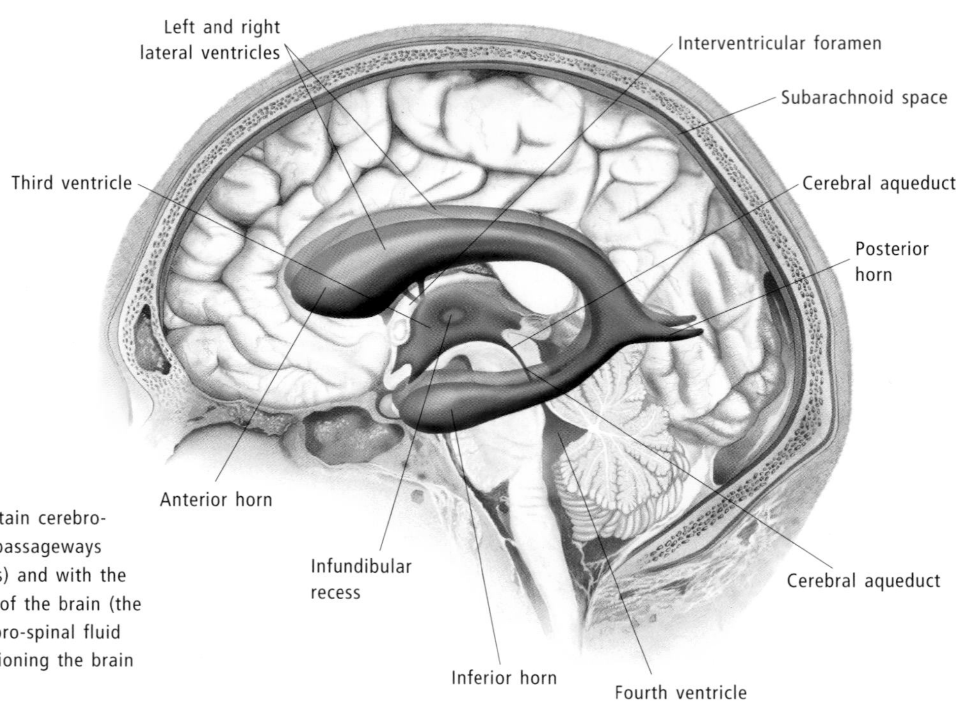

Brain ventricles

The ventricles of the brain contain cerebro-spinal fluid. They connect via passageways (called foramina and aqueducts) and with the space surrounding the outside of the brain (the subarachnoid space). The cerebro-spinal fluid acts as a shock absorber, cushioning the brain from mechanical forces.

tal lobe is not only important in movement but also has a large area devoted to thinking, behavior and personality. The overall patterns of electrical activity in the cortex can be measured in an electroencephalogram (EEG), which is obtained by recording responses from electrodes placed on the scalp.

Beneath the gray matter of the cerebral cortex is a thick mass of white matter, formed by fibers, which transmits information between different parts of the cortex or between the cortex and other parts of the brain. Embedded within the white matter of each hemisphere are some islands of gray matter known as the basal ganglia, which play a role in the control of movement and are affected in disorders such as Parkinson's disease or cerebral palsy.

The diencephalon

The diencephalon lies beneath the cerebral hemispheres and has two main structures, the thalamus and the hypothalamus. The thalamus, which is about the size of a walnut, is an important relay station, distributing sensory information from the periphery to different regions of the cortex. The hypothalamus lies on the underside of the thalamus and is surprisingly small, considering its importance as the control center for body functions such as eating, drinking, defence and reproduction. It also plays a role in behavior, particularly in the expression of emotions, such as fear and anger.

The brain stem

The brain stem, which is continuous with the spinal cord below it, consists of the midbrain, pons and medulla. Passing through the brain stem are ascending pathways, carrying sensory information from the spinal cord to the brain, and descending pathways, carrying motor commands down to the spinal cord. The brain stem contains many important reflex centers which control vital functions such as heartbeat and respiration. It is also important in regulating levels of consciousness—injury to the brain stem can result in prolonged loss of consciousness or death.

The cerebellum

The cerebellum (Latin for "little brain") is attached to the brain stem and resembles a cauliflower in appearance. Like the cerebrum, its surface is formed by a highly folded cortex. The cerebellum is important in the control of movement, particularly in the coordination of voluntary muscle activity and in the maintenance of balance and equilibrium. It is particularly sensitive to excess alcohol, and the effects of severe drunkenness (poor balance and coordination) to some degree mimic cerebellar disease.

Damage to the brain

In the adult brain there are structures called ventricles (derived from parts of the embryonic brain). These ventricles contain a watery substance called cerebrospinal fluid (CSF), which provides buoyancy and protection. Under certain conditions the volume of the CSF may be increased, causing a rise in pressure and hence damage to adjacent brain structures. This is known as "water on the brain" (hydrocephalus).

Although the brain only makes up 2 percent of the average body weight it uses 20

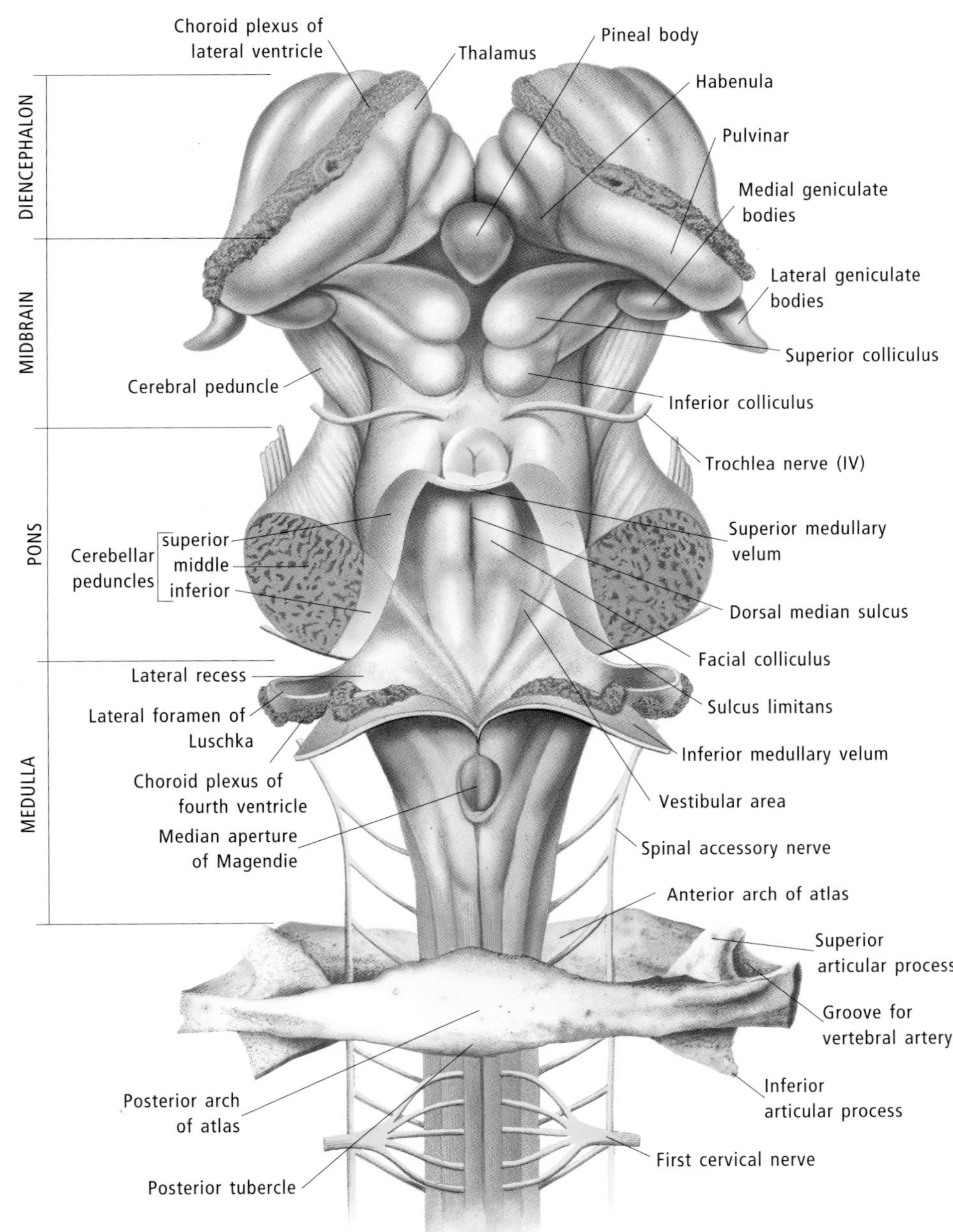

Brain stem

Centers in the brain stem regulate many vital functions including breathing, heartbeat and blood pressure. Damage to it from stroke or other injury may result in death.

B

percent of the available oxygen, and its cells will start to die if they are deprived of oxygen (via blood) for only a few minutes. This could result from cessation of breathing (as in drowning) or from a stroke, in which brain tissue is damaged due to lack of blood.

The effects will depend on the size of the affected blood vessel and the location of the damaged cells. Occasionally a small floating body (embolus) lodges briefly in a brain artery then frees itself, causing a transient ischemic attack (TIA), lasting a few minutes.

SEE ALSO *Brain wave activity, Cerebellum, Cerebral palsy, Electroencephalogram, Hydrocephalus, Neurons, Parkinson's disease, Stroke, Thalamus, Transient ischemic attack*

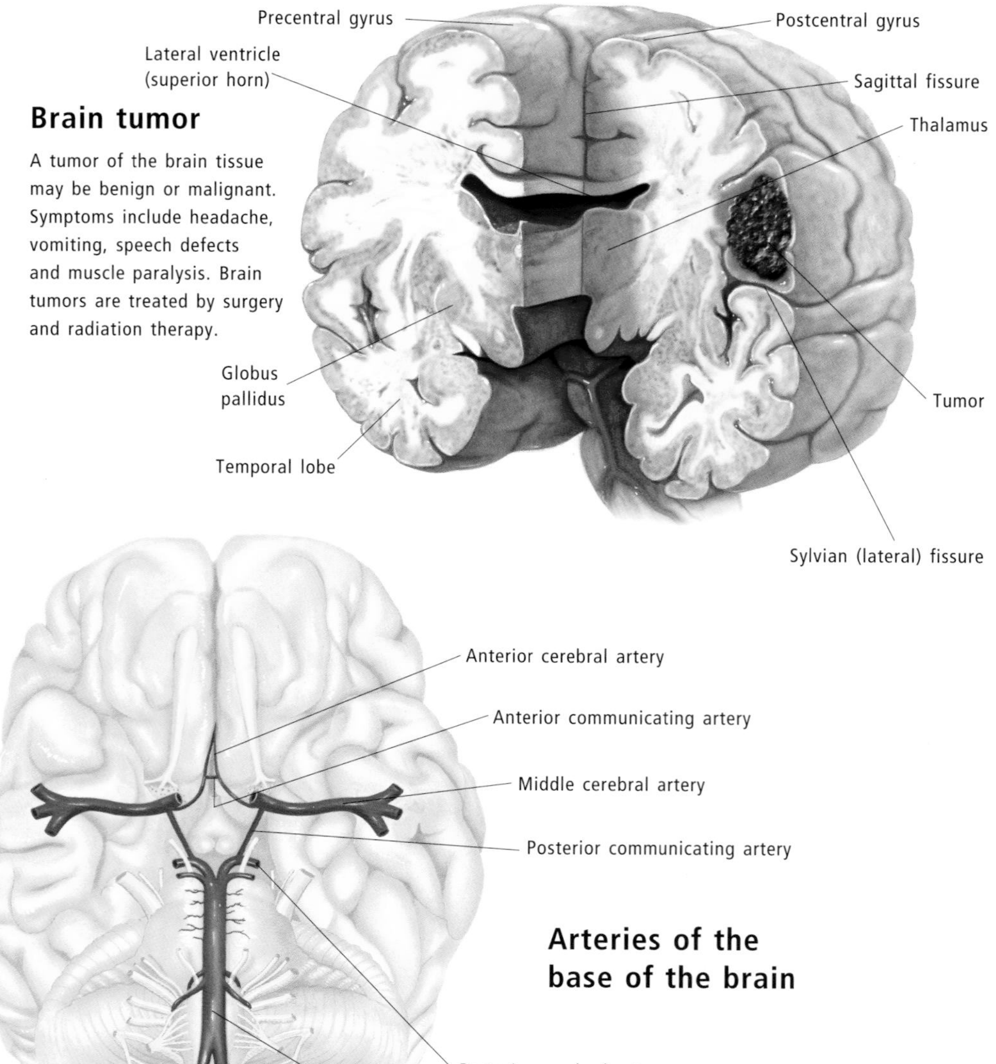

Brain tumor

A tumor of the brain tissue may be benign or malignant. Symptoms include headache, vomiting, speech defects and muscle paralysis. Brain tumors are treated by surgery and radiation therapy.

Arteries of the base of the brain

BRAIN WAVE ACTIVITY

Because nervous impulses are transmitted electrically, it is possible to record the activity of cells in the brain by placing electrodes on the scalp. The resulting graph, the electroencephalogram (EEG), shows wavelike patterns of activity, known as brain waves, which vary with different states of consciousness. Alpha waves indicate a relaxed awake state, beta waves are typical when we are mentally alert, theta waves are common in children but not adults, and delta waves appear during sleep. Brain wave activity becomes intensified during epileptic seizures. Prolonged absence of brain wave activity is an indication of brain death.

SEE ALSO *Brain, Electroencephalogram*

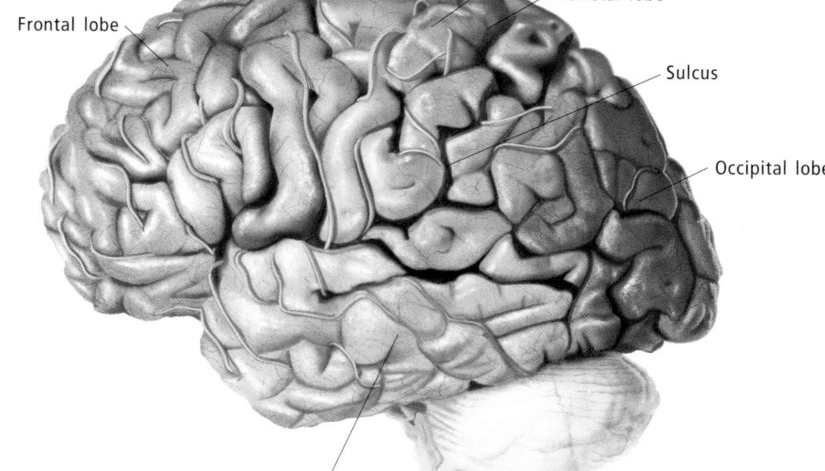

Lobes of the brain

The surface of the cerebral cortex (also called the cerebrum) is heavily folded. A ridge on the surface of the cortex is called a gyrus. A groove is called a sulcus if shallow, or a fissure if deep. Fissures and sulci divide the cortex into separate functional areas called lobes.

B

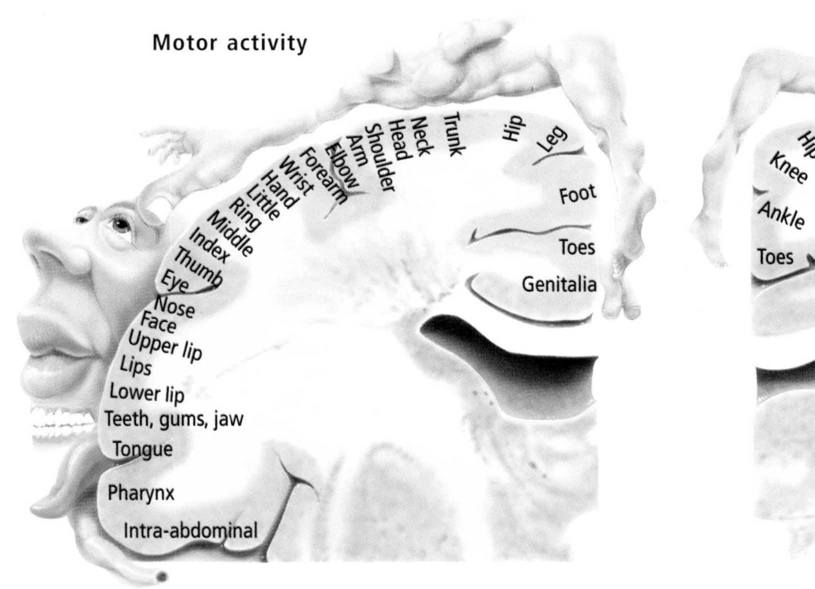

Organization of the motor and sensory areas of the cerebral cortex

The varying sizes of the body parts (top left) show the proportions of the precentral gyrus involved in motor activity in particular parts of the body, and (top right) the proportions of the postcentral gyrus involved in sensory activity in particular parts of the body.

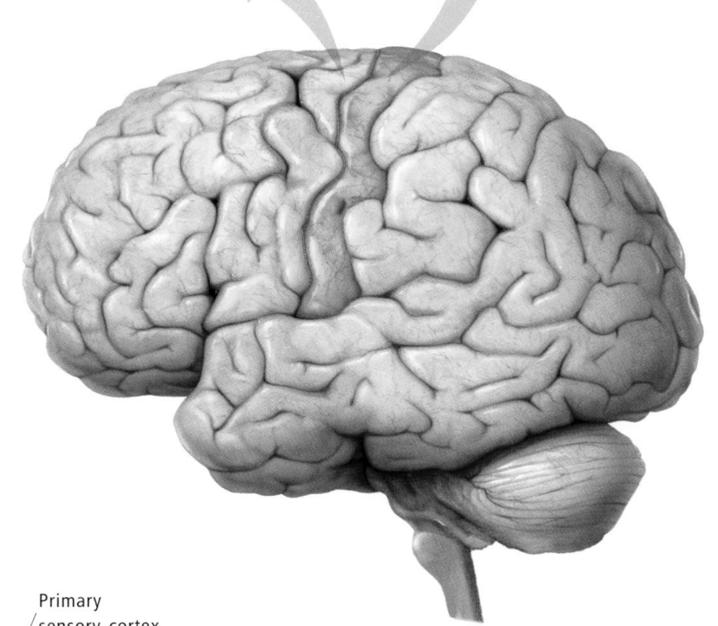

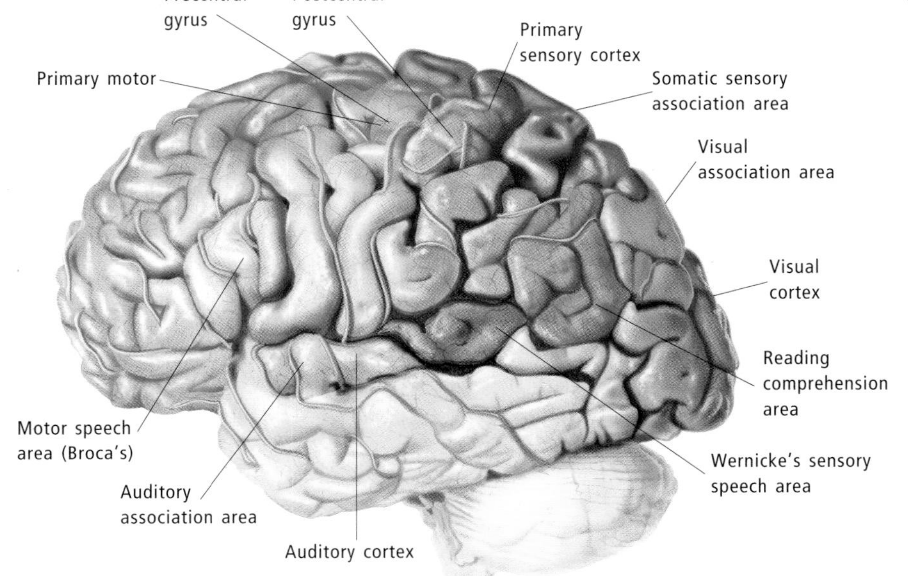

Functional areas

Particular regions of the cerebral cortex are associated with certain functions. For example, the precentral gyrus (motor cortex) is associated with the voluntary control of skeletal muscles, while the postcentral gyrus (sensory cortex) is associated with sensations from skin, muscles and joints.

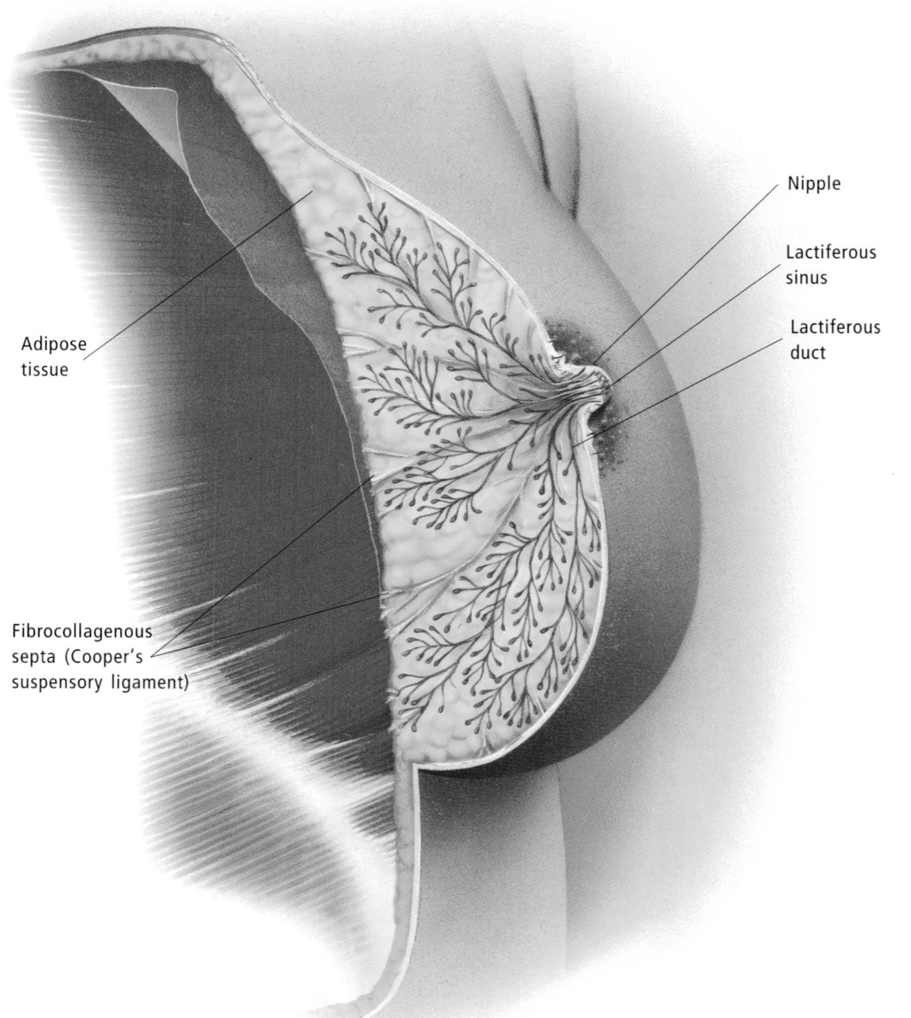

Normal breast

The development of breast tissue is governed by hormones, in particular the sex hormone estrogen. Towards the end of each menstrual cycle the breasts tend to swell and may become painful, but after menstruation, return to their normal size. After the menopause, the breasts usually shrink in size.

Breast abscess

A red, swollen, painful lump in the breast is usually a sign of a breast abscess. It often occurs if the nipples are cracked or inflamed, as bacteria can more easily enter the breast tissue.

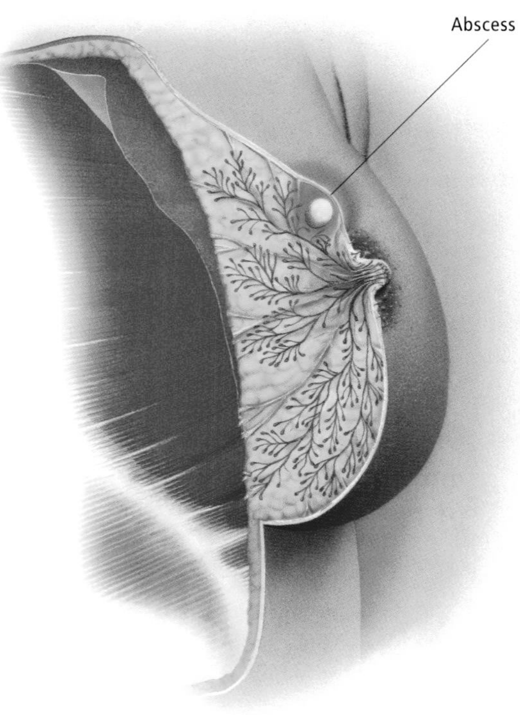

BRANCHIAL CYST

A branchial cyst is an abnormal cyst that lies just in front of one of the muscles (the sternocleidomastoid) in one side of the neck. It is caused by defective embryonic development of the second branchial cleft in the neck. Though present at birth, it is often not recognized until adolescence, when it tends to enlarge and become more noticeable. It may be left alone if it causes no symptoms, but if it makes an opening in the skin it may become infected or cause mucus to drain, so should be removed surgically.

BREAST

The breasts, or mammary glands, are two milk-producing organs situated on the chest. Normally only functional in the female, they are composed mainly of fat cells (cells capable of storing fat) interspersed with sac-like structures called lobules. These lobules are glands that can produce milk in females when stimulated by certain hormones such as prolactin. The lobules empty into a network of ducts (channels) that transport milk from the lobules to the nipple.

Differences in breast size and shape are largely due to inherited factors; also, being overweight increases the amount of fatty tissue in the breasts and hence their size. During puberty, the sex hormone estrogen causes the breasts to grow in size, due to the laying down of fat deposits. The breasts also get larger during pregnancy under the influence of estrogen. In pregnancy, the breasts grow in size by the same amount, regardless of whether the woman is normally small- or large-breasted.

Every woman should examine her breasts every month to check for any unusual lumps or other changes that might indicate cancer. It is best carried out a few days after menstruation, when the breasts are least swollen by estrogen. A woman who detects a lump should see her physician immediately.

Most breast lumps are not cancer, but are either solid fibroadenomas or fluid-filled cysts. Multiple cysts are often more prominent just before menstruation and are known as fibrocystic disease. A malignant (cancerous) lump feels hard, may be fixed to surrounding breast tissue, and may cause retraction of the skin or nipple. There may be a nipple discharge or bleeding. Lymph nodes under the armpit (axilla) on the same side may be enlarged and hard. Investigations, such as needle biopsy, mammography, ultrasonography and thermography, will confirm whether a lump is malignant or not.

Cancer and other conditions

The cause of breast malignancy is unknown. Risk factors include having a family history of breast cancer, early menarche (starting menstruation before age 12), late menopause (after age 55), never being pregnant, or having a first pregnancy after 30 years of age. Treatments may include lumpectomy, mastectomy (partial, total, or radical, i.e. extending to the armpit) and radiation therapy. Chemotherapy and hormonal therapy with antiestrogen drugs such as tamoxifen may also be used. After the procedure, except in the case of radical mastectomy, a breast implant or prosthesis may be inserted.

Reconstructive breast surgery is also used to enlarge or reshape breasts for cosmetic purposes. Breast implants consist of a silicone envelope with additional silicone gel or saline. While implants are not thought to cause autoimmune or connective tissue diseases as has been claimed, there are risks involved, including breast scarring, pain and misshapen breasts.

Mastitis is an inflammation of the breast. Acute mastitis is caused by a bacterial infection, which usually enters through a cracked nipple after childbirth, when the breast is swollen with milk. The breast feels hot, swollen and tender and the woman may have a fever. Treatment is with antibiotic drugs and analgesics. Breast feeding should continue if possible, as this keeps the breast ducts clear. Mastitis may progress to a breast abscess, in which case breast feeding should be stopped and the abscess treated.

Gynecomastia is the appearance of an enlarged breast or breasts in a male, usually occurring at puberty. It disappears naturally after six to twelve months, so needs no treatment. In older men, gynecomastia may be due to treatment with estrogens or steroids.

SEE ALSO *Breast cancer, Breast feeding, Estrogens, Fibroadenoma, Fibrocystic disease of the breast, Mammary glands, Mastectomy, Mastitis, Nipple, Pregnancy, Puberty*

BREAST CANCER

Cancer of the breast is the most important malignant tumor in women. It is by far the most common cancer in women in the economically developed nations of the world, where approximately one woman in ten will develop the disease. (Cancer of the cervix is almost as common in many developing nations.) Breast cancer is also one of the leading causes of cancer death in women (the other is lung cancer). Men can develop breast cancer, but this is approximately 100 times less common than in women.

Causes

Except during pregnancy and breast feeding, there are no functional milk-producing glands in the breast. There are, however, branching tubes called ducts which radiate out from the nipple and subdivide into smaller and smaller ducts. It is the layer of cells lining these small ducts that gives rise to almost all breast cancers. As is the case for most cancers, not enough is understood about how breast cancers develop, but two influences do seem to be important. Firstly, the growth and division of the lining cells of the ducts is controlled by hormones (especially estrogen), and stimulation of cell growth by a relative excess of estrogen (without a counterbalancing effect of progesterone) may create an environment in which breast cancer is more likely to develop. This could explain why breast cancer is often associated with other non-cancerous lumps in the breast. It could also account for the greater risk of breast cancer later in life, in association with early onset of menstruation and late menopause, in women who have not had children and in women whose first child was born relatively late.

Secondly, some breast cancers arise because of genetic factors. Genes associated with a familial risk of developing breast cancer have been identified. Despite this, environmental influences are probably much more important in causing breast cancer, but we have very little knowledge about exactly which factors play a role or how they affect an individual's risk of developing the tumor.

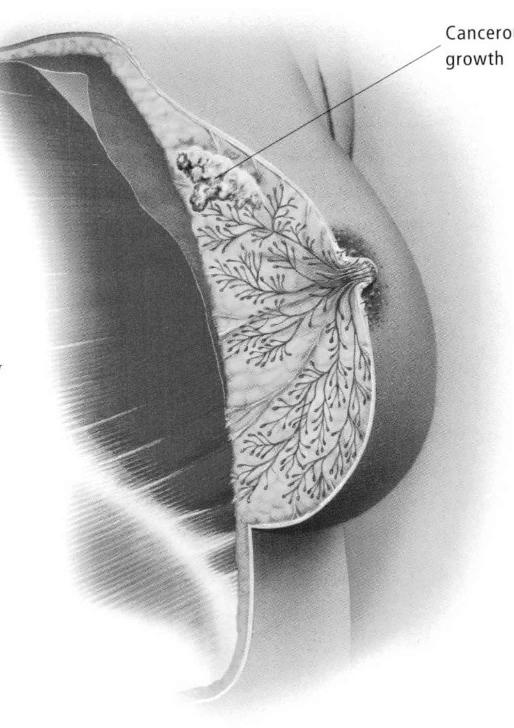

Breast cancer

The most common indication of a breast cancer is a hard lump in the breast that is often immovable. The skin over the lump may look dimpled, the nipple may turn inward and there may be lumps under the arm.

How breast cancer develops

Most breast cancers develop in women aged over 30 years and arise either in the upper outer part of the breast (which includes tissue that extends into the armpit) or in tissue immediately underlying the nipple. At first, the tumor cells grow entirely within the ducts of the breast, but later they invade through the walls of the ducts and into the surrounding fat and connective tissue. Still later, breast cancer cells enter the lymphatic vessels and spread to the nearest groups of lymph nodes which include nodes present in the connective tissue of the armpit and nodes in the area above the collar bone. At about the same time, the cells may enter blood vessels and thus spread to the lungs, or throughout the body.

Early diagnosis is critical to the outcome of breast cancer. Some of these tumors are more rapidly growing than others and more likely to spread. However, the stage at which a breast cancer is diagnosed is the single most important factor that determines the course of the disease and the patient's chances of survival. Tumors diagnosed at the stage where the cancer cells are still confined to the walls of the ducts can be treated very effectively. In such cases, the likelihood of the patient surviving at least five years from the time of diagnosis is over

90 percent. Once the cancer cells have spread to nearby lymph nodes, the survival figure drops considerably. When tumors are diagnosed at the stage when secondary cancer is widespread, the five-year survival rate is less than 15 percent.

Unfortunately, breast cancers may not produce obvious symptoms until relatively late, by which time they may have spread too far for effective treatment. Therefore, an active effort to identify them at an early stage must be made. Two useful approaches to achieving early identification are self-examination for the presence of a lump, and screening by mammography. To make a reliable diagnosis, any mass that is detected must be sampled for microscopic examination. This may involve removal of cells using a fine needle, removal of a core of tissue using a biopsy needle, or complete removal of the lump. The pathologist can provide information about the likely behavior of an individual cancer based on the appearance of the cells.

Current treatment for breast cancer involves much less removal of tissue by surgery than was the case 20 or 30 years ago. Radiation therapy, chemotherapy and hormonal therapy all have a place in modern management. Newer treatments being tested include drugs and antibodies that can block signals to cancer cells.

SEE ALSO *Biopsy, Breast, Cancer, Lumpectomy, Mammography, Mastectomy*

BREAST FEEDING

Breast feeding means feeding a baby with milk directly from the mother's breast. Within each breast are about 15 to 20 milk glands, or lobules, in clusters. It is here that the milk is produced. From the alveoli, canals called ductules lead into larger canals called milk ducts and the milk flows through these to pools which lie under the areola, the brown circle around the nipple. The baby takes the whole of the nipple into its mouth and milks the breast by pressing and pumping the milk from these pools.

One of the first actions of the healthy human baby after birth is to seek its mother's nipple. The first "milk" is actually a nutrient- and antibody-rich yellowish substance known as colostrum. Only after two or three days will real milk start to appear. This will provide all the nourishment, both food and drink, which the baby will need for the next four to six months. Ideally, babies should be breast fed for six to twelve months, but even just a few weeks of breast feeding will get them off to a good start.

Breast feeding is a learned skill for both mother and baby, and without some family support and knowledgeable advice many mothers encounter difficulties. However, many more mothers have no problems and find breast feeding a very pleasurable and rewarding experience. Breast milk is a unique, constantly changing substance containing antibodies, hormones, enzymes, growth factors and immunoglobulins, as well

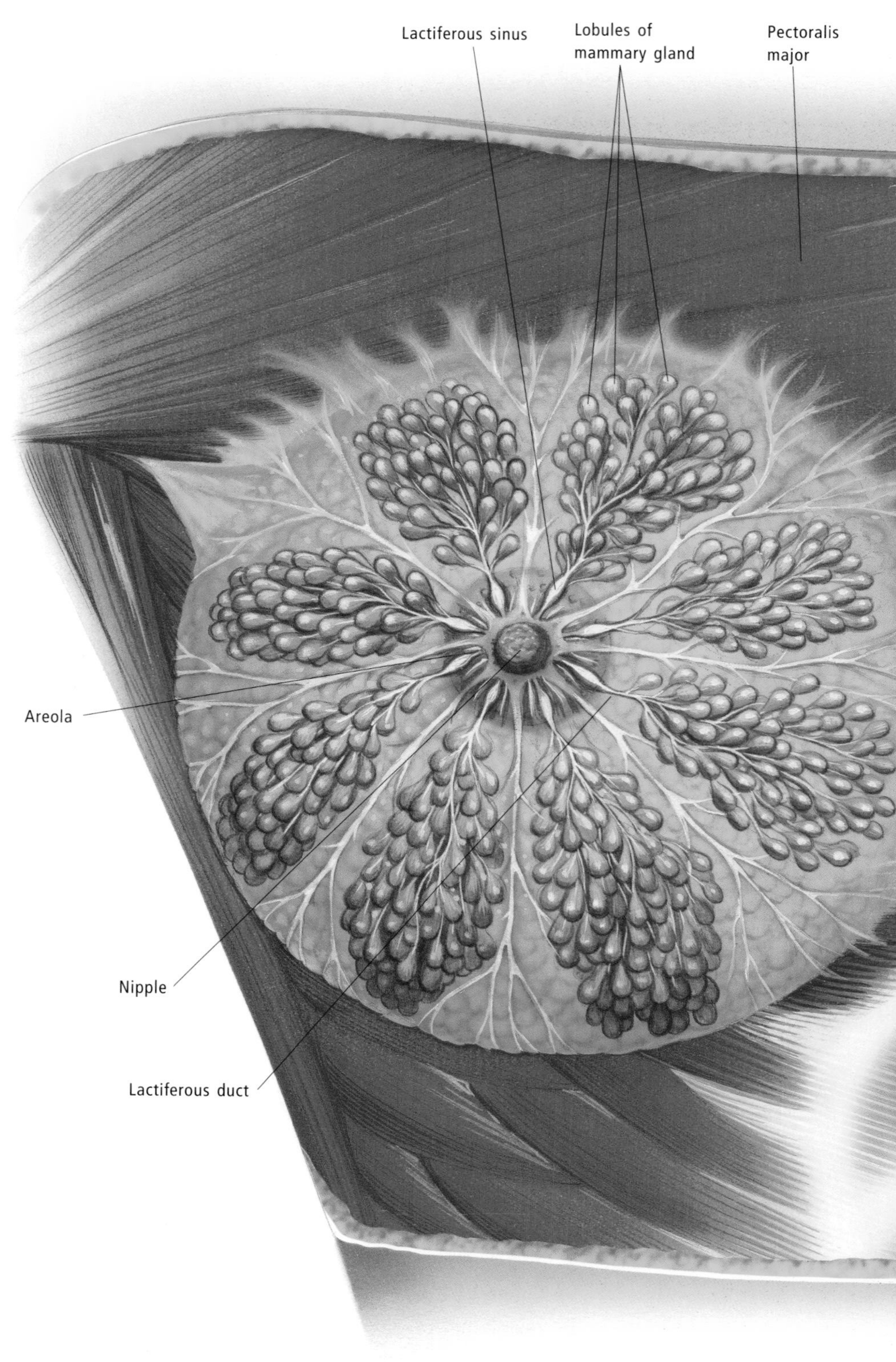

as vital nutrients. The keys to successful breast feeding are correct positioning of the baby—chest to chest and chin to breast—in a relaxed and comfortable environment, allowing the baby to feed for as long and often as necessary, understanding how the human body produces milk and how it is released, and having the support and advice of someone who understands how to breast feed. The breast feeding mother knows her baby is getting enough milk if the baby wets six to eight diapers a day, has pale yellow urine, is bright-eyed, grows steadily and feeds well at the breast.

One of the most common reasons women stop breast feeding is reduced milk supply: very few women are actually unable to breast feed. The only way to increase the amount of breast milk available is to breast feed. Supplementing a baby's feeds with artificial baby milk will decrease the demand for breast milk and result in a subsequent drop in supply. To keep up her milk supply, it is important that the mother drinks plenty of water, gets as much rest as possible, and eats healthy, nutritious food. Women also stop breast feeding because of sore, cracked nipples or breast infection (mastitis). However, these problems can be remedied with medical treatment.

Breast milk can be "expressed" (pumped) by hand or by using a hand-operated or electric pump. This milk, if stored correctly, can then be fed to the baby in a bottle, or for sick or premature (pre-term) babies via a tube. Expressing milk allows the mother some time away from her baby, which is important if she must return to the workforce. Many companies in industrialized countries now make provisions for women to continue to breast feed their babies after they return to work.

Artificial baby milks, if mixed according to directions, can be bottle fed to babies if breast feeding is unsuccessful or not desirable. They are nutritionally complete but they do not contain all the properties of breast milk. The woman who breast feeds has a lower risk of breast and ovarian cancer, osteoporosis and heart disease. Breast feeding is convenient, costs little or nothing and helps the mother's body to return to its pre-pregnant shape. Both mother and baby benefit from the intimacy of the close physical contact, which is an important part of the bonding process.

SEE ALSO *Breast, Bottle feeding, Infancy, Mastitis, Newborn, Nipple, Nutrition*

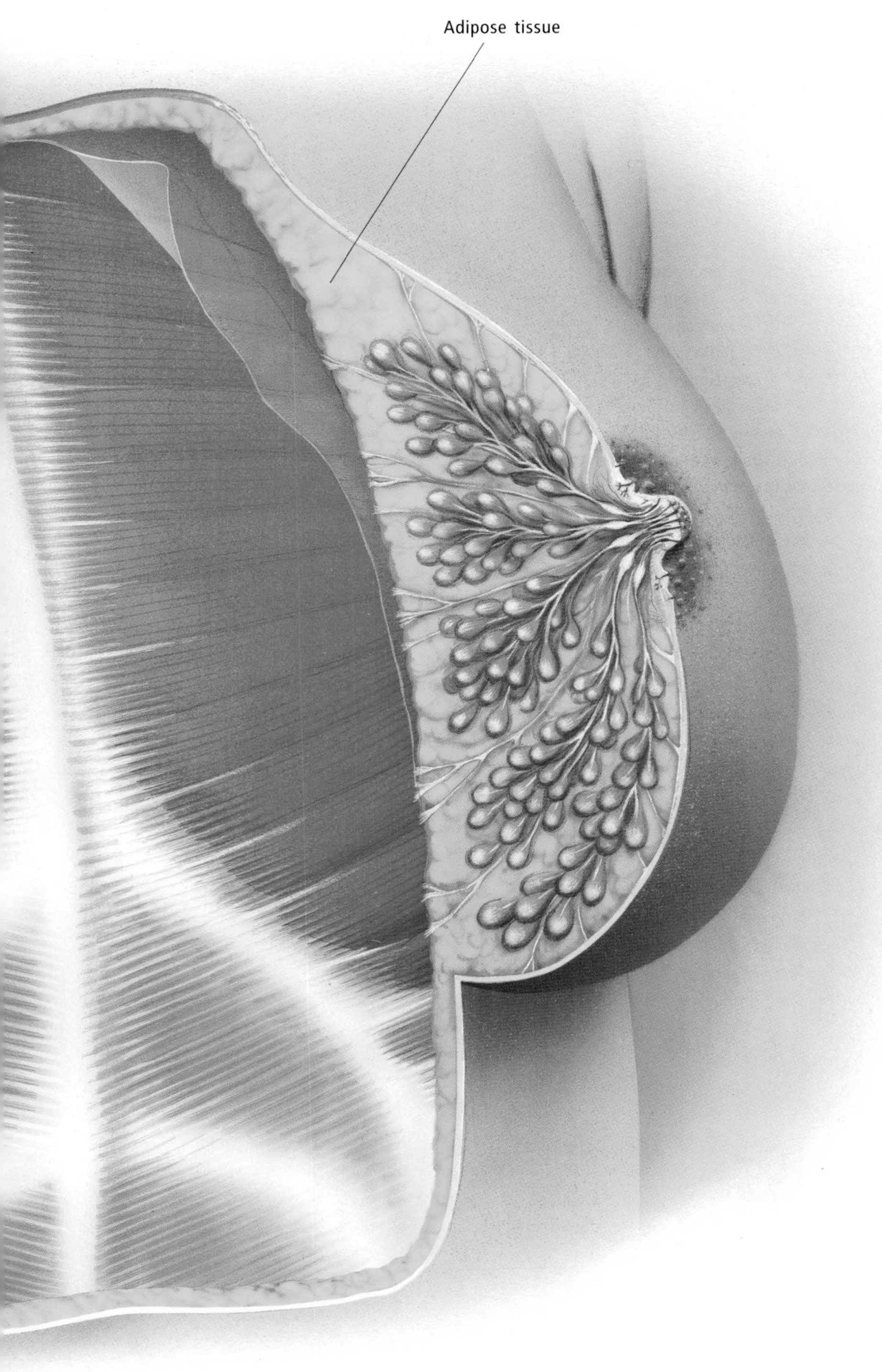

Breast feeding

In the days following childbirth the alveoli and ducts of the mammary glands fill with milk, a process controlled by a pituitary hormone called prolactin. When the baby sucks at the nipple another pituitary hormone, oxytocin, causes cells in the lactiferous ducts and sinuses to contract, ejecting milk.

BREATHING

Breathing—also known as respiration or ventilation—is the inspiration and expiration of air into and out of the lungs, by the contraction and relaxation of the diaphragm, the chest wall and abdominal wall. Breathing is the means by which a person absorbs oxygen from the air through the lungs into the bloodstream, and exhales carbon dioxide from the bloodstream through the lungs into the air.

At rest, the average person (at sea level) breathes 10 to 15 times a minute. In times of stress, or during exercise or other physical activity, the demand for oxygen by tissues is greater, and breathing is deeper and faster. Respiration is more labored at higher altitudes (unless the person is acclimatized) and during the later stages of pregnancy. Lung disorders such as asthma, chronic bronchitis, pneumonia or cancer may interfere with breathing and cause shortness of breath (dyspnea). An inhaled foreign body in the lung can also cause dyspnea. Breathing may also be slowed or may cease (apnea) in brain damage, poisoning, drug overdose or cardiac arrest. If breathing stops, oxygenation of the blood ceases, and irreversible brain damage or even death may occur in four to six minutes.

Breathing problems

In some situations, a person may breathe too fast. Rapid breathing (hyperventilation) is most commonly caused by anxiety, and produces dizziness, lightheadedness, a sense of unsteadiness and tingling around the mouth and fingertips. Symptoms subside when the person breathes in and out of a paper bag (to increase carbon dioxide levels in the blood). Hyperventilation can also occur in a condition known as metabolic acidosis, associated with diabetes, kidney disorders or starvation.

Cheyne-Stokes respiration is an abnormal breathing pattern with shallow, infrequent breathing that progresses to deep rapid breathing and then back to shallow breathing. It is seen in seriously ill patients with brain or heart disorders or during sleep.

Tests are available that can measure whether ventilation is adequate. Spirometry is a test using an instrument called a spirometer, which measures how well the lungs take in air, how much air they hold, and how well the lungs exhale air. A peak flow meter is a smaller device that measures resistance to breathing seen in disorders such as asthma and bronchitis. Both tests can be performed in the doctor's office. In cases of severe dyspnea, a blood test can determine oxygen and carbon dioxide levels in the blood.

Resuscitation

Artificial respiration (mouth-to-mouth or mouth-to-nose resuscitation) is a lifesaving method used to restore breathing to a person whose breathing has stopped, usually because they have almost drowned or have suffered a cardiac arrest. It may also be used in cases of poisoning, stroke, smoke inhalation, electrocution, suffocation and coma.

Mechanical ventilation is the use of a machine called a ventilator (or respirator) to introduce air into the airways. The patient is connected to the ventilator by a tube passed through the nose or mouth into the trachea (windpipe). The tube is sometimes inserted through an opening made in the trachea.

SEE ALSO *Asthma, Bronchitis, Dyspnea, Lungs, Respiratory system, Tracheostomy*

Moving oxygen around the body

Blood travels continuously through two different types of circulatory systems: the pulmonary (lung) and the systemic (body) circulations. The heart pumps deoxygenated blood from the veins of the systemic circulation into the arteries of the pulmonary circulation. This blood is oxygenated by the lungs and then flows back to the heart to be pumped into the arteries of the systemic circulation. Once the oxygen has been extracted by the body's tissues, the blood flows back to the heart and is pumped again into the pulmonary circulation.

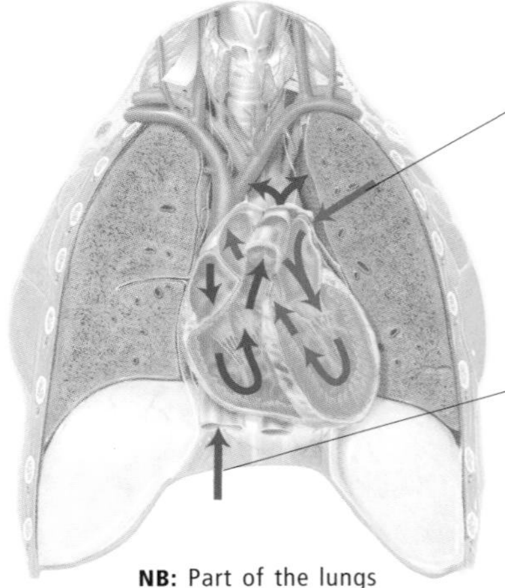

NB: Part of the lungs has been removed to reveal the pleura covering the diaphragm

Gas exchange in the alveoli

At the ends of the airways are tiny sacs full of air called alveoli. They are surrounded by small blood vessels called capillaries. It is here that oxygen passes from the air into the bloodstream and carbon dioxide passes from the blood into the alveoli to be breathed out.

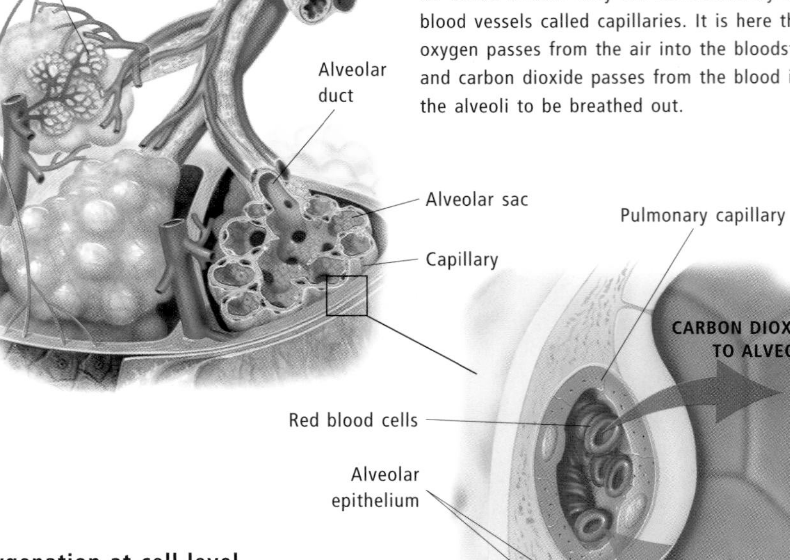

Oxygenation at cell level

Red blood cells carry oxygen into the bloodstream by combining it with a protein called hemoglobin. In the alveoli, red blood cells carry oxygen away to the tissues and pass carbon dioxide back to the alveoli. When it reaches the tissues, the oxygen is released, absorbed by the cells and used in cellular metabolism.

Breathing

Respiration is the name given to the act of breathing. It also refers to the transfer of oxygen from the lungs to the body's tissues, and of carbon dioxide from the tissues to the lungs.

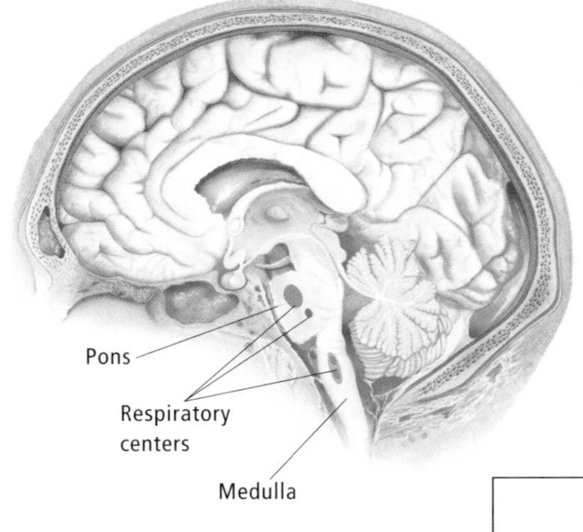

Respiratory centers in the brain

Specialized areas in the pons and the medulla receive information about blood carbon dioxide and blood oxygen levels from monitors elsewhere in the body. These respiratory centers send messages to the respiratory muscles to increase or decrease the rate and depth of breathing.

Respiratory centers

Air is inhaled

Oxygen is absorbed by the alveoli in the lungs, and passes into the bloodstream

Air moves down trachea and passes into lungs

Ribs and muscles mechanically move the lungs when we breathe

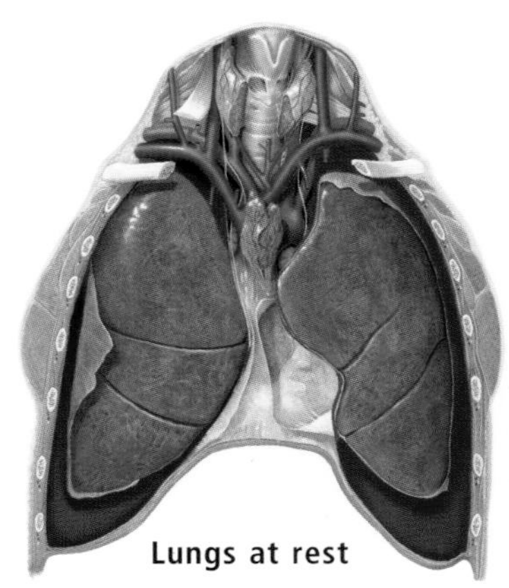

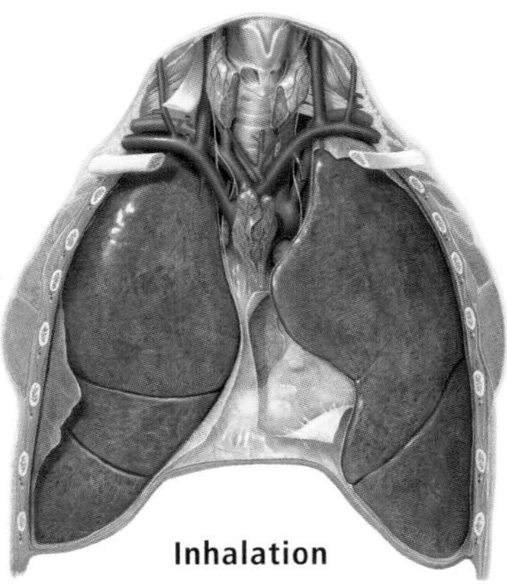

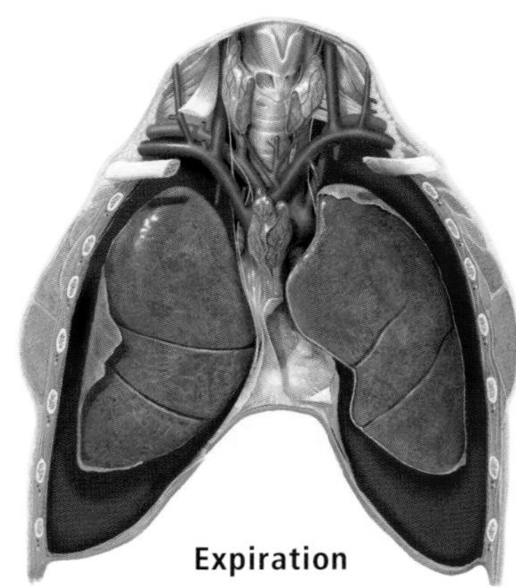

When we breathe in, the intercostal muscles move the ribs upwards and outwards and the diaphragm pushes downwards. This draws air into the expanded lungs.

Breathing muscles

Breathing is caused by the actions of the intercostal muscles (the muscles between the ribs) and the diaphragm, a muscular dome that separates the abdomen from the chest.

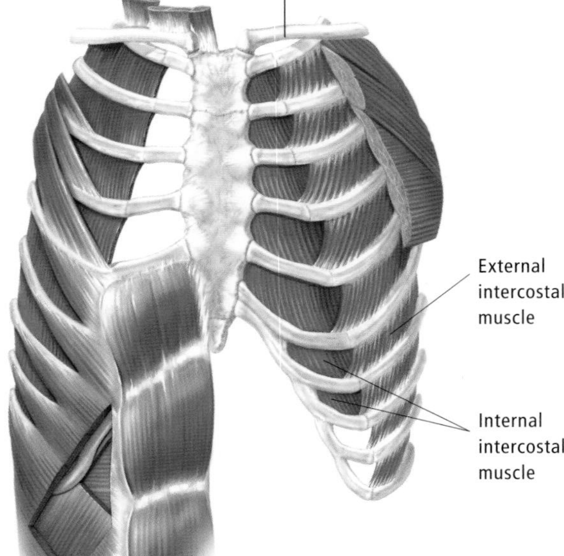

B

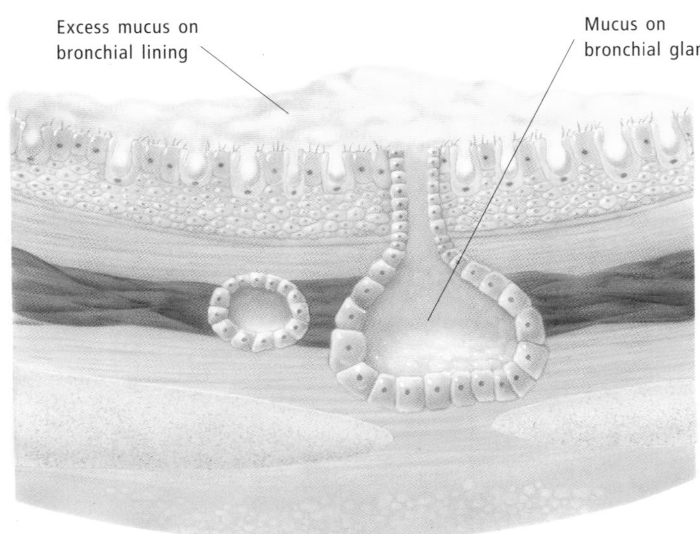

Bronchitis

In bronchitis, the walls of the airways (the bronchi) become inflamed. The glands then secrete excessive amounts of mucus, which may be coughed up as sputum. Bacterial bronchitis produces thick, yellow or greenish sputum; in viral bronchitis the sputum is thin and clear.

BRONCHITIS

This term bronchitis literally refers to inflammation of the large airways (bronchi). In practice, it is used to describe two quite separate disease processes.

Acute bronchitis is an inflammation of the major airways, usually following upper respiratory infection by a virus such as influenza, causing cough and production of sputum. It generally clears up by itself, unless a bacterial infection also occurs, in which case the sputum usually becomes thick and yellow. Because acute bacterial bronchitis can lead to the development of pneumonia, especially in elderly patients, treatment with antibiotics is advisable.

Chronic bronchitis results from inhalation of airborne irritants over a long period. By far the most common cause of this disease process is cigarette smoking, although it can also be triggered by repeated exposure to high levels of dusts, irritant gases or other pollutants. In the early stages of chronic bronchitis (simple chronic bronchitis) the main change in the large airways is not inflammation, but rather an increase in mucus secretion by cells lining the airways and glands within the airway walls. This leads to cough and the production of white or clear sputum (mucus secretion). There is often also bacterial infection and inflammation, which may cause coughing up of yellowish or greenish sputum that is a mixture of mucus and pus (mucopurulent bronchitis).

In some people, continuing exposure to the inhaled irritant leads to progressive involvement of smaller airways. This is an important complication because it causes widespread inflammation and scarring of the walls of these airways, leading to narrowing which limits the flow of air (chronic obstructive bronchitis). The person becomes increasingly breathless. To make matters even worse, the damage is usually not limited to the airways. The irritants that trigger chronic bronchitis usually also damage and destroy the alveoli of the lung in parallel, leading to the development of emphysema, which causes even more breathlessness.

The combination of chronic bronchitis and emphysema, which is referred to by terms such as chronic obstructive lung disease and chronic airflow limitation, may also overlap with asthma (asthmatic bronchitis). Eventually, these forms of chronic respiratory disease may be complicated by development of heart failure. They are major causes of chronic disability and death.

Because damage to the small airways and the lungs is difficult or impossible to reverse, stopping smoking or avoiding exposure to other inhaled irritants is by far the most important step a person can take to ensure that severe disease does not develop. In the early stages of chronic bronchitis, stopping smoking can lead to complete disappearance of symptoms. In the late stages, treatment with antibiotics, anti-inflammatory agents, bronchodilators and oxygen may be required.

SEE ALSO *Asthma, Bronchus, Cough, Emphysema, Pneumonia, Smoking*

BRONCHODILATORS

These are drugs used for treatment of asthma. Following inhalation, they provide rapid relief of breathlessness by relaxing the smooth muscle that surrounds the airways. Most bronchodilators are short-acting and are used for temporary relief of acute symptoms—more than one dose may be necessary. These drugs do not treat the airway inflammation that is the basis of asthma and so should be used in combination with anti-inflammatory agents.

Long-acting bronchodilators are also used but they are not rapidly effective, and therefore are not useful for treating an acute attack of asthma. They can, however, be used in combination with anti-inflammatory drugs.

SEE ALSO *Anti-inflammatory drugs, Asthma*

BRONCHOSCOPY

In bronchoscopy, the patient is anesthetized and the airways are examined by insertion of a tube called a bronchoscope. Modern bronchoscopes are flexible and equipped with a fiberoptic illumination system.

Tissue and cell samples can be obtained from the major airways and, by infusing and removing fluid, from the more peripheral parts of the lung as well. This makes the bronchoscope a valuable tool for the diagnosis of a variety of diseases of the airways and lungs, especially lung cancer. In addition, foreign bodies or other causes of obstruction of the airway tube can be removed using this instrument.

SEE ALSO *Lungs*

BRONCHUS

The trachea, or windpipe, branches at its lower end into two large (primary) air tubes—the right primary bronchus leading into the right lung, and the left primary bronchus serving the left lung. The route from the trachea through the right primary bronchus is more vertical, wider and shorter than it is to the left, and so inhaled objects are more likely to end up in the right lung.

The outer wall of each bronchus is supported by cartilage. The interior is lined with mucous membrane and many microscopic, mobile, hair-like projections called cilia that shift mucus and trapped particles upwards. An inflammation of the mucous membrane of a bronchus is called bronchitis.

At the lung's entrance, the primary bronchus branches into smaller (secondary) bronchi. These are also called lobar bronchi because one of them serves each lung lobe, of which there are usually three in the right lung and two in the left.

Each secondary bronchus divides into smaller (tertiary) bronchi. These split into bronchioles that separate into hair-like terminal bronchioles (of which there are about 64,000) ending at microscopic bubbles known as alveoli, where the exchange of carbon dioxide for oxygen occurs.

Together, all these branching air passages are referred to as the bronchial tree.

SEE ALSO *Alveolus, Bronchitis, Lungs, Trachea*

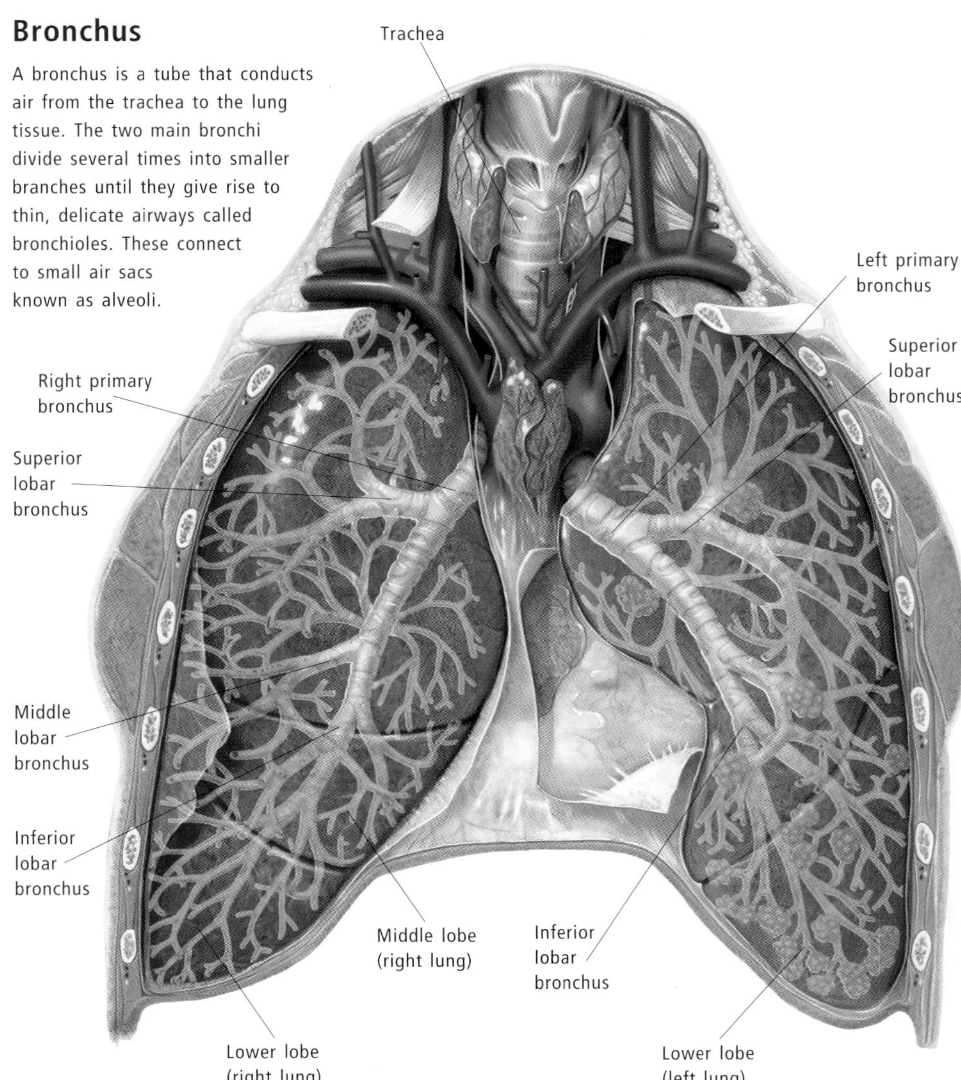

Bronchus

A bronchus is a tube that conducts air from the trachea to the lung tissue. The two main bronchi divide several times into smaller branches until they give rise to thin, delicate airways called bronchioles. These connect to small air sacs known as alveoli.

BRUCELLOSIS

Common in Spain, Mexico and South America but rare elsewhere, brucellosis is caused by contact with farm animals carrying the *Brucella* bacterium—usually cattle, goats, dogs or pigs.

Transmission to humans occurs through swallowing unpasteurized milk or other dairy products, or meat products, or by farm workers coming into contact with the placenta of an infected animal. Symptoms are mild fever, chills, sweating, muscle aches, tiredness and aching joints. Typically, the fever peaks every afternoon; hence the name "undulant fever". The disease may relapse and last for years.

Treatment is with antibiotics such as tetracycline or an aminoglycoside, often in combination. Pasteurization of dairy products and preventive measures for farm workers (such as vaccination of cattle and wearing of protective clothing) will generally prevent the disease.

BRUISE

A bruise (or contusion) is a discoloration of the skin. It occurs when blood vessels are damaged or broken as the result of a blow to the skin, such as bumping against something. The discoloration is caused by blood leaking out from damaged vessels into the skin. It first appears reddish, then, one or two days later, blue or purple. By day six, the color changes to green and after a week or so, the bruise will appear yellowish-brown. The skin color will return to normal in two to three weeks.

Bruising is usually more extensive in older persons, because of the greater fragility of blood vessels in older age groups. Some medications, especially those that cause bleeding such as aspirin and anticoagulants, make bruising more likely. Cortisone medications such as prednisone, clotting disorders like hemophilia, or liver diseases can also cause serious bruising and bleeding.

To prevent or minimize bruising after an injury, apply ice to the affected area. Apply pressure by hand or with a bandage, but do not use a tourniquet.

Bruise

Bruising is a discoloration of the skin that takes place after an injury. If bruising occurs frequently, for no apparent reason, it may indicate an underlying bleeding disorder.

B

BUNION

A bunion is a solid growth that forms a lump at the base of the big toe, or hallux. The lump results from friction and distortion of the first metatarsal bone, plus fluid and bony growths, where the bone meets the base of the big toe.

Although susceptibility to bunions is often inherited, there is no precise cause. They usually develop in middle age. Bunions can be tolerated and are not usually painful unless cramped by badly fitting footwear. Over-tight shoes will cause pain but have not been proven to actually cause bunions. Treatment is by surgery and is usually successful but recovery can be painful.

SEE ALSO *Foot*

Bunion

A bunion is a lump at the base of the big toe. If painful, it can be treated by wearing properly fitted shoes. If that does not ease the pain, surgery may be required.

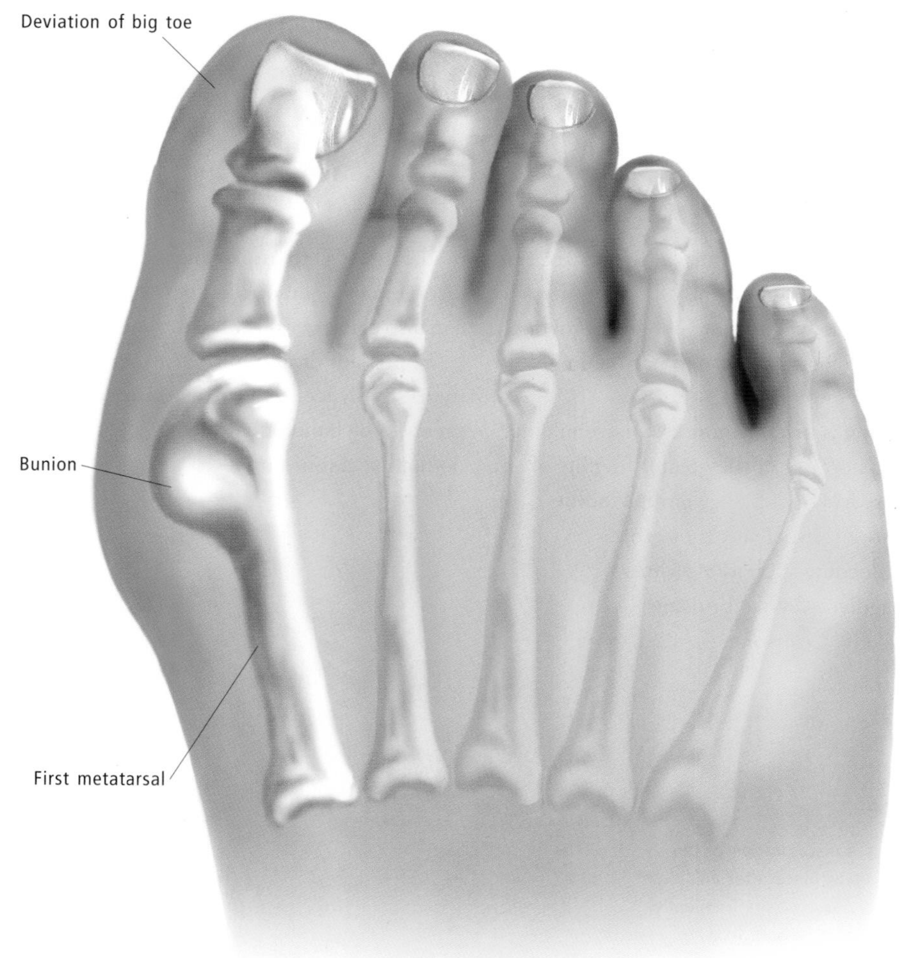

BURKITT'S LYMPHOMA

Burkitt's lymphoma, also known as B cell lymphoma, is a tumor of the lymph glands. It arises from a type of white blood cell called a B lymphocyte, although it is a different type of lymphoma from a Hodgkin's lymphoma. It is often associated with the Epstein-Barr virus (EBV), which causes infectious mononucleosis (glandular fever).

Burkitt's lymphoma is usually first noticed as a painless but rapid swelling of the lymph nodes in the neck or below the jaw (though lymph nodes in other areas may be affected). The diagnosis can be confirmed by biopsy of the node. Treatment involves a combination of radiation therapy and chemotherapy. The disease is often curable if it is treated in the early stages.

SEE ALSO *Biopsy, Infectious mononucleosis, Lymph nodes, Lymphocytes, White blood cells*

BURSITIS

A bursa is a small, fluid-filled sac-like structure, found mainly around joints, that protects bones and tendons from friction. Bursitis is inflammation of a bursa.

Bursitis often occurs in the shoulder, but it may also affect the knee (infrapatellar bursitis), elbow (olecranon bursitis), the back of heel (retrocalcaneal bursitis) or other areas. In most cases the cause is unknown, but it can be caused by injury, infection and repeated friction. Repeated attacks of bursitis or injury can cause chronic inflammation. Symptoms are pain and swelling over the area involved. Nearby joints are tender.

Bursitis is treated by rest, alternating cold and heat treatments and oral anti-inflammatory drugs. Occasionally, fluid may need to be aspirated from, and corticosteroids injected into, the bursa. Surgery is rarely required. If bursitis is caused by bacterial infection, it must be treated with antibiotics and surgical drainage of the infected bursa. As the pain eases, exercises are needed to build strength and increase mobility, especially if disuse or prolonged immobility has caused muscle wasting.

SEE ALSO *Joints*

BUTEYKO BREATHING TECHNIQUE

The Buteyko breathing technique was developed in the 1950s by Konstantin Buteyko, a Russian medical scientist, to treat asthma. This technique is based on the premise that asthma is the result of over-breathing (hyperventilation), which causes an activation of the defence mechanisms of the body in an attempt to constrict the abnormal breathing patterns. Asthmatic patients are therefore taught to recognize their own hyperventilation patterns and to return their breathing levels to normal. In encouraging nasal breathing the Buteyko technique also reduces inhalation of allergens. The technique is taught in a consecutive five-day course, and it is claimed that results can be achieved within the first three days.

SEE ALSO *Asthma, Breathing*

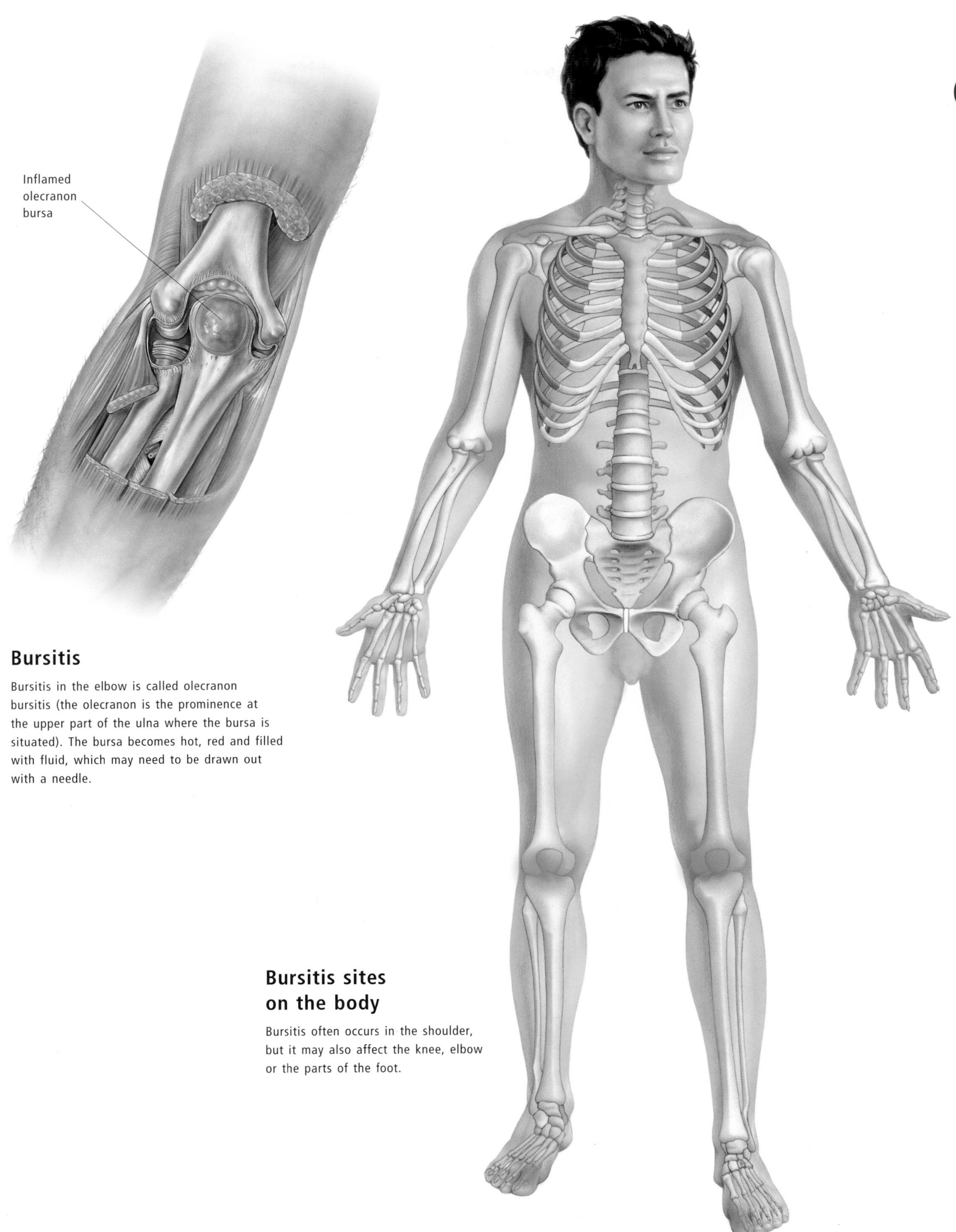

Bursitis

Bursitis in the elbow is called olecranon bursitis (the olecranon is the prominence at the upper part of the ulna where the bursa is situated). The bursa becomes hot, red and filled with fluid, which may need to be drawn out with a needle.

Bursitis sites on the body

Bursitis often occurs in the shoulder, but it may also affect the knee, elbow or the parts of the foot.

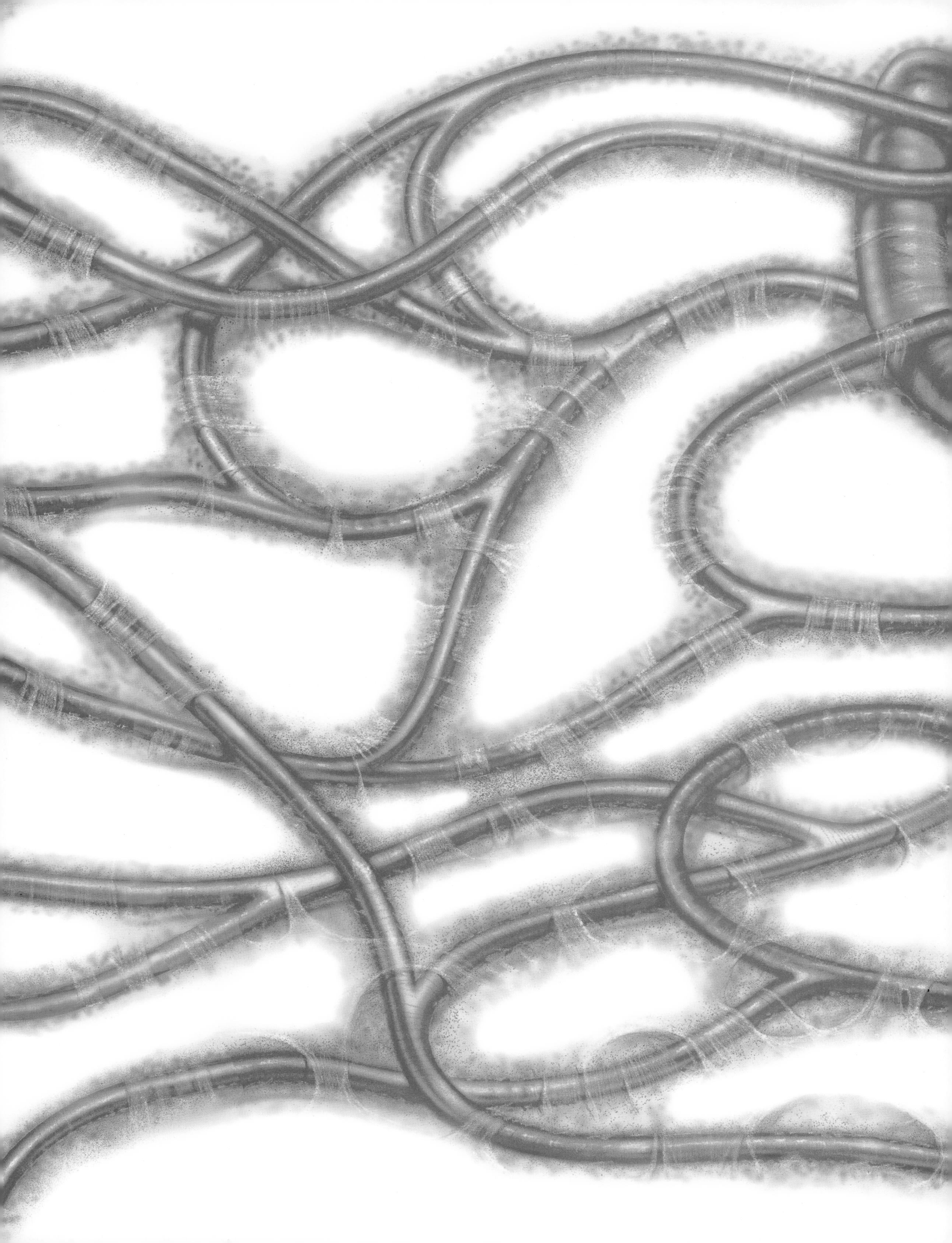

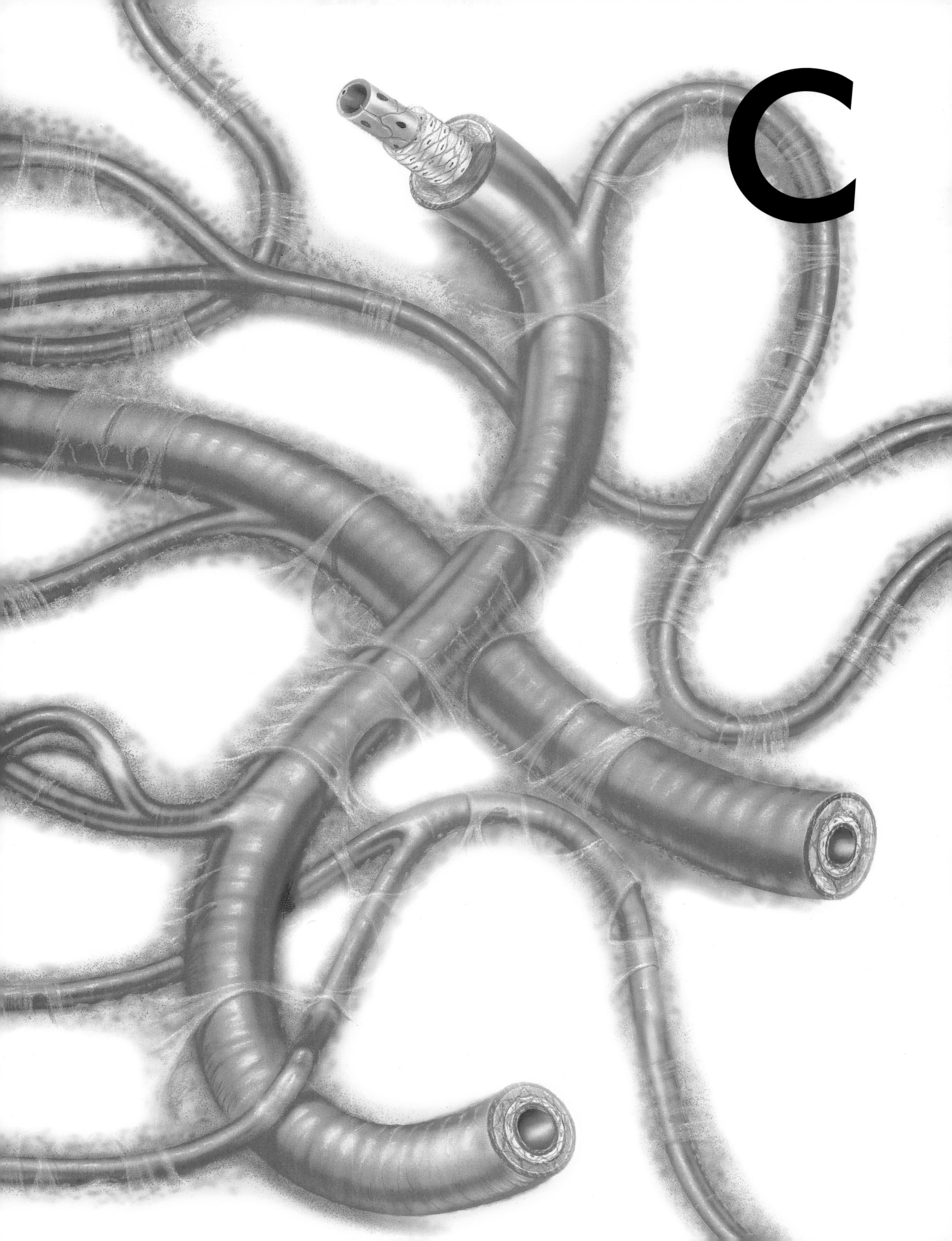
C

C

CAFFEINE

Caffeine tops the list of the world's most widely consumed drugs. It is a component of many foods and drinks, including coffee, tea, soft drinks (particularly colas), chocolate and guarana. Caffeine is also an ingredient in an extensive array of over-the-counter medications, such as treatments for allergies, headaches, migraines, muscle tension and colds. In some preparations it is designed to help people diet or stay awake.

Chemically, caffeine is an alkaloid—an organic compound containing nitrogen and derived from plants. Medically, it is regarded as a mild stimulant of the central nervous system. The physiological effects of caffeine include raised blood pressure and heart and respiration rates. It also increases the need to urinate.

A cup of coffee usually contains between 65 milligrams and 115 milligrams of caffeine. Behavioral impacts of low to moderate daily consumption of between 50 milligrams and 300 milligrams of caffeine are elevated alertness, energy and concentration levels. At higher doses, caffeine can cause adverse health effects such as anxiety, depression and insomnia. It is also possible to overdose on caffeine. A dose of about 10 grams of caffeine (equivalent to about 100 cups of strong coffee) would be fatal to most people.

Caffeine is widely considered within the medical profession to be a drug of both physical and psychological dependence. Like most addictive chemicals, people can develop tolerance to it and may suffer from withdrawal symptoms when they cease to use it. Physiological and behavioral reactions to caffeine withdrawal may include drowsiness, headaches, irritability, nausea, vomiting and depression.

SEE ALSO *Stimulants, Withdrawal*

CALCIUM

Calcium is found in bones and teeth, where it provides strength and rigidity. It is also found (in much smaller amounts) circulating in the blood and the cells, where it performs several important functions, including the regulation of the heartbeat, the transmission of nerve impulses, the contraction of muscles and the clotting of blood. Calcium occurs naturally in dairy products such as milk, cheese and yoghurt, leafy green vegetables such as broccoli, and fish such as salmon and sardines.

The absorption of calcium from the intestine is dependent on the presence in the body of sufficient quantities of vitamin D. The absorption and incorporation of calcium into bone from the bloodstream is regulated by parathyroid hormones, secreted by the parathyroid glands, and calcitonin, secreted by the thyroid gland.

Too little calcium in the blood (hypocalcemia) is usually caused by a parathyroid hormone deficiency or a vitamin D deficiency (rickets) in the body. Hypocalcemia causes muscle spasms (tetany), twitching or cramps, numbness and tingling in the extremities, seizures, and irregular heartbeat. Over the longer term, hypocalcemia causes thinning of the bones (osteoporosis) or the softening of bones (osteomalacia). The treatment is calcium and vitamin D supplements.

Too much calcium in the blood (hypercalcemia) can be caused by over-secretion of parathyroid hormones (hyperparathyroidism); by excessive ingestion of vitamin D; or by failure of the kidneys to secrete calcium (kidney failure). Symptoms of hypercalcemia are lethargy, delirium, and seizures. Over time, hypercalcemia may cause calcium deposits in soft tissues of the body, kidney stones, and hardening of the blood vessels. The treatment is to correct the underlying condition.

SEE ALSO *Bones, Hypocalcemia, Kidney, Nutrition, Osteomalacia, Osteoporosis, Parathyroid glands, Rickets, Teeth, Thyroid gland*

CALCIUM CHANNEL BLOCKERS

Calcium channel blockers (CCBs) are a group of prescription medications commonly used in the treatment of a range of heart and vascular (blood vessel) disorders. These include hypertension (high blood pressure), angina (chest pain caused by lack of oxygen to heart muscles) and certain types of arrhythmias (abnormal heart rhythms). They are also sometimes effective in treating certain types of migraines. CCBs work by obstructing the flow of calcium ions into vascular and heart muscle cells. This causes the muscle cells to relax. As a result the arteries dilate, which improves blood flow to the heart and leads to a drop in blood pressure. The heart rate is also slowed by some CCBs. There can be side effects associated with certain CCBs. These vary according to the drug used but may include swelling in the legs and dizziness.

SEE ALSO *Angina, Arrythmia, Arteries, Blood vessels, Heart, Hypertension, Migraine*

CANCER

Cancer (also called malignancy) is a disease in which normal cells become abnormal and grow uncontrollably, often metastasizing (spreading from the site of origin to other sites). A leading cause of death in many countries, only diseases of the heart and blood vessels kill more people than cancer in developed countries. It affects people of any age but is more common in middle and old age. There are over a hundred forms of cancer; most are named for the type of cell or the organ in which they arise. Almost any tissue in the body may become malignant, but the skin, the digestive organs, the lungs and the female breasts are particularly prone to cancer.

There are three main classifications of cancer. Carcinoma is cancer of the epithelial tissue that forms the skin and the linings of the internal organs. Sarcoma is cancer of connective tissue, such as cartilage, muscle or bone. Cancers of the bloodstream (leukemia) and the lymph system (lymphoma) are a third category.

A cancer by definition is malignant, that is, capable of spreading beyond its site of origin. (A benign tumor does not spread and is not malignant.) Cancer spreads by infiltrating the tissue around it, or by distant spread to other parts of the body via blood or lymph vessels, or both. Frequently it spreads to the lymph nodes that drain the tissues in which the tumor has arisen; breast cancer, for example, tends to spread to the lymph nodes in the axilla (armpit). When a cancer spreads beyond the tissue of origin to a distant site and forms a tumor, the new tumor is called a metastasis. Metastases are common in the liver, lung, bone and brain. They generally indicate a poorer expectancy or prognosis. Most cancers, if left alone, are fatal. However, advances in diagnosing and treating cancer have improved greatly over the past few decades. About one-third of all persons treated for cancer now recover completely (defined as surviving five years) or live much longer than they would have lived without treatment.

Skin cancer (including melanoma) is the most common type of cancer for both men and women in developed countries. The next most common type among men is prostate cancer; among women, it is breast cancer. Lung cancer is the leading cause of death from cancer for both men and women. Brain cancer and leukemia are the most common cancers in children and young adults.

The causes of cancer are not fully understood. Some cancers (including melanoma and cancers of the breast, ovary, and colon) tend to run in families. Others are known to be associated with certain risk factors; tobacco smoking is known to cause oral cancer and cancers of the larynx, lung, esophagus, pancreas, bladder, kidney, and cervix. Passive smoking, or exposure to smoke in the environment, increases the risk of lung cancer for non-smokers. A deficient diet may make cancer more likely. A high-fat diet may contribute to cancer of the breast, colon, uterus, and prostate. Obesity is associated with increased rates of cancer of the prostate, pancreas, uterus, colon and ovary, as well as increased rates of breast cancer in older women. Ultraviolet radiation from the sun and from other sources (such as sunlamps and tanning booths) may cause skin cancer, especially in those people with fair skin. Excess alcohol consumption may cause cancer of the mouth, throat, esophagus, larynx and liver. Chemicals and other substances in the workplace can cause cancer. Asbestos, nickel, cadmium, uranium, radon, vinyl chloride and benzene are examples of occupational carcinogens (cancer-causing substances). Radiation from medical x-rays can increase the risk of cancer.

In general, the sooner cancer is diagnosed and treated, the better the chance of survival. Regular medical checkups and self-examination of organs such as skin, testicles (in men) and breasts (in women) will increase the chance of early detection. Depending on age and gender, screening tests may be advised. These include Pap tests (a smear taken of cells of the cervix), mammograms (x-rays of the breast) and sigmoidoscopy (examination of the sigmoid colon). If there are signs and symptoms that suggest the possibility of cancer, the physician may order tests such as x-rays, ultrasound, MRI or CAT scans, endoscopy, and blood tests. A biopsy may be taken for examination by a pathologist. The tests will allow a cancer to be "staged", that is, rated according to how far it has spread. Local lymph node involvement or distant metastases indicate more advanced disease, with a correspondingly poorer outlook.

There are several approaches to treating cancer, which may be used alone or in combination with each other, depending on the type and location of the cancer, the stage of the disease, the person's age and general health. Surgery is frequently used to remove a primary tumor. The tissue around the

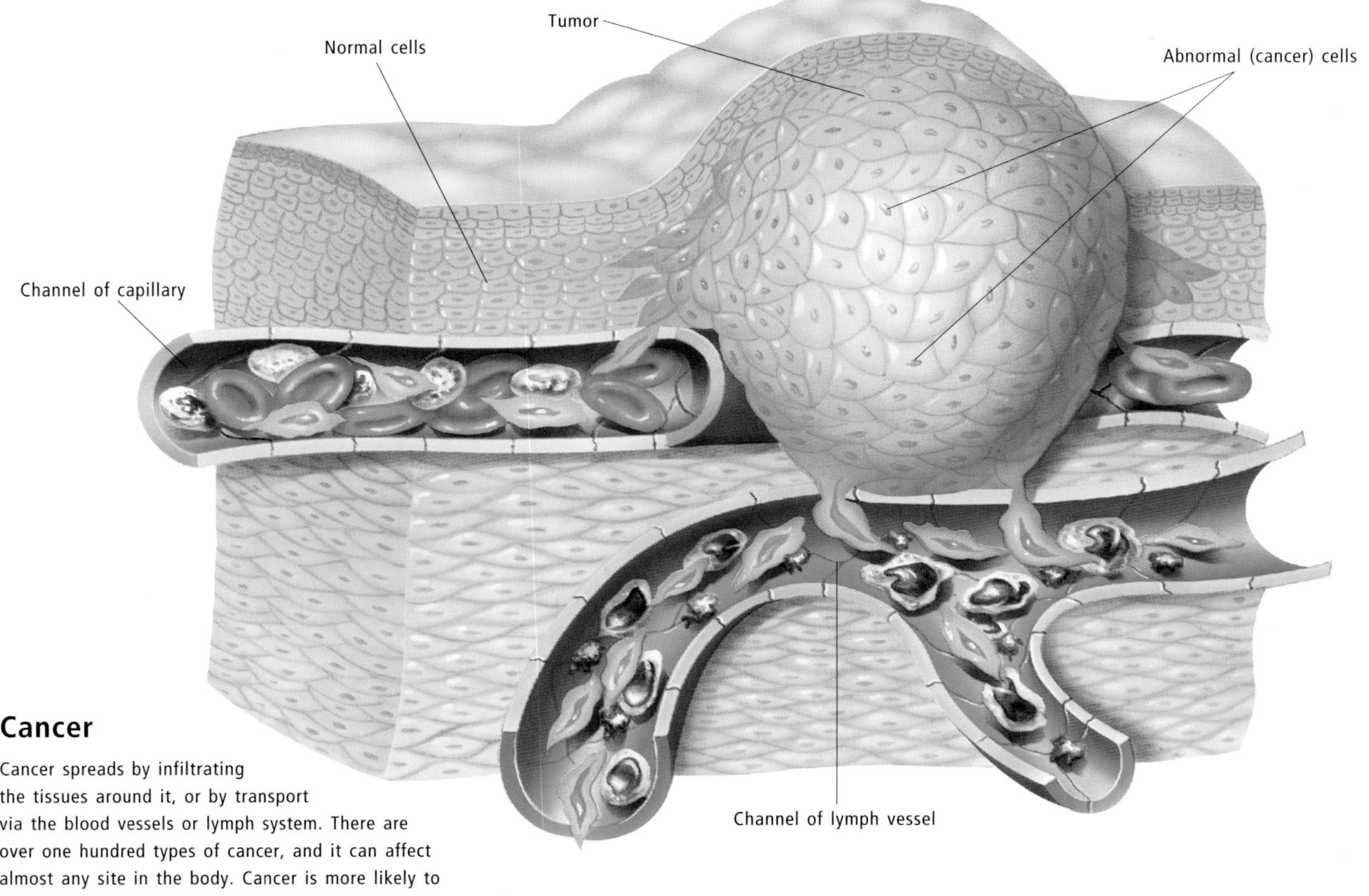

Cancer

Cancer spreads by infiltrating the tissues around it, or by transport via the blood vessels or lymph system. There are over one hundred types of cancer, and it can affect almost any site in the body. Cancer is more likely to develop when the immune system is not functioning normally.

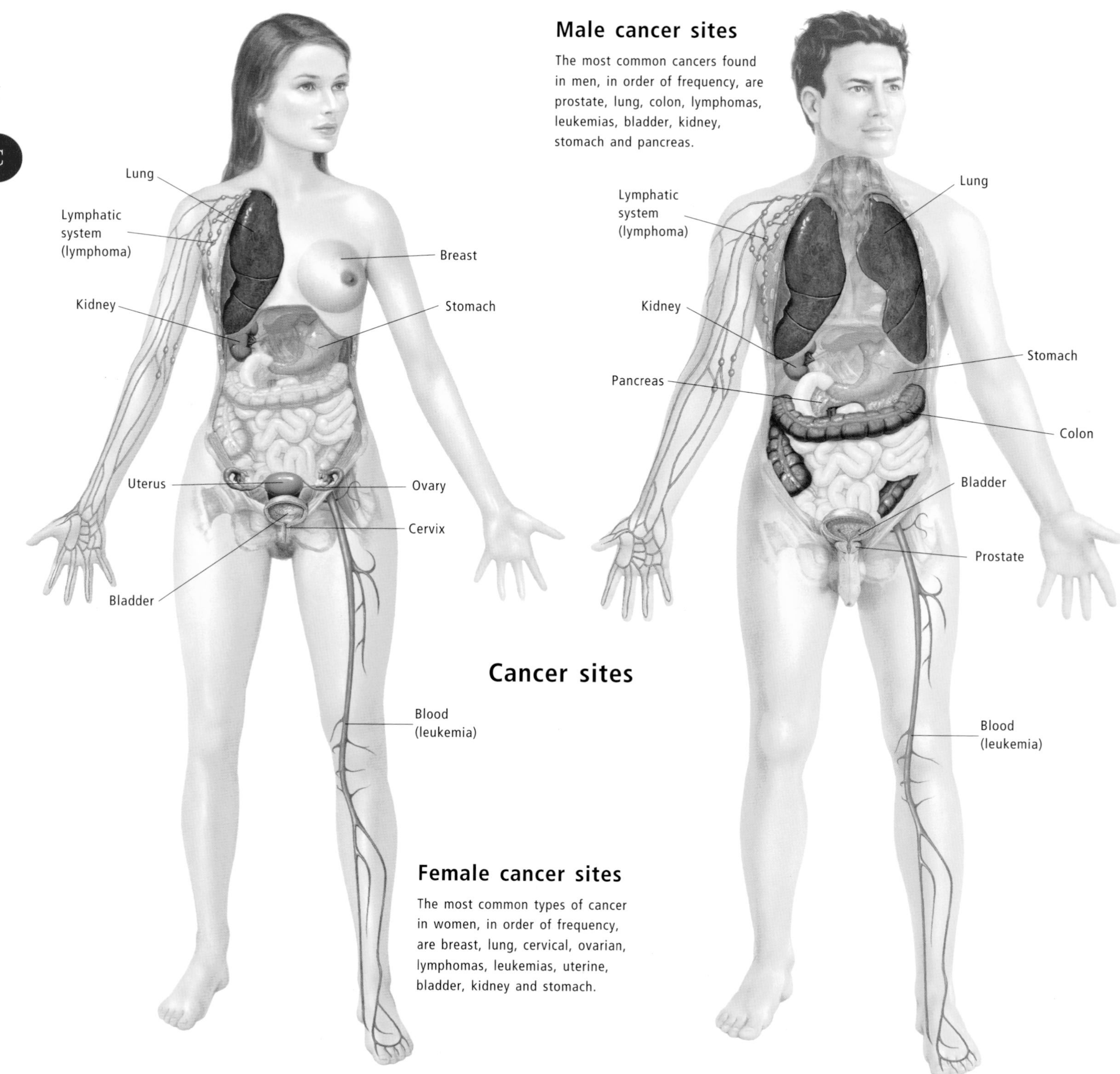
Male cancer sites
The most common cancers found in men, in order of frequency, are prostate, lung, colon, lymphomas, leukemias, bladder, kidney, stomach and pancreas.
Lung
Lymphatic system (lymphoma)
Kidney
Breast
Stomach
Uterus
Ovary
Cervix
Bladder
Blood (leukemia)
Lymphatic system (lymphoma)
Lung
Kidney
Stomach
Pancreas
Colon
Bladder
Prostate
Blood (leukemia)
Female cancer sites
The most common types of cancer in women, in order of frequency, are breast, lung, cervical, ovarian, lymphomas, leukemias, uterine, bladder, kidney and stomach.

Cancer sites

tumor and nearby lymph nodes may also be removed during the operation. Radiation therapy (radiotherapy) involves high-energy rays used to directly destroy or slow the growth of cancer cells. Chemotherapy is treatment with cytotoxic (cell-killing) drugs, introduced either directly into the tumor, or via the bloodstream. Hormone therapy and immunotherapy are used in certain cancers sensitive to these treatments. As cancer treatments affect normal cells as well as cancer cells, they often cause unpleasant side effects such as nausea, skin rashes, loss of hair, and bone marrow suppression.

Prevention is important in managing cancer. Physicians recommend giving up smoking and avoiding smoke and other environmental carcinogens. A good diet will include foods that are low in fat, rich in vitamins A and C and high in fiber such as whole-grain cereals, fruits, and vegetables. Alcoholic beverages should be taken in moderation, and overexposure to the sun avoided, particularly by fair-skinned people.

SEE ALSO *Bowel cancer, Breast cancer, Chemotherapy, Leukemia, Lung cancer, Melanoma, Metastasis, Prostate cancer, Radiation therapy, Skin cancer; information on cancers of other parts of the body is included in the entry for the body part*

C

CANDIDIASIS

Candidiasis, also called moniliasis, is an infection caused by the candida fungus (usually *Candida albicans*). This organism normally grows harmlessly in the intestinal tract, mouth and the vagina, but under certain conditions it can proliferate and cause infection. These conditions include damaged skin, moisture and warmth. A person is also more susceptible to candidiasis during pregnancy, when taking antibiotics or corticosteroids, or when the immune system is weakened as in AIDS.

In the mouth and the vagina, candidiasis appears as small, white patches on a red, inflamed background. In the skin, candida forms moist, bright red flat patches with poorly defined borders. These occur usually in the groin, around the anus, beneath the breasts (particularly in overweight women with pendulous breasts), in folds of skin of obese people, and in the armpits. In babies, they may occur as diaper rash.

It is important to keep the affected areas cool, dry and exposed to sunlight where possible. Eating yoghurt, buttermilk or sour cream, or taking acidophilus helps prevent candidiasis. A physician may prescribe antifungal topical medications such as nystatin, haloprigin, miconazole, or clotrimazole. These drugs are also available as vaginal pessaries and creams, and as suppositories.

SEE ALSO *Antifungals, Diaper rash, Opportunistic infection, Vaginitis*

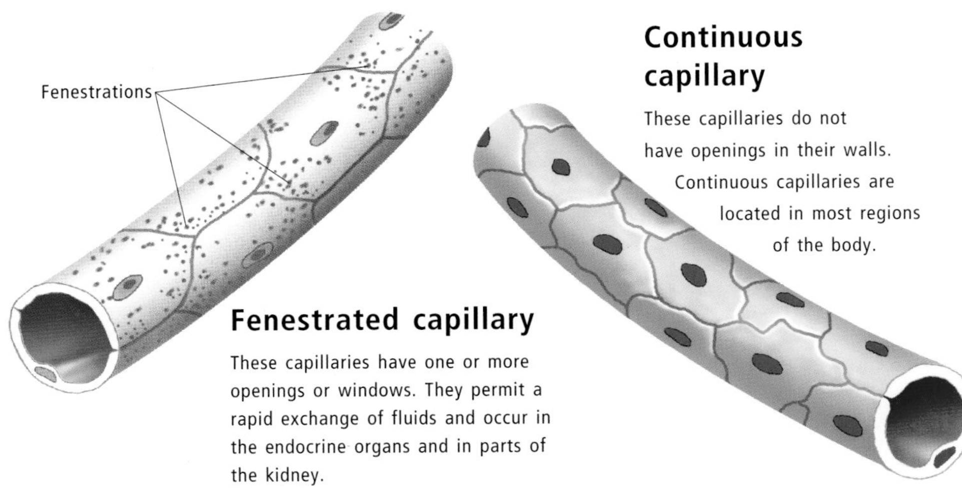

Fenestrated capillary

These capillaries have one or more openings or windows. They permit a rapid exchange of fluids and occur in the endocrine organs and in parts of the kidney.

Continuous capillary

These capillaries do not have openings in their walls. Continuous capillaries are located in most regions of the body.

CAPILLARIES

A capillary is the smallest type of blood vessel in the vascular system. Capillaries connect the smallest arteries with the smallest veins; most are so narrow they have the same diameter as a single blood cell. The function of capillaries is to carry oxygen-rich blood to the tissues, to pass food substances to tissue cells, and to carry away waste products, such as carbon dioxide and nitrates, back to the lungs and kidneys for elimination from the body.

During inflammation of body tissues, the capillaries become more permeable. They allow white blood cells and proteins into the tissues to fight infections and stimulate inflammation. Capillaries can also become more permeable as a result of some allergic reactions. In serious reactions, such as anaphylaxis, the blood can lose volume and the person can go into shock.

Microangiopathy is a term used to describe a disorder of capillaries in which the capillary walls become so thick and weak that they bleed, leak protein, and slow the flow of blood. For example, diabetics may develop microangiopathy with thickening of capillaries in the eye and the kidney.

SEE ALSO *Arteries, Blood vessels, Circulatory system, Veins*

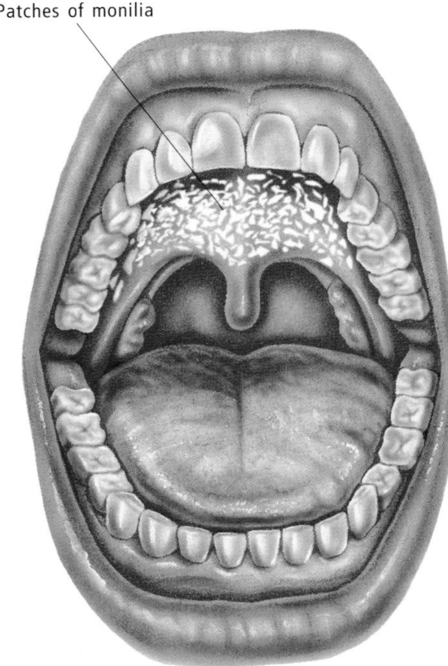

Candidiasis

Candidiasis is a fungal infection that affects the mucous membranes of the body. Infection of the mouth (thrush) causes red, inflamed areas and creamy, white, painful patches to form inside the mouth. It can be treated by applying antifungal drugs directly to the area or by taking medications orally.

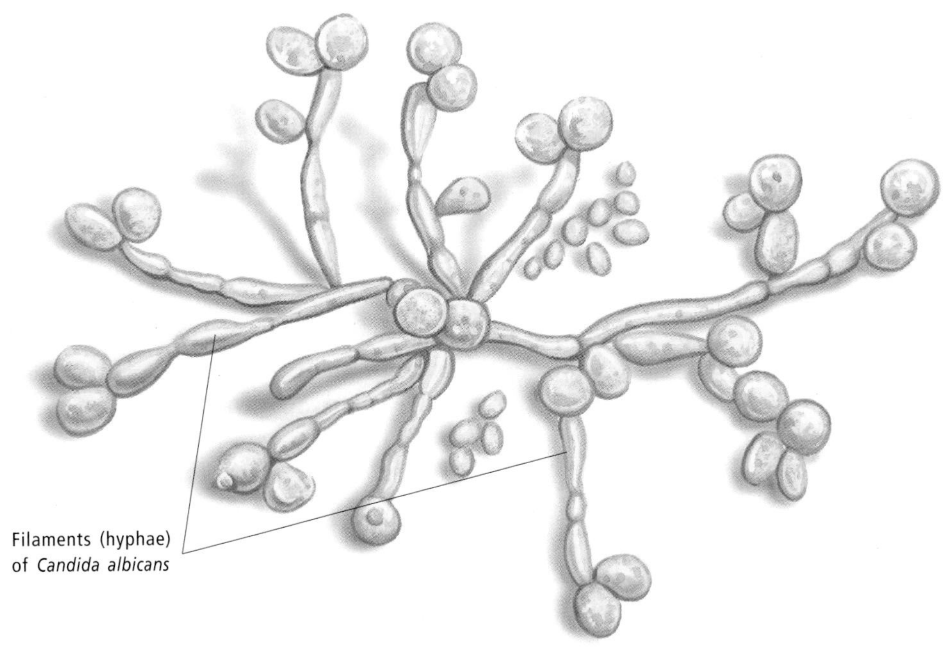

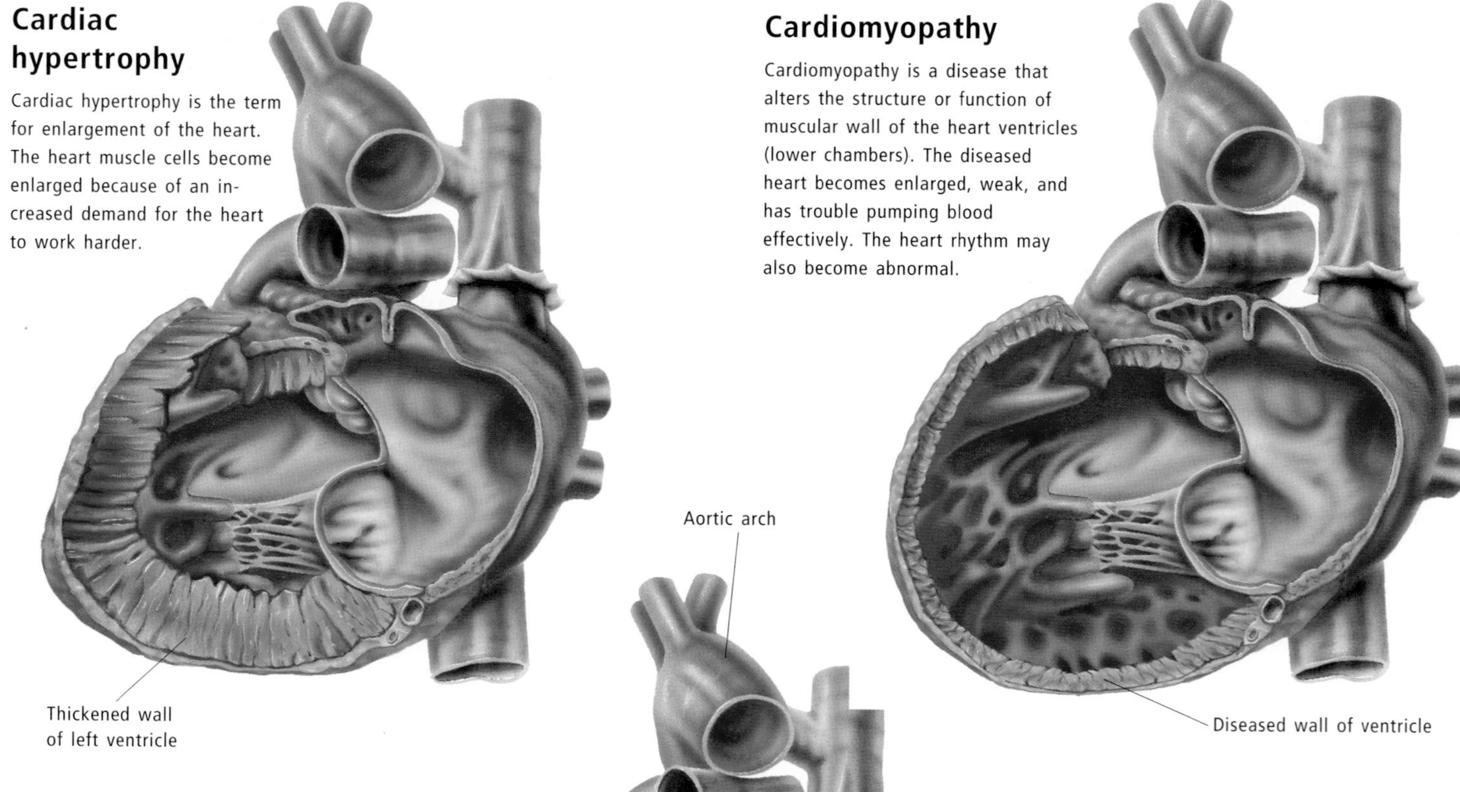

Cardiac hypertrophy
Cardiac hypertrophy is the term for enlargement of the heart. The heart muscle cells become enlarged because of an increased demand for the heart to work harder.
Thickened wall of left ventricle
Cardiomyopathy
Cardiomyopathy is a disease that alters the structure or function of muscular wall of the heart ventricles (lower chambers). The diseased heart becomes enlarged, weak, and has trouble pumping blood effectively. The heart rhythm may also become abnormal.
Diseased wall of ventricle
Aortic arch
Left ventricle
Normal heart

CARDIAC HYPERTROPHY

Cardiac hypertrophy is enlargement of the heart. It is caused by enlargement of heart muscle cells in response to a need for the heart to pump harder over months or years, in conditions such as hypertension or restricted flow of blood from the heart to the aorta (aortic stenosis). Because the heart must work harder, it requires more oxygen than normal; therefore, someone with cardiac hypertrophy is more vulnerable to conditions such as angina and myocardial infarction. It is necessary to treat the underlying cause.

Hypertrophic cardiomyopathy (formerly known as hypertrophic subaortic stenosis) is a group of diseases in which the cardiac muscle enlarges for no apparent reason. About half the cases are inherited and the disease affects mainly young adults. Symptoms are breathlessness, tiredness, fainting and chest pain. The condition is treated with beta adrenergic and calcium channel blocking drugs. In severe cases, an operation to cut or excise the muscle may be required.

SEE ALSO *Angina pectoris, Calcium channel blockers, Cardiomyopathy, Heart, Hypertension, Myocardial infarction*

CARDIAC TAMPONADE

Cardiac tamponade (also called pericardial tamponade) is a potentially life-threatening condition in which blood or fluid accumulates in the pericardium (the sac enclosing the heart), causing pressure on the heart. This prevents the ventricles from expanding fully, so they cannot adequately fill or pump out the blood.

The condition may result from a wound which ruptures blood vessels in the heart muscle, from bacterial or viral inflammation of the pericardium (pericarditis), or from cancer invading the pericardial sac. It may also be caused by radiation therapy to the chest, hypothyroidism, or systemic lupus erythematosus (SLE).

Symptoms involve chest pain radiating to the neck, shoulder, back or abdomen, difficulty in breathing, a weak or absent pulse, and low blood pressure. A chest x-ray, echocardiogram or CAT or MRI scans of the chest may show blood or fluid in the pericardium if there is any.

Cardiac tamponade is a medical emergency. Treatment is aimed at stabilizing the patient, removing the fluid by means of a needle with a suction syringe inserted through a surgical puncture, and correcting the underlying cause.

SEE ALSO *Heart, Pericarditis, Pericardium*

CARDIOMYOPATHY

Cardiomyopathy is a general term for diseases of the muscle of the heart (the myocardium). As cardiomyopathy progresses, the heart becomes weakened, enlarged and beats irregularly. In the terminal stages, the heart fails and the person may require a heart transplant. The condition may be caused by chronic diseases such as coronary atherosclerosis, excessive alcohol intake, infection due to viruses, or beriberi and other vitamin B deficiency disorders. In less common cases it is caused by the inflammation of heart muscle due to rheumatic fever or other immune disorders.

To begin with, the person notices a shortness of breath (dyspnea) and a decreasing ability to tolerate physical exertion. Chest pain, fainting (syncope), and palpitations (a sensation of feeling the heart beat) may be present. When the heart fails, swelling of the ankles and abdomen may occur.

Tests such as a chest x-ray, echocardiogram, coronary angiography, chest CAT or MRI scan will show the extent of the condition. Blood tests and a biopsy of the heart muscle may be needed to find the cause. Treatment is aimed at correcting the underlying cause. Medication will relieve the workload of the heart and stabilize the patient's condition. Rest and oxygen (given by mask) will reduce the workload of the damaged heart muscles. Hospitalization is advised if symptoms of severe heart failure are present. A heart transplant may be necessary if the patient is suitable and a donor is available.

SEE ALSO *Cardiac hypertrophy, Heart*

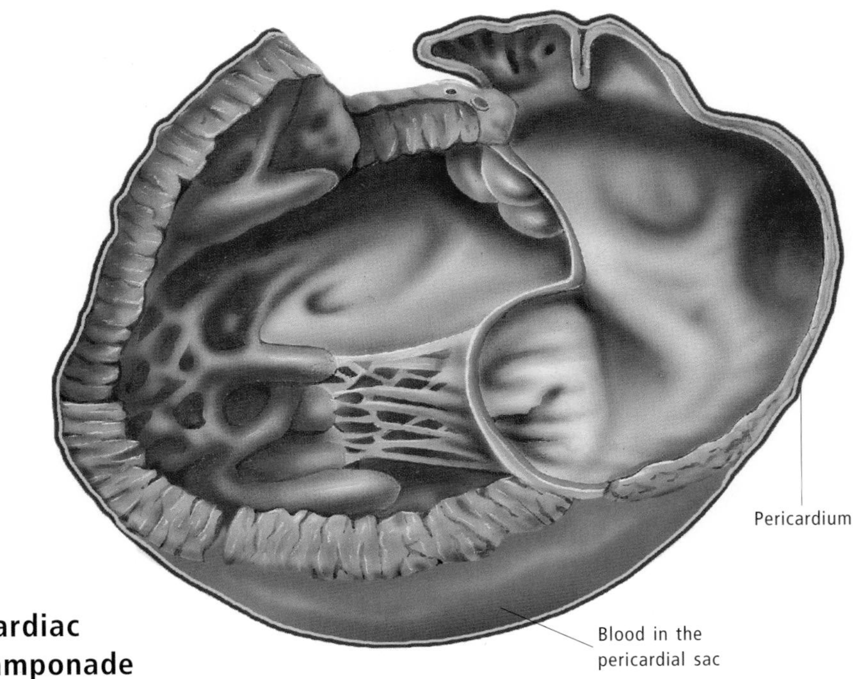

Cardiac tamponade

Cardiac tamponade is a condition in which blood or fluid accumulates in the area surrounding the heart (the pericardium). The fluid puts pressure on the heart and interferes with its ability to pump blood efficiently. This is a serious condition requiring urgent treatment.

CARDIOVASCULAR ISOTOPE SCANNING

Using a small amount of radioactive tracer injected into the circulation, an image of the blood flow through the chambers of the heart, or through the heart muscle, can be recorded with a highly sensitive scanning camera. This technique is used to define an area of heart muscle which does not receive adequate blood flow, as well as to measure cardiac performance.

SEE ALSO *Heart*

CAROTID ARTERY

The carotid arteries are the main arteries of the neck. The right and left carotid arteries are situated on either side of the neck and carry blood from the aorta to both sides of the neck, head and brain. Stenosis (narrowing) of the carotid artery caused by atherosclerosis can result in transient ischemic attacks (TIAs)—passing symptoms of a restricted blood flow to the brain—and stroke if the narrowing is severe.

SEE ALSO *Arteries, Cerebrovascular disorders, Stroke, Transient ischemic attack*

CARPAL TUNNEL SYNDROME

This is a syndrome resulting from compression of the median nerve in the carpal tunnel in the wrist. The carpal tunnel is a gap formed by the wrist bones (called the carpal bones) and the tough ligament that forms the roof of the tunnel (the flexor retinaculum). The passageway is rigid, so swelling of any of the tissues in this area can cause compression of the nerve, causing a numbness or pain in the wrist, hand, and fingers (except the little finger). The symptoms are usually worse at night.

Carpal tunnel syndrome is most commonly found in middle-aged women. It may occur during pregnancy, before the menstrual period, or during menopause. The condition is also found in diseases such as rheumatoid arthritis, acromegaly and hypothyroidism, or following injury or trauma to the area.

Treatment consists of splinting the wrist to immobilize it for several weeks. Anti-inflammatory drugs may help to improve the condition. If these fail, a physician may inject a corticosteroid drug into the ligament. In severe cases, surgical excising (resection) of the flexor retinaculum may be needed to relieve the pressure on the nerve.

SEE ALSO *Wrist*

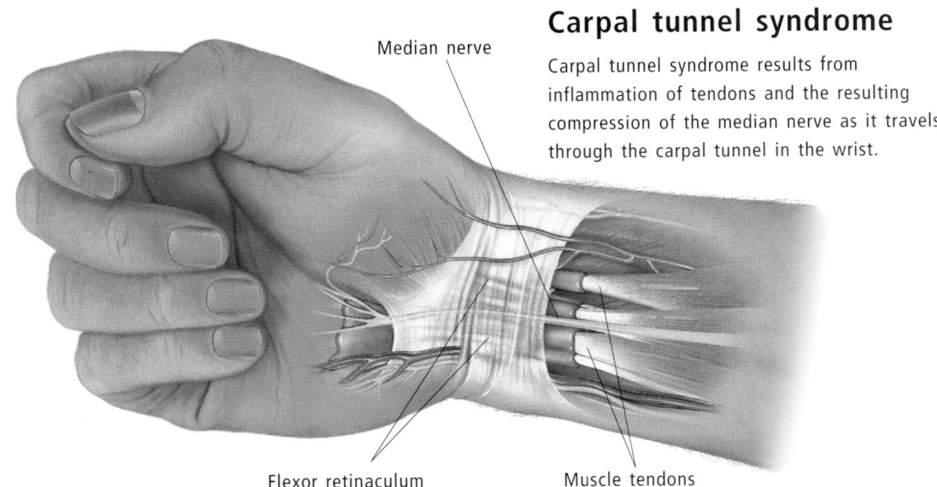

Carpal tunnel syndrome

Carpal tunnel syndrome results from inflammation of tendons and the resulting compression of the median nerve as it travels through the carpal tunnel in the wrist.

C

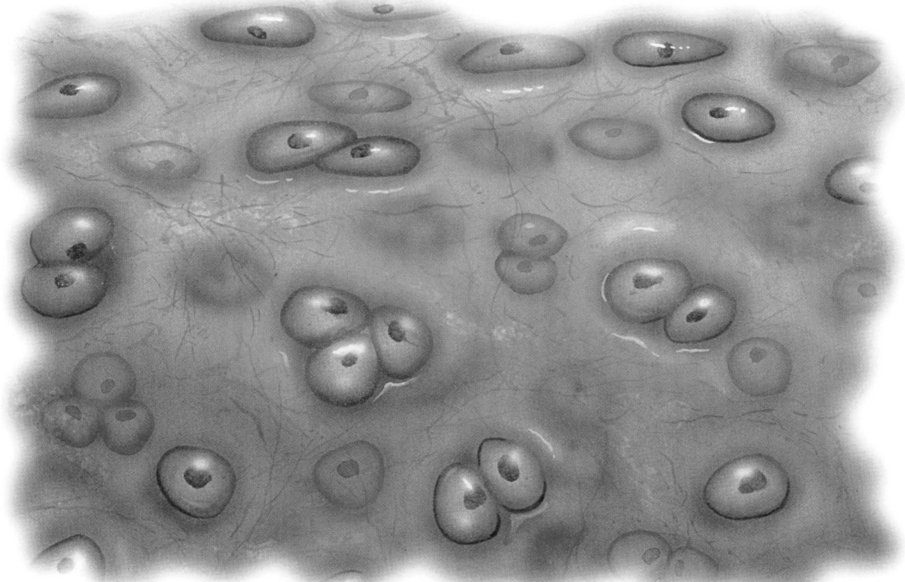

Elastic cartilage

Elastic cartilage is strong but supple cartilage containing proteins called elastin and collagen embedded in ground substance. Elastin gives it a distinctive yellow color. Elastic cartilage makes up the springy part of the outer ear, and also forms the epiglottis (the flap of tissue in the throat that prevents food from entering the airways).

Fibrocartilage

Fibrocartilage contains large amounts of collagen, making it both resilient and able to withstand compression. It is found between the bones of the spinal column, hip and pelvis.

Hyaline cartilage

Hyaline cartilage is a tissue which contains collagen fibers. It forms the skeleton in the embryo and remains as a thin layer on the end of bones which form joints. It also forms the end of the nose, and the stiff rings around the windpipe. It is found on the ends of the ribs and supports the larynx.

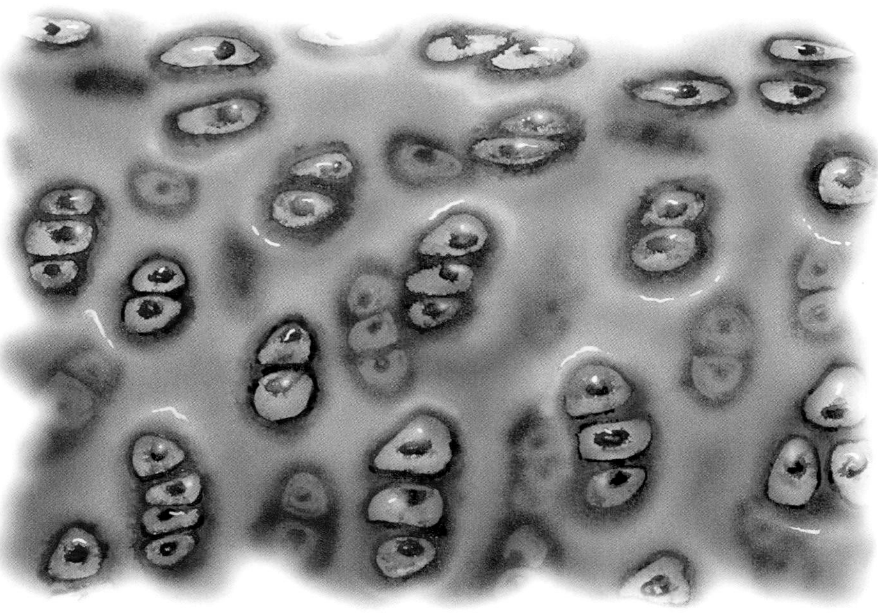

CARTILAGE

Cartilage is a tough, semi-transparent, elastic, flexible connective tissue consisting of cartilage cells (chondrocytes and chondroblasts) scattered through a glycoprotein material strengthened by collagen fibers. The exterior part of cartilage is covered by a dense fibrous membrane called the perichondrium. There are no nerves or blood vessels in cartilage, and when damaged it does not heal readily.

Cartilage has several functions. It covers the surfaces of joints, allowing bones to slide over one another, thus reducing friction and preventing damage; it also acts as a shock absorber. It forms part of the structure of the skeleton in the ribs, where it joins them to the breastbone (sternum). Cartilage is found in the tip of the nose, in the external ear, in the walls of the windpipe (trachea) and the voice box (larynx) where it provides support and maintains shape. In an embryo, the skeleton is formed of cartilage which is gradually replaced by bone as the embryo grows. Cartilage is known as elastic cartilage, fibrocartilage or hyaline cartilage, depending on its different physical properties.

A "torn cartilage" commonly refers to a disorder of the knee. A section of cartilage pad inside the knee joint known as the meniscus tears, and may move around in the knee joint, causing pain, swelling, and preventing weight being placed on that knee. A minor tear can be treated effectively with rest and a firm bandage around the knee. More serious tears require the surgical removal of part or all of the cartilage. This can often be done through an arthroscope—a tube that is passed into the knee joint, allowing visualization of the interior of the joint. Osteoarthritis later in life is a common complication of a torn meniscus.

Costochondritis (Tietze's syndrome) is a painful inflammation of the cartilage of the ribs (commonly the third or fourth rib). It causes pain in the chest wall, which may be mistaken for cardiac pain. The cause is often unknown, though it may be the result of trauma (such as a blow to the chest), unusual physical activity or an upper respiratory infection. It usually clears up in a short time with rest and mild anti-inflammatory medications such as aspirin, acetaminophen (paracetamol) or ibuprofen.

Chondrosarcoma is an uncommon cancer that may arise from cartilage associated with bone or outside of bone. The affected person notices a painful lump, usually in the long bones of the limb, pelvis or ribs. The diagnosis is confirmed with x-ray, CAT or MRI scans, biopsy and laboratory examination. The treatment is surgical removal of the tumor. If the tumor is slow growing and detected and treated early, the chances of survival are good.

SEE ALSO *Connective tissue, Joints, Knee, Osteoarthritis*

CAT SCAN

CAT or CT scan (computerized axial tomography) is an x-ray technique that can produce a three-dimensional image of a body part. The patient is placed inside a cylindrical-shaped scanner, around which an x-ray tube revolves. From multiple pictures taken from many angles, a computerized image is formed. The contrast resolution is much better than that displayed by conventional x-ray.

CAT scanning has revolutionized the diagnosis of many diseases. Tumors and other brain disorders can be delineated accurately, although a contrast fluid may occasionally still be required to outline the associated blood vessels. Lung cancers may be discovered earlier, making surgery more successful. The small coronary arteries of the heart can be checked closely for the degree of blockage when considering bypass surgery. In the abdomen, sometimes in conjunction with contrast solutions in the bowel or stomach, pathology or other abnormalities can be more accurately diagnosed without need of a major operation.

Bone disorders such as fractures (especially stress fractures of the small bones of the feet and the scaphoid bone in the wrist) can be checked more quickly and accurately than with conventional x-ray. Bone disease and spinal pathology such as slipped disks are also more clearly depicted. However, soft tissues such as muscles, ligaments and cartilages are more easily demonstrated by using the newer magnetic resonance imaging (MRI) machines.

SEE ALSO *Contrast x-ray, Magnetic resonance imaging, X-ray*

CAT-SCRATCH FEVER

Cat-scratch fever is a mild infectious disease, common in children, and caused by a small bacterium, *Bartonella henselae* (or CSD bacillus). The bacterium is carried on the claws or in the saliva of a healthy cat (usually a kitten) and transmitted by a scratch or bite.

Between three days and two weeks after the scratch or bite, a lump develops at the site of the injury and the person feels unwell with fatigue, headache and a mild fever. Lymph nodes draining the area swell, and although the lump soon disappears, the lymph nodes may remain swollen for several months. No specific treatment is necessary.

CATARACTS

Cataracts are cloudy spots which develop in the lens of the eye, sometimes due to injury but more often to age. As the cloudiness gradually increases, vision becomes hazy and a halo may be seen around bright objects. As the cataract grows, vision worsens to the point where it is severely restricted and surgery is needed. Cataracts are very common—about 20 percent of people over 60 will be subject to them—but they are not painful. During surgery the cloudy lens is removed and a plastic or silicone lens implant inserted. Certain types of cataract may respond to medication that dilates the pupil.

SEE ALSO *Eye*

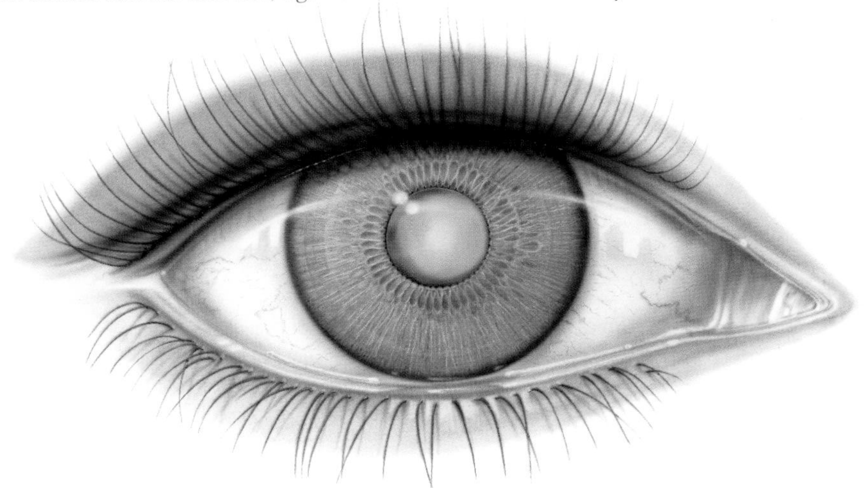

Cataracts

A cataract is a cloudiness (opacity) in the lens of the eye that produces a progressive, painless loss of vision. It causes the lens to look like a misty pane of glass. A cataract impairs vision by reducing the amount of light that reaches the lens of the eye and distorting the light being focused onto the retina. Cataracts are more common in older people because the lens becomes thicker, less resilient, and less transparent with ageing.

CATARRH

Catarrh is a term used for an inflamed mucous membrane, usually in the nose or throat, which causes a discharge of mucus. It occurs as a symptom of various upper respiratory tract infections such as hay fever, rhinitis, laryngitis, or the common cold.

SEE ALSO *Common cold, Hay fever, Laryngitis, Rhinitis*

CATATONIA

Catatonia, or catatonic motor behavior, is seen in people afflicted with catatonic schizophrenia. It is characterized by total immobility, holding unnatural postures for long periods, failure or refusal to speak, and sometimes by meaningless physical activity. Schizophrenia is treatable with drugs and psychotherapy, and about a third of cases achieve a lasting improvement.

SEE ALSO *Schizophrenia*

CATHETERIZATION

A catheter is a flexible, hollow tube that is introduced into a cavity through a narrow opening, in order to discharge the fluid in the cavity or to unblock a vessel. It may be made of glass, metal, hard or soft rubber, rubberized silk, or plastic. A catheter may be inserted into the bladder temporarily during an operation, or permanently after a brain or spinal injury to relieve an underactive or overactive bladder, or because of paralysis.

A catheter may also be inserted into an artery or vein or directly into the heart in order to inject drugs, to measure blood flow or pressure, to use in the diagnosis of congenital heart disease, to explore narrow passages, or to pass electrodes into the heart so that the heartbeat can be restored or made regular.

SEE ALSO *Bladder, Heart*

CELIAC DISEASE

Celiac disease, also known as nontropical sprue, is a true allergic reaction to gluten in the diet. This hypersensitivity results in the destruction of the food-absorbing surface of the jejunum in the small intestine; only rarely is the cecum involved. Gluten is a protein found in many grains, especially wheat, rye, barley and oats. Normally the immune system cells, known as T lymphocytes, protect the body against invaders, but in celiac disease they attack gluten, thus inflaming the small intestine lining and resulting in inefficient absorption of nutrients.

Celiac disease is considered to be inherited, though the actual cause is not known. It is rare in non-Caucasians but affects 1 in 1,500 to 2,000 Caucasians, being particularly common in people of western Irish descent, of whom it affects around 1 in 300. About half of those suffering from the disease are diagnosed during childhood. It usually manifests itself between the ages of 6 and 21 months, often following an infection. Symptoms in children are diarrhea, failure to thrive (stunted growth) and weight loss. Teenagers can suffer delayed puberty and loss of some hair (alopecia areata). In adults, symptoms include flatulence, chronic diarrhea (which does not respond to treatment), weight-loss and chronic fatigue. Vitamin deficiency can also result and produce symptoms including scaly skin, bruising, blood in the urine, tingling and numbness, muscle spasms and bone pain. It is usually diagnosed through screening blood tests. Osteoporosis is a serious illness which often occurs in people with celiac disease and symptoms can include night-time bone pain. Five percent of adults with celiac disease will also have anemia, and lactose intolerance is a common feature of celiac disease at all ages.

Once the disease is diagnosed, gluten must be totally eliminated from the diet. This is not easy as gluten is found in a surprising number of prepared foods, including canned foods, peanut butter, dips, luncheon meats, candy and yoghurt, among others. It is important to read the labels on all prepared foods to ensure they do not contain gluten. The diet needs to be under the supervision of a specialist who will suggest certain strategies and there are support groups offering valuable resources, and cookbooks that feature gluten-free products. In young babies, breast feeding and postponing the introduction of foods containing gluten can offer some protection.

Celiac disease can go into spontaneous remission in children at about the age of five years and in others, strict adherence to the diet can heal the intestine. However, for most people it will be necessary to stay on a gluten-free diet for the rest of their lives.

SEE ALSO *Anemia, Baldness, Intestines, Osteoporosis, Sprue*

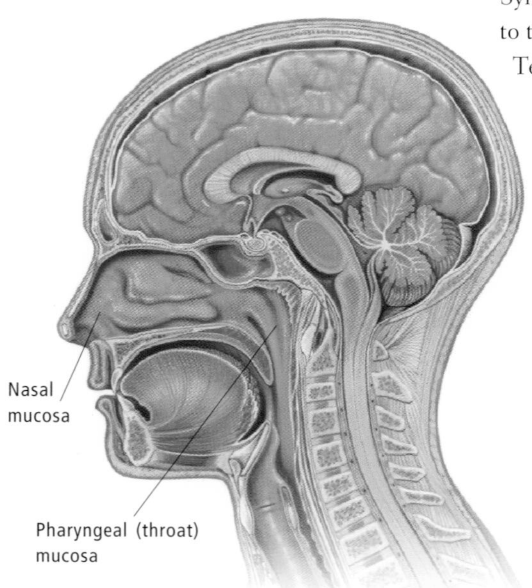

Catarrh

Catarrh is a term used to describe inflammation of the mucous membranes of the nose or throat, leading to an increased discharge of mucus (runny nose, mucus in the throat).

CELLS

Cells are the basic structural units that make up all living organisms. Cells are organized into tissues, and tissues into organs. Typical cells are surrounded by a cell membrane. Within the cell membrane lies the cell's cytoplasm, which is a fluid containing many important structural units called organelles. Some organelles are concerned with the manufacture of protein (rough endoplasmic reticulum), the generation of energy (mitochondria), the packaging of manufactured products (Golgi apparatus) and the process of cell division (centrioles). The control of the cell's function is directed by the nucleus, which contains genetic information in the form of DNA. In larger and more complex cells, the nucleus is separate from the cytoplasm.

Cell division

Many (but not all) types of cells undergo a process called mitosis, or cell division, by which a mother cell divides into two daughter cells. This is particularly well seen in the cells lining the gut and the skin. In these sites, cells are continually being shed and must therefore be replaced. When cells are dividing continuously, they pass through a series of stages called the cell cycle. This cycle consists of four individual stages: a growth stage (G1), a synthetic stage (S), another growth stage (G2) and a cell division stage (M).

When cell division runs out of control and the daughter cells invade other tissues, a cancer results. Cancers usually arise in sites where cell division is already occurring rapidly, such as the skin, gut and airway lining. Most cells are formed through this process of cell division.

In sexual reproduction, sex cells (the egg and sperm) are produced by a different type of cell division. This process is called meiosis. At fertilization, the sperm and egg unite (fuse) to form a zygote.

Specialized cells

Many cells are specialized to perform particular functions. For example, blood is made up of two broad types of cells (red and white blood cells) and specialized cell fragments called platelets.

Red blood cells develop in the red bone marrow of bones such as the sternum and hip. During their development, red blood cells lose their nucleus and their cytoplasm becomes filled with a protein called hemoglobin, which carries oxygen and carbon dioxide.

White blood cells can be of several types. Granulocytes are so called because their cytoplasm contains granules. Another type of white blood cell is the agranulocyte, which has no granule in its cytoplasm.

Agranulocytes include lymphocytes and monocytes. Lymphocytes are further divided into T and B types. T lymphocytes (T cells) are involved in the so-called cell-mediated immune response, which is a defence reaction of the body against viruses and cancer cells. B lymphocytes (B cells) are involved in the humoral immune response, which is directed mainly against bacteria.

Another type of defense cell, which travels through the blood, but also can enter and move through the tissue outside the blood stream is the macrophage (phagocytic or scavenger cells). These cells have the ability to engulf foreign material (bacteria, inorganic foreign bodies) and either destroy the bacteria or prevent escape of the invaders to the rest of the body.

Other specialized types of cells include nerve cells (neurons), which are electrically active and transmit information to other

Celiac disease

Celiac disease is an inherited disorder in which an allergic intolerance to gluten in the diet causes changes in the small intestine. This results in difficulties in the absorption of food.

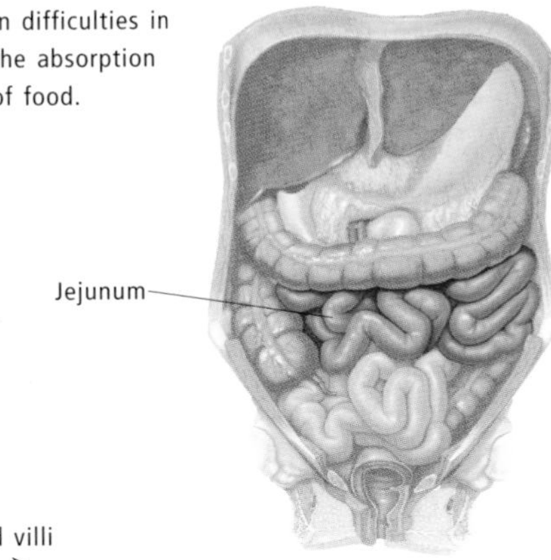

Villi

In the small intestine, tiny, finger-like projections, known as villi, stand out from the lining to increase the surface area available for absorption of nutrients. In celiac disease, the villi in the jejunum in the small intestine are flattened, making it harder for the nutrients in food to be absorbed.

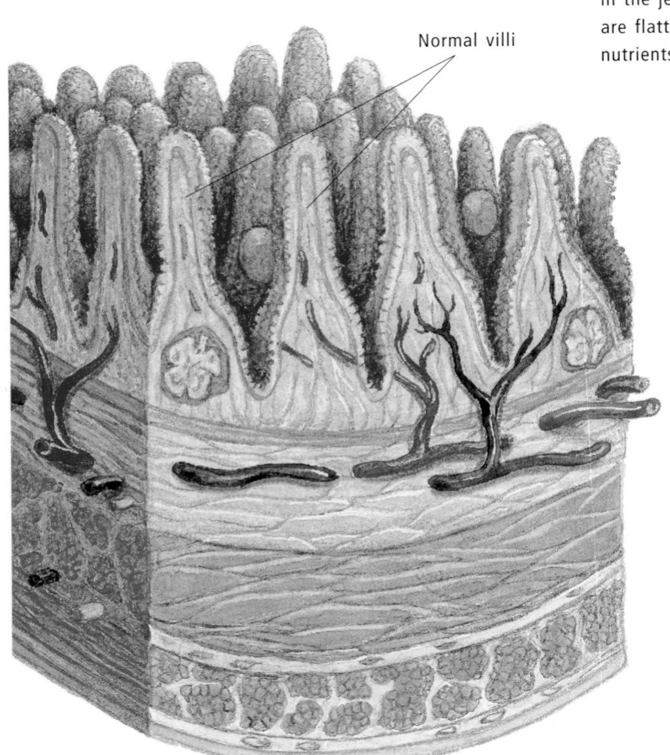

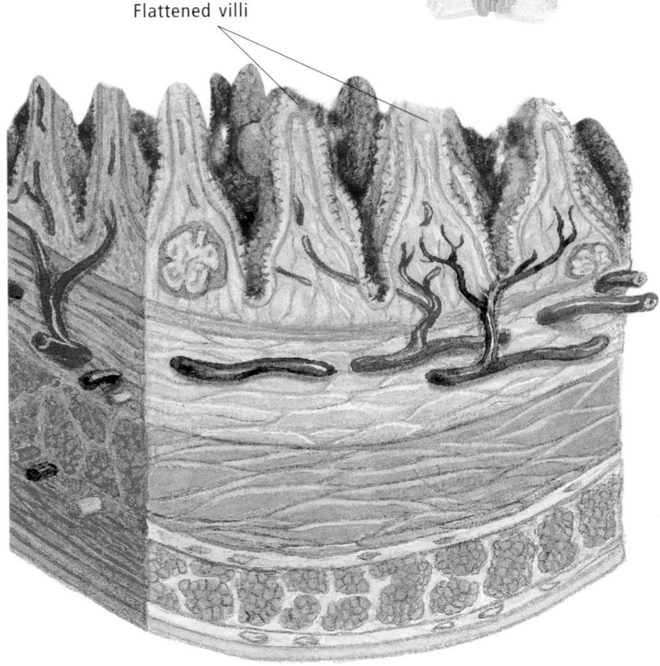

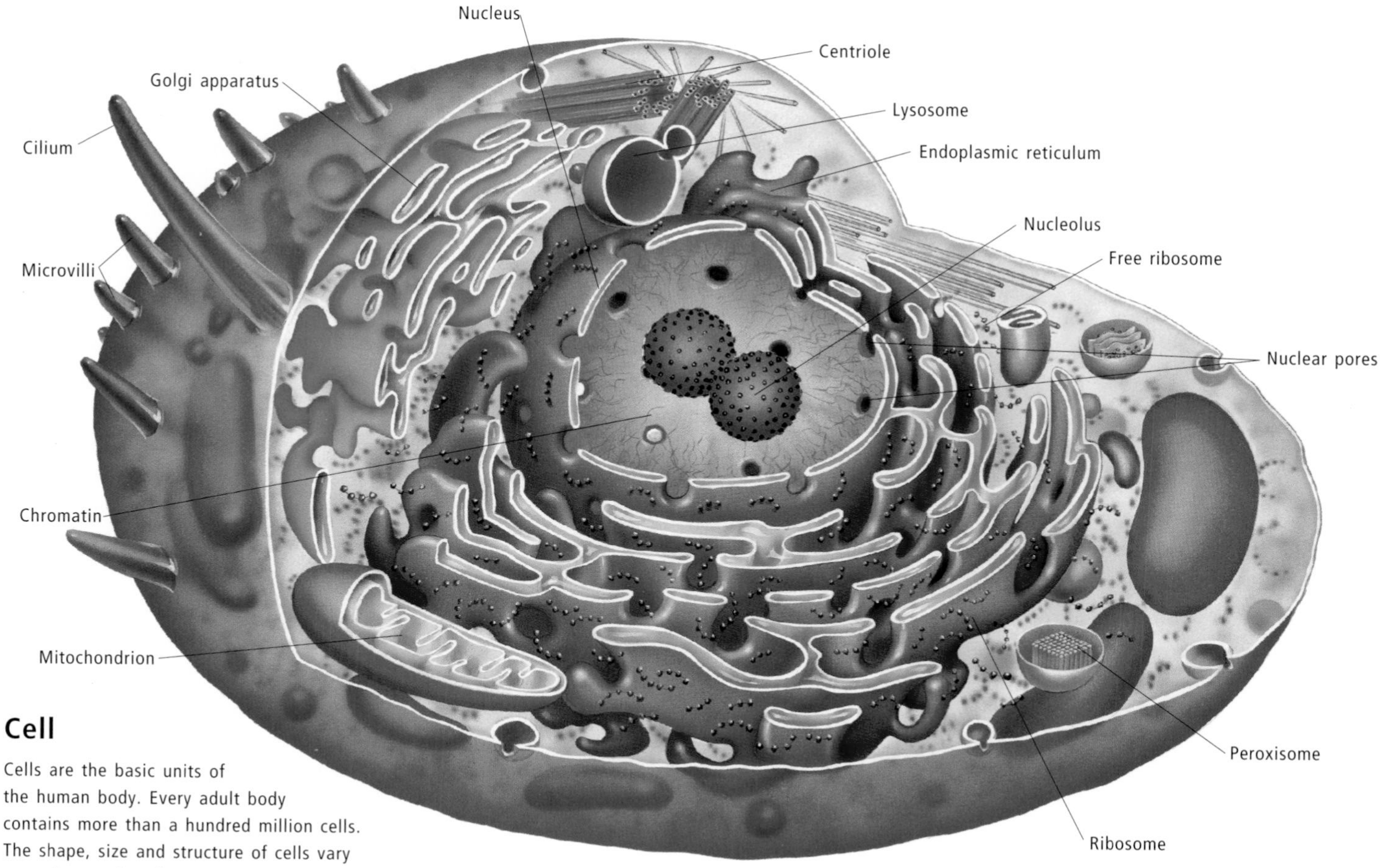

Cell

Cells are the basic units of the human body. Every adult body contains more than a hundred million cells. The shape, size and structure of cells vary according to their functions within the body.

nerve cells across special junctions called synapses. Another type of electrically active cell is the muscle cell, which contracts in response to nervous or hormonal stimulus.

Skin cells are also highly specific. They are designed to be progressively shed, because they are continuously exposed to the damaging effects of the harsh external environment with its ultraviolet radiation, physical wear and tear, extremes of temperature and low humidity. To replace shed cells, the lower layer of the skin contains cells that divide rapidly.

SEE ALSO *Blood, DNA, Skin, Tissues*

CELLULITE

Cellulite is a popular (non-medical) term for the fatty tissue that puckers and dimples just beneath the skin. The dimpling indicates that fat cells are not being strongly supported by the connective framework of the adipose (fatty) tissue. Weight reduction may not improve the appearance of cellulite and in some cases cosmetic surgery is effective.

SEE ALSO *Cosmetic surgery*

CELLULITIS

Cellulitis is a bacterial (usually streptococcal) infection of the skin and underlying tissues. Cellulitis can arise after dermatitis, ulcers, injury or animal bites. The symptoms are redness, swelling and tenderness of the skin, swollen lymph nodes which may be accompanied by fever, chills and rapid heartbeat. Medical assistance should be sought.

SEE ALSO *Streptococcal infections*

CEREBELLUM

The cerebellum (Latin for "little brain") is a cauliflower-shaped structure that lies at the back of the brain and is important in the control of movement. It coordinates movement by regulating the timing, direction and force of muscle contractions, and it regulates muscle activity in order to maintain balance and posture.

SEE ALSO *Brain*

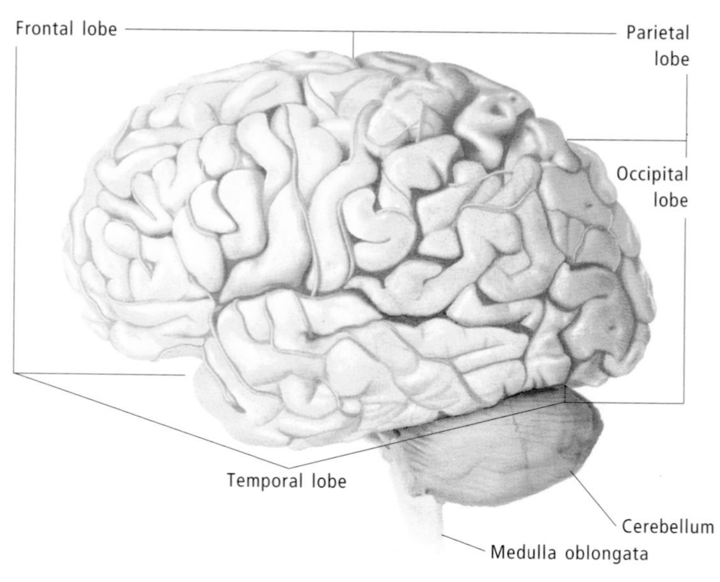

Cerebellum

The cerebellum is the part of the brain that coordinates the movements of the body and helps to maintain balance. It is situated at the back of the skull, beneath the cerebrum (largest part of the brain).

C

CEREBRAL ARTERIES

The cerebral arteries are blood vessels in the head that transport blood (containing oxygen and other nutrients) to the cells of the hemispheres of the brain. Three cerebral arteries on each side arise near the base of the brain and give branches to deep structures before supplying the cerebral cortex.

SEE ALSO *Brain, Cerebral cortex*

CEREBRAL CORTEX

The cerebral cortex in the human brain is a highly folded sheet of nerve cells (neurons) that forms the outer surface of the hemispheres of the brain. It enables a person to store memories, think, make decisions, speak and carry out voluntary movements, and to consciously perceive and understand sensations, such as vision, hearing and touch.

SEE ALSO *Brain, Neurons*

CEREBRAL HEMORRHAGE

A cerebral hemorrhage is a form of stroke which occurs when a blood vessel in the brain suddenly ruptures, releasing blood into the brain. Within a few minutes the patient will experience decreased consciousness, headache and vomiting. Other symptoms depend on which part of the brain is affected.

SEE ALSO *Brain, Stroke*

Cerebral arteries

The brain is supplied by a network of arteries (cerebral arteries). The carotid arteries supply the front and middle of the brain; the vertebral and basilar arteries supply the back of the brain, cerebellum and brain stem. The vertebral arteries join up at the back of the head and become the basilar artery. The three cerebral arteries are linked by communicating arteries to form the circle of Willis.

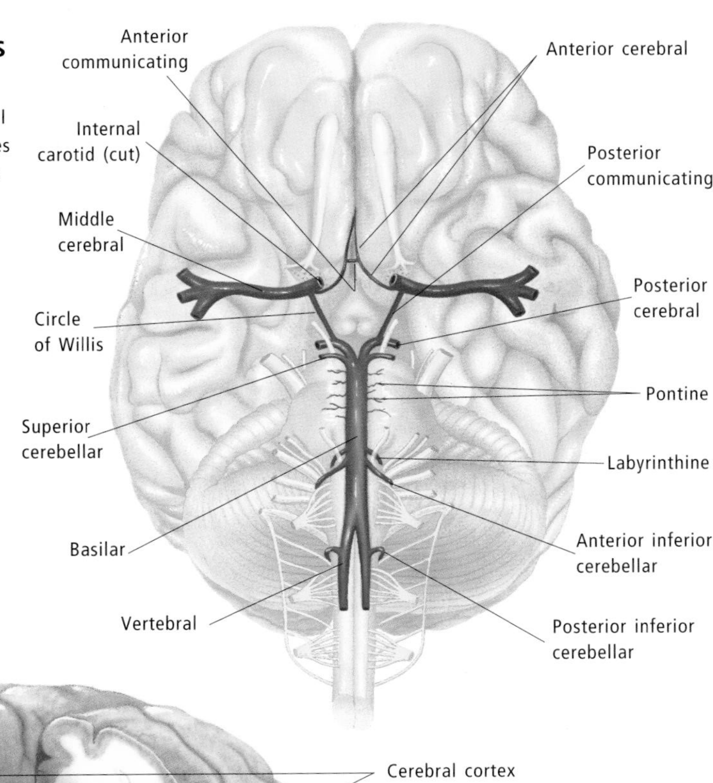

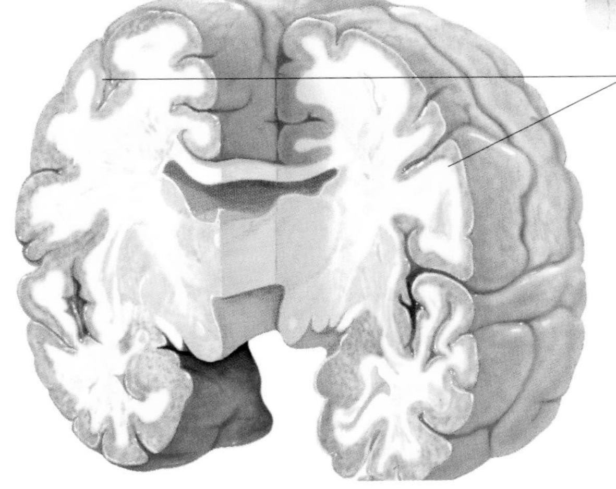

Cerebral cortex

This is the outer layer of the brain; it is made up of a vast network of nerve cells. Most messages from the brain start in the cerebral cortex, and this is where the higher functions of the brain, such as thinking, talking, seeing and hearing occur.

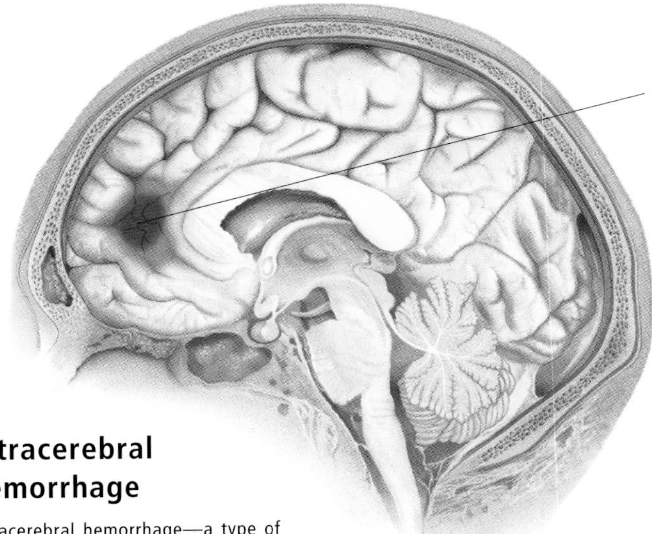

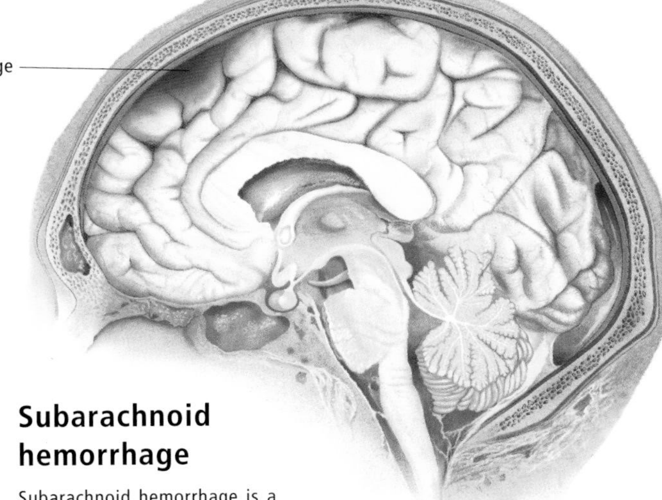

Intracerebral hemorrhage

Intracerebral hemorrhage—a type of stroke—is caused by bleeding inside the brain. It is the most dangerous type of stroke because the hemorrhage is usually large. The symptoms begin abruptly with a headache, followed by steadily worsening neurological problems, such as weakness, paralysis, loss of speech or vision. Loss of consciousness and seizures are common.

Subarachnoid hemorrhage

Subarachnoid hemorrhage is a sudden bleed into the space between the brain and its covering (meninges). The usual cause is a weak blood vessel that suddenly ruptures. The rupture usually produces a sudden, severe headache followed by a loss of consciousness. Surgery is usually necessary to repair the damaged vessel.

C

Cervical rib

Occasionally, a small extra rib is formed, attaching to the seventh cervical vertebra in the neck. This so-called cervical rib can compress the nerves in the neck, causing tingling, pain, weakness or numbness on the affected side of the neck and arm.

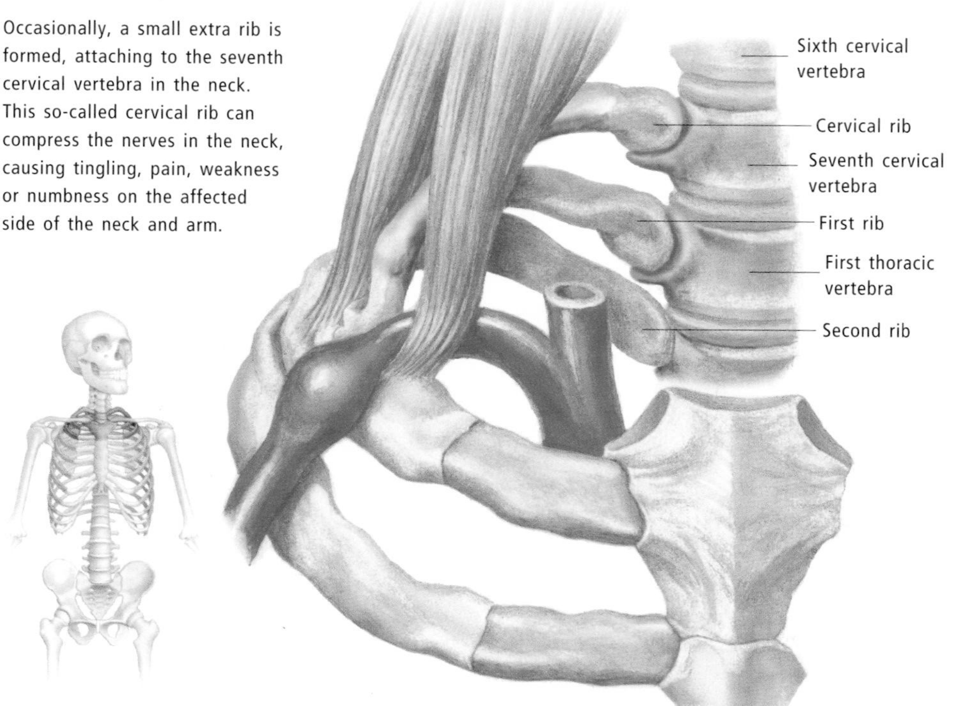

CEREBRAL PALSY

Cerebral palsy is a general term used to describe a group of disorders in which there is faulty development or damage to motor areas in the brain, which impair the brain's ability to adequately control movement and posture. The damage may result from disease, faulty growth, or injury, which may occur before, during, or shortly after birth. Rubella (German measles) in pregnancy, premature birth and brain damage due to a difficult delivery are common causes. Often, the cause is never found. The condition is never inherited.

The symptoms differ from one person to the next. Someone with cerebral palsy may have difficulty with fine motor tasks, have trouble maintaining balance and walking, or be affected by involuntary movements such as uncontrollable writhing motion of the hands, or drooling. In some persons, there is also intellectual disability, learning difficulties, slow growth, seizures, and hearing and vision problems. Usually, the condition is not apparent until the child is between one and two years old.

There is no cure for cerebral palsy. Treatment is aimed at helping affected people make best use of their abilities and may include physical therapy, speech therapy, and psychological support. Drugs to help control seizures and muscle spasms, special braces to compensate for muscle imbalance, and other mechanical aids may be required. The earlier treatment begins, the better a child will do. Many people with cerebral palsy can enjoy near-normal lives if their problems are properly managed.

CEREBROVASCULAR ACCIDENTS

Cerebrovascular accidents (strokes) are caused by damage to the arteries which supply oxygenated blood to the brain and are characterized by a sudden loss of neurological function.

There are two main types of cerebrovascular accident. The first involves occlusion or blockage of an artery, resulting in a lack of oxygen (ischemia) and consequent death (infarction) of the brain tissue supplied by that artery. Occlusion of an artery results from either a thickening of the arterial wall (arteriosclerosis) or, more commonly, from blockage by a floating body. The functional loss experienced by the patient will depend on which region of the brain is damaged. Sometimes the blockage is only temporary and the effects pass after a few minutes or hours; the patient is said to have suffered a transient ischemic attack (TIA).

The second and more common type of cerebrovascular disorder involves a sudden rupture (hemorrhage) of one of the brain's arteries, causing large quantities of blood to accumulate in the brain tissue (cerebral hemorrhage) or in the space surrounding the brain (subarachnoid hemorrhage). This leads to a sudden increase in pressure within the skull, causing severe headache, decreased consciousness and vomiting. Other signs, which vary in their severity, depend on the specific location of the rupture.

SEE ALSO *Brain, Cerebral hemorrhage, Ischemia, Stroke, Subarachnoid hemorrhage, Transient ischemic attack*

CERVICAL RIB SYNDROME

Some people are born with a small extra rib known as a cervical rib, which is an appendage to the seventh cervical vertebra in the neck. It generally causes no problems, but in some cases it can compress the nerves in the neck, causing pain, numbness and tingling in the neck, shoulders, arms and hands and weakness in the arms and fingers. If these symptoms occur, the rib should be surgically removed. The condition is sometimes called thoracic outlet obstruction syndrome. A similar disorder may be caused by an injury to the neck (often while someone is unconscious or asleep). That disorder can be treated with physical therapy.

SEE ALSO *Neck, Vertebrae*

CERVIX

The cervix is the lower part of the uterus. It is situated between the body of the uterus and the vagina. It has a centrally placed cervical canal, which leads into the cavity of the uterine body at one end and opens to the vagina at the other.

Sperm must pass through the cervix on their way to the uterine body, and menstrual blood passes down the cervix to the external environment. In labor, the cervix must dilate as much as 4 inches (10 centimeters) during the passage of the baby's head down the birth canal. The sensitive surface tissue of the cervix is in contact with the external environment, especially during sexual intercourse when the penis may introduce viruses and bacteria to the vagina. Two viruses of particular concern are the human papilloma virus (HPV) and the herpes simplex type II virus. HPV may cause warts to grow on the vaginal and cervical tissue. Herpes simplex type II is believed to cause cervical cancer (carcinoma), by inducing changes in the cells of the cervix.

Cervical cancer is the second most common cancer affecting women, accounting for almost 10 percent of cancers in females in developed countries. The incidence of the disease is more common in those women who have frequent intercourse with many different partners and is also more common in women who have given birth. During the early stages the cancer may be confined to the cervical tissue and can be easily removed by cutting out a cone-shaped block of tissue. For this reason early detection, by regular use of the Papanicolou ("Pap") smear test, is very important.

Cervical polyps are small tear-shaped structures that protrude through the vaginal opening of the cervical canal. They are composed of tissue derived from the inner lining of the cervical canal. They can cause bleeding and may be removed surgically.

Colposcopy is the medical term for the examination of the upper vagina and cervical opening. Colposcopy is used principally for diagnosis, whereby samples of cervical tissue and fluid are taken for further examination.

Cervical incompetence is a condition where the fetus is in danger of being lost during pregnancy because the cervix is not tight enough to hold the fetus and its membranes inside the uterus. This problem is more common in women who have had many surgical terminations of pregnancy (abortions). Damage to the cervix during abortions may stretch or tear the fibers that help to hold the cervix closed.

In some women, the fluid of the cervix (cervical mucus) may be resistant to the penetration of sperm cells. This may be because the mucus is too thick or because it contains antibodies (biological defence chemicals), which bind to the sperm and interfere with their movement or survival. This will lead to infertility (an inability to conceive a child) and may require sperm to be artificially introduced higher up.

SEE ALSO *Miscarriage, Pap smear, Reproductive systems*

CHALAZION

A chalazion (also known as a meibomian or tarsal cyst) is a small cyst that forms when a meibomian gland (a gland which secretes oils that lubricate the eyelids) becomes blocked with oil secretion. It is harmless, but can be surgically removed if it becomes painful or unsightly.

SEE ALSO *Eyelids*

CHANCROID

Chancroid, or soft chancre, is a sexually transmitted disease (STD) most common in tropical regions. Shallow painful ulcers appear in the infected areas, usually the genitals, three to five days after exposure through sexual contact. They are caused by the bacterium *Haemophilus ducreyi* and can be mistaken for the first symptoms of syphilis, in which similar but hard and painless chancres appear. In chancroid, localized swelling and inflammation of lymph glands follow the appearance of ulcers. The disease is often associated with HIV transmission.

Chancroid can be treated successfully with sulfonamides, or the antibiotics azithromycin and erythromycin, although the ulcers may leave scars.

SEE ALSO *Sexually transmitted diseases, Syphilis*

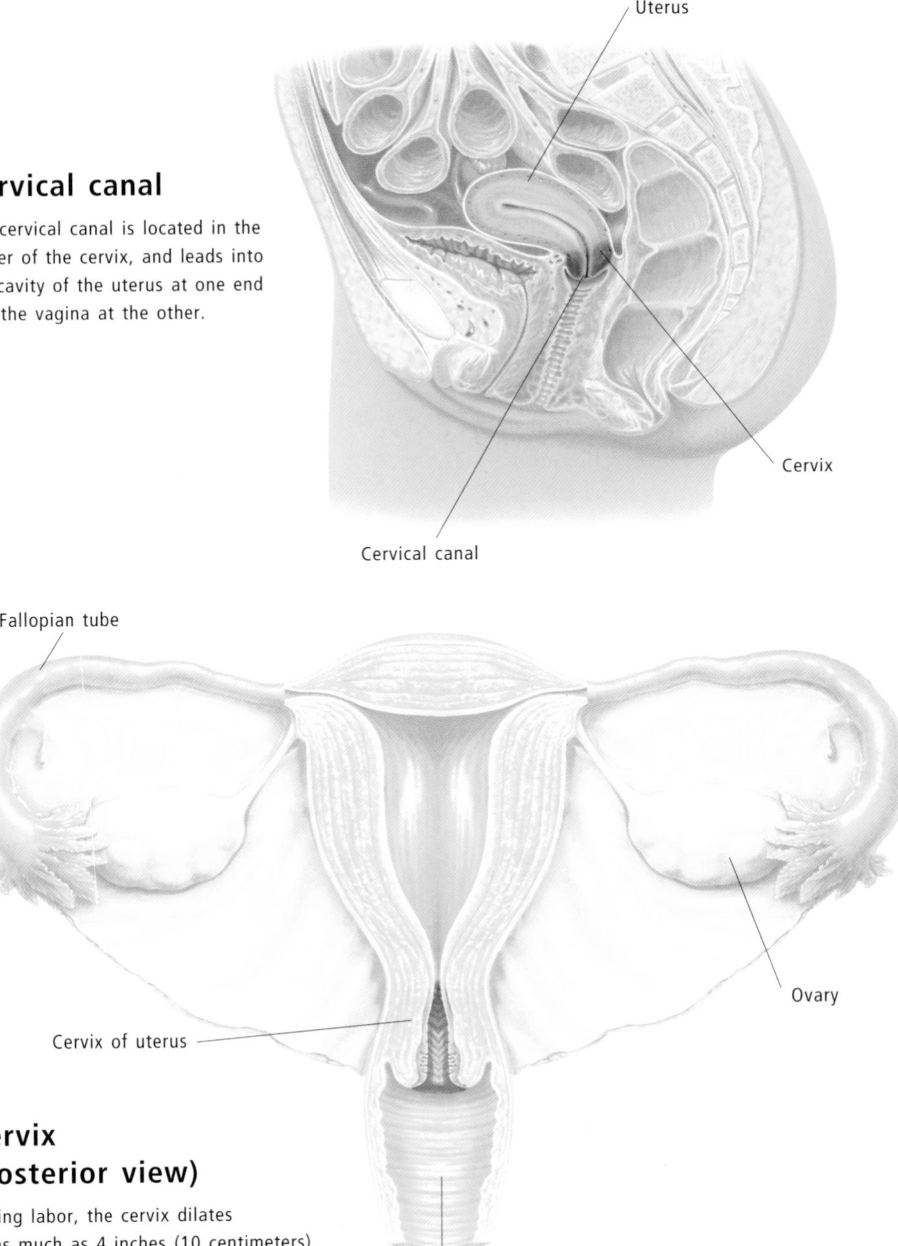

Cervical canal

The cervical canal is located in the center of the cervix, and leads into the cavity of the uterus at one end and the vagina at the other.

Cervix (posterior view)

During labor, the cervix dilates to as much as 4 inches (10 centimeters) to allow the baby's head to pass down the cervical canal.

C

CHEMOTHERAPY

Chemotherapy is the use of chemicals to kill cancer cells. There are many different anti-cancer drugs; some are given by mouth and some are injected. There is no drug yet available which is 100 percent effective in killing cancer cells, nor is there one which does not potentially harm healthy cells.

Research is constant, and treatment methods are improving to minimize the harmful effects. Chemotherapy may be given over a brief period, or may extend over several years; it can be given in hospital, outpatient clinics, at a doctor's rooms or even at home. There are many different courses of treatment and all are being improved through sharing scientific knowledge and by international trials of new drugs and procedures.

The drugs used in chemotherapy are basically poisons, some of which developed out of research into chemical warfare. Standard combinations, or cocktails, of drugs have been set for treating most forms of cancer. After starting treatment and observing the patient's response, the combinations and doses are adjusted. This has made chemotherapy less unpleasant and more effective as cancer treatment skills improve.

Hormone therapy can be used to restrict the growth of certain cancers. Immunotherapy uses substances such as interferon to attack specific tumors. Combination therapy uses surgery or radiation as well as chemotherapy to fight cancer: surgery or radiation to treat the cancer directly, chemotherapy to wipe out cancer cells that have spread to other parts of the body.

Anti-cancer drugs attack all fast-dividing cells, so that normal, healthy fast-dividing cells are killed along with the cancer cells. Most of the side effects are due to the killing of healthy cells. The major side effects of chemotherapy include the following.

Nausea and vomiting are common, but are now less severe than in the past since drug doses are constantly adjusted to a patient's responses. Vomiting can often be controlled with drugs called anti-emetics. Sometimes eating small quantities at a time and avoiding any foods which cause upset can help.

Hair loss is also common, and some cancer patients choose to shave their heads before hair loss occurs, or wear a wig. Hair usually grows back after chemotherapy.

Low blood cell count (cytopenia) does not always need treatment but, if it is thought necessary, red blood cell deficiencies can be corrected by transfusion, and the production of white blood cells can be stimulated if needed.

Damage to liver and kidneys can be caused by anti-cancer drugs and is minimized by adjustment of dosages.

Mouth ulcers and digestive disorders occur because the cells of the mucous membranes which line the mouth and the digestive tract are fast-dividing cells. Painful mouth ulcers or diarrhea can occur during treatment and can cause nutritional deficiencies when patients do not eat or the food is not properly absorbed.

Infertility and fetal abnormalities can be caused by chemotherapy, so birth control is essential while taking the drugs. Some treatments can cause permanent infertility in men and women.

Chemotherapy today involves careful monitoring of patients, including regular blood tests. As a result, problems are quickly detected and drug doses can be adjusted and other treatments given to minimize any side effects and discomfort. Success in this has meant many people now have chemotherapy as outpatients, and do not require a stay in hospital.

SEE ALSO *Cancer, Radiation therapy*

CHEST X-RAY

Early detection and diagnosis of lung disease relies initially on chest imaging by x-ray. This will also reveal an outline of the heart and major blood vessels, but as x-rays pass easily through soft tissues they show only gross abnormalities and enlargements of these organs. Conditions such as pneumonia, tumors of the lung, and emphysema can be detected, and where abnormalities are suspected, the x-ray results will help physicians to decide which further examinations and tests will be needed. Identification of a condition is increased by the use of a contrast medium such as iodine.

X-ray examinations expose subjects to very low dosages of radiation. In some countries, levels are limited to the equivalent of the amount received from natural exposure to sunlight and radio waves over six months.

SEE ALSO *X-ray*

CHICKENPOX

Chickenpox (varicella) is a highly contagious, airborne viral disease. It is most common among school-age children, though it can occur at any age, and one attack usually protects a person for life, unless it is very mild.

The main symptom, which usually appears 13–17 days after contact, is a rash which is at first apparent on the trunk and then spreads over the body. This rash has three stages: little red itchy bumps, followed by a clear blister on each bump and finally crusts or scabs. The infection lasts until all bumps have crusted, which takes seven to ten days from when the rash first appears. Headache and cold symptoms can also accompany chickenpox but these usually occur before the rash appears.

Treatment revolves around relieving the itching, as scratching of the scabs can lead to life-long scarring. A lukewarm bath with cornflour or an oatmeal preparation added can provide relief. Calamine lotion can also be applied and the fingernails should be kept very short. Some children may need antihistamines, but these should only be taken on medical advice. Acetaminophen (paracetamol) may reduce fever, but aspirin must never be given as it can lead to the complication of Reye's syndrome.

Anyone who is pregnant, has a chronic illness or weak immune system should seek medical advice if they have been in contact with someone with chickenpox. After chicken pox clears, the virus which causes the disease may lie dormant and later cause shingles.

SEE ALSO *Infections, Reye's syndrome, Shingles*

CHILBLAIN

Chilblain is an inflammation of the skin, usually occurring on the ears, face, toes or fingers. The inflammation is due to cold, damp weather that can damage small blood vessels and nerves in the skin. The condition causes pain, itching, swelling, redness, and sometimes blistering and ulceration of the skin. People with poor circulation are more susceptible to chilblains. Treatment is to gently warm the affected areas and provide warm, protective clothing.

Chickenpox areas

Chickenpox is a contagious viral illness that produces a characteristic itchy rash. The trunk is usually affected first (and most severely), and spots then spread to the arms, face, and legs.

CHILD ABUSE

Child abuse is the non-accidental harming of a child by an adult. This can be in one of four ways: physically, when the child's body is injured; emotionally, when behavior towards the child damages or destroys self-esteem; through neglect of the child's welfare and health; and through sexual abuse.

The statistics on child abuse are alarming. Despite the fact that child abuse is almost universally condemned by criminal statutes, millions of children throughout the world are abused and neglected each year, with thousands dying. Child abuse could have increased in recent times, or it could simply be that more cases are being reported; even so, it is believed that it is generally considerably under-reported. Child abuse occurs across all social and economic strata. One of the first countries to adopt laws to protect children was the USA where the state of New York legislated for their protection in 1875. National laws to protect children from cruelty were passed in Great Britain in 1884, establishing the National Society for the Prevention of Cruelty to Children.

Child abuse, in all its forms, is widespread. In many cases it is not detected until the child reaches adulthood and becomes an abusing parent. Without proper treatment, abused children can be damaged for life. There are a number of signs that may indicate a child is being abused, including: physical signs such as bruises, burns, broken bones or damaged organs; poor self-image; inability to trust other people; aggressive, disruptive behavior; anger; self-destructive or abusive behavior, including suicide; withdrawal; fear of new activities or relationships; school problems; symptoms of depression; nightmares; and drug and alcohol abuse.

Abusers have not necessarily been abused themselves; they can be grandparents, older siblings, other relatives, neighbors, teachers, church or sporting group leaders, child care workers or baby-sitters. Those who abuse children often do not see themselves as abusers. Some even consider that what they were doing was for the child's benefit—parents especially often say this.

Child abuse occurs for many reasons: inadequacies in the adult, which may be stress- or tension- related (an inability to cope with the caring of their children together with complications in their own lives); too high expectations often coupled with a misunderstanding of the mental and physical development of the child; a belief in physical punishment as a method of discipline; sexual attraction to children; pedophilia (knowingly seeking to perform sexual acts with children for self gratification); and being abused themselves as children. Children who are disabled are considered to be at greater risk. Babies, because they are unable to communicate on an adult level, can be abused—babies can suffer severe damage as a result of being shaken. Shaking a baby can stretch the skull and move the brain so that blood vessels between the brain and skull shear off, bleed, swell and eventually atrophy, causing damage and even leading to death.

People in the community have a moral duty to report any serious suspicions they have to the appropriate authority. Managing child abuse involves a multi-disciplinary team working with the family, identifying the causes and helping the family to deal with the issues. If a parent suspects their child is being abused it is important for them to realize that it is never too late to protect their child. Children need to be valued, spoken to respectfully, listened to, taken seriously, and made to feel safe.

Chickenpox

The chickenpox rash usually begins as small flat spots, which then become raised and form fluid-filled blisters. These then crust over to form scabs. The virus is contagious until all spots have crusted over.

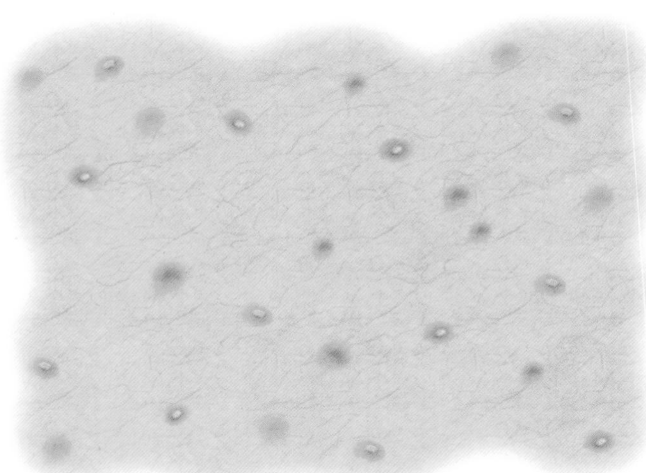

Umbilical cord
Head engaged in pelvis
Pubic symphysis of pelvis
Cervix
Vagina
Cervical canal
Sacrum
Placenta

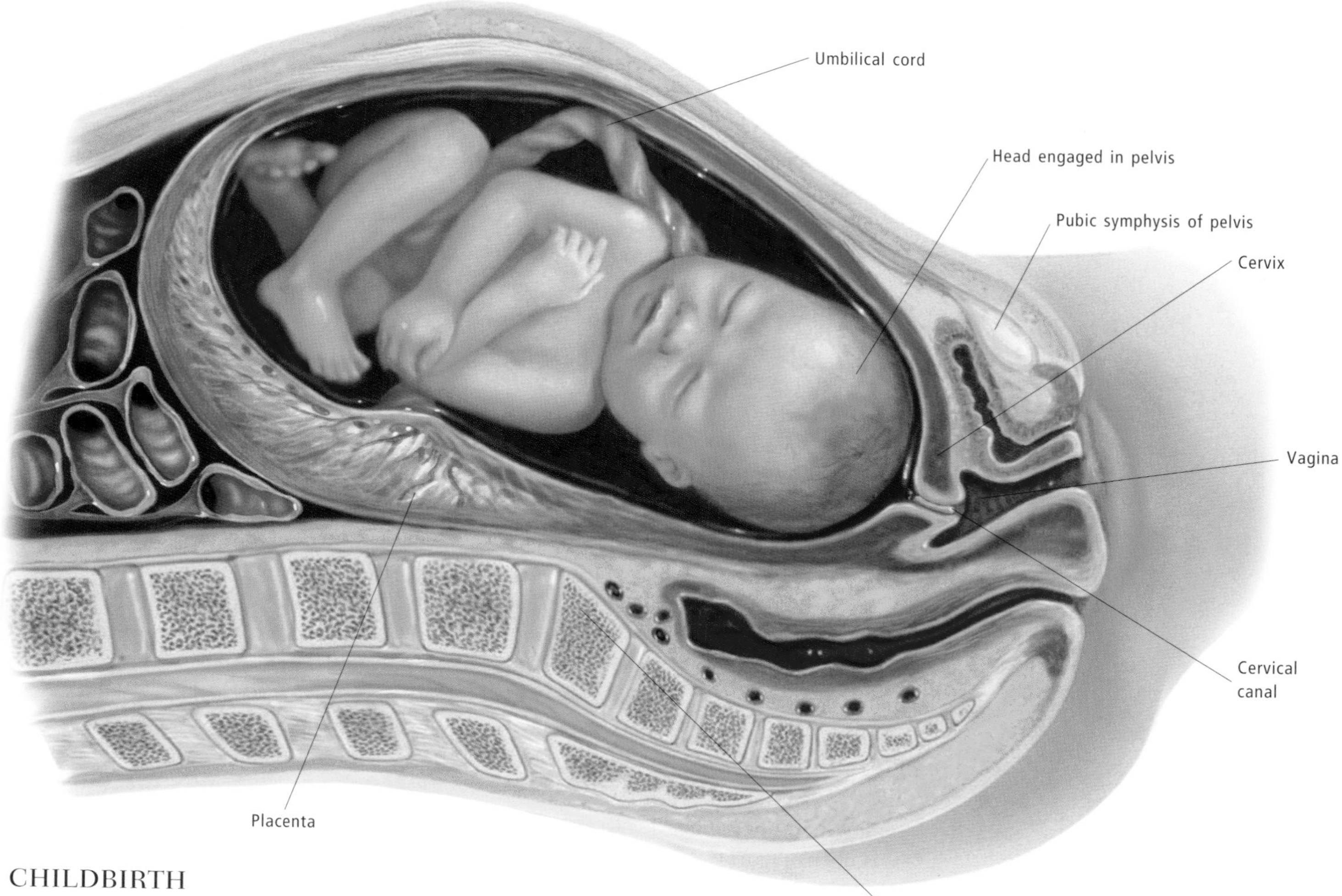

Full term

CHILDBIRTH

Childbirth is the act of giving birth to a baby, and can be done with varying degrees of assistance and intervention. Most babies born in industrialized societies are born in hospitals, under the direction of the medical profession. This has been associated with huge drops in maternal death rates. The rate of maternal death is 5 per 100,000 births for normal vaginal delivery; for cesarean section it is approximately 40 per 100,000 births. In many countries, home birth is also an option. In the Netherlands, for example, a country where home birth has always been an option for all women, about a third of births occur at home.

Home birth has a very low rate of medical intervention (a priority of many women) and a low rate of complications and hospital transfers. If a mother is prepared, and informed and supported by qualified carers, home birth can be a good choice. Many women choose home birth not just because of the familiar environment but also because they are able to have other members of the family present and can create an environment which helps them to feel relaxed.

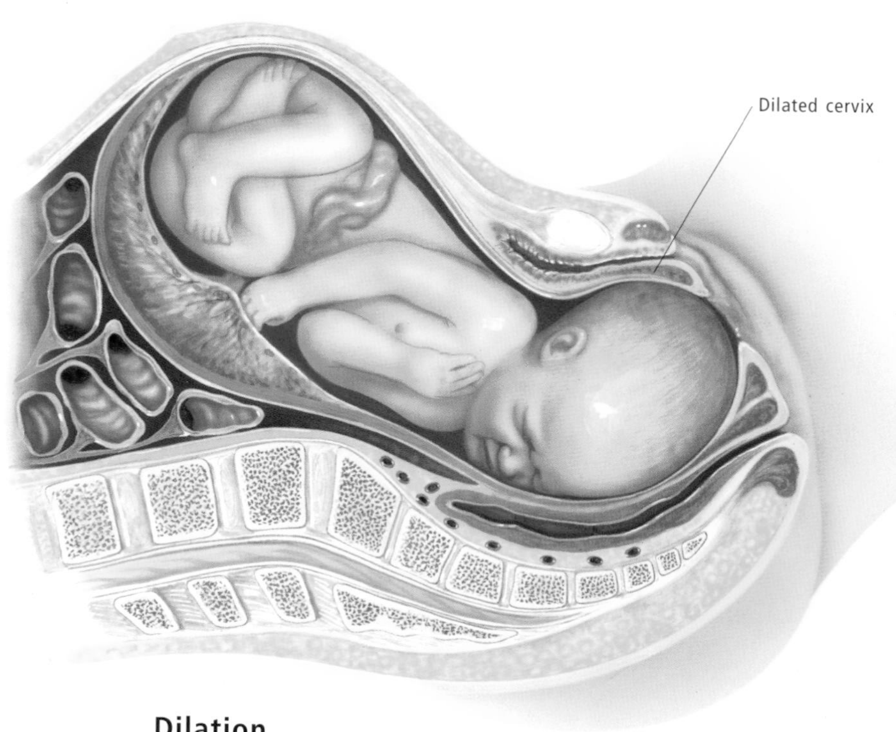

Dilation

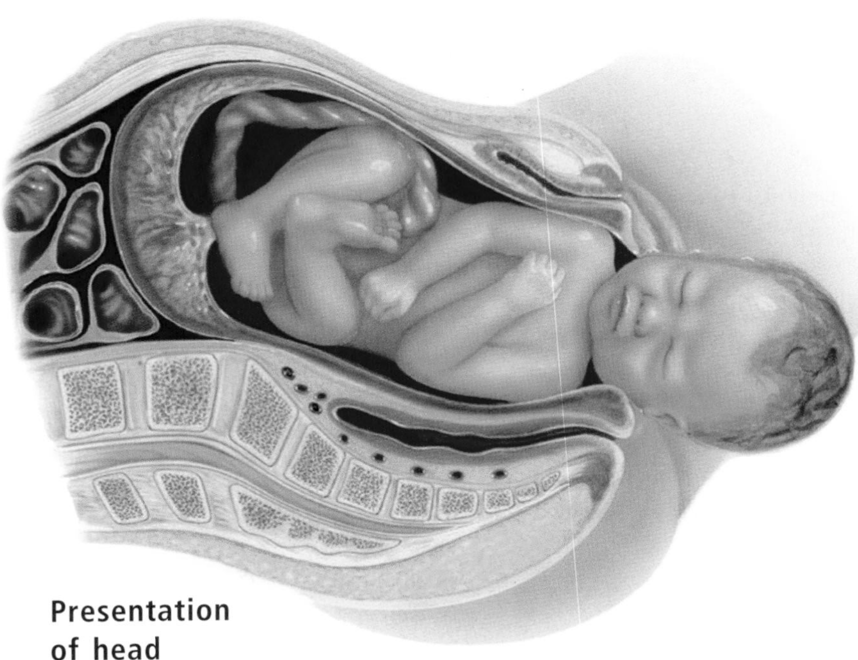
Presentation of head

There are, however, medical reasons why a home birth may not be possible—or sensible—and these include complications such as toxemia or sudden unpredictable hemorrhage, medical problems such as heart disease, and fetal problems such as the baby presenting in transverse (across the uterus) position.

Some mothers favor a water birth, which is often only possible in the home environment. For those women who want to go through labor and give birth in water, some birth centers and hospitals will provide a large enough bath. As soaking in a warm bath can relieve pain, many institutions have a protocol which allows laboring in water, but not birthing. However, around half the women who labor in water will also give birth in water. When this occurs, the baby is lifted straight from the birth canal, out of the water and into a warmed room where both mother and baby are kept warm.

In the 1970s, in industrialized countries, fathers-to-be first began to attend the births of their babies, and this is now accepted in most birth centers. The man who has attended antenatal classes with his partner and learnt how he can support her during the birth is a valuable companion. A woman who is knowledgeable and supportive also makes an excellent birth companion for the mother; in some countries these women are known as *doulas*. Research has shown that the presence of a trained female support person can reduce medical intervention in the birth process and enable the birthing woman to have a more satisfying experience. Some families choose to have their baby at home or in a birth center so the baby's siblings can be present during the birth. Preparing the children for the experience, and supporting them, helps ensure it will be a rewarding experience for all.

Labor

Labor—the process of giving birth—is described in three stages. The first stage is actual labor, during which the cervix is thinned and dilated, and is followed by a period known as transition; the second stage is the birth of the baby; and the third stage is the expulsion of the placenta, which nourished the baby during the pregnancy.

During the first stage of labor, the cervix must dilate fully to allow the baby to move into the birth canal. The endocrine signal that the baby sends to the placenta stimulates the production of estrogen. The uterus then produces prostaglandins and contracts more strongly and more frequently as it works to shorten and soften (efface) the cervix by pressing the baby's head against it. This effacement and stretching of the cervix then triggers the posterior pituitary gland to produce oxytocin; the contractions become stronger, working the uterus to stretch and dilate the cervix.

Once the cervix is fully dilated the baby can move into the birth canal. This stage of labor can be very short or last as long as 36 or more hours. In many hospitals, labor is augmented and accelerated after 12 hours.

The second stage of labor begins when the mother feels an urgent need to bear down and push the baby into the birth canal. This stage is much shorter than the first, with an average three to five "pushes" before the baby's head presents at the opening to the vagina. This is known as the "crowning". The baby's head then passes beneath the pelvic bone, with the face

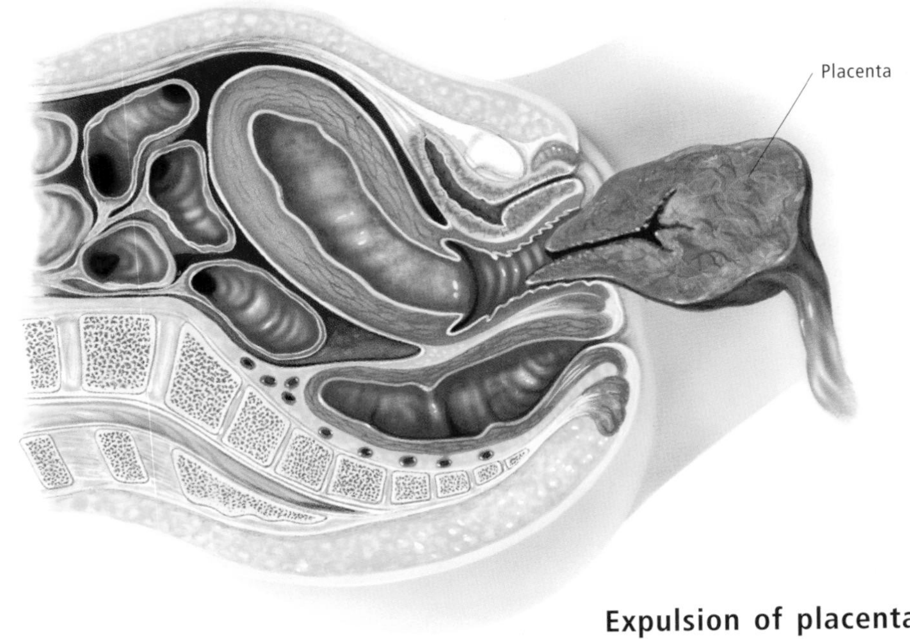

Expulsion of placenta

towards the mother's spine. The shoulders will quickly follow the head and the baby will soon be born.

The third stage of labor is the expulsion of the placenta. Once the baby is born the uterus continues to contract and there is a rush of oxytocin that prompts the placenta to separate from the uterus in a peeling action. The umbilical cord will still be joined to the placenta and may still be attached to the baby at this stage. Once the placenta has separated from the uterus it will slide down the birth canal of its own accord.

Labor, though it can be circumvented with a cesarean birth, is beneficial for the wellbeing of the baby. Stress hormones, known as catecholamines, surge through the baby's system during a vaginal delivery in response to the contractions of the uterus and the baby's head being squeezed. This surge both protects the baby from asphyxia and prepares the baby for the environment outside the uterus. It also clears the baby's lungs and prepares them to breathe, and sends a rich supply of blood to the baby's heart and brain.

Position

Advocates of natural childbirth encourage women to labor in an upright position, either standing supported by others (partner, support person such as a midwife) or squatting. Lying prone, often with legs in stirrups, is known to slow the birth and increase the likelihood of the baby's delivery by instrument (forceps or vacuum extraction). The upright position, with the woman responding to her body's signals, leads to a lower incidence of episiotomy.

Though women are given an estimated date of confinement or delivery calculated from the date of their last menstrual period, and often confirmed by the use of ultrasound, only 4 percent of babies are actually born naturally on this day.

Signs of labor

Signs of labor include: the show, which is the expulsion of a mucous plug at the mouth of the uterus (the cervix) and which can appear as many as two or three weeks before actual labor; contractions, which can be regular or irregular but which indicate labor when they become stronger and more painful as they progress; and the waters breaking, which means the amniotic sac which is holding the baby has broken.

Pain control

Labor is a painful experience and many women in industrialized societies who have little or no experience of pain use medication to help them cope with it. Epidural anesthesia is a very common form of pain relief, as are nitrous oxide gas and pethidine (a narcotic). Less invasive methods include acupuncture, aromatherapy, hypnosis, massage, relaxation, transcutaneous electrical nerve stimulation, nipple stimulation, and warm baths and showers.

Assisted births

Some obstetricians believe in active management of labor which involves breaking the waters (amniotomy), the use of synthetic oxytocin to speed up labor and continuous monitoring of the labor's progress. This can involve electronic fetal monitoring, an epidural anesthetic, episiotomy (an incision in the perineum to facilitate the delivery of the baby's head and shoulders) and instrument delivery either with forceps or by vacuum extraction. In an episiotomy the woman's perineum is cut under local anesthetic, ostensibly to give the baby an easier passage and to prevent tearing. The World Health Organization says the systematic use of episiotomy is unjustified and advises protecting the perineum in other ways. When labor is allowed to progress naturally and the woman gives birth in an upright position (squatting, sitting or standing), a tear is less likely and gravity helps the birth of the baby.

Problems and complications

The most common position (85 percent of births) for a baby to be born in is the occipito anterior position (head down, facing the mother's spine). However, babies can also be born in various positions, including: occipito posterior (with the spine against the mother's, a position which causes long backache during labor); breech (bottom first); or transverse (lying across the uterus). Breech babies can be buttocks first or have a foot presenting; this is known as footling breech. Breech babies are sometimes turned in the uterus by the obstetrician or midwife or by using natural therapies prior to the birth; they are then born by cesarean section or born naturally.

Even a baby in the most natural position for birth can present problems that require medical help. Cesareans are life-saving in an emergency and are often used with breech babies, though this is not always justified. Other methods, such as forceps and vacuum extraction, can assist the delivery of a baby. Forceps (two instruments shaped like large flat spoons that fit over the baby's head) are often used when the mother's blood pressure rises and the baby needs to be delivered, or when there are signs of fetal distress, or when the baby is in an unusual position. Vacuum extraction is used in similar situations. It involves using a suction instrument to guide the head down the canal.

Despite all the best intentions and most sophisticated calculations, babies are still born unexpectedly. When this happens it is important to make the environment as warm as possible, to support the laboring woman both physically and emotionally, and to be ready to assist if necessary. This can involve gently unlooping the cord from around the newborn baby's neck and making sure there is no membrane over the baby's face preventing breathing. It may also involve keeping both mother and baby warm and comfortable until assistance arrives. It is not vital to clamp and cut the cord which attaches the baby to the placenta; so long as the placenta detaches from the wall of the uterus during the third stage of labor without problems. The placenta can remain attached to the baby for some time. However, if the placenta does not detach then hemorrhage can result.

In the normal progress of labor, the expulsion of the placenta occurs in the third stage, often passing almost unnoticed. The uterus continues to contract, the placenta separates from the lining, the contractions of the uterus prevent excess bleeding, and the placenta slides out. Some attendants will pull on the cord to help the placenta to separate and in other situations the woman will be given an intravenous injection of ergotamine to induce powerful contractions and help the placenta separate. This, however, is considered a controversial treatment.

C

Breech birth

By the end of gestation, the fetus has usually rotated within the uterus, with its head towards the birth canal and face towards the mother's sacrum. If the fetus faces the mother's pubis instead (6 percent of deliveries) and the legs and buttocks enter the vaginal canal first, then this is called a breech birth.

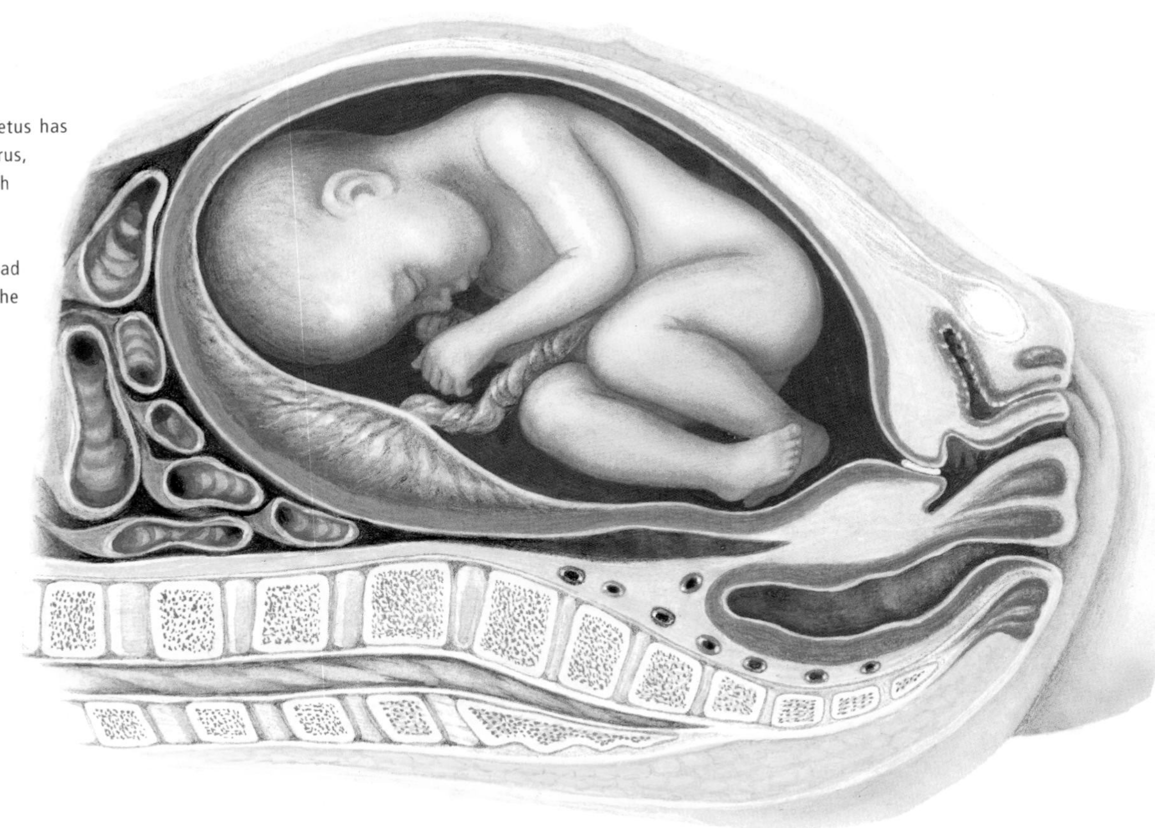

Hemorrhage is still a major cause of maternal disease and death, and a retained placenta may need manual removal. Clamping the cord early has not been found to have any effect on blood loss or hemorrhage.

Cesarean section

Cesarean section, the delivery of the baby through an incision made across the abdomen, in a line just below the pubic hair line, is the surgical alternative to vaginal birth. In many industrialized countries the cesarean rate has risen due to fear of litigation (about deaths of babies born vaginally). The World Health Organization has found that cesarean rates should not be higher than 10–15 percent, but in many industrialized countries, apart from the Scandinavian countries, the rate is climbing through the 20s, and this climb is attributed to clinical practice. Cesarean birth is a major operation. The potential benefits are great when done appropriately, but there are also substantial risks for both mother and baby. Cesareans are often used for the delivery of multiple pregnancy though the indications have not been properly established.

Premature and overdue births

Nearly half of all multiple births will occur prematurely. Other causes of prematurity are maternal illness or placental problems, such as placenta previa, smoking, anxiety, distress or excess tension, and poor nutrition. However, many premature births have no known cause. Around 6 percent of babies are born underweight and the majority of these are premature—the rest are termed small-for-dates. Prematurity is defined by the baby's gestational age (the time the baby has been in the uterus), not by birth weight.

It is unreasonable to expect all babies to spend 280 days *in utero;* just as some are premature, some will naturally be overdue. Only around 5 percent of babies are born on the estimated date of delivery or estimated date of confinement. With ultrasound, pregnancies can be closely monitored and a pregnancy can be allowed to go two or more weeks past the due date through the use of this technology, which can monitor the baby and the uterine environment. Babies born overdue are termed postmature.

After giving birth

During the labor and birth the woman's hormones help her to cope physically and emotionally with the whole experience. Once the baby is born, if there have been no drugs, she is usually in a state of euphoria. She can cuddle, caress and gaze into her baby's eyes as she grows accustomed to holding this little person she has been carrying *in utero* for nine months. This euphoria can continue for some time and in some women it buoys them along through the early days and weeks of motherhood. For others there is an emotional drop in mood sometime in the first week, which is often called the "baby blues", and for a few there is the trauma of postnatal depression. A hospital environment is not conducive to maternal–infant bonding and often restrictive hospital practices will not allow the mother to spend precious time with her baby, thus interfering with the establishment of breast feeding and the forming of this bond. This, together with the hormonal changes and a new mother's lack of experience with babies, can lead to postnatal depression. Postnatal psychosis is a rare mental illness that needs medical treatment.

The postpartum period is the first days after the delivery of a baby. In this time a woman's body will change again as it returns to the non-pregnant state. Excess fluid will be excreted and muscle tone will begin to return. The body will also adapt to its new role of feeding the baby. Women who are supported by friends and others find that coping with being a new mother is easier.

SEE ALSO ***Bottle feeding, Breast feeding, Episiotomy, Infancy, Labor, Newborn, Placenta, Postnatal depression, Pregnancy***

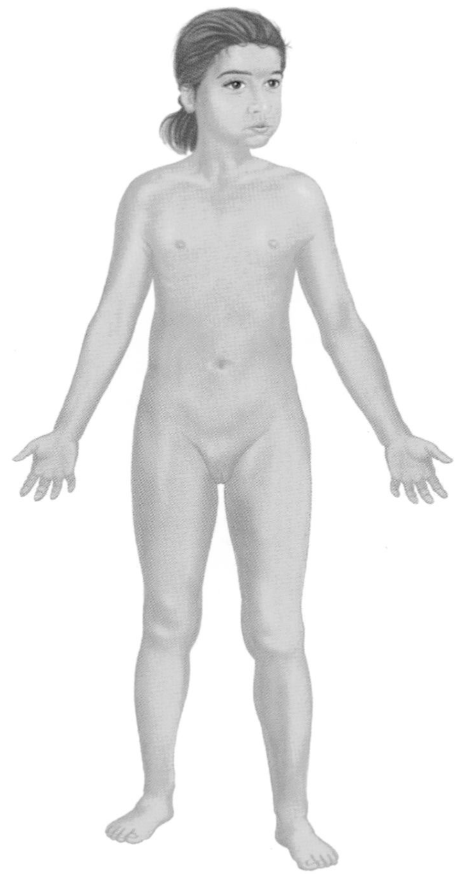

5-year-old girl

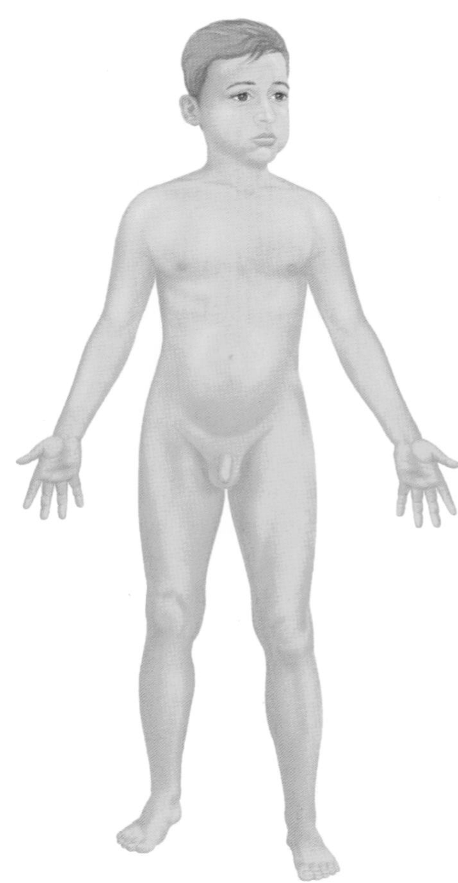

5-year-old boy

CHILDHOOD

Childhood is regarded as the period between infancy and puberty. It is the beginning of the journey towards full independence, a period of fast physical and mental growth during which education and experience build a foundation for adulthood. Childhood ends in the teenage years when growing sexual maturity brings a marked change in appearance, attitude and interests.

Each child is an individual and will develop as determined by genetic inheritance, familial traits and environmental input. Physical, emotional, social and spiritual developments will impact on each other, and, though highly complex, the changes a child undergoes are ordered and specific.

In most children growth occurs in irregular spurts. Some children will be larger or smaller than their peers. Build is a factor in growth, and overweight children may appear to grow slowly in height compared to their weight; adolescents who reach puberty later than their peers usually catch up eventually.

At 12 months old a child will be able to sit without support, crawl or move around, come up to a standing position, smile and babble, and say words which have meaning, or appear to. In the second year a child will learn to walk alone, drink from a cup, wave goodbye, understand simple commands and questions, and combine words.

By around the age of 3 or 4 years, most children will have mastered the major physical tasks, including walking, jumping, running, climbing stairs, grasping and manipulating objects. By the third year, the child will able to use sentences containing 5 or 6 words, and can understand grammar and meaning by 6 years old. At the age of 3 or 4, the child will have a vocabulary of several hundred words. Between 2 and 6 years of age the child develops cognitive skills such as knowing how to perceive, think, recognize, and remember. There is growing awareness of the child's own emotions as well as empathy with feelings and perspectives of others.

Overall, growth is a steady process, with weeks or months of slightly slower growth alternating with mini "growth spurts". After the first year, a baby's growth slows considerably, and by 2 years, growth usually continues at a fairly steady rate of approximately 2½ inches (6 centimeters) per year until adolescence.

Boys grow slightly faster than girls at birth but at about 7 months growth rates are even after which girls grows faster until about 4 years. From then until adolescence growth rates are the same. On average girls are slightly shorter than boys until adolescence and weigh less than boys until about the age of 8, after which they are heavier until about 14 years of age.

By the time a child is 6 years of age all the primary teeth will have appeared and the secondary teeth are starting to emerge. The primary (baby) teeth appear in a pattern from as early as 6 months old until around 3 years. Likewise, the secondary teeth erupt in a pattern, gradually replacing the primary teeth.

During childhood the long bones, such as those in the arm and leg, start as cartilage "models" which are then gradually converted into bone (ossified). The centers of ossification are the shaft (diaphysis) and regions near the ends of the bone (epiphyses). Between the diaphysis and epiphyses is a growth plate where increase in length of the bone takes place. By the age of about 20, ossification reaches and includes the growth plate, at which time growth stops.

Similarly the skull has certain bones which develop directly from the soft connective tissue membrane through the process of ossification. Other parts of the skull are derived from pre-existing cartilage. As the brain grows, the flat bones of the skull enlarge by expansion at the margins. The brain (along with the skull, the eyes and the ears) develops earlier than other parts of the body. At birth the brain is already 25 percent of its adult weight, at age 5 about 90 percent, and at age 10, about 95 percent. Other internal organs such as the liver, the spleen, and the kidneys grow in line with the child's general increase in height.

The different bones of the wrist ossify at known times during development, so that x-rays of a child's wrist are used as a measure of a child's growth compared to chronological age. These can also be used to estimate the expected height of a child during investigation of height problems.

Normal growth depends on a sufficient intake of nutrients and vitamins, exercise

Bone formation during childhood

Long bones begin as cartilage in the embryo. By birth, ossification (development of bone) has reached almost to the ends of the cartilage models. New centers for bone growth then develop at either end of the bone. A plate of cartilage (growth plate) develops between these two areas of bone, and is where the increase in bone length occurs. The growth plate moves steadily away from the center of the bone towards the ends until all cartilage has ossified. Growth in bone length is then complete. Long bones are modeled to be wider at the ends than the middle, providing extra support at the joints where it is needed.

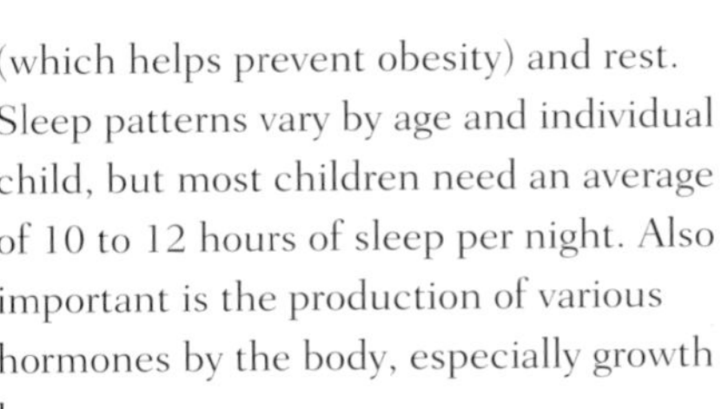

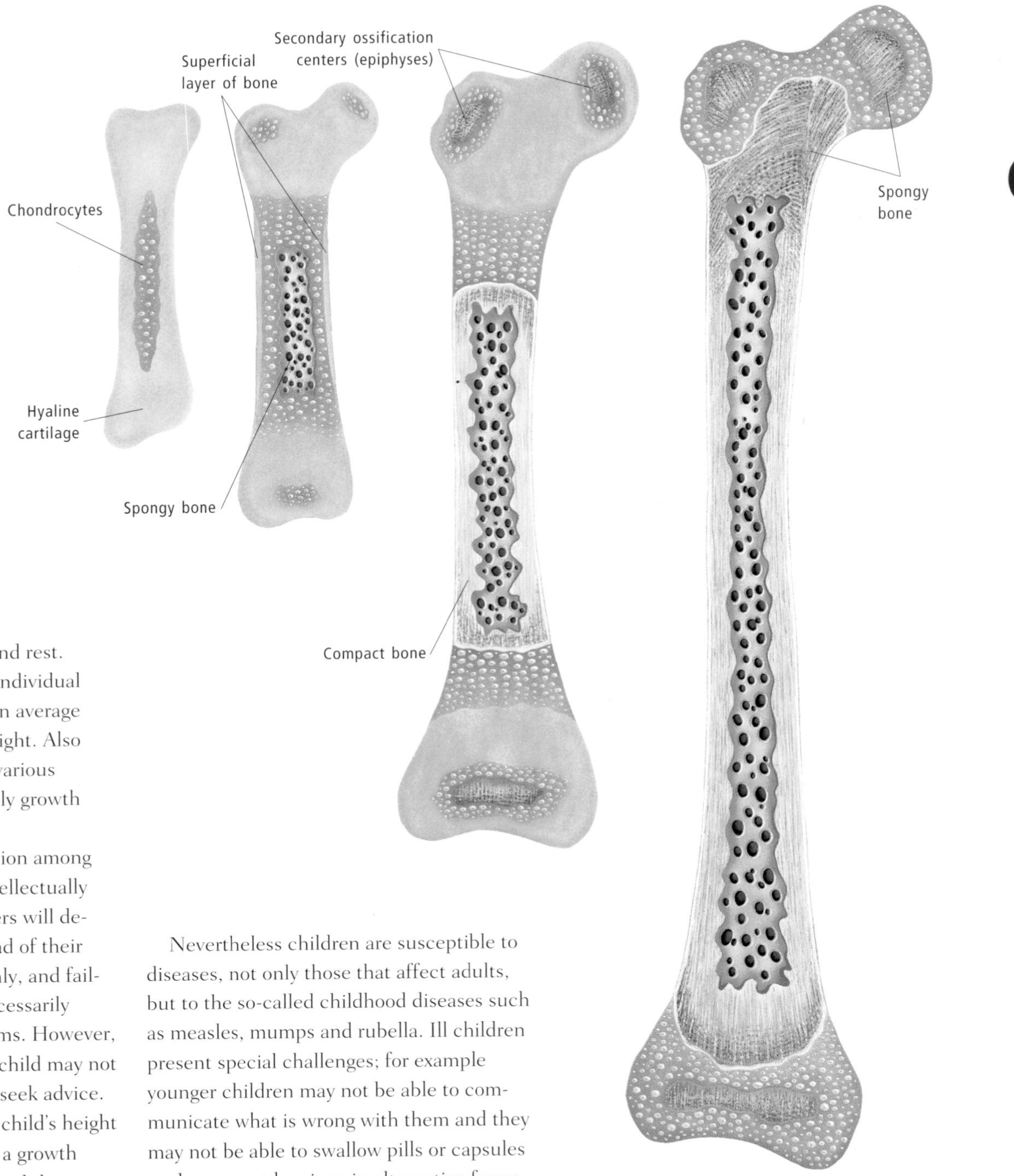

(which helps prevent obesity) and rest. Sleep patterns vary by age and individual child, but most children need an average of 10 to 12 hours of sleep per night. Also important is the production of various hormones by the body, especially growth hormone.

There is a great deal of variation among children. Some will develop intellectually ahead of their peers, while others will develop physically or socially ahead of their peers. Milestones are guides only, and failure to match them does not necessarily mean that there are any problems. However, parents who suspect that their child may not be developing normally should seek advice. During visits to the doctor, the child's height and weight can be recorded on a growth chart. This enables the doctor and the child's parents to compare the child's height and weight compared with that of other children the same age, and determine whether the child is growing at an appropriate rate. Most children who are short or delayed in development are healthy and normal.

Childhood health

Infant and childhood mortality rates over the past decades have declined dramatically, thanks to preventive measures such as better maternal nutrition and obstetrical care, and improved housing, water supply, and sewage disposal.

Nevertheless children are susceptible to diseases, not only those that affect adults, but to the so-called childhood diseases such as measles, mumps and rubella. Ill children present special challenges; for example younger children may not be able to communicate what is wrong with them and they may not be able to swallow pills or capsules so drugs must be given in alternative forms. Fortunately, because they are still growing, children tend to recover faster than adults from many conditions. Bone fractures for example tend to heal better because in childhood bone is still being remodelled and reshaped.

Behavioral problems

Although behavioral problems cause parents to worry they are not usually serious, and unless there are severe underlying emotional disorders, the children will usually grow out of them. However, counseling may be needed in some cases.

Aggression

When children play together some aggressive behavior is normal until they learn from the adults in whose care they are how to get on with others, when to stand up for themselves, when to wait and how to share. Children who grow up in a violent family environment often grow up into violent adults who are unable to solve their problems, except in an aggressive manner. Adults who never learn these skills usually carry on with their aggressive physical behavior of hitting, fighting or being unable to share. By the time children reach school age they should be able to control aggressive behavior; if it is still a problem then it is wise to seek skilled advice from a counselor.

C

Biting

Children who bite others do so for differing reasons, perhaps out of frustration because they feel powerless, as an experiment, or because they are feeling stressed. In the first two instances if they get a response, or the biting gives them a sense of power, they may do it again. If the action seems to be an experiment, such as when they are breast feeding, they must be prevented from biting and told "no" firmly. If they are biting because of stress, that stress must be eased. Whatever the circumstances, the biter needs to know that such behavior is inappropriate and that there are no rewards.

Bullying

Being bullied is not just a problem among children. The deliberate act of hurting other people—frightening them with words or deeds—can be practised by adults, teenagers and children. Bullying is a problem for both the victim and the perpetrator. People who bully will choose a victim who seems to be easy to hurt, and being bullied can destroy someone's self-esteem. At the same time, research has found that it is people who already have low self-esteem who are the targets of bullies. Strategies which help to avoid bullying include learning empowerment. Adults should be involved in the case of a bullied child. Bullies have also been found to have low self-esteem and low self-confidence and likewise need strategies—usually from professional counselors—to help them find ways of being accepted.

Lying

In order for an untruth to be told, the difference between fact and fantasy must be understood. Young children, especially children who have not yet started school, cannot do this. They are unable to make moral judgments: to them, getting caught is wrong, getting out of trouble is right. Even up to the age of eight or nine some children have trouble grasping such concepts—pleasing adults is important, telling lies is not. Once children understand what telling an untruth is, they may lie in many different situations: if they are afraid of being punished or of affection being withheld; if they have low self-esteem and want attention; if they want to impress their peers; if people they look up to tell lies; or if they need to feel independent—this last circumstance is especially the case with adolescents. To help reduce the telling of lies, mistakes should be dealt with without harsh punishments; the difference between fantasy and truth should be taught; and an understanding shown that some lies are really heart-felt wishes. Children need to be taught why it is important to tell the truth, and praising children who tell the truth and giving adolescents some privacy will contribute to minimizing the telling of lies.

Tattle (tale) telling

When someone tattle tells it is important to decide what is behind the telling. Is it jealousy, meanness or is there a real danger? Having assessed the situation, it can either be sorted out by dealing with the cause of the jealousy or by offering the tattle-teller strategies to cope with whatever is causing the unhappiness. If there is danger involved, then the situation should be resolved and the informer's helpfulness acknowledged.

Tantrums

These are not just the province of toddlers. Tantrums are thrown by people—adults, teenagers as well as children—who have no other outlet for their frustration or stress. The frustration can be mixed with other emotions such as jealousy or feeling unwanted and these can add to the fury. Tantrums in young children can be dealt with by an adult who stays in control, is ready to come to the child's assistance, and who does not give in to the demands. With older children the causes and consequences of their behavior should be discussed. Tantrums in adults generally are the sign of deeper problems and may need counseling.

Whining

On the whole, it is unhappy children who whine. Causes can be tiredness, ill health, boredom, frustration or a feeling of insecurity. Reacting swiftly to deal with the cause of the problem and not giving in to the demands of the person who exhibits this behavior, together with providing a secure emotional environment, will help to avoid any whining.

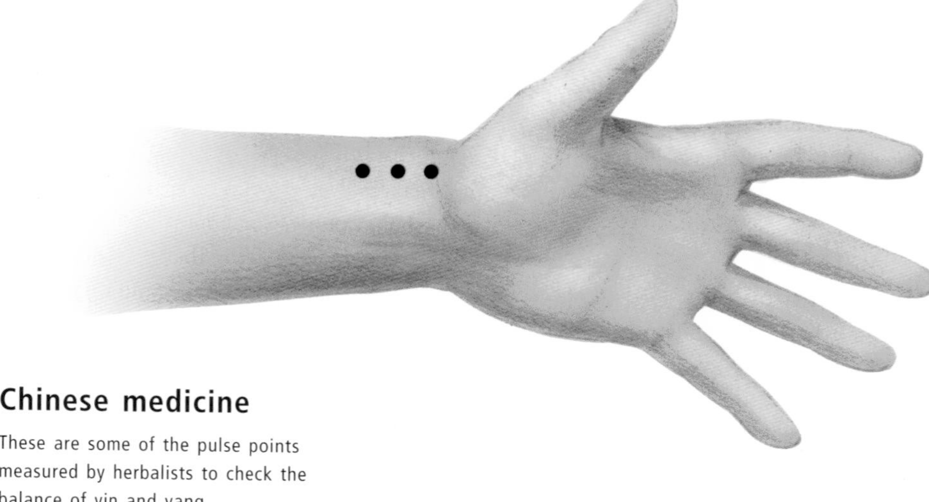

Chinese medicine

These are some of the pulse points measured by herbalists to check the balance of yin and yang.

CHINESE HERBALISM

Chinese herbalism, also known as Chinese internal medicine, is an important aspect of traditional Chinese medicine. The history of Chinese herbal medicine is believed to date back at least 5,000 years to a time when medicine was practised by shamans. The first written records date back to 1500 BC, when medicine was largely a matter of magic and superstition.

A major advance had taken place by around 200 BC when the *Huang Ti Nei-Ching*, or the *Yellow Emperor's Manual of Internal Medicine* was written. Written records, experiment and observation are emphasized; diagnosis distinguishes between the "root" of a disease and its manifestation. By the seventh century AD there were over 800 remedies classified in Chinese herbals. Today there are over 5,000 remedies, many of which have attracted interest from both Western herbalists and medical researchers. Chinese herbalism is still widely practised in China, and is gaining popularity in the West.

Philosophy

Traditional Chinese medicine is based on the Taoist philosophy that emphasizes the importance of balance in life. Herbs are used in this system to help establish and maintain the body's internal balance. *Qi* or *ch'i* refers to the life energy or force which is thought to circulate throughout the body and its organs. This energy is composed of the *yin* and the *yang*—polarities which counterbalance each other while being in a constant state of movement.

Illness is seen as a result of imbalance where overall blockages and deficiencies have developed in the flow of *ch'i*, and hence in the balance between *yin* and *yang*. These "patterns of disharmony" are said to manifest in the body's organs resulting in a particular set of physical, mental and emotional symptoms.

Herbs

Chinese herbs are drawn from a wide range of plant, mineral and animal substances. Great care is given to the correct method of growing, harvesting and processing of each herb to maximize its healing properties. Chinese herbalists classify herbs according to their nature (e.g. warming, cooling or neutral), their taste, their appearance and their properties (e.g. dispersing, consolidating, nourishing, or toning). Herbalists therefore believe they understand not only how the herb may affect a symptom (e.g. diarrhea), but also how it will address the underlying pattern of disharmony (e.g. strengthening the spleen and clearing "damp").

Diagnosis

Chinese herbalists assess a patient's condition by studying the patient's medical history, lifestyle and appearance, particularly of the eyes, skin, hair and tongue. Twelve pulses, six in either wrist, are felt, to measure the flow of *ch'i* through the organs. This gives the herbalist a picture of the underlying disharmony beneath the presenting symptom. The same symptoms may stem from a completely different imbalance within the body; for example, a headache may be caused by an imbalance of either the liver or the stomach.

After diagnosis, the Chinese herbalist prescribes a combination of herbs that may come in the form of powders, pills or raw herbs. The latter are mixed specifically for the client who then makes a decoction out of them by simmering them for between 20–40 minutes, preferably in a traditional Chinese clay pot. Usually a few courses of treatment over weeks or even months, are required to firmly rebalance the body's *ch'i*.

Chinese herbalism is said to be suitable both for general health maintenance and for treatment of specific conditions. It is particularly recommended for chronic conditions such as skin problems, migraine, chronic fatigue syndrome, respiratory and digestive disorders, arthritis, and disorders of the reproductive system.

Chiropractic

Chiropractic is a system of treating musculoskeletal and other ailments based on the manipulation of the spinal joints.

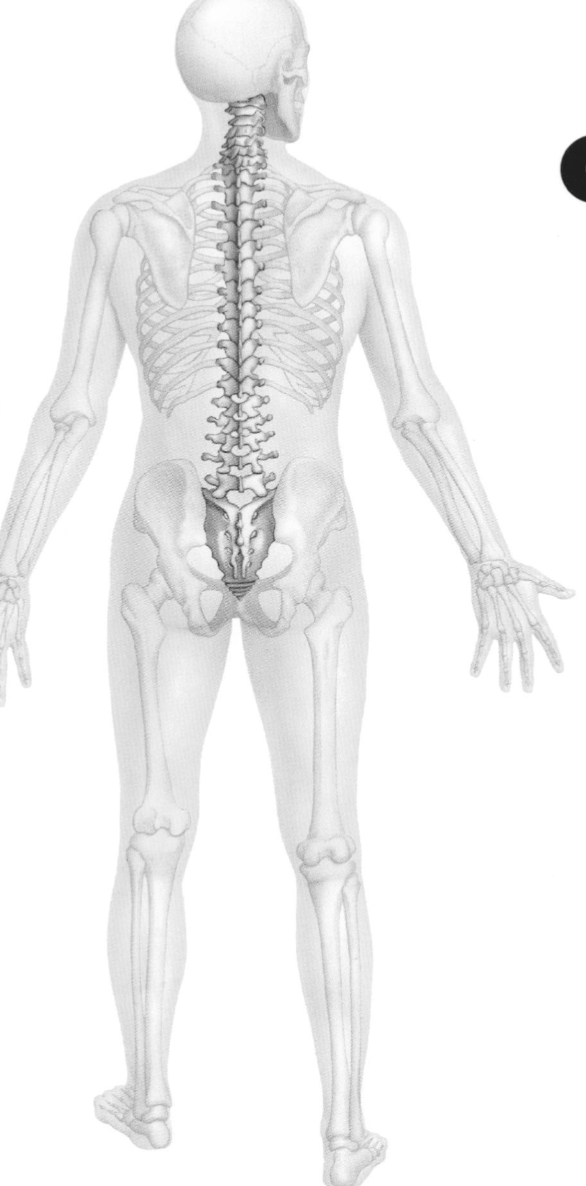

CHIROPRACTIC

Chiropractic is a system of healing based upon the manipulation of the spine and joints. It was pioneered by Daniel David Palmer (1845–1913), an American healer, who developed the premise that illness is essentially due to malfunction in the spine which affects the body's nervous system and organ function, a premise made after he cured a patient's deafness with spinal adjustments in 1895. Palmer coined the word chiropractic from the Greek *cheiro*, (hand) and *praktikos* (to do), meaning "done" by hands, and in 1897 he founded the Palmer Institute and Chiropractic Infirmary to teach his skills. Since that time chiropractic has spread rapidly, and gained acceptance for its therapeutic benefits. It is the second largest health care system in the USA.

Principles

Chiropractic works from the principle that modern life produces abnormalities in the musculoskeletal system, most especially the spine, as a result of trauma, ageing, physical and mental stress and tension. A spinal displacement which upsets the nervous system is known as subluxation; this is said to reduce neural signals and inhibits the body's natural healing ability. Chiropractors work to locate and adjust variations along the spine in order to free up the nervous system's pathways to the brain which govern the function, repair and regeneration of the body's tissues. Chiropractic care is said to enhance the body's function resulting in an improved immune response and resistance to diseases.

Diagnosis

Before any treatment is given the chiropractor needs to have a full picture of the spine's state of function. This is done through a combination of medical history, physical examination (including tissue and organ palpation), postural analysis, muscle testing and spinal x-rays. Where there is a chronic health problem a series of treatments is usually prescribed.

Treatment

Chiropractic adjustment involves changing the position of the vertebrae by specific direct force in a way that causes the vertebrae to move normally with both the vertebrae above and below. The adjustment is delivered with a controlled speed, depth and force, and requires considerable practice and training; treatment should only ever be undertaken by a qualified professional.

The most common forms of chiropractic adjustment are mobilization and manipulation. Mobilization encourages movement by rotation, stretching and pressure to the extent which is possible for the patient without causing discomfort or pain. In manipulation, movement is forced beyond the limit of normal range by a sudden thrust, often accompanied by "clicking" sounds.

Some chiropractors choose to follow a more conservative philosophy of limiting their treatment solely to spinal manipulation. But most chiropractors combine spinal manipulations with various other treatment methods such as soft tissue manipulation, acupressure, heat, and breathing and postural exercises. Many chiropractors employ massage therapists to loosen and warm the back's soft tissue before making any adjustments.

Chiropractors are most commonly consulted for specific musculoskeletal ailments such as back pain, repetitive strain and sports injuries, sciatica, arthritis, rheumatism, and whiplash, as well as migraines and tension headaches. In addition, chiropractic treatment can be used to treat asthma, digestive disorders, menstrual problems and muscular tension where postural problems and spinal misalignments are involved.

SEE ALSO *Massage, Nervous system, Skeletal system, Spine, Vertebrae*

Chlamydia bacteria

CHLAMYDIA

Chlamydia is a genus of three bacterial parasites: *Chlamydia psittaci*, which causes psittacosis; *Chlamydia trachomatis*, which causes trachoma, conjunctivitis and a variety of sexually transmitted diseases; and *Chlamydia pneumoniae*, which causes respiratory tract infections.

It is estimated that up to 30 percent of sexually active women have had a sexually transmitted chlamydial infection, which is six times as common as genital herpes and thirty times as common as syphilis. There may be no symptoms, or mild ones: women may suffer urethritis, slight menstrual-like discomfort and vaginal discharge; men may notice a frequent urge to urinate, a whitish yellow discharge and redness at the tip of the penis. The relative absence of symptoms increases the possibility of unknowingly passing the disease to others. Chlamydia has been linked with pelvic inflammatory disease, ectopic and premature birth, conjunctivitis in babies or pneumonia. A test for chlamydia in those planning a baby is wise.

Chlamydia pneumonia, which was identified as a separate species in the 1980s, causes a mild atypical pneumonia with fever, cough and sore throat.

Fortunately, most forms of chlamydia infection are easily treated with antibiotics.

SEE ALSO *Pelvic inflammatory disease, Pneumonia, Psittacosis, Trachoma, Urethritis*

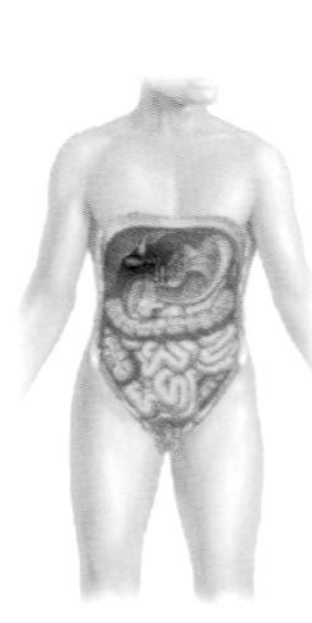

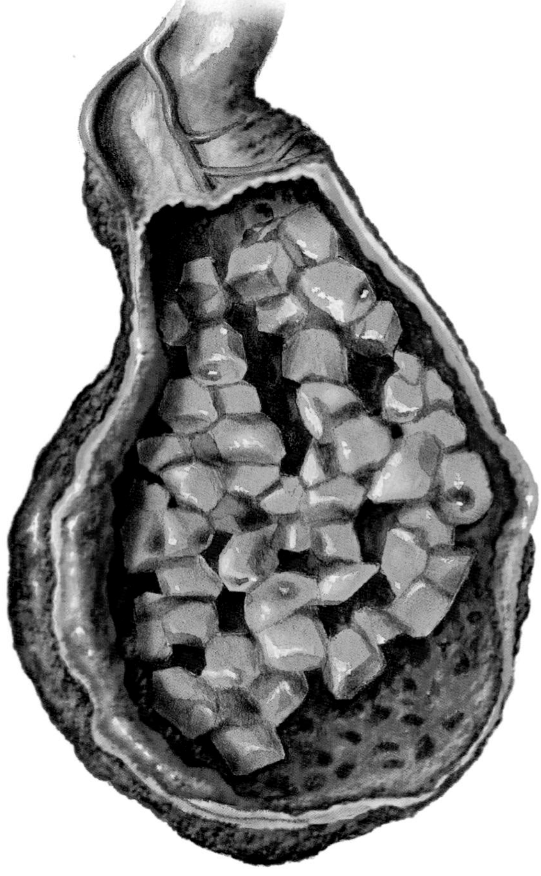

Cholecystitis

Cholecystitis is inflammation of the gallbladder, resulting in attacks of severe, sharp abdominal pain. It is usually caused by gallstones, which will be visible on ultrasound examination.

CHOLANGIOGRAPHY

A cholangiogram is an x-ray of the gallbladder and bile ducts used to identify the presence of gallstones. It involves injection into the body of a dye that is opaque to x-rays; the dye becomes concentrated in the gallbladder and bile ducts, outlining the gallstones. The dye can be injected into a vein (intravenous cholangiogram) or into the hepatic ducts (bile ducts around the liver) though the skin (transhepatic cholangiogram). Alternatively, it may be injected via an endoscope into the opening where the bile duct joins the duodenum (endoscopic retrograde cholangiography).

SEE ALSO *Endoscopy, Gallbladder, Gallstones*

CHOLANGITIS

Cholangitis is inflammation of the bile ducts. It is usually caused by an obstruction of the duct that transports bile from the gallbladder to the small intestine. The obstruction is usually caused by gallstones or a tumor in the pancreas. Pain in the upper abdomen is accompanied by a high fever and chills, often with vomiting and jaundice. The urine may be dark and the feces pale. Treatment with antibiotics may cure the condition, but a severe obstruction may require surgical removal of the gallstones. Sclerosing cholangitis is a chronic disorder of the liver in which the bile ducts become inflamed, thickened, scarred (sclerotic) and obstructed, leading to cirrhosis of the liver. It is fatal without a transplant.

SEE ALSO *Cirrhosis of the liver, Gallbladder, Gallstones, Liver, Pancreas*

CHOLECYSTECTOMY

Cholecystectomy is the surgical removal of the gallbladder. It is a common treatment in severe cases of pain due to gallstones or acute cholecystitis.

Traditionally, cholecystectomy involved removal of the gallbladder through a surgical incision in the abdomen under general anesthesia. However, laparoscopic cholecystectomy has now largely replaced it. In this procedure, the gallbladder is surgically removed through a small incision in the abdomen with the aid of a fiberoptic tube called a laparoscope. It can be performed under local anesthetic, and greatly reduces the hospital stay and recovery time, although there can often be more complications.

SEE ALSO *Cholecystitis, Gallbladder, Gallstones, Laparoscopy*

CHOLECYSTITIS

Cholecystitis is an inflammation of the gallbladder. It is usually caused by gallstones obstructing the outlet of the gallbladder into the cystic duct, which empties into the bile duct system. It may be chronic (long term), or acute (sudden) when there is often accompanying bacterial infection of the gallbladder. Cholecystitis occurs in middle-aged people, especially women who are overweight and who are on the contraceptive pill. The condition causes severe pain in the right upper abdomen with nausea, chills, vomiting and high fever. Ultrasound shows gallstones in the gallbladder and cystic duct.

Treatment is with antibiotics and intravenous fluids in hospital. If the inflammation does not settle down, surgical removal of the gallbladder (cholecystectomy) is required.

SEE ALSO *Cholecystectomy, Gallbladder, Gallstones*

CHOLERA

Cholera is a bacterial infection of the intestines. It is spread in contaminated water supplies, in contaminated food and, rarely, by person-to-person contact. The disease occurs one to five days after ingesting the vibrio cholerae bacteria. The sufferer passes large volumes of pale watery diarrhea, and this can quickly lead to dehydration and to death if not treated. Cholera is particularly dangerous to young children whose relatively small body mass results in a more rapid onset of dehydration. Treatment is oral rehydration through salt solutions by mouth, or drip, which may be combined with antibiotics.

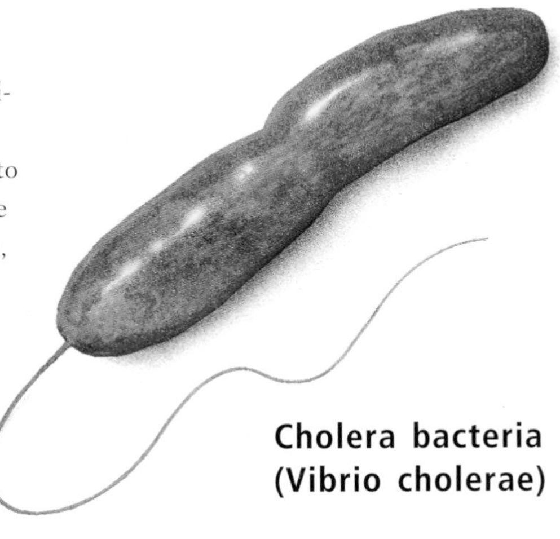

Cholera bacteria (Vibrio cholerae)

SEE ALSO *Dehydration, Diarrhea, Infectious diseases, Intestines*

CHOLESTEROL

Cholesterol is a fatty substance manufactured in the body and also absorbed from foods. It circulates in the blood in substances called lipoproteins. A high level of low-density lipoprotein (LDL) is linked to atherosclerosis—a condition where cholesterol sticks to the inside walls of arteries and

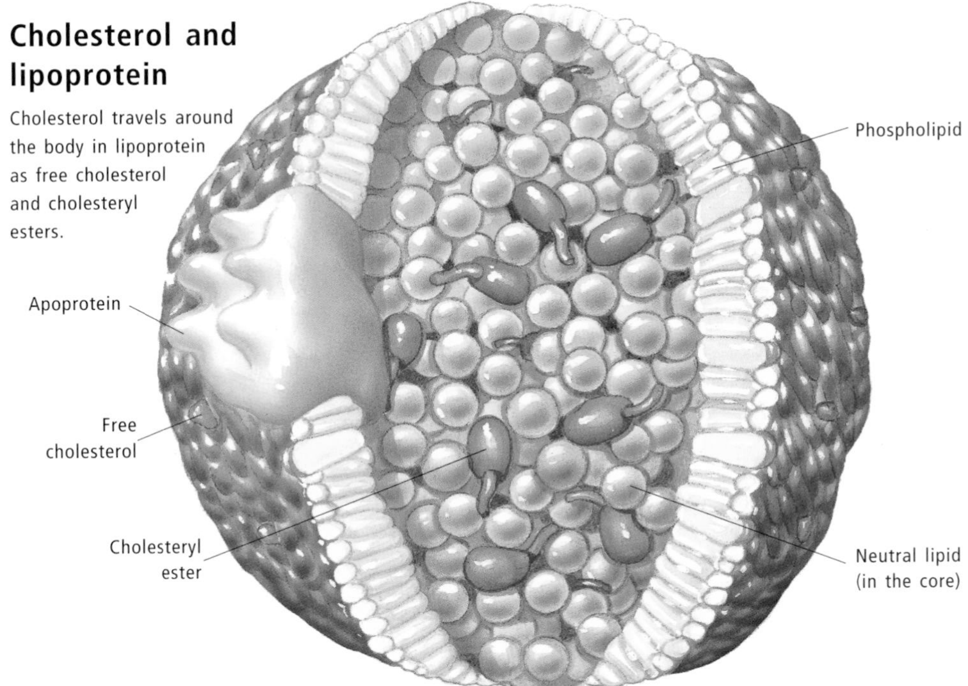

Cholesterol and lipoprotein

Cholesterol travels around the body in lipoprotein as free cholesterol and cholesteryl esters.

C

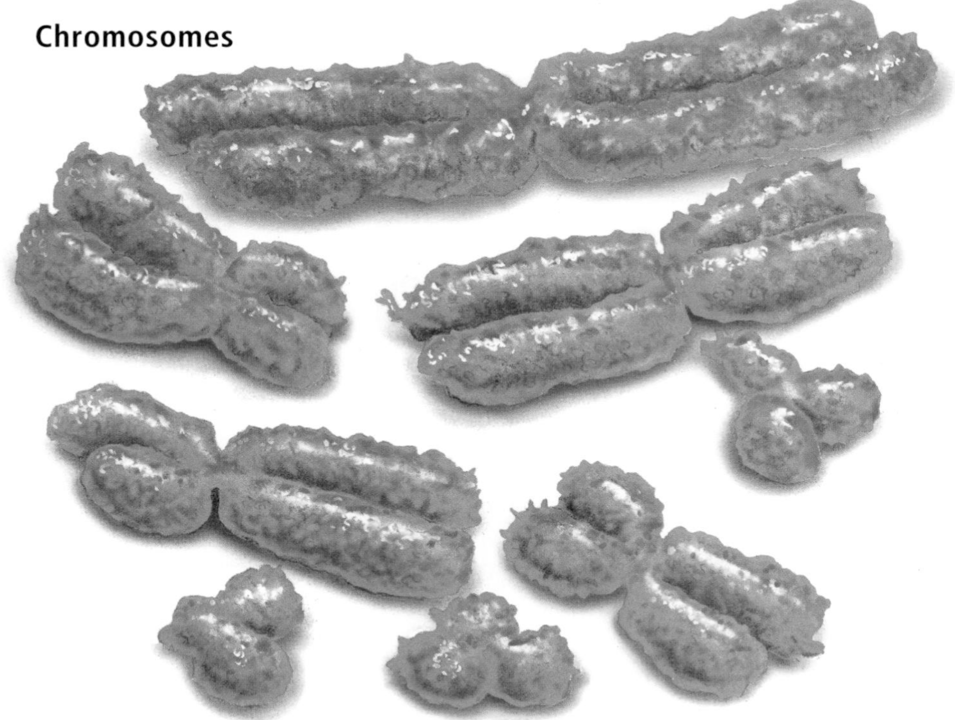

restricts blood flow. Arteries can become completely blocked, and where this happens in the arteries inside the heart the person will suffer myocardial infarction (heart attack). If arteries to the brain are blocked, a cerebral infarction (stroke) may result.

High-density lipoprotein (HDL) is believed to help remove cholesterol from the body by carrying it to the liver for processing and excretion.

International guidelines suggest that levels of LDL cholesterol in the blood should be below 200 milligrams per 100 milliliter (deciliter)—but levels differ with personal profile. In a small number of people, high cholesterol levels can be genetically inherited and the family's history plus a full medical examination will allow a doctor to consider all factors. Modifying the diet to exclude foods high in saturated fats can reduce levels of cholesterol in the blood.

This means eating less meat, butter and other dairy foods and eating more fruit, vegetables and cereals. Other risk factors, such as smoking, high blood pressure, being overweight, and not taking regular exercise need to be considered, as they further increase the chance of a heart attack.

As well as the dietary changes already mentioned, naturopaths suggest adding fish, onions, garlic, oat, barley and rice bran and vegetable proteins, especially soy products and dried legumes. Coffee, especially percolated, is to be avoided. Naturopaths recommend filtered water, as well as supplements of fish oil, nicotinic acid, calcium, vitamins C and E, lecithin and brewers' yeast.

SEE ALSO *Arteries, Diet, Fats, Heart, Myocardial infarction, Nutrition*

CHORIOCARCINOMA

Choriocarcinoma is a malignant, rapidly growing tumor that develops from embryonic tissue and may metastasize (spread to distant sites in the body). The tumor develops from the outer layer of the membrane (chorion) that had surrounded an embryo in an earlier pregnancy. It is most commonly seen after hydatidiform moles (molar pregnancies). Occasionally it appears in males in the testes.

A rare condition, choriocarcinoma tends to occur in women over the age of 40. The symptoms are irregular vaginal bleeding and discharge. It is often diagnosed by measuring levels of human chorionic gonadotropin (HCG) in the blood. Biopsy and laboratory examination confirms the diagnosis.

Choriocarcinomas are treated with chemotherapy (alone or in conjunction with radiation therapy) and prognosis is generally good. Hysterectomy is not usually needed.

SEE ALSO *Cancer, Hydatidiform mole, Pregnancy, Tumors*

CHORIONIC VILLUS SAMPLING

Chorionic villus sampling (CVS) is a prenatal test used to diagnose genetic defects in the fetus. Prenatal testing is recommended for mothers over 35, as they are at increased risk of having a child with a chromosomal abnormality such as Down syndrome. CVS has an advantage over amniocentesis in that it can detect problems much earlier in the pregnancy, but it has a slightly higher incidence of miscarriages due to the procedure (about 1.5 percent) and has been associated with limb deformities.

The procedure involves inserting a catheter through the cervix and into the uterus and sampling the chorion, a membrane that forms around the embryo in early stages of pregnancy before the placenta forms. The catheter is guided by abdominal ultrasound.

SEE ALSO *Amniocentesis, Chromosomal abnormalities, Congenital abnormalities*

CHROMOSOMAL ABNORMALITIES

Chromosomal abnormalities may arise through mutation of chromosomes during sperm production or ovum (egg) fertilization, or they may be genetically inherited. Most chromosomal abnormalities cause premature death of the fetus in the uterus, leading to spontaneous abortion (miscarriage). Some abnormalities are compatible with life, though physical or metabolic abnormalities may shorten or affect quality of life. In trisomy 21, for example, there are three number 21 chromosomes instead of two. This causes Down syndrome, a condition in which the child survives into adulthood but with developmental defects.

Suspected chromosomal abnormalities can be detected during pregnancy by amniocentesis, a procedure in which a small amount of amniotic fluid is removed from the amniotic sac around the fetus, which is then tested for specific defects in fetal cells. It is usually performed between the fifteenth and eighteenth weeks of pregnancy. It is recommended for some pregnant women known to be at risk, for example those with a family history of the abnormality or women over 35 years of age. Chorionic villus sampling (CVS) is another technique used during the first trimester of pregnancy; a tissue sample is taken from the placenta and analyzed for evidence of genetic defects in the fetus. If parents are concerned about possible chromosomal abnormalities in an unborn child—if there is a family history, or if an abnormality has occurred in a previous child—they should seek genetic counseling.

SEE ALSO *Amniocentesis, Chorionic villus sampling, Chromosomes, Down syndrome, Genetic counseling*

CHROMOSOMES

A chromosome is a threadlike structure in the nucleus of a cell. Every chromosome consists of a double strand of deoxyribonucleic acid (DNA), arranged in a helical shape. Each chromosome contains many hundreds of genes.

The nucleus of every cell in the normal human body cell contains 46 chromosomes arranged as 23 pairs. The exceptions are the ova (eggs) and sperm cells, which have only 23 single chromosomes. At fertilization, the two sex cells fuse to form an embryo cell with 23 pairs of chromosomes. One pair of the 23 pairs of chromosomes are the sex chromosomes. In males, one of the two sex chromosomes is shorter and contains fewer genes than the other; this is the Y chromosome. The other, longer, sex chromosome is the X chromosome. Males have an X and a Y sex chromosome, while females have two X sex chromosomes.

Chromosomal abnormalities may arise through mutation of chromosomes or may be inherited. Some abnormalities are compatible with life, though usually the affected person has physical or metabolic abnormalities that may be severe. Trisomy 21, in which there are three number 21 chromosomes, not two, causes Down syndrome.

SEE ALSO *Cells, Chromosomal abnormalities, DNA, Down syndrome*

CHRONIC FATIGUE SYNDROME

Chronic fatigue syndrome (CFS), also known as myalgic encephalo-myelitis (ME) or Tapanui flu (and also "yuppie flu"), is not fully understood. There is much debate as to whether this is a disease, but general agreement is that the syndrome does exist and the cause is unknown.

CFS may begin suddenly after an illness similar to flu or following surgery, accident, or bereavement. It affects the immune system and strikes more women than men. Said to exist where a person suffers chronic tiredness over at least six months and cannot gain relief through rest, the symptoms must be severe enough to prevent normal functioning at home and at work. Pain in muscles and abdomen, painful lymph nodes, and mild mental confusion are among the symptoms. Sufferers may develop sensitivity to certain foods, and to medications. Diagnosis is made after excluding pre-existing conditions such as psychiatric illness, depression, eating disorders, substance abuse and physical abnormalities.

Research has not found a cause, nor a cure, but stress seems to trigger the disease and worsen the symptoms. CFS can last for several years and some people never get better, although others recover in under a year. Treatment includes bed rest, avoiding stress, and prescription medications which help to alleviate anxiety.

There are a number of alternative therapies that may help to ease the symptoms of CFS. Acupuncture is thought to restore life energy known as *ch'i* and treats energy imbalance contributing to symptoms such as digestive weakness, muscle aches and mental cloudiness. It may also boost the immune system. Chinese herbs can also be given. Counseling or psychotherapy are often suggested to treat the depression that frequently accompanies chronic fatigue. Herbalism aims to boost the immune system with echinacea, garlic, and digestive tonics such as dandelion and chamomile. Ginkgo biloba may improve brain function and St John's wort may relieve depression. Homeopathy prescribes individual remedies, based on the patient's physical, mental and emotional profile, intending to facilitate a long-term healing process. Naturopathy treats with a detoxification diet, eliminating food additives and pesticides. An anti-candida diet may also be suggested. Patients are tested for food allergies and advised to avoid exposure to chemicals and perfumes. Various vitamins and minerals are prescribed along with exercise.

CIRCUMCISION

The operation of cutting away all or part of the foreskin of the penis is called circumcision. The operation of removing part or all of the female genitalia is known as female circumcision, clitoridectomy or female genital mutilation.

Circumcision of boys is done before or at puberty or, in some Arab peoples, just before marriage. A rite since the time of the ancient Egyptians, circumcision is today an important religious ritual in Islamic and Jew-

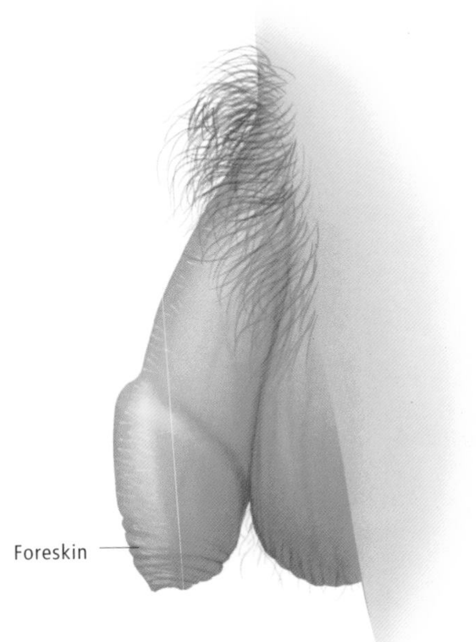

Uncircumcised penis

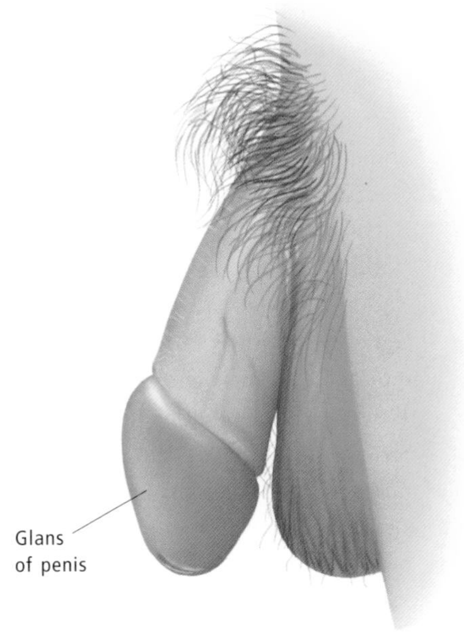

Circumcised penis

ish communities worldwide. It became popular in many industrialized cultures in the early 1900s in the belief that it promoted good hygiene and also discouraged masturbation. Generally, the arguments in favor of circumcision are that there is less likelihood of penile cancer, urinary tract infections or sexually transmitted diseases; the penis is easier to clean; the rest of the males in the family are circumcised; or problems with the foreskin. The arguments against are that it is an unnecessary, painful operation with the possibility of complications, the sensation at the tip of the penis (the glans) is diminished, it is just as easy to clean under a foreskin as without, and that problems with the foreskin are most often caused by adults forcibly attempting to retract it in a young boy before it is ready.

Female circumcision has been performed for centuries in parts of Africa, the Middle East and Southeast Asia with the purpose of preserving virginity, improving hygiene or as a religious ritual. It is usually performed by non-medical practitioners in non-medical settings and has a high risk of complications and long-term consequences including sterility. The procedure can involve infibulation which is the removal of the clitoris, the labia minora and the anterior two-thirds of the labia majora with a join made leaving a small opening. It can also involve the introduction of corrosive substances to cause bleeding for the purpose of narrowing the vagina; or any or all of the above. Even when the wounds heal normally, urination and sexual intercourse can be painful and unreleased menstrual blood can cause problems. In societies where clitoridectomy is practised, male circumcision is usually also practised and it is considered to be an important religious ritual or ethnic tradition.

The World Health Organization, the United Nations Population Fund and the United Nations Children's Fund have drawn up a plan to reduce female genital mutilation, with the aim of eliminating it completely. Strong lobby groups against female genital mutilation exist in many industrialized countries who view it not only as a major health risk but also as the subjugation of women so that they will never enjoy sexual relations.

SEE ALSO *Clitoris, Glans, Penis*

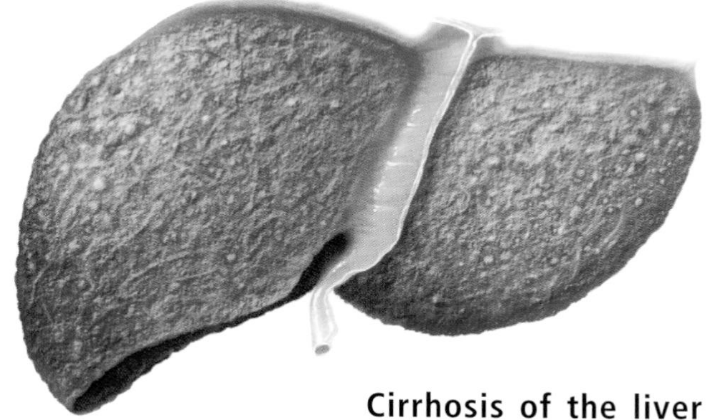

Cirrhosis of the liver

Cirrhosis is the destruction of normal liver tissue. The liver becomes shrunken and filled with fibrous tissue. It functions poorly, and the flow of blood through the liver may become restricted. Eventually, a liver transplant may be needed.

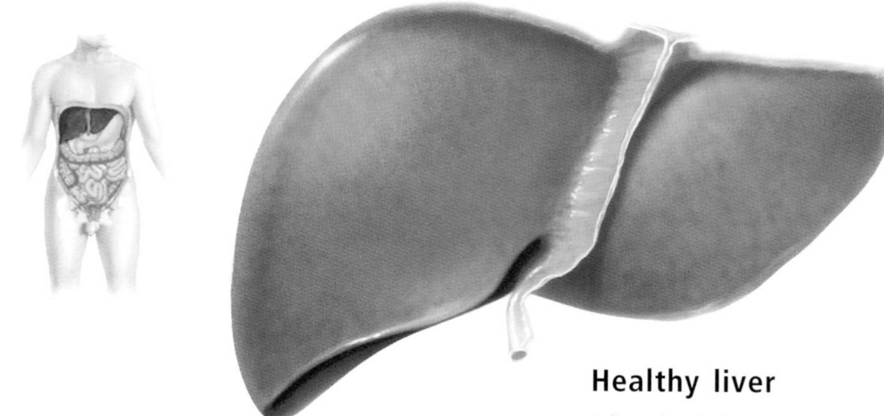

Healthy liver

A liver that is functioning properly has a number of important tasks to perform for the body, including filtering the blood, secreting bile, and converting sugars into glycogen.

Cirrhosis and liver cells

Cirrhosis disrupts the regular microstructure of the liver. Scarring of the liver occurs when cells become misshapen and form nodules, and the bands of tissue that divide the lobules become fibrous or fatty. As the structure of the lobule breaks down, the blood vessels may become blocked, leading to increased blood pressure and hypertension.

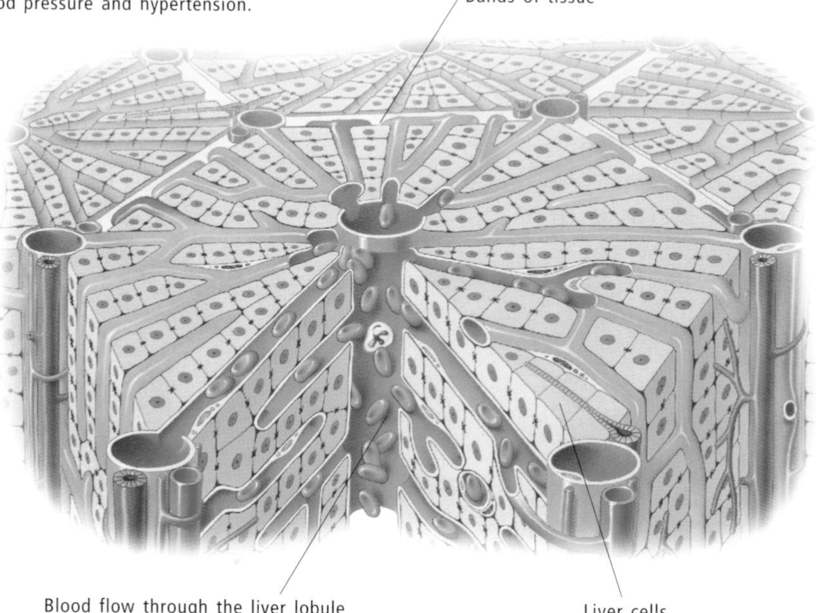
Bands of tissue
Blood flow through the liver lobule is compromised by cirrhosis.
Liver cells

C

CIRRHOSIS OF THE LIVER

Cirrhosis of the liver is a disease in which there is death of liver cells followed by production of fibrous tissue and regeneration of liver cells in lumps or nodules. The nodules distort the normal structure of the liver and prevent the easy flow of blood through the liver. Cirrhosis may be caused by excessive and prolonged consumption of alcohol. In this case the damage to the liver cells is probably due to the direct toxic effects of alcohol, although a poor diet may also contribute. Patients with alcoholic cirrhosis may also show Dupuytren's contracture, a contraction of connective tissue in the hand, deterioration of the brain, heart problems and enlargement of the parotid salivary gland in the cheek. Men may develop breast enlargement (gynecomastia) and wasting of the testes. Other causes include problems with the storage of iron (hemochromatosis) and an inherited disease to do with copper metabolism (Wilson's disease).

Complications which may arise from cirrhosis include vomiting blood from the esophagus, swelling of the abdomen and ankles, drowsiness, confusion and unconsciousness. About 20 percent of patients with cirrhosis will develop liver cancer.

Treatment of cirrhosis will depend on the cause of liver damage. Alcoholics must abstain from alcohol. Hemochromatosis is treated by removal of blood, while Wilson's disease is treated by drugs which serve to bind the excess copper.

SEE ALSO *Alcoholism, Dupuytren's contracture, Hemochromatosis, Liver, Wilson's disease*

CLAUSTROPHOBIA

Claustrophobia is a specific type of anxiety disorder—an unrealistic and extreme fear of closed places or of being confined. The thought of confinement, or a memory of a confined place, may be all that is needed to trigger the symptoms, which can be physically debilitating. Symptoms include nausea, vomiting, racing heartbeat, diarrhea, and throat constriction. A fear becomes a phobia when the condition interferes with the ability to lead a normal life. Sufferers may know that their reactions are irrational and out of proportion, but whether they are conscious of this or not, the fears are real and must be treated as such.

SEE ALSO *Anxiety, Anxiolytics, Phobias*

CLEFT PALATE AND CLEFT LIP

Cleft palate is a congenital abnormality, in which there is an abnormal opening in the roof of the mouth. Normally as the fetus develops, separate tissues from either side of the mouth fuse together to form the palate, upper lip and upper jaw. If the tissues do not fuse, an abnormal gap connecting the nasal passages with the mouth is the result. The gap is called a cleft palate; it can be closed by surgery, but a series of operations is often required.

Often, a cleft palate is accompanied by a similar gap in the upper lip—this is known as a cleft lip, or harelip. Cleft lip may occur on its own or with cleft palate. Normally, both sides of the upper lip should fuse in the first 35 days in the uterus. If it fails to fuse, a cleft lip is the result. The cleft may vary in size from a notch to a fissure that extends across the whole lip. Usually, it extends from the mouth up into the nostril. It can be on one side only (unilateral) or on both sides (bilateral). The treatment for cleft lip is surgery, usually when the infant is about 10 weeks old or weighs 10 pounds (4.5 kilograms).

Both cleft palate and cleft lip affect females more often than males and sometimes run in families. A cleft palate may occur in combination with heart defects, and an abnormal face, and also learning problems in the congenital disorder known as Shprintzen syndrome (also called the velo-cardio-facial syndrome).

SEE ALSO *Lip, Mouth*

CLITORIS

The clitoris is part of the external female genitals. The shaft of the clitoris is about half an inch (approximately 1 centimeter) in length. The clitoris lies about ½–1 inch (1–2 centimeters) in front of the external opening of the urethra, which carries urine from the bladder. The tip of the clitoris has a glans or head, usually hidden within a fold of thin skin known as the prepuce. The prepuce of the clitoris is a forward extension of the hairless folds of skin (labia minora) which lie on each side of the vagina. Much like the penis, the clitoris is extremely sensitive to sexual stimuli.

SEE ALSO *Reproductive systems, Vulva*

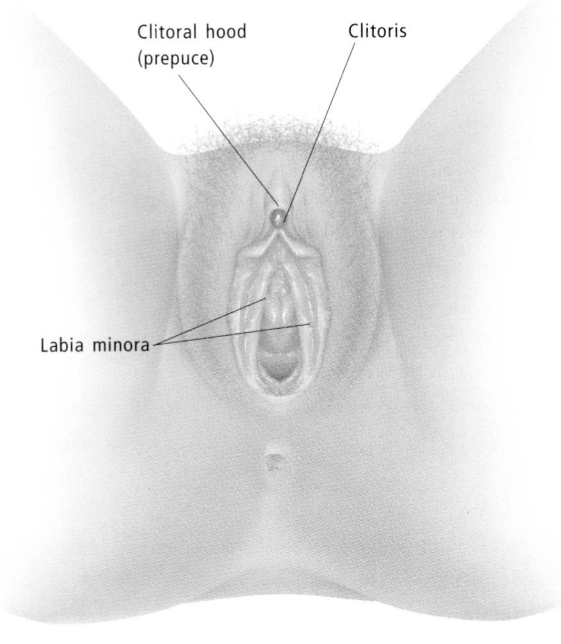

Clitoris

The clitoris is a small protrusion that is very sensitive to stimulation. When a woman becomes aroused, the clitoris fills with blood, enlarges and becomes erect.

COCAINE

Cocaine is a stimulant drug illegal in most countries. Extracted from the leaves of the coca plant, it is processed into cocaine hydrochloride, a white powder that can be inhaled or injected. Crack is a modified form of cocaine that can be smoked. Historically, cocaine was used for medicinal purposes as an anesthetic for surgery of mucous membranes.

Cocaine speeds up the central nervous system producing a faster heartbeat, a rise in temperature, feelings of exhilaration, anxiety, or even panic, loss of concentration, and unpredictable or violent behavior. Large quantities can cause paranoia, heart attack and even death. Likewise, long-term use can induce paranoia and hallucinations, repeated injections can block and inflame blood vessels, and inhalation can damage the lining of the nose and the septum (the barrier between the nostrils).

SEE ALSO *Anesthesia, Drug dependence, Stimulants*

C

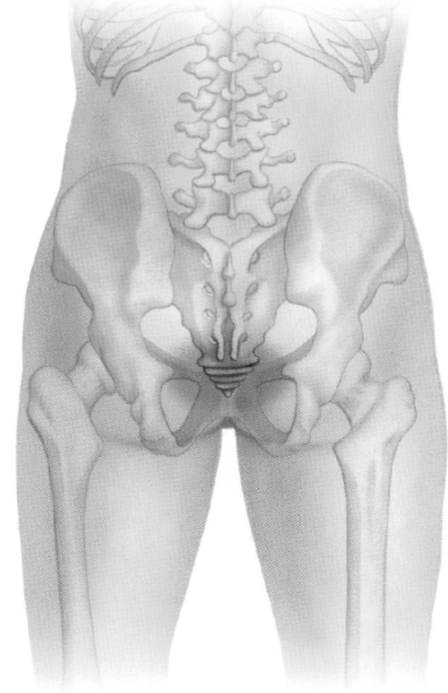

Coccygodynia

Coccygodynia is a painful inflammation of the coccyx (tailbone) that usually occurs following a direct fall onto the area. Treatment with anti-inflammatory drugs may be necessary to relieve the symptoms.

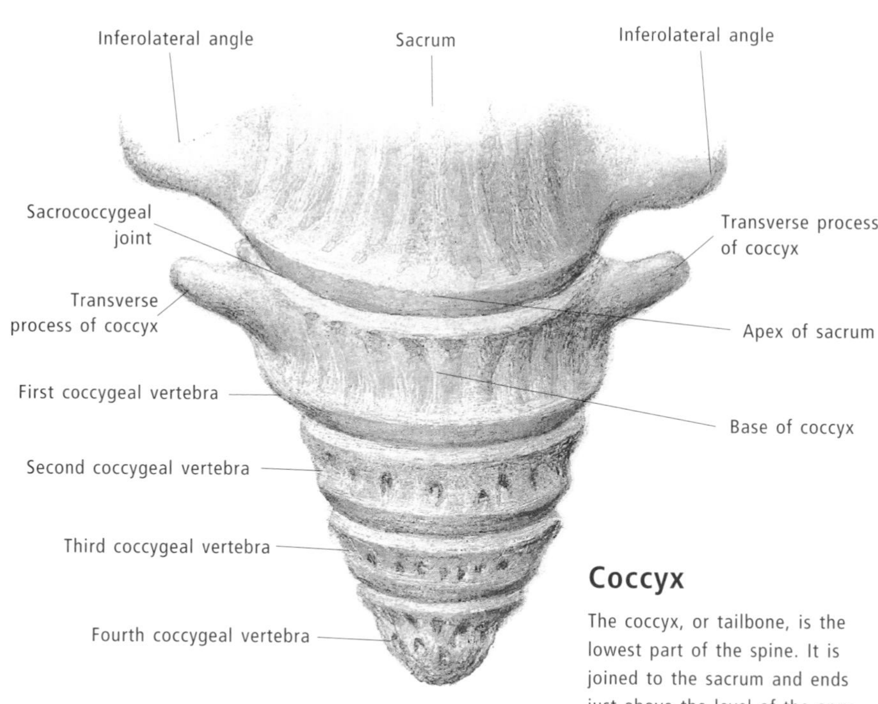

Coccyx

The coccyx, or tailbone, is the lowest part of the spine. It is joined to the sacrum and ends just above the level of the anus.

COCCYGODYNIA

Coccygodynia (also called tailbone pain) is inflammation of the bony area (tailbone or coccyx) located at the lowest part of the spine. It may occur for no apparent reason, but more usually follows an injury to the coccyx—for example when someone falls heavily backward in a sitting position. The pain is worse when sitting or passing feces, but goes when the person stands.

Treatment with anti-inflammatory and analgesic drugs can relieve the symptoms. People with coccygodynia should avoid long periods of sitting and when they do sit, they should use a padded cushion or seat. Persistent coccygodynia can be treated with cortisone injected into the area. In severe cases that don't respond to other treatments, the coccyx can be surgically removed.

SEE ALSO *Coccyx, Spine*

COCCYX

The coccyx is the lowest bone of the spine. Situated just above the anus, it is formed from three to five rudimentary vertebrae, which are fused and joined to the sacrum above. The coccyx is also called the tailbone. The word "coccygeal" derives from the Greek *kokkyx* meaning "cuckoo bird" as the coccyx was thought to look like a cuckoo's bill.

Coccygodynia is persistent, severe pain in the coccyx. It usually follows an injury to the coccyx. Treatment with analgesic and anti-inflammatory drugs can ease the symptoms on many cases.

SEE ALSO *Coccygodynia, Spine*

COCHLEA

The cochlea is a small, spiral-shaped structure in the inner ear containing fluid and special hair cells which serve as sound sensors.

Sound waves entering the ear set up a chain of vibrations, beginning with the eardrum (tympanic membrane). These continue with the middle ear bones (ossicles), which transmit vibrations to the cochlea, where they cause waves to form in the cochlear fluid. The waves in turn stimulate tiny hair cells in the cochlea, which transform vibrations into nerve impulses for transmission to the brain. These are recognized by the brain as sounds.

A cochlear implant (also known as a bionic ear) is a system of tiny electrodes which is surgically inserted into the inner ear and which transmits sound vibrations to the auditory nerve. It restores hearing to a person whose cochlea has been damaged, for example by trauma, drug toxicity or infection.

SEE ALSO *Ear, Hearing*

COGNITIVE THERAPY

Cognitive therapy is a widely practised form of psychotherapy used to treat emotional and behavioral disorders, particularly depression and anxiety. The word cognize, from which the term cognitive comes, means "to know or perceive".

A simple interpretation of the underlying basis of cognitive therapy is that thoughts affect a person's behavior and emotions. Practitioners using this treatment help patients turn around their way of thinking from being negative, destructive and sometimes harmful to being positive and constructive. As fundamental as it may sound, changing the way someone thinks about events can, however, be a complex process.

Patients with depression or anxiety often fail to understand that thoughts which enter their mind in response to experiences in their lives may be based on errors in reasoning—that is, cognitive errors or distortions. They may, for example, place all blame for a relationship breakdown on themselves or believe they are personally responsible for a tragedy beyond their control. A fundamental component of cognitive therapy involves helping patients recognize and modify cognitive distortions.

Another aspect of this form of therapy is aimed at modifying, when necessary, a patient's core beliefs or "schemas". These are regarded as the basic rules the mind uses for interpreting information.

Frequently, cognitive therapy involves the use of intervention techniques for dysfunctional behaviors, in the belief that what patients do reinforces the way they think, as well as the other way around.

SEE ALSO *Anxiety, Behavioral therapy, Counseling, Depression, Psychotherapy*

COLD SORES

A cold sore, also known as herpes simplex type 1 or HSV-1, results from a viral infection. It attacks the skin and nervous system producing small, sometimes painful, fluid-filled blisters around the mouth and nose. After a first infection the virus will continue to live in the nerve system in a dormant state from which it can be reactivated by a trigger. These triggers may include sunlight, physical or emotional stress, hormonal changes, certain foods or drugs. The trigger can also be unknown.

An attack begins with a tingling sensation at the spot where the sore will erupt, followed by a rash, then blisters or spots. These can come in clusters, fill with fluid, rupture and form crusts. Cold sores can take up to three weeks to disappear and are highly contagious until healed. Anyone with a cold sore must be diligent about washing hands and scrubbing fingernails, and avoid kissing and other oral contact. It is important not to touch the eye after touching a sore as this can cause an infection or corneal ulceration.

While cold sores are unpleasant to look at, they are not a serious risk to general health. Most cold sores will clear up without treatment; however, acyclovir, an anti-viral drug, can be prescribed. It is most effective if used at the first signs of a sore. Aromatherapists recommend neat lavender oil.

Once the herpes virus has entered the system it stays with the person for life, though attacks usually diminish and often disappear over time. From 10 to 15 percent of cases of genital herpes are caused by the cold sore virus (herpes simplex type 1) and it is possible to sexually transmit cold sores to the genitalia.

SEE ALSO *Genital herpes, Herpes simplex*

COLIC

Colic is pain resulting from the distension of a hollow internal organ, usually the intestine. Babies and children are especially prone, but adults can suffer too. Typically colic in babies begins at two to four weeks and lasts until around three months. Symptoms are excessive crying (three hours or more a day, three days a week is excessive) and curling up the legs. Older children complain of pain. One common cause is wind that has passed into the stomach or intestine rather than being released through a burp. Colic can also be caused by a groin hernia.

There is no safe medicine for babies with colic. Aromatherapy and osteopathy are said to help. If the baby is being breast fed, this should be continued as ceasing will not solve the problem. If the baby's crying is causing tension in the mother and it affects her breast feeding, then relaxation and reassurance that the colic will pass may help. Making sure the baby has a routine and learning what the baby's cries mean can also help. It is also important that the mother of a colicky baby has regular breaks herself and is offered support.

SEE ALSO *Breast feeding, Infancy, Newborn*

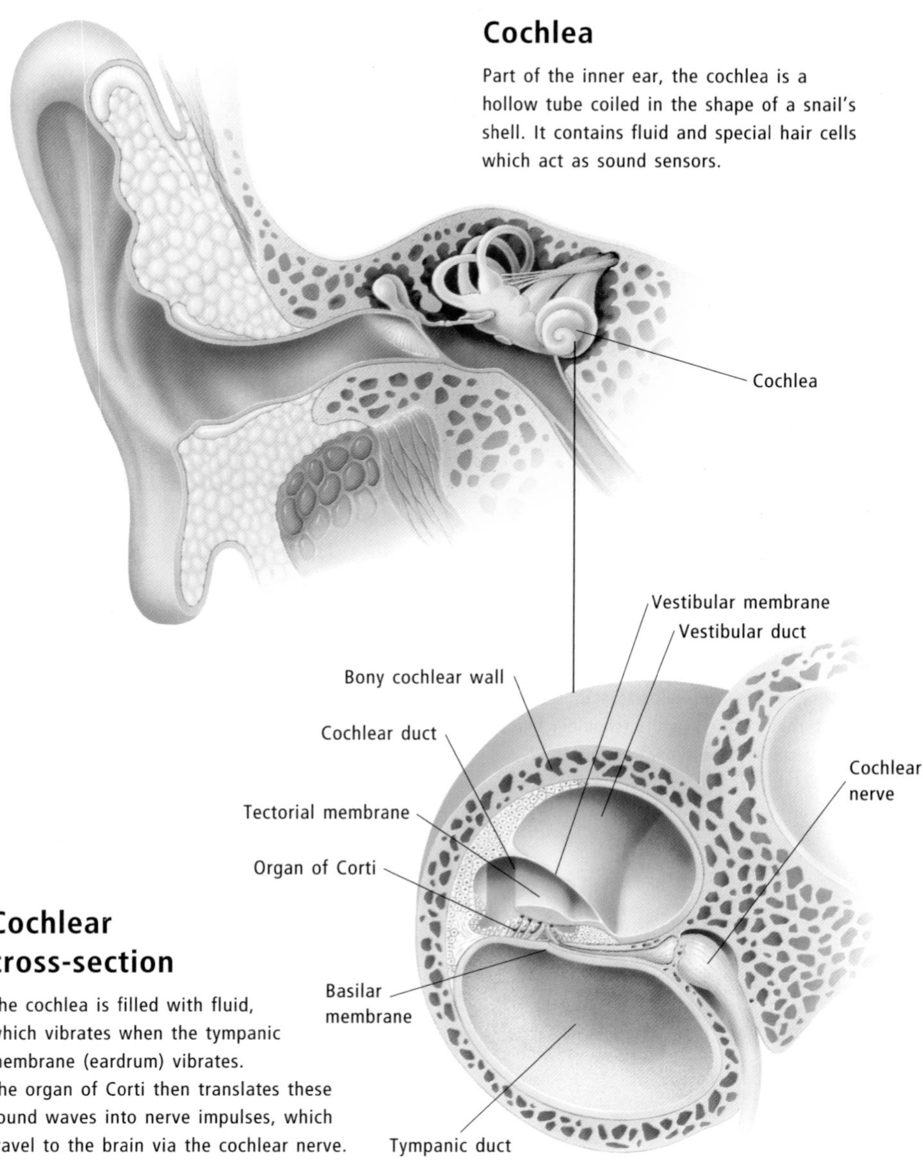

Cochlea

Part of the inner ear, the cochlea is a hollow tube coiled in the shape of a snail's shell. It contains fluid and special hair cells which act as sound sensors.

Cochlear cross-section

The cochlea is filled with fluid, which vibrates when the tympanic membrane (eardrum) vibrates. The organ of Corti then translates these sound waves into nerve impulses, which travel to the brain via the cochlear nerve.

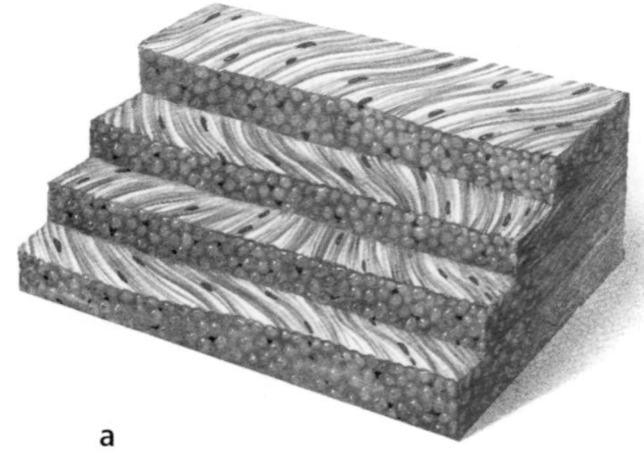

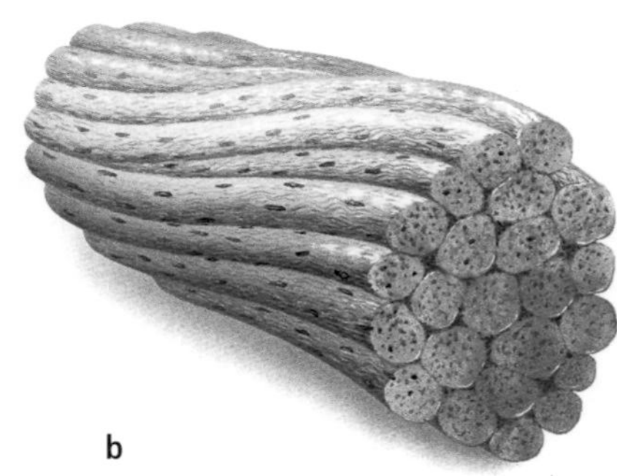

Collagen

Collagen is a tough, flexible protein, found in different arrangements, in structures such as ligaments (a), tendons (b), and the supporting capsules of internal organs (c).

COLITIS

Colitis is inflammation of the large intestine (colon). It may be mild or it may be more serious with severe symptoms, as in ulcerative colitis or Crohn's disease. Symptoms of colitis tend to come and go unpredictably. They can include diarrhea, fever, and crampy abdominal pain. In Crohn's disease or ulcerative colitis there may be intermittent bleeding from the rectum.

Diagnosis is confirmed by a barium enema, or better still, direct viewing by sigmoidoscopy or colonoscopy, which allows a sample of the lining of the large bowel to be taken for laboratory analysis.

Crohn's disease can involve both the colon and small intestine, whereas ulcerative colitis usually involves only the colon. Both are thought to be autoimmune diseases. Crohn's disease may cause ulcers in the lining of the colon, causing scarring, narrowing of the bowel, obstruction, perforation and peritonitis. It is treated with anti-inflammatory, immune suppressant and antibiotic drugs.

Ulcerative colitis can also be associated with inflammation in the joints, spine, skin, eyes, liver and bile ducts. Long-standing ulcerative colitis increases the risk of colon cancer. Mild attacks are usually treated with drugs, a low-fiber diet and rest.

SEE ALSO *Barium enema, Bowel, Crohn's disease, Colon, Intestines, Irritable bowel syndrome, Ulcerative colitis*

COLLAGEN

Collagen is an important structural protein in the body. It is made up of chains of amino acids, with glycine, proline and hydroxyproline being the most common. Collagen is often organized in long parallel bundles of fibers, forming connective tissue, which has a very high tensile strength (for example ligaments and tendons). Collagen may also be formed into sheets (such as mesenteries of the abdominal cavity).

Collagen diseases are a group of diseases (also known as connective tissue diseases), in which there is an attack by the body's immune system on the structural protein of the patient's body. One example is systemic lupus erythematosus.

SEE ALSO *Autoimmune disease, Connective tissue*

COLLAR BONE

The collar bones, or clavicles, are a pair of short horizontal bones above the rib cage. They are attached to the breast bone (sternum), and the two shoulder blades (scapulas) on either side. The function of the collar bones is to stabilize the shoulders.

A fracture of the collar bone is common in childhood. It is usually caused by a fall onto an outstretched hand or the point of a shoulder. Following the fall, the arm on the injured side is limp, and a lump or deformity can be felt or seen over the fracture site.

Treatment involves stabilizing the clavicle with a figure-of-eight splint, which holds the shoulders back and allows the two broken ends of the clavicle to knit and heal.

Collar bone

The collar bone, or clavicle, helps to stabilize the shoulder joint. It is attached to the scapula (shoulder blade) at one end and the sternum (breastbone) at the other.

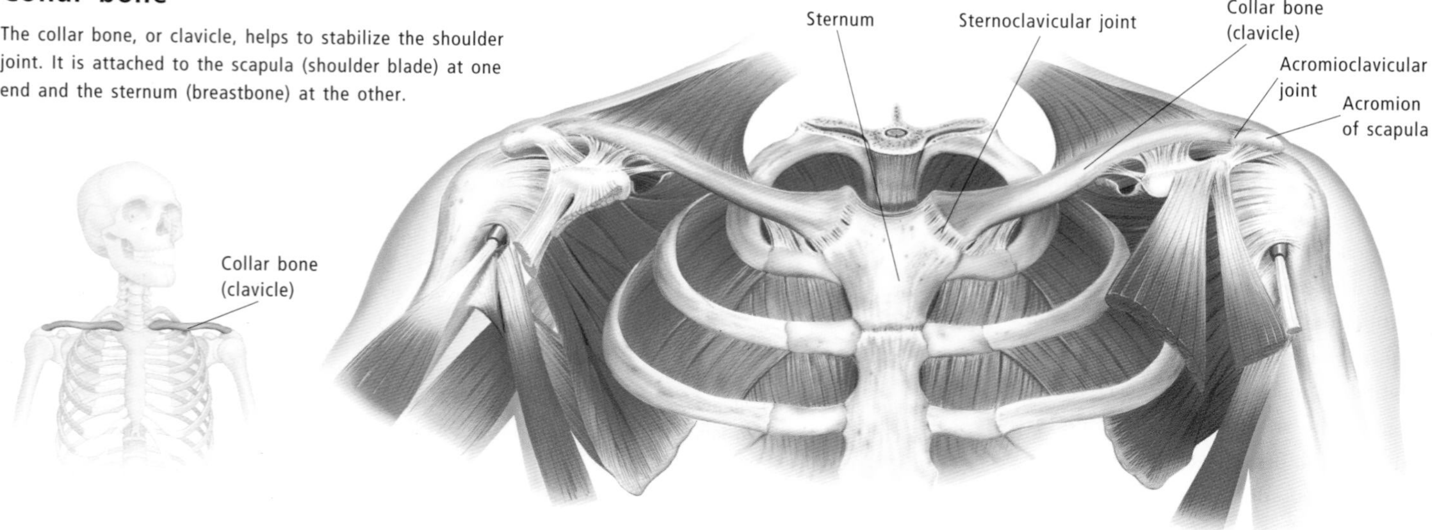

To heal completely takes eight to twelve weeks. Fracture of the clavicle is especially common in the newborn infant. It is prone to breakage so as to allow the infant's shoulders to pass through the narrow birth canal. No treatment is needed as the fracture heals by itself in a few weeks.

SEE ALSO *Ribs, Scapula, Shoulder*

COLON

The colon is part of the large intestine and moves waste material to the anus, absorbing salt and water. It is composed of various organs: the cecum, ascending colon, transverse colon, descending colon and sigmoid colon. The appendix is attached to the cecum.

Ulcerative colitis is a disease that can affect the colon. It occurs in the 15 to 20 age group, or in people over fifty. Patients present with rectal bleeding and diarrhea. They may have frequent discharges of watery stools mixed with pus, blood and mucus. Many patients have cramping abdominal pain, fever, vomiting and weight loss. The disease may have a family history, but is thought to involve some infective or toxic agent interfering with the immune system function in the bowel, causing the body's own defence cells to attack the lining of the colon. Complications include anal problems, perforation of the colon, bleeding from the colon and an increased risk of cancer of the colon.

Hirschsprung's disease is a congenital condition in which the nerve cells controlling the large bowel are missing. The bowel is unable to propel feces along its length, so that obstruction results.

Polyposis of the colon is a rare genetic condition. Patients develop multiple polyps (mushroom-shaped lumps which usually have a stalk, by which they attached to the bowel lining) in the large intestine. Polyps develop in other conditions, but not as many as seen in polyposis. The danger is that each polyp has a chance of cancer developing within it; the more polyps there are, the greater the chance of cancer. This means that patients with polyposis are almost certain to develop cancer within their lifetime. The only cure is to completely remove the colon.

Common investigations of the colon include barium enema and colonoscopy. In a barium enema, the colon is filled with a barium compund which is opaque to x-rays. An x-ray is taken both while the colon is full of barium and after evacuation, and can detect abnomalities of the colon lining. Colonoscopy involves the insertion of a fiberoptic or electronic instrument into the colon to inspect its interior.

SEE ALSO *Barium enema, Colitis, Colonoscopy, Hirschsprung's disease, Intestines*

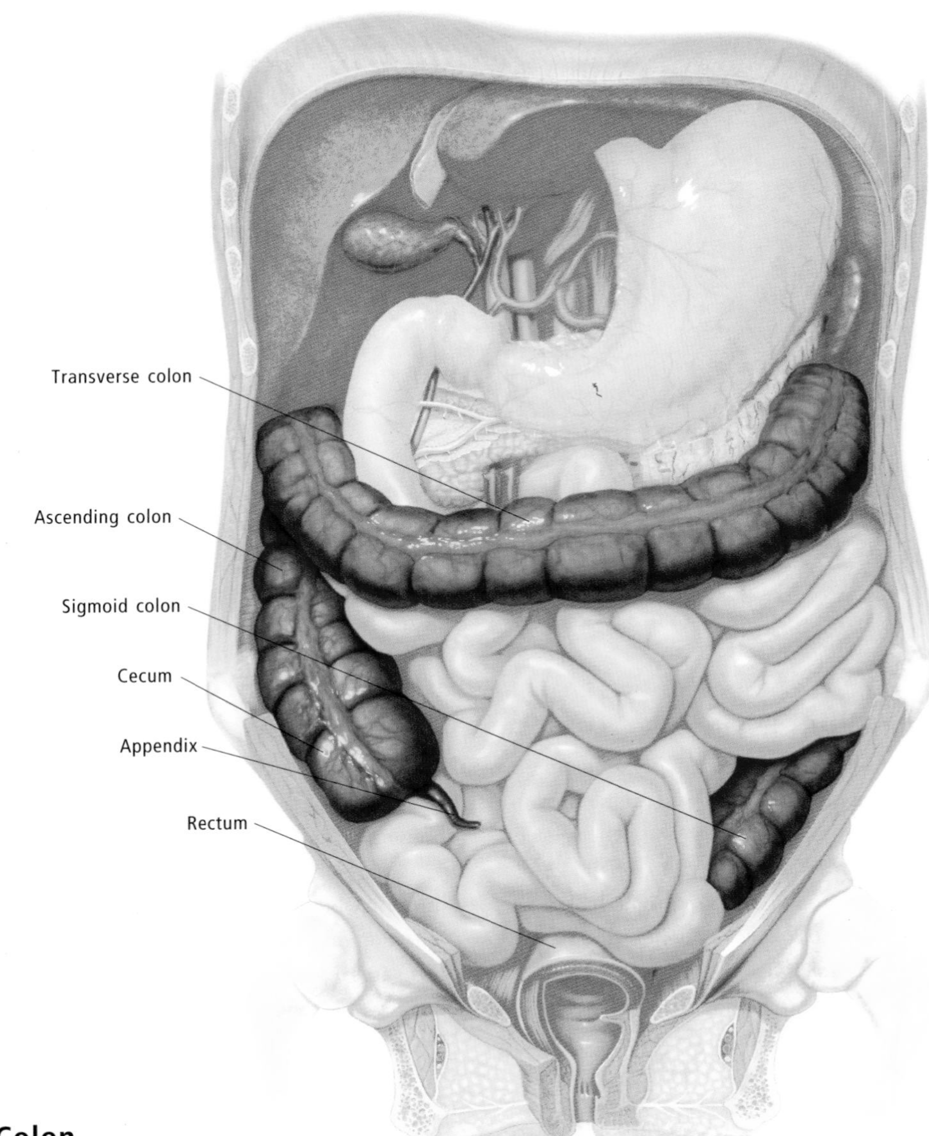

Colon

The colon is part of the large intestine. It stretches from the end of the small intestine through to the rectum and is made up of several parts. The function of the colon is to move solid material to the anus and to absorb salt and water remaining after passage through the small intestine.

COLONIC IRRIGATION

Colonic irrigation is a detoxification technique recommended by some natural therapists. It involves cleansing the large intestine with purified water introduced through the anus via plastic or rubber tubing.

During this procedure the patient lies in a knee-to-chest position on a specially designed table for the 30–40 minutes it takes for the irrigation to take place either manually or by machine. To be safe, this procedure must be performed by qualified staff using sterilized equipment. It is prescribed for chronic bowel conditions and digestive discomfort. Colonic irrigation is considered to help restore the bowel's muscle tone and circulation.

SEE ALSO *Bowel, Colon, Intestines*

C

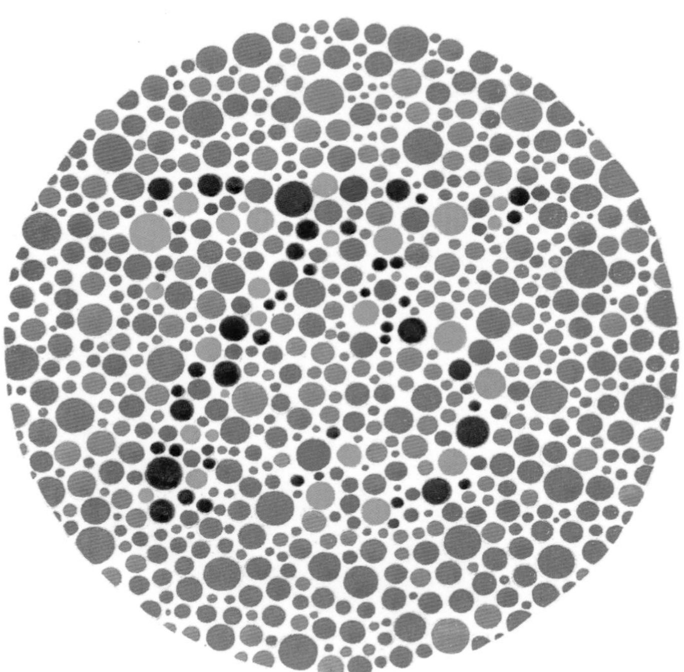

Color blindness

This is a classic test for color blindness. Those with red-green color blindness would not be able to see the number in this image. Tests like this are known as Ishihara tests.

COLOR BLINDNESS

Color blindness is an inability to distinguish between certain colors. A total inability to see color—achromatic vision, where everything appears as black, white or shades of gray—is rare in humans, although about 10 percent of males are believed to have impaired color vision.

The ability to distinguish colors is the job of cone cells in the retina of the eye. There are three types of cone cells, each absorbing different wavelengths. When one type is missing it may cause red blindness, with difficulty telling red from green, or blue blindness where it is difficult to distinguish between blue and yellow, or there may be various grades of difficulty, depending on the impairment.

Color blindness is primarily an inherited condition, caused by a gene linked to the Y (male) chromosome. The gene can be carried by both males and females, but is more likely to be inherited by male children. Another factor is age—the lens darkens with age and colors become more difficult to distinguish. Some medications and various eye diseases can also affect color vision.

Children having learning difficulties at school, and anyone with a family tendency, should be tested for color blindness. People are often ignorant of their impairment until tested. There are no cures for color blindness and sufferers will be unable to perform certain jobs where normal color vision is vital.

COLOSTOMY

A colostomy is a surgical procedure in which the interior of the bowel is opened and brought to the surface of the body. The resulting opening is called a stoma. Colostomies may be used to relieve pressure in an obstructed bowel, to divert the stream of feces in preparation of the bowel for surgery, to allow for removal of feces from the lower bowel when a portion is removed, and to protect surgically repaired bowel further down the gut. Colostomies may be temporary or permanent and may be performed by opening either the side of the bowel, or one end of the bowel, onto the skin surface. The most common type of permanent colostomy involves the sigmoid part of the colon, which is located in the pelvis. This is usually performed at the time of removal of the rectum for cancer. Usually patients can eat the same types of food which they enjoyed before colostomy, except that fruits may cause diarrhea.

SEE ALSO *Bowel, Colon, Intestines*

COMA

Coma is a deep, often prolonged, state of unconsciousness. It may be caused by a disease (such as diabetes), liver or kidney failure, head injury, stroke, reaction to drugs or alcohol, or an epileptic seizure. It differs from sleep in that the subject cannot be roused by external stimulation.

Anyone found to be unconscious should be laid on their side in the so-called recovery position. Emergency services should be called at once, as the comatose person will need to be hospitalized, where treatment will be aimed at reversing whatever is causing the coma. In the meantime, airways must be kept open, and artificial respiration and cardiopulmonary resuscitation started if pulse and breathing are absent.

SEE ALSO *Unconsciousness*

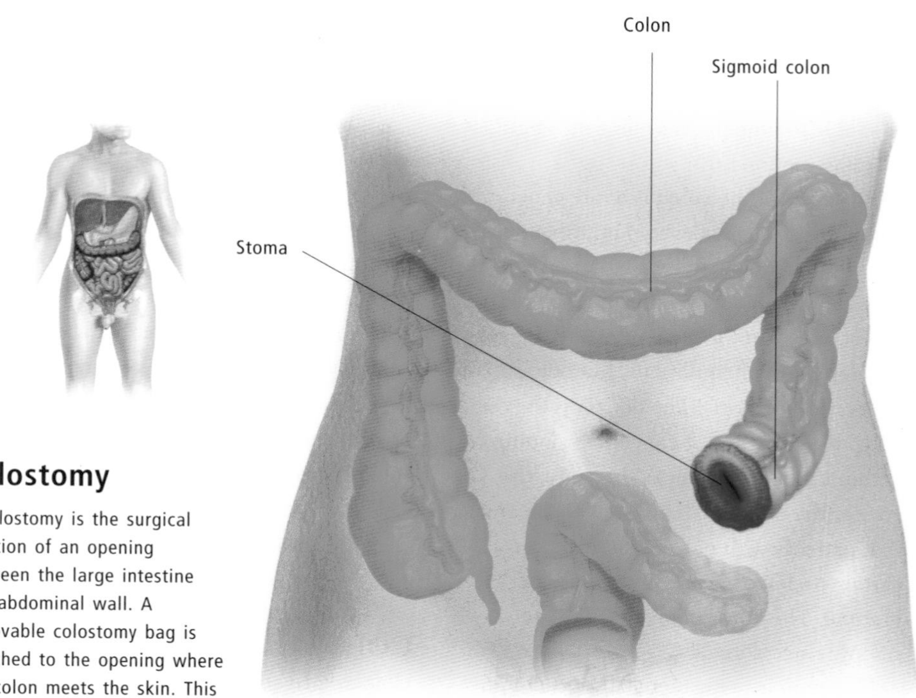

Colostomy

A colostomy is the surgical creation of an opening between the large intestine and abdominal wall. A removable colostomy bag is attached to the opening where the colon meets the skin. This opening is known as a stoma.

C

COMMON COLD

The common cold can be caused by one of five viral families that, between them, encompass a couple of hundred unique viral strains. Most typical of these are the rhinoviruses and coronaviruses, which affect the upper respiratory tract. Secondary infections may occur in the eye or middle ear, particularly in children. Adults may also suffer from inflamed sinuses. The main difference between the common cold and other respiratory infections, including the flu, is the absence of fever (except in children), as well as the general mildness of the symptoms.

Because the viral strains are sufficiently different from one another it is possible to catch one and later be infected by another. So children are particularly susceptible, especially if they mix socially with large numbers of people; they can have between four and ten colds in a year, or more if they suffer asthma attacks. The cold is spread by contact between people, which is thought to be the reason why colds are more prevalent in winter when people spend more time indoors and in contact with each other. Colds are transmitted by droplets breathed, coughed or sneezed onto another person. The incubation period is short—between one and four days. First symptoms can be a sore throat, feeling tired, nasal discharge and/or aching muscles followed by sneezing, coughing, headaches, a chill and nasal discharge. Cold symptoms will vary from person to person, but will usually take from seven to ten days from start to finish.

Treatment consists of easing the symptoms; plenty of fluids and acetaminophen (paracetamol) or ibuprofen may help. Children should never be given aspirin because of the possibility of Reye's syndrome, which can be fatal. Antibiotics are of no value against a virus, though they may be prescribed for an infectious complication. Over-the-counter preparations are plentiful for treatment of cold symptoms. Some contain drugs to constrict the blood vessels, others contain antihistamine which relieves stuffiness and can help induce sleep. There have been over sixty trials of vitamin C and its effects on the common cold, with different and confusing results. The majority, however, show that taking vitamin C has little effect on reducing the incidence of colds.

The reason it is difficult for researchers to come up with a cure is the number of different viruses. An additional factor is that the cold is only common to humans, which makes it difficult to test possible cures.

Although there is no cure, precautions can be taken: these include a nutritious diet with plenty of fruit, vegetables and legumes; regular exercise; avoiding smoky environments; getting enough sleep; staying away from people with colds and other illnesses; washing hands frequently and teaching children to do likewise, particularly after touching the nose or mouth; keeping warm and dry; and avoiding crowds.

There are a number of alternative therapies that may help to alleviate the symptoms of the common cold. Acupuncture is said to speed recovery and boost the immune system in cases of repeated bouts of cold. Aromatherapy uses decongestant oils such as eucalyptus or peppermint in inhalations, baths or oil burners. Herbalism prescribes anti-inflammatory and antiviral herbs such as echinacea, garlic and astralagus, as well as ginger and cayenne for warming. Sweating is encouraged with diaphoretic herbs such as peppermint or yarrow. Naturopathy views colds as a natural detoxification process which should not be suppressed. To ease the severity of a cold, naturopaths recommend vitamin C and zinc along with a light cleansing diet, plenty of fluids and rest.

SEE ALSO *Asthma, Viruses, Respiratory system, Reye's syndrome*

Cold virus

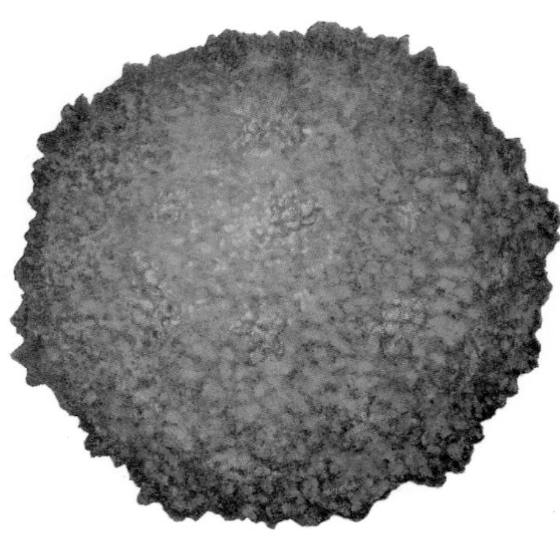

Viral attack at cell level

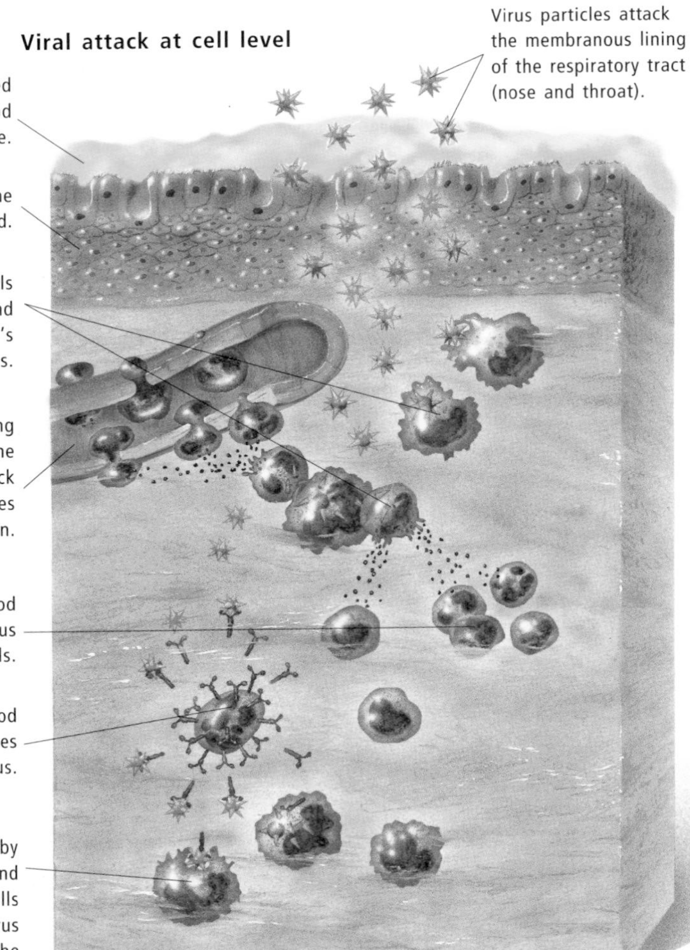
Virus particles attack the membranous lining of the respiratory tract (nose and throat).
Mucus is secreted by inflamed cells, causing congestion and nasal discharge.
The respiratory membrane becomes inflamed.
White blood cells encounter the virus and stimulate the body's defenses.
Blood vessels bring white blood cells to the infected lining to attack the virus. This causes swelling and congestion.
Some white blood cells attack the virus with chemicals.
Some white blood cells make antibodies against the virus.
Virus particles captured by antibodies are consumed and destroyed by white blood cells called phagocytes. The virus has been destroyed and the body can recover.

C

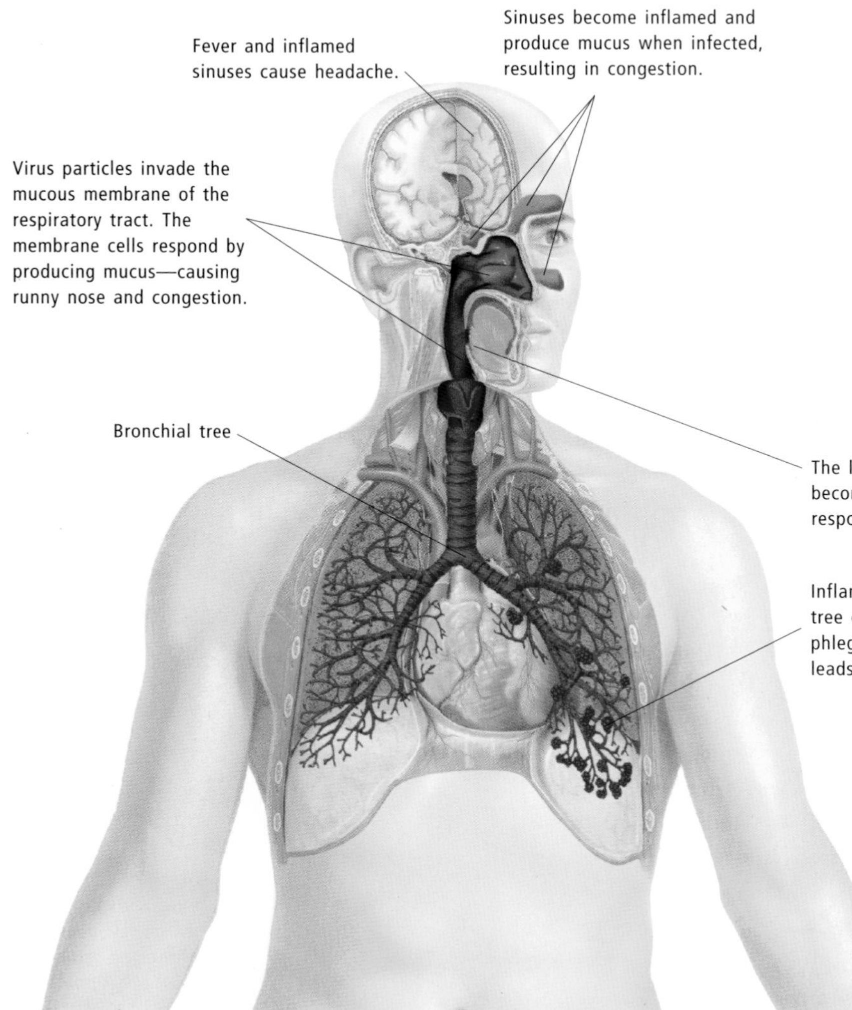
Fever and inflamed sinuses cause headache.
Sinuses become inflamed and produce mucus when infected, resulting in congestion.
Virus particles invade the mucous membrane of the respiratory tract. The membrane cells respond by producing mucus—causing runny nose and congestion.
Bronchial tree
The lining of the throat becomes inflamed in response to infection.
Inflammation of the bronchial tree causes production of phlegm and mucus, which leads to coughing.

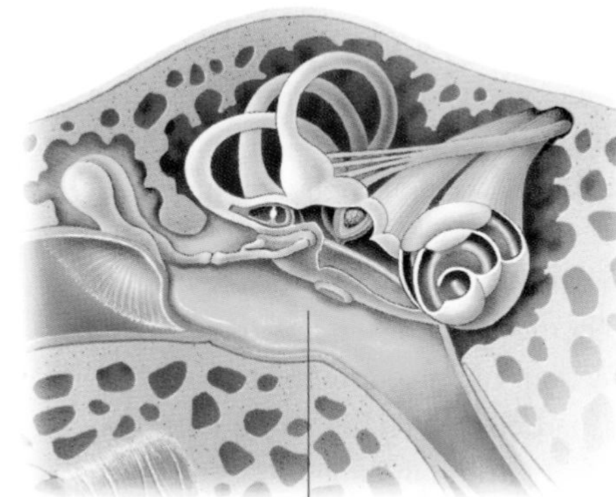

Ear infection

Virus particles traveling into the middle ear cause infection, leading to swelling and accumulation of fluid. This causes earache.

Cold

The common cold is caused by one of many viruses. Millions of cold viruses are easily transmitted via infected droplets that are coughed or sneezed into the air. When a droplet is inhaled, the virus attacks the lining of the upper respiratory tract, causing cold symptoms to develop.

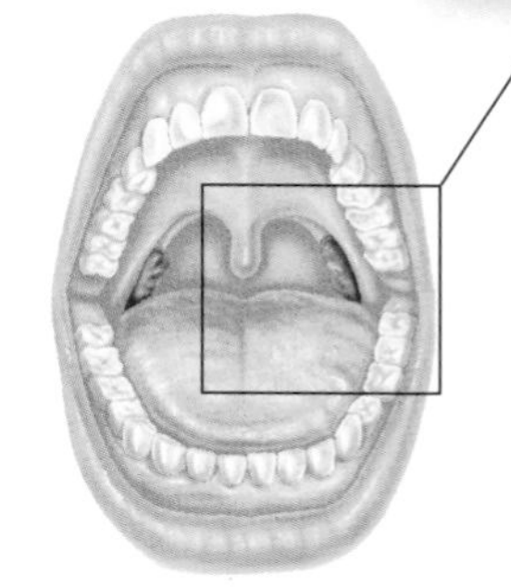

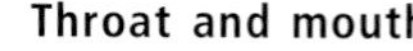

Throat and mouth

Tonsillitis

The tonsils protect the membrane of the mouth and throat from invading cold viruses. They become swollen and inflamed as part of the body's defense system to stop infection moving from the exterior to the interior of the body.

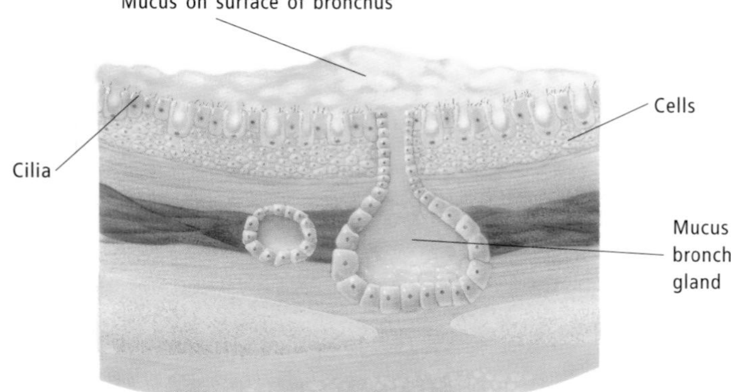
Mucus on surface of bronchus
Cells
Cilia
Mucus in bronchial gland

Lungs and bronchial tree

The cold virus attacks the tiny hairs (cilia) and cells on the lining of the bronchial tree in severe cases of cold. The tissue swells and glands produce mucus, resulting in coughing.

COMPARTMENT SYNDROME

The muscles of a limb are grouped into compartments, separated by connective tissue (intermuscular septum). In a muscle injury or strain, these compartments can become swollen with blood and fluid leaking from blood vessels. The rising pressure in the compartment compresses blood vessels; nerves and muscles may become ischemic (deprived of oxygen) and rapidly die. Treatment is surgical relief of the pressure inside the compartment, often by cutting the fibrous connective tissue.

SEE ALSO *Muscle*

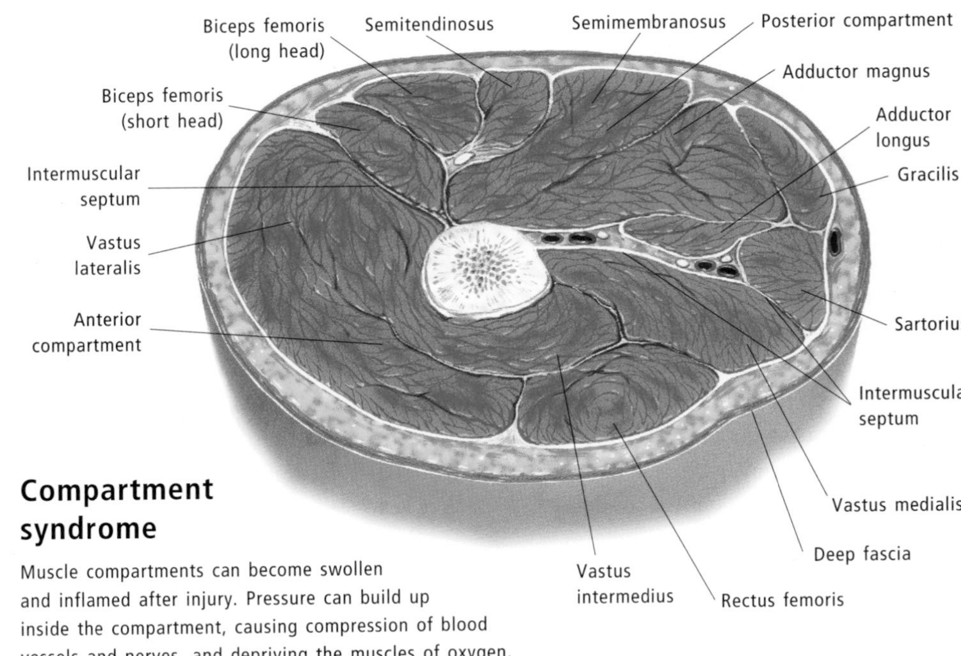

Compartment syndrome

Muscle compartments can become swollen and inflamed after injury. Pressure can build up inside the compartment, causing compression of blood vessels and nerves, and depriving the muscles of oxygen. This illustration shows the compartments in the thigh.

CONCUSSION

Concussion is a sudden alteration in levels of brain function following a blow to the head, often resulting in unconsciousness. It may be caused by a fall in which the head strikes against an object, or by a moving object striking the head. It frequently occurs in contact sports, and in auto, motorcycle or bike racing. Often, the injured person may not be aware of the problem; it may be teammates or observers who notice the confusion and disorientation. The injured person must be made to abandon the sport or activity, especially if there has been loss of consciousness.

Following the injury, the sufferer may have temporary retrograde amnesia; that is, for a time there will be no memory of events preceding the injury. There also may be headache, difficulty in concentrating and focusing, nausea, vomiting, and depression.

Usually concussion is temporary and causes no permanent brain damage. However, if the concussion is severe, there may be prolonged unconsciousness and persistent confusion. The level of consciousness is the single most important indicator of the severity of a brain injury; the more severe the concussion, the longer the period of unconsciousness. In more serious cases, there may be convulsions, vomiting, a weakness of the muscles, and permanent brain damage, depending on the extent of the injury. Loss of memory of events following the concussion (anterograde memory loss) also signifies a more serious concussion.

Concussed persons should seek medical treatment. A physician or neurologist will order x-rays of the head and neck to rule out the possibility of a skull fracture, and a CAT scan of the head if internal bleeding is suspected. If the injured person recovers and there are no signs of complications, rest at home and analegsics may be sufficient treatment. However, serious after-effects may be delayed and can appear 48 to 72 hours after injury, so a responsible person must watch the patient for serious symptoms. The first 24 hours are the most critical. Danger signs include repetitive vomiting, unequal pupils, confused mental state or varying levels of consciousness, seizures, or the inability to wake up (coma). If these signs are present, urgent medical advice should be sought.

If there are no further signs or symptoms, the patient can rest in bed for a few days, after which time, normal activity may be resumed. However, sporting and athletic activities should be avoided for three months. A second or subsequent concussion is particularly dangerous, especially if it occurs before the symptoms of the earlier concussion have cleared. Even though the second injury may be milder than the first, together they have a compounding effect that may cause acute brain swelling and rapid death.

To prevent concussion, protective head gear such as helmets should be worn when engaging in contact sports or any other activity that may result in head injury.

SEE ALSO *Amnesia, Unconsciousness*

CONFUSION

Confusion is a mental state in which a person is unsure of time, place or identity. A confused person is easily bewildered and has trouble making decisions and thinking in an orderly way. The condition is more common in elderly people, especially at night, when there are fewer stimuli to provide orientation. Confusion often occurs in hospitalized patients. It may come on suddenly (as in acute confusion or delirium) or gradually over time. The condition may be temporary, or permanent and irreversible, depending on the cause. It is often a symptom of physical illness.

Common causes of confusion include alcohol intoxication or withdrawal, low blood sugar, head trauma or head injury, concussion, fluid and electrolyte imbalance, nutritional deficiencies (such as niacin, thiamine, vitamin C or vitamin B_{12} deficiency), hyperthermia (fever), hypothermia (a drop in body temperature), hypoxia (inadequate oxygenation of the blood as seen, for example, in lung diseases), heat stroke, drugs (such as atropine or central nervous system depressants), and withdrawal from narcotics and barbiturates.

Acute confusion, or delirium, develops over a few hours or days. Delirious people may be confused about where they are or what time of day or year it is; they have a poor attention span and become easily distracted. Memory may be poor and there may be trouble speaking or understanding what others say. There may also be impaired concentration, restless excitement, senseless activity, hallucinations and fragmented delusions. Older people with delirium sometimes have mood swings and can become frightened and may try to run away.

Common causes of delirium include severe infections and high fevers (especially in the elderly or very young), drugs, alcohol, or prescription medications, dehydration, seizures, hypoxia (lack of oxygen) and head injury. Delirium can occur in the period immediately after surgery.

If a person becomes confused or delirious, medical advice should be sought. A physician may examine brain and nervous system function and may order investigations such as CAT scan, blood tests, x-rays and other tests, depending on the likely cause. Hospitalization may be necessary if the underlying condition is serious or is not easily reversible. The treatment of confusion is to correct the underlying cause, if possible. Sedatives or tranquilizers may be useful in the short term. A friend or relative should stay close by to prevent the patient from coming to any harm. Familiar surroundings, and conversation about familiar things in a calm voice will reassure the confused person. Visitors should always identify and introduce themselves. A calendar and clock can help with orientation. In order to ensure the patient's safety, physical restraints are recommended in some situations.

A permanently confused patient could be suffering from dementia, a mental deterioration due to age or from gradual changes in the brain tissue resulting from disease.

SEE ALSO *Delirium, Dementia, Memory*

CONGENITAL ABNORMALITIES

A congenital abnormality is one that is present at, and usually before, birth. It arises from the faulty development of a fetus in the uterus. The abnormality may be caused by a genetic disorder, so that it is inherited, or it may be acquired while the fetus is growing in the uterus, due to exposure to an agent that causes abnormal development. Though they are generally rare, the range of possible congenital abnormalities is wide. Limbs or organs may be absent, duplicated or malformed. Organs may fail to move to the correct place, as in cryptorchidism (undescended testes), they may fail to open properly as in imperforate anus, or may fail to close at the correct time, as in patent ductus arteriosus. Congenital abnormalities may be obvious at birth, or they may take months or years to become evident, as in the case of Huntington's disease, which does not manifest itself until middle age.

Inherited congenital anomalies are caused by abnormal genes. There are over 2,000 known inherited congenital anomalies. Some are common, for example achondroplasia (a form of dwarfism), hemolytic disease of the newborn, sickle-cell disease, Down syndrome, and cleft palate. Others, such as phenylketonuria, an inherited metabolic disorder, are very rare.

Children with genetic abnormalities can be born to normal parents if the condition is caused by an abnormal recessive (non-dominant) gene, and both parents have that recessive gene—in other words, they are both carriers. In this case there is a one in four chance that the child will inherit both genes and so manifest the disorder. Hemophilia is an example of such a condition.

Sometimes, genetic abnormalities occur if there is a spontaneous mutation of the parental genes, which may take place during sperm production or egg fertilization. In this case the affected child also has normal parents. Acquired congenital abnormalities can be caused by a variety of agents that affect the fetus in the uterus, including drugs, infections and toxins. Infection in the mother is a common cause of congenital abnormality. Rubella (German measles) contracted in the first three months of pregnancy may cause deafness, cataracts, heart disease, jaundice, or other abnormalities. Cytomegalovirus and toxoplasmosis are two other organisms that cause congenital anomalies.

Some drugs taken by a woman during pregnancy are responsible for abnormalities in the child. Corticosteroids, anticonvulsants, anti-cancer drugs, narcotics, sedatives, tranquilizers, antidepressants, antibacterials,

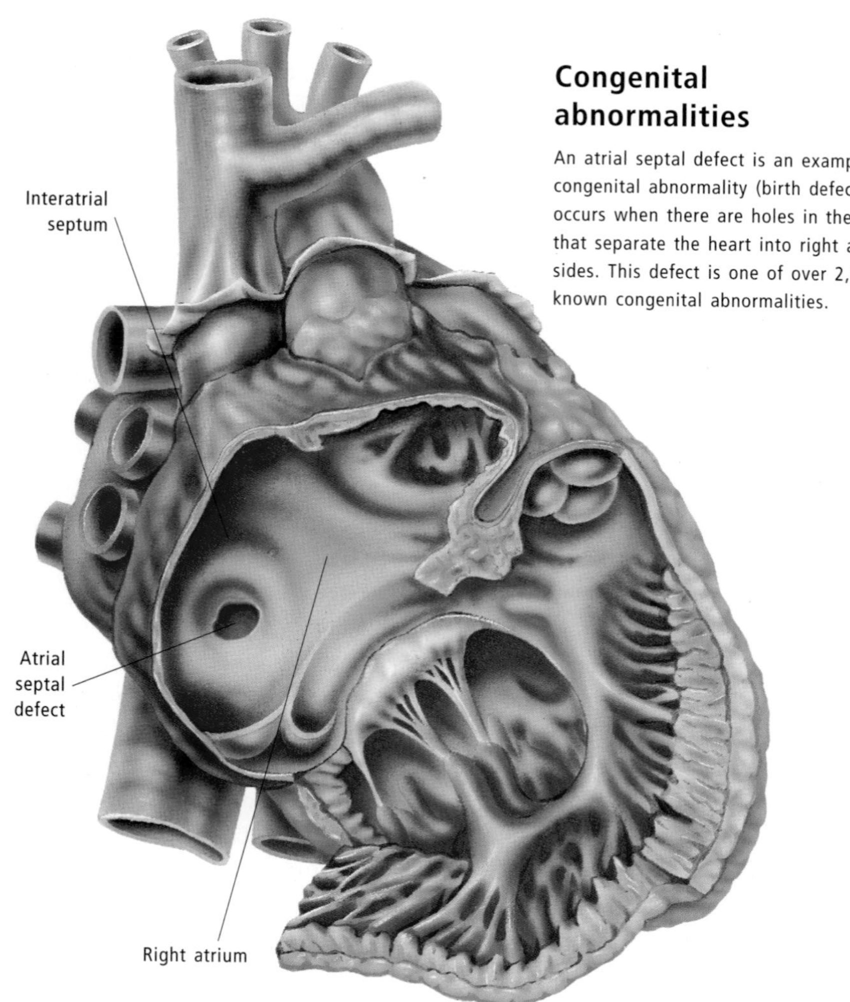

Congenital abnormalities

An atrial septal defect is an example of a congenital abnormality (birth defect) that occurs when there are holes in the walls that separate the heart into right and left sides. This defect is one of over 2,000 known congenital abnormalities.

(especially tetracycline), anticoagulants, and drugs prescribed to treat cardiac conditions and hypertension can all cause congenital defects. A pregnant woman should avoid taking any medication without first obtaining medical advice as to whether it is safe to take in pregnancy. Environmental toxins, x-rays, or injury to the fetus (for example from an intrauterine device), may cause an abnormality in the fetus. The age of the mother may be a factor (with Down syndrome, for example). Congenital abnormalities cannot be reversed, but can often be successfully treated with surgery, hormone treatment, diet, and physical therapy, depending on the condition and its severity.

If there is a known or suspected risk of a congenital abnormality developing, it can often be detected during pregnancy by a screening procedure. The most reliable procedure is to examine a sample of fluid from the amniotic sac obtained by amniocentesis between the fifteenth and eighteenth week of pregnancy. Microscopic examination of the cells in the fluid then reveals possible abnormalities in the chromosomes. The amniotic fluid can be tested for abnormal substances, for example alpha-fetoprotein, abnormally high levels of which are found in anencephaly or spina bifida. Chorionic villus sampling (CVS) is a technique used in the first trimester of pregnancy in which a tissue sample is taken from the placenta and analyzed for genetic defects in the fetus.

Termination of pregnancy (abortion) may be considered if fetal disorders are found early in a pregnancy. The decision to abort rests with the parents and is taken after they have been made aware of the nature of the disorder and the consequences of abortion. Genetic counseling should be considered by anyone who has a history of chromosomal abnormalities and all pregnant women aged 35 and over. There may be a higher risk than normal of congenital abnormality in a second child if the first is born with an abnormality; parents should have genetic counseling if they want another child.

SEE ALSO *Achondroplasia, Amniocentesis, Chromosomal abnormalities, Cleft palate and lip, Down syndrome, Genetic counseling, Hemolytic disease of the newborn, Huntington's disease, Phenylketonuria, Sickle cell disease*

CONJUNCTIVITIS

The conjunctivum is the membrane that lines the inner part of the eyelids and covers the whites of the eyes. Conjunctivitis, also called "pinkeye", is inflammation of the conjunctivum. The eye looks red and is painful and itchy with a watery discharge. The condition is common in childhood. Acute conjunctivitis may be caused by bacterial or viral infection, allergy or irritation. In bacterial conjunctivitis, the discharge from the eye is a yellow or greenish color. It accumulates during sleep, so the person wakes with the eyelids "stuck together". A warm wash-cloth applied to the eyes will remove the discharge. Antibiotic eye drops prescribed by a physician will cure the condition.

Viral pinkeye is usually associated with a more watery discharge and other viral "cold-like" symptoms. There is no treatment for viral conjunctivitis, though decongestant drops will help relieve the symptoms.

Allergic conjunctivitis is frequently seasonal, occurring in the spring and summer, and the sufferer has typical allergy symptoms such as sneezing and runny nose. The eye is intensely itchy and the conjunctiva is swollen. Decongestant, antihistamine or corticosteroid eye drops will bring relief.

Conjunctivitis may be caused by irritation—for example by dust, cosmetics, or smoke. Prompt, thorough washing of the eyes with large amounts of water will relieve the symptoms. If conjunctivitis is caused by a bacteria or virus, do not to rub the eye because the infection may be transmitted to the other eye. Anyone with conjunctivitis should wash their hands often and use their own towel so as not to transmit the disease.

Conjunctivitis may also be caused by the eye disorder trachoma or by other rare conditions such as rheumatic diseases and some inflammatory bowel diseases.

SEE ALSO *Allergies, Eye, Eyelids, Trachoma*

Allergic conjunctivitis

In allergic conjunctivitis, the eye becomes intensely itchy and the conjunctiva are swollen. This condition is typically seen in conjuction with other allergy symptoms such as sneezing and runny nose.

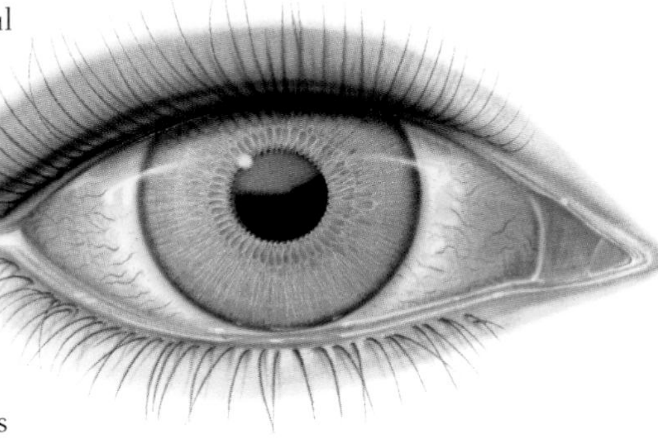

Bacterial conjunctivitis

Bacterial conjunctivitis causes a yellow or green discharge from the eye that builds up when the eyes are closed. This often causes the eyelids to stick together upon waking.

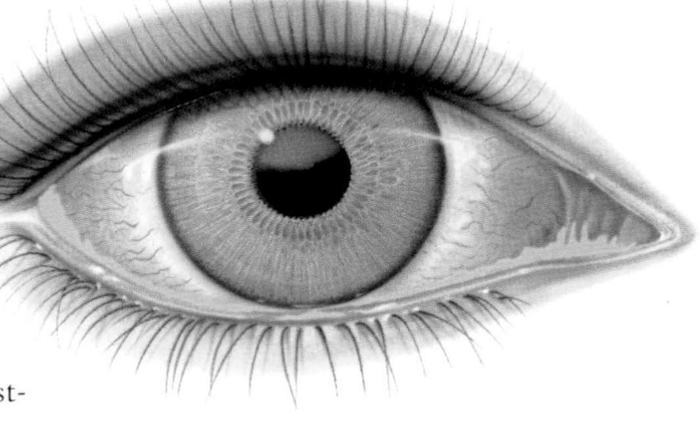

CONNECTIVE TISSUE

Connective tissue is tissue made up of cells and protein fibers arranged in a framework which provides support for other body tissues and holds them together. It is composed of two major structural proteins, collagen and elastin. Collagen is the principal protein of tendons, cartilage, bone and other connective tissue. Elastin is a protein which can stretch and return to its original length.

Connective tissue diseases attack the collagen or other components of connective tissue. Some are genetically inherited, such as Marfan's syndrome and Ehlers-Danlos syndrome. Others are part of the group of diseases known as autoimmune diseases, in which the body's defence mechanisms attack its own tissues. Autoimmune diseases include systemic lupus erythematosus, rheumatoid arthritis, scleroderma, polymyositis and dermatomyositis. A malignant (cancerous) tumor formed from connective tissue is called a sarcoma. The usual treatment for sarcoma is surgical removal, which is often followed by the use of radiation therapy.

C

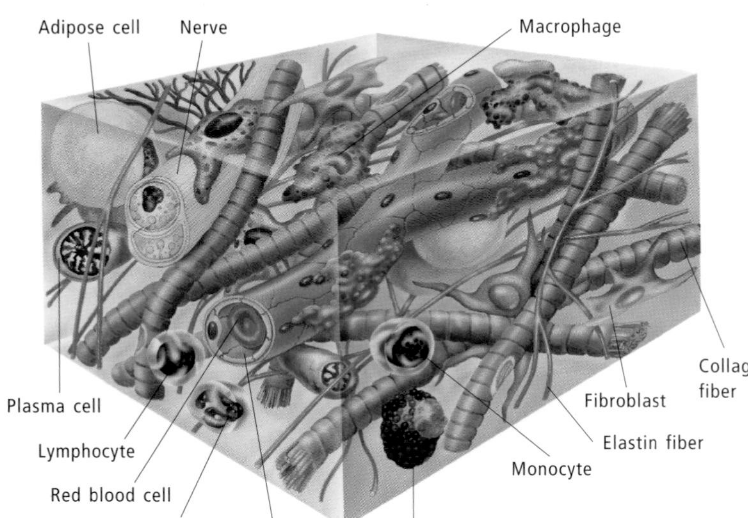

Connective tissue

Connective tissue is the framework that supports, connects and fills out body structures. Made up of collagen and elastin, it is found throughout the body. Tendons and ligaments are examples.

Vitamin C (ascorbic acid) is essential for connective tissues to function properly. Lack of vitamin C causes scurvy, with a weakening of the blood capillaries and bleeding, and bone defects. Scurvy can be prevented by eating fresh vegetables and fruits regularly.

SEE ALSO ***Autoimmune disease, Collagen, Dermatomyositis, Lupus erythematosus, Polymyositis, Rheumatoid arthritis, Scleroderma, Scurvy***

CONSTIPATION

Constipation is a condition in which a person will have hard feces and infrequent bowel movements. The bowel contents do not move and excess fluid is absorbed, leaving hard feces that are difficult to pass. They gradually dry out more and more until eventually the bowel opens through sheer weight of the material, usually leaving the sufferer feeling that the rectum is still full.

Many people think a daily bowel movement is necessary; however, this is not the case. For some, two or three movements a day are normal; for others one every two or three days. Constipation is often the result of a low-fiber diet with not enough consumption of water. Stress, anxiety or lack of exercise contribute to the problem. Constipation can also be a feature of irritable bowel syndrome.

Often a problem during pregnancy, constipation can be avoided with a high-fiber diet and plenty of water (around eight glasses a day). In breast-fed babies, constipation is rare and a baby may go from one bowel movement every few days to four a five in a day. Babies who are fed artificial baby milks can become constipated; professional help may be advisable in this situation.

Among the other causes are diseases of the central nervous system or typhoid, the taking of drugs such as codeine or morphine, and the overuse of laxatives. People who are bedridden and who have suffered a head or spinal injury can also suffer from constipation. Occasionally it is a symptom of a problem such as a bowel obstruction. It can also occur temporarily when lifestyle is changed such as when travelling.

Changes to diet will often fix the problem, especially increasing fluid intake. Laxatives and enemas are only temporary solutions.

SEE ALSO ***Bowel, Intestines, Irritable bowel syndrome, Laxatives***

CONTACT LENSES

Contact lenses are artificial lenses worn on the eyes' surface to correct vision defects, commonly astigmatism, aphakia (absence of the eye's crystalline lens) and myopia (short or near sightedness). They are a popular alternative to glasses because in many cases they provide better vision, and some people think they are more attractive. Today's lenses are also comfortable and easy to wear and care for. However, they are not suitable for everyone: elderly people and those with arthritis often find them difficult to use.

The first lenses were made of glass in 1887, but today's lenses are made of plastic. They were originally made on a mold taken from an impression of the eye; now a measurement of the curvature of the cornea is made and the plastic lens sits on a cushion of tears covering the iris and the pupil. They need to be individually prescribed and must be disinfected and cleaned regularly. Those who wear the lenses need more frequent eye examinations than those who wear glasses.

There are two types of plastic lenses available: soft, which are the most common, and rigid. Soft lenses can be tinted and are quickly adapted to and comfortable to wear. They include disposable lenses, which are designed to be replaced every two to four weeks, and extended wear lenses which can be kept in the eye for up to thirty days. These are specially designed to allow a large amount of oxygen to pass to the eye and are not suitable for all. Rigid lenses, while they give the wearer better vision, require more adaptation and are typically less comfortable. On the other hand, they last longer.

SEE ALSO ***Astigmatism, Cornea, Eye, Myopia, Sight***

CONTRACEPTION

Contraception (birth control) is, quite simply, any action taken to avoid conception. The only sure guarantee against pregnancy is to avoid vaginal intercourse. For conception to occur, the female's egg (ovum) must be met by sperm-loaded semen from the male. In natural conception the semen is deposited in the vagina. It then travels through the cervix and uterus to fertilize the egg. This egg must then implant itself into the lining of the uterus (endometrium).

Written details of birth control—a term first used by the reformer Margaret Sanger in 1915—date back to 1550 BC in Egypt. Classical writers such as Pliny the Elder and Soranus of Ephesus wrote about methods like washing the vagina after intercourse. A major advance came with the condom, which was first made from animal intestines. Vaginal barriers such as diaphragms and caps were mentioned in 1823 by the German physician F. A. Wilde. Vasectomy was used in the nineteenth century and the first documented female sterilization was performed in 1881. An Australian couple, the Billings, first used the monitoring of changes in cervical mucus to determine fertile times in the

1960s, about the same time as the first contraceptive pills became available.

Contraception should be discussed with qualified medical professionals in order to determine which method should be used, according to current lifestyle, medical history and future plans.

Intrauterine device

This is a small device inserted into the uterus to prevent conception. It is still not sure how it works but it seems that almost any foreign body in the uterus will prevent conception. Made of plastic, metal or other material, and inserted under sterile conditions by a trained professional, intrauterine devices (IUDs) have a failure rate of between 1 and 6 pregnancies per 100 women.

Barrier methods

These are the condom (for both males and females), the diaphragm and the cap.

The male condom, which is a penile sheath, acts by catching and collecting the semen so it does not get into the vagina. The female condom is a thin silicone membrane which partly or completely covers the outside of the female genitals, acting as a barrier.

Diaphragms and caps are placed inside the vagina to cover the entrance to the uterus and stop sperm getting into the womb. They come in a range of sizes and must be fitted to the user by a trained health professional. Many family planning clinics and doctors recommend the use of a spermicide (which kills the sperm) at the same time. When used carefully, barrier methods have about the same effectiveness as IUDs.

Fertility awareness methods

Not having sexual intercourse at a fertile time is the basis of the methods variously described as fertility awareness, periodic abstinence, the Billings method, the rhythm method and the temperature method.

Changes in a woman's body during the menstrual cycle can be interpreted to indicate fertility. The cervical mucus changes under the influence of estrogen and at the time a woman is most fertile is plentiful, clear and sticky. The woman's basal body temperature, taken with a special thermometer, also rises slightly for around three days. Most women have cycles which can be documented so that they can work out when they are most likely to be fertile. There is a wide range of pregnancy rates depending on the method used and the couple involved.

Hormonal contraceptives

More than 70 million women around the world use this method which involves taking an oral contraceptive pill regularly and diligently, or using slow-release implants under the skin, injections into the muscle, or using devices such as IUDs which contain hormones. Combination pills contain estrogen and progestin (progestogen); mini-pills contain progestin only. The combination pill prevents the release of an egg and both types of pill thicken the cervical mucus to prevent the sperm from reaching the egg. They can also prevent fertilized eggs from implanting. The combination pill, when taken as directed, is more than 99 percent effective in preventing pregnancy. The mini-pill has higher rates of failure.

Injections of progestin work by stopping ovulation and theoretically they are the most effective way to prevent pregnancy apart from abstinence from intercourse. Contraceptive implants, which are not available in all industrialized countries, are also highly effective and can be removed at any time, as can hormone-releasing vaginal rings and IUDs. The male pills and contraceptive injections are still being studied and researched.

The emergency pill (also called the morning-after pill) is a short course of hormones which must be started within 72 hours of unprotected intercourse. These hormones delay ovulation and change the lining of the uterus. Fewer than 5 in 100 will conceive when this method is used correctly. Emergency IUD insertion or copper IUD insertion, if done within five days of unprotected sex, will prevent conception and also provide on-going contraception.

Spermicide

This kills or immobilizes sperm. The spermicide should be inserted into the vagina at least 15 minutes before intercourse and can be a foam, cream, jelly, film or suppository. It can also be a sponge which carries the spermicide. Spermicides can be used together with a barrier method or on their own when they have about a 30 percent failure rate.

Coitus interruptus or withdrawal

This is the act of withdrawing the penis during sexual intercourse before ejaculation takes place. It has a high failure rate and is not a recommended method.

Breast feeding

Another "method" with a high failure rate is breast feeding. Thought by many to be a natural way to plan families, it is only likely to work if the baby is being breast fed at least 5 times in a 24-hour period and is not being fed solid foods, and the woman has not started to menstruate.

Female sterilization and vasectomy

Permanent contraception methods such as sterilization and vasectomy continue to be popular. A woman is sterilized by blocking both fallopian tubes (through which sperm reach the egg). This tubal ligation is

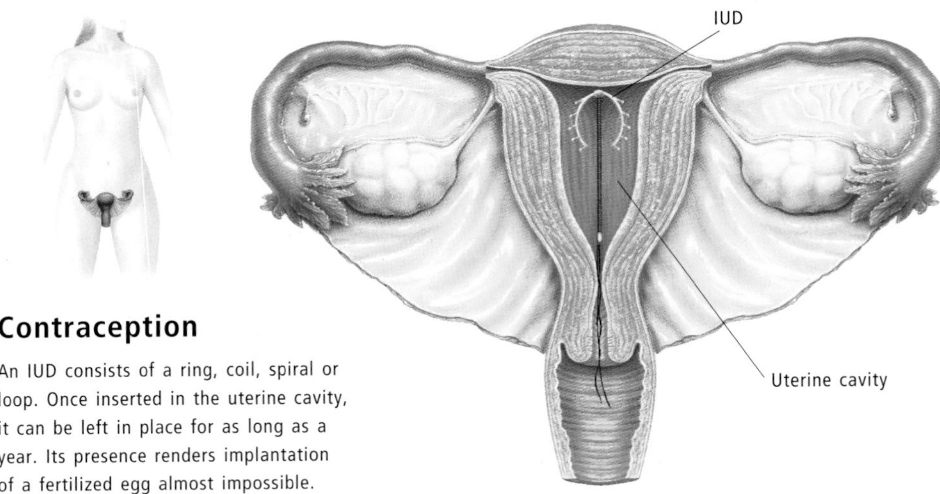

Contraception

An IUD consists of a ring, coil, spiral or loop. Once inserted in the uterine cavity, it can be left in place for as long as a year. Its presence renders implantation of a fertilized egg almost impossible.

C

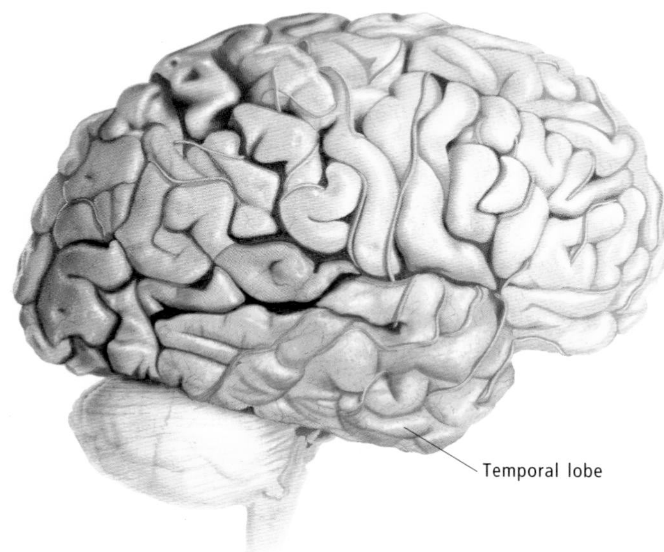

Convulsions

Convulsions, or seizures, are the result of abnormal electrical discharges in the brain. Anything that irritates the brain can cause a convulsion. Temporal lobe epilepsy is a condition that causes recurrent convulsions that may be triggered by flashing lights, repetitive sounds or even touching certain parts of the body.

a surgical procedure which is now commonly carried out by endoscopy using an optical instrument through an abdominal incision. A vasectomy blocks the tube (the vas deferens) which carry the sperm from the testis to the semen. This is a simple operation done via a small incision in the front of the scrotum.

While the success rate in reversing these methods can be as high as 70 percent, they are not recommended birth control methods for people who may want children one day.

SEE ALSO *Breast feeding, Oral contraceptives, Reproductive systems, Sterilization, Tubal sterilization, Vasectomy*

CONTRAST X-RAY

Contrast x-ray is a diagnostic technique which can outline organs and blood vessels, and reveal abnormalities of anatomy. The x-rays are obtained after injecting a solution that is opaque to x-rays into blood vessels, introducing it by means of an enema tube, or by giving the patient a solution of barium sulfate to swallow. Contrast x-ray is useful in demonstrating the function of various organs, such as the peristaltic waves of the esophagus when swallowing, or the emptying of the gallbladder and kidney.

When the solution is injected into the blood vessels of the brain, aneurysms or blow-outs of the arteries can be identified, as can shifting of the blood vessels by tumors. The physician is able to assess the degree of narrowing of coronary arteries when considering bypass operations. Barium is sometimes used during CAT scanning to allow separation of bowel shadows from associated tumors.

SEE ALSO *Barium enema, Barium meal, CAT scan*

CONVULSIONS

Convulsions—fits, epileptic attacks or seizures—are characterized by abnormal, often violent and uncontrolled spasmodic contractions and relaxations of the voluntary muscles. The eyes may roll, the teeth clench and the sufferer will twitch and shake. Convulsions can be a symptom of a disease and vary in severity, in some cases being accompanied by a loss of consciousness. Around 1 in 100 people will have a convulsion of some kind during their lifetime and about half of these will occur during childhood, most commonly between the ages of 3 months and 5 years. Seizures, particularly the first one, can be particularly worrying to parents of young children; however, they are rarely harmful.

Simple febrile convulsions (convulsions caused by a high fever) usually last less than a minute and are not repeated, though the child does have a slightly increased chance over children who never have a seizure of having subsequent attacks not associated with fever. Complicated febrile convulsions will last longer than 15 minutes and recur 2 or more times in 24 hours. Children who suffer from these have a greater risk of subsequent attacks and around 25 percent of cases will have a family history of seizures.

When people have convulsions, the most important thing is to make sure they do not injure themselves. They should be placed on a flat surface with the head to one side. It is not appropriate to put anything in the sufferer's mouth: it is more likely to cause harm. It is also not appropriate to attempt expired air resuscitation if children hold their breath in the early stages as this too can cause damage. When the convulsion has passed, medical help should be sought immediately.

Reducing and controlling fever with tepid sponge baths and acetaminophen (paracetamol) or ibuprofen—never aspirin—may prevent a convulsion. A child who suffers convulsions may be prescribed anticonvulsant medicine; however, such medication can affect a child's ability to learn so it is prescribed with care. Most children outgrow febrile convulsions.

There are a number of other types of convulsion. They can occur because of scarred brain tissue after a head injury, or can be triggered by flashing lights. They can be partial, only affecting one part of the body, or general, involving the entire body. Petit mal convulsions are not violent and show as a sudden cessation of activities. Epilepsy is diagnosed when an electroencephalogram (EEG) shows more than one convulsion. Prevention of these types of convulsion depends on the cause, and requires specialist advice.

SEE ALSO *Electroencephalogram, Epilepsy, Fevers*

COR PULMONALE

Cor pulmonale is a condition in which the right side of the heart enlarges, weakens and may fail. It is caused by high blood pressure in the pulmonary (lung) circulation, which forces the right ventricle (which pumps blood into the lungs) to overwork. Usually the high blood pressure in the pulmonary circulation is caused by lung diseases such as chronic bronchitis or emphysema.

Cor pulmonale is usually chronic (long term) and incurable, though affected people may live 10 or 15 years with the condition. In the meantime, symptoms can be relieved or controlled with medications such as diuretics, digitalis, antibiotics, and vasodilators. Plenty of rest and a low-salt diet are recommended. Oxygen (inhaled using a mask) may be needed in later stages of development. Ultimately, only a lung transplant will cure the condition.

SEE ALSO *Bronchitis, Circulatory system, Emphysema, Heart, Hypertension, Lung*

CORNEA

Lying at the front of the eye, the cornea is the transparent part of the outer layer of the eyeball. The cornea is responsible for most of the bending of light which enters the eye, but as it cannot change its shape readily, the focusing of the image on the retina is achieved by the lens. The surface of the cornea may be ulcerated through injury by foreign bodies or by infection with bacteria (*Streptococcus pneumoniae, Pseudomonas aeruginosa*) or viruses (*herpes simplex*). Corneal ulcers will impair sight and may require corneal transplantation. Examination of the inner parts of the eye is made through the cornea with the aid of an instrument known as an ophthalmoscope.

SEE ALSO *Eye, Sight*

CORONARY ARTERIES

Coronary arteries are the arteries that supply the heart with oxygenated blood. The right and left coronary arteries arise from the aorta and branch out into smaller arteries supplying the right and left sides of the heart. Arteriosclerosis, or hardening of the arteries, may result in stenosis (narrowing) of the coronary arteries and ischemic heart disease.

SEE ALSO *Arteriosclerosis, Coronary artery disease, Heart*

CORONARY ARTERY ANGIOGRAPHY

Coronary artery angiography is an x-ray technique used to show the nature and extent of disease in coronary arteries. Dye that is opaque to x-rays is injected through a thin flexible tube (or catheter) placed into the aorta or the heart. A succession of x-rays is taken to view the flow of the dye through the coronary arteries. Any sections that are narrowed (stenosed) can be clearly seen.

SEE ALSO *Coronary arteries, Coronary artery disease*

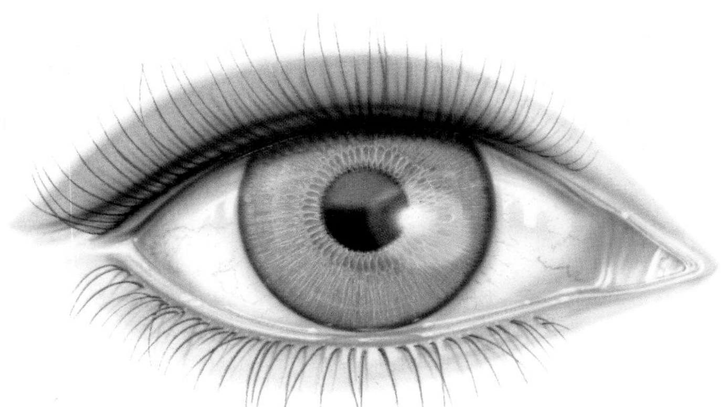

Corneal ulcer

A corneal ulcer is a sore or break in the surface layer of the cornea. It causes pain, redness, and sensitivity to light as well as blurred vision.

CORONARY ARTERY DISEASE

Coronary artery disease is a disease in which the walls of the coronary arteries thicken, cutting off blood and oxygen to the heart muscle and causing angina, arrhythmias, myocardial infarction, heart failure, or cardiac arrest. The disease is caused by atherosclerosis (also known as arteriosclerosis) in which fatty deposits called plaques are deposited within the endothelium (the inner lining) of blood vessels, including the arteries of the heart. Risk factors include smoking, hypertension, high blood cholesterol and obesity. The affected person suffers a range of cardiac symptoms such as chest pain on exertion or at rest, sweating, palpitations, breathlessness, fainting or even sudden death.

Investigations include chest x-ray, electrocardiogram (EKG), stress test, ultrasound (echocardiography) and nuclear scanning. Coronary angiography, in which a series of x-rays of the heart is taken after dye is injected into the coronary arteries, is useful in showing the extent of the disease.

Coronary artery disease—damage to heart tissue

Heart attack (myocardial infarction) occurs when some of the heart's blood supply is suddenly severely restricted or cut off. This causes part of the heart muscle to die from lack of oxygen.

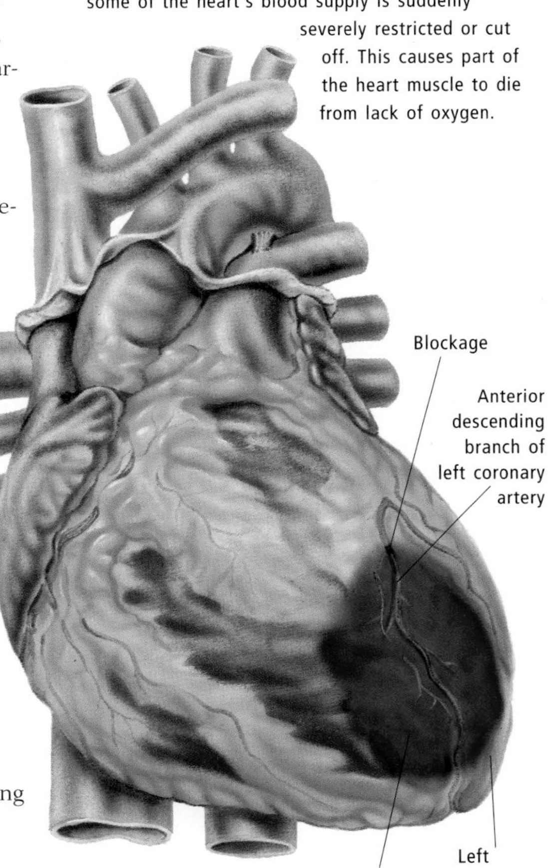

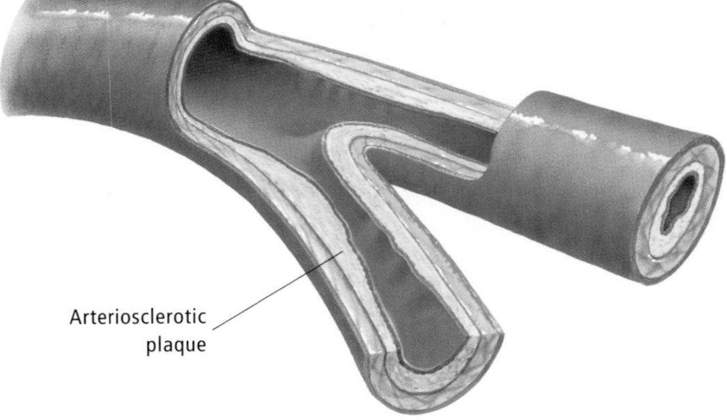

Coronary heart disease—damage to arteries

Fatty deposits (plaques) are deposited within the lining of the blood vessels. The flow of blood through the vessels is restricted, which may decrease the blood supply to vital organs.

The effects of angina can be relieved with medications such as nitrates (nitroglycerin), beta-blockers or calcium channel blockers. If one or more arteries are severely blocked, coronary bypass surgery may be needed to relieve blockages of the blood vessels of the heart muscle. The disease may be prevented by exercise, a low-fat diet, cessation of smoking and control of blood pressure with medications.

SEE ALSO *Angina pectoris, Arrythmia, Arteriosclerosis, Cholesterol, Coronary arteries, Heart, Hypertension, Myocardial infarction, Obesity, Smoking*

CORONARY THROMBOSIS

Thrombosis is the presence of a blood clot (thrombus) in an artery or vein. Coronary thrombosis is due to a blood clot blocking a coronary artery, often resulting in myocardial infarction and/or cardiac arrest (heart attack) and death. The condition is usually seen in people whose coronary arteries have been damaged by atherosclerosis. A thrombus forms at the site of the damaged arterial wall, cutting off the blood supply to the heart muscle. The affected person may feel crushing chest pain, palpitations (awareness of heart beat), abnormal heart rhythms, dizziness and sweating. The person may die suddenly.

Coronary thrombosis is an emergency and may require resuscitation, immediate transport to hospital and treatment in a cardiac unit. Treatment is with oxygen, pain relief, drugs called thrombolytics that activate natural clot-dissolving processes in the blood, and anticoagulant drugs such as heparin which prevent further clot formation. If the person is well enough, coronary bypass surgery may be needed to bypass the blockage and restore adequate blood flow to the heart muscle.

SEE ALSO *Arteries, Coronary arteries, Heart, Myocardial infarction, Veins*

CORTICOSTEROIDS

Corticosteroids, or corticoids, are steroid hormones produced in the outer layer (cortex) of the adrenal glands. The most important steroid hormones are aldosterone, which regulates the excretion of sodium and potassium salts through the kidney, and cortisol (hydrocortisone), which promotes the synthesis and storage of glucose and regulates fat distribution within the body. The production of the hormones is controlled by the pituitary gland via the hormone ACTH. Insufficient production of corticosteroid by the adrenal gland causes Addison's disease, while excessive production causes Cushing's syndrome. The term corticosteroid is also used for a number of synthetic derivatives with similar properties to naturally occurring corticosteroids, used to treat allergies, rheumatic disorders and inflammation.

SEE ALSO *Addison's disease, Adrenal glands, Cushing's syndrome, Pituitary gland*

COSMETIC SURGERY

Cosmetic surgery is undertaken in order to reshape normal parts of the body with the intention of improving the patient's appearance and usually self-esteem. It is generally not covered by health insurance because it is elective, though some countries accept psychological stress as a sufficient reason for an insurance claim.

Cosmetic surgery makes up around 10 percent of plastic surgery, a specialty which also treats cancers, reconstructs damage after trauma such as hand injury or burns, and repairs congenital abnormalities such as cleft palate.

Some common cosmetic surgery procedures are rhinoplasty, which involves changing the shape of the nose via the nostrils or the tip so that no external scars are obvious; face lift, which is quite a complicated procedure as it can involve the whole facial structure; breast reduction; breast augmentation or reconstruction which can be complicated procedures depending on whether artificial implants or body fat are used; hair transplants; and liposuction. The latter consists of smashing the fat cells with a steel bar which is stuck into the area to be suctioned, and the fat is then sucked out. Other procedures involve lasers and heat.

Face lifts have become fairly common operations and are usually carried out on women between 40–60 years of age. Technically known as rhytidectomy, the procedure involves simple scalpeling and reshaping of the fat and the skin, or more sophisticated laser techniques which remove layers of wrinkled skin. Other facial reconstructions are ear reduction (ostoplasty), and the removal of fatty tissue and skin from and around the eyelids (blepharoplasty).

The essence of effective cosmetic surgery is in the planning of the incisions—so that they are in the line of where the skin folds naturally—and in the appropriate way of closing the wound. The use of fine material

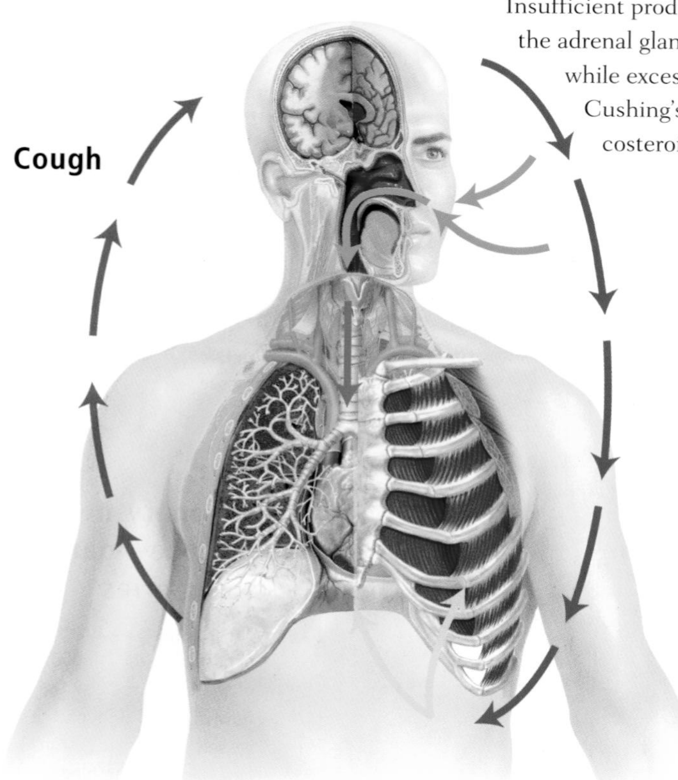

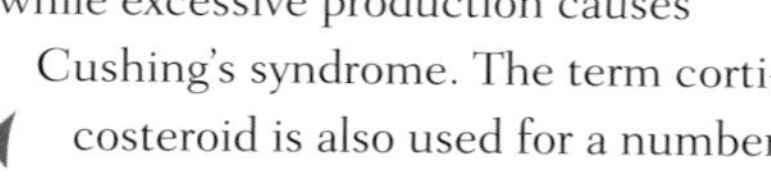

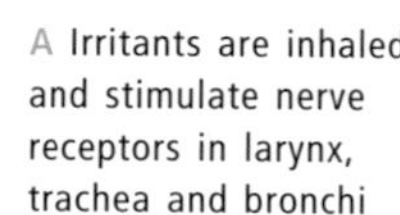

A Irritants are inhaled and stimulate nerve receptors in larynx, trachea and bronchi

B Nerve receptors in larynx, trachea and bronchi send signals to brain stem via vagus nerve

C Brain stem triggers coughing reflex via phrenic nerve

D Diaphragm rises and chest muscles contract, forcing air out of lungs as a cough

to suture and the early removal of exposed stitches so that the wound is kept closed by hidden sutures aid the healing with minimal scarring. Techniques which can be used in both cosmetic and plastic surgery include chemosurgery, electrosurgery, laser surgery and dermabrasion.

These procedures are not without risk of complications which can include scars and swelling, hematoma (blood clots requiring removal under anesthetic), and nerve damage, which will result in loss of feeling.

SEE ALSO *Plastic surgery*

COUGH

A cough is one of the most common symptoms of lung irritation or disease; almost any lung disease will cause a cough. A cough is a reflex action resulting in contraction and a sharp expiration of the diaphragm to expel something that is causing irritation to the lining of the bronchi (airways). It may be provoked by irritants such as smoke, allergens, viral or bacterial infection or other inflammation, foreign bodies or a growth in the bronchi.

In children and adults, a cough is commonly caused by bronchitis (inflammation of the airways). This commonly follows an upper respiratory tract infection such as the common cold or a viral throat infection. A bacterial bronchitis may result, especially in those with asthma or other lung disease. In adults, smoker's cough may be due to emphysema and chronic bronchitis, conditions caused by damage to the airways and connective tissue of the lung as the result of smoking. A cough may also be a symptom of lung cancer, or pulmonary fibrosis, and seen in a variety of lung disorders and connective tissue diseases.

If a cough lasts longer than a few weeks, the physician may wish to investigate further, with x-rays, CAT scans and MRI scans of the lung. Sputum can be collected and sent to the laboratory for microbial analysis. To cure a cough, the underlying cause must be treated. Cough symptoms can usually be suppressed by medications such as codeine. Often a cough suppressant will be combined with anti-flu preparations for greater effectiveness.

SEE ALSO *Bronchitis, Common cold, Emphysema, Lung*

COUNSELING

While the knowledge of the healing virtues of a good talk with an understanding person is as old as humanity, the professional practice of counseling is very much a twentieth-century phenomenon. Much of contemporary counseling theory and technique has its foundation in the work of the American psychiatrist Carl Rogers, who pioneered the "client-centered" approach.

Counseling usually takes place over a number of sessions. The general aim of counseling is to help clients review problematical situations in their lives and to explore the options they have to deal with them. Counselors aim to facilitate their clients' insight into themselves and their problems, not to direct or manage their clients' lives.

In a counseling session, clients are able to talk freely about themselves and their difficulties. The counselor listens and responds to the client with a sensitive receptivity. Fundamental to the success of the counseling relationship is the counselor's ability to be empathetic and non-judgmental.

There is no standard form of counseling. Many counselors today augment their basic counseling skills with a wide range of psychotherapeutic techniques such as Gestalt therapy, transactional analysis, art therapy, hypnotherapy, somatic (body) awareness and visualization methods. The various techniques are secondary to the basic requirement which is that counselors treat their clients with dignity and respect.

Basic counseling skills are increasingly being taught to a wide range of health professionals who can utilize them during their consultations. Alternatively, medical practitioners may refer their patients to a counselor if they feel the health condition of the patient could be improved by psychological support and insight. Counselors can help people identify and deal with any psychological issues contributing to their illness, as well as with emotional challenges posed by having the illness.

Counseling can be useful in managing stress-related illnesses, depression, alcohol and drug addictions, chronically debilitating conditions and life-threatening illnesses. In the case of the latter two categories, carers as well as patients may be helped by being involved with the counseling.

When looking for a counselor, it is a good idea to seek recommendations and talk to a few different ones before making a decision. The client should consider who they would feel most comfortable with and would be able to trust, as well as the amount of compassion and insight the counselor is able to offer.

SEE ALSO *Behavior therapy, Psychotherapy*

CRADLE CAP

Cradle cap, a skin condition that can occur on a baby's scalp, looks unpleasant, especially if it is yellow and crusty. However it is not infectious. It is a form of seborrheic dermatitis and occurs if a baby's head is not cleaned properly, usually because the parents are concerned that they may damage the soft spot (fontanelle) on the baby's head. Sebum, which is secreted from the sebaceous glands, forms in layers on the scalp, creating patches or a "cap" on the head.

Treatment is simple and usually effective if carried out when the crusts first appear: the affected areas should be rubbed with a little olive oil or paraffin in the evening. The next morning the area should be washed gently with soap and warm water and the scales should lift off easily. This should be repeated until the crusts disappear.

Careful shampooing will prevent cradle cap from returning. Persistent cases may require a special preparation available from a pharmacist or prescribed by a doctor.

SEE ALSO *Seborrheic dermatitis*

CRAMP

Cramp is a painful, involuntary contraction or spasm of muscles that can affect healthy people. It can involve any muscles and may occur suddenly while awake or asleep.

Poor circulation can be responsible, especially in the elderly, as can taking exercise without a warm-up. Swimmers can get cramps in cold water. Heavy work in hot conditions can induce heat cramps. Contraction of the uterus during or prior to menstruation is responsible for menstrual cramp (dysmenorrhea). Spasm of muscles controlling the stomach and large intestine can produce abdominal cramps. Repetitive use of muscles can cause cramps. Abdomi-

Cranial nerves

There are 12 cranial nerves that lead directly from the brain to various parts of the head. They control movements of the face, tongue, eyes and throat, and receive sensory input from the organs of hearing, sight, smell and taste.

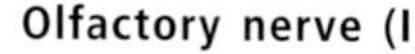

Olfactory nerve (I)

The first cranial nerve is concerned with the sense of smell. Nerve fibers starting in the mucous membranes of the nose carry messages to the cerebrum.

Optic nerve (II)

Visual impulses from the retina are sent along the optic nerve (the second cranial nerve) to the brain.

Trigeminal nerve (V)

The trigeminal nerve (fifth cranial nerve) has three sections: the ophthalmic, maxillary and mandibular divisions. They supply sensory fibers to areas such as the forehead, skin of the cheek and the muscles used for chewing.

Oculomotor (III), trochlear (IV) and abducent (VI) nerves

These cranial nerves control movement of the muscle which moves the eyeball and eyelids, and allows focusing.

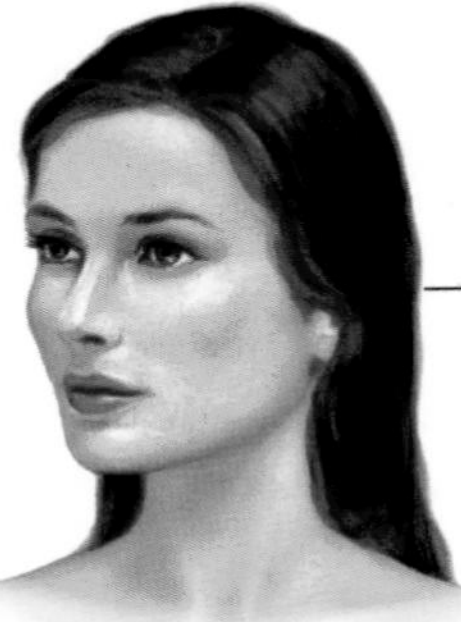

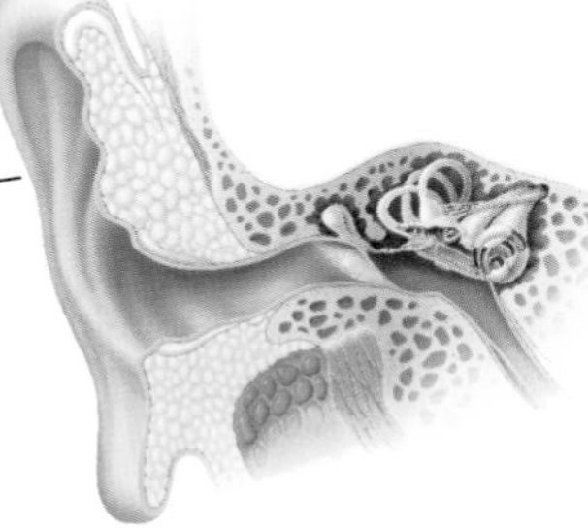

Facial nerve (VII)

The facial nerve is the seventh cranial nerve. It provides the motor fibers for facial expression. It is also responsible for the sensation of taste in the front part of the tongue.

Vestibulocochlear nerve (VIII)

Located behind the facial nerve, the eighth cranial nerve carries impulses for the sense of balance.

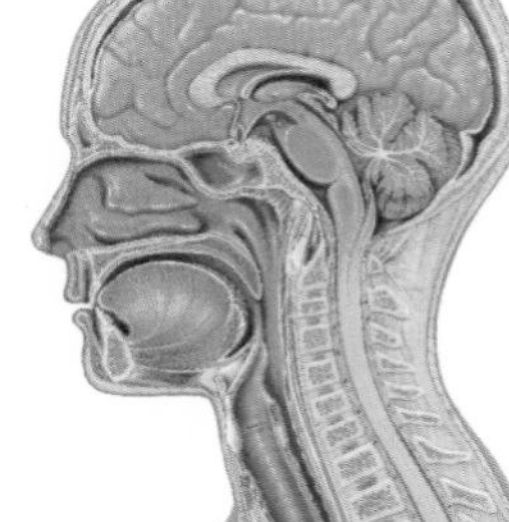

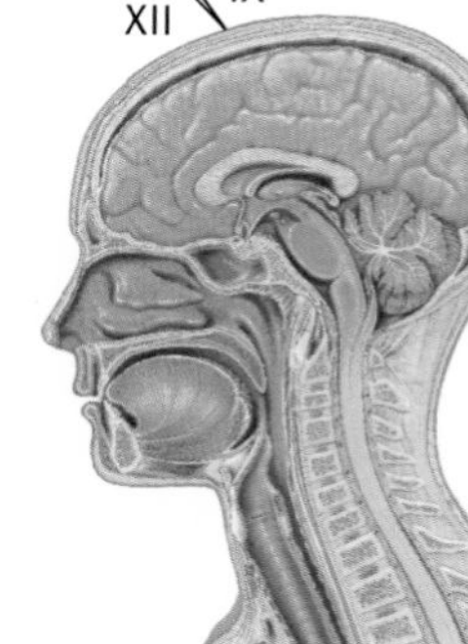

Glossopharyngeal (IX) and hypoglossal (XII) nerves

Supplying the carotid sinus, the ninth cranial nerve is responsible for the reflex control of the heart. It also supplies the back part of the tongue and the soft palate. The twelfth controls movement of the tongue.

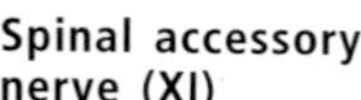

Spinal accessory nerve (XI)

The eleventh cranial nerve is primarily responsible for movement of the muscles of the upper shoulders, head, neck, and larynx and pharynx.

Vagus nerve (X)

The tenth cranial nerve is involved with functions such as coughing, sneezing, swallowing, speaking, secretions from the glands of the stomach, as well as the sensation of hunger.

nal cramps are common in pregnancy. Those occurring in the first 20 weeks may precede miscarriage. Light, irregular cramps later in a pregnancy (Braxton-Hicks contractions) may be mistaken for true labor.

Cramps can be prevented by stretching muscles before strenuous work or exercise, and by having adequate fluid in order to prevent dehydration. Cramps may be relieved by massaging and stretching the muscle, or by applying warmth from a safe source, such as a covered hot water bottle. Salt tablets (to replace salt lost in sweat) may ease cramps associated with exertion.

SEE ALSO *Muscle*

CRANIAL NERVES

The cranial nerves provide innervation (distribution of nerves) to the muscles and sensory structures of the head and neck (including skin, membranes, eyes and ears). They also distribute nerves to the organs of the chest (trachea, bronchi, lungs and heart) and the upper part of the gastrointestinal tract. The twelve pairs of cranial nerves arise mainly from the brain stem.

SEE ALSO *Brain, Nerves*

CRETINISM

Cretinism is a metabolic disorder that results from inadequate secretion of thyroid hormones during early life. It is characterized by a low metabolic rate with retarded growth and mental development. It occurs most commonly in populations whose diet is iodine deficient, and is preventable by administering iodine to pregnant mothers. Lack of thyroid hormones must be detected and treated as soon as possible after birth to prevent permanent brain damage.

SEE ALSO *Iodine deficiency, Thyroid gland*

CREUTZFELDT-JAKOB DISEASE

Creutzfeldt-Jakob disease is a rare, degenerative, invariably fatal brain disorder that causes movement abnormalities and a rapid decrease of mental function. The disorder first appears about age 60 and progresses rapidly to loss of brain function similar to that of Alzheimer's disease. There may be muscle tremors, rigid posture and changes in coordination. It may occur spontaneously with no known cause. In a small number of cases the disease is hereditary. In rare instances, it is acquired through exposure fo brain or nervous system tissue during medical procedures; it is thought to be transmitted via a viral-like protein called a prion. Adolescents who have received growth hormone derived from cadavers have contracted the disease; the use of synthetically manufactured growth hormone has meant contagion is no longer a problem. The disorder is fatal in a short time, usually within a year.

SEE ALSO *Alzheimer's disease*

CROHN'S DISEASE

Crohn's disease is a long-term, progressive disease that may involve both the small and large intestine. Most patients develop the disease in their twenties or early thirties. The disease involves swelling of lymphoid (immune system) tissue in the wall of the gut. This leads to ulcers on the inner lining of the bowel and cracks or fissures in the wall itself. Patients complain of diarrhea, lower abdominal pain, weakness, weight loss and fever. Many patients develop anemia (defined as reduced number, size and/or hemoglobin content of red blood cells in the blood) due to iron or vitamin B_{12} deficiency. Complications include bowel obstruction, abscesses in the bowel wall and bleeding from the bowel.

SEE ALSO *Anemia, Autoimmune disease, Bowel, Intestines*

CROUP

Difficulty inhaling, combined with making a noise like a barking seal (known as stridor), is the most obvious symptom of croup. It can be caused by bacterial or viral infections and in the early stages is contagious. Occasionally stridor is caused by a more serious condition known as epiglottitis which is caused by a bacterium and is life threatening. If the child is very distressed, sits bolt upright and has a high fever, emergency medical attention should be sought. Usually associated with a cold, croup is normally worse at night and upsets the child.

If the child has difficulty breathing and is distressed, then medical attention should be sought; otherwise, the usual treatment is a session in a steamy room, such as a bathroom. This can be created by turning on the hot water. Ideally the child should be sitting up on an adult's lap. Caution with hot water is important. Nothing can be done to prevent a child getting croup, although using a humidifier or vaporizer may help.

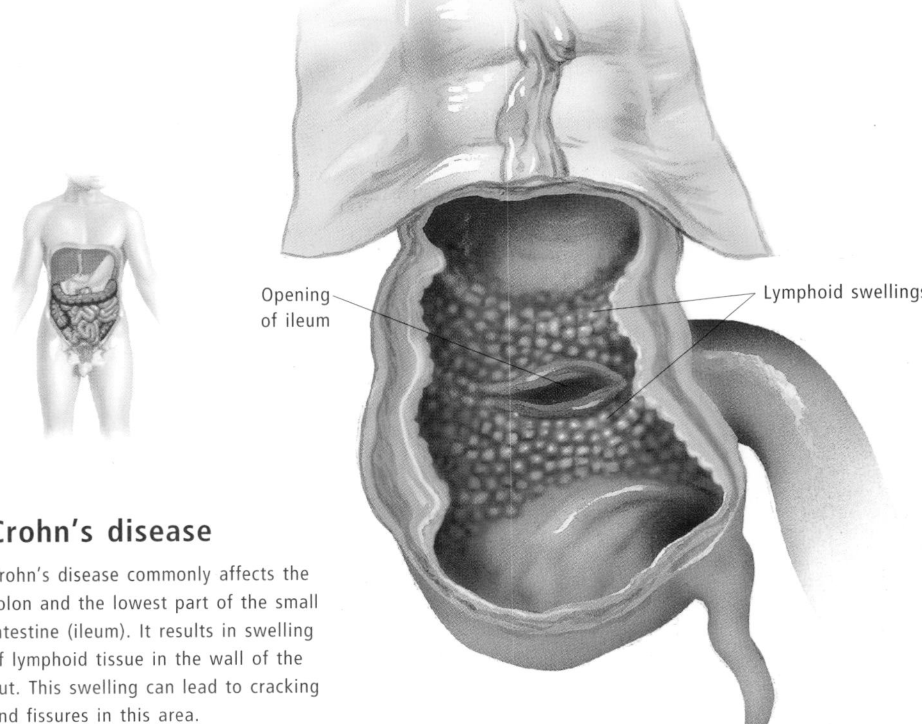

Crohn's disease

Crohn's disease commonly affects the colon and the lowest part of the small intestine (ileum). It results in swelling of lymphoid tissue in the wall of the gut. This swelling can lead to cracking and fissures in this area.

C

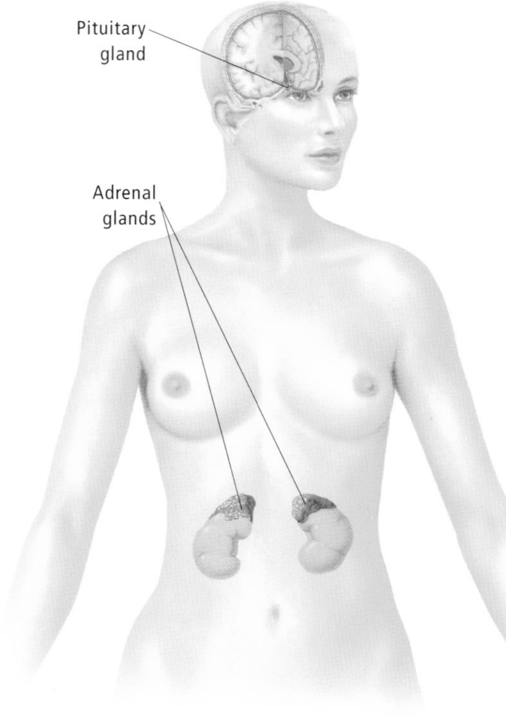

Cushing's syndrome

Symptoms produced by an excessive production of cortisol include fatty swellings of the face and trunk, and general weakness. It is usually a result of a tumor in the pituitary gland, which overstimulates the adrenal glands. The tumor may be removed surgically to cure the condition.

CROWN AND BRIDGE

These are two dental procedures, often used in combination, to fill a space created by one or more missing teeth. A crown is an artificial tooth or covering for the remains of a natural tooth, made of metal or porcelain. The teeth either side of a gap may be crowned in order to act as an anchor for a bridge. A bridge consists of false teeth on a mounting, and is often made of gold or porcelain on gold. It functions as normal teeth would and may prevent adjacent teeth from moving into an empty space. The crowns and bridge become one solid piece designed to look like individual natural teeth.

SEE ALSO *Teeth*

CRYOSURGERY

Cryosurgery is a medical technique in which extreme cold is used to destroy tissue. A part of the body is rapidly cooled to minus 76°F (-60°C) . The targeted tissue freezes and ice crystals form, breaking up and destroying the cell structure. Freezing can also stimulate the immune system to produce antibodies which attack diseased cells.

Cryosurgery is used to destroy skin cancers, warts, hemorrhoids, cataracts and difficult-to-reach internal tumors (such as in the kidney or brain). It is less invasive, less traumatic and involves less blood loss than traditional surgery. When treating growths on internal organs, liquid nitrogen is delivered through a small incision, thus avoiding major surgery.

CRYPTOSPORIDIOSIS

Cryptosporidium is a parasite of domestic and wild animals. In people with normal immune systems, it causes no illness or only mild symptoms. In people with deficient immune systems, for example those with AIDS or those on long-term corticosteroid or immunosuppressive medication, it may cause severe diarrhea, abdominal pain, malnutrition, dehydration, weight loss, and, occasionally, death. The organism is transmitted by the oral–fecal route, by person-to-person contact or through ingestion of contaminated water. Treatment for people suffering from the condition includes rehydration and antidiarrheal medications. There is no effective drug treatment for cryptosporidiosis.

CUSHING'S SYNDROME

Cushing's syndrome is a rare hormonal disorder caused by excessive production of cortisol. It is usually the result of a tumor in the pituitary gland which overstimulates the adrenal glands, but may be a side effect of corticosteroid drugs.

The affected person has fatty swellings on the back of the neck, a characteristic "moon face", fatigue, weakness, obesity of the trunk (while the limbs remain thin), and skin discoloration with pink streaks. In addition, there may be diabetes mellitus, hypertension, excessive hair growth and reduced sex drive in men; in women, menstruation may cease. The diagnosis can be confirmed by means of blood and urine tests for glucose and cortisol. Surgical removal of the pituitary tumor will cure the condition.

SEE ALSO *Adrenal glands, Pituitary gland*

CUTICLE

At the point on a finger or toe where skin meets nail, the skin grows back underneath itself, creating a fold. The topmost, visible tissue of this fold is the eponychium, commonly called the cuticle. The "true cuticle", however, is the non-living, unseen part of the fold underneath that seals off the site of new nail growth to protect it from infection.

SEE ALSO *Nails*

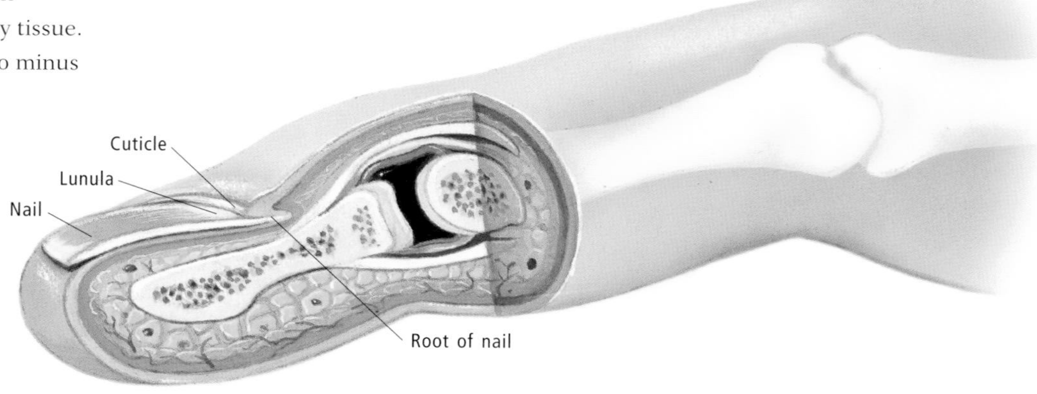

Cuticle

The cuticle is the fold of skin where the nail meets the skin. The top layer is visible, while the unseen bottom layer seals off the site of new nail growth to prevent infection.

CYANOSIS

Cyanosis is a bluish discoloration of the skin and mucous membranes (such as the lips). It is a sign that arterial blood is inadequately oxygenated. When it occurs in the whole of the body (central cyanosis) it is usually due to heart or lung disease.

Cyanosis often occurs in the terminal phases of a cardiac arrest, drug overdose, drowning or pneumonia, in fact whenever oxygenation of blood is not occurring. In rare cases it can be caused by abnormal hemoglobin (such as methemoglobinemia) and toxins such as cyanide.

Cyanosis of an area of the body, such as the feet or hands, can be caused by arterial disease. Arterial spasm in cold environments may cause cyanosis, which clears when the extremities are warmed. Arteriosclerosis may cause ischemia and cyanosis of extremities; angioplasty or amputation may be needed.

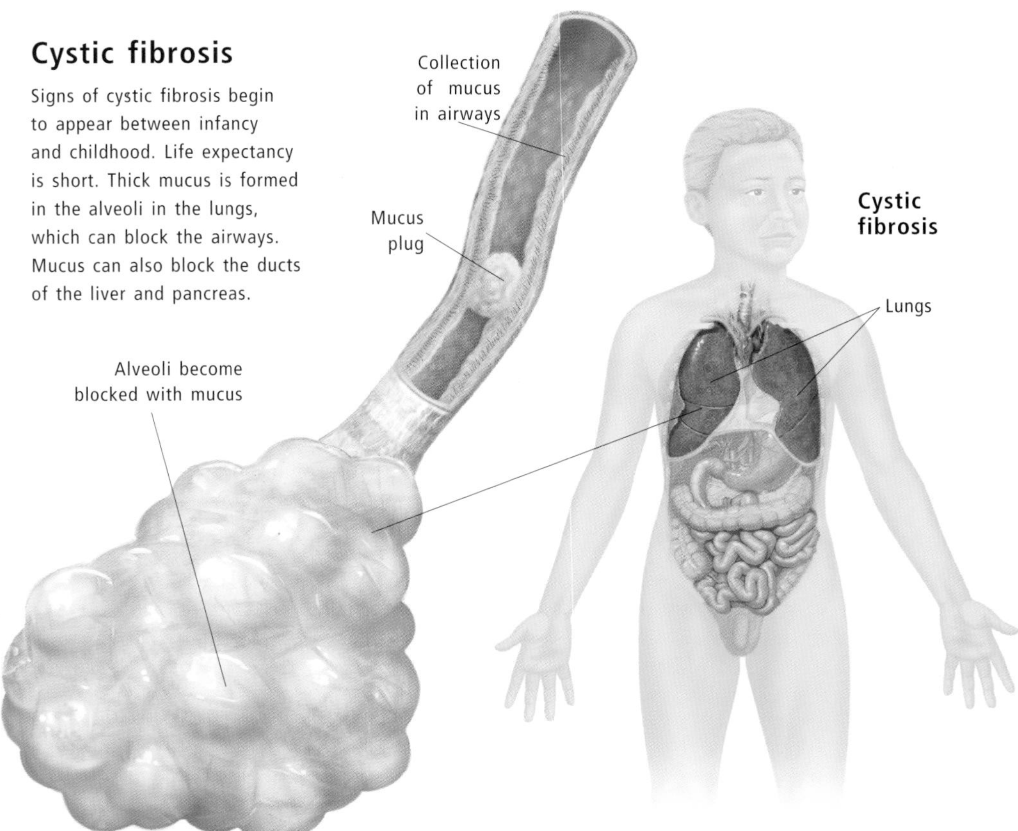
Cystic fibrosis
Signs of cystic fibrosis begin to appear between infancy and childhood. Life expectancy is short. Thick mucus is formed in the alveoli in the lungs, which can block the airways. Mucus can also block the ducts of the liver and pancreas.
Collection of mucus in airways
Mucus plug
Alveoli become blocked with mucus
Cystic fibrosis
Lungs

CYST

A cyst is an abnormal swelling that is sac-like in structure, with an outer wall of cells or fibrous tissue enclosing liquid or semi-liquid material. Cysts may contain a range of substances including blood, fat, pus or parasites. They are very common and can occur virtually anywhere in the body but are most often noticed in the skin, ovaries, breasts or kidneys.

Although usually benign, cysts can sometimes create complications. For example, symptoms caused by ovarian cysts (fluid-filled lumps on the ovaries) can include abdominal pain, abnormally heavy and irregular menstrual periods and increased growth of facial and body hair. If ovarian cysts rupture, they can cause severe pain, nausea, vomiting and shock. These cysts are usually benign in women during their reproductive years, but frequently are found to be malignant when they occur in young girls or post-menopausal women.

A cyst in the kidney may sound ominous, but more than 50 percent of people aged over 50 are thought to have these usually harmless and symptomless lesions. Only occasionally do cysts impair kidney function and require treatment. Likewise, cysts in the breasts are very common and mostly benign, although it is extremely important that each and every breast lump is assessed medically before being dismissed as harmless. Breast cysts can be as small as pin heads or as large as walnuts. They feel hard and round and move easily when touched.

Hydatid cysts are formed by the larvae of the dog tapeworm. In humans they occur most often in the liver and tend to be more common where people have close associations with dogs and sheep. They can survive for many years growing very slowly without major consequences, but they have the potential to cause serious illness. They are usually treated with potent medications or removed surgically.

SEE ALSO *Fibrocystic disease of the breast, Hydatid disease, Ovarian cysts, Tumors*

CYSTIC FIBROSIS

Cystic fibrosis is an inherited disorder, caused by a defective gene. In cystic fibrosis, mucous secretions in several organs become thick and sticky, and interfere with normal functioning. Thick mucus is formed in the lung airways which predisposes the person to chronic lung infections. Mucus can also block the ducts of the liver and the pancreas, causing inadequate absorption of nutrients from the intestinal tract (malabsorption) and malnutrition.

Cystic fibrosis affects about 1 in 2,500 people, although 1 in 25 people are carriers. Most affected people are born healthy, but begin showing signs of the disorder between infancy and adolescence. They gradually develop a chronic cough, persistent wheezing and recurrent respiratory infections. Their feces becomes greasy and foul-smelling and they fail to gain weight or thrive.

There is no known cure for cystic fibrosis. Treatment usually involves relieving and treating symptoms. Antibiotics, postural drainage, chest percussion and other breathing treatments will help fight infection in the lungs. Digestion can be improved with special diet and enzyme supplements. Advances in genetic engineering may one day provide a cure for cystic fibrosis. But for now the prognosis is poor; only about 50 percent of children with cystic fibrosis live beyond age 20 and few live beyond 35 years of age. Death usually occurs from lung complications. Screening of family members of a cystic fibrosis sufferer may detect the cystic fibrosis gene in up to 75 percent of carriers.

SEE ALSO *Genetic counseling, Liver, Lungs, Malnutrition, Pancreas*

C

C

CYSTINOSIS

About 2,000 people in the world are thought to suffer from cystinosis, a very rare inherited disorder in which abnormal levels of the amino acid cysteine accumulate and crystallize in the cells. Potentially, every organ may be affected but kidney and eye functions tend to be impaired first.

Of the three forms of the disease, infantile nephropathic cystinosis, which affects young children, is the most severe. Babies often appear normal at birth but tell-tale symptoms, such as excessive thirst and urination, usually appear by about 10 months. Growth and development are affected and death by the age of 10 years due to kidney failure was once inevitable. These days, kidney transplants and other treatments may prolong life.

In late-onset nephropathic cystinosis, symptoms first appear between the ages of 2 and 26 years and most commonly in the early teens. Without a transplant, death due to kidney failure commonly occurs within a few years of diagnosis.

In the third and mildest form of this disease, known as benign non-nephropathic cystinosis, symptoms often don't appear until middle age and do not include the kidney dysfunction that characterizes the other forms of cystinosis.

SEE ALSO *Amino acids, Kidney*

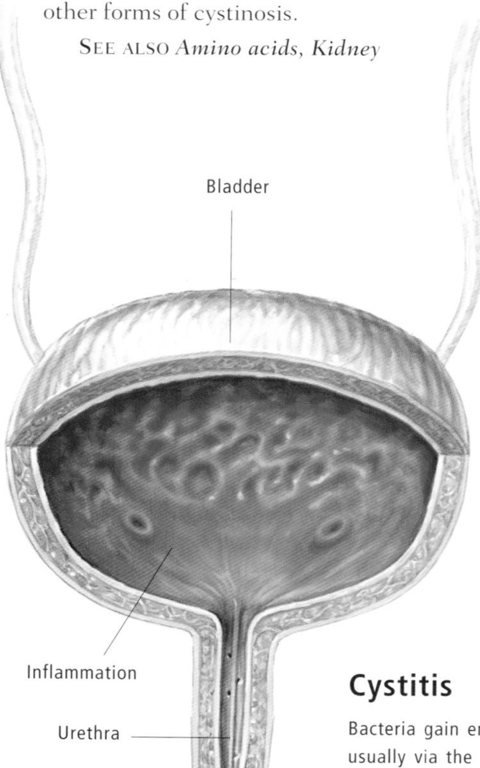

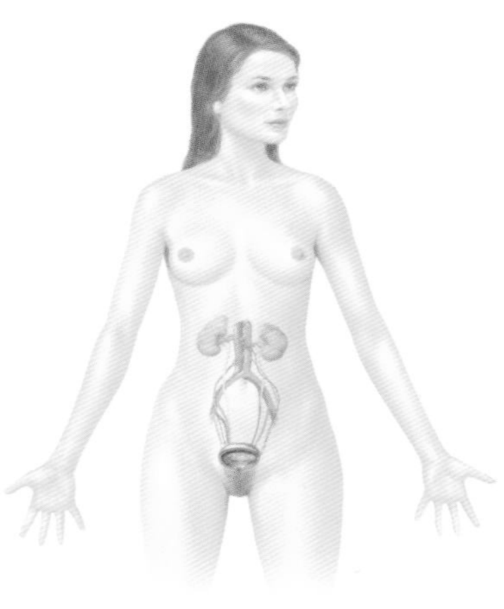

Cystitis

Bacteria gain entry to the bladder, usually via the urethra, leading to inflammation of the bladder–this is known as cystitis.

CYSTITIS

Cystitis is inflammation of the bladder, usually from bacterial infection. Bladder infections cause the sufferer to urinate more frequently than normal. Urination is accompanied by a burning or stinging sensation and there may be blood in the urine. If the infection spreads upstream to the kidneys, inflammation of the kidneys (pyelonephritis) may occur, with fever and back pain.

Cystitis is usually caused by bacteria gaining entry into the bladder via the urethra. Because the urethra is shorter in women than in men, cystitis is more common in females. It sometimes occurs in women after sexual intercourse. Any abnormality in the bladder makes cystitis more likely. A tumor or stones in the bladder, an enlarged prostate, or a distended uterus during pregnancy may obstruct the normal flow of urine and cause the disorder.

Cystitis is confirmed by a urine test which isolates the bacteria responsible and determines which antibiotic(s) will be the most effective. A short course of the correct antibiotic usually clears up the infection. The patient should drink copious amounts of water to help flush the bacteria out of the urinary tract. Should another attack of cystitis occur, it may be because of an abnormality, in which case the bladder should be more fully investigated. This may involve blood tests, an intravenous pyelogram (IVP) and cystoscopy.

There are a number of alternative therapies that may help to alleviate the symptoms of cystitis. Aromatherapy uses urinary antiseptic oils such as sandalwood and juniper in baths or massage. Herbalism dispenses urinary antiseptic herbs (uva ursi, buchu); antibacterial herbs (echinacea, goldenseal); demulcent herbs (marshmallow, cornsilk) to treat cystitis. Naturopathy advises eliminating sugar, coffee, tea, alcohol and acidic fruits while keeping to a low-protein whole-food diet. Fluids should be increased, including water, vegetable broth, barley water and cranberry juice. Sodium bicarbonate, non-acidic vitamin C, vitamin A and zinc are commonly prescribed as are alternating hot and cold sitz baths. An allergy-free diet or anti-candida diet may be prescribed for recurring urinary tract infections.

SEE ALSO *Bladder, Pyelonephritis, Urinary systems*

CYSTOCELE

A cystocele may occur in post-menopausal women who have lost hormonal support of the pelvic floor tissues. The pelvic floor becomes weak and the base of the urinary bladder pushes the front wall of the vagina backwards and downwards, making a urine-filled pocket bulging from the front wall of the vagina. It is sometimes associated with rectocele, which is a similar condition involving the posterior vaginal wall and the rectum. Patients are advised to do pelvic floor exercises; however, in more severe cases, surgery to repair the bladder may be considered necessary.

SEE ALSO *Bladder, Urinary incontinence, Urinary systems*

CYSTOGRAPHY

A cystogram is an x-ray taken of the bladder after radiopaque dye has been injected into a vein. The dye is filtered out by the kidneys into the bladder, where it outlines calculi (stones), papillomas (benign tumors), cancers and other problems.

SEE ALSO *Bladder, Kidneys*

CYSTOMETOGRAPHY

Cystometography is a medical procedure used to assess bladder function in people who are experiencing problems with urination. It is also commonly known as filling cystometography.

The patient normally lies down and remains as relaxed as possible while the bladder is filled with sterile water. Abdominal pressure is also applied to the bladder via the rectum. Throughout the procedure the patient reports on the sensations that they are feeling, and bladder pressure is monitored continuously.

SEE ALSO *Bladder*

CYSTOSCOPY

Cystoscopy is the examination of the bladder with a cystoscope, a special fiberoptic tube equipped with a lens and a light. The cystoscope is introduced through the urethra into the bladder. Through it, a surgeon or urologist can visualize the interior of the bladder. Special attachments can be used to crush stones, take a biopsy of a tumor, or to cauterize diseased tissue.

SEE ALSO *Bladder, Urethra*

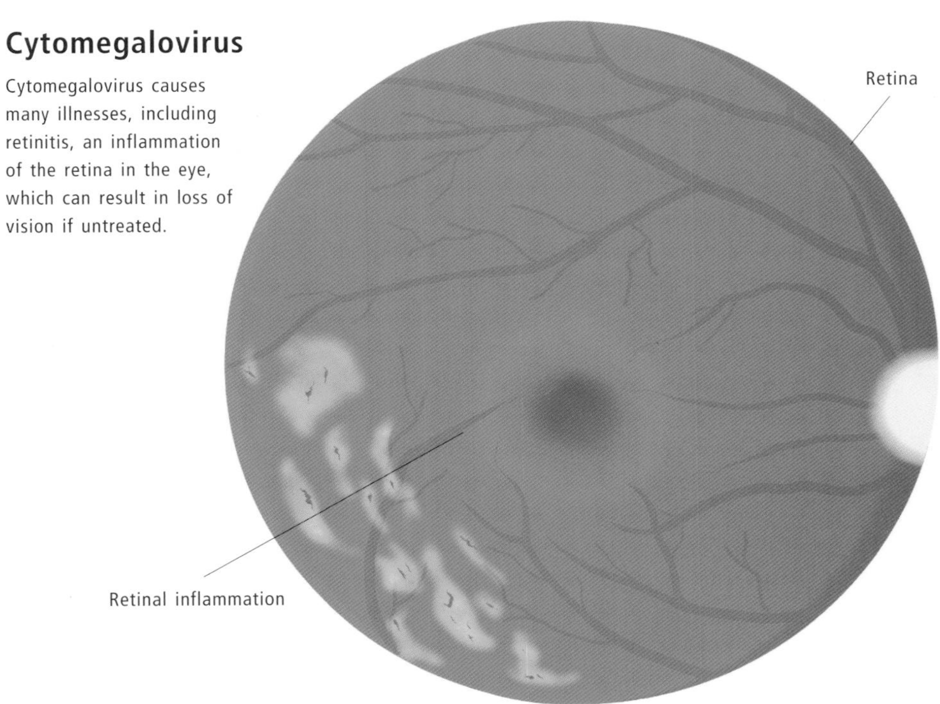

Cytomegalovirus

Cytomegalovirus causes many illnesses, including retinitis, an inflammation of the retina in the eye, which can result in loss of vision if untreated.

CYTOMEGALOVIRUS

The human cytomegalovirus (CMV), a member of the herpes family of viruses, causes cytomegalic inclusion disease. This is an extremely common virus and some 90 percent of people in the over-70s population have antibodies to CMV in their blood.

Infants commonly acquire the virus from their mother in the uterus, during birth or through breast feeding. It can be spread by close contact later in life and can be reactivated in adults after a period of dormancy.

Most healthy people do not develop any significant symptoms to CMV, though it may a cause a flu-like illness lasting a few weeks. However, people with suppressed immune systems (such as those on immunosuppressive drugs or with AIDS) who become infected with CMV may develop serious diseases such as pneumonia, hepatitis, encephalitis (brain inflammation), colitis, and retinitis (inflammation of the eye). They may need to be hospitalized and receive treatment with antiviral drugs.

Congenital cytomegalovirus is caused when an infected mother passes the CMV virus to the fetus through the placenta. In a fetus, it can cause a range of defects and may result in miscarriage. The baby may eventually develop minor impairments affecting hearing, vision or mental capacity. A small percentage are born with severe neurologic damage, causing intellectual disability or profound hearing loss. There is no specific treatment.

SEE ALSO *Immunity, Viruses*

CYTOTOXIC DRUGS

Cytotoxic drugs destroy cells or prevent their multiplication. Penicillins or other antibiotics used in the treatment of bacterial infections are cytotoxic, but the term usually refers to drugs used in the treatment of cancer, such as methotrexate and cyclophosphamide. They are sometimes used to treat other disorders such as rheumatoid arthritis.

Cytotoxic drugs affect not only cancer cells but also other cells, especially those that grow rapidly such as cells of the skin, gastrointestinal tract and bone marrow. They may cause side effects such as serious blood disorders, hair loss (alopecia) and reduced resistance to infection. Dosages and side effects of cytotoxic drugs need to be carefully monitored by the physician.

SEE ALSO *Cancer, Cells*

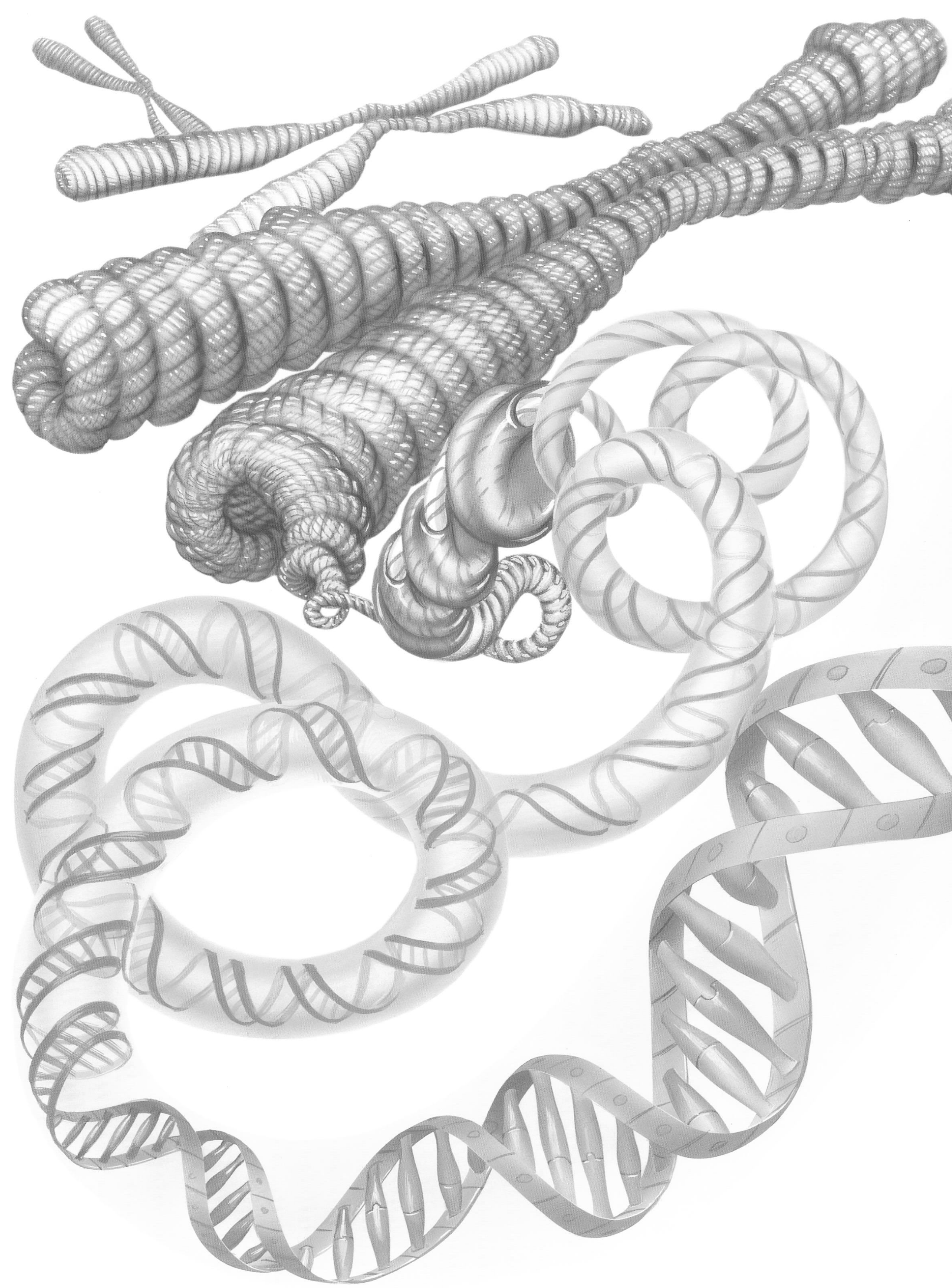

D

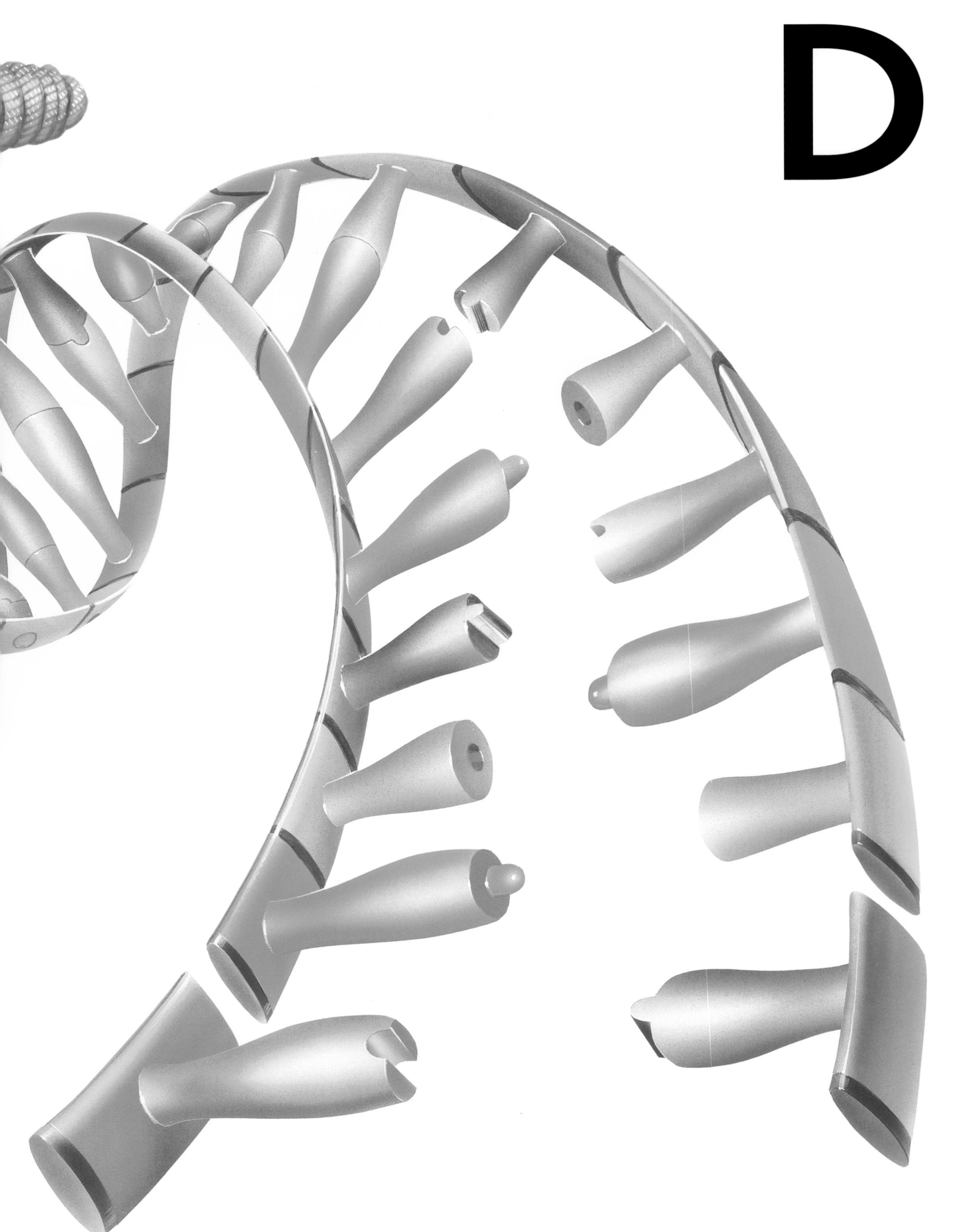

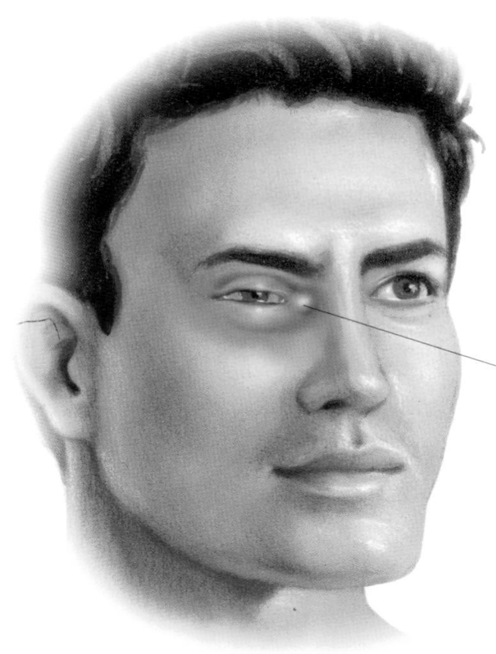

Dacryocystitis

Infection of the lacrimal sac usually results from blockage of the lacrimal duct. The area around the sac becomes red, swollen, and painful. The eye becomes red and watery and oozes fluid. An abscess may develop in which the lacrimal sac is swollen and filled with pus.

Lacrimal sac

D

DACRYOADENITIS

Dacryoadenitis is inflammation of the lacrimal gland, which is situated above the eye. It is usually caused by bacteria from other infection such as conjunctivitis or upper respiratory tract infection, resulting in a blockage of the lacrimal duct, the duct that drains tears from the eye into the nasal cavity. It often occurs along with dacryocystitis. The eye is red, and the lacrimal gland is swollen and tender. The condition is treated with oral antibiotics.

SEE ALSO *Conjunctivitis, Dacryocystitis, Eye, Lacrimal glands*

DACRYOCYSTITIS

Dacryocystitis is inflammation of the tear (lacrimal) sac, caused by a blockage of the lacrimal duct, which normally drains tears from the eye into the nasal cavity. It is most common in children, and may follow sinus or nasal infection, nasal polyps, eye injury or infection, especially conjunctivitis. It may also occur as an inherited condition, usually appearing in infants at 3 to 12 weeks of age.

The symptoms of dacryocystitis are pain, swelling and tenderness in the corner of the eye, with a discharge of pus and tears. Treatment is required to prevent infection spreading to the cornea, or permanent scarring of the tear duct (dacryostenosis). Irrigation of the infected ducts, massage of the tear duct and the application of antibiotic ointments will usually cure the condition.

Severe cases may require surgery to dilate and probe the tear duct canal to clear the infection and prevent recurrences. Complete obstruction may require a surgical opening from the eye into the nasal passage.

SEE ALSO *Eye, Lacrimal glands*

DANCE MOVEMENT THERAPY

In many ancient cultures illness is seen to be caused by a loss of soul and dance is viewed as an important way of bringing people who are sick back to themselves and their life energy.

In modern Western culture, Isadora Duncan became a pioneer of early dance movement therapy by championing dance as a spontaneous form of emotional expression. Also in the USA around the 1920s there was another contributor to the beginnings of dance therapy, Rudolph van Laban. A dancer and a theoretician, he explored the space and dynamics of movement, offering a movement-based model for human wholeness that reflected both conscious and unconscious processes.

In the aftermath of World War II the need to deal with large groups of traumatized veterans led to the development of a number of creative therapies suited to group work. In Washington DC, Marian Chace used dance in her work with psychiatric patients, finding it particularly helpful for encouraging withdrawn patients back into the present. Chace's view was that dance is a form of communication that fulfils a basic human need. She recognized that both dancers and psychotic patients used symbolic body movements to communicate emotions and ideas. Chace moved with her patients using rhythm as an ordering principle, and the circle as a means of containment. She also made a study of the movement patterns of different diagnostic categories.

Another early dance therapist pioneer, Mary Starks Whitehouse, was inspired by the psychiatrist Carl Jung who believed that all psychological complexes have a physical component. She encouraged patients to find their "authentic movement".

Practice

Dance movement therapy is based on the assumption that body and mind are inter-related. In practice dance is used psychotherapeutically to bring about changes in feelings, behavior, cognition and physical functioning. Everyday and creative movement are used through processes that help patients learn more about themselves and their interaction with others.

How dance therapy is actually practised varies widely. Generally the emphasis is on exploring and expanding movements as patients discover and express their own resources and feelings. Patients may also be encouraged to find individual movements to themes and music given by the therapist.

There is no stress on competence or experience nor do patients have to be fit or fully physically able. Some of the benefits of dance movement therapy include the development of a positive body awareness and self-image, anger management, improved communication skills and the stimulation of creativity and playfulness. This is a particularly effective therapy for children especially those with behavioral or learning problems or with physical disabilities.

Dance movement therapy is used in psychiatric hospitals, mental health care clinics, rehabilitation facilities and special schools as well as in private practice. Practitioners believe it can help with severe emotional disorders, autism, cognitive delays, neurological disorders, the elderly, those suffering trauma from physical or sexual abuse, or those in substance abuse recovery programs. Preventive health schemes also make use of dance movement therapy to relieve stress and assist movement function. It is most commonly practised in groups.

SEE ALSO *Alexander technique, Feldenkrais method, Music therapy*

D

DANDRUFF

Dandruff is the everyday term for mild seborrheic dermatitis of the scalp. It is related to cradle cap in infants, and in adults, manifests as greasy or dry, white scales that are shed from the scalp. Other areas may also be affected, including eyebrows, forehead, and behind the ears.

Dandruff is also sometime associated with excessive production of grease or oil from the sebaceous glands, and sufferers tend to have oily skin. The cause is unknown, but it tends to be worse in hot, humid weather or cold, dry weather and in periods of stress and fatigue.

Dandruff is a chronic condition with periods of improvement followed by deterioration. It is not dangerous, but it can be annoying and socially embarrassing. Shampooing should be frequent (daily), prolonged (at least 5 minutes) and vigorous enough so that the scales are loosened with the fingernails. As well, a non-prescription dandruff shampoo containing selenium sulfide or zinc pyrithione should be used at least once a week. If the condition worsens, a doctor should be consulted, as corticosteroid creams or ointments may be needed.

SEE ALSO *Cradle cap, Dermatitis, Scalp*

DEAFNESS

Deafness can be simply defined as an inability to hear. It can be partial, in which a person has an inability to hear in one ear, or inability to hear sounds at a certain frequency or below a certain volume (intensity). Or it can be profound, meaning a total inability to hear.

Unlike partially deaf people, people with a profound deafness have a hearing loss so severe that a hearing aid is useless. About 10 percent of people with deafness are profoundly deaf.

There are two main types of hearing loss: conductive hearing loss and sensorineural hearing loss.

Conductive hearing loss occurs when sound is not properly transmitted to the cochlea (a small, spiral-shaped structure in the inner ear) because of a blockage, disease or disorder of the middle ear. A person with a conductive hearing loss can generally benefit from a hearing aid.

Sensorineural hearing loss is caused by damage to the cochlea or auditory nerves. This type of deafness occurs, for example, when the tiny hair cells of the cochlea in the inner ear become damaged, with the result that sound reaching the cochlea is not adequately processed, and faulty nerve signals are sent to the brain. A hearing aid is often of no use to a person with a sensorineural loss.

Some experts recognize two other categories of deafness. Mixed hearing loss is caused by illness or injury in both the outer or middle ear and the inner ear. Central hearing loss is caused by damage to the neural pathways or parts of the brain concerned with hearing.

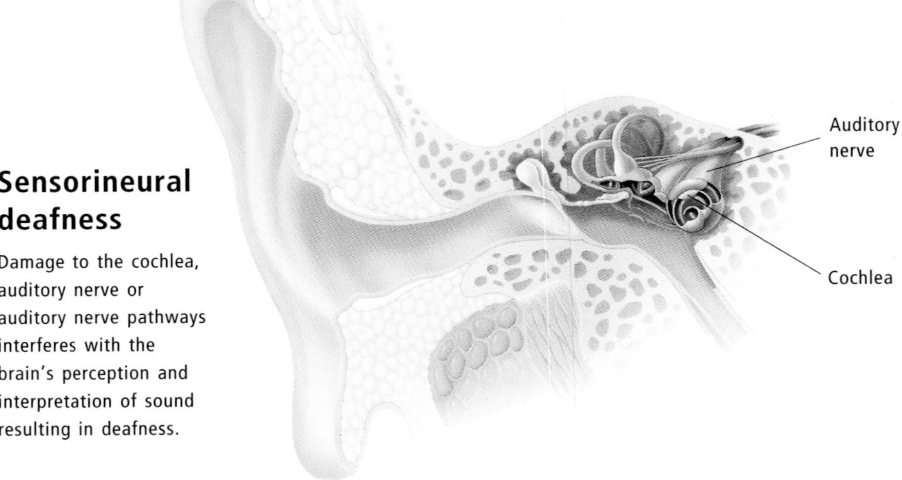

Sensorineural deafness

Damage to the cochlea, auditory nerve or auditory nerve pathways interferes with the brain's perception and interpretation of sound resulting in deafness.

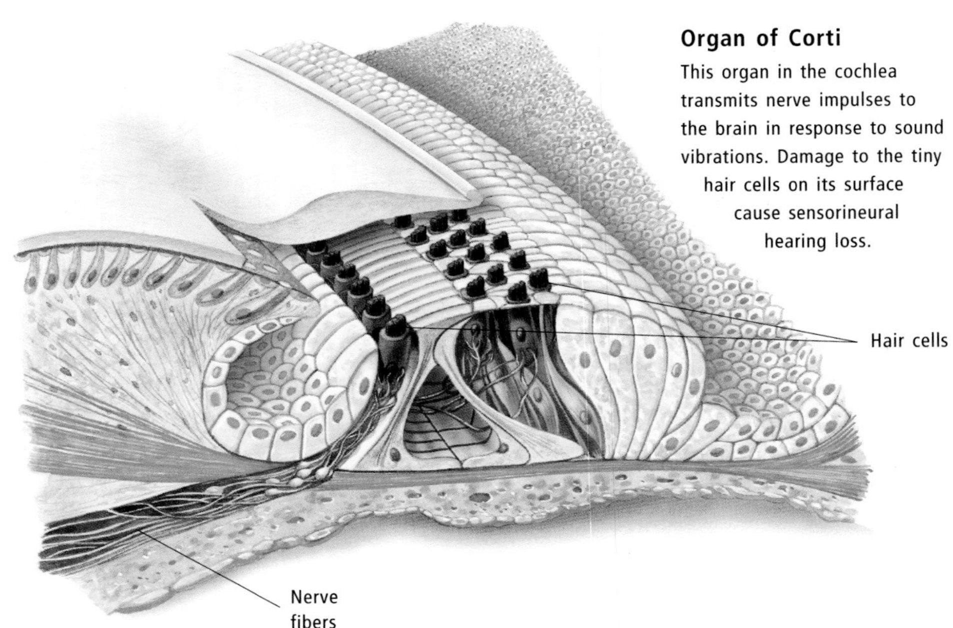

Organ of Corti

This organ in the cochlea transmits nerve impulses to the brain in response to sound vibrations. Damage to the tiny hair cells on its surface cause sensorineural hearing loss.

Factors affecting hearing loss

Babies will respond to sound soon after birth and speech begins to develop at two to three months, words following from eight to twelve months. If these developments do not occur, a hearing problem may be the reason.

Hearing problems can appear at any age but they are particularly serious in childhood as the ability to hear affects the development of speech. Hearing enables the reception of sounds and recognition of language, and allows self-monitoring when those sounds are imitated, which is an essential part of the learning process.

Birth defects causing loss of hearing can be inherited, or are the result of injury or disease. Lack of oxygen or Rh disease (Rh incompatibility) can damage the auditory nerve and inner ear. The likelihood of a child suffering birth defects that affect hear-

D

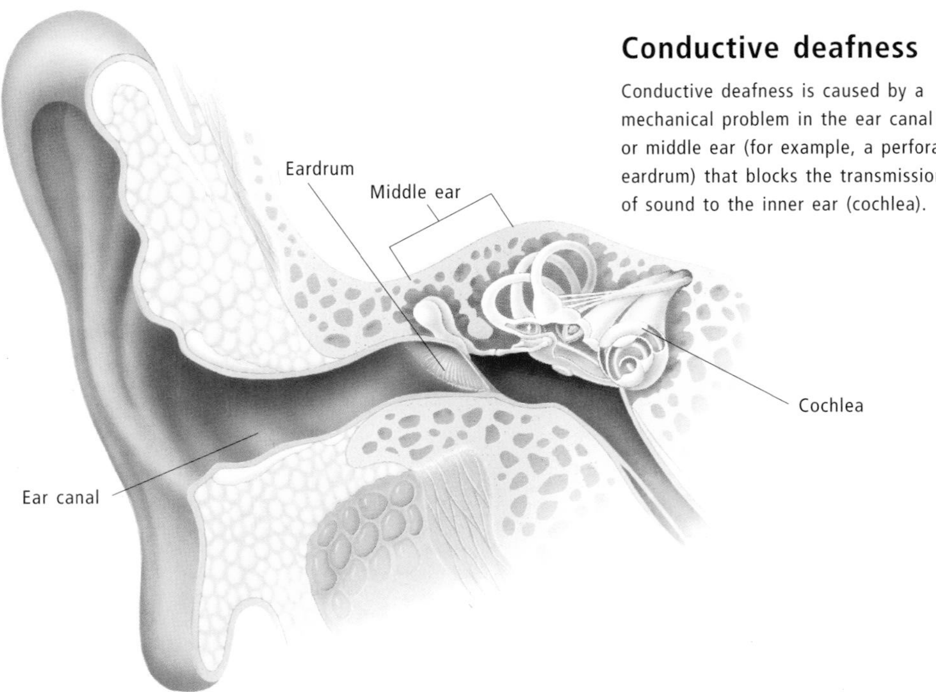

Conductive deafness

Conductive deafness is caused by a mechanical problem in the ear canal or middle ear (for example, a perforated eardrum) that blocks the transmission of sound to the inner ear (cochlea).

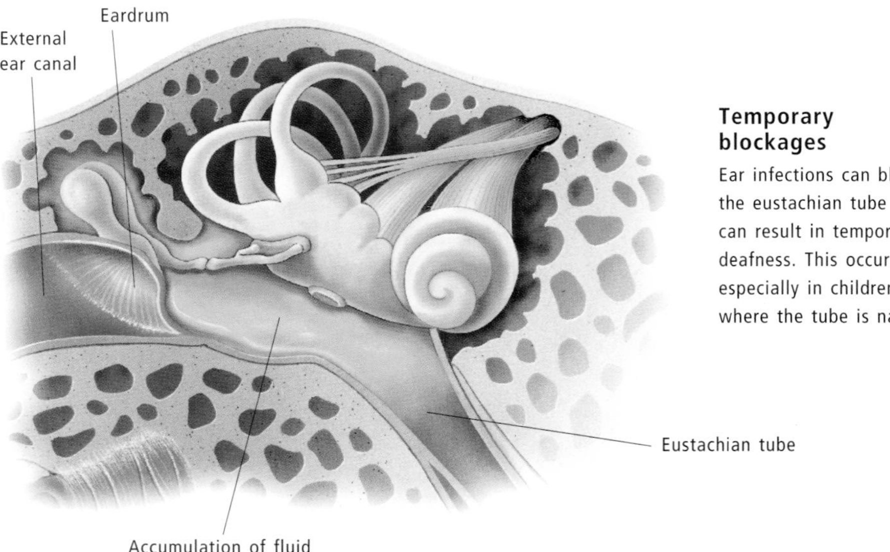

Temporary blockages

Ear infections can block the eustachian tube and can result in temporary deafness. This occurs especially in children where the tube is narrow.

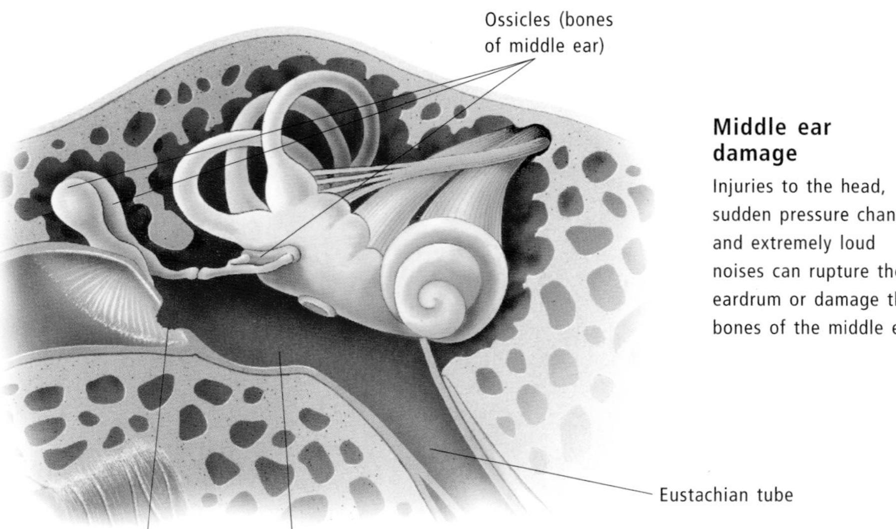

Middle ear damage

Injuries to the head, sudden pressure changes and extremely loud noises can rupture the eardrum or damage the bones of the middle ear.

ing is greater where other family members were born with hearing defects or where there is exposure before birth to infection by toxoplasmosis, syphilis, rubella, herpes or cytomegalovirus.

Down syndrome and other genetic problems can result in impaired hearing, as can exposure of the mother to certain antibiotics, quinine or radiation during pregnancy. Risk factors at birth are greater for babies with a low birth weight; those who need to spend more than ten days on a ventilator; those with an Apgar score below three; and those with high levels of bilirubin, indicating possible liver dysfunction.

Childhood illnesses including measles, mumps, meningitis and ear infections—all of which can cause scarring that restricts the movement of the ossicles—can permanently impair hearing. Head injury, exposure to very loud noises and side-effects of certain antibiotics are all possible causes of hearing loss.

Normal hearing can be affected temporarily in children by a blockage in the ear canal, which can be due to excessive ear wax, or a foreign body such as a bead or piece of food. Ear infections can infect or block the eustachian tube very easily in children as the tube is narrow. Hearing can also be lost temporarily after exposure to loud noise.

Injuries to the head, blows, sudden pressure changes (for example when divers rise too quickly to the surface) and extremely loud noises (such as explosions) can rupture the eardrum and damage the bones of the middle ear or the delicate inner ear. Repeated exposure to loud noise can also produce gradual hearing loss. Noise intensity greater than 85 decibels can destroy hair cells in the inner ear. Damage is permanent and may be accompanied by tinnitus, a high-pitched noise heard in one or both ears.

Age-related hearing loss (presbycusis) can begin in early adulthood and usually diminishes ability to hear high frequency sounds first. It can advance to profound deafness and affects men more often than women.

Sudden attacks of vertigo, nausea and vomiting, possibly preceded by hearing loss and tinnitus may indicate Menière's disease, which is a chronic disease of the inner ear. There may be pressure in one or both ears, and hearing ability gradually diminishes. The cause is unknown, but vertigo can be treated temporarily with drugs, or more permanently, by surgery to the nerves of the inner ear.

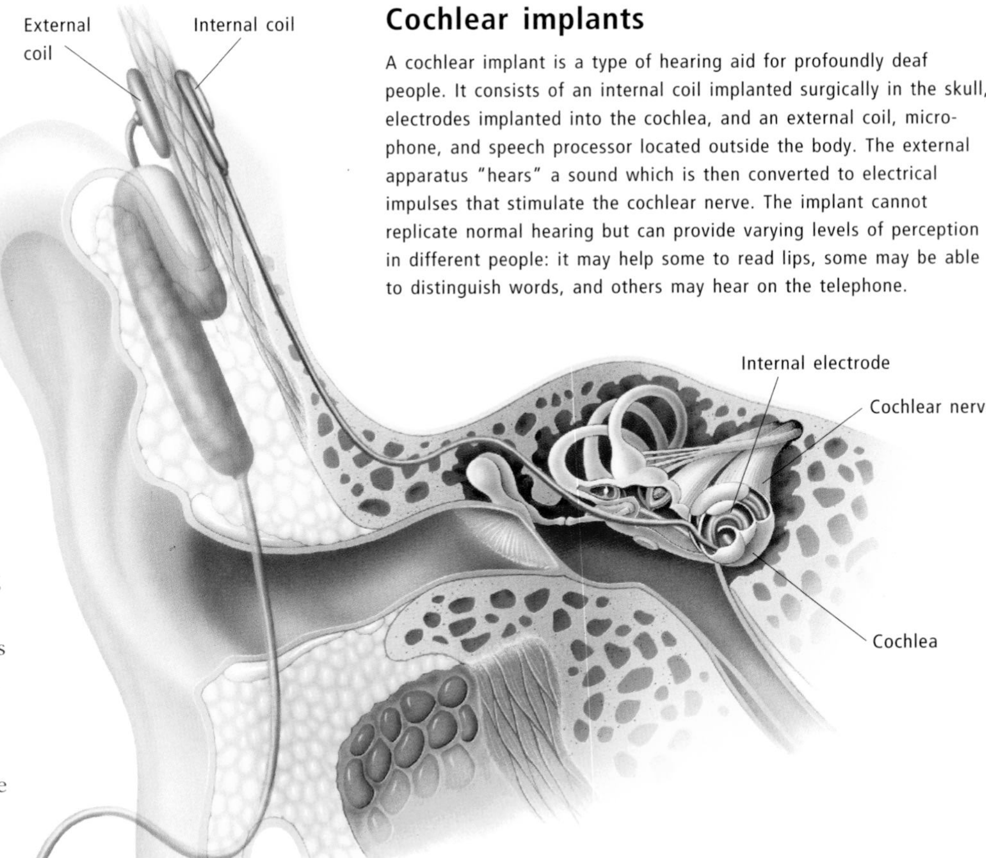

Cochlear implants

A cochlear implant is a type of hearing aid for profoundly deaf people. It consists of an internal coil implanted surgically in the skull, electrodes implanted into the cochlea, and an external coil, microphone, and speech processor located outside the body. The external apparatus "hears" a sound which is then converted to electrical impulses that stimulate the cochlear nerve. The implant cannot replicate normal hearing but can provide varying levels of perception in different people: it may help some to read lips, some may be able to distinguish words, and others may hear on the telephone.

Hearing tests

Hearing tests can show the intensity (in decibels) at which various frequencies can be heard, and at which speech is correctly understood. Testing for deafness seeks to determine whether the loss is conductive or sensory, temporary or permanent, and congenital or acquired later in life. The ears can also be checked for blockages or structural abnormalities.

Bone-conduction hearing tests include tuning-fork tests where the vibrating tuning fork is held against the mastoid process, which is part of the skull. The patient reports how long a sound is heard for, then the test is repeated with the tuning fork held close to the ear canal. If the first part of the test registers a longer audible period, conductive hearing loss is suspected.

Audiometry testing usually includes a separate test that involves a calibrated bone-conduction vibrator. The test aims to reveal any loss in hearing ability by comparing what is heard by bone conduction alone with the hearing of airborne sounds through the middle ear.

Deafness is treated by specially trained physicians called otolaryngologists (ear, nose and throat specialists). Their approach to treating deafness is to correct the underlying condition if possible. For example, infections can be treated with antibiotics, and wax can be removed by ear syringing. However, many causes of deafness are irreversible or degenerative and cannot be treated. In these cases the aim is to augment hearing with electronic devices where possible.

Hearing aids

A hearing aid is an electronic device that improves hearing. It consists of a microphone, amplifier, receiver and power source (usually batteries). It is adjustable for pitch (frequency response) and volume (saturation response) by the prescribing audiologist. Some aids have external volume controls which the user can adjust, and switches for when using the aid with a telephone and other listening devices.

Aids are usually miniaturized to fit in or behind the ear or wholly within the ear canal. Where those aids are unsuitable or the most powerful amplification is needed, larger aids using a microphone and power pack worn on the chest can be used.

The cochlear implant is a recently developed aid that is surgically implanted in profoundly deaf people. It converts sounds to electrical impulses that are sent to electrodes implanted in the cochlea and thence to the brain.

A bone-conduction hearing aid is mounted on a headband which holds it securely in contact with the head for the greatest possible sound conduction through the skull bone.

Treatment

Profoundly deaf people must communicate by means other than spoken language. There are several ways in which this can be accomplished, including lip reading (known also as speech reading), sign language, finger spelling, cued speech, manually coded language as well as writing, typing, gesture and mime. Each deaf person has a preferred method of communication that may change from situation to situation; for example they may prefer lip reading with some persons but not with others.

Deaf people face unique problems. Unemployment or underemployment is higher than in the general population and they may be discriminated against in the workplace. However, deaf people are employed in almost every type of job, and increasingly employers are hiring deaf people and adapting the workplace to accommodate them, for example by providing sign language interpreters. Deafness does not affect a person's intellect or learning ability. However, deafness may make the learning of language more difficult. Consequently, a hearing-impaired child's progress at school may be slower than that of a child who can hear. However the hearing-impaired child who is taught lip reading and sign language at an early age is more likely to do well.

SEE ALSO *Cochlea, Ear, Hearing, Menière's disease, Newborn, Speech, Tinnitus*

D

DEATH

Death is the inevitable end for all living organisms, the final and permanent shutdown of all the functions and processes that maintain life.

In past centuries identifying death was reckoned to be an easy task. A container of water balanced on the chest, or a feather held before the lips or nostrils were standard aids to show that heartbeat and breathing had stopped. If further proof was needed, bodies were allowed to lie for several days before burial to let putrefaction provide its evidence. Absence of circulation was another observable fact taken as proof of death, and a finger might be cut off to show that blood had ceased to flow. Such observations were the only tools available, and the more extreme measures allayed widespread fears of people being buried alive.

In the absence of movement, heartbeat and breathing, life was pronounced extinct. But in the last century, with the knowledge that signs of life might reappear in people apparently dead, and with medical technology evolving to sustain vital processes well beyond the point of irreversible brain death, a more exact description and definition of the moment of death were needed.

A definition was provided in 1966 by the National Academy of Medicine in France, stating that death could be certified when the brain was no longer able to take control of the body's vital functions and the brain had shown no signs of activity as measured by electroencephalogram for 48 hours. The concept of death as irreparable and irreversible loss of function and reflexes in the brain stem was accepted and enshrined in medical practice and in law in the USA, the UK and generally throughout the world.

The test for brain stem death is applied to people who have lapsed into apnea coma; that is, they are unconscious, normal breathing has stopped and they are on a ventilator. A senior medical specialist normally carries out this type of examination and, for ethical reasons, would not be in any way concerned with use of the person's organs for transplants after death.

In this process the cause of the coma is established, the presence of irreversible brain damage is confirmed, all possible curable or reversible causes (such as drug overdose, intoxication or hypothermia) are eliminated and no brain stem reflexes can be detected. After these inquiries, a series of tests is applied to stimulate the reflexes of the eyes and airways, and of the responses that induce breathing.

Diagnosis of brain stem death made in this manner is generally accepted and has been proven reliable. It is a vital step before any decision can be made to cease using a life support system.

A diagnosis of brain stem death will raise moral, ethical, religious and legal questions for everyone involved in treatment. The decision must be taken to continue or refrain from further treatment, including those measures that mechanically support life. The issues are complex and difficult to resolve. The rights of the patient must always be considered.

After death, the body is treated according to law and the wishes of the deceased. Permission may have been given for organs to be donated for transplants, in which case the organs are removed from the donor as speedily as possible after death has been certified. Arrangements may have been made for the cadaver to be used for medical research or teaching.

After death

After death, the skin becomes pale and loses elasticity, and the muscles lose their tone and flatten where they are pressed, particularly under the body's weight. Breathing and pulse stop. The body cools down and its rate of cooling can be predicted, allowing forensic pathology to determine the approximate time of death. A postmortem examination, or autopsy, may be made to establish the cause of death, if unknown.

After a few hours, muscles stiffen in rigor mortis, then relax again after three to four days. Blood clotting and the death of individual cells in the body begin within a few hours of death. Decomposition starts within 48 hours, depending on the surrounding temperature, as bacteria in the gut multiply and consume dead cells. In low temperatures this process may not start and bodies can be preserved in ice or peat bogs for centuries. In high temperatures and dry atmosphere bodies may dessicate, shrivel and mummify.

Preparation for dying

When a terminal disease is diagnosed it is now accepted practice to inform the patient of the diagnosis. The medical profession has in the past shied away from sharing this information with patients, but now the benefits of informing them are acknowledged. Despite the initial pain, truthful communication allows the sharing of grief and the full expression of emotions between loved ones, and gives patients time to put their affairs in order, not only financialy but emotionally as well.

Acceptance of approaching death does not always come immediately, but knowledge and time may help terminally ill people to find peace, which may be denied them if they are not told the truth.

The period before death can also be used to make important decisions on organ donation, disposal of assets and any other matters of concern. The dying person may choose to prepare a living will, where power is conferred on relatives to make decisions such as when to remove life support in case of coma prior to death.

The question of the "right to die" may arise, where terminally ill patients can decide to be put painlessly to death; this is known as euthanasia, or mercy killing, which is an illegal act in most of the countries of the world.

Attitudes to death vary widely, as many people in the industrialized nations have little knowledge of or familiarity with it. The death of an elderly person may be readily accepted, whereas that of a child may be seen as unjust and cause untold grief. Counseling can aid acceptance and assist the natural process of grieving.

DECOMPRESSION SICKNESS

Decompression sickness, also called the bends or caisson disease, is a disorder caused by bubbles of nitrogen gas coming out of solution in the bodily fluids and tissues, due to a sudden drop in environmental pressure. It is usually seen in divers who surface too quickly, or in people in a nonpressurized aircraft that climbs too rapidly.

The bubbles of nitrogen gas block arteries and cause loss of blood (ischemia) and death (infarction) of tissues. The person experiences joint pain (especially in the

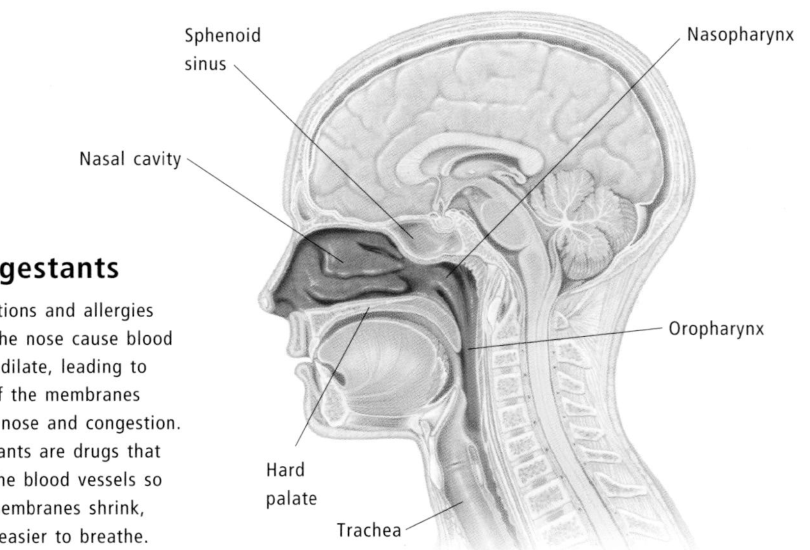

Decongestants

Viral infections and allergies affecting the nose cause blood vessels to dilate, leading to swelling of the membranes inside the nose and congestion. Decongestants are drugs that constrict the blood vessels so that the membranes shrink, making it easier to breathe.

elbow, shoulder, hip and knee), vomiting, giddiness, abdominal pain, and visual disturbances. Convulsions, paralysis and death may follow in severe cases.

Treatment involves placing the affected person into the high-pressure atmosphere of a decompression chamber. The nitrogen bubbles dissolve into the blood, and as the pressure is gradually lowered in the chamber, are safely breathed out as nitrogen gas via the lungs.

DECONGESTANTS

Decongestants are drugs that shrink swollen membranes in the nose and make it easier to breathe. They are useful in relieving the symptoms of a stuffy or runny nose in cold and flu infections, sinusitis and nasal allergies. Decongestants can be taken orally or by nasal spray.

Oral medications usually contain pseudoephedrine and phenylpropanolamine; they are effective, but may cause insomnia. People who suffer from high blood pressure (hypertension) should seek advice from a medical practitioner before taking oral decongestants, as they may cause an increase in blood pressure.

Many decongestant nasal sprays have a rebound effect if used for along time, resulting in irritation and inflammation of the nasal membranes when the treatment is stopped. A doctor's advice should be sought if treatment with a nasal decongestant is to be continued for more than five days.

SEE ALSO *Allergies, Common cold, Sinusitis*

DEEP VENOUS THROMBOSIS

Deep venous thrombosis is clotting in a deep vein, usually in the leg or pelvis. It may occur after surgery or periods of prolonged bed rest. It is more common in the elderly, people with arterial disease or diabetes, and women on some types of contraceptive pill. The calf of the leg may be swollen, warm, red and tender.

Complication occurs if a piece of the blood clot breaks off to form an embolus which can lodge in the vessels of the heart or lungs; this is potentially fatal. Treatment involves intravenous anticoagulant drugs in hospital, followed by oral anticoagulants for several months or permanently.

SEE ALSO *Anticoagulants, Embolism, Thrombosis, Vein*

DEFIBRILLATION

Fibrillation is rapid, irregular twitching of muscle fibers. In the heart it may be caused by heart disease, such as coronary artery disease, by drugs (such as digitalis), or by electrocution. Defibrillation is the term used for stopping fibrillation of the heart muscle.

If fibrillation affects the lower chambers (ventricles) of the heart, it causes cardiac arrest, which will rapidly lead to death because a heart that is fibrillating will pump little or no blood around the body's circulatory system.

Sometimes, normal heart contractions can be restored by electric shocks from a machine called a cardiac defibrillator. Cardiac defibrillation is an emergency procedure, and is combined with cardiopulmonary resuscitation (CPR). If cardiac arrest and defibrillation occur in a hospital, the survival rate is high; elsewhere it is very low. Defibrillation must occur within about five to seven minutes to be successful.

There are three types of defibrillators: the manual defibrillator; the automated external defibrillator (AED), which can read a patient's heart rhythm and deliver the shock automatically; and implantable cardiac defibrillators (ICDs), which are surgically implanted and are suitable for people with recurrent fibrillation.

SEE ALSO *Coronary artery disease, Fibrillation, Heart, Ventricle*

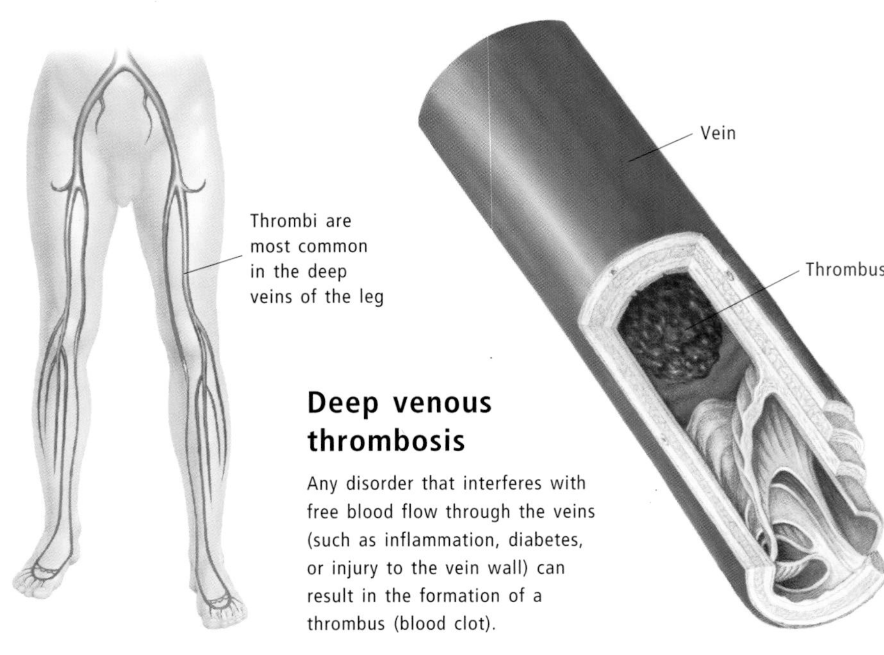

Deep venous thrombosis

Any disorder that interferes with free blood flow through the veins (such as inflammation, diabetes, or injury to the vein wall) can result in the formation of a thrombus (blood clot).

Controlling and maintaining fluid balance

The pituitary gland works with the kidneys to control water balance. When too much water is lost and dehydration occurs, the posterior part of the pituitary secretes larger than normal amounts of antidiuretic hormone (ADH) which make the kidneys retain fluid. The hypothalamus monitors water levels in the blood. When levels drop too low the hypothalamus instructs the pituitary to release antidiuretic hormone (ADH). This hormone makes the kidneys reabsorb water into the blood and decreases urine production. When the body is rehydrated, the hypothalamus tells the pituitary to slow ADH secretion, the kidneys keep less water in the blood and the bladder releases urine again.

D

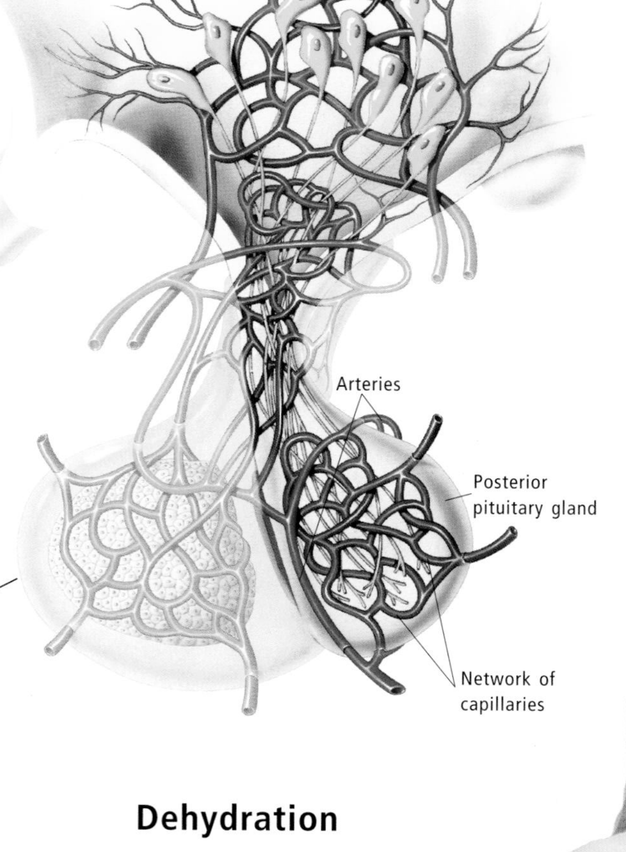

Causes of dehydration

Disorders of the gastrointestinal tract (diarrhea and vomiting), the kidney and the skin (such as sunburn) can all cause fluid loss and dehydration. Children are especially vulnerable to dehydration because water constitutes a higher percentage of their body weight (about 80 percent) than adults.

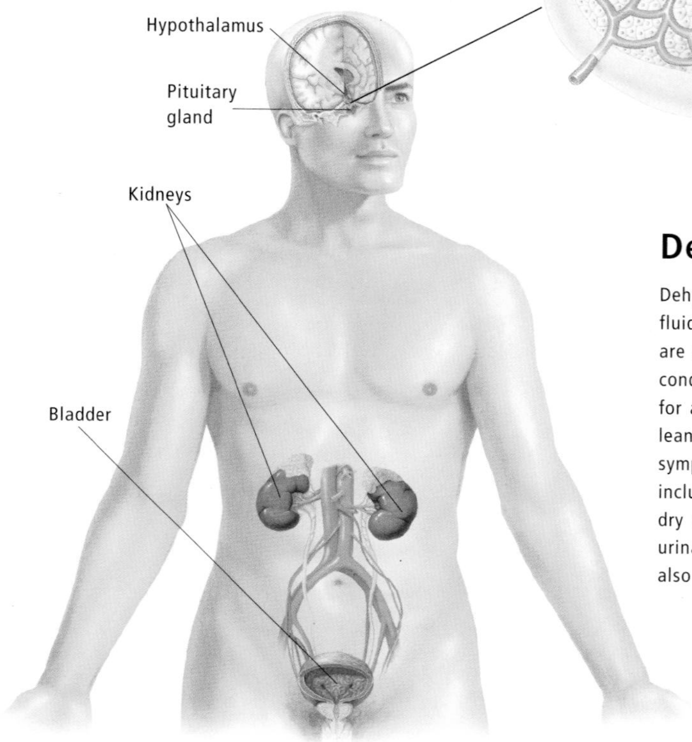

Hypothalamus

Pituitary gland

Kidneys

Bladder

Dehydration

Dehydration occurs when fluid levels in the body are depleted. Under normal conditions water accounts for around 70 percent of lean body mass. The symptoms of dehydration include thirst, sunken eyes, dry mouth and infrequent urination. The skin may also lose elasticity.

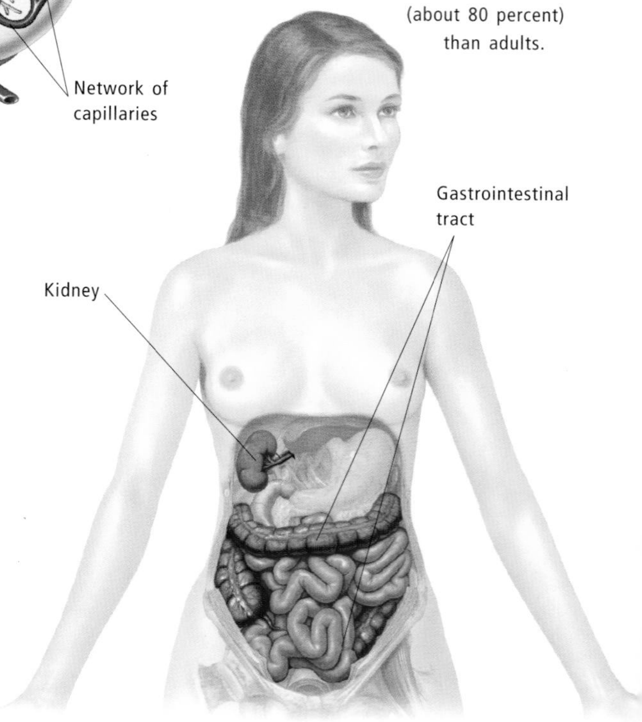

Kidney

Gastrointestinal tract

DEHYDRATION

Dehydration—the depletion of the body's water content—is a life-threatening condition. Babies and small children, who need more fluid relative to their body weight than adults, can become dehydrated—and be rehydrated—more easily.

The most common causes of dehydration are not drinking enough liquid (the deprivation of water is even more serious than the deprivation of food), vomiting, diarrhea (commonly associated with gastroenteritis), the use of diuretics which cause the kidneys to excrete excess water and salt, overheating and fever. Dehydration as a result of diarrhea is a major cause of death in children of developing countries. Some diseases such as diabetes mellitus and Addison's disease can also lead to dehydration.

Overheating or heat stress can cause severe problems, even death in the elderly, babies and young children who are not protected against high temperatures. People in conditions where the heat is severe and there is little or no water can dehydrate quickly. Babies and children die every year when they are left in cars in the summer sun.

On average the human body loses around 2.5 percent of its total body water each day, which is equal to 2½ pints (1.2 liters) in urine, expired air, perspiration and from the gastrointestinal tract. Drinking plenty of water before, during and after exercise helps prevent dehydration.

Symptoms of dehydration include thirst (which the most obvious), eyes that look sunken and dark (in a baby the fontanelle will also look sunken), dry mouth, infrequent dark urination (fewer wet diapers), lethargy and irritability. Skin tone will deteriorate so that when the skin is pinched it will not spring back as normal skin does. Blood in the stools, a high fever, extreme weakness or collapse are a medical emergency and require immediate treatment.

Since dehydration is almost invariably associated with some loss of salt (sodium chloride), rehydration also requires the restoration of the normal concentration of salt within the body fluid. Mild cases can be treated with an oral rehydration fluid. However, more severe cases need to be under medical supervision so that the correct amounts of salts and water are given to restore the normal osmotic relationships between cells, allowing the kidneys to once again begin to work properly.

SEE ALSO *Addison's disease, Diarrhea, Diabetes, Diuretics, Gastroenteritis, Heatstroke, Kidney*

DELIRIUM

Delirium is a mental disorder marked by confusion and disorientation. A mental abnormality with a sudden onset, sometimes confused with dementia, delirium is not a disease and is potentially reversible.

The common symptom is confusion. People who are delirious may suffer hallucinations, be drowsy, be gripped by imaginary fears or impelled by sudden visions of catastrophe. They may be unable to recognize their surroundings, their speech may ramble and their memory of recent events may be poor or completely missing. They will have trouble concentrating and be unable to take in new information.

Delirium can result from a number of conditions or disorders. These include injury, intoxication, drug overdose, abrupt cessation of drug taking, dehydration and disease. It is common to find the person has deteriorated physically prior to the onset of delirium.

The most common causes are alcohol, illegal drugs and poisons, high fever, stroke, brain injuries and disorders, or severe physical injury. Treatment will be dictated by diagnosis of the exact cause. If delirious people seem likely to injure themselves through physical agitation, they may have movement restricted with padded restraints.

SEE ALSO *Alcoholism, Confusion, Delirium tremens, Drug dependence*

DELIRIUM TREMENS

Delirium tremens (DTs) is a severe effect of alcohol withdrawal and is evidence of acute alcoholic dependency. It can occur after heavy bouts of drinking or several days after alcohol intake ceases.

Symptoms include sweating, shaking, nausea and anxiety and may worsen to confusion, sleeplessness and fever. Pulse rate may increase and there may be increasing tremors affecting the hands or the whole body. Movement becomes uncoordinated. There is a strong craving for alcohol. Hallucinations and disorientation may occur, inducing terror. If left untreated, the physical disorders underlying delirium tremens can be fatal.

Alcoholics who suffer DTs treat their own symptoms by drinking. Sometimes alcohol tolerance will be so high that relief is not possible. Seeking medical assistance may mean the person has taken a decision to stop drinking or that the symptoms have become too severe to endure.

Treatment will aim first to control the high fever and anxiety, then to restore nutritional and fluid balance. Alcoholics are often dehydrated and suffer thiamine deficiency and other nutritional deficiencies that can cause brain disorders. These must also be remedied to save life and minimize chances of permanent damage to the brain and nervous system.

Lastly, a process of detoxification as well as a program of alcoholic rehabilitation must be undertaken in order to treat the alcohol dependence.

SEE ALSO *Alcoholism, Delirium*

DELTOID MUSCLE

The deltoid muscle is situated on top of the shoulder joint and upper arm. This powerful, triangular muscle serves to lift the arm away from the side of the body, as well as allowing forward, backward and sideways movement of the upper arm.

The muscle is comprised of three divisions—lateral (top), anterior (front) and posterior (rear)—which all work to give the arm movement in different directions. The muscle stems from the upper part of the collar bone at the front and from the shoulder blade at the back, and attaches to the middle of the outer side of the arm bone. Underneath the muscle is a fluid-filled cavity which is designed to reduce friction between the muscle and shoulder joint.

SEE ALSO *Arm, Collar bone, Muscle, Shoulder*

D

DELUSIONS

Delusions are a feature of mental disorders where irrational and bizarre false beliefs are held with absolute conviction. People so affected may believe they are a queen or president, or that they are being persecuted. Delusions occur in paranoia, schizophrenia, major depressive illnesses, and in various types of psychosis.

SEE ALSO *Paranoia, Psychosis, Schizophrenia*

DEMENTIA

Dementia is a condition in which there is a long-term loss of intellectual function, with little or no disturbance of consciousness or perception. It involves a deterioration of memory and reasoning ability and changes in personality, and usually results from degeneration of cells in the cerebral cortex of the brain.

Dementia generally occurs in elderly people and is becoming more common as the life-expectancy of the population increases. In the USA, about 1 in 15 people over the age of 65, and 1 in 3 people over the age of 85 suffer from dementia. It is, however, not an inevitable consequence of ageing, as was previously thought. (The majority of people will not develop dementia in their old age.) Rather, it is a condition which develops in association with some diseases which happen to be more common in old age.

By far the most common cause of dementia is Alzheimer's disease, which accounts for up to 70 percent of dementia cases and currently affects approximately 2 million Americans. The onset and progression of this form of dementia (also known as senile dementia) is very gradual, usually extending over a period of 5–10 years.

The affected person becomes increasingly forgetful, disoriented and confused, and intellectual functions, such as reading, writing and decision-making, gradually diminish. As the disease progresses the person may also undergo a personality change, becoming aggressive, paranoid or depressed.

Alzheimer's disease can be distinguished from other forms of dementia by characteristic changes which occur in the cerebral cortex, in particular the presence of dying cells, abnormal protein deposits (plaques), knotted fibers (tangles), and degenerate neurons.

At present the cause of Alzheimer's disease is not well understood but it is thought to be the result of a combination of genetic and as yet unidentified environmental factors. Although it is a very active area of research, no treatment has been found.

The second major type of dementia, multi-infarct or arteriosclerotic dementia, is caused by numerous episodes in which tiny blood vessels supplying the frontal and temporal lobes of the cerebral cortex become blocked due to cardiovascular disease, resulting in death of nerve cells (neurons) in these areas because of the lack of oxygen.

These episodes (mini-strokes) may go undetected at the time but they have a cumulative effect on the cortex and make up for 10–15 percent of dementia cases. The symptoms are sometimes difficult to distinguish from those seen in Alzheimer's disease, but they often tend to appear in a more step-by-step fashion (as the mini-strokes occur).

Other causes of dementia are numerous and include chronic alcoholism, degenerative diseases such as Huntington's disease and AIDS, nutritional and metabolic disorders, infections and tumors. Some of these disorders are treatable and recovery from the dementia can be expected but in most cases dementia is a chronic ongoing condition.

When a person suffers a temporary loss of intellectual function, such as may occur when they have a very high fever or are withdrawing from alcoholism, they are said to be suffering from delirium, not dementia.

SEE ALSO *Alcoholism, Alzheimer's disease, Confusion, Memory, Stroke*

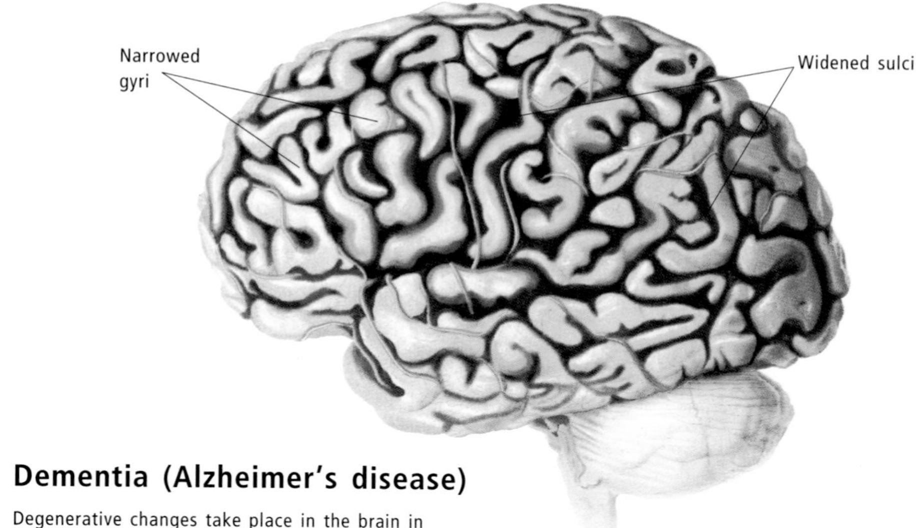

Dementia (Alzheimer's disease)

Degenerative changes take place in the brain in dementia. In Alzheimer's disease, the brain has shrunk slightly and the gaps between the folds of the cerebral cortex have widened.

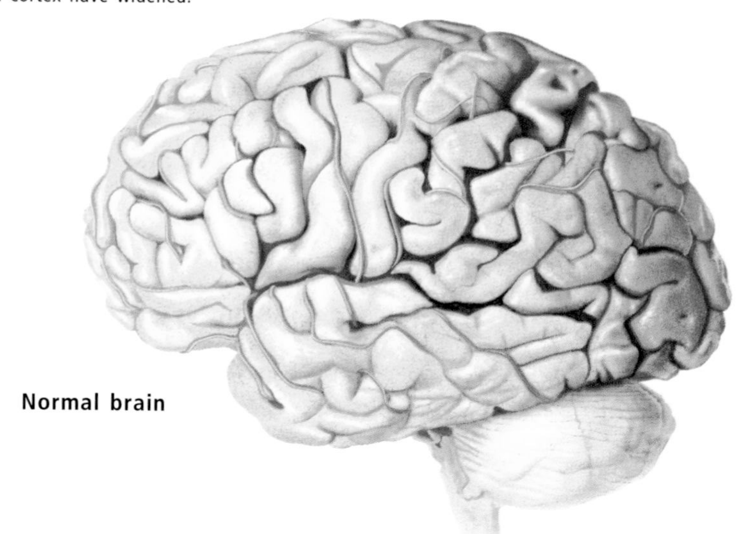

Normal brain

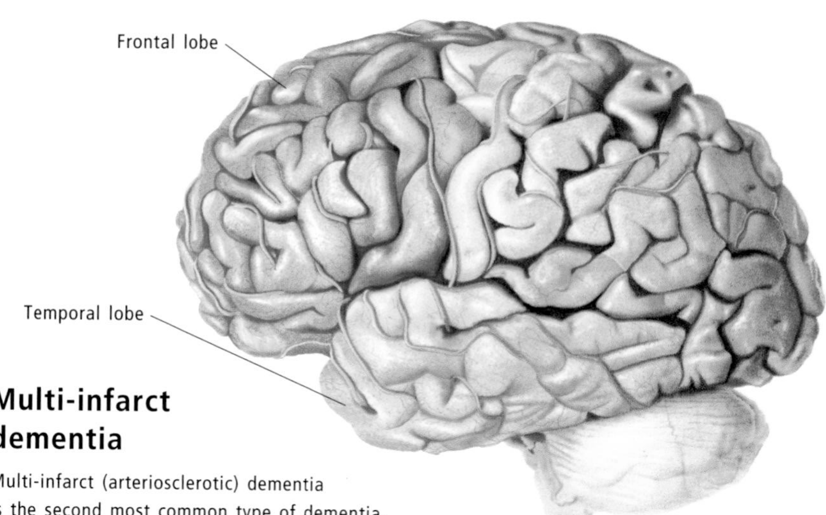

Multi-infarct dementia

Multi-infarct (arteriosclerotic) dementia is the second most common type of dementia. It is caused by repeated mini-strokes that block the blood supply to parts of the brain, eventually destroying brain tissue. The frontal and temporal lobes are most commonly affected.

DENGUE

Dengue fever is an acute viral infection of the body, transmitted by mosquitoes. It is similar to malaria in that it is a very common cause for hospitalization of children in tropical countries. It is spread from animals to humans by mosquito bites. There are two types of this disease— ordinary dengue fever (DF), which is usually a mild disease with no serious complications, and hemorrhagic dengue fever (HDF), which is a much more virulent form.

The incubation period from the mosquito bite to the appearance of the first symptoms is about 5 to 6 days. In DF, the symptoms are headache, fever, vomiting, muscle pain, joint pain, and enlarged lymph nodes. The fever rises and falls in cycles of 1 to 2 days, and the illness usually lasts about 10 days.

HDF is mostly only common in Southeast Asia. This form causes the capillaries in the skin and body organs to rupture resulting in a petechial rash (hemorrhaging in the skin), bleeding from the nose, bowels and kidneys, and can lead to serious and even fatal complications. Treatment for DF is symptomatic—analgesic for the fever, and rest and fluid replacement. There is no vaccine and the most important advice for travelers is to prevent being bitten by mosquitoes.

SEE ALSO *Infections, Viruses*

DENTURES

Dentures, also known as plates or false teeth, are composite artificial replacements of teeth and gums. A complete denture is required when all the teeth in the upper or lower jaw have been removed. Partial dentures are used to replace one or more missing teeth. Complete dentures are usually removable; partial dentures may be removable or fixed. An overdenture is a partial denture that takes support from any remaining teeth roots and gum near the missing teeth.

Titanium implants can be surgically inserted into the jawbone; replacement teeth are attached later which provide a fixed denture. This process helps to prevent resorption, which is shrinkage of the jawbone with loss of nerve and surrounding tissue, a common situation where all the teeth have been removed.

SEE ALSO *Gums, Teeth*

DEPRESSION

Depression (also known as clinical depression) affects thoughts, feelings, physical health and behaviors. Depression is not just feeling sad, it is a medical disorder, like high blood pressure.

Depression is not the same as grief—though extreme grief can bring on depression in susceptible people. Depression can be caused by many things, including genetic inheritance, an illness, certain medicines, drugs, alcohol and other psychiatric conditions. A major trauma or loss during childhood is also thought to increase a person's vulnerability to depression. There are also biochemical causes, the main one being the defective regulation of the release of naturally occurring monoamines (neurotransmitters) in the brain.

Someone suffering from depression will experience one or more of these symptoms: sadness or hopelessness, low self-esteem, an inability to enjoy daily life, low energy, lethargy, loss of appetite, or sleep problems.

This is the most common psychiatric complaint and for centuries was known as melancholia. More common in women than men, it occurs most often in the 35 to 45 age group. Many people mistakenly believe depression is normal for certain people including the elderly, teenagers, pregnant women, new mothers and the chronically ill.

While mood swings are common during pregnancy and in the early days of mothering, depression is not normal. Depression during pregnancy can occur in the last trimester as the woman begins to feel tired and apprehensive about her forthcoming role as a mother. It is important to seek advice and support if the low mood does not lift as it can carry over into the postpartum period when it can also affect the newborn child.

Postnatal depression is not the "baby blues" which frequently affects new mothers when the hormone surge their bodies experienced during the pregnancy and birth drops. Postnatal (or postpartum) depression has been found to be more common in single women who lack support, women with an unwanted pregnancy, and professional women with unrealistic expectations of how they will cope. It can also occur in women who lack emotional and physical support systems.

Research has found that both parents need help and guidance in the early days of parenting and that where the father is supportive, the mother is less likely to suffer real depression. In industrialized societies where women have little experience of mothering (apart from how they were mothered) some women suffer feelings of inadequacy at this time.

Bipolar depression or disorder, when moods swing from extreme mania to depression, is also known as manic-depressive illness. This condition requires psychiatric care and also hospitalization at certain times; bipolar disorder responds well to salts of lithium. Winter depression or seasonal affective disorder (SAD) has only recently been recognized as the cause of depression directly related to the loss of natural light.

Depression often goes untreated because people do not recognize the symptoms, are too embarrassed to seek treatment or think they can cure it themselves. Major depression can often lead to suicide.

Over 80 percent of sufferers can be treated successfully by a qualified health professional. There are three forms of treatment: psychotherapy, which seeks to resolve underlying problems which may be causing the depression as well as providing support; antidepressant drugs which affect the chemistry of the brain; and electroconvulsive therapy (ECT) which is a brief application of an electric stimulus which produces a generalized seizure. ECT is normally used for severe cases, in combination with psychotherapy and/or drug therapy.

There are a number of alternative therapies that may help to alleviate the symptoms of depression. Acupuncture practitioners regard some depressions as "liver" disorders and treat with appropriate points to release "stagnant" energy. Aromatherapists prescribe oils such as basil, clary sage, jasmine or rose. Herbalists principally prescribe St John's wort (*Hypericum*), as well as tonics such as oats, vervain or rosemary. Naturopaths will often prescribe vitamin B complex with extra B_3 (niacinamide) and magnesium. Flower essences, such as the Bach flower remedies, may be used. Counseling, exercise and a detoxifying diet are sometimes recommended.

SEE ALSO ***Antidepressants, Bipolar disorder, Counseling, Electroconvulsive therapy, Emotions, Postnatal depression, Psychotherapy, Seasonal affective disorder***

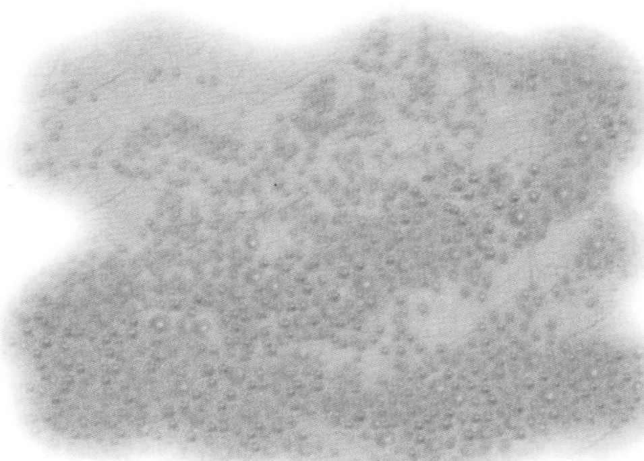

Atopic dermatitis

Seborrheic dermatitis

Dermatitis

Symptoms of atopic dermatitis include itching rash and dry thickened skin. Seborrheic dermatitis mainly appears on the head and trunk. Skin becomes greasy or dry and red patches appear topped by white scales.

DERMATITIS

Dermatitis means inflammation of the skin. Though dermatitis is not contagious, and not usually life threatening, it can be debilitating as it tends to recur and become chronic (a long-term problem).

There are many different types of dermatitis. Seborrheic dermatitis is characterized by greasy or dry, white scales over reddish patches that form on the skin of the scalp, eyebrows, forehead, face, behind the ears, or on the trunk.

Dandruff and cradle cap are both forms of seborrheic dermatitis. Both sexes and all ages are affected; the cause is unknown and the condition is usually chronic. Treatment is a steroid cream for the affected skin. Dandruff can be controlled with frequent shampooing with preparations containing selenium sulfide or zinc pyrithione. If the condition does not improve, shampoos that contain coal tar or scalp creams that contain cortisone may be used.

Atopic dermatitis affects mostly children, and is often associated with asthma or hay fever. It causes an itching rash and dry, thickened skin in the creases of elbows, knees, neck, face, hands, feet, and groin. The cause is unknown though it tends to run in families. It may disappear with age. Sufferers are advised to wear loose-fitting cotton clothing. Petroleum- or lanolin-based ointments and topical steroids or coal-tar creams relieve the itching. Scratching must be avoided, because it causes secondary bacterial infection.

Contact dermatitis is caused by contact with an irritating substance that damages the skin, causing itching, redness, cracks and fissures and in severe cases, bright red, weeping areas. The hands, feet and groin are commonly affected.

Many substances can cause contact dermatitis, including topical drugs, cosmetics, chemicals, soaps, detergents, bleaches, metal cleaners and paint removers. Treatment is to avoid contact with the irritant, wear protective gloves and other protective clothing, bathe in lukewarm water, and apply topical creams, ointments or lotions. These may include lubricants to preserve moisture, or steroid preparations to reduce inflammation. Contact dermatitis usually clears up within two or three weeks.

Stasis dermatitis is the result of fluid build-up under the skin. It is caused by varicose veins, poor circulation, and other conditions that cause swelling of the extremities, especially the feet and ankles (peripheral edema). The swelling causes surrounding tissue to become fragile; the skin darkens and becomes thin and inflamed. Ulcers may form and are slow to heal. Itching and scratching of the area may cause the skin to thicken. Elevation of the affected limbs, the wearing of elastic stockings and gentle exercise such as walking will help relieve the swelling. The underlying condition must be controlled, which may involve surgical correction of varicose veins, and diuretics in order to remove excess fluid.

SEE ALSO *Cradle cap, Dandruff, Eczema, Seborrheic dermatitis, Varicose veins*

DERMATOMES

Each of the 31 segments of the spinal cord gives rise to a pair of spinal nerves, which carry messages into and out of the central nervous system. These nerves branch into and service particular areas of the body. Ultimately, each ends up innervating a different region of the skin called a dermatome.

The location of dermatomes across the body forms a pattern that is significant when

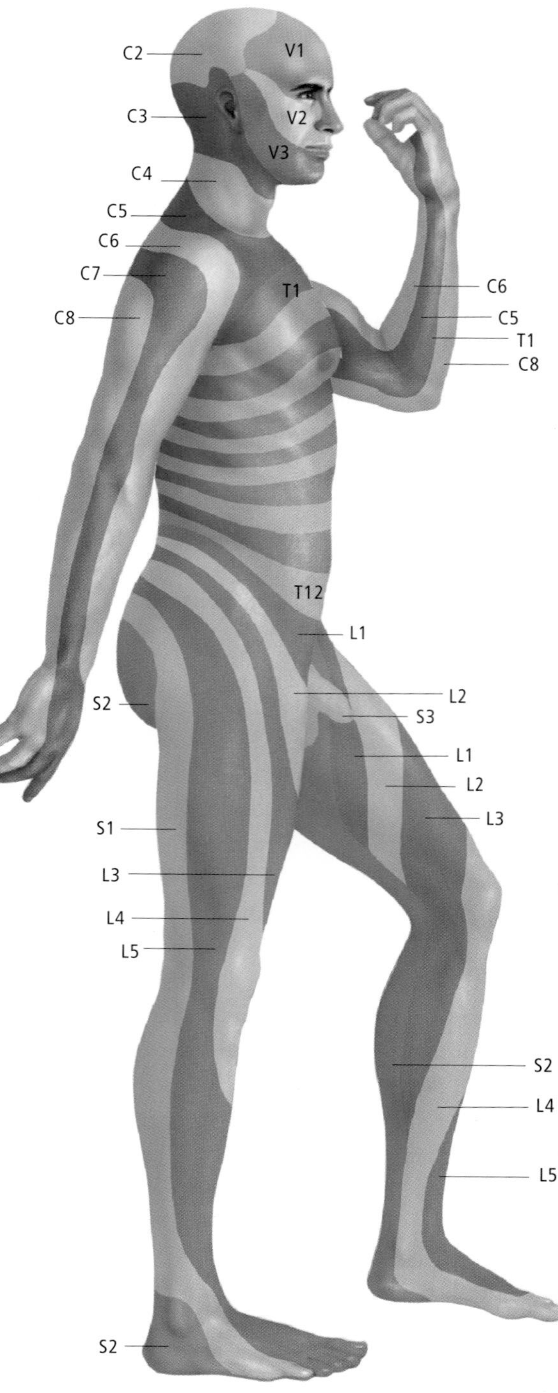

certain parts of the body require anesthesia. It indicates specific nerves that need to be blocked to cut sensations in a region. It is also of relevance in spinal cord injuries—identifying dermatomes with abnormal or no sensations helps isolate the location of damage to spinal nerves or the spinal cord.

SEE ALSO *Nervous system, Spinal cord, Spinal nerves*

Nerve to skin link

The spinal nerves are numbered and correspond closely to the spinal vertebrae. Each pair of nerves supplies a specific dermatome (skin area) of the body. The face is supplied by branches of the trigeminal nerve (V1, V2, and V3).

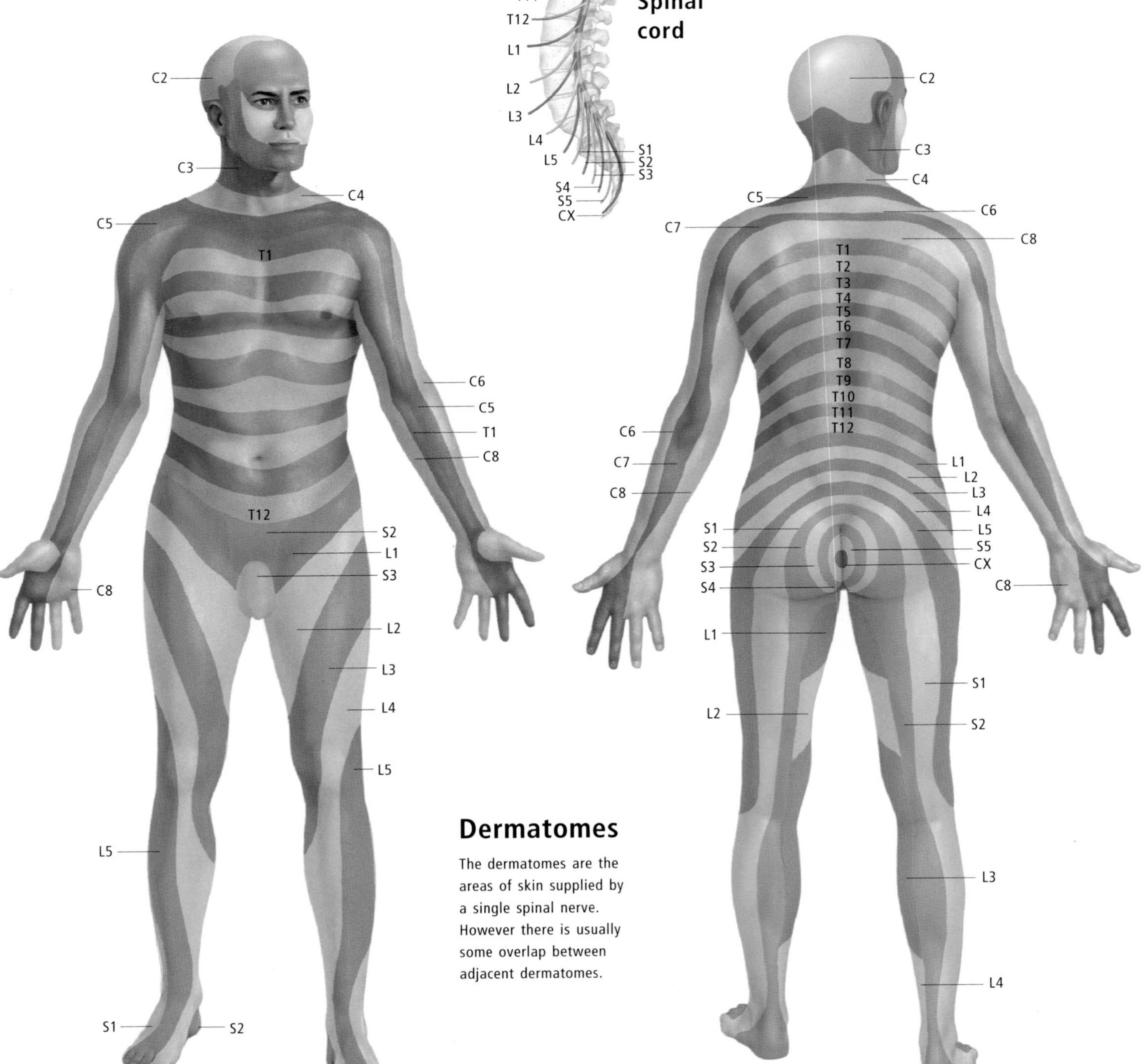

Dermatomes

The dermatomes are the areas of skin supplied by a single spinal nerve. However there is usually some overlap between adjacent dermatomes.

D

DERMATOMYOSITIS

Dermatomyositis is a rare connective tissue disease that is characterized by inflammation and degeneration of the skin and the muscles throughout the body. It causes muscle weakness and a dusky red rash over the face, neck, shoulders, upper chest and back. Joint, heart and lung disease may occur. Treatment may include physical therapy and prednisone (a steroid hormone) or immunosuppressant drugs such as azathioprine and methotrexate.

SEE ALSO *Autoimmune disease, Connective tissue*

DESENSITIZATION

Desensitization is a method of treating allergies by attempting to reduce the sufferer's allergic reaction. This is done after establishing exactly which allergen is causing the reaction. The sufferer is exposed to a minute quantity of the substance; exposure may take the form of a regular injection of small quantities of the allergen over a period of perhaps a month or two. The injected dose is increased gradually to a point where the body produces specific antibodies to block the effect of the allergens. The goal is to block enough of the allergens till a point is reached where they do not provoke the allergic reaction. Desensitization attempts to reverse the process of sensitization that originally created the allergy.

SEE ALSO *Allergies, Antigen tests*

DETACHED RETINA

Retinal detachment occurs when the retina of the eye, which contains light-sensitive cells, becomes separated from the choroid, or middle layer of the eyeball. Separation may be partial or complete. The detachment usually occurs without any obvious cause, but some cases may be due to trauma, such as a blow to the head. The patient usually complains of progressively blurred vision.

Many of the nerve cells in the separated retina will die if they remain detached from the choroid, so it is important to reattach the retina as soon as possible. Patients must rest in a position such that gravity will encourage reattachment. Surgical treatments include draining fluid below the retina, fusing the retina to the choroid with lasers, electrical diathermy or very cold probes.

SEE ALSO *Blindness, Eye, Retina, Sight*

DETOXIFICATION

Detoxification is the removal of toxins from the body. Drug taking causes toxins (poisons) to accumulate in the body tissues. When a drug-dependent person enters withdrawal, and ceases to use the substance of dependence, detoxification begins.

Dependency is an overwhelming craving for something, which is felt after a period of non-use. The most common drugs of dependency are alcohol, nicotine, amphetamines, opiates and barbiturates.

Detoxification is usually undertaken as a program managed by medical and psychological professionals.

The success of the program depends on a high level of commitment from the drug user. Withdrawal of drugs of any kind should only be started, and continued, under medical supervision.

The symptoms of detoxification vary according to the substance of dependency, and can be quite severe.

Alcohol withdrawal starts within 48 hours after alcohol intake stops. The symptoms include shaking, sweating and nausea, seizures and hallucinations. If physical effects are acute they can lead to death if not treated.

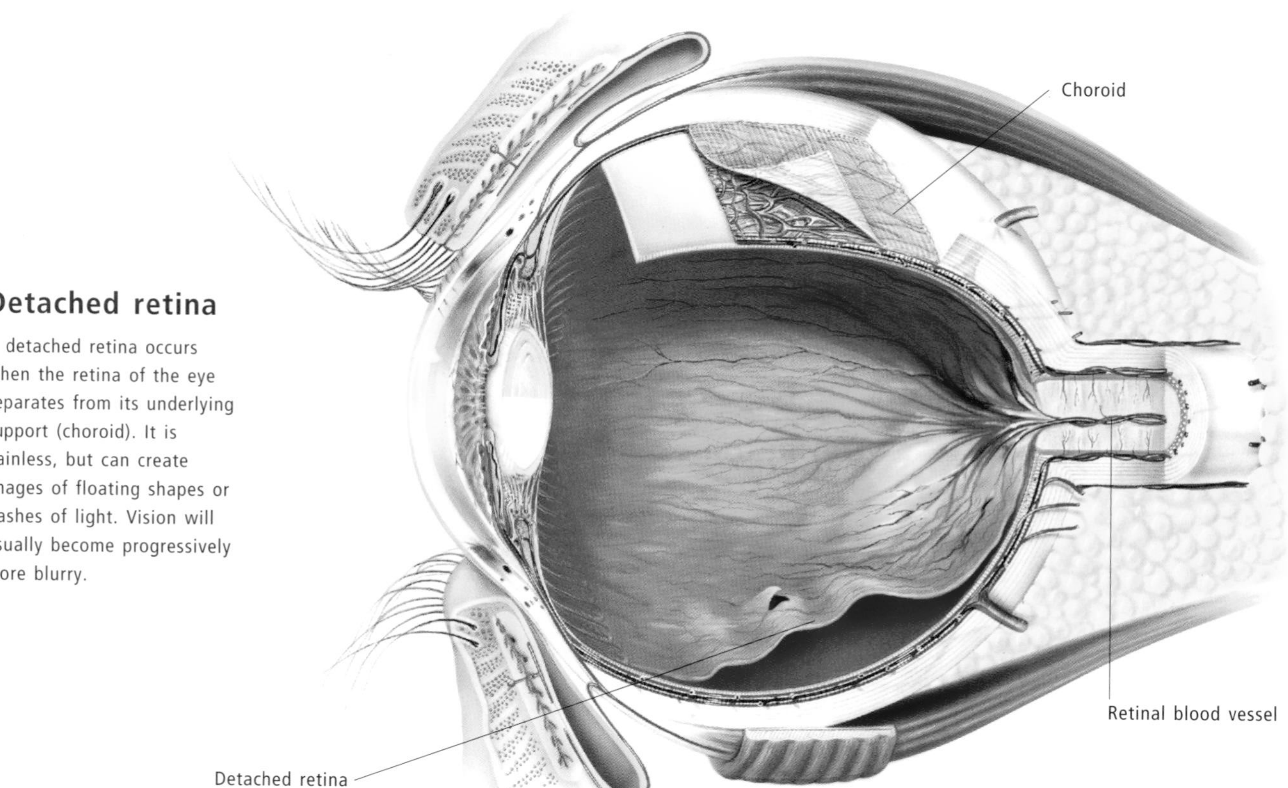

Detached retina

A detached retina occurs when the retina of the eye separates from its underlying support (choroid). It is painless, but can create images of floating shapes or flashes of light. Vision will usually become progressively more blurry.

Amphetamine withdrawal may bring on severe drowsiness or accentuate symptoms of depression that may have existed before taking the drugs. Chronically depressed users may attempt suicide and should be under close medical supervision while in detoxification.

Anti-anxiety drugs (anxiolytics, barbiturates, tranquilizers) can cause physical and psychological dependence, decreasing or depressing bodily functions and activity as well as slowing down thought processes. Abruptly stopping use can bring on symptoms of nervousness, shaking and weakness within 24 hours. Symptoms can worsen over the following three or four weeks to include seizures, delirium, sleeplessness, confusion and hallucinations.

Cocaine withdrawal will produce reactions opposite to those induced by taking the drug. Users can become extremely tired, depressed and suicidal, and may be given antidepressant drugs.

Marijuana can induce psychological dependency, and detoxification may induce insomnia in heavy users. It may take up to a year to overcome psychological dependence on the drug.

Narcotics such as morphine and heroin are pain relievers that may induce a sense of relaxation and well-being. Long-term users who withdraw may very quickly experience the opposite effects, including a falsely heightened sense of alertness, fast heartbeat, fever and rapid breathing. Dilated pupils, runny nose and stomach cramps are other common symptoms.

Nicotine withdrawal is characterized by feelings of anger and irritability. Some people increase their intake of food and drink as oral substitutes for smoking. Nicotine gum or patches, used in gradually decreasing doses, may lessen the severity of the symptoms.

Measures that help in detoxification are drinking plenty of water, taking exercise, following a balanced diet, and gaining the support of family and friends. Supportive therapies such as massage and acupuncture may be helpful.

Physical detoxification is only the first step in treatment, since psychological dependency is a major factor in substance abuse. The alcoholic or drug-dependent person needs to learn how to live without drinking or using. Many specialists believe that detoxification needs to be followed up with long-term rehabilitation, which includes spending time in a treatment center, follow-up counseling, and regular attendance at self-help groups such as Alcoholics Anonymous and Narcotics Anonymous.

SEE ALSO *Alcoholism, Anxiolytics, Barbiturates, Cocaine, Drug dependence, Hallucinogens, Heroin, Hypnotics, Marijuana, Methadone, Morphine, Narcotics, Nicotine, Psychosis, Psychotropic drugs, Sedatives, Stimulants, Tranquilizers, Withdrawal*

Detoxification, natural health

The liver and kidneys are the main organs of detoxification in the body. Toxins pass through the alimentary canal (esophagus, stomach and intestines), are processed in the liver, and excreted by the kidneys. The body's processes of toxin metabolism may be aided by detoxification programs.

NB: In this illustration part of the liver has been removed to show the kidney.

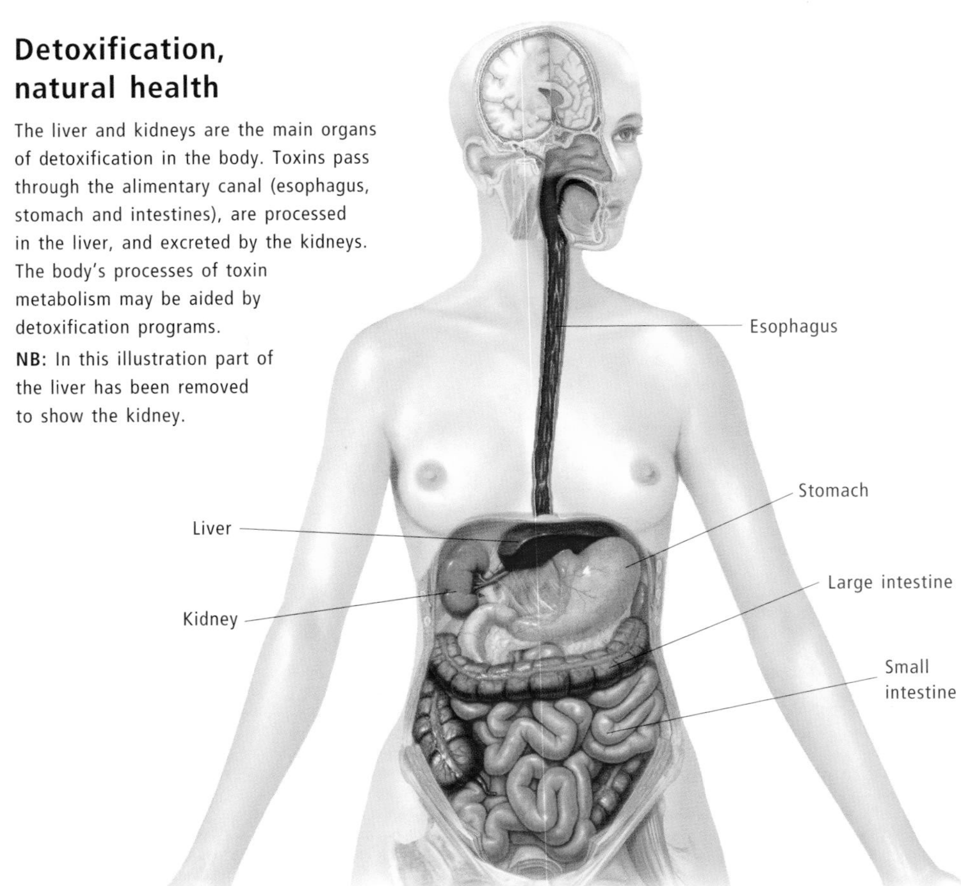

DETOXIFICATION, NATURAL HEALTH

Many of the natural therapies incorporate the belief that a process of detoxification of the body is of great benefit in the attaining and maintaining of good health. It is considered that the increasing level of pollutants, chemicals and food additives encountered by anyone living in an industrialized society can create a toxic overload in the body which can lead, in turn, to disturbances in metabolism, the immune system, respiratory function and mental outlook.

Natural therapists prescribe a range of detoxifying treatments, the most favored being fasting. Abstaining from solid foods for a set period of time is believed to give the body an opportunity to cleanse itself of toxins. Juice fasts are most commonly advised, and like any fast should only be undertaken under professional guidance. Patients are warned to expect some initial symptoms of detoxification such as headaches and bad breath. Enemas are often prescribed to help clear the bowel of toxins.

Other means of detoxification prescribed by natural therapists include colonic irrigation, mono diets (e.g. grapes only or rice only), dry brush massage, saunas, hydrotherapy, and liver/gallbladder flushes with olive oil and lemon juice. Regular detoxification is considered to be very important in Ayurvedic medicine where specific hatha yoga techniques are used to cleanse the entire intestinal tract.

SEE ALSO *Ayurvedic medicine, Colonic irrigation, Hydrotherapy, Naturopathy*

DIABETES

Diabetes mellitus is a disorder caused by decreased production of insulin by the pancreas, or by a decreased ability on the part of the body to use insulin. It is a serious, sometimes fatal, disorder and remains a leading cause of death in Western societies. The cause of diabetes mellitus is not known, though it may run in families and is more common in obese individuals.

Normally, food digested in the body releases glucose, a form of sugar, into the blood. This in turn causes certain cells called beta cells in the pancreas to release insulin into the bloodstream. The insulin aids in transporting glucose from the blood into storage in liver and muscle cells; it can be later released from these cells into the blood and used in metabolism.

However, if the pancreas is producing insufficient amounts of insulin, or if there is a failure of the mechanism of transporting glucose into the cells (so-called "insulin resistance") then diabetes results.

Types of diabetes

There are two types of diabetes. Type I, sometimes called insulin-dependent or juvenile-type diabetes, is caused by insufficient amounts of insulin being produced by the pancreas. It is usually found in persons under 25 years of age. Type II, sometimes called non insulin-dependent, maturity onset or adult-type diabetes, is more common. It is found in persons over age 40, and is usually caused by insulin resistance.

In both types, there is excess sugar in the blood (hyperglycemia) which then needs to be removed by the kidneys. Symptoms of excessive thirst, frequent urination, and hunger develop. The metabolism of carbohydrates, fats, and proteins is altered. Fatty acids released from tissue throughout the body are converted by the liver into chemical compounds called ketones which enter the bloodstream causing the blood to become dangerously acidic (ketoacidosis). Especially in juvenile Type I diabetes, this can lead to diabetic coma and, if untreated, to death. Diabetic coma is a medical emergency requiring urgent treatment in hospital.

A physician can diagnose diabetes by testing for sugar in urine and blood. A glucose tolerance test determines how well the body uses and stores sugar, by measuring blood glucose levels periodically for up to six hours after the patient swallows a glucose solution.

Regulation of diabetes

Type I diabetics need daily injections of insulin (the hormone is not available in an oral form). Most diabetics self-administer their insulin by subcutaneous injection (below the skin) from one to four times per day, though some diabetics use a portable pump that delivers insulin directly to the body through an implanted cannula.

Careful regulation of activity and a strict diet are important to keep the levels of insulin and sugar in the blood within as normal a range as possible. Both the physician and the diabetic when at home should monitor their blood glucose levels regularly to make sure the dosage of insulin is correct. During periods of stress, such as surgery and infection, the insulin dosage may need to be temporarily increased.

Type II diabetes is usually easier to control than Type I. Type II diabetes is usually treated with diet alone, or with diet plus oral antidiabetic drugs. In some cases, insulin treatment is needed. Weight control and regular exercise are also important.

Imbalance of insulin and glucose

Too much insulin or too little glucose in the diet causes hypoglycemia, or insulin shock. The signs of hypoglycemia are mild hunger, dizziness, sweating, and heart palpitations followed by mental confusion and coma. Diabetics can stop hypoglycemia by eating sugar, sweets or candy, or by injecting glucagon, a hormone that raises blood sugar.

Diabetics should be familiar with the symptoms of both hypoglycemia and hyperglycemia so as to be able to treat themselves or seek help to prevent the onset of coma. They should wear an identification card, tag or bracelet in case they need emergency care.

Diabetes and pregnancy

Diabetes can be aggravated by pregnancy, so good management during pregnancy and labor is essential. Infants of women with poorly controlled diabetes are at risk for birth defects, but if the condition is well controlled, the risk is the same as for a non-diabetic mother.

Glaucoma

Glaucoma often occurs in diabetes. In glaucoma, pressure inside the eyeball rises, damaging the retina and causing loss of vision.

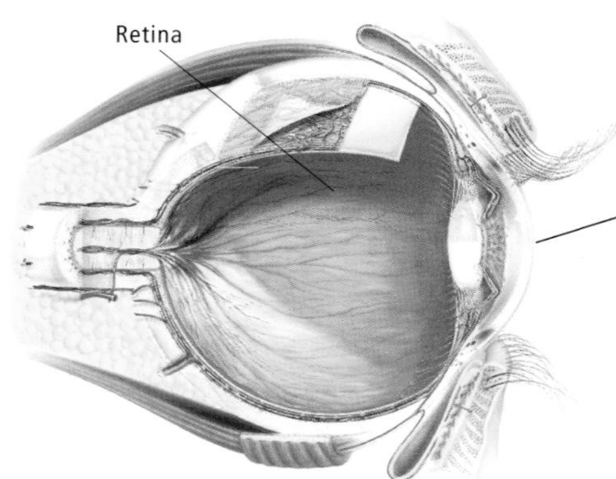

Diabetic nephropathy

Diabetic nephropathy damages the glomeruli and small blood vessels of the kidneys, due to high levels of blood glucose. This results in the loss of necessary proteins through the urine, swelling of body tissues and eventually renal failure.

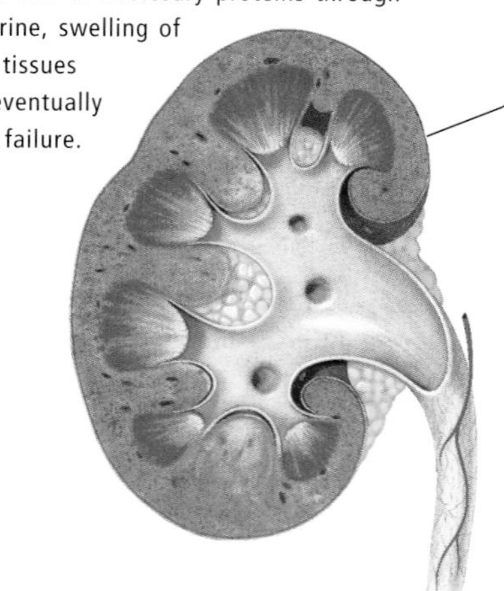

Foot ulcer

Diabetes slows the healing of body tissues and also causes degeneration of the peripheral nerves (neuropathy). These two factors act together to cause foot ulcers in diabetics.

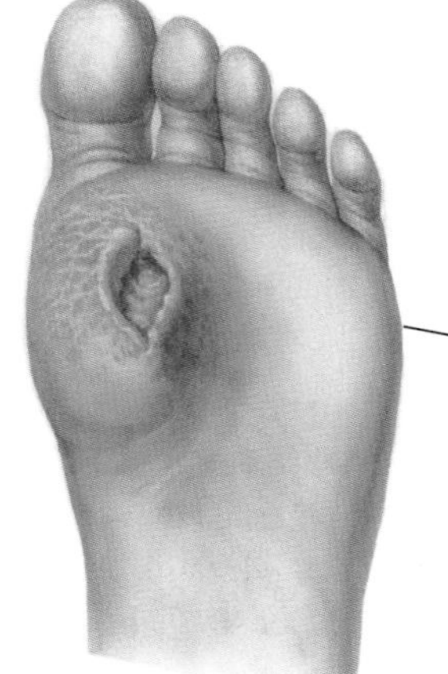

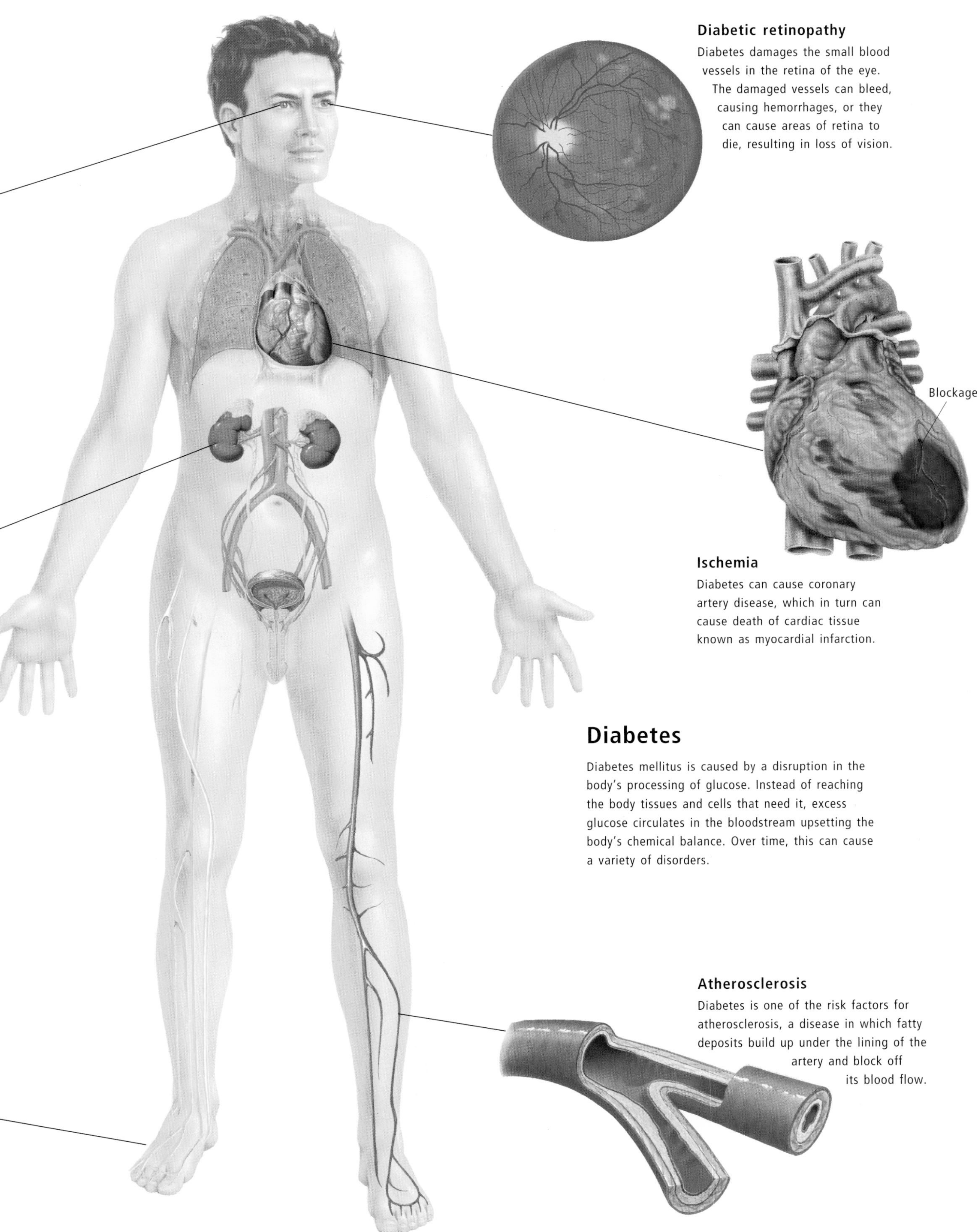

Diabetic retinopathy

Diabetes damages the small blood vessels in the retina of the eye. The damaged vessels can bleed, causing hemorrhages, or they can cause areas of retina to die, resulting in loss of vision.

Ischemia

Diabetes can cause coronary artery disease, which in turn can cause death of cardiac tissue known as myocardial infarction.

Diabetes

Diabetes mellitus is caused by a disruption in the body's processing of glucose. Instead of reaching the body tissues and cells that need it, excess glucose circulates in the bloodstream upsetting the body's chemical balance. Over time, this can cause a variety of disorders.

Atherosclerosis

Diabetes is one of the risk factors for atherosclerosis, a disease in which fatty deposits build up under the lining of the artery and block off its blood flow.

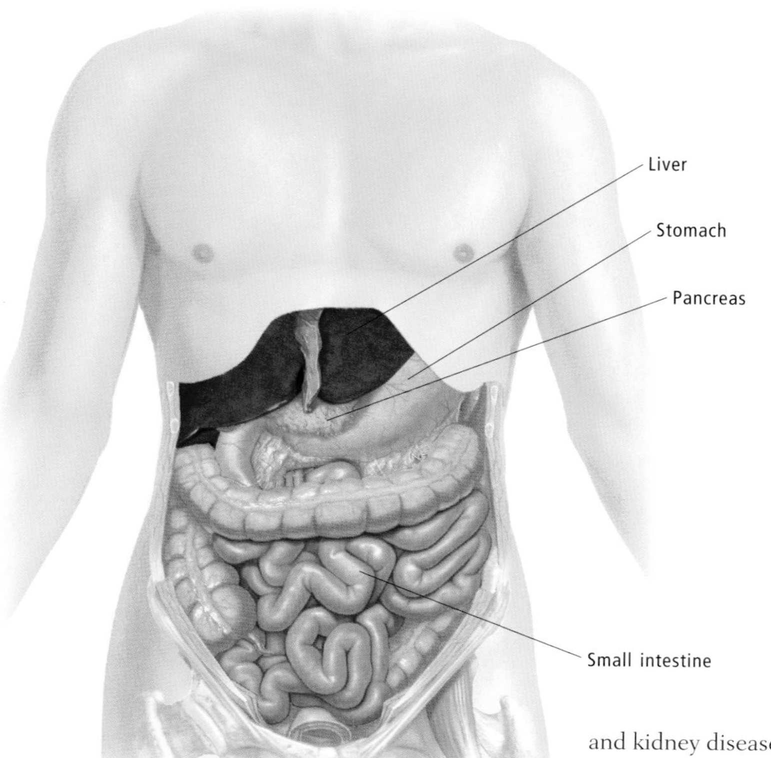

Diabetes and glucose metabolism

The hormone insulin helps the body process glucose—the sugar needed for energy by all body cells. In normal insulin production:

(a) Carbohydrates are broken down in the stomach and small intestine and converted into glucose.

(b) Glucose travels in the blood from the intestine to the liver, which releases it to body tissues for energy when needed.

(c) The pancreas controls how much glucose is stored in the liver and how much is released into tissues. When the pancreas registers increased levels of glucose in the blood it secretes insulin. Insulin instructs the liver and other tissues to absorb more glucose, lowering blood sugar levels. In Type I diabetes, insufficient amounts of insulin are produced by the pancreas. In Type II diabetes, the body either produces too little insulin, or insulin receptors in liver cells and other tissues do not respond to the hormone. In both forms of diabetes too much glucose circulates in the blood, a condition known as hyperglycemia.

Gestational diabetes is diabetes that only appears during pregnancy. It usually becomes apparent during the weeks 24–28. In many cases, the blood glucose level returns to normal after delivery. However, there is a risk the mother may develop full-blown diabetes in the future.

Long-term complications

Diabetes mellitus has long-term complications as well. Generally, the longer the diabetic condition exists, the greater the complications. Atherosclerosis is the most serious, damaging small and large blood vessels especially in the retina of the eye (diabetic retinopathy) and in the kidney (diabetic nephropathy), causing eventual blindness and kidney failure. Nerve degeneration resulting in loss of sensation in peripheral nerves, and reduced resistance to infections are other common complications.

People with diabetes are prone to foot problems because of complications caused by damage to large and small blood vessels, damage to nerves, and decreased ability to fight infection, so diabetics need to learn the techniques of foot care.

With good diabetic control, the onset of complications such as retinopathy and kidney disease can be delayed. However, they cannot be prevented, especially in the case of Type I diabetes and long-standing Type II diabetes.

SEE ALSO *Blood sugar tests, Hyperglycemia, Hypoglycemia, Insulin, Pancreas*

DIABETES INSIPIDUS

Diabetes insipidus is a rare condition causing pronounced thirst and the passage of large quantities of dilute urine. It is unrelated to diabetes mellitus.

The most common type is so-called "central" diabetes insipidus, which is caused by a lack of antidiuretic hormone (ADH or vasopressin). This hormone is produced in the hypothalamus of the brain and controls the way the kidneys filter blood to make urine. Lack of this hormone (or failure of the kidneys to respond to the hormone), allows too much fluid to pass through the kidneys.

A person with diabetes insipidus must drink large quantities of water to compensate for the fluid loss in order to avoid dehydration. The lack of ADH secretion can be caused by damage to the hypothalamus as a result of surgery, infection, tumor or head injury. There is no cure for the condition; however, synthetic ADH injections will correct the hormone deficiency. ADH is also

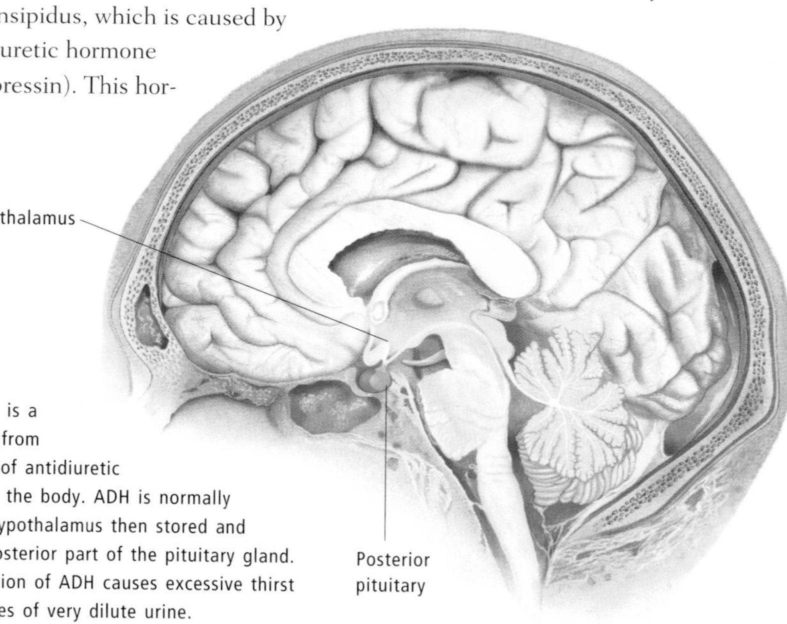

Diabetes insipidus

Diabetes insipidus is a disorder resulting from insufficient levels of antidiuretic hormone (ADH) in the body. ADH is normally produced in the hypothalamus then stored and released by the posterior part of the pituitary gland. Decreased production of ADH causes excessive thirst and large quantities of very dilute urine.

available as a nasal spray.

Diabetes insipidus can also be caused by a rare hereditary defect in the tubules of the kidney. The condition is called nephrogenic diabetes insipidus and produces symptoms similar to those of central diabetes insipidus. It may be treated with diuretic drugs.

SEE ALSO *Diuretics, Hypothalamus, Kidney*

DIALYSIS

Dialysis is a method of removing toxic substances (impurities or wastes) from the blood when the kidneys cannot do so. This is usually because of kidney disease, but dialysis may sometimes be used to quickly remove drugs or poisons from the bloodstream in people who have been poisoned or who have overdosed on drugs.

If the kidneys are unable to fulfil more than 10 percent of their normal function, this situation is considered end-stage kidney disease and dialysis is necessary. There are two types of dialysis: peritoneal dialysis and hemodialysis.

Peritoneal dialysis uses the person's abdominal peritoneal membrane to act as a dialysis mechanism. It involves filling the abdominal cavity (via a catheter) with a special solution, using the peritoneal membrane inside the abdomen as the semipermeable membrane. The fluid is allowed to absorb wastes for several hours, and then the waste-filled fluid is exchanged for a fresh batch of solution.

Hemodialysis involves filtering the blood slowly through an artificial kidney machine called a dialyzer. Inside the dialyzer, blood is run through tubes with semipermeable membranes, and the tubes are bathed with solutions that will remove small soluble molecules (such as urea) from the blood. The purified blood is then fed back into one of the patient's veins.

For hemodialysis to be successful, there must be adequate access to the circulation. A normal vein is not big enough to carry a wide bore IV (intravenous) line, so special types of arterial and venous access have to be constructed. A common method is to surgically join an artery and vein together under the skin; this is called an AV (arteriovenous) fistula. The increased blood volume stretches the elastic vein to allow a larger volume of blood flow into which a wide bore IV line can be inserted.

In people whose veins are not suitable for an AV fistula, a graft from an artery to a vein may be used. The graft may come from the person's own saphenous vein (in the leg), or it may be a synthetic graft.

Usually, dialysis needs to be performed three times a week for periods of four to six hours. Dialysis may take place in a hospital, at a special dialysis center, or at the patient's home. It needs to be continued until the kidneys recover their normal function. In chronic renal failure, this usually means for the rest of the person's life or until a kidney transplant is performed.

SEE ALSO *Hemodialysis, Kidney, Peritoneal dialysis*

DIAPER RASH

Diaper rash (nappy rash) is a common inflammation of the skin in babies mainly due to wetness and heat beneath the diaper, resulting in red blotches, spots or lesions. It can also be caused by contact friction, chemical allergies and the blockage of sweat glands and may be exacerbated by the interaction of the skin with feces and the ammonia in urine. The rash tends to be worse in the creases of the skin.

Diaper rash can be treated or prevented by keeping the skin as dry as possible, changing diapers frequently, air drying between changes and leaving the diaper off for as long as is practical each day. Plastic pants used to cover diapers can make the condition worse, and wipes containing potential irritants such as alcohol should be avoided. Simply cleanse with mild soap, water and a soft cloth. Ointments containing zinc oxide are helpful for reducing any friction between the diaper and the baby's skin.

Secondary infections can be caused by fungi (such as *Candida*) or bacteria (such as *Staphylococcus* or *Streptococcus*) which are normally found in the skin and which thrive in damaged areas. These infections can be treated with topical antibiotics.

Diaper rash is also known as baby rash, miliaria, diaper dermatitis and nappy rash.

SEE ALSO *Candidiasis, Staphylococcal infections, Streptococcal infections*

DIAPHRAGM

The diaphragm is a muscular layer which separates the chest cavity from the abdominal cavity. It is attached at the back to the vertebral column (spine), to the ribs along the side of the chest, and to the sternum at the front of the chest. The diaphragm is essential for life because it is the main muscle used for breathing.

When the diaphragm is at rest (i.e. not contracting) it forms a high dome; when the diaphragm contracts, this dome descends, thus increasing the height of the chest cavity. Increasing the height of the chest cavity in turn draws air into the lungs within the chest. This means that the diaphragm is the main muscle for inspiration (drawing air into the lungs).

Expiration, or the passage of air out of the chest cavity, is usually passive, i.e. it occurs because of the relaxation of tension in the soft and hard tissues of the chest and abdomen. The diaphragm does not play any active part in expiration.

The phrenic nerves controlling the diaphragm come from the upper parts of the spinal cord in the neck. If the nerve cells which control the diaphragm are separated from the brain stem control centers for breathing (e.g. by a high spinal cord injury), then the patient will be unable to breathe without assistance from a ventilator. High spinal injuries can occur if someone dives into a too-shallow pool, falls onto the crown of the head from a height, or experiences a violent whiplash injury in a car accident.

The diaphragm is pierced by several structures which pass between the chest and abdominal cavities. The three largest of these are the esophagus, carrying food to the stomach; the aorta, carrying oxygenated blood from the heart to the lower body; and the inferior vena cava, a large vein which carries deoxygenated blood from the lower body back to the heart. Several other nerves and lymphatic channels also pass through the diaphragm.

The central part of the diaphragm is called the central tendon. It is fibrous rather than muscular and has the pericardial sac, which surrounds the heart, firmly attached to its upper surface. The central tendon descends with every inspiration.

The stomach and abdominal part of the esophagus may be forced through the esophageal opening of the diaphragm and into the chest cavity—this is known as hiatus hernia. This condition may cause discomfort after meals, reflux of stomach acid into the chest part of the esophagus (gastroesophageal reflux) leading to heartburn, and a sense of pressure in the lower chest. Medical treatment could include antacids, change of diet, and maintaining upright posture. Surgical treatment involves fixing the esophagus and stomach firmly into the abdominal cavity with sutures.

SEE ALSO *Abdomen, Aorta, Breathing, Esophagus, Hiatus hernia, Gastroesophageal reflux, Lungs, Ribs, Spinal cord, Spine, Stomach*

Diaphragm

The diaphragm is the muscular layer that separates the chest cavity from the abdominal cavity. It is the main muscle used for breathing.

DIARRHEA

When food reaches the intestinal tract it is a liquid mush with a volume of around 1 gallon (almost 4 liters) per day. The water content is reabsorbed in the large intestine, making the feces solid or semi-solid. When the bowel fails to reabsorb fluid the feces are liquid, and this condition is known as diarrhea. It may be accompanied by abdominal cramps, low-grade fever, vomiting, blood in the stools and dehydration.

In developing countries diarrhea caused by the unsanitary preparation of artificial baby milk kills more than a million babies annually. In total, diarrhea that is caused by an infection kills nearly 8 million children under 5 years of age, worldwide. Chronic diarrhea causes an abnormal loss of essential nutrients which results in malnutrition.

Less severe forms of diarrhea, which can be caused by having too much fiber in the diet (especially unprocessed bran), lactose intolerance, or artificial sweeteners such as sorbitol or mannitol, does not require specific treatment.

Diaphragm

The heart and the lungs rest on the upper convex surface of this muscle. The lower concave surface forms the roof of the abdominal cavity, lying over the stomach on the left and the liver on the right. This illustration shows the diaphragm as seen from below.

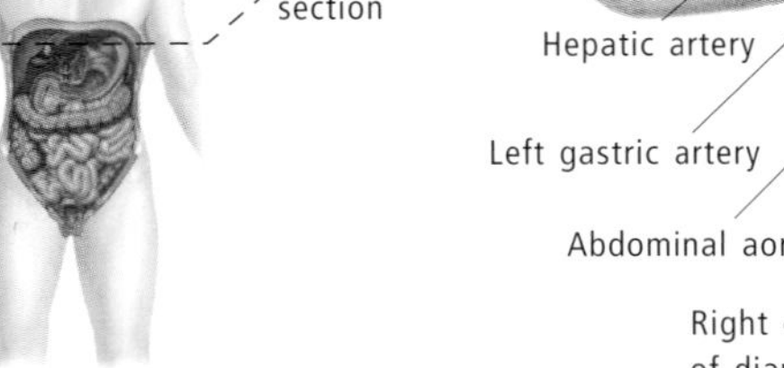

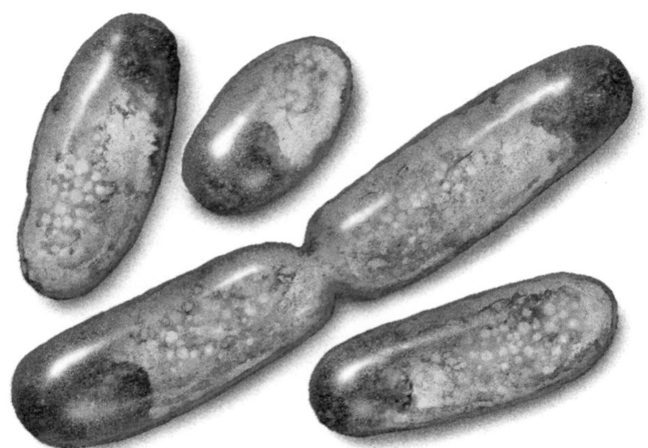

Diarrhea

The bacterium *Escherichia coli* shown here is a common cause of diarrhea in children. It can also lead to other infections such as urinary tract infections and conjunctivitis.

Causes of more severe diarrhea can be a temporary inflammation brought on by common viruses (this is especially common in children); food poisoning; infections (bacterial, viral or parasitic); eating highly spiced food; drinking large quantities of alcohol; emotional stress; poisons such as arsenic or mercury bichloride; gastroenteritis; medications such as laxatives, antibiotics and antacids; diseases such as dysentery or cholera (unusual in the industrialized world); and benign or cancerous growths in the bowel.

Diarrhea is also a symptom of conditions such as celiac disease and colitis. It is also the main cause of illness among travelers when it occurs as a result of a bacterial infection from the unsanitary handling of food and eating utensils.

Babies and children with diarrhea need medical attention if the condition does not resolve within 24 hours or if they are showing signs of dehydration, have bloody or slimy bowel movements (feces), an extremely high temperature, or are aged under six months. Treatment includes a diet of clear liquids and oral rehydration fluids which replace the lost electrolytes.

SEE ALSO *Celiac disease, Cholera, Colitis, Constipation, Dysentery, Dehydration, Gastroenteritis, Giardiasis, Irritable bowel syndrome, Lactose intolerance, Malnutrition*

DIET

Diet is a person's regular nutrition: it represents the total intake of food and drink. A balanced or normal diet is one that will maintain good health. In Western societies this means eating foods from each of the four main food groups: cereals, fruits and vegetables, protein foods, and dairy products, in proportions laid down in generally agreed dietary guidelines.

Governments around the world have recognized the links between diet and health, and many have issued guidelines to inform people as to what constitutes a healthy diet, and the benefits of good eating habits. The quantities recommended will differ according to the age, general health and energy requirements of the person.

An unbalanced diet, for example one high in fat, will have a negative effect on health, increasing weight or bringing a greater risk of dietary disorders such as diabetes.

Individual diets are influenced by cultural factors as well as by what is locally or seasonally available. People tend to eat the foods they were brought up on. Migrants from dissimilar cultures may find their preferred foods are not available in their adopted country and will have to choose unfamiliar manufactured foods with many hidden ingredients. They may unwittingly change the balance of nutrients in their diet, increasing the amounts of salt, sugar or fats they eat, with harmful effects on weight and health.

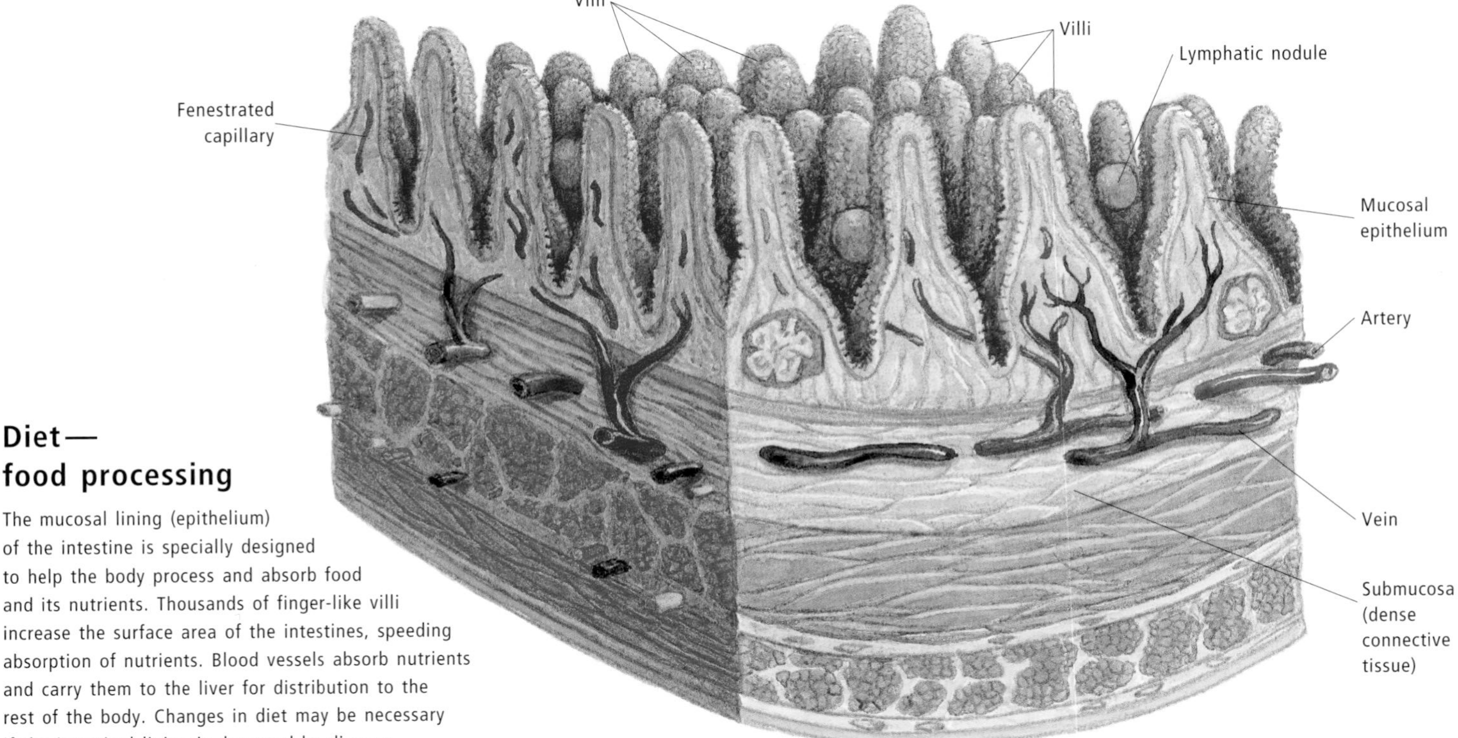

Diet—food processing

The mucosal lining (epithelium) of the intestine is specially designed to help the body process and absorb food and its nutrients. Thousands of finger-like villi increase the surface area of the intestines, speeding absorption of nutrients. Blood vessels absorb nutrients and carry them to the liver for distribution to the rest of the body. Changes in diet may be necessary if the intestinal lining is damaged by disease.

Special diets are those prescribed by a dietitian to meet the needs of a particular condition or illness; to prepare for a surgical procedure; to reduce weight; to lower the cholesterol levels of the blood; to eliminate foods which might trigger an allergic reaction; to improve digestion; or to improve health in a poorly fed person.

Diet and obesity

As lifestyles in industrialized societies have become less active, daily energy requirements have fallen. Because individuals walk less and perform less manual labor, food intake should be correspondingly lower, but where food is more affordable and more plentiful, and with many foods being dense energy sources, overeating is common.

The result is that many people are overweight, suffer poor health and increased incidences of weight-related diseases such as diabetes mellitus, high blood pressure, and heart disease.

The energy provided by food is measured in kilocalories or kilojoules—1 kilocalorie is equal to 4.2 kilojoules. Women who are overweight may adjust their diet by limiting the total energy value of their foods to approximately 1,500 kilocalories (equal to 6,300 kilojoules) per day and most will lose excess weight at this level of intake. Men may lose weight with a higher energy intake of 1,800 kilocalories (equal to 7,560 kilojoules) per day.

Fiber in diet

Diets that are lacking in fiber and high in fat have been linked with digestive diseases and certain types of cancer. Cereal foods are the major source of dietary fiber in Western societies except where fiber is removed by the refining process. This fact has been recognized in many countries and minimum requirements have been set for dietary fiber intake.

Elimination diet

An elimination diet is a therapy for suspected food allergies. Foods suspected of causing the allergic reaction are first excluded, then re-introduced one by one. When the food that triggers the reaction is identified, it can be avoided by following an exclusion diet, which allows all foods to be eaten except those containing this particular substance.

SEE ALSO *Allergies, Appetite, Celiac disease, Constipation, Diabetes, Nutrition, Obesity*

DILATION AND CURETTAGE

Often called D & C, dilation and curettage is the most commonly performed gynecological procedure. It involves the surgical opening (dilation) of the cervix (the neck of the uterus), and the removal of the contents of the uterus with a curette, an instrument with a long handle and an end shaped like a spoon. This is used to obtain tissue from the uterus lining (endometrium) for examination or to remove fragments of placenta after a miscarriage. The procedure can be performed under a general or a local anesthetic and has few side or after effects.

SEE ALSO *Abortion, Dilation and evacuation, Miscarriage*

DILATION AND EVACUATION

This procedure is used in abortions when the pregnancy is into the second trimester, or from 12 to 20 weeks, and is usually done under a general anesthetic. It involves dilating the cervix more widely than for a dilation and curettage to allow the removal of fetal parts. The fetus is removed with suction, a curette and forceps.

SEE ALSO *Abortion, Dilation and curettage*

DIPHTHERIA

Diphtheria is an acute infectious disease of the larynx, tonsils, and throat, caused by the bacterium *Corynebacterium diphtheriae*. As a result of widespread immunization against diphtheria over many years, this disease is now rare and usually seen in non-immunized children, under ten.

Diphtheria is transmitted from person to person by airborne droplets from infected persons or asymptomatic carriers, that is, people who carry the disease but do not show symptoms. The illness develops after a period of one to four days after exposure to the bacterium. The child feels weak and unwell with fever and a sore throat, and may find the lymph nodes in the neck will become swollen.

A toxin produced by the infection damages the lining of the throat, causing a tough, fibrous gray or greenish yellow membrane to form at the back of the throat, which may obstruct breathing. The toxin may enter the bloodstream and cause damage to the heart, kidneys and nervous system. Treatment involves bed rest in hospital and administration of diphtheria antitoxin and antibiotics such as penicillin or erythromycin.

Diphtheria immunization is usually carried out in the first year of life. It is usually combined with pertussis and tetanus immunization (DPT). Falling childhood immunization rates in some Western countries have led to a resurgence of the disease.

SEE ALSO *Immunization, Infectious diseases, Larynx, Throat, Tonsils*

DISK, INTERVERTEBRAL

The intervertebral disks are flexible, cartilaginous structures, which lie between adjacent vertebrae and make up approximately 25 percent of the length of the vertebral column in a young person. Intervertebral disks form joints between the bodies of the vertebrae, which serve both to unite adjacent vertebrae and to permit movement between them. They also play a role as shock absorbers when force is transmitted along the vertebral column during standing and movement.

Each disk is formed of two parts, a central mass called the nucleus pulposus (soft center), and a surrounding fibrous layer (the annulus fibrosus). The nucleus pulposus has a semi-fluid, gelatinous consistency which allows it to become deformed when pressure is placed upon it, enabling the disk to change shape as the vertebral column moves.

The surrounding annulus fibrosus is formed by concentric layers of fibers which are firmly attached to the adjacent vertebrae. These fibers pass in an oblique direction between the vertebrae and are arranged in such a way as to resist excessive movement in almost any direction. The joints formed by the intervertebral disks are reinforced in front and behind by ligaments, which pass along the length of the vertebral column.

The thickness and shape of the disks varies in different parts of the vertebral column. They are relatively thin and flat in the chest (thoracic) region, thicker in the neck (cervical) region and thickest and wedge-shaped in the lower back (lumbar) region.

Intervertebral disks in young people have a high water content (80–90 percent). This gradually reduces during the day because water is squeezed out of each disk as it bears weight during standing and movement. The lost water is however reabsorbed into the disk during sleep when lying down. The average young adult is around ¾ inch (2 centimeters) taller upon waking than at the end of the day. As a person ages, the ability to replace this water gradually reduces and the disks become drier and thinner. This partly explains why people lose height, or appear to shrink, as they get older.

The fibers of the fibrous annulus become more fragile with age and may be torn by excessive force on the joint, such as sudden twisting or flexion, causing the nucleus to protrude into or through the damaged part of the annulus. Because the annulus is thinner and weaker behind, the damaged disk usually bulges in this direction and may compress nearby spinal nerves. This condition is commonly known as a herniated disk, or slipped disk.

Herniation of the disk can occur in part of the vertebral column but is most common in the lumbar region where the nerves to the lower limbs originate. When herniation is mild and only irritates local structures, it causes pain in the lower back and buttocks ("lumbago"). If the herniation is severe enough to press on the spinal nerve roots as they emerge from the spinal cord and pass over the herniated disk, this will cause sciatica, which is pain, numbness, "pins and needles", or muscle weakness down the leg.

Treatment is usually conservative (anti-inflammatory drugs, rest, physical therapy) but in severe cases surgery may be necessary to release pressure on the nerve.

SEE ALSO *Back, Sciatica, Spine, Vertebrae*

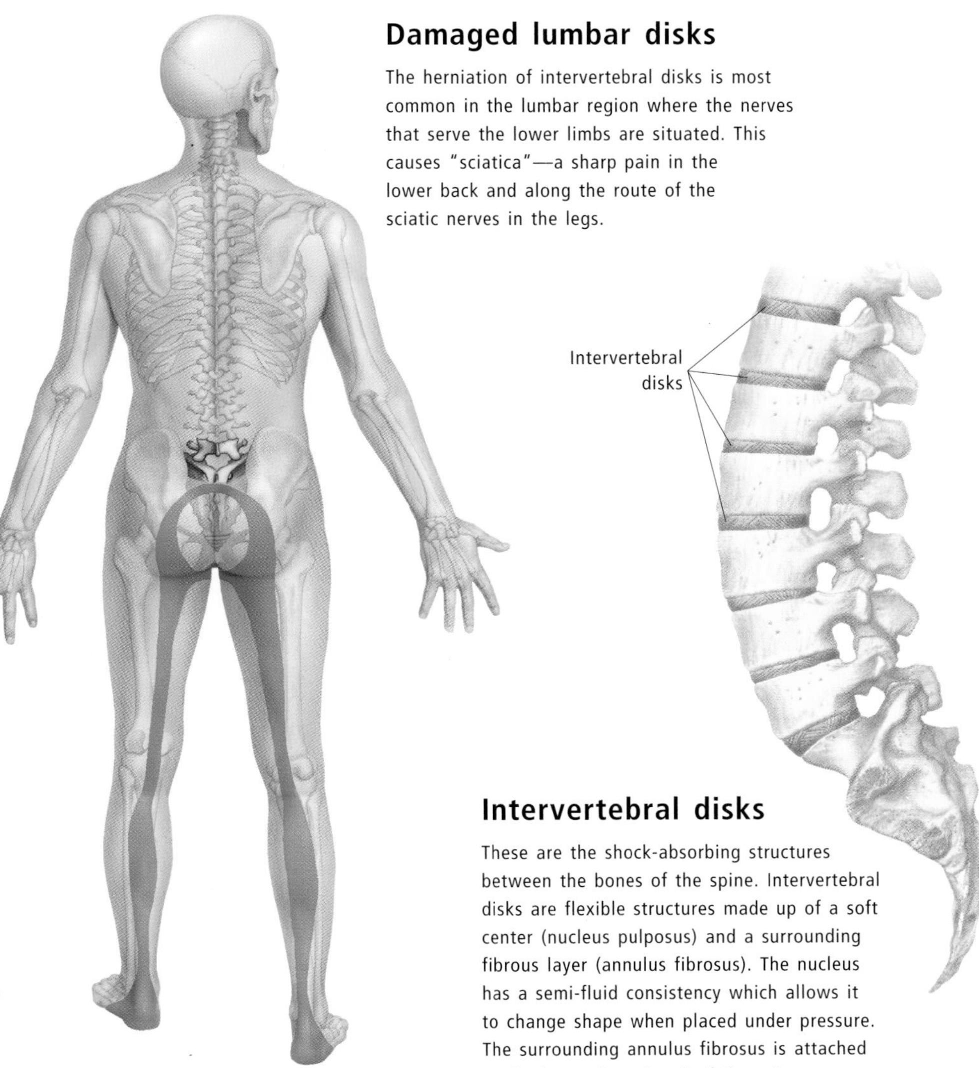

Damaged lumbar disks

The herniation of intervertebral disks is most common in the lumbar region where the nerves that serve the lower limbs are situated. This causes "sciatica"—a sharp pain in the lower back and along the route of the sciatic nerves in the legs.

Intervertebral disks

These are the shock-absorbing structures between the bones of the spine. Intervertebral disks are flexible structures made up of a soft center (nucleus pulposus) and a surrounding fibrous layer (annulus fibrosus). The nucleus has a semi-fluid consistency which allows it to change shape when placed under pressure. The surrounding annulus fibrosus is attached to the bones (vertebrae) of the spine.

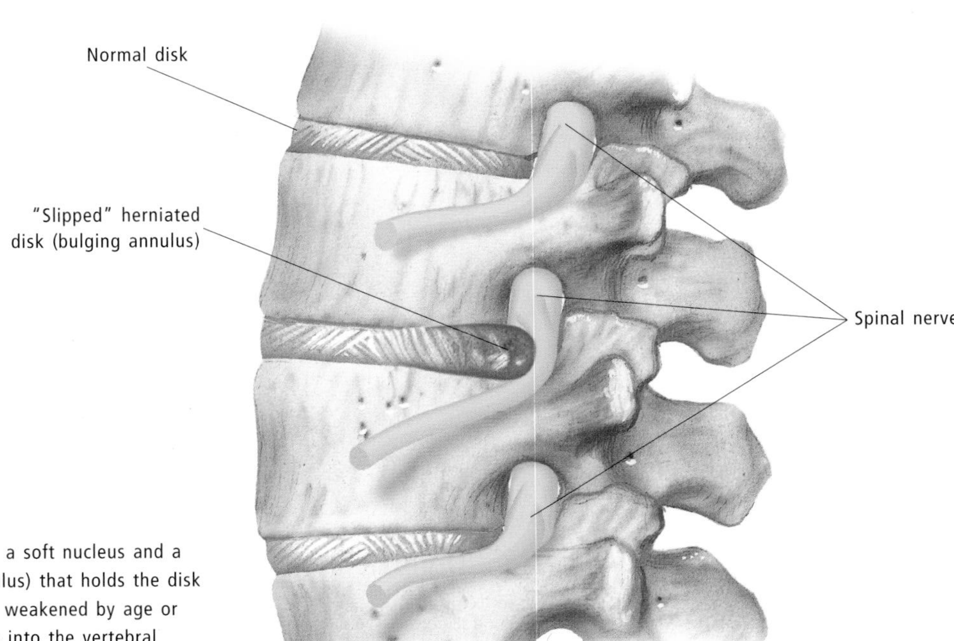

Herniated disk

Invertebral disks comprise a soft nucleus and a fibrous outer casing (annulus) that holds the disk in place. If the annulus is weakened by age or injury, the disk may bulge into the vertebral canal compressing nearby spinal nerves, referred to as a "slipped" or herniated disk.

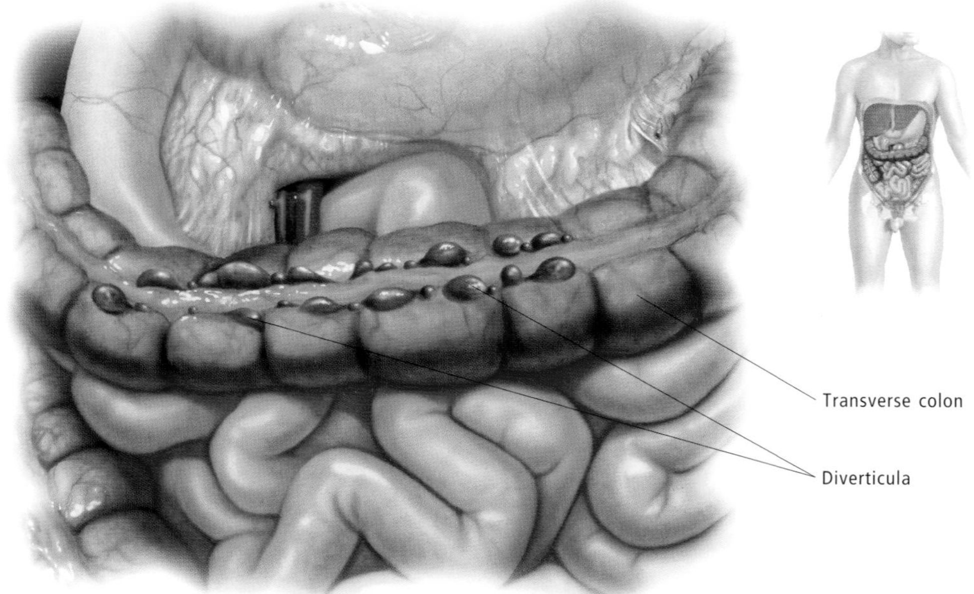

Diverticulosis

In diverticulosis, inner layers of the colon wall bulge out to form small pockets (diverticula).

DIVERTICULITIS

Diverticulitis is a disease of the large bowel or colon, which arises when small outpockets (protrusions) in the wall become inflamed; these outpockets are called diverticula, hence the name.

The patient experiences pain usually in the lower left part of the abdomen, which is mild to severe in intensity and may be either persistent or cramping in nature. Patients may also have mild fever, tenderness in the lower abdomen, swelling of the lower abdomen, constipation and, sometimes, blood in their feces.

Occasionally diverticula rupture, and the contents of the bowel leak into the tissues of the bowel wall and, sometimes, into the cavity of the abdomen. The bacteria from the bowel multiply within these regions. Complications include abscesses in the bowel wall and nearby abdominal cavity; fistulas, where the infection forms a communication between the interior of the bowel and other nearby organs; peritonitis, where bacteria spread freely through the abdominal cavity; and obstruction of the bowel.

About one-quarter of patients with acute diverticulitis require surgical treatment to either drain or remove abscesses, relieve obstruction or close fistulas.

SEE ALSO *Bowel, Colon, Diverticulosis, Peritonitis*

DIVERTICULOSIS

In diverticulosis, the wall of the bowel "blows out", forming outpockets which protrude between the muscle bands of the bowel wall. A diet low in dietary fiber and high in fat, typical of many people in Western societies, is thought to contribute to this condition of the colon.

SEE ALSO *Bowel, Colon*

DIVERTICULUM

Most commonly, a divertivulum is an outpocketing or protrusion of the wall of the colon. This may also occur in the upper part of the esophagus, where the lower throat (or pharynx) gives way to the esophagus. This type of diverticulum is called Zenker's diverticulum and occurs when the pressure generated by swallowing forces the wall of the upper esophagus outwards.

SEE ALSO *Esophagus, Pharynx*

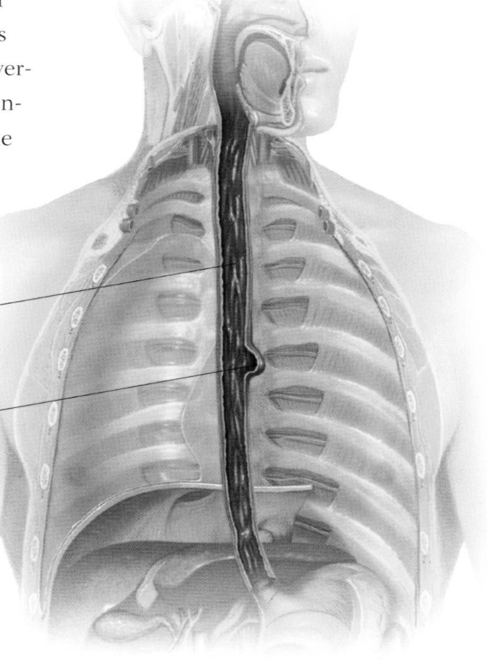

Diverticulum

A diverticulum is the formation of a small pouch or protrusion in the wall of a mucous membrane. It often occurs in the esophagus or colon.

DIURETICS

Diuretic drugs act on the kidneys to increase urine output. They cause the kidneys to increase the amount of salt and water eliminated from the body in the urine, and so are often called "water pills". Alcohol, tea and coffee also have a mild diuretic effect.

Diuretics are used to treat excessive buildup of fluid in the body (edema) or the lungs (pulmonary edema). Edema can be caused by disorders of the heart (such as congestive heart failure or heart attack), liver dysfunction (by not producing protein) or kidney dysfunction (by leaking protein). Diuretics are used to treat hypertension (high blood pressure), congestive heart failure and also high fluid pressure within the eye (glaucoma).

Some diuretics, such as thiazide diuretics, cause the kidneys to lose potassium, which must be replaced by adding foods rich in it to the diet, or by taking potassium supplements.

SEE ALSO *Edema, Glaucoma, Hypertension, Kidney, Potassium, Urinary systems*

DIZZINESS

Dizziness is a feeling of light-headedness, unsteadiness or falling, accompanied by weakness and swaying, or a sensation of whirling rotation and general loss of balance.

Low blood pressure (hypotension) can cause dizziness as the brain may not receive

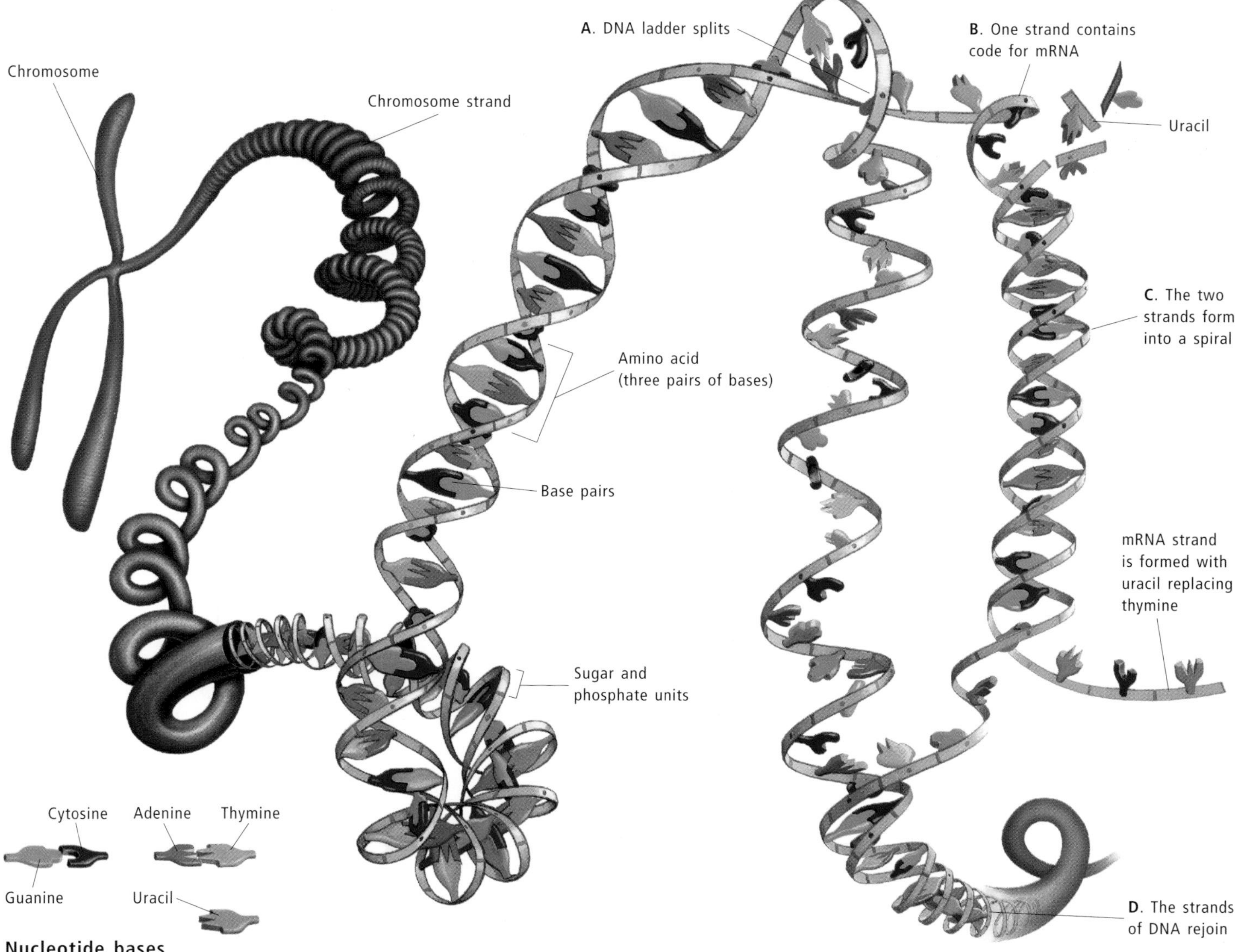

DNA

Deoxyribonucleic acid (DNA) molecules, found in the chromosomes in the nucleus of every cell, carry the genetic information that determines inherited traits (such as hair and skin color and body function). This information dictates the formation of proteins used by the body for growth and chemical processes.

Unravelling a chromosome shows that DNA comprises a spiral ladder consisting of two chains of phosphate and sugar units attached to nitrogenous bases. The chains are joined together at the bases—like the rungs in a ladder. There are four bases in DNA—adenine, thymine, cytosine and guanine—which bind together in limited combinations (adenine always binds with thymine; cytosine always binds with guanine). Proteins are made up of chains of amino acids. DNA passes on its information to protein factories (ribosomes) in the cytoplasm of the cell by creating a messenger acid—messenger ribonucleic acid (mRNA).

A. To make mRNA, the DNA ladder separates lengthwise, separating the bases of each strand.

B. One of the newly separated DNA strands is used as a template to make an mRNA strand.

C. The mRNA strand contains the bases of DNA, but thymine is replaced with a new base: uracil. mRNA leaves the nucleus of the cell and passes into the cytoplasm where it gives the ribosomes the information they need to produce proteins.

D. The two chains of DNA now join back together to form a spiral ladder once more.

enough blood and not enough oxygen.

Orthostatic or postural hypotension occurs when a person stands up quickly and causes a temporary fall in blood pressure, enough to cause dizziness or sometimes fainting. Sitting, or lying down will make it easier for blood to reach the brain, increasing the flow and relieving the dizziness.

Infections, damage and tumors of the inner ear, brain disorders, head injuries, brain tumors, and medications used to relieve high blood pressure are all possible causes of dizziness.

SEE ALSO *Hypotension, Menière's disease, Vertigo*

DNA

Deoxyribonucleic acid, commonly known as DNA, is a code for life found in almost every living organism. It is found in strands known as chromosomes in the interior part of a cell—the nucleus. Each chromosome contains genes, which are blueprints of genetic information and are made up of segments of DNA. DNA also contains the blueprints for making proteins and for replicating itself.

The structure of DNA was discovered in 1953 by Francis Crick and James Watson, who were awarded the Nobel prize for medicine in 1962 for their discovery.

The DNA molecule is a double helix, resembling a spiral ladder. The sides of the ladder are made up by alternating units of phosphate and a sugar, deoxyribose. Attached to the sugar units are the rungs of the ladder, which are made up of combinations of bases. There are four bases: adenine, cytosine, guanine and thymine (A, C, G, and T).

Each rung in the ladder consists of two bases. Because of chemical attractions, only a few combinations of bases are possible: A–T, T–A, C–G, or G–C. Lengthwise up and down the ladder, the bases form different patterns, for example ATCGAT. Three of these bases together form a codon which encodes a single amino acid of a protein. The order of the bases in one strand (half) of the ladder determines the order of the bases in the other strand. For example, if the bases in one strand are ATCGAT, the bases in the opposite strand would be TAGCTA.

Before a cell divides, the DNA duplicates. The ladder splits lengthwise, separating the bases of each strand. Then, with the help of special enzymes, the bases in each half ladder pick up their matching mates. The As attach to Ts, the Ts to As, the Gs to Cs, and the Cs to Gs. In this way, each new ladder becomes a duplicate of the original ladder. When the cell divides, the two new cells have identical DNA molecules.

DNA also determines the proteins a cell makes. It does this by encoding a messenger ribonucleic acid (mRNA) with information needed to make proteins in "cell factories" called ribosomes in the cytoplasm of the cell. The amino acid structure of each protein made by a ribosome corresponds to a particular sequence of bases in the DNA.

If there is a mistake made during DNA replication and a sequence is altered (known as a mutation) the composition of a protein may be also be changed. The result may be a genetic disorder. There are an estimated 4,200 diseases caused by genetic defects.

The Human Genome Project is mapping the entire genetic code of DNA. It will be completed early in the twenty-first century, holding out the promise of an understanding, and possibly a cure, for inherited disorders.

SEE ALSO *Cells, Chromosomes, Genes*

DOMESTIC VIOLENCE

Any abuse in a relationship situation can be described as domestic violence. The abuse is most commonly perpetrated by a male towards his female partner. It can be physical assault, rape or other sexual assault, and emotional or psychological abuse such as demeaning and making threats. Very often the abuse is a combination of these.It occurs in all socioeconomic, cultural and educational backgrounds.

Domestic violence is the major cause of injury to women in the 15 to 44 age group in the US; 15- to 24-year-olds are most commonly the victims of sexual assault and domestic violence is the cause of one-third of the murders of women. It was not until the women's movement of the 1970s that domestic violence became a matter for the courts.

Experts believe that it is widely underreported because family matters are still thought of by many as private, even when they include violence. There is often an element of denial of the situation, and those involved are frightened of the legal consequences. Some research indicates that nearly 30 percent of relationships are believed to have suffered from violence at some stage.

Men can also experience domestic violence. Because they are more likely to report it than women are, it can seem that the percentage of men who suffer from domestic violence is higher than the actual incidence of abuse. However, data indicate that women are six times more likely to be victims than men.

Historically women have been regarded as the property of men, and wife-beating was acceptable and even considered necessary in medieval times. Patriarchal (male-dominated) societies with traditions which allow husbands to punish wives physically and afford women a lower socioeconomic status than men still exist in many parts of the world, and where these traditional laws have been replaced there are still vestiges of male proprietorial rights over the women and children in their family.

There is usually more than one reason why violence occurs in a relationship. Causes include low income, alcohol or substance abuse, growing up in a violent family, unemployment and low job satisfaction, sexual difficulties, and not knowing other ways to cope or behave. The age of the couple involved can also be a factor: violence is more common in couples under 30 years of age.

The effects of domestic violence are both physical and emotional. Physical injuries include bruises, cuts, burns, stab wounds, broken bones and miscarriage. Consequent emotional problems include eating disorders, alcohol and substance abuse, psychological disturbances, anxiety and depression.

A woman who wants to leave an abusive relationship, particularly if she comes from a lower socioeconomic background, may often have to choose between the abuse or living on the streets. Shelters and refuges which have been established for women and children in this situation are frequently filled to capacity. This situation can add to the woman's dilemma. Victims will often leave a violent relationship and then return because of the economic, emotional, cultural and social difficulties which they encounter when they leave.

Escaping from a violent situation is the best course of action when children are involved. Research reveals that in the US domestic violence is the crime which is increasing the fastest. It also indicates that children who come from violent homes where they are either the witnesses to domestic violence, or the victims of it, or both, are likely to grow up to become violent adolescents and adults.

Once a woman, with or without children, has found a place in a shelter or refuge she will then have access to a number of different programs, including legal aid and counseling. There is also an increasing number of treatment programs being established to which courts may send offenders.

SEE ALSO *Child abuse*

DOPPLER ULTRASONOGRAPHY

Named after Christian Doppler (Austrian physicist, 1803–1853), Doppler ultrasound is used to measure the flow of a liquid, usually blood flow. It is based on the principle that when a source of sound or light moves rapidly the pitch of sound appears to get higher as the object approaches and lower as the object recedes. It can measure the rate and quantity of the flow and therefore highlight any abnormalities or obstructions in the circulatory system.

SEE ALSO *Ultrasound*

DOUBLE VISION

Double vision, known clinically as diplopia, occurs when the movements of the two eyes are not properly coordinated. The eyes are moved by a number of "extraocular" muscles in the bony cavity known as the orbit. Normally when we choose to view an object, both eyes are directed towards the object. If the muscles moving one eye are weakened or paralyzed the patient will not be able to turn that eye in the correct direction. Consequently, the good eye looks at the object, the bad eye looks elsewhere, causing two quite different images to reach the brain which results in double vision.

SEE ALSO *Eye, Sight*

DOWN SYNDROME

Down syndrome, or trisomy 21, is a congenital defect: a person with Down syndrome has three number 21 chromosomes instead of two. An affected person survives into adulthood, but with a range of physical and mental abnormalities.

There are several characteristic physical features of Down syndrome. The head is round, flat and may be smaller than normal (microcephaly). The ears are small and low-set, the nose is flattened and the eyes slant upwards (Mongolian slant). The inner corner of the eyes may have a rounded fold of skin rather than coming to a point. The hands are broad with short fingers and often have a single palmar crease (simian crease). Normal growth and development is retarded; most Down syndrome children never reach average adult height.

The most significant feature of the condition is that intellectual development is retarded; an affected child will have an IQ (intelligence quotient) of about 60 although some are borderline retarded or have low average range IQs. Adult Down sufferers have an average mental age of about eight years. Nearly all Down syndrome adults will develop Alzheimer's disease and become prematurely senile.

Down syndrome is often associated with other congenital disorders such as heart and intestinal defects, chronic respiratory and ear infections, and visual problems. About half of Down syndrome children are born with a heart defect, often a hole between the two sides of the heart. Hirschsprung's disease (congenital aganglionic megacolon), which can cause intestinal obstruction, occurs more frequently in Down syndrome. Children with Down syndrome also have a higher than average incidence of acute lymphocytic leukemia.

The older a woman becomes, the greater her chance of having a Down syndrome child. Between the ages of 35 and 39, a mother has a 1.5 percent chance of having a child with Down syndrome; over the age of 40 she has a 5 percent chance. Down syndrome can be detected in the first few months of pregnancy by examination of fetal chromosomes from a sample of the fluid surrounding the fetus obtained by amniocentesis. Chorionic villus sampling (CVS) can provide the same information. If Down syndrome is detected, the woman may then be offered the chance to terminate the pregnancy.

There is no cure for Down syndrome. But with specialized education and training, most affected children can learn to look after themselves and to lead useful lives. Heart and gastrointestinal defects may require surgical correction. Down syndrome can be inherited, so the mother of a child with Down syndrome could be at increased risk of having another. However, inherited Down syndrome is rare: in most cases, subsequent children will be normal. It is advisable for parents to seek genetic counseling before they begin another pregnancy.

SEE ALSO ***Amniocentesis, Chorionic villus sampling, Chromosomal abnormalities, Chromosomes, Genetic counseling, Intellectual disability***

Down syndrome

The physical features of Down syndrome are easily recognizable. The head is round and flat, eyes slant upwards and the nose is flat. The hands are broad with short fingers.

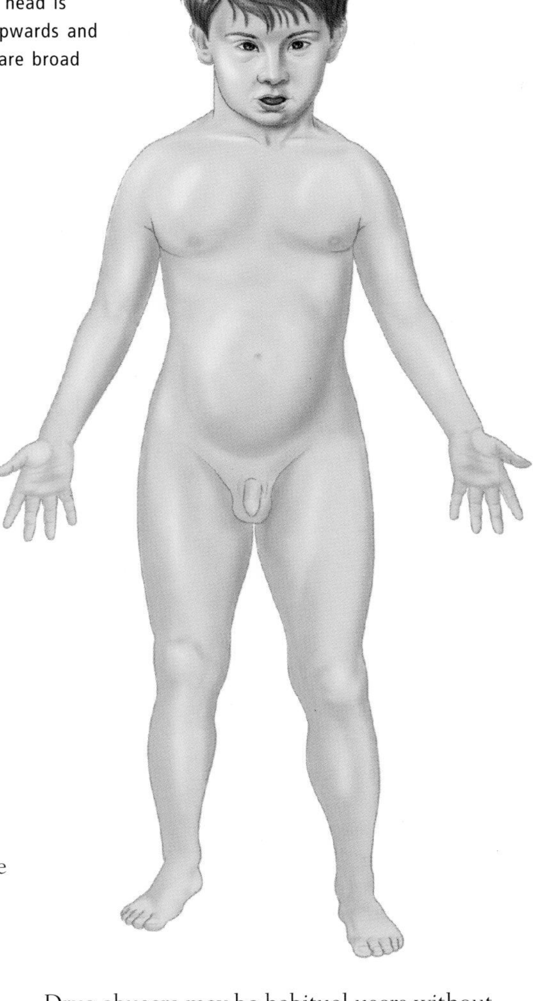

DRUG DEPENDENCE

The use of drugs in a harmful way is described as "drug abuse". Many substances can be abused, from prescription drugs to petroleum vapors inhaled to gain a "high". Drug abusers may be habitual users without being dependent, or addicted ("dependence" is currently the term used instead of "addiction", and a dependent person is a drug "user" rather than an "addict"). Dependence is usually considered to involve both psychological and physical dependency. Often a description includes the name of the drug, e.g. "morphine type" drug dependence.

Physical dependence arises as the user's body adapts to the repeated use of the drug. Tolerance to the drug is high (meaning there is a need to continually increase the dose to obtain the original effect). Psychological dependence is present when users believe they cannot cope without the drug. This compulsion can be extremely strong and may be due to underlying emotional issues.

Drug dependence is characterized by loss of control over the use of a drug. The voluntary decision to take a drug is replaced by a craving that arises as the effects of the last intake wear off. The craving can be so great that the user's thoughts and activities are directed solely toward getting more of the drug. This is destructive of other facets of life.

Dependence may dramatically alter behavior. Work, social responsibilities and personal hygiene may be neglected as more time is spent under the influence of drugs or in chasing further supplies. Drug users often lose jobs, families and friends this way. Health will suffer if drugs replace normal food intake. The person may suffer nutritional disorders or acquire diseases from contaminated syringes. Dependence is often a route to crime and prostitution, since drugs, especially street drugs, are very costly.

Personality problems, social pressures, inability to deal with relationships, and life crises all may provide impetus to use drugs.

Types of drugs and their effects

Drugs of dependence can be grouped as depressants, stimulants and hallucinogens.

Depressants include alcohol, opiates (morphine, heroin, methadone, codeine, pethidine), barbiturates, tranquilizers, anxiolytics, hypnotics and inhalants such as petroleum, glue, paint thinners and lighter fluid. Effects vary from mild (relaxation, euphoria) to extreme (slurred speech, uncoordinated movement, reduced breathing and heart rate) with large doses causing nausea, vomiting and occasionally death.

Stimulants are drugs that affect the nervous system. Depending on the strength and type of the particular substance, stimulants generally make you more alert and active, help you stay awake, reduce hunger and elevate mood. Legal stimulants include caffeine and nicotine, and ephedrine, which is an ingredient in some medicines used for respiratory conditions. Illegal stimulants include Ecstasy, amphetamines and cocaine.

Hallucinogenic drugs include lysergic acid diethylamide (LSD), mescaline and psilocybin. Marijuana also has hallucinogenic properties. All of these drugs can produce psychological dependency and offer an altered perception of reality, providing complete, if temporary, escape. Hallucinogens can be the cause of psychosis in certain people.

How dependence develops

Just as there are many different types of drugs, there are many different types and

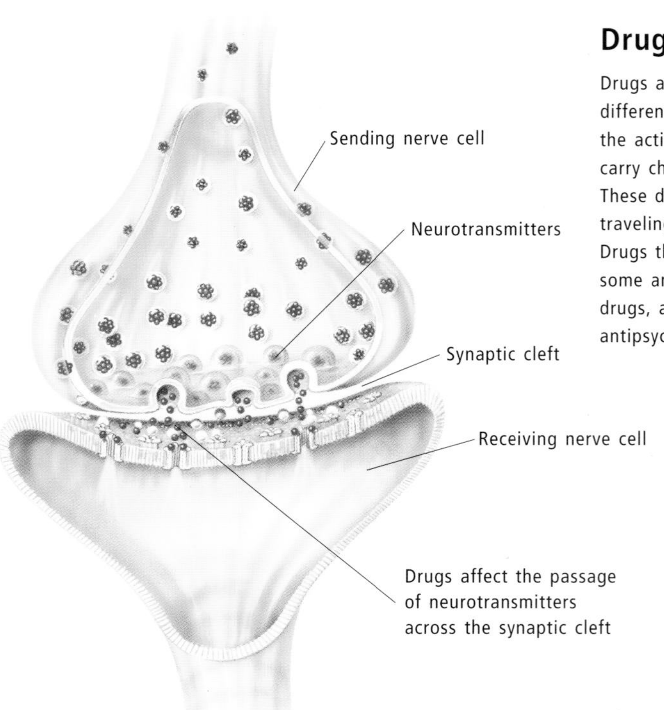

Drug mechanisms

Drugs act on the body in a number of different ways. Some work by blocking the action of neurotransmitters, which carry chemical signals between nerves. These drugs prevent an impulse from traveling from one nerve to another. Drugs that work in this way include some anesthetics and cardiovascular drugs, antihypertensives and antipsychotics.

Drug dependence

With frequent and prolonged use of many drugs, tolerance develops and the user must take more of the drug to get the required effect. In the case of some depressants, such as narcotics, increased doses may depress the respiratory centers in the brain stem, ultimately causing overdose and death.

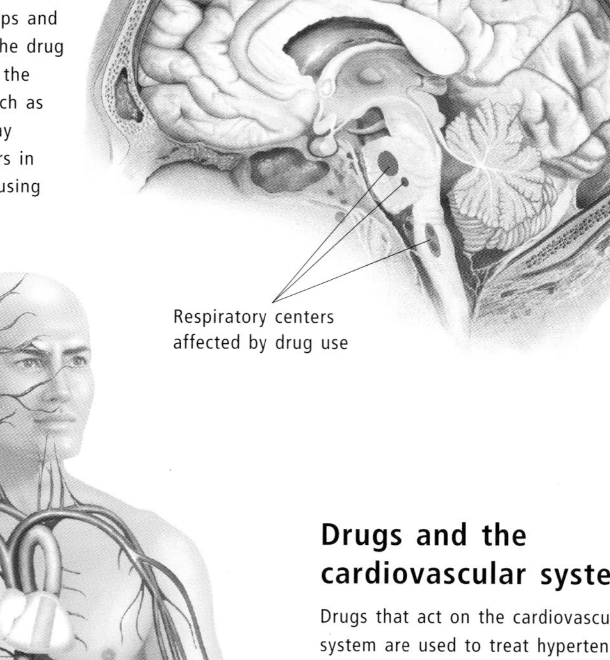

Drugs and the cardiovascular system

Drugs that act on the cardiovascular system are used to treat hypertension, heart disease and peripheral vascular disease. They usually work by acting on the muscle in the heart and the blood vessels, for example by slowing the heart rate, making the heart pump harder, or by relaxing the blood vessels and lowering the blood pressure in the circulatory system.

patterns of dependence, as well as a variety of causes. Explanations put forward suggest that users display personalities that make them more vulnerable to dependence. Certain types of dependence seem to be inherited and are described as familial because no clear genetic cause has yet been found.

There is no such thing as instant dependence, although the period of use before becoming dependent may be very short. With many drugs, but not all, the user develops a rising level of tolerance to the drug. This may result in the person using an increasing quantity of the drug each time.

Detoxification and treatment

Repeated drug use causes the level of substances derived from the drug in body tissues and bloodstream to rise. When use stops, these substances are excreted and blood levels fall. This is the process of detoxification, which is the body's natural process of breakdown and excretion of waste products. But in the drug-dependent person, this fall in toxin levels triggers craving and often results in severely unpleasant physical and psychological withdrawal symptoms. These can include nausea, cramps, sweating, restlessness, seizures, insomnia, headaches, tremors, delirium, depression and suicidal impulses—all varying with the particular drug and its quantity and strength.

It is extremely dangerous to come off any drug of dependence without professional help. Sometimes heroin users are given methadone under medical supervision as a substitute for heroin. Although methadone is a drug of dependence, it is safer than heroin and users are able to live relatively normal lives. Medical treatment can also include admission to a hospital detoxification unit. The patient may be given drugs such as mild tranquilizers to aid withdrawal, and naltrexone to help stop the physical cravings. Patients who are dependent on tranquilizers or anxiolytics are given gradually decreasing doses before complete withdrawal happens.

Physical detoxification is only the first step—the next challenge is to learn how to live without drugs. Many experts believe that no dependent person is ever able to use again with safety, and recommend total abstinence from all drugs, including alcohol. There is a much greater chance of long-term recovery if detoxification is followed by several weeks in a treatment or rehabilitation center. These centers offer residential programs and provide psychological counseling, education, group therapy and nutritional guidance. Sometimes extended rehabilitation (six months to a year) in a long-term center or halfway house is advised.

Recovery is likely to be more successful if treatment is followed up by further counseling (particularly if there are underlying mental and emotional disorders), and regular attendance at Narcotics Anonymous (NA) meetings. NA is a self-help program run along similar lines to Alcoholics Anonymous. At NA meetings, recovering drug users share their stories, and support each other in leading healthy, fulfilling lives.

Social consequences

Drug dependence is a social problem imposing massive personal and social costs. It is perpetuated by a constant supply of illegal drugs which has become a worldwide industry fueled by criminal activity in drug agriculture and manufacturing, the transfer of huge sums of money between countries, and the distribution to users. The huge illegal rewards of this trade provide funds and opportunity for corruption of officials at every stage. The cost to nations is increased medical care, loss of productivity, street crime and violence.

SEE ALSO *Alcoholism, Anxiolytics, Barbiturates, Cocaine, Detoxification, Hallucinogens, Heroin, Marijuana, Methadone, Morphine, Narcotics, Nicotine, Psychosis, Psychotropic drugs, Sedatives, Solvent sniffing, Stimulants, Tranquilizers, Withdrawal*

DRUG INTERACTIONS

Drugs can interact with other chemicals in the body, and these include other drugs. Chemical interactions between drugs may change the make-up of those drugs and render them ineffective, less (or more) effective, or toxic (poisonous).

The risk of adverse drug interactions is higher in older people, because their vital organs process drugs less easily and because they tend to have more diseases and take more drugs than younger persons.

The following types of drugs commonly interact with other medications: antibiotics, anticoagulants, anticonvulsants, antidepressants, antihypertensives, decongestants, and sedatives. Common antibiotics (such as ampicillin, amoxycillin, neomycin and tetracycline) and anticonvulsants can interfere with the effect of oral contraceptives (birth control pills), and increase the risk of pregnancy.

Special care should be taken with heart drugs. The combination of beta-blockers and calcium channel blockers, for example, may slow the heart rate excessively or cause heart failure. Beta-blockers can aggravate asthma and prevent diabetic patients from recognizing the signs of low blood pressure due to an insulin reaction. The combination of calcium channel blockers and digoxin can also slow the heart rate. Angiotensin-converting enzyme (ACE) inhibitors can cause dangerously high potassium levels in people who use potassium supplements. Diuretics combined with digoxin can cause dangerously low potassium or magnesium levels, which can cause heart arrhythmias.

Certain foods or beverages can interfere with drugs as well. Foods most likely to interfere with medications include dairy products, alcohol, caffeine, salt, and fruit juices. For instance, some antidepressants (those known as MAO inhibitors) are dangerous when consumed with anything containing tyramine (such as red wine, cheese and beer). It is advisable not to take over the counter drugs with other medications. Many common medications contain the same antihistamines as anti-cold preparations; you can get an unexpected double dose by taking an allergy drug along with some cold remedies.

Harmful interactions can also occur between herbal products and drugs. Warfarin taken with ginseng, garlic, ginkgo, ginger and feverfew may result in bleeding. Echinacea and zinc may negate the effects of cyclosporine. Ginseng may interfere with digoxin. It may also cause headaches, trembling, or manic episodes if taken with phenelzine sulfate. Saint John's wort and saw palmetto may inhibit anemia drugs. Drugs can also interact with alcohol and tobacco; smoking reduces the effectiveness of many medications.

Always ask your physician or pharmacist if the drug you have been prescribed can interact with any foods, other medications, or herbal remedies you may be taking.

SEE ALSO *Antibiotics, Anticoagulants, Anticonvulsants, Antidepressants, Antihistamines, Beta-blockers, Diuretics, Sedatives*

D

DRUGS

A drug (also called a medication or a pharmaceutical) is a compound that is introduced into the body for a therapeutic effect, to cure a disease or to relieve or control the symptoms of a disease. There are thousands of drugs available. Common types of drugs include antibiotics, vaccines, antiserums and immunoglobulins, cardiovascular drugs, analgesics, anesthetics, sedatives, hypnotics, diuretics, hormones and vitamins.

Some drugs are available only with a prescription from a physician, while others are available "over the counter" from a drugstore, pharmacy or other outlet. Drugs may be sold under a particular brand name, or they may be "generic"; that is, sold unbranded. Generic drugs are often cheaper than branded drugs. Drugs (for example, antibiotics) may need to be taken for a short period, e.g. an acute chest infection, or they may need to be continued for life, for example insulin for certain diabetics.

Administering drugs

Drugs are usually administered either orally or by injection. Oral medications can be taken as syrup, capsules or tablets. They are absorbed in the small intestine along with food. Injected drugs can be administered via intramuscular or intravenous routes; drugs administered intravenously begin acting almost immediately, while those administered intramuscularly can take minutes or hours to take effect, depending on the drug.

Occasionally a drug many be given subcutaneously, that is, injected into the tissue below the skin. Some drugs can be inhaled, such as asthma medications. Others can be administered as suppositories, placed into and absorbed via the rectum.

Side effects

Drugs may have side effects, which differ from person to person. Some are minor and can be tolerated; nausea and a skin rash, for example, are common to many drugs. In other cases side effects can cause serious illness. If side effects are not outweighed by the medical benefits of taking the drug, the drug should be discontinued. Drugs may produce allergic reactions in some people.

Allergic reactions may range from a slight rash to a fatal shock. It is not possible to predict whether someone will have an allergic reaction to a prescribed drug, though they are more common in older persons. One of the biggest risk factors is a previous reaction to a drug, since drug-induced immune responses may persist for years. A drug that causes an allergic reaction should be discontinued. The reaction may require antihistamines or corticosteroids.

Some medications can cause birth defects, especially when taken early on in pregnancy. A physician should always be consulted before taking a drug during pregnancy. In general, physicians are reluctant to prescribe drugs unless necessary, though some believe reluctance to take drugs during pregnancy does more harm than good.

Drug resistance

Drug resistance has emerged as a major problem in recent years, particularly in the case of antibiotics. Increasingly, disease-causing organisms are able to resist eradication, making infections more difficult to treat. To avoid resistance, antibiotics should only be used against microorganisms sensitive to them (and not against viruses, for example). Inadequate duration of treatment also leads to resistance, so the full course of antibiotics should always be completed.

SEE ALSO *Allergies, Analgesics, Anesthesia, Antihistamines, Corticosteroids, Diuretics, Hormones, Hypnotics, Immunization, Insulin, Sedatives, Vitamins*

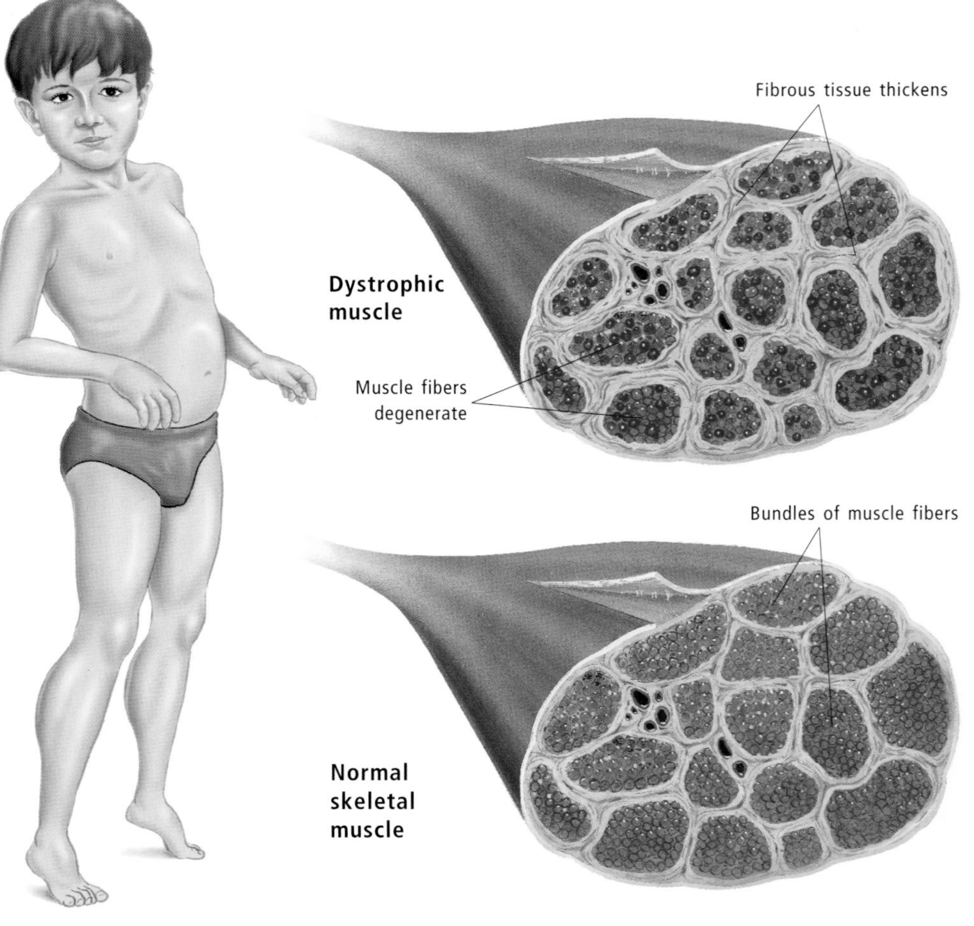

Duchenne muscular dystrophy

This disease affects young boys, and usually presents as muscle weakness in and around the pelvis. The weakness spreads to the limbs and as muscles weaken they also enlarge. Progressive muscle wasting and weakness occurs in Duchenne muscular dystrophy when the normal structure of skeletal muscle deteriorates. Individual muscle fibers degenerate, while the tissue that surrounds them thickens.

D

DUCHENNE MUSCULAR DYSTROPHY

This is a rare inherited disorder caused by an abnormal gene that causes rapidly progressing weakness of the muscles. It is the most serious of the muscular dystrophies, a group of disorders that cause malfunction and degeneration of voluntary muscles.

Duchenne muscular dystrophy occurs in boys from infancy to age six. There is progressive muscle weakness and wasting of muscles, especially in the legs and pelvis. Heart muscle is damaged and the bones of the chest become malformed, causing respiratory difficulty. By their teens, most sufferers are confined to a wheelchair. There is no known cure, and sufferers usually die by their mid-teens. The disorder can be detected in the fetus by genetic studies performed during pregnancy.

SEE ALSO *Congenital abnormalities, Genetic counseling, Muscle, Muscular dystrophy*

DUMPING SYNDROME

Dumping syndrome is a digestion disorder that occurs in a patient who has had an operation to remove part or all of the stomach. Most patients experience the problem to a minor degree for one to six months after the surgery, but in about 1–2 percent of cases, symptoms persist. The cause of dumping syndrome is not fully understood; however the symptoms result from the remnants of the stomach "dumping" its contents too quickly into the small intestine after a meal. The affected person experiences explosive diarrhea, abdominal cramps, belching and vomiting. There may also be headache, dizziness and sweating.

The condition can be relieved by eating several small meals instead of one or two large ones per day. The meals should be low in carbohydrates and high in fat and protein. Most affected persons recover spontaneously within a few months to a year.

SEE ALSO *Diarrhea, Digestive system, Intestines, Stomach*

DUODENAL ULCERS

The duodenum is that part of the gut immediately beyond the stomach. Ulcers are formed when the mucus and internal epithelium (lining) of the gut are broken down, e.g. by aspirin-like drugs or the *Helicobacter* bacterium, thus exposing the deeper layers of the gut wall. Duodenal ulcers belong to a group of diseases of the gut called peptic ulcers. These peptic ulcers arise when the highly damaging stomach juices, which contain acid and enzymes designed to break down protein, erode the surface of the stomach or duodenum.

Patients with duodenal ulcers often complain of pain in the upper abdomen, which is usually relieved by food, milk or antacid preparations. They may also be tender in the upper abdomen and may occasionally experience vomiting. Complications of duodenal ulcers include heavy bleeding, obstruction of the duodenum, or perforation of the duodenal wall with spilling of the duodenal contents into the abdominal cavity. The last complication may cause life-threatening peritonitis, or inflammation of the tissues of the abdominal cavity.

SEE ALSO *Duodenum, Peptic ulcers, Stomach*

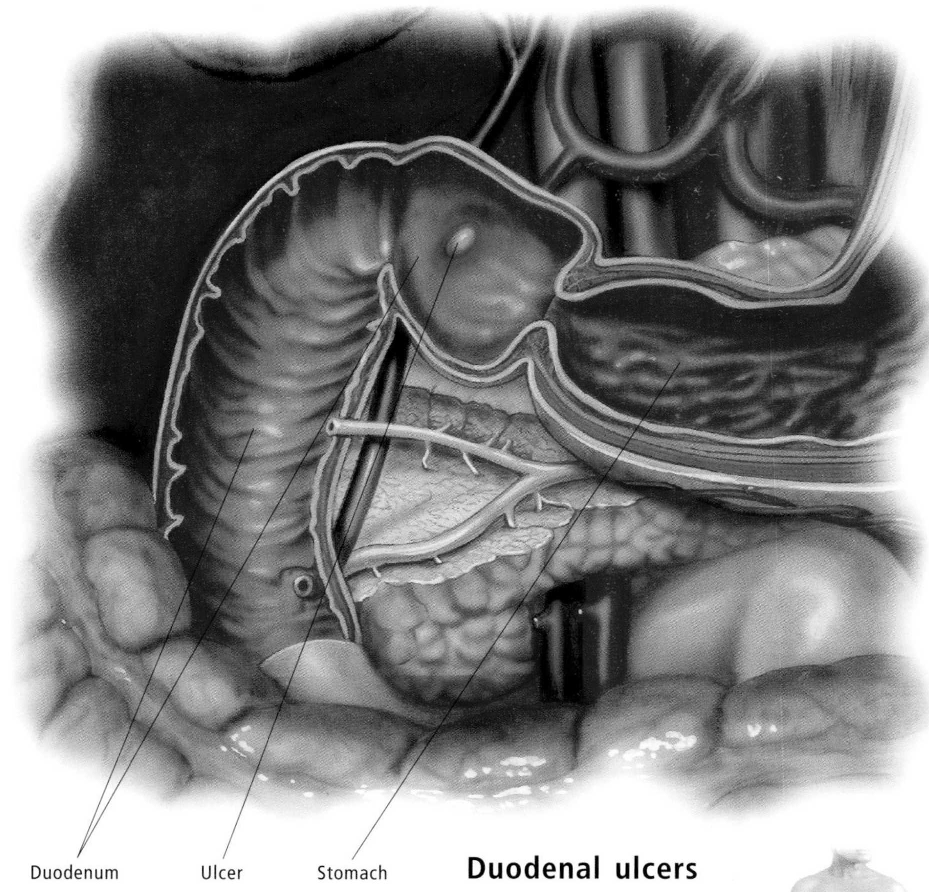

Duodenal ulcers

A round or oval sore is formed when the lining of the duodenum is eroded by stomach juices. These ulcers are the most common type of peptic ulcer.

DUODENUM

The duodenum is the part of the gut directly beyond the stomach and is the first part of the small intestine. It has a "C" shape, with the curvature of the "C" encircling the head of the pancreas. The duodenum receives the contents of the stomach once the stomach has added digestive enzymes and acid to the food and begun the digestion of protein. This means that the duodenum must be able to withstand periodic exposure to the highly acid stomach contents. The duodenum is also the site where bile, from the liver and gallbladder, and pancreatic enzymes, from the pancreas, are brought into contact with food.

The interior of the duodenum has a folded surface, which increases the available surface area for absorption of sugars, fats and amino acids. While some of the absorp-

D

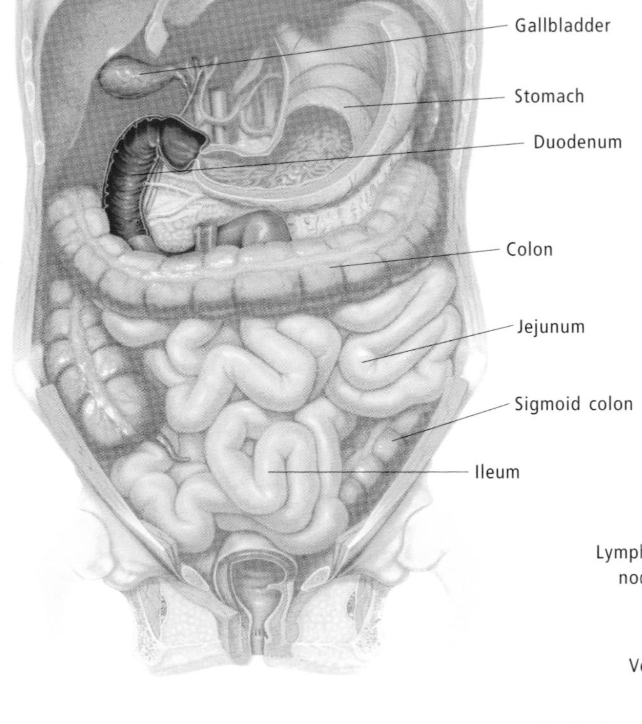

Duodenum

The first 10 inches (25 centimeters) of the small intestine is known as the duodenum. It receives the contents of the stomach, including digestive enzymes and acid, and is the site where bile is brought into contact with food.

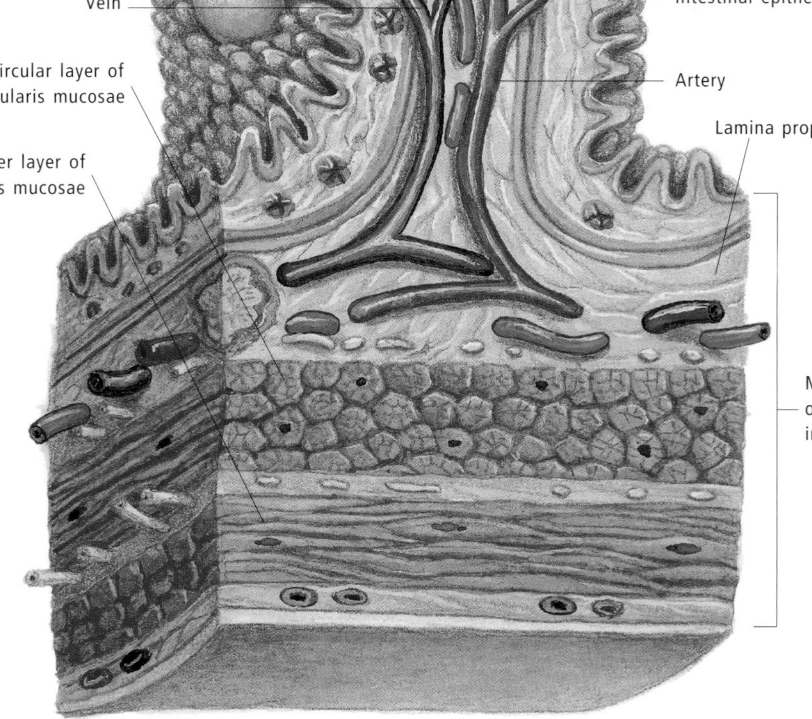

Duodenal lining

The wall of the duodenum has folds covered in tiny finger-like villi which increase the surface area available for the absorption of sugars, fats and amino acids. Fat and lipids are absorbed by the lymphatic nodules; sugars and amino acids are absorbed into the bloodstream through the arteries.

tion of these nutrients will begin in the duodenum, the other parts of the small intestine, the jejunum and ileum, will continue the process.

The duodenum is a common place for ulcers to occur because of its periodic exposure to stomach juices. It is only very rarely the primary site of malignant disease (cancer).

SEE ALSO *Duodenal ulcers, Gallbladder, Ileum, Intestines, Liver, Pancreas*

DUPUYTREN'S CONTRACTURE

Dupuytren's contracture is a painless thickening and contracture of the connective tissue beneath the skin on the palm of the hand. A small, painless nodule eventually develops into a cord-like band, which prevents the fingers from straightening. The fourth and fifth fingers are the most affected. In advanced cases, the hand looks like a claw. One or both hands may be affected. Sometimes it can affect the soles of the feet as well.

The cause is not known, but it may be inherited. It is more common in men over the age of forty, and in alcoholics and persons with diabetes or epilepsy. Treatment may involve an operation to remove the thickened fibrous tissue and release the ligaments, followed by physical therapy. This usually restores normal movement of the fingers.

SEE ALSO *Connective tissue, Finger, Hand*

DWARFISM

Dwarfism is the condition of being abnormally small in physical stature. A dwarf may be born normal, but growth is arrested during the childhood years because of malnutrition, chronic illness or growth hormone deficiency. The affected person (also known as a midget) has normal body proportions but is smaller than normal.

So-called "true" or genetic dwarfism is congenital (present at birth) and results in abnormal body proportions, that is, disproportionate stunting. Achondroplasia, in which growth of the bones of the limbs is retarded, is the most common form of congenital dwarfism. An achondroplastic dwarf has a normal-sized head and trunk, but proportionally short arms and legs.

SEE ALSO *Achondroplasia, Growth disorders, Pituitary gland*

DYSARTHRIA

Dysarthria is difficulty in speaking. It differs from dysphasia (aphasia) in that in dysarthria, the speech impediment is due to inability to articulate speech rather than inability to recognize and formulate speech.

Dysarthria may be caused by poorly fitting dentures, alcohol intoxication, stroke affecting the part of the cortex which controls face or larynx muscles, or damage to the nerves that supply those muscles. It may be temporary and reversible as in alcohol intoxication, or permanent as in nerve injury. In irreversible cases, speech therapy may improve the symptoms.

SEE ALSO *Aphasia, Dysphasia, Speech*

DYSENTERY

Dysentery is an inflammatory disease of the large bowel, common in tropical areas where living conditions are crowded and sanitation is poor. In areas of Africa, Latin America, Southeast Asia and India, it is endemic.

In humans there are two main forms: bacterial dysentery (caused by the bacterium *Shigella sonnei*), and amebic dysentery (caused by an ameba, *Entamoeba histolytica*). Both forms are transmitted by fecally contaminated drinking water or food, or hand to hand contact. Amebic dysentery is also spread by flies and cockroaches.

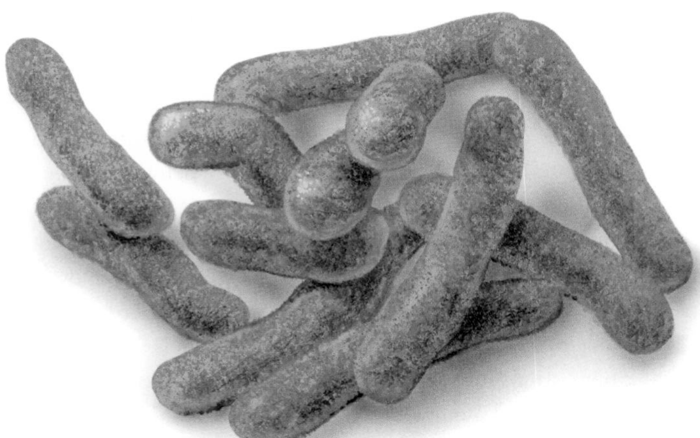

Dysentery

There are two main forms of dysentery: bacillary, caused by *Shigella* bacteria (shown here) and amebic, caused by *Entamoeba histolytica*.

Both forms of dysentery cause severe diarrhea often with blood and mucus in the stools, abdominal pain and sometimes contracting spasms of the anus with a persistent desire to empty the bowels. The infection may spread through the blood to the liver, lungs, brain or other organs.

Shigella infections are mild and usually curable in a week or so with antibiotics such as ampicillin or trimethoprim. However, in a severe attack, excessive dehydration can be fatal (especially in infants and young children); serious cases require hospital care and intravenous fluid supplements.

Amebic dysentery causes attacks that come and go for months before the diagnosis is made, and which may be complicated by abscesses, particularly liver abscesses. Drugs such as metronidazole or idoquinol are usually successful in treating the condition. In tropical areas where food or water may be contaminated, one should avoid eating uncooked foods and ensure that foods are hygienically prepared. Drinking water should be boiled and foods covered to prevent flies from contaminating them.

SEE ALSO *Bacteria, Bowel, Dehydration, Diarrhea, Intestines*

DYSKINESIA

Dyskinesia is a syndrome in which there are dysfunctional involuntary movements of various body parts. These abnormal movements usually occur as side effects of medications taken to treat psychiatric or neurological conditions such as schizophrenia or Parkinson's disease. They may manifest as writhing, wriggling or jerking of body parts such as the body trunk, legs, arms, fingers, mouth, lips, or tongue. There may be facial tics, grimacing, eye blinking, lip smacking, tongue thrusting, moving one's head back or to the side, foot tapping, ankle movements, shuffled gait, and head nodding. As well as being socially embarrassing, these abnormal movements may cause difficulty walking and standing, eating and breathing. There are various forms of dyskinesia, including acute dystonia, tardive dyskinesia, akathisia and Parkinsonian syndrome. The most common is tardive dyskinesia, which is associated with long-term use of antipsychotic medications such as haldoperidol, fluphenazine, and chlorpromazine. Tardive dyskinesia may appear anywhere from three months to several years after initial use of these medications, and withdrawal from these drugs often makes the symptoms worse. If dyskinesia appears, the drug(s) which caused the symptoms must be discontinued.

Medications such as propanalol, amantadine, bromocriptine and diazepam can be given to counteract the symptoms of dykinesia but their effect is variable. The dosage of antipsychotic drugs and other medications that may cause dyskinesia should be kept as low as possible to prevent the syndrome from developing.

SEE ALSO *Antipsychotics, Parkinson's disease, Schizophrenia*

DYSLEXIA

Dyslexia is a disability which makes learning to read difficult. It can affect both children and adults despite a normal intellect and satisfactory education. Originally a catchword which covered various disorders, the term dyslexia came to refer to all types of reading, writing and spelling problems.

D

There is currently no internationally agreed definition of dyslexia and for that reason not all educators and psychologists will use the term. Dyslexia, as it is now generally understood, refers to its key feature: a substantial difficulty in gaining effective reading skills. Dyslexia was originally thought of a as a disability produced by poor sight, but it is now seen as result of abnormal brain function. There is no proven genetic basis for the condition, but current research into families with many affected members suggests that it may be inherited. The degree of intellectual ability plays no part, as dyslexia sufferers often score above average in non-language based intelligence tests. Unlike the ability to speak, which is innate in humans, reading skills are learned.

Children with normal vision learn to read after a gradual acquisition of pre-reading skills—the ability to follow a sequence of characters, the development of a vocabulary of language, the identification of sounds, and the recognition that sounds can be represented by letters.

This last process is one which dyslexic children are unable to develop. They are unable to decode speech into the individual sound components (phonemes) used to build words. There are 40 or more phonemes in the English language. The word pit, for example, is a combination of three sounds: "puh", "ih" and "tuh". It is essential to understand this and be able to associate the individual letters *p, i* and *t* with the sounds they represent before one can recognize the written word. Where the brain cannot hear the individual sounds it cannot make the association between sounds and letters, and reading skills will not properly develop.

Dyslexia is suspected when reading skills fail to match a child's intellectual level, with the key indicator being the inability to decode phonemes. This inability may affect one child in five severely enough to persist into adulthood, and at this level it may not improve with time or instruction, causing academic standards to fall gradually behind.

Identification

Before confirming a diagnosis of dyslexia it is important to investigate other possible reasons for delayed reading development, including poor hearing, poor sight, emotional disorders, environmental or family problems and poor teaching. Dyslexia produces poor readers and writers in children who are otherwise intellectually able, even above average. It has been identified in other cultures with written languages different in form and structure from English, notably Chinese, and it can affect speech.

Although dyslexia has previously been identified more in boys than girls, recent research indicates that both sexes may be represented equally and that girls with problems are simply not being identified.

Treatment

Treatment should always be attempted. It will usually take the form of special instruction aimed at developing awareness of phonemes before moving on to improving word recognition, pronunciation and reading comprehension. With early identification and special instruction it is possible to make dramatic improvements in reading ability in most affected children. Without help, problems may become extremely difficult to fix, with devastating effects on academic achievement, adult life and future employment. Specialist remedial help should always be considered to minimize the possibility of problems extending into adulthood, when they may be considerably more difficult to alleviate.

Famous people with dyslexia include screen actor Tom Cruise, and US decathlon athlete and 1996 Olympic gold medallist, Dan O'Brien.

DYSPHAGIA

Dysphagia refers to difficulty when swallowing. This constant or recurring condition can be caused by a throat disorder, lack of muscle coordination, anxiety disorder, esophageal spasm, or radiation treatment. Medications for treating other illnesses may be a trigger, as can neurological disorders such as stroke, or infections such as diphtheria. Dysphagia can also be an early symptom of cancer of the esophagus or stomach.

Dysphagia often affects elderly people and can cause chronic dehydration and malnutrition if not diagnosed and monitored. It may also cause aspiration pneumonia due

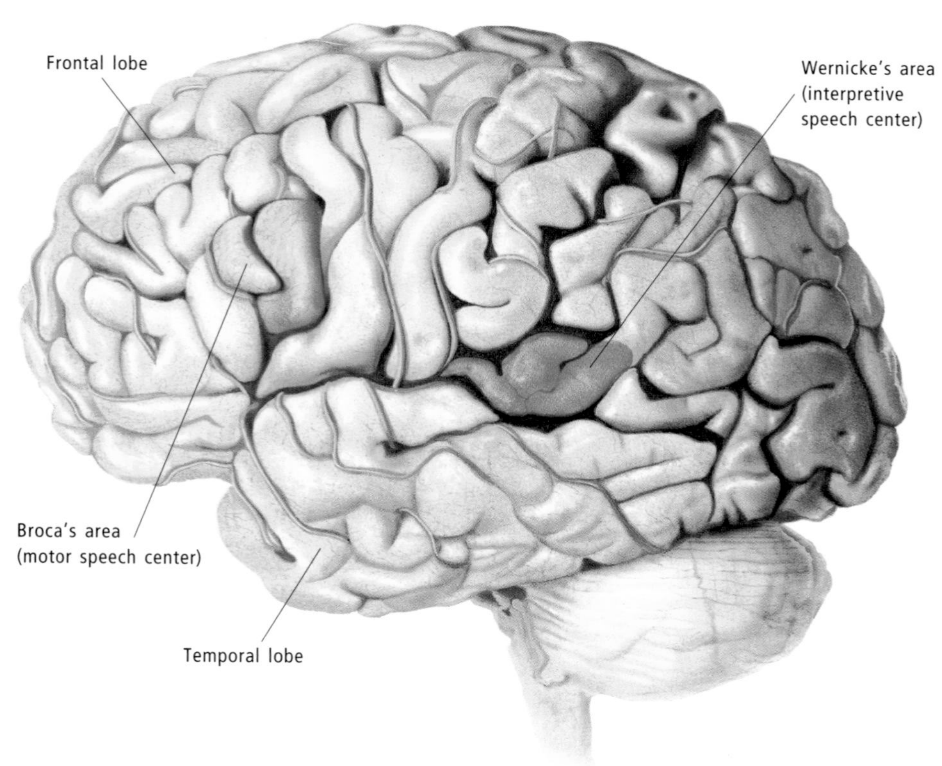

Dysphasia

Damage to the temporal and frontal lobes of the brain can result in impaired speech, known as dysphasia. The type of dysphasia varies depending on which part of the cortex is affected. Damage to Broca's area, for example, causes problems in the formation of words as this area controls motor function. Damage to Wernicke's area affects speech comprehension.

to the inhalation of food, drink, vomit or saliva into the airway. Treatment depends on the cause, though eating slowly and chewing food thoroughly may help.

SEE ALSO *Esophagus, Throat*

DYSPHASIA

Dysphasia is an impairment of speech due to damage to the brain (usually the temporal or frontal lobes). It differs from dysarthria in that the speech impediment in dysphasia is due to damage to the parts of the brain that recognize and formulate speech, whereas dysarthria is an inability to articulate speech.

Dysphasia may be caused by stroke, transient ischemic attack (TIA), head trauma or Alzheimer's disease. The impairment may vary according to which part of the brain is affected. Damage to Wernicke's area in the temporal lobe (the interpretative center) results in trouble understanding speech and the written word. Damage to Broca's area in the frontal lobe (the motor speech area) results in difficulty in mentally constructing written and spoken language. In total dysphasia, both comprehension and language formation are impaired. Speech therapy may improve the symptoms.

SEE ALSO *Aphasia, Dysarthria, Speech, Stroke*

DYSPNEA

Dyspnea is the medical term for the sensation of breathlessness or shortness of breath. The word comes from the Greek "dys-", difficulty + "pnoia", breathing. It may be a normal reaction to greater than usual exertion, such as vigorous physical exercise. However, if shortness of breath occurs without undue physical exertion, it may a sign of serious disease of the airways, lungs, or heart requiring medical attention.

See also Breathing, Lungs

DYSURIA

Dysuria is a medical term for painful or difficult urination. Dysuria is most often a symptom of urinary disorders such as cystitis or stones in the bladder. It may indicate that there is prostate disease such as prostatitis or enlarged prostate. In males, dysuria can be a symptom of gonococcal urethritis or other sexually transmitted diseases.

SEE ALSO *Bladder, Cystitis, Prostate, Urethritis, Urinary systems*

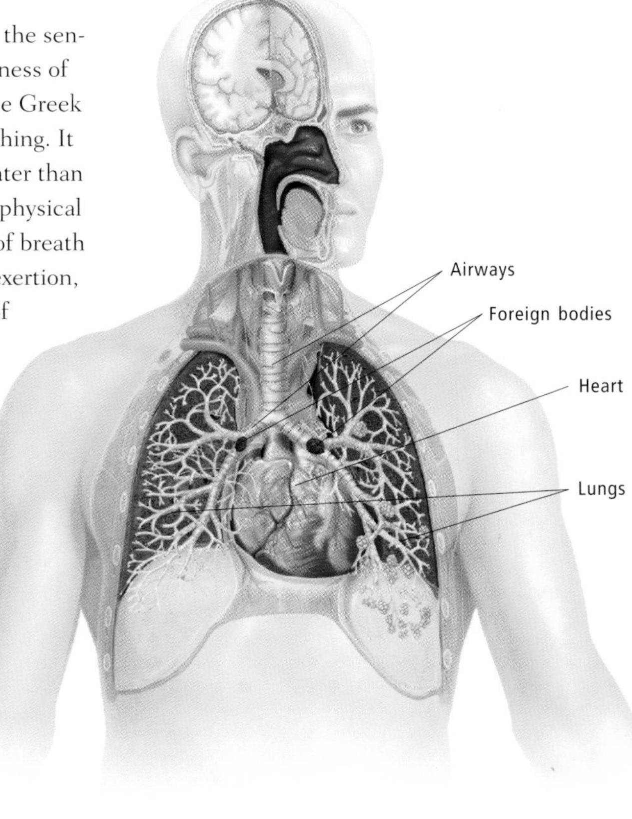

Dyspnea

Shortness of breath may be a sign of disease of the airways, lungs or heart, or obstruction of an airway by a foreign body.

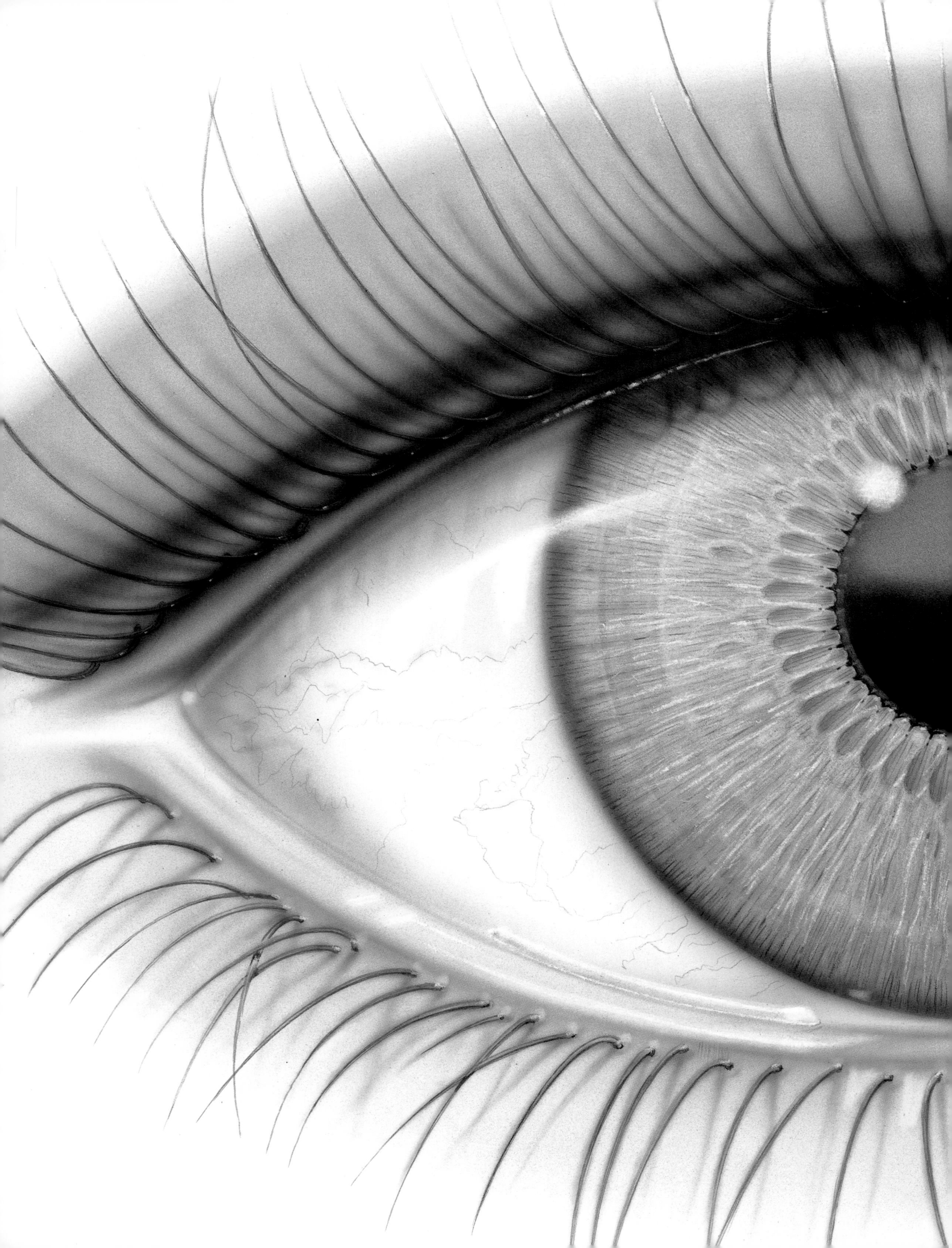

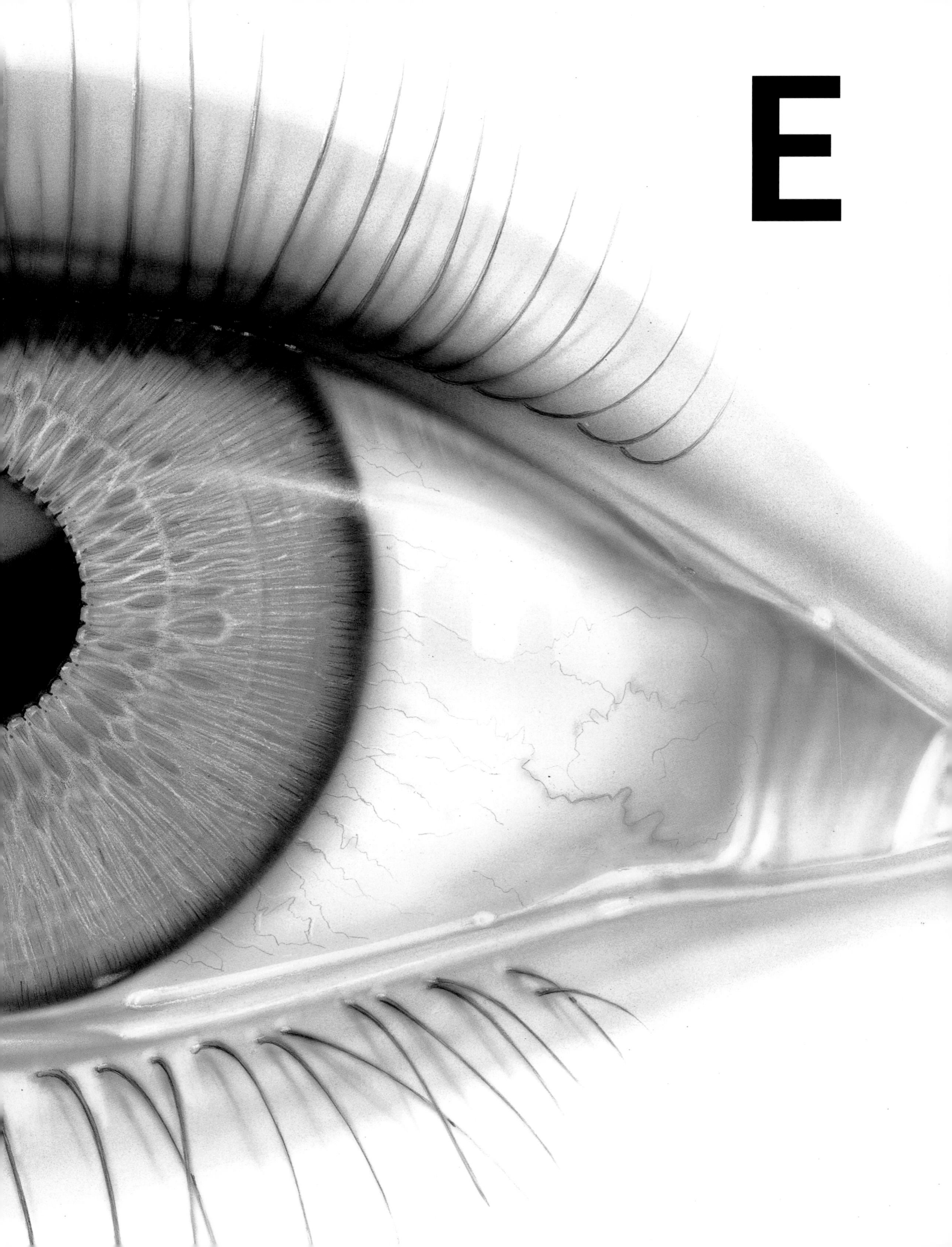
E

EAR

The ear is the organ of hearing and balance. It receives sound waves traveling through the air and changes them first into mechanical vibrations and then into electrical nerve impulses which are sent to the brain and interpreted as sounds. The ear also senses the body's position relative to gravity, sending information to the brain that allows the body to maintain postural equilibrium.

Structure and function

The ear is positioned in a hollow space in the temporal bone of the skull. It is comprised of three separate sections: the outer ear; the middle ear; and the inner ear. Each section has its own function.

The purpose of the outer ear is to collect sound waves and guide them to the tympanic membrane (the eardrum). The outer ear has three parts. The auricle (also called the pinna) funnels sound waves into the external acoustic meatus (or ear canal), a narrow canal that leads to the eardrum.

The eardrum, or tympanic membrane, is a thin, semitransparent membrane, approximately ⅓ inch (9 millimeters) in diameter. It separates the external ear from the middle ear. Wax (also called cerumen) is secreted by glands lining the auditory canal, protecting the eardrum from damage by trapping dust and dirt.

The middle ear is an irregular-shaped, air-filled space, about ¾ inch (19 millimeters) high and ⅕ inch (5 millimeters) wide. It is spanned by three tiny bones: the malleus (hammer); the incus (anvil); and the stapes (stirrup), collectively known as the ossicles.

When sound waves strike the outer surface of the eardrum, they cause the tympanic membrane to vibrate. These vibrations are mechanically transmitted through the middle ear by the ossicles, which relay them to a membrane that covers the opening into the inner ear. This opening is called the oval window.

Connecting the middle ear to the throat is a short narrow passage called the eustachian tube, which helps to ensure equal air pressure on both sides of the eardrum.

The function of the inner ear is to turn the mechanical vibrations received from the ossicles of the middle ear into nerve impulses. The inner ear contains a structure

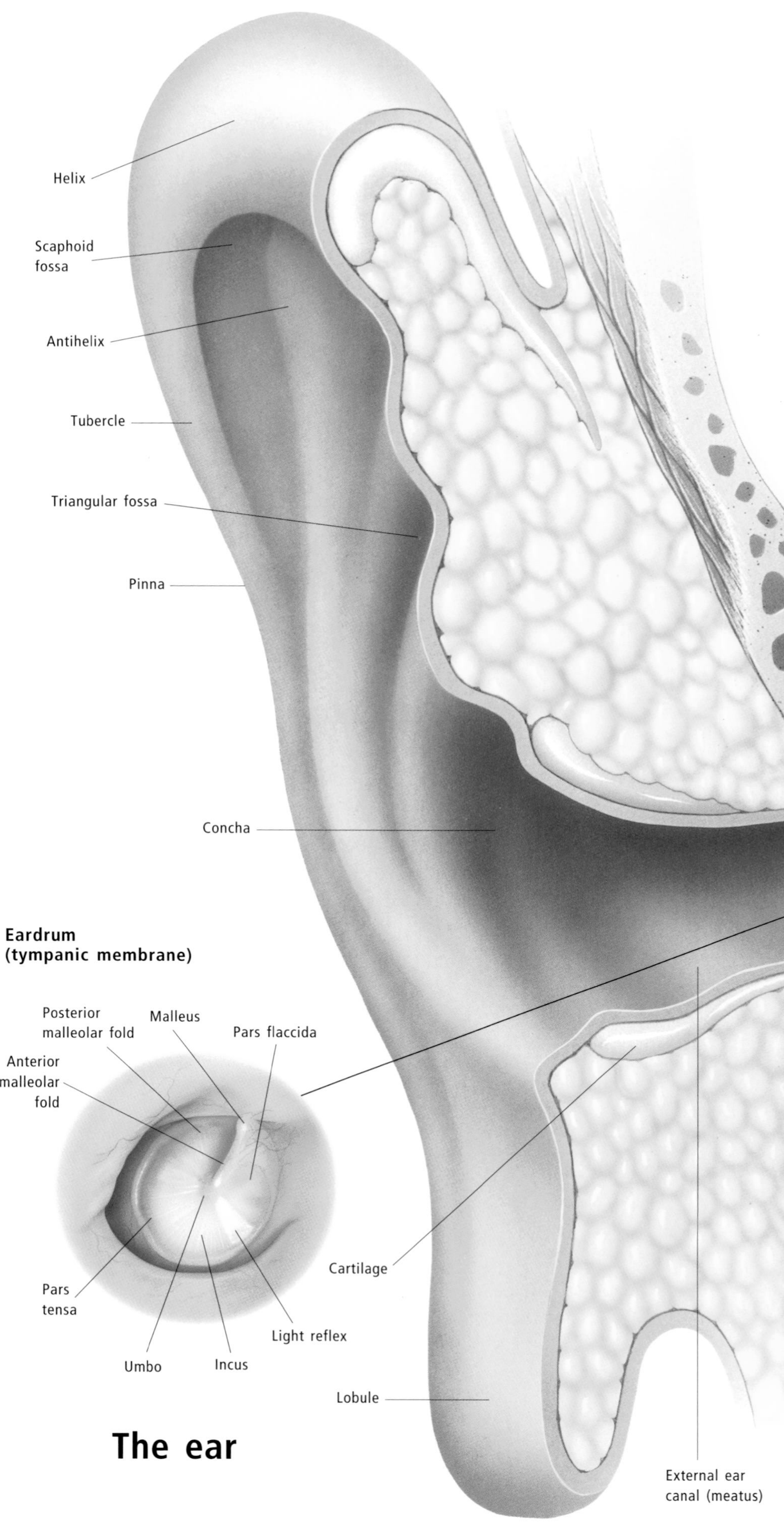

The ear

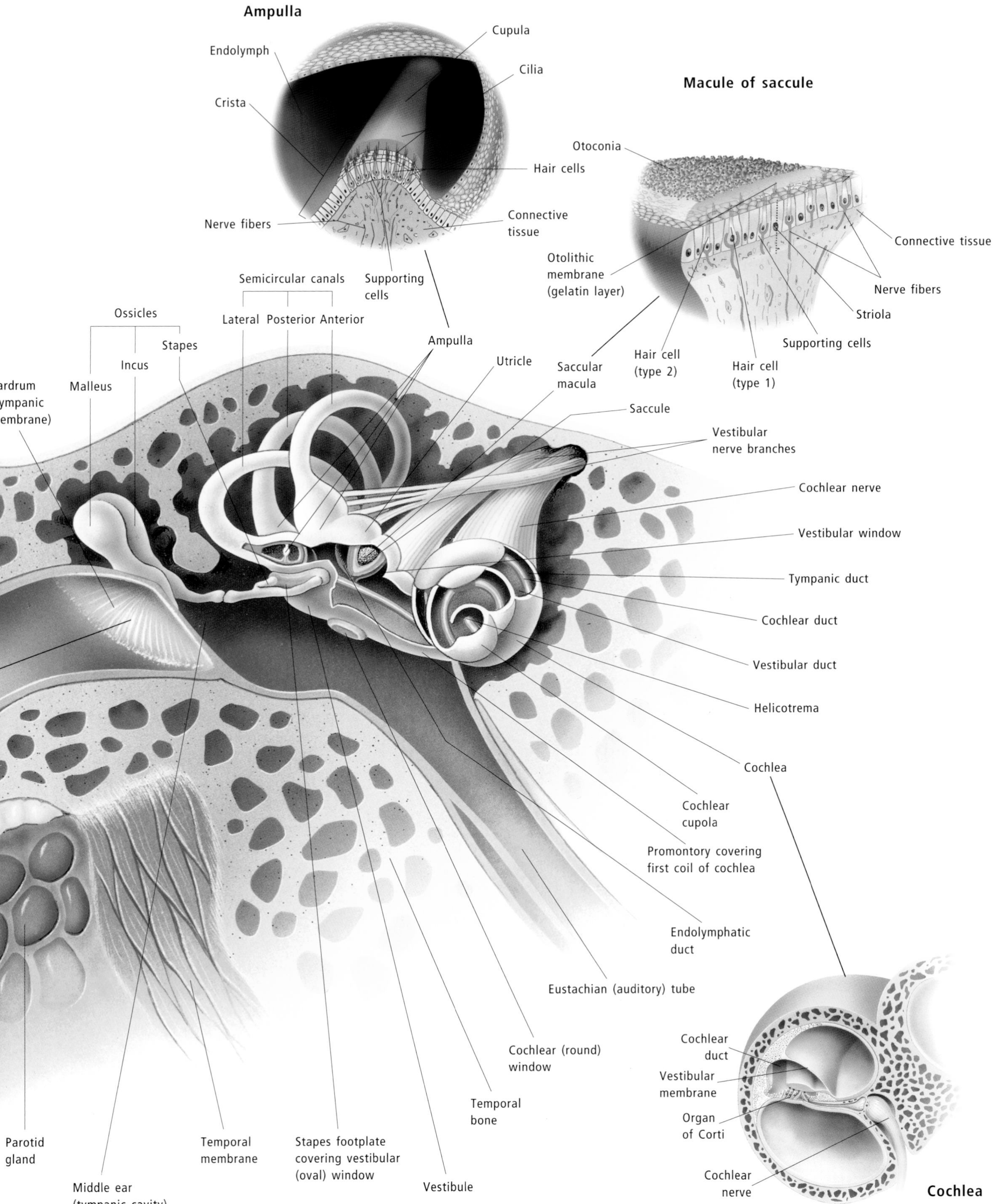
Ampulla
Endolymph
Cupula
Cilia
Crista
Hair cells
Nerve fibers
Connective tissue
Supporting cells
Macule of saccule
Otoconia
Connective tissue
Otolithic membrane (gelatin layer)
Nerve fibers
Striola
Supporting cells
Hair cell (type 2)
Hair cell (type 1)
Semicircular canals
Lateral
Posterior
Anterior
Ossicles
Stapes
Incus
Malleus
ardrum
tympanic
nembrane)
Ampulla
Utricle
Saccular macula
Saccule
Vestibular nerve branches
Cochlear nerve
Vestibular window
Tympanic duct
Cochlear duct
Vestibular duct
Helicotrema
Cochlea
Cochlear cupola
Promontory covering first coil of cochlea
Endolymphatic duct
Eustachian (auditory) tube
Cochlear (round) window
Temporal bone
Parotid gland
Temporal membrane
Stapes footplate covering vestibular (oval) window
Vestibule
Middle ear (tympanic cavity)
Cochlear duct
Vestibular membrane
Organ of Corti
Cochlear nerve
Cochlea

E

called the cochlea, a small, spiral-shaped structure containing fluid and special hairs which serve as sound sensors.

The vibrations of the membrane covering the oval window cause waves to form in the cochlear fluid. These vibrations are picked up by the organ of Corti, the hearing organ housed in the cochlea. The organ of Corti contains tiny hairlike nerve endings anchored in a membrane that extends the length of the cochlea.

These nerve endings are highly specialized endings of the eighth cranial nerve, also called the vestibulocochlear nerve. When vibrations in the fluid reach them, these nerve endings fire off electrical impulses, which are sent along the nerve to the brain to be interpreted as sounds.

The inner ear is also the organ of equilibrium, or balance. It contains tiny organs that sense the body's relationship to gravity. A person knows which way is up because these organs send information to the brain about the body's position. Comprised of the utricle, the saccule and the three semicircular canals, they are collectively known as the vestibular organs.

Both the utricle and the saccule are hollow sacs filled with a gelatinous fluid called endolymph. Fixed into the inner surface of each of them are tiny, hair-like structures, the free ends of which project into the hollow space. Crystals of calcium carbonate, known as otoliths, lie over the hair cells; when the head is tilted, the otoliths change position. In shifting, they pass over the hair cells, which in turn generate impulses which are sent to the brain. The brain then triggers the body's reflex mechanisms to correct the position of the body.

The three semicircular canals act in a similar way. Fluid-filled tubes, they are placed at right angles to each other. They connect with the utricle and contain hair cells in the ampulla. When the head turns, fluid flows through the canals, stimulating the hair cells to send signals to the brain about the position of the body.

Diseases of the ear

The three parts of the ear are affected by disease or injury in different ways. Disorders of the outer ear are mainly related to disorders of the skin, glands and hair follicles in the outer ear canal. Infection and inflammation can affect the middle ear and (rarely) the inner ear.

Inflammation of the outer ear is called otitis externa and is usually caused by a bacterial or fungal infection, most commonly from swimming in polluted water. Symptoms are itching and pain and a slight discharge from the ear. The condition is treated with antibiotic ear drops in the affected ear.

Some people may experience some degree of hardened wax build-up in the ear. Wax in the outer part of the ear can be removed by wiping it away with a clean, damp washcloth. Never try to reach the wax in the ear canal with a cotton swab or a finger, as you may push the wax deeper into the ear canal. Instead, the wax must be removed by a physician who will syringe it out with warm water. The wax may be softened first with a warm solution of olive oil, bicarbonate of soda, or an over-the-counter solution for softening earwax.

After swimming or washing the hair, water may be trapped in the ear canal if there is wax in it, causing temporary deafness. If this happens, tip your head to one side and gently pull the external ear forward. The water will then flow out of the ear.

Children commonly push small objects into the ear. Parents should never try to remove anything lodged in the ear, but instead should seek professional aid. Similarly, if an insect lodges in the ear, see a physician.

A perforated or "burst" eardrum is a painful injury which can lead to partial hearing loss and discharge of fluid or blood from the

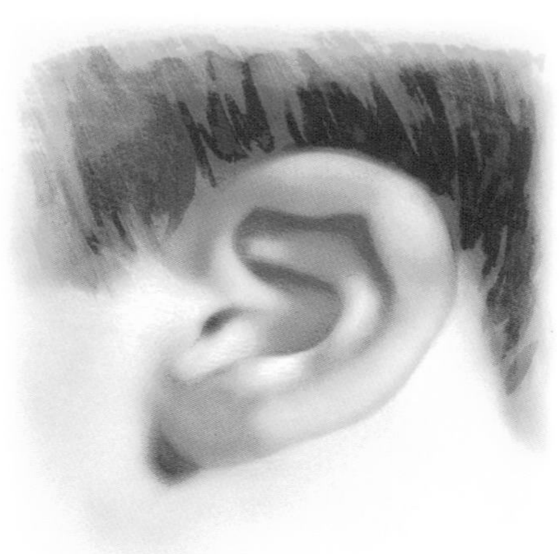

Child

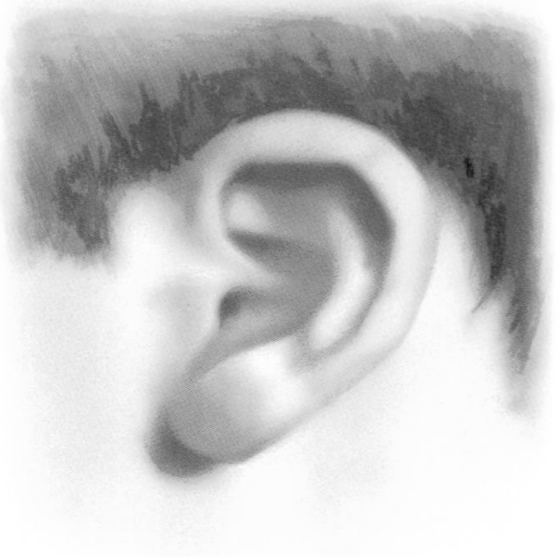

Adolescent

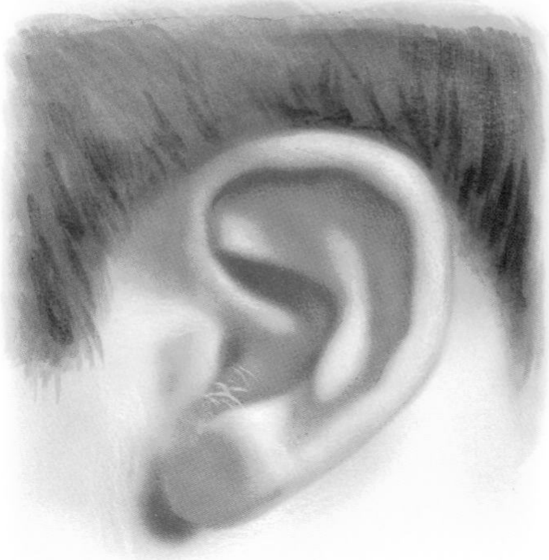

Adult

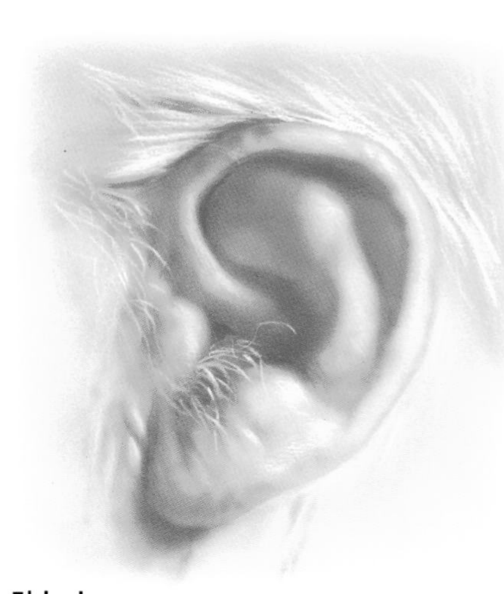

Elderly

Ageing of the ear

As the ear ages, the lobe becomes fleshier and longer. Hairs begin to grow on the lobes and in the ear canal. The skin becomes dryer, thinner and wrinkled. Brown age spots may appear. The ear is one of the few body organs that can continue to grow throughout the body's lifetime.

ear. It is caused by a sudden inward pressure on the eardrum such as that from an explosion, a foreign object being pushed into the ear, a slap or diving too deep when scuba diving. If left alone, the eardrum is often able to repair itself, but sometimes surgery may be required if it does not heal. Those with a perforated eardrum can expect to have their hearing restored in one to two weeks, but in some cases healing may take up to two months.

Many conditions of the outer ear are treated with ear drops. Warm the drops by placing the container in a bowl of warm water (though antibiotic drops should not be warmed). Lie the person on their side with the affected ear uppermost. Pull back the earlobe to create as large an opening into the canal as possible. Rest the end of the dropper over the ear opening and allow the drops to trickle gently into the ear. Place a small plug of cotton in the outer ear to prevent the drops from leaking out. The person should continue to lie in this position for about five minutes.

Unless the physician advises otherwise, do not administer ear drops if the eardrum is perforated or if a child has plastic tubes in the ears.

The most common disease of the middle ear is bacterial infection. The medical term for inflammation of the middle ear is otitis media. This condition is very common in children and is most commonly caused by the spread of bacteria from the throat into the middle ear via the eustachian tube (which is shorter in childhood). Usually there is an associated infection of the throat.

Otitis media causes fever, sometimes deafness in the affected ear, and earache that may be severe or mild, due to an accumulation of pus in the middle ear which continues to accumulate until it may rupture the eardrum. Treatment with painkillers and antibiotics cures the condition.

However, some children experience recurrent attacks of otitis media; in others the condition may become persistent (chronic). This is known as glue ear, and it may cause deafness. This is a very common in some populations, and can have a detrimental effect on children's learning and development. Treatment is with antibiotics and the insertion of a small plastic tube (grommet) into the affected ear(s) to allow pus to drain.

Glue ear

When children have glue ear (persistent otitis media), a grommet is inserted to allow drainage.

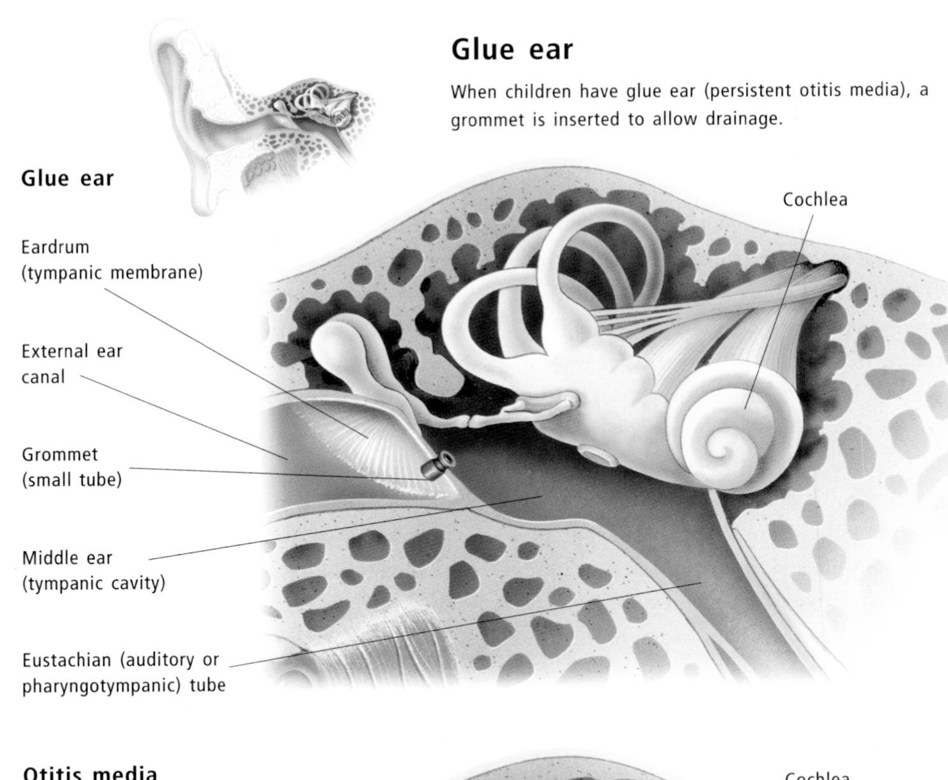

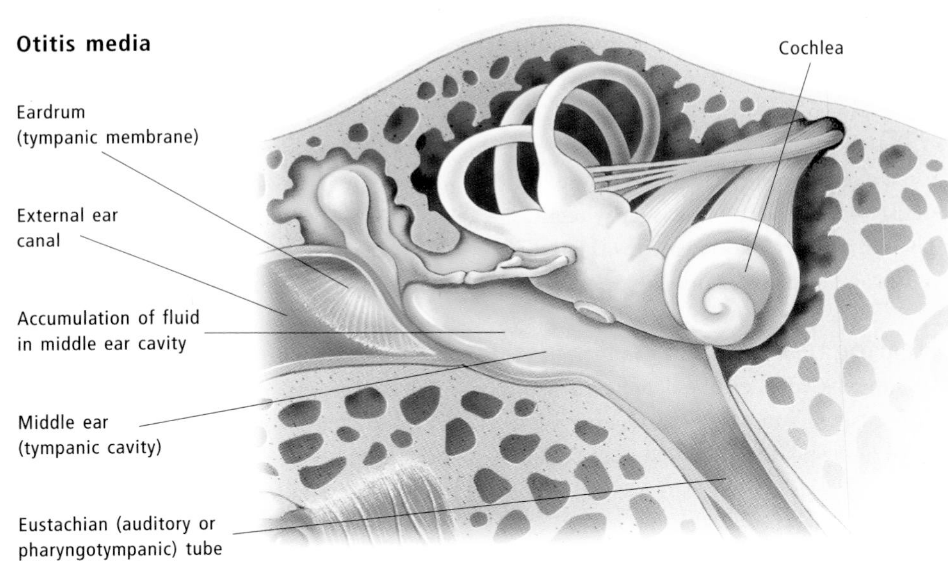

In some cases, an acute infection in the middle ear may spread to the mastoid bone, located behind the ear (mastoiditis). The symptoms include fever and a throbbing earache. The mastoid bone may be tender, and the ear may discharge pus. Treatment with antibiotic drugs cures most cases, but if treatment has been delayed and there is necrosis (death) of bone, surgical removal of part of the mastoid bone may be necessary.

Otosclerosis is a disorder of the middle ear in which there is a gradual build-up of abnormal spongy bone tissue around the footplate of the stapes (one of the ossicles), impeding their function and causing gradual deafness. It is most commonly seen in women between the ages of 15 to 30, and may be triggered by pregnancy. A family history of the condition is common, though the exact cause is unknown. It is treated by surgical replacement of most of the rigid stapes bone with a prosthesis (stapedectomy).

Diseases affecting the inner ear may cause deafness, tinnitus (ringing in the ear) and vertigo (the sensation that one's self or surroundings are spinning). A common inner ear disease is congenital nerve deafness, which is caused by a defect of the hearing nerves in the cochlea. This may be present at birth or may develop during, or soon after, birth. Usually both inner ears are affected, causing (often severe) deafness.

Some drugs, such as aspirin and some antibiotics, can cause damage to the hair cells in the inner ear, which may be permanent. Exposure to loud noise may also cause temporary or permanent hearing damage. A single loud noise such as an explosion may produce severe and permanent deafness. Repeated exposures to sounds that reach more than 80–90 decibels (for example, listening to rock bands) may cause a more gradual loss of hearing. Anyone who is likely to be exposed to noise levels greater than this should wear earplugs or ear protectors.

Labyrinthitis is inflammation of the labyrinth (another term for the inner ear). It is usually caused by a virus and is accompanied by vertigo, nausea and vomiting. Menière's disease is a disorder of the inner ear arising from changes in the pressure of fluid within the vestibular organs. Symptoms include attacks of severe dizziness, nausea, vomiting, tinnitus and fluctuating hearing loss in the affected ear. The cause is not known.

Both labyrinthitis and Menière's disease usually clear up spontaneously in one to six weeks, but Menière's disease may recur. The symptoms can be treated with antihistamines and antinausea drugs.

Hearing tests and aids

Hearing disorders can be detected by a physician using a tuning fork. Audiometry is a more sophisticated technique that demonstrates the extent of hearing loss, and determines whether it has occurred in the upper or lower frequencies.

Abnormal hearing can frequently be improved by hearing-aid devices. If hearing loss is permanent and disabling, the use of sign-language and lip-reading may also become necessary.

A cochlear implant is a system of tiny electrodes which are surgically inserted into the inner ear and which transmit sound vibrations to the auditory nerve. It restores hearing to a person whose cochlea has been impaired by congenital deafness, trauma, drug toxicity or infection.

SEE ALSO *Audiometry, Balance, Cochlea, Deafness, Hearing, Labyrinthitis, Mastoiditis, Menière's disease, Otitis externa, Otitis media, Otosclerosis, Semicircular canals, Tinnitus, Vertigo*

EATING DISORDERS

An eating disorder exists where there is persistent abnormal behavior related to meals, specific foods or the intake of food. Eating disorders are always serious because they will almost certainly lead to malnourishment and poor health, and have been the cause of death. People of any age, male or female, can suffer from an eating disorder, but young women seem to be particularly at risk.

When there is strong pressure to conform to the looks and body shapes dictated by fashion, this can set up unrealistic goals and expectations. Dissatisfaction with looks, body shape or weight can cause an obsession with dieting or exercise and a quest for the perfect body. There may be no real need to lose weight, and no possibility of changing basic body shape.

Although friends and family may clearly see that the weight loss is unnecessary and excessive, the person affected may persist, perhaps in secret to avoid interference or criticism, to the point where health is at risk. Before this point is reached, an eating disorder may be suspected.

Diagnosis

It is necessary to differentiate between an eating disorder and what may only be a temporary change in habits. Eating habits may change, especially during periods of physical illness, and this makes it very important to have an accurate diagnosis from a medical practitioner.

Severe under-nourishment will almost certainly require specialized medical help, and a person with an eating disorder may also need counseling or closely supervised psychiatric treatment and dietary re-education in order to establish healthy eating habits.

The most serious and most widely known eating disorders are anorexia nervosa and bulimia nervosa. The disorders have also been associated with severely low self-esteem, obsessive-compulsive disorder and other mental and emotional problems.

Anorexia nervosa

Consciously deciding not to eat, anorexia sufferers are deliberately starving. Refusing food while still feeling hunger, they may be constantly thinking of food but are terrified of gaining weight. The self-image may be distorted: sufferers will persist in believing themselves to be overweight despite a painfully thin appearance. The fear of becoming fat may cause anorexics to deny the pain of hunger, to be excessively choosy about which foods they will eat, and to exercise obsessively. Adolescent girls are the most likely sufferers, but boys, adults, even athletes, can become anorexic.

The causes are widely thought to be cultural—that is, the pressure from society and peer groups to conform to what is currently thought fashionable or beautiful. This pressure is felt strongly by young adults who may become obsessive dieters, reducing weight well below healthy levels.

Anorexics often feel that they are not in charge of their own lives—losing weight is one way of achieving control. Anorexia may also follow weight loss dieting or can result from weight loss after illness.

It is also thought that there may be a biological component to anorexia nervosa, stemming from hormonal or metabolic disorders.

Bulimia nervosa

Overeating or binge eating followed by self-induced vomiting or by purging with laxatives is known as bulimia nervosa. Bulimia sufferers may be of normal weight but are afraid of becoming overweight. Rather than simply starving themselves, they may eat uncontrollably, consuming a large amount of food in a short time. They may then purge themselves by vomiting or taking laxatives, exercise excessively or deny themselves food. They may do one or all these things in secret.

The behavior of bulimia sufferers is out of their control. The cycle of binge eating, followed by purging, then fasting, is a hard one to break. Not being in control may produce feelings of shame, guilt and self-hatred; many sufferers may become depressed and even suicidal.

Either anorexia or bulimia can cause severe weight loss: anorexia because the food intake is too low for the body's needs, and bulimia because the food is ejected before the nutrients can be absorbed by the body. People can suffer from anorexia at some stages in their lives, and bulimia at other stages.

Symptoms
Symptoms of eating disorders may include obsession with eating, exercise or weight loss, and obvious and continuing weight loss below normal levels. The person may become excessively picky about food; could have unusual rituals or quirky behavior around foods or meals; or will not be eating regular meals or will be eating unusually small amounts. The person appears to be eating well but is losing weight, perhaps by secretly vomiting after meals or by constant use of laxatives. Other symptoms include refusal to eat with the family, inability to concentrate and constant tiredness. Girls may cease menstruation—note that starvation in puberty can stop proper physical development, including the start of periods. Feelings of guilt, anxiety or depression may accompany these behavior patterns.

Effects
The effects of eating disorders may include excessive weight loss, weakness, dry skin, and fine hair growth all over the body. Some cases result in death, either from excessive starvation or by suicide due to depression.

The lack of vital nutrients in the body produces the same effects as plain starvation: poor health, dry skin, hair loss and brittle nails are early signs. With constant vomiting, tooth enamel is eroded. Purging through constant use of laxatives can cause stomach cramps—this is common with senna-based laxatives.

Treatment
Early diagnosis of anorexia or bulimia is vital. Specialist treatment can then be considered. The first priority is to remedy the damage from unhealthy eating, then to correct problems that have caused the disorder.

People who suffer eating disorders generally recover under treatment, but are likely to have continuing problems or adverse health effects throughout their lives. Early diagnosis and treatment will minimize the damage. A stay in hospital or treatment as an outpatient may be needed. Group therapy or self-help programs can be beneficial.

The prospect of recovery is good if the person receives specialized help and is willing to work hard. Adolescents can recover spontaneously, but it is important to seek medical assistance early and to recognize that it can take time to get well.

It is always wise to seek the advice and supervision of a qualified medical practitioner or dietitian before modifying the diet of a child, adolescent, pregnant or lactating woman, or when aiming to significantly reduce food intake for weight loss.

SEE ALSO *Diet, Laxatives, Malnutrition, Nutrition*

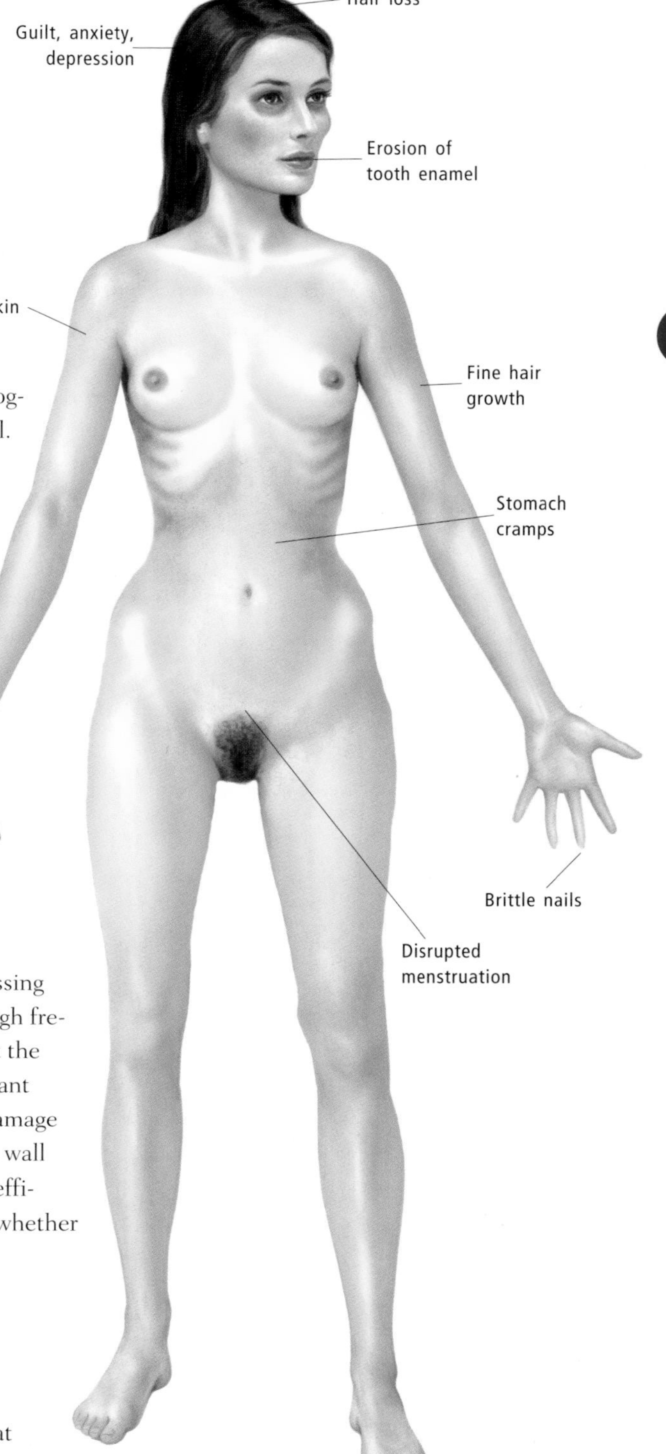

Eating disorder

As well as weight loss, effects of eating disorders can include dry skin, brittle nails, stomach cramps and hair loss. Menstrual periods often cease, and there may be a fine growth of hair over the body.

ECHOCARDIOGRAM
This is a diagnostic method of assessing cardiac health using ultrasound. High frequency sound waves are directed at the heart wall and valves and the resultant echo used to detect an infection, damage or tumors and to measure the heart wall and chamber. The test shows how efficiently the heart pumps blood and whether valves are working properly.

SEE ALSO *Heart*

ECLAMPSIA
Eclampsia is a serious condition that can occur in pregnant women anywhere between the fifth month of pregnancy and the end of the first week after delivery. It is characterized by headaches, high blood pressure, visual disturbances, irritability, abdominal pain and convulsions.

In the most severe cases eclampsia causes coma and death. It is one of the most dangerous complications of pregnancy, and the best treatment is prevention. Regular measuring of blood pressure and testing of urine during pregnancy is used to detect pregnancy-induced hypertension (PIH).

If detected and treated early, complications can be prevented. When eclampsia does occur, expert hospital care is absolutely essential as the sufferer will need heavy sedation. Any woman who suffers from preeclampsia is at risk of eclampsia.

SEE ALSO *Hypertension, Preeclampsia, Pregnancy*

Eczema

Eczema is an allergic condition that most commonly affects the face, scalp, neck, hands and feet, and the creases of the trunk, elbows and knees.

Atopic eczema

Eczema is characterized by itching, redness, blisters, oozing and crusting. Scratching can cause further irritation.

ECZEMA

Also known as atopic dermatitis, eczema is a chronic (long term) allergic skin disorder, occurring most commonly in infants, beginning between the ages of one month and one year. Most infants will outgrow it by the time they are two to three years old, but it may flare up again at any age. In adults, it is generally a chronic or recurring condition.

The condition is a hypersensitivity reaction similar to an allergy, causing chronic inflammation of the hands, scalp, face, back of the neck or skin creases of elbows and knees. The inflammation causes the skin to become itchy and scaly. Chronic irritation and scratching can cause the skin to thicken and become leathery-textured. There may be blisters with oozing and crusting, and the skin may become secondarily infected through scratching.

Eczema may occur for no known reason, or as an allergic reaction to a wide variety of things including foods (such as eggs, wheat, milk or seafood), woolen clothing, skin lotions and ointments, soaps, detergents, cleansers, plants, tanning agents used for shoe leather, dyes, topical medications, moisture, overheating, common house dust, dog or cat dander, cigarette smoke and stress.

There is often a family history of asthma, hay fever, eczema, psoriasis or other allergy-related disorders.

The first step in treating eczema is to identify whatever it is that causes the reaction and if possible remove or avoid it. Next, the skin itself should be cared for.

Dry skin makes the condition worse, so to keep the skin healthy, reduce the frequency of bathing to once or twice a week in lukewarm water, and use a small amount of very mild soap (or better still, use no soap at all). Bath oils and soap substitutes are often recommended. Apply a moisturizing lotion to the affected areas as least twice a day and after bathing; this keeps the skin moist and protects it from other irritants.

If this doesn't improve the condition, a physician may prescribe mild cortisone cream or ointment; for example, 1 percent hydrocortisone cream. The physician may also prescribe antihistamines to reduce itching (in rare cases, sedatives or tranquilizers may be needed). Keep nails short and wear soft gloves at night to minimize scratching. Sometimes exposure to sunlight helps heal the rash.

Chronically thickened areas may be treated with ointments or creams that contain tar compounds, or medium-to very high-potency steroid creams. In very severe cases, corticosteroids by mouth may be needed. Antibiotics may be prescribed for areas of infection. These measures are usually successful in controlling the disorder.

There are a number of alternative therapies that may help to alleviate the symptoms of eczema. Ayurvedic and traditional Chinese medicine prescribe herbs and a change of diet. Counseling, hypnotherapy or psychotherapy may be of use if there are emotional or stress-related factors. Herbalism prescribes alterative herbs such as burdock, nettle and red clover to cleanse and boost the lymphatic system, and liver tonics, such as dandelion, to aid in the detoxification process. Homeopathy views eczema as a constitutional illness and prescribes remedies to match the patient's overall constitution, as well as to treat individual symptoms. Naturopathy prescribes evening primrose oil, flaxseed oil, zinc and a range of vitamins. Patients are advised on eliminating allergens, additives and colorings from their diet and a supervised fast may be suggested (not for children). Oatmeal or Epsom salt baths are traditional home remedies used to ease symptoms. Reflexology treats eczema by massaging skin and liver zones, and by helping the patient to relax.

SEE ALSO *Allergies, Dermatitis*

EDEMA

Edema is swelling caused by the build-up of fluid in the tissues. It can be localized (limited to a part of the body), or generalized (occurring throughout the body).

Localized edema may result from injury or infection, sunburn or varicose veins. Slight edema of the legs commonly occurs in warm summer months and during pregnancy.

More generalized edema can be caused by heart failure or by a lack of protein in the blood from cirrhosis of the liver, chronic nephritis or malnutrition. It can also occur as a result of toxemia of pregnancy (preeclampsia).

Edema is treated by correcting the underlying cause. Diuretic drugs, which make the kidneys eliminate excess salt and water, are often used to relieve the symptoms. Elastic stockings will help prevent edema caused by pregnancy, failure of lymphatic drainage, or varicose veins.

Pulmonary edema is a complication of heart disease in which the failing heart allows fluid to accumulate in the lungs, which eventually seeps into the air spaces (alveoli). This interferes with the exchange of oxygen and carbon dioxide, causing severe breathlessness. Pulmonary edema is a medical emergency, requiring immediate hospitalization and treatment with oxygen, diuretics, morphine and drugs for the underlying heart failure.

SEE ALSO *Diuretics, Pulmonary edema*

ELBOW

The elbow is the joint between the expanded lower end of the bone of the upper arm (the humerus) and the two bones of the forearm (the radius and ulna). The radius is on the thumb side of the arm and the ulna on the side of the little finger. When the arms are placed by the side with the palms facing forwards, the ulna is closest to the body (medial) and the radius is away from the body (lateral).

The radius and ulna articulate with the expanded end of the humerus. There are bony swellings on the humerus, either side of the joint, called the lateral and medial epicondyles. These bony protrusions can be felt through the skin on either side of the elbow.

The brachial artery is the main artery of the upper arm, which runs down the medial side of the humerus and across the inside surface of the elbow, below which it divides into radial and ulnar arteries. The brachial artery is compressed against the humerus by means of a cuff when blood pressure is checked using a sphygmomanometer and stethoscope.

A number of superficial veins cross the front of the elbow (the cubital fossa). These vary considerably in arrangement but their position just under the skin makes them suitable for obtaining a sample of blood or for cardioangiography. This involves insert-

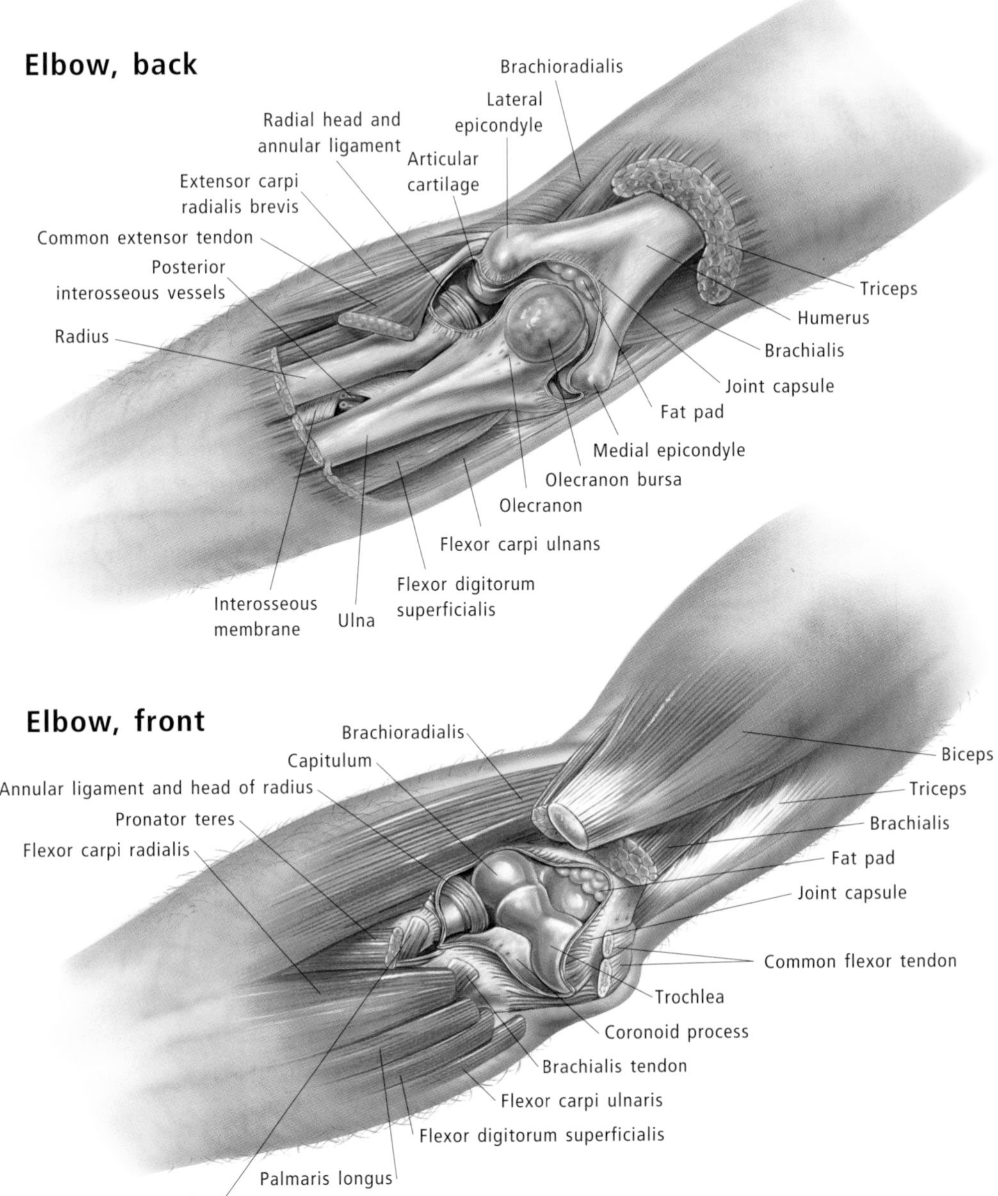

Elbow, articular

Cross-sectional view of the elbow joint.

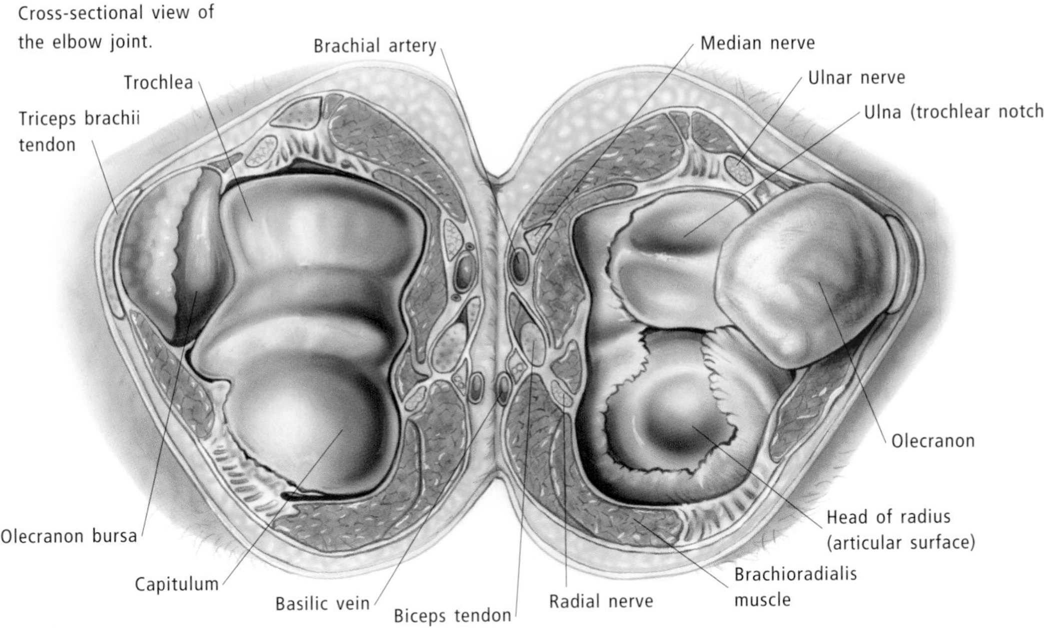

ing a fine tube (catheter) into the vein and threading it through the vessels of the arm and ultimately into the heart where blood samples can be taken or an opaque dye injected prior to taking an x-ray.

Elbows are prone to certain types of sports injuries, commonly called "tennis elbow" and "golfer's elbow".

Tennis elbow is a painful sensation in the vicinity of the lateral epicondyle (lateral epicondylitis). The pain may also radiate down the forearm. Some of the muscles which extend (straighten) the wrist attach to the lateral epicondyle and it is thought that repetitive wrist movements cause strain or damage to this attachment.

Golfer's elbow is pain in the vicinity of the medial epicondyle where some of the muscles which flex (bend) the wrist attach. Repetitive movements of the wrist are believed to place stress on this part of the elbow. A similar condition can arise from excessive throwing using poor technique.

Despite the common names for the two conditions, tennis and golf can affect either epicondyle, and epicondylitis can also result from other sports requiring repetitive wrist or forearm movements, including bowling, gymnastics, baseball, fencing, swimming and karate. Epicondylitis does not usually resolve without some sort of treatment.

Therapies include laser treatments, injections of botulinum toxin or steroids, oral or topical non-steroidal anti-inflammatory agents, elbow support bands, remedial exercise and acupuncture. Some of these remedies seem to give relief in many cases.

There is no universal agreement as to which method is best, nor do there seem to have been any clinical trials which satisfy the majority of practitioners treating these conditions.

SEE ALSO ***Arm, Humerus, Radius, Tennis elbow, Ulna***

ELECTROCARDIOGRAM

The activity of the heart can be measured through minute electrical impulses from the cardiac muscle that reach the skin surface.

This electrical activity can be detected through the taping of electrodes to the skin in positions dictated by the information required. The ankles, wrists and the chest wall are the standard sites for applying the electrodes. Electrical signals are amplified and the details are recorded on an electrocardiogram, a chart scribed on a moving strip of paper.

Results show the efficiency of the heart's ability to transmit the electrical impulses that control the cardiac cycle, and its rate and rhythm. In a person with a normal heart, the EKG tracing has a characteristic pattern, showing upward and downward deflections. The first upwards deflection, called a P wave, is known as the atrial complex and is due to the electrical activity associated with the contraction of the upper chambers (atria) of the heart. A further series of deflections, the Q, R, S and T waves, are the ventricular complexes and are due to the electrical activity associated with the contraction of the lower chambers (ventricles). Delayed transmission of electrical impulses, abnormally-shaped complexes and abnormal rhythms in the EKG tracing may indicate heart disease.

Some EKG changes only become apparent when the subject is exercising. An EKG carried out in a physician's office when a person is exercising vigorously is called a stress test. Other abnormal electrical activity in the heart may occur intermittently and may not be present when an EKG is performed. A Holter monitor is a device that makes a 24-hour EKG recording which can be used to detect sporadic arrhythmias.

SEE ALSO ***Arrythmia, Heart, Heartbeat***

ELECTROCONVULSIVE THERAPY

Electroconvulsive therapy (ECT) is a psychiatric treatment that involves bringing on a seizure by administering an electric shock to the brain. The patient is first anesthetized and given a muscle relaxant, then an electrode is placed on each temple and an electric current is passed through the brain between the two electrodes.

The patient usually experiences some memory disturbance immediately after treatment, but this usually passes with time. Exactly how or why ECT works is still unclear but it is known to be effective in the treatment of certain types of depression.

ECT is probably the most controversial psychiatric treatment in use today, the controversy revolving around its effectiveness versus its side effects. The major side effect is the risk of prolonged memory loss and confusion in some patients.

Although ECT was widely used in the 1940s and 50s to treat cases of severe psychiatric illness, it was subsequently found to be relatively ineffective in many cases, particularly those involving psychosis. Today its use is more limited but it is still being used, usually in conjunction with medication, to successfully treat cases of severe depression and sometimes to interrupt manic episodes. Generally, a number of treatments are required over a period of several weeks for ECT to be effective.

SEE ALSO ***Bipolar disorder, Depression, Psychosis***

ELECTROENCEPHALOGRAM

An electroencephalogram (EEG) is a record of the overall activity occurring in the cerebral cortex of the brain. It is obtained by recording electrical signals from electrodes placed at various points on the surface of the head and appears as a series of spikes on a graph. These spikes, known as brain waves, can be classified according to their frequency into four groups known as alpha, beta, theta and delta waves. Their pattern varies during different types of brain activity such as rest, sleep and mental concentration.

In certain brain conditions the EEG reading is found to be abnormal. An EEG can be used in the diagnosis of epilepsy (the test will help determine the type of epilepsy), brain injuries, abscesses, meningitis, encephalitis and brain tumors. The procedure is usually carried out in a hospital clinic or a doctor's office. A sleep encephalogram, performed on a person after they have been kept awake the previous night, can help evaluate some types of sleep disorders.

Absence of electrical activity in an EEG is sometimes used as legal proof of brain death in a person who is in a coma and is being kept alive only by artificial means.

SEE ALSO ***Brain wave activity, Coma, Epilepsy***

E

ELECTROLYTES

Electrolytes are ions in solution in the blood and other body fluids. They play an essential role in all body functions. The major electrolytes are sodium, potassium, calcium, phosphate, chloride and bicarbonate. Derived from food, their concentration in the blood is regulated mostly by the kidneys and lungs and can be measured by laboratory studies of serum (the clear liquid in plasma).

Different fluids in the body have different concentrations of electrolytes. For example, the concentration of sodium in serum is 142 millimoles/liter whereas the potassium concentration is only 4 millimoles/liter. Inside the cell, the concentration of sodium is 10 millimoles/liter while the concentration of potassium is 160 millimoles/liter. This difference in concentration is maintained by special ion pumps in cell membranes which continuously move sodium ions out of the cell and potassium ions into the cell. The difference in concentration of electrolytes in different fluids is important for some metabolic processes, for example, the conduction of electrical impulses along nerve fibers.

The concentration of electrolytes in body fluids depends on an adequate intake of electrolytes in the diet, adequate absorption from the intestine, and proper functioning of the kidneys and lung, which also regulate electrolyte concentration in body fluids. Diseases that interfere with these processes can cause disturbances of electrolyte concentration. For example, kidney disease may cause the body to retain too much sodium, chloride, bicarbonate and calcium. Electrolyte concentrations in the body are also controlled by hormones, and diseases which affect the production of these hormones also cause electrolyte disturbances, which can have severe effects on the body's metabolism.

Different electrolytes play different roles in the body's metabolism. Sodium helps regulate the body's water balance, and maintains normal heart rhythm, blood pressure and blood volume. Increased intake of sodium may contribute to high blood pressure, so people with high blood pressure may be advised to reduce their sodium intake. Sodium also plays a part in the conduction of nerve impulses and muscle contraction.

Too much sodium in the blood and body fluids (hypernatremia) or too little sodium (hyponatremia) can cause confusion, restlessness, anxiety, weakness, muscle cramps, edema and, in severe cases, stupor or coma.

Potassium assists in the regulation of the acid-base and water balance in the blood and the body tissues. It assists in protein synthesis from amino acids and in carbohydrate metabolism. It is necessary for the building of muscle and for normal body growth. Along with sodium and calcium, it maintains normal heart rhythm, regulates the body's water balance and is responsible for muscle contractions and nerve impulses.

Tissue cells usually have a high concentration of potassium, while blood usually has a low concentration. Too much or too little potassium in the blood can cause weakness and paralysis and affect the heartbeat.

Sodium and potassium levels in the blood and body fluids are regulated by aldosterone, a hormone secreted by the adrenal gland, which increases sodium resorption from the kidneys and promotes potassium loss by the kidneys. A tumor of the adrenal gland may cause excess secretion of aldosterone (hyperaldosteronism), leading to hypernatremia, hypokalemia and fluid imbalance.

Calcium is a mineral component of blood which, along with phosphate, forms bone and teeth. Calcium also helps in the regulation of the heartbeat, transmission of nerve impulses, contraction of muscles and clotting of blood. Calcium and phosphate levels in the blood are regulated by parathormone, a hormone secreted by the parathyroid gland, which requires vitamin D to function. Calcium levels are also regulated by calcitonin, a hormone secreted by the thyroid gland. Too much calcium causes lethargy, delirium and seizures; too little causes muscle spasms, twitching, cramps, numbness and tingling in extremities, seizures and irregular heartbeat.

Chloride is necessary in the maintenance of the body's acid-base and fluid balance. It is an essential component of the secretions of the stomach, aiding in digestion. Fluid loss due to excessive sweating, vomiting or diarrhea can cause a deficiency of chloride, resulting in excessive alkalinity of body fluids (alkalosis), low fluid volume (dehydration) and loss of potassium in the urine.

Bicarbonate acts as a buffer in blood and body fluids, keeping the pH (acidity) to within a narrow range of 7.35–7.45. The concentration of bicarbonate is regulated by the kidney and the lungs.

SEE ALSO *Adrenal glands, Calcium, Kidney, Potassium, Sodium*

Electrolytes

The concentration of electrolytes in the blood is regulated by various organs. For example, the pituitary gland releases hormones which contribute to the regulation of the electrolyte balance; the adrenal glands regulate sodium and potassium; the parathyroid glands regulate calcium and phosphate; the kidneys and lungs regulate bicarbonate; and the kidney regulates chloride.

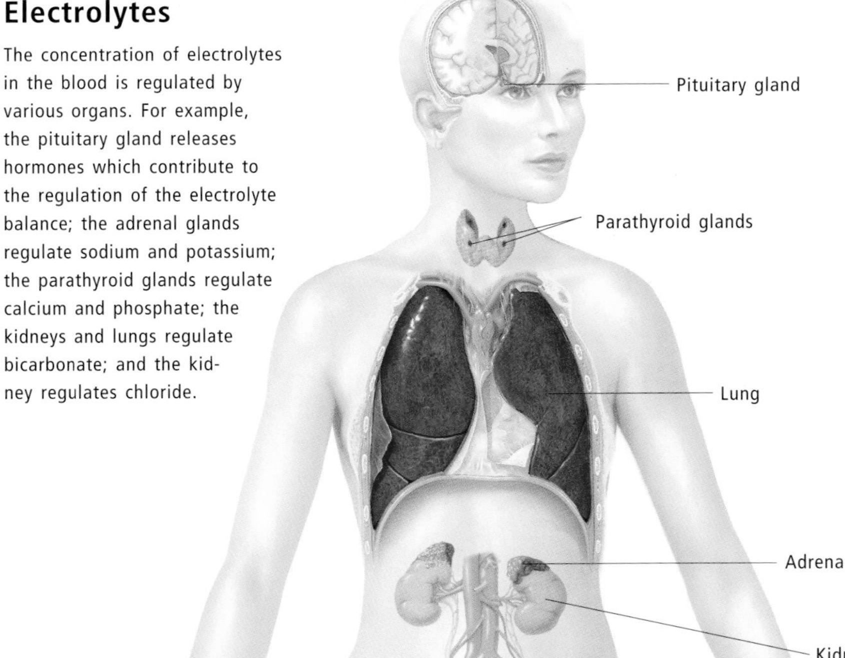

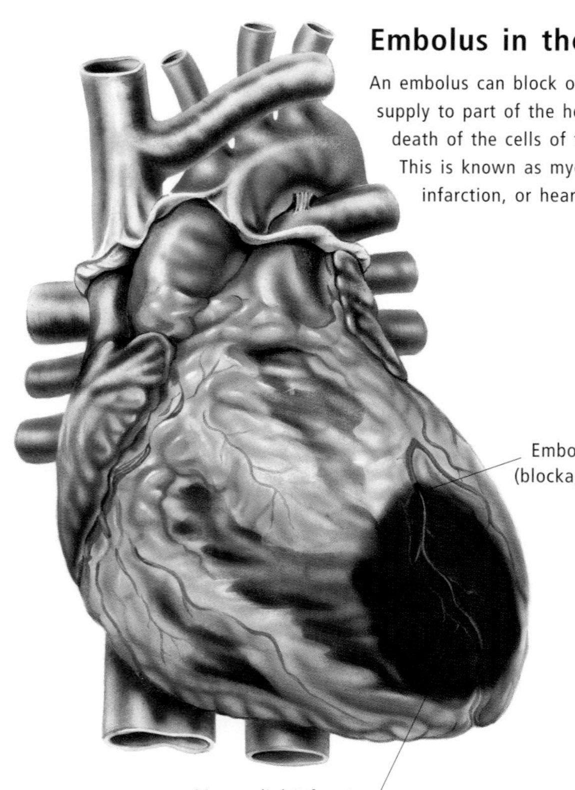

Embolus in the heart

An embolus can block off the blood supply to part of the heart, resulting in death of the cells of the heart muscle. This is known as myocardial infarction, or heart attack.

Cerebral infarction

Embolus in the brain

An embolism in a cerebral artery can block the blood supply to areas of the brain, resulting in death of brain tissue (cerebral infarction)—this is a common cause of stroke.

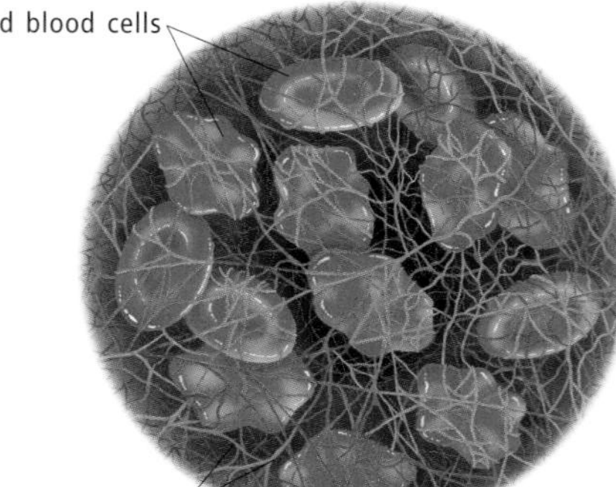

Embolus

Emboli are usually clots composed of strands of fibrin and red blood cells (erythrocytes). They form most commonly in the arteries of the brain, heart, kidney, legs and intestines.

ELECTROMYOGRAPHY

Electromyography is a method of diagnosing the health of muscle tissue by measuring its electrical activity. At rest, muscles are electrically silent, producing no electrical impulses, but when stimulated or voluntarily contracted they generate an electrical current. These impulses are recorded on a cathode ray tube by continuous tracing in the form of a wave and monitored as a sound through a loudspeaker.

The visual tracing or electromyogram records the electrical impulses, and these can be interpreted to evaluate the health of the muscle, to reveal any weakness or wasting indicating impairment of nerve functions or muscle disease.

SEE ALSO *Muscle*

ELECTROSURGERY

Electrosurgery is the use of electrical current to destroy healthy or diseased tissue. It is used to make incisions in healthy tissue (for example, to excise skin lesions), to destroy diseased tissue such as tumors, or to coagulate bleeding blood vessels during surgery. There are several electrosurgery techniques, all of which use the principle that as electrical current is converted into heat by tissue resistance, it destroys tissue.

Electrosurgery has largely been replaced by laser surgery, which is more accurate and can be used in areas where electrosurgery cannot, for example in eye surgery.

ELEPHANTIASIS

Elephantiasis is a condition associated with infectious disorders known collectively as filariasis. The filarial worm in tropical and subtropical regions is transmitted to humans as larvae by mosquitoes. After about a year the larvae mature into nematodes which live in lymph nodes and vessels, mainly those draining the legs and genital regions, where they impair circulation and induce allergic reactions in surrounding tissues.

The disease progresses as attacks with fever and increasing swelling, usually of the legs. Over time, gross hardening and enlargement give the skin an appearance similar to elephant hide, hence the name of the condition. Treatment may kill the worms but drugs and surgery are the only recourse for advanced symptoms. The disease is not curable.

SEE ALSO *Filariasis*

EMBOLISM

Embolism is the sudden obstruction of blood flow to an organ or body part by an embolus. Usually the embolus is a blood clot that has formed in an artery and has traveled in the blood and lodged in a smaller artery downstream.

An embolus may sometimes be composed of fat globules from the site of a bone fracture (fat embolus), infected material from an abscess, cancer cells, or an air bubble (air embolus).

The effect of an embolus is to block off the blood supply and cause ischemia (damage caused by lack of oxygen) to the organ supplied by that artery.

An embolus may cause myocardial infarction (in the heart), stroke (in the brain) or leg pain and ulcers.

Treatment for embolism depends on the size, nature, and location of the embolus. An embolus in one of the major organs, such as the heart, lung or brain, will require emergency treatment at a hospital. Surgery or drug treatment with thrombolytics and anticoagulants may considered to be necessary.

SEE ALSO *Anticoagulants, Ischemia, Myocardial infarction, Stroke*

EMBRYO

The term "embryo" covers the time from fertilization to the end of week 8 of gestation. After this, the term "fetus" is used. During the first eight weeks the embryo grows from a single cell to a complex multicellular organism. The placenta and fetal membranes develop and all the major organ systems are acquired, although not necessarily in functional form. External features are sufficiently developed by the end of week 8 that the fetus has a recognizably human form, including head, arms and legs.

Fertilization results in a single-celled embryo called a zygote. This divides rapidly as it passes down the fallopian tube. When it reaches the uterus a cavity forms with an inner mass of cells on one side of the cavity, which will become the embryo and the embryonic membranes. The cells on the outside will form the placenta. Implantation begins on about day 7.

Formation of embryo and amnion

The inner mass of cells undergoes rearrangement to form a flat elongated sheet covered by a hollow balloon-like structure (rather like a gondola under a hot air balloon). The hollow structure will form the amnion, a fluid-filled sac in which the embryo will eventually float, connected to the placenta by the umbilical cord. The flat sheet of cells will become the embryo. The amnion does not form part of the embryo's body but its normal functioning is important in development. If the amniotic sac is punctured prematurely, loss of amniotic fluid may lead to miscarriage or infection.

Damage to the amniotic membrane may cause the formation of strands of tissue (amniotic bands) within the sac. If one of these becomes wrapped around a developing body part it may cause constriction of its blood supply and distortion or loss of the part. Amniotic bands can be detected by ultrasound in some cases.

If there is insufficient amniotic fluid the loss of its cushioning effect can also result in pressure damage to the developing embryo; this mostly results in spontaneous abortion (miscarriage). A sample of amniotic fluid (obtained by amniocentesis, a common test for fetal abnormalities) contains molecules and cells shed from the embryo which can be used to detect some abnormalities such as Down syndrome and spina bifida. It is difficult prior to week 14 to

Embryo

Three days after conception, the fertilized egg (zygote) begins its journey down the fallopian tube. On entering the uterus, the zygote sheds its protective, jelly-like covering before implanting itself in the uterine lining. In just 8 weeks, the embryo will have transformed from a single cell to a tiny (1 inch/2.5 centimeter) yet recognizably human entity with limbs, facial features and all the major organ systems.

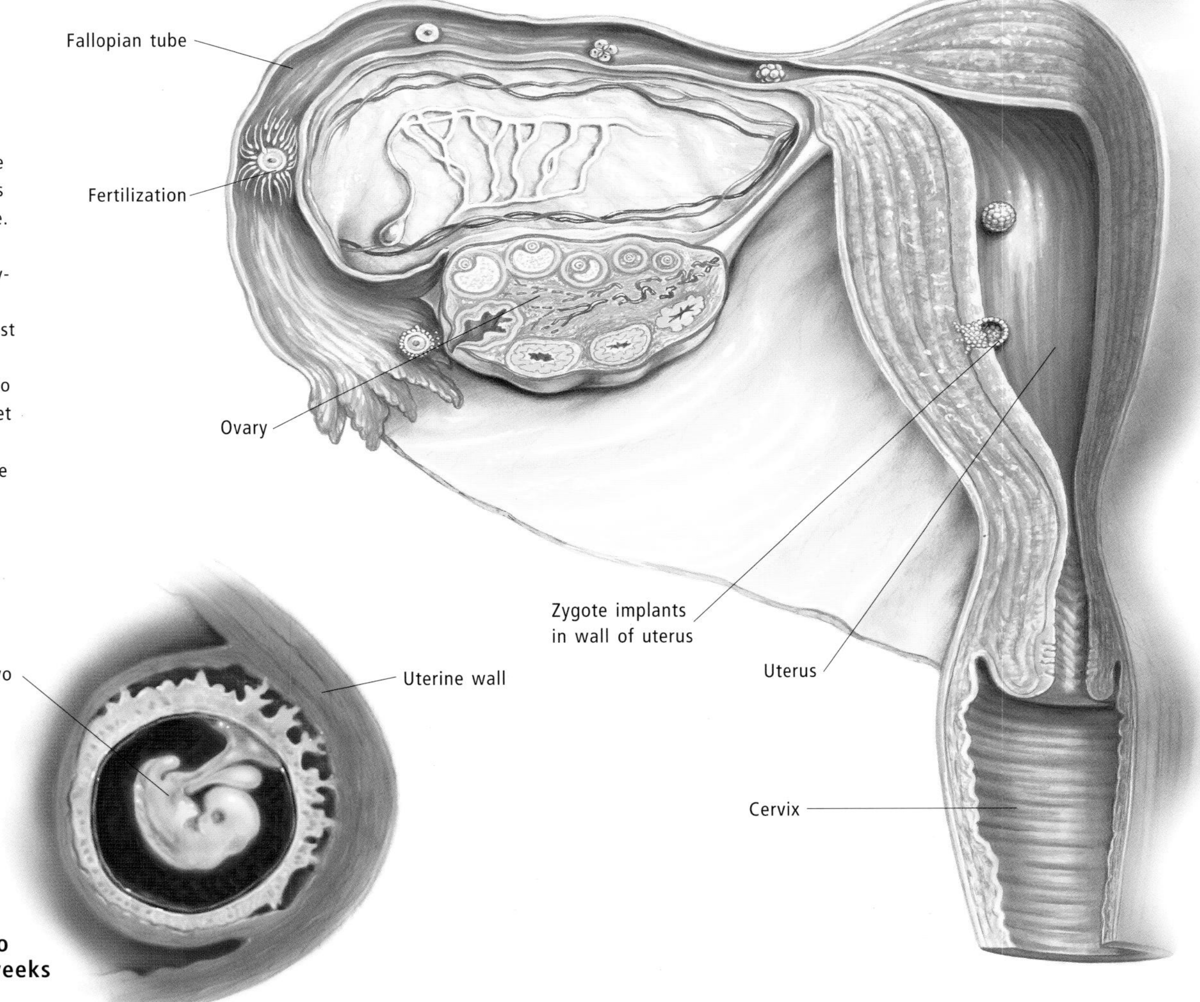

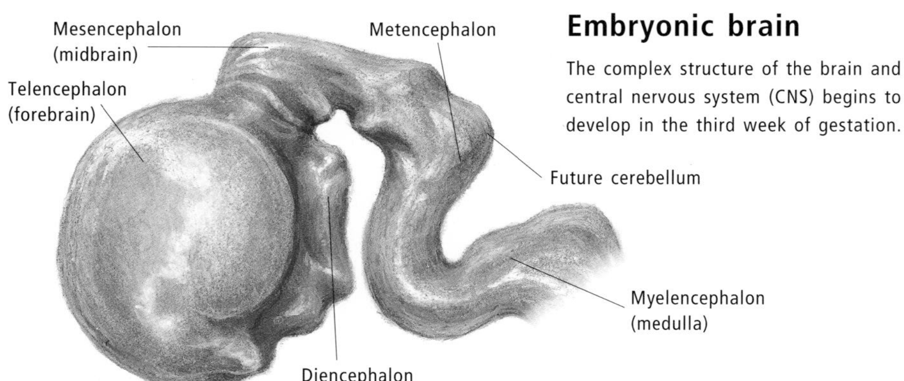

Embryonic brain

The complex structure of the brain and central nervous system (CNS) begins to develop in the third week of gestation.

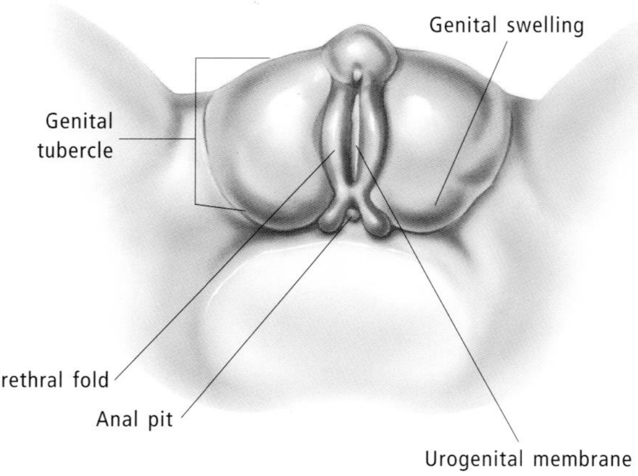

Gender difference

In the first few weeks of life the sex organs are undifferentiated. As the embryo develops, the genital tubercle will become part of the penis (the glans) if the embryo is male, and the clitoris if it is female.

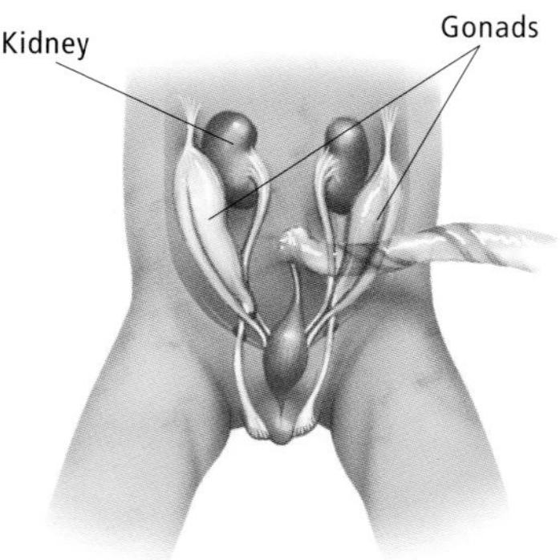

Development of testes

As the gonads (the sex glands) develop in the embryo, it is possible to distinguish between ovaries and testes as early as week 7. The testes start to form in the body cavity near the kidneys, gradually descending into the scrotum during fetal development.

safely remove enough amniotic fluid for diagnosis, so this is not done during the embryonic period.

Organ development

Considerable rearrangement is required for a flat sheet of cells to become a recognizably human embryo. Folding and growth during week 3 results in a rolling under of the sides, head and rear of the embryo so that it becomes a hollow tube with the gut suspended inside it. This coincides with the start of formation of many of the organ systems. The diaphragm and the compartments in the chest cavity which contain the lungs and heart begin to develop just after folding. These are important for normal postnatal function and in embryonic development. For example, if the diaphragm fails to form completely there may be herniation of abdominal organs into one of the pleural (lung) cavities and these may compress the lung and prevent its proper development.

Heart and blood vessels

The heart and blood vessels are the first organs to function. This is important as even a small embryo is so functionally active that it requires a good blood supply.

During week 3, groups of blood vessels form throughout the embryo and, as they grow, join and form a network. This network communicates with the heart which develops separately. The heart then starts to beat. Heartbeat can be detected by ultrasound during week 5 of gestation. The heart is initially a simple tube; the partitions which will convert it into a 4-chambered structure develop later. If one of these partitions is incomplete a "hole in the heart" (septal defect) results, which will misdirect the flow of blood through the postnatal heart. These defects can usually be corrected surgically.

Brain and spinal cord

Development of the brain and spinal cord (the central nervous system or CNS) is initiated during the third week when a shallow groove forms along the back of the embryonic disk. This groove becomes deeper and the edges fuse together to form a tube. The fusion starts in the region of the neck and extends forwards and backwards to fully enclose the tube by the end of week 4 of gestation. Sometimes an abnormal opening remains at one or, rarely, both ends.

If the tube fails to close at the end which should form the brain, then normal brain and skull do not form and there is either a portion of brain protruding from an opening in the skull or, in extreme cases, an open undeveloped structure where the brain and cranium should have been. This is called anencephaly. A defect in the closure of the rear end of the neural tube leads to spina bifida.

After closure of the tube, there is extensive further growth and development of the CNS which continues during the first two years of postnatal life. It is important to realize that the CNS is prone to abnormal development in the embryonic period due to extensive cell division. A common cause of CNS malformations is heat stress, which can be caused by infections or strenuous exercise in early pregnancy. The hollow center of the neural tube remains and becomes filled with cerebrospinal fluid. The vertebrae and skull form around the developing CNS.

Continuing growth of the CNS is possible after bone formation because of remodeling, i.e. resorption of old bone from the inside and laying down of new bone on the outside, which results in a larger structure of the same shape. In the case of the developing brain, the fontanelles and the flat bones of the skull also play a role in permitting growth.

Some nerves grow out from the CNS to innervate muscles and organs of the body. Other nerves, including those carrying sensory information, develop separately and later make communication with the appropriate parts of the CNS.

Digestive system

The digestive system starts as a simple tube, formed when the underside of the flat embryo is rolled inwards during folding. The upper part becomes the esophagus and this joins to the mouth when it develops. The part of the tube below the diaphragm expands to form the stomach. Outgrowths from this region will also form the liver, gallbladder and pancreas. The rest undergoes enormous change to form the intestines.

The growth of the intestines is so considerable that they temporarily herniate into the body cavity in the umbilical cord during weeks 6 to 10. After this the abdominal cavity has enlarged sufficiently to permit return of the intestines to their normal position. This procedure occasionally fails and the infant is born with a type of umbilical hernia.

Respiratory system

The respiratory system arises at the end of week 4 as a tubular outgrowth from the front of the upper digestive tract. The first part of the respiratory system remains unbranched and forms the larynx and trachea. Development of the other respiratory structures involves a process of repeated branching and later differentiation. The first branches are the main lower airways (bronchi). Later branching forms the smaller airways and the alveoli where, in postnatal life, oxygen is supplied to the blood.

The lungs are immature until around 32 weeks of gestation; an infant born before this has a reduced chance of survival, though with sophisticated treatment some do survive from as early as 23 weeks. The lungs develop slowly because the embryo lives in a fluid rather than a gaseous environment, and the lungs are non-functional before birth, oxygen being obtained from the placenta via the umbilical arteries.

Face and jaws

The face and jaws start to develop during week 4, arising from a series of thickenings on either side of the developing head, which fuse in the midline and rearrange to form small but recognizable jaws, mouth and nose by the end of the embryonic period.

The main problem encountered with this process is the formation of a cleft lip or palate, resulting from failure of fusion of the thickenings which would normally form these structures.

The eyes and the ears

The retina of each eye starts as an outgrowth of the brain, which elongates towards the surface of the head. As the retina develops, it assumes a shape rather like a cup on the end of a stalk. The cup becomes the retina and part of the iris, and the stalk becomes the optic nerve. The presence of the developing retina induces superficial structures of the head to form lens, cornea and eyelid. Final maturation of the retina takes place after birth as a result of exposure to light.

The inner, middle and external ears all develop from surface structures on the side of the developing head. The precursor to the inner ear (which contains the organs of hearing and balance) starts as a hollow vesicle which sinks into the underlying tissues, undergoes profound development and connects to nerves from the brain during weeks 5 to 7 of gestation. The middle ear is filled with air and contains three tiny bones (the ossicles), which transmit sound from the external ear to the organ of hearing. These bones develop near a tubular outgrowth from the pharynx, which will become the eustachian tube. The external ear grows inwards to make contact with part of the middle ear to form the eardrum.

Many noxious influences, such as rubella (German measles) or heat stress, can disrupt the normal development of these complex organs. Rubella or heat stress during the embryonic period can cause congenital cataract (lens opacity) and deafness.

Limbs

Limbs start as small protrusions from the surface of the embryo during week 4. The ends of the limb buds become paddle-shaped and during week 6 develop thickenings where the fingers and toes will develop.

Controlled (or programmed) cell death is an important mechanism in many parts of the embryo for disposing of tissue which is no longer required. The skeletal support of both the limbs and digits is initially cartilage, which is replaced by bone from week 7. It is not known what determines the development of an arm rather than a leg or why particular fingers or toes form where they do.

Limb abnormalities are common and most are caused by genetic factors. Drugs such as thalidomide can be involved as well. The most critical time is during weeks 5 to 7, when the basic pattern of the limbs is being structured.

Kidneys

Three successive sets of kidneys develop in intrauterine life. The first is rudimentary and the second, the mesonephros, functions from weeks 4 to 9, being gradually replaced by the final pair of kidneys, the metanephrons. Renal function is important in intrauterine life as the urine helps to maintain the correct volume of the amniotic fluid.

Reproductive system

The gonads develop at about the same time and in the same region of the posterior body wall as the mesonephros. By week 7 it is possible to distinguish ovaries from testes. Most of the development of the gonads and other reproductive organs takes place during fetal life, including relocation of the ovaries into the pelvis and testes into the scrotum.

Chemical factors and development

The process of embryonic development as a whole is a highly coordinated affair. Much of the early embryo consists of cells which can develop along one of many lines rather than being committed to form a particular organ from the very beginning. This flexibility only lasts while the tissue is primitive and is lost once development is initiated.

As the tissues develop they either produce a chemical signal or modify their surrounding environment. These signals attract cells from other parts of the body. These cells in turn start to develop and produce their own chemical factors, and so on. In many cases the critical time during which normal development of a particular structure is determined is only a matter of a few days.

SEE ALSO *Amniocentesis, Fertilization, Fetal development, Placenta, Pregnancy*

E

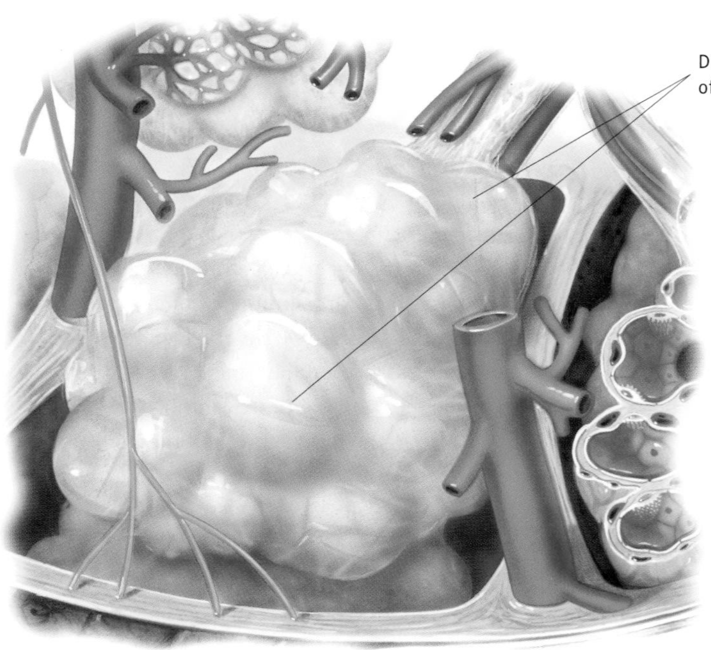

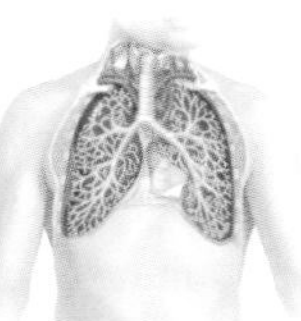

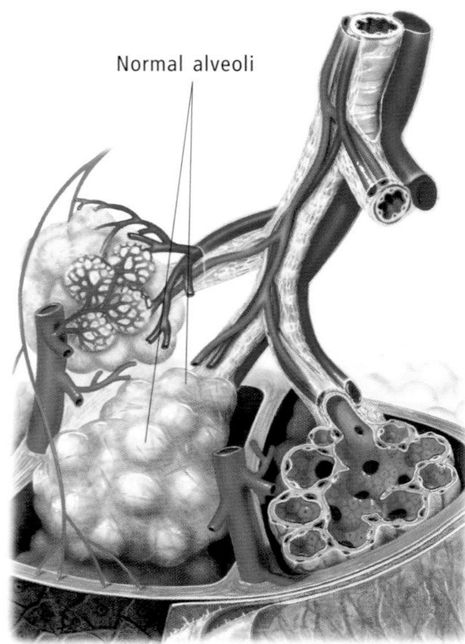

Emphysema

In emphysema, the air sacs in the lungs (the alveoli) become damaged and distended. As a result, the lungs are less able to supply the oxygen that the body requires.

EMBRYOSCOPY

Using the same high-resolution fiberoptic equipment as employed in fetoscopy, embryoscopy allows surgeons to see the embryo and fetus (two stages of a growing baby) in early pregnancy in order to identify abnormalities. Fetal blood sampling can also be performed using this technique, known as embryofetoscopy.

SEE ALSO *Embryo, Fetoscopy*

EMOTIONS

Emotions or feelings influence the way humans react to and interpret the world they live in; they affect thoughts, words, actions and bodily functions. The basic emotions are anxiety, fear, anger, happiness and sadness. Emotions are activated by neural processes, bodily changes and mental activity. They may or may not be reflected by a person's outward appearance.

Anxiety and fear are the ways our body signals that something is wrong and that action is needed to alleviate those feelings. Usually, a person experiencing fear can identify the source; anxiety, however, may be felt only as vague uneasiness. Both emotions may be rational or irrational, which can cause psychological and bodily tension in anticipation of something which is not really a threat.

Anger, which can be caused by external or internal events, can vary from intense fury to mild irritation and, like other emotions, is accompanied by physiological and biological changes. Heart rate and blood pressure go up, as does the level of the energy hormones epinephrine (adrenaline) and norepinephrine (noradrenaline).

Sorrow or grief can often encompass other emotions such as anger and fear. Triggered by a loss the feelings can, depending on the cause, last for a long period. Happiness, together with love, is a complex emotion, which may be triggered by many factors. The causes underlying most complex emotions, such as joy, grief and anxiety, are not known.

Mood refers to a sustained emotional state; for example, elation or depression. Mood disorders are a cluster of mental disorders outside the normal emotions of sadness or elation, and are characterized by excessive depression or mania.

SEE ALSO *Anxiety, Body language, Depression, Grief, Mania*

EMPHYSEMA

Emphysema or pulmonary emphysema is a chronic obstructive lung disease marked by wheezing, breathlessness and increasing loss of lung function. The disease occurs most commonly in smokers and people exposed to polluted air and airborne dust or similar irritants, but can also affect children who suffer asthma or bronchitis.

In the early stages of emphysema the lining of the lung's airways, the bronchi and bronchioles, is stimulated by irritation of smoke or other pollutants to produce abnormal quantities of mucus. Mucus is produced in the lungs to trap dust and it is normally removed by the movement of specialized cells. Over time, the greater quantity of mucus leads to persistent coughing, "smoker's cough", and a greater susceptibility to colds, which can lead to chest infections.

The early symptoms are similar to those of bronchitis: coughing and bringing up mucus combined with asthmatic wheezing as the airways narrow. In emphysema, there is the added complication that the alveoli decay. Alveoli are the tiny sacs at the end of the bronchioles where blood gives up carbon dioxide and takes on fresh oxygen from inhaled air.

As the alveoli become less efficient, air is trapped in the lungs and the lung tissue decays. The trapped air decreases the volume of fresh air that can be inhaled and the lungs may expand permanently in the effort to counter this, resulting in a permanently expanded chest and a "barrel-chested" appearance that is characteristic of the disease. The lungs are unable to supply the oxygen the body needs, and the smallest exertion may produce severe breathlessness.

In addition to breathlessness, the symptoms of emphysema include a bluish tinge to the skin, a build-up of carbon dioxide caused by inefficient reoxygenation of the blood, loss of weight, swelling in hands and feet, tightness in the chest and increased respiratory distress in cold or smoky air. Reduced oxygen intake causes the heart to pump faster, and the strain can lead to heart failure. Bullous emphysema is a condition in which the alveoli distend and form cysts on the lungs that may rupture causing lung collapse.

The exact cause of emphysema is not known, but it is commonly associated with cigarette smoking and long-term exposure to air pollutants in mining and industrial processes. A deficiency in a protein in the liver (alpha$_1$-antitrypsin) has been found in some sufferers. Antitrypsin counteracts trypsin, an enzyme produced by many types of bacteria that decays tissue.

When emphysema is diagnosed it is essential to stop further damage by giving up smoking and avoiding exposure to pollutants and dust. No treatment can reverse the lung damage but existing lung function can be improved with the use of drugs such as bronchodilators, which relax muscles that restrict the airways, and by supplying oxygen to the sufferer for inhalation at home. Steroids can reduce lung inflammation and antibiotics are used to clear up infections. A more recent development is the surgical removal of damaged lung tissue to allow the functioning tissue room to expand and work better. Lung transplantation is also an option.

SEE ALSO *Asthma, Breathing, Bronchitis, Lungs, Respiratory system, Smoking, Wheezing*

ENCEPHALITIS

Encephalitis is inflammation of the brain, causing swelling of brain tissue (cerebral edema), bleeding within the brain (intracerebral hemorrhage) and, sometimes, brain damage. Encephalitis is usually caused by one of a number of viruses. A virus may be transmitted to humans by mosquitoes or ticks, especially in rural areas. It can also follow other viral disorders such as measles, mumps, chickenpox, rubella, infectious mononucleosis (glandular fever) and coxsackievirus illnesses. Symptoms range from a mild illness with fever and tiredness to headache, stiff neck, vomiting and, in more serious cases, seizures, paralysis and drowsiness progressing to coma.

A laboratory analysis of blood and cerebrospinal fluid (taken via lumbar puncture) will confirm the presence of the virus. Electroencephalography, cranial magnetic resonance imaging (MRI) or a CAT scan of the head may be needed to determine the extent of the infection.

Mild viral encephalitis is common and often requires no treatment other than bed rest and painkillers (analgesics). Severe cases are uncommon and usually require hospitalization and treatment with antiviral drugs such as acyclovir or amantadine, corticosteroids and drugs to control seizures, if needed.

Most cases make a full recovery within two to three weeks. A small percentage of cases suffer permanent brain damage—usually infants or the elderly.

SEE ALSO *Brain, Lumbar puncture, Viruses*

ENCEPHALOMYELITIS

Encephalomyelitis is an inflammation of the brain and the spinal cord, usually caused by a viral infection. It is closely related to encephalitis, which is an acute inflammatory disease of the brain, but without involvement of the spinal cord. Causes, symptoms, treatment and prognosis are the same as for encephalitis.

SEE ALSO *Brain, Encephalitis, Spinal cord*

ENDOCARDITIS

Endocarditis is inflammation of the smooth inner lining of the heart (the endocardium). It is caused by bacteria or fungi that enter the blood and infect and damage the endocardium of the heart chamber as well as the

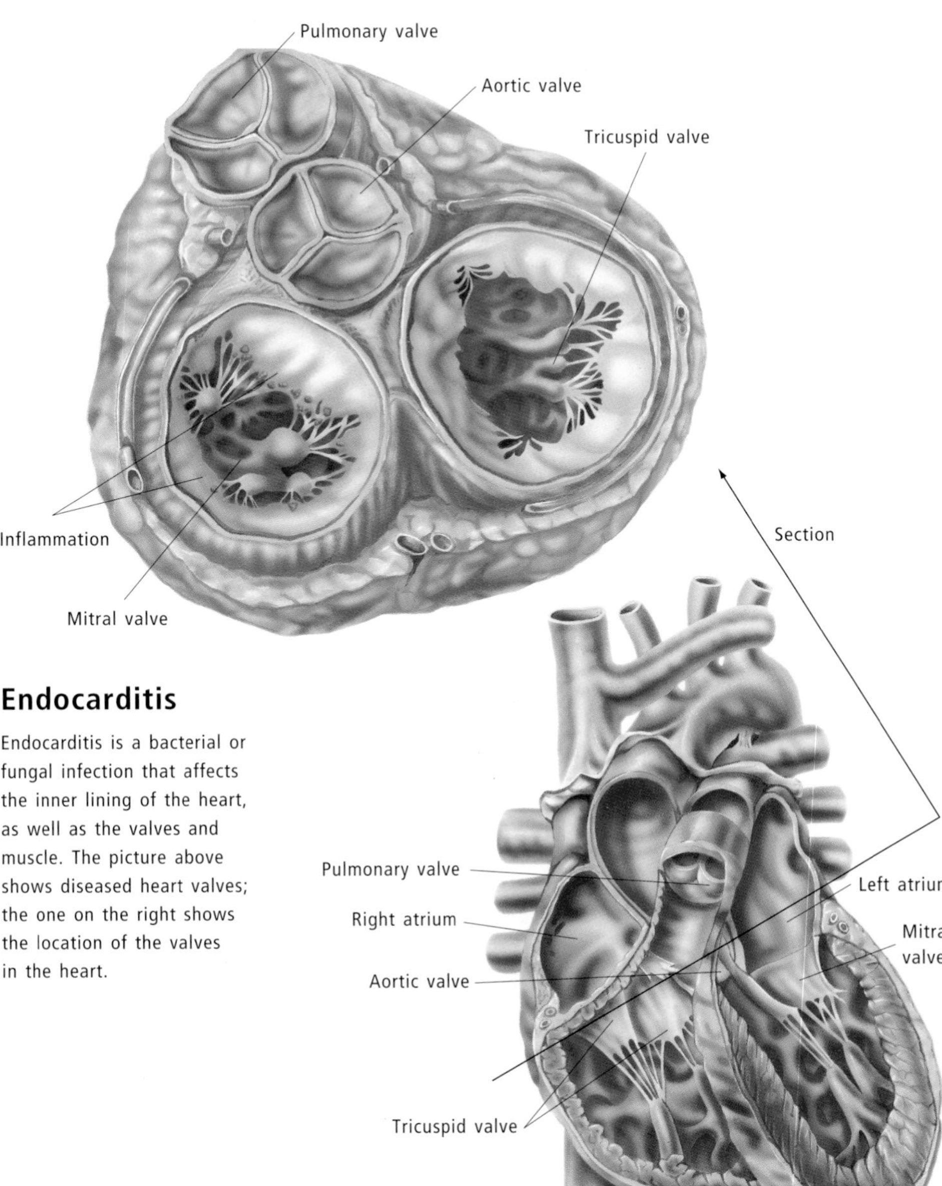

Endocarditis

Endocarditis is a bacterial or fungal infection that affects the inner lining of the heart, as well as the valves and muscle. The picture above shows diseased heart valves; the one on the right shows the location of the valves in the heart.

valves and the heart muscle itself. Endocarditis is more likely if there is pre-existing damage to the heart such as a congenital heart deformity, an artificial heart valve, or rheumatic heart disease. It may follow the delivery of a baby, surgery or dental work, or the use of intravenous drugs, all of which may introduce organisms into the bloodstream.

Symptoms begin gradually with fatigue, chills, aching joints and intermittent fever. Blood culture of the bacterium or fungus confirms the diagnosis. Treatment is with antibiotics which may be given intravenously. If untreated, death from heart failure is usual, but, with early treatment, most patients survive. Persons who have pre-existing heart valve disease should take antibiotic drugs before any dental or surgical procedure.

SEE ALSO *Heart*

ENDOCRINE GLANDS

The endocrine glands secrete hormones into the blood which determine growth and structure of many organs (such as during growth and maturation). They also control many vital body functions. The endocrine glands include the anterior and posterior pituitary gland, the pineal gland, thyroid and parathyroid glands, pancreas, adrenal glands, ovaries (in women) and testes (in men).

The pituitary gland is often considered the master controller, regulating the function of the thyroid, adrenal glands, pancreas, ovaries and testes. Over- or under-production of hormones from any of these glands is associated with many different types of disease. Disorders of the pituitary include dwarfism, acromegaly, diabetes, gigantism and diabetes insipidus.

Disorders of the thyroid include cretinism, myxedema, goiter and thyrotoxicosis. Disorders of the adrenal glands can cause Addison's disease, adrenogenital syndrome, Cushing's syndrome or pheochromocytoma, while disorders of the parathyroid glands cause tetany, kidney stones (renal calculi) and abnormal loss of minerals from bone. Disorders of the pancreas include diabetes mellitus and hypoglycemia.

Underproduction of sex hormones by the testes and ovaries causes lack of sex development. Underproduction of hormone is usually treated by hormone replacement therapy. Overproduction may be treated with surgery, radiation therapy or medications which suppress production of hormone by the gland.

SEE ALSO *Adrenal glands, Endocrine system, Hormones, Ovaries, Pancreas, Pituitary gland, Testes, Thyroid gland*

ENDOMETRIAL BIOPSY

During an endometrial biopsy a sample of tissue is removed from the uterine wall for testing in a laboratory. This is usually done to determine the cause of abnormal bleeding. A small tube is passed through the cervix and into the uterus and the sample taken from the uterine lining, the endometrium.

If the purpose of the test is to exclude the likelihood of endometrial cancer, a curette may be preferred. This is a different procedure which requires anesthetic, usually general, and involves removing tissue by scraping the wall with a curette. A biopsy can be performed with no anesthetic.

SEE ALSO *Biopsy, Dilation and curettage, Endometrium*

Endocrine glands

The endocrine glands produce hormones that regulate growth, sexual development and other important body functions.

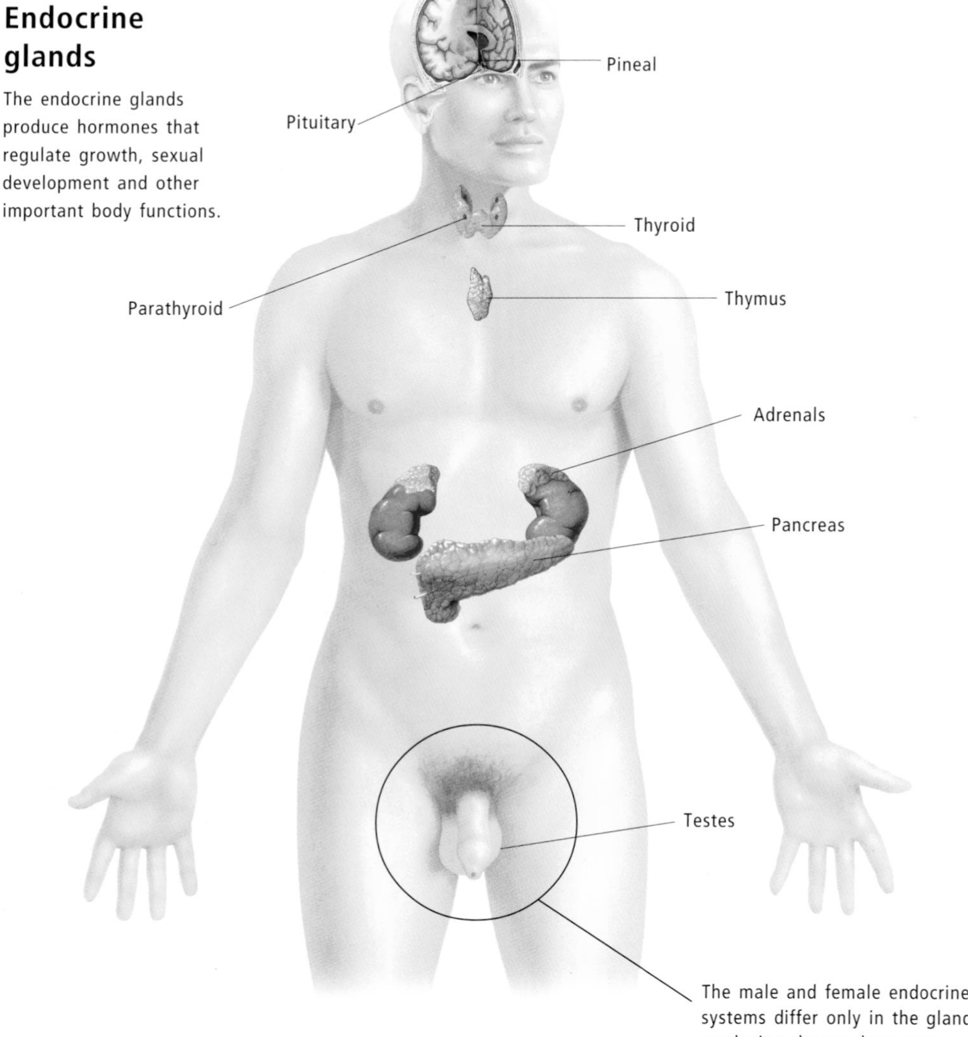

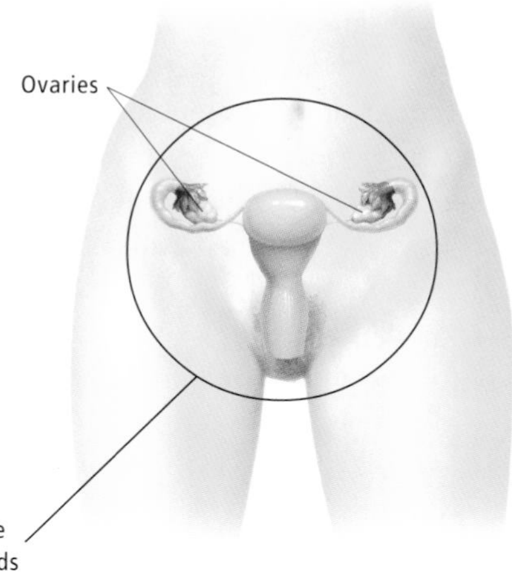

The male and female endocrine systems differ only in the glands producing the sex hormones

E

ENDOMETRIOSIS

Endometriosis is a condition in which tissue normally found on the lining of the uterus grows in other parts of the body such as the pelvic cavity, ovaries, bowel, bladder and rectum. This tissue (called the endometrium) acts in the same way as it would in the uterus, swelling before each period as if to prepare for nourishing a fertilized egg and then bleeding. The result is scarring and adhesions (clusters of endometrial cells) which may implant in the ovaries and fallopian tubes and obstruct the passage of the ovum.

Symptoms include increasingly painful and abnormal periods, lower back pain, pelvic cramps, pain during intercourse, abdominal pain before or during menstruation, blood in the urine, fatigue, bloating, diarrhea and constipation. Some women may experience no pain at all. Serious side effects include blood cysts in the ovaries and infertility.

The cause of endometriosis is not known, though women whose mother or sisters have had the condition have a greater chance of suffering from it. Mild cases are treated with painkillers. Symptoms may be reduced by creating a state of pseudo-pregnancy or menopause using hormonal drugs or oral contraceptives. Where pregnancy is not desired, options include removal of the ovaries or a hysterectomy. Scar tissue and adhesions may be surgically removed in some cases. Pregnancy has been known to cure the condition.

SEE ALSO *Adhesions, Endometrium, Hysterectomy, Menstruation, Reproductive systems, Uterus*

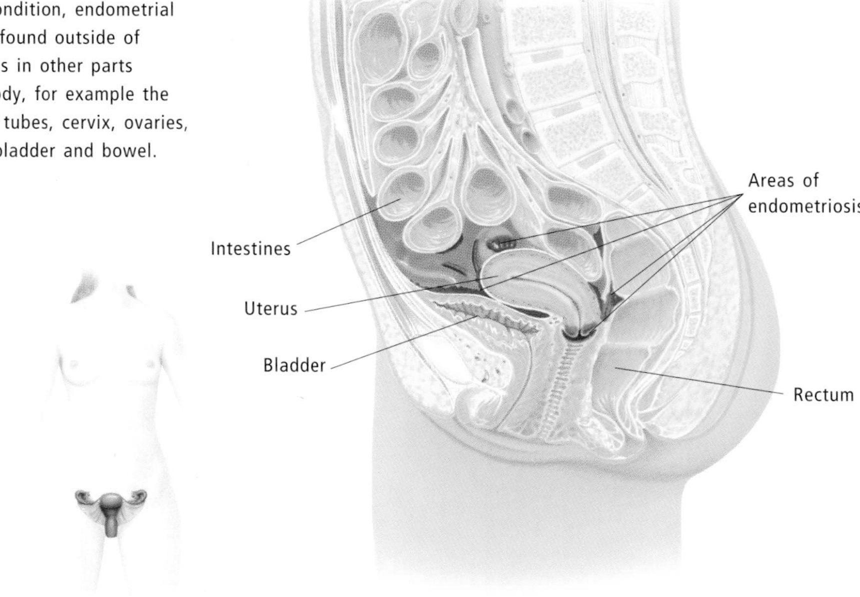

Endometriosis

In this condition, endometrial tissue is found outside of the uterus in other parts of the body, for example the fallopian tubes, cervix, ovaries, rectum, bladder and bowel.

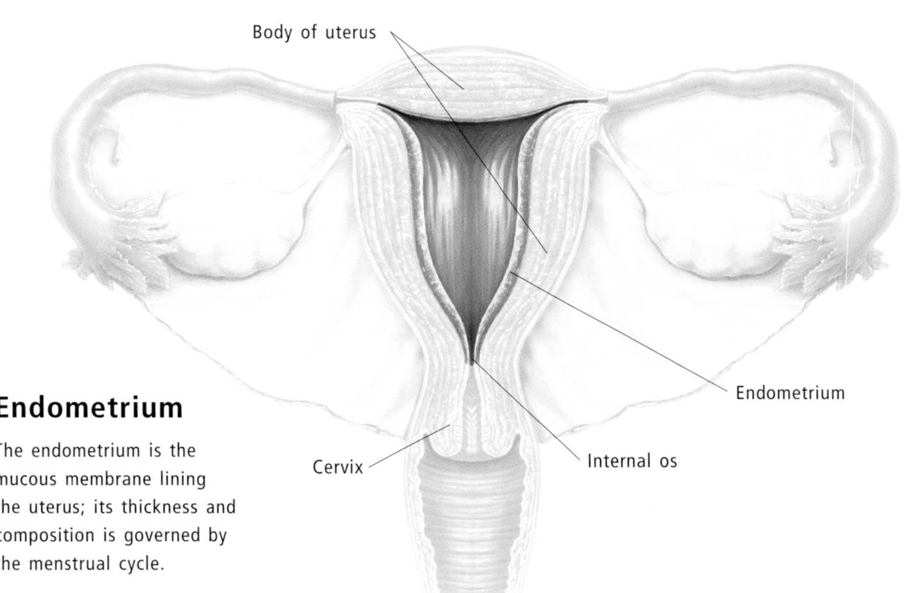

Endometrium

The endometrium is the mucous membrane lining the uterus; its thickness and composition is governed by the menstrual cycle.

ENDOMETRIUM

The endometrium is the inner glandular layer of the uterus. It consists of simple, tubular-shaped glands overlying a layer of connective tissue called the lamina propria. In a woman of reproductive age (approximately 13 to 50 years), the endometrium undergoes cyclical changes in its thickness and composition as part of the 28-day menstrual cycle.

During the first part of the cycle (the proliferative phase—lasting from 5 to 14 days after the appearance of menstrual blood), estrogen from the ovaries makes the endometrium thicker by inducing the multiplication of gland cells.

The second part of the cycle (the secretory or luteal phase—from 15–28 days after the appearance of menstrual blood) starts after the release of the egg from the ovary and the formation of the corpus luteum, which secretes progesterone. Progesterone makes the glands of the endometrium secrete and blood vessels of the endometrium be more coiled.

The final stage is the menstrual phase, which begins at the end of the secretory phase, lasts 4 days, and ends when the proliferative phase of the next cycle begins. The menstrual phase occurs only if the egg is not fertilized and no embryo embeds in the endometrium. During the menstrual phase, hormonal support for the endometrium is lost and the endometrium breaks down with bleeding. Blood and discarded endometrium are expelled from the cervix into the vagina as menstrual fluid.

The effect of oral contraceptives is to inhibit secretion of the pituitary hormone (follicle stimulating hormone, or FSH) which stimulates the maturation of eggs in the ovary. Oral contraceptives also produce cyclical changes in the endometrium.

The endometrium is also where the embryo will implant to continue its development into a fetus during pregnancy. It is the tissue of the endometrium that contributes blood vessels to the maternal part of the placenta, supplying the fetus with nutrient-rich blood.

After menstrual cycles have ceased (usually at about 50 years of age—a stage of a woman's life called menopause), the hormonal support of the endometrium is lost and the endometrium becomes thinner, less vascular and not prone to cyclical changes.

Cancer of the endometrium is usually seen only in post-menopausal women. The most common symptom is bleeding after menopause. In fact, about 40 percent of women who have vaginal bleeding after menopause have a cancer of the reproductive tract. Pain is not a common symptom, but mild uterine cramping may occur.

Diagnosis is made by taking a scraping of the uterus wall (curetting) after cervical canal dilation, and examining the tissue under a microscope. Treatment consists of removal of the uterus (hysterectomy), which is curative if the cancer is confined to the uterus, or radiation therapy combined with hormone therapy and surgery, if some spread has occurred to areas outside the uterus.

SEE ALSO *Endometriosis, Hormone replacement therapy, Menopause, Menstruation, Oral contraceptives, Placenta, Pregnancy, Reproductive systems, Uterus*

ENDORPHINS

Endorphins are a group of naturally occurring opiates with pain-relieving properties found in the brain. They are related to painkilling opiates such as opium, morphine and heroin; the word "endorphin" comes from the word "endogenous" (meaning "produced within the body") and the word "morphine".

Endorphins were discovered in 1973, following the discovery of receptors in the brain that morphine binds to. This led to the belief that the body must contain its own naturally occurring opiates; since then, several related molecules called enkephalins have also been discovered.

Endorphins and enkephalins are released into the circulation during vigorous physical exercise, such as running and jogging, and are believed to account for the painkilling (analgesic) and euphoric effect which exercise can produce in people (the "runner's high"), especially if they are mildly depressed or anxious. (Acupuncture is also thought to work by stimulating the production of endorphins.)

Dependence on and tolerance to morphine and other narcotic analgesics is thought perhaps to be caused by suppression of the body's normal production of endorphins by these opiates. When the effects of morphine wear off, it is thought that withdrawal symptoms occur because the body lacks endorphins.

SEE ALSO *Acupuncture, Exercise, Heroin, Morphine, Narcotics*

ENDOSCOPY

An endoscopy involves looking inside the body through an endoscope to investigate suspected abnormalities. Endoscopes are narrow tubes containing optical fibers and lights, and are extremely flexible. Many can also remove tissue samples or destroy abnormal tissue.

Endoscopy is used to examine the esophagus (esophagoscopy), the stomach

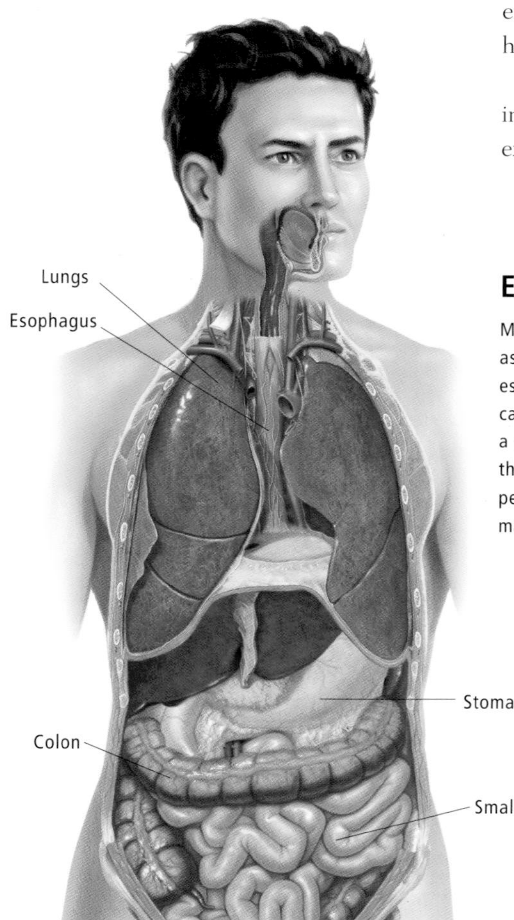

Endoscopy

Many internal organs, such as the lungs, stomach, esophagus and intestine, can be viewed by passing a narrow fiberoptic tube through the mouth, anus or penis, or through a small cut made in the abdominal wall.

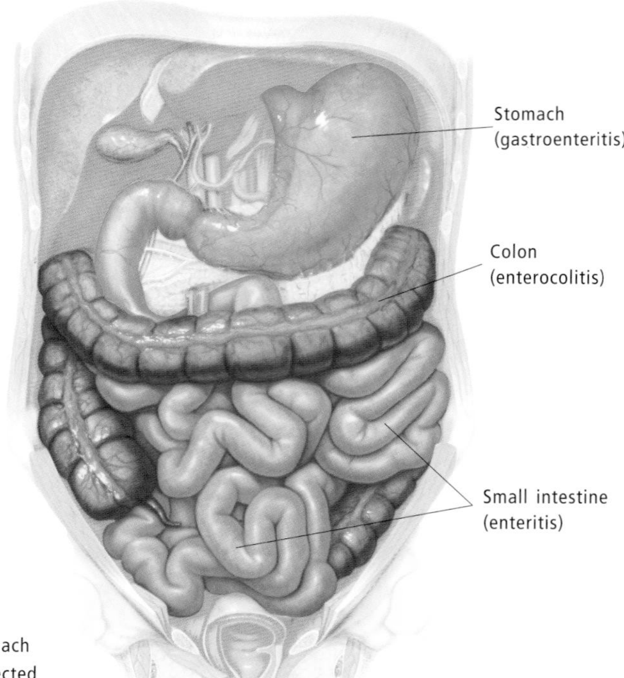

Enteritis

The small intestine, stomach and colon can all be affected by a form of enteritis, an inflammatory condition usually caused by bacterial or viral infection.

(gastroscopy), the lungs (bronchoscopy), the small intestine (upper gastrointestinal endoscopy), the lower portion of the large intestine (sigmoidoscopy), and all the large intestine (colonoscopy). Some conditions can also be treated during an endoscopy.

The use of the endoscope has simplified diagnosis and treatment of a number of problems which in the past required barium meals and enemas, though these are still used. Complications from an endoscopy are rare.

SEE ALSO *Barium enema, Barium meal, Bronchoscopy, Colonoscopy, Gastroscopy*

ENEMA

Enema is the injection of fluid into the rectum via the anus to expel the rectum's contents. Enemas were once routine for pregnant women but are more commonly used to treat cases of constipation or colonic inertia that have caused fecal impaction—the compaction of hard stools in the rectum which can cause painful cramps and block normal defecation. Enema fluids may be a saline solution or contain an oil such as olive oil.

A barium enema is given to outline the lower portion of the large intestine in x-ray procedures. It is expelled by taking a mild laxative.

SEE ALSO *Barium enema, Colonic irrigation, Constipation*

ENTERITIS

Enteritis is inflammation of the small intestine, caused by a bacterial or viral contamination of ingested food or liquids. The stomach is often also involved; the condition is then known as gastroenteritis. If the colon is involved, it is called enterocolitis. Symptoms of abdominal pain, diarrhea, fever and dehydration can begin as soon as four hours or as late as 72 hours after exposure.

Mild cases usually need no treatment and clear up in one to three days. Clear fluids such as apple juice or broth are recommended, and milk should be avoided. Anti-diarrheal medications may be useful in relieving symptoms. Diarrhea can cause rapid and extreme dehydration in infants and in such cases medical advice should be sought immediately.

SEE ALSO *Dehydration, Diarrhea, Gastroenteritis, Intestines*

ENZYME DEFICIENCIES

An enzyme is a protein produced by a living cell that speeds up chemical reactions. There are hundreds of them in the human body. Some release energy to make the heart beat and the lungs expand and contract. Many help convert sugar and foods in the digestive tract into simpler compounds so they can be absorbed and used to build tissue, replace dead cells and release energy to move muscles.

There are many diseases caused by deficiencies of enzymes. Most of them are genetic and most are rare. Two examples of enzyme-deficiency diseases are phenylketonuria (PKU) and lactose intolerance.

Phenylketonuria is caused by the absence of the enzyme phenylalanine hydroxylase, which prevents the build-up of the amino acid phenylalanine by converting it to tyrosine. If this does not happen, intellectual disability and seizures can eventuate. The enzyme deficiency can be detected at birth by a PKU test (Guthrie's test). The treatment is a diet that limits the intake of phenylalanine.

Lactose intolerance is caused by deficiency or absence of the enzyme lactase. Lactase breaks down lactose, the main sugar in milk. Without lactase, the stools become foamy and loose, with nausea and abdominal cramps and bloating. The disorder usually develops in adulthood, and can be diagnosed by examination of the stools and a lactose-tolerance test. Though not curable, the condition can be controlled with a milk-free diet.

SEE ALSO *Lactose intolerance, Phenylketonuria*

ENZYME-LINKED IMMUNOSORBENT ASSAY

Enzyme-linked immunosorbent assay (ELISA) is a family of very versatile immunologic techniques which rely on the binding of an antibody or antibodies to their corresponding antigen. An enzyme linked to one of the antibodies (either directly or indirectly) is used to generate a reaction product, usually colored, and measurement of this product allows the amount of bound antibody to be determined. Uses of ELISA techniques include detection of antibodies in blood serum, which is valuable in the diagnosis of infections, and measurement of minute amounts of circulating proteins or drugs.

SEE ALSO *Antibodies*

EPIDERMIS

The skin has three layers of tissue: epidermis, the outermost layer; dermis, the middle layer; and subcutaneous tissue, the innermost layer. The epidermis is made up of five sublayers, each with its own function. As cells in the

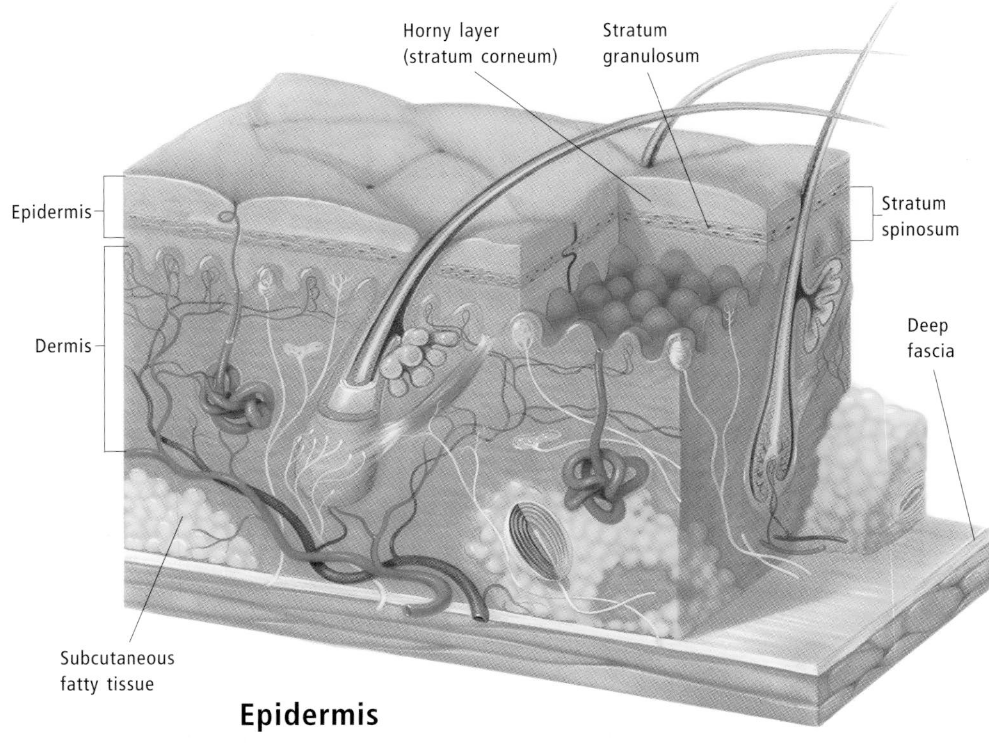

Epidermis

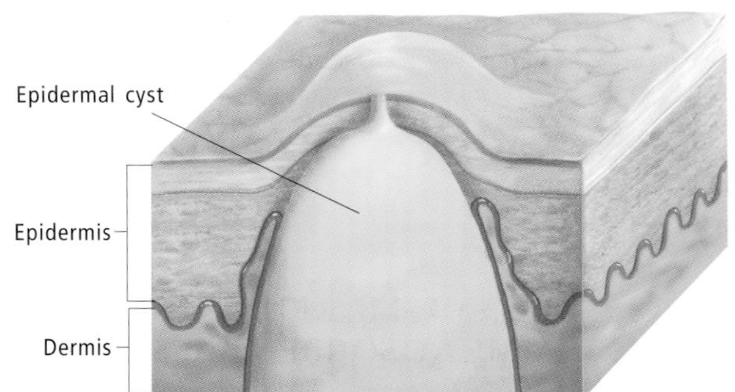

Epidermal cyst

Epidermal cysts (also known as sebaceous cysts) contain the fatty secretions of the sebaceous gland, and most commonly occur on the scalp, neck, face and trunk.

top layer die and are sloughed off, they are continually replaced by cells from the lower layers. It takes approximately four weeks for cells formed in the bottom layer to reach and replace those in the top layer.

The bottom layer of the epidermis is the basal layer (*stratum basale* or *stratum germinativum*). This layer is three to five cells thick; cell mitosis, or cell reproduction, occurs here, and it is also the layer in which pigment-producing cells called melanocytes are found. They produce the pigment melanin, responsible for absorbing dangerous ultraviolet light and for giving skin its dark appearance in dark-skinned races.

Sunlight stimulates the production of melanin, resulting in a tanned appearance following prolonged exposure to sunlight.

On top of the basal layer lies the spiny layer (*stratum spinosum*), which is eight to ten cells thick and is made up of flattened cells with spiny projections. Above this is the grainy layer (*stratum granulosum*). This layer is three to five cells thick; cells in this layer produce keratin, a waxy substance that forms a tough surface layer in the outermost epithelial cells.

Next is the clear layer (*stratum lucidum*), a thin, clear, keratin-rich layer three to four cells thick, which is thickest on areas subjected to heavy wear and tear, such as the palms of the hands and the soles of the feet.

The outermost layer is the horny layer (*stratum corneum*). Most of the cells in this layer (25–30 cells thick) are dead; it takes about two weeks for cells to reach the surface, where they are sloughed off. Thus, the skin is in a constant process of renewal. The stratum corneum is the main barrier to skin infection; if a bacterium, virus or fungus manages to penetrate this layer, dermatitis (inflammation of the skin) may follow.

Epidermal cysts, also called sebaceous cysts, are benign cysts containing fatty or keritanous material. They occur from adolescence onwards, most commonly on the trunk, face, neck and scalp. They may become infected, turning bright red and painful. Symptomless cysts may be left alone, but if they become a source of infection or are unsightly, medical advice should be sought.

SEE ALSO *Dermatitis, Keratin, Sebaceous cyst, Skin*

EPIDIDYMITIS

Epididymitis is inflammation of the epididymis, an oblong structure attached to the upper part of each testis in the male. The inflammation causes the epididymis to become swollen and painful. The condition may be caused by the spread of a bladder infection (cystitis), or it may be a complication of a sexually transmitted disease.

The affected person experiences pain when urinating and increased frequency of urination. The scrotum may be painful, enlarged and tender. Treatment with antibiotic drugs and painkillers (analgesics) is usually effective.

SEE ALSO *Cystitis, Sexually transmitted diseases, Testes, Urinary systems*

EPIDURAL ANESTHESIA

Epidural anesthesia is used to eliminate pain in childbirth and involves the administration of an anesthetic near the base of the spinal cord. It numbs the lower part of the body, either completely or partially, and allows the woman to remain conscious. An epidural may be used on request or on the advice of the doctor or other caregiver; an epidural is sometimes to lower high blood pressure (hypertension).

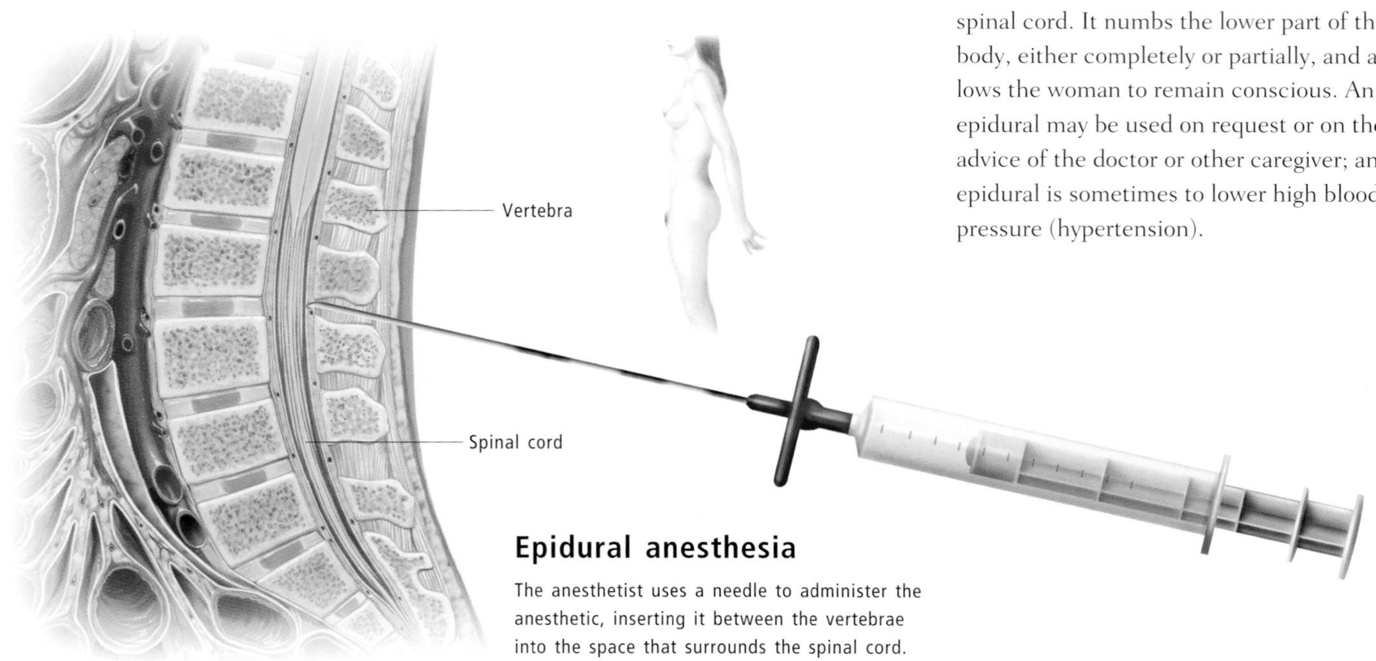

Epidural anesthesia

The anesthetist uses a needle to administer the anesthetic, inserting it between the vertebrae into the space that surrounds the spinal cord.

It is a more effective method of pain relief than the alternatives but carries with it an increased likelihood of cesarean section and, if used in the second stage of labor, an increased likelihood of instrumental delivery. There is little data available on its effects on the baby or long-term effects on the mother.

SEE ALSO *Anesthesia, Childbirth*

EPIGLOTTIS

The epiglottis is a leaf-shaped flap of tissue in the throat that lies just behind the base of the tongue and over the opening of the voice box (larynx) and windpipe (trachea). It closes off the trachea when swallowing, preventing food and liquids from accidentally passing into the trachea, directing them instead into the esophagus.

Epiglottitis is inflammation of the epiglottis. It is most common in children between two and six years old and is usually caused by the bacterium *Hemophilus influenzae*, although it may be caused by other bacteria or viruses. It begins with a high fever and sore throat, followed by rapid swelling of the epiglottis and difficulty swallowing. The swollen epiglottis can obstruct breathing and very quickly becomes a medical emergency. No attempt should be made to look in the throat if epiglottitis is suspected. Emergency medical help should be sought immediately.

The condition is treated in intensive care in hospital with antibiotics and oxygen therapy. Surgery may be needed to make a temporary opening in the trachea or to place a tube in the trachea to allow breathing until the condition improves, which may take up to a week or ten days.

SEE ALSO *Esophagus, Larynx, Trachea*

EPILEPSY

Epilepsy is disturbance in the normal electrical functions of the brain, causing seizures that may range from brief attacks of unusual behavior, a change in consciousness, erratic movements, or major seizures involving loss of consciousness. The condition affects between 0.5–1 percent of people in Western countries, and usually begins between two and fourteen years of age.

The cause is usually unknown, though there is often a family history of seizure dis-

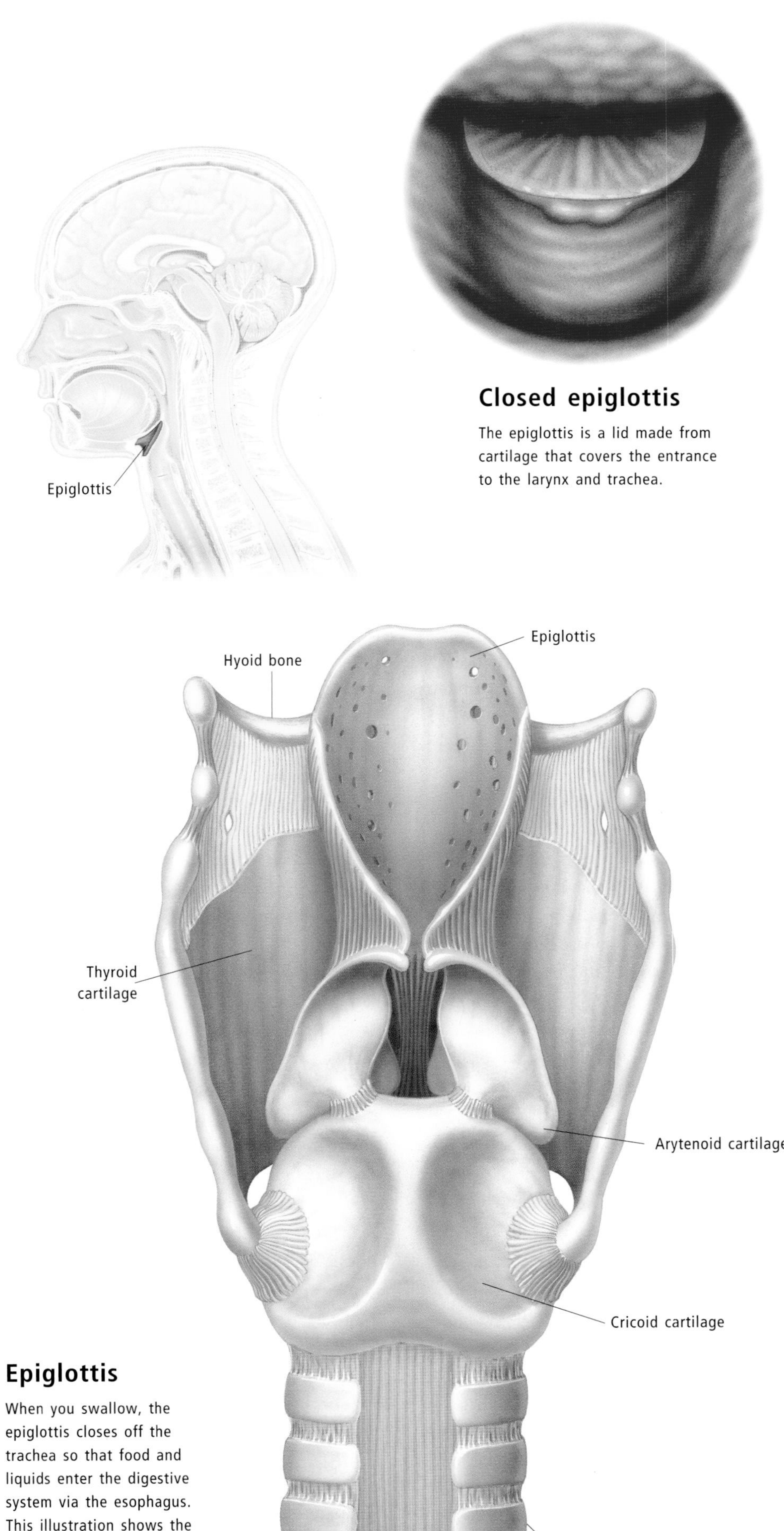

Closed epiglottis

The epiglottis is a lid made from cartilage that covers the entrance to the larynx and trachea.

Epiglottis

When you swallow, the epiglottis closes off the trachea so that food and liquids enter the digestive system via the esophagus. This illustration shows the back of the epiglottis.

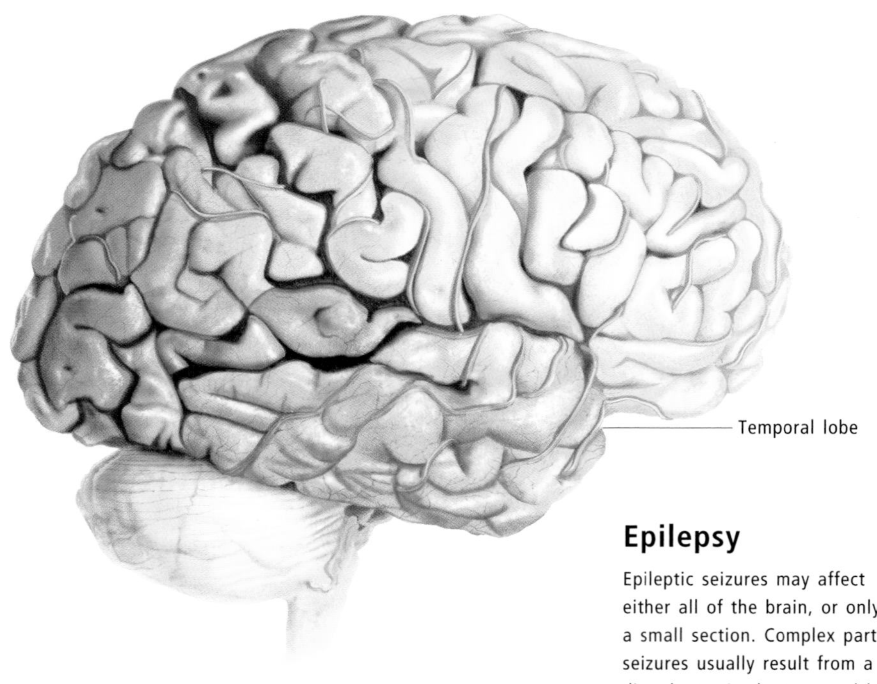

Epilepsy

Epileptic seizures may affect either all of the brain, or only a small section. Complex partial seizures usually result from a disturbance in the temporal lobe.

orders. In about a quarter of cases, there is an organic brain disorder such as a head injury, brain tumor, cerebral palsy, meningitis or encephalitis.

Seizures may occur in a generalized form (affecting all or most of the brain) or in a partial form (affecting only a portion of the brain). Generalized seizures cause loss of consciousness and include grand mal or tonic-clonic seizures (major seizures) and petit mal (minor) seizures (which occur mostly in children). Partial seizures that are termed focal result from a disturbance in the cortex; there may be abnormal movements or sensations, but the sufferer usually remains conscious. Complex partial seizures most commonly result from a disturbance in the temporal lobe.

Generalized tonic-clonic seizures begin with a sudden loss of consciousness. The person falls and the muscles become rigid (the tonic phase). As the abdominal muscles contract, forcing air from the lungs through the larynx, the person may give a shrill scream. Respiration ceases briefly, and the skin may turn blue. The lower limbs become extended and the upper limbs flexed. After about a minute, the clonic phase follows, consisting of jerking contractual movements of muscles in all four limbs. Breathing starts again, but is heavy and irregular, with frothing of saliva at the mouth. Incontinence (loss of bowel and bladder control) is common and the tongue may be bitten. Recovery occurs after 3–5 minutes. A period of confusion follows, when the person feels sleepy and may have a headache. Afterwards, there is no recollection of the seizure or the period of confusion after it.

A petit mal seizure is much shorter than a grand mal seizure. It generally lasts less than 15 seconds and is characterized by loss of consciousness, but there are no involuntary movements and the person does not fall over. After the seizure, the person is alert and can resume their previous activity.

Other symptoms and signs may accompany the seizures; including headache, changes in mood or energy level, dizziness, fainting, confusion and memory loss. An aura (a sensation such as a peculiar smell, vision or other sensation) may occur just before a generalized seizure. In some people, seizures may be triggered by hormone changes such as pregnancy or menstruation, illness, or by sensory stimuli such as lights, sounds and touch.

An electroencephalogram (EEG) which measures electrical activity in the brain will confirm the diagnosis; it shows abnormal patterns of electrical activity and may show where the seizure is emanating from. A CAT or MRI scan of the brain may help to rule out an organic cause. Unless there is a reversible cause, epilepsy is considered a chronic, incurable condition. Nevertheless, anticonvulsant drugs can prevent most seizures and allow a near-normal life.

Grand mal seizures are usually treated with phenytoin, carbamazepine, valproic acid, phenobarbital or primidone. Petit mal seizures usually respond best to valproic acid, ethosuximide or clonazepam. Focal seizures or partial complex seizures are treated with phenytoin or carbamazepine.

If the sufferer has been free of seizures for a period (usually some years), the medications may be withdrawn gradually; many sufferers (especially children) will then stay free of seizures without medication.

Any circumstance that has triggered a seizure should be avoided and sufferers should wear a bracelet or pendant that identifies the condition. If someone has a seizure, clear the area of objects that might get in the way. Do not attempt to restrain the person. Turn the person onto the side if vomiting occurs. When the seizure is over, keep the person on their side as they sleep.

Epilepsy is a serious, potentially life-threatening condition, usually defined as recurrent major convulsions that last for more than twenty minutes. Permanent brain damage or death can result if the seizure is not treated effectively; the longer the seizure lasts, the greater the danger. Treatment with intravenous anticonvulsants should be given as soon as possible.

SEE ALSO *Anticonvulsants, Brain, Cerebral palsy, Electroencephalogram, Encephalitis, Meningitis*

EPINEPHRINE

The hormone epinephrine (adrenaline) is released by the central part (medulla) of the adrenal glands in response to stress. Epinephrine increases heart rate, blood pressure, and flow of blood to the muscles. It causes the liver to release glucose into the blood. These changes enable the body to perform under conditions of stress and danger.

Epinephrine can be produced chemically and used as a drug to treat shock, allergy attacks, anaphylaxis and asthma. It is used in surgery to decrease bleeding or prolong the effect of local anesthetics, and can be given as a heart stimulant during cardiac arrest.

Pheochromocytoma is a tumor of the adrenal medulla which secretes abnormally high amounts of epinephrine and norepinephrine. It causes headaches, palpitations, anxiety and high blood pressure. The treatment is surgical removal of the tumor.

SEE ALSO *Adrenal glands, Anaphylaxis, Allergies, Asthma*

EPISCLERITIS

Episcleritis is inflammation of the episclera, a thin layer of loose connective material that covers the sclera (the white of the eye). The cause is unknown, but is often associated with diseases such as rheumatoid arthritis, Sjögren's syndrome and herpes zoster. The affected eye is sensitive to light, and is painful and bloodshot.

Episcleritis clears up in one to two weeks without treatment, sometimes sooner with corticosteroid eyedrops.

SEE ALSO *Eye, Rheumatoid arthritis, Sjögren's syndrome*

EPISPADIAS

Epispadias is a congenital defect of the penis. The urethra—the duct connecting the bladder to the tip of the penis—opens abnormally on the top of the penis, either in the head or along the entire length. The result is abnormal leakage of urine (incontinence) and sexual dysfunction. Reconstructive surgery usually cures the defect.

SEE ALSO *Bladder, Hypospadias, Incontinence, Penis, Urethra, Urinary systems*

ERECTION

Erection is a state in which the erectile tissue of an organ or body part has become distended and rigid by the accumulation of blood. Though the nipple and clitoris contain erectile tissue, the term usually refers to the distension of the penis.

The penis is comprised primarily of two cylinders of sponge-like vascular tissue. (A third cylinder contains the urethra, a tube that carries the urine and the ejaculate.) After physical or psychological sexual stimulation, the cylinders become engorged with blood and the penis becomes erect and hard. This enables the male to insert the erect penis into the female's vagina during sexual intercourse. The blood is unable to drain out through the veins because they are temporarily closed by pressure from arterial blood in the spongy tissue of the penis.

Inability to produce or maintain an erection of the penis is called impotence. It is more common in older men and can be caused by psychological problems, alcohol, drugs, surgery, or disorders such as diabetes and stroke. Depending on the cause it can be successfully treated with sex therapy, penile implants, needle injection therapy, vacuum cup devices or medications such as sildenafil (Viagra).

Peyronie's disease (curvature of the penis) is a bend in the penis that occurs during erection. It cannot be cured but it can be helped with hormone (corticosteroid) injections into the penis.

SEE ALSO *Impotence, Penis, Peyronie's disease, Reproductive systems*

EROGENOUS ZONES

An erogenous zone is any part of the body that, when stimulated, can produce sexual arousal or pleasure.

In the mid-twentieth century, the American researcher Alfred Charles Kinsey found that there is no part of the human body that is not able to bring about sexual arousal in some individuals. He estimated that in about half of all females the breasts and nipples were erotically sensitive enough for stimulation to result in orgasm. Conversely, his research found about 2 percent of females had never found themselves to be sexually aroused under any conditions.

Obvious erogenous zones in men are the external sex organs: the penis, particularly the glans which is the sensitive head above the shaft; the skin of the scrotum and inner thighs; the buttocks and external skin around the anus; and in some men, the nipples. In women the clitoris, vulva, nipples, areolae, breasts and inner thighs are the main areas sexually responsive to stimulation.

Every part of the body can be sexually aware, and respond to stimulation, as our experience of sexual pleasure is largely mental. When injury or disablement affects the touch-receptive nerve endings in one area, new areas can replace them, and relocate the traditional erogenous zones.

The hypothalamus, the part of the brain that regulates the autonomic nervous system, receives nerve impulses generated by manual stimulation of the nipples and genitalia. It responds to sexual desire by releasing hormones that increase heart rate, blood circulation and respiration rates and dilate the pupils of the eyes, bringing about a state of sexual arousal or readiness for sexual intercourse.

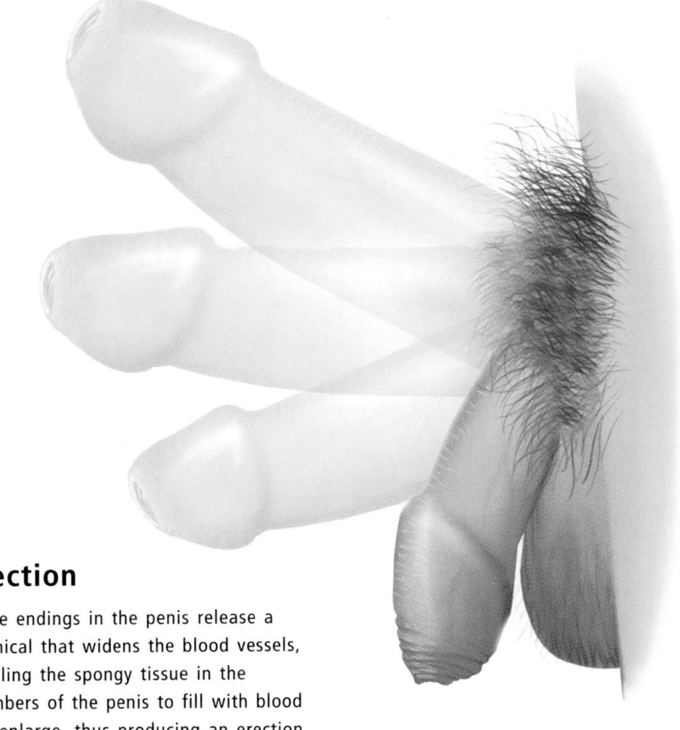

Erection

Nerve endings in the penis release a chemical that widens the blood vessels, enabling the spongy tissue in the chambers of the penis to fill with blood and enlarge, thus producing an erection.

E

E

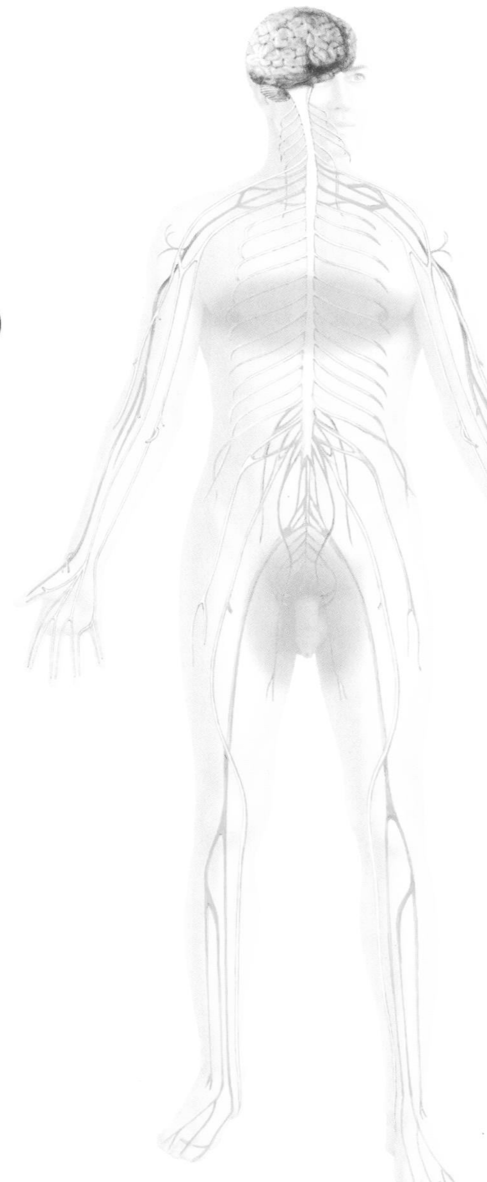

Erogenous zones

Although any part of the body can be an erogenous zone, the main areas for both men and women include the genitals, inner thighs, buttocks, breasts and nipples.

Sexual arousal is a complex emotional and physical response to stimulation of the senses—sight, smell, hearing and touch. What a person finds stimulating will be a combination of individual preferences, personal history, memories and influences from culture and conditioning. A person's response at any one time can be influenced by their physical and emotional condition.

Under stress, such as financial pressures or relationship problems, sexual drive and response to normal stimulus may be very low. Tiredness, physical disorders and pain, mental attitudes and conditioning can also reduce or eliminate normal sexual arousal. The person may have no interest in sexual contact, although they may still need the physical and emotional reassurance given by the loving touch of a partner. Under these conditions, stimulation may not produce sexual arousal.

SEE ALSO ***Sexual activity, Sexuality***

ERYSIPELAS

Erysipelas is an acute inflammation of the tissues below the skin, usually on the face, caused by infection by *Streptococcus* bacteria. The bacteria enter via a break in the skin, often following a respiratory infection such as a cold. A bright red spot appears on the nose or cheeks, enlarges and becomes hot and painful, accompanied by fever, chills, muscle pains and malaise. Infection of the blood (septicemia) may follow if the condition is not treated. Erysipelas can also occur in the legs, where veins have been cut.

The inflammation subsides over a week or ten days with antibiotics. Painkillers and anti-febrile medications (antipyretics) help relieve the symptoms.

SEE ALSO ***Septicemia***

ERYTHEMA

Erythema is a condition in which there is reddish discoloration of the skin or mucous membrane. Blushing and mild sunburn are examples of erythema. More serious forms of erythema are associated with inflammation, and include erythema nodosum and erythema multiforme.

Erythema multiforme

Erythema multiforme is a type of hypersensitivity (allergic) reaction that occurs usually in children and young adults. It is caused by infection (especially with the herpes simplex virus), drug sensitivity or other allergic reactions. Spots, pimples or vesicles appear on the face, hands and legs, caused by damage to the blood vessels of the skin and to underlying skin tissues.

Usually the condition subsides in two to three weeks with oral corticosteroid treatment and skin dressings. In one variant, Stevens-Johnson syndrome, lesions are extensive, involving multiple body areas and requiring treatment in a burns unit in hospital.

Erythema nodosum

In erythema nodosum, painful, red, oval nodules appear on the skin, usually on the shins. The nodules turn purple, then brown, and disappear after several weeks. Fever and malaise are accompanying symptoms.

The condition usually follows a streptococcal throat infection, but may be associated with diseases such as tuberculosis or ulcerative colitis. Certain drugs such as penicillin, salicylates and birth control pills may also cause the condition. Treatment is with oral hormones (corticosteroids), bed rest and aspirin; topical creams have no effect on the nodules.

SEE ALSO ***Corticosteroids, Herpes simplex, Stevens-Johnson syndrome, Tuberculosis, Ulcerative colitis***

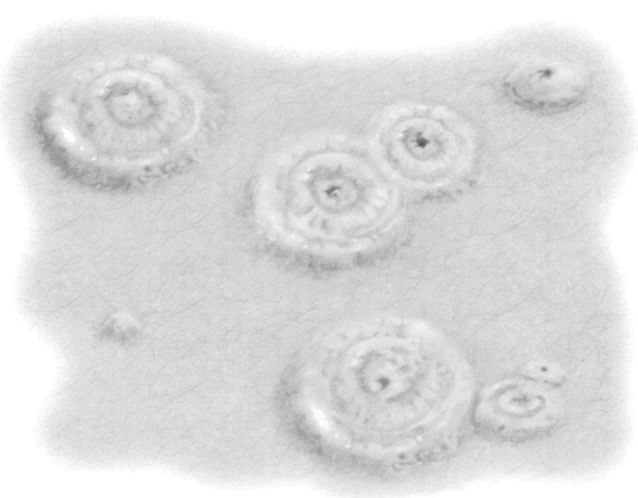

Erythema multiforme

Erythema multiforme is characterized by spots, pimples or blisters that usually appear on the face, hands and legs.

E

ERYTHRASMA

Erythrasma is a chronic, slowly spreading skin infection. It occurs mostly in adolescents, in overweight people and in those with diabetes, especially in hot areas like the tropics. Reddish-brown, slightly scaly patches with sharp borders appear in moist areas such as the groin, axilla and skin folds, and between the toes. They resemble a fungal infection, but in fact are caused by a bacterium, *Corynebacterium minutissimum.*

Antibacterial soaps and oral antibiotics (such as eythromycin or tetracycline) clear the infection, but it tends to recur.

SEE ALSO *Intertrigo*

Erythema nodosum

Erythema nodosum is a painful condition in which red nodules appear, usually on the shins, fading to bruise-like patches that disappear after several weeks.

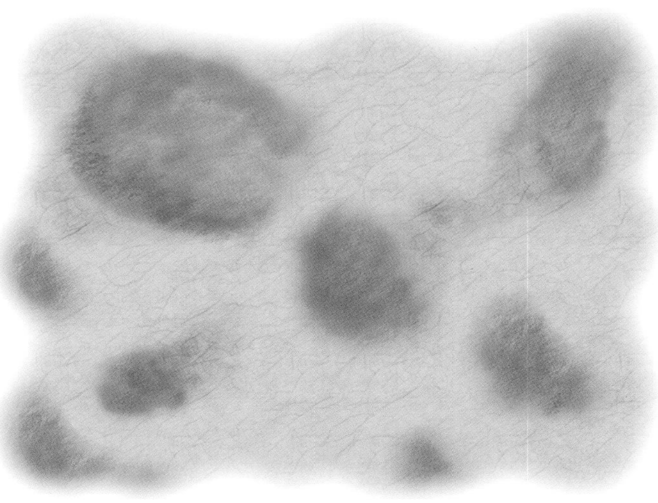

ERYTHROCYTE SEDIMENTATION RATE

A commonly requested pathology test, erythrocyte sedimentation rate (ESR) is a measure of the rate at which red cells settle in a column of blood standing in a thin tube.

Infections, anemia, certain rheumatic diseases and other autoimmune disorders are all associated with a rapid rate compared to normal ESR (1–20 millimeters/hour). Certain cancers such as multiple myeloma can also, though not invariably, produce a high ESR reading.

The efficacy of treatment of infections can be monitored over a period until cure—judged by a normal ESR—has occurred. Therapy for tuberculosis and bone infections is checked in this way.

SEE ALSO *Red blood cells*

ESOPHAGITIS

Esophagitis literally means inflammation of the esophagus, the tube connecting the back of the throat (pharynx) with the stomach. An inflammation of the esophagus usually damages the inner, or epithelial, lining most of all. It may be due to the accidental swallowing of corrosive chemicals such as caustic soda or concentrated acid (corrosive esophagitis), or due to reflux of acidic stomach juices into the lower esophagus (reflux esophagitis). The latter may occur in sliding hiatus hernia when the mechanism which keeps stomach juices in the stomach, is impaired.

Reflux esophagitis is a serious disease and may be accompanied by heartburn and regurgitation. In severe cases, surgery to treat the sliding hiatus hernia may be necessary.

SEE ALSO *Esophagus, Hiatus hernia*

ESOPHAGUS

The esophagus is a muscular tube that allows food to be transported from the throat (pharynx) to the stomach. It passes through the neck and chest and into the abdomen, with the portion through the chest being the longest. The esophagus must pass through the diaphragm on its way to the stomach.

Three areas of the esophagus are relatively narrow and may be sites where swallowed corrosive substances (such as caustic soda or sulfuric acid) are slowed up and may cause major damage. These sites of narrowing are at the beginning of the esophagus, where the esophagus crosses the arch of the aorta just above the heart, and where the esophagus passes through the diaphragm.

Sometimes the esophagus does not form properly during development and may be obstructed; this condition is known as esophageal atresia. The infant has great difficulty in swallowing milk; the regurgitated milk may be inhaled, causing pneumonia.

Achalasia of the esophagus is a condition in which nervous control of the esophageal muscle is impaired, due to degeneration of nerve cells in the esophageal wall. It results in difficulty in swallowing (dysphagia), retention of food in the esophagus and dilation of the esophagus.

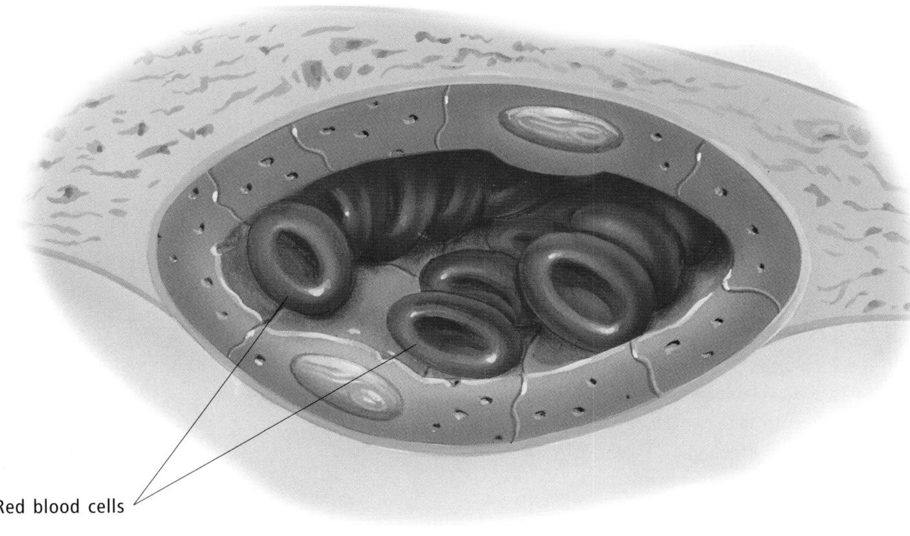

Erythrocyte sedimentation rate

Erythrocyte sedimentation rate (ESR) measures the rate at which red blood cells (erythrocytes) settle in a column of blood standing in a tube. It is a test used to help diagnose many illnesses.

Cancer of the esophagus is a relatively rare, but serious, condition, usually involving the malignant growth of the cells lining the esophagus. The patient complains of progressive difficulty in swallowing, beginning with solids and eventually involving liquids. There can be progressive weight loss and, occasionally, bleeding. Complications of the disease include fatal bleeding, pneumonia, obstruction of the trachea and problems with heart rhythm.

Infection of the esophagus itself is rare, but infection by yeast cells (candidiasis) can affect the esophagus. This is more common in those patients whose immune defenses against fungus are impaired.

As already mentioned, the esophagus may be damaged by swallowed corrosive substances such as strong acids or caustic soda (corrosive esophagitis). These substances cause chemical burns to the lining of the esophagus, which may cause perforation of the esophagus with spilling of food into the chest cavity, bleeding from esophageal ulcers and constriction (esophageal strictures) when scar tissue forms several weeks after injury.

A diverticulum or out-pocketing of the esophagus may occur when the esophagus "blows out" between strands of encircling muscle. This usually occurs in the upper part of the esophagus.

The esophagus leads into the stomach. In some situations, stomach juices may regurgitate from the stomach into the lower esophagus (gastroesophageal reflux). This usually occurs when part of the stomach slides through the diaphragm into the chest cavity (sliding hiatus hernia), thus interfering with the ability of the diaphragm to prevent reflux of stomach juices into the esophagus.

In cirrhosis of the liver, often caused by chronic alcoholism or viral hepatitis, small veins in the lower end of the esophagus may become enlarged (esophageal varices). These varices protrude through the inner surface lining of the esophagus and may rupture, discharging large amounts of blood into the lower esophagus. This blood is either vomited (hematemesis), or passed out through the anus as a dark, black, tarry stool. This is a very serious condition, because most patients who have massive bleeding from esophageal varices die as a result of the initial bleed.

SEE ALSO *Achalasia, Candidiasis, Cirrhosis of the liver, Diaphragm, Digestive system, Dysphagia, Gastroesophageal reflux, Hiatus hernia, Pharynx, Stomach*

ESTROGENS

Estrogens are a group of steroid hormones produced in the ovaries and, in lesser amounts, by other organs such as the adrenal glands. Steroid hormones are fatty substances derived from cholesterol and are taken up from the blood. The conversion of cholesterol to estrogens takes place via a series of steps, each of which is controlled by an enzyme. Intermediate substances in the pathway include both progesterone and testosterone; if one of the enzymes is deficient or inactive, testosterone may be secreted instead of estrogen.

The estrogens produced in the ovary are estradiol and a related substance, estrone. These are both released into the circulation

Esophageal diverticulum

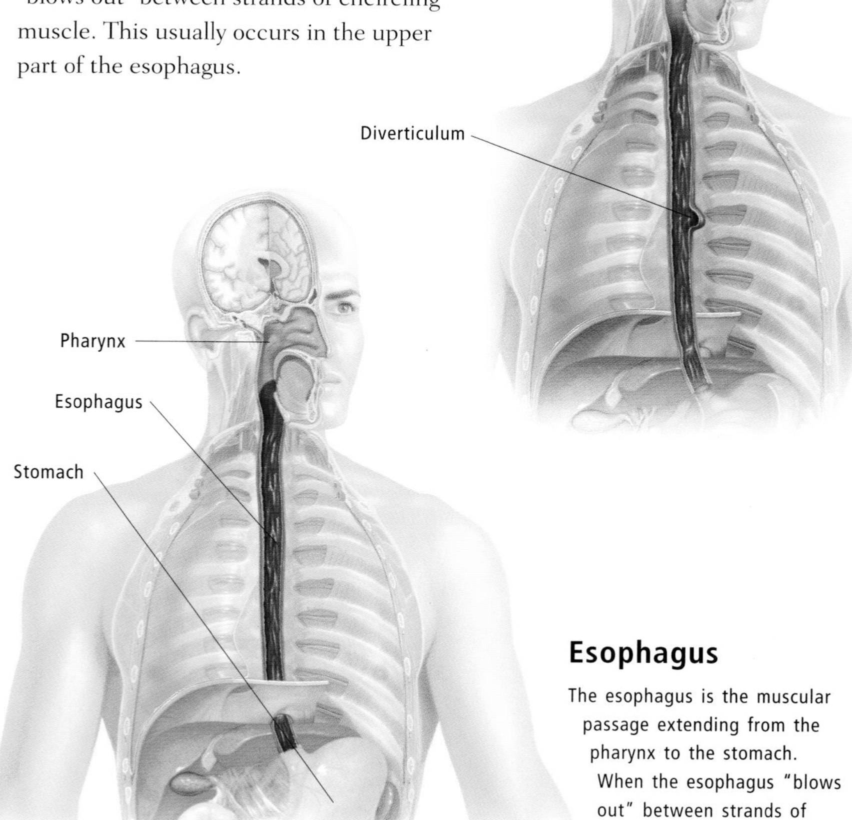

Esophagus

The esophagus is the muscular passage extending from the pharynx to the stomach. When the esophagus "blows out" between strands of encircling muscle, a diverticulum may occur.

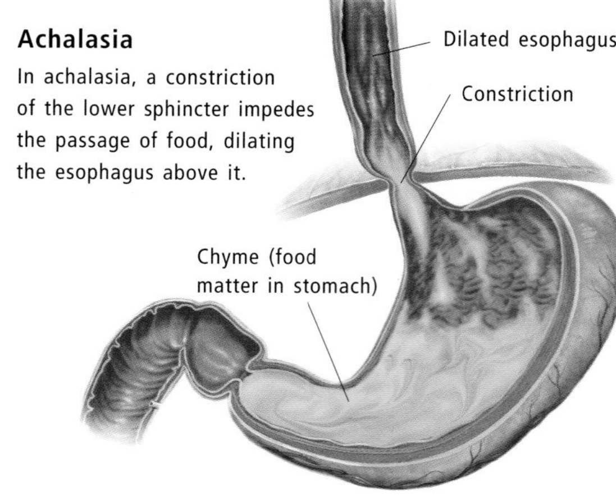

Achalasia

In achalasia, a constriction of the lower sphincter impedes the passage of food, dilating the esophagus above it.

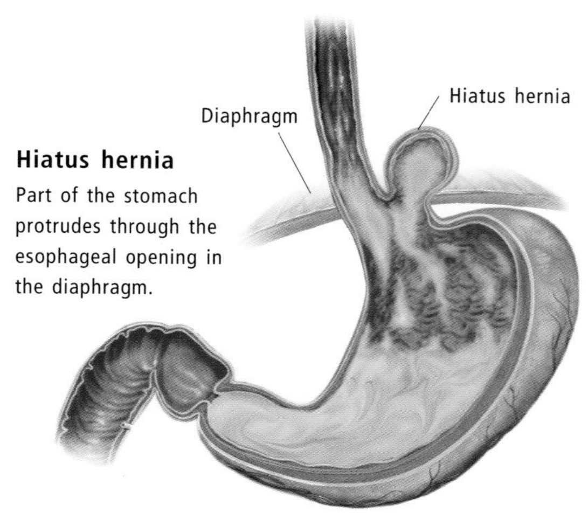

Hiatus hernia

Part of the stomach protrudes through the esophageal opening in the diaphragm.

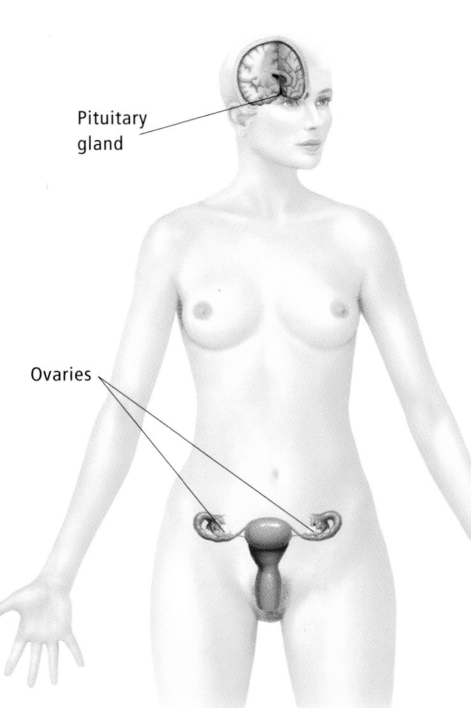

Estrogens

Estrogens are female sex hormones produced mainly by the ovaries. Their production is controlled by the pituitary gland. They control the development of the female sex characteristics and reproductive system.

and are broken down in the liver to form estriol, found in urine. The ability of target organs, such as the uterus, to respond to estrogens and other hormones is determined by whether the cells of that organ have receptors for the hormone on their surfaces.

Estrogens are secreted in high quantities in pregnancy. The placenta and the fetal and maternal adrenal glands are all involved. Estrogen levels fall a few days after giving birth. Estrogen production declines before and during menopause, and its loss may cause thinning of the lining of the vagina, vulvitis, osteoporosis and increased risk of cardiovascular disease. Hormone replacement therapy, using a combination of estrogen and progesterone, reduces or eliminates these effects.

Estrogens are involved in the development of fibroids (benign tumors in the muscle wall of the uterus and the most common pelvic tumor in women). Fibroids tend to grow rapidly during pregnancy when estrogen levels are high and may cause complications or miscarriage. Fibroids decrease in size following menopause.

Abnormally early breast development (gynecomastia) can result from ovarian tumors, which produce large amounts of estrogens, or from estrogens in oral contraceptives mistakenly ingested by young children. Gynecomastia may also occur in boys because of the transient increase in the amount of estrogens produced during puberty. It disappears when testosterone secretion is established in normal amounts.

SEE ALSO *Adrenal glands, Cholesterol, Fibroids, Hormones, Hormone replacement therapy, Menopause, Oral contraceptives, Ovaries, Pregnancy, Testosterone*

EWING'S SARCOMA

Ewing's sarcoma is the second most common type of bone cancer. It occurs in children and adolescents (usually Caucasians) between 10 and 20 years of age. A person will experience pain and sometimes swelling at the tumor site, usually in the long bones of the arms and legs (especially the femur), or the pelvis or ribs. The tumor grows quickly and spreads to other bones and the lungs.

Treatment involves a combination of intensive radiation therapy and chemotherapy, and (in some patients) surgical removal. If treated before it has spread, 60 percent of children with the tumor will survive.

SEE ALSO *Cancer, Metastasis*

EXERCISE

Exercise is physical activity undertaken to develop, maintain or improve physical fitness. People need exercise because humankind evolved leading a much more active life than is normal in industrialized societies today.

The nomadic existence of hunters was a necessity as they traveled to follow their food supplies, migratory animal herds and wild food sources that waxed and waned with the seasons. As agricultural societies evolved, a life of physical exertion and manual labor was normal for most. Only since the Industrial Revolution has the less active lifestyle largely become the norm, and this has made regular exercise a necessity to maintain good physical condition.

The mechanics of exercise

All exercise involves tension or contraction of muscles. Because muscles can only actively contract (shorten) they can only pull in one direction. They are arranged in opposing pairs to enable active extension and flexion, as in the biceps and triceps that contract to bend and straighten the elbow.

Energy for muscular contraction comes from glycogen, a form of the sugar glucose, stored in muscle tissue. When the stored energy is required, the glycogen reacts with oxygen in the blood to metabolize its energy. If oxygen is not present, which can happen during heavy workouts, the glycogen can still be metabolized, but this process creates an oxygen debt and a build-up of lactic acid in the muscles being worked. The oxygen

Exercising muscles

Muscles are arranged in antagonistic pairs to allow opposing movements such as flexion of a joint in one direction and extension in another. For example, the biceps controls flexion of the elbow, while the triceps controls elbow extension.

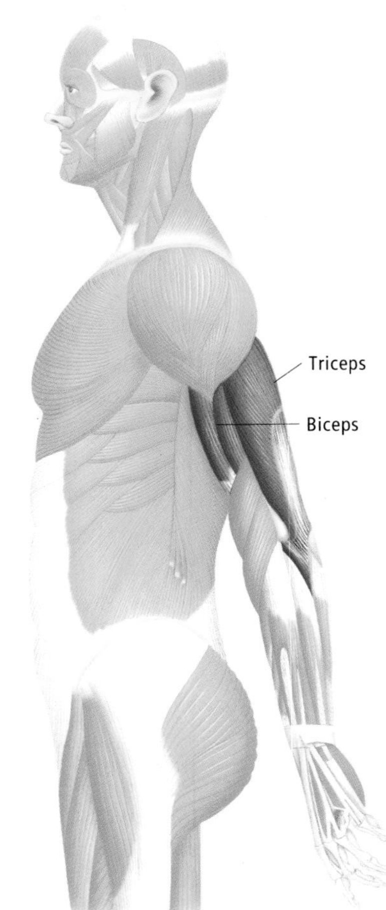

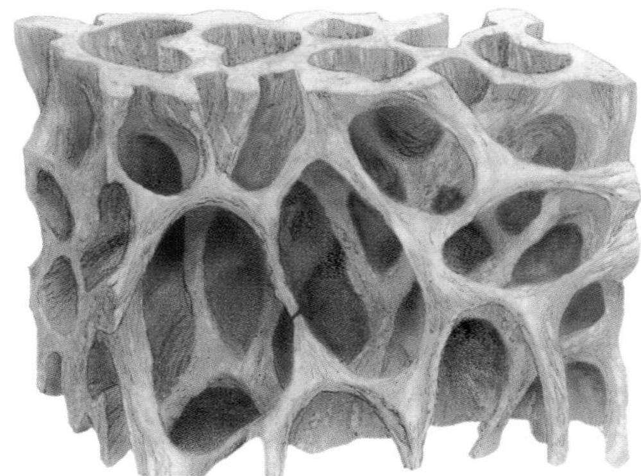

Osteoporotic bone

It is important to maintain exercise levels in later life to prevent diseases such as osteoporosis—a progressive bone disease in which bone density decreases, causing weakness and a greater likelihood of fracture.

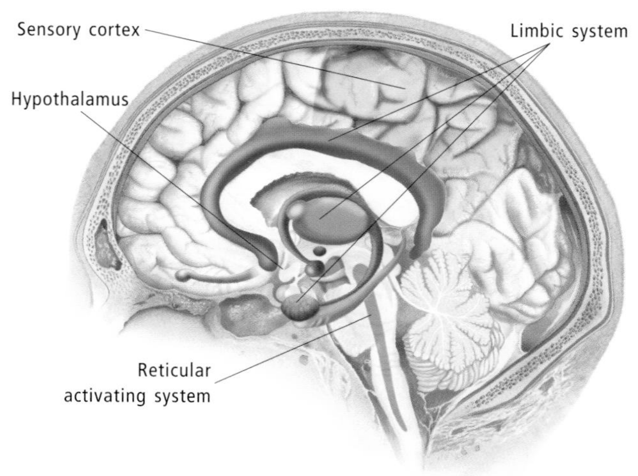

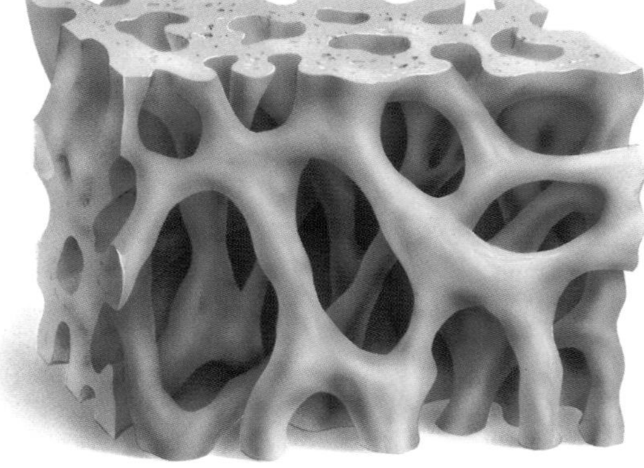

Normal bone

Exercise, particularly weight-bearing exercise, can help to maintain or increase bone density.

Role of the brain in exercise

Endorphins are found in the hypothalamus, limbic system and reticular formation. The hypothalamus influences the blood supply to muscles through the autonomic system and spinal nerves. Endorphin release increases during exercise. These neurotransmitters inhibit the conduction of pain impulses to the sensory cortex and their release can induce a feeling of well-being.

debt is repaid when oxygen becomes available. The lactic acid build-up may lead to muscle soreness.

Exercise programs are directed specifically at a performance task, or at improving flexibility, strength or endurance. The type of exercise must relate to the outcome required. Progression is another feature of exercise. A sedentary person just beginning a fitness walking program needs to start at a very modest, easily achievable level of activity, then aiming to cover a few hundred yards (meters) more every day until a goal distance is reached.

Exercise relies for improvement on continually increasing the demands put upon the muscles being exercised. Weightlifters make heavier lifts and sprinters aim to shave tenths of seconds from their timed runs.

Warming up and cooling down are vital steps in an exercise session. A gradual start allows the body's various systems to adjust to the higher demands being made: heart rate increases, pumping more blood around the body and muscle temperatures rise.

As the session draws to a close, it is important to let activity tail off and reduce intensity. This lets the heart rate slow and avoids complications such as lowered blood pressure which can cause fainting or even cardiac arrest. Target heart rate for the cool-down period is 120 to 100 beats per minute, depending on age and fitness level.

To be effective, exercise must be frequent. A minimum level of frequency is generally agreed to be three times a week or every second day. While exercising every day may be the goal for some, others may find this excessive.

Effect on health

Exercise changes the body's composition to increase the proportion of lean muscle tissue and proportionally reduce fat.

A recent study has found a marked difference in body composition with significantly lower levels of visceral fat (fat around the trunk and internal organs) between those whose daily routine included walking 7,500 paces—approximately 2½ miles (4 kilometers)—each day and those who did less. It was not important whether the walking was planned as exercise or part of their daily living routine, the effect was the same. This research, although not yet scientifically proven, seems to confirm that a sedentary lifestyle is the greatest enemy of health.

Babies, from the moment they are born, begin to exercise their muscles. As they play and experiment they are learning how to use their muscles until they can crawl, walk and run. Children also exercise when they are involved in activities such as running and bicycle riding. Obesity is a major problem for children today as the time spent on sedentary tasks has reduced the time exercising in active play. Exercise and sport need to be a natural part of childhood and adolescence, both for physical and emotional well-being and to protect against diseases in later life such as osteoporosis.

Adults who continue to exercise as they grow older will continue to benefit. Women can continue to exercise during and after pregnancy: it is wise to consult a doctor about exercise when pregnant, but most forms can usually be adapted for pregnancy. Exercises that help the woman's body to return to its pre-pregnant state are often taught during the early postpartum period and most forms of exercise can be resumed from around six weeks after the birth.

Kegel or pelvic floor exercises will often be taught to women at this time in order to strengthen pelvic floor muscles and prevent urinary incontinence, which can occur when the hormones of pregnancy relax these muscles. Women can practice these exercises throughout their adult life to help prevent urinary incontinence, which can also occur in menopause.

In later life both men and women will benefit from continuing weight-bearing types of exercise, either in daily life by walking as much as possible or by involving themselves in an activity such as swimming, cycling, golf, dancing, yoga or bowling. Exercise is important to general well-being—it can elevate mood, relieve anxiety, improve sleep and enhance mental alertness.

Aerobic exercises

Such exercises include activities like walking and jogging which involve moving muscles throughout their full range over a relatively long period, during which rates of respiration and heart rate increase, building to a desired maximum level and sustaining that for 15 to 20 minutes. This type of exercise is used to improve cardiovascular fitness, which increases blood flow and transport of oxygen to the muscles, and has a beneficial effect on general health.

Aerobic exercise programs are planned to improve heart–lung capacity by raising heart rate to about 70 percent of its maximum, which is calculated as 220 minus the person's age in years. Thus at 45 years of age, the heart should be capable of 175 beats per minute and should be 120 during exercise.

Anaerobic exercises

These are the body-builders' methods of adding bulk and involve high-intensity activity by a small group of muscles and a limited range of movement over short periods of time. Weightlifting is an example where the energy demand on muscles outstrips the body's ability to aerobically metabolize glycogen and creates an oxygen debt. Anaerobic activities increase muscle mass and strength but deliver little benefit to heart, lungs and overall health.

Beginning an exercise program

When undertaking exercise, beginners should ideally be supervised as they must initially be made aware of potential strains on the heart and circulatory system. Loading muscles to the point of pain or exhaustion is dangerous, and where heart health is already poor this can bring on collapse or cardiac arrest.

In the beginning, even moderate exercise will require effort and create an oxygen debt. After a few weeks or months, heart and lung function may improve, allowing more efficient conversion of glycogen to muscle energy and increasing capacity for sustained effort.

Regular exercise is a necessity for everyone and particularly important for those whose daily lives include little physical effort. Starting an exercise program for the first time or after a period without regular exercise should be done cautiously to lessen risks of injury.

SEE ALSO *Heart, Muscle, Muscular system, Obesity, Osteoporosis, Pilates, Respiratory system, Sports medicine, T'ai chi ch'uan, Yoga*

EXOPHTHALMOS

Exophthalmos is abnormal protrusion or bulging of one or both eyeballs. It may be accompanied by double vision and eye pain. The condition is usually a symptom of an overactive thyroid gland (hyperthyroidism), but may have other causes, such as a tumor or blood clot behind the eye. It improves after the underlying cause is corrected; surgical correction may be necessary.

SEE ALSO *Eye, Hyperthyroidism*

EXPECTORANTS

Expectorants are compounds used in cough and cold products to help loosen phlegm and make coughing more productive. They can be bought over-the-counter without a doctor's prescription. Guaifenesin is the most widely used expectorant and is found in a range of over-the-counter preparations.

Expectorants cause mucus and other substances blocking the airways to become thinner, so they are easier to cough up. Coughing becomes easier and less irritating, and chest congestion is relieved. For example, someone with pneumonia may find an expectorant helps clear the airway of mucus, making breathing easier.

Some medical professionals question whether using an expectorant speeds recovery or really does relieve symptoms of respiratory illness. Some compounds commonly sold as expectorants do not in fact have expectorant properties at all; these include ammonium chloride, a bitter plant extract called horehound, pine tar and spirits of turpentine. Moreover, if the cough does not produce mucus, then an expectorant is of no use. In this case, a cough suppressant may be more appropriate because it allows the sufferer to cough less, feel more comfortable and sleep better.

It is important to follow label instructions on cough suppressants to avoid over-use and possible side effects. If a cough persists, medical advice should be sought.

SEE ALSO *Cough*

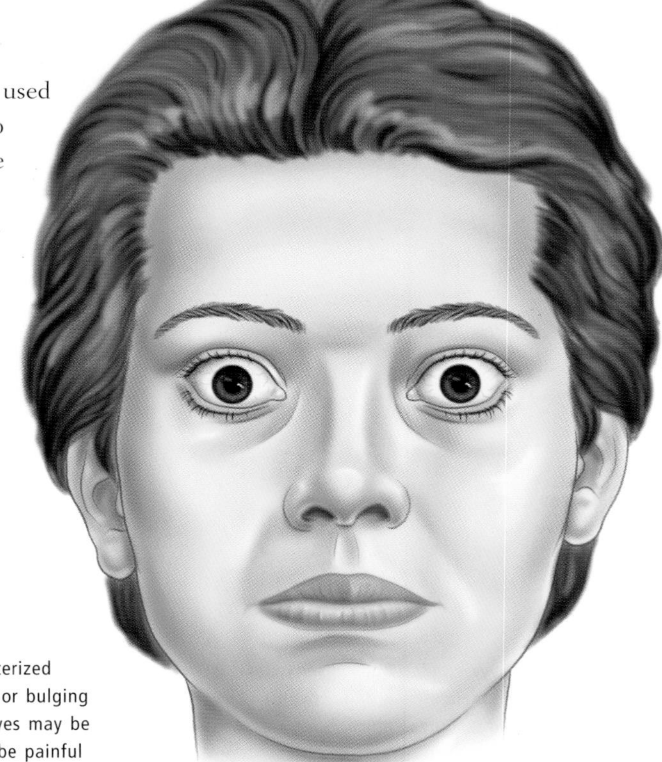

Exophthalmos

This condition is characterized by abnormal protruding or bulging eyeballs. One or both eyes may be affected. The eyes may be painful and double vision can occur.

E

EYE

The eye is the organ of sight: a complex, versatile and delicate structure.

Eyeball

Every time we look at a scene, an image is formed on the retina of the eye and sent to the brain for analysis. The eyeball can be compared to a camera. A camera has three main parts: the camera body, the lens and the film.

The eyeball is made up of three layers. The outer layer consists of the sclera and cornea, the middle layer is the uvea and lens, and the inner layer is the retina.

Sclera and cornea

The eyeball is a sphere formed by a white layer called the sclera. The front part of this sphere is cut off and replaced by a section of a smaller sphere. This section is more curved and formed by a transparent layer called the cornea.

The sclera gives the eyeball its shape and maintains a constant distance between the cornea and the retina at the back of the eye. It serves the same function as the camera body. When the eye is focused on infinity, the image should fall on the back of the eye. If the sphere of the sclera is slightly too large, images of close objects will fall exactly on the back of the eye but distant objects will not, and so the eye can only clearly see close objects, a condition known as near-sightedness or myopia.

The opposite condition is far-sightedness or presbyopia, occurring when the scleral sphere is too small.

The sclera has a hole near the posterior pole of the eyeball through which the optic nerve, which connects the retina to the visual area of the brain, passes.

The cornea is transparent because its fibers and cells are organized in a very orderly fashion. Opacity results when this arrangement is disrupted by injuries and scarring.

Just like the camera lens, the cornea must have a perfect and adequate curvature, because it is the front element of the optic system of the eye. The cornea bends the light and works together with the lens to form an image on the retina. Vision is very poor in the condition called keratoconus (the cornea, *kerato-*, is shaped like a cone, *conus*). In this condition, the image is distorted because the cornea does not have the profile of a sphere but is more pointed at the center.

In astigmatism, the image on the retina is distorted because the cornea is not exactly spherical.

The cornea is very sensitive to pain and temperature. We all experience that pain when a tiny speck of dust gets in our eyes.

The junction between the sclera and the cornea is called the limbus (meaning the rim) and contains Schlemm's canal, a circular channel which drains the fluid from the front part of the eye. Its significance is discussed below.

Uvea and lens

The uvea is the middle layer of the eye and has three parts: the choroid, ciliary body and iris.

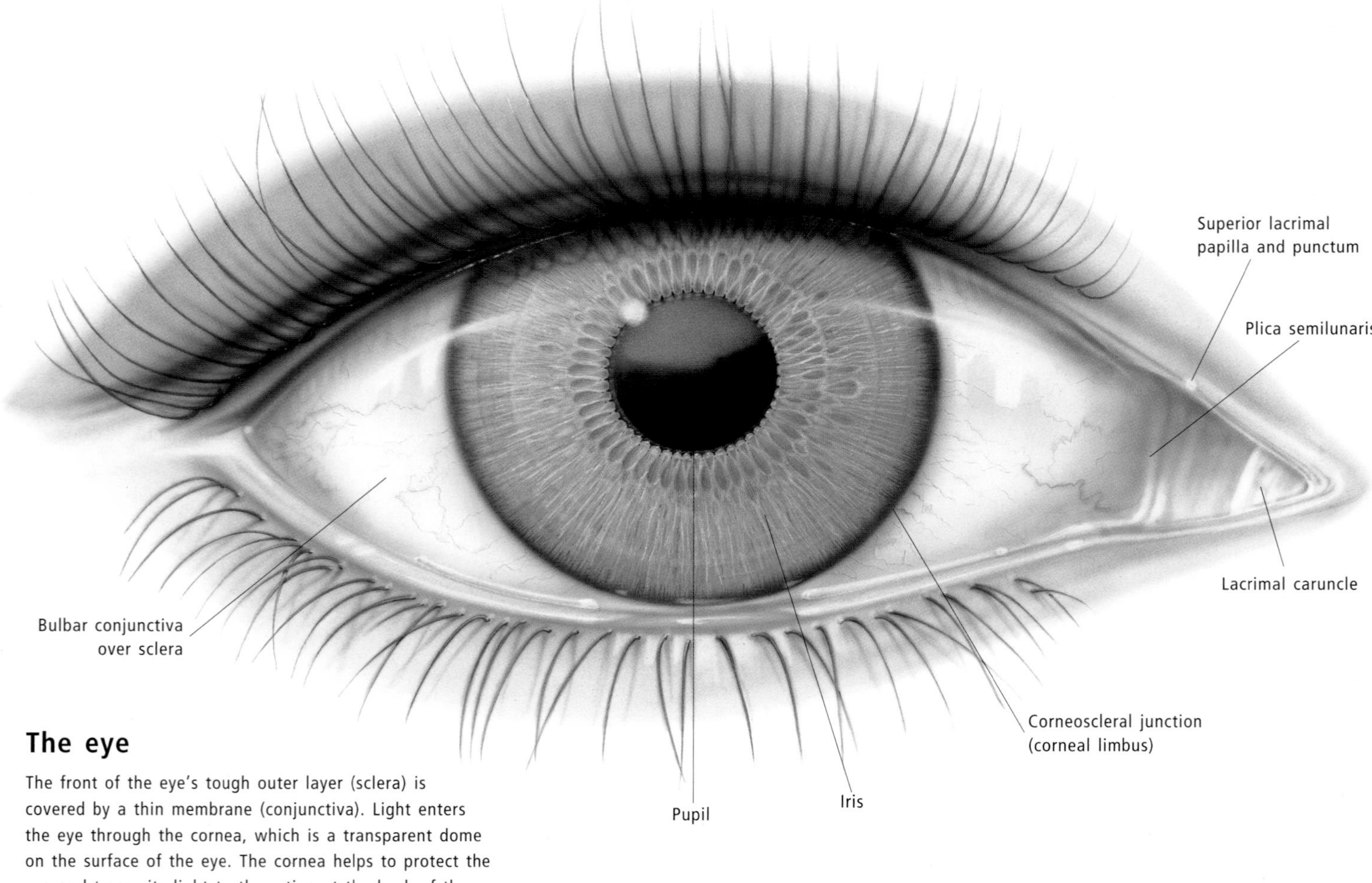

The eye

The front of the eye's tough outer layer (sclera) is covered by a thin membrane (conjunctiva). Light enters the eye through the cornea, which is a transparent dome on the surface of the eye. The cornea helps to protect the eye and transmits light to the retina at the back of the eye.

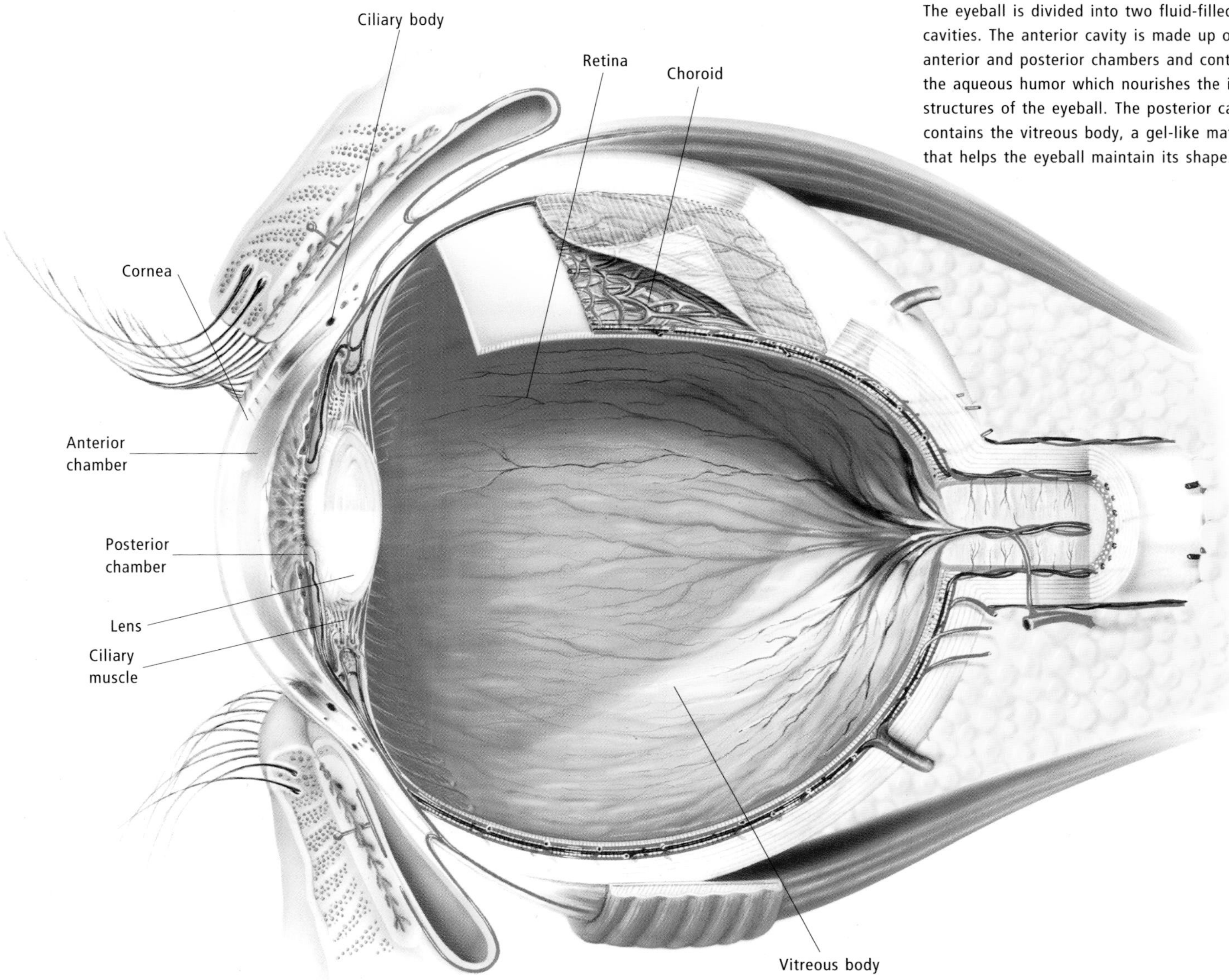

Eyeball

The eyeball is divided into two fluid-filled cavities. The anterior cavity is made up of the anterior and posterior chambers and contains the aqueous humor which nourishes the internal structures of the eyeball. The posterior cavity contains the vitreous body, a gel-like material that helps the eyeball maintain its shape.

The choroid is the back part of the uvea. It contains many blood vessels and gives passage to nerves going to the cornea, ciliary body and iris.

The choroid continues forwards as the ciliary body. If you were to cut the eye in two and look at the inside of the front half, you would see the ciliary body as a dark ring which gradually becomes thicker at the front. When the lens is removed, one can see that the ciliary body joins a flat ring that stretches down in front of the lens, the iris. The hole in the center of the iris is the pupil.

The ciliary body contains ciliary muscles. Tiny fibers that look like nylon strings run from the ciliary body to a ring near the equator of the lens. They form a suspension mechanism for the lens called the zonule.

The lens is a clear structure that looks and works as a magnifying glass. It does not bend the light as much as the cornea (i.e. its refractive power is not as great), but it can change its curvature. When the lens is in place in a normal eye which is looking into the distance, it is stretched and flattened by the pull of the zonule.

An experiment with a magnifying glass will help us understand how the eye focuses. Point the magnifying glass towards a tree far away outside a window and collect the inverted image on a piece of white cardboard. Move the cardboard back and forth until the tree looks sharp. The image of the window frame (which is nearer to us) is blurred. To get a sharp image of the window, we must either move the lens slowly further from the cardboard or add another lens in front of it to increase its refractive power.

The first conclusion is that the image of a close object is further from the lens than that of a distant object. That is why someone whose eyeball is slightly too large will not be able to see distant objects—their images fall in front of the retina. Corrective glasses must be concave to effectively reduce the refractive power of the lens of the eye to bring the image further back, onto the retina.

The second conclusion is that when we want to get a sharp image of a nearer object without moving the lens, we have to increase the thickness of the lens. This is achieved in the eyeball by the action of the ciliary muscles. The ciliary muscles contract, causing a movement of the ciliary body, which slackens the tension on the zonule. The lens shrinks back by its elasticity, becomes thicker (more rounded) and the image of the object is pulled back to the retina. As we age, the lens loses its elasticity and fails to achieve the thickness required. We can no longer focus on a near object and need reading glasses to add refractive power to our lenses.

If you have used manual cameras, you will be familiar with the diaphragm which controls the amount of light entering the lens. You will also know that when the opening of the diaphragm is small, depth of field is increased— objects closer to and further from the distance set on the lens will be acceptably sharp in the photograph. Photographers always use a small diaphragm opening to photograph close objects.

The iris works as the camera's diaphragm. It is heavily pigmented to block the light. It has circular muscle fibers around the pupil which contract in bright light to constrict the pupil. The iris also has contractile cells radiating out from the pupil. In darkness, these cells contract and the pupil is dilated.

The adjustment of pupil size and actions of the ciliary muscles is controlled by the autonomic nervous system, the part of our nervous system that operates without conscious effort. If this system is disrupted, the pupils will not constrict when a light is shone on the eyes.

Retina

The retina lines the inside of the back part of the eyeball. It receives and converts the image cast on it by the eye's optic system into neural signals. The retina develops the same way in the embryo. The outside layer is pigmented to reduce light reflection just like the black paint inside a camera. The inside layer is light sensitive like film in a camera.

A blow to the eyeball may result in a "retinal detachment" (this may also occur from no obvious cause); the two layers are separated from each other and vision is lost at the detached area.

The optical axis of the eye is a straight line between the center of the lens and the center of its image on the retina. The point where all the nerve fibers from the retina converge into the optic nerve is called the optic disk.

Photoreceptors

Light is converted into neural impulses by specialized cells called photoreceptors. These are classified into two types based on their shape: rods and cones. Cone receptors are not as sensitive to light as the rods but they can detect colors. Signals from individual cones are not mixed together much because only a few cones are connected together before the signal is sent to the brain. They are therefore responsible for detailed vision.

According to the laws of optics, the image made by a lens is sharpest around the optical axis of the lens. The area of the retina around the optical axis is designed for high resolution perception with a high concentration of cones. At the central point, each cone is connected by one optic nerve fiber to one point on the cortex of the brain. This point-to-point projection to the brain ensures the highest resolution possible. When you read this page, you really only see clearly the words in the center of your visual field. You cannot recognize the words on the rest of the page.

Rod photoreceptors are more sensitive to light, but a large number of them are connected together before the sum of signals is sent to the brain. Thus they are good for sensing brightness and movement, not for color or detailed vision. The rods are almost nonexistent around the optical center of the retina, but they are the only type of photoreceptor in the periphery of the retina. That is why we can only see movements of a friend from the "corner of the eye", not the facial expression.

There is no light detection at the optic disk where there are no photoreceptors. Light falling on the optic disk it will not be perceived by that eye, it is in the "blind spot".

When the photoreceptors are exposed to light, they lose an amount of a light-sensitive pigment called rhodopsin which has to be replaced by synthesis in the cell. After staring at a bright light, the eye is blinded for a short while because the photoreceptors are depleted of their rhodopsin.

Central artery of the retina

The central artery of the retina enters the eyeball by running in the center of the optic nerve. As it emerges from the optic disk it fans out into four main branches accompanied by their veins. These branches run on the inside of the retina and spread out into a capillary network.

Observation of these blood vessels through an ophthalmoscope is not only important for the diagnosis of disorders of the eye but also tells the doctor much about the general condition of arteries in diseases such as high blood pressure or diabetes.

Vitreous body

The cavity behind the lens and its zonule is filled up by a viscoelastic gel which is called the "vitreous body" because it is as clear as glass. In old age, tiny particles may form in the vitreous body and these are visible as floating spots in the visual field because they cast shadows on the retina.

Anterior and posterior chambers

The space in front of the lens and zonule is divided by the iris into the anterior and posterior chambers. The ciliary body secretes into the posterior chamber a fluid called aqueous humor which passes through the pupil into the anterior chamber.

The lens and cornea do not receive any blood vessels and rely entirely on aqueous humour for nutrition. Aqueous humor is drained into Schlemm's canal, located in the anterior chamber, and from there into the veins.

The pressure in the eye, the intraocular pressure, depends on the balance between the rate of production and drainage of aqueous humor. This pressure is often measured when you have your eyes examined by your doctor or optometrist. Excess intraocular pressure is seen with glaucoma, which can lead to blindness.

Appendages of the eye

The eyeball is moved by extraocular muscles and is protected by the eyelids and the lacrimal apparatus.

Movements of the eyeball

We move our eyes to look around us or to follow a moving object. Movement must be precise because the eye turns only a tiny angle to fixate on a person walking across the visual field a hundred yards (or meters) away. Moreover, movement of both eyes have to be coordinated to maintain stereoscopic vision.

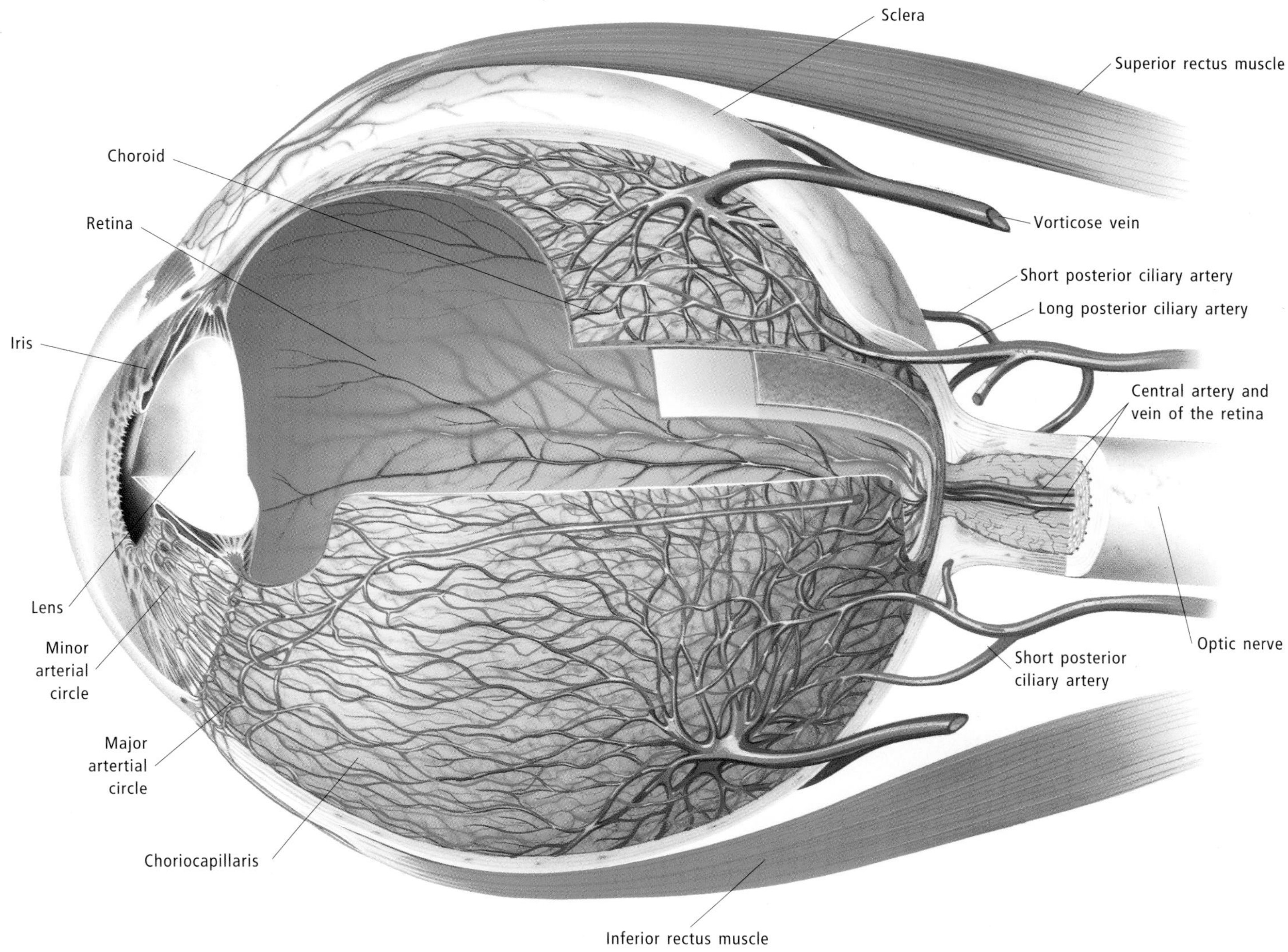

E

Sclera
Superior rectus muscle
Choroid
Retina
Vorticose vein
Short posterior ciliary artery
Long posterior ciliary artery
Iris
Central artery and vein of the retina
Lens
Minor arterial circle
Optic nerve
Short posterior ciliary artery
Major artertial circle
Choriocapillaris
Inferior rectus muscle

Arteries of the eye

The central artery of the retina enters the eye through the center of the optic nerve. It fans out into four main branches, each accompanied by veins. These arteries spread out to form a capillary network within the eye. The arteries can be adversely affected by conditions such as high blood pressure or diabetes.

Blind spot

Cover your right eye and focus on the red cross with your eyes at about 12 inches (30 centimeters) from this page. You can vaguely see the black dot in the periphery of your visual field. Move the page slowly closer, still focusing on the cross. At a certain distance, the black dot will disappear (when its image falls on the blind spot). With both eyes open, we see no blind spot as objects falling on the blind spot of one eye do not fall on the blind spot of the other eye.

The eyeball in its resting position is suspended by six muscles that run from the bones of the orbit (the cavity of the skull which accommodates the eyeball) to the eyeball. To simplify their actions, we can think of them as working in pairs to move the eyeball. For example, when the right eye looks to the right, the lateral rectus on the right side of that eye contracts and the medial rectus on the left side of the same eye relaxes to allow for the movement. In actual fact every movement of the eyeball involves actions of all six muscle. The neural mechanism of control is thus extremely complex.

If one muscle is too long (take the example above, the lateral rectus of the right eye), the eye is deviated to the opposite side (the left) by the pull of the unopposed muscle of the pair (the medial rectus) and this eye does not move in harmony with the other eye. This squint is known by the medical term strabismus. It can be repaired surgically by shortening the muscle or moving its attachment on the eyeball.

Eyelids

The eyelids are shutters that protect the eyes. The framework of each eyelid is a plate of connective tissue called the tarsus which is covered on the outside by the skin and on the inside by conjunctiva. The eyelid margin carries a few rows of eyelashes and has openings of numerous glands. Inflammation of these glands is the cause of chalazion while a stye (hordoleum) is caused by their infection. Inflammation of the conjunctiva is called conjunctivitis.

E

Disorders of the eye

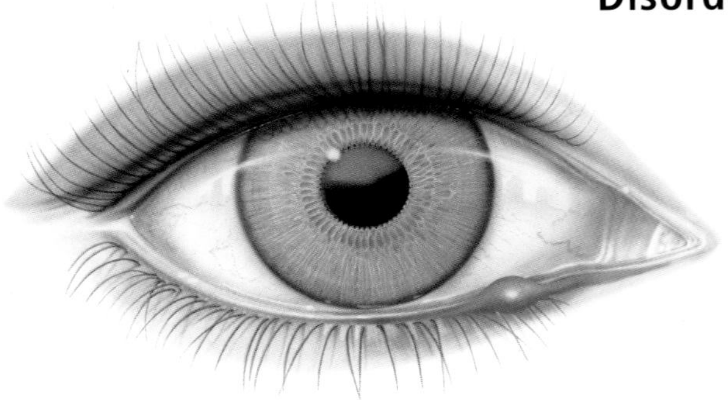

Stye

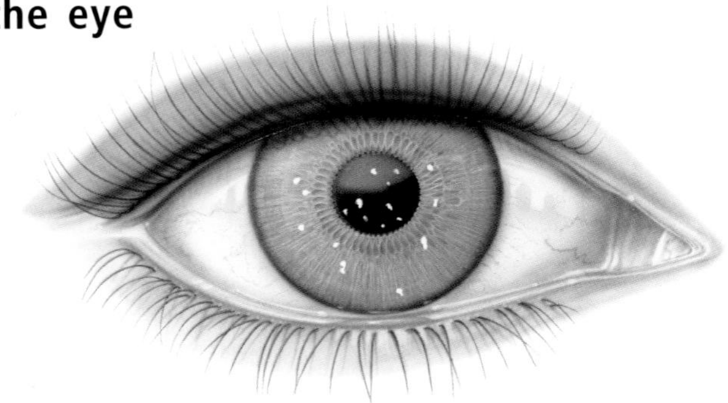

Punctate keratitis

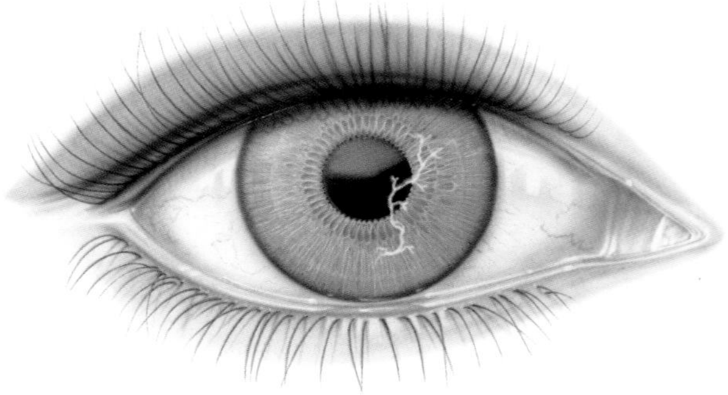

Dendritic keratitis

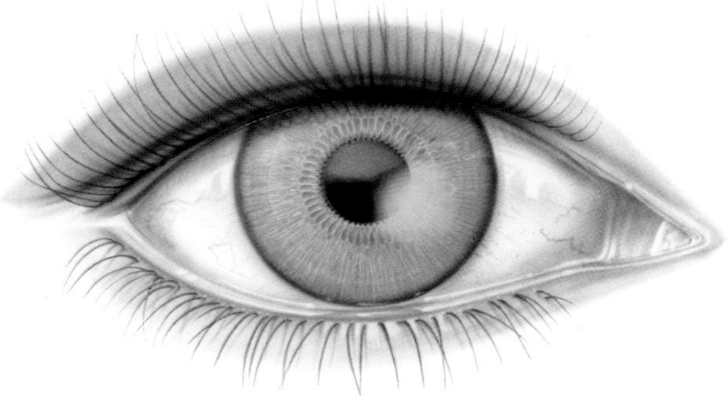

Diskiform keratitis

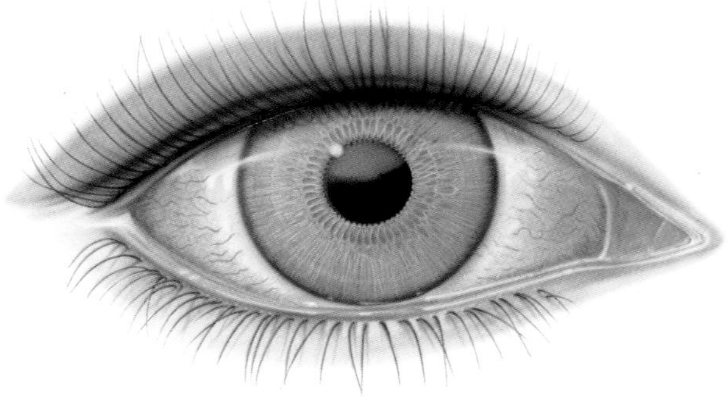

Allergic conjunctivitis

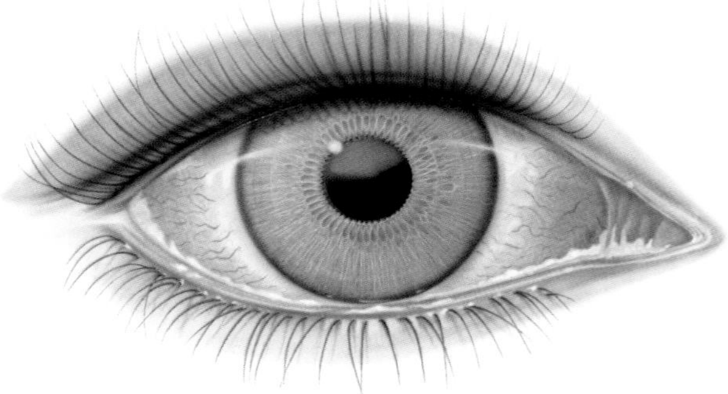

Bacterial conjunctivitis

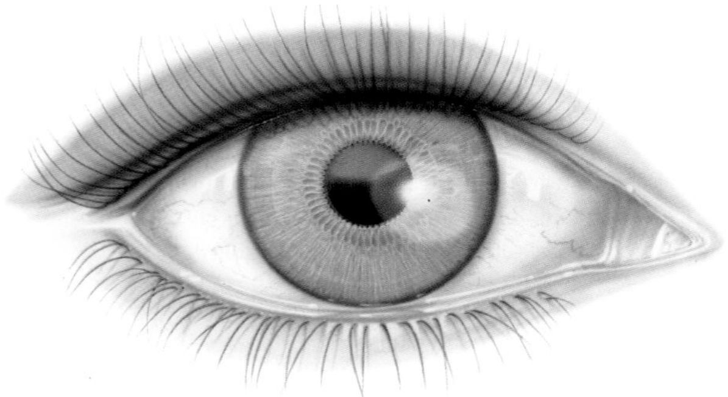

Corneal ulcer

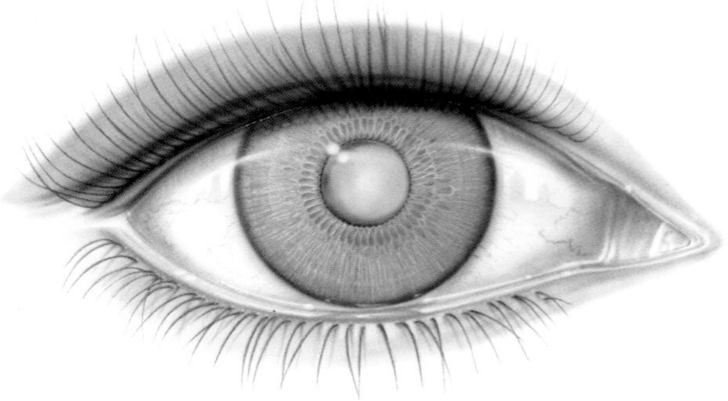

Cataract

Lacrimal apparatus

Tears keep the eye moist as well as providing lubrication and protection against infection. They are secreted by the lacrimal gland which is located at the upper outer corner of the orbit.

Tears form a film over the eye and flow down across the cornea towards the inner corner of the eye to be collected by two tiny canals which open near the inner end of each eyelid. Tears go from these canals into the lacrimal sac and flow down the nasolacrimal duct, a small tube which opens into the nose. This is why we can taste bitter eye drops—they get into the nose and drip onto the back of the tongue.

Movement of tears is facilitated by blinking. Tears overflow when we cry, when we have hay fever or when smoke gets into our eyes, because their production exceeds the draining mechanism.

Tears are essential in maintaining the integrity of the eye. The cornea may be ulcerated if it is dry. When their production is deficient, in conditions such as Sjögren's syndrome, patients have to instil artificial tears every few hours.

Eye disorders

The eye is subject to infection, inflammation, structural disorders and tumors. Some disorders are illustrated here, but more information is to be found under their specific entries.

SEE ALSO *Autonomic nervous system, Blindness, Cataracts, Chalazion, Color blindness, Conjunctivitis, Cornea, Eyelashes, Eyelids, Glaucoma, Iris, Keratitis, Lacrimal glands, Myopia, Pupil of eye, Retina, Sclera, Sight, Sjögren's syndrome, Squint, Stye*

EYELASHES

The eyelashes are hairs that extend out from the eyelids. They have a protective as well as a cosmetic function. Trichiasis is a condition in which the eyelashes grow inward and rub against the cornea of the eye, causing irritation, watering of the eyes, and a feeling of a foreign body in the eye. It is usually caused by entropion, in which the eyelids curl inward. It is treated by removing the inturned eyelash or by surgical correction.

SEE ALSO *Cornea, Eyelids*

EYELIDS

Eyelids are folds of skin that protect the front of each eyeball. When the eye is open, the upper eyelids retract above the eyeball; when closed, both upper and lower eyelids cover the visible area of the eye. The margins of the eyelids contain meibomian glands which secrete oils that lubricate the eyelids. The conjunctiva, a mucous membrane covering the surface of the eyeball, also extends to cover the undersurface of the eyelids.

Eyelid disorders include black (bruised) eye, blepharitis, chalazion, conjunctivitis, ectropion, entropion, ptosis and stye. The skin of the eyelids is also affected by skin disorders such as eczema.

Blepharitis is a disorder caused by an increased oil secretion from, or infection of, the meibomian glands. The eyelids become red and inflamed; the treatment is to cleanse the eyelids regularly with a warm solution of salt water.

A chalazion, or meibomian or tarsal cyst, is a small cyst formed when a meibomian gland becomes blocked with oil secretion. Chalazions are harmless but can be surgically removed if painful or unsightly.

Ectropion of an eyelid is a condition where the eyelid (usually the lower eyelid) turns outwards instead of remaining close to the eyeball. Common among the elderly, it is usually caused by the degeneration of the muscles of the eyelid.

Entropion of the eyelids is the opposite of ectropion: the eyelid curls inward toward the eye and may rub against the cornea, causing pain and redness of the eye. Both of these conditions can be corrected with minor surgery.

A stye is a small abscess of hair-follicle glands in the eyelid caused by a bacterial infection. The symptoms include swelling, redness and pain. Eventually the stye bursts and the symptoms subside. Treatment is to bathe the stye repeatedly with warm water. Antibiotic drops and ointments may also be prescribed.

SEE ALSO *Chalazion, Conjunctivitis, Eye, Stye*

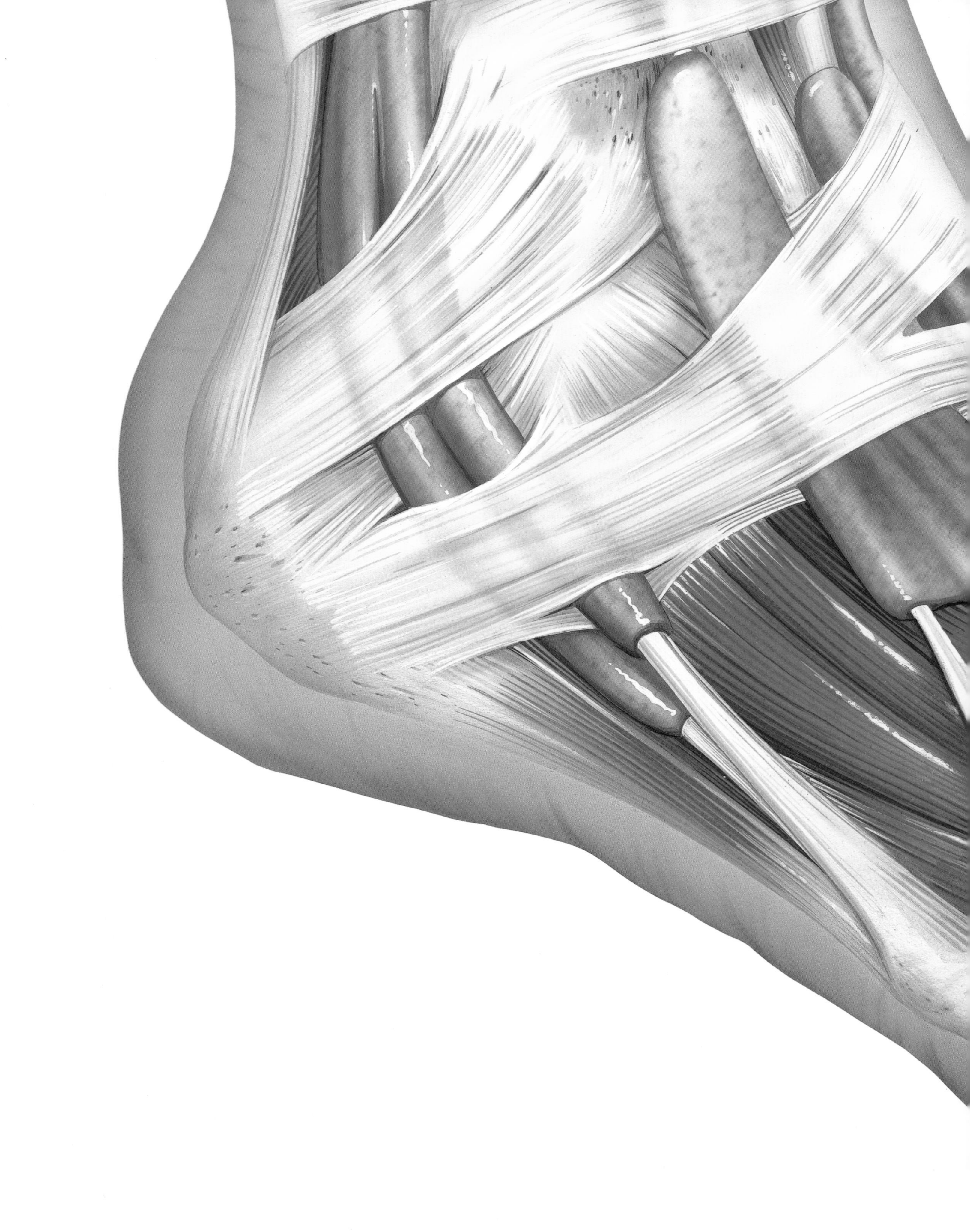

F

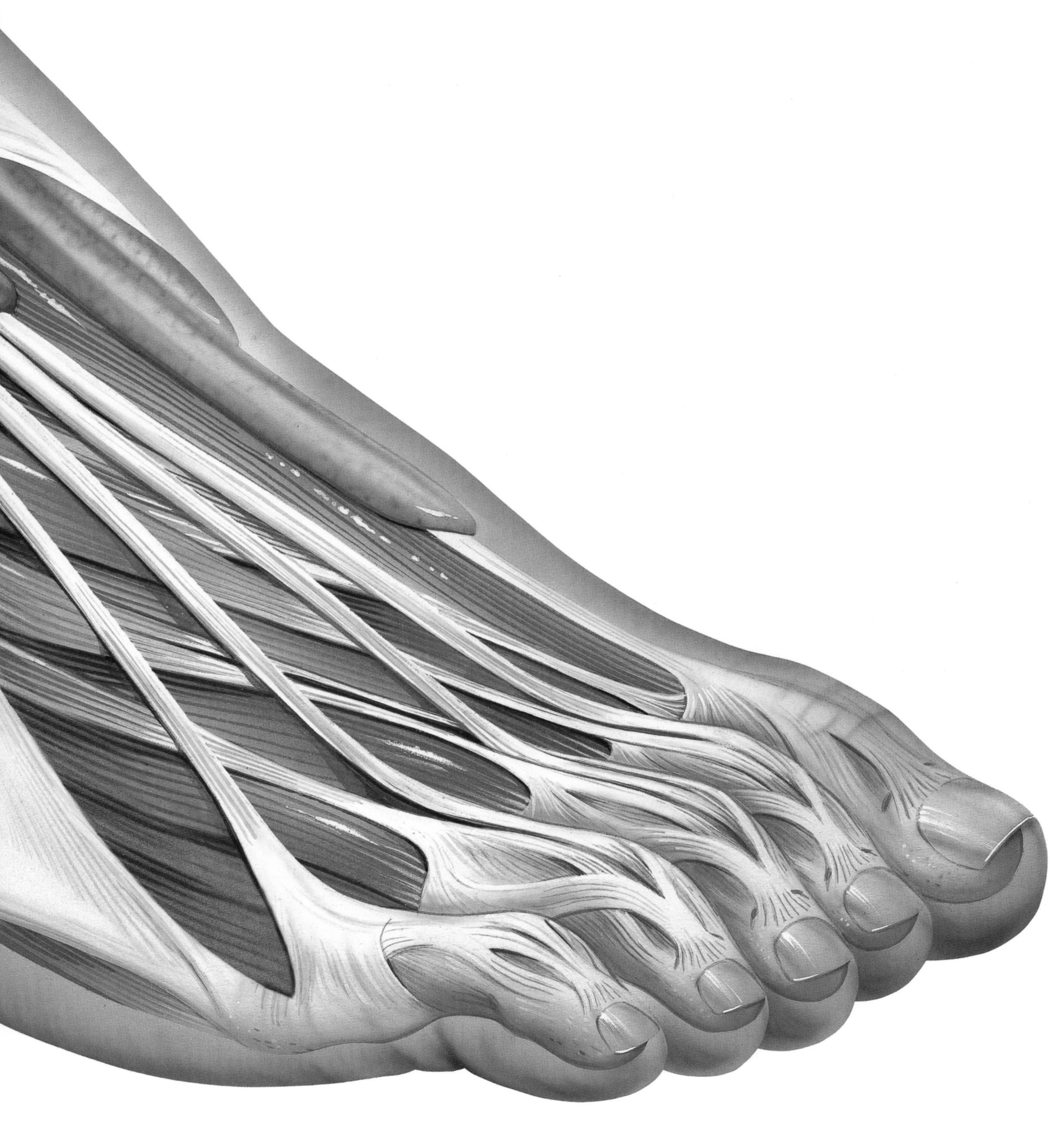

F

FACE

The face is made up of facial bones, muscles, skin, eyes, nose, jaws, cheeks and chin, as well as the nerves and blood vessels supplying these structures. The facial bones are covered with muscles and skin. Variations in these features account for our individual appearance; thanks to these variations we can recognize each other and tell one another apart. Much of what we think and feel is expressed in the face.

Evolution and development

During evolution from the prehuman *Australopithecus* to modern human (*Homo sapiens*), the face became smaller compared to the overall size of the head. The brain and the cranium (braincase) tripled in volume, but the jaws became shorter and the teeth smaller. In consequence, the face receded beneath the forehead. As a result, the modern human face exhibits an essentially vertical profile, in marked contrast to the protruding facial muzzle of the gorilla and the chimpanzee. As the jaws receded, they left the distinctive modern human features of a prominent nose and a sharply defined chin.

By the age of six years, the brain and the cranium have reached 90 percent of their adult size. But the face grows more slowly; at birth it is less than one-fifth the size of the braincase; by adulthood it has increased to nearly half. Facial dimensions increase most in depth, next in height (length), and least in width. Facial musculature increases and the nasal sinuses enlarge during adolescence, especially in males.

Parts of the face

The facial skeleton is made up of 14 bones. The frontal bone forms part of the forehead. The facial bones include the two nasal bones, forming the upper portion of the bridge of the nose; two lacrimal bones, which are located in each eye socket (orbit) next to the nose and close to the tear ducts; two maxillary bones (upper jaw); the mandible (lower jaw); the two palatine bones of the hard palate; the vomer, which, with a part of the ethmoid bone, makes up the nasal septum; and the two inferior turbinates of the nose.

The eyes are the organs of sight. Shaped like a ball, with a slight bulge at the front, each eye lies within a bony socket of the skull, protected from glare and dust by the eyelids, lashes and eyebrows. When the eyelids are closed as in sleep, the surface of the eye is covered; when awake, the eyelids blink roughly once every six seconds, washing the eye with salty secretions from the lacrimal (tear) glands, which are situated at the outer corner of the eye behind the upper eyelid. These secretions drain through the tear duct at the inner corner of the eye and into the nose; in certain emotional states, secretions from the lacrimal glands overwhelm the ducts and tears spill out over the eyelids. If an object suddenly moves too close to the eye, the eyelids automatically close.

The nose is a protuberance consisting of two cavities around a wall of cartilage called the nasal septum. The skeleton of the nose is cartilage at the tip, but bony closer to the skull. The nose functions as part of the breathing apparatus—filtering, warming, and moistening incoming air on its way to the lungs. The nose also contains olfactory nerve endings that detect smells. Just inside the nostrils grow short, coarse hairs which filter dust particles from the incoming air.

There are also a number of muscles in the face. There is a circular muscle around the mouth and one around each eye. Other muscles spread out over from the face from the edge of the circular muscles.

The mouth is the opening between the maxillae and the lower jaw. It is used for ingesting food, breathing air and for making sounds, especially speech. Lips, which form the mouth's muscular opening, contribute to formation of words during speech and also help hold food in the mouth. They also help form facial expressions, such as smiling and frowning. The sides of the mouth are formed by the cheeks. These are composed of muscle tissue covered on the outside by skin and on the inside of the mouth by mucous membrane. The cheeks also play an important

Bones of the face

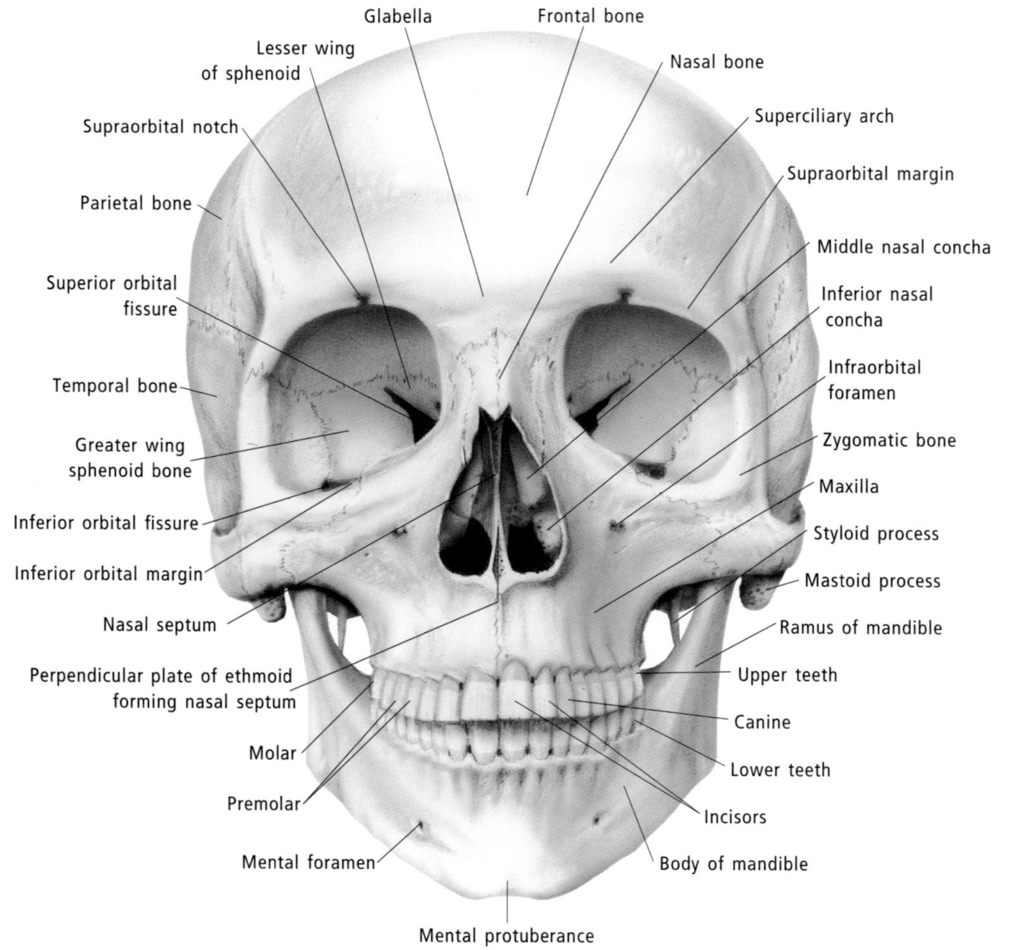

Face

A complex range of thoughts and emotions is expressed in the face—this requires an intricate system of muscles and nerves. The special sense organs (eyes, nose, ears and tongue) are all part of the facial structure.

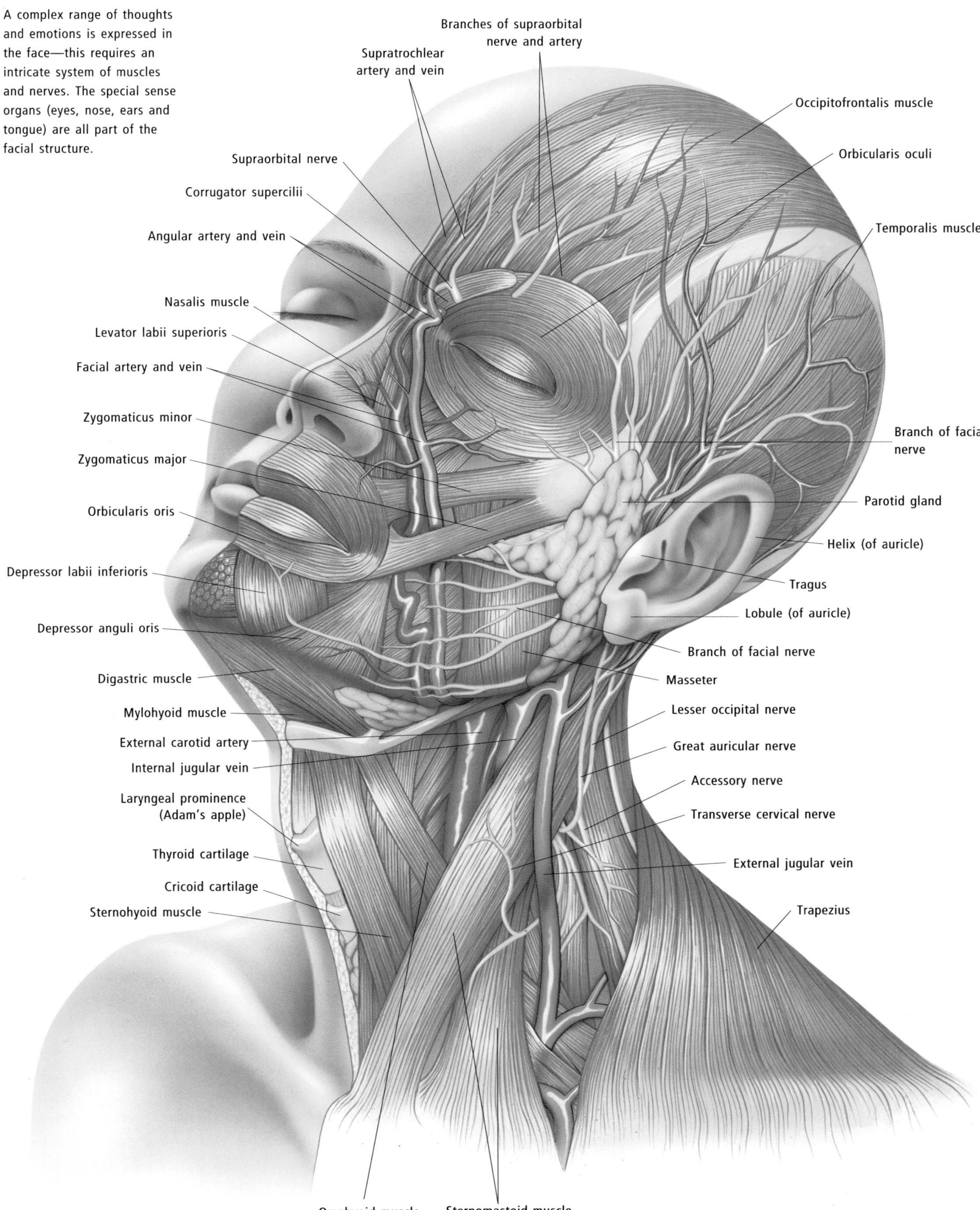

F

role in speech and help hold food as it is chewed and then swallowed.

The jaws are three bones making up the bony framework of the mouth. The two upper jaw bones (maxillae) are fixed, while the lower jaw (mandible) is moveable. By moving in opposition to each other, jaws can bite and chew food to prepare it for swallowing.

Fixed to the bottom of the maxillae and the top of the mandible are the teeth, which are used for biting into and chewing food. Children have 20 primary teeth, which first appear about age six months and are replaced at the age of about six years by the 32 permanent teeth.

Problems

The face can be affected by a variety of problems. Diseases including infections of the skin such as herpes zoster (shingles), herpes simplex, tinea and impetigo can affect the face. Conditions of inflammation of the skin (dermatitis), such as eczema and psoriasis, can also occur. Acne may occur, especially in adolescence, and can cause unsightly scarring. Cancers of the skin such as squamous cell carcinoma, basal cell carcinoma and melanoma commonly occur on the face. Many systemic (generalized) diseases affect the face. Endocrine diseases such as Graves' disease, hypothyroidism, Cushing's disease or acromegaly may affect the features by altering the soft tissues or bones of the face. Muscle movements and facial expressions may be affected in neurological diseases such as myasthenia gravis, Parkinson's disease and Bell's palsy. Infections such as tuberculosis, leprosy and cellulitis can damage the tissues of the face and its features.

A number of conditions can cause facial pain. Inflammation of the joint in the jaw (the temporomandibular joint) can cause aching pain over or around the jaw. Infection around a tooth can cause a throbbing pain on one side of face that worsens at night, when eating, or when touching a particular tooth. Sinus infection can cause pain or tenderness around the eyes and cheekbones which worsens when bending the head forward. It commonly follows a recent cold or nasal allergy. Headache may be caused by migraine, tension or stress, meningitis, or high blood pressure (hypertension). Herpes zoster may also cause severe facial pain.

Fractures of the facial bones are common, and are usually due to a sporting injury or a blow to the face. The facial bones that most commonly fracture are those of the upper jaw, the cheekbones, the bones that form the eye sockets, and the nose. There is severe pain at the injury site, swelling and bruising of soft tissue around the fracture (including black eyes), and deformity if the fracture is complete and bone fragments separate enough. Often no treatment is needed, as the fracture heals spontaneously within six weeks. If there has been displacement of bones, surgery may be needed to realign fractured bones and reconstruct normal facial contours. Fractures to facial bone can often be avoided by wearing protective face masks and headgear when playing contact sports.

Hairs are particularly numerous in the skin of the face, especially in males. A condition called folliculitis, or infection of the hair follicles with staphylococcus bacteria (also known as beard rash), is common on the face. Characteristic yellow-white pustules surrounded by reddish rings form on areas of beard. The condition is treated by avoiding hot moist conditions, using an antibacterial cream on affected areas, and, if the infection is severe, antibiotics which are taken orally.

Cosmetic surgery

Cosmetic procedures can be performed by a plastic or cosmetic surgeon to alter the features of a person's face. Rhinoplasty (nose surgery) can correct or alter a nose; otoplasty (ear surgery) can be used to correct protruding ears; blepharoplasty can remove excess fat and skin from the eyelids. So-called "face-lifts" can eliminate skin wrinkles; the surgeon makes an incision in the scalp and behind the ears, then pulls the skin taut to remove the wrinkles.

SEE ALSO *Acne, Acromegaly, Basal cell carcinoma, Bell's palsy, Brain, Cellulitis, Cosmetic surgery, Cushing's syndrome, Dermatitis, Eye, Facial nerves, Folliculitis, Graves' disease, Head, Headache, Herpes simplex, Hypothroidism, Impetigo, Jaw, Lacrimal glands, Leprosy, Lip, Melanoma, Migraine, Mouth, Myasthenia gravis, Nose, Parkinson's disease, Plastic surgery, Shingles, Sinusitis, Squamous cell carcinoma, Teeth, Tuberculosis*

FACIAL NERVES

The facial nerves, one on either side of the face, are the nerves that control the muscles of the face. They also supply the salivary glands below the mouth and the lacrimal glands in the eye, and carry taste sensations from the front two-thirds of the tongue. They are the seventh pair of the twelve pairs of cranial nerves. The facial nerves emerge from the brain stem, pass through the temporal bone in the skull (which houses the middle and inner ears), exit the skull through a small hole called the stylomastoid foramen, and then fan out over each side of the face anterior to (forward of) the ear.

Disorders of the facial nerves may be caused by fractures of the base of the skull, injuries to the face or middle ear, and birth or surgical trauma. The result is paralysis, weakness, or twitching of the face on the affected side; also, facial features lose their symmetrical arrangement, the mouth droops at one corner, the eyelid may not close properly, and there may be dryness of the eye or mouth and loss of taste. When the condition occurs with no known cause it is called Bell's palsy. This condition may come on suddenly or develop over several days; often there is a preceding condition such as stress, fatigue or the common cold. In most cases it improves by itself over a few months. Prompt treatment with corticosteroid drugs will help recovery.

SEE ALSO *Bell's palsy, Cranial nerves, Face*

FAINTING

Fainting (syncope) is usually triggered by severe deep-seated pain, or sudden shock or grief. It can often follow a period of acute anxiety. Fainting may also be caused by prolonged standing, particularly in a crowd and especially if the person has not eaten before going out. Early pregnancy may be a contributing factor.

Sudden blood loss can cause a fall in blood pressure followed by a fainting episode, as can the sight of severe trauma in others.

The experience of fainting can include a sudden drop in blood pressure, slowing of the heart, and pooling of blood in the extremities due to reflex dilation of their blood vessels. The person usually feels anxious, becomes clammy, and then falls unconscious to the ground. If the person is

Activating the face

The brain controls the motor and sensory activity of the body from different parts of the cerebral cortex. The sensory activities associated with the skin and muscles of the face are processed by the postcentral gyrus and the motor activities associated with the voluntary muscles, such as smiling, are processed by the precentral gyrus.

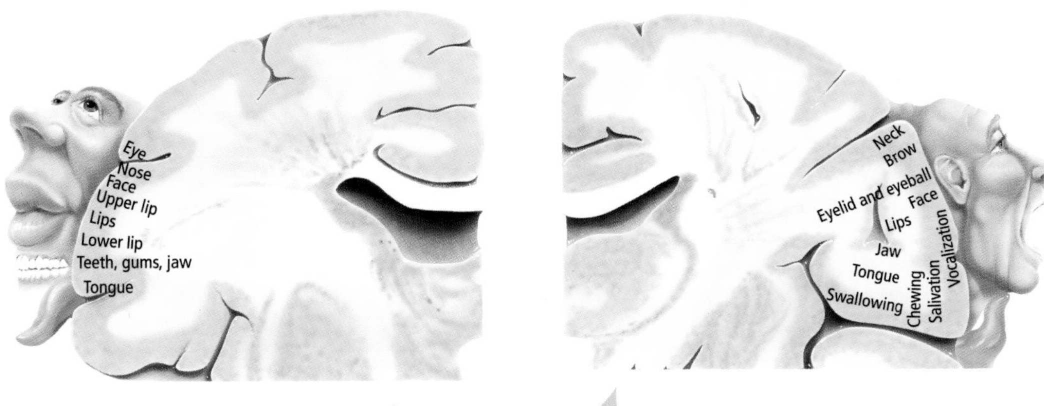

Sensorimotor areas of cortex

surrounded by a crowd of people and is not able to fall over, the brain becomes starved of sufficient blood supply and a seizure might occur.

Once the head is at or below the level of the heart, consciousness rapidly returns. Lying the patient flat and elevating the legs hastens the process. Traditionally a fainting person would be given spirits of ammonia to inhale. However, by the time anyone can find a bottle of ammonia these days, the patient will have already returned to consciousness (also, ammonia can be very dangerous if inhaled).

SEE ALSO *Blood pressure, Hypotension, Unconsciousness*

FALLOPIAN TUBES

Each of the two fallopian (uterine) tubes leads from its corresponding ovary, which lies on the lateral wall of the pelvis, to the body of the uterus. They are shaped a little like an alpine or medieval trumpet, with a narrow end joined to the uterus and a broad, flared end next to the ovary. In fact, the anatomical term for them is *salpinx*, which is Latin for trumpet.

The fallopian tubes convey the woman's egg (ovum) to the uterus. Also, shortly after sexual intercourse, sperm cells may reach the fallopian tubes, travelling in the opposite direction. In fact, the fallopian tubes are a common site for

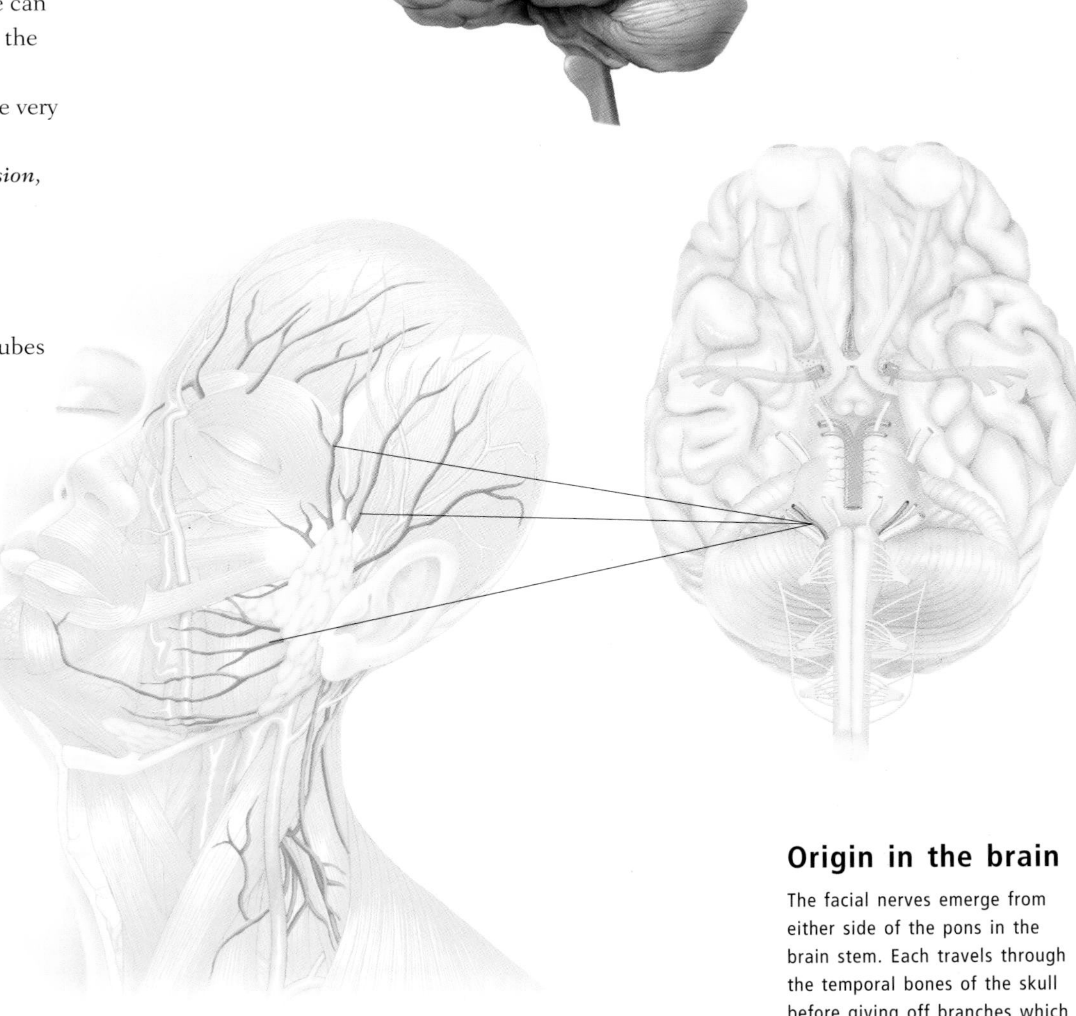

Origin in the brain

The facial nerves emerge from either side of the pons in the brain stem. Each travels through the temporal bones of the skull before giving off branches which fan out across the face.

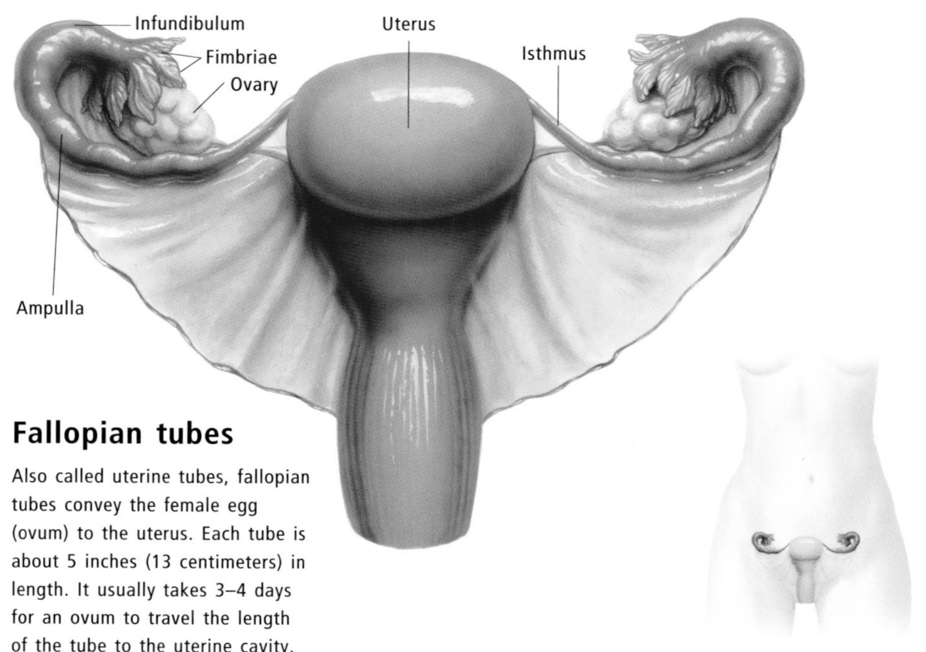

Fallopian tubes

Also called uterine tubes, fallopian tubes convey the female egg (ovum) to the uterus. Each tube is about 5 inches (13 centimeters) in length. It usually takes 3–4 days for an ovum to travel the length of the tube to the uterine cavity.

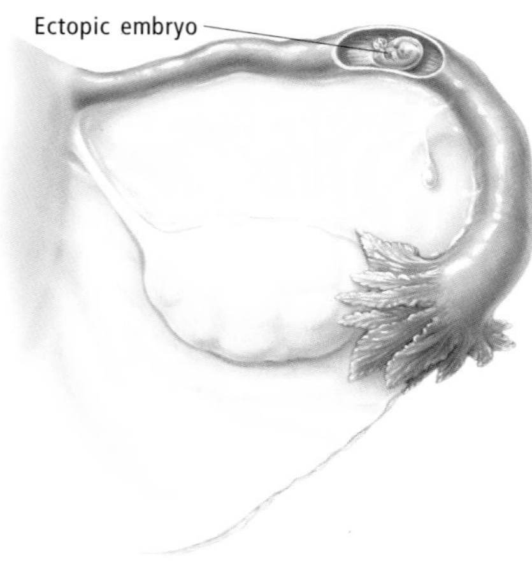

Ectopic pregnancy

An ectopic pregnancy occurs when a fertilized egg implants in the wall of the fallopian tube instead of in the wall of the uterus. At first it feels like a normal pregnancy until severe pelvic pain and vaginal bleeding occur. If not quickly treated, the condition can turn into a life-threatening medical emergency.

fertilization (the junction of the egg and sperm) to occur. The fertilized egg becomes an embryo, and moves down the tube and implants in the wall of the uterus.

Occasionally the embryo may implant in the wall of the tube itself, a type of ectopic pregnancy. Ectopic pregnancies are unable to proceed to full term, because the embryo quickly outgrows the available blood supply and may rupture the tube. The mother's life may also be at risk when this happens, because profuse bleeding into the mother's abdominal cavity may occur, leading to potentially fatal blood loss. Surgery to remove the damaged tube may be required. Fortunately, this procedure normally leaves the other tube intact and capable of performing its reproductive function.

SEE ALSO *Embryo, Fertilization, Ovaries, Ovum, Pregnancy, Reproductive systems, Salpingitis, Sperm, Uterus*

FAMILY HISTORY

A doctor will, during a first consultation, take a record of the patient's family medical history in order to form an overall picture of their state of health. It is an essential tool, as many illnesses, such as heart disease, run in families.

A family history is necessary before certain procedures take place. For instance, adverse reactions to anesthetics can run in families. These reactions may only become apparent when a family member needs surgery. Two such rare conditions are pseudocholinesterase deficiency, which is a reaction to a muscle relaxant; and malignant hyperthermia, which affects people who have a defective gene. When there is a possibility of a genetic abnormality, family history is also important. For an accurate assessment, the family history of three generations is required.

SEE ALSO *Genetic counseling*

FARMER'S LUNG

This condition is a hypersensitivity reaction to a mold-like bacterium found dwelling in hay. The reaction causes inflammation or irritation of the lungs (pneumonitis). The hay handler, usually a farmer, initially feels generally unwell then develops a fever, chills, breathlessness and a cough within the next four hours. Up to 5 percent of farmers in the United Kingdom develop this condition, generally during the wet part of the summer months. Though the condition is mostly self-limiting (tends to run its own course for a limited time without need for treatment), occasionally steroids, to be taken orally or inhaled, may be required.

SEE ALSO *Lungs*

FATS

Fats (also called lipids) are an extremely rich source of energy that can be used by the body as an alternative to carbohydrates. Fats are ingested in food and stored in layers of fatty (adipose) tissue under the skin, in the liver and around internal organs. Fats are broken down in the small intestine by lipases (fat enzymes) and are transported, stored and utilized in the body as triglycerides, cholesterol, lipoproteins and other fatty molecules.

Food high in animal fats (such as red meat, dairy products and eggs) can produce high levels of cholesterol and triglycerides in the blood, which may lead to various disorders including atherosclerosis, a common cause of heart disease and stroke. Some lipoproteins have also been linked to heart disease in recent years, especially high-density lipoproteins (HDL) and low-density lipoproteins (LDL). A low HDL to LDL ratio has been shown to protect against developing heart disease. People who exercise regularly and eat less animal fats are more likely to have a low HDL to LDL ratio.

A lipoma is a benign (non-cancerous) tumor made up of fat cells. Lipomas commonly occur in the limbs, abdomen or breasts, and feel like soft swellings under the skin. They seldom cause problems but may be surgically removed if preferred.

SEE ALSO *Atherosclerosis, Cholesterol, Lipoma*

FELDENKRAIS METHOD

Dr Moshe Feldenkrais (1904–1984) was a Russian-born Israeli physicist and Judo master who devoted more than 40 years to developing his method of movement education. His system of learning through movement, the Feldenkrais method, focuses on conscious thinking, moving, sensing and feeling. It is a gentle form of physical training which works the mind as much as the body.

The method is taught through two processes. The first process is a series of lessons called "awareness through movement". In these lessons, students are talked through a series of "movement explorations" that aim to increase awareness of habitual movement patterns (that is, patterns they use, and which may be inappropriate, but are unaware of) and develop more efficient and appropriate options. These explorations are achieved by having students focusing their attention on subtle differences in movement and by experiencing the interconnectedness of body movements.

In the second process, known as "functional integration", the practitioner helps the student to move through postures and exercises that benefit the nervous system and the skeletal structure. The goal is for the student to instinctively find postures and movements that require less energy and improve flexibility. Feldenkrais taught that developing body awareness enables the brain's signals to change, facilitating a shift away from rigid patterns of behavior, thought and movement.

Supporters of the Feldenkrais method recommended it particularly for people who suffer from recurring injuries, breathing disorders, chronic pain or anxiety.

SEE ALSO *Alexander technique, Pilates method*

FEMINIZATION

Feminization, the normal sexual development of females, occurs during puberty. It is a process which is governed by the sex hormones estrogen and progesterone. Under the influence of the sex hormones, the breasts develop, the hips widen, hair appears on the underarms and around the vulva, the uterus grows, and menstruation begins. Feminization can be delayed in certain circumstances, or be absent if the female is suffering from certain diseases, such as Turner's syndrome and hypopituitarism.

Testicular feminization syndrome is the development of female sex characteristics in a male, giving rise to a genetic male with the appearance of a female. It is caused by lack of response of tissues to male hormones produced by the testes.

SEE ALSO *Estrogens, Hormones, Turner's syndrome*

FEMORAL ARTERY

Most of the blood supplied to the legs travels from the aorta to the external iliac artery. This becomes the femoral artery as it enters the thigh by passing deep to the ligament (known as the inguinal ligament) at the groin. A major branch of the femoral artery, called the profunda femoris artery, supplies blood to much of the thigh.

The femoral pulse is one of four pulses that can be felt in the leg. It can be felt in the groin at the mid-inguinal point, that is, midway between the uppermost part of the pubic symphysis (joint) and the anterior limit of the ilium (a pelvic bone).

SEE ALSO *Aorta, Arteries*

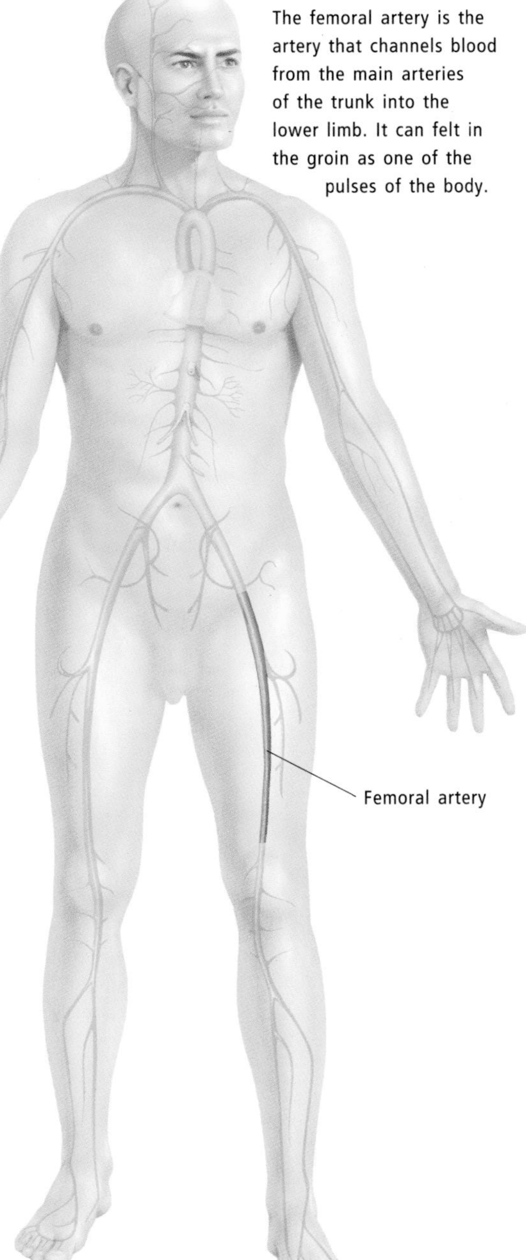

Femoral artery

The femoral artery is the artery that channels blood from the main arteries of the trunk into the lower limb. It can felt in the groin as one of the pulses of the body.

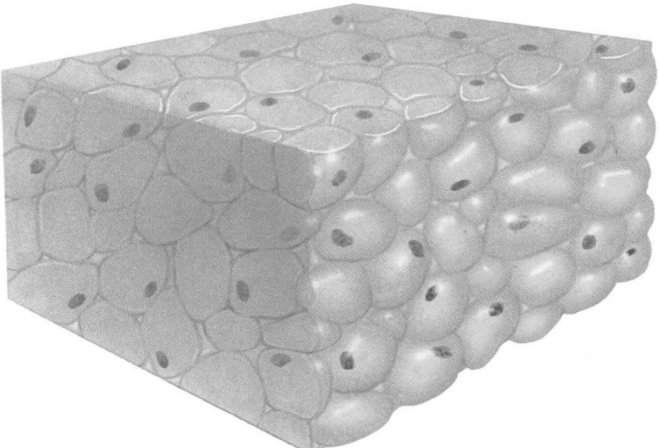

Fat

Fatty (adipose) tissue is found just under the skin, in the liver and around the internal organs. It helps to insulate the body from extremes of temperature, and serves as an energy store.

FEMUR

Extending from the hip to the knee, the femur (thighbone) is the longest and strongest bone in the body. It articulates (joins with) the hip bones above, and the tibia (shinbone) and patella (kneecap) below. The tendons of the powerful muscles that move the leg are attached to the femur.

Fracture of the neck of the femur (hip fracture) often follows a fall, and is common in the elderly, especially those with osteoporosis. Surgery followed by physical therapy is the recommended treatment. Fracture of the shaft of the femur is caused

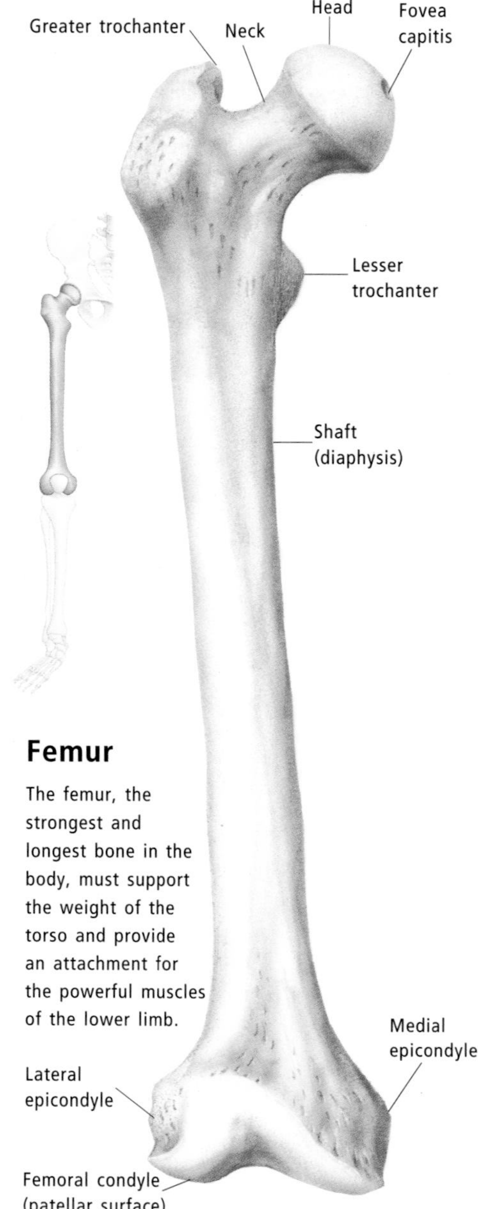

Femur

The femur, the strongest and longest bone in the body, must support the weight of the torso and provide an attachment for the powerful muscles of the lower limb.

by a blow to or a fall on the knee or leg, for example in a sporting injury. The fracture must be re-aligned under anesthesia and then held by traction, a splint, or surgical device (such as a nail inserted into the bone) while healing takes place.

SEE ALSO *Hip, Knee, Tibia*

FERTILITY

Fertility is the ability to conceive a child; it depends on several factors in both male and female reproductive function.

Males must have an adequate number of vigorous sperm cells. Normal human semen has a volume of approximately 0.1 fluid ounces (3 milliliters) per ejaculate, with 60 to 100 million sperm per milliliter. At least 50 percent of sperm should be moving four hours after ejaculation and at least 60 percent of sperm should be normal in shape.

In women, the vagina must be hospitable to the sperm and the mucus of the cervix must be thin enough for the sperm cells to penetrate. The interior of the uterus and uterine tube must allow movement of sperm to the egg. Egg production depends on many factors, including the normal cyclical production of sex hormones by the hypothalamus of the brain and normal production of eggs by the ovary. Once the egg has been fertilized, there must be a favorable environment for implantation of the early embryo into the wall of the uterus; infections and tumors in the uterus may prevent the early embryo developing.

Subfertility is defined as the failure to conceive after a year of normal intercourse. Of 100 women wanting to become pregnant, 70 will usually do so within a year, and 85 within two years. If a woman has never conceived then the problem is said to be one of primary subfertility. If she has conceived before, the problem is one of secondary subfertility. A common factor reducing fertility is blockage of the fallopian tube, which is caused by pelvic inflammatory disease.

Fertility tests include an examination of a sample of the man's ejaculate, looking at the percentage of sperm with normal shape and movement as well as the absolute number; a hysterosalpingogram and/or a laparoscopic examination of the woman to ensure that the fallopian tubes will allow the passage of sperm cells and fertilized egg; a cervical mucus sperm penetration test to determine if the cervical mucus is hostile to the sperm cells; and analysis of blood levels of the woman's pituitary hormones and progesterone to check for normal hormonal control of egg production and evidence of ovulation. It is also thought to be advisable for a woman to prepare a body temperature chart to help identify times of egg release.

SEE ALSO *Cervix, Embryo, Fallopian tubes, Hormones, Ovum, Pelvic inflammatory disease, Reproductive systems, Semen, Sperm, Uterus, Vagina*

FERTILIZATION

Fertilization is the fusion of ovum and sperm to form a zygote, which is essentially a one-celled embryo. This usually takes place in the ampulla (middle region) of the fallopian tube.

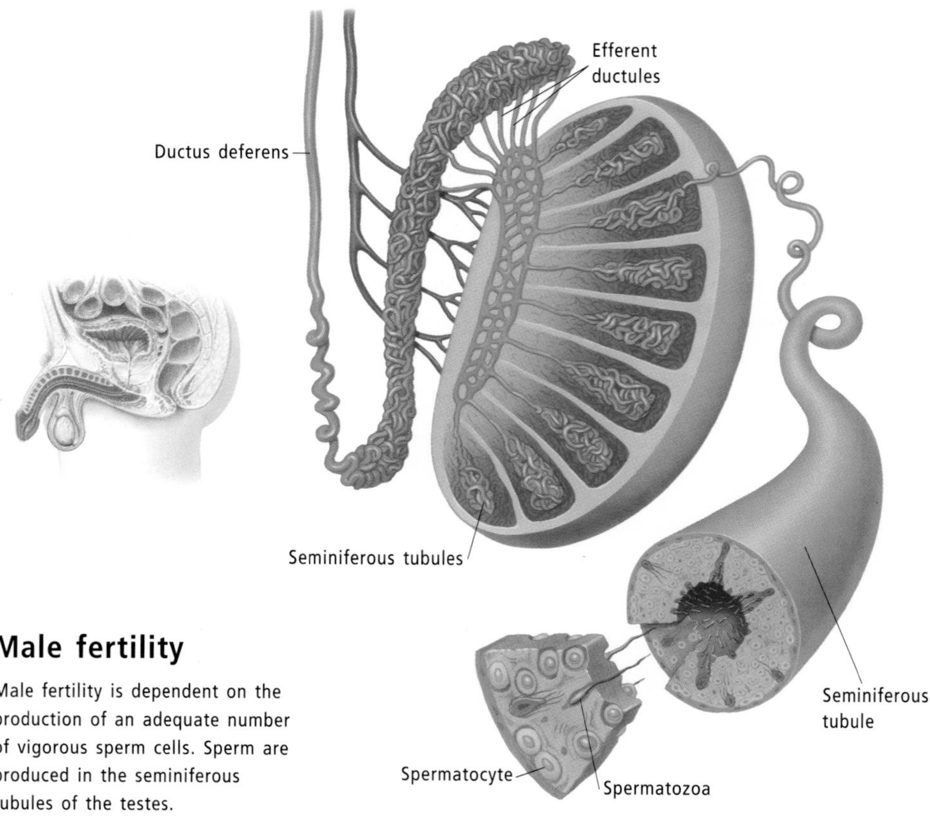

Male fertility

Male fertility is dependent on the production of an adequate number of vigorous sperm cells. Sperm are produced in the seminiferous tubules of the testes.

The ovum is released from the ovary along with two important coverings: a thin non-cellular membrane called the zona pellucida, which forms around the ovum while it is still in the ovary and, outside this, some of the cells from the outer wall of the ovarian follicle. The unfertilized ovum can remain in the ampulla for only two days, after which it degenerates.

At ejaculation, 60 to 100 million sperm are deposited in the vagina, but only a few of these travel through the female reproductive tract, with just 200 or so sperms reaching the ampulla. A major barrier to sperm travel for most of the menstrual cycle is the cervical mucus, but this becomes watery and readily penetrable around the time of ovulation. If this does not happen, or if the original number of sperm in the ejaculate is abnormally low, fertilization is unlikely to occur. Sperm motility is also an important factor, as transport to the ampulla is dependent on sperm movement, as well as on contractions of the muscular walls of the female reproductive tract.

Sperm undergo some maturation in the male reproductive tract and a process called capacitation in the female reproductive tract completes maturation. Capacitation takes about seven hours and is induced by secretions produced in the uterus and fallopian tube. The process is mainly concerned with changes in the outer surface of the sperm which will allow it to penetrate the ovum. Most sperm remain viable for only two days in the female reproductive tract.

Fertilization includes safeguards which ensure that just one sperm penetrates the ovum. The first barrier is the layer of cells adhering to the ovum. A few of the sperm which pass through these cells will adhere to the zona pellucida, the layer covering the egg. The first sperm to release enzymes allowing it to penetrate the zona pellucida will trigger an immediate reaction which makes the zona impenetrable to other sperm. The sperm thus selected then fuses with the ovum, and the chromosomes of ovum and sperm blend to form the nucleus of a new cell, the zygote. This starts dividing almost immediately and begins to move down the fallopian tube towards the uterus.

Penetration of the ovum by two sperm occasionally happens. The resulting embryo has 69 chromosomes in each of its body cells instead of the normal 46 and has severe development problems which in almost all cases lead to early spontaneous abortion (miscarriage). Occasionally, infants with this problem are born alive but all die very shortly after birth.

Fertilization with the combination of genetic material from two different individuals has the advantage of providing genetic variability in the embryo. This is enhanced by the rearrangement of genes on both maternal and paternal chromosomes during meiosis. It also allows for both male and female individuals. Development of a new individual from an ovum alone is called parthenogenesis and occurs naturally in certain insects and a few reptiles, and can also be induced artificially, using chemicals. The offspring are always female. Parthenogenesis has never been verified in humans.

SEE ALSO *Embryo, Fallopian tubes, Genes, Reproductive systems, Ovaries, Ovum, Sperm, Uterus*

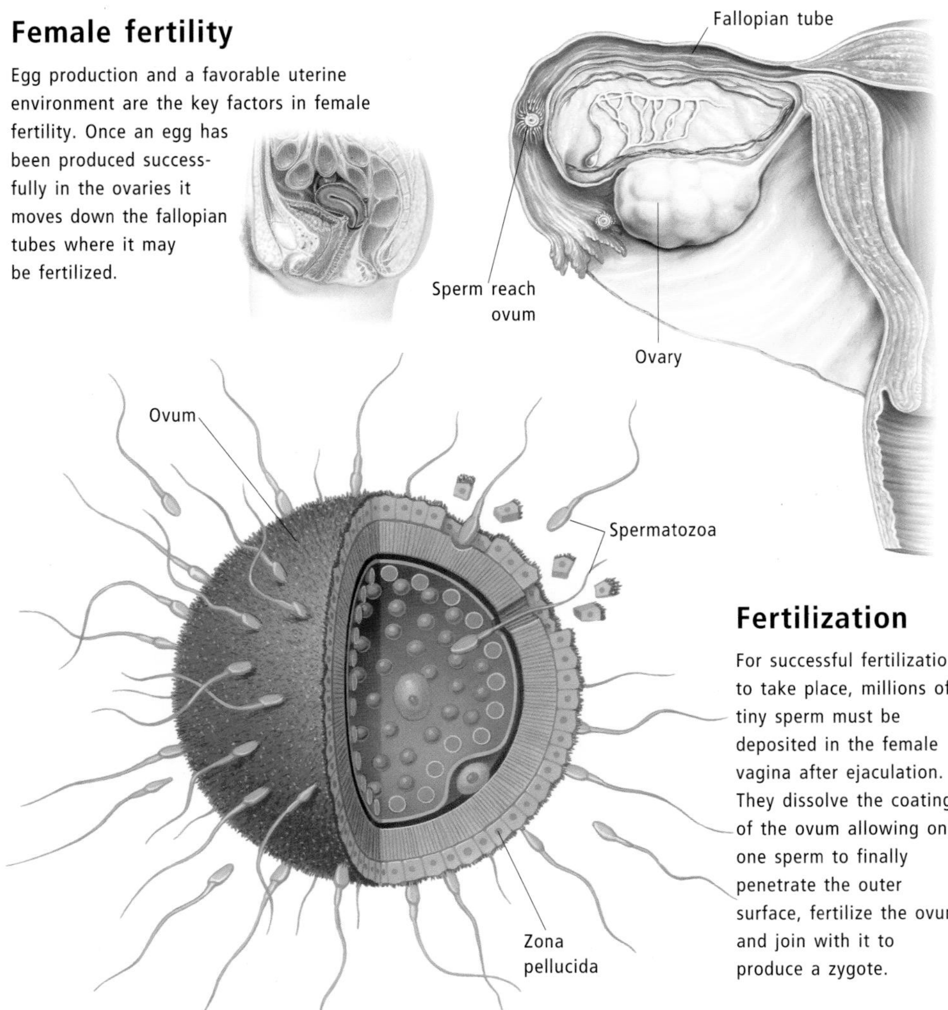

Female fertility

Egg production and a favorable uterine environment are the key factors in female fertility. Once an egg has been produced successfully in the ovaries it moves down the fallopian tubes where it may be fertilized.

Fertilization

For successful fertilization to take place, millions of tiny sperm must be deposited in the female vagina after ejaculation. They dissolve the coating of the ovum allowing only one sperm to finally penetrate the outer surface, fertilize the ovum and join with it to produce a zygote.

FETAL ALCOHOL SYNDROME

Fetal alcohol syndrome (FAS) is the name given to a group of symptoms characterized by physical and mental abnormalities in an infant, and linked to alcohol consumption by the mother during pregnancy.

Opinions differ as to how much alcohol is too much, and many doctors recommend abstinence for this reason. It is known that binge drinking, particularly in the first trimester (12 weeks) of the pregnancy, is potentially dangerous and the baby may be born with varying degrees of fetal alcohol syndrome.

A baby born with the most severe form of FAS will suffer from intellectual disability, growth deficiencies (most babies with FAS are shorter and weigh less than normal babies), and facial abnormalities, such as narrow eyes, low nasal bridges and thin upper lip. Heart and joint abnormalities are also likely. The child will not recover from these defects.

SEE ALSO *Alcoholism, Fetal development*

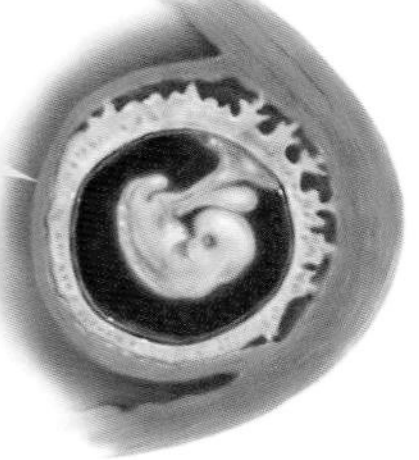

5 weeks

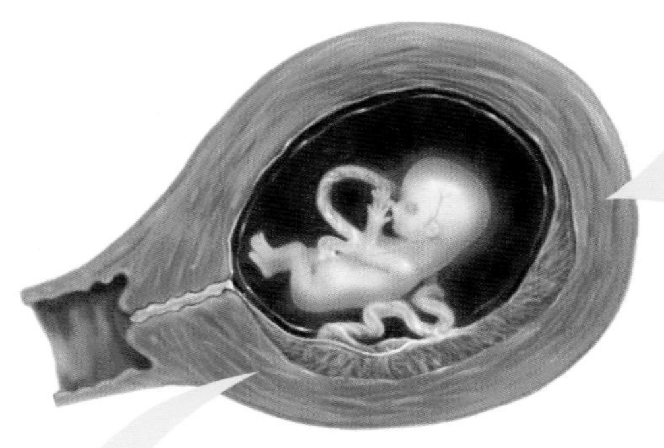

11 weeks

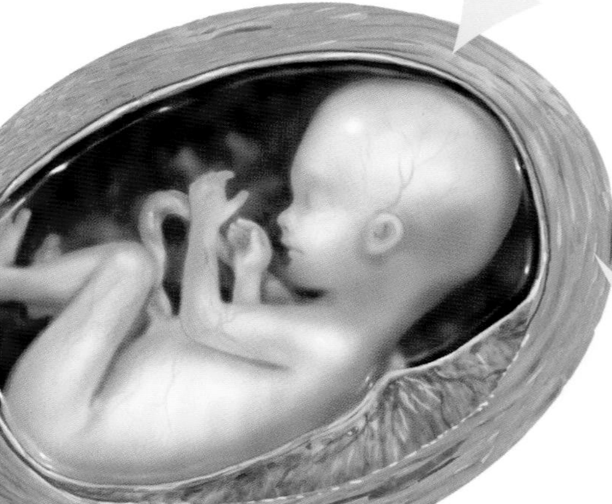

20 weeks

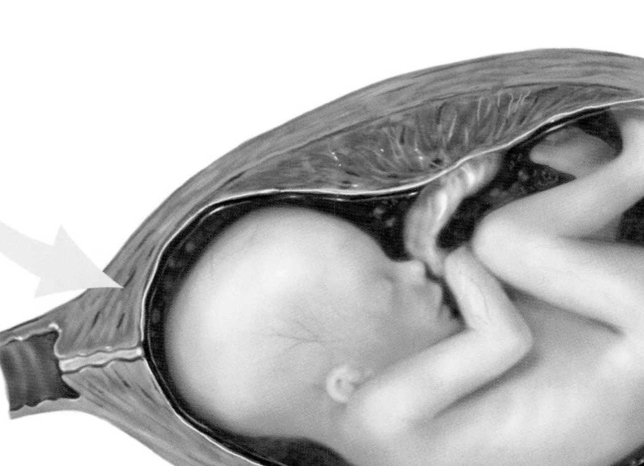

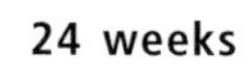

24 weeks

32 weeks

Fetal development cycle

Fetal development is a gradual process, but certain events take place at particular times. At 5 weeks, facial features have formed. At 11 weeks, the organs have developed. By week 20 the fetus is active, and movements are easily felt. By 24 weeks most of the organ systems become ready to function normally. At 32 weeks the growth rate has slowed down but weight has markedly increased. At 40 weeks, the fetus weighs 6–9 pounds (2.5–4 kilograms) and is ready for birth.

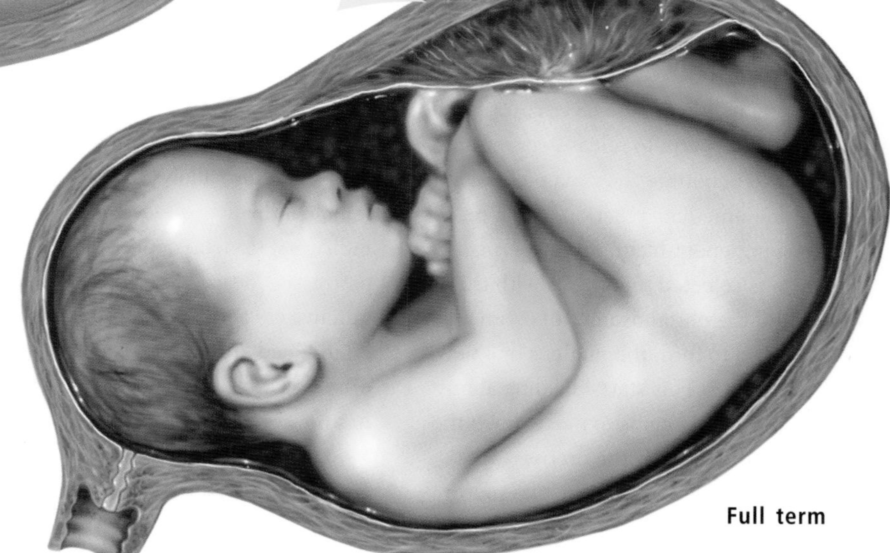

Full term

FETAL DEVELOPMENT

Fetal development is the process of the development of the individual in the uterus, from fertilization to the formation of the embryo and the fetus, to birth.

Fertilization and early development

Fetal development begins with the fertilization of the egg, when the head of a sperm penetrates a mature ovum high in a fallopian tube. Both sperm and ovum have 23 chromosomes each, but after fertilization, the resulting cell, which is called the zygote, has the full complement of 46 chromosomes.

The zygote grows by dividing its cells, a process called mitosis. This process continues as the zygote travels down the fallopian tube, brushed along by fine hairs (cilia). After division has occurred several times, the solid cluster of cells is called the morula, which, after several more days of dividing, becomes a hollow sphere called the blastocyst. Eventually, after about three to five days, the blastocyst reaches the uterus.

Further division sees the blastocyst separate into a cluster of inner cells in one part of a fluid-filled sac with an outer layer known as the trophoblast. The cluster of inner cells continues to divide until three separate layers of cells have formed. These are the so-called germ layers from which organs will form. The outermost layer is called the ectoderm; the innermost, the endoderm. Between these two layers develops a third layer, the mesoderm.

Now the blastocyst implants itself in the lining of the uterus (endometrium) until, about ten days after fertilization, it is completely buried. By this time, from the germ cells, unique tissues and organs begin to take shape. From the mesoderm, bone, muscle, heart, connective tissue, blood cells and vessels begin to grow. From the endoderm, digestive and respiratory tracts form, and from the ectoderm, skin, hair, and the tissues of the central nervous system. A cavity forms between the layers of germ cells and the outer trophoblast; this is the amniotic cavity, and it is filled with amniotic fluid.

Development of the embryo

The embryo grows inside the amniotic cavity, floating in the amniotic fluid, which acts as a water cushion, absorbing jolts and allowing the embryo to change posture. About two weeks after fertilization, blood vessels begin to develop within the embryo. At the same time, tiny extensions from the outer trophoblast layer of the blastocyst reach out into the endometrium and become blood vessels, joining with the mother's circulation. They develop into an organ called the placenta.

Across the placenta, separated by only a few layers of cells, the mother's circulation and that of the embryo come into close proximity. Across this barrier, oxygen, nutrients and antibodies (infection-fighting proteins) are able to pass from mother to embryo and waste products can pass from embryo to mother. The placenta also secretes hormones that help maintain the endometrium.

Securely floating within the amniotic fluid, and nurtured by the placenta, the embryo's cells continue to divide. By the third week, a closed tube called the neural tube has formed, which will become the brain and spinal cord. The front part of the neural tube enlarges; this enlargement will become the brain; the rest will be the spinal cord.

The brain itself forms into three separate parts: the prosencephalon, the mesencephalon, and the rhombencephalon. These areas will differentiate into the various parts of the mature brain. The relative positions of these areas of the brain to each other will change over time, as the brain flexes and doubles up on itself.

Meanwhile, as the alimentary canal is forming, another tube is developing into the heart. The embryo forms a circulation system different from that of an adult, as it includes short circuits which bypass the liver and lungs (these organs are not needed as their function is being performed by the placenta). At birth, these circuits will close.

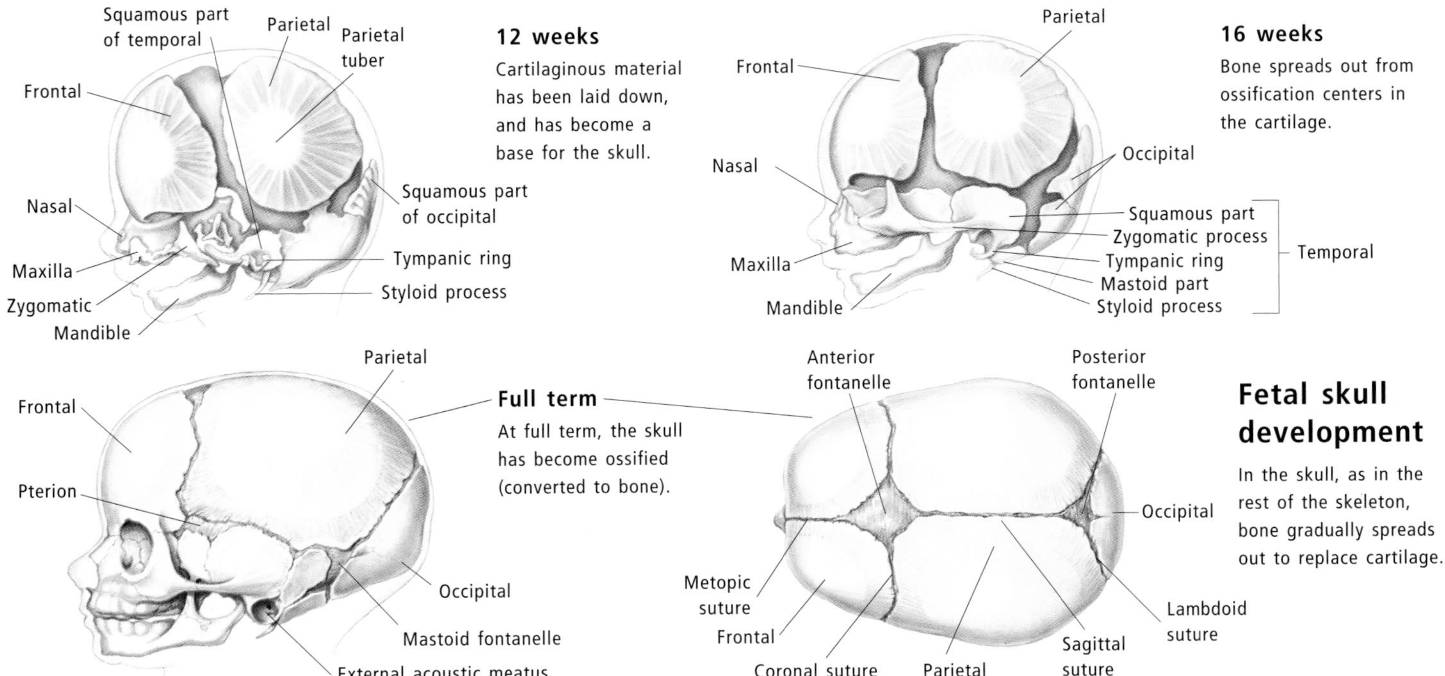

Fetal skull development

In the skull, as in the rest of the skeleton, bone gradually spreads out to replace cartilage.

At the start of its fourth week, the embryo has the beginnings of eyes and ears. Early in the second month, the major internal organs begin to take shape, and at about week six, bones and muscles begin to form. The buds of the arms and legs appear in week six; by week seven they are well defined.

Development of the fetus

From eight weeks, the embryo is described as a fetus. It is only tiny, at 1 inch (2.5 centimeters) long, and weighing about 1 gram, but all the human features are present. Limbs, eyes, ears, nose, mouth can all be seen, and the internal organs such as the heart, kidneys, liver, lungs, brain and digestive tract have formed. The limbs have begun to move (though the movements are not discernible by the mother until the twentieth week). From now on the main changes will be in size. Growth becomes more rapid; from now on it grows at about $\frac{1}{20}$ inch (1.5 millimeters) each day.

During the embryonic stage, material (either cartilage or membrane derived from mesenchyme) is laid down, becoming a template for the skull. The base of the skull develops from cartilage, which gradually becomes ossified (bony) as bone spreads out from ossification centers in the cartilage.

The rest of the skeleton develops in a similar way. Gradually, bone spreads out and replaces the cartilage until, by birth, much of the skeleton is fully ossified.

The genital organs begin to develop in the second month, but there is no difference in appearance between the sexes until about the seventh week. After this the sex glands develop differently, becoming the testes in the male and ovaries in the female. Both the testes and the ovaries gradually move to lower positions in the body, with the testes coming to lie in the scrotum by the end of the eighth month. In the male, a pair of tubules form which join up to the testes, and then open into the urethra; pouches in the ducts become the seminal vesicles. In the female, a pair of ducts also develops; one end of these ducts comes to lie alongside the ovaries, while the other end fuses into a common tube that becomes the uterus and vagina.

In both sexes, the external genital organs develop from a genital tubercle, along with a pair of urogenital folds with genital swellings on either side of the fold. At twelve weeks these differentiate into external male or female genitalia; in the male the tubercle and the united urogenital folds become the penis and the genital swellings fuse together and become the scrotum, while in the female, the tubercle becomes the clitoris and the urogenital folds and genital swellings become the lesser and greater lips of the vulva.

By twelve weeks, the fetus has a definite face with discernible facial expressions, though the head is disproportionately large because of development of the brain. In the eleventh or twelfth week the external geni-

Fetal brain development

Over a period of 9 months, the primitive neural tube forms into the prosencephalon, the mesencephalon and the rhombencephalon, which in turn develop into the various sections of the mature brain. By 4 weeks the prosencephalon has become the telencephalon and the diencephalon, and the rhombencephalon has become the myelencephalon and the metencephalon. The telencephalon develops into the cerebral hemispheres. At full term, all the surface features of the adult brain are already present.

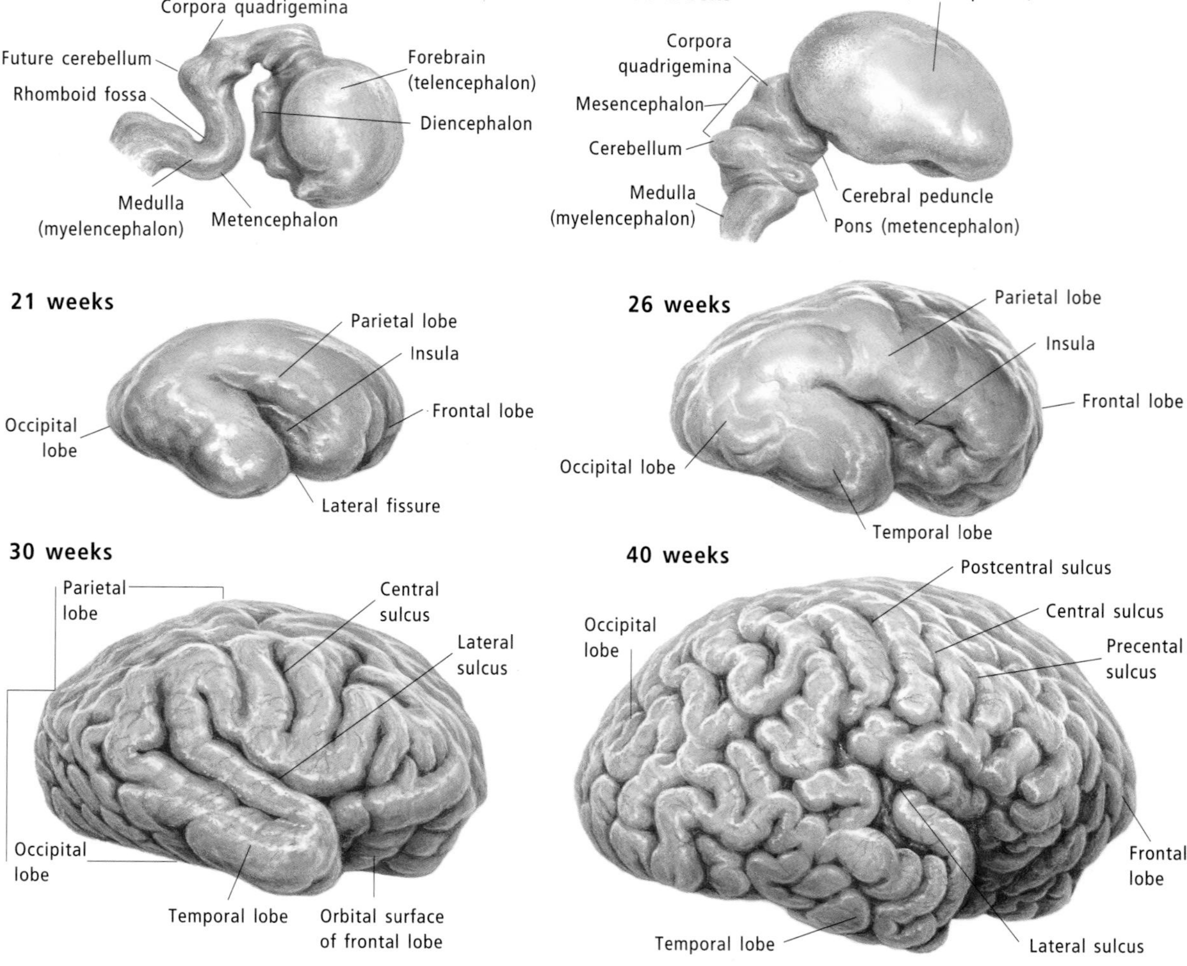

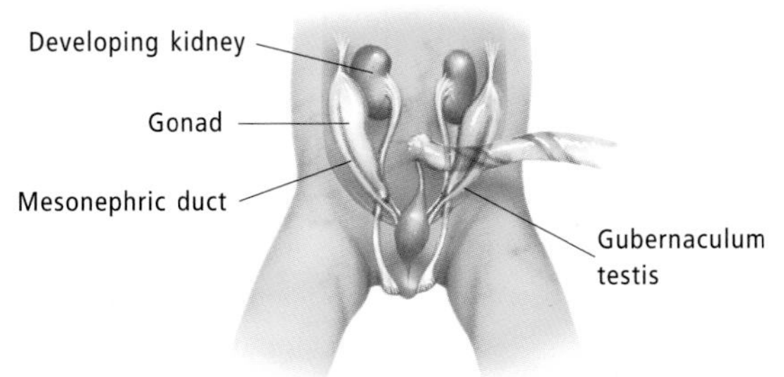

7 weeks

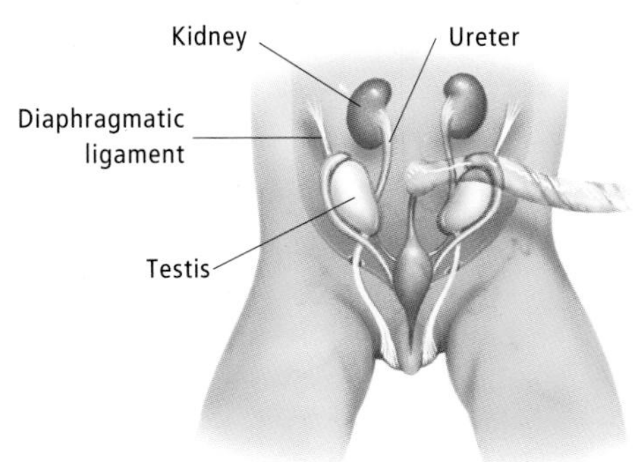

16 weeks

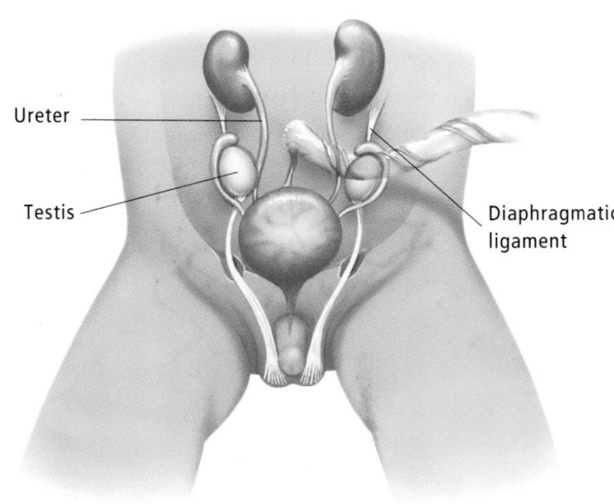

30 weeks

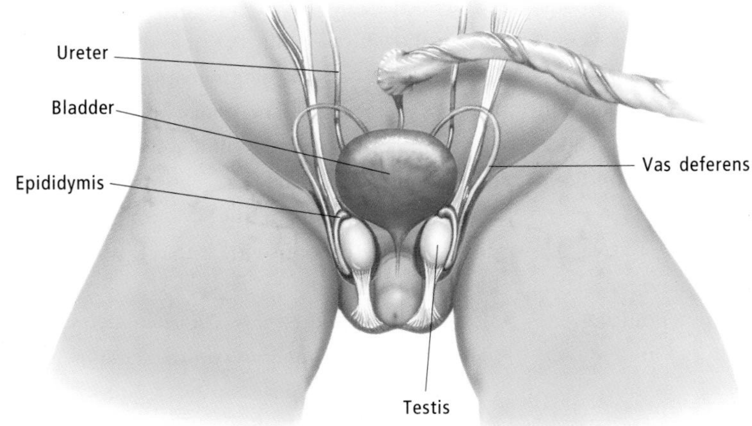

Fully developed

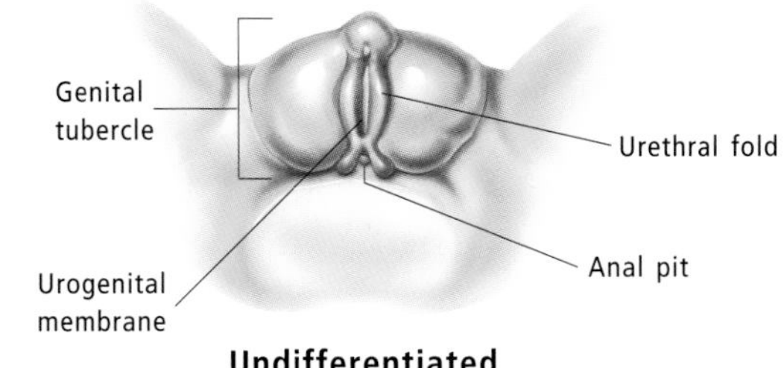

Undifferentiated

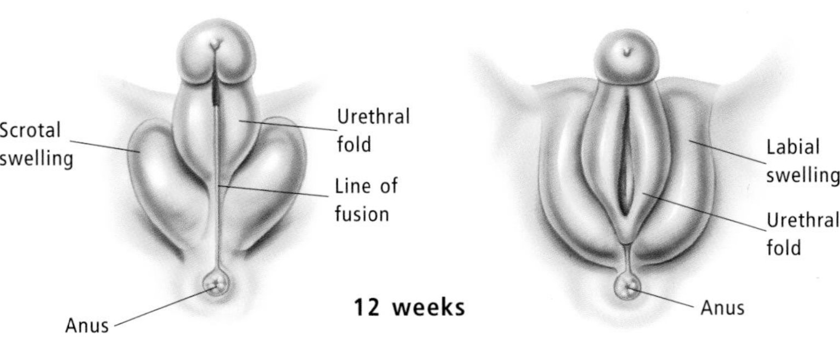

12 weeks

Male

Female

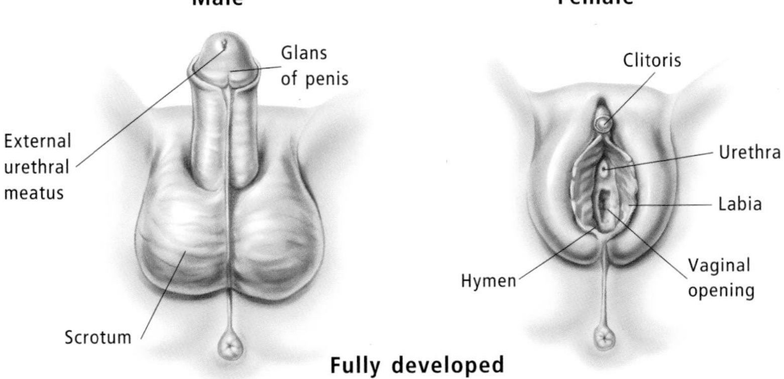

Fully developed

Fetal sex differentiation (above)

Up to 12 weeks, there is no difference between the male and female external genital organs, which consist of a genital tubercle, a urogenital membrane, a pair of urogenital folds and a genital swelling. After 12 weeks, these differentiate into the penis and scrotum in the male, and the clitoris and vulva in the female.

Descent of testes (left)

The testes (male gonads) form in the embryo from a piece of tissue at the back of the abdomen, near the kidneys. When they are fully developed at about 30 weeks, the testes make their way down the inguinal canal, reaching the scrotum as the time of birth approaches.

tals become evident, and by the fourth month the fetus is clearly recognizable as human. By twelve weeks, tiny nails are growing on its fingers and toes. The external ears, the eyelids (which will remain fused until the sixth month or so), and 32 permanent teeth buds have formed.

During the fourth month, simple reflexes have developed, and the mother first becomes aware of the movements of the fetus. The fetus will now respond to stimuli, such as a loud noise or a change in the mother's position, by moving vigorously. During the fifth and sixth months a downy covering (lanugo) develops on the body, and the body becomes increasingly larger in proportion to the head.

Weight gain begins during the seventh month, when fat is deposited under the skin all over the body. In the last few weeks before birth a special type of fat called brown fat will also be deposited in the upper part of the body. During the seventh month the skin, which is red and wrinkled, is covered with a creamy white substance known as vernix, manufactured by glands under the skin. This keeps the fetus waterproof. At 40 weeks, the fetus weighs 6–9 pounds (2.5–4 kilograms), is about 20 inches (50 centimeters) long, and is mature and ready for birth.

The physician or the obstetrician will monitor fetal development in various ways —through measurements of the mother's weight and abdominal girth, by listening to the fetal heartbeat through a special stethoscope, and by ultrasound, which is performed routinely during pregnancy.

Fetal abnormalities

Several factors can cause delayed growth of an otherwise normal fetus. These include poor nutrition, heart disease or high blood pressure, smoking, drug dependence, multiple pregnancies, heart disease in the mother, preeclampsia or eclampsia, and high altitude. Babies born to these mothers may be below normal weight. The general outlook for the development of these infants is poorer than for normal weight children.

Sometimes the fetus may develop abnormally. A disorder of development while the fetus is growing in the uterus is known as a congenital abnormality. It may be caused by a genetic disorder, so that the abnormality is inherited, or it may be acquired while the fetus is growing, due to exposure to an agent that is teratogenic, that is, causes abnormal development. Though they are generally rare, the range of possible congenital abnormalities is wide. Limbs or organs may be absent, duplicated or malformed. Organs may fail to move to the correct place, as in undescended testes (cryptorchidism); they may fail to open properly, as in imperforate anus, or fail to close at the correct time, as in patent ductus arteriosus (when the channel bypassing the lungs does not close).

Congenital abnormalities may be obvious at birth, or they may take months or years to become evident, as in the case of Huntington's disease (a degenerative brain disease), which doesn't manifest until middle age.

Inherited congenital anomalies are caused by abnormal genes. There are over 2,000 known inherited congenital anomalies; some are common, for example sickle cell disease, Down syndrome, and cleft palate, while others such as phenylketonuria, an inherited metabolic disorder, are rare.

Sometimes genetic abnormalities may occur if there is a spontaneous mutation of the parental genes, which may happen during sperm production or egg formation. Severe mutations are not compatible with life and result in miscarriage. Others allow the fetus to survive to birth but it may not live long. Other abnormalities, such as Down syndrome, are compatible with life well into adulthood, but the affected person may have disabilities.

Acquired congenital abnormalities can be caused by a variety of agents that affect the fetus in the uterus, including drugs, infections and toxins. Infection in the mother is a common cause of acquired congenital abnormality. Rubella (German measles) contracted in the first three months of pregnancy may cause deafness, cataracts, heart disease, jaundice or other abnormalities in the child. Cytomegalovirus (CMV) and *Toxoplasma* are two organisms that cause congenital anomalies.

Some drugs taken by a woman during pregnancy are responsible for abnormalities in the child. Corticosteroids, anticonvulsants, anti-cancer drugs, narcotics, sedatives, tranquilizers, antidepressants, antibacterials (especially tetracycline), anticoagulants, and drugs prescribed to treat cardiac conditions and hypertension can all cause congenital defects in a few cases. A pregnant woman should avoid taking any medication without first obtaining medical advice.

Environmental toxins, x-rays, or injury to the fetus may cause an abnormality in the fetus. The age of the mother may also be a factor. Down syndrome (trisomy 21), for example, occurs more frequently when conception takes place after about 35 years of age.

Congenital abnormalities cannot be reversed, but they can often be successfully treated with surgery, hormone treatment, diet and physical therapy, depending on the condition and its severity. In the future, gene therapy may provide a treatment.

If there is a known or suspected risk of a congenital abnormality developing, it can often be detected during pregnancy by screening procedures. The most reliable procedure is to examine a sample of fluid obtained by amniocentesis from the amniotic sac between the fifteenth and eighteenth week of pregnancy. Chorionic villus sampling (CVS) is a technique used in the first trimester of pregnancy in which a tissue sample is taken from the placenta and analyzed for evidence of genetic defects in the fetus. Ultrasound can also reveal some abnormalities.

Termination of pregnancy (abortion) may be considered if fetal disorders are found early in a pregnancy. The decision to abort rests with the parents and should be taken after they are made fully aware by their physician of the nature of the disorder and the consequences of abortion.

Genetic counseling should be considered by anyone who has a history of chromosomal abnormalities, and by all pregnant women over 35 years of age. There may be a higher risk than normal of congenital abnormality in a second child if the first is born with an abnormality; parents in this situation should undergo genetic counseling if they wish to have another child.

SEE ALSO ***Amniocentesis, Chorionic villus sampling, Congenital abnormalities, Embryo, Fertilization, Genetic counseling, Lanugo, Miscarriage, Ovum, Placenta, Sperm, Ultrasound, Uterus***

FETOSCOPY

Fetoscopy is the use of high-resolution fiberoptic equipment in surgery on a pregnant woman. It is used when performing operations on the growing baby (fetus) or its environment, in the first and early second trimester of the pregnancy. The surgery is performed through a small incision in the abdomen and uterus. It is sometimes referred to as embryofetoscopy.

SEE ALSO *Embryoscopy, Fetal development*

FEVER

Fever is an abnormal increase in body temperature. Normal temperature, taken orally, is 98.6°F (37°C). Someone with fever has a temperature at least 0.5°F (about 0.3°C) above normal, on two recordings taken at least two hours apart to be certain. Fever can occur in otherwise healthy people through exercise or dehydration, or following childhood immunizations. Usually fever is a symptom of illness, particularly viral or bacterial infection. It may be accompanied by shivering, sweating, headache, restlessness, weakness and loss of appetite. An overactive thyroid gland, certain cancers and connective tissue disorders can be responsible for prolonged fever.

If the fever is less than 24 hours old, and the temperature is less than 102°F (39°C), it is recommended that the patient drink plenty of fluids and take an oral antipyretic drug like acetaminophen (paracetamol) or ibuprofen every four hours. Children under the age of 16 should not take aspirin.

If the fever persists, if there is mental confusion or disorientation, if the temperature rises above 102°F (39°C) or if there is vomiting or diarrhea, consult a physician. In very young children, fevers above 102°F (39°C) may trigger a febrile convulsion, requiring immediate medical attention.

SEE ALSO *Body temperature, Viruses*

FIBRILLATION

Fibrillation is irregular electrical activity of the heart muscle, with the result that the heart muscle cannot contract effectively. It may occur in either the atria or ventricles of the heart. Atrial fibrillation may be due to disease of the mitral valve, myocardial infarction, infections or thyroid disease. The great danger of atrial fibrillation is that stagnant blood in parts of the atrium may coagulate. Small fragments of coagulated blood may then break off and become lodged in the arteries of the brain or kidneys. Ventricular fibrillation is even more serious, because the ventricles are unable to pump blood while fibrillating. Patients with ventricular fibrillation will have no pulse and will die in minutes unless resuscitation and electrical defibrillation are used.

SEE ALSO *Arteries, Defibrillation, Heart, Mitral valve, Myocardial infarction, Ventricle*

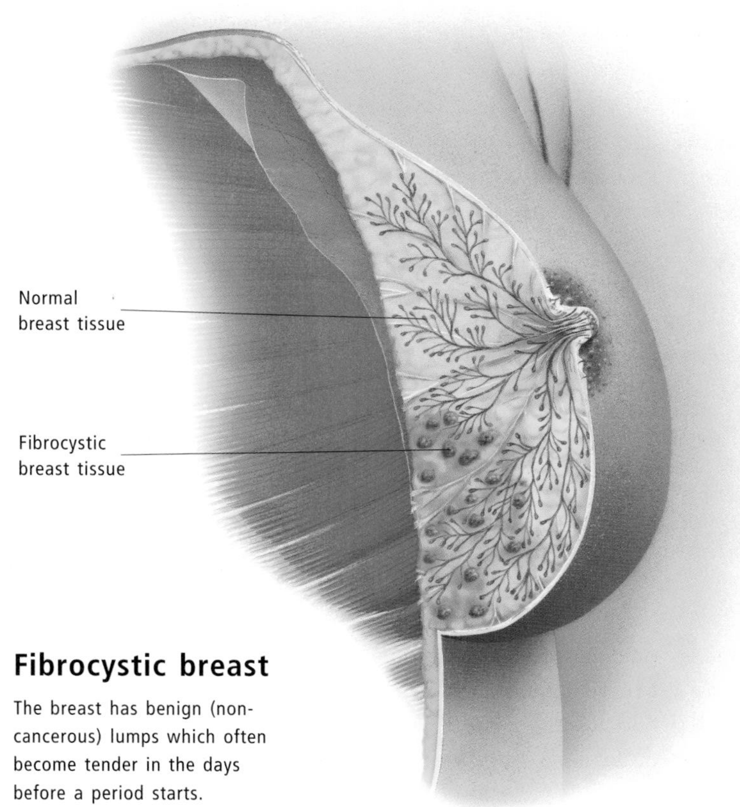

Fibrocystic breast

The breast has benign (non-cancerous) lumps which often become tender in the days before a period starts.

FIBROADENOMA

A fibroadenoma is a benign tumor formed from glandular tissue. It occurs most commonly in the female breast, most often among women who are in their reproductive years. Fibroadenomas are not usually tender. However, they generally need to be surgically removed to confirm they are benign, and because they can continue to grow and cause an unsightly lump. Usually a fibroadenoma can be removed under local anesthesia.

SEE ALSO *Breast, Tumors*

FIBROCYSTIC DISEASE

Fibrocystic disease is a very common condition of women in their reproductive years. It is characterized by a number of small cysts (fluid filled sacs surrounded by fibrous tissue) that give the breast a dense, irregular and bumpy consistency. Usually both breasts are involved.

The breasts become enlarged and tender just before the menstrual period, with symptoms improving after the period finishes. The condition improves after menopause and often after commencing the contraceptive pill. No treatment is required, though any single lump that stands out should be investigated by a physician.

SEE ALSO *Breast, Menopause, Menstruation, Oral contraceptives*

FIBROIDS

Leiomyomata uteri, known colloquially as fibroids, are benign (non-malignant) tumors of the uterus which are believed to arise from smooth muscle cells of the wall of the uterus. They are extremely common, occurring in 20 percent of Caucasian women and 50 percent of African-American women.

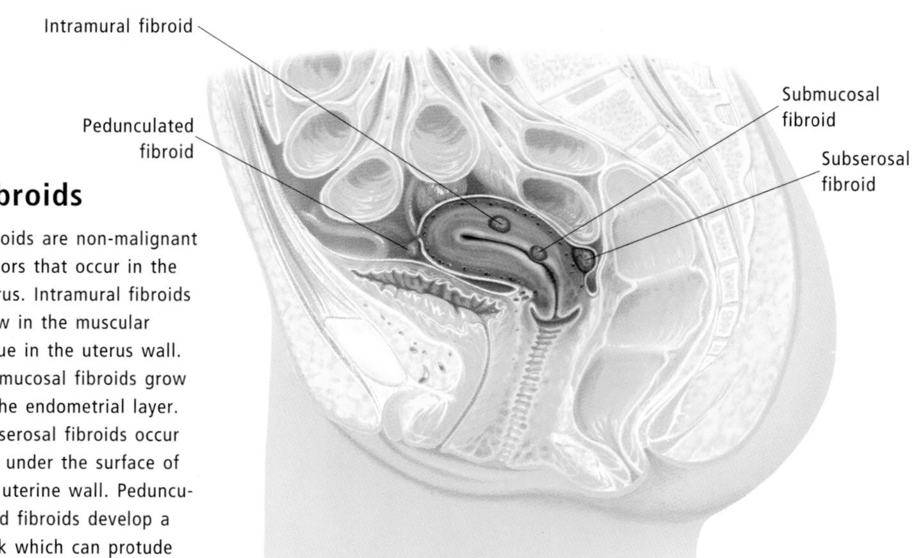

Fibroids

Fibroids are non-malignant tumors that occur in the uterus. Intramural fibroids grow in the muscular tissue in the uterus wall. Submucosal fibroids grow in the endometrial layer. Subserosal fibroids occur just under the surface of the uterine wall. Pedunculated fibroids develop a stalk which can protude from the uterus or cervix.

The cause is unknown and most tumors have no symptoms. Where symptoms do occur, they include abdominal distension (swelling), abdominal discomfort, constipation, heavy periods (hypermenorrhea), increased frequency of urination, and bleeding between periods.

Pregnancy may occur in women with fibroids, but complications may arise, such as miscarriage, premature labor, prolonged labor and excess bleeding after birth (postpartum hemorrhage). Some patients with fibroids may suffer from anemia (reduced hemoglobin in the blood) due to excessive blood loss associated with the heavy menstrual periods.

Treatment of fibroids is not necessary where there are no symptoms, but such tumors should be carefully watched to determine the rate of growth. If the woman is experiencing symptoms, the uterus may be removed (hysterectomy) or the individual lump cut out (myomectomy). Myomectomy is used in younger women who wish to retain the ability to have children. Unfortunately, myomectomy is usually less effective than hysterectomy and fibroids may recur.

SEE ALSO *Anemia, Hysterectomy, Menstruation, Tumors, Uterus*

FIBROMYALGIA

Fibromyalgia is a common rheumatic condition consisting of painful muscles, body aches and pains, and sleep disorders. The cause is unknown; the muscles themselves are not weak, nor is there any sign of inflammation or disease in them. Fibromyalgia is usually mild and improves with treatment in the form of stretching exercises, application of heat and/or gentle massage, and taking of anti-inflammatory drugs, and, in some cases, antidepressant drugs.

SEE ALSO *Anti-inflammatory drugs, Antidepressants, Massage, Muscle, Rheumatism*

FIBROSIS

Fibrosis is the formation of fibrous scar tissue. It normally follows after infection, injury and inflammation. Too much scarring can cause a disorder, such as adhesions in the peritoneum following peritonitis, or keloid tissue, an overgrowth of scar tissue at the site of a skin injury. Scarring can also be a result of chronic inflammatory diseases such as interstitial lung disorders (a group of disorders characterized by scarring and thickening of the deep lung tissues) and hepatitis, which can cause cirrhosis, or scarring of the liver.

SEE ALSO *Adhesions, Cirrhosis of the liver, Hepatitis, Keloid, Peritonitis*

FIBULA

The fibula is the long, slender bone on the outside of the lower leg. It extends from just below the knee to the ankle, where its lower end forms the outer side of the ankle joint.

Fibula

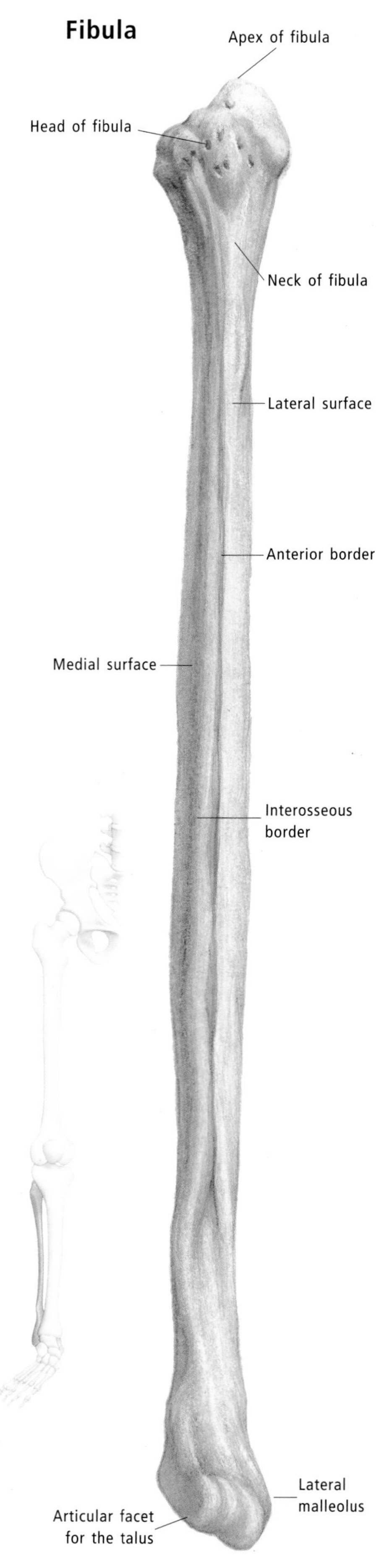

It does not bear weight like the shinbone (tibia), but instead serves as an attachment for some of the leg muscles. Fracture of the fibula is common, especially in children, often occurring in contact sports such as football or hockey. It can occur with an ankle sprain. In most cases fractures are not serious, and setting is usually unnecessary; surgery is occasionally necessary.

SEE ALSO *Ankle, Knee, Leg, Tibia*

FILARIASIS

Characterized by irregular swinging fevers, and swelling and inflammation of lymph nodes and vessels, this tropical disease is due to infection by the larvae of the nematode *Wuchereria bancrofti*.

Monkeys, cats and human beings may be infected by the bites of mosquitoes, after which the larvae develop into adult worms, which may grow up to 3 inches (8 centimeters). Over time the adult worms invade the lymph nodes and vessels causing both inflammation and obstruction. Massive swelling of legs, arms, breasts and scrotum can occur (known as elephantiasis).

In the early stages, antibiotics may be required for secondary infection. While drugs can suppress, if not always cure, the disease, surgery may be required when swelling or elephantiasis occurs.

SEE ALSO *Elephantiasis, Lymphatic vessels*

FILLINGS

Fillings are metal, porcelain or plastic material used to replace decayed parts of teeth and to halt the growth of dental cavities. The process of filling a tooth may begin by drilling into the cavity to remove the decayed matter. Smaller cavities may not require drilling. The hole is then filled with gold, silver alloy, porcelain or plastic, depending on the desired effect. Plastic and porcelain look more like the natural tooth and may be preferred for fillings in front teeth. Metal fillings are usually stronger. Fillings may be done with the aid of local or general anesthetic, or nitrous oxide gas.

SEE ALSO *Teeth*

FINGER

A finger is any of the digits of the hand. Each finger has three bones (phalanges), separated by joints, except the thumb, which has only two phalanges.

Powerful movements of the fingers and thumb are carried out by muscles in the forearm, whose long tendons run in front of and behind the wrist and along the front and back of the phalanges, where they attach. Precision movements of the fingers and thumb are made by small muscles in the hand.

Finger joint sprains and dislocations are common in sporting injuries. They are usually treated by splinting the broken finger to an adjacent finger. If the fracture is unstable or cannot be reduced, then surgery may be felt to be necessary. "Mallet finger" results from damage to the tendon attaching to the tip of the finger, resulting in an inability to straighten the fingertip. It is usually treated with a special splint for six to nine weeks.

SEE ALSO *Hand*

FISSURE

A fissure is a crack or a groove in the skin or the surface of an internal organ. It may be a normal feature, or it may result from an injury or disease and be abnormal.

The most common pathological (abnormal) fissure is an anal fissure, which occurs when skin around the anus is torn when passing hard feces. Most common in infants and children, the condition is very painful, and there may be bleeding while passing feces.

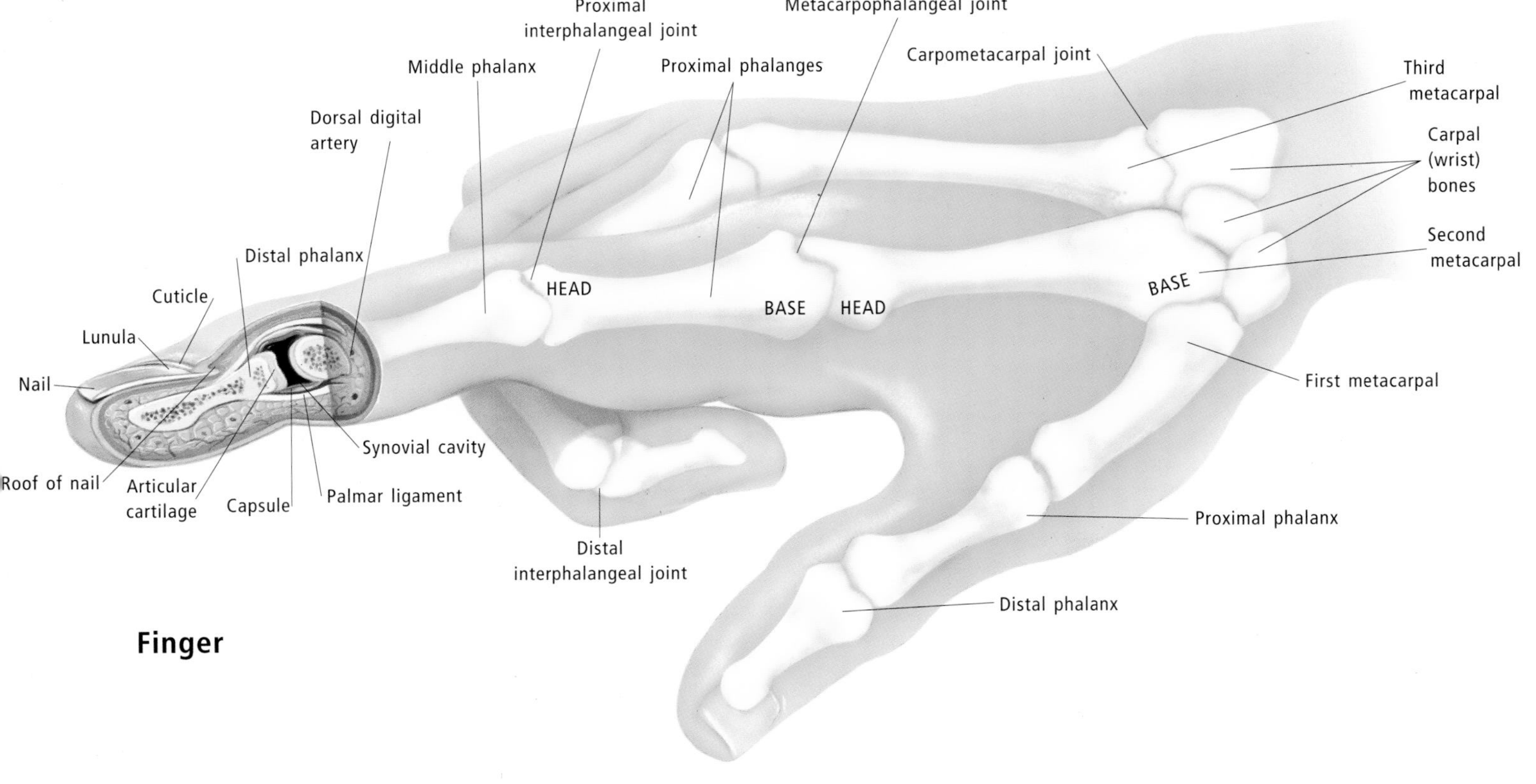

Finger

Fissure

A fissure is a split or crack in the skin or on the surface of an organ, often resulting from disease or injury.

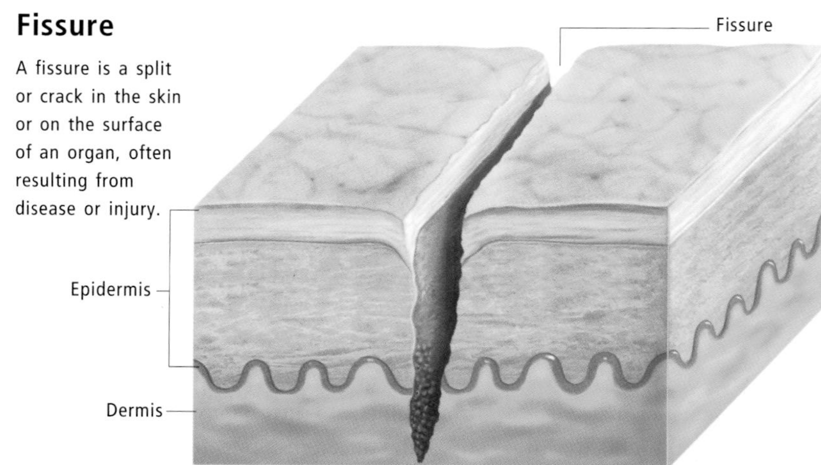

Anal fissures usually heal after several days when the constipation ceases. A laxative may help constipation. An anesthetic ointment applied to the anus will help relieve pain. If the fissure does not heal by itself, surgery may be needed.

SEE ALSO *Anus*

FISTULA

A fistula results from an abnormal communication between the inner surface linings of two adjacent organs. It may occur, for example, between the rectum and the bladder, where urine may pass from the bladder to the rectum, or between the rectum and the vagina, which can lead to feces passing into the vagina. A fistula may be caused by malignant (cancerous) tumors, inflammation or infection. Treatment is by the use of surgery.

Anorectal fistula

Anorectal fistula (or "fistula in ano") is a condition in which there is an abnormal passage between the inner surface of the anus and the surface of the skin around the anus. It is due to infection on the anus, usually by pus-causing bacteria that results in a break in the wall of the anal canal or rectum. Other cases may be due to cancer of the anus and rectum, Crohn's disease or diverticulitis. An untreated anorectal fistula may lead to bacterial infection throughout the body, and some may become the sites of origin of cancers. Small anorectal fistulas may repair themselves, but for larger ones the site of infection should be removed and the fistula opened to allow pus to drain.

SEE ALSO *Anus, Bladder, Crohn's disease, Diverticulitis, Rectum*

FLAT FEET

"Flat feet" is a musculoskeletal disorder characterized by loss of the arches of the feet.

Normally, the arches of the feet are formed by the arrangement of the tarsal and metatarsal bones and are flexible to assist weightbearing and shock-absorbency. The head of the talus bone is the keystone of the arch and is supported by a ligament. The plantar or longitudinal arch runs from the ball of the foot to the heel; the metatarsal arch runs across the ball. Under load, the arches may flatten slightly.

Flat feet can occur in adolescence or adulthood and may result from abnormally stretched ligaments, a condition that can be caused by standing for long periods. The head of the talus bone is unsupported and rotates excessively, flattening the arch. When weight is taken off the foot the arch may become visible again.

At birth, a newborn's feet appear to be flat, but this is simply the appearance produced by thick pads of fat under the skin layer in the soles of the feet, and does not indicate flat feet. The arches will be visible a few months after the child begins walking.

Diagnosis of flat feet will consider stress fractures and arthritis as possible causes. Treatment for flat feet in children used to be to wear arch supports inside the shoes but this is now considered of little value, though adults may wear them to reduce shoe wear.

SEE ALSO *Foot*

FLATULENCE

Flatulence is excessive build-up of gas in the gastrointestinal tract. It may produce a bloated feeling and is expelled through the mouth or through the anus. Air can be swallowed when eating or gas can be ingested with foods that have a high gas content, such as fizzy drinks. Also gases, such as hydrogen, methane and carbon dioxide, can be

Fistula

For a woman, a problematic labor may lead to the formation of a fistula between the rectum and the vagina, which can lead to feces passing into the vagina.

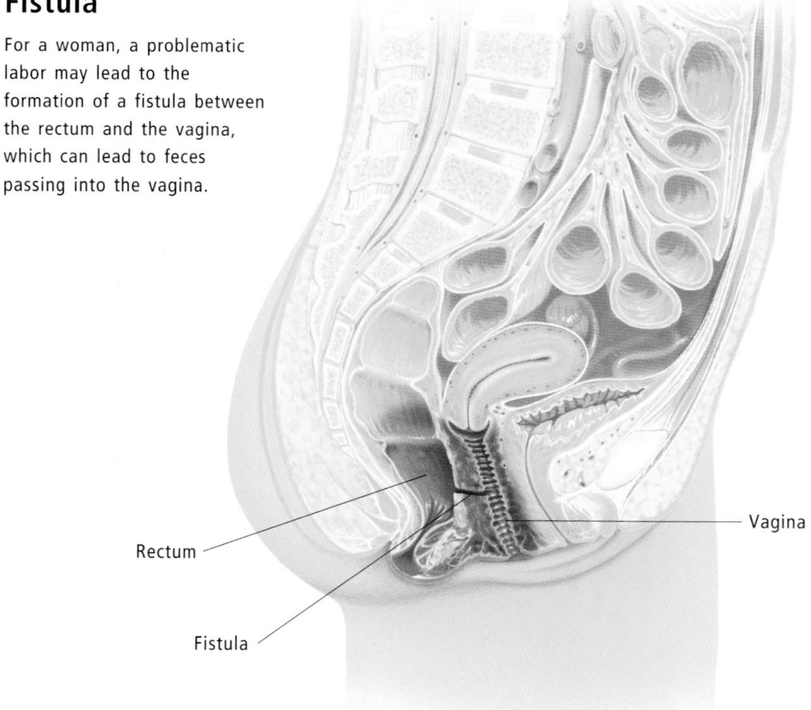

produced by the various bacteria in the colon or the lower part of the large intestine.

Intestinal gas may have an offensive smell, or be odorless, depending on the bacteria, and the volume produced can be affected by the foods eaten. Beans, cabbage, unprocessed wheat bran and other foods high in dietary fiber may produce large quantities of gas, while an inability to digest foods, such as milk products, may also produce gas.

SEE ALSO *Colon, Digestive system, Intestines, Lactose intolerance*

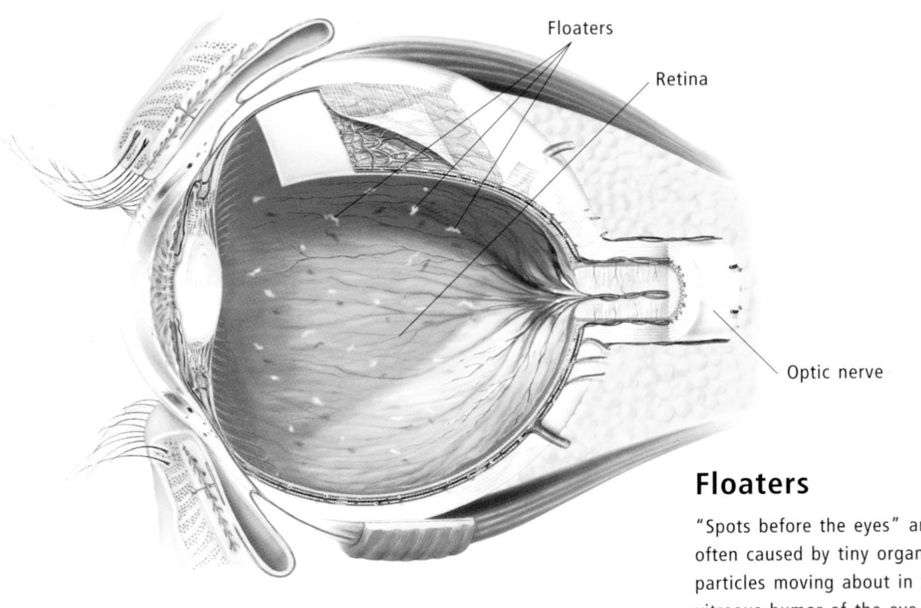

Floaters

"Spots before the eyes" are often caused by tiny organic particles moving about in the vitreous humor of the eye.

FLOATERS

Also known as muscae volitantes or "spots before the eyes", floaters appear as small shadows that seem to float over the fields of vision. Most common among the aged, they are caused by anything that breaks into the jellylike portion (vitreous humor) of the eyeball. Such breaks may be due to a few blood cells floating away from a broken capillary at the back of the eye, degenerative deposits, escaped fluid from blood vessels (exudates), and contraction of the vitreous gel and its detachment from the retina. These agents cause shadows to fall on the retina, characteristically perceived by the patient as tiny shadows, usually trailing just behind the center of vision. They are most often noted while reading across a page. A sudden shower of floaters may indicate detachment of the retina (the inner lining of the eyeball), which may result in flashing lights and disturbed vision.

The majority of floaters are not overly serious and generally occur when the patient is tired. A major problem, however, can be the cause and early referral to an eye specialist is required to ensure that this is not the case.

SEE ALSO *Eye*

FLOTATION THERAPY

The purpose of flotation therapy, also known as restricted environmental stimulation therapy (REST), is to introduce patients to states of deep mental and physical relaxation. In this therapy, patients float for 30 to 60 minutes on very salty water heated to around 94°F (34°C) in a tank a little larger than a bathtub. Alternatively, in dry flotation systems, a membrane separates the patient from the fluid underneath. There may be no lighting or sound, or there may be dim lights and relaxation music or guided visualizations. Practitioners consider flotation therapy to be effective for stress-related disorders and for the management of chronic pain.

SEE ALSO *Relaxation techniques*

FLOWER REMEDIES AND ESSENCES

The original flower remedies were the work of the English physician Dr Edward Bach (1880–1936). A distinguished Harley Street doctor and bacteriologist, Bach became disillusioned with orthodox medicine, believing that it treated symptoms rather than causes of illness. He became interested in homeopathy and worked at the London Homeopathic Hospital for many years.

Bach believed in treating a person's temperament rather than their physical symptoms. He urged his patients to search within themselves for the emotional and psychological origins of their illness, and to address them. At the same time Bach sought natural healing remedies that would facilitate emotional shifts to bring increased vitality and inner peace.

Bach devoted the final six years of his life to walking the countryside in search of his healing flower remedies. He believed that the essence of a plant was concentrated in a flower before it seeded. Holding a flower in his hands he would intuitively sense its essence and the effect it had on him. From his observations he identified 38 flower remedies which he believed could heal through releasing their particular qualities, thereby bringing about a change of outlook.

Rescue remedy

The best known of all the Bach flower remedies is the combination rescue remedy, which is thought to relieve the effects of any kind of trauma, from physical shock to mental anxiety. It has often been noted that it is particularly effective when given to children and animals. Rescue remedy consists of: star of Bethlehem for shock, rock rose for panic and terror, impatiens for mental stress, cherry plum for fear of losing control and clematis for feeling "out of the body".

Remedy preparation

Bach believed that his remedies worked on a vibrational level and devised a method of preparation to release the flower's vibrational essence. Wild flowers are placed in a bowl of spring water and left in the sun for three hours to transfer their essence to the water. This water then becomes the concentrated remedy, or stock, with the addition of brandy to stabilize it. The stock is further diluted to make up an individual remedy, often containing several remedies. This is taken a few times a day in drop doses.

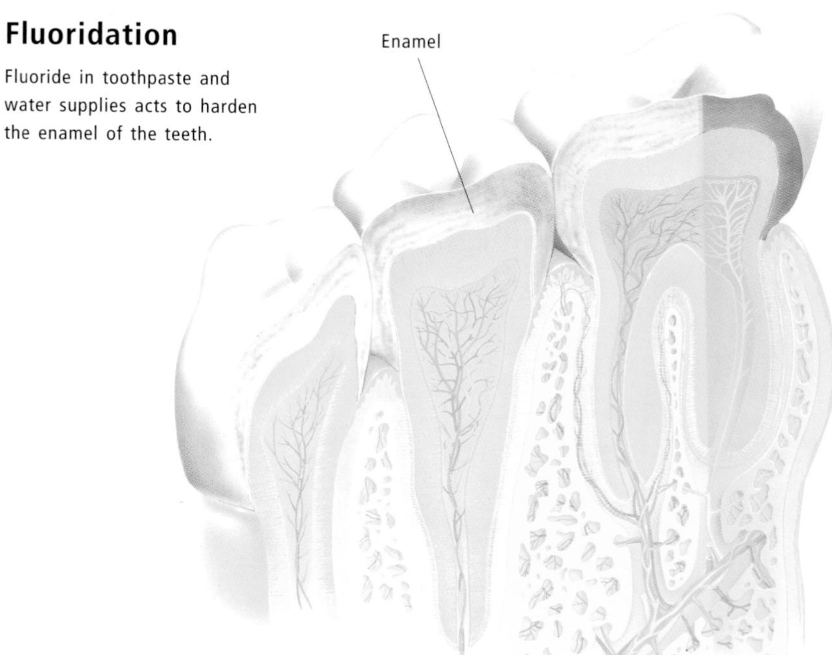

Fluoridation

Fluoride in toothpaste and water supplies acts to harden the enamel of the teeth.

The use of flower remedies has spread worldwide, although there is as yet no scientific explanation as to how they work. Researchers in more than 50 countries have followed the work of Bach in making flower essences from their native wildflowers. Flower remedies and essences can be self-prescribed, or may be prescribed by natural therapists, counselors or psychotherapists in conjunction with other treatments.

FLUID RETENTION

Fluid retention is the abnormal accumulation of the fluid that surrounds cells and is a symptom of an underlying disorder of kidney function and fluid balance.

The balance of fluid in the body is regulated by the hypothalamus, which triggers the release of hormones to control the functions of the kidneys and bladder. Normal fluid balance can be upset by excessive blood loss, and by various disorders, including kidney malfunction, which can cause an excess of sodium in the blood. When sodium levels rise the blood volume also rises and the excess fluid results in edema and swelling in the feet and legs. Dietary salts can aggravate fluid retention, and heart patients particularly are advised to follow low-sodium diets. Hormonal changes during the menstrual cycle may cause retention of sodium and fluid and produce a bloated feeling. Heart, liver or kidney failure may also cause fluid retention.

In pregnancy, swelling caused by fluid retention is common and can usually be relieved by resting with the legs up; if it is severe it can also be a sign of a more serious condition and a doctor should be advised.

Other causes include certain drugs used in the treatment of heart disease (notably calcium channel blockers), head injuries, stroke, and any surgery or disorder that interferes with normal drainage of lymphatic fluid and its return to the blood.

Diuretic drugs may be prescribed to increase urine output and decrease fluid volume throughout the body. They are prescribed with care since they cause dilation of blood vessels and loss of potassium.

SEE ALSO *Angioedema, Edema, Hypothyroidism, Myxedema, Papilledema, Pre-eclampsia, Pulmonary edema, Varicose veins*

FLUORIDATION

Fluoride is an inorganic ion found in seawater and in most fresh groundwater. It is added to water, foods or toothpaste to increase dietary intake to levels at which it is known to reduce tooth decay.

Numerous studies throughout the world have shown that fluoridation of water supplies significantly reduces tooth decay or dental cavities. Fluoride, added to water as sodium fluoride, or to toothpaste as stannous fluoride, increases the ability of tooth enamel to replace minerals lost when the teeth are attacked by the bacterial acids that produce decay.

Public health authorities in many countries have acted on this information. Fluoride is applied by dentists or added to foods such as salt, or to mouthwash. The most effective, and most economical, method of distribution is through water supplies. Fluoridated water is supplied to over half the population of the USA and Canada, and to two in every three people in Australia, reducing the need for dental treatment and particularly benefiting people who are less able to afford preventive treatment. Fluoridation of water supplies also reduces the needs for restorative work later in life. Concerns about fluoride added to the water supply are usually related to water purity and freedom of choice.

The role of fluoride

When teeth are being formed, fluoride in the diet of the mother-to-be will be incorporated into the developing baby's tooth enamel, improving its structure and making it less vulnerable to acid dissolution. From birth, and up to adolescence as teeth continue to develop, fluoride in saliva, from water, toothpaste, or when applied as part of dental treatment, has been shown to increase resistance to acids, help teeth to repair themselves by remineralization after attack by acids, and reduce the formation of acids by the bacteria which promote decay. In adults, these benefits continue to apply as the presence of fluoride in saliva reduces decay on exposed root surfaces of teeth. High concentrations of fluoride are used to inhibit the growth of decay-causing bacteria.

SEE ALSO *Minerals, Teeth*

FOLLICLE STIMULATING HORMONE

This is one of two hormones produced by the pituitary gland which are collectively called gonadotropins and which stimulate the sex glands (the gonads). In females, FSH stimulates the development of ovarian follicles up to the time of ovulation. The other gonadotropic hormone, luteinising hormone (LH), is involved in ovulation. In males, FSH is one of the hormones stimulating the production of sperm while LH induces testosterone production.

SEE ALSO *Hormones, Ovulation, Pituitary gland*

FOLLICULAR CYST

Following degeneration of an ovum (egg), the unruptured Graafian follicle enclosing the ovum begins to secrete fluid from its lining cells. This leads to the formation of a cyst in the ovary, which may grow to up to 2 inches (5 centimeters) in diameter. When this happens, the menstrual cycles sometimes become longer and excessive menstrual bleeding can ensue. Multiple cysts (Stein-Leventhal syndrome) may also be associated with obesity, hirsutism, infertility and lack of periods. If the cyst is larger than 2 inches (5 centimeters) in diameter, it needs to be surgically removed.

SEE ALSO *Menstruation, Ovaries, Ovum, Stein-Leventhal syndrome*

FOLLICULITIS

Folliculitis is a bacterial or fungal infection of the hair follicles. It can occur anywhere on the body and often arises when follicles are damaged by shaving or wearing tight clothing. The condition is marked by itching, reddened skin, a rash and pustules around the follicles that may dry out and crust over. It is treated with antiseptic creams and antibiotics.

SEE ALSO *Hair*

FONTANELLE

Known as the "soft spot" on a newborn baby's skull, the fontanelle is a gap between the bones due to the normal delay in the joining together of several flat bones making up the skull. (There are actually two—one at the top of the skull and a smaller one at the back—with the one at the top known as "the fontanelle".) Examined with the baby sitting quietly, the fontanelle shows a slight depression in the skull, but when the baby cries, or if infection or hemmorhage has occurred, the fontanelle will bulge.

Normal closure of the gap occurs by about one year. If the fontanelle appears closed at birth or shortly thereafter, it may indicate failure of underlying brain growth (craniosynostosis). Craniosynostosis can not only distort the shape of the skull and limit its growth, but can also lead to intellectual disability and deafness. Surgery to reopen the closed gaps is imperative.

Delayed closing of the fontanelle is occasionally associated with thyroid gland deficiency (cretinism).

SEE ALSO *Cretinism, Newborn, Skull*

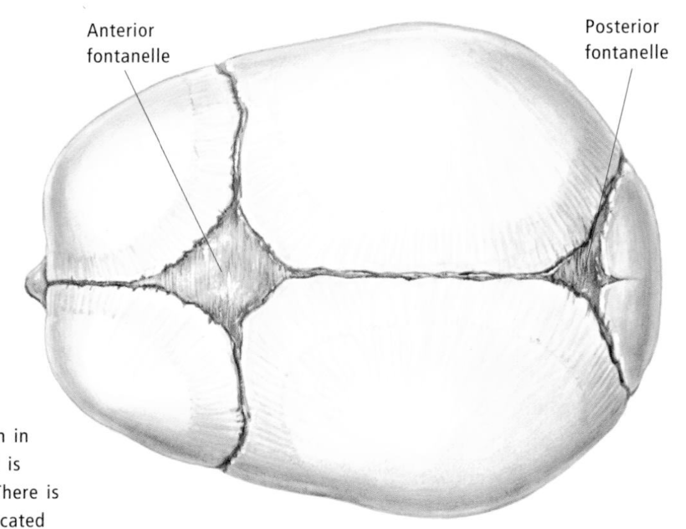

Fontanelle

The soft spot or depression in the top of the baby's skull is known as the fontanelle. There is also a second soft spot, located at the back of the skull.

FOOD ADDITIVES AND PRESERVATIVES

Food additives and preservatives have been known and used in human society for thousands of years. As humans formed fixed settlements and cultivated their food they gave up their nomadic existence and learned to live with the extremes of seasons in one location. This produced the necessity for preservatives to help in storing food for use during the winter months or in unproductive seasons.

Microorganisms such as *Lactobacillus bulgaricus* were used to produce yoghurt, and wild yeasts were used to make beer and bread. Common salt is one of the oldest food additives and has been used widely for thousands of years in cooking for flavor enhancement and as a preservative. It reduces the availability of water to bacteria and fungi. Drying, smoking and pickling in brine are also traditional techniques of preserving food. Smoking is an effective preserving technique because it reduces the water content (minimizing bacterial growth) and deposits chemicals toxic to bacteria on the food surface. Honey, spices and vinegar also have a long history of use as food additives and preservatives.

Today there are over 2,500 additives used in food manufacture. There are substances that preserve foods against deterioration during storage and distribution; add flavor or color to enhance appetite appeal; improve

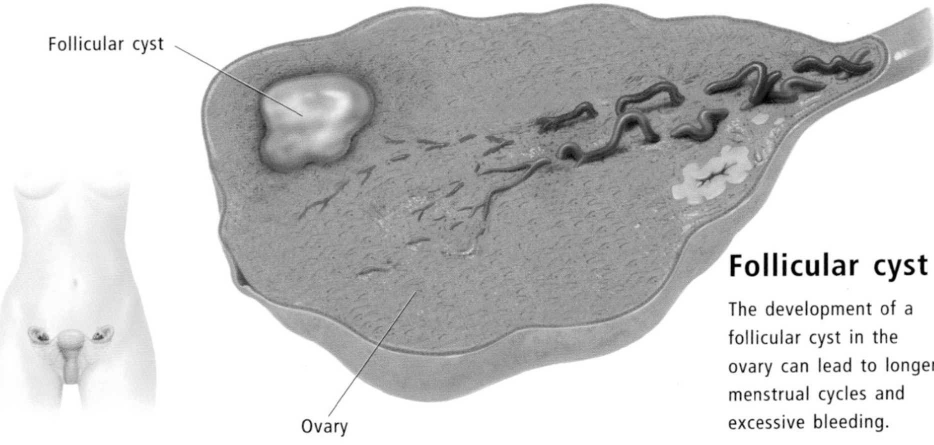

Follicular cyst

The development of a follicular cyst in the ovary can lead to longer menstrual cycles and excessive bleeding.

nutritional content; and assist in processing. Their use is subject, in the industrialized countries, to stringent tests before approval, and to close regulation when incorporated into foods. But there is no completely harmless substance—only safe quantities. Many individuals and consumer groups keep a watch on what they see as a threat to nutritional standards and to possible sources of nutritional deficiencies and allergy problems.

Processing additives may be: emulsifiers, which help to maintain a mixture that might otherwise separate, such as oil and water; stabilizers and thickeners, which make products more viscous, or foamy, or stop ice crystals forming; propellants, such as those used in pressurized foods; and chelating agents, which protect foods from enzyme action which would cause deterioration.

Preservatives can be antioxidants or antimicrobials. Antioxidants, such as ascorbic acid (vitamin C), citric acid and sulfite compounds, prevent food spoilage due to oxidation and enzyme action that causes browning on cut surfaces. Antimicrobials, such as common salt, nitrites, acetic acid, sulfites and preservatives produced by microorganisms, prevent or inhibit the growth of bacteria, molds and yeasts that spoil food.

Coloring directly influences perceptions of taste as well as quality and visual appeal. Processing foods often diminishes their natural colorings, so colorant additives, which may be natural (derived from plant sources) or synthetic, are then included to achieve the desired appearance. Bleaching agents remove unwanted coloring, as in the manufacture of white flour.

Sweeteners as additives are either nutritive or non-nutritive. Nutritive sweeteners, such as glucose, fructose, corn syrup and sucrose, provide energy in the form of carbohydrates or as sugar alcohols. Non-nutritive sweeteners are used in low-calorie foods suitable for dieters or for diabetics, or in sweet foods to reduce tooth decay. They include aspartame and saccharine.

SEE ALSO *Nutrition, Food poisoning*

FOOD POISONING

Food poisoning is an acute gastroenteritis caused by eating contaminated or poisonous food. Though not common in the Western world thanks to health regulations governing food vendors, it still occurs when food preparation is poor or when food is reheated or partly refrigerated. Food poisoning can be caused by bacteria (*Salmonella*, *Shigella* or *E. coli*, for example) which survive in poorly cooked or unrefrigerated meats. The bacteria are swallowed and produce toxins which affect the gut. *Staphylococcus* bacteria, for example, can be transmitted from someone who has a boil, abscess or other infection. These bacteria produce a toxin which may survive the cooking process.

One to eight hours after ingesting the contaminated food, the patient experiences nausea, followed by vomiting, abdominal cramping, and sometimes diarrhea, along with general symptoms such as fever and chills, weakness and headache. Other people who ate the same food may be similarly affected. Children, the elderly, and those with poor immune systems (for example, with HIV infection) are worst affected.

Fortunately, food poisoning is rarely fatal (with the exception of botulism) and recovery usually takes place after about 6–24 hours. Affected people should avoid dehydration by drinking electrolyte solutions to replace fluids lost by diarrhea. Those unable to take oral fluids due to nausea, and young children who can dehydrate very rapidly, may need intravenous fluids administered in hospital.

Food poisoning is best prevented in the first place by storing and preparing food carefully and cooking it thoroughly. It is advisable to wash all uncooked fruits and vegetables and refrigerate them. Picnic coolers containing cold or frozen food should be packed with ice packs on top. On a hot day, eat perishables or refrigerate them within an hour. It is best not to buy seafood that is not on ice.

Botulism is a dangerous form of food poisoning caused by a toxin that affects the nervous system. The toxin is produced by *Clostridium botulinum,* a bacterium found in contaminated or incompletely cooked canned foods (such as home-canned vegetables and fruits), undercooked sausage, smoked meats, and fish. Eighteen to 36 hours after eating the contaminated food, vomiting and diarrhea occur, which is then followed by signs of nervous system damage such as blurred or double vision, drooping eyelids, dry mouth, slurred speech, weakness of the arms and legs, and paralysis. The condition is a medical emergency requiring treatment in hospital with intravenous fluids and injections of the botulism antitoxin. Botulism has a 10–25 percent mortality rate.

SEE ALSO *Diarrhea, Gastroenteritis*

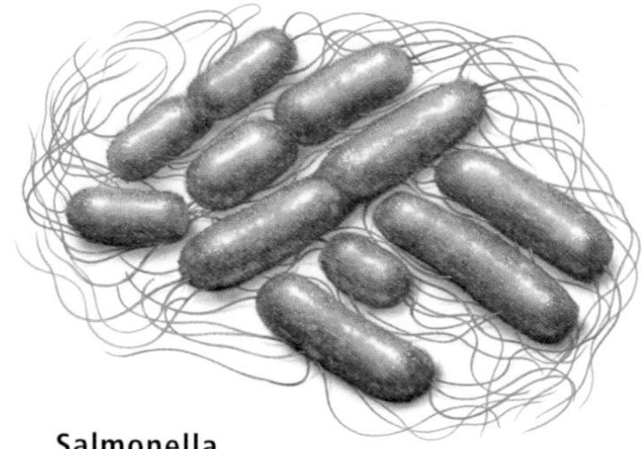

Salmonella

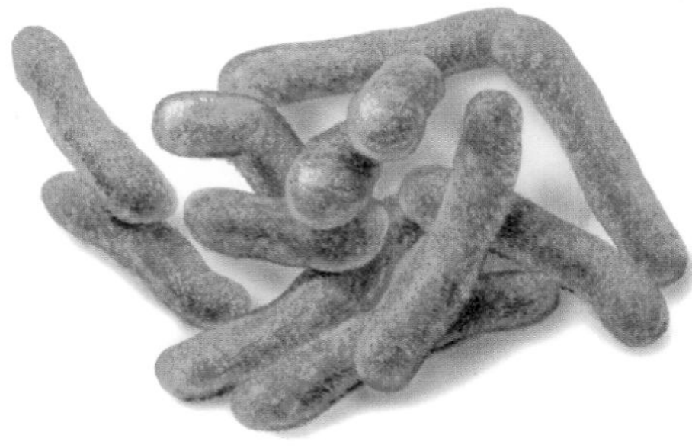

Shigella

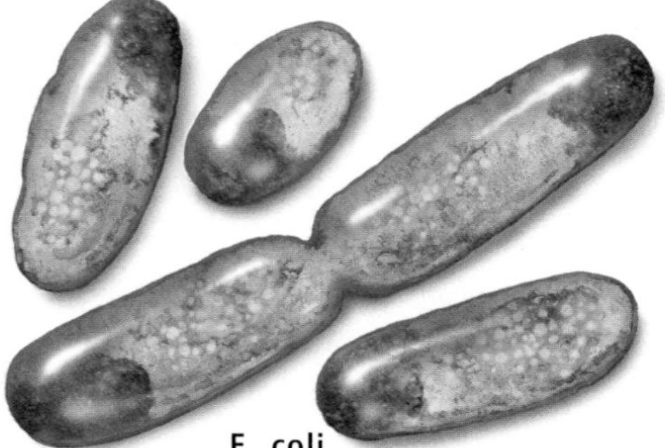

E. coli

Food poisoning

Bacteria such as these can cause food poisoning, producing vomiting, abdominal pain, headache and diarrhea.

FOOT

The foot is designed to support the body weight and to act as a lever to propel the body forwards during walking. Rather than being just one rigid bone, its skeleton is segmented, allowing it to adapt to the shape of any surface and to enhance its propulsive effect during running.

Bones and tissues of the foot

The back half of the foot (the tarsus) is formed by seven irregularly shaped tarsal bones. One of these, the talus, fits into a socket formed by the bones of the leg to form the hinge-like ankle joint. The talus sits on top of the largest tarsal bone, the calcaneus, which forms the heel and has the

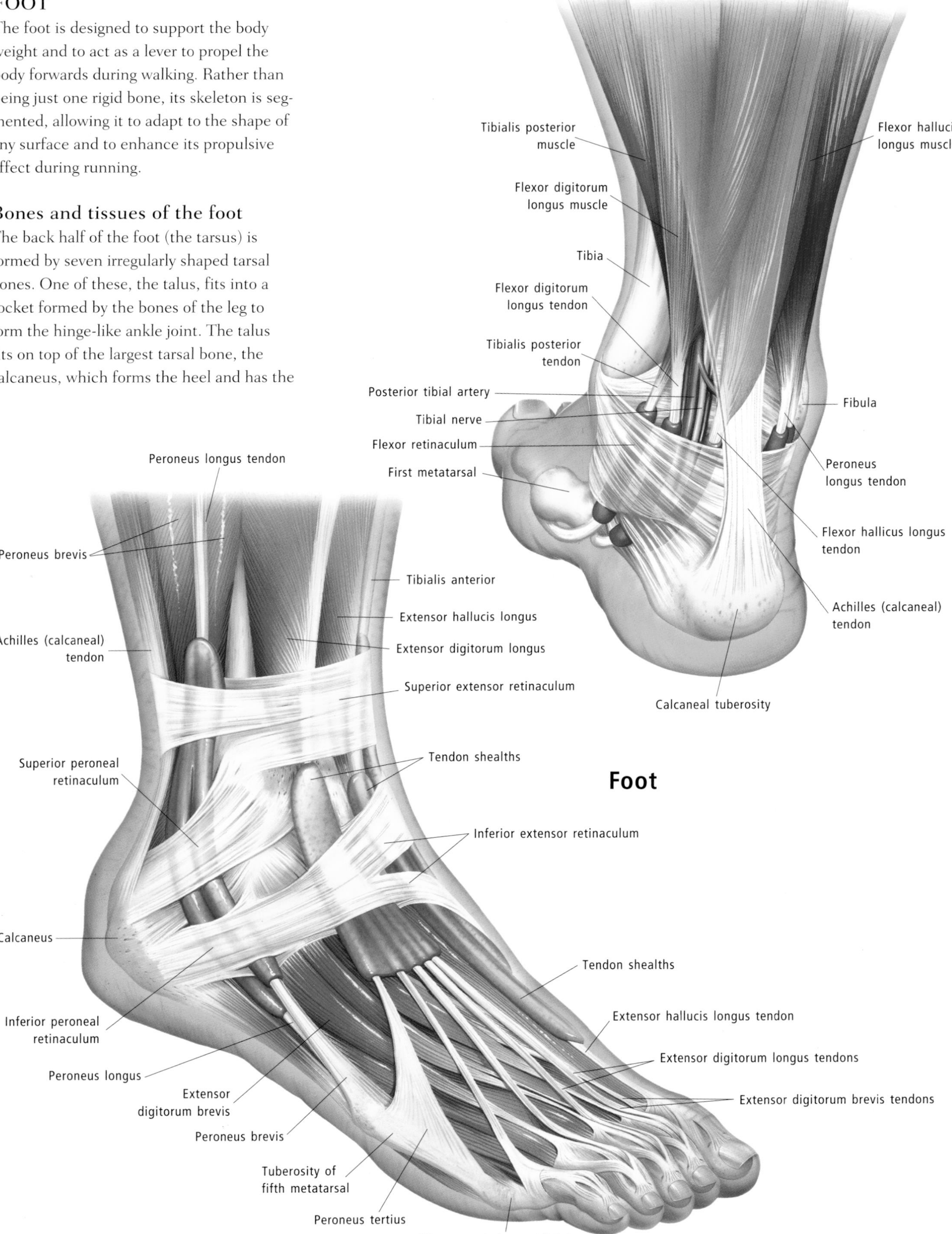

Foot

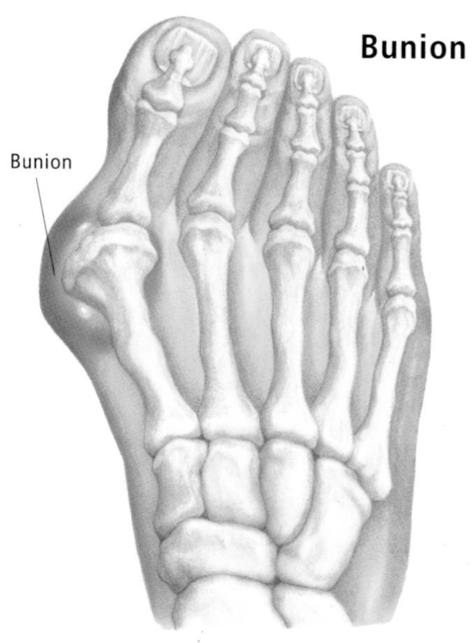

Achilles tendon attached to it. The other tarsal bones are the navicular, the cuboid and the three cuneiform bones. The bones of the tarsus are separated from each other by joints, which allow gliding movements to occur between them.

The skeleton of the front of the foot is formed by the metatarsals and phalanges. The metatarsals are long bones which form joints behind with the tarsus, and in front with the phalanges, or toe bones. The big toe has only two phalanges, the other toes have three phalanges each.

The upper surface of the foot is formed by thin skin, which overlies tendons extending from the front of the leg to the tarsus and toes. In contrast, the sole of the foot is covered by thick skin which is separated from the underlying tissues by fat pads. Fibrous tissue extends longitudinally along the sole, deep into the fat pads, from the calcaneus to the toes. It is important in binding the overlying skin and fat firmly to the deeper bones and ligaments of the foot, so it does not slip around during walking. The plantar fascia, which also acts like a bowstring to maintain the longitudinal arches of the foot, becomes stretched when the foot is flattened after the heel hits the ground. Repeated excessive stretching of this structure, which may occur in dancers, athletes or obese people, causes it to become inflamed, resulting in heel pain, especially in the mornings or at the commencement of exercise.

The sole of the foot contains long tendons and a number of small muscles which are arranged in four layers. Unlike on the hand, the big toe is prevented from coming into contact with the other toes. However, the toes do have the potential to be used for grasping; this can be seen in people born without arms, who can learn to write, draw and manipulate objects with their feet.

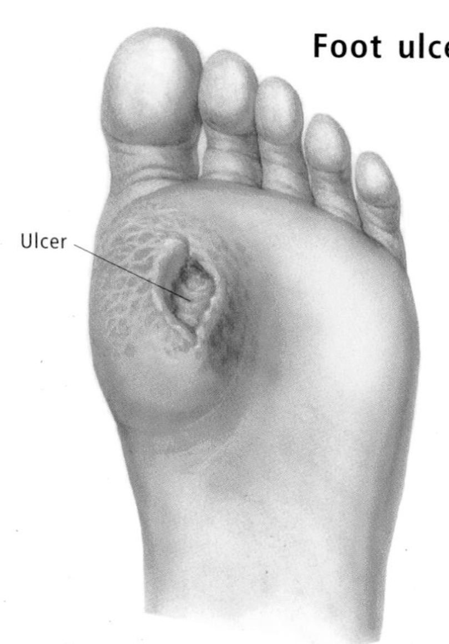

Problems

Arthritis or tight-fitting shoes can deform the metatarsophalangeal joint of the big toe, causing the toe to be forced against the other toes and the head of the metatarsal to protrude onto the medial side of the foot, forming a lump known as a bunion. Ill-fitting footwear can also cause bunions on the outside of the foot, as well as deformities of the toe joints, or thickening of the skin (corns). Deformities of the toe joints, usually caused by shoes which are too short, include hammer toe and mallet toe.

Clubfoot is a relatively common condition in which the foot is turned so that the sole faces inward, the toes point downwards (inverted and plantarflexed) and the foot cannot be straightened. It usually occurs in newborn babies as a result of genetic factors or, more commonly, from the developing foot being forced into an abnormal position in the uterus. If treated early, clubfoot is curable by gradually straightening the foot over time using a series of plaster casts.

Movement

Movements of the foot can be defined as dorsiflexion (feet point upwards), plantarflexion (feet point down), inversion or supination (sole faces inwards) and eversion or pronation (sole faces outwards). The ankle joint, between the talus and the bones of the leg, is the most commonly injured joint in the body, with injury usually resulting from a fall which forces the ankle into a position of excessive inversion. This causes damage to the ligaments which reinforce the outside of the ankle (ankle sprain) and swelling around the joint. More severe sprains may also involve fractures of the fibula or base of the fifth metatarsal.

SEE ALSO *Achilles tendon, Ankle, Bunion, Flat feet, Heel spur, Joints*

FRACTURES

A fracture is a break in a bone, usually caused by excessive stress being applied to the bone.

There are several types of fractures. In a complete fracture, the two parts of the bone are completely separated. In an incomplete fracture, the two parts are partially separated. An incomplete fracture in a long bone in a child is often called a greenstick fracture. If there are more than two bone fragments at the fracture site, it is called a comminuted fracture. If the fractured bone has broken the skin and is exposed to the air, it is a compound or open fracture; if it hasn't broken the skin, it is a simple, or closed fracture. In an impacted, or compression fracture, the break occurs from extreme pressure on the bone. A stress fracture is a crack in a bone caused by repetitive and prolonged pressure on the bone, usually from exercise. A pathologic fracture is one that occurs in bone that is weakened or destroyed by disease such as osteoporosis or a tumor; the injury itself may be minor. A compression fracture is an example of this.

The symptoms and signs of a fracture are pain, swelling and deformity at the fracture site, weakness of movement, and inability to bear weight on the affected parts. The arteries around the fracture may be damaged, causing bleeding or bruising at the site. In a limb especially, there may be loss of pulse, with cold white extremities. Nerves around the fracture sometimes become damaged; there may be numbness, tingling or paralysis in the extremity below the fracture.

A fracture can usually be seen clearly in an x-ray. The treatment of a fracture is to reduce (realign) the bone back into its normal position, then immobilize the bone fragments to prevent movement and so they can join back together. Immobilization can be achieved by means of a plaster cast, traction (usually in hospital), or surgical insertion of rods, plates or screws. After the bones have healed (which may take from six weeks to six months), physical therapy and rehabilitation are required.

First aid is vital in the treatment of fracture. Follow the procedure for bleeding, and cover any open wounds. Do not move the person—especially if the injury is to the hip, pelvis, or upper leg—unless necessary. Do not try to straighten a bone or change its position, or give the person anything by mouth. Arrange emergency transport to the hospital immediately.

SEE ALSO *Bones*

FRAGILE X SYNDROME

The fragile X syndrome is the most common cause of inherited intellectual disability and is due to a defect involving a gene called the FMR1 gene. The syndrome most often involves males, although females may also be affected. The abnormality occurs in the X chromosome, of which females have two and males only one. Boys with the defective chromosome will be intellectually disabled; women with only one damaged X chromosome will be carriers of the disease, with the chance of having intellectually disabled boys. If parents are at risk of having boys with this disease, the fragile X mutation can be detected by prenatal sampling of fetal tissue, and abortion may be offered.

SEE ALSO *Chromosomes, Congenital abnormalities, Genes, Genetic counseling, Intellectual disability*

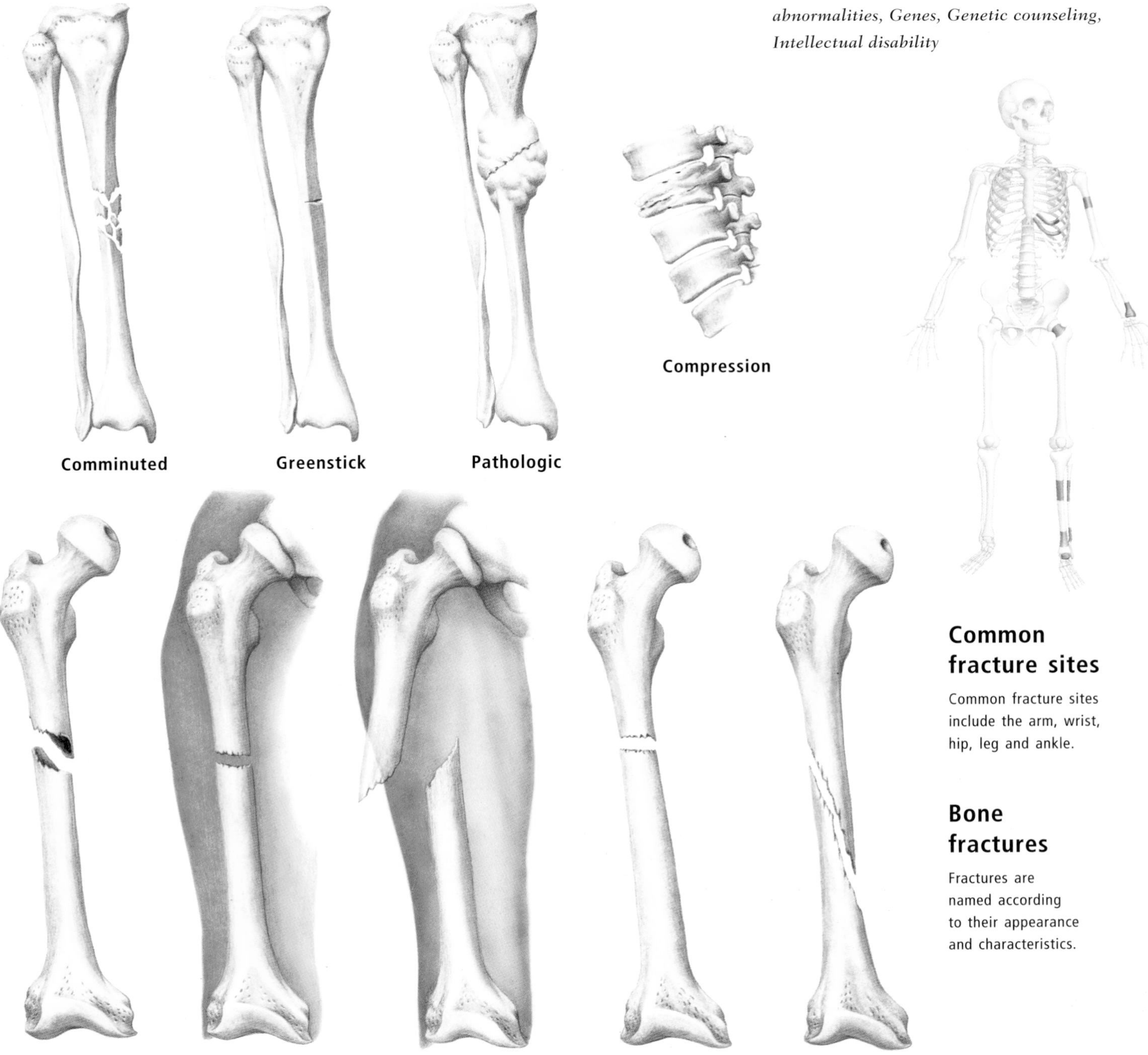

Common fracture sites

Common fracture sites include the arm, wrist, hip, leg and ankle.

Bone fractures

Fractures are named according to their appearance and characteristics.

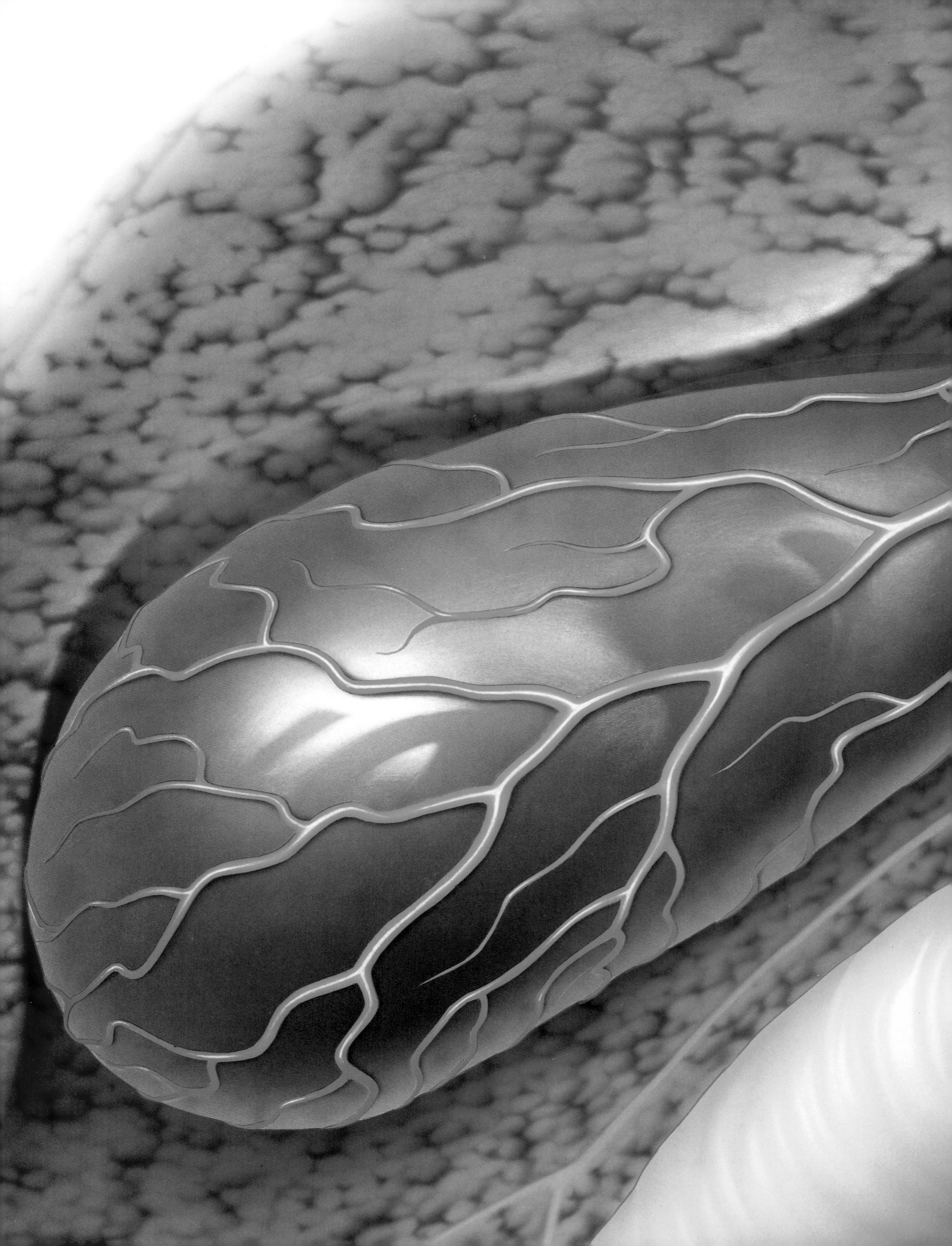

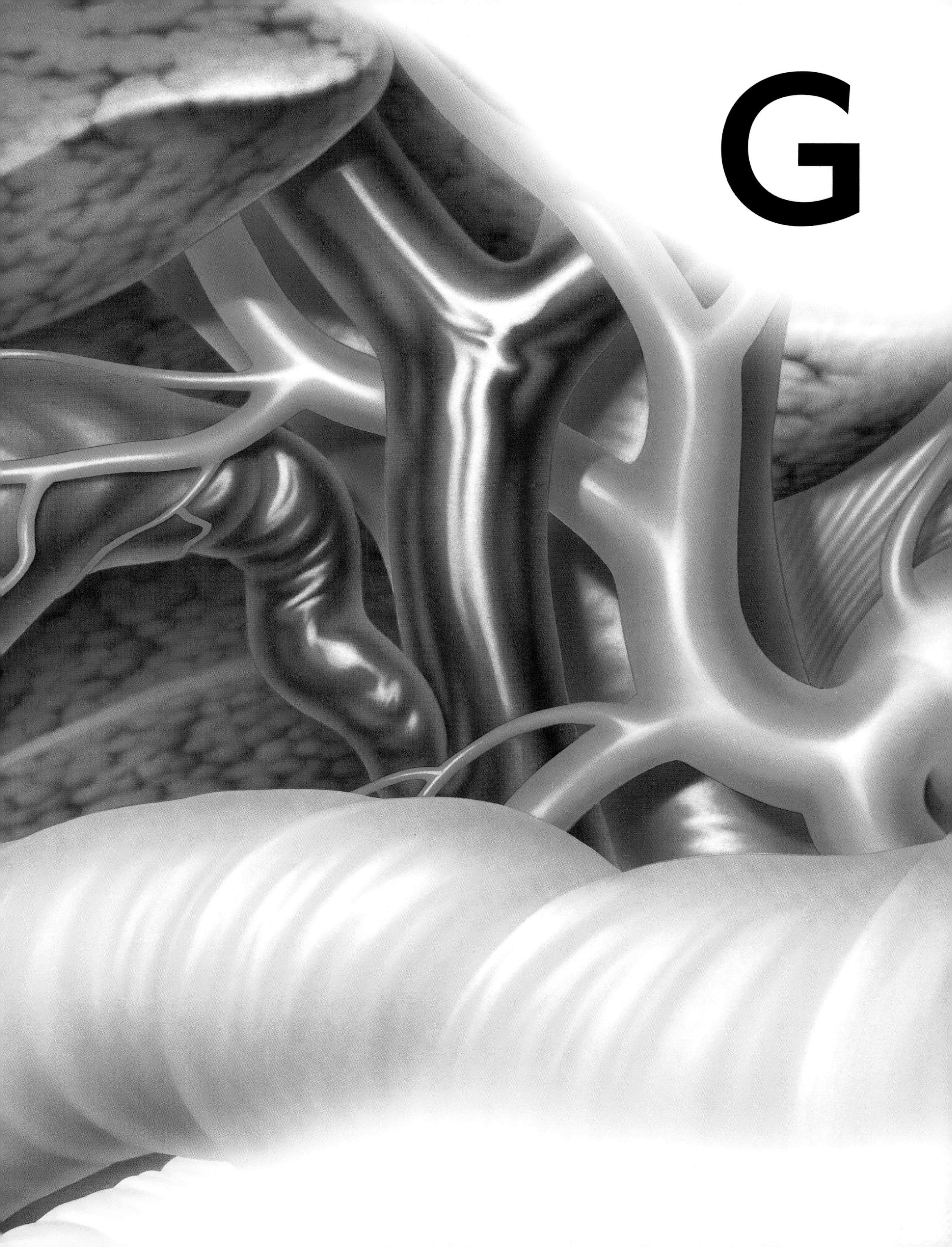
G

GALACTOSEMIA

Galactosemia is an uncommon inherited disorder, caused by a deficiency of an enzyme in the intestine that breaks down galactose, a sugar normally found in milk. It is seen mainly in newborn infants in whom the condition is not yet diagnosed.

The infant feeds poorly, vomits, and fails to thrive or gain weight. If milk feeding continues, the infant may develop jaundice, cirrhosis, cataracts and brain damage.

The condition is confirmed by special blood and urine tests that show the lack of the enzyme. Treatment consists of eliminating all milk and milk-containing products from the diet for life, using milk substitutes such as soy formula instead. If the diet is modified, life expectancy is normal. A potential parent with a family history of galactosemia may need to seek genetic counseling before having children.

SEE ALSO *Genetic counseling*

G

GALLBLADDER

The gallbladder is a sac-shaped organ that stores and concentrates bile prior to its release into the small intestine. It is part of the biliary tree, a series of ducts that conveys and stores bile. The gallbladder is usually firmly attached to the lower surface of the liver and lies on the right side of the abdomen just below the ribs at the front.

Bile is a body fluid which contains pigments, lecithin and bile salts. The pigments are made from cholesterol and bilirubin, and give the bile fluids a yellow to orange color during life. Bile is very important because, when it is released into the small intestine, it serves to break down relatively large globules of fat into smaller droplets, thus increasing the available surface area of the fat particles so as to improve their digestion and absorption.

Bile is produced by liver cells, then passes along the bile ducts, and is stored and concentrated in the gallbladder before being released into the initial part of the small intestine, known as the duodenum. Once digestion and absorption of fats has taken place, the bile is reabsorbed in the end of the small intestine, carried back to the liver by a group of veins known as the portal system, and there re-excreted into the bile ducts to begin the process again. This is known as the enterohepatic biliary circulation.

The gallbladder is joined to the bile duct by the cystic duct. The bile duct passes from the junction with the cystic duct down through the head of the pancreas to drain bile into the duodenum. Just before it enters the duodenum, the bile duct is joined by the main duct of the pancreas. The passage of the bile duct through the pancreas means that a tumor (cancer or, more correctly, carcinoma) in this pancreatic head can obstruct the lower bile duct and cause a build-up of bile in the biliary tree. This back-up eventually reaches as far up the biliary tree as the gallbladder and liver, causing an enlarged gallbladder and leading to jaundice, when the bile salts reach the blood.

Another more common disease of the biliary tree is cholelithiasis, or gallstones. This condition commonly affects women in their reproductive years who are fair-skinned and overweight, but it may affect men and women of all ages. Gallstones are formed when bile chemicals come out of solution to form crystals in the gallbladder. These stones may irritate the inner lining of the gallbladder, causing a condition known as cholecystitis.

The gallbladder does not usually enlarge in cholecystitis, because the inflammation causes the formation of fibrous tissue in the gallbladder wall. Sometimes gallstones may enter the cystic and bile ducts and be passed down to the duodenum. The pain that results when the smooth muscle of the bile duct attempts to squeeze the stones along the duct is known as biliary colic. Characteristically, the pain is severe, located on the upper right side or in the upper middle parts of the abdomen, and occurs minutes after eating a meal, particularly one with a high fat content. The pain may subside over 12–18 hours, only to recur after a subsequent meal. Other common symptoms include fever, nausea, vomiting, chills and shaking. Sometimes a stone does not give rise to pain but silently obstructs the bile ducts, causing jaundice.

Certain x-ray examinations help to diagnose disorders of the biliary tree. During these examinations, the patient swallows a chemical similar in structure to normal bile constituents, and one that is also opaque to x-rays. The chemical is absorbed from the small intestine and transported to the liver by the portal system. It is subsequently excreted into the biliary tree and concentrated in the gallbladder. X-rays taken at this stage will reveal the ducts of the biliary tree (cholangiography) and gallbladder (cholecystography) standing out against the darker upper abdominal contents.

Further investigations include ultrasound and retrograde cholangiography, which involves back-filling the biliary tree from the duodenum with a chemical opaque to x-rays. This test requires the insertion of an endoscope, a device for viewing the interior of the gut. The endoscope is inserted through the stomach and into the duodenum, in order to place a catheter into the lower bile duct.

Removal of the gallbladder is known as cholecystectomy—this may be done by open surgery or by laparoscopy, a technique whereby instruments are inserted into the abdomen through small punctures in its wall. Laparoscopic surgery results in a shorter hospital stay and faster recovery, as the abdominal scar is much smaller than with surgery via the open method. Gallbladder disease can be prevented or minimized by losing weight and reducing one's intake of fatty foods.

SEE ALSO *Bile duct, Cholangiography, Gallstones, Intestines, Jaundice, Liver, Pancreas*

GALLSTONES

These are very common—as many as 7 percent of adults in the USA have gallstones (cholelithiasis) in their gallbladders. Each year in the USA approximately 350,000 people have operations for gallstones, and as many as 6,000 people die from associated complications. Gallstones are more common in women in the 40–65 years age group than any other group in the community, suggesting a hormonal link. In fact, taking the contraceptive pill contributes to formation of gallstones in susceptible women.

About 75 percent of gallstones are made of cholesterol, while the remainder are composed of bile pigments. Problems arise when cholesterol or bile pigments come out of solution in the bile fluids concentrated in the gallbladder. This means that gallstones are usually encountered in the gallbladder itself, where they may cause chronic inflammation of the gallbladder lining (chronic cholecystitis). Occasionally the gallstones may leave the gallbladder and become lodged in the bile duct, where they can cause obstruction to bile flow. Jaundice results as bile builds up in the liver and eventually the bloodstream.

Actually, 70 percent of people with gallstones never require surgery, but several problems can arise. Chronic cholecystitis is the most common form of gallbladder disease. Patients experience episodes of abdominal pain (biliary colic) whenever the gallstones cause transient obstruction of the cystic duct, which leads out of the gallbladder. This pain is usually felt in the upper right part of the abdomen and is sometimes accompanied by nausea and vomiting.

Patients may not be able to tolerate fatty foods, and may complain of indigestion, heartburn and flatulence.

If the impaction of the gallstone in the cystic duct leads to inflammation, the abdominal pain may become more severe and persistent. The pain may be accompanied by fever and increased numbers of white blood cells in the blood. This is known as acute cholecystitis. Resulting complications include gangrene of the gallbladder, formation of pus in the gallbladder (empyema, or suppurative cholecystitis), perforation of the gallbladder with spilling of infected contents into the abdominal cavity, or the formation of abscesses around the gallbladder.

Gallstones may pass through the cystic duct into the bile duct. In this situation, known as choledocholithiasis, patients experience biliary colic pain accompanied by moderate to severe jaundice, chills and fever. The pancreas may become inflamed (pancreatitis).

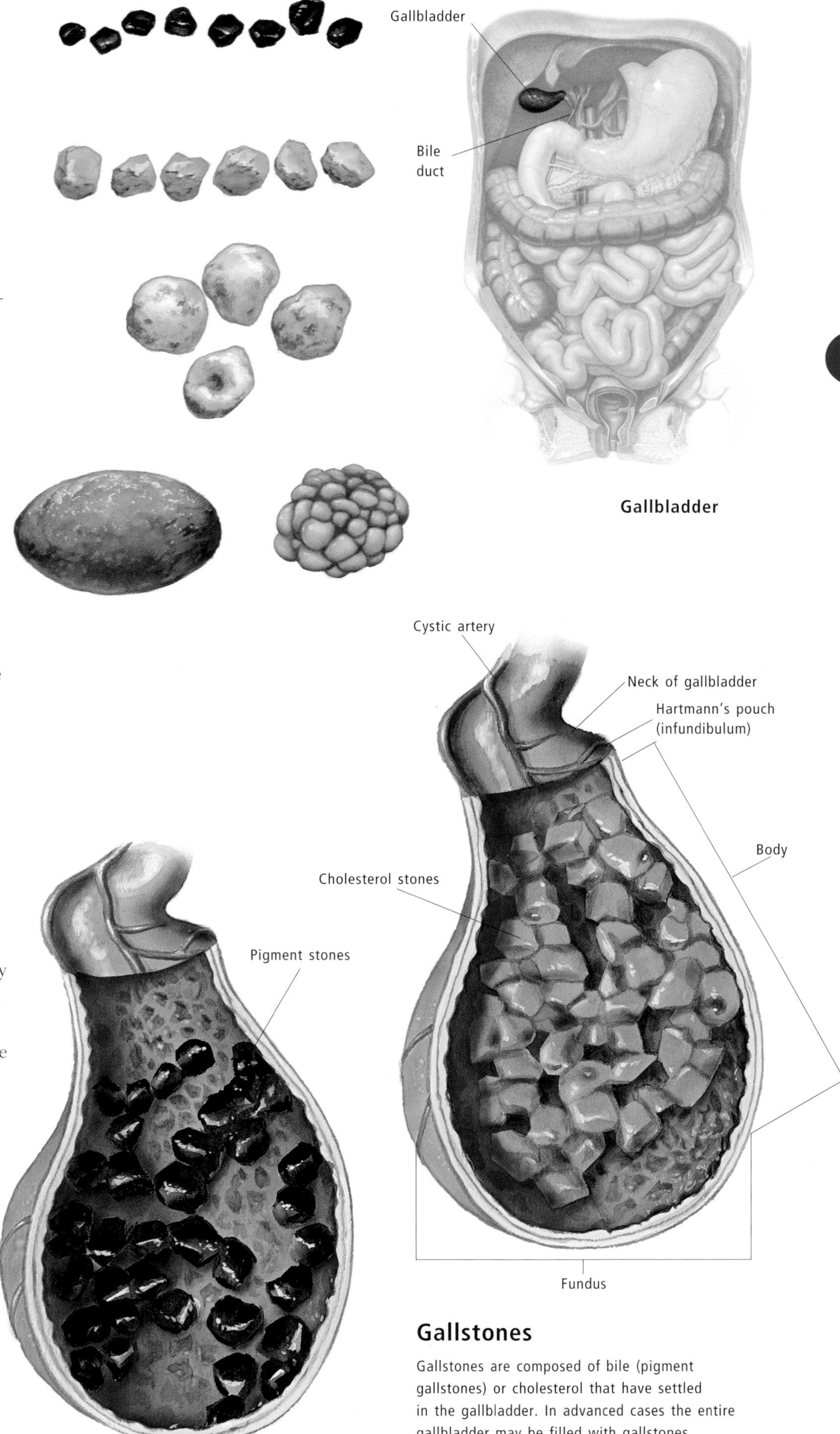

Gallstones

Gallstones have different shapes and sizes. They can be multifaceted or round, and vary in color from yellow to brown to black. Small black gallstones are made of calcium bilirubinate. Yellow-brownish gallstones are made from cholesterol and can range from about $\frac{1}{2}$–$1\frac{1}{2}$ inches (1–4 centimeters) in size. A single gallstone can grow large enough to fill the gallbladder. These illustrations are all actual size.

Gallbladder

Gallstones

Gallstones are composed of bile (pigment gallstones) or cholesterol that have settled in the gallbladder. In advanced cases the entire gallbladder may be filled with gallstones.

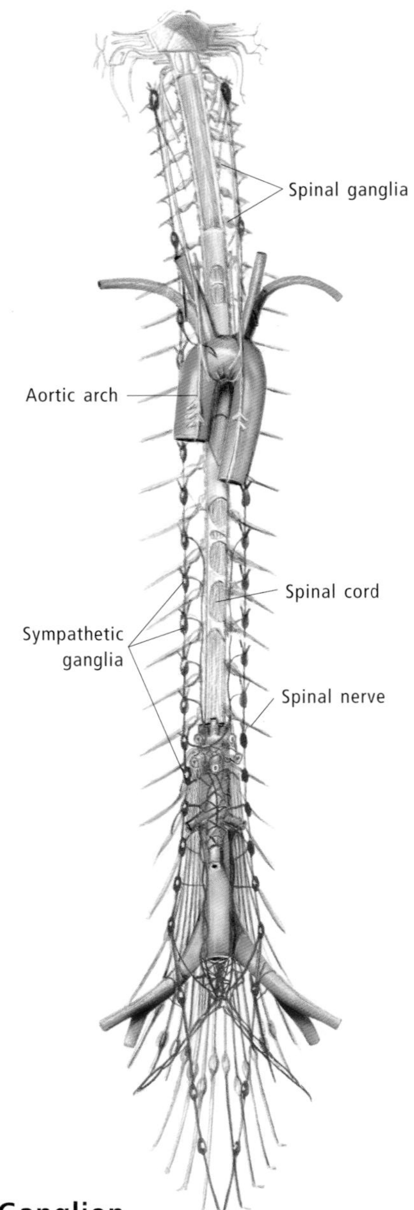

Ganglion

A ganglion (plural ganglia) is a cluster of nerve cell bodies found in the peripheral nervous system. Spinal ganglia contain the cell bodies of sensory nerve fibers in the peripheral nerves. Sympathetic ganglia are part of the autonomic nervous system.

G

Gallstone disease is detected in a number of ways. During an oral cholecystogram, the patient is given a chemical that is opaque to x-rays and is excreted by the liver into the gallbladder and bile duct. Ultrasound is a technique whereby sound waves are used to form an image of the gallbladder and the stones within. Retrograde cholangiography is an investigation in which an endoscope is used to insert a catheter into the lower bile duct and back-fill the biliary tree from the duodenum.

The symptoms of gallstones can be prevented or minimized by losing weight and reducing one's intake of fatty foods. However if symptoms persist then the gallstones (along with the gallbladder) should be surgically removed, either by open abdominal operation or through a laparoscope. Laparoscopic surgery is the preferred method for most people as it results in a shorter hospital stay and faster recovery.

If there is bacterial infection of the gallbladder (for example cholecystitis) urgent treatment in hospital with intravenous antibiotics is necessary; after the inflammation has subsided, the gallbladder can be removed at a convenient time in the subsequent weeks or months.

SEE ALSO *Cholecystitis, Gallbladder, Liver, Pancreas, Pancreatitis*

GANGLION

The word "ganglion" refers to two different things. Firstly, a ganglion is a group of nerve cell bodies outside the central nervous system. For example, a spinal ganglion is a cluster of sensory nerve cell bodies found along the spinal cord at the root of a spinal nerve. Secondly, a ganglion is a cyst in or around a tendon or joint, especially in the hands, wrists and feet. Ganglion cysts can be treated with ice packs applied directly to the affected area, together with oral medication for pain. A ganglion cyst may be removed by a ganglionectomy or cyst aspiration.

SEE ALSO *Nerves, Nervous system, Spinal cord*

GANGRENE

This term refers to death of tissue, with secondary growth of bacteria that derive their nutrition by breaking down the dead tissue. In practice, gangrene is often used to refer to death of a large area of tissue (frequently as a result of loss of blood supply or in wounds infected by anaerobic bacteria), whether or not it has undergone significant bacterial decomposition.

Gangrene occurs most often in the extremities, for example in the foot or toe resulting from blockage of an artery, though it can also involve internal organs, such as with hernias. Fever, pain, darkening of the skin and unpleasant odor are common symptoms. Correcting the initial causes, medication and surgery may be required.

SEE ALSO *Bacteria, Circulatory system*

GAS GANGRENE

In this form of gangrene, dead tissue is invaded by bacteria called *Clostridium welchii* which break it down and in the process release bubbles of gas into the tissue. Bacteria are frequently found in soil and include a variety of organisms that are able to secrete very powerful toxins. For example, the bacteria causing tetanus and the serious food poisoning known as botulism are members of this group. Despite its name, it is the toxins and the tissue-destroying enzymes released by the bacteria, not the gas bubbles, that make gas gangrene so dangerous. Progressive breakdown of tissue, damage to blood cells and other effects of the toxins can eventually kill the patient.

Clostridia prefer a low-oxygen environment and therefore grow well in deep wounds with considerable tissue damage, especially if contaminated by soil and dirt. This is why gas gangrene is such a feared complication of wounds during war. It may also develop after injury in an accident or after surgery. Attention to wound care is essential to prevent the onset of gas gangrene.

SEE ALSO *Bacteria, Food poisoning, Gangrene*

GASTRECTOMY

Gastrectomy is the surgical removal of part or (very rarely) all of the stomach. It is used for treatment of gastric cancer, and gastric ulcers that do not respond to medical treatment. Partial gastrectomy involves removal of the lower parts of the stomach, while keeping other parts (the fundus and cardiac parts) intact.

SEE ALSO *Gastric ulcer, Stomach*

GASTRIC ULCER

Gastric ulcers involve the loss of the inner lining (mucous layer) of the stomach to produce a lesion (wound). Most patients with gastric ulcers are aged 40 to 60 years, about 10 years older than patients who develop duodenal ulcers. Most gastric ulcers develop on the inner surface of the right edge of the stomach, usually within a few inches (5–6 centimeters) of the last part of the stomach (pylorus). Some gastric ulcers are associated with duodenal ulcers, but most appear separately. Some gastric ulcers develop in conjunction with gastric cancers and it is of the utmost importance that these are identified early to improve the patient's chance of survival.

Causes vary, but environmental and genetic factors play important roles. Gastric ulcers can be related to a number of drugs (aspirin, non-steroidal anti-inflammatory drugs and steroids) and dietary and personal factors. It is now recognized that infection of the stomach with acid-resistant bacteria (*Helicobacter pylori*) is an important contributing factor in the development of gastric ulcers. Also, people with a family history of gastric ulcers are at greater risk.

Patients with gastric ulcers usually complain of experiencing pain in the upper abdomen within 30 minutes of eating a meal. With duodenal ulcers, the pain usually comes on more than one hour after meals.

The severity and duration of attacks of pain from the gastric ulcer are usually more severe than that from duodenal ulcers, but in both cases food and antacids often temporarily relieve the pain. Some patients with gastric ulcers experience vomiting, loss of interest in (or aversion to) eating, and pain aggravated by meals. Treatment is by antibiotics, antacids or surgery.

SEE ALSO *Duodenal ulcer, Stomach*

Gastric ulcer

When the mucous lining of the stomach wall is damaged, the acid in the stomach erodes the wall and an ulcer forms.

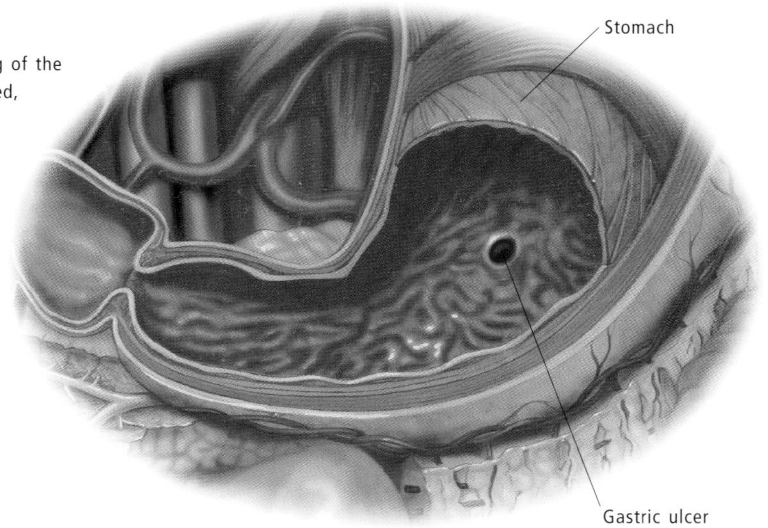

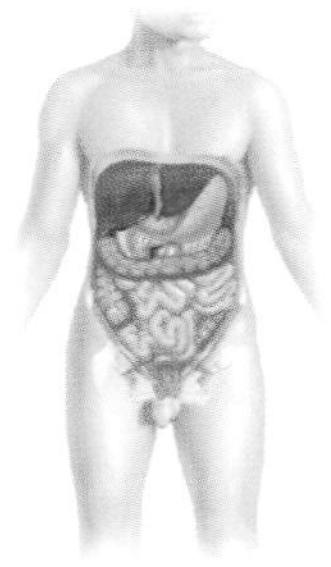

Gastritis

Inflammation of the stomach (gastritis) is a common disorder. It often manifests as a sudden pain resulting from the irritation of the stomach wall.

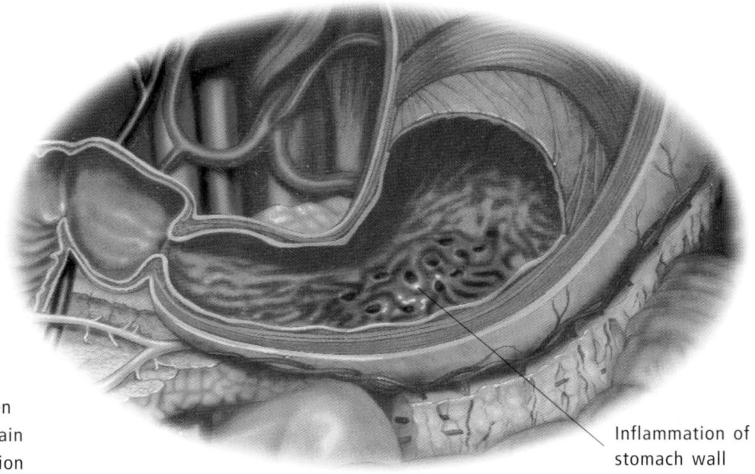

GASTRITIS

Gastritis is an inflammation of the stomach lining. It tends to become more prevalent with age and can appear as a short-lived acute (sudden onset) condition or may be ongoing and chronic (long term).

Depending on the cause and type of gastritis, symptoms can range from mild stomach aches and cramps, burping, diarrhea, a swollen abdomen, chest pain, loss of appetite and an unpleasant (often acidic) taste in the mouth due to vomiting. Although gastritis is a common and usually minor ailment, signs that may indicate the need for medical attention include black tarry feces (melena) due to bleeding in the stomach, vomit containing blood, a fever and severe pain.

Potential causes of acute gastritis include alcohol, caffeine, nicotine, overeating, medications that irritate the stomach lining (such as aspirin and non-steroidal anti-inflammatory drugs), physiological stress brought on by another illness or major surgery, food allergies and bacterial or viral infections.

Treatment depends on the cause, but the symptoms of acute gastritis usually disappear within a few days with rest and avoidance of drugs or food that irritate the stomach. Over-the-counter antacid medications usually provide short-term relief of symptoms. The use of aspirin or related drugs should be avoided but, if painkillers are required, alternatives such as acetaminophen (paracetamol) may help.

The only definitive way to identify the cause (and sometimes, to confirm the presence) of chronic gastritis is through medical tests such as endoscopy and biopsy. An endoscopy involves passing a long, thin, flexible tube down the esophagus into the stomach to view and often photograph the appearance of the stomach wall. A biopsy, taking a small piece of the stomach wall for analysis, is often performed with an endoscopy. The two procedures normally require the patient to be mildly sedated.

These days, one of the most common causes of chronic gastritis is widely acknowledged to be a bacterium called *Helicobacter pylori,* first described in the medical literature in the 1980s by two Western Australian medical researchers. Not all people infected with these bacteria develop symptoms. Many people become infected in childhood and live normal lives without ever developing any complications. However, *H. pylori* infections (which are readily treated with antibiotics) are now understood to be a major cause of stomach ulcers and cancers.

Chronic gastritis can also be due to an autoimmune disorder in which the cells in the stomach lining are attacked by the body's own immune system. This causes a loss of stomach cells and a reduction in a person's ability to absorb vitamin B_{12}, which leads to a condition known as pernicious anemia. The gastritis itself may not cause any symptoms but may be identified when causes of the anemia are investigated.

Another type of chronic gastritis is hypertrophic gastritis, in which the folds of the stomach wall become enlarged and inflamed. Ménétrier's disease, a rare form of this condition, is most often seen in elderly patients; protein loss is a common complication. Drug treatments are available but, if they fail, surgery may be required.

SEE ALSO *Anemia, Autoimmune disease, Biopsy, Digestive system, Endoscopy, Stomach*

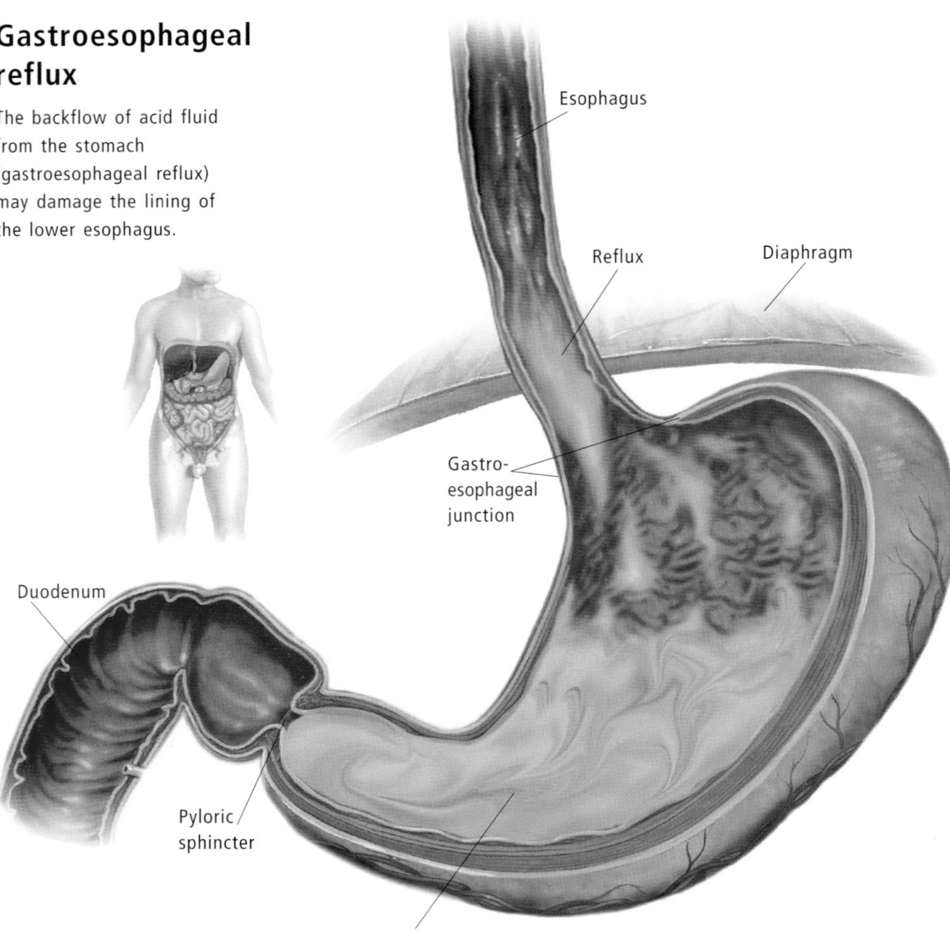

Gastroesophageal reflux

The backflow of acid fluid from the stomach (gastroesophageal reflux) may damage the lining of the lower esophagus.

GASTROENTERITIS

Gastroenteritis is characterized by infection—usually of the entire gastrointestinal tract—and diarrhea is the hallmark, generally with associated nausea and often vomiting.

Death from gastroenteritis is greatest among young children and the old or debilitated, particularly in developing countries. Rotavirus and certain forms of *Escherichia coli* (*E. coli*) are the main causes, closely followed by cholera and amebic dysentery. The major problem lies in dirty food handling or inadequate sewerage management, particularly when polluted river water or well water is not boiled before use. Like the toxin of *E. coli,* rotavirus can produce watery diarrhea, rapidly leading to dehydration and death. Fluid replacement, either orally or intravenously, may be required, particularly if vomiting is a feature. If dehydration is present, as characterized by sunken eyes, diminished skin tone and sunken fontanelle (in babies), similar urgent fluid and electrolyte replacement is required.

Frequent causes of diarrhea among travelers are giardiasis and amebic dysentery. Giardiasis is caused usually by swallowing water contaminated by animal feces, and produces nausea and foul-smelling, pale, frothy and bulky stools, that usually float. Diarrhea may persist for many weeks but is neither watery nor likely to cause dehydration. Due to a flagellate protozoa (*Giardia lamblia*) in the small intestine, giardiasis is diagnosed by either small bowel biopsy via endoscopy or else from the presence of the flagellate in the stools. Because of the difficulty of diagnosing giardiasis, the physician will often presume its presence, based on symptoms, and prescribe medication accordingly.

Amebic dysentery is caused by a protozoan (*Entamoeba hystolytica*), usually passed on from an infected carrier. The condition develops slowly, leading to frequent sloppy bowel movements with a foul odor. Blood is occasionally seen in the stool. The illness can be debilitating but is rarely overwhelming. Liver abscess can be a complication and must always be considered. Treatment is with metronidazole, while liver abscesses also respond to chloroquine (a drug used for malaria).

Shigella infections, that can cause dysentery, range from mild to severe and are characterized by high fever, severe colic and bloody diarrhea. Nausea is the usual accompaniment. The condition is normally short lived, generally lasting no more than three or four days following a short incubation period. Rarely fatal, the condition usually responds rapidly to medication. If the infection is severe, intravenous fluids may be necessary.

Cholera remains a major problem, with epidemics occurring in developing countries and sporadically elsewhere, particularly where there has been strife and war. Poor hygiene and inadequate sewerage are the major factors. Sufferers dehydrate extremely rapidly and can die within hours unless intravenous replacement fluids are given immediately.

Helicobacter infection can cause acute gastroenteritis and is commonly reputed to occur after eating undercooked chicken. Nausea and colic are usual symptoms, together with foul-smelling bowel movements. The infection is mostly self-righting after two or three days, but occasionally an antibiotic is required for cure.

Many viruses have associated diarrhea. However, the gastroenteritis with these infections tends to be a minor part of the illness overall and usually subsides spontaneously within a day or so.

SEE ALSO *Cholera, Dehydration, Dysentery, Food poisoning, Giardiasis*

GASTROESOPHAGEAL REFLUX

Gastroesophageal reflux is the movement of stomach fluid up into the lower esophagus. It occurs quite normally during the waking hours, especially after meals. In some people, however, reflux of stomach acids is excessive and causes symptoms. Usually in these people the band of muscle fibers that closes off the esophagus from the stomach (called the lower esophageal sphincter) is incompetent.

This happens most commonly in pregnancy, obesity, or with a hiatus hernia (when part of the somach has moved up into the chest).

The symptoms are heartburn (pain felt under the breastbone, or sternum) which is made worse by bending, stooping, or eating, and is relieved by milk or antacids. There may be other symptoms such as belching, nausea, vomiting, and difficulty swallowing.

A specialist physcian will usally confirm the diagnosis by performing an endoscopy (a tube placed down into the esophagus to enable it to be visualized), which will show inflammation and possibly ulceration of the esophagus lining due to stomach acid. A barium swallow may show the reflux occurring.

Other specialized tests may demonstrate that stomach acids are in the esophagus, and that the sphincter is incompetent.

In most cases the symptoms improve after simple preventive measures have been taken. These include losing weight, avoiding lying down after a meal, and avoiding foods like fat, chocolate, caffeine, alcohol and tobacco, which seem to make the condition worse. When sleeping, the head of the bed should be elevated.

Medications such as antacids (taken after meals and at bedtime) and histamine H2 receptor blockers will relieve the symptoms. In a small percentage of cases, surgery to correct the sphincter is needed.

Recurrent gastresophageal reflux may cause a pre-cancerous condition of the lower esophagus called Barrett's syndrome.

SEE ALSO *Esophagus, Heartburn, Hiatus hernia, Stomach*

GASTROSCOPY

Gastroscopy is one of a number of tests that use fiberoptic tubes called endoscopes to see inside the body and perform minor procedures such as taking samples or destroying diseased or abnormal tissue. The tubes are flexible, carry a light, and can also be fitted with small surgical instruments. This technique is used to examine the stomach. Patients are required to fast for several hours before endoscopy to ensure that food does not obstruct the internal examination. Endoscopy can cause irritation and minor internal bleeding, and in rare instances may damage the bowel.

SEE ALSO *Endoscopy*

GENES

Genes are the units of genetic information, passed from parent to offspring and found on chromosomes in the nucleus of each cell. Humans have 23 pairs of chromosomes, and at conception each parent contributes one chromosome of each pair. These chromosomes are then copied into each cell in the body.

Chromosomes consist of deoxyribonucleic acid (DNA), with each gene being a section of DNA that instructs the cell how to make a particular protein. (Proteins are extremely important functional and structural molecules in cells.)

The instruction is contained in the order, or sequence, of nucleotide bases (adenine, guanine, cytosine and thymine) of the DNA, which codes the sequence of amino acids in the protein.

Humans have approximately 100,000 genes, with each of us having different combinations giving us our unique characteristics. Not all genes are active at any one time; gene expression can be inhibited or induced, depending on the function of the cell and the body's needs.

Because each person has a unique genetic makeup, DNA analysis ("DNA fingerprinting") can be used to identify individuals, as in forensic medicine.

Since we inherit half our genetic makeup from each parent, the DNA of close family members contains more similarities than that of unrelated people. This can be used to establish relationships, in paternity cases for instance.

Mutations

Mutations occur when there is a change in one or more nucleotides in the DNA molecule in a cell. Mutations can occur if the DNA is damaged, for instance by excess radiation or by harmful chemicals, such as those in cigarette smoke. The change in the DNA sequence in a gene may result in a change in the amino acids in the protein that the gene encodes.

Mutations are relatively rare and may be beneficial, but are more often harmful. Sickle cell disease, for example, is due to a change in one base in the gene that controls hemoglobin, the protein that carries oxygen in red blood cells. This causes a change in one amino acid in the hemoglobin, leading to poor oxygen transport. Mutations can also occur when DNA is copied, as in cell

Chromosomes

There are about 100,000 separate genes in the human genome (or genetic blueprint), spread across 23 pairs of chromosomes (coiled, double stranded DNA material of varying lengths). In the gamete (sperm or egg), these are separated into 23 single chromosomes through a process called meiosis. Once an egg is fertilized by a sperm new pairs of chromosomes are formed.

division. Cells have mechanisms to repair damaged DNA, but some degree of mutation is desirable since it may produce new proteins and useful variability.

If harmful mutations occur in the germ cells (ova and sperm), they may be passed to the offspring. If that offspring survives and reproduces again, the mutation may be passed onto the next generation, and so on, to eventually become established in the population.

Many disorders are inherited. Some disorders run in families but occur irregularly. Environment, diet, smoking and other factors are often as important as genetic influences in causing a number of diseases.

However, there are over 3,500 diseases that are known to be linked to a defect in a single gene and are strictly genetically inherited. In some of these diseases, the defective gene is "dominant"—only one parent needs to pass on the gene to give their offspring the disease, for example, myotonic dystrophy, a type of muscular dystrophy associated with muscle wasting and loss of muscle tone. In others, the defective gene is "recessive", requiring the gene from both parents for the disease to be genetically expressed, for example, cystic fibrosis, a disease of the exocrine glands of the lung, skin and pancreas.

Other defective genes are "X-linked", (also called sex-linked); that is, they are located on the X chromosome. This means that usually only males get the disease; women have two X chromosomes and X-linked diseases are usually recessive, so the disease is not expressed. The women become carriers, however. Hemophilia is an X-linked disease.

Prospective parents with a genetic disorder in the family may not want to risk passing it on to their future offspring. Genetic counseling for the parents may be valuable so that they can discuss the genetic risks and possible options. For some inheritable disorders such as Down syndrome, screening during pregnancy can provide a prenatal diagnosis, and allow the parents to consider terminating the pregnancy.

Gene mapping

Gene mapping refers to the sequence and spacing of genes along a chromosome.

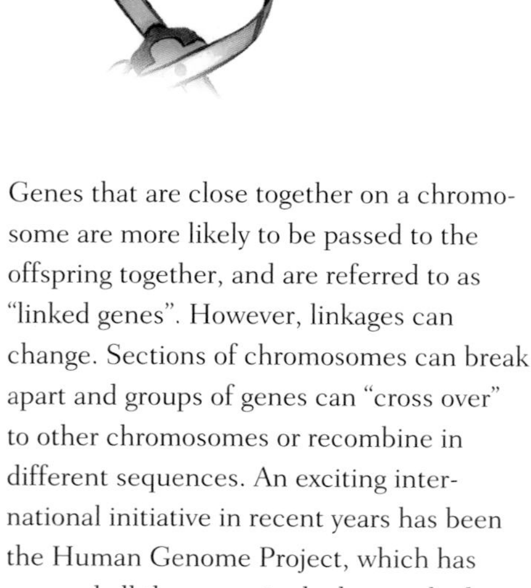

Gene sequencing

Each nucleotide base interlocks with a specific partner to form a base pair. Three base pairs form a codon and code for one amino acid. The order in which the bases are carried on a DNA strand determines the information contained in that strand.

Genetic code

Genetic information is contained in the myriad combinations of bases that exist along the length of the DNA molecule. A gene is a particular sequence of bases which codes for a specific protein. Proteins catalyze chemical reactions, build cells and tissues, and ultimately confer characteristics on an individual. Even a single base alteration can lead to disease.

Genes that are close together on a chromosome are more likely to be passed to the offspring together, and are referred to as "linked genes". However, linkages can change. Sections of chromosomes can break apart and groups of genes can "cross over" to other chromosomes or recombine in different sequences. An exciting international initiative in recent years has been the Human Genome Project, which has mapped all the genes in the human body.

Genetic engineering

Genetic engineering refers to our ability to manipulate DNA, for instance to sequence a gene and recombine it to make the code for a new or modified protein. Such techniques have been used to make new vaccines, as for the hepatitis B virus, or to synthesize in yeast proteins, such as human insulin.

Using modern techniques of molecular biology, individual genes can be removed from a cell, or new genes inserted. These techniques are increasingly opening the way for "gene therapy", allowing defective genes to be replaced with normally functioning ones, thus providing new molecular treatments for previously incurable diseases.

Advances in genetic engineering also makes possible the cloning of organisms, that is, the manufacture of a organism from a single body cell of its parent which is genetically identical to it. Cloning has been known to agriculture since ancient times, but because of their greater biodiversity, cloning of animals has proved more difficult.

A breakthrough came in 1996 when researchers were able to produce a cloned lamb called "Dolly" using DNA from an adult sheep. The possibility exists that humans beings may also one day be cloned, a prospect raising many ethical and moral dilemmas.

SEE ALSO *Chromosomes, Congenital abnormalities, DNA, Down syndrome, Genetic counseling, Heredity, Sickle cell disease*

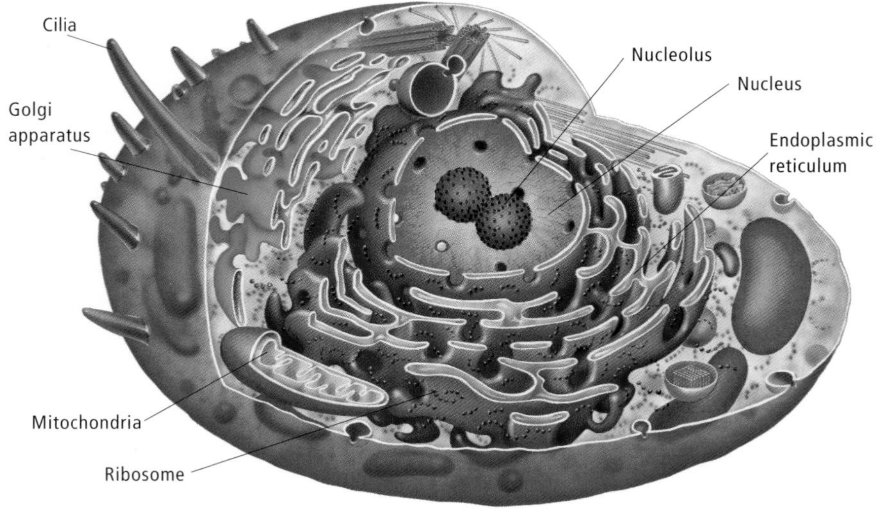

Passing on genetic information

DNA, containing genetic information, is found within the nucleus of the cell. It is transcribed to mRNA within the nucleolus of the cell. The genetic information is then translated, by ribosomes in the endoplasmic reticulum, into a sequence of amino acids which form a protein. The proteins are then incorporated by the Golgi apparatus into small packets (vesicles) and released at the cell membrane.

G

GENETIC COUNSELING

Genetic counseling is the education of individuals (and the community) about inherited disorders. It usually stems from an inquiry from a couple about whether a given disease is likely to recur in a planned family. Genetic counseling usually involves a session in which a medical practitioner will explain to prospective parents the probability of producing a child with a disorder. They can then make responsible and informed decisions from a range of options. One option might be for example to accept the risk and take a chance that the baby will be unaffected or the condition will be treatable. Alternatively the parents may decide against conceiving and adopt a baby instead. The aim of counseling is to educate, not advise.

Couples with a genetic disease in their family history, or who are first cousins, or in which the woman is over 35, may seek genetic counseling before they attempt pregnancy. Cousins share 25 percent of the same gene pool, and older women have a greater risk of a chromosomal disorder, the risk rising with age.

Women who have had three or more miscarriages may also benefit from genetic counseling. Genetic counseling is also available for pregnant women; where tests discover an abnormality in the fetus, abortion may be discussed.

SEE ALSO *Chromosomes, Genes*

GENITAL HERPES

Genital herpes is a virus infection of the genitals by one of two types of herpes simplex virus. The type that usually causes genital herpes is called herpes simplex type 2, and it is most often transmitted by sexual intercourse (including oral sex).

The initial infection usually follows contact with a partner who has an active herpes lesion. An itching and irritation of the skin follows, which reddens. Multiple vesicles (blisters) then appear, filled with a clear straw-colored fluid. The blisters break, leaving shallow painful ulcers which eventually crust over and slowly heal over a period of one to two weeks. The vaginal lips or penis, less commonly the thigh and buttocks, are affected. During the acute stage, there may be a fever, and the lymph nodes in the groin may be swollen. The infection then goes into a latent stage with the virus lying dormant in nerve cells in the skin. At any time—but most often in times of stress, menopause, sunburn, or following another illness—the lesions erupt again. Recurrent attacks may be rare or be so frequent that the symptoms seem continuous. In some people they can last many years. Fortunately, attacks tend to get milder and less frequent over time.

Recurrent herpes is a diffucult condition to treat. Oral acyclovir (an antiviral medication) reduces the duration and severity of the attacks, but it doesn't cure the infection, which persists for life.

Genital herpes may increase the risk of cervical cancer, and it can be a traumatic and psychologically damaging condition.

The best cure is prevention. Avoid sexual intercourse if either partner has blisters or sores. Use a condom if either has had herpes lesions in the past. Condoms are a barrier to transmission of the virus.

Pregnant woman need to tell their physician about previous herpes infection as a cesarean delivery may be advised to prevent infection of the baby.

SEE ALSO *Herpes simplex, Sexually transmitted diseases*

GENITAL WARTS

Genital warts are a sexually transmitted infection, caused by the human papilloma virus. The warts occur on the penis and on the vulva, vagina and cervix. They are also common in the anal region in homosexual men. The warts have a cauliflower-like appearance. They can be removed surgically or by laser or cryotherapy. In women, follow-up treatment is particularly important, as genital warts can lead to cervical cancer.

SEE ALSO *Sexually transmitted diseases, Warts*

Genital herpes

Genital herpes is caused by the herpes simplex virus which invades nerve cells. Mostly spread by sexual intercourse, it is highly contagious. There is no known cure.

GERIATRIC MEDICINE

Geriatric medicine, or geriatrics, is an area of medical specialization that deals with health care of the elderly, and the disorders and diseases that arise with age. It is not to be confused with gerontology, which is the study of the ageing process and its social effects.

Industrialized countries have experienced a change in their population structure throughout the last century. As standards of nutrition and public health have improved, life expectancy for men and women has also improved, and the proportion of aged persons has increased. People over 70 years make up an increasing percentage of the population in Western countries.

Although people in the industrialized nations are living longer, they still experience the declines associated with ageing, and many diseases requiring full-time or nursing home care are becoming more common. In the UK, one-third of all hospital beds are occupied by people over age 65, about half of those being psychiatric patients. Aged patients often have more than one disorder, and more often suffer from chronic (long term) or incurable conditions, meaning they require proportionately more specialized attention. Women tend to live longer than men and constitute over half of the aged population. Geriatric medicine is increasingly concerned with disorders affecting women.

Complicating the provision of health care to elderly people are factors such as unreported illness, multiple disorders, loneliness and potential loss of independence. As infirmity grows, people may be reluctant to visit their doctor with what seem only minor symptoms. These may grow to become major problems by the time they are reported and may be complicated by other disorders that have arisen in the meantime. If mobility or normal dexterity is affected, elderly persons may be unable to care for themselves or to leave the home alone. This can result in depression, which may require treatment as well as the underlying causes. Care may therefore involve a team of health professionals as well as the family doctor.

Geriatric medicine developed in response to the special health needs of the elderly and infirm. Fast help in emergencies, a thorough

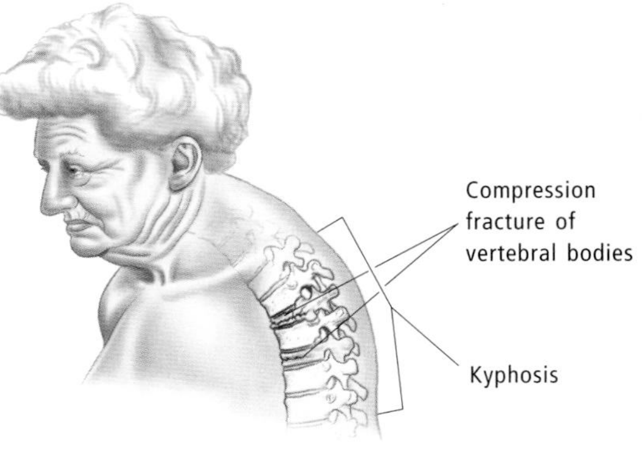

Dowager's hump

Older women with severe osteoporosis may develop dowager's hump. The vertebrae in the spine compress and become distorted, leading to a forward curvature of the thoracic spine which may worsen progressively.

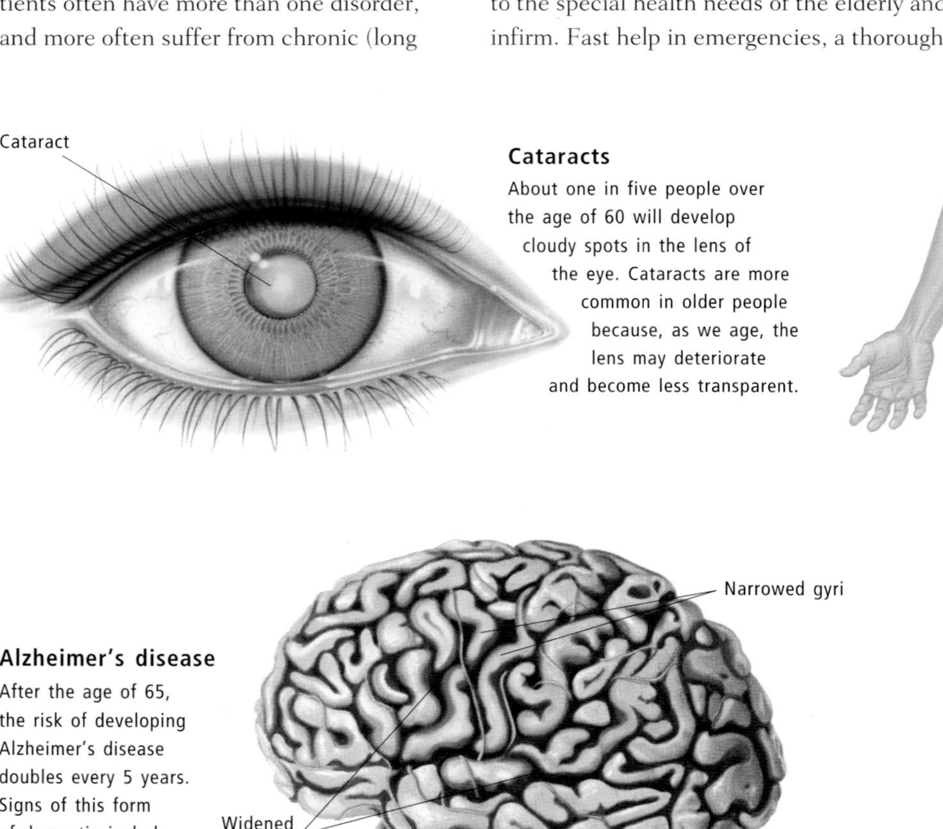

Cataracts

About one in five people over the age of 60 will develop cloudy spots in the lens of the eye. Cataracts are more common in older people because, as we age, the lens may deteriorate and become less transparent.

Alzheimer's disease

After the age of 65, the risk of developing Alzheimer's disease doubles every 5 years. Signs of this form of dementia include increasing forgetfulness, diminished intellectual capacity, personality changes and loss of motor skills and coordination.

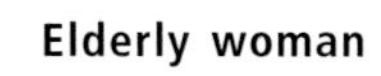

Elderly woman

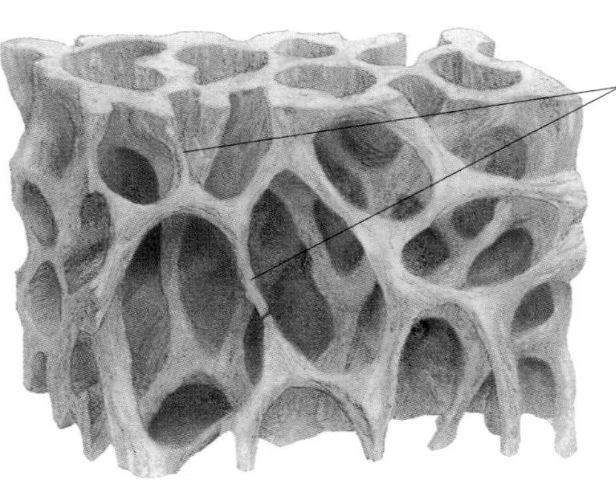

Osteoporosis

Both elderly men and women can suffer from osteoporosis. As we age, new bone growth no longer replaces old bone as quickly as it used to, so the bones become porous and brittle.

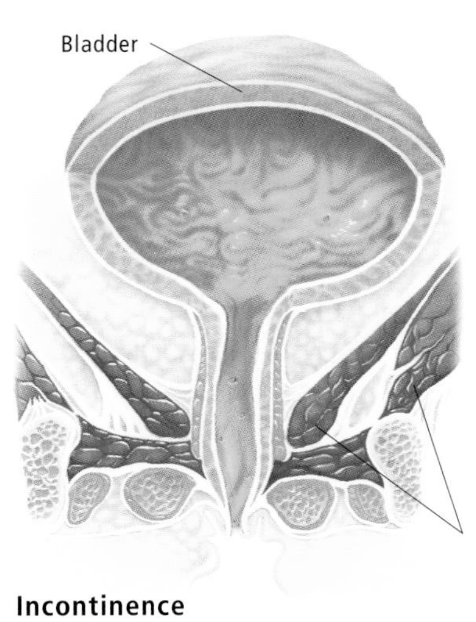

Incontinence

In the elderly, incontinence can be caused by a number of different factors. The muscles that support the bladder and floor of the pelvis can weaken with age, or incontinence may be associated with disorders such as senility, stroke or diabetes mellitus.

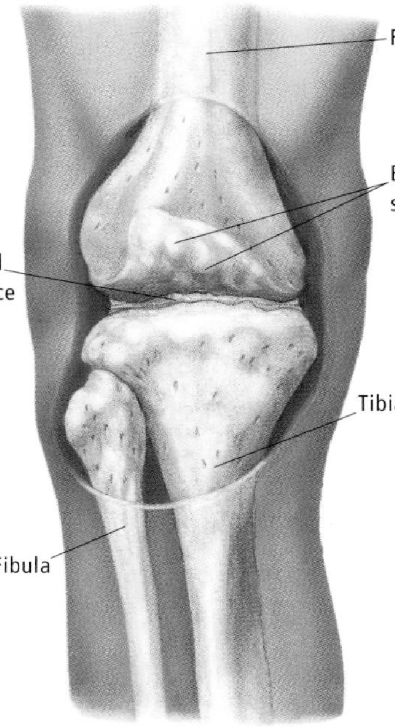

Femur

Bony spurs

Narrowed joint space with damaged cartilage

Tibia

Fibula

Osteoarthritis

As part of the ageing process, the cartilage that covers the ends of the bones begins to disintegrate, and the bones themselves may wear down. Symptoms of osteoarthritis include pain, stiffness and discomfort in joints such as fingers, knees, hips, toes and the spine.

Geriatrics

As people grow older their bodies become less flexible and more inefficient. There is a loss of height—women shrink more than men—and muscle tone is reduced and fat deposits increase.

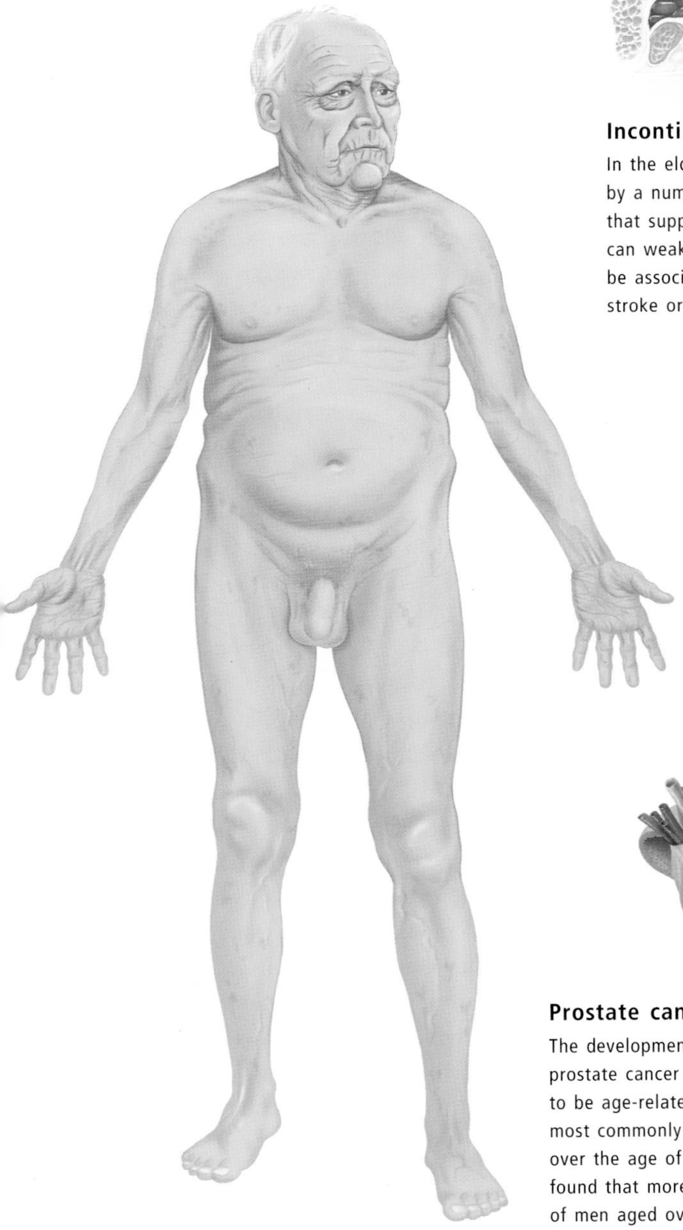

Ankle fracture

Fibula

Tibia

Fracture sites

Talus

Calcaneus

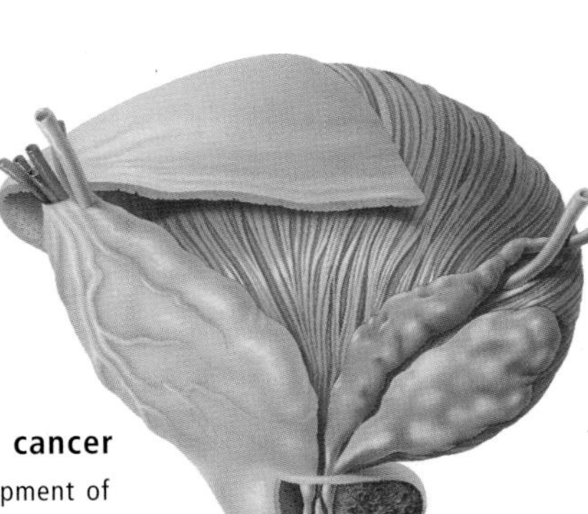

Prostate cancer

The development of prostate cancer appears to be age-related, as it is most commonly found in those over the age of 60. It has been found that more than 50 percent of men aged over 80 years have latent tumors of the prostate.

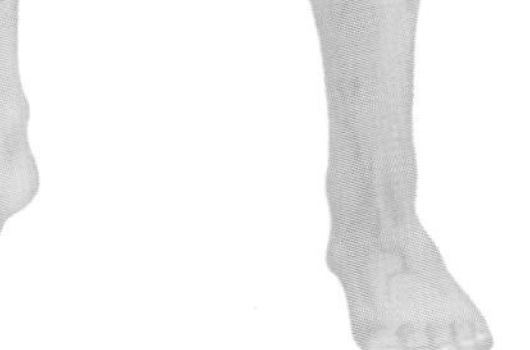

Elderly man

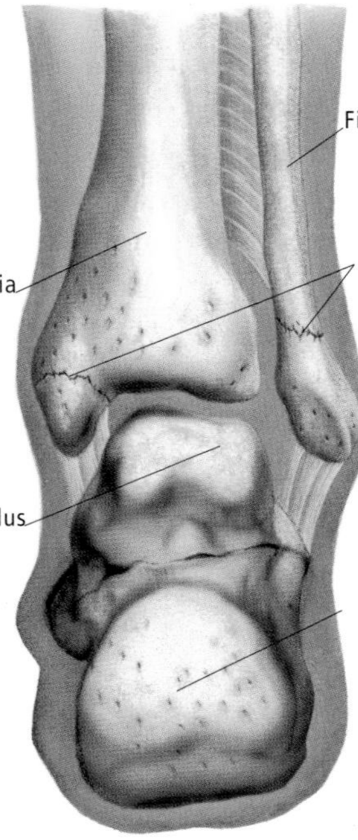

Fractures

In older age groups, especially women after menopause and people suffering from osteoporosis, bones lose calcium and phosphate and become less dense. Consequently they become weak and prone to fracture. Wrist, humerus, ankle, hip and vertebral fractures as a result of falling are particularly common.

G

assessment of each patient's needs, comprehensive treatment aimed to reduce disability (or minimize its effects) and assistance in keeping patients in their homes while addressing the needs of their caregivers are all elements of this medical specialty. The practice of geriatric medicine is based on acceptance that medical disorders in elderly people are not necessarily curable. Treatments prescribed may be different than in general medicine. The emphasis is on retaining quality of life for patients, rather than solely achieving a cure. The aims and expected outcomes of any treatment must be clearly defined.

Physicians and health professionals dealing with the elderly aim to relieve discomfort and treat symptoms, no matter what the predicted outcome or the nearness or apparent certainty of death. Disorders or their effects are kept under control in order to allow patients to live as well as possible and maintain physical mobility and independence for as long as possible. It is important to maintain access to all medical services in order to fulfil these aims.

Central to geriatric medicine is the provision of care in the home. This relieves the pressure on hospital beds and in many cases retains the quality of life that comes from familiar surroundings and maintenance of domestic routines. In financial terms it is less costly to provide or subsidize a range of services aimed at maintaining elderly people in their homes than to create places in hospitals and attempt to provide services in that environment. Home care includes nursing, many forms of therapy, counseling, providing special equipment, rehabilitation, personal care services, preparation or delivery of meals, and even making modifications to the home.

Palliative care for the terminally ill and bereavement counseling for relatives are also part of a web of services which support health workers in geriatric medicine.

Ageing is an inescapable fact of life, and a process that begins at conception. Cells mature, die and are replaced. Life expectancy and general health are products of our genetic heritage, from parents, grandparents and their parents, and of our environment, particularly nutritional standards in childhood years, and health care.

As age advances, soft tissues become less flexible and the internal organs lose their efficiency. Sharpness of the senses is lost or gradually declines. Eyes lose their ability to focus on close objects and reading glasses become necessary. Hearing high-pitched tones becomes more difficult, taking some of the impact and enjoyment out of listening to music and affecting how speech is heard and understood.

Statistically, humans grow fatter with age. Fat becomes a greater proportion of body weight and is distributed differently, subcutaneous fat decreasing while abdominal fat and fat around internal organs increases—but these changes are statistical observations and may only tell us what is happening in society, rather than what should happen as we age. There is ample reason to suppose that an active lifestyle and balanced nutrition can maintain good health and physical abilities well into old age.

Although the effects of age can be reduced, delayed and deferred, they cannot be eliminated. As the body ages, circulatory and respiratory ailments become more common. Blood flow to the liver, kidneys and brain is reduced, affecting the clearance of waste products from the bloodstream. Lung capacity decreases, reducing the effective reoxygenation of blood and leaving increasing amounts of unexpired air in the lungs. Intellectual impairment is a common problem in the elderly and is a serious problem, affecting many aspects of an elderly person's life, including the ability to live independently, manage financial affairs, or drive a vehicle. About 10 percent of persons over the age of 65 years have some degree of mental impairment. It may be due to irreversible conditions, such as Alzheimer's disease or multiple small strokes, or it may be treatable, as in diseases of the thyroid gland, sleep disorders, or depression.

Decreasing mobility is also a feature of old age. Decreased balance, poor gait, muscle weakness, poor coordination and arthritis in the joints may also restrict movement. Basic functions such as bathing and dressing become more difficult and there is an increased incidence of falls and injuries. As elderly people become more sedentary, medical problems may develop; those who are bed- or chair-bound may develop edema, contractures, incontinence or pressure sores.

As a person ages, the senses deteriorate. Most older adults have at least some degenerative disease of the eye; 16 percent of those aged 75 to 84, and 27 percent of those older than 85 are blind in both eyes. Visual impairment reduces the ability to drive, read, shop, and even walk.

Hearing loss affects one-third of 65 year olds, two-thirds of those over age 70, and three-quarters of those 80 years of age and older. Typically, elderly people have difficulty hearing sounds in the higher frequencies. Visual and hearing losses increase their sense of alienation and loneliness and are often a contributing factor in falls and injuries.

Maintaining adequate nutrition is essential in the elderly, who are often malnourished because of poverty, social isolation, depression, dementia, pain or immobility. As a consequence of malnourishment, they tend to suffer pressure sores and take longer to recover from illnesses.

As a rule, elderly people tend to take too many medications. It has been estimated that an elderly person over the age of 65 takes on average 13 different medications in a year. These may interact, with toxic effects. To make matters worse, the kidneys don't function as well in old age, so toxic levels of the drugs may build up.

The immune system functions more poorly in old age, making elderly people more susceptible to cancers and infections. Progressive diseases also tend to become more severe in old age. Other diseases that are common in the elderly include fracture, (hip, ankle); heart attack; incontinence; kidney disorders; osteoarthritis (painful degenerative disease of the joints); osteoporosis (decalcification of bones, making them fragile and prone to fracture); Parkinson's disease; prostate problems (cancer or enlargement of the prostate gland); shingles (painful skin rash); and stroke.

Geriatric medicine can now ensure a comfortable and functional independent life for sufferers of some chronic conditions that previously resulted in death or disability.

SEE ALSO ***Ageing, Cataracts, Diabetes, Glaucoma, Incontinence, Kidney, Osteoarthritis, Osteoporosis, Palliative care, Parkinson's disease, Prostate cancer, Shingles***

GIARDIASIS

Caused by the flagellate protozoa (*Giardia lamblia*) that is found in contaminated water, giardiasis is a common infection of the small intestine. It is characterized by stomach ache and large, bad-smelling, frothy stools containing mucus. It is infectious and is usually transmitted as cysts through oral-fecal contact or by ingesting food or water contaminated by feces.

Giardia is one of the most common intestinal parasites, and it is estimated that up to 20 percent of the world's population is infected with it at any one time. It is most common in tropical regions and in developing countries with poor sanitary conditions, inadequate water quality control and overcrowding.

Children are more likely to be affected than adults, and families with young children who attend preschool or day care centers, as well as homosexual men and women, and anyone who drinks untreated water from creeks or rivers, are at most risk.

The period from infection to the onset of acute symptoms ranges from several days up to two weeks, distinguishing it from food poisoning. Without treatment, the disease can go on for months, with recurrent mild symptoms, such as digestive troubles, intermittent diarrhea, and weight loss. Diagnosed by laboratory testing of fecal matter, giardiasis is treated with drugs.

SEE ALSO *Diarrhea, Intestines*

GIGANTISM

Gigantism is a rare condition of bone, muscle and organ overgrowth in childhood, caused by overproduction of growth hormone (GH), usually due to an overactive pituitary gland. The result is an adult of excessive size and stature. If the hyperpituitarism begins after puberty, the condition is known as acromegaly, and is characterized by excessive enlargement of the jaw, hands and feet.

Gigantism is treated with combinations of surgery, radiation therapy and the drug bromocriptine. Hormone replacement therapy with pituitary hormones may be needed after surgery. Early diagnosis in childhood is essential for successful treatment.

SEE ALSO *Acromegaly, Growth disorders, Pituitary gland*

Gingivitis

The accumulation of food particles in the crevices between teeth and gums can cause gingivitis (inflammation of the gums). Symptoms include gum bleeding and swelling.

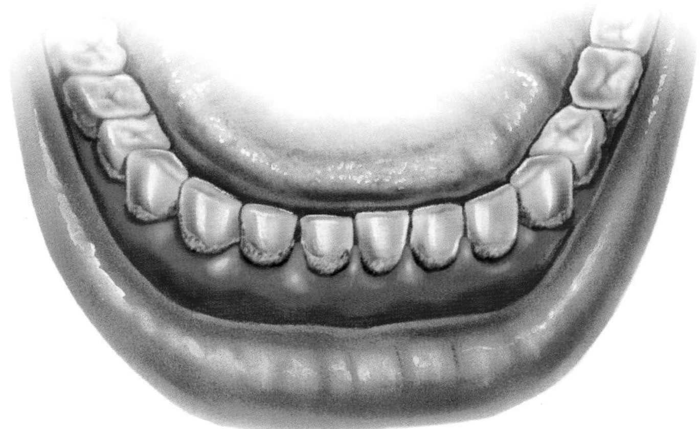

GINGIVITIS

Gingivitis is an inflammation of the gums. It commonly occurs when small particles of food get trapped between the tooth and gum, causing the build-up of bacteria in these areas. The gums become swollen and red, and bleed easily.

Chronic gingivitis is often the result of poor oral and dental hygiene, with build-up of debris and plaque (tartar) around the teeth, although it may also occur with poorly fitting dentures, or with tooth decay or abscesses.

If left untreated, gingivitis can lead to periodontitis, where the infection spreads to deeper tissues such as the tooth socket and bone. This causes bone loss, and leads to enlarging of the tooth socket, so that teeth become loose and may eventually fall out. Regular visits to the dentist and improved tooth brushing, with flossing between teeth, are recommended.

Acute ulcerative necrotizing gingivitis is a more severe inflammation caused by a gum infection. The infected areas bleed heavily and are very painful and ulcerated, and the breath smells foul. Again the inflammation can spread to deeper tissues and eventually inflammation will lead to the destruction of periodontal tissues and tooth loss. An urgent dental referral is recommended.

SEE ALSO *Gums, Periodontitis, Teeth*

GLANDS

Glands are a type of tissue that is made up of cells specialized for the production of a fluid secretion. These special secretions may contain mineral salts, protein, fats or complexes of carbohydrates and proteins.

There are two broad types of glands: exocrine glands, which drain their secretions to the surface of the body or the interior of the gut, lungs or reproductive organs; and endocrine glands, which release their secretions directly into the blood stream or tissue spaces for circulation to other places in the body.

Exocrine glands have a secretory part, which makes the secretory product, and a tubular duct, which carries the secretion to the body or the gut surface. It is the presence of the duct that distinguishes these glands from endocrine glands. In some types of exocrine glands, the cells release their secretion without any loss of cellular material, while in other types the entire cell becomes filled with the secretory product and is completely shed with the secretion.

Examples of exocrine glands include the sweat and sebaceous glands of the skin. Sweat glands are responsible for helping in the control of body temperature, while the fats of sebaceous gland secretions (sebum) prevent water loss from the skin and help to control the growth of microorganisms like bacteria and fungi.

Mammary glands, found only in mammals, are a modified type of sweat gland. They produce milk, which is rich in many secretory products (protein, fats, carbohydrates, immune system proteins and vitamins).

Other types of exocrine glands include: the salivary glands of the oral cavity; the exocrine part of the pancreas, which produces digestive enzymes; the mucus-secreting cells of the lining of the gut and respiratory tract; enzyme secreting cells of the stomach and small intestine; and secretory cells lining the uterus. The pancreas is unique in that it contains both exocrine and endocrine glands.

Endocrine glands, or ductless glands, produce hormones which travel to all tissues of the body via the bloodstream. The main endocrine gland is the pituitary, located immediately below the brain and receiving commands from the hypothalamus in the brain by special nerve pathways and blood channels. The pituitary gland produces a number of important hormones with diverse functions. These include growth hormone (GH), which controls the growth of bones by affecting the cartilage at growth plates; thyroid stimulating hormone (TSH), which controls the production of thyroid hormones by the thyroid gland; follicle stimulating hormone (FSH); luteinizing hormone (LH); adrenocorticotropic hormone (ACTH); and prolactin.

Other endocrine glands are scattered throughout the body (such as the adrenal glands, thyroid gland, parathyroid glands, ovaries and testes). The adrenal gland is divided into two parts: an outer cortex and an inner medulla. The outer cortex produces corticosteroids, which control carbohydrate, lipid and protein metabolism, mineralocorticoids, which control the resorption of sodium in the kidney, and sex steroids, which play a minor role under normal conditions. The adrenal medulla produces epinephrine and norepinephrine (adrenaline and noradrenaline), released in times of acute physical or emotional stress. The parathyroid gland produces a hormone that controls blood calcium. The ovaries and testes produce sex hormones (estrogen and testosterone), responsible for the bodily changes associated with sexual maturity (for example, growth of pubic hair, development of sexual organs and breasts). The placenta is also an endocrine gland, secreting chorionic gonadotropin.

The thymus is often called a gland, but is more accurately described as a lymphoid organ. During early childhood it produces a type of white blood cell known as the "T" lymphocyte. These cells are later distributed throughout the body, going to lymph glands (lymph nodes), the spleen and the gut wall.

The lymph glands are positioned along the lymphatic vessels—on both sides of the neck, in both armpits and on both sides of the groin, as well as the internal body cavities. They act as filters, inhibiting the spread of infection.

During a reaction to infection, the cells in a lymph gland multiply, and the gland becomes large and painful.

SEE ALSO *Adrenal glands, Endocrine glands, Estrogens, Hypothalamus, Lymph glands, Mammary glands, Ovaries, Parathyroid glands, Pituitary gland, Sebaceous glands, Sweat glands, Testes, Testosterone, Thymus gland, Thyroid gland*

Glands

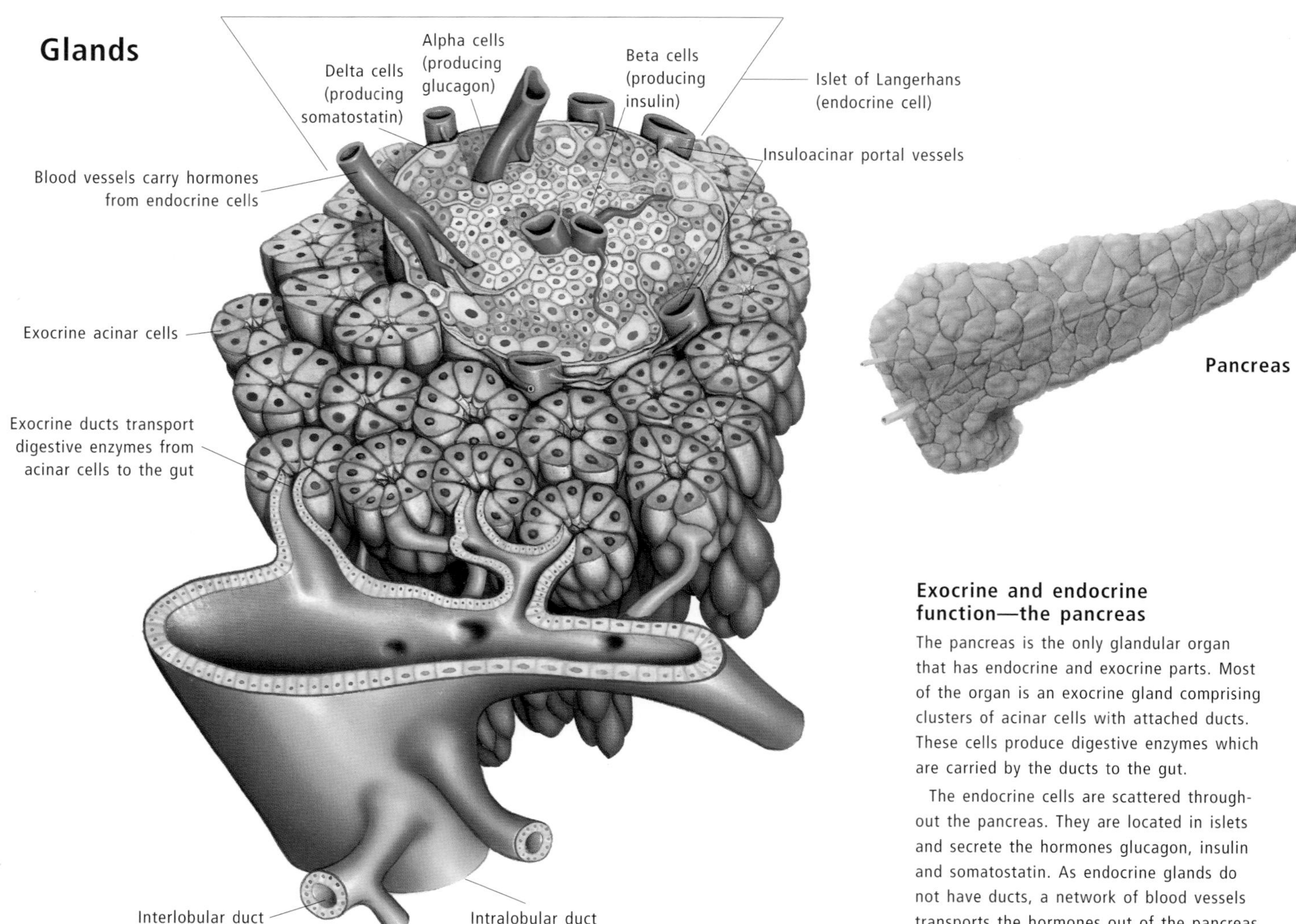

Exocrine and endocrine function—the pancreas

The pancreas is the only glandular organ that has endocrine and exocrine parts. Most of the organ is an exocrine gland comprising clusters of acinar cells with attached ducts. These cells produce digestive enzymes which are carried by the ducts to the gut.

The endocrine cells are scattered throughout the pancreas. They are located in islets and secrete the hormones glucagon, insulin and somatostatin. As endocrine glands do not have ducts, a network of blood vessels transports the hormones out of the pancreas.

Glands

Exocrine glands

These glands drain their secretions to the surface of the body or into the gut, lungs or reproductive organs. They are comprised of secretory cells and ducts which carry the secretion to the body or gut surface. They include sweat and mammary glands and part of the pancreas.

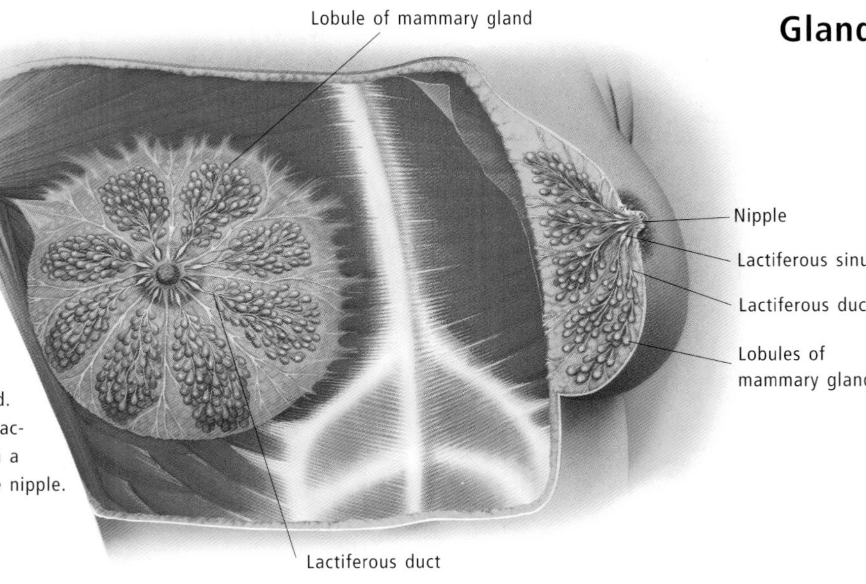

Mammary glands (exocrine)

The mammary glands (breasts) are modified sweat glands. They produce milk when stimulated by the hormone oxytocin, secreted by the pituitary gland. The mammary lobules secrete into the lactiferous ducts, which carry milk through a wider tube (the lactiferous sinus) to the nipple.

Pituitary gland (endocrine)

The pituitary is the main endocrine gland.

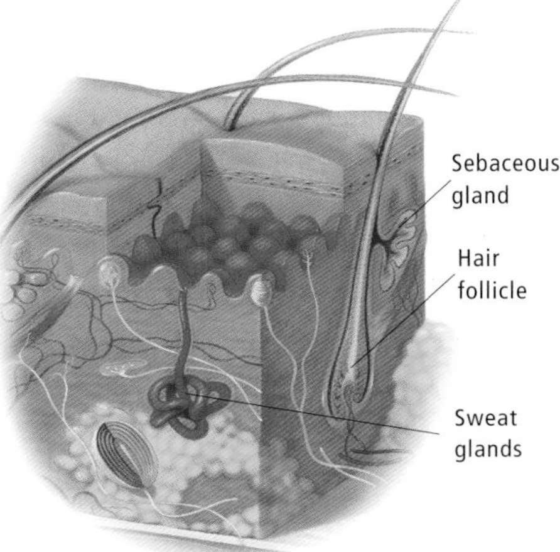

Sweat and sebaceous glands (exocrine)

The sweat and sebaceous glands of the skin are two examples of exocrine glands.

Endocrine glands

These glands secrete hormones directly into the bloodstream or into tissue spaces for circulation to other places in the body. They include the pituitary, thyroid, parathyroid, adrenal and pineal glands and part of the pancreas.

The skin (exocrine)

The skin contains two types of exocrine glands—the sweat and sebaceous glands—that secrete in different ways. Sweat glands release perspiration to the surface of the skin without losing any cellular material. The sebaceous glands which are mostly attached to hair follicles release an oily substance called sebum which moisturizes the skin and hair.

GLANS

The glans is a small mass of erectile tissue found in both the female and male genitals. In women it is known as the glans clitoris, and is located at the tip of the clitoris.
In men the glans penis is the smooth, expanded end of the penis. The glans penis is usually partly covered by the foreskin and contains the slit-like opening of the urethra, the tube carrying the urine and sperm. In both sexes the glans is composed of tissue that can engorge with blood when sexually aroused. It is highly sensitive to physical stimulation, since it contains many sensory nerve endings.

SEE ALSO *Clitoris, Penis, Urethra*

G

GLAUCOMA

This is a group of eye diseases that can cause damage to the optic nerve. Glaucoma is typically, although not invariably, associated with increased pressure within the eyeball. If untreated, it causes progressive loss of vision and may ultimately lead to blindness. Glaucoma ranks with diabetic eye disease, macular degeneration and cataracts as a major cause of blindness today.

Of the various forms of glaucoma, the most common is known as open-angle glaucoma. In this form of the disease, the angle between the iris and the cornea, through which the nutrient fluid (the aqueous humor) drains, remains open. Despite the open angle, drainage of the fluid (into an area called the canal of Schlemm) is inadequate, for reasons that remain unknown. The resulting tendency towards accumulation of fluid within the eye causes pressure (known as the intraocular pressure) to rise above the normal range of 12–21 millimeters of mercury. However, increased intraocular pressure is not synonymous with glaucoma and the pressure may be normal in some forms of glaucoma.

In its early stages, open-angle glaucoma produces few symptoms and may not be recognized or treated. Over time the increased pressure causes death of the photoreceptor (light-receiving) cells within the retina and their nerve fibers. This change first affects the peripheral (side) vision so that the patient progressively develops what is termed tunnel vision, but eventually sight may be completely lost. The exact mechanism by which elevation of intraocular pressure damages the retinal nerve cells is not yet well understood.

In closed-angle glaucoma, a blockage between the iris and cornea prevents the drainage of aqueous humor. Intraocular pressure increases rapidly and sharply and may result in severe pain. Other less common forms of glaucoma, such as congenital glaucoma and glaucoma secondary to injuries or other eye diseases, are also usually associated with noticeable symptoms.

Although glaucoma is not yet curable, it can be controlled by a variety of measures, including drug treatment, laser surgery to increase drainage through the angle, and conventional surgery to establish a new pathway for drainage. For control of the disease to be effective, it is essential that the diagnosis is made as early as possible. This can be achieved by regular eye examination, especially for individuals at risk, such as persons over 60 and those with a family history of the disease. Measurement of intraocular pressure, known as tonometry, is part of such an examination. Examination of visual sharpness, changes in the visual fields and changes in the optic disk viewed through a dilated pupil are very helpful in determining whether significant damage to the eye has occurred.

SEE ALSO *Cornea, Eye, Iris, Retina, Sight, Tonometry*

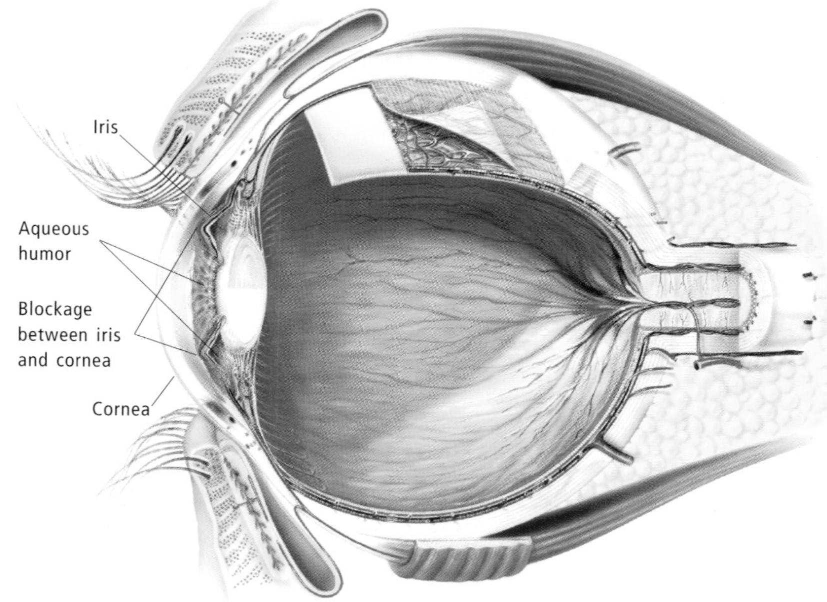

GLOBULINS

Globulin is one of two types of proteins in the blood plasma, the other being albumin. Globulins can be divided into alpha, beta, and gamma subgroups. Alpha and beta globulins include fibrous and contractile proteins, transport proteins, and enzymes. Gamma globulins play a vital role in natural and acquired immunity to infection; they are manufactured by the immune system to help destroy or neutralize infection-causing bacteria. Gamma globulin (also known as antibodies) derived from blood of other humans can be used to induce temporary immunity to some diseases, for example hepatitis A.

SEE ALSO *Immunity, Plasma*

GLOMERULONEPHRITIS

Glomerulonephritis is inflammation of the glomeruli, the clusters of tiny blood vessels in the kidney that filter waste products from the bloodstream to form urine. Damaged glomeruli cannot filter these waste products, leading to serious kidney complications. The disease may be caused by specific problems with the body's immune system, but the precise cause of most cases is unknown. There are two types; acute and chronic.

Acute (sudden) glomerulonephritis sometimes follows a sore throat caused by a streptococcal infection and is more common in children than in adults. A few weeks after the onset of infection, the affected person notices smoky or slightly red urine, puffy eyes and ankles, a general ill feeling, drowsiness, nausea or vomiting, and headaches. Blood tests for kidney function reveal biochemical abnormalities in the blood, and the urine is found to have blood and protein in it. Mild cases are treated with bed rest, and by restricting salt and fluid intake.

Glaucoma

The buildup of pressure in the eye may result in the loss of side vision, blurred or fogged vision and the appearance of colored rings or halos around bright objects. In closed angle glaucoma, the drainage of aqueous humor from the chamber in front of the lens is disrupted by the narrowing of the exit channel at the angle between the iris and cornea.

Sometimes, and especially in adults, kidney dialysis is necessary until the kidneys recover.

Chronic glomerulonephritis develops slowly, and may not be detected until the kidneys fail, which may take 20–30 years. Because symptoms develop gradually, the disorder may only be discovered during a medical examination for some other problem. Or it may be discovered as an unexplained cause of hypertension. In other cases, there are symptoms, such as blood in the urine, or unexplained weight loss, nausea, vomiting, a general ill feeling, fatigue, headache, muscle cramps, seizures, increased skin pigmentation, bruising, confusion, or delirium. There may be signs of chronic renal failure such as edema and fluid overload.

The diagnosis can be confirmed with blood tests that show reduced kidney function, and a urine test that may show blood and proteins in the urine. Abdominal ultrasound, CAT scan, or intravenous pyelography may show scarred, shrunken kidneys. A kidney biopsy will reveal inflammation of the glomeruli.

In some cases of glomerulonephritis there is spontaneous remission. In other cases, treatment with corticosteroid or immunosuppressive drugs will bring about an improvement. However, many cases cannot be cured so the goal will be to manage symptoms for as long as possible.

Glomerulonephritis

Due to the inflammation of the capillary loops in the glomeruli, the kidneys are unable to filter waste products from the blood. This may lead to fluid retention in the legs, face and arms.

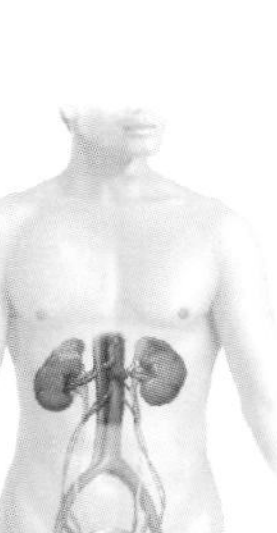

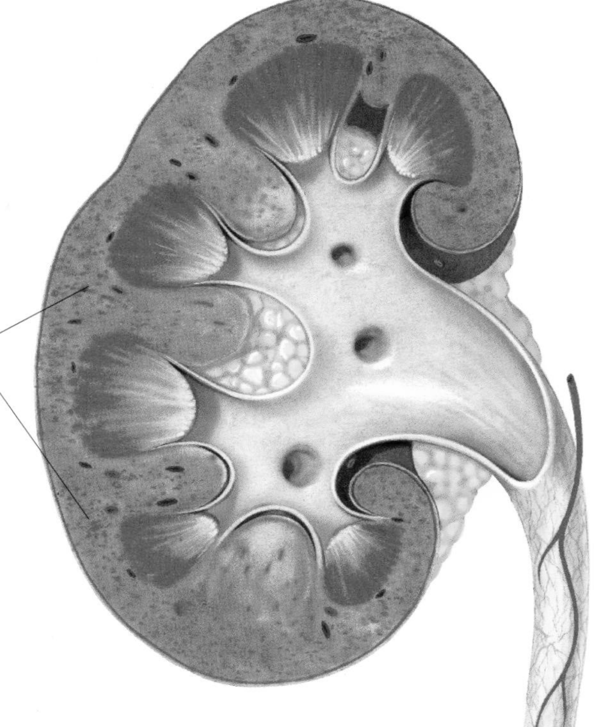

Various antihypertensive medications may be used to control high blood pressure along with dietary restrictions on salt, fluids and protein. In the end stages, regular kidney dialysis or kidney transplantation may be necessary.

SEE ALSO *Dialysis, Hypertension, Kidney, Urinary systems*

GLOSSITIS

Glossitis is inflammation of the tongue. Acute (sudden) glossitis often occurs in children; symptoms of acute glossitis include a painful, bright red, swollen tongue, which is sometimes ulcerated. There may be difficulty in swallowing, and the child may complain of an unpleasant taste in the mouth. Other mouth disorders such as gingivitis (inflammation of the gums) and stomatitis (inflammation of the mouth) may be present. Acute glossitis is treated with antiseptic mouthwashes and an anesthetic solution to reduce pain.

Chronic (long term) glossitis is associated in an adult with chronic ill health, anemia, poor nutrition, vitamin deficiencies, tooth infections, smoking, alcohol consumption, and occasionally as a side effect of antibiotic drugs. Chronic glossitis is treated by correcting the underlying cause.

SEE ALSO *Gingivitis, Tongue*

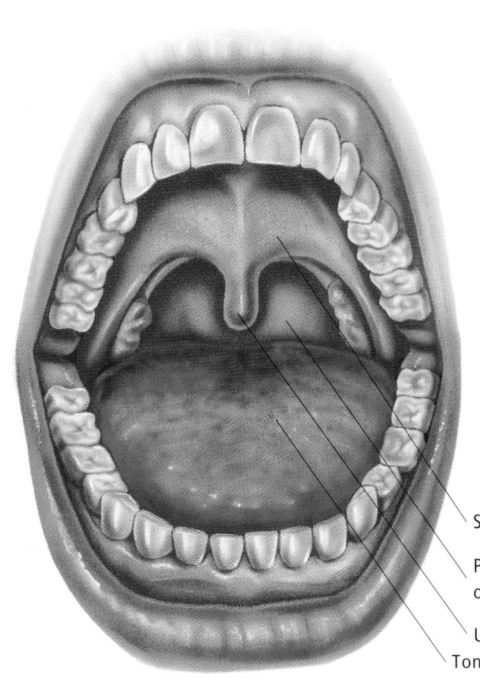

Glossitis

In glossitis the tongue becomes bright red and swollen.

GOITER

Goiter is an enlargement of the thyroid gland, which is located in the front of the neck. The thyroid gland makes the hormone thyroxine, that regulates the body's metabolism. Goiters can be associated with high, low and sometimes even normal thyroxine levels. Symptoms of goiter depend on thyroxine levels (too much leading to thyrotoxicosis; too little leading to myxedema); the goiter itself is only a problem if it affects breathing or swallowing.

The amount of thyroxine produced is regulated by a hormone from the pituitary gland called the thyroid stimulating hormone (TSH). If there is insufficient thyroxine, TSH will be released to stimulate the thyroid to produce more, and this can lead to enlargement of the gland (goiter). A common cause of goiter is a lack of iodine in the diet. With insufficient iodine, and low thyroxine levels, TSH production will increase to stimulate

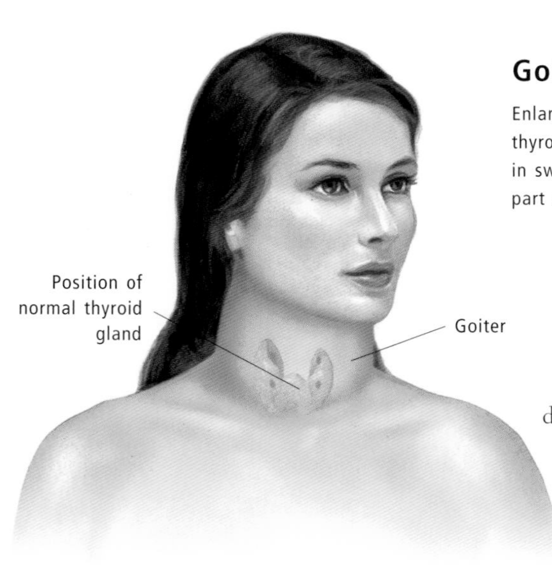

Goiter

Enlargement of the thyroid gland may result in swelling of the front part of the neck.

the thyroid to make more thyroxine. This type of goiter can be treated by addition of iodine to the diet.

Goiter can be caused by excess stimulation of the thyroid gland from other causes, such as abnormally high levels of TSH ocurring with pituitary tumors. Similarly, excess thyroid stimulation occurs in Graves' disease, an autoimmune disorder in which abnormal antibodies are produced that mimic TSH. Treatment can include medication, radioactive iodine, or surgery. Another autoimmune disorder, Hashimoto's disease, is associated with inflammation of the gland, goiter and low thyroxine levels.

SEE ALSO *Graves' disease, Hashimoto's disease, Myxedema, Thyroid gland, Thyrotoxicosis*

GONORRHEA

Gonorrhea is a common sexually transmitted disease caused by a bacterial infection (*Neisseria gonorrhoeae*). It is frequently transmitted during sexual intercourse, including both oral and anal sex. Gonorrhea is most common in people aged 15–30 years. Risk of infection increases with multiple partners, partners with a history of infection, and unprotected intercourse.

In women the infection usually involves the cervix, although it may also spread to the vulva and vagina, urethra and fallopian tubes. Signs of infection include a vaginal discharge and pain on urinating although, in about half the cases, no symptoms may be noted. In some cases the rectum may become infected, causing discomfort in the anal region. Throat infections can occur following oral sex. Symptoms start 1–3 weeks after infection.

If the bacteria spread to the fallopian tubes (as happens in 10–15 percent of untreated cases) the condition is termed pelvic inflammatory disease (PID). PID can cause abdominal pain and may lead to blocked fallopian tubes and infertility. Approximately 50 percent of women will be unaware they have the disease and therefore may pass it on to unsuspecting sexual partners. On rare occasions the disease may be transmitted from mother to baby during childbirth, and may result in infection of the baby's eyes.

In males, gonorrhea usually affects the urethra and is associated with a discharge and pain on urinating. In homosexuals, infections of the throat, anus and rectum are common. In men the infection can spread to other regions of the reproductive tract, such as the epididymis and the prostate. In both sexes gonorrhea can occasionally (in about 1 percent of cases) lead to more widespread infection of the peritoneum, joints and blood, with abdominal pain, arthritis and fever.

Gonorrhea bacteria

Gonorrhea

Gonorrhea in men

A painful burning sensation during urination is an early sign of disease.

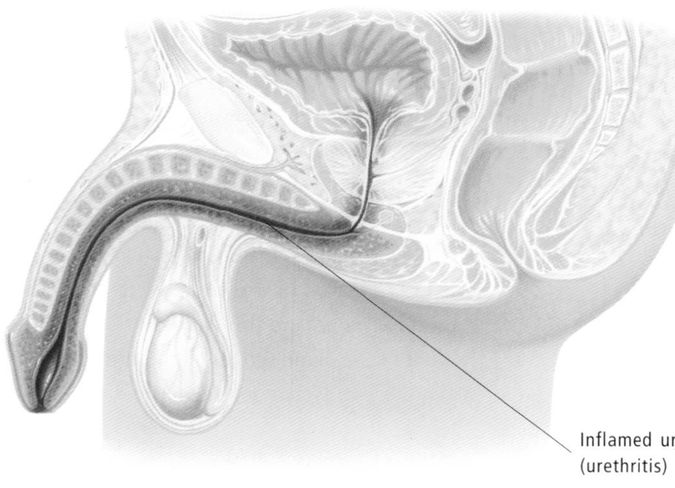

Gonorrhea in women

Women may experience no early symptoms, making gonorrhea difficult to diagnose.

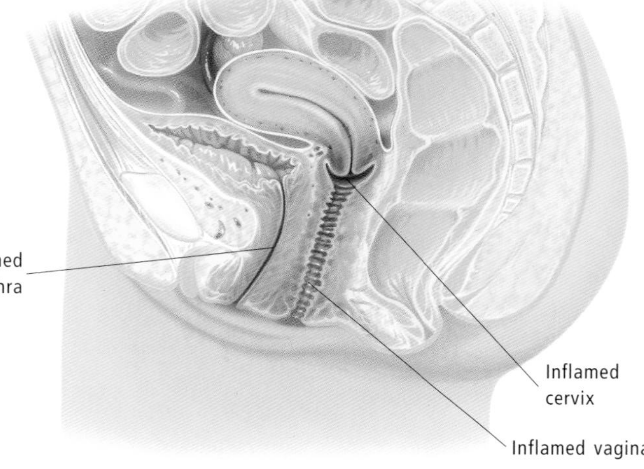

Diagnosis of gonorrhea is made by identifying the bacteria in the discharge, for example from the cervix, urethra or rectum. As many strains of gonorrhea have become resistant to common antibiotics, specific antibiotic courses are used. If the disease is treated early the prognosis is good. Gonorrhea is often associated with other sexually transmitted infections, including HIV, which should also be tested for. Patients should be advised to abstain from sexual contact until treatment for gonorrhea has been successfully completed. Also, all sexual contacts should be traced and tested for infection.

SEE ALSO *Pelvic inflammatory disease, Sexually transmitted diseases*

GOODPASTURE'S SYNDROME

Goodpasture's syndrome is a form of rapidly progressive inflammation of the kidney (glomerulonephritis) which results in progressive decrease in kidney function. The alveoli of the lung are also involved, producing a cough with bloody sputum. It is an autoimmune disorder, triggered in some cases by a viral illness or by sniffing glue or inhaling gasoline, resulting in the formation of antibodies by the body's immune system, which are deposited in the glomeruli of the kidneys and in lung tissue, damaging them. It is a rare disorder, seen most often in men ages 16–60, usually around 20 years old. It may develop after a recent viral respiratory infection, and smoking is known to increase the risk of developing the disorder.

The symptoms are blood in urine, poor urinary output, cough with blood in the sputum, difficulty breathing after exertion, and weakness and weight loss. As kidney function deteriorates there may be signs of kidney failure such as edema and fluid overload.

A blood test may show antibodies to the kidney and lung tissue. Lung and kidney biopsies will show the deposits in the lung and kidney tissue. Treatment is with corticosteroids, electrophoresis dialysis (a procedure by which blood plasma, which contains antibodies, is replaced with plasma free of antibodies), and kidney transplant. The prognosis is variable but is better if the condition is diagnosed and treated early.

SEE ALSO *Autoimmune disease, Glomerulonephritis, Kidney*

GOUT

Gout is an inflammation of the joints that is usually accompanied by the presence of excess uric acid (one of the body's waste products) in tissues in the body. If the uric acid level gets sufficiently high, needle-shaped crystals develop within a joint, leading to an inflammatory response in the joint. Gout most commonly occurs in the joint at the base of the big toe but it can affect other joints such as the hands, wrist, elbow and ankle. The attack usually starts suddenly, often at night, with the joint becoming red, swollen and very painful.

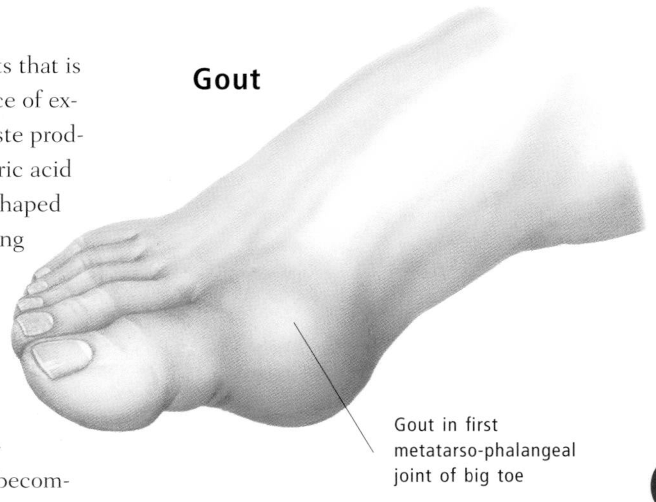

Gout

Gout in first metatarso-phalangeal joint of big toe

Gout is most common in middle-aged men, but can occur in women after menopause. The high levels of uric acid are basically due to either its overproduction or to not excreting enough, or a combination of both. Uric acid is formed from the breakdown of purines in the diet, which particularly come from offal, shellfish and some vegetables and fruits. Gout can also be aggravated by too much alcohol, which inhibits the excretion of uric acid by the kidneys. In rare cases, the overproduction of uric acid can be due to an inherited disorder of protein synthesis or to diseases which increase cell turnover.

The most common finding is reduced excretion of uric acid in the urine. Although the cause is often unclear, it can be aggravated by some drugs, such as diuretics, commonly used in the treatment of high blood pressure, and aspirin.

Besides being deposited in joints, crystals of urate may also be deposited in tissues around the joints and under the skin, for instance in the hands, elbows and around the ear. These deposits are called tophi; those under the skin can be felt as hard nodules. The presence of tophi in the joints, which can be seen on x-rays, can lead to arthritis and joint erosion. Crystals can also be deposited in the kidneys, where they are known as kidney stones. These may cause kidney damage, obstruction of urine flow, or painful renal colic as the stones are passed out of the body.

The diagnosis of gout can be made by measuring the uric acid levels in the blood, and by finding urate crystals within a joint. Gout is treated by anti-inflammatory drugs to reduce the pain and joint inflammation. Aspirin should not be used because it actually inhibits uric acid excretion. After the acute attack passes, long-term medication with drugs such as allopurinol can reduce the production of the uric acid. This can help to prevent future attacks, and if uric acid levels can be lowered sufficiently, may lead to resorption of some tophi and therefore prevent further joint destruction. High fluid intake is also helpful, especially for patients with kidney stones. If uric acid levels are untreated attacks usually become more common, and can lead to permanent joint damage and deformity.

SEE ALSO *Arthritis, Joints*

GRAAFIAN FOLLICLE

At puberty the average woman has about 300,000 egg cells (ova) lying dormant within her ovaries. When she becomes sexually reproductive, some 20 ova (each contained within its own sac-like structure known as a follicle) begin to ripen at the beginning of each menstrual cycle. Usually just one follicle becomes dominant and continues development while the others, and the eggs they contain, shrivel up. This remaining follicle ultimately matures into a Graafian follicle, named after the seventeenth-century Dutch physician Reijnier de Graaf.

The Graafian follicle has a diameter of about $^1/_2$ inch (12 millimeters), is composed of an outer wall three to four cells thick surrounding follicular fluid, and a mature ovum; it produces the hormone estrogen which prepares the uterus for pregnancy. During ovulation it ruptures, releasing the ovum which is then swept into the

G

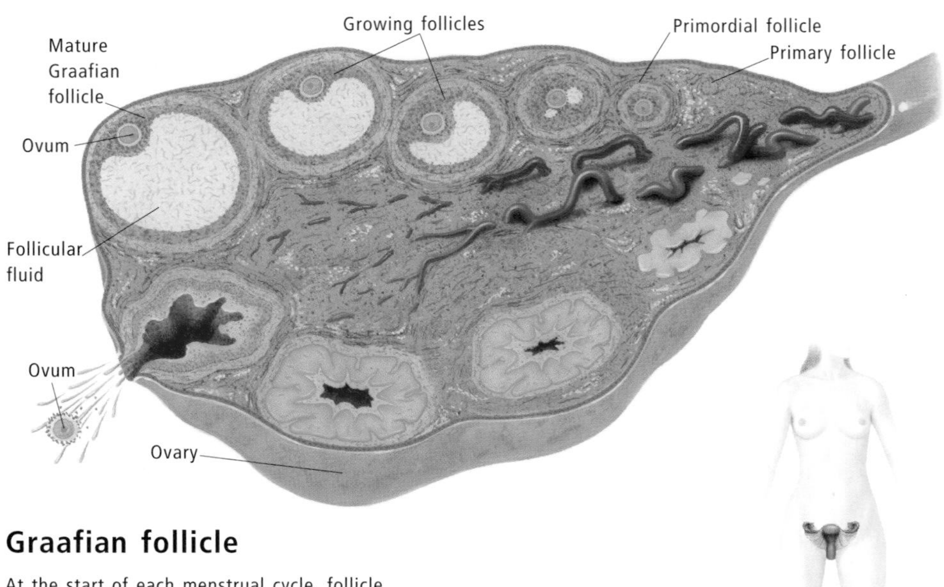

Graafian follicle

At the start of each menstrual cycle, follicle cells in the ovaries begin to divide and produce the hormone estrogen which prepares the uterus for pregnancy and stimulates an ovum (egg) to mature. By days 8–10 one follicle is dominant and develops into a Graafian follicle—a sac-like structure containing a mature ovum. The follicle releases its ovum into the fallopian tube during ovulation, then collapses.

fallopian tubes where it may be fertilized by a sperm. The remaining follicle collapses on itself, its cells enlarge and the structure develops into the corpus luteum, or yellow body, which produces the hormones progesterone and estradiol.

If conception fails to take place, the corpus luteum ceases development after about 14 days and degenerates. If, however, the ovum is fertilized, the corpus luteum continues development and plays an important role during pregnancy.

SEE ALSO *Fertilization, Menstruation, Ovaries, Ovulation, Ovum, Pregnancy, Reproductive systems*

GRAFTING

Grafting is a medical procedure used to repair or replace damaged, defective or diseased parts of the body. It usually involves isolating and removing living tissue and joining it to other living tissue in either the same or a different person. (In some cases, the grafted tissue may come from an animal or it may be produced synthetically.)

Grafts, which are also known as transplants, may be portions of tissue such as skin, bone, nerves, blood vessels or muscle, or they may be complete organs, such as the heart, liver or kidneys. When a graft is intended as a permanent transplant it should grow and fuse with other tissues at its new location and ultimately function as normal.

There are several different types of grafts. In an autograft, tissue is taken from the body of an individual and relocated to another area on the same person. Skin, bone and cartilage are tissues commonly used in autografts. An allograft or homograft is tissue removed from one person (known as the donor) and implanted in another person (the recipient). Some organs used as allografts can be provided by living people. These include bone marrow and kidneys. But organs such as the heart and corneas (in the eyes) can only be used after a person has died.

Whenever tissue is taken from one person and grafted into another, there is always a risk the recipient's immune system will treat the donated material as foreign and trigger a serious response known as rejection. This often occurs between 4 and 15 days after a graft, though it may not appear for a year or more. Rejection is characterized by fever, and pain and function loss in the grafted area. A system of cross-matching the tissues of donors and recipients, similar to blood typing, helps reduce the severity of rejection. Powerful immunosuppressive drugs are also used to reduce rejection reactions.

SEE ALSO *Immunosuppression, Lymphatic/Immune system, Transplant surgery*

GRANULOMA INGUINALE

Granuloma inguinale is a sexually transmitted disease (STD) marked by the appearance of painless red ulcers on or close to the genitals that appear within 60 days of infectious contact. Lymph nodes are not affected but the ulcers will bleed easily on contact. They may also be subject to futher infection.

Rare in industrialized nations, granuloma inguinale is a bacterial infection caused by *Calymmatobacterium granulomatis* and is found mainly in tropical areas, including India, Africa and Papua New Guinea. Treatment with streptomycin and broad spectrum antibiotics is usually successful although relapse can occur any time from 6–18 months later.

SEE ALSO *Sexually transmitted diseases*

GRAVES' DISEASE

Graves' disease is associated with overactivity of the thyroid gland. The thyroid gland secretes thyroid hormones important for the control of body metabolism. The thyroid gland is regulated by the pituitary gland, which secretes thyroid stimulating

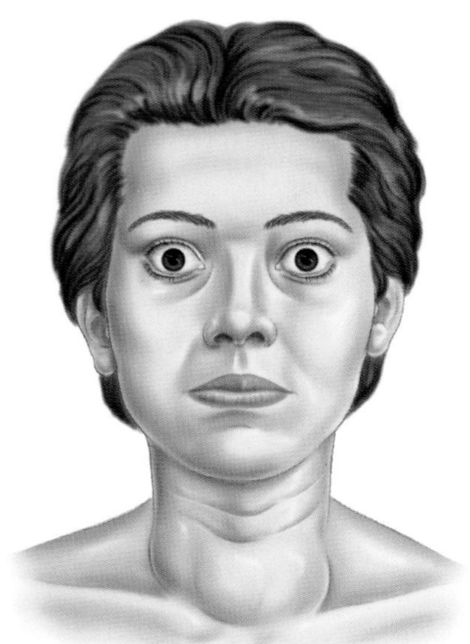

Graves' disease

Exophthalmos (abnormally protruding eyes, as if staring) is a common feature of this disease.

hormone (TSH). Graves' disease is due to the body producing antibodies which mimic TSH and stimulate the thyroid gland to secrete large amounts of thyroid hormone. The thyroid gland enlarges (causing a goiter) and symptoms include feeling hot, and having increased sweating, weight loss and muscle weakness, rapid heart rate and palpitations, frequent bowel movements, nervousness and anxiety. Exophthalmos (abnormally protruding eyes, as if staring) is another common feature of this disease.

Graves' disease can be treated with antithyroid drugs, radioactive iodine or surgery to remove a portion of the thyroid gland.

SEE ALSO *Exophthalmos, Goiter, Pituitary gland, Thyroid gland*

GRIEF

Grief is an intense basic emotion, described as a feeling of sharp sorrow at a potential or real loss. Grief may be felt for many reasons, such as the loss of a loved one, job, possessions, home, or body part or function. Each person experiences grief differently, but there are reactions which most experience.

The initial reaction is usually shock at the loss. Sometimes, in the case of death, if the loved one has died from a prolonged illness, the shock will be less as people will have had time to prepare themselves for the loss.

Emotional release through crying is a healthy expression of grief and a beneficial release of tension. Depression, loneliness and a feeling of isolation may also accompany feelings of grief. This can be particularly true for someone who has lost their life partner. Physical reactions to a severe loss such as death may also be experienced. This can include loss of appetite, overeating, sleeplessness and sexual difficulties. Panic may follow. It is important to avoid using drugs and alcohol at this time as not only is there a risk of dependence, but the substances may also hinder the necessary grieving process.

Guilt, real or imagined, is another common reaction. Feelings of "if only" may be thought or expressed. Anger, which, like guilt, needs to be expressed and worked through, is another common reaction. Some find that they are unable to return to usual activities. In most cases, however, the person will start to heal, with a gradual regaining of hope and acceptance as they adjust their lives to the reality of their loss.

Children experience grief differently to adults. Although they may feel the loss acutely, they commonly show it in less direct ways than adults do and can move in and out of grieving—sometimes showing what seems like a callous disregard for the loss. Very young children do not understand that death is permanent. Children in the early years of school will likewise not understand the permanency and may worry about their own situation and ask lots of questions. By the time they are ten, children will be able to understand the permanency of death. Their strong sense of right and wrong will be challenged and they may be interested in religious explanations. Children need careful attention and support when they are grieving; just because they appear not to be suffering does not mean they are not feeling the loss.

Groin

This is the name given to the junctional region between abdomen and thigh. Groin strain occurs in this area when the muscles are overextended.

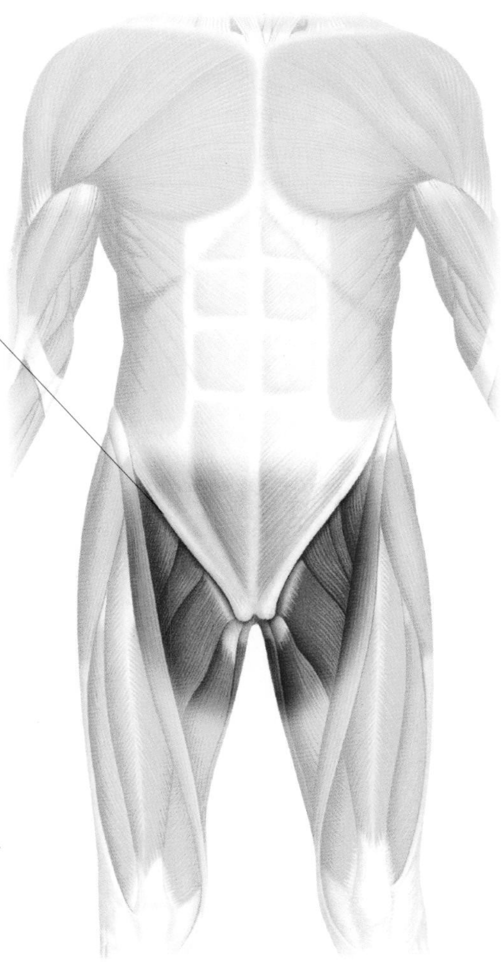

GROIN

The groin (inguinal region) is where the abdomen joins the front of the thigh. Groin strain occurs when muscles in this region are pulled. Groin swellings may be the result of a hernia, which occurs when part of the gut is forced into the front of the thigh under pressure through a weakness in the abdominal wall in the region of the inguinal canal. If painful, medical advice should be sought, because the gut may become damaged. The groin also contains lymph nodes (also known as lymph glands), and these can swell if inflamed, for instance with infections in the leg. Tinea cruris (jock itch) is a fungal infection that occurs in the groin, particularly in men.

SEE ALSO *Hernia, Lymph glands*

GROWTH

Growth is the process by which the body and its various parts increase in size and reach maturity. It is largely controlled by hormones, the secretion of which is influenced by a large number of interrelated factors, ranging from genetics and nutrition to environment, hygiene and disease.

Most people continue to grow in height until the long bones of the body cease expanding, which usually occurs around the age of 18 years. Although the rate and times at which individuals grow vary considerably, most people experience two significant periods of accelerated growth en route to reaching adulthood. The first of these periods occurs during the 12 months after birth. On average, a healthy baby triples its birth weight by the age of one year, while increasing its height by about 50 percent. The other notable growth spurt occurs during puberty, in the early to mid-teens, when most people shoot upwards by about 20 percent of their final adult height. Growth rates for boys during this period can reach as much as $3\frac{1}{2}$ inches (9 centimeters) a year.

Among the many hormones affecting growth in the body, the most significant is human growth hormone (hGH) which is released by the pituitary gland in the brain. Too little hGH during childhood and adolescent development leads to dwarfism. Too much causes gigantism.

SEE ALSO *Dwarfism, Gigantism, Growth disorders, Hormones, Infancy, Pituitary gland, Puberty*

GROWTH DISORDERS

Human growth is controlled by hormones, especially growth hormone. Excessive production of growth hormone by the anterior part of the pituitary gland in adulthood causes acromegaly, a disorder in which the bones in the arms and legs, hands, feet, jaw, and skull get thicker and longer. Facial features become coarser, and the voice may become deeper. If the condition occurs before puberty, it results in gigantism, causing excessive size and stature. Treatment is surgery or radiation therapy on the pituitary gland.

A deficiency of growth hormone causes dwarfism. The affected person has normal body proportions but is smaller than normal. Administration of growth hormone to patients with pituitary dwarfism may induce skeletal growth. Dwarfism may also be caused by malnutrition and chronic illness.

SEE ALSO *Achondroplasia, Acromegaly, Dwarfism, Gigantism*

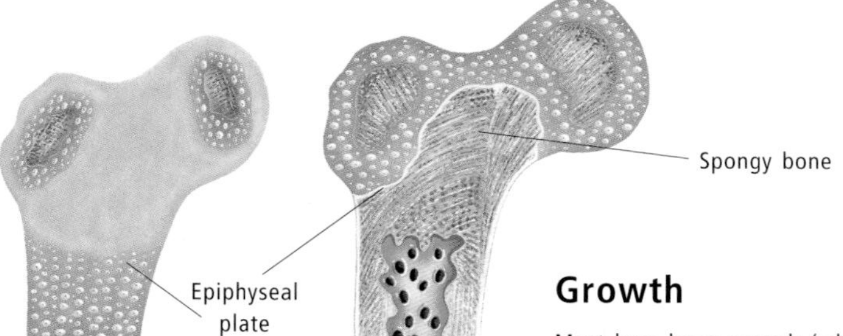

Growth

Most long bone growth (which determines height) occurs before the age of 18 years. As bones elongate, cartilage is replaced by compact bone and the epiphyseal (growth) plate moves upwards towards the end of the bone shaft. New cartilage is produced on the other side of the plate (at the bone ends) until late adolescence, when the epiphyseal plate calcifies and growth ceases.

GUILLAIN-BARRÉ SYNDROME

Guillain-Barré syndrome (also called acute inflammatory polyneuropathy) is an inflammatory disorder of the peripheral nerves. It starts suddenly (usually over days) with muscle weakness in the legs and arms, associated with numbness in the feet and hands. The weakness may spread to muscles in the face and trunk, and there may be difficulty swallowing or breathing. The syndrome usually follows an infectious illness and is thought to involve an autoimmune attack on the nerves. Damage to the nerves involves loss of the myelin sheath surrounding nerve fibers. This results in the loss of signals going along the nerves to control the muscles or provide sensation.

Guillain-Barré syndrome can be diagnosed by observing the rapid onset of weakness and the loss of reflexes and sensation on both sides of the body. Diagnosis is confirmed by lumbar puncture, from which cerebrospinal fluid is withdrawn for protein analysis; increased protein concentration indicates disease. If the disease progresses rapidly with serious complications, patients need to be hospitalized and monitored constantly. The airway must be kept clear and respiration supported artificially if necessary. Treatment may involve exchanging the patient's blood plasma for normal plasma, or replacing albumin and blood cells. Most patients recover but some may be left with muscle weakness and may require physical therapy and rehabilitation. If symptoms are relieved within three weeks of their onset the outcome is usually good.

SEE ALSO *Nerves, Neuropathy*

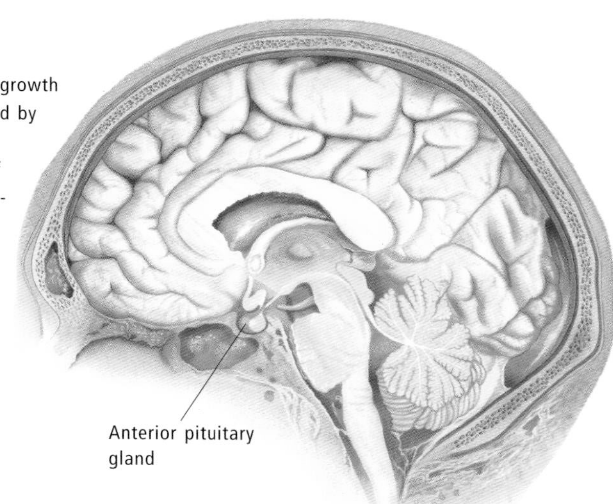

Growth disorders

Growth hormone controls cell growth and replication and is produced by the anterior pituitary gland. A deficiency in the production of growth hormone inhibits development, causing disorders such as dwarfism. The production of too much growth hormone stimulates abnormal growth of bones and muscles as in gigantism and acromegaly.

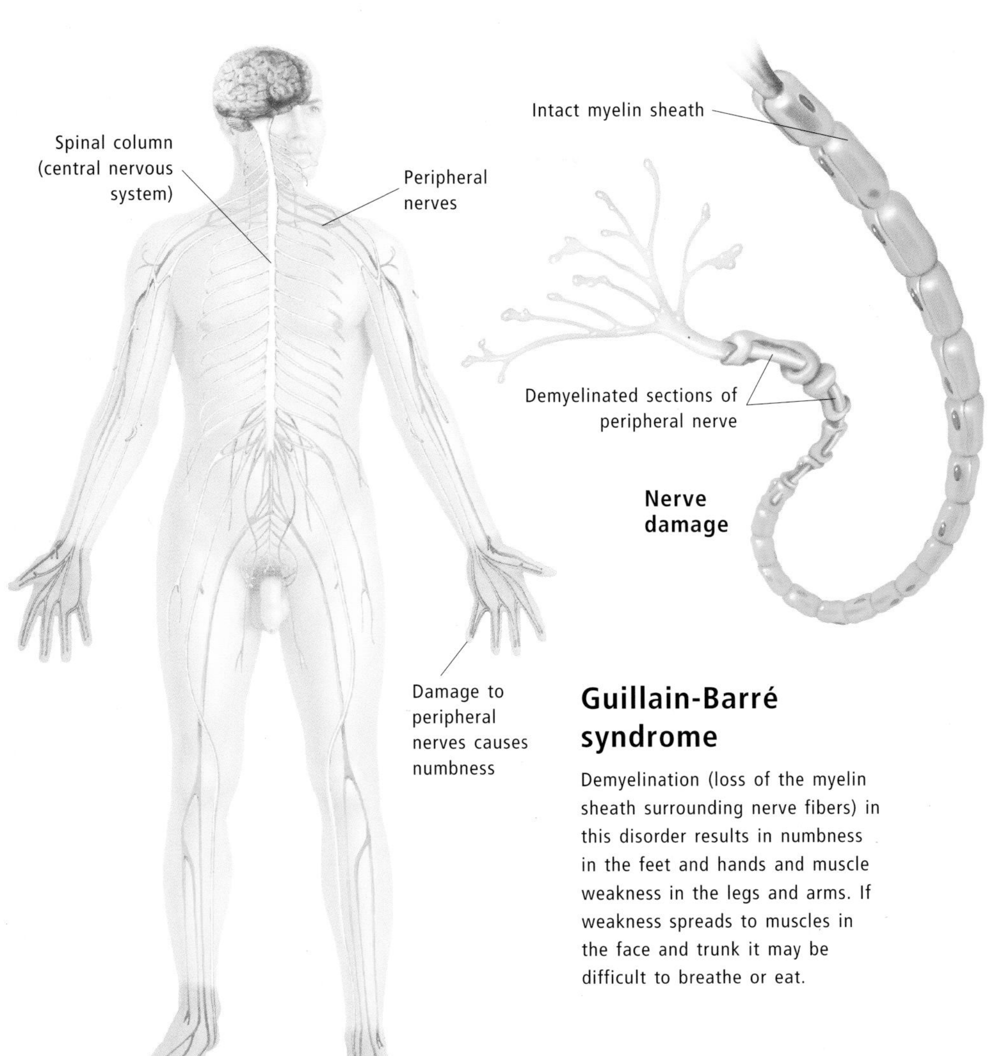

Guillain-Barré syndrome

Demyelination (loss of the myelin sheath surrounding nerve fibers) in this disorder results in numbness in the feet and hands and muscle weakness in the legs and arms. If weakness spreads to muscles in the face and trunk it may be difficult to breathe or eat.

GUMS

The gums (gingivae) are the soft tissue covering the upper and lower jaws, inside the mouth. They extend from inside the lips, around and between the teeth, to the floor of the mouth (lower jaw) and the palate (upper jaw). The gums are kept moist by saliva and receive sensory nerves, similar to the skin. The gums are attached around the neck of the teeth, where food particles can become lodged and cause gum inflammation (gingivitis). Swelling, ulcers or discoloration of the gums may indicate more widespread disease and should be investigated. Severe lack of vitamin C (scurvy) also leads to swollen and bleeding gums and loose teeth.

SEE ALSO *Gingivitis, Teeth*

G

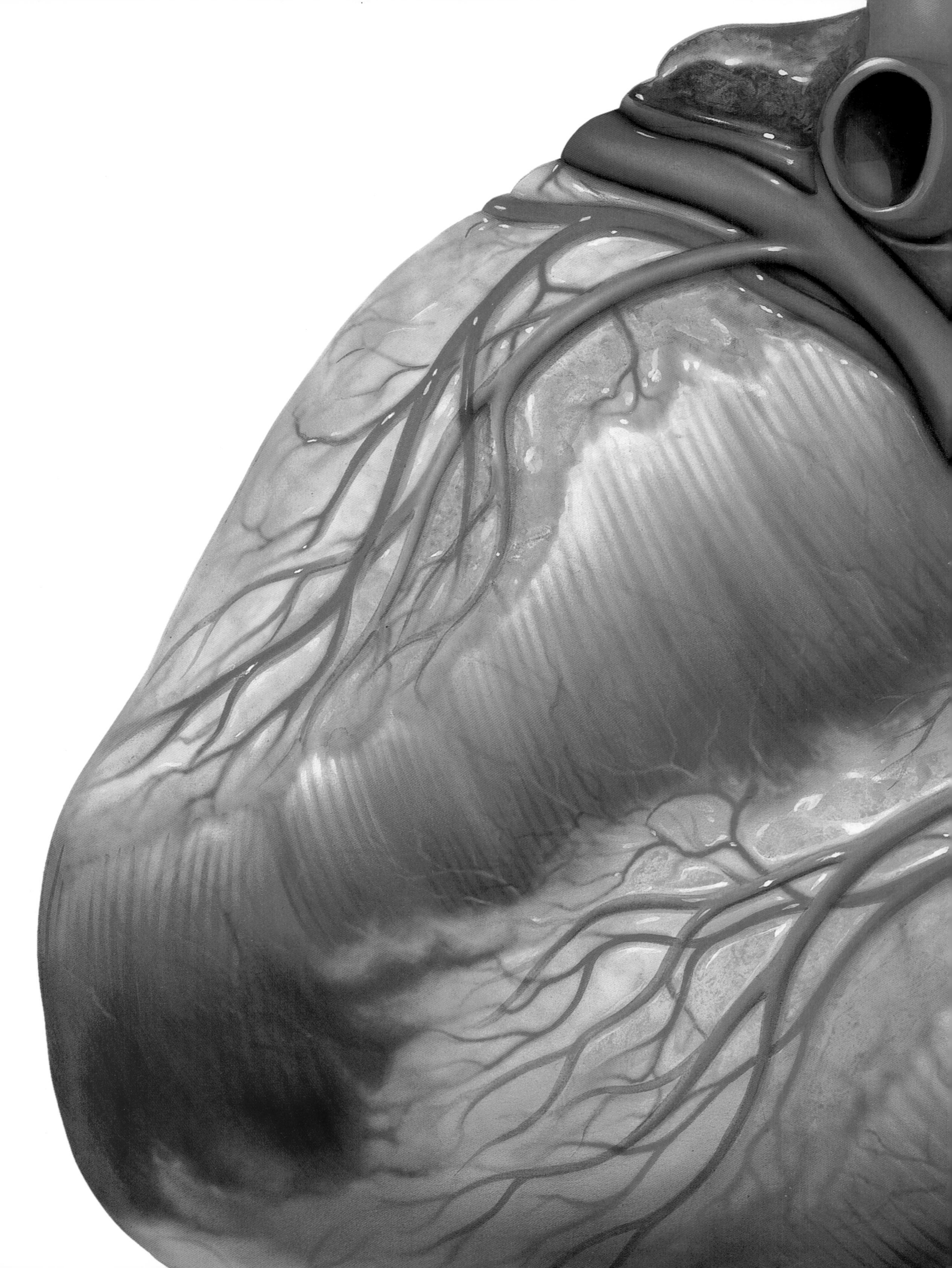

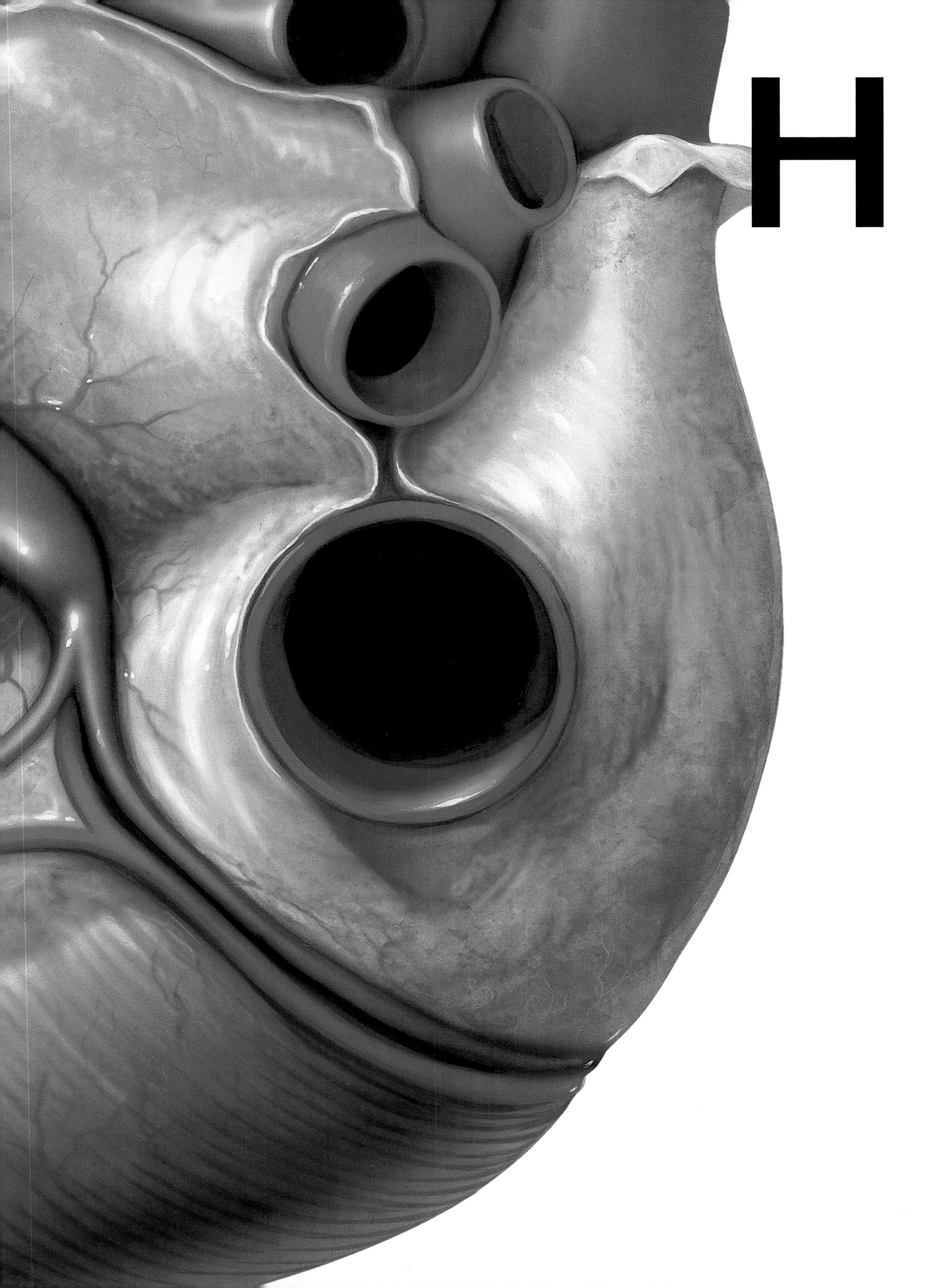
H

HAIR

Hair is a fine, threadlike structure, made of a tough protein called keratin. It is produced only by mammals and is an identifying character of that group of animals. Hair consists of a root, embedded in the skin, and a shaft, projecting from the skin surface. The root ends in a soft, whitish enlargement, the hair bulb, which is lodged in an elongated pit in the skin, called the follicle.

The hair grows upwards from the base of the follicle at the rate of about ⅓ millimeter a day. Blood vessels arranged in a small protrusion known as a papilla extend up into the follicle and the root of the hair and nourish it. Attached to each hair follicle is a tiny muscle called the erector pili. This muscle is under the control of the autonomic nervous system and under certain conditions, for example in the cold, it contracts to make the hair stand on end.

Individual hairs are composed of dead epithelial cells containing keratin, arranged in columns around a central core. The cells also contain varying amounts of the dark pigment melanin, which is responsible for the color of the hair. With age, less pigment is deposited into these cells, so hairs tend to become white.

Hair has a protective function. Hair around the eyes, ears and nose serves to prevent dust, insects and other matter from entering these organs. The eyebrows decrease the amount of light that is reflected into the eyes.

Hair color is genetically determined. Dark hair color usually dominates over light hair color. For example, if a child has one parent with black or brown hair and one with red or blond hair, the child's hair is likely to be dark.

Hair loss

All body hair falls out gradually and is replaced by new hair. Baldness (alopecia) results when hair replacement fails to keep up with hair loss. It may have several causes, including ageing and genetic factors. It occurs more frequently in men than in

H

Hair follicle

The shaft of the hair projects from the skin's surface. The root is embedded in the skin—it ends in a bulb, which is lodged in a pit known as the follicle.

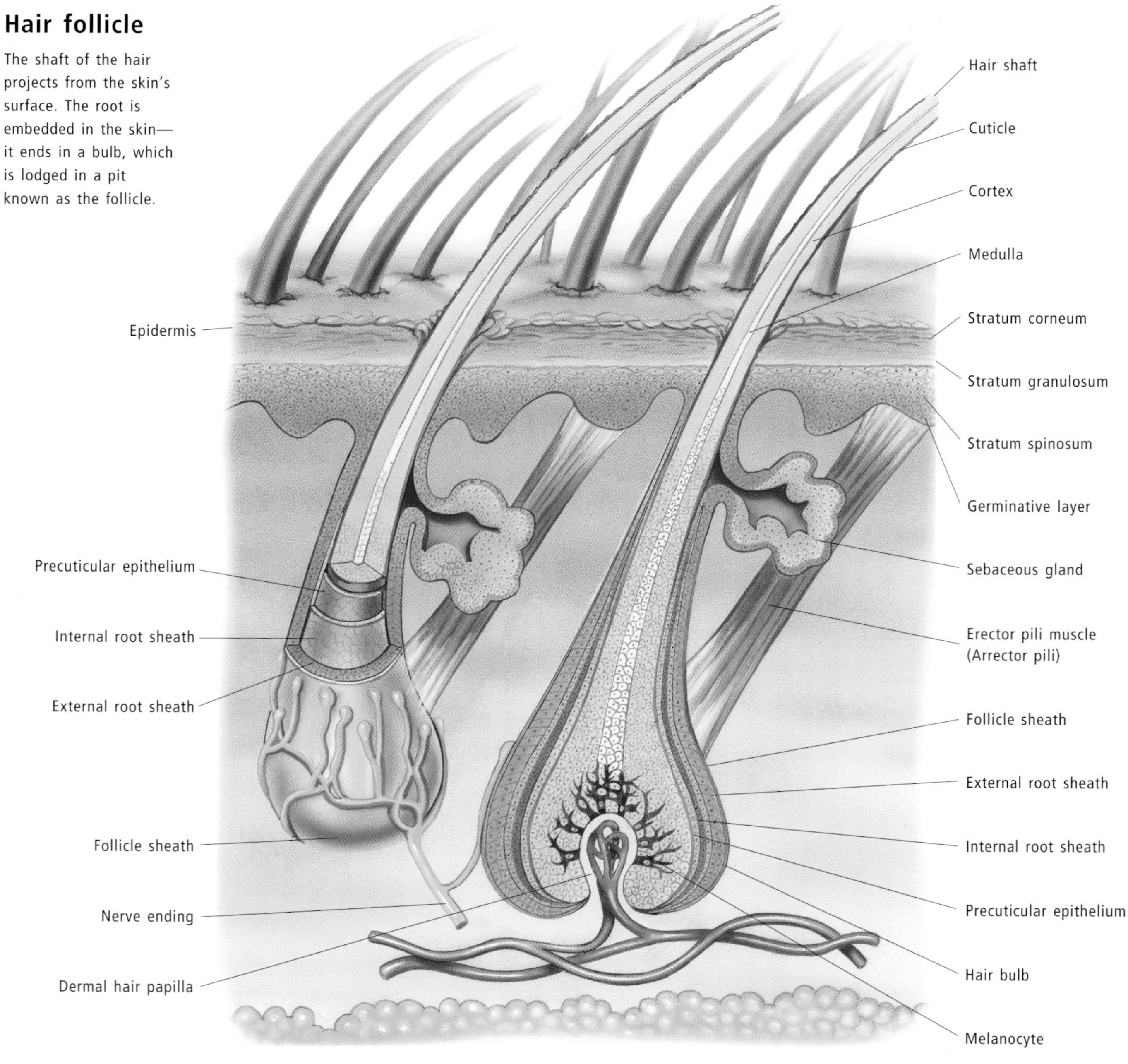

women. Partial hair loss may affect women after menopause. Sometimes hair loss occurs after a severe emotional shock, a severe illness, or childbirth.

Some medications, such as Minoxidil, may slow or prevent hair loss. Minoxidil must be used continually, as hair loss resumes when the drug is stopped. A hair transplant involves surgically replacing non-productive hair follicles with productive follicles from another area of the scalp. The procedure is expensive and the results vary.

SEE ALSO *Baldness*

HALITOSIS

Halitosis is an unpleasant, disagreeable or offensive breath odor. Poor oral hygiene is the leading cause of halitosis, though it may also be due to eating smelly foods such as onion or garlic, or to smoking. It may be a symptom of an underlying illness, such as alcoholism, throat infection, sinusitis, lung infection, gum disease (gingivitis), tooth abscess, or a foreign body in the nose (usually in children). Occasionally it may be due to more serious disease such as acute renal failure, chronic renal failure or bowel obstruction.

The condition is treated by improving oral hygiene (brushing teeth more frequently, rinsing with a mouth rinse, and visiting a dentist regularly) and by treating any underlying disorder.

SEE ALSO *Gingivitis, Gums, Teeth*

HALLUCINATION

A hallucination is a false perception of vision, sound, taste, smell or touch. Though the person experiences the sensation as real, no stimulus actually exists. Visual hallucinations are the most common type. Hallucinations may occur in a variety of states of altered consciousness such as prolonged wakefulness, while under hypnosis, in delirium, or after taking mind-altering drugs such as marijuana, mescaline or lysergic acid diethylamide (LSD). Alcoholics can also experience hallucinations.

Auditory hallucinations may occur in schizophrenia, in which a sufferer hears what are believed to be "voices". These hallucinations may lead to panic attacks or even suicide.

The exact cause of hallucinations is unknown, but it is thought that, like dreams, they may be unconscious expressions of memories that erupt when the normal attention mechanisms of the brain are diminished.

SEE ALSO *Alcoholism, Delirium, Hallucinogens, Schizophrenia*

HALLUCINOGENS

An hallucinogen, or hallucinogenic drug, sometimes called a psychedelic or mind-expanding drug, temporarily changes the functioning of the brain.

Hallucinogens affect the senses, emotions, and reasoning, distorting the perception of self and surroundings.

In Western countries, laws prohibit the manufacture, distribution and possession of these drugs, except in government-approved research. Nevertheless, hallucinogens such as LSD are available on black markets, sold as "trips". Less widely available are hallucinogens derived from plants, for example, peyote and mescaline.

Some drug users claim that, during a trip, they have gained a new understanding of themselves. Others have "bad trips"—acute panic or paranoid reactions which may resemble schizophrenia.

Some users of hallucinogens afterwards suffer "flashbacks", which can last for months or years.

SEE ALSO *Drug dependence*

HAMMER TOE

A hammer toe is a deformity in which the toe is bent in the shape of a hammer. Although any toe may be affected, it usually affects the second toe.

The condition may be congenital or it may be acquired, occurring most often in children who have outgrown their shoes. In older people it may be caused by pressure from a bunion.

Hammer toe is best prevented by making sure footwear fits correctly. A physician can treat mild cases by manipulating the toe and then splinting it. Corns can be treated with corn pads. In severe cases, surgery may be needed to straighten the joint.

SEE ALSO *Foot*

Hamstrings

The hamstring muscles are able to straighten the hip joint and bend the knee joint. They are susceptible to tearing and sprain injuries.

Biceps femoris
Semitendonosus
Semimembranosus

HAMSTRING MUSCLES

The hamstrings are a group of muscles that form the muscle mass on the back of the thigh. They are so-named because butchers would use these tendons to suspend "ham" (thigh and leg muscles of a pig) while it was being cured.

The hamstring group consists of 3 muscles—the semimembranosus, the semitendinosus and the biceps femoris—which are all attached above to the ischium (part of the pelvis). In the middle of the thigh they separate so the biceps femoris tendon passes behind the outside of the knee to reach the fibula, and the semimembranosus and semitendinosus tendons pass behind the inside of the knee to reach the tibia. These tendons can be easily felt on either side, just behind the knee when it is bent.

Because the hamstrings pass behind both the hip and knee joints they are able to cause movements at both joints but they are also more vulnerable to injury (tearing). The hamstrings function to extend (straighten) the hip joint and flex (bend) the knee joint.

A hamstring muscle may be torn or strained when it is suddenly and forcefully contracted, usually when it is either not properly warmed up, or fatigued.

SEE ALSO *Fibula, Hip, Knee, Tibia*

HAND

The hand is designed to grasp and manipulate objects. It consists of the palm, or front of the hand, the dorsum or back, and the thumb and fingers. Between the wrist bones (carpals) and finger bones (phalanges) are five metacarpal bones. The metacarpals join the bones of the fingers, the phalanges ("phalanx" is the term for a single one) in the metacarpophalangeal (MCP) joints.

The metacarpal bones can be easily felt through the skin over the back of the hand. The first metacarpal, between the wrist and thumb, is particularly mobile, allowing the thumb a wide range of movements. The fifth metacarpal can be fractured relatively easily. Between the metacarpals and the dorsal skin of the back of the hand are long tendons which pull the fingers and thumb backwards (extension) and a network of veins draining blood from the fingers and hand.

The palm has a slightly hollowed surface, that helps with gripping objects, and it is covered by thick skin which is tightly bound to the tissue below. The creases on the skin of the palm are the result of flexing the thumb and fingers and their joints. The palm also contains tendons, which bend the fingers forward (flexion), and two soft bulges due to the thenar and hypothenar muscles.

The thenar muscles form the fleshy prominence between the wrist and the thumb and contribute to thumb movements. These include the important movement of opposition by which the thumb can be touched to the tips of the fingers.

The hypothenar group lies along the side of the palm, between the wrist and little finger. The interosseus muscles lie between each of the metacarpal bones and move the fingers apart (abduction) and back together (adduction), as well as helping with flexion of the MCP joints and extension of the fingers. The thumb has a separate adductor muscle to move it towards the palm.

Besides these muscle groups there are four thin, worm-like muscles, the lumbricals, which connect between the long flexor tendons and the fingers and also assist with MCP flexion and finger extension.

Sheets of connective tissue, known as septa, separate the palm into compartments: the thenar and hypothenar compartments; a central compartment containing the long flexor tendons, blood vessels and nerves; and an adductor compartment for the thumb adductor. These compartments can become infected, but can also help to contain infections within their boundaries. Treatment with antibiotics is needed.

The long tendons are surrounded by synovial sheaths containing fluid which lubricates the tendons. These sheaths can become inflamed (tenosynovitis) through injury or excess use (in repetitive strain injury, for example). Treatment is by immobilization of the limb.

The four fingers are referred to as the index, middle, ring and little finger. They each contain three bones or phalanges, with hinge joints between them. The thumb has only two bones, the proximal and distal phalanx, again with a hinge joint between. The fingers contain no muscles, and are moved by tendons connected to muscles in the palm or forearm. Their tips are protected by nails on the dorsal (back) surface.

The fingertips are covered in a unique

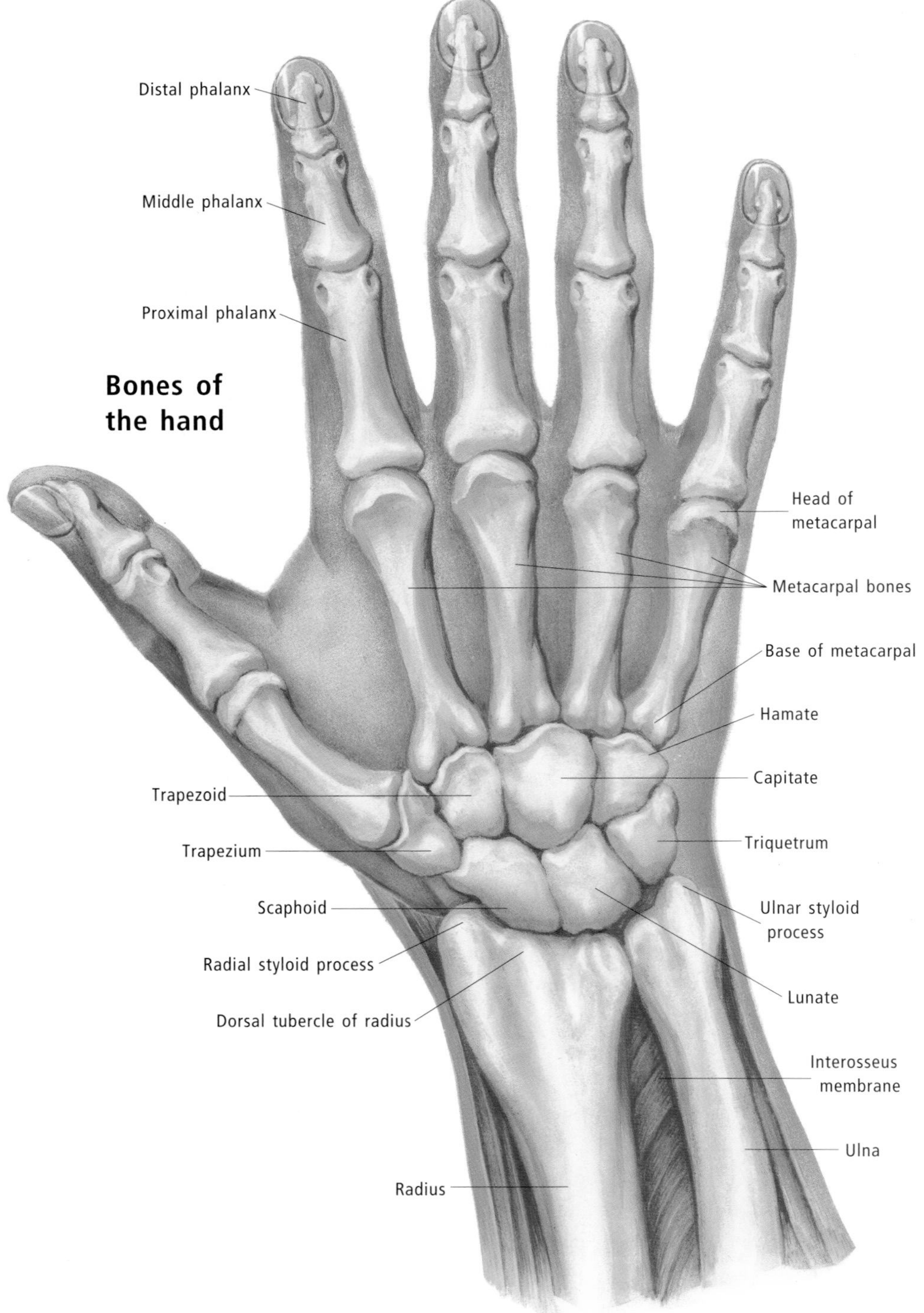

pattern of skin ridges, and these ridges give us our fingerprints.

The hand is supplied by two arteries, the radial artery on the same side as the thumb, and the ulnar artery on the other side. These two arteries join to form two arches in the palm. The digital arteries branch off from these arches and run down each side of the fingers.

Three large nerves—the ulnar, median and radial—supply the muscles and skin of the hand. The ulnar nerve supplies the hypothenar, interosseus muscles, the thumb adductor and two of the lumbricals, as well as the skin over the little finger and the adjacent side of the ring finger. The median nerve supplies the thenar muscles and the remaining two lumbricals, together with the skin of the palm, thumb, index, middle and adjacent side of the ring finger.

The sensory nerve supply (innervation) of the fingertips is particularly rich, providing for sensitive, delicate tactile discrimination. The radial nerve does not supply any hand muscles, but innervates the skin over most of the back (dorsum) of the hand and the back of the thumb.

The hand is involved in holding objects in two rather different ways, referred to as the power grip and precision grip.

In the power grip, used for carrying heavy bags or for holding tight to a support, objects are grasped in the palm, with much of the muscle power coming from flexor muscles in the forearm. Long flexor tendons run from the forearm to the fingers and thumb, so that the digits can be held tightly around the object. Muscles within the hand may also be active but the large forearm flexors are particularly important.

The precision grip is used for delicate manipulation of an object, for example, when writing, sewing or drawing. The thumb is opposed to one or more of the fingertips, involving the thenar and adductor muscles. Precision grip particularly involves muscles within the hand, most of which are controlled by the ulnar nerve, except for the thenar muscles of the thumb, controlled by the median nerve.

Injury to any of the hand nerves causes a unique group of problems. Damage to the ulnar nerve causes loss of abduction and adduction movements of the fingers, and loss of sensation in the little finger. The hand develops a deformity called clawhand in which the fourth and fifth MCP joints are extended and the fingers flexed.

The median nerve can be damaged by cuts to the wrist or by compression, such as in carpal tunnel syndrome. This causes weakness or loss of opposition of the thumb, and loss of sensation in the thumb and fingertips.

Radial nerve injury in the hand only affects sensation over the back of the hand. However, radial nerve injury in the arm leads to inability to extend the hand, and the hand flexes at the wrist (wrist drop). Since it is not possible to have a firm power grip when the wrist is flexed, wrist drop makes it difficult to hold implements (knife, fork, hairbrush, etc). This can be helped by a brace which holds the wrist in a slightly extended position.

SEE ALSO *Adduction and abduction, Arteries, Carpal tunnel syndrome, Finger, Muscle, Nerves, Radial nerve, Skeletal system, Tenosynovitis, Ulnar nerve, Wrist*

Muscles and tendons of the hand

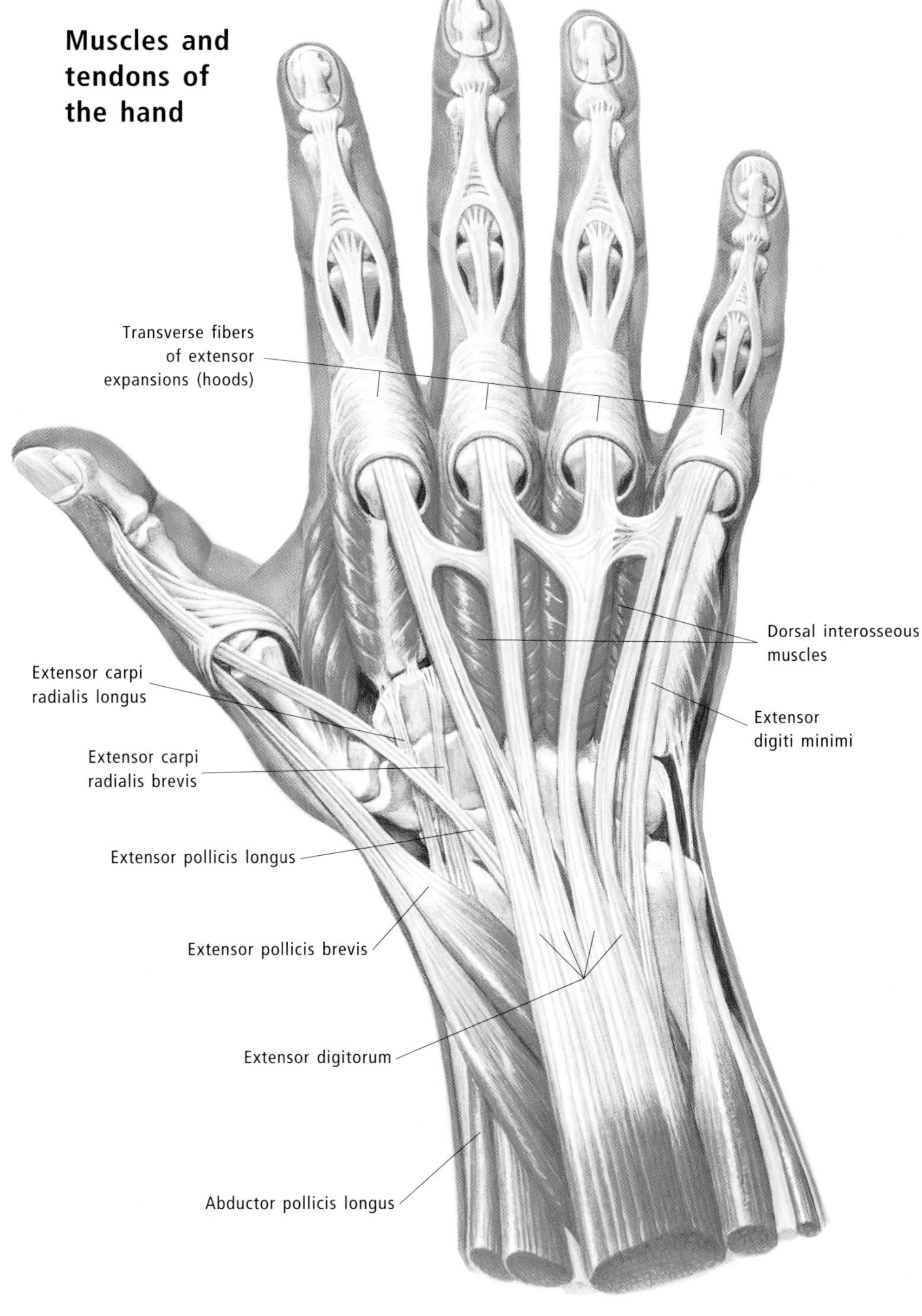

Hay fever

Sensitivity to pollen in the air, particularly during spring, triggers an allergic reaction in those who suffer from hay fever. This often results in blocked sinuses, a runny nose, red eyes and sneezing.

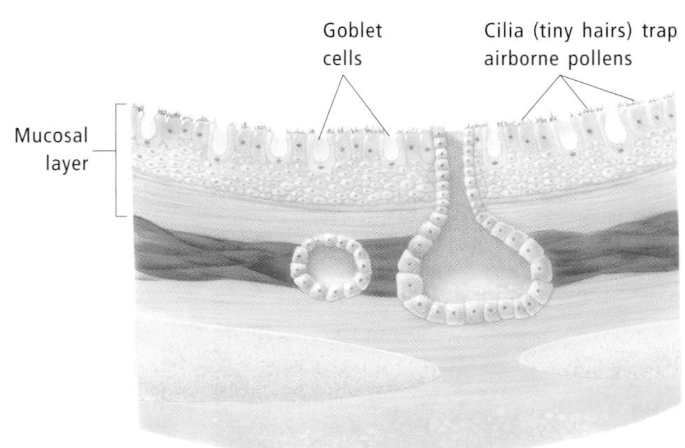

Mucous membrane

The lining of the nasal passages, trachea and lungs is covered in a sensitive mucosal lining that intercepts airborne particles. When pollen is inhaled and trapped in this lining it can trigger an allergic reaction—causing inflammation and mucus production.

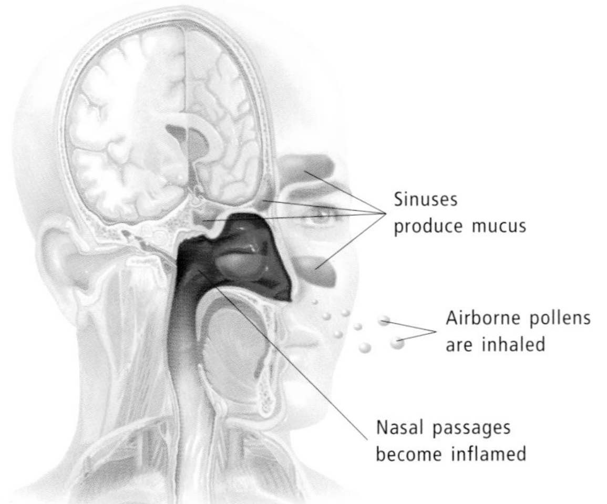

Allergic response

Each time pollens (allergens) enter the body of a hay fever sufferer, they are captured by antibodies attached to mast cells. These cells release histamine—an inflammatory substance which produces the symptoms of hay fever.

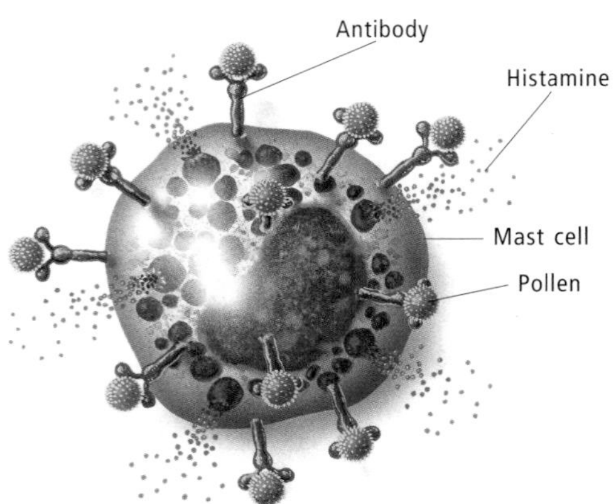

HASHIMOTO'S DISEASE

Hashimoto's disease is a destructive inflammation of the thyroid gland, most commonly affecting women, which is believed to be the result of autoimmunity and may be associated with other autoimmune disorders. Initially, it causes painless enlargement of the thyroid, but the loss of functioning thyroid tissue eventually leads to hypothyroidism, requiring treatment with thyroxine.

SEE ALSO *Autoimmune disease, Hypothyroidism, Thyroid gland*

HAY FEVER

Hay fever or seasonal allergic rhinitis (also sometimes called pollinosis) is caused by extreme sensitivity to airborne pollen, and is common through spring and summer. Hay fever may affect up to 10 percent of the population and tends to run in families, as do many allergies. It can develop at any age.

Pollen is the fine powdery yellow dust that is the fertilizing agent of plants. Airborne pollen from grasses, weeds and trees is the major cause of hay fever. In the USA and Australia, the pollen of common ragweed is well known as a hay fever allergen. Russian thistle, another plant known to cause allergic reactions, is widespread in mid-western USA, while ryegrass is a common source in Europe. A combination of pollen with pollution from vehicle exhaust gases can produce irritation similar to hay fever.

There are many airborne substances that can trigger hay fever. Besides pollen, molds and fungal spores can cause or worsen seasonal symptoms, and most are light enough to be carried hundreds of miles if the wind is right. This is what makes airborne allergens almost impossible to avoid. If you suffer from hay fever it helps to know which substances you are most sensitive to, and this can be established by observation and through specialized tests.

It is almost impossible to eliminate contact with airborne allergens in your local area, but avoiding heavy concentrations of whatever you are most sensitive to will certainly limit the amount of the allergens you are exposed to, which can decrease the severity of your allergic reaction.

In some countries the pollen count is often broadcast by local radio stations. This can alert sufferers to take medication before the onset of symptoms. The pollen count is a figure that expresses the number of pollen grains per cubic yard (cubic meter) of air and is highest in the spring and summer months. But pollens from different plants can be airborne and present even in winter and still produce symptoms at low concentrations.

When pollen or dust is inhaled, it is trapped in the lining of the trachea (windpipe). This triggers a reaction in a sensitized or allergic person. The release of histamine then causes the typical signs of hay fever: a runny nose, red and swollen mucous membranes in the nose and eyes, and sneezing. Symptoms present at times when pollens are not may be caused by sensitivity to household dust mites, or animal hairs. This condition is called perennial rhinitis.

Antihistamines, the medication most often used to control hay fever, block the action of histamine, which is responsible for the runny nose and other symptoms. Possible side effects are drowsiness, nausea and dryness of the mouth. Some of the newer antihistamines do not cause drowsiness; these can be used for daytime medication, under medical supervision.

SEE ALSO *Allergies, Antigen tests, Antihistamines, Asthma, Desensitization, Respiratory system, Rhinitis*

HEAD

The head contains the brain, encased in the cranium within the skull. There are five special senses in the head associated with cranial nerves: smell, vision, taste, hearing and balance (semicircular canals, inner ear).

The tongue is contained in the oral cavity (mouth). At the back of the oral cavity is the pharynx, which allows food to pass to the esophagus and air to pass into the trachea. Muscles in the neck allow the head to be flexed, extended and partially rotated.

Skull

The skull is the most complex bony structure in the body. With the exception of the lower jaw (mandible), the numerous bones of the skull are joined to each other by fibrous joints called sutures. Many of the skull bones develop separately from a membrane which covers the embryonic head.

At birth a significant amount of this membrane is still present between the partially formed bones, allowing them to slide over each other as the head passes through the birth canal. This means the bones are not crushed during the birth process. For descriptive purposes the skull is divided into two parts, the cranium and the face.

Cranium

The cranium surrounds and protects the brain. It is formed, from front to back, by the frontal bone, the paired parietal and temporal bones and the occipital bone with the sphenoid bone also forming part of the cranial joint. The lobes of the cerebral hemispheres of the brain are named according to the bone which overlies them—the frontal, parietal, temporal and occipital lobes. The temporal bone contains a system of spaces within it, which form the middle and inner parts of the ear (see below). Each bone (except the parietal) also contributes to the floor of the cranium, which is divided into three terraces known as the anterior, middle and posterior cranial fossae.

The anterior fossa is occupied by the frontal lobes of the brain, the middle one by the temporal lobes and the posterior one by the cerebellum and brain stem. The floor of the cranium contains many holes (foramina) through which the spinal cord, cranial nerves and blood vessels enter or leave.

The brain is separated from the skull by three layers of membrane, which are known as the meninges. The outermost layer, the dura mater, is a tough, fibrous membrane which adheres to the inner surface of the skull. The middle layer, the arachnoid mater, lines the inner surface of the dura, to which it is loosely attached. The innermost layer, the pia mater, adheres to the brain and follows its contours. Between the arachnoid and pial layers is the fluid-filled subarachnoid space, which forms a cushion around the brain, providing buoyancy and protection.

Arteries which supply the skull and meninges, and veins draining blood from the brain, lie between the dura and the skull. An extradural hemorrhage occurs when these vessels are torn (usually in association with a skull fracture) and blood rapidly accumulates between the dura and the skull, putting pressure on the underlying brain. This is a potentially fatal condition which must be treated quickly, usually by making a hole in the skull to release the pressure.

Subdural hemorrhage occurs when veins are ruptured as they pass through the dura mater, causing blood to accumulate between the dural and arachnoid layers. This can occur from a bump on the head but is not as serious as an extradural hemorrhage because the blood accumulates at a much slower rate. The major arteries supplying the brain run through the subarachnoid space before entering the brain. A sudden increase in blood pressure in patients with cardiovascular disease can cause these arteries to rupture, causing blood to accumulate in the subarachnoid space (subarachnoid hemorrhage).

Face

The bones of the front of the skull constitute the face. The frontal bone forms the forehead, the zygoma forms the cheek bone, the maxilla forms the upper jaw, palate and outer walls of the nasal cavity, and the mandible forms the lower jaw.

Unlike most other parts of the body, the skin of the face, lips and scalp contains numerous small muscles, known as the muscles of facial expression, which enable us to open and close the mouth, smile, blink and frown. The skin of the face and scalp is extremely sensitive to touch and pain and is also very vascular, so that while wounds may bleed profusely they also heal quickly.

Temporomandibular joints

Each side of the mandible has a head which fits into a socket on the base of the skull, forming the temporomandibular joints. These joints, located just below and in front of each ear, permit both the hinge-like and gliding movements of the mandible that occur during eating and speech. When the mouth is forced open beyond its normal range the joints can dislocate forwards, becoming locked in the open position.

Orbit

Each eye and its associated structures (muscles, nerves and blood vessels) occupies a cavity on the front of the skull known as the orbit. The walls of the orbit are relatively thin and fragile and can be easily fractured if a small object is inadvertently poked into the orbit, or by a blow to the front of the eye. The outer margin of the orbit, however, is thick and strong, protecting the eye from damage by larger objects. The eyelids function to protect and lubricate the eye. The lacrimal gland, which produces tears, is located just behind the upper eyelid.

Nose (nasal cavity)

The walls of the nasal cavity are formed by bone at the back and by the nasal cartilages at the front; the cartilages surround the nostrils. The cavity is divided into halves by the nasal septum and its floor is formed by the palate, which is also the roof of the mouth.

The inner lining of the nostrils is formed by hairy skin; the membrane at the roof of the nasal cavity contains specialized olfactory cells, which are responsible for detecting smells. The remainder of the nasal cavity has a specialized lining called respiratory epithelium, which has a very rich blood supply and numerous mucous glands to warm and moisten the air as we breathe.

In order to maximize the available surface area for this epithelium, the walls of the nasal cavity contain coiled inward-projecting bones, known as conchae or turbinate bones. The nasal cavities open behind into a space known as the pharynx, through which air passes on its way down to the lungs.

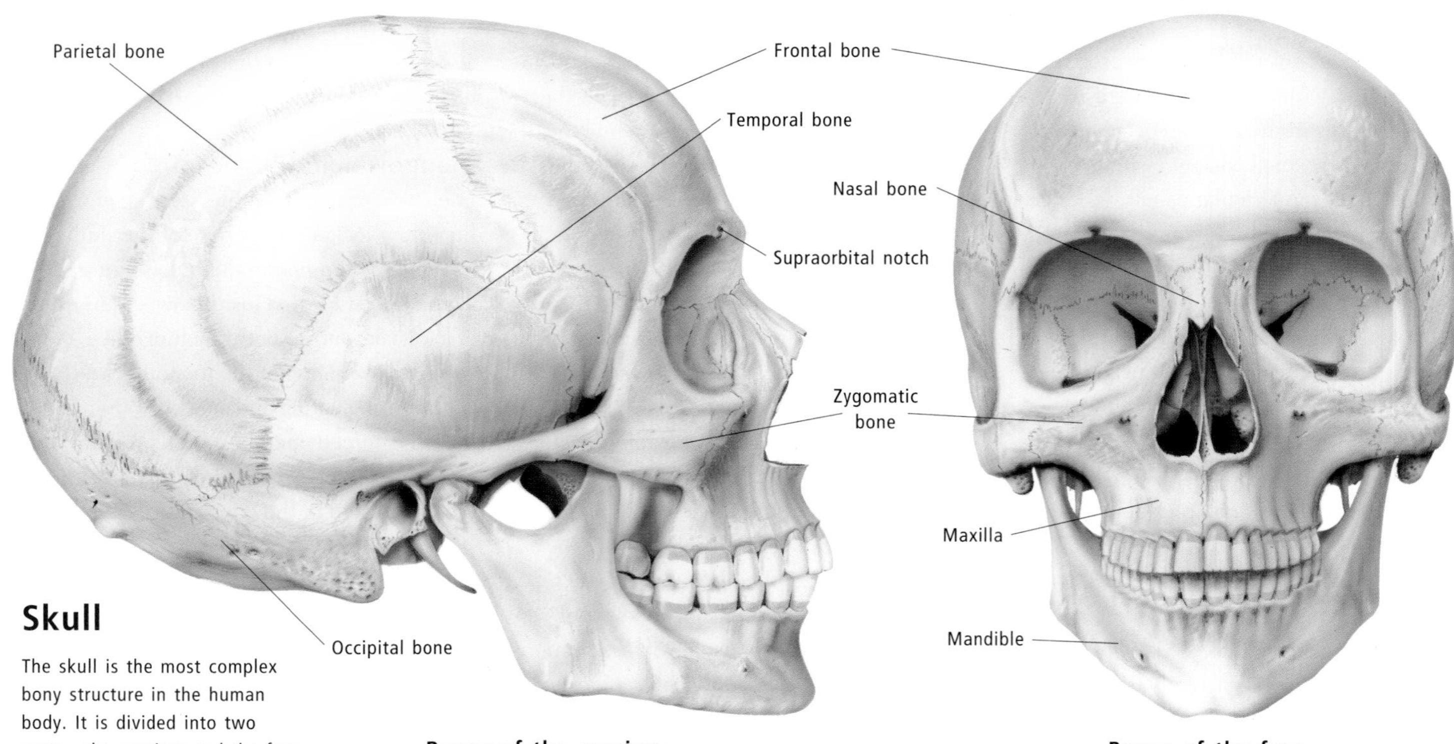

Skull

The skull is the most complex bony structure in the human body. It is divided into two parts—the cranium and the face.

Bones of the cranium

Bones of the face

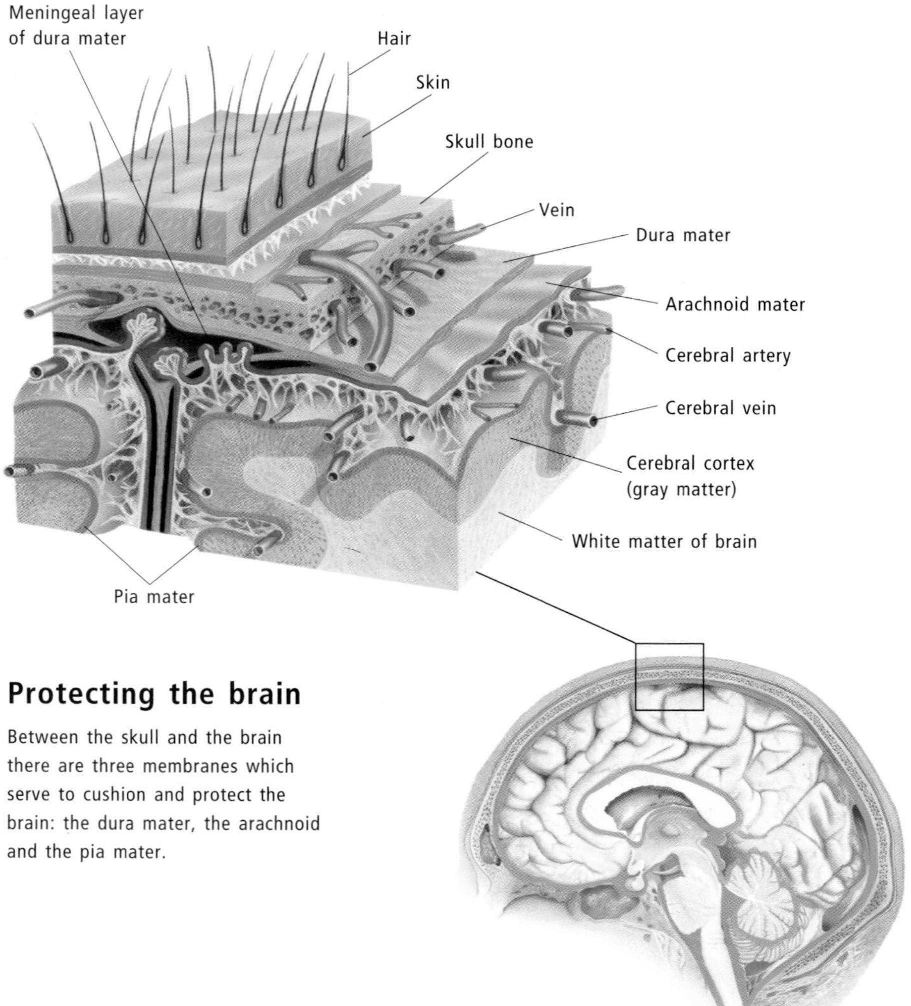

Protecting the brain

Between the skull and the brain there are three membranes which serve to cushion and protect the brain: the dura mater, the arachnoid and the pia mater.

Paranasal sinuses

The nasal cavity also communicates with spaces known as the paranasal sinuses, which occupy the major bones adjacent to the nasal cavity (the maxillary, frontal, ethmoid and sphenoid sinuses, named after the bones in which they are located). These sinuses are also lined by respiratory epithelium and infection can spread to them easily from the nose, causing congestion and pain (sinusitis).

The maxillary sinuses, which lie to the sides of the nose, are the largest and most susceptible to infection, from either the nose or the upper teeth.

Oral cavity (mouth)

The oral cavity or mouth extends from the lips at the front to the throat (pharynx) behind, and is bounded at the sides by the cheeks. Its roof is formed in front by the hard (bony) palate and behind by the soft (muscular) palate. Its floor is formed by muscle. Its major contents are the teeth and the tongue.

There are a total of 20 baby (deciduous) teeth, which usually appear between the ages of 6 and 24 months. From approximately 6 years of age onwards, the deciduous teeth are gradually replaced by permanent or adult teeth. The mature adult has a total of 32 teeth. Each jaw contains 4 incisors (for cutting), 2 canines (for tearing), 4 premolars and 6 molars (for grinding). The third molars, or wisdom teeth, are the last to appear and cause problems in people whose jaws are not long enough to fit them comfortably.

The tongue is a muscular organ essential for normal swallowing and speech. It is also a very important sensory organ; it is extremely sensitive to touch and contains taste buds, special cells which detect different tastes.

The tongue, which is attached below to a small bone in the neck called the hyoid bone, consists of a root (in the throat), dorsum (the main part in the mouth) and an apex or tip. It is formed by numerous muscle fibers which lie in different planes, allowing it to change shape and move in almost any direction.

The sides and upper surface of the dorsum and apex are rough because they contain numerous tiny projections called papillae, which enable the tongue to grip food and move it around during chewing. Taste buds are located on the sides of the papillae. The root of the tongue has a smooth, slippery surface so food can slide freely over it as it passes down the throat during swallowing.

Pharynx (throat)

The pharynx (throat) is a muscular tube, which is suspended from the base of the skull. It is a common passageway for both food and air, being continuous at the front with the nasal and oral cavities, and below with the trachea or windpipe (for air) and esophagus (for food and liquids). During swallowing, the muscular walls of the pharynx contract to force food down to the esophagus. At the same time the soft palate is pulled upwards to prevent food passing into the nasal cavity, and the epiglottic cartilage flips down like a lid to prevent food entering the larynx and trachea.

The walls of the upper part of the pharynx contain the palatine tonsils and the adenoid tonsils. These are islands of lymphatic tissue which are important in the immune system, particularly in children.

Inflammation of the palatine tonsils is known as tonsillitis, and is usually treatable by antibiotics or, in recurring cases, surgical removal. Inflammation of the adenoid tonsils can block off the nasal cavity, causing breathing difficulties and snoring. They may also be surgically removed.

Ear

The ear contains sensory organs necessary for both hearing and balance. It consists of outer, middle and inner parts.

The outer ear is located on the side of the skull and consists of the auricle and ear canal. The auricle directs the sound waves down the ear canal where they cause vibration of the tympanic membrane.

The middle ear is an air-filled cavity in the temporal bone. It is separated from the outer ear by the tympanic membrane. The middle ear contains a chain of three tiny bones or ossicles (hammer, anvil and stirrup) extending across the cavity from the tympanic membrane to the oval window. Vibration of the tympanic membrane causes movement of the ossicles, which is then transmitted to the inner ear through the oval window.

The inner ear is filled with a fluid called perilymph. Suspended in this fluid is a system of membrane-covered ducts which are filled with a different fluid (endolymph). These ducts include the cochlear and semicircular ducts, and the utricle and saccule. Specialized receptors in the cochlear duct respond to vibrations of the fluid (caused by the stirrup vibrating in the oval window) and enable us to detect different frequencies and intensities of sound. Receptors in the semicircular ducts detect the direction of head movements and those in the utricle and saccule can detect head position, even when the head is not moving.

Some viral infections, as well as alcohol, can change the pressure of the fluid, causing abnormal stimulation of the receptors and consequent dizziness and nausea, as well as ringing in the ear (tinnitus).

SEE ALSO *Brain, Ear, Esophagus, Eye, Face, Lacrimal glands, Nose, Pharynx, Sinuses, Sinusitis, Skull, Subarachnoid hemorrhage, Teeth, Throat, Tinnitus, Tongue, Trachea*

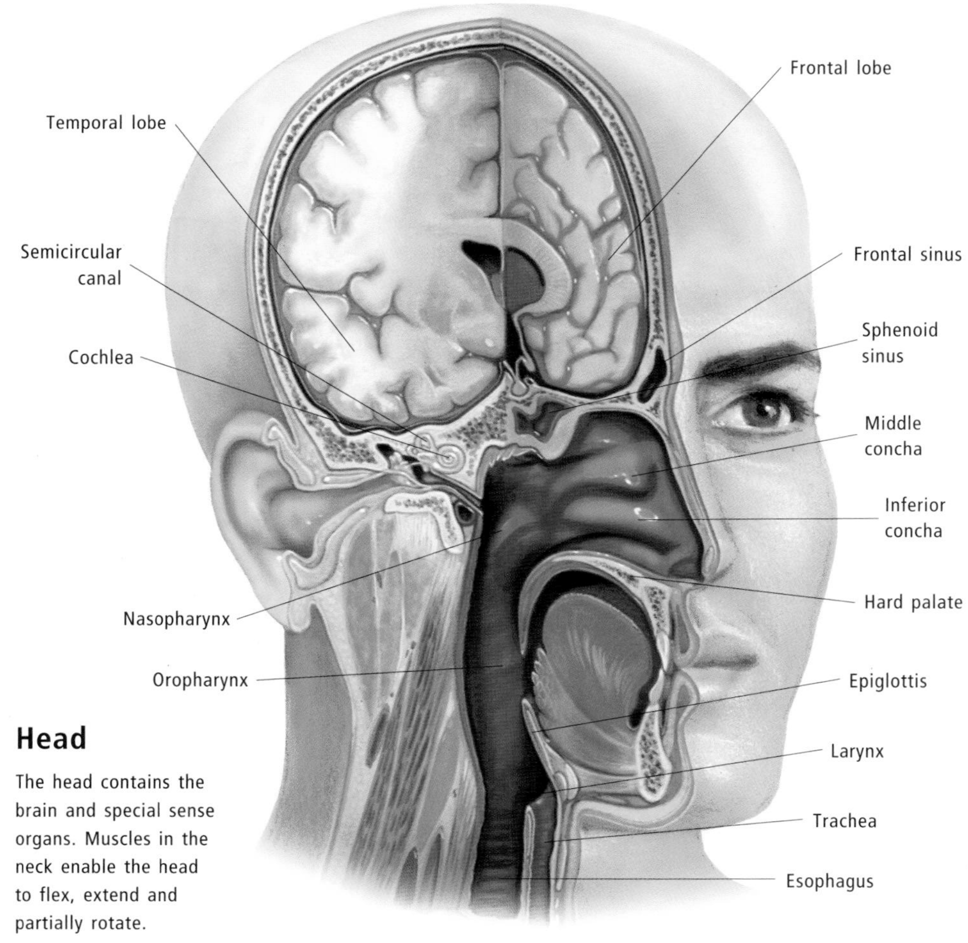

Head

The head contains the brain and special sense organs. Muscles in the neck enable the head to flex, extend and partially rotate.

HEAD LICE

Tiny wingless insects that live on the scalp and suck blood, head lice are spread through direct contact and by sharing hats and combs. Though anyone can have them, young children, particularly those who attend preschool, school or child care, are more likely to suffer because of the contact they have with other children. Lice are attracted to clean rather than dirty hair, and are very common (parents should not feel that their children having head lice is a sign of neglect).

Head lice cause itching. Their presence can be confirmed by a fine black powder of louse feces or pale flecks on the pillow, by the lice themselves, and by their eggs (nits—white specks stuck to hairs, near their roots).

Head lice can be eradicated by the use of special shampoos, which everyone in the household should use. Wash the hair, then have the sufferer sit in the sunlight. Check behind the ears and the back of the neck, then comb the hair carefully using a special lice comb, rinsing or wiping the comb between strokes. Dry the hair with a hair dryer, as the heat will also help to eradicate the pest. Daily combing is important once you are sure the lice have been eradicated. Hair brushes, combs, pillow cases, hair accessories and hats should also be washed.

SEE ALSO *Lice*

HEADACHE

Headache is a very common problem which can seriously interfere with a person's normal activities. It is not usually the result of another, more serious, underlying disease but severe or persistent headache, especially in children, requires medical investigation to exclude the presence of any such disorder.

By far the most common headaches are those referred to as tension headaches. Most persons experience occasional headaches of this type, often related to emotional stress or fatigue, but not necessarily triggered by tension. Tension headaches can also be triggered by caffeine, alcohol, certain foods, stress, fatigue, and skipping meals. The precise mechanics behind the development of these common headaches remain unclear. There can be associated tightening and tenderness of the muscles of the scalp, neck or jaw. Pain is usually moderate but may be severe with a sensation of the head being "gripped in a vise."

Episodic tension headaches usually respond to over-the-counter analgesics such as acetaminophen (paracetamol) or aspirin. Chronic tension headache can be associated with depression, anxiety, insomnia or other medical problems. Chronic or severe tension headaches should be investigated by a primary care physician, as they can be due to another cause, and there are other treatments that are available.

Vascular headaches make up a second large and important group, in which there is an associated dilation of the blood vessels supplying the head. The specific mechanisms involved are again poorly understood.

Migraine and its many variants are in cluded in this category. Most migraine sufferers develop pain that usually affects one half of the head and lasts for several hours, often with throbbing and sometimes accompanied by nausea and vomiting. A number of precipitating factors for migraine headaches are

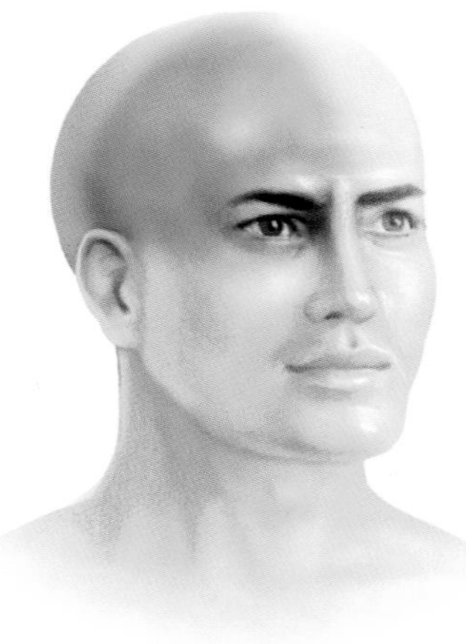

Headache—migraine

A migraine headache is characterized by severe, throbbing pain, usually on one side of the head.

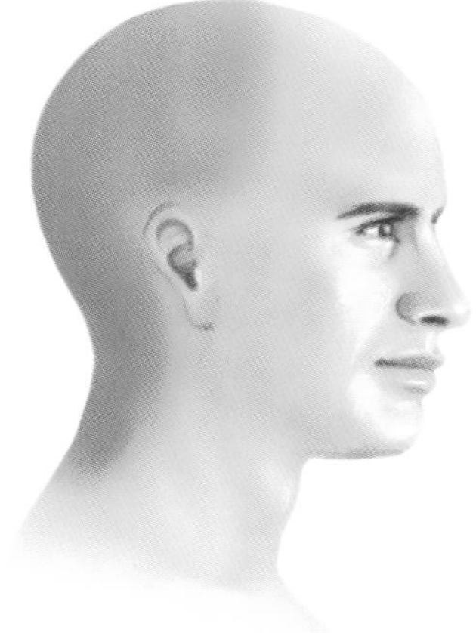

Headache—occipital neuralgia

Occipital neuralgia is a painful, stabbing sensation in the back part of the head (occiput).

Headache

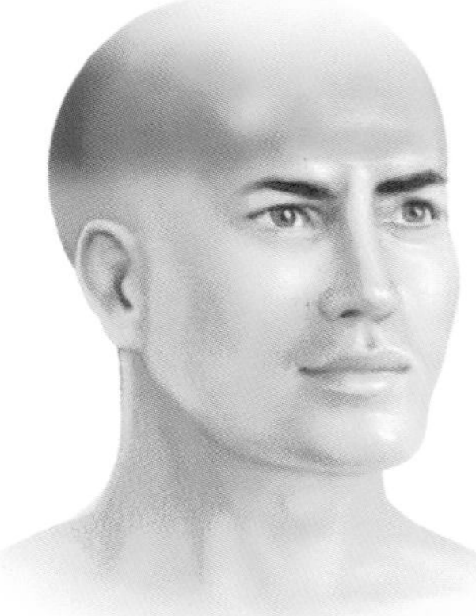

Headache—tension

A tension headache usually occurs in the front part of the head and is often accompanied by tightness in the muscles of the scalp, neck and jaw.

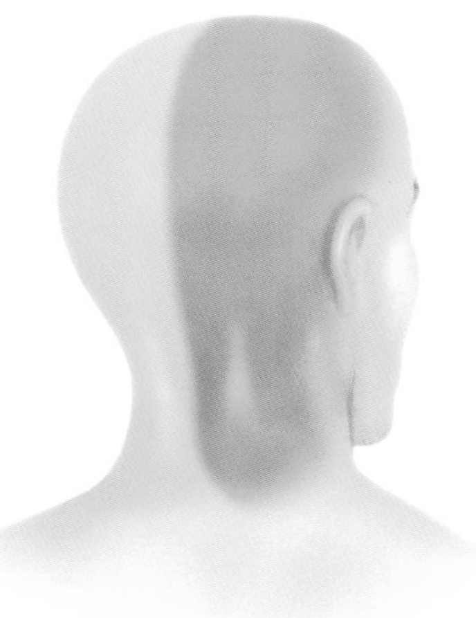

Occipital neuralgia—back view

recognized and several types of migraine can be distinguished. So-called hormonal headaches, associated with menstruation, pregnancy, oral contraceptive therapy and menopause, are forms of migraine headache.

Another important, although much less common, type of vascular headache is known as cluster headache. They are of relatively short duration, but very severe attacks occur in clusters over periods of several weeks.

Headache is sometimes a manifestation of an underlying disease, although such headaches occur much less commonly than either tension or vascular headaches. Among the specific disease processes that may initially appear as headache are: inflammation of the blood vessels supplying the head and neck (known as cranial or temporal arteritis), which is of particular concern in older persons; pain originating from inflamed nasal sinuses, inflamed teeth, osteoarthritis of the vertebrae in the neck, or injured or inflamed nerves; inflammation of the meninges covering the brain; very high blood pressure; and pain caused by masses within the cranium, including various brain tumors.

Excessive self-medication for headaches can cause further headache, sometimes referred to as rebound headache. This is especially true of overuse of analgesics such as aspirin and acetaminophen (paracetamol).

The varieties of headaches that develop in children are similar to those in adults; both tension headaches and migraines commonly occur. Children's headaches can frequently be the first sign of underlying diseases (such as inflammation of eyes, ears, nose, head trauma, meningitis, and brain tumors), so severe or recurrent headaches should always be investigated by the family doctor.

SEE ALSO *Brain, Depression, Hypertension, Meningitis, Migraine, Osteoarthritis, Sinusitis*

HEALING

Healing is the restoration of structure and function of damaged tissues. Different processes are involved depending on the nature and extent of the injury, and the type of body tissue involved.

Inflammation

Inflammation is the body's natural response to tissue damage. It takes place after infections, burns, frostbite, or radiation exposure. The process begins with dilation of blood vessels and increased blood flow to the area. The vessels become more permeable, allowing plasma to escape from the blood into the extracellular fluid. This produces swelling of the affected region. Leukocytes (white blood cells) also escape from blood vessels in the region, and release chemicals that may cause pain. These changes together produce the classic signs of inflammation: heat, redness, swelling, and pain and tenderness.

As inflammation progresses, leukocytes migrate in increased numbers from the bloodstream into the injured area. The inflammatory response proceeds until the dead tissue and invading organisms have been removed. The inflammation then resolves—the excess fluid is drained from the area by the lymphatics, the blood vessels constrict and become less permeable, and the swelling, heat and redness subside.

If there has been damage of the tissue as well, then healing also involves regeneration of tissue—that is, the repeated division of surviving tissue cells to take the place of those damaged. Not all tissue can regenerate, however (e.g. brain and nerve cells). Moreover, if the damage is extensive, it may not be possible for regeneration to occur.

Surgical intervention sometimes may be necessary to aid the healing process. In some cases, dead bacteria, cells and tissue may collect to form pus, which may collect and form an abscess. This may need to be drained. If there are large areas of dead tissue, the dead tissue needs to be removed.

Wound healing

If an injury causes a wound such as a laceration, then healing takes place by a different mechanism. If the edges of the wound are close together, wound healing takes place by "primary intention". A blood clot forms in the wound which contracts, bringing the edges still closer together. From the edges, fibroblasts produce granulation tissue, which is gradually replaced with connective tissue. Meanwhile, epithelial tissues grow over the surface of the wound. If the edges of the wound are far apart, healing takes place by "secondary intention". Granulation tissue forms at the base and sides of the wound and "fills up" the wound until it reaches the level of the skin. The granulation tissue is gradually replaced with (often unsightly) scar tissue.

Healing

For a wound to heal, leukocytes (white blood cells) must first migrate from blood vessels to the injured tissues in order to remove dead cells and invading organisms. A blood clot comprising fibrin strands, platelets and red and white blood cells then forms to bring the edges of the wound together. Finally, fibroblasts produce new granulation tissue.

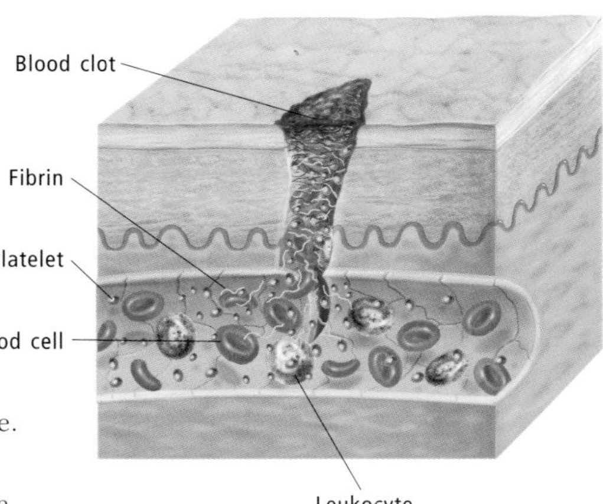

Bone healing

Healing of bone is similar to that of other injured tissue, but uses specialized cells and materials. Immediately after a fracture, bone forming cells called osteoblasts begin to produce a tough binding material called callus, which knits the bones together. Once this is accomplished, the bone is remodeled as the callus is absorbed and replaced by true bone, which is gradually remodeled into its previous shape.

The process of bone healing is greatly helped if displacement of the ends of the fractured bone is minimal. Several general factors can influence the healing process. The younger the person is, the faster healing takes place. Someone who is in good general health will heal faster than someone in poor general health or who is malnourished. Sufferers from liver or kidney disease or diabetes do not heal as well as healthy individuals. Someone who is immunosuppressed or on cytotoxic, immunosuppressant or corticosteroid drugs may take longer to heal. Poor blood supply to damaged tissues also slows or prevents healing.

HEARING

Hearing is the ability to perceive sound vibrations, which are transmitted in waves through gas, water or solid matter. Sounds can vary in frequency (be pitched high or low) and in intensity. Frequency is measured in hertz (cycles per second); sounds are audible from a low frequency of about 50 hertz to a high frequency of about 16,000 hertz. Intensity is measured in decibels, ranging from inaudible at zero to the devastatingly loud (above 140 decibels). Sound is conducted to the brain through the delicate and complicated mechanisms of the ear. Binaural hearing (i.e. with both ears) gives information about direction and distance of the source of sound.

The ear contains the sensory organ that perceives the sound through a process called audition, and converts the mechanical energy of the sound wave into nerve impulses which are transmitted to the brain and interpreted. Hearing is present before birth, the inner ear developing in the fetus at around 9 weeks.

The ear has three parts—the outer, middle and inner ear—each of which plays a special role in the hearing process.

The outer or external ear consists of the pinna or auricle and the auditory canal, a tubular passage lined with fine hairs and glands which secrete earwax (cerumen). The passage connects the external ear to the eardrum.

The middle ear includes the eardrum and the chain of three bones, the ossicles, whose individual names are derived from the Latin for hammer, anvil, and stirrup (malleus, incus and stapes, respectively) which connect across the tympanic cavity to the oval window, in the cochlea.

The eustachian or auditory tube connects the air space of the tympanic cavity with the pharynx and allows air pressure in the middle ear to be equalized with atmospheric pressure. The tube is lined with mucous membrane and can be blocked by swelling due to head colds or similar viral infections. This can cause discomfort and pain in the ear on changes of pressure, such as when flying, and hearing can be severely reduced. Swallowing or chewing can help unblock the tube and equalize pressure.

The inner ear (labyrinth) contains the major organ of hearing, the fluid-filled cochlea, and the semicircular canals, the organs of balance.

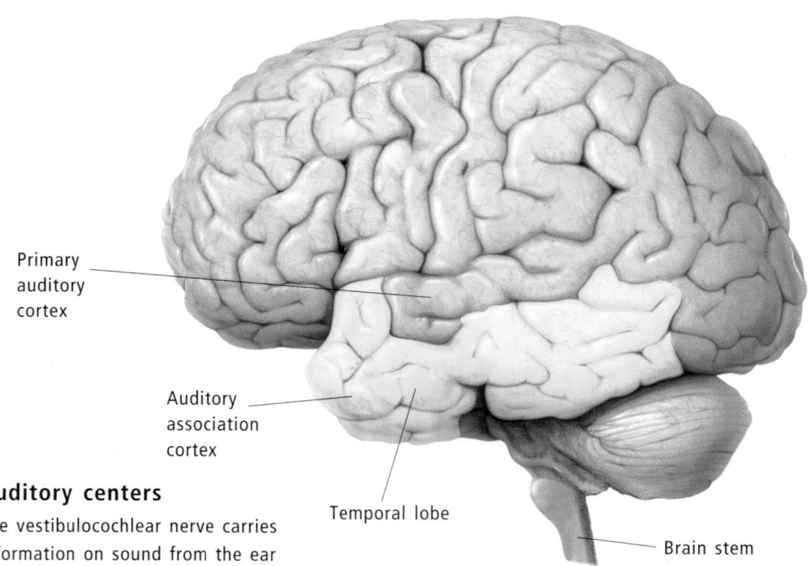

Auditory centers
The vestibulocochlear nerve carries information on sound from the ear into the brain stem. From here, the information passes through the midbrain and on to the auditory cortex in the temporal lobe of the brain. This is where we recognize and interpret sounds. High frequency sounds activate one part of the cortex, low frequency sounds activate another part.

How we hear **(opposite page)**
(a) Sound waves enter the ear canal and hit the eardrum. **(b)** The eardrum vibrates and passes vibrations to the ossicles (three tiny bones in the middle ear). **(c)** The ossicles intensify the pressure of the sound waves and transmit vibrations to the oval window (a membrane that covers the entrance to the cochlea). **(d)** The vibrations pass into the cochlear spiral where fluid displaces tiny hair-like receptor cells in the organ of Corti. **(e)** These cells send nerve impulses along the cochlear nerve to the brain stem, midbrain, then the hearing center in the temporal lobe of the brain where sounds are interpreted.

Airborne sounds or sound waves are captured by the auricle (outer ear), which directs them through the auditory canal to the eardrum (in the middle ear). From here waves are relayed by vibration of the ossicles to the organ of Corti, which is in the cochlea (the inner ear). There they disturb the cochlear fluid, exciting thousands of tiny hair cells which transduce mechanical energy to electrical impulses that are relayed via the cochlear nerve to the brain. Different hair cells relay high- and low-pitched sounds, those in the deepest part of the cochlea receiving the lowest pitches.

Conductive hearing is the reception of sound through the bones of the skull and is the main transmission route for one's own voice. Sound waves go direct to the cochlea, bypassing the middle ear.

The loudness of sound is measured in decibels, and the lowest sound of a certain pitch that can be heard is expressed as the hearing threshold for that pitch. Sounds below 10 decibels (dB), the volume of a whisper, are difficult to hear, and those above 140 dB will cause actual pain. Constant or regular exposure to sounds above 70 dB in volume can accelerate hearing loss, and those above 100 dB may inflict permanent damage on a single exposure.

Hearing sensitivity has some protection from the acoustic reflex which, in response to loud noise, stiffens the chain of bones, the ossicles, in the middle ear to diminish the strength of vibrations transmitted to the inner ear. This protection, however, is not enough to prevent damage caused by repeated exposure, which permanently destroys hair cells in the cochlea.

SEE ALSO *Deafness, Ear*

Hearing

Auditory ossicles

The ossicles in the inner ear (the malleus, incus and stapes) are three tiny bones that act as an amplifier by magnifying the movement of the eardrum. This allows us to hear even very faint sounds. The malleus is attached to the eardrum; when the eardrum vibrates the malleus vibrates the incus which in turn vibrates the stapes. The base of the stapes covers the oval window, a membrane that passes vibrations into the spiral of the cochlea.

Ossicles
Malleus
Incus
Stapes
Semicircular canals
Cochlea
Eardrum
Stapes footplate covering vestibular (oval) window

Ossicles
Malleus
Incus
Stapes
Eardrum
Vestibular nerve branches
Cochlear nerve
Cochlear duct
a
b
c
d
e
Cochlea
Middle ear
Stapes footplate covering vestibular (oval) window
External ear canal

Inside the cochlea

Three channels run through the spiral of the cochlea. Inside the central channel—the cochlear duct (scala media)—lies the organ of Corti. When fluid in the central channel pulses with sound waves, it moves the membrane and hairs of the organ of Corti which send signals to the cochlear nerve and on to the brain.

Organ of Corti

The organ of Corti consists of rows of cells with fine hair-like projections under a layer of membrane. Movement of the hairs provides the brain with information on the volume or intensity of sound. Soft sounds stimulate only a few cells; loud sounds stimulate cells in many of the rows. The cells stimulate the cochlear branch of the vestibular nerve which carries information to the brain.

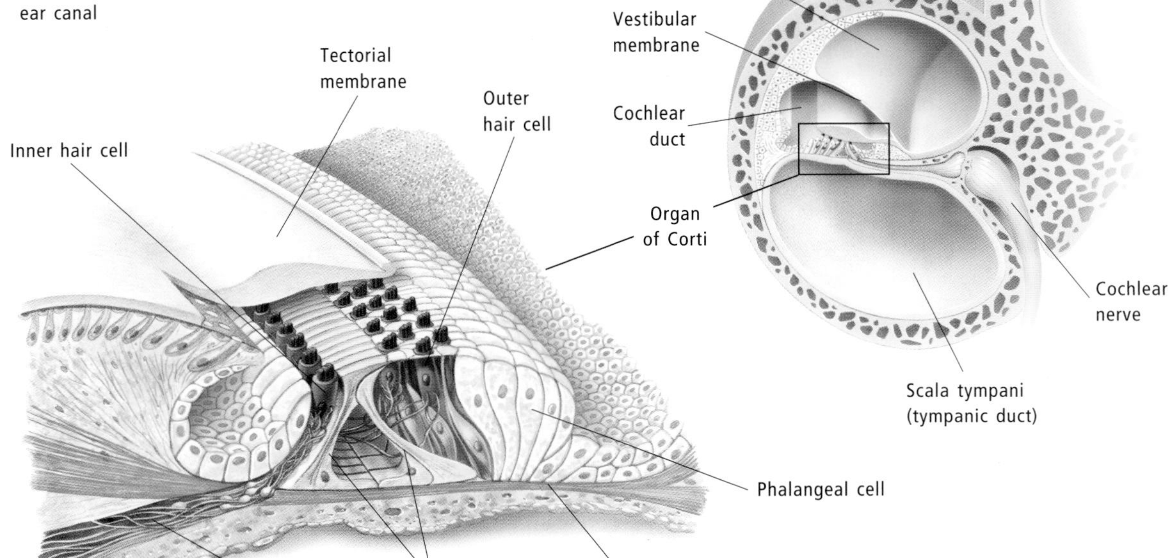

HEART

The heart is essentially a muscular pump, which is responsible for moving blood around the vessels of the body. It is made up of two halves, separated by the septum, a thick muscular wall. Each half is again divided into an upper and lower chamber.

The two chambers on the left side of the heart (left atrium and ventricle) are responsible for receiving oxygen-rich blood from the lungs and pumping it out to the body along its largest artery, the aorta. The two chambers on the right side of the heart (right atrium and ventricle) are responsible for receiving relatively deoxygenated blood from the body and distributing it via the pulmonary trunk to the lungs for gas exchange to occur. These two circuits of blood flow are called systemic and pulmonary circulations respectively.

Within the heart there are four valves that ensure blood flows in one direction: from atrium to ventricle and out through its appropriate artery. The two atrioventricular valves are located between the atria and ventricles on each side of the heart. Between the right atrium and right ventricle lies the tricuspid valve, while the mitral valve lies between the left atrium and left ventricle. The function of atrioventricular valves is to prevent backflow of blood from the ventricles to the atria during ventricular contraction.

The other two cardiac valves (semilunar valves) are located at the outlets from the ventricles: the pulmonary valve lies at the point where the right ventricle expels blood to the pulmonary trunk, while the aortic valve lies at the outlet of the left ventricle. The role of semilunar valves is to prevent backflow of blood from the aorta and pulmonary trunk into their respective ventricles when the ventricles relax.

The heart muscle receives a rich blood supply from the coronary arteries, which branch from the aorta. Cardiac blood is returned to the right atrium by the cardiac veins.

The pumping action

The heart has a system of specialized cells, which either set the rhythm of cardiac contraction or allow for rapid spread of electrical impulses through the heart.

The sinoatrial node, in the right atrium, is a specialized tissue that acts as the heart's pacemaker; it controls the frequency of the heart's rhythmic contractions. Electrical impulses are then transmitted through the atria to the atrioventricular node, which then passes the impulse down the atrioventricular bundle, resulting in coordinated contractions of the ventricles.

Although divided into a left and right side, with distinct functions, the heart is organized in such a way that its pumping action serves both sides at once. In the relaxation phase (diastole) blood pours from the left and right atrium into its corresponding ventricle. In the next contraction phase (systole) the blood is forced from the left and right ventricles into the aorta and the pulmonary artery, respectively. The valves control the direction of blood flow. At the beginning of each contraction, the atrioventricular valves close and the pulmonary and aortic valves open. At the end of each contraction the aortic and pulmonary valves close and the atrioventricular valves open.

Diseases of the heart

Heart disease can be congenital (existing from birth), or can develop later in life.

Diseases of the coronary arteries

Disease of the coronary arteries usually leads to narrowing and reduced blood supply to the cardiac muscle. The most common type of coronary artery disease is due to atherosclerosis, which involves the accumulation of fats (atheroma) within the vessel wall leading to the formation of fatty/fibrous plaques and deposition of calcium. This disease may also occur in arteries of the neck, legs and abdomen, but is particularly dangerous in the brain and coronary arteries. Lifestyle factors, such as smoking and a diet rich in saturated fats, increase the risk of atherosclerosis. High blood pressure is also an important contributing factor.

The interior of a vessel may be blocked by fatty plaques, which cause thickening and loss of elasticity in the wall. Plaques may also lose their surface, with the result that blood coagulates on them (thrombus formation) which also contributes to obstruction of coronary arteries (coronary heart disease).

Partial obstruction of the coronary artery may severely limit the patient's ability to perform physical activity. Such patients will complain of chest pain that has a crushing feeling and is usually located in the center of the chest (angina pectoris). Angina pectoris is usually felt when the patient is climbing stairs or walking up a hill. It will pass in a few minutes once the patient stops to rest.

Complete obstruction of a coronary artery (coronary thrombosis) will lead to the death of the heart muscle supplied by that artery (myocardial infarction). This is commonly known as a "heart attack" or "coronary". In this case the patient will experience a crushing pain in the center of the chest which does not pass with rest and may last for several hours. The pain may spread into other parts of the body such as the left arm, neck, back and upper abdomen. The patient may also experience severe breathlessness. If the death of cardiac muscle causes abnormal electrical activity then the remaining heart muscle may not be able to contract effectively (ventricular fibrillation).

Obstruction of the coronary arteries may be treated before too much damage has occurred by several techniques. Partial or mild obstructions may be treated by dilating the blocked segment with a balloon, removing the obstructing matter (plaque) with laser pulses, or inserting a "stent" to hold the artery open. These are all methods of angioplasty. More severe obstructions may be bypassed surgically by grafting a piece of leg vein or chest wall artery alongside the obstructed segment (coronary artery bypass).

If the death of cardiac muscle occurs slowly, the patient may develop congestive cardiac failure. In such cases, the heart is unable to move blood around the body effectively, so that blood accumulates in the veins of the legs, abdomen or lungs. This leads to swelling of the ankles or swollen liver due to pooling of fluid in the tissue spaces of those sites. Pooling of fluid in the lungs will cause shortness of breath. Treatment of congestive cardiac failure is usually aimed at improving the strength of the heart and removing excess fluid from the body by increasing the output of urine.

Electrical abnormalities

Problems with the conducting and pacemaking tissues of the heart may lead to abnormalities of the cardiac rhythm (cardiac arrhythmias) or delayed and ineffective contraction of cardiac muscle (bundle branch

The heart

Heart—front

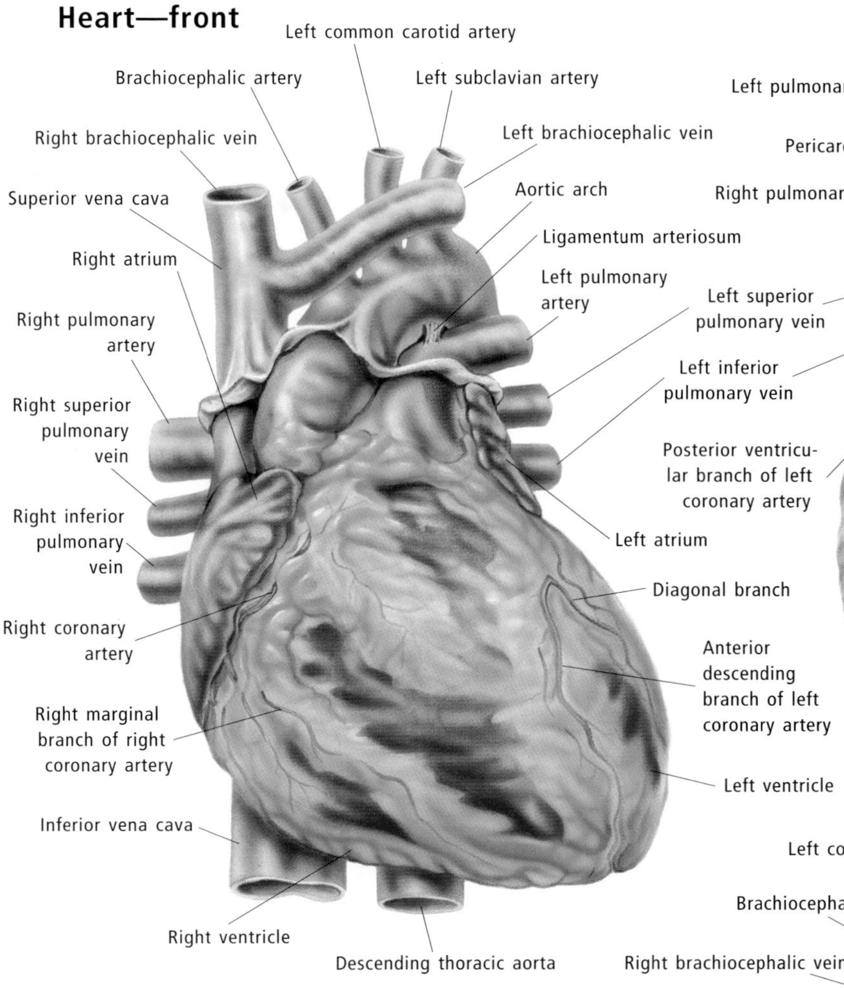

Left common carotid artery
Brachiocephalic artery
Left subclavian artery
Right brachiocephalic vein
Left brachiocephalic vein
Superior vena cava
Aortic arch
Ligamentum arteriosum
Right atrium
Left pulmonary artery
Right pulmonary artery
Left superior pulmonary vein
Right superior pulmonary vein
Left inferior pulmonary vein
Right inferior pulmonary vein
Left atrium
Diagonal branch
Right coronary artery
Anterior descending branch of left coronary artery
Right marginal branch of right coronary artery
Left ventricle
Inferior vena cava
Right ventricle
Descending thoracic aorta

Heart—back

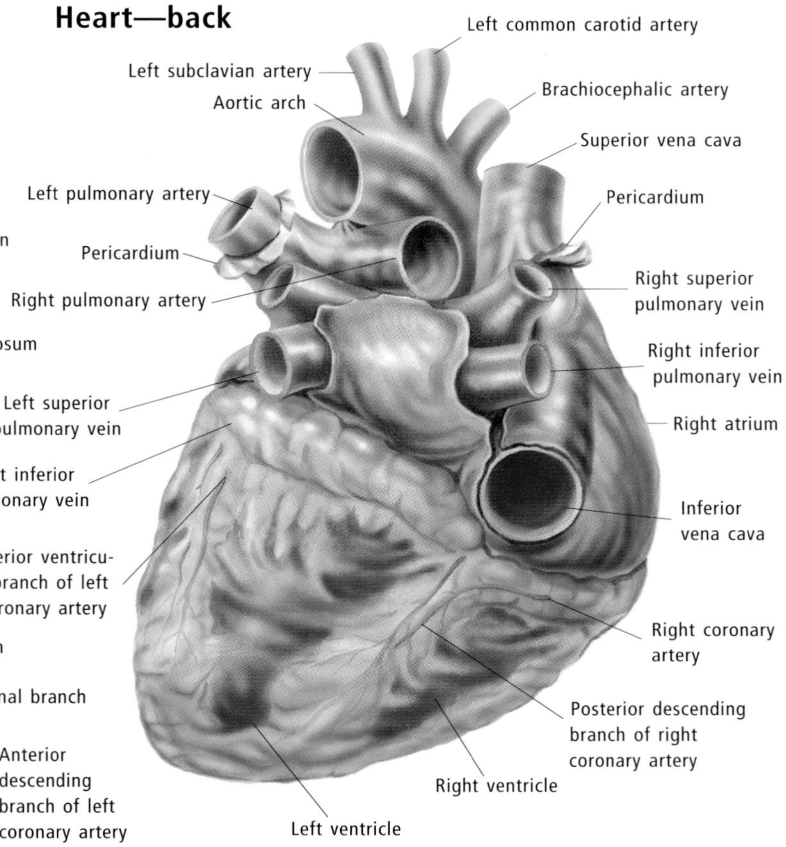

Left common carotid artery
Left subclavian artery
Brachiocephalic artery
Aortic arch
Superior vena cava
Left pulmonary artery
Pericardium
Pericardium
Right superior pulmonary vein
Right pulmonary artery
Right inferior pulmonary vein
Left superior pulmonary vein
Right atrium
Left inferior pulmonary vein
Inferior vena cava
Posterior ventricular branch of left coronary artery
Right coronary artery
Posterior descending branch of right coronary artery
Right ventricle
Left ventricle

Heart—section
showing all four chambers

Left common carotid artery
Brachiocephalic artery
Left subclavian artery
Right brachiocephalic vein
Left brachiocephalic vein
Superior vena cava
Aortic arch
Ascending aorta
Left pulmonary artery
Right pulmonary artery
Pericardium
Right superior pulmonary vein
Left superior pulmonary vein
Right inferior pulmonary vein
Left inferior pulmonary vein
Right atrium
Left atrium
Leaflet/cusp of tricuspid valve
Pulmonary valve
Leaflet/cusp of mitral valve
Right ventricle
Chordae tendineae
Aortic valve
Chordae tendineae
Papillary muscle
Inferior vena cava
Papillary muscle
Descending thoracic aorta

blocks or heart block). Cardiac arrhythmias may affect the atria (atrial tachycardia, atrial fibrillation) or the ventricle (ventricular tachycardia, ventricular fibrillation). Many electrical abnormalities are linked with problems with the coronary arteries, although some can be caused by rheumatic heart disease, fever, excess thyroid hormone, coffee and alcohol.

Ventricular fibrillation is a particularly serious cardiac arrhythmia. It often arises shortly after myocardial infarction and is a common immediate cause of death. In ventricular fibrillation chaotic electrical activity in the ventricles prevents effective pumping of blood to the body. The patient will have no pulse, breathing will stop and loss of consciousness will occur. The patient will die within minutes unless the normal rhythm is re-established.

This can often be achieved by delivering a powerful electrical current across the chest cavity (cardioversion or defibrillation). If a

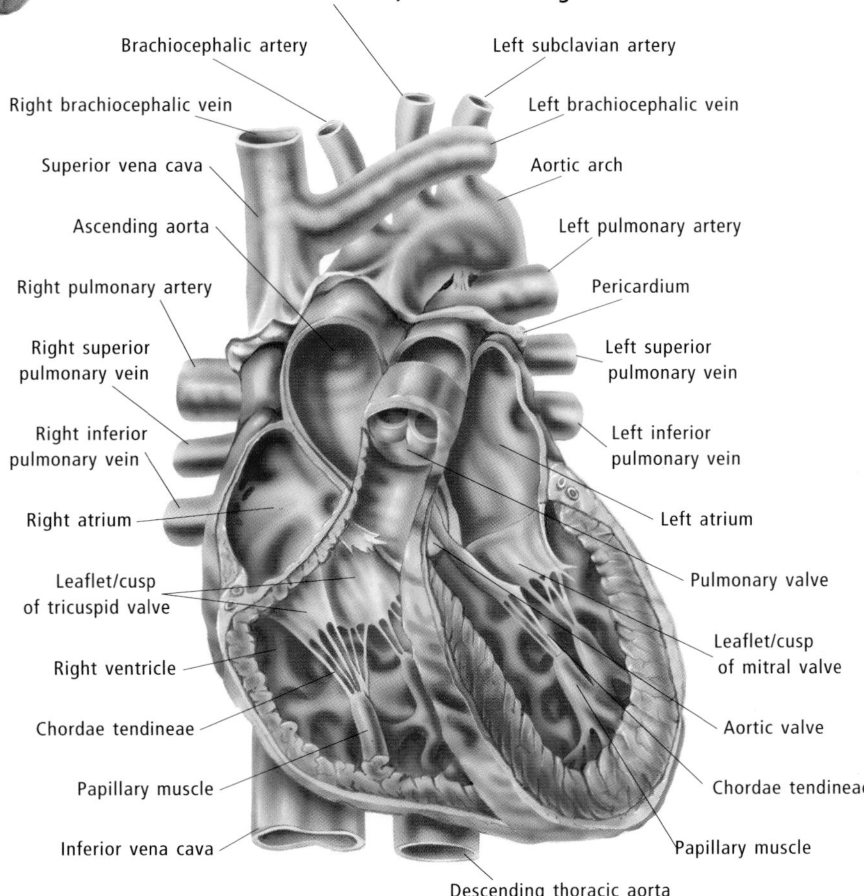

Heart cycle

In the cardiac cycle, the chambers of the heart pass through a relaxation phase (diastole) and a contraction phase (systole).

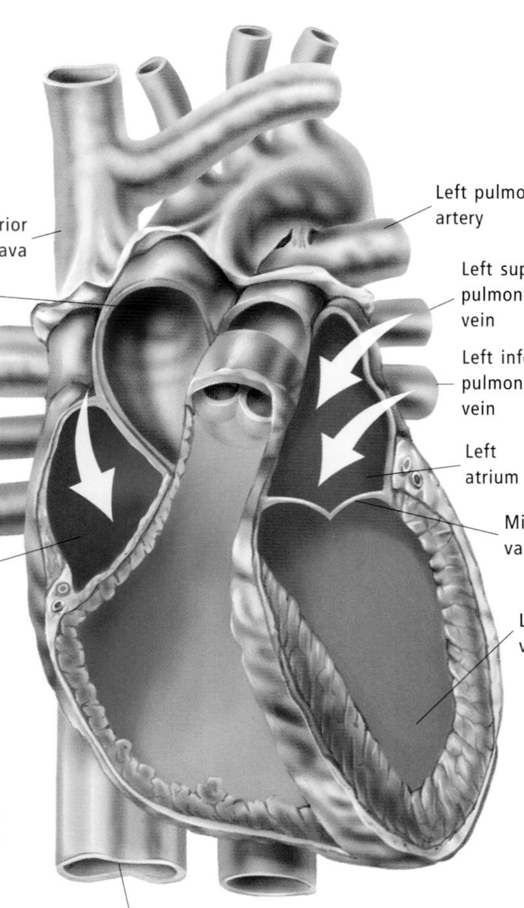

Heart cycle 1

In atrial diastole (at the beginning of ventricular diastole), deoxygenated blood from the systemic circulation and oxygenated blood from the lungs enter the left and right atria (upper chambers) of the heart.

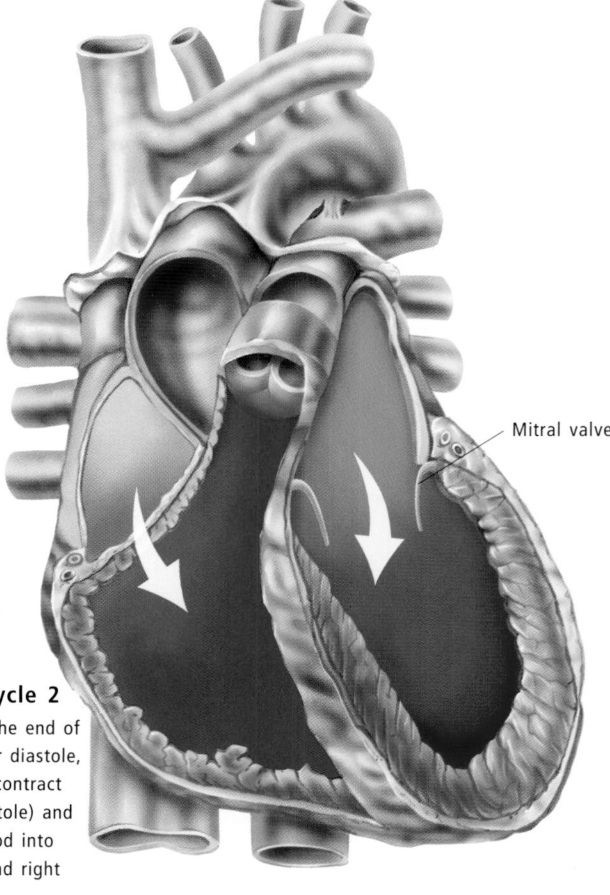

Heart cycle 2

Towards the end of ventricular diastole, the atria contract (atrial systole) and pump blood into the left and right ventricles.

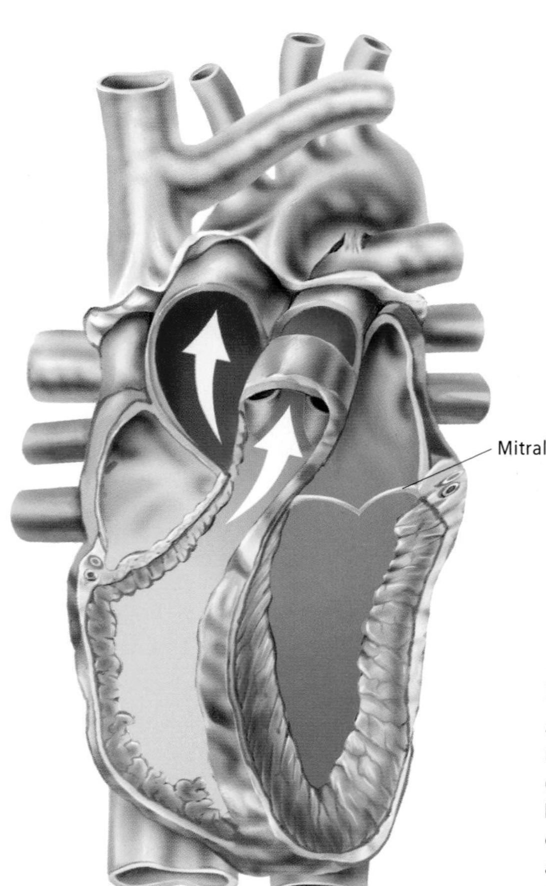

Heart cycle 3

In ventricular systole, the right and left ventricles contract and eject blood into the aorta and pulmonary arteries.

Mitral valve

Heart cycle 4

As the ventricles relax and ventricular diastole commences, blood once again enters the two atria and the cycle begins again.

Heart in ventricular systole

The ventricles of the heart contract, pushing oxygenated blood into the aorta (for circulation around the body) and deoxygenated blood into the pulmonary artery (to be sent to the lungs).

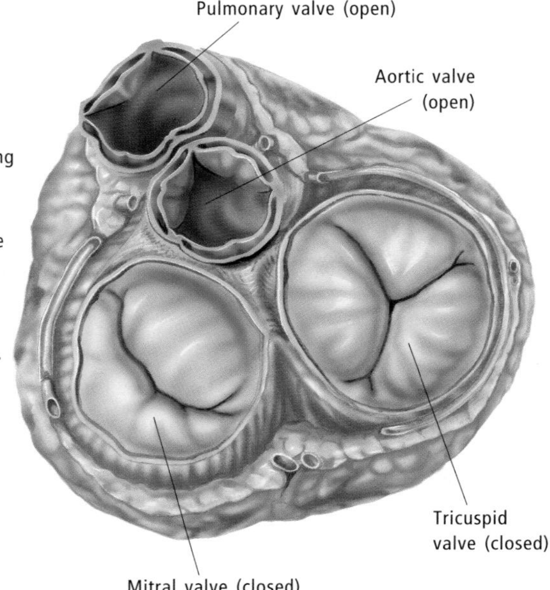

Heart in ventricular diastole

After a contraction the mitral and tricuspid valves open, allowing blood to fill the left and right ventricles of the heart.

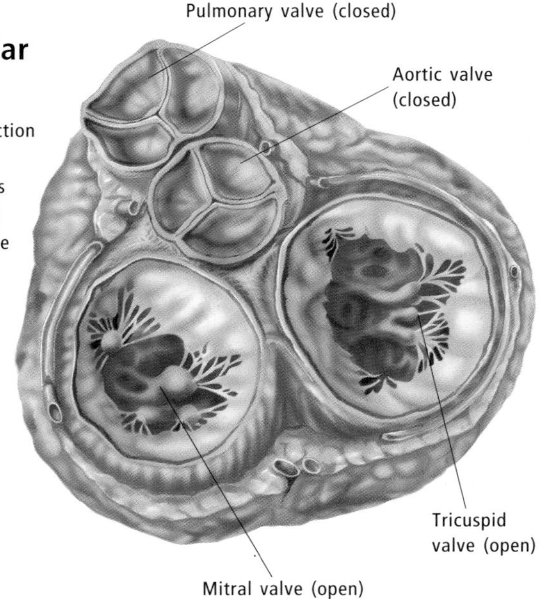

defibrillator is not available, the patient may be kept alive for a short time by compressing the heart between the breastbone and the vertebral column (external cardiac massage) and breathing into the patient's mouth (expired air ventilation). Together these techniques are called cardiopulmonary resuscitation (CPR). In abnormalities of the conducting and pacemaking tissues of the heart, the condition may be treated using drugs or by use of an artificial pacemaker).

Congenital heart diseases

Congenital heart diseases arise before birth, and affect about 1 in every 100 babies born in developed countries. About half of all babies born with a congenital abnormality of the heart will die during the first year of life. Often there is no known cause, but some may be due to abnormal genes, viruses (rubella) or drugs (thalidomide). Congenital heart disease may accompany other congenital abnormalities.

Congenital heart disease is usually due to one (or a combination) of the following defects: abnormal openings between the two sides of the heart (atrial or ventricular septal defect), blockage of large arteries or valves (coarctation of the aorta, pulmonary stenosis), or abnormal positioning of heart chambers or vessels.

Another type of congenital heart disease is patent ductus arteriosus. The ductus arteriosus is a normal opening between the aorta and pulmonary trunk in unborn babies. It usually closes shortly after birth, but in patent ductus arteriosus it remains open into adult life; it can be connected surgically.

Diseases of the valves

The valves of the heart may be involved in disease. The valve openings may become narrowed (valvular stenosis) with the result that blood does not readily flow through; or be unable to prevent the backward flow or regurgitation of blood (valvular incompetence or insufficiency).

Many valve diseases give rise to murmurs—sounds produced by the turbulent flow of blood across roughened valve surfaces, or the excessive movement of blood through normal valves. These may be heard with the aid of a stethoscope, or if loud enough, the vibrations may be felt on the chest wall. Often the presence of a heart murmur may not indicate serious disease, but any murmur should be investigated.

Rheumatic heart disease

Rheumatic heart disease is a condition which follows throat infection with a particular type of bacteria (group A streptococci). The patient's body mounts an immune reaction which damages connective tissues in the heart and joints.

Other heart diseases

Most disease of the heart muscle is due to blockage of the coronary arteries, but there are some rare but serious heart diseases that primarily affect the heart muscle itself. One of these, myocarditis, involves infection or toxic damage of the heart muscle, usually as a result of viral or parasitic infections or toxins from infectious agents, such as diptheria toxin.

Cardiomyopathy is a term used for diseases of the heart muscle of unknown origin. Some cardiomyopathies appear to be caused by alcohol or genetic disorders.

Endocarditis is inflammation of the inner lining of the heart (endocardium). It may occur in rheumatic heart disease and in some connective tissue diseases. It may also be due to infection by bacteria, fungi or viruses.

Pericarditis is an inflammation of the membranes that enclose the heart (the pericardium). If fluid or blood accumulates in the pericardium the heart may be unable to pump effectively (pericardial tamponade). If the pericardium contracts as it heals, the heart may be squeezed (constrictive pericarditis). There are many forms of pericarditis, and it can often be the result of some other disease, such as renal failure.

SEE ALSO *Angina pectoris, Aorta, Arteries, Arrhythmia, Atherosclerosis, Atrial septal defect, Cardiomyopathy, Circulatory system, Coronary arteries, Coronary artery disease, Coronary thrombosis, Endocarditis, Fibrillation, Heartbeat, Hypertension, Myocardial infarction, Myocarditis, Pacemaker, Pericarditis, Rheumatic fever, Stenosis, Tachycardia, Ventricle, Ventricular septal defect*

HEARTBEAT

The beating of the heart against the chest wall is known as the apex beat. It results from the contraction of the ventricles of the heart and can be felt on the lower left side of the chest, immediately below the left nipple. The rate and rhythm of the contraction of the heart can also be assessed by feeling the pulse, a pressure wave conducted down the main arteries of the body with each beat of the heart. The pulse is usually felt at the wrist (radial artery pulse), the neck (common carotid artery pulse), the groin (femoral artery pulse) or the back of the knee (popliteal artery pulse).

The rate and rhythm of contraction of the heart chambers is normally determined by the sinoatrial node, located near the entrance of the superior vena cava into the right atrium. The sinoatrial node is known as the pacemaker of the heart, as the regular electrical impulses it sends out produce the orderly contraction of the heart chambers. It, in turn, is under the influence of sympathetic and parasympathetic nerves, which tend to increase or reduce the heart rate, respectively, and is also influenced by circulating hormones like epinephrine (adrenaline).

Disorders of the rhythm of the heart are called arrhythmias. Abnormalities of heart rhythm can range in severity from mildly annoying to life-threatening. A quite common type of minor arrhythmia is the ventricular ectopic beat (ventricular extrasystole). These occur when an abnormal focus of electrical activity in the ventricles causes a premature contraction. This may occur in healthy people, particularly if they are tired or have consumed a lot of caffeine. The patient may feel nothing or may notice the occasional heavy heartbeat.

More serious types of arrhythmia include atrial fibrillation, in which irregular electrical impulses in the atria cause an uncoordinated contraction of the atria; or ventricular tachycardia in which an abnormal electrical focus in the ventricles drives the heart rate up to 140–220 beats per minute. Atrial fibrillation may arise as a result of mitral valve disease and can have serious consequences. Blood may coagulate (thrombose) in the left atrium and throw off small fragments (thrombotic emboli) that can become lodged in arteries to the brain or legs. Ventricular tachycardia usually accompanies serious heart disease and often causes a feeling of breathlessness and chest pain. The most serious arrhythmia, however, is ventricular fibrillation, which may occur after electrocution, drowning or the death of heart muscle (myocardial infarction). Ventricular fibrillation causes chaotic, uncoordinated and ineffectual contraction of the ventricles. Patients will die within minutes unless cardiopulmonary resuscitation (CPR) is commenced immediately. If available, an electrical defibrillator may be used to reset the heart rhythm (cardioversion).

Another type of disorder involving electrical conduction in the heart is heart block. In this condition the conduction of electrical impulses from the atria to the ventricles is blocked (AV block) so that the atria beat at a faster rate than the ventricles. Conduction blocks may also occur within the conduction pathways of the ventricle.

Many drugs are now available that can help control arrhythmias. These drugs may act to stabilize the electrically excitable membranes of heart cells (such as with quinidine, procainamide, lignocaine, disopyramide and phenytoin), slow the rate of ventricular response to atrial arrhythmias (for example, digitalis) or block the effects of circulating sympathetic substances on the rate and excitability of heart tissue (beta-blocking drugs).

SEE ALSO *Antiarrhythmic drugs, Arrythmia, Beta-blockers, Fibrillation, Heart, Mitral valve, Pacemaker, Pulse, Tachycardia*

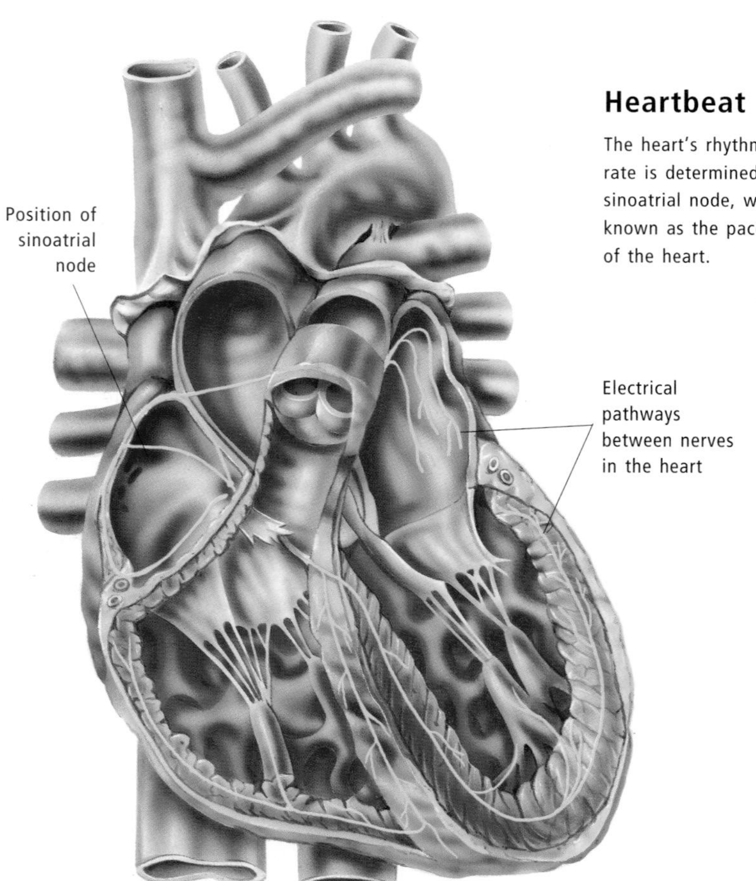

Heartbeat

The heart's rhythm and rate is determined by the sinoatrial node, which is known as the pacemaker of the heart.

HEARTBURN

Heartburn is a feeling of burning pain in the chest behind the breastbone combined with a sour or bitter taste at the back of the throat. These symptoms are caused by the regurgitation (reflux) of stomach contents, a mixture of food and digestive acids which flows back up the esophagus causing pain and irritation. Gastroesophageal reflux is common in otherwise healthy people although it can also be a symptom of an underlying disorder.

Chronic cases of heartburn are termed GERD (gastroesophageal reflux disease) and may be associated with intestinal disorders.

Chronic exposure of the esophegeal lining to stomach acids can lead to a number of complications such as ulceration of the esophagus, scarring and narrowing (strictures), and changes in the lining (epithelium) that can lead to cancer.

Relaxation of the lower esophageal sphincter, a muscle which closes after allowing swallowed food to pass to the stomach, is the cause of reflux. The sphincter may be weakened, or may react to stimulus from certain foods, alcohol or tobacco, or may open under pressure from the stomach that results from overeating or from sitting, lying or taking up activity too soon after eating.

Heartburn is common in the overweight, can be caused by hiatus (hiatal) hernia, and is also common in pregnancy through the displacement of the stomach by the developing baby and the hormonal changes which reduce the tone of all muscles, including the stomach and esophageal sphincters.

The symptoms are usually treated with antacids or, for more severe cases, anti-ulcer drugs. It is also important to reduce or avoid coffee, very spicy foods and curries, give up smoking, lose weight, eat smaller and less-rich meals, reduce alcohol, not lie down or bend over until food is digested. Certain drugs such as aspirin, anti-inflammatory or anti-arthritic drugs should be avoided. Raising the head of the bed when you sleep may help avoid heartburn at night.

There are a number of alternative therapies that may help to alleviate the symptoms of heartburn. Acupuncture treats heartburn at points that are believed to improve gastric function, relieve pain and reduce feelings of stress and anxiety. Herbalism prescribes alfalfa and meadowsweet to alkalize stomach acids, marshmallow and licorice to soothe mucous membranes and chamomile for dyspepsia associated with nervous tension.

Naturopathy suggests a low acid, non-spicy wholefood diet of frequent, small meals, eaten in a calm environment. Possible food allergens such as gluten need to be eliminated and smoking, coffee, citrus or alcohol should be avoided. Slippery elm or barley water taken before eating may help soothe the stomach. The biochemic tissue salt Nat Phos may reduce acidity and relieve nausea.

SEE ALSO *Esophagus, Gastroesophageal reflux, Hiatus hernia, Intestines, Pregnancy*

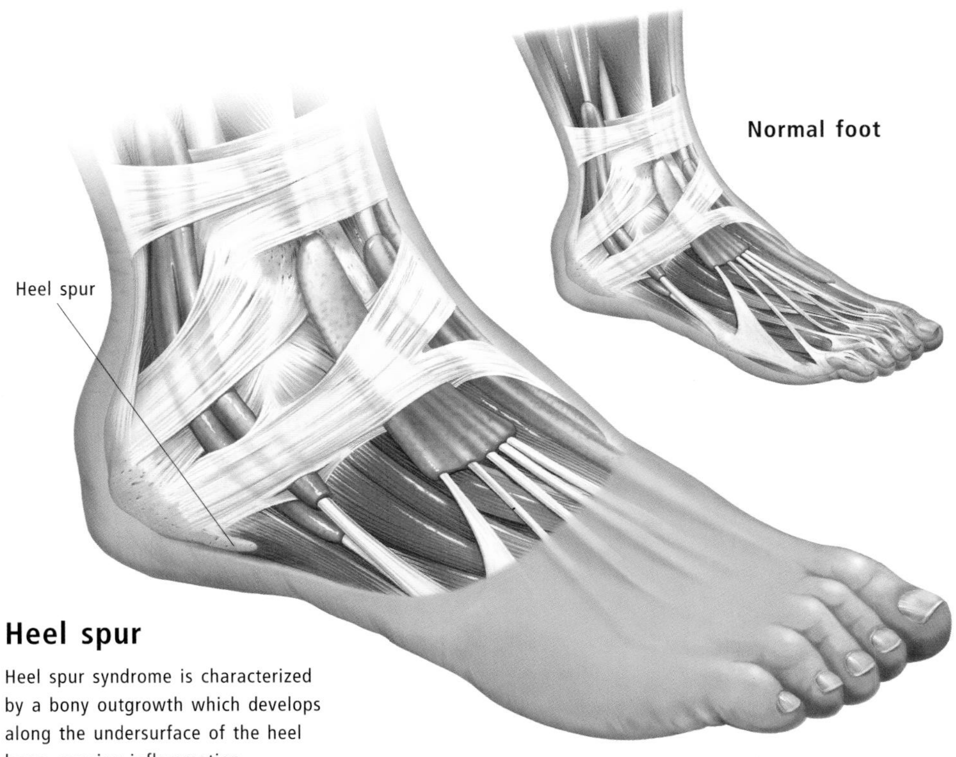

Heel spur

Heel spur syndrome is characterized by a bony outgrowth which develops along the undersurface of the heel bone, causing inflammation.

HEAT RASH

Also known as miliaria or prickly heat, heat rash consists of tiny blisters at the site of sweat pores. When the sweat ducts become blocked, the sweat escapes into other levels of the skin and the blisters result. Extremely hot weather is usually the cause. In newborn babies the sweat glands are not fully developed and will become blocked if the baby is overheated. Babies may also suffer heat rash when they have a fever.

Treatment for babies is a tepid bath, fresh air and lightweight clothing; sometimes calamine lotion may also be necessary. The rash usually disappears in a couple of days, if not then check with a health professional.

Other types of heat rash include miliaria crystallina, seen in people who have a fever or are suffering from sunburn. These blisters are tiny and dewdrop shaped. Miliaria rubra, commonly called prickly heat, is the most common form of heat rash and produces dense, itchy red papules (solid cone-shaped lumps), which appear on the trunk. Miliaria pustules are blisters filled with pus, and miliaria profunda are firm papules found in the vascular layer of the skin.

Treatment for heat rash concentrates on reducing heat, minimizing sweating, and avoiding irritants such as tight clothing.

SEE ALSO *Newborn, Rash, Skin*

HEATSTROKE

Heatstroke, or sunstroke, is a potentially fatal reaction to heat caused by the body's inability to regulate its own temperature. Its onset may be gradual or sudden with headache, weakness and nausea followed by mental confusion and high body temperature around 104–115°F (40–46°C). Shock, convulsions, brain damage, coma and death may follow.

Treatment is to reduce the temperature below 102°F (39°C) by moving the person to a cooler place, removing clothing where possible, and cooling with fans and ice packs to the head, neck, armpits and groin.

SEE ALSO *Body temperature, Fever*

HEEL SPUR

A painful condition, heel spur syndrome is often most severe upon standing after a period of rest. It is typically associated with development of a spur-like projection from the bone of the heel, visible on x-ray

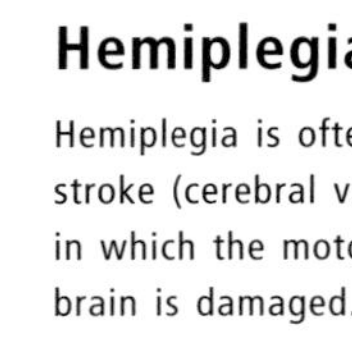

Hemiplegia

Hemiplegia is often the result of stroke (cerebral vascular accident) in which the motor area of the brain is damaged.

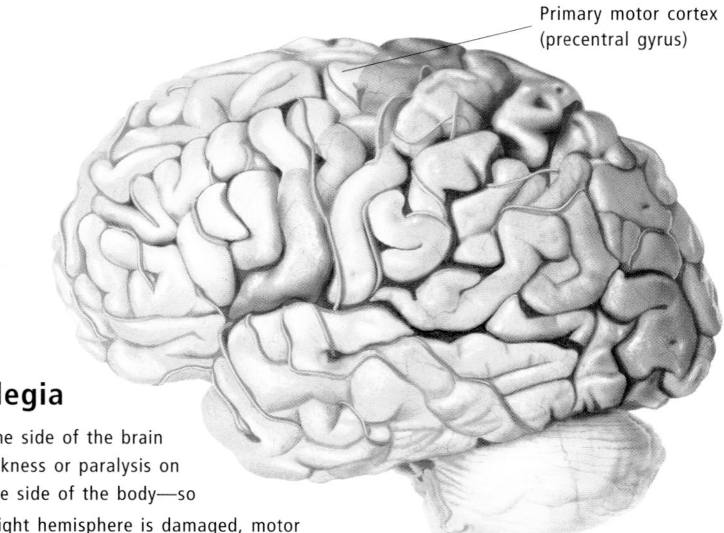

Hemiplegia

Injury to one side of the brain causes weakness or paralysis on the opposite side of the body—so when the right hemisphere is damaged, motor control on the left side of the body is affected.

examination. The spur itself is not the cause of the pain—it is usually secondary to injury or inflammation of the plantar fascia (a ligament that extends from the heel bone across the sole of the foot) which becomes calcified to form the visible spur. Other causes of heel pain include stress fractures and bursitis.

Treatment of the heel spur syndrome may involve providing suitable physical support to the heel, anti-inflammatory drugs or injections, or surgery.

SEE ALSO *Bursitis, Foot, Fractures*

HEMANGIOMA

A hemangioma is a benign, congenital tumor consisting of a cluster of blood vessels. There are two main types: capillary and cavernous.

Capillary (strawberry) hemangiomas are raised red lumps that look like strawberries and are caused by dilated blood vessels. They usually disappear between the ages of five and ten but laser treatment is also available if it is considered necessary.

Cavernous hemangiomas are raised large purple or dark red patches, which can occur anywhere on the body. Treatment may involve surgical removal or, for children, corticosteroids.

SEE ALSO *Birthmarks*

HEMIPLEGIA

Paralysis of two limbs on the same side of the body is known as hemiplegia. When it is the result of a stroke (cerebral vascular accident), the weakness or paralysis occurs on the side of the body opposite to the side of the brain which has been injured by the stroke. Hemiplegia can make it difficult for the affected person to sit, walk or stand, even when their muscles are strong enough.

Acute alternating hemiplegia in children is a rare disorder which occurs before the age of 18 months. The disorder is identified by frequent attacks of paralysis on alternate sides of the body. These paralysis attacks are treated with drugs.

SEE ALSO *Paralysis, Stroke*

HEMOCHROMATOSIS

Hemochromatosis is a disease state characterized by excessive retention of iron within the body, most commonly the result of a recessive genetic disorder associated with increased iron absorption. It can lead to liver damage, pancreatic injury leading to diabetes, and skin pigmentation. Treatment requires repeated bleeding of the patient to deplete body iron stores.

SEE ALSO *Iron*

HEMODIALYSIS

Also known as kidney dialysis, hemodialysis is the filtration of the blood through semipermeable membranes to remove waste materials in patients lacking renal function (renal failure). Blood from an artery is pumped through the artificial kidney, known as a dialyzer, and then returned to the body via a vein. Intermittent dialysis has kept some patients alive for nearly 20 years and though it is mostly carried out in hospitals, some patients, using automatic equipment, can carry out the procedure at home.

SEE ALSO *Dialysis, Kidney*

HEMOGLOBIN

Hemoglobin is a compound found in red blood cells. It consists of an iron-containing pigment, called heme, which combines with the protein globin to form hemoglobin. Oxygen combines readily with hemoglobin: so-called oxyhemoglobin looks bright red, while deoxygenated hemoglobin looks much darker. The role of hemoglobin is to carry oxygen in the blood from the lungs to the body tissues and transport carbon dioxide back to the lungs. Hence hemoglobin is essential to metabolism.

Normal levels of hemoglobin in the blood are approximately 14–17 grams per 100 milliliters (deciliter) for males and 12–15 grams per 100 milliliters for females.

People with anemia have lower than normal levels of hemoglobin. They feel tired and weak and look pale. Anemia may be due to blood loss, inadequate manufacture of hemoglobin in the bone marrow, or the production of abnormal hemoglobin. Sickle cell disease and thalassemia, for example, are genetic diseases caused by different, abnormal forms of hemoglobin.

SEE ALSO *Anemia, Red blood cells, Sickle cell disease*

HEMOLYTIC ANEMIA

Hemolytic anemia is a condition in which red blood cells (erythrocytes) are rapidly destroyed in the blood (a process called hemolysis). It can happen in hereditary conditions where red blood cells are abnormal, such as in sickle cell disease, hereditary spherocytosis or thalassemia. Hemolysis may be caused by antibodies, for example after a mismatched blood transfusion, or it may be a side effect of some drugs.

Treatment for hemolytic anemia involves replacing the blood with blood transfusions and correction of the cause if possible. Sometimes splenectomy (surgical removal of the spleen) is required.

SEE ALSO *Red blood cells, Sickle cell disease, Spleen, Thalassemia*

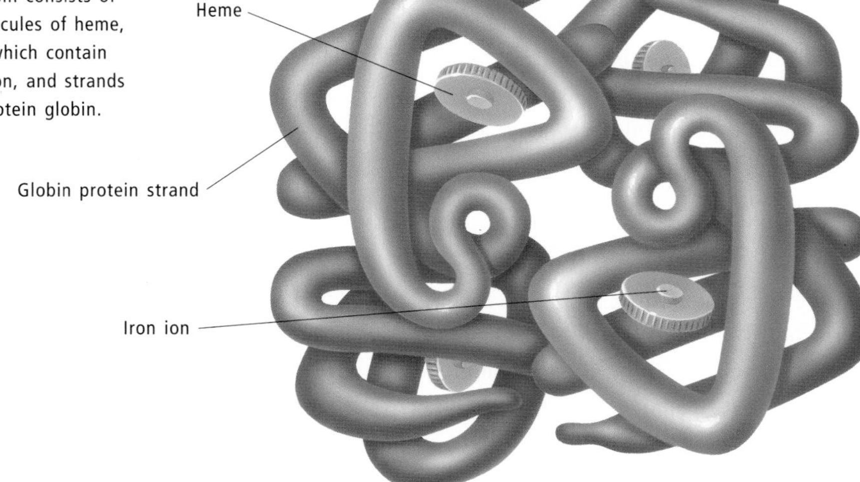

Hemoglobin

Hemoglobin consists of four molecules of heme, each of which contain an iron ion, and strands of the protein globin.

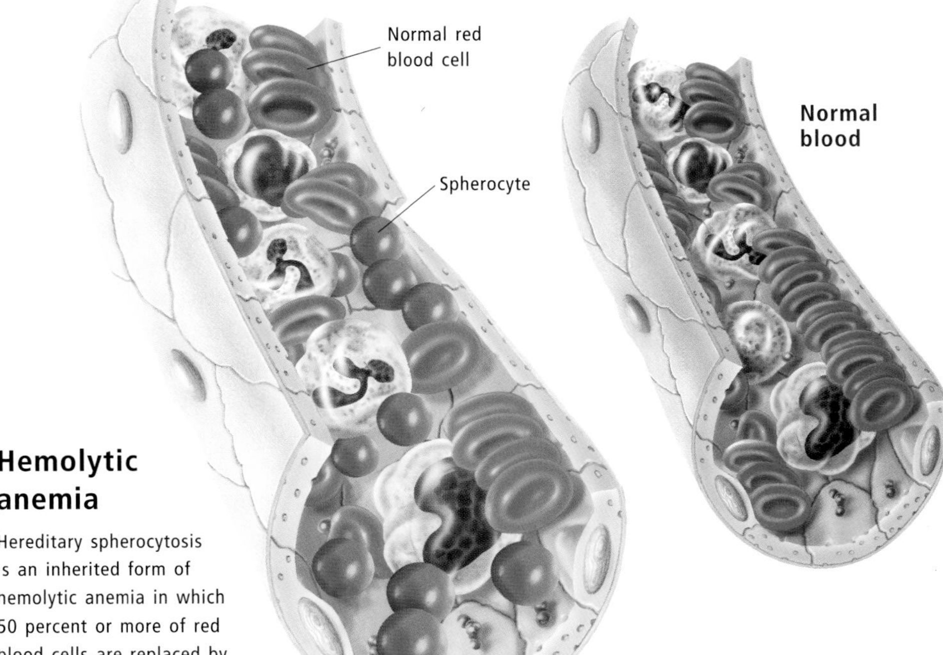

Hemolytic anemia

Hereditary spherocytosis is an inherited form of hemolytic anemia in which 50 percent or more of red blood cells are replaced by abnormal, small round spherocytes.

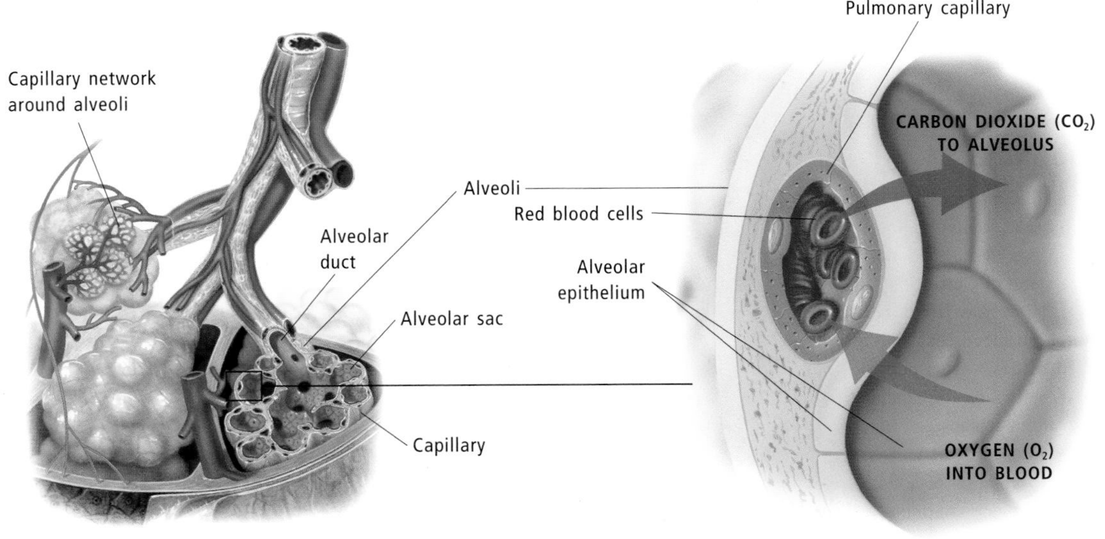

Hemoglobin and oxygen transport

Hemoglobin is the main component of the red blood cell and serves as the oxygen-carrying protein. In the lungs, hemoglobin carries oxygen from the alveoli (air sacs) to the body tissues and transports carbon dioxide back to the alveoli.

HEMOLYTIC DISEASE OF THE NEWBORN

Also called erythroblastosis fetalis, hemolytic disease of the newborn is a condition that develops in an unborn infant when there is an incompatibility between the mother's blood type and the baby's.

As a result of the incompatibility (usually of the Rh blood factor), antibodies that are formed in the mother's blood attack the red blood cells of the fetus. The incompatibility of the blood cells usually leaves the first child unharmed, affecting subsequent pregnancies. It can still affect the first pregnancy if the mother has formed antibodies from a previous blood transfusion. The child may be born with anemia (because of the destruction of fetal blood), jaundice (because the yellow pigment bilirubin is released when the red blood cells break down), an enlarged liver and/or spleen, and generalized swelling (edema).

If too much bilirubin is released, brain and nerve damage (kernicterus) may result. If there is too much edema, fatal heart failure may result (hydrops fetalis).

The condition can be prevented by screening the mother with a blood test during pregnancy. If she is Rh negative, and if the father is Rh positive (meaning there is a chance of an Rh positive fetus and hence incompatibility), then an injection of gamma globulin should be given to the mother during the pregnancy and within a few days of delivery. These injections prevent the development of maternal antibodies against the fetal blood. Babies born with hemolytic anemia may need to be given blood transfusions after delivery.

SEE ALSO *Antibodies, Rhesus (Rh) factor*

HEMOPHILIA

Hemophilia refers to a group of inherited disorders which can result in severe bleeding. An abnormal gene is carried on an X chromosome of unaffected females and produces the bleeding disorder in their affected male children, who have no additional normal X chromosome. Affected males cannot transmit hemophilia to their sons. Fifty percent of the sons of carrier females will be affected, and 50 percent of daughters of carrier females and affected males will be carriers.

In about a quarter of cases, hemophilia develops in a male without a family history of it, due to a new abnormal gene. The abnormal gene can result in decreased production of factor VIII (classical hemophilia) or factor IX (Christmas disease).

Hemophilia varies in severity, depending on the level of the clotting factor involved. If severe, it may cause bleeding in the newborn, from the umbilical cord or at circumcision. More often it appears when the boy starts to walk, causing painful bleeding into joints, especially the knee joint. Milder forms may not be detected until surgery, or until a major injury results in large bruises in the muscles.

The treatment of hemophilia involves preventing excess bleeding when injury occurs by giving the person an infusion of clotting factors obtained from normal blood donors. In the past, giving clotting factor transfusions (and blood transfusions in general) was complicated by the transmission of hepatitis B and HIV (the AIDS virus). In most countries plasma is now treated to destroy viruses and the risk of this is very small, and factor VII can be produced synthetically.

SEE ALSO *Chromosomes, Congenital abnormalities, Genes*

HEMORRHAGE

Hemorrhage is the technical term for bleeding. Bleeding can be a normal process, as with menstrual bleeding, but it is usually abnormal. The commonest cause of bleeding is trauma, such as from a cut. Bleeding is often a sign of damage to a blood vessel. This may be due to minor trauma, such as most nosebleeds; trauma can also cause subconjunctival hemorrhage under the white part of the eye.

Damaged blood vessels may be due to infection; cystitis, for example, can produce blood in the urine, and bronchitis can cause blood to appear in the sputum. Erosion of the vessel wall by acid can cause bleeding from peptic ulcers. Sometimes damage to the blood vessel is the result of a more serious disease, such as inflammation of the blood vessel (vasculitis) or a tumor invading it.

Bleeding can result from increased pressure in veins or arteries. An example of the former is bleeding from hemorrhoids and of the latter is subarachnoid hemorrhage, which is bleeding on the surface of the brain; this is often associated with high blood pressure.

Some types of bleeding can have serious or life-threatening effects, due either to the volume of blood lost or the site of the hemorrhage. Massive blood loss can result from major trauma, such as a car accident or, less often, from deficiencies of platelets or clotting factors. Bleeding that can be serious due to its location includes cerebral hemorrhage and bleeding before (antepartum), during (intrapartum) or just after (postpartum) childbirth.

SEE ALSO *Blood vessels, Bronchitis, Cystitis, Hemorrhoids, Peptic ulcer, Platelets, Subarachnoid hemorrhage, Vasculitis*

Hemophilia

In hemophilia, an important clotting factor in blood, known as factor VIII, is missing due to an abnormal gene. The first stage of clotting (a), in which platelets, leukocytes (white blood cells) and red blood cells spill into the damaged tissues, occurs normally, but in the second stage (b), coagulation between fibrin strands and blood cells fails to occur. This means that the normal formation of a clot cannot occur and bleeding continues instead.

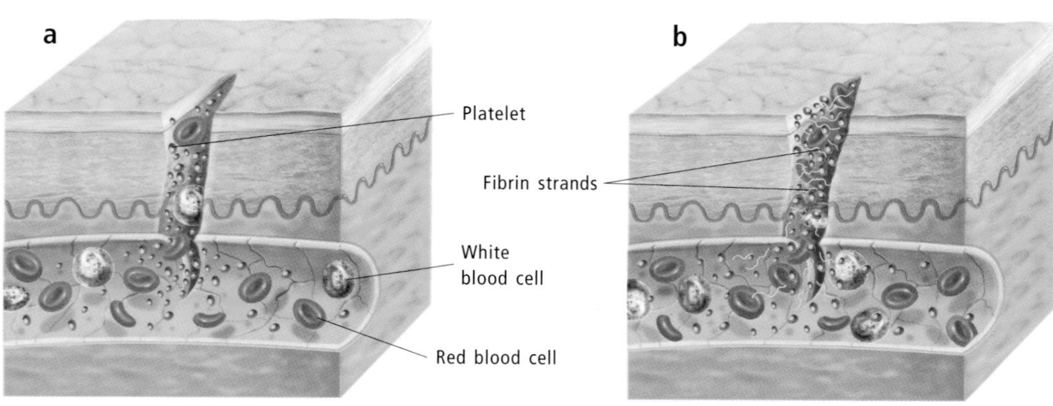

HEMORRHOIDS

Often known as piles, hemorrhoids are enlarged veins in the lower portion of the rectum and anus, which become swollen due to straining when passing feces. They occur frequently in people who suffer constipation and those who sit down for prolonged periods.

Hemorrhoids are common, affecting 1 in every 500 persons. They are especially common during pregnancy, after childbirth and in hepatic hypertension, caused by tumors or cirrhosis. Though not dangerous, they can cause irritation by bleeding or passing through the anus. Symptoms include bright red blood in the stool, anal itching and pain during bowel movements. Painful thrombosis (clotting of blood in the veins) sometimes occurs.

The diagnosis is usually made by a primary care physician (general practitioner), who may use a small tube called an anoscope or proctoscope to visualize the hemorrhoids in the anal canal. More serious conditions such as colonic or rectal polyps and cancer, which can also cause bleeding, must be ruled out.

Hemorrhoids are treated with a high-fiber diet, topical steroid ointment, and surgery in troublesome cases. Surgical techniques include rubber band ligation, cryosurgery and hemorrhoidectomy. These treatments are usually effective, but the condition may recur unless preventive measures—treatment of constipation and a more active lifestyle—are adopted.

SEE ALSO *Anus, Constipation, Rectum, Thrombosis, Veins*

Hemorrhoids

Hemorrhoids are swollen veins in the lower part of the rectum or anus, often due to constipation or prolonged periods of sitting.

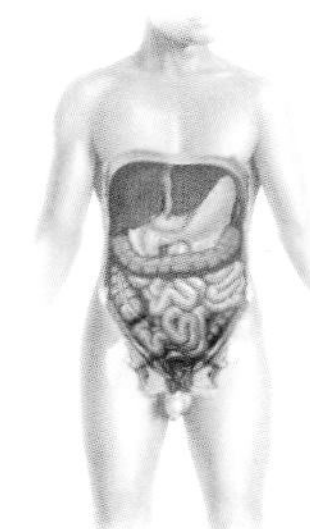

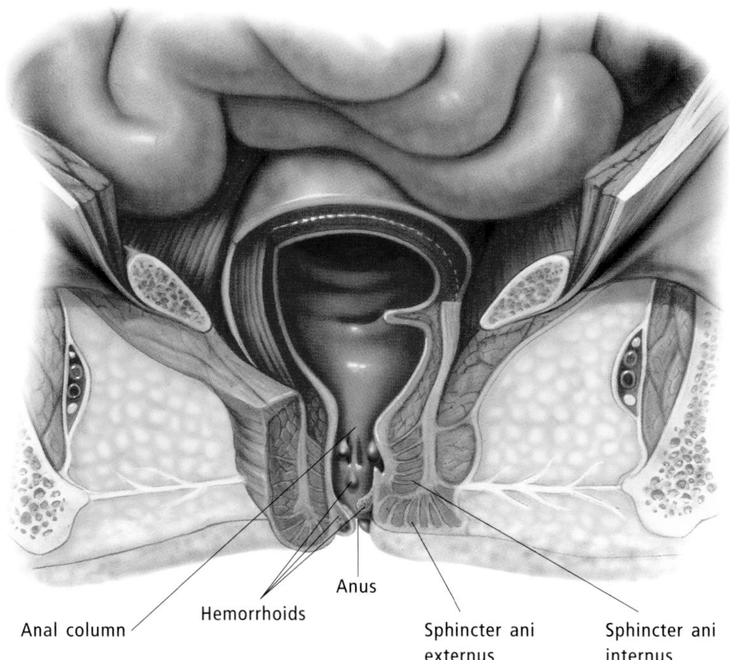

HEPATIC ARTERY

The hepatic artery supplies 30 percent of the liver's blood supply, the rest coming from the portal vein. The common hepatic artery divides into right and left hepatic arteries to supply both sides of the liver with oxygenated blood. The portal vein delivers venous blood from the gut.

SEE ALSO *Liver*

HEPATIC ENPHALOPATHY

Hepatic encephalopathy is an acute complication of liver disorders in which the nitrogen wastes such as urea and other toxins build up in the body and affect the brain and nervous systems.

When liver cells are damaged due to conditions such as alcoholic cirrhosis or hepatitis they cannot effectively do their job of cleansing the body of toxins. This causes metabolic abnormalities marked by symptoms ranging from confusion and memory loss to muscular tremors and speech impairment.

Hepatic encephalopathy may be chronic, leading to dementia, coma and death. It is due to liver failure as a result of diseases like hepatitis, alcoholic cirrhosis, some medications, and cancer, or eating too much protein when you have those diseases.

Treatment involves addressing contributing causes and may include removing toxins from the intestinal tract, preventing ammonia absorption from the intestines, adopting a reduced-protein diet and avoiding medications that are normally metabolized by the liver. Those who are suffering from hepatic encephalopathy may require hospitalization with respiratory and cardiovascular support.

SEE ALSO *Cirrhosis of the liver, Hepatitis, Liver, Nervous system*

Hepatic artery

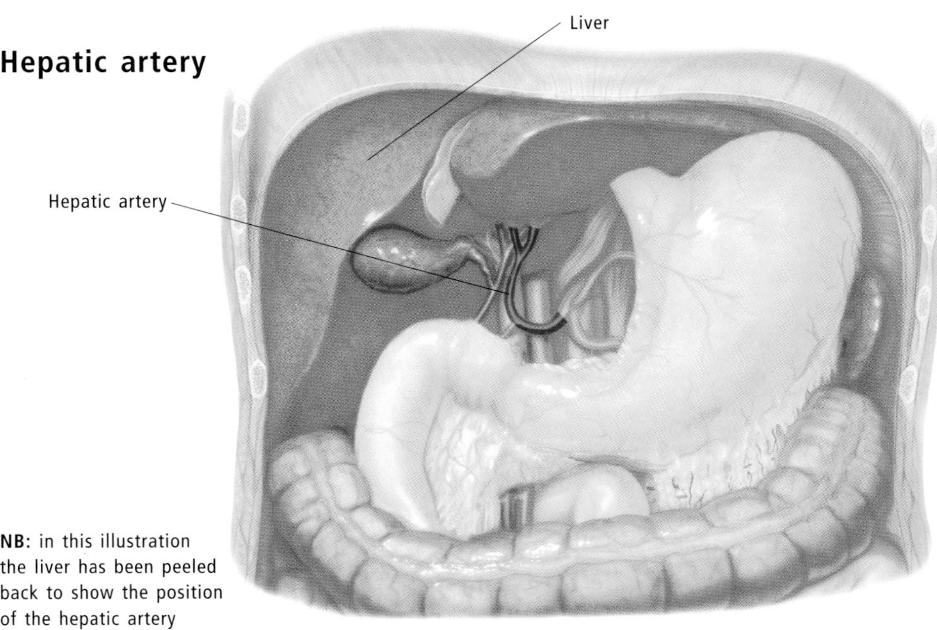

NB: in this illustration the liver has been peeled back to show the position of the hepatic artery

HEPATITIS

Hepatitis is an inflammation of the liver which reduces its ability to function. It can be infectious, when caused by viruses and parasites, or non-infectious, when caused by alcohol, certain drugs and toxic agents such as chemicals found in aerosol sprays and paint thinners. Alcoholic hepatitis is the result of sustained consumption of excessive quantities of alcohol. If caught early enough it can be reversed, if not, it leads to alcoholic cirrhosis.

Hepatitis can also be caused by an autoimmune disorder when the body mistakenly fights its own healthy tissue with its own cells, and can be associated with some illnesses such as Wilson's disease. Most cases are caused by a viral infection.

Some cases of hepatitis are difficult to recognize, but when symptoms are present there may be general weariness, loss of appetite, fever, vomiting, abdominal pain and jaundice (a yellowing of the skin and eyes). This yellowing is a result of the damage the virus inflicts on the liver cells. Viral hepatitis in its acute phase usually lasts from a few days to several weeks. In about 5 percent of cases the symptoms will subside into chronic hepatitis, which can continue for years.

There are seven known hepatitis viruses, labeled A, B, C, D, E, F and G. Hepatitis A (HAV), the most common form worldwide, is spread through oral–fecal transmission. For example, it can be spread via an infected person with fecal matter on their hands handling food that is to be eaten by non-infected people. This virus can also be transmitted in drinking water, or water in contact with food which is infected with raw sewage. Time between exposure and developing symptoms is around 28 days. Treatment is usually bed rest and adequate intake of fluids and most patients recover completely. A vaccine against the disease (made from inactivated hepatitis A virus) is available to those considered at risk. This provides at least ten years protection. Otherwise, good personal hygiene and avoiding raw seafood in areas where hepatitis A is prevalent is recommended.

Hepatitis B (HBV), though not as common as HAV, is becoming increasingly frequent. Spread through blood transfusions, intravenous drug use or unprotected sexual intercourse, this virus remains in the body for many years. Babies born to a mother with HBV have a 95 percent chance of being infected. A more serious disease than hepatitis A, it can become chronic and can lead to permanent liver damage such as cirrhosis or liver cancer. Symptoms appear between 40 days to six months after exposure, and include fatigue, abdominal pain, loss of appetite, nausea, diarrhea, dark urine and jaundice. Treatment is bed rest. A vaccine is available which provides protection for at least 5 years.

Hepatitis C (HCV) was first identified in the 1980s and initially was known as non-A or non-B. It is spread through blood, most commonly through sharing needles among intravenous drug users, occasionally during sexual acts or from an infected mother to her baby. It can also spread through sharing toothbrushes or razors. Symptoms are rarely acute and may be similar to HBV. Of 100 people infected with HCV about 20 will find the virus has cleared up of its own accord after about six weeks, the other 80 will suffer chronically. Treatment is via interferon formulations, which are effective in about 30 percent of patients. In many countries blood and sperm donors are screened for HCV. There is no vaccine.

Hepatitis D (HDV), also known as delta agent, is a parasite of HBV using the B virus to survive and can therefore occur only at the same time as HBV. Transmitted only through infected blood, it has similar symptoms to HBV. Between 70 and 80 percent of those infected will develop cirrhosis. It can be prevented with the same vaccine used against HBV and treatment is with alpha interferon, though this is not always effective.

Hepatitis E (HEV) is similar to HAV. Transmitted in the same way, via feces and oral ingestion, it is found mostly in countries where sanitation is poor or among travelers returning from high-risk areas. It is particularly dangerous for pregnant women, in whom infection can prove fatal. The symptoms of fatigue, abdominal pain, loss of appetite, nausea, diarrhea, dark urine and jaundice are similar to HAV. There are few chronic cases and treatment is rest for two weeks.

Hepatitis F (HFV), was first reported in 1994 and is spread in the same way as HAV and HEV.

Hepatitis G (HGV) is thought to be the cause of large numbers of sexually transmitted and blood-borne cases of hepatitis. Symptoms are not yet fully determined though it does cause both acute and chronic forms of the disease and can infect a person already infected with HCV. There is no vaccine and treatment is rest.

When symptoms associated with hepatitis are present, tests will be conducted on liver function to determine whether the illness is hepatitis or some other problem, such as gallstones, or even cancer. Laboratory tests, including a biopsy, may be necessary.

Anyone who is wanting to travel to areas where hepatitis is a risk needs to consider vaccination and to be aware of the need for good hygiene practices. People who are working in high-risk professions, such as physicians, nurses and dentists, also need to consider vaccination. In some countries, immunization is also advised for newborns and adolescents.

SEE ALSO *Alcoholism, Cirrhosis of the liver, Jaundice, Liver, Viruses, Wilson's disease*

HEPATOMA

Hepatoma, or hepatocellular carcinoma, is a malignant tumor of the liver. It is a primary tumor, that is, originating in the liver rather than spreading to the liver from another site. It is usually associated with an underlying liver disease such as alcoholic cirrhosis or by hepatitis B or C infection, and it is especially common in South Africa and Southeast Asia.

The symptoms are a hard mass in the right upper abdomen, unexplained weight loss and appetite loss, abdominal aches and pains and sometimes jaundice with yellow skin. Blood tests for liver function, an abdominal CAT scan and a liver biopsy may be used by the physician to confirm the diagnosis.

Treatment is not usually successful; in only about 25 percent of cases can the tumor be fully removed and it tends to spread to other organs such as lungs and bones. It is usually considered incurable.

SEE ALSO *Cancer, Cirrhosis of the liver, Hepatitis, Liver*

Cirrhotic liver

If it is not treated, chronic hepatitis can lead to cirrhosis of the liver. When this occurs, nodular, fibrous tissue replaces damaged liver cells and connective tissue in the liver, distorting its smooth surface and internal microstructure.

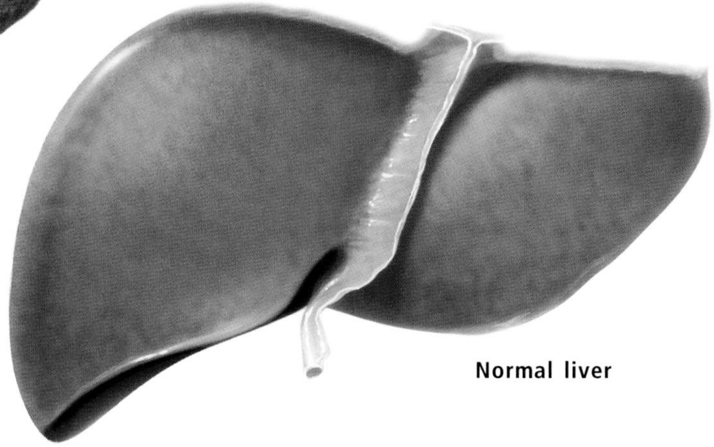

Normal liver

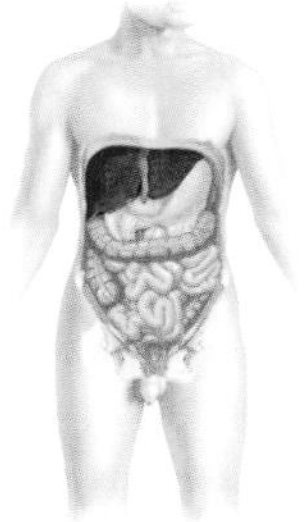

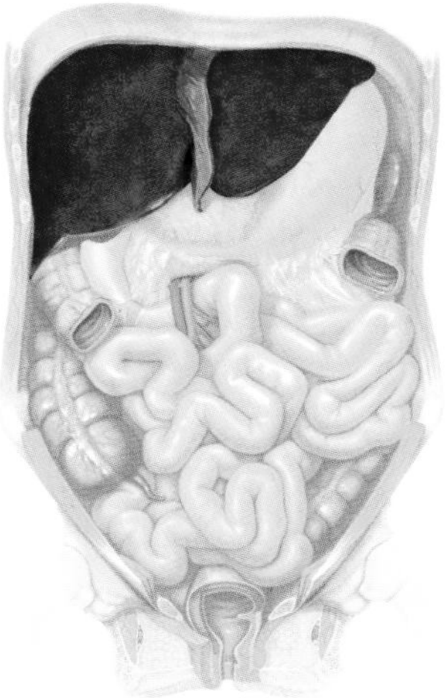

H

Damaged liver microstructure

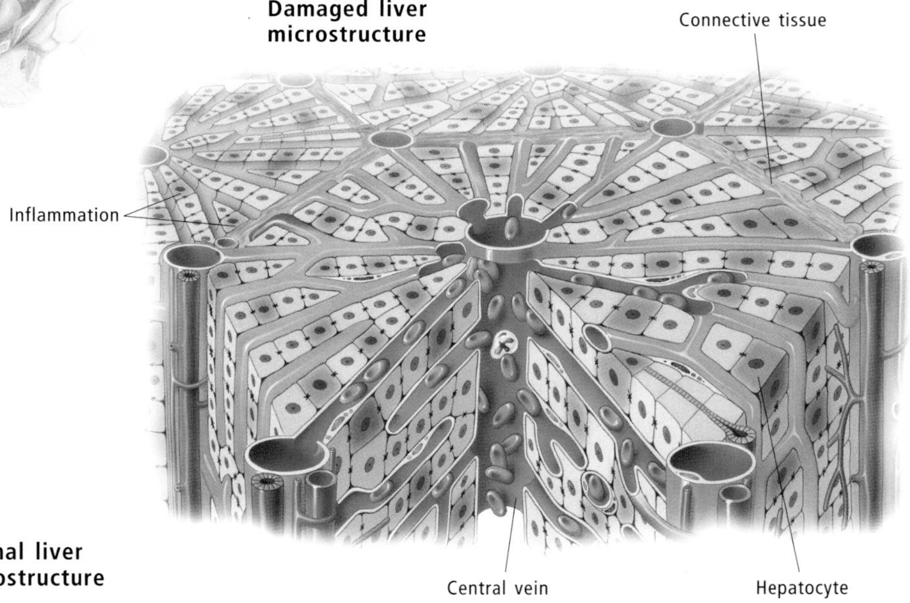

Connective tissue

Inflammation

Central vein

Hepatocyte

Normal liver microstructure

Hepatitis virus

Hepatitis is inflammation of the liver. When caused by a virus, it is called viral or infectious hepatitis. Sometimes viral hepatitis can be transmitted in drinking water.

Scarring of the liver microstructure

Chronic hepatitis causes cirrhosis, a disease in which the normal microscopic lobular architecture of the liver is destroyed. Scarring and distortion of the hepatocytes (liver cells) and connective tissue that form each hexagonal lobule can disrupt the flow of blood through the liver.

HEPATORENAL SYNDROME

This is a syndrome that occurs when a person who has liver dysfunction undergoes a decrease in kidney function as well. The cause is unknown but is thought to involve a reduction of blood flow to the kidney. As in acute renal failure, there is decreased urine production and abdominal swelling. Nitrogenous wastes build up in the bloodstream, causing nausea, dementia, delirium, confusion, and jerky muscle movements.

Hepatorenal syndrome is diagnosed when other causes of kidney failure are ruled out. The treatment is the same as for other types of renal failure and dialysis may be necessary. The underlying liver disease must be corrected and liver transplantation may be necessary.

Despite failing, the kidney itself remains normal in structure and if the liver disease is corrected, or following liver transplantation, kidney function improves. More often, though, the syndrome is a terminal stage of liver failure, cirrhosis, or alcoholic hepatitis, and death occurs from secondary infections or internal bleeding.

SEE ALSO ***Cirrhosis of the liver, Hepatitis, Kidney, Liver***

HERBALISM

The use of herbal medicine is as old and as widespread as humanity. Paleontologists have found bunches of medicinal herbs among the fossilized remains of our Neanderthal ancestors. In traditional societies knowledge of the healing properties of plants, probably originating from an intuitive animal instinct and then continuously tested and evaluated, has been passed down through the millennia.

The earliest written records of herbal medicine, found in the Middle East, India and China, date back over 3,500 years. From these beginnings herbal treatment developed into an important branch of Traditional Chinese Medicine, still widely practiced today, and Ayurvedic medicine in India also makes use of an extensive herbal dispensary.

Traditional European herbalism developed under the ancient Greeks, most particularly Hippocrates (460–380 BC) who emphasized careful diagnosis, minimalist intervention and the use of simple herbal drugs. During the Dark Ages, Greek medicine was kept alive in monasteries, and developed by Arab physicians, most notably Avicenna (AD 979–1037), whose research influenced the practice of herbal medicine from India to Europe for many centuries.

In Renaissance Europe herbalism was augmented by herbs brought from the New World where native Americans had an impressive knowledge of plant remedies. The printing press led to the publication of many self-help herbals; the best known of these, the seventeenth century's Nicholas Culpeper's *Complete Herbal,* is still in print today.

With the Industrial Revolution people lost touch with their herbal folklore as they moved into the cities, turning to herbally based pharmaceutical preparations. In the nineteenth century a number of traditional herbs, such as the quinine-containing Peruvian bark, were analyzed and their active ingredients extracted to make potent drugs.

Professional herbal associations and colleges have sprung up in the twentieth century to pass on the traditions of herbal medicine and to bring them up to date. In Europe the term herbalism has been replaced by "phytotherapy", from the Greek *phyton* (plant) and *therapeuein* (to heal). This renaming reflects a shift by medically-orientated herbalists towards the scientific proof of their plant-based medicines. In Western societies there has been a huge revival of interest in herbal medicine by both people seeking alternatives to drug therapy and by pharmaceutical researchers investigating the active principles of plants for new medicines. In the less industrialized nations locally produced herbs continue to be used as the main source of medicine.

Philosophy

Herbalists use plant-based medicines to encourage the body to make its own corrective healing processes. They favor the use of the whole herb as medicine, rather than its isolated active ingredients, arguing that this provides a gentler, safer and more natural form of treatment than pharmaceutical drugs do.

Where herbalism is based on a holistic philosophy, such as in Traditional Chinese Medicine or Ayurveda, illness is viewed as a result of imbalance and the herbal remedies are given to restore overall harmony within the body. Western herbalists usually work from a dual understanding of both naturopathic principles and orthodox medical diagnosis. They prescribe herbal remedies by matching their therapeutic properties with the patient's symptoms, as well as by seeking to strengthen the body's systems that are under-functioning.

In order to make the right choice of herbs for their patient's condition, professional herbalists undertake a comprehensive assessment of the patient's medical history, lifestyle and physical and psychological symptoms.

Herbal constituents and actions

A herbal medicine may comprise whole plant, part of a plant (root or flower) or an extract of a plant, such as a tincture or oil. Chemical analysis of herbs show up a range of active principles, the most common being tannins, glycoside and alkaloids. Other chemicals are produced as plant hormones, volatile oils, gums or resins. Herbs also contain vitamins, minerals and enzymes in small amounts.

Herbs are classified medicinally according to their specific actions. There are many herbs that may be used, but the main ones include the following.

Alterative herbs are believed to restore healthy function and stimulate the body's nutrition and elimination processes, e.g. yellow dock *(Rumex crispus),* red clover *(Trifolium pratense).*

Antiseptic herbs aim to prevent or reduce infection, e.g. echinacea *(Echinacea angustifolia),* garlic *(Allium sativum).*

Antispasmodic herbs are prescribed to ease muscle tension and spasm, e.g. passion flower *(Passiflora incarnata),* cramp bark *(Viburnum opulus).*

Astringent herbs are said to bind the proteins of the skin and mucous membranes, reducing inflammation, e.g. witch hazel *(Hamamelis virginiana),* sage *(Salvia officianalis).*

Bitter herbs may help to stimulate saliva and gastric juices, aiding digestion and appetite, e.g. dandelion *(Taraxacum officinale),* gentian *(Gentian lutea).*

Nervine herbs

It is thought that some herbs can affect the body's nervous system, restoring harmony and balance. Herbs such as lavender and St John's wort may have a calming effect, whereas other herbs, such as oats, may be stimulating.

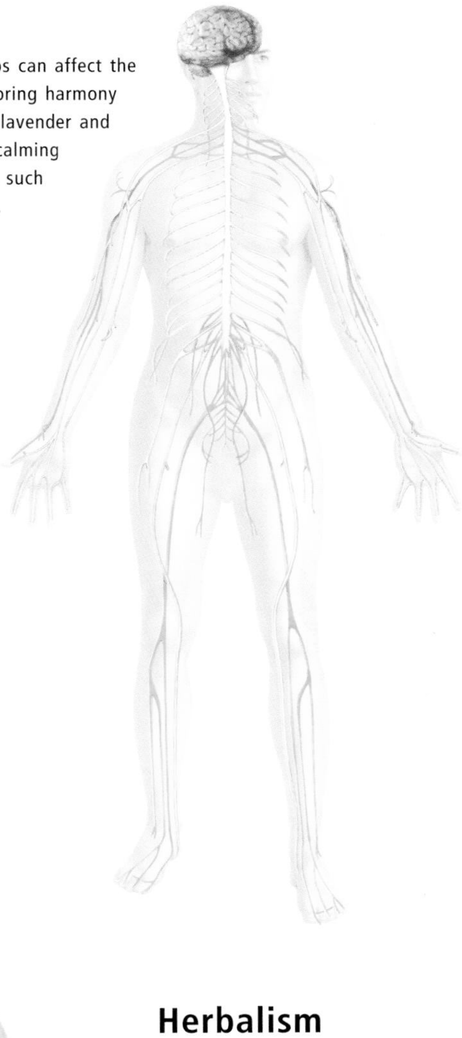

Muscle health

Herbalists prescribe damiana and goldenseal to nourish muscle and tissue. Antispasmodic herbs such as passion flower and cramp bark may help ease muscle spasm.

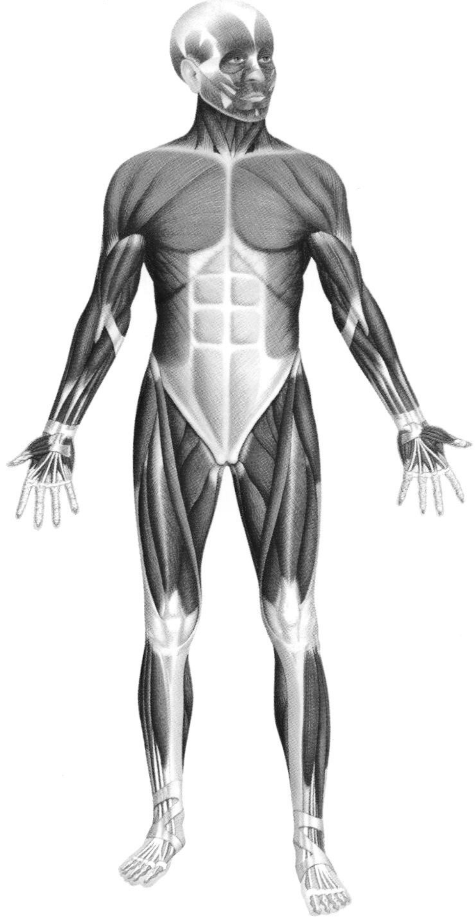

Herbs and digestive disorders

Practitioners of herbal medicine treat disorders of the digestive system with herbs such as red clover, peppermint, fennel and senna. These alterative, carminative and laxative herbs are thought to stimulate the body's nutrition and waste elimination processes.

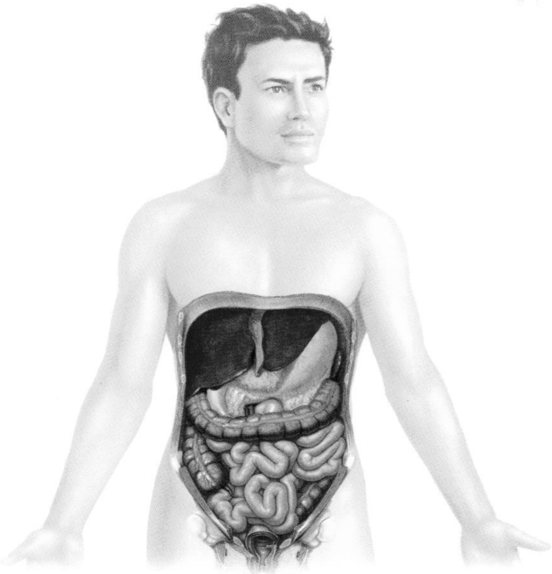

H

Herbalism

Carminative herbs may relieve digestive pain and flatulence, e.g. peppermint *(Mentha piperita)*, fennel *(Foeniculum vulgare)*.

Demulcent herbs are said to form a soothing and protective coating over mucous membranes, e.g. slippery elm *(Ulmus fulva)*, marshmallow *(Althaea officinalis)*.

Diuretic herbs are thought to promote excretion of urine, e.g. parsley *(Petroselinum crispum)*, nettle *(Urtica dioica)*.

Expectorant herbs may aid the softening and expulsion of lung secretions, e.g. licorice *(Glycyrrhiza glabra)*, horehound *(Marrubium vulgare)*.

Laxative herbs may help to promote bowel movements when constipation is a problem, e.g. senna leaves *(Cassia angustifolia)*, aloe vera *(Aloe vera)*.

Nervine herbs aim to soothe and restore the nervous system, and may be sedating, e.g. lavender *(Lavendula officianalis)*, or stimulating, e.g. oats *(Avena sativa)*.

Nutritive herbs may assist assimilation and nourish and build tissues, e.g. alfalfa *(Medicago sativa)*, fenugreek *(Trigonella foenum-graecum)*.

Stimulant herbs are used to temporarily raise the energy level of organs, e.g. chilli *(Capsicum minimum)*, ginger *(Zingiber officinalis)*.

Tonic herbs can help restore and nourish muscle and tissue tone and build energy, e.g. damiana *(Turnera diffusa)*, goldenseal *(Hydrastis canadensis)*.

Herbal preparations

Preparation begins with the correct cultivation and harvesting of a plant to maximize its healing properties. The choice of preparation depends on both the type of active ingredients in a plant and the purpose of the medicine. A herbal medicine may consist of one plant, known as a simple, or it may consist of a combination of herbs. The most common herbal preparations are infusions, decoctions, tinctures, powders and ointments.

Infusions are fresh or dried herbs steeped in boiling water in a pot covered with a lid. Decoctions are usually used for the tougher parts of the herb, such as the root, which is brought to the boil in water and simmered slowly. In a tincture, the herb is steeped in a solvent, usually alcohol or gycerol, and strained off. Powders are pulverized dried herbs mixed in water or put into capsules. Ointments are made with fresh or dried herbs, or tinctures in an oily base.

SEE ALSO ***Ayurvedic medicine, Chinese herbalism, Naturopathy***

H

HEREDITY

Heredity is the genetic transmission of biological traits from one generation to the next. Millions of traits, ranging from eye color and facial features to information the body needs to develop organs and tissues, are transmitted via heredity.

Heredity operates via structures in the nucleus of the cell known as chromosomes, of which there are 46 in humans. The chromosomes contain deoxyribonucleic acid, or DNA, a complex molecule capable of duplicating itself exactly. The chromosomes carry thousands of units of DNA called genes, which contain the hereditary "code". These codes cover the physical, biochemical and physiological traits of a person. For example, some genes govern the development of tissues and organs. Others govern certain traits such as straight or curly hair, color vision and blood type.

Chromosomes are found in pairs, that is, 23 pairs of chromosomes, or 46 in all. When a normal body cell divides, each chromosome produces a duplicate of itself. In this way, newly formed cells have the same DNA, contained in 23 paired chromosomes with the same genes, as the other cells in the body. Sex cells, the male sperm cells and female ova (egg cells), however, have only 23 single chromosomes rather than pairs.

During fertilization a sperm cell and an ovum unite to form a fertilized ovum, or zygote, with the full number of chromosomes. The zygote then begins to reproduce itself by the normal process of cell division, mitosis. As the genetic material in the original cell has come from different parents, it will be a new, unique individual, developing with traits from both parents.

The expression of some traits in the new individual depends on how the parents' genes interact. Some genes are dominant, while others are recessive. The presence of one or two dominant genes results in expression of the dominant trait; for example, the gene for brown eyes in humans is dominant over the gene for blue eyes. To exhibit a recessive trait, such as blue eyes, both genes, one from each parent, must be recessive.

Many characteristics are influenced by more than one gene; skin color, for example, is controlled by several genes. Some depend on other input besides the genes. Although intelligence may be genetically influenced, it is also determined by environmental influences. Sex-linked traits refer to those hereditary traits that are carried on the X chromosome, such as color blindness.

Genetic defects, passed on by heredity from one generation to the next, are the cause of many human diseases and disorders. There may a single defective gene as in muscular dystrophy, phenylketonuria and sickle cell disease, or there may be a predisposition in the genetic make-up for a certain condition, such as arteriosclerosis or some types of cancers. More and more diseases, for example hypertension, are now thought to be made much more likely by particular combinations of genes.

Many genes that cause disease have now been identified, allowing parents the option of genetic counseling and testing during pregnancy. Advances in DNA mapping hold out the promise of one day eliminating or curing many hereditary diseases.

SEE ALSO *Chromosomes, Congenital abnormalities, DNA, Genes, Genetic counseling*

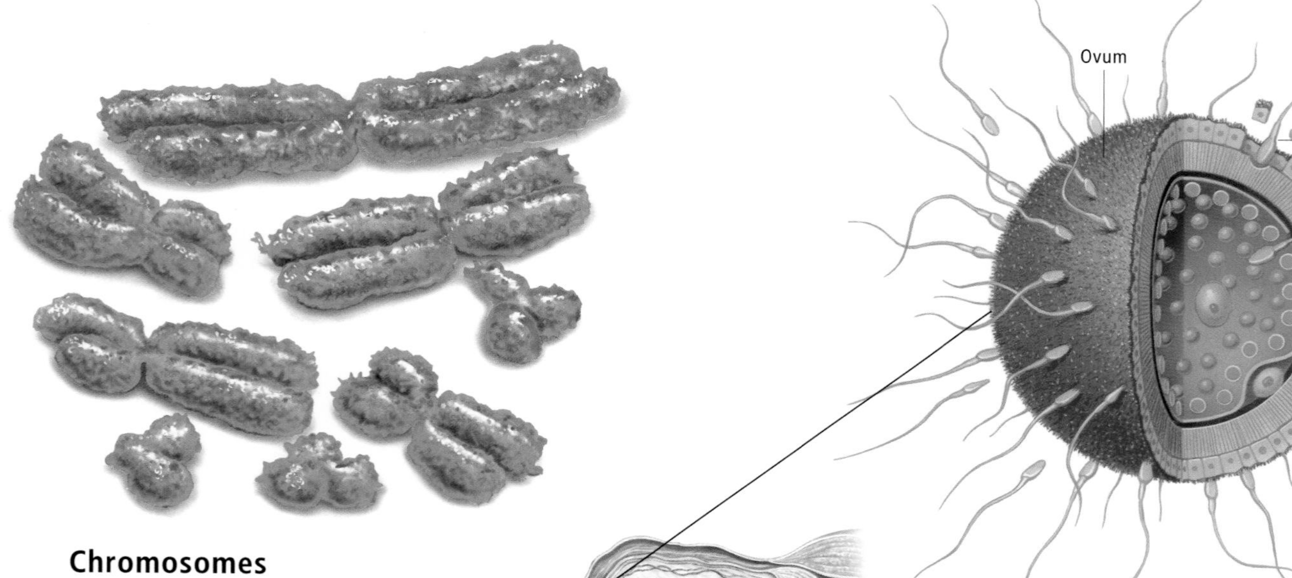

Chromosomes

Chromosomes consist of genes which carry the hereditary code that determines a person's physical and psychological make-up. We all have 46 chromosomes arranged as 23 pairs; one of these pairs is the sex chromosomes. Women have two X chromosomes and men have an X chromosome and a Y chromosome which carries the male features. One sex chromosome from each parent determines the sex of a baby—the embryo inherits an X chromosome from the mother; if it inherits the X chromosome from the father it is a girl, and if it inherits the Y, it is a boy.

Sex cells

Every cell in our bodies contains 46 chromosomes except for sex cells, the sperm (male sex cell) and ovum (female sex cell), which contain only 23 chromosomes. When a sperm fertilizes an ovum the 23 chromosomes from each parent join together to form a zygote containing 46 chromosomes. These chromosomes are then copied into every cell that forms the new embryo. In this way, a child inherits characteristics from each parent.

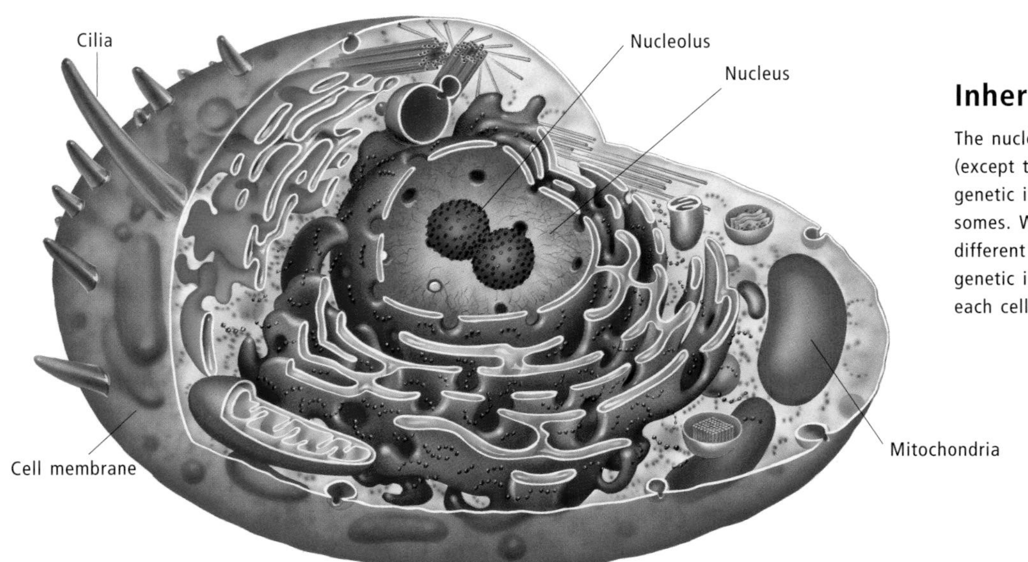

Inherited information

The nucleus of every body cell (except the sex cells) contains genetic information on 46 chromosomes. When cells replicate to form different body parts and organs this genetic information is copied into each cell structure.

Dominant and recessive genes

Most characteristics result from a mixture of two sets of genetic instructions contained in one or more gene pairs, but some features, such as eye color, are determined by a single gene. This dominant gene overrides the instructions of the other recessive gene. A recessive trait can only emerge when two recessive genes for that trait are inherited. The gene for brown eyes is dominant over the recessive gene for blue eyes. This means that two parents with brown eyes can only have a child with blue eyes if the child inherits a recessive blue gene from each parent (a). If one parent with brown eyes has two dominant brown-eye genes, all children will inherit at least one dominant gene (even if one parent is blue eyed) and will all have brown eyes (b). If both parents have blue eyes, neither will have the dominant gene and all children will have blue eyes.

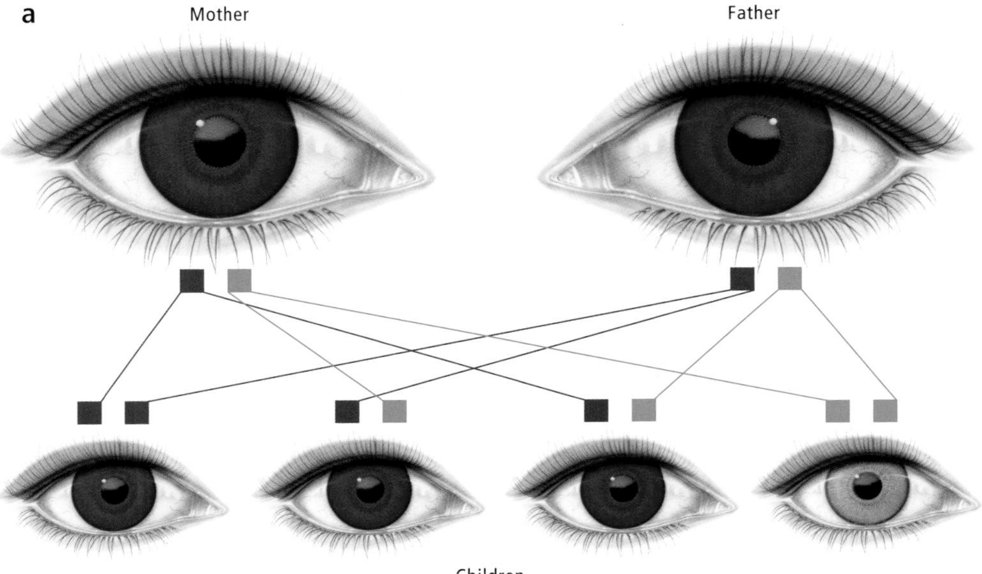

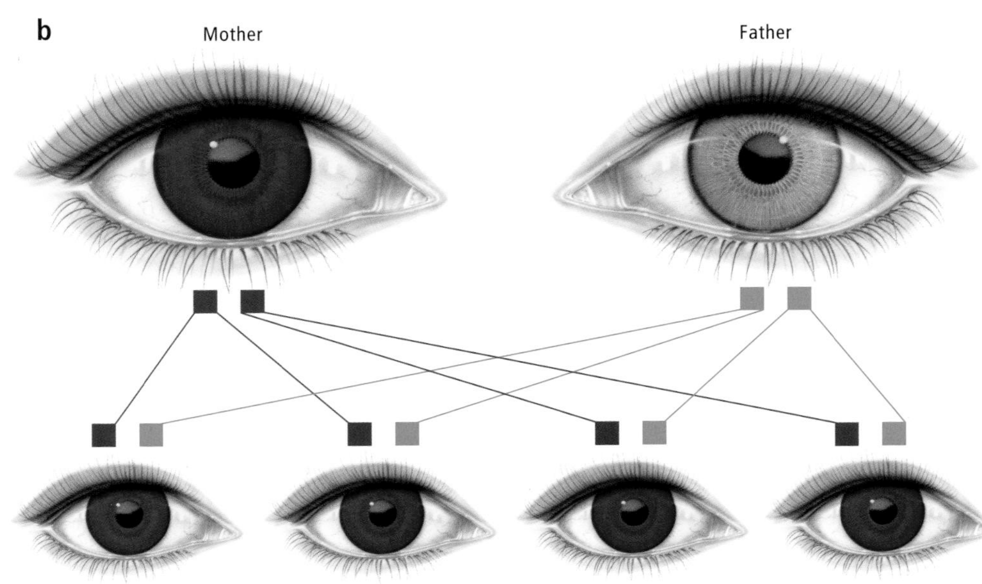

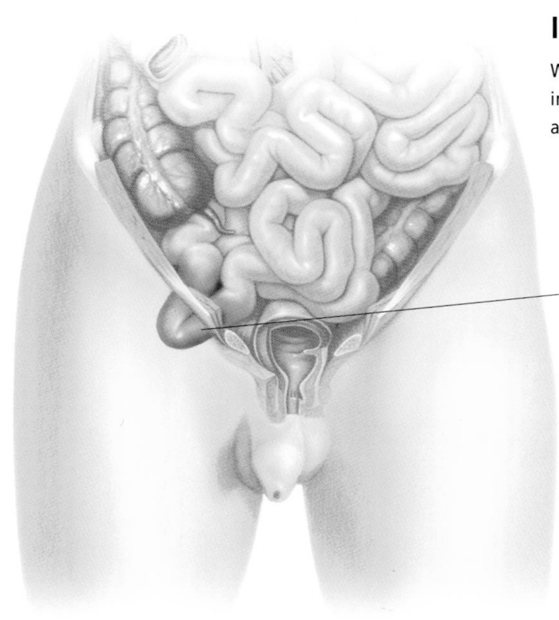

Inguinal hernia

When a hernia occurs, the intestine protrudes through a weakened muscle in the abdominal wall, causing a lump under the skin of the groin.

HERNIA

A hernia is a protrusion of tissue or an organ through an abnormal opening. A hernia may be acquired or congenital, and may occur in various parts of the body, though most hernias involve the abdomen. They occur most often when pressure in the abdomen, during coughing or lifting a heavy weight, for example, forces the soft abdominal tissue through a weakness in the muscles of the abdominal wall.

The most common types of hernia are inguinal and femoral hernia. Both involve protrusion of the small intestine from the abdomen into the groin. Inguinal hernias are more common than femoral, and more common in men than women, as the hernia can enter the inguinal canal more easily. Femoral hernias occur below the inguinal canal at the top of the thigh. Hiatus hernia, in which the stomach protrudes through the diaphragm muscle into the chest, is also common. An incisional hernia is one where tissue has protruded through the site of a previous surgical operation. An umbilical hernia is usually seen in newborn infants and involves protrusion of tissues through the navel.

Some hernias are reducible—they can be pushed back into the abdomen. A hernia which cannot be pushed back is called irreducible, and such a hernia may become pinched ("strangulated"). If the blood supply is cut off, the hernia may become gangrenous and cause death. If there is intestine caught in the hernia, intestinal obstruction, infection and gangrene may follow. These conditions require emergency surgery. Nonurgent treatment of a hernia depends on where it is located. In an infant, an umbilical hernia will usually disappear by itself by the age of about four; if not it can be surgically corrected. An inguinal, femoral or incisional hernia is treated with an operation called a hernia repair, in which a surgeon closes the weakness in the abdominal wall under general or local anesthesia. Hernias in the midline of the abdomen usually do not need treatment. If a person with an inguinal hernia is too old or too unwell for an operation, wearing a truss will sometimes help.

SEE ALSO *Abdomen, Groin, Hiatus hernia*

HEROIN

Heroin (diacetylmorphine) is a drug developed from morphine and was used in the late nineteenth century as a painkiller. When it was found to be highly addictive, its use was prohibited, and it is now illegal in most countries.

Heroin can be inhaled or injected, intravenous injection producing the most rapid uptake. The early effect is a warm feeling known as a "rush". This is followed by a range of reactions that can include drowsiness, relaxation, poor concentration, restlessness, nausea and depression. A heroin "habit" is dangerous to health, is expensive and also has social and legal risks. A heroin dependent person often has to inject several times a day, and can die from contaminated drugs or overdose, or may contract hepatitis B or C, or HIV (AIDS virus) from sharing infected needles.

SEE ALSO *Detoxification, Drug dependence, Hepatitis, Morphine, Narcotics*

HERPES SIMPLEX

The family of herpes viruses includes the herpes simplex viruses (two closely related types) as well as the viruses responsible for chickenpox and for infectious mononucleosis (glandular fever). All these viruses may produce symptoms at the time of initial infection, but in 50 percent of people they persist indefinitely in a dormant form in the sensory nerve cells of an infected person, with later reactivation and recurrent disease.

Herpes simplex virus types 1 and 2 (HSV-1 and HSV-2) infect the skin and mucous membranes. Transmission requires close personal contact, but the initial infection is often inapparent. Both HSV-1 and HSV-2 infect the cells of the nerves that supply the infected area and persist in these cells. Reactivation of herpes simplex virus infections may be triggered by stress, menstruation, exposure to sunlight or by other illnesses. Severe disease may develop if reactivation follows suppression of the immune response.

Most initial infection by HSV-1 occurs in children and is symptomless, although it may be associated with fever, a sore throat, or ulceration of the mouth. Because infection with HSV-1 usually involves the skin and mucous membrane of the mouth, recurrences are manifested as "cold sores" that typically develop on the lip margins.

In contrast, HSV-2 is mainly spread by sexual transmission and thus produces genital herpes, although some 10–15 percent of cases of genital herpes are due to HSV-1. The initial infection usually produces small blisters which burst and turn into sores that are often painful or itchy. These involve the genital area, buttocks and thighs, and can be accompanied by

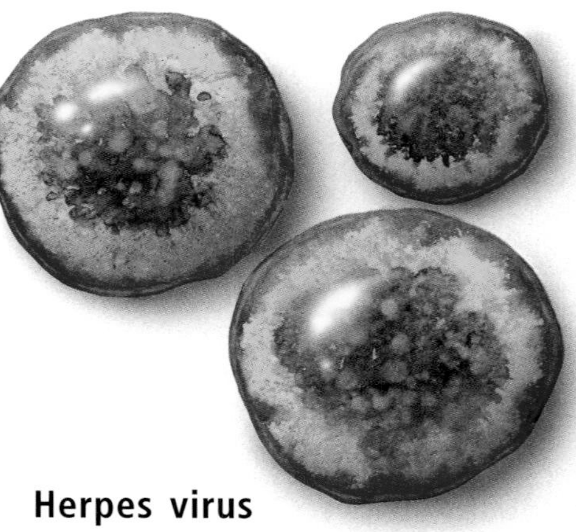

Herpes virus

fever, headache and a flu-like illness. Recurrences are associated with similar skin and mucous membrane changes and may be preceded by flu-like symptoms.

Diagnosis of the common forms of herpes virus infection is largely based on medical history and physical examination; in addition, various laboratory tests are available. While there is no treatment available that will eliminate the infection, it can be quite effectively controlled using different antiviral drugs, which need to be administered as early as possible in the course of the primary infection or episode of recurrence.

Severe forms of infection are uncommon but include inflammation/ulceration of the cornea of the eye (mostly HSV-1); encephalitis (brain inflammation and tissue destruction) (also mostly HSV-1); and disseminated infection in the newborn (mostly HSV-2) and in individuals with HIV (AIDS).

There are a number of alternative therapies that may help to alleviate the symptoms of herpes. Acupuncture may help to relieve the symptoms and may also strengthen the immune system against the virus, reducing the frequency and intensity of subsequent attacks. Herbalism prescribes echinacea and garlic internally, and aloe vera gel, St John's wort *(Hypericum)* or calendula externally to soothe pain and itching. Homeopathy prescribes specific remedies according to the patient's symptom picture. Naturopathy prescribes vitamins B and C, zinc, lactobacillus acidophilus, lauric acid and lysine during an attack to weaken the virus. Dietary measures include fruits, vegetables and foods high in protein, and avoidance of chocolate, coconut, peanuts, wheat, soy beans and peas. One can bathe or wash in warm salty water and apply zinc cream to the affected areas.

SEE ALSO *Antiviral drugs, Chickenpox, Cold sores, Infectious mononucleosis, Viruses*

HIATUS HERNIA

Hiatus (hiatal) hernia is a condition in which part of the stomach protrudes through the opening through which the esophagus passes, through the diaphragm, into the chest cavity. There are two types of hiatus hernia: sliding and rolling.

Sliding hiatus hernia is the most common (about 90 percent) and involves the sliding of the upper stomach (cardiac part and cardioesophageal junction) through the esophageal opening in the diaphragm.

Patients complain of heartburn, a burning pain in the lower front of the chest and the upper abdomen, particularly after meals and when lying down. They may also experience regurgitation of bitter or sour-tasting fluid (waterbrash) as far as the throat and mouth, particularly at night. Difficulty in swallowing may also occur due to swelling of the lining of the lower esophagus. Continued regurgitation of stomach juices into the esophagus can result in reflux esophagitis.

Sufferers are often advised to take antacids, eat smaller meals more frequently, elevate the head of the bed and avoid lying down after meals. Surgical treatment of sliding hernias is aimed at anchoring the gastroesophageal junction in the abdomen and tightening the esophageal opening through the diaphragm. Most patients will experience a good outcome from surgical treatment.

Rolling hiatus hernia is also known as paraesophageal hiatus hernia. The cardioesophageal junction, where the esophagus and stomach join, stays within the abdominal cavity; it is usually the fundus of the stomach which protrudes into the thorax. Patients complain of gaseous eructations (burping), a sense of pressure in the lower chest and, occasionally, irregular heartbeat.

Rolling hiatus hernia is usually treated by the use of surgery which aims to fix the part of the stomach which herniates to the back of the anterior abdominal wall.

SEE ALSO *Diaphragm, Esophagitis, Esophagus, Heartburn, Hernia, Stomach*

HICCUPS

Hiccups are spasmodic involuntary contractions of the diaphragm that cause a disturbance in the rhythm of breathing. They develop when some stimulus, such as rapid eating, triggers a sudden spasm of the diaphragm. The irregular rhythm causes a sudden closure of the vocal cords, resulting in the characteristic hiccup noise.

Hiccups are most likely to occur after a meal when the stomach is stretched. They usually begin without warning and stop in the same way. There are dozens of folk remedies—from taking a tablespoon of sugar to drinking from a glass of water backwards—but most do not work and the hiccups disappear of their own accord. Remedies which do work involve increasing the carbon dioxide in the blood, and include holding the breath, and breathing into a paper bag (though this is not advised as it is dangerous). Persistent hiccups may require medication.

Far less commonly, hiccups may also be caused by irritation of the diaphragm during pneumonia, or after surgery; or from harmful substances in the blood, such as those which result from kidney failure; or from interference with the part of the brain that controls the breathing, due to a stroke.

SEE ALSO *Breathing, Diaphragm*

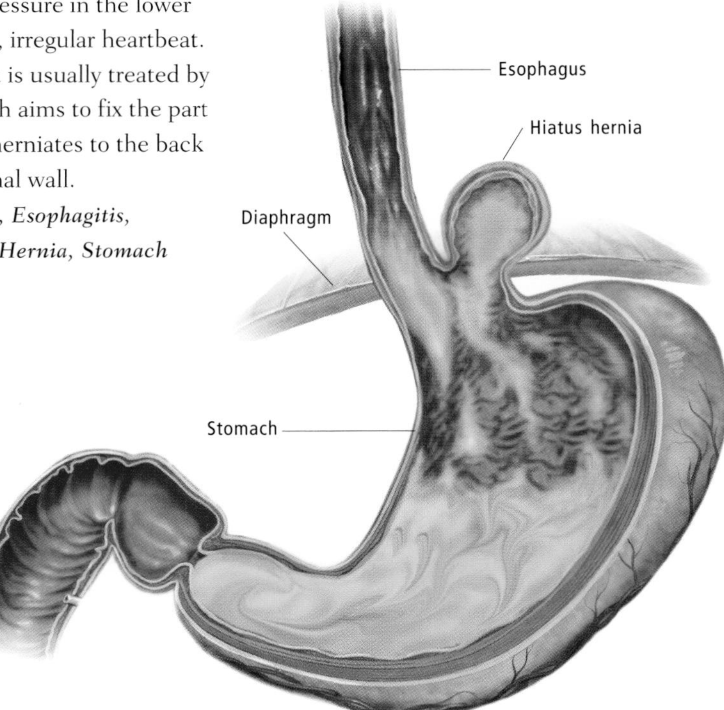

Hiatus hernia (rolling type)

The stomach bulges out of the weakest part of the diaphragm, through which the esophagus passes. Sufferers can experience heartburn and indigestion.

HIP

The hip (coxal or innominate) bone is made up of three bones: the ilium, ischium and pubis. The three bones fuse with each other at the acetabulum (part of the hip joint) at 14–16 years of age.

The crest of the ilium is found at the waist, laterally, below the ribs. The tuberosities of the two ischia are the bony knobs that we sit on. The pubic bones are at the front at the lower limit of the soft anterior abdominal wall. The left and right hip bones and the sacrum form the bony pelvis. The hip joint is formed by the acetabulum, a cup-shaped socket and the rounded head of the femur.

The head of the femur is covered with cartilage and lubricated by synovial fluid. The whole joint is enclosed in a fibrous capsule which is loose enough to permit free movement yet strong enough to hold the femoral head securely in place. The muscles of the hip joint are large and powerful to hold the joint firm and to move the thigh for walking and running. They include the gluteus maximus and the gluteus medius at the back, and the rectus femoris at the front.

More than half the round head of the femur is held within the acetabulum and surrounding cartilage, making the hip joint extremely stable and strong, with capability of rotation second only to the shoulder joint and limited only by the flexibility of its supporting ligaments. The hip transmits the entire weight of the upper body to the head and neck of each femur and is at its most solid during weight-bearing activities.

The strength and flexibility of the pelvis and hip allows the femur to descend vertically while bearing the body's full weight, an ability vital for the development of standing, running and jumping.

Blood supply to the hip joint is from the femoral arteries. Several nerves supply the hip joint and pain in the hip can be misleading as it may be generated from the spinal column. Loss of blood supply due to accident or dislocation can result in pain which radiates to the knee.

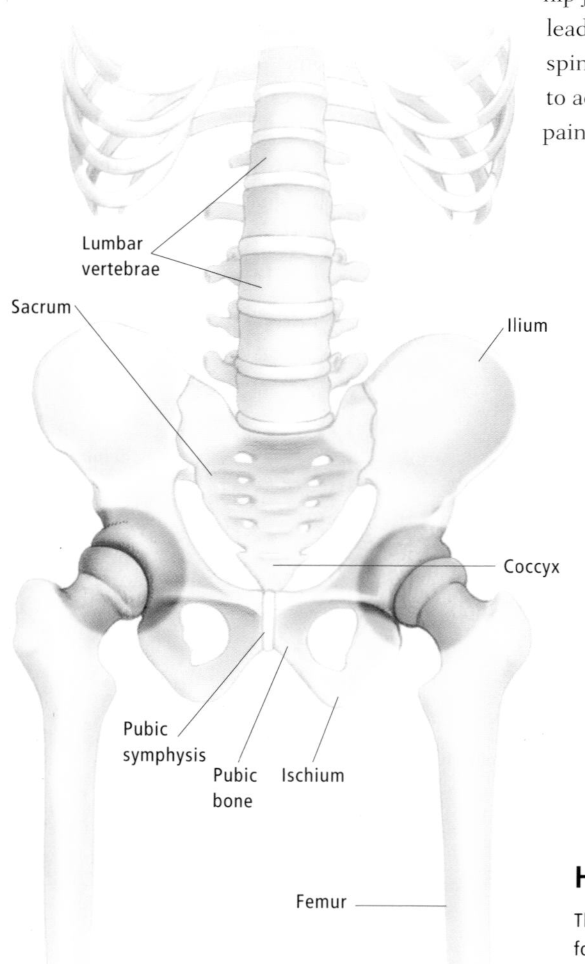

Hip bone and joint

The hip is a ball-and-socket joint formed at the point where the thigh bone (femur) meets the pelvis. The rounded end of the thigh bone fits into the cup-shaped socket.

Disorders

Joint abnormalities, deformities or malalignments are revealed by radiography or, in newborns, by observation. Congenital dislocation of the hip is found in approximately 15 babies per 10,000 births and may affect one or both joints. It is eight times as common in girls as boys. In such cases, the end of the femur is not properly located in the socket (acetabulum).

To test for congenital dislocations of the hip, the baby is laid face upwards and the thighs are moved sideways to see if movement produces a clunk as the head of the femur enters the pelvic socket. Instability of the joint at this stage can right itself but if present after five days, treatment will usually be recommended. The pelvic harness, which holds the thighs so that the head of the femur is securely in its socket, is worn for a few months, until radiography reveals that the abnormality has been corrected.

If further treatment is required, the baby may wear abduction splints for a further few months. Clicks or noises heard on moving a baby's hips should always be investigated as untreated abnormalities can lead to limping and permanent deformity.

Disorders affecting growth of bones during childhood, such as rickets, can affect the formation of the head of the femur and the joint. Slipped epiphysis of the femur may occur in late childhood and adolescence and is a dislocation of the growing head (epiphysis) of the femur from the femoral neck. Perthe's disease also occurs around this age. Symptoms are increasing discomfort at the hip with pain referred to the knee.

Osteoarthritis is a degenerative disorder common in adults of middle age, which involves the abrasion and loss of cartilage at the surfaces of joints with outgrowths of bony ridges at abraded surfaces.

Osteoarthritis of the hip joint may be secondary to a structural abnormality, or of a primary nature, involving no underlying abnormality. One underlying cause is congenital dysplasia, dislocation or subluxation of the hip, where the head of the femur and socket fit badly, which can arise in infancy due to genetic factors or swaddling, which leaves the thighs extended. This delays development of the hip joint, which can become deformed once the child begins to walk.

Osteoarthritis of the hip joint in people under age 40 often follows from disease or disorder and may require surgery to correct it. This may involve osteotomy, reshaping the end of the femur, or removal of diseased tissue and replacement with an artificial hip. As age advances, degenerative diseases and hip replacements become more common.

Injuries

Trauma or violent stresses can result in dislocation or fracture of the hip bone or fracture of the neck of the femur. Such injuries commonly result from falls onto hard surfaces in sports such as ice-skating or athletics. Automobile accidents are also a common cause because of the high velocity of secondary impacts, such as when the knee strikes the dashboard. This type of stress can dislodge the head of the femur from its socket, causing dislocation with injury to surrounding tissues. Where there is greater force, or in persons with osteoporosis, the neck of the femur may fracture with far greater damage to surrounding tissues.

Persons over 60 are at risk of serious fracture from even trivial falls, because their bones and supporting tissue structures are likely to be weaker than those of younger persons, especially if the person has osteoporosis. The femur is the largest bone in the body and its fracture is one of the most serious, sometimes taking a year to heal.

Hip replacement

This is an increasingly common and successful option in instances where a joint has deteriorated through rheumatoid arthritis, osteoarthritis or osteoporosis. The materials used are constantly improving, extending the useful life of replacement joints and reducing the possibility of an adverse response from the body's tissues. Stainless steel in early artificial joints has been replaced by titanium alloys, which are usually lighter and more stable.

The artificial hip usually consists of a highly polished metal (cobalt-chromium) ball, which replaces the head of the femur, and a cup made of extremely tough polyethylene, to replace the socket (acetabulum). It is important to avoid abrasion between the two surfaces as small particles of debris can cause inflammation. The materials used must simulate the mechanical properties of bone to avoid uneven stresses which would weaken bones and induce reshaping.

SEE ALSO *Femur, Fractures, Joints, Osteoarthritis, Osteoporosis, Pelvis, Rheumatoid arthritis, Rickets, Skeletal system, Synovial fluid*

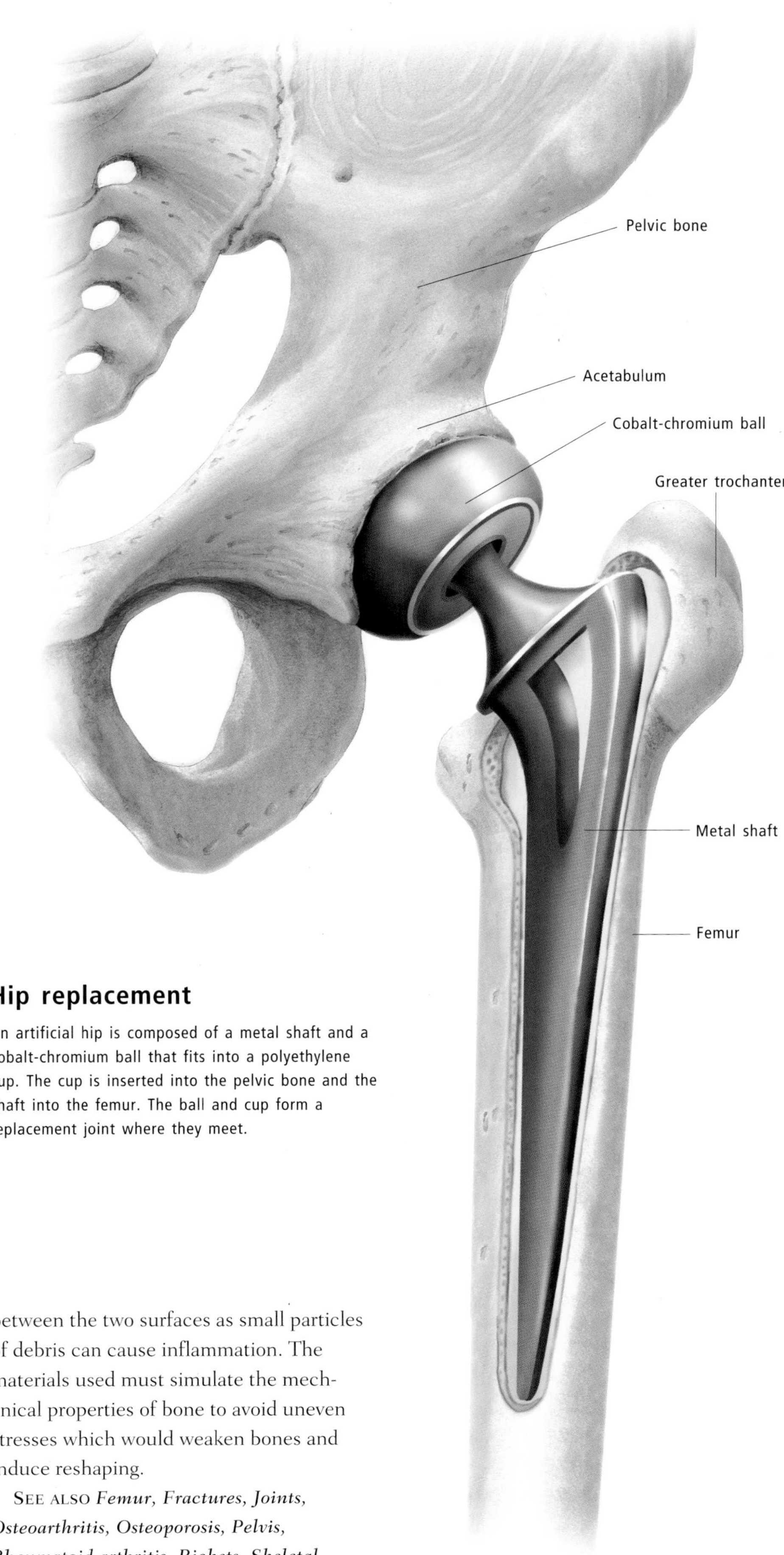

Hip replacement

An artificial hip is composed of a metal shaft and a cobalt-chromium ball that fits into a polyethylene cup. The cup is inserted into the pelvic bone and the shaft into the femur. The ball and cup form a replacement joint where they meet.

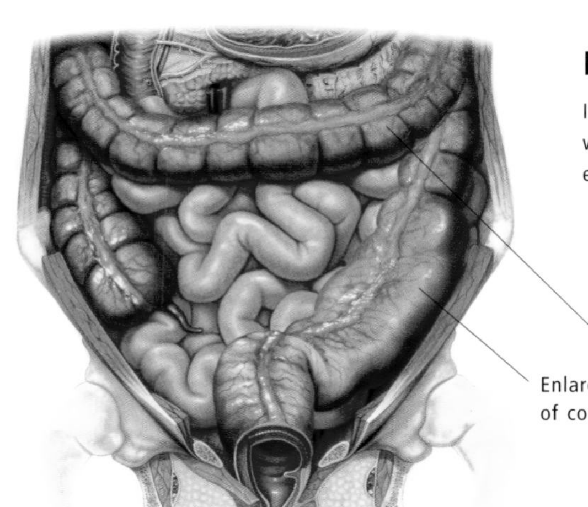

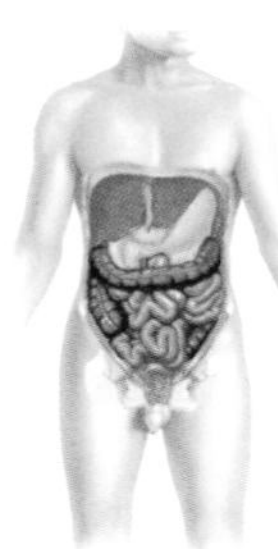

Hirschsprung's disease

In this condition, the nerve cells in the wall of the colon are absent, resulting in enlargement, constipation and obstruction.

H

HIRSCHSPRUNG'S DISEASE

Hirschsprung's disease is a congenital condition (present at or before birth). The basic abnormality is the absence of nerve cells in the wall of the lower large bowel. Without these nerve cells, the bowel is unable to make the peristaltic movements which propel the feces towards the anus. Consequently, the infant will have constipation, abdominal swelling, reluctance to feed and vomiting.

Temporary relief may be obtained by washing out the colon with a saline solution, but in the long term the child may need a colostomy to allow evacuation of the large bowel.

SEE ALSO *Bowel, Colon, Congenital abnormalities, Intestines*

HIRSUTISM

Hirsutism is the excessive growth of hair, or the presence of hair in areas that are not usually hairy. It is more common in women, when unwanted hair may appear on the face, chest, around the nipples, lower back and buttocks and inner thighs.

The cause is usually a hormonal disturbance, such as polycystic ovarian syndrome, or, less commonly, an ovarian tumor or a disorder of the adrenal gland. Drugs may also cause the condition, especially steroids, phenytoin, minoxidil and diazoxide. Mild hirsutism may occur naturally after menopause. Other signs of virilization (such as clitoral enlargement and baldness) are usually absent.

The treatment depends on the cause. Hormonal causes often respond to oral contraceptives or spironolactone, though it may take 3–6 months before an improvement is noticed. Meanwhile, unwanted hair can be removed by shaving, waxing, tweezing, use of depilatories, and/or electrolysis. Also, as obesity seems to worsen the condition, losing 10–15 percent of body weight may ease hirsutism in obese persons.

SEE ALSO *Adrenal glands, Hormones, Virilization*

HISTAMINE

Histamine is a chemical messenger found in all body tissues that reacts with histamine receptors on cell surfaces causing change in certain specific bodily functions. Histamine affects smooth muscles, such as those in the intestine, heart and lungs, causing them to contract; or can cause the smaller blood vessels to dilate resulting in a fall in blood pressure and release of lymphatic fluid into surrounding tissues, as when redness and swelling follows a sting or bite.

Overproduction of histamine can occur when the body comes into contact with something to which it is allergic, e.g. pollen in hay fever sufferers. Extreme cases can be life threatening.

SEE ALSO *Allergies, Anaphylaxis, Antihistamines, Hay fever*

HISTOPLASMOSIS

Histoplasmosis is infection caused by the fungus *Histoplasma capsulatum*, which grows in bat or bird droppings. Humans may inhale dust containing the spores; this causes no problems for most people but in people with damaged immune systems (such as AIDS sufferers) the fungus multiplies in the lungs and may spread to other organs. The disease can cause lung damage with weight loss, cough, and breathlessness, fever, fatigue and muscle pains. Treatment is with anti-fungal medications.

HIV

HIV (human immunodeficiency virus) is a retrovirus, one of a unique family of viruses consisting of RNA surrounded by a protein envelope. It attacks a type of white blood cell critical to the immune system known as helper T lymphocytes, or T4 helper cells. This may eventually cripple the immune system and leave the body vulnerable to a variety of life-threatening illnesses that are ordinarily harmless. Transmission of the virus can occur through sexual contact, via blood through transfusions or needle sharing, and from a pregnant woman to the fetus.

A person may be HIV-positive for many years before developing illnesses that indicate a serious deterioration of the immune system. At that stage, a person is said to have acquired immunodeficiency syndrome (AIDS). There is, at present, no cure for AIDS, but drugs have been developed that suppress replication of HIV virus in the body, and so effectively arrest or stop the progress of the disease.

SEE ALSO *AIDS, Viruses*

Histamine

When allergens (like pollen) enter the body, antibodies to the allergen trigger histamine release from circulating mast cells, causing symptoms such as runny nose and sneezing.

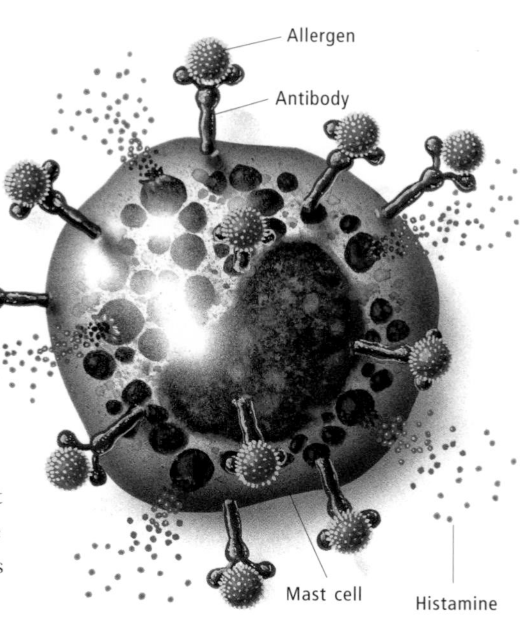

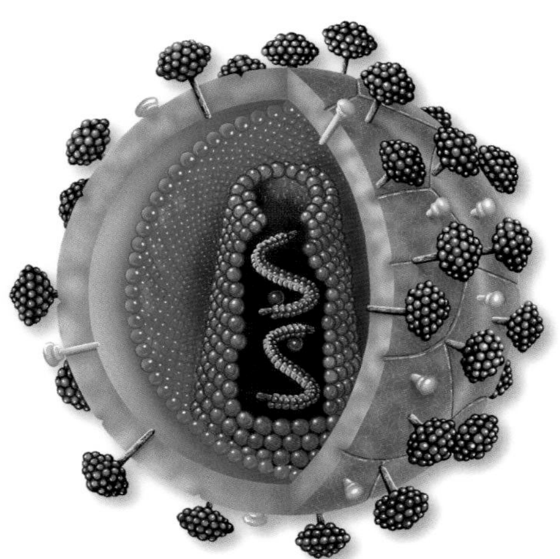

Human immunodeficiency virus (HIV)

HODGKIN'S DISEASE

Hodgkin's disease is a type of lymphoma (a cancer arising in lymph nodes), which was first described by Thomas Hodgkin in 1832. Lymphomas are a relatively common group of cancers (typically ranking fifth or sixth in frequency among both men and women) of which Hodgkin's disease makes up a variable proportion (approximately one-fifth in most economically developed nations). What makes Hodgkin's disease distinctive is that it usually develops in young to middle adult life, when most other types of cancer are rare.

Hodgkin's disease is more enigmatic than many other cancers. As is true for most tumors, the exact cause of its development remains unknown. There is a strong suspicion that certain viral infections may contribute to its emergence, at least in a proportion of cases, but the sequence of events by which this might occur is not clear. Even the specific cell type that gives rise to Hodgkin's disease remains uncertain and it appears quite likely that more than one type of cell is involved.

Hodgkin's disease typically produces enlargement of the lymph nodes early in the disease. The patient may notice a swelling, for example in the neck, but the nodes are usually not painful. Quite often, patients with Hodgkin's disease develop symptoms such as fever, weight loss and night sweats as part of their illness, which are triggered by chemical signals released by the cancer cells and by the patient's response to the tumor. In addition, some patients develop complicating infections, because Hodgkin's disease is associated with suppression of the immune response, although the reason for this is not entirely clear.

The microscopic appearance of Hodgkin's disease is quite distinct from other types of lymphoma, which allows it to be diagnosed by examination of a sample of involved tissue. Unlike most other lymphomas, it usually does not spread far and wide at an early stage, but instead extends progressively from one group of nodes to the next, with later involvement of the spleen and other tissues. This relatively slow and orderly progression may be one reason why Hodgkin's disease is more responsive to treatment with anti-cancer drugs than many other varieties of lymphoma.

The extent of spread at the time of diagnosis is the most important determinant of the patient's likely response to chemotherapy. Also relevant is the specific variety of Hodgkin's disease that the individual has developed. With modern combination chemotherapy, the disease is controlled in the great majority of patients with early stage disease, and a substantial proportion can expect to be cured.

SEE ALSO *Cancer, Chemotherapy, Lymph glands, Lymphatic/Immune system, Non-Hodgkin's lymphoma*

HOLTER MONITOR

Worn over one shoulder, the Holter monitor consists of electrodes (EKG wires) attached to the chest and a monitor which correlates heart rhythm disturbances with symptoms such as dizziness or palpitations. The patient is required to keep a diary for 24 to 48 hours and record any symptoms and activity taking place during moments of rhythm irregularities. The information gained is used to determine the pattern and severity of disturbance in heart rhythm.

SEE ALSO *Electrocardiogram, Heart*

HOME NURSING

Home nursing or home care can include nursing care; care by a physician, social worker, physical therapist, occupational therapist or speech therapist; and housework and other home help services. Community services may also be available.

Many types of care, which were originally undertaken by hospitals, are now often conducted in the home, with family members performing many of the duties of nursing and hospital staff. Apart from the rising costs of hospitalization, many patients also prefer home care to hospital care when given the choice.

Being cared for at home often helps patients to feel more comfortable and secure than they would in a hospital environment, particularly if education for the patient and family, as well as home health care services, is available. Transportation to appointments or services is often available using community or health resources for those who need the service. Home nursing is often an option for the elderly, cancer sufferers and those who have had a stroke.

SEE ALSO *Palliative care*

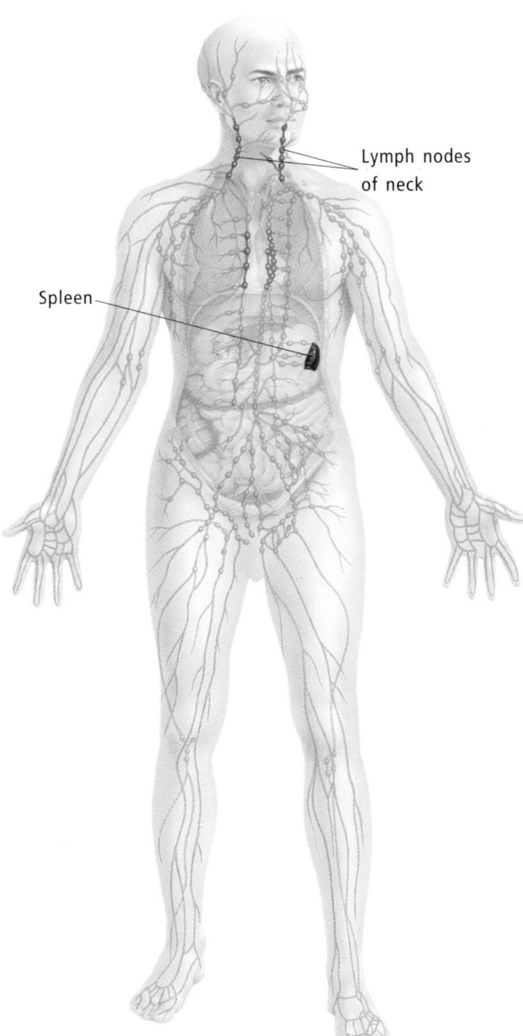

Hodgkin's disease

This type of lymphoma produces enlargement of the lymph nodes, often starting with the lymph nodes in the neck and spreading progressively to other nodes in the body, the spleen and other tissues. Symptoms include fever, night sweats and infections.

HOMEOPATHY

The pioneer of homeopathy was Samuel Hahnemann (1755–1843), a German physician. After working as an orthodox doctor, Hahnemann became dissatisfied with the medical practices of his day and turned to research.

For one of his experiments he dosed himself with Peruvian bark, or cinchona, a known remedy for malaria. To his surprise he found that he quickly developed malaria-like symptoms: drowsiness, trembling, heart palpitations, flushed cheeks, fever and thirst. This outcome suggested to him that substances which produced a specific set of symptoms in a healthy person could also cure the same set of symptoms in an ill person.

Hahnemann recognized the connection between his idea and the references made by the ancient Greek physician Hippocrates to a medicine of "similars": substances which could both cause and cure an illness. It was an idea utilized soon after by Edward Jenner in his development of a smallpox vaccine; Hahnemann supported Jenner, who was widely condemned as a quack.

Early developments

Hahnemann continued to experiment on himself and healthy colleagues, recording his observations rigorously. A range of plants, herbs, animal and mineral matter were tested in a process known as "proving". The provings produced remedy "pictures" which described the first line, or keynote symptoms, the second line or less common symptoms, and the third line or idiosyncratic symptoms of each substance.

Finding a cure

Homeopathy uses the principle of "like cures like"—the idea that the same substance can both cause and cure an illness. Edward Jenner's development of a vaccine against smallpox in the nineteenth century was based on a similar principle.

Smallpox virus

Next Hahnemann and his colleagues trialed the remedies in their clinics. Patients were physically examined and questioned closely about their symptoms, general health, way of life and attitudes. This process produced a "symptom picture" which was then matched with a "remedy picture", i.e. the symptoms of the patient were similar to those produced by the chosen remedy's "proving". These remedies worked.

Hahnemann concluded that from these trials that "like should be treated by like" according to a theory he called the "law of similars", naming his new form of medicine homeopathy from the Greek *homios* (similar) and *pathos* (suffering).

A further refinement to homeopathy was made when Hahnemann observed that in some patients there was a worsening of symptoms before an alleviation took place. To prevent this, he started to dilute his remedies by 1:100 and then to mix them by repeatedly banging (succussing) the vials against a hard surface, which he believed released the energy of the substance. Remedies prepared in this way, known as "potentization", proved to be even more successful. The complications produced by each remedy were reduced while at the same time the healing power of the remedy was increased.

Later developments

In the nineteenth century homeopathy quickly spread from Germany across Europe and to the Americas as well as Asia. Its reputation grew in Europe when Hahnemann's prescription of homeopathic doses of camphor proved successful in treating cholera.

By the early twentieth century two schools of homoeopathy had emerged. The classical homeopaths, following the work of American homeopath Dr James Tyler Kent, prescribed high-potency remedies according to the patient's emotional make-up and appearance, as well as their physical symptoms. Other homeopaths, following the English homeopath Dr Richard Hughes, prescribed lower potencies according to purely physical symptoms.

In recent times homeopathy has enjoyed a resurgence, and the practice of classical homeopathy in particular has gained popularity with both homeopaths and medical doctors. Self-treatment for minor physical ailments has also become popular as low potency remedies have become available commercially, e.g. arnica in 6x potency to treat physical shock and injury.

Homeopathic treatment

Homeopathy views illness as a unique manifestation of a specific disease in the patient. Symptoms are believed to be the body's way of trying to maintain an equilibrium as it instinctively seeks healing, and thus should not be suppressed. A homeopathic remedy prescribed in accordance with the patient's total symptoms, constitution, temperament and disease state will hasten recovery by stimulating the body's innate vital force.

Finding the right homeopathic remedy to treat a person is a complex procedure. It starts with the homeopath taking a lengthy personal history which covers medical history, emotional reactions, food preferences, reactions to weather, state of mind and personal beliefs. An understanding of the patient's unique physical and psychological make-up is crucial to the homeopath making a correct diagnosis and choice of remedy.

Homeopaths treat chronic illnesses and their symptoms by stages, giving progressive remedies to peel back ailments layer by layer. The homeopathic "Laws of Cure" state that symptoms will disappear first from the most important organs to the least important, and in reverse chronological order to the onset of symptoms. Thus homeopaths approach all the patient's physical and mental health problems as related, rather than treating any one ailment in isolation.

The homeopath chooses remedies that match the patient's basic constitution to unravel the underlying causative factors of an illness. For example, the constitutional remedy "Nat Mur" is often prescribed to serious, conscientious people who are inclined to suppress their emotions.

In the course of treatment the patient may experience an "aggravation", or brief worsening, of symptoms. This signals to the homeopath that the body is in the process of healing itself and that an improvement will soon follow. As well as prescribing remedies, homeopaths advocate that the body's vital force be supported with adequate sleep, regular exercise, proper hygiene and a nutritious diet.

H

The remedies

In today's homeopathic *Materia Medica* up to 3,000 remedies are listed, made from plants, minerals and animals, many of which would be poisonous in large doses. For example the deadly plant *Aconite napellus,* used throughout history as an arrow poison, is made up into homeopathic doses of aconite to treat sudden and acute onsets of fever, inflammation or fear.

Once the remedy is chosen, its potency has to be decided—ideally the minimum dose necessary to stimulate the patient's self-healing process. In homeopathy the greater the dilution the more potent the remedy. Homeopathic remedies are given either in liquid form as drops or as small pills, usually one to ten doses over a period of one to seven days.

HOMOSEXUALITY

Homosexuality is defined as sexual attraction between persons of the same sex. Homosexual or gay are the terms used for men; gay or lesbian are the terms used for women. Some people are neither totally homosexual nor heterosexual, but attracted to both sexes (bisexual).

Homosexuality is not considered a psychological disorder and does not need treatment. However individuals who are not happy with their sexuality can benefit from counseling. The outbreak of HIV (AIDS) has had a devastating effect on homosexual communities.

SEE ALSO ***AIDS, Bisexuality, HIV, Sexuality***

HOOKWORM

The hookworm (*Ancyclostoma duodenale*) is a common parasitic roundworm found in tropical and subtropical climates, and flourishing in unsanitary conditions. The eggs are found in infected human feces, and hatch into infective larvae which can then infect another human, either by direct contact, usually through bare feet, or by swallowing contaminated soil—a common source of infection for children in areas with poor sanitation.

Where the hookworm enters the skin it creates an itchy patch, hence its other name, "ground itch". Upon entering the body, it travels to the intestines where it attaches to the intestinal wall and sucks blood from it for nourishment.

In severe cases, symptoms can include abdominal pain, diarrhea, loss of appetite and weight loss. A stool sample will determine if the infection is great enough to cause anemia or protein deficiency as a result of the blood loss. This can retard growth and mental development in children, and hookworm infection can be fatal in babies. Treatment is usually drugs over a one to three day period, sometimes with an iron supplement.

SEE ALSO ***Worms***

HORMONAL THERAPY

Hormones are natural chemicals produced by the body to regulate various processes such as blood sugar metabolism, bone growth or milk production. Some cancers will only grow in the presence of certain hormones; for example, certain types of breast cancers need the female hormones estrogen and progesterone to grow. Hormonal therapy seeks to prevent these cancers from growing by altering the hormonal environment around them. It is usually used in conjunction with other cancer treatments such as surgery and radiation therapy.

Cancers that are stimulated by hormones have certain areas on their surface called receptor sites. By using a drug that blocks these receptor sites, the growth of the cancer can be slowed or even stopped. For example, many breast cancers have estrogen and progesterone receptors, and are stimulated by these hormones. This means they may respond to treatment with a drug such as Tamoxifen, which blocks the effects of estrogen on breast cancer. Treatment with Tamoxifen reduces cancer recurrence and is used after surgery or radiation therapy. Not all breast cancers respond to the drug; before commencing treatment with Tamoxifen a section of breast cancer must be tested in a pathology laboratory to see whether it will respond to the drug.

In males, prostate cancer grows more quickly when exposed to the male hormone testosterone. By reducing the amount of testosterone in the environment around the prostate, hormone therapy can be used to reduce the growth and spread of these cancers. This is done by surgically removing the testicles or treating the patient with drugs that block the action of testosterone on the prostate. Alternatively estrogens or luteinizing-hormone-releasing hormones may be given. The treatment is also effective in slwong the progress of prostate cancer metastases (secondaries). It is usually used in conjunction with surgery, radiation therapy, or chemotherapy.

Side effects associated with hormonal therapies include loss of libido, weight gain, diarrhea, tiredness, hot flashes, bone loss, and, in women, irregular menstrual periods and vaginal dryness or bleeding.

SEE ALSO ***Breast cancer, Cancer, Hormones, Prostate cancer***

HORMONE REPLACEMENT THERAPY

At menopause, the ovaries start to regress and women produce less of their reproductive hormones, estrogen and progesterone. The decrease in the quantity of these hormones can cause a variety of symptoms, which include hot flashes (sudden feeling of heat, usually over the face and neck, often with redness and sweating), headaches, vaginal dryness, anxiety and sleep problems. The hot flashes are probably the result of sharp surges in pituitary hormones as a result of falling ovarian hormone levels while vaginal dryness is a direct result of estrogen withdrawal.

Estrogen loss also increases the risk for other health problems such as heart disease. Loss of bone substance also increases after menopause, and can lead to osteoporosis where the bones lose calcium and are easily fractured.

Most of the problems associated with menopause can be prevented by hormone replacement therapy (HRT). HRT involves supplementing the patient's hormone levels with doses of estrogen, often in combination with progesterone. HRT can be very effective in relieving symptoms such as hot flashes and vaginal dryness, while also aiding in reducing the risk of heart disease and osteoporosis.

In some cases HRT is taken cyclically to allow for monthly bleeding, much like a

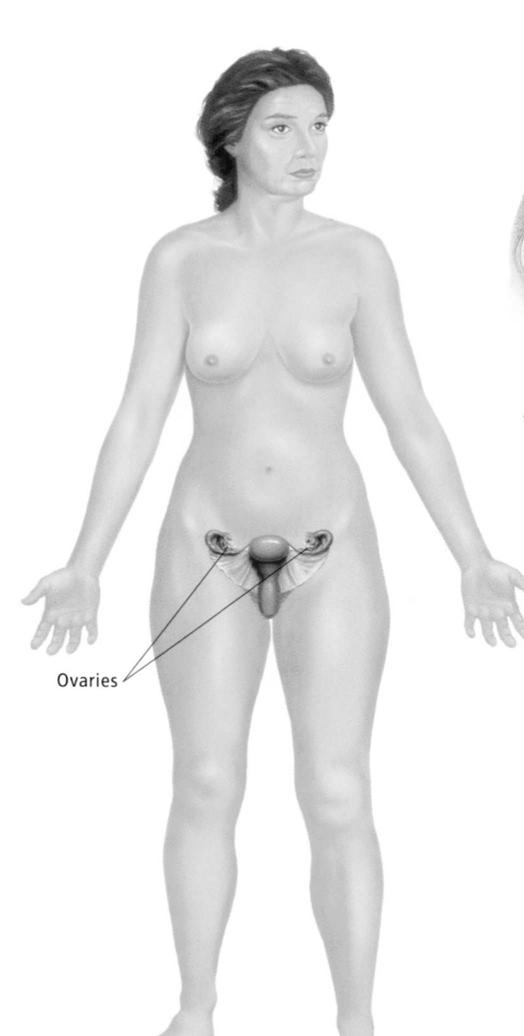

Hormone replacement therapy

At menopause, the ovaries produce less estrogen and progesterone. A woman may choose to supplement her hormone levels with hormone replacement therapy. HRT can reduce the risk of osteoporosis, heart disease and bladder problems such as incontinence.

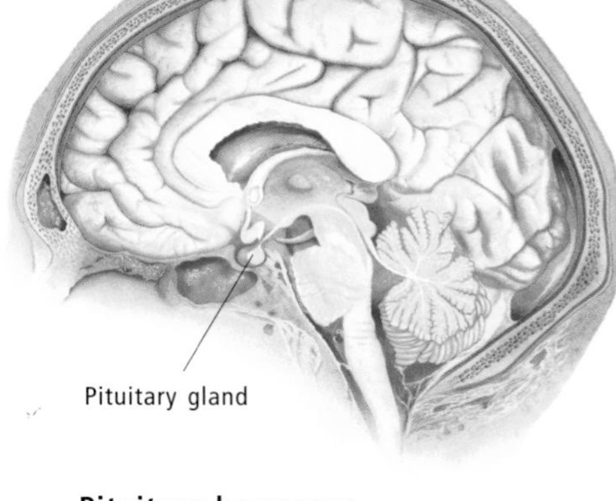

Pituitary hormones

Surges of pituitary hormones as a result of falling ovarian hormone levels cause the hot flashes often experienced during menopause.

Incontinence

Weakening of the pelvic floor muscles is common after menopause and may result in incontinence. Estrogen treatment can improve symptoms.

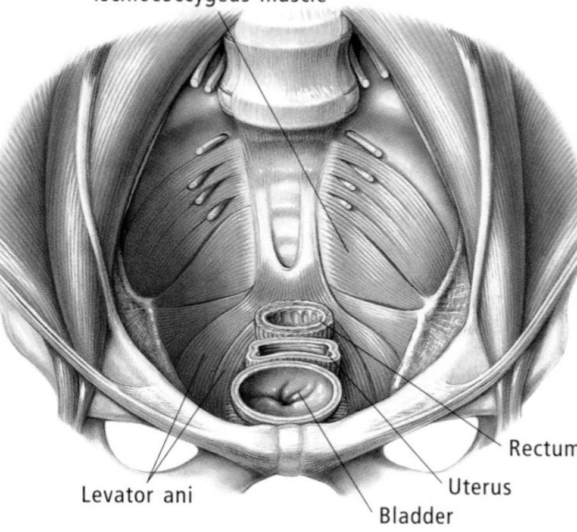

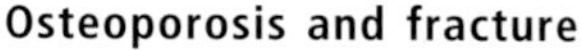

Osteoporosis and fracture

The risk of osteoporosis and resulting bone fractures increases greatly when estrogen levels fall after menopause. HRT can slow down calcium loss preventing loss of bone density.

menstrual cycle, and in other cases it is taken without pause, which will cause regular bleeding to cease. The HRT regimen is tailored to suit each patient, depending on her symptoms and other health problems.

HRT can also be useful in some cases of incontinence, where there is a loss of bladder control leading to leakage of urine. This is known as "stress incontinence", where increases in abdominal pressure can force urine out, for instance when coughing or sneezing. This is common in postmenopausal women, due to a weakening of the pelvic floor muscles. Estrogen treatment may be helpful, as may pelvic muscle exercises and other medications. Changes in the lower urinary tract after menopause can also predispose a woman to cystitis (bladder infection). This causes frequent and sometimes painful urination and can be helped by HRT.

HRT can lead to a number of unwanted side effects. Women may experience breast tenderness and swelling, unwanted vaginal bleeding, nausea, fluid retention and a degree of weight gain.

The levels of estrogen and progesterone used in HRT are generally lower than those used in the oral contraceptive pill. Thus complications which have been associated with taking the pill (particularly the higher doses used in early pill preparations), such as increased blood pressure and increased risk of pulmonary embolism, are not considered to be problems with HRT. However HRT may not be considered appropriate in people who have already had these problems.

Estrogen given on its own has been shown to increase the risk of uterine (endometrial) cancer. Combination therapy (estrogen and progesterone) is not associated with an increased risk of uterine cancer, so it is the preferred treatment for women who have not had a hysterectomy. HRT is not recommended in certain conditions. For instance, many breast cancers are sensitive to estrogen, which stimulates their growth, so HRT should not be used in these cases. A full breast examination and mammogram is therefore recommended before HRT treatment begins.

SEE ALSO *Cystitis, Estrogens, Hormones, Menopause, Osteoporosis, Progesterone, Urinary incontinence*

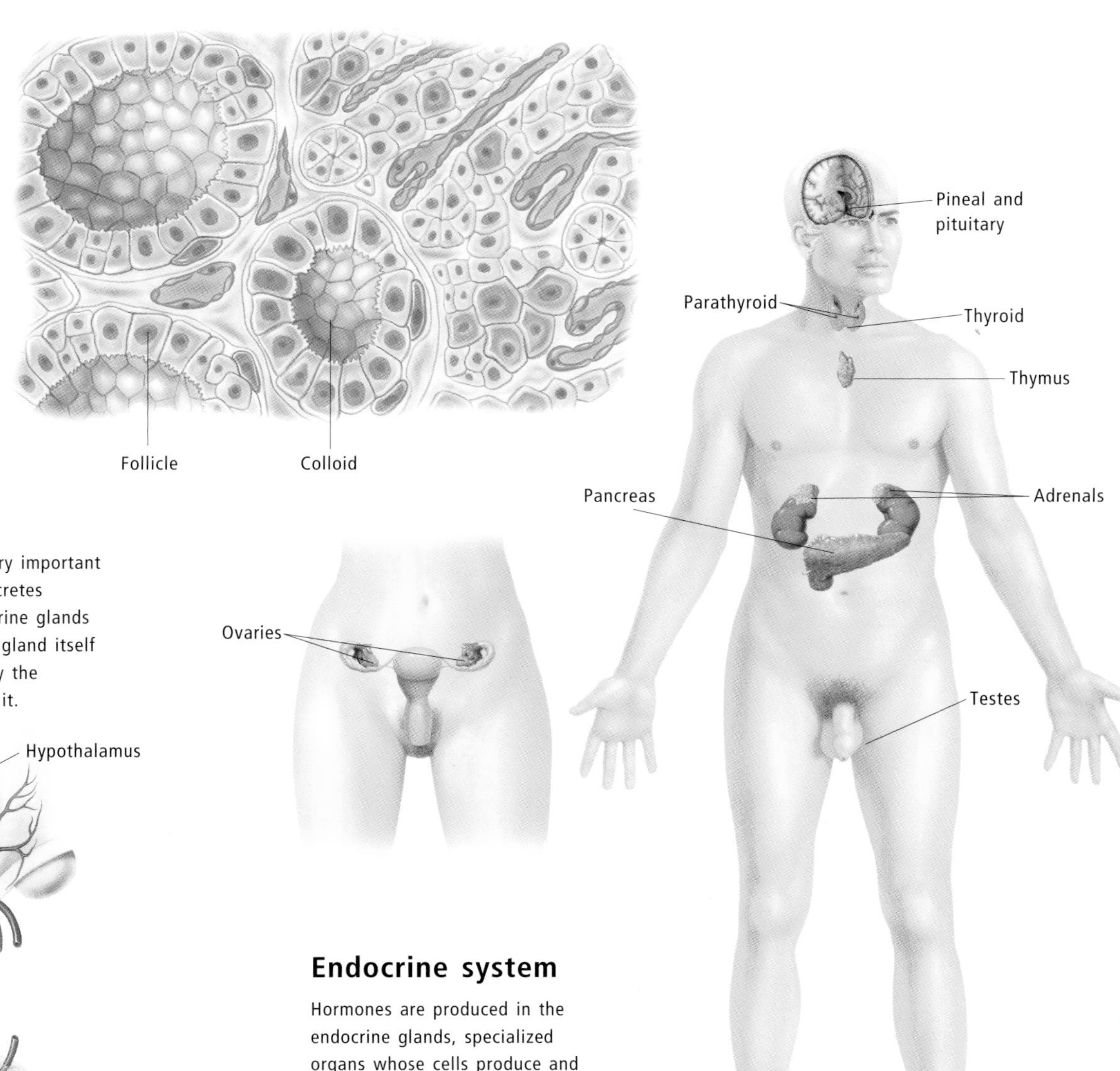

Thyroid microstructure

The thyroid is the only endocrine gland that does not release its hormones straight into the body. It stores thyroid hormones (which control metabolism) in colloid fluid held in the follicles of the gland. The hormones are then secreted gradually into the blood when needed.

Pituitary gland

The pituitary gland is a small but very important gland in the base of the brain. It secretes hormones which control other endocrine glands elsewhere in the body. The pituitary gland itself is regulated by hormones secreted by the hypothalamus, which lies just above it.

Endocrine system

Hormones are produced in the endocrine glands, specialized organs whose cells produce and release hormones directly into the bloodstream. The thyroid gland, for example, is made up of cells producing and secreting thyroid hormones.

HORMONES

Hormones are chemical substances that are produced by endocrine organs, including the pituitary, thyroid, parathyroid, adrenal, pancreas, gonads (the testes in males and the ovaries in females) and the placenta (during pregnancy). They are released into the bloodstream and carried to other regions called target organs, where they alter the activity of target cells.

Hormones control a whole range of body functions including growth, metabolism and reproductive activity. They are divided into three main classes, according to their chemical structure: peptide and protein hormones, such as growth hormone and insulin; hormones made from the amino acid tyrosine, such as epinephrine (adrenaline) and thyroxin; and steroid hormones, which include corticosteroids and the sex hormones.

The way hormones are produced depends on their type. Peptide and protein hormones are made from an mRNA (messenger RNA) sequence, like cellular proteins, and stored in the cell in membrane-bound vesicles until released. Thyroxin and epinephrine are made by specific chemical reactions within the thyroid and adrenal glands. Steroid hormones, such as estrogen and testosterone, are made from cholesterol; they are not stored in vesicles but are found free in the cell cytoplasm.

Hormones work by combining with specific receptors in the target cells. These receptors are usually proteins and may be in the cell membrane (for peptide hormones) or in the cell cytoplasm or nucleus (for steroid hormones). Having bound to the receptor, the hormone may stimulate or inhibit specific metabolic pathways in the cell, for example, they may change the activity of an enzyme, or stimulate production of a new protein. Receptors for some hormones (for example, thyroxin) are present on many body cells and hence the effects of the hormone are widespread. For other hormones (such as thyroid stimulating hormone) the receptors are only present

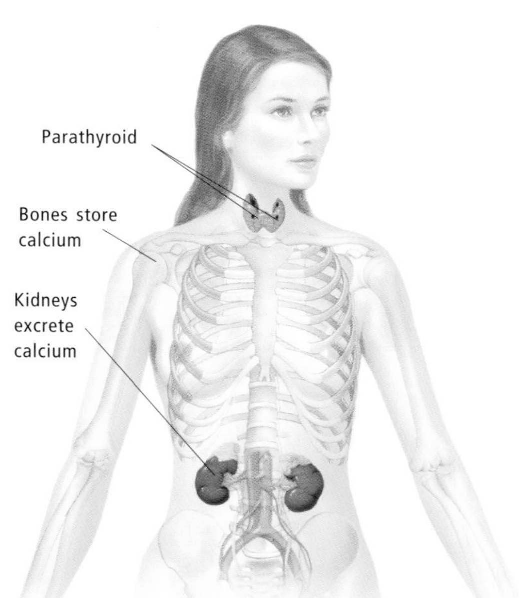

Negative feedback mechanism

The body uses the mechanism of the negative feedback loop to regulate hormone levels. In this system, an excess or deficit of a particular hormone triggers a response to normalize hormone levels. Calcium levels in the blood, for example, are controlled by parathyroid hormones which instruct the bones to store calcium or the kidneys to excrete it, depending on circulating levels. If levels fall too low, for example, the parathyroid registers the deficit and releases parathyroid hormone which tells the bones to release calcium, increasing blood calcium levels.

on specific tissues (the thyroid gland) and thus their effects are very localized.

While many hormones are carried in the blood, some cells are known to release secretions which act locally, generally referred to as paracrine secretions. Yet others, called autocrine secretions, can act on the same cell (that is, the secretory cell itself has receptors).

Hormones can have long-lasting effects, for instance growth hormone from the pituitary acts on a wide range of tissues to stimulate growth during childhood. Other hormones can cause very rapid changes, such as epinephrine (adrenaline). Produced in the adrenal medulla, it is important in the "fight or flight" response to stress and can cause an increase in heart rate, widening of the airways and release of glucose.

Besides regulating many body functions throughout our lives, some hormones are important at specific times, such as during pregnancy, childbirth and lactation. These include sex hormones like estrogen and progesterone, and hormones from the placenta (for example, chorionic gonadotropin) and pituitary (for example, prolactin).

Hormone levels, and thus their impact on the body, are controlled in different ways, depending on the hormone, but a common mechanism is called negative feedback. This is a system whereby either an excess or deficit of a hormone prompts a response that results in that hormone's return to normal levels. For example, calcium levels are controlled by parathyroid hormone from the parathyroid gland, which acts on tissues such as the bones and kidneys, to mobilize or excrete calcium. If calcium levels fall, this stimulates the parathyroid gland to increase the secretion of parathyroid hormone, which activates the bones to release calcium, thus increasing blood levels.

Conversely, if blood calcium rises, parathyroid hormone secretion is decreased, calcium in bones is retained and calcium excretion by the kidney is increased. Similar negative feedback loops operate for many hormones (such as the control of glucose by insulin), although several hormones often interact for the final outcome.

Hormone imbalance can occur when there is an excess or deficiency of one hormone, which can often affect the function of others. Imbalances can also occur when there is sufficient hormone produced, but the target tissue fails to respond properly, usually because of changes in the receptors. The effects of hormone imbalance will differ depending on the particular hormone and its target area.

During the menopause in women, when menstruation ceases, there are surges in pituitary hormones (FSH and LH) as a result of falling levels of ovarian hormones, due to the increasing unresponsiveness of the ovaries. These surges in pituitary hormones can result in hot flashes.

Female and male sex hormones

The development of the gonad into an ovary or testis occurs early in fetal life, and is dependent on the sex chromosomes (XX in females, XY in males).

During childhood, the ovaries and testes are relatively dormant. At puberty, the hypothalamus in the brain releases gonadotropin-releasing hormone (GnRH) which starts the changes leading to sexual maturity. This in turn stimulates the pituitary to release the gonadotropins, lutenising hormone (LH) and follicle stimulating hormone (FSH) in both men and women.

These hormones stimulate the ovaries in females for follicle maturation and ovulation, and the testes in males for sperm production and testosterone secretion. The ovary and testes secrete sex hormones; testosterone in males, and estrogen and progesterone in females.

At puberty, sex hormones are involved in the development of the external genitalia and secondary sexual characteristics. For the male this includes enlargement of the penis and testes, growth of body and facial hair, development of body musculature and growth of the larynx, causing a deepening of the voice. For the female the changes include development of the breasts, growth of body hair, and the beginning of menstruation (menarche).

After puberty has begun, the production of sex hormone is continuous in the male; in females, however, production occurs in cycles (menstrual cycles) which last until women reach menopause.

SEE ALSO *Adrenal glands, Endocrine glands, Endocrine system, Menopause, Ovaries, Parathyroid glands, Pituitary gland, Placenta, Puberty, Testes, Thyroid gland*

HORNER'S SYNDROME

Horner's syndrome is the result of damage to the sympathetic nerves which supply the face. It is characterized by a small pupil, drooping eyelid and loss of sweating on the face.

It may be a pointer to more serious disease. It is most commonly caused by Pancoast syndrome, when cancer in the apex of the lung invades the nerve.

SEE ALSO *Eye, Pupil of eye*

Greater tubercle
Head of humerus
Anatomical neck
Intertubercular sulcus
Lesser tubercle
Surgical neck
Deltoid tuberosity
Humerus
Lateral supracondylar ridge
Lateral condyle
Radial fossa
Lateral epicondyle
Capitulum
Coronoid fossa
Trochlea
Medial supracondylar ridge
Medial condyle
Medial epicondyle

Humerus

Humerus

The humerus forms the skeleton of the upper arm. It is a long bone comprised of a cylindrical shaft and two enlarged extremities.

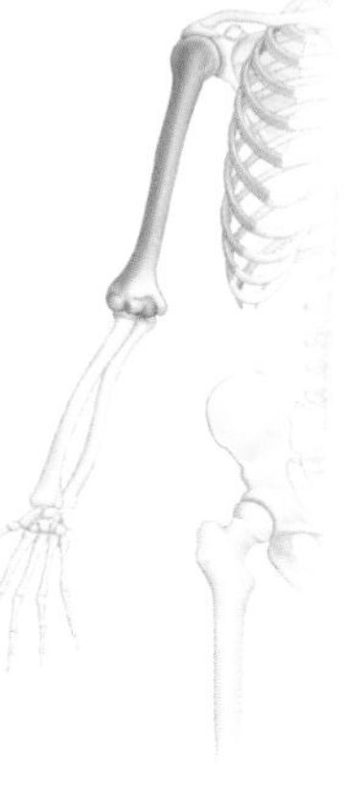

HUMERUS

The humerus is a long bone that forms the skeleton of the arm. It consists of a cylindrical shaft, a rounded head (upper end), which articulates with the scapula to form the shoulder joint, and paired condyles (lower end), which articulate with the radius and ulna to form the elbow joint.

Several major nerves lie in contact with the humerus and are at risk in fractures or blows to the bone. The familiar tingling sensation which we experience in our hand when we "hit our funny bone" is actually caused by hitting the ulnar nerve as it passes behind the humerus on its way to the hand.

SEE ALSO *Arm, Elbow, Radius, Skeletal system, Ulna, Ulnar nerve*

HUNTINGTON'S DISEASE

Also known as Huntington's chorea, Huntington's disease is a rare genetic disorder involving degeneration of nerve cells in the cerebrum (the largest portion of the brain). It is inherited as a dominant condition; this means that it is inherited from only one parent and there is a 50 percent chance that someone with the condition will transmit it to an offspring.

Some people with the disorder are affected more severely and earlier in life than others. Usually, however, it begins between the ages of 35–50 when the affected person notices the gradual onset of involuntary, jerky and contorted movements of the limbs ("chorea" refers to the tendency to writhe and twist in a constant, uncontrollable motion, similar to a dance). Mental deterioration and severe personality change follows. The affected person may eventually need institutionalized care.

There is no cure for Huntington's disease and it is usually fatal within 10–20 years. Treatment is aimed at maximizing the ability to function for as long as possible. Medications have been found to be only partially successful at reducing abnormal behaviors and movements. A blood test is available that can identify the defective gene before any symptoms appear. Genetic counseling may be advised if there is a family history of the disorder.

SEE ALSO *Brain, Congenital abnormalities, Genetic counseling, Nerves*

HOUSEMAID'S KNEE

Housemaid's knee is one example of bursitis, inflammation of a bursa. A bursa is a fluid-filled sac that helps to protect ligaments, tendons, skin or muscle where they rub across bone. In this case, it is the prepatellar bursa in front of the patella that becomes inflamed. Bursitis may result from injury, pressure or overuse. The condition is painful and limits movement. It may be relieved by rest or anti-inflammatory drugs.

SEE ALSO *Bursitis, Knee*

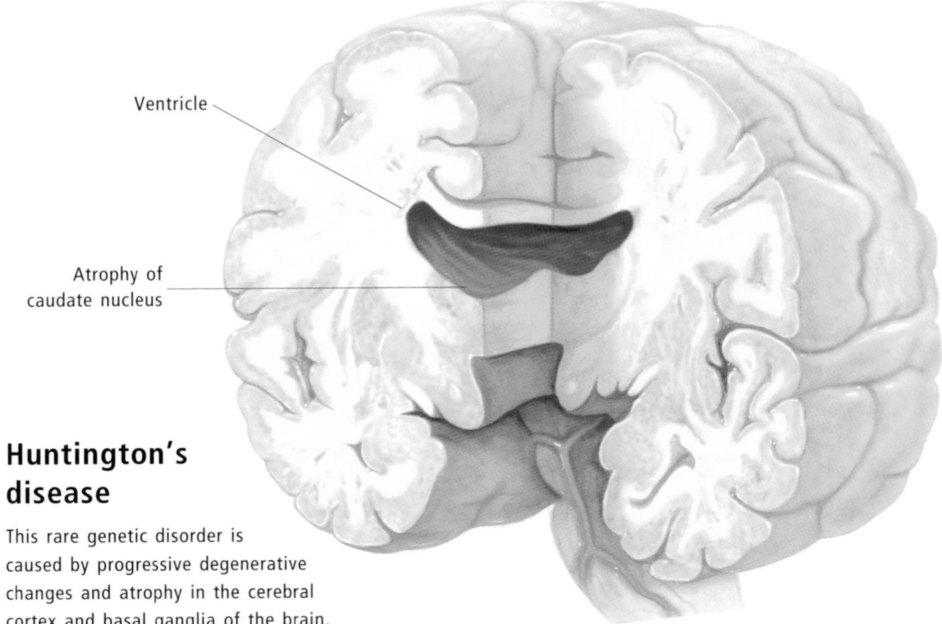

Huntington's disease

This rare genetic disorder is caused by progressive degenerative changes and atrophy in the cerebral cortex and basal ganglia of the brain.

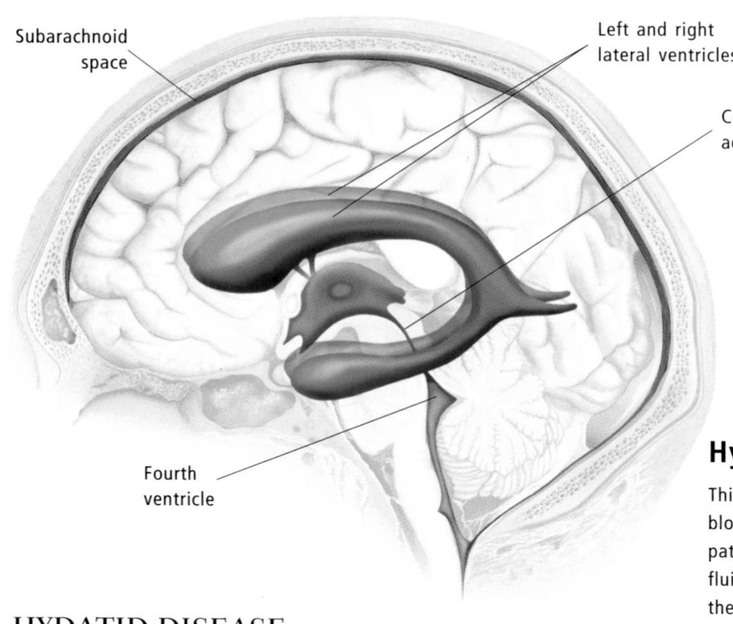

Hydrocephalus

This disorder is caused by blockage or narrowing of the pathways for cerebrospinal fluid (CSF). This results in the accumulation of CSF in the ventricles, which exerts pressure on the brain.

H

HYDATID DISEASE

Hydatid disease is an infection, usually of the liver, that is common in southern South America, the Mediterranean, the Middle East, central Asia and Africa. It is caused by the larvae of a type of tapeworm *(Echinococcus granulosus)*, which can infest dogs, foxes, wolves, cattle and sheep.

Humans become infected when they swallow food contaminated with tapeworm eggs. The larvae lodge in the liver, where they form cysts which grow slowly for 10–20 years before producing symptoms of a lump and a dull ache on the right side of the abdomen. Occasionally other organs such as the lung, brain and bones are also affected. X-rays and CAT scans will highlight the cyst(s), which must be surgically removed.

SEE ALSO *Liver, Tapeworm*

HYDATIDIFORM MOLE

A hydatidiform mole is a benign (noncancerous) growth that develops within the uterus from a degenerating embryo. The abnormal growth produces multiple cysts, often resembling a bunch of grapes. The tumor usually causes bleeding similar to that from a threatened miscarriage. It may be spontaneously expelled from the uterus; if not, a dilation and curettage (scraping) is performed to surgically remove it. In some cases, a hydatidiform mole will progress to form a malignant tumor called a choriocarcinoma.

SEE ALSO *Dilation and curettage, Miscarriage, Pregnancy*

HYDROCELE

Hydrocele refers to an accumulation of fluid in the sac which covers the testes, the tunica vaginalis. It is a common cause of swelling in the scrotum and may be due to injury or inflammation in the testes, or obstruction of drainage. The fluid can be removed, but may reappear. Hydroceles are usually painless, but, if causing discomfort, they can be treated surgically.

SEE ALSO *Scrotum, Testes*

HYDROCEPHALUS

Hydrocephalus ("water on the brain") is a condition in which there is an excess of fluid within or surrounding the brain. This fluid, known as cerebrospinal fluid or CSF, is produced at a constant rate within the ventricles (cavities) of the brain. It circulates from the ventricles into the space surrounding the brain (subarachnoid space) and from there it drains into the venous system. The total volume of CSF is replaced about three times per day so, if CSF circulation is blocked (e.g. by a tumor) or its drainage is defective, the CSF accumulates and exerts pressure on the brain.

Occasionally, in some infants, the openings between the ventricles and the subarachnoid space fail to develop, and the resulting hydrocephalus causes the head to enlarge, because the skull bones have not yet fused. In adults, where the skull has fused and cannot expand further, nearby structures can become compressed and CSF pressure builds up inside the skull, which can affect consciousness and result in headache and vomiting.

Hydrocephalus is usually treated by placing a tube (shunt) into the ventricles, which enables the excess CSF to drain into the internal jugular vein in the neck.

SEE ALSO *Brain*

HYDROTHERAPY

The term hydrotherapy covers a broad range of health treatments involving the use of water. The use of hydrotherapy goes back to antiquity, with many cultures advocating bathing in hot mineral springs and sea water to restore health. Modern hydrotherapy spa treatments were pioneered in the nineteenth century by Father Sebastian Kneipp, a Bavarian monk.

Central to hydrotherapy is the idea that water is naturally healing because it is both essential to life and is the major component of our bodies. The temperature of the water is of crucial significance in many treatments. Hot water is used to encourage relaxation and sweating, and to draw blood to the surface of the skin. Cold water constricts the blood vessels, reduces surface inflammation and stimulates blood flow to the internal organs.

Different forms of hydrotherapy are used by a variety of health professionals. Physical therapists recommend gentle exercise in warm water or whirlpool baths in order to relax muscles, and recommend iced water compresses for physical trauma, such as tendinitis. Naturopaths prescribe sitz baths for pelvic problems, steam baths for congestion, foot or hand baths for insomnia, hot and cold water showers for menstrual problems and colonic irrigation to cleanse and tone the bowel. Aromatherapy treatment uses essential oils in baths or inhalations.

SEE ALSO *Aromatherapy, Naturopathy*

HYMEN

In a female infant the vaginal opening is closed by a thin membrane called the hymen. This membrane usually ruptures before puberty to allow menstrual blood to escape. An intact hymen used to be considered evidence of virginity but in fact in most cases the hymen commonly ruptures, at least in part, during physical exercise. Further rupture usually occurs during the first sexual intercourse.

After childbirth there is little of the hymen left in the mother. In rare cases the hymen will fail to rupture before puberty, causing menstrual blood to accumulate in the vagina. The hymen then must be cut surgically.

SEE ALSO *Reproductive systems, Vagina*

HYPERGLYCEMIA

Hyperglycemia is a condition in which the blood sugar level is higher than normal. It occurs in diabetics, in pancreatic disorders, as a complication of extensive burns and in cases of acute stress. People who find it difficult to control their diabetes probably have hyperglycemic periods every day. In diabetics, hyperglycemia is caused by missing or miscalculating doses of insulin or by overeating or drinking too much alcohol. If untreated, it can lead to coma.

Symptoms are thirst and blurred vision together with numbness and tingling. When diabetes mellitus is first diagnosed, the symptoms of hyperglycemia are likely to be present. These include increased urination, increased thirst, weight loss despite increased food intake, fatigue and increased susceptibility to yeast infections.

Once diabetes has been diagnosed, patients are taught how to test their own blood glucose levels at home so that they can control hyperglycemia with either insulin injections or oral medications.

SEE ALSO *Blood sugar tests, Diabetes, Insulin, Pancreas*

HYPERTENSION

Hypertension is the term for high pressure (tension) in the arteries (i.e. high blood pressure). The average normal blood pressure at rest is about 120/80 mm Hg, and is usually between 100/60 and 140/90. Systolic blood pressure (the upper number) represents the maximum pressure in the arteries as the heart contracts and ejects blood into the circulation. Diastolic pressure (the bottom number)

Arteriosclerosis

Hypertension may lead to the development of arteriosclerosis, a condition in which fatty deposits form beneath the lining of arteries and cause them to narrow.

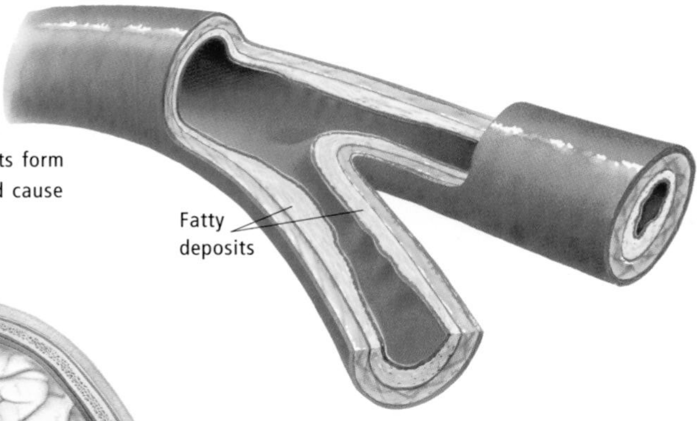

Fatty deposits

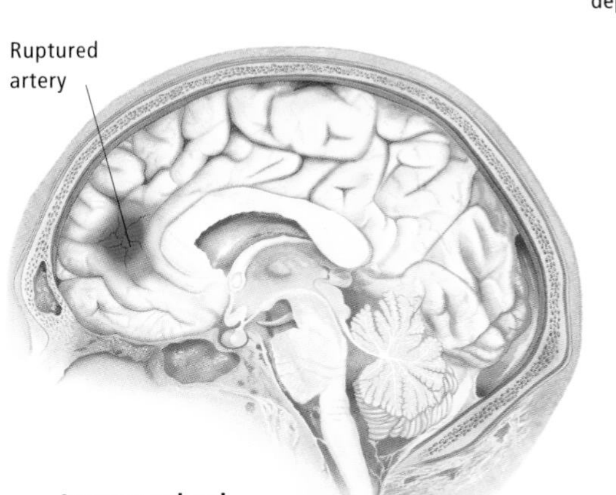

Intracerebral hemorrhage

Hypertension may cause an artery to rupture and bleed, especially if it is already affected by arteriosclerosis. A ruptured artery in the brain for example may cause an intracerebral hemorrhage.

Hypertension

High blood pressure (hypertension) describes a condition in which the pressure of the blood in the arteries is too high. This can occur when the heart pumps blood too forcefully around the body, or when arterioles narrow, inhibiting blood flow. Hypertension causes a number of (often fatal) complications including arteriosclerosis, stroke and heart disease.

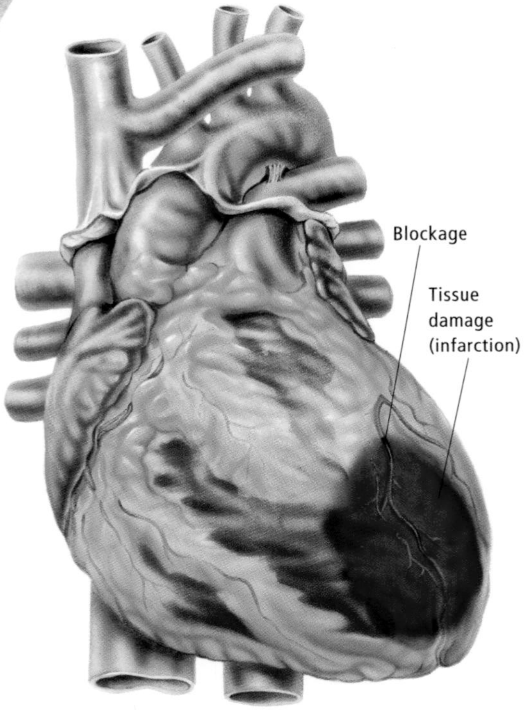

Blockage

Tissue damage (infarction)

Ischemia/myocardial infarction

Hypertension is one of the causes of myocardial infarction. It causes the arteries to harden and narrow (arteriosclerosis) which obstructs the blood supply to the heart muscle.

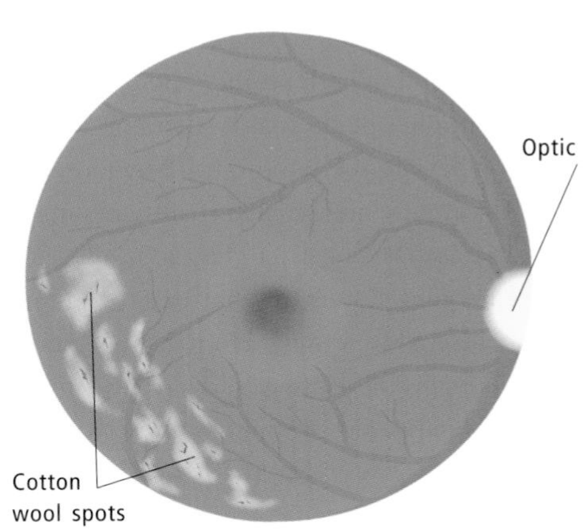

Retinopathy

After many years, hypertension can cause eye damage and even blindness. The arteries of the retina may narrow, small hemorrhages can occur and areas of damaged retina appear, seen here as pale-colored areas called "exudates" and "cotton wool spots".

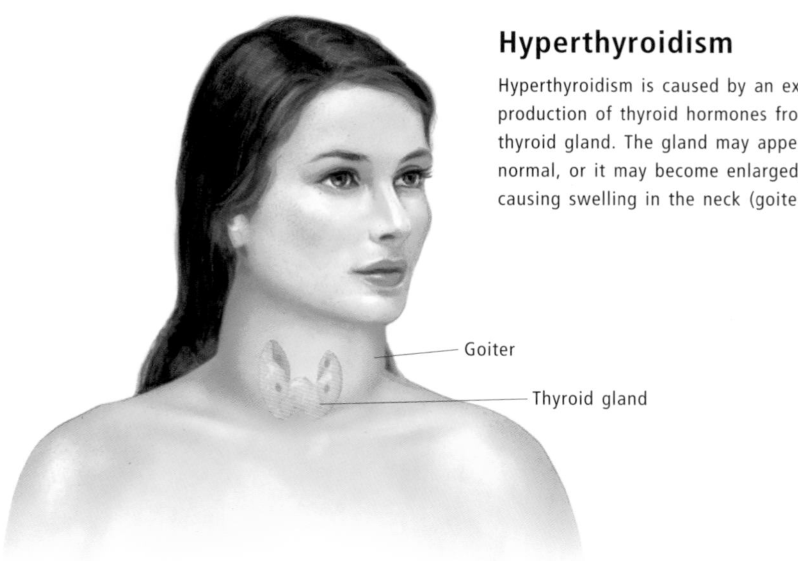

Hyperthyroidism

Hyperthyroidism is caused by an excess production of thyroid hormones from the thyroid gland. The gland may appear normal, or it may become enlarged, causing swelling in the neck (goiter).

represents the minimum blood pressure as the heart relaxes following a contraction.

Although blood pressure varies from person to person and from time to time, someone is said to have hypertension when the blood pressure is 140/90 or above. High blood pressure is one of the causes of arteriosclerosis which in turn can cause heart attack, stroke, intermittent claudication and kidney failure. Hypertension can exist silently for decades; by the time it is diagnosed, the damage has already occurred. Hence, hypertension is sometimes called "the silent killer".

In 90 percent of cases, no-one knows what causes hypertension. People with a family history of hypertension, who smoke, are overweight or obese, and consume a diet high in salt are at particular risk. Stress and excess alcohol consumption are also thought to be contributing factors. In 10 percent of cases there is a predisposing medical condition such as kidney disease or a tumor of the adrenal gland.

The diagnosis of hypertension can be made by a primary care physician (general practitioner) using simple blood pressure measurements, repeated to confirm the diagnosis. Additional tests may be required if the physician suspects an underlying disease is causing hypertension.

Because of its role in stroke, heart attack and kidney failure, it is important to bring hypertension under control. Preventive measures are the first line of treatment. Smoking and alcohol use should be stopped, or at least reduced, regular aerobic exercise and weight control introduced, and intake of salt and animal fats reduced. These measures can reduce blood pressure by about five points in 50 percent of sufferers. If this fails to control the hypertension, drug therapy is the next step. Drugs used for treating hypertension include diuretics, beta-blockers, alpha-adrenergic blockers, angiotensin-converting enzyme (ACE) inhibitors, and calcium channel blockers.

About 1 percent of people with hypertension have a severe form of the condition called accelerated or malignant hypertension. In these people, diastolic blood pressure exceeds 140 and is associated with headache, nausea and dizziness. This condition requires urgent hospital treatment to prevent stroke or brain hemorrhage.

High blood pressure in pregnancy can indicate preeclampsia, or toxemia of pregnancy. Other symptoms are fluid retention and albuminuria (protein in the urine). If the blood pressure is not quickly reduced to normal, there is an increased chance of the mother developing eclampsia, which can be fatal to both mother and fetus.

A number of alternative therapies may help alleviate the symptoms of hypertension. Acupuncture and shiatsu treatments may help relax the constricted artery walls, calm the nervous system and balance the kidney and adrenal functions. Herbalism prescribes hypotensive herbs (e.g. garlic or linden), with sedative nervines (e.g. motherwort), arterial cleansers (e.g. nettle or hawthorn) and diuretics (e.g. uva ursi or dandelion).

Naturopathy advises a vegetarian low-fat wholefood diet with restricted tea, coffee, alcohol, salt and sugar intake, and regular consumption of ginger and garlic. Supplements prescribed include vitamins B and C plus a range of minerals. Meditation, biofeedback or other relaxation techniques, as well as gentle exercise such as qigong, t'ai chi or yoga may help in the management of hypertension by relieving stress.

SEE ALSO *Arteriosclerosis, Blood pressure, Preeclampsia, Toxemia*

HYPERTHERMIA

Hyperthermia is the term for abnormally high body temperature. High temperatures are used as part of an experimental approach to controlling and eliminating cancer. This is a non-ionizing, non-invasive radiation therapy which kills cancer cells through the use of high temperatures. Hyperthermia during pregnancy may cause abnormal development of the fetus.

SEE ALSO *Body temperature*

HYPERTHYROIDISM

Hyperthyroidism (or thyrotoxicosis) occurs when overactive thyroid tissue secretes too much thyroid hormone into the bloodstream. The thyroid tissue may be overactive as a result of abnormal stimulation, as in Graves' disease; there may be an isolated overactive thyroid nodule or an entire overactive gland.

Symptoms of thyrotoxicosis include nervousness, increased appetite with weight loss, poor tolerance of hot weather, increased sweating, palpitations, increased frequency of bowel motions, menstrual problems, infertility and muscular weakness. An enlarged thyroid gland (goiter), increased heart rate, fine hair and warm, moist skin may also occur. Patients with Graves' disease will often have a wide-eyed staring appearance, due to the protrusion of the eyeballs (exophthalmos).

Blood tests usually reveal elevated levels of thyroid hormone and the absence of thyroid stimulating hormone (TSH), which is produced by the pituitary. If left untreated, hyperthyroidism can cause heart attacks, arrhythmias and heart failure, progressive weight loss and death.

Treatment is with antithyroid drugs to interfere with thyroid hormone production, radioactive iodine to destroy hyperactive thyroid tissue or surgery to remove excessively active thyroid tissue. The choice of treatment depends on the age and state of health of the patient and the size of the goiter.

SEE ALSO *Goiter, Graves' disease, Pituitary gland, Thyroid gland, Thyrotoxicosis*

HYPNOTHERAPY

The use of hypnotism in medicine began with the Austrian doctor Franz Anton Mesmer (1734–1815), a flamboyant character who put his patients into a light hypnotic trance . The word "mesmerize" is derived from the name of Dr Mesmer. His work was largely discredited, but some of his trance-inducing techniques were researched, most notably by James Braid, a Scottish surgeon who coined the term "hypnotism" in the mid-1800s. Braid performed some of his surgery using hypnosis but the development of quicker forms of anesthesia, such as chloroform, eclipsed his achievements.

The use of hypnotic states in treating psychological disorders was investigated by a few European doctors, most notably Jean-Martin Charcot and Sigmund Freud, in the latter part of the nineteenth century.

Widespread recognition of the therapeutic applications of hypnosis developed in the mid-twentieth century, when its use was endorsed by both the British and American Medical Associations. In recent times hypnotherapy has been used for a number of physical and psychological disorders including stress-related problems, addictions and phobias, as well as sleep disorders, respiratory conditions and pain management.

The word hypnotherapy is derived from the Greek *hypnos*, meaning "to sleep". This is somewhat misleading as the hypnotic state is actually an altered state of consciousness that falls somewhere between waking and sleeping, similar to when a person daydreams. To help induce this state in a patient the hypnotherapist uses a progressive relaxation technique, such as a step-by-step countdown procedure, or the patient is asked to focus on a particular object, image or light.

Hypnotherapists stress that a hypnotic state will only be achieved if the patient chooses to go along with the process, and that for this reason all hypnosis is in fact "self-hypnosis".

Once the patient reaches the hypnotic state the hypnotherapist guides their attention to a particular health issue such as reducing pain or anxiety. The patient's mind is both more focused and more receptive so that health problems are able to be approached from a fresh mental perspective. Phrases and images are given to the patient to focus on which generate feelings of mental and physical well-being. Suggestions for behavioral or attitudinal change made by either the patient or the hypnotherapist are more likely to be taken up and acted upon when received under hypnosis.

Hypnotherapy aims to combine a state of concentration with a state of relaxation so that patients can focus on something that would normally distress them and yet stay relaxed. This may help alleviate traumas, fears and anxieties in everyday life. During the course of treatment the hypnotherapist often teaches patients a method of self-hypnosis which they can practise when at home.

Hypnotherapy should only be practised by a fully qualified practitioner, as it can do harm when improperly used.

SEE ALSO *Relaxation techniques*

HYPNOTICS

Hypnotics are a group of drugs used to ease anxiety or to produce sleep. They function by depressing the central nervous system. Hypnotics are sometimes called sedatives or tranquilizers, though neither of these induces sleep, as hypnotics do.

In the past, barbiturates and chloral hydrate were often used as hypnotics, but they have been replaced with benzodiazepines, which are safer and have less likelihood of overdose.

Hypnotics can be useful in cases where sleep is important to recovery. Nevertheless, they are not without dangers.

While overdose is very rare with benzodiazepines, it may occur where benzodiazepines are taken in combination with alcohol or other drugs.

Because of possible side effects such as drowsiness, loss of co-ordination, and loss of judgement, these drugs should not be used with alcohol and other similar types of drug. The dose should be kept low when prescribed for the elderly. Warnings should also be given about driving and working with machinery.

SEE ALSO *Anxiety, Anxiolitics, Detoxification, Drug dependence, Insomnia, Sedatives, Sleeping pills, Tranquilizers, Withdrawal*

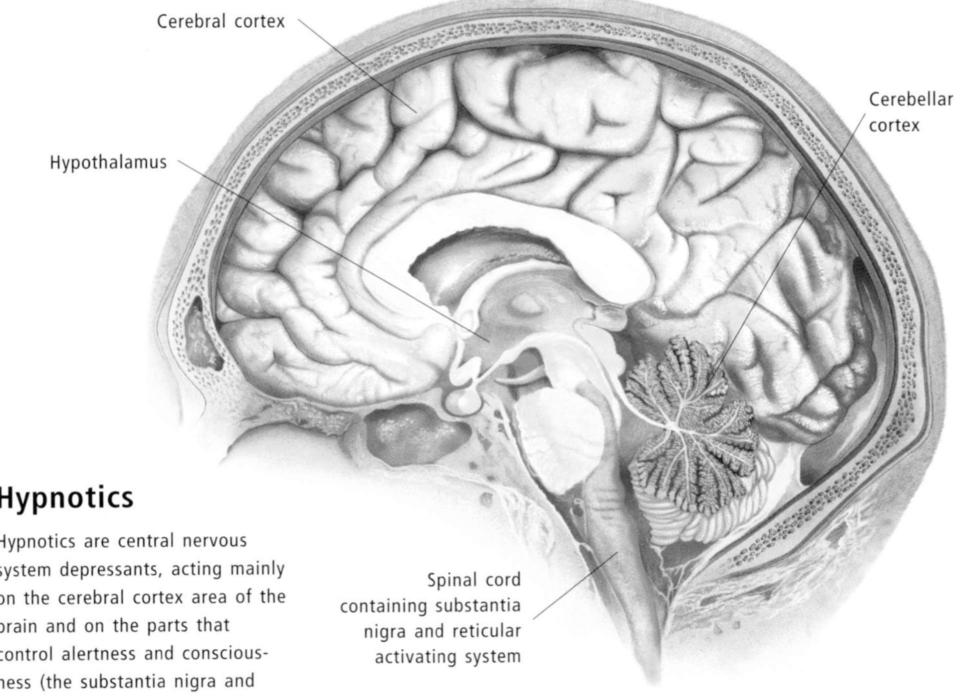

Hypnotics

Hypnotics are central nervous system depressants, acting mainly on the cerebral cortex area of the brain and on the parts that control alertness and consciousness (the substantia nigra and reticular activating system).

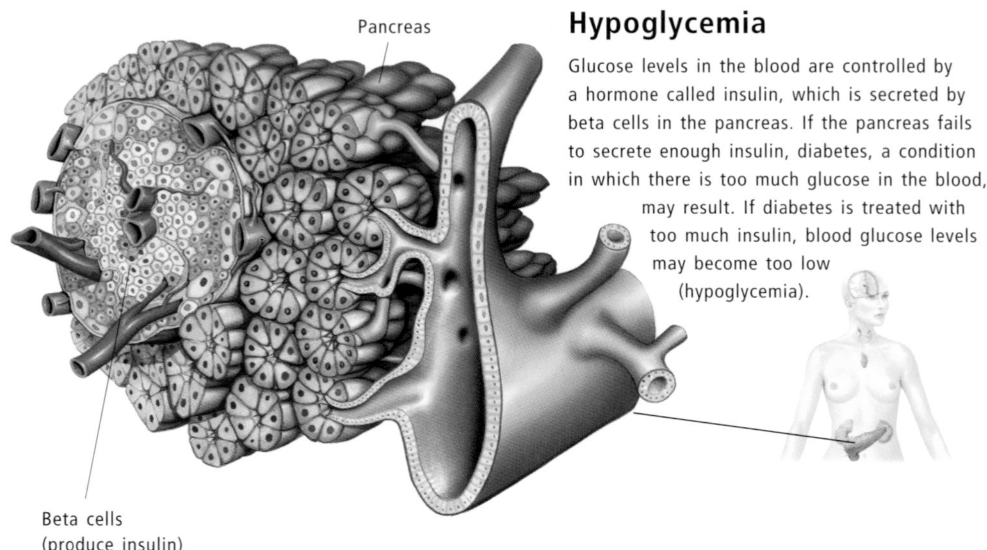

Hypoglycemia

Glucose levels in the blood are controlled by a hormone called insulin, which is secreted by beta cells in the pancreas. If the pancreas fails to secrete enough insulin, diabetes, a condition in which there is too much glucose in the blood, may result. If diabetes is treated with too much insulin, blood glucose levels may become too low (hypoglycemia).

HYPOCALCEMIA

Hypocalcemia is the medical term for abnormally low levels of calcium in the blood. It may be caused by underactivity of the parathyroid glands (hypoparathyroidism), or by vitamin D deficiency. Mild hypocalcemia causes no symptoms and may only be detected after a routine blood test. More severe hypocalcemia causes muscle twitching and seizures. Over time, chronic calcium deficiency contributes to poor mineralization of bones (osteoporosis), soft bones (osteomalacia) and rickets in children.

Treatment is with oral or intravenous calcium and oral vitamin D supplements.

SEE ALSO ***Calcium, Osteomalacia, Osteoporosis, Rickets, Parathyroid glands, Vitamins***

HYPOGLYCEMIA

Hypoglycemia is a condition caused by abnormally low levels of glucose (sugar) in the blood. This may be due to glucose leaving the blood at an excessive rate, or to decreased secretion of glucose into the blood. It most often occurs in persons with diabetes mellitus. For example, the condition may occur if a diabetic taking insulin (or other diabetic medication) has not eaten enough or has increased their amount of exercise without increasing the intake of food, or it may occur if the dosage of their medication is too high. In rare cases, hypoglycemia may be caused by an insulinoma, a tumor in the pancreas which secretes insulin. Occasionally, hypoglycemia may occur without any apparent cause.

Hypoglycemia deprives the body's cells of nutrients necessary for normal metabolic functioning. It causes dizziness, weakness, sweating, hunger, mental confusion, and/or personality changes. Severe hypoglycemia, which may cause coma, brain damage or death, is a medical emergency.

A diabetic learns to recognize the symptoms of hypoglycemia and takes sugar by mouth (by sucking candy, for example). In more serious cases, such as a coma, an injection of glucose or glucagon (a hormone that raises blood glucose levels) may be needed. After recovery, the diabetic's medication and/or diet will need to be adjusted by the physician.

SEE ALSO ***Blood sugar tests, Diabetes, Insulin, Pancreas***

HYPOKALEMIA

Potassium is crucial to the normal functioning of our cells. Classified medically as an electrolyte, it is involved in the maintenance of a normal heartbeat, regulation of the body's water balance and the activities of nerves and muscles. A deficiency of potassium in the blood and body tissues is known as hypokalemia, a dangerous and potentially life-threatening condition most often associated with chronic illness and ageing. It may also occur as a side effect of certain drugs.

Symptoms of a deficiency may include high blood pressure, abnormal heartbeat rhythms, depression, fatigue, slow reflexes, muscle weakness and paralysis. Depletion of the body's potassium can be caused by excessive vomiting, diarrhea or sweating, kidney disease or certain medications, such as digitalis (for heart problems) and diuretics.

Most people can obtain sufficient potassium through a balanced diet, and minor deficiencies can be treated by increasing your intake of potassium-rich foods, such as oranges, tomatoes, bananas, potatoes with their skins on, carrots, dried apricots and fish. More severe deficiencies may require oral or intravenous potassium supplements and hospitalization.

SEE ALSO ***Electrolytes, Nutrition, Potassium***

HYPONATREMIA

Publicity about the dangers of high-salt diets has made many people aware of the health risks of too much sodium. But an abnormally low concentration of sodium in the blood—known as hyponatremia—can also cause some problems. Usually the condition occurs when too much water is consumed in relation to sodium, or the body fails to excrete excess water. Both situations can create an imbalance in the body.

People who are more likely to be susceptible to hyponatremia include the elderly, the very young and the mentally ill patients who may not be able to respond appropriately to their thirst, and people with certain kidney disorders.

Hyponatremia can also be a problem for athletes, particularly distance and marathon runners, who can develop the condition if they drink too much water without also replacing sodium lost in sweat during excessive physical exertion. The problem can be avoided by quenching thirst with sports drinks that contain electrolytes, rather than just water alone.

Symptoms of hyponatremia range from nausea, muscle cramps, weakness and fatigue to seizures and a loss of consciousness in severe deficiencies. In extreme cases the condition can be fatal.

SEE ALSO ***Sodium***

HYPOPARATHYROIDISM

Hypoparathyroidism is a rare disorder in which production of parathyroid hormone—which helps regulate blood calcium levels—is either reduced or non-existent due to dysfunctional or absent parathyroid glands. It may be a congenital condition or, less commonly, acquired later in life (usually due to surgical damage to or removal of the parathyroids).

Hypoparathyroidism leads to abnormally low blood calcium levels (hypocalcemia) which can trigger a nerve disorder called tetany, characterized by painful muscle spasms and twitches. People born with hypoparathyroidism can also suffer from dry skin, hair loss and a susceptibility to yeast (*Candida*) infections.

Without treatment, hypoparathyroidism in children can lead to impaired physical and mental development. The condition is treated with calcium and vitamin D supplements, which need to be taken for life.

SEE ALSO ***Parathyroid glands***

HYPOPHOSPHATASIA

Hypophosphatasia is an inherited metabolic disorder caused by abnormally low levels in the body of the enzyme serum alkaline phosphatase which is critical in the development of the bones. The severity of the condition can vary widely from patient to patient.

Symptoms of the mildest forms may not appear until late childhood or adulthood. In the most severe cases, newborns can suffer from impaired growth and eventually die. In all sufferers, the skeleton is affected in some way and the teeth are often involved. There is no known treatment for hypophosphatasia.

SEE ALSO ***Congenital abnormalities, Enzyme deficiencies***

HYPOPLASIA

Incomplete or defective development of a body organ or tissue is known as hypoplasia. Potential causes are many and varied and may depend on the particular part of the body affected.

Cartilage-hair hypoplasia, in which the cartilage is affected leading to bone abnormalities, has a genetic cause. This condition is characterized by dwarfism. Enamel hypoplasia, which affects the teeth, can also be a genetic disorder. Pulmonary hypoplasia can occur when other organs have compressed the lungs during their development in the uterus. The cause of optic nerve hypoplasia remains unclear but it is sometimes blamed on substances taken by a mother during pregnancy. Sufferers of this disorder are missing 10–90 percent of the 1.2 million nerve fibers usually found in an optic nerve, impairing vision in the affected eye.

SEE ALSO ***Congenital abnormalities***

HYPOSPADIAS

This is a relatively common male birth defect of unknown cause, in which the development of the penile urethra is abnormal. Instead of forming a tube that extends the full length of the shaft and opens at the tip of the glans penis, the urethral opening (the meatus) develops at some point on the underside of the penis, interfering with normal voiding of urine.

Hypospadias may be accompanied by a downward curve of the shaft of the penis, known as chordee. There is no associated abnormality of the testes, and the condition can be corrected surgically, usually with good results.

SEE ALSO ***Penis, Reproductive systems, Urethra, Urinary systems***

HYPOTENSION

Hypotension, or low blood pressure, is a condition in which the blood pressure is below the average measurement of 120/80 mm Hg. Often a low blood pressure is of little significance, being a statistical variant from the average, and normal for a particular person (it may even indicate a prolonged life expectancy).

Sometimes hypotension may be caused by disease, such as vasovagal syncope, hypoaldosteronism, diabetes mellitus, tabes dorsalis or Parkinson's disease. Some drugs, especially antidepressants, may have hypotensive effects.

Often hypotension has no symptoms and is diagnosed during a visit to the doctor for a routine checkup or for some other reason. The sufferer may go to the doctor complaining of feeling dizzy and fainting, especially when standing up quickly. Most cases get better without treatment. If there is an underlying cause, treating it will reverse the condition. If hypotension is due to drug treatment, the drug(s) should be stopped if possible.

SEE ALSO ***Blood pressure***

HYPOTHALAMUS

The hypothalamus is a small but vital region at the base of the brain, which is essential for the maintenance of life. It contains specialized receptor cells, which can detect changes in the properties of circulating blood (for example, temperature, hormone levels, osmotic pressure). The pituitary gland, or hypophysis, is attached to its exposed surface.

By regulating hormone production in the pituitary gland, and through neural connections with other parts of the brain and spinal

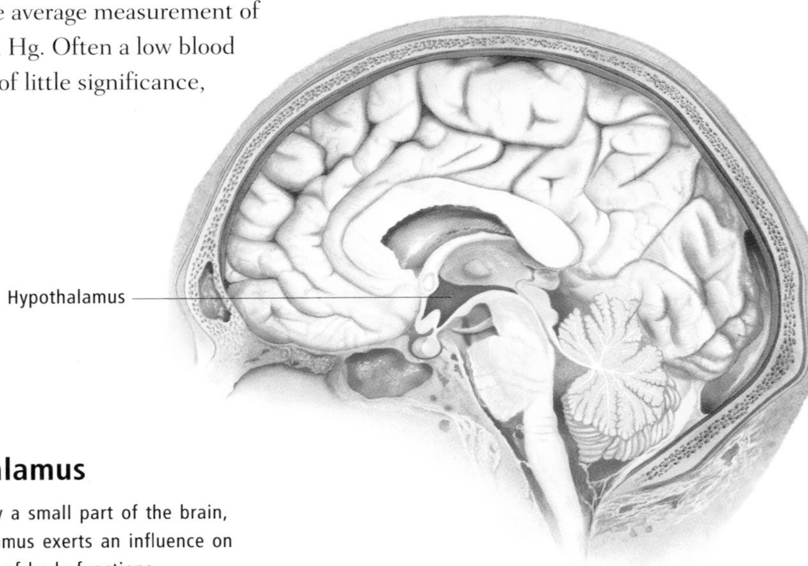

Hypothalamus

Although only a small part of the brain, the hypothalamus exerts an influence on a wide range of body functions.

H

cord, the hypothalamus provides overall control of the autonomic nervous system, which coordinates activity in the body's internal organs. It contains centers which regulate the heart and blood pressure, body temperature, water balance, food intake, growth and sexual reproduction. It is also important in the expression of emotions such as fear, anger and pleasure.

Activity in the hypothalamus may be disrupted by tumors, vascular disease or head injury. The most common disorder of the hypothalamus is diabetes insipidus, a condition in which there is excessive urine production, accompanied by constant drinking (up to 10 quarts or 10 liters per day). Inability to maintain a constant body temperature, eating disorders (such as obesity and bulimia), sleeping problems and memory loss may also associated with disorders of the hypothalamus.

SEE ALSO ***Autonomic nervous system, Brain, Diabetes insipidus, Hormones, Pituitary gland***

HYPOTHERMIA

Hypothermia results from exposure (usually accidental) to cold. It occurs commonly in the elderly and children (who have difficulty shivering to keep warm), in ill or alcohol-dependent people. Healthy people, for example, mountaineers, caught out in the cold can also develop hypothermia especially when conditions also involve snow, wind and/or rain.

In hypothermia, the body's core temperature gradually drops below the normal level of 98.6°F (37°C) to as low as 80°F (27°C). When this happens, the body's metabolism, respiration and heartbeat all slow down and the person becomes mentally confused, with slurred speech and muscle cramps. If untreated, coma and death may follow.

Any wet and frozen clothing should be removed and the person's body needs to be gradually warmed in layers of dry, warm clothing. Hospitalization may be necessary.

SEE ALSO ***Body temperature***

HYPOTHYROIDISM

This refers to the reduced secretion of hormones by the thyroid gland, principally involving the underproduction of thyroxine. It may be caused by insufficient thyroid tissue, inhibition of hormone synthesis or by decreased production of thyroid stimulating hormone by the pituitary gland. If untreated, infants develop a condition called cretinism, while in adults hypothyroidism leads to myxedema.

SEE ALSO ***Cretinism, Myxedema, Pituitary gland, Thyroid gland***

HYPOXIA

Hypoxia is a shortage of oxygen in the cells and tissues. There are many potential causes. It can result from a variety of disorders or substances, such as carbon dioxide or carbon monoxide, which reduce the blood's ability to transport and circulate oxygen throughout the body. It can be caused by environmental factors, particularly high altitudes. Or it may be due to a disease or injury that affects a tissue's ability to use oxygen.

Hypoxia can be isolated to a particular organ or it may be widespread in the body. The tissues that are most sensitive to reduced oxygen levels are the heart, brain, liver and blood vessels to the lungs. In severe or protracted episodes of hypoxia, permanent tissue damage due to cell death can occur. The onset of the condition can often appear without warning. Early symptoms may include a rise in heart and respiration rates in response to falling oxygen levels in the blood. Another early symptom can be a sense of euphoria, or well-being—something like an alcohol-induced high. Dizziness and mental confusion may follow.

Treatment for hypoxia will depend on the cause. A patient may require mechanical ventilation, drugs to stimulate respiration, or oxygen therapy.

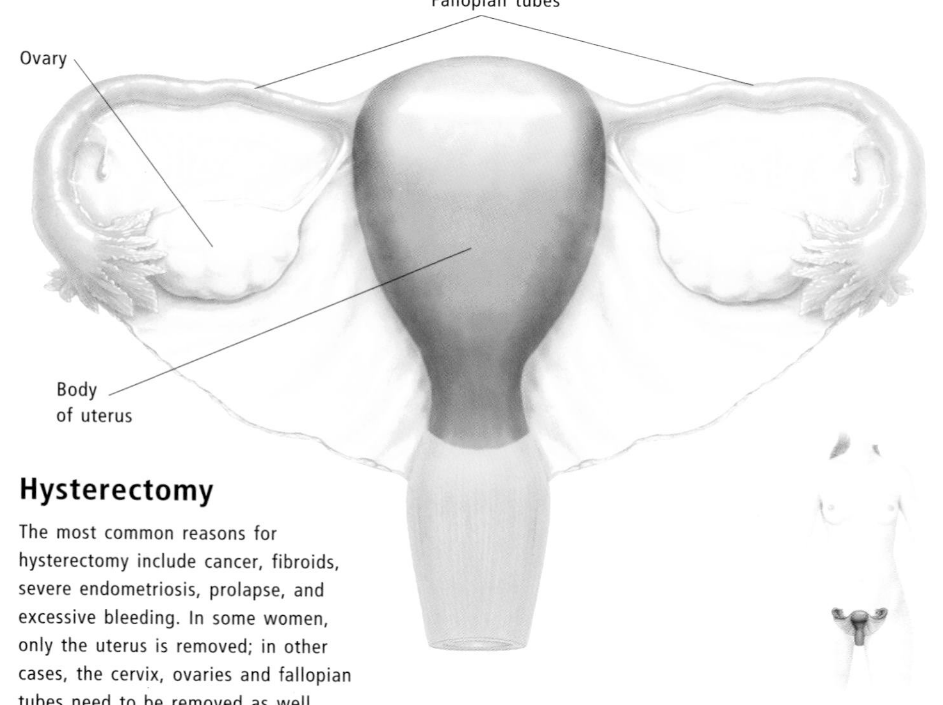

Hysterectomy

The most common reasons for hysterectomy include cancer, fibroids, severe endometriosis, prolapse, and excessive bleeding. In some women, only the uterus is removed; in other cases, the cervix, ovaries and fallopian tubes need to be removed as well.

HYSTERECTOMY

Hysterectomy is the surgical removal of the uterus and it is the second most common operation on women in the industrialized world after dilation and curettage. It may be performed for a number of reasons. These include cancer of the uterus, the cervix or the ovaries; benign tumors, such as large fibroids; extreme cases of endometriosis; a severe prolapse of the uterus; excessive blood loss that is not responding to treatment; and, very rarely, after childbirth or gynecological surgery.

There are several forms of this operation. A total hysterectomy is the removal of the entire uterus plus the cervix. A subtotal hysterectomy removes the uterus but not the cervix. A radical hysterectomy removes the uterus and the associated lymph glands in the pelvis. A hysterosalpingo-oophorectomy removes the uterus, ovaries and tubes on both sides.

The operation can be performed through an abdominal incision or through the vagina; the latter method is now more common. A laparoscope, a narrow tube with a fiber-optic light on one end, is often used in the operation. It is inserted through a small incision just below the navel and enables the surgeon to view the reproductive organs and to operate using small instruments guided by the laparoscope.

Risks include infections and damage to other organs. An abdominal hysterectomy is major surgery which will require post-operative painkillers and a convalescence period of around six weeks. Vaginal hysterectomy causes less post-operative pain and requires a shorter convalescence. Laparoscopic hysterectomy has more complications but a very short recovery time.

Once the woman has recovered from the operation, hysterectomy will not affect her ability to have sexual intercourse and, in many cases, will improve her quality of life. A serious operation, a woman may require adequate support and counseling, if necessary. Side effects include no more menstrual periods and no risk of pregnancy. A woman who must have a hysterectomy before she has reached menopause will need hormone replacement therapy, if her ovaries are not left in place.

Fewer hysterectomies are performed now than in the 1970s, when there was some controversy over unnecessary operations.

SEE ALSO *Endometriosis, Fibroids, Hormone replacement therapy, Hysterosalpingo-oophorectomy, Ovaries, Reproductive systems, Uterus*

HYSTEROSALPINGOGRAPHY

Hysterosalpingography is a medical x-ray investigation *(-graphy)* aimed at visualizing the uterus *(hystero-)* and fallopian tube *(salpingo-)*. The investigation involves introducing a fluid which is opaque to x-rays into the uterine cervix, under gentle pressure.

This fluid fills the interior of the uterus and tube, making it possible, using x-rays, to detect tumors or obstructions which might cause infertility.

In most modern investigations of infertility, hysterosalpingography has largely been superseded by laparoscopic examination, where a fiberoptic instrument allows the practitioner to see the interior of the pelvis, combined with colored dye injection.

SEE ALSO *Fallopian tubes, Laparoscopy, Salpingitis, Uterus*

HYSTEROSALPINGO-OOPHORECTOMY

This is the surgical removal of the uterus, fallopian tube and ovaries. It may be used in combination with radiation and hormone therapy to treat advanced cases of carcinoma (cancer) of the cervix and uterus.

SEE ALSO *Cervix, Fallopian tubes, Hysterectomy, Ovaries, Uterus*

HYSTEROSCOPY

Hysteroscopy is the use of a hysteroscope, a uterine speculum with reflector, to remove by excision a fibroid tumor that is bulging into the uterine cavity. It is also used in visual examination of the canal of the uterine cervix and the uterus.

SEE ALSO *Cervix, Fibroids, Hysterectomy, Uterus*

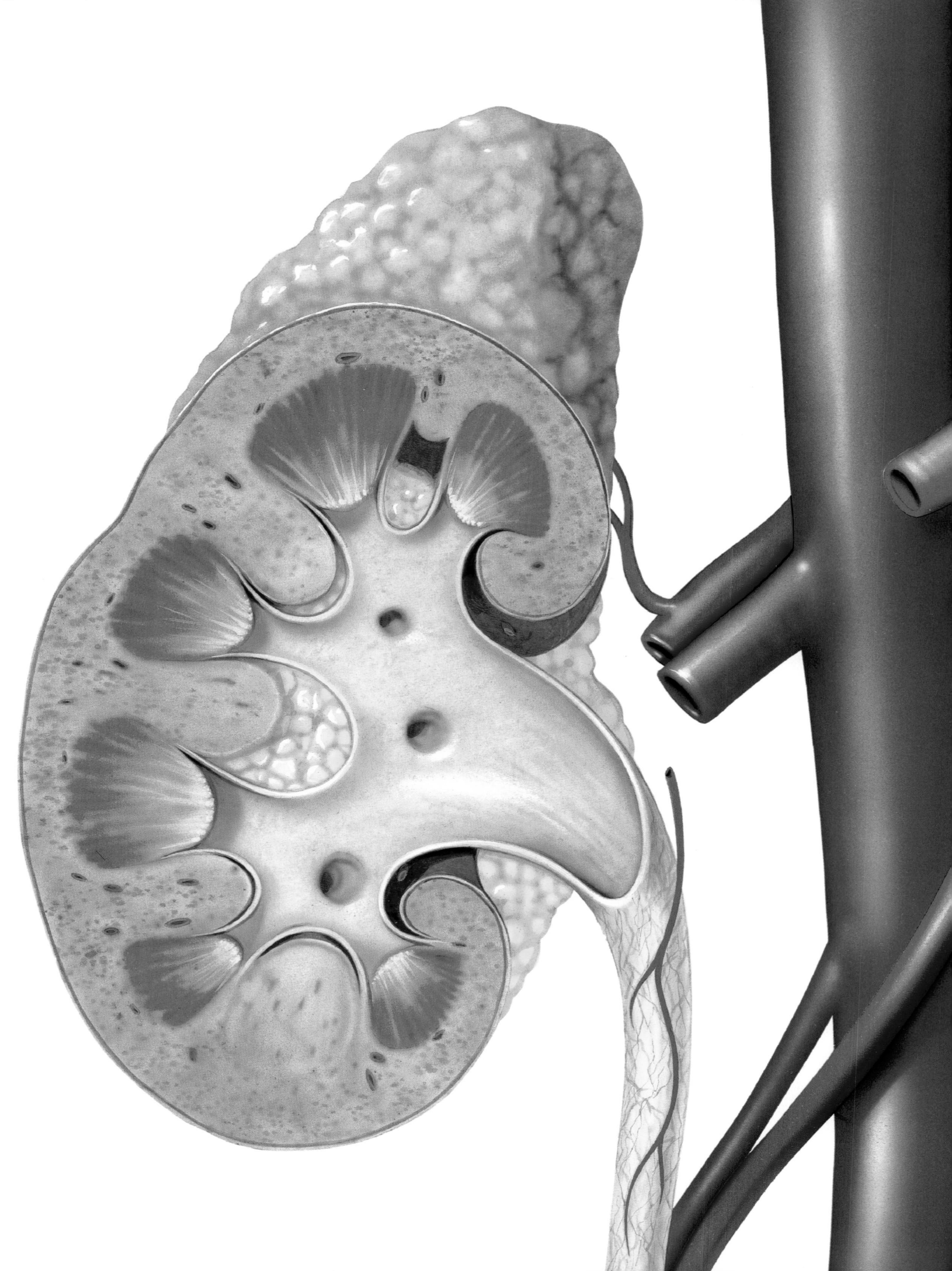

IJK

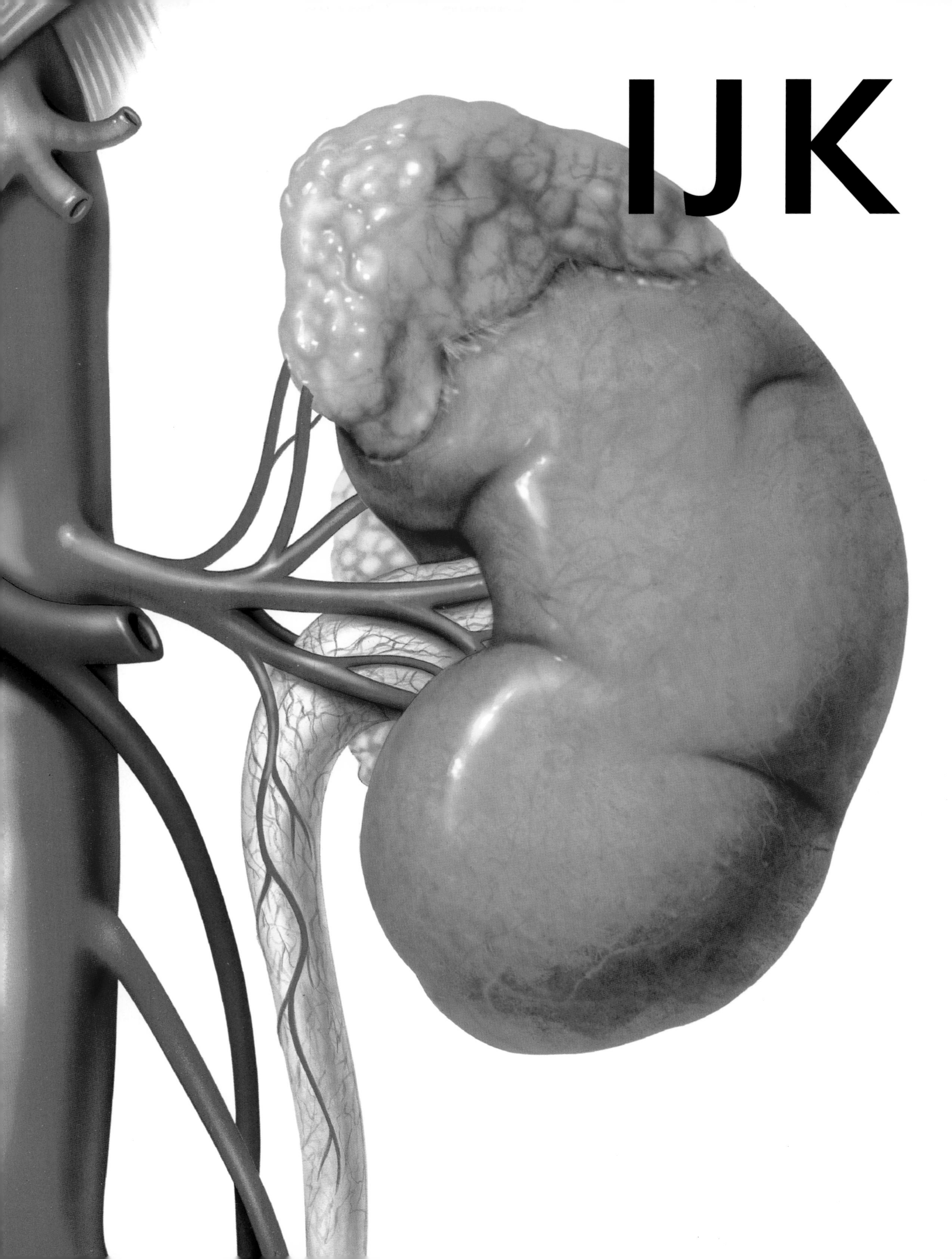

IATROGENIC DISEASE

Iatrogenic disease is disease caused by medical treatment or resulting from the effects of a doctor's words, treatments or actions on the patient. It may be an unavoidable side effect of the treatment or occur because the treatment was inappropriate.

The word iatrogenic comes from the Greek *iatros* ("physician") plus *genic* ("produced by"). Iatrogenic diseases are estimated to cause between two and four times as many fatalities annually as road accidents in developed countries. The elderly are twice as much at risk as young people. It can occur in orthodox and alternative medicine.

Prevention strategies include seeking treatment outside of hospital where appropriate, obtaining information about treatment options, reading consent forms carefully, obtaining a second opinion about a proposed treatment, and delegating a relative to liaise with staff in hospitals.

ICHTHYOSIS

Ichthyosis is an inherited disorder in which the skin becomes thickened, forming cracks and fissures, which give it a fish-scale appearance.

Legs, arms, hands and trunk are the areas most affected. The condition typically begins in childhood before the age of four and improves during adulthood; however, it may recur when a person becomes elderly. There are various types of ichthyosis, but most are inherited genetic traits. Some forms may be acquired or develop in association with other diseases.

There is no cure for ichthyosis, but the use of mild, non-drying soaps and moisturizing creams and ointments will help the condition. Ointments that contain catalytic agents, such as lactic acid and salicylic acid, are especially useful, as these chemicals help the skin to shed.

SEE ALSO *Skin*

ILEITIS

Ileitis is literally inflammation of the ileum, which is the furthest end of the small intestine. Inflammation can occur as the result of infection with viruses or bacteria, and includes common conditions such as viral gastroenteritis and rarer conditions such as tuberculosis of the intestine, which affects the ileum more commonly than other parts of the bowel.

Crohn's disease is an inflammatory disease of the gastrointestinal tract, which most commonly affects the ileum. Its cause remains unknown, but appears to involve a combination of genetic and environmental factors.

Ileitis may also occur following radiation therapy of the abdominal organs. A person suffering from ileitis may experience pain in the abdomen and loss of appetite and weight. Treatment involves medication to remove the source of infection.

SEE ALSO *Crohn's disease, Ileum, Intestines*

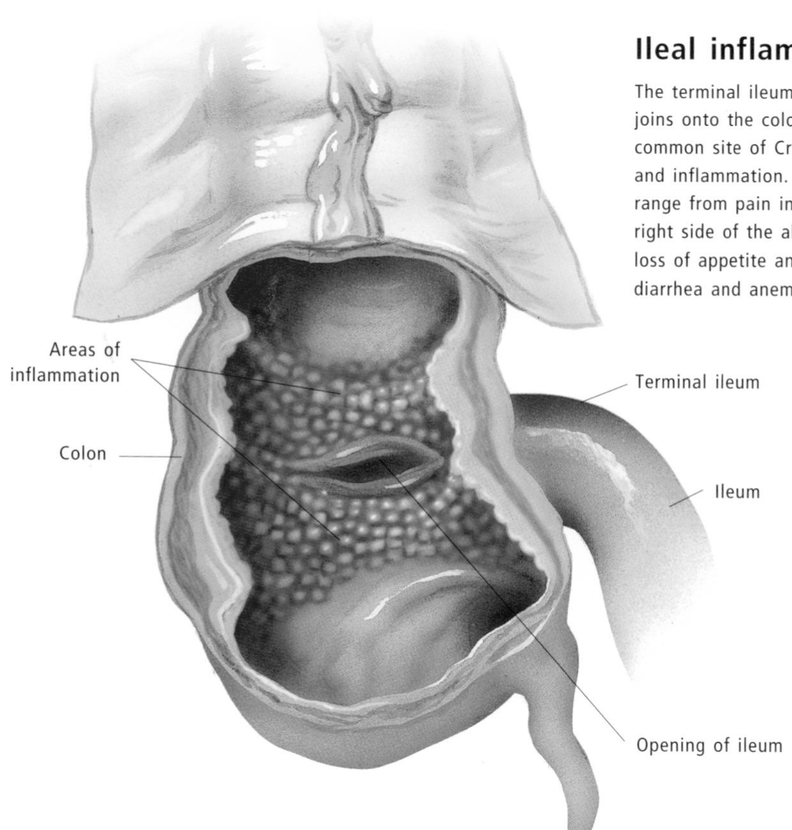

Ileal inflammation

The terminal ileum—where it joins onto the colon—is a common site of Crohn's disease and inflammation. Symptoms range from pain in the lower right side of the abdomen to loss of appetite and weight, diarrhea and anemia.

ILEOSTOMY

Ileostomy is a surgical procedure in which the last part of the small intestine (the ileum) is permanently opened and brought to the surface of the abdomen. Fecal matter leaves the body through this opening which is called a "stoma". The stoma is located in the right lower quadrant of the abdomen. The procedure is usually performed after removal of the entire colon and rectum for the treatment of ulcerative colitis, Crohn's disease or familial polyposis coli.

Fecal matter will be more liquid and will pass more frequently than fecal matter from a colostomy. The procedure is performed under general anesthesia in a hospital. Full recovery takes about six weeks.

SEE ALSO *Colostomy, Ileum, Intestines*

ILEUM

The ileum is the last part of the small intestine. It leads on from the jejunum and empties into the cecum at the ileocecal junction. The ileum is about 10 feet (3 meters) long and, along with the jejunum, is suspended from the back abdominal wall by a fold of membrane called the mesentery.

While most nutrients (fats, sugars and amino acids) are absorbed from the duodenum and jejunum, there are important substances absorbed primarily from the ileum. These include bile acids, which are produced by the liver and secreted into the duodenum to break up fat globules. The bile acids are then recycled by being reabsorbed from the ileum and returned to the liver. The ileum is also important as the absorption site for vitamin B_{12} (cyanocobalamin).

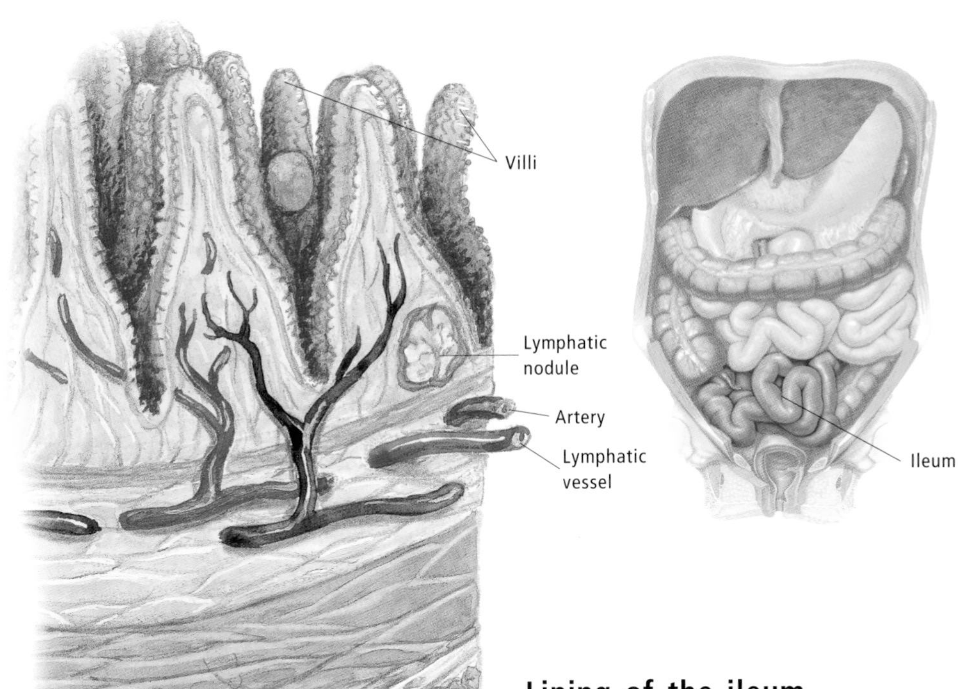

Ileum

The ileum is the last part of the small intestine, which absorbs bile acids and vitamin B_{12}. The working of the ileum can be affected by a number of illnesses, such as gastroenteritis and Crohn's disease.

Lining of the ileum

The villi and microvilli increase the surface area of the small intestine. Each villus contains lymph and blood vessels and it is through these villi that bile acid is absorbed from the ileum and returned to the liver.

The ileum can be affected by bowel obstruction, Crohn's disease and gastroenteritis. Crohn's disease is most common in the terminal ileum, with patients usually complaining of diarrhea, recurrent abdominal pain, weakness, weight loss and fever. Obstruction of blood vessels supplying the ileum may cause gangrene of the bowel, requiring immediate surgery.

Tumors are rare in the small intestine, comprising only 1–5 percent of all tumors of the gastrointestinal tract.

SEE ALSO *Crohn's disease, Digestive system, Duodenum, Gastroenteritis, Intestines, Jejunum*

ILEUS

Ileus refers to paralysis of bowel movement (a normal function known as peristalsis). It may arise in several different situations: after major abdominal surgery, infection in the abdomen, low output of blood from the heart, and even as a result of pneumonia. The abdomen is distended and bowel sounds are usually absent, although occasional faint or irregular bursts of bowel movement may be heard. When an x-ray is taken, the loops of bowel appear to be distended.

In newborn infants with cystic fibrosis, ileus may occur due to the presence of a thick plug of meconium (meconium ileus). In normal newborn infants the meconium, which is a paste filling the bowel before birth, is cleared from the bowel within a few days. Surgical intervention may be required to remove the blockage.

SEE ALSO *Bowel, Intestines, Peristalsis*

IMAGING TECHNIQUES

These are techniques used in the production of diagnostic images. Since the discovery of x-rays (electromagnetic radiation) in 1895, imaging techniques have played an important role in diagnosis.

Radiography uses x-rays to produce a negative photographic image of the internal bones and organs. The various parts of the body allow the x-rays through to differing degrees; the film creates an image by recording these variations in contrast. Often, to outline organs and tissues, opaque substances are used as well; for example, in a barium meal, the patient drinks a barium compound, which outlines the stomach and increases its contrast with surrounding tissue.

New technologies offer more precise images and are safer than x-rays. Ultrasound is a sonar technique that bounces sound waves off internal bodily structures and measures their density. The resulting picture can be used to visualize organs and body structures and detect movement. Ultrasound is especially useful in investigating pregnancy because it does not harm the fetus or the mother.

Computerized axial tomography (CAT) scanning is a technique in which a machine passes x-rays through a patient's body from various angles. A computer then creates a three-dimensional image of internal organs and structures inside the body. Using CAT scanning, a physician can tell the difference between a solid tumor, a fluid-filled cyst and a blood-filled hematoma in brain tissue.

Magnetic resonance imaging (MRI) uses an external magnetic field created by a series of powerful electromagnets in a scanner to excite hydrogen atoms in the body, which give off radio signals to the scanner. These signals are read by a computer and converted into a detailed image. By using magnetism instead of x-rays, MRI scanning avoids exposing people to radiation.

Nuclear scans are scans in which radioactive material such as thallium is injected into a vein. The isotope passes through the body, to be selectively taken up by organs such as the heart, bone and kidneys, depending on which isotope is used. A scintillation camera or scanner then detects radiation emitted from the isotope, converts them into images and displays them on a video screen for interpretation to help assess defects in the organ's structure and function. Nuclear scans are usually perfomed in the nuclear medicine department of a hospital.

SEE ALSO *Barium meal, CAT scan, Magnetic resonance imaging, Ultrasound, X-ray*

IMMUNITY

Immunity is the body's ability to protect itself from disease. It is achieved via the immune system, a complex network of organs, cells and proteins that recognizes foreign substances (such as viruses, bacteria, fungi and other pathogens) in the body and destroys them. This process is called the immune response.

There are two broad parts to the immune system. One part is called the humoral immune system, so called because the immune response takes place in the body fluids (humors). When a foreign body, or antigen, is identified, proteins called antibodies are produced by B lymphocytes (white blood cells) in the blood and body fluids which then attack the antigens or render them more easily attacked by other white blood cells.

The second component is the cell-mediated immune system, involving the different types of T lymphocytes. Some ingest and destroy invading pathogens while other T lymphocytes destroy them directly. Antibodies are not involved.

The first time an individual is exposed to a pathogen, or antigen, there is a delay while the immune system responds and overcomes the pathogen. The next time the individual is exposed to that same pathogen, the response is much faster, and the individual may not develop the disease. This is due to "memory" B and T cells, stored since the first encounter with that particular pathogen. The individual is then said to have immunity to that pathogen.

Immunity can be artificially induced by vaccination. A vaccine is a weakened or killed form of the pathogen. It causes the body to manufacture antibodies against the pathogen, so that if it is later exposed to the live form of the pathogen, the body can then launch a prompt and effective immune response.

Immunity is acquired through either active or passive means. Active immunity refers to those situations where the body itself has created the immunity, either as a result of past exposure to the disease, or because it has been vaccinated against it. In cases of passive immunity, the response has come from elsewhere, either from an injection of antibodies for example, or, in the case of the fetus, from the mother. Unlike active immunity, which has "memory" and can mount future responses to the same pathogen, passive immunity is usually only temporary.

Immunodeficiency

When the immune system fails to work properly and is deficient, a person is said to have an immunodeficiency. This can be due to a genetic disease or may be acquired—for example, in acquired immunodeficiency syndrome (AIDS) due to the human immunodeficiency virus (HIV). If the immune system is severely damaged, serious infections, called "opportunistic infections" may develop after exposure to pathogens that would not normally cause disease.

Allergy

An allergy is a condition in which the immune system reacts with unusual hypersensitivity to a substance or substances (called allergens). In the process, a compound

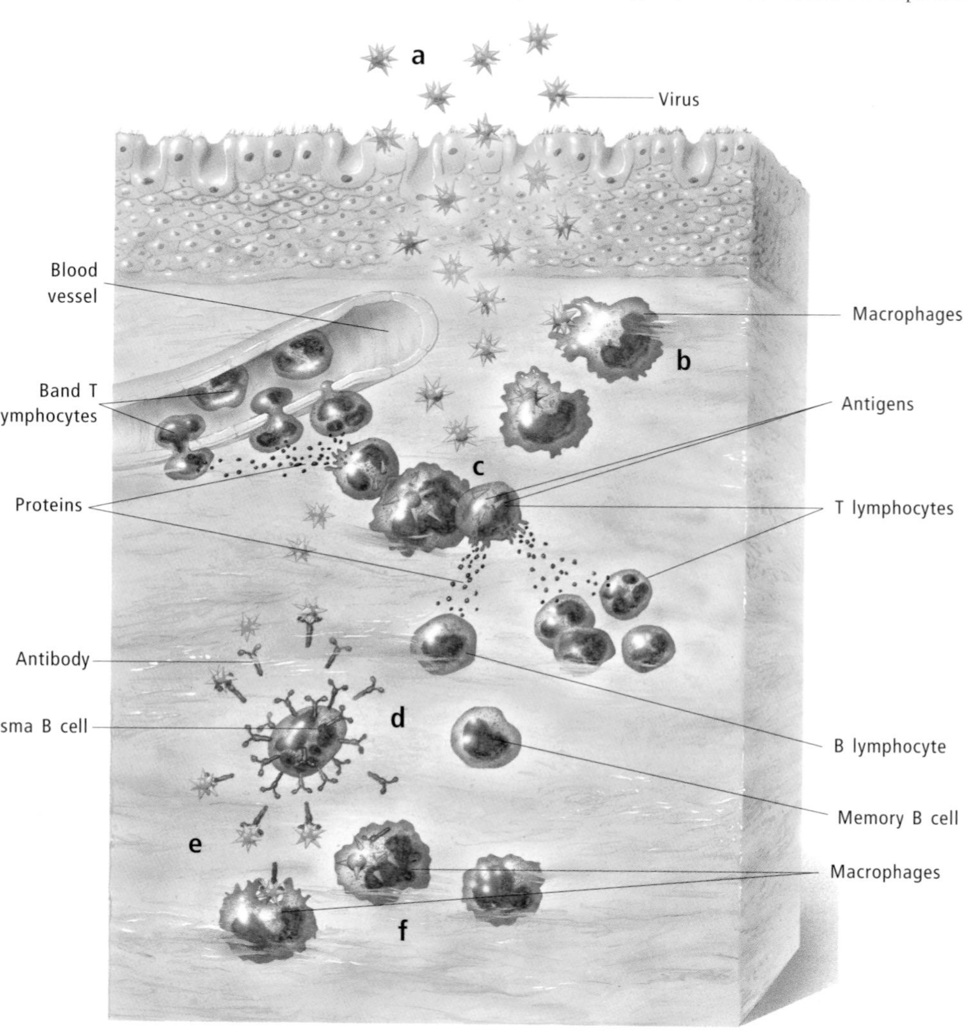

Humoral immune response

B lymphocytes (white blood cells) produce antibodies to help identify and eliminate invading antigens (carried by bacteria or viruses). They are helped in the body's defenses by circulating T lymphocytes and macrophages (scavenging white blood cells).

(a) Virus particles invade tissue through surface cells and multiply.

(b) Virus particles are consumed by macrophages.

(c) The macrophages break down the virus and present antigens to circulating T lymphocytes. These release proteins to recruit more T and B lymphocytes from nearby blood vessels and tissue to help defend the body.

(d) B lymphocytes divide into memory B cells (which remember the invading virus for future attacks) and plasma B cells which make antibodies specific to the invading virus.

(e) The circulating antibodies attach onto the virus particles.

(f) Macrophages primed to recognize the antibody consume the virus and break it down, saving the body from infection.

called histamine is released from special body cells called mast cells. This excess of histamine irritates the surrounding tissues and causes allergy symptoms, such as coughing, sneezing, wheezing and rash.

There are several common allergic conditions. Hay fever causes a runny nose and watering or itching eyes. In urticaria (hives) there is itching, redness and lumps in the skin. An allergy to antibiotics, especially penicillin, may cause a skin rash, while asthma causes a wheezing in the chest. An allergic person can undergo desensitization with injections of the allergen known to cause the symptoms, however, the results are very variable and may not last.

Autoimmune diseases

Autoimmune diseases develop when the body's immune system fails to recognize tissues belonging to the body and attacks and destroys them as though they were foreign. The cause is not fully understood, but in some cases it is thought to be triggered by exposure to microorganisms and drugs, especially in people with a genetic predisposition to these disorders.

Autoimmune disorders and the tissues they attack include: Hashimoto's thyroiditis (thyroid), pernicious anemia (blood), Addison's disease (adrenal cortex), diabetes mellitus (pancreas), rheumatoid arthritis (joints), systemic lupus erythematosus (connective tissues), and myasthenia gravis (muscles).

Organ rejection

After organ transplantation, the immune system of the body may not recognize the transplanted tissue as part of the recipient's body tissues and may mount an immune response against it. This is known as organ rejection, and is a common complication of transplantation. It is less likely if the donor is a close relative of the recipient.

SEE ALSO *AIDS, Allergies, Antibodies, Autoimmune disease, HIV, Immunization, Lymphatic/Immune system, Opportunistic infection, White blood cells*

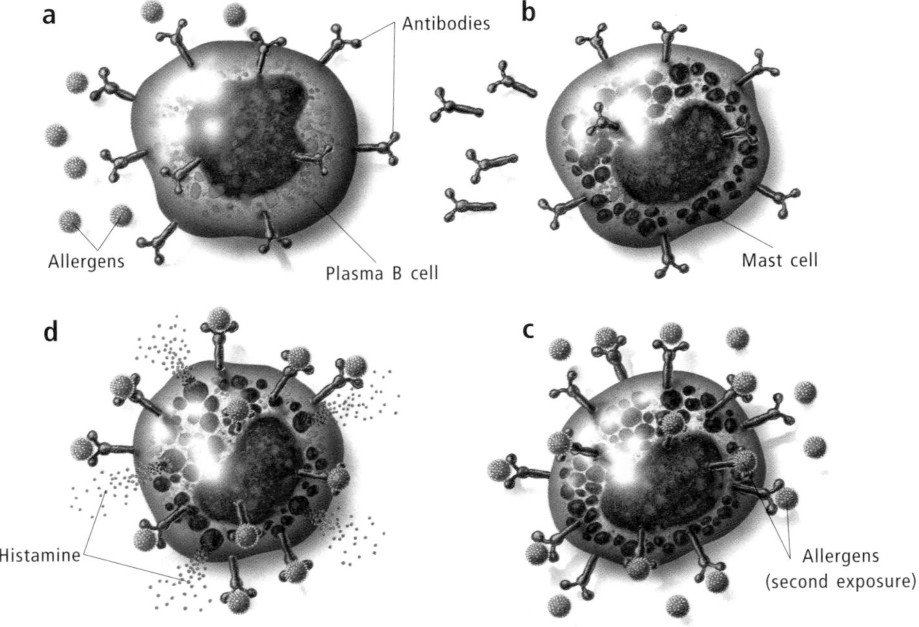

Allergic reaction

Exposure to invading allergens (that the body is sensitive to) leads to the release of histamine, which irritates tissues and causes sypmtoms such as sneezing and rash.

(a) On the body's first exposure to an allergen, plasma B cells produce antibodies.

(b) The antibodies attach to mast cells circulating in the body's tissues.

(c) The next time allergens enter the body they are captured by the antibodies on the mast cells.

(d) The mast cells respond by releasing histamine, a chemical that causes inflammation and the symptoms of allergy.

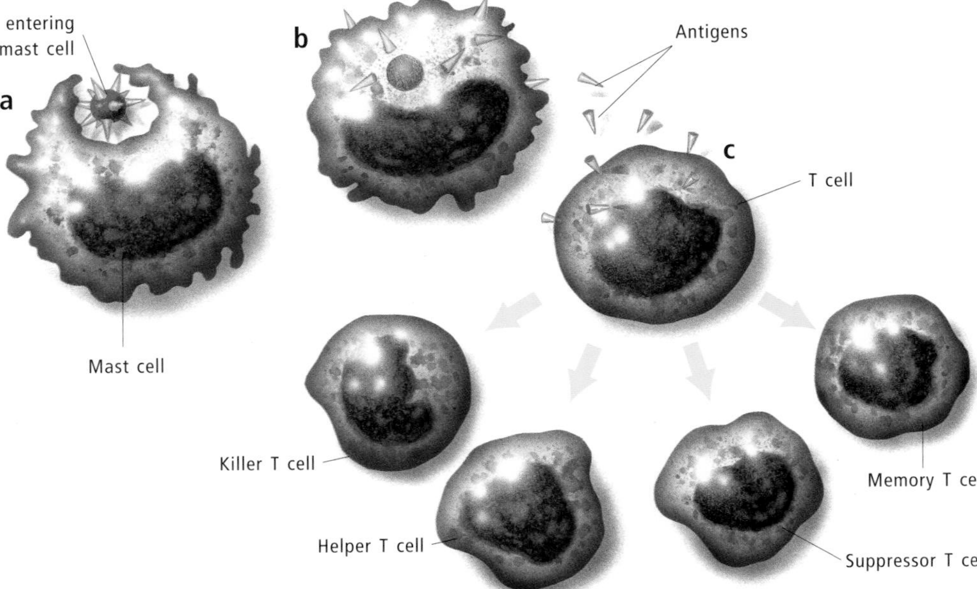

Cell-mediated immune response

T lymphocytes (a type of white blood cell) are responsible for the delayed action of the cell-mediated response.

(a) Circulating mast cells ingest invading virus.

(b) Mast cells process the virus and present antigens to T cells.

(c) The T cells produce clones which each play a special role in the immune response: memory T cells remember the invading antigen for future attacks; helper T cells recruit B and T cells to the site of antigen attack; suppressor T cells inhibit the action of B and T cells; and killer T cells attach onto invading antigens and destroy them.

I

IMMUNIZATION

Immunization uses a killed virus or bacterium, a weakened strain ("attenuated"), a deactivated toxin ("toxoid"), or sometimes a synthetically or genetically engineered vaccine to help the body build up its immunity to certain diseases. After being immunized, the body's immune system manufactures antibodies which are special proteins that can recognize and help destroy viruses and bacteria or foreign toxins when they invade the body. In addition, other parts of the immune system are also activated to combat an infection.

A single dose of some vaccines will give immunity for life, however others need to be given according to a specific schedule and need boosters or additional reinforcing doses to maintain immunity. When children are immunized against diphtheria, tetanus and pertussis (whooping cough) they are given a vaccine known as DTP. This has recently been replaced with a newer vaccine called DTaP, which contains a different form of pertussis vaccine called "acellular pertussis" vaccine and has fewer side effects than the older form. When children are immunized against measles, mumps and rubella, they are given a vaccine called MMR. A vaccine is available in some parts of the world for varicella (chickenpox), and a vaccine that against all four of these , called MMRV, is being developed. Vaccinations against *Haemophilus influenzae* type b and poliomyelitis are also part of the usual childhood immunization schedule in most countries. It is important that when children are being immunized, that they receive the full schedule of initial and booster vaccinations so that the immunization process is effective. The timing is also important in immunization. Schedules have been established by health authorities to achieve the most effective results.

There are other vaccines which are available or being developed, and many of these are also intended for travelers and people at high risk of infection such as the elderly or people with underlying diseases, who may have weakend immune systems. Some of these vaccines include hepatitis A, Japanese encephalitis, yellow fever, tuberculosis (BCG vaccine), pneumococcal infection, meningococcal infection, influenza, varicella-zoster (chickenpox and shingles), plague and typhoid. Some of these are not available in all countries, and there are other vaccines currently under development. There are as yet no effective vaccines for dengue fever, malaria or HIV (AIDS).

It is advisable for travelers to be aware of the schedule for certain immunizations when they are traveling to countries where vaccine-preventable diseases are a risk.

The vaccines used in immunization have been tested thoroughly and are safe and effective. Though minimal risks have been found with some vaccines, serious reactions are rare. The complications associated with the disease far outweigh the risks of complications from the vaccine.

Immunization against infectious diseases of all types has probably saved more lives than any other public health measure, apart from the provision of sanitation and clean water. Research into new vaccines is ongoing with a vaccine for infants against meningitis and blood poisoning being among the newest to become available.

SEE ALSO *Antibodies, Chickenpox, Diphtheria, Hepatitis, Measles, Mumps, Poliomyelitis, Rubella, Smallpox, Tetanus, Whooping cough*

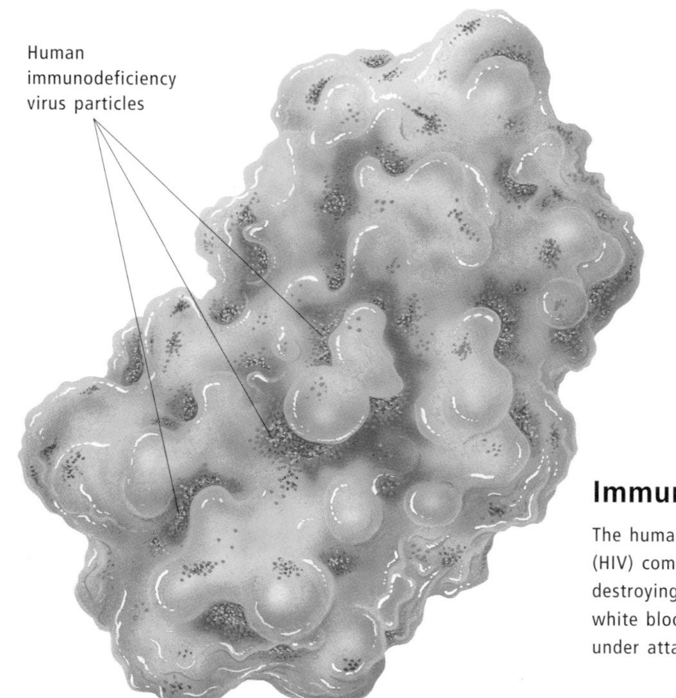

Immunodeficiency

The human immunodeficiency virus (HIV) compromises immunity by destroying T4 helper cells—a type of white blood cell. Here a T4 cell is under attack.

IMMUNODEFICIENCY

When an individual's immune system has been damaged and is deficient, that person is said to have an immunodeficiency. Immunodeficiency can be congenital (due to a genetic disease), or it can be acquired, as in cancer, leukemia or infection with the human immunodeficiency virus (HIV). Congenital immunodeficiency is relatively rare and involves inborn defects in the production of B and T lymphocytes.

If the immune system is severely damaged, exposure to pathogens that would not normally cause disease in healthy people may cause serious infections; these are called opportunistic infections. Examples include candidiasis (thrush); herpes simplex viruses, which can cause oral herpes (cold sores) or genital herpes; and *Pneumocystis carinii* pneumonia which can cause a fatal pneumonia. People with damaged immune systems are also prone to developing cancers such as Kaposi's sarcoma.

Immunodeficiency can be detected by measuring the levels of white blood cells in the blood. In HIV infection, for example, there is a fall in the number of white cells called T4 cells, which can be monitored. The T4 cell count gives an indication of how far the HIV infection is progressing.

SEE ALSO *AIDS, Cancer, HIV, Leukemia, Lymphatic/Immune system, Opportunistic infection*

IMMUNOSUPPRESSION

Immunosuppression is inhibition of the immune system. It may occur as a side effect of drugs used to treat cancer, or in radiation therapy, when the bone marrow or other tissues of the immune system are damaged. It may also occur as a rare side effect of commonly used drugs.

Immunosuppression also refers to the use of certain drugs to prevent the body's immune system destroying its own tissues. This may be necessary, for example, after transplantation of organs or in autoimmune diseases. Examples of immunosuppressant drugs are corticosteroids and azothiaprine.

SEE ALSO *Autoimmune disease, Corticosteroids, Radiation therapy*

Impetigo

This contagious bacterial infection of the skin involves blister-like spots that fill with pus, rupture and become itchy yellow crusts.

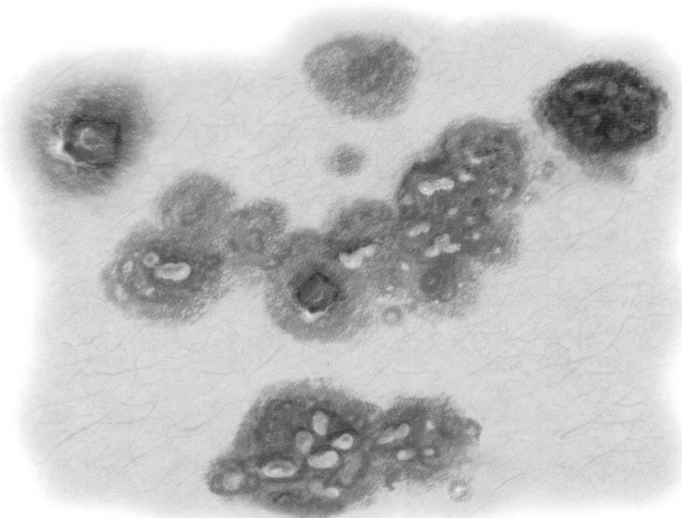

IMPETIGO

Also known as "school sores" in some parts of the world, impetigo is a bacterial skin infection which is highly contagious and occurs mainly in young children. It affects in general the mouth and nose area, but can also occur under diapers in babies, or anywhere else on the body. It is not painful, but it can be itchy and lead to scratching which will spread the infection. The surface of the skin is infected with bacteria, either *Streptococcus pyogines* or *Staphylococcus aureus*, which feed on a wound such as a cut or insect bite, or a skin condition such as eczema.

Appearing first as red blisters, the spots become filled with pus and form a scab. Impetigo is treated with a course of antibiotics and/or antibiotic ointment prescribed by a physician. If the sore is surrounded by red skin or the person is unwell, then further medical attention should be sought.

As impetigo is highly contagious, the sufferer needs to bathe or shower daily, keep linen and towels separate, be scrupulous about cleaning under fingernails and washing hands, and stay away from other people, at least outside the family, until the sores have healed.

SEE ALSO *Staphylococcal infections, Streptococcal infections*

IMPOTENCE

Impotence is a man's inability to produce or maintain an erection of the penis, so that he is unable to engage successfully in sexual intercourse. It can occur at any age, but is more common in older men. Impotence may be temporary, or long lasting.

Impotence often has a psychological origin, such as stress, anxiety, depression or marital conflict. There may be a physical cause, such as a stroke, atherosclerosis, diabetes mellitus or alcoholism. Brief bouts of impotence may follow illnesses such as influenza, or after taking drugs or alcohol. It may occur as a side effect of some medications or following surgery, or from a combination of factors.

If the condition has a psychological basis, discussion (together with the affected male's sexual partner) of the condition with a qualified sex therapist or relationship counselor may be of benefit. If the cause is a physical disorder, the underlying cause must be treated first. If this is not possible, there are several treatments available. A prosthesis (which may be inflatable) can be surgically inserted into the penis. Non-surgical treatments include needle injection therapy, vacuum cup devices and medications such as sildenafil (Viagra).

SEE ALSO *Erection, Penis, Sexual dysfunction*

IN VITRO FERTILIZATION

In vitro fertilization (IVF)—the fertilization of an ovum ("egg") in vitro ("in glass") and the return of the resulting embryo to the woman's uterus—is the pioneer procedure which produced what were originally called "test tube babies". This technique was first used in the 1970s to offer hope to women who were infertile because something interfered with the passage of the ovum from the ovary to the uterus via the fallopian tube. It is now available to treat infertility arising from most causes.

IVF begins when the woman takes ovary-stimulating drugs for about 10 days. Ultrasound checks determine the number and size of the ovarian follicles in which eggs are developing. The eggs are collected using a trans-vaginal probe when the woman is under local or general anesthetic.

The man will be required to masturbate to produce a semen sample. A small amount of this semen will be processed to remove debris and then added to the dish which holds an egg. Fertilization can take up to 18 hours, and one to five days later the embryos—which at this stage are technically known as blastocysts—will be ready for implanting into the woman's uterus.

Generally up to three fertilized eggs are transferred to the uterus to increase the chances of pregnancy, and most transfers are done on day two. The transfer is done using a fine catheter and the woman does not need to be sedated. The woman may be prescribed hormones to increase the chances that the fertilized eggs will successfully implant.

Only between 15 and 20 percent of embryos created in this artificial environment are truly viable—that is, have the potential to continue their development.

SEE ALSO *Embryo, Fertilization, Infertility, Ovum, Semen*

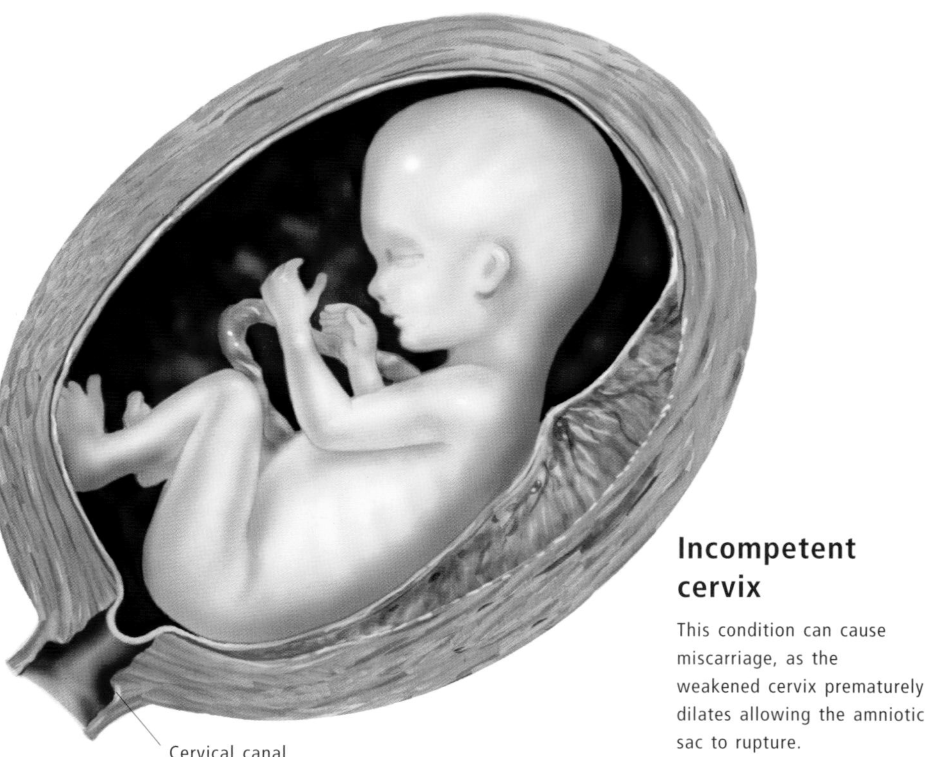

Incompetent cervix

This condition can cause miscarriage, as the weakened cervix prematurely dilates allowing the amniotic sac to rupture.

INCOMPETENT CERVIX

During pregnancy, the cervix (the entrance to the uterus) is sealed with a plug of mucus and remains tightly shut, keeping the fetus safely within the uterus, until labor begins. However, in some cases, especially where the cervix has been damaged by surgical procedure such as a cone biopsy, the cervix can be weakened and may open prematurely during the third or fourth month of pregnancy. When this happens, the amniotic sac may pass through the cervix into the vagina and may rupture, causing loss of amniotic fluid and miscarriage.

The condition is not usually diagnosed until a miscarriage has occurred; however, subsequent miscarriages can be prevented by a procedure in which the cervix is stitched closed with strong thread which tightens the cervix and keeps it from dilating prematurely. The stitches are removed at about 37 weeks to allow delivery of the fetus to take place.

SEE ALSO *Cervix, Childbirth, Miscarriage, Pregnancy, Reproductive systems, Uterus*

INCONTINENCE

In an infant, daytime control of the bladder is achieved around the age of two, and nighttime control some years later. Lack of voluntary control of the bladder beyond this age is called incontinence. It is a problem most common in the elderly.

There are several causes of incontinence in adults. Shortening of the urethra and loss of the normal muscular support for the bladder and floor of the pelvis, for example, may cause incontinence. This occurs during pregnancy, after childbirth (especially after multiple pregnancies) and as a consequence of ageing. Any neurological disorder affecting the bladder such as spina bifida, multiple sclerosis, and the nerve degeneration that occurs with conditions like diabetes mellitus can cause incontinence.

Stress incontinence is the involuntary leakage of urine during exercise, coughing, sneezing, laughing, lifting heavy objects, or during other body movements that put pressure on the bladder. Urge incontinence is the inability to hold urine back long enough to reach a toilet. It is a major complaint of patients with urinary tract infections. Overflow incontinence is the leakage of small amounts of urine from a bladder that is always full. In older men, this can occur when the flow of urine from the bladder is blocked, for example in enlargement of the prostate gland (prostatomegaly) or following surgery or cancer.

Most people with incontinence can be cured or helped. For mild incontinence, the use of a portable urinal or bedside commode, and wearing sanitary pads or panty liners may be sufficient to manage the disorder. Other treatments include strengthening of bladder muscles and pelvic floor muscles, and surgery to tighten relaxed or damaged bladder muscles, or to remove a blockage due to an enlarged prostate.

Incontinence of the bowels can also occur. In young children, lack of bowel control may simply be resistance to toilet training. In older children, it may occur because of stress or a psychological disorder. In adults it may be caused by chronic constipation, diarrhea or stress. It may follow childbirth (when the anal sphincter muscle may be torn), or an operation for anal fistula or fissure. In the elderly, it may be associated with senility, or with neurological disorders such as a stroke, multiple sclerosis or diabetes mellitus. Treatment options include rectal muscle strengthening and surgery to the rectal sphincter.

SEE ALSO *Bladder, Urinary incontinence, Urinary systems*

INDIGESTION

Indigestion is defined as abdominal discomfort experienced within a few hours of eating. It may be characterized by heartburn, cramps, flatulence and belching. It may be of no clinical significance (no more than a normal consequence of over-eating) or it may indicate serious disease (for example, upper abdominal pain following a meal may be a symptom of gastric ulcer or cancer).

The symptom of indigestion on its own is no clear indicator of the type of problem: it is the accompanying symptoms and signs and subsequent clinical investigations that will indicate the presence or absence of serious disease. Upper abdominal discomfort or pain following a meal may be the result of a wide variety of diseases involving the esophagus (reflux esophagitis), stomach, duodenum (duodenal ulcer) or gallbladder (chronic cholecystitis due to gallstones). Indigestion may also arise as a side effect of several common drugs, such as aspirin (acetylsalicylic acid), non-steroidal anti-inflammatory drugs and antibiotics.

SEE ALSO *Cholecystitis, Digestive system, Duodenal ulcer, Duodenum, Esophagus, Gallstones*

Incontinence

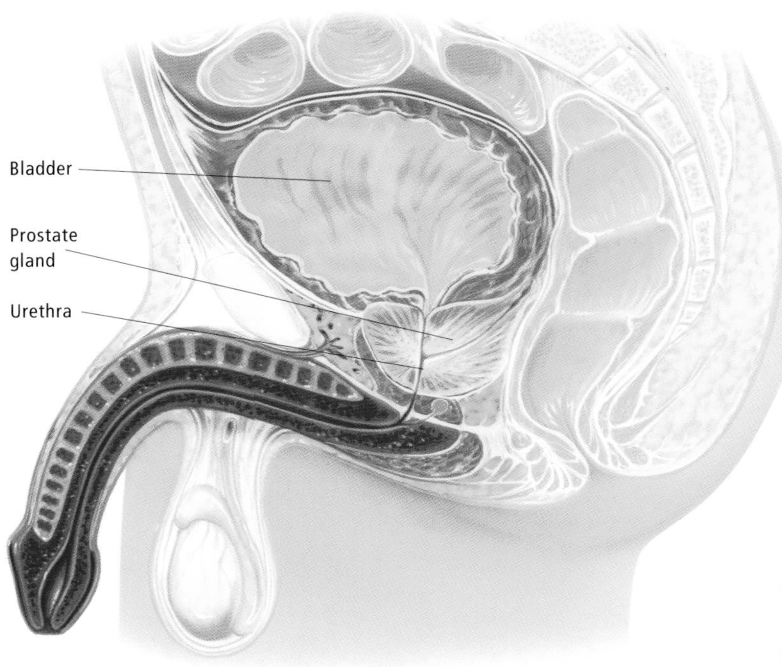

Male incontinence

Incontinence in men is often caused by an enlarged prostate gland which compresses the urethra, obstructing the flow of urine. Urine then collects in the bladder and eventually leaks out.

Female incontinence

Women may suffer incontinence during pregnancy and after childbirth due to a weakening of the muscles which support the bladder and the floor of the pelvis.

Urine in bladder

Pelvic bone

External urethral sphincter

Urethra

Pelvic muscles

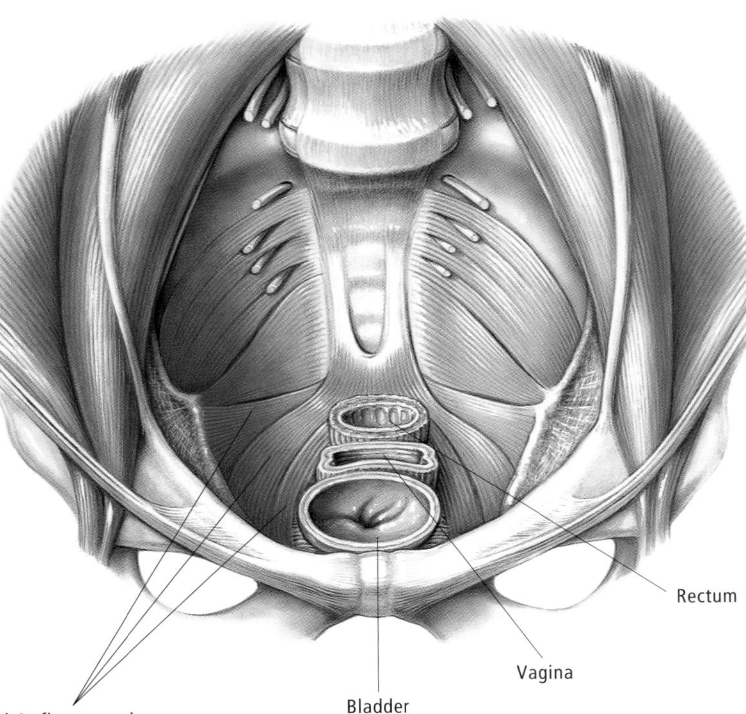

Muscle control in incontinence

Performing a series of appropriate exercises daily can strengthen pelvic floor muscles and help to avoid incontinence.

INFANCY

An infant, or baby, is a child of 12 months of age or less (although some authorities define this stage as 2 years or less). It is an important period, during which the child gains in weight and height, begins to walk and talk, begins teething, and develops sensory discrimination.

A baby grows and develops more rapidly in the first 12 months than at any other time. At birth, an average newborn infant weighs 7½ pounds (3.4 kg) and is about 20 inches (51 cm) long and gains weight at an average of 6 to 7 ounces (170 to 200 grams) per week for the first 3 months. After this the rate declines to an average of 2 ounces (60 grams) per week by 12 months.

A baby's skeleton includes a greater percentage of cartilage than an adult skeleton in that some parts are still made of cartilage and have not yet ossified. Some cartilagenous parts do not become bone until the child is almost an adult.

A baby's brain also grows at a remarkable rate in the first year, doubling in weight as the number of brain cells (glia) increases, together with increases in the number of connections between cells and parts of the brain.

Developmental stages

Babies develop individually. Some develop physically more quickly than others, others develop mental or social skills sooner than their peers. Skills develop in a particular order because of the way the body and the nervous system mature, but not every child will go through every stage.

The infant's means of exploring and understanding the world begins with reflex movements—sucking, grasping, throwing and kicking. By 4 months of age the infant can reach out and grasp an object, and can hold a small object between thumb and forefinger by the tenth month. At 4 months most babies are able to sit up for a short while without support, and can do so without support for 10 minutes or longer by the age of 9 months. Crawling begins between 7 and 10 months, and by 12 months most infants can stand up alone. With help, most babies can walk by 12 months and can walk by themselves at 14 months.

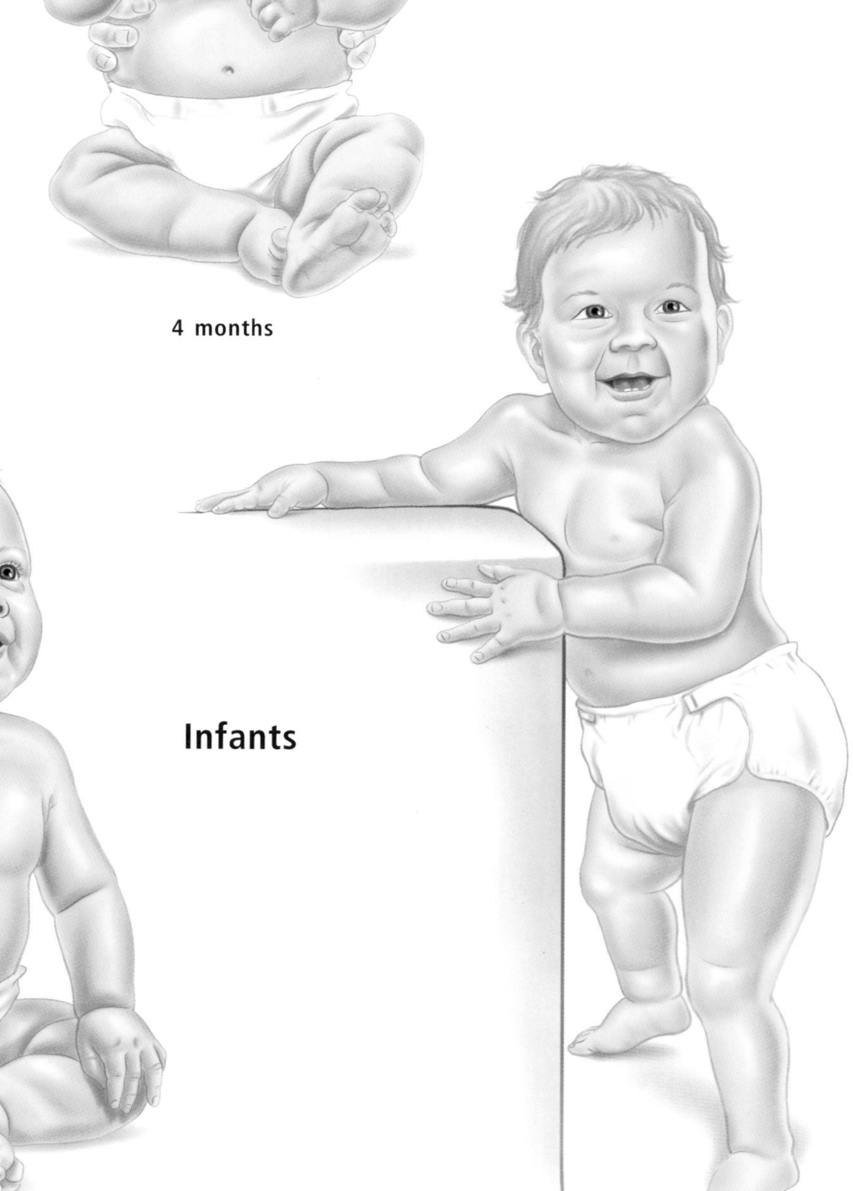

Infants

4 months

8 months

12 months

Infancy

Infants develop at their own rate, but there is a specific order of developmental changes. For example, babies must learn the muscular skill of head control before they learn to sit up.

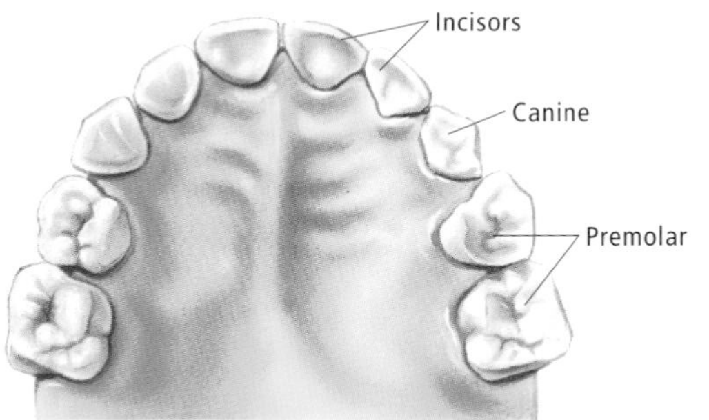

Infancy—teething

The first teeth usually appear when the infant is approximately 6–8 months of age; by the age of 3, a full set of "baby teeth" should be present.

Fontanelle

The fontanelles are gaps between the bones in a baby's skull due to the normal delay in the joining together of several flat bones.

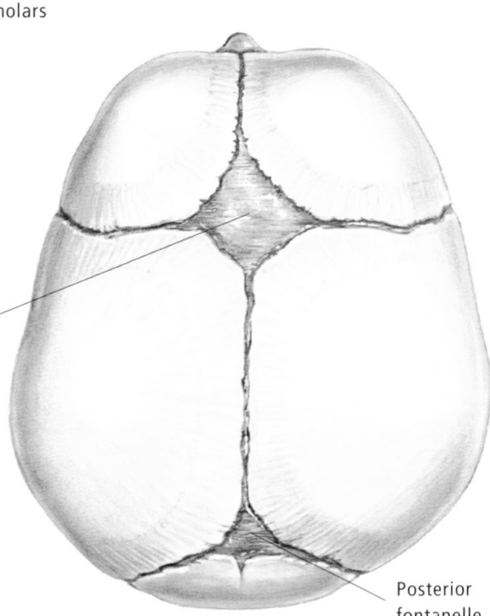

Fetal bone **Infant bone**

Chondrocytes

Cortical bone

Spongy bone

Hyaline cartilage

Bone development

Bone growth begins very early in fetal development. At 6 weeks, chondrocytes in the center of the cartilage begin to enlarge—the first stage in bone development. By the time the baby is born, bone has been laid down in the center of the shaft and in a collar around the middle of the shaft.

The senses also develop rapidly during the first 3 months of life. Newborns can distinguish between sounds and objects close to their face; within 3 months the infant can distinguish color and form. Mimicking of sounds begins soon after birth, but the infant's first full words will not be uttered until between 12–18 months.

A baby born before week 37 of pregnancy is classified as premature. Premature babies' development stages generally need to be corrected to the age the baby would be if born full term—thus a baby born 3 weeks early will be developmentally 3 weeks behind a full-term baby born at the same time.

Immunization and illnesses

Regular checkups to ensure that a baby is growing and developing normally will allow any problems to be detected and treated quickly if necessary. Checkups are also important to ensure that the baby is protected against a range of childhood diseases which can have serious repercussions, including death.

Immunization programs have been designed to protect children against a number of diseases, including diphtheria, measles, mumps, poliomyelitis, rubella (German measles), tetanus (which can cause lockjaw), whooping cough (pertussis), *Hemophilus influenzae* type B (which can result in meningitis) and hepatitis B.

Other common illnesses which babies can suffer in the first year include bronchiolitis, bronchitis, conjunctivitis (also known as pink eye), croup, ear infections, encephalitis, gastrointestinal upset, hand, foot and mouth disease, herpes simplex, hepatitis, influenza, pneumonia and roseola infantum.

Feeding

Problems can arise with breast feeding, often because the new mother has not received the right advice and information from those around her. Bottle feeding has its own set of problems, including the possibility of infection and under or over feeding, if correct procedures are not followed. Weaning onto family foods may not proceed as expected for numerous reasons, including allergy, too early introduction of food or unrealistic expectations on the part of the parents.

Breast milk is the ideal food for a human baby for the first 6 months of life, and for up to 12 months gives many benefits. Breast milk changes for each feed and within each feed to meet the individual baby's needs. It is a unique substance which has not been duplicated artificially. Breast milk contains antibodies, which provide immunity against infections, and many other important nutrients including choline, which aids in the development of the brain. The action of the baby's mouth during breast feeding facilitates the optimum development of the facial muscles.

Babies who are not breast fed need an infant formula (artificial baby milk) which is appropriate to their age and fortified with iron. These formulas are nutritionally complete, but do not contain the antibodies found in human breast milk.

Some time after the age of 4 months, and ideally around the age of 6 months, a baby should begin to eat family foods. A baby has to learn how to eat, and new tastes and textures (from puree to lumpy to mashed and chopped) need to be introduced quite quickly. Iron is very important in a baby's food intake after about 6 months. By the time children are a year old they need to be eating a wide variety of healthy foods.

Sleeping

Understanding *how* a baby sleeps (which is very different from the way adults sleep) and how *much* sleep is needed, is the second greatest problem faced by parents and care givers. Many sleep problems are really problems of adults' perceptions of a baby's sleep needs. A baby sleeps better in the presence of others and with some noise around; baby sleep is much more restless than adult sleep; a baby's brain is more alert during sleep than an adult's and in the first 3 months a baby will generally wake after an REM (rapid-eye-movement) stage of sleep. Not until the end of month 3 can a baby fall into a deep sleep. By 6 months a baby has the ability to sleep for longer periods, but will still need adult comfort and attention when awake.

Bedtime routines, including story reading, bathing and soft singing, work for some families; other families sleep together or in the same room and find that this gives everyone the required night sleep. There are many theories and methods to help parents come to terms with, and develop strategies for, getting the night's sleep they want.

Teething

Babies' first teeth usually appear between 6 and 8 months of age. Already formed inside the gums at birth, the teeth slowly push and twist their way through. Teething can be painful and may cause drooling, irritability, swollen gums, difficulty sleeping and a strong biting urge. Signs include rosy cheeks, frantic finger sucking and ear pulling. Recent research suggests that teething does not cause diarrhea or fever as was commonly thought.

Discomfort can be alleviated by rubbing the gums with a clean finger or offering rusks, teething rings, a cold wet washcloth, a cool spoon or slushy frozen fruit juice to chew on. Also available are teething salves containing anesthetic and non-prescription oral pain relievers. Alternatively, simply distracting the child with walks and new play activities can help.

By one year of age, up to 12 of the 20 "milk" teeth are usually in place. The two lower front teeth or central incisors are often first, followed by the upper central incisors, then the lower and upper lateral incisors either side of the front teeth. The large back molars and the sharp canine teeth either side of the incisors usually erupt between 12 and 30 months. There is no "normal" teething timetable, however—parents may find it starts as early as 3 months and end as late as 3 years.

Communicating

Babies are born with the ability to communicate with the adults responsible for their care. From day one, babies can gaze into the eyes of a person holding them at chest height (if drugs are used during labour it may take a little longer). They can imitate their carers' facial expressions and one day, some time in the first 6 weeks, will smile. In order to thrive, babies need the love and attention of those who care for them; this ability to smile and gaze at parents or carers is vital in establishing emotional bonds between baby and carer.

Crying is babies' other method of communication and the most important way they communicate in the first 12 months. Many adults have little experience of a baby's cries until they have responsibility for a baby for the first time. Some babies cry more than others and need more attention. This is normal, but crying can sometimes become a problem in itself and it is important that parents learn strategies to help them cope with their babies' needs without being overwhelmed.

Babies cry for one or more of the following reasons: they are hungry, they are too hot or too cold, they have a pain in the stomach, they need their diapers changed, they are feeling insecure or lonely, they are bored, or they have become over-excited and need to be calmed. Unfortunately, determining which of these problems it is can sometimes be difficult.

Over the age of 6 months one of the most common reasons for crying is boredom. A stimulating environment with changing patterns, shapes, sounds and colors will amuse a baby, as will the presence of an adult or older child who spends time interacting with the baby.

Parental concerns

Sudden infant death syndrome (SIDS) is an issue which frightens many parents. Understanding and taking heed of the risk factors are the best safeguards parents can have to protect their child.

Teething is often blamed for illnesses such as diarrhea, stomach upsets and infections, but these are not symptoms of this normal part of development. Teething can cause considerable discomfort and unhappiness but not illness.

Failure to thrive is another issue that often confronts parents. A baby who has not gained weight in accordance with standardized baby growth charts may be described as "failing to thrive". In many instances it can be explained that parents' expectations are unrealistic, but in some infants there can be feeding or malabsorption problems which are affecting growth rate.

Apart from feeding and sleeping, babies require a great deal of time. Their physical needs, including comfort and warmth, must be met. This means changing diapers up to ten times in a 24-hour period, as well as bathing once a day. On top of this, taking a baby out requires safety devices for car travel, a stroller for shopping trips and baby carriers for other outings. Parents are generally concerned to give the babies they bear the best possible beginning in life.

SEE ALSO ***Breast feeding, Bottle feeding, Newborn, Reflexes, Sudden infant death syndrome***

INFECTIOUS DISEASES

An infectious disease is a disease caused by the invasion of and multiplication in the body's tissues of microorganisms that have been passed from one person (or animal) to another. These microorganisms include bacteria, viruses, fungi, protozoa or rickettsiae. Some diseases may be caused by the toxins (poisons) these microorganisms produce.

For infection to occur, a number of factors must be present: an infectious agent; an environment in which it can reproduce, such as contaminated food; a mode of transmission; and a susceptible host.

Transmission can occur in many ways. Infectious agents can be spread in droplets through the air when infected persons sneeze or cough. Whoever inhales the droplets can then become infected. Some diseases can be passed through contaminated eating or drinking utensils. Similarly, ingesting contaminated food or liquids exposes a healthy person to the disease. Other diseases can be spread through sexual activity. Common entry routes into a host are the skin (especially if it has been injured) and the mucosal surfaces of other body openings. A pregnant mother may also transmit infections from her blood supply to that of the fetus. Occasionally, infections can be spread in the course of medical or surgical treatment, or through using dirty injection equipment, as occurs with some drug users.

Every infectious disease has an incubation period. This is the length of time between the entry of the infectious agent into the body and the appearance of the first symptoms of the disease. It may be as short as a few days, as with the common cold, or it may be months or years, as in some slow viral diseases that affect the brain.

Not everyone who has an infectious agent contracts the disease. The virulence of the microorganism may be insufficient for the exposed person to develop the disease. However, this person (known as an asymptomatic carrier) may be harboring the disease and may spread it to another. Carriers may also include someone who is incubating the disease and is yet to develop it, or someone who may have recovered from the disease but is still capable of transmitting it to others.

A person whose immune system has been damaged by diseases of the immune system, leukemia and cancer is more likely to prove susceptible to disease. A disease which a normal person would fight off easily but which causes often serious illness in someone with a damaged immune system is called an opportunistic infection.

An infection may be local and confined to one area or it may be generalized. If it is localized it often produces characteristic symptoms of pain, swelling and reddening at the site of infection. This response is the body's way of fighting the infection and is known as inflammation. If the infection is generalized it will spread through the blood and affect the whole body, causing fever, chills, and a rapid pulse.

Different types of infectious agents (pathogens) cause different types of disease.

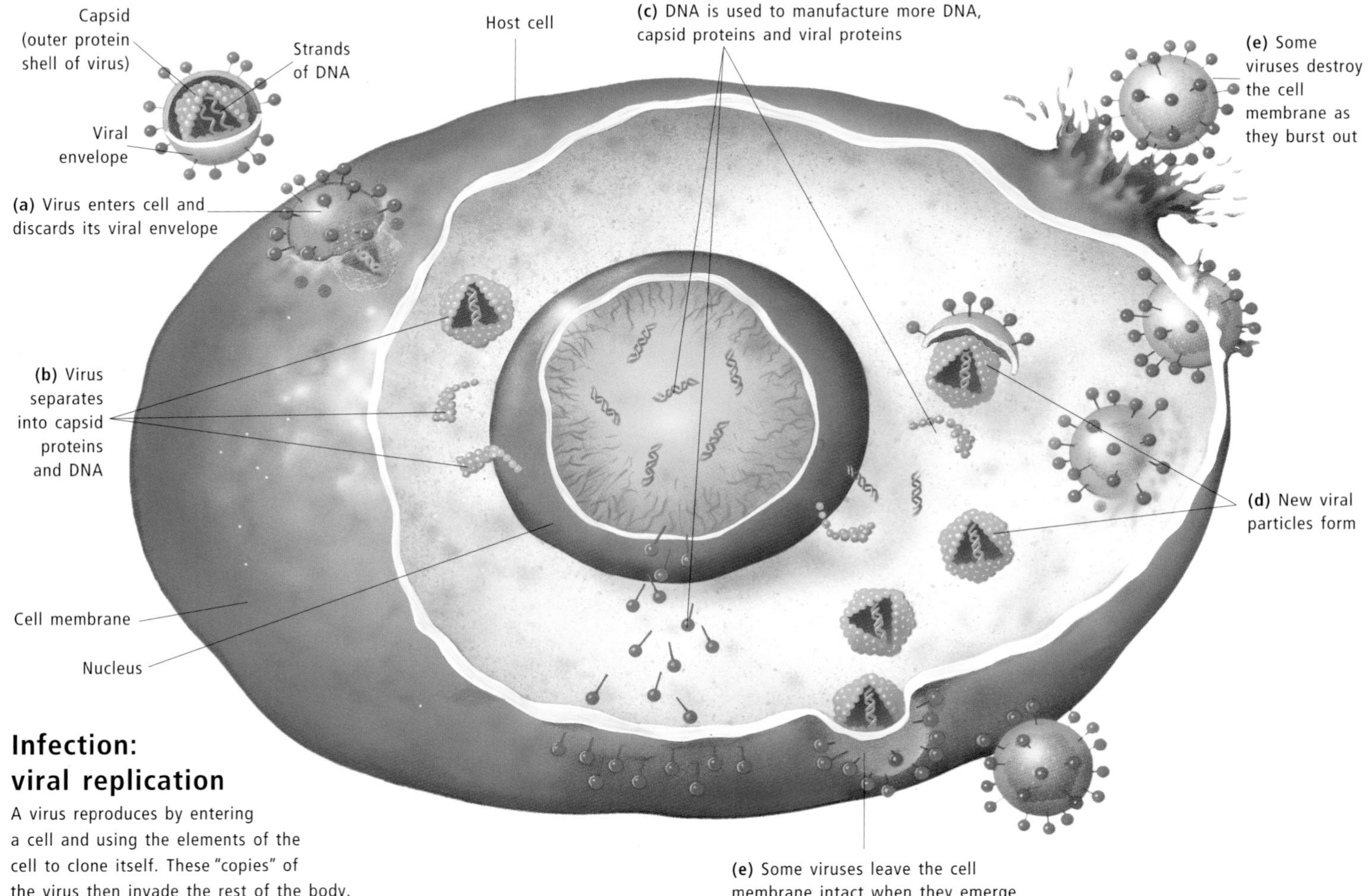
Capsid (outer protein shell of virus)
Strands of DNA
Viral envelope
Host cell
(c) DNA is used to manufacture more DNA, capsid proteins and viral proteins
(e) Some viruses destroy the cell membrane as they burst out
(a) Virus enters cell and discards its viral envelope
(b) Virus separates into capsid proteins and DNA
(d) New viral particles form
Cell membrane
Nucleus
(e) Some viruses leave the cell membrane intact when they emerge

Infection: viral replication

A virus reproduces by entering a cell and using the elements of the cell to clone itself. These "copies" of the virus then invade the rest of the body.

I

Fungal infections

Fungal infections are diseases caused by the growth of fungi in or on the body. Fungal infections are usually mild, normally involving only the skin, hair, nails or other superficial sites, and they clear up spontaneously. Such infections include athlete's foot and ringworm. In someone with a damaged immune system, fungi may invade internal organs of the body and cause serious disease. Fungal disease can usually be treated with antifungal drugs, which are administered intravenously, orally, or applied to the skin.

SEE ALSO *Antibiotics, Bacteria, DNA, Inflammation, Lymphatic/Immune system, Opportunistic infection, Viruses*

Infectious mononucleosis

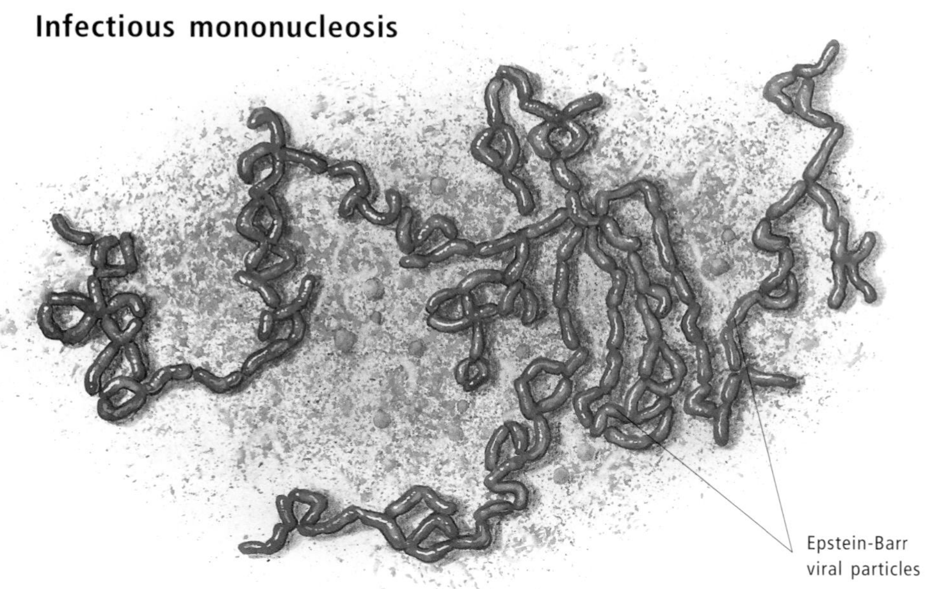

Bacteria

Bacteria are tiny, single-celled organisms with a cell wall but no nucleus. They may need oxygen to live (aerobic bacteria) or they may be able to live without oxygen (anaerobic bacteria). Some bacteria are spherical *(cocci)*, corkscrew-shaped *(spirilla* or *spirochetes)* or rod-shaped *(bacilli)*. They are also classified as gram-negative or gram-positive, according to whether their cell wall holds a special laboratory stain called Gram's stain.

Bacteria are responsible for many epidemic diseases, such as cholera, dysentery, plague, tuberculosis and typhoid fever. Many cause skin diseases, such as dermatitis, erysipelas, leprosy and yaws. They may also cause infections of other organs, such as gastroenteritis (infections of stomach and intestine), cystitis (bladder infection), pneumonia (lung infection), meningitis (infection of the meninges, the membranes that cover the brain), osteomyelitis (infection of bone), conjunctivitis (infection of the conjunctiva, the membrane that covers the eyeball) and many others. Some bacteria, especially *Staphylococcus*, may form a collection of pus, comprised of dead cells, bacteria and white blood cells, known as an abscess.

Most bacteria can be treated by antibiotics, which kill bacteria by interfering with their metabolism. Antibiotics can be injected or taken orally. Certain antibiotics work only against a certain type of bacteria, for example, they may work against gram-positive but not gram-negative bacteria. Bacteria tend to develop resistance to antibiotics over time.

Public health measures have led to much quality lengthening of life in industrialized countries. In many emerging countries these measures need to be introduced to control infectious diseases that continue to kill millions of people.

Viruses

Viruses are between 20 and 100 times smaller than bacteria. They contain either deoxyribonucleic acid (DNA) or ribonucleic acid (RNA). They are not considered to be alive, since they cannot reproduce outside a living cell. However, a virus can reproduce by entering a cell and using the cell's parts to make more copies of itself, which then leave the cell and spread elsewhere in the body, causing disease. These are called intracellular infections.

Common viral illnesses include hepatitis, influenza, the "common cold", measles, herpes and HIV (which causes AIDS). Many common childhood diseases are caused by viruses, including measles, mumps, rubella and chickenpox.

Viruses have also been implicated in causing some types of cancers. Antibiotics are ineffective against viruses, although antiviral drugs are available for some viral diseases. However, many viral diseases can be vaccinated against, including poliovirus, influenza, rabies, rubella, yellow fever, measles, mumps, and chickenpox.

INFECTIOUS MONONUCLEOSIS

Infectious mononucleosis (also known as glandular fever) is an illness commonly resulting in swollen lymph nodes (also known as lymph glands), fatigue, fever and a sore throat. Often referred to as "the kissing disease", infectious mononucleosis is thought to be spread through saliva, as well as through nasal secretions, sexual contact, blood transfusions and respiratory droplets. The disease is called mononucleosis as the blood of sufferers contains unusually large numbers of the white blood cells known as mononuclear leukocytes or monocytes, which are formed in the spleen and bone marrow.

The illness is caused by the Epstein-Barr herpes virus (EBV) which often produces no symptoms in young children and can stay in the body without effect for a long time before being activated by, for instance, a weakening of the immune system due to disease. EBV commonly results in mononucleosis in people aged 15–35 years.

Lethargy is often the first sign of illness. Other symptoms include muscular aches, loss of appetite, enlarged spleen and, occasionally, a faint pink rash. After about ten days acute symptoms subside, but fatigue, a general feeling of discomfort and sometimes depression may continue for up to about three months. Bed rest may cure the illness within six weeks, while painkillers and other non-prescription medications may be used to treat symptoms.

SEE ALSO *Spleen, Viruses, White blood cells*

Infertility

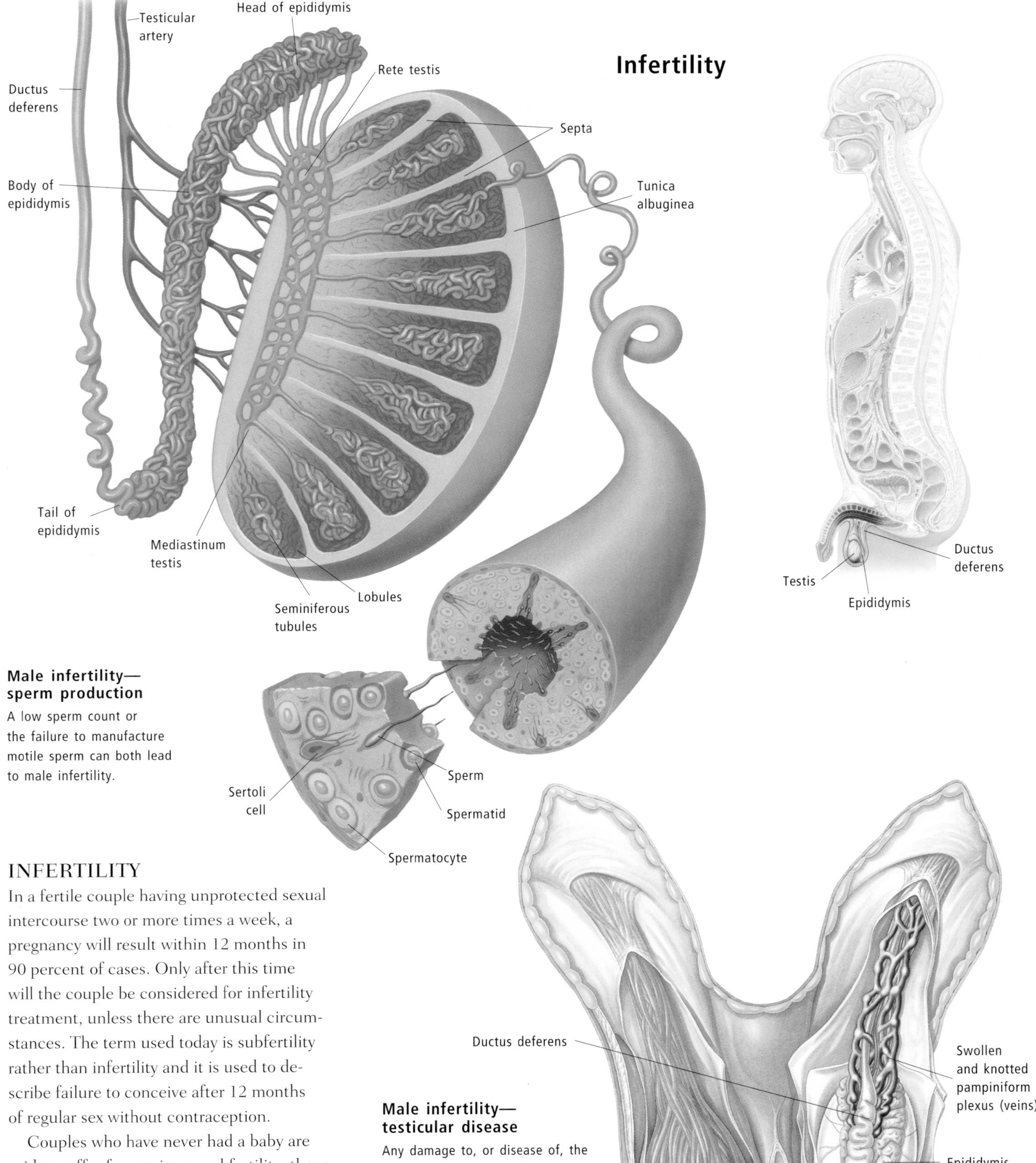

Male infertility—sperm production

A low sperm count or the failure to manufacture motile sperm can both lead to male infertility.

Male infertility—testicular disease

Any damage to, or disease of, the testes and the vas or ductus deferens (which link the testes to the seminal vesicles) can cause infertility. In varicocele, veins in the testes become swollen and knotted, disrupting blood flow and affecting the production and movement of sperm.

INFERTILITY

In a fertile couple having unprotected sexual intercourse two or more times a week, a pregnancy will result within 12 months in 90 percent of cases. Only after this time will the couple be considered for infertility treatment, unless there are unusual circumstances. The term used today is subfertility rather than infertility and it is used to describe failure to conceive after 12 months of regular sex without contraception.

Couples who have never had a baby are said to suffer from primary subfertility; those who have had one or more children are said to have secondary subfertility. After treatment, around half of these couples will achieve a pregnancy and in most cases this takes about 12 months—though it can take up to 10 years. In about 35 percent of cases it is the man who has a fertility problem, in 35 percent it is the woman, while in the remaining 30 percent both have problems.

Subfertility rates in industrialized countries are rising alarmingly, mostly, it is thought, because women are delaying childbearing. Discovering that conception will need medical assistance and may even be impossible has a profound effect on the lives of couples who have planned a child. Counseling as well as medical assistance is important.

Causes

One of the causes of subfertility can be recurrent miscarriage or recurrent spontaneous abortion (RSA). The two main reasons for these are, firstly, a chromosomal abnormality that prevents normal development of the embryo or, secondly, something wrong with woman's reproductive system. Hormonal and anatomical problems, such as a structural abnormality of the uterus, can be responsible. For some, miscarriage is "unexplained", which may be due to immunological factors or could be due to environmental factors such as pollution or chemicals.

Male causes may be the failure to manufacture sperm (azoospermia); the sperm may be weak or few in number (oligospermia: fewer than 20 million per milliliter), or the tubes (vas deferens or ductus deferens) that link the testicles to the seminal vesicle where the sperm is stored may be damaged. Problems may be caused by testicular disease; a varicocele (a lump of varicose veins in the scrotum); occupational factors such as working with certain chemicals; general health disorders; mumps; treatment such as radiation therapy; excessive smoking or alcohol intake.

The woman may not produce an ovum; or the fallopian tube (oviduct) along which the sperm and fertilized ovum must travel may be blocked. In some cases it is thought that the cervical mucus is hostile to the sperm, thus preventing them from reaching the ovum.

Problems with sexual intercourse and disorders with the lining of the uterus (the endometrium) can also prevent conception.

Treatment

Before treatment can commence, tests must be done to establish the cause. Treatments include improving the sperm count,

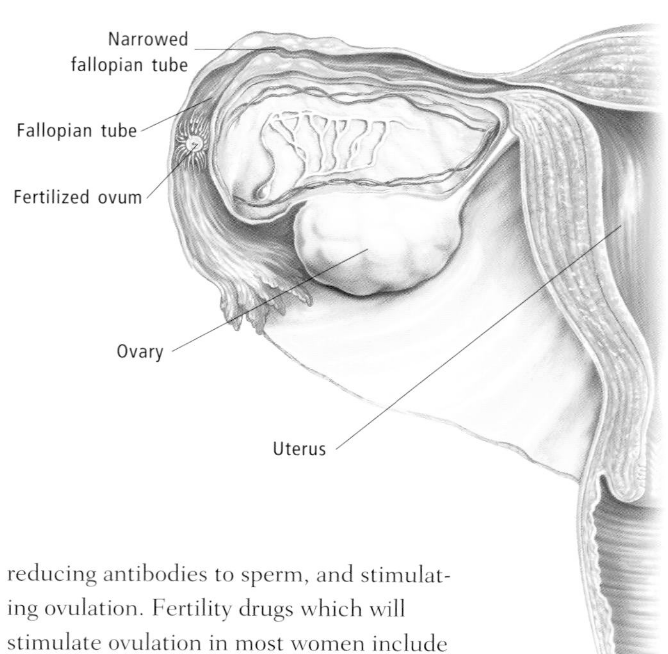

Female infertility

Women may suffer infertility if they cannot produce an ovum, or if one of the fallopian tubes is blocked or infected.

reducing antibodies to sperm, and stimulating ovulation. Fertility drugs which will stimulate ovulation in most women include gonadotrophin-releasing hormone (GnRH). Surgery to unblock the fallopian tubes (tuboplasty) is not guaranteed to be successful as scar tissue may form a barrier even if the tube can be opened.

Other treatments are assisted conception, such as artificial insemination or in vitro fertilization, used when the woman's reproductive system is functioning; semen from her partner or from a donor may be used. In vitro fertilization (IVF) involves uniting ova with sperm in a glass dish and then placing the fertilized ova in the uterus. Gamete intrafallopian transfer (GIFT) involves ova being taken from the ovary and being placed with sperm in the fallopian tube where fertilization may take place. It has a better success rate than IVF.

MIFT (microinjection fallopian transfer), PROST (pronuclear stage transfer), TEST (tubal embryo stage transfer), ZIFT (zygote intrafallopian transfer) are all acronyms for treatments which begin the same way as IVF but transfer the fertilized ova to the tube rather than to the uterus. The difference between these methods and GIFT is that the ovum is fertilized before transfer. In MIFT, using a microscope, sperm is injected into the ovum and when fertilized the ovum is transferred to the fallopian tube; in PROST the fertilized ovum is transferred as soon as the sperm has penetrated the ovum but before the ovum and sperm have united; in TEST the embryo is transferred when it reaches the two, four or eight cell stage; in ZIFT a single-cell embryo is transferred.

Future methods

Future methods of dealing with subfertility are likely to include the use of frozen ova which have been harvested from young women planning a career before a family, or women undergoing potential infertility-inducing treatment; ova would be thawed and fertilized at a later date. Another method is to use frozen ovaries, which will involve sections of ovaries containing immature ova being frozen, then thawed and matured when needed.

DNA transfer is a process which will bypass problems with older ova by swapping the nucleus of the older ovum with that of a younger one. Cytoplasmic donation, whereby cytoplasm from a younger ovum will be added to an older one, improves the chances that the older ovum will develop properly. A further method is to use improved growth media in which chemical solutions that mimic the female reproductive tract make it easier to implant embryos because they are more mature and hardier.

In order to cope with both the treatment itself and the chances of success or failure, counseling is vital for both partners. If a cause for infertility is found, this can result in feelings of guilt and blame which can be very destructive to a relationship and a person's emotional stability. Sex may be no longer pleasurable and this too can affect the relationship. If treatment fails and a pregnancy is not forthcoming, the

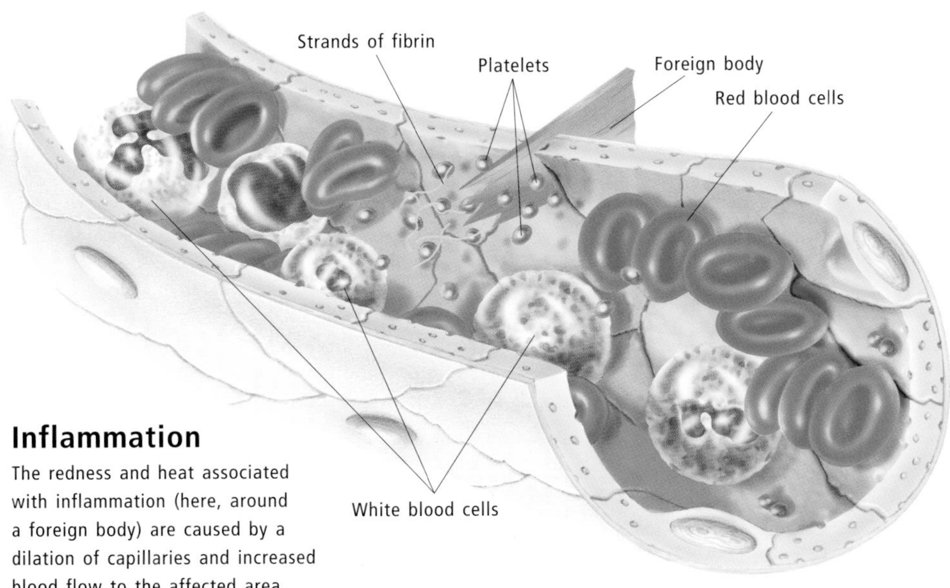

Inflammation

The redness and heat associated with inflammation (here, around a foreign body) are caused by a dilation of capillaries and increased blood flow to the affected area.

ouple will need to work through feelings of grief and loss.

SEE ALSO *Artificial insemination, Fertility, Fertilization, In vitro fertilization, Miscarriage, Pregnancy, Reproductive systems, Sperm*

INFLAMMATION

Inflammation is a reaction of body tissue to disease, injury or irritation, producing swelling, pain, redness and an increase in temperature of the affected area. Exposure to chemicals, allergens, radiation, heat and cold can cause inflammation, as well as physical trauma, surgery and diseases such as rheumatoid arthritis. It is part of the healing process and helps the body to rid itself of irritants and damaged tissue. A build-up of pus may occur and if severe can cause an abscess if not discharged through the skin during healing.

Inflammation may be acute or chronic. If acute it may happen suddenly, is often short-lived and produces characteristic redness, swelling, pain, increased temperature and loss of function. If chronic it may last months or years, beginning slowly and causing dull pain without visible symptoms.

Redness and increased temperature are caused by increased blood flow due to the dilation of blood vessels in the affected area. Swelling is brought about by fluid passing from capillaries into the fluid between cells and tissues. White blood cells also pass out of the capillaries into surrounding tissue to help fight infection or remove debris. They release chemicals which may also cause pain.

Treatment depends on the body part involved and the severity. For mild cases it may be sufficient to wash and rest the affected part; the use of aspirin or acetaminophen (paracetamol) may help.

SEE ALSO *Tissue*

INFLUENZA

This viral disease is quite distinct from the common cold and other upper respiratory infections that are often incorrectly referred to as "the flu", although the symptoms of influenza are varied and can resemble a severe common cold.

Influenza is usually transmitted by airborne droplet infection and occurs more commonly in winter. The virus is remarkable because of the frequency with which its outer coat proteins change. Since immunity to viral infections depends on the binding of antibodies to such proteins, the immune system of a previously infected person cannot recognize the influenza virus with a new outer coat and thus infection can recur.

Relatively minor variations in the recognizable surface proteins (antigens) of the influenza virus occur almost every year, producing new infective strains. Major antigenic shifts occur much less frequently, but effectively produce completely new viruses, leading to large-scale epidemics of influenza that can spread worldwide (known as pandemics).

Influenza typically causes acute onset of fever with chills, headaches, aching muscles and extreme tiredness. There may also be a dry cough, a sore throat and loss of appetite. Fever usually reaches 100–104°F (38–40°C) and persists for 3 or 4 days. Other symptoms last for 1 to 2 weeks. Although influenza is usually self-limiting, the patient usually feels most unwell and the illness is responsible for considerable time lost from work and school.

What makes influenza potentially dangerous are the major complications that are associated with this infection. Persons with pre-existing chronic lung disease may suffer exacerbations of their condition when they develop influenza. The virus itself can affect the lungs, producing a pneumonia with severe breathlessness, which may develop in patients of any age. A complicating bacterial infection, leading to typical pneumonia with cough and sputum production, is especially common in older persons. Pneumonia associated with influenza can cause death, especially during major outbreaks.

It is important for persons at high risk of developing influenza to be immunized. High-risk groups include individuals aged 65 or more, persons with chronic heart or lung disease, diabetics and immunosuppressed persons. Immunization is also recommended

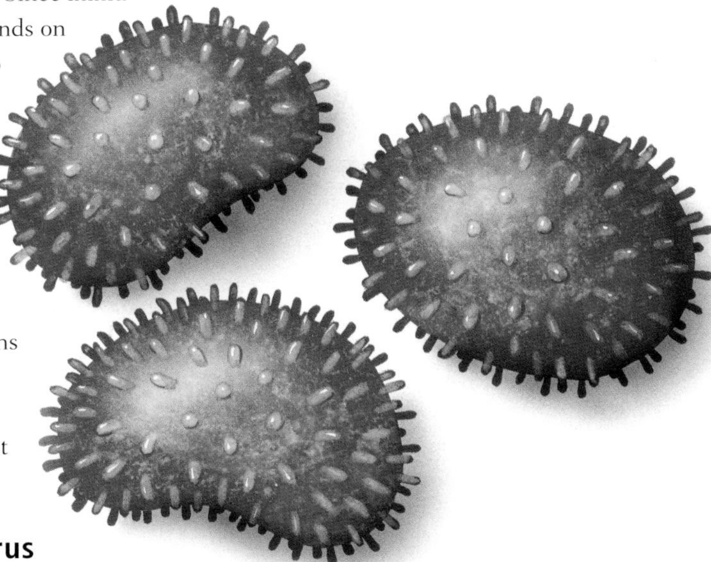

Influenza virus

I

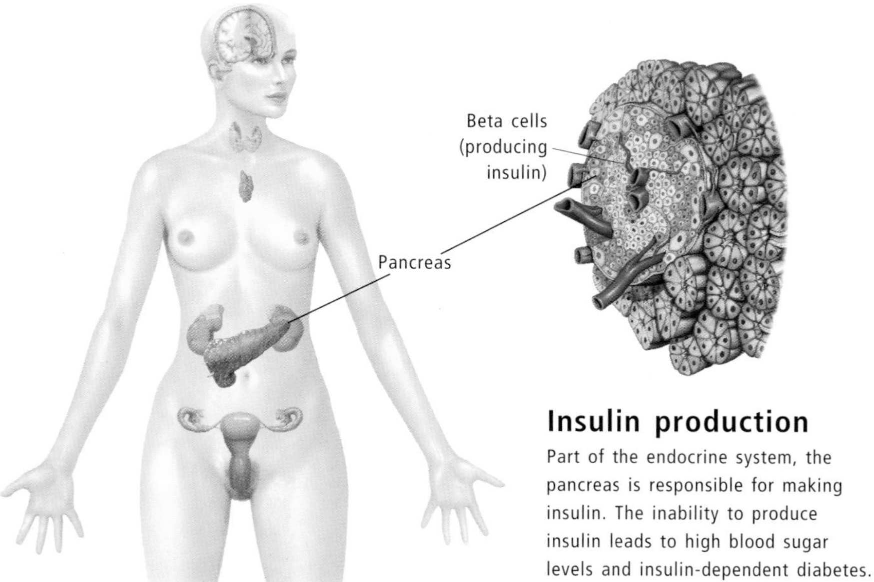

Insulin production

Part of the endocrine system, the pancreas is responsible for making insulin. The inability to produce insulin leads to high blood sugar levels and insulin-dependent diabetes.

for persons in nursing homes because of the likelihood of transmission of infection in such an environment. Killed influenza virus vaccines provide a high level of protection against development of influenza and its complications. Because of the constant antigenic variations that the virus undergoes, it is essential that individuals be reimmunized each year with the vaccine developed against the most recent infective strains.

The diagnosis of influenza is usually presumptive, based on the clinical features. Making a specific diagnosis of influenza used to be quite difficult, because of the need for complex laboratory tests which took several days to yield a result, but methods for rapid and precise diagnosis are now available. These are of particular interest because of the recent release of specific antiviral drugs that can treat influenza in its early stages. These drugs do not prevent the development of serious complications, so they are clearly not a substitute for immunization and should only be used where appropriate.

SEE ALSO ***Common cold, Immunity, Immunization, Infectious diseases, Pneumonia, Respiratory system, Viruses***

INSOMNIA

Insomnia is defined as difficulty falling asleep or staying asleep—it is not the number of hours a person sleeps or how long it takes to fall asleep. When it occurs only occasionally it is not generally harmful and is described as transient insomnia, when it occurs more frequently it is called intermittent insomnia, and when it occurs night after night it is referred to as chronic insomnia.

There are many causes but the most common are stress, noise, extreme temperatures, change in the environment, changes in sleep/wake schedules such as those caused by jet travel and shift work, and side effects of medication. It can happen to both men and women but is more likely to occur in women who have reached menopause, the elderly (the ability rather than the need to sleep diminishes with age) and those with depression.

Diseases that can cause insomnia are arthritis, kidney disease, heart failure, asthma, sleep apnea, narcolepsy, restless legs syndrome, Parkinson's disease, hyperthyroidism and depression. Controllable influences include caffeine, alcohol, worrying about not sleeping, and sleeping too much during the day or early evening.

Chronic insomnia is often caused by a number of different factors. It needs treatment in order for the person to resume a normal life. Identifying and reducing behavior which aggravates the situation, sleeping pills and relaxation therapy are among the common forms of treatment.

A number of alternative therapies may help to alleviate the symptoms of insomnia. Acupuncture and shiatsu treatments may help break the cycle of insomnia by calming the mind. Treatments can be supported by Chinese herbs. Traditional Chinese Medicine advises going to bed before 11 p.m. to sleep well. Aromatherapy suggests massages and baths with relaxant oils such as lavender, ylang-ylang or sandalwood. Counseling or psychotherapy may be helpful where insomnia is due to emotional distress. Herbalists prescribe sedative nervines such as hops, linden, skullcap, chamomile, valerian or passiflora, usually to be taken as teas. Hypnotherapy may help with anxiety and teach specific self-hypnosis techniques to induce sleep. Light therapy may help to break cycles of insomnia or balance sleep patterns in shift workers. Naturopathy suggests regular exercise and bedtimes, avoiding tea, coffee, chocolate or alcohol at night, eating a low-protein dinner at least three hours before retiring, and having a relaxing warm bath with Epsom salts at night. One can also try relaxation techniques, such as autogenic training. Yoga teaches yoga nidra relaxation which may help insomnia, as may a few gentle yoga postures done in the evening.

SEE ALSO ***Jet lag, Relaxation techniques, Sleep disturbances, Sleeping pills***

INSULIN

Insulin is a hormone produced in the pancreas that affects the body's ability to use sugars. Produced in either abnormally high or abnormally low quantities it can have a severe effect on the body's metabolism. Too much insulin leads to low blood sugar levels (hypoglycemia); too little causes high blood sugar levels (hyperglycemia).

Normally, when food is digested, carbohydrates are broken down into sugars such as glucose and absorbed into the bloodstream. This triggers the secretion of insulin into the blood by clusters of cells in the pancreas known as the islets of Langerhans. The pancreas is part of the body's endocrine system, a network of glands that secrete various hormones into the blood to chemically regulate body functions. Insulin aids the absorption of glucose into body cells, for immediate use or storing.

In insulin-dependent diabetes, the insulin-producing cells are destroyed, causing sugars to remain in the blood and pass out of the body in the urine. This causes weight loss, weakness, hunger and thirst, and insulin injections are needed for the body to function properly. The insulin for these injections may be synthetic or obtained from cattle or pig pancreases. It is injected under the skin at regular intervals daily.

SEE ALSO *Blood sugar tests, Diabetes, Endocrine system, Hyperglycemia, Hypoglycemia, Islets of Langerhans, Pancreas*

INTELLECTUAL DISABILITY

Formerly known as mental retardation, intellectual disability affects around 2 percent of the population. It can be defined as limited intelligence or cognitive potential. Those who have this condition have a reduced capacity to learn, to solve problems and possibly to perform other functions, depending on the degree of disability.

Intellectual disability is classified according to severity, and is usually measured by intelligence quotients (IQ) or scores.

In the general population the average intelligence quotient is 100. The upper range of intellectual disability, known as mildly disabled, falls in an IQ range of around the low 50s to high 60s. These people comprise the majority of intellectually disabled persons and they are able to learn basic academic skills with some difficulty and to be employed, usually in unskilled or semi-skilled jobs; they are also able to function independently.

Those who are classified from the high 30s to mid 50s are described as moderately disabled. They are able to care for themselves, to live in a sheltered workshop situation and to live in a home with supervision.

The severely disabled fall into the low 20s to high 30s, and have slow motor development and limited communication skills. They may also have physical disabilities but will be able to care for their basic needs and contribute to their own care in work and living situations.

The last and smallest group are the profoundly disabled, with IQs below the low 20s. These people need full-time care because they have poor motor development and communication skills and are unable to care for themselves or to work except in highly structured activities.

Caused by events before, during or after birth, intellectual disability can be found in those with genetic disorders, such as Down syndrome; infectious disease, for example meningitis; metabolic disorders; fetal alcohol syndrome; physical malformations; poisoning, for example lead poisoning; trauma or injuries to the head; and malnutrition.

Diagnosis

Children with the more severe disabilities will usually be diagnosed before they reach their first birthday, often as a result of parental concerns. Mildly intellectually disabled children are sometimes not diagnosed until they are attending preschool or school, when it is the abstract areas of reasoning, problem solving and use of language which indicate a problem.

A comprehensive evaluation is very important. Tests which are coordinated by a pediatrician or a child psychiatrist, in areas such as neurology, psychology, psychiatry, special education, hearing, speech, vision and physical therapy, may be necessary to determine the extent of intellectual disability.

Treatment

Intellectual disability cannot be cured, but early diagnosis may lead to early treatment and help the family to establish appropriate expectations for their child and to handle the stresses which this level of disability can bring to both child and family. Children diagnosed as intellectually disabled will benefit from an education that is tailored to their needs and from continued monitoring and evaluation.

In many countries it was believed that mental health problems could be solved by deinstitutionalizing and that the ordinary health care system could give the same or better care than that provided by institutions. However, recent research has found that governments need to address the problem of the stress a disability causes to a family and the decrease in the quality of life for both the family and the disabled person that this stress can bring. It has been found that the majority of mental health problems are not solved by deinstitutionalization and this is no substitute for professional assistance.

SEE ALSO *Down syndrome, Fetal alcohol syndrome, Learning disorders*

INTERTRIGO

Intertrigo is an inflammatory condition in which moisture and bacteria accumulate in a skin fold, causing the skin to become red and inflamed. Skin folds of the inner thighs, armpits and underside of the breasts are most often involved, especially in obese people. Treatment involves keeping the skin clean and dry, and dieting and exercise to lose weight.

INTESTINES

The intestines consist of two parts: the small intestine (duodenum, jejunum and ileum) and the large intestine (colon and rectum). The intestines occupy the lower two-thirds of the abdominal cavity. The small intestine (or small bowel) leads on from the stomach, and is mainly concerned with absorption of nutrients from food after digestion (simple sugars, amino acids from protein, fatty acids and glycerol from fats). Some vitamins are also absorbed here (for example, vitamin B_{12}, which is absorbed from the end of the ileum).

The large intestine leads on from the small intestine and is concerned with absorption of water and salts (electrolytes), thereby forming the stool or fecal mass by the time the rectum is reached. It is arranged like a picture frame around the margins of the abdomen and is composed of an initial part called the cecum, with the small vermiform appendix attached. It also includes the ascending colon, transverse colon, descending colon, sigmoid colon and rectum.

The small intestine occupies the central part of the frame provided by the large bowel. It contains about 3½ fluid ounces (100 milliliters) of gas, while the large intestine has considerably more. In fact the average person produces up to approximately 1 quart (about 1 liter) of gas per day as flatus. This gas is mainly nitrogen with some carbon dioxide, oxygen, hydrogen and methane. The last four are produced by bacteria in the large bowel, while nitrogen may enter the bowel from the bloodstream.

Diseases and disorders

Cancer of the large intestine arises when the cells forming the lining of the gut multiply out of control. Bowel cancer cells

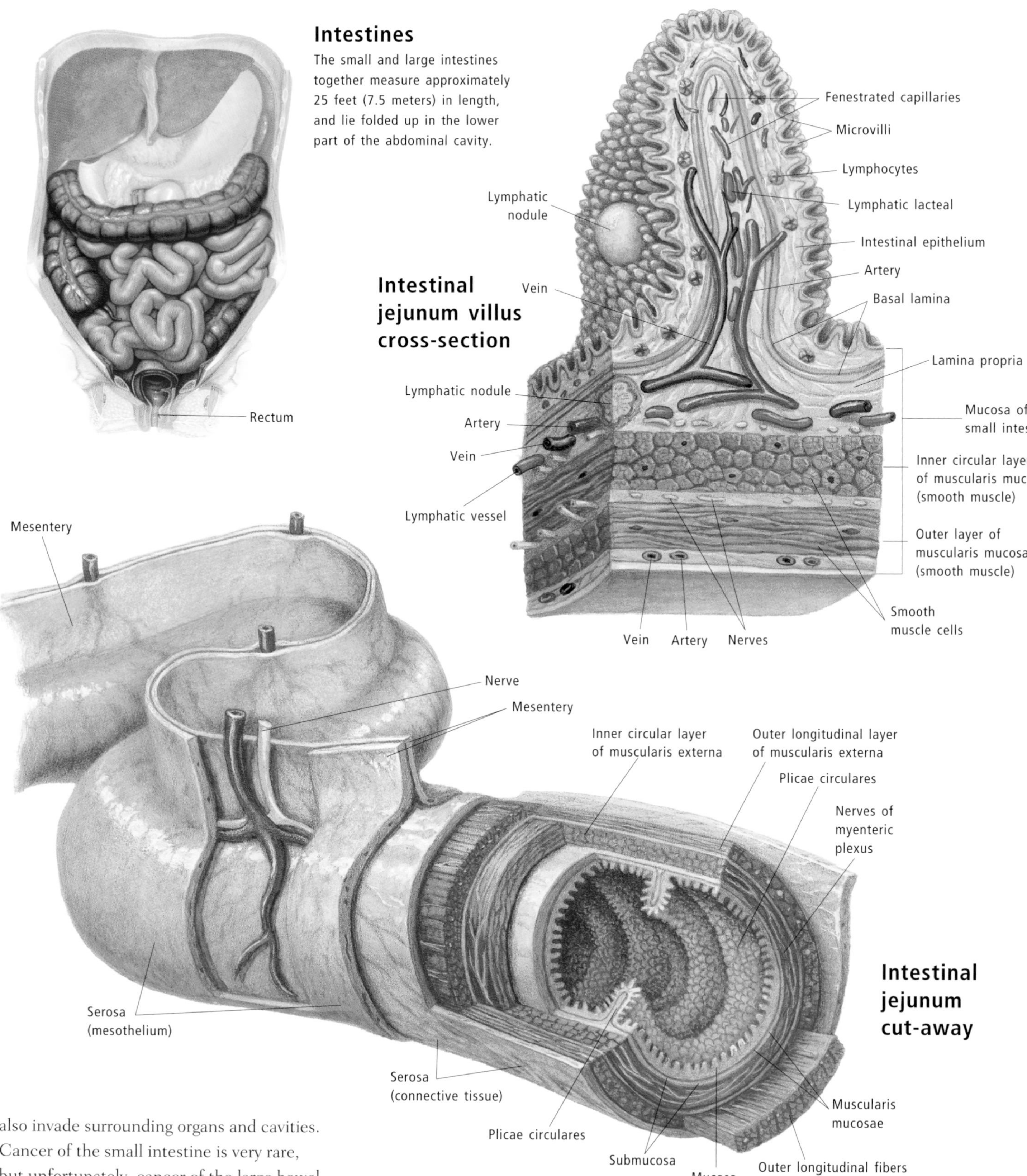

Intestines

The small and large intestines together measure approximately 25 feet (7.5 meters) in length, and lie folded up in the lower part of the abdominal cavity.

also invade surrounding organs and cavities. Cancer of the small intestine is very rare, but unfortunately, cancer of the large bowel is very common in Western societies. In fact, each year in the USA more than 100,000 new cases of bowel cancer are diagnosed and about half that number of people die from the disease each year. The causes may be genetic, with some families being particularly at risk, and/or dietary; diets high in protein and fat are shown to be contributing factors. Greater consumption of meat may change the type of bacteria present in the bowel, favoring bacterial species that turn bile acids and other chemicals into cancer-causing agents (carcinogens).

The most common site for cancer of the large intestine is in the rectum, which accounts for more than a third of cases. Symptoms and signs vary depending on the actual part of the bowel involved, but commonly patients complain of bleeding from the anus, change in bowel habit (i.e. less or more frequent), a feeling of incomplete emptying when a motion is passed, weakness and sometimes abdominal pain and discomfort.

Irritable bowel syndrome is a condition in which the patient experiences bloating, abdominal cramping, diarrhea and sometimes constipation. There are no obvious changes in the structure of the bowel, so it appears that the disease involves changes in the function of the colon, in particular the function of the smooth muscle and nerve cells in the bowel wall. Patients appear to have increased sensitivity to several factors, but the actual source of this increased sensitivity is so far unclear.

Obstruction may occur in either the small or large intestine. Small bowel obstruction leads to profuse vomiting, upper abdominal distension, often severe discomfort, and constipation. It is usually caused by adhesions between the small bowel and other structures within the abdominal cavity; involvement of a length of bowel in a hernia; twisting of a loop of bowel around itself (volvulus); or intussusception, the infolding of one length of bowel into another. Large bowel obstruction may be caused by twisting of the sigmoid colon (volvulus), bowel cancer, or adhesions to other organs. It gives rise to constipation, pain in the lower abdomen and eventually vomiting.

Fecal incontinence may result when there is a neurological problem with the anorectal region (such as lack of sensation or lack of control of muscles around the anus). It can also occur when there has been trauma or surgery to the area, or when the patient has constipation with obstruction and overflow incontinence around a hardened fecal mass. The latter may occur in children with poor bowel habit.

SEE ALSO *Anus, Bowel, Bowel cancer, Colon, Digestive system, Duodenum, Ileum, Incontinence, Intussusception, Irritable bowel syndrome, Rectum*

INTUSSUSCEPTION

Intussusception is a condition in which one part of the bowel telescopes inside an immediately adjacent segment (forming a tube within a tube). It is the most common cause of bowel obstruction in children under two and is more common in boys than girls. The disease can have serious consequences if left untreated, because gangrene may arise in the telescoped part of the bowel due to loss of blood supply.

Intussusception appears to be associated with previous viral infection which causes enlargement of clumps of immune system cells (Peyer's patches) in the bowel. Often the cause is not known, and the condition may only become apparent when an otherwise healthy infant experiences sudden and severe abdominal pain.

Treatment of the disease involves reversal of dehydration, therapeutic barium enema to distend the intussusception, or surgery if bowel perforation and/or peritonitis occur.

SEE ALSO *Bowel, Intestines*

IODINE DEFICIENCY

This is the cause of some types of goiter (a swelling of the thyroid gland), in particular the form that is widespread among people living in the foothills of the world's major mountain ranges (such as the Himalayas and the Andes). Leaching of iodine from the soils in these areas is the reason for deficiency of iodine in the diet. Iodine is essential for hormone production by the thyroid gland. When its availability is limited, the gland attempts to compensate for reduced hormone output by increasing in size.

If iodine deficiency persists for many years, the goiter may become nodular and massive. Extreme iodine deficiency may cause hypothyroidism and children may suffer significant mental impairment, referred to as cretinism. Dietary supplementation, for example by providing iodized salt, can eliminate these problems.

SEE ALSO *Cretinism, Goiter, Hypothyroidism, Thyroid gland*

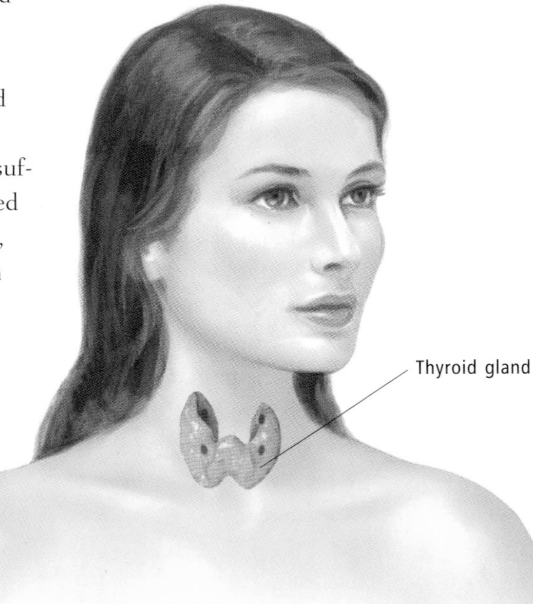

Iodine deficiency
Iodine is found in thyroid gland hormones. A deficiency of iodine can cause swelling of the thyroid gland (goiter) or physical and mental retardation in children (cretinism).

IRIDOLOGY

Iridology, or iris analysis, is a diagnostic technique used by a range of natural therapists; it was pioneered in the late nineteenth century by Ignatz von Peczeley, a Hungarian doctor. In this technique, the pigmentation, texture, patterns and rings of the iris of the eye are closely examined to gain an indication of the overall constitution of the patient.

Iridology is based on the belief that different areas of the iris are linked to different organs of the body through the nervous system, so that markings in any particular part of the iris can give information about the past and present health of the linked organ.

IRIS

The iris is a colored ring positioned in front of the lens and behind the cornea of the eye. The center of the ring is the hole through which light is admitted into the interior of the eye, the pupil. By opening and closing, the iris controls the amount of light entering the eye through the pupil. In bright light, muscles of the iris make the pupil smaller, reducing the amount of light that passes through. In dim light, these muscles make the pupil larger to admit more light. The color of the eyes is determined by pigments in the iris; eye color is inherited. An albino person has no

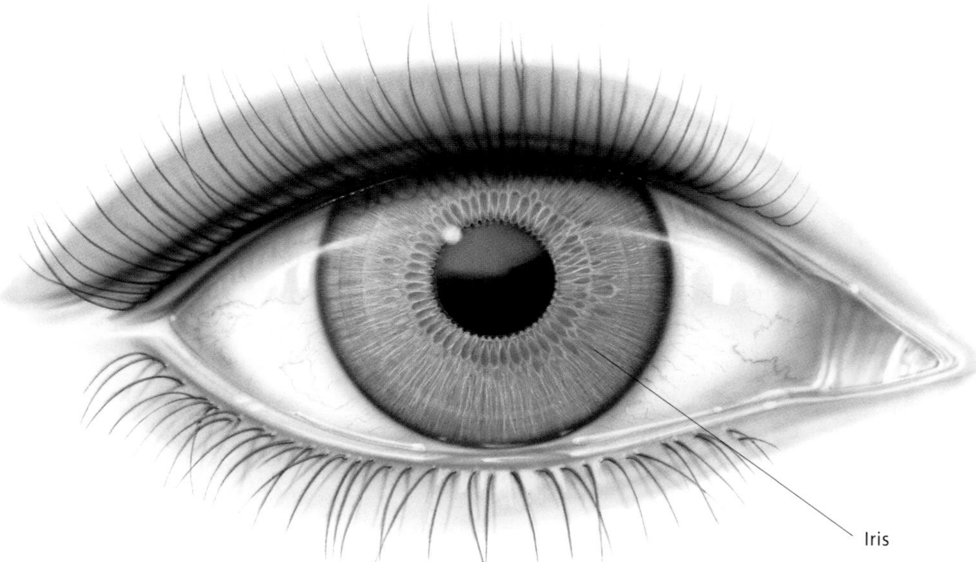

Iris
The iris is the colored part of the eye, encircling the black pupil.

pigmentation in the iris so the eyes look pink due to the small blood vessels in the retina.

The iris can become inflamed (iritis), producing pain, sensitivity to light (photophobia), and redness in the eye.

SEE ALSO *Cornea, Eye, Iritis, Pupil of eye*

IRITIS

Iritis is inflammation of the iris, the colored ring positioned in front of the lens and behind the cornea. Iritis causes pain, photophobia (intolerance to light), redness, blurred vision, and a small, irregular iris. A foggy-looking cornea may develop. It is associated with various illnesses, including ankylosing spondylitis, collagen disease and toxoplasmosis. Treatment is with eye drops that dilate the pupil, such as atropine sulfate and homatropine, and corticosteroid drops.

SEE ALSO *Cornea, Eye, Iris, Photophobia*

IRON

A chemical element, iron is a metal essential for the formation of hemoglobin, the component in red blood cells that transports oxygen and carbon dioxide to and from the body's cells. It is also required for the formation of myoglobin (a muscle protein) and certain enzymes needed in respiration.

The body needs a small but constant supply of iron, which it gets from foods. Foods rich in iron include liver, eggs, spinach, and lean meat. The average adult needs about 15 milligrams of iron a day; a female between puberty and menopause needs about twice that amount. Pregnant women and growing children also need additional iron.

Iron deficiency anemia is a condition that occurs when iron is being lost from the body, for example in a bleeding peptic ulcer, heavy menstrual bleeding, or bleeding caused by bowel cancer. Treatment is to cure the underlying condition and replace the body's depleted iron reserves by taking iron tablets regularly.

Too much iron can be toxic to the body; in a hereditary disease called hemochromatosis, excess absorption of iron by the body leads to damage to organs such as the pancreas, liver, and skin.

SEE ALSO *Anemia, Hemochromatosis, Hemoglobin, Red blood cells*

IRRITABLE BOWEL SYNDROME

Irritable bowel syndrome (IBS) is a common condition, affecting between 15 and 25 percent of people in Western societies. Symptoms include abdominal pain (especially cramps and spasms), bloating and abnormal function of the bowel. Some patients may have hard stools and difficulty in passing motions, whereas others may have loose stools and a feeling of urgency to pass motions. Patients with IBS appear to have a greater degree of pain sensitivity in the lower bowel compared with the general population. The cause remains obscure, but appears to involve some increased sensitivity of the bowel to the sensations of bowel function.

The diagnosis is usually made in the absence of other physical evidence of gut disease: the condition is thought to be a functional, rather than a structural or biochemical, change in the bowel.

Treatments which have been used include antidepressants and drugs which

Irritable bowel syndrome
Irritable bowel syndrome is characterized by cramping abdominal pain and spasms plus unusual diarrhea or constipation, but does not have the inflammation associated with other diseases of the intestinal tract.

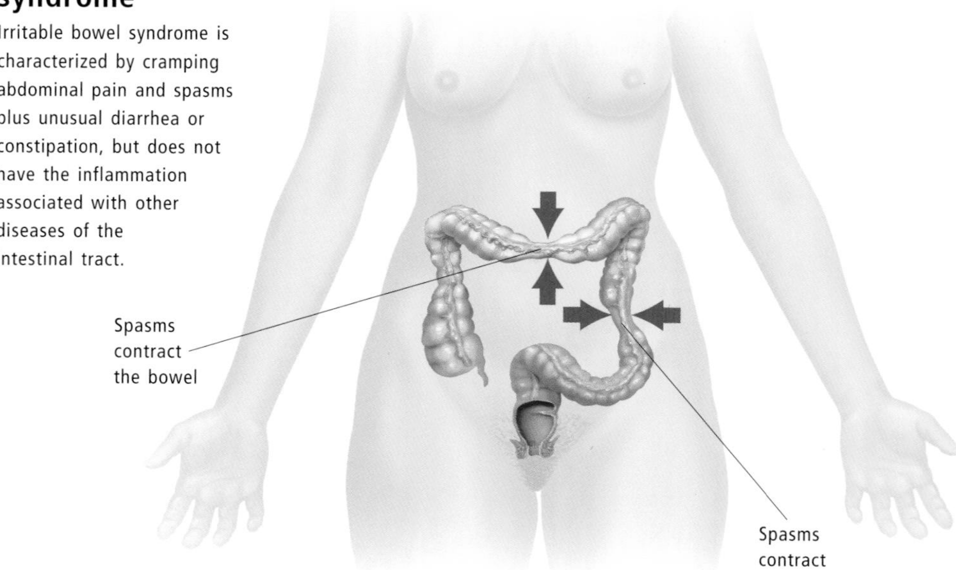

inhibit the function of a neurotransmitter known as serotonin.

There are a number of alternative therapies that may help to alleviate the symptoms of IBS. Acupuncture may relieve symptoms and help with anxiety levels. Chinese herbs can be given in support of treatment. Chiropractic or osteopathic treatment can be given where spinal maladjustment or a trapped spinal nerve is a contributing factor. Herbalism prescribes peppermint and chamomile teas and slippery elm powder. Homeopathy uses a number of remedies that address the specific symptoms of irritable bowel syndrome. Hypnotherapy or psychotherapy may help patients identify and deal with stress. Massage of the abdomen may relax the area, and can be self-administered. Reflexology massage works on colon zones. Shiatsu massage attempts to balance colon function. Any relaxing style of massage may help with anxiety levels. Naturopathy prescribes a wholefood diet to maintain bowel action, and fiber or bulk laxatives such as linseed or psyllium seeds. Relaxation techniques are also recommended. One should avoid irritants such as tea, coffee and alcohol, and check for possible allergies, particularly dairy or wheat.

SEE ALSO *Bowel, Digestive system, Intestines*

ISCHEMIA

Ischemia is the lack of supply of oxygenated blood to a particular part of the body. It is usually caused by disease in the blood vessels (most commonly arteriosclerosis), but it may also result from the blockage of an artery following an injury or a blood clot. If lower limb arteries are affected, ischemia produces leg cramps and intermittent claudication (pain on walking). If the heart is affected, angina pectoris or myocardial infarction can occur. In the brain, ischemia causes transient ischemic attack (TIA) or stroke.

SEE ALSO *Angina pectoris, Arteriosclerosis, Circulatory system, Myocardial infarction, Stroke, Transient ischemic attack*

ISCHEMIC HEART DISEASE

Ischemic heart disease refers to a group of conditions where there is insufficient blood supply to the heart muscle. This is usually due to partial or complete blockage of the coronary arteries supplying the heart by a disease called atherosclerosis. Atherosclerosis is a common condition in Western society and involves the accumulation of fatty and fibrous tissue in the vessel wall.

If coronary artery obstruction is only partial, the patient will experience pain in the center of the chest (angina pectoris) during exercise or emotional excitement. If coronary artery obstruction is complete, there may be death of heart muscle (myocardial infarction).

SEE ALSO *Angina pectoris, Arteriosclerosis, Atherosclerosis, Coronary arteries, Coronary artery disease, Heart, Myocardial infarction*

Ischemia

Ischemia results from a constriction or blockage of a blood vessel, so that oxygenated blood does not reach a particular part of the body. Obstruction of the arteries to the heart can lead to angina or a heart attack.

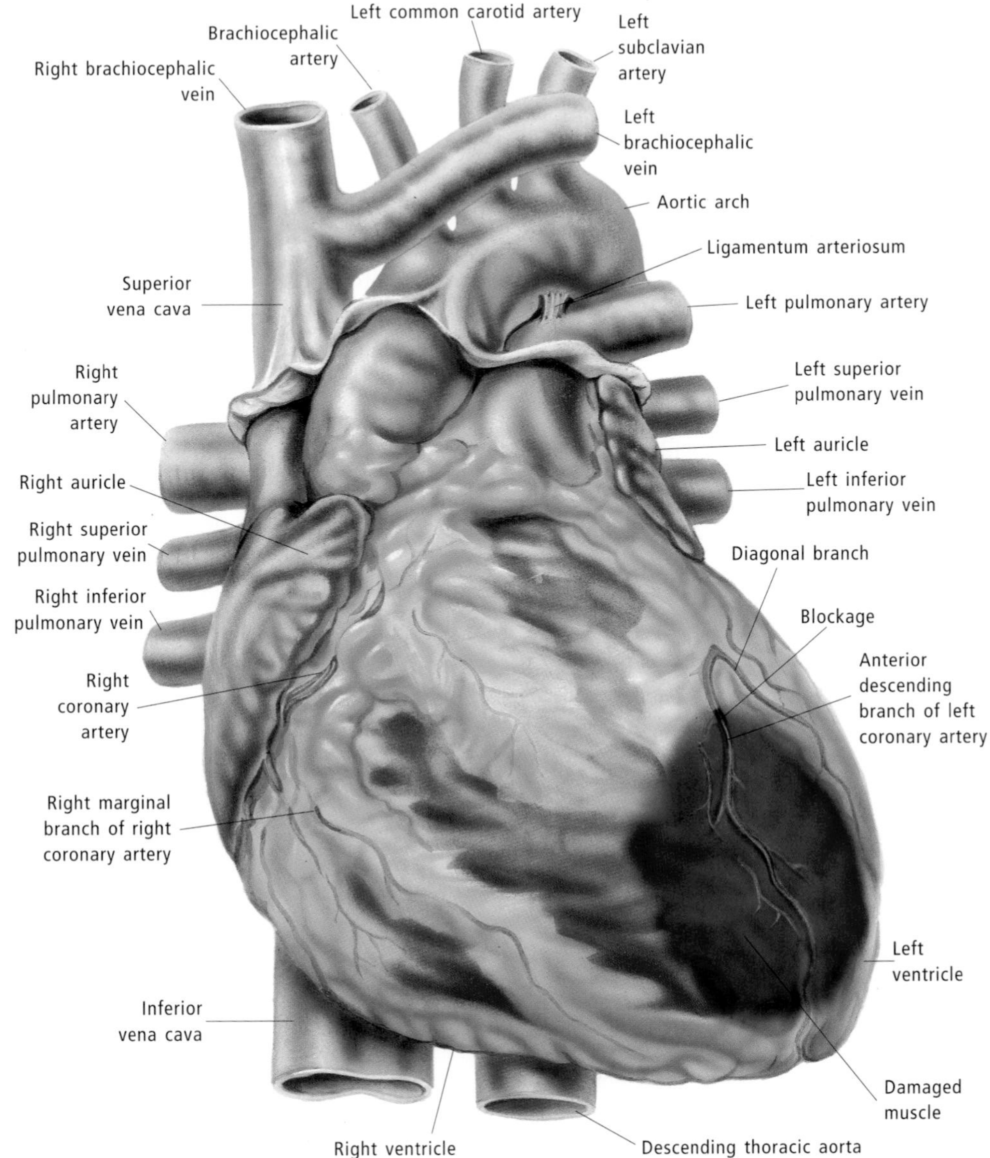

ISLETS OF LANGERHANS

These are many spherical clusters of specialized cells within the pancreas. They are a type of endocrine gland, i.e. a gland that secretes hormones directly into the bloodstream rather than onto the surface of the gut or skin. The islets are made up of several different types of cell. The first two types (alpha and beta cells) are involved in the control of blood sugar concentration and are responsive to changes in that concentration. The alpha cell type produces a

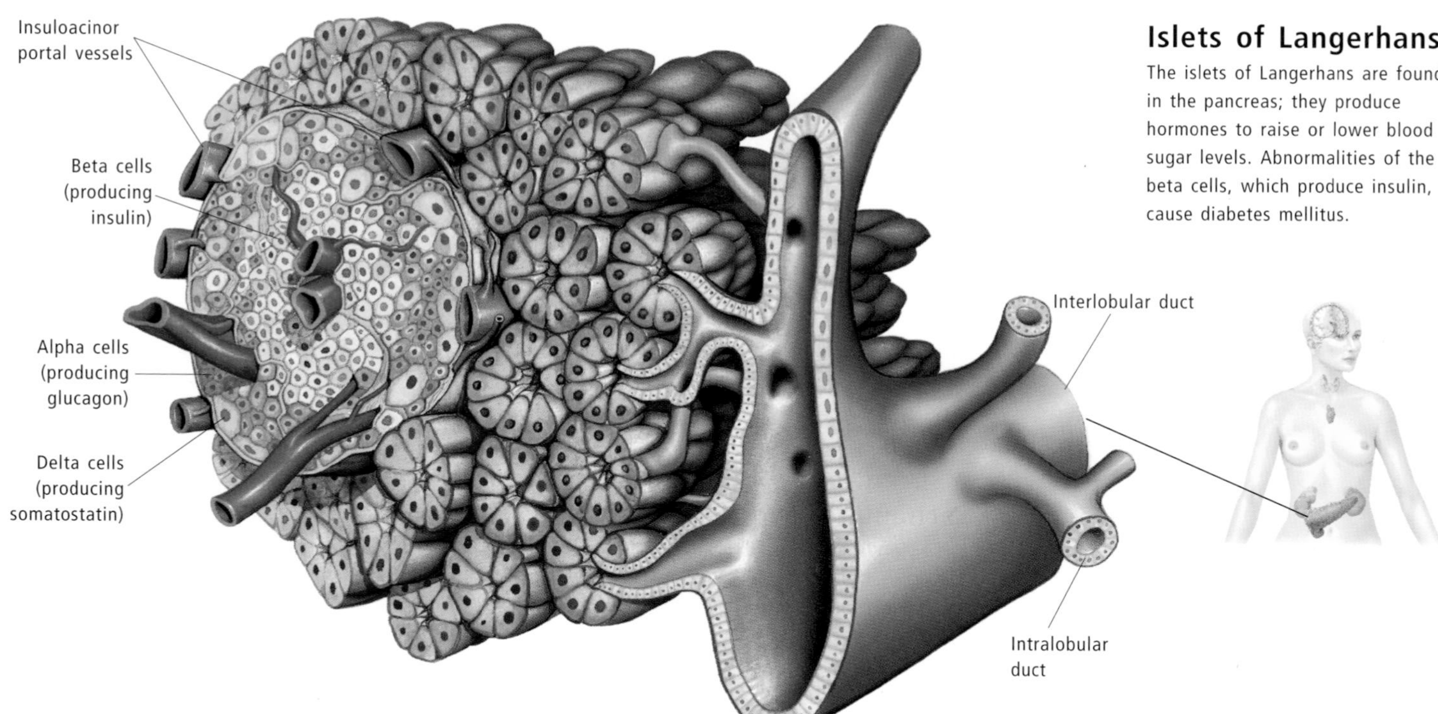

Islets of Langerhans

The islets of Langerhans are found in the pancreas; they produce hormones to raise or lower blood sugar levels. Abnormalities of the beta cells, which produce insulin, cause diabetes mellitus.

hormone known as glucagon, which acts to increase blood sugar level. The beta cell type produces the hormone insulin, which has the effect of reducing blood sugar level. A third type, the delta cell, secretes somatostatin, which inhibits the release of glucagon and insulin.

SEE ALSO *Endocrine glands, Endocrine system, Insulin, Pancreas*

JAUNDICE

Jaundice is a condition in which there is yellowing of the skin and eyes due to an increased concentration of bilirubin in the blood. The condition may be due to excessive breakdown of blood cells (hemolytic jaundice), excessive production of pigments (pigment overload), problems with liver cells (hepatocellular jaundice), or obstruction of the ducts leading from the liver to the gut (obstructive jaundice). In practice, many cases of jaundice present a mixture of these types.

Hemolytic or pigment overload jaundice is due to abnormalities of red blood cells or the metabolic pathways involved in the production of hemoglobin. Red blood cells are normally broken down and recycled, but patients with hemolytic jaundice have a higher than normal rate of destruction of blood cells. The excess hemoglobin is converted into excess amounts of bilirubin.

Hepatocellular jaundice is due to damage to liver cells, as seen in hepatitis and alcoholic cirrhosis, or a result of inherited problems with enzymes in the liver. In this type of jaundice the liver cells are unable to process bile pigments and excrete them into the bile duct system. Bilirubin builds up in the blood to produce jaundice. Destruction of liver cells releases enzymes, which can be detected in the patient's blood.

Obstructive jaundice is often due to the presence of gallstones in the biliary duct system, although tumors in the head of the pancreas, parasites in the bile duct, inflammation of the pancreas, drugs and pregnancy may also cause the condition. Patients develop pale stools and dark urine. The stools are pale because the pigments which normally pass down the bile duct to color the feces are no longer reaching the gut. The dark urine is due to excretion of bile salts by the kidney. Blood tests may show elevated concentrations of an enzyme called alkaline phosphatase. If the obstruction is caused by a gallstone, the gallbladder is unlikely to be enlarged; if it is due to a cancer in the head of the pancreas which is compressing the lower part of the bile duct, the gallbladder may be enlarged and easily felt just below the ribs on the right side of the abdomen. Patients with obstructive jaundice will often experience itching of the skin due to deposition of bile salts.

All normal newborn infants have a small degree of jaundice which is due to immature enzyme systems in the liver. This "physiological" jaundice, will usually disappear over a few days, but may become a serious problem in infants who are born prematurely or who have increased destruction of red blood cells due to other diseases. If the concentration of bilirubin in the blood rises too high, the brain may be damaged in a condition called kernicterus.

Jaundice may also be caused by drugs including phenacetin, paracetamol, sex steroids, anti-psychotic drugs, some anesthetics, selected antibiotics and anti-tuberculosis drugs. Some toxic chemicals like carbon tetrachloride can also damage the liver and cause jaundice.

SEE ALSO *Cirrhosis of the liver, Gallbladder, Gallstones, Hemoglobin, Hepatitis, Liver, Newborn, Red blood cells*

JAW

The jaw consists of two parts: a moveable lower jaw, formed by the mandible, and a fixed upper jaw, formed by the maxillae. The mandible is made up of a thickened body (which forms the lower border of the face); an alveolar part (which contains sockets for the lower teeth); and a ramus (which projects upwards from each end of the body). The top of each ramus has a small rounded head, which fits into a socket on the base of the skull to form the temporomandibular joint. This joint, which is reinforced by a capsule and strong ligaments, allows gliding (backwards, forwards and sideways) movements, as well as a hinge movement, which occurs during opening and closing of the jaw. Sometimes, when the jaw is opened too far, the mandible can be pulled forwards out of its socket, causing it to dislocate.

The movements of the temporomandibular joint are brought about by a group of muscles known as the muscles of mastication. These muscles include the medial and lateral pterygoid, masseter and temporalis muscles. The medial pterygoid and masseter muscles cover the medial (inner) and lateral (outer) surfaces respectively of the ramus of the mandible and, with the temporalis muscle, act to elevate (close) the mandible. They can all be palpated when the teeth are clenched. It is interesting to note that the masseter muscle is said to be the strongest muscle in the body (based on force per unit of mass). The lateral pterygoid muscle is the major depressor (opener) of the mandible.

The upper jaw is formed by the maxillae. It has an alveolar part (which contains sockets for the upper teeth); a palatine part (which forms the hard palate in the roof of the mouth); and a hollow body (which forms part of the cheek). The cavity in the body is known as the maxillary sinus, and is a frequent site of minor infections (sinusitis) which can spread to it from the nose, or in some cases from the upper teeth.

The alveolar parts of the maxilla and mandible contain sockets for the teeth (alveolar sockets). The base of each socket contains a hole through which branches of the superior and inferior alveolar nerves and blood vessels reach the inside (pulp cavity) of the teeth. In an adult, each jaw contains sockets for 16 teeth, including 4 incisors (for cutting), 1 pair of canines (for tearing), 2 pairs of premolars and 3 pairs of molars (for grinding). In many people the alveolar parts of the mandible and/or maxilla are not long enough to accommodate the third pair of molars (often called the wisdom teeth) causing them to become "impacted".

SEE ALSO *Face, Sinuses, Sinusitis, Teeth*

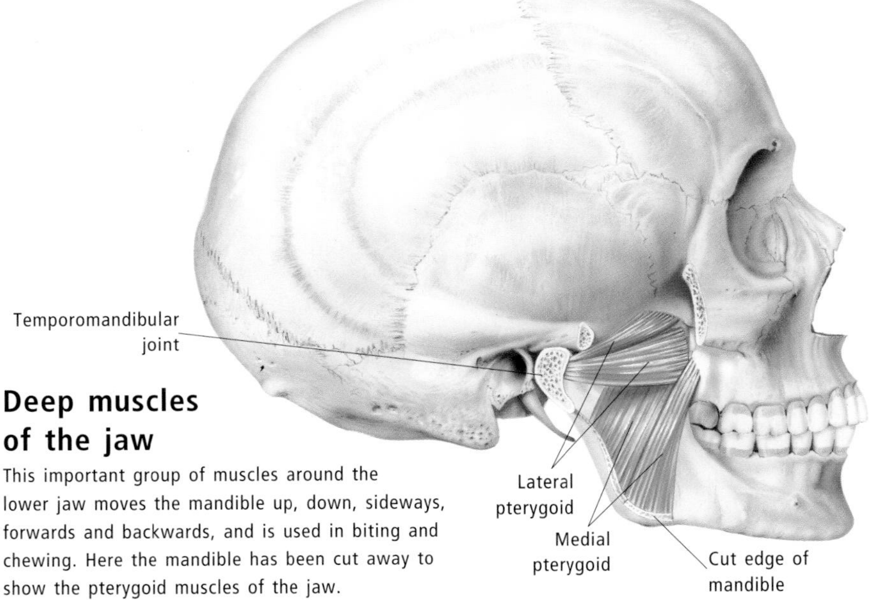

Deep muscles of the jaw

This important group of muscles around the lower jaw moves the mandible up, down, sideways, forwards and backwards, and is used in biting and chewing. Here the mandible has been cut away to show the pterygoid muscles of the jaw.

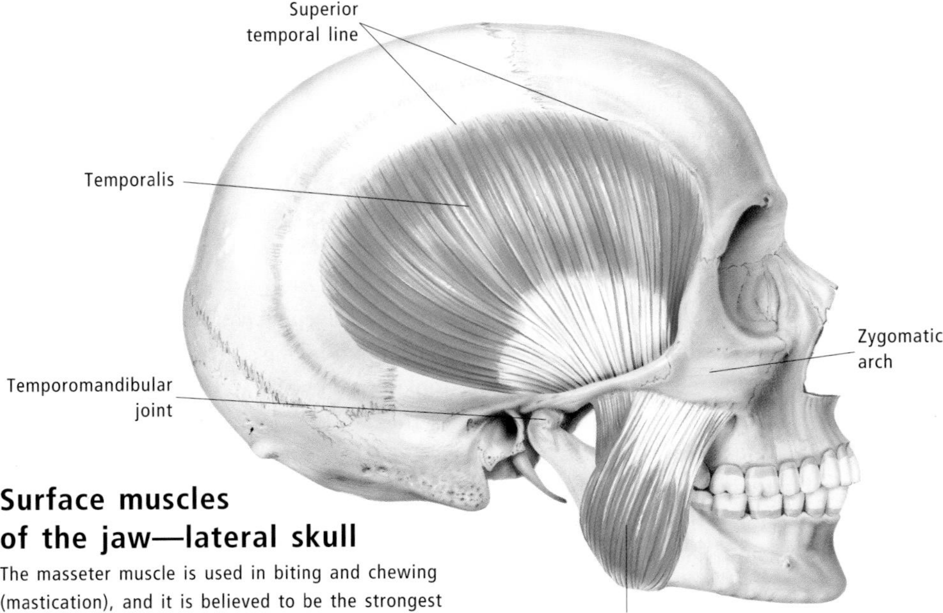

Surface muscles of the jaw—lateral skull

The masseter muscle is used in biting and chewing (mastication), and it is believed to be the strongest muscle in the human body based on force per unit of mass.

JEJUNUM

Located in the upper left part of the abdomen, the jejunum is the middle part of the small intestine, extending from the duodenum to the ileum. It is about 4 feet (1.2 meters) long and together with the duodenum, makes up about two-fifths of the length of the small intestine.

The jejunum, like the rest of the small intestine, is covered by smooth muscle with an inner, circular layer that is thicker than the outer, longitudinal layer. Food passes from the duodenum into the jejunum by a series of muscular contractions and relaxations known as peristalsis. In the jejunum, as in the duodenum, food is digested and absorbed, passing though the lining of the walls of the jejunum into the lymphatic vessels and the hepatic portal vein to the liver.

The jejunum is one part of the small intestine that is either partially or completely bypassed during gastric bypass operations, which are sometimes performed as a treatment for obesity.

Like the duodenum, the jejunum is suspended from the back of the abdominal wall by a fold of membrane called the mesentery. Blood vessels, nerves and lymphatic vessels travel through the mesentery and supply the jejunum.

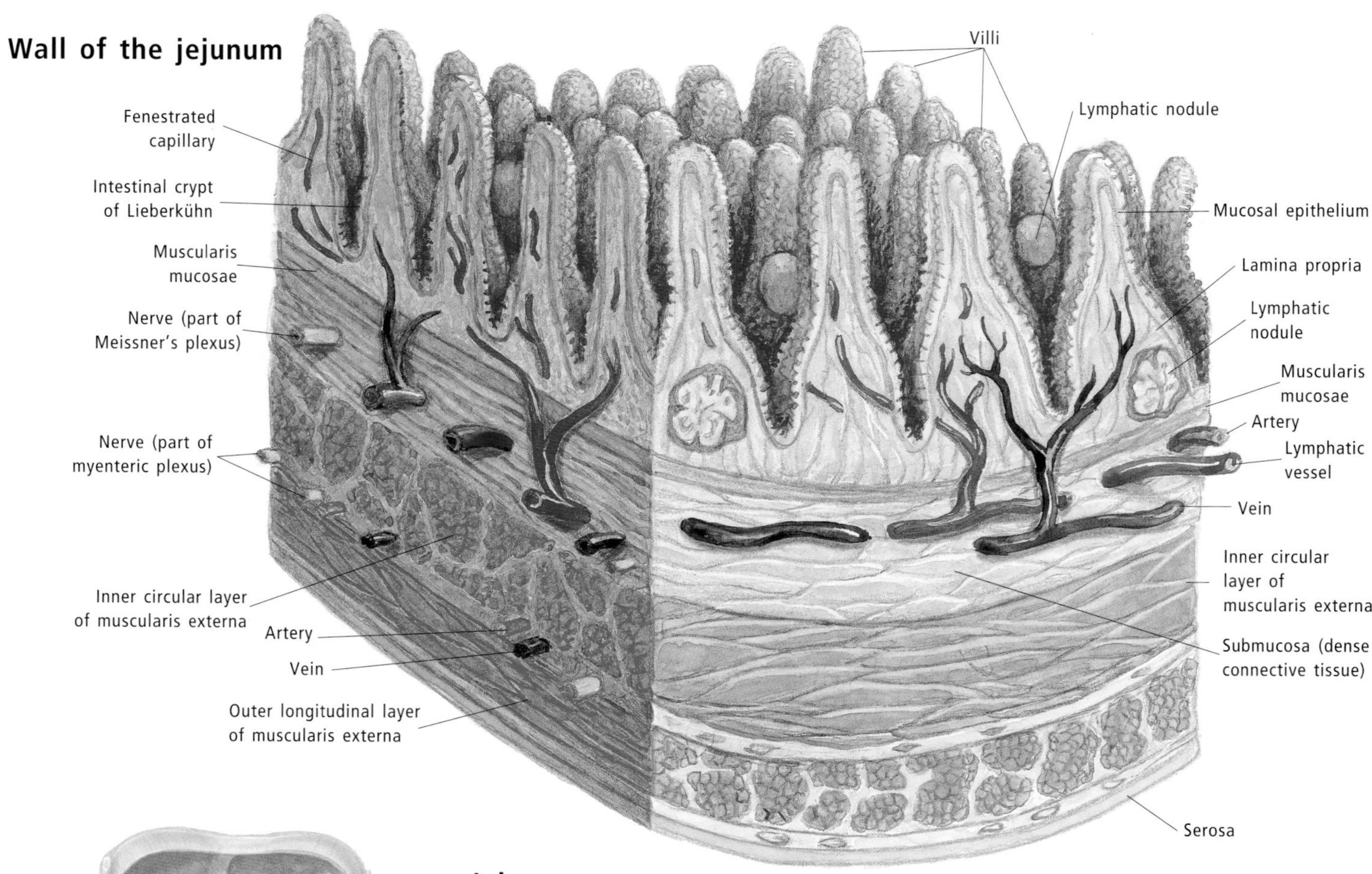

Jejunum

The jejunum is the part of the small intestine between the duodenum and the ileum. It digests and absorbs food, sending nutrients to the lymphatic vessels and liver.

The jejunum can be affected by several diseases, including bowel obstruction, gastroenteritis, celiac disease and Crohn's disease. Peptic ulcers, though occurring commonly in the duodenum, do not occur in the jejunum. Tumors are rare in the jejunum.

The jejunal button and jejunostomy tube (J-tube) are surgically installed feeding devices that deliver nutrients directly into the jejunum. They are used to assist patients with nutritional inadequacies or who are unable to eat due to illness.

SEE ALSO *Celiac disease, Crohn's disease, Digestive system, Duodenum, Gastroenteritis, Ileum, Intestines, Peristalsis*

JET LAG

Symptoms of jet lag are daytime drowsiness, fatigue, difficulty sleeping and a general feeling of vagueness. The person who travels across time zones in a jet plane will suffer varying degrees of jet lag. The person who travels from north to south will not experience jet lag, though they may be tired.

Many hormones change in level at approximately 24-hour intervals: these periodic changes are called circadian rhythms. Cortisol, the major steroid hormone secreted by the adrenal cortex, is at a low level during sleep, rising rapidly in the early morning hours and gradually descending during the day, with spurts during meal times. The rhythm of this hormone is dependent on night–day cycles and lasts for some days after jet travel into different time zones. The period when the body is adjusting to the change of these patterns is characterized by jet lag. One of the problems with jet lag is that all the body's rhythms are upset. After a few days (this differs from individual to individual) the body will have settled into the new time frame; heart rate will adjust ahead of body temperature.

There are dozens of theories on how to prevent or stave off the effects of jet lag. These include keeping to the same sleep hours you would normally follow in the new destination (this is only possible for short stays); taking melatonin, a human hormone available in tablet form (this is controversial) and taking sleeping pills (these result in their own form of grogginess).

Other ways to minimize jet lag are getting a good night's sleep before the trip; flying in the late afternoon and evening; anticipating the new time zone by trying to follow its eating and sleeping patterns while on the plane; not drinking alcohol or caffeine, but drinking plenty of water; immediately adopting the new time on arrival; keeping the room cool so you can sleep at night; making sure the morning is bright (if there's no sun turn on all the lights); exercising in the morning when you wake up and eating lightly for the first days after arrival.

SEE ALSO *Insomnia, Sleep disturbances*

JOINTS

A joint is an area in the body at which two bones articulate. The bones may be fixed and immobile, such as the connections between the bones of the skull. These joints, (which are also called synarthroses) occur where two bones are fused or fixed together before or shortly after birth. Joints may be slightly mobile, such as the junction of the bones making up the front of the pelvis. These joints (also called symphyses) have a layer of cartilage between them and are held together by strong fibrous ligaments. Joints may also be freely mobile, such as the bones of the limbs. These joints (also called diarthroses) are held together and moved by muscles, ligaments, and tendons.

The bony surfaces of movable joints are covered with smooth cartilage. A thin fluid called synovial fluid, which is produced by the synovial membrane which lines the joint capsule, lubricates the joints.

There are several different kinds of mobile joints. In a ball-and-socket joint, such as the hip and the shoulder, free movement occurs in all directions. The elbow and the knee are essentially hinge joints, allowing movement mainly in one plane only. A saddle joint, such as the base joint of the thumb, allows sliding movement in two directions. A plane (or gliding) joint, such as those found between the carpal bones of the wrist allows only slight sliding movements. Pivot joints allow rotation about a single axis and are found between the first two vertebrae.

A mobile joint may have more than one type of joint movement; the elbow, for example, includes a hinge joint and a pivot joint.

Diseases and disorders

Displacement of the bones at a joint is called dislocation, and is more common in some joints, such as the shoulder, than in others which are more stable, such as the elbow. In some cases the dislocation is present from birth; this is called a congenital dislocation. This is common at the hip joint ("clicky hip") and, if not treated, will prevent the joint from developing normally.

Inflammation in the joints is called arthritis. There are two common types of arthritis, with different causes. In osteoarthritis, long-term heavy use of a joint causes the cartilage to become rough

Gliding joint

Aided by synovial fluid, the bones in the joint slide across each other in a limited movement.

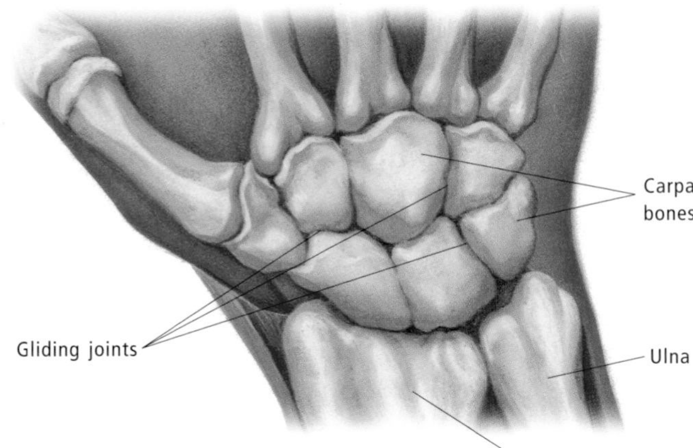

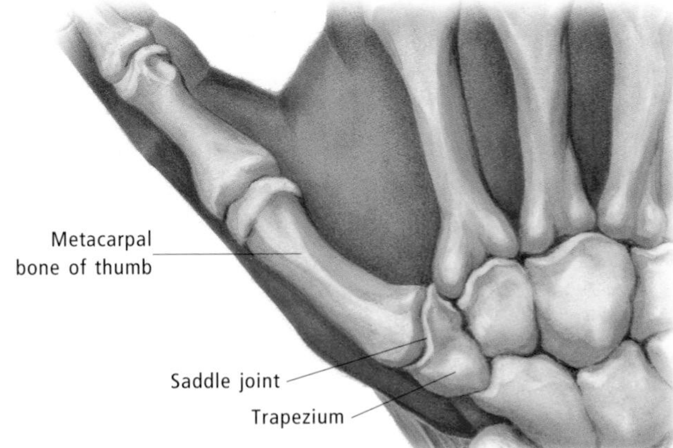

Saddle joint

A saddle joint allows almost as much movement as a ball-and-socket joint.

Ellipsoidal joint

This is a joint structure which allows movement in two directions, such as that which takes place at the wrist joint.

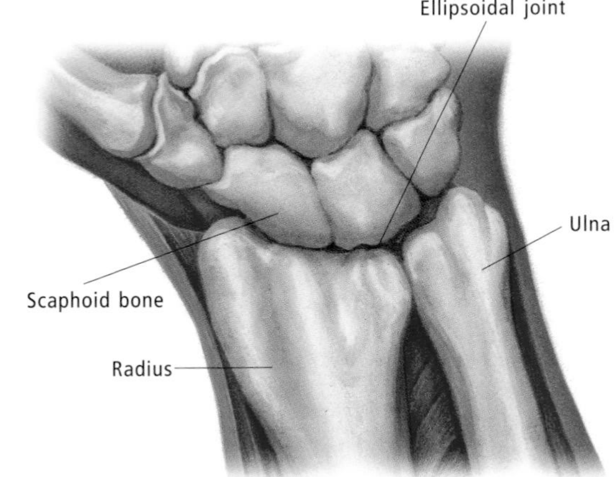

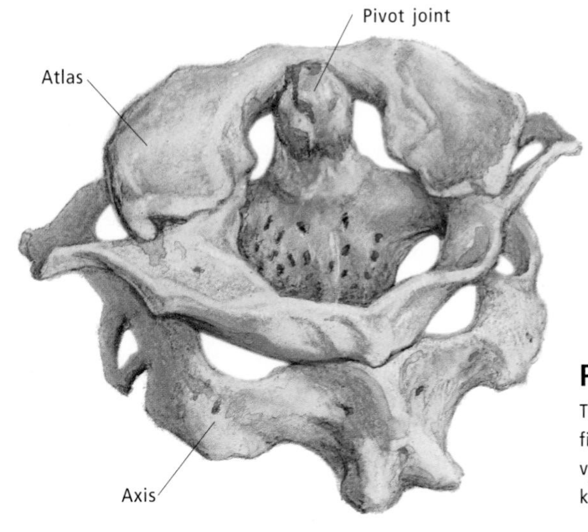

Pivot joint

The joint between the first and second cervical vertebrae rotates—this is known as a pivot joint.

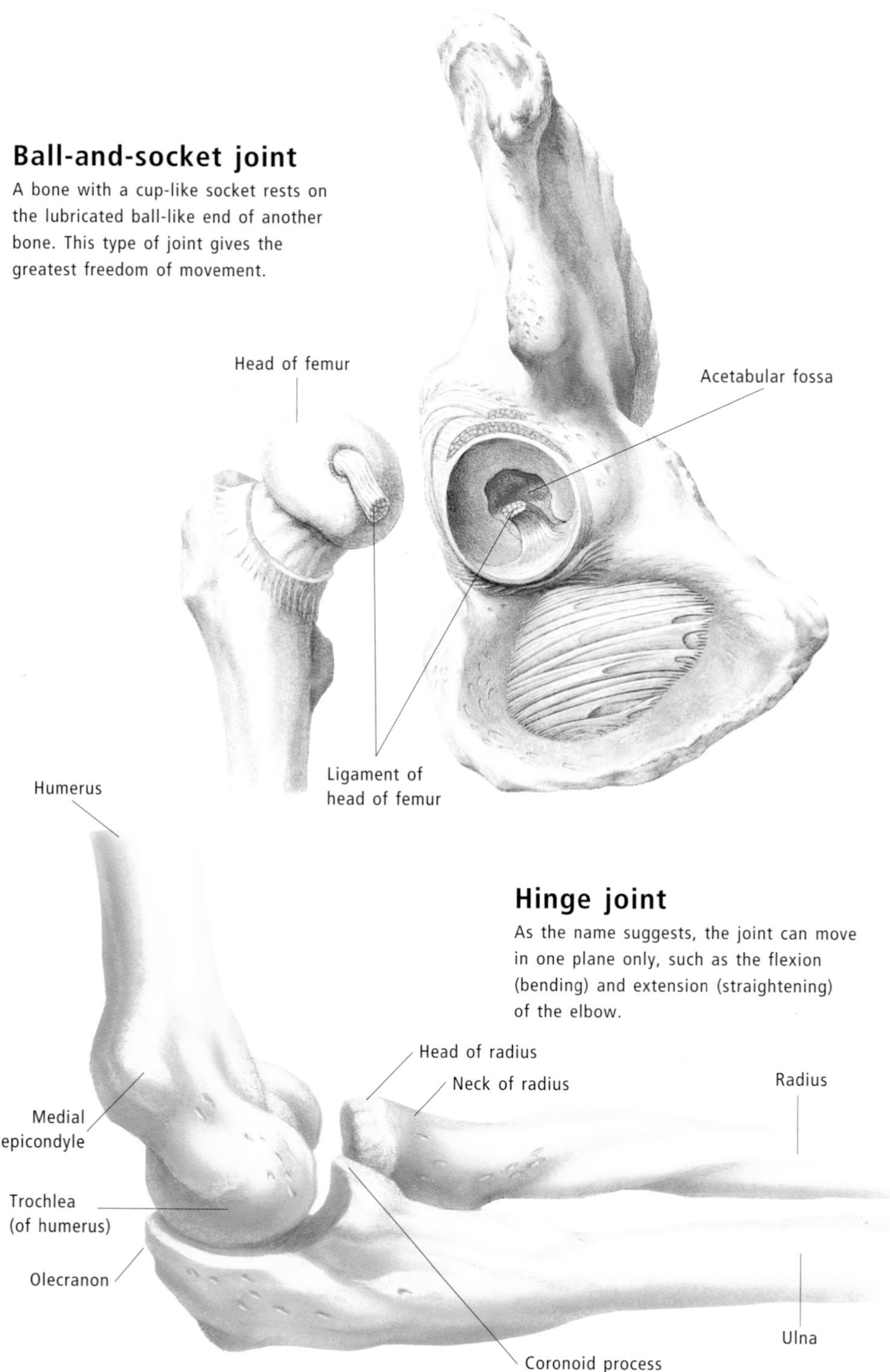

Ball-and-socket joint

A bone with a cup-like socket rests on the lubricated ball-like end of another bone. This type of joint gives the greatest freedom of movement.

Hinge joint

As the name suggests, the joint can move in one plane only, such as the flexion (bending) and extension (straightening) of the elbow.

and frayed and gradually worn away. This is particularly common in the hip and knee joints, which get heavy use. It is usually seen in older people, but can also occur earlier in sportspeople such as football and netball players. The joint is painful to use and movement is limited. If damage is severe the joint can be replaced by an artificial hip or knee, which relieves the pain and restores movement.

The other type of joint inflammation is rheumatoid arthritis, an immune disorder which involves the synovial membrane and cartilage within the joint. It is particularly common in women, and usually affects the small joints in the wrists and fingers. The joints are very painful and gradually become deformed. Treatments include anti-inflammatory drugs, sometimes injected directly into the joint.

Besides developing rheumatoid arthritis and osteoarthritis, joints can also become infected, when an increase in synovial fluid in the joint makes it swell and become hot and painful. Joints also become swollen, hot and painful in gout, where crystals of uric acid precipitate within them. Excess fluid in a joint can be removed by aspiration, in which a needle is inserted into the joint cavity. This can relieve the pain. The fluid can be used to diagnose the infective agent or to confirm the presence of crystals.

Joints can also be investigated by arthroscopy, a technique in which a small tube is inserted into the joint to transmit images of the interior to a screen; arthroscopy can be used to guide surgical procedures within the joint, such as taking a biopsy of synovial membrane.

The disease ankylosing spondylitis particularly affects the joint between the spine and hip bone (sacroiliac joint) and the small joints of the spine. It can cause severe back pain and reduced movement. It is a long-term disease, most common in young men. Diagnosis is confirmed by x-rays and blood tests, and treatment includes anti-inflammatory medication and physical therapy.

Pain in the angle of the jaw may be due to excess tension in jaw muscles, often with tooth grinding, referred to as the temporomandibular joint syndrome. The pain is usually on one side and may spread to the ear, temples and back of the head. Treatment includes a dental visit to check tooth alignment, a soft diet and medication to relax muscles and relieve stress.

Many joints, such as the elbow and knee, have blind sacs, or bursae, which allow tendons or skin to move smoothly over the joint. Like the joint cavity itself, these sacs can become inflamed, swollen and painful. "Student's elbow" and "housemaid's knee" are common names for bursitis of the elbow and knee. The shoulder is also a frequent site for bursitis, leading to pain with certain movements (the painful arc).

The capsule of the shoulder joint can become inflamed and thickened, causing movements to gradually become more limited, a condition referred to as frozen shoulder. This requires pain relief; physical therapy can also be useful.

SEE ALSO *Ankylosing spondylitis, Arthritis, Bones, Bursitis, Gout, Housemaid's knee, Osteoarthritis, Rheumatoid arthritis, Skeletal system, Synovial fluid, Synovial membrane, Temporomandibular joint syndrome*

JUGULAR VEIN

A jugular vein is any one of the four large veins in the neck (two on either side) that drain venous blood from the brain, face and neck into larger veins that eventually drain into the heart. Sometimes the jugular veins are used to gain access for intravenous administration of fluids and drugs to a patient in hospital by insertion of an intravenous cannula. Jugular veins can be affected by thrombophlebitis (inflammation of the vein and clotting). If a jugular vein is severed, rapid loss of blood will occur and immediate action is required.

SEE ALSO *Thrombophlebitis, Veins*

KALA-AZAR

Kala-azar is a form of leishmaniasis, a protozoal infection spread by the bite of a bloodsucking sandfly found in tropical regions. The disease is transferred in the saliva of the fly after biting an infected animal. The symptoms include fever, weight loss, and enlargement of liver and spleen. It is usually fatal unless treated. Kala-azar is treated with amphotericin B (an antifungal medication) or pentamidine.

SEE ALSO *Leishmaniasis*

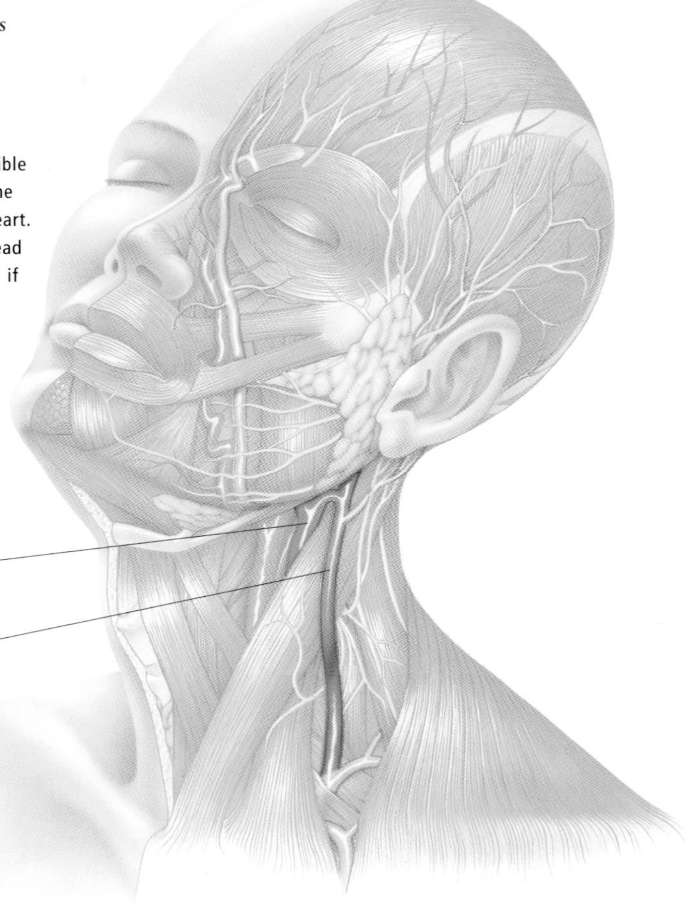

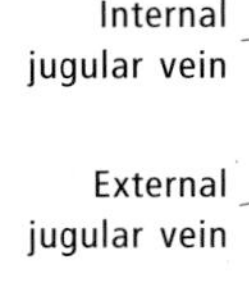

Jugular vein

The jugular veins are responsible for transporting blood from the head and neck back to the heart. Severing a jugular vein will lead to rapid blood loss and death if the wound is not attended to immediately.

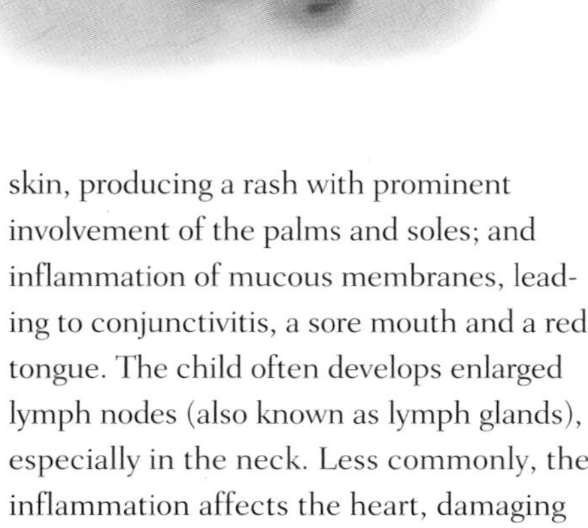

Kaposi's sarcoma

These cancerous growths on the skin first appear on the lower extremities and then spread up the body.

KAPOSI'S SARCOMA

A malignant skin tumor most often seen in late-stage AIDS, Kaposi's sarcoma is possibly caused by an unknown virus. It is the most common cancer seen in AIDS. Flat, reddish brown or purple patches appear first on the toes or feet and then slowly spread over the skin and in the mouth, developing into plaques or nodules. They may also occur in the digestive tract or lungs. Treatment is with radiation therapy and anti-cancer drugs.

SEE ALSO *AIDS*

KAWASAKI'S DISEASE

This disease, which is of unknown cause, usually affects children under five years. Typically there is fever; inflammation of the skin, producing a rash with prominent involvement of the palms and soles; and inflammation of mucous membranes, leading to conjunctivitis, a sore mouth and a red tongue. The child often develops enlarged lymph nodes (also known as lymph glands), especially in the neck. Less commonly, the inflammation affects the heart, damaging and weakening the walls of the coronary arteries or injuring the heart muscle itself.

Treatment with anti-inflammatory drugs such as aspirin helps to control the disease and the development of complications.

SEE ALSO *Inflammation*

KELOID

Overproduction of collagen in scar tissue at the site of a wound creates a keloid, or keloid scar. People with darkly pigmented skin have a greater tendency than others to develop keloids. Firm, raised, hard and slightly pink, keloids usually arise following surgery or after a burn, but sometimes arise from a minor scratch. They may appear anywhere on the skin, but most commonly form on the breastbone, upper back and shoulder. They may itch, cause pain or be tender to the touch; although of cosmetic concern they are otherwise harmless. In some cases the keloid scar continues to grow and may develop claw-like projections into the surrounding skin.

Keloids can be treated by surgical excision, cryosurgery, or injection of corticosteroids into the keloid. Unfortunately they may recur.

SEE ALSO *Collagen, Scar, Skin*

J K

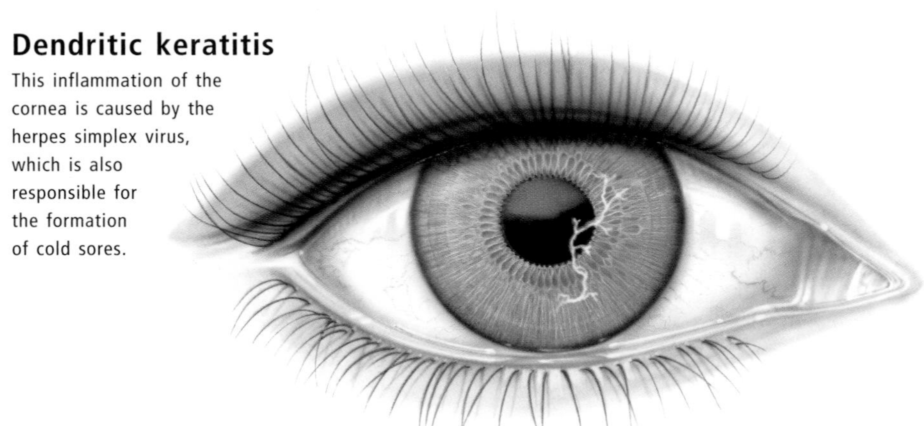

Dendritic keratitis
This inflammation of the cornea is caused by the herpes simplex virus, which is also responsible for the formation of cold sores.

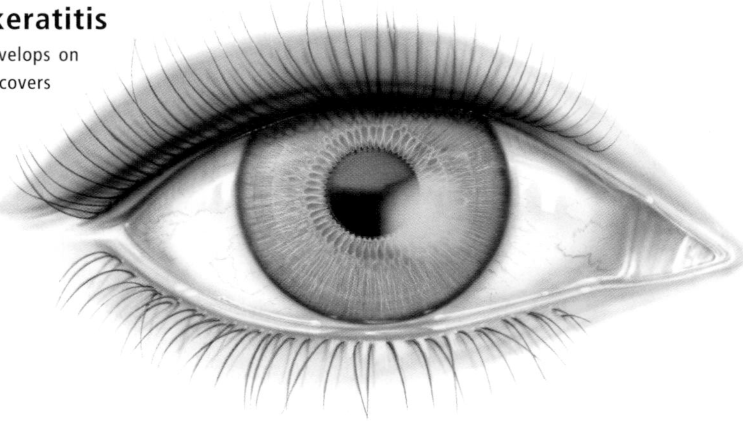

Diskiform keratitis
An opaque disk develops on the cornea. If this covers the pupil, light is restricted from entering the eyes and sight may be lost.

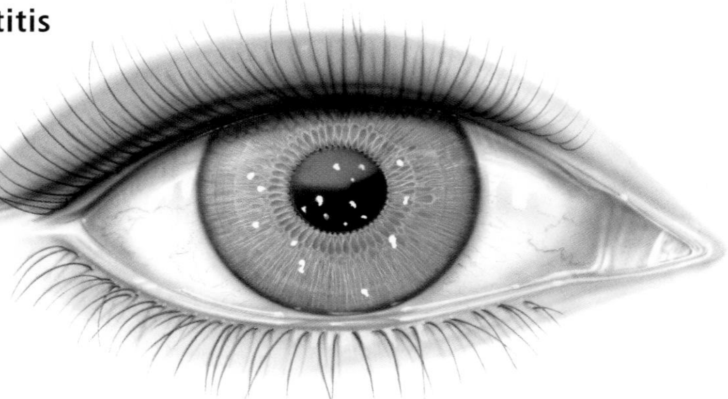

Punctate keratitis
Small lesions caused by foreign bodies on the surface of the cornea can result in painful inflammation.

KERATIN

Keratin is a tough, highly fibrous, protein that is rich in sulfur. It is the main component of our hair, nails and tooth enamel, and forms part of our epidermis (the outermost layer of the skin).

Keratin is also found throughout the animal kingdom in feathers, beaks, horns and hooves.

In our skin, this protective substance helps prevent injury and microbial invasion and, because it is insoluble in water, provides waterproofing.

SEE ALSO *Epidermis, Skin*

KERATITIS

Inflammation of the corneal surface is known as keratitis. This may be caused by chemicals (acids or alkalis) splashed into the eye, ultraviolet radiation (arc welding, sun exposure or snow blindness), bacterial, viral or fungal infections (especially herpes simplex virus type 1), or sensitivity to cosmetics, air pollution, or allergens such as pollen. Symptoms vary, but pain and an inability to tolerate light are usual. Treatment depends on the original cause. A temporary eye patch is often needed. Antibiotic or antiviral eye drops and ointments may be indicated for infection. Non-prescription eye drops containing topical corticosteroids should not be used as they may worsen the condition or perforate the eyeball. With early treatment, most types of keratitis can be cured. Severe cases may cause corneal scarring, and corneal replacement may be necessary.

SEE ALSO *Cornea*

KERATOSIS

A keratosis is a thickened lesion of the outermost skin layers. There are several different forms. Small lumps on the upper arms, and less commonly the thighs, characterize a harmless condition known as keratosis pilaris. It tends to run in families and can be controlled but not cured.

Seborrheic keratoses—sometimes called "barnacles of ageing"—are harmless, slightly raised, dark spots that appear as the skin ages. Usually, they first appear after the age of 30. They may thicken and become wartlike in appearance but do not require treatment, although they can be cut or burned off. They only occasionally turn malignant.

Actinic or solar keratoses are precancerous lesions caused by sun exposure. Because they inevitably develop into skin cancer they should be removed.

SEE ALSO *Skin, Skin cancer*

KETOSIS

Ketosis is a condition in which there is a high concentration of a type of chemical called ketone bodies in the blood. Ketone bodies are produced during starvation, but ketosis is most often seen in the Western world in diabetics who have insufficient insulin to control their blood sugar concentration. This causes the blood to become dangerously acidic (ketoacidosis).

Common symptoms are thirst, frequent urination, nausea and weakness. The affected person is dehydrated, has rapid pulse and breathing, is confused or comatose, and has a fruity breath odor (indicating the presence of ketones). Ketoacidosis is a medical emergency requiring urgent treatment in hospital with intravenous insulin and fluid and electrolyte replacement. The condition has a 10 percent mortality rate.

SEE ALSO *Acidosis, Diabetes*

KIDNEY

The kidneys are a pair of bean-shaped, red-brown organs whose function is to dispose of the waste matter produced by the normal functioning of the body, and to keep the salts and water of the body in correct balance. They do this by filtering excess water and chemicals from the blood and excreting them as waste in the form of urine.

The kidneys are located at the back of the abdomen, one on each side of the spine, at the level of the lowest ribs. Because of the position of the liver, the right kidney in most people is located slightly lower than the left. Each kidney is about 4 inches (10 centimeters) long and 1 inch (2.5 centimeters) thick and weighs about 5 ounces (140 grams). Each has an outer layer (the cortex), an inner layer (the medulla), and a pelvis, a hollow inner structure that joins with the ureters, the tubes that conduct urine to the bladder.

At the center on one side of each kidney is an indentation known as the renal hilus, the exit point for the ureter and the location where nerves, blood and lymphatic vessels enter and exit. Enclosing each kidney is a protective membrane, the renal capsule. Surrounding each capsule is a cushion of fatty tissue and a layer of connective tissue which attaches the kidneys to the back wall of the abdomen. An adrenal gland sits on top of each kidney.

The renal medulla contains between 8 and 18 renal pyramids, triangular shaped as their name implies and with a striped appearance. The pyramids are positioned with their tips, the renal papillae, facing towards the renal hilus and their bases aligned with the edge of the renal cortex. The cortex continues in between each pyramid creating areas known as renal columns.

The functional units of the kidneys are microscopic structures called nephrons, of

Kidney

The two kidneys filter the blood and send the waste products (as urine) to the bladder via the ureters. Kidney stones sometimes block one of the ureters, causing intense abdominal pain.

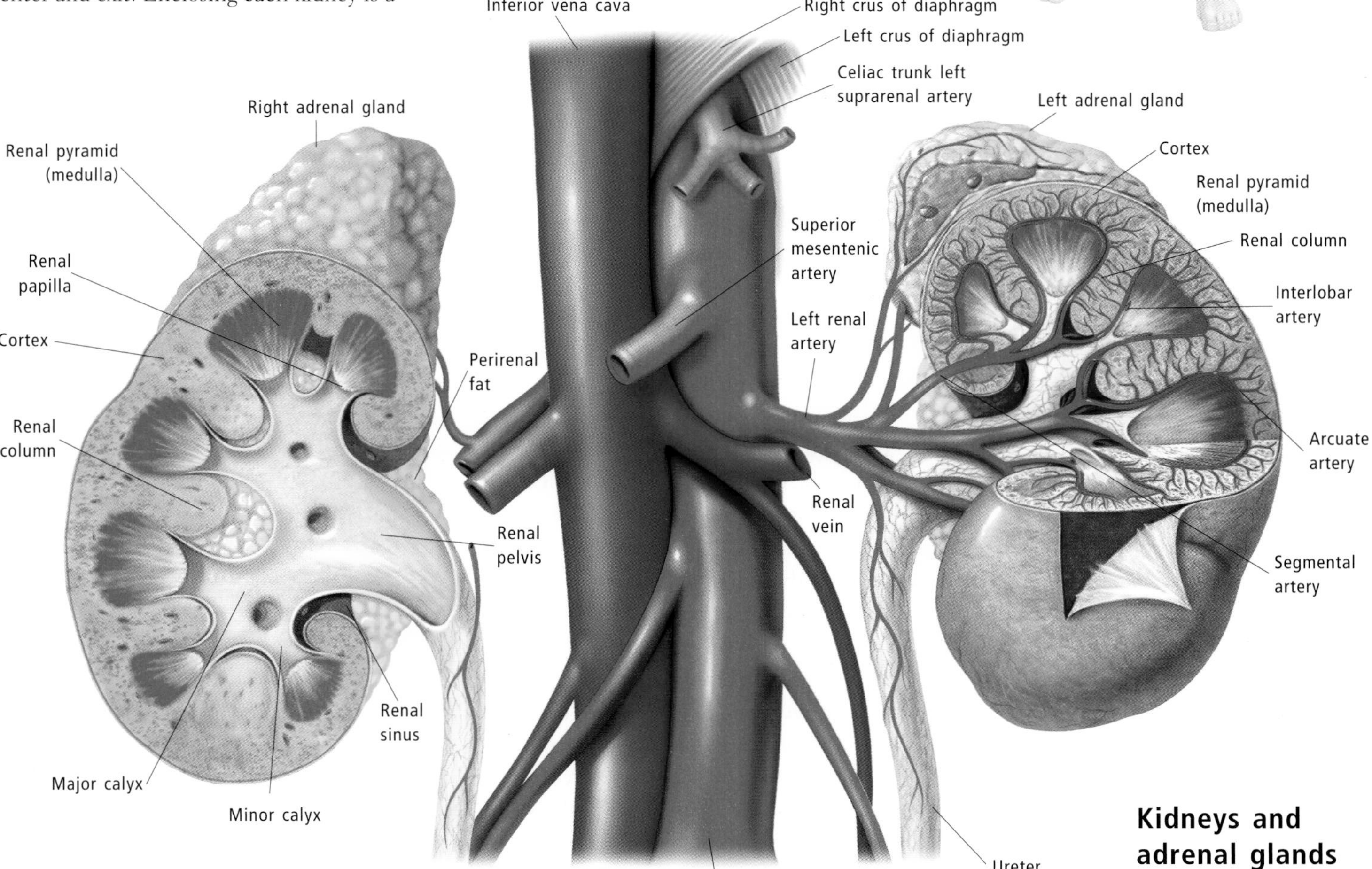

Kidneys and adrenal glands

which there are estimated to be about 1.2 million in each kidney. Each nephron has a renal corpuscle, which lies in the renal cortex, and a renal tubule which runs through a renal pyramid. The renal corpuscle is comprised of an extensive ball-shaped capillary network called the glomerulus surrounded by a double-walled cup of epithelial tissue—the glomerular or Bowman's capsule. Together, these structures filter the blood, producing a liquid (the filtrate) containing minerals, wastes and water.

The purified blood is returned to the body while the filtrate passes into the renal tubule, which comprises the proximal convoluted tubule, the descending limb of the loop of Henle, the ascending limb of the loop of Henle and the distal convoluted tubule. As the filtrate passes along the renal tubule, a network of tiny blood vessels called the peritubular capillaries reabsorbs useful substances from it and secretes additional wastes into it. About 99 percent of the filtrate is reabsorbed in this way and returned to the general circulation. The rest—1 percent, or about 1–1½ quarts or 1–1¼ liters a day—collects in the pelvis and is transported to the bladder as urine.

If the body needs to conserve water (or needs to dilute salt in the blood), the kidneys return more water to the capillaries. If the body has more water than it needs, more is excreted in the urine. In this way, the precise balance of salts and water in the body is maintained. Toxins, such as urea, are not reabsorbed but are excreted in the urine and in this way the body rids itself of the unwanted products of metabolism.

Kidney disease may be caused by many factors, such as injury, infection, cancer, or be part of a more generalized disease affecting other parts of the body. In some cases, there may be no obvious cause of kidney disease. Treatment depends on the cause and may involve the care of a nephrologist, a specialist in kidney diseases.

The symptoms of kidney disease vary and may be vague until the disease is well advanced. One common symptom is generalized edema (swelling of tissues such as ankle, abdomen and face), which is due to the accumulation of water in body tissues. The formation of either abnormally large quantities of urine (polyuria) or of diminished amounts of urine (oliguria) are also features of kidney disease. Blood may be found in the urine (hematuria), or there may be severe abdominal pain (colic).

If damage to the kidney is severe, toxic wastes build up and cause a range of ailments including hypertension, heart failure, anemia, disturbances of calcium metabolism, acidosis, nerve damage, bleeding, confusion, coma and death.

Several different types of diagnostic test will reveal the presence of kidney disease. Abnormal substances in the urine such as protein (proteinuria), sugar (glycosuria), blood (hematuria), or abnormal levels of white blood cells (which indicate infection) may be detected by examining a urine sample. A blood test may reveal excess levels of urea, creatinine, calcium and other biochemical abnormalities in someone with chronic renal failure.

Radiological examination may also be used to detect disease in the kidneys. For an intravenous pyelogram, dye is injected into the bloodstream. The kidneys concentrate and excrete the dye, which shows up the outlines of the kidney (and any stones or tumors) in an x-ray. For a retrograde pyelogram, the dye is injected via a tube that is passed into the urethra, bladder and ureters. Renal ultrasound, a less invasive test, shows the size and shape of the kidneys and may detect stones or obstructed ureters. Abdominal CAT scan, MRI examination, arteriogram and renal biopsy are other techniques used to diagnose kidney disease.

Diseases and disorders

Nephritis is a general term for any inflammation of the kidney. It may involve the glomeruli, the kidney's tiny filtration units (glomerulonephritis), the spaces within the kidney (interstitial nephritis), or the main tissue of the kidney and pelvis (pyelonephritis). Nephritis may be acute (sudden onset) or chronic (slow onset). Glomerulonephritis is inflammation of the glomeruli. Inflamed and scarred glomeruli are unable to filter the blood to make urine, which may lead to poor kidney function and kidney failure.

Pyelonephritis is an infection of the kidney and the renal pelvis. Acute pyelonephritis is usually the result of upstream spread of a bladder infection.

Chronic pyelonephritis is caused by destruction and scarring of the kidney tissue as a result of recurrent or untreated bacterial infection.

Stones may form in the kidneys (nephrolithiasis). They may be caused by an underlying metabolic disorder, or may form for no obvious reason. Stones may form in the tissue of the kidney and cause damage, or they may form in the kidney and pass into the ureter, causing severe colicky pain. Sometimes they may not cause pain at all, but instead silently obstruct the ureter, raising the pressure in the renal pelvis and producing distension of the pelvis (hydronephrosis) and progressive loss of kidney function.

Sometimes kidney stones may be passed spontaneously. If not, they need to be surgically removed. This may sometimes be done via cystoscopy. Lithotripsy is a new technique in which a machine called a lithotriptor sends sound waves into the body to break up stones which then pass out in the urine.

Cancer of the kidney may occur in the renal pelvis, or in the body of the kidney itself. Hypernephroma, or Grawitz's tumor, is the most common form of kidney cancer and occurs mainly in adults. Less common is nephroblastoma (also called Wilms' tumor) which usually occurs in children under the age of seven. Treatment of both malignant cancers is nephrectomy (surgical removal of the affected kidney) plus radiation treatment and anti-cancer drugs.

Polycystic kidney disease is an inherited condition in which cysts form in the kidney, enlarging the kidneys and reducing their function. It may appear soon after birth or, more commonly, in adulthood. Symptoms include blood in the urine (hematuria), hypertension (high blood pressure), kidney infection and pain in the lower back. The function of the kidneys gradually deteriorates until, after several years, chronic kidney failure occurs, and the patient requires dialysis or a kidney transplant.

Nephrosis, or nephrotic syndrome, is an abnormal kidney condition in which there is excess protein in the urine and edema (swelling of the body tissues). Other symptoms include fatigue, weakness and loss of appetite. The condition usually begins in children under the age of six.

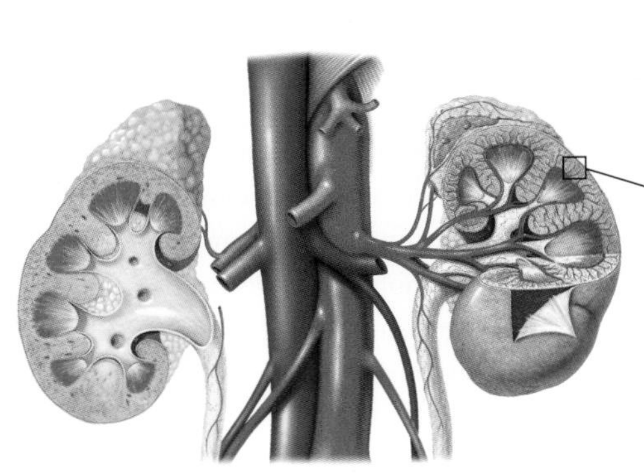

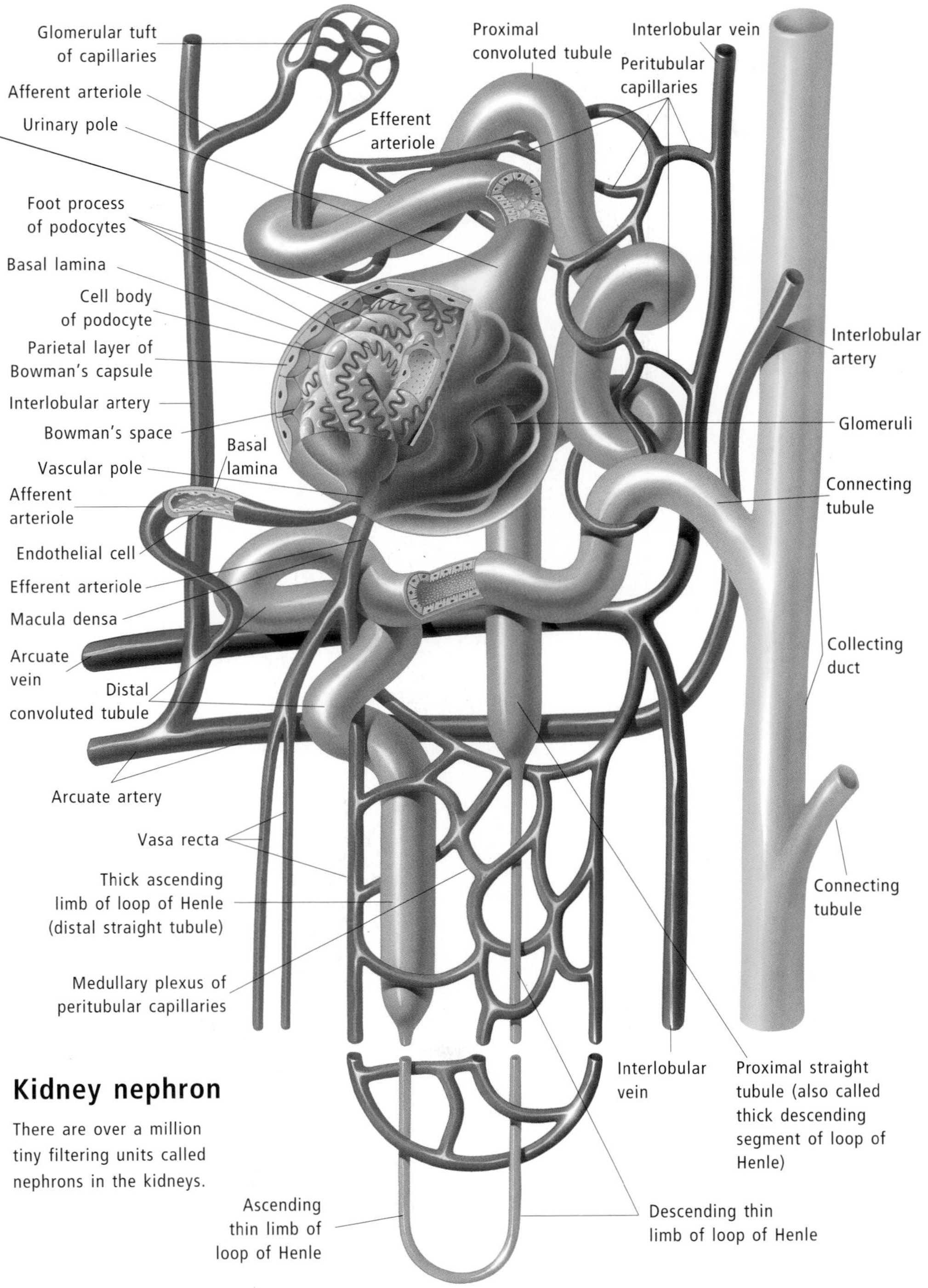

Kidney nephron

There are over a million tiny filtering units called nephrons in the kidneys.

Disorders elsewhere in the body may affect the kidney. As well as producing excess sugar in the urine, diabetes mellitus can, over time, cause damage to the glomeruli or to the blood supply to the kidney. High blood pressure damages the small vessels of the glomeruli and can cause renal failure. Hormone disorders, such as Cushing's syndrome, hyperthyroidism and hyperparathyroidism, can affect the functioning of the kidneys.

Treatment

Early stage kidney failure can be controlled through the restriction in the diet of salt, fluid and protein. However, if the kidneys are unable to fulfil more than 10 percent of their normal function, this is considered end-stage kidney disease and dialysis is necessary. Dialysis is a method of removing toxic substances (impurities or wastes) from the blood when the kidneys cannot do so.

There are two types of dialysis: hemodialysis and peritoneal dialysis. Hemodialysis involves slowly filtering the blood through an artificial kidney machine called a dialyzer which removes specific soluble materials from the blood. The purified blood is then fed back into one of the patient's veins. Peritoneal dialysis uses the person's abdominal peritoneal membrane to act as the dialyzer. It involves filling the abdominal cavity via a catheter with a special solution that absorb toxins.

Usually, dialysis needs to be performed three times a week for periods of four to six hours. Dialysis may take place in a hospital, at a special dialysis center, or at the patient's home. In chronic renal failure, it will need to be performed for the rest of the person's life or until a kidney transplant is performed.

Renal transplant is the surgical implantation of a healthy kidney into a patient with kidney disease or kidney failure. It allows a patient suffering from kidney disease to live a life without dialysis. Transplantation is usually preceded by a period of dialysis while a donor can be found. The donor may be living (usually a blood relative) or someone recently deceased. As with other transplants, the main problem with kidney transplantation is rejection of the new kidney by the recipient's immune system. Hence, the recipient needs life-long treatment with medications that suppress the immune response. Transplants from a blood-related living donor are slightly less likely to be rejected. Other problems include finding a donor, and the high expense.

SEE ALSO *Adrenal glands, Dialysis, Edema, Glomerulonephritis, Hemodialysis, Hypertension, Nephritis, Peritoneal dialysis, Polycystic kidney disease, Pyelonephritis, Pyelogram, Urinary systems*

K

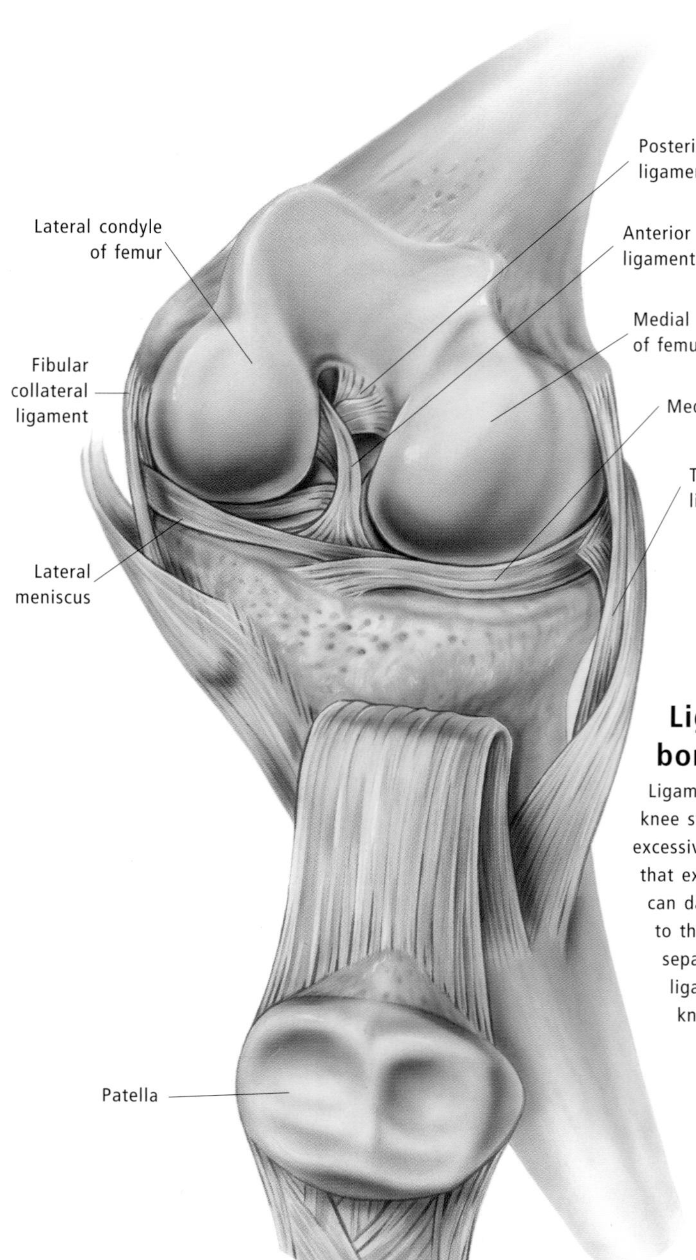

Ligaments and bones of the knee

Ligaments and muscles keep the knee strong and stable, but excessive force on the joint, like that experienced during sport, can damage it. In the illustration to the left, the patella has been separated to show the inner ligaments and bones of the knee joint.

KNEE

The knee joint, between the thigh and the lower leg, is one of the most important and complicated joints in the body. Because its adjacent surfaces do not fit closely together, it relies mainly on ligaments and muscles for stability. As a mobile but weight-bearing joint, the knee is under a great deal of strain and is vulnerable to injury when excessive force is put on it.

The knee is essentially a hinge type of joint with its main movements being flexion (bending) and extension (straightening), but some backward and forward gliding movements also occur in association with the hinge movements of flexion and extension. A small amount of rotation also occurs at the end of extension (to "lock" the knee) and at the beginning of flexion (to "unlock" the knee).

The knee joint is formed by three bones: the femur above, the patella (kneecap) in front and the tibia below. The lower end of the femur has a concave surface at the front, into which the back of the patella fits, and two rounded bulges at the bottom called condyles. The upper surface of the tibia has two rounded slightly concave areas (also

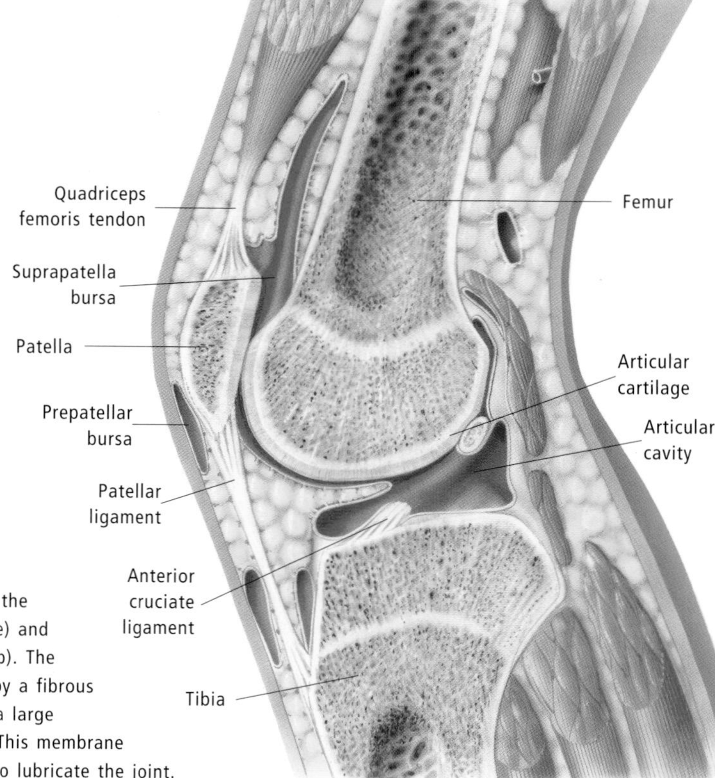

Knee joint

The knee is a complex hinge joint between the femur (upper leg bone), the tibia (the lower leg bone) and the patella (the knee cap). The three bones are united by a fibrous capsule which encloses a large membrane-filled cavity. This membrane produces synovial fluid to lubricate the joint.

KLINEFELTER'S SYNDROME

Klinefelter's syndrome is a genetic disease of males, caused by the presence of one or more extra X (female sex) chromosomes. An affected infant appears normal at birth, but at puberty the breasts may become enlarged and the testicles remain unusually small. The affected person remains infertile. Varying degrees of intellectual disability may also be present. There is no specific treatment for the disorder.

SEE ALSO *Chromosomal abnormalities, Chromosomes*

called condyles) separated by an intercondylar space. Each of the rounded condyles of the femur fits into the shallow sockets formed by the corresponding condyle of the tibia. The adjacent (contacting) surfaces are lined by cartilage.

The knee joint capsule

The three bones are united by a fibrous capsule (the knee joint capsule) which encloses a single, large joint cavity between the bones. The inside of the capsule is lined by a membrane, which produces an oily fluid called synovial fluid that acts to lubricate the joint surfaces to keep them friction-free. In some areas, pouches of synovial membrane extend beyond the confines of the joint capsule forming sacs known as bursae, and making the synovial membrane of the knee joint the most extensive of any joint in the body. Consequently, when the knee is traumatized, and the synovial membrane responds by producing more fluid to protect the joint, the swelling that occurs can be quite considerable.

Some bursae, which are not continuous with the synovial cavity of the knee, may become swollen due to friction on the overlying skin. These include one between the skin and the front of the kneecap, which becomes inflamed in a condition known as "housemaid's knee", and one between the skin and the upper surface (tuberosity) of the tibia, which becomes inflamed in "clergyman's knee".

The knee joint capsule is continued in front by the quadriceps tendon above, the kneecap and the patellar ligament below (attaching the kneecap to the tibia). The kneecap is incorporated into the joint, fitting into a concavity on the front of the femur. It glides up and down on the femur during contraction and relaxation of the quadriceps muscle and may be fractured in falls onto the front of the knee.

The knee joint cavity contains two circular fibrocartilaginous disks, or menisci, which are attached to the top of each tibial condyle. These are the "cartilages" often referred to in descriptions of injuries. Each disk is wedge-shaped in cross-section, with the thicker surface on the outside, so they act to deepen the sockets on top of the tibia and to allow a small amount of rotation to

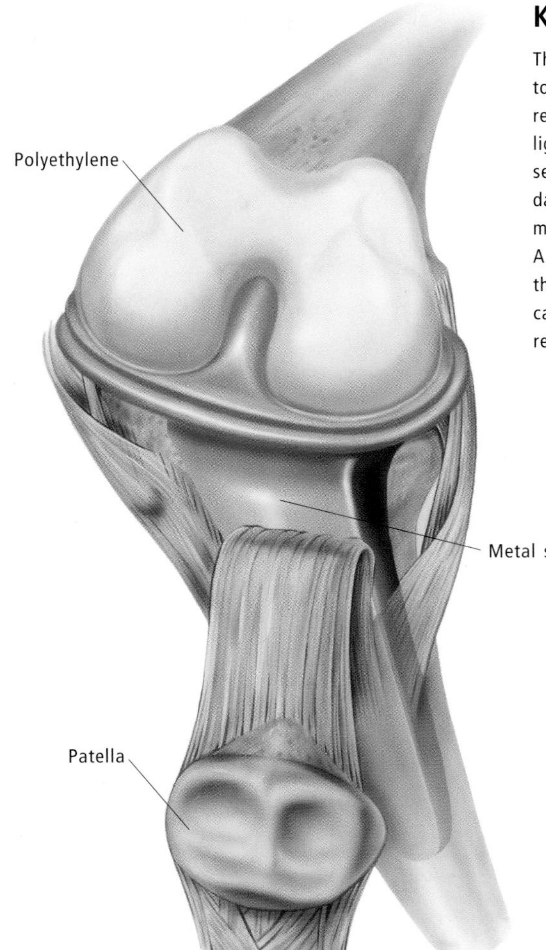

occur between the tibia and femur. The menisci may be torn if they get caught between the tibia and femur when the knee is forcibly rotated in the flexed (bent) or semiflexed position, as may occur when someone is tackled or tripped around the ankles or legs, and their thighs and body twist forward.

In osteoarthritis the cartilage that protects the bone surfaces from rubbing against each other degenerates and the joint may become so damaged and painful that it needs to be replaced with a prosthesis. A knee replacement may also be needed after damage from rheumatoid arthritis or injury. Although it will greatly reduce the pain and restore full mobility to the joint, a replacement joint is not as strong as a natural one. Extensive physical therapy will help rebuild muscle.

Ligaments

Because the sockets on the tibia are so shallow, the ligaments are important in strengthening the knee joint and limiting excessive or unwanted movements. The inner (medial) side is reinforced by the medial collateral ligament, which is a long flat band of fibers, about ½ inch (1 centimeter) wide and 4½ inches (10 centimeters) long, extending from the sides of the femoral condyle down onto the shaft of the tibia. As it

Knee replacement

The knee joint is particularly vulnerable to stress injuries, and reconstruction or replacement may be necessary if the ligaments have been badly torn or severed. In knee replacement the damaged joint is repaired by inserting metal shafts into the tibia and femur. A strong polyethylene coating covers the end of the shafts (in place of cartilage) and the knee ligaments are re-attached to hold the joint together.

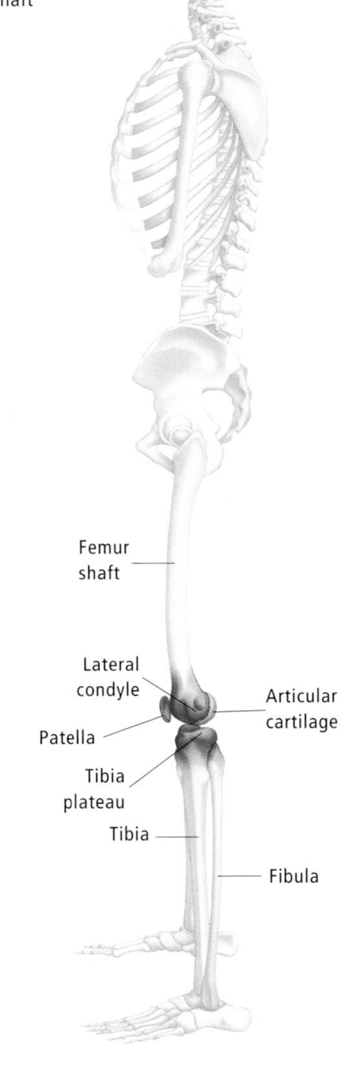

passes the joint it is fused to the capsule and the medial meniscus. The medial ligament can be stretched and torn when the knee is struck forcefully from the outer (lateral) side. In serious injuries the medial meniscus, which is fused to the ligament, may also be damaged.

The outer (lateral) side is reinforced by the lateral collateral ligament, a narrow cord-like band about 1–1½ inches (2–3 centimeters) long, which extends from the lateral femoral condyle down to the head of the fibula. Damage to this ligament is much less common than to the medial ligament but can occur when the knee or leg is struck from the inner side.

Two important ligaments also exist internal to the joint capsule, in the space between the medial and lateral pairs of condyles. Because the two internal ligaments cross over each other in the form of an X they are known as the cruciate ligaments. The anterior cruciate ligament passes from the front of the tibia up and backwards to the back of the femur. The posterior cruciate ligament passes from the back of the tibia upwards and forwards to the front of the femur. The cruciate ligaments guide the tibia in its movement around the end of the femur and prevent excessive forward and backward gliding during flexion and extension of the knee. The anterior cruciate ligament may be damaged when the knee is hit from the front and overextended or in twisting injuries of the knee. The anterior cruciate ligament is only half as thick as the posterior cruciate ligament and so is more frequently damaged.

If the ligament is completely severed a "knee reconstruction" may be performed, in which parts of tendons surrounding the knee are used to replace the damaged ligament.

Muscles

The muscles that surround the knee joint are also important in maintaining its stability. The tendons of the hamstrings, which pass over the inner and outer sides of the joint, help to reinforce it, but the most important muscle is the quadriceps femoris muscle on the front of the thigh, whose tendon reinforces the front of the joint and ensures correct movement of the patella on the femur. Weakness in the inner side of the quadriceps muscle, which occurs when the knee has been inactive after previous injury, can cause the patella to dislocate to the outer side.

SEE ALSO *Bursitis, Hamstring muscles, Housemaid's knee, Joints, Knock-knee, Leg, Ligaments, Muscles, Synovial fluid, Synovial membrane*

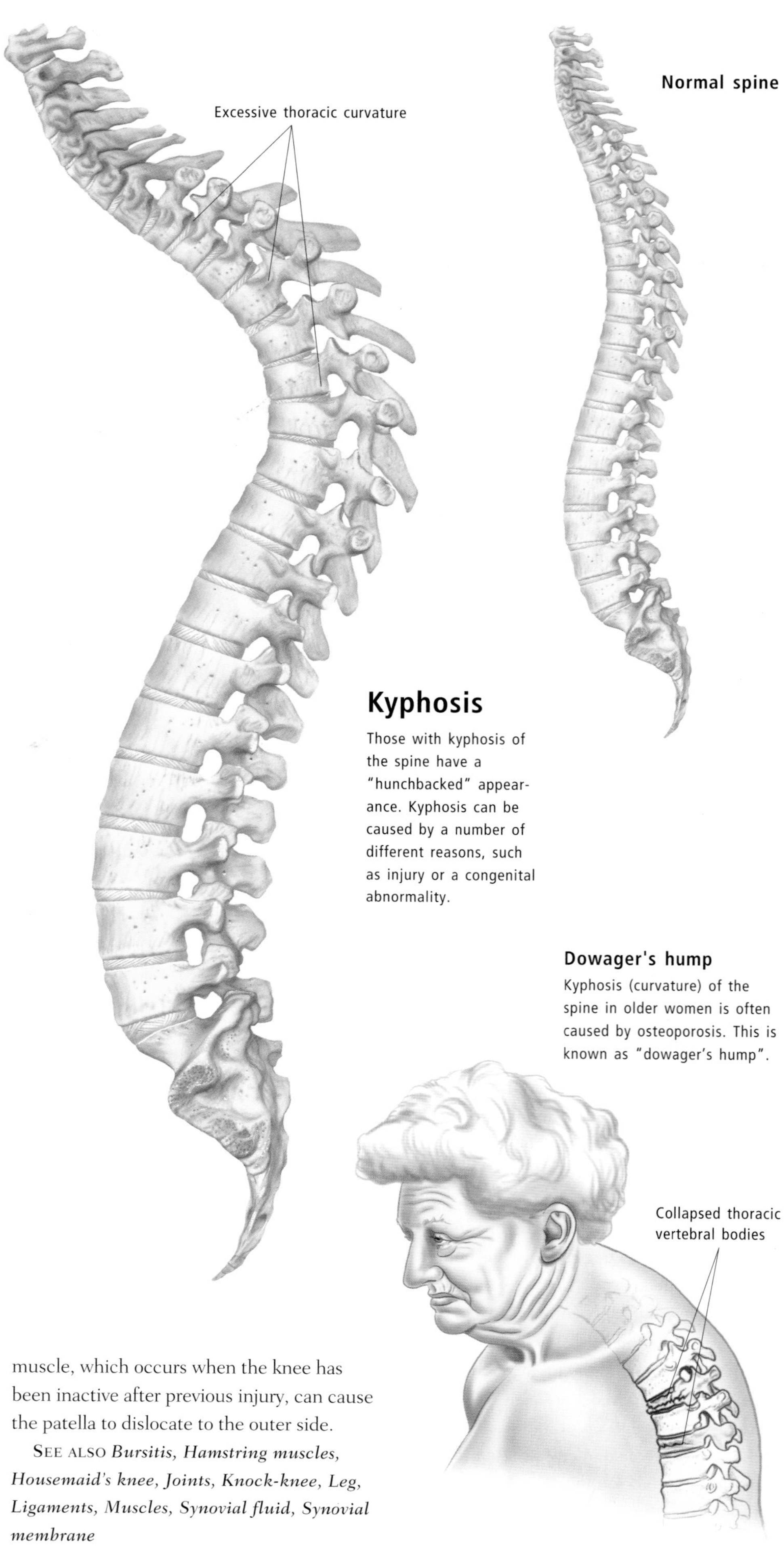

Kyphosis

Those with kyphosis of the spine have a "hunchbacked" appearance. Kyphosis can be caused by a number of different reasons, such as injury or a congenital abnormality.

Dowager's hump

Kyphosis (curvature) of the spine in older women is often caused by osteoporosis. This is known as "dowager's hump".

KNOCK-KNEE

Knock-knee (genu valgum) is a condition in which there is a significant space between the ankles when the knees are touching in the normal stance position; it is commonly seen in childhood. This outward angulation of the lower legs causes the knees to knock together when walking.

Knock-knee often appears at about three years of age as a normal part of development and usually corrects itself by the time a child reaches puberty. The condition may also be symptomatic of disease, irregular bone growth or weak ligaments, however. It is rare that knock-knees cause difficulty walking, although they may lead to foot and back pain, and damage to the knees. Most problems are associated with low self-esteem due to the appearance of the legs.

While knock-knee is usually not treated, strengthening exercises or braces may be used to encourage correct bone alignment. Surgery may be considered in severe cases to prevent or correct excessive abnormal wear on the cartilage of the knee joint.

A procedure known as osteotomy may be performed, where a wedge of bone is taken from the inside of the upper leg bone just above the knee. The bone is then fixed with plates and screws.

SEE ALSO *Knee*

KWASHIORKOR

Kwashiorkor is a type of malnutrition affecting children fed diets high in starch and low in protein, particularly when weaned directly onto these foods. Common in rural areas of developing countries, the condition develops through starvation, or at times of rapid growth or recovery from illness when the body needs more protein.

Symptoms are a lack of energy, reddening of the hair and fluid retention causing a distended belly and a moon-shaped face. Diarrhea, anemia and skin rash are common, behavioral development is slowed and growth may be permanently retarded.

Kwashiorkor, in which the body accumulates fluid, is often combined with another form of low-protein malnutrition—marasmus—where the body breaks down its own tissues for energy and proteins. The condition is treated with protein supplements or a high-protein diet.

SEE ALSO *Malnutrition*

KYPHOSIS

Kyphosis is an abnormal curvature of the spine in an anterior or forward direction. It usually occurs in the upper part of the spine, causing a hunched back and shoulders, with back pain and stiffness. It may be a congenital condition, appearing in children or adolescents, but more commonly it develops later in life (in older women it is sometimes known as "dowager's hump").

Kyphosis is caused by compression fractures of the spine, due to osteoporosis, ankylosing spondylitis, infection, endocrine diseases, arthritis, Paget's disease, cancer or tuberculosis of the vertebrae. The curvature, along with any degenerative changes in the vertebrae, is easily seen in an x-ray of the spine.

Treatment aims to reverse the underlying cause; back pain and stiffness may be helped by exercises, a firm mattress for sleeping, and a back brace. Bed rest and sometimes traction are recommended for severe pain. Surgery can be used to correct the defect, but is not usually feasible if the condition is due to osteoporosis or other degenerative disease.

SEE ALSO *Lordosis, Scoliosis, Spine*

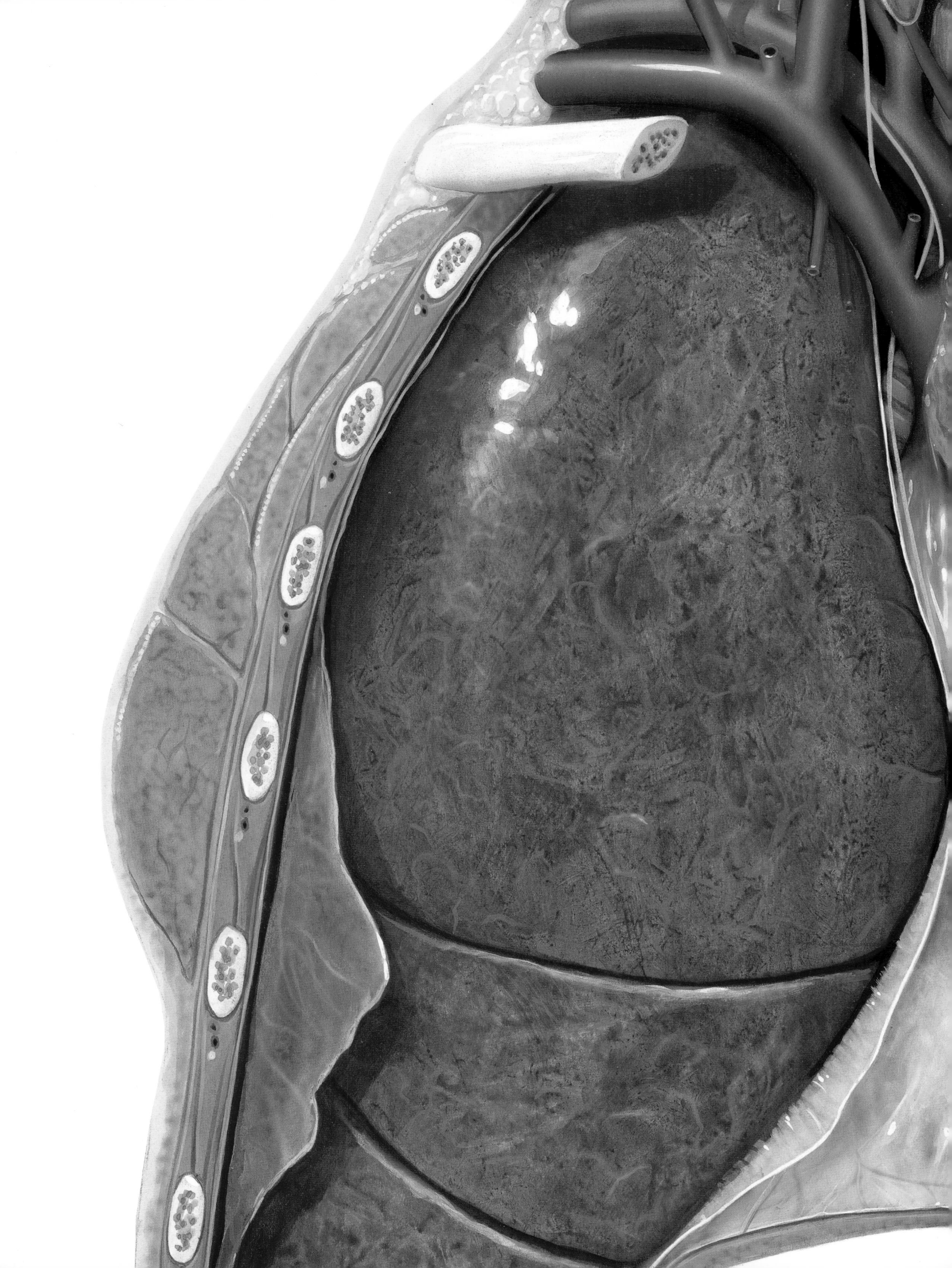

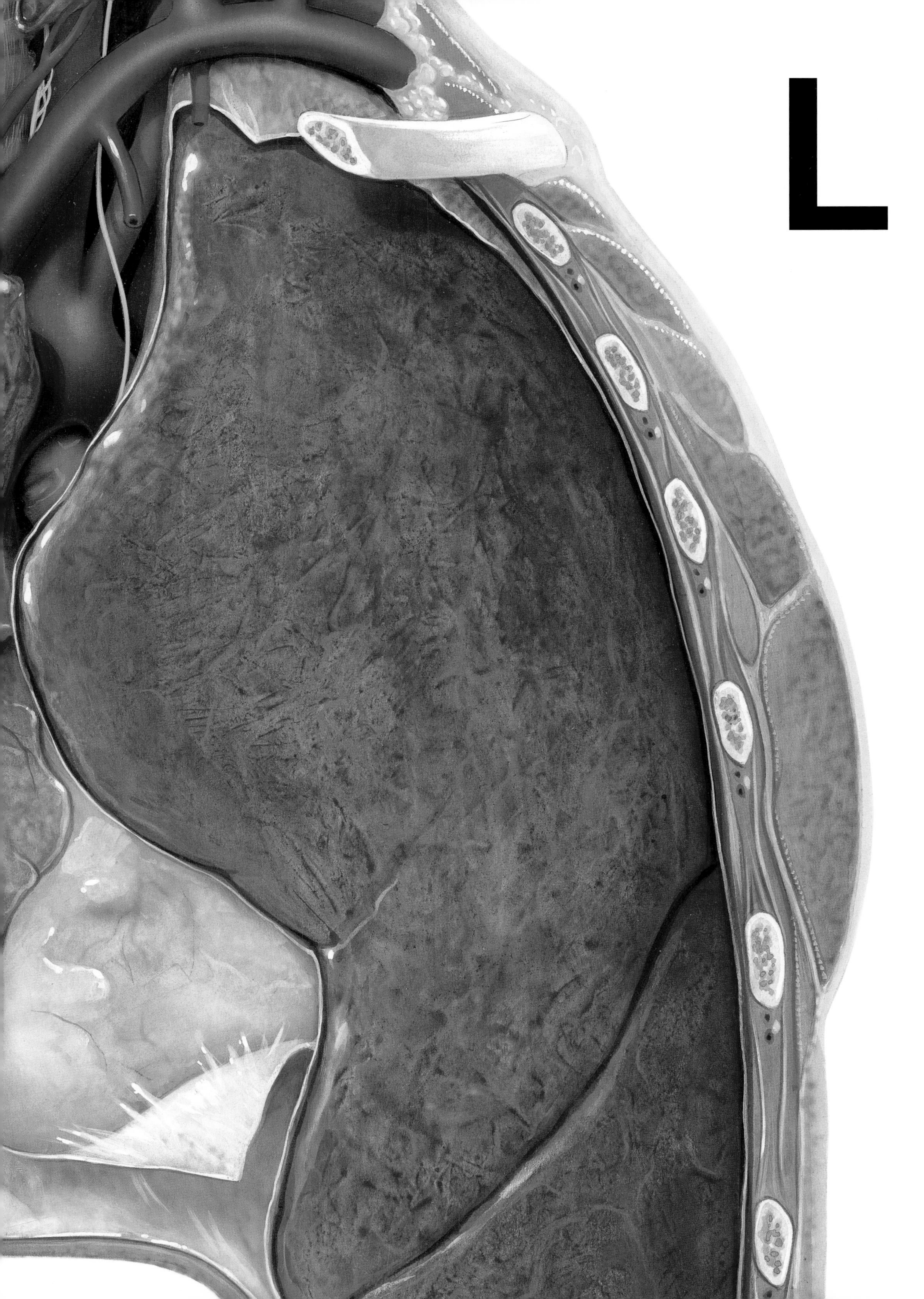

L

LABYRINTHITIS

Labyrinthitis is inflammation of the labyrinth, the network of fluid-filled semicircular canals in the inner ear that is responsible for monitoring the body's position and movement, and helping the brain to maintain equilibrium and balance. Labyrinthitis is usually caused by a virus, but may also be caused by bacteria spreading from a middle ear infection (otitis media), meningitis or following an ear operation.

Symptoms of labyrinthitis include vertigo (sensation that you or your surroundings are spinning around), dizziness, especially with head movement, loss of balance, nausea and vomiting, and sometimes temporary deafness and tinnitus (ringing in the ear).

Viral labyrinthitis is treated with anti-nausea (or anti-motion sickness) drugs and bed rest; recovery usually takes several weeks. Bacterial labyrinthitis is treated with antibiotics. Surgical drainage of the ear may be necessary if the condition is associated with serious otitis media ("glue ear").

SEE ALSO *Balance, Deafness, Ear, Semicircular canals, Tinnitus, Vertigo*

LACRIMAL GLANDS

The lacrimal glands, one above each eye, produce fluid (tears), which moves across the eye from the outer corner toward the nose, lubricating the eyeball. The tears eventually drain into the nose through the nasolacrimal duct and are swallowed or blown out with other nasal fluids. Tears keep the eye moist and clean and may be produced in response to irritation of the eye or emotion.

Sjögren's syndrome (also called dry eye syndrome) is a condition in which the lacrimal glands become inflamed and are unable to produce enough tears. It is an autoimmune disorder, which also affects the salivary glands. The treatment is to administer artificial eye drops frequently.

Dacryoadenitis is inflammation of the lacrimal gland or glands. It is most commonly seen in younger children, often due to bacterial infection. Antibiotic eye drops can help clear the condition.

SEE ALSO *Eye, Glands, Sjögren's syndrome*

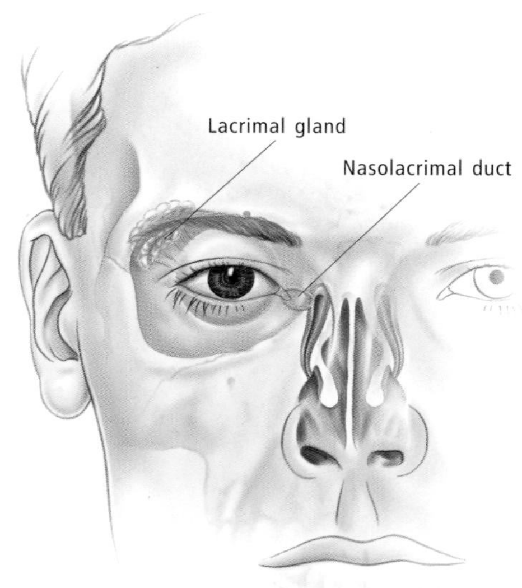

Lacrimal secretions

The lacrimal glands excrete a complex fluid (tears) to the eye surface. The fluid moves across the eye surface, lubricating the eyeball and keeping it moist.

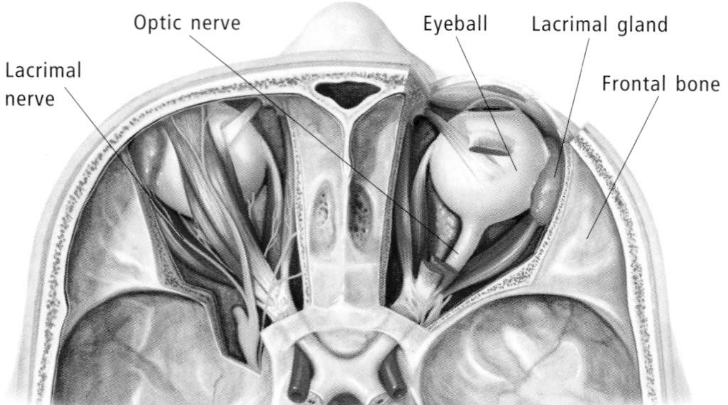

Lacrimal glands—orbital cavity

The lacrimal glands sit in the orbital cavity just above each eye. Their nerve supply comes from the lacrimal nerve.

LACTOSE INTOLERANCE

Lactase, the enzyme that helps break down lactose, the sugar in milk, is found in the brush border cells of the small intestine. If the enzyme is missing, the lactose cannot be digested and so produces increased gas, colic and sometimes violent, watery and acid diarrhea.

There are several forms of lactose intolerance. Premature infants of under 30 weeks are often unable to cope even with breast milk because the lining of the intestine is immature. There is also a form of lactose intolerance that runs in families and can be extremely severe. It is usually associated with intractable vomiting from infancy.

Temporary damage to the lining of the small intestine often follows an episode of gastroenteritis in children, and results in temporary lactose intolerance. The lining heals in a week or so; until then, the child should avoid milk and dairy products.

The commonest form of lactose intolerance is genetic: up to 90 percent of Asians, 70 percent of African-Americans and up to 25 percent of Caucasians have lactase deficiency in varying degrees.

Diagnosis is made by the lactose tolerance test, when after ingesting lactose blood glucose does not rise, while the patient becomes flatulent and develops diarrhea.

Treatment means avoiding milk and milk products; soy milk is often used instead. In many instances of the genetic form, sufferers can tolerate up to a cup of milk each day.

SEE ALSO *Digestive system, Gastroenteritis, Intestines*

LANUGO

From the third month of pregnancy, the unborn child (fetus) develops hair follicles which initially produce very delicate hairs over much of the body, mainly on the forehead, cheeks, back and shoulders. These hairs are called lanugo (from the Latin *lana*, meaning wool). The lanugo is shed before birth except in the region of the eyebrows, eyelids and scalp, where it persists until it is replaced by stronger hairs a few months after birth. No more hair follicles are formed after birth.

The presence of a larger than usual amount of lanugo on a newborn infant may be an indication of prematurity.

SEE ALSO *Fetal development, Hair*

LAPAROSCOPY

Laparoscopy is a procedure for examining the abdomen internally, which is sometimes referred to as "keyhole" surgery.

Two rods inserted through small incisions in the abdominal wall below the navel, one for viewing and one with lighting, allow intricate operations and diagnostic surveillance to be undertaken. After the incision is made, carbon dioxide gas is pumped into the abdomen to elevate the abdominal wall. This makes it easier for the surgeon to see and manipulate organs in order to collect tissue samples. When the female reproductive organs are being examined a dye may be injected through the cervical canal so that the fallopian tubes are easier to see.

Through the same incision, surgical procedures can also be carried out. These include gallbladder removal, hernia repair, removal of ectopic pregnancies, sterilizing procedures and even removal of uterus, ovaries and fibroids. In vitro fertilization is also undertaken by this method.

The laparoscopy procedure is much less invasive than normal surgery and, depending on the severity of the medical problem involved, may be performed on an out-patient basis. The greater risk of perforation of organs than in conventional surgery is counterbalanced by far shorter convalescence.

SEE ALSO *Fibroids, Gallbladder, Hernia, Hysterectomy, In vitro fertilization, Sterilization*

LAPAROTOMY

Laparotomy is the exploration of the abdominal cavity by surgical means and is used in unexplained illness where a diagnosis remains obscure despite investigation with ultrasound and CAT scans. Laparotomy may also be used following trauma such as motor vehicle accidents, or puncture wounds from implements such as knives and bullets, to check for bowel perforation.

Laparotomy can detect conditions such as an inflamed appendix, various infections and cancer of the liver, ovary, colon and pancreas. It can be used to correct hernias in the abdominal wall and to remove diseased organs and abnormal tissue. During the procedure the surgeon may take samples of fluid in the abdominal cavity for laboratory examination. Where internal bleeding is suspected in ectopic pregnancies, laparatomy may also be carried out.

Laparotomy has now largely been superseded by laporoscopy.

LARYNGECTOMY

This operation involves the surgical removal of the voice box (larynx), and is most commonly performed when the larynx has been irretrievably damaged by injury or invaded by cancer. The patients most at risk of needing a laryngectomy include heavy smokers and drinkers.

Air travels past the vocal cords upon exhaling, causing them to vibrate, and it is this vibration that causes sounds. However, after a laryngectomy the passage of air between lungs and mouth cannot occur as the connection between the mouth and windpipe no longer exists.

The operation leaves an opening from the windpipe to the outside. This permanent opening, or stoma, allows air to pass directly into the trachea and on to the lungs. Sometimes a tracheostomy tube is inserted in the stoma temporarily to help it stay open during the healing process. It is important that the stoma does not become blocked as it is the only existing air passage.

In most cases the laryngectomy procedure does not affect the swallowing of food and liquid as the connection between mouth and esophagus remains.

After a laryngectomy, laryngeal speech is no longer possible. In the past, patients who underwent the procedure were taught to "speak" again by trapping air in the esophagus. Patients now often speak through the use of electronic devices that are held against the throat. Artificial vocal cords may also be surgically implanted.

SEE ALSO *Esophagus, Larynx*

LARYNGITIS

Laryngitis is usually an acute illness that is characterized by hoarseness due to an inflammation of the voice box (larynx). It is caused by a viral upper respiratory infection which normally lasts up to a week. During the acute phase talking should be limited. If a high temperature persists, a doctor should be consulted. Small children may develop croup (noisy difficult breathing) from swelling of the vocal cords and windpipe.

The most common form of laryngitis is an infectious condition caused by a virus. It may be associated with a bacterial infection or illnesses such as the common cold, influenza, bronchitis, pneumonia and upper respiratory infection.

Allergies, trauma, malignant tumors and laryngeal polyps are among other causes. Fever and upper respiratory infection may accompany the characteristic hoarseness or loss of voice.

Diphtheria-type laryngitis is a rarity nowadays but if undiagnosed, it can be fatal. Tubercular laryngitis is very painful, as is epiglottitis or bacterial inflammation of the epiglottis and larynx. The latter condition is a medical emergency; typically the patient isunable to swallow due to pain, and drooling and a high fever are other symptoms.

Chronic laryngitis can be caused by overuse of the voice, or the frequent inhalation of chemical fumes and other irritants. For all types of laryngitis, the initial treatment is rest. The use of a humidifier may offer some relief from the discomfort felt in the throat. Associated upper respiratory infection may be alleviated with the help of analgesic or decongestant medication. If the condition does not improve, medical advice should be sought.

SEE ALSO *Croup, Epiglottis, Larynx, Respiratory system, Throat, Trachea, Vocal cords*

LARYNGOSCOPY

Laryngoscopy is an examination of the interior of the larynx or voice box. Indirect laryngoscopy is the simplest type and involves holding a small mirror against the back of the palate, with the mirror angled down towards the larynx. This procedure may not be suitable for those with a strong gag reflex. Direct laryngoscopy is another option and, as the names suggests, is a way of looking directly at the larynx. It is usually performed under general anesthetic because of problems with the gag reflex, and involves the insertion of an instrument called a laryngoscope in the mouth. During this procedure a microscope can be used for a magnified view of the vocal cords and other parts of the larynx. Tissue biopsies can also be taken.

Other optical instruments can also be used to examine the larynx. A flexible nasopharyngoscope can be inserted through the nose to look at the vocal cords during normal speech. This may cause a little gagging and

Larynx

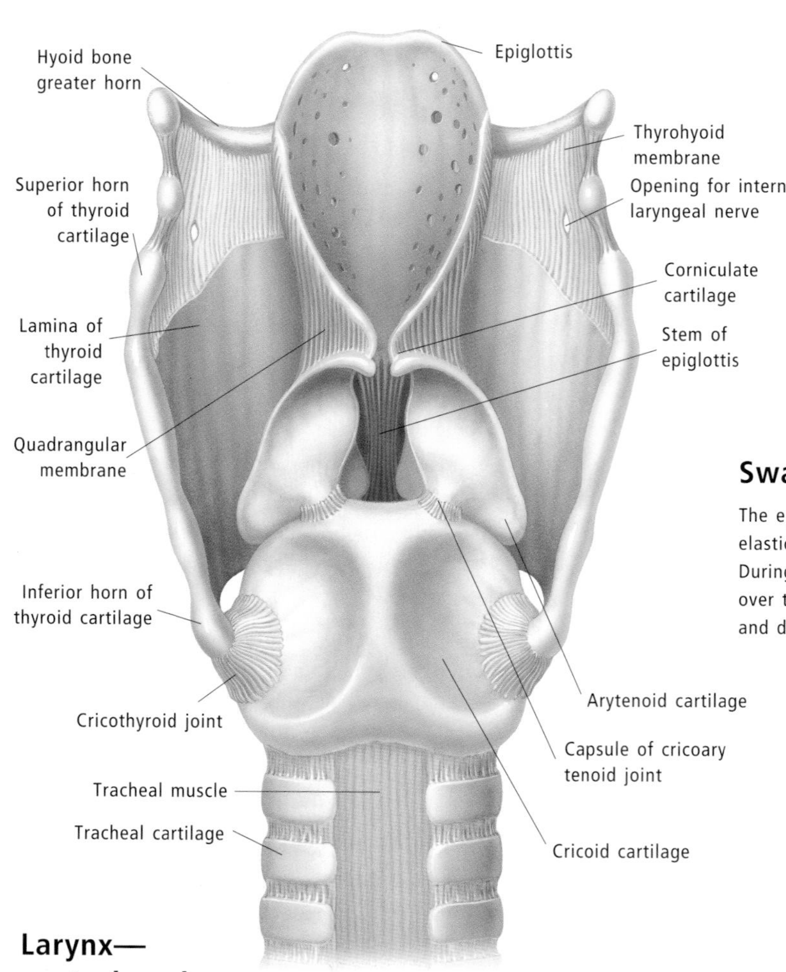

Larynx—posterior view

The larynx is a triangular box composed of nine cartilages that are joined by ligaments and controlled by skeletal muscles. It serves as a passageway for air between the pharynx and the trachea, and provides a framework for the vocal folds (vocal cords). Muscles in the larynx close the air passage while food is pushed into the esophagus.

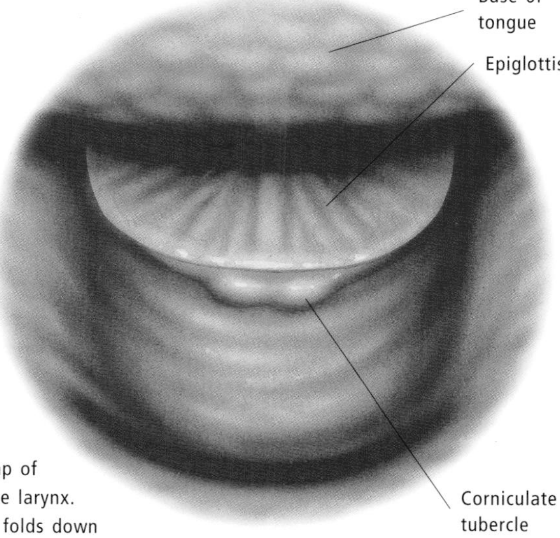

Base of tongue
Epiglottis
Corniculate tubercle

Swallowing

The epiglottis is a flap of elastic cartilage in the larynx. During swallowing it folds down over the glottis to prevent food and drink passing into the airway.

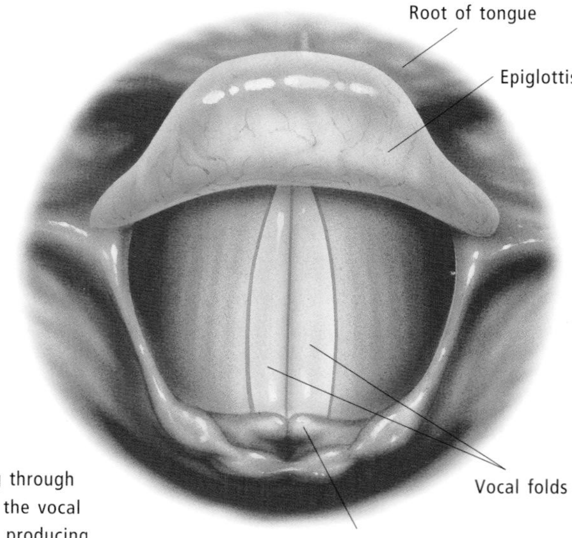

Root of tongue
Epiglottis
Vocal folds
Vocal process of arytenoid cartilage

Speaking

Exhaled air flowing through the larynx vibrates the vocal folds (vocal cords), producing sound. The tension and length of the cords determines the pitch of the sound.

Position of the larynx

This passageway lies in the middle of the neck below the hyoid bone and in front of the laryngopharynx.

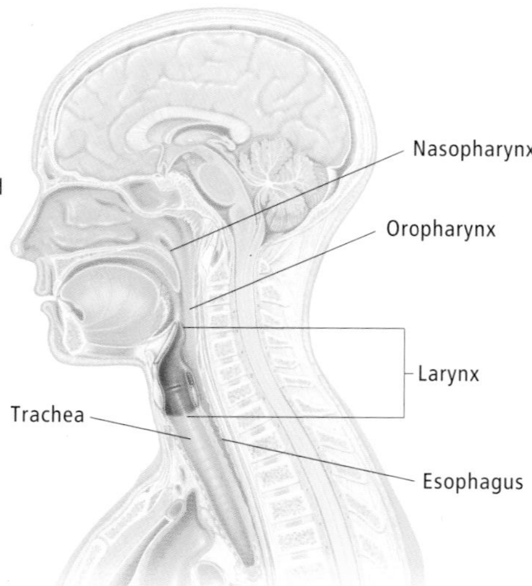

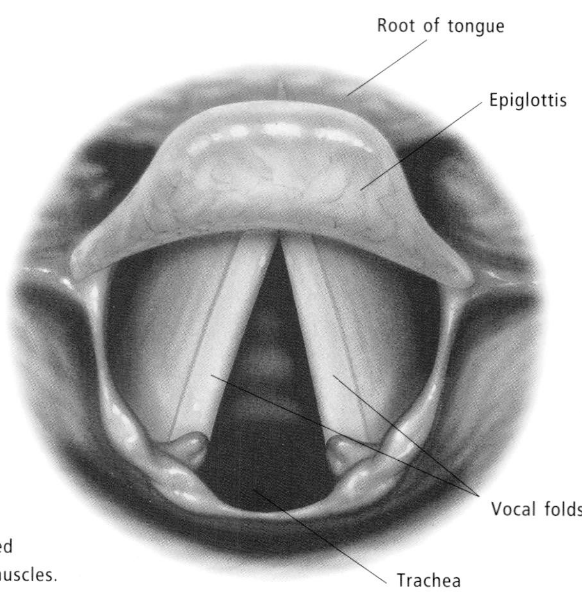

Breathing

In breathing, the vocal folds are moved apart by laryngeal muscles.

the image obtained is not as clear as when looking at the larynx directly. A rigid instrument called a 90 degree telescope may be placed at the back of the throat for a clear, magnified image of the vocal cords. A camera may be attached to these instruments to record information during the examination.

SEE ALSO *Larynx*

LARYNX

The larynx (or voice box) is the part of the throat that leads from the pharynx to the trachea (windpipe) and lungs. The larynx serves two main functions: to protect the airway to the lungs from inhalation of food and water; and to produce a source of air vibration for the voice. The larynx is composed of nine cartilages which provide strength for the airway and attachments for the various muscles, ligaments and membranes of the larynx.

The uppermost cartilage is the epiglottis, which lies immediately behind and below the tongue and can be bent downwards and backwards by muscles to close off the entrance to the larynx during swallowing. The largest cartilage of the larynx can be felt at the front of the throat and is called the thyroid cartilage, because the thyroid gland lies in front of its lower part. This cartilage consists of two slightly curved plates, which meet in the midline at a prominent ridge. Above the ridge lies a notch, called the thyroid notch.

In males, the thyroid cartilage grows rapidly after puberty, resulting in an increased prominence of the ridge and notch of the thyroid cartilage (the Adam's apple). This enlargement elongates the vocal ligament, which is attached to the back of the thyroid cartilage and vibrates to produce the sound of the voice. A longer vocal ligament vibrates with a lower frequency (pitch), thus making men's voices lower in pitch than those of women and children.

The other cartilages of the larynx include the cricoid, which lies below the thyroid cartilage and encircles the airway; the arytenoids, which are paired cartilages lying on top of the cricoid; and the tiny corniculate and cuneiform cartilages, which strengthen the folds of membrane around the laryngeal entrance.

The voice depends on several key elements for its production. The first is that the column of air above the larynx must be set vibrating. The larynx contains the vocal cords, which are the source of the sounds we produce. The vocal cords consist of a tent-shaped fold that extends upwards on each side from the cricoid cartilage to attach to the thyroid and arytenoid cartilages. The paired upper free edges of this membrane (vocal ligaments) are covered by mucous membranes to form paired vocal folds. When these folds are brought together across the larynx, they can be set vibrating by forcing exhaled air between them and thus producing sound waves.

In speech, sound is modified by the complex action of muscles in the throat, larynx and mouth. Vowels are usually produced by modifying the shape of the air column in the throat, mouth and nose, while consonants are produced by introducing noise into the pure tone of the vibrating column (for example, by touching the tongue to the back of the teeth or the roof of the mouth). The length and tension of the vocal ligaments can be adjusted to produce sounds of different pitch. Volume is determined by the force used when breathing air through the vocal cords.

Laryngitis is inflammation of the inner lining of the larynx, usually produced by viral infection. Cancer of the larynx is much more common in those who drink and smoke heavily. It may be treated, firstly, by surgery to remove both the actual tumor and any lymph nodes to which the cancer may have spread, and secondly, by irradiation of the throat.

SEE ALSO *Epiglottis, Laryngitis, Pharynx, Respiratory system, Trachea, Vocal cords*

LAXATIVES

A laxative is a drug that speeds the passage of stool or feces through the intestinal tract and causes a bowel movement. Laxatives are used to treat or prevent constipation (infrequent bowel movements), thereby relieving associated abdominal discomfort.

Some laxatives, such as senna and cascara, act by directly stimulating the nerves and muscle of the bowel. This starts a series of contractions known as peristalsis which encourage a bowel movement. Others, called hyperosmotics, work by attracting water into the bowel from surrounding tissues, increasing the bulk and volume of the stool, which speeds its passage through the bowel. These do not increase the number of bowel movements and are more for preventing constipation than treating it. They are recommended for people who need to avoid straining while defecating, such as those recovering from childbirth and certain types of abdominal surgery. Hyperosmotics include milk of magnesia, Epsom salts (magnesium sulfate) and Glauber's salts (sodium sulfate). Bulk laxatives such as bran, psyllium and vegetable fiber, and general roughage absorb water in the intestinal tract, swelling, and forming soft, bulky stool. They are the safest and most effective forms of laxatives and are available in powder form for mixing in a drink, or as wafers, granules or tablets containing bran. To be safe and effective, these must be taken with a least one glass of water, so are not suitable for people suffering from other conditions that demand a restricted fluid intake such as kidney failure.

Using natural measures, such as increasing the amount of fiber and fluid in the diet, is preferable to taking laxatives.

Laxatives should be a short-term treatment for constipation only, particularly harsh stimulant varieties which may be habit-forming and in large doses can cause side effects such as cramps, dehydration and malnutrition. If taken for too long, abnormalities of the bowel wall may occur. Laxatives should not be taken if constipation occurs with abdominal pain or fever as these symptoms may indicate a bowel obstruction.

SEE ALSO *Bowel, Constipation, Intestines*

LEAD POISONING

Lead is widely distributed in the earth's crust and is a "heavy metal", which accumulates in and is toxic to humans. Adults may be exposed to increased levels of lead through their work, and children through contamination of the home environment. Occupational exposure through inhalation of fumes or dusts occurs in mining of lead ore, smelting operations, soldering or oxy-cutting of lead alloys, lead-acid battery manufacture and the use of lead pigments. Children may be exposed to lead released from lead paints in pre-1950 houses during renovations. Paint fragments settle as a fine dust after sanding and may contaminate the house and soil for many years afterwards. Lead dust particles are so small that they can often pass through protective masks and filters.

Since the 1980s there has been a reduction in environmental lead exposure through the use of unleaded gasoline and the discontinuation of lead soldering of tin cans. Water is also safer, although the use of lead pipes or lead-lined galvanized tanks increases lead levels in the water supplies of some countries. Wine contains more lead than other beverages, probably due to the previous use of lead arsenate as an insecticide on vines.

The symptoms of lead poisoning generally occur late in the course of exposure. The earliest effects are on the nervous system and include impairment of memory and learning ability, and decreased attention and reaction time. Affected persons may exhibit fatigue, personality changes, pins and needles sensations, and muscle weakness. Later effects include abdominal pain, constipation or diarrhea, anemia and kidney failure.

Since these effects occur late, the current approach is preventive; for example by monitoring blood lead levels in workers at risk. During fetal life and the first 4 years of childhood, lead can affect the developing brain, resulting in intellectual impairment. It is important, therefore, for women to avoid occupational lead exposure during pregnancy and lactation. Environmental lead exposure should be minimized for young children. Infants aged 1–3 years who often put their hands in their mouth during play are particularly at risk. Some children may show no symptoms while others are obviously suffering from the effects of lead poisoning which can inhibit growth, impair hearing and damage the central nervous system, reproductive organs and kidneys. In severe cases of lead poisoning they may suffer from seizures or coma, and even die.

Lead gradually accumulates in the body with continued exposure and is carried in the blood on the surface of red blood cells. It inhibits several red blood cell enzymes, resulting in anemia. Over 90 percent of the total body lead is contained in the bones.

Treatment of lead poisoning is difficult, due to the large amount of lead that has accumulated by the time symptoms occur. Removal from the place of occupational exposure is essential. As lead leaves the body through the kidneys, this can be accelerated by the use of chemicals which bind to lead (chelation therapy). Patients must be well hydrated and their kidney function closely monitored during such treatment.

SEE ALSO *Poisoning*

LEARNING DISORDERS

A learning disorder affects a person's ability either to link the information within the brain or to interpret what they see and hear, resulting in the person learning differently from someone without a malfunction. This type of disorder can involve spoken and written language; memory and reasoning; coordination; social competence; or emotional maturation, including self-control or attention span.

Learning disorders affect around 15 percent of school children—more often boys than girls. The disorders may be caused by a problem in the nervous system that affects the receiving, communication and processing of information. Some children with learning disabilities also have a short attention span or are hyperactive. Children with reading problems are sometimes described as dyslexic though many professionals no longer use this term.

Some children may be developmentally delayed, intellectually disabled or suffering from a physical problem such as cerebral palsy. Others who have been, or are, chronically ill will be at risk of learning problems as they miss or drop behind in schoolwork.

Signs that a child has a learning disability are: difficulty following and understanding simple instructions; an inability to master reading, writing and/or mathematical skills (these children may have difficulty processing words as they hear them, or they may have difficulty with word-finding); a difficulty differentiating left from right; a lack of coordination which indicates difficulties with motor functions—using pens and scissors may pose a problem; an inability to understand the passage of time (these children have a visual memory problem which makes the understanding of sequential organization a difficulty); difficulty remembering what they have been told (these children may have suffered from recurrent ear infections which can mean their auditory memory is not intact and they find it difficult to work or sound out new words).

The longer a learning disability is left untreated, the worse it will become. Once it has been determined that a child has a learning disability and any underlying health problems have been treated, treatment by a remedial teacher or a psychiatrist trained in working with children suffering from learning disabilities may help the child to overcome the disability.

SEE ALSO ***Attention deficit hyperactivity disorder, Autism, Dyslexia, Cerebral palsy, Memory, Speech***

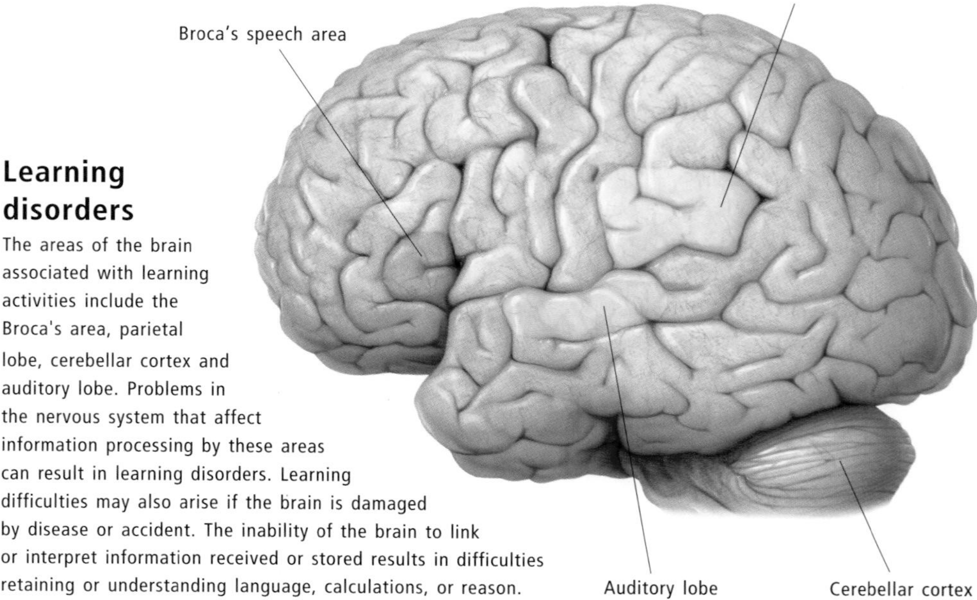

Learning disorders

The areas of the brain associated with learning activities include the Broca's area, parietal lobe, cerebellar cortex and auditory lobe. Problems in the nervous system that affect information processing by these areas can result in learning disorders. Learning difficulties may also arise if the brain is damaged by disease or accident. The inability of the brain to link or interpret information received or stored results in difficulties retaining or understanding language, calculations, or reason.

LEG

In anatomical terms, the leg refers only to the area between the knee and the ankle, while the term lower leg includes the thigh, leg and foot. However, in general usage "leg" refers to the whole limb, except for the foot. The leg is designed on a similar structural plan to the arm, but in humans is adapted to bipedal locomotion, that is, walking upright on two legs. The bones are long to increase the stride, the joints are large and bound by strong ligaments, and the muscles controlling locomotion are powerful.

Bones and joints

The two hip bones (the pelvic girdle) connect the lower limb to the vertebral column and join in front at the pubic symphysis. Together with the sacrum, they are known as the bony pelvis. Body weight is transferred from the vertebral column, through the relatively immobile sacroiliac joints to the hip bones, and from the socket of each hip bone to the femur.

The femur is the longest bone in the body. It has an almost spherical head and a long neck (a common site of fracture in the elderly), at the end of which are two enlargements (trochanters) for muscle attachment. The shaft angles inward, so that the knees come to lie together in the midline below the trunk. This arrangement reduces lateral body sway, and hence reduces energy expenditure in walking. The two femoral condyles at the lower end take part in the knee joint. The femur articulates with the kneecap (patella), a bone within the tendon of the quadriceps muscle. It also articulates with, and transfers weight to, the tibia.

The tibia is the second longest bone in the body. The tibia and fibula comprise the bones of the lower part of the leg. The tibia is the bone most commonly fractured, often breaking though the skin (compound fracture) as it is just below the skin (subcutaneous) through much of its length. The fibula is thin, and bears little weight. It serves as a structure for muscle attachment, and stabilizes the outside of the ankle joint.

The tibia and fibula articulate with the talus bone at the ankle joint. It is a mortice-like joint, with the tibia and fibula projecting down on either side of the talus to prevent sideways movement. The bones of the foot are the tarsals (7, including the talus and the calacaneus), metatarsals (5) and phalanges (14 of these constitute the toes).

In bow legs, the lower part of the leg angles outward towards the knee. It may occur as a consequence of injury (such as a fracture) or disease (such as rickets, osteomalacia, Paget's disease, or osteomyelitis affecting growth plates in children).

Bones of the leg

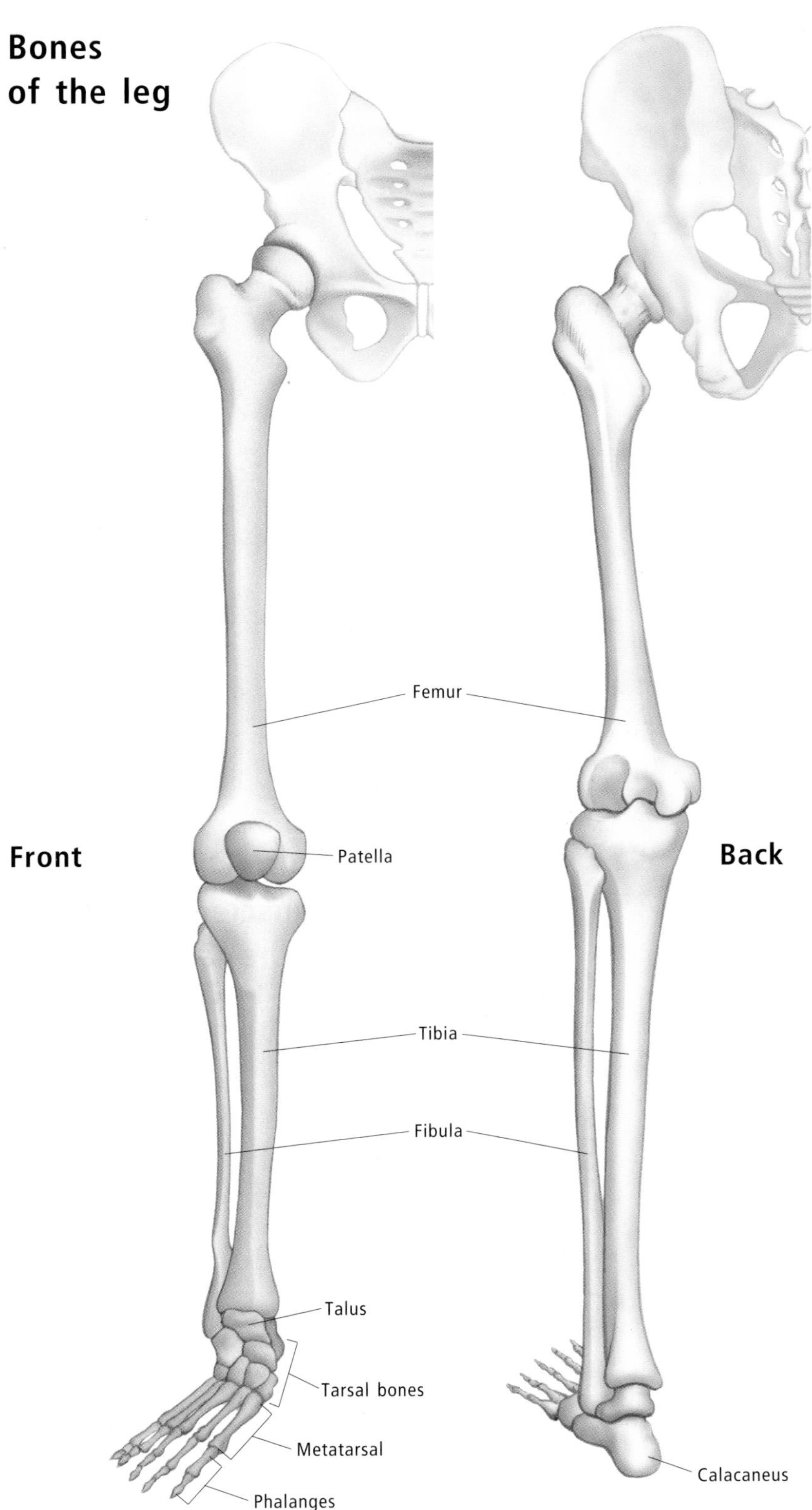

Muscles

Powerful muscles surround and stabilize the hip region. The gluteal region is situated posteriorly and the characteristic shape of the buttocks in humans is a result of the gluteus maximus muscle.

This is the largest muscle in the body and powerfully extends the thigh when

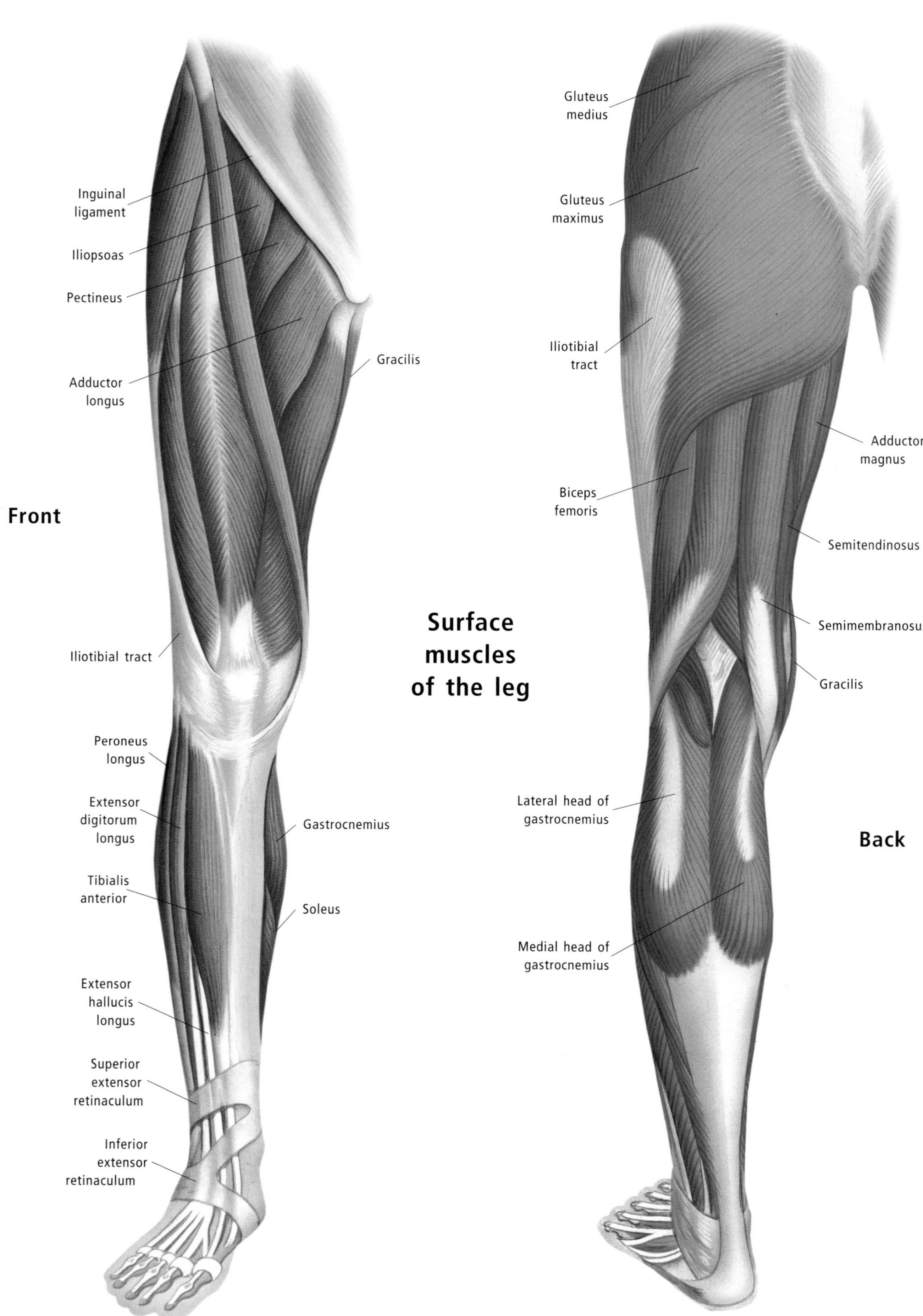
Front
Inguinal ligament
Iliopsoas
Pectineus
Adductor longus
Gracilis
Iliotibial tract
Peroneus longus
Extensor digitorum longus
Gastrocnemius
Tibialis anterior
Soleus
Extensor hallucis longus
Superior extensor retinaculum
Inferior extensor retinaculum
Surface muscles of the leg
Gluteus medius
Gluteus maximus
Iliotibial tract
Adductor magnus
Biceps femoris
Semitendinosus
Semimembranosus
Gracilis
Lateral head of gastrocnemius
Back
Medial head of gastrocnemius

L

Deep muscles of the leg

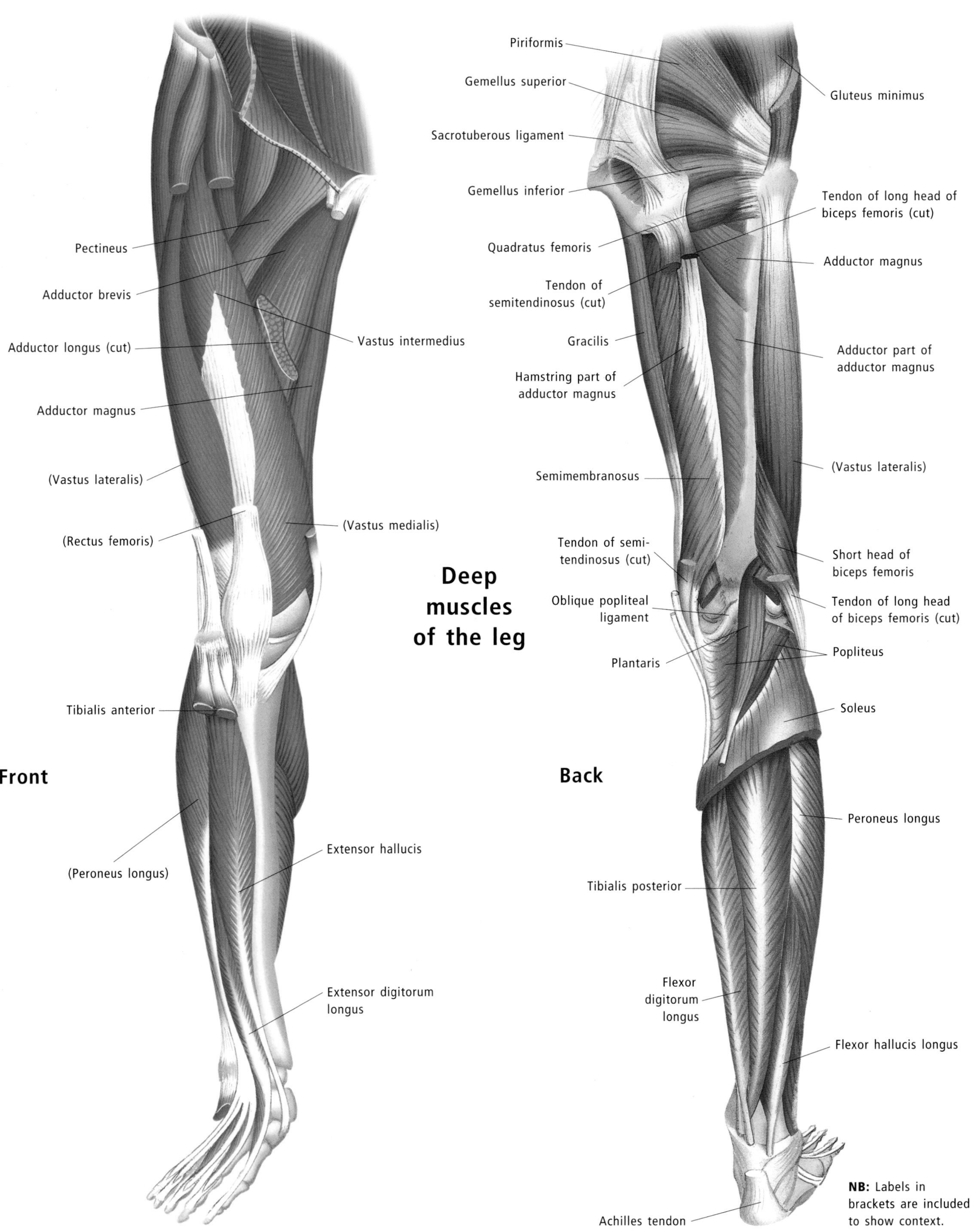
Pectineus
Adductor brevis
Adductor longus (cut)
Vastus intermedius
Adductor magnus
(Vastus lateralis)
(Rectus femoris)
(Vastus medialis)
Tibialis anterior
Front
(Peroneus longus)
Extensor hallucis
Extensor digitorum longus
Piriformis
Gemellus superior
Sacrotuberous ligament
Gemellus inferior
Quadratus femoris
Tendon of semitendinosus (cut)
Gracilis
Hamstring part of adductor magnus
Semimembranosus
Tendon of semi-tendinosus (cut)
Oblique popliteal ligament
Plantaris
Back
Tibialis posterior
Flexor digitorum longus
Achilles tendon
Gluteus minimus
Tendon of long head of biceps femoris (cut)
Adductor magnus
Adductor part of adductor magnus
(Vastus lateralis)
Short head of biceps femoris
Tendon of long head of biceps femoris (cut)
Popliteus
Soleus
Peroneus longus
Flexor hallucis longus

NB: Labels in brackets are included to show context.

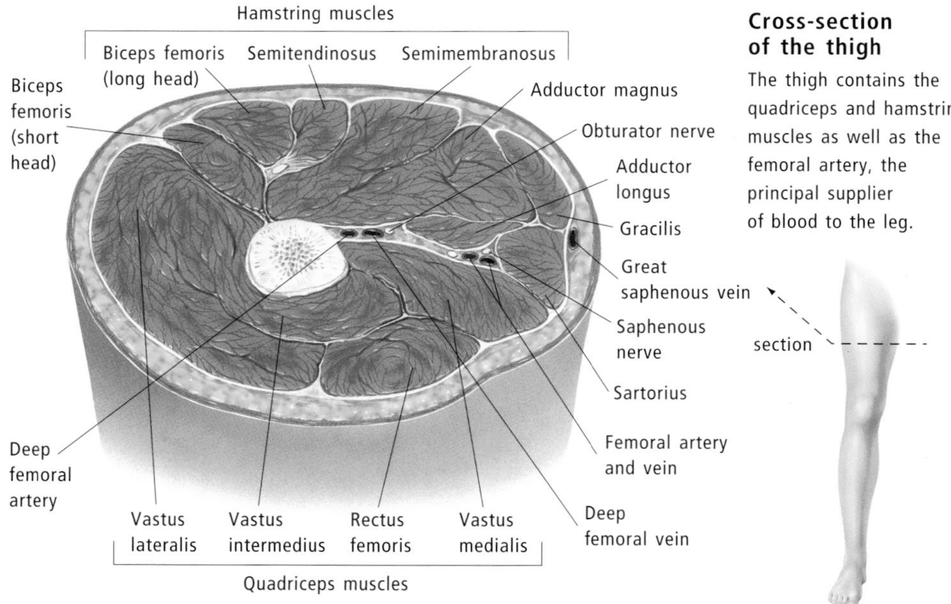

Cross-section of the thigh
The thigh contains the quadriceps and hamstring muscles as well as the femoral artery, the principal supplier of blood to the leg.

running or climbing. Gluteus medius and minimus muscles are laterally placed and are important in keeping the pelvis level, and swinging the opposite side forward, during walking.

The thigh has two distinct muscle compartments, separated by connective tissue (deep fascia). The quadriceps (Latin for "four heads") muscle lies in the anterior (front) compartment and extends the knee joint. The hamstring muscles lie in the posterior compartment (at the back). They extend the hip joint and flex the knee. The posterior compartment also contains the adductor muscles, which pull the leg toward the midline. They are important in counterbalancing the action of the gluteus medius and minimus muscles (adductors) when walking.

The lower part of the leg is divided into three compartments by deep fascia. The anterior (front) compartment contains muscles that move the foot upwards (dorsiflex the ankle), an action that is important in allowing the toes to clear the ground when swinging the leg forward in walking. The lateral compartment (on the outside of the lower leg) contains only two muscles, that turn the sole of the foot outwards (eversion). The calf region (posterior compartment) contains the greatest number of muscles, and is divided into two groups—those closest to the skin (superficial) and the deeper group. The superficial group contains the powerful gastrocnemius and soleus muscles, both critical to pushing off from the ground (plantarflexion of ankle joint—in which the foot moves downwards) during walking, running and jumping, and when standing on one's toes.

The deeper group of muscles pass behind the ankle joint and attach to bones of the foot. The largest of these, flexor hallux longus muscle, is critical to pushing off from the big toe during walking.

Due to the inelastic nature of the fascia bounding the compartments of the lower part of the leg, any swelling in a compartment results in pressure build-up, which can impair the blood supply. This is called compartment syndrome and may result from inflammation of muscles caused by excessive exercise in an unfit person, or trauma, such as fracture. With muscle overuse, it commonly involves the anterior, or deep posterior, compartments of the lower part of the leg and is characterized by shin pain (commonly known as shin splints) that increases during exercise and reduces at rest. Compartment syndrome may also be associated with pins and needles sensations and muscle weakness.

Nerve and blood supply

The femoral, obturator and sciatic nerves are the principal nerves of the leg, supplying the muscles and much of the skin. The sciatic nerve and its branches (tibial and common peroneal nerves) supply the hamstrings and all the muscles of the lower part of the leg and foot.

The femoral artery is the principal artery of supply to the leg. It descends in the front of the thigh. Two-thirds of the way down, it passes backward behind the knee and is renamed the popliteal artery. It then divides into anterior and posterior tibial branches that descend in the anterior and posterior compartments of the lower part of the leg. The femoral artery in the groin is easily exposed and is often used in cardiac catheterization (in coronary bypass surgery).

Veins are divided into two groups: the deep group and the superficial group. The deep group of lower limb veins travel with the arteries and are similarly named. The superficial veins (e.g. great and small saphenous) travel in the superficial tissue just below the skin. Lower limb veins have numerous valves directing blood toward the heart, and when muscles in the leg contract, the veins are squeezed and blood is forced upward. When the muscles relax, blood can flow from the superficial veins into deep veins via perforating or communicating veins. Faulty valves in the communicating veins can cause the superficial veins to become elongated, tortuous and enlarged (varicose veins).

Stasis of blood in veins may result in the formation of clots (thrombosis). When formed in the deep veins of the lower part of the leg it is called deep vein thrombosis (DVT). Increased risk is associated with advanced age, bed rest, immobilization and oral contraceptives. The greatest risk of thrombosis is that a piece of clot may dislodge and become lodged in the lung; this is called a pulmonary embolus, and is a major cause of death in the USA. Painful white leg ("milk leg") from venous thrombosis can also occur in the last three months of pregnancy or in the postdelivery period. Thrombophlebitis is the tenderness associated with a blood clot in a vein.

If blood in the skin of the lower part of the leg becomes stagnant (for example, from valve incompetence or venous thrombosis) even minor trauma to the poorly nourished skin can result in a varicose ulcer. It is especially common over the subcutaneous surface of the tibia. Leg ulcers can also result from arterial disease, underlying systemic disease (such as diabetes), neuropathy, malignant changes and infection.

SEE ALSO ***Ankle, Compartment syndrome, Embolism, Foot, Hamstring muscles, Hip, Knee, Muscles, Pelvis, Thrombophlebitis, Thrombosis, Varicose veins, Veins***

LEGIONNAIRES' DISEASE

Named after an occasion when several members of the American Legion (ex-servicemen) became ill at a reunion in Philadelphia, USA in 1976, this disease has symptoms that are similar to pneumonia. More severe in heavy smokers with lung disease and in those who lack immunity, the disease is caused by a bacterium of the *Legionella* species. The strain identified in the original outbreak was *L. pneumophila*, but other strains can also cause the disease. It has been attributed to contaminated water, particularly in air-conditioning units and is contracted by breathing in fine water droplets or aerosols that contain bacteria. It cannot be acquired by drinking contaminated water and is not passed from person to person.

Legionella bacteria may also thrive in spa pools, humidifiers, garden potting mix and reticulated water systems where water temperature is kept between 20 and 45 degrees.

The flu-like symptoms of Legionnaires' disease usually appear 2–10 days after infection. These include headache, loss of appetite, muscle aches, a dry cough progressing to grey or blood-stained sputum, disorientation, fever, and sometimes stomach cramps and diarrhea. Diagnosis is confirmed by a sputum culture and many antibiotics appear to be effective. Untreated, the condition can be fatal.

SEE ALSO *Lungs, Pneumonia, Sputum tests*

LEISHMANIASIS

Leishmaniasis is a parasitic disease caused by various protozoan parasites of the genus *Leishmania*, which live on dogs and rodents in many parts of world, especially tropical and subtropical countries. The parasites are transmitted from infected animals or people to new hosts by sandfly bites.

There are two main types. One is visceral leishmaniasis, also called kala-azar, which attacks the internal organs, and causes fever, enlargement of the spleen, anemia and skin darkening. Symptoms include cough, fever, weight loss, diarrhea, general abdominal discomfort, thinning hair and scaly, ashen skin. Not all symptoms appear at the same time, however, and as many of them are associated with other diseases it increases the difficulty of diagnosing leishmaniasis. After a sandfly bite the bone marrow, spleen and lymph nodes are invaded by parasites. In children there may be a sudden onset of vomiting, diarrhea, fever and cough, while adults may suffer fever for up to 2 months, as well as general fatigue, loss of appetite and weakness. As the disease progresses the immune system is damaged and death may occur within 2 years from complications such as infection. It can be fatal if untreated.

The other type is cutaneous leishmaniasis, also known as Delhi boil or oriental sore, which attacks the skin, causing skin lesions and ulcers. It can attack the mucous membranes, causing nasal congestion, nose bleeds, mouth and nose ulcers, and difficulty breathing and swallowing. The characteristic skin lesions may look like those of cancer, tuberculosis or leprosy. They can cause disfigurement requiring plastic surgery.

Treatment of both types is with antimony compounds or pentamidine. There is a good chance of a cure if the disease is diagnosed before the immune system is damaged. Some cases of cutaneous leishmaniasis heal spontaneously and do not require treatment.

Leishmaniasis has been reported in all continents except Australia. Travelers to endemic areas should avoid sandfly bites by using insect repellent, wearing appropriate clothing, and ensuring that windows and beds are screened with fine netting.

SEE ALSO *Kala-azar*

LENTIGO

Lentigines ("lentigo" is the singular form) are flat, round, light-brown spots that appears mostly on sun-affected areas such as the face and hands, and are frequently found on Caucasians and Asiatics. Though often confused with freckles, they do not fade during the winter months. Liver spots (solar lentigines) on the back of the hands of people who have spent a lot of time outdoors rarely become malignant. Lentigines are occasionally up to an inch (2.5 centimeters) across, irregular in shape and staining. If they change in size or shape, indicating possible melanomas, they need immediate attention from a doctor. Sun protection such as a hat, long sleeves, sunglasses and sunscreen with at least SPF15 may reduce the occurrence of lentigines. Skin bleaching creams may help fade them.

SEE ALSO *Melanoma*

LEPROSY

Leprosy is caused by a rod-shaped bacterium, *Mycobacterium leprae*, a relative of the tuberculosis bacillus. It is prevalent in Central and South America, in East Asia, and in the tropical countries of Asia and Africa. There are two main forms: tuberculoid leprosy and lepromatous leprosy.

Tuberculoid leprosy is an infection in the deep skin layers, which destroys the hair follicles, sweat glands and nerve endings at the site of infection. The skin above the site becomes dry and discolored and loses the ability to sense touch, heat and cold, and pain. Fingers and toes are easily injured and may become mutilated and fall off.

In lepromatous leprosy, the organism multiplies freely in the skin. Large, soft bumps, or nodules, appear over the body and face. The mucous membranes of the eyes, nose, and throat may be invaded. In extreme cases the voice may change drastically, blindness may occur, or the nose may be destroyed.

Both types of leprosy are only mildly contagious (via the respiratory tract) and the infection is very slow to develop, ranging from 6 months to 10 years. Typical early

Legionnaires' disease

The bacteria *Legionella pneumophila* found in contaminated water (for example in air-conditioning cooling towers) causes Legionnaires' disease.

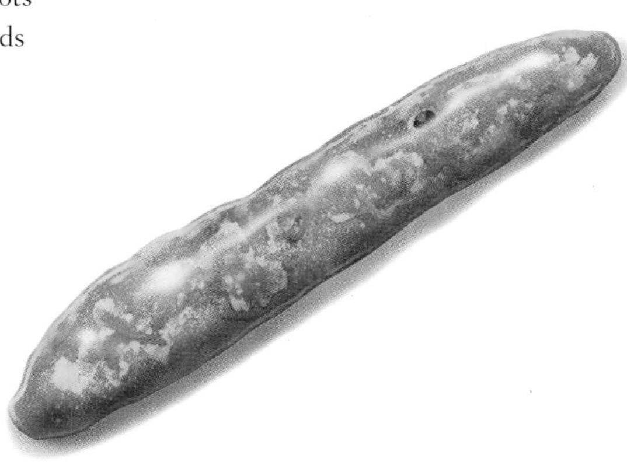

signs of the disease include one to three slightly raised patches on the skin which are non-itching, may be reddish in color and on which there is sensory loss. The diagnosis can be confirmed through a biopsy of the edge of an affected skin area or nerve.

Leprosy most commonly strikes people aged 10–20 years, and is seen more in men than women. It is thought to be transmitted through the inhalation of dust particles laden with bacilli. It is particularly prevalent in poorer countries where overcrowding and malnutrition make the spread of the disease easier.

Leprosy has existed for thousands of years and has a huge stigma attached to it because of the dreadful deformities that can result from infection. For this reason it is now often referred to by another name—Hansen's disease—in an effort to avoid fear and hysteria that may disadvantage efforts to treat the disease and reduce its incidence.

Early treatment is important in preventing deformities and other physical handicaps. Drugs such as dapsone, rifampin and clofazimine are used in combination to prevent drug resistance and may cure the disease within a year. Treatment usually needs to be continued for several years after the disease becomes inactive.

LEPTOSPIROSIS

Also called icterohemorrhagic fever, leptospirosis is a rare bacterial infection caused by *Leptospira*, a spiral-shaped microorganism (spirochete). It is contagious, being transmitted to humans mostly via liquids, soil, contaminated with the urine of infected wild or domestic animals—mainly rats, dogs, pigs and cattle. It may also be passed on by direct contact with the urine or tissue of an infected animal. The bacteria may enter the body through an open cut on the skin, through the intact mucous membrane of the mouth or when contaminated water is swallowed.

After an incubation period of 1–3 weeks, in a mild case the victim experiences a sudden onset of fever, shivering attacks (rigor), headache, muscle aches and pains (myalgia). These symptoms usually last 4–7 days, after which there may be a period where the sufferer feels well. The fever then recurs and 2 –4 weeks later may be accompanied by inflammation of the nerve to the eye, brain and spinal column (meningitis), and less commonly disease of the gallbladder, lungs and heart.

In about 10 percent of cases a severe form of the illness develops (known as Weil's syndrome), involving symptoms such as jaundice, mental confusion, kidney failure and bleeding abnormalities. The condition may be fatal, sometimes by drowning as the lungs fill with blood or fluid after the illness attacks the respiratory system.

Leptospirosis is diagnosed by testing of the blood, urine or spinal fluid. Treatment with antibiotics such as penicillin or doxycycline may be effective if commenced early in the illness.

LESION

This is a general term given to changes that occur in organs or tissues following injury or disease. An open wound is a lesion, as is the resulting scar. A birthmark or a mole is a superficial lesion, while a change from a mole to a melanoma produces a new lesion.

There are a number of ways of categorising lesions, one of which is size. A gross lesion is one that can be seen by the naked eye, and a microscopic or histologic lesion may only be viewed with the help of a microscope. Some lesions are known for their characteristic shape, such as bull's-eye or target lesions which are symptoms of a number of diseases and appear as well-demarcated raised red concentric circles. Round shadows that may appear on chest x-rays are sometimes referred to as coin lesions.

Some lesions are benign, while others are malignant. Inflammations or infections are not lesions, although lesions may be produced, such as the scar which can be seen on x-ray following an episode of tuberculosis. Other common examples of skin lesions are blisters, scabs, ulcers and boils.

SEE ALSO ***Birthmarks, Melanoma, Moles, Scar***

LEUKEMIA

Leukemia is a progressive, malignant disease arising from the white cells in the blood. It occurs in both adults and children, and is the most common type of malignant disease in children. The disease is characterized by an increase in white cells in the blood and in the blood-forming organs, the bone marrow and spleen. The leukemic white cells do not perform the normal function of fighting infection, but rather they interfere with the function of the normal white cells. They also interfere with the development of red blood cells and platelet cells in the bone marrow.

There are many types of leukemia, but they can be grouped according to the following criteria: duration (acute or chronic); the type of proliferating white cell; and the fluctuations in the number of abnormal cells in the blood.

Acute leukemia is a form of leukemia that develops rapidly, over weeks, and is quickly fatal if not treated. Patients develop infections, which are persistent and fail to respond to usual antibiotic treatment. The infections are generally due to bacteria and result in fever with or without local symptoms. Common sites of infection are the throat, gums, chest and skin.

Acute leukemia also causes exceptional fatigue and shortness of breath, due to anemia from decreased production of red blood cells. Easy bruising and spontaneous bleeding, from the nose and gums or from cuts, results from the interference with the production of platelet cells. The rapid expansion of white cells in the bone marrow can cause severe bone pain in the ribs and spine.

No single cause has been identified for acute leukemias and the cause of most cases is unknown. Exposure to high doses of ionizing radiation, such as in nuclear accidents like Chernobyl, resulted in increased cases of leukemia. However, it is not known whether low-level exposure to ionizing or other forms of radiation also increases the risk. The use of some toxic chemicals increases the occurrence of leukemia; benzene and its derivatives have the strongest association. Acute leukemia can also occur after the use of certain chemotherapy drugs recommended for other cancers, or after the use of certain drugs designed to suppress the rejection of kidney and other transplants.

There is a possibility that some drugs or chemicals affecting a woman during pregnancy can increase the risk of acute leukemia later developing in the child; these include alcohol, cannabis, benzene and pesticides. There is increasing interest in the possible role of viruses in causing leukemias in humans. Hereditary leukemia is rare but there is an increased incidence in conjunction with some genetic diseases, such as trisomy 21 (Down syndrome).

Acute lymphoblastic leukemia is the common form of childhood leukemia. It is derived from the type of white blood cells called lymphocytes. Blast cells are the immature cells from which the different types of blood cells normally develop. In acute lymphoblastic leukemia the blast cells that normally develop into lymphocytes do not do so and accumulate instead. Specific chromosomal or genetic abnormalities have now been identified in 60–75 percent of patients with acute lymphoblastic leukemia, giving hope for improvements in the understanding and treatment of this disease.

Acute myeloid leukemia is the common form of adult leukemia, whose incidence increases with age. It arises from an increase in myeloblasts in the bone marrow. At least six types of acute myeloid leukemia are recognized. Many are associated with specific chromosomal abnormalities and almost all patients have some chromosomal abnormality in their leukemic cells. In one type, acute promyelocytic leukemia, this knowledge has led to a major breakthrough in treatment with the use of a form of vitamin A.

Treatment of acute leukemia involves combinations of chemotherapy drugs and supportive treatment to prevent infections and bleeding. The initial chemotherapy is administered by intravenous injection and in tablet form over several days. Often a plastic catheter is inserted into a large vein to make repeated injections more convenient. The purpose of the initial treatment is to achieve apparent eradication of the leukemic cells; this is known as a remission. Once remission has been achieved, it is followed by consolidation chemotherapy and, in the case of lymphoblastic leukemia, more prolonged maintenance chemotherapy.

The results of treatment have improved with the development of powerful antibiotics, platelet transfusions and the use of growth factors to stimulate recovery of the

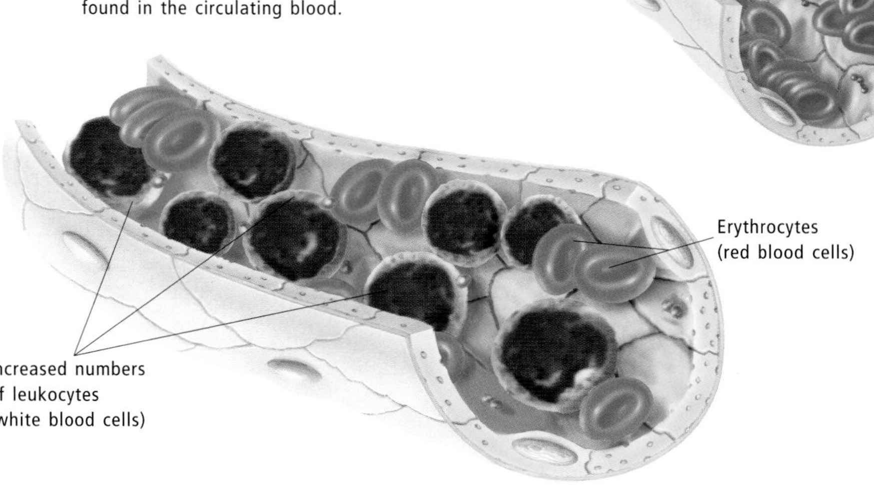

Leukemia

This malignant disease involves the rapid and uncontrolled proliferation of leukocytes (white blood cells) in the blood-forming organs. The white cell count is greatly elevated and large numbers of immature cells are found in the circulating blood.

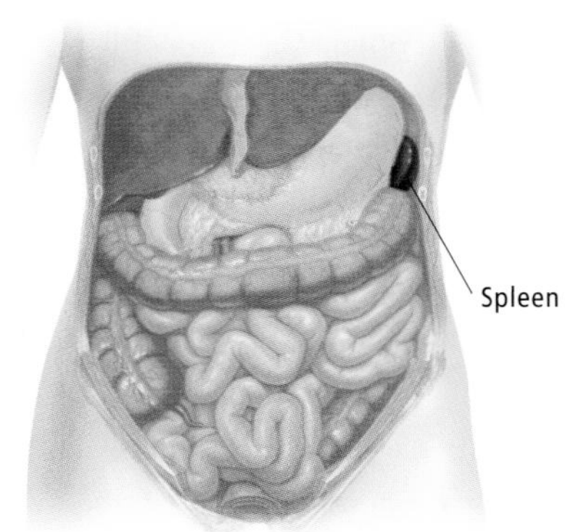

Leukemia—spleen

The spleen produces lymphocytes (one type of white blood cell) which are essential to the body's immune system. Overproduction of lymphocytes results in the most common form of leukemia—chronic lymphocytic leukemia. This can cause enlargement of the spleen.

Branch of nutrient artery

Marrow cavity

Bone marrow

Cortical bone

Leukemia—bone marrow

The bone marrow is the most important site for the storage and production of white blood cells (leukocytes) in the body. Leukocytes are produced mainly in the long bones, spine, skull, ribs, and sternum. In acute leukemia, the rapid expansion of white cells in the bone marrow can cause severe pain.

normal white cells. With current best methods of treatment, remission can now be achieved in 70–80 percent of adults up to 60 years of age and 97–99 percent of children. Bone marrow transplantation in remission can achieve cure rates of 50–60 percent in adults and 75–80 percent in children.

Chronic, as differentiated from acute, leukemias are leukemias which run a more gradual and prolonged course. They are often detected by chance, such as through a routine blood test, in which the raised white cell count appears. These leukemias involve an increase in mature white blood cells.

The most common leukemias is chronic lymphocytic leukemia, in which there is an increase in the number of lymphocytes. This occurs mainly in men over 50 years of age. It can cause enlargement of the lymph glands and spleen. Often there is an increased susceptibility to bacterial infections, due to reduced production of antibodies by normal lymphocytes. However, some patients may be completely asymptomatic and may not require treatment for years.

Chronic myeloid leukemia has its peak incidence at 20–40 years and involves an increase in mature myeloid cells, or granulocytes, in the blood and bone marrow. Enlargement of the spleen is an important feature of this condition, as is the association with a chromosomal abnormality in the bone marrow cells, called the Philadelphia chromosome, after the city in which it was first described. This form of leukemia generally requires treatment and can be cured in young patients with bone marrow transplantation. In those not suitable for this procedure, the use of injections of interferons (agents that inhibit cellular growth) can decrease the number of Philadelphia-positive cells and prolong patient survival.

SEE ALSO *Cancer, Lymphocytes, Spleen, White blood cells*

LEUKOPLAKIA

Leukoplakia refers to a whitish-looking patch on the mucous membrane of the cheeks, gums or tongue that cannot be removed by scraping. It is most often the result of thickening of the surface layer of cells (the epithelium), and is a response to injury or chronic irritation. This may be a result of friction caused by rough edges on teeth, fillings, and ill-fitting dentures and crowns. It occurs most often in smokers (especially pipe smokers) and in users of chewing tobacco, but other irritants can also trigger leukoplakia.

A white or gray colored lesion usually develops slowly over a period of weeks or months. This area may be sensitive to touch, heat and spicy foods. In a small proportion of patients, the change is either pre-cancerous or represents an early cancer of the mouth, both of which can only be excluded by microscopic examination of a biopsy sample.

Other forms of this condition include hairy leukoplakia, which involves fuzzy patches on the tongue and occasionally other parts of the mouth. It is a symptom of AIDS. A rare form of leukoplakia of unknown cause has also been reported on the external genital area (vulva) of women.

SEE ALSO *Mouth, Tongue*

LEUKORRHEA

It is natural for all women to have some relatively odorless vaginal mucus or leukorrhea (white fluid discharge). Most vaginal secretions come from the cervix with a lesser amount coming through the vaginal walls. Normally, the glands secrete a clear mucus which combines with bacteria, discarded vaginal cells and other secretions. The amount of leukorrhea secreted by the cervical glands fluctuates during the menstrual cycle and may vary in consistency from thick to pasty to thin. It may be clear, cloudy or colored and in some cases, perhaps where infection is present, may be malodorous.

The production is largely under hormonal control: an excess of estrogens produces too much. Women who take the contraceptive pill as well as those who are pregnant often have excessive moisture, as do women in an excited sexual state. The possible causes of significant changes in the color, smell, consistency and amount of vaginal discharge include yeast infection, sexually transmitted disease, the use of certain medications and irradiation of the reproductive tract. Itchiness can be associated with excessive mucus production.

If there is no infection present, reassurance is usually all that is needed.

SEE ALSO *Cervix, Estrogens, Vagina*

LICE

Lice are tiny parasites, about the size of sesame seeds, which live on the skin of the human body where they suck blood for food.

Head lice

Head lice (*Pediculus humanus capitis*) live in human hair. They hatch out from tiny eggs known as nits which are attached with a glue to the human hair, and can affect anyone. Contrary to popular belief, they do not thrive on dirty hair in unsanitary conditions; they prefer clean hair and are no respecters of social or economic status. Once laid the nits will stay attached to the hair shaft, unless dislodged, for 10 days, when they will hatch and reach maturity in about 2 weeks. A female louse can live for up to 30 days and lay about 6 eggs a day.

Lice are passed from one person to another by direct contact, which is why young children in constant contact with each other are most likely to spread them. They can be transmitted on combs, brushes, hats, pillowcases and towels. Scratching and occasionally small white specks are the signs.

More easily seen in sunlight and on dark hair than light, nits and lice can be difficult to eradicate. They are mostly found on the scalp behind the ears and near the neckline at the back. Eradication involves the use of a fine "nit" comb, insecticidal shampoo, a warm to hot hairdryer and disinfecting everything the head may have come in contact with—by washing in hot water and drying in hot air or strong sunlight. Head lice and nits on the eyelids need to be physically removed. Bed linen and stuffed toys that cannot be washed or dry cleaned should be placed in sealed plastic bags for 2 weeks. Carpet and furniture should be thoroughly vacuumed. It is important that other household members ensure they have not been infected.

Pubic lice

Pubic lice or crabs (*Phthirus pubis*) live in the hair in the pubic and thigh area. Crabs can be a problem in crowded living conditions. They are mainly contracted during sexual activity but can also contaminate bedding and clothing. Lice on toilet seats are usually injured and not likely to be looking for a new host. They can live in wet towels and be passed on in a gym or household.

Pubic lice can be easily visible attached to or moving in the pubic hairs, and look like a crab under magnification. They feed on blood and can live up to 30 days, mating frequently in that time. The most common symptom is an itch in the genital area; a rash, or tiny blue spots, may also be evident.

Treatment is with an insecticidal lotion or shampoo (often permethrin). The itching continues for some days after the lice have been killed and all bed linen and clothing must be disinfected in hot water and dried in hot conditions. Bathrooms, towels and linen need to be disinfected by washing with hot, soapy water and hot drying. Sexual contact should be avoided until the infection has been treated successfully so that the lice are not passed on to partners.

Body lice

Larger than head and pubic lice, body lice (*Pediculus humanis corpons*) usually live on people in unhygienic, crowded conditions.

These are the lice responsible for carrying diseases such as typhus, trench fever and relapsing fever (or tick fever). They too can be eradicated by hot washing of everything that has come into contact with the body and by the use of an insecticidal shampoo.

SEE ALSO *Head lice, Relapsing fever, Scabies, Typhus*

LICHEN PLANUS

Lichen planus is a rare and recurrent skin inflammation characterized by small, slightly raised bumps that itch. It usually starts at the wrists or on the legs and may spread to the trunk. Lesions may also appear in the mouth, vulva or penis, and the nails may be affected.

The exact cause of the condition is unknown, but is thought to be a result of an allergic or immune reaction. Exposure to potential allergens such as certain medications, dyes and other chemical substances has been implicated. It has also been reported that symptoms worsen with emotional stress, which is thought to affect the immune system.

This disease is extremely rare in children, mostly affecting the middle-aged and elderly. The dark red-purple lesions may be almost 1½ inches (4 centimeters) long, with distinct borders and a shiny or scaly appearance. They may appear singly or in clusters. Other symptoms include a dry mouth with a metallic taste, ridges on the nails and hair loss.

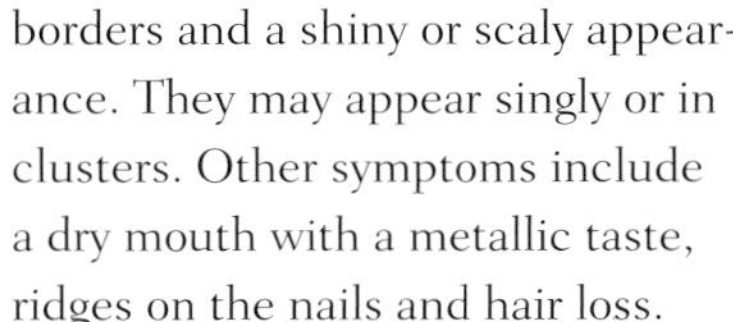

Lichen planus
Small slightly raised bumps with an accompanying itch characterize this inflammation of the skin.

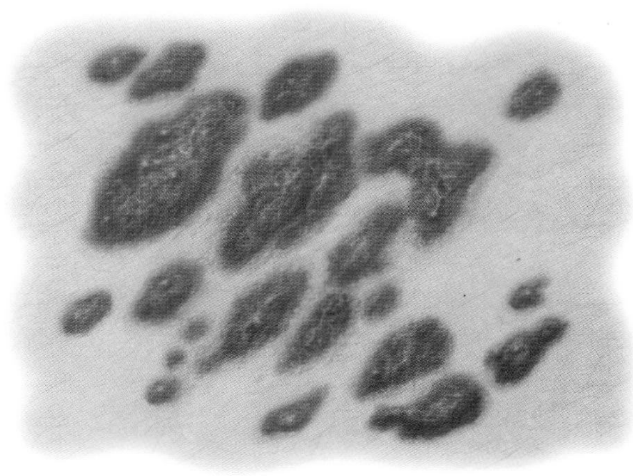

Creams or lotions containing corticosteroid drugs are used to control the condition, which may subside after a few months. However, symptoms may recur for years.

In some instances lichen planus may be a precursor to squamous cell cancer. Mouth ulcers that do not clear up may develop into oral cancer.

LIFE SUPPORT

Life support is the term generally given to the efforts to maintain vital body functions, such as respiration, circulation and fluid and nutrient intake, in patients who are comatose and cannot maintain these functions naturally. Life support involves the use of mechanical ventilation, intravenous fluids, physical therapy and round-the-clock nursing care in an intensive care unit in hospital.

Ethical questions have been raised regarding the quality of life of people kept alive by artificial life support. When the patient is unlikely to make any recovery, physicians—with the cooperation of the patient's relatives—may elect not to continue life support, especially where the patient has been declared brain dead. Some indivduals draw up what is known as a "living will" in which they specify how they wish to be treated if accident or illness leaves them in a vegetative state.

SEE ALSO *Death*

LIGAMENTS

Ligaments (from the Latin *ligamentum*, meaning a band or tie) are tough, white, fibrous, slightly elastic tissues. They support many internal organs, including the uterus, the bladder, the liver and the diaphragm, and they also help in shaping and supporting the breasts. Their main function is to support and strengthen joints, preventing excessive movement that might cause dislocation and breakage of the bones in the joint.

A ligament may be damaged or torn if a joint, through injury or accident, is moved into a position it was not designed for. The tear may be a complete tear of all the strands of the ligament or a partial tear, where only some of the ligament strands are torn. A tear in a ligament is sometimes called a sprain.

Sprains most often occur in the ankle and knee joints, but may also occur in the fingers, wrist, shoulder and the spine.

Sprains are treated with the application of cold compresses, immobilization of the joint, elevation of the joint to allow fluid around the joint to drain away, and the application of a bandage or splint. Nonsteroidal anti-inflammatory drugs (NSAIDs) may be given for pain relief and to aid healing.

Ligaments tend to heal very slowly because of their poor blood supply. Healing takes 7–10 days for mild sprains and 3–5 weeks for severe sprains. Surgery may be required if a ligament is completely torn or severed from its point of attachment to the bone.

An ankle sprain is a common injury and usually results when the ankle is twisted, or inverted. The foot turns inward, towards the other foot, causing the ligaments on the outside of the ankle (the lateral ligaments) to stretch and tear. The ankle swells and becomes painful and bruised. It is treated with ice, elevation, rest, painkillers, a bandage,

Ligaments

The main function of ligaments is to mobilize joints and prevent excessive movement. This strengthening and support system saves joints from fractures and dislocations.

Ligament microstructure
The direction of fibers within ligaments is related to the stress that is applied to them. The considerable interweaving increases structural stability and resilience.

Posterior cruciate ligament

Anterior cruciate ligament

Tibial collateral ligament

Fibular collateral ligament

and crutches, to keep the weight off the affected foot. Healing of the ligaments usually takes about 6 weeks.

The anterior cruciate ligament is a strong ligament that provides stability to the knee. It is often damaged during sporting activities. A sudden change in direction while running or jumping, as occurs in football and squash, for example, may result in a partial or complete tear, dislocation or stretch of the ligament.

Treatment involves rest, analgesics and physical therapy. In fit and active people, surgical repair is often performed with excellent results. This is often done via arthroscopy, involving a tube with a microscope inserted into the knee joint. Injury to the medial and to the lateral collateral ligaments of the knee may also occur.

SEE ALSO *Ankle, Joints, Knee, Sprain*

LIGHT THERAPY

Since 1981, intense artificial light therapy has been used in the USA and Europe, principally for the treatment of seasonal affective disorder (SAD) or winter depression. Light therapy affects the body's circadian rhythms by lengthening the day with bright light. Exposure to the light suppresses secretion of the night-time hormone melatonin and may enhance the effectiveness of serotonin and other neurotransmitters, producing an antidepressant effect in those whose depression is caused by a sensitivity to the reduction in sunlight.

The lamps used for this therapy produce a high intensity light, far brighter than normal lighting—at least eight times brighter than normal household lighting—and equal to standing outside on a sunny spring day. The individual with SAD sits in front of this lamp, usually for half an hour upon first waking. It is not necessary to stare at the lamp, but the patient may be advised to look at the lamp at regular intervals whilst carrying on with activities such as reading or watching television. Treatment for SAD commences in early autumn as the days begin to shorten and ends in spring when longer hours of daylight diminish the symptoms of SAD.

Light therapy is also used to treat sleep disorders, since exposure to light in the morning advances the circadian rhythm. This means that a person who is unable to fall asleep until very late at night can fall asleep earlier. Exposure to light at night delays the circadian rhythm, normalizing the sleep of those who are fatigued in the early evening and then wake early in the morning.

Light therapy can help shift workers and jet-lag sufferers to reset their body clocks. It may give SAD sufferers some relief from symptoms such as irritability, fatigue, low energy levels and weight gain. With regular light therapy treatment symptoms may disappear and the length of the sessions may be reduced.

SEE ALSO *Seasonal affective disorder, Sleep disturbances*

LIMBIC SYSTEM

The limbic system is a collective term for a group of interconnected brain structures that are involved in behaviors associated with survival, including the expression of emotion, feeding, drinking, defense and reproduction, as well as the formation of memory. The term "limbic system" comes from the fact that the earliest parts of this system to be identified were observed to form a ring or "limbus" around the central structures of the brain (cingulate, parahippocampal and hippocampal gyri), but later definitions include a number of other structures. The key components of this system are the hippocampus, amygdala, septal area and hypothalamus.

The hippocampus is located deep in the temporal lobe and is continuous with the cortex on the inner part of the lower surface of that lobe. It is connected to other parts of the cerebral cortex, thalamus and hypothalamus and is essential in the formation of new memories.

When the hippocampus is damaged, patients are able to recall old memories but are unable to remember what they did or said 5 minutes before. In other words, they cannot transform newly acquired knowledge into a memory, but old memories are intact—this condition is known as anterograde amnesia. This form of amnesia is seen in Alzheimer's disease, in which degeneration of the hippocampus is a characteristic feature. Because the hippocampus is very sensitive to oxygen deprivation, patients who recover from near-drowning or suffocation may suffer from anterograde amnesia for some time after the incident.

The amygdala is located in the temporal lobe, just in front of the hippocampus. It is strongly linked to the olfactory (smell) system, hippocampus, cerebral cortex and hypothalamus, and is an important center for the expression of emotions. People or animals in which the amygdala is removed fail to react to stimuli that would normally cause fear. In other words they are unable to recognize a fearful or threatening situation. Conversely, electrical stimulation of the amygdala in cats, for example, causes a full-blown defensive reaction. In humans it causes feelings of anxiety and irritability.

The septal area, a small region of the inner surface of the brain, beneath the front of the corpus callosum, is linked to the hippocampus, amygdala and hypothalamus. It is thought to be a pleasure or reward center and is a focus of some studies investigating addictive behavior.

The hypothalamus is a small but vital region that regulates the activity of the body's organs (viscera) through connections with other parts of the brain and through regulating the production of hormones. It is interconnected with all parts of the limbic system and is responsible for bringing about visceral changes associated with emotions, such as the increase in blood pressure, heart and breathing rate which occurs when scared or anxious, or blushing when embarrassed. The behavioral and cognitive changes associated with emotional expression are brought about mainly through projections from the various limbic structures (hypothalamus, amygdala, hippocampus) to the cortex of the frontal and temporal lobes.

SEE ALSO *Alzheimer's disease, Amnesia, Brain, Hypothalamus, Thalamus*

LIP

Part of the face, the lips are the muscular borders of the mouth. They are covered in front with skin, and at the back by a mucous membrane that forms part of the lining of the oral cavity. The free edges of the lips are covered by a type of very thin skin called the vermilion border which, due to its dense nerve supply and thinness, is extremely sensitive to touch. The vermilion border itself is

Lip

The lips play an essential role in speech by modulating sounds into recognizable words. They are an important part of the expressiveness of the face and contain many nerve endings, making them highly sensitive.

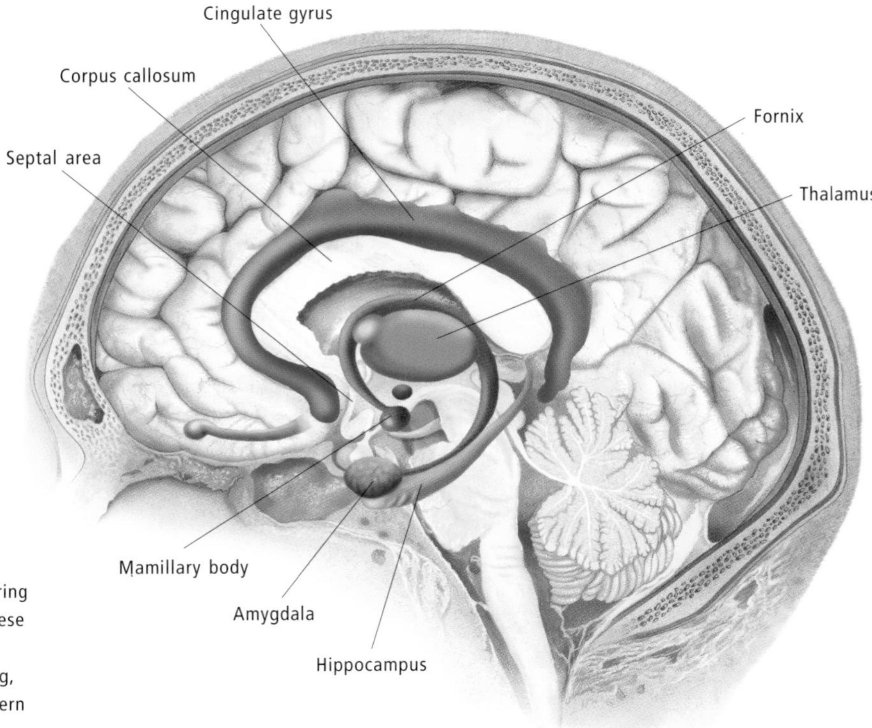

Limbic system

This "system" is a collective term referring to a group of elements in the brain. These structures are involved in behaviors associated with survival, such as feeding, defense and reproduction, and also govern emotional states and memory storage.

unpigmented, but blood from the blood vessels shows through it, giving the lips their characteristic red color.

The muscles of the lips are divided into two groups. The fibers of one group run concentrically around the mouth like purse strings and act to close it. The other muscles have fibers that run radially and are used to open the mouth. The lips serve to make a watertight and airtight closure of the mouth for drinking, swallowing and chewing. The muscular movements of the lips form an important part of the expressiveness of the face and, in infants, are essential for suckling on the breast. The lips and teeth form the embouchure (mouthpiece), by which musicians play wind instruments.

The delicate surface of the vermilion border is especially liable to injury. Lips may also require sunscreen and moisturizing preparations to protect against painful sunburn and chapping.

SEE ALSO *Face, Mouth, Mucous membranes*

L

LIPIDS

Lipids include fats and cholesterol. They are organic chemical substances of biological origin, and are usually esters (alcohol and acid compounds) of fatty acids. Lipids are characterized by not mixing with water. This gives them important physical properties, especially in the formation of cell membranes and the myelin sheaths of nerves. Lipids are widely distributed in the body, and form an important part of the diet.

SEE ALSO *Fats, Nutrition*

LIPODYSTROPHY

The lipodystrophies are a group of rare disorders causing loss of fat (adipose) tissue under the skin due to a disturbance of normal fat metabolism. Other metabolic disorders such as diabetes may be present. Lipodystrophy may be congenital (present at birth) or acquired, and may be generalized (affecting the whole body), partial or local, affecting just one area of the body.

One type of lipodystrophy is seen in people who are being treated with protease inhibitor drugs for AIDS-related illness. Their face, arms and legs become thin due to loss of fat, while fat builds up on the back of the neck, and the breasts and stomach become enlarged with tissue. Other symptoms include cracked lips, dry skin, weight loss and protruding veins. It is not known why these drugs have this effect.

Generalized lipodystrophy may be congenital or it may occur after an infectious illness, especially measles, chickenpox or whooping cough. The main feature is loss of fat; the affected person looks as though their skin is drawn tightly over their bones. There is also associated growth disorder; the affected person appears to be suffering from acromegaly, as they have coarse facial features and large feet and hands, and their internal organs are enlarged. Intellectual disability is common. There is no treatment and affected persons often die at an early age. Insulin may be needed to control the diabetes that is also associated with the condition.

Acquired partial lipodystrophy affects females in the first decade of life. The loss of fat usually affects only the upper half or, less commonly, one side of the body. This variation is not as severe as the generalized form and the outlook is better.

SEE ALSO *Acromegaly, Diabetes, Fats, Metabolism*

LIPOMA

A lipoma is a benign tumor composed of fatty tissue which is often found just under the skin. Lipomas manifest as soft swellings that can occur in multiples and are commonly seen in the back, thighs, buttocks and breasts. Lipomas in the breast are sometimes mistaken for malignant tumors if they are firmer than usual to the touch.

Lipomas are more prevalent in adults than children. As they are generally benign they do not invade nearby tissue and may be left untouched for many years. Medical advice should be sought, however, if they increase in size or shape in case they are malignant. Lipomas are usually easily removed by surgery to improve cosmetic appearance or reduce discomfort if they are inconveniently located.

Lipomas may also form inside the body. They may be found in muscle tissue, where they can grow quite large before detection. They may attach to the spinal cord, causing complications such as paralysis, and in rare instances may attach to the pancreas.

SEE ALSO *Tumors*

LIPOSUCTION

Liposuction (also known as lipolysis or suction lipectomy) is the surgical removal of fat from the body for cosmetic purposes using a suction apparatus inserted into the body through an incision.

The most common method is tumescent liposuction. In this procedure, several quarts (liters) of saline solution are pumped under

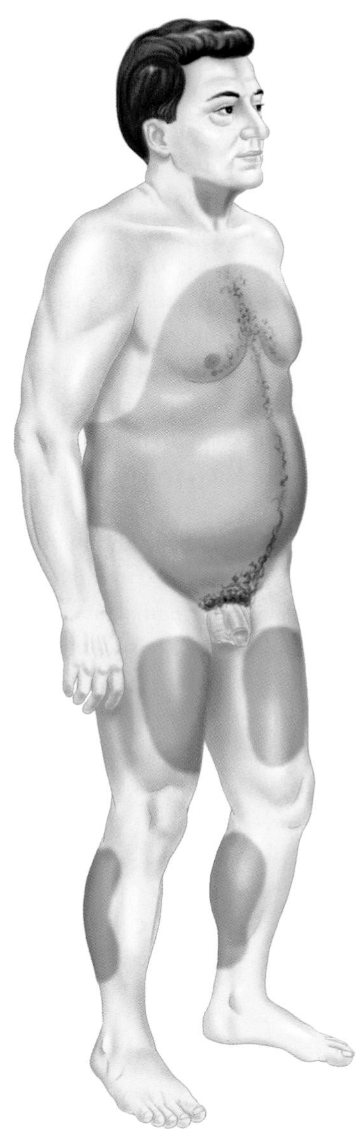

Liposuction

Liposuction involves the removal of unwanted fat from the body. The most commonly treated areas include the thighs, buttocks, hips, chin, and abdomen.

the skin, then the fat is sucked out using a tube, or cannula, to which a high-pressure vacuum is applied. The saline solution also includes a local anesthetic to numb the area being treated and a substance that constricts blood vessels to minimize bleeding. With ultrasonic-assisted liposuction, a wand-like instrument is energized with ultrasonic energy to liquefy fat. This method—known as lithotripsy—is often used to re-treat areas of the body that have already undergone liposuction. However, it may require longer incisions, takes more time to complete and be more expensive. It also carries a greater risk of burns to the skin or inside of the body.

The most commonly treated areas are the buttocks, thighs, hips, knees, abdomen, upper arms, back and chin. The procedure may also be used to "contour" the neck, calves and ankles. It is not used for breast reduction, for removing fatty tumors or as a treatment for obesity. Nor will it eliminate the dimpled appearance of skin caused by cellulite.

Serious and potentially fatal complications can occur while undergoing tumescent liposuction as a result of blood clots (thrombosis), fluid overload resulting in the collection of fluid in the lungs (pulmonary edema) and slowed heart rate in combination with lowered blood pressure.

SEE ALSO Cosmetic surgery

Lithotripsy

Stones that have formed in the gallbladder, kidneys or bladder can be shattered using shock waves. This avoids the need for invasive surgery. Once shattered, gallstone fragments pass out of the body via the bile duct and bowel; kidney and bladder stone fragments are passed with urine through the ureter.

Gallstones

Bladder stones

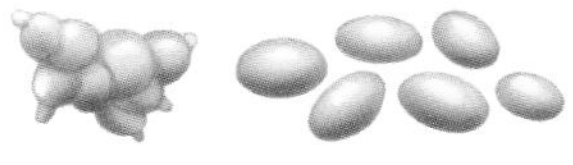

Stones shattered with lithotripsy

Stones no larger than ⅝ of an inch (1.5 centimeters) are ideal candidates for lithotripsy.

Gallbladder

Kidneys

Bladder

LISPING

Lisping is the term broadly used to describe a range of speech impediments, the most common of which is pronounciation of the sibilant sounds of "s" or "z" as "th". This happens when the tip of the tongue is positioned too far forward in the mouth, instead of against the hard palate. Lisping may be treated with speech therapy.

SEE ALSO *Speech*

LISTERIOSIS

Listeriosis is an infection caused by *Listeria monocytogenes*, a bacterium found in nature and in some foods. Infection is not common and there are usually few or no symptoms in healthy people though it can cause a flu-like illness. In pregnancy, however, listeriosis is dangerous to the fetus and can cause miscarriage, stillbirth or premature birth.

About half of the babies infected at or near birth will die. Signs that a newborn is infected include a red skin rash, whitish nodules on mucous membranes, respiratory distress, shock, vomiting, lethargy and jaundice. The condition often manifests as meningitis in babies aged 2 weeks or older.

In adults, the infection can take many forms depending on the body part affected. It may manifest as meningitis, septicemia, pneumonia, endocarditis or, in less severe cases, skin lesions, conjunctivitis or abscesses.

The organism can be found in such foods as soft cheese, cold cooked chicken, cold meats and paté, raw seafood, pre-prepared salads and smoked seafood. Observing good hygiene and avoiding these foods during pregnancy minimizes the risk of infection.

SEE ALSO *Bacteria, Food poisoning*

LITHOTRIPSY

The procedure known as lithotripsy is used to shatter stones (calculi) that have formed in the bladder, gallbladder, ureter or kidney. Extracorporeal shockwave lithotripsy is a common technique that involves the creation of shock waves outside the body which are targeted at the stone to break it up. This technique is generally used on stones no more than ⅝ inch (1.5 centimeters) in diameter and some sort of anesthesia is given. The patient may be positioned in water during the procedure. X-rays or ultrasound are used to ensure the accurate location of the stone.

While surgical stone removal once required a lengthy stay in hospital, lithotripsy may take only 45 minutes and can sometimes be performed on an out-patient basis. Depending on the size of the stone and the strength and duration of the shock waves needed, anesthesia may be used to alleviate pain. It may take between 800 and 2000 shocks, for example, to break up a kidney stone. Stone fragments are sometimes passed from the body with the aid of a catheter inserted in the ureter.

Another type of lithotripsy involves the insertion of an instrument called a lithotrite through the ureter which shatters or crushes stones using an electrical spark.

Complications of lithotripsy include blood in the urine for a few days after treatment, bruising on the abdomen or back, and pain or discomfort as stones pass out of the body in the urine. More than one treatment may be required if the stone is not completely shattered the first time.

SEE ALSO *Bladder, Gallbladder, Kidney, Ureter*

LIVER

The liver is an organ associated with the digestive tract. It is the heaviest single organ in the body, weighing about 3½ pounds (1.5 kilograms) in an adult, and makes up about one-fiftieth of total body weight. The liver is normally reddish brown in color and lies under the cover and protection of the lower ribs on the right side of the upper abdomen.

The liver has an upper (diaphragmatic) surface, which is in contact with the diaphragm, and a lower (visceral) surface, which is in contact with organs in the abdominal cavity. The two surfaces are separated at the front by a sharp inferior border, which may sometimes be felt when the liver becomes enlarged and protrudes below the line of the ribs. The visceral surface of the liver is in contact with the gallbladder (which is usually attached to the liver by connective tissue), with the kidney, part of the duodenum, the esophagus, the stomach and a part of the large bowel.

The liver is attached to the diaphragm—the muscle which separates the chest and abdominal cavities—by a series of folds of membrane called the falciform, triangular and coronary ligaments.

The liver is also joined to the stomach and duodenum by folds of membrane called the gastrohepatic and hepatoduodenal ligaments respectively.

On the visceral surface of the liver lies a region known as the porta hepatis. This is the site at which vessels and ducts enter and leave the liver. Within the porta hepatis are the portal vein, which carries blood from the gut to the liver, the hepatic artery, which carries blood from the aorta to the liver, and the common hepatic, cystic and bile ducts, all of which are part of the biliary system of ducts concerned that store bile and deliver it to the duodenum.

Microscopic structure

Microscopically, the liver contains sheets of cells (hepatocytes) arranged in hexagonal prism-shaped lobules. Each hepatocyte is about one-thousandth of an inch (25 thousandths of a millimeter) across and they are piled up in sheets one cell thick, much like bricks in a wall. Hepatocytes contain a large amount of glycogen, which is an energy storage chemical made from glucose.

The space between the sheets of hepatocytes is filled with small blood vessels called liver sinusoids. In the walls of the liver sinusoids are special cells called macrophages (Kupffer cells) that are capable of engulfing debris. A system of bile ductules runs between the hepatocytes. These ductules carry bile, which is produced by the hepatocytes. The ductules eventually join together to form hepatic ducts, which in turn join together to form the bile duct.

At the corners of each hexagonal liver lobule lie branches of the portal vein, hepatic artery and hepatic ducts, while the center of each lobule is occupied by a central vein.

Venous blood from the gut flows past the sheets of liver cells on its way to the central vein. Nutrients, bile salts and toxic and waste substances are removed from the portal blood by hepatocytes and processed as necessary. The central veins of all the lobules join together and contribute blood to the hepatic veins. These in turn drain into the inferior vena cava, which carries blood back to the heart.

Metabolic functions

The liver serves many metabolic functions. It receives all the blood returning from the gastrointestinal tract, which is laden with glucose derived from the breakdown of food. The liver converts much of this glucose to a storage molecule called glycogen. Glycogen can be converted back to glucose for release into the blood whenever it is required. This means that the liver plays a key role in maintaining a relatively constant concentration of glucose in the blood, regardless of the time of day or the energy demands of the body. Two hormones released from the pancreas, insulin and glucagon, are important in the control of this function.

The liver also plays a key role in the metabolism of other sugars, as well as fats and proteins. Liver cells have much of the cellular machinery (granular endoplasmic reticulum) associated with making proteins and glycogen. Under the electron microscope, granules of glycogen with the appearance of berries are often visible in liver cells. Liver cells also contain many mitochondria—tiny chemical power houses whose presence indicates very high metabolic activity in the liver. The position of the liver in the flow of blood from the gut also allows it to remove and destroy any toxic substances that may be ingested along with food and water. These toxic substances include alcohol, drugs and the chemicals produced by microorganisms. Bacteria entering the body from the gut must also get past the defensive scavenger cells (Kupffer cells) of the small vessels of the liver before they can reach the body at large.

The liver makes and stores vitamin A, which is essential for the well-being of the surface-lining tissues of the body, and stores iron, used in the production of hemoglobin in the blood. Bile, which is used to aid the digestion of fats, is made in the liver and released into the duodenum through the biliary system of ducts. The liver also produces albumin, an important plasma protein in the blood, which helps to control fluid movement between the inside of blood vessels and the spaces between the cells throughout the body. Finally, the liver makes several important substances involved in the control of blood clotting, including the clotting factors prothrombin and fibrinogen.

Bile is a yellow-orange fluid produced and excreted in the liver. It consists of water, bile salts and a chemical called bilirubin. Bile is produced by the hepatocytes and flows along tiny channels (bile canaliculi) towards the bile duct branches at the corners of the lobules. Bile is also continually recycled, as it is reabsorbed from the gut once the digestion of fats has taken place. About 90 percent of bile secreted by the liver is actually recycled from the gut. The bile flows back to the liver in the portal vein blood, where it is transferred by hepatocytes to the bile duct branches for delivery back to the gut for further fat digestion.

Diseases and disorders

Several congenital diseases may affect the liver. These include congenital bile duct atresia, in which the bile ducts fail to develop, and problems with the enzymes responsible for bile metabolism. Children with these disorders develop jaundice, or yellowing of the skin, during the first few days to weeks of postnatal life. This should be distinguished from the normal mild jaundice that occurs to some extent in all infants shortly after birth, and which disappears within a few days.

The liver may be damaged by penetration or blunt injury. Laceration of the liver or its blood vessels by bullets or knives can cause dangerous blood loss. Blunt injury occurs when there is a direct blow to the upper abdomen, such as in a car accident. Treatment involves the surgical control of bleeding by repairing torn vessels and maintaining the patient's blood volume by blood transfusion.

Hepatitis is inflammation of the liver, which can be caused by viruses (such as hepatitis A, B, and C), bacteria, parasites, nematodes, drugs or alcohol. The different types of viral heptatitis are transmitted in different ways; for example, heptatitis A by

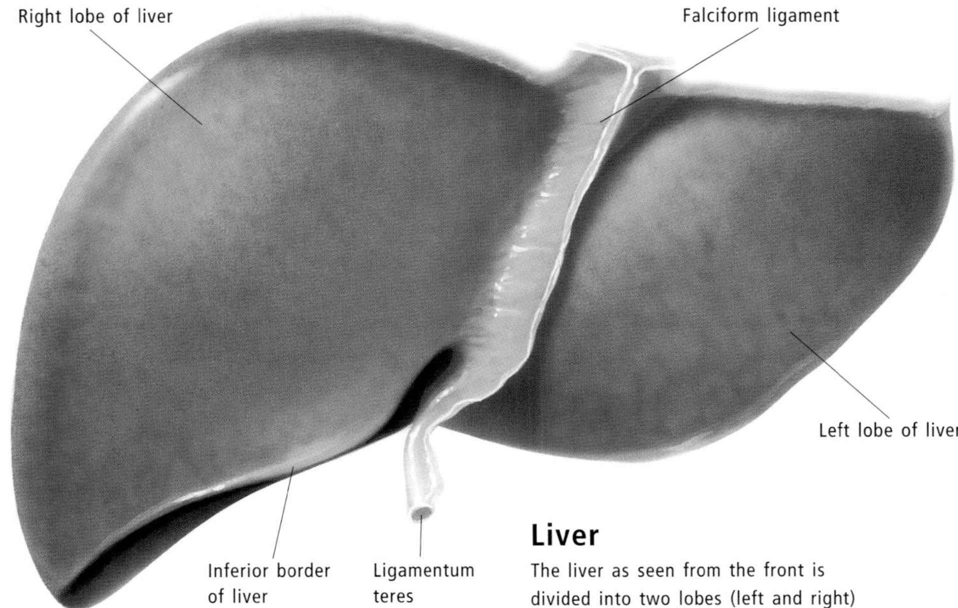

Liver

The liver as seen from the front is divided into two lobes (left and right) by a fold of peritoneum called the falciform ligament. The lower edge of the falciform ligament is called the ligamentum teres and is a remnant of a structure important before birth—the left umbilical vein. The left umbilical vein carries blood from the placenta back to the developing fetus and shuts down shortly after birth.

Liver

The liver lies in the upper right side of the abdomen under the cover of the ribs. In a healthy person it should not be possible to feel the liver. The liver covers part of the stomach and other organs of the upper abdomen and is in contact with the right kidney, right large bowel and the beginning of the duodenum.

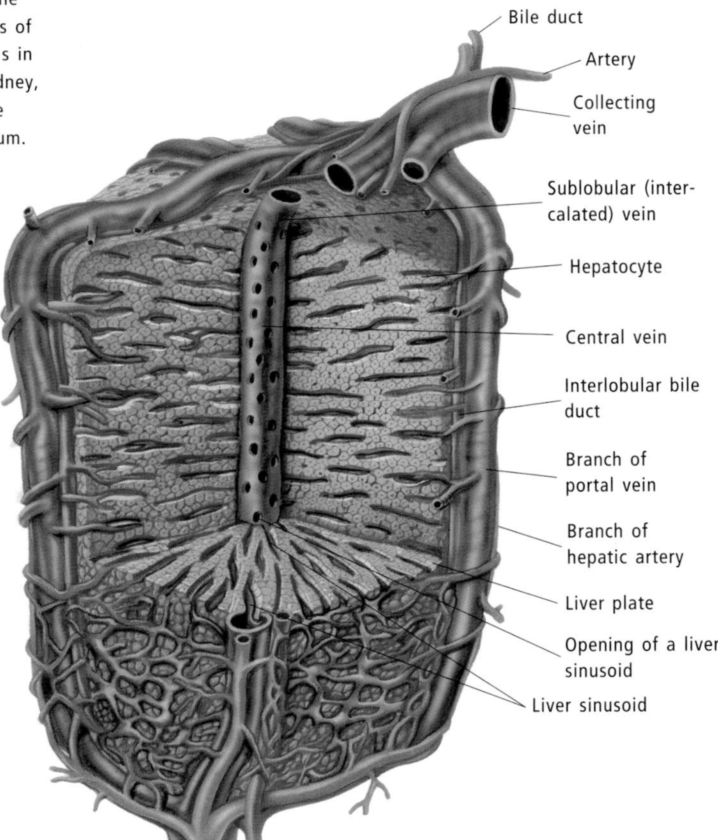

Liver lobule

The liver is made up of many hexagonal structures called liver lobules. Each liver lobule has a central vein at its core, which drains blood from the lobule to the hepatic veins that lead out of the liver. Blood arrives in the liver from the gut via the portal vein, which has branches at the corners of the liver lobule. More blood is brought into the liver by the hepatic artery and its branches. The bile produced by liver cells passes into the branches of the bile duct, which eventually drains towards the duodenum.

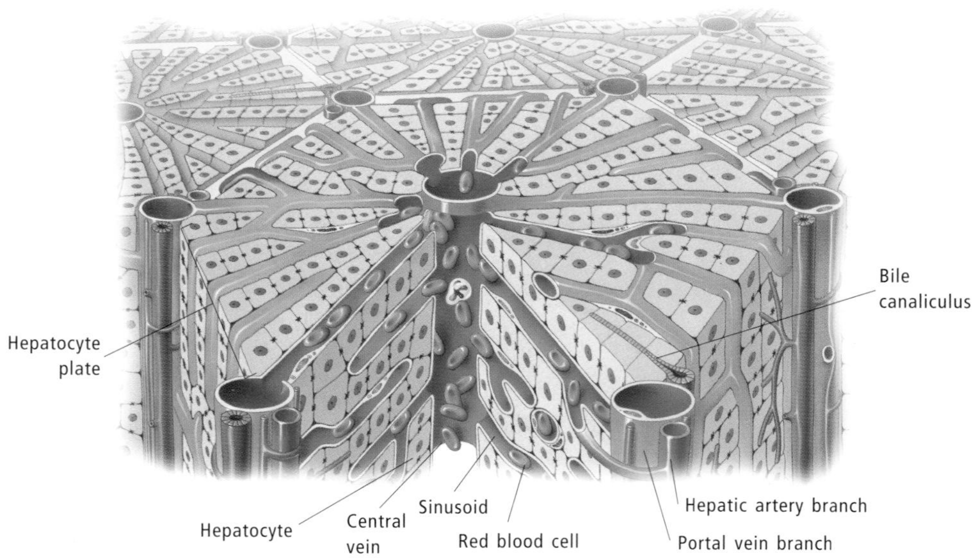

Liver—microstructure

Each liver lobule consists of radially arranged sheets of specialized epithelial cells interpenetrated and ensheathed by supporting connective tissue. Small blood vessels called liver sinusoids run past the sheets of liver cells. Branches of both the portal vein and hepatic artery feed into these sinusoids. Nutrients and toxic substances are drawn from the passing blood by liver cells and processed appropriately. Other fine tubular structures between the liver cells, called bile canaliculi, collect bile and carry this fluid towards the branches of the bile duct located at the corners of the liver lobule.

the gut through contaminated food or water and hepatitis B and C by blood, intravenous drug use with shared needles, or sexual intercourse. The incubation period for hepatitis A is 2–6 weeks, while type B and C have longer incubation periods of about 6 weeks to 6 months. Patients experience a period of feeling generally unwell, followed by nausea, vomiting and disinterest in eating. They may also develop fever, upper abdominal pain and yellowing of the skin and eyes (jaundice) due to high levels of a chemical called bilirubin in the blood. Sometimes, widespread destruction of liver cells occurs, with a progression to complete liver failure, coma and even death (though fortunately this is rare).

The liver can be infected by parasites, bacteria or fungi, resulting in the production of pus-filled cavities (abscesses). Liver abscesses may form in patients with diverticulitis of the bowel, or they may appear on their own. Patients with liver abscesses develop high fevers, up to 106°F (41°C), and chills. The liver is enlarged and may be tender. Treatment is by an appropriate antibiotic and surgical drainage of pus from the abscess.

Cirrhosis of the liver is a condition involving the death of liver cells, followed by fibrosis and regrowth of the liver cells in small lumps or nodules. Causes of cirrhosis include alcoholism; hemochromatosis, an iron storage disease; Wilson's disease, an inherited disease of copper metabolism; heart problems and immunological disorders.

Patients with cirrhosis often commonly develop jaundice. They may also experience swelling of the abdomen and ankles, breast enlargement and testicular wasting in men, mental confusion, disorientation and coma. The disordered regrowth of liver cells interferes with blood flow through the cirrhotic liver. This raises the pressure of blood in the portal vein, leading to a condition known as portal hypertension, which can have serious consequences because small veins in the lower esophagus swell (esophageal varices) and may rupture. Patients with cirrhosis can die from blood loss due to bleeding from esophageal varices, or they may develop low blood pressure, high levels of ammonia in the blood, coma and ultimately kidney failure.

Cancer in the liver may have spread from other parts of the body, including the large bowel, breast, lung, pancreas, stomach, kidney and uterus, or arise in the liver itself (primary cancer of the liver). In Western countries, cancer which has spread from other sites to the liver is about 20 times as common as primary liver cancer. Cancer may be spread to the liver by blood from the gut, along lymphatic vessels, or by arterial blood. Treatment may include surgery, if only an isolated nodule of tumor is present, or chemotherapy delivered directly to the liver. Life expectancy once a tumor has spread to the liver is very low.

Primary cancer of the liver is a very serious disease with a very low life expectancy after diagnosis. It is not common in Western countries, but has a high incidence in Africa and Asia, where the causes seem to be environmental and cultural rather than racial. The incidence of liver cancer among people from those regions living in Western countries is no different than in Caucasians.

Liver cancer commonly occurs in patients with previous cirrhosis of the liver. In developing countries, infestation with liver flukes or ingestion of a fungal toxin (aflatoxin) on grains and peanuts probably play important roles in its initiation. A particular type of liver cancer (angiosarcoma of the liver) is caused by industrial exposure to vinyl chloride. With primary liver cancer, removal of part or all of the liver is the only hope of a complete cure. Chemotherapy may also delay the advance of the tumor.

Diagnostic tests

Investigation of liver disease often involves taking blood specimens to test for liver enzymes, which are released from damaged liver cells. Removal of a small specimen of liver for examination (liver biopsy) may be performed to investigate jaundice, liver enlargement or suspected cirrhosis. Patients are given medication to calm nervousness, and a special biopsy needle is inserted between ribs 8 and 9 on the right side of the body below the nipple. The tissue is examined by a pathologist to assist in making a diagnosis. Other diagnostic tools for liver disease include ultrasonography, which uses sound waves to form images of internal organs; computerized tomography and magnetic resonance imaging techniques; and isotope scans to detect regions of high blood flow and metabolic activity.

SEE ALSO *Cirrhosis of the liver, Digestive system, Hemochromatosis, Hepatitis, Insulin, Jaundice, Liver function blood tests, Portal hypertension, Wilson's disease*

LIVER FUNCTION BLOOD TESTS

Liver function blood tests are tests on the blood which give information about the health of the liver. The liver performs many essential functions. It makes many important proteins, such as albumin and clotting factors. Albumin is the major protein in the blood, responsible for keeping fluid in the blood vessels and transporting chemicals.

Liver function blood tests will reveal levels of albumin in the blood. In severe liver disease, the albumin level decreases and fluid leaks into the limbs (edema) and abdominal cavity (ascites). A reduction in clotting factors also occurs, resulting in easy bruising and a tendency to bleed.

Other abnormalities may also be detected, such as abnormal enzyme levels. Liver cells contain enzymes which are released into the blood when they are damaged. An alcoholic binge will produce this, as well as damage by viruses or chemicals.

SEE ALSO *Liver*

LORDOSIS

Lordosis, often described as swayback, is one of a group of spinal deviations. It is an exaggeration of the normal forward or inward curvature of the lumbar (middle to lower) spine. It can be caused by diseases of the hip joint, obesity or abdominal enlargement. Physical therapy and exercises may be beneficial.

SEE ALSO ***Kyphosis, Scoliosis, Spinal curvature, Spine***

Normal spine

Lordosis

Exaggerated forward or inward curvature of the spine can be caused by disease of the hip joint, obesity or abdominal enlargement.

LUMBAGO

Although lumbago means simply "backache", it is usually applied to an ache in the lower portion of the back associated with spinal disk damage. When humans first stood upright, the spine became a weight-bearing organ, something for which it was not designed. As a consequence, awkward weight bearing and unusual strains can disrupt the disks between the vertebrae. When damaged disk tissue projects into the spinal canal, nerves are frequently comrpressed, producing neuralgia (such as sciatica). An operation to remove the displaced piece of disk or injections of an enzyme into the disk to make it shrink back into position may be required. Surgery is imperative if muscle weakness occurs.

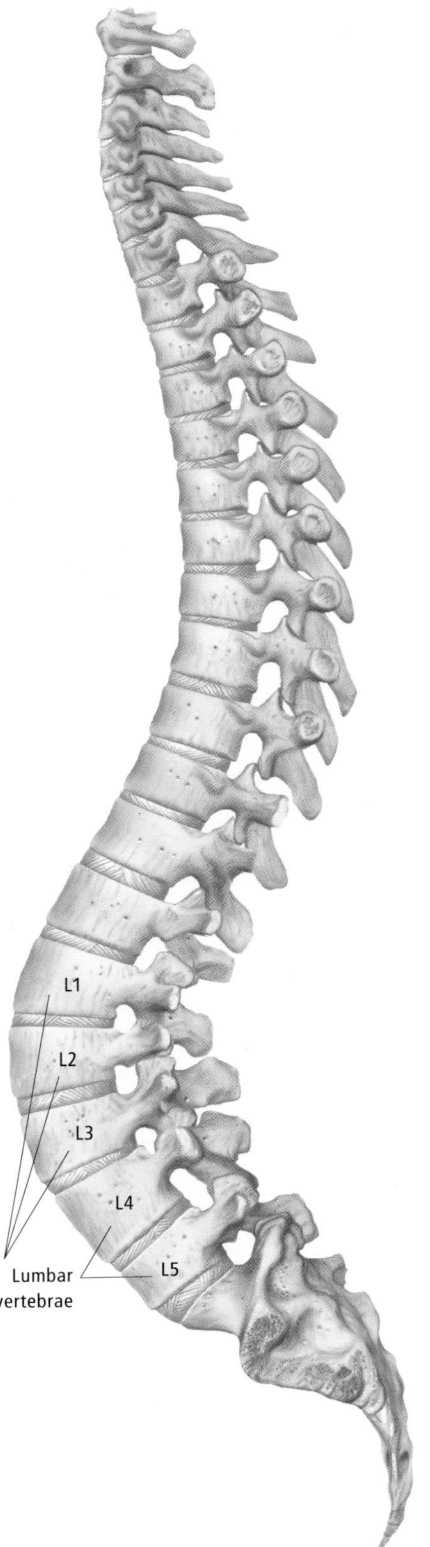

Diagnosis depends largely upon the result of CAT scan, x-rays or MRI (magnetic resonance imaging). The patient may need advice on the best methods of lifting as well as back-strengthening exercises.

Lumbago may also be due to referred pain from pelvic organs, such as prostate inflammation and cancer, or associated with menstrual pains or uterine or ovarian disease.

SEE ALSO ***Disk, intervertebral, Pain, Sciatica, Spine***

LUMBAR PUNCTURE

Lumbar puncture is a procedure that involves the insertion of a needle into the spinal cavity (usually below the third lumbar vertebra) to take a sample of cerebrospinal fluid or to administer drugs or an anesthetic. The five lumbar vertebrae are situated in what is known as the "small" of the back. The procedure is also known as a spinal tap.

SEE ALSO ***Disk, intervertebral, Spine***

LUMPECTOMY

A lumpectomy is a surgical procedure to remove a small tumor or lump (benign or malignant) while disturbing as little of the surrounding tissue as possible. Lumpectomy is particularly associated with the treatment of breast cancer and is a more conservative form of surgery than a mastectomy where the whole breast may be removed.

A lumpectomy may be followed by radiation therapy and possibly chemotherapy to kill any remaining cancer cells. Depending on the type and development of the tumor, it may be the only treatment necessary. It may also act as a diagnostic tool through which physicians can decide whether more radical surgery is needed.

SEE ALSO ***Breast cancer, Mastectomy***

LUNG CANCER

Lung cancer is a common cancer, ranked second in frequency in both men (after prostate cancer) and women (after breast cancer). It is usually more aggressive than other cancers and is thus the most common cause of cancer death in most countries.

Tobacco smoking plays a very important role in causing lung cancer. A variety of precancerous changes can be seen in the inner layer of cells (the epithelium) lining the major airways of smokers. Cigarette smoking is particularly incriminated, although pipe and cigar smoking also increase the risk of developing lung cancer. Long-term heavy smokers have at least a 20-fold higher risk of lung cancer than non-smokers.

The risk decreases for those who stop smoking, approaching that of non-smokers after 15 years, with a progressive disappearance of the abnormalities in the epithelium. Lung cancer can therefore be regarded as a preventable disease. Given that there is also a strong association between smoking and vascular disease, and increased risk of a number of other cancers in smokers, the implementation of public health strategies in this area is still only partially successful. Other risk factors for the development of lung cancer include exposure to asbestos, a variety of metal dusts, ionizing radiation and certain industrial chemicals.

Although most lung cancers develop in the epithelium of the airways, lung cancer is not a single type of tumor. Several different varieties can be recognized microscopically, of which one known as small cell cancer is of particular importance. As they grow, lung cancers usually invade through the airway wall, causing cough and sometimes the coughing up of blood. The cancer may also grow into the airway tube, which tends to cause obstruction leading to wheezing, repeated chest infections or breathlessness.

In a proportion of patients, the first evidence of lung cancer is the appearance of secondary growths, especially in the bones (causing pain), in the liver (causing enlargement) and in the brain (causing seizures and various other complications). This pattern is especially likely to occur in small cell lung cancer, which is spread quickly through the body via the blood. Unusual symptoms can also develop as as a result of hormone secretion by the tumor cells.

Early diagnosis is the key to effective treatment of cancers. In the case of lung cancers, however, few symptoms develop early in the course of the disease. There is as yet no available diagnostic test that is sensitive, easy to perform and inexpensive. While x-rays, examination for cancer cells in the sputum, biopsy via bronchoscope and other techniques allow a specific diagnosis to be made, these techniques are unsuitable for population screening. As a result, by the time symptoms become obvious and a diagnosis is made, the tumor is already quite large and has typically invaded into surrounding structures, spread via the lymphatics and the blood, or both. This is why the success rate for the treatment of lung cancer is still very poor.

Surgery and radiation therapy are used for most types of lung cancer, but early blood-borne spread of small cell cancers means that these tumors can only be treated with chemotherapy.

SEE ALSO *Cancer, Lungs, Smoking*

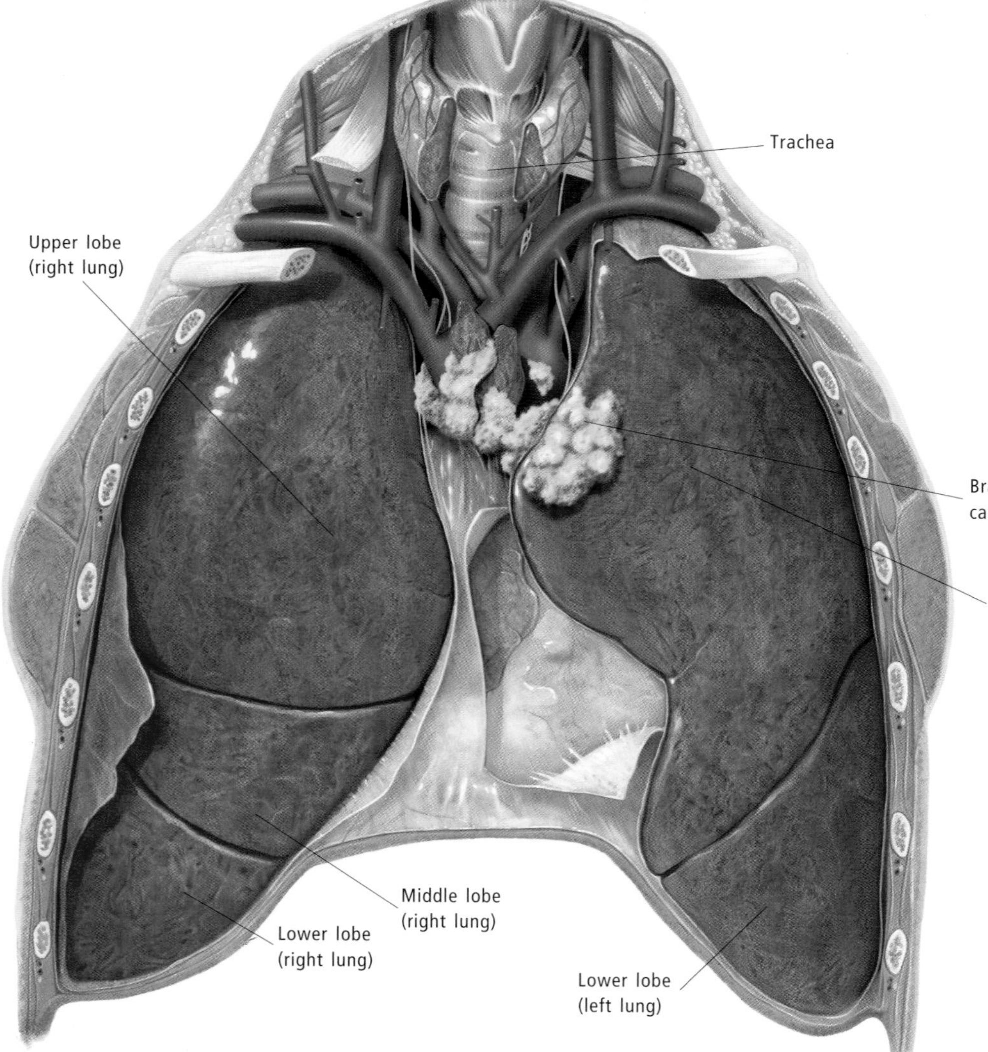

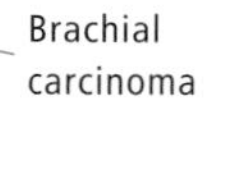

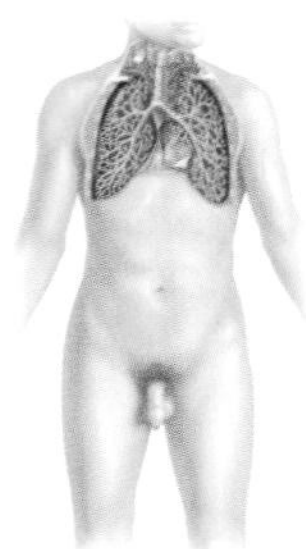

Lung cancer

Malignant growths of the lung are among the most common types of cancer. Most lung cancers arise in the cells that line the major airways, but the disease encompasses a number of different tumor types. The cancer usually progresses through the walls of the airway and may then spread through the blood to other organs.

LUNGS

The lungs are paired organs in the chest that are responsible for gas exchange between the atmosphere and the blood. Inhaled oxygen is supplied to the blood, and carbon dioxide is exhaled. The lungs are enclosed within pleural sacs, which provide a smooth, low friction surface so that the lungs can move freely inside the chest. Between the two pleural sacs, with their enclosed lungs, lies the mediastinum, a group of organs in the central part of the chest cavity. The mediastinum contains the heart, esophagus, trachea and major vessels and nerves.

Each lung has a roughly conical or pyramidal shape, with a base sitting on top of the diaphragm; sides in contact with the rib cage (costal surface), the mediastinum (mediastinal surface), and the backbone (vertebral surface); and an apex. The lung apex is encircled by the first rib and actually lies above the first rib in the hollow at the angle between the neck and the shoulder.

On the mediastinal surface of each lung is a region known as the lung hilum, where the large airways (left and right main bronchi) enter the lung and the major lung vessels (pulmonary arteries and veins) enter and leave, respectively. The bronchi subdivide into the bronchioles—smaller tubes which in turn subdivide into the alveoli (tiny clusters of air sacs). The lungs are divided into lobes, usually three in the right lung and two in the left lung, by a series of clefts or fissures (the horizontal fissure in the right lung and the oblique fissures in both the left and right lungs).

Inflation and deflation of the lungs

Most of the expansion of the lungs with each intake of breath, or inspiration, is due to the contraction of the diaphragm, the muscle separating the chest and abdominal cavities. Breathing out air from the lungs depends mainly on the passive recoil of elastic tension built up in the lungs and chest during inspiration. Some lung expansion is produced by the intercostal muscles, which lie in the space between the ribs and can actively raise or lower the ribs. As the lungs compress and expand, the pressure within also rises and falls in relation to the outside atmospheric pressure. The pleural sacs are at a pressure below that of the outside atmosphere. This ensures that when the chest expands or the diaphragm muscle descends, the lungs are also expanded as air flows in to equalize the pressure.

To reach the lungs, air must flow through the mouth or nose, pharynx, larynx, trachea and main bronchi. The walls of the windpipe (trachea), the main, lobar and smaller bronchi are strengthened by the presence of cartilage either as incomplete rings around the airway (as in the trachea and main bronchi) or as large plates (as in the finer divisions of the bronchi). Air reaches the lungs via the two main bronchi entering at the hilum of each lung. There the bronchi divide repeatedly, as many as 23 times, into finer and finer divisions (bronchioles), until the tiny air sacs known as alveoli are reached.

The inner surfaces of the larger airways are lined with special cell types. Some of these cells produce mucus to trap inhaled debris and bacteria, while others have fine hairs, called cilia, on their surfaces which beat rhythmically towards the larynx, thus wafting the debris towards the throat, where it may be swallowed or coughed up as sputum. In the air passages, particularly concentrated towards the alveoli, are scavenger cells called macrophages, which clean up debris and defend against invasion by bacteria. The inner surfaces of the alveoli are covered with a thin film of fluid, which contains a special chemical known as pulmonary surfactant. The surfactant helps to reduce the surface tension in the alveoli and thus prevent the tiny air sacs from collapsing when air is breathed out.

Gas exchange

The alveoli are the sites where gas exchange between blood and inhaled air occurs. The walls of the alveoli are extremely thin—less than a few ten-thousandths of an inch (hundredth of a millimeter) thick, and are richly supplied with thin-walled capillaries, filled with blood. Venous blood from the right side of the heart, which has relatively high levels of carbon dioxide and low levels of oxygen, flows through the lung's capillaries. As it does so, carbon dioxide in the blood diffuses into the air spaces of the alveoli, and oxygen diffuses from the air spaces to the blood.

Oxygen entering the blood is bound to a protein called hemoglobin in the red blood cells. Hemoglobin contains another type of chemical called the heme group. It also contains several bound iron atoms, each within a heme group, which assist with the transport of oxygen. Hemoglobin is the chemical that gives blood its red color.

Gas exchange in the lungs is most effective at sea level and is driven by the pressure difference for that particular gas between the alveolar air and the blood. At higher altitudes the partial pressure of oxygen in the air is lower, so that oxygen loading of hemoglobin may not be complete. People traveling from low to high altitude within a few hours will experience shortness of breath and be easily fatigued. In a healthy person, these symptoms will disappear after a few days to weeks as the body acclimatizes to the changed conditions.

Diseases of the lungs

Asthma is a very common lung disease characterized by recurrent attacks of wheezing due to obstruction of the airways. The airway obstruction arises because of a combination of spasms in the smooth muscle of the airway and excessive amounts of secretions in the airways. The underlying problem seems to be hyper-reactivity of the bronchial tree to a variety of inhaled stimuli. These stimuli include the house dust mite (*Dermatophagoides*), flower and grass pollens, feathers, animal dander, some drugs, foods, cold air, exercise, infection and wood dust.

Another important group of lung diseases in Western countries is chronic obstructive pulmonary disease (COPD). There are two serious diseases within this classification: chronic bronchitis and emphysema, which can occur together.

Chronic bronchitis is characterized by cough and sputum production, occurring on most days during at least three consecutive months for more than two successive years. The sputum may contain just mucus or may include some pus in it if additional infection is present. Chronic bronchitis is more likely to be found in people who smoke.

Emphysema often accompanies chronic bronchitis. Whereas chronic bronchitis mainly involves the larger airways, emphysema involves the destruction of very fine airways and alveoli. This is caused by a combination of repeated infection, tissue

Lungs

The lungs are divided into lobes. The left lung has only two lobes and is smaller than the right lung as the heart and its vessels take up more space in the left side of the chest. The trachea carries inhaled air down into the bronchial tree within the lungs, where oxygen and carbon dioxide are exchanged.

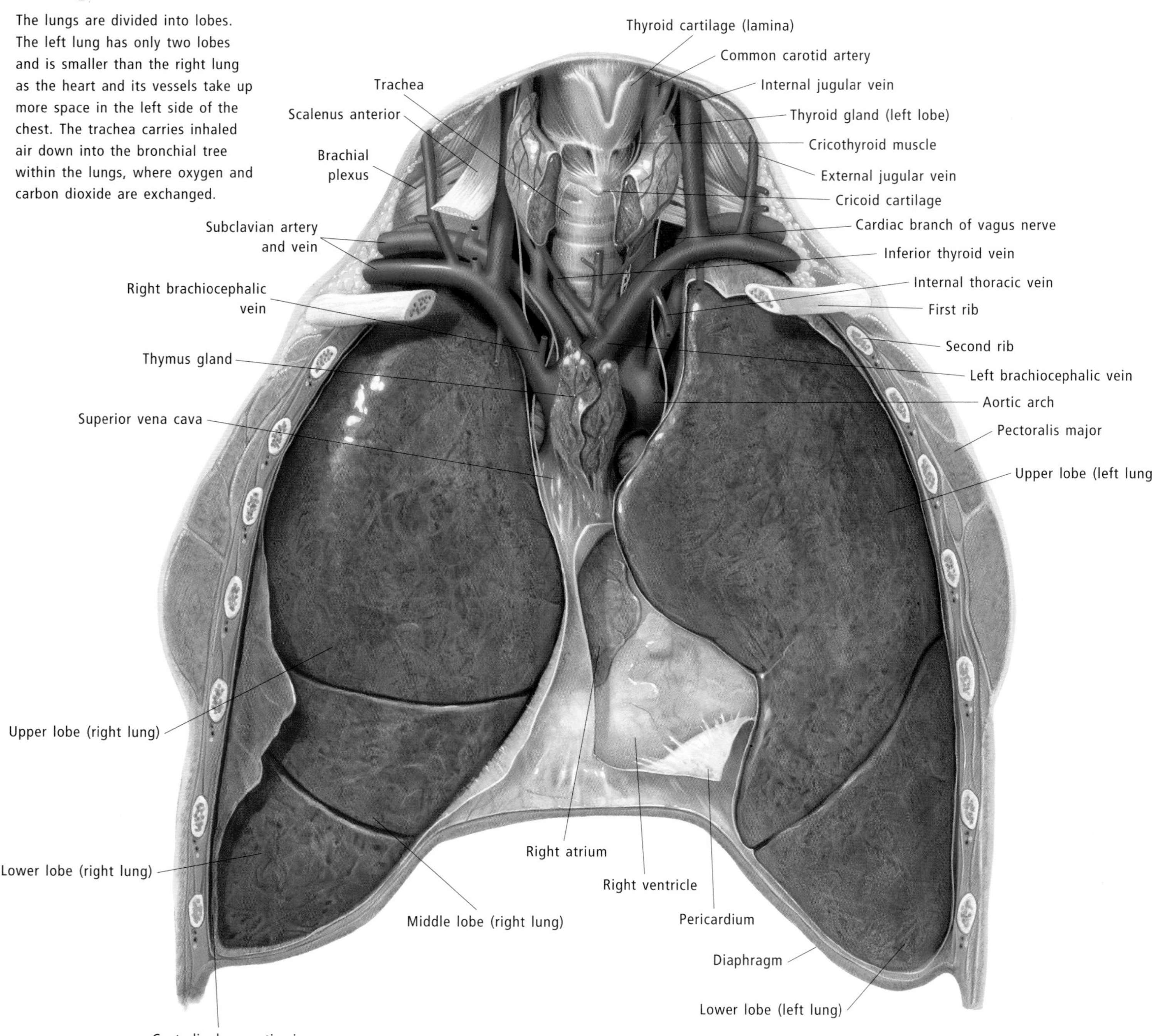

degeneration and over-distension of alveoli due to obstruction of the larger airways in chronic bronchitis.

Infections of the lung are of many different types and are named according to the lung sites affected. Bronchitis is infection of the large airways by bacteria and may follow viral infections of the upper respiratory tract. Bronchiolitis is infection of the finer airways (bronchioles) in infants and is usually due to respiratory syncytial virus. Bronchiectasis is the dilation of the large airways with the accumulation of secretions and chronic infection. The disease is usually seen in childhood. The incidence of bronchiectasis has declined considerably since the introduction of antibiotics, but is still seen in cystic fibrosis, congenital immune system deficiency, and after measles and whooping cough. Pulmonary tuberculosis is due to infection of the lung by mycobacteria. Tuberculosis is now much rarer than in the nineteenth century, but is still a serious public health problem.

Tumors or cancers of the lung most commonly arise from cells lining the large airways (bronchial carcinoma). There is little doubt that many bronchial carcinomas are caused by smoking. Nicotine does not by itself cause cancer, although it is very addictive and toxic to airway cells in other ways.

Lungs

The lungs are the two main organs of the respiratory system, lying on either side of the heart within the chest cavity. The trachea and a network of tubes (the bronchial tree) supply the lungs with air. Alveoli, tiny sacs at the end of the bronchioles, transfer oxygen from the air into the bloodstream.

NB: In this illustration the top two-thirds of the lungs and pleura have been cut away to show the heart and the bronchial tree.

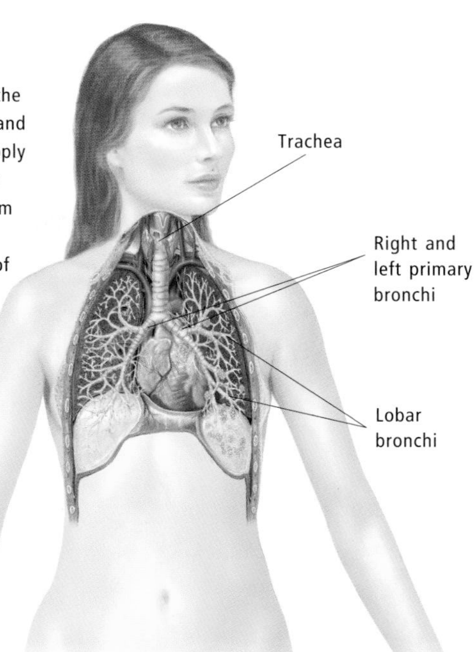

Lungs at rest

Breathing

When we breathe in, the intercostal muscles move the ribs upwards and outwards and the diaphragm pushes downwards. This draws air into the expanded lungs.

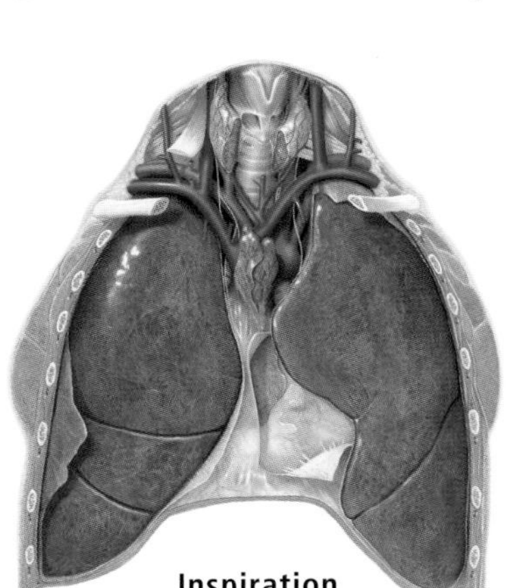
Inspiration

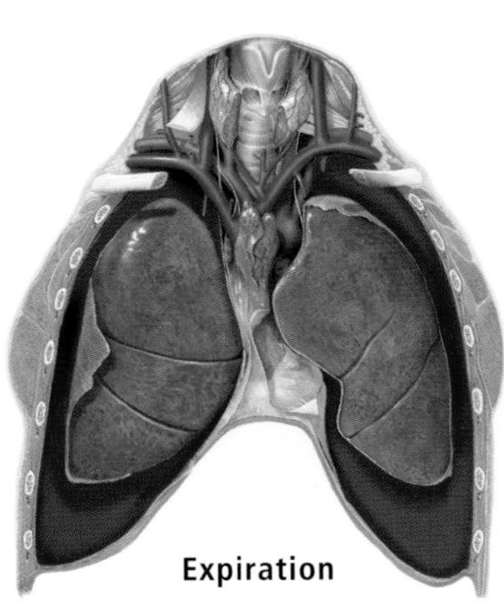
Expiration

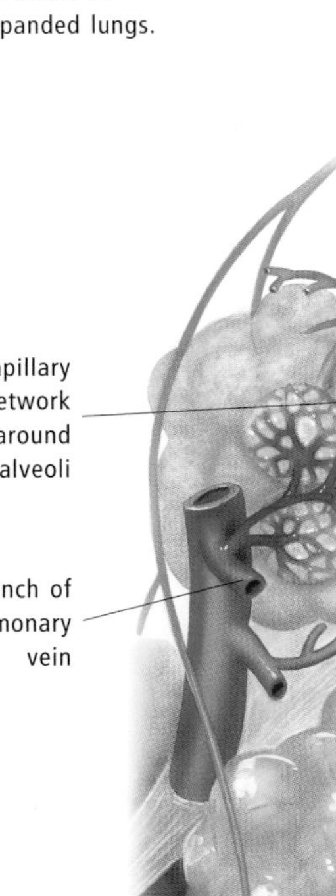

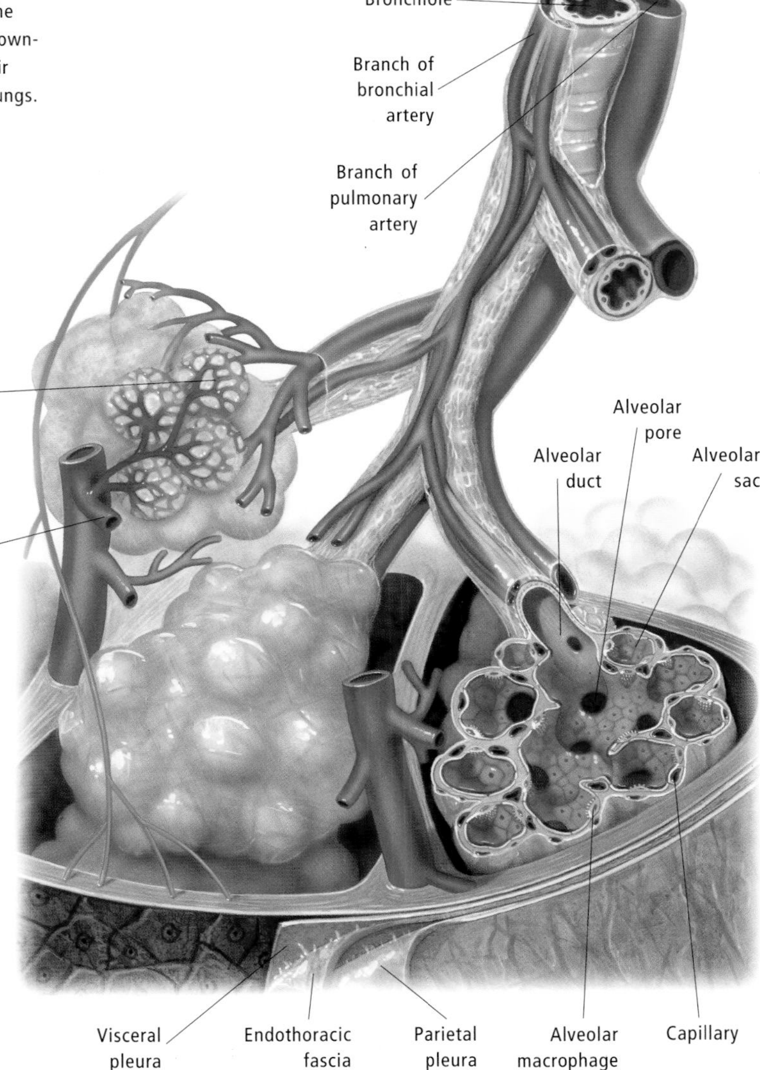

Lung function—gas exchange

The lungs contain millions of tiny air sacs (alveoli) which are located at the ends of the branches of the bronchial tree. The alveolar walls are extremely thin and coated with capillaries. This allows oxygen to pass into the blood from inhaled air and carbon monoxide to pass from the blood to the alveoli so it can be exhaled.

Other contributing factors are atmospheric pollution and the inhalation of uranium or asbestos during mining, although these are of small significance compared to smoking.

Occupational lung diseases are a varied group of disorders caused by exposure to dusts, gases or fumes. The largest group are the pneumoconioses, which are caused by prolonged inhalation of inorganic dusts such as coal dust, silica and asbestos. Asbestosis is a particularly serious form, because asbestos fibers can cause both fibrosis of the lung and cancer of the pleural sac (mesothelioma) and lung (bronchial carcinoma).

Another important occupational lung disease is extrinsic allergic alveolitis, caused by inhalation of organic dust which produces an allergic reaction in the lung (for example, "farmer's lung", due to moldy hay; "bird fancier's lung", due to pigeon and budgerigar droppings; and "malt worker's lung", due to moldy barley and malt).

Other occupational respiratory conditions include occupational asthma, in which dusts and fumes cause constriction of the airways within a few minutes to hours of exposure (for example, cedar dust asthma among carpenters), and toxic reactions to irritant gases like chlorine.

Trauma may also cause lung problems. Pneumothorax, where air at atmospheric pressure enters the normally airtight pleural cavity surrounding the lung, is one example. It may follow a penetrating injury to the chest or rupture of a lung airspace following blast injury. The lung of the affected side collapses, making lung ventilation impossible.

Some lung disorders are inherited. The best-known example is cystic fibrosis, a genetic disorder affecting one in every 2,500 live births.

Some lung problems arise because of disease of other organs. One example is pulmonary edema, which is the accumulation of fluid in the lower lungs due to failure of the heart to pump blood effectively.

SEE ALSO *Asbestosis, Asthma, Breathing, Bronchitis, Bronchoscopy, Cystic fibrosis, Emphysema, Farmer's lung, Lung cancer, Pneumothorax, Pulmonary function tests, Respiratory system, Smoking, Tuberculosis*

Lungs and heart

Pleural sacs around the lungs provide a smooth, low friction surface, allowing the lungs to inflate and deflate freely within the chest. Here the front of the lungs has been cut away to show the organs of the mediastinum—the heart, trachea and blood vessels.

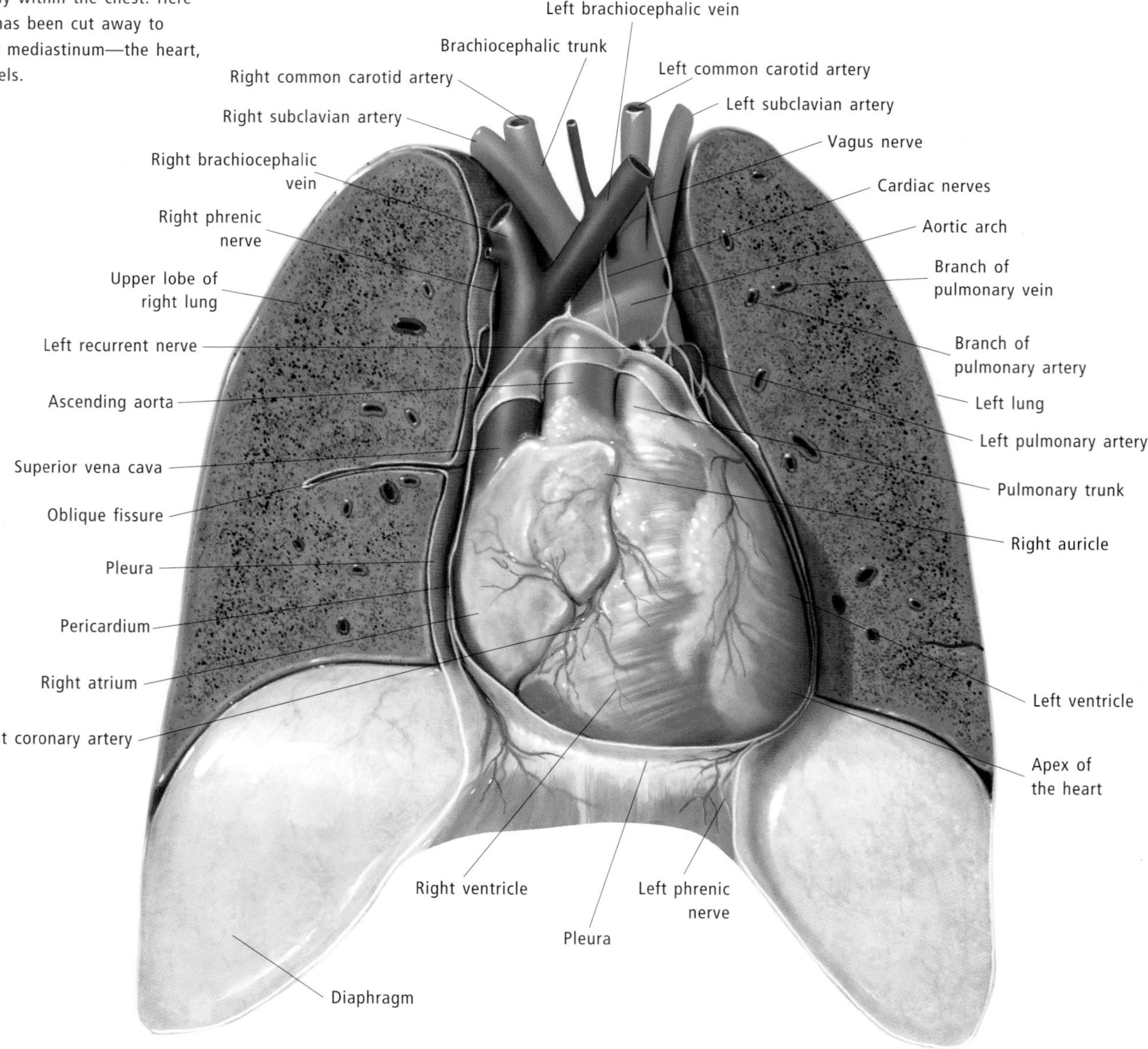

LUPUS ERYTHEMATOSUS

Lupus erythematosus is an autoimmune connective tissue disease in which the body's immune system attacks its own tissues. There are two forms: discoid lupus erythematosus (DLE), which affects only the skin, and systemic lupus erythematosus (SLE), which attacks joints and internal organs as well as the skin.

DLE is a chronic skin disorder that occurs most commonly in middle-aged women. It produces thickened, reddish patches on the face, cheeks and forehead. Sunlight makes the condition worse, so patients with DLE should wear hats and sunscreen to protect their skin. Corticosteroid skin creams are helpful. In severe cases, the antimalarial drug hydroxychloroquine may be beneficial.

In SLE, not only is the skin involved (in a similar way to DLE) but other organs are involved too. Generalized symptoms of fever, fatigue, weight loss and nausea are common. Arthritis usually develops in the fingers, hands, wrists and knees. A malar (butterfly-shaped) rash over the cheeks and bridge of the nose is a characteristic feature and may be made worse by sunlight. There may also be kidney, nervous system, blood, heart and lung damage.

No cure exists for SLE, but symptoms can be treated. Nonsteroidal anti-inflammatory medications (NSAIDs) are used in mild cases to treat arthritis. Corticosteroid creams are used to treat skin rashes. Antimalarial drugs (hydroxychloroquine) are sometimes prescribed for skin and arthritis symptoms. Severe or life-threatening cases may require the use of corticosteroid therapy, immunosuppressants (medications to suppress the immune system) or cytotoxic drugs, which block cell growth.

SEE ALSO *Autoimmune diseases*

LYME DISEASE

A multisystemic recurrent inflammatory disease, Lyme disease (also known as Lyme borreliosis or Lyme arthritis) is transmitted by tick bite, with symptoms ranging from skin lesions to chronic arthritis. It is caused by a corkscrew-shaped bacterium or spirochete called *Borrelia burgdorferi* which ticks, especially the *Ixodes* variety, collect from the bodies of white-footed field mice and other rodents. The ticks are dispersed by deer and migratory birds.

First documented in Europe in the 1880s as a skin rash, the full arthritic disease was named in the 1970s when a group of mothers from three towns in southeastern Connecticut—including Lyme and Old Lyme—became aware that their children all suffered from what was thought to be rheumatoid arthritis. The condition has now been reported in many other countries around the world.

Lyme disease is difficult to diagnose due to the variety of symptoms, which are similar to those seen in many other disorders, and to the fact that most sufferers do not recall the tick bite. The most recognizable symptom is a rash which may have concentric red rings and is accompanied by chills and fatigue. Days to weeks afterwards, there may be joint pain and problems with the nervous system or heart, and up to a year later skin disorders, arthritis and neurological problems such as facial palsy may appear.

Treatment with antibiotics in the early stages may prevent these later symptoms. However, if the disease has progressed, long-term treatment (including several weeks of intravenous antibiotics) may be necessary.

People living, traveling or working in tick-infested areas should wear light-colored long-sleeved shirts, long pants, socks, closed shoes, and a hat; tick repellent is also advisable.

SEE ALSO *Ticks*

LYMPH

The body's tissues are bathed in an almost-clear liquid called interstitial fluid, which filters out from blood vessels. It is collected (along with tissue and cellular wastes), drained away, cleaned in lymph nodes and

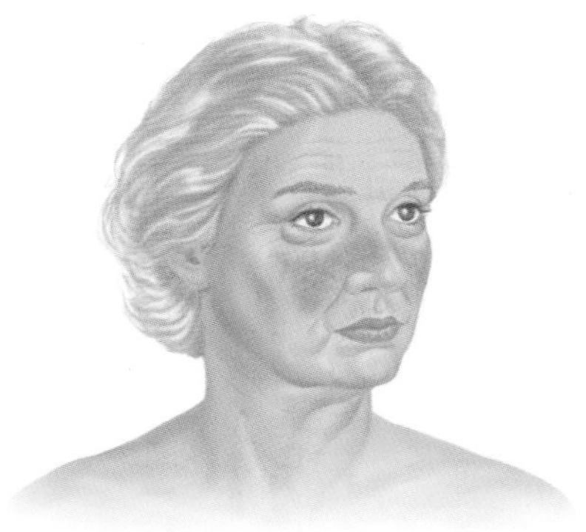

Lupus erythematosus

The body's immune system attacks its own tissues in this disease, producing a distinctive red rash on the face. Middle-aged women are most commonly affected.

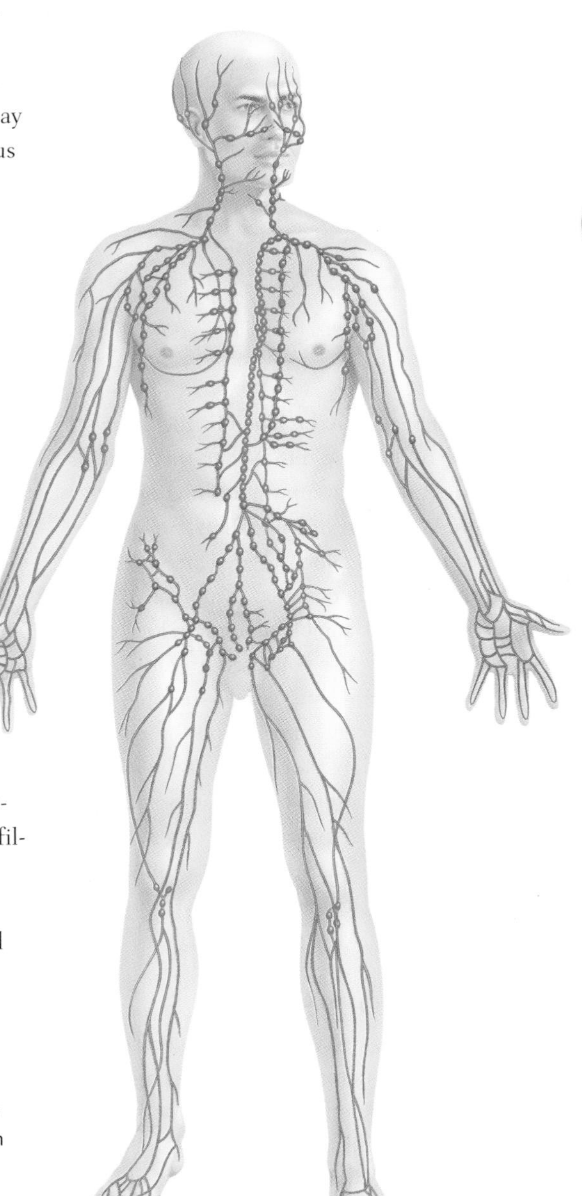

Lymph transport

Lymph fluid passes round the body via a network of transparent lymph vessels, known as the lymphatic system. Lymph is transported from tissues, filtered in the lymph nodes and then returned to the blood.

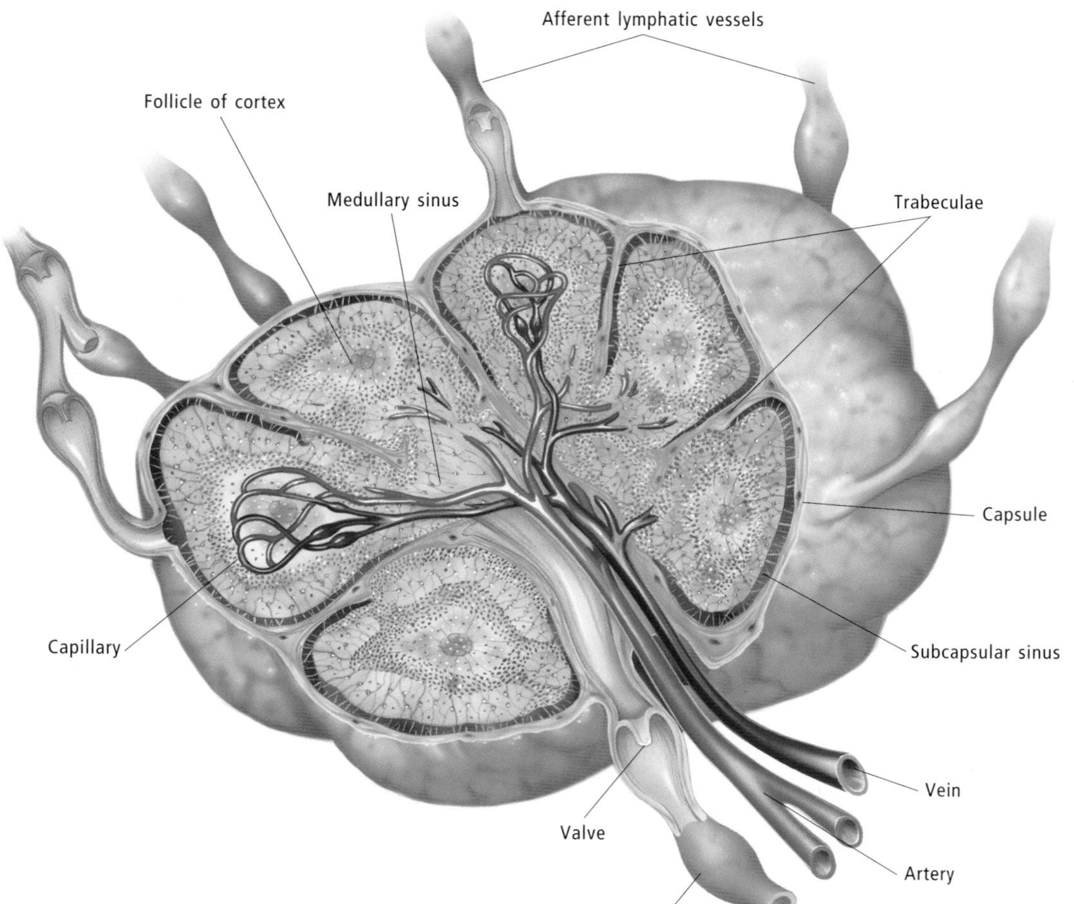

Lymph nodes

Lymph fluid is filtered and cleaned by white blood cells in the lymph nodes or glands. The nodes cluster in groups along the lymphatic vessels. Each node is enclosed in a fibrous capsule and has compartments divided by partitions of collagen fibers (trabeculae). Afferent lymphatic vessels bring lymph fluid to the node from surrounding tissues; efferent vessels transport lymph to the veins.

Lymphatic vessel

Numerous valves prevent the backflow of lymph as it passes through the lymphatic vessels. Blockage of the vessels can cause a buildup of lymph fluid, which may result in swelling of body parts.

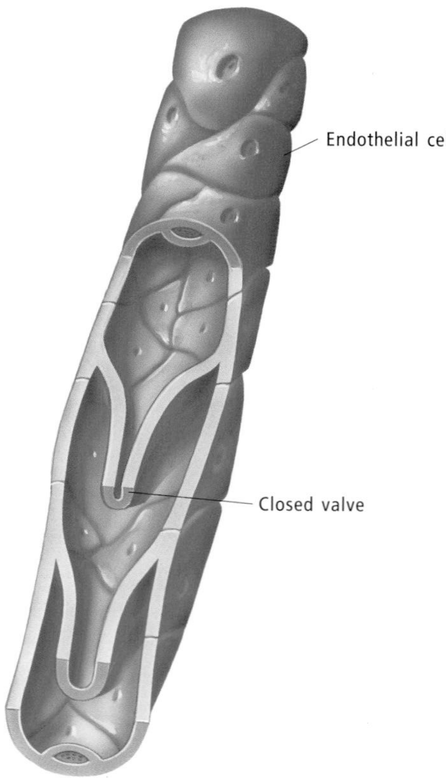

recycled back into the blood by the vessels of the lymphatic system. When this liquid is flowing through lymph vessels it is called lymph. It contains mainly water, protein molecules, salts, glucose, urea and disease-fighting white blood cells. Lymph also carries, en route to the blood, certain fats and fat-soluble vitamins collected from the digestive tract. The lymphatic system has no pump. The movement of lymph through the body is assisted by the actions of the skeletal muscle and breathing contractions and is slower than the movement of blood.

SEE ALSO *Lymphatic vessels, Lymphatic/Immune system, Lymph nodes*

LYMPH NODES

Lymph nodes, also called lymph glands, are nodular structures occurring along the course of the lymphatic vessels. They are composed of cells of the immune system, mainly lymphocytes. When foreign substances, such as bacteria, enter the body's tissues, they are conveyed via the lymphatic vessels to the regional lymph nodes. It is here that the body's immune system mounts the first defense against infection.

Normal lymph nodes are generally up to about ¾ inch (2 centimeters) in diameter, and can be felt under the skin in thin people. They are located on both sides of the neck, in the armpits and groin area, as well as in the internal body cavities. During a reaction to infection, the cells within a lymph node multiply and the node becomes enlarged and painful. Lymph nodes can also enlarge when tumor cells grow there. This occurs most often when cancers spread to regional nodes but may also occur in tumors arising in nodes—these are known as lymphomas.

If enlargement of the lymph nodes is detected and this persists without any apparent cause, a lymph node biopsy is performed to obtain cells for the pathologist to examine under the microscope. The biopsy can be performed either surgically or using a fine needle.

SEE ALSO *Lymphatic/Immune system, Lymphatic vessels, Lymphoma*

LYMPHATIC VESSELS

Lymphatic vessels form a parallel circulation to the veins and arteries throughout the body. Lymphatic capillaries drain fluid that has oozed out of capillaries into body tissues. The fluid, called lymph, is conveyed through larger lymphatics to regional lymph nodes. In the lymph nodes, the cells of the immune system can respond against invading bacteria or can ingest foreign particles, such as tattoo dyes. The protein-rich lymph is then channeled to the upper part of the chest cavity, where it passes through the thoracic duct to re-enter the venous circulation. Lymph from the intestinal tissues has a creamy color, due to absorbed fats.

The blockage or disruption of lymphatic vessels can result in the accumulation of lymph—this is known as lymphedema. Occasionally this occurs asthe result of hereditary underdevelopment of the lymphatic vessels. More often it is a consequence of repeated infection spreading to the lymphatics (lymphangitis), damage from tumors, or damage caused by the treatment of tumors. For example, surgery to remove lymph glands in the armpit involved by breast cancer can result in lymphedema of that arm.

Worldwide, blockage by filarial worms is the commonest cause of lymphedema, which may be so severe it results in elephantiasis. Treatment of lymphedema includes skin care, preventive antibiotics, elevation and compression of the affected limb and, more recently, microsurgery.

SEE ALSO ***Elephantiasis, Filariasis, Lymph, Lymph glands***

LYMPHOCYTES

Lymphocytes are one of the major white cell types in the body and are the main cells responsible for our immunity. They circulate in the blood and are also found in the organs of the immune system—the lymph nodes and spleen. Several types of lymphocytes are now recognized. Most of the lymphocytes in the blood are T cells, which help the body fight certain difficult infections and also cancers. These are the cells ravaged by the AIDS virus, which leaves sufferers prone to opportunistic infections. The other main type of lymphocyte is the B cell, which produces antibodies to help fight bacteria and viruses.

SEE ALSO ***Lymphatic/Immune system, Spleen, T cells, White blood cells***

LYMPHOGRANULOMA VENEREUM

Lymphogranuloma venereum (also called LGV, lymphogranuloma inguinale, climatic bubo or Nicolas-Favre disease) is a sexually transmitted disease common in tropical areas and spread by unprotected sexual intercourse. It is caused by the bacterium *Chlamydia trachomatis* and develops between 3–12 days after contact with the infection.

First symptoms are a small painless blister on the penis or in the vagina, which may become an ulcer and heal without being noticed. Lymph glands then become swollen and tender and may develop sinuses—openings to the skin surface which discharge fluid. Fever, headaches and joint pains may develop without treatment, which is normally the antibiotic tetracycline or, in pregnant women, erythromycin.

SEE ALSO ***Granuloma inguinale, Sexually transmitted diseases***

Lymphocytes

Essential to the functioning of the body's immune system, lymphocytes are a type of white blood cell. Found in lymph, lymphatic tissue and the blood, they identify and destroy invading bacteria and viruses.

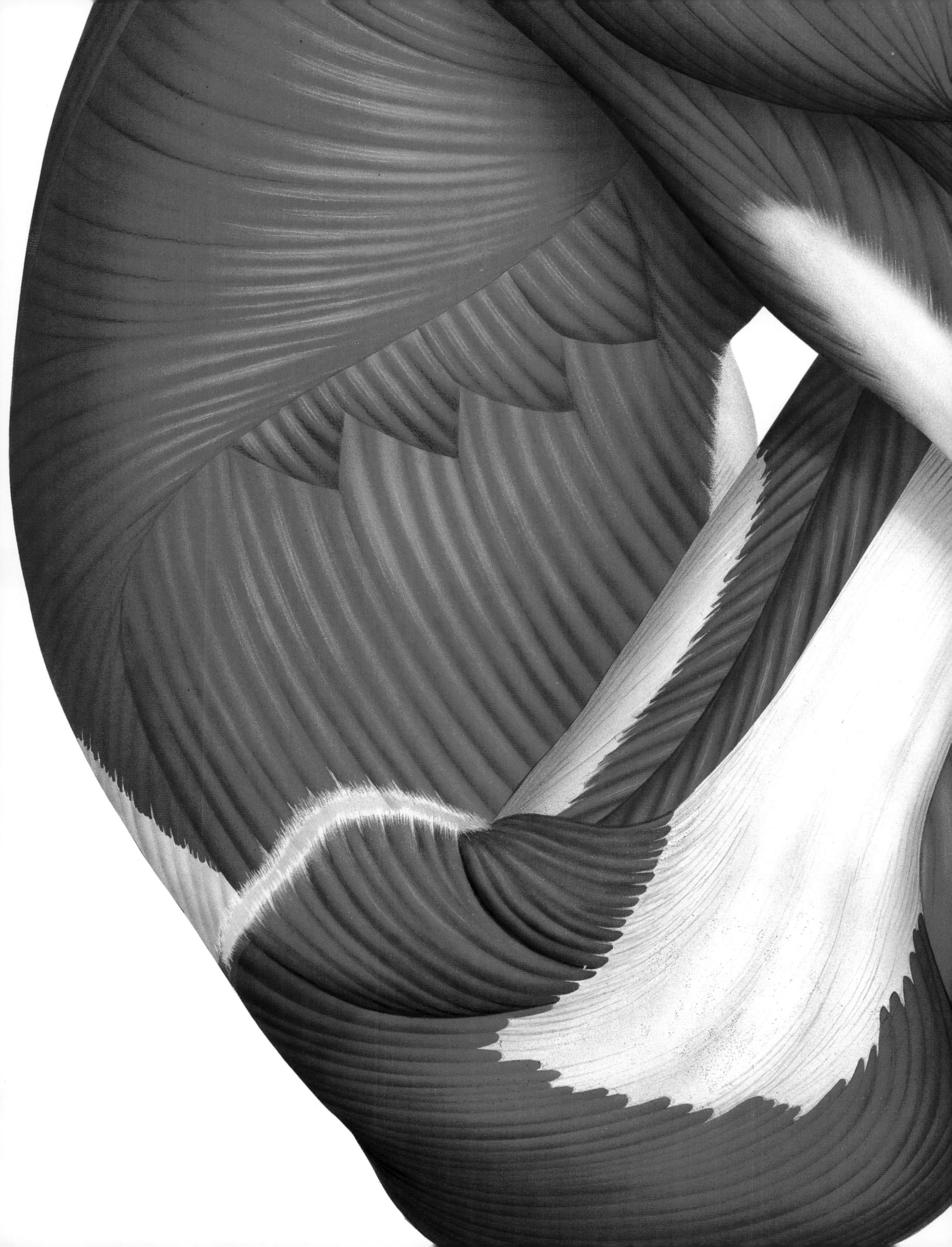

M

MACULAR DEGENERATION

A condition of the macula in which impaired blood supply causes gradual vision loss. The macula is the area on the retina that provides fine visual acuity, used in driving, reading, watching television or activities that require focusing on very small objects. The disorder results in the loss of central vision only; peripheral visual fields are always maintained. It usually develops over a long period, often going unnoticed in its early stages. The cause is often not known.

Macular degeneration is one of the leading causes of blindness in Western countries and is common in the elderly. There is no treatment; though laser surgery in some cases can slow the progression of the disease.

SEE ALSO *Blindness, Eye, Retina*

MAGNETIC RESONANCE IMAGING

Magnetic resonance imaging (MRI) is a non-invasive procedure used for imaging tissues that have a high water and fat content. MRI uses an external magnetic field created by a series of powerful electromagnets in a scanner to excite hydrogen atoms in the body, which give off radio signals to the scanner. These signals are read by a computer and converted into a detailed image. Because it uses a magnetic field instead of x-rays, MRI scanning does not expose people to radiation.

During an MRI, the patient lies on a table that slides into a cylindrically shaped machine, and must remain motionless for up to 90 minutes. The test is painless but noisy, and can cause claustrophobia in some people; a mild sedative can relieve the anxiety.

SEE ALSO *CAT scan, Imaging techniques, Ultrasound, X-ray*

MALARIA

Malaria is a tropical febrile illness caused by the protozoan parasite *Plasmodium*, transmitted to animals and humans by the *Anopheles* mosquito. There are four varieties of the parasite, the most common being *Plasmodium vivax*, followed by *P. falciparum* (which causes malignant or cerebral malaria), and then *P. malariae* and *P. ovale*. Usually two weeks after a bite by an infected mosquito, the patient develops violent chills and shivering, high fever and drenching sweats. Headache, muscle pains, cough and diarrhea may all occur. *P. falciparum* may also produce "blackwater" (dark urine) from the massive breakdown of red blood cells and the excretion in the urine of the blood pigment (hemoglobin).

Malaria causes over 1 million deaths yearly worldwide, especially from cerebral malaria due to *P. falciparum*. This type may progress rapidly, with confusion, convulsions and coma possibly leading to death within a day.

Diagnosis of malaria is made by the examination of blood films taken over three days. As malaria may not appear for between four weeks and several months after infection, tourists are advised to treat any unexplained fever on their return as potential malaria (or other possibile infections like dengue fever).

Many countries where malaria is common regularly spray insecticides to eliminate mosquitoes. As the mosquito needs water and animals to breed, malaria is not likely to be present in major cities and most holiday resorts. Even so, travellers should take precautions against being exposed to malaria and other diseases caused by mosquitoes. They should use mosquito repellent, especially at dawn and dusk, wear long sleeves and pants, wear light-colored clothing, avoid perfumes, perfumed soaps and deodorants, have mosquito nets on the beds, and use an insecticide coil in the room.

There are now kits for self-diagnosis and treatment. Travelers into malarial areas are advised to take prophylactic tablets such as doxycycline, chloroquine, primaquine or mefloquine. Unfortunately, resistance to these drugs is developing rapidly. For the treatment of an acute attack, quinine and artemisin-type drugs may be used together with combinations of the prophylactic drugs. Malaria, especially the *P. vivax* type, can become a chronic illness, recurring over many years.

SEE ALSO *Infectious diseases*

Macular degeneration

This condition involves the breakdown of the cells in the eye that allow the perception of detail. Those with macular degeneration can compensate for this partial loss of vision by using a magnifying glass.

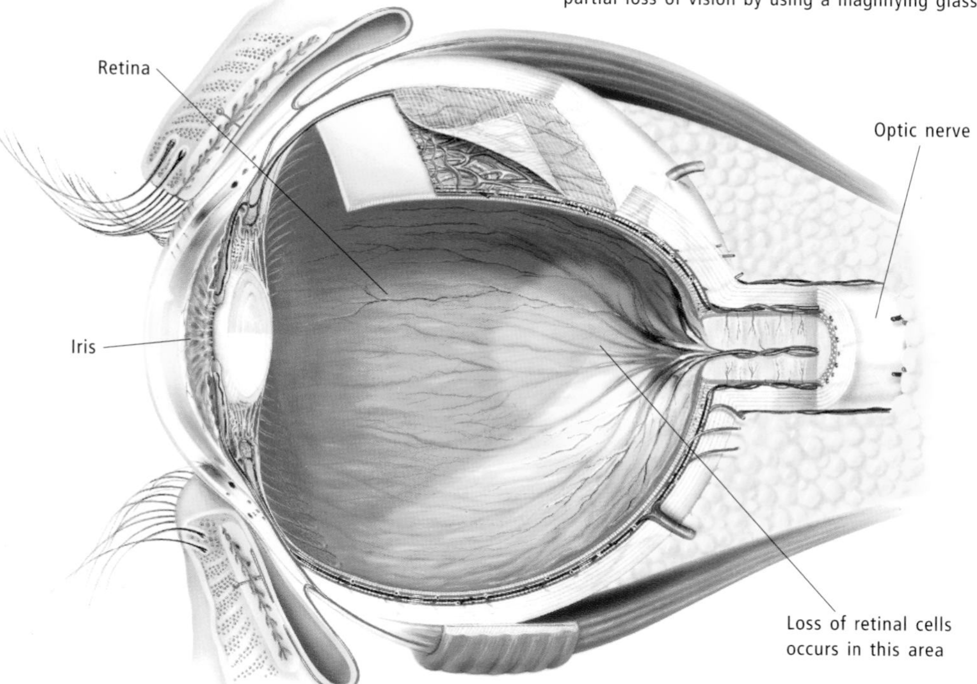

MALNUTRITION

Malnutrition is a condition caused by one of three types of dietary deficiency. Firstly, an inadequate intake of energy-producing food, such as carbohydrates, fats and proteins, which provide the calories needed for work. Secondly, inadequate intake of tissue-building food, particularly protein, especially in children and after illness. Thirdly, an inadequate intake of vitamins and minerals, needed for health.

Malnutrition is normally taken to refer to inadequate intake, but excessive intake is also a problem, leading to nutritional disorders such as obesity and heart disease.

Nutritional disorders can arise from, for example, defective intake of food (starvation); defective digestion and absorption (malabsorption syndrome); defective utilization of nutriment (such as cancer, which in later stages produces wasting); and loss of nutrients from the body (for example, nephrotic syndrome, where protein is lost in the urine).

Severe malnutrition is manifested by loss of body weight, particularly fat and muscle, together with the symptoms of associated vitamin deficiencies such as rickets and scurvy. Iron deficiency leads to anemia, and copper deficiency is believed to be an important contributory cause of heart disease.

Malnutrition is an economic and social problem affecting a large proportion of humanity. Even in regions where sufficient food is available for purchase, nutritional disorders may occur because of poverty, prejudice and ignorance. Malnutrition can also be associated with alcoholism.

SEE ALSO *Eating disorders, Minerals, Nutrition, Pellagra, Rickets, Scurvy, Vitamins*

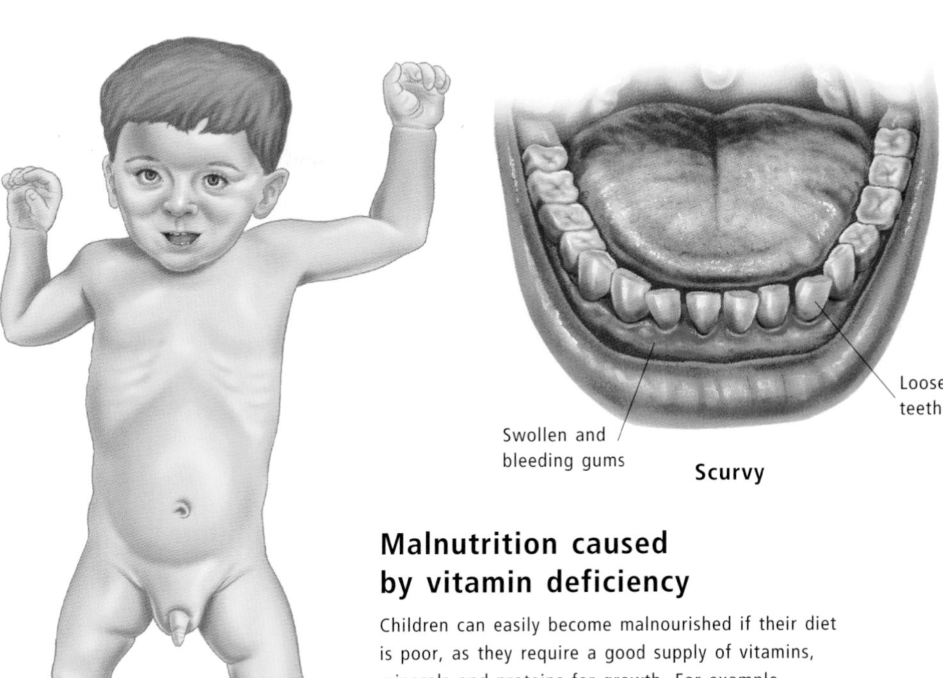

Malnutrition caused by vitamin deficiency

Children can easily become malnourished if their diet is poor, as they require a good supply of vitamins, minerals and proteins for growth. For example, a child lacking vitamin D may have weakened or deformed bones (rickets). Scurvy, which is caused by a lack of vitamin C in the body, can cause gums to swell and bleed, and teeth to become loose.

MALOCCLUSION

Ideally, with the mouth closed, the middle lower teeth should abut against the back of the middle upper teeth. Any deviation of the teeth forwards, backwards or sideways will produce malocclusion. Although usually a problem with growing children—particularly if the teeth are too large for a small mouth—adults who have teeth removed from one side of the mouth may find that the remaining teeth drift sideways towards the gap and result in malocclusion. Other causes include unbalanced contractions of the muscles responsible for chewing, and prolonged thumb sucking. Tooth decay, inability to chew properly and tension headaches can all result.

Treatment is provided by orthodontists who, by bracing or banding the teeth and applying gentle but prolonged pressure, eventually straighten the teeth. In older children and adults, wisdom teeth must occasionally be removed to allow adequate room for the remaining teeth.

SEE ALSO *Braces, Orthodontics, Teeth*

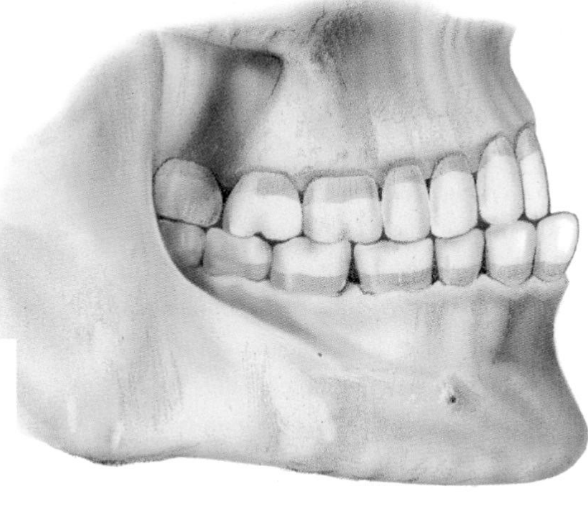

Malocclusion (underbite)

When the mandible (lower jaw) juts out further than it should, the teeth become misaligned and malocclusion occurs.

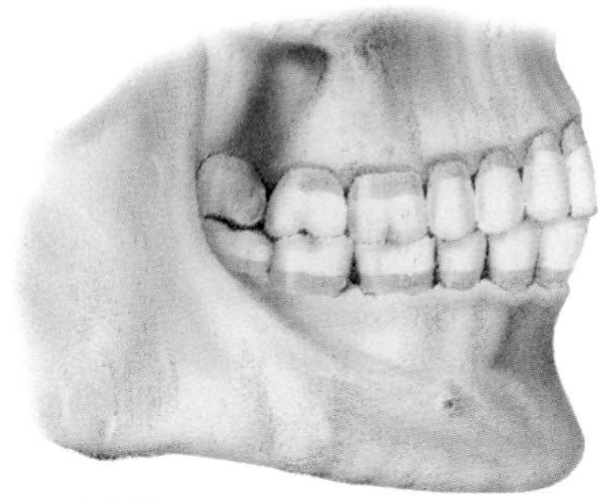

Normal bite

When teeth are correctly positioned, the middle lower teeth should abut against the back of the middle upper teeth.

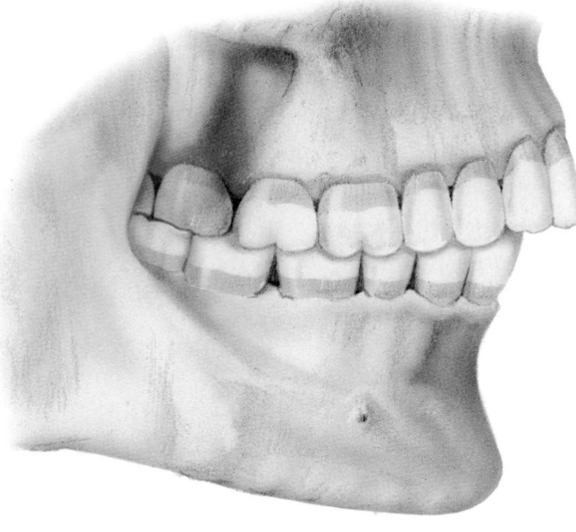

Malocclusion (overbite)

When the maxilla (upper jaw) protrudes over the mandible (lower jaw), or in some cases when the mandible is underdeveloped, an overbite malocclusion occurs.

M

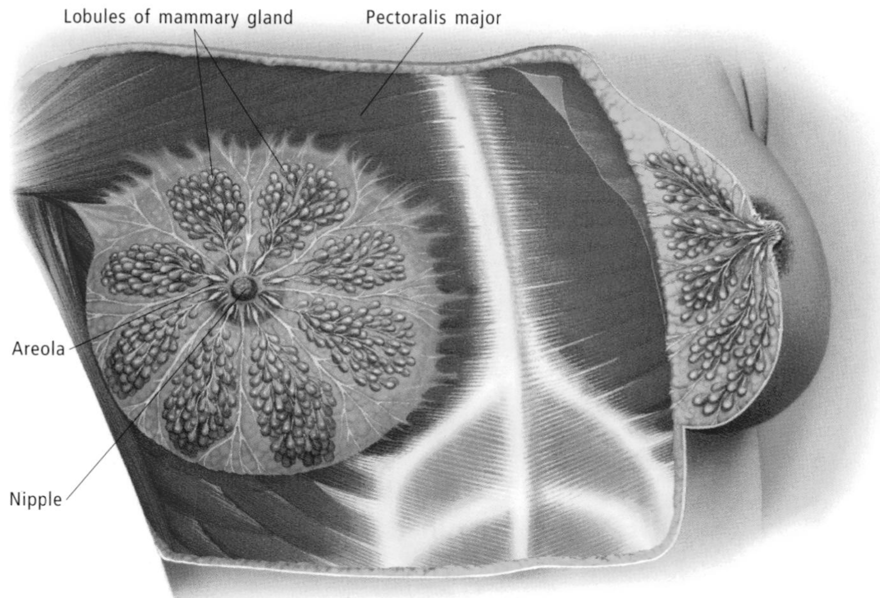

Mammary glands

In women, the hormones secreted during and after pregnancy stimulate the mammary glands to produce milk.

MAMMARY GLANDS

Mammary glands, or breasts, are modified sweat glands and are present in all mammals. They develop in the embryo along two narrow elongated regions (milk lines) extending from the armpit (axilla) to the groin. In humans a single pair of mammary glands develops under the skin of the upper chest although it is not uncommon for rudimentary extra mammary glands to develop elsewhere in the milk line.

Female mammary glands undergo considerable changes during the individual's life. At birth the mammary glands of both sexes are alike, consisting of a limited amount of glandular tissue leading into 15–20 openings in the nipple (some domestic animals have only one opening into the nipple). There is little fat or fibrous tissue. Some temporary secretory activity, traditionally known as witch's milk, may occur briefly just after birth under the influence of placental hormones.

After puberty, development involves elevation and pigmentation of the nipple and a considerable increase in fat and fibrous tissue. There is also some proliferation of the glandular tissue. Transient changes such as swelling may occur towards the end of each menstrual cycle.

During pregnancy, under the influence of placental hormones, there is a decrease in the amount of fat and fibrous tissue and an enormous increase in the amount and complexity of the glandular components. During the third trimester a liquid called colostrum is secreted. Colostrum contains milk fat and immunoglobulins but few nutrients. It continues to be secreted for the first few days after birth and then is followed by the production of true milk, induced by a lactation-stimulating hormone, prolactin.

Release of milk from the mammary glands is controlled by another pituitary hormone, oxytocin. Breast milk is rich in lactose, protein, calcium and fat, and also contains vitamins and immunoglobulins. Lactation can continue for several years if suckling is maintained. After weaning, most of the glandular tissue breaks down and is replaced by increased amounts of fat and fibrous tissue.

The glandular and fibrous components of mammary glands gradually decrease with age up to and after menopause, and there is an increased amount of fat. Fat is more translucent to x-rays which facilitates mammograms in older women.

The mammary glands in males have a similar structure throughout life to that of prepubescent females. Male mammary tissue is, however, sensitive to a variety of hormonal influences with temporary enlargement sometimes occurring at puberty and more permanent enlargement in ageing males. Considerable development may also accompany certain pituitary tumors which secrete excessive amounts of prolactin. Mammary enlargement in males or prepubescent girls is called gynecomastia.

SEE ALSO *Breast, Breast feeding, Colostrum, Estrogens, Menstruation, Oxytocin, Progesterone*

MAMMOGRAPHY

A mammogram is an x-ray picture of the breasts. It is used to detect tumors and cysts and help differentiate malignant (cancerous) tumors from benign (non-cancerous) ones. Any woman with breast symptoms such as a lump, nipple discharge, breast pain, dimpling of the skin on the breast, or a recent retraction of the nipple, should have a mammogram. Approximately 90–95 percent of breast cancers are detected with mammography. The test is also used to screen for breast cancer in women with no symptoms. The American Cancer Society recommends a screening mammogram around age 40; annually or every two years between the ages of 40 and 49; and every year thereafter.

SEE ALSO *Breast, Breast cancer*

MAMMOPLASTY

Mammoplasty is an operation to reconstruct a breast after removal of a tumor, or to change the size and shape of the breasts for cosmetic purposes.

Reduction mammoplasty involves reducing the size of the breasts and is commonly done to relieve pain and discomfort from enlarged breasts. A plastic surgeon removes some of the breast tissue together with excess skin under general anesthesia, and may relocate the nipples higher on the breasts. The operation can take up to six hours.

A breast uplift procedure is a shorter procedure in which skin is removed from a section of the breast; the areola, nipple, and underlying breast tissue are then moved up to a higher position.

Augmentation mammoplasty is an operation to increase breast size, shape and fullness. A plastic surgeon places breast implants—bags filled with saline or silicone gel—either above or below the pectoralis major muscle in the chest. The implant should last indefinitely, but if it leaks or ruptures, it can cause the formation of lumps in the breast. There is no evidence currently that breast implants cause autoimmune diseases.

Mammoplasty does not predispose a woman to breast cancer, and it should not interfere with normal breast feeding.

SEE ALSO *Breast, Cosmetic surgery, Plastic surgery*

MANIA

Mania is a form of mental disorder characterized by emotional excitement and lack of self-control and judgment, often resulting in impulsive, bizarre or violent behavior. Other symptoms include excessive euphoric feelings, a decreased need for sleep, an unrealistic belief in one's abilities and power, increased sexual drive and abuse of drugs (particularly cocaine, alcohol and sleeping medications).

Mania is one of the phases of bipolar disorder (manic-depressive illness), a psychiatric disorder characterized by severe swings in mood from mania to depression. An early sign of bipolar disorder may be hypomania, a mild form of mania in which the person shows a high energy level, excessive moodiness, and impulsive or reckless behavior.

Lithium-based drugs help to lessen the mood swings of bipolar disorder. They may be combined with an antidepressant. Certain anxiolytics or sedatives may be used where lithium therapy is not tolerated or effective.

SEE ALSO *Bipolar disorder, Depression*

MANTOUX TEST

The Mantoux test is a test for tuberculosis in which a solution made from dead tuberculosis bacteria is injected between the skin layers, usually on the forearm. If a slight swelling or redness develops at the site within two to three days, this indicates the presence of infection-fighting antibodies which in turn indicate a past or present infection with tuberculosis. Infections less than two weeks old may not show up with this test. Named after French physician Charles Mantoux, who developed the test in 1908, the Mantoux test is also known as a purified protein derivative (PPD) test.

SEE ALSO *Tuberculosis*

MANUAL LYMPH DRAINAGE

The technique of manual lymph drainage was pioneered in the 1930s by Danish therapists Astrid and Emil Vodder. This alternative therapy is a gentle pumping massage that claims to help the circulation of the lymph and its flow in the blood circulation. The massage rhythm is slow and only light pressure is used because the lymph vessels are close to the skin's surface.

The sequence of the massage through the body is crucial, since the therapist follows the flow of the lymphatic system. First the superficial lymphatic nodes are emptied with circular movements over the main lymph node of each section of the body (located in the neck, armpit, groin, knees and elbows). Then rhythmical pumping movements are performed up towards the nodes. The whole procedure takes around an hour.

Alternative therapists believe that manual lymphatic drainage will speed up the removal of waste products through the lymphatic system. They recommend it for the treatment of edema, acne, eczema and cellulitis, and to help reduce swelling and scarring resulting from injuries. This treatment may also be used for rheumatism or neurological disorders such as migraine or neuralgia. It is most commonly performed by massage therapists and naturopaths.

SEE ALSO *Lymph, Lymphatic/Immune system, Massage*

MARIJUANA

Marijuana (cannabis) is a drug derived from Indian hemp that is now in widespread—and mostly illegal—use in Western society. The dried leaves and flowers are used to make cigarettes, or the tarry resin (hashish) smoked in a pipe or eaten cooked in cakes or bread. Marijuana is a sedative-type drug which produces a euphoric or tranquilized state, and colors, sounds and pleasurable sensations may appear heightened. Motor abilities decrease, making driving unsafe. Early use during pre-adolescence may affect development of visual abilities and produce permanent attention disorders. Other effects may include arterial disease, even in adolescent users. Heavy or chronic use can lead to mental disorders and has been known to precipitate or worsen psychiatric conditions such as schizophrenia and panic attacks. Bronchitis is common in heavy smokers, and there is an increased risk of lung cancer as with cigarette smoking. Marijuana is used in some countries as a pain killer and anti-nausea drug, especially in cancer, where its use is strictly controlled.

SEE ALSO *Drug dependence*

MASSAGE

The practice of massage is as old as humankind, with many variations being found throughout the world. Chinese artifacts point to the practice of massage as far back as 3000 BC. An Indian Ayurvedic medical text written about 1800 BC describes how to rub and "shampoo" the body to aid its recovery after injury. In ancient Greece and Rome, massage was a principal method of medical treatment. The Greek physician Hippocrates wrote in 400 BC that "The physician must be experienced in many things, but assuredly in rubbing... for rubbing can bind a joint which is too loose and loosen a joint that is too hard".

After the collapse of the Roman Empire, massage fell out of favor in Europe as it was associated with the sinful pleasures of the flesh. It was not until the early nineteenth century that massage became more popular, due to the development of the Swedish massage technique by Per Henrik Ling, a medical professor and gymnastics instructor. Ling studied ancient Greek and Roman massage techniques as well as those from Asia where the use of massage was highly respected and well-developed. In Stockholm, massage studies were offered by a Western college for the first time in 1813. Massage was incorporated into other natural therapies that were being pioneered around this time, such as naturopathy, hydrotherapy and chiropractic.

Benefits of massage

Massage aims to work on both body and mind. On a physical level, massage generates a mechanical heat which has beneficial effects throughout the body. It is believed to relax the muscles and the central nervous system and stimulates sluggish body systems, aiding digestion and the elimination of waste products. Massage aims to reduce swelling, stimulate blood and lymph flow, soften skin and scar tissue and break down fibrous tissue around joints.

Emotionally, massage helps people to relax and feel "cared for", which relates back to the infant's instinctive need to be touched.

Techniques

Massage can vary from being a relaxing sensuous experience to a vigorous workout on the muscles. The more common forms of massage techniques include the following.

Stroking is used at the beginning of the massage to gently establish contact with the patient and to spread oil over the areas to be massaged.

Effleurage uses long, even strokes with steady pressure which increase warmth and circulation.

Massage

Massage—manipulation of parts of the body by rubbing, kneading or tapping—can relax muscles, stimulate blood flow, invigorate the skin and reduce stress.

Petrissage involves rolling and squeezing to loosen knotted muscle fibers; it may help to relieve muscle fatigue and release built-up toxins.

Kneading is used to relax and invigorate large areas of flesh not close to the bone.

Frictions are small circular movements made by the thumbs, fingers or heel of the hand which work on a deep level where there is a tension build-up.

Hacking is a light percussive chopping stroke, done with the side of the hands, that may increase circulation and stimulate the nerve endings.

Cupping is a percussive movement with a slightly cupped palm; it draws blood to the surface and is extremely invigorating.

Styles

There are a huge range of different massage styles available now throughout the world. The most common are the following.

Swedish massage

This is a system of soft tissue and muscle movement using stroking and pulling to relieve tension and relax bound muscle fibers. Swedish massage aims to loosen fibrous thickenings around the joints and to help the elimination of toxic and acidic deposits, and fatty accumulations. It is used in health spas and gyms to break up cellulite deposits before applying stronger stimulation using connective tissue massage and vibration. It is also often used by physical therapists, especially to restore blood circulation and limb movement to stroke patients or people confined to bed for long periods. In Swedish massage, fixed oils are used to reduce friction on the skin. Essential oils may also be used to give an aromatherapy massage.

Connective tissue massage

This is a vigorous massage involving strong upward stroking and pulling move

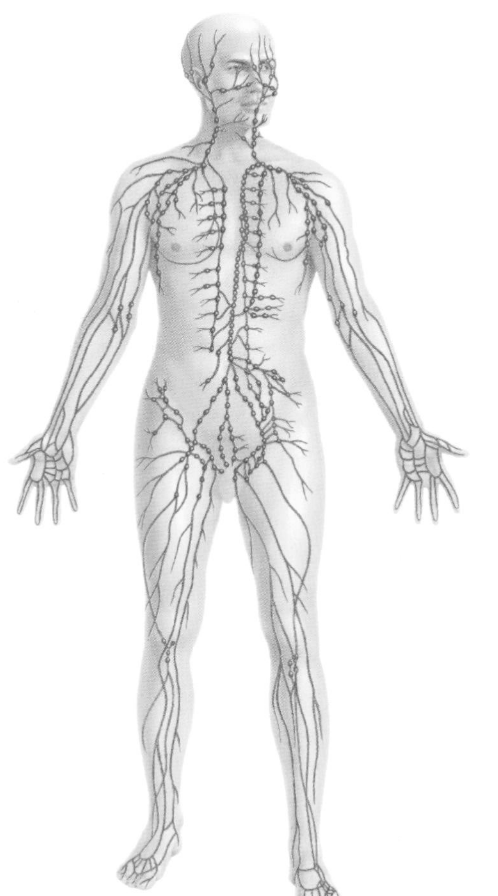

Lymphatic benefits

Massage can increase the flow of lymph in the body, improving circulation and reducing inflammation.

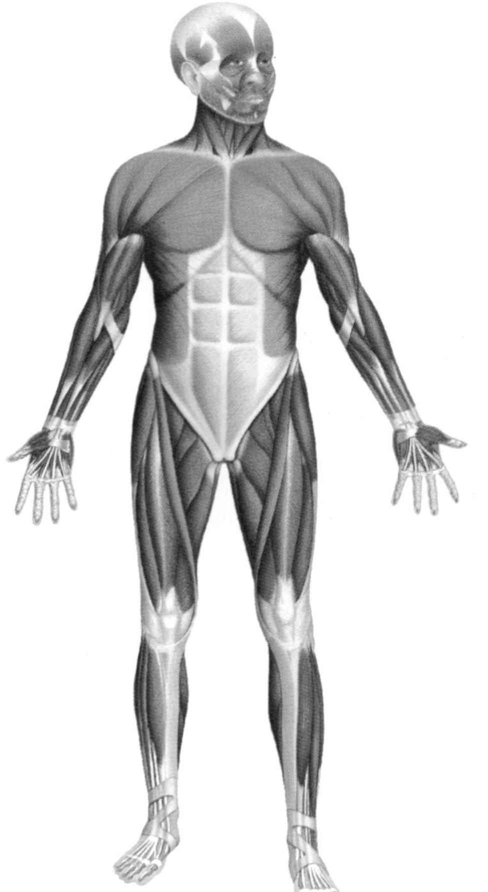

Muscular benefits

Tense or tight muscles all over the body can be relaxed, stretched and made more flexible with massage.

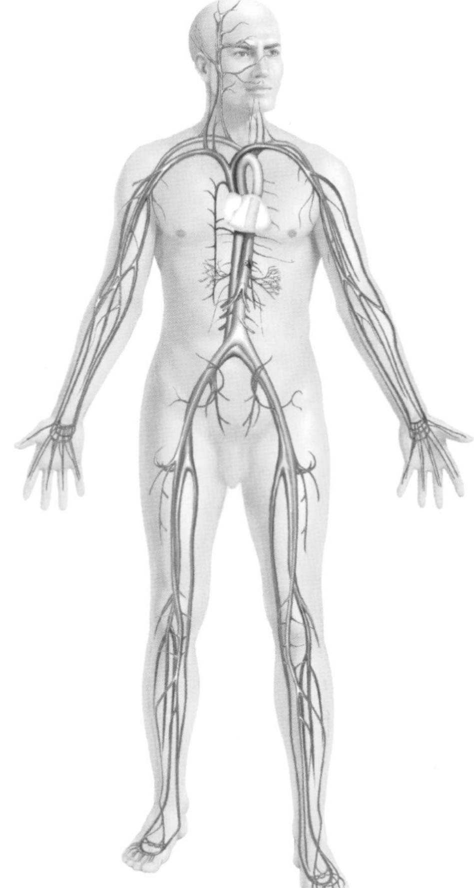

Circulatory benefits

The rubbing action of massage encourages blood to circulate around the body, increasing vitality and energy.

ments that may stimulate lymphatic drainage, decongest areas of fluid retention and break up localized fatty deposits. It is also used as a cellulite treatment.

Remedial massage

In remedial massage, Swedish massage techniques are combined with other remedial work such as stretches, exercises, acupressure or reflexology. It is used to treat muscular problems of the back and neck. Sports massage is a form of remedial massage which helps prepare the muscles for vigorous activity and aids their recovery after such activity.

Deep tissue massage

Deep pressure is used to help the body realign itself to regain its natural posture. Deep tissue massage works specifically on areas which have been injured or misused to reduce muscle pain and tightness and to improve flexibility.

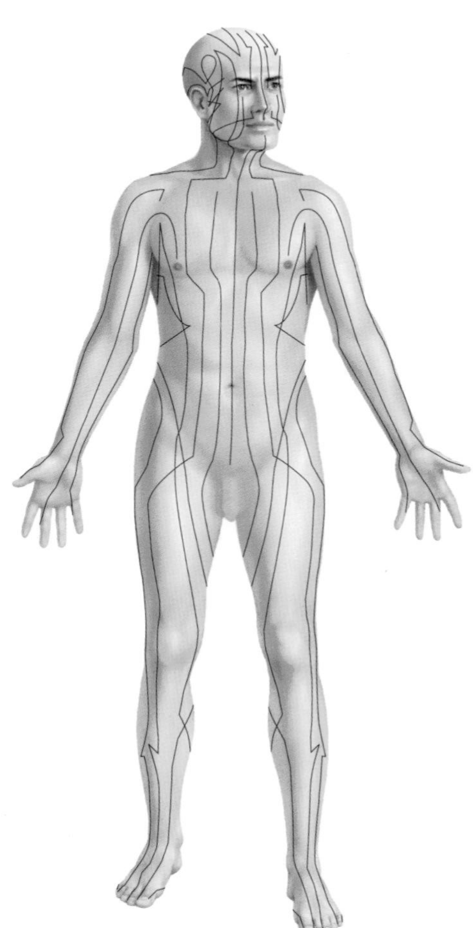

Eastern medicine

Practitioners of Eastern massage utilize the traditional Chinese meridian system, dividing the body into sections with a number of pressure points in each section.

Rolfing (also known as "structural integration" or "postural integration") and Hellerwork both utilize deep tissue massage in their treatment plans.

Polarity therapy

Developed by Randolph Stone, a chiropractor, osteopath and naturopath, polarity therapy uses manipulation and touch to balance the body's vital energy. Stone drew on the Eastern concept of "life energy" (known as *prana* or *ch'i*) and combined it with his studies of electromagnetic flows in the body. He mapped the body's positive, negative and neutral energies and devised hands-on techniques that he believed would stimulate their flow throughout the body to achieve an overall balance. Polarity therapy techniques can be integrated into other styles of massage.

Asian massage

Eastern massage styles are usually vigorous and deep. Pressure is applied on points mapped out by the meridian system of Traditional Chinese Medicine. Styles include Japanese *shiatsu* and Chinese *tui na*.

Ayurvedic massage

Ayurvedic massage is commonly practised at home in India, where there is a tradition of massaging babies every day for the first three years. Massage is done with essential oils to nourish the body internally and externally, and works through energy points in the body, known as *marmas*, using light, steady strokes.

Uses

Massage is believed to help relieve stress-related illnesses and muscular pain as well as aiding general preventive health care. In pregnancy, massage can be used to relieve insomnia and to ease back pain. Baby massage results in a calmer and more content baby while massage given to the elderly and sick provides both physical and emotional comfort.

SEE ALSO *Acupressure, Aromatherapy, Ayurvedic medicine, Manual lymph drainage, Shiatsu, Somatic therapies*

Mastitis

A sore and inflamed breast can result from a hormone imbalance or an infection of the tissues in the breast.

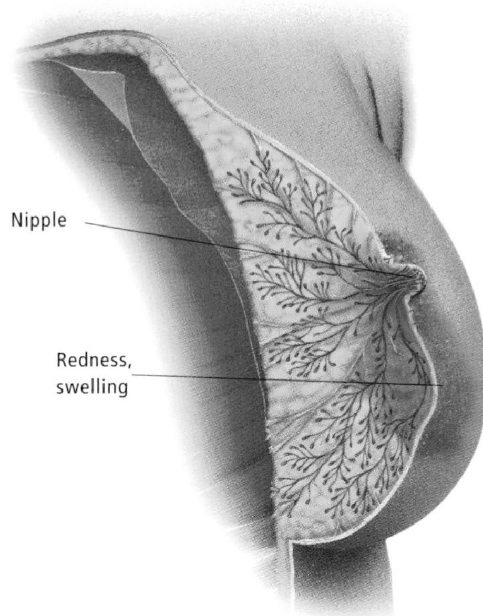

MASTECTOMY

Mastectomy is the surgical removal of the breast to treat diseased breast tissue, usually cancer. There are several approaches to removing diseased breast tissue, depending on the type of tumor present, its size, how fast it has grown, how widely the cancerous cells have spread, and the patient's general health. Lumpectomy is the surgical removal of a lump only. Simple mastectomy is the removal of the breast only. Radical mastectomy is the removal of the breast and the surrounding lymph nodes, muscles, fatty tissue and skin. Modified mastectomy is the removal of the breast and part of the muscles. A breast implant (prosthesis) can often be inserted at the time of the surgery (except in the case of radical mastectomy).

SEE ALSO *Breast, Breast cancer, Lumpectomy*

MASTITIS

Mastitis is inflammation of the breast. Acute mastitis is caused by an infection that enters the breast through a cracked nipple, most commonly while breast feeding. The breast becomes hot and swollen and there may be a fever. Mastitis is treated with antibiotic drugs, painkillers and bandaging of the breast. Breast feeding should be continued if possible. If an abscess forms, breast feeding should cease and the abscess must be incised and drained. Chronic mastitis is another name for fibrocystic disease of the breast.

SEE ALSO *Breast, Breast feeding, Fibrocystic disease of the breast*

M

MASTOIDITIS

Inflammation of the air-filled spaces encased in the mastoid part of the temporal bone behind the ear can follow inadequately treated inflammation of the middle ear (otitis media). The acute phase can often be reversed with antibiotics. However, should the infection become chronic, the patient will complain of severe pain behind the ear with associated fever, local redness and swelling. Appropriate antibiotics chosen on the basis of a culture from the inflamed middle ear may control the infection, but more often an operation to drain the area is necessary. Diagnosis is made both clinically and by confirmatory x-rays or CAT scans.

SEE ALSO *Ear, Otitis media*

MASTURBATION

Masturbation is the erotic stimulation of one's own, or a sexual partner's, genital organs for pleasure. It is a natural expression of human sexuality that begins in childhood and which can be an important part of self-discovery and satisfaction in a sexual relationship with a partner. Once the subject of taboos and superstitions, masturbation was said to cause numerous ill effects, ranging from hairy palms to insanity, none of which had any foundation in fact. Most people will masturbate at some time, some more often than others.

While children need to know the social etiquette of not masturbating in public, preventing them from masturbating can affect natural exploration of their own sexuality and lead to guilt and associated problems.

SEE ALSO *Sexual activity*

MEASLES

An extremely infectious viral disease, measles is spread by droplet infection. It is normally a childhood illness, but adults can also contract it. The incubation period is 10–14 days. Initially a high fever develops, accompanied by a runny nose and dry cough. Two days before the characteristic rash appears, small white spots, called Koplik's spots, may be seen inside the cheeks or in the region of the back teeth.

The spots fade within two or three days, by which time the rash will have appeared. The rash begins on the face and behind the ears, then spreads sequentially onto the body and limbs, including the palms and soles. The rash tends to be irregular and in patches. The lymph glands enlarge generally, while the eyes become inflamed, bleary and sensitive to light.

The eyes may discharge secretions. There is a dry cough, unproductive and exhausting. Within a week the patient begins to improve rapidly, though bronchitis, frequently appearing as a secondary infection, may persist. The rash fades but can leave temporary brown staining and may flake slightly.

Complications include middle ear infections, bronchitis, pneumonia and, most seriously, encephalitis or meningitis. If encephalitis occurs, usually three to seven days after the rash begins, the patient may sink into coma, have convulsions and vomit. Up to one in five people with measles encephalitis can die. Those who survive may remain epileptic or become retarded.

Measles

Measles is usually a childhood disease. It begins with flu-like symptoms such as headache, fever, runny nose and cough, before a rash appears on the face and spreads to the rest of the body.

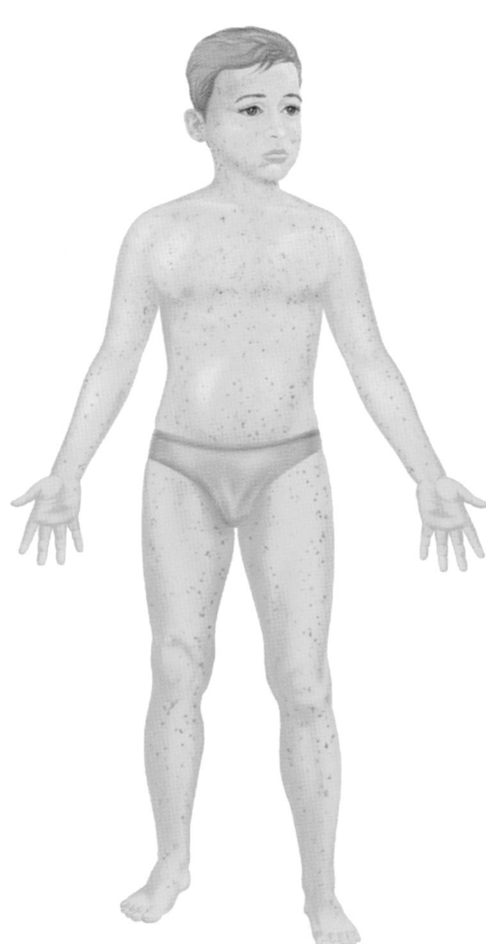

Beyond general nursing measures and controlling extreme fevers, little can be done to treat measles. Antibiotics may be of value if a middle ear infection or pneumonia occurs (as happens in 15 percent of cases). Vitamin A may be beneficial.

Since the introduction of immunization with an attenuated live measles virus in infancy (12–15 months), the periodic epidemics seen earlier are now rare. A booster dose is recommended at the age of 10–12, while people over 20 traveling into developing countries are advised to have a further booster. When immunized the child may develop a mild fever, slight cough and even a transient rash. However, this is not infectious. The measles vaccine is nowadays combined with mumps and rubella (German measles) vaccine (MMR). The vaccine, because it contains a live virus, should not be given in pregnancy or immune deficiency.

Measles has an average mortality rate in industrialized countries of about 1 in 1,000, more if contracted in infancy. In developing countries mortality is much higher because of coexisting malnutrition, other diseases and infections, and lack of access to medical care.

SEE ALSO *Immunization, Infectious diseases, Viruses*

MEDITATION

While meditation is an integral part of many of the world's religions, it is not in itself a religion. It is a method of resting the mind from its habitual involvement in the "busyness" of thinking in order to achieve a state of relaxation and detached observation. This state may be seen as a prelude to experiences of self-realization, or it may be seen as an end in itself, bringing with it the benefits of inner peace and mental refreshment.

In the East, Traditional Chinese Medicine and Ayurvedic medicine have advocated meditation for thousands of years as an essential means of maintaining health of mind and body through its ability to bring about an emotional and mental equilibrium.

M

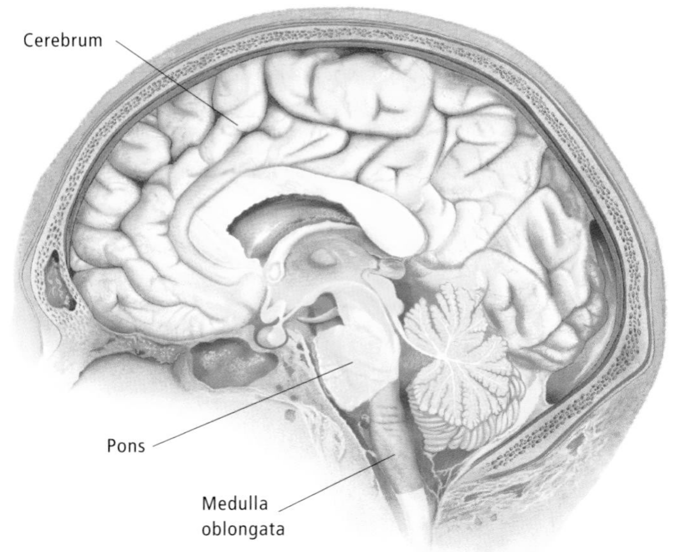

Medulla oblongata

The medulla oblongata sits above the spinal cord and below the pons. It is an important part of the brain, as it contains the nerve centers for vital functions such as breathing and heartbeat.

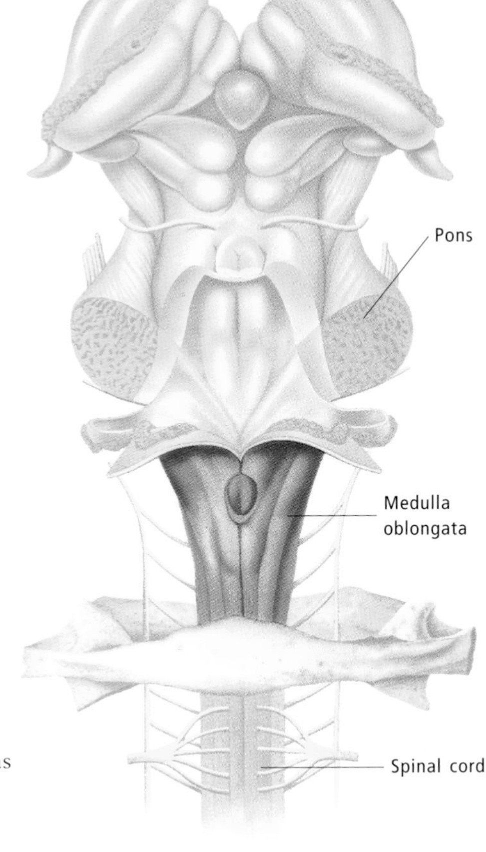

The health benefits of meditation began to be studied in the West in the 1960s when transcendental meditation (TM) started to become popular. In TM a personal secret phrase, called a mantra, is repeated, inducing a state of deep relaxation. Research showed this practise to lower blood pressure, protect against heart and circulation problems, and increase perceptual abilities.

TM is one of a range of meditation techniques which aims to achieve states of deep relaxation through the power of concentration, either by focusing on a mantra or an image such as a mandala or a flame, or on one's own pattern of breathing. Other forms of meditation, such as Vipassana, aim for a detached awareness by observing all that is going on outside and inside the meditator—sounds, thoughts, and sensations—without judging or getting involved in them.

The Vietnamese Buddhist monk Thic Nhat Hanh teaches a form of mindfulness meditation which can be done by bringing full attention to simple daily acts such as washing the dishes or answering the phone. In all cases meditation attempts to help the busy mind let go of all of its usual fretting over past and future concerns so as to become receptive and open to the present moment.

Meditation does not have to be done cross-legged on the floor. It can be done sitting in a chair or lying down, or in whatever position best supports the stillness of the body so that attention can then be directed to the relaxing of the mind. In some cases meditation teachers combine the deeply relaxed state of meditation with guided visualizations to induce feelings of peace and well-being.

One of the first doctors to study the positive effects of meditation on health was Australian psychiatrist Dr Ainslie Meares, who observed that it brought about a significant reduction of stress and discomfort in his cancer patients. Today doctors may suggest that their patients meditate as part of their health program, particularly those being treated for heart disease, cancer, AIDS and immune disorders, since the regular practise of meditation is believed to enhance immune function. Meditation is also taught in substance abuse recovery programs to build self-discipline as well as decrease anxiety.

MEDULLA OBLONGATA

The medulla oblongata is the upward continuation of the spinal cord which forms the lower part of the brain stem. It contains pathways taking information between the brain and spinal cord and gives rise to the hypoglossal, accessory, glossopharyngeal and vagus nerves. It contains a central core of gray matter called the reticular formation, which is involved in regulating sleep and arousal, and in pain perception. The reticular formation also includes vital centers that regulate breathing and heart activity. Trauma to the medulla oblongata may occur from a fracture of the skull base and is often fatal.

SEE ALSO *Brain, Skull, Spinal cord*

M

MEGALOMANIA

Megalomania, also known as delusions of grandeur, is an unrealistic and exaggerated belief or paranoia that one's self is of utmost importance. It is usually combined with the conviction that others do not recognize how important one is. Well-known megalomaniacs include the Roman emperor Caligula; the World War II Fascist dictator, Mussolini; and Shakespeare's fictional King Lear.

SEE ALSO *Paranoia, Personality disorders*

MELANIN

Melanin is responsible for the brown to black or golden coloring of the hair, skin and eyes. The melanins are a group of pigments found mainly in the skin, hair and the retina of the eye, and are also widely distributed in nature. There are two main types: eumelanin (dark) and pheomelanin (golden yellow). In the skin, the dark melanins serve to protect the skin against sunburn. Melanin is produced by cells called melanocytes, which pass the pigment on to the more numerous surrounding cells (keratinocytes, which produce keratin).

SEE ALSO *Keratin, Melanoma*

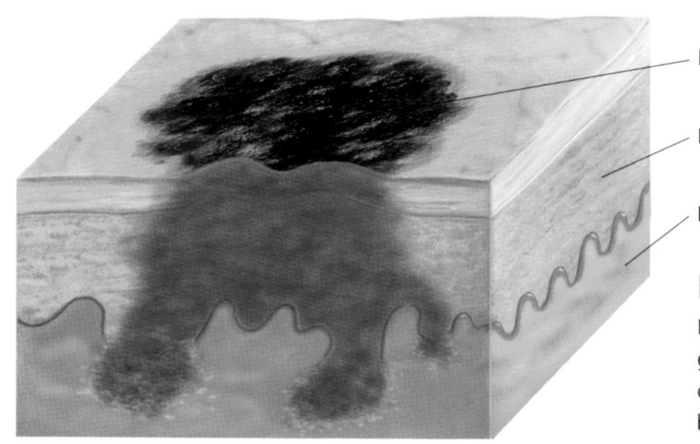

Melanoma

Melanomas are dark, cancerous growths found on the skin. They can begin as ordinary moles which become malignant.

MELANOMA

This is a dangerous form of cancer, which arises from pigment-producing cells (melanocytes), normally located in the deepest part of the surface layer of skin cells (the epithelium). The melanoma tumor is frequently referred to as malignant melanoma, which emphasizes its cancerous growth pattern (the term is now redundant because benign tumors of the melanocytes are no longer called melanomas, but are called "nevi"). Melanomas most commonly occur in the skin, but can also develop at other sites.

These tumors have the potential to spread via the lymphatic system and the blood, with a fatal outcome. On the other hand, melanoma can be cured if diagnosed early and treated appropriately by surgical removal. Thus it is most important for any individual who develops a pigmented area or lump on the skin to seek early medical attention.

Development of a melanoma of the skin is related to exposure to sunlight, especially in fair-skinned persons who lack protection against injury by ultraviolet rays. This is not the only predisposing factor, as a tumor may arise in a pre-existing mole (nevus) or in skin that has not been subjected to repeated or prolonged sun exposure. Heredity plays a role in a minority of cases.

Because melanomas arise from pigment-producing cells, they may have a dark color, but this is by no means necessary. Distinguishing a melanoma from a mole may not be easy, especially in children, in whom one variety of nevus used to be referred to as juvenile melanoma. In adults, recognition of an early melanoma is most effectively achieved by careful self-examination.

Development of an enlarging new mole in an adult, increase in size of an existing mole, changes in the surface or color, development of irregularity of the borders or additional pigmented areas around the edges, itching or pain, and bleeding are all important warning signs. The diagnosis can only be established by microscopic examination of a biopsy sample.

In the early stages of a melanoma, the tumor spreads radially, meaning that it grows outwards from its origin to form a larger but still superficially located collection of tumor cells. Later, it shows vertical growth, in that the tumor cells invade the deeper layers of the skin. If a melanoma is found microscopically to still be in the phase of radial growth, the likely outcome is much better than if it shows vertical growth. The greater the depth of invasion into deeper tissues, the higher the likelihood of spread to lymph nodes (lymph glands) or distant sites and the poorer the response to treatment.

SEE ALSO *Moles, Skin cancer, Sun exposure*

MELASMA

Light-skinned women who become pregnant frequently acquire dark tan staining of their cheeks or foreheads, called melasma or chloasma. After the birth of the baby the staining persists and darkens each summer if exposed to the sun. Though melasma occurs in darker skinned people, it is not as obvious. The estrogen-containing contraceptive pill has a similar side effect.

Other causes of this staining include menopausal changes, certain types of ovarian tumors, and endocrine disorders such as Addison's disease where changed pigmentation is also noted inside the mouth and in the creases of the palms.

It has been found that the use of sunscreen creams all year round before one ventures out will allow the staining to fade in time.

SEE ALSO *Addison's disease, Menopause, Pregnancy, Sun exposure*

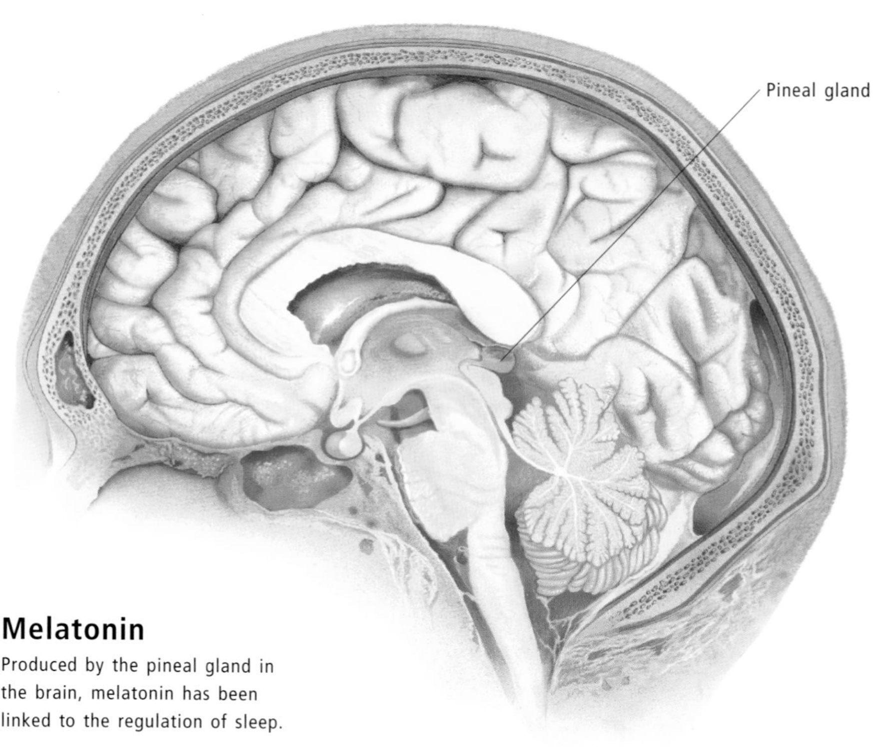

Melatonin

Produced by the pineal gland in the brain, melatonin has been linked to the regulation of sleep.

MELATONIN

Melatonin is a hormone secreted by the pineal gland, located deep inside the brain. Thought to be involved in regulating the body's sleep–wake "clock", melatonin production is highest during a person's normal sleeping hours and drops off as the body begins waking. There is evidence that melatonin supplements may help some forms of insomnia and ease the symptoms of jet lag by hastening the body's return to its usual sleep–wake cycle.

Research investigating a wide range of potential applications suggests melatonin supplements could also be useful in birth control, boosting the immune system, treating cancer and depression and in the management of many other disorders.

SEE ALSO *Insomnia, Jet lag*

MELIOIDOSIS

Melioidosis (Whitmore disease) is a predominantly tropical disease caused by the bacterium *Pseudomonas pseudomallei*, which is found in soil and stagnant water. Most cases occur in Southeast Asia and northern Australia. Symptoms range from headache and fever to chest pain, appetite loss and cough. Melioidosis commonly affects the lungs and can be fatal. Treatment is with antibiotics.

SEE ALSO *Bacteria*

MEMBRANE

Membranes are thin and flexible sheets of tissue that line surfaces or divide spaces in the body. Three of the four main types—mucous, serous and cutaneous membrane—are composed of an epithelial cell layer overlaying a connective tissue layer. In synovial membranes the epithelial layer is modified as a mesothelial layer.

SEE ALSO *Connective tissue, Mucous membranes*

MEMORY

Memory is a cognitive process which allows humans to retain and retrieve information about previously experienced events, impressions, sensations and ideas. Humans acquire knowledge and store it as memory.

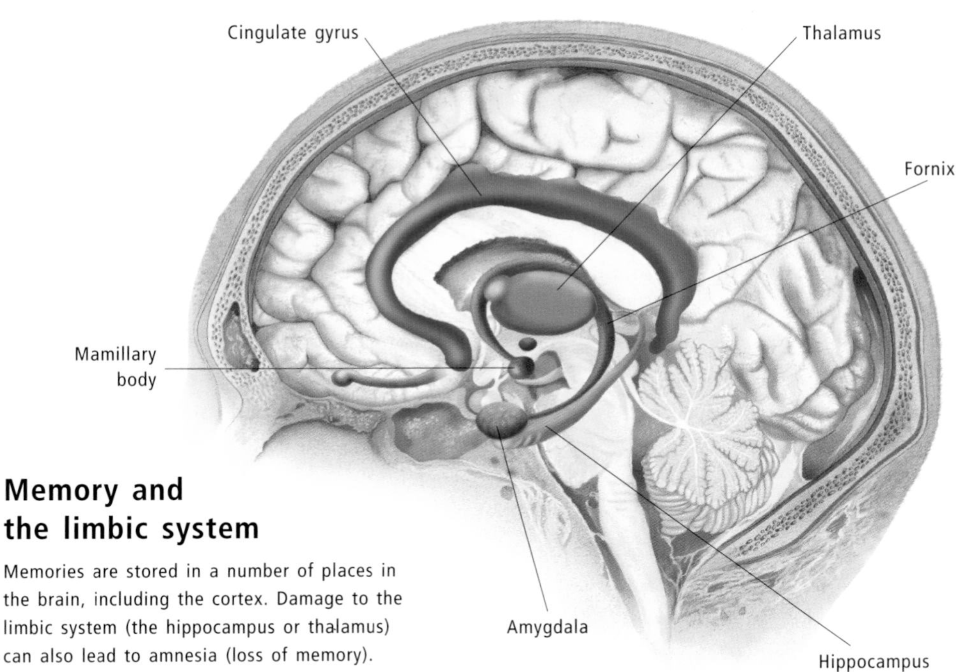

Memory and the limbic system

Memories are stored in a number of places in the brain, including the cortex. Damage to the limbic system (the hippocampus or thalamus) can also lead to amnesia (loss of memory).

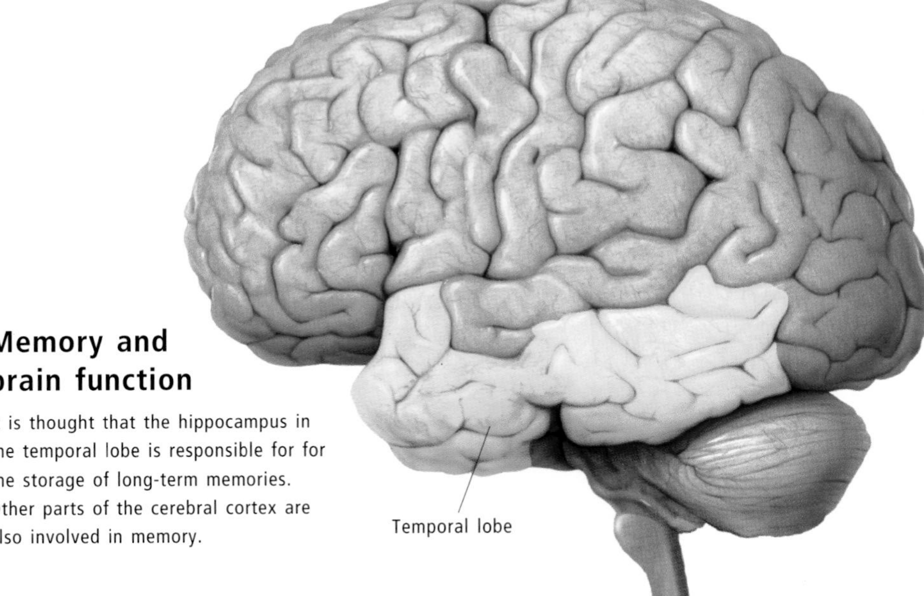

Memory and brain function

It is thought that the hippocampus in the temporal lobe is responsible for for the storage of long-term memories. Other parts of the cerebral cortex are also involved in memory.

The ability to learn or the ability to reason is largely dependent on the ability to remember. For example, the ability to perform a simple task, such as making a cup of coffee or crossing the street, is based on remembering earlier experiences. In solving a problem or even simply recognizing that a problem exists, one is depending on memory.

Although not exactly understood, neuroscientists describe the storing of memory in three ways: sensory memory, which lasts from milliseconds to seconds; short-term memory, which lasts seconds to minutes; and long-term memory, which lasts days to years.

Different storage mechanisms are said to exist for short-term and long-term memory. In short-term memory, a limited amount of information (from five to ten separate items) can be held for a few seconds, after which they must be transferred to long-term memory or they will be lost. For example, we use short-term memory to remember a phone number after looking it in up in a directory, but only for as long as it takes to dial the number. The capacity of long-term memory is large—certain items, especially important events, can be stored for life.

Psychologists also divide memory into four different categories: recollection, recall, recognition and relearning. Recollection is the mental reconstruction of previous events from reminders that "jog" the memory. Recall is the unprompted active remembering of events or incidents from the past. Recognition is the identifying of a stimulus as being familiar from the past. Relearning is the ability to commit to memory with relative ease something that has been forgotten previously, the learning process being easier than the first time.

Memory is thought to be stored over wide areas of the brain rather than in any single location. However, the limbic system, notably the hippocampus on the medial side of the temporal lobe and some parts of the thalamus, are thought to be particularly important in the laying down of memories and in their recall when required. Injury to these areas of the brain results in amnesia, a disorder of memory.

Learning, and thus remembering, begins in the uterus. Ultrasound observations of twins have shown the development of gestures and habits as early as 20 weeks gestation, which continue into early childhood.

The fetus also becomes familiar with the native language of its mother; for example, in tests, French babies look to persons who are talking French. Taste is also learned in utero, as the baby becomes familiar with its mother's diet by inhaling and swallowing the amniotic fluid it lives in. Emotion too is learned; studies have found that babies whose mothers were depressed during pregnancy also exhibited symptoms of depression at birth.

Problems

Forgetting is normal, and apart from a rare few, everyone forgets. Over time something which is not practised will be forgotten. The ability to forget, however, is also important to the process of learning. One is continually adjusting the ability to learn with the ability to forget in order to adapt to new learning experiences and learn new skills. Those who are unable to forget have been found to be extremely confused.

Certain situations, conditions or illnesses can affect memory. Depression, if it includes agitation and psychomotor retardation,

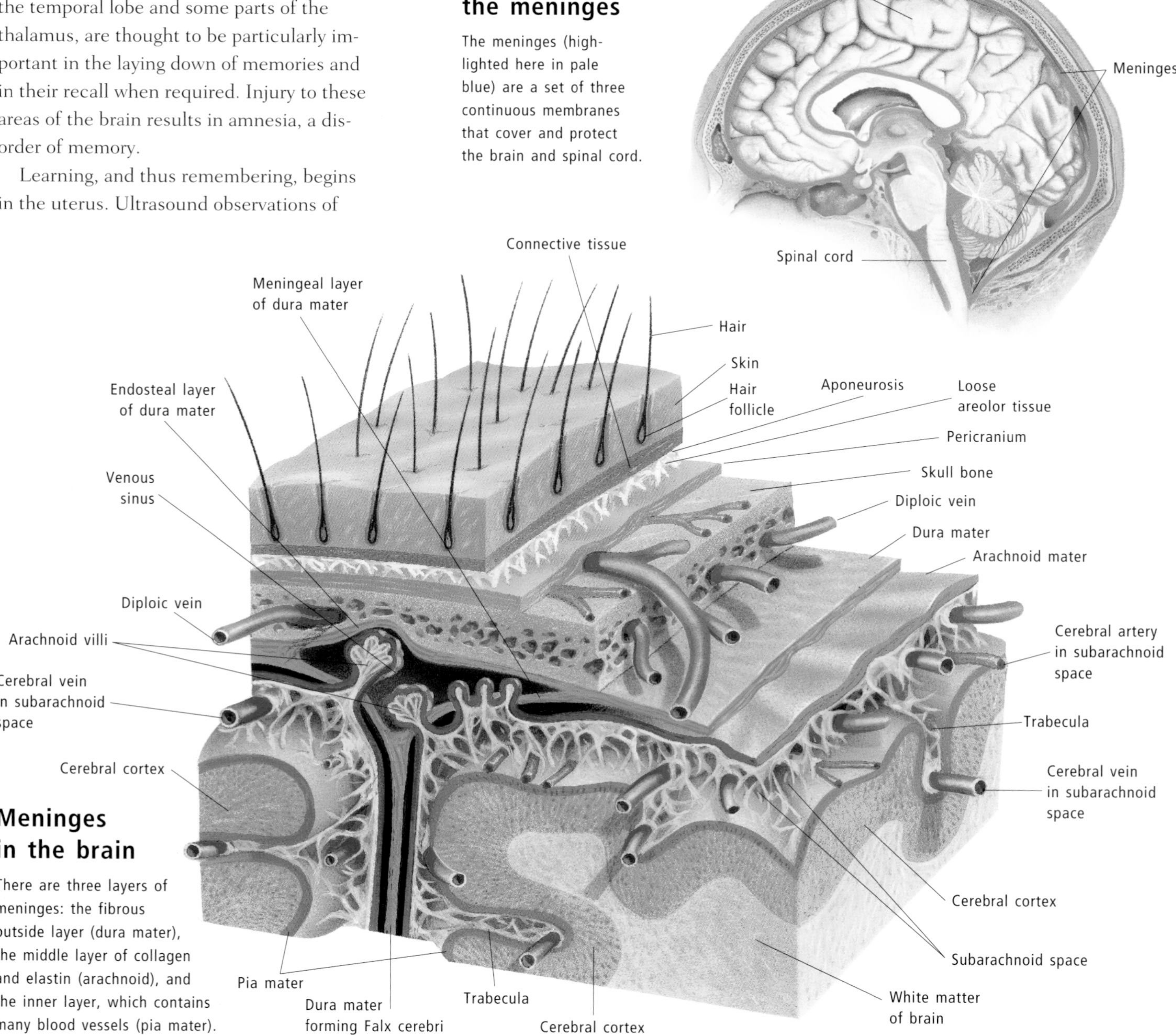

Location of the meninges

The meninges (highlighted here in pale blue) are a set of three continuous membranes that cover and protect the brain and spinal cord.

Meninges in the brain

There are three layers of meninges: the fibrous outside layer (dura mater), the middle layer of collagen and elastin (arachnoid), and the inner layer, which contains many blood vessels (pia mater).

makes it difficult for people to remember as well as they would normally, and such depression can lead to pseudo-dementia. Anxiety can reduce the ability to concentrate, for instance in an examination situation, and can affect memory. With age, the ability to learn new skills and to recall information from one's memory can diminish. This may be partly because the memory store is greater in the elderly than in younger persons, thus making recall more complicated. This has been described as age-associated memory impairment (AAMI). Boredom, tiredness, hearing and sight impairment, alcohol, drugs and pain can all reduce the ability to remember and thus learn.

Infections, particularly of the brain (such as meningitis), can cause memory problems, as can an under-active thyroid gland, which will slow down the body's processes. Severe heart or lung disease will affect memory by reducing the supply of oxygen to the brain, and untreated, or poorly treated, diabetes with high or low levels of sugar in the blood can affect the brain's workings.

The most serious cause of memory problems is dementia. Rarely a problem for people under 65 years of age (when it is usually associated with conditions such as Creutzfeld-Jakob disease), the risk of dementia increases with age. One in five people over the age of 80 will suffer from dementia, the most common cause being Alzheimer's disease.

Memory improvement

It is possible to assist memory by using certain strategies. There are many programs available aimed at teaching people to maximize the ability to remember and learn. Strategies include the following.

- Being selective: deciding what it is that one wants to learn. Taking notes, writing things down, and being organized are recognized memory aids.
- Learning by rote: repeating and memorizing important facts and formula is essential for some subjects.
- Reciting out loud: this has been found to be one of the most powerful tools in transferring knowledge from short-term to long-term memory.
- Having a good basic background: learning new skills depends a great deal on what a person already knows.
- Using memory aids such as mnemonic devices: for example, "homes", a word that contains the first letter of each of the Great Lakes (Huron, Ontario, Michigan, Erie and Superior).
- Applying and practising what has been learnt: for example, when the concepts are abstract, discussion will aid understanding; when it is a dance step, repetition will imprint the movements on one's memory.
- Keeping fit and healthy: healthy people who enjoy regular exercise, eat a nutritious diet, drink alcohol moderately and do not take unnecessary drugs help their minds to stay alert. Those who have hearing or sight defects need to ensure they have the correct aids to maximize their ability to experience and learn.
- Keeping the brain active: using the mind and continuing to exercise it by learning new skills, practising those already learnt, and including hobbies such as doing crosswords and playing word games helps to keep the brain working.

Well-educated people seem to experience fewer memory problems as they age than others, which may be because they have a better memory to begin with than those who are having problems, or it may be that because they continue to solve problems, study and learn, their brains remain active.

SEE ALSO *Alzheimer's disease, Creutzfeld-Jakob disease, Dementia, Wernicke-Korsakoff syndrome, Learning disorders*

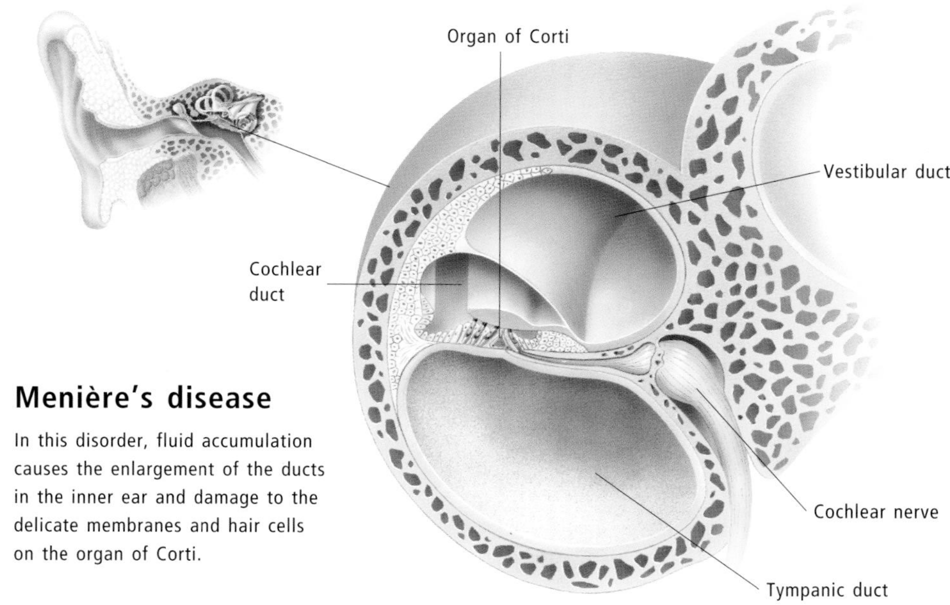

Menière's disease

In this disorder, fluid accumulation causes the enlargement of the ducts in the inner ear and damage to the delicate membranes and hair cells on the organ of Corti.

MENIÈRE'S DISEASE

Menière's disease is a disorder of unknown cause characterized by periodic attacks of vertigo and hearing loss. The first symptom can be a ringing or hissing sound in the ears, known as tinnitus. This is followed by debilitating vertigo, nausea and vomiting that may last up to 24 hours. There may be a feeling of pressure or fullness in the ears. There is progressive hearing loss over time. The vertigo can be treated temporarily with drugs or more permanently by surgically cutting the nerves of the semicircular canals, the organs of balance within the inner ear.

SEE ALSO *Deafness, Ear, Hearing, Semicircular canals, Tinnitus, Vertigo*

MENINGES

The meninges are three thin, protective, continuous membranes surrounding the brain and spinal cord. The outermost is a tough, fibrous layer called the dura mater. The middle membrane, the arachnoid, is a fragile network of collagen and elastin fibers with a cobweb appearance. The innermost membrane, the pia mater, is a layer of collagen and elastic fibers containing many blood vessels. Cerebrospinal fluid fills the space between the arachnoid and pia mater.

A meningioma is a tumor originating in the meninges. It is usually benign but may cause problems by placing pressure on the brain. Surgical removal is often successful.

SEE ALSO *Brain, Meningitis, Spinal cord*

Meningitis bacteria

Meningitis can be caused by a number of different agents, including fungi, viruses or bacteria. The condition causes inflammation of the tissues (meninges) which encase the brain and spinal cord.

MENINGITIS

Meningitis is an infection in the meninges, the membranes which cover the brain and spinal cord. It can be caused by fungi, protozoa, a virus or, in its most serious and potentially fatal forms, by a number of different bacteria.

Bacterial meningitis can be caused by *Meningococcus (Neisseria meningitidis), Haemophilus influenza* type B (HIB), *Pneumococcus, Streptococcus* or *Staphylococcus*.

Meningococcal meningitis is found in all countries and primarily affects adolescents and children under age 10, as does the type of meningitis produced by *Haemophilus influenzae*. In adults, the most common cause is *Streptococcus pneumoniae*. It is an infection which can be only a very mild disturbance and therefore difficult to diagnose, or can make the sufferer extremely ill.

Bacterial infections of the middle ear or of another region of the body can be carried to the meninges via the blood. The bacteria then multiply quickly, causing the first symptoms to appear very rapidly. The first symptom is usually vomiting, followed by a severe headache, which is due to inflammation of the meninges and increased pressure of the cerebrospinal fluid. The neck may be very stiff, even arched and drawn backwards in young children. Fluid may accumulate in the brain, causing coma and death unless relieved.

Other symptoms include moderate to high fever, headache, vomiting, collapse, convulsions, lethargy, inability to tolerate bright light, bulging fontanelle in children under two, and a purple rash all over the body. (This kind of purple rash is associated with *Meningococcus* infection, which is a very virulent form of meningitis.) In very young children, the fever may be the only sign until the child is suddenly critically ill.

The various forms of bacterial meningitis are spread through the secretions of the nose and throat, by coughing or kissing, but not by less intimate contact or in the air. Prolonged contact, such as between people sharing the same room or house, or children at the same daycare centers or school classroom, can cause infection and these people would be considered at risk in an outbreak.

A diagnosis is made by taking a sample of spinal fluid and testing for bacteria and abnormal chemical components. This is in order to differentiate between meningitis and encephalitis, and to establish which type of organism is responsible for the infection. Early diagnosis is vital in preventing death from the more serious bacterial forms of the disease.

Safe and effective vaccination is available against HIB, some strains of meningococcal meningitis (also known as *Neisseria meningitidis*) and forms of *Streptococcus pneumoniae*. HIB vaccines should be given routinely to infants with three doses before age 6 months, and a fourth between 12 and 18 months. Vaccines against meningococcal meningitis are not effective in children under 18 months. Available vaccines against pneumococcal meningitis were, until recently, not effective in children under the age of 2 years, the major group at risk. However, a vaccine developed and approved for use in the USA offers hope for a dramatic improvement in protection against brain damage, hearing loss and death rates—currently 10 percent of those infected—for babies and infants up to the age of 5 years.

Adults may be vaccinated during outbreaks of the disease and should consider vaccination prior to travel in infected areas.

SEE ALSO *Brain, Encephalitis, Immunization, Meninges, Spinal cord*

MENINGOCELE

The neural tube develops in the human embryo as the precursor of the spinal cord. Normally, the tube closes to produce the nervous system structures; if it does not, the membranes or meninges covering the nerve tissue of the cord may protrude through the skin in the form of a fluid-filled sac.

Meningocele is a term that encompasses any congenital abnormality involving inadequate closure of the spine.

Sometimes parts of the spinal cord also protrude into the hernia. This is known as a meningomyelocele, and is more common, and also more serious, than meningocele because the spinal cord and nerve roots may be damaged, causing weakness or paralysis below the defect.

Both conditions occur in the lower lumbar or sacral areas of the back, which are the last parts of the fetal spine to close. Other congenital disorders such as hydrocephalus or dislocated hip may also be present. Both types require surgical treatment shortly after birth to repair the defect. Any neurological damage is often irreversible and physical therapy will be needed to minimize future disability.

SEE ALSO *Congenital abnormalities, Hydrocephalus, Spinal cord*

MENINGOCOCCAL DISEASE

Meningococcal disease is a rapid, potentially fatal form of bacterial infection, due to *Neisseria meningitidis*. It is most commonly seen in children under 5 years of age, and its incidence has increased in recent years. As a general rule, meningococcal disease is a combination of meningitis and septicemia.

The illness develops rapidly, with a flu-like infection, headache, confusion, and the appearance of a blotchy, purplish rash. Early treatment with intravenous antibiotics can be lifesaving.

The infection occurs mainly in winter, is spread through respiratory secretions and can occur in epidemics. People who are in close contact with the patient require preventive antibiotics. Vaccination against meningococcal disease is advised for travelers to epidemic areas and those with reduced immunity.

SEE ALSO *Meningitis, Septicemia*

MENOPAUSE

Menopause literally means "pause in menstruation". Menopause does not accurately describe what is happening to a woman's body at the time when ovarian function and hormonal production decline and the body adjusts itself. Climacteric is a more accurate term because it describes a time of life, just as puberty describes the time after the menarche, the first menstruation.

During the climacteric period, which can last several years, the woman's body goes through three phases. The premenopause is the time before the menstrual cycle ceases; this term can also refer to most of a woman's fertile years, but more commonly to the years when the menstrual periods are irregular and heavy. The next phase, the perimenopause, are the years on either side of the menopause when a woman may experience some of the symptoms commonly associated with menopause, including hot flashes (also known as hot flushes), depression and loss of interest in sexual intercourse. The menopause is defined as starting after the final menstrual period, which can only be determined when 12 months have passed without a menstrual bleed. After the menopause comes the postmenopause, which extends to the end of the woman's life.

There are three important hormones produced by the ovaries: estrogen, progesterone and relaxin. Once a woman has passed the menopause, estrogen and progesterone will no longer be produced by the ovaries, though in some obese women estrogen may still be produced by fat tissue, thus reducing some of the symptoms. Estrogen is needed to maintain healthy body tissues and long term estrogen deficiency can result in stroke, dowager's hump, angina, genital degeneration and fractures, commonly of the hip, due to osteoporosis.

Physical effects

Around the time a woman reaches menopause she may experience some or all of the following symptoms: hot flashes, night sweats, palpitations and sleep problems (which are a result of changes in the normal working of the blood vessels), anxiety and depression, vaginal dryness, and decreased or no interest in sexual intercourse.

There are many physiological changes that accompany the climacteric and many women will be unaware of most of them. They include the following.

- Changes to the urogenital tissue. A reduction in the blood supply to the tissues leads to an alkaline environment, with the possibility of infections and itching.
- Changes to the reproductive organs. The ovaries, which produced eggs during the woman's reproductive years, no longer do so and, because it is the egg follicle which produces progesterone, production of this hormone ceases. The inner part of the ovary known as the stroma continues to produce hormones, most importantly, androstenedione and testosterone. Androstenedione converts to estrone, which is important in maintaining pelvic organs, the vagina, skin and hair. Testosterone, a male hormone, is important in maintaining energy levels; however, this hormone also increases the risk of heart disease.
- Poor bladder control. The pelvic floor muscles lose their elasticity and strength. This can result in continence problems, which can be combated by doing pelvic floor exercises.
- Changes to the menstrual cycle. Bleeding may become heavier, lighter, or more irregular for several years prior to the final menstrual period. This is a symptom of the alteration in the pattern of female and pituitary hormones at this time.
- Dry skin that is more prone to wrinkles. The skin will lose much of its elasticity and because of a decrease in collagen, wrinkles will appear. A loss of melanocytes, cells which manufacture melanin and give the skin a tanned appearance, means the skin is also more likely to burn under the sun's rays.
- Changes in hair growth patterns. Hair on the head loses its body and thickness and becomes finer. This hormonally-related hair loss occurs around 40 years and there is no known cure. It is not the same as alopecia (baldness). Hair on the body, on the other hand, can become thicker and darker as a result of the hormonal changes. This can lead to masculine-like hair growth on the face, arms and legs, which can be counteracted with estrogen therapy.
- Osteoporosis. This is a disease in which the amount of bone calcium in the skeleton reduces to the point that the bones are thin, brittle and prone to fracture. Osteoporosis can result after the menopause because insufficient estrogen leads to calcium loss. Hormone replacement therapy can prevent bones from deteriorating.
- Loss of muscle strength and mobility. Weak muscles lead to poor coordination. This, together with lack of exercise

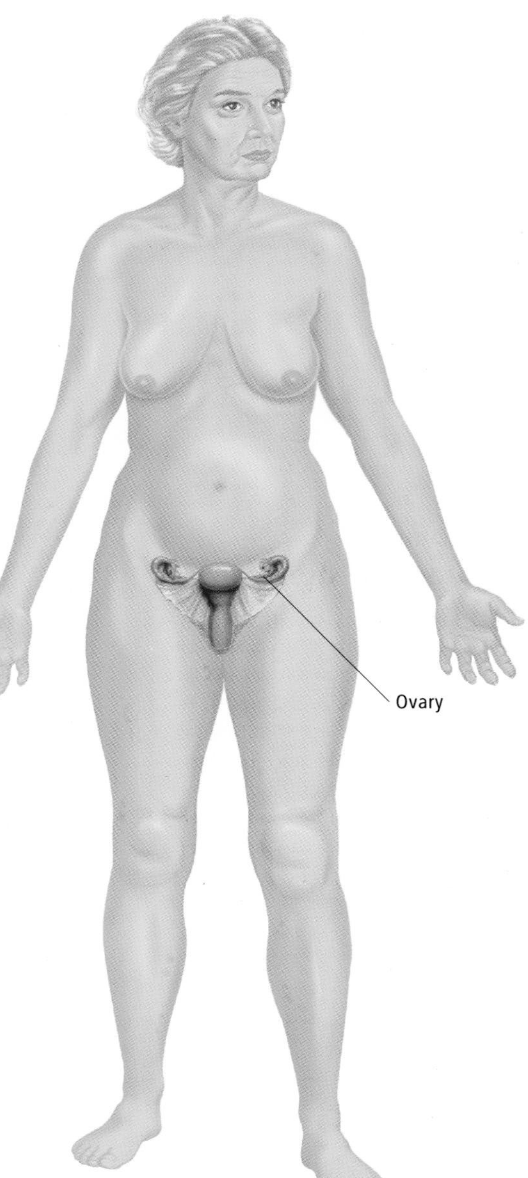

Menopause

At menopause, ova (eggs) are no longer produced by the ovaries, and menstruation ceases. Hormone replacement therapy may be undertaken to compensate for hormones which are no longer produced by the body.

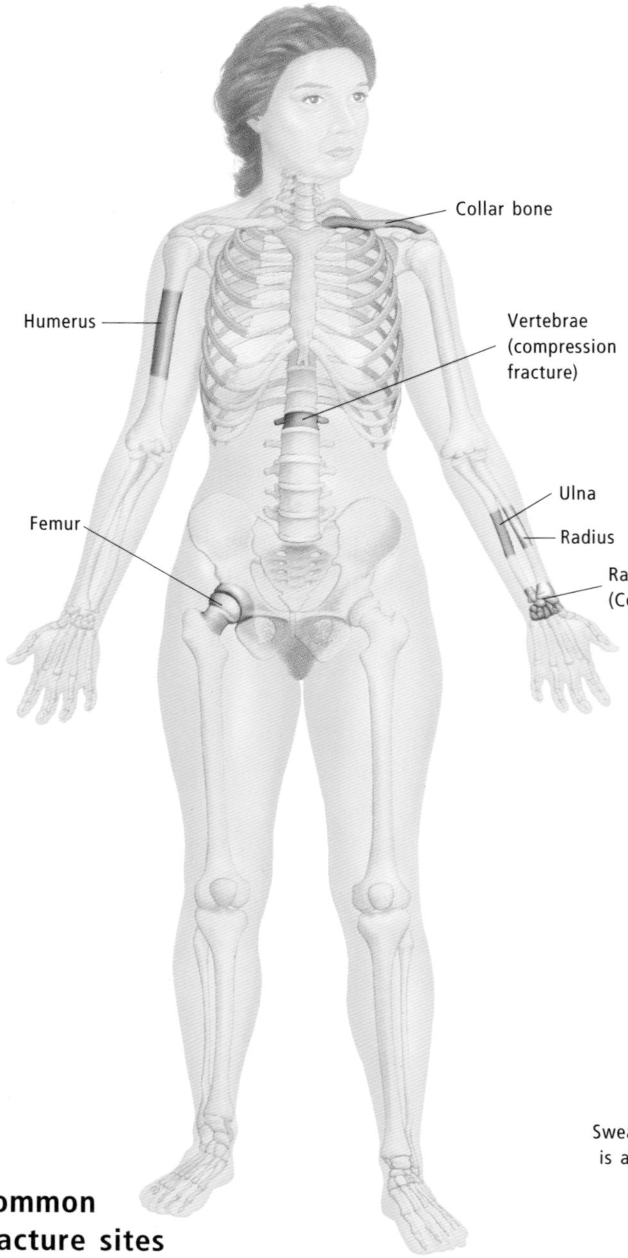

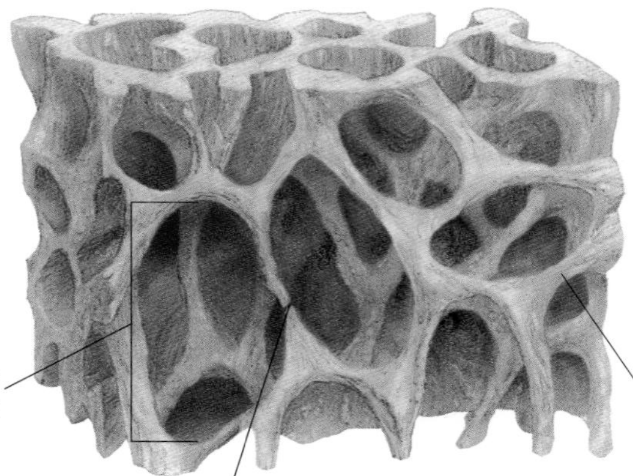

Collar bone
Humerus
Vertebrae (compression fracture)
Ulna
Femur
Radius
Radius (Colles' fracture)

Bone increases in porosity
Connecting network weakens
Loss of bone mass causes breakdown

Osteoporosis

Women entering menopause are encouraged to take calcium and vitamin D supplements and to maintain exercise levels, to avoid bones becoming porous and weak.

Common fracture sites

A reduction in the level of estrogen in the body during menopause can result in a loss of calcium and lead to brittle bones (osteoporosis). There is an increased risk of fractures during this period of life; the most common include fractures of the collar bone, upper and lower arm, radius (Colles' fracture), femur, and compression fractures of the spine.

During a hot flash

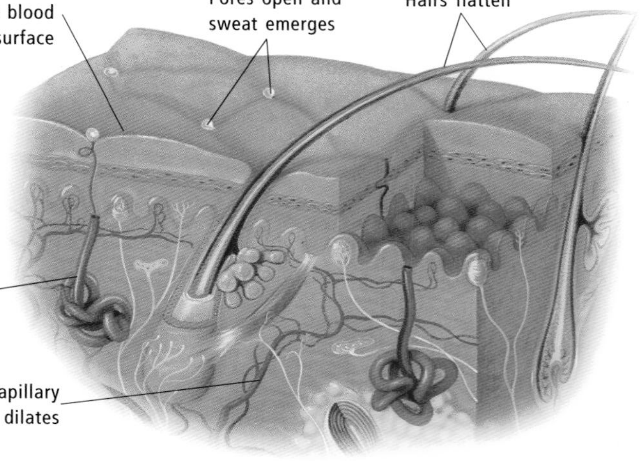

Skin becomes flushed as blood rushes to surface
Pores open and sweat emerges
Hairs flatten
Sweat gland is activated
Capillary dilates

After a hot flash

Skin becomes pale
Pores close
Hairs rise for insulation
Sweat gland
Capillary contracts and blood drains from skin

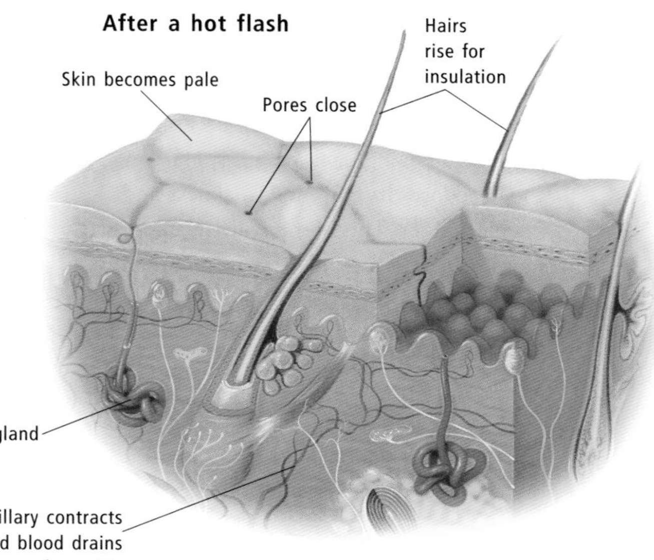

Hot flash

Hormone imbalances during menopause cause the capillaries of the skin to dilate, sending a sudden flood of warm blood to the surface. After the flash has passed, the capillaries rapidly constrict, the skin becomes pale and cold as blood drains away and hairs rise to provide insulation.

Menopausal fat distribution

Falling estrogen and progesterone levels during menopause affect fat distribution in women. Before menopause, most women have some fat deposits around the thighs, hips, breasts and upper arms. After menopause, fat tends to collect around the breasts, abdomen and waist.

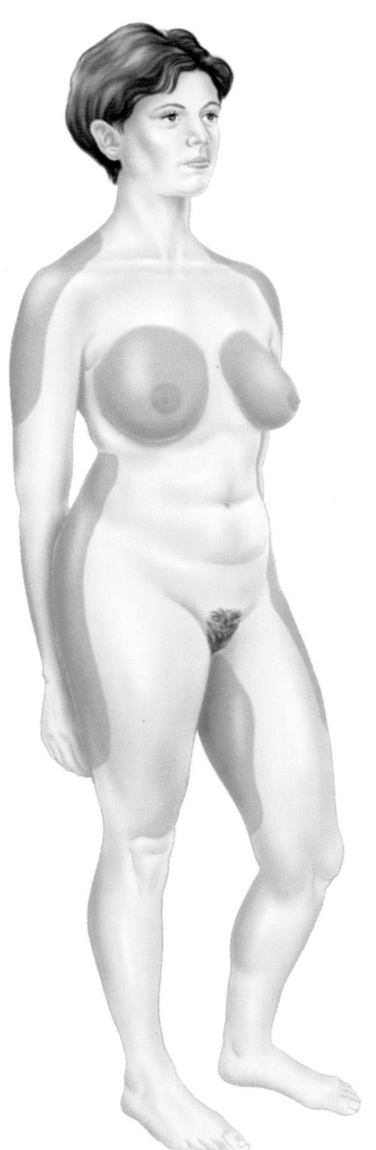

Fat distribution before menopause

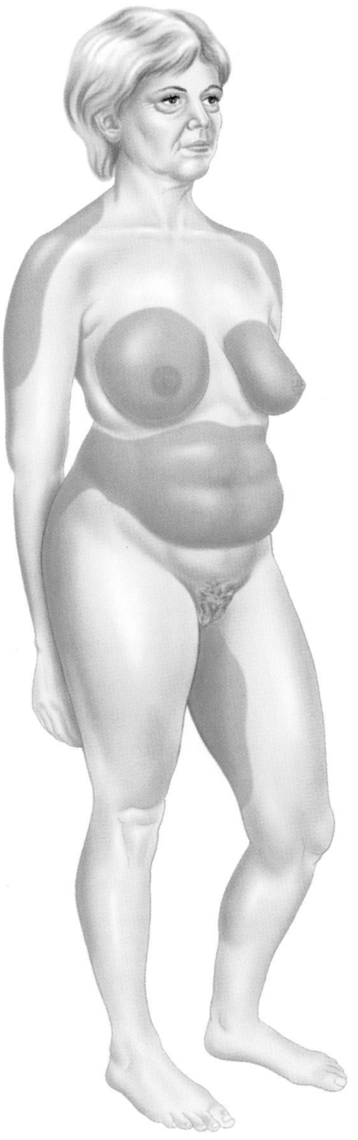

Fat distribution after menopause

and the decline in estrogen and progesterone, can lead to a sedentary lifestyle which may bring its own set of problems and diseases.

- Increased chance of heart disease. Once a woman reaches menopause she is at much greater risk of cardiovascular disease than she was before, because her ovaries are no longer producing estrogen. Hormone replacement therapy (HRT) can reduce these risks.
- Breasts flattening and losing their fullness. This too can be prevented with the use of HRT. Breast cancer, however, is a concern with HRT and the risk factors need to be discussed with a medical practitioner when this therapy is considered.

Other effects

The menopause can produce many different responses in a woman. Some of the above symptoms, together with a decline in the male hormones, can be responsible for a loss of interest in a sexual relationship. For some women, male hormone replacement may be of benefit. However, if a woman maintains a healthy lifestyle and seeks help for any symptoms she encounters, she often finds the menopause brings a new lease of life in some ways, such as a sex life where contraceptive worries are removed.

Researchers have found that most women who had an enjoyable sex life before they reached the menopause continue to enjoy sex afterwards.

In some cultures, menopause confers new power and prestige on the woman, while in other societies it is seen as a decline in femininity and sexuality. An understanding of what to expect, and support and recognition of changes, can greatly help a woman feel at ease with what is an entirely natural phase of every woman's life.

The climacteric is a natural life event and the hormone deficiency state that accompanies it may, or may not, need medication.

Alternative therapies

There are a number of alternative therapies that may be helpful during menopause. Aromatherapy massage may help alleviate dry skin, anxiety and insomnia. Fennel, cypress and sage oils are recommended by aromatherapists for menopausal symptoms. Herbalism treats with herbs that may support liver function (dandelion, milk thistle), herbs that are high in plant estrogens and progesterone (red clover, wild yam, sage, agnus castus, dong quai) and sedative nervines (passiflora, skullcap, chamomile). Calendula ointment is prescribed for vaginal dryness. Naturopathy suggests a wholefood diet rich in calcium and phyto-estrogens (found primarily in soy products). Caffeine, alcohol and cigarettes should be avoided, as well as foods rich in oxalic acid (e.g. spinach and rhubarb), which bind with calcium in the body. A regular weight-bearing exercise program is suggested to counteract bone loss. Supplements of vitamins B, C and E, calcium, magnesium, flaxseed oil and fish oils may help. Various flower essences and remedies may help with emotional issues. Traditional Chinese Medicine uses acupuncture and Chinese herbal treatments to correct energy and hormonal imbalances.

SEE ALSO *Ageing, Angina, Breast, Estrogens, Hormone replacement therapy, Urinary incontinence, Menstruation, Osteoporosis, Progesterone, Reproductive systems, Testosterone*

M

MENSTRUATION

Menstruation is the cyclic vaginal discharge of blood and tissue debris derived from breakdown of the uterine lining. The menstrual cycle is considered to start with the onset of menstruation, which occupies approximately 5 days out of the complete cycle of about 28 days (both these figures can vary considerably from the average). Apart from menstruation, the cycle can be divided into two phases, the days before (proliferative phase) and the days after ovulation (secretory phase). The menstrual cycle is an unusual type of reproductive cycle found only in humans and a few other primates.

The most obvious changes during the menstrual cycle take place in the uterine lining (endometrium). Menstruation involves the degeneration and loss of a large amount of endometrium along with about 1–2 fluid ounces (35–50 milliliters) of blood from broken endometrial vessels. At the end, a small amount of the lining (about 1 millimeter thick) remains, which is essential for regeneration. Regeneration of the endometrium occurs under the influence of estrogen from follicles developing in the ovary during the proliferative phase, and proceeds until the lining is about 1/10 inch (3 millimeters) thick. The fully formed endometrium is a richly vascular tissue that also contains glands.

Progesterone derived from the corpus luteum (the follicle that matured and released its egg) is the predominant hormone from just after ovulation to about 2 days before menstruation (approximately day 26). The main function of progesterone is to stimulate the endometrial glands to produce a secretion capable of nourishing the embryo for the first few days of pregnancy, before a functional placenta has formed. The secretion occurs regardless of whether pregnancy has taken place or not.

If the woman is not pregnant, the corpus luteum lasts until about day 26 of the cycle when it starts to degenerate and progesterone production decreases rapidly. The blood vessels in the uterine lining are sensitive to levels of circulating progesterone and respond to reduced levels by contracting and cutting off the blood supply to all but the deepest parts of the endometrium. This results in tissue breakdown and bleeding from the damaged blood vessels, which leads to the onset of the next menstruation. Menstrual flow is facilitated by muscular contractions and by substances produced in the endometrium which prevent clotting of menstrual blood.

Menstruation does not take place if the woman has become pregnant because the corpus luteum survives and continues to secrete progesterone under the influence of hormones derived from the early placenta. This is essential to maintain the pregnancy until the placenta is able to produce its own progesterone towards the end of the first trimester. Only then does the corpus luteum gradually cease to function.

Menarche

The first menstruation normally occurs between 10 and 16 years and is called the menarche. Puberty is a more general term describing both the onset of menstruation and the development of secondary sexual characteristics, which usually precedes menarche. This includes the growth of pubic hair, breast development and a spurt in body growth. The hormonal events leading up to puberty are not fully understood but changes in the pituitary a couple of years before puberty result in increased secretion of the sexual hormones, the gonadotropins.

The age of menarche appears to be related to a number of social factors. Menstruation tends to occur earlier in urban girls of higher socioeconomic status and also relates to heredity and better nutrition. It was widely believed in the past that menarche took place earlier in tropical climates, but

Cycle regulation

The hypothalamus and the pituitary gland in the brain regulate the menstrual cycle. At the start of the cycle they release luteinizing hormone (LH) and follicle stimulating hormone (FSH) which trigger follicles (egg sacs) in the ovaries to release estrogen and progesterone. The follicles then mature and finally release an egg.

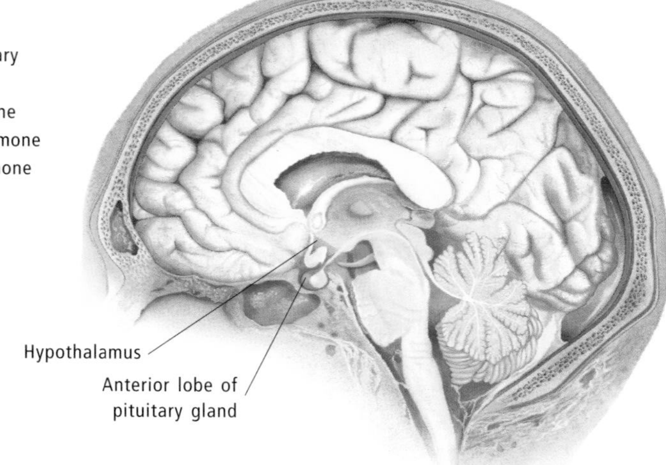

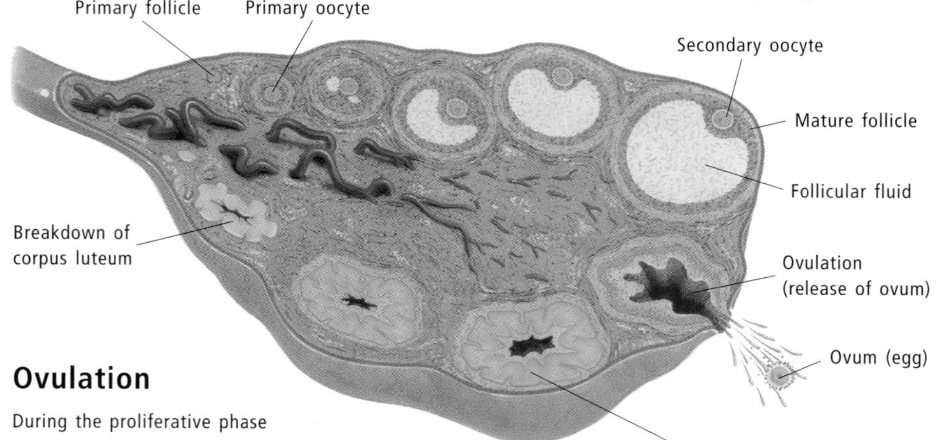

Ovulation

During the proliferative phase of the cycle (days 8–10), follicle cells in the ovary divide and increase in size, creating a sac that contains an oocyte (female sex cell). By days 10–14, a mature follicle holding a secondary oocyte (mature egg) has formed. A surge of hormone from the pituitary gland triggers ovulation—the follicle releases its ovum into the fallopian tube. The ruptured follicle then transforms into the corpus luteum, which secretes progesterone and estrogen. If the egg is not fertilized the corpus luteum breaks down, hormone levels fall and menstruation occurs.

this seems to be a racial rather than a climatic effect. The age of puberty has dropped by several years over the last hundred years but this trend now seems to have slowed down.

Puberty is considered to be precocious or abnormally early if it occurs before 8 or 9 years. This may be due to ovarian cysts or rare hormonal disorders, but in many cases there is no obvious cause.

Menstrual problems

The days preceding menstruation are a time of discomfort for some women; this is known as premenstrual tension or premenstrual syndrome and should be differentiated from dysmenorrhea, which is discomfort or pain during menstruation. Dysmenorrhea is usually most severe for the first 12 hours or so of the period. It is most prevalent in younger women and usually appears 2–4 years after the onset of menstruation and is uncommon after the thirtieth year. It is widely believed that childbirth will cure dysmenorrhea but this is not always the case.

The pain characterizing dysmenorrhea ranges from a dull ache to a severe ache with colic. It is usually located in the lower abdomen but may also be referred to the inside and front of the thighs. Nausea, vomiting, diarrhea and migraines sometimes accompany the pain. It is now generally accepted that the pain is the result of the actions of a group of substances produced in the endometrium, called prostaglandins. These are involved in both endometrial breakdown and control of excessive bleeding during menstruation. They also stimulate contractions of the uterine and cervical muscle during menstruation which may become painful (prostaglandins are involved in uterine contractions during labor). Oral administration of prostaglandin inhibitors for the first few days of the period help to alleviate the dysmenorrhea. Prostaglandin production does not occur without previous stimulation of the uterus by progesterone, so an alternative therapy is to use oral contraceptives which suppress ovulation.

Dysmenorrhea most commonly occurs in the absence of any recognizable abnormality, when it is called primary dysmenorrhea. It may also be a symptom of a number of gynecological disorders including endometriosis, a condition in which fragments of endometrium are relocated and become attached to other organs. These fragments remain functional and

Menstruation

(a) During menstruation (days 1–6) the lining of the uterus (endometrium) breaks down and is discharged.
(b) At the start of the proliferative phase (days 7–13), cells begin to repair the endometrium and
(c) Follicles in the ovary begin to form an ovum (egg).
(d) Ovulation takes place (around day 14) and the ovary releases its ovum into the fallopian tube.
(e) The secretory phase (days 15–28) follows ovulation. The ovum travels up the fallopian tube towards the uterus and hormones thicken the endometrium in readiness to support a fertilized ovum. If the ovum is not fertilized, hormone levels fall and blood vessels in the uterus constrict. This causes the unused endometrial blood and tissue to be discharged from the body and the menstrual cycle begins again.

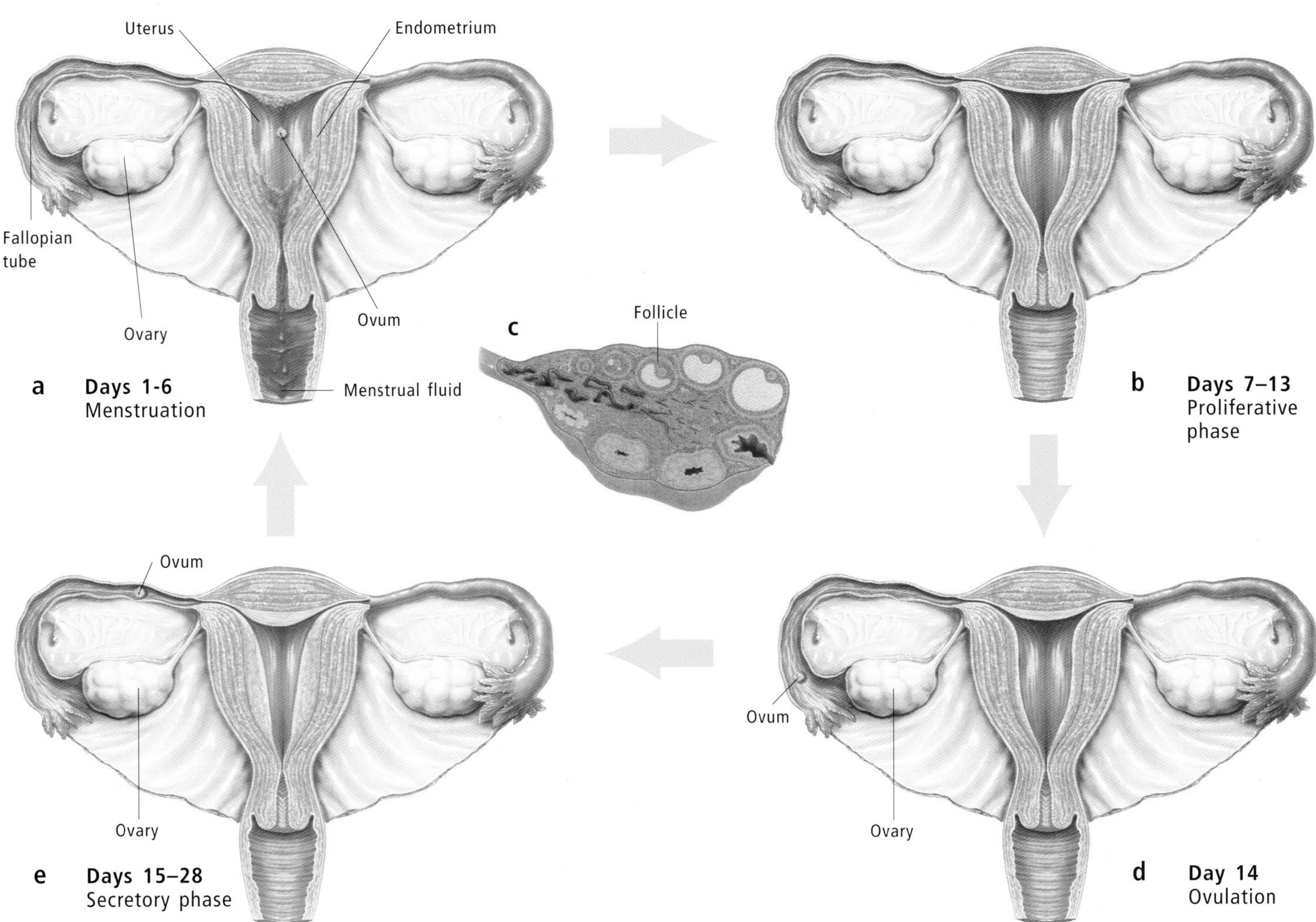

M

hormonally responsive and undergo variable amounts of hemorrhage at menstruation. The pain is due to build-up of blood in the displaced fragments and is thus usually worse at the end of the period than at the beginning, as with dysmenorrhea.

Amenorrhea is absence of menstruation, either primarily in women who have never menstruated or secondarily, when menstruation ceases after having occurred previously. Amenorrhea of either sort may be the result of pituitary malfunction due either to injury or to a tumor or, rarely, to the congenital inability of the pituitary to produce gonadotropins. Stress, excessive or heavy exercise or low body weight are also implicated. Primary amenorrhea may be the result of chromosomal or genital abnormalities or ovaries that are insensitive to gonadotropins.

Uterine bleeding

Uterine bleeding, similar to normal menstruation, may occur even if ovulation has not taken place. The hormonal environment prior to endometrial breakdown in an anovulatory cycle will clearly be different from that in a normal cycle. If ovulation does not occur, there is no corpus luteum to produce progesterone and so the bleeding is not the result of progesterone withdrawal. Instead the follicle which should have ovulated continues to secrete estrogen for a variable length of time until it degenerates and blood estrogen levels drop. The endometrial response is to undergo breakdown in a similar way to that which occurs under progesterone withdrawal, although often to a lesser extent, so that loss of blood and tissue debris is noticeably lighter than with a normal period. Withdrawal bleeding when an oral contraceptive is stopped for a few days occurs in a similar way.

Anovulatory cycles are normal for the few months after menarche and just before menopause. Anovulation may be established by biopsy of the uterine lining and looking for changes in the tissue which indicate the influence of progesterone.

Uterine bleeding is considered to be abnormal if menstruation is excessively heavy, of normal intensity but occurring too frequently, or if bleeding or spotting occurs consistently between normal periods. This can be the result of disturbances to the normal production of pituitary gonadotropins, ovarian hormones or prostaglandins. Other possible factors include cancer of the uterus, cervix, ovary or fallopian tube, retained fragments of placenta, an infection such as pelvic inflammatory disease, ectopic pregnancy, polycystic ovary syndrome and, occasionally, coagulation disorders which prevent normal blood clotting (e.g. von Willebrand's disease).

Irregular abnormal bleeding may be associated with the use of an intrauterine device for contraceptive purposes. Emotional disturbances affect bleeding in some women. Occasionally bleeding may be associated with ovulation. Benign tumors in the uterine muscle called fibroids or leiomyomas are found in perhaps 50 percent of all women over 40 years of age. Most are symptomless but they can also be a common cause of excessively heavy menstruation (sometimes called "flooding") in older women.

Irregular or heavy bleeding is frequently associated with menopause. In the absence of any abnormality this is a symptom of the alteration in the pattern of female and pituitary hormones at this time. Bleeding occurring after menopause should be investigated thoroughly as it may be a symptom of a malignant disease of the uterus.

Social and cultural aspects

Menstrual bleeding is a normal functional event but it is also a biological oddity, as bleeding is usually a sign of trauma. This may partly account for the numerous beliefs, customs and rituals that have been associated with menstruation since ancient times.

Almost all tribal cultures have restrictions and taboos on the activities of menstruating women. Most of these are based on the concept that either menstrual fluid or menstruating women are contaminating or harmful to others. Cultural practices may include the maintenance of special places of residence ("menstrual huts") to which women retire for the duration of their menstrual period. Other customs aimed to restrict the activities of menstruating women by preventing them from collecting or handling food, touching hunting equipment, planting crops or having sexual intercourse.

The early religious writings of Zoroastrianism, Judaism, Christianity and Islam provided rules for most aspects of living. These included codes of behavior for both the menstruating woman and the people with whom she came into contact, and were usually based on the concept that menstruation was unclean. Many of these rules are now either forgotten or disregarded.

The physiology of the menstrual cycle was described early in the twentieth century and the hormones responsible for the cyclic changes in the uterine lining were discovered and synthesized in the laboratory shortly afterwards. Despite this, prior to the introduction of the oral contraceptive in the late 1950s, numerous beliefs regarding the danger of menstruation prevailed. These beliefs perceived the danger as being directed towards the menstruating woman herself, rather than towards others. Bathing, swimming, washing hair or indulging in vigorous physical exercise were considered to be harmful at this delicate time. Even having the hair permed was to be avoided in case the perm did not "take". Menstruation was described as "the curse" or as being "unwell", a concept which persists, with some justification, up to the present time in the expectation that the premenstrual and menstrual phases of the female cycle will be uncomfortable or even incapacitating.

Attempts were also made during the early twentieth century to establish whether menstrual fluid was actually toxic. These scientific studies have since been discredited but, at the time, some claimed to have isolated a substance named menotoxin present in menstrual blood and sweat, tears, urine, saliva and other bodily secretions of menstruating females, which was responsible for the ancient belief of harm.

Despite the inconvenience and possible discomfort, menstruation is still accepted as a necessary part of female function, even for women who suppress their natural cycles by taking the contraceptive pill. The pill is almost always administered in an intermittent pattern which mimics the menstrual cycle, although there is little medical evidence to support this as being a better or healthier approach than continuous use which would exclude bleeding altogether.

SEE ALSO *Fibroids, Menopause, Mittelschmerz, Ovaries, Ovulation, Premenstrual syndrome, Progesterone, Prostaglandins, Puberty, Reproductive systems*

M

MERCURY POISONING

Mercury poisoning is caused by ingestion, inhalation or absorption through the skin of mercury compounds. Although it is a naturally occurring metal, mercury is used at potentially dangerous concentrations for a wide range of industrial purposes. Effects on the body depend on exposure levels. Acute poisoning occurs when large amounts are ingested in a short space of time. Symptoms include a burning sensation in the throat, a metallic taste in the mouth, abdominal pain, vomiting, excessive saliva production and blood-tinged diarrhea. Kidney failure may lead to death. Mercury can also cross the placental barrier and cause birth defects.

Mercury accumulates in body tissues, particularly the liver, kidney, brain and blood. Chronic poisoning results when small quantities are swallowed or absorbed gradually through persistent low-level exposure. Symptoms include red and swollen extremities ("pink disease"), irritability, fevers, hair loss, nail damage and eventually tremors, convulsions, personality changes and brain damage.

In one tragic incident of mass poisoning during the 1950s, many residents in the Japanese fishing village of Minamata died after eating seafood that had been contaminated by mercury-laden industrial waste. Workers making felt hats in the 1800s routinely used mercury and frequently suffered symptoms of chronic poisoning, leading to the expression "mad as a hatter". These days, however, mercury poisoning is rare although there is debate about the potential for mercury in teeth fillings to cause chronic poisoning.

SEE ALSO *Poisoning*

MESOTHELIOMA

Mesothelioma is a rare and malignant form of cancer of the membranes lining the lungs (the pleura), abdomen (the peritoneum) or heart (the pericardium). It is almost always caused by previous exposure to asbestos, which may have taken place 20 years or more before the symptoms of the disease appear. Those symptoms are cough, shortness of breath, weight loss and chest pain. There is often an accompanying pleural effusion (fluid in the pleural sac of the lung). A chest x-ray, thoracic CAT scan and a lung biopsy will confirm the diagnosis. The disease is usually incurable, though surgery, radiation therapy, and chemotherapy may control symptoms.

SEE ALSO *Asbestosis, Lung*

METABOLISM

Everything that happens in the human body is dependent upon chemical reactions in the cells. These complex biochemical events or pathways that drive all of the body's systems are collectively referred to as metabolism. There are two fundamental phases or processes involved in metabolism—one is constructive and uses energy, the other breaks down compounds and creates energy.

During the building-up phase, called anabolism, simple molecules are used to create more complex molecules and substances. For example, amino acids are bonded together to build proteins and simple sugars are packaged up to produce polysaccharides. Anabolic reactions require energy and occur during the growth, repair and maintenance of body cells and systems.

During the reverse process, catabolism, complex substances such as food are broken down into simpler compounds. Catabolic reactions produce energy, which is stored in a substance known as ATP until required for use in anabolic reactions. Chemical diges-

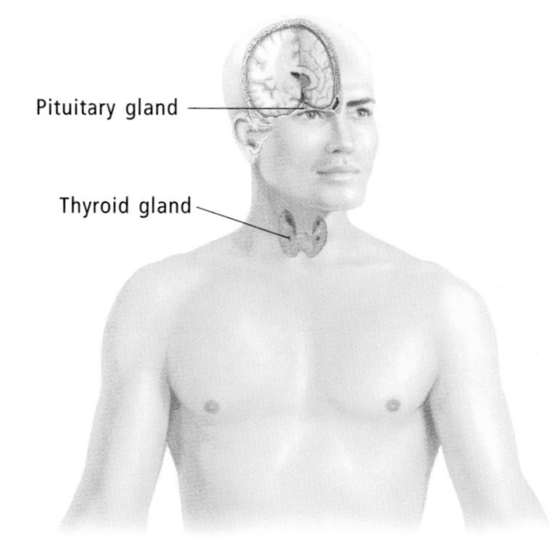

Metabolism—regulating mechanisms

Metabolism is the collective term for all the chemical processes that run our body. Thyroid hormones regulate the metabolic rate, so under- or over-activity of the thyroid can disrupt the body's metabolism. The pituitary gland controls the release of thyroid hormones.

Chemical metabolism

One of the most important chemical processes in the body is the breakdown of carbohydrates into glucose, and the subsequent conversion of glucose into energy. Chemicals in the pancreas, stomach and intestines break down carbohydrates and other nutrients to allow the body to run efficiently. The liver metabolizes food and stores glucose to provide energy for body cells and muscles.

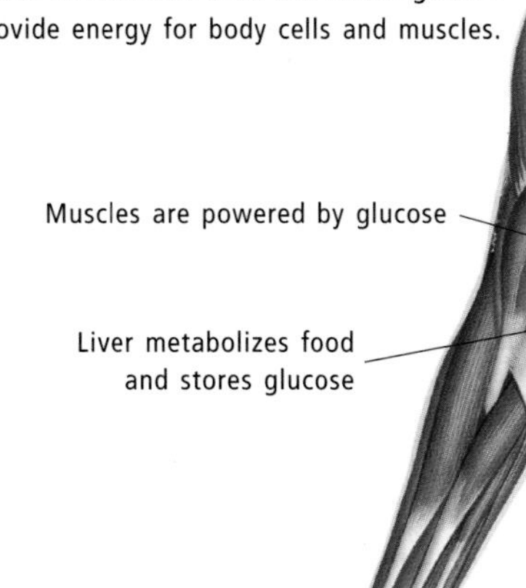

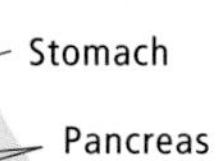

M

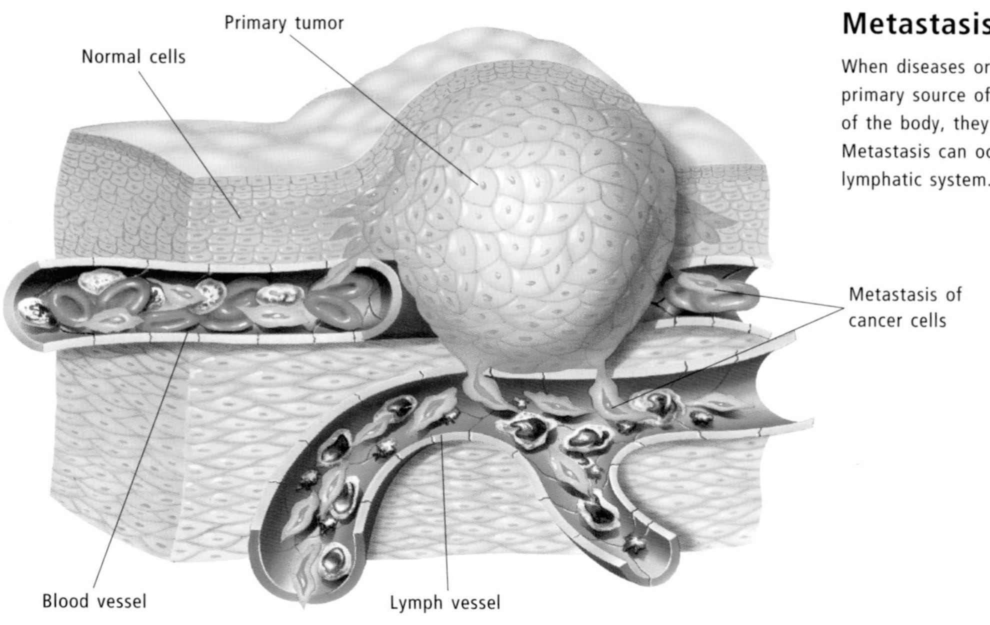

Metastasis

When diseases or cancerous cells spread from the primary source of infection or tumor to another part of the body, they are said to have metastasized. Metastasis can occur via the bloodstream or the lymphatic system.

tion, during which food molecules are broken down and energy released, is an example of a catabolic process.

Substances that are crucial to the chemical reactions that run our bodies include enzymes, which are produced by the body itself, and nutrients, which are extracted from the foods we eat. Nutrients include carbohydrates, lipids, proteins, minerals and vitamins. Many metabolic disorders involve an inability of the body to produce or use particular enzymes or to break down or use certain nutrients from foods.

Fortunately, most serious metabolic disorders are exceptionally rare. Many are congenital (present from birth). These include fructose intolerance, galactosemia, maple sugar urine disease and phenylketonuria (PKU). Early recognition of such diseases is crucial because their impacts on the body can often be controlled or limited by strict nutritional or dietary regimes.

Basal metabolic rate is the lowest rate of energy use required by the body to sustain its essential functions, including respiration, blood circulation and temperature maintenance. It is measured between 14–18 hours after the last meal, when the person is awake but at complete rest in a comfortable environment. The resulting measurement is known as the basal metabolic rate (BMR), which is ultimately an expression of the pace at which a particular person's body breaks down food. On average, a healthy human uses 1,500–2,000 kilocalories (6,000–8,000 kilojoules) per day in the maintenance of basic body functions.

A person's overall metabolism is regulated internally by hormones, particularly those secreted by the thyroid gland. Too much or too little of these can alter the metabolic rate and may cause serious health problems.

There are, however, many other factors that also affect metabolic rate. For example, our metabolism slows with age and increases with exercise. The metabolic rate of women tends to be lower than that of men, although it increases during pregnancy and lactation. Stress hormones raise the metabolic rate, as do other hormones such as testosterone. High temperatures, associated with illness, will also cause an increase in metabolic rate. The metabolic rate slows during sleep and when we are malnourished.

SEE ALSO *Amino acids, Diabetes, Enzyme deficiencies, Hormones, Phenylketonuria*

METASTASIS

Metastasis is the general term for the spread of cancer from one part of the body to another. A single tumor that has spread is called a metastasis (also called a "secondary"); more than one are referred to as metastases (or "secondaries"). Metastases are caused by cancer cells that have separated from a primary tumor, have spread through the veins or lymphatic system (less commonly via an artery) and have lodged in distant tissue and grown to form tumors themselves. Metastases are commonly found in the liver, lung, bones and brain. The cancer cells in a metastasis are the same as in the primary tumor.

A metastasis may also spread across the surface of a body cavity such as the peritoneum (the lining of the abdomen) or the pleura surrounding the lungs. Occasionally, metastases result from surgery and may be found in the scar of the wound through which a tumor has been removed. A metastasis usually indicates advancing spread of the cancer, and a generally poorer prognosis.

Treatments such as radiation therapy, surgery and chemotherapy are usually aimed at relieving the symptoms rather than curing the cancer. Occasionally it may be the metastasis rather than the primary tumor that causes the initial symptoms of cancer. Sometimes the primary tumor is never found.

SEE ALSO *Cancer*

METHADONE

Methadone is a synthetic narcotic painkiller (analgesic) similar to morphine. It blocks the effects of heroin withdrawal, and so is used primarily in the treatment of heroin users, though it may sometimes be used in the management of cancer pain. It can be given once a day as an oral preparation. Side effects are similar to those other narcotics and include nausea, constipation and urinary retention. Methadone is itself addictive but it is thought to be easier to withdraw from than heroin, though still not easy.

Though not a cure for drug dependence in itself, methadone gives people the opportunity to manage their lives and reduces their dependence on crime and the illegal drugs market, and therefore minimizes the social and legal consequences and the risks of transmission of infections such as HIV (AIDS), hepatitis B and C.

SEE ALSO *Drug dependence, Heroin*

M

MICROCEPHALY

Microcephaly is a rare disorder in which a child's head circumference is below the normal size range for age and sex. There are a variety of causes, including premature closing of the fontanelles, genetic abnormalities and disease. Microcephaly can be present at birth, or it may develop during a child's early years. Some degree of intellectual disability and impaired physical development are common. Life expectancy is often low.

MICROSURGERY

Microsurgery is a surgical technique in which a surgeon uses a microscope and specially adapted hand-held miniaturized instruments to operate on tiny structures, such as very small blood vessels and nerves. It is used for operations that require extreme delicacy, such as plastic surgery, reconstruction and transplantation. Microsurgery is frequently used in surgery of the ears, the eyes, or the brain.

MIDBRAIN

The midbrain is located deep inside the brain, below the cerebrum. It sits directly above the pons and, together with this structure and the medulla oblongata, forms the brain stem, the part of the brain attached to the spinal cord. The brain stem is the most primitive part of the brain and is involved in many basic body functions. The midbrain itself relays motor signals from the cerebral cortex to the pons, and sensory transmissions in the other direction, from the spinal cord to the thalamus. Cranial nerves III and IV, which service the eye muscles, start in the midbrain, making this area important in eyelid, eyeball, lens and pupil movements. The midbrain is also referred to as the mesencephalon.

SEE ALSO *Brain, Eye, Medulla oblongata, Spinal cord*

MIDDLE EAR

The middle ear is part of the mechanism for sensing sound. It is situated within the skull, adjacent to the outer ear. A thin tympanic membrane (eardrum), which vibrates under the influence of sound, covers the inner end of the ear canal. A sound wave striking the ear causes the membrane to vibrate. The vibrations are transmitted to a sensory region, the cochlea, from which the auditory nerve conveys the sensation of sound, now in the form of nerve impulses, to the brain.

SEE ALSO *Cochlea, Ear, Hearing, Otitis media*

Midbrain

Also known as the mesencephalon, the midbrain relays information between the medulla oblongata and the cerebral hemispheres. It contains the nerve centers for the third and fourth cranial nerves, and includes the colliculi and cerebral peduncles.

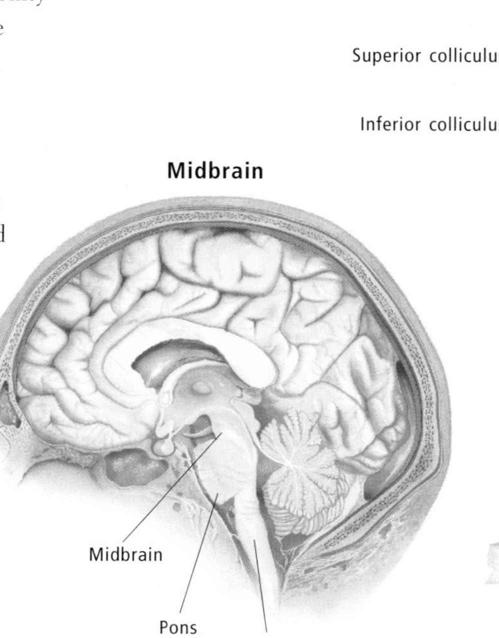

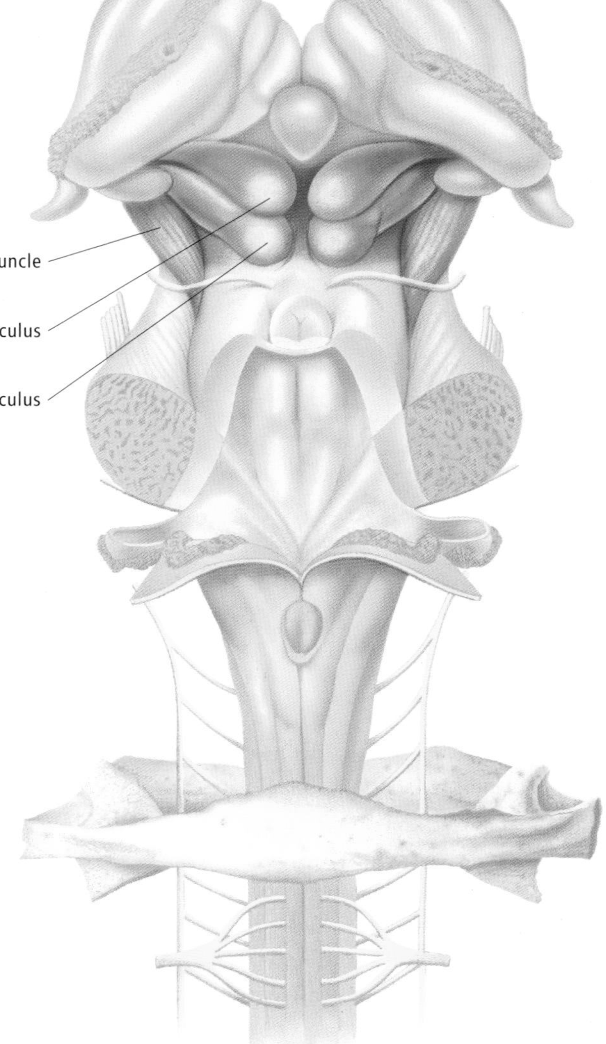

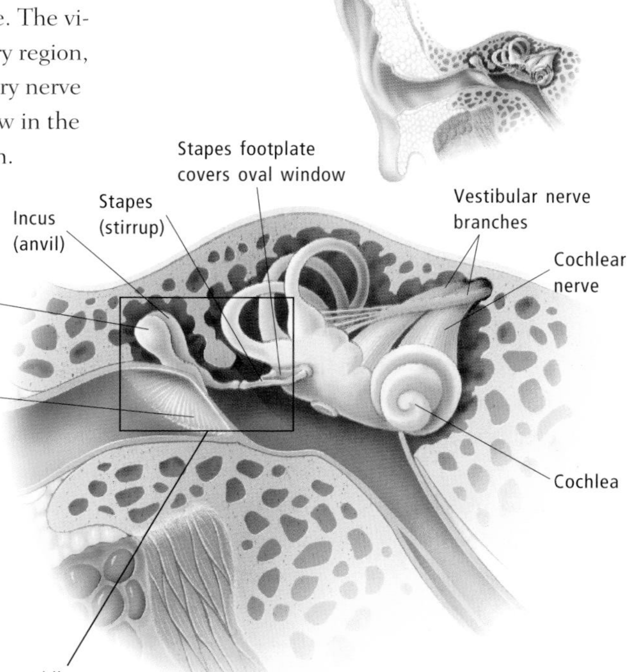

Middle ear

The middle ear is a short chamber between the eardrum and the oval window of the inner ear. It contains a chain of three small bones or ossicles (malleus, incus and stapes), which carry sound waves from the vibrating eardrum to the cochlea.

M

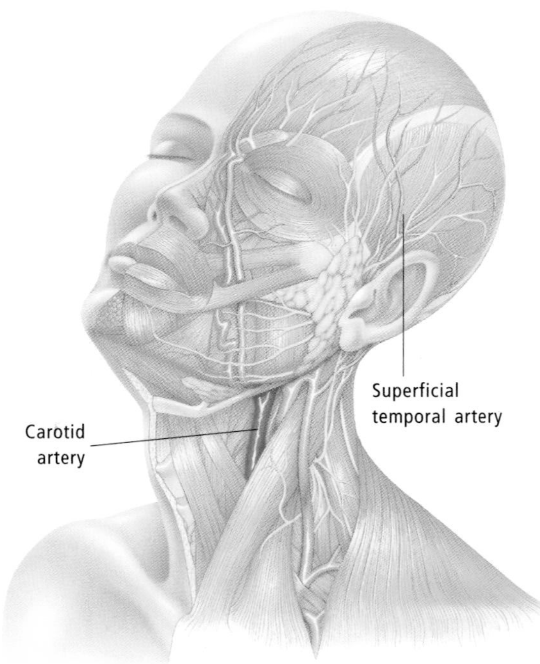

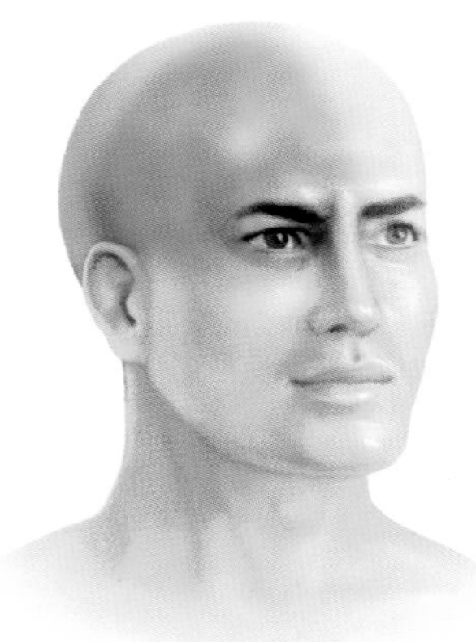

Migraine

Migraines have been linked to the dilation of cerebral blood vessels such as branches of the the carotid arteries. Pain relief may be obtained from drugs that stop the dilation of blood vessels, but only if taken in the early stages of the migraine.

MIGRAINE

Migraine headaches are the most common and serious variety of vascular headaches, estimated to affect over 10 percent of the population. They are associated with dilation of one or more branches of the carotid and vertebral arteries, which supply the scalp and structures within the skull. Migraine is not a single disease entity. Although most migraine headaches share a number of clinical features, several varieties of the migraine syndrome are recognized. The precise cause of migraine headaches remains unknown, as does the mechanism of development of the clinical features. Recent research indicates that abnormalities with serotonin (a neurotransmitter) or with serotonin receptors in the brain may be involved.

Migraine headaches typically cause severe, often throbbing pain that usually affects one half of the head or behind one eye (although sometimes it can be on both sides). The sufferer may wake up with a headache, which usually lasts several hours, sometimes a whole day or longer. There may be associated nausea and vomiting, as well as tenderness of the scalp (sometimes overlying the involved dilated arteries). After the headache subsides, the person is usually exhausted.

The common form of migraine affects women approximately three times more often than men. A tendency to develop migraine runs in families. Many precipitating factors have been identified, such as fatigue and stress, oversleeping or missing a meal; consumption of certain foods (especially chocolate, drinks containing caffeine, alcoholic drinks, especially red wine, and nuts, beans, lentils and cheeses); and various food additives (such as nitrates/nitrites in processed meats, monosodium glutamate in processed foods and some Asian foods, as well as certain food colorings.

Hormonal factors apparently play a very important role; migraine headaches are often related to menstrual periods, and may occur in the first trimester of pregnancy, during menopause and as a side effect of oral contraceptive therapy.

A less common variety of migraine is known as classic migraine or migraine with aura. In this form, the patient develops symptoms suggestive of interference with normal brain function, for periods of 5–30 minutes before the onset of the headache. The symptoms may include visual disturbances, such as seeing flashing lights or partial loss of vision; disruptions in hearing, taste or smell; or, rarely, speech disturbances, partial paralysis, dizziness or loss of balance. These abnormalities are temporary and reversible, usually disappearing as the headache worsens. The headache is otherwise similar to common migraine. Other variant forms of migraine are quite rare but may be associated with more severe neurological disturbances.

Migraine headaches are difficult to treat, although some effective drugs are available. Prevention is best, so, where possible, known precipitating factors should be avoided. If avoidance of dietary triggers and modifications of lifestyle do not help to reduce the frequency of headaches, a number of drugs can be used to prevent the onset of migraine, although their effectiveness is variable.

There are a number of alternative therapies that may be used to alleviate the symptoms of migrane. Acupuncture and shiatsu treat points to relieve the pain and correct imbalances of the liver and gallbladder meridians. Aromatherapy prescribes a 5-minute hot water foot bath with chamomile, melissa, lavender or rosemary, or regular massage as a preventive measure. Psychotherapy or somatic therapies may help to pinpoint and release underlying tensions. Herbalism prescribes chamomile, ginger and feverfew. Homeopathy treats migraine with constitutional remedies prescribed according to an overall patient "picture". Naturopathy eliminates possible food allergies or other triggers.

Low blood sugar levels or hormonal imbalances are treated with diet and supplements; emotional upsets are treated with flower essences. Qi gong, t'ai chi or yoga seek to prevent migraine by helping release accumulated stresses held within the body.

SEE ALSO *Headache*

MINERALOCORTICOIDS

Mineralocorticoids are a class of hormones produced by the adrenal gland. They are concerned with maintaining adequate fluid volume, blood pressure and heart output in the body. The main mineralocorticoid is aldosterone. A deficiency of mineralocorticoid, for example in Addison's disease, can cause reduced cardiac output and fatal shock.

SEE ALSO *Hormones*

MINERALS

Minerals, in the present context, are inorganic substances found in the body or diet. In general, minerals are required for the formation of bone, for use as electrolytes in intracellular and extracellular fluids, and for incorporation into the molecules of hemoglobin, enzymes and coenzymes.

Minerals important for health include calcium, chloride, magnesium, phosphorus, iron, potassium and sodium. Some minerals, such as those mentioned above, are required in relatively large quantities; others, generally known as trace elements, are required only in very small amounts and may be toxic if taken in large amounts. Many mineral substances are toxic in any dose, notably lead, mercury and all radioactive substances.

Electrolytes are chemical substances, which when dissolved in fluids, dissociate into electrically charged ions. They are so-called because in their ionic form they can conduct electricity. The main minerals required as electrolytes are sodium, potassium, magnesium, calcium and chloride.

Sodium is a major electrolyte of all fluids in the body. Potassium is an important electrolyte in intracellular fluid. Fruit juices are an important dietary source of potassium. Some medications cause loss of potassium, but overdose of potassium is serious and may be fatal. Magnesium is another important intracellular electrolyte. Calcium is an important intracellular electrolyte, playing a vital role in muscle action and nerve transmission. Chloride is a major anionic (negatively charged) electrolyte, occurring in all body fluids. Electrolytes are lost in sweat, vomiting and diarrhea. Excessive intake of salt (sodium chloride) may be harmful in heart disease and pregnancy.

Calcium, besides acting as an electrolyte, is a major constituent of bone, which is a hydroxyapatite (a mixture of calcium phosphate and calcium hydroxide) deposited in an organic matrix. The adult body typically contains about 42 ounces (1,200 grams) of calcium. Milk is an important source.

Iron is required for the synthesis of hemoglobin (the red pigment of the blood) and myoglobin (a similar pigment found in muscle). Iron deficiency, usually due to poor absorption of iron, leads to anemia. Paradoxically, excessive iron is also harmful. Phosphorus is required for bone, DNA,

Minerals

Minerals cannot be manufactured by the body and hence must be ingested. They perform three important functions: they play a role in physiological processes, such as the movement of muscles and skeletal development; they determine the concentration of fluids in body cells; and they are important for enzymatic reactions.

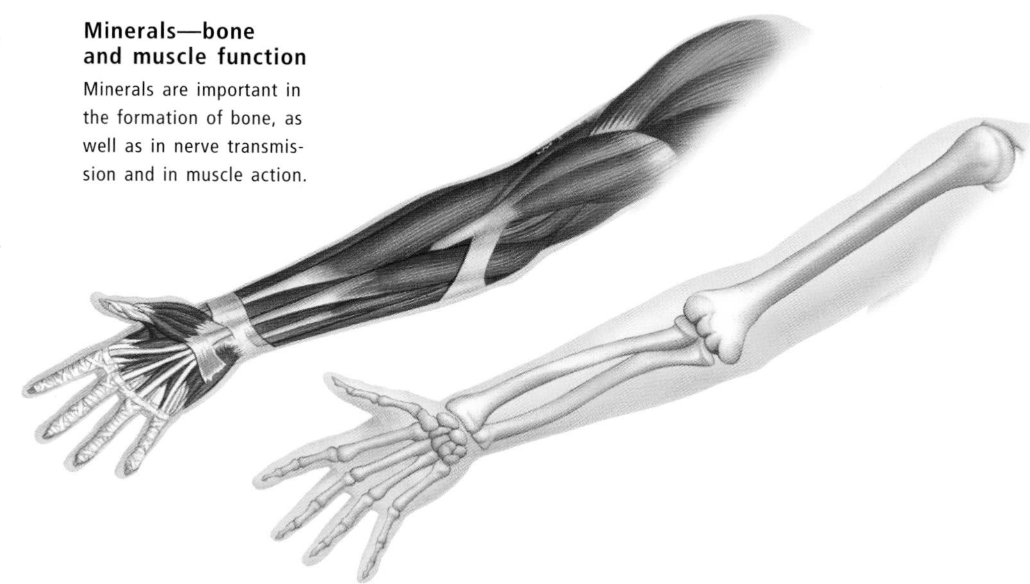

Minerals—bone and muscle function

Minerals are important in the formation of bone, as well as in nerve transmission and in muscle action.

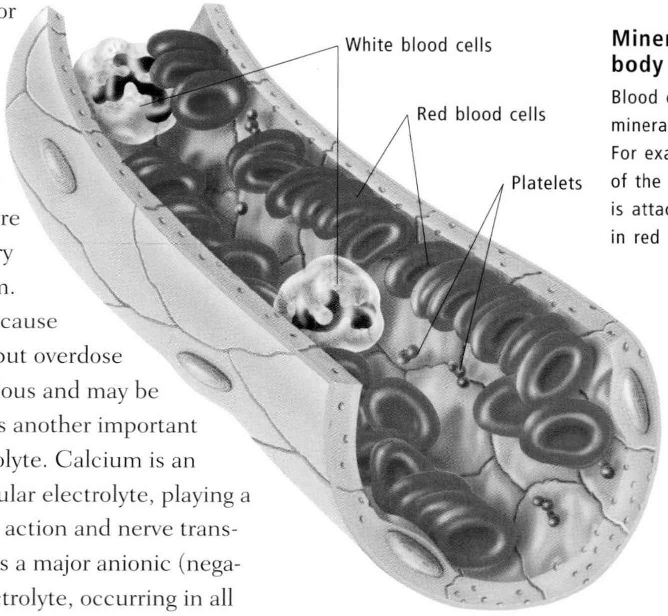

White blood cells

Red blood cells

Platelets

Minerals—body fluids

Blood carries the various minerals around the body. For example, two-thirds of the iron in the body is attached to hemoglobin in red blood cells.

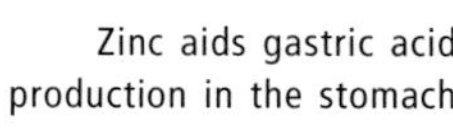
Zinc aids gastric acid production in the stomach

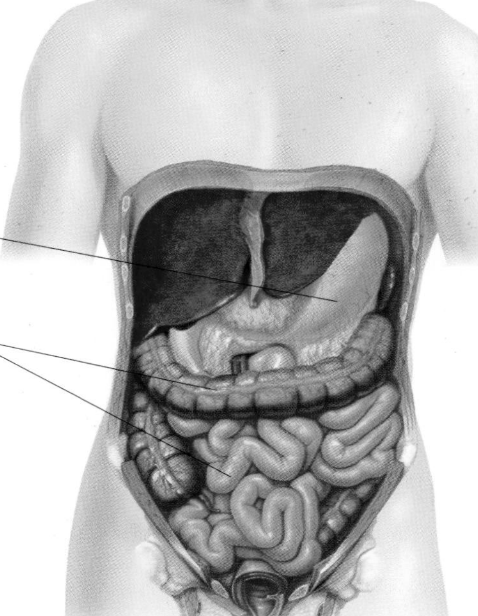
Minerals assist enzyme production in the intestines

Minerals—enzyme reactions

Minerals are required for the body to produce enzymes. These are needed for food processing and absorption. Zinc, for example, is needed for the production of gastric acid.

M

RNA and some coenzymes, playing an important role in all metabolic processes. Sulfur is an essential constituent of proteins, such as the amino acids cysteine and methionine. It is found particularly in the hair.

There are several other minerals which are essential, but needed only in small quantities. Iodine is required for thyroid hormone. Its main dietary sources are seafood (for example, fish and seaweed), and artificially iodized salt. Deficiency causes goiter. Zinc is an essential component of some enzyme systems, required for important functions including wound healing, immune responses and reproduction. Copper deficiency is believed to be an important cause of heart disease. Cobalt is a component of vitamin B_{12}. Manganese is a component of several enzyme systems.

Fluorides are deposited in the enamel of the developing teeth of children, giving increased resistance to dental caries. Dietary sources are naturally or artificially fluoridated water, tea, and sea-fish.

Diet during pregnancy and lactation must include the additional minerals necessary for the needs of the growing fetus and baby, notably calcium, phosphorus and iodine.

SEE ALSO *Calcium, Electrolytes, Fluoridation, Iodine deficiency, Iron, Lead poisoning, Nutrition, Potassium, Sodium*

MISCARRIAGE

A miscarriage or spontaneous abortion generally occurs before week 12 of a pregnancy. Miscarriage occurs in one in every five pregnancies. Before week 20 of the pregnancy the loss of a fetus is a miscarriage; after that date it is a stillbirth.

Around 85 percent of miscarriages are related to fetal abnormalities. Of the remaining 15 percent, two-thirds are due to problems in the mother and one-third have an unknown cause. Miscarriage can follow a severe fever, particularly if it is caused by a virus. It can be due to some abnormality of the uterus. It is less common in women under 25, and more likely after the age of 35.

Bleeding, first spotting then a heavier discharge, is usually the first sign of a miscarriage, though some minor bleeding can also occur as part of a normal pregnancy. Cramping of the uterus follows. If an ultrasound detects a fetal heartbeat, then there is around a 90 percent chance that the pregnancy will proceed. Although some doctors still recommend bed rest there is no evidence that this is necessary. When the fetus is no longer viable, cramping will continue and pieces of tissue may be expelled. It is important to seek medical advice if miscarriage seems possible. Sometimes a curette may be suggested to scrape out any remaining contents of the uterus; however, ultrasound will usually indicate that this is not necessary.

Late miscarriage (between weeks 12 and 20) can be caused by a weak cervix (in approximately 20 percent of women). If this is found to be the cause, a stitch (cervical cerclage) may be used. After 20 weeks a miscarriage can be the result of placental insufficiency. Recurrent miscarriage (after a woman has had three or more miscarriages in succession) will need investigation by a specialist. The next pregnancy will need careful monitoring.

SEE ALSO *Abortion, Dilation and curettage, Placenta, Pregnancy*

MITRAL VALVE

The mitral valve is one of the valves in the heart; it prevents the backflow of blood from the left ventricle to the left atrium during systolic contraction of the heart. The mitral valve gets its name due to the distinctive shape of the valve, which resembles the miter worn by bishops. The mitral together with the tricuspid valves are called atrioventricular valves because they lie between the atria and ventricles. Both atrioventricular valves have parachute-like valve cusps, which have tough fibrous cords (chordae tendineae, the "heart strings") attached along the free edge.

The other ends of the chordae are attached to small tongue-shaped elevations of the heart muscle of the ventricle (papillary muscles) which are designed to pull down on the chordae and the valve cusps when the ventricle contracts, thus keeping the tricuspid and mitral valves shut as the ventricles rapidly decrease in size during contraction.

Mitral valve disease usually is divided into two types: mitral stenosis, where the valve opening is too narrow, and mitral insufficiency (or incompetence) where the mitral valve is unable to prevent backflow of blood from the left ventricle to the left atrium. Most mitral valve disease is due to rheumatic heart disease, but mitral insufficiency may be caused by ruptured or defective chordae tendineae or papillary muscles.

Patients with mitral stenosis usually present to their doctor with symptoms of failure of the left side of the heart, including shortness of breath, breathlessness while lying down, and coughing up blood. They may develop palpitations (the sensation of rapid heart beating in the chest) and chest

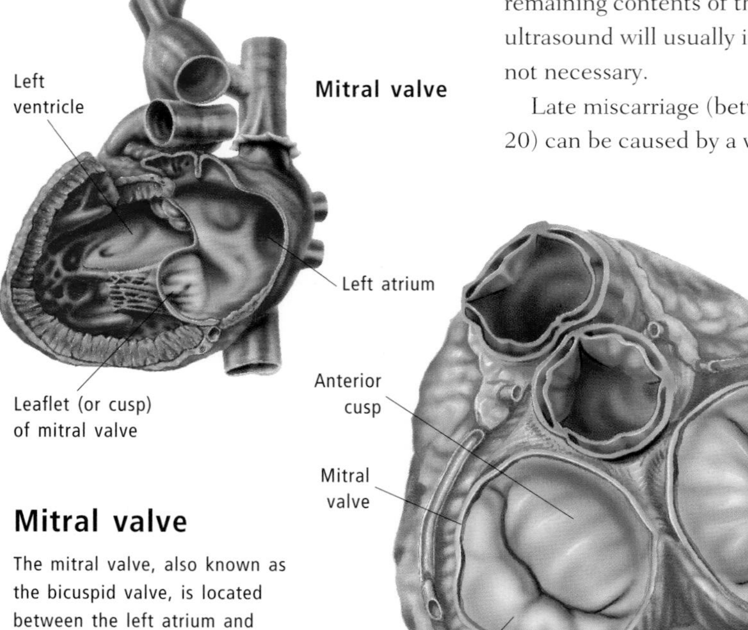

Mitral valve

The mitral valve, also known as the bicuspid valve, is located between the left atrium and left ventricle. Prolapse of the mitral valve may result in chest pain, dyspnea, palpitations, fatigue and fainting.

pain. Patients may also develop atrial fibrillation (the chaotic and ineffectual contraction of the left atrium) which can have serious consequences if blood coagulates in the left atrium and throws off tiny fragments to block arteries in the brain, limbs or kidneys. There will be a murmur (a sound produced by abnormal blood flow through the heart) heard best on the lower left side of the chest.

Medical treatment for mitral stenosis is aimed at treating arrhythmias (abnormal rhythm) and usually includes digoxin, beta-adrenergic blocking drugs and maybe quinidine in various combinations, but would depend on the clinical circumstances. Anticoagulants like warfarin prevent formation of thrombosis in the atrium which can dislodge and block other arteries. Antibiotics are used to treat infections on valve surfaces.

Surgical treatment involves separating the valve cusps (valvotomy), which are often stuck together along their edges. In some cases, the entire valve may need to be replaced by an artificial valve (prosthesis), or a valve graft from pig heart.

Patients with mitral insufficiency often complain to their physician of fatigue, shortness of breath and episodic breathlessness at night. Symptoms may start suddenly if the condition is due to sudden rupture of the chordae tendineae. A murmur is also present, but the timing of the sound differs from that heard in mitral stenosis. Medical treatment may be similar to that used in mitral stenosis; surgical treatment involves replacing the damaged mitral valve with a prosthetic valve or graft.

Replacement of the mitral valve in either mitral stenosis or insufficiency will require open-heart surgery, in which the patient's body is cooled and the function of the heart is temporarily taken over by a heart–lung machine. This will allow the heart to be stopped and opened, so that the surgeon may reach the damaged valve.

SEE ALSO *Heart, Ventricle*

MITTELSCHMERZ

Of German origin, mittelschmerz is a term used to describe the pain experienced by women mid-way through the menstrual cycle, at around day fourteen. It is thought to be caused by the stretching of the nerves around the ovary as it increases in size. It is often accompanied by bloating, mood changes, headache, and fluid retention. Mittelschmerz can be treated if necessary with diuretics and painkillers, or, in severe cases, by suppressing ovulation through the use of oral contraceptives.

SEE ALSO *Menstruation, Ovulation*

MOLES

A mole is the common term for a nevus, a congenital pigmented skin marking. Moles are also known as birthmarks because they usually appear shortly after birth. Moles can also appear during childhood and early adolescence. They may be round and raised or flat. They range in color from brown or black to bluish or blue-gray. Most people have twenty to thirty—some people have several hundred. There are many varieties, including cafe-au-lait spots, congenital nevi, hairy nevi and sebaceous nevi.

Cafe-au-lait spots are light tan, the color of coffee with milk. Multiple cafe-au-lait are associated with neurofibromatosis, a genetic disorder causing abnormal growth of nerve tissues.

A mongolian spot (or mongolian blue spot) is usually bluish or bruised-looking. It appears most commonly over the lower back or buttocks, but may also occur in other areas such as the trunk or arms. Mongolian spots may persist for months or years but are benign and do not become cancerous.

Congenital nevi (those present at birth) have an increased risk of developing into malignant melanoma, a form of skin cancer. Those with a mixture of colors, those that are irregular in shape, and those that are large have the highest potential for malignancy. People living in areas with high levels of ultraviolet radiation such as Queensland in Australia are also at high risk, as are those with moles in trauma areas such as the palms of hands, soles of feet, under nails, on the genitals, inside the mouth, or belt and bra areas. All congenital nevi should be examined periodically; if there are changes in the size, color, or surface texture, or sudden ulceration, bleeding, or itching in the birthmark, a physician should be consulted and the mole should be removed.

Diagnosis of the type of mole is made by a physician based on the appearance of the mole, when it appeared, and any symptoms or pre-cancer type features. Usually the mole doesn't need to be treated; however, if it looks ungainly and is causing concern, it can be covered with cosmetics. Alternatively, it can be surgically removed.

If a mole has an increased risk of cancer, surgical removal is desirable. Usually, moles can be removed under local anesthesia in a physician's office. Alternatively a mole can be removed using liquid nitrogen, electrotherapy or radiation therapy.

A hydatidiform mole is a benign (noncancerous) growth that develops within the uterus from a degenerating embryo and causes bleeding similar to that from a threatened miscarriage. It may be spontaneously expelled from the uterus; if not, a dilation and curettage (scraping) is performed to surgically remove it. In some cases, a hydatidiform mole can become malignant, when it is called a choriocarcinoma.

SEE ALSO *Birthmarks, Choriocarcinoma, Hydatidiform mole, Melanoma, Sun exposure*

MOLLUSCUM CONTAGIOSUM

Characterized by multiple little blisters or blebs $\frac{1}{10}$ inch (2–3 millimeters) across with a central dimple, molluscum contagiosum is an acutely infectious disease transmitted by skin to skin contact.

Due to a pox-type virus, it is common to find the infection on the body and limbs of children where it is probably spread by skin contact with other children. In adults, it can be spread by sexual contact and is commonly found in the genital area in this case.

People with AIDS may develop florid molluscum all over the face, with the blebs being up to $\frac{1}{5}$ inch (5 millimeters) across. The incubation period is relatively long, ranging from a week to several months.

Treatment includes freezing with liquid nitrogen, using electric high-frequency currents (diathermy), or applying various chemicals injected into each spot with a sharpened sterile toothpick.

SEE ALSO *Sexually transmitted diseases, Viruses*

MORNING SICKNESS

Nausea and vomiting experienced generally in the first trimester of pregnancy are commonly referred to as morning sickness. At least 50 percent of pregnant women are affected by it to some degree, and many also experience headaches, dizziness and exhaustion. Symptoms may be more common in the morning but can be present at any time of day.

Although the exact cause is not known, major contributing factors are thought to be hormonal changes and lower blood sugar levels in early pregnancy. The condition may be aggravated by excess stomach acid, traveling, an enhanced sense of smell, fatigue, stress and some foods. Drinking small amounts of fluid between meals may prevent stomach distension which can cause vomiting, and eating dry toast or crackers before getting out of bed may settle the stomach.

In cases of excessive vomiting in pregnancy, known as hyperemesis gravidarum, anti-nausea drugs may be prescribed by a physician or fluids may be administered intravenously to prevent dehydration and malnutrition.

There are a number of alternative therapies that may be used to alleviate the symptoms of morning sickness. Acupuncture or acupressure treat specific points for morning sickness. Herbalism prescribes slippery elm bark, or ginger, lemon balm or chamomile teas. Homeopathy has a number of remedies for morning sickness prescribed according to specific symptoms. Naturopathy prescribes vitamin B complex and a diet of frequent small meals of plain food. Coffee, orange juice, and oily or fried foods should be avoided.

SEE ALSO *Nausea, Pregnancy*

MORPHINE

Morphine is a bitter-tasting crystalline alkaloid derived from the opium poppy and related to codeine and meperidine. It was discovered in 1803 and called morphine after Morpheus, the Greek god of dreams. A powerful narcotic painkiller (analgesic), it is usually prescribed for people in severe pain, such as the pain associated with terminal cancer. It is also used in the treatment of acute heart failure and shock.

Morphine may be taken orally, but because of its slow and poor absorption by the intestine, it is more usually injected or given via an infusion pump. If used for longer than a week or two, withdrawal symptoms may be experienced on ceasing the treatment.

Because morphine depresses respiration, it should be used with care in people with lung disease such as chronic bronchitis, and in the elderly or the very young (who are particularly sensitive to the drug's respiratory depressant effects). Constipation is another common side effect.

SEE ALSO *Narcotics*

MOTION SICKNESS

Most people experience motion sickness at some stage in their lives—on a boat or ship tossed on the ocean, in an aircraft struck by turbulence, in a long car or train trip or on an amusement park ride. Even astronauts in space get motion sickness. It begins with sweating, headaches and fatigue and culminates in nausea, dizziness and vomiting. In most cases, symptoms disappear rapidly when the motion stops. In some people, however, it can continue for days after.

Motion sickness is associated with the way the brain assesses the body's balance and movement, which relies on a stream of information from various nervous system components. Signals from the inner ears, the eyes and stretch receptors in the muscles allow the brain to establish where the body is in space. When the brain receives conflicting messages, the symptoms of motion sickness develop. For example, when a person reads in a moving car, the eyes signal no motion while the inner ears indicate movement.

A range of medications is available for motion sickness, from ginger tablets to antihistamines.

SEE ALSO *Balance, Sea sickness*

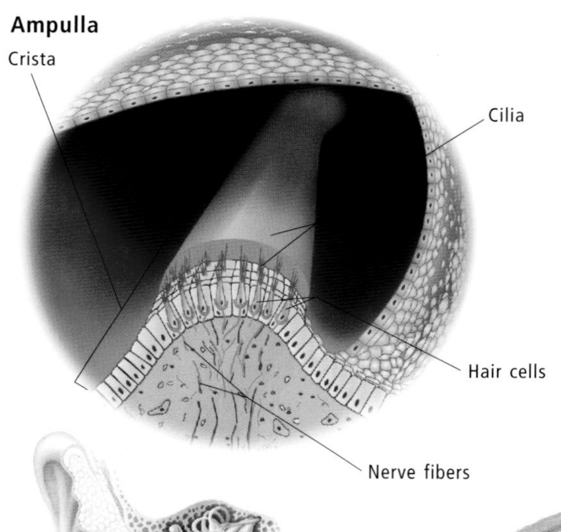

Motion sickness—balance

Changing the position of the head moves fluid in the inner ear, which stimulates hairs on the surface of the ampulla. These hairs send signals to the brain. When these signals are disrupted or confused, such as when traveling in a car, plane or boat, you may suffer from motion sickness.

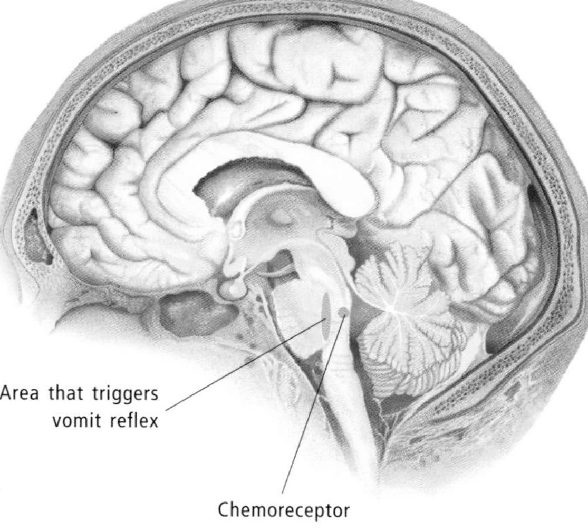

Vomiting and nausea centers

Two points in the brain instigate the nausea associated with motion sickness. The chemoreceptor triggers the vomit reflex when the brain receives conflicting messages about the position of the body in space and time.

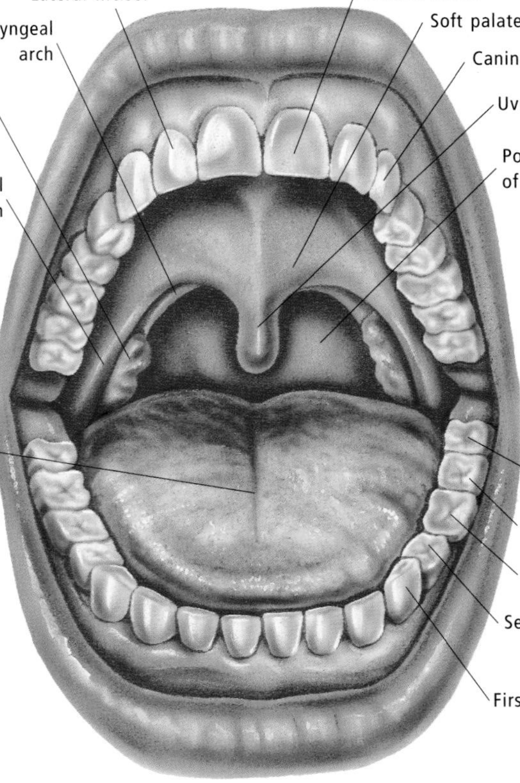

Lateral incisor
Central incisor
Palato-pharyngeal arch
Soft palate
Canine
Palatine tonsil
Uvula
Posterior wall of pharynx
Palatoglossal arch
Median sulcus
Third molar
Second molar
First molar
Second premolar
First premolar

Structure of the mouth
(with tongue down)

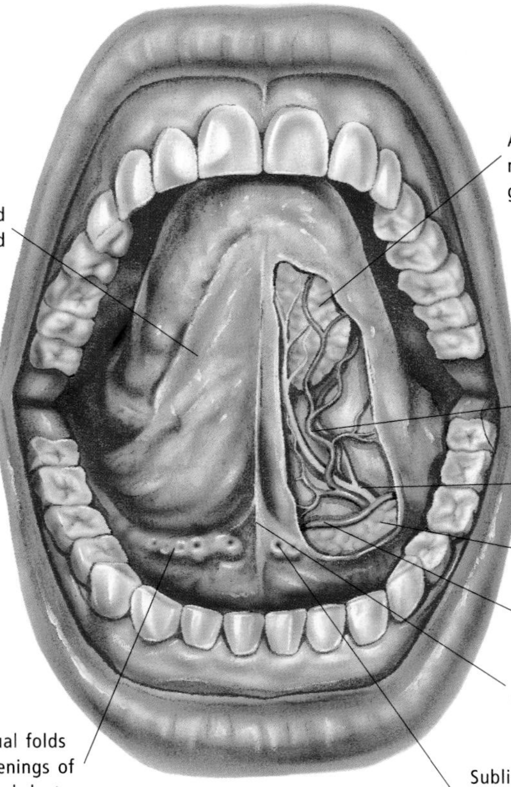

Anterior lingual minor salivary gland
Fimbriated fold
Deep lingual artery and veins
Lingual nerve
Sublingual gland
Submandibular duct
Frenulum of tongue
Sublingual folds with openings of sublingual ducts
Sublingual caruncle with opening of submandibular duct

Salivary glands
(with tongue up)

M

MOUTH

The mouth is the first part of the digestive tract. It consists of an outer vestibule, which lies between the teeth and the cheeks or lips, and an inner true oral cavity within the arches formed by the teeth. The true oral cavity has a roof formed by the hard palate in the front and the soft palate at the back, which separate the mouth from the nasal cavity. The hard palate is bony; the soft palate is formed of muscle covered by mucous membrane. The prominent droplet-shaped fleshy structure which hangs from the rear edge of the soft palate is called the uvula. The floor of the oral cavity is made up of the tongue and the tissue between the tongue and the teeth. At the back, the oral cavity leads into the oropharynx, which is part of the throat. The external opening and the lips are encircled by a muscle called the orbicularis oris, which allows the lips to be pursed for whistling and sucking on straws. Each cheek is formed by another facial muscle, the buccinator, whose fibers run forward into the orbicularis oris.

Body of tongue
Respiratory tract
Digestive tract

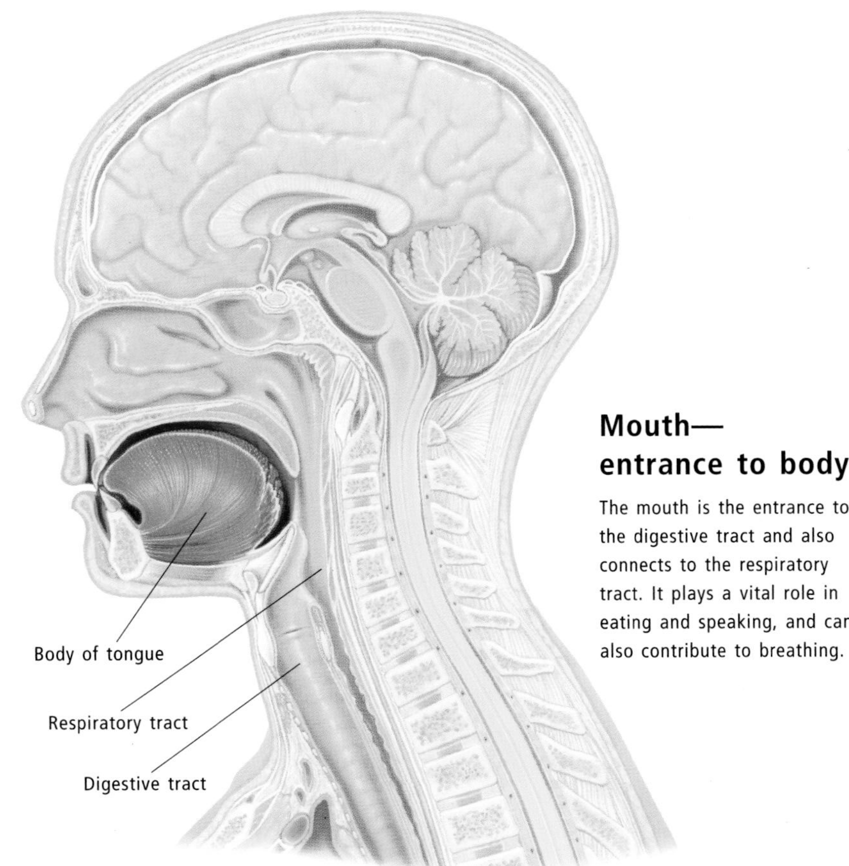

Mouth—entrance to body

The mouth is the entrance to the digestive tract and also connects to the respiratory tract. It plays a vital role in eating and speaking, and can also contribute to breathing.

Teeth and gums

In the adult, 32 permanent teeth are arranged in two arcades of 16 teeth. On each side of each jaw are 8 teeth, which fall into four types. At the front on each side lie 2 incisors, specialized chisel-shaped teeth for cutting food into segments. Further to the side lies the canine, a sharp dagger-tooth designed for gripping food. The canine ("dog" tooth) is not particularly large in humans, but can be very prominent in males of other primate species (e.g. baboons) and in carnivores. Behind the canine lie the 2 premolars or bicuspids and at the back are 3 molars. Premolars and molars are specialized for grinding food. The last molars, often called the wisdom teeth, emerge from the gum at about the eighteenth year of life.

During infancy a set of 20 deciduous or milk teeth is arranged as 5 teeth (2 incisors, 1 canine and 2 molars) in each jaw on each side. They emerge between 6 months and 2 years of age and are progressively replaced by permanent teeth between 6 and 18 years, in a rough sequence from front to back.

Each tooth consists of a central pulp cavity containing nerves and blood vessels. This is surrounded by dentine, which is in turn capped by enamel, the hardest substance in the body. Dentine is constantly exposed to intense physical wear during chewing. Dentine is similar to bone elsewhere in the body and is composed mainly of collagen and calcium. Enamel is 97 percent calcium salts and 3 percent organic material. The enamel does not cover the tooth below the gum line, where a bone-like structure called cementum covers the tooth. A periodontal membrane or ligament, a collagen-rich fibrous structure, surrounds the cementum of the root, and helps to fix the tooth firmly into the jaw.

Tongue

The tongue is a muscular organ which helps to move food around the mouth and assists in speech. Muscles of the tongue are arranged in three directions—vertical, horizontal and longitudinal. When the vertical fibers are activated the tongue becomes flat, when the longitudinal fibers contract the tongue becomes shorter, when the transverse fibers are contracted the tongue becomes narrower. Some people have a genetically determined ability to activate discrete sets of transverse muscle fibers and are able to curl their tongue.

The tongue is attached to the floor of the mouth and is divided into two main regions by a V-shaped groove (the sulcus terminalis). The front part consists of about two-thirds of the tongue and is covered with specialized projections and taste buds. The tongue is covered with projections called papillae, which come in three main types. The filiform papillae are elongated cone-shaped projections from the upper tongue surface, which are designed for gripping food. They are very prominent on the tongues of many animals and can be felt when a cat licks your hand. Fungiform papillae are mushroom shaped projections from the upper tongue surface, which contains taste buds. The circumvallate papillae are shaped like small castles, with a central bulge and a surrounding moat. The circumvallate papillae are arranged in a V in front of the sulcus terminalis and contain taste buds. The back one-third of the tongue is covered by lymphoid tissue called the lingual tonsil, which is important for the defence of the body from microorganisms. On each side the tongue is joined to the palate by arches of tissue (palatoglossal arches). Immediately behind these lie the palatine tonsils, which are lymphoid organs like the lingual tonsil.

Salivary glands

The mouth is kept moist by the secretions of two types of salivary glands. The minor salivary glands are either very small or microscopic while the major salivary glands (parotid, submandibular and sublingual) are large structures which drain into the mouth through relatively long ducts. The parotid glands lie in front of the ears and have ducts which drain forward to open opposite the upper second molar. The sublingual and submandibular glands lie below the floor of the mouth. The ducts of the submandibular glands open below the tongue, while the sublingual glands lie below paired ridges under the tongue and open by many shorter ducts into the oral cavity.

Diseases of the mouth

The oral cavity may be involved in a variety of infections, which may be due to viruses like herpes simplex and Coxsackie virus type A, or yeast. Infection with yeast can result in oral thrush or candidiasis, particularly in those people whose immune systems are functioning poorly due to chemotherapy for tumors or leukemia. Infection of the tooth pulp with pus-forming bacteria can result in abscesses of the jaw.

Mouth ulcers may result from herpes simplex or from diseases elsewhere in the body such as aplastic anemia, a condition where the bone marrow ceases to produce red and white blood cells. Mouth ulcers may also accompany leukemia, erythema multiforme and Stevens-Johnson syndrome. Erythema multiforme is a generalized disease of the whole body characterized by fever, sore throat, headache, gastroenteritis, joint pains and gastroenteritis. Stevens-Johnson erythema is a particularly severe form of erythema multiforme with lesions in the mouth, eyes and genital region.

Disease of the gums (gingivitis) may cause separation of the gum from the enamel, exposing the cementum and dentine of the tooth neck to plaque-forming bacteria and resulting in tooth decay (caries) and possibly tooth loss. Caries are partly (up to 60 percent) preventable by ensuring adequate levels of dietary fluoride during tooth development.

Cancer of the oral cavity often occurs between the ages of 45 and 85 in association with heavy smoking and high alcohol intake, or poor oral hygiene. Many cancers arise around the edge of the tongue or in the gutter between the tongue and the gums of the lower teeth (the "cancer gulch"). Often the cancers develop as ulcers which are found by dentists. Final diagnosis is made by taking a biopsy.

Oral cancer can be treated by surgery in combination with radiation therapy. All patients with oral cancer should be carefully examined for tumors of the nose, airways, esophagus and larynx. Cancer of the lip is more frequent in farmers, sailors and others exposed to sunlight over prolonged periods. Treatment of lip cancer is by surgery or radiation therapy. The chances of survival are quite good for lip cancer, with about 90 percent of patients still alive after five years. Survival rates are lower if the tumor has spread to local lymph nodes.

SEE ALSO *Gingivitis, Gums, Jaw, Lip, Palate, Salivary glands, Teeth, Tongue*

MUCOUS MEMBRANES

Mucous membranes form the lining of many of the hollow internal cavities of the body, notably the nose and mouth, the larger respiratory passages and the gut. A mucous membrane (mucosa) consists of several layers of cells, and is kept moist by secretions (mainly mucus) from glands found in or underneath the mucous membrane. The cells on the surface are adapted to the functions of that particular organ. For example, the surface of the mucous membrane of the mouth has many layers of flattened cells which give some resistance to abrasion from food, whereas that of the respiratory passages carries hair-like cilia to sweep foreign particles away.

SEE ALSO *Mouth, Nose, Respiratory system*

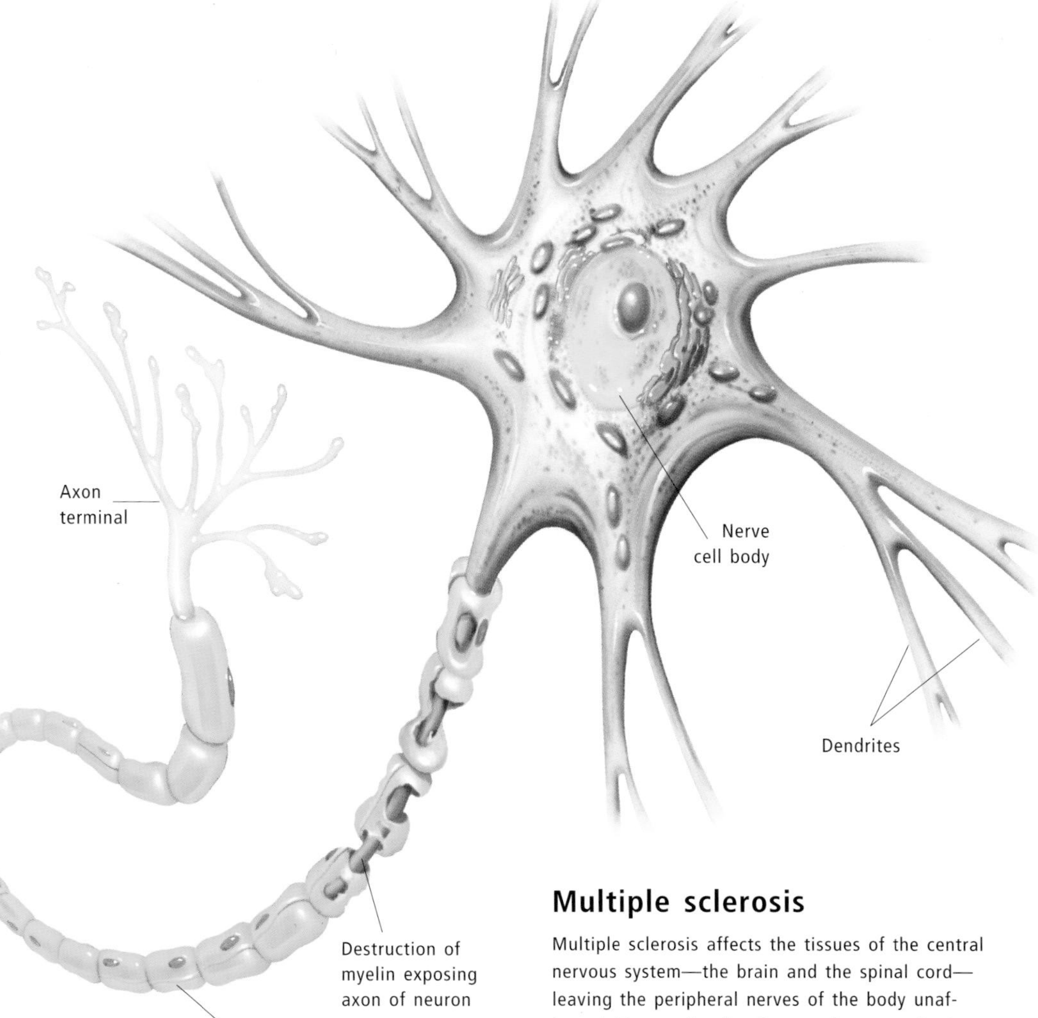

Multiple sclerosis

Multiple sclerosis affects the tissues of the central nervous system—the brain and the spinal cord—leaving the peripheral nerves of the body unaffected. The myelin sheath around neurons in the central nervous system is progressively destroyed. This leads to symptoms such as blurred vision, fatigue, poor coordination and tingling sensations.

MULTIPLE SCLEROSIS

Multiple sclerosis (MS) is a progressive and frequently debilitating disease of the central nervous system (CNS). It involves the ongoing destruction of the protective myelin sheaths around neurons in the brain and spinal cord. This interferes with the transmission of impulses by neurons, and disrupts signals sent throughout the CNS.

The cause of MS is unknown, although evidence suggests the trigger may be viral. Whatever the trigger, it is thought to stimulate an autoimmune response in which T cells mistakenly identify the myelin of the CNS as foreign. The T cells, which normally fight disease, then set up an immune response that leads to myelin destruction.

Just over 1 million people worldwide suffer from MS. Statistics reveal it to be far more prevalent in women than men, most common in people of northern European descent (particularly those with Scottish ancestry), extremely rare in people of Asian or African descent, and far less common in the tropics than in temperate areas. Aside from ethnicity and ancestry issues, there are other indications that genetics may predispose a person to developing MS. Children of a parent suffering from MS are 30 to 50 times more likely to develop the disease than the general population.

MS is not fatal, although the life span of sufferers is usually reduced by an average of six years due to complications of the disease, with lung and kidney infections being the principal life-threatening risks. MS can also have a debilitating impact on a person's quality of life. Because the symptoms and progression of the disease vary widely between sufferers, however, it is hard to predict how an individual will be affected.

At one end of the range, between 20 percent and 35 percent have such a mild form of the disease that they suffer little, if any, impact. Up to 12 percent of patients fall into the category at the other end of the spectrum and suffer from a serious and particularly aggressive form of the disease which may involve paralysis and dementia.

The first signs vary and do not always immediately suggest a serious disorder. They usually appear some time between the ages of fifteen and forty, but the disease most often strikes for the first time when the sufferer in the twenties or thirties. Blurred or double vision is frequently one of the earliest indicators. Pain and involuntary movements in the eyes are also common in people who later go on to develop MS. Extreme tiredness, clumsiness and tingling sensations are other early symptoms.

The disease usually takes years to progress, with sufferers often experiencing periods of remission when symptoms apparently disappear, followed by relapses. In advanced-stage MS, symptoms can include spasticity, poor coordination and vertigo, loss of bladder control, constipation, uncomfortable but short-lived sensations in the extremities, sexual problems including impotence in men, tremors in the arms or legs and mental dysfunction that can range from simple memory lapses to impaired problem-solving abilities.

There is no cure for MS and symptoms are often difficult to treat, although there is a range of therapies and medications available that can help make life more tolerable, including drugs which prevent muscle stiffness.

SEE ALSO *Brain, Neurons, Nervous system, Spinal cord*

MUMPS

In its simplest form, mumps is a viral illness of childhood due to a paramyxovirus which produces a mild febrile condition lasting a few days and characterized by painful swelling of the salivary glands that lie under and in front of the ears. After a 2–3 week incubation period, the patient becomes infectious a day or so before the swelling occurs and for 3 or 4 days thereafter. The illness is spread by droplets transmitted by coughing or breathing. Occasionally one side of the neck only will swell. The other side may swell up several days later. Adults usually suffer more than children. Occasionally the other salivary glands will also enlarge.

Complications are not uncommon, the most frequent being aseptic meningitis, which is usually mild and often not suspected unless an examination of the fluid around the brain and spinal cord (cerebrospinal fluid) is carried out. Twenty-five percent of adult males can develop swelling of one or both testes, occasionally leading to sterility. Similar painful swelling of the ovaries occurs in adult women. Inflammation of the pancreas in the abdomen can produce severe upper abdominal pain, sometimes with nausea and vomiting.

Far less common complications include encephalitis (often with high fever and disorientation), inflammation of the thyroid gland, inflammation of the heart muscle (myocarditis), arthritis, kidney inflammation (nephritis) and thrombocytopenia, a condition in which the platelet cells in the blood decrease in number, leading to otherwise unexplained bruising. Deafness can also be a complication.

As far as is known, the fetus is not affected. Mortality is minimal, most deaths resulting from encephalitis.

Diagnosis of mumps is largely clinical, the result of a physical examination. Isolating the virus from saliva is possible, especially if pancreatitis is present.

Other viral infections, including influenza type A, coxsackie infections and infectious mononucleosis (glandular fever), can produce swelling of the salivary glands. However, the general symptoms are sufficiently different to allow a proper diagnosis.

Treatment for mumps is largely simple nursing in bed. Testicular swelling (orchitis) may need surgical intervention, although high doses of hydrocortisone may help. The pain is often lessened if the scrotum is suspended in a scrotal support.

Live virus vaccine is available and usually given in conjunction with live measles and rubella vaccines, at the age of 12–15 months. Complications of immunization are rare but can include mild fever and minor swelling of one or both salivary glands. Even so the child is not infectious. A booster dose is recommended when the child is about 14 years old. It should not be given to people who lack immunity (HIV infected people or cancer patients undergoing treatment), or to pregnant women.

SEE ALSO *Immunization, Meningitis, Viruses*

Glands affected by mumps

Mumps most commonly causes swelling and tenderness in one or both of the parotid (salivary) glands that lie just under and in front of the ears. Occasionally the other salivary glands, testes and ovaries may also be affected.

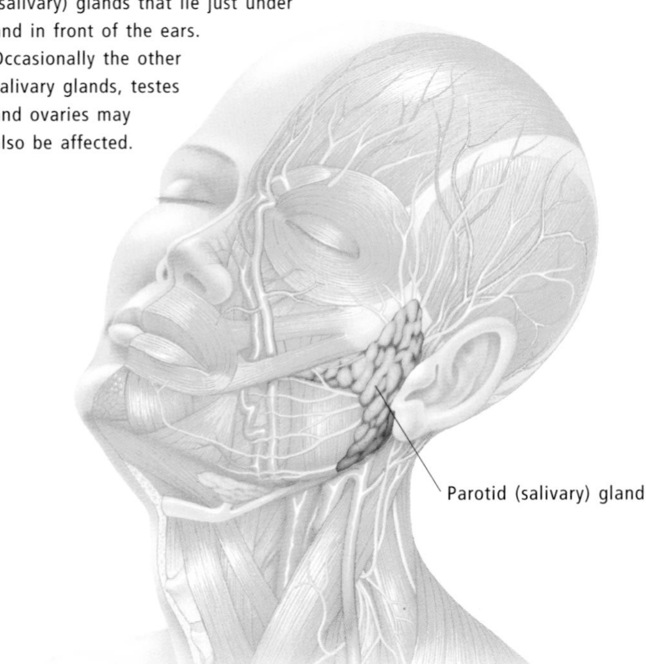

Mumps in childhood

Mumps is usually a childhood disease and symptoms are often more severe if it is contracted by adults. Immunization against mumps, measles and rubella is generally given at age 12–15 months.

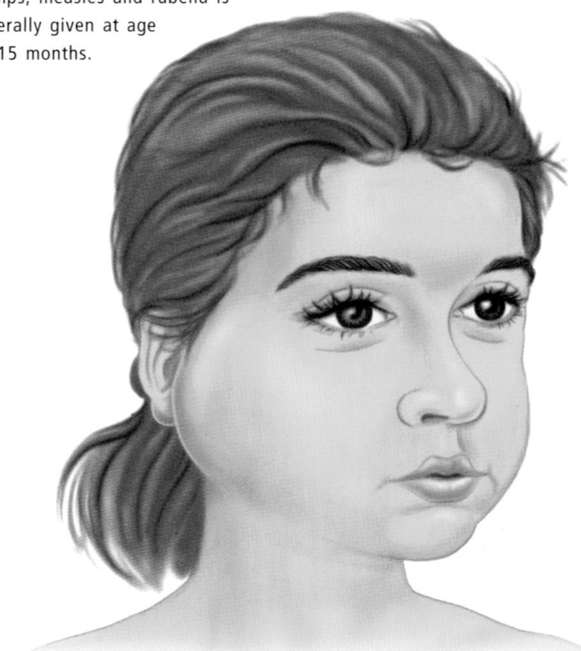

MUSCLE

Muscle is a type of body tissue responsible for the movement of the bones and joints. Muscle movement is normally controlled by the central nervous system (CNS). Smooth muscle is responsible for motility (movement) of some internal organs such as the intestine and blood vessels.

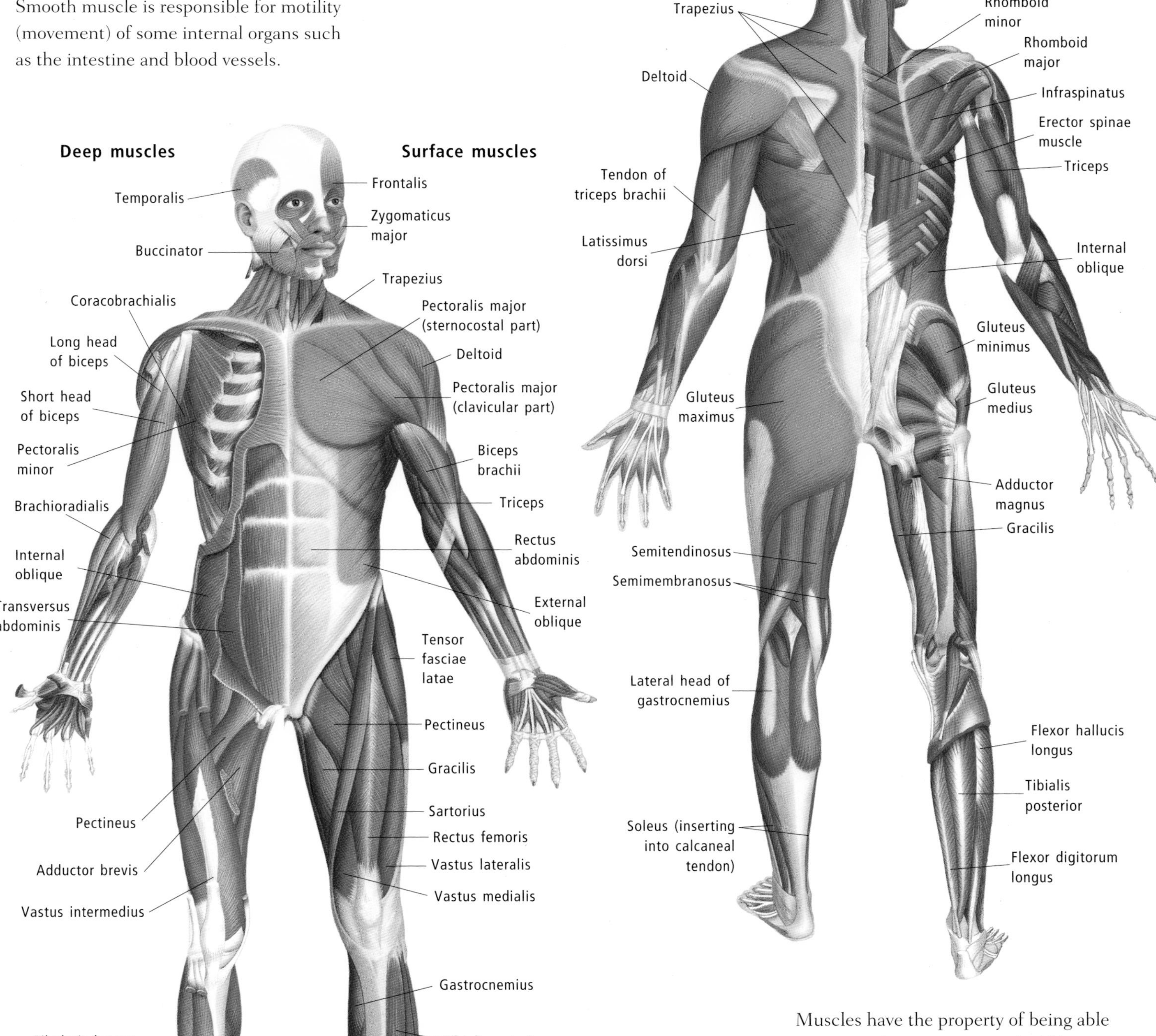

Muscles have the property of being able to contract. They are composed of fibers, which are elongated cells containing tiny, threadlike structures made of complex proteins, myofibrils. Myofibrils consist of regularly arranged protein strands called myofilaments; the so-called "thick" myofilaments contain the protein myosin, while "thin" filaments contain the proteins actin, troponin and tropomysin. Thick and thin myofilaments lie side by side with their ends

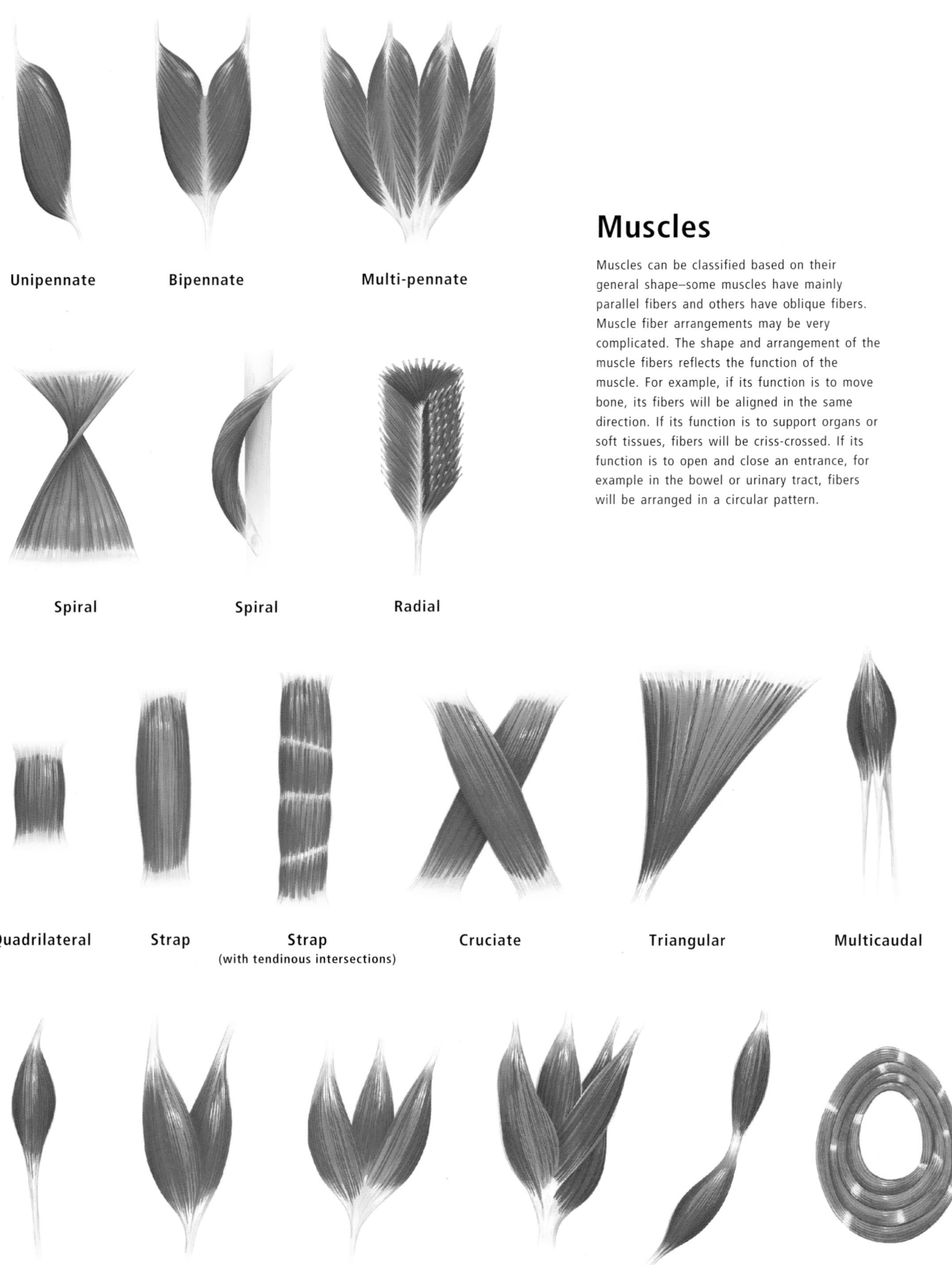

Muscles

Muscles can be classified based on their general shape–some muscles have mainly parallel fibers and others have oblique fibers. Muscle fiber arrangements may be very complicated. The shape and arrangement of the muscle fibers reflects the function of the muscle. For example, if its function is to move bone, its fibers will be aligned in the same direction. If its function is to support organs or soft tissues, fibers will be criss-crossed. If its function is to open and close an entrance, for example in the bowel or urinary tract, fibers will be arranged in a circular pattern.

interlinked by chemical cross bridges. When stimulated, they slide along each other and the result is a muscle contraction.

If the force of a muscle contraction is greater than the force that is resisting the contraction, the contraction is said to be isotonic. If, however, the resistance to contraction is equal to the force generated in muscle tissues, the muscle will not contract. This is called an isometric contraction.

Types of muscles

The human body has three types of muscle: cardiac, smooth and skeletal. Each has different characteristics.

Cardiac muscle is found only in the heart and consists of a network of branches of muscle fibers that do not contract voluntarily and are not under the control of the central nervous system. A heart muscle contraction originates with an electrical impulse in a natural pacemaker called the sinoatrial node, located within the heart itself. This node and the electrical conducting system that runs through the muscle control the heart rate. The heart is, however, supplied with nerves from the autonomic nervous system, but these nerves speed or slow the heart rate rather than originate contractions.

Smooth muscle is found in the digestive system, reproductive system, major blood vessels, skin and some internal organs. Smooth muscle contraction is involuntary and not under the control of the central nervous system (CNS), being influenced by the autonomic nervous system. Peristalsis—the regular and rhythmic contraction of smooth muscle in the gastrointestinal tract which propels food along the tract—is an example of the autonomous contraction of smooth muscle.

Skeletal muscle is the most prominent type of muscle and may account for up to 60 percent of the mass of the body. It is attached to the bones of the skeleton at both ends by tendons. It acts voluntarily: nerve endings that carry electrical impulses from the CNS control its movement. These nerve endings terminate at the cell membrane of the muscle fibers. The contraction of a muscle cell is activated by the release of calcium from inside the cell in response to electrical changes at the cell's surface.

Muscle tissue

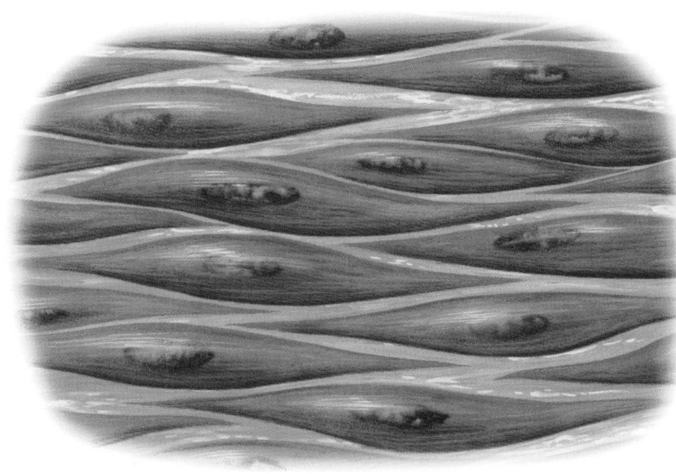

Smooth muscle tissue

Smooth muscle is controlled by the autonomic nervous system, and is found in the skin, the blood vessels, and the reproductive and digestive systems.

Skeletal muscle tissue

Skeletal muscles allow the body to move. They are voluntary muscles, controlled by the brain and spinal cord.

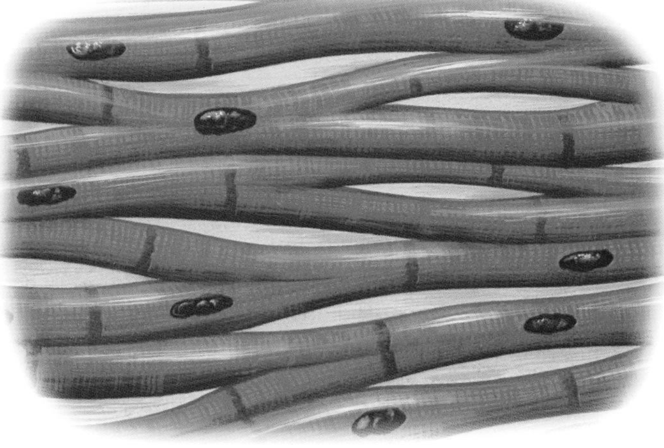

Cardiac muscle tissue

Cardiac muscle is the heart muscle, which contracts and relaxes rhythmically in an involuntary manner.

Skeletal muscle is usually found in bundles, forming characteristic shapes and sizes, depending on where it is located in the body and what bones and joints it moves. When skeletal muscle contracts, it usually thickens and shortens.

Most skeletal muscle is clearly visible below the surface of the skin and is responsible, together with the skeleton, for an individual's physique.

Skeletal muscles that are exercised regularly may hypertrophy, that is, increase in

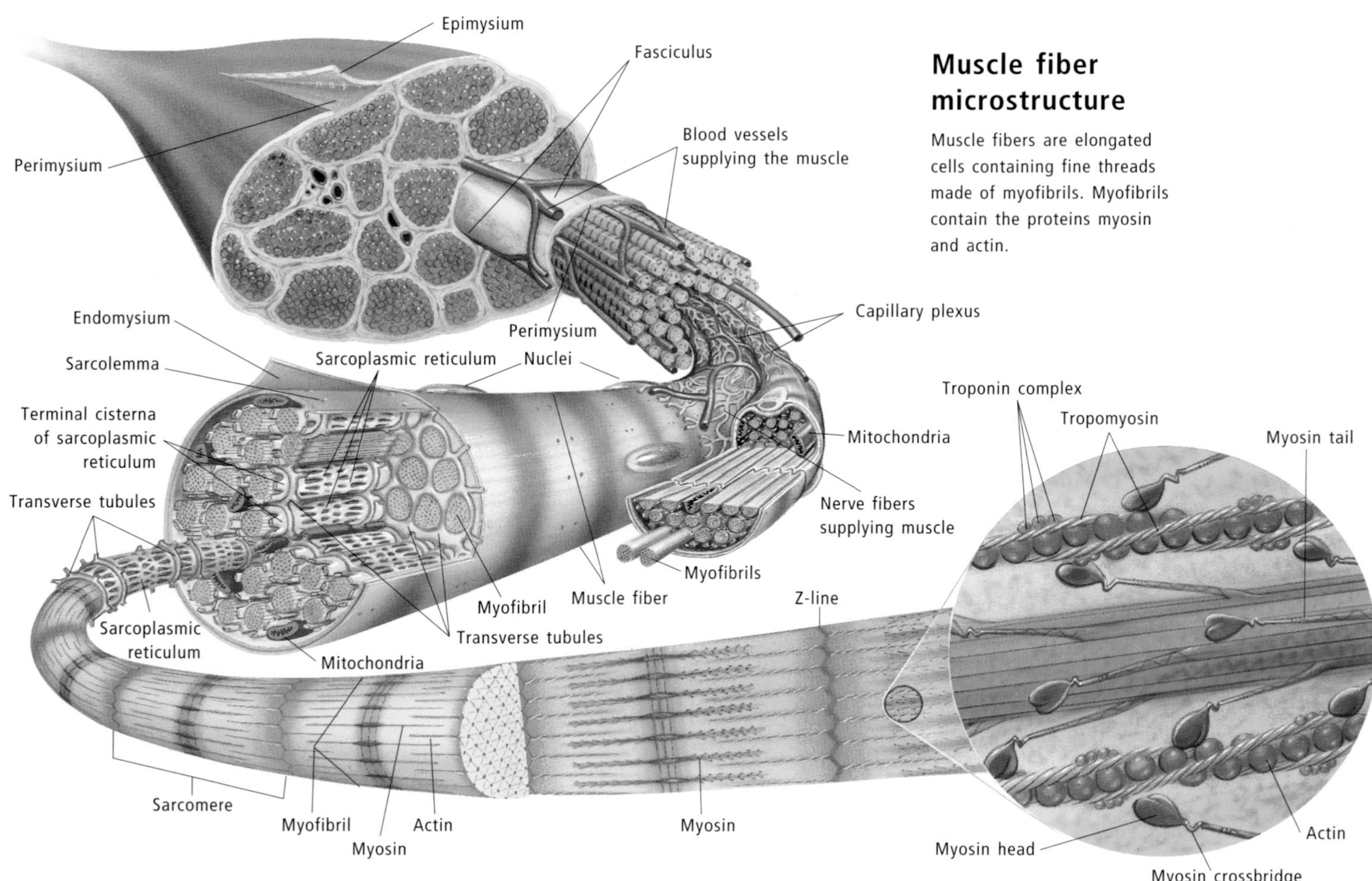

Muscle fiber microstructure

Muscle fibers are elongated cells containing fine threads made of myofibrils. Myofibrils contain the proteins myosin and actin.

size and strength. If these muscles are not used sufficiently (for example in paralysis or disease), they may atrophy, or diminish in size, and become weaker.

Muscle injuries and diseases

A pulled muscle, also known as a strained muscle, is a common term for a muscle that has been damaged by a sudden rupture of fibers within the muscle tissue. It is common in sporting and work-related injuries. The pulled muscle causes pain and stiffness that gradually improves over a number of days. It is treated with rest, ice packs and painkillers (analgesics).

Muscle cramps are painful, involuntary contractions of muscles experienced during exercise. They are caused by changes in the chemistry of muscle cells that occur during exercise brought on by lack of oxygen. They are treated with applications of ice or heat, gentle massage or physical therapy.

Muscles are subject to a variety of diseases. They may become inflamed, a condition known as myositis. The muscle becomes hot, tender, painful and there may be fever. Dermatomyositis is inflammation of muscle and skin; polymyositis refers to inflammation of multiple muscle groups.

Muscles may become infected with bacteria such as *Staphylococcus*. Disruption or damage to the blood supply may cause muscle tissue to die, a condition called gangrene. Muscles may become paralyzed by injury or disease. Poliomyelitis and polyneuritis are viral diseases that result in paralysis and muscular wasting. Muscular dystrophies are hereditary diseases characterized by progressive muscular weakness and wasting.

Myasthenia gravis is a condition in which transmission of nerve impulses is incomplete and paralysis follows. Sometimes individual muscles or muscle groups may be affected by injury or disease; Bell's palsy is paralysis of all the muscles on one side of the face, caused by acute malfunction of, or damage to, the facial nerve that supplies them.

Drug treatments

Muscle relaxant drugs relax skeletal muscles by blocking the transmission of nerve impulses that cause muscle contraction. They are used to relieve painful muscle spasms that sometimes occur in stroke, in some muscle and rheumatic disorders, and in some skeletal muscle disorders. Neuromuscular blocking drugs are drugs that paralyze skeletal muscles by blocking nerve impulses completely and are used in general anesthesia.

Muscles can gain greater bulk and strength through the use of anabolic steroids such as testosterone, methandrostenolone and nandrolone. These drugs are sometimes used by athletes to enhance performance. Over time, however, these drugs can be responsible for a range of side effects such as depression, arterial disease, liver cancer, reduced sperm count in males and masculinization in females.

SEE ALSO *Anabolic steroids, Bell's palsy, Bones, Cramp, Gangrene, Joints, Muscular dystrophy, Myasthenia gravis, Peristalsis, Poliomyelitis, Skeletal system*

M

MUSCULAR DYSTROPHY

Muscular dystrophy (MD) is the name of a group of chronic hereditary disorders, which cause a gradual deterioration of the body's muscles. Different types affect different areas of the body, such as shoulders, hips or face, and also differ in their type of inheritance (dominant genes, recessive genes and so on), and in the age when symptoms appear.

The affected person suffers gradual weakening of muscles and loss of muscle bulk, giving rise to walking and other movement difficulties. Muscle contractures are common, caused by shortening of the muscle fibers and fibrosis of the connective tissue. Some types of muscular dystrophy involve the heart muscle, causing cardiomyopathy or arrhythmias.

Muscular dystrophy affects males more than females, usually between 5–12 years of age. The condition is incurable and persons with the condition rarely reach adulthood. Physical therapy can maintain muscle strength and functioning and the use of orthopedic appliances, such as braces and wheelchairs, may improve mobility.

The most common and severe form is Duchenne muscular dystrophy, a rapidly progressive type. Other forms include limb-girdle, Becker, facioscapulohumeral and myotonic dystrophies. In these types, progression of the disease is generally slow.

Muscular dystrophy is a genetic abnormality. Carriers can be detected with medical testing. If there are relatives with the disorder, genetic counseling and prenatal testing in pregnancy are advisable.

SEE ALSO *Congenital abnormalities, Duchenne muscular dystrophy, Muscle*

MUSIC THERAPY

In traditional societies music is an important component of healing rites and ceremonies. In the West, music was introduced into hospitals for its therapeutic effects in the nineteenth century. Today music therapists treat people with mental illness, physical disabilities, learning disabilities and chronic illnesses such as Alzheimer's disease.

There are a number of ways in which music can be used therapeutically. It has been found that music stimulation can increase endorphin release which helps to relieve pain and anxiety. In neonatal intensive care units in the USA, lullaby tapes which echo the sound of a human heartbeat are played to calm the babies and help them sleep. Carefully selected music is also played to patients before, during and after surgery in many hospitals.

In vibroacoustic therapy, a form of music therapy popular in Europe, selected music is played to children with physical and mental disabilities to induce physical and mental relaxation. In India traditional ragas have been researched and found to be beneficial in the treatment of hypertension and mental illness.

Another form of music therapy involves encouraging patients to sing and play instruments in an improvised manner for free emotional expression. The therapist and patient relate to each other through their shared music making. Singing and playing may help the physically disabled to improve breath control and physical movement.

SEE ALSO *Dance movement therapy*

MYASTHENIA GRAVIS

Most often an autoimmune disorder, myasthenia gravis may also be due to a tumor of the thymus gland (thymoma). Characterized by fluctuating but progressive weakness of the voluntary muscles, early symptoms can include double vision (diplopia) and lid-droop after prolonged reading, fading of the voice during a speech, difficulty swallowing the latter part of a meal and tiredness of the legs and arms. The weakness is reversed by resting the affected muscles, but the condition is slowly progressive.

Diagnosis is made when there is a rapid reversal of the weakness after the administration of certain drugs.

Treatment may be continued with drugs but the removal of the thymus gland will produce the greatest improvement. The occasional patient may require steroids or other immunosuppressive drugs. Myasthenia gravis may be associated with other autoimmune disorders such as thyrotoxicosis (overactive thyroid), rheumatoid arthritis and lupus erythematosis. Small cell cancer of the lung and botulism can produce a somewhat similar myasthenia.

SEE ALSO *Autoimmune disease, Muscle, Thymus gland*

MYCOSIS FUNGOIDES

Mycosis fungoides can be mistaken initially for a simple fungal rash. It is, however, a rare and frequently fatal form of cancer of the immune system that often takes years to progress. The first outward indications are raised, scaly, red or brown, itchy skin lesions that tend to form open sores. As the disease

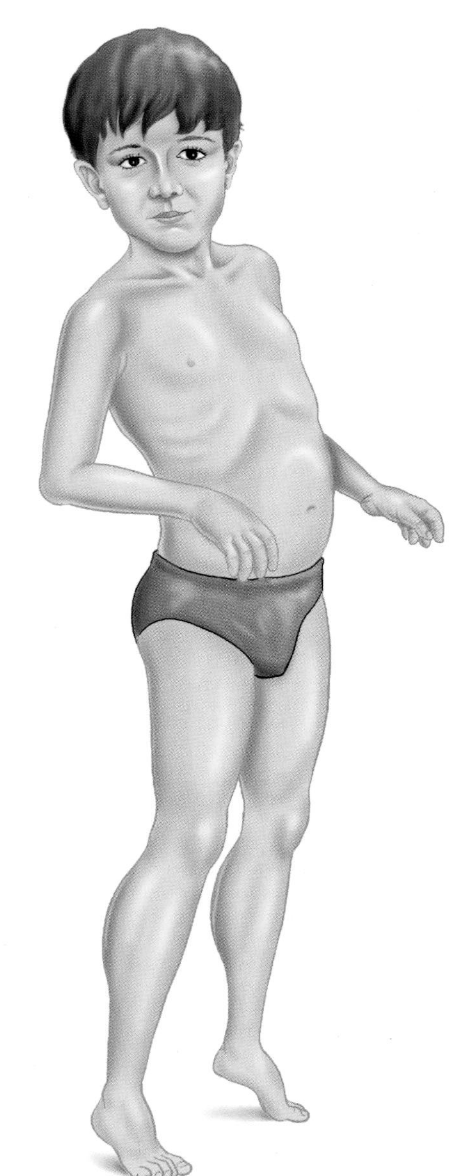

Muscular dystrophy

An early sign of muscular dystrophy in children is bulging calf muscles, which are caused by excessive fat rather than healthy muscles.

M

Mycosis fungoides
Mycosis fungoides generally develops over three stages commencing with itchy skin lesions, followed by large raised skin lesions and finally mushroom-like tumors which frequently ulcerate.

advances, the patient develops swollen lymph glands and then tumors on the skin. During the late stages, much of the skin reddens, peels and becomes scaly and extremely itchy. Eventually, cancer cells spread to the lymph glands and internal organs. If treated early enough, mycosis fungoides can sometimes be cured. Remission brought about by various cancer treatments is also possible in later stages.

SEE ALSO *Cancer, Lymphatic/Immune system*

M

MYELITIS

Myelitis is a general term for inflammation of the spinal cord. It involves the loss of fatty tissue (myelin) around the nerves. One of the most common types is acute transverse myelitis, a neurological syndrome that involves inflammation through one level of the spinal cord. This rapidly developing condition obstructs the path of motor nerve fibers, causing low back pain, muscle spasms, dysfunction of the spinal cord, headache, numbness and tingling in the legs. It can be brought on by viral infection, spinal cord injuries and immune system abnormalities in which the spinal cord is attacked.

SEE ALSO *Spinal cord*

MYELOGRAPHY

Myelography refers to x-ray photography of the spinal cord, as well as the biopsy examination of cells in bone marrow. The spinal x-rays are called myelograms and are used in the diagnosis of disorders such as herniated disks and spinal tumors. They are taken after injecting a radiopaque dye into the fluid around the spinal cord.

SEE ALSO *Spinal cord, X-ray*

MYELOMA

Myeloma is a tumor of plasma cells in the bone marrow, which results in pain and weakness of the bones, anemia and the production of an abnormal protein. It is the commonest tumor actually arising in bone, rather than spreading to bone as other cancers may do. It occurs most often in men over 65 years of age. There is an increased risk after exposure to high-dose ionizing radiation or pesticides. There have been recent reports of the possible role of a virus.

Myeloma may be detected by the finding of anemia and other blood abnormalities, or by the presence of severe, persistent bone pain. The pain is often in the spine or ribs and can be due to the myeloma itself or to fractures resulting from weakening of the bones. X-rays will typically show punched-out holes in the bones. If myeloma is suspected, testing of blood and urine is done to detect an abnormal protein produced by the malignant plasma cells. The diagnosis is confirmed by bone marrow biopsy.

The treatment of myeloma is initially pain control and treatment of complications, such as infection, high blood calcium or reduced kidney function. Then chemotherapy is given in the form of tablets or injections, usually as monthly cycles, for periods of up to 12 months. Myeloma is not curable but can be controlled for several years on average. Recent advances in treatment include bone marrow transplantation and the use of the drug, thalidomide.

SEE ALSO *Bone marrow biopsy, Bones*

MYOCARDIAL INFARCTION

The myocardium is the name for the muscle of the heart, while infarction is the death of tissue due to interference with its blood supply. Myocardial infarction is the death of heart muscle due to loss of arterial blood supply. This generally occurs as a result of blockage of the coronary arteries which supply the heart with blood, usually due to a disease known as atherosclerosis, which leads to the accumulation of fatty and fibrous tissue in the walls of arteries in discrete patches called plaques.

If plaques lose their surface layer, blood may coagulate on the rough surface of the vessel wall, causing sudden obstruction of the entire vessel. A patient with a myocardial infarction will experience a crushing pain centered mainly in the middle of the chest, but possibly spreading to the left arm, neck or upper abdomen. The pain will not be relieved by rest or prescription medication, and patients should immediately seek medical help.

With very early intervention it may be possible to dissolve the coagulated blood, but in most cases treatment is aimed at minimizing the amount of heart muscle lost, supporting the heart and providing pain relief. Patients may die if the loss of heart muscle is so great that heart function cannot be maintained, or if the electrical function of the heart is impaired.

SEE ALSO *Arrhythmia, Atherosclerosis, Coronary artery disease, Fibrillation, Heart*

MYOCARDITIS

Myocarditis is inflammation of the heart muscle, which usually accompanies a generalized disease of the body (such as diphtheria or toxoplasmosis)or a viral infection (such as poliomyelitis). Patients often experience rapid heart rate in mild cases. In more severe cases, as the heart fails, there may be shortness of breath, enlarged heart and murmurs.

SEE ALSO *Heart*

MYOMECTOMY

Myomectomy is an operation to remove a fibroid, or tumor, formed of muscle tissue in the uterus. It is performed instead of a hysterectomy when it is important to preserve the woman's fertility. About one-quarter of women who would formerly have had a hysterectomy now have a myomectomy, which leaves the uterus in place and is not a major operation. This operation can be done by vaginal incision, or abdominal incision, which may mean that a cesarean is necessary should the woman later decide to have children.

SEE ALSO *Fibroids, Hysterectomy, Hysteroscopy, Uterus*

MYOPIA

Myopia—also called nearsightedness or shortsightedness—is a condition in which close objects are clearly visible while distant objects are blurred. It is caused by an abnormality of the eye in which the image is focused in front of the retina rather than directly on it. This may happen because the eyeball is too long, or because the lens is focusing the image too strongly. The condition usually develops in school age and may run in families. Myopia is usually treated by wearing eyeglasses or contact lenses. Radial keratotomy, a surgical procedure performed on the cornea, improves or corrects the condition in many cases.

SEE ALSO *Contact lenses, Eye, Sight*

Myocardial infarction

Commonly called a heart attack, myocardial infarction occurs when the cardiac muscle and tissues are deprived of oxygen because the blood supply to the heart has been disrupted in some way.

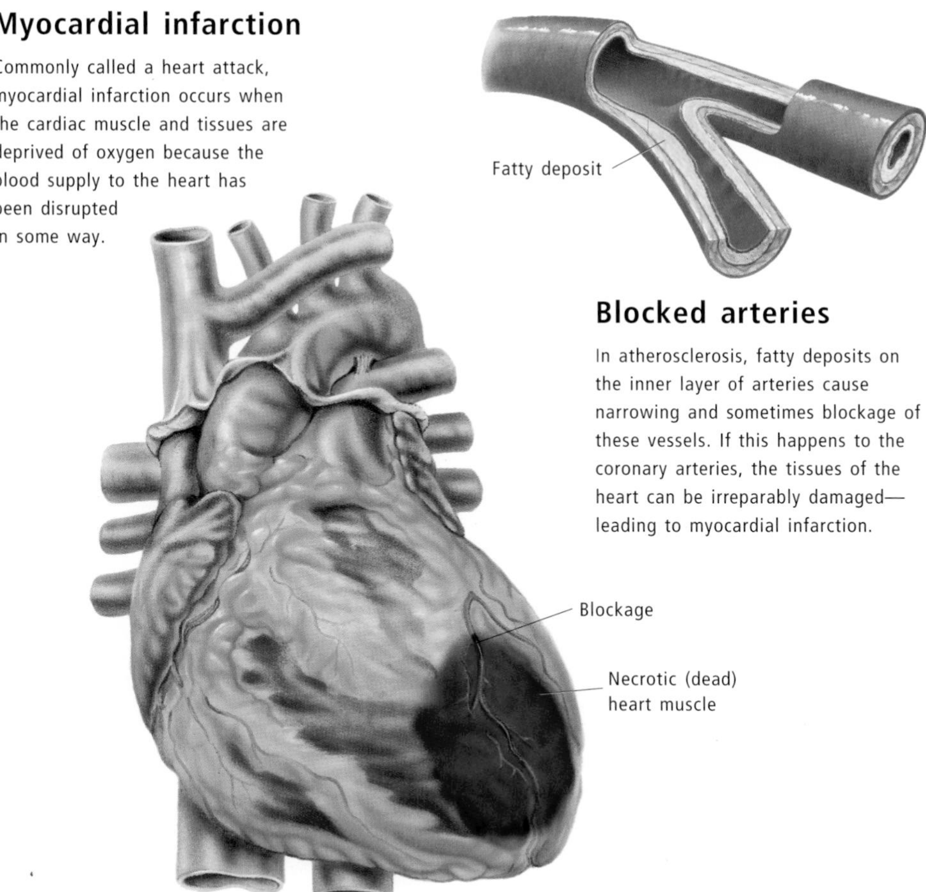

Blocked arteries

In atherosclerosis, fatty deposits on the inner layer of arteries cause narrowing and sometimes blockage of these vessels. If this happens to the coronary arteries, the tissues of the heart can be irreparably damaged—leading to myocardial infarction.

MYXEDEMA

Myxedema is a condition resulting from a reduced metabolic rate throughout the body, in turn a result of low thyroxine levels (hypothyroidism).

There is progressive slowing of mental and physical activity, and the disorder is characterized by a puffy face, coarse dry skin and hair, lethargy, sensitivity to cold, slowed heart rate and constipation. Causes include disease of the thyroid gland (such as Hashimoto's disease) or lack of stimulation (from the pituitary gland, for example). Treatment is by giving thyroid hormones to replace the low levels.

SEE ALSO *Hashimoto's disease, Hypothyroidism, Pituitary gland, Thyroid gland*

M

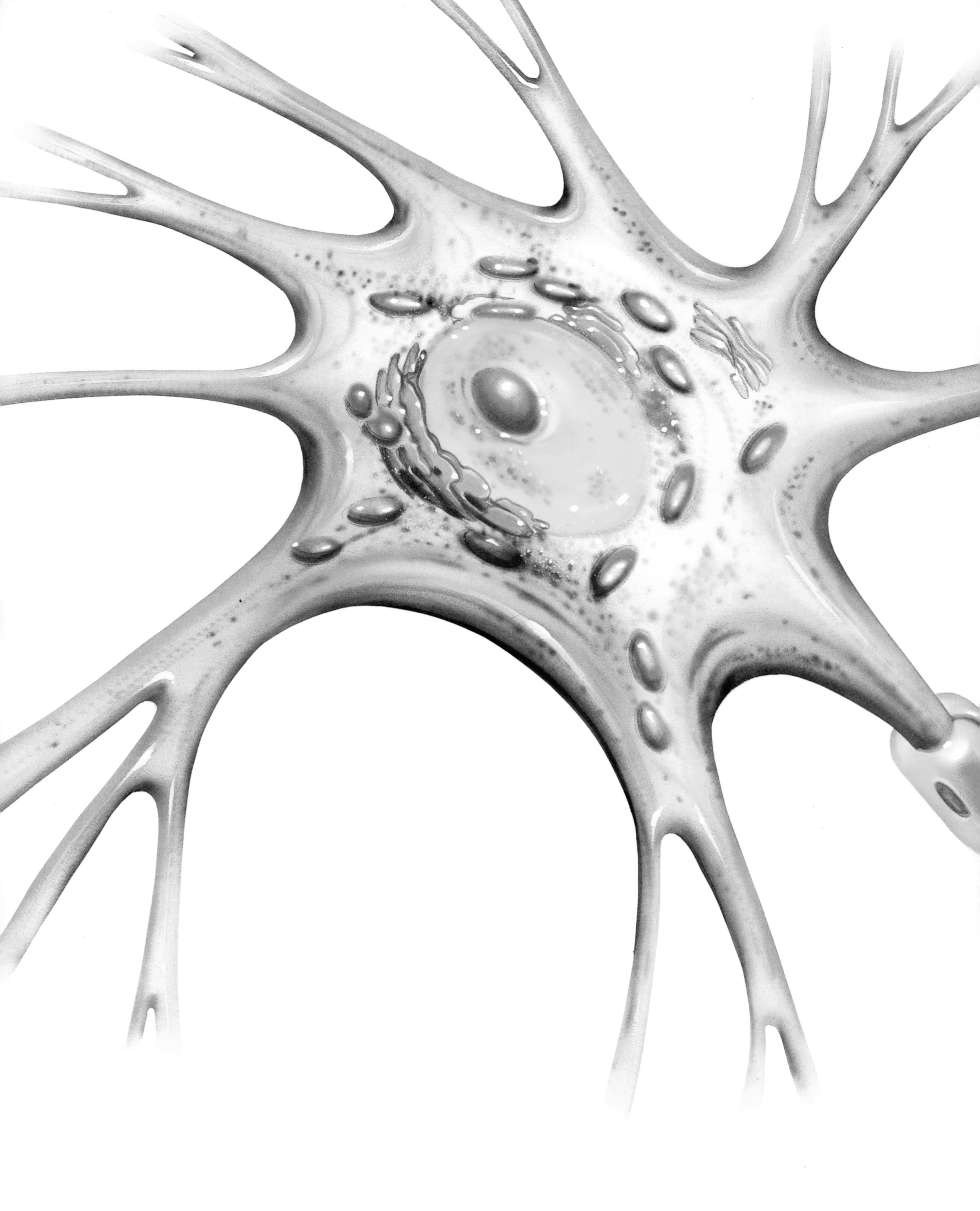

NO

NAILS

The primary function of our nails is to provide protection for the sensitive tips of our fingers and toes, and they are well-designed for the purpose. They are made mainly of the tough protein called keratin and most of what we can see of them is actually dead—attributes that make them reasonably resilient to everyday knocks.

The only living part of a nail is the root, where growth occurs. This is located under the flap of skin—the cuticle—at the nail's base. Beneath the nail is the nail bed, visibly pink through the nail in healthy circumstances due to a rich blood supply. If a nail becomes detached from the bed it is inevitably replaced. Because fingernails grow at an average rate of about 2 inches (5 centimeters) a year, it takes about 6 months for a nail to regrow fully. Toenails grow more slowly, taking 12–18 months to grow back.

Although most nail afflictions are minor and easily remedied, neglect or incorrect treatment can turn them into painful, lingering and unsightly problems. For example, tearing or biting a hangnail—a piece of partly detached skin at the side or base of a fingernail—is one way of damaging the skin near a nail and causing a tender and swollen bacterial infection, known as a paronychia. Hangnails should be cut off neatly with sharp scissors. A paronychia usually responds quickly to antibiotics.

A fungal infection in a nail—onychomycosis—is usually more persistent. This is most likely to occur on a toe, rather than a finger, and is often indicated by a discolored, brittle or peeling nail. Without treatment, onychomycosis can cause numbness or pain in the affected area. The nail may separate from the nail bed and eventually be destroyed. Treatment often includes taking an oral antifungal medication over several months.

Another normally minor problem that is far more likely to affect toes than fingers, particularly the big toe, is an ingrown nail. This occurs mostly when a nail is trimmed overly short or shoes are too tight, forcing the sharp corner of a growing nail to push into the skin. The result is a painful swelling and sometimes infection. Regular massage of the skin surrounding the ingrown corner often corrects the problem. Gently taping the skin back from the nail edge may also help, as can going barefoot for a while. In the unlikely event that the problem persists, several minor surgical procedures are available.

As well as suffering their own minor maladies, nails can also be excellent indicators of a person's more general state of health. For example, white bands running across a nail—Meet's lines—can be a sign of a particular protein deficiency caused by illness, some anti-cancer drugs or arsenic poisoning. A change in color from normally healthy pink can indicate a problem with a major organ. Hepatitis, which affects the liver, can give nails a yellow tinge. A brown discoloration can indicate kidney disease. Nails that look very white suggest anemia, a lack of iron in the blood. Small white flecks usually indicate minor injuries and normally disappear after a few weeks.

SEE ALSO *Cuticle, Finger, Keratin, Paronychia*

NARCOLEPSY

Narcolepsy is a rare sleep disorder characterized by uncontrollable episodes of falling asleep at any place or time. Attacks of sleep may last minutes or hours and may vary in frequency from an occasional episode to ten or more in a single day. On awakening, the person feels refreshed, but another attack may occur again quickly. The condition usually begins in adolescence or young adulthood and continues throughout life. There may be a family history of the disease.

The condition can be diagnosed by sleep studies (continuous recordings of brain waves, muscle movements, and pulse and breathing patterns during sleep). Narcolepsy cannot be cured, but symptoms can be controlled with regular planned naps, and antidepressant and stimulant drugs.

SEE ALSO *Sleep apnea*

NARCOTICS

Narcotics (or narcotic analgesics) are drugs that produce relief from pain, a state of stupor or sleep and often addiction or physical dependence.

Opium, produced from the opium poppy, has been in use for thousands of years; in 1803 the alkaloid compound morphine was discovered and in 1898, heroin (diacetylmorphine) was discovered and used as a treatment of morphine addiction (though it was later found to be even more addictive and dangerous than morphine).

Modern narcotics are either opium derivatives, such as morphine and codeine, or synthetic drugs known as meperidine and methadone. They are used primarily for controlling strong to severe pain, such as pain from kidney stones, cancer pain and post-operative pain.

Codeine is sometimes used in cough mixtures because it suppresses coughing and sometimes as a treatment for diarrhea. Methadone is sometimes used in the treatment of heroin addiction, though it is itself addictive. Side effects of narcotics can be problematic; they include constipation, nausea and vomiting and urinary retention.

SEE ALSO *Analgesics, Drug dependence, Methadone, Morphine*

NATUROPATHY

Ancient Greek physicians, such as Hippocrates, were among the earliest to articulate naturopathic philosophies in their belief that the body will naturally cure itself when given pure air, water, food and exercise. Naturopathic medicine was revived and developed in association with hydrotherapy in nineteenth-century Europe. It was introduced into the USA in the 1890s by Benedict Lust after he was treated successfully at the health spa of Father Sebastian Kneipp. Today naturopathy is well established in most Western countries.

The naturopathic view is that illness stems from a biochemical or metabolic imbalance that is due to physical or emotional stress over a prolonged period. Disease is not seen as the cause of illness but as the end result of an overworked body with a weakened immune system. Symptoms of illness such as fever or vomiting are believed to be the body's attempt to move itself back into a state of health. For this reason naturopaths encourage symptoms to come out, rather than to suppress them, as part of the body's self-healing process.

Naturopaths stress the importance of giving the body time to restore itself to health. In order to devise an ongoing individualized regime of treatment, they take a detailed

Naturopathy

The holistic approach adopted by naturopathic practitioners is based on adhering to a "triad of health": psychological, biological and structural factors should all be balanced. Illness is a sign of imbalance in the system, so analysis of individual parts—the eyes, nails and tongue, for example—may be used to identify problems elsewhere in the body.

Tongue
The color and texture of the tongue is used by naturopaths to assess ill health. Red in the center of the tongue may indicate a stomach-related problem.

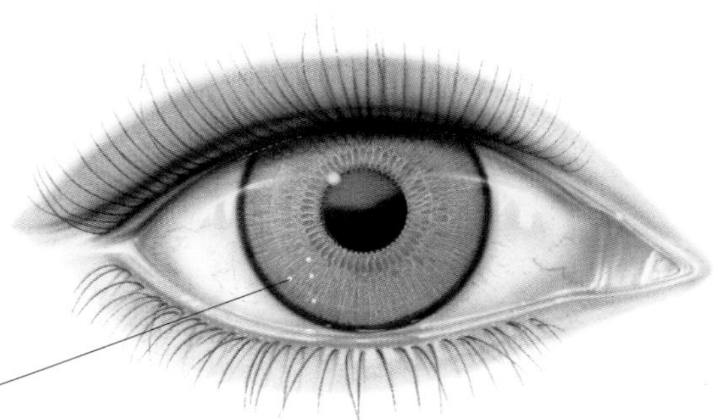

Iris
The iris is divided by naturopaths into sections that correspond to parts of the body. White spots in a particular section, for example, may indicate a disorder of the chest. A dark ring may indicate toxins.

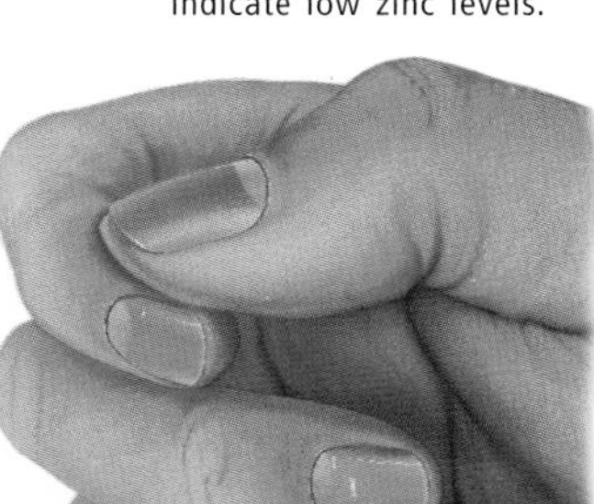

Nails
White spots on nails may indicate low zinc levels.

medical history to identify the stresses carried by the patient. Diagnosis of the iris, nail and tongue may be used and pathology tests may be carried out.

A prime area of focus in naturopathy is diet, where there is an emphasis on highly nourishing "clean" food and water, free of pesticides and preservatives and as unprocessed as possible. Typically, naturopaths suggest a diet that is high in fresh vegetables, fruits, seeds, nuts and whole grains, and low in meat, coffee and alcohol.

To aid detoxification of the body, naturopaths may prescribe fasts. Special attention is paid to the health of the bowel as this is where nutrients are absorbed into the bloodstream. Diets are given to clear the gut of yeasts and bacteria that are seen to contribute to toxicity, allergy and poor immunity. Colonic irrigation may also be prescribed.

Many naturopaths warn patients of the possibility of some kind of "healing crisis" where symptoms briefly worsen soon after the commencement of detoxification as the body's organs become overloaded by the release of toxins into the bloodstream.

As well as nutrition, naturopathy emphasizes the importance of rest, relaxation, exercise, fresh air and bathing. Treatment for illnesses may also include hydrotherapy, massage, herbs, homeopathic remedies and nutritional supplements; the latter is viewed as necessary because of the depletion of the nutrient content of soils through modern agriculture. Flower essences, relaxation techniques or counseling are recommended for psychological stress.

Naturopathic medicine, especially in its use of nutrition to strengthen the body, is gaining widespread acceptance. It is becoming more common to find medical doctors adopting naturopathic practices or working in alliance with naturopaths, especially where patients are being weaned off pharmaceutical drugs. Naturopathy is particularly suited to treating stress-related chronic illnesses including asthma, arthritis, skin and digestive disorders.

SEE ALSO *Counseling, Detoxification, Flower remedies and essences, Hydrotherapy, Massage, Relaxation techniques, Orthomolecular therapy*

NAUSEA

Nausea is the unpleasant sensation of feeling sick in the stomach and of being about to vomit. It is often followed by vomiting. It may be caused by conditions such as food poisoning and other gastrointestinal disorders, early pregnancy, or a physical or emotional shock. It may also be a side effect of medication.

The treatment of nausea depends on the cause. Lying down can often help. If vomiting accompanies the nausea, it is important to frequently drink fluids in small amounts to replace lost fluid. Antihistamines such as cyclizine or meclizine, that have an anti-nausea effect, may help. Scopolamine is also often used, but causes dry mouth, blurred vision and urinary retention.

Morning sickness is nausea and vomiting during pregnancy. It affects about 50 percent of women in pregnancy, usually from about the sixth to the twelfth week. The symptoms may be present at any time of day, not just the morning. Eating frequent, small, bland meals and avoiding an empty stomach may ease the symptoms. In severe cases, an anti-nausea drug may be required.

Motion sickness is caused by a disrupted sense of balance that occurs when the brain receives conflicting information about the body's orientation in space during movement. Air sickness, car sickness and sea sickness are all examples of motion sickness. It may be caused by amusement rides such as carousels and rollercoasters. Children are more prone to it than adults. Motion sickness is best avoided by prevention; while traveling, look at the horizon for a stable perspective rather than watching passing scenery. Anti-nausea drugs taken before a journey may help in severe cases.

SEE ALSO *Morning sickness, Motion sickness, Sea sickness, Vomiting*

Neck cross-section

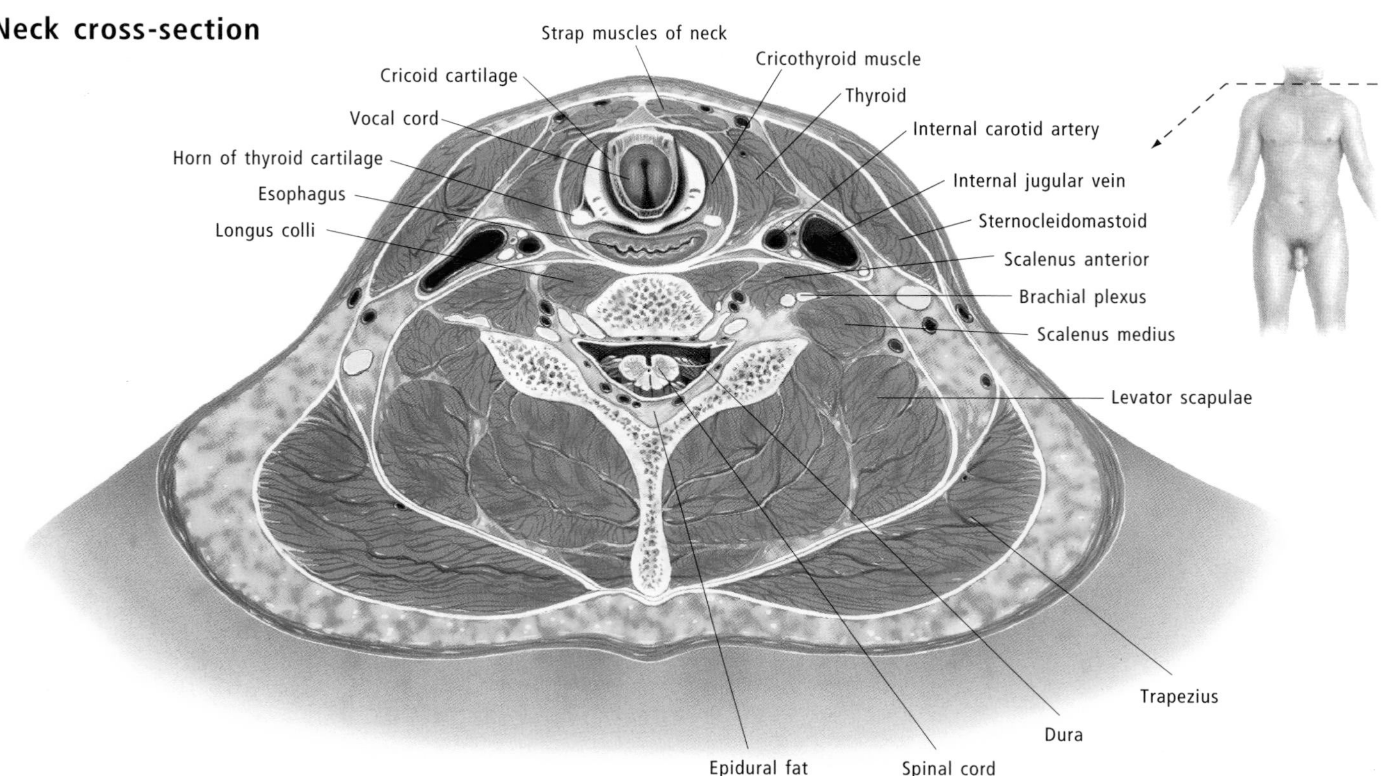

N

NECK

The neck supports and provides mobility for the head and contains a large number of important structures in a relatively confined space: the spinal cord, protected by the vertebrae; major blood vessels to the brain and face; and passageways for food and air. Important nerves course through the neck and some arise from the neck region.

The neck can be divided into two major columns. At the back, the nuchal region comprises the vertebrae of the neck (cervical vertebrae) and their supporting musculature. In front, it comprises a "visceral" column containing the larynx and trachea and behind them the pharynx and esophagus. On either side of these are major blood vessels.

The thyroid gland is attached to the front and sides of the trachea and larynx, and covering these structures at the front are thin strap-like muscles and skin. There are two large muscles, the sternocleidomastoid and trapezius.

Surrounding the muscles and visceral structures in the neck are a series of connective tissue sheaths that can affect the spread of infection.

Musculoskeletal column

The vertebrae in the neck are small (compared to those of the spine), since they carry very little weight, but the opening in the vertebrae for the spinal cord is relatively large. The two upper cervical vertebrae are specialized.

The first vertebra, the atlas, is a bony ring, and forms two joints (atlanto-occipital joints) with the base of the skull, allowing a nodding action.

The next vertebra, the axis, has an upward projecting bony element that forms a joint in the midline with the atlas. This, together with a joint on either side, allows a pivoting movement to occur, as in shaking the head when saying no. About 45 degrees of rotation in the neck occurs at these joints alone (the atlantoaxial joint).

The remaining vertebrae have a typical vertebral pattern with a body in front, a bony arch behind and spines projecting backward (spinous processes) and to the sides (transverse processes). The intervertebral disks that separate and cushion neighboring vertebrae from each other are relatively thick in the cervical region of the spine, permitting great freedom of movement.

Blood vessels

A feature of cervical vertebrae is that an artery (vertebral artery) passes through openings in the bony transverse processes. It ascends on the left and right, protected by the vertebrae, and supplies blood to the lower parts of the brain (cerebellum, brain stem and lower posterior part of the cerebral hemispheres).

Muscles

Muscles attach to the front, back and sides of the vertebrae, producing forward, backward and sideways movements. Those with an oblique orientation also produce rotation (turning). The largest musculature lies to the back. Some of these muscles are exclusively related to moving the head and neck (for example, splenius capitis and cervicis, semispinalis capitis and cervicis), while others are related to moving the shoulder (for example, trapezius, levator scapulae) or raising the upper two ribs (the scalene muscles).

Nerves

The spinal cord in the neck region gives origin to nerves (cervical nerves C1–C8) that pass to the skin and muscles of the neck (C1–C4) and upper limb (C5–C8). They

The neck

Dens
Superior articular surface of lateral mass for occipital condyle
Anterior tubercle
Anterior arch
Transverse foramen
Transverse process, C1
Lateral mass
Body of C2
Posterior arch
Transverse foramen
Posterior tubercle
Transverse process, C2
Inferior articular process
Spinous process, C2

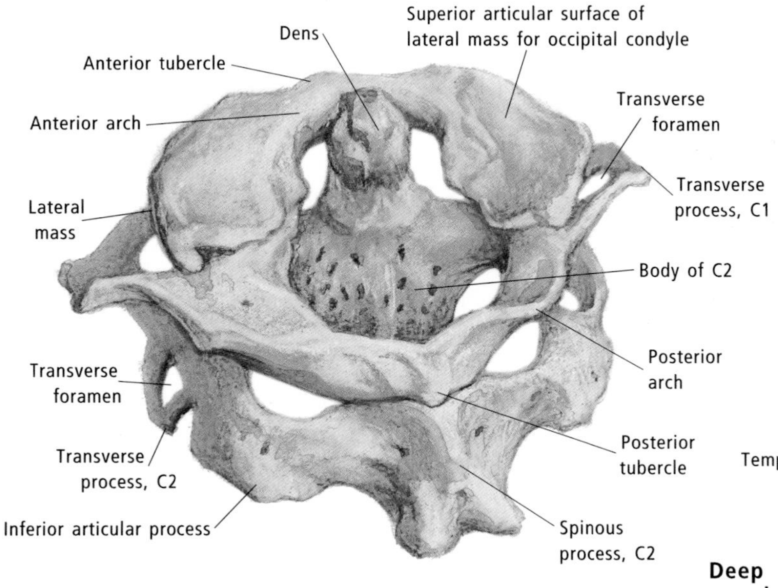

Atlas and axis

There are 7 vertebrae in the neck—the first 2 are more specialized than the others. C1, the atlas, supports the head and allows it to have a nodding movement. C2, the axis, articulates with the atlas and gives the head its ability to rotate.

Musculoskeletal column

The various muscles of the neck have fibers arranged in a number of different directions, giving the head and upper spine great freedom of movement.

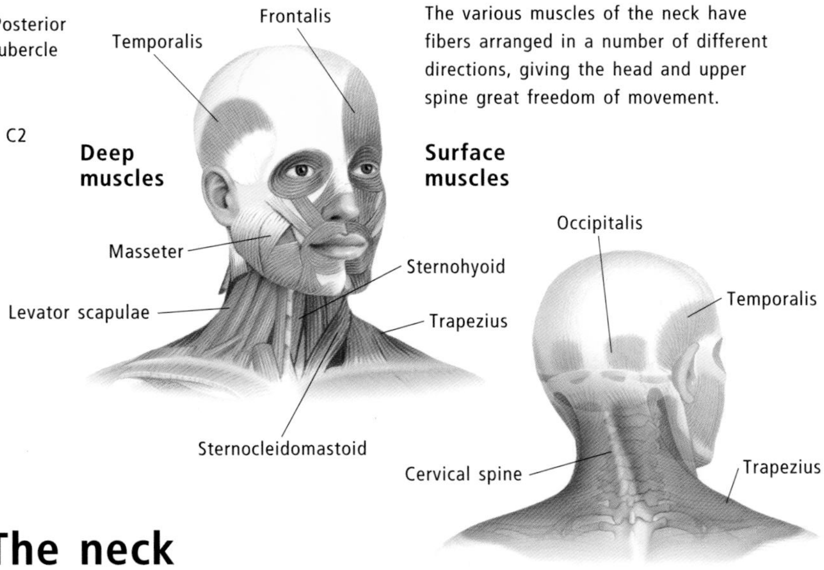

Frontalis
Temporalis
Deep muscles
Surface muscles
Masseter
Sternohyoid
Levator scapulae
Trapezius
Sternocleidomastoid
Occipitalis
Temporalis
Cervical spine
Trapezius

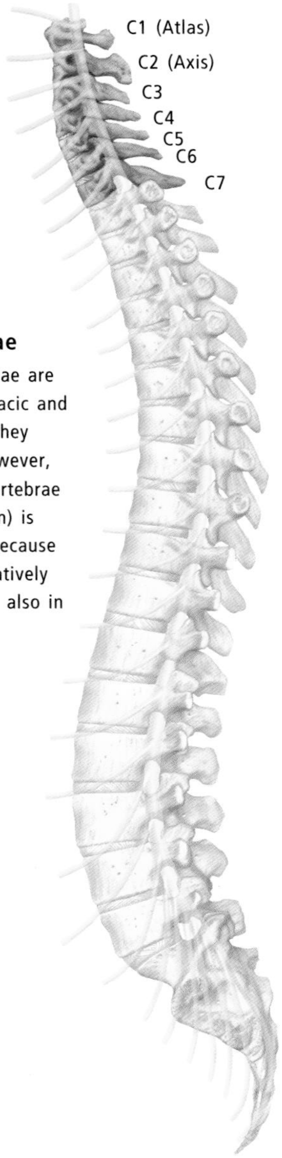

C1 (Atlas)
C2 (Axis)
C3
C4
C5
C6
C7

Cervical vertebrae

The 7 cervical vertebrae are smaller than the thoracic and lumbar vertebrae as they carry less weight. However, the opening in the vertebrae (the vertebral foramen) is comparatively large because the spinal cord is relatively thick at the neck and also in the lumbar regions.

C1
Pharynx
Epiglottis
Thyroid cartilage
Larynx
Cricoid cartilage
Trachea
C7
Esophagus

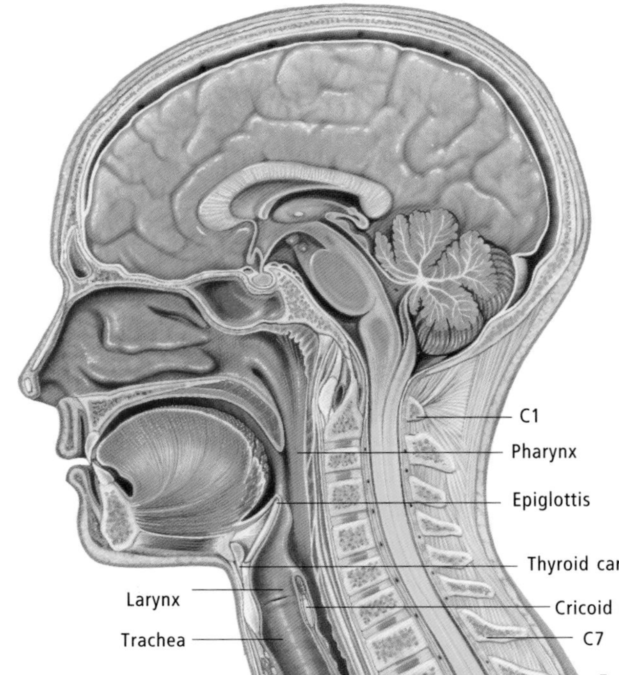

Neck column

The front of the neck houses several important structures in a relatively small area. These include the larynx (voice box), the upper part of the trachea (windpipe), the thyroid gland, and the pharynx (throat) which leads to the esophagus. Running beside these are large blood vessels, one of which is the carotid artery.

N

pass out through openings between the vertebrae (intervertebral foramen) and can be compressed here by bony outgrowths of the vertebrae (osteophytes), giving rise to symptoms such as tingling, numbness and weakness in the arm and hand.

The phrenic nerve is formed in the neck. It supplies the diaphragm, the muscle that contracts on inspiration. Damage to one or both phrenic nerves will affect breathing. Fracture of the cervical vertebrae may affect the spinal cord and/or cervical nerves. If damage occurs at spinal cord level C4 or higher it can be fatal, because the diaphragm is paralyzed.

Visceral column

At the angle in the upper part of the front of the neck is a small, U-shaped bone called the hyoid bone and, suspended from this, the voice box (larynx). The larynx is part of the upper respiratory tract, and a cartilaginous framework serves to keep the airway open. In males, the thyroid cartilage forms a distinct prominence called the laryngeal prominence or Adam's apple. The epiglottis, a piece of flexible cartilage at the inlet to the larynx, helps to prevent food and fluids from entering the airway when swallowing. The vocal cords, or vocal folds, are located within the larynx and control the size of the aperture between them (the rima glottidis). The folds lie close together and vibrate during speech, move wide apart in deep breathing, and may stop the flow of air completely (for example, when holding the breath).

The trachea commences at the lower end of the larynx and descends into the thoracic cavity to connect with the lungs. It can be felt, and moved from side to side, in the lower part of the neck. Wrapping around the upper trachea and extending onto the sides of the larynx and trachea is the thyroid gland. It has a narrow piece in front and expanded lobes on either side. It is bound to the larynx and trachea by connective tissue and so moves with them on swallowing, a feature that allows an enlargement of the thyroid gland to be distinguished from other swellings in the neck (such as an enlarged lymph node, which does not move with swallowing).

The pharynx lies behind the larynx. It is connected below to the esophagus, which lies directly behind the trachea, and empties into it when food is swallowed. The pharynx and esophagus have muscular walls that contract in a milking action to move food toward the stomach.

Blood vessels

On either side of the pharynx, larynx, trachea and esophagus are large blood vessels bound together by a connective tissue sheath (carotid sheath).

Within the sheath, in the lower part of the neck, is the common carotid artery, that divides into an internal and external carotid arteries at about the level of the laryngeal prominence. The internal carotid artery supplies the brain and the external carotid artery supplies the face and neck.

The pulse of the common carotid artery may be felt at the side of the larynx, and can be compressed against a bony outgrowth of the sixth cervical vertebrae (the carotid tubercle), stemming its flow. Carotid comes from the Greek word *karoo*, meaning "to put to sleep".

Within the carotid sheath, on the outer aspect of the internal and common carotid arteries, is the internal jugular vein, that drains the blood from the brain. Veins from the face and neck drain into it. At its lower end is a valve that prevents backflow of blood toward the brain. Behind and between the blood vessels and within the sheath is the vagus nerve, an important nerve supplying the larynx, trachea, pharynx, esophagus, heart, lungs and much of the gastrointestinal tract. Branches of the vagus (external laryngeal nerve and recurrent laryngeal nerve) pass to muscles controlling the vocal cords and may be damaged in thyroid surgery.

Muscles

In front of the visceral tubes and thyroid gland are thin strap-like muscles (infrahyoid muscles) that move the larynx and hyoid bones. Attaching to the skin of the neck is a wide, thin muscle, the platysma muscle, that is involved in facial expression, and tenses in anger. A large muscle that extends from the skull to the clavicle and sternum is the sternocleidomastoid muscle. It contracts when one lifts the head, and can be subject to spasm, as occurs in the condition torticollis or wryneck. The spinal nerves which supply the arm (C5 to T1) come together in the brachial plexus and separate into the nerves of the arm. They then pass obliquely down and outward, just below the skin, in the angle between this muscle and the clavicle. The outer margin of the neck is defined by the trapezius muscle, and the degree of development (bulk) of this muscle, can affect the shape and appearance of the neck.

Injuries

The neck is easily traumatized in whiplash injuries, where the muscles are not able to protect the neck from excessive movement. Damage to ligaments, muscles and joints may produce pain and instability. Following severe trauma, the neck needs to be immobilized and assessed for spinal cord damage, that can result in quadriplegia, or may be fatal if damage occurs to the highest part of the spinal cord.

Stiff neck is a condition of strained ligaments and muscles in the neck. It may be caused by a sudden twisting of the neck, by sleeping in an awkward position, or by stress or injury. The symptoms are neck pain and stiffness. Aspirin or non-steroidal anti-inflammatory drugs and physical therapy (heat, massage and exercise) will help relieve the symptoms.

Cervical osteoarthritis is a gradual deterioration of the cervical vertebrae. It affects mainly people over 50, developing slowly over many years. The symptoms are neck pain and stiffness. Sometimes a spinal nerve may be pinched by a damaged vertebra or herniated disk, causing numbness or pain that radiates down the neck and shoulders.

A neck x-ray usually shows the degenerative changes of osteoarthritis. Aspirin or non-steroidal anti-inflammatory drugs may help the symptoms. Physical therapy including heat and massage will also help. A neck collar that supports and immobilizes the neck may be needed intermittently, and traction may be required in severe cases. Surgery is sometimes an option, though the results are variable due to the poor condition of the vertebrae.

SEE ALSO ***Carotid arteries, Disk, intervertebral, Epiglottis, Esophagus, Jugular vein, Larynx, Pharynx, Quadriplegia, Spinal cord, Thyroid gland, Torticollis, Trachea, Vagus nerve, Vertebrae, Vocal cords, Whiplash injury***

N

NEEDLE BIOPSY

A needle biopsy is a procedure to sample an abnormal lump or mass in the body. It may also be used to determine whether disease is present in normal tissue, for example in the lung or liver. A needle biopsy is usually performed by a radiologist.

During the procedure, the radiologist inserts a small needle into the abnormal area and removes a sample of the tissue, which is then sent to a pathologist. The pathologist then determines what the abnormal tissue is: cancer, non-cancerous tumor, infection or scar. The procedure is quicker and causes much less damage to normal tissue than an open biopsy, which leaves a surgical scar.

SEE ALSO *Biopsy*

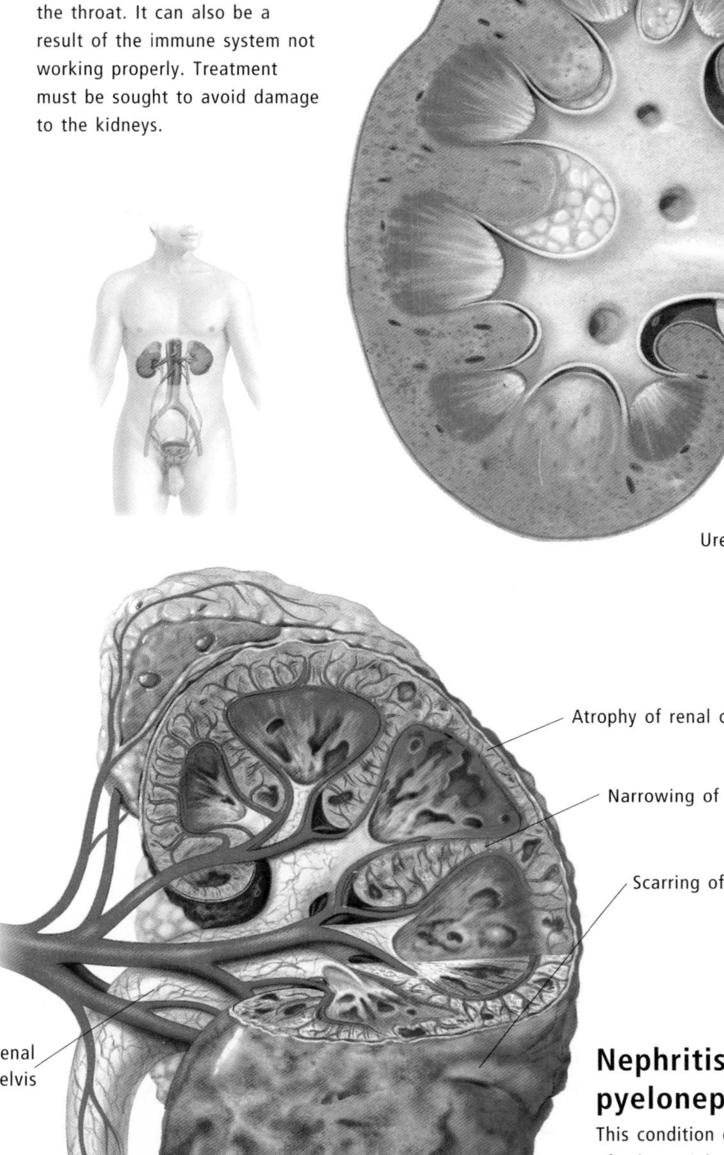

Nephritis—glomerulonephritis
This type of kidney disorder may begin with an infection, often of the throat. It can also be a result of the immune system not working properly. Treatment must be sought to avoid damage to the kidneys.

Nephritis—chronic pyelonephritis
This condition can be the result of a bacterial or viral infection of the renal pelvis. If untreated, severe kidney damage may occur. The main symptoms are high fever, intense pain, vomiting, diarrhea and blood in the urine.

NEPHRITIS

Nephritis is a general term for any inflammation of one or both kidneys and may be acute or chronic. It may involve the glomeruli (glomerulonephritis), the main tissue of the kidney and pelvis (pyelonephritis), or the spaces within the kidney (interstitial nephritis).

Glomerulonephritis

Glomerulonephritis is inflammation of the glomeruli, which are clusters of renal capillaries. Damage to the glomeruli results in an inability to filter the blood properly, so that blood and protein pass out into the urine. This may lead to poor kidney function and kidney failure.

Acute (sudden) glomerulonephritis sometimes follows a throat infection or other streptococcal infection and is more common in children than in adults. There may be no symptoms but, usually, the affected person notices smoky or slightly red urine, puffy eyes and ankles, a general ill feeling, drowsiness, nausea or vomiting and headaches. Analysis of the urine reveals it to contain blood and proteins. Mild cases are treated by a carefully controlled diet and bed rest. Sometimes, and especially in adults, kidney dialysis is necessary until the kidneys recover. Recovery is usually complete.

Chronic (slow onset) glomerulonephritis may develop after a case of acute nephritis, even after a long interval, or the affected person may have never had the acute form. Symptoms vary greatly, but may include poor appetite, fatigue, anemia and high blood pressure. Treatment involves a strict diet low in proteins and sodium. High blood pressure may require treatment with antihypertensive drugs. In severe cases, cortisone or cytotoxic drugs, kidney dialysis and, eventually, kidney transplantation, may be necessary. There is no known cure for chronic glomerulonephritis, but the progress of the disease can be delayed.

Pyelonephritis

Pyelonephritis is an infection of the kidney and the renal pelvis. It develops from pyelitis, a less severe inflammation of the renal pelvis. Acute pyelonephritis is usually the result of a bladder infection that has spread to the kidney. It is characterized by the sudden onset of pain in the lower back, fever with chills, nausea and vomiting. A urine

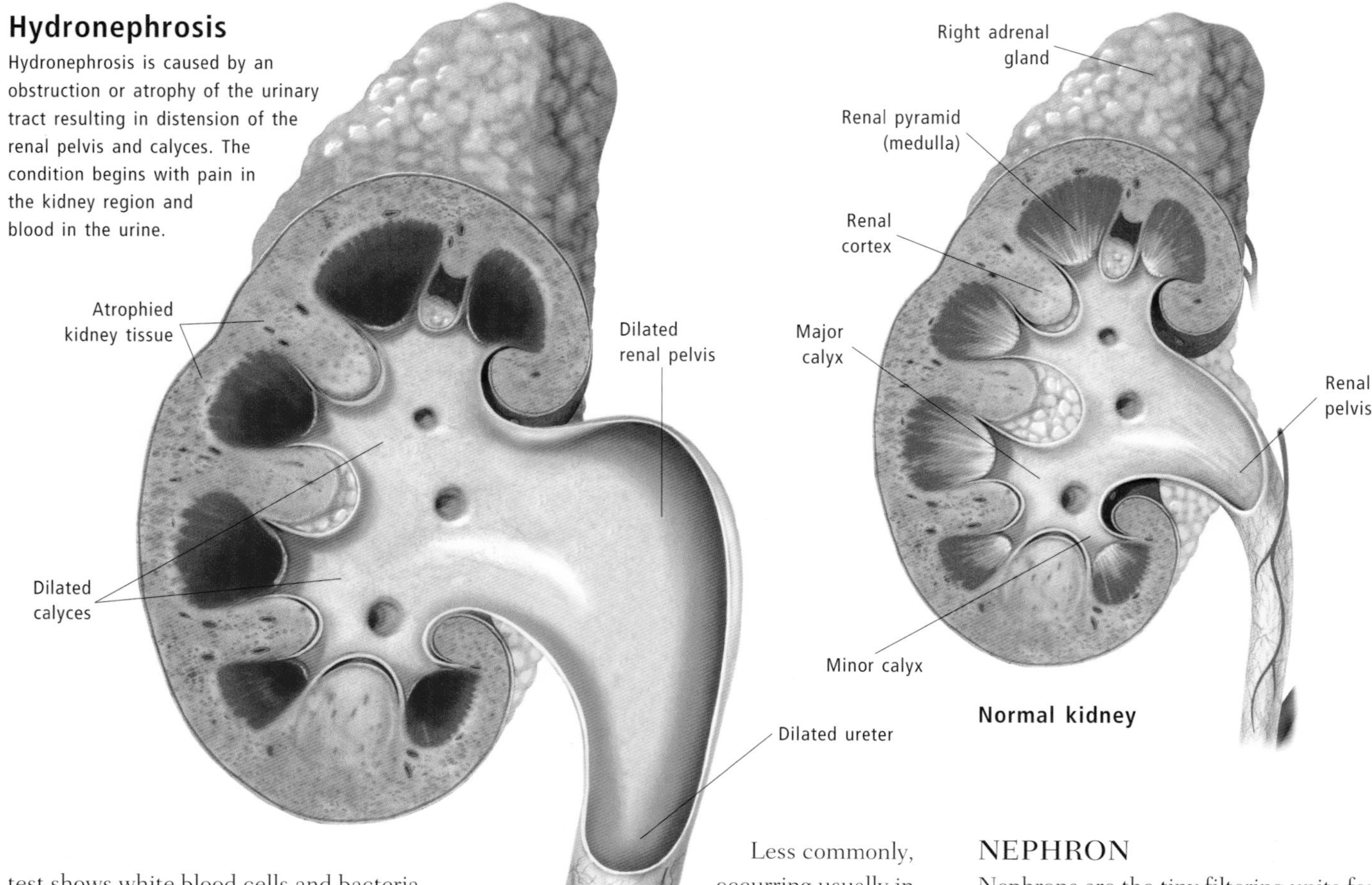

Hydronephrosis

Hydronephrosis is caused by an obstruction or atrophy of the urinary tract resulting in distension of the renal pelvis and calyces. The condition begins with pain in the kidney region and blood in the urine.

Normal kidney

test shows white blood cells and bacteria in the urine and, once the bacteria involved is identified, antibiotics can be chosen accordingly. Acute pyelonephritis generally responds to treatment with antibiotics given intravenously in hospital.

Chronic pyelonephritis is caused by destruction and scarring of the kidney tissue as a result of recurring or untreated bacterial infection. This may be due to an abnormality of the urinary tract, that leads to repeated infection. Treatment is via a course of antibiotics to treat the infection, and surgical correction of any underlying abnormality. If left untreated, renal failure may occur, requiring dialysis or transplantation.

Interstitial nephritis

Interstitial nephritis is inflammation of the spaces between the renal tubules and (sometimes) of the tubules themselves. It is usually a temporary, reversible condition, occurring as a side effect of certain drugs such as analgesics or antibiotics. Interstitial nephritis causes varying degrees of impaired kidney function; if severe, dialysis may be needed temporarily. Corticosteroids or anti-inflammatory medications may be of benefit in some cases.

Less commonly, occurring usually in the elderly, it may be chronic and progressive, when eventually long-term dialysis or renal transplantation may be necessary.

SEE ALSO *Dialysis, Glomerulonephritis, Kidney, Pyelitis, Pyelonephritis, Urinary systems*

NEPHROBLASTOMA

Nephroblastoma, which is also called Wilms' tumor, is a rapidly developing malignant tumor of the kidney. It occurs mainly in children under the age of seven and most often in children with congenital abnormalities.

Symptoms are an enlarged abdomen (a large, firm, smooth tumor can be felt in the child's abdomen), high blood pressure, blood in the urine, weight loss and, sometimes, abdominal pain. An ultrasound, CAT scan or MRI scan of the abdomen will show the tumor.

Treatment is with surgery, radiation therapy and anti-cancer drugs. In most cases the child can be cured, especially if the tumor is detected before it spreads to other organs.

SEE ALSO *Cancer, Kidney*

NEPHRON

Nephrons are the tiny filtering units found in the kidney. There are millions of tiny nephrons located within the cortex of both kidneys. Each is composed of a ball-shaped cluster of capillaries (the glomerulus) and a narrow, hairpin-shaped little tube (the tubule). An extension of the tubule forms a cup-shaped capsule part of the way around the glomerulus called Bowman's capsule.

From the arterial circulation, blood passes into the capillaries of the glomerulus. Because the capillary membranes are thin and permeable, a fluid composed of blood minus red and white blood cells and proteins filters readily through the glomerulus and capsule membranes into the tubule.

This filtrate passes along the tubule, which twists and turns, and contains a U-shaped section called Henle's loop. As the filtrate passes along the tubule, a network of capillaries reabsorbs water, glucose and salts from the filtrate, and secretes unwanted substances into the filtrate. The remaining filtrate, that contains the wastes such as urea that are toxic to the body, drains from the tubules into the renal pelvis and is then transported to the bladder via the ureters as urine.

SEE ALSO *Bladder, Kidney, Plasma, Ureter, Urinary systems*

N

NEPHROSIS

Also called nephrotic syndrome, nephrosis is any abnormal kidney condition in which damage to the glomeruli leads to high loss of protein in the urine. Other symptoms include edema (swelling of the body tissues), fatigue, weakness and loss of appetite. The condition usually begins in children under six years of age.

The leakage of protein, especially albumin, out of the glomeruli and into the urine lowers the concentration of protein in the blood, causing a shift in osmotic pressure. Because of this change in pressure, fluid then leaks out of the blood and into the tissues, causing puffy eyes and ankles, a swollen abdomen and other signs of edema.

Nephrosis can be caused by damage to the glomerulus in conditions such as glomerulonephritis, diabetes, systemic lupus erythematosus and other autoimmune disorders. It is likely that several, not just one, pathologic processes are involved, all of which affect the glomeruli. Nephrosis may also be caused by any condition that causes an increase in the pressure of blood in the vessels of the glomerulus, such as heart failure or following a thrombosis in the renal vein. Elevated pressure in the blood vessels of the kidney also forces protein out into the urine. In some cases there is no obvious cause.

The condition cannot be cured but the symptoms can be controlled with cortisone or immunosuppressive drugs, which reduce kidney inflammation; diuretics, which reduce fluid retention and edema; and a low salt diet. In severe cases dialysis or kidney transplant may be needed.

Hydronephrosis is a different condition that occurs when the kidney's pelvis and calyces become distended because urine is unable to drain into the bladder. This distension occurs because ureter is blocked, for example by a tumor or a stone in the ureter or bladder or by enlargement of the prostate gland. If the condition progresses unchecked, this distention destroys the tubules in the cortex of the kidney, which may become atrophied and scarred. Urinary tract infection is a common accompaniment, leading to further kidney damage. If both kidneys are affected, kidney failure may be the end result. The symptoms are recurrent back pain, pain on passing urine, fever and chills. The urine may be cloudy and may contain blood. Sometimes the condition presents no symptoms and is discovered only during investigations for something else. Diagnosis can be confirmed with a pyelogram (x-ray investigation in which the kidney is outlined with the use of dye), ultrasound, CAT scan of the kidneys or abdomen or abdominal magnetic resonance imaging. These tests will also reveal the underlying cause.

The treatment is to treat the underlying cause. It may be necessary to surgically drain the dilated renal pelvis and remove the cause of the blockage. If there is a urinary tract infection it must be treated with antibiotics.

SEE ALSO *Diabetes, Glomerulonephritis, Kidney, Lupus erythematosus, Urinary systems*

NERVE CONDUCTION TESTS

Nerve conduction tests evaluate the health of a nerve by recording how fast an electrical impulse travels through it. Two electrodes are placed on the skin at different points along the path of a nerve being tested. One electrode initiates a nerve impulse which travels along the nerve and the other records the impulse. The time between the stimulus and response is recorded to determine how quickly and thoroughly the impulse travels along the nerve.

In a number of nerve conditions, such as nerve entrapment syndromes or degenerative nerve diseases, the transmission of nerve impulses is slowed. Different nerve diseases will affect conduction in different ways, and the test can be used as a diagnostic aid. The person being tested feels a small electric shock, but most people tolerate the test well.

SEE ALSO *Nerves*

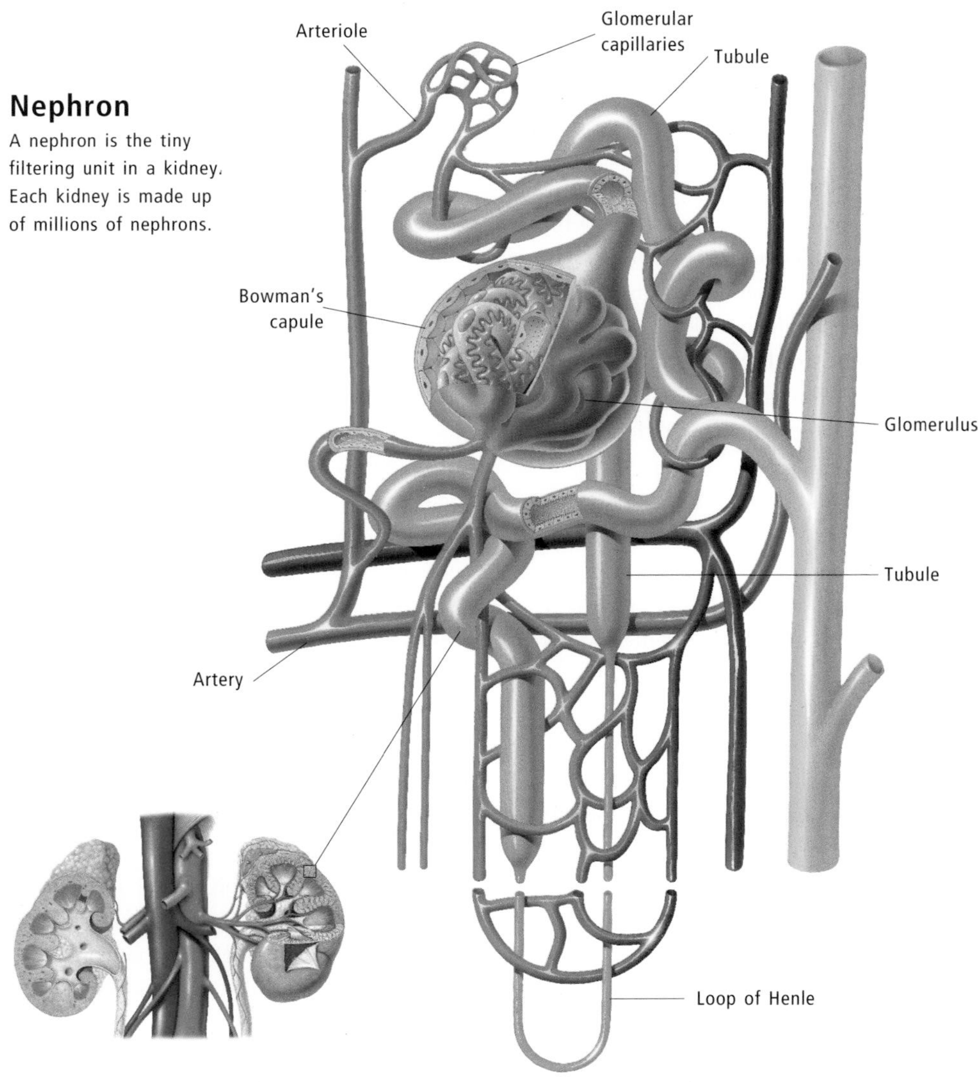

Nephron
A nephron is the tiny filtering unit in a kidney. Each kidney is made up of millions of nephrons.

NERVES

Nerves connect the brain and spinal cord (central nervous system, CNS) with peripheral regions such as the muscles, skin and viscera. Their role is to carry signals which provide us with sensations or control our muscles. Twelve pairs of nerves arise from the brain and are called cranial nerves; they include the trigeminal and facial nerves and the vagus nerve. Nerves arising from the spinal cord, between the vertebrae, are known as spinal nerves. There are 31 pairs of spinal nerves, supplying the trunk and limbs.

A special branch of the peripheral nervous system, the autonomic nervous system, is concerned with controlling muscles in the viscera, such as the gut, bladder, heart and blood vessels. The autonomic nervous system has two parts, the sympathetic and parasympathetic. Some axons of the sympathetic system (e.g. those serving blood vessels in the limbs) travel with ordinary (somatic) nerves to reach their targets. Other autonomic, sympathetic and parasympathetic axons travel in special visceral nerves, such as the splanchnic nerves, to the gut and pelvic organs.

Nerve cells

Nerves contain the long processes of the nerve cells called axons, with one nerve containing many thousands of axons, running together in parallel bundles. Each axon extends all the way from the CNS to the tissue it supplies. Thus an axon can extend from the spinal cord to the hand or foot, a distance of over a meter, although others (e.g. to muscles and skin on the back) may be much shorter. There are two types of axons, sensory and motor. Sensory axons carry signals coming into the CNS from structures such as the skin, muscles, joints and viscera. They carry information about touch, temperature, pain, joint and muscle position. The nerve cell bodies of these axons (sensory neurons) lie in ganglia close to the CNS. Motor axons carry signals coming from the CNS to muscles in the body wall, limbs and viscera, to control our body movements. Their nerve cell bodies, known as motor neurons, lie in the CNS.

The signals carried by axons consist of short pulses of electrical activity, called action potentials, each about 0.1 volt and lasting about one-thousandth of a second. Action potentials in sensory axons start in the periphery (e.g. skin) with a stimulus (e.g. touch) which activates particular receptors (e.g. hair receptors). The action potentials then travel to the CNS where they activate other nerve cells, in sensory centers, to cause sensations. For motor outputs, action potentials start in motor cells in the CNS and travel out along the motor axons to muscles, causing the muscle to contract.

Most nerves contain both sensory and motor axons, with signals going both to and from the CNS in the different axons. Because each axon is like a separate insulated wire it does not interfere with its neighbors. A few nerves are purely motor in function, such as the hypoglossal nerve controlling muscles in the tongue. Similarly, a few nerves are purely sensory, such as the sural nerve to the skin on the lateral side of the foot. Activity in a nerve can be blocked by a local anesthetic, which prevents action potentials from passing through the block. This can be useful for stopping pain signals, for instance from the teeth during dental repairs.

Nerves also contain supporting cells called Schwann cells that envelop the axons. The combination of axon and Schwann cell is often referred to as a nerve fiber. A Schwann cell extends just a short distance along the axon, with the next cell looking after the next section of axon, from one end to the other. Larger axons are completely surrounded by the Schwann cells, that wrap their cell membranes around the axon, making a special layer known as myelin. This acts as an electrical insulator, and is important for increasing the speed at which action potentials can travel (conduction velocity). These axons are called myelinated axons. Smaller axons do not have any myelin (unmyelinated axons). They are still surrounded by Schwann cells which help to insulate them, but the cell does not wrap them in layers of membrane, and their signals travel more slowly.

In sensory axons there is a relationship between the size of an axon and the type of sensation it carries. Large myelinated axons carry information for fine tactile discrimination (e.g. texture of a surface), vibration and limb position. They can transmit signals at about 16–230 feet (5–70 meters) per second (e.g. it takes less than one-tenth of a second for action potentials to reach the spinal cord from the foot). Smaller unmyelinated axons carry signals about cold, warmth and pain, as well as a crude sense of touch. Being smaller and lacking a layer of myelin, their signals are carried more slowly, at about 3 feet (1 meter) per second. In these axons, action potentials from the foot, for example, take about 1 second to reach the spinal cord.

The activity traveling along a nerve can be recorded at certain sites by electrodes on the skin surface. Assessing the function of nerves in this way (nerve conduction testing) can be used to detect the slowing of conduction velocity which may occur when the nerve is injured or the myelin is damaged. This is similar to the evoked potential tests that can be used to detect slowing of conduction in central pathways, as with multiple sclerosis.

Connective tissue

Nerves also contain several layers of connective tissue, which protect the nerve and carry blood vessels. Connective tissue surrounds individual axons and groups them into bundles (fascicles) as well as surrounding the whole nerve. Blood vessels to nerves have a special barrier, the blood–nerve barrier, that is similar to the blood–brain barrier. The blood–nerve barrier prevents certain chemicals in the blood from entering the nerve, thus providing further protection for the axons. When the blood supply to a nerve is restricted or there is pressure on a nerve, strange sensations, usually called paresthesias, can be felt in the area supplied by the nerve. These include tingling sensations, "pins and needles" and numbness. If such a sensation is due to tight clothing or a particular posture (e.g. sitting in a squatting position), it usually disappears when the pressure is relieved. Other paresthesias may need treatment, e.g. pressure to the median nerve at the wrist can give pins and needles in the thumb, that may require surgery.

Nerve damage and disease

Nerves can be damaged by mechanical injuries, such as fractures or stab wounds. Some nerves are particularly vulnerable. For example, the radial nerve can be injured in fractures of the arm, where the nerve passes close to the bone; the median nerve can be injured when the wrist is cut, for instance in suicide attempts. Severing the nerve breaks the continuity of the axons and prevents them from transmitting signals to or from the periphery, thus loss of control of movement and loss of sensation occur in the affected area. The part of the axon separated from the nerve cell body in the CNS dies, but the part connected to the cell body is able to regenerate. As it grows at approximately 1⁄25 inch (1 millimeter) per day, it may take many weeks to recover.

In order to grow back to the appropriate region, it is important for the separated ends of the nerve to be rejoined. Even very careful repair is not able to reconnect individual axons, however, so that regeneration is often rather inaccurate, and recovery may be limited. Other nerves, such as the sural nerve in the leg, can be used for a nerve graft if the damage is extensive or part of the nerve is missing. Crush injuries to nerves usually recover better than injuries where the nerve is cut because the nerve is left in continuity after crushing, which can improve the extent and accuracy of the regeneration.

If nerve continuity is not re-established, the growing axons form a tangled ball of sprouts (neuroma) at the cut end of the nerve. This can occur after amputations and may be painful or contribute to phantom sensations that the limb is still present.

Diseases of peripheral nerves are usually called neuropathies, although if they involve inflammation the term neuritis may be used. Another term, neuralgia, refers to pain along the course of a nerve. Nerve disorders may affect just one nerve, for instance in carpal tunnel syndrome and Bell's palsy. More often, neuropathies involve many nerves, often symmetrically on the two sides of the body. Guillain-Barré syndrome is an example of an acute inflammatory neuropathy. Other examples include nerve damage as a result of diabetes, that particularly involves sensory fibers, and alcoholic neuropathy, that affects both sensory and motor fibers.

The optic nerve is unusual in that it is actually an extension of the brain, and therefore part of the CNS rather than a peripheral nerve. Inflammation of the part of the nerve close to where it leaves the eye is called optic neuritis. It causes partial or complete loss of vision in the affected eye and is frequently associated with multiple sclerosis.

A disease that affects only motor pathways, but involves both the CNS and peripheral nerves, is amyotrophic lateral sclerosis (motor neuron disease). The cause is unknown, but the disease leads to a gradual loss of motor neurons and their axons, with associated weakness and paralysis.

SEE ALSO *Autonomic nervous system, Bell's palsy, Brain, Carpal tunnel syndrome, Guillain-Barré syndrome, Multiple sclerosis, Nerve conduction tests, Nervous system, Neuritis, Neuroma, Neuropathy, Radial nerve, Sciatic nerve, Spinal cord, Sympathetic nervous system, Trigeminal nerve, Ulnar nerve, Vagus nerve*

Spinal cord—cross-section

Nerve fibers leave the spinal cord and their signals travel along axons. Bundles of nerve fibers (with thousands of axons) are called fascicles and are surrounded by connective tissue.

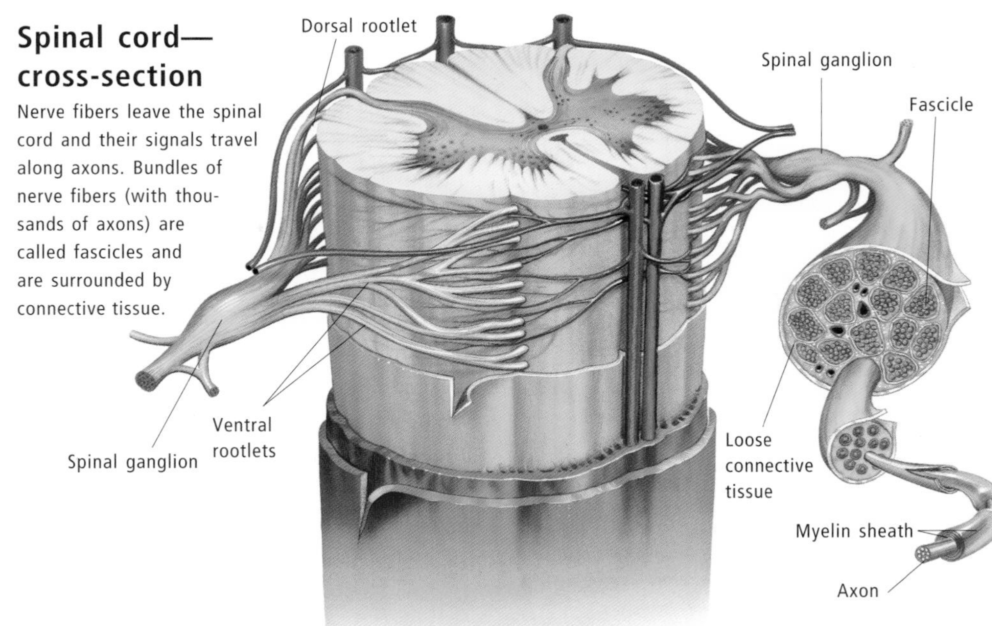

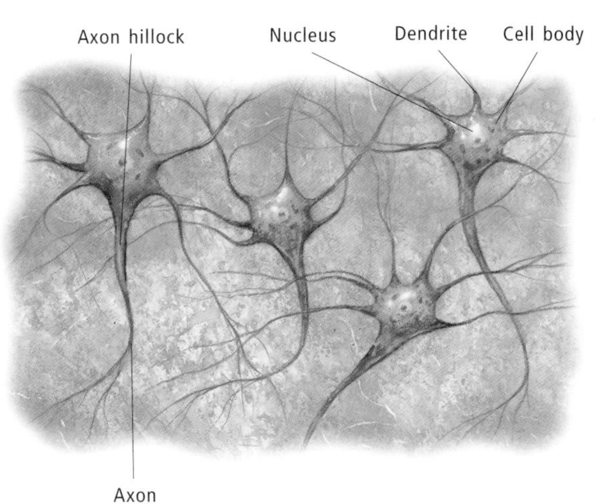

Neural tissue

Neural tissue processes neural data and conducts electrical impulses from one part of the body to another part. Ninety-eight percent of neural tissue is located in the brain and spinal cord.

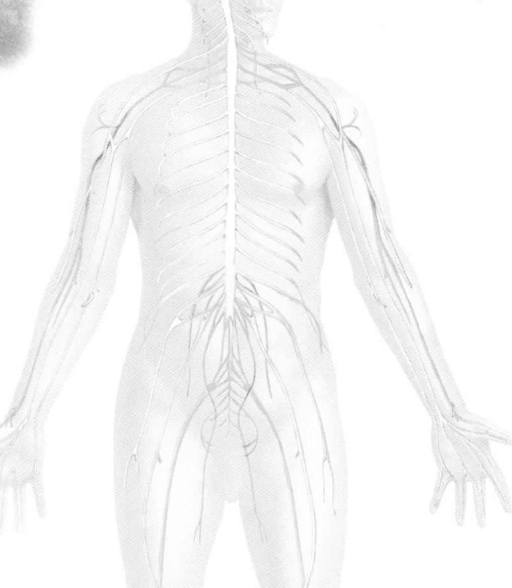

Peripheral nervous system

The peripheral nerves branch out from the central nervous system (the spinal cord) to carry messages to and from all parts of the body.

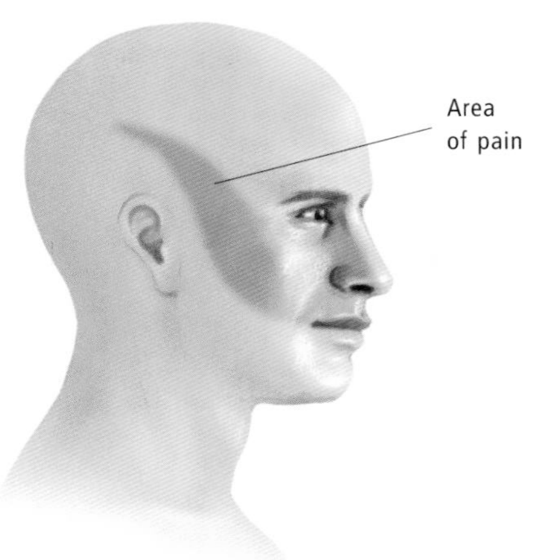

Neuralgia

Neuralgia is pain in or along the course of a sensory nerve. Trigeminal neuralgia causes severe pain in the face and cheek on one side of the face. The pain is often triggered by chewing, brushing the hair, washing the face, drinking cold liquids, and cold winds.

NEURAL TUBE DEFECT

Neural tube defects are disorders resulting in the abnormal development of the brain and spinal cord, and/or the membranes (meninges) surrounding them, in the embryo. In week 3 or 4 of pregnancy, a narrow sheath normally folds and closes to form what is known as the neural tube. This is the first stage of development of the central nervous system (brain and spinal cord); if the tube fails to close perfectly such defects as spina bifida, anencephaly and hydrocephalus can occur. Anencephaly is a condition in which a large part of the brain, skull and scalp are absent due to the incomplete closure of the end of the neural tube nearest the head. Incomplete closure of the bottom end of the tube results in spina bifida, a defect in which the spinal cord and its membranes are exposed and may protrude through a gap in the vertebrae.

Research has shown that ensuring a daily intake of 0.4 milligrams of folic acid (vitamin B_9) before and during pregnancy can halve the risk of neural tube defects. Folic acid occurs naturally in foods such as dark green leafy vegetables; supplements may be taken in tablet form. Neural tube defects can be detected by prenatal tests.

SEE ALSO *Brain, Fetal development, Hydrocephalus, Nervous system, Spinal cord, Spina bifida*

NEURALGIA

Pain in or along the route of a sensory nerve is known as neuralgia. The pain is often sudden, severe and stabbing. Although any part of the body may be affected, the most common sites are the face, arms and chest. An infection such as tooth decay can trigger neuralgia. So too can pinching or pressure on a nerve, as occurs briefly with a knock on the "funny bone" at the elbow. Carpal tunnel syndrome, in which there is inflammation of soft tissues in the forearm, produces a more sustained form of neuralgia. A nervous system disorder can be responsible or it may be associated with other conditions such as diabetes mellitus, some vitamin deficiencies and arthritis. In many cases, however, it is not always possible to identify an underlying cause for neuralgia.

One of the most common forms of neuralgia is trigeminal neuralgia, involving the trigeminal nerve that carries sensory impulses to the brain from the jaws, nose, mouth and eyes.

The sensations associated with this condition occur as very short but overwhelmingly painful repetitive stabs along the path of the trigeminal nerve on one side of the face. Pain may be short-lived, lasting only a few seconds, or can persist for minutes at a time. Trigeminal neuralgia also tends to occur in a series of episodes over several days, disappearing for a brief period and then returning.

Because the facial muscles often twitch in response to the pain, as if in a "nervous tic", trigeminal neuralgia is sometimes known by the French term *tic douloureux*. It usually occurs in the middle-aged and elderly and is also common in people who have advanced multiple sclerosis. Episodes of pain may be sparked by eating or by touching certain trigger zones on the face.

Glossopharyngeal neuralgia is another form of neuralgia affecting the head region. In this case, however, the pain occurs deep inside the throat, starting near the tonsils and extending into an ear. Chewing and swallowing are frequent triggers. The cause is usually a blood vessel pressing on the nerves involved in swallowing.

A form of neuralgia known as postherpetic neuralgia sometimes occurs following episodes of shingles, a condition caused by the chickenpox virus. After a bout of chickenpox, the virus responsible can hide in nerve roots along the spinal cord, later in life making its presence felt as shingles at times of physical or emotional stress. During an episode of shingles the virus multiplies and spreads along the nerve, causing the tissues it supplies to experience pain and sensitivity. Blisters and a rash form on the skin serviced by the affected nerve. In postherpetic neuralgia, pain along the nerve can persist for weeks or months after the shingles rash disappears.

Treatment for neuralgia depends on the cause, if one can be found. Sometimes the condition rights itself spontaneously. Analgesics such as aspirin and ibuprofen usually help to ease the pain. Pressure on affected nerves may be relieved by using anti-inflammatory drugs to reduce tissue swelling. In severe and persistent cases of neuralgia, when drug treatments fail to bring relief, various surgical options are available.

SEE ALSO *Carpal tunnel syndrome, Nerves, Shingles, Tic douloureux, Trigeminal nerve*

NEURITIS

Neuritis is an inflammation of a nerve or group of nerves. When more than one nerve is affected the disorder is sometimes referred to as polyneuritis. When the condition involves the root of a spinal nerve, it is termed radiculitis.

Symptoms of neuritis vary, depending on which nerves are affected and the severity of the condition. The impacts can range from strange but mild sensations, such as pins and needles, to the severe complications of paralysis. There may be pain (often in the form of a burning sensation), defective reflexes and either a loss of sensitivity or heightened sensitivity in the area supplied by the affected nerves.

The symptoms may not always, however, readily point to nervous system involvement. In some cases, for example, muscles served by inflamed and dysfunctional nerves may weaken and degenerate over time. Similarly, problems in joints may be caused by neuritis. Low blood pressure is a possible outcome when neuritis affects the autonomic nervous system; in this case abnormal nerve signals lead to the failure of veins and leg muscles

Neuritis

Neuritis is the inflammation of a nerve or a group of nerves. Vestibular neuritis affects the vestibular nerves in the ear and can cause dizziness.

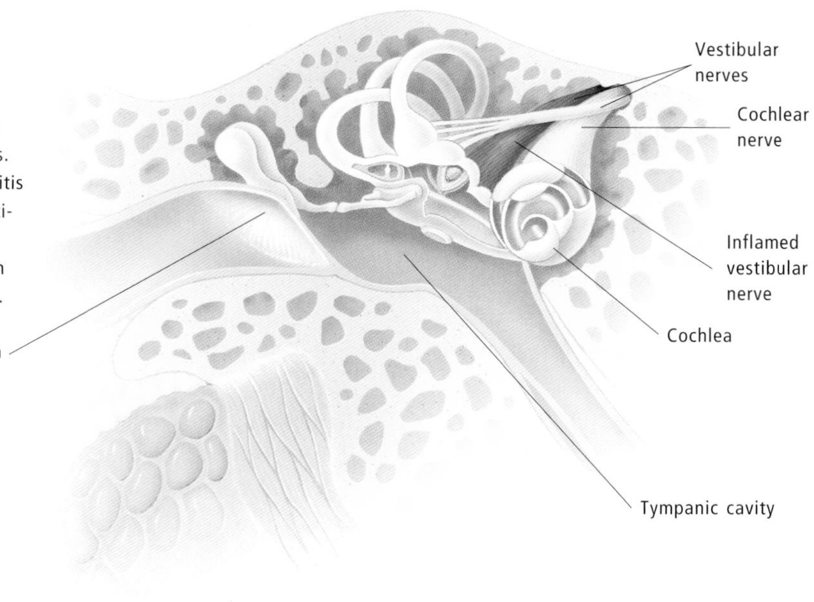

to return venous blood to the heart. This causes pooling of blood in the legs.

There are many different potential causes for neuritis, including injury, nutritional deficiencies and disease. Toxins produced by the bacteria responsible for the diseases diphtheria and leprosy can cause neuritis. Vitamin B deficiencies, associated with diseases such as beriberi and alcoholism, commonly cause neuritis. Other factors that can underpin the condition include diabetes mellitus, lung cancer, industrial poisoning and autoimmune diseases such as multiple sclerosis (MS).

Optic neuritis, which involves inflammation of the optic nerve serving the eye, can affect a person's vision. It occurs more commonly in women than men and normally afflicts one eye rather than both (although it often occurs in both eyes simultaneously in children). Optic neuritis is also known as retrobulbar neuritis. It can be caused by encephalitis or an infection that has spread from the sinuses or may arise after an injury to the eye area. In adults, the condition is often an early sign of MS. Statistically, about 40 percent of people who develop optic neuritis later go on to develop MS.

The symptoms of optic neuritis usually appear over several days, often beginning with a blurring of vision in the affected eye, followed by a loss of color vision and the appearance of blind spots. Eye movements may be painful. Although effects on vision can be so extreme that a patient may be barely able to detect light with the affected eye, optic neuritis usually gets better and full vision is restored. Treatment commonly involves anti-inflammatory medications but the condition often improves on its own without intervention.

Vestibular neuritis is a condition involving inflammation of a vestibular nerve, which is integral to the sense of balance. The vestibular nerves convey messages about head movements from the inner ear to the brain. Neuritis in one of these nerves is usually caused by an infection due to a virus, possibly a member of the herpes family. The main symptom is dizziness. Hearing is not affected but a slight sensitivity to head movements can persist in some people for months, even years.

SEE ALSO *Multiple sclerosis, Nerves, Optic nerve*

NEUROBLASTOMA

Neuroblastoma is a cancer that affects fetal nerve cells, causing a tumor in early childhood. It often begins in the adrenal gland in the abdomen and may spread quickly to parts of the body such as the bone marrow and lymph nodes. Surgical removal of the tumor, radiation therapy, chemotherapy and bone marrow transplant are treatment options.

SEE ALSO *Cancer*

NEURODERMATITIS

Neurodermatitis is a general term used to describe an itchy skin disorder thought to have emotional or "nervous" causes. Disorders such as atopic dermatitis (a type of eczema) and lichen simplex chronicus, which leads to thickening of the skin, are often grouped under this heading although they may have other contributing causes.

SEE ALSO *Dermatitis, Eczema*

NEUROFIBROMATOSIS

Neurofibromatosis refers to a range of hereditary nervous system disorders caused by chromosomal abnormalities that result in multiple benign fibrous tumors (fibromas) on the peripheral nerves, internal organs, spine and skin. Type 1 neurofibromatosis (sometimes known as von Recklinghausen's disease) is also characterized by brown (café-au-lait) spots on the skin. Type 2 neurofibromatosis usually involves less spots and may include tumors of the acoustic nerves in the ear (acoustic neuromas). Learning disabilities may result from the disease. There is no specific treatment, although tumors that cause pain, affect the function of a body part or turn malignant are surgically removed if possible.

SEE ALSO *Chromosomal abnormalities, Nerves, Nervous system, Neuroma*

NEUROMA

Neuromas are benign tumors formed from nerve cells, sometimes referred to as schwannomas. They may occur singly, or in multiples, along with pigmented patches on the skin (neurofibromatosis or von Recklinghausen's disease).

Neuromas may occur between the bones in the ball of the foot (plantar or Morton's neuroma). This is due to compression of the nerves between the metatarsal bones where the toes join the foot, causing swelling, inflammation and a sharp burning sensation that may radiate to the toes. Surgery may be needed to remove severe tumors. Otherwise, rest, ice packs and anti-inflammatory medications should offer pain relief.

Painful neuromas sometimes form on the stumps of amputated limbs where severed nerves grow back abnormally.

Acoustic neuromas are benign tumors of unknown cause that grow on the acoustic nerve in the ear canal and are sometimes associated with hereditary neurofibromatosis

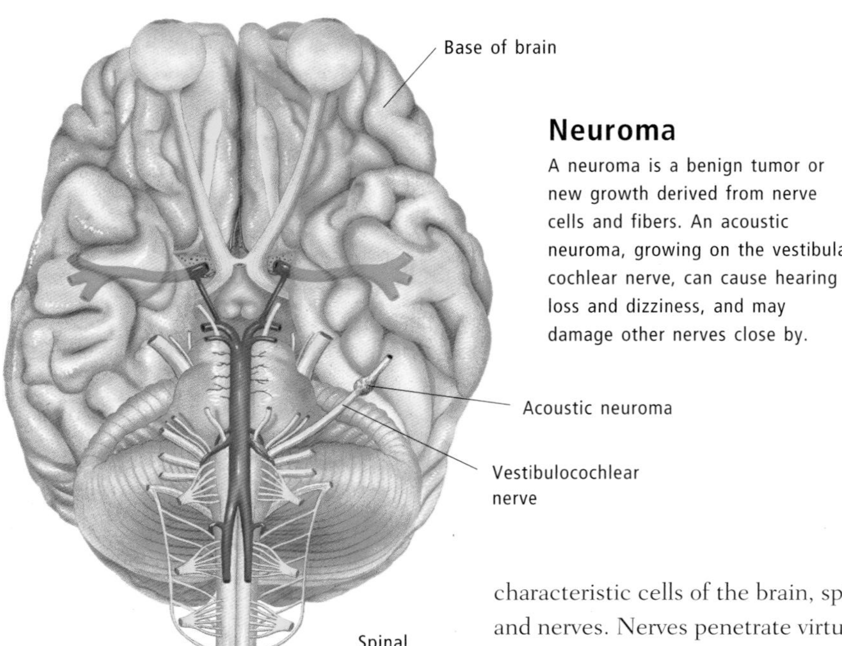

Neuroma

A neuroma is a benign tumor or new growth derived from nerve cells and fibers. An acoustic neuroma, growing on the vestibular cochlear nerve, can cause hearing loss and dizziness, and may damage other nerves close by.

Type 2. They may cause hearing loss and ringing (tinnitus) in the affected ear, loss of balance, dizziness, pain and numbness. Large acoustic neuromas may cause complications by pressing on the skull. Surgical removal may result in total hearing loss in the affected ear and paralysis of facial muscles.

SEE ALSO *Ear, Nerves, Neurofibromatosis, Tinnitus, Tumor*

NEURONS

Neurons, also known as nerve cells, are specialized cells involved in sensation, information processing and cognition, and control of muscle and gland activity. Neurons are the characteristic cells of the brain, spinal cord and nerves. Nerves penetrate virtually all parts of the body.

Every neuron consists of a cell body (perikaryon), a cell nucleus, contained within the cell body, and one or more narrow projections, known as processes. The processes, which radiate from the cell body, are of two types: dendrites, which convey impulses to the cell body; and axons, which normally convey impulses away from it. Neurons usually have a single axon, and a variable number of dendrites, depending on the cell's function.

The central nervous system (CNS) is composed of nerve cells whose axons are situated in the brain, eye and spinal cord. The peripheral nervous system is composed of nerve cells whose axons are situated outside the CNS. The brain consists of a mass of neurons of various types, together with supporting cells (glia) and blood vessels. Nerves consist of bundles of axons, together with supporting cells (Schwann cells) and connective tissue.

Some axons and dendrites are protected by a covering of Schwann or glial cells containing a fatty substance called myelin. Myelinated axons and dendrites carry impulses faster than unmyelinated ones.

Impulses are conveyed along dendrites and axons by the passage of a wave of chemical and electrical changes affecting the cell membrane of the dendrite or axon. The point at which an impulse is transmitted from one neuron to another is called a synapse: chemical transmitter agents, such as glutamate, norepinephrine (noradrenaline) and serotonin, convey impulses from one cell to another. There is no direct contact between the axon of one neuron and the dendrite of another.

Sensory neurons receive sensations from the outside environment and carry them to the spinal cord or brain. They generally have terminals specialized for the reception of specific sensations, such as touch, vibration, temperature, pain and movements.

Motor neurons carry impulses in the opposite direction: that is, away from the brain and spinal cord, and towards muscles. They function by stimulating muscles. In addition, they produce and control both voluntary and involuntary movements of muscles, and maintain muscle tone. Motor nerves connect to muscle cells by structures called motor end plates.

Intermediate neurons (interneurons), which are the most numerous in the brain,

Neuron

Neurons are specialized cells found in the nervous system which conduct nerve impulses. Each neuron has three main parts: the cell body, the branching projections (dendrites) that carry impulses to the cell body, and one elongated projection (the axon) that conveys impulses away from the cell body.

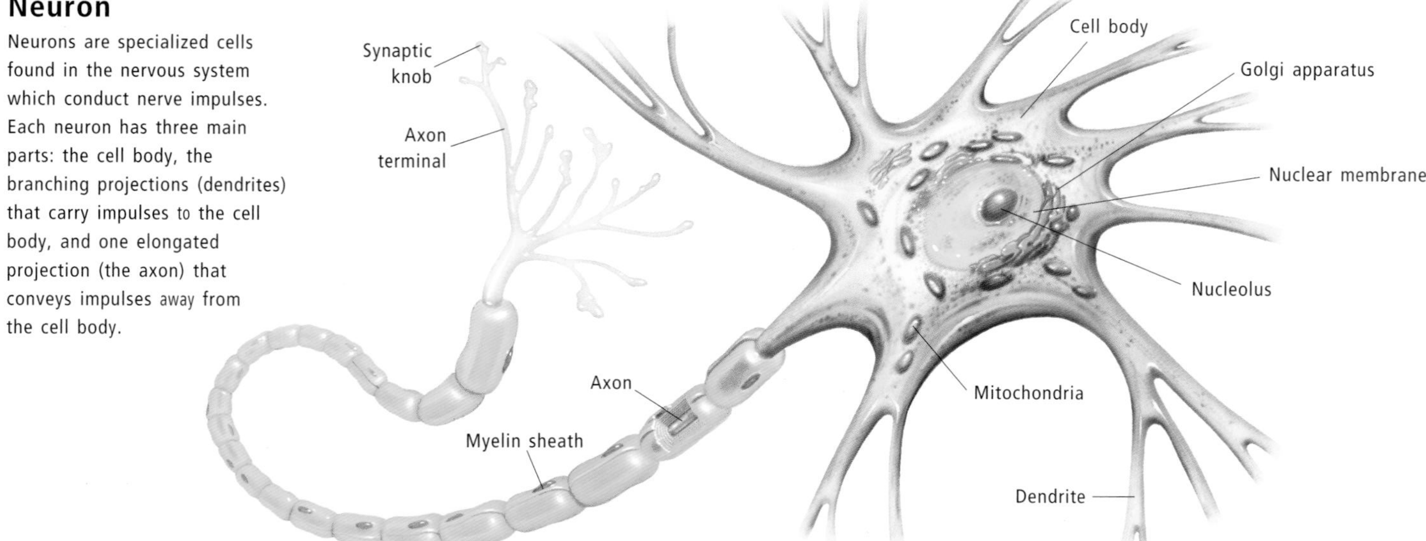

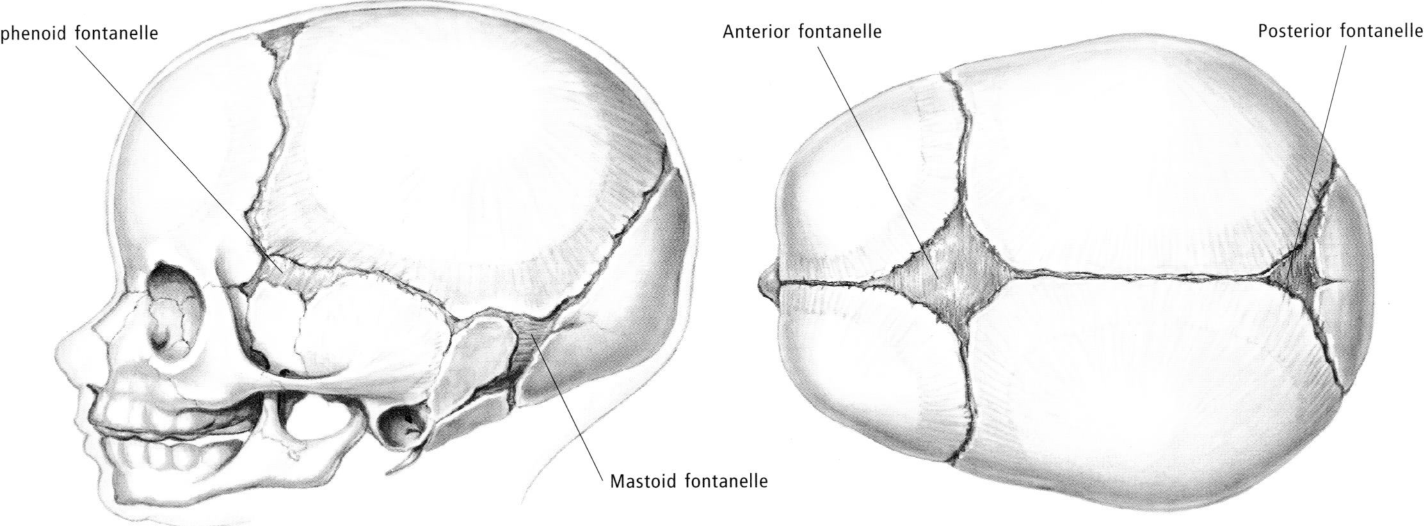

Newborn's skull

There are six "soft spots" on a baby's skull, which allow some compression of the skull during birth. These regions are called fontanelles. By a baby's second birthday these bones have joined together.

connect sensory and motor neurons either directly or by networks of cells. Cell networks are responsible for cognition and memory.

Reflexes, such as the knee jerk, involve a minimum of two neurons: a sensory neuron (which, in this case, detects stretching of the quadriceps muscle) and a motor neuron, which is stimulated by the sensory neuron and fires to initiate muscle contraction (in this case, contraction of the quadriceps muscle). Usually there is at least one intermediate neuron in between the sensory neuron and the motor neuron.

The total number of neurons is greatest before birth, and decreases during life. Once lost, neurons do not regenerate, but cut axons in damaged nerves may regenerate.

Disorders affecting neurons may include injury, congenital defects, cancer, infections, vitamin deficiency and degeneration. Epilepsy is due to the inappropriate generation of impulses by neurons in the cerebral cortex.

SEE ALSO *Brain, Epilepsy, Nervous system, Reflexes, Spinal cord*

NEUROPATHY

Neuropathy refers to disorders of the peripheral nerves. Causes include diabetes, lead poisoning, vascular disorders and damage due to penetrating injury, broken bones, mechanical pressure or exposure to cold or radiation. Weakness, numbness, tingling and pain in the feet, legs, hands or forearms are symptoms. Treatment depends on the cause.

SEE ALSO *Nerves, Peripheral nervous system*

NEWBORN

A newborn is a baby less than 6 weeks old. Healthy newborn babies begin to breathe almost as soon as they reach the outside world and before the umbilical cord, which attaches the navel to the placenta that has been their life support, has stopped pulsating. Usually the cord is left intact until it has stopped pulsating, then it is clamped, or in some countries it is bound.

The head of a newborn is disproportionately large in relation to the body, the hair, if present, is wet, the skin is peeling, wrinkly or furry, or all three, and the complexion may be red, pink or blue. The baby may be alert or crying, quiet or sleepy.

A newborn baby has more individual bones than an adult. (Many bones ossify and fuse together with growth.) A newborn baby's skull is made up of a number of individual bones held together by fontanelles, the most obvious being the soft spot (often called the fontanelle) in the top of its skull. A newborn has a low sloping forehead, a receding chin and often a slightly misshapen head which is from pressure and only temporary when the baby is born vaginally. The newborn's skin may be covered in a creamy substance known as vernix. The molding of the skull may be high and pointed if the baby was delivered in the posterior position (with its spine against the mother's); the face may be swollen and bruised if the baby was born face first. If the contractions of the uterus pushed the baby's head against a cervix that was not fully dilated, the baby may have a large bump on the head like a blister (called a caput).

Enlarged genitals, a slight menstrual-like bleeding in some girls, and "milk" in the breasts of both sexes are all caused by the presence of the mother's hormones in the baby's bloodstream, and disappear quite soon.

A baby born before week 37 is termed premature or pre-term. These babies are immature, smaller than full-term babies, and usually need special care. They are more likely than full-term babies to be covered in dark hair (lanugo). They are more likely to suffer from breathing and cardiovascular problems, anemia, jaundice and feeding problems, and to be unable to control their body temperature. Premature babies are also prone to infection.

A baby born after the normal length of gestation is described as postmature and may have dry, peeling skin and long finger and toe nails. Some postmature babies will be undernourished with disproportionately large heads, and may be described as "small-for-dates".

Immediately after birth a test called the Apgar test (named after Virginia Apgar, the US anesthesiologist who devised it) is performed on newborns in many industrialized countries. The Apgar test scores an aggregate of observations about the baby's vitality based on heart rate, breathing, skin color, muscle tone and reflex response. It is repeated 5 minutes after the first test.

Another test, the Neonatal Behavioral Assessment Scale, is now used in hospitals worldwide. Devised by American pediatrician T. Berry Brazelton, it assesses the baby's behavioral response to human and non-human stimuli.

Other checkups done on a newborn include measuring the diameter of the head and the length from head to foot, recording the weight, checking hips and jaws for dislocation and the mouth for cleft palate. Babies' reflexes are also tested.

A pH test may be done to test the blood in the umbilical cord artery for acidity. A low pH indicates that blood and tissues contain too many metabolic products and that the newborn's oxygen supply is lacking.

Vitamin K may be administered, either intravenously or orally, to prevent vitamin K deficiency bleeding (hemorrhagic disease of the newborn). Newborns have only minimal stores of vitamin K, which is essential to the clotting of blood. Bleeding from the umbilicus, intracranially, or from a circumcision, can occur up until week 26 after birth, and is most likely to occur between weeks 4 and 6 after birth in babies who are deficient in vitamin K.

SEE ALSO *Infancy, Reflexes, Sudden infant death syndrome, Umbilical cord*

N

NICOTINE

Nicotine is a poisonous alkaloid found in tobacco smoke and in other tobacco products. Like other alkaloids, such as cocaine and morphine, it is habit-forming and narcotic, producing physical and psychological dependence and tolerance.

If delivered via a cigarette, nicotine acts as a stimulant when inhaled in short puffs, but it acts as a tranquilizer when inhaled in deep drags. Hence, tobacco may be used by smokers for the relief of symptoms of depression, anxiety, attention deficit disorder or stress. However, studies have shown that nicotine does not enhance performance. Moreover, nicotine is known to constrict the blood vessels and raise blood pressure, and smoking is linked to some forms of cancer as well as to heart disease.

Nicotine withdrawal is characterized by feelings of stress, anger and irritability. Nicotine replacement therapies are frequently used in smoking cessation treatments. They include nicotine gum, nicotine patch, nicotine nasal spray and the nicotine inhaler.

Because nicotine depresses the appetite, people who give up smoking often find they are eating more and putting on weight. Chewing gum is recommended by some therapists.

SEE ALSO *Smoking, Withdrawal*

NIGHT BLINDNESS

Night blindness is a condition which can be caused by the disease retinitis pigmentosa. It can occur in people who have normal daytime vision but cannot see properly in reduced light. Some of the light-sensitive cells (rods) in the retina degenerate, and vision in low light gradually diminishes. The field of vision narrows, resulting in tunnel vision in the later stages of the disease. Deterioration progresses to total blindness. Ophthalmic examination may show early signs.

Night blindness is believed to be an inherited condition and at present there is no treatment to slow or reverse the damage to the retina.

SEE ALSO *Blindness, Eye, Retina, Retinitis pigmentosa*

NIPPLE

The nipple is the raised area in the center of a breast. It is surrounded by a disk-shaped pigmented area called the areola. The milk ducts of the breast empty into the nipple. The nipples, which contain some erectile tissue, can be an erogenous zone, common to both men and women.

Tenderness in the nipple may result from local trauma or friction or be a feature of lactation (breast feeding). A milky-looking nipple discharge may normally occur during or shortly after pregnancy, or during breast feeding. It may also be caused by endocrine (hormonal) disorders and some drugs. Less commonly, a discharge may indicate underlying breast cancer. Bleeding from the nipple may also indicate breast cancer and should be investigated by a physician. Treatment aims at correcting any underlying cause.

The nipples need extra care when a woman is breast feeding. Good breast hygiene and the use of breast pads will maintain dryness between feedings and relieve symptoms of tenderness and irritation. Breast creams may be used to help keep the nipple area lubricated and supple.

Occasionally the nipple and areola may be affected by a rash; most are benign and easily treated, but a rash (especially with a discharge) may indicate an underlying carcinoma known as Paget's disease of the breast.

SEE ALSO *Breast, Breast feeding, Paget's disease of the breast*

NON-HODGKIN'S LYMPHOMA

Non-Hodgkin's lymphoma is a tumor of the lymph glands, which is distinct from Hodgkin's lymphoma (also called Hodgkin's disease). It is a group of malignant diseases

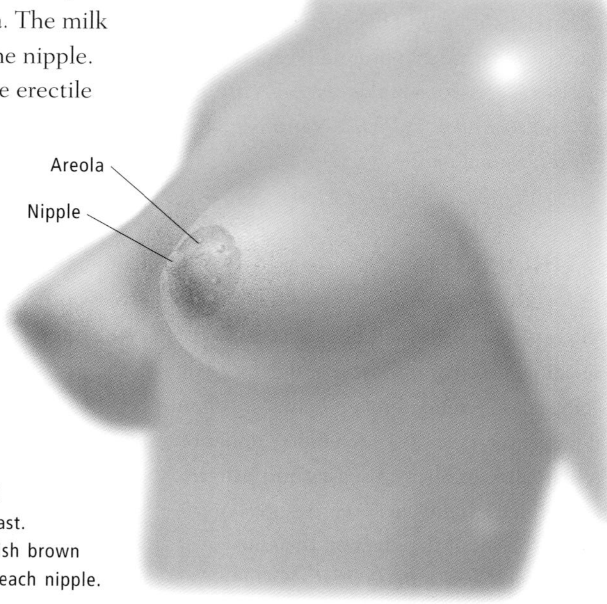

Nipple

The nipple is a conical projection of each breast. The areola is the reddish brown region of skin around each nipple.

arising in the lymph glands (also called lymph nodes) rather than spreading there, such as cancers do. Microscopic examination of a lymph gland by the pathologist accurately distinguishes between the two conditions.

Non-Hodgkin's lymphomas are more common than Hodgkin's disease, and the average age of patients is 50 years. The cause is generally unknown, although several possible causes have been identified. Exposure to high-dose ionizing radiation increases the risk, as do chemicals such as benzene and pesticides.

The risk of lymphoma is increased in certain occupations, such as farmers and forestry and timber workers, from exposure to herbicides. Chemotherapy drugs can lead to later development of lymphoma, which is also increased in patients with reduced immunity, either from medication or acquired immune deficiency syndrome (AIDS). Other viruses than HIV of AIDS have also been associated with lymphoma, including Epstein-Barr virus, the cause of infectious mononucleosis (glandular fever).

The main symptoms of lymphoma are persistent fever, drenching night sweats and severe unexplained weight loss. Patients may notice enlarged lymph glands in the neck, under the armpits or in the groin area and there may be enlargement of the spleen. The diagnosis is made by biopsy of an enlarged lymph gland, either using a fine needle or by a minor operation. Sometimes lymphoma causes a tumor that is not in the glands, such as lymphoma of the stomach or brain.

There is a variety of treatments for non-Hodgkin's lymphomas, depending on the particular type. Some lymphomas are very slow-growing and may not require treatment, particularly if the patient is elderly. If such a tumor causes symptoms, it can often be treated with mild chemotherapy tablets or radiation therapy to the affected area. Although such lymphomas are compatible with survival for years, they are not currently curable.

An important new development has been the production of antibodies directed against the cells causing lymphomas. These antibodies can kill the lymphoma cells without the side effects caused by most chemotherapy drugs. Other types of lymphoma are rapid-growing and require strong chemotherapy for treatment. The treatment consists of a combination of tablets and injections given on a cycle of three to four weeks for a total of six to nine treatments, generally given as an outpatient. Common side effects include nausea, hair loss and reduction of the normal white blood cells, leading to increased risk of infection. Injections are now available to stimulate the white cells to recover sooner, reducing the risk of infection. With such treatments, a proportion of aggressive lymphomas can be cured.

Currently, doctors are assessing higher doses of chemotherapy with the use of the patient's own (autologous) marrow or stem cell transplants. In this procedure the patient's normal cells are collected and stored in liquid nitrogen, so that they can be returned to "rescue" the patient following doses of chemotherapy so high that they destroy both lymphoma and healthy bone marrow cells.

SEE ALSO *Cancer, Hodgkin's disease, Lymph glands, Lymphatic/Immune system*

Non-Hodgkin's lymphoma

Non-Hodgkin's lymphoma is a group of malignant diseases that cause tumors of the lymph glands (nodes). The nodes of the neck, armpits, and groin area are most commonly affected. Enlargement of these nodes may be the first signs of disease.

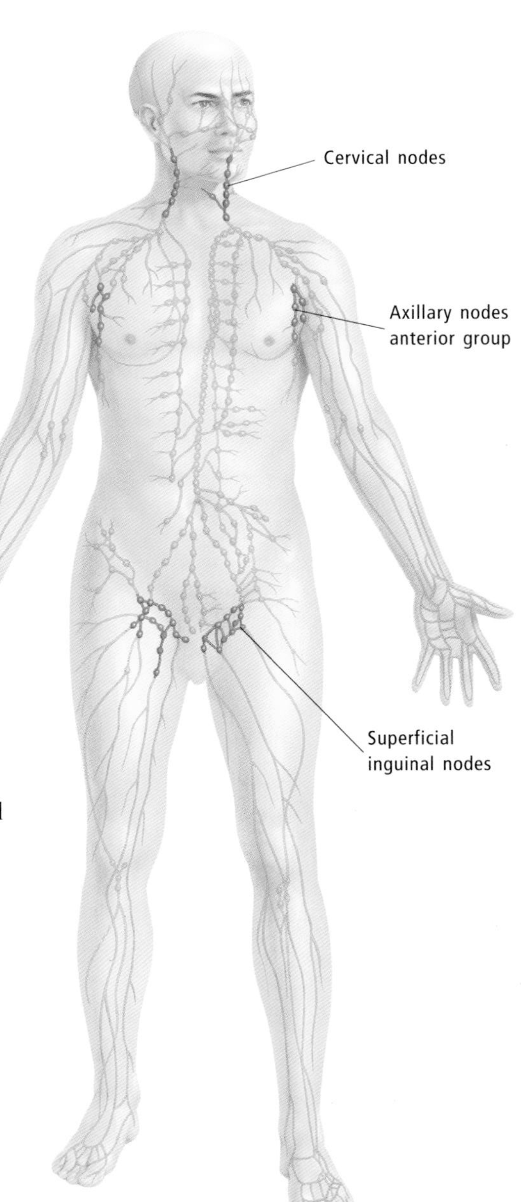

NONSTEROIDAL ANTI-INFLAMMATORY DRUGS

Along with aspirin and acetaminophen (paracetamol), nonsteroidal anti-inflammatory drugs (NSAIDs) are the drugs most commonly used to treat mild-to-moderate pain, fever and inflammation. NSAIDs work by inhibiting prostaglandin synthesis in body tissues, which in turn reduces pain, fever and inflammation. They are used in acute injuries and conditions such as rheumatoid arthritis, osteoarthritis, ankylosing spondylitis, menstrual cramps, tendinitis, bursitis and gout.

There are many NSAIDs on the market. Many are available over the counter, as well as on prescription from a physician. The most commonly used include ibuprofen, naproxen, indomethacin, mefanamic acid and phenylbutazone. They are non-habit forming and most are taken by mouth as a pill or liquid.

Side effects of NSAIDs include nausea and heartburn and, after long-term use, peptic ulcers. They can also cause clotting disorders and kidney disease. Anyone suffering from indigestion, stomach ulcer, kidney or blood diseases should consult a physician before taking NSAIDs.

SEE ALSO *Analgesics*

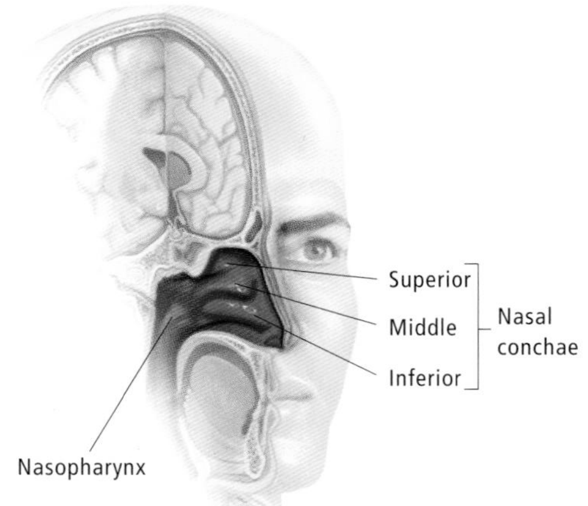

Nose

The main passageway for air entering the body is the nose. Air enters the nostrils and passes through the nasal cavities into the nasopharynx, trachea and down into the lungs.

NOSE

The nose is a part of the respiratory system. Its bony structure forms part of the skull. The bones of the external nose consist, on each side, of a nasal bone and the maxilla. The framework of the nostrils is made of cartilage, while the nasal septum, which separates the nostrils in the midline, is part bone and part cartilage.

Inside, the nose contains cavities which form part of the respiratory tract. The nose serves to warm and humidify inhaled air, and to filter out particles of dust. Air is normally breathed into and out of the body through the nose, via the nostrils. The nostrils are guarded by hairs (vibrissae) whose function is to prevent entry by insects and larger particles of dust. The nostrils lead to the nasal cavities, one on each side, which in turn lead to the pharynx and thence to the voice box (larynx) and windpipe (trachea). The nasal cavities are also connected to the paranasal sinuses and receive drainage of tear fluid through the nasolacrimal ducts; the eustachian tubes connect the ears to the pharynx.

In each nasal cavity, three curved plates, called the conchae (also known as turbinates), project from the side wall. These increase the surface area of the cavity, exposing inspired air to a greater amount of warm, moist surface due to a rich supply of blood vessels.

The bones surrounding the nasal cavities are the vomer and portions of the frontal, ethmoid, maxillary and sphenoid bones. The floor of the nasal cavities forms the roof of the palate. The two nasal cavities are separated by a partition called the nasal septum, which is commonly deviated to one side, thereby enlarging one nasal cavity at the expense of the other.

Most of each nasal cavity is lined by a specialized type of mucous membrane called respiratory mucosa. This is characterized by the presence of cilia, which are minute hairs that waft foreign particles on a sheet of mucus towards the nasopharynx. In the upper region of each nasal cavity, the mucous membrane changes to olfactory mucosa, containing specialized nerve cells for the reception of smell. Glands of the mucous membrane produce a watery secretion which both protects the walls of the nasal cavities and is evaporated to humidify the inspired air.

Problems affecting the nose include the common cold (a viral infection predominantly affecting the nasal mucosa), hay fever (an allergic reaction to pollen particles in inhaled air) and bleeding. Besides injury, nose bleeding may be associated with high blood pressure.

SEE ALSO *Common cold, Hay fever, Mucous membranes, Nosebleed, Olfactory system, Smell*

NOSEBLEED

A nosebleed (epistaxis) is a common occurrence, and is due to rupture of the delicate blood vessels just beneath the mucous membrane covering the nasal septum. In this position the blood vessels are susceptible to damage from fingers or trauma. Nosebleeds are common in childhood and are often related to upper respiratory infection, which results in sneezing or vigorous noseblowing. In children, the possibility of a foreign object in the nose needs to be considered.

Nosebleeds can also be due to more serious medical conditions. They can result from clotting disorders, similar to hemophilia, or a low number of platelet cells. Blood-thinning drugs, nasal polyps, tumors, or, occasionally, abnormally fragile blood vessels are other causes. Some believe that high blood pressure can cause nosebleeds. Most nosebleeds are minor and, although alarming and distressing, they are not harmful. The bleeding usually comes from the front part of the nose and can be controlled by firm finger pressure on the nostril against the nasal septum for several minutes. An icepack over the bridge of the nose can be helpful also. If the bleeding is severe or is not controlled with these simple measures, medical attention must be sought. Such bleeding is treated with nasal packing or special balloon catheters, and a cause is then investigated.

SEE ALSO *Blood, Nose, Platelets*

NUCLEIC ACID TESTING

Nucleic acids are present in body cells as well as in viruses, bacteria and other agents of infection. Tests exist that can detect the presence of foreign nucleic acids in the body, and are a very useful diagnostic tool.

NUMBNESS

Numbness is the absence of sensation in a part of the body. It is usually due to damage or degeneration of a peripheral nerve, though it may also be caused by injury to the central nervous system (brain and spinal cord).

Total loss of sensation means all of the nerve is damaged. But if the nerve is partly injured, there may be partial numbness, accompanied by tingling (also known as paresthesia).

Numbness may be temporary, as when the blood supply to a hand or foot is temporarily cut off because of the position a person is in, causing the hand or foot to fall asleep. When the blood supply is restored, normal sensation returns. Or the numbness may be permanent and irreversible. Conditions causing permanent nerve injury include diabetes, degenerative nerve diseases, local injury to the nerves under the skin, pressure on the nerves caused by a herniated disk, nerve damage from the effect of toxins (lead, alcohol or tobacco) or as the side effects of drugs.

It is necessary to treat the underlying condition where possible. A numb hand or foot is prone to accidental injury, so care must be taken to protect it from cuts, bumps or other injuries.

SEE ALSO *Nerves, Nervous system*

NUTRITION

Nutrition is the intake of food and its use by the body. Nutritional research extends into genetics, which examines how differences in genetic makeup can influence the body's reactions to food components; into psychology and eating disorders; into the influence of various foods on mental functions and physical performance; into the reasons why people eat what they do and their personal and cultural beliefs; and into the attitudes, habits and preferences which influence food intake.

Weight is affected by nutrition. If the diet supplies too little energy, body tissues are metabolized and weight generally falls. If too much energy is supplied by the diet, the excess is often stored as fatty tissue under the skin or around major organs, which may lead to high blood pressure and circulatory problems.

Nutritional standards

Good nutrition is fundamental to good health. Many diseases are directly related to either excessive or insufficient intake of certain foods or food types, or to identifiable patterns of food intake. Poor health and the onset of disease are costly to communities as health care services are funded in part or whole by taxes, thus many governments are concerned to raise nutritional standards which in turn will eventually improve the general health of the population. Laws which control the manufacture or supply of certain basic foods are one example of this involvement. The fluoridation of water is a public health measure which is practised in many countries, including the USA, UK and Australia.

The international bodies, the Food and Agricultural Organization (FAO) and the World Health Organization (WHO) jointly publish dietary guidelines in the form of RDAs (recommended dietary allowances) which set nutritional standards based on daily consumption of the basic food components. These figures are used by health professionals to compile or assess diets and may be found as consumer information on food labels or on diet sheets.

Government agencies in most industrialized countries have worked with nutrition scientists to specify the foods and quantities needed to make a healthy diet. These guidelines differ from country to country because they rely on using foods that are locally available and commonly eaten in that country. They all recognize the need to limit consumption of fats, oils and foods high in proteins and generally aim for a diet where around 70 percent of daily energy (calorie or kilojoule) needs are supplied by dietary carbohydrates, mainly from grain and cereal foods.

As developing nations turn away from agriculture to industry and grow in prosperity, their populations change their diets. They turn away from traditional eating habits, generally based on cereals and relatively little protein and fat, and abandon practices such as breast feeding, which ensures the best available nutrition for infants. They can afford to eat more of the foods they like and think of as luxuries, which generally means diets become higher in fat, higher in protein and correspondingly lower in carbohydrates. Infants are raised on breast milk substitutes, bottle feeding sometimes being mistakenly seen as more "advanced" than breast feeding. This inevitably has harmful effects on health, with a rise in dietary diseases caused by high intakes of protein and fat, rising infant malnutrition and higher death rates.

Because of the huge number of food products available in the industrialized nations, it is essential that consumers are aware of the ingredients. Labelling laws ensure that some details are given, including basic nutritional values and the presence of additives, synthetic and natural, which may trigger allergies in sensitized people. The increasing number of additives used to assist in marketing foods and food products has led to regulations intended to avoid potentially harmful consequences.

Energy

Energy derived from nutrients is measured in calories or kilojoules, one calorie being equal to 4.2 kilojoules. The human body at rest consumes energy at the rate of approximately 1.25 calories (5.25 kilojoules) per minute for males and 0.9 calories (3.78 kilojoules) per minute for females; this is known as the basal metabolic rate (BMR). Activity will increase consumption to approximately 5 calories (21 kilojoules) per minute for walking, and up to 15 calories (63 kilojoules) per minute for high-performance sports.

Daily energy needs vary according to lifestyle. A manual worker in a non-mechanized society may need as much as 5,000 calories (21,000 kilojoules) each day, and even more during periods of exceptionally heavy labor. In contrast, a worker in a sedentary occupation in an industrialized society may need as little as 2,000 calories (8,400 kilojoules). Women generally have lower requirements than men, but actual needs vary widely, depending upon body mass and daily activity.

While it is burning food for energy, the body must also replenish dead cells, grow new tissue and maintain all the chemical processes which sustain life. The nutrients in food which must supply all these needs must also include the chemicals and organic compounds which the body cannot manufacture for itself.

A balanced diet

The essence of good nutrition is variety, with expert advice suggesting people should eat up to 30 different foods in the course of a week to ensure they obtain a wide range of nutrients. The food we eat must supply certain basic nutrients which will be available after digestion in a form the body can use. Digestion begins as we chew food, generating saliva which contains enzymes, chemical substances that break down food. Digestion continues as the food enters the stomach where it is bathed in acids and other secretions, and as it passes through the small and large intestines. Nutrients pass through the walls of the intestines into the bloodstream which distributes them throughout the body. Unwanted or undigested food and waste products accumulate in the rectum and pass out of the body through the anus.

Good nutrition in youth lays a groundwork that is an investment in future health, particularly in middle and old age. It starts with a diet based on a wide variety of natural or basic, non-manufactured, foods including meats, fish, nuts, cereals, fruits, vegetables and water. A balanced diet means limiting the intake of fats, oils and protein-rich foods in favor of cereals, fruits and vegetables, and eating in moderate quantities. A modest

Digestion and absorption of nutrients

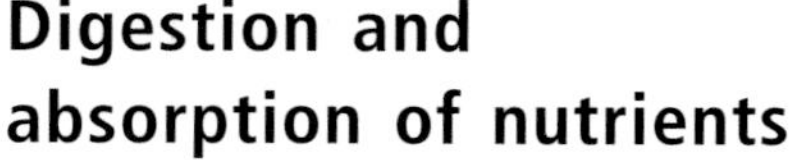

All the nutrients needed to maintain vital body functions are absorbed into the body via the gastrointestinal tract (or alimentary canal). As it travels along the tract, food is progressively broken down and the proteins, fats, carbohydrates, vitamins and minerals needed by the body are absorbed, leaving the remaining material to be excreted as waste. Many diseases of the digestive tract interfere with these processes and result in nutritional deficiencies.

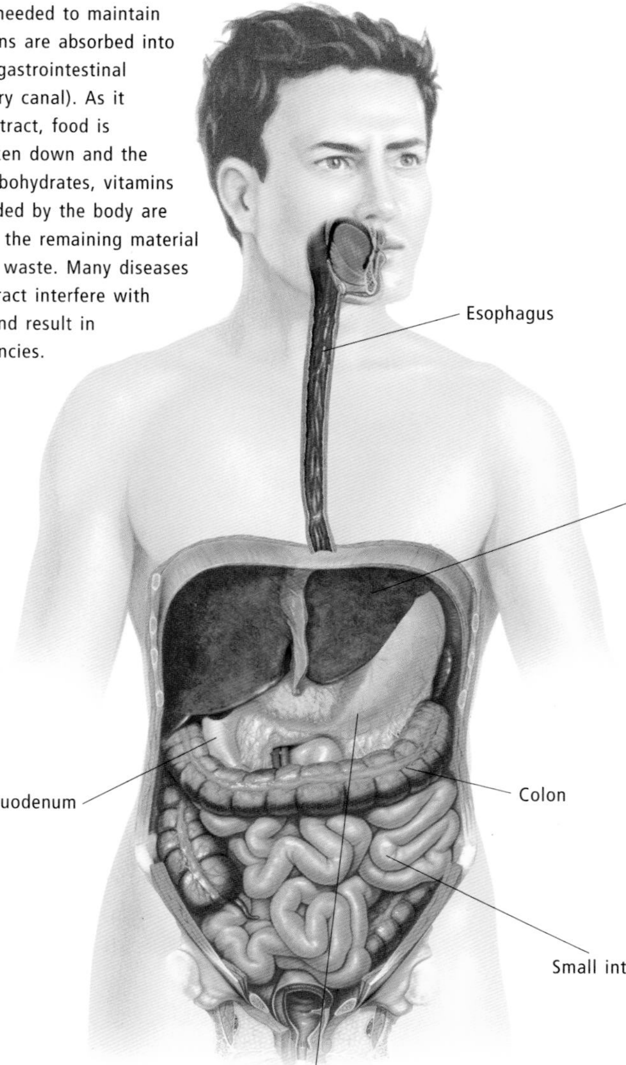

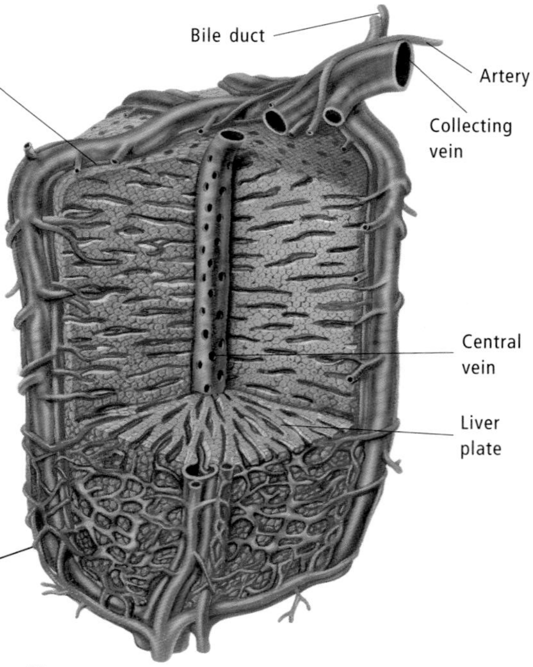

Liver

The absorbed nutrients pass from the small intestine via the bloodstream into the liver. A liver lobule is full of hepatic cells arranged around a vein. The hepatic cells extract nutrients from the blood that flows along the branches of this vein and extract oxygen and fat from the branches of the hepatic arteries. These nutrients are used for metabolism (energy supplies for the body) and to produce bile (for digestion).

Stomach

Food is swallowed via the mouth, travels down through the esophagus and enters the stomach, where it is mixed with acid and pepsin, an enzyme that breaks down proteins into amino acids.

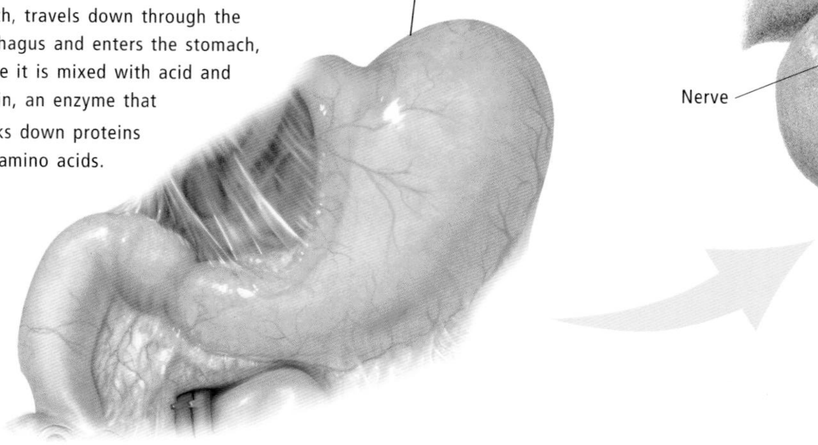

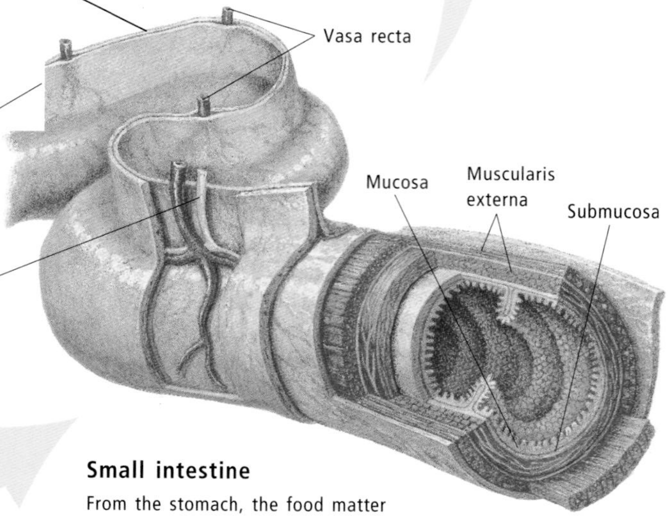

Small intestine

From the stomach, the food matter (now in a semiliquid form called chyme) passes into the small intestine where it mixes with enzymes from the pancreas and bile from the gallbladder. The chyme, containing carbohydrates, proteins and fats, is broken down into simple sugars, amino acids, and fatty acids, which are small enough to be absorbed through the lining of the small intestine. What is left over will pass along the colon (large intestine) and be excreted as feces.

amount of exercise each day is also considered essential in regulating the appetite, which helps to set correct levels for food intake. Exposure to sunlight is important in manufacturing vitamin D, essential for building strong bones.

Nutrients

The nutrients from food are categorized broadly as carbohydrates, fats and oils, cholesterol, proteins, water, minerals and vitamins.

Carbohydrates

Carbohydrates supply 4 calories (16.8 kilojoules) per gram and are the main sources of fuel energy for the body. They include sugars and starches, which are compounds of carbon, hydrogen and oxygen. These are easily and quickly digested, except for their cellulose or fiber content, which humans cannot digest but which is valuable in stimulating the muscular action of the intestine and in carrying waste products out of the body.

Carbohydrates are mainly supplied by plant foods such as fruits and vegetables, and cereals such as wheat, oats and corn, and come in company with many other nutrients of which the body needs only small quantities, like minerals and vitamins. Carbohydrates also come from sugars such as cane sugar, golden syrup and honey, which provide mainly energy for fuel. Sugars are sometimes called "empty calories" and may be a cause of overweight. Carbohydrates should supply about 65 percent of daily calorie intake.

Fats and oils

Fats and oils are necessary only in small quantities. Fats and oils are the most difficult food components to digest and have the highest energy rating by weight at 9 calories (37.8 kilojoules) per gram. They are a hidden component in many manufactured snack foods in which they can easily be eaten to excess, contributing to overweight. They contribute vitamin E but few other micronutrients. Fats and oils may be used as an energy source in very active people, but in others any excess is stored, contributing to overweight. Fats in food carry flavors and provide fatty acids which the body cannot manufacture, the most important of which is linoleic acid, used in building cell structure.

Fats, solid at room temperatures, and oils, liquid at room temperatures, are essentially similar substances which are classified according to their structure as saturated, monounsaturated or polyunsaturated. Fats or oils should supply between 15 and 30 percent of daily calorie needs.

Saturated fats are mostly animal fats, found in meat and dairy products. This group is believed to aid the deposition of cholesterol on arterial walls, impeding blood circulation and increasing the risk of heart attack.

Monounsaturated fats are found mainly in olive, canola and peanut (groundnut) oils. These fats are considered to have the most beneficial effect in lowering cholesterol levels in the bloodstream.

Polyunsaturated fats are found in sunflower, safflower, corn and soybean oils, and the oils used in making margarine. These also can have a beneficial effect on cholesterol levels, but only when their consumption accounts for 10 percent or less of the daily calorie intake. When eaten in excess they may contribute to raising blood cholesterol levels.

Cholesterol, a substance similar to fat, is manufactured by the liver from the breakdown of saturated fats ingested in the diet; it is also supplied in small quantities in eggs and animal foods. It is important in building and repairing cells, the production of sex hormones and the bile acids which aid digestion. Dietary fats provide the mechanism for transporting cholesterol in the bloodstream to cells, and to the liver for excretion.

Cholesterol is incorporated into compounds called lipoproteins for circulation in the bloodstream. There are two types, high-density lipoprotein (HDL) and low-density lipoprotein (LDL). HDL helps to excrete waste cholesterol from the body and is associated with a low risk of heart and circulatory disorders. LDL forms deposits on the walls of arteries, leading to atherosclerosis, which carries a high risk of heart disease. This condition may result from a diet too high in saturated fats.

Proteins

Proteins are complex substances made up of over 20 amino acids, many of which, the essential amino acids, cannot be synthesized inside the body and must be supplied by foods. Proteins are used to build and repair cells in every part of the body, from hair to internal organs, bones, muscle, skin and toenails; they also transport oxygen from lungs

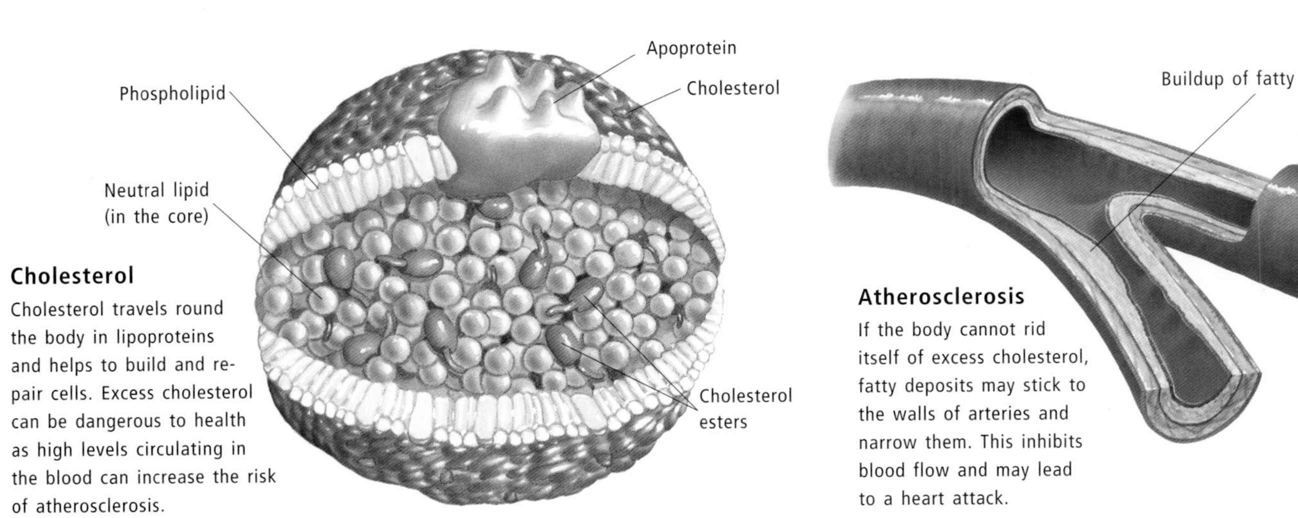

Cholesterol
Cholesterol travels round the body in lipoproteins and helps to build and repair cells. Excess cholesterol can be dangerous to health as high levels circulating in the blood can increase the risk of atherosclerosis.

Atherosclerosis
If the body cannot rid itself of excess cholesterol, fatty deposits may stick to the walls of arteries and narrow them. This inhibits blood flow and may lead to a heart attack.

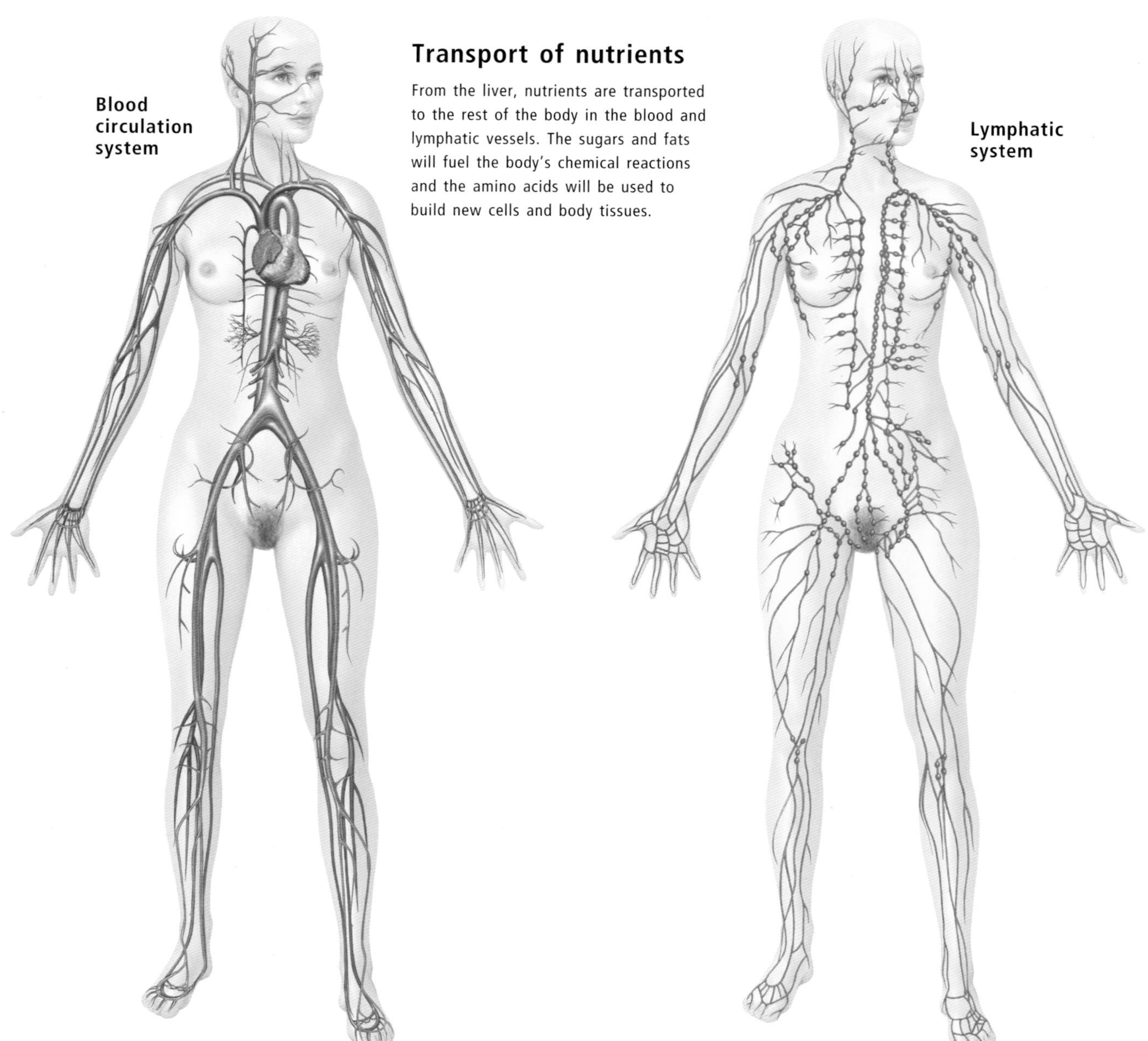

Blood circulation system
Transport of nutrients
From the liver, nutrients are transported to the rest of the body in the blood and lymphatic vessels. The sugars and fats will fuel the body's chemical reactions and the amino acids will be used to build new cells and body tissues.
Lymphatic system

N

to cells and act as chemical messengers. Animal foods (meat, eggs, milk, fish and poultry) in the diet supply complete proteins containing all the amino acids that cannot be synthesized. Plant foods such as soybeans, cereals and nuts each lack one or more essential amino acid and thus must be eaten in combinations which supply all the amino acids to provide a complete source of protein. Excess protein can be burned as energy if required but is likely to be stored as excess weight in many individuals. Proteins should supply up to 20 percent of daily calorie needs.

Water

Water is essential for life. It forms part of every cell in the body and is a major component of blood. The human body is about two-thirds water, men's bodies containing a greater percentage of water than women's, and that level must be maintained for health. Loss of only 1 or 2 percent of bodyweight in fluids causes dehydration with headache, fatigue, loss of appetite, dizziness, dry mouth and eyes. Loss of 10 percent bodyweight brings severe illness and of 20 percent almost certain death. Chronic dehydration may cause permanent damage to internal organs.

One problem in maintaining fluid levels is that signals of thirst do not arise until after mild dehydration has begun. The body loses water constantly through sweat, urine, feces and respiration.

For proper hydration, males should drink about 3 quarts (3 liters) of water each day and females at least $2\frac{1}{4}$ quarts (2.5 liters); recent research in North America, however, has indicated that people drink only about half that amount.

Water aids efficient removal of the body's waste matter. Excretion of toxins from the bloodstream depends on the availability of water for production of urine. Water is a major component of foods, particularly vegetables and fruits, and has a nil calorie value. As food sources will not supply the body's needs, adults should aim to drink about eight glasses of plain water a day, regardless of any other fluids ingested.

Minerals

Minerals are inorganic chemical elements that occur in small amounts in most foods.

More than twenty are required for good nutrition and health and are better obtained from eating a wide variety of foods than taken as supplements.

Iron, supplied by meat, milk and some plant foods, is vital in binding oxygen to red blood cells. Blood loss increases the need for iron and extra amounts may also be needed in pregnancy and throughout breast feeding. Calcium is present in bones and blood plasma and its levels are maintained by hormones. Absorption of calcium is inefficient and the diet must contain more than is theoretically needed. Sodium is required in very limited amounts to maintain intracellular fluid volume. Too much causes edema or fluid retention and may contribute to high blood pressure. Iodine, magnesium, phosphorus, potassium, sulfur and selenium are other minerals vital to good nutrition.

Vitamins

Vitamins are organic compounds identified by the letters A through K, most of which cannot be synthesized within the body. When vitamins are not supplied by the diet, symptoms of deficiency will occur. A deficiency of vitamin C (a vitamin found only in fresh fruits and vegetables) often produced scurvy on early voyages of exploration, causing bleeding gums and general ill health; in 1754 orange or lemon juice was found to prevent it. A lack of vitamin D will prevent proper bone development in children, a condition known as rickets, with gross deformities in limbs. Night blindness is one effect of a vitamin A (retinol) deficiency, because it directly affects the adjustment of the eye to dim light.

Nutrition through life

Pregnancy is a time to give special attention to good nutrition as the developing fetus needs a rich supply of nutrients for proper growth. It is not necessary to eat more but much more important to eat foods of good nutritional value. Energy value from foods should be from 1,700 to 2,100 calories (7,140 to 8,820 kilojoules) per day. Nutrient deficiencies will be made up from the mother's body tissues before the fetus is deprived. Folic acid requirements increase in pregnancy when it is needed in forming hemoglobin, the oxygen-carrying component of red blood cells and for proper neural tube development. Folate deficiency can cause anemia, and in pregnancy can result in premature birth, low birth weight or neural tube defects in the baby.

Children's growth and mental development are strongly influenced by nutrition, from the moment of conception. Good nutrition is important in laying the foundation for healthy bones, muscles and teeth. Poor nutrition and an unbalanced diet can result in obesity very early in life, in abnormal cholesterol levels and high blood pressure. These disorders lay a poor foundation for health in adulthood. Children are particularly at risk of deficiency diseases as their reserves are low and their nutrient needs high. Deprivation of nutrients over a long period may cause permanent physical or mental damage. Hydration is also very important, as children's bodies lose fluid fast during episodes of vomiting and diarrhea.

Adolescence is also a time of rapid growth and high nutritional needs, and a time when good nutrition can suffer through outside influences such as fad diets. Eating disorders that restrict food intake, such as anorexia, can delay the onset of the menarche in girls and severely affect growth. Disorders which involve vomiting can deplete the body's reserves of fat and protein, producing all the symptoms and health risks of starvation.

Women going through menopause should pay particular attention to their calcium intake as estrogen levels decrease at this time, reducing calcium levels in the body and decreasing bone strength. Osteoporosis in older people is the eventual consequence of seriously depleted calcium levels; it can become evident earlier in life as a consequence of poor diet. Medical advice may prescribe hormone replacement therapy and calcium supplements at menopause.

Ageing does not necessarily bring special nutritional needs. Energy requirements at any age are regulated mostly by body weight and activity levels. Nutrients are required throughout life to replenish body tissues and rebuild cells. Illness or disability are likely to be factors affecting the desire to eat and the absorption of nutrients from foods, and may have more severe consequences in an older person than in a younger person with greater reserves. Attention to diet and daily exercise are important for men and women as age advances. It is important to eat a variety of foods to ensure a good supply of vitamins and minerals.

Vegetarianism

Vegetarianism is the practice of avoiding animal foods in the diet, eating only foods of plant origin. It is generally seen as a healthful alternative. Properly constructed vegetarian or vegan diets supply all the body's needs and contribute very little to overweight or dietary disease. Ovo-lacto vegetarians eat eggs, cheese, milk and milk products as well as plant foods. A vegan diet is more strictly vegetarian and adherents neither eat nor wear anything of animal origin.

A macrobiotic diet incorporates many Japanese foods into a diet based on beans, vegetables and whole-grain foods combined with a lifestyle philosophy that seeks harmony between body and mind. Foods are classed as *yin* or *yang* and these elements are balanced to achieve optimum health. The principles of food combinations used in vegetarianism are applied to ensure the diet provides complete proteins.

SEE ALSO *Breast feeding, Cholesterol, Digestive system, Eating disorders, Fats, Minerals, Obesity, Proteins, Vitamins, Weight*

NYSTAGMUS

Nystagmus is involuntary circular movement of the eyes. It may occur normally, for example, when a person is looking out the window of a moving vehicle: the slow phase of the nystagmus occurs as the eyes drift while maintaining the gaze at the object outside, the quick phase takes place when the eyes dart back to their original position.

Nystagmus may be horizontal (side to side movements), vertical (in an up and down direction) or rotary (in a circular pattern). It may occur without any underlying disorder and usually does not affect vision. Nystagmus may also be a symptom of disease; it can be the result of injury to the cerebellum in the brain, injury to the labyrinth of the inner ear, hereditary diseases or ingestion of toxins (poisons). The underlying condition will need to be treated.

SEE ALSO *Eye*

OBESITY

Obesity is the build-up of excess fat in the body, the simple cause being consistent overeating (consuming more calories in food than the body needs). The underlying reasons for obesity may be far more complex.

The presence of obesity is usually obvious overweight, but overweight and obesity are not synonymous. Athletes and body-builders and those who inherit a large skeletal frame can register weights well above average for their height. This may be due to development of muscle tissue rather than fat. When weight is 20 percent or more above the optimum, obesity is the most likely cause. Weight-for-height tables and calculation of the Body Mass Index (BMI) are not definitive but can be used as a guide to individual optimal weight, with a BMI greater than 30 indicating a need for treatment (normally BMI should be about 20–25).

Adipose or fatty tissue is present throughout the body, and is stored mainly at sites of the greatest numbers of fat cells—the hips, thighs, buttocks and abdomen. Fat also accumulates in a layer beneath the skin and in membranes coating internal organs and lining cavities such as the abdominal cavity, one of the body's main fat stores.

Obesity in childhood results in the creation of an abnormal number of fat cells, which do not disappear when weight is reduced. The fat cells lose only some of their fat content, but they retain their capacity for fat storage, giving the individual a tendency to overweight in adolescence and adult life.

An overweight child can be disinclined to take part in physical activities. Overweight can be worsened by the inactivity which results from spending time on sedentary leisure pursuits such as playing computer games and watching television. When activity levels are low, fewer calories are burned and more are stored as fat. The overweight child who is unable to keep up with peer-group sports and games may suffer low self-esteem, a factor which can lead to seeking comfort in food, aggravating the problem. Puberty and adolescence bring increasing body awareness and fast growth, which can turn mild obesity into a more serious problem.

Other factors in the development of obesity include the following.

Disorders of the hypothalamus, the part of the brain which regulates appetite, can result in obesity.

Genetic influences (inherited physical traits) can favor weight gain.

Hormonal disorders may upset hormone levels and cause weight gain.

Low levels of physical activity can be a problem at all ages, as walking and manual labor give way to car transport, sedentary occupations and leisure time spent in front of the television.

Side effects from drugs can cause weight gain; corticosteroid drugs, in particular, have been identified as having this effect.

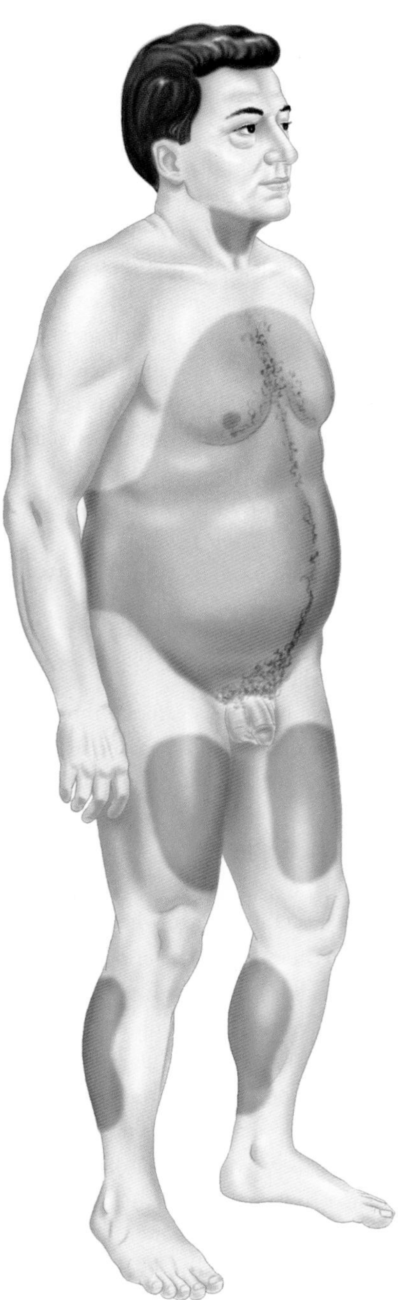

Obesity—male fat distribution

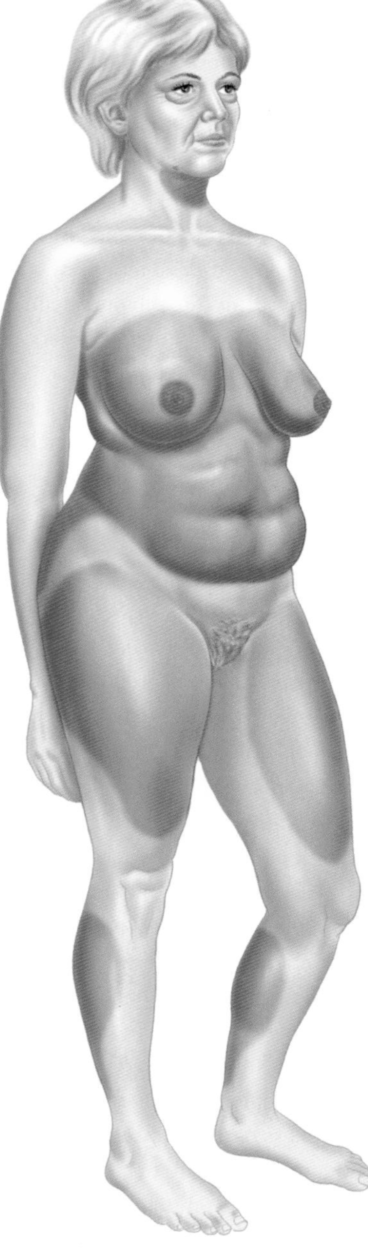

Obesity—female fat distribution

Obesity

Obesity is defined as an abnormal increase of the percentage of fat in the body. It may be a symptom of a physical or behavioral disorder, or the result of genetic influences. Fat tends to be mainly deposited around the abdomen and top of the legs.

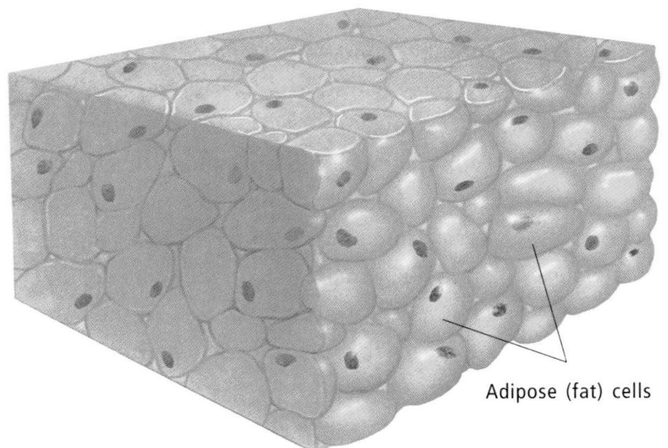

Fatty tissue

Adipose (fat) cells occur in greater numbers around the hips, thighs, buttocks and abdomen, creating deposits of fatty tissue. The number of fat cells in the body is determined during the first few years of childhood.

Obesity generally brings greater risk of cancer, gallbladder disease, menstrual disorders, adult-onset diabetes, high blood pressure and raised blood cholesterol levels which can lead to heart disease. Overweight increases the load on the heart, lungs, spine and all the weight-bearing joints. Upper body obesity, common in men, is a greater health risk than lower body obesity, more common in women. Paradoxically, women are 8 times more likely to seek help with weight reduction than are men. Treatment may involve both increasing physical activity and reducing weight.

Successful weight loss must be followed with a long-term regime to ensure that weight is maintained at optimal levels. Weight loss clinics, self-help groups and individual supervision by dietitians are common methods. Prescription drugs may be used to assist initial weight loss but must be combined with therapy and diet re-education for long-term success. Surgery, to reduce stomach size and eating capacity, is a more drastic choice, carrying risks of complication and death alongside the promise of a permanent solution to a distressing and life-threatening condition.

SEE ALSO *Body Mass Index, Eating disorders, Fats, Hypothalamus, Nutrition*

OBSESSIVE-COMPULSIVE DISORDER

Obsessive-compulsive disorder (OCD) is a psychiatric illness in which obsessive thoughts lead to compulsive actions such as repeated counting, cleaning or checking. Sufferers are plagued by persistent unwelcome thoughts or images that can sometimes be of a violent or sexual nature. Many are obsessed with germs or dirt and may continually wash their hands. Others spend hours rearranging objects. However, they derive little, if any, relief from their compulsive behavior.

The exact cause is not known. Once thought to have psychological origins, recent research suggests that OCD could be genetic and that damage to the basal ganglia, a part of the brain that controls automatic activities, could be a contributing factor. Streptococcal infection is also thought to trigger the disorder in some sufferers.

Symptoms fluctuate and may last for decades. OCD produces a high level of anxiety, interrupts the normal flow of life and may be accompanied by depression. It can also contribute to other problems, such as eating disorders.

Treatment is by a combination of antidepressant medication and behavioral therapy. One behavioral treatment is exposure and response prevention, where sufferers voluntarily expose themselves to the trigger of their disorder and are encouraged to avoid their compulsive action for as long as possible.

SEE ALSO *Antidepressants, Behavior therapy, Depression, Personality disorders*

OBSTRUCTIVE JAUNDICE

Jaundice is a condition in which there is yellowing of the skin and eyes due to an increased concentration in the blood of a

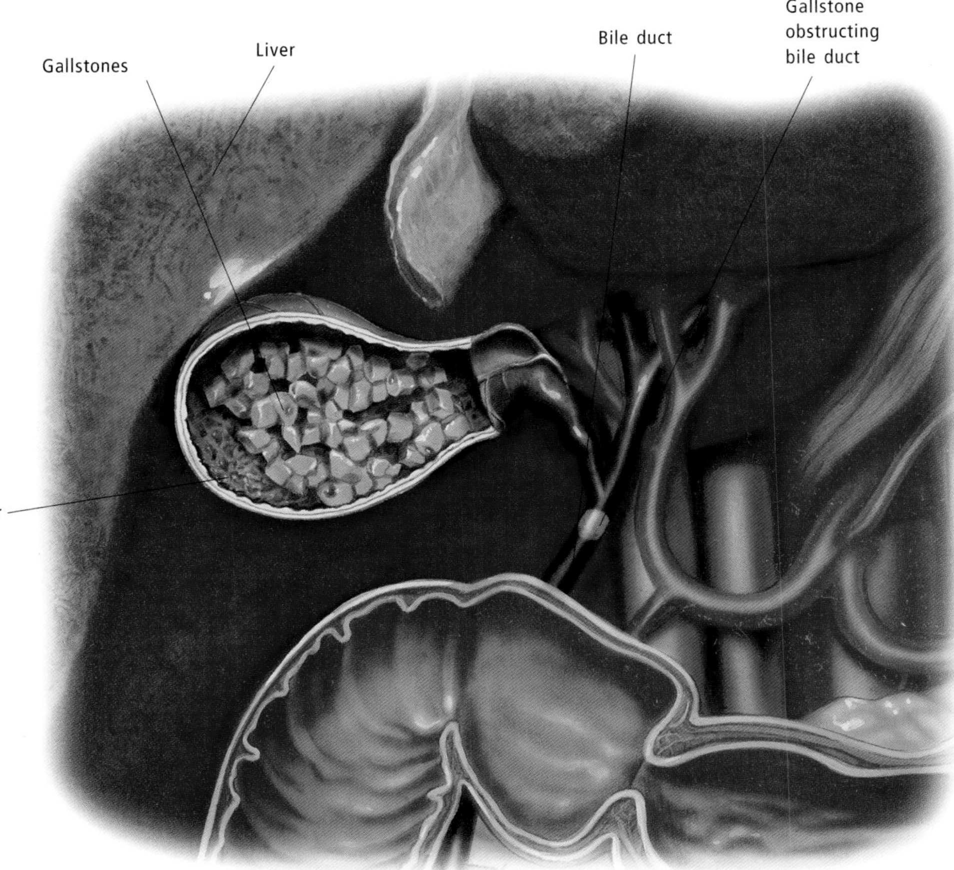

Obstructive jaundice

Obstructive jaundice results when bile is unable to be discharged through the bile ducts into the intestine. Causes include gallstones and cancer of the pancreas and bowel.

O

chemical called bilirubin. If the bilirubin gets into the blood because of obstruction of the ducts leading from the liver to the duodenum, the condition is known as obstructive jaundice. Common causes of obstruction of these ducts include gallstones, cancers of the gallbladder or pancreas, hepatitis, pregnancy, parasites and inflammation of the pancreas (pancreatitis). Patients with obstructive jaundice will experience itching of the skin due to accumulation of bile salts in the skin. Treatment will depend on the cause: gallstones should be removed, ducts obstructed by cancer should be dilated.

SEE ALSO *Duodenum, Gallstones, Hepatitis, Jaundice, Liver, Pancreas, Pancreatitis*

OLFACTORY SYSTEM

The olfactory system is concerned with the sense of smell, through the detection of airborne chemical substances in the nose. Odors are sensed by special nerve cells in the lining of the nose. Sensations of smell are conveyed by the olfactory nerves to a part of the brain, lying above the nose, referred to as the rhinencephalon or limbic lobe. The senses of smell and taste act together for the assessment of food.

In the roof of the nasal cavities, the mucous membrane contains nerve cells that are specialized for the reception of odors. This region of the mucous membrane is known as the olfactory epithelium or olfactory organ, and has a total area of about 1 square inch (5 square centimeters). The surface of the epithelium is kept moist, to dissolve odors from passing air. The olfactory receptor cells, of which there are about 100 million, are modified neurons. A dendrite extends from each cell body towards the surface of the epithelium, where it terminates as a swelling termed an olfactory vesicle. This vesicle is specialized for the reception of smell. The sensation is carried by an unmyelinated axon (nerve fiber) from each receptor cell into the connective tissue beneath the epithelium, where it joins with others to form bundles of olfactory nerve fibers, called the olfactory nerves. These, about 20 in number, pass through holes (foramina) in the cribriform plate of the ethmoid bone, to terminate in the brain at the olfactory bulbs.

The olfactory bulbs are ovoid structures forming forward extensions of the olfactory area of the brain. In the olfactory bulbs, axons from olfactory sensory cells converge and end (synapse) on dendrites of cells known as mitral cells because of their shape (conical). Each mitral cell receives approximately 1000 axons. These synapses between olfactory sensory cells and mitral cells are grouped to form conspicuous clusters known as glomeruli. The axons of the mitral cells run back (posteriorly) to terminate in the cerebral cortex and adjacent parts of the forebrain, providing a pathway for conscious perception of smell. The pathway from the olfactory receptors to the cerebral cortex therefore has only one synapse (in the olfactory bulb), a more direct connection than that for any other type of sensation. Other cells (interneurons) in the olfactory bulb link one glomerulus with another, and also link the two olfactory bulbs across the midline. Axons from mitral cells and other cells of the olfactory bulb travel through the

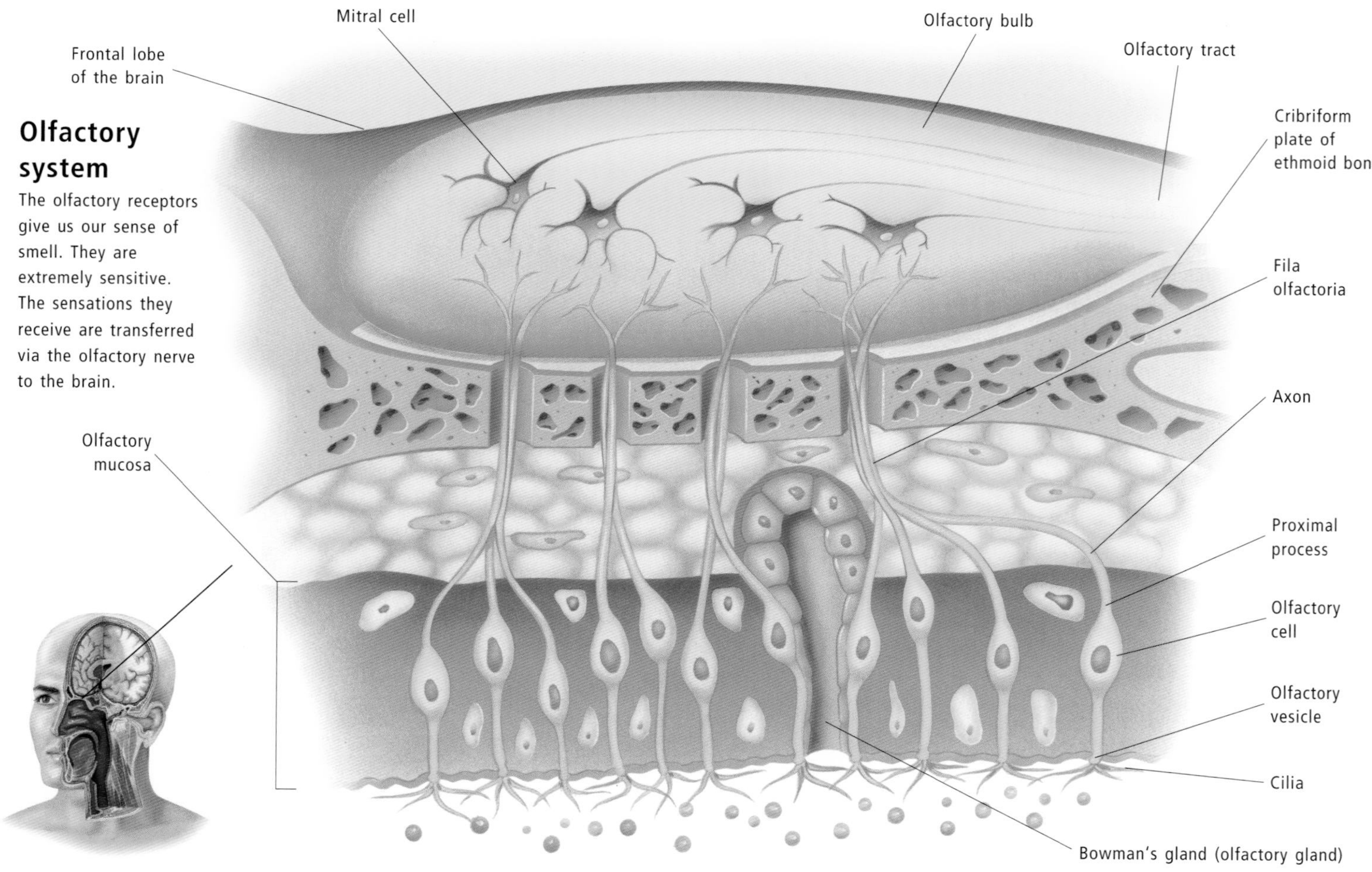

Olfactory system

The olfactory receptors give us our sense of smell. They are extremely sensitive. The sensations they receive are transferred via the olfactory nerve to the brain.

olfactory tract and terminate, either directly or through relay neurons, in two areas of the brain called the medial olfactory area and the lateral olfactory area.

Both medial and lateral olfactory areas have neural connections to the hypothalamus, hippocampus and brain stem nuclei. These latter areas control automatic responses to smells, particularly feeding activities (such as salivation) and also emotional responses (such as pleasure, fear, and sexual drives).

Loss of the sense of smell (anosmia) is most commonly due to blockage of the nose, for example, by a common cold. Hallucinations of smell may be due to physical or psychological causes, including tumors of the temporal lobe.

SEE ALSO *Neurons, Nose, Smell*

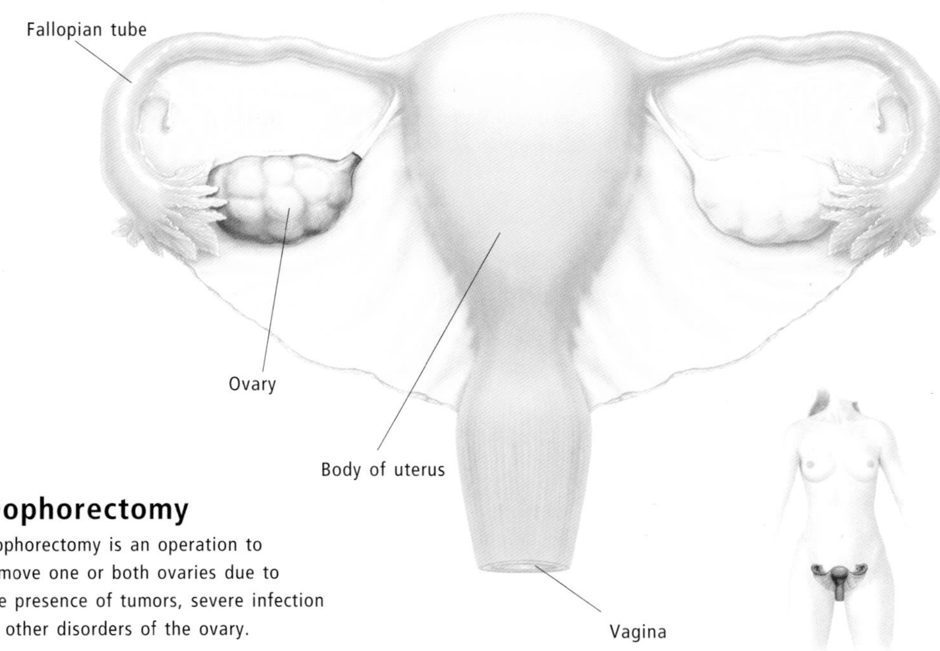

Oophorectomy

Oophorectomy is an operation to remove one or both ovaries due to the presence of tumors, severe infection or other disorders of the ovary.

OMPHALOCELE

An omphalocele is a congenital abnormality of the abdominal wall occurring in approximately one out of every 5,000 births. The normal layers of the abdominal wall are missing at the navel; only the thin peritoneal membrane lies between the intestines (which protrude through the opening) and the air. Urgent surgery is required to repair the defect so as to prevent peritonitis and dehydration of the intestines.Other birth defects that may be associated with the condition will require treatment.

SEE ALSO *Abdomen, Congenital abnormalities, Intestines*

OOPHORECTOMY

Oophorectomy means surgical removal of one or both ovaries (unilateral or bilateral oophorectomy). Ovaries are removed for a variety of reasons, including extensive or very large cysts, or ovarian cancer. Oophorectomy may sometimes accompany hysterectomy, even though the ovaries are not diseased. It has been argued that removing the ovaries avoids possible future problems of cysts or ovarian cancer. However, the advantage of leaving at least one ovary in premenopausal women is the avoidance of symptoms of premature menopause and the possible need for hormone replacement therapy.

SEE ALSO *Hysterectomy, Ovarian cysts, Ovaries*

OPHTHALMOSCOPY

Ophthalmoscopy is examination of the interior and the retina of the eye with an ophthalmoscope, an instrument about the size of a flashlight, which projects a beam of light through the pupil. The instrument allows the physician to view the interior and back portion of the eye, including the retina, optic disc and blood vessels, and to detect and evaluate symptoms of eye disease such as glaucoma, or the effect of other diseases such as diabetes, atherosclerosis or hypertension on the eye.

SEE ALSO *Eye*

OPPORTUNISTIC INFECTION

Infections that take advantage of a weakness in the immune defenses are called "opportunistic". They are common in HIV/AIDS, cancers, blood disease such as leukemia, bone marrow disease and aplastic anemia.

Examples of opportunistic infections include candidiasis (thrush)—a fungal infection of the mouth, throat, or vagina, cytomegalovirus, a viral infection that causes eye disease that can lead to blindness, herpes simplex, viruses which can cause oral herpes (cold sores) or genital herpes, *Pneumocystis carinii*, which can cause a fatal pneumonia, and toxoplasmosis, a brain infection.

Treatment involves correcting (if possible) the underlying condition and treating the invading organism with antibiotic, antifungal or antiviral medications—usually by intravenous injection in an isolation ward in hospital. In the absence of a normal immune system, opportunistic infections are often fatal.

SEE ALSO *AIDS, Candidiasis, Cold sores, Cytomegalovirus, Genital herpes, Herpes simplex, HIV, Pneumonia, Toxoplasmosis*

OPTIC ATROPHY

Optic atrophy is wasting or degeneration of the optic nerve, the nerve that transmits the impulses for the sense of sight. It can occur in one or both eyes, and is the end result of some type of injury or damage to the optic nerve, such as severe head injury or anoxia (lack of oxygen). It may also occur as a hereditary disorder appearing in childhood. Optic atrophy usually results in blindness and there is no cure.

SEE ALSO *Blindness, Eye, Optic nerve*

OPTIC NERVE

The optic nerve connects the eye to the brain and is the second of the 12 cranial nerves. It contains the long processes (axons) of ganglion cells in the retina, the light-sensitive layer at the back of the eye. The retina and optic nerve grow out from the brain and are actually part of the central nervous system. The axons of the ganglion cells converge at the optic disk (blind spot), where the optic nerve leaves the eye. The nerve continues to

Optic nerve

The optic nerve carries impulses for the sense of sight. Damage to the optic nerve may be the result of infections, metabolic or nutritional disorders, or an accident. Diabetes mellitus and anemia may affect the optic nerve and lead to loss of sight.

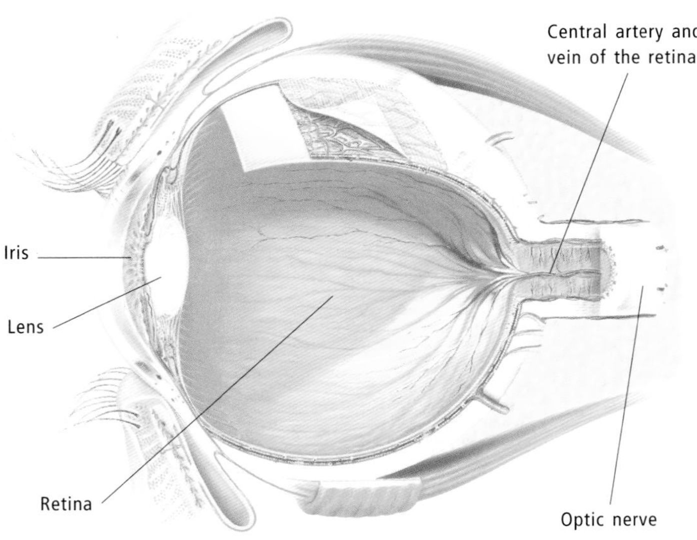

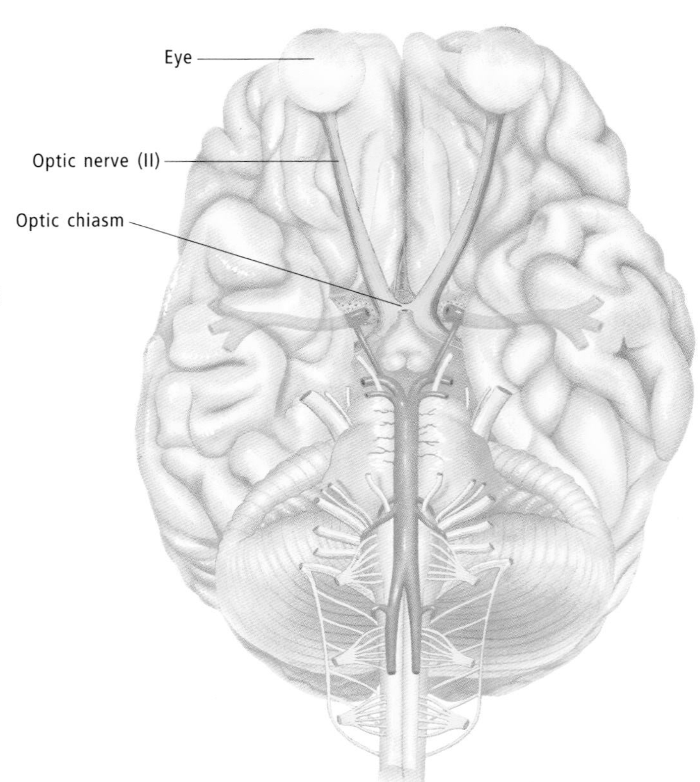

the optic chiasm, where it joins the nerve from the other eye. There are about a million axons in each optic nerve, as well as blood vessels supplying the retina. Action potentials in the nerve are transmitted to the brain to provide visual sensations.

Damage to the optic nerve can cause partial or complete blindness in the affected eye. The nerve can be inflamed at the optic disk where it leaves the eyeball (optic neuritis). This can occur in multiple sclerosis as well as in some diseases of blood vessels, such as temporal arteritis. When viewed through an ophthalmoscope, the normal optic disk looks like a cup, but in optic neuritis it appears swollen and red. Treatment to reduce the inflammation is important, to prevent blindness. The optic disk is also swollen (papilledema) when there are increases in pressure within the brain (increased intracranial pressure).

SEE ALSO *Cranial nerves, Eye, Nerves, Nervous system, Neuritis, Papilledema, Retina*

OPTIC NEURITIS

Optic neuritis is inflammation of the optic nerve, causing sudden partial blindness in the affected eye. It may occur as the result of a viral infection, an autoimmune process or in multiple sclerosis. The symptoms are a sudden loss of vision in one eye and pain on movement of the affected eye. Fortunately, vision often returns to normal in a few weeks. If intravenous steroids are given, visual acuity may return earlier than this. However, if the condition is due to herpes zoster or systemic lupus erythematosus (an autoimmune disease), then complete recovery is less likely.

SEE ALSO *Autoimmune disease, Eye, Lupus erythematosus, Multiple sclerosis, Neuritis, Sight*

ORAL CANCER

Oral cancer is a term that encompasses cancer of the lips, tongue, the floor of the mouth, the inside of the cheek, the gums and the palate. Oral cancers occur most commonly in older people, more commonly in men than in women, in people whose dental and oral hygiene is poor and who smoke cigarettes, cigars or pipes, or who are heavy users of alcohol. The cause is thought to be the irritant effect of these toxins.

Oral cancers are malignant squamous cell carcinomas. They begin as a small, painless lump or ulcer on the tongue, lips or elsewhere in the mouth. They grow and spread rapidly, ulcerating and bleeding, and as they become larger they cause difficulties in talking, chewing and swallowing.

The diagnosis is conformed by a biopsy of the cancer. Treatment is surgical removal, which may involve radical head and neck surgery if the cancer has spread to the lymph nodes in the neck. Surgery is sometimes combined with radiation therapy. Early detection gives the best hope of a cure, but unfortunately most cancers are advanced by the time of diagnosis. About 50 percent of people with oral cancer will survive longer than 5 years.

SEE ALSO *Cancer, Mouth, Smoking, Squamous cell carcinoma*

ORAL CONTRACEPTIVES

The most common oral contraceptive in current use is the low-dose combination pill containing both estrogen and progesterone. Progesterone-only pills are also available but tend to be used only when the combined pill is contraindicated. Some combination pills contain the same concentrations of estrogen and progesterone throughout the dose cycle, in others the relative amounts of the hormones are varied in pills to be taken at different times of the cycle. The rationale of these latter preparations is that variable hormone levels resemble the natural situation more closely.

Estrogen and progesterone in the oral contraceptive have to be in a form which can be taken by mouth and still remain active, which precludes use of natural hormones. If natural hormones are taken by mouth they are broken down in the liver before they enter the general blood circulation of the body.

Synthetic hormones resemble the natural ones closely but have a slight modification to their molecular structure which overcomes this problem. The estrogens are either ethinyl estradiol or mestranol. The most commonly used synthetic progesterones are levonorgestrel, norgestrel and norethindrone.

Oral contraceptives are usually taken for 21 days and then stopped for 7 days, during which time withdrawal bleeding occurs. This mimics but is not the same as a period. The regimen may be varied if it is desired to avoid withdrawal bleeding at a particularly inconvenient time. Anecdotal evidence also suggests that at least some women elect to take the pill continuously rather than cyclically and thus avoid the nuisance of withdrawal bleeding altogether. During a normal menstrual cycle, a few follicles develop in the ovaries during the first half of the cycle (the follicular phase) under the influence of follicle stimulating hormone (FSH) from the pituitary. These follicles produce increasing amounts of estrogen and this in turn stimulates a surge of luteinising hormone (LH) from the pituitary which induces ovulation. The amount of estrogen and progesterone in the pill is approximately the same as that present at the beginning of the follicular phase.

Estrogen levels in a normal cycle would rise by about six- to ten-fold during the natural follicular phase, but this does not occur with the contraceptive pill. Low levels of estrogen and progesterone result in decreased production of FSH and LH by the pituitary, which in turn suppresses ovarian function and prevents ovulation.

Oral contraceptives affect other parts of the reproductive tract besides the ovary. Progesterone makes the cervical mucus thick and impermeable to sperm, and both estrogen and progesterone affect the motility of the fallopian tube and thus may reduce gamete or zygote transport. Changes occur in the endometrium that render it hostile to implantation and it also becomes thin after prolonged contraceptive use. These changes are reversible when the pill is stopped and regular ovulations are restored in the vast majority of women within 3 to 6 months.

Progesterone-only pills often do not inhibit ovulation but instead function by causing changes in cervical mucus and the endometrium as described above. It is also thought that they may interfere with capacitation of sperm in the female tract.

The most obvious advantage of the pill is its almost 100 percent reliability and it is thought that the occasional failures are more often due to non-compliance than to method failure. The pill also offers many non-contraceptive benefits, including relief from a wide range of menstrual disorders and reduction in the incidence of ovarian cysts, rheumatoid arthritis, ectopic pregnancies and pelvic inflammatory disease. There is also decreased risk of endometrial and ovarian cancer. The most serious of the reported disadvantages are disorders of the cardiovascular system in some individuals. These include abnormal blood clots (thromboembolism), stroke and some elevation of blood pressure. Risks appear to increase slightly with age but are reduced considerably in non-smokers and with low-dose pills. Many of the other problems reported in the past have been shown to be due to other causes or of minimal significance with the low-dose pill. Some drugs, including certain antibiotics and anticonvulsants, may reduce the effectiveness of oral contraceptives to some extent.

SEE ALSO *Contraception, Estrogens, Follicle stimulating hormone, Hormones, Hypertension, Menstruation, Ovulation, Reproductive systems, Stroke, Thromboembolism*

ORCHITIS

Orchitis is an inflammation of one or both of the testicles. It is caused by viruses (especially mumps), bacteria and sexually transmitted organisms, such as those that cause gonorrhea or chlamydia. Orchitis often occurs with infection of the prostate (prostatitis), infection of the urethra (urethritis) and infection of the epididymis (epididymitis).

Symptoms of orchitis are pain in the groin and testicle, pain with urination (dysuria), pain with intercourse or ejaculation and, sometimes, a discharge from the penis. Lymph nodes in the groin may be tender and enlarged and, when a rectal examination is performed, the prostate gland may be tender and enlarged as well.

Urinalysis and blood tests will confirm the diagnosis and isolate the organism responsible. The condition is treated with analgesics and antibiotics (if caused by bacteria). If the condition is sexually transmitted, sexual partners must also be treated. A full recovery is usual, though sterility may follow mumps orchitis.

SEE ALSO *Chlamydia, Epididymis, Gonorrhea, Mumps, Prostatitis, Testes, Urethritis*

O

ORTHODONTICS

Orthodontics is a branch of dentistry concerned with the diagnosis, prevention and correction of misaligned teeth and jaws. This involves the fitting of braces, plates, retainers

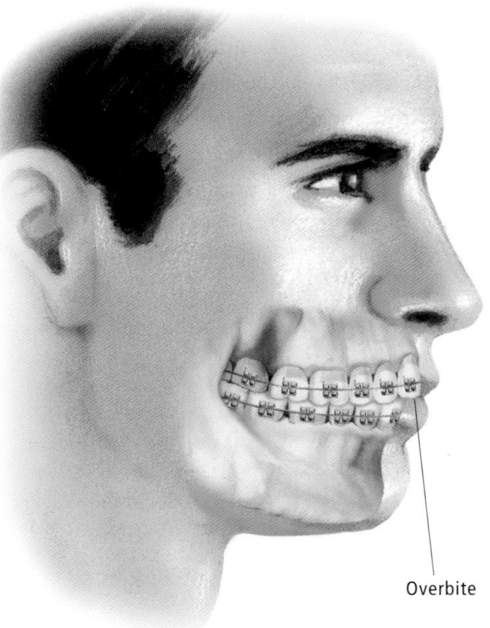

Orthodontics

The misalignment of teeth and jaws can be corrected by orthodontic appliances. Many teenagers are fitted with braces to rearrange the position of their teeth within the jaw to obtain a more favorable even line of teeth.

and other dental appliances to reposition and straighten teeth. The result is improved appearance, function and dental health.

Most orthodontic procedures are performed on children whose jaws, unlike those of adults, are not fully developed. This early treatment makes it easier to manipulate the teeth and jaw and prevent malocclusion, or a bad bite, from developing or worsening.

When upper and lower teeth do not meet correctly, problems with biting and chewing can arise. Teeth may wear unevenly or excessively due to grinding or clenching. They may also become overcrowded, making cleaning difficult and increasing the risk of inflammation, gum disease and tooth loss. In severe cases, where the teeth and/or jaw develop incorrectly, or where they have suffered trauma, results can be infection, difficulty with speech and poor nutrition. Aside from the physical aspects of poor dental development, many orthodontic procedures are carried out for cosmetic reasons as a means of improving self-confidence.

Common orthodontic problems

A common type of malocclusion is overbite, where the upper jaw juts out past the bottom jaw, making teeth more prone to damage. An underbite is where the lower jaw protrudes further than the upper jaw and can wear down the front teeth. With a normal bite, the top teeth close over the bottom teeth slightly. In some instances the top teeth may completely cover the bottom teeth. This is known as a deep bite and can damage the gum behind the top front teeth. Cross-bite is when the upper jaw is too narrow, causing the bottom jaw to swing to one side so that the teeth can meet. An open bite occurs when some teeth don't meet and is a common cause of eating and speech problems. Orthodontic procedures may also be recommended in order to fill gaps made by missing teeth or where teeth or jaw are crooked or misshapen due to such things as thumb sucking in infancy.

Treatment

The orthodontist assesses each dental problem with the help of x-rays to decide how the teeth and bone can be manipulated. Treatment may involve the extraction of some teeth or surgical manipulation of the jaw. With children, assessment usually takes place at 8–10 years of age when most adult teeth have appeared. Treatment, usually involving braces, is a slow process during which teeth are gradually moved over a period of about 18–24 months. It is slower and perhaps a little more painful for adults as the fully developed adult jaw is more difficult to manipulate.

Braces usually consist of brackets fitted over individual teeth and connected by wires. Rubber bands attached to the braces, or an appliance fitted to the head, may also be needed. Every 4–8 weeks the orthodontist adjusts the wires. Traditional designs are made of stainless steel, though less conspicuous clear ceramic types are now available. When the braces are taken off, a removable appliance called a retainer, or plate, is worn for a certain period to help keep the teeth in the correct position.

SEE ALSO *Braces, Malocclusion, Teeth*

ORTHOMOLECULAR THERAPY

The term orthomolecular, referring to a system of medicine which treats with vitamin, mineral and amino acid supplements, was coined in the 1960s by American biochemist Dr Linus Pauling. The Greek word *ortho* meaning "to correct", refers in this case to the body's restoration of good health through achieving the right balance of nutrients.

In Pauling's view, individual requirements for nutrients vary widely and can be a good deal higher than the minimum recommended doses for good health. He became famous for advocating very high doses of vitamin C to counter infections and to strengthen the immune system, views which provoked considerable controversy in the medical community. His view has been upheld to some extent by later research into the use of all the antioxidant vitamins for the prevention and treatment of degenerative diseases.

Another American researcher into megavitamin doses, Dr Abram Hoffer, advocated the use of high doses of vitamin B_3 in the treatment of schizophrenia. His work has led to the subfield of orthomolecular psychiatry, where B group vitamins in particular have been used for the treatment of certain kinds of depression and also for drug dependencies.

Orthomolecular therapy should only be used under professional guidance as some nutritional supplements are toxic in high doses. They may be prescribed by either doctors or naturopaths.

SEE ALSO *Amino acids, Antioxidants, Minerals, Vitamins*

OSGOOD-SCHLATTER DISEASE

Osgood-Schlatter disease is a relatively common, minor ailment of late childhood and early adolescence. It is characterized by pain, tenderness and often swelling at the attachment of the quadriceps tendon just below the knee on the front of the shin (the tibial tuberocity) and usually affects both legs. The disease is more common in boys than girls and usually occurs in highly active or athletic children. It is caused by excessive use of the quadriceps muscles and inflammation in the quadriceps tendon where it inserts into the front of the tibia. Avoidance of strenuous exercise, particularly jumping, usually corrects the problem although, in severe cases, the affected limb may need to be immobilized in a cast for several weeks.

SEE ALSO *Knee, Tibia*

OSTEOARTHRITIS

Osteoarthritis is the most common form of joint disease, where progressive deterioration of cartilage is accompanied by the formation of bony spurs and growth of dense bone at the margins of the joint. This condition does not necessarily involve the inflammation common in other forms of arthritis, many of which occur as a result of infection or accident trauma.

Symptoms of osteoarthritis have been found in skeletons of Neanderthal man and are consistently found in humans over the age of 70, but can occur much earlier. It is a condition common in all vertebrate animals, including birds and fish and all mammals except bats and sloths, which spend their lives hanging upsidedown placing little weight on their joints. Estimates are that over 40 percent of the adult population of the USA and the UK have symptoms which show under x-ray, and a considerable number of children also suffer the condition.

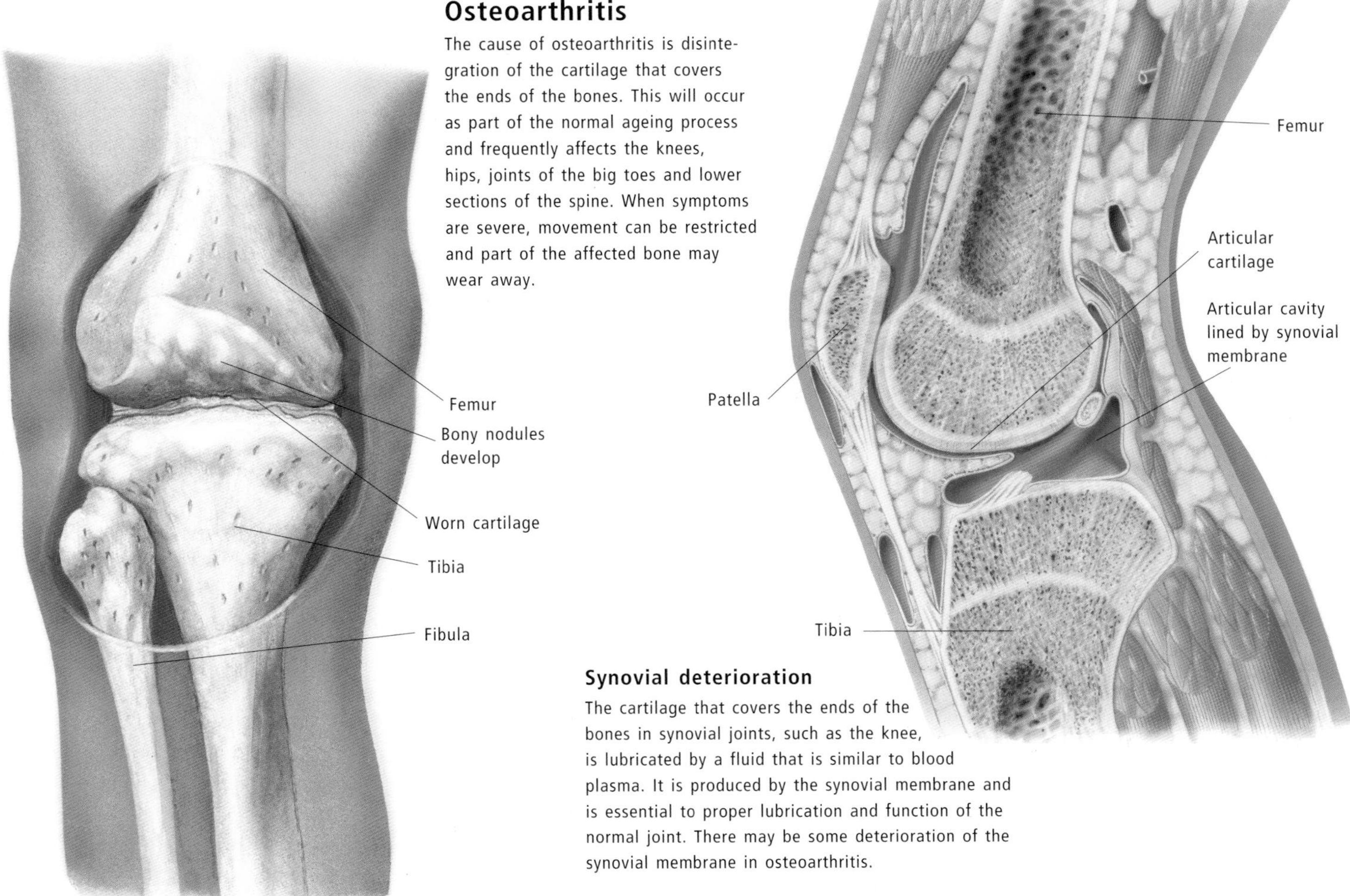

Osteoarthritis

The cause of osteoarthritis is disintegration of the cartilage that covers the ends of the bones. This will occur as part of the normal ageing process and frequently affects the knees, hips, joints of the big toes and lower sections of the spine. When symptoms are severe, movement can be restricted and part of the affected bone may wear away.

Synovial deterioration

The cartilage that covers the ends of the bones in synovial joints, such as the knee, is lubricated by a fluid that is similar to blood plasma. It is produced by the synovial membrane and is essential to proper lubrication and function of the normal joint. There may be some deterioration of the synovial membrane in osteoarthritis.

Joints are formed where two bones meet. Synovial joints have cartilage on the adjacent surfaces that cushions the adjoining surface of each bone, reducing friction on movement and protecting from shock. Synovial joints are lubricated by synovial fluid and enclosed within a fibrous capsule. Heavy use and the passage of time causes wear and tear on the cartilage coating bone ends, sometimes eroding it completely together with the underlying bone surface.

Ageing of the cartilage normally begins in early adult life and most commonly affects joints of the hip, knee, spine and hands. This degenerative damage is irreversible. Gradually the cartilage becomes less well lubricated and less effective as a shock absorber, with increased friction and pain on movement. There may be increasing stiffness and discomfort, particularly on rising.

Osteoarthritis in older individuals most commonly affects the major weight-bearing joints, such as the hips and knees. The degree of pain and stiffness involved can vary widely from person to person.

Although osteoarthritis is a more common ailment in older age groups, factors other than age are the primary cause. Sites of sports injuries in youth, an injured knee for example, often become the first reported site of osteoarthritic effects such as limited mobility, pain and stiffness. Such damage can occur to weight-bearing joints of large-framed or overweight people early in life, yet go unnoticed until distinct symptoms are felt. Genetic factors may also be involved and twice as many women suffer as men.

Symptoms include swelling and pain at the joint in response to activity or a change in position, limited flexibility, and a condition known as Heberden's nodes, which are bony lumps, particularly noticeable at the joints nearest the ends of the fingers, and are thought to be genetic in origin. There may be tenderness at joints, and x-rays may show a change in shape and a reduction in the thickness of cartilage in the joint. Diagnosis may include blood tests.

Sufferers often complain of a deep ache in the center of the joint, worsened by use and relieved by rest. This pain may become constant and severe enough to interfere with sleep. Pain and discomfort may respond to analgesics and to corticosteroids if there is accompanying inflammation. Pain-relieving therapies include application of heat by taking hot baths or applying heat pads, or the application of cold by the use of ice packs. Further damage to the joint may be preventable through exercise to strengthen supporting muscles and improve flexibility and range of movement. Excess weight should be reduced where this is a contributing factor. A common and increasingly successful solution is joint replacement, with artificial hip, knee and finger joints being recommended in some cases.

SEE ALSO *Arthritis, Hip, Inflammation, Joints, Knee*

OSTEOCHONDRITIS DISSECANS

Osteochondritis dissecans is a disorder that usually affects young adults, who have recurrent attacks of mild pain and "locking" of a joint, usually the knee but sometimes the elbow. The symptoms are caused by a loose fragment of cartilage and underlying bone breaking off and moving about freely in the joint. It is thought that a disruption to the blood supply of the bone causes the fragment to break off. The fragment usually needs to be removed by an orthopedic surgeon under general anesthesia, followed by physical therapy to restore the movement of the joint.

SEE ALSO *Elbow, Joints, Knee*

OSTEOCHONDROSIS

Osteochondrosis is an abnormal condition of bone and cartilage formation in children, affecting growth plates at the ends of bones. It may occur at areas where tendons or ligaments attach to bones, or in areas that receive a lot of impact stress. This may be the hip (Perthes' disease), the tibial tuberosity (Osgood-Schlatter disease), or the calcaneus, the bone in the heel of the foot (Sever's disease).

In all cases, degeneration of bone and cartilage occurs; this is thought to be caused by an interruption to the blood supply of the bone, which is followed by spontaneous regeneration. The child feels pain and sometimes a lump at the site where the degeneration has occurred.

Treatment is aimed at protecting the bone and joint while spontaneous healing takes place, through bed rest and the use of appliances such as a brace, cast or splint. In most cases the bone heals without any resulting deformity.

SEE ALSO *Bones, Cartilage, Osgood-Schlatter disease, Perthes' disease*

OSTEOGENESIS IMPERFECTA

Osteogenesis imperfecta, also called brittle bones, is a rare inherited condition in which the bones are abnormally brittle. It is usually present at birth. Bone fractures and deformities occur easily, especially once the child begins to walk. There may be deafness and the whites of the eyes can appear bluish. There is no specific treatment; when bones fracture they must be repaired quickly to avoid deformities.

There are four separate genetic types, each with different manifestations and a prognosis. The disorder is fatal in some types, in others there is a normal life expectancy.

SEE ALSO *Bones, Fractures*

OSTEOMALACIA

Osteomalacia is softening of the bones caused by lack of vitamin D. It can be caused by poor dietary intake of vitamin D, poor absorption of vitamin D from the intestine, or too little exposure to sunlight, which is necessary for the formation of vitamin D in the body. Other causes include hereditary or acquired disorders of vitamin D metabolism, and kidney failure. In children, the condition is called rickets.

Common symptoms are aching bones, fractures and deformities, muscle weakness and spasms. The condition is diagnosed with x-rays of the bones, and blood tests for calcium, vitamin D and phosphorus. Treatment depends on the cause and may include vitamin D, calcium and phosphorus supplements.

SEE ALSO *Bones, Rickets*

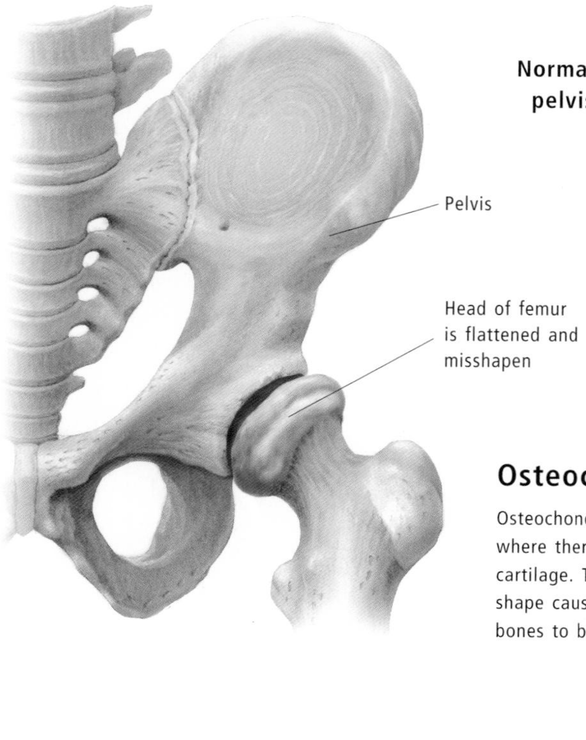

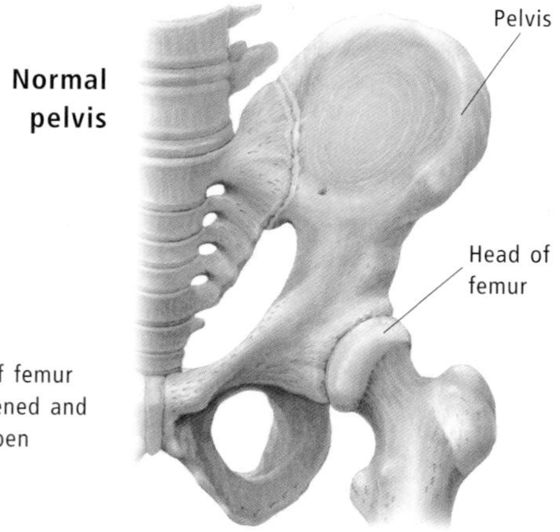

OSTEOMYELITIS

Osteomyelitis is an infection of bone. Acute (sudden onset) osteomyelitis occurs most often in children, is usually caused by a bacterium or fungus which has traveled from an infection elsewhere in the body—a boil, or an ear infection, for example—to the bone. In children, the long bones are usually affected. In adults, the vertebrae and the pelvis are most commonly affected. It can also follow injury, such as an open fracture.

Symptoms are fever and general illness followed a few days later by pain, swelling, redness, warmth and tenderness in the area over the infected bone. X-rays of the bone are normal in the early stages, but the infection will show up in a bone scan. A bone biopsy and culture will grow the organism causing the infection and thus determine what antibiotic to use. Treatment is with intravenous antibiotics in massive doses for at least six weeks. If an abscess has formed, surgery will be needed to remove the abscess and drain any pus.

Slow onset (chronic) osteomyelitis results when bone tissue has died (become necrotic) following an acute infection. An opening to the skin (sinus) may form and drain pus, which may persist intermittently for years. Chronic osteomyelitis is treated by surgical removal of dead bone tissue, which is replaced with bone graft or other material, which promotes the growth of new bone tissue. In some cases amputation is required.

SEE ALSO *Bones*

Pelvis
Head of femur is flattened and misshapen
Normal pelvis
Pelvis
Head of femur

Osteochondrosis

Osteochondrosis occurs mainly in children, where there is degeneration of bone and cartilage. The bone may be moved out of shape causing a deformity. The most likely bones to be affected are the hip and shin.

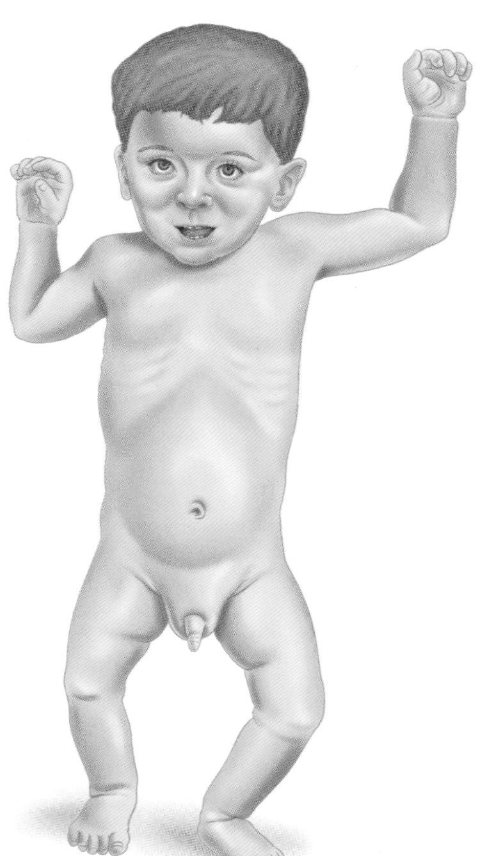

Osteomalacia

Osteomalacia is the result of insufficient vitamin D, either due to an inadequate diet or poor absorption by the individual. The condition inhibits the uptake of calcium by the body and this causes pain in the bones and sometimes also muscle weakness.

OSTEOPATHY

The term osteopathy derives from the Greek words *osteo*, meaning "bone", and *pathos*, meaning "suffering". Osteopathy was pioneered as a form of medical treatment in the late nineteenth century by the American Dr Andrew Taylor Still. A deeply religious man, he believed that the body was created in perfect harmony, with a capacity to self-heal when correctly adjusted and balanced.

Dr Still believed that dysfunctions in the body structure (that is, the muscles, joints and skeleton) affected the health of the body's organ systems by disrupting the nerve and blood supply. He diagnosed various health conditions by touching parts of the body, and assessing the speed and quality of blood flow to that area while noting the changes in position and movement of the musculoskeletal system. Through massage and manipulation he corrected the body's dysfunction and set up the right conditions for self-healing.

Osteopathic treatment is largely done with the hands. Practitioners use a combination of gentle techniques including soft tissue stretching, joint articulation and manipulation, and deep pressure. Minimum force is used in line with the tensions found within the body itself.

Osteopathy is similar to chiropractic treatment in its use of manipulation of the body to correct postural misalignments, but differs in its philosophy and treatment approaches. Whereas chiropractic focuses on the spine and nerve supply in the body, osteopathy focuses on the full musculoskeletal system and improvement of blood and lymph circulation.

Osteopaths make their diagnosis through taking a detailed medical history and assessing the patient's current lifestyle, including diet and exercise. They closely examine body structure and posture by observing the patient standing, sitting, lying and walking. By palpating different parts of the body the osteopath observes muscle tone and joint movement while also noting the skin's health.

As well as treating through the gentle pulling and pushing of bones and muscles, osteopaths often advise on diet, exercise, posture and lifestyle. Osteopaths commonly treat back pain, headaches, arthritis, sciatica and cartilage injuries, as well as digestive problems and chronic respiratory ailments accompanied by chronic muscular tension.

Osteopathy is widely accepted within the USA where it is practised by medical practitioners. Outside the USA osteopaths train in colleges or universities which teach

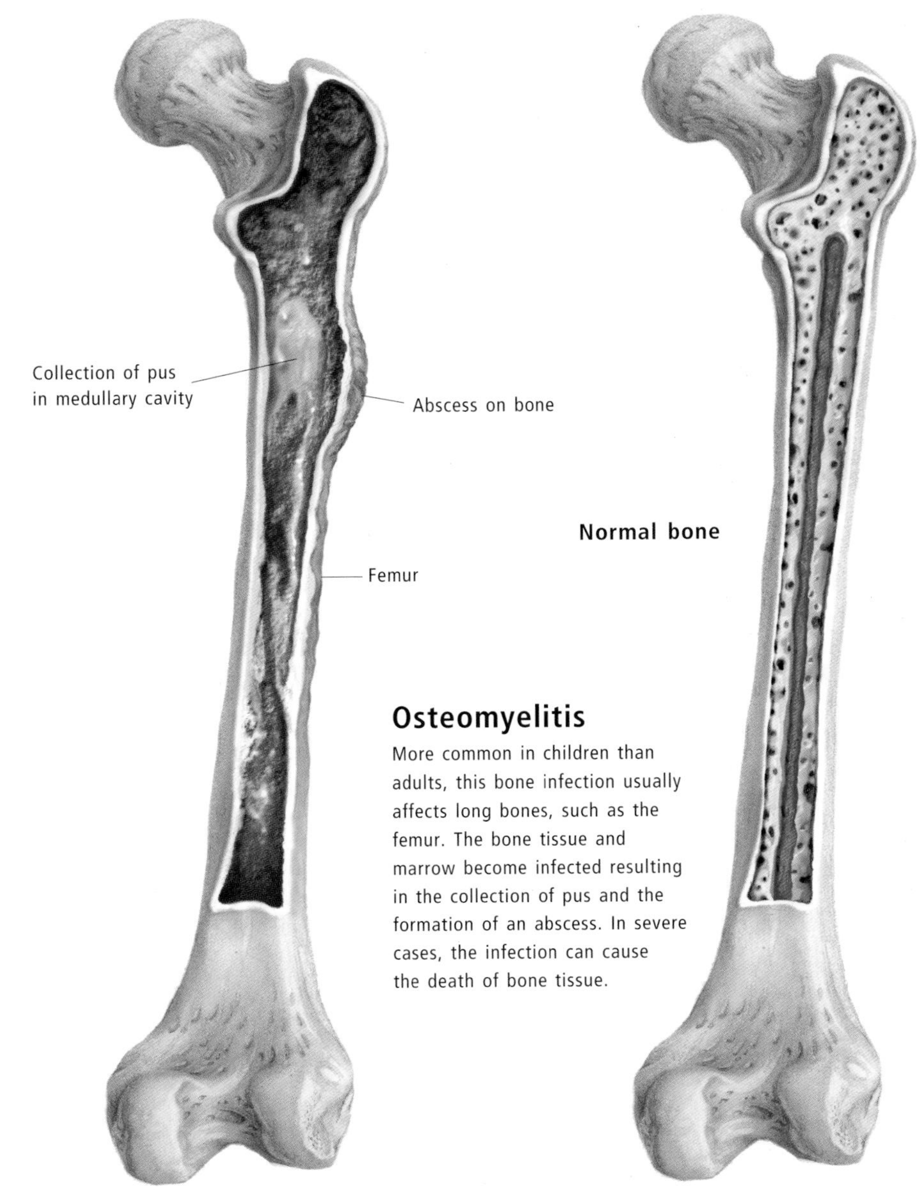

Osteomyelitis

More common in children than adults, this bone infection usually affects long bones, such as the femur. The bone tissue and marrow become infected resulting in the collection of pus and the formation of an abscess. In severe cases, the infection can cause the death of bone tissue.

O

Osteoporosis

Osteoporosis occurs in both older men and women, however the incidence is higher for women. The condition occurs when bone mass is severely reduced, resulting in porous, weak and brittle bones which break easily.

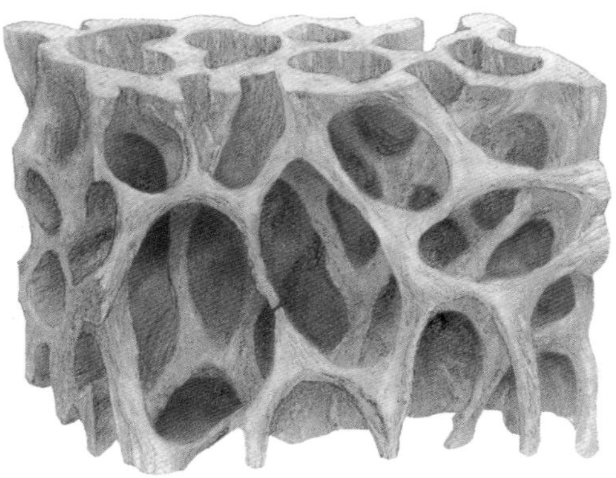

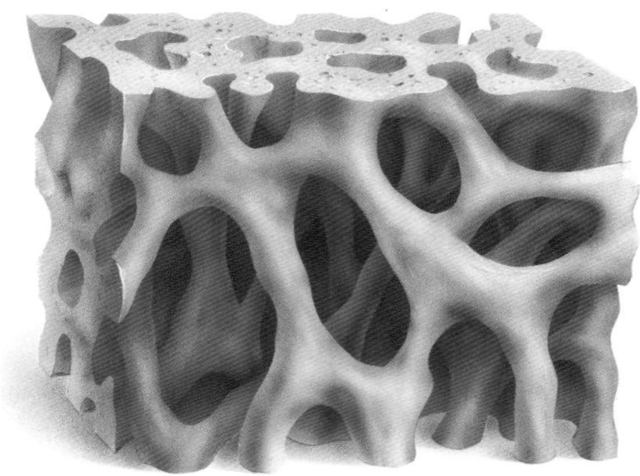

Normal bone

osteopathy in conjunction with naturopathic techniques and orthodox medical diagnosis.

Cranial osteopathy and its latest variant, cranio-sacral osteopathy, are methods of balancing the body through very slight movements of the bones of the skull and spinal column. This form of osteopathy was pioneered by Dr William Garner Sutherland, who believed that the bones in the skull are designed to allow very little movement, being interlocking and held together by dense connective tissue. The inside of the skull bones is lined by the dura mater, one of the membranes surrounding the brain and containing the cerebrospinal fluid. Sutherland's belief was that if the flow of cerebrospinal fluid becomes interrupted or distorted for any reason, an imbalance leading to disease can result. The cranial osteopath gently releases any tensions between the skull bones to allow the cerebrospinal fluid to pump correctly.

This treatment is particularly recommended for children and babies, especially where there has been birth trauma. It can also be helpful for treating both old and recent injuries to the head, neck or back, recurring ear or sinus infections and headaches.

SEE ALSO *Chiropractic*

Dowager's hump

Dowager's hump develops in older women with severe osteoporosis. The vertebrae in the spine may compress, so that the normal curve of the spine is exaggerated. This condition may progressively worsen.

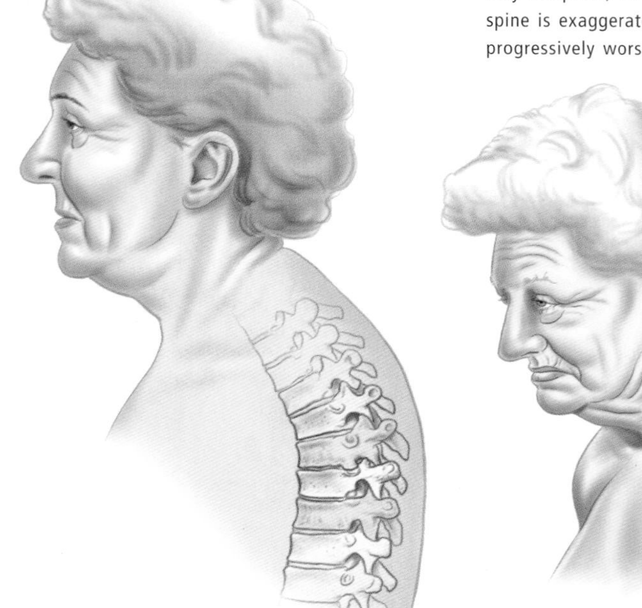

OSTEOPOROSIS

Osteoporosis is a disorder in which bones lose their density and become weak and brittle. The condition gets worse with age and is seen most commonly in postmenopausal women. The bone loss is greatest in bones containing a large percentage of spongy (trabecular) bone, found in the vertebral column, the hips and the wrist. The bones lose calcium and phosphate, as well as the connective tissue that is the matrix of the bone. Consequently they become brittle and prone to fracture. Osteoporosis is different from osteomalacia, which is caused by vitamin D deficiency, and in which only calcium, but not the matrix, is lost from the bone.

The cause of osteoporosis is unknown. However, some factors are known to accelerate the condition; they include a diet low in calcium, lack of exercise, cigarette smoking, excessive alcohol consumption and prolonged bed rest. In women, estrogen appears to protect against osteoporosis, but levels of estrogen fall after menopause and so from the age of 50 or so, osteoporosis is more common in women than men.

Some diseases can cause or accelerate osteoporosis. They include Cushing's syndrome (overactivity of the adrenal glands) and hyperparathyroidism (overactivity of the parathyroid glands). Liver, kidney or heart disorders can also accelerate osteoporosis. Other possible causes include eating disorders, such as anorexia, and some drugs, such as thyroid hormones and corticosteroid medication taken over a long period.

Typically the sufferer has no symptoms but gradually loses height over the years, finally becoming stooped with forward curvature of the thoracic spine (also known as dowager's hump, or kyphosis). Back pain can be severe and a back brace may be needed for support. Fractures, especially of the hip and wrist, are common in the elderly, and can happen without warning. Compression fractures of the vertebrae may compress the surrounding nerves and cause severe pain.

The diagnosis can be confirmed with x-rays and photodensitometry (a scanning technique that measures bone density). These tests show bones with diminished density, and may be used to predict future fractures. There is no treatment for osteoporosis. Instead, management is directed at preventing further bone loss, and treating fractures and other complications. Calcium and vitamin D supplements and adequate protein will prevent further bone loss.

In postmenopausal women, hormone replacement therapy is often used. Estrogen taken orally halts bone demineralization, as well as protecting against heart disease and stroke, and relieving the hot flashes and mood swings of menopause. To prevent the possibility of cancer of the endometrium (the lining of the uterus), estrogen is usually given along with the hormone progesterone.

There are several drugs available, including the hormone calcitonin, which prevent loss of bone mineral and allow the bone to gain density. Calcitonin must be given daily by injection.

The best approach to the problem of osteoporosis is prevention. Adequate calcium in the diet (at least three to four glasses of milk per day or the equivalent), regular exercise, giving up tobacco and reducing alcohol consumption will prevent or slow the progression of the disease. Women should begin these measures in their teens.

SEE ALSO *Bones, Calcium, Estrogens, Hormone replacement therapy, Kyphosis*

OTITIS EXTERNA

Otitis externa is inflammation of the outer ear, that is, the skin of the ear canal extending from the eardrum to the outside of the ear. Symptoms of otitis externa include itching, ear pain that worsens when the earlobe is pulled, a slight discharge and (sometimes) deafness. The cause is usually a bacterial or fungal infection resulting from a number of causes, including swimming in dirty, polluted water (the condition is also known as swimmer's ear), scratching the ear, the use of ear plugs for prolonged periods, or excessive sweating. It may also occur in people with eczema (an inflammation of the skin) or diabetes mellitus.

Treatment is with ear drops that contain antibiotics to fight infection and cortisone drugs to control inflammation. Oral antibiotics may be needed in severe infection. Any dead skin, pus or wax should be removed by a physician.

SEE ALSO *Ear*

OTITIS MEDIA

Otitis media is inflammation of the middle ear. It is most commonly caused by the spread of bacteria from the throat into the middle ear via the eustachian tube. Usually there is an associated infection of the throat, such as the common cold or tonsillitis.

The sufferer, usually a child, develops fever, deafness in the affected ear, and severe earache, due to an accumulation of pus in the middle ear which can build up until it ruptures the eardrum, releasing the pus and relieving the earache. Diarrhea, abdominal pain, and vomiting accompany the symptoms—in infants they may be more obvious than the earache.

Treatment is with painkillers and antibiotics. If the eardrum has ruptured or been surgically opened and is discharging pus, the ear should be kept clean and dry until the eardrum has healed. Sometimes, pus under pressure may need to be released surgically via an incision in the eardrum (myringotomy). In some children, otitis media becomes recurrent and may become chronic (glue ear), when the insertion of a drainage tube becomes necessary. If untreated, chronic otitis media can cause deafness.

SEE ALSO *Deafness, Ear*

OTOSCLEROSIS

Otosclerosis is a disorder of the middle ear that leads to progressive deafness. It is caused by the gradual build-up of abnormal spongy bone tissue around one of the small bones (the stapes) in the middle ear. The abnormal bone prevents the stapes from vibrating, thereby preventing the transmission of sound vibrations from the eardrum to the inner ear. The result is progressive deafness in the affected ear and, sometimes, ringing in the ear (tinnitus). Eventually both ears become affected. Otosclerosis is most commonly seen in women between the ages of 15–30 and may be triggered by pregnancy. A family history of otosclerosis is common.

The condition is treated by a surgical procedure called a stapedectomy, in which

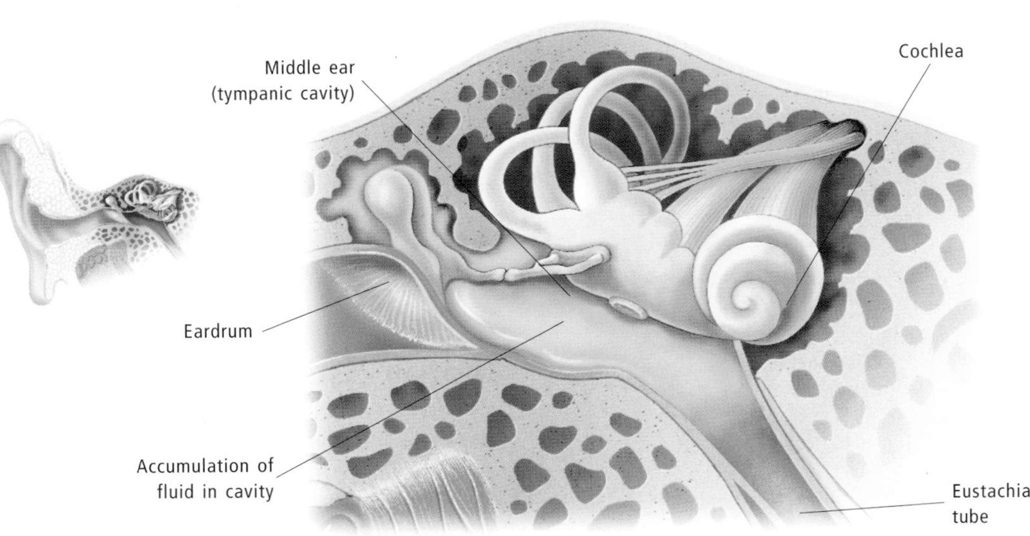

Otitis media

Otitis media is inflammation of the middle ear, which occurs frequently in infants and young children. Fluid accumulates in the ear behind the tympanic membrane. There is hearing loss, which ceases after treatment.

O

the diseased stapes bone is replaced with a prosthesis, which restores hearing in most cases. A hearing aid may be used as an alternative to surgery.

SEE ALSO *Deafness, Ear, Hearing*

OVARIAN CYSTS

Ovarian cysts are relatively common and can occur in females of all ages, including both newborns (neonates) and those who have been through menopause. They are hollow, fluid-filled structures which may be derived from abnormal development of ovarian follicles or of a corpus luteum (an ovarian follicle that has matured and released its egg).

Ovarian cysts are usually multiple and affect both ovaries. They contain a watery or bloody fluid and are usually quite small although some may be as large as 2 inches (5 centimeters) or more in diameter. They are often symptomless and ovulation may occur in their presence; however, complications are not uncommon. These include pain, disturbances to the menstrual cycle and to ovulation with resulting infertility, excessive hair growth, rupture of one or more of the cysts and degeneration of adjacent normal ovarian tissue. Larger cysts may damage the ovarian blood supply with possible loss of the entire ovary.

The cause of ovarian cysts of this type is complex but has been linked to imbalances in the production of certain pituitary hormones, collectively called gonadotropins, which are involved in the control of ovarian function. In women of childbearing age some of the complications of ovarian cysts may be reduced with weight loss. Estrogen and/or progesterone or fertility drugs are other possible treatments. In some instances, drainage or surgical removal of the larger cysts or even of the whole ovary may be necessary.

Certain types of cystic ovaries may be inherited. One of the best known is polycystic ovary syndrome or Stein-Leventhal syndrome, which is characterized by numerous small cysts and excessive thickening of the tissues forming the covering of the ovary. There are also higher than normal amounts of male sex hormones in circulation (ovaries produce these hormones normally but they are generally converted to estrogens).

Certain ovarian cysts are frequently associated with endometriosis (a condition in which tissue-like uterine lining is found outside the uterus). These cysts are lined with fragments of displaced uterine lining (endometrium) and are known as chocolate or tarry cysts because they contain a viscous brown material, arising from bleeding into cavities of the cysts during menstruation. Chocolate cysts are commonly multiple, large and affect both ovaries. These can be treated by giving hormones for the endometriosis, removing the cysts surgically or by using laser treatment.

Several forms of cystic tumors also exist and, unlike other types of ovarian cyst, may become malignant. One of the most common is multilocular cystadenoma. Usually only one ovary is affected, with a mass of tiny, mucus-filled cysts surrounding a single very large cyst. This can grow to enormous size, 44 pounds (20 kilograms) or more, which will distend the abdomen. The cyst may either be drained, or surgically removed. Sometimes the whole ovary will need to be removed. Other types of cystic tumor do not reach the considerable size of an untreated multilocular cystadenoma.

SEE ALSO *Endometriosis, Endometrium, Ovaries, Stein-Leventhal syndrome*

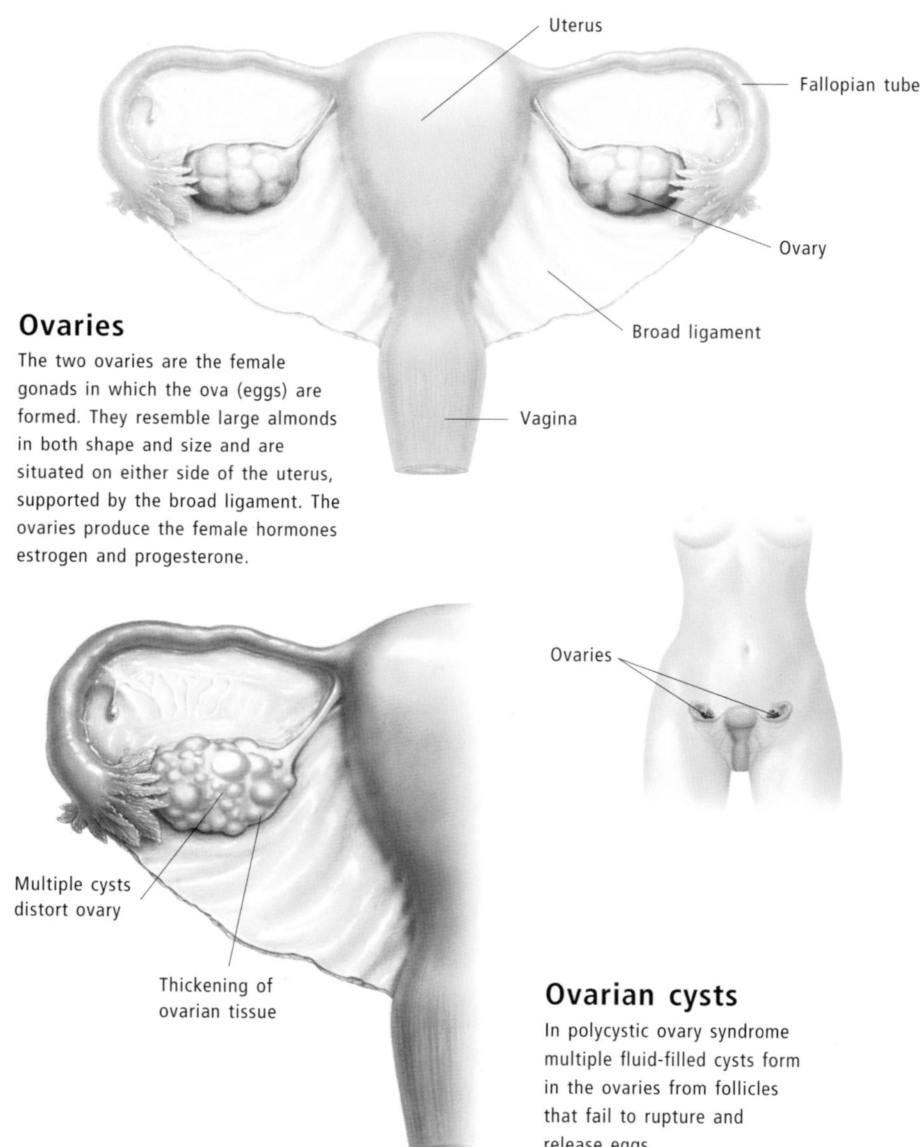

Ovaries
The two ovaries are the female gonads in which the ova (eggs) are formed. They resemble large almonds in both shape and size and are situated on either side of the uterus, supported by the broad ligament. The ovaries produce the female hormones estrogen and progesterone.

Ovarian cysts
In polycystic ovary syndrome multiple fluid-filled cysts form in the ovaries from follicles that fail to rupture and release eggs.

OVARIES

The ovaries are elliptical organs roughly 1½ inches (3 centimeters) long and ½ inch (1 centimeter) wide. They are situated close to the side walls of the pelvis and are sup-

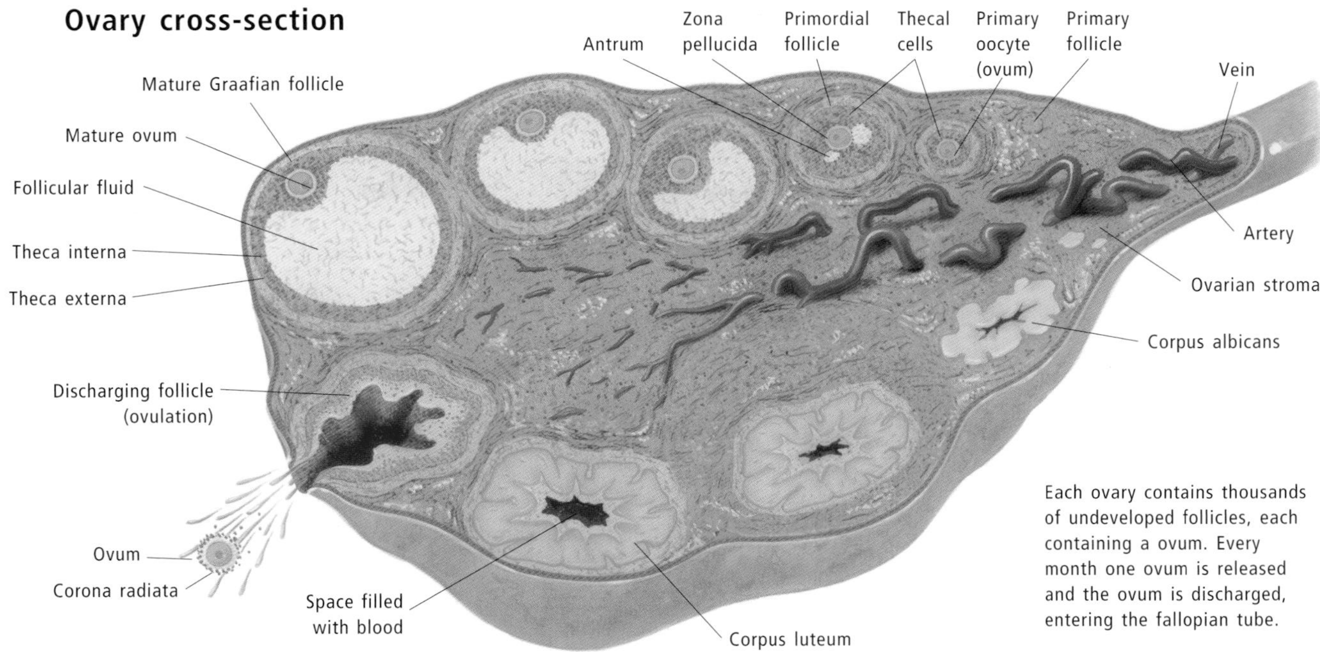

ported by the broad ligament of the uterus.

Ovaries contain thousands of small undeveloped follicles, each of which consists of an ovum surrounded by specialized secretory cells that produce female hormones. Ovaries in women of reproductive age also contain a few follicles undergoing enlargement and development prior to each ovulation. Most of these developing follicles will degenerate so that only a single ovum from one of the ovaries will finally be ovulated.

After ovulation, a corpus luteum is formed from the remains of the ovulated follicle. About two days before the start of the next menstrual cycle it will begin to degenerate. Degenerating follicles and corpora lutea persist for a number of cycles and in some women continue to produce small amounts of estrogen and progesterone.

There are changes in the normal structure and function of the ovaries associated with age. Several years prior to menopause the number of follicles (both undeveloped and developing) begins to decrease, there is a decline in the overall amount of estrogen in circulation and loss of other ovarian tissue, resulting in an overall decrease in size of the ovaries.

Ovarian abnormalities are likely to cause infertility, for example if the ovary is unable to respond normally to the stimulating gonad hormones (gonadotropins) from the pituitary. This occurs in the polycystic ovary syndrome (Stein-Leventhal syndrome). Individuals with this syndrome have infrequent or absent menstruation, infertility, excessive facial and body hair and are usually obese. Both ovaries are smooth and enlarged with numerous small cysts. The condition is caused by a congenital inability to produce normal amounts of estrogen. Instead testosterone-like substances, which precede estrogen, are released into the blood. Decreased estrogen secretion is involved in the failure to ovulate and menstruate normally. Other types of ovarian cysts may also affect ovulation.

In some individuals, ovaries do not develop normally (gonadal dysgenesis). This occurs in certain genetic disorders, for example Turner's syndrome, where the ovaries are often fibrous streaks without follicles. No estrogens are produced, resulting in total amenorrhea and absence of secondary sex characteristics, including breast development and axillary and pubic hair.

Ovarian malignancies are the commonest cause of death from gynecological cancers and can occur at any age, although they are rare in childhood. Ovarian cancers are often diagnosed late because they are relatively asymptomatic until well developed or have spread to other organs. It is common for ovarian cancer to be described as if it were a single entity but there are many different types with different rates of spread and response to therapy. There is even a particular type of tumor called a teratoma, usually benign but sometimes malignant, in which fragments of skin, hair, cartilage, thyroid-like tissue and even teeth develop. Some types of cancer are more common after menopause and they can cause postmenopausal bleeding. Ovaries are also a fairly common site for secondary cancers arising from other organs.

SEE ALSO *Estrogens, Menstruation, Ovarian cysts, Ovulation, Progesterone, Reproductive systems, Stein-Leventhal syndrome, Turner's syndrome*

OVERDOSE

Excessive doses of medication or drugs, taken either by accident or deliberately, usually constitute an overdose. Accidental overdoses are generally taken by curious children and confused elderly people, or as a result of doctor, pharmacist or patient error; deliberate overdoses are often attempted suicide or even homicide.

If there are several equally effective drugs to treat a particular condition, doctors will generally prescribe the one with the lowest risk of toxicity should an overdose occur.

Substances which people can and do overdose on include the following.

Amphetamines, also known as speed because these drugs seem to speed up the central nervous system, have severe effects in overdose including brain hemorrhage, heart attack, coma and occasionally death.

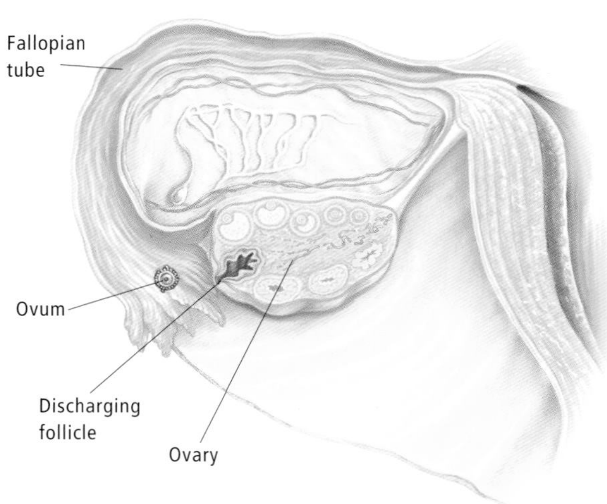

Ovulation

The release of an ovum (egg) from the ovary is known as ovulation and takes place on about day 14 of the menstrual cycle. A surge of hormone encourages the follicle that carries the mature ovum to burst open. The ovum is discharged and is swept up into the fallopian tube.

Barbiturates, which are drugs classed as sedative hypnotics, are used to manage seizures or sometimes as a sedative. Intoxication with barbiturates slows a person's movements and breathing and can cause coma and loss of most reflexes.

Cocaine is a stimulant drug produced from the leaves of the coca plant. Overdose can happen to anyone and very small amounts can have an overdose effect on susceptible persons. Death can result.

Heroin, a drug made from the opium poppy and originally used as a painkiller, is very easy to overdose on. Even small amounts can result in an overdose for some people, and the longer the drug is used the more likely it is that an overdose will be taken. Symptoms of overdose include a slowing of breathing, a very low pulse rate or blood pressure, and drowsiness or unconsciousness. Coma and death can result.

Methadone is an opioid painkiller used to treat people dependent on heroin. Overdose to methadone happens when more than the prescribed dose is taken or when the substance is injected or taken with alcohol or minor tranquilizers.

MethyleneDioxyMethAmphetamine (MDMA), commonly known as Ecstasy, is a synthetic drug used as a stimulant. Overdose can result in death.

Minor tranquilizers, drugs in the benzodiazepine group, including diazepam, tempazepam and clonazepam, can cause overdose. Many sleeping pills fall into this category.

It is also possible to overdose on some substances that are generally considered safe, such as vitamin supplements.

Vitamin A is a fat-soluble vitamin found pre-formed in animal foods such as egg yolk, fatty fish and full-fat dairy foods. Excess vitamin A is toxic. Overdosing on supplements can cause headache, joint pain and itchy skin and can be fatal to the developing fetus. Vitamin B_6 in large quantities is also dangerous. Vitamin D is the most toxic vitamin and large doses as supplements lead to loss of appetite, nausea, vomiting and even death.

Prescription and over-the-counter medicines can also be taken in overdose; some are far more dangerous than others.

Acetaminophen (paracetamol) is a common cause of accidental poisoning in children, but such overdoses also occur in other age groups and need immediate medical treatment. Ibuprofen can also be taken in overdose and medical attention must be sought if this occurs.

SEE ALSO ***Amphetamines, Barbiturates, Cocaine, Detoxification, Drug dependence, Heroin, Methadone, Poisoning, Sleeping pills, Stimulants, Tranquilizers, Vitamins***

OVULATION

Ovulation is the release of an ovum from the ovary on about day 14 of an average menstrual cycle. It can take place from either ovary; the selection of left or right ovary seems to be a random process.

Prior to ovulation, during the first half of each menstrual cycle, a few follicles, each consisting of an ovum and the secretory cells which surround it, start to develop. Most of these follicles will degenerate at various stages of maturity until usually just one is left to undergo ovulation. Development of the follicles is stimulated by the follicle stimulating hormone (FSH), a gonadotropin, released by the pituitary gland.

As the follicles develop, the secretory cells produce increasing quantities of estrogen which is released into the blood. When blood estrogen reaches a particular concentration, the pituitary is stimulated to produce a surge of another gonadotropin called luteinising hormone (LH). This induces ovulation through a temporary break in the surface of the ovary. The open end of the fallopian tube adjacent to the ovary draws the ovum inside the tube. The ovum is either fertilized here or degenerates within the next few days. Transport into the uterus occurs if fertilization has taken place. Occasionally the fallopian tube may fail to collect the ovum, which then falls into the peritoneal cavity. If fertilization then occurs, ectopic implantation may result on one of the pelvic or peritoneal organs.

After ovulation, the secretory cells remaining in the ovary become a corpus luteum which will produce progesterone and small amounts of estrogen until day 26 of a non-pregnant cycle. The corpus luteum degenerates at this time with a rapid decline in concentrations of progesterone in the blood resulting in menstruation.

Determining whether and when ovulation has taken place is important in establishing the cause of infertility and also in "natural" methods of birth control and in timing intercourse to maximize the possibility of conception. Tests should be made over a number of cycles in order to establish a pattern of ovulation. The simplest method is to take daily body temperature readings and to record these on a temperature chart. Temperatures should be lower during the first half of the cycle and there may be a further drop at the time of ovulation. Alternatively, cervical mucus may be sampled throughout the cycle. This dries in a characteristic fern-like pattern around the time of ovulation, a pattern not seen during the rest of the cycle.

Other techniques rely on the fact that a functional corpus luteum and progesterone production can only occur if ovulation has taken place. These can be established either by measuring blood progesterone levels during the second half of the cycle or by biopsy of the uterine lining in order to see if changes consistent with progesterone production have occurred. Monitoring of the developing follicles with ultrasound is sometimes used. In some women pelvic pain ("mittelschmerz"), possibly accompanied by bleeding, may be associated with ovulation.

An anovulatory cycle is one in which ovulation does not occur and therefore a corpus luteum does not form. Uterine bleeding may still take place but is the result of the withdrawal of estrogen rather than of progesterone and is often irregular. Ovulation failure in women of reproductive age may be caused by a malfunction of organs, such as the pituitary, which produce hormones affecting the ovaries. It can also be the result of certain therapeutic drugs, obesity, starvation or may have a psychological basis. In some cases ovulation may be restored by fertility drugs such as clomiphene citrate. Doses are kept low in order to avoid multiple ovulations. Oral contraceptives are used to deliberately introduce anovulatory (not related to ovulation) cycles.

Anovulatory cycles are common for the first few months after menstruation first occurs (menarche), before a mature hormone pattern is established. They also occur in increasing frequency prior to menopause as a result of normal hormone changes at that time. Occasionally ovulation can occur several years after assumed menopause.

SEE ALSO *Estrogens, Fertility, Fertilization, Follicle stimulating hormone, Infertility, Menstruation, Mittelschmerz, Ovaries, Ovum, Progesterone, Reproductive systems*

OVUM

The ovum is the mature female germ cell. The ovaries of women of reproductive age contain about 800,000 immature ova (oocytes), each surrounded by a covering of specialized cells which secrete female hormones. Only about 400 of these will be ovulated. The rest degenerate sometime during the reproductive years or just after menopause.

Normal body cells are diploid, that is, they contain 23 pairs of chromosomes and divide by mitosis to produce daughter cells which also have 23 pairs of chromosomes. Germ cells (oocytes and sperm) are haploid, that is, they contain only one of each pair of chromosomes (23 single chromosomes). This is possible because oocytes are produced in the embryo by a special form of cell division called meiosis (reduction or division) which halves the number of chromosomes. Sperm are also produced by meiosis. When fertilization takes place and ovum and sperm join together, the chromosome number in the new individual is restored to the normal 23 pairs (46 single chromosomes).

The development of normal ovaries and oocytes takes place only if the individual is a normal female and two conditions are fulfilled: the individual does not have a Y chromosome (carrying the normal gene for maleness), and there are two normal X chromosomes. If one X chromosome is missing, as is the case in Turner's syndrome, the oocytes degenerate and the ovaries do not develop in the embryo.

SEE ALSO *Cells, Chromosomes, Embryo, Fertilization, Hormones, Ovaries, Reproductive systems, Sperm, Turner's syndrome, X chromosome, Y chromosome*

OXYTOCIN

Oxytocin is a hormone secreted by the pituitary gland and also by the ovary and placenta. Secretion of this hormone results from stimulation of nerves in the nipple during suckling. Oxytocin is responsible for the release of milk during breast feeding (lactation), whereas the manufacture of milk by the glandular tissue is under the control of a different pituitary hormone, prolactin.

It is also thought that oxytocin is important in maximizing uterine contractions during the later stages of labor. It may also help to reduce bleeding after delivery by causing mild uterine contractions which compress damaged blood vessels. However, oxytocin does not seem to be involved in the initiation of labor.

SEE ALSO *Breast feeding, Childbirth, Hormones, Mammary glands, Pituitary gland*

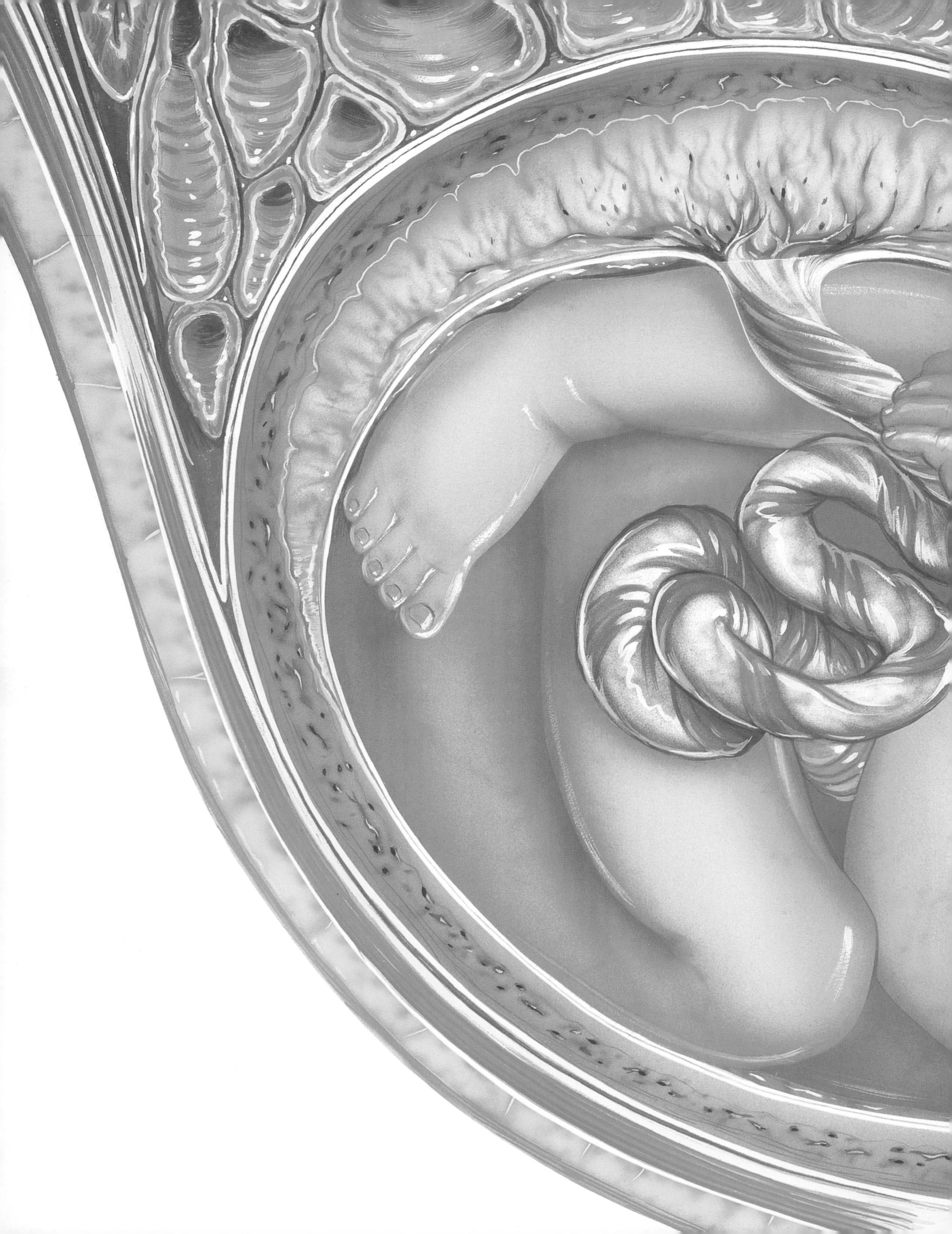

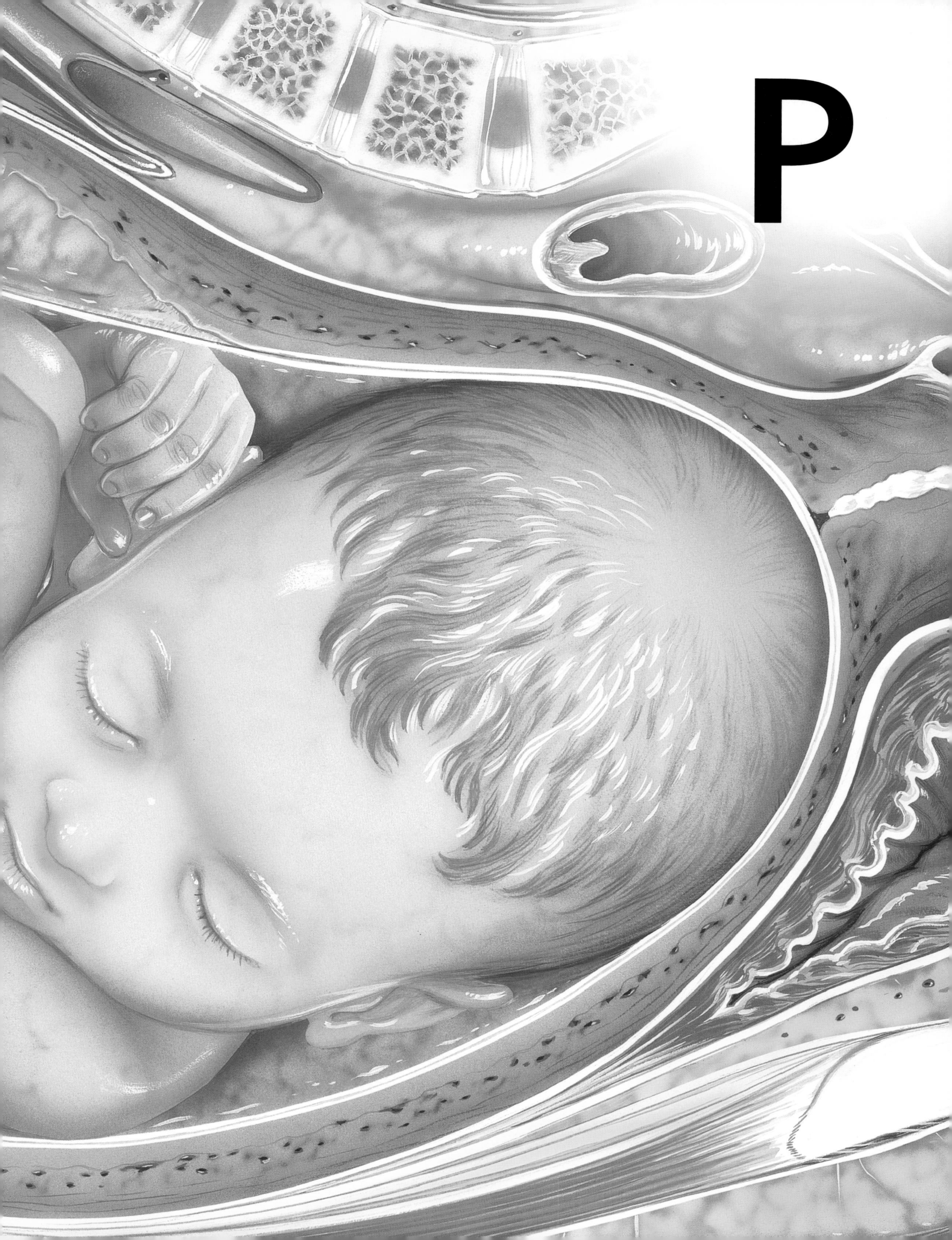
P

PACEMAKER

This term is usually used in reference to the heart, although other organs (such as the uterus and bowel) may also have specialized tissue which controls rhythmic contraction. There is a naturally occurring pacemaker, called the sinoatrial node, which directly controls the rhythmic contraction of the heart.

The sinoatrial node is located in the wall of the right atrium near the superior vena cava and has its own rhythmic cycle of electrical activity. This activity is transmitted to surrounding heart muscle and through specialized conducting cells to all parts of the heart, thus initiating heart muscle contraction. The electrical rhythm of the sinoatrial node may be slowed by the vagus nerve, or quickened by the sympathetic cardiac nerves and circulating hormones such as epinephrine (adrenaline).

If the heart is unable to maintain an adequate rhythm due to disease, then artificial pacemakers may be used. They give the heart small stimulant shocks by delivering electrical impulses at a pre-determined rate. These impulses trigger contractions of the heart muscle which cause blood to pump through the heart.

Artificial pacemakers usually consist of two main components: a transducer for generating electrical impulses and tiny wires, or electrodes, which are fed into veins and make contact with the heart muscle. The transducer is a small device weighing about 1 ounce (28 grams) and powered by a lithium battery that may not need changing for at least five years. The transducer is usually implanted beneath the skin just below the collar bone via a small incision. This is a relatively minor procedure carried out using mild sedation and local anesthetic. Transducers are often encased in titanium, which usually does not irritate the body. Alternatively, the transducer may be worn externally on a belt around the body.

Electrical impulses from the transducer travel along the electrodes to the heart muscle at a rate that may be preset or controlled externally by a remote switch. Depending on the heart condition involved, the transducer may monitor the heart's rate of contraction and send out electrical impulses only when it beats abnormally. In this way, pacemakers can be used to stimulate a heart that beats too slowly due to such problems as blocked arteries, metabolic abnormalities or the side effects of certain medications. They can also help to stabilize a heart that beats too fast or to re-establish the heart's rhythm after cardiac arrest.

SEE ALSO *Heart*

PACHYDERMOPERIOSTOSIS

Pachydermoperiostosis is a rare condition marked by thickening of the skin and enlargement, or clubbing, of the fingers and toes due to the build-up of a fibrous covering on the bones. Thought to be hereditary, it usually develops during childhood or adolescence and progresses slowly over about 10 years.

Symptoms include the formation of skin folds or furrows on the scalp, coarsening of facial features and excessive sweating of feet and hands. The nails of the fingers and toes may become increasingly curved. Despite the apparent severity of the condition, there is usually little associated pain.

SEE ALSO *Skin*

PACHYONYCHIA

Pachyonychia (literally "elephant nails" and also known as nail-bed hypertrophy) is a rare condition involving the overgrowth and excessive thickening of the nails. It is often a congenital disorder and may be combined with other disorders of the skin and mucous membrane.

Jadassohn-Lewandowski syndrome is a type of pachyonychia in which abnormally curved and thickened nails are accompanied by other symptoms such as white plaques in the mouth, thickening of the skin on the elbows, palms, soles and knees, and excessive sweating of feet and hands.

SEE ALSO *Nails*

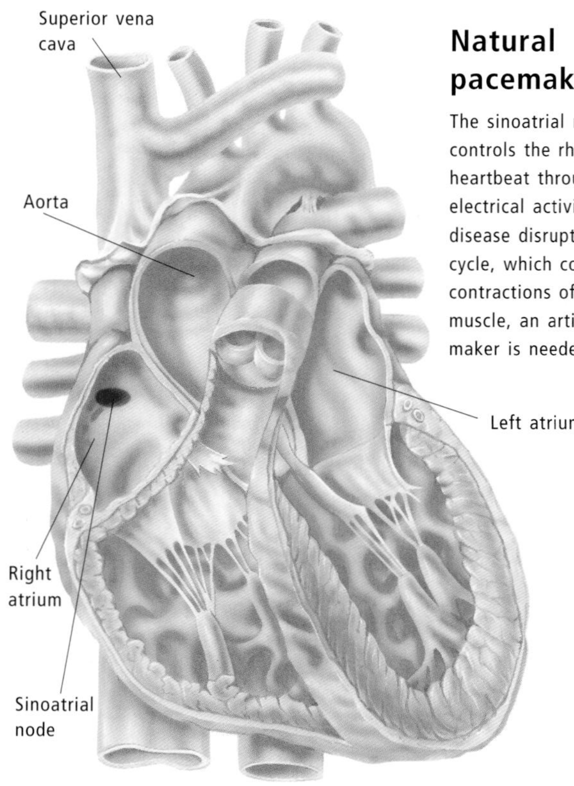

Natural pacemaker

The sinoatrial node usually controls the rhythm of heartbeat through its own electrical activity. When disease disrupts this electrical cycle, which controls contractions of the heart muscle, an artificial pacemaker is needed.

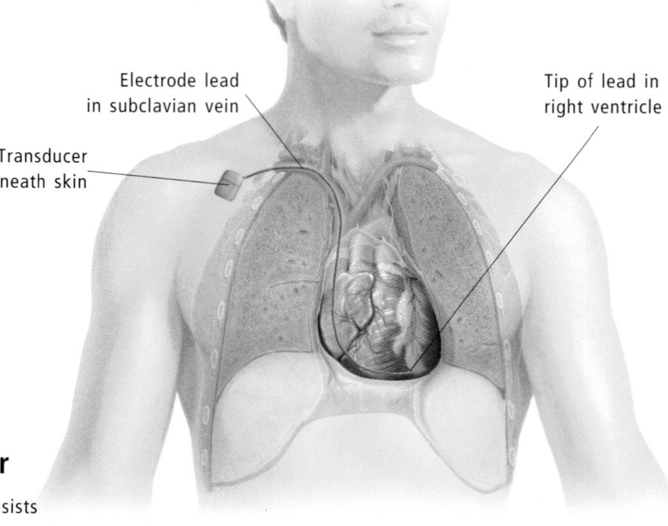

Artificial pacemaker

A pacemaker consists of two main components: a transducer to generate electrical impulses, and electrodes (tiny wires) to make contact with and stimulate the heart muscle.

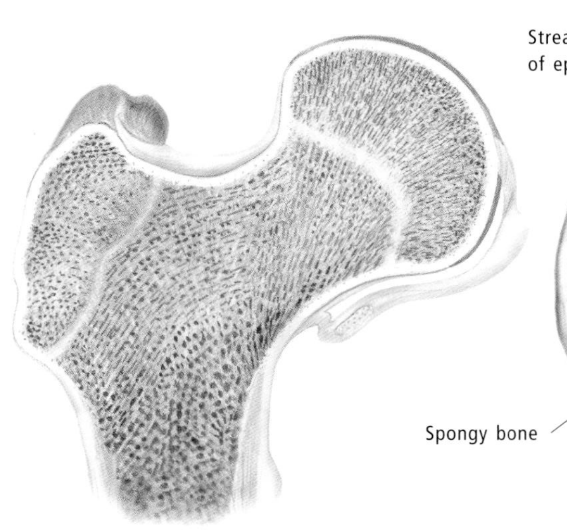

Normal bone

Paget's disease of bone

In Paget's disease, the growth of new bone tissue is disrupted, resulting in bones becoming coarse and soft.

PAGET'S DISEASE OF BONE

Paget's disease of bone, or osteitis deformans, is a disorder in which several bones, most often the pelvis, the lower limbs and the skull, gradually thicken. The disease involves abnormally fast bone destruction and reformation where the new bone matter is structurally abnormal and fragile. This is a chronic, slowly progressive disease that mostly affects elderly people. It may be localized in one or two parts of the body or become widespread. The cause of the disorder is unknown, though recent research points to genetic causes or viral infection. It is known to be common in Europe, Australia and New Zealand.

The disorder (which has no connection with Paget's disease of the breast) often has no symptoms, and is generally discovered during examination or x-ray for some other complaint. In advanced cases, it can cause thickening of the skull, spinal curvature, barrel-shaped chest, bowing of the legs and leg pain. When the skull is affected the head may become enlarged, and hearing loss and blindness may occur if bone growth damages cranial nerves. Radiating sciatic pain in the lower extremities may be felt if the bones of the lumbar spine thicken. Bones affected by Paget's disease fracture more easily than normal bones. Osteosarcoma, a cancer of bone, may sometimes arise from the affected bones.

X-rays and bone scans help diagnose the condition, showing increased bone density and thickening. Blood tests show normal serum calcium with raised serum levels of the bone enzyme alkaline phosphatase. If treatment is required, anti-inflammatory drugs such as aspirin and ibuprofen may be used to relieve pain. Drugs such as calcitonin which suppress bone loss and relieve pain may be prescribed if symptoms persist. If there is extensive damage to the hip, a total hip replacement may be needed.

SEE ALSO *Bones, Paget's disease of the breast*

PAGET'S DISEASE OF THE BREAST

Paget's disease of the breast is an uncommon form of breast cancer, characterized by a lesion on the skin of the nipple similar to moist eczema. Paget's disease does not respond to standard treatments for eczema and is distinguished pathologically by the presence of large pale cells (Paget's cells) never seen in healthy nipple tissue. Since these cells may accumulate pigment, the disease is sometimes mistaken for melanoma.

The affected nipple may be slightly firmer than usual. Other symptoms include nipple discharge, redness or itching around the nipple and a lump or thickening under or near the nipple or areola.

Paget's disease is almost invariably accompanied by or is a precursor to malignant growth (carcinoma) in the underlying breast. It usually affects only one nipple. Rare cases have been reported in male breast cancer.

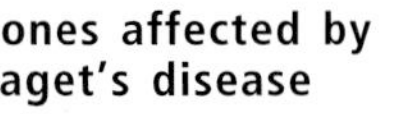

Bones affected by Paget's disease

In the advanced stages of this disease, the bone may be so weakened that even a light blow may cause a fracture. Paget's disease most often affects the pelvis, the lower limbs, and the skull.

Treatment is similar to that for breast cancer without Paget's disease. This may include surgery to remove at least the nipple, areola and some underlying tissue. Alternatively, a mastectomy may be performed as there is a risk that the disease may have spread to other parts of the breast. The risk of this occurring is higher if there is a lump in the nipple area. This disease has been known to occur in the skin areas of the anus and genitals, where it is called extramammary Paget's disease.

SEE ALSO *Breast, Breast cancer, Melanoma, Nipple*

PAIN

Pain is an unpleasant experience associated with real or potential damage to the body. Pain usually serves as a signal that tissues are being damaged, and that the sufferer needs to move away from the painful stimulus as quickly as possible. It also urges rest and recovery from any damage that has been done, to allow healing to take place.

There are two main types of pain. If pain does not outlast its cause, such as a burn or cut, then it is often referred to as acute pain. Such pain serves a useful warning function. For example, there are some rare people born without a sense of pain. While this might seem to be a blessing, such people die relatively young because they do not receive warning of potential damage, and may experience burns, fractures and joint damage.

Unfortunately, however, pain does not always serve a purpose. It may outlast the initial injury and the healing process. It may have a cause which cannot be removed, such as cancer or a malfunction of nerve cells. This is chronic pain and may involve hyperalgesia (increased sensitivity to painful stimuli), allodynia (pain caused by stimuli which would not normally be painful) and spontaneous pain, which has no obvious cause. Chronic pain is debilitating and difficult to treat.

Pain receptors and stimuli

The sensory neurons that mediate pain sensation are known as nociceptors. They have endings or receptors in skin, muscles, joints and internal organs. These nerve endings are connected to the spinal cord or brain stem by nerve fibers which generally lack the myelin sheath which insulates most other sensory nerve fibers.

Nociceptors are activated by a range of potentially damaging (noxious) stimuli which may be mechanical (such as a pinch or cut), thermal (such as a burn) or chemical (such as exposure to acid). Once nociceptors have been activated, signals are conducted along their nerve fibers to the spinal cord or brain stem, and from there to parts of the brain such as the thalamus and cerebral cortex.

Nociceptors have properties which depend on the tissue in which they are located. Nociceptors in the skin are readily activated by pinching or cutting, but internal organs, such as the liver or appendix, can be pinched with forceps without causing pain. This does not mean that the internal organs are entirely insensitive to pain. It is more likely that many of the nociceptors in the viscera are so-called "sleeping" nociceptors. These are only activated by mechanical stimuli when they have already been stimulated by chemicals produced when tissue is inflamed. Sensitization of nociceptors in this way contributes to the increased pain sensitivity felt following tissue damage.

Most of us are familiar, for example, with increased sensitivity of the skin due to sunburn, or how ordinary movement becomes painful following a joint injury. Many analgesics, such as aspirin or acetaminophen (paracetamol), help relieve pain in damaged or inflamed tissues by preventing the production of chemicals which sensitize nociceptors.

Transmission and recognition of pain

Nociceptors form only part of a complex network of nerve cells that give rise to the sensation of pain. Nociceptors send signals to neurons in the spinal cord or brain stem. These neurons receive information not only from nociceptors, but also from mechanoreceptors. These sensory receptors transmit information about muscle length, skin pressure or joint angle—information which normally has nothing to do with pain. Signals from mechanoreceptors do not normally activate spinal neurons which deal with pain. However, in chronic pain, the spinal neurons which deal with painful stimuli receive excessive input from nociceptors. This sensitizes the spinal neurons, which now overreact to inputs from nociceptors or even from mechanoreceptors. The body can therefore become more sensitive to painful stimuli, and can often perceive harmless stimuli as painful as well. The changes in spinal neurons which contribute to chronic pain are often long-lasting and difficult to reverse.

Drugs that have proven useful for acute pain relief include non-narcotic analgesics such as aspirin and acetaminophen (paracetamol), and for more severe pain, narcotic (opioid) drugs such as morphine, codeine and pethidine. There is a common misconception that using opioids for pain relief carries a risk of addiction, but this risk is negligible when they are used purely for the relief of pain in prescribed doses. Chronic pain is often more difficult to relieve than acute pain, but may be treated with anti-epileptics and tricyclic antidepressants as well as non-steroidal anti-inflammatory drugs and opioids such as morphine and methadone.

Once pain signals have been processed in the spinal cord, they are transmitted to the thalamus and cerebral cortex. Relatively little is known about the role of the cortex in pain perception, but recent techniques of brain imaging have been very useful in showing that several areas of the cortex are involved, probably dealing with different aspects of pain. Objective aspects of a painful stimulus (intensity and location) appear to be represented in the somatosensory cortex, while emotional aspects (unpleasantness, associations with other events) are represented in other parts of the cortex, such as the anterior cingulate cortex. Decisions about what sort of action to take in order to avoid the pain may involve the motor cortex.

People (including many doctors) tend to think that the pain they experience depends simply on the intensity of the painful stimulus. This is often not the case. While the nociceptors themselves are very simple, their connections within the spinal cord and brain are complex, and include circuitry which can suppress or even enhance pain sensation. Some people are very sensitive to painful stimuli, while others are quite insensitive. It is also often thought that there are significant cultural differences in pain sensitivity, but such differences are probably more to do with the expression of pain rather than the sensation itself.

Pain sensation can also depend on circumstance. For example, someone injured in a football game or in the heat of battle may hardly notice even a severe injury; conversely pain may be exaggerated by fear or anticipation—an injection may be more painful if there is time to worry about it in advance. Some of these differences in pain perception are due to the control that parts of the brain can exert on pain sensation.

Treatment of pain

Drugs are perhaps the most common measure employed to relieve pain. However, these are not always effective, particularly for chronic pain, and many people turn to alternative therapies, such as chiropractic or acupuncture, for the relief of pain which conventional medical treatment has not been able to alleviate. People may be helped by these alternative treatments, although there is little firm clinical evidence to prove their efficacy.

SEE ALSO *Analgesics, Brain, Narcotics, Neurons, Nerves, Nervous system, Spinal cord*

Processing pain

The brain controls our perception of pain in a number of different areas. Pain signals are relayed to the brain via the thalamus. The sensation and location of pain is registered in the sensory cortex and emotional responses are governed by the limbic system.

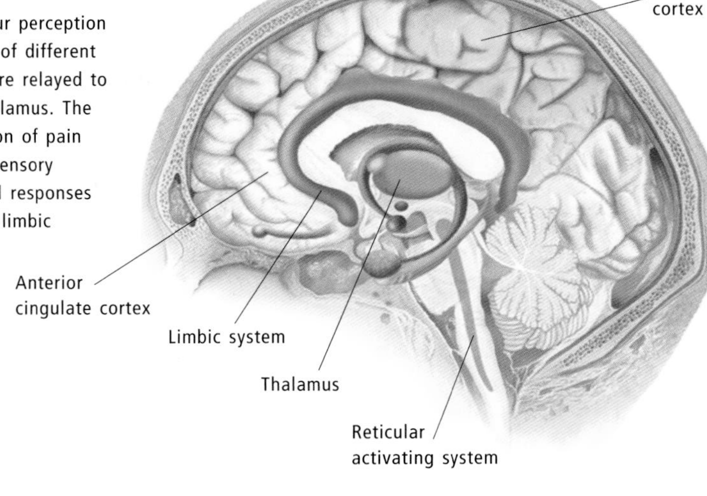

Referred pain

The pain from internal organs may be felt on the surface of the skin as well as internally. This is because the skin and internal organs may share the same pain pathways. When an organ sends pain signals to the spinal cord, the brian may perceive the signal as coming from an area of the skin.

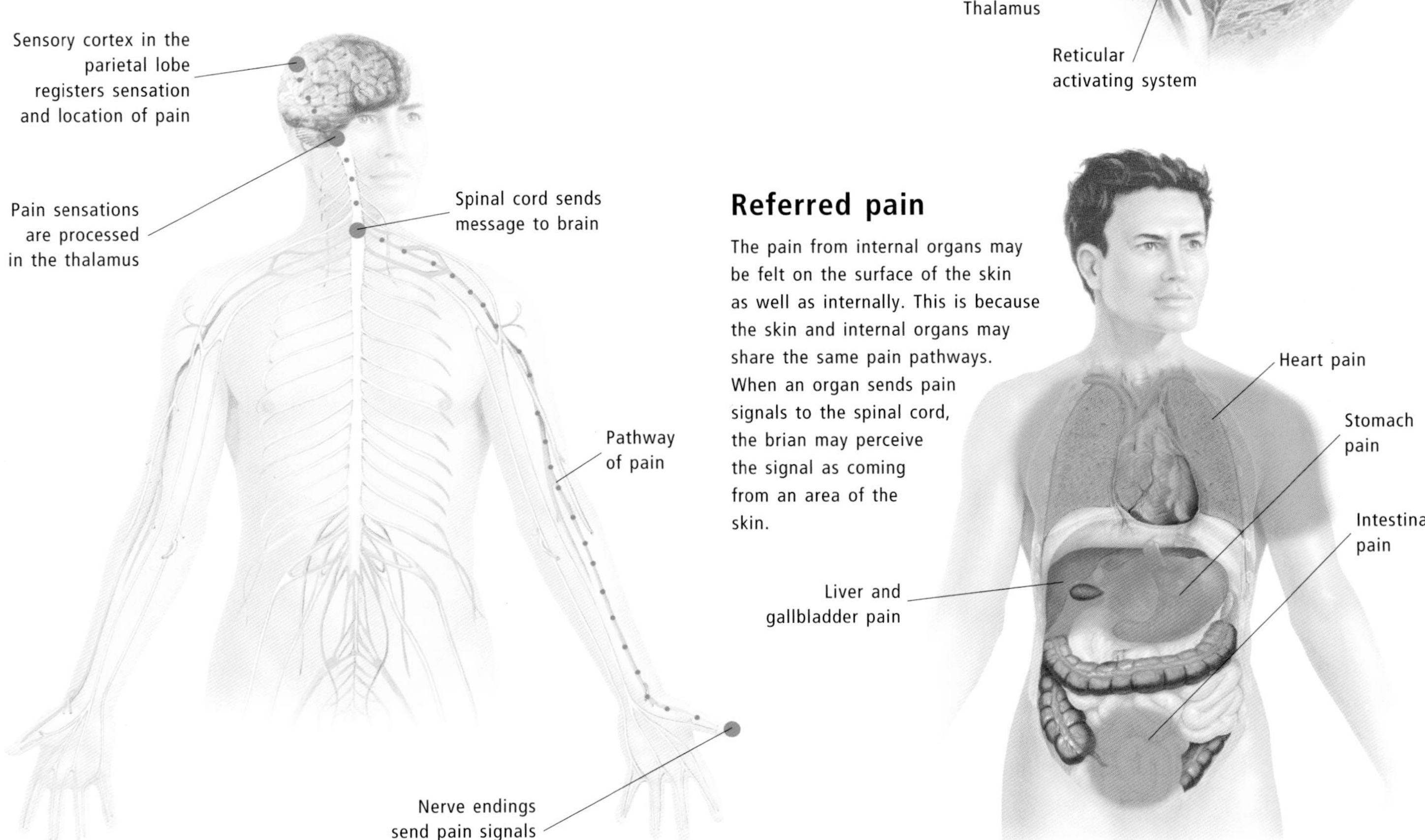

Pain pathways

When sensory neurons (nociceptors) in skin, muscles, joints or internal organs are activated by pain they send signals along nerve fibers to the spinal cord. From there the signals pass up the spinal cord to the brain stem and on to the thalamus and cerebral cortex where the sensation of pain is registered.

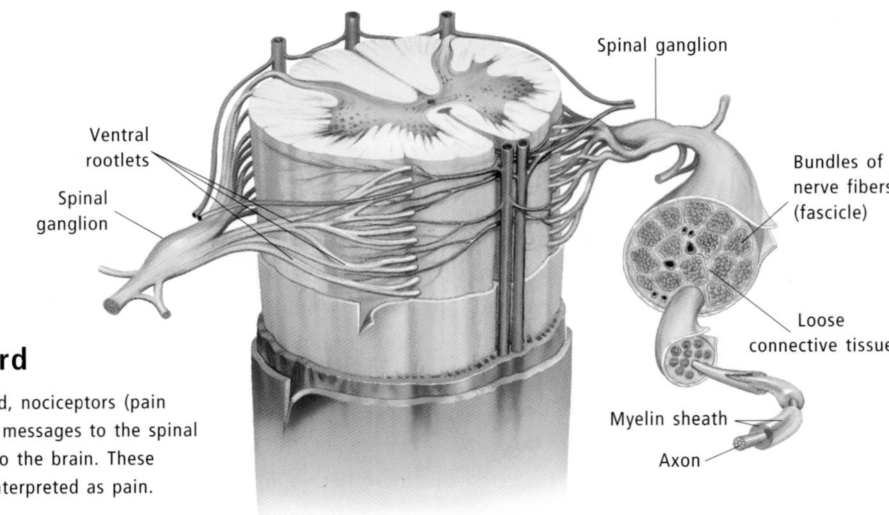

Spinal cord

When stimulated, nociceptors (pain receptors) send messages to the spinal cord and then to the brain. These messages are interpreted as pain.

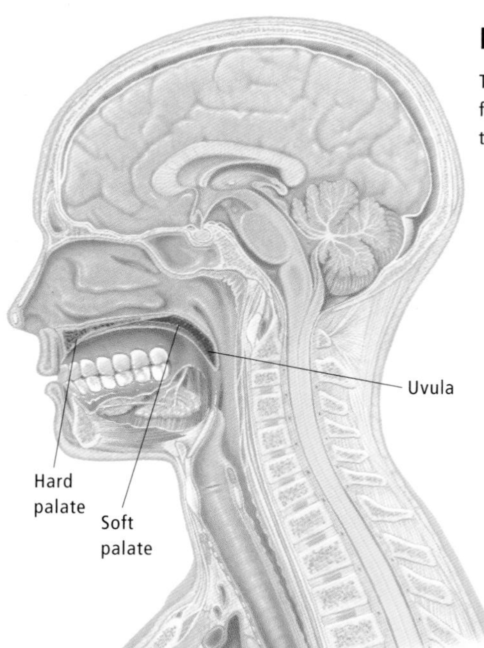

Palate

The hard palate extends back from the top teeth, separating the oral and nasal cavities.

Posterior wall of pharynx
Soft palate
Uvula
Palatoglossal arch

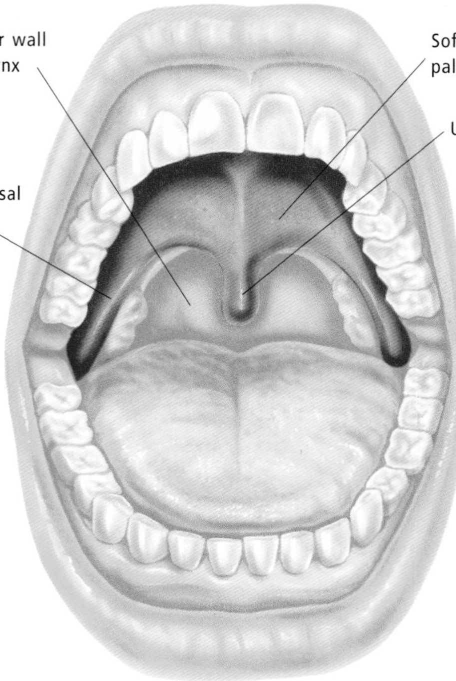

Palate—front view

The soft palate is mainly composed of muscle fibers and mucous membrane. The uvula is its most prominent feature.

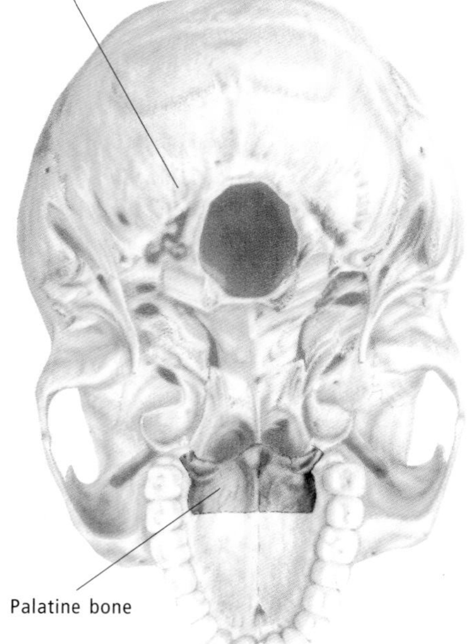

Palatine bone

Situated at the back of the nasal cavity, the palatine bone forms part of the hard palate.

PALATE

The roof of the mouth, separating the oral and nasal cavities, is called the palate. It comprises two sections—one hard, the other soft. Both are covered by mucous membrane containing numerous lubricating glands that keep the mouth and throat moist.

Much of the hard palate, extending from directly behind the top teeth, is formed by parts of the upper jaw bones, or maxillae. These normally fuse at the midline during fetal development. If this fails to occur, it leaves an opening or cleft along the midline which may extend from the teeth to the nasal cavity. This is known as cleft palate and is usually surgically repaired during early childhood. The posterior section of the hard palate is formed by the two L-shaped palatine bones of the skull. Ridges on the hard palate help with maneuvering food in the mouth during chewing and swallowing. When the mouth is closed, the tongue rests on the hard palate.

The soft palate is the fleshy structure that extends from the edge of the hard palate at the back of the mouth. Its own edge is like an incomplete curtain suspended between the back of the mouth and the beginning of the throat (pharynx). The soft palate is composed of muscle fibers and mucous membrane. A small cone-shaped projection, the uvula, hangs from the middle of the soft palate. Both the soft palate and uvula move up during swallowing or sucking to stop food entering the nasal cavity.

SEE ALSO *Jaw, Mouth, Teeth*

PALATINE BONE

The palatine bone is an irregularly shaped bone at the back of the nasal cavity that forms part of the hard palate. It consists of a horizontal plate in the bony palate and a vertical plate that has three projections, or processes, which help form the floor of the eye socket, the outer wall of the nasal cavity and other adjoining parts of the skull.

SEE ALSO *Nose, Palate, Skull*

PALLIATIVE CARE

Palliative care is defined by the World Health Organization as "the active total care of a person whose disease is not responsive to curative treatment". The aim of palliative care is to meet the needs of the whole person—their physical, psychosocial and spiritual needs—as well as those of their family in order to give them the best quality and quantity of life possible under the circumstances. Palliative treatments relieve but do not cure.

Many treatments and therapies for terminal illnesses can prolong the life of the patient for many years, which makes palliative care a complex mix of managing symptoms and therapies, and providing emotional support to prepare the patient and their family for the inevitability of death.

To be effective, palliative care must provide for the needs of the patient coping with the rigors of therapy as well as maintain, as much as possible, a level of physical, mental and social functioning which is satisfactory to the patient. Palliative care has become a subspeciality of medicine in many countries.

When a person is dying, the most important goal is comfort. Forms of comfort include: pain medication which is tailored to the needs of the individual patient; drugs, oxygen therapy and emotional support to relieve shortness of breath; the management of incontinence with drugs, catheters or disposable products; products to relieve dry mouth, such as fluids, humidified air, ice to suck on, or medication; the support and care needed in order to sleep as much as necessary; and an understanding that a patient's appetite may alter or fluctuate.

Other factors that can enhance comfort and dignity are personal grooming—a daily bath, change of sheets or clothes, hair styling or manicure if that is important to the patient; attention to skin care to ensure the avoidance of bed sores; and proper care of teeth, mouth and dentures.

Emotional and spiritual support is also very important. Family, friends and community and health care professionals who can offer honest, compassionate communication about the treatment as well as arranging personal affairs and helping the person to prepare for death are paramount. Patients benefit from being involved in treatment decisions for as long as possible. Working through any unresolved issues is also important for both the patient and their family and carers. People with religious or spiritual beliefs may find they receive support and comfort from priests or counselors. It is common for a person who is dying to feel depressed and this can be alleviated with counseling and medication. The patient and family may need help talking about their needs, wants and expectations and may also need assistance getting any necessary documents, such as a will, finalized.

SEE ALSO *Death*

PALLIDOTOMY

Pallidotomy is a surgical procedure used in the treatment of nervous system disorders such as Parkinson's disease, during which a part of the globus pallidus in the brain is destroyed. It is used to reduce symptoms such as involuntary movements, tremors, slow movement and rigidity.

A wire probe is inserted into the globus pallidus, which lies deep within the brain in the corpus striatum. Radio waves are transmitted via the probe, causing surrounding tissue to heat up, destroying cells in a precisely targeted area of the sensorimotor section of the globus pallidus.

Pallidotomy may be used when medication fails. Possible side effects include impaired vision.

SEE ALSO *Brain, Nervous system, Parkinson's disease*

PALPITATIONS

Usually, a person is not aware of the beating of their heart. However, when the heart beats rapidly or irregularly, there may be an awareness of the heartbeat, and these noticeable beats are referred to as palpitations.

Palpitations are often a normal response to anxiety, fear, exertion, excitement, excessive smoking, or drinking too much coffee. They may also be a symptom of abnormal heart rhythms (arrhythmias), such as fibrillation or tachycardia.

These may be caused by disease of the heart, such as coronary artery disease, or by other diseases, such as anemia or thyrotoxicosis. Palpitations may be accompanied by other symptoms such as chest pain, shortness of breath, or feelings of lightheadedness or dizziness.

Some arrhythmias, such as atrial fibrillation and ectopic beats, are usually not life threatening. Others, such as ventricular fibrillation and ventricular tachycardia, can cause cardiac arrest, a severe decrease in blood flow to tissues and organs, and death. Anyone with palpitations should therefore seek medical advice.

A physician or cardiologist may perform tests such as an electrocardiogram (EKG) and 24-hour Holter monitoring to determine the cause of palpitations. Drugs such as digitalis, quinidine, beta-blockers, calcium antagonists or disopyramide may need to be taken to control an arrhythmia.

SEE ALSO *Arrhythmia, Fibrillation, Heart, Heartbeat, Tachycardia*

PANCOAST'S SYNDROME

Pancoast's syndrome is a complex of symptoms stemming from a malignant tumor known as Pancoast's tumor in the upper part of the lung. It is brought about as neural structures in the lung are invaded and destroyed by the cancer.

Symptoms includes nerve pain (neuralgia) in the arm due to pressure on the brachial plexus, a network of nerves supplying the shoulder and arm. This pain is usually felt in the shoulder area.

Often associated with Pancoast's syndrome is another complex of symptoms known as Horner's syndrome, which includes drooping eyelids, narrowed pupils and facial dryness. Symptoms are relieved by treatment of the underlying cancer.

SEE ALSO *Cancer, Horner's syndrome, Lungs*

P

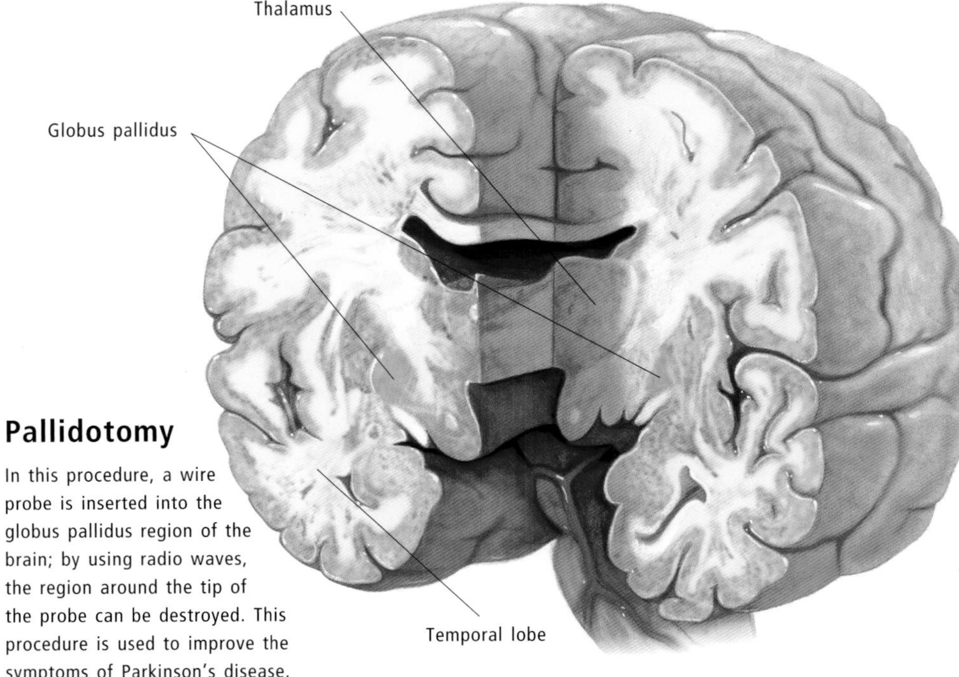

Pallidotomy

In this procedure, a wire probe is inserted into the globus pallidus region of the brain; by using radio waves, the region around the tip of the probe can be destroyed. This procedure is used to improve the symptoms of Parkinson's disease.

PANCREAS

The pancreas is a mixed gland, which has some cells which secrete enzymes into the gut (exocrine pancreas) and other cells which produce hormones which enter the bloodstream (endocrine pancreas). In other words, the pancreas is part of both the digestive and endocrine systems of the body.

The pancreas lies within the abdominal cavity, behind the stomach and in front of the large artery and vein which pass down the center of the abdomen (the aorta and inferior vena cava respectively). The pancreas has a head region which is encircled by the four parts of the duodenum. Leading off to the left from the head region are the neck, body and tail of the pancreas. The tail meets the spleen on the left of the abdomen.

The pancreas has a series of ducts within it which allow digestive enzymes to flow into the interior of the duodenum. The point at which the larger of these ducts enters the duodenum is called the ampulla of Vater. The exocrine secretions of the pancreas are slightly alkaline to neutralize the acid juices coming into the duodenum from the stomach. Enzymes in the pancreatic juices help to digest protein, fat and starch in the food.

P

Under normal circumstances, the enzymes of the pancreas are prevented from digesting the pancreas itself by three mechanisms. Firstly, the enzymes are stored within cells of the pancreas in separate compartments from the other cell proteins. Secondly, the enzymes are secreted in an inactive form. Thirdly, there are chemical inhibitors of the enzymes present within the pancreatic ducts and tissue.

The endocrine function of the pancreas is concerned with both foodstuff storage after meals and foodstuff release during fasting. The two pancreatic hormones responsible for these functions are respectively insulin and glucagon, which are produced in special cell types within many tiny spherical clumps of pancreatic tissue—these are known as the pancreatic islets, or the islets of Langerhans.

The pancreatic islets are a type of endocrine gland, that is, a gland that secretes products directly into the bloodstream rather than onto the surface of the gut or skin. Insulin release is stimulated by rising blood levels of glucose and amino acids. The hormone in turn stimulates the uptake of sugars, protein and nucleic acids by the body's cells. Glucagon is released in response to low blood glucose and amino acid concentration. It, in turn, stimulates release of glucose, amino acids and fats from body stores.

Damage to the endocrine part of the pancreas by viruses or unknown agents may be one cause of diabetes mellitus, a condition of inadequate control of blood sugar level. In fact, some patients with chronic pancreatitis may develop diabetes mellitus as a complication.

Diseases of the pancreas

Some congenital conditions involve the pancreas. One of these is annular pancreas, in which a ring of pancreatic tissue surrounds the descending duodenum, causing upper gut obstruction in infants and adults. These patients present with vomiting after meals and x-rays often show a dilated stomach and upper duodenum. Surgery to bypass the obstructed segment will correct the problem.

Cancer of the pancreas is a very serious disease, which is a significant cause of death among men aged between 35 and 60 years. It appears to be more frequent in cigarette smokers and diabetics. It is particularly serious because early spread of the disease to nearby structures, lymph nodes and the liver is common, thus making complete surgical removal of the cancer impossible. Cancer in the head of the pancreas may obstruct the duct system of the pancreas, causing weight loss and jaundice from build-up of bile salts.

Other pancreatic cancers located in the tail of the pancreas, away from the pancreatic duct system, will produce weight loss and abdominal pain as the initial symptoms. The prognosis for pancreatic cancer is poor, with most patients dying within a year of diagnosis. Only about 10 percent of patients will survive 5 years, and complete cures are extremely rare.

Occasionally tumors may arise from the islet cells of the pancreas. Insulinomas, for example, arise from the beta cells of the islets. They produce insulin in excess amounts, which gives rise to symptoms of low blood sugar level. Patients show bizarre behavior, memory lapses, palpitations, sweating and unconsciousness. Some may even be mistakenly treated for psychiatric illness. Symptoms are relieved by food, so patients often gain weight from overeating. Treatment may be by drugs, which suppress release of insulin from the tumor, or by surgical removal if the tumor can be located.

Very rarely, gastrin-producing tumors may arise in the pancreas or duodenum. Gastrin is a hormone which controls the amount of stomach acid produced, and it is usually released in response to distension of the stomach by food. These gastrin-producing tumors are often cancers of pancreatic islet cells. They cause a condition known as Zollinger-Ellison syndrome, in which the patient develops peptic ulcers from increased gastric acid secretion, abdominal pain and diarrhea. Treatment should ideally involve locating and removing the gastrin-producing tumor, although removal of the stomach may be necessary if the tumor cannot be found.

The pancreas may be involved in a non-infective inflammatory disease known as pancreatitis. This disease may be short-term or chronic and is often due to gallstones or excessive alcohol intake. The precise sequence of events leading to the disease is poorly understood, but damage to the pancreas is known to be due to release of pancreatic enzymes into pancreatic tissue, with digestion of the pancreas by the patient's own digestive enzymes. Patients will experience nausea, vomiting and upper abdominal pain which may radiate through to the back.

Complications of the disease include the formation of pus-filled abscesses, and cysts filled with digestive enzymes. Treatment is usually medical for acute cases, and is aimed at relieving pain, correcting fluid imbalance and reducing the production of digestive enzymes by the pancreas. Surgery may be necessary for chronic cases.

SEE ALSO *Amino acids, Diabetes, Digestive system, Endocrine system, Islets of Langerhans, Insulin, Pancreatitis, Zollinger-Ellison syndrome*

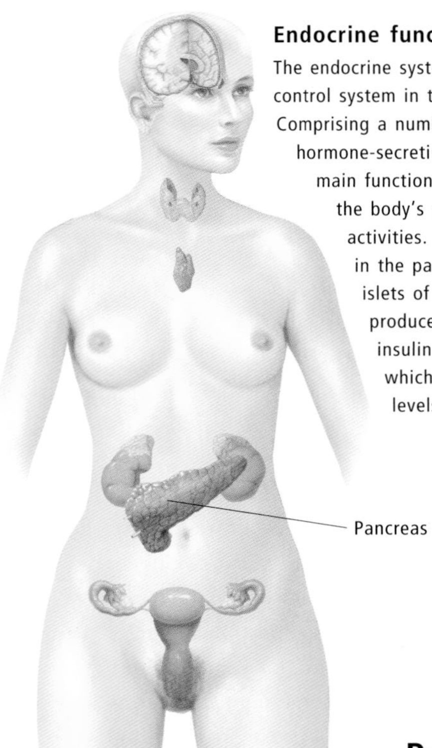

Endocrine function

The endocrine system is a major control system in the body. Comprising a number of hormone-secreting glands, its main function is regulating the body's metabolic activities. Endocrine cells in the pancreas—the islets of Langerhans—produce the hormones insulin and glucagon which control sugar levels in the body.

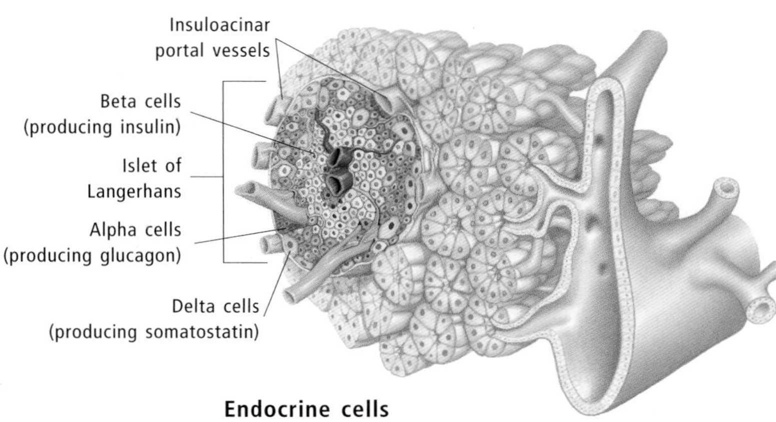

Endocrine cells

Clusters of hormone-producing endocrine cells—the islets of Langerhans—are scattered throughout the pancreas. Alpha cells secrete glucagon which elevates blood sugar. Beta cells secrete insulin which affects the metabolism of fats, proteins and carbohydrates. Delta cells secrete somatostatin which can inhibit the release of both glucagon and insulin.

Pancreas

The pancreas plays two different roles in the body. Most of its cells (the exocrine acinar cells) secrete enzymes into the gut and are part of the digestive system. Other cells (in the islets of Langerhans) produce hormones which enter the bloodstream and are part of the endocrine system.

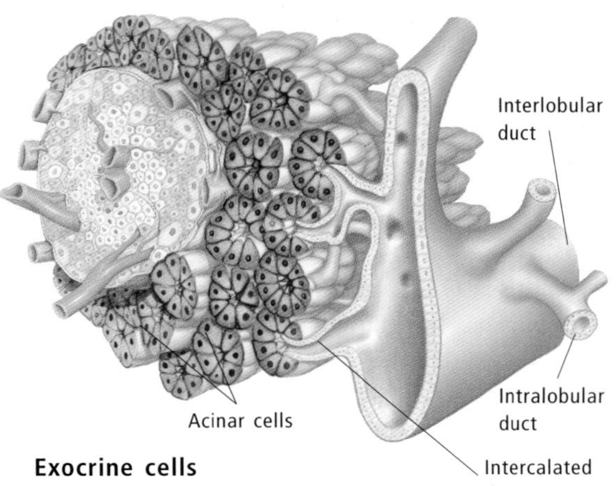

Exocrine cells

Most of the pancreas consists of acinar cells which secrete digestive enzymes that aid in food processing. The enzymes flow from the cells into the small intestine along a network of attached ducts.

Stomach

Pancreas

Small intestine

Pancreas—digestive function

The pancreas lies in the abdominal cavity just behind the stomach. The exocrine part of the pancreas secretes enzymes which flow into the small intestine and help the body break down food and extract nutrients.

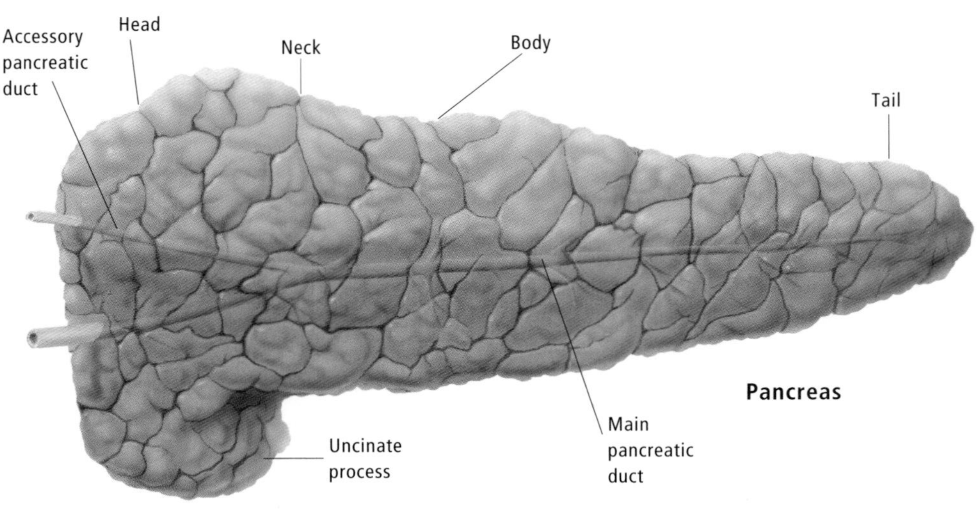

Pancreas

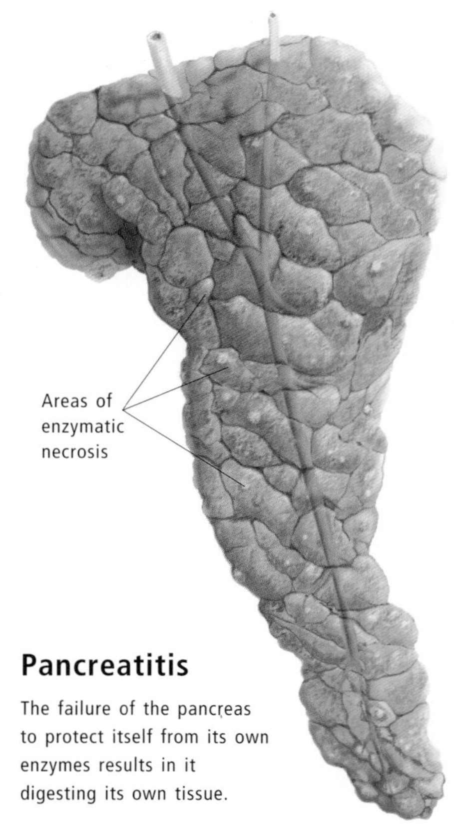

Pancreatitis

The failure of the pancreas to protect itself from its own enzymes results in it digesting its own tissue.

PANCREATITIS

Pancreatitis is a non-bacterial inflammation of the pancreas. It is caused by the digestion of the tissue of the pancreas by its own enzymes. Pancreatitis may be acute, with a sudden onset and relatively short duration, or chronic, lasting for weeks to months with frequent relapses.

Individuals suffering acute pancreatitis experience a sudden onset of pain in the upper abdomen, nausea and vomiting, and have increased concentrations of the digestive enzyme amylase in their blood. Acute pancreatitis may be caused by gallstones (about 40 percent of cases), excessive alcohol intake (a further 40 percent of cases), increased levels of calcium or fats in the blood, surgery or drugs, such as corticosteroids, diuretics and oral contraceptives.

Complications of acute pancreatitis include the formation in the pancreas of abscesses, or pus-filled cavities, and a pancreatic pseudocyst (a cavity filled with fluid rich in digestive enzymes). Treatment does not usually involve surgery unless complications are experienced. Medical treatment can include fluid replacement, pain relief, gastric suction and the control of blood calcium levels.

Chronic pancreatitis is often caused by alcoholism. Patients with chronic pancreatitis suffer recurrent bouts of abdominal pain and problems with absorbing food, and frequently develop diabetes mellitus. Treatment may be medical, as described for acute pancreatitis, or involve surgery to relieve chronic pain.

SEE ALSO *Alcoholism, Diabetes, Gallstones, Pancreas*

PANIC ATTACKS

Panic attacks are a form of anxiety disorder. They can occur in people who also suffer agoraphobia but may happen without warning to people with no previous history or symptoms of such disorders.

A panic attack is characterized by all the physical and emotional signs of a body in danger. The nervous system is activated where no obvious danger exists; there may be chest pain, shortness of breath, irregular or accelerated heartbeat, sweating, dizziness, trembling, weakness, nausea and feelings of fear and a desire to escape. With no apparent reason for the attack, there is no obvious means of escape, and fear of further attacks can lead to staying only in safe areas. The sufferer may stay home through fear of having an attack in a public place, or may only leave home if accompanied. There is a loss of confidence and inability to cope.

Specialist treatment is readily available and should be sought before the disorder creates further problems. Treatment may involve drugs in combination with behavior therapy to help the sufferer understand what causes the attacks and to control the fear of having them.

SEE ALSO *Agoraphobia, Anxiety, Anxiolytics, Behavior therapy*

PAP SMEAR

The Pap smear (or Papanicolaou smear) is a cervical cell sample prepared for viewing under a microscope.

It can reveal the presence of precancerous and cancerous cells in the cervix and is regarded as a crucial screening test that should be performed regularly throughout a woman's life, starting from the time she becomes sexually active.

Since its introduction in the 1940s, the Pap smear has contributed to a massive worldwide reduction in deaths due to cervical cancer.

Taking the smear is a simple and painless procedure that can be performed in a doctor's office. Medical advice should be sought on the frequency with which Pap smears need to be taken because it may vary according to a patient's personal history.

SEE ALSO *Cervix, Reproductive systems*

PAPILLEDEMA

A serious eye disorder, papilledema involves inflammation and swelling of the optic disk, at the point where the optic nerve joins the eye. It is caused by increased pressure inside the brain, often due to a tumor, infections such as meningitis, or cerebral hemorrhage. Symptoms may include blurred or double vision, headaches and nausea. Partial blindness can develop quickly. Papilledema requires immediate medical attention.

SEE ALSO *Eye, Optic nerve*

PAPILLOMA

A papilloma is a non-cancerous growth or tumor on the skin or a mucous membrane. Usually, it is covered by a thickened outer skin layer (epidermis). Warts are among the best known papillomas and are caused by viruses (human papilloma virus, or HPV). Corns, which develop with repeated rubbing of the skin, are also regarded as papillomas.

SEE ALSO *Epidermis, Warts*

Papilloma

Warts and corns are two types of papilloma—a non-cancerous growth on the skin or a mucous membrane.

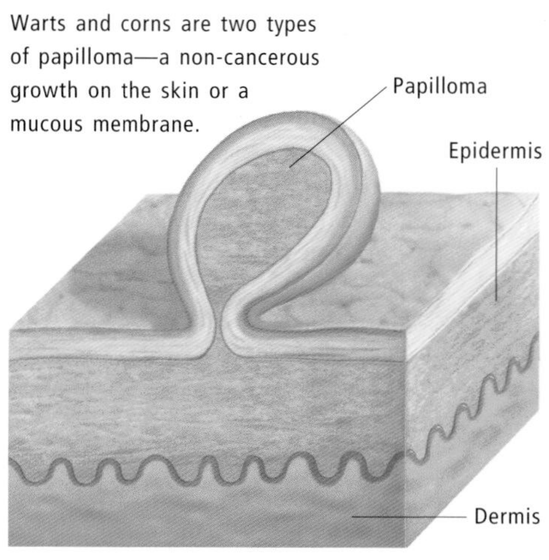

PARACENTESIS

Paracentesis (also known as abdominal tap or peritoneal tap) is a medical procedure which involves removing fluid from a body cavity, usually from within the abdomen. It can be performed in a doctor's treatment room or a hospital. A specialized needle is inserted through the body wall, after the area has first been numbed with a local anesthetic, and fluid is then drawn off. An incision may be needed to assist insertion of the needle.

Paracentesis is commonly used to sample excessive abdominal fluid (ascites) to test for its cause, check for internal bleeding or relieve the effects of fluid build-up.

SEE ALSO *Abdomen, Ascites*

PARALYSIS

Paralysis is the loss of the ability to move a part of the body. It is caused by the inability to contract one or more muscles and usually results from injury to the brain, the spinal cord, a nerve or a muscle. It may be partial or full, and is usually accompanied by a loss of sensation.

There are many causes leading to paralysis; all of them involve an injury or disruption to the nerve pathway through which signals are sent from the brain to the muscles to instruct them to move. The disruption may be in the brain, for example, as a result of stroke (the most common cause), brain tumor, hemorrhage or infection (encephalitis). It may be in the spinal cord, for example, due to injury from trauma (also very common), or pressure on the spinal cord from disk prolapse (herniation) or from spondylosis.

Diseases of the spinal cord, such as multiple sclerosis, poliomyelitis, motor neuron disorders of the peripheral nervous system (neuropathies) and muscle disorders, such as muscular dystrophy, are less common causes of paralysis.

The kind and degree of paralysis differs according to whether the damage is to a peripheral nerve or to the central nervous system (brain and spinal cord). Damage to a peripheral nerve can cause loss of the ability to move a particular muscle or muscles, and a consequent wasting away of those muscles. Damage to the central nervous system, by comparison, produces weakness or loss of the use of a group of muscles, frequently affecting an entire limb. The muscles are stiff when moved (spasticity) but there is no wasting.

Paralysis of the cranial nerves in the head and neck causes paralysis of the facial, throat and eye muscles, causing difficulty speaking and swallowing, and blurred or double vision.

If there is partial or complete paralysis of both legs (and sometimes the trunk), the condition is known as paraplegia. If the arms are also affected, it is called quadriplegia (also called tetraplegia). These conditions are caused by damage to the spinal cord, usually from trauma (most commonly road accidents and sporting injuries), but may also be caused by spinal cord tumors or birth defects. An injury to the neck results in quadriplegia, while an injury to the chest or lower back can result in paraplegia. Hemiplegia is paralysis of the limbs on the same side of the body, often the result of a brain tumor or stroke. The weakness or paralysis occurs on the side of the body opposite to the side of the brain which has been affected.

When the spinal cord is damaged, other disabilities usually occur, such as loss of

Paralysis

The disruption of nerve pathways by disease or injury, especially in the brain and spinal cord, can result in the paralysis of body parts.

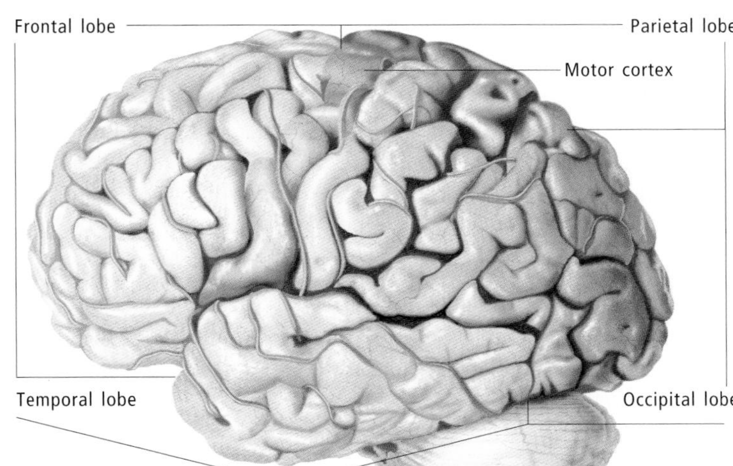

Paralysis—hemiplegia

A brain tumor or stroke may damage the motor cortex of the brain, causing hemiplegia. Paralysis occurs on the side of the body opposite to the damaged side of the brain.

P

urinary and bowel control, impaired sexual function, loss of normal blood pressure, loss of control of body-temperature, constipation, and breathing difficulties.

Treatment of paralysis requires treating the underlying cause, where possible. Immediate treatment may mean hospitalization, which may take place in intensive care with artificial ventilation if breathing muscles are affected.

Surgery may be possible to limit further spinal-cord damage or to remove bone fragments or a tumor if necessary. Peripheral nerve injuries can be helped by nerve transplants, orthopedic operations to immobilize a joint (arthrodesis), or the transplant of the tendon of a working muscle to aid paralyzed muscles.

Physical therapy and rehabilitation play an important part in the treatment of paralysis. With rehabilitation, many lost functions can be compensated for or restored. Passive exercises for paralyzed muscles will help prevent contractures. Physical therapy will prevent joint stiffness.

Someone who has been in an accident and has neck pain or possible spinal cord injury should not be moved unless absolutely necessary. The injured person's neck should be immobilized with splints or pillows to prevent movement until an ambulance or other emergency service arrives.

SEE ALSO *Brain, Hemiplegia, Nerves, Nervous system, Paraplegia, Quadriplegia, Rehabilitation, Spinal cord*

PARANOIA

Paranoia, or paranoid disorders, are usually classified as personality disorders. People with psychotic disorders, such as schizophrenia or bipolar disorder, may also suffer from paranoid delusions.

Individuals with paranoia suffer from delusions of persecution and are always searching for evidence to support their suspicions. Hostility towards others and angry reactions to perceived insults are also characteristic of paranoia.

In some cases, delusions of grandeur may accompany the feelings of persecution.

SEE ALSO *Personality disorders, Psychosis*

PARAPLEGIA

Paraplegia is partial or full paralysis of the body below the chest or waist, involving the trunk and lower limbs. If all four limbs are affected the condition is known as quadriplegia or tetraplegia.

Paraplegia is caused by damage to the spinal cord, usually from trauma (most commonly the result of road accidents or sports injuries), which disrupts the nerve pathways that connect the brain and muscles. Males between 15 and 35 years old are the group most commonly affected. Less frequently, paraplegia is caused by spinal cord tumors or birth defects.

In paraplegia, all body parts below the level at which the spinal cord is damaged are affected. In addition to paralysis, this may mean constipation, problems with blood pressure and sexual function, as well as the inability to control body temperature or bowel and urinary movements. Treatment as soon as possible

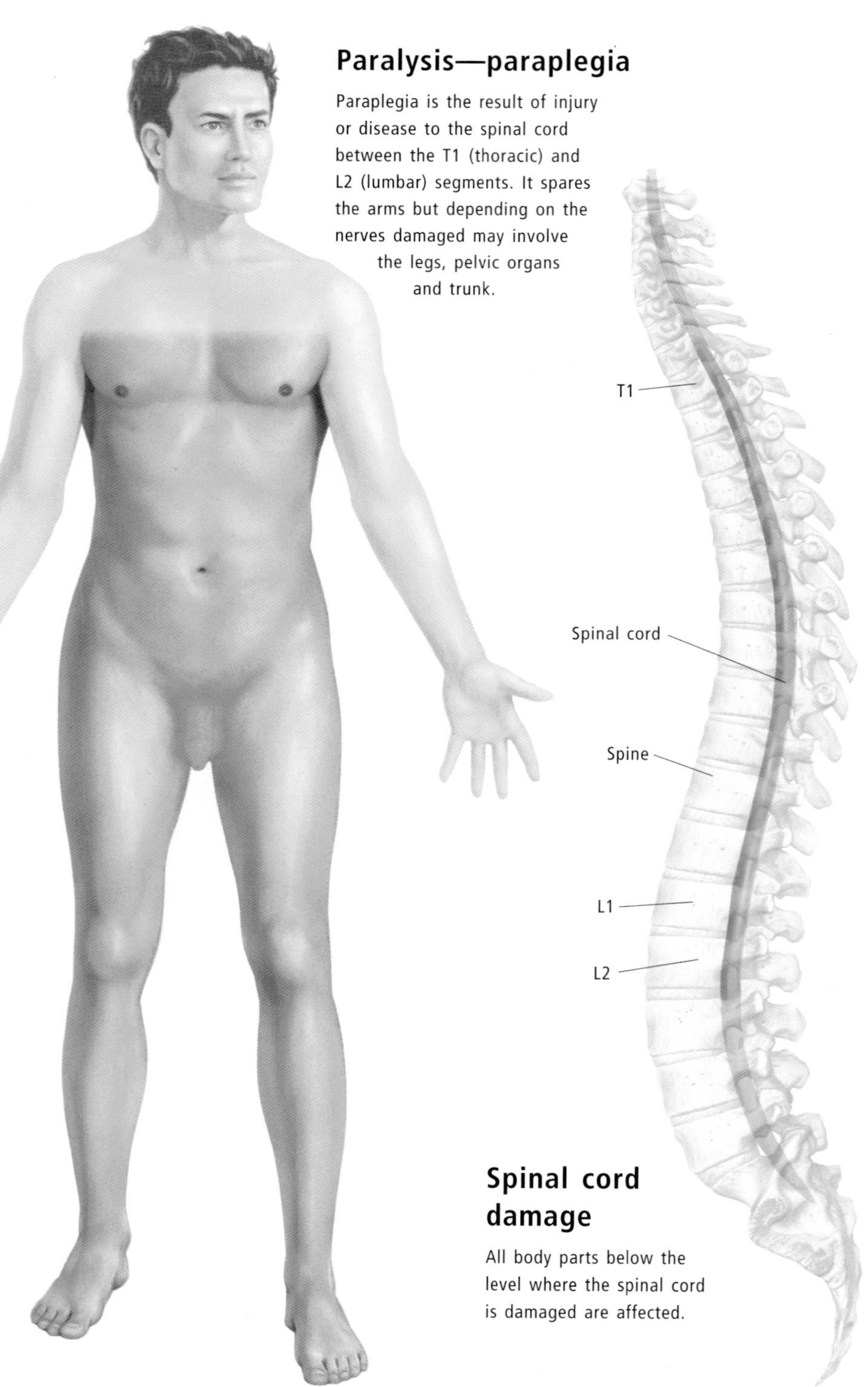

Paralysis—paraplegia

Paraplegia is the result of injury or disease to the spinal cord between the T1 (thoracic) and L2 (lumbar) segments. It spares the arms but depending on the nerves damaged may involve the legs, pelvic organs and trunk.

Spinal cord damage

All body parts below the level where the spinal cord is damaged are affected.

after the injury will provide the injured person with the greatest chance of recovering some function. Treatment may include surgery in order to remove fluid or tissue that presses on the spinal cord (decompression laminectomy), to remove bone fragments or foreign objects, or to stabilize fractured vertebrae by fusion of the bones or insertion of hardware. Bed rest and spinal traction (which immobilizes the spine and reduces dislocation) will promote healing.

If movement or sensation return within 1 week after the injury, then most function will eventually be recovered (although this may take 6 months or more). Losses that remain after 6 months are likely to be permanent. Approximately one-third of sufferers remain permanently wheelchair-bound.

Most treatment for paraplegia is therefore centered around rehabilitation. Passive exercises for paralyzed muscles will help prevent contractures. Physical therapy will prevent joint stiffness. Occupational therapy and psychotherapy or counseling may help depression or sexual problems. Prolonged immobility can cause serious complications; for this reason, frequent position changes and good skin care are very important. Complications such as bed sores, kidney stones, muscle spasms and leg ulcers need to be treated immediately.

Paraplegics will need to come to terms with permanently reduced mobility and may require help with accommodation, employment, transport, access to buildings, and in dealing with the financial costs and isolation. Life expectancy for a paraplegic is on average 90 percent of that expected by the able-bodied population.

In many cases, paraplegia can be prevented. Paraplegia often results from road accidents, so drinking alcohol or using mind-altering drugs before or during driving should always be avoided. Seat belts should be worn in cars. In the case of sporting accidents, it is advisable to wear protective headgear for contact sports or while riding a bicycle or motorcycle. Do not dive into shallow swimming pools or into water of unknown depth.

SEE ALSO *Nervous system, Paralysis, Quadriplegia, Rehabilitation, Spinal cord*

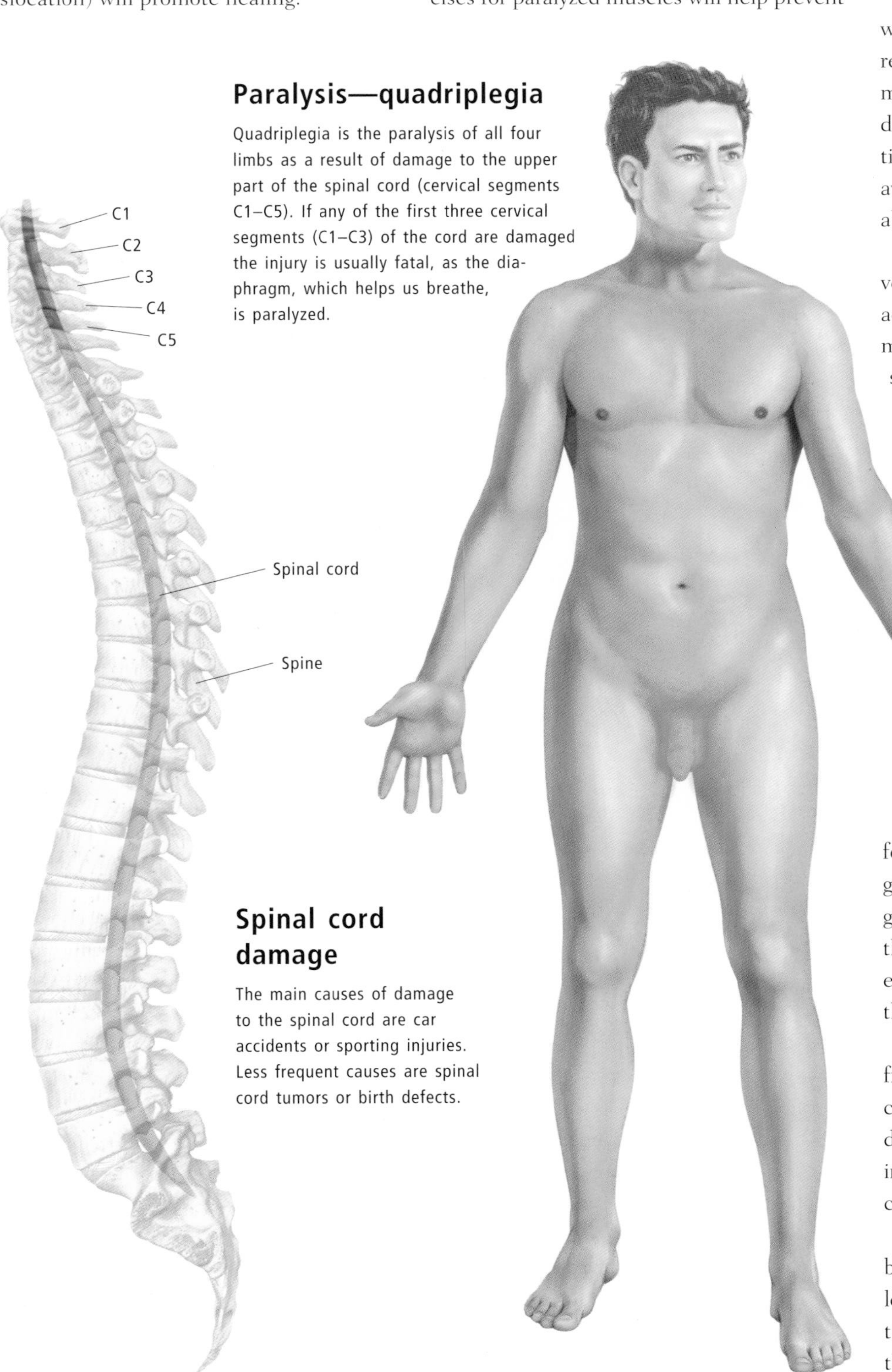

Paralysis—quadriplegia

Quadriplegia is the paralysis of all four limbs as a result of damage to the upper part of the spinal cord (cervical segments C1–C5). If any of the first three cervical segments (C1–C3) of the cord are damaged the injury is usually fatal, as the diaphragm, which helps us breathe, is paralyzed.

Spinal cord damage

The main causes of damage to the spinal cord are car accidents or sporting injuries. Less frequent causes are spinal cord tumors or birth defects.

PARATHYROID GLANDS

The parathyroid glands are four (or occasionally three) small endocrine glands, which lie just behind the thyroid gland in the neck. The glands are only about the size of peas. Sometimes these glands are embedded within the thyroid gland itself; they may occasionally be found in the chest.

Each parathyroid gland comprises a fibrous tissue capsule and two types of cell called chief and oxyphil cells. Chief cells produce parathyroid hormone, which is involved in the control of calcium and phosphate concentrations in the blood.

A reduction in the levels of calcium in the blood stimulates the parathyroid gland to release parathyroid hormone. This hormone in turn stimulates the release of calcium from the bones by increasing the activity of cells

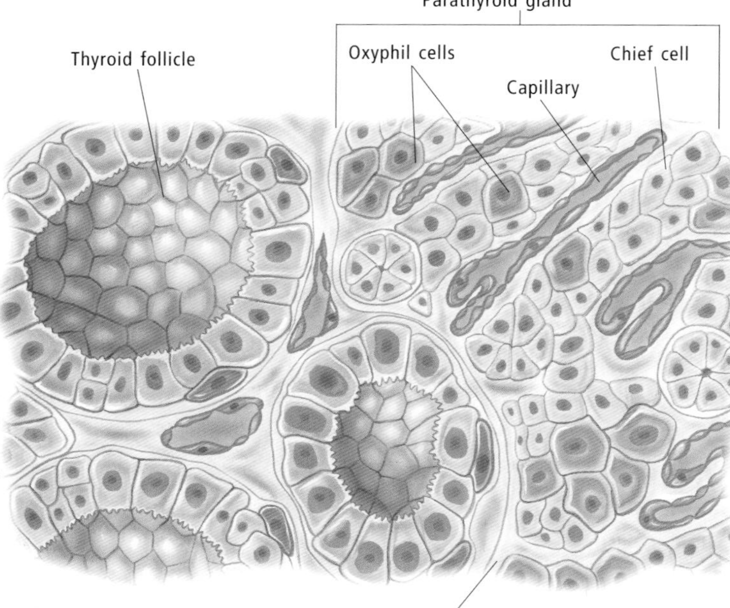

Parathyroid gland microstructure
The cells of the parathyroid are separated from thyroid cells by a dense capsule of fibers. The parathyroid contains two different cells: chief cells and oxyphil cells. Chief cells produce parathyroid hormone when blood levels of calcium fall.

Parathyroid glands
These tiny glands lie behind the thyroid gland at the base of the neck. They secrete parathyroid hormone which controls calcium levels in the blood.

called osteoclasts, which break down the mineral part of bone.

If levels of blood calcium are too high, another hormone called calcitonin is released by the thyroid gland and acts to decrease the levels. If the parathyroid gland is too active (hyperparathyroidism) excess parathyroid hormone causes decreased concentration of phosphate and increased concentration of calcium in the blood. Reduced parathyroid activity (hypoparathyroidism) causes an increase in blood phosphate and decreased blood calcium.

SEE ALSO *Calcium, Endocrine glands, Glands, Hormones, Thyroid gland*

PARATYPHOID

Paratyphoid is a gastrointestinal disease caused by certain forms of *Salmonella* bacteria. It occurs throughout the world but, because it is spread via food or water contaminated by feces or urine from an infected person, outbreaks occur mainly where sewerage and sanitation systems are inadequate. Symptoms, similar to but usually less severe than those of typhoid, appear between one and ten days after consuming a contaminated product. They include headaches, watery diarrhea, a rosy chest and abdominal rash, and dry cough. In severe cases, the disease can cause intestinal bleeding, mental fogginess and minor deafness. Death is rare when medical attention is provided. Treatment commonly involves antibiotics.

SEE ALSO *Gastroenteritis, Typhoid*

PARKINSON'S DISEASE

First described in 1817 by the British physician James Parkinson, Parkinson's disease is a disease of the central nervous system, characterized by gradual, progressive muscle rigidity, tremors and clumsiness.

The affected person suffers muscle stiffness and slowness, has a mask-like expression and an awkward or shuffling walk with a stooped posture, and talks in a slow, monotonous voice. Walking, talking, or completing other simple tasks becomes progressively more difficult. The symptoms are made worse by tiredness or stress. Some people with Parkinson's disease become severely depressed. In the later stages of the disease, mental deterioration and dementia may occur.

Parkinson's disease affects approximately two out of 1,000 people, and most often develops after age 50; it is one of the most common neurologic disorders of the elderly. The exact cause is unknown, but common to all is a progressive deterioration of the nerve cells in the part of the brain that controls muscle movement. As a result, there is a deficiency of a neurotransmitter (a chemical that relays messages across the nerve pathways) called dopamine that is normally found in this area of the brain. Without dopamine, the nerve cells cannot properly transmit messages, and this results in abnormal firing of neurons and consequently, abnormal muscle movement. The disorder may affect one or both sides of the body, with varying degrees of loss of function.

Parkinsonism refers to those cases where Parkinson's disease occurs as a result of another disorder. It can be caused by medications (especially the phenothiazine tranquilizers), and brain disorders such as post-influenza encephalitis and some slow virus infections.

Parkinson's disease is incurable. However, symptoms can be relieved or controlled by medications, which work by increasing levels of dopamine in the brain. They include levodopa, which is converted by the body to dopamine, and carbidopa, which reduces the side effects of levodopa. These drugs are successful in decreasing tremors and reducing muscle rigidity, but they often have significant side effects. These may be controlled with antihistamines, antidepressants, bromocriptine, monoamine oxidase inhibitors, and other drugs.

Most people respond to medications, but to a variable degree. The therapeutic effect of the medications tends to wear off after a few years. Surgery to destroy parts of the nerve pathways in the brain responsible for tremors may reduce symptoms in some people. A new technique involves surgical grafting of dopamine-secreting neurons into the brains of Parkinson's sufferers. The long-term success of this technique is not yet established.

Regular rest periods and avoidance of stress will help symptoms such as tremor. Physical therapy, speech therapy, occupational therapy, social work and other counseling services help the affected person to function as normally as possible.

SEE ALSO *Nerves, Nervous system, Neurons, Palliodotomy*

PARONYCHIA

Paronychia is an infection of the skin around a nail. It is caused by bacteria, fungi (especially candida) or both. Usually the infected skin is already damaged, from biting, picking or trimming nails or from immersing hands in water for long periods, for example. The skin around the nail becomes red and swollen, and in the case of bacterial paronychia, there may be tiny abscesses. The nail is often infected as well, becoming discolored and misshapen. Treatment is with antibiotic or antifungal creams or ointments. Fungal paronychia may take some months to clear.

Paronychia is best prevented by caring for nails and the skin around them. Protective gloves should be worn to prevent exposure to detergents and chemicals. Nails should be kept smooth and should be trimmed regularly. Biting or picking at the nails, trimming the cuticles and the use of cuticle removers may worsen the condition. Diabetics are especially prone to paronychia and need to take special care.

SEE ALSO *Nails*

Parkinson's disease

Nerve cells in the substantia nigra (part of the brain stem) control muscle tone and movement. The progressive deterioration of these cells is the most common cause of Parkinson's disease, which causes muscle rigidity and tremors.

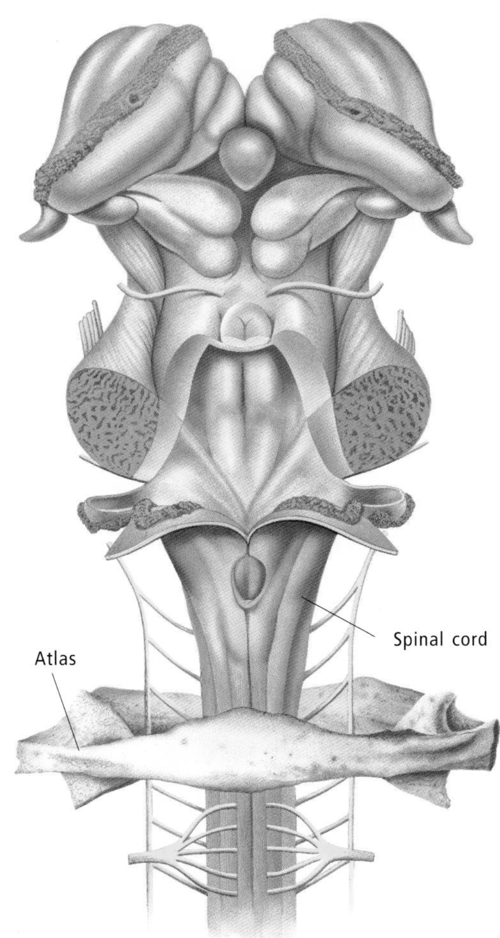

PATENT DUCTUS ARTERIOSUS

Normally the fetus receives oxygen from the placenta via the umbilical cord, so the lungs are not needed. Hence, there is a channel between the pulmonary artery and the aorta called the ductus arteriosis. The function of this duct is to allow the blood flowing through the fetal heart to bypass the lungs and be pumped straight into the systemic circulation and around the body.

Shortly after birth the duct normally closes, and the heart commences pumping blood into the lungs as well as the rest of the body. In about 60 out of 100,000 infants, the duct doesn't close properly—this condition is known as patent ductus arteriosus. It is similar to atrial septal defect except that in that condition, the hole that fails to close is between the two upper chambers of the heart (the atria). The cause is unknown, but it is more common in premature infants. Patent ductus arteriosus causes mild shortness of breath and failure to thrive, which may progress over time to heart failure.

The condition is diagnosed by a physician using a stethoscope (usually a heart murmur is audible) and an echocardiogram (ultrasound of the heart). Surgical ligation of the patent ductus corrects the condition and is usually done between 6 months and 3 years of age, earlier if heart failure develops.

SEE ALSO *Atrial septal defect, Fetal development, Heart, Lungs, Placenta*

Pectoral muscles

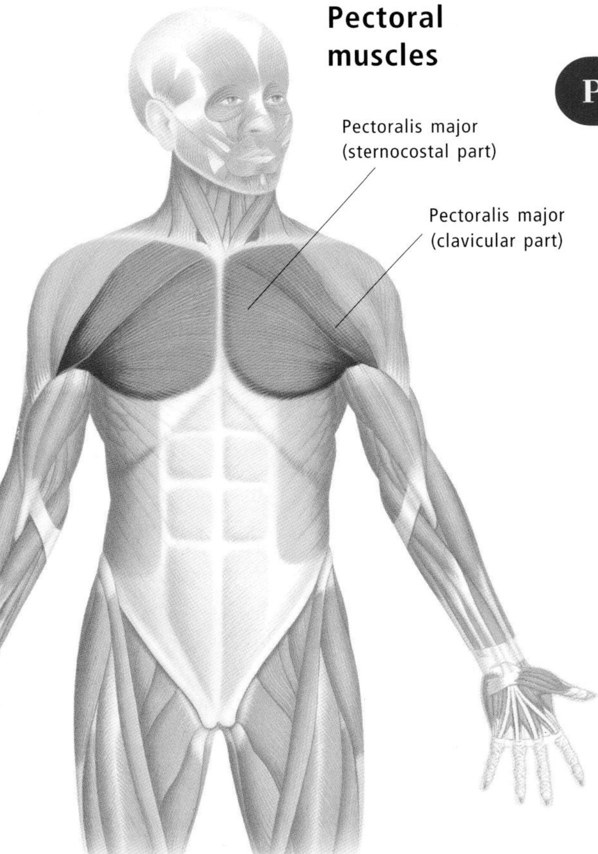

PECTORAL MUSCLES

The pectoral muscles lie in the front of the chest, under the breasts. There are two on each side: the pectoralis major and pectoralis minor. They arise mainly from the collar bone (clavicle), sternum and rib cage, and are attached to the humerus in the upper arm and the

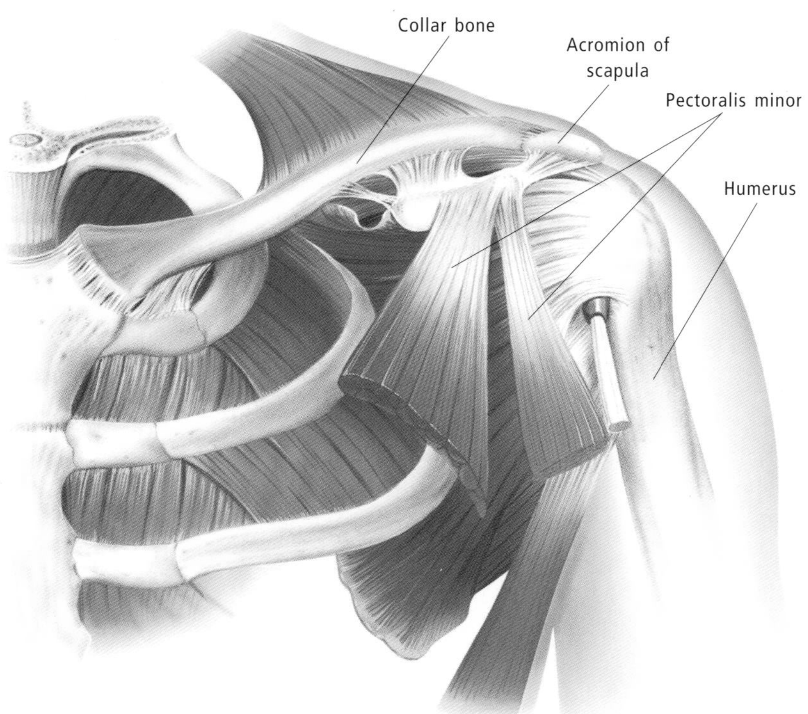

Pectoral muscles

The pectoral muscles cover the front of the chest and are attached to the shoulder and humerus. They work in combination with the scapula to control the movement of the humerus (the upper arm bone).

coracoid process of the shoulder blade (scapula). The pectoralis major can be felt under the breast when the muscle is tensed by attempting to pull a fixed object sideways towards one's midline.

SEE ALSO *Chest, Collar bone, Muscle, Ribs, Scapula, Sternum*

PELLAGRA

Due to the progressive nature of its symptoms, pellagra is sometimes called the disease of the four Ds: dermatitis, diarrhea, dementia and death. It is caused by a deficiency in niacin (one of the B group vitamins) or the amino acid tryptophan, which is used by the body to make niacin. It usually stems from poor diet and can develop rapidly—within 8 weeks in people with severe deficiencies.

Loss of appetite, falling weight, irritability and lack of energy are early signs. A scaly, sun-sensitive skin rash and diarrhea follow. Mental disturbances, including depression, delirium and ultimately dementia, appear in chronic cases. Without treatment, death is inevitable. Oral vitamin B supplements, however, are a simple and effective remedy, usually evoking a rapid turnaround of symptoms within 24 hours.

These days pellagra is rare in industrialized countries, although it is occasionally seen in alcoholics. It is more common in poor nations where people have inadequate nutrition. African populations that rely on a diet of corn, and little else, are particularly susceptible because this grain, unlike wheat, contains virtually no tryptophan. Foods rich in niacin or tryptophan include liver, eggs, milk, red meat, fish, wholegrain products, yeast, peas, beans and nuts.

SEE ALSO *Amino acids, Vitamins*

PELVIC FLOOR MUSCLES

The pelvic floor muscles form a "floor" or diaphragm across the pelvis, running from the back to the front and in from the sides. Strung like a hammock between the sacrum at the back and the hip bones at the front and sides, these muscles support the bladder and bowel and, in women, the uterus.

The pelvic floor muscles have openings for the urethra (the tube that connects the bladder to the outside of the body), the anus (anal canal) and, in women, the vagina.

In some conditions, the pelvic floor muscles can become overstretched and weakened. These conditions include pregnancy (especially repeated pregnancy), advanced age, and menopause; disorders that increase pressure in the abdomen, such as tumors, chronic coughing and chronic constipation; or activities such as continuous lifting. Stretched and weak pelvic floor muscles can have several consequences: uterine prolapse (a disorder in which the uterus moves down, out of its normal position); urinary incontinence (the leaking of urine during coughing, straining or physical exertion); rectal prolapse; and in women, difficulty keeping tampons in place.

The treatment of weakened pelvic floor muscles involves exercises to strengthen and tighten them. The exercises should be performed daily and may need to be continued indefinitely. These exercises include tightening one at a time, the openings from front to back, or back to front, or interrupting urination in mid-stream. The exercises should be practised during and after each pregnancy. An exercise program can be obtained from a physician, a physical therapist or from a childbirth clinic.

SEE ALSO *Bladder, Bowel, Hip, Intestines, Pelvis, Prolapse, Sacrum, Urinary incontinence, Uterus*

PELVIC INFLAMMATORY DISEASE

Pelvic inflammatory disease involves infection of the female reproductive organs above the level of the uterine cervix. This type of infection is serious for several reasons. Firstly, infection may spread throughout the abdominal cavity, giving rise to peritonitis. Secondly, infection may spread to nearby pelvic organs to create an abscess. Thirdly, pelvic inflammatory disease is a common cause of infertility because the fallopian tubes may become blocked by scar tissue during healing.

Most pelvic infections are caused by bacteria. They may occur after childbirth or termination of pregnancy, in which case invasion of the tissues by bacteria (*Clostridium, E. coli, Streptococcus*) is rapid and the patient may be at great risk of dying from septicemia. Where the infection is due to the bacteria *Neisseria gonocccus* (gonorrhea), the progress is usually slower, with the patient complaining of vaginal discharge, fever, burning when passing urine, and pelvic pain.

Long-term pelvic infection may cause abnormal periods, menstrual pain, painful intercourse and infertility. Treatment for pelvic inflammatory disease includes the appropriate antibiotic and pain relief, although surgery may be required for complications of chronic infection.

Pelvic inflammatory disease is an important social problem because of its link to sexually transmitted diseases such as gonorrhea, and the increasing incidence of infection with drug-resistant bacteria.

SEE ALSO *Cervix, Fallopian tubes, Gonorrhea, Infertility, Peritonitis, Reproductive systems*

PELVIS

The term pelvis (from the Latin meaning "basin") encompasses a number of structures. It can refer to the bony pelvis, a ring of bone between the trunk and thigh. It can refer to the lesser or true pelvis, the part of the bony pelvis below the pelvic inlet, or may refer to the pelvic cavity, a funnel-shaped region within the lesser or true pelvis that contains pelvic organs, including the bladder, rectum and internal genitalia. Usually the term refers to the lesser pelvis.

Bony pelvis

The bony pelvis forms the skeletal framework for the pelvis and is mostly covered by muscles. It functions to transfer weight from the vertebral column to the lower limbs as well as to provide protection for the pelvic and lower abdominal organs. It comprises the hip bones, sacrum and coccyx. Each hip bone is made up of three bones (ilium, ischium and pubis) that are separate in a child, but later fuse. Each hip bone unites in front at the pubic symphysis and joins the sacrum behind at the sacroiliac joints. The coccyx (tail bone) forms a joint with the lower end of the sacrum.

The pelvic inlet demarcates a region called the greater or false pelvis above (part of the abdominal cavity) and the lesser or true pelvis below. The lower borders of the bony pelvis form the pelvic outlet.

Lesser pelvis

The lesser pelvis (or true pelvis) is bounded behind and above by the sacrum and coccyx. Muscles of the wall include the piriformis muscle toward the back, and the obturator internus muscle on the side wall. The pubic bones and pubic symphysis lie in front and below, and the floor is formed by the pelvic diaphragm; below this is the urogenital diaphragm. The lesser pelvis is open above to the abdominal cavity.

Pelvic cavity

Within the lesser pelvis is a funnel-shaped cavity or region, known as the pelvic cavity. It is defined as the area between the pelvic inlet above and the thin, sheet-like muscle of the pelvic diaphragm below. It contains and protects the pelvic organs: the bladder and rectum in both sexes; the uterus and vagina in the female; and the prostate and seminal vesicles in the male.

The bladder lies in the front of the pelvic cavity and rests partly on the pubic bones. The rectum lies to the back against the curve of the sacrum and coccyx.

The uterus and vagina lie between the bladder and the rectum in the female, and in the male, the prostate lies below the bladder while the seminal vesicles and vas deferens can be found behind the bladder. Abdominal organs (small and large intestines) hang down into the pelvic cavity, and expansile pelvic organs, such as the full bladder and pregnant uterus, are able to rise up through the pelvic inlet and extend into the abdominal cavity.

Pelvic diaphragm

The pelvic diaphragm (pelvic floor) is important in supporting the pelvic organs. It is formed by the coccygeus and the levator ani muscles, and has a sphincteric (constrictive) action on the rectum and vagina, and assists in increasing intra-abdominal pressure. The puborectalis part of the pelvic diaphragm is important in fecal and urinary continence.

The pelvic diaphragm reflexly contracts when coughing, sneezing, laughing and straining. Poor muscle tone can lead to urinary incontinence when intra-abdominal pressure rises suddenly.

Damage to the pelvic diaphragm or to the perineal body (for example during childbirth) may lead to prolapse (herniation) of pelvic organs such as the bladder, uterus or rectum. The perineal body is a fibrous and muscular structure into which many muscles of the region attach, including the pelvic diaphragm, urogenital diaphragm and anal sphincter.

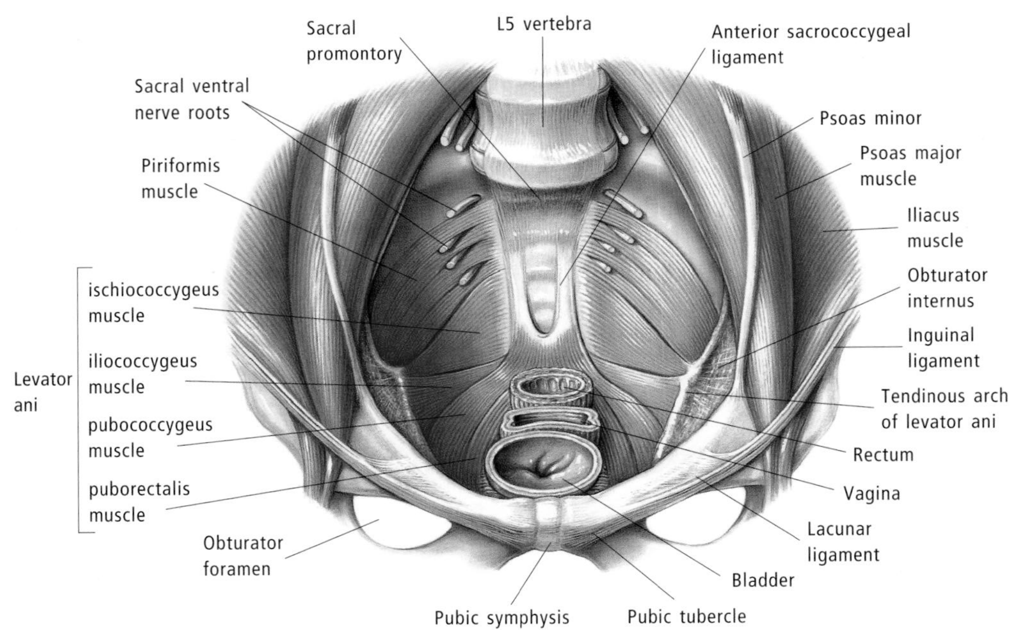

Pelvic floor muscles

Stretching from the sacrum at the back to the hip bones at the front, the pelvic floor muscles form a muscular floor across the pelvis.

The integrity of the structure of the perineal body is therefore critical in pelvic support.

Male and female pelvis

In women, the pelvis is constructed to accommodate the fetus during childbirth. Therefore, the pelvic inlet and outlet are larger than in the male pelvis, the length of the canal is shorter and its walls are more parallel than those of the male.

In men, the pelvis has a smaller, heart-shaped inlet, a small pelvic outlet and a more cone-shaped, longer cavity. In addition, the male pelvis is distinguished by its larger bones, more defined muscle markings and larger joint surfaces, reflecting the generally stronger build and heavier weight of men.

A quick reference for differentiating between the male and female bony pelvis is the subpubic angle (angle below the pubis). This is at about 80–85° in the female, and 50–60° in the male.

One example of how knowledge of these differences is used, is that bicycle seat design reflects the difference in the size of the pelvic outlet in men and women. The sitting bones (ischial tuberosities), which form part of the pelvic outlet, are closer together in the male pelvis and further apart in the female.

The dimensions of the lesser pelvis, particularly the inlet and outlet, are very important in women as they must be large enough for the infant's head to pass through during childbirth.

These dimensions are usually measured carefully by the obstetrician. The greatest dimension of a baby's head is front to back. The typical "gynecoid" female pelvic inlet is slightly wider than it is deep, hence the infant's head will pass through this opening transversely (face directed to the side). The outlet is normally deeper than it is wide, so that the baby's head rotates within the pelvic cavity so that the back of the infant's neck lies against the pubic bones, and the face is directed backward at birth.

Not all women have a gynecoid pelvic inlet, however. Some have an android shape (heartshape, similar to the male), anthropoid shape (narrow from side to side, and deep front to back) and, less commonly, a platypelloid shape (excessively wide, and shortened front to back). Awareness of these differences in shape is essential for anticipating any possible complications during labor.

Injuries

A direct blow or compression injury may cause the pelvic bones to fracture and/or the joints to dislocate. Falls on the feet may fracture the part of the hip bone associated with the hip joint—this is called fracture of the acetabulum.

Soft tissue injury must be considered in pelvic fractures, as there is potential for damage to bladder, urethra, rectum, blood vessels and nerves.

SEE ALSO *Coccyx, Hip, Prolapse, Sacrum, Skeletal system*

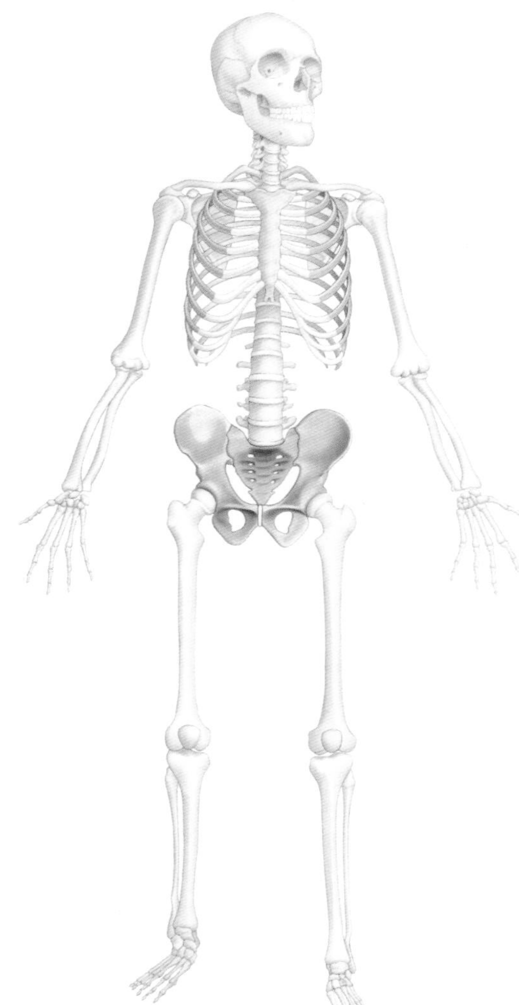

Pelvis

The pelvis helps protect the lower abdominal organs and transfers weight from the vertebral column to the lower limbs.

PEMPHIGOID

In the autoimmune disease pemphigoid (or bullous pemphigoid), large blisters appear on the skin. Uncomfortable, but rarely fatal, the condition can be controlled by strong drug treatments. It is incurable, but sometimes disappears after several years. Pemphigoid usually occurs in the over-50s, and more often in women than in men. The cause is unknown but it is not contagious.

SEE ALSO *Autoimmune disease*

PEMPHIGUS

Formerly, the rare and incurable autoimmune disease pemphigus was invariably fatal. These days, treatment with steroids and immunosuppressive drugs make it possible for sufferers to lead a near-normal life. Characterized by large blisters on the skin and mucous membranes, pemphigus may initially appear similar to the disease pemphigoid but it is not related.

People of all ages and both sexes can develop pemphigus although it is rarely seen in children. The blisters are extremely painful and tend to appear mostly on the scalp, face, chest, armpits, groin, navel area, nose, mouth, throat and, in women, the vagina. The cause is unknown.

SEE ALSO *Autoimmune disease*

PENICILLINS

First discovered by British physician Alexander Fleming in 1938, penicillins are a class of antibiotics used to kill bacteria. They were originally extracted from molds of the genus *Penicillium*, but are now synthesized. They work by preventing bacterial cells from forming a cell wall, killing them in the process. Penicillins can be given orally via tablet, syrup or capsule, or by injection. In some people, they may cause allergic reactions such as skin rashes, swelling of the joints, and in rare instances, anaphylaxis, which may be fatal.

Excessive use of penicillins has resulted in the development of bacterial strains that are resistant to them. Newer penicillins such as amoxycillin, methicillin, oxacillin and dicloxacillin have been developed that are effective against many resistant strains.

SEE ALSO *Antibiotics, Bacteria*

Pelvis—female

Unlike its male counterpart, the female pelvis is designed to support the fetus during pregnancy. The inlet and the outlet are larger than the male, while the canal is shorter.

Sacroiliac joint
Median sacral crest
Promontory
Alar part of sacrum
Articular process
Iliac crest
Ilium
Anterior superior iliac spine
Anterior superior iliac spine
Iliopectineal eminence
Pelvic sacral foramina
Obturator foramen
Coccyx
Femur
Pubic tubercle
Pubic symphysis
Ischiopubic ramus

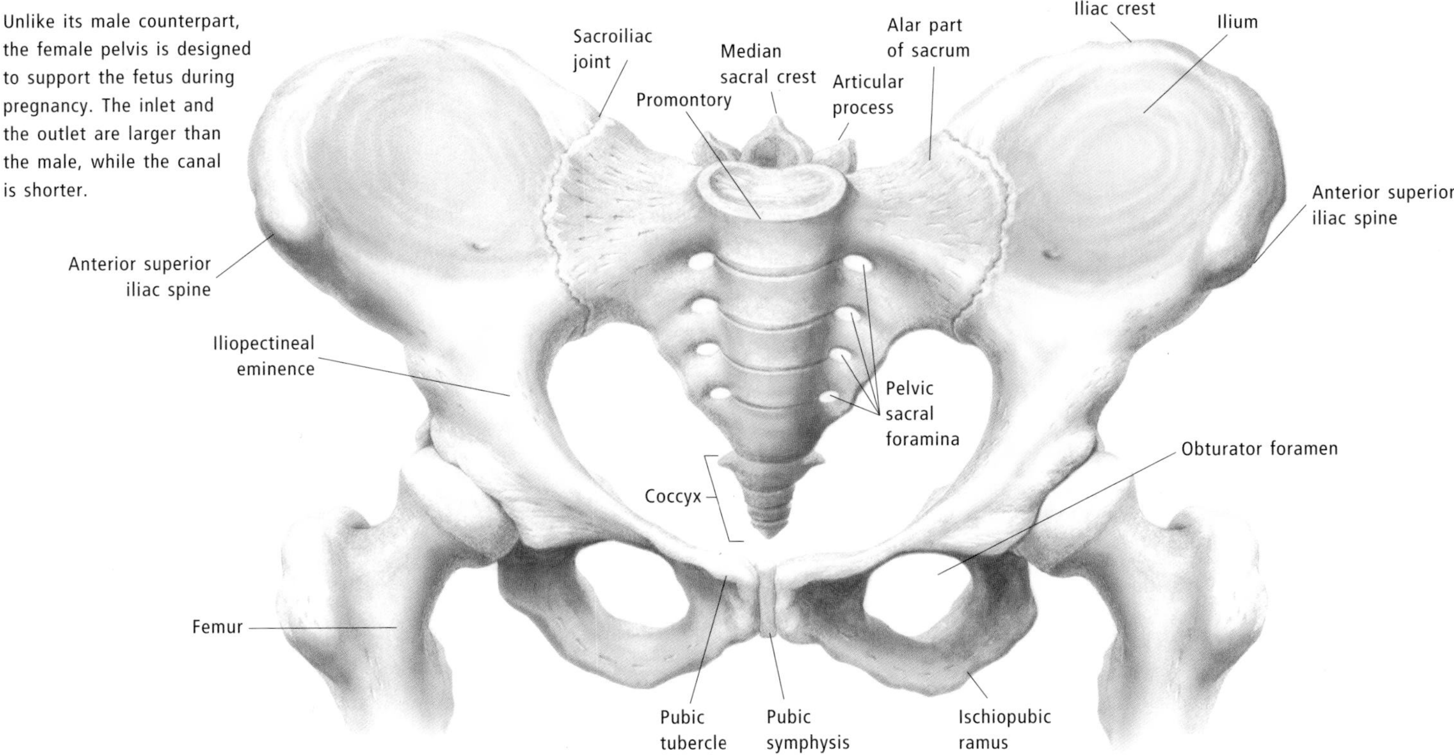

Pelvis—male

The male pelvis is easily distinguished from the female by the presence of stronger bone and larger joint surfaces.

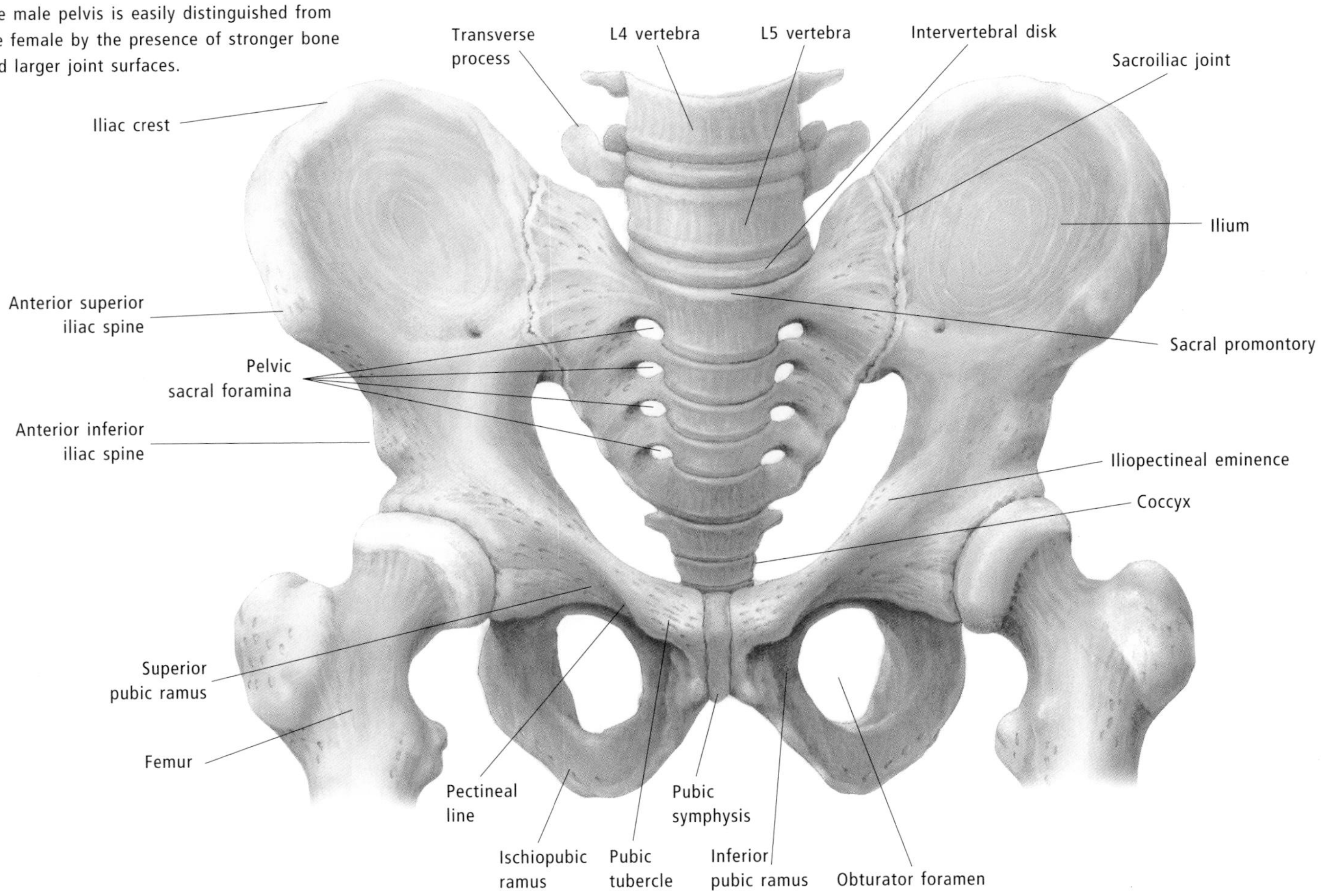

Transverse process
L4 vertebra
L5 vertebra
Intervertebral disk
Sacroiliac joint
Iliac crest
Ilium
Anterior superior iliac spine
Pelvic sacral foramina
Sacral promontory
Anterior inferior iliac spine
Iliopectineal eminence
Coccyx
Superior pubic ramus
Femur
Pectineal line
Pubic symphysis
Ischiopubic ramus
Pubic tubercle
Inferior pubic ramus
Obturator foramen

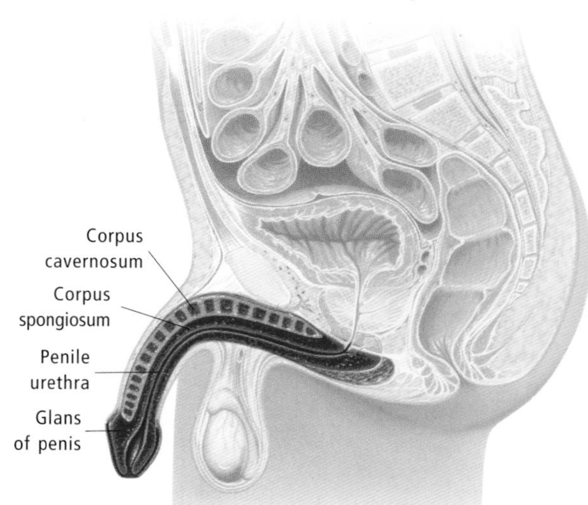

Penis

The penis is the male urinary and reproductive organ comprising three cylinders. Two cylinders (the corpus cavernosum and corpus spongiosum) are composed of sponge-like vascular tissue which allow erection; and the third cylinder contains the urethra—part of the urinary system.

Penis—reproductive system

The penis is attached to the pelvic bone by connective tissue, and usually hangs flaccid unless sexually stimulated. Stimulation increases the blood flow in the network of vessels that surround the spongy cylinders of the corpus cavernosum, allowing erection.

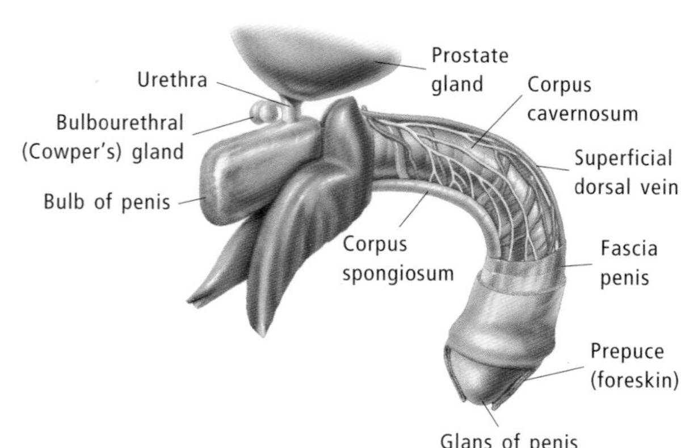

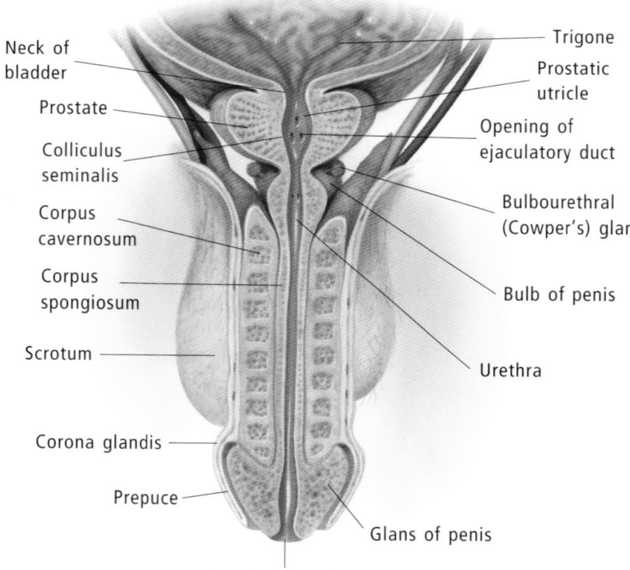

Penis—urinary system

The largest part of the urethra—the tube that carries urine from the bladder out of the body—passes through the penis. The urethra ends in an external swelling at the tip of the penis (the glans) where urine passes out through the urethral meatus. Urinary tract infections may cause discharge or pain in the penis.

PENIS

The penis is the external male reproductive and urinary organ, through which semen and urine leave the body. It is attached at its base to the pelvic bone by connective tissues. It is comprised primarily of two cylinders of sponge-like vascular tissue (corpora cavernosa). A third cylinder contains the urethra, a tube that carries the urine and the ejaculate. The urethra ends in an external swelling at the tip of the penis, the glans. The glans is particularly sensitive and, in an uncircumcised penis, is covered by a protective foreskin (prepuce).

After physical or psychological sexual stimulation, the two spongy cylinders become engorged with blood and the penis becomes erect and hard. This enables the male to insert the erect penis into the female's vagina during sexual intercourse. The blood is unable to drain out through the veins in the penis because they are temporarily closed by pressure from arterial blood in the corpora cavernosa. An erection ceases when the veins open, allowing the blood to flow back into the body's circulation. Sildenafil (Viagra) works by closing these same veins.

Circumcision is the surgical removal of all or part of the foreskin of the penis. In infancy it is usually performed (often without anesthetic) for social or cultural reasons, as there are no medical reasons for routine circumcision of newborn boys. In adults, it may be performed for medical reasons, for example for phimosis or paraphimosis.

Diseases and disorders

Balanitis is inflammation of the glans of the penis. It is usually caused by a yeast such as candida (thrush), and is more common in males who have not been circumcised, and who have not been keeping the glans clean. Symptoms are a red, shiny glans with itchiness and a slight discharge. It is treated with antifungal creams or ointments and by keeping the glans washed and clean.

The penis is often affected by venereal (sexually transmitted) diseases. Syphilis or chancroid form ulcers (chancres), on the skin of the penis; other venereal diseases, such as gonorrhea, cause infections of the urethra (urethritis). Symptoms of urethritis are pain on urinating (dysuria) and a discharge from the penis. Treatment is with an antibiotic appropriate for the particular microorganism causing the disease.

Cancer of the penis occurs most commonly in elderly, uncircumcised males who have had chronic balanitis (infection of the glans). It manifests as a small ulcer that bleeds easily and does not heal. It is treated either by amputating the end of the penis or by radiation therapy.

Phimosis is a condition in which the foreskin of the penis is so tight that it cannot be easily pulled back over the tip (the glans). Balanitis may accompany it. Circumcision is the usual treatment. Paraphimosis is a condition in which the foreskin of the penis is retracted and "stuck" and cannot be returned to its normal position. As a result, the glans becomes swollen and painful. Circumcision under general anesthetic is the usual treatment.

Peyronie's disease (curvature of the penis due to a band of fibrous tissue) is a bend in the penis that occurs during erection. It cannot be cured but it can be minimized with corticosteroid injections into the penis.

Epispadias is a congenital defect in which the urethra, the duct connecting the bladder to the tip of the penis, opens abnormally on the top of the penis, either in the head or along the entire length. In hypospadias, another congenital defect, the urethral opening appears on the underside of the penis. Both conditions cause abnormal leakage of urine (incontinence) and sexual dysfunction in adulthood. Reconstructive surgery usually cures both defects.

Priapism is a condition where the penis remains persistently and painfully erect without any sexual arousal or desire. It may be caused by excessive sexual stimulation or by certain drugs, including corticosteroids, anticoagulants and antihypertensives. Injuries to the spinal cord or to the penis may also result in priapism. Treatment options include surgery, spinal anesthesia, and aspiration of blood from the penis.

Impotence is an inability to produce or maintain an erection of the penis sufficient for successful sexual intercourse. It is more common in older men and often has a psychological origin, such as stress, anxiety, depression or relationship problems. Brief bouts of impotence may follow illnesses such as influenza, or after taking drugs or alcohol. There may be a physical cause, such as a stroke, atherosclerosis, diabetes mellitus or alcoholism. In other cases, it may occur as a side effect of certain medications or following surgery.

If the cause of impotence is a physical disorder, the underlying cause must be treated first. If not, sex therapy with a qualified sex therapist may be of benefit. Possible treatments include a prosthesis surgically inserted into the penis, needle injection therapy, vacuum cup devices and medications such as sildenafil.

SEE ALSO *Circumcision, Epispadias, Erection, Glans, Gonorrhea, Impotence, Peyronie's disease, Priapism, Reproductive systems, Sexual intercourse, Sexually transmitted diseases, Syphilis, Urethra, Urethritis, Urinary systems*

PEPTIC ULCER

Peptic ulcers result from the damaging action of acidic stomach juices on the vulnerable mucosal lining of the esophagus, stomach or duodenum. They affect men three times more often than women. Among patients under 50 years of age, duodenal ulcers are ten times more common than stomach (gastric) ulcers.

A patient with peptic ulcer will experience pain in the upper abdomen, which may be relieved by food or antacid preparations. In some patients, the ulcer may erode through a blood vessel, leading to the vomiting of large amounts of blood. If left untreated, the ulcer may perforate the gut wall, spilling stomach or duodenal juices into the abdominal cavity and causing painful chemical peritonitis. Swelling and scarring of the gut wall, which may cause obstruction of the gut, may arise with ulcers in the lower esophagus and pyloric sphincter.

At one time it was thought that peptic ulcers arose from excessive acid secretion as a result of psychological stress. It is now recognized that infection of the upper gut with acid-resistant bacteria and use of nonsteroidal anti-inflammatory drugs play a major role in their initiation. Treatment of peptic ulcers makes use of antacid preparations, antibiotics and drugs to control acid secretion (triple therapy).

There are a number of alternative therapies that may help to alleviate the symptoms of peptic ulcers. Acupuncture treats ulcers along points said to improve gastrointestinal function, relieve pain and reduce feelings of stress and anxiety. Herbalism treats with demulcent herbs (marshmallow, for example), antibacterial herbs (such as echinacea), astringent herbs (like golden seal) and herbs which may aid tissue healing (such as calendula). Hypnotherapy, meditation and other relaxation therapies treat anxiety and stress

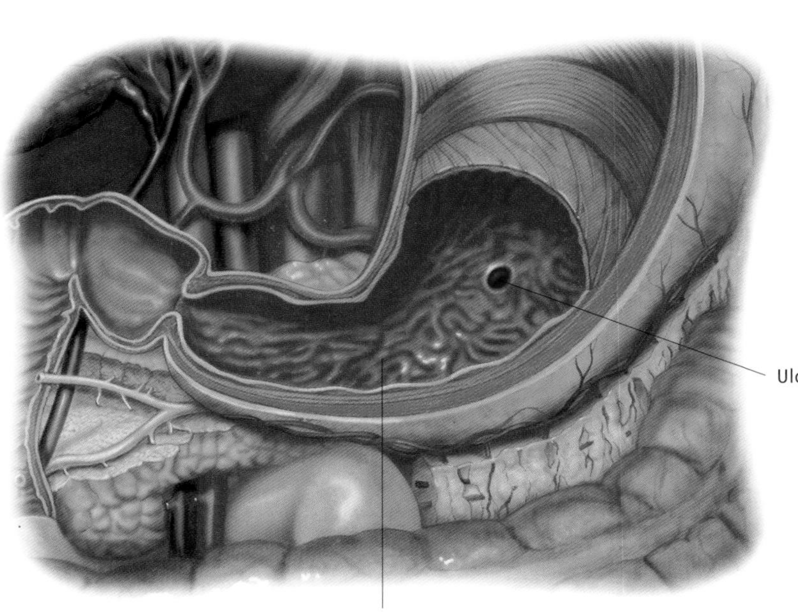

Peptic ulcer

Damage to the mucous membrane can result in the formation of a peptic ulcer. Ulcers can form in the lining of the stomach, esophagus and duodenum.

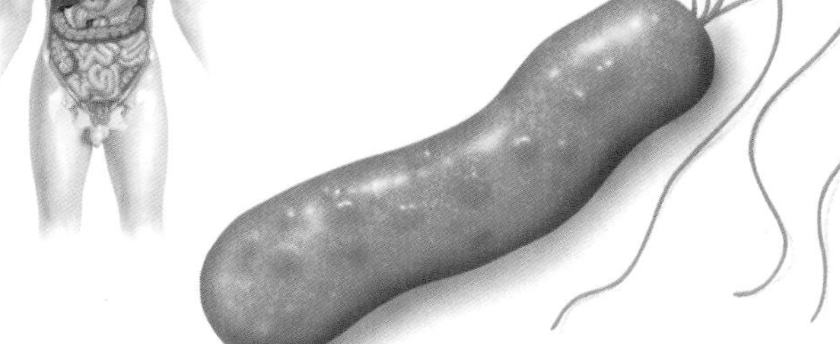

Ulcer-causing bacteria

The presence of an acid-resistant bacteria *(Helicobacter pylori)* in the upper intestine plays a major role in the formation of peptic ulcers.

associated with ulcers. Psychotherapy is also thought to be beneficial. Naturopathy suggests a low-fat wholefood diet of small meals that are thoroughly chewed. Smoking, coffee, tea, sugar, citrus and alcohol should be avoided. Cow's milk should be substituted with soy or rice milks. Possible food allergies such as wheat need to be eliminated. Supplements prescribed include vitamins A, C and E, zinc, *Lactobacillus acidophilus*, digestive enzymes and slippery elm. Reflexology massage aims to relax the nervous and gastrointestinal systems while stimulating the stomach and duodenal zones.

SEE ALSO *Digestive system, Duodenum, Esophagus, Stomach*

PERICARDITIS

The pericardium is the tissue sac that surrounds the heart. The sac consists of an inner double-layered part and an outer tough fibrous part. Pericarditis is literally inflammation of the pericardium and may be the result of infection (viruses, tuberculosis or pus-forming bacteria), invasion by cancer cells (leukemic infiltration), connective tissue diseases (rheumatoid arthritis, systemic lupus erythematosus) or changes in blood chemistry (kidney failure and gout). Patients complain of sharp, strong pain in the center of the chest. Unlike myocardial infarction, the pain is made worse by breathing in, moving and lying flat on the back. Patients also commonly have fever and an audible friction rub, heard when a stethoscope is applied to the chest; they may develop failure of the right ventricle.

SEE ALSO *Heart, Pericardium*

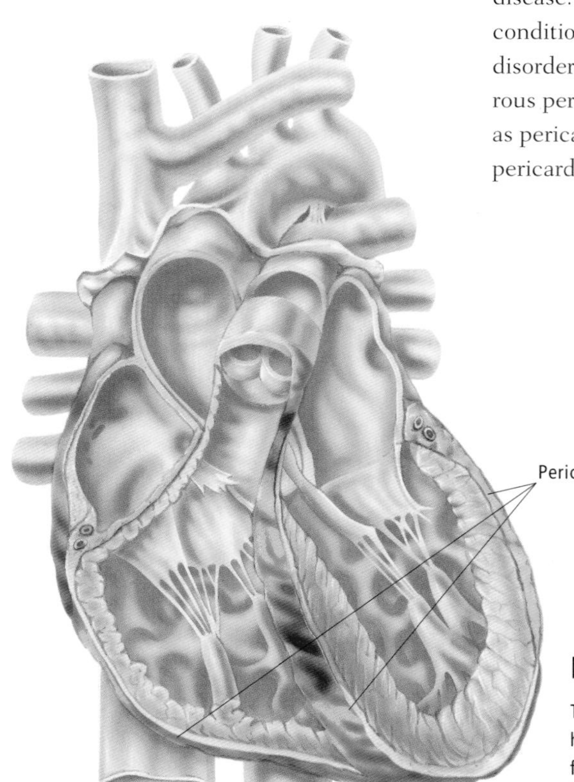

Pericardium

The pericardium surrounds the heart, providing a low-friction fluid-filled space in which the heart can beat freely.

PERICARDIUM

The pericardium is a series of sacs that enclose the heart. The inner set of sacs is called the serous pericardium and provides a low-friction, fluid-filled space to permit the beating heart to move freely. The serous pericardium has an inner visceral layer and an outer parietal layer, separated by a thin film of fluid. Outside the parietal layer of the serous pericardium lies the fibrous pericardium. This is a tough layer of connective tissue that is attached at the top around the great vessels entering and leaving the heart, and is fused below with the central part of the diaphragm. The fibrous pericardium provides a strong mechanical support to maintain the position of the heart within the center of the chest.

The pericardium may be involved in disease. When it becomes inflamed the condition is known as pericarditis. In some disorders, fluid may accumulate in the serous pericardial sac. This condition is known as pericardial effusion and may accompany pericarditis. If a large volume of fluid accumulates in the pericardial space, then the normal distension of the ventricle during the rest phase of the cardiac cycle may be impaired. This is known as cardiac tamponade and may be fatal unless the excess fluid is drained urgently.

SEE ALSO *Cardiac tamponade, Heart, Pericarditis*

PERINEUM

The perineum encloses the base of the pelvis in both men and women. It consists of a sheet of fibrous tissue and muscle and provides support for the pelvic floor muscles immediately above. It also contains the urethral and anal sphincters. Tears in the perineum are not uncommon during childbirth and may result in prolapse of the vagina.

SEE ALSO *Anus, Childbirth, Pelvic floor muscles, Prolapse, Urethra*

PERIODONTITIS

Periodontitis is inflammation of the gums that leads to the infection of the ligaments and bone supporting the teeth. The condition is usually caused by a build-up of plaque on the teeth due to poor dental hygiene. If untreated, the teeth become loose and fall out. Warning signs include swelling and a red-purple coloring of the gums, blood on the toothbrush, tenderness and bad breath. Bone structure can be damaged before the condition is realized as there is usually little or no pain.

Treatment involves thorough cleaning by a dentist and perhaps surgical trimming of scar tissue and reshaping of bone. In severe cases, some teeth may need to be removed to stop the spread of infection.

SEE ALSO *Gums, Teeth*

PERIOSTEUM

Periosteum is a thin, fibrous membrane that covers all bone surfaces, except those that are involved in joints (which are covered by cartilage).

Periosteum is made up of two layers. The inner layer comprises osteoblasts or bone-producing cells) which produce bone when a fetus or child is growing. Following a fracture, they produce new bone in order to

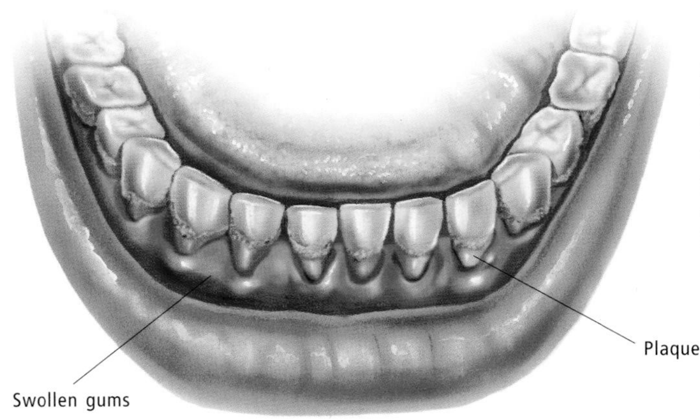

Periodontitis

In this condition, a painful inflammation of the tissues supporting the teeth is caused by bacteria, food particles and calcium deposits collecting in the spaces between the teeth and gum.

mend the two ends of the broken bone together. Fibers from this inner layer also penetrate the underlying bone and help bind the periosteum to the bone. The dense outer layer contains nerves and blood vessels. Branches of these blood vessels penetrate the bone to supply the cells with nutrients.

Periostitis is inflammation of the periosteum. It usually occurs along with infection of bone (osteomyelitis). A periosteoma (also called a periostoma) is a benign tumor arising from the periosteum.

SEE ALSO *Bones, Joints, Osteomyelitis, Periostitis*

PERIOSTITIS

Periostitis is inflammation of the periosteum, the thin, fibrous membrane that covers bone surfaces. It may occur from overuse, especially along the medial side of the shin bone (a form of "shin splints"), in people who are physically active. Treatment involves rest and anti-inflammatory drugs. Periostitis may also occur with infection of bone (osteomyelitis) when it is caused by bacteria. In these cases, treatment is with intravenous antibiotics.

SEE ALSO *Bones, Joints, Osteomyelitis, Periosteum*

PERIPHERAL NERVOUS SYSTEM

The peripheral nervous system (PNS) is one of the two main divisions of the nervous system, the other being the central nervous system (CNS). The PNS is the network that collects signals from sensory receptors throughout the body's periphery and carries them back into the CNS (spinal cord and brain), that interprets the data and formulates a response. The instructions from the CNS are then carried to the muscles and glands by the PNS. The nerve cells of the PNS that transmit messages into the CNS are known as sensory (afferent) neurons. The nerve cells that carry messages out from the CNS are called motor (efferent) neurons.

The PNS includes peripheral parts of two systems, called the somatic nervous system (SNS) and the autonomic nervous system (ANS).

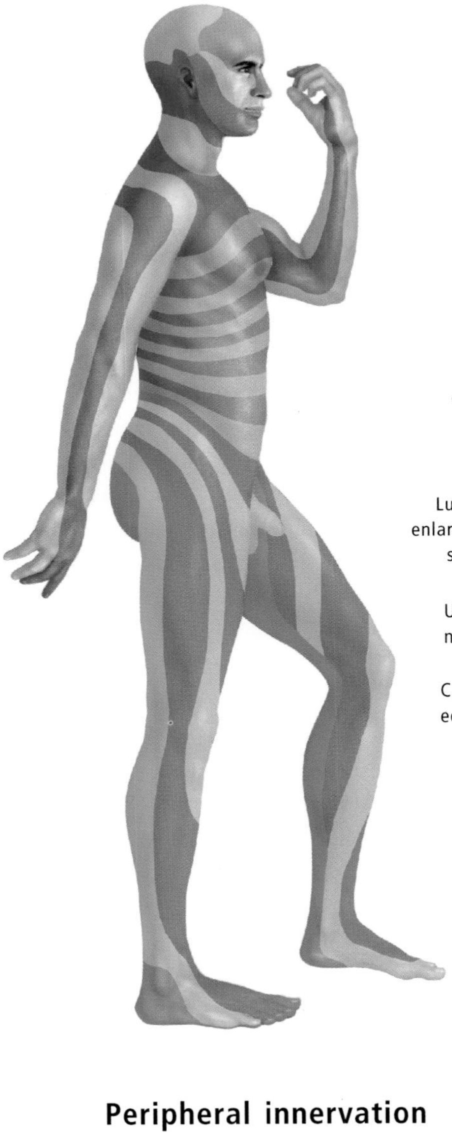

Peripheral nervous system

The peripheral nervous system is a network of nerves that transports signals between sensory receptors in the peripheral areas of the body (skin and muscles, for example) and the central nervous system (brain and spinal cord).

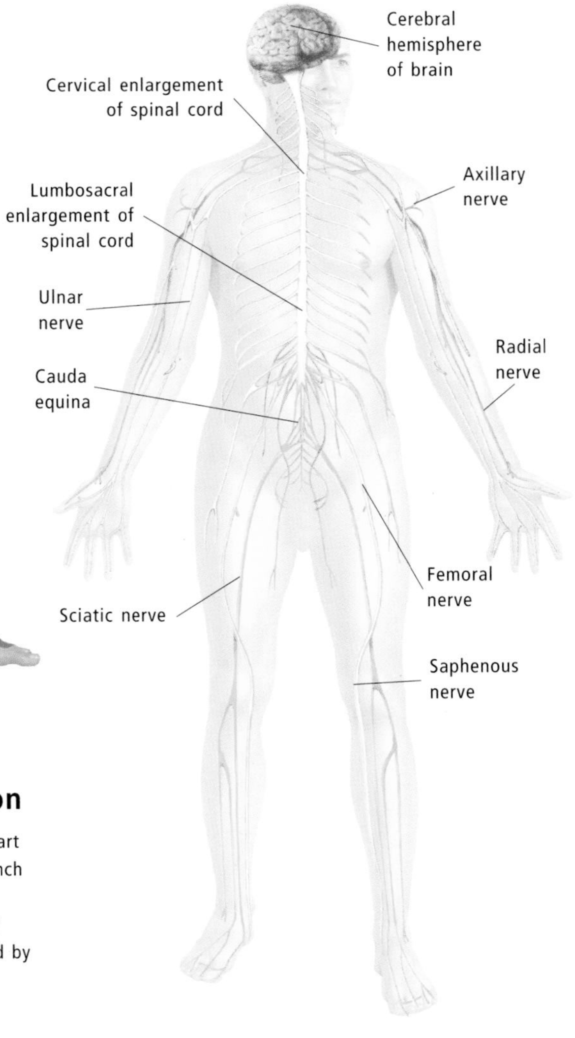

Cerebral hemisphere of brain
Cervical enlargement of spinal cord
Axillary nerve
Lumbosacral enlargement of spinal cord
Ulnar nerve
Radial nerve
Cauda equina
Femoral nerve
Sciatic nerve
Saphenous nerve

Peripheral innervation

The nerves from the spinal cord (part of the central nervous system) branch out along a network of peripheral nerves that serve different parts of the body. The area of skin supplied by a given spinal nerve is called a dermatome.

P

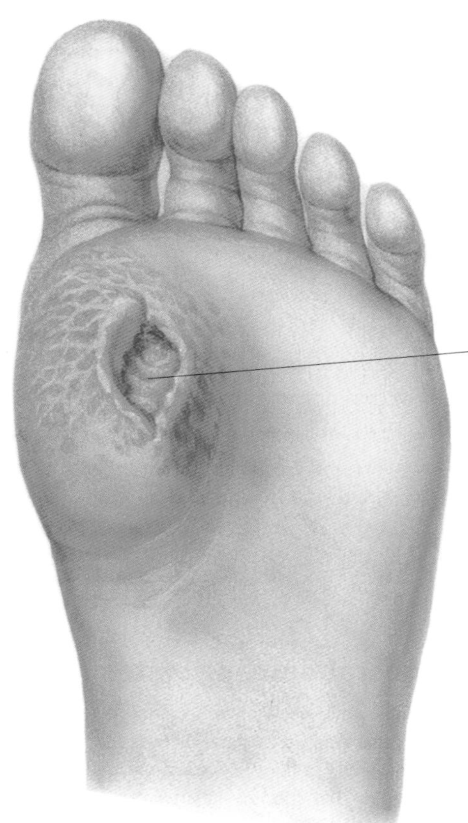

Peripheral vascular disease

The deterioration of arteries can cause disruption to the flow of blood to arms and legs. Reduced blood supply can cause pain in the limbs and, in severe cases, ulcers can develop.

Somatic nervous system (SNS)

The motor neurons of the SNS transmit signals directly to the skeletal muscles. These are the muscles people can normally move and control consciously or voluntarily, such as those attached to the bones in the arms and legs. For this reason, the SNS is also known as the voluntary nervous system. It stimulates the muscle activity needed to run, jump, flick a switch to turn on a light and perform the many other movements that people choose deliberately to make.

Autonomic nervous system (ANS)

In contrast, the ANS transmits messages to the glands and cardiac (heart) and smooth muscle. Smooth muscle is found in the walls of internal organs such as the stomach and intestines, around blood vessels, in the skin around hair follicles and in the eye. The actions of cardiac and smooth muscle are mostly out of a person's conscious control and so the ANS is also often referred to as as the involuntary nervous system. It maintains and controls heartbeat, blood pressure, breathing, digestion and the many other fundamental functions of the body necessary to maintain life.

The ANS consists of two components, the sympathetic nervous system and the parasympathetic nervous system, which essentially create complementary but opposite actions. The sympathetic components mostly stimulate activities that use energy. The parasympathetic side of the system switches the same activities down and conserves energy. For example, when faced by a sudden threat the body responds instinctively with a range of reactions that together are known as the "fight or flight" response, the sympathetic nervous system automatically preparing the body to confront or run from danger. The pupils dilate. Heart rate and blood pressure rise. The hairs on the back of the neck stand up. Digestion slows as blood is diverted from the intestines and made available for use by the skeletal muscles. The adrenal glands are stimulated to produce hormones that accelerate all of these activities.

When the danger has passed, the parasympathetic nervous system calms the body down and switches on what are sometimes called "rest and digest" activities. Most of these are directly opposite to those of the "fight or flight" responses. Heart rate and blood pressure fall, the pupils constrict and digestive processes restart.

SEE ALSO *Adrenal glands, Brain, Nerves, Nervous system, Neurons, Spinal cord, Sympathetic nervous system*

PERIPHERAL VASCULAR DISEASE

Peripheral vascular disease refers to deterioration of the arteries supplying blood to the arms and legs. This is almost always due to atherosclerosis and tends to affect the legs and feet most severely.

Atherosclerosis, commonly referred to as hardening of the arteries, results from deposition of fatty material, such as cholesterol, in the arterial wall. This causes gradual narrowing of the artery and weakening of its wall, decreased blood flow to the legs and, sometimes, an enlargement of the weakened part of the artery, called an aneurysm. Narrowing of the arteries causes pain in the affected leg muscles supplied by that artery, due to insufficient oxygen supply for their metabolism. This type of pain is called intermittent claudication, since it occurs only upon commencing walking and is relieved by stopping. Reduced blood supply to the legs can make them look pale and feel cool to the touch. The skin becomes shiny and there is hair loss and thickening of the nails. In severe cases ulcers develop and gangrene may occur.

Atherosclerosis is caused by a combination of factors, including high cholesterol, high blood pressure, diabetes and smoking. It is most common in men over the age of 40 but is also common among women who smoke. Smoking is a most important factor in the development of peripheral vascular disease. Once it develops, the continuation of smoking will lead to gangrene of the affected limb. Medical treatment is unsatisfactory and surgical by-pass grafting is required if symptoms worsen. Gangrene is treated by amputation and the fitting of prosthetic limbs.

SEE ALSO *Aneurysm, Arteries, Atherosclerosis, Cholesterol, Diabetes, Gangrene, Hypertension, Smoking*

PERISTALSIS

Peristalsis consists of wave-like contractions in the muscular walls of the esophagus, stomach, intestines, ureters and fallopian tubes that propel the contents of the tube along. The walls of many tubular structures in the body are composed of smooth muscle whose contractions, like those of the heart muscle, are involuntary, that is, controlled by the autonomic nervous system. When food is swallowed, muscular contractions in the esophagus push the food downwards into the stomach. There, peristalsis in the stomach mixes the chewed food with gastric juices and moves it through the pyloric

P

sphincter to the small intestine, where peristalsis continues to move gut contents into the large intestine.

Esophageal spasm is a disorder in which muscle spasm affects normal swallowing, causing chest pain, with the potential for achalasia to develop. Ileus is failure of intestinal peristalsis caused by blockage, surgery, drugs or trauma.

SEE ALSO *Achalasia, Digestive system, Esophagus, Fallopian tubes, Ileus, Intestines, Muscle, Ureter*

PERITONEAL DIALYSIS

Peritoneal dialysis is a technique in which the abdominal peritoneal membrane is used as a dialysis mechanism to remove toxic substances from the blood. The abdominal cavity is filled (via a catheter) with a special solution that absorbs toxins, using the peritoneal membrane inside the abdomen as the semipermeable membrane. The solution is allowed to absorb wastes for several hours, and then the waste-filled fluid is exchanged for a fresh batch of solution.

SEE ALSO *Abdomen, Dialysis*

PERITONITIS

Inflammation of the peritoneum (the membrane that lines the wall of the abdomen and covers the organs) is known as peritonitis. It can result from infection (such an abdominal abscess), injury or occasionally other diseases. Symptoms include abdominal pain, distension and tenderness, fever, nausea and vomiting. The cause must be quickly identified and treated, for example with intravenous antibiotics in the case of bacterial peritonitis. Untreated, the mortality rate is high.

SEE ALSO *Abdomen*

PERSONALITY DISORDERS

A personality disorder is not easy to define because there is no clear line between what is and is not a disorder. However, behavior that significantly deviates from societal or cultural expectations, or behavior that is an extreme variant of normal behavior and thus hampers an individual's ability to function in society, may be defined as characteristic of a personality disorder. In many instances, a person with a personality disorder does not seek treatment unless ordered by a court or pressured by relatives. It is estimated that about 20 percent of people in the general population has one, or more than one, personality disorder.

In medical practice, there are ten defined personality disorders.

Antisocial personality disorder People with this disorder disregard the feelings and rights of others. They often break the law, lie, act impulsively and get into violent fights. Their behavior towards others, including their partners and children, may be violent. They can also be called sociopaths or psychopaths. People with this disorder may be a major danger to society and often die a violent death themselves.

Avoidant personality disorder is often seen as intense shyness, coupled with anxiety. Sufferers avoid occupations or activities that bring them into contact with others and see themselves as socially inadequate.

Borderline personality disorder is a condition characterized by intense emotional instability. Those who suffer from this disorder are thought of as unstable and are unable to maintain relationships. They may attempt suicide or self-mutilation. Alcoholism, depression, drug dependence and eating disorders are common among people with this disorder.

Dependent personality disorder People with this disorder allow others to make most of their important life decisions and are severely emotionally dependent on others. They are not comfortable with themselves and are often preoccupied with thoughts of being abandoned.

Histrionic personality disorder This state is characterized by the need to be the center of attention. Sufferers often display inappropriate sexual behavior, and they are easily influenced.

Narcissistic personality disorder is characterized by a grandiose sense of self-importance. Sufferers of this disorder seek and expect excessive attention from others. They believe they are special and often have very fragile self-esteem.

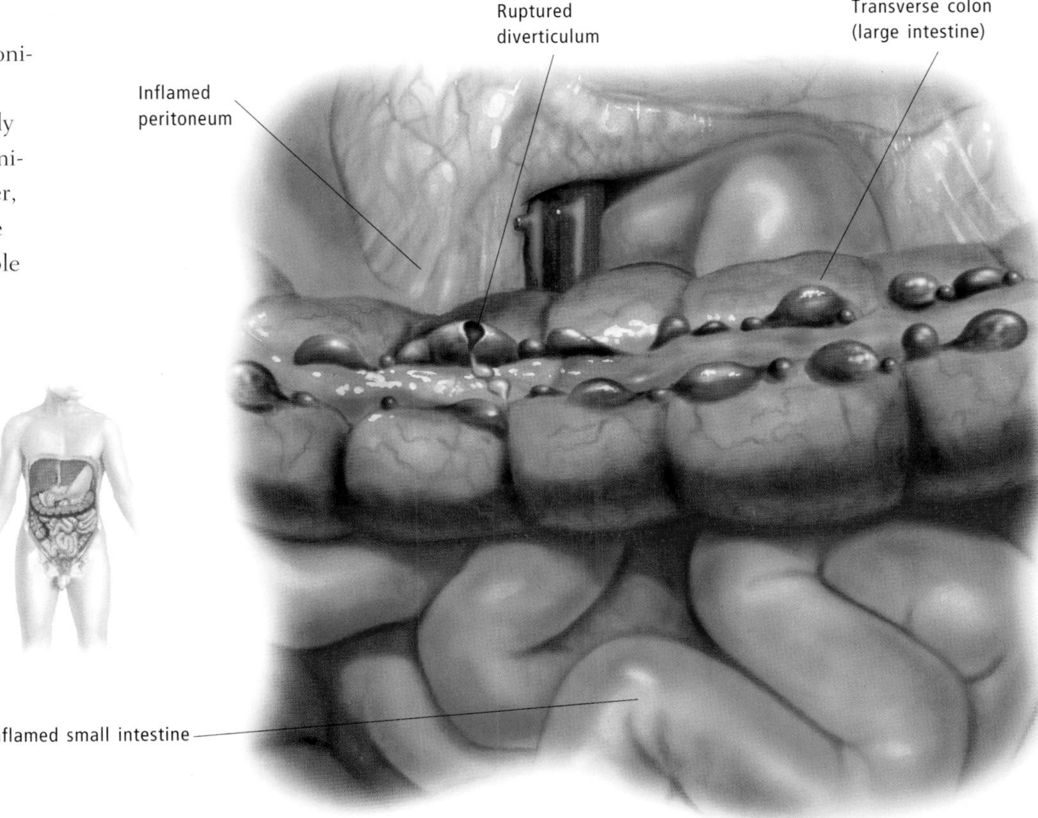

Peritonitis

An infection in the abdomen, if untreated, can lead to inflammation of the peritoneum—peritonitis—as in this example of a ruptured diverticulum.

Obsessive-compulsive personality disorder is marked by a preoccupation with details, rules, lists, order, organization or schedules to the point where the purpose is lost. These people are rigid, formal and serious and their behavior is often marked by strange rituals.

Paranoid personality disorder is a state of constant suspicion and distrust of others. A person suffering from such a disorder is always on the lookout for evidence to support their suspicions and believes that everyone is against them.

Schizoid personality disorder involves a lack of desire for close relationships, including sexual relationships, and an emotional detachment resulting in social isolation.

Schizotypal personality disorder is marked by odd thinking and behavior. People with this disorder speak in a disjointed fashion and sometimes believe they have magical powers. Close relationships make them uncomfortable. It is thought this form of personality disorder could be a less severe form of schizophrenia.

Other personality disorders exist, sometimes described as depressive personality disorder and passive-aggressive personality disorder. A sufferer may exhibit traits of more than one disorder, making diagnosis difficult.

Personality disorders are the result of a combination of life experience and inherited characteristics. They are often the result of unresolved conflicts, which may date back to childhood. Because patients often refuse to admit that there is anything wrong, such disorders are difficult to treat and therapists will often try a range of methods including psychoactive drugs and psychotherapy.

SEE ALSO *Obsessive-compulsive disorder, Paranoia, Schizophrenia*

PERTHES' DISEASE

Perthes' disease is a chronic disorder that affects children, in which the head of the femur (the ball part of the ball-and-socket hip joint) becomes inflamed and flattened, due to an interruption in its blood supply. The cause of the condition is unknown. Movement of the affected joint becomes limited, resulting in a limp, with pain in the thigh and groin. The condition occurs most frequently in boys aged 4–10 years and tends to run in families. In most cases, the bone heals itself without any resulting deformity. Treatment is aimed at protecting the bone and joint while healing takes place. Bed rest and the use of appliances such as a brace, cast or splint is usually recommended. Osteoarthritis of the affected hip may develop in adulthood.

SEE ALSO *Femur, Hip, Osteoarthritis*

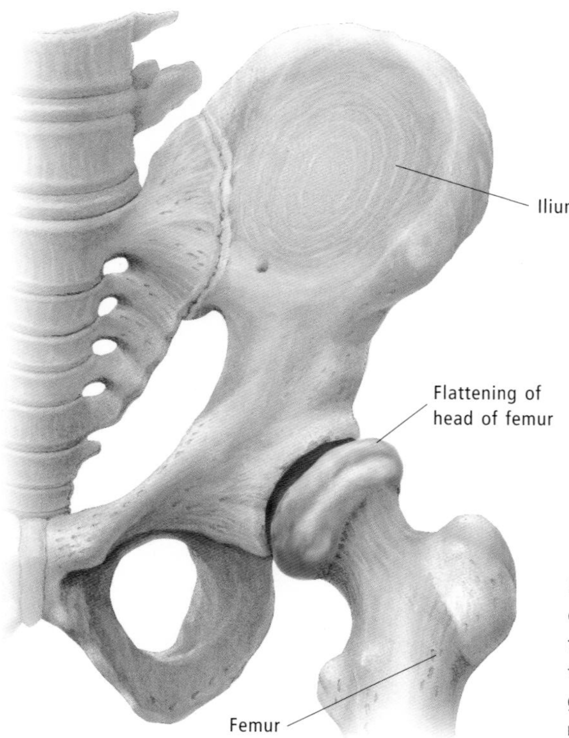

Perthes' disease

In this condition, the ball part of the femur degenerates due to an interruption to the blood flow, resulting in pain in the groin and thigh. Osteoarthritis may occur in affected adults.

PEYRONIE'S DISEASE

Peyronie's disease (curvature of the penis) is a bend in the penis that occurs during erection. It is caused by the abnormal presence of fibrous tissue in the vascular sheath that runs the length of the penis (corpora cavernosa). The obstruction causes the bend in the penis to form during erection which is painful and interferes with intercourse.

The condition is uncommon, affects older males and is sometimes associated with Dupuytren's contracture. It cannot be cured but can be alleviated somewhat with radiation therapy or the injection of hormones (corticosteroids) into the fibrous tissue in the corpora cavernosa.

SEE ALSO *Dupuytren's contracture, Erection, Penis*

PHARYNGITIS

Pharyngitis is an inflammation of the throat (pharynx). The symptoms of pharyngitis include a sore throat and discomfort or pain on swallowing. Acute pharyngitis may be caused by the viruses which cause such conditions as the common cold, laryngitis, infectious mononucleosis (glandular fever), tonsillitis and sinusitis. It may also be caused by the streptococcal bacterium, when the infection is known as strep throat. Other bacterial causes of acute pharyngitis include gonorrhea and mycoplasma.

When a physician examines the affected throat, it is seen to be red and swollen. The lymph nodes in the neck may be enlarged and tender and there may be a fever. If the cause is bacterial, antibiotics will cure the condition (antibiotics are ineffective in viral pharyngitis). Painkillers and decongestants will help the symptoms, which clear up in a week or so.

Chronic pharyngitis may be caused by smoking cigarettes or drinking too much alcohol. It may also be caused by postnasal drip resulting from chronic nasal or sinus inflammation. Treatment involves improving oral hygiene, giving up smoking and alcohol, and using antiseptic gargles.

SEE ALSO *Common cold, Infectious mononucleosis, Laryngitis, Pharynx, Sinusitis, Throat, Tonsils*

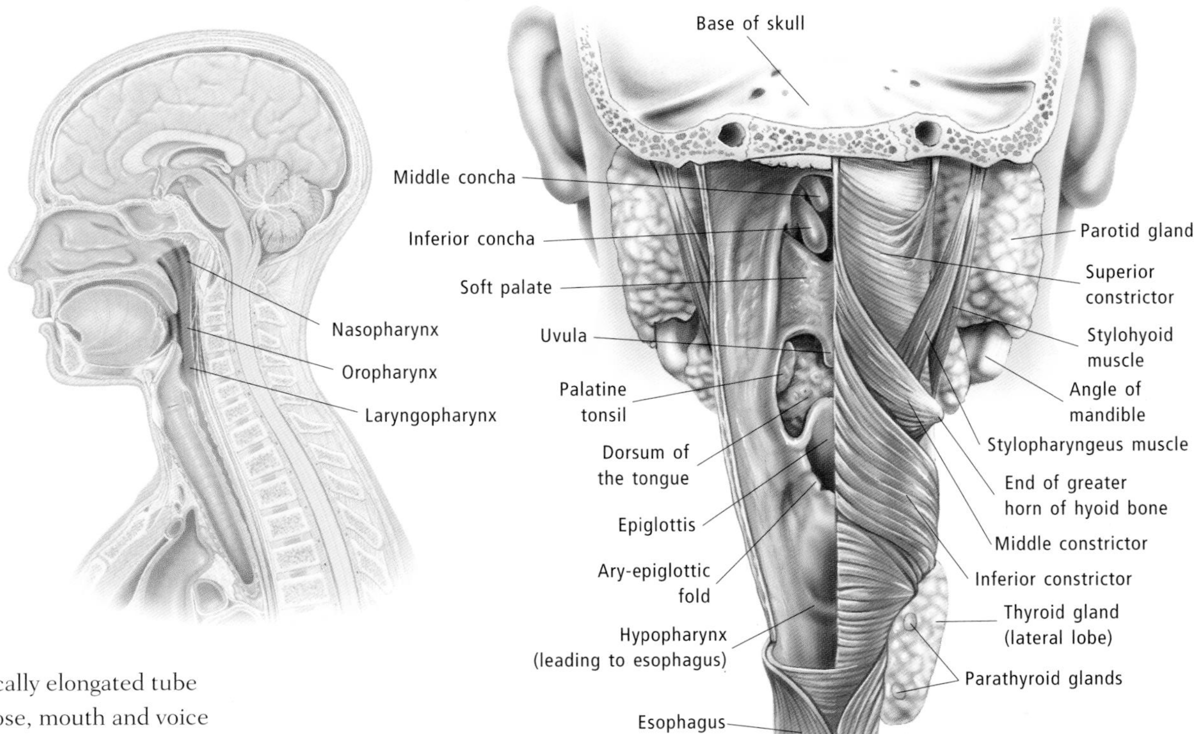

PHARYNX

The pharynx is a vertically elongated tube that lies behind the nose, mouth and voice box (larynx). The pharynx has openings to all three of these regions and is a common passage for air, water and food. The pharynx is divided into three parts. From the top down, these are the nasopharynx, the oropharynx and the laryngopharynx.

Nasopharynx

The nasopharynx lies immediately beneath the base of the skull and behind the nose. Air from the nose passes through the nasopharynx on its way down to the lungs. In the side walls of the nasopharynx lie the openings of the auditory (eustachian) tubes, which connect the pharynx with the middle ear. These tubes allow air pressure in the middle ear to be equalized with the outside environment, thus allowing the eardrum to move freely in response to air vibrations.

The auditory tubes are particularly important when one is changing altitude, as in an aircraft flight, or ascending in an elevator to the top of a tall building. If the auditory tube becomes blocked by mucus, as in a head cold, discomfort or pain will be felt in the ear and hearing may be temporarily impaired.

The nasopharynx also contains tonsillar tissue in the form of the nasopharyngeal tonsils or adenoids. These tissues of the immune system protect the body from any disease-causing organisms that may enter the body via the nose.

Oropharynx

The oropharynx lies behind the mouth and provides a passage for air, water and food. It is separated from the mouth by paired arches of tissue on each side. The entrance from the mouth to the pharynx is guarded by the palatine tonsils, which lie in a ditch (fossa) between the paired arches on each side and serve a similar function to the tonsillar tissue in the nasopharynx. The oropharynx receives air and nasal mucus from the nasopharynx above and opens into the laryngopharynx and laryngeal inlet below.

Laryngopharynx

The laryngopharynx, or hypopharynx, is the lowest part of the pharynx and extends from the tip of the epiglottic cartilage to the lower edge of the larynx. The laryngopharynx has an opening into the larynx in front, and air may pass through the upper laryngopharynx on its way to the larynx. Food from the oropharynx passes through the laryngopharynx on its way to the esophagus and stomach. Chicken and fish bones sometimes become lodged in pockets in the sides of the laryngopharynx. These pockets are called the piriform recesses and have an important nerve, the internal laryngeal nerve, lying in their floor. The internal laryngeal nerve supplies sensation to the upper larynx.

Cancer of the pharynx

Cancer may arise in the pharynx and, like mouth and tongue cancers, is usually associated with heavy smoking and drinking. These cancers need to be treated early and aggressively, with surgery and irradiation, for the patient to have a good chance of survival. Spread of the cancer to nearby lymph nodes is often present at diagnosis.

SEE ALSO *Adenoids, Ear, Larynx, Mouth, Nose, Pharyngitis, Respiratory system, Tonsils*

PHENYLKETONURIA

In most Western countries, 1 in every 10,000 to 20,000 children is born with the hereditary genetic disorder phenylketonuria (PKU). Despite its rare occurrence, all newborns are routinely tested for PKU using a simple blood analysis, the Guthrie test. This is because PKU can produce devastating affects without early intervention. People with PKU produce little or none of the enzyme phenylalanine hydroxylase, which breaks down the amino acid phenylalanine found in many foods. As a result, phenylalanine, which is toxic to brain tissue, accumulates in the body. The most serious impact is progressive mental retardation. This can be avoided, however, by a strict diet and regular monitoring.

SEE ALSO *Enzyme deficiencies*

P

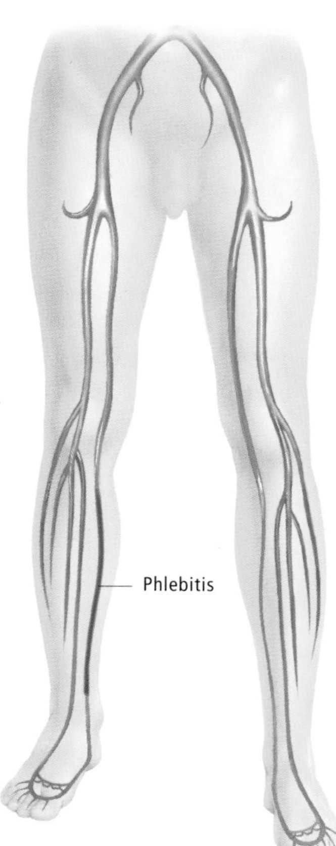

Phlebitis

Phlebitis is an inflammation of the veins, occurring mainly in the legs. The inflamed area swells and can become red and warm, and the blood flow may slow or stop.

PHLEBITIS

Phlebitis, or inflammation of the veins, is most commonly seen in the superficial veins of the legs. It results in pain and redness at the sites of inflammation, along the course of the vein. Inflammation of the vein wall causes the blood to clot at that point, and a lump can be felt under the skin. This condition is known as thrombophlebitis.

Phlebitis is most often a complication of varicose veins and may occur after prolonged standing or during pregnancy. Sometimes it occurs due to trauma to the vein or a reaction to a plastic cannula inserted for intravenous therapy.

Generally phlebitis is resolved with simple measures, such as rest and elevation of the leg, pain relief and anti-inflammatory medication. Sometimes it may extend to the deep venous system or be a sign of underlying malignant disease.

SEE ALSO *Thrombophlebitis, Varicose veins, Veins*

PHLEBOTOMUS FEVER

A virus transmitted by the bite of a female sandfly is responsible for phlebotomus fever. Symptoms appear suddenly, between three and six days after the bite, and include a general feeling of weariness, stomach pain, fever, headaches, muscle aches and sensitivity to light. Phlebotomus fever is prevalent throughout hot dry areas of the tropics and sub-tropics, where sandflies occur. The recommended treatment is simply bed rest and plenty of fluids. The disease runs its course after a few days and has never been known to have resulted in a fatality. Other names for phlebotomus fever include sandfly fever, pappataci fever and three-day fever.

SEE ALSO *Viruses*

PHOBIA

A phobia is a persistent, irrational fear, often recognized as such by the sufferer. A phobia may be triggered by specific objects, activities or situations and produces feelings of anxiety which can be overwhelming, often interfering with the sufferer's capacity to cope with everyday life. Typically, the anxiety is out of proportion to reality, but the fear is real and the person may be unable to control their feelings, even in cases where they are aware that they are overreacting.

Phobias are a form of anxiety disorder specific to physical objects or circumstances, and they produce all the symptoms characteristic of fear in other situations. Symptoms may involve heart palpitations, sweaty palms and breathing difficulties, and the sufferer may faint or feel dizzy.

There are various known phobias, for example, acrophobia is a fear of heights, arachnophobia is fear of spiders, claustrophobia is fear of enclosed spaces, agoraphobia is fear of open spaces—chronic agoraphobics may fear to leave their own homes—and social phobia causes a dread of being embarrassed in front of others.

Development of a phobia may result from a spontaneous panic attack, and the situation where that first attack was experienced may become the focus of phobic fear in the future. Behavioral therapy is successful in treating many phobias and involves gradual confrontation, under controlled conditions, with the fear and the objects or circumstances which produce it. After continued increasing exposure, the sufferer may become accustomed to the cause and lose their fear.

SEE ALSO *Acrophobia, Agoraphobia, Anxiety, Behavior therapy, Claustrophobia, Panic attack*

PHOTOCOAGULATION

Photocoagulation is a form of laser surgery used to correct certain eye disorders. It involves an intense beam of light directed into the eye to destroy damaged blood vessels and seal off leaking ones. Photocoagulation usually takes about 30 minutes, is relatively painless and is performed in a medical center or doctor's office by a specially trained ophthalmologist.

SEE ALSO *Eye*

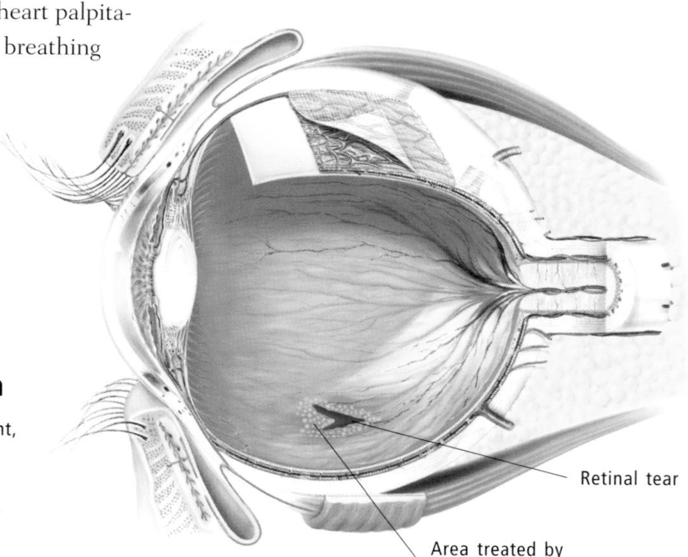

Photocoagulation

In cases of retinal detachment, photocoagulation can be used to "weld" the edges of the torn retina to the deeper layers of the eyeball and prevent further detachment.

PHOTOPHOBIA

Photophobia is an abnormal fear of or intolerance to light. It may develop as a result of infection, such as iritis, which causes pain and extreme sensitivity to light.

SEE ALSO *Iritis, Phobia*

PHOTOSENSITIVITY

Photosensitivity is a reaction to sunlight or ultraviolet light. It can be the cause of some skin conditions such as solar urticaria where itching wheals appear. Photosensitivity can cause blistering in people diagnosed with the enzyme deficiency disease porphyria cutanea tarda. It can also cause rosacea, a type of acne sometimes related to long-term exposure to sunlight. Light can be a source of pain and discomfort to migraine sufferers. Certain chemicals or drugs, such as some antibiotics, can produce photosensitivity.

SEE ALSO *Porphyria, Rosacea, Sun exposure, Urticaria*

PHYSICAL THERAPY

Physical therapy (physical medicine or physiotherapy) involves the use of physical modes of treatment—such as heat, massage, exercise and electrical currents—in the treatment of people physically disabled by pain or disease.

Physical therapy is an important part of the treatment of many conditions, including fractures, back pain, stroke, nerve and spinal cord injuries, and arthritis. The physical therapist (physiatrist or physiotherapist) is one of a team of health professionals involved in the rehabilitation of patients suffering from these illnesses; such a team may also include speech and occupational therapists, psychologists and counselors.

The objectives of physical therapy are to relieve pain and/or improve functions such as muscle strength, joint mobility, muscular coordination and breathing capacity. Heat may be used to stimulate circulation and to relieve pain. Heat may be applied by infrared lamps, short-wave radiation, high-frequency electrical currents (diathermy), immersion in hot water (hydrotherapy), application of hot moist compresses or by ultrasound. Exercise is used to increase the range of motion of a joint, to increase the strength in a muscle, or to improve muscle coordination. Breathing exercises may be used to improve the breathing of patients with lung disorders and correct faulty posture. Massage to an injured or diseased area aids circulation and relieves local pain or muscle spasm.

SEE ALSO *Hydrotherapy, Massage, Rehabilitation*

PICA

People with pica crave and eat non-food substances, such as clay, dirt, gravel, glue, ice, plaster and hair. The disorder occurs mostly in pregnant women, children aged between one and six years, people afflicted with certain forms of mental illness, and some people with intellectual disability. The cause may be an underlying nutritional problem. For example, an iron deficiency may prompt a person to crave and eat clay, or there may be psychological reasons. Treatment depends on the cause. Psychological or psychiatric counseling may help. In the case of a nutritional deficiency, the cravings may be dispelled by dietary adjustments or nutritional supplements.

PIGEON TOES

The condition known as pigeon toes or intoeing is characterized by feet that turn in during walking or running. It is seen commonly in toddlers and sometimes older children and is due to a temporary twist in a leg or foot bone, usually caused by the way a child lay in the uterus. It is uncommon in adults. In the past, the condition was often treated with corrective bracing or special footwear. These days this is rarely done as it is understood that, in all but a few cases, pigeon toes gradually improve by exercising the foot, and the condition usually disappears by the time a child starts school.

SEE ALSO *Foot*

PILATES METHOD

The Pilates method of exercise was devised by Joseph Pilates in the 1920s to aid in the rehabilitation of people injured in World War I. It is based on developing an awareness of the positioning of the body during exercise to achieve better muscle control, and aims to achieve pelvic stability, improve posture and safeguard the back from injury.

In Pilates exercises muscle groups are isolated to achieve maximum performance with minimal expenditure of energy. By strengthening and elongating muscles the exercises can help treat back injuries or pain.

SEE ALSO *Alexander technique, Feldenkrais method*

PILONIDAL SINUS

Pilonidal sinus (or cyst) is a common disorder that occurs most frequently in hairy young males. The affected person has a minor congenital abnormality, a small skin sac (sinus) at the base of the spine in the cleft between the buttocks. It causes no problems, unless it is infected (pilonidal abscess), causing pain and swelling in the area and a discharge of pus. The condition is treated with antibiotics, surgical drainage, and later, when the infection has subsided, surgical removal of the sinus.

SEE ALSO *Cyst*

PIMPLES

A pimple is an eruption in the skin, most commonly of the face, chest or upper back, which shows as a white spot (pustule), possibly surrounded by a reddened and inflamed area. Pimples form where skin pores are

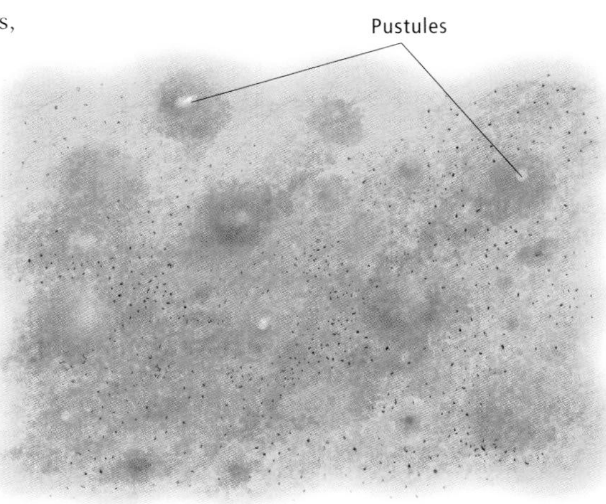

Pimples

Pimples form when skin pores become blocked by dried sebum from the sebaceous glands.

clogged by dried sebum (the oil from the sebaceous glands), flaked skin and bacteria. Bacterial growth in the blocked pore irritates the skin and a white head of pus forms from debris, largely white blood cells. A blackhead may form from dead skin cells if there is no bacterial infection in the pore.

Drugs such as anabolic steroids, corticosteroids, iodides, bromides and phenytoin can cause acne and eruptions of pimples. Keratosis pilaris is a disorder causing small pointed pimples on upper arms, thighs and buttocks.

SEE ALSO *Acne, Acne rosacea*

PINS AND NEEDLES

Pins and needles (parasthesia) is the sensation of tingling and pricking felt in the skin, usually in the hands and feet. It is due to a problem with the peripheral nerve supplying that region of the skin. Often the problem is pressure on the nerve, and will disappear when body position is changed and the pressure is relieved. Sometimes the pressure may be due to the nerve being trapped in a confined space, as in carpal tunnel syndrome, which causes pins and needles in the thumb, index and middle finger. Pins and needles also occur in diseases like diabetes and kidney failure which affect the nerves.

SEE ALSO *Carpal tunnel syndrome, Diabetes, Nerves*

PINWORMS

Pinworms *(Enterobius vermicularis)* are common gut parasites which usually cause only mild symptoms such as itching around the anus, and minor diarrhea. They infect people when their eggs are swallowed and hatch inside the colon. Adult pinworms, which look like white threads up to ½ inch (1 centimeter) long, lay their eggs in the rectum. Poor personal hygiene, particularly among children, is responsible for their spread—typically, an infected person scratches their anus, picks up the eggs on their fingers and reinfects themselves or passes the parasite on.

Effective medications are available but, even without treatment, infections usually disappear within weeks if strict personal hygiene measures are taken. Other names include seatworm and threadworm.

SEE ALSO *Worms*

PITUITARY GLAND

The pituitary gland (hypophysis) is a small organ lying immediately below the hypothalamus of the brain. It weighs only about $\frac{1}{60}$ of an ounce (0.5 gram), but plays a very important role in the control of endocrine gland function throughout the body. Endocrine glands are those glands that secrete special chemicals called hormones into the bloodstream or body cavities.

The pituitary gland is divided into two basic parts, each of which has a different

Pituitary function

The pituitary gland controls all the other endocrine glands in the body. It has two parts: the neurohypophysis (posterior pituitary), which secretes two hormones (vasopressin and oxytocin), and the adenohypophysis (anterior pituitary), which secretes hormones that control the thyroid and adrenal glands, and the follicles and corpus luteum in the ovaries.

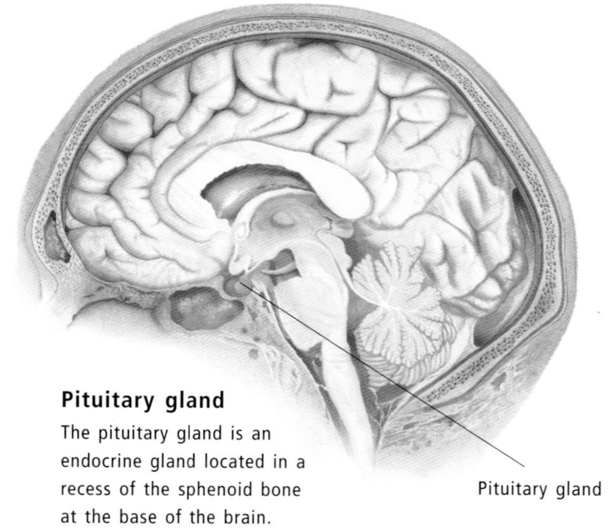

Pituitary gland
The pituitary gland is an endocrine gland located in a recess of the sphenoid bone at the base of the brain.

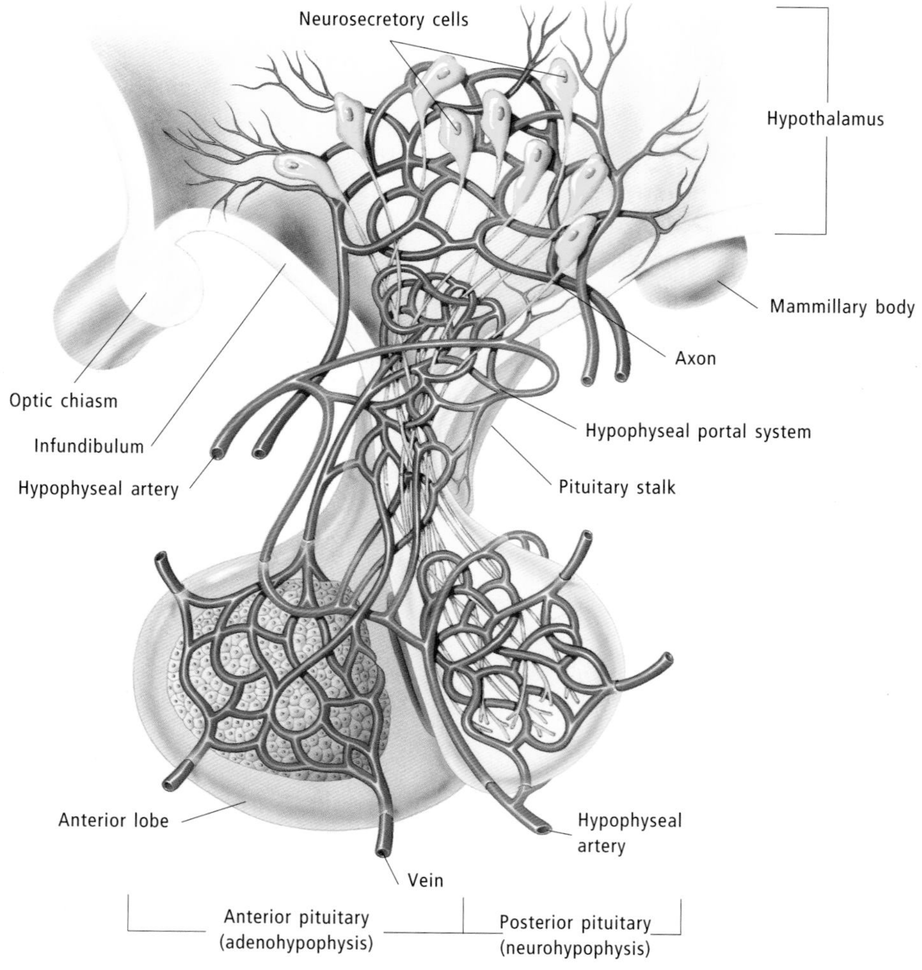

origin during embryonic life. The part towards the back of the gland is derived from the embryonic brain and is called the neurohypophysis (posterior pituitary). It is connected to the brain by a stalk called the infundibulum. The other part of the gland towards the front is derived from a pouch in the roof of the developing mouth (Rathke's pouch) and is called the adenohypophysis (anterior pituitary).

Neurohypophysis

The neurohypophysis is responsible for the release of two hormones: vasopressin (antidiuretic hormone—ADH) and oxytocin. Both hormones are polypeptides (chains of amino acids) that are made in the hypothalamus, a part of the brain immediately above the pituitary. Vasopressin increases water reabsorption from the urine as that fluid is being formed by the kidneys, thus making the urine more concentrated. The ultimate effect of this is to dilute the blood. Not surprisingly, vasopressin release is regulated in response to blood concentration, with special parts of the hypothalamus detecting changes in that concentration. Oxytocin causes contraction of smooth muscle cells in the uterus during childbirth and in the breasts during milk release (the milk ejection reflex).

Adenohypophysis

The adenohypophysis is also under the control of the hypothalamus, but is regulated by the release of hormones which flow in a special blood vessel system from the hypothalamus to the pituitary. The adenohypophysis releases many important hormones, with functions implied by their names. Growth hormone (GH) is important in the control of cartilage growth in long bones. Thyroid stimulating hormone (TSH) stimulates the production of thyroid hormone. Prolactin (lactogenic hormone) triggers the secretion of milk by the breasts (lactation). Adrenocorticotrophic hormone (ACTH or corticotropin) stimulates the production of hormones (corticosteroids and sex hormones) from the outer part of the adrenal glands (adrenal cortex). Follicle stimulating hormone (FSH) stimulates the development of egg follicles in a woman's ovaries and sperm cells in a man's testes. Luteinizing hormone (LH) stimulates the rupture of egg follicles in the ovary, and the formation of a corpus luteum in the ovary to produce progesterone during the latter half of a woman's menstrual cycle. The proper functioning of many of these hormones is essential to the correct growth, maturation and reproduction of an individual.

Tumors of the adenohypophysis usually grow slowly, but may damage nearby structures such as the visual pathways, causing partial blindness in the outer parts of the visual fields for each eye. Some endocrine diseases may arise due to abnormalities in hypothalamic/pituitary function (for example, failure to reach sexual maturity, some types of infertility, gigantism and acromegaly). Hypophysectomy is the surgical removal of all or part of the pituitary gland. It is sometimes necessary in the treatment of a pituitary tumor.

SEE ALSO *Adrenal glands, Endocrine system, Follicle stimulating hormone, Glands, Growth disorders, Hormones, Hypothalamus, Oxytocin*

PITYRIASIS ROSEA

A common and harmless skin disorder, pityriasis rosea is of unknown cause. It occurs mostly in adolescents and young adults, is slightly more common in females than males, and is more prevalent in spring and autumn.

The condition is characterized by a skin rash that follows a distinctive pattern. It begins on the trunk, upper arms, neck or thighs with a single, raised, oval-shaped, scaly, dark-red "herald patch" which can be mistaken for ringworm. Within three weeks many similar but smaller lesions appear, mainly in lines following the ribs, creating a Christmas-tree pattern. The rash may spread to other parts of the body but is rarely seen on the face, palms or soles of the feet. Treatment is not necessary although calamine lotion, cortisone creams and oral antihistamines should provide relief for people who experience itching from the rash.

Pityriasis rosea always clears by itself, usually after four to eight weeks, although the rash can persist for up to three months. It leaves no scars but darkly pigmented skin may bear discolored spots for several months. People rarely contract pityriasis rosea more than once. Although it is a minor affliction, a doctor should be consulted to rule out more serious conditions.

PLACEBO

A placebo is a "medicine" with no pharmacological action, sometimes given as make-believe medicine. Placebos are occasionally used in clinical trials of new medicines: consenting patients are divided into two groups, one of which is given the medicine, and the other group a placebo. The placebo will resemble the real medicine in appearance and taste but lack its pharmacological action. The trial is successful if patients taking the new medicine do significantly better than those taking the placebo.

PLACENTA

An organ of pregnancy, the placenta joins the mother and offspring, providing for selective exchange of substances through its membrane.

Formation

At conception, the ovum and sperm combine to form a single-celled embryo, the zygote. This divides rapidly and forms a hollow structure called a blastocyst upon reaching the uterus on day 4 of gestation. Some of the cells inside the blastocyst will become the embryo and fetal membranes, the outer cells will form the placenta.

On about day 6 the blastocyst adheres to the lining of the uterus (the endometrium). The outer cell mass undergoes changes which make it highly invasive and the entire blastocyst burrows its way into the endometrium which heals over it. That part of the outer cell mass which will form the placenta becomes elaborately folded and, as further erosion into the endometrium occurs, maternal blood vessels are broken down and maternal blood seeps into the spaces between the folds. Gradually a circulation is set up with maternal blood flowing in from the ends of arteries and out via the veins. Fetal blood vessels develop within the folds of the placenta and these connect with the blood vessels in the body of the embryo via the umbilical cord.

P

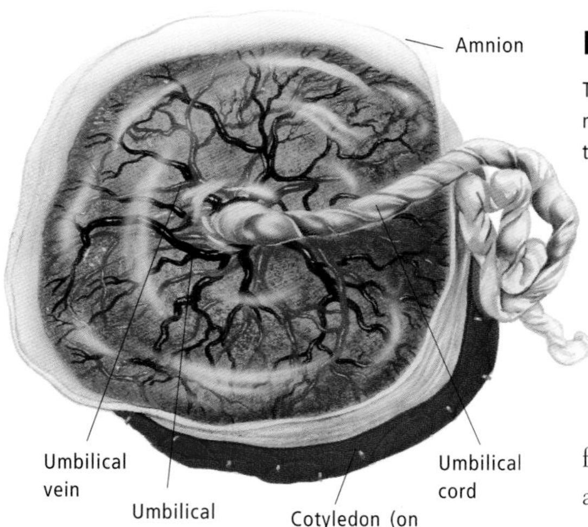

Placenta

The placenta connects the baby to the mother via the umbilical cord. It keeps the baby in position and ensures the baby receives adequate nutrients and oxygen. The placenta also acts as an endocrine organ, producing hormones such as placental prolactin, estrogen, and human chorionic gonadotropin during the pregnancy.

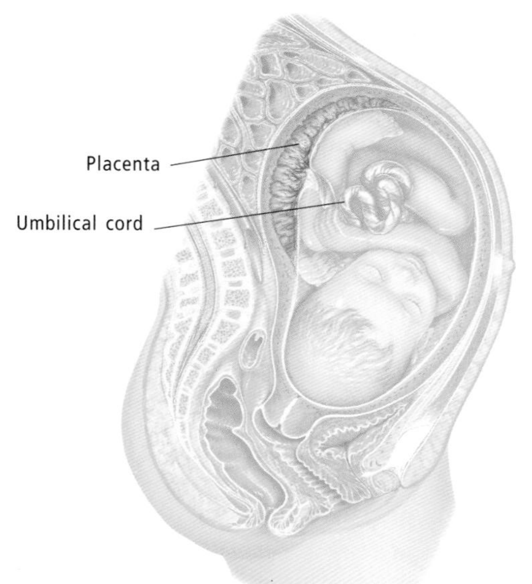

The parts of the placenta overlying the fetal capillaries become very thin in order to allow for diffusion of nutrients and oxygen from the maternal blood into the fetal blood and for fetal wastes to pass back to the mother's blood. Despite their close proximity, the two bloodstreams never actually have direct contact. As pregnancy proceeds, the fetus and the amnion enlarge so much that the cavity of the uterus is totally filled.

The blastocyst can implant anywhere in the uterus but most commonly in the upper posterior wall. Implantation near the opening of the cervix results in a placenta previa which partly or wholly covers the cervical opening. This forms a physical barrier at birth between the fetus and the birth canal; a placenta previa may also prematurely separate from the uterine wall. This can cause severe or fatal hemorrhaging of the mother's blood, either before or just after birth.

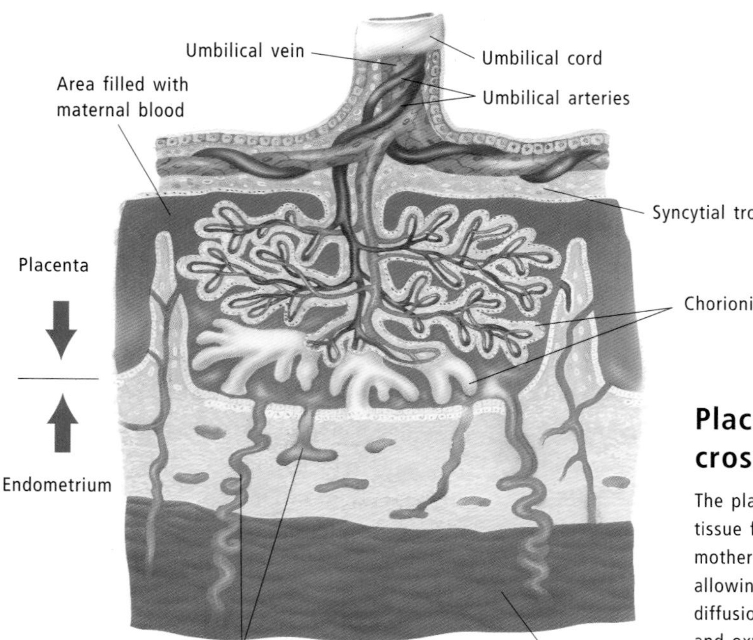

Placenta cross-section

The placenta contains tissue from both the mother and baby, allowing for the diffusion of nutrients and oxygen and the removal of fetal waste.

Other functions

The placenta produces many hormones including human chorionic gonadotropin (HCG), estrogen, progesterone, growth hormone and placental prolactin. HCG is the earliest placental hormone to be produced and is first secreted on day 6 of gestation. HCG maintains the corpus luteum (the ovarian follicle from which the ovum burst) and ensures that it continues to manufacture progesterone and estrogen until the placenta is able to produce adequate amounts of both, usually by the third month of gestation, when HCG levels decline. Progesterone is secreted by the placenta in increasing amounts during the last two trimesters and is necessary for the maintenance of pregnancy. HCG crosses the placenta into the maternal blood and is the basis for many of the tests for pregnancy.

The placenta forms a protective barrier between the maternal and fetal blood although certain noxious agents can travel across it and infect the fetus. These include many (though not all) viruses, notably rubella and HIV, anti-Rhesus factor antibodies, alcohol, pesticides, drugs such as thalidomide, and hormones such as diethylstilbestrol. Microbes larger than viruses usually cannot cross the placenta but exceptions include the bacterium of syphilis and the protozoan parasite which causes toxoplasmosis.

Tumors

Hydatidiform mole and choriocarcinoma are tumors arising from the placenta. Hydatidiform moles are characterized by some, or all, of the placental folds undergoing abnormal proliferation to form a mass of watery cysts. The embryo is usually missing, especially when the mole affects the whole placenta. These tumors grow rapidly and can cause severe hemorrhage if they invade deep into the uterine wall or the adjacent pelvic vessels. They produce large amounts of HCG which is used to diagnose the condition. Choriocarcinoma is a rare, highly malignant tumor formed from placental tissue; it may follow a hydatidiform mole or occur after a spontaneous abortion or normal pregnancy.

SEE ALSO *Embryo, Estrogens, Fetal development, Hydatidiform mole, Pregnancy, Progesterone, Reproductive systems, Toxoplasmosis*

P

PLANTAR FASCIITIS

A common cause of heel pain, plantar fasciitis often occurs in athletes and people who walk a lot on hard surfaces. It is an inflammation of the thick band of fibrous tissue on the bottom of the foot—the plantar fascia—and can persist for months. Treatment includes anti-inflammatory medications and resting the affected foot.

SEE ALSO *Foot*

PLASMA

Plasma refers to the fluid component of the blood. It consists of water, salts and proteins and contains all the chemicals which circulate between body tissues, including glucose, hormones, enzymes and growth factors. Plasma generally contributes approximately half the blood volume, the rest being due to red and white blood cells.

The major plasma protein is albumin, synthesized by the liver and important in maintaining the blood's osmotic pressure. The liver also makes some of the blood clotting proteins, which are found in the plasma. Another group of plasma proteins are the globulins, which include immunoglobulins produced by the immune system and are responsible for fighting infection.

Plasma is lost together with red and white cells during bleeding and may need to be replaced if loss is severe. Initial replacement can be with plasma substitutes, followed by the infusion of fresh frozen plasma. This is produced from donated blood, the plasma being separated by centrifugation and frozen until required.

In some diseases the patient's plasma may be exchanged with normal plasma or albumin solution as part of the treatment. The procedure is known as plasmapheresis and is performed using an apheresis machine.

SEE ALSO *Blood, Globulins, Liver, Lymphatic/Immune system, Plasmapheresis*

PLASMAPHERESIS

Plasmapheresis is a technique in which plasma is passed through a filtration device that removes certain antibodies and abnormal protein elements and returns the plasma, free of antibodies and these protein elements, to the patient. It is used in the treatment of certain autoimmune diseases (caused by antibodies attacking the body's own tissue), such as systemic lupus erythematosus (SLE), myasthenia gravis and multiple myeloma.

SEE ALSO *Antibodies, Autoimmune disease, Plasma*

PLASTIC SURGERY

Plastic or reconstructive surgery is a versatile specialty which includes the correction of disfigurement, restoring impaired function and improving physical appearance (cosmetic surgery). Reconstructive surgery is performed on abnormalities caused by congenital defects, developmental abnormalities, trauma, infection, tumors or disease. One of the possible sources of the term is the Greek word *plastikos*, which means "to mold or give form".

The driving force behind most developments in plastic surgery was war. World War I (1914–18) resulted in outstanding developments in plastic surgery. At this time doctors were required to treat many extensive facial and head injuries, ranging from shattered jaws and blown-off noses to gaping skull wounds. At first this specialty had no formal training. Then in the 1930s the American Society of Plastic and Reconstructive Surgeons was launched. In the 1940s, during World War II, the skills of plastic surgeons were again in great demand.

In the 1960s silicone emerged as a tool for plastic surgeons. Initially it was used to treat skin imperfections. However, in 1962 it was first used by an American surgeon, Thomas Cronin, in a breast implant device. It was not until 1990 that concerns about silicone implants came to a head and patients began to sue manufacturers, leading to the ban of silicone breast implants in the USA in 1992.

Plastic surgery repairs or reshapes tissue structures, removes tissues and grafts or transfers tissue. Grafting is used to treat cases of trauma such as severe burns, injuries from automobile accidents and gunshot wounds. If the circumstances are favorable, plastic surgeons may also reattach a severed body part. Congenital deformities—commonly cleft lip and palate—can also be corrected by plastic surgery.

SEE ALSO *Cosmetic surgery, Mammoplasty*

PLATELETS

Platelets are small cell fragments in the blood that prevent bruising and bleeding. They adhere to small breaks in blood vessels and form a plug, which blocks the defect. Platelets release chemicals which attract more platelets to the affected area and trigger the clotting system to form a clot, or thrombus.

Thrombocytopenia is a condition in which there are too few platelets, and results in a tendency to bleed. Having too many platelets, a condition known as thrombocytosis, increases the risk of thrombosis, which can cause heart attack or stroke.

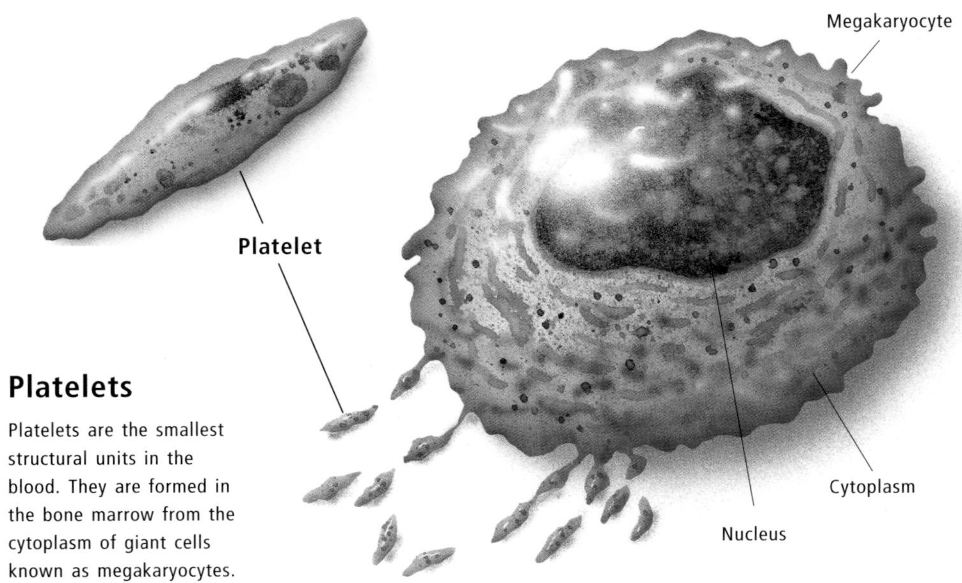

Platelets

Platelets are the smallest structural units in the blood. They are formed in the bone marrow from the cytoplasm of giant cells known as megakaryocytes.

Aspirin blocks the release of chemicals by platelets and can cause easy bruising in some people. It is widely used to reduce the risk of thrombosis as it makes platelets less sticky or adherent.

SEE ALSO *Blood, Thrombocytopenia, Thrombocytosis, Thrombosis, Thrombus*

PLAY THERAPY

Play therapy was recognized in the 1930s as a valuable way of helping troubled children. Through play children develop, integrate and communicate their emotions, thoughts and sense of self. In play therapy, children are encouraged to play freely in the safe environment provided by a psychotherapist. The therapist learns about the children's concerns by observing their play.

Discussion between the child and the therapist about the play allows the therapist to support the child and understand the child's feelings. Play also helps the therapist make diagnoses, and establish rapport with the child. Play therapy is helpful for children with emotional, behavioral and learning difficulties.

SEE ALSO *Counseling, Psychotherapy*

Viral pneumonia
The influenza virus is one of several viruses that can cause pneumonia.

Bacterial pneumonia
Culture of the sputum of pneumonia sufferers will reveal bacteria. These need to be tested for sensitivity to antibiotics before treatment.

Pneumonia
In pneumonia, air spaces in the lungs fill with fluid and cellular debris preventing gas exchange. This can result in respiratory or cardiac failure.

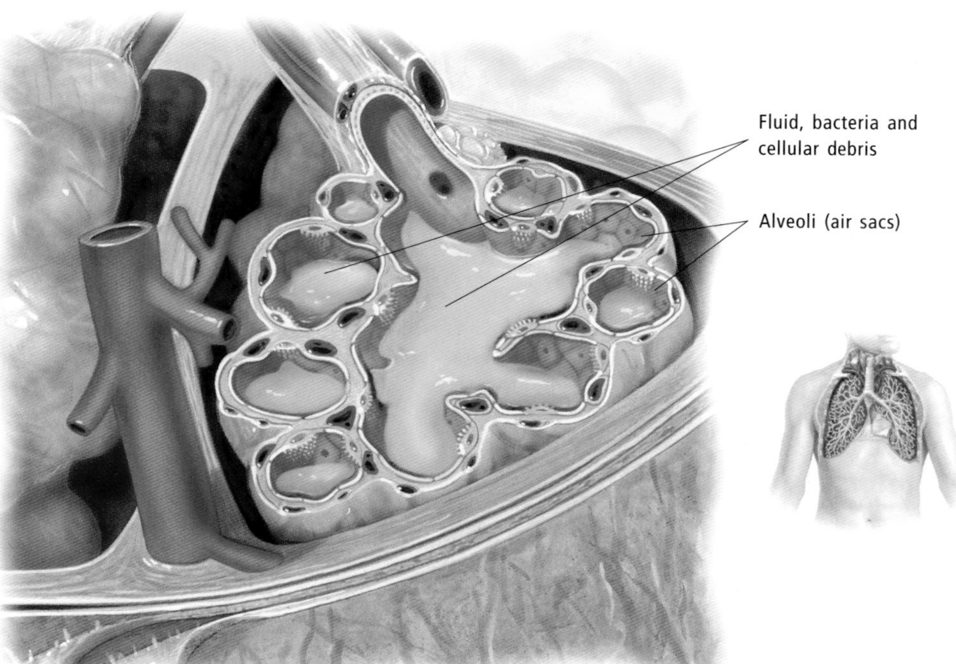

PLEURISY

Pleurisy is inflammation of the pleura, a thin, two-layered membrane that lines the lung and chest cavity and enables the lungs to move smoothly against the chest wall during breathing. Pleurisy is a consequence of other lung conditions rather than a disease in itself. Conditions that may lead to the development of pleurisy include bronchitis, pneumonia, a blood clot in the lung, lung cancer, collagen vascular diseases (such as systemic lupus erythematosus or rheumatoid arthritis), congestive heart failure or kidney and liver disorders.

The symptoms of pleurisy are sudden chest pain that worsens with breathing, and coughing. Other symptoms of the underlying disease may also be present; for example, chest pain, cough and fever.

Depending on the cause, pleurisy may occur with a pleural effusion (fluid that has collected in the pleural cavity). A pleural effusion may show up on a chest x-ray, which may also show evidence of the disorder causing the pleurisy—pneumonia or lung cancer, for example. Other investigations may be ordered by the physician, depending on the cause. Treatment is directed toward the underlying cause and may include painkillers, anti-inflammatory drugs and antibiotics.

SEE ALSO *Breathing, Lungs, Respiratory system*

PLEURODYNIA

Also known as Bornholm disease or epidemic myalgia, pleurodynia is a temporary inflammation of the pleura, the tissue lining the lungs, occurring most often in children. The condition is caused by the Group B coxsackie viruses. The patient suffers severe pain in the lower chest (worsened by breathing and coughing), muscle pain, fever, sore throat, and headaches. Symptoms usually clear up in 2–4 days without treatment, though relapses may occur. Acetaminophen (paracetamol) may help relieve pain and fever .

SEE ALSO *Lungs*

PNEUMOCONIOSIS

Pneumoconiosis is a group of diseases caused by prolonged inhalation of inorganic dusts, which collect in the lungs. These dusts (coal, silica or asbestos) are usually inhaled in the course of particular occupations, such as coal mining, sand blasting, pottery, stone dressing or asbestos mining. Symptoms vary slightly according to the type of dust, but all patients with pneumoconiosis experience breathlessness.

SEE ALSO *Lungs*

PNEUMONIA

Pneumonia is a serious lung disease in which inflammation, caused by bacteria and/or viruses, results in the accumulation of fluid and cellular debris in the air spaces of the lungs. This prevents the exchange of carbon dioxide and oxygen in the lungs. Pneumonia is very common, affecting about 1 percent of the population every year. It is most common in winter and spring because of sudden drops in air temperature, overcrowding in poorly ventilated rooms and the prevalence of bacteria and viruses. Smoking, alcoholism, a poor immune system and air pollution are associated with an increased risk of pneumonia. As many as 5–10 percent of those developing pneumonia may die from the disease, usually the very young or the elderly. Bedridden patients with dementia, hip fractures or chronic heart disease are particularly prone to developing pneumonia, which is often the ultimate cause of death.

Depending on the site involved, different types of pneumonia may be described: lobar pneumonia affects an entire lobe of the lung; lobular pneumonia affects lung tissue around the major airway branches; bronchopneumonia is lobular pneumonia affecting both lungs.

The microorganisms responsible for pneumonia include bacteria, such as *Streptococcus pneumoniae*, *Staphylococcus aureus*, *Klebsiella pneumoniae* and *Haemophilus influenzae*, and viruses, such as influenza, adenovirus and respiratory syncytial virus. Occasionally pneumonia may be caused by unusual microorganisms such as fungi, rickettsiae and mycoplasma. Unusual microorganisms like fungi and mycoplasma are more likely to be found to be responsible when the patient's immune system is functioning poorly, as in those with AIDS.

Patients with pneumonia may at first complain of cough and sputum (coughed-up lung fluid), breathlessness, sharp chest pain aggravated by coughing or by taking a deep breath, fever and a general feeling of being unwell. The sputum is usually yellow or green and may occasionally contain blood, particularly if vessels in the lung have been ruptured by vigorous coughing. A chest x-ray will show loss of the normal air-filled spaces, so that the lung fields appear white, either uniformly, within a lobe of the lung (lobar pneumonia) or in patches (bronchopneumonia). Culture of the sputum will reveal bacteria, which may be the actual causative organism or present as secondary bacterial infection of a pneumonia caused by a virus. The bacteria need to be tested for sensitivity to antibiotics, because in recent years many bacteria have developed resistance to some of the available antibiotics (such as the penicillin family). The concentration of oxygen in the arterial blood may be reduced, and in the severely ill the concentration of carbon dioxide in the blood may rise.

Treatment of pneumonia involves prescribing the appropriate antibiotic for the causative microorganism. The patient should be supported by inhaled oxygen, receive physical therapy to clear the airways and analgesics to relieve pain. Complications which may arise include respiratory failure, cardiac failure, abscesses (pus-filled cavities) in the lung and fluid in the pleural sacs around the lung (pleural effusion). Occasionally pus may collect in the pleural sacs around the lung (pleural empyema).

SEE ALSO *Bacteria, Lungs, Sputum tests, Viruses*

Pneumothorax

In this condition, air enters one or both of the pleural sacs which enclose the lungs. This may occur if the chest wall is pierced. When air is trapped in the chest cavity, increased pressure can result in the collapse of the lungs.

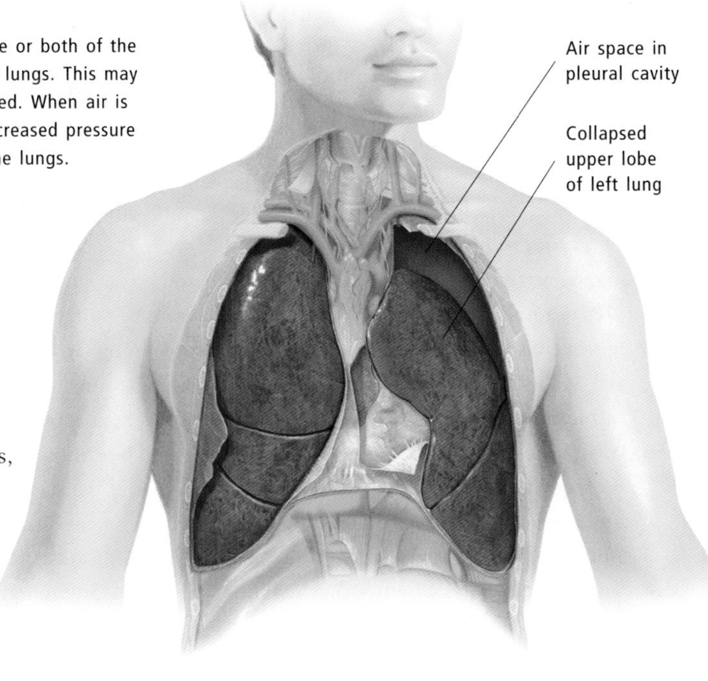

PNEUMOTHORAX

Pneumothorax literally means "air in the chest". It occurs when air enters one or both of the pleural sacs which enclose the lungs. Pneumothorax may occur spontaneously, due to rupture of an air space in the outer part of the lung, or as a result of injury, which leads to perforation of the chest wall. Traumatic pneumothorax may follow penetrating chest wall injuries, blast injuries and diving accidents.

A particularly dangerous type of pneumothorax is tension pneumothorax, which occurs when a flap-valve effect in the damaged pleural membrane allows air to enter the pleural sac, but not escape. Pressure in the pleural sac rises rapidly, causing complete collapse of the lung on the affected side and a movement of the organs in the center of the chest to the opposite side of the chest, thus compressing the other lung. Both heart and lung function may be seriously affected, and rapid reduction of the air pressure in the pleural sac may be required.

Pneumothorax is treated by insertion of a tube into the affected side of the chest. This tube is connected to a drain and water valve mechanism, which allows air to leave the pleural sac but prevents re-entry. Often pneumothorax is accompanied by bleeding into the pleural sac (hemothorax), which may require drainage if a large amount of bleeding has occurred.

SEE ALSO *Lungs*

POISONING

Any substance that can cause illness or death is a potential poison. Poisons can be swallowed, inhaled, injected, absorbed through the skin or developed within the body. Some substances are more toxic than others and only a small quantity may be needed in order to poison a person; other poisons may need to be ingested in large quantities before they produce an effect.

Different poisons operate in different ways and will affect different parts of the body. Some poisons will act immediately, other substances are only poisonous once they reach certain levels in the body—lead poisoning is a good example of this.

For some substances, how they enter the body can also determine whether they will be poisonous or not; some are harmless when eaten but deadly if injected into a vein. In other cases, a substance which is harmless to an adult may poison a baby or child, for example, a dose of aspirin or alcohol. Listeria (listeriosis), not usually noticeable in adults, is particularly dangerous to an unborn child if the mother should be infected.

Food poisoning

One of the most common types of accidental poisoning is food poisoning. Symptoms of vomiting, diarrhea, abdominal cramps and general nausea result from consumption of foods which are contaminated by bacteria (*Salmonella, Shigella, Staphylococci, Clostridium* and *E. coli*) or their toxic products. Cooking destroys salmonella but cooked foods can be recontaminated if they come in contact with raw foods.

Strict personal hygiene standards when preparing and serving foods are essential, because bacteria can be transferred through the oral-fecal route—for example, by not washing hands after defecating or urinating and then working with food. It is also important to keep hot food very hot and to refrigerate food immediately at temperatures of 41°F (5°C) or lower after cooking, if it is not being eaten. Utensils and equipment used for preparing food needs to be kept scrupulously clean.

Food poisoning can also be caused by toxins from plants and animals or chemical poisons. Healthy adults usually recover quickly from food poisoning, though it can lead to chronic illness such as Reiter's syndrome and reactive arthritis. In young children, the elderly and those with a compromised immune system, food poisoning demands immediate treatment.

Mussels, clams, certain other shellfish and some fish can be poisonous when ingested by humans. Examples include tetraodon poisoning (which is poisoning from certain puffer-like fish) and scombroid poisoning (from fish in the mackerel family, such as tuna and bonito, which have lost their freshness). Mussels and clams can become poisonous, particularly in the Pacific Ocean, feeding on microorganisms that appear in the warmer months of the year.

Other foodstuffs which can poison, if taken in large quantities, include dietary supplements such as iron tablets and the vitamins D and A.

Environmental poisoning

Carbon monoxide poisoning is the most common cause of poison-related deaths in the USA. Carbon monoxide is a tasteless, colorless, odorless gas produced by the incomplete burning of fuel containing carbon—automobile exhaust, coal gas and furnace gas are all sources of carbon monoxide.

Lead poisoning—contamination from lead paints, dust, contaminated soil, and automobile gases—affects the blood, nervous system and digestive system. A blood test will reveal a person's lead level, although simple precautions, plus a diet which is low in fat and includes sufficient iron, are effective methods of minimizing the risks.

Other sources of environmental poisoning are pesticides and herbicides, often ingested through their accidental contact with foodstuffs. Toxic chemicals used around the home include soap and detergents, mothballs, bleaches and cleaners, rat or mouse bait, cosmetics, eucalyptus and tea-tree oil. Any of these can poison children who ingest them accidentally.

Poisonous plants, while sometimes attractive to children, are not considered to be a major cause of poisoning. Poisoning can result from eating any of several species of mushroom or toadstool. Plant poisoning can also occur from eating green or sprouting underground roots which contain solanine, sometimes found in green potatoes.

Treatment

First aid for poisoning varies depending on the poison ingested. The best course for the untrained person is to call a Poison Information Hotline or Control Center. A knowledge of first aid including cardiopulmonary resuscitation may be helpful. Inducing vomiting can worsen the damage and should only be done on the advice of a medical practitioner. Victims of an inhaled poison should be removed to fresh air, and when poisoning is via the skin, the area affected should be repeatedly rinsed with water.

SEE ALSO *Listeriosis, Overdose, Reiter's syndrome*

POLIOMYELITIS

Poliomyelitis (commonly known as polio) is a viral illness, usually affecting young children. It is spread from the infected individual to others by fecal-oral infection (which may occur if hands are not washed properly after defecating or urinating) or droplet infection (such as with sneezing). It is usually a mild illness; symptoms are slight fever, malaise, headache, sore throat, and vomiting 3–5 days after exposure. Complete recovery normally occurs in 24–72 hours. In about 10 percent of cases, however, it causes inflammation of the spinal cord and the brain stem.

Symptoms are fever, severe headache, stiff neck and muscle pain. In some cases, this may progress to weakness or paralysis of muscle groups, causing difficulty swallowing and breathing, and paralysis of the muscles of the legs and lower torso.

The condition is diagnosed by identifying the virus in cerebrospinal fluid, in the throat or in feces. Treatment involves physical therapy to aid muscle function. In severe cases, a tracheostomy (cutting an opening in the windpipe to insert a breathing tube) and an artificial respirator may be necessary.

The disease can be prevented by immunization. Polio vaccine may be given by injection, or (more usually) by mouth, at the ages of 2 months, 4 months, 6–18 months and 4–6 years. The development of polio vaccines has almost eliminated the disease in industrialized countries.

SEE ALSO *Immunization, Paralysis, Spinal cord, Viruses*

Poliomyelitis

The success of vaccines against the polio virus has greatly reduced the incidence of poliomyelitis. Jonas Salk developed the first effective vaccine, which has been largely superseded by an oral vaccine developed by Albert Sabin.

POLYCYSTIC KIDNEY DISEASE

The most commonly inherited disorder in the USA, polycystic kidney disease (PKD), is characterized by pain in the back and side of the body, frequent kidney infections, blood in the urine and high blood pressure. In this condition, cysts grow in the kidneys causing symptoms and damaging the kidneys. There is no treatment for the cysts themselves, but the symptoms of the disease can be treated. Over half of those suffering from PKD will suffer from kidney failure at some time in their life.

Genetic counseling is generally available for couples with a family history of PKD, and tests such as chorionic villus sampling and amniocentesis can determine whether a fetus will have the disease.

SEE ALSO *Amniocentesis, Chorionic villus sampling, Kidney*

POLYCYTHEMIA

Polycythemia, literally "many blood cells", refers to a group of blood conditions in which the numbers of cells in the blood increases. This may involve the red cells, white cells and/or the platelets. The most common and important form is an increase in the red cells, causing facial redness and increased viscosity of the blood. The affected person may have a sensation of fullness in the head and of itching, particularly after a hot bath or shower, which releases histamine from the white cells. The increased red cells and platelets result in a greater tendency to clotting in the veins and arteries, leading to deep venous thrombosis, heart attack or stroke.

Treatment is based on reducing blood viscosity through regular venesection, which is removal of blood from a vein—a needle is inserted into a large vein at the front of the elbow. Sometimes medication is required to control the increased cell production by the bone marrow.

SEE ALSO *Blood, Platelets, Red blood cells, White blood cells*

POLYMYOSITIS

Polymyositis is an autoimmune inflammatory disease of muscle. It causes muscle weakness, especially around the shoulders and hips. The muscles ache and may be tender to the touch. Fatigue, weight loss and a low-grade fever are common. The cause is unknown. The condition is treated with physical therapy and corticosteroids or immunosuppressant drugs.

SEE ALSO *Autoimmune disease*

POLYPS

A polyp is a growth or tumor protruding from a mucous membrane. It may be shaped like a grape on a stalk or may be a small lump. While polyps are usually benign (non-cancerous), they may lead to complications. They are most commonly found in the colon (large intestine), the nasal passages, the cervix of the uterus and within the uterine cavity.

Intestinal polyps are found most often in the rectum and sigmoid colon. They usually cause no symptoms, though in some cases there may be bleeding from the rectum. They should be removed, as they may become malignant. Surgery to remove a polyp is usually done via a proctoscope or

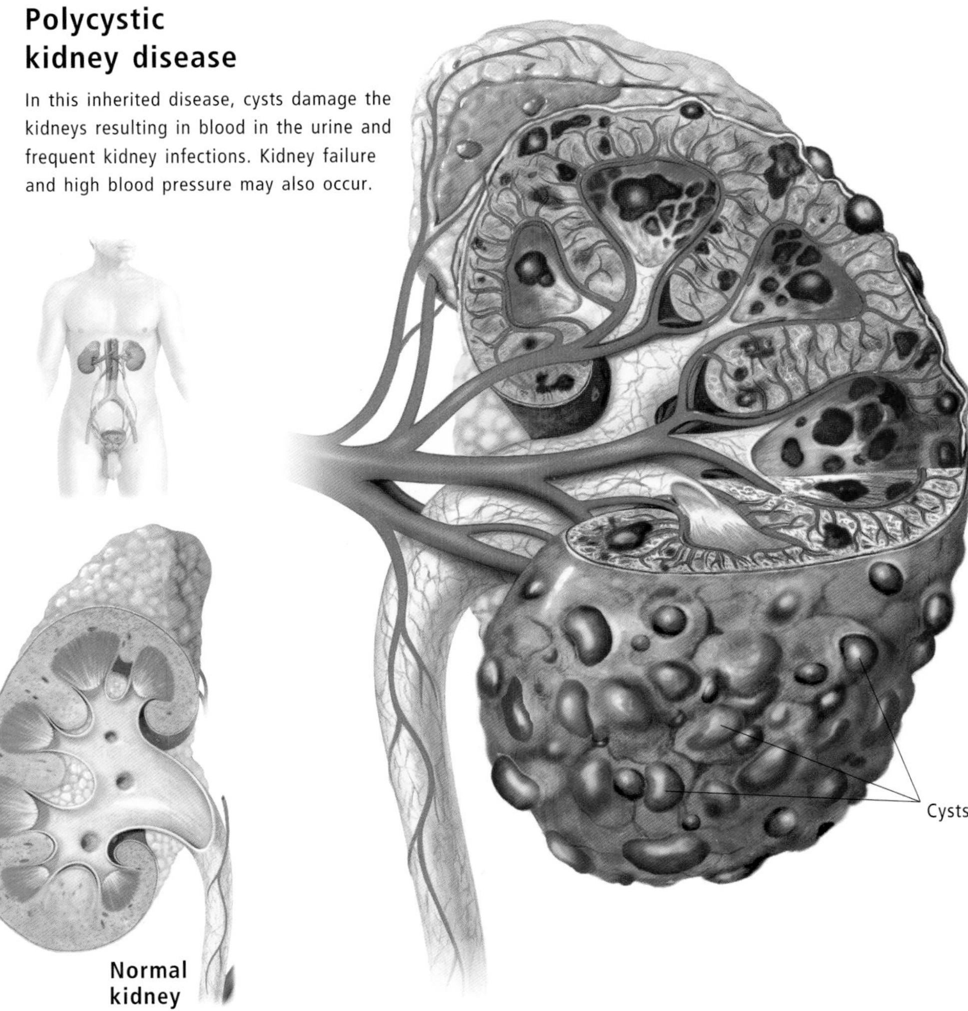

Polycystic kidney disease

In this inherited disease, cysts damage the kidneys resulting in blood in the urine and frequent kidney infections. Kidney failure and high blood pressure may also occur.

P

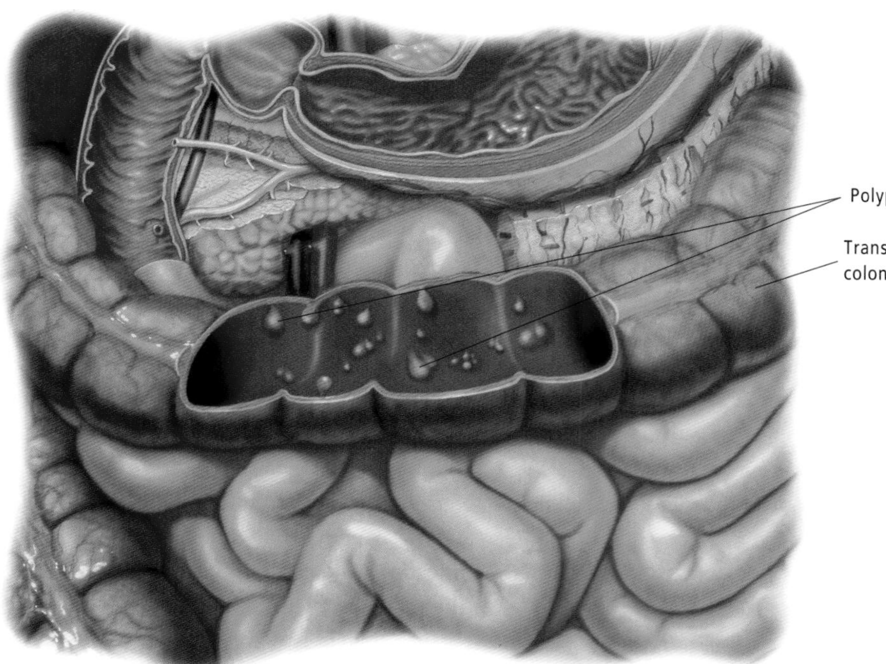

Polyps

Most commonly found in the colon, polyps are growths or tumors which protrude from the mucous membrane. A polyp may be a small lump, or shaped like a grape with a stalk.

sigmoidoscope inserted via the rectum; the polyps are snipped off or destroyed by electric cauterization. Anyone with a personal or family history of polyps should have regular sigmoidoscopic examinations.

Familial polyposis is a rare hereditary condition in which multiple polyps cover the colon and rectum. It usually develops into cancer, so the rectum and colon must be removed surgically. Relatives should have periodic sigmoidoscopic examinations.

Nasal polyps are caused by chronic infection or allergy in the nose (allergic rhinitis). They cause a nasal discharge and chronic stuffiness. They are easily removed with minor surgery under local anesthesia.

SEE ALSO *Colon, Nose, Proctoscopy*

PORPHYRIA

Porphyria is a rare group of disorders resulting from defects in the production of heme, the oxygen-carrying portion of hemoglobin. An accumulation of chemicals called porphyrins results in attacks of abdominal pain and mental disturbance in one type of porphyria (King George III was thought to suffer from this), and blistering of the fingers in another. Symptoms can be triggered by a variety of factors including alcohol, certain drugs, hormonal irregularities and exposure to the sun. There is no cure—sufferers should avoid the offending substance, wherever possible.

SEE ALSO *Blood, Hemoglobin*

PORTAL HYPERTENSION

Portal hypertension is an increase in the pressure of the blood in the portal venous system. This is the system of veins that drains blood from the intestines to the liver.

The most common cause of this condition is chronic liver disease leading to cirrhosis, which obstructs blood flowing through the liver. This causes life-threatening bleeding into the lower esophagus and stomach. The patient may vomit copious amounts of blood (hematemesis) or pass black, tar-like feces containing altered blood (melena). The associated swelling of the abdomen is due to the accumulation of fluid in the abdominal cavity (ascites). Fluid collects in the abdomen and lower legs because the diseased liver is unable to produce a protein called albumin which helps to control fluid movement between the tissues of the body and the bloodstream.

SEE ALSO *Cirrhosis of the liver, Liver, Portal vein*

PORTAL VEIN

The portal vein is a wide but short vein that collects nutrient-rich blood from the veins leading from the large and small intestines, the stomach, the spleen, the pancreas and the gallbladder. It then transports this collected blood to the liver. The portal vein enters the liver through a slit called the porta hepatis (Latin for "door to the liver") and ends as a network of capillaries in the liver called sinusoids, which permeate the entire liver. There, ageing red cells, bacteria and other debris are removed from the blood, and nutrients are added to the blood or removed from it for storage. The blood then leaves the liver via the hepatic veins, which empty into the inferior vena cava.

Portal hypertension is increased pressure in the portal vein, and the veins that supply it, resulting from increased resistance to the blood flow into the liver, usually from scarring due to cirrhosis. A portacaval shunt is a surgically produced junction between the hepatic portal vein and the inferior vena cava, bypassing the liver. It is performed in cases of severe portal hypertension to improve the flow of blood through the portal vein to the inferior vena cava.

SEE ALSO *Portal hypertension*

POSITRON EMISSION TOMOGRAPHY

Commonly referred to as a PET scan, positron emission tomography is an imaging technique for monitoring body processes such as blood flow and metabolism. Chemical compounds containing radioactive isotopes are injected into an organ, and the body is scanned using a special machine. Positrons (positively charged electrons) emitted by the isotopes collide with electrons within the body, creating gamma radiation that is detected by the scanner. The resulting information is converted to computer images to give a cross-sectional view of the organ being studied. This technique is used to assess such things as muscle damage after a heart attack and the effects of chemotherapy drugs on body tissue.

SEE ALSO *Imaging techniques*

POSTNATAL DEPRESSION

Postnatal depression, also known as postpartum depression, is experienced by some women after giving birth. It is characterized by mood swings, insomnia, despondency, feelings of hopelessness and an inability to cope with normal situations. The condition is thought to result from extreme hormonal changes after birth, combined with the stress of looking after a new baby. It affects about 3 percent of mothers, even those with no history of psychological illness.

Many mothers suffer from a milder, short-lived depression known as "baby blues" in the week following a delivery, during which they may cry and feel anxious and moody. About 10 percent of mothers develop full-blown symptoms of postnatal depression, sometimes up to a year after the birth. They may have a preoccupation with their baby's health, feel guilty about not loving the child enough and appear detached from the baby. There may also be physical symptoms, such as headaches, chest pain, lethargy, heart palpitations and hyperventilation. Behavior can be extreme and hostile, and may include having nightmares, hallucinations and panic attacks. The condition usually lasts anywhere from 3–6 months.

Family problems or stressful events can put a woman at greater risk of suffering from postnatal depression. In some cases, the condition may resolve itself spontaneously. Where necessary, treatment is with a combination of counseling and medication (although some drugs can affect the baby via breast milk).

SEE ALSO *Childbirth, Depression, Infancy, Newborn*

POSTPOLIO SYNDROME

Postpolio syndrome is a condition that occasionally affects individuals who have previously had poliomyelitis. Sufferers experience weakness, fatigue and muscle twitches, as late as 20–30 years after the initial illness. The symptoms develop gradually; muscle groups that were not originally affected may become involved. In most cases, symptoms of the disease reach a plateau and do not deteriorate further.

Postpolio syndrome is not a recurrent bout of polio, but is thought to be due to death of nerve cells (neurons) that survived the original disease. There is no specific treatment but physical therapy may help manage the symptoms.

SEE ALSO *Poliomyelitis*

POST-TRAUMATIC STRESS DISORDER

Post-traumatic stress disorder (PTSD) is a debilitating condition that follows a terrifying event. First recognized as a condition of war veterans, called "shell shock" or "battle fatigue", it can be caused by any traumatic incident, such as car or train wrecks, natural disasters such as floods or earthquakes, or violent attacks against a person.

Symptoms usually begin within 3 months of the trauma, and may include recurrent, intrusive and distressing recollections of the event, flashbacks and dreams of the event, difficulty in concentrating, and memory impairment. The disorder can be accompanied by chronic anxiety, insomnia, depression and substance abuse. Not everyone who experiences a traumatic event suffers from PTSD, and many who do experience such an event may display these symptoms for only a short time. The diagnosis of PTSD is usually only made if the symptoms last longer than 1 month.

The recommended treatment is psychotherapy and counseling on an individual or group basis, as needed. Several different methods of therapy are available, including behavior therapy, desensitization, and hypnotherapy. The earlier the therapy takes place after the incident, the better the outcome. Psychiatric hospitalization may be needed for a suicidal patient or one who is severely dysfunctional.

The prognosis of PTSD is variable; some sufferers recover within six months, while in others symptoms last much longer. In some cases the condition may be ongoing.

SEE ALSO *Anxiety, Behavior therapy, Counseling, Depression, Psychotherapy, Trauma*

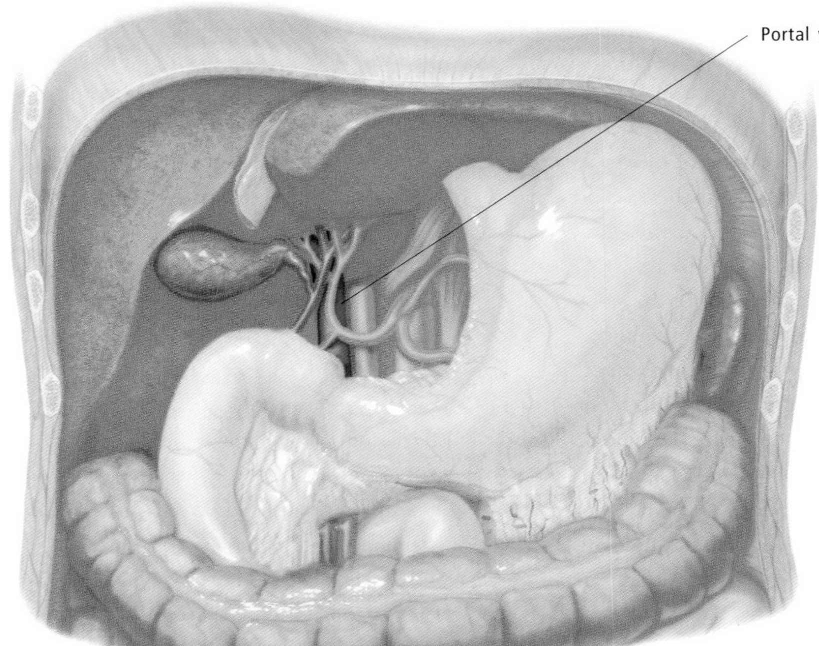

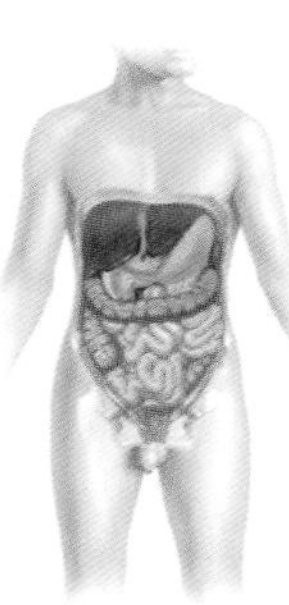

Portal vein

The portal vein collects blood from the veins that lead from the digestive tract. It transports this collected blood into the liver, where sugars and amino acids are removed.

NB: In this illustration the liver has been lifted up to show the portal vein.

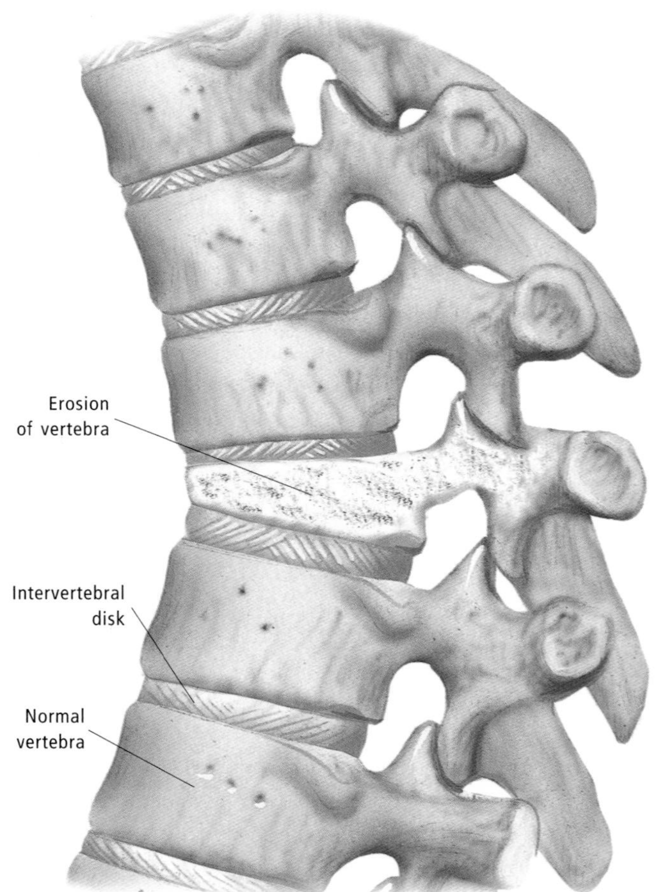

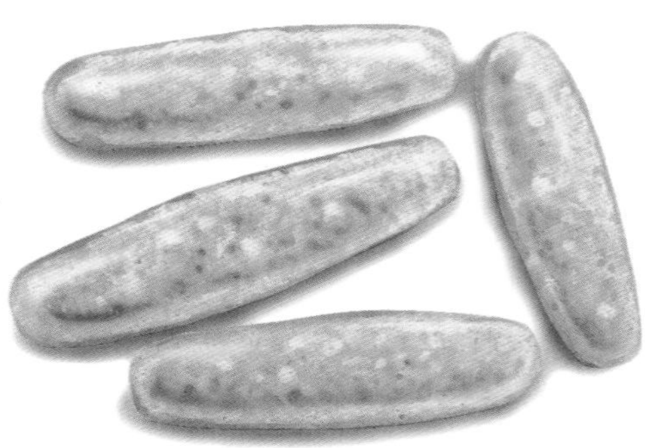

Tuberculosis bacteria

Pott's disease

Caused by the tuberculosis bacteria, Mycobacterium tuberculosis, this disease of the spine first affects the vertebrae, then attacks the intervertebral disks. Spinal curvature may result if the disease is left untreated.

POTASSIUM

Potassium occurs in the body in the form of the positively charged ion (K^+). A small amount of potassium is essential in the diet. It plays an important role in metabolic processes, including those involved in changing food into the energy used for repairing body cells and tissues.

Together with sodium, potassium works inside cells to regulate the balance of acidity and water in the blood. This action is controlled by the kidneys. As potassium is found in vegetables, fruit, meat, chicken, dairy and grain foods, potassium deficiency does not generally occur in healthy individuals eating a varied diet.

Potassium deficiency can occur as a result of diarrhea, vomiting, taking laxatives or diuretics, or from fasting. A diet that is higher in sodium than potassium can draw water out of muscle cells and lead to high blood pressure. A low intake of potassium can also alter heart rhythm. People who exercise more than normal, such as those who play competitive sport, should increase their potassium intake.

Foods which are high in potassium, such as chickpeas, lean steak, baked beans, fish, potatoes, sweet corn, spinach and prunes, can be eaten in order to balance the high levels of sodium which are often difficult to avoid.

SEE ALSO *Kidney, Minerals, Nutrition, Sodium*

POTT'S DISEASE

Pott's disease is a form of tuberculosis of the spine which affects the vertebrae and may progress to include damage to the intervertebral disks. If untreated, it may cause a hunchback curvature of the spine, pain on motion, and pain and swelling of a knee or hip, usually resulting in a limp.

Diagnosis of Pott's disease is confirmed by the presence of the tubercle bacillus (*Mycobacterium tuberculii*) and treatment is with antibiotics.

Surgery may be required to correct any damaged to the spine, for example, if kyphosis results.

SEE ALSO *Spine, Tuberculosis*

PREECLAMPSIA

A condition that may develop in the second half of pregnancy, preeclampsia is characterized by edema, high blood pressure, and protein in the urine. It occurs in about 5 percent of pregnancies and the exact cause is unknown, although poor nutrition is possibly involved.

Particularly at risk are first-time mothers, those carrying multiple babies, women in their teens or over 40 years of age, those with high blood pressure or chronic nephritis (kidney inflammation or infection), and those who have had preeclampsia before.

There are no symptoms in the early stages so it is important that women in these risk categories have regular antenatal check-ups to screen for the condition.

Initial signs include a sudden increase in edema (some swelling is normal in pregnancy), sudden weight gain, nausea and dizziness. Then there may be abdominal pain and vomiting, severe headaches and disturbed vision. If left untreated it may develop into eclampsia, a condition that can trigger life-threatening seizures.

Preeclampsia is potentially fatal for the fetus as it restricts the blood supply to the placenta, causing the baby to grow more slowly. The only cure is the birth of the baby. If the pregnancy is not far enough advanced for the baby to be delivered, bed rest or hospitalization may be recommended. Preeclampsia is also known as toxemia or pregnancy-induced hypertension.

SEE ALSO *Blood pressure, Eclampsia, Fetal development, Hypertension, Kidney, Nephritis, Placenta, Pregnancy, Toxemia*

PREGNANCY

Pregnancy is the state of having a developing fetus in the uterus, which, in the human female and other mammals, extends from conception (union of an ovum and spermatozoon) to labor (parturition).

In the human female a pregnancy takes approximately 283 days (10 lunar months) from the first day of the last menstrual period or approximately 267 days from conception. Only 5 percent of babies whose mothers go into labor and give birth naturally are born on their estimated date of delivery—in the majority of cases, the baby will born within the 10 days either side of this date.

There are about 24 hours in every menstrual cycle when a woman is fertile, and sperm can survive for up to 5 days in the woman's reproductive system; this means that for about 5 days in every 28 sexual activity could result in pregnancy. Approximately 1 in 4 women who are planning pregnancy will conceive in the first 3 months. When a couple is fertile and have unprotected sexual intercourse at least 2 or 3 times a week, a pregnancy will result within 12 months in 90 percent of cases. If fertilization does take place, within 5–6 days the fertilized egg will have implanted itself into the womb's lining (the endometrium) and the placenta will have begun to develop and to produce hormones.

A pregnancy that ends prematurely with the loss of the embryo or fetus either spontaneously or by artificial induction is an abortion. A spontaneous abortion is also known as a miscarriage.

Tests and signs of pregnancy

Blood tests can confirm a pregnancy from the ninth day after ovulation, or 4 or 5 days before the monthly period is due. Urine tests can confirm a pregnancy from the eleventh day after ovulation. Generally, tests are conducted when the period is missed; this is often the first indication of the pregnancy.

Many women, however, may notice changes in their body at or before this time that indicate they are pregnant. These can include enlarged and tender breasts, enlarged nipples, nausea (which can occur in the morning or any other time), increased frequency of urination, tiredness, dizziness, moodiness and skin changes—acne can either break out or clear up as a result of the pregnancy hormones.

In medical terminology, a pregnancy is divided into three trimesters (periods of 3 months) and many of the symptoms described above have usually passed by the second trimester. During this trimester, the woman generally feels fit and well, and it is often now that it becomes more obvious to others that she is pregnant. Sometime between weeks 18 and 22 she will feel the fetus move for the first time, and a woman may have an ultrasound to determine whether the fetus is developing according to the dates calculated.

In the last two months of the pregnancy new symptoms of discomfort may appear or worsen. These include practise contractions of the uterus (known as Braxton Hicks contractions), which can be quite painful; constipation, which can be alleviated by increasing the intake of fiber and water in the diet; hemorrhoids, which may need a cream prescribed; varicose veins, which, like hemorrhoids, are due to the relaxing or softening of the vein walls by the pregnancy hormones and are best relieved with rest and support hosiery; edema or swelling of the ankles, which also responds to rest; increased frequency of urination; leg cramps, particularly at night; itchy skin; stretch marks due to breaks in tissue deep below the skin (not removable by massage or creams); backache, which can be the result of poor posture; skin changes, including the linea nigra (a brown line down the middle of the abdomen); and chloasma, or pregnancy mask, which is a brown patch on the face.

Antenatal care

This includes regular checkups by qualified health care providers and information about a healthy lifestyle, and has reduced many of the problems which women previously encountered during pregnancy. With modern obstetrics the risks to both mother and baby have been greatly reduced.

Medical checks

There are many tests which can be conducted during a pregnancy. Tests to monitor the health of mother and baby include urine tests for the presence of protein, to exclude the possibility of abnormal kidney function, and for sugar, to test for diabetes. Blood tests may also be carried out to determine blood group, to screen for blood group antibodies, and to test for anemia and rubella.

Tests which are available but not routinely performed are the alpha-fetoprotein test, which can detect a multiple pregnancy and spina bifida, and screening for syphilis, a disease which can cause malformations in the fetus. An HIV antibody test for AIDS can also be performed. Other tests that are performed on women whose fetuses are at risk of abnormalities include chorionic villus sampling and amniocentesis.

Complications can arise during pregnancy and regular antenatal checks will often detect these and treatment can be prescribed. Vaginal bleeding during pregnancy, depending on the severity and timing, can be a breakthrough bleed caused by hormonal changes; in late pregnancy it can be a sign that labor is about to begin; or it can be a hemorrhage or a placental abruption in which the placenta has separated from the lining of the womb—the last two eventualities are both medical emergencies. Urinary tract infections are common and can lead to premature birth and low birth-weight babies so antibiotic treatment is generally prescribed. Diabetes can be caused by the pregnancy and needs dietary monitoring. Preeclampsia, which occurs in 5–10 percent of pregnancies, can lead to life-threatening eclampsia if not treated. Preeclampsia is dangerous to the unborn baby and can cause the placenta to fail and labor to begin prematurely. Hypertension (high blood pressure) will occur in 1 in 6 women and is defined as blood pressure of 190/140, or more, that persists or increases—the normal value is 120/80.

Most Caucasians (about 85 percent) have red blood cells which are Rhesus positive (Rh+). The remaining 15 percent are Rhesus negative (Rh-). This incidence of Rh- is higher than in any other human group—Southeast Asians have the lowest incidence of Rh- blood, at 1 percent. Rhesus factor incompatibility may become a problem if the woman is Rhesus negative and the baby is Rhesus positive. The woman's body manufactures antibodies against the blood of the new baby, which can become a

Pregnancy—early stages

Once fertilized, an ovum (egg) is called a zygote and begins to divide immediately. This developing mass moves along the fallopian tube and reaches the cavity of the uterus 5–6 days after fertilization. The mass of cells (now called a blastocyst) implants in the wall of the uterus and begins to develop into an embryo.

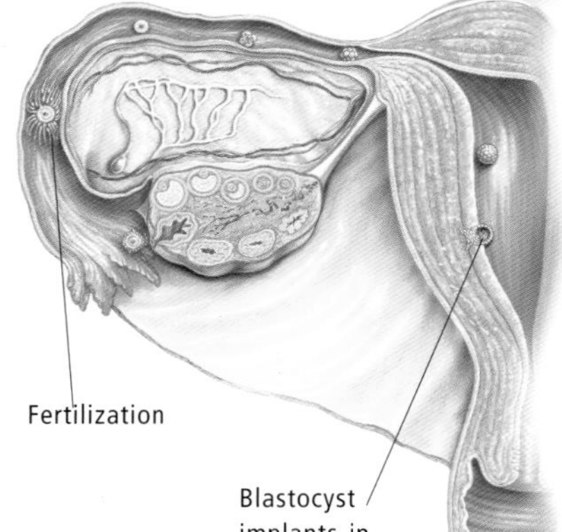

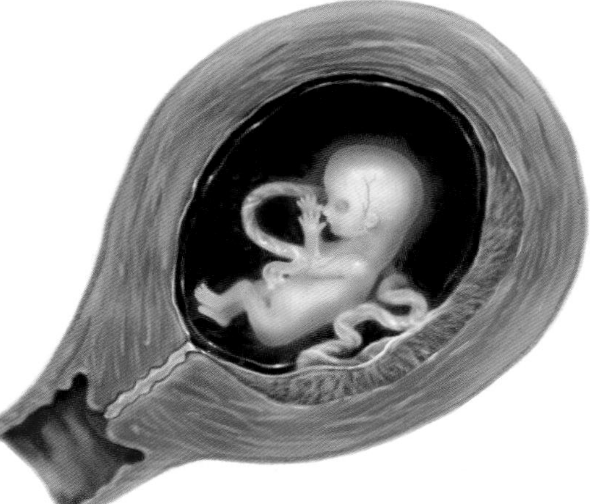

Fetus

By the eleventh week, the fetus is distinguishable as a human.

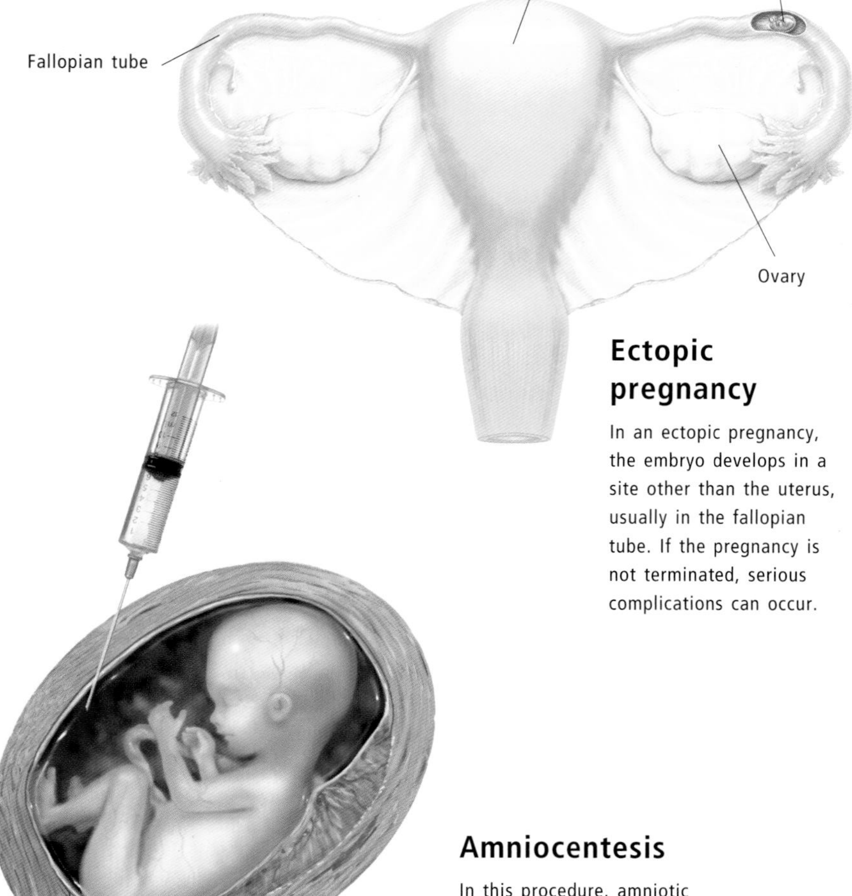

Ectopic pregnancy

In an ectopic pregnancy, the embryo develops in a site other than the uterus, usually in the fallopian tube. If the pregnancy is not terminated, serious complications can occur.

Amniocentesis

In this procedure, amniotic fluid is extracted and tested for fetal abnormalities.

problem in later pregnancies when the antibodies attack the "foreign" cells of the baby. Future Rhesus factor problems can be prevented with an injection of anti-D immunoglobulin to the mother within about 72 hours of the birth of the first baby or after a spontaneous miscarriage or termination of a pregnancy.

A pelvic ultrasound is a common test that can predict the length of the pregnancy and also detect multiple pregnancy suspected ectopic pregnancy and some fetal abnormalities. Because pelvic ultrasound itself has not been found to improve the outcome for either mother or baby, it is not recommended as routine. Ectopic pregnancy (ectopic literally means "out of place"), is a pregnancy that implants itself in the fallopian tubes or occasionally on the ovary or in the abdominal cavity. It is dangerous to the mother and is treated as a medical emergency. It is extremely rare for an ectopic pregnancy to be viable.

The chance of a multiple pregnancy increases with the age of the mother and the number of children she has already borne. Heredity and race are also factors. A multiple pregnancy is more likely when the woman has received treatment for subfertility that involves stimulation of ovulation. Without medical assistance, the chance of having twins is 1 in 90; of triplets, 1 in around 8,000; and of quadruplets, 1 in 750,000. With a multiple pregnancy the woman is at increased risk of pregnancy-induced hypertension, premature labor, abnormal presentation—the baby not presenting for birth head-first and facing the mother's spine—difficult labor and birth, and low birthweight babies.

Antenatal care also monitors the position of the baby. Labor and birth are extremely painful for many women, though perception of pain depends on the woman's preparation for and education about the processes as well as her pain threshold. A baby who is not presenting head first, facing towards the mother's spine and with the head tucked in, will cause a more painful and often a more difficult delivery. The most common abnormal presentation is breech or bottom first. Because the baby's soft bottom rather than its firm head is pressing against the cervix, the first stage of labor can be prolonged. Some obstetricians and midwives will turn breech babies if they do not turn of their own accord. In many instances, a cesarean delivery will be advised.

Other abnormal presentations are face or brow first, or posterior presentation with the baby facing outwards and its spine against the mother's spine. Both these positions can cause a long, painful labor. Shoulder presentation, which is rare, and transverse lie (the baby lying across the uterus) necessitate a cesarean delivery in both cases.

Healthy lifestyle

Though a pregnant woman does not need to eat twice as much food as she would normally, she does need a daily intake of between 1,700 and 2,100 calories (7,000–9,000 kilojoules). This should consist of a minimum of four servings of bread and cereals; a minimum of four servings of vegetables and fruit; one or two servings of lean meat, eggs, fish, chicken or nuts; approximately three servings of dairy foods, but no more than the equivalent of four tablespoons of fats (butter, oil, spreads); six to eight glasses of water and no more than two cups of tea and coffee. Foods high in fat or sugar should be reduced or eliminated. While excess weight during pregnancy can be a problem, being underweight can also lead to fetal and maternal complications.

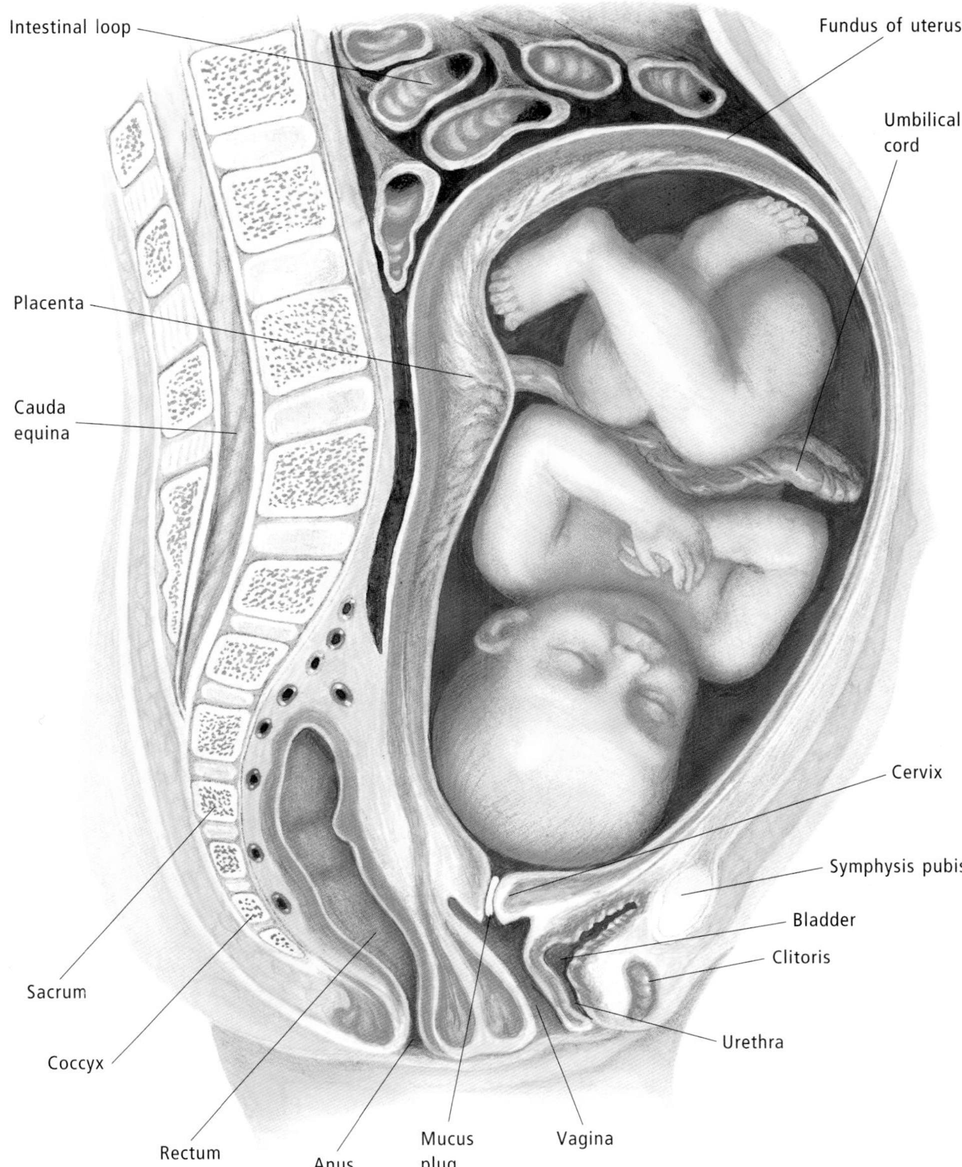

Pregnancy—full term

A full-term pregnancy lasts about 40 weeks. At the end of the pregnancy, waves of rhythmic contractions sweep through the uterus, moving the baby through the cervical canal.

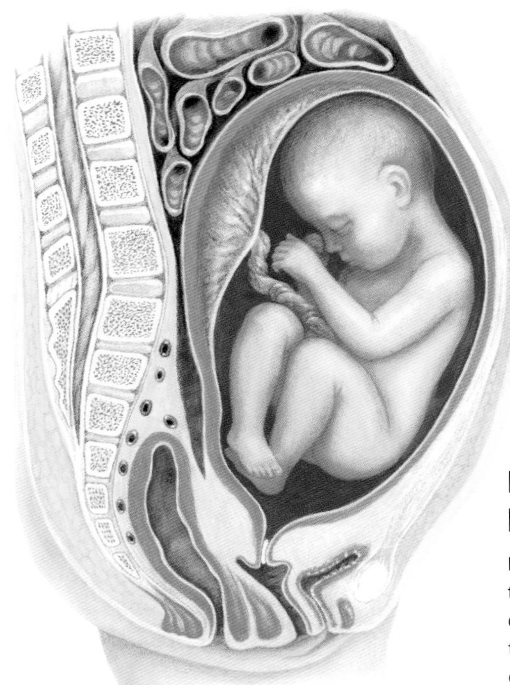

Pregnancy—breech

In a breech presentation the baby's bottom, instead of its head, faces down towards the uterus. This can cause prolonged labor and a higher risk of complications.

Drugs, including tobacco, alcohol, over-the-counter preparations and herbal and alternative remedies, are best avoided, except on the advice of a health care provider who is aware that the woman is pregnant. Alcohol, if not avoided completely, should be limited to no more than one drink a day. Abnormalities in the developing fetus have been linked with regular consumption of just two standard drinks per day.

Fitness and exercise also need to be maintained during pregnancy. Most forms of exercise, if carried out before the pregnancy, can continue throughout, though confirmation of this with a doctor, midwife or physical therapist is essential. Sports which are generally advised against include both high-impact sports such as strenuous aerobics and competitive contact sports such as basketball

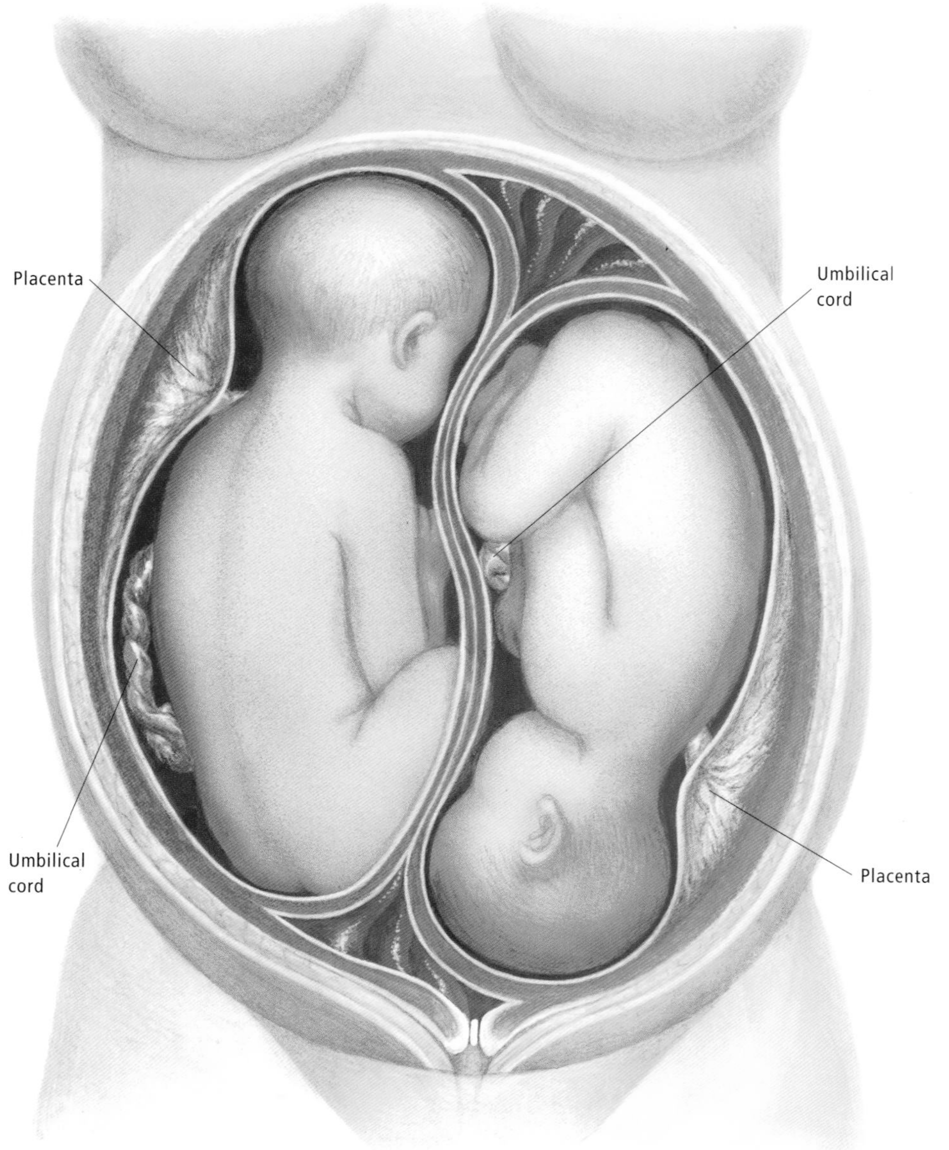

Pregnancy—twins

Fraternal (non-identical or dizygotic) twins develop when two eggs are fertilized independently by two different sperm. Unlike identical (monozygotic) twins, who come from the same egg and share a placenta, fraternal twins have separate placentas.

and netball, horse-riding, skiing and competitive tennis. Taking precautions against overheating, over-exertion and back strain is also recommended. Swimming, t'ai chi, yoga, belly dancing and walking are generally considered to be suitable during pregnancy.

In a healthy pregnancy, prohibition of sexual activity is quite inappropriate and many women find that their libido increases due to the hormones active throughout pregnancy. Others find that it diminishes—that too is normal. Sex during pregnancy can be fun, carefree (no worries about contraception) and a chance to experiment as the woman's growing abdomen means trying out different ways to sexually satisfy both partners. Sex can also be beneficial in inducing an overdue baby. The woman's orgasm coupled with the prostaglandins in the man's sperm can induce a birth when the cervix is beginning to dilate and labor is imminent.

Pregnancy is a state of wellness, not an illness. While it is important for the woman and her health care providers to monitor any problems, the medicalization of pregnancy, labor and birth can lead to its own set of problems. A woman and her partner who plan their pregnancy and prepare themselves mentally and physically by abstaining from alcohol, giving up smoking, having medical checkups and adopting a healthy lifestyle give themselves the best possible chance of conceiving a healthy baby.

SEE ALSO *Abortion, AIDS, Amniocentesis, Chorionic villus sampling, Contraception, Eclampsia, Embryo, Fertilization, Fetal alcohol syndrome, Fetal development, Hemorrhoids, Infertility, Miscarriage, Newborn, Placenta, Preeclampsia, Reproductive systems, Rhesus (Rh) factor, Rubella, Twins, Ultrasound*

PREMATURE DELIVERY

The birth of a live baby or babies at less than 37 weeks gestation is described as a premature (or preterm) birth; prematurity is not defined by birth weight. Around 5 percent of babies are born prematurely and usually the cause is unknown. Nearly half of all multiple births will occur prematurely. Other causes of prematurity are: maternal illness; placental problems such as placenta previa; premature rupture of the membranes, often with no explanation; cervical problems such as cervical incompetence; health problems in the mother such as diabetes, smoking, anxiety, distress or poor nutrition; health problems in the baby; maternal age—for those over 40 and under 17 years the risk is greater; and a previous low birth weight baby. Around 6 percent of all babies are born underweight, the majority of these being premature—the rest are termed small-for-dates.

A pregnancy that ends prematurely with the loss of the embryo or fetus either spontaneously or by artificial induction is an abortion. A spontaneous abortion is also known as a miscarriage.

There is little that can be done to prevent premature delivery. Drinking plenty of fluids, particularly water (about 8 glasses a day), has been found to prevent premature labor in some instances. A woman who lives in an industrialized country and who goes into premature labor will be closely monitored in a hospital environment. Attempts will be made to continue pregnancy and if that is not possible, then the baby will be cared for after birth in a neonatal intensive care unit.

SEE ALSO *Abortion, Childbirth, Miscarriage, Placenta, Pregnancy*

PREMATURE EJACULATION

Premature ejaculation is a condition in which male orgasm and ejaculation occurs too quickly for satisfactory intercourse—often happening before penetration has taken place. It is the most common sexual complaint, and is especially common in younger men and adolescents for whom sex is a new experience. It may cause feelings of self-doubt, inadequacy and guilt in the man and may lead to sexual dissatisfaction and tensions in the relationship for both members of the couple.

Often an explanation of the condition from a sympathetic physician is enough to solve the problem. If the problem persists, therapy from a qualified sex counselor may be needed.

There are several techniques that can be used to help the man delay ejaculation. One common approach is the "stop and start" method, in which the man recognizes that he is about to ejaculate; the couple simply ceases stimulation for about 30 seconds, after which time stimulation can begin again. These steps are repeated until the woman is ready to achieve orgasm, at which point stimulation is allowed to end in ejaculation.

The "squeeze" method is a similar technique whereby, after recognizing that he is about to ejaculate, the man (or his partner) gently squeezes the end of the penis (where the glans meets the shaft) for several seconds, withholds further sexual stimulation for about 30 seconds, and then resumes stimulation again.

SEE ALSO *Erection, Penis, Sex therapy, Sexual dysfunction, Sexual intercourse*

PREMENSTRUAL SYNDROME

Premenstrual syndrome (PMS) describes a range of physical and psychological symptoms which usually occur for a few days prior to menstruation. About 80–90 percent of women experience PMS at some time during their reproductive lives, although only about 5 percent report severe symptoms. In some cases PMS may extend as far back as ovulation; a few women may experience PMS-like symptoms only around the time of ovulation and not later in the cycle. PMS is most common in women over 30, especially those who have had years of natural menstrual cycles uninterrupted by pregnancies or oral contraception.

It has been suggested that PMS is less common in non-Western societies but this is probably related to more frequent pregnancy and lactation than to any other social factors. Behavior characteristic of PMS has also been reported in non-human primates (rhesus monkeys and baboons) which also have menstrual cycles.

Physical disturbances commonly associated with the syndrome may include weight gain, fluid retention, a sensation of pelvic heaviness or bloating, breast tenderness or enlargement, skin blemishes, headaches, constipation, frequency of urination, gingival bleeding and mouth ulcers. Preexisting conditions such as varicose veins, migraine and acne may become worse. The thyroid gland may be enlarged and blood sugar slightly elevated.

Psychological or behavioral changes may include an inability to concentrate, tiredness, mood swings, irritability and depression. PMS has been taken as a mitigating circumstance in certain criminal trials but this also undermines female responsibility in other spheres. Suicide or suicidal thoughts and accidental death have been reported as being more common in the latter part of the menstrual cycle. Symptoms should be classified as due to PMS only where they occur between ovulation and menstruation and are resolved within a few hours of the onset of menstruation.

Many theories have been put forward to explain PMS. Possible psychological causes include negative social or cultural attitudes towards menstruation and the unconscious association of menstruation with preexisting psychological or psychiatric problems. It has been hypothesized that endocrine imbalances involving prolactin, insulin, cortisone and androgens may be the cause.

Many practitioners believe that a simple explanation can be found in progesterone deficiency or in altered progesterone-to-estrogen ratios. However, studies of hormone levels of women suffering from PMS have failed to conclusively confirm these theories, although the occurrence of PMS at times of hormonal fluctuations, such as at puberty or after pregnancy, indicates at least some involvement of endocrine factors.

The wide range of symptoms and the uncertainty regarding their cause makes effective treatment of PMS difficult. Keeping a daily chart of physical and psychological symptoms may help in deciding which symptoms should be considered for treatment. Vitamin B_6, fluid tablets, prostaglandin inhibitors, antidepressants and low doses of progesterone have all been tried but, although they give relief in some women, are not uni-

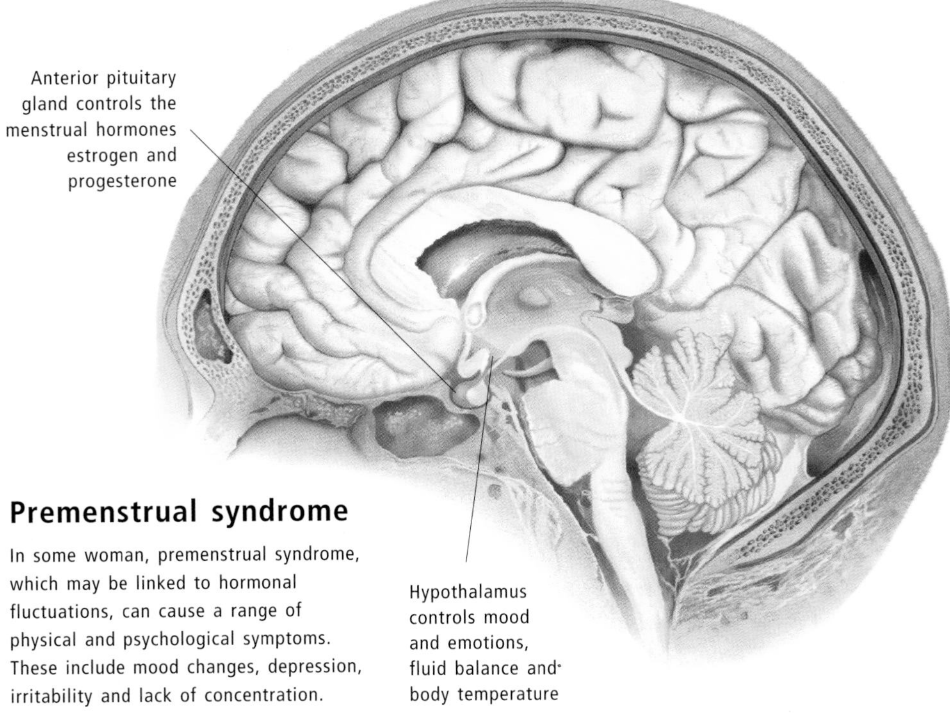
Anterior pituitary gland controls the menstrual hormones estrogen and progesterone
Hypothalamus controls mood and emotions, fluid balance and body temperature

Premenstrual syndrome

In some woman, premenstrual syndrome, which may be linked to hormonal fluctuations, can cause a range of physical and psychological symptoms. These include mood changes, depression, irritability and lack of concentration.

versally successful. Altering the hormonal pattern of a normal menstrual cycle with oral contraceptives may alleviate PMS in some women but others report aggravation of symptoms. Some success has also been reported with dietary changes, including reduction in caffeine or salt intake, and with increased exercise. Surgical removal of the ovaries (oophorectomy, also known as ovariectomy) has occasionally been used as a last resort in severe cases. There is little evidence that pregnancy or tubal ligation have any effect on PMS.

There are a number of alternative therapies that may help to alleviate premenstrual symptoms. Acupuncture, shiatsu and Chinese herbal treatment given regularly are said to reduce premenstrual tension by regulating blood and energy flows, especially through spleen and liver meridians. Chinese medicine advises women with menstrual disorders to avoid exposure to cold or eating too much cold or raw food. Aromatherapy suggests massage or baths with oils such as clary sage, lavender, juniper or rose.

Herbalism prescribes agnus castus for hormonal balance, and diuretics (horsetail, dandelion). Estrogenic herbs (sage, parsley, dong quai) are prescribed for those with a tendency towards premenstrual depression, confusion or memory loss. Naturopathy suggests a wholefood diet with increased soy products, reduced salt and dairy intake and avoidance of caffeine, sugar, animal fats and alcohol. Supplements prescribed include vitamin B with additional B_6, vitamin E, zinc, calcium, magnesium and evening primrose oil. Regular aerobic exercise is also suggested.

SEE ALSO *Estrogens, Hormones, Menstruation, Ovulation, Progesterone, Prostaglandins, Reproductive systems*

PRIAPISM

Priapism is a condition in which the penis remains persistently and painfully erect without any sexual arousal or desire. It is caused by a blockage of the veins that carry blood from the penis, trapping blood in the penis and causing its engorgement. It may be brought on by excessive sexual stimulation or by certain drugs, including corticosteroids, anticoagulants and antihypertensives.

Treatment options include surgery, the injection of anesthesia into the spinal cord, and the draining (aspiration) of blood from the penis. Without treatment the penis may be permanently damaged, making normal erections impossible.

SEE ALSO *Erection, Penis, Sexual dysfunction*

PROCTITIS

Proctitis is inflammation of the rectum. It can occur as part of ulcerative colitis. It may also be due to bacterial infection, as is sometimes seen in male homosexuals with gonorrhea of the rectum from anal intercourse. These patients will complain of rectal irritation, itching, pain and pus-containing (purulent) discharge. Gonorrhea of the rectum is treated with the appropriate antibiotic (penicillin and/or tetracyclines).

Occasionally proctitis may be due to physical factors, as seen in radiation proctitis, a side effect of radiation therapy of tumors in the uterine cervix, bladder, uterus or prostate. In those patients the inflammation may be reduced with steroids.

SEE ALSO *Gonorrhea, Radiation therapy, Rectum, Ulcerative colitis*

PROCTOSCOPY

Proctoscopy is an internal examination of the anal canal and rectum using a short rigid speculum (proctoscope); sometimes, to include an examination of the colon, a flexible or fiberoptic tube (sigmoidoscope) is used. This painless procedure allows the bowel lining to be examined, biopsies to be taken and other medical procedures to take place. It is used to aid in the diagnosis of such diseases as rectal cancer and diverticulosis.

SEE ALSO *Colon, Diverticulosis, Rectum*

PROGESTERONE

Progesterone is a steroid sex hormone produced in the corpus luteum (ruptured follicle) in the ovaries during the second half of the menstrual cycle. Progesterone is one of the main hormones of pregnancy (or gestation). It stimulates the endometrium to secrete a fluid which protects and nourishes the fertilized ovum in the uterus before implantation. It also fosters placental growth.

If pregnancy does not occur, then the corpus luteum only functions until about day 26 of an average cycle, after which progesterone production decreases rapidly; this causes changes in the lining of the uterus which lead to menstruation. If the woman becomes pregnant, the placenta secretes human chorionic gonadotropin (HCG), which prolongs the production of ovarian progesterone until the end of the first trimester, after which progesterone is secreted by the placenta.

Progesterone drops to very low levels a few hours after birth. The pituitary gland during lactation produces large amounts of prolactin and this often disrupts development of follicles in the ovary and suppresses ovulation. Even when menstruation is restored, which can be as early as three months after birth, the first few cycles are often anovulatory. Anovulatory cycles do not produce a corpus luteum. Diminished secretions of progesterone can lead to spontaneous abortion (miscarriage) in pregnant women.

Synthetic progesterone is used as an oral contraceptive, most commonly in combination with estrogen but sometimes on its own if use of estrogen is inadvisable.

SEE ALSO *Estrogens, Hormones, Menstruation, Oral contraceptives, Ovulation, Pituitary gland, Placenta, Pregnancy*

PROGESTOGENS

Progestogens are a group of natural and synthetic steroid hormones derived from cholesterol. Natural progestogen is progesterone produced by the ovary which is inactive if given by mouth and only slightly active if injected and is thus unsuitable for therapeutic use. Slight modifications of the natural molecule can be made, which produces a range of hormones which can either be taken by mouth or injected.

Synthetic progestogens, including levonorgestrel, norgestrel and norethindrone are used in oral contraceptives, either alone or in conjunction with a synthetic estrogen. Contraception with oral contraceptives is due to anovulation (prevention of ovulation). Synthetic progestogens are also used, along with estrogen, in hormone replacement

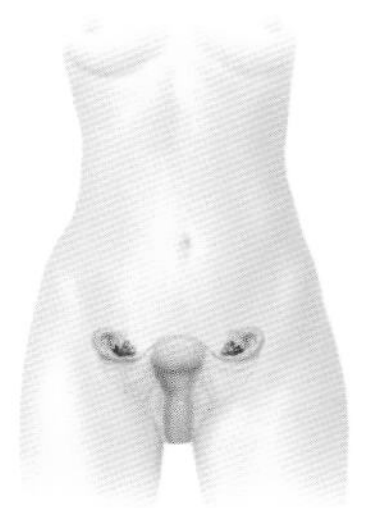

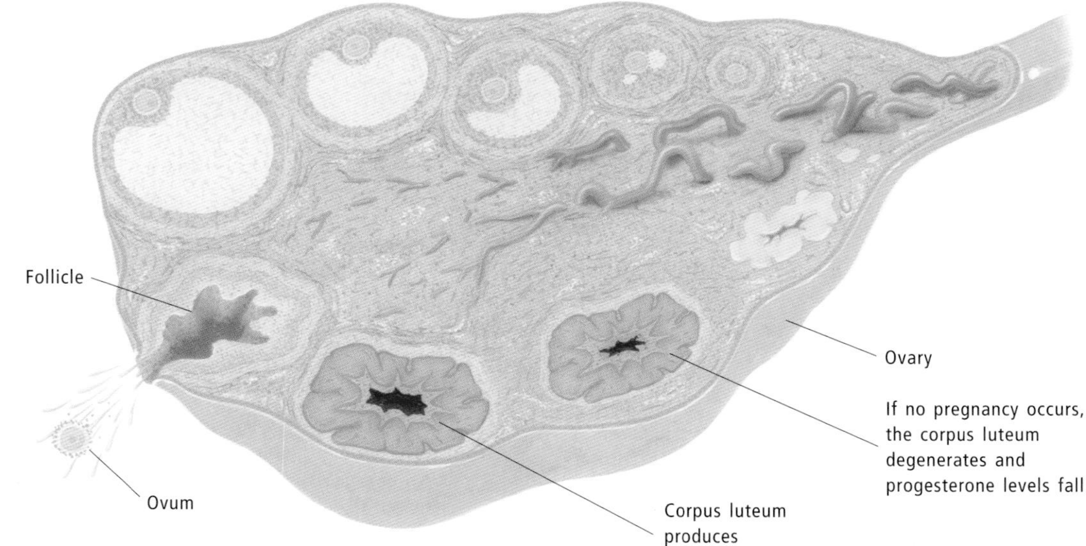

Progesterone

After releasing its ovum (egg), an ovarian follicle turns into a gland-like structure, the corpus luteum. This produces progesterone which prepares the uterus for pregnancy.

therapy (commonly referred to as HRT). HRT consisting of estrogen alone has been linked to an increased risk of endometrial carcinoma. This increased risk is removed if a progestogen is added to the HRT.

SEE ALSO *Cholesterol, Estrogens, Hormone replacement therapy, Hormones, Oral contraceptives, Progesterone*

PROLAPSE

A prolapse is the outward movement, or slipping, of any one of a number of body parts from its normal position.

Prolapsed intervertebral disk

A prolapsed intervertebral disk (also known as slipped disk or herniated nucleus pulposus) occurs when the soft center of a disk (nucleus pulposus) ruptures through a tear or fracture in the fibrous tissue of the disk. This can happen in the lumbar (lower back) or cervical (neck) regions, putting pressure on spinal nerves (radiculopathy).

Lumbar radiculopathy (sciatica) is characterized by severe lower back pain that radiates to the buttocks, legs and feet, and may be combined with tingling in the legs, muscle weakness, muscle spasms and groin pain. Cervical radiculopathy brings pain in the sides and back of the neck, down the shoulders and arms and sometimes the hands and fingers.

The natural ageing and degeneration of the spine cause most prolapsed disks. Middle-aged and older men are most at risk, especially those who undertake strenuous physical activity. Bed rest on a firm mattress, medication and perhaps physical therapy are usually prescribed to reduce inflammation; surgery may be needed in extreme cases.

Prolapsed rectum

A prolapsed rectum is an abnormal movement of the internal mucous membranes of the rectum, the end section of the large intestine, down to or through the anus. It appears as a red mass up to several inches (about 10 centimeters) long, which may bleed. Prolapsed rectums are most common in children under the age of 6 years. The condition usually corrects itself in young children—a physician may gently push the protruding mass back inside. Surgery is often needed when the condition occurs in adults and may involve attaching the rectum to surrounding muscle for support. Alternatively, the anus may be tightened via the insertion of a circle of wire or nylon.

Prolapsed rectum may be associated with conditions such as cystic fibrosis, constipation, malnutrition and infestation with pinworm or whipworm.

Prolapsed uterus

A prolapsed uterus is the displacement of the uterus into the vaginal canal as a result of weakness in the supporting ligaments. Slackening of the ligaments may be due to the normal ageing process or the result of stretching during childbirth, particularly with large babies or rapid deliveries. Hormonal changes during menopause are also thought to be a cause and, rarely, a pelvic tumor. Obesity, chronic bronchitis, excessive coughing, chronic constipation and asthma may increase the risk of developing the condition. Sufferers may experience feelings of pressure or pulling in the pelvis, pain in the anus or lower abdomen, urinary tract infections, excessive vaginal discharge and difficulty having sexual intercourse. They may also urinate when coughing, laughing, or straining to lift heavy objects. In severe cases the neck of the uterus (cervix) protrudes from the vagina. A pelvic examination will determine the severity of the prolapse. Treatment may be via vaginal pessary, a ring-shaped object that is inserted into the vagina, or by surgery.

SEE ALSO *Anus, Disk, intervertebral, Hernia, Intestines, Pelvic floor muscles, Rectum, Spine, Uterus*

PROPRIOCEPTION

Proprioception is perception of one's own body, which is of vital importance for everyday activities. Activities such as standing, walking, and picking up objects require information on the position and movement of each part of the body and of muscle activity, which is provided by sensors in joints and muscles. The sense of balance is provided by the semicircular canals and otolith organs of the inner ear. Visceral sensations include hunger, thirst, the feeling of food being swallowed, and the necessity to defecate or

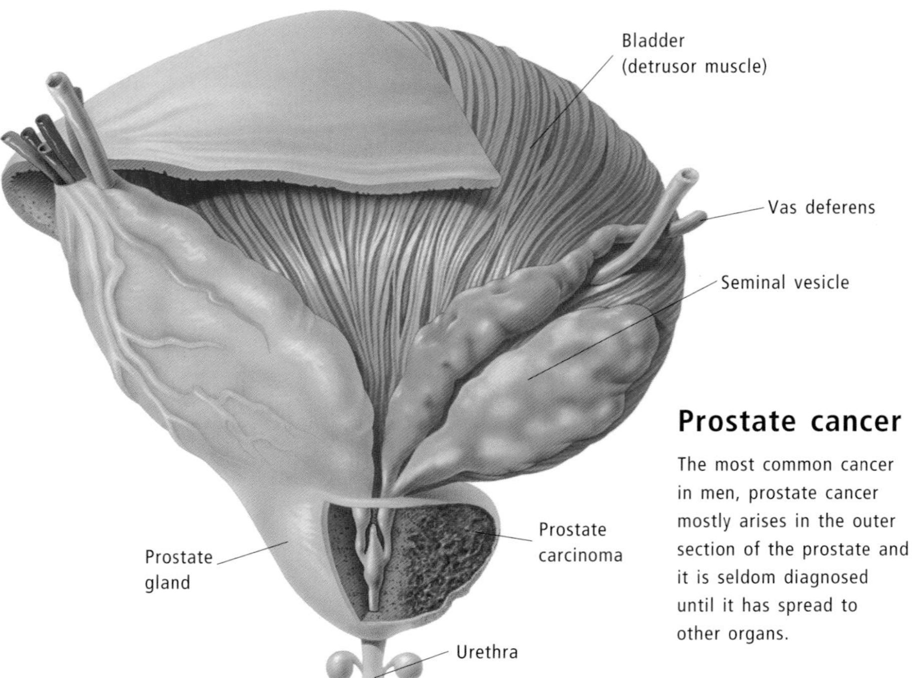

Prostate cancer

The most common cancer in men, prostate cancer mostly arises in the outer section of the prostate and it is seldom diagnosed until it has spread to other organs.

urinate. Other proprioceptive sensations include palpitations (awareness of the beating of the heart), and (on occasion) the necessity to breathe.

SEE ALSO *Balance, Breathing, Palpitations, Semicircular canals*

PROSTAGLANDINS

Prostaglandins are an important group of chemicals produced in many tissues of the body, including platelet cells, blood vessels, the uterus and stomach. They play an important role in inflammation and pain.

Prostaglandins produce contractions of the uterine muscle, which can induce labor, abortion or painful menstrual periods (dysmenorrhea). Anti-inflammatory medication is a common treatment prescribed to inhibit the painful uterine contractions which cause dysmenorrhea. Prostaglandins in platelets cause them to clump together, resulting in the formation of blood clots, as in a heart attack or stroke. Aspirin inhibits prostaglandin production in platelets, making them less sticky.

SEE ALSO *Anti-inflammatory drugs, Platelets, Prostate gland, Uterus*

PROSTATE CANCER

Prostate cancer is the most common cancer in men, typically occurring in individuals aged over 60 years. It is also one of the most common causes of death from cancer in men. Despite its frequency, almost nothing is known about the causes of prostate cancer, although genetic factors may play a role.

Development of prostate cancer appears to be age-related and latent tumors (tumors which are demonstrable by microscopic examination of the prostate but do not produce any clinical effects) are present in more than 50 percent of men aged over 80 years.

The growth of prostate cancer cells depends at least in part on stimulation by testosterone, but the exact role of hormones in the development of this cancer remains poorly understood.

Prostate cancer commonly produces discomfort during urination or symptoms suggesting obstruction of urine flow. Because the cancer usually arises in the outer part of the prostate gland, whereas the urethra runs through the central portion, symptoms relating to urinary outflow may not develop until quite late in the course of the disease. In some patients, prostate cancer first becomes apparent as a result of spread to other organs, in which case the outcome is less favorable.

A major site of spread of prostate cancer is into bone, especially the spine and pelvis, producing pain. Unlike most other tumors, prostate cancer that has spread to bone is typically associated with new bone formation around the secondary deposits, making these easily visible on x-rays.

Benign (non-cancerous) enlargement of the prostate is very common among men in the same age group (much more common than cancer of the prostate) and causes similar urinary obstruction. This makes it quite difficult to distinguish the two conditions, a situation that is complicated by the fact that they often co-exist. However, much as is the case for other cancers, early diagnosis is critically important in achieving a good response to treatment.

One way of demonstrating the possible presence of a cancer of the prostate is by digital rectal examination (DRE), because many cancers can be felt directly by the medical practitioner by examination through the rectum. Specific diagnosis usually requires needle biopsy of the gland under ultrasound guidance.

Unfortunately there is no effective screening test that allows an early diagnosis of prostate cancer to be made easily and cheaply. A blood test for prostate-specific antigen (PSA), an antigen produced by prostate cells, is available but is not considered to be sufficiently sensitive or specific for use as a screening test for early prostate cancer. The PSA test is still valuable in following the progress of prostatic cancer after a person has had treatment for the cancer.

The extent of spread at the time of diagnosis has an important bearing on the approach to treatment of prostate cancer. Surgical removal or radiation therapy may be the initial treatment of choice. Because tumor cell growth is partly controlled by testosterone, treatments that reduce the levels of testosterone or block its activity are also valuable. Patients with early cancers often have an excellent response to therapy but those with late-stage disease have a poor outcome.

SEE ALSO *Cancer, Prostate gland, Testosterone, Urethra*

PROSTATE GLAND

The prostate gland is a part of the male sex organs. About the size of a walnut, it surrounds the neck of the bladder and the urethra, the tube which carries urine from the bladder to the tip of the penis, and is composed of both glandular and muscle tissue.

Secretions from the prostate and the seminal vesicles make up the seminal fluid ejaculated during sexual orgasm that contains the glucose and enzymes which provide the energy spermatozoa need for their journey toward the ovum. Secretions from the prostate can also be tested to reveal the presence of infections that may affect sperm count and quality.

By the age of 50, it is common for the prostate to show some signs of enlargement. It may increase in weight from less than an ounce (20 grams) to five or six times this. Known as benign prostatic hypertrophy, this enlargement may eventually obstruct flow of urine from the bladder, and if uncorrected, can cause bladder and kidney damage.

Symptoms of urethral obstruction include nocturia (the need to empty the bladder often at night); dysuria (pain or difficulty with urination); and the sudden urgency for urination. Usually, the bladder will not empty completely and urine may stagnate, causing infection or the formation of stones. Straining to pass urine may make things worse and can cause bleeding and abdominal pain. A catheter may be inserted to drain the bladder.

Diagnostic procedures to confirm abnormality include excretory urography, which is an x-ray of the urinary tract, and cystourethroscopy, an internal visual examination of the bladder.

Prostatic cancer is more common as age advances but it is generally slow-growing and may be well advanced before producing detectable symptoms. Some prostate cancers, however, can grow aggressively and cells often spread to nearby lymph nodes and then to bone, kidneys or the brain. Early detection increases the chances of a cure. Older patients with slow-growing cancers may opt for "watchful waiting" to avoid the negative effects of treatment.

Surgical removal of part or all of the prostate is common to correct hypertrophy and for treating cancer. In serious cases, the entire prostate, seminal vesicles and ejaculatory ducts are removed. Surgical techniques aim as far as possible to retain sexual function and normal urinary control and success rates are constantly improving. Cancers that have spread are not usually curable but their growth may be slowed by blocking the effects of testosterone. Side effects include loss of sexual drive, impotence and breast enlargement.

Testing for prostate cancer can include the prostate-specific antigen test (PSA) and digital rectal examination (DRE). The PSA tests for antigens which are produced by prostate cells at higher than normal levels in benign enlargement of the prostate, and at much higher levels in prostatic cancer. Neither method is totally effective at detecting cancer of the prostate, but men aged over 50 are advised to have PSA and DRE regularly.

There are a number of alternative therapies that may help to alleviate the symptoms of enlarged prostate. Herbalism prescribes saw palmetto, nettle root and epilobium to treat enlargement, couch grass and horsetail to ease symptoms. Naturopathy advises hot and cold compresses or sitz baths and regular exercise; vitamin E, evening primrose oil and zinc supplements, and a low-fat wholefood diet eliminating tea, coffee and alcohol are also prescribed. Reflexology advises the massaging of the "prostate zone", located on the inner (medial) side of the foot beneath the ankle. Yoga suggests a number of traditional hatha yoga poses, particularly the thunderbolt or kneeling pose. Acupunture and shiatsu treatments are also said to ease symptoms.

SEE ALSO *Bladder, Penis, Prostate cancer, Prostatitis, Reproductive systems, Urethra, Urinary systems*

PROSTATITIS

Prostatitis is inflammation of the prostate gland, the walnut-sized organ that encircles the urethra at the base of the bladder. It is caused by bacteria such as *E. coli* (transmitted from the bowel) or gonorrhea, chlamydia or trichomoniasis (transmitted through sexual contact with an infected partner). Prostatitis commonly occurs along with urethritis (inflammation of the urethra), epididymitis (inflammation of the epididymis), and/or orchitis (inflammation of the testis).

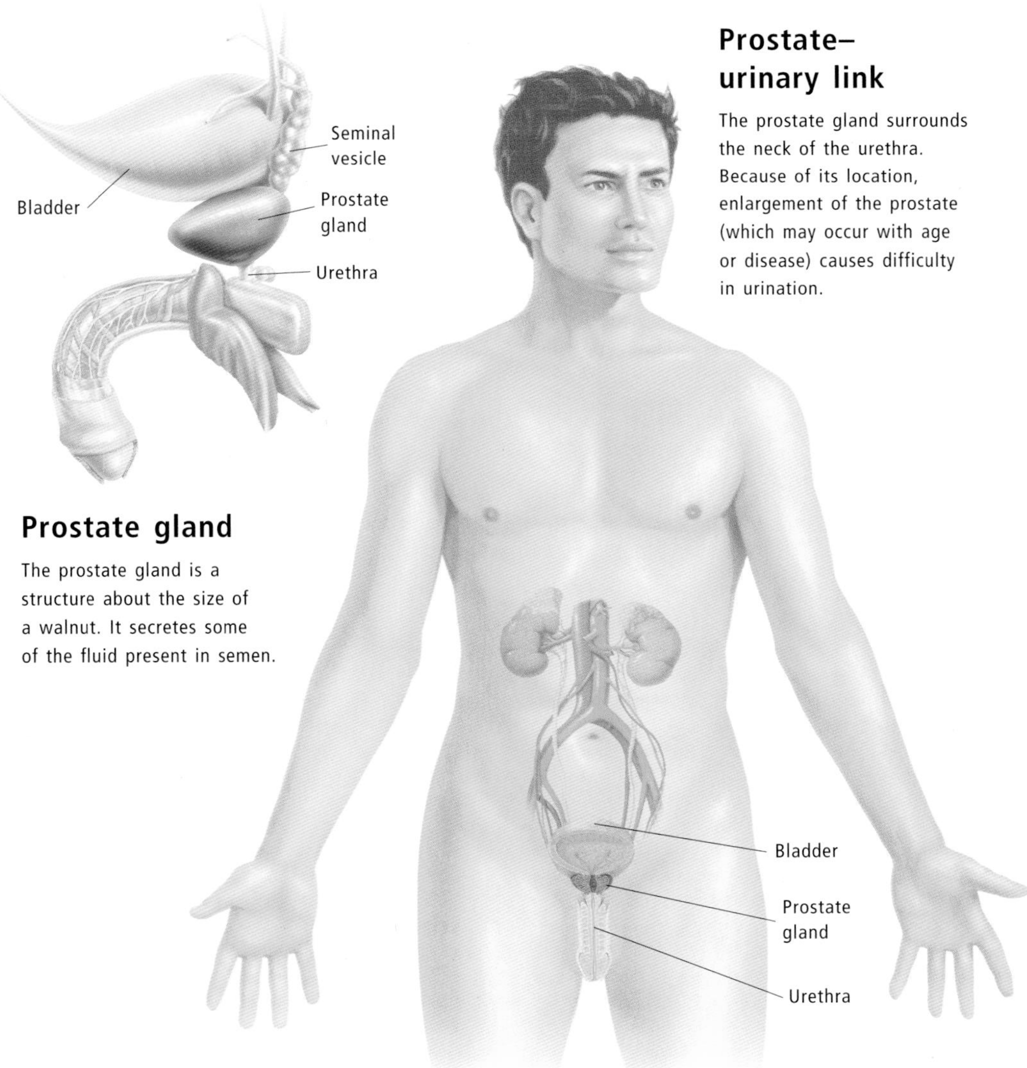

Prostate gland

The prostate gland is a structure about the size of a walnut. It secretes some of the fluid present in semen.

Prostate–urinary link

The prostate gland surrounds the neck of the urethra. Because of its location, enlargement of the prostate (which may occur with age or disease) causes difficulty in urination.

The symptoms of prostatitis are a burning pain on urination, a diminished urine stream and pain on ejaculating. There may be fever, chills and low back pain. Blood may be found in the urine or the semen, and there may be a frequent desire to urinate urgently. The testes may be painful.

A physician will diagnose the condition after finding an enlarged and tender prostate on rectal examination. A urethral swab and a urine sample are taken to determine which bacteria are involved, and their sensitivity to antibiotics. Oral antibiotic therapy will need to be continued for 6–8 weeks. Most cases are successfully treated, but recurrence is common and in some men the condition becomes chronic.

SEE ALSO *Prostate gland*

PSITTACOSIS

Psittacosis is a common infectious disease of many bird species that is sometimes contracted by humans. It is caused by the bacterium *Chlamydia psittaci*. Psittacosis can be aquired by inhaling dust from dried infected bird droppings or from handling affected birds. Symptoms usually appear within 10 days of contact and include fever, headache, fatigue, chills, muscle aches, chest pains and a cough.

A severe form of pneumonia can develop that, if left untreated, may be fatal, particularly among the elderly. The disease is, however, treatable with tetracycline antibiotics. Psittacosis is also known as ornithosis and parrot fever.

SEE ALSO *Pneumonia*

PSORIASIS

With up to 3 percent of the world's adult population suffering from psoriasis, this mostly mild but frequently distressing skin disorder is considered common. Its exact cause remains a medical mystery, although it is known to involve an abnormal reaction by the body's immune system against the skin.

Genetic factors influence the likelihood of developing the disorder. A person with a father suffering from psoriasis has about a 30 percent chance of developing the disease. The child of a mother with psoriasis has a 20 percent chance. The disease is rarely seen during childhood years, often making its first appearance with the onset of puberty.

The impact of the disease varies widely between sufferers. Typically, it causes a rash of sensitive red patches covered by silvery-white scales on the elbows, knees, lower back and scalp. The outer layer of skin at the sites of these flaking sores grows approximately seven times faster and thicker than normal. These areas can range in diameter from a few millimeters to several centimeters. In severe cases they may join to form very large "plaques" that can cover large areas of skin, such as a person's entire back.

Psoriasis does not normally affect the face, is not contagious, does not cause scars and rarely leads to hair loss. It does, however, often affect the nails, causing pitting, discoloration and separation from the nail bed. About 10 percent of sufferers develop a form of arthritis that causes swollen and painful joints and can become debilitating. A very rare, but potentially fatal, form of the disease is erythrodermic psoriasis, in which the skin becomes inflamed and red all over and sufferers have problems regulating body temperature.

Contrary to popular belief, psoriasis is not an allergic reaction and avoidance of certain foodstuffs will not control the disease. It is, however, aggravated by excessive alcohol intake. It also has a tendency to repeatedly appear and disappear, with possible triggers including stress, streptococcal throat infections, certain medications and skin wounds.

Although the condition is incurable and difficult to treat, there is a great array of therapies and medications available to help control symptoms. Complete remission is rare.

Sufferers usually need to experiment to find the treatment that works best for them. Careful exposure to ultraviolet light may help some people. Soaking in warm water with bath oil or a coal tar solution can soften and loosen the scale. Special shampoos can control a scaly scalp, and simple moisturizing creams, such as sorbolene, can also help keep the scales soft and prevent the skin from cracking.

A variety of creams and ointments, intended to reduce the scaling, is available, ranging from simple products based on coal tar preparations to high-strength steroid preparations so strong that they can only be used for short periods of time. Oral medications for psoriasis are normally prescribed in only the most serious cases because they often have dangerous or unpleasant side effects.

SEE ALSO *Lymphatic/Immune system, Skin*

PSYCHOSIS

Psychosis is a severe mental illness in which a person loses contact with reality. Psychotic people suffer from poor judgment and insight and a disordered thinking process. They may experience acute distress, confusion, hallucinations and delusions, which may include the belief that someone will harm them or their family. Usually they do not realize they have the condition.

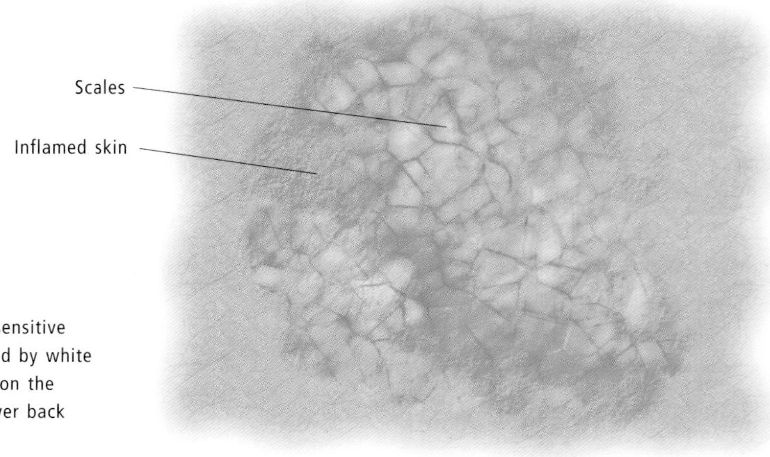

Psoriasis

In this condition, sensitive red patches covered by white scales can appear on the elbows, knees, lower back and scalp.

Psychoses may be organic or functional. Organic psychoses are those with a physical cause such as dementia, a brain tumor, alcoholism, poisoning or a head injury. The symptoms improve if the underlying condition can be treated.

Functional psychoses are those with no organic cause. Schizophrenia is the most common, and involves a withdrawal from reality, hallucinations, delusions and an inability to feel normal emotions. The onset is usually in the teens and there may be only one episode, or there may be recurrent episodes. In some individuals the illness is chronic and they may need to be hospitalized permanently. The cause of schizophrenia is unknown, although there is a genetic predisposition to develop the disease. Schizophrenia cannot be cured but the symptoms can be controlled with antipsychotic drugs. Psychotherapy may be useful in some cases.

Other psychiatric disorders such as depression and bipolar disorder (manic depression) may have a psychotic element to them, especially if they are accompanied by delusions, hallucinations or paranoia. Psychosis can be caused by certain drugs such as LSD and cannabis. Usually the symptoms disappear when the effects of the drug wear off. A brief psychosis lasting from several hours to a week may occur in an otherwise normal person after an extremely stressful event, such as a death in the family.

SEE ALSO *Bipolar disorder, Depression, Hallucinations, Paranoia, Schizophrenia*

PSYCHOTHERAPY

The term psychotherapy describes a broad range of treatments for mental or emotional disorders that use psychological methods to focus on a person's thoughts, behavior and emotions.

Central to this practice is the theory that the mind is comprised of conscious and unconscious components, and the unconscious state of mind affects conscious thoughts and behavior. Psychotherapy works to bring unconscious thoughts, behaviors and emotions into consciousness to allow the patient greater choice.

Psychotherapy may use the analysis of fantasies and dreams to uncover unconscious thoughts and feelings. The building of trust and rapport between the psychotherapist and the patient is crucial.

Common psychotherapeutic approaches include the following.

Psychoanalysis was pioneered by the Viennese psychiatrist Sigmund Freud (1856–1939). This approach focuses on the repressed material found in the unconscious which expresses itself in disguised forms known as defense mechanisms. Psychoanalysis aims at freeing the patient from repeating past conflicts. Techniques used include free association, dream interpretation and the interpretation of the relationship between analyst and patient. This form of therapy is sometimes used for chronic neurosis, traumatic pasts or relationship difficulties.

Analytical psychotherapy, based upon the work of the Swiss psychiatrist Carl Jung (1875–1961), views the unconscious as the container of all conscious life. The therapy works with the theory of archetypes (such as the "mother" or the "hero") contained within the "collective unconscious". It utilizes dream work, active imagination and the relationship between patient and therapist to free the patient from being driven by either unconscious forces or the expectations of external environments. It can help with non-clinical depression and adjustment to midlife crisis and the ageing process.

Existential therapy focuses on the fundamental questions of what it means to be alive and how to address the issues of self and life with openness. This psychotherapy seeks to understand the patient's experience and process and its aim is personal authenticity. The main technique is reflection. It can help with life dissatisfaction.

Cognitive behavioral therapy (CBT) aims at changing the patient's negative thinking and behavior patterns. Patients are helped to identify the link between the assumptions they make about themselves and their lives, and the outcomes in their life. The therapy helps the patient to achieve greater self-esteem and self-care through adopting positive thought and action. The therapist takes an active role, teaching strategies and setting homework assignments. This form of therapy can help phobias, obsessive-compulsive disorder, post-traumatic stress disorder, and depression and anxiety states.

Humanistic psychotherapy is based on belief in the individual's innate capacity to realize their true self and become fully functioning. The main focus is on current problems and the patient's feelings towards themselves and their lives. The patient is encouraged to develop self-knowledge, communicate thoughts and feelings honestly and to achieve a positive self-esteem and view of the world. The therapist aims to create a safe place for the patient that is free of judgmental criticism, probing for hidden motives or personality interpretation. Humanistic psychotherapy can help address issues arising from traumatic pasts, relationship difficulties, bereavement or other major life changes.

SEE ALSO *Art therapy, Behavior therapy, Counseling, Dance movement therapy, Music therapy*

PSYCHOTROPIC DRUGS

Medications that affect the mind and behavior are called psychotropic drugs. They include antidepressants, neuroleptics, mood stabilizers, and benzodiazepines. These drugs may be prescribed by a psychiatrist to treat conditions such as depression, anxiety, phobias and insomnia. They may be used in conjunction with psychotherapy.

Determining the right medication(s) and doses that work best for a particular person is usually a matter of trial and error. The drugs do not always work, but when they do the effect may be dramatic, allowing a sufferer to function in day-to-day living. However, in many cases people may become dependent on them, or use them after they are no longer needed. Also, withdrawal from psychotropic drugs may cause unpleasant symptoms. (On the other hand, some drugs must be continued indefinitely.) It is important to seek medical advice before coming off these drugs.

Medication alone can not solve a psychological problem and will not substitute for learning the coping skills necessary to adapt to and enjoy life.

SEE ALSO *Antidepressants, Anxiety, Anxiolytics, Depression, Detoxification, Drug dependence, Insomnia, Phobias, Psychotherapy, Tranquilizers, Withdrawal*

PUBERTY

Puberty is the 2–6 year period between childhood and adolescence when hormonal changes cause a rapid increase in body size, changes in the shape and composition of the body, and rapid development of the reproductive organs and the secondary sexual characteristics.

In females, this process includes the development of the breasts, widening of the hips, rapid growth of the uterus, and the appearance of hair on the underarms and around the vulva. Menstruation, a monthly discharge of blood and uterine tissue, begins about 2 years after the onset of puberty and continues to be irregular for 2 years or so before becoming more regular. The changes are caused by the actions of the sex hormones, estrogen and progesterone, released by the ovaries under the control of hormones from the pituitary gland.

In males, secondary sexual characteristics include rapid growth in the size of the testes and the penis; an increase in the size of the larynx, which deepens the voice and gives the "Adam's apple" look to the front of the neck; and the appearance of facial, underarm, pubic and body hair. Height increases rapidly and the first ejaculation occurs, usually about a year or so after the penis begins enlarging. These changes are governed by the male sex hormone testosterone.

In both females and males, there is also increased glandular activity. The apocrine glands, located in the underarms, the anus, the genitals and the breasts, become active at this time, giving off their characteristic odors. The sebaceous glands increase their production of sebum—an oily substance that lubricates the skin. This may lead to the familiar problem of acne in adolescence.

Although girls undergo greater physical change during puberty than boys, they tend to reach puberty earlier and take less time to reach maturity. Puberty in girls begins around age 11 and continues until about age 16. In boys, the corresponding period begins about age 13 and continues until about age 18. Differences in the times and rates of growth and sexual maturity are caused by a combination of inherited tendencies, nutrition, and the environment.

Emotional and behavioral changes accompany these physical changes. Hormonal

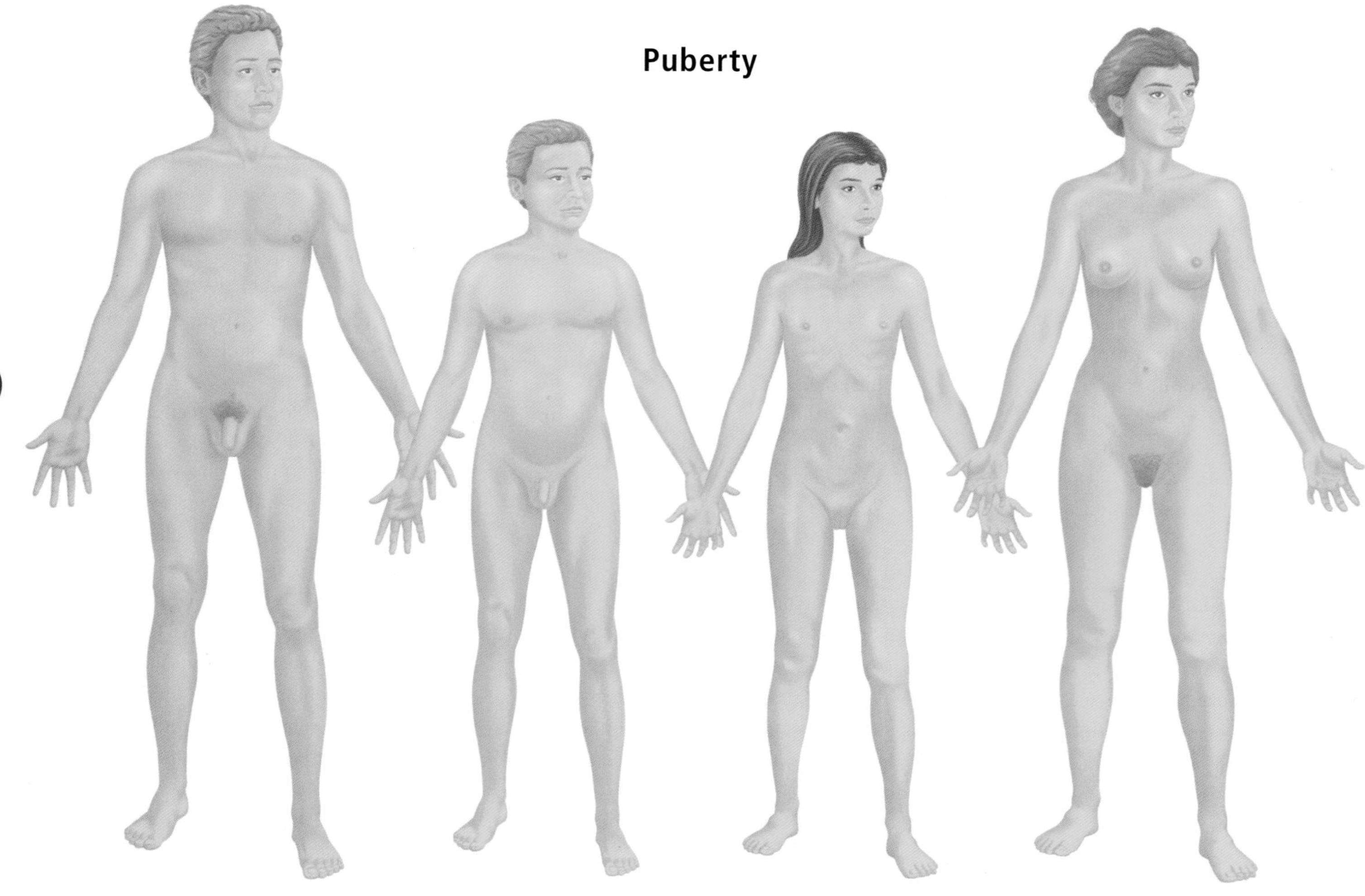

17-year-old male
Appearance of facial hair along with body and pubic hair, and increase in the size of the testes and penis are the predominant signs of male puberty. The larynx also increases in size creating the "Adam's apple" look at the front of the neck.

12-year-old male
Puberty in males occurs about 2 years later than in females. At age 12, a boy has little or no body hair, a small penis and testes, and still appears childlike.

10-year-old female
There is little or no breast development, no pubic hair and an almost boyish appearance at this age.

17-year-old female
Fully developed breasts, hair growth around the vulva and widening of the hips are the outward signs of female puberty.

changes awaken sexual feelings, and many adolescents have some sexual experience. Dating normally begins during puberty.

In some cases puberty occurs later than usual or does not occur at all. Sexual development can be retarded by many different factors, including metabolic defects, hereditary conditions, hormonal disorders and poor nutrition.

SEE ALSO *Acne, Adolescence, Hormones, Menstruation, Reproductive systems*

PULMONARY ARTERY

The pulmonary trunk or pulmonary artery is the large vessel which carries relatively deoxygenated blood from the right side of the heart into the lungs. Blood from the right ventricle of the heart is expelled into the pulmonary trunk through the pulmonary valve, which prevents regurgitation of the blood back into the ventricle when the heart muscle relaxes.

The pulmonary trunk is quite short, about 1 inch (2–3 centimeters) long. It divides into the left and right pulmonary arteries to enter each lung. During fetal life, the pulmonary trunk is joined to the aorta by a duct (ductus arteriosus) which allows blood to flow from the right side of the heart to the aorta, bypassing the uninflated lungs. After birth, the duct closes up, leaving a ligament called the ligamentum arteriosum.

SEE ALSO *Aorta, Circulatory system, Fetal development, Heart, Lungs*

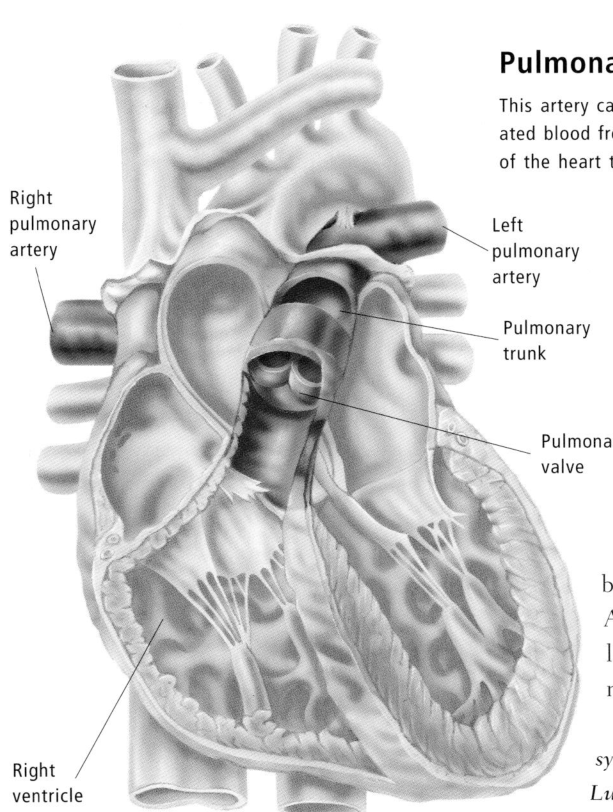

Pulmonary artery

This artery carries the deoxygenated blood from the right side of the heart to the lungs.

PULMONARY CIRCULATION

In the human body, blood passes through the heart twice during each complete passage of the circulatory system. In this so-called "double circulation" system, found in all mammals, the blood follows two complementary but separate routes from the heart. Systemic circulation takes the blood around the body and back; pulmonary circulation transports the blood to the lungs and back.

The purpose of pulmonary circulation is to pass the blood close to the thin-walled air sacs (alveoli) of the lungs so that the blood can exchange carbon dioxide collected from the body for oxygen. Before being sent into the pulmonary blood vessels, the blood returns, deoxygenated and dark red, from the head, limbs and internal organs, to the heart. The oxygen-depleted blood enters the right atrium then passes, via the tricuspid valve, to the right ventricle located immediately below. From there the blood is pumped out along the route of the pulmonary circulation.

The right ventricle sends the blood through the pulmonary valve and on to the lungs via the pulmonary arteries, the only arteries that carry deoxygenated blood after birth. The right pulmonary artery runs to the right lung and the left goes to the left lung. Each pulmonary artery divides repeatedly to culminate in a network of tiny, thin-walled capillaries around the air sacs of a lung. Here, carbon dioxide diffuses out of the blood into the lungs, from where it is exhaled. At the same time, oxygen contained in air breathed into the lungs diffuses into the blood.

From each lung the oxygenated blood (now bright red) flows from the capillaries to venules and eventually into the two pulmonary veins. Most veins after birth carry deoxygenated blood but the pulmonary veins, transporting oxygenated blood from the lungs back to the heart, are the exception.

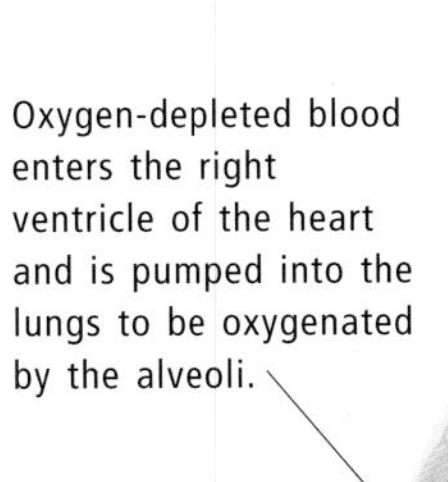

Oxygen-depleted blood enters the right ventricle of the heart and is pumped into the lungs to be oxygenated by the alveoli.

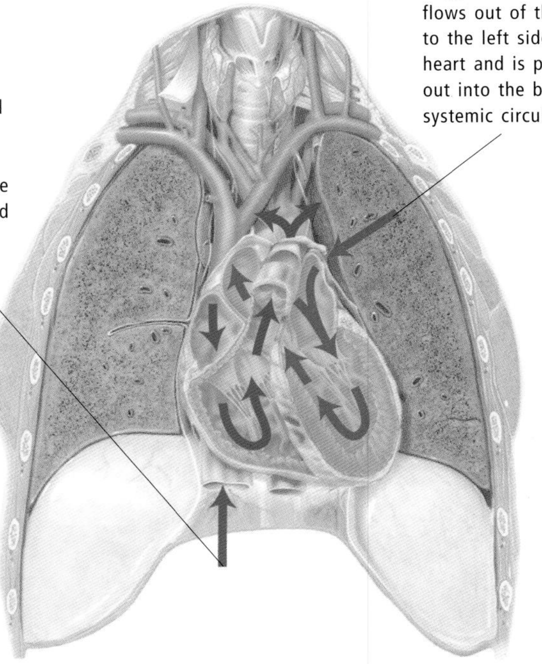

Oxygenated blood flows out of the lungs to the left side of the heart and is pumped out into the body for systemic circulation.

Pulmonary circulation

The primary purpose of pulmonary circulation is to offload carbon dioxide, which the blood has collected from the body, and pick up oxygen through the thin-walled air sacs of the lungs.

NB: In this illustration the top two-thirds of the lungs and pleura have been cut away to show the heart.

P

The pulmonary circulation is completed when blood is delivered back to the heart at the left atrium. From there the oxygenated blood passes through the mitral valve to the muscular left ventricle and then on to the rest of the body via the systemic circulation.

Pulmonary circulation comes "on-line" in humans only after birth. Before that, the lungs (along with the gastrointestinal tract) do not function. Instead, the fetal blood collects oxygen from and dumps carbon dioxide into the mother's circulation through the placenta.

Pulmonary hypertension and pulmonary embolism are two of the most commonly encountered serious disorders of the pulmonary circulation. Pulmonary hypertension is abnormally high blood pressure in the lungs. It is not necessarily related to high blood pressure in the systemic circulation and can interfere with oxygen levels in the blood. Possible causes include tissue damage in the lungs due to disease or the inflammation of blood vessels in the lungs.

In pulmonary embolism, a condition requiring urgent medical attention, a pulmonary artery becomes blocked by fat, an air bubble, tumor or blood clot (which will usually have arisen in the deep leg veins). Symptoms include breathing discomfort, sudden chest pain, shock and a blue discoloration to the skin caused by an excess of deoxygenated blood in the body. Very large pulmonary embolisms are often fatal.

SEE ALSO *Circulatory system, Deep venous thrombosis, Lungs, Mitral valve, Placenta, Pulmonary embolism, Veins, Ventricle*

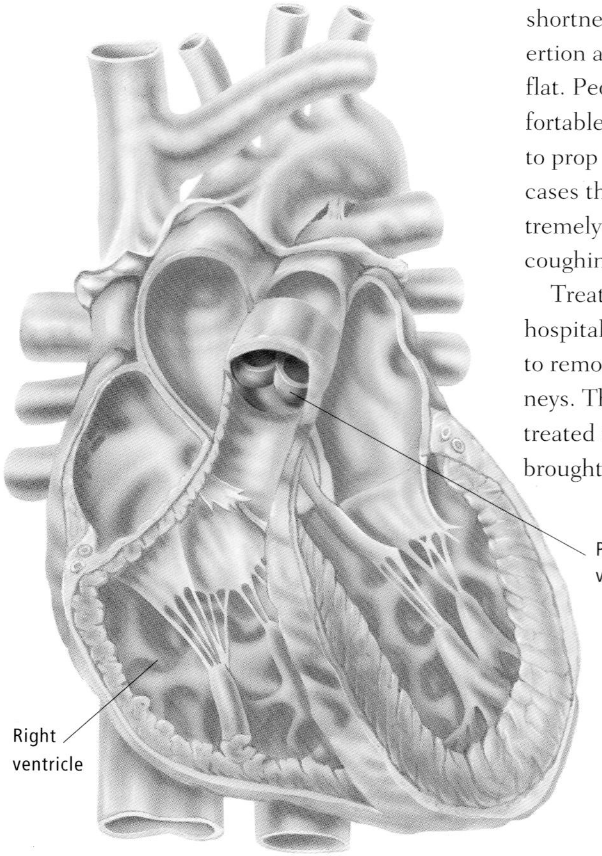

PULMONARY EDEMA

Pulmonary edema is a build-up of fluid in the lungs, most often due to heart failure, which may be a complication of a myocardial infarction (heart attack), myocarditis (disease of the heart muscle), mitral or aortic valve disease, or other heart disorders.

Pulmonary edema may also occur in cases of fluid overload, for example, in someone who has been given too much intravenous fluid in hospital. It may result from a major allergic reaction such as anaphylactic shock. As the heart muscle weakens, it becomes less able to pump blood forward into the arterial system and thus pressure rises in the veins of the lungs, the pulmonary veins. This results in leakage of fluid into the air spaces in the lungs.

The symptoms of pulmonary edema are shortness of breath, occurring initially on exertion and later at rest, especially when lying flat. People with heart failure are more comfortable sitting up and may use extra pillows to prop themselves up at night. In severe cases they may wake during the night extremely short of breath, gasping for air and coughing frothy pink fluid.

Treatment requires urgent admission to hospital for intravenous diuretic medication to remove fluid from the lungs via the kidneys. The patient is given oxygen, and is treated for any underlying condition that has brought on the heart failure, such as infection, irregular heartbeat or heart attack. Medication may be given to increase the pumping ability of the heart.

SEE ALSO *Circulatory system, Edema, Heart, Lungs*

PULMONARY EMBOLISM

Pulmonary embolism is obstruction of the pulmonary circulation by solid or cellular material that has traveled from the venous circulation through the right side of the heart and lodged in an artery of the lungs, blocking the blood supply. It is usually caused by a blood clot from a vein in the lower leg (a deep vein thrombosis). Less commonly the embolus may be air, fat, or bone marrow.

Not only does the embolus cut off the blood supply to the lungs, but just as importantly, it disrupts the flow of blood through the left side of the heart and the rest of the body. If the blockage is large enough, the cardiac output falls and the body tissues die.

The risk of a pulmonary embolus is greatest in people with deep vein thrombosis or those with a propensity to clotting—that is, those who are immobile, bedridden, pregnant, taking oral contraceptives, or who have had recent surgery, especially pelvic surgery.

The symptoms of pulmonary embolism are sudden chest pain (as the heart is deprived of oxygenated blood), difficulty in breathing, a pale skin, a rapid heart rate, and faintness. The condition is a medical emergency and must be treated in hospital. Pulmonary embolism will be confirmed by a lung scan; blood tests should be done to measure the levels of oxygen in the blood. Angiography (an x-ray test in which dye is injected into the veins) or Doppler ultrasound studies of the veins can confirm whether there is a deep vein thrombosis.

The treatment is with intravenous drugs that dissolve the clot (thrombolytic drugs). Further clotting is prevented with intravenous anticoagulant drugs. In the meantime the patient is given oxygen by mask. With adequate treatment, the death rate is low.

After surgery the condition is best prevented by patients walking around as soon as possible, combined with the use of elastic support stockings. Heparin (an anticoagulant)

Pulmonary valve

This valve prevents the backflow of blood into the ventricle when the heart muscle relaxes.

P

can be given in small doses under the skin to patients requiring prolonged bed rest.

SEE ALSO *Anticoagulants, Circulatory system, Lungs, Thrombosis*

PULMONARY FUNCTION TESTS

Pulmonary function tests (also known as lung capacity tests) measure the effectiveness of ventilation. They are used in lung diseases such as asthma, bronchitis, emphysema and fibrosis of the lung to determine the severity of the disease.

Spirometry is a test using an instrument called a spirometer, which measures how well the lungs take in air, how much air they hold, and how well the lungs exhale air. A peak flow meter is a smaller device that measures how quickly the lungs can expel air. Both tests can be performed in the physician's office.

SEE ALSO *Asthma, Bronchitis, Emphysema, Lungs*

PULMONARY VALVE

The pulmonary valve is situated where the blood from the right ventricle of the heart flows out into the large artery to the lungs, the pulmonary trunk. The pulmonary valve prevents backflow of blood from the pulmonary trunk into the right ventricle when the heart muscle relaxes. Both the pulmonary valve and the aortic valve are said to be semilunar valves, because they each consist of three half-moon shaped valve cusps.

Disease may affect the pulmonary valve, resulting in either pulmonary stenosis or pulmonary insufficiency (incompetence). Pulmonary stenosis is usually a congenital disease in which the cusps of the pulmonary valve are fused in the form of a membrane or diaphragm with a narrow central opening, rather than the normal semilunar (half-moon) shaped cusps.

Pulmonary insufficiency means that the pulmonary valve is unable to prevent the backflow of blood from the pulmonary trunk into the right ventricle when the ventricle stops contracting. It most often arises in individuals who have had rheumatic heart disease, in which the valve cusps become contracted and fused with the wall of the artery, or in cases of increased blood pressure in the lung circulation.

SEE ALSO *Circulatory system, Heart, Lungs*

PULSE

As the heart beats, each beat causes a quantity of blood to be forced under pressure into the arterial system. These beats cause a pulse or shock wave that travels along the walls of the arteries. This pulse can be felt in several parts of the body by placing the finger over an artery. Arteries in which the pulse can normally be felt particularly easily are the carotid arteries (in the neck) and radial arteries (at the wrist).

Clinically, the pulse rate is normally measured by feeling the radial pulse, found near the thumb side of the front surface of the wrist. Sometimes the carotid pulse (in the neck) is used instead. The number of pulse beats counted in 10 seconds is multiplied by 6 to obtain the rate in beats per minute. The pulse must, however, be felt for a longer period to check for irregular pulse rate. The strength or weakness of the pulse is also noted.

The pulse rate in healthy adults at rest is typically about 60–70 beats per minute. Athletes and those on beta-blocker medication may have slower pulse rates, while children and babies have faster pulse rates. The pulse rate increases during exercise to increase the output of blood from the heart. The rate is also increased by excitement.

SEE ALSO *Carotid arteries, Heart, Palpitations, Radial artery*

Pulse points

The pressure created by a beat of the heart can be felt quite easily where arteries are close to the skin.

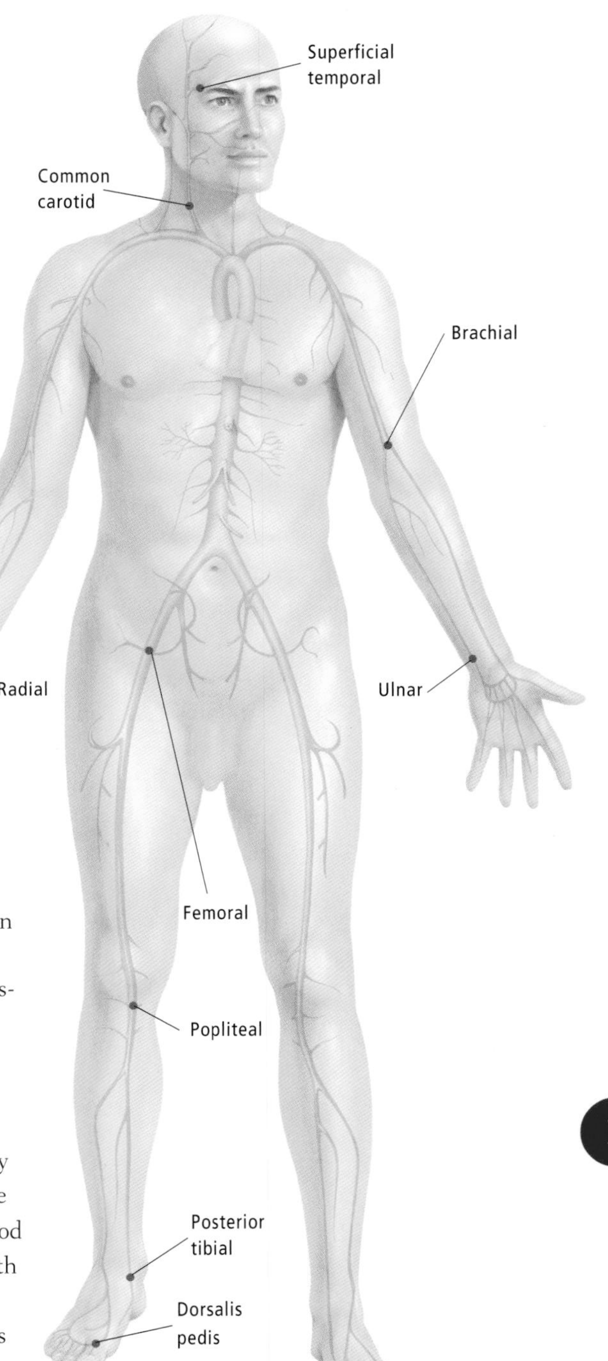

PUPIL OF EYE

The pupil of the eye is the central hole in the iris through which light enters the eye. Tiny muscles in the iris control the size of the pupil. In daylight, the pupil is typically about $\frac{1}{10}$ inch (3 millimeters) in diameter. In dark conditions, it opens to about $\frac{1}{3}$ inch (7 millimeters) in diameter to allow more light to enter the eye. Adaptation to dark also involves adaptation in the retina. When using an optical instrument, such as a telescope or binoculars, the diameter of the exit hole of the instrument should be matched to that of the pupil. For this reason, binoculars intended for night use have a larger exit hole than those intended for daylight use.

SEE ALSO *Eye, Iris, Retina*

PURPURA

Purpura is a disease in which hemorrhages occur in the skin and mucous membranes. It manifests itself as small red spots on the skin. There are two main types: thrombocytopenic purpura, involving a decrease in platelet count in the blood; and nonthrombocytopenic purpura, which does not involve any such decrease.

Causes of purpura include exposure to drugs or chemical agents; cancerous diseases such as leukemia; and infectious diseases such as rubella.

Schönlein's purpura is a nonthrombocytopenic purpura characterized by pain and tenderness in the joints and often accompanied by mild fever and hive-like skin eruptions. Henoch's purpura is an allergic nonthrombocytopenic purpura marked by attacks of gastrointestinal pain, bleeding and hive-like skin eruptions.

Allergic purpura, also known as Schönlein-Henoch purpura, is an uncommon allergic disorder manifesting itself as an inflammation of blood vessels in the skin, joints, gastrointestinal tract or kidneys. It mainly affects young children and is more common in boys (from 2–8 years) than in girls. It usually develops as the result of an infection but may be drug related. Treatment depends on the cause.

SEE ALSO *Hemorrhage, Thrombocytopenia*

PYELITIS

Pyelitis is an inflammation of the pelvis of the kidney. It is most often caused by bacteria that make their way to the kidney via the blood or the bladder.

Pyelitis is reasonably common, particularly in children. It is easily treated but requires prompt attention to ensure that it does not lead to the development of the more serious kidney infection known as pyelonephritis.

SEE ALSO *Bladder, Kidney, Pyelonephritis, Urinary systems*

PYELOGRAM

A pyelogram is the film produced by a radiology technique (pyelography) in which a contrast medium (iodine-containing radiopaque dye) is introduced into the kidneys and the urinary collecting system, after which an x-ray is taken. There are two main types; intravenous pyelography (IVP) and retrograde pyelography.

In intravenous pyelography, dye is injected into the bloodstream at designated intervals. As the kidneys excrete the dye, a series of x-rays are taken which reveal the rate of excretion; detail the outlines of the kidney and ureters, showing their shape and size, and highlight any abnormalities, such as stones, tumors, scarring, or hydronephrosis, for example.

In retrograde pyelography, the dye is injected via a tube that is passed through the urethra and bladder and into the ureters where the dye is injected. The dye is then forced along the tube to the kidneys. Retrograde pyelography has been found to be most suitable for highlighting specific parts of the urinary tract, such as the ureters and the renal pelvis. Both procedures are performed in a radiology department of a hospital or in a radiology clinic.

SEE ALSO *Bladder, Kidney, Ureters, Urethra, Urinary systems*

PYELONEPHRITIS

Pyelonephritis is an infection of the kidney and the renal pelvis. Acute (sudden onset) pyelonephritis is usually the result of the

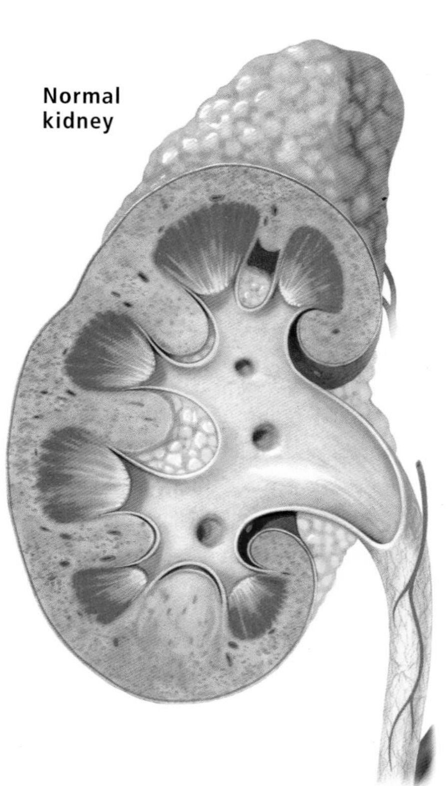

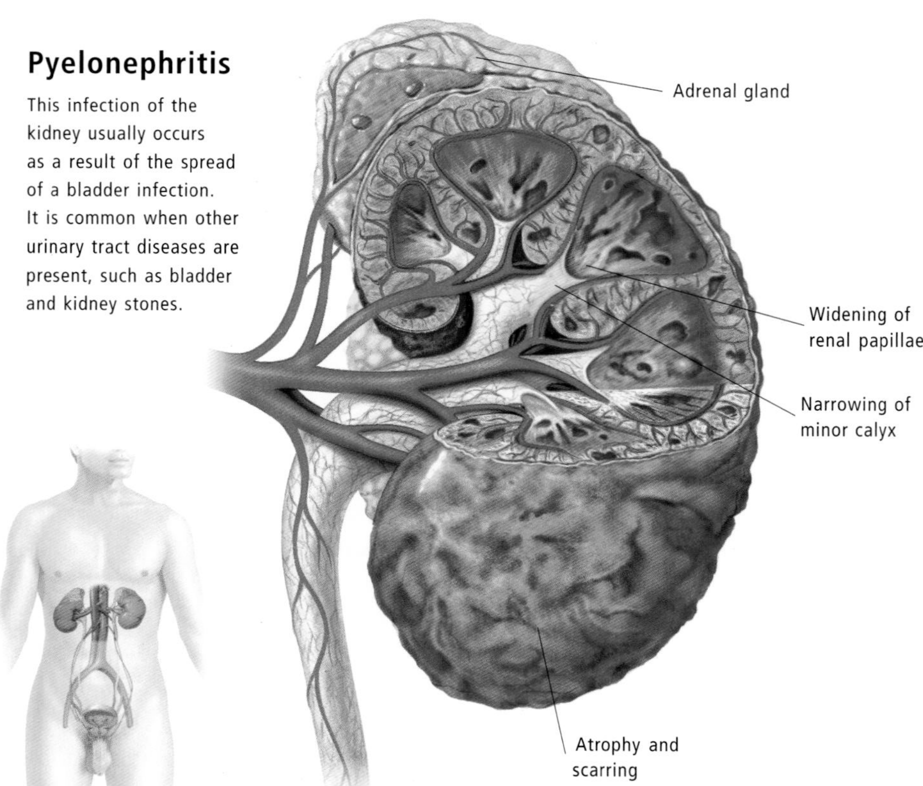

Pyelonephritis

This infection of the kidney usually occurs as a result of the spread of a bladder infection. It is common when other urinary tract diseases are present, such as bladder and kidney stones.

upstream spread of a bladder infection (cystitis). It is more common if there is pre-existing urinary tract disease, such as kidney or bladder stones. It is characterized by the sudden onset of pain in the lower back, fever with chills, nausea, and vomiting, pain passing urine (dysuria) and frequent urination. In children, the symptoms may be milder and less obvious. A urine test shows white blood cells and bacteria in the urine, while a culture of the urine will show the specific bacteria that is causing the infection (most commonly *E. coli*), and also its antibiotic sensitivity. Acute pyelonephritis generally responds to treatment with antibiotics given intravenously in hospital. The infection usually clears in 10–14 days.

Chronic pyelonephritis is caused by destruction and scarring of the kidney tissue as a result of recurrent or untreated bacterial infection. There is often an associated abnormality of the urinary tract, which leads to repeated infection. Treatment is surgical correction of any abnormality and a prolonged course of antibiotics. Eventually there may be renal failure requiring dialysis or transplantation.

SEE ALSO *Bladder, Cystitis, Dysuria, Kidneys, Ureter, Urinary systems, Urinary tract*

Pylorus

This ring of muscle prevents the contents of the intestines re-entering the stomach.

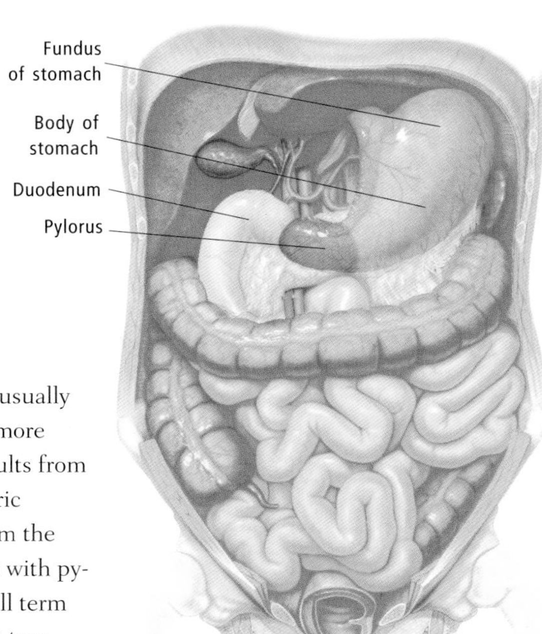

PYLORIC STENOSIS

Pyloric stenosis is a disease which usually affects only newborn infants. It is more common in boys than girls and results from the thickening of the muscle (pyloric sphincter) surrounding the exit from the stomach to the duodenum. Infants with pyloric stenosis are usually born at full term and feed and grow well for the first two weeks of life. After this time they begin to regurgitate milk with increasing force over the next few days until the vomiting becomes projectile. Unless the problem is corrected, the infant may become dehydrated, lose weight and die.

Treatment may be by antispasmodic drugs and rehydration with intravenous fluids, but usually surgery to sever the fibers of the enlarged pyloric sphincter will be required.

SEE ALSO *Newborn, Pylorus*

PYLORUS

The pylorus is a cone-shaped gate of muscle between the stomach and the small intestine (duodenum). Its role is to prevent the contents of the intestine from re-entering the stomach and also to prevent large food particles and undigested food from entering the small intestine prematurely.

SEE ALSO *Duodenum, Intestines, Stomach*

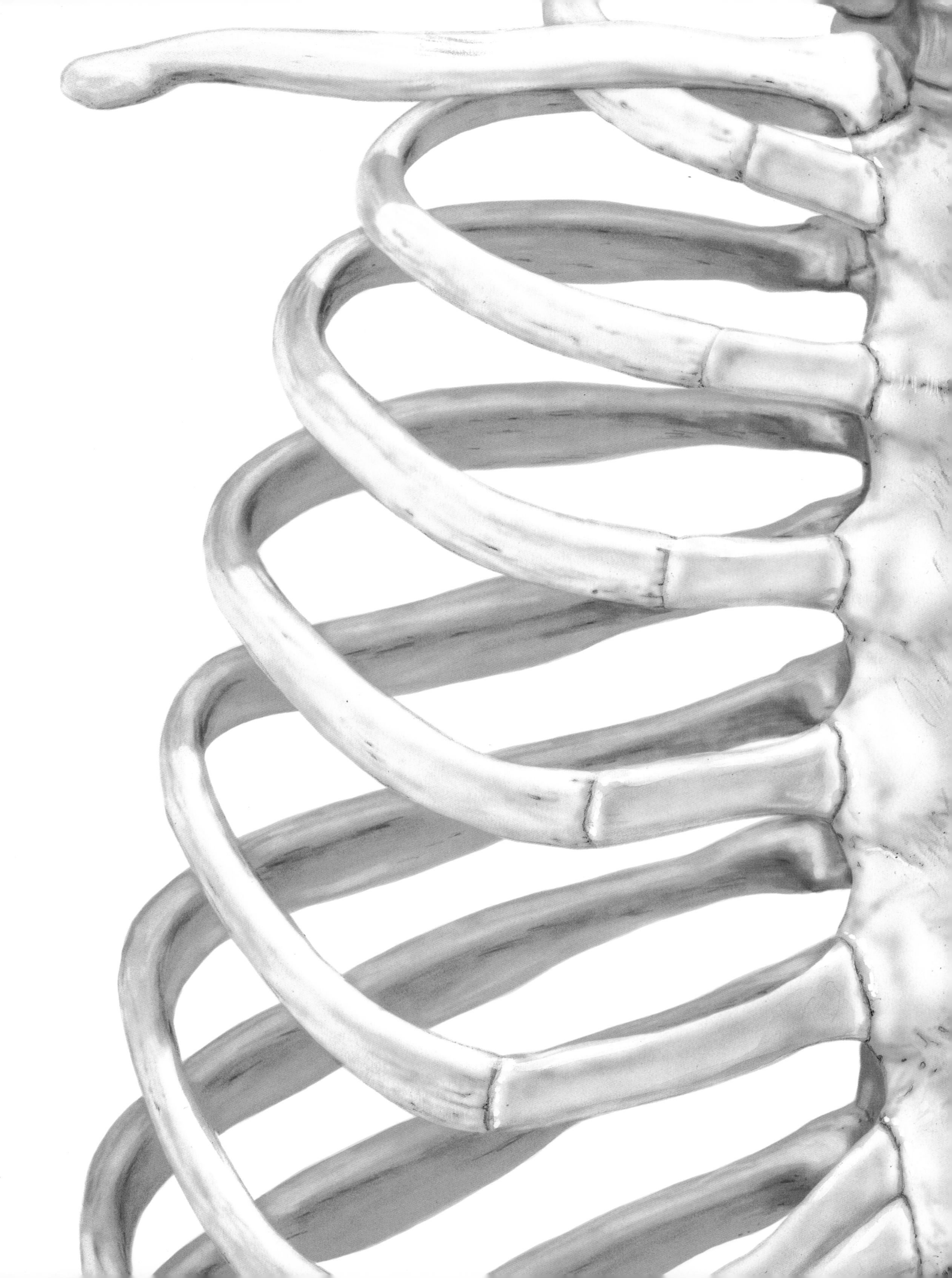

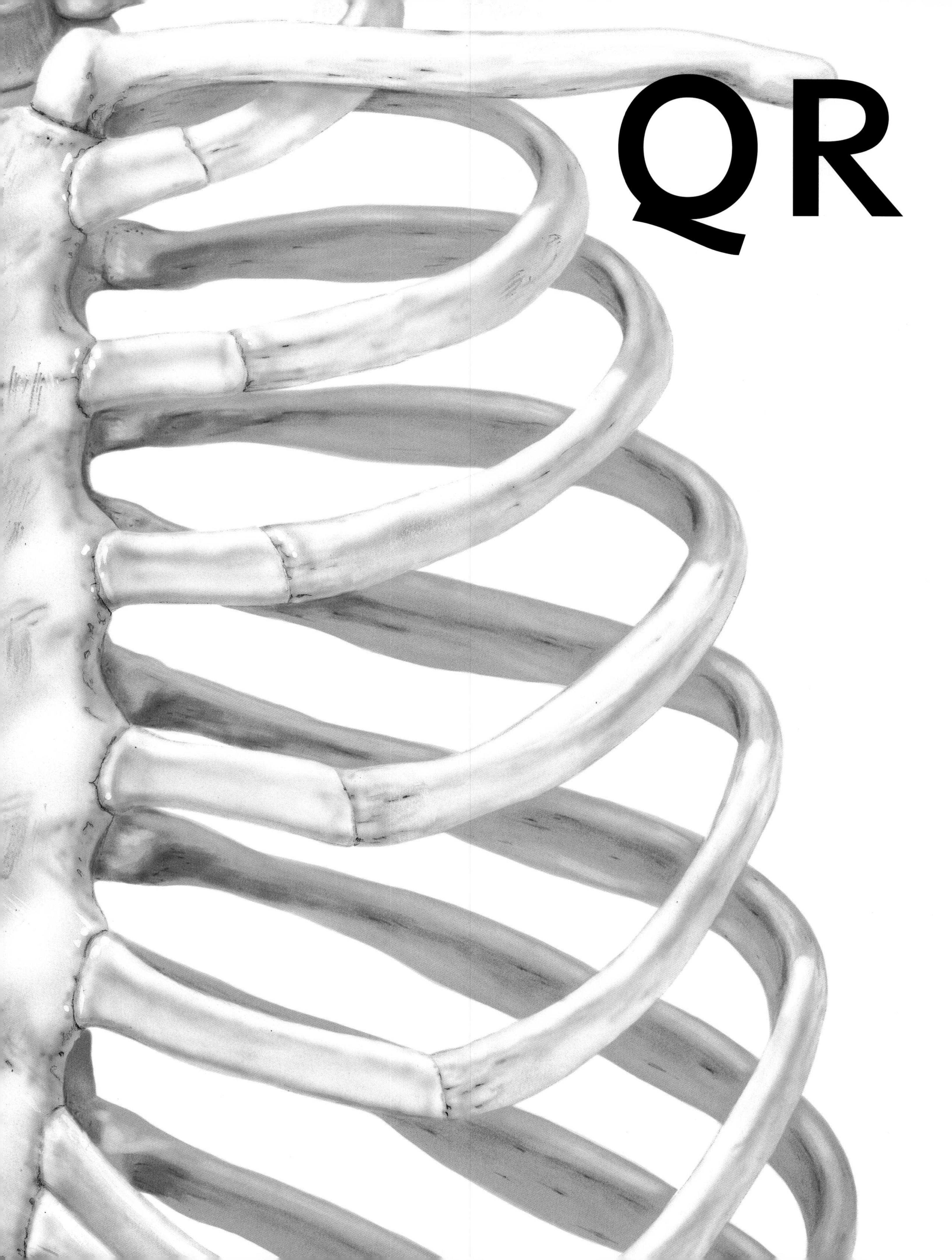
QR

Q FEVER

Q fever is an infectious disease acquired from animals; it causes fever, chills and muscular pains and sometimes more serious illnesses such as pneumonia, chronic hepatitis and encephalitis. It is caused by the microorganism *Coxiella burnetii*, which is found in domestic animals such as cattle, sheep, goats and cats, as well as in wild animals and ticks. The disease may be passed to humans when they inhale contaminated dust or droplets, consume contaminated food or unpasteurized milk or come into contact with materials, such as soil, which are contaminated with infected blood or feces.

The incubation period is 9–28 days after which a fever suddenly occurs, accompanied by symptoms resembling influenza, such as severe headaches, shivering, muscle pain and sometimes chest pain. After a week a dry cough may develop and the fever may continue for up to 3 weeks. This early form of the disease is known as Q fever (early) and may include complications such as pneumonia and hepatitis. Q fever (late) is a rare relapse of the illness that may cause problems with the aortic heart valve.

People who work with animals, such as farmers and veterinarians, are most at risk. Q fever rarely causes death and is treated with antibiotics. It is widely found in Europe, North America and parts of Africa.

SEE ALSO ***Encephalitis, Hepatitis, Infectious diseases, Pneumonia***

Q

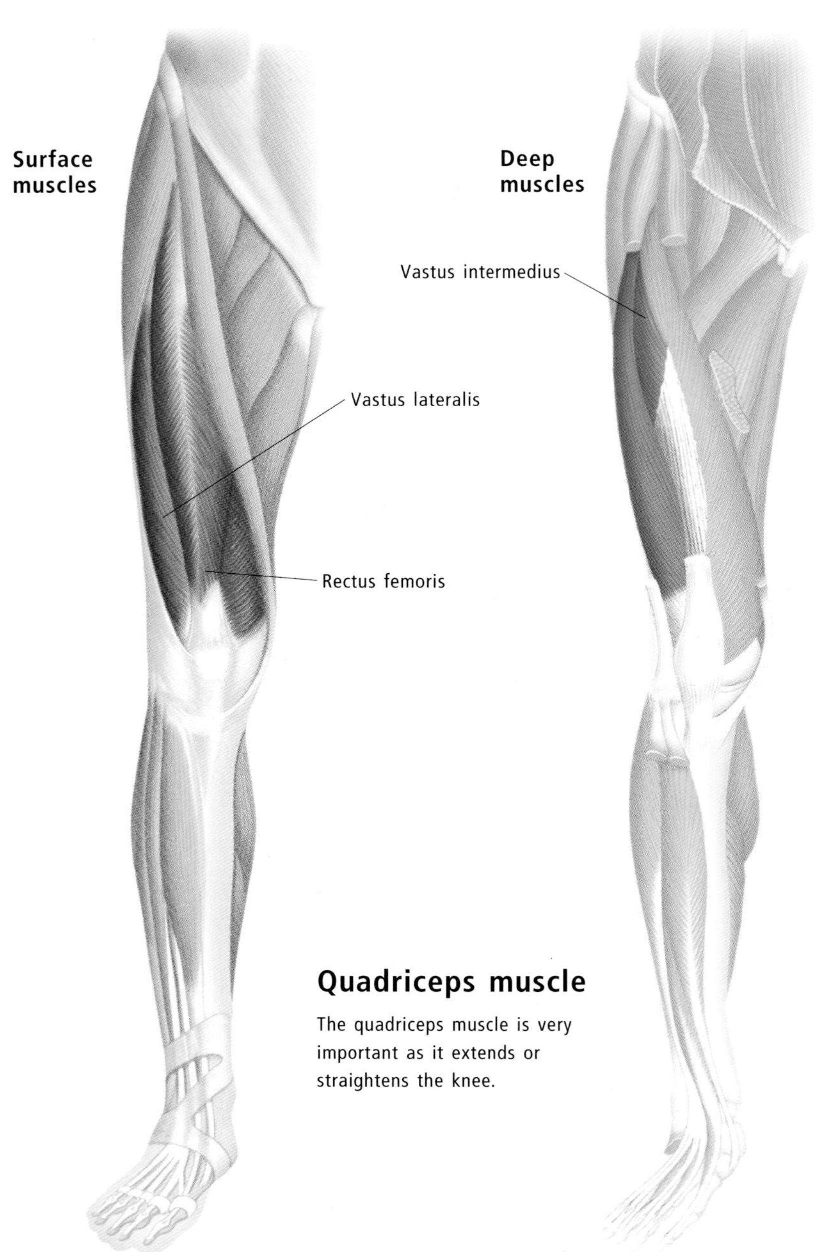

Quadriceps muscle

The quadriceps muscle is very important as it extends or straightens the knee.

QI GONG

Qi gong, also known as chi kung, is an ancient Chinese healing technique which combines movement, meditation and breath regulation to improve the flow of *qi (ch'i)* or life energy throughout the body. Practitioners trace the acupuncture meridians through the body with their hands, using visualization and breath control to cleanse and activate the vital organs, and to facilitate the flow of blood, lymph and energy.

Qi gong is widely practised in China, where it is combined with conventional medical treatments, and it is also used in Western countries. It is considered to be particularly beneficial for stress-related disorders and respiratory and circulatory problems.

SEE ALSO ***Acupuncture, Meditation***

QUADRICEPS MUSCLE

The quadriceps muscle forms the major muscle mass of the front and outer side of the thigh, covering most of the front and sides of the thigh bone (femur). The muscle is properly known as the quadriceps femoris muscle, so called because it has four parts, each with separate names. These are the rectus femoris, vastus lateralis, vastus medialis and vastus intermedius.

The quadriceps muscle arises mainly from the upper two-thirds of the thigh bone, and also from the bony pelvis. At its lower end, the tendons of the component muscles blend together to form a single tendon, which is attached to the upper surface of the kneecap (patella). The tendon extends below the patella as the "patellar ligament", which is attached to the tubercle of the shin bone (tibia) and is spread out on both sides to strengthen the capsule of the knee joint.

The quadriceps serves to straighten the knee. It also flexes the thigh on the pelvis. Both of these actions can be produced simultaneously. The quadriceps is also involved in the knee jerk reflex.

The quadriceps and hamstring muscles contribute to the stability of the knee joint, and recovery from knee injuries is assisted by strengthening these muscles.

SEE ALSO ***Knee, Leg, Muscle***

QUADRIPLEGIA

Quadriplegia (also referred to as tetraplegia) is partial or full paralysis and loss of sensation below the neck, involving all four limbs and the trunk of the body. (If only the lower limbs and trunk are affected, the condition is called paraplegia.)

Quadriplegia is caused by damage to the spinal cord in the neck, usually at the level of the fourth and fifth cervical vertebrae (if injuries occur above this level the diaphragm is often paralyzed and the victim may die). The injury is usually from trauma, most commonly road accidents and sporting injuries. Males between 15 and 35 years old make up the group most likely to be affected.

Less frequently, quadriplegia may be caused by spinal-cord tumors or birth defects. As well as muscle paralysis, quadriplegia leads to dysfunction of other organs and body systems whose nerve supply from the spinal cord has been disrupted. There may be loss of urinary and bowel control, impaired sexual function, loss of normal blood pressure, loss of body-temperature control, poor healing of tissues, and constipation.

Treatment as soon as possible after the injury gives the injured person the greatest chance of minimizing the extent of the damage and of recovering some function. Surgery may be performed to remove fluid or tissue that is pressing on the spinal cord (decompression laminectomy); to remove bone fragments or foreign objects; or to stabilize fractured vertebrae by fusion of the bones or insertion of hardware. Bed rest and spinal traction (which immobilizes the spine and reduces dislocation) promotes healing.

If movement or sensation return within a week after the injury, then most function will eventually be recovered (although it may take 6 months or more). Losses of function that remain after 6 months are likely to be permanent. Approximately one-third of sufferers will be permanently wheelchair-bound.

Thus, rehabilitation remains the mainstay of treatment. Physical therapy can help joint stiffness, and passive exercises will help prevent contractures.

Prolonged immobility can give rise to complications such as constipation, pressure sores and ulcers, so frequent position changes and good skin care are important. Other complications, such as bladder and lung infections and kidney stones, will also need to be treated. Psychotherapy or counseling may relieve depression and sexual problems.

With rehabilitation, some lost functions can be restored or compensated for. However, quadriplegics will have permanently reduced mobility and will require help with many facets of their lives, including accommodation, employment, transport, and access to buildings.

The condition can often be prevented by following commonsense safety precautions such as the wearing of seat belts in cars and of protective headgear for contact sports.

SEE ALSO *Paralysis, Paraplegia, Rehabilitation, Spinal cord*

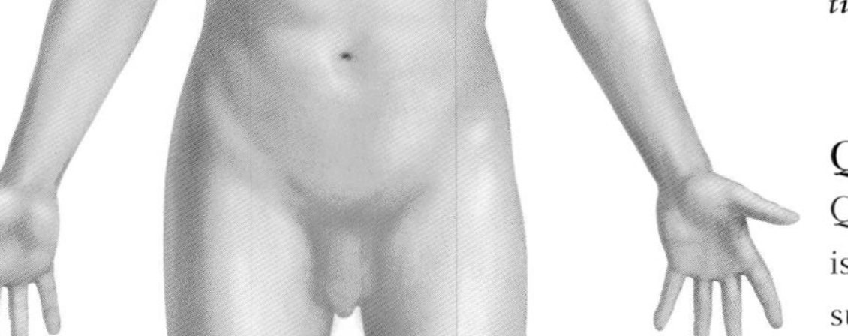

Quadriplegia

Quadriplegia is the paralysis of the torso, both arms and both legs. It is most often caused by injury to the fourth or fifth segment in the spinal cord through sporting or car accidents.

QUINSY

Quinsy, also known as peritonsillar abscess, is a relatively uncommon infection of the tissue surrounding the tonsils that results in an abscess or collection of pus. Often caused by spreading infection from tonsillitis, its symptoms include fever, severe pain when swallowing, and difficulty opening the mouth. It may be treated with antibiotics if caught in the early stages.

More severe conditions may require draining of the pus via a surgical incision. The infection can recur and if left untreated may spread to the mouth, neck, chest and lungs, causing life-threatening tissue swelling that can block airways. Quinsy is most common in older children, teenagers and young adults.

SEE ALSO *Abscess, Tonsils*

RABIES

Rabies is an acute viral disease that affects the nervous system of animals and is transmitted to humans via saliva, commonly after being bitten or licked on broken skin by a rabid animal, such as a bat, dog or cat. The average incubation time is 1–2 months, though it may occasionally be more than a year. It starts with fever, depression, nausea and vomiting. In "furious" rabies the victim becomes highly agitated, with uncontrollable behavior, spasms of the throat muscles, excessive saliva and frothing at the mouth which makes them unable to drink water. For this reason, rabies was once known as hydrophobia, which means "fear of water". "Dumb" rabies is characterized by sluggishness, weakness and paralysis. Once symptoms appear death is inevitable, usually within a week.

Vaccination soon after exposure to infection offers protection. An injection of rabies immune globulin is followed by a course of rabies vaccine over 28 days. Vaccination does not cancel out the risk of infection but reduces the intensity of the disease in those infected. Possible side effects of vaccination include headache, dizziness, nausea, muscle aches and, less commonly, neurological disorders and paralysis. Family pets should also be vaccinated.

SEE ALSO *Immunization, Viruses*

RADIAL ARTERY

The radial artery is a medium-sized artery which conveys blood through the forearm to the hand. It is one of two major arteries of the forearm, the other being the ulnar artery. It runs superficially through the muscular part of the forearm towards the thumb. The radial artery provides blood to muscles of the forearm and, together with the ulnar artery, contributes to the palmar arches in the hand, from which the digital arteries arise to supply the fingers.

The superficial course of the radial artery makes it easily accessible to the clinician taking the pulse during assessment of a patient. The examiner's fingers are placed over the radial artery at the wrist, just beside the tendon of flexor carpi radialis. Information can be obtained this way regarding the pulse rate and rhythm, whether it is strong or weak, and about the firmness of the arterial wall. With the ageing process the arterial wall hardens (arteriosclerosis) and this can be felt in the radial artery. The radial artery's superficial position also makes it vulnerable to injury at the wrist, before it descends into the space between the radius bone and the base of the thumb.

SEE ALSO *Arms, Arteries, Arteriosclerosis, Hand, Radius*

RADIAL NERVE

The radial nerve is one of the major nerves in the arm. It starts in the armpit (axilla) from a network of nerves (the brachial plexus). It supplies extensor muscles in the back of the arm, such as the triceps and extensors for the wrist, fingers and thumb. It also supplies skin over the back of the arm and hand, on the thumb side.

The radial nerve can be compressed in the armpit, for instance by the arm being draped over the back of a chair in sleep or when one is intoxicated, causing pins and needles or even temporary paralysis ("Saturday night palsy"). It can also be damaged by fractures of the humerus or injuries in the forearm. These injuries can lead to wrist-drop, in which the hand and fingers cannot be extended.

SEE ALSO *Arm, Hand, Nerves, Radius, Wrist*

RADIATION

Radiation is the emission or transfer of radiant energy as a stream of ions (electrically charged atoms), subatomic particles or electromagnetic energy waves. Heat, sound, light, radio waves and microwaves all come under the banner of radiation and are known as nonionizing radiation.

Ionizing radiation, including x-rays and gamma rays, is so named because it can cause substances such as human tissue to break into ions. It is used in medicine to treat cancers by damaging the cancerous cells so they are unable to grow and divide. This practice, known as radiation therapy or radiotherapy, may involve radiation created by a machine outside the body or by radioactive material, such as radium, implanted in the body. Radiosensitive cancers include leukemias and lymphomas.

Ultraviolet radiation from the sun, or ultraviolet light, has a wavelength shorter than the violet end of the visible spectrum of light, making it invisible to the eye. It is now known that prolonged exposure to ultraviolet radiation, especially over a lifetime, can be harmful to the skin and is associated with

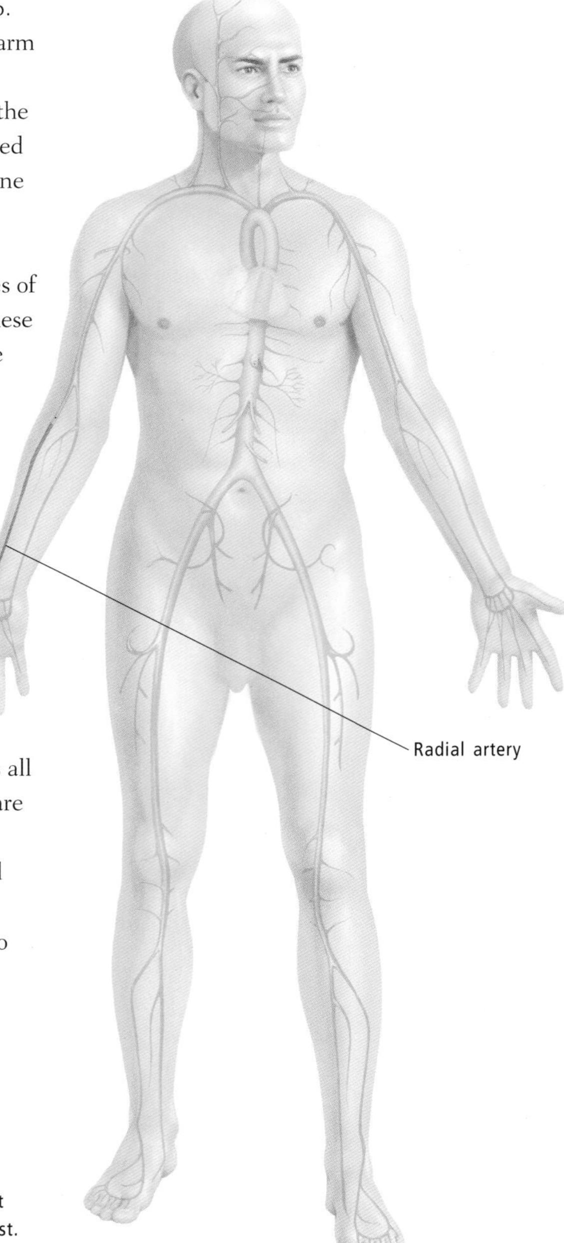

Radial artery

Passing through the forearm to the hand, the radial artery comes closest to the surface of the skin at the wrist. This allows the pulse to be taken easily.

solar keratoses ("sun spots"), skin cancer, melanoma and cataracts of the eye. Ultraviolet light is classified as UVA, UVB, or UVC depending on the wavelength. These different wavelengths are also be used in the treatment of skin diseases (phototherapy) such as acne vulgaris and psoriasis.

SEE ALSO *Cancer, Radiation therapy, Skin cancer, Ultraviolet therapy, X-ray*

Radiation therapy

In this treatment, high energy rays are directed towards a specific area of the body (such as a cancerous tumor) in order to target damaged cancer cells. Applying localized radiation in this way minimizes damage to normal tissues.

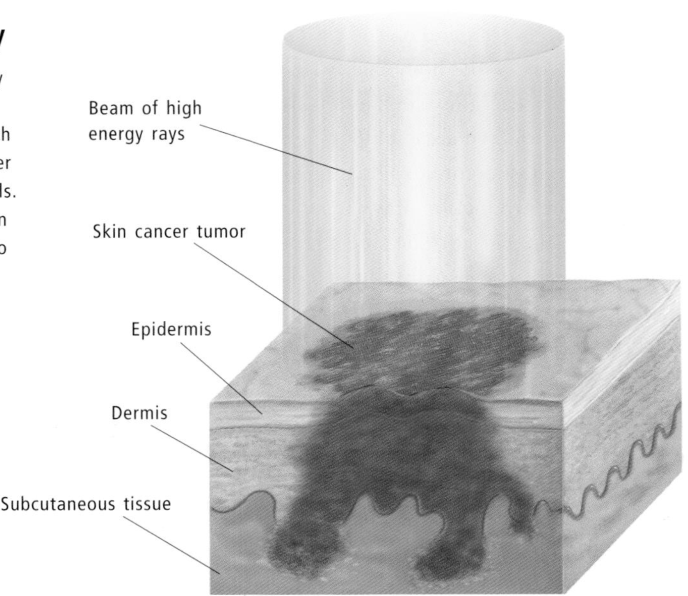

RADIATION SICKNESS

Accidental or intentional overexposure to ionizing radiation, either from x-rays or contact with radioactive substances can cause radiation sickness. Symptoms depend on the type of radiation, the length of exposure, the amount of radiation received and the parts of the body exposed.

Symptoms usually begin with fatigue, nausea, vomiting, diarrhea and burns. The victim may then suffer from the loss of hair and teeth, conjunctivitis, an unsteady gait, convulsions and open sores. In extreme cases, blood-forming tissue can be damaged, causing anemia and bleeding; inflammation of the stomach and intestinal lining (gastroenteritis) may also develop.

Radiation sickness affects the body's immune system, leaving the sufferer vulnerable to infection. It can cause miscarriage in pregnant women or result in damage to the fetus.

Exposure to low doses of radiation over an extended period may cause what is known as delayed radiation sickness. This is characterized by cataracts, a reduction in fertility, premature ageing and an increased risk of developing cancer or leukemia. It is also known as radiation poisoning or radiation syndrome.

SEE ALSO *Radiation, X-ray*

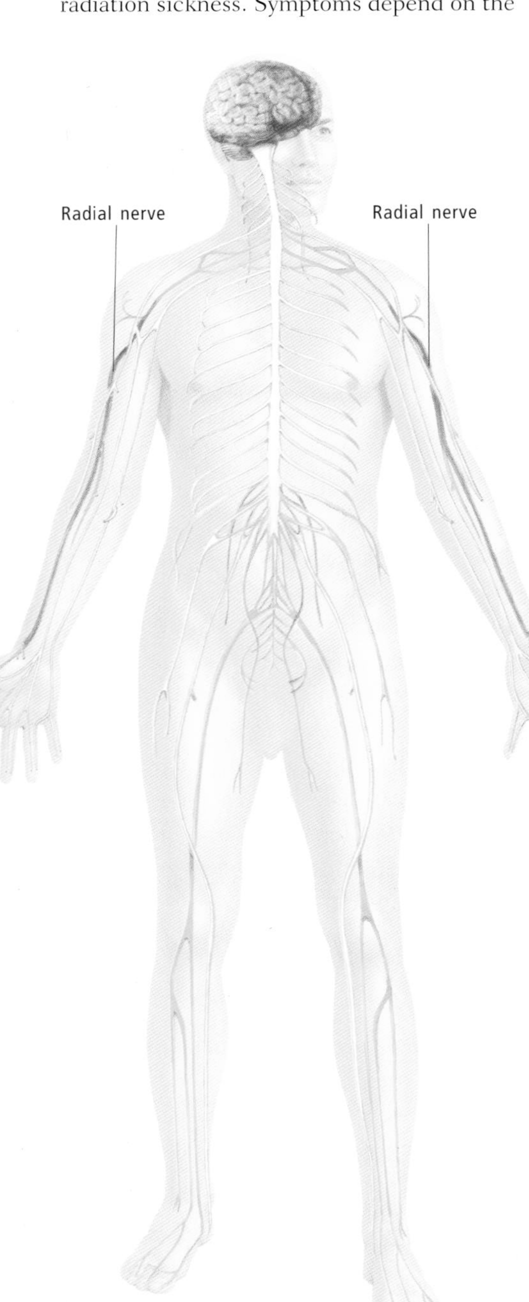

Radial nerve

The radial nerve controls the muscles that straighten the elbow and extend the wrist. Damage to this nerve can lead to wrist-drop, a paralysis of the extensor muscles of the hand.

RADIATION THERAPY

Radiation therapy (or radiotherapy) is the treatment of disorders using radiation. It is most widely used in the treatment of many different types of cancer. High-energy rays are used to damage cancer cells and stop them from growing and dividing. Like surgery, radiation therapy is a local treatment; it affects cancer cells only in the treated area. It may be used with other forms of treatment, like chemotherapy and surgery. Often it is used to shrink a tumor, which is then removed during surgery. It may also be used to provide temporary relief of symptoms, or to treat malignancies not accessible to surgery.

The machinery used is similar to x-ray equipment, but it contains a source of high-energy radiation, such as radium or a radioactive isotope of cobalt. Treatment is usually given on an outpatient basis in a hospital over several weeks. Patients are not radioactive during or after the treatment. Alternatively, the radiation can be administered via an implant, a small container of radioactive material placed directly into or near the tumor. Some patients receive both kinds of radiation therapy.

Radioimmunotherapy is a form of radiation therapy in which radioactive particles (radionuclides) are attached to antibodies. These antibodies are introduced into the body, travel to tumor cells, attach to them and kill them. The technique has the advantage of other types of radiation therapy in that normal (non-cancer) cells are unaffected.

R

The side effects depend on the treatment dose and the part of the body that is treated. Tiredness, skin reactions (such as a rash or redness) in the treated area, and loss of appetite are the most common side effects. Sometimes the production of white blood cells may be suppressed. The side effects of radiation therapy can usually be treated or controlled and are not permanent.

SEE ALSO *Cancer, Chemotherapy, Radiation, X-ray*

RADICULOPATHY

Radiculopathy is the name given to any disorder of the radicular nerves (spinal nerve roots). Spinal tumors and abscesses may cause radiculopathy, but by far the most common cause is a slipped or herniated intervertebral disk which compresses one or more of the roots; some people incorrectly take the term radiculopathy to refer to this condition alone.

In old age, the gelatinous material in the interior of the disk between the vertebra may degenerate. Under strain, such as when bending and lifting, it may herniate or rupture, becoming displaced from its normal position. In the process it tends to impinge on a nearby spinal nerve root, causing pain, numbness in the skin and weakness in the muscles supplied by that nerve root. Any part of the spine may be affected, but it is most common in the lumbar region, followed by the cervical region of the spine.

It occurs most often in the disk between the fifth lumbar vertebra and the sacrum, causing severe low back pain (which radiates to the buttocks, legs, and feet), tingling or numbness in legs or feet and, if severe, muscle weakness in the legs. The treatment is bed rest, analgesics and anti-inflammatory drugs, and physical therapy. If the condition persists, back surgery may be needed.

SEE ALSO *Disk, intervertebral, Sacrum, Spine, Vertebrae*

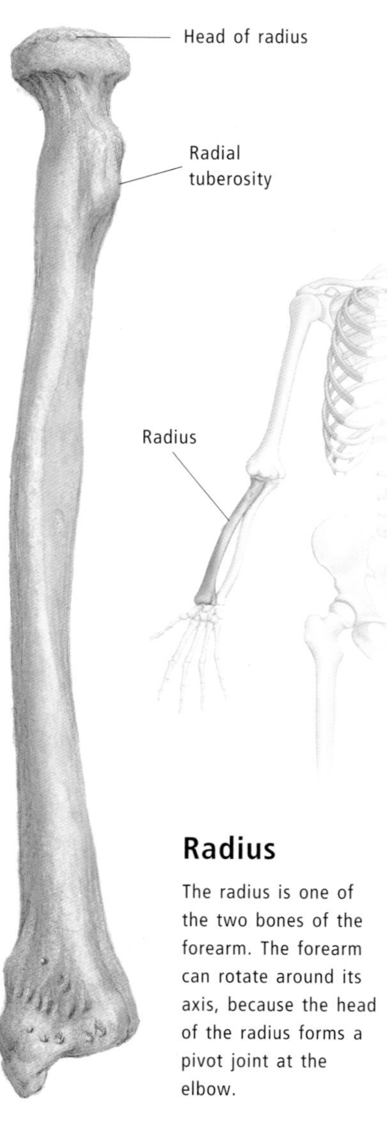

Radius

The radius is one of the two bones of the forearm. The forearm can rotate around its axis, because the head of the radius forms a pivot joint at the elbow.

RADIOLOGY

Radiology is a branch of medicine that uses various imaging techniques to generate pictures of the body that can detect a huge range of diseases and conditions. Originally, radiology involved the use of x-rays, a form of electromagnetic radiation that penetrates the body to form an image on film. Later, contrast materials such as barium were introduced to give a clearer picture of blood vessels and organs. In more recent years, other forms of diagnostic imaging have been utilized. These include: computerized axial tomography (CAT) scanning, which uses x-rays to give a three-dimensional view of the body; ultrasound, which uses sound waves; radioisotope scanning; nuclear magnetic resonance imaging (MRI); and positron emission tomography (PET) scanning.

SEE ALSO *CAT scan, Imaging techniques, Magnetic resonance imaging, Positron emission tomography, Ultrasound, X-ray*

RADIOISOTOPE SCAN

Also known as a nuclear scan, a radioisotope scan uses radioactive isotopes in the diagnosis of disorders of the bones, the heart, the lungs, thyroid gland and kidney. It can measure the size, shape, position and function of an organ, and can detect abnormalities such as cysts, abscesses, tumors or other diseases in these organs.

During the test, the radioactive isotope is introduced into the body in one of two ways: either it is swallowed and concentrated by the organ being examined, or it is introduced into the organ via a catheter that is inserted into a vein or artery and guided to that organ. A camera, which can detect the gamma rays emitted by the isotope, then takes an image of the organ, and a physician interprets this picture.

The patient is exposed to a small amount of radiation, but this is outweighed by the benefits of the scan; the dose is not considered dangerous. The test takes a few hours and usually takes place in a physician's office or hospital radiology clinic.

SEE ALSO *Imaging techniques, Radiation, X-ray*

RADIUS

The radius is one of the two bones of the forearm. Located on the thumb side, it lies parallel to and rotates around the other forearm bone, the ulna. Near the uppermost end of the radius, which forms part of the elbow, is a raised and roughened area called the radial tuberosity. This is an attachment point for the biceps brachii (commonly called the biceps), the long muscle of the upper arm. At its other, larger end, the radius forms part of the wrist. A fracture of the radius just above this joint, known as a Colles' fracture, forces the wrist into an unnatural upwards position.

SEE ALSO *Arm, Ulna, Wrist*

RASH

Rash is a general term used to describe the temporary occurrence of raised or differently colored spots or patches on the skin. Rashes have a variety of causes and will vary in appearance depending on how severely the person is affected. Detailed information on the various rashes illustrated on the page opposite will be found under the specific entries for the various conditions.

Rashes

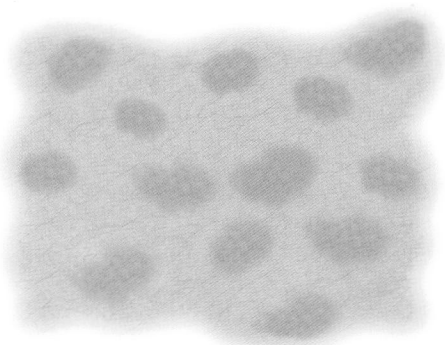

Measles
Small, white spots in the mouth, followed by reddish spots on the face and then the rest of body.

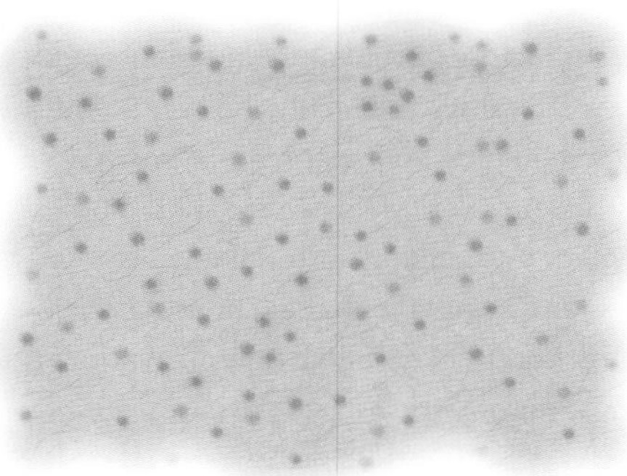

Rubella (German measles)
Like measles, but a fainter pink rash, spreading from the face to the rest of the body.

Chickenpox
Small itchy fluid-filled blisters appear on the chest and back, then spread to the rest of the body.

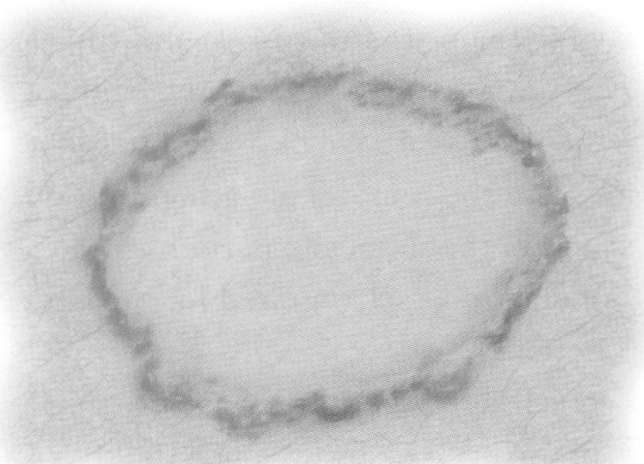

Ringworm
Reddish, ring-shaped patches of blisters or scales on the skin, caused by fungi.

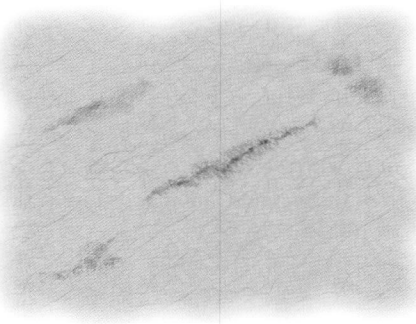

Scabies
A rash of tiny red lumps around a wavy line caused by mites burrowing under the skin.

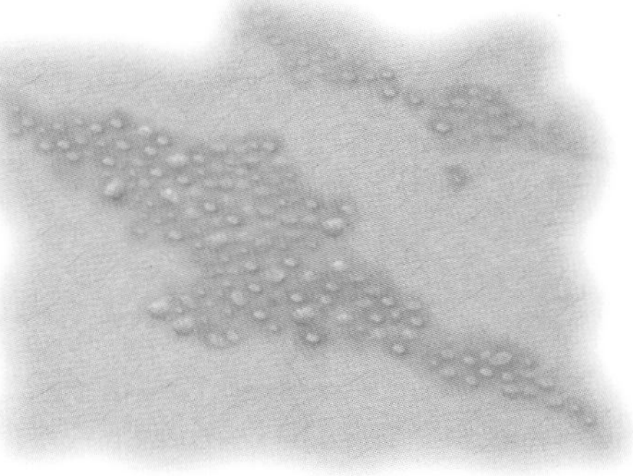

Shingles
Itchy blisters form on a part of the body, on one side, breaking down into a painful ulcerative rash.

Atopic dermatitis
Itchy and dry inflammation of the skin, usually on the face, neck, arms and legs.

Seborrheic dermatitis
Itchy red scaly patches, usually seen on the scalp as dandruff, and on the face, forehead and chest.

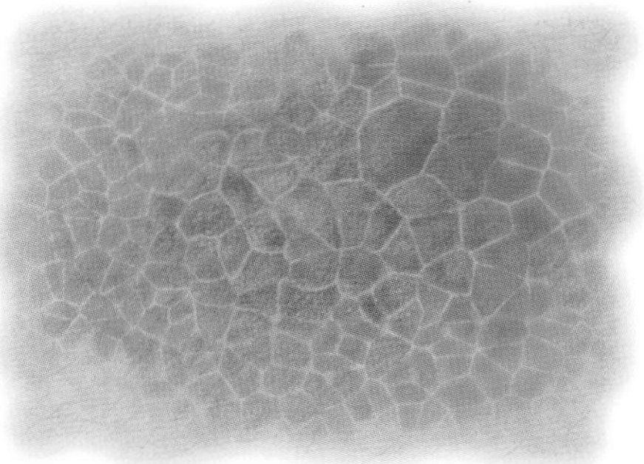

Ichthyosis
Inherited disorder resulting in skin that appears dry, rough, thick and scaly.

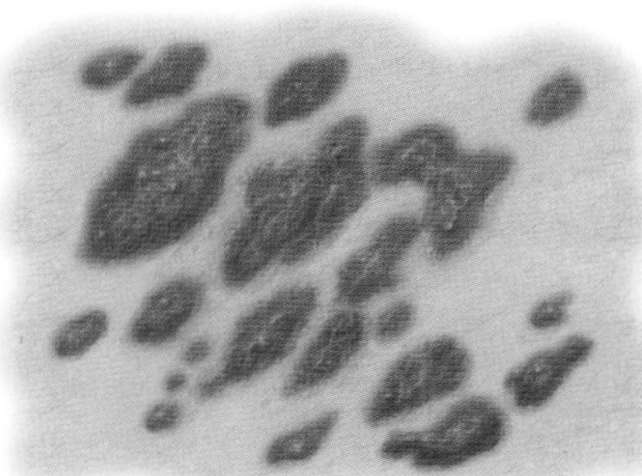

Lichen planus
Raised shiny pink or purple itchy spots, which may become scaly and spread to join together.

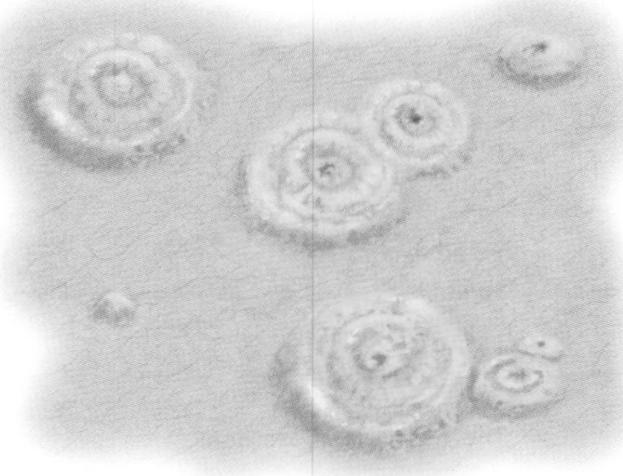

Erythema multiforme
Characterized by the reddening of the skin in circles around a central lesion.

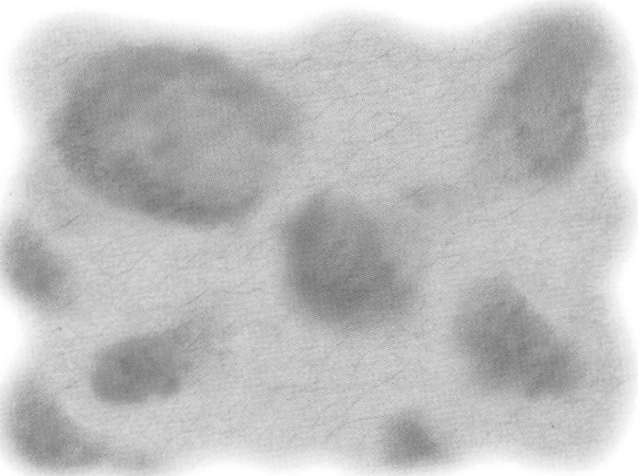

Erythema nodosum
Tender, red nodules which commonly appear on the shins; in time they become bruise-like patches.

RATBITE FEVER

Ratbite fever is a rare infectious disease carried by rats (and other rodents such as mice and squirrels), which is transmitted to humans via a bite, a scratch or the ingestion of food or water contaminated by the animal's feces. The infection may take the form of septicemia, with symptoms including rashes on the hands and feet, headaches, relapsing fever, weakness, muscular pain and arthritis. Alternatively, it may be marked by swollen lymph glands, muscular pain and an open sore on the bite mark. The disease is treated with antibiotics and can sometimes be fatal. Potential complications include pneumonia and heart problems.

SEE ALSO *Fever, Infectious diseases, Septicemia*

RAYNAUD'S DISEASE

In Raynaud's disease, the smaller blood vessels go into spasm, especially those of the fingers and toes. The digits become progressively cold and white, then blue, and then turn red as they warm up again. Attacks may last from a few minutes to several hours and are usually set off by cold or emotional upset. In severe cases, ulcers and gangrene of the fingers or toes may develop. The cause is usually unknown, though it may occur as a complication of other conditions such as connective tissue disease, vascular disease, or trauma.

Treatment involves giving up smoking if the sufferer is a smoker, and avoiding the trigger factors of cold and emotional stress. The extremities,especially the hands and feet, should be kept warm and covered in winter. Any underlying cause should be treated. Vasodilators (arterial muscle relaxants) and sympathectomy (surgical excision of the sympathetic nerves supplying the arteries) may be tried in severe cases.

The symptoms that are associated with Raynaud's disease are also known as Raynaud's phenomenon.

SEE ALSO *Blood vessels*

RECTUM

The rectum is the second last part of the digestive tract and leads into the last part, the anus. The rectum receives fecal material from the sigmoid colon and stores it for a short time until it is convenient to expel the stool. It also receives gas, which is passed as flatus. The upper rectum has a series of folds in its wall called the rectal valves. At the lower end of the rectum are longitudinally running folds called anal (or rectal) columns. The lower ends of these columns are joined together by anal valves to form the pectinate line. Immediately above each valve lies an anal sinus, into which open the anal glands. These glands may become sites of infection to form anorectal abscesses. Below the pectinate line is the anal canal, which leads to the external environment.

The exterior anus and rectum are common sites of disease and can be involved in hemorrhoids (dilated veins of the anorectal junction), cancer and inflammatory disease (proctitis). In rectal prolapse, the rectum may be turned inside out through the anal canal. This may occur as a congenital problem in babies or in adults whose pelvic muscles are weakened, injured or paralyzed.

SEE ALSO *Anus, Colon, Digestive system, Hemorrhoids, Proctitis, Prolapse*

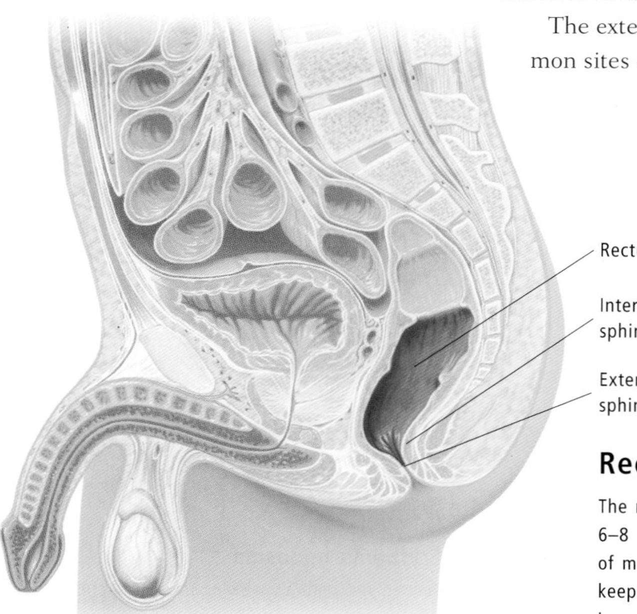

Rectum

The rectum and the anal canal measure 6–8 inches (15–20 centimeters). Rings of muscle called the anal sphincters keep the anus closed when fecal matter is not being expelled.

RED BLOOD CELLS

Red blood cells are the most numerous cells in the blood and their production rate by the bone marrow the highest in the body. They are highly specialized cells, devoted to the carriage of oxygen to the tissues and the removal of carbon dioxide. This allows the tissues to perform the metabolic processes required for the body to function.

Red cells are produced from early stem cells in the bone marrow, which multiply rapidly. The more mature red cells accumulate a red pigment, hemoglobin, which has special properties that ensure the efficient binding and release of oxygen. The fully mature red cell extrudes its nucleus and appears in the circulation full of hemoglobin. Its shape is that of a biconcave disk, which allows it to deform and squeeze through narrow spaces, such as in the small capillaries. Red cells are stored in the spleen which discharges them as needed. In emergencies, such as hemorrhage, some of the stored cells are released. After an average lifespan of 120 days the ageing red cell loses its ability to change shape and is destroyed in the spleen.

The number of red blood cells normally remains fairly stable, despite their constant production and destruction. The normal red cell count ranges between 4,000,000 and 6,000,000 per cubic millimeter, with the amount of hemoglobin in blood ranging between 14 and 18 grams per 100 milliliters in normal adults.

A deficiency of red cells results in anemia. There are many causes of anemia, which may result from diseases of the bone marrow, vitamin or mineral deficiencies affecting red cell production, diseases causing increased breakdown of red cells, or simple bleeding.

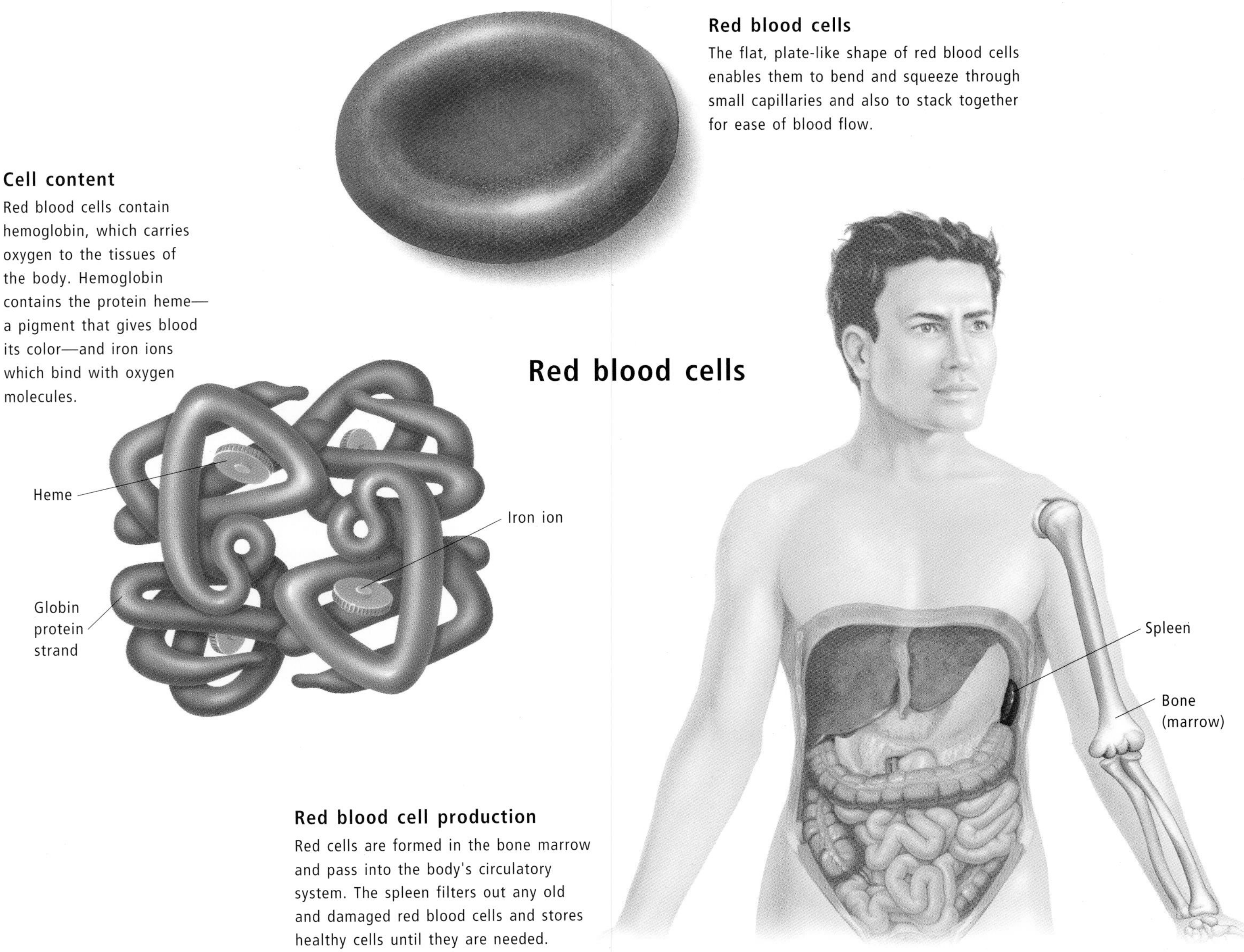

Red blood cells
The flat, plate-like shape of red blood cells enables them to bend and squeeze through small capillaries and also to stack together for ease of blood flow.
Cell content
Red blood cells contain hemoglobin, which carries oxygen to the tissues of the body. Hemoglobin contains the protein heme—a pigment that gives blood its color—and iron ions which bind with oxygen molecules.
Red blood cells
Heme
Iron ion
Globin protein strand
Spleen
Bone (marrow)
Red blood cell production
Red cells are formed in the bone marrow and pass into the body's circulatory system. The spleen filters out any old and damaged red blood cells and stores healthy cells until they are needed.

The most common cause of anemia is iron deficiency. Iron is a central part of the hemoglobin molecule, responsible for the binding of oxygen. It is obtained from the diet, red meat being especially rich in iron. Iron deficiencies in developing countries are mainly due to a combination of poor diet and chronic blood loss from hookworm infection. In industrialized countries, iron deficiency may result from heavy periods in menstruating women, or from chronic gastrointestinal bleeding.

Another cause of anemia is decreased production of the globin molecules which make up hemoglobin. This form of anemia is known as thalassemia, of which the major forms are alpha- and beta-thalassemia, corresponding to the globin chain affected. Thalassemia is an inherited disorder that involves mutations in the globin chain genes. It is most prevalent in the Mediterranean and Southeast Asia. The minor forms of this condition do not result in physical symptoms but the major forms of thalassemia can cause severe anemia and even the death of a fetus.

Sickle cell disease is another inherited abnormality of the globin gene, which results in abnormal sickle-shaped red cells. As well as causing anemia, sickle cell disease can result in the blockage of small blood vessels, causing severe, painful secondary conditions.

An increase in the rate of breakdown of red cells occurs in various conditions and is termed hemolytic anemia. Released hemoglobin is converted in the liver to bilirubin; a more rapid rate of red cell destruction can result in abnormally high levels of bilirubin. This may result in yellow coloration of the skin and eyes, called hemolytic jaundice. Increased breakdown of red cells in the spleen results in enlargement of the spleen.

The most common cause of hemolytic anemia worldwide is malaria, caused by a group of parasites which infect red blood cells and destroy them. The malaria parasites breed in certain mosquitoes and are transmitted to humans by the bite of the mosquito. The occurrence of malaria throughout the equatorial parts of the world is due to the presence of these mosquitoes. It is thought that thalassemia and sickle cell disease may have evolved as adaptations to malaria in those regions, since they make the red cell relatively resistant to infection by the parasite.

SEE ALSO *Anemia, Blood, Hemoglobin, Hemolytic anemia, Iron, Malaria, Sickle cell disease, Thalassemia*

R

Reflexes

Reflexes are quick and automatic responses to stimuli, whereby a nerve impulse travels to a nerve center in the spinal cord. The nerve center then sends a message outward to a muscle or gland to effect a response without the person being consciously aware of it.

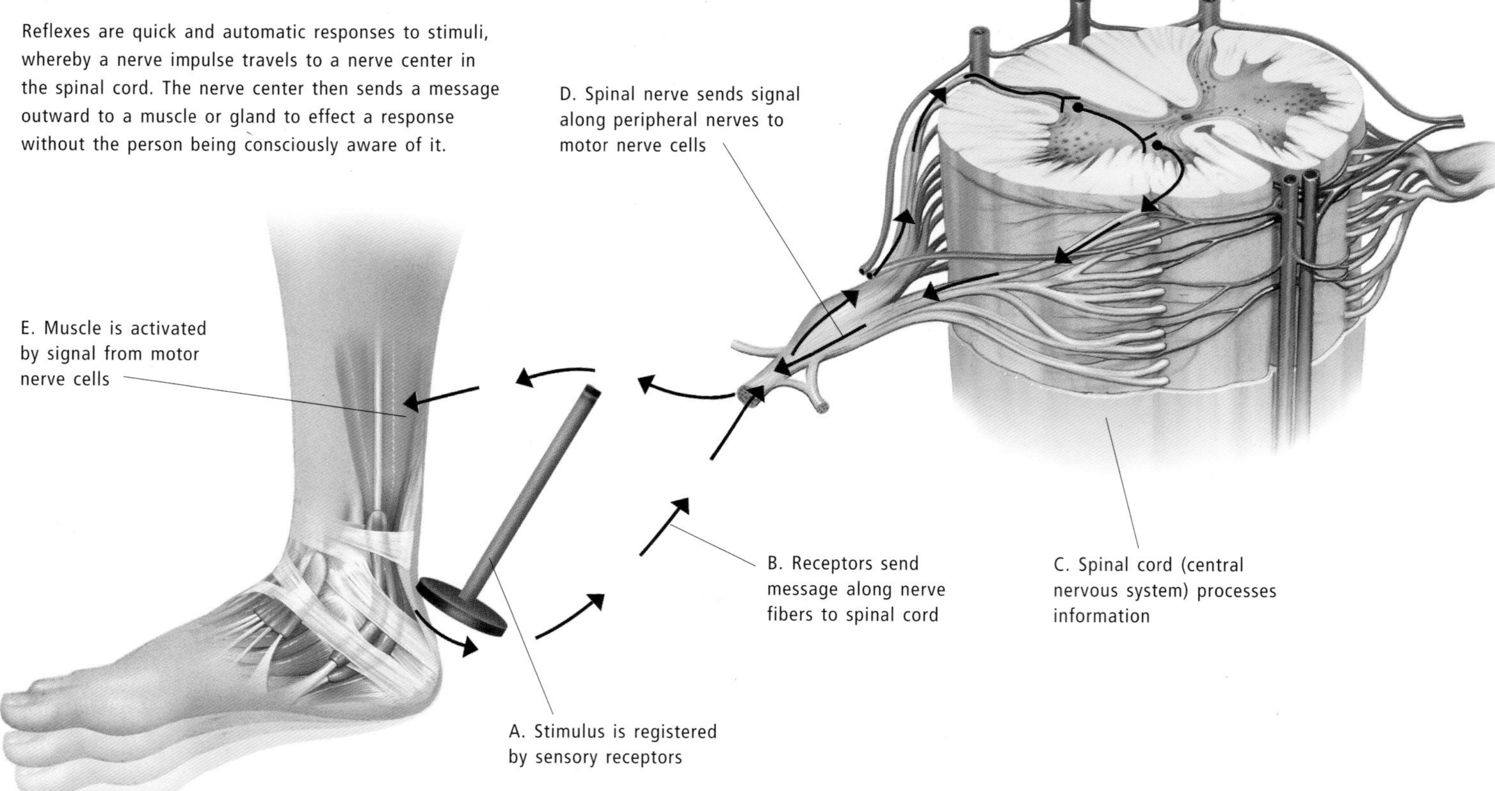
D. Spinal nerve sends signal along peripheral nerves to motor nerve cells
E. Muscle is activated by signal from motor nerve cells
B. Receptors send message along nerve fibers to spinal cord
C. Spinal cord (central nervous system) processes information
A. Stimulus is registered by sensory receptors

REFLEXES

A reflex is an involuntary immediate movement or other response to an appropriate stimulus, which occurs unconsciously (without being willed). If you touch a sharp spike or a hot surface you will pull your hand away in a reflex action. There are many everyday reflexes that we take for granted.

When a bright light is shone into a person's eyes the pupils will contract; a blink is a reflex action that protects the eye; a cough or a sneeze protects the lungs and the respiratory system, and there are many other reflexes. Four things happen when a reflex acts—reception, conduction, transmission and response—and all of these involve the nervous system.

The well-known knee-jerk or patellar reflex is the sudden kicking out of the lower leg when the patellar tendon, just below the knee, is tapped sharply. This reflex is used to test for damage to the central nervous system and the peripheral nerves and in recognizing thyroid disease. Many other reflexes can also be tested to evaluate the nervous system.

The concept of the conditioned reflex is attributed to the Russian physiologist Ivan Pavlov, who won the Nobel Prize in 1904 for his work. After noting that a hungry dog salivated at the sight of food, he rang a bell when the food appeared. After some time the dog would salivate at the sound of the bell when no food was present—thus the "conditioned" reflex.

There are three groups of reflexes found in a newborn. The first group, which are vital for survival, include the rooting reflex—when a baby's cheek is gently stroked it will turn its head and open its mouth on that side; the sucking reflex, which is triggered by pressure on the upper palate of the baby's mouth; the swallowing reflex; the gagging reflex, which is triggered if the baby swallows too much fluid; and the labyrinthine reflex, which makes the baby raise its head when lying on the stomach. Newborns also have protective reflexes. For example, if a cloth is held over a baby's face the baby will brush the cloth away. Medication during labor, brain damage and prematurity can affect these survival reflexes and these will be tested if there is any doubt about the newborn's state of health.

The second group of reflexes are found in the newborn. The stepping reflex, activated when a baby's foot touches the ground, is usually gone by the time a baby is two months old. The crawling reflex is displayed when a newborn is placed in a face-down position. The Babinski reflex comes into play when the sole of the foot is stroked from heel to toe, resulting in the toes curling up and the foot turning in. It will generally last until the baby is around 2 years old. In older age groups, the Babinski reflex may also be used as a diagnostic tool to determine disorders of the central nervous system.

The third group of reflexes are behavior patterns that no longer appear to serve a function. These include the grasp reflex, which can also be found in the baby's foot; the Moro or startle reflex, which is used by doctors to test muscle tone; and the galant reflex, which is tested by gently stroking a finger along one side of the baby's back while the baby is being held under the stomach. The baby's body will bend like a bow, pulling the pelvis towards the side stroked. It indicates the development of the spinal nerves and will last until the baby is about 9 months old.

SEE ALSO *Nervous system, Newborn*

R

REFLEXOLOGY

Modern reflexology, also known as reflex zone therapy, was developed by American ear, nose and throat specialist Dr William Fitzgerald in the early twentieth century. In a system known as zone therapy he divided the body into 10 vertical zones through which he believed vital energy flowed. He found when he applied pressure to a point in the hand or foot of one zone that an analgesic response occurred in other body parts that lay within that same zone.

Fitzgerald's work was developed further by Eunice Ingham, an American masseur, who devised the Ingham reflex method of compression massage, in which points on the feet are massaged, using an alternating pressure, with the aim of stimulating the related organ or body system (for example, massaging the toes helps to clear the sinuses).

Reflexology massage aims to stimulate nerve endings and energy flow while also breaking up lactic acid, uric acid and calcium crystals accumulated beneath the skin's surface. A particularly tender point on the foot is believed to be an indication that the related organ is in some kind of difficulty. Reflexologists believe that their system increases the body's overall state of relaxation and helps improve circulation; it may also be used in the treatment of minor pain and stress-related disorders.

REHABILITATION

Rehabilitation is a branch of medicine concerned with helping people recover as fully as possible from a physical disability, and then helping them to live with physical challenges that do remain. It is integral to the treatment of many conditions, including stroke, neurological conditions, accidents, heart attacks, and drug and alcohol dependence.

Successful rehabilitation involves health professionals from a number of disciplines: family physicians, social workers, physical therapists, occupational therapists, rehabilitation nurses, speech pathologists, psychologists and vocational counselors.

Physical therapies include exercise, heat and ultrasound, massage, diathermy (the use of high-frequency electrical current) and hydrotherapy. Physical therapy also involves teaching the use of such aids as braces, artificial limbs and wheelchairs.

Occupational therapy involves activities to increase independent function and prevent disability. The therapist may help adapt the home or work environment to maintain function and independence as much as possible. The occupational therapy departments of many hospitals have facilities in which the patient may be trained to use tools for trades and light industrial work, or for clerical duties.

Speech therapists treat speech disorders caused by physical malformations, diseases, injuries, or psychological disorders, and work with the patient to develop or improve communication skills: speaking, reading, and writing techniques.

In some disorders, rehabilitation is an essential part of the treatment, without which recovery cannot hope to take place. For example, rehabilitation is a necessary part of recovery from disorders of the musculoskeletal system, such as back pain, whiplash, tennis elbow, on-the-job or sports injuries, and fractures. Rehabilitation should start immediately after the initial treatment. Programs with a multidisciplinary approach using physical therapy together with physical and mental training yield the best results. If the injury is not serious, the individual may be encouraged to participate in an alternative sport to maintain overall conditioning.

Patients with spinal cord injuries may never fully recover, but rehabilitation will allow them to adapt physically and psychologically to their disability. Passive exercises for paralyzed muscles will help prevent contractures. Physical therapy will prevent joint stiffness. Occupational therapy and psychotherapy or counseling may help depression or sexual problems.

Children with spina bifida and cerebral palsy learn to take care of themselves and their bodily needs; many are able to attend school and achieve vocational goals with the use of crutches and wheelchairs.

In stroke victims, rehabilitation therapy is crucial; the goal is to teach the patient to make the best use of remaining skills and to compensate for those lost. Further strokes can sometimes be prevented and there will be recovery as other areas of the brain take over functioning for the damaged areas. Patients with stroke may learn to walk and perform daily activities using mainly their remaining abilities. Speech therapy, occupational therapy, physical therapy and other interventions may be used.

Many medical centers now offer cardiac rehabilitation programs for heart attack survivors and people who have undergone heart surgery. These programs help patients make the necessary changes in their daily

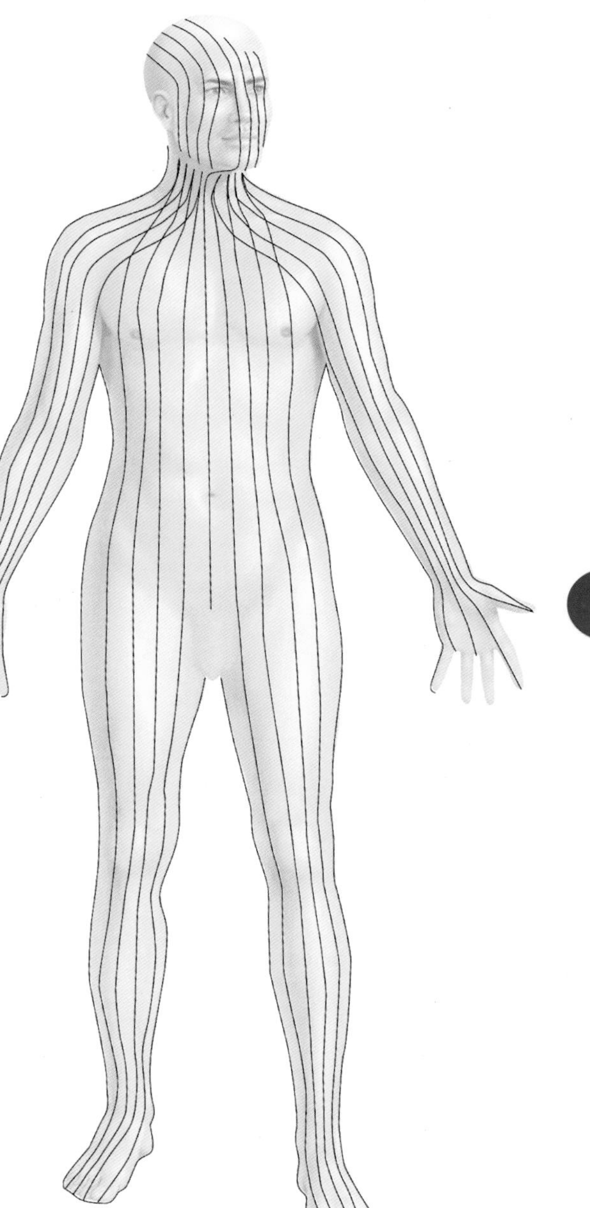

Reflexology

Reflexology is based on the idea that massaging or simply applying pressure to certain points within each of the 10 energy zones stimulates other parts of the body within the same zone.

Rehabilitation

Rehabilitation aims to help those who are sick or injured to regain physical and psychological strength in order to return to their normal lives, or to deal with any permanent disabilities. Rehabilitation may include education about healthy eating for a heart attack victim, teaching a paraplegic how to be independent, or physical therapy for someone recovering from a hip replacement operation.

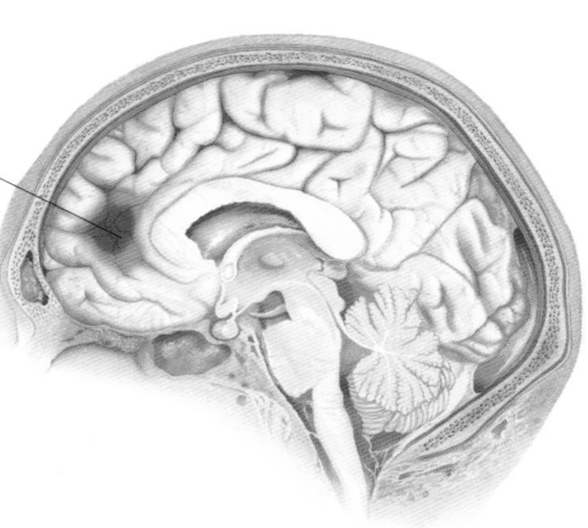

Stroke

Rehabilitation allows stroke patients to make the best use of their remaining skills and to compensate for those lost. It may include physical therapy, occupational therapy, speech therapy and psychotherapy.

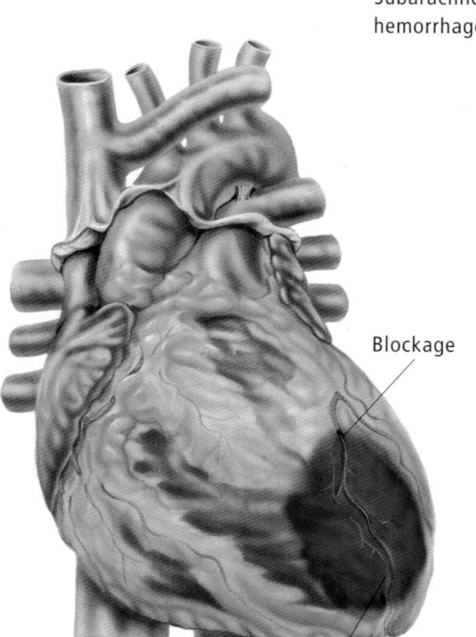

Heart attack

Rehabilitation is an important part of treatment after a myocardial infarction (heart attack). It usually includes exercise, the modification of diet to eliminate fat, cholesterol and salt, and the cessation of smoking.

Whiplash

Physical therapy, such as exercise, heat and electrical current therapy, plays an important role in the treatment of soft tissue injuries such as whiplash, although many resolve naturally over time.

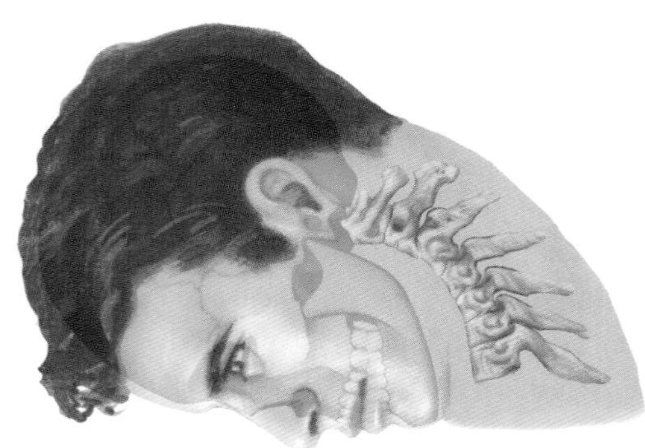

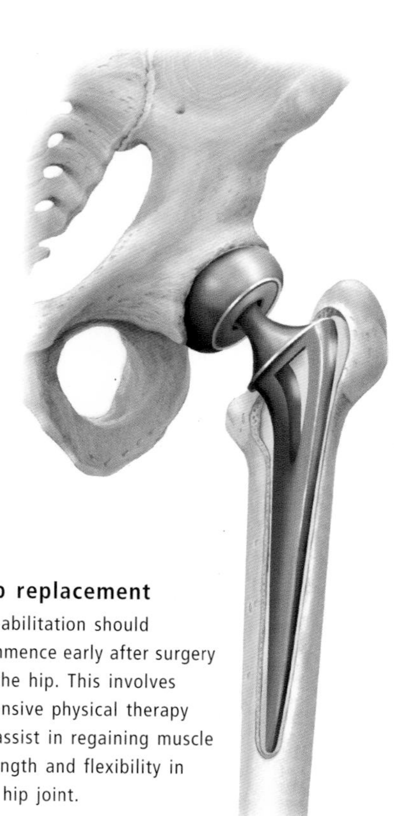

Hip replacement

Rehabilitation should commence early after surgery to the hip. This involves intensive physical therapy to assist in regaining muscle strength and flexibility in the hip joint.

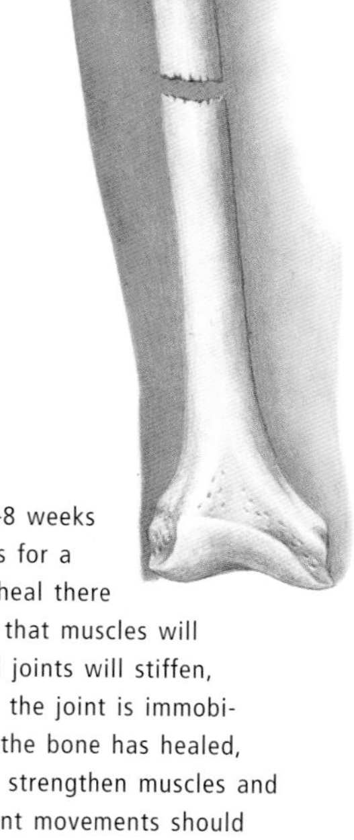

Fracture

Over the 6–8 weeks that it takes for a fracture to heal there is a danger that muscles will atrophy and joints will stiffen, especially if the joint is immobilized. Once the bone has healed, exercises to strengthen muscles and maintain joint movements should begin as soon as possible.

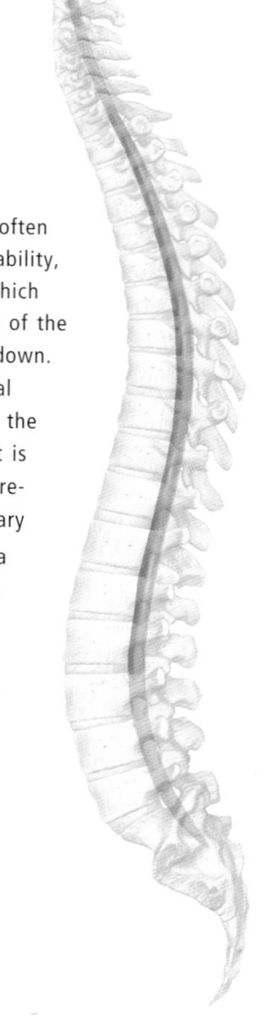

Paralysis

Injuries to the spine often result in physical disability, such as paraplegia which may involve paralysis of the body from the arms down. The degree of physical disability depends on the part of the spine that is damaged. Long-term rehabilitation is necessary and usually involves a team of professionals including a physical therapist, an occupational therapist, a rehabilitation engineer and a psychological counselor.

lives and improve recovery. Rehabilitation begins in the hospital and can continue for weeks to months after returning home. Most programs offer group therapy. Cardiac rehabilitation improves the quality of life and extends the life expectancy of heart patients, but lifelong follow-up is usually necessary.

SEE ALSO *Alcoholism, Drug dependence, Paraplegia, Quadriplegia, Spinal cord, Sports medicine, Stroke*

REIKI

The word *reiki* means "universal life force". It describes a form of healing founded early in the twentieth century by Dr Mikao Usui, a Japanese Christian minister, from his studies of an ancient Tibetan healing technique. Reiki practitioners are taught through a series of initiations by Reiki masters to draw in *ki,* or life force, and to redirect it to the patient through their hands. A higher power is believed to direct the life force to wherever it is needed in the patient's body to remove blockages to the energy flow and to rebalance it. Reiki practitioners claim that their treatment relaxes and energizes the patient, without promising specific cures.

REITER'S SYNDROME

Reiter's syndrome is a potentially chronic disease marked by arthritis, conjunctivitis and urethritis (inflammation of the urethra), along with lesions of the skin and mucous membranes. The exact cause is not known, although it is thought that certain people are genetically predisposed. The syndrome often occurs after severe diarrhea or a sexually transmitted infection, such as chlamydia. It is most common in men under the age of 40. Arthritic symptoms tend to dominate and may recur over several years. The infection is treated with antibiotics, anti-inflammatory medications and pain relievers.

SEE ALSO *Arthritis, Chlamydia, Conjunctivitis, Urethritis*

RELAPSING FEVER

Relapsing fever, also known as recurrent fever or tick fever, is a bacterial infection transmitted by ticks and lice that causes repeated bouts of fever. Symptoms include vomiting, headache, chest pain, muscle aches and rapid heartbeat, which set in after an incubation period of about 7 days. These may be accompanied by a rash, nosebleeds, and blood in the urine and vomit. After about a week the fever passes, causing blood pressure and body temperature to drop, accompanied by excessive sweating and extreme weakness. Symptoms recur within a week and keep recurring in a progressively milder form until immunity is built up.

The disease often has severe effects on the central nervous system of children, causing seizures and neuritis. It may also cause inflammation of the heart muscle and liver.

The bacteria that causes relapsing fever are usually carried by the *Ornithodorus* tick, which is common in the western USA. The disease is also found in West Africa and tropical regions of the world. Preventive measures include avoiding wooded areas where ticks live, covering exposed skin and using insect repellent. Antibiotics will cure most cases of relapsing fever, although the condition can sometimes be fatal.

SEE ALSO *Fever, Lice, Ticks*

RELATIONSHIP COUNSELING

At some time almost anyone in a relationship may find they need assistance to help deal with problems; to learn how to improve a relationship or even how to form one; to cope with a relationship which is in crisis or to change a relationship when there is violence involved. Everyone in a relationship experiences problems. It is the people who know how to deal with these problems and meet the challenges who have successful relationships.

It can often strengthen a relationship to talk about it. Relationship counselors, formerly called marriage guidance counselors in many places, are trained to help people sort out problems, to learn to understand and accept the differences in people and to handle conflict.

SEE ALSO *Counseling*

RELAXATION TECHNIQUES

Modern research has shown that learning how to consciously relax can have a powerful healing effect on body and mind. When a person relaxes in this way, heart and respiratory rates slow, blood pressure drops, muscle tension decreases, blood flow to skin and internal organs increases and brain wave patterns alter, leading to mental and emotional peace. The body's nervous, endocrine and immune systems, which all feel the direct impact of stress, are rested. It has been found that even a short period of relaxation can increase mental clarity, emotional stability and physical energy.

Relaxation techniques are highly valued and well developed in many ancient Eastern spiritual and healing traditions, where deep

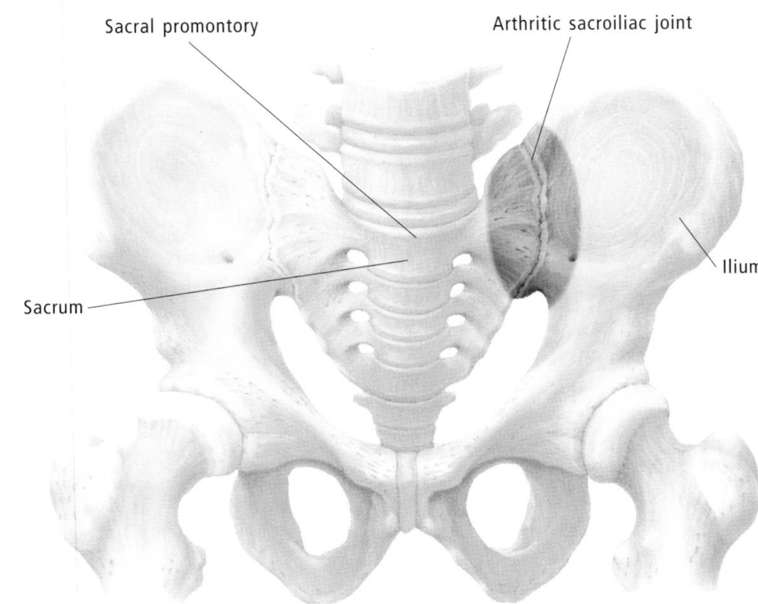

Reiter's syndrome

Arthritis (such as in the sacroiliac joint) is the most obvious symptom of Reiter's syndrome; it is accompanied by conjunctivitis, urethritis and lesions. Young men are most commonly affected.

states of relaxation are achieved through a variety of practices including meditation, yoga, t'ai chi, shiatsu and acupuncture. In the West, relaxation therapies developed during the twentieth century often incorporated the more accessible of the Eastern techniques.

In his book *The Relaxation Response*, Herbert Benson, an American physician, identified four basic components he found common to a range of traditional and modern relaxation techniques—quiet environment; a mental device, such as a repeated word, sound or phrase, to help avoid distracting thoughts; a passive attitude, which disengages from distracting thoughts as they arise; and a physically comfortable position.

In the 1920s Dr Johannes Schultz, a German neuropsychologist, developed a relaxation therapy known as autogenic training, sometimes also called Western meditation. This technique resulted from his quest to find an alternative to hypnotism which would equal its results. It has elements in common with meditation and yoga as well as with self-hypnosis.

Autogenic training uses a sequence of six standard exercises that involve focusing the mind on the body while silently repeating a series of statements to oneself (for example, "my right arm is heavy"). This form of relaxation consists of becoming progressively aware of sensations of heaviness in different parts the body, such as arms, legs, neck; feelings of warmth in the limbs; the calmness and regularity of the heartbeat; the calmness and regularity of breathing; feelings of warmth in the abdomen; and a coolness in the forehead.

Relaxation

Response to relaxation

Relaxation techniques such as meditation and massage may help to reduce tension, anxiety, stress and chronic pain. When a person relaxes, heart and respiratory rates slow, blood pressure drops, muscle tension decreases, and blood flow to the skin and organs increases. Much of this effect is coordinated by the parasympathetic nervous system, the part of the autonomic nervous system that promotes physiological relaxation.

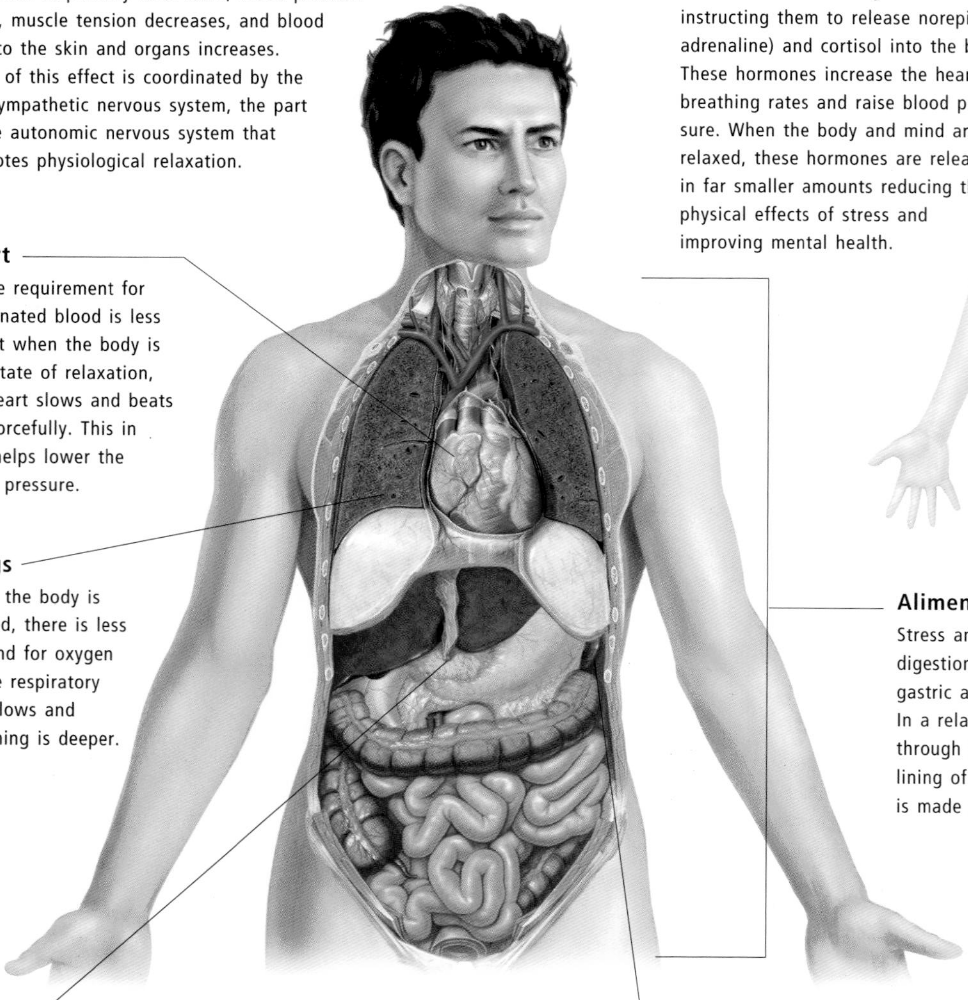

Heart

As the requirement for oxygenated blood is less urgent when the body is in a state of relaxation, the heart slows and beats less forcefully. This in turn helps lower the blood pressure.

Lungs

When the body is relaxed, there is less demand for oxygen so the respiratory rate slows and breathing is deeper.

Blood glucose

Less glucose is needed in the bloodstream when the body is relaxed. Hence, the pancreas secretes more insulin and the liver releases less glucose than normal, both of which act to lower glucose levels in the blood.

Relaxing the brain

Stress affects the body's endocrine system, which produces the hormones that control many body functions. Under stress, the pituitary gland in the brain sends messages to the adrenal glands instructing them to release norepinephrine (noradrenaline) and cortisol into the bloodstream. These hormones increase the heart and breathing rates and raise blood pressure. When the body and mind are relaxed, these hormones are released in far smaller amounts reducing the physical effects of stress and improving mental health.

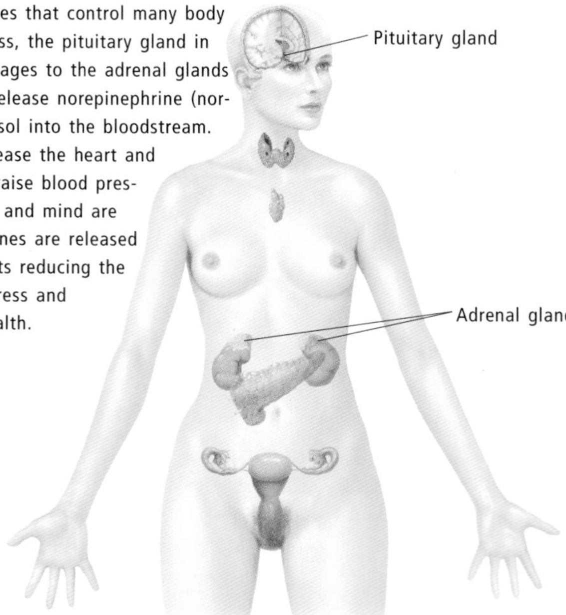

Alimentary tract

Stress and anxiety can interfere with digestion and increase the production of gastric acid, which may cause stomach pain. In a relaxed state, food moves more slowly through the bowel. Blood flow through the lining of the bowel increases, and digestion is made more efficient.

Immunity

Stress leads to higher circulating levels of the hormone cortisol, which compromises the immune system. When the body is relaxed, the immune system functions more efficiently increasing the body's ability to fight off infection.

NB: In the main illustration the top two-thirds of the lungs and pleura have been peeled away to show the heart.

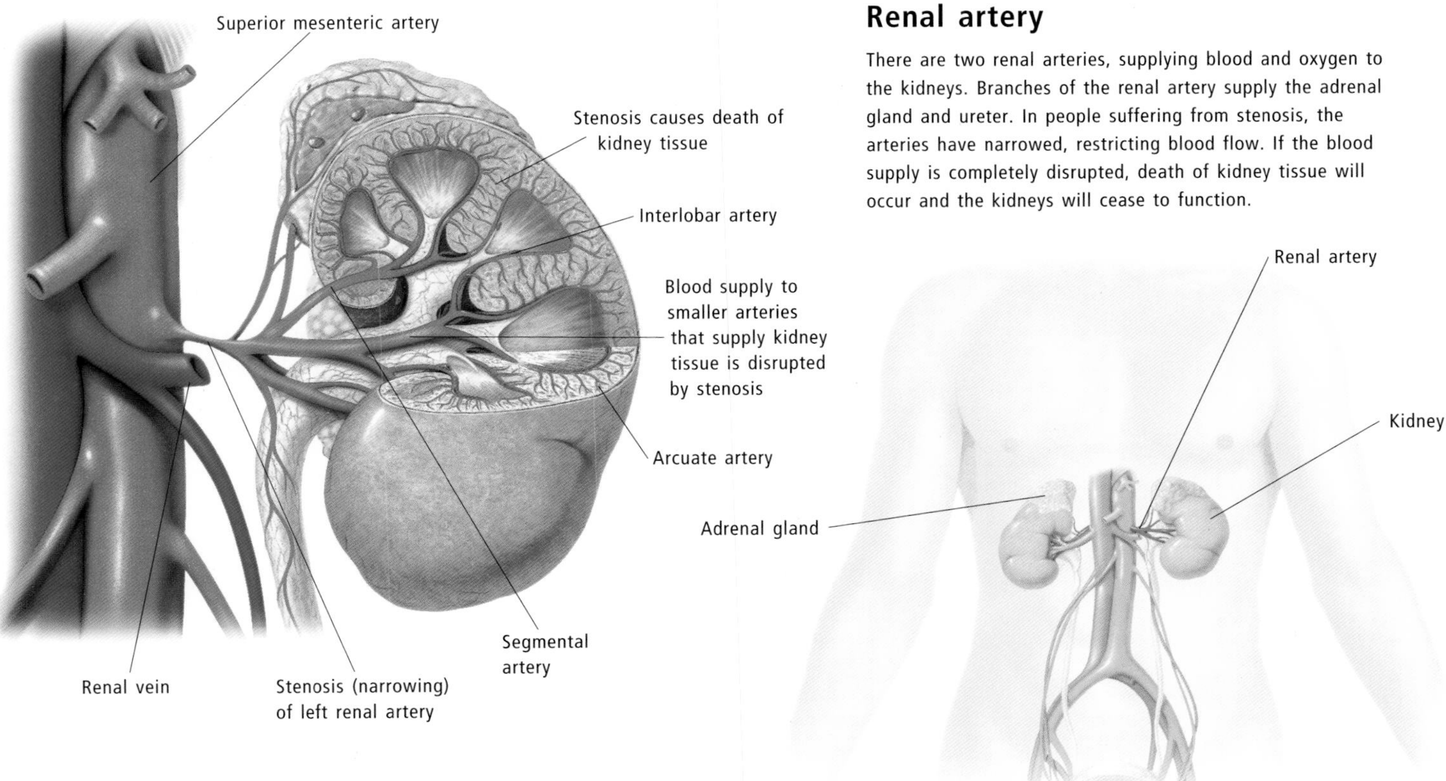

Renal artery

There are two renal arteries, supplying blood and oxygen to the kidneys. Branches of the renal artery supply the adrenal gland and ureter. In people suffering from stenosis, the arteries have narrowed, restricting blood flow. If the blood supply is completely disrupted, death of kidney tissue will occur and the kidneys will cease to function.

Autogenic training is usually taught by trained practitioners in weekly sessions. It is recommended that it be practised three times a day after eating. This form of relaxation is useful for those wishing to reduce or stop tranquilizer medication as well as for all stress-related disorders. It may be also be helpful in the management of chronic pain.

The technique of focusing on breathing to induce a state of relaxation is well known from meditation and yoga practice. Breathing exercises which encourage deep rhythmic breathing are known as diaphragmatic breathing. In this type of breathing an individual focuses on the rib muscles and their role in expanding the diaphragm while breathing deeply and slowly. This helps avoid the panting or shallow breathing from the upper chest which accompanies states of tension or anxiety.

SEE ALSO *Meditation, Stress, T'ai chi ch'uan, Yoga*

REMISSION

Remission is the disappearance or reduction of symptoms during the course of an illness. When this happens, the illness is said to be "in remission". This condition may be permanent or temporary, sometimes lasting for years before symptoms recur.

RENAL ARTERY

The renal arteries are two large blood vessels that branch off either side of the abdominal aorta to supply the two kidneys. They pass through the hilum, or entrance, of the kidney, where each artery gives off small branches to the adrenal gland and ureter and then divides into two large branches, which are called the anterior and posterior divisions of the artery.

Each branch divides into smaller and smaller branches, eventually forming the capillaries which supply oxygen to the kidney tissue and take part in kidney filtration via their role in the nephrons.

The renal arteries can be affected by arteriosclerosis, which may cause clots (thrombi), or a narrowing (stenosis). Blockage of the arteries can disrupt the blood supply to the kidneys, causing death of kidney tissue and loss of function. Treatment is by angioplasty (for example balloon angioplasty) or bypass surgery.

Less commonly, arteriosclerosis may cause an aneurysm in the artery, which may rupture, causing abdominal pain and sometimes death. Treatment is by surgical repair of the aneurysm.

Renal angiography is a radiological test designed to show abnormalities in the structure and function of the renal arteries and the kidneys. It is routinely undertaken prior to angioplasty or other renal artery surgery. Under local anesthesia, a catheter is inserted through an artery in an arm or a leg, passed through the aorta and into the renal artery. A dye which is opaque to x-rays is injected via the catheter, and as the dye passes through the renal artery and its divisions, a series of x-rays is taken. Any blockages or clots are highlighted by the dye.

SEE ALSO *Aneurysm, Angiography, Angioplasty, Arteries, Arteriosclerosis, Kidney*

RESTLESS LEGS SYNDROME

This is a neurological disorder marked by unpleasant sensations in the lower legs which compel the sufferer to move their legs, sometimes involuntarily. The exact cause is not known but conditions such as iron-deficiency anemia, arthritis and pregnancy may play a part. There is no specific treatment but treatment of any suspected underlying cause may alleviate discomfort.

SEE ALSO *Legs, Nerves*

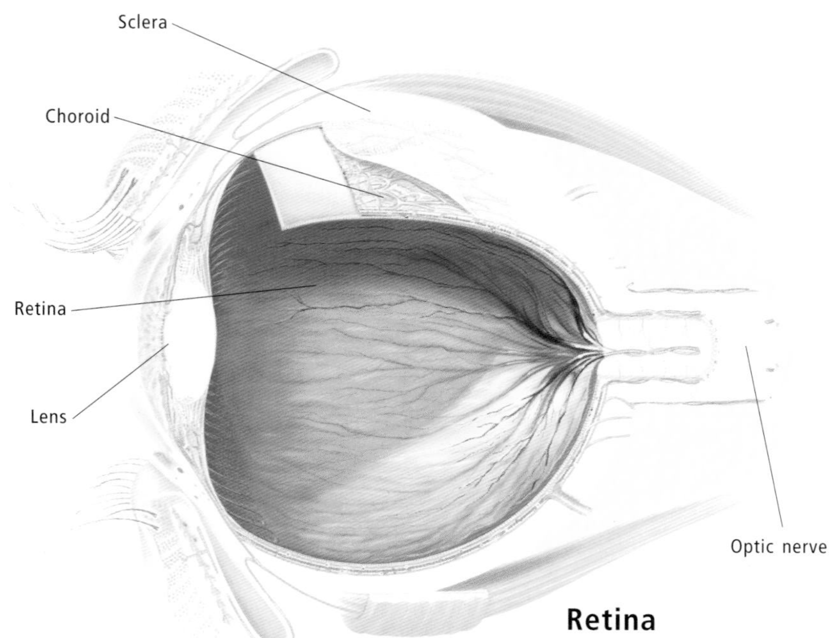

Retina

The retina is a light-sensitive layer at the back of the eye. It transforms the image formed by the lens into nerve impulses which are sent to the brain via the optic nerve. Detachment of the retina from the choroid, either by disease or injury, can lead to blindness.

RETINA

The retina is a light-sensitive layer at the back of the eye; it has photoreceptors that send visual information to the brain via the optic nerve. Light reaches the retina after passing through the cornea into the pupil, then through the optic lens and vitreous humor. The retina contains light-sensitive cells called rods and cones, which specialize in perceiving light intensity and color vision.

Disorders of the retina

The retina draws a rich blood supply from a vascular layer called the choroid. A hole or tear in the retina may lead to partial or total detachment from the choroid. Vision in the eye may be lost completely if the retina cannot be reattached. The hole may be caused by natural degeneration of the retina, disease or a blow to the eye. Symptoms include specks in the field of vision, flashes of light, blind spots and blurred vision. Laser surgery may be used to close the hole.

Retinoblastoma is a potentially fatal malignant tumor on the retina, usually found in children under the age of five. It may strike one or both eyes, giving the pupil a whitish glow and leading to impaired vision, pain and inflammation. Removal of the eye may be necessary in severe cases, though the disease may still return in the other eye. Other treatment options include laser surgery, and a combination of radiation therapy and chemotherapy.

Retinopathy is a non-inflammatory disease of the retina which manifests in a number of ways. Retinopathy of prematurity affects premature infants, causing extreme vision impairment or blindness due to rapid tissue production and retinal detachment. The exact cause is unknown and symptoms include white spots in the pupil, cross eyes, and cataracts. The condition is treated by surgical reattachment of the retina, or by reducing unwanted tissue via laser therapy or cryotherapy (a treatment involving the application of extreme cold).

Diabetic retinopathy involves damage to the blood vessels nourishing the retina, causing cloudy vision and possibly blindness. It usually strikes diabetics aged 25 years or older, and is marked by the sudden onset of blurred vision, loss of vision in either eye, decreased color perception and flashing lights or black spots. Laser surgery may be used to seal or destroy abnormal or bleeding blood vessels, though this may not improve vision.

Hypertensive retinopathy is caused by high blood pressure and may result in hemorrhaging, lesions, permanently impaired vision or blindness. Blood pressure needs to be controlled to arrest progression of the disease.

Diagnosis

In order to diagnose retinal disorders and diseases, a bright beam of light is shone through the pupil using an instrument called an ophthalmoscope. It gives a magnified view of the retina to help check for conditions such as retinal or macular degeneration and cataracts. During an eye examination, a procedure called retinoscopy may also be used to determine how light is refracted in the eye. A retinoscope measures how a projected beam moves over the surface of the retina, helping to detect refractive errors such as near- and farsightedness (or short- and longsightedness). This also determines the prescription for glasses or contact lenses to correct or neutralize refractive errors.

SEE ALSO *Blindness, Cataracts, Diabetes, Eye, Ophthalmoscopy, Retinitis pigmentosa, Sight*

RETINITIS PIGMENTOSA

This is a rare degenerative disease of the retina in which the progressive breakdown of pigment stops the eye from responding to light and color in the usual way. Night blindness is usually the first indication of the disease, followed by the loss of peripheral vision, a reduction in color sensitivity, deterioration of daytime vision and narrowing of the field of vision from the edges inward, or tunnel vision. In some instances the disease may result in blindness.

Retinitis pigmentosa is thought to be hereditary and there is currently no definitive treatment or cure.

SEE ALSO *Blindness, Eye, Night blindness, Retina, Sight*

RETROVERSION OF THE UTERUS

The uterus is usually tilted forward in the pelvis (anteverted). Retroversion, where the uterus is tilted backwards, exists in about 20 percent of women. The condition may be present from puberty but, providing the uterus remains mobile and is able to expand during pregnancy, no symptoms or complications are likely to occur.

In some instances retroversion may occur later in life because the pressure of either a tumor or adhesions fixes the uterus in an abnormal position. In such cases symptoms such as backache and pelvic pain may be experienced and there may be difficulties in conception and pregnancy. These symptoms can arise from a variety of other conditions, however, which must be eliminated before surgery is considered.

There is little evidence to support the idea that retroversion may cause prolapse of the uterus.

SEE ALSO *Uterus*

REYE'S SYNDROME

Reye's syndrome (RS) is a disease that occurs mostly in children; it most seriously affects the brain and the liver, but also affects all other body organs. In its most serious form it can be fatal.

The syndrome was first reported by Australian pathologist R. D. K. Reye in 1963. It causes an acute increase of pressure within the brain, together with massive accumulations of fat in the liver and other organs. It can develop in children following or during influenza, chickenpox or other viral infections.

Reye's syndrome has been misdiagnosed as encephalitis, meningitis, diabetes, poisoning, drug overdose, sudden infant death syndrome or a psychiatric illness. This is because the symptoms include nausea, vomiting (though babies do not always have this symptom), lethargy, drowsiness, disorientation, seizures, respiratory arrest and coma.

The precise cause of the illness is still unknown, although studies have found that aspirin or medications which contain salicylate can increase the risk of the disease developing. A decline in the incidence of the illness in the 1980s was attributed to the reduction in the use of these drugs in children.

RS does not have a cure. Early diagnosis is important to survival and complete recovery, and treatment is aimed at protecting the brain against irreversible damage. Not all sufferers will recover completely; some may suffer brain damage because of the severity of the swelling of the brain.

SEE ALSO *Diabetes, Encephalitis, Meningitis, Non-steroidal anti-inflammatory drugs, Overdose, Poisoning, Sudden infant death syndrome*

RHESUS (Rh) FACTOR

Rhesus (Rh) factor is named after an antibody produced in 1940 in the blood of a rabbit after immunizing it with red blood cells from a rhesus monkey. This antibody was shown to be the same as one found the previous year in the blood of a woman who had a stillborn child. The child was born with hydrops fetalis, or generalized swelling, due to severe anemia.

What had been discovered was a new blood group system, separate from the ABO system already known. Eighty-five percent of Caucasians are now known to have the Rh antigen on the cell membrane of their red blood cells and are Rh positive; the other 15 percent lack this antigen and are Rh negative. The presence or absence of an Rh factor is important when considering the compatability of blood types, especially in pregnancy and blood transfusions.

When an Rh negative woman and Rh positive man have a baby, there is a possibility that the baby will be Rh positive and that its red cells will be destroyed by Rh antibodies. The Rh positive cells of the baby are introduced into an Rh negative woman via the placenta. This Rh incompatibility stimulates the woman's immune system to produce antibodies, a process called isoimmunization, which destroy the foreign, introduced cells, or antigens. Of real concern is that the antibodies then travel from the mother to the baby, where they continue to attack the Rh positive red cells. This may result in increased physiological jaundice of the newborn, in neonatal anemia or, if severe, in hydrops fetalis.

Immunization to Rh antigens can also result from the transfusion of Rh positive blood to an Rh negative recipient, leading to destruction of the transfused cells in a blood transfusion reaction.

The discovery of the Rh blood group system has resulted in safer blood transfusion, through testing for the Rh factor during crossmatching of blood. It has also led to measures to prevent Rh isoimmunization in pregnancy. Before the development of DNA sequence analysis, the Rh system contributed to the identification of blood or body fluids at the scene of crimes or accidents and was also used in testing for disputed parentage.

The Rh system consists of six major antigens, the most important being the D antigen, which results in the most severe isoimmunization. Initial exposure to the D antigen results in sensitization of the immune system; a second exposure produces a strong antibody response. It is now routine practice to test women during pregnancy for the Rh antigen. If a woman is Rh negative and her partner Rh positive, there is a possibility of isoimmunization. If this is the woman's first pregnancy, it is unlikely that she will become sensitized until delivery, when small numbers of fetal red cells enter the maternal circulation.

If she delivers an Rh negative baby, she will receive an injection of anti-D globulin to prevent her immune system reacting and

R

Retroverted uterus

One-fifth of all women have a retroverted uterus, in which the uterus is tilted backwards in the pelvis.

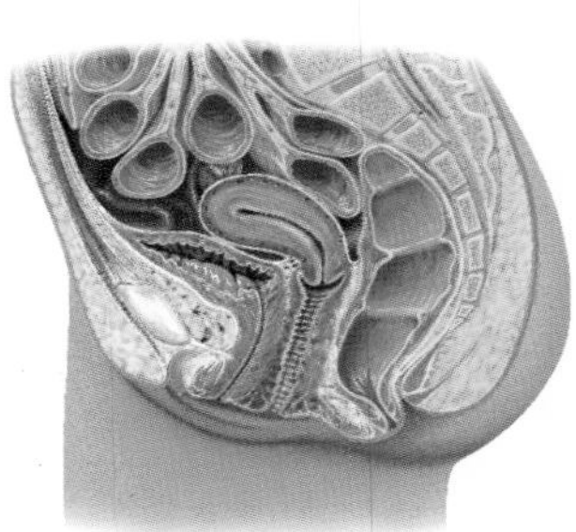

Normal uterus

A normal uterus is tilted forward in the pelvis.

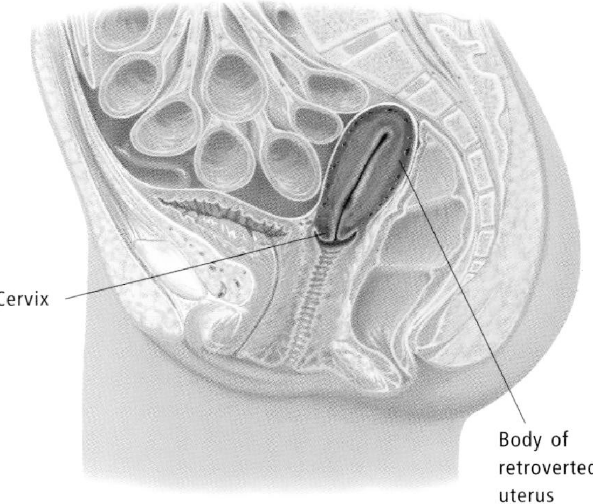

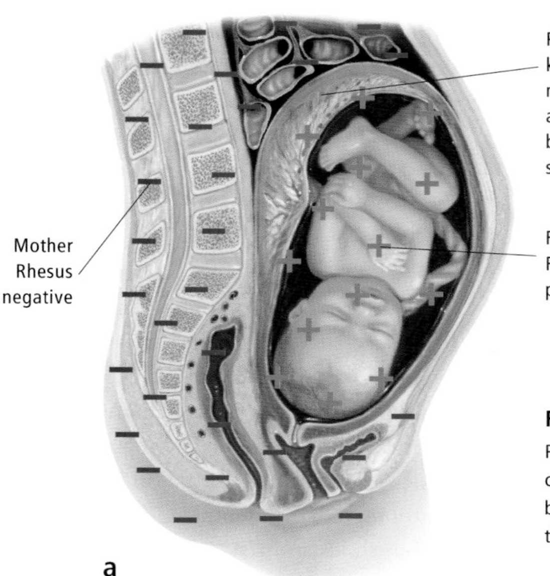
Placenta keeps maternal and fetal blood separate
Mother Rhesus negative
Fetus Rhesus positive
a

Rhesus (Rh) factor

In pregnancy, problems may occur if the mother is Rh negative and the fetus is Rh positive. The red blood cells of the fetus may be destroyed by the mother's Rh antibodies, which can lead to hydrops fetalis (swelling in the fetus due to excessive fluid).

First pregnancy

Problems rarely occur during the course of the pregnancy, as the bloodstreams of the mother and the fetus do not mix.

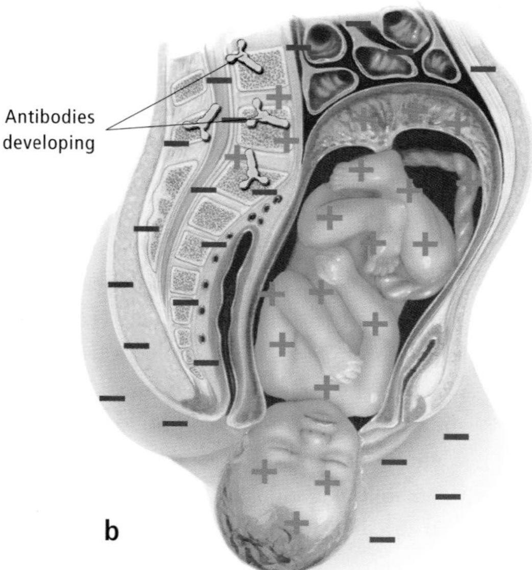
Antibodies developing
b

First pregnancy—delivery

During delivery, the baby's blood can leak into the maternal bloodstream; this causes the Rhesus-negative mother to develop antibodies which destroy Rhesus-positive blood cells.

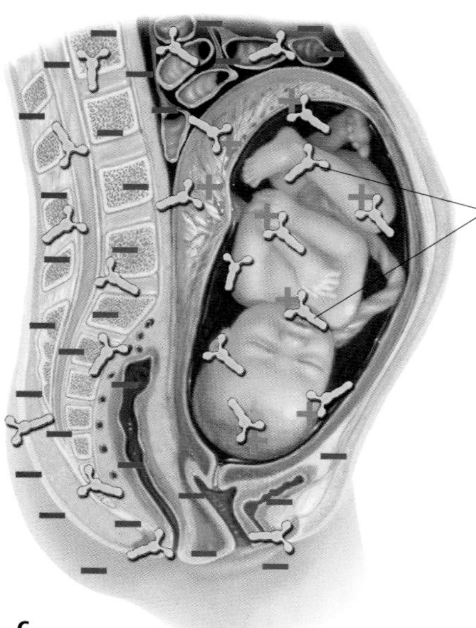
Rhesus-positive antibodies produced during the first pregnancy attack the cells of the next Rh-positive fetus.
c

Second and subsequent pregnancies

If the mother does not receive an Anti-D globulin injection following the first pregnancy (to halt the production of antibodies), her antibodies may attack the blood cells of subsequent Rhesus-positive babies.

forming Rh antibodies that could affect future pregnancies. Anti-D is also given to Rh negative women following an abortion, miscarriage or amniocentesis. The other means of preventing Rh isoimmunization is through the transfusion of Rh negative blood to Rh negative women of childbearing age.

These precautions have resulted in a marked decrease in the incidence of Rh immunization and its effects on the newborn. Hemolytic disease of the newborn (anemia caused by excessive destruction of red blood cells) does still occur, either due to episodes of sensitization not treated by anti-D globulin or due to other Rh or ABO antibodies. However, it is unusual now to see increasingly severe cases in successive pregnancies, as in the past, resulting in fetal death.

SEE ALSO *Anemia, Antibodies, Blood groups, Hemolytic disease of the newborn, Newborn, Pregnancy*

RHEUMATIC FEVER

In some children between the ages of 5 and 15, streptococcal infection of the tonsils or throat may be followed 2 weeks later by an immune reaction called rheumatic fever. It manifests as fever and arthritis; the joints become tender, swollen and red. It can also damage the tissues of the heart, central nervous system and skin.

With bed rest, treatment with aspirin (and sometimes corticosteroid drugs), the symptoms usually resolve in a matter of weeks. However, the endocardium (the internal lining of the heart) may be permanently scarred, resulting in heart murmurs and valvular heart disease.

People with rheumatic heart disease should take antibiotics before undergoing medical and dental procedures to prevent bacterial endocarditis (infection of the internal lining of the heart).

SEE ALSO *Arthritis, Endocarditis, Fever, Heart, Streptococcal infections*

RHEUMATISM

Rheumatism is a name given to several conditions which involve inflammation of connective tissues in joints and muscles, causing pain and stiffness. The term includes degenerative disorders such as

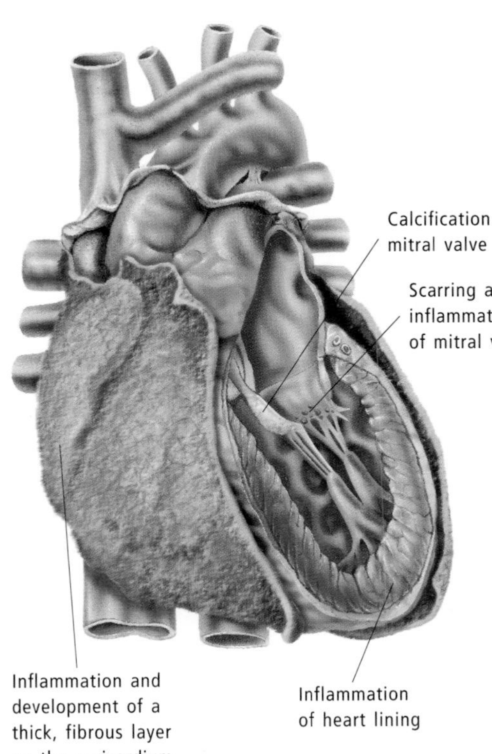

Rheumatic fever

Symptoms of rheumatic fever include fever, lethargy, painful swelling of the joints, and the formation of nodules under the skin and in the heart. Permanent heart damage may result from inflammation of the lining, valves and muscles of the heart, scarring of the valves and the development of a fibrous, thickened layer around the pericardium.

rheumatoid arthritis and osteoarthritis, septic or infectious arthritis resulting from tuberculosis, and bacterial, viral or fungal infections of the synovial fluid in joints.

Desert rheumatism is a condition involving inflammation of the eye surface and joints, as well as formation of skin nodules. It develops with coccidioidomycosis, a lung infection caused by inhalation of fungal spores found in soil. The disease has a mild form, which usually clears up without treatment, and a progressive form, which may be fatal and often requires lifelong treatment.

SEE ALSO *Connective tissue, Joints, Muscle, Osteoarthritis, Rheumatoid arthritis, Synovial fluid*

RHEUMATOID ARTHRITIS

Rheumatoid arthritis (RA) is a chronic and progressive condition which inflames connective tissue throughout the body. It most commonly affects both sides of the body simultaneously and involves the small joints of fingers, wrists, toes, ankles and elbows where the adjoining bone ends are enclosed in a membrane containing fluid for lubrication to ease movement.

Lungs and kidneys may also be affected; the spleen may enlarge; heart membranes, conjunctiva and sclera of the eyes or arteries may become inflamed; anemia, dry eyes and reduced secretion of saliva are also possible effects. RA is one of many forms of arthritis, a group of around 100 disorders which may affect up to 20 percent of people in industrialized society, making it possibly the most common chronic cause of continuing or permanent disability.

Symptoms of RA most commonly arise in women between ages 35 and 55 and in men between ages 40 and 60, but children and the elderly can suffer attacks. A minority recover after only one attack, but for others the disease is progressive, needing continual treatment. The major effects are aching and stiff joints, fatigue and anemia, weight loss and wasting muscles, with the onset of the disease marked by inflammation and redness around the affected areas.

Repeated attacks may produce problems such as carpal tunnel syndrome, with pain and numbness in the hand and wrist; permanent swelling of finger joints, knuckles and wrist; inflamed tendons; tenosynovitis; and nodules under the skin of the arms. When attacks subside, joints may become excessively loose and mobile, and it is in this state that they are most susceptible to further damage through overuse.

Diagnosis involves a blood test used to distinguish RA from similar conditions such as rheumatic fever, infectious arthritis and gout, and to detect the presence of a distinctive antibody called rheumatoid factor, carried by about 70 percent of people, some of whom will never suffer the disease.

The exact cause of the disease is unknown, but since the rheumatoid factor antibody is found in most sufferers, RA is thought to have an autoimmune mechanism, a reaction which causes the body's defense system to attack its own tissues. It is also thought that susceptibility to RA is a genetically inherited trait, with the disease being triggered by infection or possibly by environmental factors.

Treatment can involve rest, diet therapy, drugs and surgery, depending on individual symptoms. Rest may relieve pain and is recommended during attacks because movement aggravates the inflamed joints. Supports and splints can be used to immobilize joints for limited periods but regular use

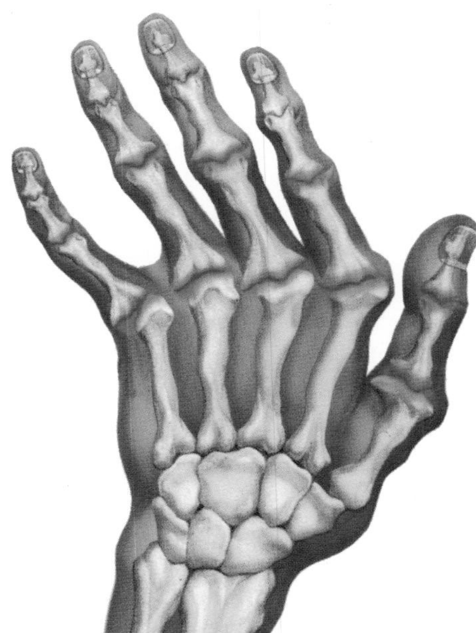

Rheumatoid arthritis

One of the most common areas of the body to suffer rheumatoid arthritis is the hands. The joints become stiff, painful, inflamed and swollen, making even the most simple of tasks such as picking up an object—difficult or impossible to do.

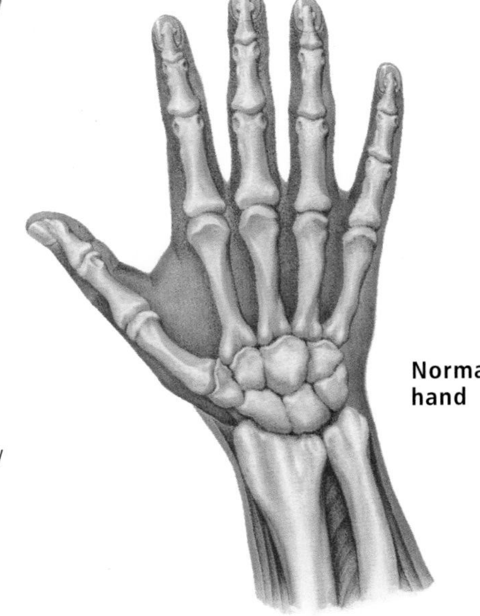

and movement of the joints is essential to prevent stiffness and preserve mobility. Certain foods can cause attacks in some people and paying careful attention to a balanced diet may help.

The drugs prescribed for the relief of rheumatoid arthritis are mainly non-steroidal anti-inflammatories (NSAIDs), including aspirin and ibuprofen. These should not be taken by those with gastric ulcers, however, as side effects may include digestive upsets as well as headaches, increased blood pressure and edema. There are also specific antirheumatoid drugs including steroids, penicillamine, gold preparations and methotrexate, but most of these have potentially severe side effects.

Lack of movement in joints and muscle weakness can create difficulties in walking and accomplishing everyday tasks. A range of aids is available, from orthopedic shoes to specially designed household appliances and hand tools. Fusion of small joints or replacement of hips or knees are options of last resort where other treatments have failed.

SEE ALSO *Arthritis, Autoimmune disease, Connective tissue, Osteoarthritis, Rheumatism, Synovial joints, Tenosynovitis*

RHINITIS

Rhinitis is the inflammation of the mucous membranes lining the nose and is usually accompanied by an excessive production of mucus, which may be watery or thick. There may be difficulty breathing through airways restricted by swelling and mucus.

Infection with the common cold or other viruses, bacterial infections, irritation by smoke or airborne pollutants, and allergic reactions can all produce similar symptoms.

Symptoms can be treated with nasal sprays or orally administered drugs which constrict the blood vessels in the swollen membranes and return them to near normal size, freeing up the airways. These drugs should be used for a few days only as their prolonged use may actually produce symptoms of congestion. If the mucous membrane itself is infected, nasal mucus may be yellow and pus-like and the nose will bleed easily. Antibiotics may be prescribed, depending on the cause.

Allergic rhinitis results from inhaling a substance to which the individual has been sensitized, whether or not there has been a previous allergic reaction. There is increased production of mucus, and there may also be redness and irritation of the eyes. Severe reactions can bring feelings of tightness in the chest and difficulty breathing. These changes are caused by the body's production of histamine, a substance used to help fight invading organisms.

The main culprit is pollen, rye grass pollen in particular, and symptoms can arise very quickly following contact. Seasonal allergic rhinitis is an almost permanent affliction for many allergy sufferers from spring through summer as airborne pollen levels rise in the growing season. Animal hair and skin flakes, mold, dust and the feces of the household dust mite are also known causes.

Medication with antihistamines may counter the immediate symptoms; for more serious reactions, corticosteroids may be prescribed. Identification of the allergenic substance is important to therapy which aims to desensitize chronic sufferers.

SEE ALSO *Allergies, Antihistamines, Histamines, Nose*

Rhinitis

Viruses, bacteria and allergens can all cause the mucous membranes of the nose to become inflamed. Acute rhinitis (or the common cold) is treated with decongestants to relieve nasal congestion.

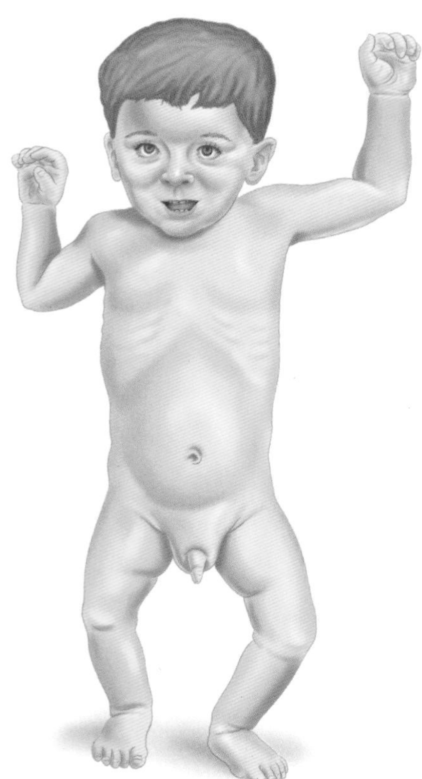

Rickets

A lack of vitamin D in children can cause soft and deformed bones, as without this vitamin, calcium and phosphorus cannot be utilized by the body's cells.

RHINOPHYMA

Rhinophyma is a rare condition in which the nose becomes enlarged and red, with thickened skin and the appearance of veins near the surface. The nose takes on a bulb-like shape and oil-producing glands become enlarged. Once thought to be the result of excessive alcohol consumption, rhinophyma strikes just as many non-drinkers. It usually only affects men and is associated with the skin disease, acne rosacea. While antibiotics may be successful in reducing symptoms in the early stages, surgical reshaping of the nose is the only other treatment.

SEE ALSO *Acne rosacea, Nose*

RIBS

The rib cage helps shield the heart and lungs from injury. Movement of the rib cage also assists the diaphragm in controlling the intake and expulsion of air during breathing.

Typically, the human skeleton has 24 ribs, arranged in 12 pairs. At the back, they join the thoracic vertebrae in the spine. At the front, each of the upper seven pairs connects to the sternum (or breastbone) directly by a costal cartilage. Pairs 8, 9 and 10 also connect to costal cartilages but these join with each other and then join the cartilage of the seventh rib. As they are not directly attached to the sternum, they are termed false ribs. The top seven pairs are directly attached to the sternum, and so are called true ribs. Pairs 11 and 12 are not attached at all at the front and are called floating ribs.

Occasionally a person may have a small additional rib, joined only at the back to a vertebra in the neck, usually the seventh cervical vertebrae. This so-called cervical rib may often go unnoticed but if it comes to place pressure on nerves and blood vessels it may need to be removed surgically.

SEE ALSO *Cervical rib syndrome, Skeletal system*

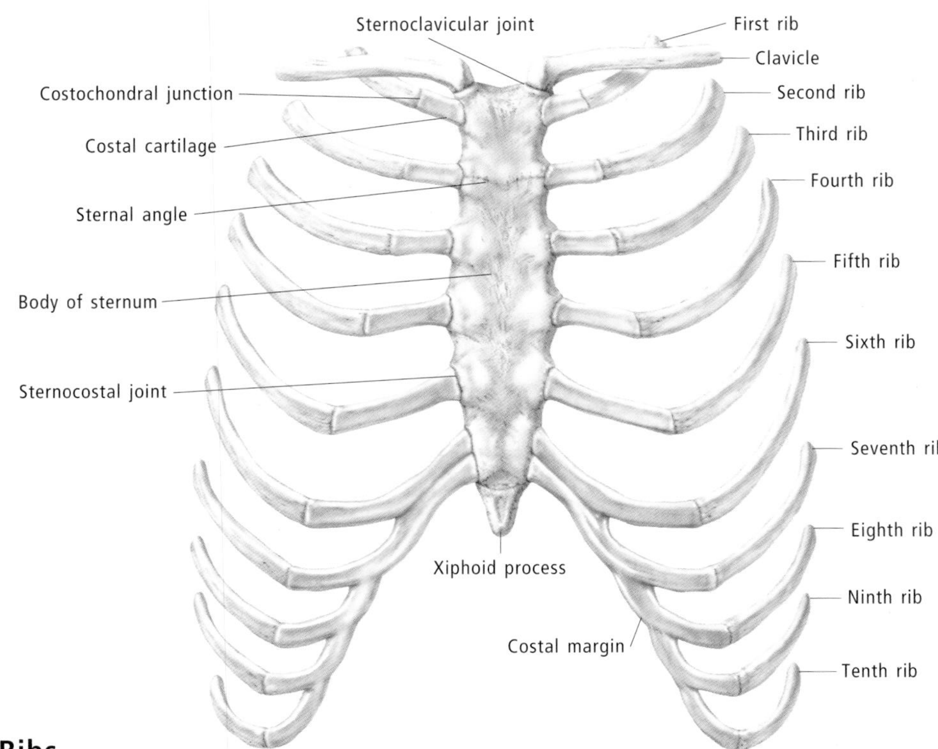

Ribs

The 24 ribs are arranged in 12 pairs. The first 7 pairs are referred to as "the true ribs" because they are directly attached to the breastbone (sternum). Pairs 8–10 are known as "false ribs" because they are not attached to the sternum. the lowest two pairs (11 and 12) are not attached at the front and are called "floating ribs".

Rib cage

The rib cage is designed to protect the organs within the chest, particularly the heart and lungs. Damage to the rib cage may lead to serious problems, such as a punctured lung.

RICKETS

Rickets is a bone disease of infants and children that is caused by a lack of vitamin D from either insufficient sunlight or inadequate diet. Occasionally, it may be caused by disorders of the kidney, liver or biliary system. The lack of vitamin D causes progressive softening and weakening of the bone structure which can result in deformity.

Infants with rickets grow more slowly than normal, and take longer to begin crawling or walking. When the infant does start to walk, the legs may bend, resulting in either bowlegs or knock-knees. The chest may also be deformed, producing a pigeon chest, and small knobs may develop on the ends of the ribs.

Rickets is treated by giving the child a concentrated supply of vitamin D, calcium and phosphorus; an adequate diet is essential. Deformities usually disappear if the condition is treated in the early stages.

SEE ALSO *Bones, Vitamins*

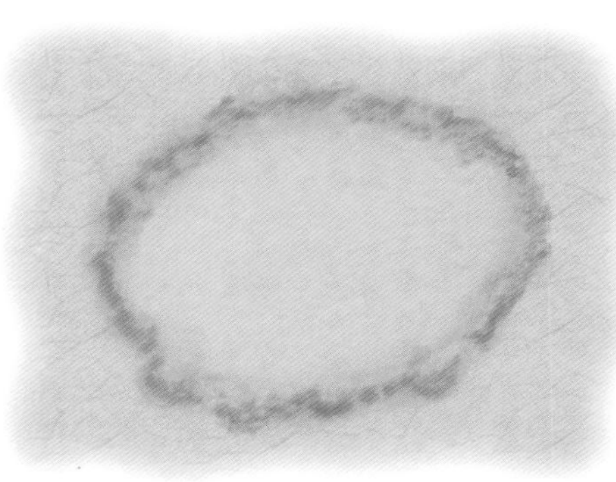

Ringworm

Also called tinea, this disease is caused by a fungus, not a worm as the name suggests.

RINGWORM

Ringworm is a skin infection caused by various fungi, which results in a characteristic red, ring-shaped rash. The fungi, called dermatophytes, invade the top layer of skin and affect the tissue underneath. Ringworm is particularly common among children and is usually treated with non-prescription antifungal creams and powders. Oral medications and stronger topical creams may be used for more severe and persistent cases.

Preventive measures include attention to personal hygiene and keeping the skin clean and dry.

Because the infection is highly contagious, hairbrushes, clothing and other personal items should be cleaned and dried after use. The complications of ringworm include secondary skin infections and spread of tinea to other parts of the body. Tinea is ringworm of the feet (athlete's foot), scalp, groin and nails.

SEE ALSO *Antifungals, Tinea*

ROOT CANAL THERAPY

Root canal therapy is a dental procedure in which the center, or pulp, of a dead or infected tooth is removed. The pulp includes nerves, blood vessels and lymphatic tissue which pass through the root canal. Root canal therapy is usually needed to avoid severe toothache and abscesses that can result from infection or trauma such as a blow to the mouth. It may save a tooth that would otherwise be extracted. The empty tooth is usually filled with a plastic substance. A crown may be fitted to improve the strength of the tooth, which may become weak as a result of the treatment.

SEE ALSO *Crown and bridge, Teeth*

ROSEOLA INFANTUM

A common infection of early childhood, roseola infantum is caused by a type of herpes virus and marked by a temperature which rises rapidly to a high fever of 39–40°C (102–104°F). This fever lasts 3–4 days and then suddenly disappears. Other symptoms may include febrile convulsions, mild diarrhea, a cough, enlarged lymph glands (lymph nodes) in the neck and earache. The fever is followed by a rash which is mildly itchy and spreads from the trunk and neck to behind the ears and lasts for about 2 days. Roseola infantum is highly contagious and can incubate for 5–15 days.

Treatment is aimed at relieving the symptoms, particularly the high fever; it is important to seek medical attention when a child's temperature rises to this level. This disease is sometimes confused with measles, the difference being the height and duration of the fever which precedes the appearance of the rash. A child who has a suppressed immune system may develop hepatitis or pneumonia. Recovery is generally rapid, however, and once the rash has disappeared the child will return to normal.

SEE ALSO *Convulsions, Fever, Hepatitis, Herpes simplex, Pneumonia*

ROTATOR CUFF MUSCLES

The rotator cuff muscles are dynamic stabilizers of the shoulder joint. They hold the head of the humerus securely in its shallow socket, while muscles attaching further from the joint powerfully move the arm. The subscapularis muscle forms the anterior part of the cuff, the infraspinatus and teres minor form the posterior part, and the supraspinatus the superior part. All four cuff muscles arise from the shoulder blade (scapula) and attach to bony elevations (tubercles) close to the head of the humerus.

The subscapularis muscle rotates the front of the arm inward, as in a forehand stroke in tennis. The infraspinatus and teres minor muscles rotate it outward, as in a backhand stroke. The supraspinatus muscle assists the deltoid muscle in raising the arm (abduction). The tendon of the supraspinatus passes under a bony and ligamentous arch (coracoacromial arch) and is separated from it by a bursa that allows the structures to glide easily against each other. Sometimes the tendon and bursa become inflamed, causing pain when the arm is raised.

SEE ALSO *Humerus, Shoulder*

ROUNDWORMS

Roundworms belong to the class Nematoda, a group containing over 10,000 species, many of which are parasites. Roundworms infecting humans live mostly in the intestine, range in length from a millimeter to many centimeters, and include hookworms, pinworms and whipworms. The most common roundworm is a long pale yellow worm with the scientific name of *Ascaris lumbricoides*, which infects the human gastrointestinal tract and lungs.

Root canal therapy

A damaged tooth may be saved by root canal therapy. First the tooth is opened up to allow access to the abscess and all pulp is removed (a). Then the abscess and canal is cleaned and sterilized (b). Finally the canals are sealed with filling (c).

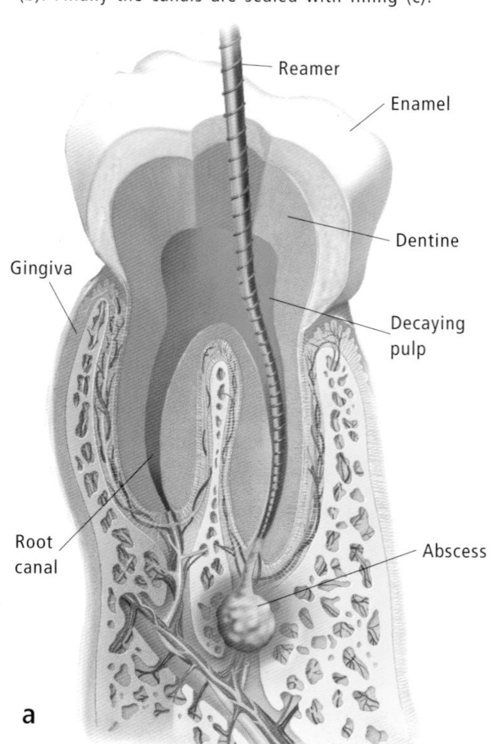

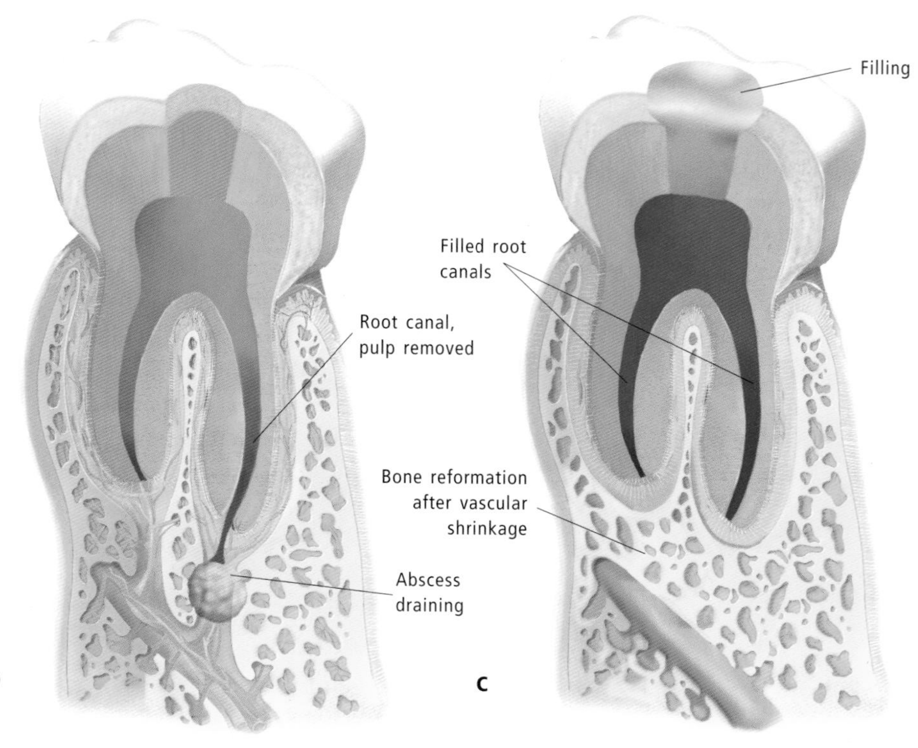

R

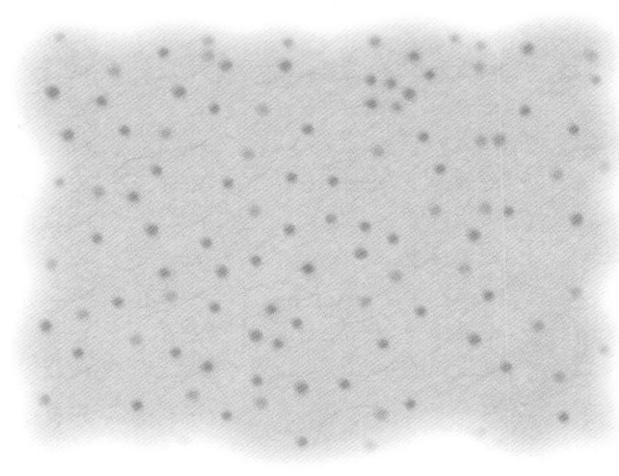

Rubella

Also known as German measles, rubella is similar to but less contagious than measles. The rash begins on the face and scalp, and then quickly spreads to the body and arms.

Ascariasis infection affects an estimated 1 billion people worldwide, mainly in developing nations where untreated human sewage is used to fertilize food crops. It develops when people consume food, water or soil traces contaminated with roundworm eggs.

In heavy infestations, adult worms can cause intestinal obstructions or malnutrition, and larvae can irritate the lungs. Oral medications are usually effective in eradicating infections although surgery may be needed to clear blockages.

SEE ALSO *Hookworm, Strongyloidiasis, Threadworms, Whipworm, Worms*

RUBELLA

Rubella (German measles) is caused by a virus which is transmitted by droplet inhalation. The incubation period for rubella is 2–3 weeks. Highly infectious, rubella is usually a mild illness lasting days only, but may be occasionally complicated by arthritis. If an expectant mother develops rubella during early pregnancy there is a high risk of congenital abnormalities developing in the fetus.

In childhood the condition usually begins with slight irritability and minor but tender enlargement of lymph glands in the back of the neck and head. A transient spotty rash will usually appear initially on the face and behind the ears, and then spread rapidly over the body. Occasionally the rash is noted when a child is being bathed in warm water, yet will have faded by the time the child is seen by the doctor and not recur. A few spots may be seen on the palate at the same time. There may be mild fever but the child is usually only minimally ill, with a runny nose. Adults often, and children rarely, develop various painful joints, particularly in the fingers. Occasionally it is noted that a child develops bruising due to a transient shortage of platelet cells in the blood. A very low percentage of patients develop an encephalopathy where there is inflammation and damage to the brain. Mortality in that instance may be 20 percent but recovery otherwise is usually complete.

If a woman is planning a pregnancy she is advised to have her rubella antibody level checked well beforehand. If there are adequate antibodies present, then there is no problem; if antibodies are absent, she is advised to be vaccinated at least three months before starting on a pregnancy.

If the embryo is infected before 14 weeks, a variety of different problems can occur, ranging from miscarriage to congenital heart defects, cataracts, glaucoma and deafness. The brain may not develop adequately and retardation can occur, even if the developing infant is past 14 weeks.

Rubella vaccination, usually combined with measles and mumps vaccines, is given initially at the age of 12–15 months. A second vaccination may be given in the early teens. Arthritis is an occasional complication with older children and women but otherwise there are few complications following immunization.

SEE ALSO *Congenital abnormalities, Infectious diseases, Immunization*

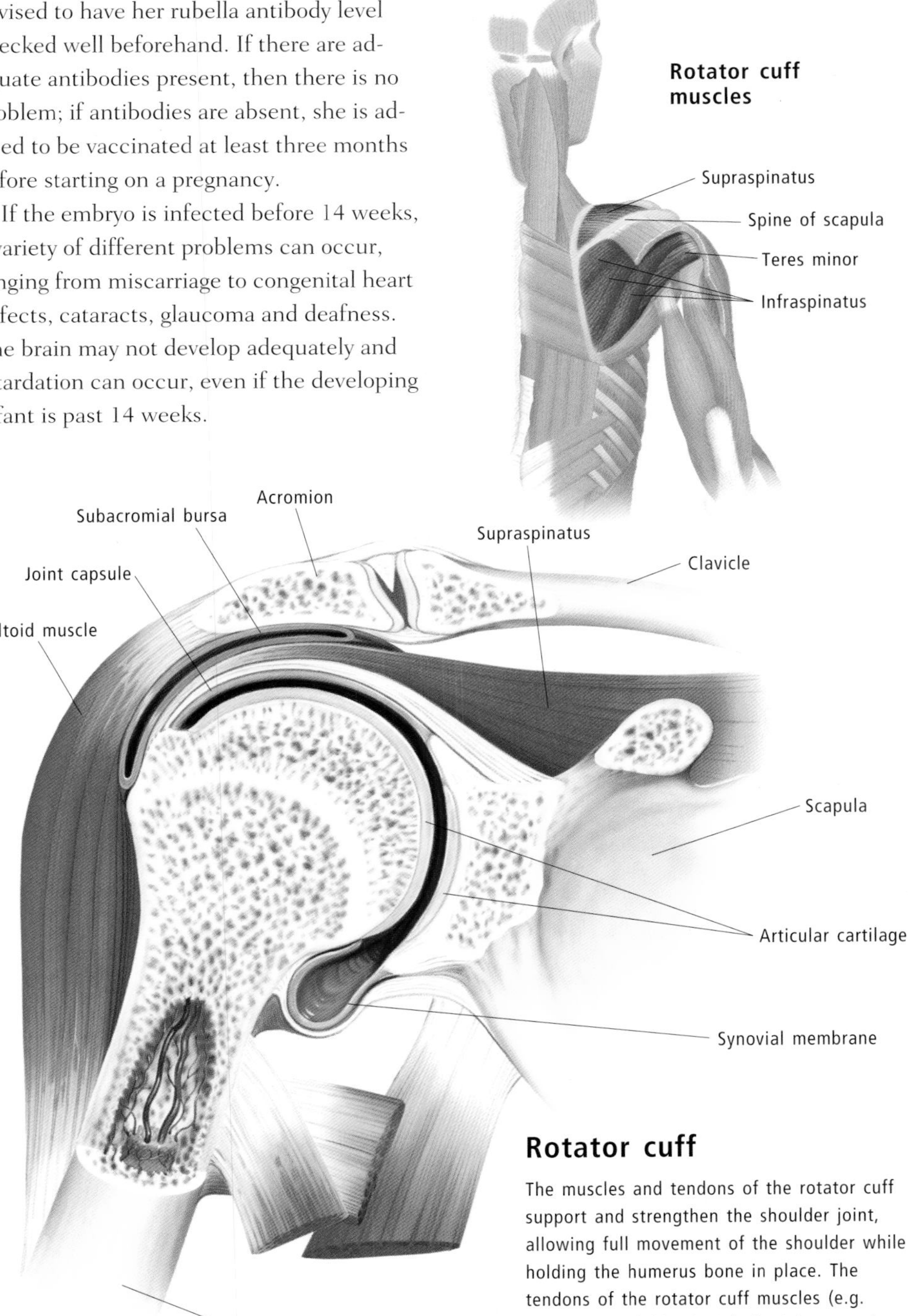

Rotator cuff

The muscles and tendons of the rotator cuff support and strengthen the shoulder joint, allowing full movement of the shoulder while holding the humerus bone in place. The tendons of the rotator cuff muscles (e.g. supraspinatus) blend with the joint capsule.

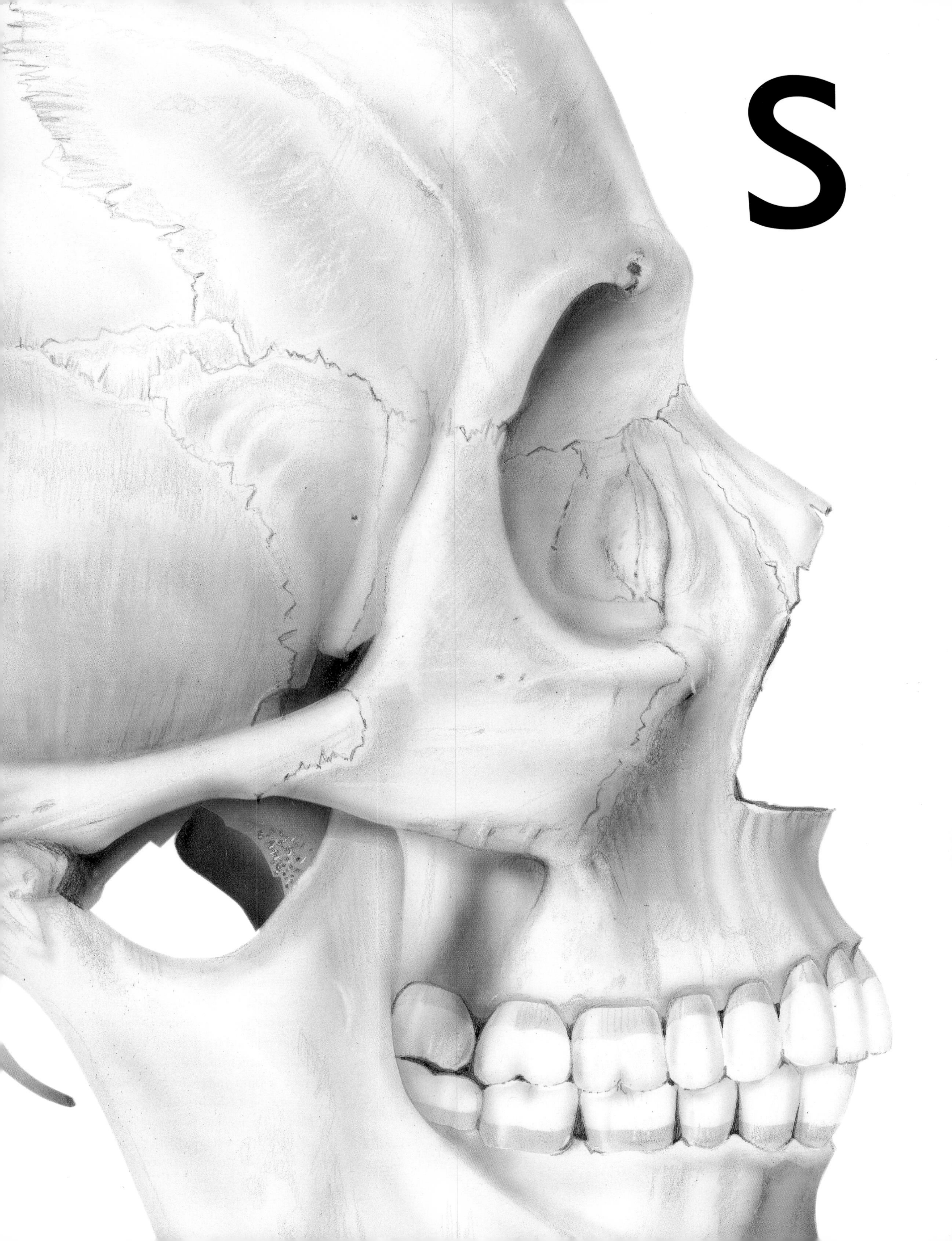

S

SACROILIAC JOINT

The sacroiliac joint is located where the ilium of the hip bone and the sacrum at the base of the spine meet. Because the weight of the trunk passes through this joint, powerful interosseous ligaments are required to unite the bones. At the front, the joint is synovial and at the back it is fibrous.

The synovial part of the joint has an L-shaped surface, which is usually related to the first three fused segments of the sacrum in the male and the first two segments in the female. The sacral and iliac articular surfaces are reciprocally ridged and furrowed to increase stability.

The interosseous sacroiliac ligament is strong and unites the roughened areas of bone behind the synovial part of the joint. The weight of the body tends to drive the upper end of the sacrum downward, tightening this ligament and drawing the joint surfaces together. This same force tends to tilt the lower end of the sacrum upward, which is resisted by the powerful sacrotuberous and sacrospinous ligaments.

The sacroiliac joint is capable of only a small amount of movement and is subject to great stress, from the downward pressure of the body's weight and the upward thrust of the legs and pelvis. It must also be able to cope with the movements of the body, for example as it turns, twists, pulls and pushes. Movement of the sacroiliac joint increases during pregnancy. An excess motion can cause a strain on the joint. With increasing age, the joint cavity may become partially or completely obliterated by fibrous tissue or fibrocartilage, and may even show bony fusion in the very old.

SEE ALSO *Hip, Joints, Sacrum, Skeletal system, Spine*

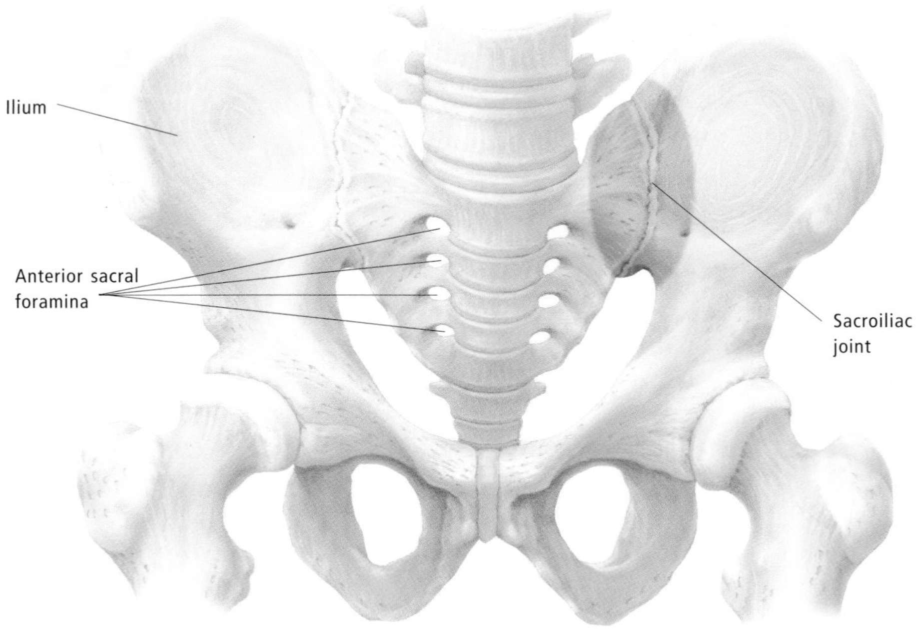

Sacroiliac joint

The sacroiliac joint articulates between the sacrum and ilium bone of the hip. It transfers body weight to the pelvis. The range of movement is relatively small.

SACRUM

The sacrum and coccyx form the lower end of the spine. The sacrum is formed by fusion of the five sacral vertebrae. The sacrum forms a part of the bony pelvis, being joined to the hip bones at the sacroiliac joints. Above, it articulates with the fifth lumbar vertebra, and below with the coccyx. Passing through the sacrum from top to bottom is the sacral canal, which is a continuation of the spinal canal of the rest of the vertebral column. The spinal roots (cauda equina) of the spinal cord pass through the sacral canal, giving off sacral spinal nerves which leave through pelvic and dorsal passages in the bone (sacral foramina).

SEE ALSO *Skeletal system, Spine, Vertebrae*

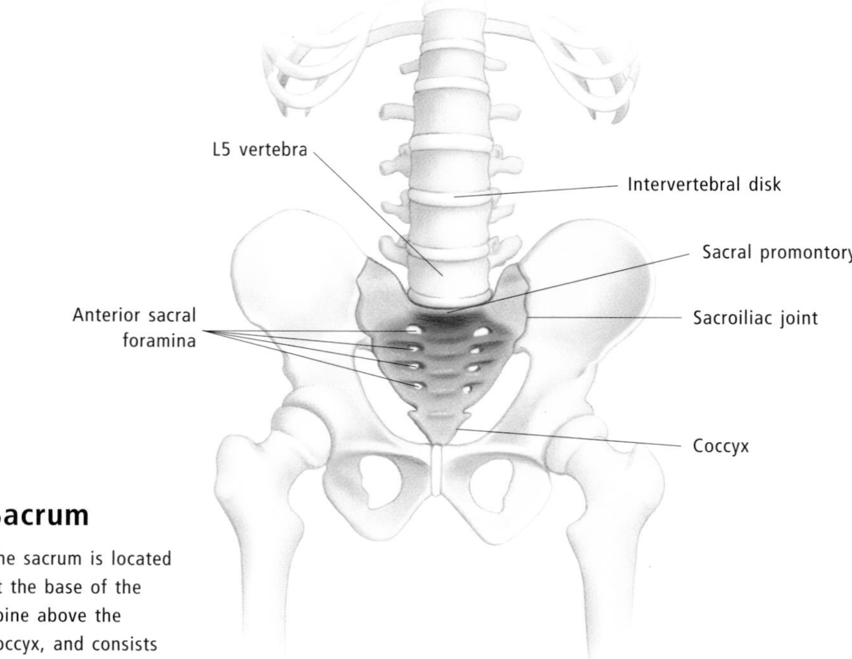

Sacrum

The sacrum is located at the base of the spine above the coccyx, and consists of five fused vertebrae.

SALIVA

Saliva is an alkaline fluid secreted by salivary glands that helps soften food, moistens the mouth and aids in digestion. Saliva is composed of mucus, water, mineral salts, proteins and amylase. The mucus helps in swallowing the food, the water dissolves some of the components of food and helps in tasting, and the amylase begins the digestion of carbohydrates. Saliva helps keep the mouth moist and clean. It is also important in helping the body to retain control of its water balance and, in its role of removing food debris, reducing tooth decay.

SEE ALSO *Mouth, Salivary glands*

S

SALIVARY GLANDS

The salivary glands are located around the beginning of the digestive tract. They produce saliva, a fluid that moistens food and enables food to be bound together into a mass called a bolus, thereby making chewing and swallowing easier. The moisture of saliva allows chemicals in the food to be dissolved and delivered to the taste buds for tasting. Saliva is also rich in digestive enzymes—chemicals that initiate the breakdown of food into simpler substances. The main enzyme in saliva is amylase, which begins the breakdown of starches into their constituent chemicals. This process will continue until the food bolus reaches the stomach and the acid of that region reduces the activity of amylase. Human saliva also contains substances such as lysozyme, and antibodies that control bacteria, thereby protecting the body against invasion by potentially disease-causing bacteria.

The salivary glands are divided into two groups. The major salivary glands are large structures that are easily seen with the naked eye. They consist of three pairs of glands: the parotid, submandibular and sublingual glands. The minor salivary glands are microscopic and are scattered around the mouth, palate and throat. Human saliva is made up mainly of secretions of the

Salivary glands

The salivary glands secrete saliva into the mouth. This fluid is needed to moisten food to ease swallowing and begins food breakdown in the preliminary stage of digestion. Infection of the salivary glands can cause swelling and pain.

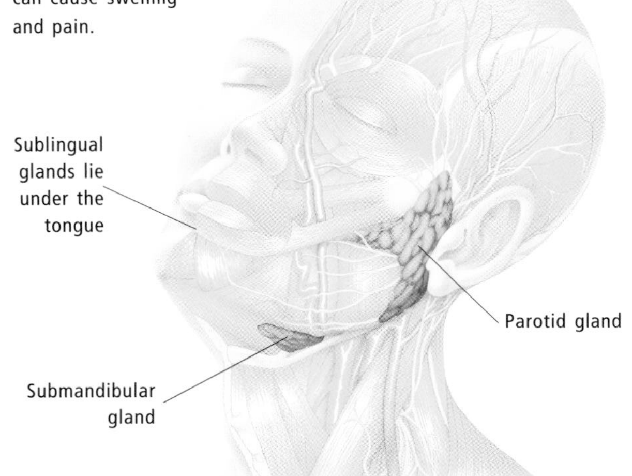

Salivary glands microstructure

There are three distinctive pairs of salivary glands—the parotid, sublingual and submandibular glands. Each pair has a unique cellular organization and produces saliva with slightly different properties.

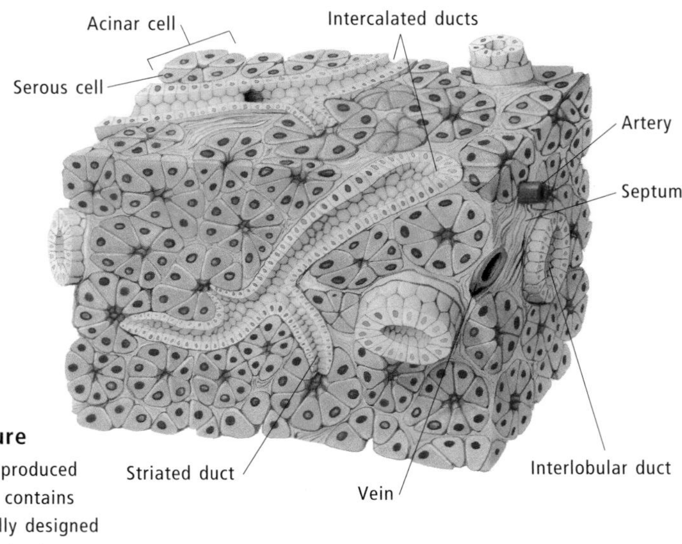

Parotid microstructure

The thin saliva produced by the parotids contains enzymes specially designed to break down starch.

Submandibular microstructure

The submandibular gland is comprised of a mixture of enzyme-producing serous cells and mucus-producing cells. Its saliva is predominantly water.

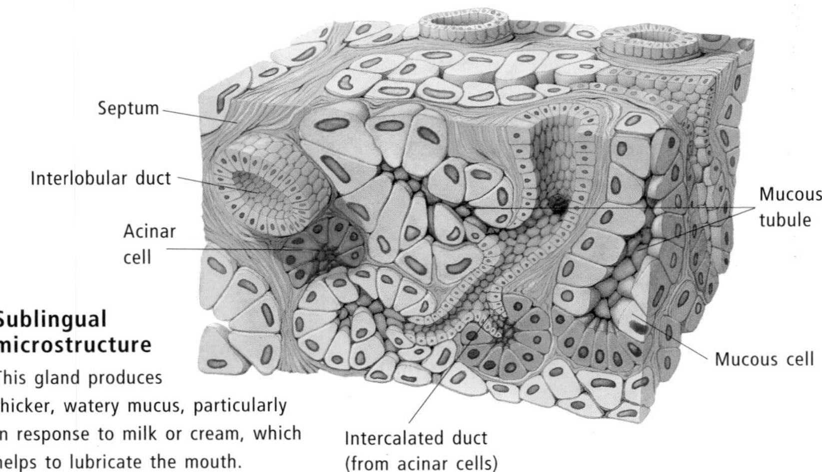

Sublingual microstructure

This gland produces thicker, watery mucus, particularly in response to milk or cream, which helps to lubricate the mouth.

S

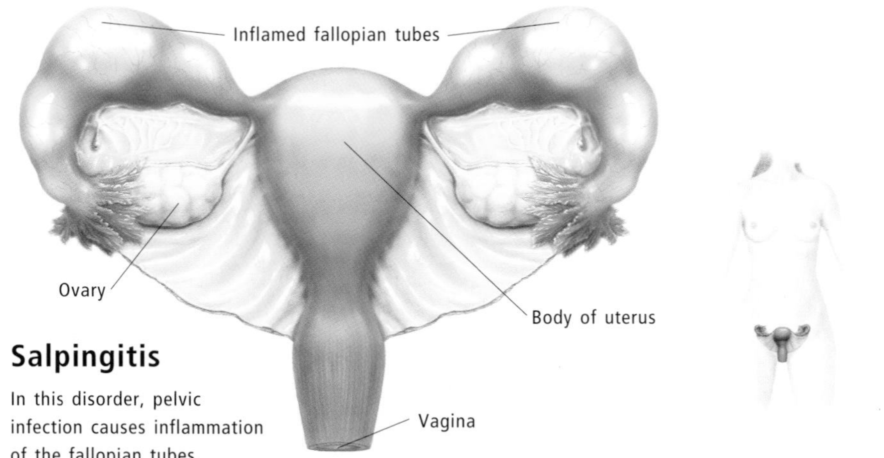

Salpingitis

In this disorder, pelvic infection causes inflammation of the fallopian tubes.

submandibular gland, with contributions from the parotid, sublingual and minor salivary glands in decreasing order of importance.

The parotid gland is located in front of the ear. It gives rise to a duct that runs forward to open into the mouth opposite the second molar of the upper teeth on each side. A flap of mucosa is present at the point where the duct opens into the mouth, and may be felt with the tip of the tongue. The submandibular gland is located below the jaw on each side, about 1 inch (2–3 centimeters) in front of the angle of the jaw. It gives rise to a duct which runs forward a short distance to open into the floor of the mouth under the tongue. The sublingual glands are small, and lie within ridges on the floor of the mouth beneath the tongue. They open by many small ducts into the floor of the mouth.

Salivary glands are mainly under the control of the nervous system, although some hormones may affect their function. The two parts of the autonomic nervous system, the parasympathetic and sympathetic divisions, both contribute nerves to the salivary glands. The parasympathetic nerves are probably most important, because they provide the stimulus to release copious amounts of saliva which is rich in digestive enzyme. This occurs in response to the smell and sight of food, as well as to the presence of food in the mouth. Sympathetic stimulation of salivary glands tends to produce a dry mouth (such as during states of anxiety or fear) with very little enzyme content in the saliva.

The salivary glands may be involved in disease. Infection with the mumps virus produces a characteristic enlargement of the parotid gland, which causes painful swelling in the face and cheek. Tumors may also arise in the salivary glands. Most tumors arise in the parotid gland, and about 80 percent of these are benign (non-invasive and less dangerous). About half of the tumors arising from the submandibular gland are benign, while the others are malignant (invasive and potentially fatal). Cancers of the salivary gland may be treated by surgical removal or radiation therapy.

SEE ALSO *Autonomic nervous system, Digestive system, Mouth, Mumps, Saliva, Sympathetic nervous system, Tongue*

SALPINGITIS

Salpingitis is inflammation of the fallopian (uterine) tubes, usually due to pelvic infection. Prolonged infection can lead to infertility due to obstruction of the tubes so that either sperm cells cannot reach the eggs, or fertilized eggs cannot reach the uterus.

SEE ALSO *Fallopian tubes, Pelvic inflammatory disease, Reproductive systems*

SAPHENOUS VEINS

The saphenous veins are the major superficial veins of the leg. The great saphenous vein returns blood from the foot and leg to the femoral vein below the groin, and the small saphenous vein returns blood from the calf to the popliteal vein behind the knee. The location of these veins requires them to return blood towards the heart against the action of gravity. Most of the venous blood in the calf is returned to the heart by the deep veins, assisted by the increased pressure applied by contraction of the calf muscles.

The deep veins receive blood from the great saphenous vein via "perforating" veins;

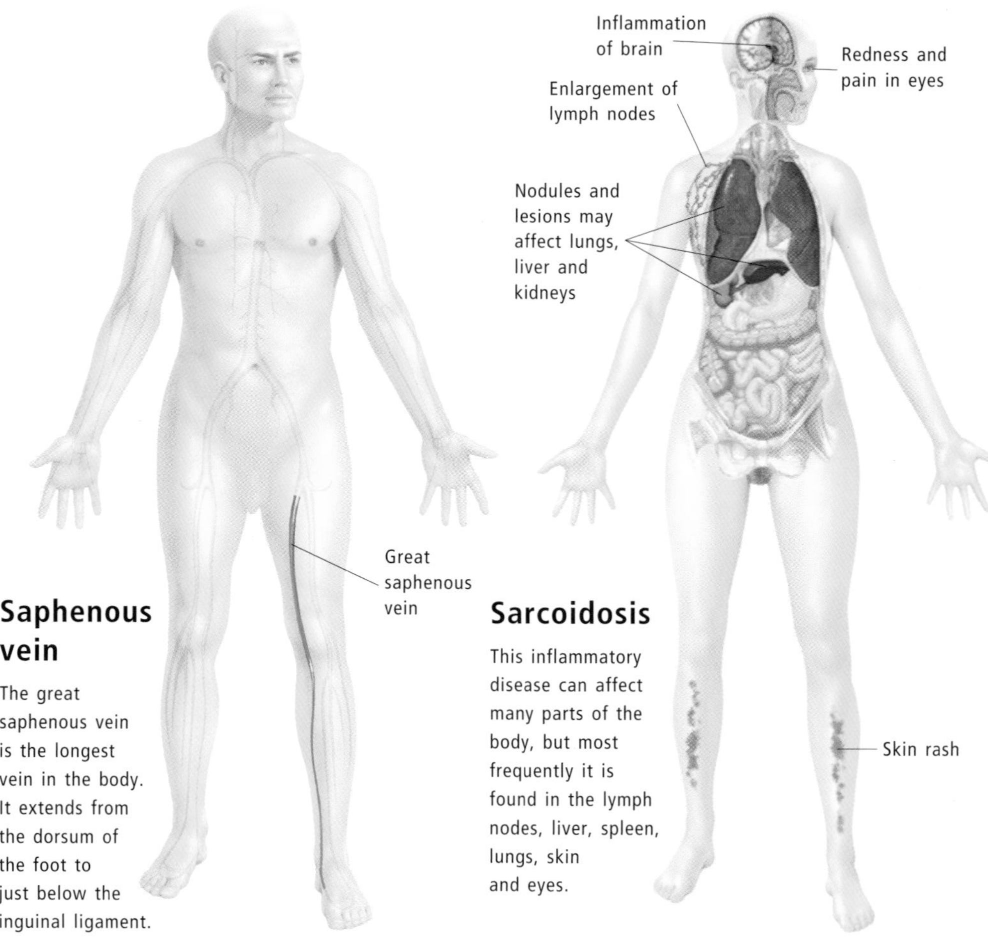

Saphenous vein

The great saphenous vein is the longest vein in the body. It extends from the dorsum of the foot to just below the inguinal ligament.

Sarcoidosis

This inflammatory disease can affect many parts of the body, but most frequently it is found in the lymph nodes, liver, spleen, lungs, skin and eyes.

these contain valves preventing backflow of blood from deep veins to the great saphenous vein. If the valves fail, blood is squeezed into the superficial veins by the muscle pump, distending the veins, which become varicose.

SEE ALSO *Leg, Phlebitis, Thrombosis, Varicose veins*

SARCOIDOSIS

Sarcoidosis is a systemic inflammatory disease of unknown origin, which may affect a variety of body organs. Most often it is detected as an incidental finding on a chest x-ray. It causes enlargement of lymph nodes in the chest and may cause shadows in the lungs. Later, symptoms such as persistent dry cough or shortness of breath may develop. Other symptoms may include a painful red rash on the shins and redness and pain of the eyes. Less commonly, sarcoidosis may affect the kidneys, heart or brain. The inflammatory cells involved can produce an increased level of calcium in the blood and urine. Young women are most often affected.

Sarcoidosis is diagnosed by x-rays, blood tests and tissue biopsy. It needs to be distinguished from other causes of enlarged lymph glands, such as lymphoma and tuberculosis. The physician will often assess the function of various organs with further tests, such as an electrocardiograph or detailed lung function studies. Often the condition is mild and may improve without treatment, especially in children. In other cases treatment is required with anti-inflammatory medication. This can range from mild drugs, such as aspirin, to cortisone or powerful immunosuppressants in severe cases.

SEE ALSO *Lungs, Lymph nodes*

Scabies

Scabies is caused by female parasitic mites burrowing under the skin to lay their eggs. An allergic reaction to the mites' feces causes an itchy rash to appear.

SCABIES

Tiny mites (*Sarcoptes scabiei*) cause the highly contagious skin condition scabies. It is spread by close personal contact with an infected person, by sharing their bed or wearing their clothes. Female mites burrow under the skin—favoring hands, toes, groin and bends of elbows and knees—to lay eggs. It takes about 10 days for the mites to mature and continue the cycle. Within weeks, the skin develops an allergic reaction and itches intensely. An eczema-like rash often develops and the mite burrows may be visible.

Treatment includes chemical washes, but the itching may persist for weeks.

SEE ALSO *Sexually transmitted diseases, Skin*

SCALP

The scalp is the skin and connective tissue covering the skull. The hair that grows from it protects against heat loss, minor abrasions and ultraviolet light. The adult human scalp contains around 100,000 hair follicles. Hair may disappear because the follicles are

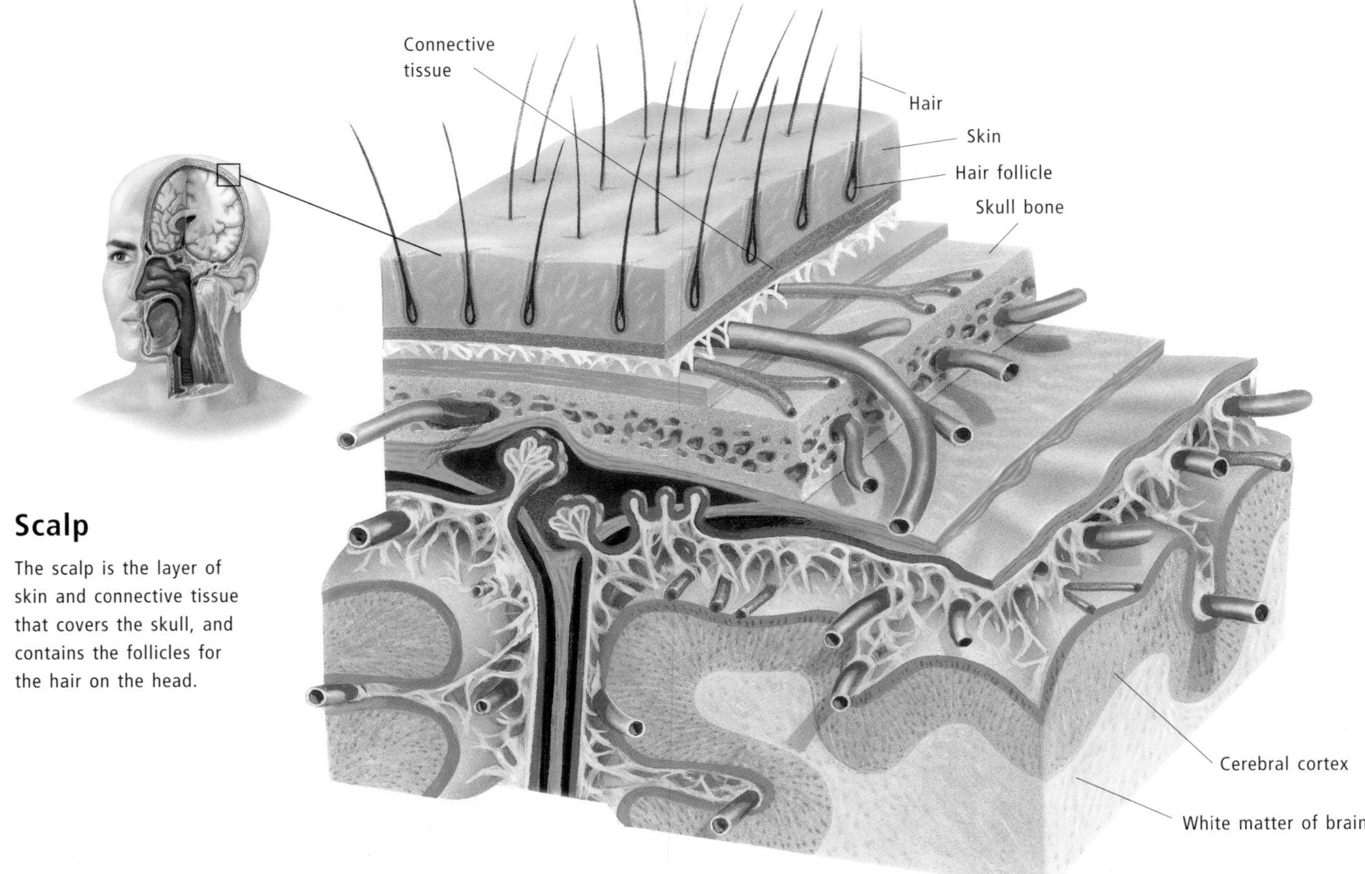

Scalp

The scalp is the layer of skin and connective tissue that covers the skull, and contains the follicles for the hair on the head.

S

damaged, either permanently or temporarily; because the person is going bald for reasons of heredity or hormonal imbalance; or because it has been voluntarily removed.

Conditions that can cause itchiness of the scalp include dandruff, scalp psoriasis and head lice. Dandruff is a mild form of seborrheic dermatitis, cause unknown, and is more of a cosmetic problem than a medical one. It can usually be controlled by a medicated shampoo. Scalp psoriasis, also cause unknown, produces scaly lesions that can be treated with shampoos and other preparations, including topical corticosteroids. Infestations of head lice require diligent fine combing, the use of an insecticidal shampoo and sometimes washing the hair with hot soapy water to remove the lice and eggs.

Cradle cap, common in babies, is a scalp condition created when sebum from the sebaceous glands forms layers on the scalp. It is generally a yellow color and feels greasy. It is not dirty. Rubbing olive oil into the crusts the night before and washing with a gentle shampoo will often remove it, though sometimes a doctor may prescribe a lotion for stubborn cases. The actual cause is unknown and older children may also suffer from it.

SEE ALSO *Cradle cap, Dandruff, Hair, Head lice, Psoriasis*

SCAPULA

The scapula (shoulder blade) forms part of the shoulder, at the back. It is a triangular, flattened bone, with several projections. The scapula is attached to the outer end of the collar bone (clavicle) at the acromioclavicular joint. Its outer end provides a socket for the head of the upper arm bone (humerus), forming the bony articulation of the shoulder joint. The scapula is held in place by strong muscles, which can move it in relation to the chest wall. It provides attachment for many of the muscles of the shoulder and upper arm, including the biceps.

SEE ALSO *Collar bone, Humerus, Shoulder*

Scapula—back view

Each scapula is connected to the humerus bone and clavicle (collar bone).

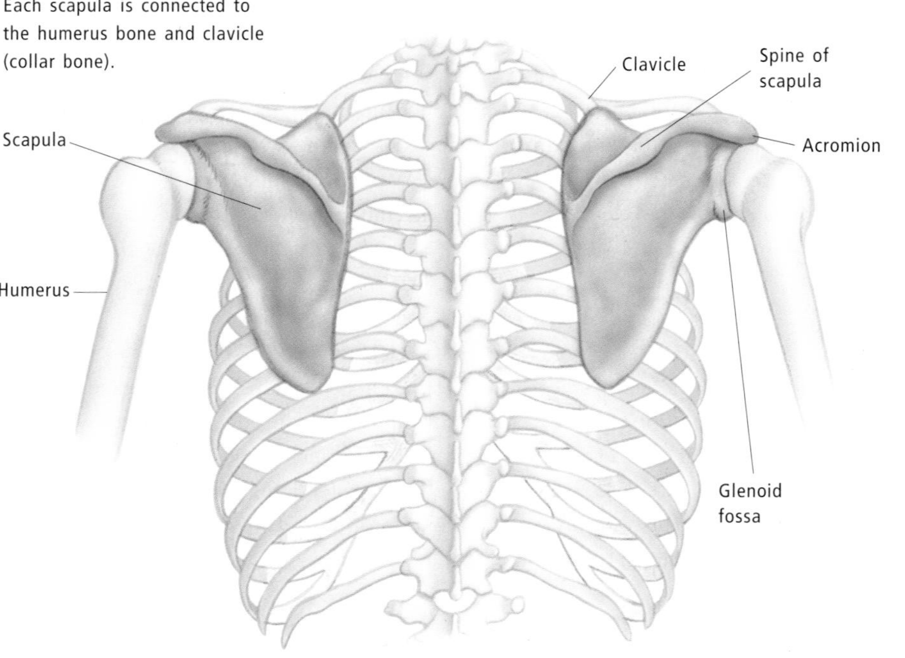

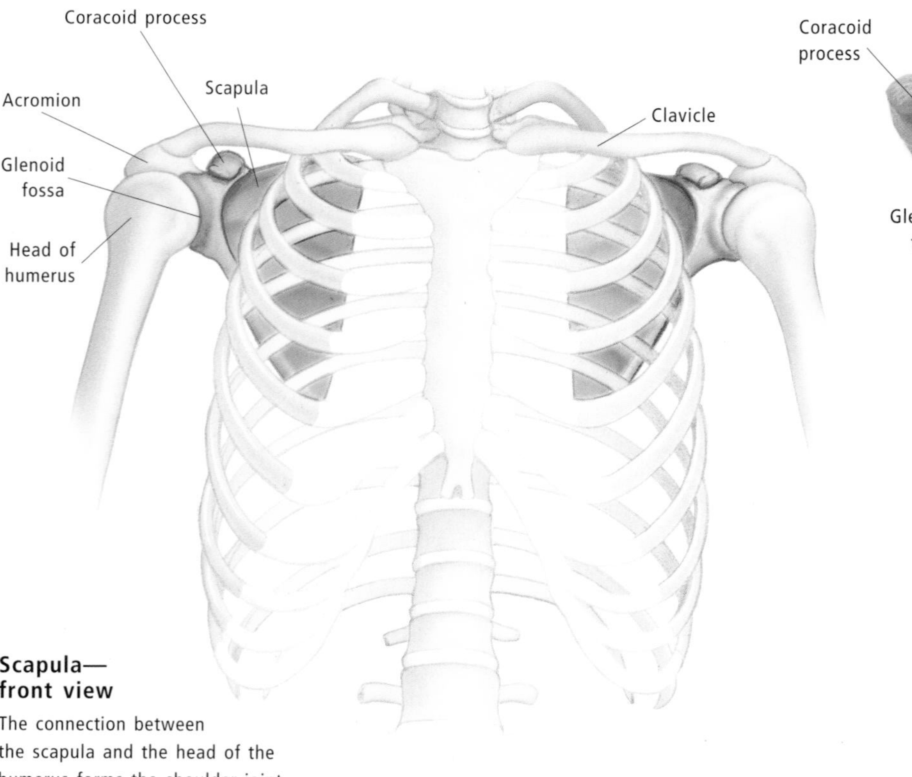

Scapula—front view

The connection between the scapula and the head of the humerus forms the shoulder joint.

Coracoid process
Acromion
Suprascapular notch
Glenoid fossa
Subscapular fossa

Scapula

The scapula (shoulder blade) is a flat triangular bone located in the back of the shoulder.

SCAR

A scar, or cicatrix, is toughened fibrous tissue that develops while a burn, wound or surgical incision heals. A scar helps knit the wound together. Inside the body, scars rarely cause problems. People are more commonly concerned about scars on the skin. The extent to which an injury will leave a scar depends on where it occurs on the body, its size and depth. Scarring will also vary with a person's age, genetic predisposition to scarring, and skin characteristics.

A range of treatments is available to minimize scarring, including dermabrasion, during which the surface of the skin is frozen with an aerosol spray and then abraded by mechanical means.

SEE ALSO *Keloid*

SCARLET FEVER

Scarlet fever is caused by bacteria known as Group A beta-hemolytic streptococci. Thanks largely to the advent of antibiotics, which offer quick and effective treatment, this once common disease is no longer the deeply feared scourge it was during the 1800s and early 1900s.

As immunity usually develops after one bout of scarlet fever, the disease tends to occur mainly in children. It begins suddenly with a fever and sore throat within two days of contact with an infected person. Shivering, headaches and vomiting may follow. Within two days of the first symptoms, a small bright red rash begins appearing, first on the neck and chest but eventually spreading to the rest of the body. The rash, which feels like sandpaper, is a reaction to a toxin released by the bacteria. It may last up to a week, after which the skin peels as if it has been sunburnt. During the early stages of scarlet fever, the tongue is coated in white and the taste buds are red and swollen—known as a "strawberry tongue". Later, the white coating disappears to leave a "raspberry tongue", which is red all over.

Before antibiotics were developed, scarlet fever was often followed by meningitis or rheumatic fever. These are now rare as complications of streptococcal infection.

SEE ALSO *Antibiotics, Bacteria, Infectious diseases*

Scar

The growth of granulation tissue during wound healing may leave a mark or scar on the skin.

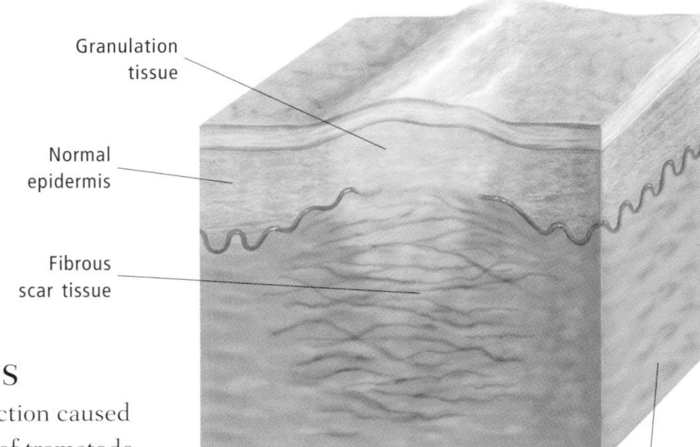

SCHISTOSOMIASIS

Schistosomiasis is an infection caused by the *Schistosoma* genus of trematode worms, and is second only to malaria in prevalence worldwide. The worms develop in snails and are released into fresh water where their larvae penetrate the skin to infect humans. The most common form of the disease occurs in South America, Africa and the Middle East, while another form occurs in the Far East.

Local inhabitants may not develop symptoms of initial infection, whereas visitors may develop intense itching (swimmer's itch). Weeks later a febrile illness occurs with cough and diarrhea, due to an immune reaction to the developing worms and their eggs in the intestines. Prolonged exposure to the worm infection can result in scarring of the liver (cirrhosis) and enlargement of the liver and spleen.

Infection is diagnosed by increased blood eosinophils, antibody tests and microscopic stool examination for eggs. Drugs are available which are active against the infection.

SEE ALSO *Swimmer's itch, Worms*

SCHIZOPHRENIA

Schizophrenia is a serious and incurable mental illness that profoundly disrupts thought patterns, thinking processes and emotions. The disorder is difficult to describe accurately because it produces a broad range of symptoms which can affect every attribute of character and personality. Language and thought, perception and response, and the individual's sense of self may all be upset; it may be impossible for sufferers to respond properly to people or events and to differentiate between what is real and what is imagined.

Schizophrenics may hold delusions or invest everyday events or actions with strange meanings. They may experience hallucinations, both visual and auditory. Their speech may be incoherent and disorganized. They may show no emotion or respond to others in a very limited emotional manner, or they may grossly exaggerate their responses. They may withdraw from all interaction with others or become deeply depressed. The effects of schizophrenia have a marked impact on the ability to carry on everyday activities.

One popular analogy to explain what is happening in schizophrenia is to liken the normal brain to a telephone switchboard where incoming perceptions are sent to the correct part of the brain, which produces an appropriate response—an action, thought, feeling or verbal reply. In the schizophrenic brain it is as if the incoming signals get jammed or sent to the wrong place and the response generated is inappropriate or nonexistent. There is a foundation for this analogy, as the brains of some schizophrenia sufferers have been found to have altered levels of chemicals called neurotransmitters which are responsible for carrying nerve impulses. This disturbance in the levels of neurotransmitters can be treated by medication under supervision.

Schizophrenia most often appears in early adulthood, in the mid to late twenties; it is found in men and women of all cultures, races and social groupings, occurring in about 1 percent of the population of industrialized societies. Onset may be gradual or quite sudden, with one or a series of psychotic episodes, and the course of the disease varies widely from person to person.

The exact cause of schizophrenia is still largely unknown but is believed to be

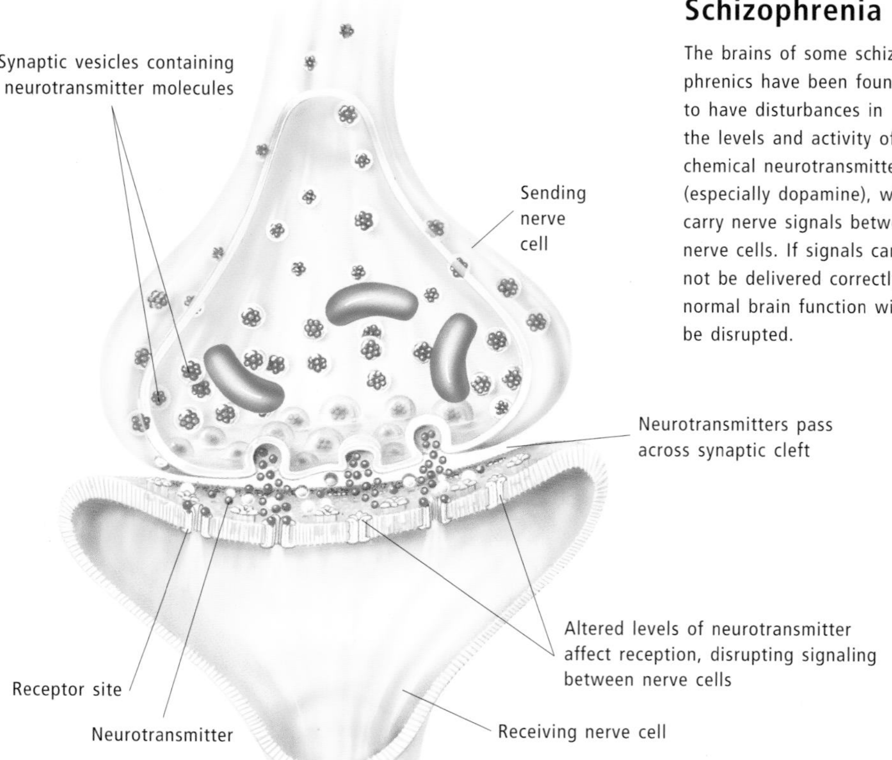

Schizophrenia

The brains of some schizophrenics have been found to have disturbances in the levels and activity of chemical neurotransmitters (especially dopamine), which carry nerve signals between nerve cells. If signals cannot be delivered correctly, normal brain function will be disrupted.

genetic or a chemical imbalance in the brain. Gradual signs of onset are usually observed by immediate family as a marked change in behavior, often believed to be temporary. Eventually it becomes obvious that something is seriously wrong, and professional help is sought.

While schizophrenia is neither preventable nor curable, an appropriate medication regime can do much to ameliorate its symptoms. People need to be encouraged to continue medication even when they feel well.

SEE ALSO *Antipsychotics*

SCIATIC NERVE

The sciatic nerve is the major nerve of the back of the thigh. At its commencement, it is the thickness of a little finger in diameter—the thickest nerve in the body. It arises from the lumbar and sacral plexus at the base of the spine. It leaves the pelvis through the greater sciatic foramen, passes under the gluteus maximus muscle and runs down the back of the thigh. In the lower third of the thigh, it divides into two branches, the tibial and common peroneal nerves. Its course in the thigh can be represented approximately by a line drawn from midway between the ischial tuberosity and the apex of the greater trochanter (both of which can be felt in the hip area), to the apex of the popliteal fossa, located behind the knee.

The sciatic nerve sends branches to supply several muscles, namely the biceps femoris, semitendinosus, semimembranosus, and the ischial head of the adductor magnus. The sciatic nerve also provides sensation for the hip joint.

Injections into the buttocks must be placed to avoid the sciatic nerve as injury or inflammation to it may cause pain that can travel down the length of the leg. Sciatica is pain experienced in the region supplied by the sciatic nerve. It is usually due either to a slipped, or herniated, intervertebral disk or to osteophytes—bony outgrowths affecting the roots of the nerve in the sacral foramina.

SEE ALSO *Nerves, Sciatica, Spine*

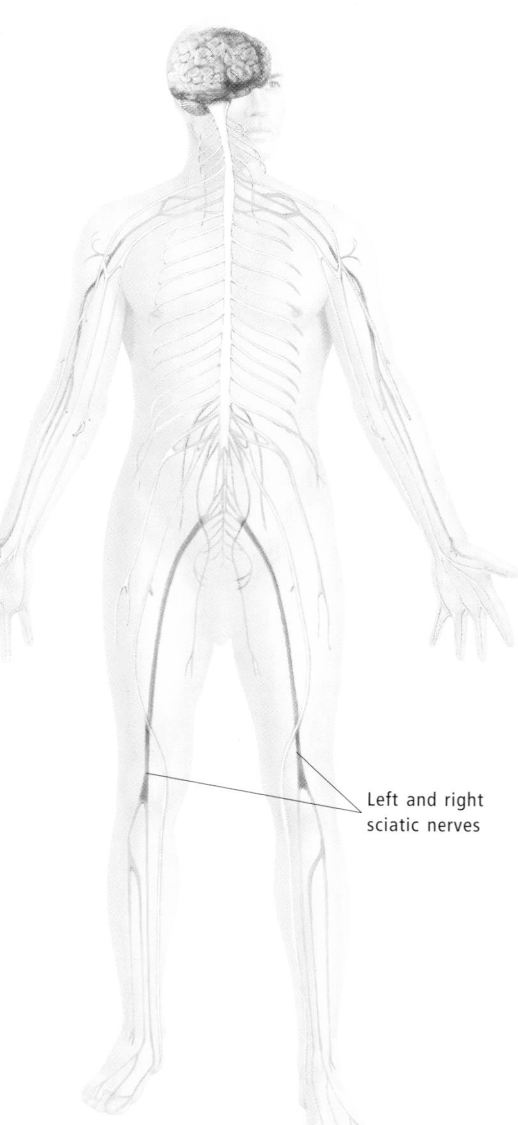

Sciatic nerve

This is the widest nerve of the body. It extends from the base of the spine down the thigh, then branches out through the lower leg and foot.

SCIATICA

Each leg is served by a sciatic nerve which begins at the base of the spine, travels through the hip and buttock, then down the length of the limb. Pain along it or its branches is called sciatica.

Sciatica is usually caused by stress on the nerve around the point where it emerges from the vertebral column.

Sciatica occurs most commonly when the nerve becomes pinched by a herniated disk between vertebrae or is placed under pressure around the base of the spine due to arthritis or pregnancy.

Occasionally, sciatica may be due to more serious conditions such as a tumor, blood clot or abscess in the spine. The severity and type of pain varies, from pins and needles in the toes to excruciating pains that run the length of the limb. Weakness in the lower leg muscles can result; in severe cases, it may be difficult to bend the knee or even move the foot, making standing near-impossible.

Sciatica usually gets better with simple treatments, often within a few days, although very occasionally surgery may be necessary. In most cases, over-the-counter pain killers and anti-inflammatory drugs ease the pain.

SEE ALSO *Nerves, Sciatic nerve, Spine*

SCLERA

The sclera and the cornea together form the outside of the eyeball. Part of the sclera is visible, the so-called white of the eye. It is composed of dense, tough fibrous tissue.

Besides containing and protecting the optical parts of the eye, the sclera provides attachment for the muscles which move the eye.

SEE ALSO *Cornea, Eye*

SCLERITIS

Scleritis is inflammation of the sclera, the dense white fibrous covering of the eye beneath the transparent conjunctiva.

A relatively mild nodular scleritis sometimes occurs in the superficial layers of the sclera; it is thought to be an allergy and it generally responds to treatment with corticosteroid eye drops.

A more severe and often painful form of scleritis is often associated with autoimmune diseases such as Crohn's disease, rheumatoid arthritis or other connective-tissue disorders. However, in some cases, no cause is found.

The symptoms are severe eye pain, blurred vision, and sensitivity to light. Purple-red, inflamed areas may appear in areas of the white of the eye.

Scleritis may affect one or both eyes. The condition usually responds to treatment with corticosteroid eye drops or oral corticosteroids, but may recur. If the underlying disease can be treated, the condition will improve. In some cases it is chronic and progressive. If there is any vision loss, it is usually permanent.

SEE ALSO *Eye, Sclera*

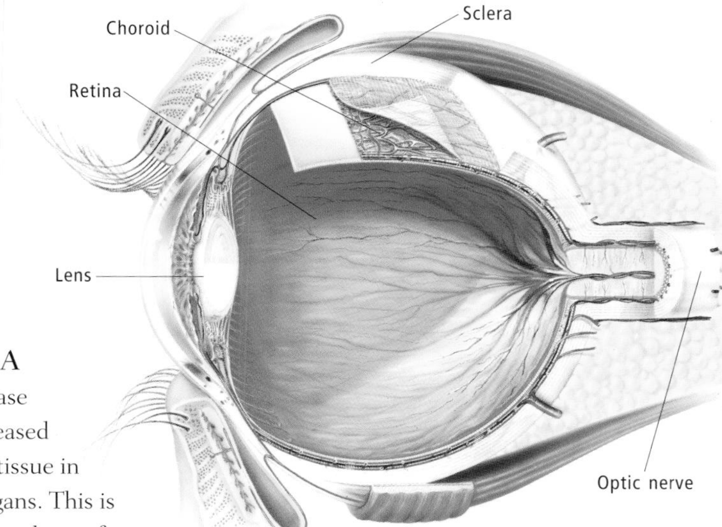

Sclera

Commonly called the "white" of the eye, the sclera is composed of dense, tough, fibrous tissue.

SCLERODERMA

Scleroderma is a disease characterized by increased deposition of fibrous tissue in the skin and other organs. This is associated with abnormalities of blood vessels, such as spasm precipitated by the cold, resulting in color change in the extremities (Raynaud's phenomenon). The fingers become swollen and small blood vessels may be prominent; gradually the skin over the fingers and face becomes thickened and tight. In severe cases the lungs, heart and kidneys can be affected.

Diagnosis is aided by the presence of autoantibodies in the blood. Treatment of scleroderma is difficult and the condition tends to progress gradually.

SEE ALSO *Raynaud's disease, Sclerosis*

SCLEROSIS

Sclerosis is the hardening or thickening of body tissue. Possible causes range from inflammation to the deposition of mineral salts to scarring. It is usually an abnormal and undesirable condition, often associated with disease. For example, the incurable and chronic illness known as progressive systemic sclerosis (also called scleroderma) is characterized by a thickening of the connective tissue causing debilitating changes to the skin, blood vessels and internal organs. In arteriosclerosis, the walls of the arteries thicken, calcify and lose their elasticity.

SEE ALSO *Arteriosclerosis, Scleroderma*

SCOLIOSIS

Scoliosis is an abnormal sideways deviation of the vertebral column (spine). It affects the muscles and ligaments connected to the spine and if left untreated can lead to

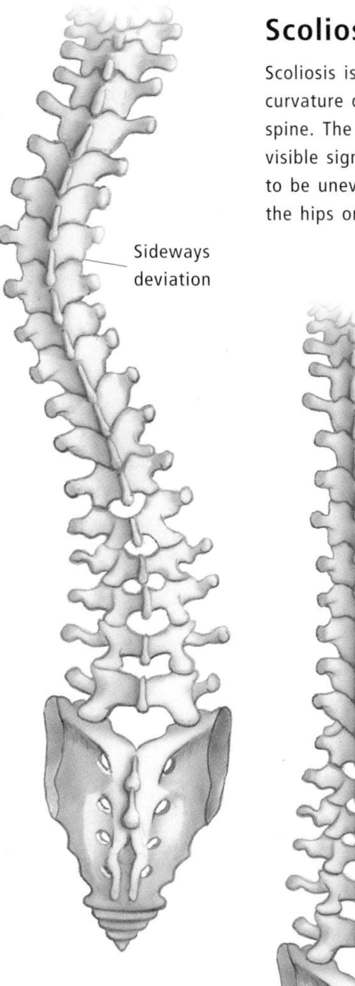

Scoliosis

Scoliosis is lateral curvature of the spine. The first visible sign is likely to be unevenness of the hips or shoulders.

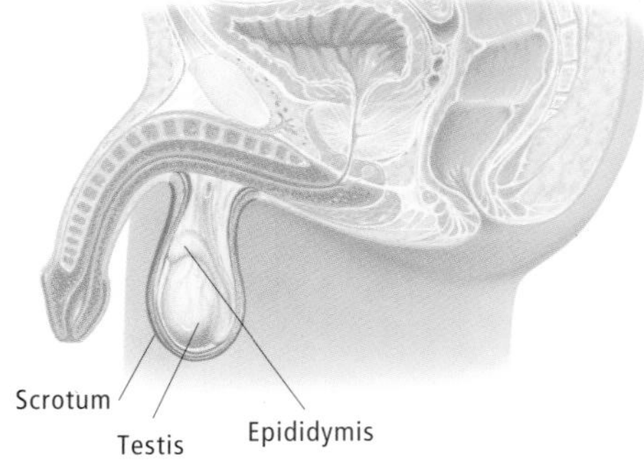

Scrotum

The scrotum is a bag of skin which hangs just behind the penis and contains the testes. The cremaster muscle adjusts the tension of the skin of the scrotum, moving the testes towards or away from the body in response to changes in temperature.

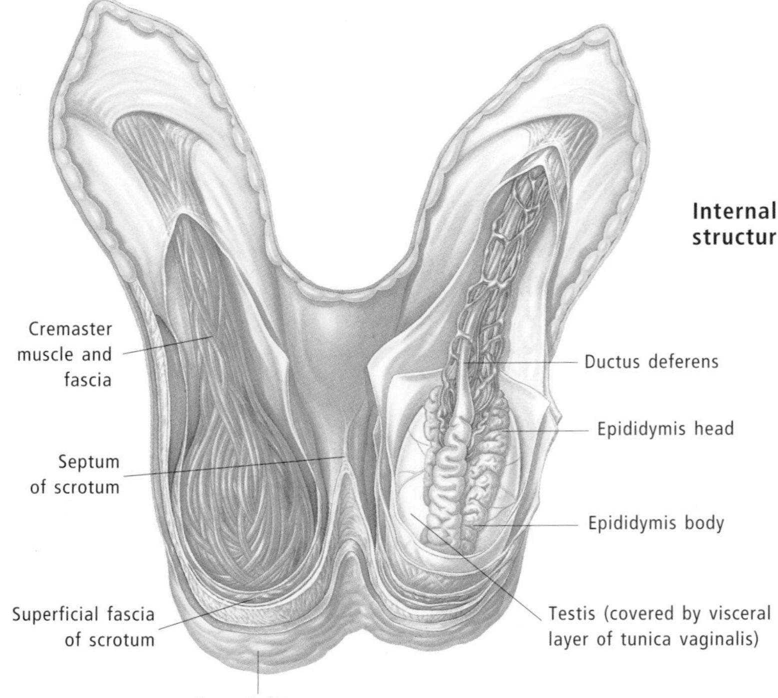

deformities of the rib cage, which in turn can result in heart and lung problems. Treatment may involve wearing a corrective back brace, the use of traction, exercise, a plaster cast or, in more severe cases, orthopedic surgery, in which a metal rod is inserted to support the spine.

SEE ALSO *Lordosis, Kyphosis, Spine*

SCROTUM

The scrotum is the bag of skin and soft tissue attached to the perineum in the male, hanging between the thighs. It contains the testes and the lower parts of the spermatic cords. Under the skin of the scrotum is a thin layer of muscle (dartos muscle), whose contractions make the skin of the scrotum wrinkle. The testes normally descend before or just after birth from the abdominal cavity, along the inguinal canal, and into the scrotum. In rare cases, the testes fail to descend into the scrotum. An inguinal hernia, particularly the indirect type, will often descend into the scrotum along the route taken by the testis and will need to be surgically corrected.

Several other conditions cause a lump in the scrotum besides an inguinal hernia. They include epididymitis (inflammation of the epididymis), tumors such as carcinoma of the testes, varicocele (a group of varicose veins in the scrotum), hematocele (a collection of blood within the scrotum) and a spermatocele (a cyst-like mass within the scrotum containing fluid and dead sperm cells).

A physician will often diagnose the lump with the help of an ultrasound of the scrotum, or a biopsy performed during surgery.

Treatment depends on the cause; most conditions can be easily treated and some such as hematoceles and spermatoceles do not need treatment. A scrotal support (jockstrap) may be worn to help relieve pain and discomfort.

It is a good idea for males to regularly self-examine each testis and the scrotum and consult a physician if a lump is found. A lump that is accompanied by sudden severe pain in a testis may be a sign of torsion of the testis, indicating that it has become twisted in the scrotum and is losing its blood supply. Urgent medical attention should be sought or the testicle may be damaged permanently.

SEE ALSO *Hernia, Reproductive systems, Testes*

SCRUB TYPHUS

Scrub typhus is an infectious disease which is caused by a microorganism called *Rickettsia tsutsugamushi*. It is transmitted from rodents to humans via the bite of mite larvae. The disease is most prevalent in eastern Asia, northern Australia and the western Pacific.

Symptoms occur suddenly between 1–3 weeks after a bite and can include severe headaches, fever, swollen and tender lymph nodes, muscle aches, eye pain and a rash. Often a dark-colored ulcer appears where the mite has attached to the skin.

There is no effective vaccine, however broad-spectrum antibiotics are effective against scrub typhus. In severe cases, serious complications such as pneumonia may occur if left untreated. Death from scrub typhus is rare.

SEE ALSO *Infectious diseases*

SCURVY

Scurvy is an illness caused by inadequate intake of vitamin C. This essential vitamin is needed by the body to make collagen, the connective tissue that helps form healthy bones, teeth and capillaries, and which is used also for wound healing.

In the late eighteenth century it was noted that scurvy in sailors was due to a dietary deficiency and could be cured by eating citrus fruits and vegetables. The disease now occurs mostly in infants or elderly people whose diets are poor, or in people following fad diets that do not include fruits and vegetables.

The symptoms of scurvy include bleeding gums, loss of teeth, rough skin, bleeding or bruising under the skin or into joints, weakness and fatigue, and mental changes.

Vitamin C deficiency can be fatal, but treatment with vitamin supplements will cure the condition. Scurvy is best prevented by ensuring the diet includes vitamin C-rich foods, such as citrus fruits (and/or their juices), tomatoes, and green vegetables, including peppers, broccoli and cabbage.

SEE ALSO *Diet, Nutrition, Vitamins*

SEA SICKNESS

Sea sickness, like other forms of motion sickness, occurs when the brain receives contrary signals about the body's state of balance and movement. Inside the cabin of a boat rolling on the ocean waves, for example, the inner ears detect the boat's movements but the eyes perceive no motion. The result is often sweating, headaches, fatigue, dizziness and vomiting. Like the motion sicknesses experienced in aircraft, cars and trains, sea sickness tends to be more common in children. For most adults it is a minor and occasional nuisance that occurs only in the roughest conditions. For some, however, it is an incapacitating experience that occurs on every boat ride.

Symptoms can be reduced by a range of over-the-counter medications. The syndrome can also be alleviated by taking a few simple measures to reduce the conflict between the body's balance and movement sensors. Sit on deck and stare at the horizon so the eyes register the same movements as the rest of the body. Sit towards the center of the vessel where the up-and-down motion is least. Avoid strongly flavored, spicy or greasy foods before embarking. Do not read while on board. Keep the body lightly and comfortably dressed, but not overheated or cold.

SEE ALSO *Balance, Motion sickness*

Scurvy

A lack of vitamin C in the diet can lead to bleeding gums and the loosening of teeth. Sufferers of scurvy bruise easily, and even simple wounds take a long time to heal.

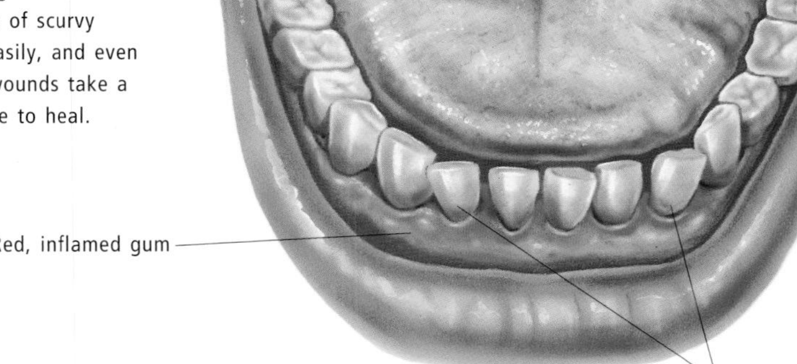
Red, inflamed gum
Discolored, loose teeth

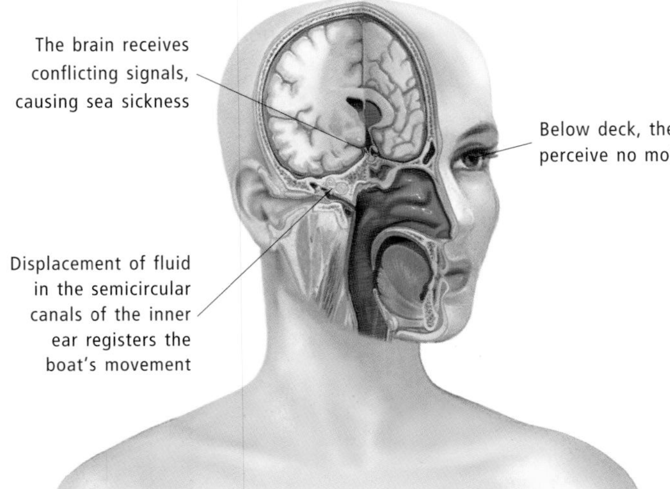
The brain receives conflicting signals, causing sea sickness
Below deck, the eyes perceive no motion
Displacement of fluid in the semicircular canals of the inner ear registers the boat's movement

Sea sickness

The motion of a boat disturbs fluid in the inner ear, stimulating nerve cells on the ampulla (the organ of balance). These nerve cells tell the brain that the body is moving. Below deck where the horizon cannot be seen, the eyes register no movement. These conflicting signals trigger feelings of nausea and dizziness.

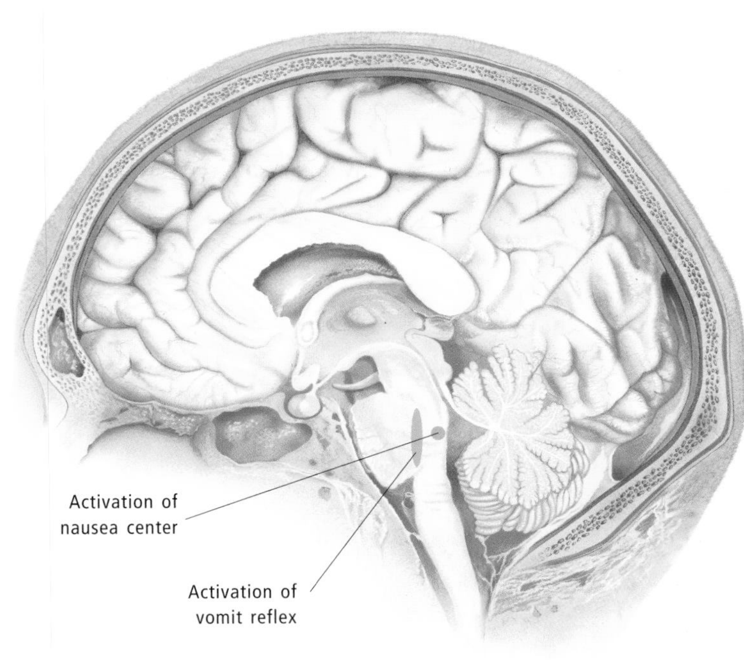
Activation of nausea center
Activation of vomit reflex

Nausea

Nausea centers in the brain are activated when messages received from the balance organs in the ear differ from those sent by the eyes.

S

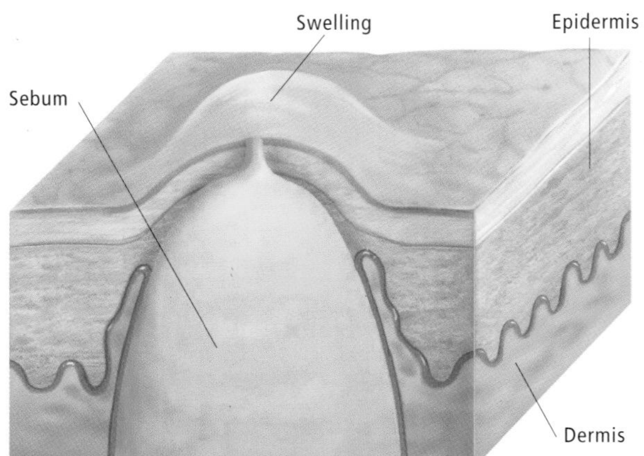

Sebaceous cyst

When a sebaceous gland becomes blocked it may fill with fatty material, forming a cyst.

SEASONAL AFFECTIVE DISORDER

Also known as winter depression, seasonal affective disorder (SAD) is caused by the lack of sunlight during the shorter days of autumn and winter. Sufferers feel gloomy, tired and irritable; however, their problems can often be relieved by light therapy. The condition is more common in the young than the old, and is seen in women more often than men.

SEE ALSO *Depression, Emotions, Light therapy, Sun exposure*

SEBACEOUS CYST

A sebaceous cyst, sometimes called an epidermal or pilar cyst, is a dome-shaped cyst just below, and attached to, the skin, containing semisolid sebum and keratin. They occur most commonly in adolescents and adults, appearing on the trunk, face, neck and scalp. Almost always benign, symptomless cysts can be left alone, but may need to be surgically removed if they are unsightly or become infected.

SEE ALSO *Keratin*

SEBACEOUS GLANDS

Sebaceous glands are skin glands which produce a fatty liquid called sebum. Sebum contains fatty acids and glycerides. Sebaceous glands are found in the lower layer of skin (the dermis) throughout the body surface, except on some hairless areas such as the soles of the feet and palms of hands. They are usually associated with hair follicles and often release their sebum along the hair shaft. In some areas of the body (for example, the lips, glans penis and clitoris), sebaceous glands release their oils directly to the skin surface. Sebum helps to minimize loss of water from the skin and to control the spread of bacteria and fungi.

Sebaceous glands are under hormonal control (testosterone in men, ovarian and adrenal androgens in women); this means that production of sebum increases after puberty. A disturbance in the normal production and flow of sebum is one of the causes of the development of acne.

SEE ALSO *Acne, Fats, Glands, Hormones*

SEBORRHEA

Seborrhea is a term covering a variety of common skin disorders that involve excessive production of sebum, the oily secretion of the sebaceous glands. Under normal circumstances sebum, which is composed mostly of keratin and fat, helps to protect the skin from drying. Too much can lead to either dry and scaly or overly oily skin.

SEE ALSO *Acne, Sebaceous glands, Skin*

SEBORRHEIC DERMATITIS

Seborrheic dermatitis is a patchy inflammation of the skin, characterized by greasy, oily, reddish areas of skin with white or yellowish flaking scales, which may appear on the skin of the scalp, eyebrows, nose, forehead, or ears. It is painless but may be mildly itchy.

Seborrheic dermatitis is a chronic condition which tends to run in families. Stress, fatigue, and cold weather make it worse, while it often improves in the summer.

In its mild form, seborrheic dermatitis causes dandruff and can be treated with

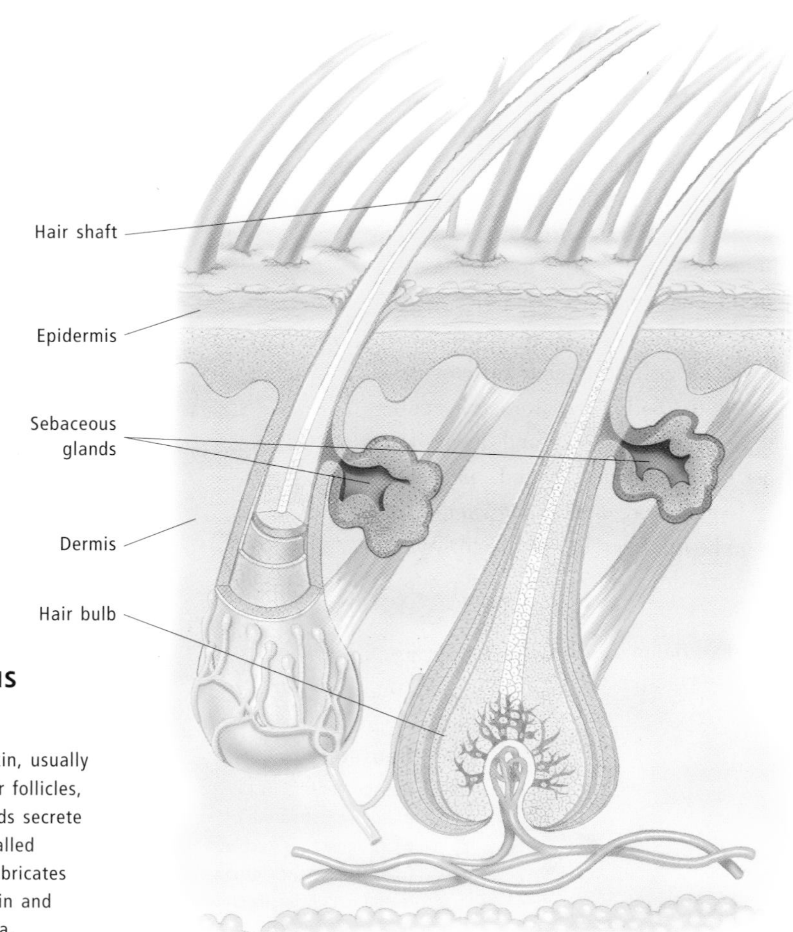

Sebaceous glands

Found in the skin, usually attached to hair follicles, sebaceous glands secrete a fatty liquid called sebum which lubricates the hair and skin and controls bacteria.

over-the-counter anti-dandruff lotions containing salicylic acid, coal tar, zinc, or selenium. The hair should be shampooed vigorously and frequently (once a day). Loosen scales with the fingers, scrub for at least 5 minutes, and rinse thoroughly.

More severe cases require treatment with shampoos or lotions containing selenium or ketaconazole, or corticosteroid creams or ointments applied directly to the scalp.

In newborns and small children up to the age of 3 years, seborrheic dermatitis appears as cradle cap. Thick, crusty, yellow scales appear over the child's scalp, on the eyelids and ears, around the nose, or in the groin.

Cradle cap can be treated with massaging of the scalp to loosen the scales, daily shampoos with mild soap, and brushing the hair several times a day. If cradle cap persists, consult a physician who may prescribe a cream or lotion to be applied to the scalp.

SEE ALSO ***Cradle cap, Dandruff, Dermatitis, Skin***

SEDATIVES

Sedatives are drugs which are prescribed to calm anxiety or mental disturbance, induce sleep or drowsiness and reduce the body's functional activity. Sedatives may also be prescribed for insomnia and epilepsy. They can be taken as tablets or by injection. Anxiety is often treated with sedative drugs because they relax muscles, thus reducing tension and allowing sleep to provide a temporary relief from symptoms. Travelers with a fear of flying or who suffer claustrophobia may use sedatives to reduce anxiety before and during a flight.

Common side effects include drowsiness, impaired judgement, lack of coordination, lowered heart rate and blood pressure, nausea and diarrhea, and dependence. More rarely sedatives produce memory defects, hallucinations, constipation, vomiting and headaches, and loss of consciousness. Sedatives should be taken only on prescription and under medical supervision, used only intermittently, and not taken in pregnancy.

Long-term use can lead to dependence, and stopping use should be a gradual process under medical supervision. All sedatives may interact with other similar drugs, such as anti-epilepsy, antidepressant and antipsychotic drugs, and especially alcohol, which increases the risk of side effects and overdose.

SEE ALSO ***Anxiety, Anxiolytics, Barbiturates, Drug dependence, Overdose, Sleeping pills***

Semicircular canals

Located in the inner ear, the semicircular canals contain the fluid-filled semicircular ducts, which provide our sense of balance.

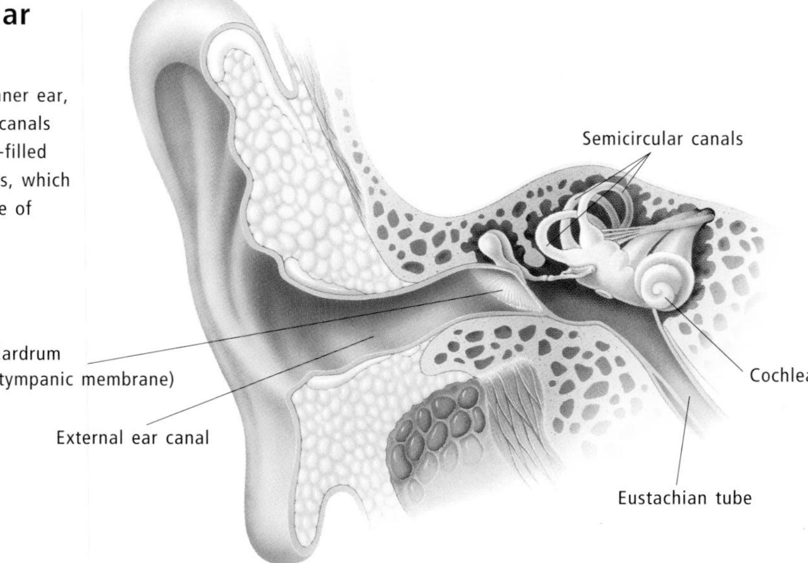

SEMEN

Also called seminal fluid, semen is a liquid that is emitted from the male reproductive tract. It comprises sperm cells and the fluids that nourish and support them. The fluids are produced and secreted by the various tubules and glands of the reproductive system, including the prostate gland and seminal vesicles. These ensure that the semen contains the correct concentration of nutrients and electrolytes needed to keep the sperm healthy. These nutrients include sugars, amino acids, phosphorus, potassium, and prostaglandin hormones. A small amount of mucus is also secreted into the semen by the bulbourethral and urethral glands. The secretions of the testes and other glands are controlled by the male hormone testosterone.

Semen contains millions of sperm cells, needed to fertilize female ova (eggs). Sperm cells are produced by the testes, stored in the epididymis, then transported down a muscular tube called the ductus deferens (or vas deferens).

During ejaculation, muscles around the epididymis and ductus deferens contract, forcing semen into the urethra. The fluid is then expelled out of the body by spasmodic contractions of the bulbocavernosus muscle in the penis.

When a man ejaculates, at the height of sexual excitation, he will normally discharge about $\frac{1}{20}$–$\frac{1}{5}$ ounce (1.5–5 milliliters) of semen from his urethra. Each ejaculation normally contains between 200 and 300 million sperm which comprise only about 2–5 percent of the ejaculate.

Semen analysis is usually carried out to assess a man's fertility—about one-third of infertility problems seen in couples are due to male problems. The semen must be tested within 2 hours of collection for a valid result. Low sperm counts or insufficient semen production may be the cause of infertility.

SEE ALSO ***Fertility, Infertility, Reproductive systems, Sperm***

SEMICIRCULAR CANALS

As well as being fundamental to hearing, the ears are also organs of balance. Head movements are detected deep inside the inner ear (labyrinth) by the semicircular ducts—three liquid-filled looped tubes in the bony semicircular canals arranged at right angles to each other. The end of each has a bulge (ampulla), containing sensory hairs which bend as the liquid in the canals moves. Nerve cells at the base of the hairs send signals to the brain about the head's movement. Each canal registers a slightly different movement: one detects the head nodding, another senses side-to-side shaking and the third perceives tilting.

SEE ALSO ***Balance, Ear***

SENSES

The senses are the faculties that enable individuals to perceive changes in their external and internal environments. These changes are detected by sense organs—specialized organs in the body consisting of receptors that can detect physical stimuli, such as light, heat, touch and sound. The organs change physical stimuli into nerve impulses

Sensory pathways

Sensory receptors provide information on conditions inside and outside of the body. When stimulated, they pass information along the peripheral nerves to the central nervous system, where the signals are recognized as a sensation.

Sensory cortex in the brain registers sensations and coordinates appropriate response

Spinal cord

Peripheral nerves pass sensations on to the central nervous system via the spinal cord.

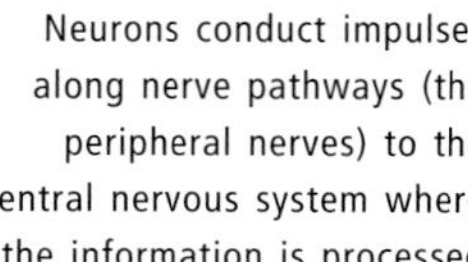

Neurons conduct impulses along nerve pathways (the peripheral nerves) to the central nervous system where the information is processed

Neuron

Nerve endings in the skin, muscles, joints and internal organs transmit signals of pain, temperature or pressure along peripheral nerves.

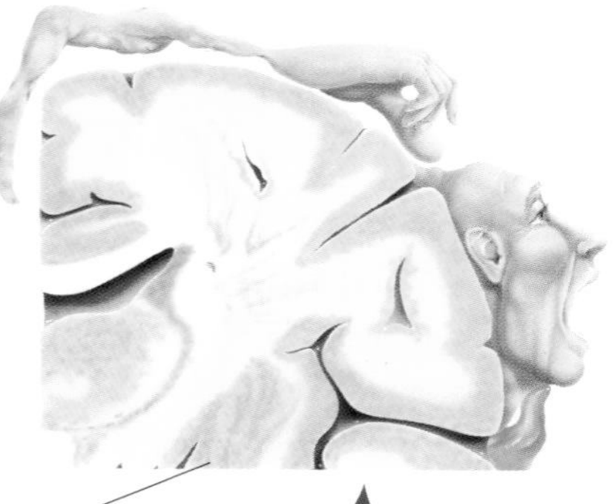

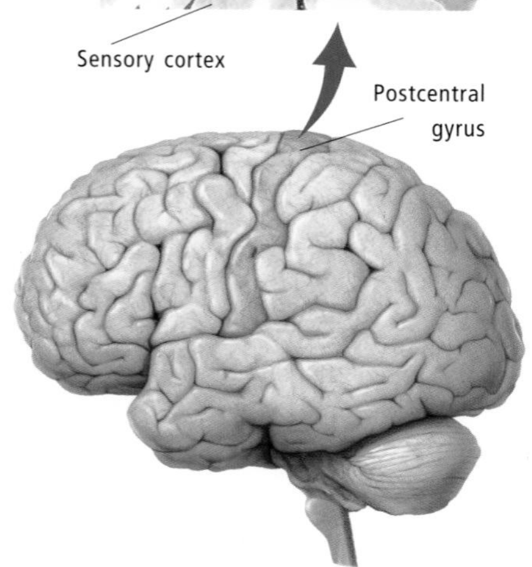

Processing centers

Sensory information from all over the body is processed in the somatic sensory cortex. Some parts of the body have a higher density of sensory receptors than others and send more information to this part of the brain. The number of nerve receptors in an organ (as opposed to its size) determines its share of the sensory cortex. This illustration, for example, shows that the lips take up an equivalent proportion of the cortex to the legs because of their greater sensitivity.

Body showing peripheral nerves

General senses

The general senses include temperature, pain, pressure, proprioception and vibration. The receptors for these sensations are distributed throughout the body. Some receptors provide information about the environment outside the body, some detect sensations in internal organs and tissues, others monitor the position and movement of joints, muscles and tendons.

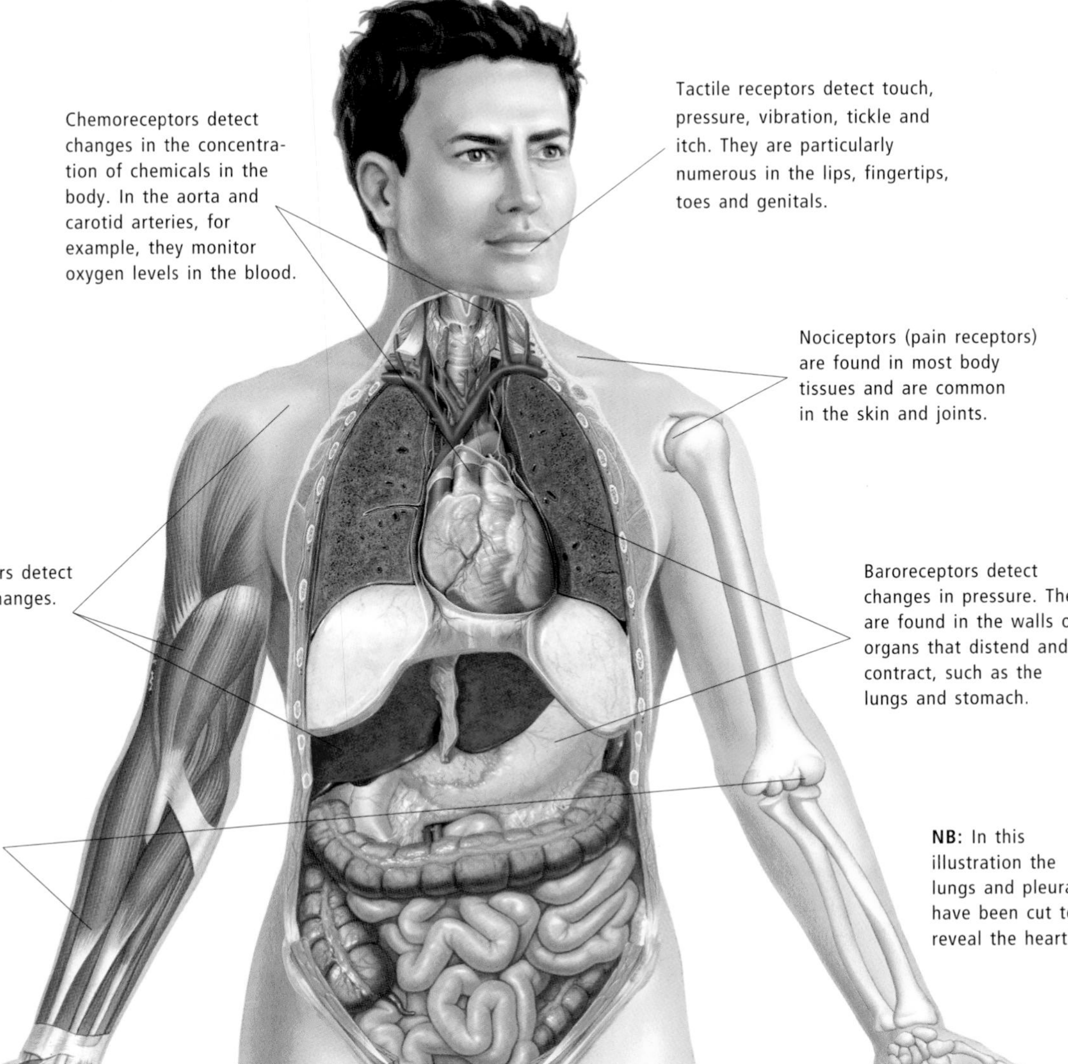

Chemoreceptors detect changes in the concentration of chemicals in the body. In the aorta and carotid arteries, for example, they monitor oxygen levels in the blood.
Tactile receptors detect touch, pressure, vibration, tickle and itch. They are particularly numerous in the lips, fingertips, toes and genitals.
Nociceptors (pain receptors) are found in most body tissues and are common in the skin and joints.
Thermoreceptors detect temperature changes.
Baroreceptors detect changes in pressure. They are found in the walls of organs that distend and contract, such as the lungs and stomach.
Proprioceptors provide information on the position and movement of joints, tendons and muscles.
NB: In this illustration the lungs and pleura have been cut to reveal the heart.

Senses

Special senses

The special senses are smell, taste, hearing, sight, and equilibrium (balance). All the special sense organs are found in the head and nerve impulses from these organs travel to the brain via the cranial nerves.

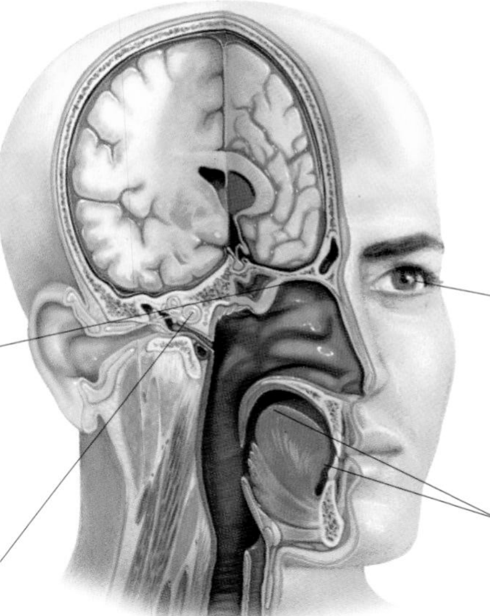

Smell

Chemoreceptors on tiny hairs in the nasal cavity send signals to olfactory areas at the base of the brain where they are interpreted as smell.

Hearing

Hair cell mechanoreceptors in the inner ear send signals along the vestibulocochlear nerve. This provides the brain with information on sound and balance.

Sight

Signals from light-sensitive photoreceptors in the eyes pass along the optic nerve, then to the occipital cortex in the brain where visual information is processed.

Taste

Taste buds (chemoreceptors) on the tongue, palate and throat send information on salty, sweet, sour and bitter flavors along the cranial nerves to the brain where the taste is recognized.

and send these impulses along sensory nerve pathways to the brain where they are interpreted as sensations.

The senses are commonly divided into general senses and special senses.

General senses include touch, pressure, vibration, proprioception, stretch, pain, heat and cold. The receptors for these senses are distributed widely throughout the body. They are nerve endings, most of which are covered by a capsule of connective tissue.

The special senses include olfaction (smell), vision, taste, hearing and equilibrium (balance). The receptors for these senses are found in very localized areas of the body and are more complex.

Receptors are often classified according to the type of stimulus they can detect. For example, sight is detected by photoreceptors; touch, sound and equilibrium are detected by mechanoreceptors; smell and taste by chemoreceptors; heat and cold by thermoreceptors; and pain by nociceptors.

General senses

Many of the receptors of the general senses are found in the skin. Tactile receptors are mechanoreceptors, which can detect touch, pressure, vibration, tickle and itch. There are at least six different types of tactile receptors found in the skin, including Ruffini endings, Meissner's corpuscles, Krause's end bulbs, Pacinian corpuscles, and Merkel's disks.

Tactile receptors are particularly numerous in certain areas such as lips, fingertips, palms, toes, nipples, the glans of the penis and the clitoris. When a stimulus, such as a pinprick or vibration, is applied to one of these receptors, it generates a nerve impulse, which then travels along a sensory (or afferent) nerve to the spinal cord. The stimulus then travels up the spinal cord along special pathways through the thalamus to the cerebral cortex, where it reaches consciousness as a vibration, pinprick or other sensation according to the nature of the original stimulus and the brain's general level of consciousness at the time.

Other types of receptors found in skin include thermoreceptors and nociceptors.

Other general sensory receptors are found deep in the tissues of muscles, tendons and joints.

Proprioceptors give rise to sensations of weight, position of the body, movements of body parts such as limbs, and the position of various joints. Proprioceptors include muscle spindles, Golgi tendon organs and joint receptors. These receptors provide the body with the sensory information needed to coordinate muscle movements and maintain body position. Most of the information from proprioceptors does not reach consciousness.

Thermoreceptors (receptors that detect changes in temperature) are widely distributed in the body. Separate thermoreceptors detect heat and cold and can detect wide variations in temperature, ranging from freezing cold to burning hot. They are especially numerous in the skin around the lips, mouth and anus.

Nociceptors (pain receptors) are also found in most tissues of the body. They may detect somatic pain (from the skin, muscles, tendons or joints) or visceral pain (from the internal organs of the body).

These receptors respond to chemicals released by damaged cells, by high temperatures, by stretched muscle fibers and other stimuli.

The nerves carrying the impulses from visceral nociceptors may enter the spinal cord at the same place as nerves from a different and separate area of skin on the surface of the body. Pain is often felt in the skin area rather than in the affected organ; this is known as referred pain. Some nociceptors, known as "silent" nociceptors, do not respond to intense stimuli unless they are sensitized by chemicals released by cells in inflamed tissue.

Special senses

The special senses are smell, vision, taste, hearing and equilibrium (balance). The special sense organs are all found in the head and the impulses from these organs travel to the brain via the cranial nerves.

The receptors for smell are found in the nasal cavity. Substances suspended in air enter the nasal cavity and react with tiny receptors on olfactory hairs in the nasal cavity. The receptors generate impulses that are transmitted via the olfactory nerve to specialized areas at the base of the brain where they are interpreted as odors. The olfactory receptors can detect thousands of different odors.

On the tongue and parts of the palate and throat are the taste buds, located in cuplike structures called papillae on the tongue, palate and throat. Receptors on the tongue are more sensitive to sweet and salty stimuli, while those on the palate and throat respond more readily to sour and bitter ones. When combined with substances dissolved in saliva, the taste buds generate impulses that travel along the facial, glossopharyngeal and vagus nerves and eventually to the cerebral cortex. The sensation of taste is complemented by that of smell; about 80 percent of the sensation of taste is actually due to smell.

The sense organs for vision are the eyes. Light enters the eye and strikes the retina at the back of the eyeball, where special photoreceptors called cones and rods convert the image to electrical impulses. These travel via the optic nerves to the occipital cortex and other parts of the brain where they are experienced as vision.

The sense organs for hearing are the ears, a pair of complex organs housed in the temporal bones of the skull. In the cochlea, the ear converts sound waves into mechanical waves and then into electrical impulses. These impulses travel via the cochlear part of the vestibular-cochlear nerve to the brain's cerebral cortex to be interpreted as sound.

Also in the ear are the organs concerned with the sense of balance, or equilibrium. These organs are known as the vestibular system and consist of the semicircular canals and the utricle and saccule of the vestibule of the inner ear. They detect changes in the body's position and relay this information via the vestibular part of the vestibulocochlear nerve to the brain.

If a person is deprived of one or more special senses, other senses will often become sharper. For example, if people lose their sight their sense of hearing may become more acute, or they may develop a heightened sense of touch.

SEE ALSO *Balance, Ear, Eye, Hearing, Mouth, Nervous system, Nose, Olfactory system, Pain, Proprioception, Sight, Skin, Smell, Spinal cord, Taste, Temperature, Tongue, Touch*

S

SEPARATION ANXIETY

Separation anxiety, the feeling of distress that comes from being separated from a loved one, most often occurs in children. From about the age of 8–9 months, many babies become upset when their parents or important carers go out of sight. This is particularly common in children who spend their time with one primary carer. It can also be a problem with babies who have been left to "cry it out". At 12 months of age many children will be able to wave goodbye but still may become distressed or miserable until distracted or occupied in play.

When children are older they learn that their carers will come back eventually. Separation can create unhappiness at any age, but for most people is a short-lived source of anxiety.

If a deeper sense of insecurity exists, children will display symptoms even after the apparent causes are resolved. These can include persistent crying or irritability, poor appetite, sleeplessness, pains or compulsive behavior. These signs should not be ignored, particularly if there is an obvious possible trigger for the distress.

Support and reassurance can help to resolve the problem. It is important to recognize the anxiety and remove any obvious causes. If the problem cannot be resolved quickly, seek expert advice.

SEE ALSO *Infancy, Childhood*

SEPTICEMIA

Septicemia (commonly called blood poisoning) is an infection of the bloodstream, which can occur directly or as a complication of infection at another site. It is a serious illness resulting in high fever and often violent shaking, called rigors. Infective organisms are more likely to gain access to the blood in people with decreased immunity or in hospitalized patients with intravenous catheters or undergoing invasive procedures. The effects of septicemia are due to the combination of bacterial toxins and the body's immune response to the infection. The elderly may fail to mount a high fever.

Treatment is with prompt introduction of intravenous antibiotics and supportive therapy in hospital.

SEE ALSO *Bacteria, Infectious diseases*

Serotonin

Serotonin is one of the key neurotransmitters in the limbic system, a collection of neural centers and tracts in the cerebrum, thalamus and hypothalamus that are involved in regulating mood and alertness levels. Low levels of serotonin have been linked to depression.

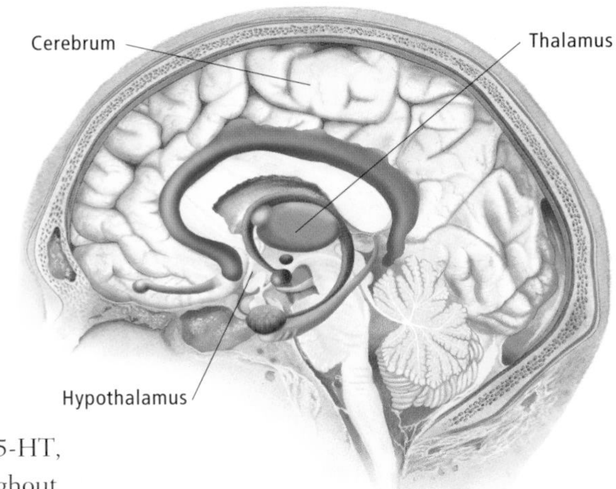

SEROTONIN

Also called 5-hydroxytryptamine or 5-HT, serotonin is a chemical found throughout the plant and animal kingdoms. In the human body it is synthesized from the amino acid tryptophan (found in many foods) and has various roles. It stimulates muscle contractions in the intestine and blood clotting at the site of wounds. Blood vessels constrict when serotonin levels rise and dilate when levels fall.

Migraine pain is thought to be caused partly by blood vessels in the brain dilating due to low serotonin levels.

Serotonin also works in the brain as a neurotransmitter responsible for regulating moods. Low levels are thought to trigger depression. The serotonin-specific reuptake inhibitor group of antidepressants help the brain optimize limited amounts of serotonin.

SEE ALSO *Amino acids, Antidepressants, Depression, Migraine*

SERUM SICKNESS

Serum is the part of the blood that contains antibodies. If you are exposed to a dangerous toxin or microorganism against which you have no antibodies, treatment sometimes involves an antiserum injection. This is produced from the serum of another person or animal already exposed to the offending toxin or microorganism; the serum contains the relevant antibodies to temporarily boost your immunity until you can develop your own antibodies.

Serum sickness is a type of allergic reaction to antiserum that can develop 2–3 weeks after having an antiserum injection. Symptoms include an itchy skin rash, joint stiffness and fever. Patients usually recover fully within weeks. Treatment often involves antihistamines and corticosteroids.

SEE ALSO *Allergies, Antibodies*

SEX

Sex is the sum of anatomical and physiological features which divides the members of a species into two groups that complement each other—male and female. In humans the two sexes, sexuality and sexual intercourse are all interwoven with the propagation and survival of the species, although each can also stand apart.

Sex is determined genetically at conception when the X chromosome from the ovum is paired with an X or Y chromosome from the sperm. An XX pairing leads to a genetic female, an XY pairing to a genetic male. Other genetic elements, as yet poorly understood, may modify the expression of the basic genetic coding.

SEE ALSO *Chromosomes, Genes, Sexual intercourse, Sexuality*

SEX EDUCATION

Sexual feelings are present from birth and sex education begins in the family situation from that moment. Baby boys can have erections and both girls and boys will get pleasure from their sexual organs. Some time before their first birthday children have usually discovered their genitals and may enjoy playing with them—it is quite natural.

By the time children reach the age of 3 or 4 they will be aware that the other sex has different genitals and be interested in looking at the human body, usually without any feelings of coyness. By this age most children are also curious about where babies come from, and are interested in body processes, but do not usually understand sexual intercourse. They will ask questions which need to be answered at their level of understanding.

Sexual organs

During sex, the man's penis penetrates the vagina, delivering sperm which travel up the cervical canal to the fallopian tubes. Eggs released by the ovaries are fertilized by incoming sperm.

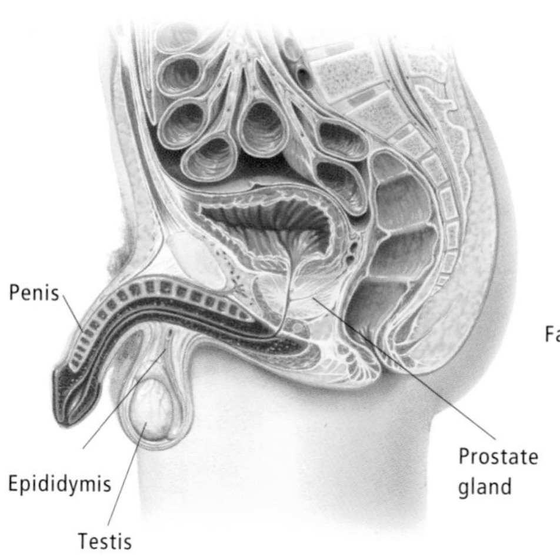

Male reproductive organs

The organs and glands of the male reproductive system are specially designed to produce sperm and deliver them to a woman's reproductive organs through sexual intercourse. Sperm are produced and mature in the testes. During sex they are ejaculated by the penis.

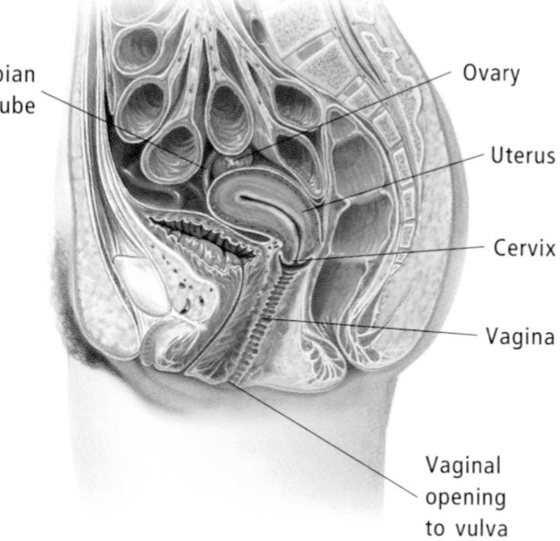

Female reproductive organs

The female reproductive system consists of the the outer genitals—the vulva—and internal parts—the ovaries, fallopian tubes, uterus and vagina.

Sex hormones and behavior

The hypothalamus and pituitary gland in the brain, together with the adrenal glands, stimulate the gonads—testes in men and ovaries in women—to produce testosterone and estrogen. The release of these hormones modulates sexual appetite and activity.

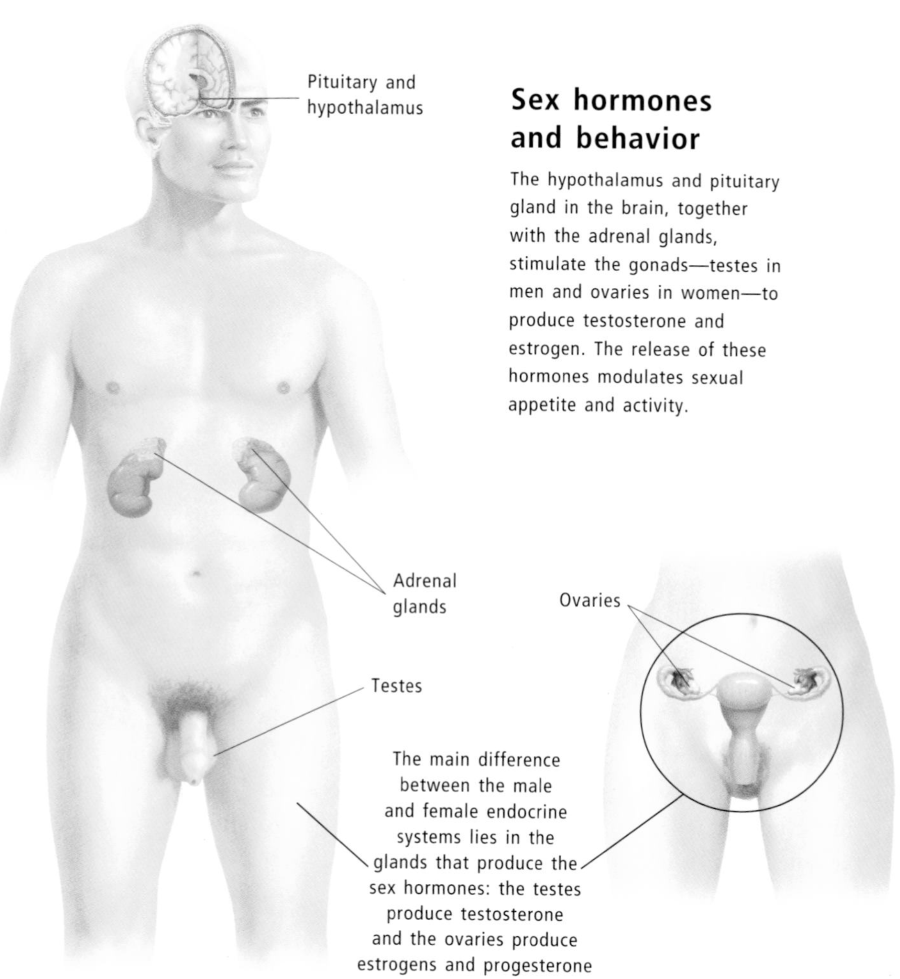

The main difference between the male and female endocrine systems lies in the glands that produce the sex hormones: the testes produce testosterone and the ovaries produce estrogens and progesterone

By the age of about 5 or 6, children become more aware of sexuality and social restraints. Children who can talk to their parents or carers about their bodies, who know the right names for the sexual parts, and who are in a loving environment, will generally grow up with a healthy attitude to sex.

Inappropriate attitudes to sex may indicate sexual abuse. Children who know more about sex than you would expect for their age, have unexplained injuries to the genitals, force other children to play sex games, talk about sex a great deal, draw sexual parts frequently, and show signs of stress or anxiety, may have been abused.

Knowledge about sexual behavior, about sexually transmitted diseases and pregnancy is important as adolescents reach the age when they are ready for a sexual relationship. Societies which provide medically accurate sex education as part of the education of their children, encourage adolescents to make responsible decisions about their sexual relationships, and provide easy access to contraception and reproductive health care, have lower rates of teenage pregnancy.

Formal sex education includes scientific information on human sexual physiology, reproduction and cultural attitudes.

SEE ALSO *Sexual behavior, Sexual intercourse, Sexuality*

SEX THERAPY

Sex therapy is a form of behavior modification or psychotherapy which endeavors to solve difficulties with sexual relationships, based on techniques pioneered by William Masters and Virginia Johnson in the 1960s. It may be done individually, as a couple or in a group. A trained counselor may use exercises and therapy to treat impotence (erectile dysfunction), rapid or inhibited ejaculation, orgasmic difficulties in women and men (anorgasmia), problems with sexual desire or dissatisfaction with sex.

Both physical and psychological issues must be addressed. If a physical problem is suspected, treatment from the appropriate specialist, such as a urologist, gynecologist or endocrinologist, is important.

SEE ALSO *Behavior therapy, Impotence, Premature ejaculation, Psychotherapy, Sexual dysfunction*

SEXUAL BEHAVIOR

Sexual behavior is any activity that leads to sexual arousal; it may be solo, between two people or in a group. The sexual appetite begins in the brain in the hypothalamus which, together with the adrenal glands, is responsible for stimulating the gonads to produce estrogen and testosterone. These hormones combine with other factors to initiate sexual activity. In many societies, romantic love is associated with the sexual act.

The contraceptive pill and the freedom it brought from the risk of an unwanted pregnancy led to a revolution in sexual behavior in many societies in the 1960s, leading to sex being seen as a recreational activity. Greater freedom has resulted in a wider knowledge and understanding of sexuality and sexual intercourse.

Women's role in these changes has been crucial, though there are still marked differences between cultures. In many industrialized societies women's attitudes have become more permissive over the past 40 years, and many girls are experimenting with sex earlier in life. Many women are also taking control of their own fertility and planning their families to fit in with other life goals.

Human sexual behavior can be divided into heterosexuality (a sexual relationship between a man and woman), homosexuality (a sexual relationship between people of the same sex) and bisexuality (sexual relationships with both sexes).

Heterosexuality is everywhere accepted as the norm, and other forms of sexuality are not accepted in many societies.

Male-to-male sexual techniques include voyeurism, mutual masturbation, kissing, body rubbing to orgasm, fellatio (oral–penile sex) and sodomy (penile–anal sex).

Female-to-female relationships (also known as lesbianism) involve sexual techniques including foreplay, body rubbing, kissing, licking, clitoral stimulation, oral sex, digital vaginal penetration, the use of both vibrators and dildos (artificial penises).

Heterosexual relationships may involve any of these practices, as well as penile–vaginal penetration.

Bisexuality is more prevalent in some cultures than others and is thought to be more prevalent in men than women. Transsexualism is seen in people who are biologically one gender but identify with the opposite.

Social taboos have made the study of sexual behavior in industrialized countries difficult. Much of the recent information available comes from the Institute for Sex Research (also known as the Kinsey Institute) and from research in Sweden.

SEE ALSO *Bisexuality, Brain, Contraception, Homosexuality, Hypothalamus, Masturbation, Sexuality, Transsexualism*

SEXUAL DISORDERS

Sexual disorders or paraphilias, a preference for unusual sexual practices, include hypersexuality, divided into satyriasis, an uncontrollable, obsessive craving by men for sex, and nymphomania, an abnormally high sex drive in women.

Other sexual disorders include exhibitionism, that is, exposing genitals to unsuspecting strangers; fetishism, sexual fantasies involving material objects; masochism, abuse or humiliation used to raise sexual excitement; necrophilia, sexual arousal induced by contact with dead bodies; pedophilia, sexual activities with children; sadism, sexual excitement achieved by physical or psychological acts of cruelty; voyeurism, observing unsuspecting people in sexual acts; and zoophilia, using an animal for sex.

SEXUAL DYSFUNCTION

Not easy to define, a sexual dysfunction could be said to be any condition which results in dissatisfaction with performance, sensation or satisfaction during any part of a sexual interaction. Men and women perceive sexual dysfunction differently, men tending to see it as associated with physical problems whereas women understand it as associated with relationship problems. Sexual dysfunctions include the following.

Anorgasmia is the inability to experience orgasm, either during sexual intercourse or sexual activity with a partner or during masturbation; this is mostly a female problem, although men may also suffer. It was originally termed frigidity. Sex therapists have discovered that the problem is mostly due to a lack of sexual knowledge or to religious or social prohibitions that have prevented the development of a sexual awareness through masturbation.

Dyspareunia or painful or difficult sexual intercourse in women is most commonly caused by insufficient arousal and lubrication of the vagina prior to penetration. Spending time in foreplay and ensuring that the woman is aroused will usually resolve the problem. Inflammation or irritation of the vulva can also cause dyspareunia and intercourse is best avoided until the condition is resolved. Pain during deep penile thrusting can be due to endometriosis; cervical infections or other infections surrounding the uterus, tubes or pelvic organs; or abdominal surgery. Vaginal dryness, often a problem for women after menopause, can usually be solved by hormone replacement therapy.

Impotence or problems with erection is one of the most common worries for men. Where impotence is due to lack of libido, the solution is often the same as for women who suffer anorgasmia (see above). Damage to the blood vessels to the penis may cause impotence; heart problems, smoking, diabetes, trauma and radiation may also cause impotence, as may the drugs used to treat these conditions.

Libido problems include the absence, temporary loss or reduction of libido and can cause sexual difficulties. Natural differences in libido can create tensions in relationships, despite romantic love. Stress, fatigue and negative feelings about a partner can be the cause of temporary loss of libido which will return when, and if, the problems are solved. (As with anorgasmia, this was previously called frigidity in women.) Some medications can also be responsible for reduced libido.

Male "menopause" is considered by some medical authorities to be an emotionally triggered mid-life crisis, while others believe it is a physical condition resulting from changing hormone levels, in particular of testosterone.

Orgasm problems. Orgasm may not always be reached during sexual intercourse, a source of concern for many women. It should be remembered, however, that orgasm can result from any sexual activity—it does not have to be sparked by sexual intercourse. Understanding and wanting sexual intercourse, a sympathetic and caring partner

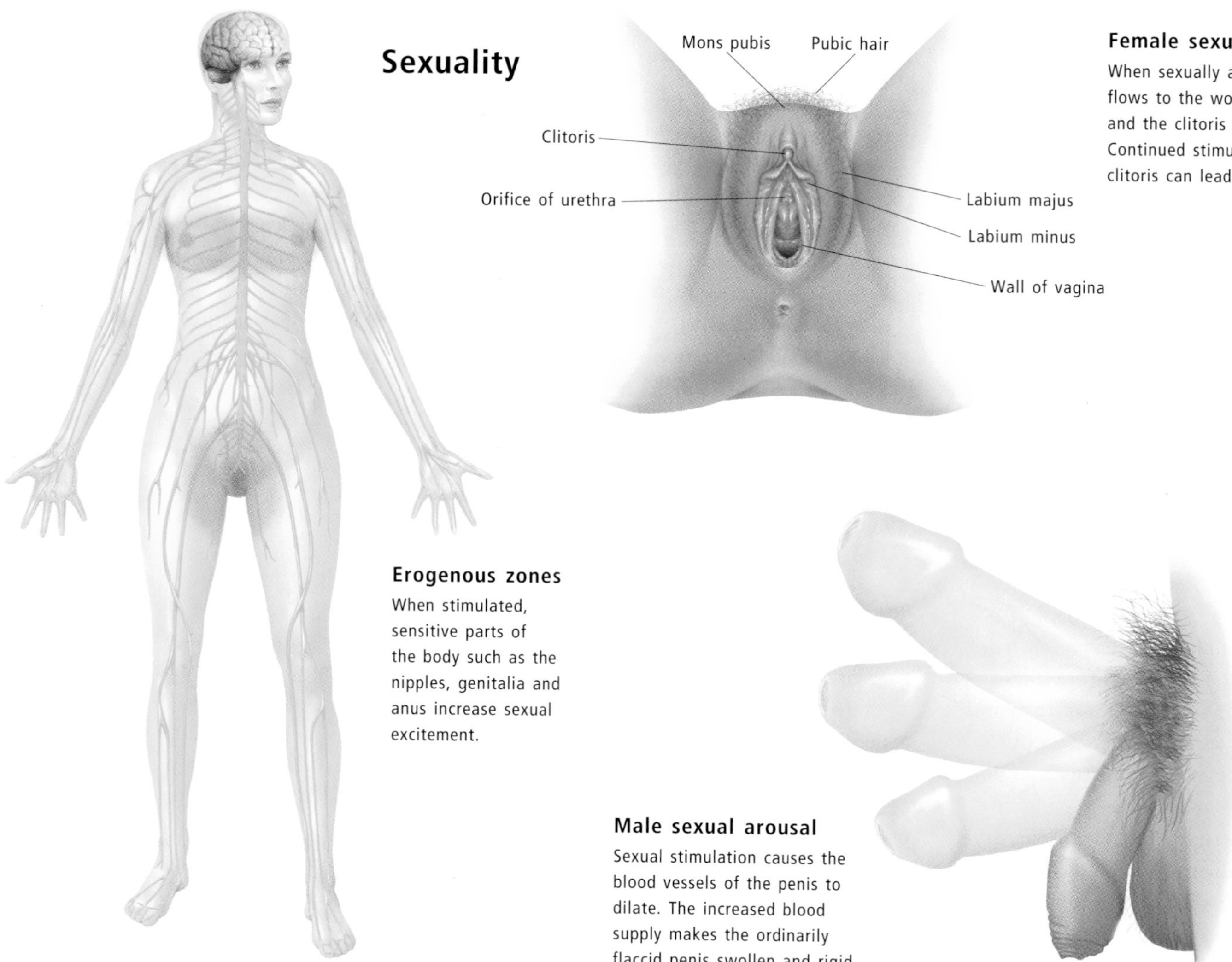

Female sexual arousal
When sexually aroused, blood flows to the woman's vulva and the clitoris becomes firm. Continued stimulation of the clitoris can lead to orgasm.

Erogenous zones
When stimulated, sensitive parts of the body such as the nipples, genitalia and anus increase sexual excitement.

Male sexual arousal
Sexual stimulation causes the blood vessels of the penis to dilate. The increased blood supply makes the ordinarily flaccid penis swollen and rigid.

who understands the need for foreplay, and experimenting with positions can help to solve this concern. Men can also have problems with orgasm, for similar reasons.

Premature ejaculation occurs when a man cannot delay orgasm or has a partial orgasm and ejaculation before he and his partner are ready. The cause can be any one of a number of psychological and physical reasons. Premature ejaculation can usually be solved with sexual therapy and a cooperative partner.

Retarded ejaculation occurs when a man cannot achieve orgasm. Similarly to premature ejaculation, it is accompanied by emotional and physical frustration, discomfort and loss of interest in sexual intercourse. Consultation with a sex therapist and an understanding partner will usually solve the problem.

Sexual headache is a relatively rare but extremely painful phenomenon. It affects four times as many men as women. It usually starts at the beginning of sexual intercourse and intensifies during orgasm and is thought to be related to tension in the head, face and neck muscles. About one in four sufferers also suffer from migraines. Drug therapy is available.

Vaginismus is involuntary spasm of the muscles round the entrance of the vagina which causes pain as soon as sex begins. A vaginal examination can also trigger this problem. An overwhelming fear of sex, often after a traumatic or violent sexual experience, is usually the cause. Sex therapy can help, although treatment is often long term.

SEE ALSO *Hormone replacement therapy, Hormones, Impotence, Menopause, Premature ejaculation, Sexual behavior, Sexual intercourse, Vaginismus*

SEXUAL INTERCOURSE

Sexual intercourse, or coitus, is the union between a male and female whereby the woman is penetrated by the man's penis, usually resulting in ejaculation. It may also be defined more widely as any sexual contact between two individuals involving stimulation of the genitals of at least one of them. Using the first definition, sexual intercourse is an integral part of the reproductive process and basic to the existence of the human species (forgetting the development of technologies that allow reproduction without sexual intercourse).

Normal sexual intercourse begins with foreplay, when a couple arouse each other sexually by caressing, kissing and stimulation, preparing their bodies for sexual intercourse. Arousal increases blood supply into the penis, causing it to extend and become erect. It also increases blood flow to the woman's vulva and vagina, which becomes coated with a lubricating mucus; the clitoris becomes erect and the nipples more sensitive.

When the woman is ready for penetration the penis enters the vagina. The man, and often the woman, will usually experience orgasm during intercourse, not necessarily at the same time. The man usually experiences orgasm as he ejaculates. After ejaculation the penis becomes limp. After intercourse the bodies of both man and woman will return to normal, although it usually takes the woman's body longer.

Anal intercourse, in which the penis is inserted via the anus into the rectum of the other person, is occasionally used by heterosexual couples, but more frequently in homosexual relationships. As the anus is not designed to accommodate a thrusting penis, damage is more likely than in vaginal sex. There is also the possibility of infectious bacteria adhering to the penis after anal intercourse, thus hygiene is important. As autoimmune deficiency syndrome (AIDS) can be transmitted by unprotected anal intercourse (among other ways), a condom should always be used.

Oral sex is the term used to describe mouth and genital contact. It has been part of sexual activity for centuries, being depicted in ancient Indian and carvings and in the *Kama Sutra*, a famous Hindu love and sex manual from the second century BC.

Contraceptives can be used to prevent unwanted pregnancy and to protect both parties against sexually transmitted diseases.

SEE ALSO ***Contraception, Reproductive systems, Sexual behavior, Sexually transmitted diseases***

SEXUALITY

A person's sexuality results from the combination of sexual attributes, behavior and tendencies. Sexual feelings are present from birth, and continue right through life.

Sexual desire is influenced by many factors and its intensity may fluctuate greatly over a lifetime. For women, sexual desire may be influenced by changes in hormone levels at different life stages (such as menopause), changes in roles and responsibilities, whether child-rearing or work outside the home, and economic and relationship factors. Men experience less fluctuation in hormone levels, but sexual desire and arousal is affected by many factors including economic problems, stress, work pressure and family situation.

Sexual feelings continue to be present as people age. Although sexual arousal may occur less often and men may find that erections are not as strong or as frequent, and women may suffer problems such as vaginal dryness, the need for, and the rewards from, an active sex life continues for many people to the end of their lives. Passing the menopause gives many women a greater sense of sexual freedom.

Sexual feelings are also important to people who suffer from physical and mental disabilities. Physically disabled or challenged people have a normal need for sexual expression and often the ability to participate in a sexual relationship is only limited by the nature of their disability. Paraplegia, however, can affect sexual function severely. While a woman's fertility is often restored when menstruation returns after spinal cord injury, anorgasmia is common. Men may suffer impotence, which can be solved with the use of external mechanical devices, but orgasm, ejaculation and the quality of sperm are usually affected and involuntary muscle spasms may be a problem.

Sexual relationships in the emotionally or intellectually disabled pose a problem for society when people are not capable of caring for a child without support. There is no easy solution to the ethical dilemmas created by such situations and the issues continue to be debated in most societies.

SEE ALSO ***Sexual behavior, Sexual dysfunction, Sexual intercourse***

SEXUALLY TRANSMITTED DISEASES

A sexually transmitted disease (STD) is any disease transmitted from one person to another through sexual contact. Such diseases may also be transferred from mother to child before, during, or immediately after birth, or through kissing, tainted blood transfusions or the use of unsterilized hypodermic syringes. The diseases may be bacterial, viral or parasitic in origin. STDs have been around for all of recorded history and up until the end of the twentieth century they were known as venereal diseases.

The annual rates of reported new cases of STDs in the USA are the highest of any country in the industrialised world, higher than in some developing countries. *Chlamydia* is the most frequently reported infectious disease in the country.

Bacterial diseases

Bacterial STDs include the following.

Chlamydia is caused by the bacterial parasite *Chlamydia trachomatis*. It has been linked with pelvic inflammatory disease, ectopic pregnancy, premature birth, and infections causing conjunctivitis or pneumonia in babies.

Bacterial disease

Chlamydia is a bacterial infection that can be treated with antibiotics. If it is not treated, it can cause sterility in both men and women.

Sexually transmitted diseases

Viral disease

Herpes is a viral disease, and as such cannot be cured. Therefore, individuals infected with herpes often suffer repeat attacks of symptoms, such as blisters on the genital area, throughout their lives.

Chancroid (or soft chancre) is an STD most common in tropical regions and often associated with HIV transmission. Shallow painful ulcers appear in the infected area, usually the genitals, 3–5 days after exposure by sexual contact. They are caused by the bacterium *Haemophilus ducreyi* and can be mistaken for the first symptoms of syphilis; localized swelling and inflammation of lymph glands follow the ulcers.

Gonorrhea is caused by the bacterium *Neisseria gonorrhoeae*. It mainly affects people aged 15–30 and is highly contagious. Many people have no symptoms. Men may have a pus-like discharge from the penis and pain on urinating. In women there may be a yellowish, smelly vaginal discharge and pain on urinating. The infection can spread into the body, causing arthritic pains and high temperatures; untreated, it can result in infertility, miscarriage or premature birth.

Granuloma inguinale (also known as donovaniasis) is characterized by deep, purulent ulcers on or near the genitals. Common in subtropical and tropical areas, and often occurring with syphilis or gonorrhea, it is not as infectious as some of the other STDs.

Lymphogranuloma venereum (LGV) is an infection of the lymph vessels and lymph nodes, caused by the same organism as chlamydia. Swollen lymph nodes, ulcers, enlargement of the genitals and rectal stricture are symptoms of the disease, relatively common in subtropical and tropical areas. Fevers and joint pains often occur.

Syphilis, a serious disease caused by the spirochete *Treponoma pallidum*, progresses through three stages, each separated by months and even years. It begins with a lesion—a painless, circular chancre which may appear on the lips, mouth, tongue, nipple, rectum or genitalia; nearby lymph nodes may enlarge but are not painful. The chancre heals and weeks or months later the secondary symptoms appear, caused by microbes spreading to every organ and tissue in the body. Non-painful skin rashes appear and disappear, sometimes in association with fever, headache and hair loss. Tertiary lesions, appearing years later, can destroy normal skin, bone and joints by ulceration. Tertiary syphilis also attacks the nervous system.

S

Viral diseases

Viral STDs include the following.

AIDS, caused by the human immunodeficiency virus (HIV), is transferred via body fluids and blood. The virus invades and multiplies within the lymphocytes (cells essential to the immune system) until it eventually destroys them. The body fluids that can pass the virus to another person are blood (including menstrual blood), semen, fluid from the vagina and cervix, and breast milk. HIV can also be spread by intravenous (IV) drug use with shared needles.

Hepatitis B (HBV) is spread through blood transfusions, IV drug use with shared needles, unprotected sexual intercourse or sharp instruments which break the skin. The virus remains in the body for many years. It can become chronic and lead to permanent liver damage through cirrhosis or cancer. Symptoms appear between 40 days to 6 months after exposure, and include fatigue, abdominal pain, loss of appetite, nausea, diarrhea, dark urine and jaundice. Treatment is bed rest. Babies born to a mother with HBV have up to a 95 percent chance of being infected. A vaccine that provides protection for at least 5 years is available.

Genital herpes is caused by one of the family of herpes viruses—Type II mainly affects the genital area. It can be spread to the mouth via oral sex. A temperature, mild headache, swollen lymph glands, small blisters on the genitals and vaginal discharge are common symptoms.

Molluscum contagiosum, contagious lumps caused by a type of pox virus, usually have a tiny dimple in the middle, are pinkish and itchy but not painful. They can be spread by close skin contact but in adults are usually transmitted sexually.

Genital warts are caused by the human papilloma virus (HPV). Reddish soft swellings that grow rapidly, they flourish in the genital area, the foreskin, the cervix and vulva being common sites. Warts can be painful during sexual intercourse. Women with genital warts should have regular gynecological checkups, including a Pap smear.

Parasitic diseases

Parasitic STDs include the following.

Pediculosis pubis (pubic lice or crabs) can be a problem in crowded living conditions. They are mainly acquired during sexual activity but can also be transmitted from contaminated bedding and clothing. Small white specks, which under a microscope look like a crab, pubic lice feed on blood. They can live up to 30 days, mating frequently in that time. The most common symptom is an itch in the genital area; a rash or tiny blue spots may also be evident.

Scabies is caused by a tiny mite known as *Sarcoptes scabiei*. It burrows under the skin, making a wavy line and causing a severe itch. It is usually spread in adults by sexual contact. The rash, which appears on the wrist, between the fingers, in the armpits or on the penis or thighs, is treated with lotions which kill the mites and their eggs.

Trichomoniasis vaginalis (TV) is another STD that causes genital ulcers. It infects the vagina, urethra, bladder and sometimes glands. Up to 90 percent of men who are infected have no symptoms, though it may cause pain on urination and itchiness.

When a test is carried out for a particular STD, it is wise to have tests for others which may have been contracted at the same time. While the female condom will provide protection from STDs, including HIV/AIDS, any person with an STD should avoid sexual intercourse while symptoms are present or until a medical practitioner advises that it is safe.

SEE ALSO ***AIDS, Chancroid, Chlamydia, Genital herpes, Genital warts, Gonorrhea, Granuloma inguinale, Hepatitis, Lice, Lymphogranuloma venereum, Molluscum contagiosum, Scabies***

SHIATSU

The Japanese word *shiatsu* means "finger pressure". It is the name of a therapy developed in Japan based on traditional massage, stretching and breathing techniques. Shiatsu therapists use the meridian system of traditional Chinese medicine to help them determine on which points in the body to apply pressure to rebalance the body's energy flow or *ki* (*ch'i* or *qi* in Chinese medicine). Shiatsu therapists use their fingers, knees, elbows, knuckles, palms and feet to release blockages of *ki*, applying a pressure which comes from body weight.

Diagnosis is done by palpating the abdomen (or *hara*), which is considered central to overall health and vitality as all the meridian pathways connect to this area. Pulses in the wrist are also read, as well as facial signs. Once the diagnosis is made the shiatsu therapist works in a series of sequences through the body to tonify and disperse *ki*, using pressure and gentle stretches combined with breathing techniques. Shiatsu is done on a clothed patient lying on a floor mat. Dietary advice according to macrobiotic principles is also often given.

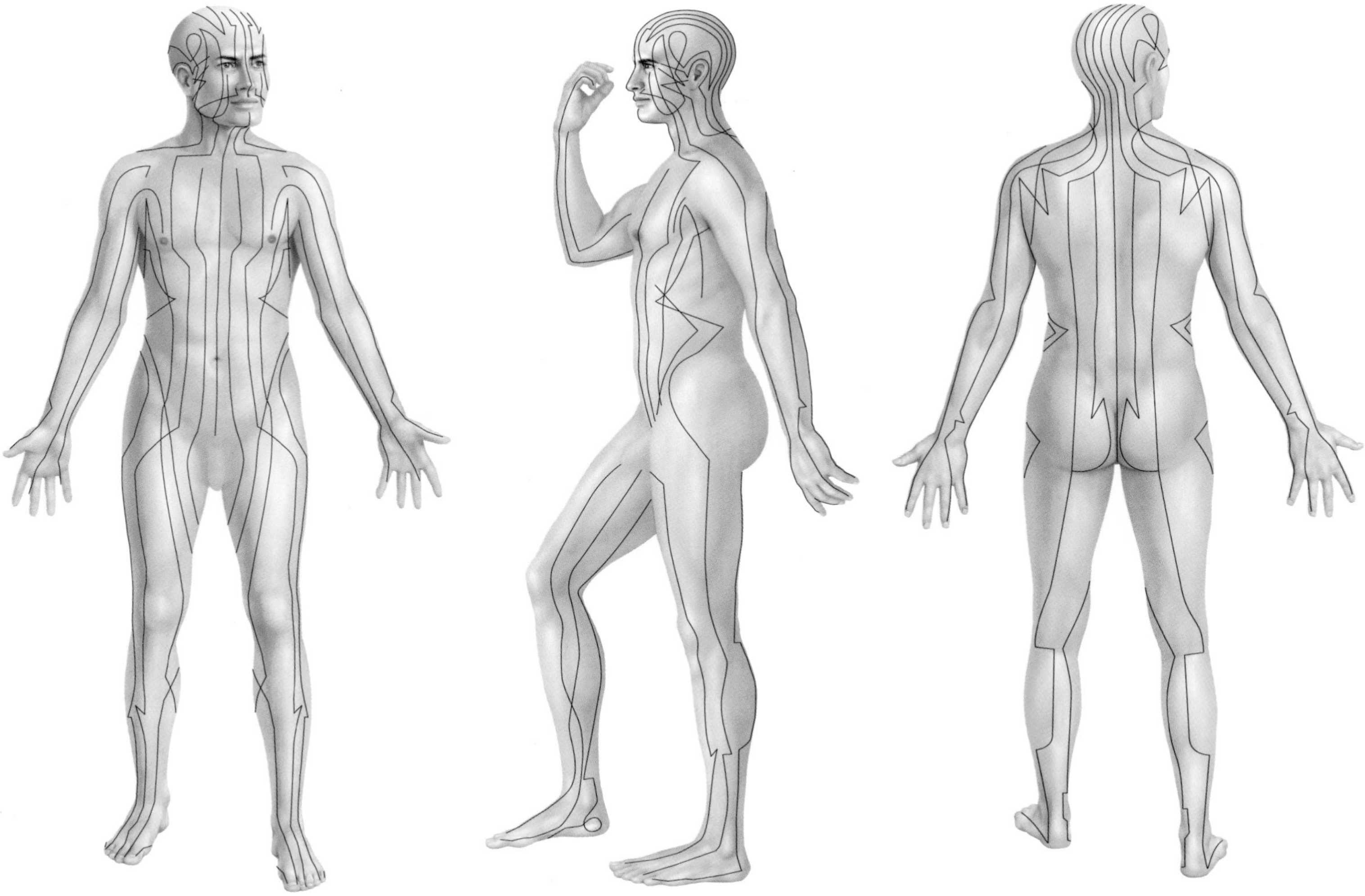

Shiatsu is a holistic treatment considered to benefit body and mind. It is said to be particularly effective in treating chronic pain, digestive and respiratory problems and stress-related illnesses.

SEE ALSO *Acupuncture, Massage*

SHIN SPLINTS

"Shin splints" is a common term that is used to refer to a variety of different conditions, all of which cause pain in the lower leg. To most medical practitioners, however, shin splints are more accurately referred to as medial tibial stress syndrome, an inflammation of soft tissues associated with the tibia which causes aching or tenderness along the shin. This is one of the most common injuries affecting joggers and is often caused by excessive walking or running, particularly on hard surfaces. Inadequate training is often blamed and susceptibility to shin splints can be reduced by improving the strength and flexibility of the lower leg. Rest is the usual treatment.

SEE ALSO *Leg, Tibia*

Shiatsu

In this Eastern therapy, pressure is applied to points along the body's meridian pathways to stimulate and balance the body's energy flow. The meridian system is thought to indicate the path of energy through different organs in the body. Disturbance or blockage of this flow can lead to illness.

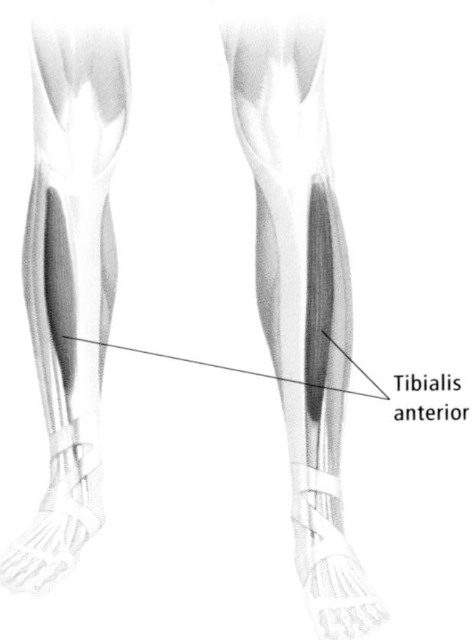

Shin splints

Running on hard surfaces such as bitumen or concrete for extended periods can cause inflammation of the tissues that join the muscles and bones of the lower leg. The soft tissues linked to the tibia (such as the tibialis anterior muscle) are most commonly affected.

Shock

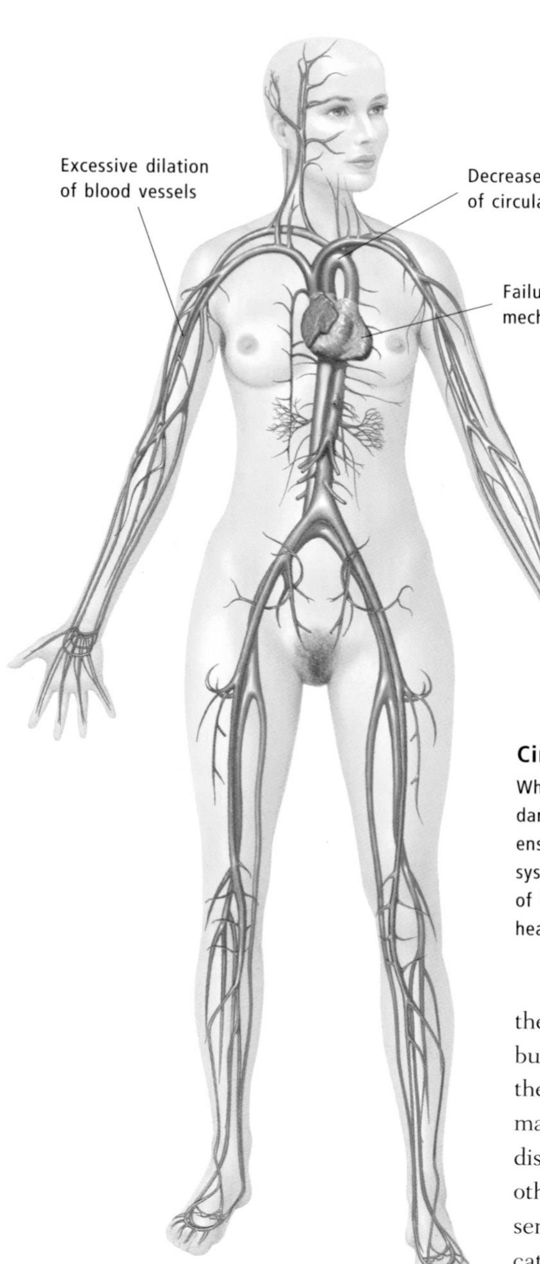

Circulatory shock
When blood pressure falls to dangerously low levels, shock ensues. This failure of the circulatory system may be caused by dilation of blood vessels, severe blood loss, heart failure or dehydration.

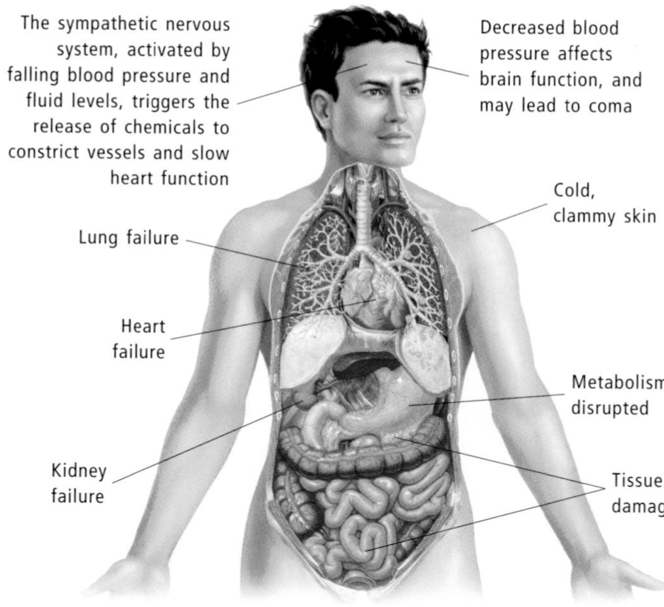

Shock—organ failure
To compensate for falling blood pressure and fluid levels, a body in shock releases chemicals to constrict vessels and slow body processes. This can lead to oxygen deprivation and damage to vital organs such as the kidneys, stomach and lungs. The effects can be fatal if not attended to immediately. **NB:** In this image part of the lungs, pleura, and liver have been cut to show the heart and kidney.

SHINGLES

Shingles is the common term for herpes zoster infection, a reactivation of the varicella-zoster virus that causes chickenpox. Following chickenpox infection the virus remains dormant in the body and reactivation can occur years later, particularly if the body's immunity decreases. This occurs most commonly with age.

While dormant the virus is located in spinal ganglia beside the spinal cord; on activation it migrates along a sensory nerve to the area of skin it supplies (its dermatome). It is here that the infection appears as a rash composed of small blisters with surrounding inflammation. The rash is therefore localized, and usually strictly confined to one side of the body. It may be associated with severe burning or sharp nerve pain, particularly in the elderly. Pain may precede the rash and may persist afterwards. This is often the most distressing aspect of the infection, since it is otherwise generally benign. More severe disseminated infection and neurological complications can occur in immunocompromised patients, such as those with lymphoma or following bone marrow transplantation.

More effective antiviral medications have been developed in recent years to treat shingles, including oral medications. When commenced soon after the rash appears, these can reduce the duration of infection and the pain during and after it.

SEE ALSO *Chickenpox, Nerves, Viruses*

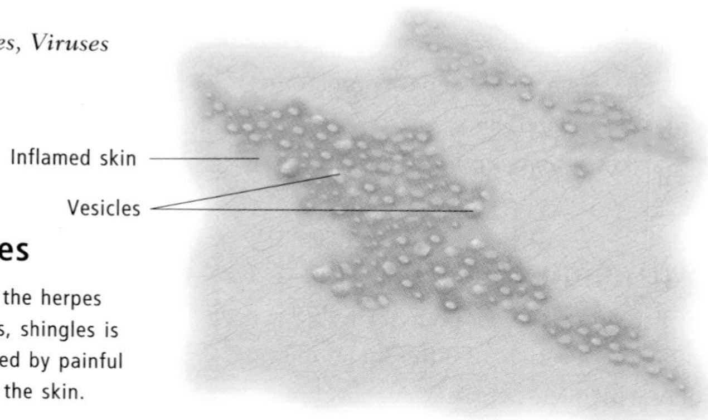

Shingles
Caused by the herpes zoster virus, shingles is characterized by painful blisters on the skin.

SHOCK

Shock is a term used in the medical sense to describe a complex sequence of events resulting in collapse of the circulatory system. Although an emotional component of fear or anxiety may also be present, it is only part of a severe body response. The most important feature of shock is failure of the circulation to maintain an adequate blood pressure to allow vital organs to continue to function.

Causes

Shock may result from a failure of the pumping ability of the heart, from a reduction in the circulating blood volume or from excessive dilatation of the blood vessels. The most common cause of shock is reduction in the blood volume, due to hemorrhage or severe dehydration. Another important cause of shock is septicemia, in which severe infection results in the release of chemicals called endotoxins, causing dilation of blood vessels. They may also impair the function of the heart. Heart diseases themselves can result in shock, particularly in the case of a major heart attack (myocardial infarction) which damages a large proportion of the heart muscle.

A number of conditions can cause dilation of blood vessels resulting in shock, including anaphylaxis and poisonings. Anaphylaxis is a severe immediate allergic reaction resulting in the release of histamine, a chemical which causes the dilation of blood vessels. Poisoning by a variety of drugs and chemicals may result in depression of cardiac function and dilation of blood vessels. Drugs include those used for the treatment of cardiovascular diseases or depression, as well as non-prescription drugs including alcohol. Exposure to high-voltage electricity can cause shock through cardiac arrest and severe electrical burns, resulting in fluid loss.

Symptoms

The symptoms of shock depend initially on the precipitating factor. They may be dramatic, such as a heart attack or an electric shock. Sometimes shock develops more gradually as a result of progressive dehydration or infection. Anaphylactic shock is associated with swelling of the lips and throat, wheezing and difficulty breathing, and the rapid appearance of an itchy raised rash.

Regardless of the initial symptoms, a common sequence of events then ensues. Decrease in the blood pressure affects brain function, resulting in confusion and even coma. The body mounts a protective defense of the circulation by releasing chemicals from the adrenal glands and activating the sympathetic nervous system. Chemicals such as epinephrine (adrenaline) increase the pumping action of the heart and constrict blood vessels. These chemicals are also responsible for symptoms of tremor and anxiety that accompany the shock syndrome.

The body's response may result in the person appearing pale, cold and clammy. While it is beneficial in maintaining the blood pressure, the compensatory response is only a temporary measure before organ function is compromised further. Constriction of blood vessels can reduce blood flow to vital organs, especially the kidneys. Also, the lack of blood supply to body tissues results in anaerobic metabolism with the accumulation of lactic acid. Ultimately shock can result in an irreversible situation, in which tissue damage has become so great that the condition becomes fatal.

Treatment

Treatment of shock relies on its early detection and institution of emergency measures, such as oxygen and epinephrine (adrenaline) in anaphylaxis. The maintenance of circulatory volume by intravenous fluids is essential and is combined with infusion of drugs to maintain blood pressure. Specific treatment, such as antibiotics for septicemia or antidotes for poisoning, is also given.

SEE ALSO ***Anaphylaxis, Circulatory system, Epinephrine, Myocardial infarction, Poisoning, Septicemia, Toxic shock syndrome***

SHOULDER

The shoulder includes three bones—the clavicle (collar bone), the scapula (shoulder blade) and the humerus—and their associated joints and muscles, as well as major nerves and blood vessels passing to and from the arm.

The arm is attached to the trunk by the pectoral girdle, which consists of the clavicle and the scapula. The clavicle acts as a strut to hold the arm away from the center of the body. It forms joints with the sternum (breastbone) at one end and with the scapula at the other end. The scapula is a flat triangular-shaped bone which covers part of the upper back. It is largely enclosed by muscle but has a prominent spine, which can be felt extending across the back towards the shoulder, where it expands to form the acromion.

Joints

The joints of the shoulder region include the following.

Acromioclavicular joint

The inner surface of the acromion meets the clavicle to form the acromioclavicular joint, which can be felt at the top of the shoulder. This joint allows a small amount of gliding movement to occur between the two bones in conjunction with movements of the arm. The acromioclavicular joint is supported by a capsule and several ligaments, the most important of which is the coracoclavicular ligament. These ligaments, which pass down from the under surface of the clavicle to the coracoid process (a part of the scapula which protrudes forward under the clavicle) also help to support the weight of the arm.

Heavy falls on to the back of the shoulder (as may occur when someone is thrown from a motorcycle) cause the scapula to be driven forwards under the clavicle and may result in rupture of the conoid and trapezoid ligaments. When this occurs, the arm is pulled down by its own weight and the affected shoulder appears lower than the shoulder on the other side, a condition known as shoulder separation. This is a serious injury and usually requires a surgical prodecure in order to repair the damaged ligaments.

Shoulder joint

The outer (lateral) angle of the triangular scapula is flattened to form a shallow cavity, in which the head of the humerus (the long bone of the upper arm) sits, forming the glenohumeral or shoulder joint. The shoulder joint is a ball and socket joint, allowing movement of the arm to occur in almost any direction. The socket, which is formed by the glenoid cavity of the scapula, is very shallow and has a small contact area, relative to the head of the humerus, which forms the ball.

Only a small part of the head of the humerus is in contact with the glenoid cavity at any time, making the joint extremely mobile but also making it relatively unstable (easy to dislocate). A ring of fibrocartilage, the glenoid labrum, which encircles the edge of the glenoid cavity, deepens the socket slightly and increases the contact area.

The joint surfaces are covered by smooth, glassy cartilage and the two bones are held together by a relatively loose capsule. The

Acromion
Acromioclavicular ligament
Subacromial bursa
Joint capsule
Clavicle
Deltoid muscle
Coracoid process
Scapula
Articular cartilage
Synovial membrane
Triceps brachii muscle
Teres major
Humerus

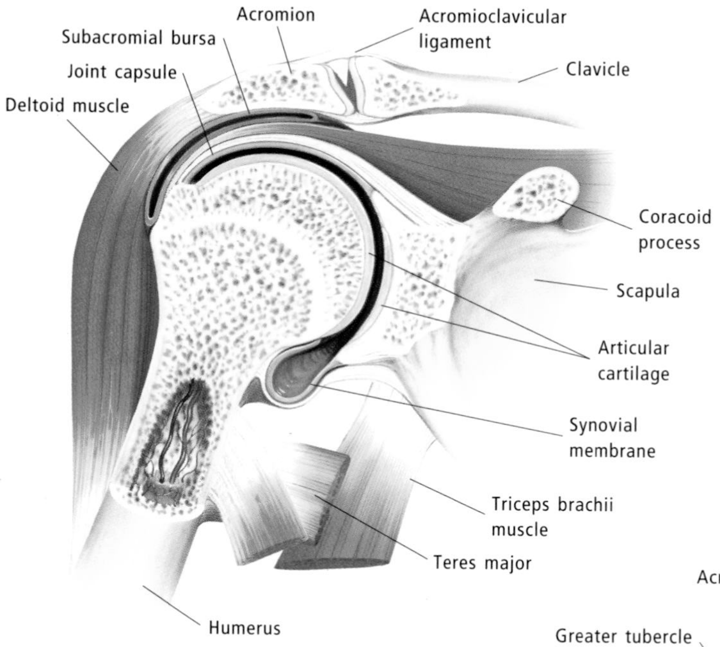

Shoulder cross-section

A loose capsule lined with a synovial membrane joins the humerus bone to the scapula. The synovial membrane secretes a fluid which lubricates the joint, reducing friction and easing movement. Damage to the synovial membrane or cartilage that cushions the joint may cause pain and stiffness in the shoulder.

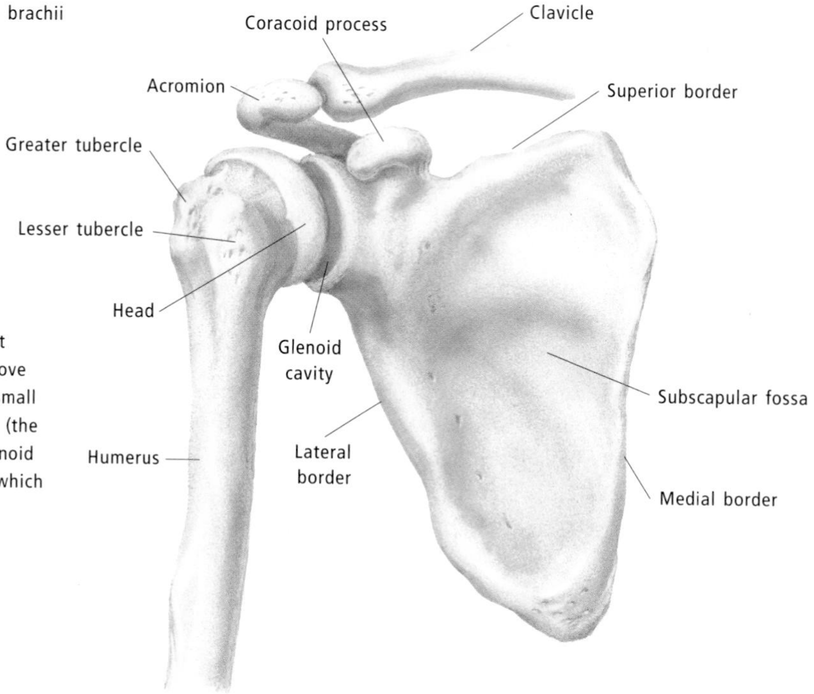

Shoulder

Coracoid process
Clavicle
Acromion
Superior border
Greater tubercle
Lesser tubercle
Head
Glenoid cavity
Subscapular fossa
Humerus
Lateral border
Medial border

Shoulder joint

The shoulder is a ball and socket joint which allows the arm to move in almost any direction. Only a small part of the head of the humerus (the ball) makes contact with the glenoid cavity (the socket) at any time, which provides maximum mobility but increases the risk of dislocation.

Pectoral girdle

The bones and muscles of the pectoral girdle provide a support network for the shoulder joint. One set of muscles attaches the humerus bone of the arm to the shoulder girdle, another set attaches the shoulder girdle to the trunk of the body.

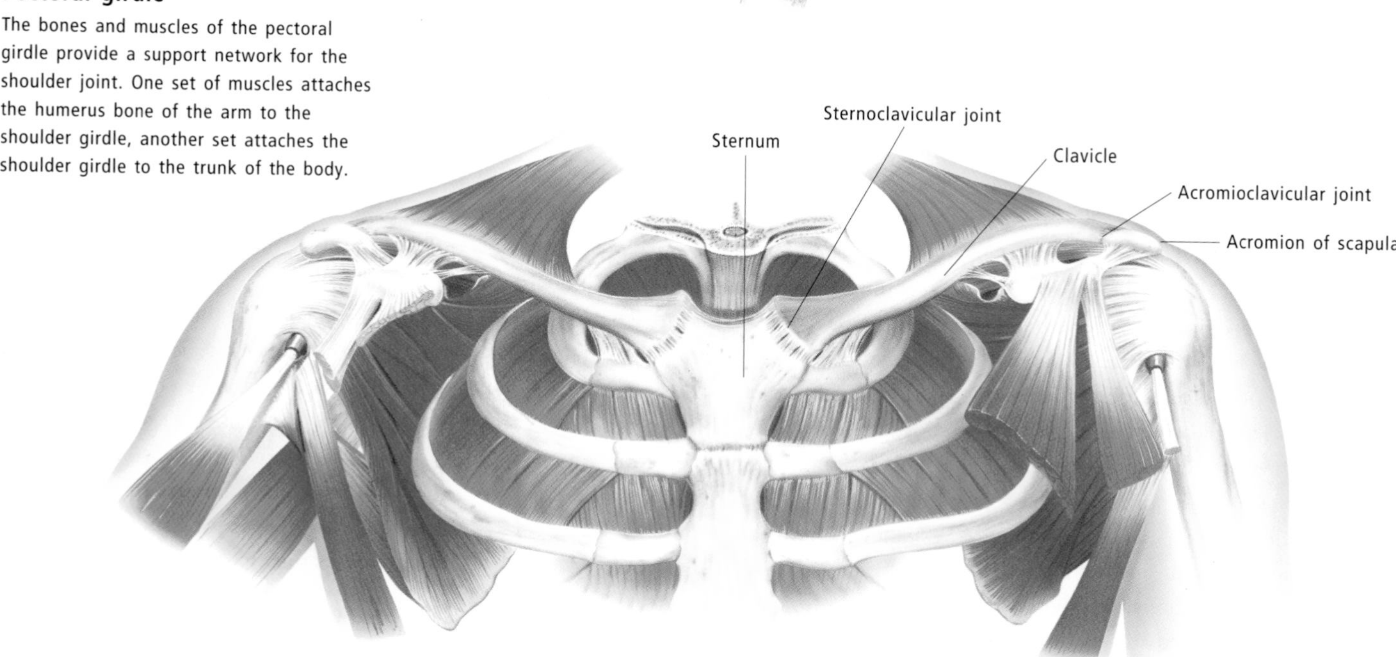

inside of the capsule is lined by a synovial membrane, which produces an oily synovial fluid that is released into the joint cavity to lubricate the cartilage surface and reduce friction. The capsule is reinforced on the top, front and back by a group of muscles known as the rotator cuff muscles, whose tendons blend with the capsule as they pass over it. In addition to enabling certain movements at the joint, these muscles are said to act as "dynamic ligaments", holding the head of the humerus in the socket during movement. The rotator cuff muscles, subscapularis covering the front, infraspinatus and teres minor covering the back and supraspinatus covering the top of the capsule, are the most important factors preventing dislocation of the head of the humerus from the socket when force is placed on the joint.

Dislocation of the shoulder is a relatively common occurrence and usually occurs as a result of a sudden force being transmitted along the arm when it is in the elevated (abducted) position. In this position, the force from the head of the humerus is transmitted to the lower part of the capsule where it is weakest and not reinforced by tendons, forcing the head to pop out of the lower part of the socket. Although the humerus can be placed back into the socket with the assistance of local anesthetic and muscle relaxants, the damage that is usually sustained by the capsule and labrum in the dislocation makes the joint vulnerable to dislocation in the future, and surgery may be required to overcome the problem.

The shoulder joint is bridged and protected above by a structure known as the coracoacromial arch, which consists of the acromion behind, the coracoid process in front and the coracoacromial ligament passing between them. A cushion of synovial fluid enclosed by a synovial membrane, and known as the subacromial bursa, lies between the supraspinatus tendon (which blends with the joint capsule) below and the coracoacromial arch above. It functions to reduce friction between the greater tubercle of the humerus and the arch when the arm is elevated.

Stress on the supraspinatus tendon in some people may cause degeneration of the tendon with age, resulting in the formation of crystalline calcium deposits in the tendon (tendinitis) which cause friction and consequent swelling of the bursa. When this occurs the person experiences pain on elevating the arm because of pressure on the swollen bursa as the humerus impinges on the acromion, a condition known as "painful arc syndrome". The syndrome is usually treated with heat, physical therapy and anti-inflammatory medication.

Frozen shoulder (adhesive capsulitis) is caused by inflammation of all the rotator cuff tendons causing generalized thickening of the shoulder capsule, which may adhere (stick) to the humerus. It may or may not be preceded by trauma to the joint. Frozen shoulder is characterized by increasing pain and stiffness of the shoulder. Over time the pain subsides but the stiffness continues to increase. The stiffness usually outlasts the pain by a few months before movement gradually returns to normal. The course of the disease may take 1–2 years, but a good recovery can usually be expected.

Movements

The shoulder is a multi-axial ball and socket joint, which allows movement in almost any direction. The arm (humerus) can be drawn forwards (flexed), drawn backwards (extended), elevated (abducted), drawn downwards (adducted) and rotated (around its own axis). Movements of the shoulder joint are always accompanied by movements of the pectoral girdle (clavicle and scapula), which increase the range of movement. For example, the arm cannot be elevated above the level of the shoulder without rotation of the scapula. This can be verified by observing someone from behind (with their shirt removed) as they lift the arm above the head—the lower angle of the scapula can be seen to move up and outwards as the arm is raised.

Muscles

The muscles associated with the shoulder and pectoral girdle fall into two groups, those attaching the humerus to the shoulder girdle and trunk wall, and those attaching the shoulder girdle to the trunk.

The first group includes the rotator cuff muscles: the deltoid (covers the shoulder and gives it its rounded contour); the pectoralis major (covering the front of the chest); the latissimus dorsi (large flat muscle covering the lower back and converging on a tendon which attaches to the humerus); and the teres major (a small bulky muscle passing from the scapula to the humerus).

The second group includes the rhomboids and levator scapulae, which pass from the inner (medial) side of the scapula to the vertebral column; the trapezius (a large triangular muscle extending from the skull and vertebral column across to the spine of the scapula and the clavicle); the latissimus dorsi (covering the lower back and converging on a tendon which attaches to the humerus); and the serratus anterior and pectoralis minor (both extending from the scapula to the front of the chest wall).

As a general rule, muscles which pass in front of the shoulder joint act to flex or rotate the humerus, those passing behind the joint extend and or rotate the humerus, and those passing above abduct the humerus. Because the large deltoid muscle passes over three sides of the joint (front, back and top), it is involved in most shoulder movements. Muscles which are most important for flexion of the shoulder joint are the pectoralis major and deltoid muscles. Muscles which are important for extension include the teres major, latissimus dorsi and deltoid muscles.

Abduction is brought about by the deltoid assisted by supraspinatus; medial rotation by subscapularis, latissimus dorsi, teres major, pectoralis major and part of the deltoid muscle. Lateral rotation is brought about by infraspinatus and teres minor; and adduction mainly by latissimus dorsi at the back and pectoralis major at the front and teres major; although teres major only adducts when the movement is resisted. The trapezius muscle has fibers passing up to the skull and across to the vertebral column and is important in shrugging the shoulders and in rotating the scapula upwards (when lifting the arm above the head). The serratus anterior is also essential for scapular rotation.

Weakness or paralysis of any of these muscles will impair shoulder movement.

Nerves and blood vessels

Most of the nerves and blood vessels supplying the arm pass through the armpit (axilla), just below the front of the shoulder joint as they travel to and from their target structures in the shoulder region and arm. They include the large axillary artery and vein and their branches, and the axillary, radial, musculocutaneous, median and ulnar nerves. In this area these structures are held together by loose connective tissue (axillary sheath). The nerves arise from a complex known as the brachial plexus, located on the side of the neck, where it can be felt as cords passing towards the arm, just above the clavicle.

The axillary nerve is of particular importance to the shoulder because it supplies the deltoid muscle from its deep surface by encircling the surgical neck of the humerus. It is vulnerable to injury in shoulder dislocations (when it is stretched) and in fractures of the surgical neck of the humerus. When injury of this nature occurs the muscle quickly atrophies due to lack of use, and the shoulder becomes angular and bony. The person experiences weakness of most shoulder movements, but particularly in elevation (abduction) of the arm. Damaged peripheral nerves will repair themselves over time, although recovery may not be complete.

SEE ALSO *Adduction and abduction, Arm, Collar bone, Deltoid muscle, Humerus, Joints, Muscle, Nerves, Rotator cuff muscles, Scapula, Skeletal system, Tendinitis, Trapezius*

Sickle cell disease

In this blood disorder, red blood cells form curved or sickle shapes, resulting in the blockage of small blood vessels. This causes tissue damage and pain can be severe.

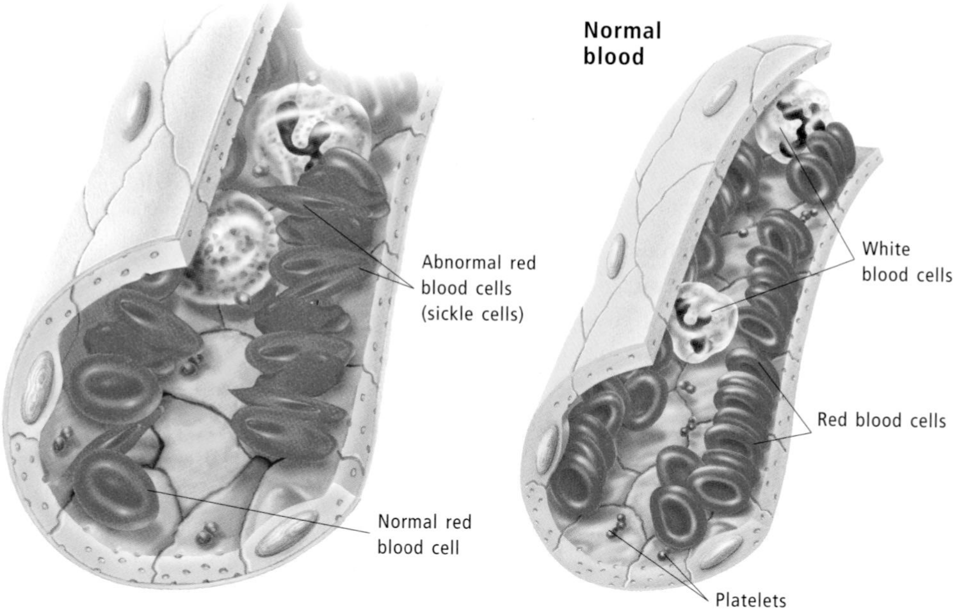

SHOULDER-HAND SYNDROME

Shoulder-hand syndrome is a condition marked by stiffness and pain in the shoulder, as well as stiffening and swelling of the hand and fingers. It is a type of reflex sympathetic dystrophy, a nervous system disorder affecting extremities which often results from an injury. The condition may also stem from myocardial infarction.

SEE ALSO *Hand, Myocardial infarction, Shoulder*

SIAMESE TWINS

Siamese (conjoined) twins are identical twins formed from a single fertilized ovum, joined together by a part, or parts, of their bodies at birth. Many are joined at the hip, head or chest, and some share limbs and internal organs such as the liver and heart. Most are delivered by cesarean section and less than half survive after birth. Siamese twins joined only by superficial tissue may be easy to separate surgically. This procedure becomes more risky and sometimes impossible, when organs and arteries are shared; in such cases, one twin may not survive.

The condition results from the failure of a zygote to fully separate into two after fertilization. Despite the difficulties of facing life joined to another person, some Siamese twins marry and have children.

SEE ALSO *Fertilization, Twins*

SICK SINUS SYNDROME

Sick sinus syndrome is a relatively rare malfunction of the heart's natural pacemaker, the sinus node, that results in abnormal heartbeat rhythms. It can be caused by a variety of diseases.

Sufferers often experience lethargy, weakness, dizziness and fainting. The only long-term treatment is implantation of an artificial pacemaker.

SEE ALSO *Heart, Pacemaker*

SICKLE CELL DISEASE

Sickle cell disease is due to the inheritance of a variant gene for the protein globin, which results in altered physical properties of the hemoglobin in red blood cells. It is the commonest variant of hemoglobin occurring worldwide.

The gene is most prevalent in equatorial regions of Africa, the Middle East and in North America in those of African descent. It is thought that the sickle gene has undergone selection by providing resistance to infection of the red cells by malarial parasites. Inheritance of one sickle gene results in the carrier state and two genes cause the disease to manifest.

Sickle hemoglobin undergoes aggregation under conditions of decreased oxygen, which causes the red cells to form a curved or sickle shape. This results in blockage of small blood vessels, causing the characteristic painful crises of the disease and resulting in tissue damage. The pain is severe and affects the bones, chest and abdomen.

Sickle cell disease may result in painful swelling of fingers and toes, leading to arthritis. Other organs can also be damaged, including the kidneys, lungs and brain. Renal complications are common.

The severity of the symptoms of sickle cell disease varies between affected individuals and can be reduced by avoiding cold conditions and by early treatment of infections.

Regular blood transfusions can reduce complications during pregnancy. In severe cases bone marrow transplantation has been used as curative treatment.

SEE ALSO *Congenital abnormalities, Genes, Hemoglobin*

SIGHT

Sight is a process in which light received by the eye triggers nerve impulses in the brain to enable the perception of the shape, size, color, movement and position of objects. The ability to see clearly defined images with the correct color and intensity depends on the way in which rays of light pass through the eye and the resulting chain of physical, chemical and electrical reactions.

The amount of light entering the eye is controlled by the iris, the colored part of the eye which lies behind the transparent curved cornea at the front of the eye. The cornea focuses light rays through the pupil to the lens, another transparent structure responsible for the fine focusing of light. As the light rays travel through the eyeball they are refracted, or bent. The degree of refraction depends on the shape of the cornea and the lens; the shape of the lens can be altered by surrounding muscles to allow the eye to focus on objects both nearby and far away.

The light rays then pass through a jelly (vitreous humor) in the center of the eye to the retina, a highly sensitive layer of cells at the back of the eye. It is here that nerve impulses are generated for transmission to the brain via the optic nerve.

Color and intensity

The retina is made up of millions of light-receptor cells known as rods and cones. The cone cells are responsible for color vision while the rod cells specialize in the perception of light intensity, enabling vision in dim light. As rod cells cannot provide color vision, objects seen in semidarkness are perceived in shades of gray. The rod cells contain a red photosensitive pigment called rhodopsin (visual purple) and the cone cells contain opsin. When light is focused on the rods and cones a chemical reaction takes place and the pigments are broken down, triggering the electrical impulses that travel to the brain.

A deficiency of rhodopsin in the rod cells can lead to a condition known as night blindness, in which vision is impaired when light intensity drops below a certain level. The deficiency is sometimes due to a lack of vitamin A in the diet but more commonly follows the disorder retinitis pigmentosa, a degenerative disease of the retina. Absent or abnormal pigments in the cone cells lead to either partial or total color blindness.

In color blindness the perception of colors is not normal, making it difficult to distinguish between them. Color perception is a result of the stimulation of three pigments in the cone cells, which react to red, green and blue. Partial color blindness usually involves the inability to distinguish between red and green, sometimes with both appearing as shades of yellow. Total color blindness or achromatism results in everything being seen as shades of gray.

The optic nerve

The rods and cones of the retina send nerve impulses to the optic nerve via a network of nerve fibers. Nerve impulses concerning the left field of vision of each eye are sent to one part of the brain's cerebral cortex, and the impulses concerning the right part of the field of vision of each eye are sent to another. When interpreting this information, the brain combines the two messages to form one image. The brain also inverts images which are focused on the retina upside down. It is not known how this occurs.

The optic nerve can become inflamed (optic neuritis) causing sudden loss of vision in the affected eye, impaired color vision and painful eye movement. The cause of this condition is uncertain but it may be due to deterioration of a fatty layer of cells known as the myelin sheath, which aids in the transfer of nerve impulses.

Binocular vision

Normal human vision is binocular, that is, the images from each eye are fused into one focused image. Each eye sees the same scene or object in a slightly different way because each sees it from a slightly different angle. Binocular vision is the ability to maintain focus on a scene or object with both eyes, blending the two pictures to create one image that is seen with depth. A person without perfect binocular vision may have difficulty visually estimating distance due to problems with the perception of depth.

The condition in which two images of an object are perceived instead of one is known as double vision (diplopia). This may be a side effect of a disorder known as astigmatism in which the curved shape of the cornea is not symmetrical, or it may be caused by the muscles of one eye being stronger or weaker than those of the other. Double vision may be a symptom of a squint (strabismus) where pairs of muscles surrounding the eyeball do not work in unison, causing abnormal movement of the eye. The result can be cross-eye, where one or both eyes turn inward toward the nose, walleye, where the eyes turn outward, or the need to peer at scenes or objects with eyes partially closed to aid focusing. The brain receives two different images, distorting depth perception.

Refractive errors

For an object to be seen clearly, light rays must focus at a precise point on the retina. When this does not happen, due to the shape of the eyeball, it leads to problems with vision known as refractive errors. These include shortsightedness (nearsightedness or myopia), longsightedness (farsightedness or hyperopia), presbyopia and astigmatism. Rather than being caused by disease or trauma, these focusing errors are due to the natural physical characteristics of the eye.

In longsightedness the eye has difficulty focusing on nearby objects but no problems with objects far away. Light rays from nearby objects focus on a point beyond the retina instead of directly on it, because the eyeball is not deep enough, or because the lens is weak. The blurred vision associated with longsightedness may lead to eyestrain and headaches.

Longsightedness caused by a decrease in the elasticity of the lens due to the normal ageing process is known as presbyopia. This makes it difficult to adjust focus for viewing close objects. Everybody suffers from presbyopia to some degree, mostly after the age of 45. Sometimes known as "old man's eyes", this condition cannot be prevented.

In shortsightedness the eye has difficulty focusing on objects far away but has no problem with those close up. This is because the eyeball is too deep or the lens too curved, causing light rays to bend too much so that visual images are focused in front of the retina instead of on it. This focusing error, like longsightedness, may be hereditary or may develop later in life as the lens becomes less elastic. An irregularly curved cornea or lens results in a condition known as

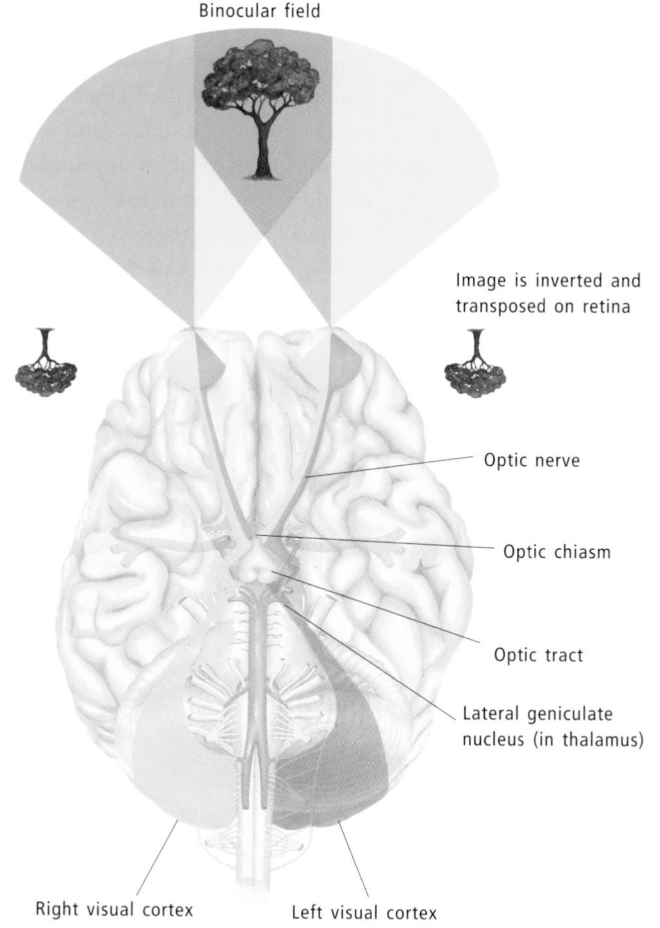

Visual pathways

The left and right eyes have slightly different, but overlapping fields of vision. The discrepancy between the images in the binocular field allows us to judge how far away an object is and its 3-D structure. Images are inverted, transposed and converted into nerve impulses. The impulses pass down nerve fibers to the optic nerves and through the optic chiasm to the lateral geniculate nuclei of the thalamus. These nuclei carry out some processing of the visual information and then send it to the visual cortex in the occipital lobes of the brain. Images are combined and interpreted in the visual cortex.

Field of vision

The structure of the eye is specially designed to bend and concentrate light rays to form a tiny image of a seen object on the back of the eye. This is then transported to the brain in the form of nerve impulses. Light rays entering the eye strike the cornea, which bends (refracts) the rays bringing them closer together. The rays then pass through the lens which focuses the rays on the back of the retina. The retina consists of a layer of light-sensitive cells—rods and cones. When stimulated by light, the rods and cones send electrical signals along the cells of the optic nerve.

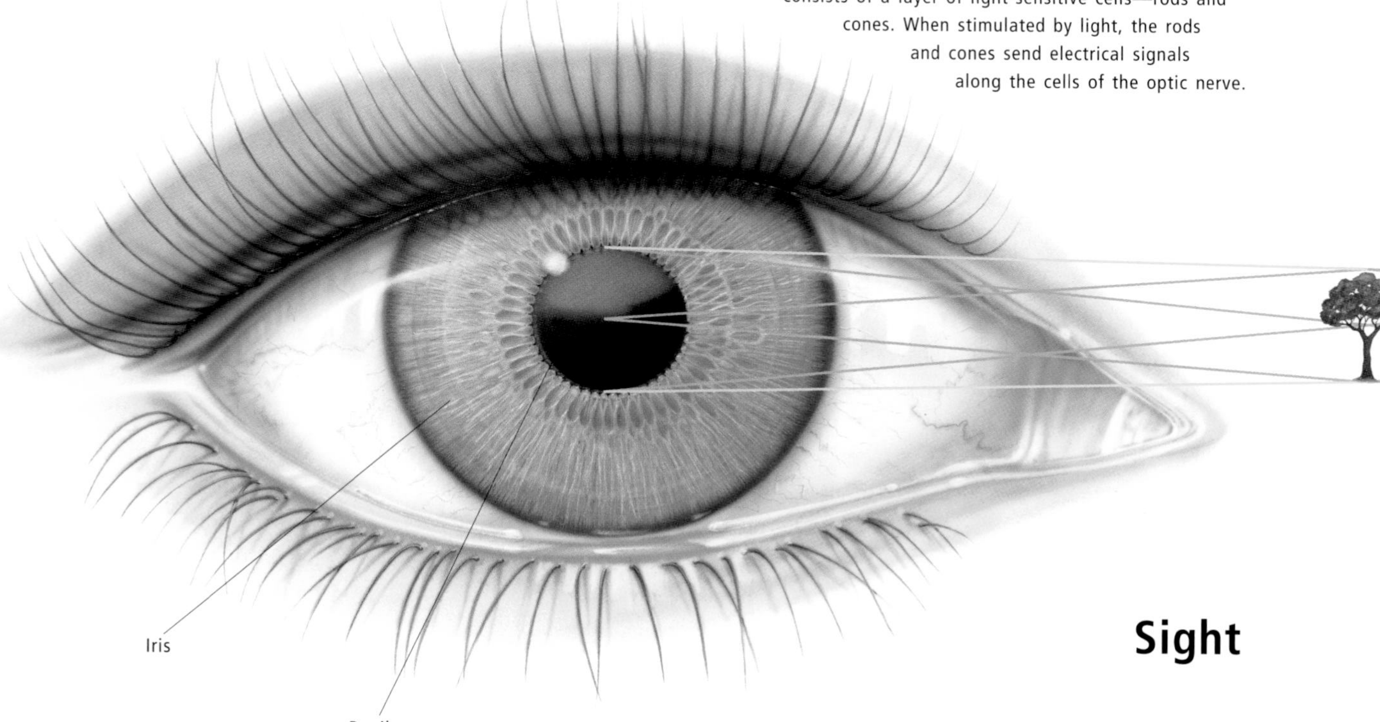

Sight

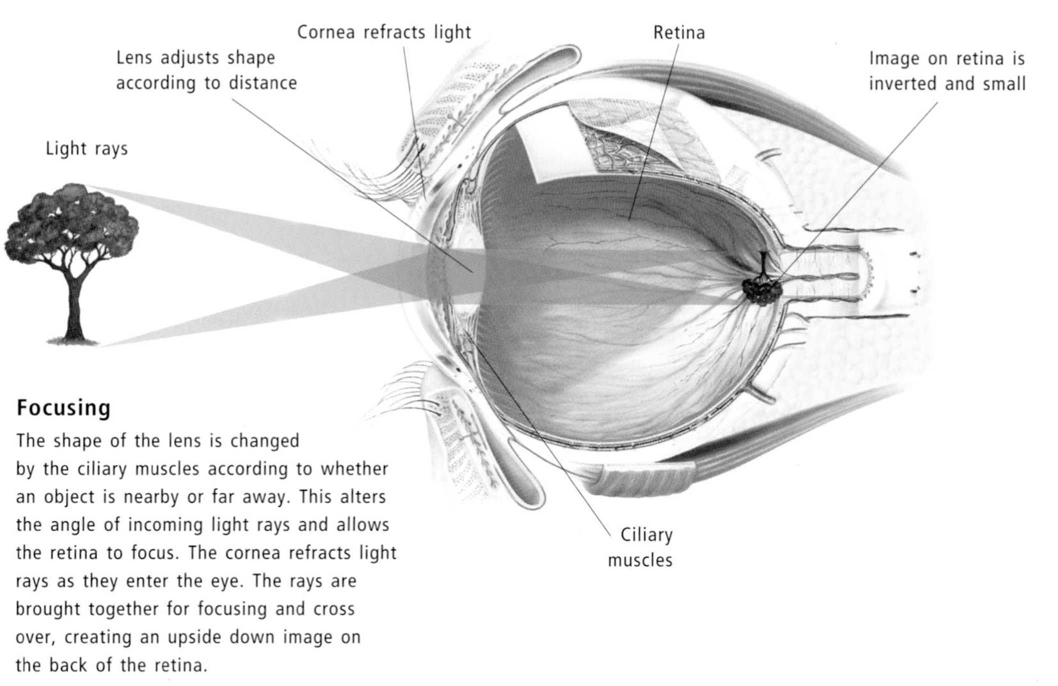

Focusing

The shape of the lens is changed by the ciliary muscles according to whether an object is nearby or far away. This alters the angle of incoming light rays and allows the retina to focus. The cornea refracts light rays as they enter the eye. The rays are brought together for focusing and cross over, creating an upside down image on the back of the retina.

Color blindness

Color perception is the result of the stimulation of three groups of cone cells in the retina which react to red, green and blue. Color blindness occurs when one group of cones is missing or not functioning. Inability to distinguish between red and green (one of the most common forms of color blindness) occurs when red cones are missing. Tests can reveal difficulties in distinguishing between colors—anyone with red–green color blindness will not be able to see the number in this image.

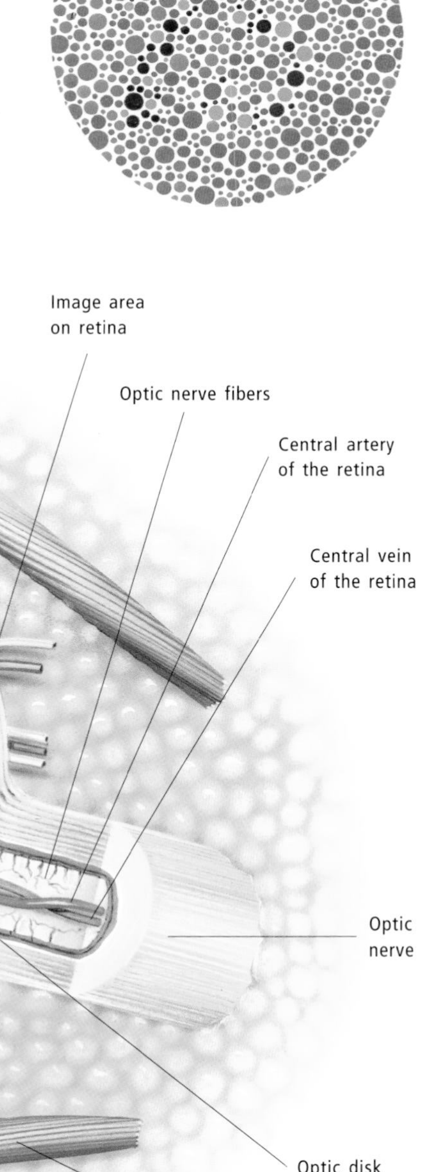

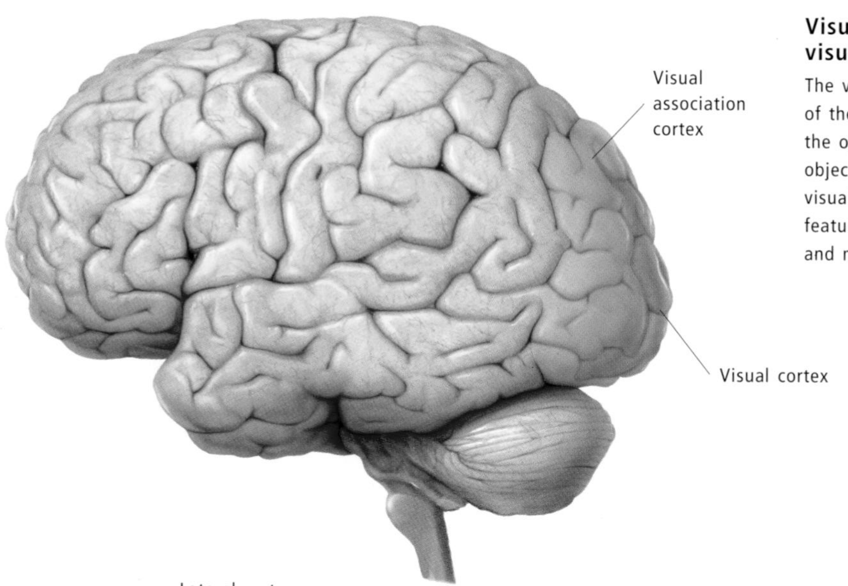

Visual cortex and visual association cortex

The visual cortex interprets and makes sense of the nerve impulses sent from the eyes via the optic nerves and thalamus. This is where objects are recognized and given meaning. The visual association cortex process more complex features of the visual stimulus such as color and movement.

Lateral rectus
Optic nerve
Superior rectus
Medial rectus
Superior oblique
Levator palpebrae superioris

Eye movement and innervation

The movement of the eyeball is controlled by six muscles, allowing the eye to look down, up, left and right. This provides a wide field of vision. The optic nerve carries sensory information, in the form of nerve impulses, from the eyes to the brain for processing.

astigmatism, where light also focuses in front of or behind the retina instead of on it. This can be hereditary or due to injury or disease and causes blurred or distorted vision.

Field of vision

Sight defects often affect the size or shape of the field of vision, the total area perceived by the eye. They include a condition called macular degeneration in which the central part of the retina (macula) deteriorates, causing blurring and a gradual loss of central vision. Peripheral vision is usually not affected by this condition. A large number of the eye's nerve endings are concentrated in the macula, the part of the eye where vision is sharpest. Macular degeneration may be a natural part of the ageing process or be due to disease or environmental factors.

Severe narrowing of the peripheral field of vision (the outside edges of the visual field), as if looking through a tube, is called tunnel vision. It often develops as a complication of the disease glaucoma, when the pressure of excess fluid in the eye damages the optic nerve. It is also a symptom of advanced retinitis pigmentosa, a degenerative disease of the retina. As a result of the restricted visual field, a person suffering tunnel vision may not see someone standing right alongside. The condition often causes night blindness, resulting in difficulty functioning normally in light below a certain level.

Hemianopia is the loss of vision or blindness in one half of the normal visual field in one or both eyes. Loss of vision usually occurs in the left or right half of the visual field, but may also manifest in the upper or lower half. The disorder often goes undetected in the early stages as the vision loss is equal in both eyes. Hemianopia is caused by a brain disorder in which images transmitted by the eyes are not received and processed properly. It often appears in people who have suffered a brain injury.

Treatment options

Glasses and contact lenses, which change the refractive power of the eye, are the most common forms of treatment for refractive errors.

Laser surgery may be used to correct or improve nearsightedness, longsightedness and astigmatism in some cases. The most common form of laser therapy for treatment of refractive errors is known as laser in-situ keratomileusis (LASIK), in which a thin flap of the cornea is surgically peeled back and a laser beam used to remove some of the cornea by heating tissue cells to bursting point. This changes the shape of the cornea according to the refractive error being treated, allowing the correct movement of light through the eye for focusing on the retina.

There is a chance, however, that best corrected vision—with the use of glasses or contact lenses—may be worse after laser surgery than it was before. Laser surgery may also be used to rid the eye of scar tissue and excess blood vessels caused by certain diseases and injuries.

Vision which is below the normal range and which cannot be corrected by the use of glasses, contact lenses, surgery or other medical treatment is referred to as partial sight or low vision. It is often caused by damage to the macula, as well as by diseases and disorders such as diabetic retinopathy, glaucoma, cataracts and retinitis pigmentosa. Many people with partial sight may appear to be blind but have some usable vision. Activities such as reading may still be possible with the aid of such things as large-print books and magnifiers.

SEE ALSO *Astigmatism, Blindness, Cataracts, Color blindness, Contact lenses, Cornea, Eye, Glaucoma, Iris, Macular degeneration, Myopia, Neuritis, Optic nerve, Retina, Retinitis pigmentosa, Squint*

S

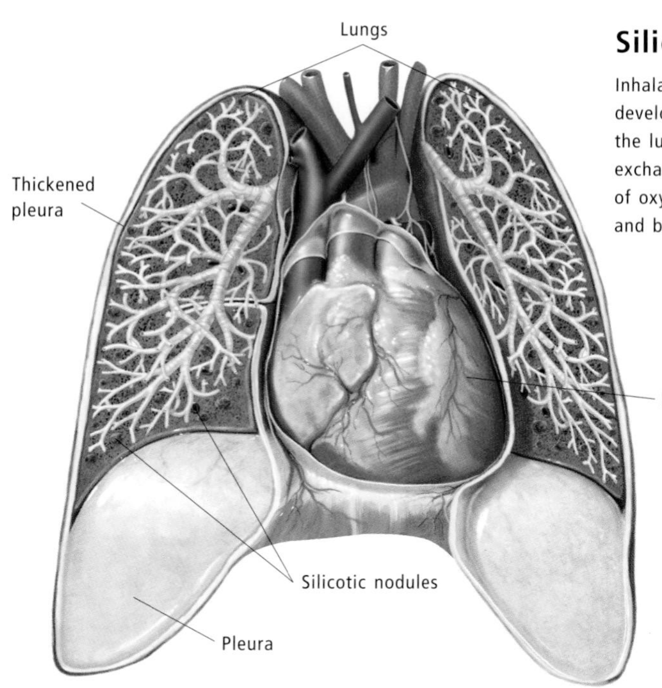

Silicosis

Inhalation of silica dust causes the development of hard nodules in the lungs. The nodules impede air exchange, depriving body tissues of oxygen and causing coughing and breathing difficulties.

NB: In this illustration the upper two-thirds of the lungs have been cut and the pleura has been peeled back to reveal the bronchial tree and heart.

SILICOSIS

Known also as grinder's disease, miner's phthisis and potter's asthma, silicosis is a respiratory disorder caused by inhaling silica, mainly in industrial situations. Occupations at risk include those involving close contact with stone, sand or ceramics such as mining, quarrying, tunneling and the manufacture of ceramics and pottery. The most serious effect of the inhaled silica dust is impaired gas exchange associated with the development of small hard nodules and fibrosis in the lungs.

The severity of the disease depends on the level and length of time of exposure. Chronic or simple silicosis develops after more than 10 years of low-level exposure. Higher levels over 5–10 years cause accelerated or complicated silicosis. Acute silicosis results from highly concentrated exposure over a short period of time.

Symptoms range from shortness of breath and a dry cough in mild forms to lethargy, restless sleep, appetite loss, chest pain, a cough that produces blood, and hypoxia (lack of oxygen in the blood) which shows as blueness of the lips and skin. There is no cure for silicosis and it commonly reduces life expectancy and quality of life. Records of the disease date back two thousand years. It was prevalent in the nineteenth and early twentieth centuries but is becoming rarer due to improved occupational health and safety standards.

SEE ALSO *Lungs, Respiratory system*

SINUSES

A sinus is, in general terms, a small passage or cavity relatively wide in relation to its length. The term is commonly applied to a cavity containing air (the paranasal sinuses) or blood (particularly the venous sinuses). A sinusoid is a small sinus: sinusoids containing blood occur in many organs, including liver, spleen and bone marrow, where they serve to facilitiate contact between blood and the cells of the particular organ.

The paranasal sinuses are air-containing cavities within the frontal, ethmoid, maxillary and sphenoid bones of the skull, which are connected by passages to the nose. They lighten the bones in which they occur, assist in cushioning blows to the head, and add resonance to the voice. These sinuses are rudimentary at birth, and develop rapidly at the age of puberty. In women, the sinuses are relatively small. Because of the narrowness of the connecting passages to the nose, and their orientation, the paranasal sinuses do not always drain properly. This may lead to acute or chronic infection (sinusitis).

The venous sinuses of the dura mater (a tough membrane covering the brain and spinal cord) are channels which collect venous blood from the brain and the bones of the cranium. They are situated inside the skull, between the two layers of the dura mater.

SEE ALSO *Nose, Sinusitis, Skull*

SINUSITIS

The paranasal sinuses are cavities lined with mucous membrane in bones around the nose and eyes. Under normal conditions mucus moves steadily from the sinuses into the nose. In sinusitis, the sinuses become inflamed and fill with mucus or pus, causing headaches, facial tenderness and minor breathing difficulties. There are two types of this disorder, which affects 35 million people in the USA alone. Acute sinusitis is caused by a disorder that causes swelling of the membranes of the nose, such as a viral respiratory infection or allergic rhinitis. The swelling prevents fluid from draining out of the sinus normally, and infection with bacteria, viruses or fungi then follows. Swimming

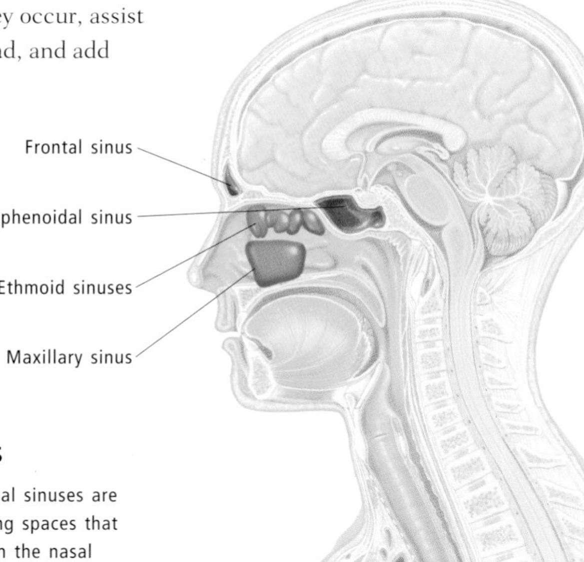

Sinuses

The paranasal sinuses are air-containing spaces that connect with the nasal cavity. They are lined with ciliated mucous membranes.

S

or immersion of the head in water may allow water and bacteria to enter the sinus, causing irritation and infection. Less commonly, dental infections such as a tooth abscess may spread into the sinus and infect it directly.

One of the symptoms of sinusitis is headache, the location of which depends on the sinus(es) involved. There may also be pain in the front of the head or around the eyes, the forehead or cheeks, or in the roof of the mouth or teeth. The pain results from the accumulation of undrained fluid which causes pressure within the sinus. There is often a thick yellow or yellow green nasal discharge and there may be fever and chills.

If the condition is due to bacterial infection, sinusitis is treated with antibiotics. Oral or nasal decongestants may help the sinuses to drain, although the use of nasal drops or sprays should be temporary, since long-term use can cause damage to the nasal lining. If sinusitis is persistent or recurrent the condition is known as chronic sinusitis. It is less common than acute sinusitis and may be caused by a deviated nasal septum or other obstruction of the nose. Chronic sinusitis can also be treated with antibiotics (if infection) and steroid or cromoglycate nasal sprays (if allergic).

If the condition is severe, surgery may be required to control it. This may involve unblocking the sinus, or repairing a deviated septum or nasal obstruction.

There are a number of alternative therapies that are used in chronic sinusitis. Acupuncture treatment is said to stimulate circulation and drainage in blocked sinuses. Aromatherapy uses hot water inhalations with added essential oils of tea tree, pine or eucalyptus. Herbalism uses horseradish, chilli, eyebright, goldenseal, garlic or olive leaf. Externally, poke root (*Phytolacca*) ointment can be rubbed over the blocked sinus region. Naturopathy suggests a light dairy-free wholefood diet, vitamin A and C supplements and exercise in fresh air. Reflexology massage is said to stimulate sinus zones located on each of the toes. Yoga practitioners use a Neti pot to pour weak salty water through the nasal passages to clear and cleanse. Pranayama or breathing exercises are also said to aid nasal decongestion.

SEE ALSO ***Allergies, Common cold, Sinuses***

SJÖGREN'S SYNDROME

The second most common autoimmune rheumatic disorder after rheumatoid arthritis, Sjögren's syndrome is a syndrome of dryness of the eyes and mouth. It is caused by a failure of the lacrimal glands, which produce tears, and the parotid glands, which produce saliva. In Sjögren's syndrome (for reasons that are not yet understood) these glands are attacked by the body's own immune system which produces antibodies against the gland tissues. The syndrome may occur on its own, or may be associated with other connective tissue disorders such as rheumatoid arthritis, scleroderma, or systemic lupus erythematous.

The symptoms of Sjögren's syndrome are dryness and grittiness of the eyes (sufferers complain of the sensation of "something in the eye", redness and burning of the eyes and sensitivity to light. Dryness of the mouth causes difficulty in swallowing and talking, abnormal taste or smell, mouth ulcers and dental cavities. A physician will confirm the condition with a special test called Schirmer's test which measures the quantity of tears produced in 5 minutes. Salivary flow studies may also be performed.

The disorder cannot be cured, but the symptoms can be managed by using artificial tears for eye dryness, and methylcellulose or saline sprays for mouth dryness. In cases of severe underlying disease corticosteroid and immunosuppressive drugs may be prescribed.

SEE ALSO ***Lacrimal glands, Salivary glands***

SKIN

The skin is a protective organ that covers the body, merging with mucous membranes at the openings of the body such as the mouth and anus. It is loosely attached to underlying tissues, and varies in thickness from 0.5 millimeter on the eyelids to $\frac{1}{7}$ inch (4 millimeters) or more on the palms and soles.

The function of skin is to protect the body from damaging external agents, extremes of temperature and invading organisms such as viruses, bacteria, fungi and parasites. Specialized nerve receptors in the skin also allow the body to sense pain, hot and cold, touch and pressure. Skin plays a role in temperature regulation, protection from ultraviolet light, in the manufacture of vitamin D and in attracting the opposite sex.

Structure

Skin is composed of two layers. The outer layer, called the epidermis or epithelium, is several cells thick. The deepest layers of the epidermis are called the basal and spinous layers and are made up of living cells. They produce cells called keratinocytes, which contain a tough insoluble protein called keratin. The hard dead outer layer of the skin, called the stratum corneum or horny layer, is made up of dead keratinocytes. This layer has a protective function and is particularly thick in the soles of the feet and the palms of the hand. Cells of the horny layer are continuously being shed and replaced by new keratinocytes from the deeper layers. In some areas, keratinocytes form specialized keratin-containing appendages such as the hair and the nails. The basal layer of the epidermis also contains melanocytes, which make the pigment melanin.

The dermis is the inner layer of the skin. It is composed of a network of fibers made from the proteins collagen and elastin, which provide strength and support to the skin. Among them are networks of blood vessels, nerves and fat lobules. The junction of the dermis and epidermis is irregular, with finger-like projections of dermis called papillae running up into the epidermis and causing elevations in the surface in the palms of the hands and the soles of the feet. In the fingers they create fingerprints.

Among the layers of the epidermis and the dermis are the specialized structures—the hair follicles, the sweat glands and the sebaceous glands. These develop from the epidermis and extend into the dermis. Beneath the dermis is a layer of fat cells arranged in lobules, which serves to insulate the body against extremes of temperature and provides a storage site for fat. The thickness of this layer varies greatly.

Specialized functions

The skin has several specialized functions. It plays a major role in temperature regulation. Tiny glands in the skin secrete sweat, a salty, watery fluid. As the sweat evaporates it cools the body surface and helps prevent overheating. Tiny hairs embedded in the skin have the ability to become erect in cold conditions, forming a fine blanket that helps insulate the skin from the cold. The skin contains fine blood vessels. In hot conditions the blood vessels dilate, allowing heat to escape from the skin. This also happens when body temperature is abnormally high, as in a fever. When outside conditions are cold, the blood vessels in the skin contract, diverting blood flow away from the skin to minimize loss of heat.

The skin contains varying amounts of a dark pigment called melanin, which protects the underlying tissues from harmful ultraviolet light by absorbing it. The amount of melanin in the skin varies according to a person's racial origins and is passed on as a genetic trait. The amount of melanin in the skin can be temporarily increased following periods of exposure to sunlight (suntanning). Sunlight also leads to the production of vitamin D in the skin—essential for the absorption of calcium from the gut and the maintenance of bone density.

Sebaceous glands in the skin open into hair follicles and secrete a material called sebum. Sebum is responsible for the waxy feel of skin; its function is to lubricate and soften the skin and to protect it from damage by water, chemicals and microorganisms.

Skin also contains specialized nerve endings that can sense hot and cold, touch, pain and pressure. Nerve impulses travel to the brain via nerves and pathways in the spinal cord, allowing the brain to experience these sensations and take appropriate action.

As the body ages, the features of skin change. In infancy the skin is soft, dry and free of wrinkles. At adolescence, pigmentation increases and body hair becomes longer and thicker, especially in the male. Exposure to the elements, along with physiological changes, result in ageing skin becoming dry, wrinkled and flaccid.

Skin may be destroyed by injury, burns or disease. In most cases regeneration takes

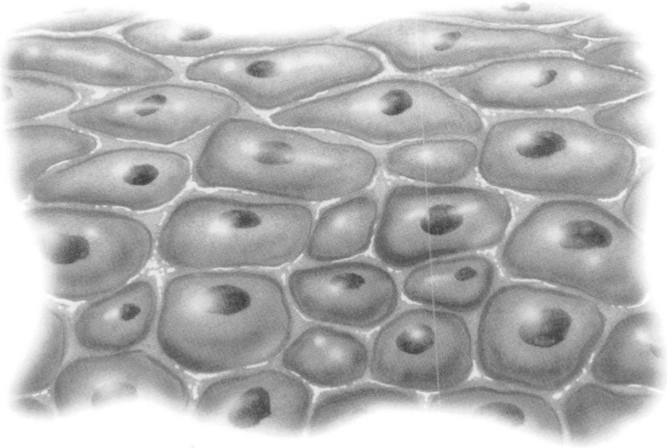

Stratified squamous skin cells

Near the surface of the skin (the horny layer), cells are flattened. The arrangement of cell layers provides a protective shield and prevents dehydration.

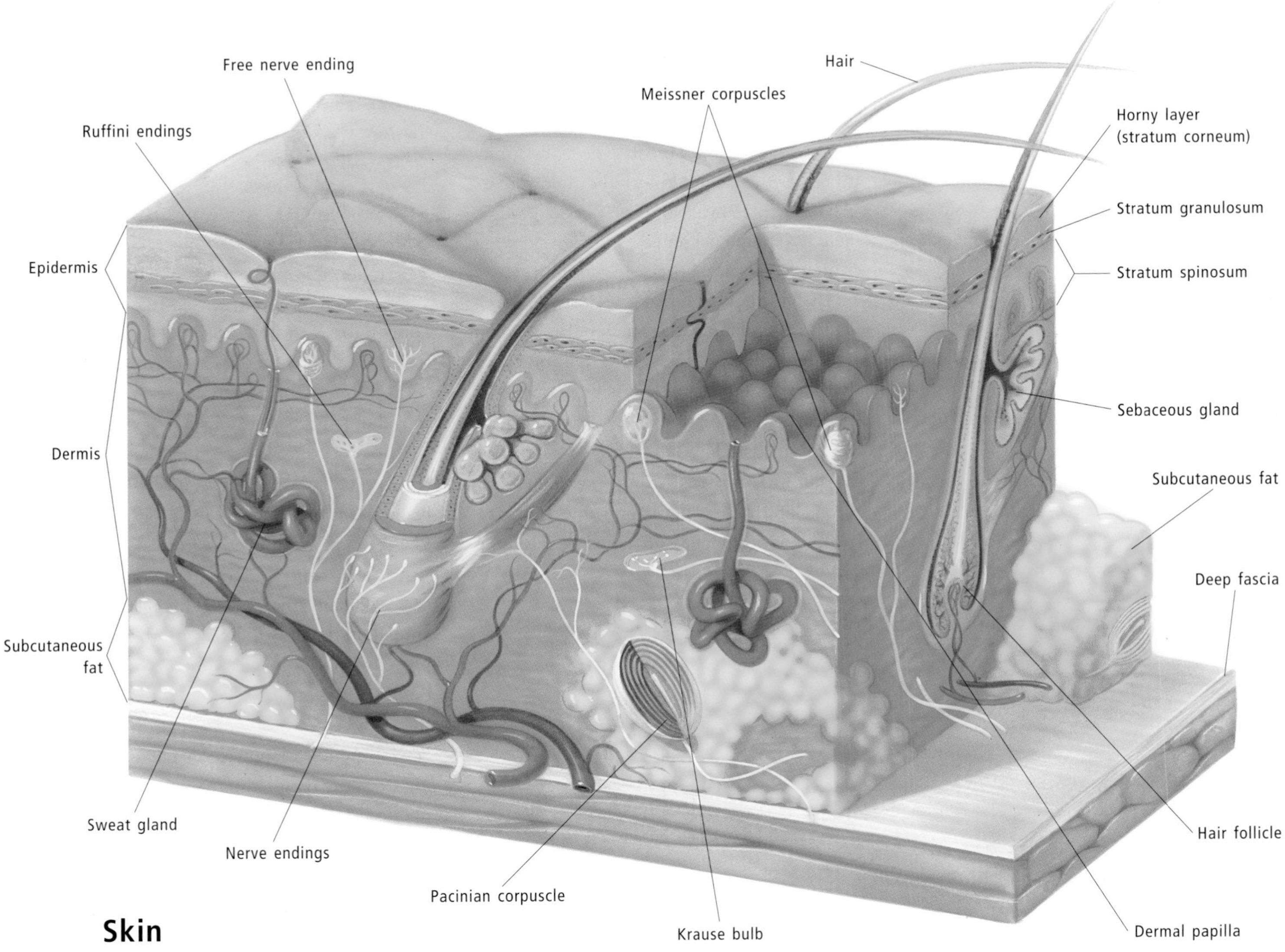

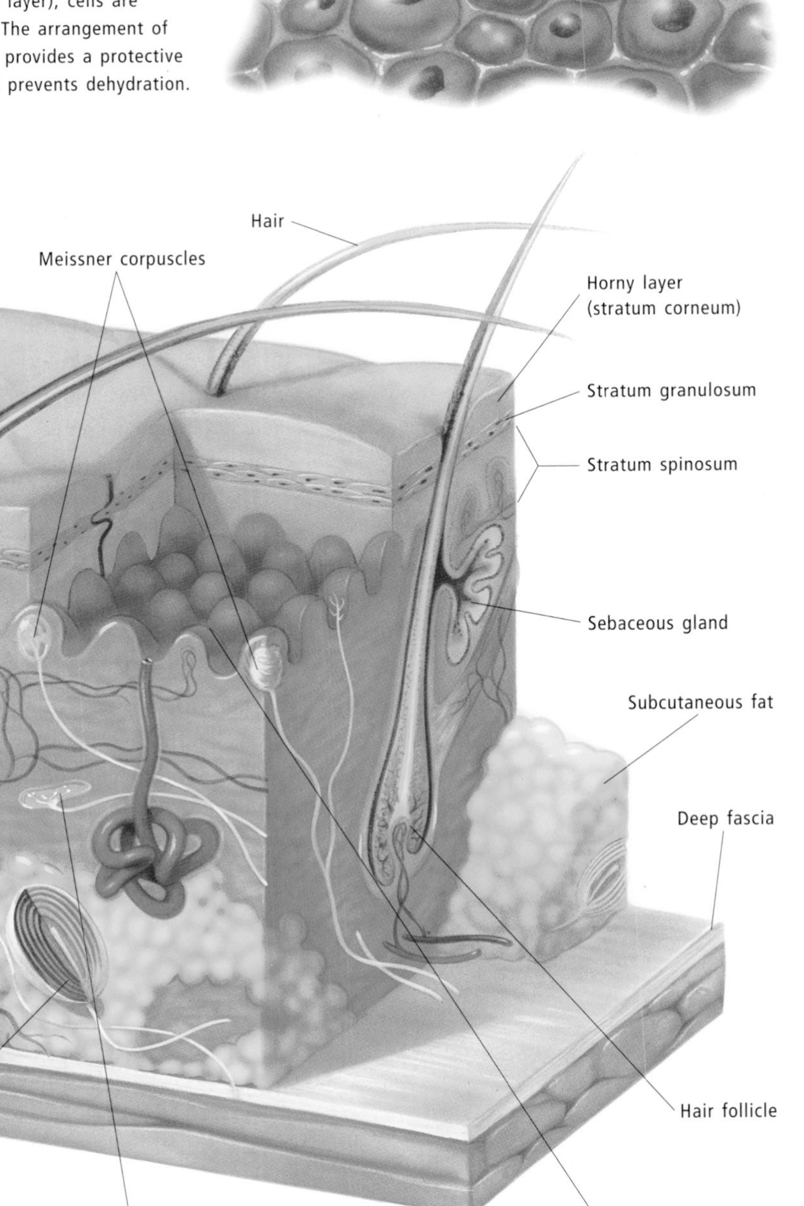

Skin

place from normal skin at the margins of the injured area. If the injury is severe enough, scar tissue forms, over which skin cannot regrow. The damaged area can be covered in skin taken from another site in the body. This is known as skin grafting.

Diseases and disorders

Skin can be affected by a number of diseases and conditions. Bacteria, viruses and fungi can cause infections such as acne, impetigo, herpes blisters and ringworm. Inflammation of the skin, dermatitis, may be caused by infection, a foreign irritant, or an allergic reaction. Many systemic diseases involve the skin, such as the so-called "childhood" diseases of measles and chickenpox. Other skin disorders include benign and malignant tumors, cysts, ulcers and frostbite. In certain conditions the skin color can change due to the presence of abnormal pigments; for example, it may appear yellow in jaundice because of high levels of the pigment bilirubin. Skin disorders are frequently treated by a primary-care physician; more difficult conditions are treated by a specialist dermatologist.

SEE ALSO *Acne, Blood vessels, Dermatitis, Hair, Herpes, Impetigo, Jaundice, Keratin, Melanin, Nails, Nerves, Ringworm, Scar, Sebaceous glands, Senses, Skin cancer, Sun exposure, Sweat glands, Temperature regulation*

SKIN CANCER

There are several different types of skin cancers. Collectively, they are among the most common cancers, especially in fair-skinned people. Exposure to the sun is the most important risk factor for development of skin cancer. In dark-skinned individuals, the skin pigment melanin provides some protection against damage by ultraviolet rays. Persons who lack this protection and/or those whose exposure to the sun is excessive may develop premature ageing of the skin, pre-cancerous skin changes such as scaly spots, and eventually cancers.

Other factors that can contribute to the development of skin cancers include exposure to certain industrial chemicals, exposure to x-rays, and certain hereditary disorders.

The three major varieties of skin cancer, known as basal cell carcinoma, squamous cell carcinoma and melanoma, arise from the surface layer of cells (the epidermis).

Basal cell carcinoma is the most common and most often develops on the upper part of the face, producing a lump or ulcer. This tumor invades locally but very rarely spreads beyond the site of origin. However, its invasive growth can destroy nearby tissues to a considerable extent.

Squamous cell carcinoma is the next most common and may develop anywhere on sun-exposed skin, including the face, neck and back of the hands. It usually appears as a scaly patch which may be red or ulcerated. Unlike basal cell carcinoma, squamous cell carcinoma of the skin will eventually spread to nearby lymph nodes or other body organs. An early (pre-invasive) form of squamous cell carcinoma is known as Bowen's disease, which looks similar but is easier to treat.

By far the most dangerous form of skin cancer is melanoma, a cancer of the pigment-producing cells of the skin. The tumor may have a dark color, but this is by no means necessary. Although the development of a melanoma is related to damage by ultraviolet rays, it may also arise in pre-existing moles or in skin that has not been subjected to repeated or prolonged sun exposure. Heredity plays a role in some cases. If untreated, this aggressive cancer spreads to lymph nodes and other organs of the body, and can cause death.

For all skin cancers—as is the case for cancers at almost all sites—the best outcomes are achieved if the diagnosis is made at an early clinical stage and treatment is begun promptly. Because the development of skin cancers is clearly related to sun exposure, minimizing ultraviolet-induced injury is the most effective approach to reducing the risk of these tumors. Wearing protective clothing and using suitable sunscreens are two obvious methods of limiting such injury to the skin. Less simple, but perhaps more important, is the changing of lifestyle and behavior to reduce risk.

Uncommonly, the skin can also be affected by a tumor known as mycosis fungoides, a variety of lymphoma that arises from T lymphocytes. This produces raised, scaly, itchy areas of skin that vary in color from bluish to brown and may develop ulcers. Mycosis fungoides can be controlled and may even be cured by treatment such as radiation therapy or chemotherapy.

SEE ALSO *Basal cell carcinoma, Melanoma, Mycosis fungoides, Squamous cell carcinoma*

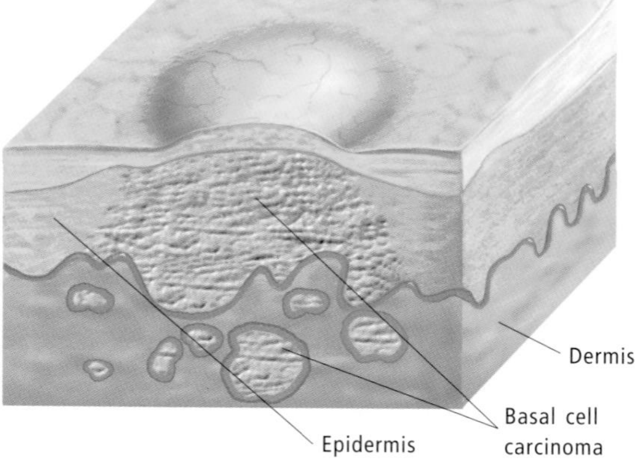

Skin cancer

Basal cell carcinoma is the most common form of skin cancer. It usually forms a localized tumor and very rarely spreads.

SKIN GRAFT

Skin grafting is a procedure in which healthy skin is taken from one area of the body and applied to area where no skin exists. It is part of the treatment of extensive wounds or burns, or in other surgery, for example, removal of large skin lesions.

The procedure is performed by a general surgeon or a plastic and reconstructive surgeon in hospital. During the procedure, healthy skin is removed using a skin-cutting instrument called a dermatome under local or general anesthesia. This healthy skin is spread on the area to be covered and held in place by a dressing or by stitches. The raw donor area is covered with a sterile dressing for a few days to prevent infection. If all goes well, new blood vessels will begin growing from the recipient area into the transplanted skin within 36 hours, though complete recovery takes 6 weeks or so. In some cases the graft does not "take" and the procedure will need to be performed again.

SEE ALSO *Grafting, Skin*

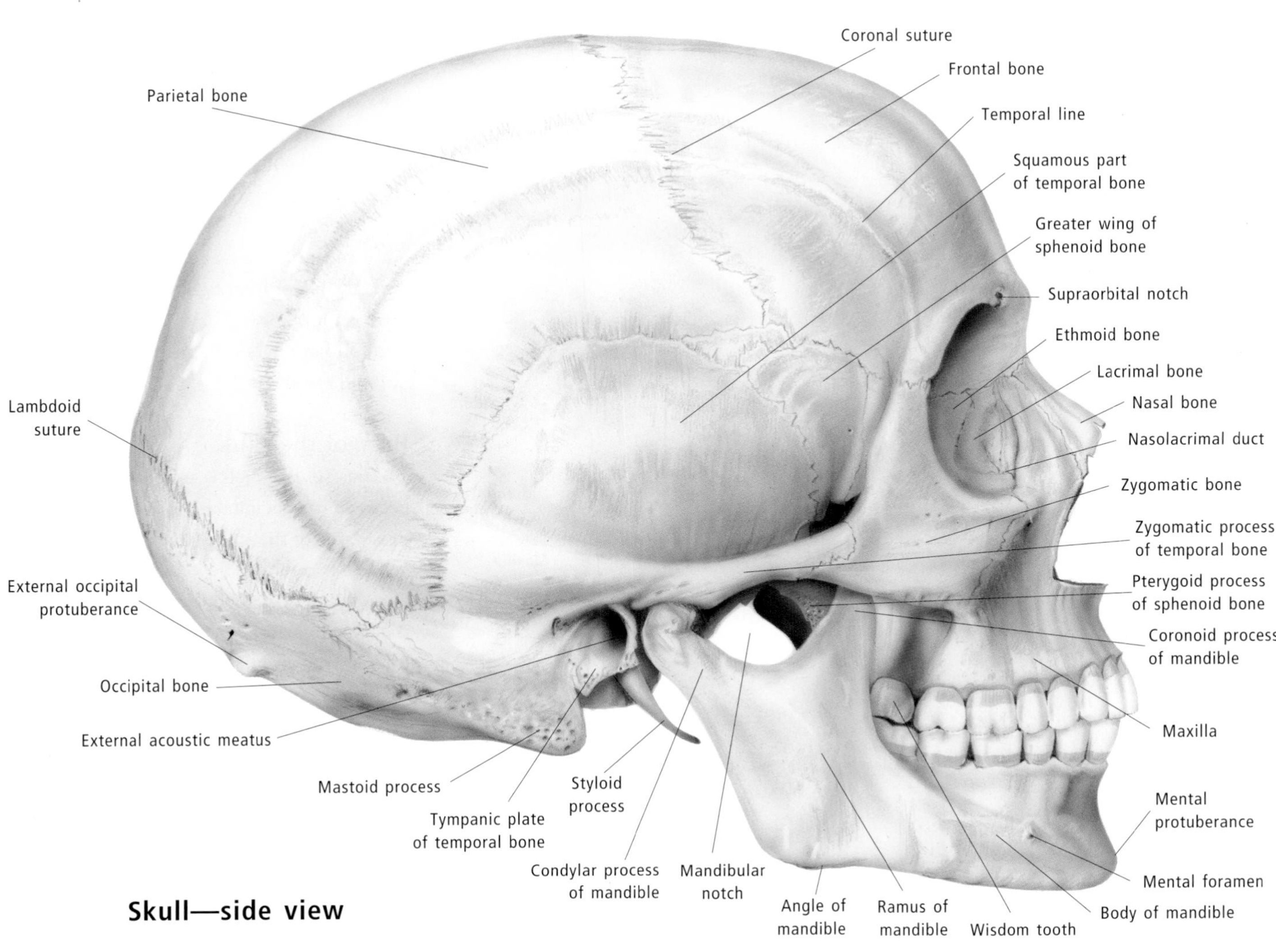

Skull—side view

SKULL

The skull forms the skeleton of the head, and is a part of the axial skeleton. It serves to protect the brain, eyes and inner ears; forms the upper and lower jaws; and provides attachment for muscles of the face, eyes, tongue, pharynx and neck.

The skull provides a strong protective case for the brain and the sensory organs for sight, hearing, balance and smell. This protective value is based on several factors, including the convex shape of the part enclosing the brain, the strength of the interlocking arches of the face, the hardness of the outer bones, and the presence of spongy bone within to absorb impact.

The skull consists of a number of small, irregular-shaped bones. There are seven unpaired, midline bones: the ethmoid, frontal, hyoid, occipital and sphenoid bones and the mandible and vomer. There are 10 pairs of paired bones, one on each side: the lacrimal, maxillary, nasal, palatine, parietal and zygomatic bones, and the temporal bone and middle ear bones (stapes, incus, malleus). There is also a variable number of sutural bones.

The forehead is formed by the frontal bone. Below that are the two nasal bones, with an opening below each. On either side are cavities for the eyes, called the orbits, so named because the eyes rotate in them. An arch of bone, the zygomatic arch, forms the skeleton of the cheek. The roof or vault of the cranium is formed by the frontal, parietal and occipital bones. The rear view of the skull is dominated by the occipital bone in the midline below, with the parietal bones above on each side. At the sides of the skull, the temporal bones contain the middle and inner ears, with the special sense organs for hearing and balance. The middle ear is unique in containing a chain of three tiny bones (ossicles) which relay sound vibrations from the tympanic membrane.

A woman typically has a smaller, lighter skull with relatively smaller paranasal sinuses and other small differences, but it is often impossible to say whether a given skull is male or female. Minor differences in the shape of the frontal, ethmoid, maxillary and sphenoid bones occur between different races.

Strictly, the skull consists of the cranium and the mandible (lower jawbone) plus the hyoid bone at the base of the tongue, but the term "skull" is often applied loosely to the cranium only.

Cranium

The cranium consists of two regions, one accommodating the brain and the other forming the skeleton of the face. The first part consists of a strong box, approximately ovoid in shape, supported by the spine. To this box is attached a series of arches, which form the skeleton of the face. From the side, the division of the skull into the larger, ovoid brain-case and the smaller, approximately triangular skeleton of the face, is clear.

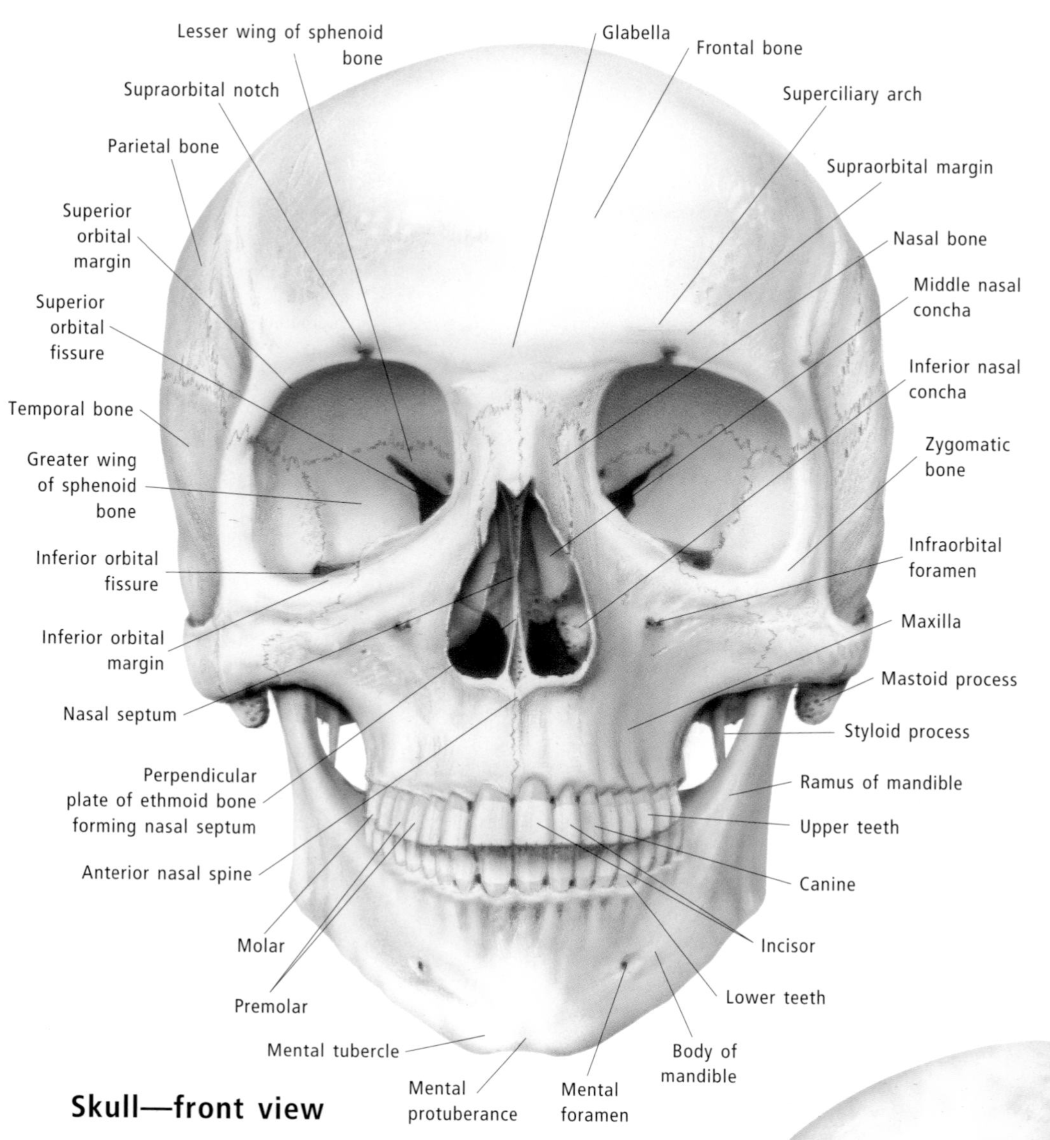

Skull—front view

The bones of the cranium are linked together by "joints" known as sutures, found only in the skull. No active movement occurs. The adjacent bones have irregular, interlocking edges (rather like a jigsaw puzzle) bound together by fibrous connective tissue. Sometimes there are small sutural bones interpolated in sutures between the bigger bones.

At birth, the cranium is relatively large and the face is small. The teeth are not fully formed and the paranasal sinuses are rudimentary. There is no mastoid process. Between some bones of the vault, ossification is incomplete, leaving gaps containing fibrous connective tissue, particularly at the angles of the parietal bones. These gaps are called fontanelles. The anterior fontanelle, easily felt in the newborn child, lies between the separate halves of the frontal bone and the two parietal bones; about 1½ inches (3 centimeters) long and 1 inch (2 centimeters) wide, it closes during the second year. The posterior fontanelle at the apex of the occipital bone, between the two parietal bones, is closed at 2 months. There are several smaller fontanelles. Growth of the skull is rapid for the first 7 years, then slows until puberty, when there is another period of rapid growth.

Base of the skull

The base of the skull is supported by joints between the occipital bone and the uppermost bone of the spine (the atlas or first cervical vertebra). The joint with the atlas permits the head a nodding motion. There is a large hole in the occipital bone, the foramen magnum, above the spinal canal of the atlas vertebra, for the passage of the medulla oblongata and meninges.

Sagittal suture
Lambda
Temporal bone
Lambdoid suture
Mastoid process
Parietal bone
Occipital bone
Ramus of mandible
Superior nuchal line
External occipital protuberance
Angle of mandible

Skull—back view

Jaw

The upper jaw and the bony roof of the mouth are formed by the maxillary and palatine bones. The mandible, the skeleton of the lower jaw, articulates with the temporal bones on each side at the temporomandibular joints. These joints are condylar synovial joints, enabling the mandible to be elevated and depressed, protruded, retracted and moved side to side. The hyoid bone lies in the root of the tongue, where it gives attachment to muscles of the tongue, floor of the mouth and neck.

The teeth are bony structures attached to the upper and lower jaws, projecting through the mucous membrane of the mouth into the mouth cavity. Their free surfaces are covered with a very hard mineral substance called dental enamel. The other end of each tooth has one or more roots embedded in sockets in the maxilla or mandible.

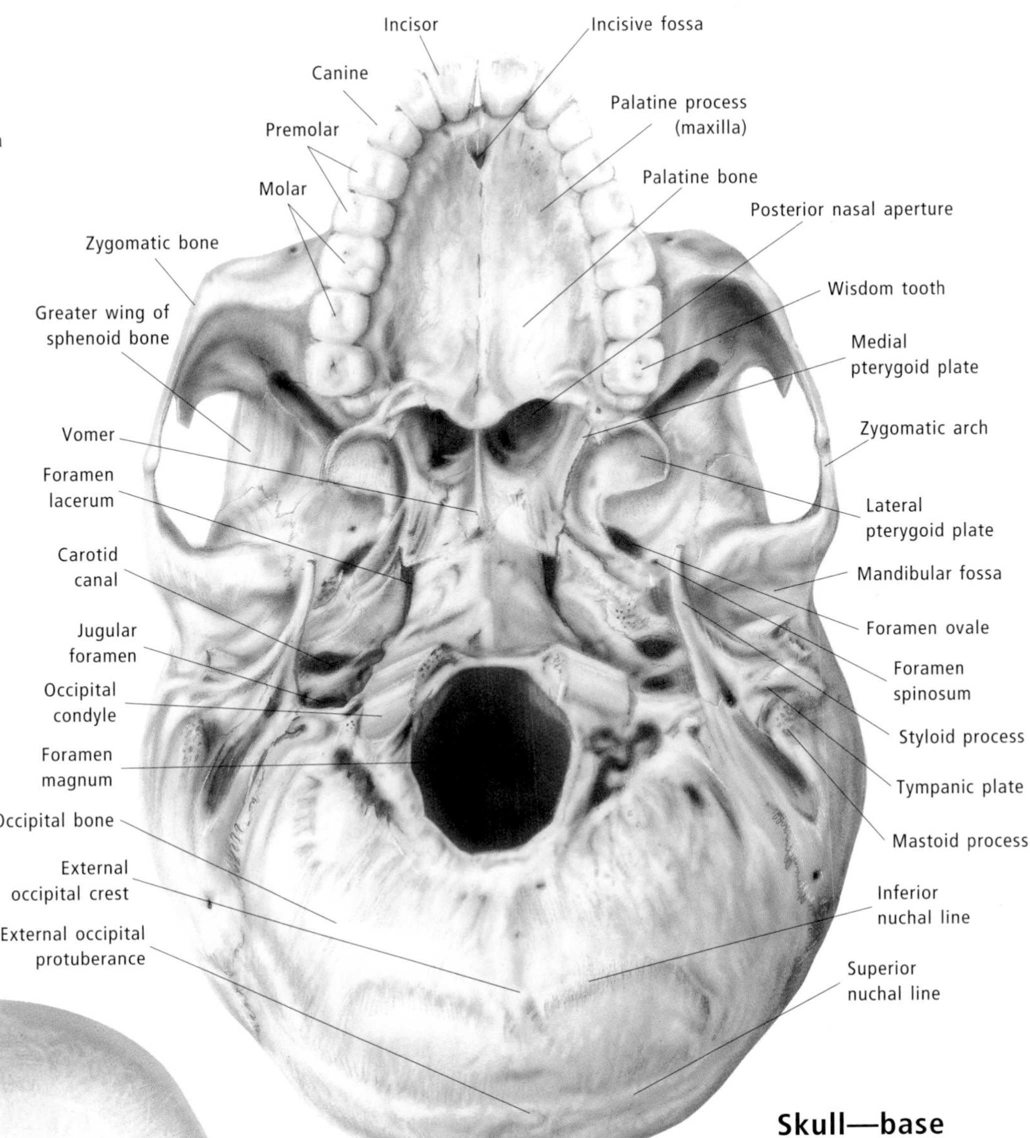

Skull—base

Frontal bone
Coronal suture
Parietal bone
Sagittal suture
Occipital bone

Skull—top

Cavities of the skull

The bones of the skull enclose several spaces. The largest cavity accommodates the brain; this is usually described as three contiguous regions, the anterior, middle and posterior cranial fossae. The orbits are pyramidal spaces (tapering backwards) on either side of the face. The nasal cavities are flattened ducts, into which protrude curved plates called conchae or turbinates, which increase the surface area of the nasal cavities. The nasal cavities are connected to paranasal sinuses in the frontal, ethmoid, maxillary and sphenoid bones.

The skull has openings to the exterior for the eyes, nostrils, ears, and mouth, as well as the foramen magnum already mentioned. There are numerous small apertures for nerves and blood vessels.

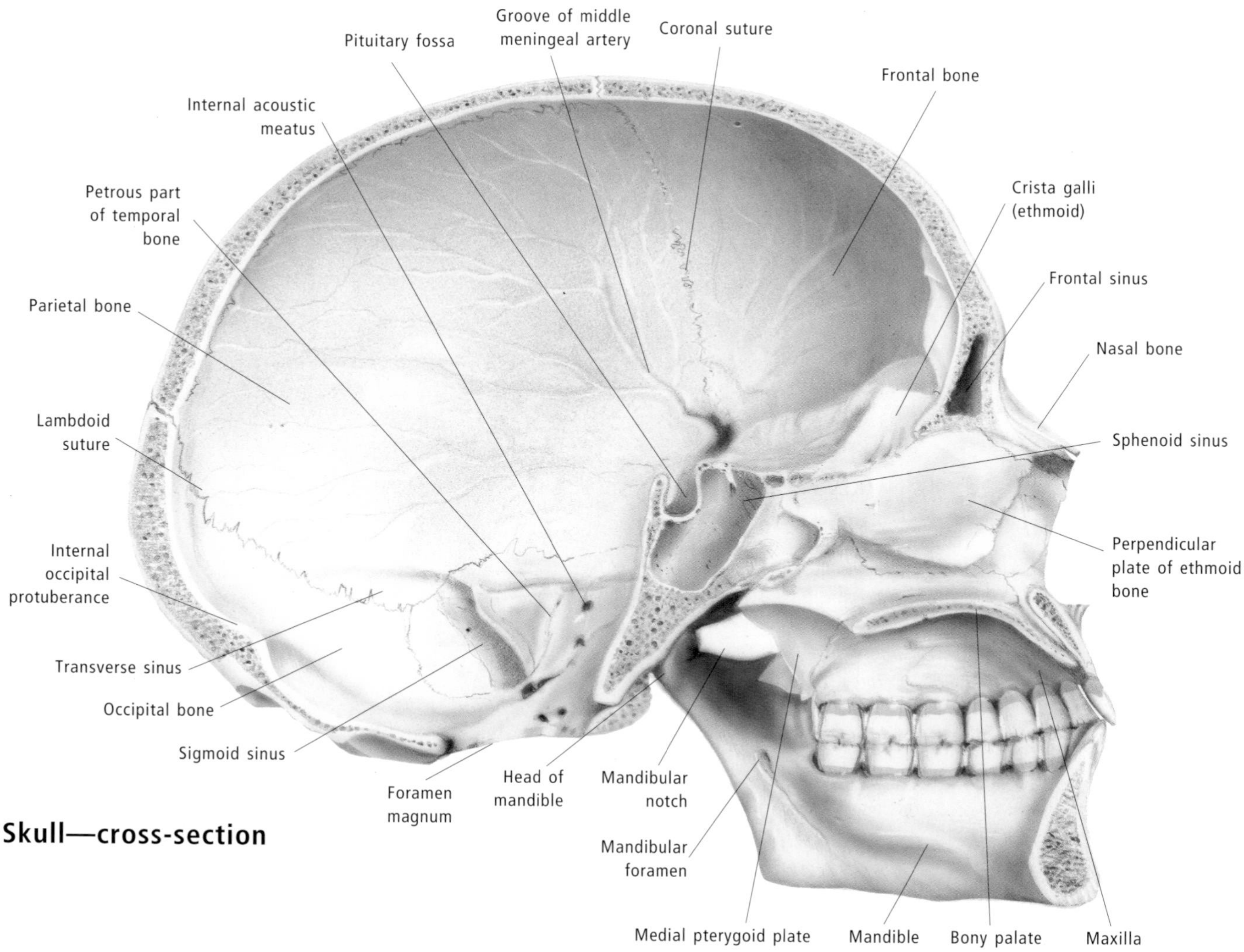

Groove of middle meningeal artery
Pituitary fossa
Coronal suture
Frontal bone
Internal acoustic meatus
Petrous part of temporal bone
Crista galli (ethmoid)
Frontal sinus
Parietal bone
Nasal bone
Lambdoid suture
Sphenoid sinus
Perpendicular plate of ethmoid bone
Internal occipital protuberance
Transverse sinus
Occipital bone
Sigmoid sinus
Foramen magnum
Head of mandible
Mandibular notch
Mandibular foramen
Medial pterygoid plate
Mandible
Bony palate
Maxilla

Skull—cross-section

Fetal skulls

The fontanelles are of great importance during the birth of a baby as they give the baby's head the capacity to change shape as it passes through the narrow birth canal.

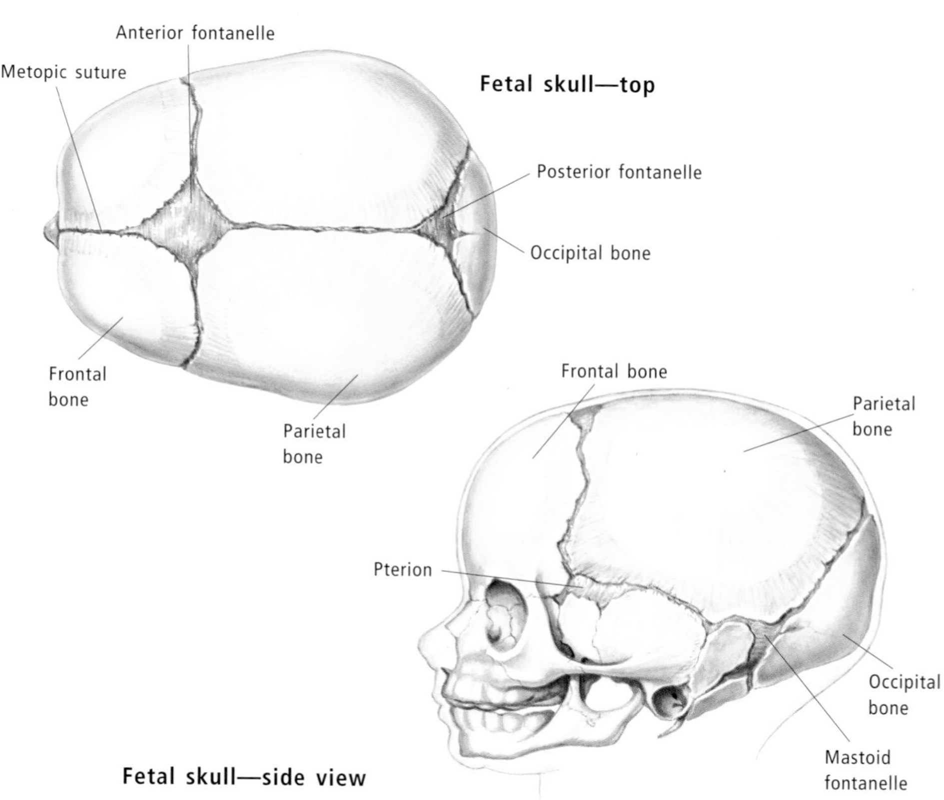

Anterior fontanelle
Metopic suture
Posterior fontanelle
Occipital bone
Frontal bone
Parietal bone

Fetal skull—top

Frontal bone
Parietal bone
Pterion
Occipital bone
Mastoid fontanelle

Fetal skull—side view

Skull injuries

Fractures of the bones of the skull can be associated with serious injury to the brain, meninges and the sensory organs for sight, hearing, balance and smell. A particular risk with skull fractures is intracranial hemorrhage, which may cause pressure damage to the brain. The most frequently fractured bones are the lower jaw and the nasal bones. The skulls of children are more elastic than those of the adult; blows to the head may produce serious injury to the underlying brain and meninges without fracturing bones.

SEE ALSO *Bones, Ear, Fontanelle, Head, Nose, Sinuses, Skeletal system, Teeth*

SLEEP

Sleep has a number of functions in keeping the human body running smoothly. A "biological clock" located in the brain regulates circadian (daily) sleeping and waking patterns. Sleep researchers have defined four stages in the way human adults sleep.

The first is the transition from wakefulness through drowsiness to real sleep. Stage two is real (but light) sleep—the sleeper can usually be aroused. Stages three and four are deep slow-wave (referring to brain-wave patterns) sleep, stage four being the deepest. A sleeper is difficult to wake during this time.

An adult sleeps in 90-minute cycles at night, starting with light sleep (about 50 percent of sleep time), going to deep sleep (about 20 percent of sleep time) and back to light sleep, with dreams (about 30 percent of sleep time). There are two distinct sleep states—rapid eye movement (REM), when the eyeballs move rapidly back and forth under the eyelids, which is associated with dreaming, and non-REM (when the body shuts down to vital functions only).

Babies sleep very differently from adults. They sleep better in a noisy environment than a quiet one; their sleep is more restless and characterized by a variety of facial expressions. REM and non-REM sleep are almost identical for a newborn baby; not until around 3–4 months does a baby fall into a deep sleep, which lasts only half the time it does in an adult. Around the first birthday a child's sleep–wake pattern begins to approximate that of an adult. Babies must learn the difference between night and day as their circadian rhythms are not naturally "tuned" at birth. Research suggesting that babies dream, beginning at 25 weeks' gestation, has led to the conclusion that dreaming is necessary to stimulate and activate the development of the brain. Research has still to establish the purpose of dreaming in older people.

Babies are unable to manage on night-time sleep alone. Most need to nap in 1–2 hour periods during the day, usually until they are aged about 2–3 years. By this time most babies will have fewer or no night wakings.

Children sleep more deeply than adults. They are not at all responsive to stimuli such as sound, light, touch or heat. Adolescents also sleep differently from adults and in most instances, because of their lifestyle, are probably sleep-deprived. Adolescents who are allowed to sleep until they wake naturally usually sleep for 10–11 hours; it has been found that their circadian rhythms shift so that they naturally go to sleep later at night, and wake later in the morning.

How much sleep people need differs among individuals. It is generally thought, however, that babies need between 9–18 hours in a 24-hour period, children and adolescents between 9–12 hours, and adults between 8–9 hours.

When humans do not get enough sleep on a regular basis they establish a "sleep debt" and are unable to perform at their best throughout the day. This applies to children as well as adults. Both children and adults are getting enough sleep when they wake up of their own accord.

SEE ALSO *Infancy, Insomnia, Sleep apnea, Sleep disturbances, Snoring*

Sleep

Neurons in the reticular formation of the brain stem are important in regulating sleep. Distinct groups of neurons trigger REM and non-REM sleep. A "biological clock" located in the hypothalamus regulates daily sleeping and waking patterns (circadian rhythm).

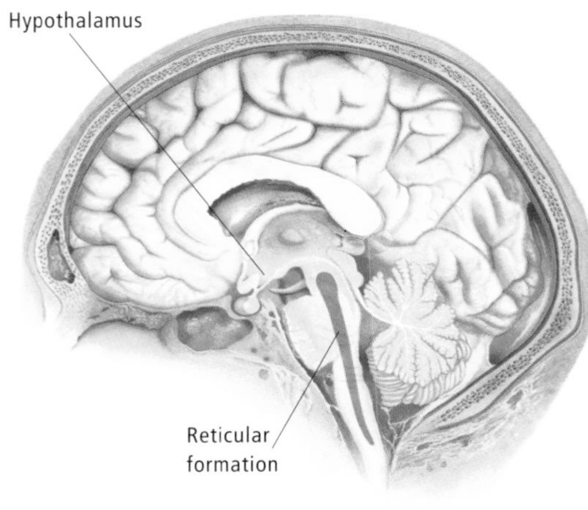
Hypothalamus
Reticular formation

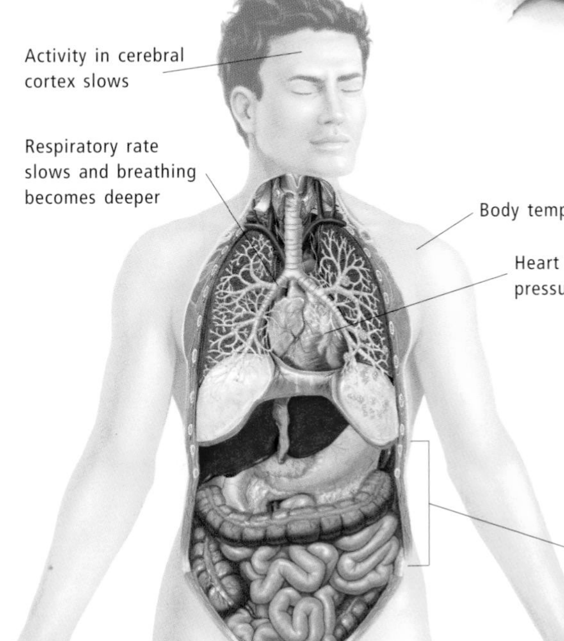
Activity in cerebral cortex slows
Respiratory rate slows and breathing becomes deeper
Body temperature drops
Heart rate and blood pressure slow
Digestion and metabolism slow

Deep sleep

During deep non-rapid eye movement (non-REM) sleep, the body slows down to perform only vital functions. The muscles relax, the rate of breathing and heartbeat slows and blood pressure decreases.

NB: In this illustration the top two-thirds of the lungs and pleura have been cut away to show the heart and bronchial tree.

SLEEP APNEA

Sleep apnea is one of the most common and dangerous types of sleep disorder, characterized by repeated episodes of the cessation of breathing during sleep. It can cause drowsiness, fatigue and loss of concentration in the day and has also been linked to hypertension and heart disease. Snoring, not in itself a sign of sleep apnea, often accompanies it.

Sleep apnea sufferers will have difficulty breathing while asleep because the airflow is blocked. The reason may be over-relaxation of the throat muscles and tongue, often a problem in people with receding chins, or those with fatty tissue in the airway (often linked to obesity). Other causes may be central sleep apnea (a dysfunction in the brain that controls breathing), smoking and excessive alcohol. Sleep apnea affects about 9 percent of men and 4 percent of women.

Treatment for sleep apnea is nasal continuous positive airway pressure (CPAP). The sufferer wears a soft plastic mask over the nose during sleep; this provides pressurized room air to prevent the airways from collapsing. Surgery is an option in extreme cases, and in children the removal of adenoids and tonsils may be recommended.

SEE ALSO *Insomnia, Sleep, Sleep disturbances, Snoring*

SLEEP DISTURBANCES

Sleep disturbances include insomnia, narcolepsy, restless legs syndrome (akathisia), night terrors, nightmares, teeth-grinding (bruxism), sleeptalking (somniloquy), sleepwalking (somnambulism), snoring, sleep apnea and bed-wetting (enuresis).

Those who describe themselves as poor sleepers are usually found, upon investigation, to sleep better than they imagine, although they usually have disturbed sleep with frequent body movements, less REM sleep than other people, and some wakeful periods. Poor sleepers are treated either with medication or behavioral programs.

Nightmares are vivid, frightening dreams which can happen at any time of life. They occur in the last third of the sleep period and can usually be recalled. They usually reflect current difficulties or anxieties. Anxiety dreams which happen occasionally to many people are often precursors to nightmares.

Night terrors (pavor nocturnus) usually occur in children, occasionally in young adults, and are quite different from nightmares. The child sits upright in bed and screams or shouts, is sometimes coherent, sometimes incoherent, and usually inconsolable. Waking the child during the terror is not recommended as it may cause confusion and distress. The episode will be forgotten in the morning. No treatment is needed unless episodes are frequent or there is some other cause for concern, in which case medical advice should be sought.

Restless legs syndrome is fairly common and occurs just before falling asleep. It is found mostly in the over-50s, in pregnant women and in people suffering from stress. In severe cases the movement of the legs may be uncontrollable; it may be treated by benzodiazepines (but not in pregnancy).

Sleeptalking is usually incoherent mumbling rather than intelligible sentences. It is common and occurs at all ages. Sometimes sleeptalking is associated with night terrors, sleepwalking or confusional arousals, but mostly it is of little consequence.

Sleepwalking happens mostly in childhood and adolescence and is a complex set of automatic behaviors. It generally lasts for less than 15 minutes and takes place in the first third of the sleep period. Sleepwalkers get out of bed and walk slowly in an automatic way. They may engage in activities such as eating or getting dressed, but their actions are automatic and uncoordinated. Sleepwalking may be associated with stress, anxiety, sleep deprivation, a full bladder, noise or medication. There is often a family history. The best action is to safeguard the sleepwalker from any accidents.

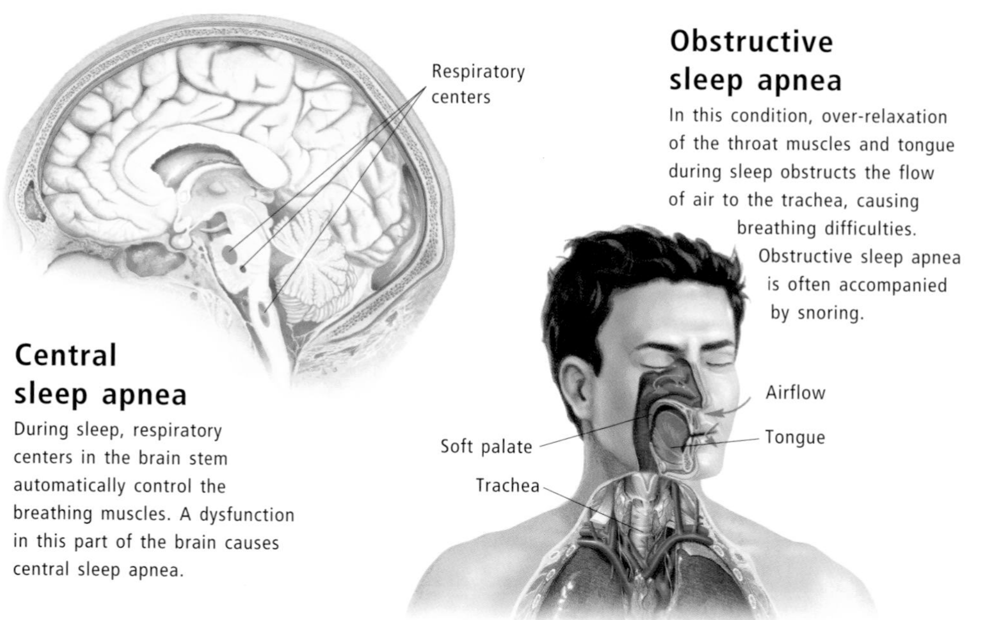

Central sleep apnea
During sleep, respiratory centers in the brain stem automatically control the breathing muscles. A dysfunction in this part of the brain causes central sleep apnea.

Obstructive sleep apnea
In this condition, over-relaxation of the throat muscles and tongue during sleep obstructs the flow of air to the trachea, causing breathing difficulties. Obstructive sleep apnea is often accompanied by snoring.

Teeth-grinding is not associated with a particular sleep stage and does not affect sleep. Other sleep problems include poor sleep hygiene, a common problem among adolescents who do not get enough sleep at the right time and so have difficulty falling asleep and staying asleep, and may also have difficulty staying awake during the day; environmental sleep disturbance, which is directly related to too much light or too much noise or both; obstructive sleep apnea, which is difficulty breathing during sleep; bed-wetting; hyposomnia (too little sleep); and hypersomnia (an increase in sleep of around 25 percent more than normal, and which may indicate a more serious problem in the individual).

SEE ALSO *Bed-wetting, Insomnia, Narcolepsy, Restless legs syndrome, Sleep, Sleep apnea, Sleeping pills, Snoring, Teeth-grinding*

SLEEPING PILLS

Drugs administered to induce sleep are usually potentially addictive and therefore dangerous over long periods. As the mechanism of sleep is understood more thoroughly, so also are the effects of medications used to induce sleep. Some drugs affect REM (rapid eye movement) sleep, and research suggests this may have far-reaching consequences. Alternative remedies such as Bach flower essences, acupuncture, aromatherapy, massage and relaxation techniques are said to be just as effective with fewer unpleasant consequences.

SEE ALSO *Acupuncture, Aromatherapy, Drug dependence, Massage, Sedatives, Sleep, Sleep disturbances*

SLEEPING SICKNESS

In tropical Africa, the bites of the tsetse fly can pass parasites called trypanosomes to humans, causing the frequently fatal sleeping sickness or African trypanosomiasis. The first sign is sometimes a red sore at the site of the bite. Other symptoms, which may not follow for weeks or even months, include headaches, fever, extreme fatigue, swollen lymph nodes and aching muscles and joints. As the parasites invade the central nervous system, confusion, seizures and impaired walking and talking occur.

There is no vaccine or preventive medication available. With drug treatment and hospitalization, patients normally recover, although it may take years to be completely free of the disease.

SEE ALSO *Infectious diseases*

SMALLPOX

Smallpox was an acute and contagious viral infection that was eradicated worldwide by a vaccination campaign launched by the World Health Organization. The program began in 1967, when smallpox caused about 2 million deaths. The last known naturally occurring case of the disease was reported in 1977.

Smallpox was spread by contact, the virus being exhaled or expelled in saliva by the infected person. The infection could cause death before the characteristic skin pustules appeared, or be so minor that symptoms went unnoticed; in those cases the virus could continue to be spread. The virus could also live in bedding, clothing or dust for up to 18 months, although it would not replicate outside the human body. The vaccination program was so successful that it has now generally been discontinued.

SEE ALSO *Immunization, Viruses*

SMELL

The sense of smell is one of the major senses, along with sight, hearing, taste and balance, and the senses of touch, proprioception (sense of movement and body position), pain and temperature. It responds to the chemical nature of airborne substances breathed into the nose, and also to odors from food and drink that reach the nose from the mouth and pharynx. It is extraordinarily sensitive to some volatile substances, such as methyl mercaptan, which is added to natural gas to give it an odor. The receptors for the sense of smell are situated in the olfactory mucosa that line the upper part of the cavities of the nose. Sensations are carried by the olfactory nerves to a part of the brain above the nose which is specialized for receiving and interpreting sensations of smell.

SEE ALSO *Nose, Olfactory system*

Smell

Olfactory path

Odor molecules enter the nostrils and pass into the nasal cavity where they dissolve in olfactory mucosa in the nasal lining. They stimulate olfactory receptors which send signals to the olfactory bulb. From here, nerve signals travel along the olfactory tract to reach the olfactory cortex, the limbic system and the hypothalamus in the brain. This is where smells are identified and the body's response coordinated. Smell has the most direct pathway to the brain of all the senses.

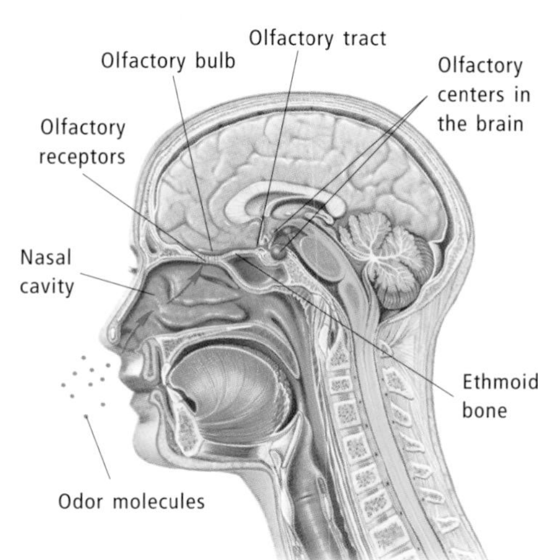

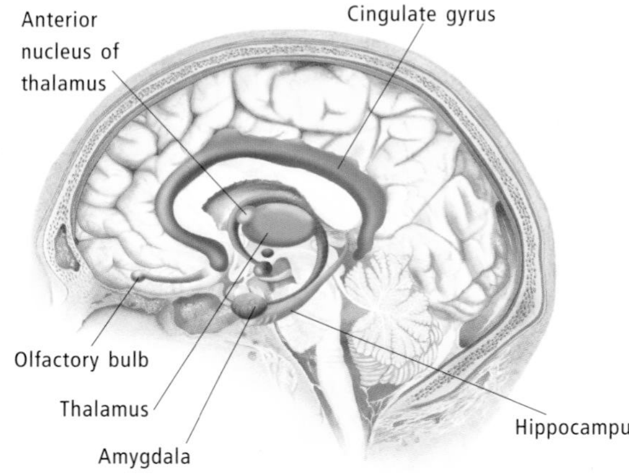

Smell and the limbic system

The olfactory bulbs are directly connected to the hippocampus and the amygdala in the limbic system, which is important for memory and emotion. This is why smells are evocative of past places and feelings. Some smells stimulate the limbic system to activate the hypothalamus and pituitary gland,which triggers the release of hor-mones associated with appetite and emotional responses including pleasure, fear, and sexual drive.

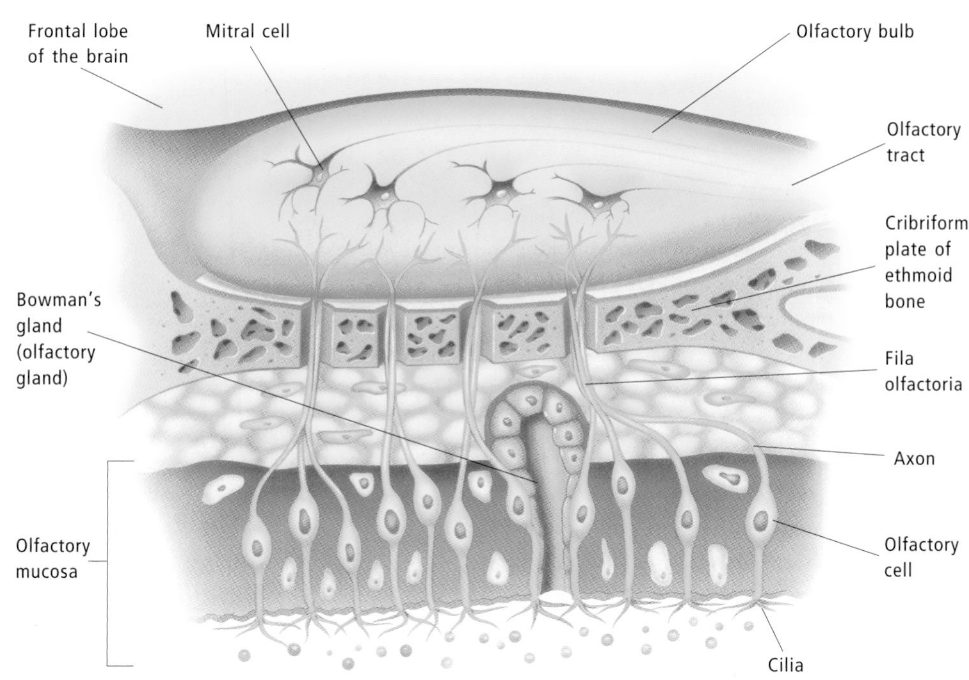

Olfactory apparatus

The olfactory receptors are located in the roof of the nasal cavity. A small area of mucous membrane (the olfactory epithelium) contains millions of nerve cells bearing cilia. When odor molecules are dissolved on the moist surface of the epithelium, they stimulate the nerve cells. Nerve impulses are transmitted along the nerve fibers through holes in the cribriform plate to the olfactory bulb under the frontal lobe of the brain.

S

SMOKING

Smoking is the drawing into the mouth, and inhalation, of smoke from burning tobacco or other plant material. Cigarettes are the most common form of smoking, with pipes and cigars in a minority. Tobacco is the substance most commonly smoked, but the use of cannabis, also smoked in cigarettes and pipes, is also widespread although it is illegal in many parts of the world.

Smoking was introduced into European society by explorers who observed its use by the peoples of Asia and the Americas, who believed it had medicinal properties. Current use of tobacco is likely to be habitual for reasons of pleasure and relaxation and to relieve the craving for nicotine, a chemical component of tobacco on which smokers become dependent.

Throughout the twentieth century evidence accumulated that smoking had harmful, even deadly, effects on health and that it delivered no physical benefits other than to relieve the cravings of those addicted. The strength of this addiction can be such that in times of economic and currency instability, or in special situations such as in the huge prison camps set up in Europe during World War II, cigarettes are used as a form of currency.

In 1964 the Surgeon General of the United States of America gave the first official warning of the health hazards of smoking. Since then the percentages of the populations of Australia, UK and the USA who smoke have declined, but current trends show an increase in women as a proportion of all smokers as more women than men take up the habit.

Smoking is now actively discouraged in many countries, both by private regulation, including organizations creating no-smoking areas, and by legislation, enforcing health warnings on product packs, prohibiting sale of tobacco products to minors and banning smoking in areas such as designated public places or on public transport. Health and life insurance premiums are generally lower for non-smokers.

That about a quarter of most populations continue to smoke illustrates just how difficult it is to overcome nicotine addiction and the aggressive marketing strategies used by cigarette companies.

Heart disease

By causing disease of the arteries that supply oxygen to the heart, smoking increases the risk of a range of heart conditions including angina, myocardial infarction, cardiomyopathy, heart failure and cardiac arrest. Cessation of smoking is an essential part of the treatment for individuals with heart disease.

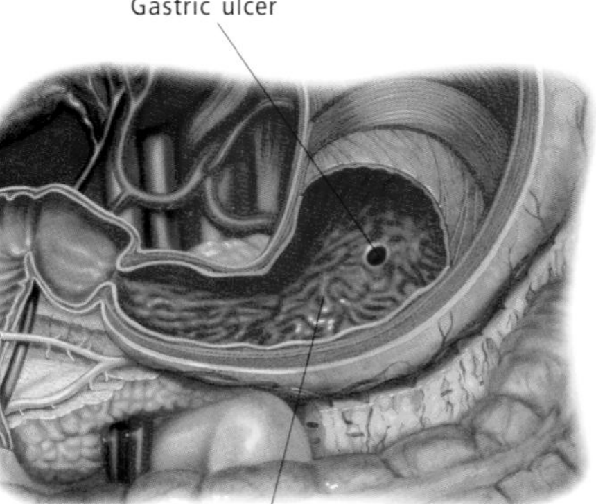

Gastric ulcers

Smokers are at increased risk of developing gastric ulcers. When tobacco smoke is inhaled it stimulates acid production by the stomach. Over time, this acid attacks the mucous membrane in the walls of the stomach causing ulceration.

Stroke and cerebral hemorrhage

When the walls of blood vessels thicken and deteriorate as a result of smoking, the arteries in the brain may narrow, blocking off the blood supply and causing a stroke. Diseased vessels may develop aneurysms and burst, causing a cerebral hemorrhage. Either condition may result in death or severe neurological disability.

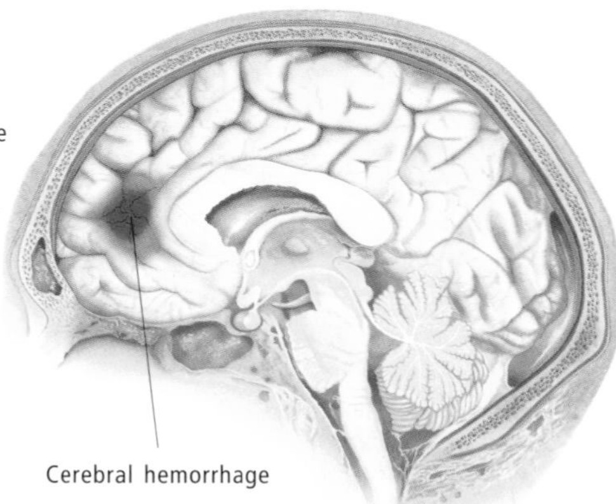

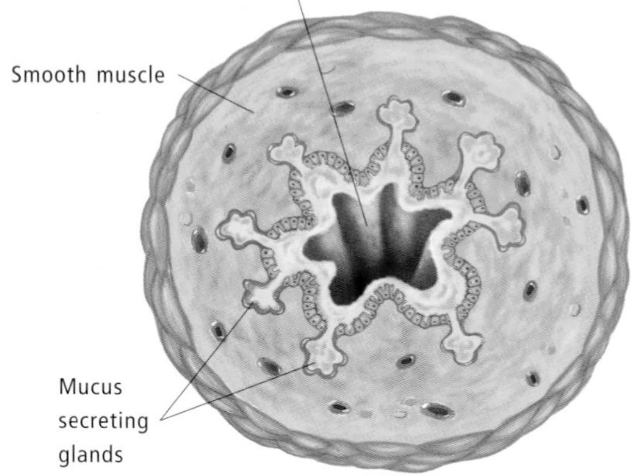

Asthma

Cigarette smoke irritates the smooth muscles of the bronchi (airways) and increases mucus secretion from the glands in the bronchi. It aggravates the symptoms of asthma including breathing difficulties, and may precipitate an asthma attack.

The effects of smoking

The immediate effects of inhaling tobacco—increased heart rate, raised blood pressure and stimulation of the nervous system—are reversible. However, the long-term effects of years of smoking are often not reversible, making smoking one of the leading causes of death and disease.

Lung cancer

Lung

Cancers

Cigarette smoke contains 43 known carcinogens (cancer-causing agents). It can cause cancers in the tissues of the lungs, mouth, pharynx and esophagus through direct contact, as well as cancers at more distant sites, such as the bladder, kidney, pancreas and cervix. Smoking causes almost 90 percent of lung cancers.

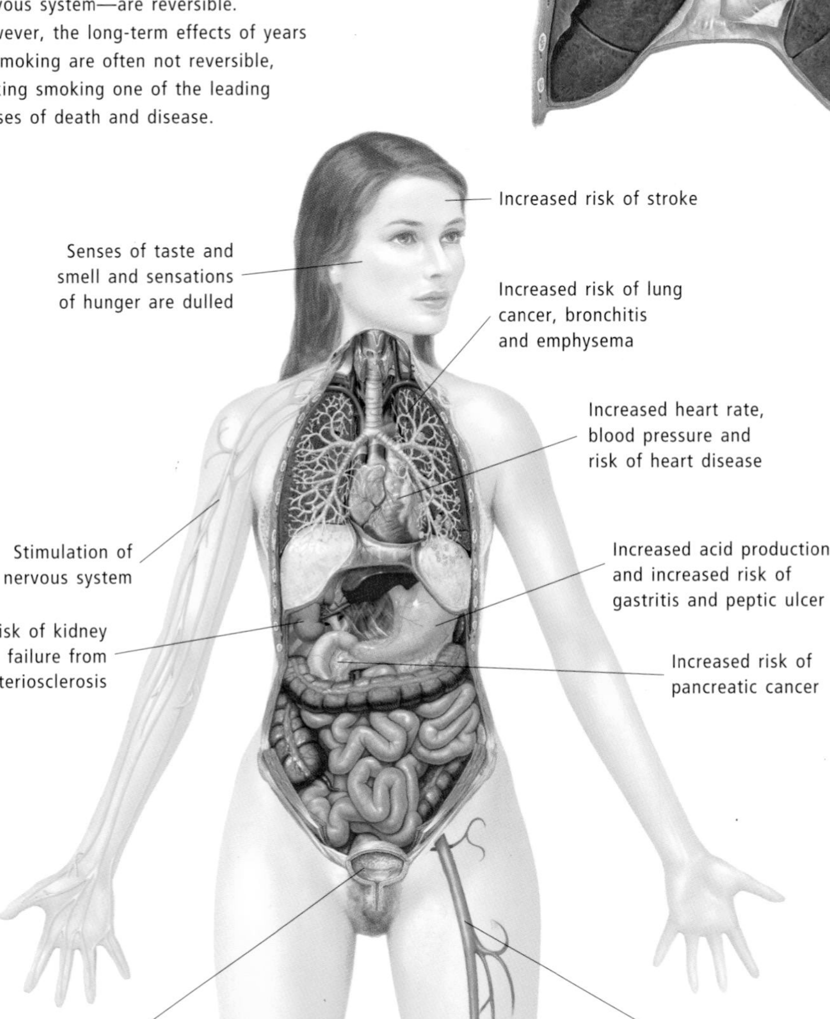

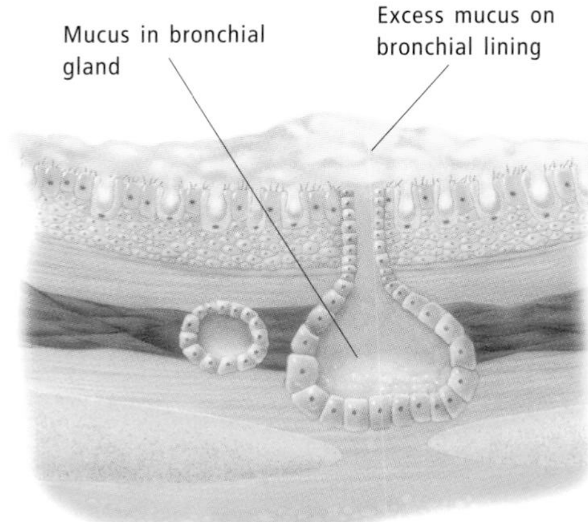

Bronchitis

Cigarette smoke damages the airways of the lungs, increasing the risk and frequency of chest infections such as acute bronchitis. Many heavy smokers develop chronic bronchitis (repeated and prolonged episodes of bronchitis) in which excess mucus secretion in the airways causes cough and sputum production.

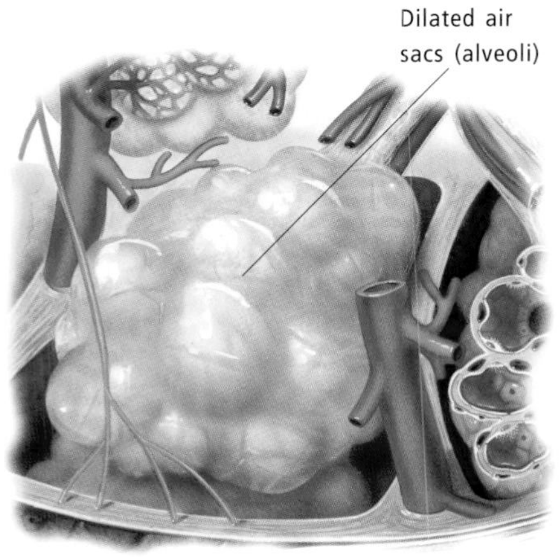

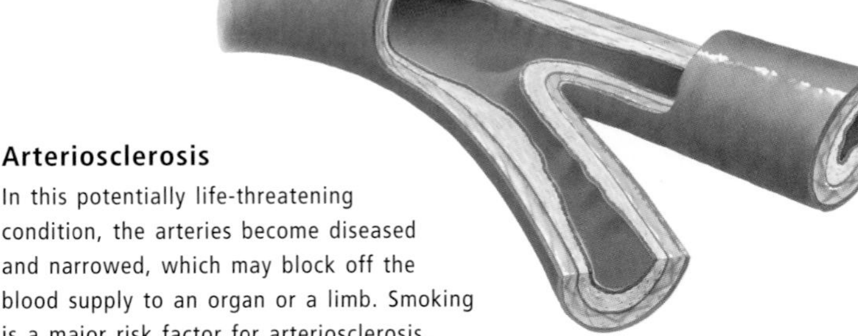

Arteriosclerosis

In this potentially life-threatening condition, the arteries become diseased and narrowed, which may block off the blood supply to an organ or a limb. Smoking is a major risk factor for arteriosclerosis.

Emphysema

Cigarette smoke destroys the delicate structure of the air sacs (alveoli) in the lungs, preventing the efficient exchange of oxygen and carbon dioxide. When advanced, this condition is called emphysema and is characterized by severe shortness of breath.

S

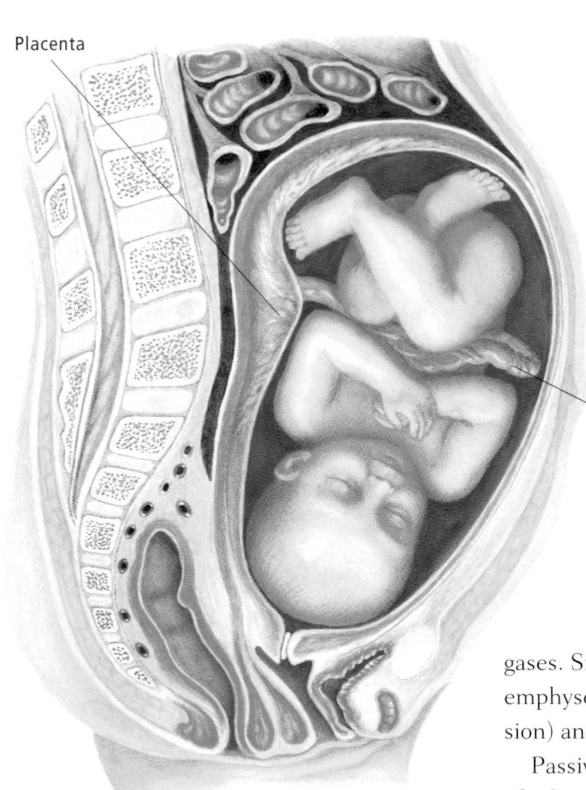

Smoking during pregnancy

Pregnant women who smoke are more likely to suffer a miscarriage, have a complicated delivery, or have a baby who is underweight, than women who do not smoke. Carbon monoxide from tobacco smoke passes into the mother's bloodstream and through the umbilical cord to the baby. This affects the amount of oxygen and blood flow to the baby, inhibiting healthy development.

Effects of smoking

Inhaling tobacco smoke immediately increases the heart rate, raises blood pressure, excites the nervous system and slows down the cilia, tiny hairs in the airways to the lungs which act as filters to clean incoming air. Other short-term effects of smoking are to increase acid production in the stomach, reduce urine produced by the kidneys, dull the senses of taste and smell and sensations of hunger, thus reducing appetite, and to reduce the efficiency of blood circulation.

Long-term smoking has been proven to increase the risks of developing cancer in those areas of the body in direct contact with inhaled smoke. Cancers of the lung, mouth, pharynx and esophagus affect more smokers than non-smokers, as do cancers of the bladder, kidney, pancreas and cervix. Smoking also increases the risks of dying from these disorders. The culprits are nicotine and the various tars which leave deposits seen as stains on teeth and fingers and on the internal surfaces of the lungs, where they reduce the flow of oxygen into the blood. Inhaled smoke contains less oxygen than normal air and more carbon monoxide, a deadly poison also found in car exhaust gases. Smokers are also more susceptible to emphysema, high blood pressure (hypertension) and heart disease.

Passive smoking is the term for inhalation of tobacco smoke by those around the smoker. This sidestream smoke has adverse effects on health that can significantly increase risks of disease in non-smokers.

Smoking in pregnancy is to be avoided. Carbon monoxide from tobacco smoke passes into the mother's bloodstream and through the umbilical cord to the baby, reducing the oxygen intake and increasing the baby's heart rate. The blood vessels in the cord narrow, reducing blood flow to the baby. Nicotine also passes to the baby, affecting the development of proper breathing movements. Pregnant women who smoke are more likely to miscarry, to have complications at birth, and to deliver a low birthweight baby, or to lose the baby shortly after birth. Smoking in pregnancy may be a factor in SIDS (crib or cot death), and the later development of asthma and respiratory infections in the baby. Quitting at any stage in the pregnancy is statistically better than smoking to full term.

Smoking while breast feeding passes inhaled poisons to the baby through the milk. Smoking near a baby may result in the development of a sensitivity to smoke which leads to asthma and breathing problems, poor lung function, frequent coughs, and chest infections, including bronchitis and pneumonia.

Smokers develop a tolerance to nicotine which produces a need to smoke more tobacco to allay cravings, the level varying with the individual. The development of serious diseases related to smoking is affected by the quantity of tobacco smoked: the more tobacco is smoked over a given period, the faster related health disorders develop. Increased intake deepens an individual's dependence and results in stronger symptoms of withdrawal when the effects of the last intake diminish.

Withdrawal symptoms make it extremely difficult to quit smoking. They include coughing, difficulty concentrating, headaches, irritability, nervous tension, and changes in taste and smell. There are psychological difficulties in withdrawing from tobacco, as many daily activities or habits trigger the desire to smoke, such as smoking after eating or lighting up immediately on rising each morning. A successful program to quit smoking must address all the factors creating dependency.

Quitting smoking

The immediate benefits of stopping tobacco use may go unnoticed under the accompanying withdrawal symptoms but they are important and significant. Only 6 hours after the last cigarette, heart rate slows to normal and blood pressure reduces. After 12 hours, nicotine has been eliminated from the body. After 24 hours, carbon monoxide has been cleared from the lungs, and there may be increased coughing as wastes are expelled. In two days many other chemicals from smoking are also expelled. After a year, the risk of heart disease falls. After 10 years, the risk of smoking-related illness is reduced to the same level as in non-smokers.

Quitting smoking is difficult and first time efforts may not be successful. Therapies include clinics and self-help groups supplemented by aids such as nicotine replacement therapy to overcome physical cravings. Hypnotherapy has also been used to reinforce the willpower needed to successfully overcome a pernicious habit, which has been called the most health-damaging single activity an individual can undertake.

SEE ALSO *Cancer, Emphysema, Heart, Hypertension, Lung cancer, Lungs, Nicotine, Pregnancy, Respiratory system, Withdrawal*

S

SNEEZING

Sneezing is a sudden, noisy and spasmic exhalation of air through the nose and mouth. A sneeze is an involuntary reflex action triggered by stimulation of nerves in the mucous membranes of the nose or by overstimulation of the optic nerve by very bright light. Sneezing often accompanies respiratory infections such as the common cold where nasal membranes become swollen and inflamed. Inhaling tiny foreign particles, such as specks of ground pepper or talcum powder, can also lead to the sort of nasal irritation that elicits sneezing.

Allergens, such as mold or pollen, are among the most common causes of persistent sneezing. For people suffering from protracted allergy-related sneezing, there are several over-the-counter medications that may offer relief. These include antihistamines, decongestants and nasal sprays.

Interrupting or suppressing a sneeze is dangerous and can result in damage to abdominal muscles or to the middle ear as air is forced up the eustachian tube. Trying to suppress a sneeze can also propel mucus into the middle ear or sinuses which may then promote the development of infections in these areas. Very occasionally, the pressure that results from stifling a sneeze can cause an eardrum to rupture.

A sneeze is sometimes also called a sternutation.

SEE ALSO *Common cold, Mucous membranes, Reflexes, Rhinitis*

SNORING

It is estimated that between 30–50 percent of people will be snoring during sleep by the time they have reached their 50s. Snoring is defined as breathing during sleep in a way that causes a vibration of the soft palate and produces a rough audible sound. It generally occurs when people sleep on their back with the mouth open. In this position, the mouth tends to fall open and the tongue comes to rest in the back of the mouth, partly obstructing the airway. This causes passing air to make the snoring sounds. In most cases, people who snore are unaware that they do so.

Usually there is nothing dangerous about snoring, but it may be annoying for a sleeping partner or others in the vicinity. Sometimes snoring can be caused by anatomical characteristics such as a small chin, by enlarged tonsils or by obesity. It can run in families, or be related to an underactive thyroid gland or sleep apnea, allergy or respiratory infection. Smoking, excessive alcohol and sedatives can cause or aggravate snoring.

There are many other simple remedies that may alleviate mild snoring and the right solutions will usually depend on the cause. Often a light snorer will cease making noise if they are rolled from their back onto their side during sleep. Increasing the humidity in your bedroom can help if snoring is caused or exacerbated by dry and swollen mucous membranes.

When obesity is a contributing factor, exercise and healthy eating can make a difference by improving muscle tone and promoting weight loss. Other people may find that modifying pre-bedtime behaviour and habits improves the situation. Avoiding meals, alcohol and medications that induce deep drug-induced sleeping (such as tranquilizers and some antihistamines) during the 2–3 hours preceding bedtime may, for example, have a beneficial effect. Some light snorers may also be able to reduce or eliminate the problem by raising their bedhead slightly. Other people have success with oral anti-snoring devices, of which there are now many different forms available, usually through pharmacies.

Although snoring is usually innocuous, adults who are heavy and persistent snorers may occasionally suffer from or develop a serious health problem. Because of this, it is usually recommended that they seek the opinion of a medical specialist to identify and treat the causes and any potentially unhealthy consequences of their snoring. In severe cases, where a person's health is affected by snoring or when snoring indicates certain underlying physical or medical conditions, there are a number of surgical procedures that may prove helpful.

Persistent heavy snoring in children or adolescents usually warrants investigation by a medical professional as it often indicates tonsil or adenoid problems that may require treatment.

SEE ALSO *Insomnia, Sleep, Sleep apnea, Sleep disturbances*

SNOW BLINDNESS

Snow blindness is sunburn on the cornea—part of the lens of the eye. It is a temporary condition caused by exposure of the eyes to ultraviolet rays reflected from snow or ice. These rays can damage the outer layers of the cornea, causing intolerance to light, temporary blindness, and/or inflammation and pain in the eye. The condition affects mostly skiers, as well as people walking or driving in snow-covered areas. A similar condition can also result in people whose unprotected eyes have been exposed to high-voltage electric sparks, the flames of arc welding or light emitted by sun or tanning lamps. Affected people should rest in a dark room. Sometimes an antibiotic ointment, eye patches or over-the-counter pain relief medications may be necessary. With proper rest, a full recovery with no lasting ill effects usually takes only 24 hours. In cases of severe or extended exposure of unprotected eyes to intense ultraviolet light, however, there may be permanent damage that irreversibly affects vision. Snow blindness can be avoided by wearing dark glasses when going out in the snow.

SEE ALSO *Blindness, Eye*

SODIUM

Sodium is a mineral element important in small quantities for proper nutrition. It helps maintain the proper water balance in the body. Sodium ions are a component of common salt, sodium chloride, which is often added to food during processing, or in domestic cooking.

The quantities ingested often add up to amounts well in excess of the body's needs and long term this can cause fluid retention (edema) and may contribute to high blood pressure, leading to strokes, heart disease and kidney failure. Conversely, an inadequate sodium intake can lower blood pressure and can lead to diuresis, or excessive excretion of fluids from the body, which causes a degree of dehydration by reducing cell fluids below healthy levels.

Disease or illness involving diarrhea or vomiting, or other massive loss of fluids, may lead to sodium depletion, which causes blood pressure to fall, the heart to beat faster and symptoms of exhaustion to occur.

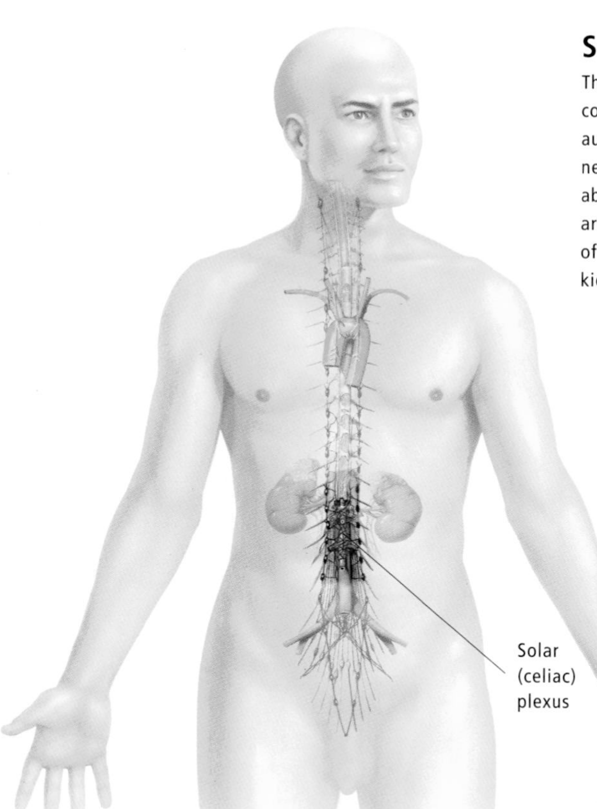

Solar plexus
The solar (celiac) plexus comprises a network of autonomic ganglia and nerves in the center of the abdomen. Nerves in this area influence the function of the adrenal glands, kidneys, liver and stomach.

Adequate amounts of sodium can be obtained from basic foods. Adding salt in cooking or at the table is a choice made largely from habit and a tolerance to salty tastes that is built up over time. Large amounts of salt added to manufactured food products and prepared meals are often hard to detect or to calculate from detailed information found on labels.

Drinking sufficient water, around eight glasses each day, is one way to assist the body in ridding itself of any excess sodium.

SEE ALSO *Dehydration, Edema, Hypertension, Hyponatremia, Hypotension, Minerals, Nutrition, Stroke*

SOLAR PLEXUS

The solar plexus is a dense network of nerve cells on the abdominal aorta behind the stomach. The solar plexus is known anatomically as the celiac plexus due to the fact that it is situated around the celiac artery just below the diaphragm.

The solar plexus is part of the autonomic nervous system and nerve fibers branch out from it to all the abdominal viscera. Through these, the solar plexus helps to regulate vital bodily functions such as intestinal contraction and adrenal secretion, as well as controlling the kidneys, spleen, liver and pancreas. The region of the solar plexus is often referred to as the "pit of the stomach." A blow to the solar plexus can cause severe pain and difficulty in breathing. This is because there is temporary paralysis of the diaphragm and chest and abdominal muscles.

A celiac plexus block (known also as a neurolytic celiac plexus block or NCPB) is a form of long-term pain relief used occasionally in the palliative care of patients terminally ill with certain forms of abdominal cancer, particularly those affecting the pancreas. The block involves a procedure during which a chemical is injected into the solar plexus, leaving it paralyzed so that the transmission of pain signals from the abdomen to the brain is impeded. This form of treatment is usually applied in conjunction with other methods of alleviating pain and discomfort in dying patients.

SEE ALSO *Autonomic nervous system, Abdomen, Diaphragm, Kidney, Nerves, Stomach*

SOLVENT SNIFFING

Solvent sniffing is a form of drug abuse in which the fumes of a volatile substance are inhaled. The act is not illegal and the substances used for sniffing are mostly legally available—gasoline (petrol), butane gas, glues, cleaning fluids, aerosol pain relief sprays, paint removers, lighter fluid and correcting fluid. Effects are felt almost immediately after inhalation because substances enter the lungs and pass directly into the bloodstream.

Solvents contain central nervous system depressants, which lower inhibitions and bring feelings of disorientation and lack of coordination, giving way to headaches and hangovers as effects wear off.

Physical damage from short-term use may be reversible. Accidents related to sniffing in hazardous situations pose greater dangers. Long-term use can damage kidneys, liver and brain, as the chemicals bind with lipids (fats) and are carried to these organs before being broken down and eliminated. Sniffing leaded gasoline can in the long term cause leukemia and other cancers as the lead cannot be broken down but accumulates in the body. Gasoline sniffing can also lead to anorexia, seizures involving spasms and loss of consciousness, and death by heart failure.

SEE ALSO *Drug dependence, Withdrawal*

SOMATIC THERAPIES

Somatic therapies explore the interface between mind and body, combining psychotherapy with techniques such as massage, breathing exercises, physical movement and postural awareness. In the somatic therapist's view emotional or psychological distress always has a bodily expression, which when worked with therapeutically has a corresponding positive effect on the psyche.

The foundations of somatic therapy were laid by the psychiatrist Wilhelm Reich (1897–1957). A follower of Freud, Reich developed his own theories and methods which primarily focused on the accumulation in the body of physical tensions resulting from psychological trauma and emotional inhibitions. In Reichian therapy the patient is asked to observe their breathing patterns, muscular tension and habitual postures while the therapist works with exercises and massages to release the "character armoring" of the body.

Reich's work was further developed and refined by his pupil Dr Alexander Lowen in the 1960s. Lowen's bioenergetic therapy focuses awareness on habitual postures and body movements, which are seen to be associated with chronic psychological states such as depression or anger. Exercises, stress positions and emotional release are used to help "unlock" the armoring, thereby mobilizing energy. Bioenergetics is said to help those with sexual dysfunction, psychosomatic or stress-related illnesses, postural difficulties or poor self-image.

Rolfing, also known as structural integration, is another somatic therapy, a form of massage pioneered by American biochemist Ida Rolf, in which the therapist's hands, elbows and knees are used with the aim of relaxing tension and softening hardened connective tissue (or fascia), resulting from incorrect posture and prolonged stress. Rolf believed that loosening the fascia helps release early memories of trauma, which in turn helps the body to regain its natural alignment. Patients are encouraged to talk about early trauma, although this is not the primary focus of the therapy. Rolf believed that realigning the body restored physical and psychological well-being. Rolfing is done over ten sessions, with each session focusing on a different area of the body.

Hellerwork, an offshoot of Rolfing, was devised in the late 1970s by Joseph Heller, an American aerospace engineer. Consisting of a series of sessions which work systematically through the body, it is recommended by its practitioners for poor posture, musculoskeletal injuries or other physical disabilities. Hellerwork combines three strands—bodywork, in which the practitioner manipulates and releases the tension in the fascia; movement education, which supports supple and tension-free movement; and dialogue, which explores links between mental attitudes and emotions and their affect on the body.

The gentle, non-invasive somatic therapy known as the Traeger approach was developed by Dr Milton Traeger. There are two aspects to this therapy, which aims to relax muscles and dissolve unconscious patterns of muscle tension. In the passive state the patient lies on a table and is gently rocked and moved by the practitioner to release holding and tension patterns. In the active state (known as pentastichs), the patient learns to make movements while releasing muscle tension. Originally developed to help those suffering from paralysis or neuromuscular disorders, the Traeger approach is also recommended by its practitioners for stress-related disorders.

SEE ALSO *Alexander technique, Feldenkrais method, Massage, Pilates method, Psychotherapy*

Producing sound

Producing sound, and turning it into speech, is a three-step process. First, the lungs expel air. Second, the vocal cords open and close to alter the air flow and cause vibrations, making a sound. Third, this sound is modified by muscles in the mouth and tongue—involving movement of the soft palate, tongue and lips.

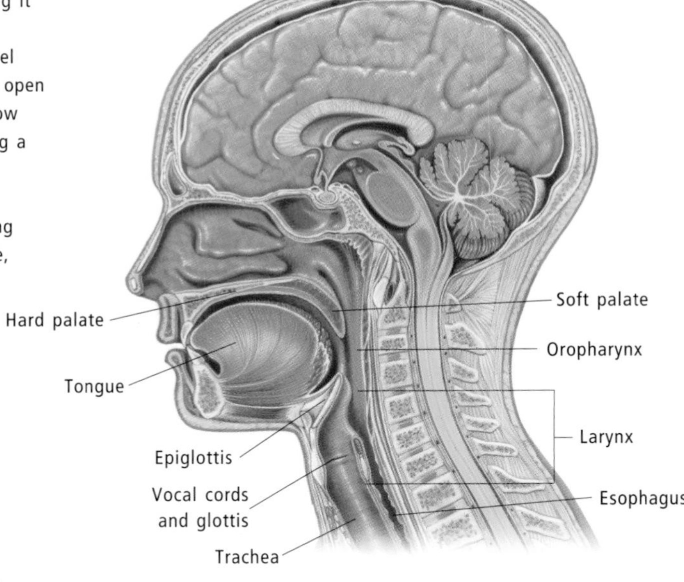

Speech

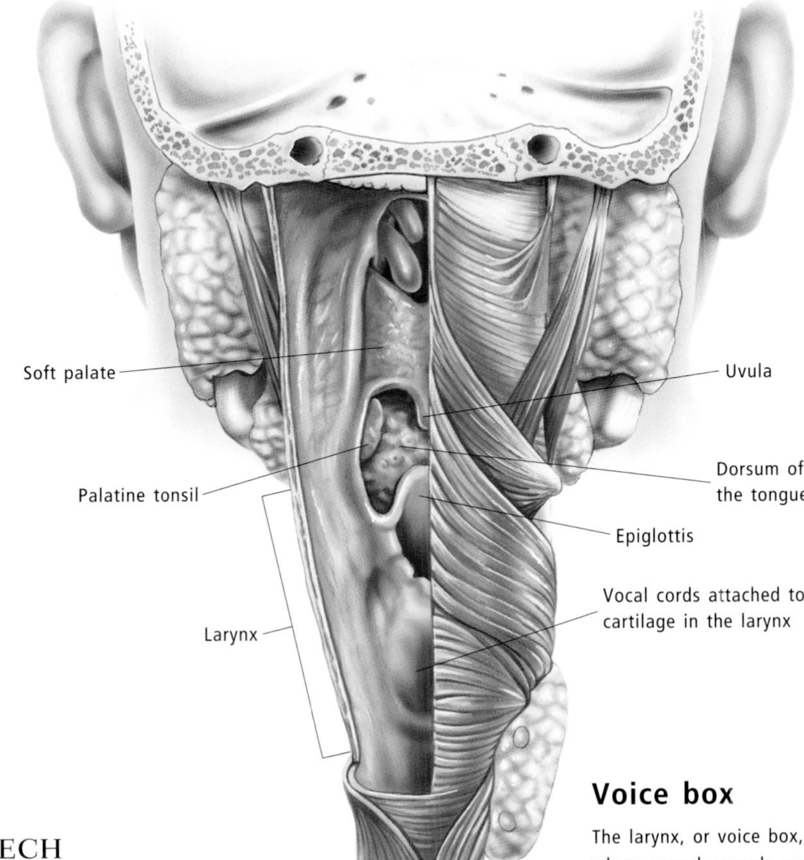

Voice box

The larynx, or voice box, is where speech sounds are made. It contains the vocal cords and extends from the back of the tongue down to the trachea. Air from the lungs passes up the trachea and through the larynx vibrating the cords. The force of the airflow determines the loudness of the voice.

SPEECH

Speech and language depend on the function of many different organs and structures within the body. These can be divided into: nervous system elements, for planning language production and control of muscles; parts of the respiratory system and larynx, for the production of the raw sound (phonation); and the mouth area, for the modification of this raw sound to produce the vowels and consonants of speech (articulation).

Within the brain, usually in the left hemisphere, there are two specialized language regions known as Broca's area and Wernicke's area. Wernicke's area is concerned with the comprehension of language, while Broca's area is involved in the expressive aspects of language. These areas act through the cerebral cortex to control the activities of neurons in the brain stem and so to produce phonation and articulation. The cerebellum at the back of the brain also plays an important role in articulation.

Raw sound is produced by expelling air from the lungs through the larynx. Within the larynx are the two vocal cords, which can be separated during intake of breath and brought close together during speech. When the vocal cords are close together, and air is forced between them, they begin to vibrate, in the same way that two leaves held close together will vibrate when air is forced between them. This raw sound can be altered by increasing or decreasing the tension or length of the vocal cords.

Vowel sounds (such as "ah" or "ooh") are produced by modifying the shape of the expelled air above the vibrating vocal cords. This is done by moving the soft palate, tongue and lips in a precisely coordinated fashion. Most consonants are produced by temporarily stopping the flow of air. Consonants are often named according to the part of the airway involved. Thus, labial consonants ("b", "p") are produced by bringing the lips (labia) together; dental consonants ("d", "t") involve the tongue touching the teeth; nasal consonants ("m", "n") involve passing air through the nose; and glottal consonants ("q", "g", "k") involve the temporary closing of the back of the tongue (the epiglottis) against the soft palate.

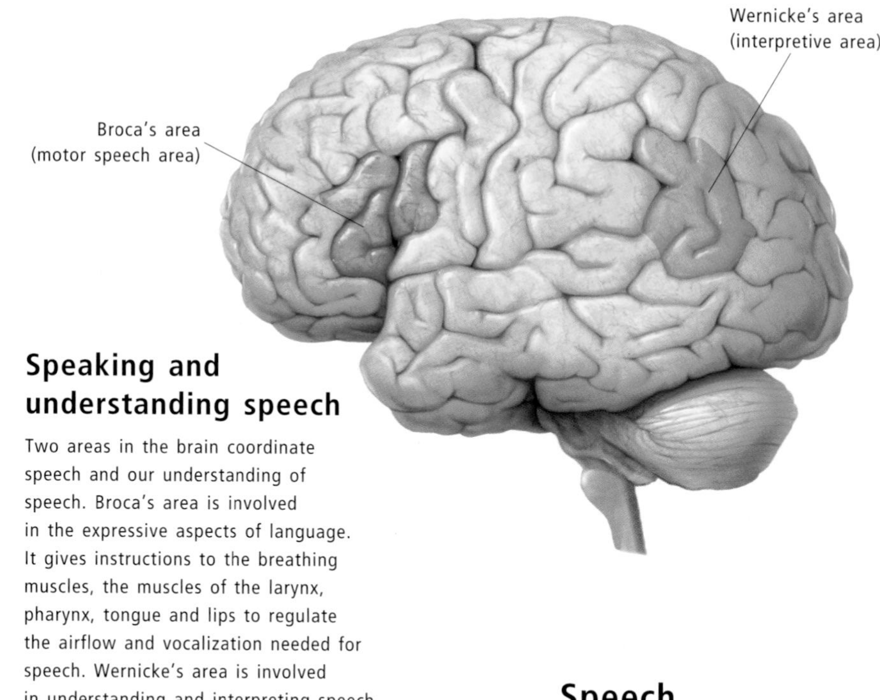

Speaking and understanding speech

Two areas in the brain coordinate speech and our understanding of speech. Broca's area is involved in the expressive aspects of language. It gives instructions to the breathing muscles, the muscles of the larynx, pharynx, tongue and lips to regulate the airflow and vocalization needed for speech. Wernicke's area is involved in understanding and interpreting speech.

Speech

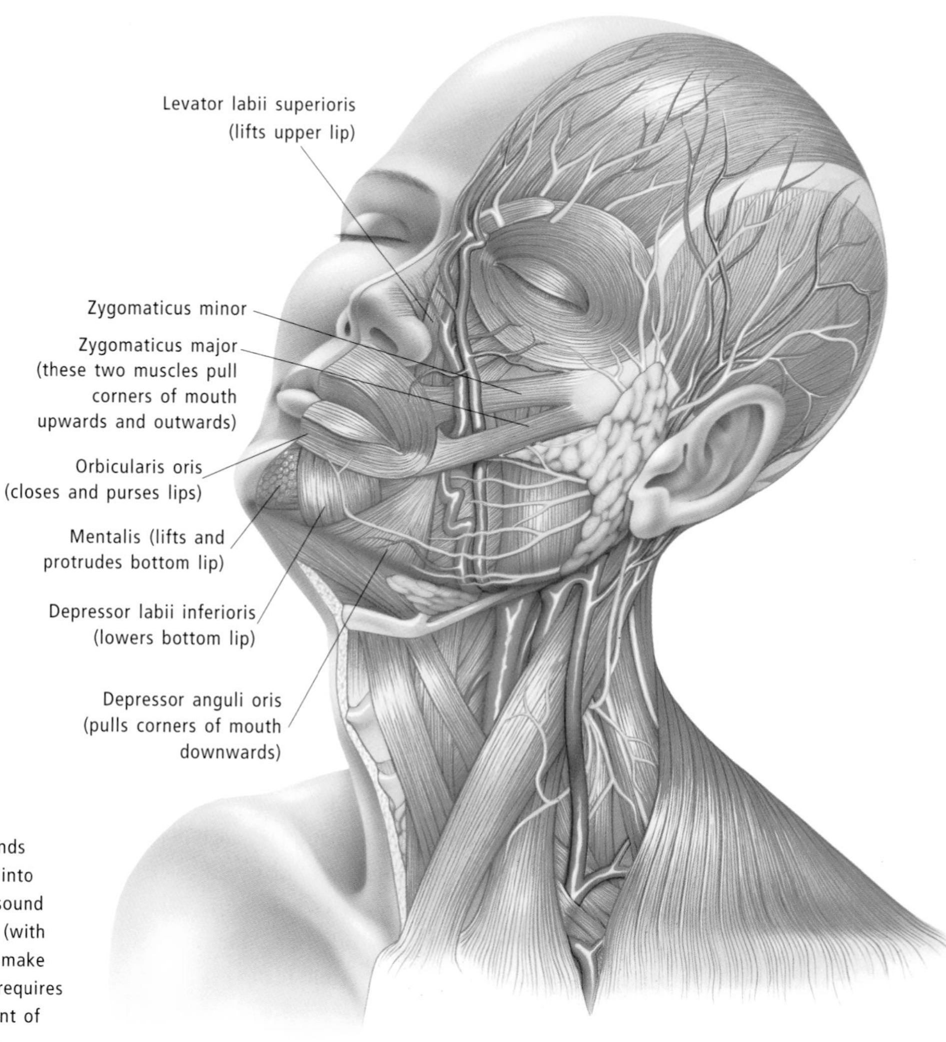

Lip movement for speech

The movement of the lips modifies the sounds that come from the larynx and vocal cords into speech. The lips need to join to make the sound "m", for example, need to touch the teeth (with the bottom lip) to make "f", and round to make "o". The accurate movements that speech requires are made possible by a complex arrangement of muscles around the mouth and cheek areas.

S

Vocal cords

The vocal cords, or vocal folds, are two folds of mucous membrane that vibrate to make sound when we speak. One end of each vocal cord attaches to cartilage at the front of the larynx. The other ends of the cords are attached to cartilages that can move freely, allowing the cords to vibrate and make sound. The folds are also very flexible—relaxing them will make low-pitched sounds and making them taut will produce high-pitched sounds

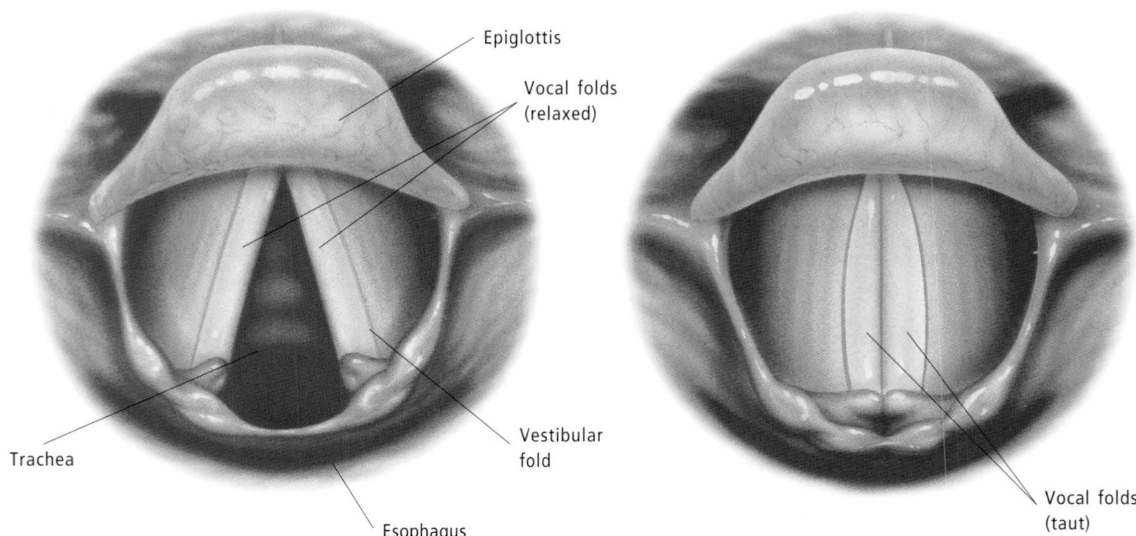

Speech development

From the time they are born, babies are listening, watching and attempting to copy actions and expressions of those around them. The human face, or any clear, large, face-shaped object, will fascinate. Babies begin by making little noises and by as early as four weeks may be squealing; by around six weeks familiar voices, particular the mother's, will bring a response. Cooing type sounds slowly develop, first one syllable, then two syllables. Around 7 months most babies will be making a sound that resembles "dada" or "papa". By 12 months the average child will normally be able to say at least one word.

Understanding precedes speech, so that in the early years children will understand much more than they can articulate. By 18 months of age a vocabulary of around 10 words is considered average. Gradually language skills develop, until some time between the age of 30 and 42 months the child begins to talk in sentences.

Speech disorders

Speech disorders have been a concern since the beginning of recorded history. It has been estimated that around 10 million Americans have a speech disorder of some kind. The major types include voice disorders (dysphonias), which can be caused by paralysis of the larynx, injury or a disease of the endocrine glands; and speech disorders, the most common being those that disrupt a child's ability to learn a language. These include an absence of speech, unintelligible speech and lisping, and may be caused by genetic factors or by damage some time before, during or shortly after birth. Poor language skills within the family, parental neglect or prolonged illness can also play a part.

It is perfectly normal for some children, particularly boys, not to talk until they are 3 years of age, when they will often talk in sentences; however, such a delay may also be caused by the factors just mentioned. Delay in language development may also be the result of intellectual disability or a delay in learning to read and write, sometimes described as dyslexia.

Difficulties in articulation come in different forms. Cluttering (tachyphemia) is mumbled, fast, sloppy speech that is difficult to understand and is hereditary. Lisping has a number of different forms and can be caused either by physical factors, such as abnormal position of the teeth or hearing loss, or by behavioral factors such as imitation of other lispers. It is not easy to outgrow and often persists into adult life. Stuttering or stammering (dysphemia) is the most common and obvious type of disturbed speech. Experts are still undecided about the causes, however it is found more in males than females and is often hereditary. Treatment is difficult and often combines psychotherapy with behavioral therapy. Emotional problems are often part of this disorder.

Physical problems can also affect speech. Injury to the part of the brain related to language results in dysphasia; it may be the result of stroke or head injury. Aphasia (speechlessness) happens when the left side of the brain is damaged. It involves the loss of memory for the meaning of language and how it is produced. Sufferers may know what they want to say but be unable to say or write it. Together with treatment for the cause of the problem, the sufferer must also re-educate the parts of the brain that still function normally.

Tongue-tie (ankyloglossia) is easy corrected with surgery, but major defects of the tongue will reduce the ability to articulate. Sufferers can be taught to speak despite these defects. Hypernasal speech, where increased nasal resonance results in a person "talking through the nose", can be caused by paralysis, congenital malformation, injury or palate defects. Treatment needs a thorough understanding of the causes. A cleft in the palate, lip or other part of the mouth is a congenital malformation which can be corrected by surgery; speech therapy will help to correct speech defects.

Symptomatic speech disorders, caused by lesions in the nervous system, are known as dysarthria. When speech development is limited by mental disorders, it is known as dyslogia.

Hearing loss in early childhood will result in distorted speech known as audiogenic dyslalia; speech problems caused by defects to the lips, teeth or mouth are known as dysglossia. Cerebral palsy, chorea, Parkinson's disease and other nervous disorders can also affect the production of speech.

SEE ALSO *Aphasia, Cleft palate, Dyslexia, Larynx, Lisping, Mouth, Stuttering, Vocal cords*

S

SPERM

Sperm are the mature male reproductive cells which combine with the ovum, the female reproductive cell, to begin the process leading to pregnancy and the development of a baby. Sperm are produced at the rate of about 50,000 every minute of every hour from puberty until late in life. They are made in the testes (or testicles) which hang outside the body in a sac of skin—the cooler scrotum (sperm do not develop properly at full body temperature).

Newly produced sperm pass into the epididymis, a tube at the back of each testis, where they mature and wait to be ejaculated. During ejaculation, muscle contractions squeeze the sperm along the sperm duct and into the urethra. Along the way, the seminal vesicles and prostate gland add seminal fluids, which mix with the sperm and mobilize them. Semen contains 90 percent seminal fluids and 10 percent sperm and epididymal fluid. On average, between 80 million and 300 million sperm are ejaculated each time a man has an orgasm.

Although sperm can live up to 72 hours in the female reproductive tract, their death rate is high; assuming ejaculation occurs when the woman is fertile, generally only

Sperm production

Sperm are produced in the seminiferous tubules—tightly coiled tubes in the testes. Sperm cells (spermatocytes) divide and produce spermatids, which mature into spermatozoa. Each tubule contains sperm cells at different stages of development and a number of Sertoli cells which support the developing sperm. Spermatozoa move through the testes and into the epididymis, a tube at the back of the testes. Here they mature and wait to be ejaculated.

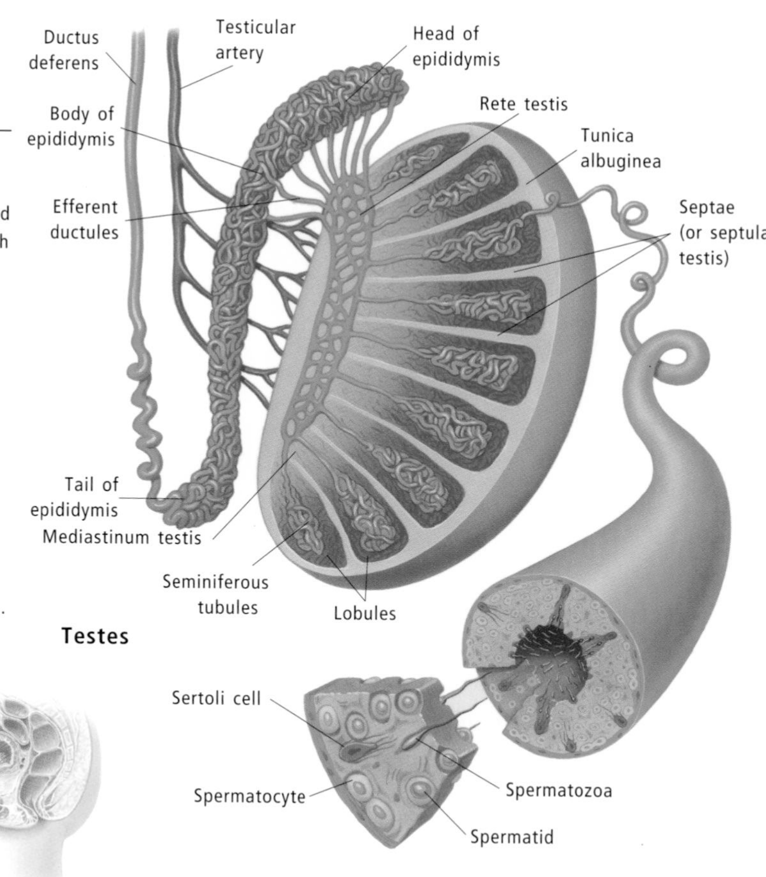

Sperm structure

The head of each sperm has a nucleus, containing chromosomes, and an acrosomal membrane which holds enzymes needed for fertilization. The tail of the sperm helps it move in a corkscrew action on its journey from the testes to the female reproductive organs.

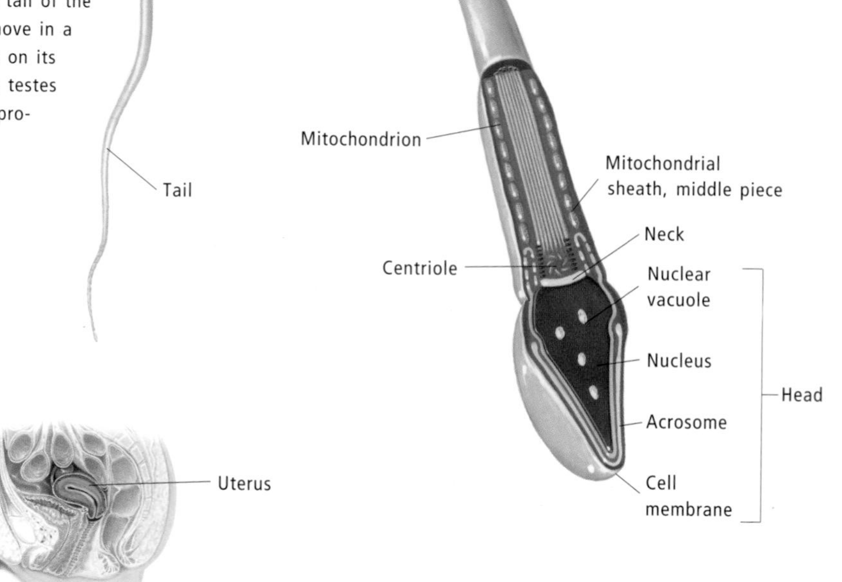

Fertilization

Millions of sperm are ejaculated into the woman's reproductive tract, but only one successfully fuses with the ovum. When the sperm reach the ovum, enzymes released from the acrosomes help to break down the shell. This allows one sperm to penetrate the ovum and fertilization to occur.

Zona pellucida

Polar body

Sperm

one sperm will penetrate the ovum. Sperm which are not ejaculated are reabsorbed into the man's lymph glands over a period of time.

Sperm carry the man's genetic potential. One half of the chromosomes which carry the genetic makeup of a new human being are to be found in the head of the sperm, the other half coming from the mother's ovum. The sperm decides the sex of the baby; one half of sperm cells contain the Y chromosome which produces a male child, the other half contain the X chromosome which produces a female child.

The microscopic sperm, often likened to a tadpole in shape, has a tail which enables it to "swim" from the vagina, through the cervix and uterus and into the fallopian tube to meet the ovum. In each sperm is a cap (acrosome) containing enzymes which can penetrate the coating around the ovum.

In the sterilization procedure known as vasectomy, a portion of the ductus deferens (or vas deferens), the tube leading from the testicles to the seminal vesicle where the sperm is stored, is removed to prevent sperm traveling from the testes and into the semen, thus rendering the man infertile. A vasectomy does not affect the production of semen, nor does it affect libido—it simply means that when the man ejaculates his semen contains no sperm. After this operation it takes about 16 ejaculations for all sperm to disappear from the semen. This means that normal contraception methods should be continued for up 2 months after a vasectomy is performed.

Where subfertility (infertility) is a problem, tests are carried out on both partners to determine the reason. A man may fail to manufacture sperm (azoospermia); sperm may be weak or few in number (oligospermia: fewer than 20 million per milliliter) or there may be damage to the ductus deferens.

SEE ALSO ***Epididymitis, Fertilization, Infertility, Reproductive systems, Scrotum, Semen, Testes, Vasectomy***

SPINA BIFIDA

Spina bifida is a congenital defect of the spinal column resulting from the abnormal formation of the neural tube very early in embryonic development (usually during weeks 3–4 of fetal life). It can appear in several forms. In its most benign form, spina bifida occulta, neither the spinal cord nor the meninges (the covering of the spinal cord) protrudes through the opening left in the vertebrae.

In its most severe form, meningomyelocele, the spinal cord and nerves are exposed. Weakness in the feet (sometimes paralysis), problems with reflexes, and spinal defects indicate spina bifida. A soft fatty deposit on the skin covering the defect, or a cyst protruding over the spine, may also be present. Babies born with meningomyelocele usually undergo surgery soon after birth. Early surgical correction of the defect is important to minimize the risk of meningitis and further neurological damage. Although surgery will improve quality of life for the child, disorders such as limb paralysis and bladder and bowel problems may still occur.

During pregnancy it is important that the mother's diet contains adequate folic acid to reduce the risk of spina bifida in the baby. Many foods are now fortified with this compound and it is also available in tablet form if prescribed.

Women of childbearing age should aim to ingest 400 micrograms of folic acid a day. It is recommended that folic acid supplementation should begin 3–4 months prior to conception and should continue for the first 3 months of the pregnancy.

Spina bifida can be screened for in pregnancy with the alpha-fetoprotein (AFP) test, ultrasound and amniocentesis.

SEE ALSO ***Amniocentesis, Congenital abnormalities, Folate, Neural tube defect, Spinal cord, Ultrasound***

SPINAL CORD

The spinal cord is a cylindrical nervous structure which occupies the vertebral canal, a cavity extending the length of the vertebral column. A series of rootlets (made up of nerve cell fibers) attaches in a line along the front and back of each side of the cord. Those attaching to the front (ventral rootlets) and to the back (dorsal rootlets) group together to form 31 pairs of spinal nerves, giving the cord a segmented appearance. These nerves supply skin, bone, muscles and joints of the limbs and trunk.

The spinal cord is usually $16\frac{1}{2}$–$17\frac{3}{4}$ inches (42–45 centimeters) long and does not extend the full length of the vertebral column. In the adult its lower end (conus medullaris) is usually located at the level of the L1 or L2 vertebra. Below this, the vertebral canal is occupied largely by the elongated rootlets of the lumbar and sacral spinal nerves (cauda equina, which is Latin for "horse's tail") traveling down to lower levels before they exit from the canal.

The spinal cord is made primarily of nerve cell bodies and their associated fibers that function to process and transmit sensory information to the brain and motor information from the brain. The cell bodies group together in the center of the cord to form a column of gray matter, which is H-shaped in cross-section, the H being formed by pairs of dorsal "horns" at the back and ventral horns at the front, separated by an inter-

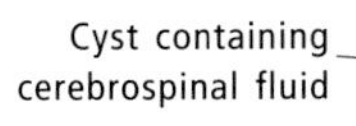

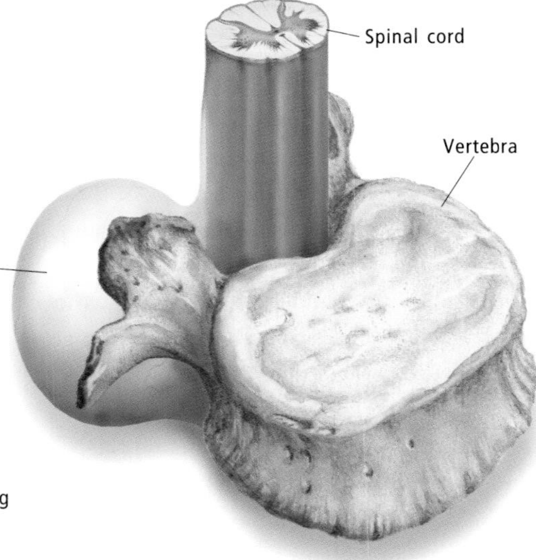

Spina bifida

Spina bifida occurs when the bony column that surrounds the spinal cord does not fuse properly during embryonic development. The spinal cord and its covering (the meninges) may then protrude through the opening between the vertebrae, creating a cystic swelling filled with cerebrospinal fluid.

S

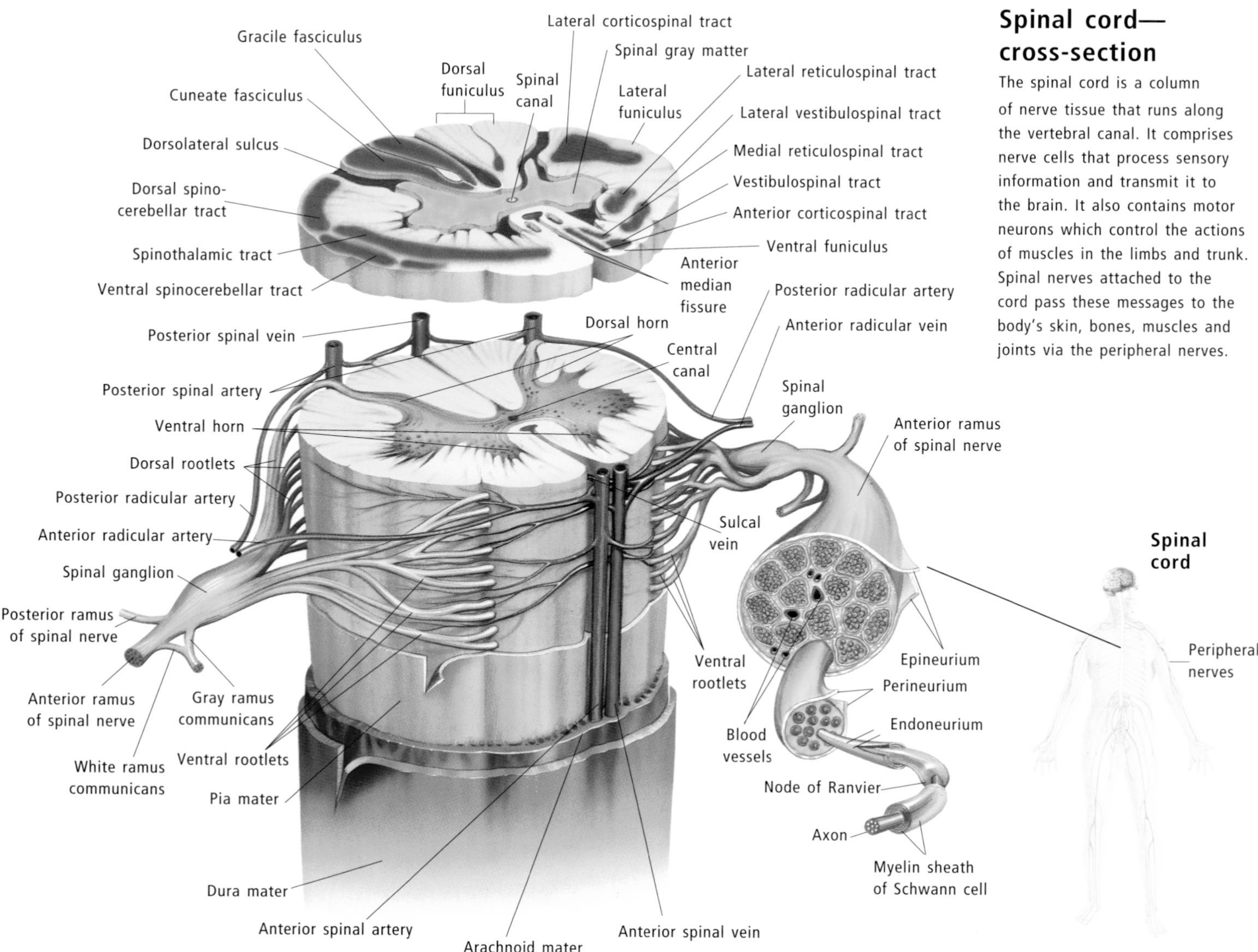

Spinal cord—cross-section

The spinal cord is a column of nerve tissue that runs along the vertebral canal. It comprises nerve cells that process sensory information and transmit it to the brain. It also contains motor neurons which control the actions of muscles in the limbs and trunk. Spinal nerves attached to the cord pass these messages to the body's skin, bones, muscles and joints via the peripheral nerves.

mediate zone. The dorsal horns are specialized to process sensory information (for example, touch, pain, temperature, joint sensation) and to relay this information up to the brain. The ventral horns contain motor neurons, which transmit messages out to the muscles via spinal nerves. The intermediate zone contains many interneurons involved in linking incoming sensory neurons with outgoing motor neurons to bring about automated (reflex) responses which do not involve the brain. Simple spinal reflexes include the stretch reflex such as the knee jerk, in which tapping the patellar ligament below the kneecap brings about contraction of the quadriceps muscle of the thigh; and the withdrawal reflex, in which a pain stimulus to the skin (such as touching a hot iron) causes a reflex withdrawal from the stimulus.

The gray matter of the spinal cord is surrounded by white matter (nerve fibers), transmitting information to and from the brain. Fibers carrying similar types of information tend to group together into bundles known as tracts. When the spinal cord is cut or damaged these tracts may be severed, meaning motor commands cannot get to levels below the damage and sensory information from these levels cannot get past the damage to the brain. If only the lower limbs are affected the person is said to be paraplegic, and if all limbs are affected they are said to be quadriplegic. Injured neurons in the spinal cord regenerate or repair themselves, so the effects are usually permanent.

SEE ALSO *Nerves, Nervous system, Neurons, Paralysis, Paraplegia, Quadriplegia, Reflexes, Spinal nerves, Spine*

SPINAL CURVATURE

The human spinal column is normally curved, but abnormal curvature is also a common condition. It can be caused by weak ligaments, poor posture, disease, injury or congenital abnormalities.

Hunchback (kyphosis) is an exaggeration of the normal curvature of the thoracic spine; swayback (lordosis) is an exaggerated forward or inward curvature of the lumbar (middle to lower) spine. Pott's disease is a form of tuberculosis which affects the vertebrae and causes deformities; a sideways deviation of the spine is called scoliosis (humpback). Treatment may include plaster jackets, traction, pads, electrical stimulation, exercise and surgery.

SEE ALSO *Lordosis, Kyphosis, Pott's disease, Scoliosis, Spine*

S

SPINAL NERVES

Spinal nerves emerge from the sides of the vertebral column and function to transmit information in both directions between the spinal cord and the peripheral structures of the body. Each nerve is made up of sensory fibers (transmitting information from skin, muscles, bones and joints to the spinal cord) and motor fibers (transmitting messages away from the spinal cord towards the skeletal muscles). Some spinal nerves also carry sympathetic (autonomic) fibers (transmitting messages to sweat glands and blood vessels) and parasympathetic fibers to mucous membrane and smooth muscle in the pelvis.

Each nerve is formed within the vertebral canal by the union of its dorsal and ventral roots. The dorsal roots, made up of sensory fibers, emerge in a line along each side of the back of the spinal cord. The ventral roots, made up mainly of motor fibers, emerge in a line along each side of the front of the cord. Once the two roots unite, the spinal nerve leaves the vertebral canal through a space on each side between each pair of adjacent vertebrae. Soon after it leaves these vertebrae, the spinal nerve divides into a small branch, which supplies structures in the back, and a large branch, which supplies the limbs and the remainder of the trunk.

The 31 pairs of spinal nerves are named according to the level that they exit from the vertebral column. There are eight cervical spinal nerves (C1–C8), twelve thoracic (T1–T12), five lumbar (L1–L5), five sacral (S1–S5) and one coccygeal nerve. Each nerve supplies a circumscribed area of skin (dermatome) and a specific group of muscles. The thoracic nerves supply skin and muscles of most of the trunk wall, whereas the ventral rami of cervical, lumbar and sacral nerves form complex networks, known as plexuses, from which branches emerge to supply the motor and sensory needs of the limbs.

Spinal curvature

The spinal column is normally curved, but abnormal or excessive curvature (as in kyphosis or lordosis) may be caused by disease, injury or congenital disease.

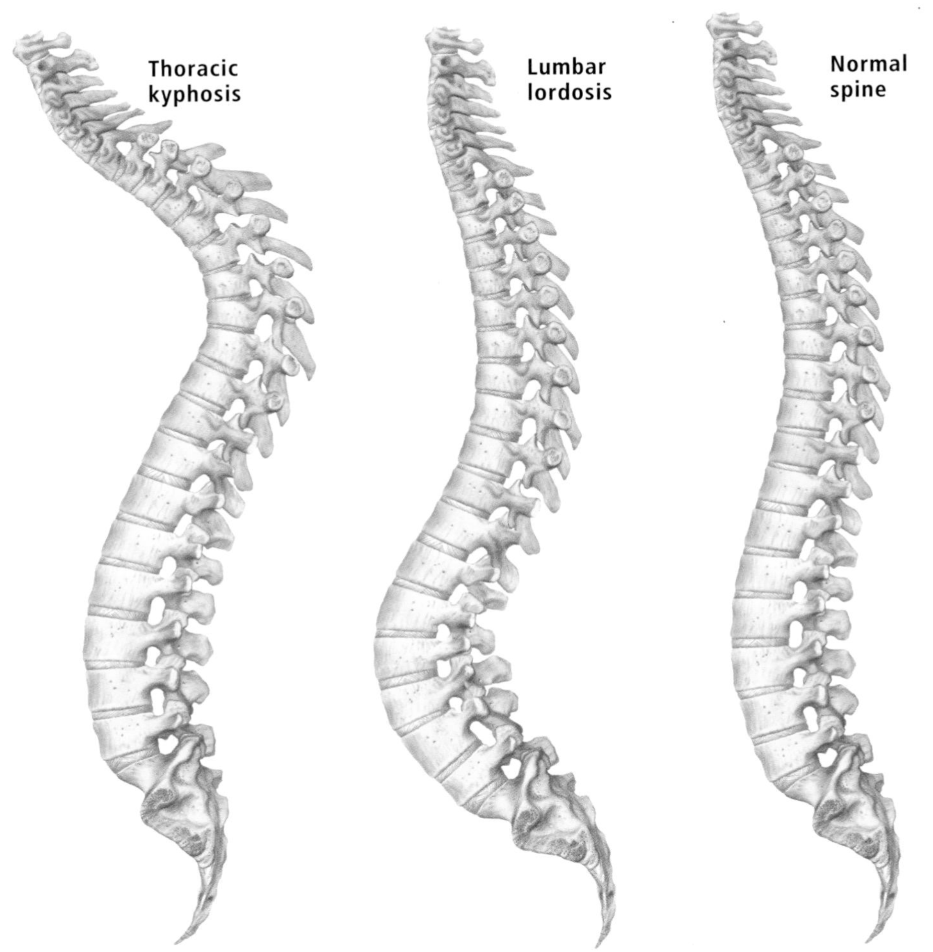

Spinal nerves and dermatomes

There are 31 pairs of spinal nerves which emerge from the sides of the vertebral column. Each spinal nerve supplies a specific group of muscles and a circumscribed area of skin (dermatome).

A spinal nerve may be torn due to excessive tension, such as a heavy fall on the shoulder, rupturing the C5 and/or the C6 nerves. When a spinal nerve is torn the person will experience a loss of sensation in the skin area and weakness in the muscles it supplies. The level at which the nerve is damaged will determine whether recovery can be expected.

One common disease which affects spinal nerves is shingles, in which the varicella-zoster virus that causes chickenpox infects the cells of the sensory roots of one or more spinal (or cranial) nerves. Painful blisters appear in the skin area supplied by the infected nerve. In recent years antiviral medications have been developed, which can alleviate the symptoms when an attack occurs.

SEE ALSO *Dermatomes, Nerves, Nervous system, Shingles, Spinal cord, Spine*

SPINE

The spine, or vertebral column, extends down the midline of the back, from the base of the skull to the pelvis, and forms the central axis of the skeleton. It also functions to protect the spinal cord, a nervous structure located in a hollow canal (the vertebral or spinal canal) which runs down the center of the vertebral column. The spine must be firm enough to support the body weight but it also requires flexibility to allow bending of the trunk. These requirements are satisfied by its curved, segmented structure made up of 26 bones (vertebrae), which are separated from each other by pads of cartilage (intervertebral disks). These disks make up 25 percent of the length of the vertebral column in a young adult.

The spine is divided into five regions—cervical, thoracic, lumbar, sacral and coccygeal. The cervical region is formed by seven vertebrae, numbered 1–7 from the top down (C1–C7). The thoracic region is formed by twelve vertebrae (T1–T12), all of which have ribs attaching to their sides. The lumbar (lower back) region has five vertebrae (L1–L5). The sacrum, a single curved bone in the adult, actually develops as five separate vertebrae (S1–S5), which fuse to each other during early development to form a single bone. Similarly, the four vertebrae of the tail region fuse during development to form the coccyx, a rudimentary bone attached to the lower end of the sacrum.

Viewed from side on, the vertical column is not straight, but curved into an S-shape. At birth the vertebral column is bent forward into a C-shape, this forward curvature remaining in the adult in the thoracic and sacral regions (primary curvatures). During childhood two reverse curves appear, in the cervical and lumbar regions, to better balance the weight of the head and body. The cervical curvature appears when the child begins to lift the head and the lumbar curvature appears as the child learns to sit, stand and walk. Because the cervical and lumbar curvatures appear after birth they are said to be secondary curvatures.

Developmental factors, poor posture or pathological changes can cause the curvatures to become abnormal. An exaggerated thoracic curvature (hunchback) known as kyphosis commonly develops in the elderly as a result of degenerative changes in the vertebrae due to osteoporosis. An exaggerated lumbar curvature (sway back) known as lordosis is commonly seen in pregnant women. Bending of the vertebral column to one side is known as scoliosis. This is quite common and may result from asymmetry in the back muscles as can occur in athletes who play predominantly one-handed sports, for example, baseball pitchers and tennis players.

Structure of vertebrae

All vertebrae have a similar structural pattern, although the size and shape of the individual features varies in different regions. Each vertebra consists of the following.

- A body at the front, which gets progressively larger from the top to the bottom of the column, because it is the weight-bearing part of the vertebra.
- An arch of bone, known as the vertebral arch, which attaches to the back of the body and surrounds a hole in the center called the vertebral foramen. The arch is divided on each side into a pedicle attaching to the body and a lamina at the back.

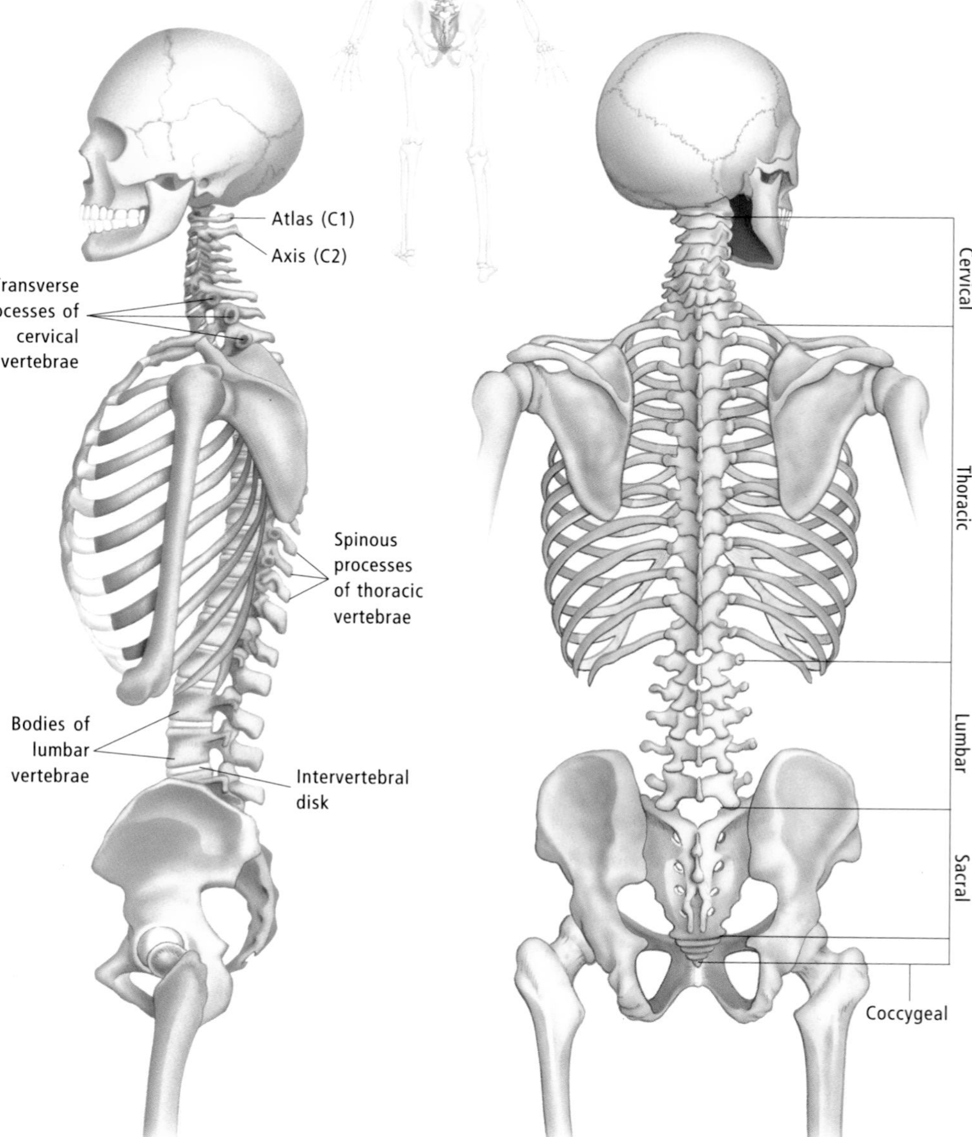

Spine

The spine forms the central axis of the skeleton and supports the weight of the head, neck and trunk. Its segmented structure provides flexibility, allowing the trunk to bend and twist.

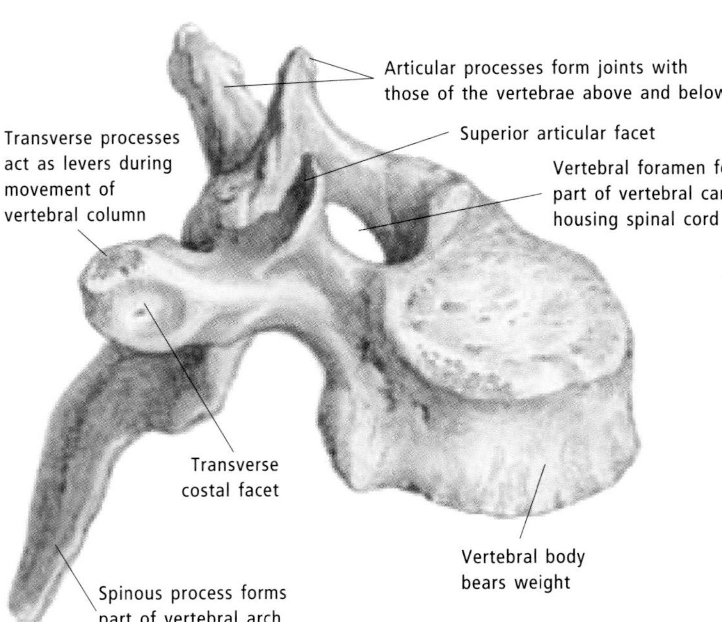

- A spinous process (spine), which extends backwards from the arch. The spinous processes can be easily felt extending down the midline of the back. That of the C7 vertebra (the "vertebra prominens") is particularly prominent at the base of the neck and can be used as a landmark for counting other vertebrae.
- A pair of transverse processes, which extend outwards from each side of the arch. The spinous and transverse processes act as levers during movements of the vertebral column.
- Two pairs of articular processes, extending from the upper and lower surfaces of each side of the arch. These processes form joints with those of the vertebrae above and below.

The atlas (C1) is atypical in that it does not have a body or spinal process.

The upper and lower surfaces of the pedicles of each vertebral arch are notched, so that when two vertebrae sit together, the adjacent notches form an incomplete ring, which is known as an intervertebral foramen. The spinal nerves enter and exit through these holes from each side of the vertebral canal.

Movements of the vertebral column

The vertebral column is a flexible structure that acts as a single unit, in which large movements result from the sum of the many small movements occurring at the joints between the vertebrae. Movements of the vertebral column are flexion (to bend

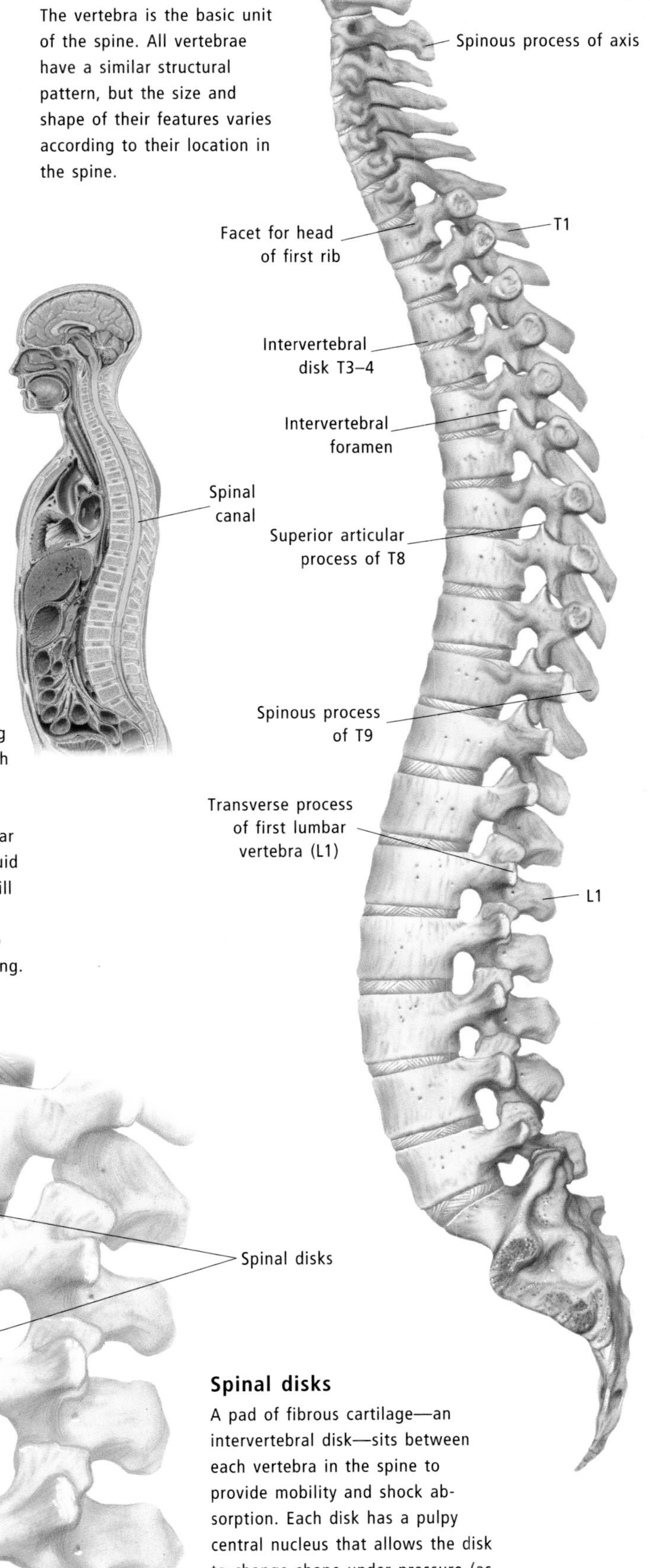

Vertebrae

The vertebra is the basic unit of the spine. All vertebrae have a similar structural pattern, but the size and shape of their features varies according to their location in the spine.

Spinal canal

The vertebral column provides a protective casing for the spinal cord, a length of nervous tissue that runs from the brain to the level of the first or second lumbar vertebrae. Cerebrospinal fluid and a layer of membrane fill the space between the vertebral canal and cord to provide additional cushioning.

Spinal disks

A pad of fibrous cartilage—an intervertebral disk—sits between each vertebra in the spine to provide mobility and shock absorption. Each disk has a pulpy central nucleus that allows the disk to change shape under pressure (as the spine bends or turns) and a tough, fibrous outer layer that holds the nucleus in position and attaches the disk to the vertebrae.

forwards), lateral flexion (to bend sideways), extension (to bend backwards), rotation (around its own axis) and circumduction (a combination of all these movements). The range of movement varies in different regions—the cervical and lumbar regions are the most mobile, with less movement possible in the thoracic region because of the presence of the ribs.

Joints

Each vertebra forms three separate joints with the vertebra above or below—a pair of facet joints and a single anterior intervertebral joint. A facet joint is formed on each side between the articular processes of the two vertebrae. The facet joints are synovial joints so they have a fluid-filled cavity between the bones, which are held together by a joint capsule. The adjacent cartilage-covered surfaces are able to glide on each other during movements of the vertebral column. The direction of orientation of the joint surfaces determines the type of movements that are permitted in different regions. For example, pure rotation of the vertebral column can only occur in the thoracic region. The facet joints are vulnerable to osteoarthritic changes in the elderly, particularly in the lumbar region, where they are one of the most common causes of localized low back pain. In some cases surgery may be required (known as a laminectomy) to relieve pain caused by bony deposits which form around the joint, compressing a nearby spinal nerve.

The anterior intervertebral joints, between the bodies of the vertebrae, are designed for strength and involve a pad of strong fibrous cartilage called the intervertebral disk. The disk sits between each pair of vertebral bodies and serves to both unite the vertebrae and permit movement between them. The disks may be relatively thin and flat in shape (as in the thoracic region) or wedge-shaped and thicker, as in the lumbar and cervical regions.

The intervertebral disks are reinforced in front and behind by the anterior and posterior longitudinal ligaments. These are bands of ligamentous fibers, which attach to the bodies of the vertebrae and extend along the length of the vertebral column. The anterior longitudinal ligament prevents excessive extension, and is commonly injured in automobile accidents, when a car is struck from behind and the head is suddenly and forcibly thrown backwards. This type of injury is known as whiplash.

Each intervertebral disk consists of two parts, a central region known as the nucleus pulposus, and a surrounding region called the annulus fibrosus. As its name suggests, the nucleus has a pulpy or gelatinous texture, and is easily able to change shape when pressure is placed upon it. The annulus is tough and fibrous, and is firmly attached to the vertebrae above and below. It consists of concentric rings of strong fibers, which pass in an oblique direction from one vertebra to the next. The fibers in adjacent rings are oriented at right angles to each other, allowing some movement to occur between the bones but also providing a strong bond between them. It also serves to hold the nucleus in position. The nucleus pulposus does not sit exactly in the center of the disk. It is located more towards the back, so the annulus is thinner behind than in front.

The fibers of the annulus become more fragile with age and can be torn during sudden, forceful movements of the joint, causing the nucleus to bulge into the damaged area of the annulus, a condition commonly known as a slipped disk. The fibers in the outer back part of the annulus are most vulnerable to injury because the annulus here is thinnest and not protected by the longitudinal ligaments. When this occurs, the bulging disk may compress a spinal nerve as it passes out of the vertebral column. This happens most commonly in the lumbar region, when nerves supplying the lower limb can be compressed, causing a type of pain known as sciatica. Sciatica can also result from osteoarthritic changes in the facet joints.

The vertebral canal

The vertebral canal is a hollow cavity that extends the length of the vertebral column and contains the spinal cord and the roots of the spinal nerves. It is surrounded at the front by the vertebral body and at the sides and back by the vertebral arch. The vertebral canal is lined by a membrane known as the dural sheath. The dural sheath consists of an outer fibrous layer called the dura mater and a thin, inner layer called the arachnoid mater. A fluid-filled space, the subarachnoid space, exists between the dural sheath and the spinal cord. It contains cerebrospinal fluid and is continuous with a similar space surrounding the brain. The spinal cord usually ends at the level of the first or second lumbar vertebrae and below this level the canal is occupied only by spinal nerve roots, passing along its sides. It is therefore reasonably safe to place a needle between the spines of the fourth and fifth lumbar vertebrae to take samples of cerebrospinal fluid for neurological examination. This procedure is known as a spinal tap or lumbar puncture.

The dural sheath is separated from the bone surrounding the canal by a narrow epidural space, which is filled with fat and some veins. The sacral spinal nerves, which supply the organs of the pelvis, can be anesthetized by placing anesthetic into the epidural space of the sacrum. This type of anesthesia, known as epidural anesthesia, is commonly used when babies are born by cesarean section, allowing the mother to remain conscious during the birth.

SEE ALSO *Coccyx, Disk, intervertebral, Epidural anesthesia, Joints, Kyphosis, Lordosis, Lumbar puncture, Neck, Osteoarthritis, Sacrum, Sciatica, Scoliosis, Skeletal system, Spinal cord, Vertebrae, Whiplash injury*

SPLEEN

The spleen is an organ about the size of a fist, which is situated high in the left side of the abdomen, beneath the diaphragm. It is an important blood-forming organ during fetal life but is not essential to life in the adult. The spleen receives a disproportionately large blood supply for its size, which it filters through channels called sinuses. Red blood cells squeeze through narrow pores in the sinuses and older, more rigid cells are destroyed there. The part of the spleen that forms blood cells in fetal life and filters the blood through the sinuses is called the red pulp. The other portion functions as part of the body's immune system and is called the white pulp.

The spleen is part of the immune system and contains large numbers of lymphocytes. It assists the body in fighting certain infections, especially pneumonia and meningitis.

S

If the spleen is removed (splenectomy), vaccinations are given to boost the body's immunity against such infections. Even so, a small risk remains of severe infection and people who have undergone splenectomy are advised to carry a medical alert card or necklace to alert medical staff of the fact in the event of a sudden febrile illness.

The spleen is a soft organ and is easily ruptured by injuries to the upper abdomen, such as occur in car collisions or contact sports, or with certain infections, such as malaria. If the spleen is enlarged, for example by glandular fever, it is even more susceptible to rupture. Rupture results in severe pain and internal bleeding and is a medical emergency. Splenectomy may need to be performed as a life-saving procedure. Sometimes it is possible for the surgeon to repair the damage and preserve part of the spleen, so that it can continue to function.

Enlargement of the spleen

There are many problems that can affect the spleen, causing enlargement.

Hemolysis

In conditions in which there is increased destruction of red blood cells, called hemolysis, the spleen becomes enlarged (splenomegaly) and can be felt below the rib cage. Hemolysis can result from a variety of disorders—some inherited, some developing during adult life. The treatment for a number of these conditions may include splenectomy.

The most common cause of hemolysis is malaria, in which there is an infection of the red blood cells by parasites transmitted by *Anopheles* mosquitoes. This results in high fevers, shaking, chills, anemia and jaundice. The damaged red cells are removed by the spleen, which becomes enlarged and painful. In countries where malaria is endemic, the spleen may eventually become very large in people exposed to repeated infections.

Other infections

Other infections can cause enlargement of the spleen, in particular infection by the Epstein-Barr virus, which causes infectious mononucleosis (glandular fever). This disease generally causes painful enlargement of the spleen, which gradually subsides as recovery occurs.

Spleen

The spleen is designed to filter blood and also functions as part of the body's immune system. Its red color and pulpy texture are due to its high blood content. The organs that surround the spleen (the stomach, colon and kidney) leave impressions on its soft surface. An enlarged spleen may indicate a disease or disorder elsewhere in the body.

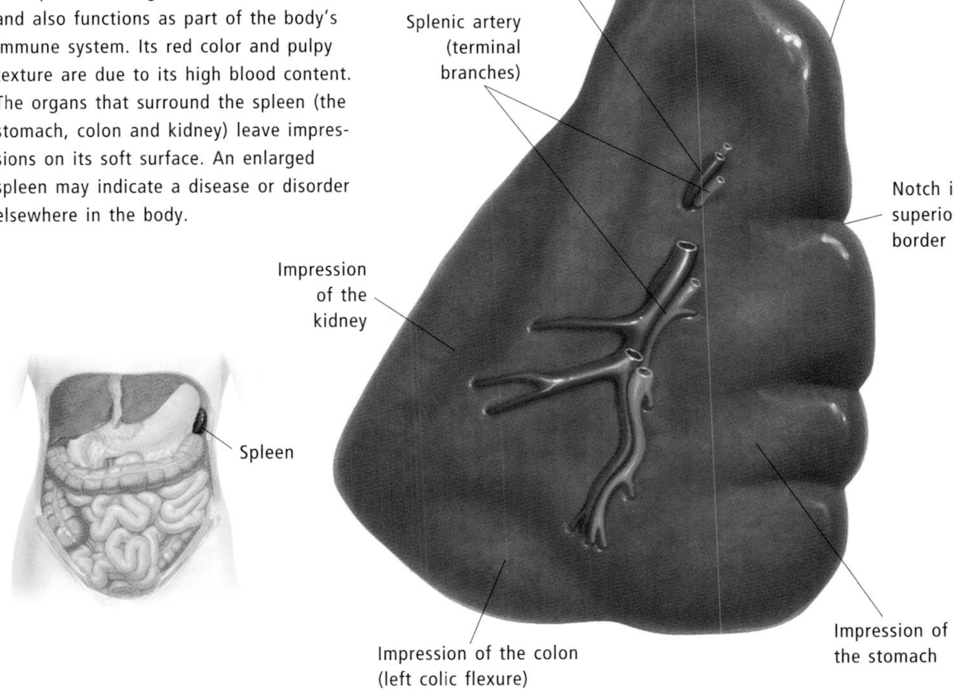

Spleen—microstructure

Red blood cells are filtered through channels, called sinuses, in the spleen which remove old and abnormal cells. The capillaries in the spleen are surrounded by lymphatic tissue.

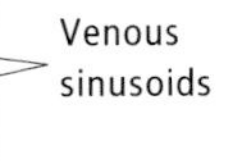

Venous sinusoids
Trabecular arteries
Red pulp
White pulp nodule
Capsule

Spleen—immune function

The spleen is the largest unit of lymphatic tissue in the body. It plays a vital role in the body's immune system by producing and storing lymphocytes, a type of white blood cell. These cells attack invading bacteria and viruses and make antibodies against them.

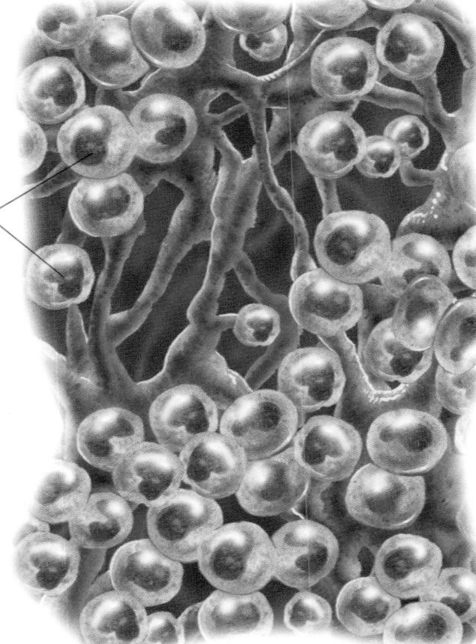

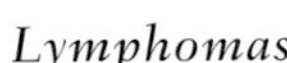

Lymphomas

Due to its link with the lymphatic system, the spleen may be affected by the same sorts of diseases that affect the lymph nodes. For example, lymphomas or tumors of the lymph nodes may cause enlargement of the spleen. Generally this does not cause pain but is detected during abdominal examination. The physician may confirm that the spleen is enlarged by ultrasound study, isotope scan or

S

CAT scan. The spleen may be involved by Hodgkin's or non-Hodgkin's lymphomas. Splenectomy is only usually performed for the diagnosis of non-Hodgkin's lymphomas that affect the spleen alone.

Leukemia

Leukemias can also cause enlargement of the spleen, which may be massive in the case of chronic myeloid leukemia. Other disorders of the blood cells that cause enlargement need to be distinguished from leukemias. In particular, a myeloproliferative disease—myelofibrosis (also called agnogenic myeloid metaplasia), can cause massive splenic enlargement. In this disease, while the adult spleen regains the capacity for blood cell formation, its massive enlargement results in a net decrease in circulating red blood cells.

Other diseases

The spleen can also enlarge due to a buildup of pressure in the splenic vein—the result of portal hypertension complicating cirrhosis of the liver. Other causes of splenomegaly include autoimmune diseases such as rheumatoid arthritis and systemic lupus erythematosus (SLE), and storage diseases such as amyloidosis and Gaucher's disease.

Whenever the spleen is markedly enlarged, a reduction in circulating red blood cell counts may occur because of the destruction or pooling of blood cells in the spleen. This condition is called hypersplenism and can result in anemia, leukopenia and thrombocytopenia.

Treatment

If the spleen is enlarged because of a blood disorder it may cause pain or hypersplenism needing treatment. In some cases the spleen can be shrunk using medication or chemotherapy. Sometimes a small dose of radiation therapy can be directed over the spleen to relieve the patient's symptoms. Otherwise splenectomy may be recommended.

It is now possible to perform splenectomy laparoscopically, through a very small incision in the abdominal wall. This allows for much quicker post-operative recovery as well as a more acceptable cosmetic result.

Following removal of the spleen, red blood cells containing small nuclear remnants (which are usually removed from the circulation by the spleen) appear in the blood. Sometimes this characteristic is found in the blood of a person whose spleen has not been removed. Occasionally this may be due to absence of the spleen from birth, but it is generally a sign of an underlying disease resulting in atrophy of the spleen. Such diseases include celiac disease (which results from an allergy to gluten protein) and autoimmune diseases such as hyperthyroidism.

Splenic atrophy is also a feature of sickle cell disease, as repeated episodes of vascular occlusion by misshapen red blood cells may damage the microstructure of the spleen. People with splenic atrophy require the same vaccinations as those whose spleens have been surgically removed.

Occasionally following splenectomy, an accessory spleen will develop from residual splenic tissue left behind at the time of surgery. This may result in a recurrence of the disease for which the spleen was removed and may require a second operation.

SEE ALSO *Anemia, Autoimmune disease, Celiac disease, Hodgkin's disease, Immunity, Infectious mononucleosis, Lymphatic immune system, Leukemia, Malaria, Non-Hodgkin's lymphoma, Red blood cells, Thrombocytopenia*

SPONDYLITIS

Spondylitis is the inflammation of one or more vertebrae in the spine. The most common form is ankylosing spondylitis, a rheumatic disorder in which the joints between the vertebrae become inflamed and the spine becomes increasingly stiff until the vertebrae fuse together.

Initial symptoms include lower back pain and/or hip pain and stiffness. There may be joint pain and swelling in the shoulders, knees and ankles, heel pain, stooping, fever and limited chest expansion as the disease spreads upwards from the lower back. About a quarter of spondylitis sufferers experience eye inflammation. In fact, this may be an early symptom of the disease, sometimes appearing years before any spinal inflammation occurs.

Spondylitis may also be associated with inflammatory bowel disease or tuberculosis of the vertebrae. About 10 percent of people who suffer from psoriasis—a condition marked by a scaly rash on the elbows, knees and scalp—also suffer from spondylitis, often years after the rash appears.

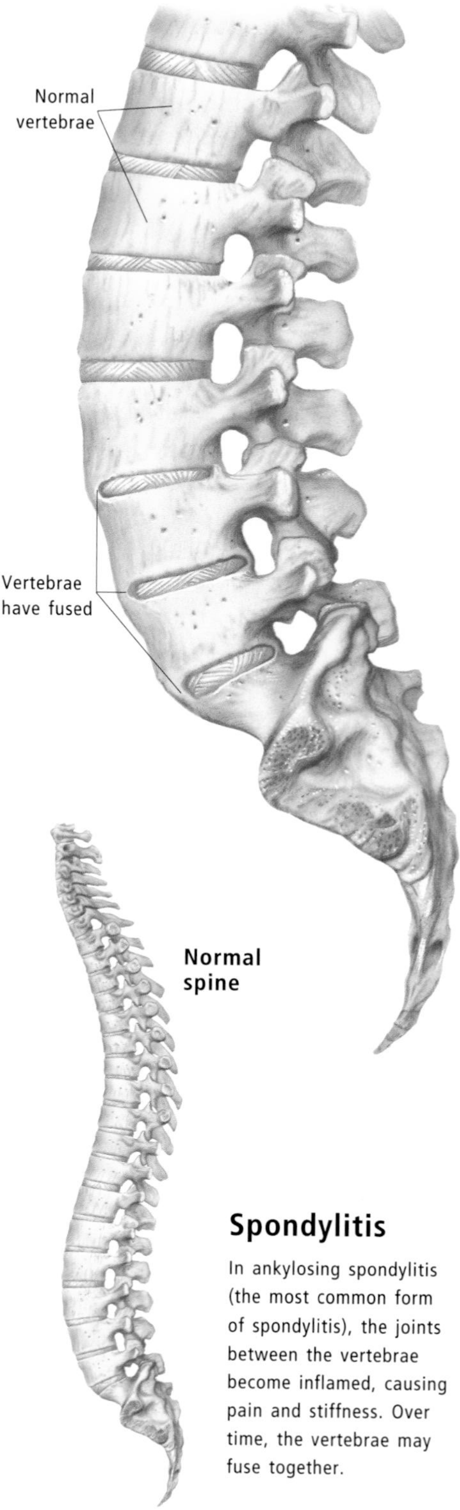

Spondylitis

In ankylosing spondylitis (the most common form of spondylitis), the joints between the vertebrae become inflamed, causing pain and stiffness. Over time, the vertebrae may fuse together.

Anti-inflammatory drugs, physical therapy and exercise are used to treat spondylitis. Ensuring good posture may also help.

SEE ALSO *Ankylosing spondylitis, Spine, Vertebrae*

SPONDYLOSIS

Spondylosis is osteoarthritis of the spine, due to natural ageing. It is also known as osteoarthritis. It often occurs in the neck (cervical) region of the spine and is caused by the degeneration of the disks located between the vertebrae. The condition can be aggravated by excessive activity or repeated injury. Abnormal bone growths (spurs) may occur, leading to compression of nerve roots and spinal cord. This can cause severe neck pain, radiating to the arms and shoulders, as well as loss of movement, function and sensation in parts of the body below the compression. There may be difficulty moving the head, buzzing in the ears, muscle weakness and loss of balance.

Treatment, if any, may include exercises to strengthen the neck and maintain good head movement, plus anti-inflammatory medication, and hospitalization and traction for severe cases.

SEE ALSO *Neck, Osteoarthritis, Spine*

SPORTS MEDICINE

Sports medicine is a field of health care focused on the prevention and treatment of sports injuries. It is primarily concerned with minimizing risk factors involved in any sport or physical activity, and offering effective treatment when injuries occur. Specialist doctors, trainers, physiologists and researchers are all involved in finding ways to improve the safety of sporting practice and in the formulation of training regimes to help athletes perform to the highest standard. Part of this doctrine is the gradual increase in stamina and strength through working muscles progressively harder over a set period, particularly after an injury.

Traumatic injuries

Most sports injuries are "traumatic". These happen suddenly and may involve immediate pain, swelling or bruising, or an open wound. Most are minor injuries to soft tissue, muscles, tendons or ligaments, such as strains and sprains. They may be due to a sudden wrenching or twisting of a body part, or have no obvious cause.

Ensuring a safe environment in which the physical activity takes place can minimize the risk of suffering from traumatic injury. For example, slippery floors are highly dangerous in basketball. Using safety gear such as mouthguards, helmets and padding where appropriate, is a priority and all equipment used must be in good condition.

Sprain

The ankle and wrist are particularly susceptible to sprains—the tearing or severe stretching of the tendons, muscles and ligaments that support the joint.

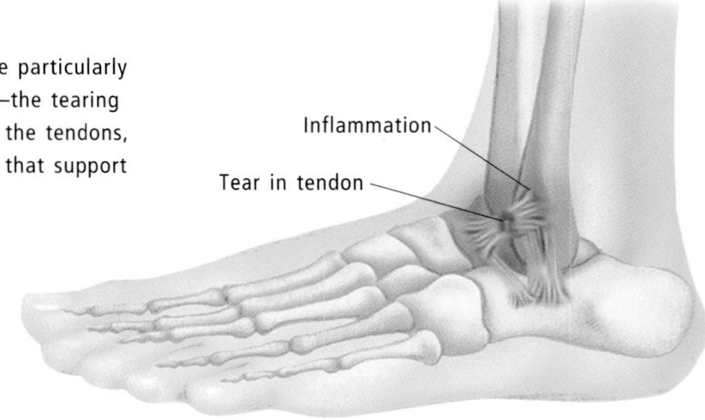

Overuse injuries

These are products of particular physical activities, especially repetitive ones, and are characterized by a gradual increase in pain and discomfort. An example is tennis elbow. These types of injuries can be avoided by building a progressive training regime that allows the body to get used to potentially damaging physical activity. For example, weight lifters start with light weights and build their bodies up so that they can cope with heavy lifting. Sudden changes in training routines may also put stress on a part of the body. Rest and recovery days are recommended if pain is experienced.

Warming up and cooling down before and after physical activity is essential to avoid muscle stiffness. Warm-ups might include stretching muscles, bouncing movements for the joints and sprints to get the heart beating. A healthy diet with energy-giving carbohydrates and plenty of fluids is also important to help avoid fatigue and dehydration.

Treating an injury

Once an injury is sustained it is important not to add extra stress by keeping up the physical activity that caused it. Treatment will depend on the type and extent of the injury. A strained muscle may require gentle stretching exercises to regain flexibility, then strengthening exercises to help avoid a recurrence of the injury. Joint injuries may also respond to exercises that strengthen surrounding muscles. This will help stabilize the joint, after which a training regime can be formulated aimed at regaining mobility and function. Training programs must be progressive to avoid risk of further injury.

There is a simple way of remembering how to give immediate treatment to acute injuries on the sports field: Rest, Ice, Compression and Elevation (RICE). Rest minimizes hemorrhage and swelling, applying ice reduces pain and inflammation, and compression and elevation limit bruising.

SEE ALSO *Exercise, Joints, Muscle, Tennis elbow, Trauma*

SPRAIN

Sprain is severe stretching or tearing of the tendons, muscles or ligaments surrounding a joint such as the ankle or wrist. This may be caused by a sudden twisting or wrenching movement and results in joint or muscle pain, swelling and sometimes bruising. Joint movement may also be impaired.

Applying cold compresses immediately after the injury and keeping the injured joint elevated above the heart will help reduce swelling. Severe cases may require bandaging and splinting. Resting the joint is the main treatment—depending on the severity of the sprain, it may be four or five weeks before normal use should be resumed.

SEE ALSO *Joints, Ligaments, Muscle, Tendons*

SPRUE

Sprue is a disorder of the small intestine marked by impaired absorption of food, especially fats. It is most common in the tropics where it is thought to be caused by infection. In other regions it can result from any illness or medical treatment that interrupts normal intestinal cell activity, such as celiac disease, pancreatitis, radiation treatment, worm infection or the surgical removal of part of the stomach or small intestine.

Symptoms include dry skin, weight loss, soreness in the corners of the mouth, a red tongue (due to vitamin B deficiency), flatulence, and foul-smelling bowel movements. Swollen ankles and abdomen and clubbing of the fingers may occur, along with weakness, fatigue, diarrhea and muscle cramps. Treatment depends on the underlying cause.

SEE ALSO *Celiac disease, Intestines, Pancreatitis, Radiation therapy*

SPUTUM TEST

Sputum is the fluid that patients cough up from their lungs, usually during infective or allergic lung conditions, or after inhaling dust. Sputum may contain a lot of clear thick mucus, as seen in asthma or chronic bronchitis; pus, as in pneumonia; frothy fluid tinged with blood, as in heart failure with pulmonary edema; or black material, found in coal-miner's lung and heavy air pollution. Sputum may be analyzed for the presence of bacteria, which can be cultured and tested for antibiotic resistance; pus cells, indicating infection; malignant cells, which indicate cancer; or asbestos bodies, seen in asbestosis.

SEE ALSO *Asbestosis, Asthma, Bronchitis, Lungs, Pneumonia, Pulmonary edema*

SQUAMOUS CELL CARCINOMA

This term describes a large group of cancers. Multiple layers of squamous (flat) cells form the normal covering epithelium (surface cell layer) in many parts of the body, including the skin, the mucous membranes of the mouth, anal canal, vagina and cervix, and the lining of the esophagus and larynx. Irritation of other mucous membranes can lead to a change in cell type from glandular epithelium to squamous epithelium, such as in the lung as a result of smoking.

When squamous epithelium turns cancerous, the resulting tumor is called a squamous cell carcinoma (SCC). It has microscopic features that allow it to be recognized by a pathologist. Squamous cell carcinomas do not all grow and spread at the same rate. The site of origin and the extent of microscopic change (compared to normal epithelium) may indicate likely behavior.

SEE ALSO *Cancer, Mucous membranes, Smoking*

Squint

Three pairs of muscles control eye movement. A squint (misalignment of the eyes) occurs when any of the pairs does not function correctly. With a squint, one or both of the eyes may look inward (cross-eyed) or outward (wall-eyed).

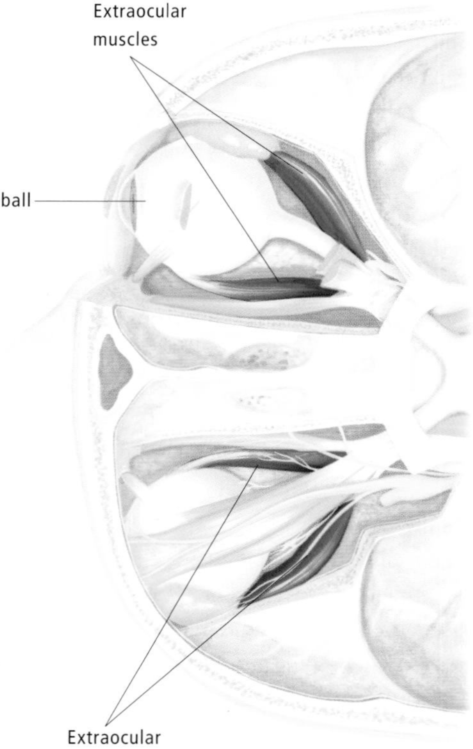

SQUINT

A squint (also known as strabismus) is a condition in which a person looks with partially closed or crossed eyes, primarily due to misalignment of the eyes. There are six muscles attached to each eye that work in pairs to allow movement; if muscle coordination is affected the eyes have trouble working in unison and can point in different directions. One eye may turn inward (cross-eye) or outward (wall-eye) while the other looks straight ahead. This sends two different pictures to the brain, which may ignore one image or allow two images to be seen, resulting in double vision. When one eye is favored over the other, vision in the nondominant eye can be lost as a consequence and the sense of depth perception distorted.

A squint may be a congenital condition, or the result of a neurological disorder, cranial nerve and eye diseases, eye trauma or cerebral palsy. Farsightedness can be a contributing factor. The condition can usually not be prevented, but exercises to strengthen muscles around the eye often improve symptoms. In severe cases, the muscles of one or both eyes may be repositioned and shortened by surgery.

This may not totally cure the condition, but the squint will be significantly reduced. Squinting generally appears at a young age and early treatment is important to avoid permanent loss of vision in one eye.

SEE ALSO *Eye, Sight*

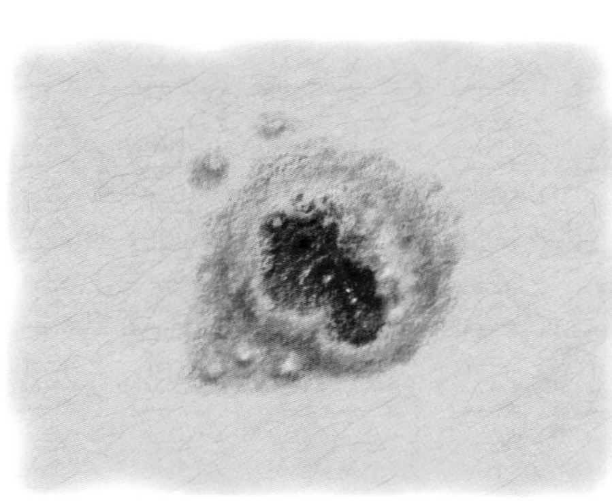

Squamous cell carcinoma

Malignant changes in the squamous cells that form the skin's surface layer can result in the formation of a cancerous tumor called a squamous cell carcinoma.

STAPHYLOCOCCAL INFECTION

Staphylococci are bacteria responsible for a wide range of human infections. Several species exist including *Staphylococcus epidermidis,* which is part of the normal bacterial flora of the skin, and *S. aureus,* commonly known as "golden staph", which has a greater potential to cause infection.

S

Staphylococcal infection most commonly involves the skin, in the form of abscesses, but the bacteria may spread to deeper tissues to cause deep abscesses, osteomyelitis or septicemia. Some strains of *S. aureus* produce a toxin that results in toxic shock syndrome—high fever, a red rash, low blood pressure and organ dysfunctions. Staphylococci are very common causes of infections in hospitals: *S. epidermidis* causes infection of intravenous cannulas and *S. aureus* can cause severe infections in diabetics, patients with renal (kidney) failure and intravenous drug users. Treatment of staphylococcal infection is with antibiotics and surgical drainage of abscesses when required. The widespread use of antibiotics in hospitals has led to the emergence of multi-resistant staphylococci, which are important pathogens in surgical and intensive care units. Prevention of cross-infection by the use of handwashing is important for reducing staphylococcal infections.

SEE ALSO *Abscess, Bacteria, Osteomyelitis, Septicemia, Toxic shock syndrome*

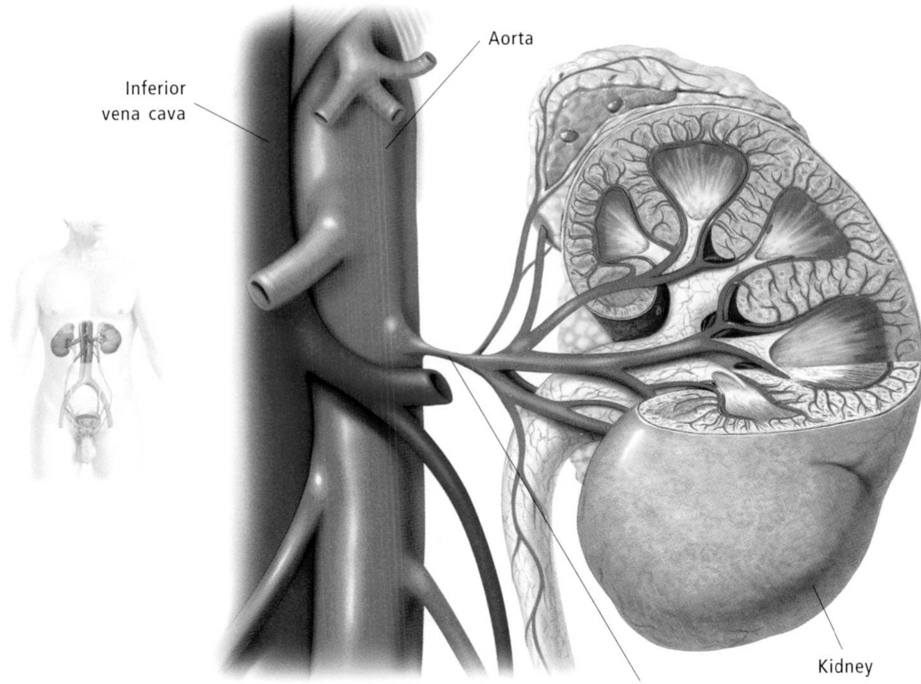

Stenosis

The narrowing of a tube, such as an artery, or duct is known as stenosis. In renal artery stenosis, constriction of the artery disrupts blood flow to the kidney and affects kidney function.

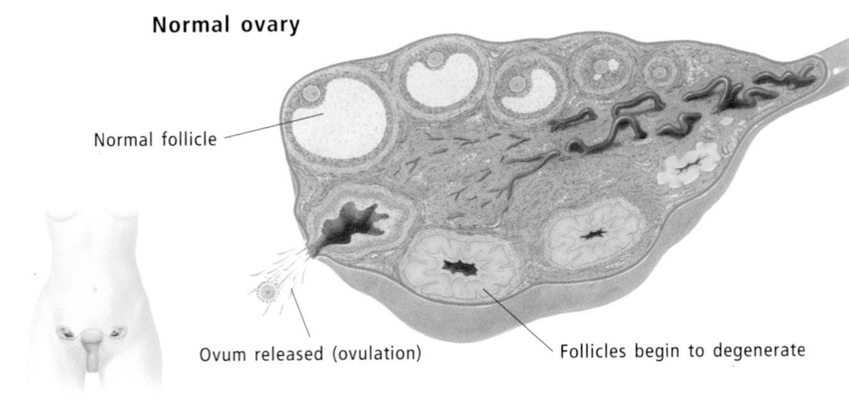

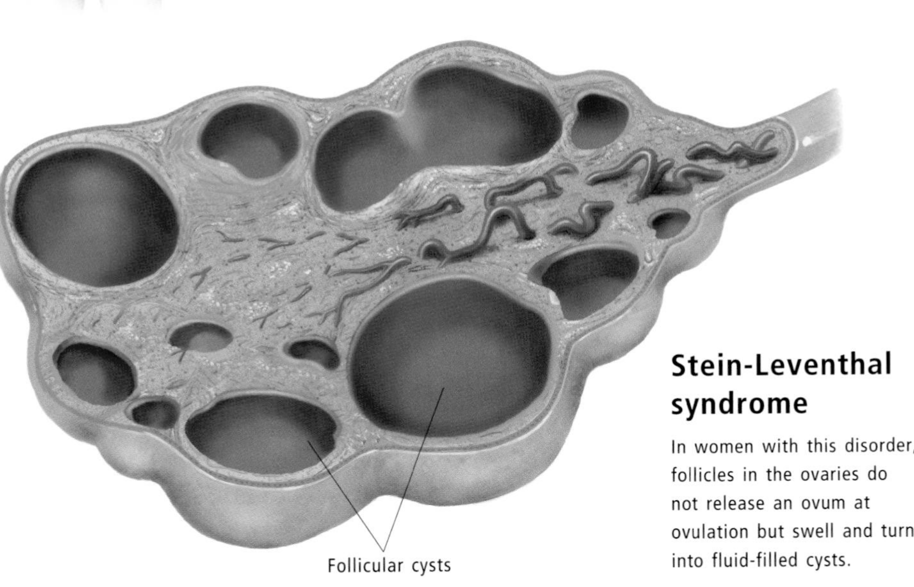

Stein-Leventhal syndrome

In women with this disorder, follicles in the ovaries do not release an ovum at ovulation but swell and turn into fluid-filled cysts.

STEIN-LEVENTHAL SYNDROME

Stein-Leventhal syndrome, also known as polycystic ovarian syndrome, is a disorder of the follicles in the ovaries characterized by multiple cysts, the absence of menstruation, obesity, infertility and increased hair growth on the face and body. Instead of releasing ova, the swollen follicles fill with fluid and turn into cysts. The ovaries can consequently become two to five times larger than normal. Abnormal hormone levels are thought to cause the condition, which commonly occurs just after puberty and appears to a have a hereditary link.

Oral contraceptives are one of the medications used to treat the disorder. Pregnancy may be possible with medical help.

SEE ALSO *Hormones, Oral contraceptives, Ovarian cysts, Ovaries*

STENOSIS

Stenosis is the constriction of a tube or duct in any one of a number of locations inside the body. One type is spinal stenosis, a condition that usually affects middle-aged and elderly people in which the spinal canal narrows due to degenerative bony overgrowth. Pyloric stenosis occurs at the exit to the stomach and in adults is commonly caused by muscle spasms. Babies may suffer from a congenital form of pyloric stenosis, in which

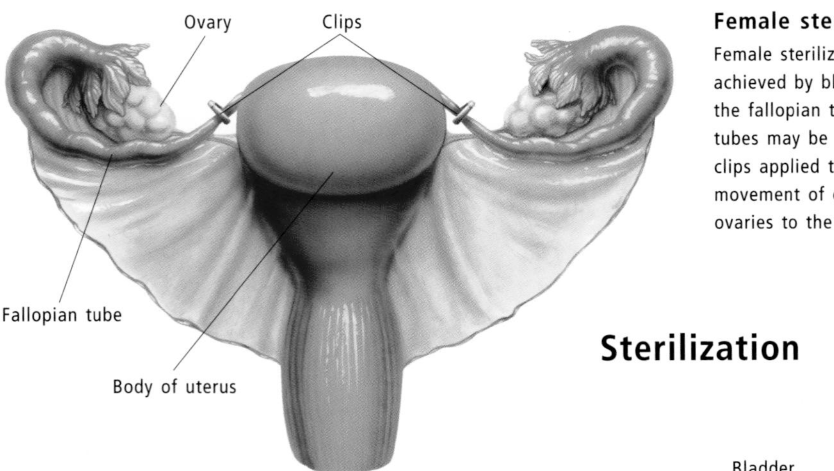

Female sterilization
Female sterilization is achieved by blocking the fallopian tubes. The tubes may be severed or clips applied to block the movement of ova from the ovaries to the uterus.

Sterilization

Male sterilization
Usually performed under local anesthetic, a vasectomy involves cutting the vas deferens tube that carries sperm from the testes to the urethra. Sterilization can be reversed if the tubes are rejoined.

case an operation may be performed to cut the muscle and thereby prevent spasms from occurring.

Stenosis may also occur in the arteries of the leg or the carotid artery in the neck. This causes reduced blood flow and, when the leg is affected, cramping and pain in the calf muscle.

Other parts of the body that may be affected by stenosis include the heart valves and salivary glands. Treatment for these and other forms of stenosis includes medication and/or surgery.

SEE ALSO *Spine, Heart, Pyloric stenosis*

S

STERILIZATION

Sterilization is a permanent surgical form of contraception involving a vasectomy in men and tubal ligation or tubal sterilization in women, the latter often referred to as tying the tubes. These procedures are commonly chosen by couples who don't want to have more or any children, and who prefer to avoid drug-based forms of birth control or those that carry a higher risk of pregnancy. It is estimated that as many as 100 million couples worldwide have opted for sterilization as a method of birth control. More female sterilizations have been performed than male, but demand is high for both.

The advantages of permanent protection against pregnancy, no effect on sexual pleasure and no lasting side effects, may outweigh any costs or the possibility of later regrets. As both of these operations should be regarded as permanent, it is a good idea for anyone contemplating sterilization to receive some counseling.

Vasectomy

Vasectomy is the quicker, simpler operation. Usually performed under local anesthetic it involves the cutting of the vas deferens (or ductus deferens), the tube that carries the sperm to the urethra from the testicles. A small opening is usually made in the front of the scrotum allowing each vas deferens to be cut and sealed. The operation takes around 20 minutes and is not effective until all the sperm in the tubes have been ejaculated, which can take up to 16 ejaculations. Samples of semen need to be tested some months after the operation to ensure that it has been successful.

The most common side effects are a slight soreness, swelling and bruising which last for a few days. A few men suffer bleeding or infection. About one in 300–500 vasectomies will fail to sterilize, usually because the tubes were not completely blocked off, the surgery healed itself or there was a third undetected vas deferens.

Tubal sterilization

Female sterilization is a more serious operation in which the fallopian tubes are blocked. Surgery can be performed by using a laparoscope (an optical instrument) inserted through an incision near the navel and into the abdominal cavity, or through the vaginal vault. The tubes, once found, are blocked by rings or clips, or by burning with diathermy or laser. A mini-laparotomy involves a small incision just below the pubic hairline.

After sterilization, the ovaries will continue to release ova, but sperm will not be able to reach them. The menstrual cycle is not affected by the procedure, with periods and menopause still occurring. There are usually no side effects after recovery from the operation, although some women have reported heavier than usual periods, strong cramps, recurrent abdominal pain and pelvic infections.

The failure rate of tubal ligation is around two per 1,000. This may be due to tubes joining themselves back together and, on rare occasions, may result in a potentially dangerous ectopic pregnancy where a fertilized ovum embeds in a fallopian tube or somewhere else outside the uterus.

While reversal of these operations is possible, the success rates differ. Although microsurgery is improving all the time, sterilization is not a procedure which should be undertaken if the person has any thoughts of producing children later in life.

SEE ALSO *Contraception, Reproductive systems, Tubal sterilization, Vasectomy*

STERNUM

The sternum (or breastbone) forms part of the skeleton of the thorax. It is situated in the front wall of the chest, in the midline. It consists of three parts, from top to

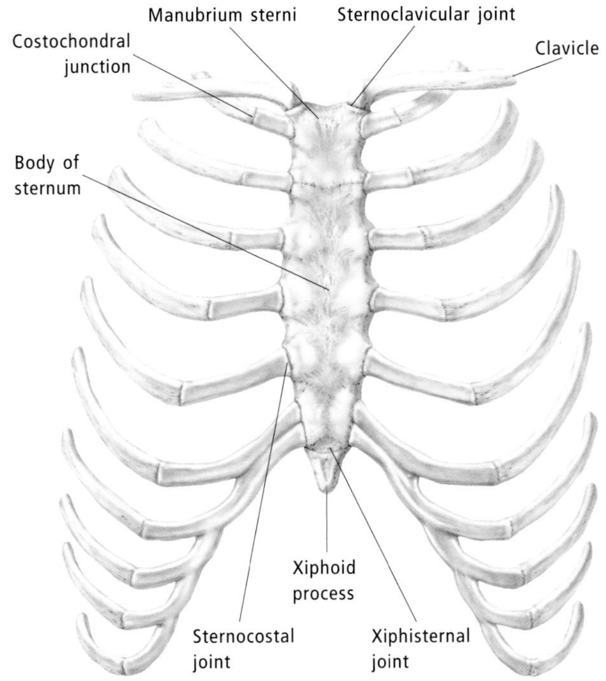

Sternum

Forming part of the anterior wall of the thorax, the sternum consists of three parts: the manubrium, the body and the xiphoid process.

bottom: the manubrium; the body of the sternum; and the xiphoid process (pronounced "ziffoid"). The manubrium articulates with the clavicles (collar bones), thereby assisting in stabilizing the shoulders. The ribs are connected to the sides of the manubrium and body of the sternum by their costal cartilages. The pectoralis major muscle is attached in part to the sternum. The sternum contains a marrow cavity, which is a convenient site for bone marrow biopsy.

SEE ALSO *Collar bone, Ribs, Shoulder*

STEROIDS

Steroids are a group of chemicals that comprise a large number of the body's hormones. They are synthesized from cholesterol mainly in the adrenal glands and gonads, and regulate a number of important body processes.

There are three main groups of steroids: glucocorticoids, mineralocorticoids and sex steroids (androgens and estrogens). The major glucocorticoid is cortisol, which is also known as the "stress hormone". It is released from the adrenal gland in response to physiological stresses such as exercise, injury or infection, or psychological stresses, such as fear or depression. Cortisol acts on many cells in the body, regulating their metabolism and activity. It prepares the body for action by mobilizing glucose stores and preventing excessive tissue reaction to injury. This anti-inflammatory action is used when cortisol-type medication is prescribed for the treatment of autoimmune diseases.

These synthetic steroid medications have a similar chemical make-up to steroids that occur naturally in the body and are designed to have the same effect. Corticosteroids were first used in the 1940s for the treatment of rheumatoid arthritis and today there are many more types prescribed by physicians to provide relief from conditions such as allergies, asthma and skin inflammation.

The wide range of effects explains the potential for many side effects from cortisol treatment. In large doses it may increase blood sugar and blood pressure, affect mood, accelerate osteoporosis, and reduce wound healing and response to infection. Patients with Cushing's syndrome, in which there is increased cortisol production from an adrenal tumor, show similar symptoms.

Mineralocorticoids help the body control salt and water balance. Androgens are produced by the adrenal glands; however, they require conversion in the testes to the main male hormone testosterone. The main female sex hormone, estradiol, is made from cholesterol by cells in the ovaries.

Synthetic anabolic steroids are different to other steroid medications. Chemically similar to the male sex hormone testosterone, they increase muscle growth and lean body mass, and they have been abused by body builders and athletes who often use dangerously high amounts in order to boost their physical performance. This overuse creates a severe imbalance in the secretion of natural hormones by the body and if the synthetic steroids are suddenly withdrawn may lead to side effects such as weakness, nausea, vomiting, weight loss and abdominal pain.

SEE ALSO *Adrenal glands, Autoimmune disease, Cholesterol, Cushing's syndrome, Hormones*

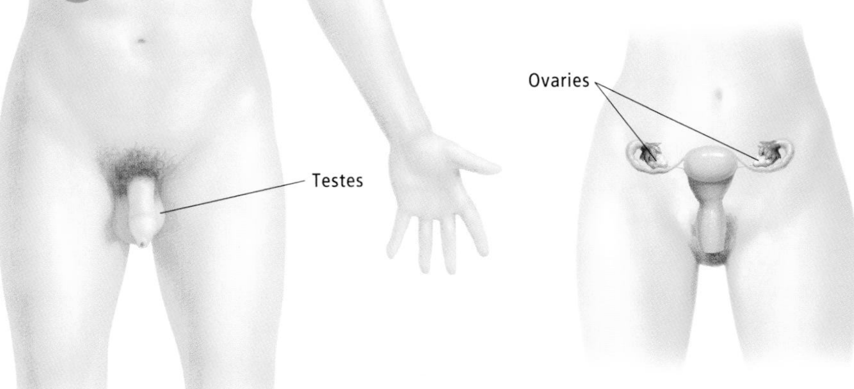

Steroids

Steroids are a group of chemicals that comprise a large number of the body's hormones, including the sex hormones testosterone and estrogen. Many are synthesized from cholesterol, mainly in the adrenal glands and in the gonads (testes and ovaries). Steroids regulate body processes, such as growth, and the repair of body tissue.

STEVENS-JOHNSON SYNDROME

Stevens-Johnson syndrome, a type of erythema multiforme, is a rare and potentially fatal skin condition marked by blisters in the mouth, throat, anal region and the mucous membranes lining the eyelid. It usually occurs after other illnesses and infections, or in response to certain medications. Ring-shaped lesions appear on the palms, hands, arms, legs and feet. These are often accompanied by fever, aching joints and itching, and sometimes mouth sores, bloodshot eyes and abnormal vision. Blisters in the throat may be extremely painful, making swallowing very difficult.

Some relief may be experienced by applying moist compresses to skin lesions. Antihistamine medications can be used to control itching and topical anesthetics applied to mouth sores to reduce pain and discomfort.

Hospitalization is often necessary, with the use of antibiotics and other medications to control inflammation and secondary infections. Skin grafts may be performed when lesions affect large areas.

Due to the severity of Stevens-Johnson Syndrome there is a high risk of death. Complications may include shock due to the loss of body fluids, systemic infection and scarring.

SEE ALSO *Erythema*

STILL'S DISEASE

Still's disease, or juvenile rheumatoid arthritis (JRA), is a form of rheumatoid arthritis that affects children under 16 years of age. As with adult rheumatoid arthritis, the cause is unknown, but it is thought to be an autoimmune connective tissue disease, as it affects not only the joints of the body, but also other organs such as the heart and pericardium (the lining around the heart), the lungs and pleura (the lining around the lungs), the eyes and the skin.

There are various forms of the illness. In one form, arthritis is the prominent feature; the joints are swollen, painful and tender to touch and may be hot and red. In another form, the joints are not affected but fever, chills and a rash are present, and the spleen may be enlarged (splenomegaly). In this type, uveitis (inflammation of the inner lining of the eyes and iris muscle) may occur, leading to visual problems or blindness.

The diagnosis of Still's disease is usually made by a specialist pediatrician or rheumatologist. Blood tests, which may reveal the presence of certain proteins such as rheumatoid factor and antinuclear antibody, help make the diagnosis easier.

Treatment is with drugs such as corticosteroids and nonsteroidal anti-inflammatory agents (NSAIDs) and in some cases gold and chloroquine. Physical therapy and exercise programs are often recommended; in severe cases, joint replacement may be needed. However, most of the time the disease burns itself out (often at puberty) without leaving any permanent loss or deformity.

SEE ALSO *Autoimmune disease, Connective tissue, Joints, Rheumatoid arthritis*

STIMULANTS

Stimulants are drugs that accelerate (excite) mental or bodily functions. Laxatives, for example, are stimulants used to overcome constipation or lack of motility in bowel functions, which work by stimulating the intestines to contract.

There are many mild stimulants readily and legally available which act on the nervous system. These include caffeine, found in coffee, tea, cola drinks, maté and guarana, and theobromine, found in cocoa. Nicotine, found in cigarettes and other tobacco products, is regarded as a stimulant as its immediate effects on inhalation of tobacco smoke are to increase heart rate, raise blood pressure and excite the nervous system.

Stronger stimulants include illegal substances (street drugs), such as cocaine, and drugs such as methylxanthines, amphetamines (also known as speed), or methylated purines, which are available on prescription.

Amphetamines stimulate the central nervous system, elevating alertness and well-being, increasing energy and self-confidence and at the same time reducing appetite. They can also induce anxiety, increased heart rate and palpitations; high intake of these drugs may result in feelings of hostility and aggression. Long-term use brings dependency and can cause hallucinations, delusions (including hearing voices) and feelings of persecution. Overdose can cause brain hemorrhage, heart attack, coma and death. Amphetamines were first prescribed for depression, narcolepsy and, because they reduce appetite, for obesity.

More recently amphetamines have been prescribed for children with some types of hyperactivity. Use without a prescription is generally illegal.

SEE ALSO *Amphetamines, Attention deficit hyperactivity disorder, Cocaine, Drug dependence, Drugs, Laxatives, Nicotine, Overdose*

STITCH

A stitch is a sharp abdominal pain usually experienced during physical exertion. It is commonly felt under the rib cage on one side of the body due to muscle cramps in the abdominal wall.

People with low fitness levels are more likely to get a stitch. The pain disappears without treatment but gently rubbing the affected area may help. Ceasing physical activity for 15 minutes or so is also recommended.

SEE ALSO *Abdomen, Cramp*

STOKES-ADAMS SYNDROME

Stokes-Adams syndrome is a form of heart block. The normal electrical impulses that regulate the heartbeat are blocked as they pass from the upper chambers of the heart to the lower chambers—usually because the heart muscle is damaged. This slows the heartbeat temporarily, reducing blood flow to the brain and causing fainting.

The condition is most common in the elderly and is associated with coronary heart disease. It results from transient or permanent heart problems and is characterized by episodes of loss of consciousness, sometimes referred to as Stokes-Adams attacks.

These attacks may last from a few seconds to a few minutes. When consciousness is regained, sufferers may experience spells of nausea, dizziness and faintness when they try to sit or stand. The heart rate may return to normal spontaneously or a complete heart block may persist.

Stokes-Adams syndrome is best treated with an artificial pacemaker. Alternatively, drug treatment may be used. The condition is also called Adams-Stokes syndrome.

SEE ALSO *Heart, Heartbeat, Pacemaker*

STOMACH

The stomach receives food from the esophagus and continues the process of digestion. It acts as a reservoir, permitting the intake of large amounts of food every few hours. When empty of food, the stomach contains only about one-twelfth of a pint (50 milliliters) of liquid, but can expand to accommodate up to 2 pints (1,200 milliliters) after a large meal is eaten. The stomach mixes the food with the acidic gastric juices, which digest protein and carbohydrates, and delivers semi-digested food to the next part of the gut, the duodenum. The stomach is also the site of absorption of some drugs such as aspirin.

Structure and function

The stomach has many parts. The cardia is located at the entrance of the esophagus into the stomach (cardioesophageal junction). The fundus lies to the left of the cardia, while the body of the stomach is the large central part which extends from the fundus to the pylorus. The pylorus is the final part of the stomach and consists of a pyloric antrum, which leads to the pyloric canal. The pyloric canal is encircled by a ring of muscle known as the pyloric sphincter, which controls the passage of stomach juices and food into the duodenum.

The inner lining of the stomach has many types of specialized cells. Some, such as the mucous cells, produce a thick layer of mucus to protect the stomach from its own acid juices. Another group, the parietal or oxyntic cells, produces the hydrochloric acid to keep the stomach interior at the optimal acidity level for protein digestion, while another group, the zymogen cells, produces the enzymes to digest protein and fat. There are also several cell types in the stomach which produce hormones for controlling acid secretion and regulating nutrient levels in the blood.

The stomach is a very muscular organ and can churn the partially digested food it receives to break it up into more easily digested fragments. Waves of muscular contraction, called peristalsis, move down the stomach from the body to the pylorus. When the food is ready to be moved on down the digestive tract, these waves propel the food into the pyloric canal and on to the duodenum.

The secretion of stomach acid is controlled in several phases or stages. The sight, smell, taste and even the thought of food act upon the brain to stimulate acid secretion. The nerve impulses which control this are carried from the brain stem by the vagus nerve. When the food reaches the stomach, local mechanical and chemical stimulation leads to the release of gastrin, a hormone which controls gastric juice secretion.

Diseases and disorders

There are many problems that can affect the stomach, including the following.

Cancer

Stomach cancer is fortunately becoming rarer in Western countries. The incidence of stomach cancer is higher in Japan and in eastern and central European countries, compared to the USA. Cancer of the stomach, rare in people aged under 40, is about twice as common in men as in women.

There are several different types of stomach cancers. About one-quarter of cancers produce ulcers and can be mistaken for peptic ulcers. A further quarter produce bulky bulbous growths in the interior of the stomach, while about 15 percent spread superficially through the surface lining of the stomach. Unfortunately, many stomach cancers are advanced at the time of diagnosis and are found to be both partly within and partly outside the stomach. Most tumors arise in the pyloric region, the bulk of the remainder developing in the stomach body.

Most patients with stomach cancer will initially note a vague feeling of heaviness after meals. Weight loss will follow and may be

Stomach

The walls of the stomach serve several purposes. The mucosa and submucosa, which form the stomach's inner lining, secrete gastric juices and other substances to aid digestion. The layers of muscle contract and expand in order to mix and expel the stomach contents. The outer coating of the wall is smooth and slippery, easing movement of the stomach.

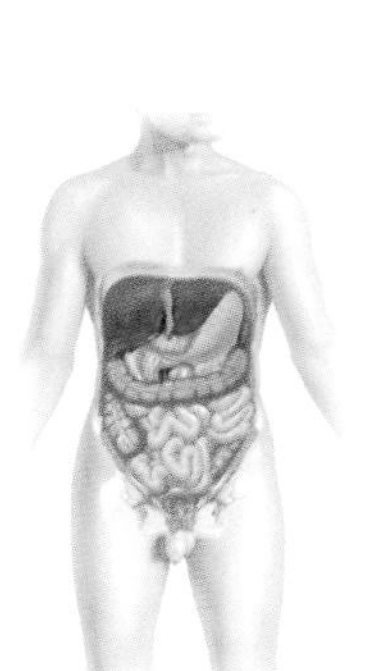

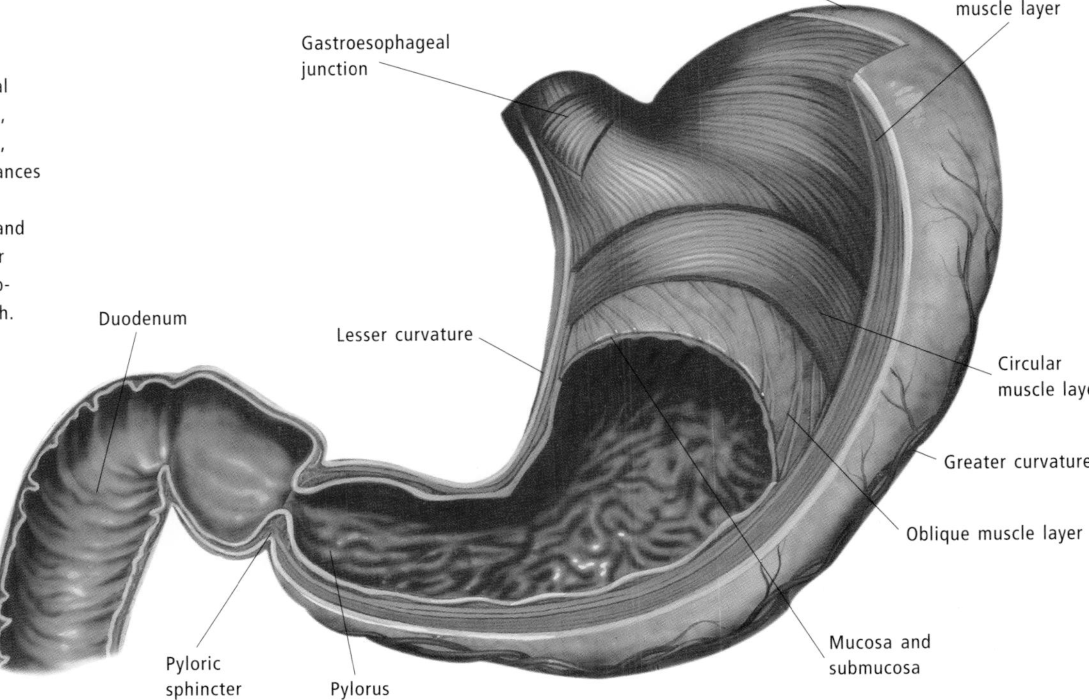

accompanied by vomiting of a coffee-ground colored material. A palpable lump may be present in the upper abdomen and the liver may be enlarged if the tumor has spread to that organ.

The diagnosis may be made by barium meal x-ray and examination with a fiberoptic instrument (gastroscopy). The only curative treatment is the surgical removal of the tumor (gastrectomy), any local lymph nodes and portions of surrounding organs if necessary. The long-term prospects for patients with this disease are poor. Of all patients with stomach cancer only about 12–15 percent will survive 5 years; of those patients where the tumor is localized at the time of diagnosis, 40–50 percent may survive for 5 years.

Ulcers

Peptic ulcers result from the action of stomach juices on the vulnerable surface lining of the stomach, duodenum or esophagus. Peptic ulcers in the stomach are usually located along the lesser curvature and most are within a few inches of the pylorus. Patients will experience pain in the upper abdomen, which is relieved by food and antacids. Complications arising from peptic ulcers include bleeding, obstruction and perforation of the stomach, duodenum or esophagus.

Ulceration of the lining of the stomach may also occur as a result of stressful illnesses such as acute blood loss, serious infection, burns, brain injury and brain tumors. Patients with stress ulcers from burns or infection typically develop bleeding from the stomach and duodenum, and some patients may have perforation of the stomach or duodenum wall. Ulcers developing in patients with brain injury or tumors are usually due to increased gastrin production and excessive stomach acid secretion. Alcohol and drugs such as aspirin, steroids and anti-inflammatories can also cause irritation and ulceration of the stomach lining. Treatment may include the eradication of any infection.

Hiatus hernia

Parts of the stomach may protrude (herniate) through the diaphragm in a condition called hiatus (hiatal) hernia. Hiatus hernia can be of two types. The paraesophageal or rolling hiatal hernia involves the herniation of the stomach fundus through the esophageal opening. Sliding hiatus hernia is more common than the rolling type and involves the movement of the cardioesophageal junction through the diaphragm into the chest cavity. Rolling hiatus hernia may may not be accompanied by any symptoms, while patients with sliding hiatus hernia usually experience heartburn, particularly on lying down, and a feeling of regurgitation.

Gastroenteritis

Infection of the stomach and intestines may occur as a result of ingesting disease-causing viruses and bacteria (food poisoning). This causes an inflammatory condition called gastroenteritis. The sufferer experiences nausea, vomiting and upper abdominal discomfort if the infection involves the upper gastrointestinal tract.

SEE ALSO *Cancer, Digestive system, Esophagus, Gastrectomy, Gastritis, Gastroenteritis, Hiatus hernia, Peptic ulcer, Peristalsis, Pylorus*

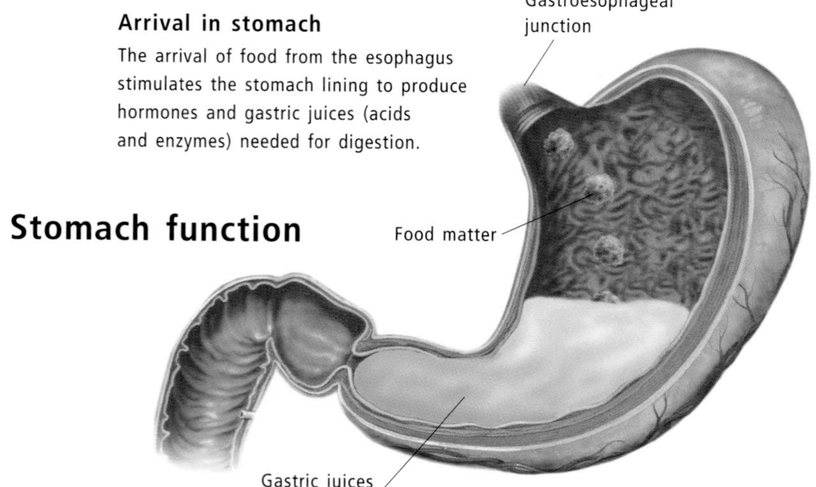

Arrival in stomach
The arrival of food from the esophagus stimulates the stomach lining to produce hormones and gastric juices (acids and enzymes) needed for digestion.
Stomach function
Gastroesophageal junction
Food matter
Gastric juices mix with food

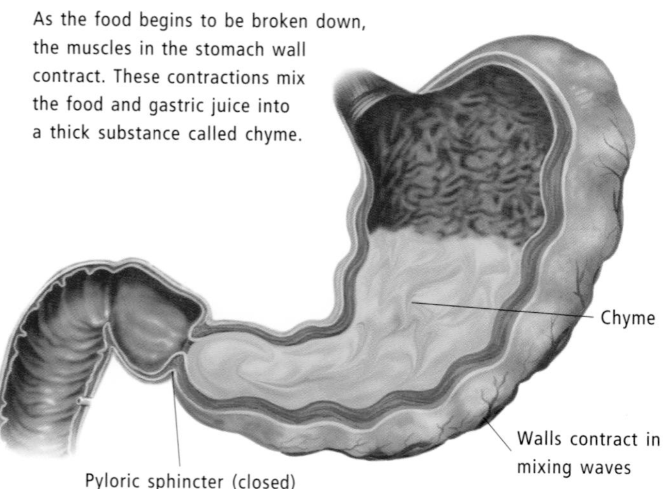

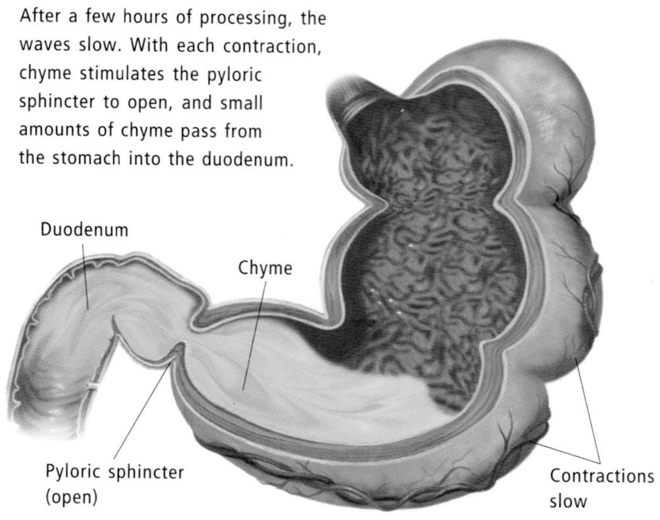

Exiting the stomach
After a few hours of processing, the waves slow. With each contraction, chyme stimulates the pyloric sphincter to open, and small amounts of chyme pass from the stomach into the duodenum.
Duodenum
Chyme
Pyloric sphincter (open)
Contractions slow

STREPTOCOCCAL INFECTIONS

Streptococcal infections are caused by perhaps the most common human bacterial pathogen, *Streptococcus*. Streptococci are classified into several groups and cause a spectrum of disease, ranging from minor to life-threatening. The same groups of streptococci that cause minor infections can occasionally cause severe disease.

The commonest streptococcal infection is streptococcal pharyngitis, or "strep throat". This is generally due to infection by Group A streptococci, which most often causes sore throat and fever in childhood. Although most cases of throat infection are viral and associated with the common cold, throat swabs should be taken if streptococcal infection is suspected, particularly in children aged 5–15 years. Antibiotic treatment can prevent the development of possible serious long-term complications. Apart from otitis media, sinusitis and abscess formation, there may be occasional immune-mediated complications. These are acute rheumatic fever and post-streptococcal glomerulonephritis. The former can be prevented by a full 10-day course of penicillin, avoiding possible later damage to the heart valves.

Another common form of superficial Group A streptococcal infection is impetigo. This causes crusted pustules, mainly on the legs, of young children in tropical climates. Occasionally Group A streptococci cause severe invasive infections, such as streptococcal toxic shock syndrome or necrotizing fasciitis ("flesh-eating bacteria").

Group B streptococci are the commonest cause of infection of the uterus after childbirth and neonatal infection. Group D streptococci are major causes of pneumonia and endocarditis (infection of the heart valves).

Streptococci

While usually causing only mild infections such as "strep throat", streptococci bacteria are also responsible for more severe disorders such as streptococcal toxic shock syndrome and necrotizing fasciitis.

STRESS

Stress is difficult to define, but it can be thought of as the body's response to a threatening or dangerous situation, or to demands arising from a new or changing situation. These stimuli may be physical, emotional or mental, internal or external.

Under these conditions, physiological changes take place. The sympathetic nervous system is activated and the body produces hormones such as epinephrine (adrenaline). Together, these increase blood supply to the muscles, raise the heart rate, increase respiration, and increase the blood sugar supply. These changes, sometimes called the "fight-or-flight" response, allow a person to cope with the threat or the demand. If the stressful situation is resolved, the symptoms disappear. If the stressful situation continues, however, its long-term effects may prove harmful.

Health can be damaged by stress in several ways. Stress can cause sleep problems, weight gain or weight loss. It may encourage unhealthy lifestyle practices. It can weaken the immune system, making a person more vulnerable to colds and other diseases. It is also an important contributing factor in diseases such as high blood pressure, cardiovascular disease, arthritis and other inflammatory diseases, asthma, sleep disturbances, and anorexia nervosa and other eating disorders. Stress is also related to migraine headaches, ulcers, respiratory or lung diseases, and skin conditions. Although the relationship between health and stress is not fully understood, medical researchers estimate stress may play a part in between half and two-thirds of all illnesses.

Everyone's tolerance of stress is different, and individuals handle various types of stress in different ways. Researchers have divided human behavior into two broad types according to how people handle stress. Type A individuals react with aggressive and competitive behavior. Type B people are more patient, easygoing, and relaxed. Type A individuals are more likely to develop heart disease and other illnesses than Type B individuals. Some experts believe there is a third group, Type C individuals, who are prone to cancer as a result of chronic stress.

Stress can be beneficial in some circumstances, as it enhances performance; an athlete in a race, for example, may perform better because of the stress of the event. However, once stress reaches a certain limit, additional stress will detract from performance levels. Stress or nervousness before a big presentation may help a speaker perform better or think with more clarity and precision; conversely, excessively high levels of stress and anxiety may cause confusion and forgetfulness. Doctors recommend recognizing individual limits and adjusting the circumstances so that the amount of stress involved in a situation will benefit, rather than hinder, an individual.

Moderate stress may be relieved by exercise and self-relaxation techniques such as deep breathing, muscle relaxation and meditation. A change of job, environment or living situation may reduce stress. Severe stress may require psychotherapy to uncover and work through the underlying causes. A form of behavior therapy known as biofeedback enables the patient to become more aware of internal processes and thereby gain some control over bodily reactions to stress.

SEE ALSO *Biofeedback, Epinephrine, Meditation, Psychotherapy, Relaxation techniques*

STRETCH MARKS

Stretch marks are streaks or lines which appear on the skin as a result of rapid growth, or as reactions to certain diseases and topical medications. They are commonly seen on the abdomen and breasts of pregnant women, but can also occur on the buttocks, hips, thighs and sides, wherever the elastic fibers in the skin stretch and rupture. Hormonal changes and the rapid growth of puberty cause them in both males and females. They appear as soft, red-purple glossy streaks and generally can't be prevented or cured by applying moisturizers. However, they often fade or disappear with time, especially when the initial cause of the skin stretching has passed.

SEE ALSO *Pregnancy*

STROKE

Stroke is loss of brain function as a result of cérebral infarction (lack of oxygen and death of tissue in some part of the brain) as a consequence of interruption to the blood supply to the brain. It is a common condition, particularly in the elderly, affecting about one in 500 people. Stroke is the third largest cause of death in industrialized countries after heart disease and cancer.

Causes

There are several causes of cerebral brain infarction. Most commonly, a blood clot forms in one of the carotid arteries (the major arteries in the neck) and obstructs blood flow to the brain. The clot usually forms in a part of the artery that has been damaged by atherosclerosis (hardening of the arteries).

A blood clot may also form in the carotids, then dislodge and travel via the bloodstream to the brain, where it causes the infarction. Similar blockages may occur in any of the multiple branches of the carotid or vertebral arteries, which supply blood to specific areas of the brain.

Less commonly, stroke is caused by bleeding (hemorrhaging) from a diseased artery. This may occur in an artery affected by atherosclerosis or one with a congenital berry aneurysm, either of which may rupture. Bleeding into surrounding brain tissue damages the tissue and causes stroke.

Symptoms

The symptoms of stroke vary according to the part of the brain affected. Common symptoms are loss of movement (paralysis) of a body area, weakness, decreased sensation, numbness, loss of coordination, vision problems and difficulty speaking. Symptoms may occur suddenly, or develop over a period of days, fluctuating in severity. With hemorrhage there may be a sudden severe headache and discomfort with bright light.

A precursor to a stroke is often a transient ischemic attack (TIA), a "mini stroke" in which the deprivation of blood is not sufficient to cause permanent damage. The symptoms are the same as those of a stroke, but are temporary, and the affected person makes a full recovery, usually within 24 hours. The episode serves as a warning of the possibility of a complete stroke in the future.

Treatment

Suffers of stroke are usually treated in hospital, and may require intensive care. The sooner the patient is taken to hospital the better the chances of effective treatment. A CAT (computed axial tomography) scan or MRI (magnetic resonance imaging) of the head may be used to rule out bleeding (hemorrhage) or other lesions and to define the location and extent of the stroke.

If there is bleeding or a blood clot, surgical removal of blood or blood clots from the brain cavity, or repair work at the source of the bleeding, may be possible. Usually, however, there is no cure for stroke; treatment is centered around rehabilitation. Programs of speech therapy, occupational therapy, physical therapy and other measures are designed to recover as much function as possible.

Part of treatment involves minimizing the risk of future strokes. This includes reducing risk factors for atherosclerosis, such as smoking, high blood pressure, high levels of lipids in the blood and diabetes. Carotid endarterectomy (removal of plaque from the carotid arteries) may be performed in some cases.

About a quarter of stroke sufferers recover most or all impaired functions, a quarter die of the stroke or its complications, and half experience long-term disabilities.

SEE ALSO *Arteries, Arteriosclerosis, Atherosclerosis, Brain, Carotid arteries, Transient ischemic attack*

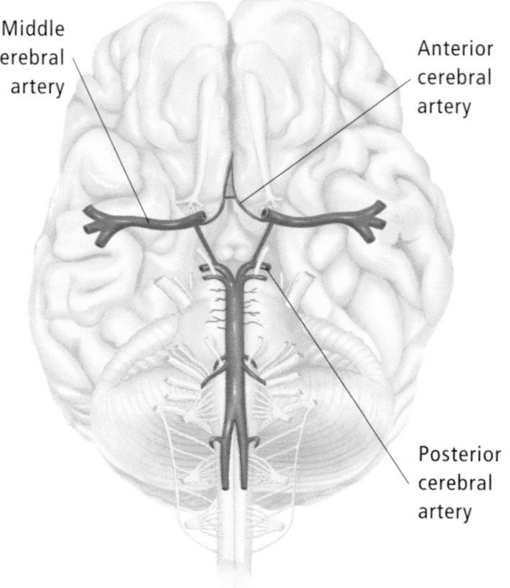

Cerebral thrombosis

Blockage of the cerebral arteries by a thrombus (blood clot) is a common cause of stroke. The clot may form in the cerebral arteries due to high blood pressure or arterial disease, or may form elsewhere and travel to arteries in the brain before blocking the blood supply.

Arteriosclerosis

In arteriosclerosis, fat and calcium deposits form in the wall of an artery, gradually narrowing it until it blocks off the blood supply to an organ or tissues. This major cause of stroke is more common in people who smoke, have a high fat content in their diet, are overweight, who have a family history of stroke or heart disease, or have high blood pressure.

Narrowing of artery

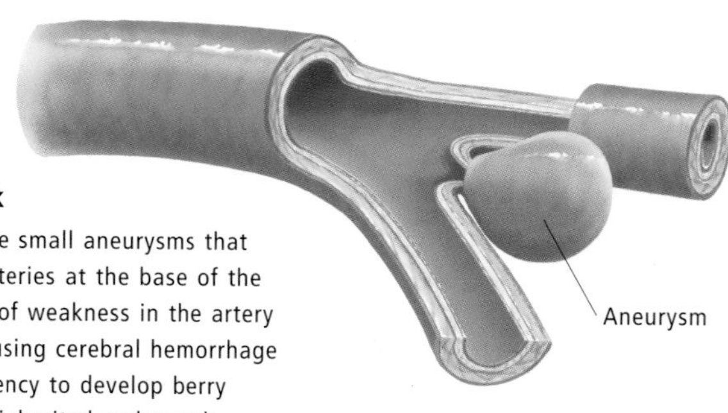

Congenital risk

Berry aneurysms are small aneurysms that can occur in the arteries at the base of the brain. These areas of weakness in the artery wall may burst, causing cerebral hemorrhage and stroke. A tendency to develop berry aneurysms may be inherited and people who have them may suffer a stroke at a relatively early age.

Cerebral infarction

Cerebral infarction is the death of brain tissue. This occurs when the brain is deprived of sufficient oxygen to keep the tissue alive and functioning normally. All the cerebral tissue may be affected if there is insufficient oxygen in the blood, for example following cardiac arrest. When localized, as in this illustration, infarction is usually due to the disease of a cerebral artery, which has blocked off the blood supply to that area.

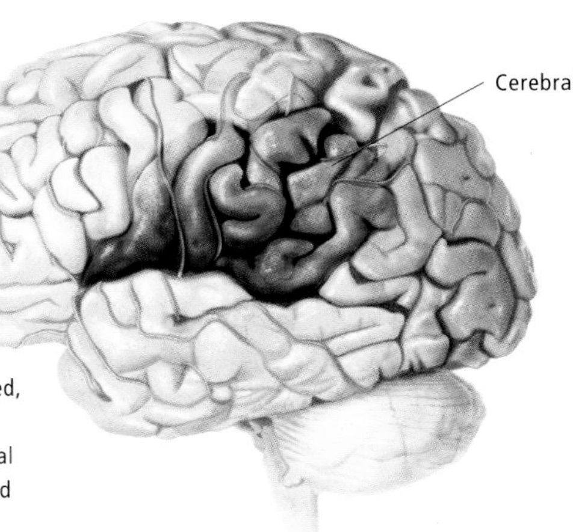

Brain stem

A stroke in the brain stem may result in coma or death, because the vital centers that regulate the basic functions of the body, such as breathing and blood pressure, are located here.

Brain stem

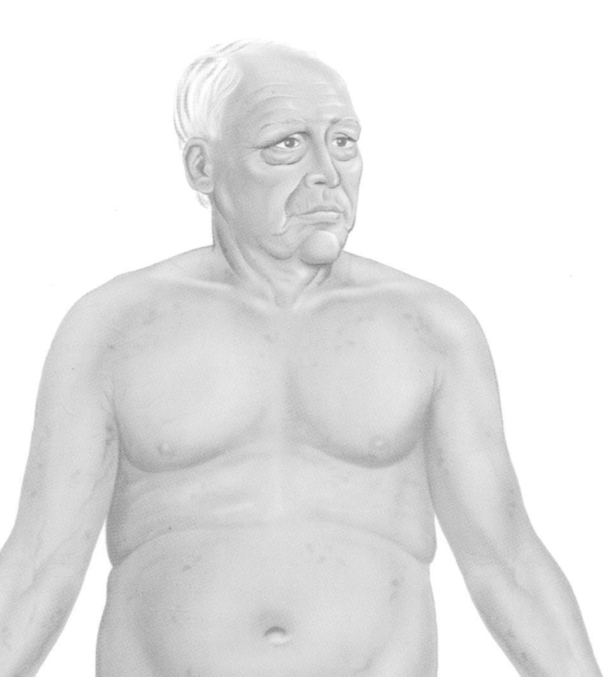

Stroke

Stroke is the term for loss of brain function arising from the death of brain tissue usually caused by arterial disease. It is one of the leading causes of death and illness in industrialized countries and particularly affects the elderly. Stroke usually cannot be cured, but preventive measures can be taken and, in some people, rehabilitation after a stroke may restore much of their former function.

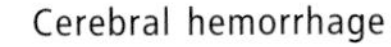

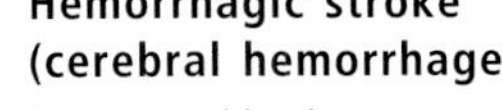

Hemorrhagic stroke (cerebral hemorrhage)

Sometimes blood may escape from an artery into the brain tissue (cerebral hemorrhage). The pressure of this bleeding destroys surrounding brain tissue, causing a stroke. Bleeding usually occurs at a section of artery that is damaged by arteriosclerosis. The diseased artery may weaken and balloon out, forming an aneurysm, which may burst. The risk of an aneurysm bursting is higher in people who suffer from hypertension (high blood pressure).

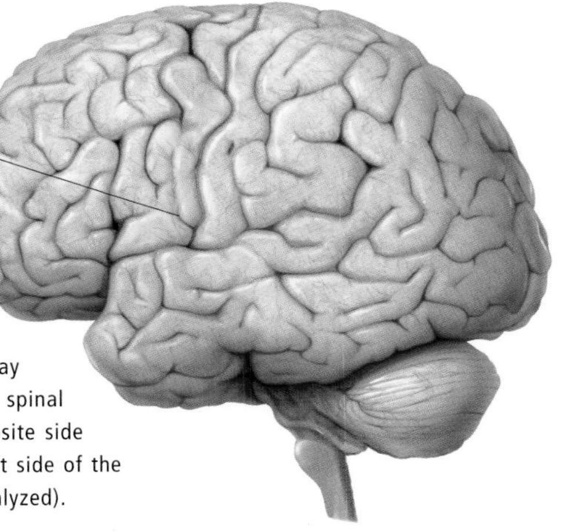

Hemiplegia

When a stroke damages the motor part of the cerebral cortex, the result is often hemiplegia, or paralysis of half of the body. Because of the way the nerve pathways are arranged in the brain and spinal cord, the part of the body affected is on the opposite side to the damaged part of the brain (i.e when the left side of the brain is affected, the right side of the body is paralyzed).

STRONGYLOIDIASIS

Strongyloidiasis is a widespread infection of humans by worms, occurring in the tropics. Microscopic worm larvae penetrate the skin and migrate through the lungs, where they may cause cough and shortness of breath. On reaching the intestine they multiply and are excreted in the stools. Diagnosis is suspected by blood eosinophilia and confirmed by microscopic examination of the stool.

SEE ALSO *Worms*

STUTTERING

Stuttering or stammering (dysphemia) is the most common and obvious type of disturbed speech. Every child will stutter at some time, as will many adults. The condition is characterized by hesitant or jerky speech and an inability to pronounce or join syllables. While experts are uncertain of the causes, it is found more in males than females and may be caused by a combination of genetic and emotional problems. In young children, stuttering can be a mechanism for the child to hold a place in the conversation while thinking of what to say and how to say it.

The time to seek help is when the child is embarrassed or worried about speaking, when the stuttering is pronounced and the child is getting stuck on words, or when there are physical signs of speech difficulty, such as tension in the neck or blinking. Parental support and cooperation are important. Some research suggests that stuttering is not really a problem and that those who stutter should seek occupations which allow them to stutter without feeling shame.

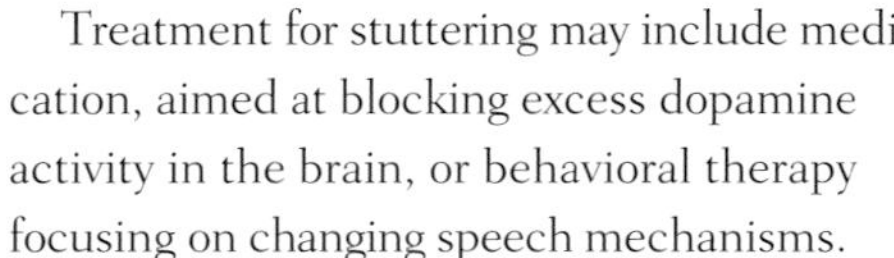

Treatment for stuttering may include medication, aimed at blocking excess dopamine activity in the brain, or behavioral therapy focusing on changing speech mechanisms.

SEE ALSO *Speech*

STYE

A stye is the inflammation of one or more sebaceous glands on or under the eyelid due to bacterial infection.

Styes occur near the roots of eyelashes and look like pimples or boils. These red, swollen lumps fill with pus over 1–2 days, causing pain, watering eyes and blurred vision. They are best left to burst on their own.

In the meantime, applying a warm, wet cloth for 10 minutes a few times each day may offer some relief. Antibiotics are used to treat persistent styes. Styes can be prevented by washing the hands before touching the eye area, particularly after treating acne and skin infections.

SEE ALSO *Eye, Eyelashes, Eyelid, Sebaceous glands*

Subarachnoid hemorrhage

An aneurysm or the dilation of an intercranial artery may cause bleeding (hemorrhage) into the subarachnoid space.

SUBACUTE SCLEROSING PANENCEPHALITIS

A rare progressive disease, subacute sclerosing panencephalitis develops months or years after measles infection in childhood. It is thought to result from persistent infection of the central nervous system by altered forms of the measles virus. There is damage to nerve cells and to the protective covering (the myelin sheaths) of nerves, as well as inflammation in the brain. The sufferer develops seizures, spasticity and impaired mental function. Treatment can include physical therapy, occupational therapy, and drugs such as anticonvulsants and muscle relaxants.

SEE ALSO *Measles, Nerves, Nervous system*

SUBARACHNOID HEMORRHAGE

Subarachnoid hemorrhage is bleeding into the subarachnoid space over the surface of the brain. This occurs mostly from an aneurysm of an intracranial artery which weakens its wall. The bleeding results in sudden severe headache with vomiting and temporary unconsciousness. It is a surgical emergency which can have serious consequences such as coma or death.

SEE ALSO *Brain*

SUBCLAVIAN VEIN

The subclavian vein is a major vein draining the arm. It is a continuation of the axillary vein. It lies beneath the collar bone (clavicle), where it may be injured by fracture of that bone, or compressed by back-

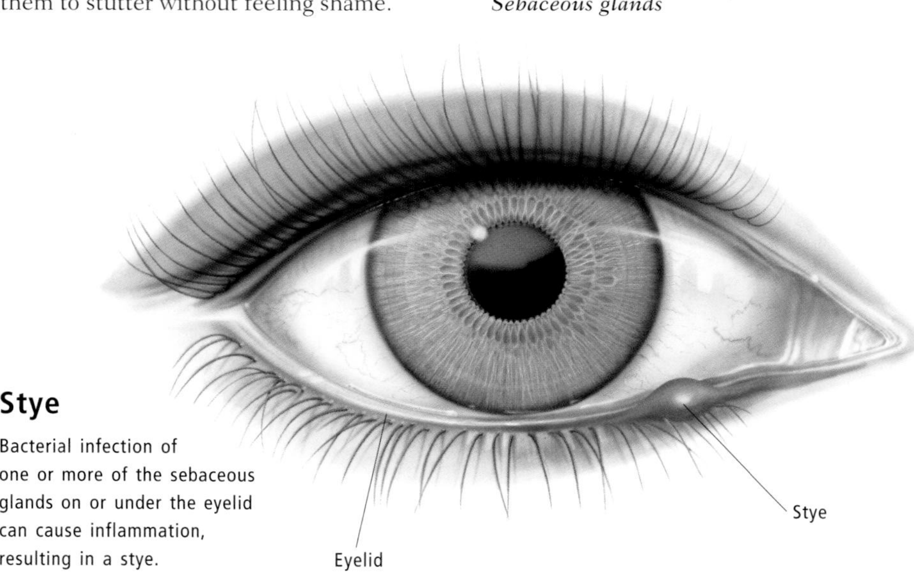

Stye

Bacterial infection of one or more of the sebaceous glands on or under the eyelid can cause inflammation, resulting in a stye.

wards pressure on the shoulder. It joins with the external and internal jugular veins, draining the superficial and deep tissues of the head and neck respectively, to form the brachiocephalic vein. Prior to its termination is the last valve which blood passes before reaching the heart.

SEE ALSO *Collar bone, Veins*

SUBDURAL HEMATOMA

Subdural hematoma is a blood clot on the surface of the brain, beneath its covering layer, the dura. It results from head injury, either from a direct blow or from sudden acceleration, as in whiplash injury. It may develop immediately (acute) or gradually (chronic), after injury.

The main sign of acute subdural hematoma is rapidly decreasing consciousness following head injury, together with enlargement of the pupil on the same side as the injury. This is a surgical emergency requiring immediate drainage of the hematoma. If drowsiness is more gradual, a CAT scan of the brain is performed to confirm diagnosis.

Chronic subdural hematoma is more likely to occur in the elderly or alcoholic person following minor head trauma. It may cause rapidly developing dementia associated with headache. Surgery is not always required for the chronic forms.

SEE ALSO *Brain*

SUDDEN INFANT DEATH SYNDROME

Sudden infant death sydrome (SIDS) is the unexpected and unexplained death of a baby while sleeping—it is also known as crib death or cot death. There are no symptoms or warning signs—the child is usually thought to be sleeping peacefully when death occurs and no struggle is evident. It is thought that respiratory and cardiac function are at the root of the syndrome, which generally affects infants between 2 weeks and 1 year of age, with most deaths occuring from 2–4 months.

While the exact cause has not been pinpointed, certain risk factors have been identified from research into the health, environment and family background of infants who have died from SIDS. For instance, it has been established that more male babies succumb to SIDS than females, and that most SIDS deaths occur in autumn and winter. Children with a greater risk of dying from SIDS include the following.

- Premature babies with low birth weight
- Children from multiple births
- Siblings of babies who have died from SIDS
- Babies with mothers who smoke or are drug dependent
- Babies with mothers under 20 years of age
- Children from pregnancies that are close together
- Children who live in overcrowded conditions
- Those whose mothers have had late, little or no prenatal care

Scientists have been researching a theory that brain abnormalities present at birth mean some children have an increased chance of dying from SIDS. A part of the brain is involved known as the arcuate nucleus of the medulla, which helps control breathing and waking during sleep. These abnormalities may stem from a lack of oxygen during pregnancy or exposure to toxic substances. Other theories have focussed on events after birth, such as excessive intake of carbon dioxide as a result of rebreathing exhaled air trapped in bedding. A metabolic disorder which prevents the proper processing of fatty acids is also thought to be a contributing factor.

Reducing the risk of SIDS

There is no definite prevention, though the following measures have been found to reduce the incidence of SIDS.

- Lying the baby on its back to sleep rather than its front. The side is also better than the front, with a rolled blanket placed near the front to stop the baby rolling forward.
- Placing the baby to sleep on a firm mattress without fluffy pillows, blankets or coverings, or soft surfaces such as sheepskins. Stuffed toys should be kept out of the crib.
- Ensuring that overheating does not occur; this may allow the baby to slip into too deep a sleep, and it may be difficult to arouse the baby. The room temperature should be comfortable and the baby should not be overdressed.
- Providing a smoke-free environment. Exposure to passive smoking is thought to double the risk of SIDS, and smoking during pregnancy to triple it by reducing the amount of oxygen available to the fetus.
- Breast feeding the baby, as this is thought to offer protection from infections.

If a baby is found to be not moving or breathing, cardiopulmonary resuscitation (CPR) should be started and an ambulance called immediately.

SEE ALSO *Infancy, Pregnancy, Smoking*

Subclavian vein

One of the major veins in the upper body, the subclavian vein lies beneath the collar bone. It carries blood from the arms towards to heart.

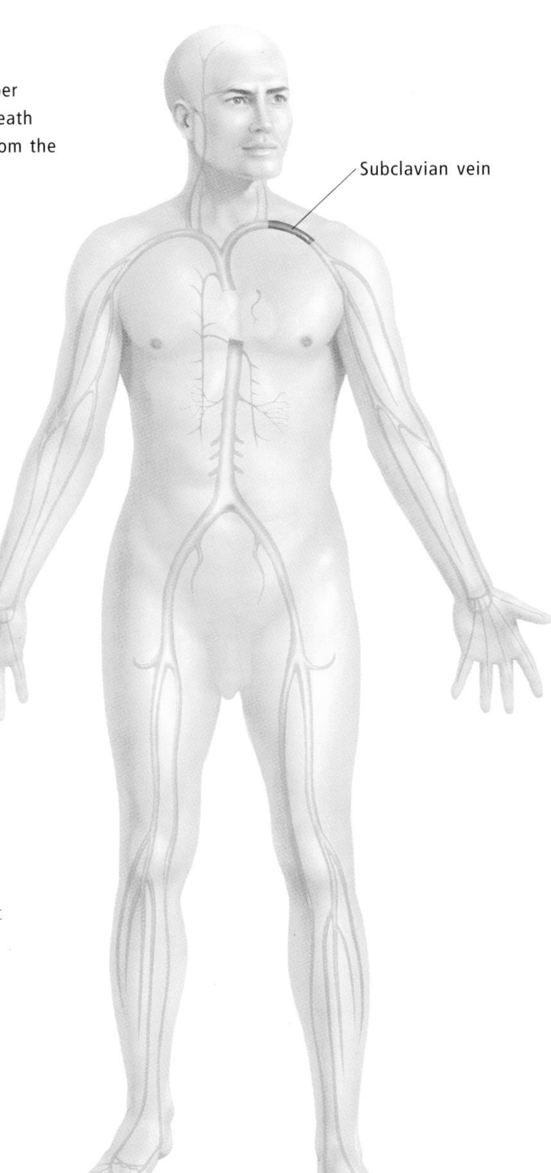

S

SUGAR

Sugar is a general term for simple sugars, organic compounds which, along with complex carbohydrates, are the main constituents of foods of plant origin. The main sources of the refined sugar (sucrose), used throughout the world as a sweetener, are sugar cane and sugar beet.

There are two kinds of sugars: monosaccharides, the simplest forms of carbohydrate, which include glucose, fructose and galactose; and disaccharides, made up of two monosaccharides, which include sucrose, lactose (found in milk) and maltose (formed from starch).

Digestion converts carbohydrates, except plant fiber or cellulose which humans cannot metabolize, into glucose to provide energy to cells. Any surplus becomes glycogen and is stored in the liver and muscles, for later use in metabolic processes; large oversupplies are stored as excess weight. Blood glucose levels, which normally rise after eating, are maintained at proper levels by the hormone insulin produced in the pancreas.

Diabetes is a disease caused by lack of insulin, leading to inability to control blood sugar levels. Hypoglycemia, or a low blood sugar level, can result in coma or death. Gluconeogenesis, the synthesis of blood sugar from the liver and kidneys, is an important part of recovery after strong physical exertion. There are several types of glycogen-storage diseases which interfere with the normal production of glycogen and result in enlarged liver and spleen.

SEE ALSO *Blood sugar tests, Diabetes, Hypoglycemia, Insulin, Nutrition, Pancreas*

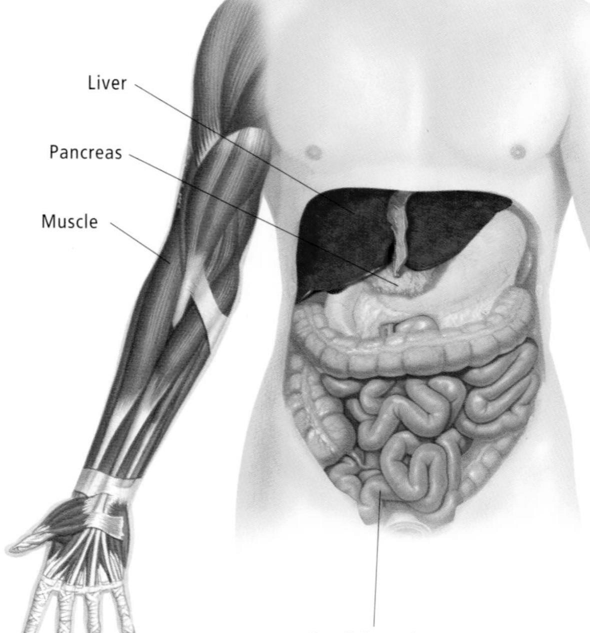

Sugar

The body needs sugar for metabolic processes. The breakdown of carbohydrates to sugars occurs mainly in the small intestine. Surplus sugar is converted to glycogen which is stored in the liver and muscles until it is needed by body cells and tissues. Levels of sugar (glucose) in the blood are maintained by the hormone insulin, which is produced by the pancreas.

SUICIDE

Suicide (literally "self-murder"), is the act of intentionally ending one's own life. Until the mid-twentieth century it was illegal in some countries, being seen as a crime against Church and State, a view formed in medieval times when laws were passed to deny suicides church services at burial. The Koran also forbids suicide. In more recent times, the stigma of an illegal act was often circumvented by sympathetic clergy, while coroners gave verdicts of death as "suicide, while of unsound mind", a way of sidestepping the issue by granting the deceased the indulgence of supposed insanity. Although in most countries suicide itself is no longer a crime, aiding a person to end his or her own life is treated as murder.

Suicide is not a modern phenomenon, shame often being an adequate reason for "falling on one's sword" in ancient times. The Vikings required the wife of a dead warrior to accompany him to Valhalla, and the same practice, known as *suttee*, survived in India until the early twentieth century. Japanese warriors practised *hara-kiri* or ritual self-disembowelment to avoid the humiliation of defeat or failure. Suicide has also been used as a protest, as seen in the self-immolation of Buddhist monks in Vietnam in the civil war prior to reunification, and as an act of defiance.

It is generally true that more men succeed in suicide than women, and that more women attempt suicide than men. In many industrialized nations, suicide ranks among the top 10 causes of death. In the USA, rates for suicide in late adolescence and early adulthood rose significantly over the last 50 years, the causes being cited as increased use of drugs, availability of guns, and a rising incidence of mental illness in that age group.

In everyday life, despair or extreme emotional suffering, mental illness, depression, hopelessness, the misery of a debilitating disease, stress and feelings of inability to cope can trigger a suicide attempt.

Depression is usually seen prior to suicide, as is a feeling of hopelessness, suicide becoming the alternative to an unbearable life. Social isolation is very common among suicide victims, who commonly live alone or lack the emotional support of family or close friends. The impact of a fatal suicide attempt is very great, often adding guilt and shame to the natural feelings of grief felt by relatives and friends at the death.

An unsuccessful suicide attempt may be seen as a cry for help, and may lead to an improvement in the situation, a result which may unconsciously have been hoped for and influenced the attempt.

People who are considering suicide often give warning signs. They may talk about dying, or express a wish to die. They may write about death in letters or essays, or depict it in drawings. There may be changes in behavior and attempts to tidy up affairs before death, such as giving away favorite things. If these signs are acted upon, by asking the person if they are thinking of suicide, the help of a trained counselor may prevent the suicide.

Suicide-prevention programs take the form of counseling, usually through phone-in services run by health-oriented charities and welfare organizations or through resident counselors in colleges and universities. But these services can help only when they

S

are called, and the evidence is that women call more often than men, who are more at risk.

SEE ALSO *Death, Depression*

SUN EXPOSURE

Exposure to the sun is essential to human growth and development, but it can also have harmful effects. Exposure to sunlight in infancy and childhood aids production of vitamin D, vital for bone formation and growth, and prevents the development of rickets, a deficiency disease marked by soft and deformed bones. The harmful effects of over-exposure to sunlight include sunburn, premature ageing of the skin and formation of skin cancers.

Ultraviolet light

The sun emits ultraviolet radiation, which is classified by wavelength from the longest, UVA radiation, to UVB radiation, to UVC radiation. UVA penetrates the most through the atmosphere and causes long-term subcutaneous damage. UVB is partially blocked by the Earth's ozone layer and causes sunburn. UVC kills living organisms and is produced artificially for sterilization and, fortunately for life on Earth, is completely blocked by the ozone layer.

Seasonal affective disorder, or SAD, is a form of depression caused by lack of sunshine that commonly occurs in winter in the northern hemisphere and is treated with artificial light. Medical use of sunlight or natural ultraviolet light includes treatments for the chronic skin conditions psoriasis and vitiligo, which combine drug therapy with controlled sun exposure.

Sun damage

Exposure to sunlight stimulates cells called melanocytes to increase production of melanin, a dark pigment that colors the skin and protects deeper tissues from UV light. Exposure to direct sunlight for more than an hour or so will bring risks of sunburn, real tissue damage similar to any other burn.

Severe or frequent sunburn in childhood increases the risks of developing skin cancers (especially melanoma). Outdoor workers and others with a lifetime of sun exposure commonly develop squamous or basal cell carcinomas, most of which are treated by removal. Fair-skinned people or those with a history of severe childhood sunburn are at considerably higher risk of melanoma, an aggressive cancer which can spread very quickly through the body.

Symptoms of sunburn often appear as redness and pain, later with swelling or blistering and subsequent peeling of dead skin cells. A cool bath or applying cool compresses to the skin may soothe symptoms. Severe sunburn may require medical assistance. Sunstroke is a form of heatstroke brought on by sun exposure and caused by the inability to sweat sufficiently to reduce internal body temperature. Developing quickly, the condition causes heart rate and breathing to speed up; internal temperature may rise markedly, bringing disorientation and loss of consciousness and a risk of death. Looking directly into sunlight can harm the eyes, producing an inflammatory condition called flash keratoconjunctivitis. Extreme sensitivity to sunlight (photosensitivity), with a reaction after very brief exposure, affects sufferers of systemic lupus erythematosus and porphyria; it can also be a side effect of certain drugs, notably isotretinoin, used to treat acne. Sun spots are smooth dark brown spots on exposed skin formed from a concentration of melanocytes that commonly appear in middle and later life.

Sun exposure

Exposure to sunlight makes skin cells called melanocytes produce pigment (melanin), resulting in a suntan. Repeated exposure may make melanocytes produce pigment uncontrollably, which can lead to melanoma, a potentially life-threatening cancer.

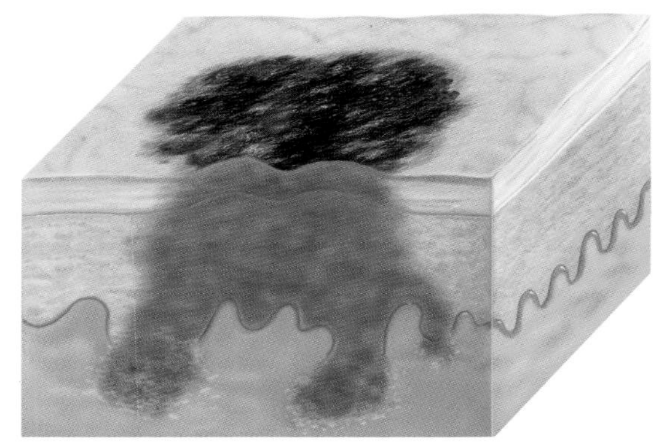

Sun protection

Sun protection is a sensible precaution for everyone and is particularly important for children. The most effective defense against sun exposure is to stay out of direct sunlight, particularly from late morning to early afternoon when the sun is at its strongest. Reflected sunlight from water or snow can also burn skin and cause eye damage. Protective clothing is a good second line of defense. Exposure to sun should be gradual, allowing the body time to produce melanin, a process which is fast for some and almost nonexistent in very fair-skinned people.

Sunscreen creams and lotions have a part to play in sun protection but are far less effective than shade or clothing because they may not be applied evenly or thickly enough to give their full potential protection, and they degrade with time and exposure to air and water.

SEE ALSO *Basal cell carcinoma, Melanoma, Photosensitivity, Seasonal affective disorder, Skin, Skin cancer, Squamous cell carcinoma, Ultraviolet therapy*

SWEAT GLANDS

Sweat glands are of two types: eccrine and apocrine. Both secrete a watery fluid—perspiration—onto the surface of the skin.

The eccrine sweat glands are distributed over the body, except on the lips and some parts of the genital regions. They are small tubular glands, opening at pores onto the surface of the skin. They can secrete large quantities of sweat, which cools the body by evaporation. The sweat glands are activated when the body becomes overheated (due to environmental conditions or exercise), and occasionally by emotions such as fear ("cold sweat").

The apocrine sweat glands are special sweat glands found in the axillary and pubic regions and in the areolae of the breasts. These tubular glands have a particularly wide lumen (internal cavity), which opens into hair follicles rather than directly onto the skin surface. They secrete an odorifer-

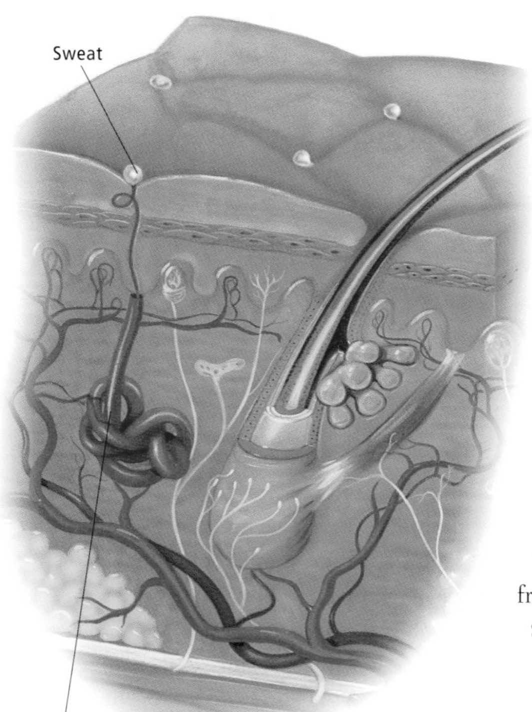

Sweat
Sweat gland

Sweat gland

Sweat glands are small tubular glands that open onto the surface of the skin. They secrete sweat (perspiration) to promote cooling.

ous secretion which probably acts as a pheromone for sexual attraction.

Body odor is determined primarily by sweat from both types of glands, and by interactions between bacteria and sweat, particularly the sweat produced by the apocrine glands.

SEE ALSO *Glands*

SWIMMER'S ITCH

Penetration of the skin by larvae of trematode worms of the *Schistosoma* genus (nonhuman schistosome cercariae) causes the skin infection swimmer's itch (also known as swamp itch, cutaneous schistosomiasis or schistosome dermatitis). The disease is contracted when swimming, as the worms are found in freshwater lakes in the USA, Canada, Europe and Asia.

SEE ALSO *Schistosomiasis, Worms*

SYDENHAM'S CHOREA

Chorea is a neurological disorder characterized by involuntary, purposeless, spasmodic movements of the body. The most common types of this disorder are Sydenham's (or rheumatic) chorea, once known as Saint Vitus' dance, and Huntington's disease. Sydenham's chorea occurs in 50 percent of children aged 5–15 who have had rheumatic fever and is more common in girls.

Triggered by emotional upset and episodes of crying, the spasms can range from mild to completely incapacitating. Attacks can last for several weeks and recurrence is frequent. Bed rest in a pleasant environment is the best treatment; some patients benefit from sedation and tranquilizers.

SEE ALSO *Huntington's disease*

SYMPATHOMIMETIC DRUGS

Sympathomimetic drugs are medications whose actions are similar to those of the hormone epinephrine (adrenaline). They work by mimicking the effects or stimulating the release of epinephrine or norepinephrine (noradrenaline). They are often used in the treatment of conditions such as asthma, shock and cardiac arrest. They are also used in over-the-counter preparations to relieve nasal congestion and allergic disorders, and to suppress appetite.

Side effects include rapid heart rate (tachycardia), high blood pressure, increased body temperature, agitation, cardiac arrhythmias and seizures. Amphetamines and ephedrine are both sympathomimetic drugs. An overdose can be fatal.

SEE ALSO *Amphetamines, Epinephrine, Nervous system*

SYNAPSES

Synapses are junctions between nerve cells (neurons), where impulses are passed from one cell to another, or from one cell to an effector organ. Synapses usually occur between the axon terminal of one cell and a dendrite or cell body of another. The neural impulse is carried across the synapse, in one direction only, by chemical molecules known as a neurotransmitters. Common neurotransmitters include glutamate and serotonin. Low levels of neurotransmitters or disruption of their action can cause neurological disorders.

SEE ALSO *Nerves, Nervous system, Neurons*

SYNOVIAL FLUID

The fluid contained within synovial joints lubricates the joint surfaces, helps to reduce friction and provides nourishment for the joint cartilage. It is normally a clear, pale yellow, viscous fluid, and is only present in small amounts. Its composition is similar to blood plasma except that it contains hyaluronate and lubricin, which are essential for viscosity and lubrication. Monocytes, lymphocytes and macrophages are also found in low numbers in the synovial fluid.

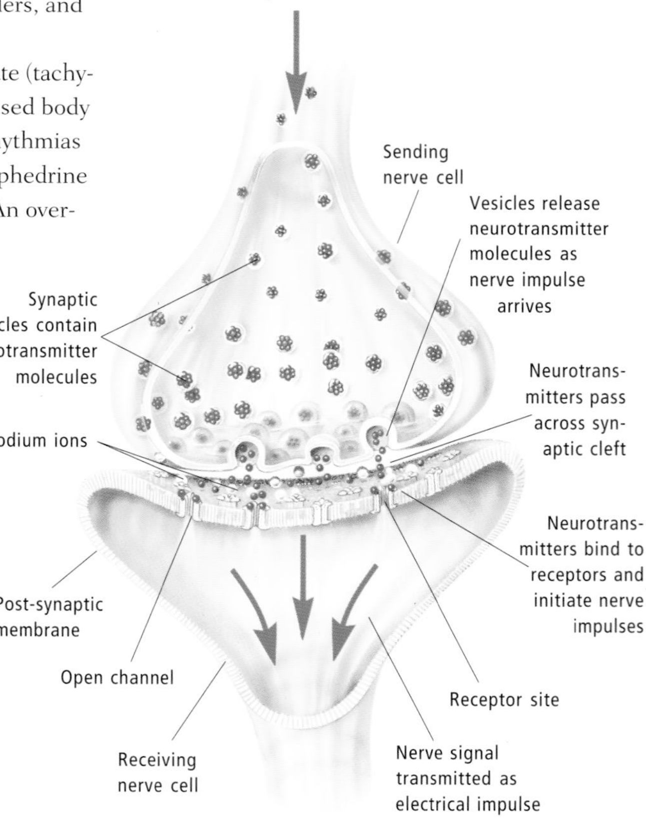

Nerve impulse arrives
Sending nerve cell
Vesicles release neurotransmitter molecules as nerve impulse arrives
Synaptic vesicles contain neurotransmitter molecules
Neurotrans-mitters pass across syn-aptic cleft
Sodium ions
Neurotrans-mitters bind to receptors and initiate nerve impulses
Post-synaptic membrane
Open channel
Receptor site
Receiving nerve cell
Nerve signal transmitted as electrical impulse

Synapses

A synapse is the junction between two nerve cells (neurons). Nerve signals are passed from cell to cell across the synaptic cleft by chemical molecules—neurotransmitters. The receiving cell has receptor sites specific to certain neurotransmitters. When the correct transmitters lock in place they open channels in the nerve membrane to let in sodium ions. This causes an electrical change which fires the receiving cell, passing on the nerve signal.

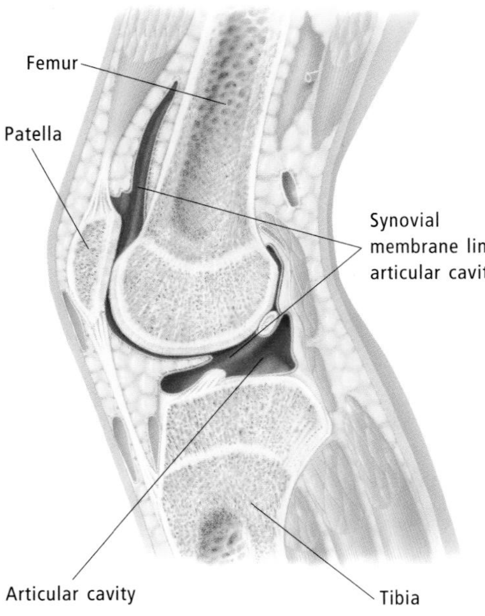

Synovial membrane

This type of membrane lines the non-cartilage areas of synovial joints such as the knee. Specialized cells in the membrane produce fluid that is critical for the lubrication of joint surfaces and the nourishment of cartilage.

Synovial fluid may be aspirated from a joint and checked for the presence of red blood cells, inflammatory cells, infectious agents and crystals (for example, gout).

SEE ALSO *Joints*

SYNOVIAL MEMBRANE

Synovial membrane is found in synovial joints, bursae and tendon sheaths. It lines the non-cartilage areas of synovial joints, such as the joint capsule and exposed bony surfaces. The membrane is very vascular. It appears pink, smooth and shiny and may exhibit folds and fringes. Accumulations of fat are found in the membrane in some joints (for example, fat pads in the knee and elbow joints).

Specialized cells of the membrane (synoviocytes) both produce and reabsorb synovial fluid, a fluid that is critical to the lubrication of joint surfaces, and nourishment of the cartilage. These cells also remove debris from the joint cavity and may initiate an immune response to foreign material in the joint.

SEE ALSO *Joints, Synovial fluid*

SYNOVITIS

The cavities of freely movable joints are lined with synovial membranes, smooth, thin sheets of connective tissue that secrete a nourishing lubricant (synovial fluid) which helps bones move freely over other bones.

When a synovial membrane becomes inflamed, the condition is called synovitis. It can often cause an entire joint to become swollen and tender. Synovitis can occur with a bacterial infection, follow an irritation or trauma to the site such as a sprain or fracture, or be a complication of diseases such as gout and rheumatoid arthritis.

Treatment depends on the cause. In many cases time and rest are sufficient but severe or chronic synovitis may need treatment with analgesics or anti-inflammatory drugs.

SEE ALSO *Joints, Synovial fluid, Synovial membrane*

SYPHILIS

Syphilis is a serious, sexually transmitted diseased caused by the organism *Treponema pallidum*. Clinically it can resemble many other diseases, including gonorrhea. A disease that progresses through three stages, each separated by months and even years, cases of infection are currently on the rise in many parts of the world, including the USA.

Syphilis begins with a lesion, a painless, circular chancre that may appear on the lips, mouth, tongue, nipple, rectum or genitalia; nearby lymph nodes may enlarge but are not painful. The chancre heals and weeks, or even months later, the secondary symptoms appear when microbes spread to organs and tissues in the body. Non-painful skin rashes appear and disappear, sometimes in association with fever, headache and hair loss. Tertiary lesions, which can appear years later, may destroy normal skin, bone and joints by ulceration.

Tertiary syphilis also affects the nervous system. It can take three forms: cardiovascular syphilis, which affects the heart severely; neurosyphilis, which affects the brain and the nervous system; and benign late syphilis.

Difficult to diagnose (a series of blood tests is often necessary), syphilis can be treated with penicillin, or an alternative for those allergic to this drug. Anyone who has sex with a person known to have syphilis, or someone known to have another sexually transmitted disease, should be tested for syphilis. It can pass into the fetus at any stage of pregnancy and cause growth deformities in the baby or stillbirth; this can be prevented by treatment early in the pregnancy.

SEE ALSO *Sexually transmitted diseases*

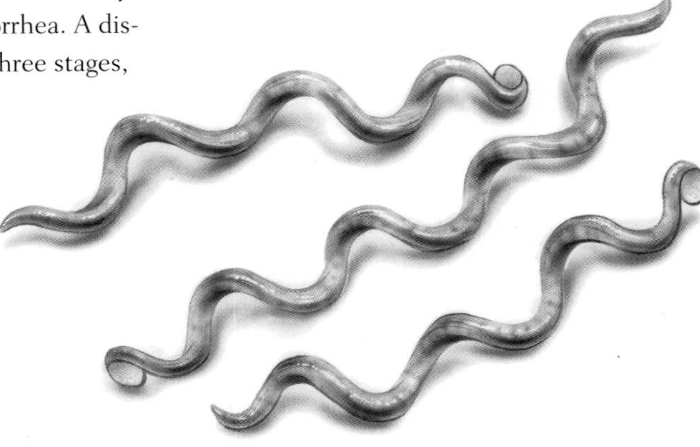

Syphilis

A serious sexually transmitted disease caused by the bacteria *Treponema pallidum*, syphilis may take years to develop fully. In its final stages, the disease affects the nervous system.

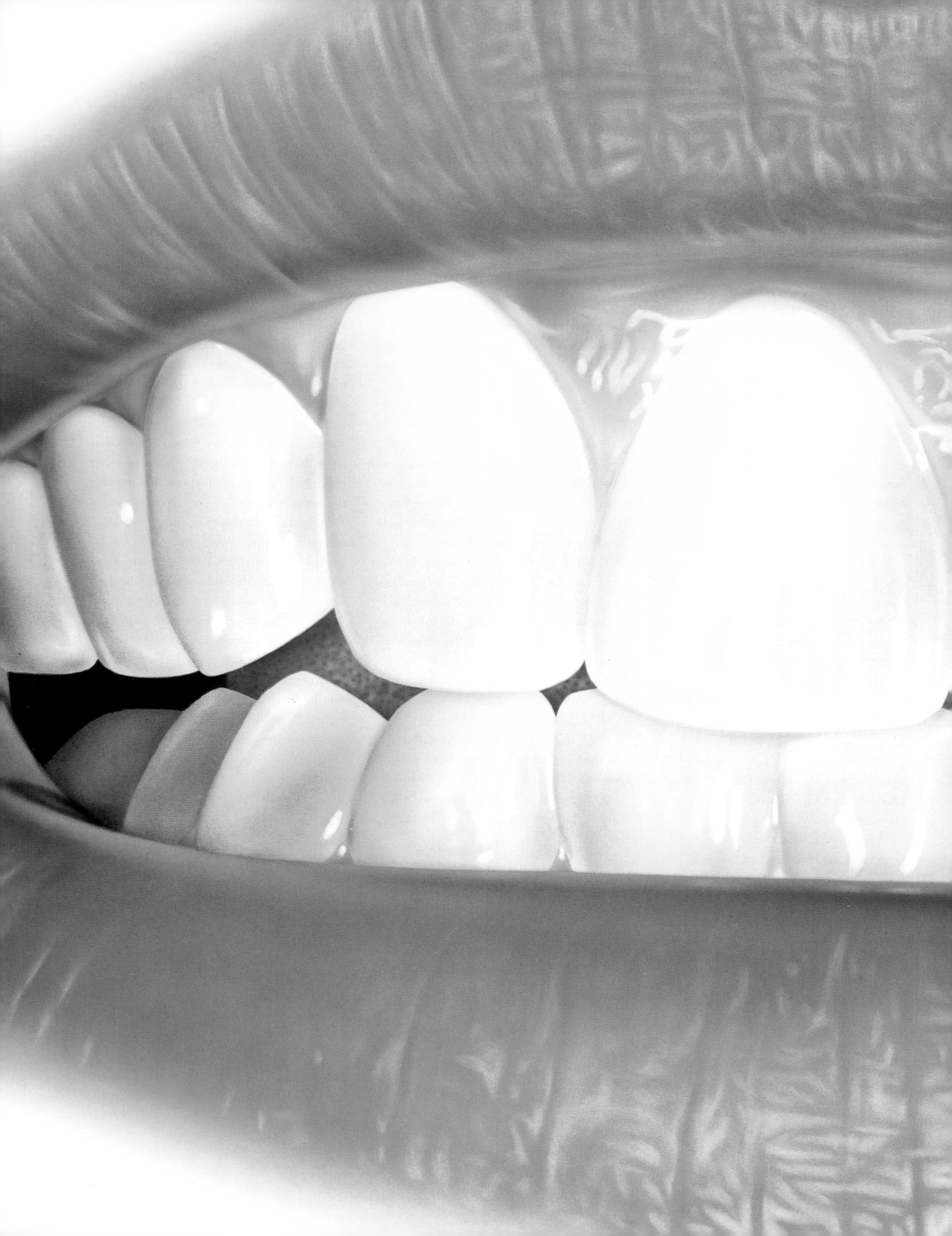

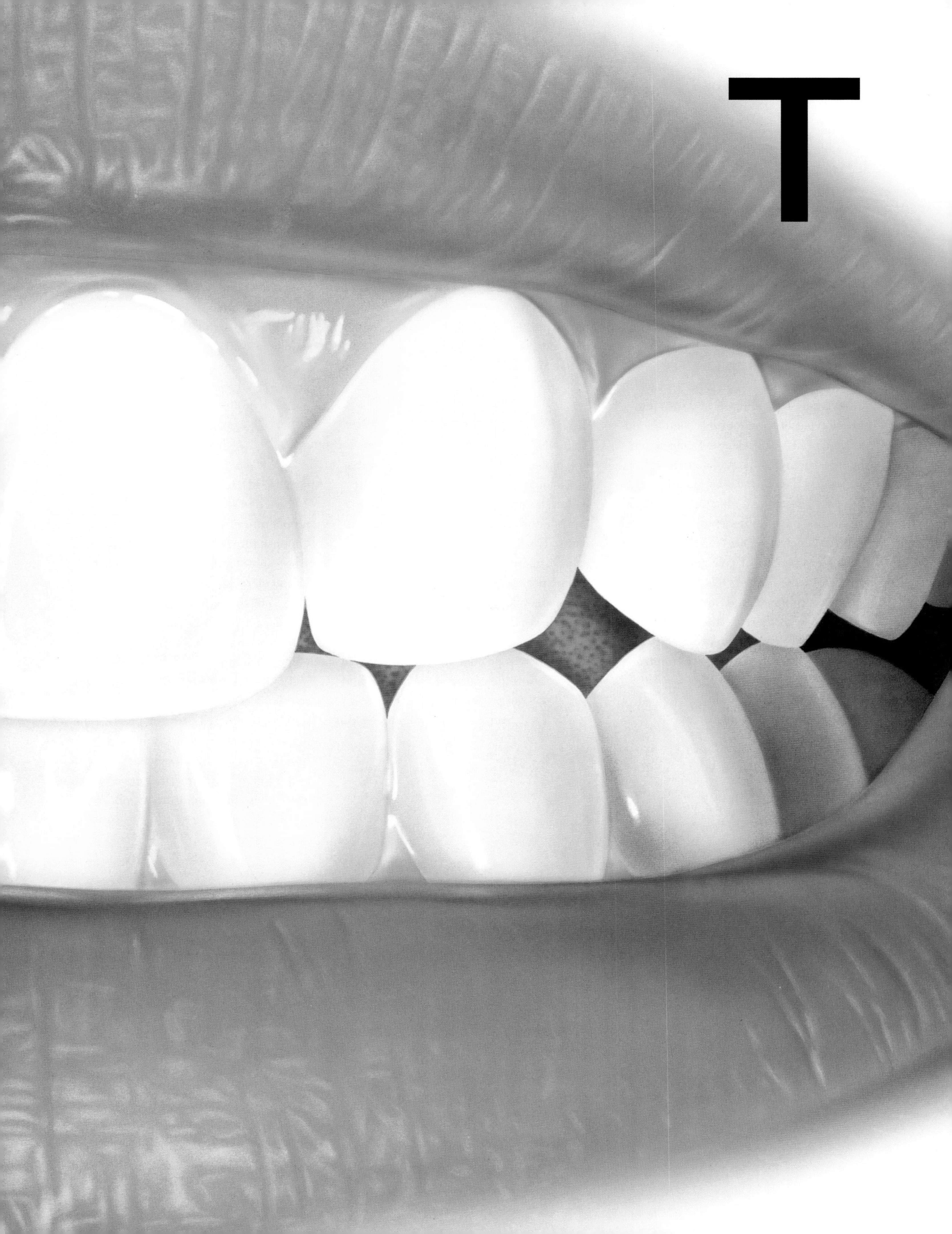
T

T CELLS

Lymphocytes are the white blood cells responsible for the body's ability to distinguish and react to foreign substances, such as bacteria, viruses and other microbes. They are part of the body's line of defense against invaders.

Lymphocytes are small rounded cells that originate in the bone marrow from primordial cells (called stem cells). Once they have matured, they pass into the bloodstream where they travel to areas of lymphoid tissue, such as the spleen, lymph nodes, tonsils, and the lining of the intestines.

Some lymphocytes enter the thymus gland, where they multiply and turn into special types of lymphocytes called thymus-derived, or "T", cells. These T cells rejoin the bloodstream and circulate to lymph tissue around the body. There, their function is to patrol the body for bacterial or viral invaders by means of receptors on their cell surfaces which recognize foreign molecules. Once identified, the T cells multiply, attack and destroy the foreign cells. This process is known as "cell-mediated" immunity. T cells are also involved in regulating B lymphocytes. These are another type of white blood cell which produce antibodies to foreign molecules in the immune process known as "humoral" immunity.

Progress of HIV (human immmunodeficiency virus) infection can be monitored by measuring the sufferer's T cell count (more specifically the T4 cell count) in the blood at regular intervals. T4 cells (also known as CD4 or T helper cells) play a specific role in the body's fight against infection and cancer.

In HIV infection, T4 cells are invaded and destroyed; a fall in blood T4 numbers gives an indication of how far the infection has progressed. The T4 cell count usually drops sharply in the late stages of AIDS; serious opportunistic infections develop at counts of below 200 cells per mm^3.

SEE ALSO *AIDS, HIV, Immunity, Thymus*

TABES DORSALIS

Tabes dorsalis is one of the later effects of syphilis, occurring 20–30 years after the initial infection. It involves damage to the part of the spinal cord involved in sensory inputs—the posterior (dorsal) roots and columns. The damage causes sudden sharp pains, usually starting in the legs. The sense of limb position is affected so that there is difficulty walking, especially in the dark. Tendon reflexes are also lost and there may be bladder and bowel incontinence, and impotence. There is no cure, but medication may slow the course of the damage and can provide pain relief.

SEE ALSO *Spinal cord, Syphilis*

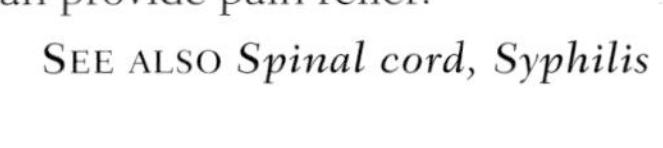

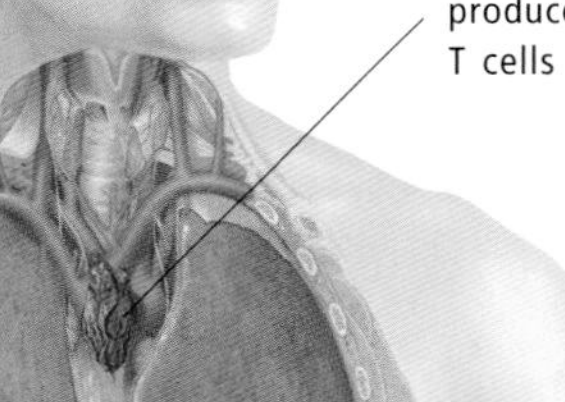

T cell production

T cells take about 3 weeks to develop in the thymus and are then released into the bloodstream.

TACHYCARDIA, PAROXYSMAL

Paroxysmal tachycardia refers to episodes of rapid heart rate (140–220 beats per minute). It may arise from problems with either the atria or ventricles in the heart. In both types the patient complains of palpitations, the sensation of a rapidly beating heart fluttering in the chest. The ventricular type is more serious, and is often a complication of severe heart disease. Ventricular tachycardia often causes chest pain and breathlessness: these symptoms are less common in atrial tachycardia. The two types can be distinguished by an electrocardiogram (EKG) and treated with appropriate antiarrhythmic medication.

SEE ALSO *Heart, Palpitations, Ventricle*

T'AI CHI CHU'AN

T'ai chi chu'an, which translates as "supreme ultimate power", is a traditional Chinese form of moving meditation which grew out of its predecessor *qi gong*. Combining elements of Chinese martial arts with Taoist breathing practices, t'ai chi's exercises incorporate mental discipline and creative visualization with a focus on deep, rhythmic breathing.

T'ai chi works through a choreographed sequence of movements, where every motion is coordinated with the breath. The movements often draw inspiration from nature with names like "embrace tiger, return to mountain", and practitioners are encouraged to visualize themselves embodying

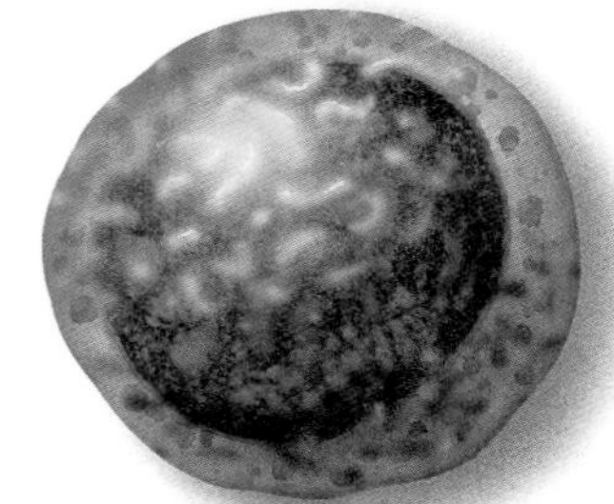

T cell

T cells are a type of white blood cell that play an important role in the body's immune system. In healthy people they circulate around the body, identifying and destroying invading bacteria and viruses.

these images. Each sequence of movements is known as a "form", and can vary from 5–60 minutes in length.

There are a number of different forms and styles of t'ai chi which are taught throughout China and increasingly in the West. The main aims of t'ai chi are to develop the *chi* (life force) in the body, relax the mind, restore balance, strengthen muscles, slow down the ageing process and reconnect the body with mind and nature. It can be learnt by people of all ages and levels of fitness and is thought to be useful in treating stress-related illnesses, as well as back pain and digestive and respiratory disorders.

SEE ALSO *Qi gong*

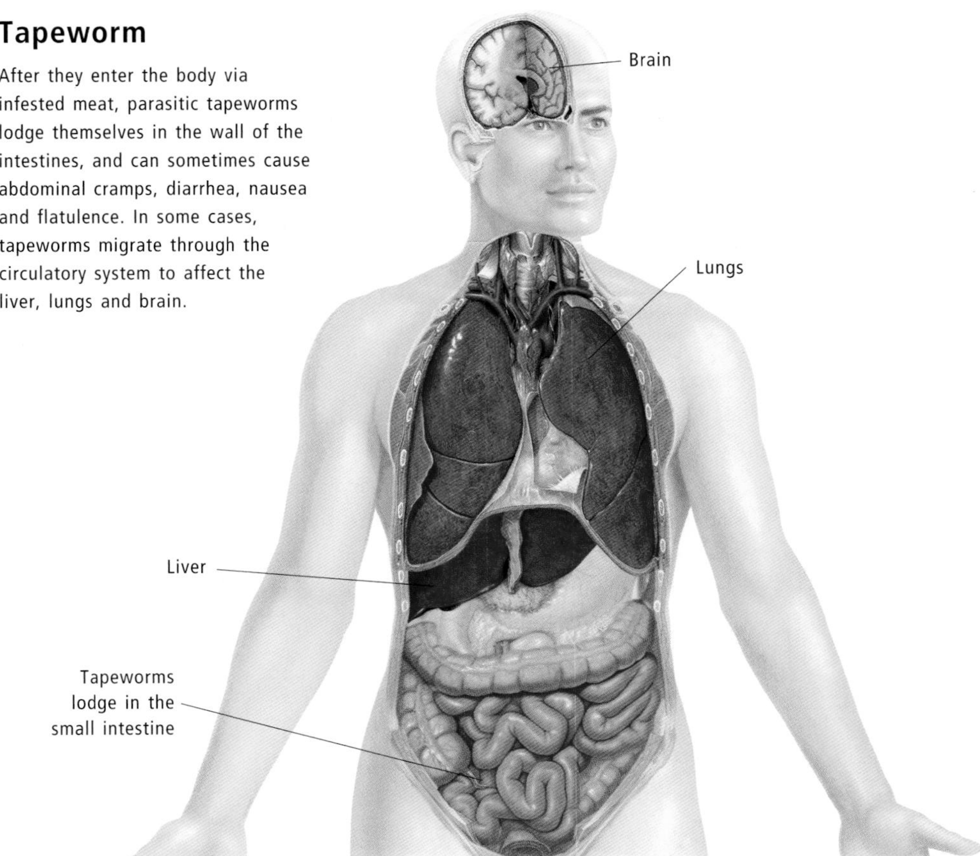

Tapeworm

After they enter the body via infested meat, parasitic tapeworms lodge themselves in the wall of the intestines, and can sometimes cause abdominal cramps, diarrhea, nausea and flatulence. In some cases, tapeworms migrate through the circulatory system to affect the liver, lungs and brain.

TAPEWORM

Parasitic tapeworms, members of a group of parasitic flatworms, can infect the intestinal tract. The condition is not contagious. Most sufferers have no symptoms; some people, however, may experience pain in the upper abdomen, diarrhea, unexplained weight loss or symptoms of anemia. Bowel movements will contain worms and worm eggs.

Tapeworm infestation results from eating infected or improperly cooked beef, pork or fish containing encysted larvae. It is most common in Africa, the Middle East, Eastern Europe and South America. A drug may be prescribed to kill the parasite. Hygiene before eating is important, as well as avoiding food which could be infected. Proper cooking provides the most certain protection.

SEE ALSO *Worms*

TARDIVE DYSKINESIA

Tardive dyskinesia is a side effect of antipsychotic drugs (neuroleptics), such as those used in the treatment of schizophrenia. The symptoms are involuntary and abnormal movements of the mouth and tongue, such as lip smacking and grimacing, which interfere with talking and swallowing, as well as writhing movements, which may continue during sleep. This neurological disorder may subside when drugs are withdrawn or may continue indefinitely. Prevention is best achieved by minimizing dosage and duration of drug intake, and close observation for early detection of symptoms.

SEE ALSO *Antipsychotics, Schizophrenia*

TARTAR

Tartar (dental calculus or dental plaque) is a hard yellowish film composed of calcium and food particles which is deposited on the teeth by the saliva. Found mostly at the line where the gum and tooth meet, and behind the lower front teeth and sides of the back teeth, it is not in itself responsible for tooth decay; rather it is the bacteria which lodge behind it that cause both decay and gum disease. Thorough brushing, preferably with an electric toothbrush, is essential to prevent build-up of tartar. Deposits should be removed regularly by a dentist.

SEE ALSO *Gums, Teeth*

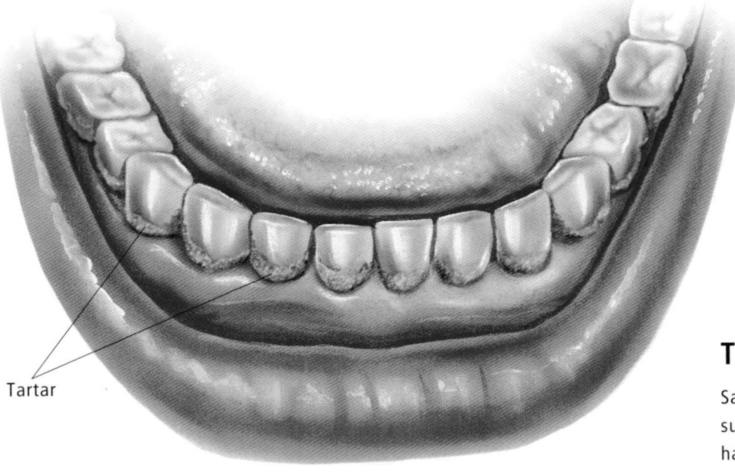

Tartar

Saliva, scraps of food and other material such as calcium carbonate form tartar, a hard, yellow deposit on the teeth.

T

TASTE

Taste, also known as gustation, is one of the five special senses. The organs of taste are the taste buds, specialized receptors made up of small clusters of cells called papillae, which are located on the surface and sides of the tongue, the roof of the mouth, and the entrance to the pharynx. At the top of each taste bud there is an opening called the taste pore. In order for food to be tasted it must be dissolved in a watery solution like saliva so that it can activate the receptors. Each person has 2,000–5,000 individual taste buds (with women having more than men). The taste buds are capable of discerning among the four basic taste sensations: sweetness, sourness, saltiness and bitterness.

Historically, it was believed that each bud could only taste one type of taste—for example, those at the tip of the tongue were thought to detect sweetness, whereas those on the sides of the tongue would detect saltiness and sourness. Researchers now believe, however, that all taste buds are capable of detecting multiple combinations of the four basic taste types. Nevertheless, different areas of the tongue are not equally sensitive to all four tastes. The back of the tongue is more sensitive to bitter, the sides of the tongue to sour, the tip to sweet, and the tip and the sides to salt. Taste can be tested by applying a salty or sweet solution to the front two-thirds of the tongue.

The exact mechanism whereby a taste bud detects a particular taste is poorly understood. However, it is thought that when a food particle is dissolved in saliva and comes into contact with the taste bud, it causes a chemical reaction within the bud. The taste bud then sends a nerve impulse via a nerve fiber attached to the base of the bud, which joins nerve impulses from other taste buds and travels via the cranial nerves to the brain.

Three different cranial nerves are involved in relaying taste: the facial nerve relays taste impulses from the front two-thirds of the tongue, the glossopharyngeal nerve supplies the back of the tongue and the vagus nerve supplies taste buds in the throat. These impulses are then relayed through nerve pathways in the brain stem and the thalamus and thence to a taste-receiving area in the anterior cerebral cortex where they are experienced as a particular taste.

The taste fibers follow a complicated route. The taste fibers of the facial nerve are distibuted to taste buds in the front two-thirds of the tongue, predominantly along the lateral borders. The taste fibers travel with the lingual nerve but cross to the facial nerve in the chorda tympani, so that taste is impaired if the facial nerve is damaged above this junction with the chorda tympani (as is often the case in Bell's palsy). These fibers enter the brain stem in the sensory root of the facial nerve (nervus intermedius). The fibers are joined by taste fibers from the glossopharyngeal and vagus nerves and terminate in the nucleus of the tractus solitarius. The part of this nucleus that receives taste fibers is often called the gustatory nucleus. Fibers ascend from here to reach the thalamus. Fibers then ascend from the thalamus to the cortical area for taste which is located at the lower end of the sensory cortex in the parietal lobe. The taste area is adjacent to the sensory area of the cortex for the tongue and pharynx.

The taste fibers of the glossopharyngeal nerve are distributed to taste buds in the back third of the tongue and the pharynx while the taste fibers of the vagus only supply the epiglottis. The vagal taste fibers are relatively unimportant because few persist into adult life. The vagal and glossopharyngeal fibers terminate in the gustatory nucleus. The fibers then ascend to the cortex from the gustatory nucleus in the same way as described above for the facial nerve.

Our state of consciousness, our cultural conditioning, our past experiences of taste and, in particular, the sense of smell, are all important in how we finally perceive a particular taste. About 80 percent of what we experience as taste is actually due to smell.

Taste abnormalities can be caused by conditions that affect the tongue and throat, the nasal passages, or the nerve pathways and brain. Conditions that can attenuate the sense of taste include the common cold, nasal infections, influenza, viral pharyngitis, mouth dryness, ageing (taste buds tend to diminish in number with age) and heavy smoking (which tends to dry the mouth).

SEE ALSO *Nervous system, Saliva, Senses, Smell, Tongue*

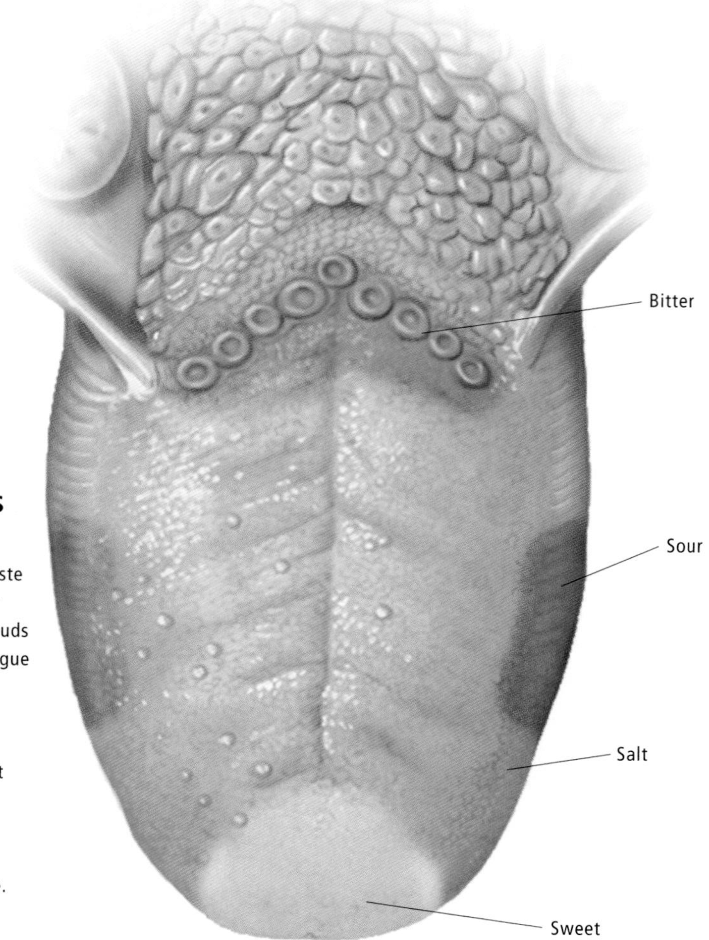

Tongue zones

There are four distinct tastes registered by taste buds: sweet, salt, sour and bitter. The taste buds at the front of the tongue are most sensitive to sweet and salty foods, the ones at the sides of the tongue are most sensitive to any sour taste, and bitterness is best registered at the back of the tongue.

Taste

Nerve stimulation

Three cranial nerves that lead directly to the brain from different parts of the head and neck are involved in our sense of taste.

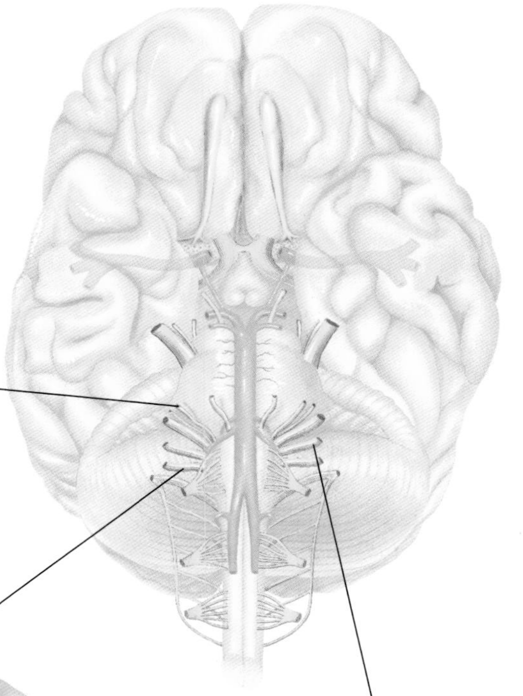

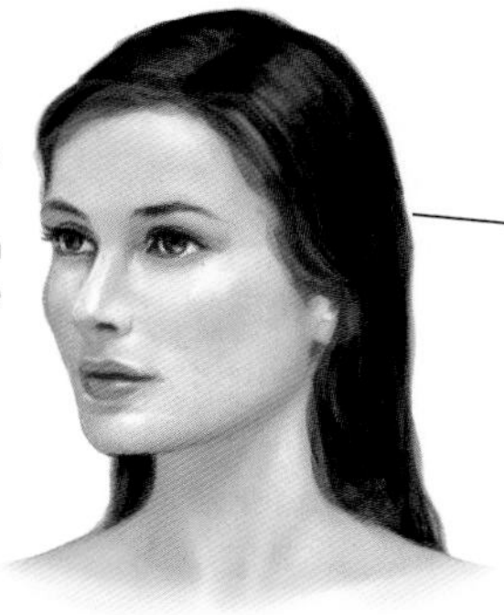

The facial nerve (cranial nerve VII) is responsible for the sensation of taste in the front part of the tongue

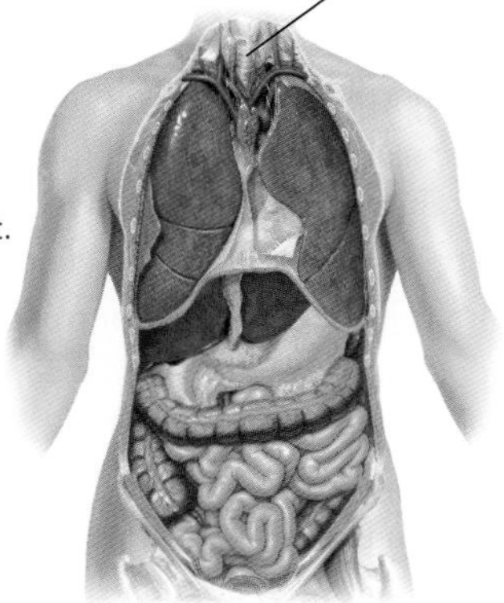

The vagus nerve (cranial nerve X) supplies the taste buds in the throat.

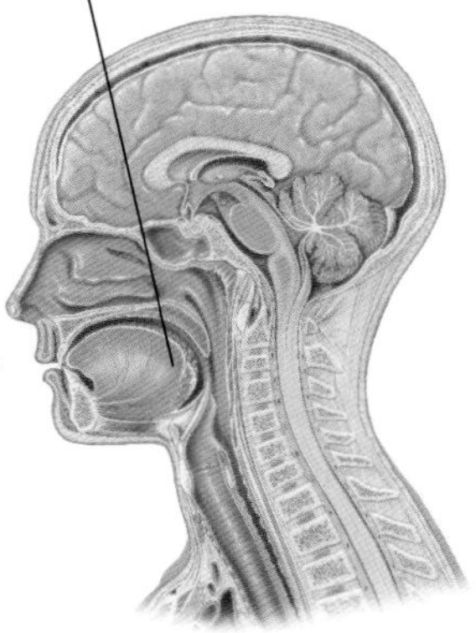

The glossopharyngeal nerve (cranial nerve IX) relays taste signals from the back part of the tongue

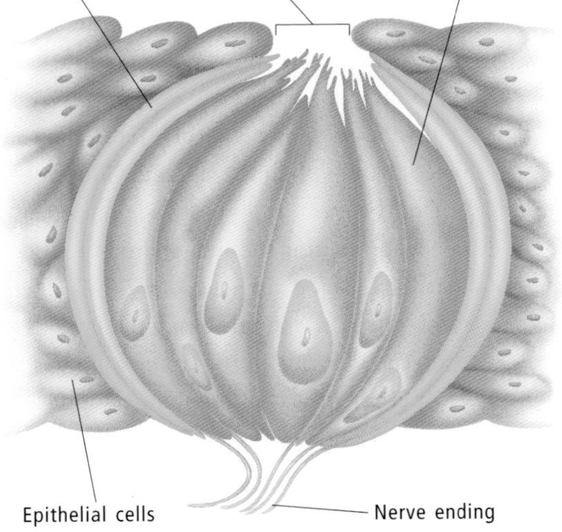

Supporting cell

Taste pore

Gustatory cell

Epithelial cells

Nerve ending

Taste buds

Taste buds are packed together in groups at various places on the tongue. These bundles of cells are sensitive to sweet, salty, bitter and sour flavors. Substances must be dissolved in a watery solution like saliva in order to activate the taste buds.

Taste pathways

Taste buds at the front and back of the tongue and in the throat send nerve impulses via the cranial nerves to the medulla in the brain stem. From here, the information passes to the thalamus and on to taste-receiving areas in the parietal lobe of the cerebral cortex where the taste is identified. The olfactory organs provide additional information vital for interpreting and appreciating different tastes.

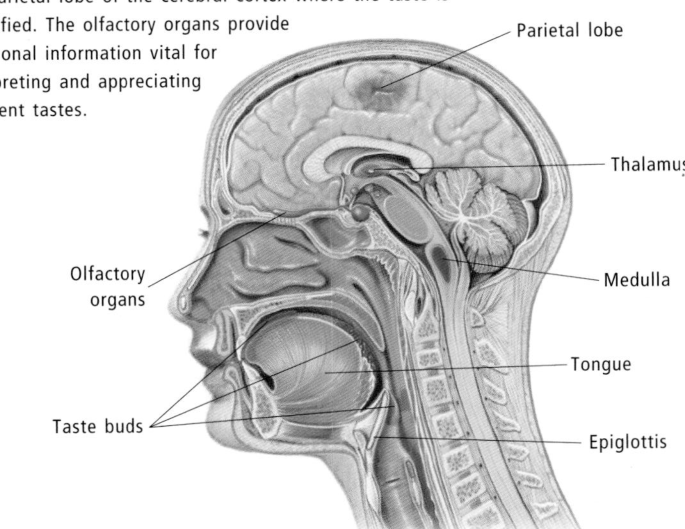

T

TATTOOING

A tattoo is a permanent pattern made on the body by introducing pigment into the dermis layer of the skin. Practised in most parts of the world for many centuries, tattooing is thought by some societies to provide protection against misfortune, and in others is seen as an indication of status or as signifying membership of a group. Tattoos may also be thought of as works of art. They have also been used to brand slaves and criminals and to identify prisoners.

It is important that tattooing be done under sterile conditions, as non-sterile needles can transmit HIV and hepatitis. Some people develop allergies to the dyes used.

Removing a tattoo is not a simple procedure; it is best to consult an experienced plastic surgeon. Every method of removal leaves at least a faint blemish on the skin, the amount of scarring depending on the age, size and depth of the tattoo and the colors used to make it. Covering one tattoo with another has been found to increase the risk of scarring when removal is attempted. Surgical removal, by cutting out the tattoo, works best with small tattoos. Dermabrasion, literally "sanding off" the tattoo, generally causes more bleeding than other methods. Lasers can also be used, but this method usually requires a number of treatments.

SEE ALSO *Hepatitis, HIV, Skin*

TAY-SACHS DISEASE

Tay-Sachs disease (TSD) is a rare genetic disorder affecting chiefly Ashkenazi Jews, Cajun communities and French Canadians. It produces progressive deterioration of the brain and central nervous system.

Afflicted babies initially appear normal, but start to decline mentally and physically at about 6 months, rapidly becoming lethargic and unresponsive. They are unable to produce the enzyme hexosaminidase A (hex A) whose function is to break down a certain type of lipid (fat); this fat accumulates in the brain cells, causing cell death and a gradual failure of the central nervous system. A variant of the disease occurs when the enzyme deficiency appears around 2 years of age.

Both forms of TSD are untreatable and invariably fatal; most of those afflicted die before the age of 5. The presence of the defective gene can be detected by a blood test measuring the level of the enzyme hex A, allowing screening and genetic counseling of potential carriers.

SEE ALSO *Congenital abnormalities, Genes, Genetic counseling*

TEETH

Teeth are calcified bonelike structures in both jaws whose role is to chew food, aid with speech and influence the shape of the face. The crown of the tooth, that part above the gum line, is covered with enamel, which is the hardest substance in the body. Under the enamel is dentine, slightly softer, which makes up the main part of the tooth. The dentine below the gum line is covered with cementum, a hard bony substance covering the roots of the teeth. Dentine is a sensitive tissue, with millions of tubules running into the central pulp or nerve, which runs from the tip of the root into the center of the tooth. The cementum is surrounded by the periodontal ligament, which contains the fibers that anchor the tooth in the bone of the gum.

Humans develop two sets of teeth in a normal lifetime. The first set, 20 in number, are known as the deciduous, primary or baby teeth. The secondary or permanent set, containing 32 teeth, begins to replace the first set around the age of 7 years; there are 16 teeth in each jaw.

There are different types of teeth. The incisors, with sharp edges for biting, are at the front of the mouth; next to them, the canines have sharp points to tear food; at the back of the mouth the molars, together with the premolars which only appear in the second set of teeth, are used to grind food.

A baby is born with the teeth already developing in the jaws. Occasionally a baby is born with some teeth already apparent. In most babies the teeth begin to erupt between the ages of 5 months and 1 year; the average age for the appearance of the first four front teeth is 7 months. It takes nearly 20 years for the complete set of permanent teeth to be established, the final set of molars (often called "wisdom teeth") erupting usually in late adolescence.

Care of the teeth

Good nutrition helps to ensure healthy teeth. Reducing the number of snacks consumed between meals reduces the amount of tooth decay (dental caries). Every time food is consumed the teeth are attacked by lactic acid, formed by the action of bacteria on carbohydrates. Other factors which lead to the development of tooth decay are inherited susceptibility (genetic make-up is partly responsible for tooth structure); the amount and frequency of consumption of fermentable sugars (carbohydrates); the presence of oral microorganisms; the flow of saliva; dental hygiene; factors in food working against decay; and fluoride.

Tooth care can help to prevent problems. From the time the first teeth appear they need to be cleaned, at first with a clean wet cloth, later with a soft baby toothbrush. A baby should never fall asleep with milk or any other fluid except water in the mouth; once the child is eating family foods, sticky, chewy foods should be avoided.

By the time a child reaches adolescence, teeth should be cleaned twice a day with fluoride toothpaste, flossed at least once a day, smoking and chewing tobacco should be avoided, the correct headgear, including mouthguards, should be used while playing sport and there should be regular dental check-ups. Adults need to continue these habits and to seek professional help when teeth problems arise.

It is better to keep natural teeth than replace them with artificial teeth. Fluoride is one of the most important weapons against decay, protecting teeth by increasing the tooth's resistance to acid attack, helping the tooth to repair and inhibiting the growth of bacteria. Fluoride in the water supply is the most efficient way of reducing dental caries in a population.

Cosmetic dentistry

Cosmetic dentistry involves repairing or improving the appearance of teeth. Teeth can be bonded with a tooth-colored plastic when the problem is chipped, stained or heavily filled front teeth or gaps that need closing up. Porcelain veneers can also be used to improve the appearance of the teeth and teeth can be whitened with bleach. A missing front tooth can be replaced with a partial

Teeth—structure

Although it looks like a solid piece of bone, a tooth contains a network of nerves, veins and arteries which enter the tooth through the root canal.

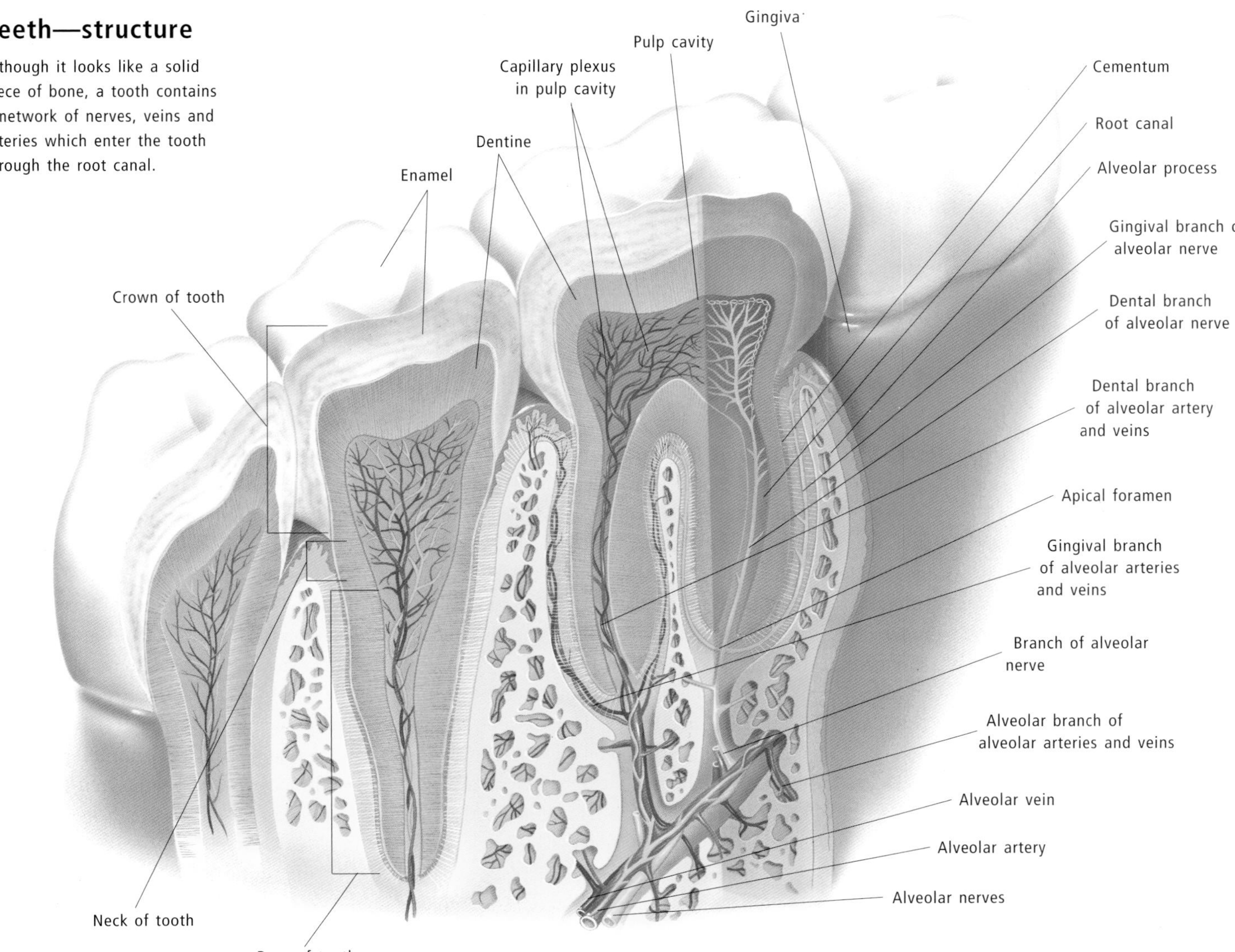

denture, bridgework or an implant. One or more missing teeth elsewhere may be replaced by a partial denture, either removable or fixed. Implants are artificial teeth, requiring surgery which can only be performed on people with healthy gums and adequate bone; implants require a commitment to meticulous ongoing hygiene.

Teeth problems

The most common problems experienced with teeth include the following.

Abscess When the pulp of a tooth becomes infected the infection can spread into the tissues near the root tip, and a pocket of pus (an abscess) can form in the gum. Treatment begins with antibiotics.

Bad breath Poor oral hygiene, gum disease, a dry mouth (xerostomia), tobacco products, various foods and medical problems are the main causes of bad breath. Once the cause has been determined, improving oral hygiene is the best method of keeping bad breath at bay.

Crooked or large teeth Orthodontic treatment will help to correct malocclusion ("bad bite") caused by overlarge, crowded or crooked teeth. Adjustable or removable appliances will help the teeth of younger children to develop in the proper positions; once all the permanent teeth have erupted fixed appliances may be used.

Decay (caries) Decay can be stopped or reversed in the early stages by appropriate use of fluoride and proper cleaning. More advanced decay can be repaired by removing damaged tissue and filling the tooth with amalgam or composite resin, which is tooth-colored. Other materials that can be used are glass ionomer cement, porcelain and gold. Crowns, which cap teeth, are usually made from porcelain and metal.

Discoloration There are many causes of unattractive blemishes on the teeth. Smoking, inherited conditions, childhood illnesses, inappropriate antibiotic treatment, injury and fluorosis, which is a superficial blemish, are some of the most common.

Fissures These are grooves on the chewing surface of the molars which are very susceptible to decay. They can be sealed.

Gum disease Periodontal or gum disease affects three out of four adults at some time. Gums that bleed, are sore, have pulled away from the teeth, persistent bad breath, loose teeth or a change in the bite are all indications of gum disease. Removing plaque or tartar is the first remedial step. Antibiotics may be necessary, as may surgery in severe cases.

Severely damaged teeth Root canal therapy may be necessary to save a tooth damaged by fracture or a deep cavity,

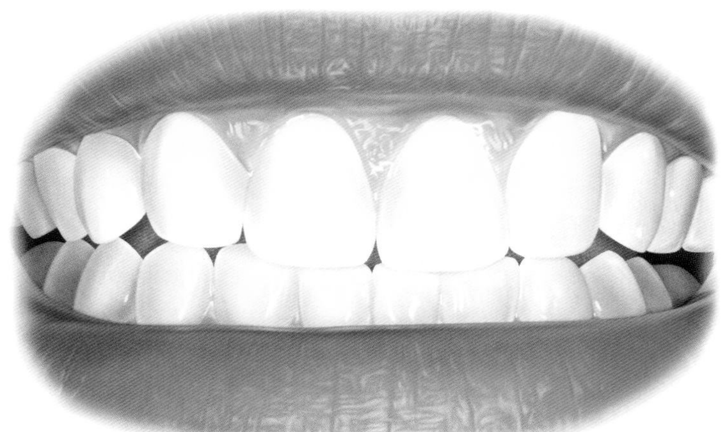

Teeth

Adults have 16 teeth in each jaw. The enamel that covers the teeth is the hardest substance in the human body.

which may cause the pulp to die. If the problem is discovered in time this treatment will save the tooth.

Wisdom teeth These are the last of the back molars to erupt and play a valuable role if they are healthy and properly positioned. If the jaw is not large enough for proper eruption (partial eruption), the wisdom teeth may damage adjacent teeth, or a cyst may form, destroying surrounding structures, and they should be surgically removed.

Yellowing As people age, teeth often become yellow, the result of plaque build-up and changes in the dentine. Gum disease and bad breath can become problems. Every effort should be made to preserve teeth.

SEE ALSO *Braces, Crown and bridge, Dentures, Fluoridation, Gums, Mouth, Orthodontics, Saliva, Teeth-grinding, Teething*

TEETH-GRINDING

Teeth-grinding (bruxism) is the act of grinding or clenching the teeth, usually during sleep. It is not associated with any particular stage of sleep and does not affect sleep—though it can damage teeth and cause face pain or headache. It seems to run in families and can occur at all ages. The most important treatment is to protect teeth and for this a mouth guard, as prescribed by a dentist, may be necessary.

SEE ALSO *Sleep disturbances, Teeth*

TEETHING

Teething is the term used to refer to the eruption of the first teeth in a baby. A baby's first tooth will generally erupt anytime between the fifth and twelfth month of the first year of life; a few babies will get their teeth earlier or later. A very small number, about 1 in 2,000, will be born with one or more teeth. The last tooth usually erupts around the age of 3 years. There are 20 primary teeth (also called deciduous or milk teeth), which are smaller and usually whiter than the permanent set of teeth.

In general, the lower central teeth (incisors) arrive first, followed by the central upper incisors, the lateral incisors (lower and upper), the first molars, the canines and the second molars, though not all children get their teeth in this order. These first teeth guide the permanent teeth into place and aid in the growth of the jawbone. It is important that they are kept healthy and clean—they are not dispensable.

A baby's first teeth can be cleaned with a clean wet cloth, sitting the baby on an adult's lap and gently rubbing the teeth. Once the child is accustomed to this routine twice a day, a very soft toothbrush can be used. Children will need assistance cleaning their teeth until middle childhood.

Signs that a tooth is about to erupt can include dribbling and a need to chew on anything and everything. A baby who is teething may also be unhappy and pull on the ear, because the ear canal is connected to the same nerve as the lower jaw. There is much folklore surrounding teething, inaccurately blaming it for fever, diarrhea, constipation, loss of appetite, diaper rash and convulsions. All these symptoms require medical attention—they are not symptoms of teething and indicate other conditions. The canines and the molars tend to cause the most distress.

The best treatment for sore gums due to teething is a cool (not cold), hard, clean teething ring or similar. The dribbling which naturally accompanies teething results in some fluid loss and babies are generally more thirsty when they are teething. Many babies wake at night while they are teething and need to drink.

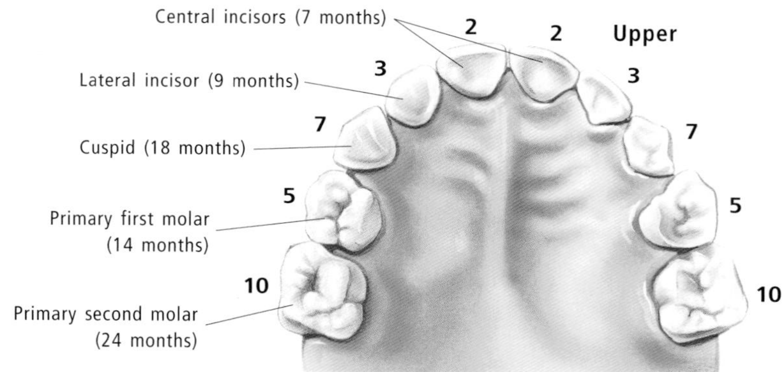

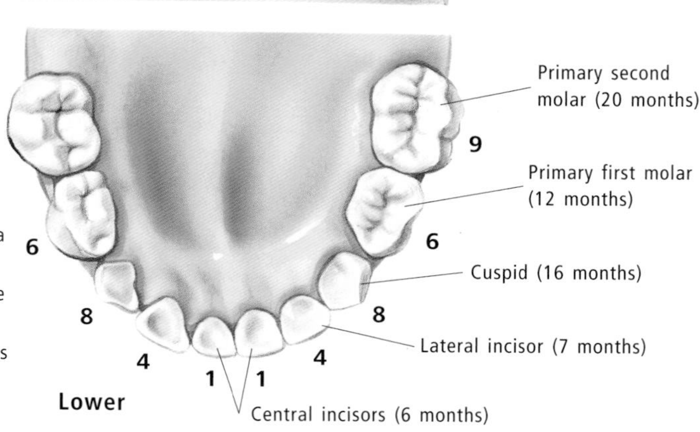

Teething

The first two deciduous teeth are usually the central lower incisors, which appear when the baby is approximately 6–9 months old. The eruption of the other primary teeth follows a set pattern, and all 20 teeth are generally present by the time the child is 24–30 months old. The number next to each tooth shows the order in which the first set of teeth appear.

The arrival of teeth is not a reason to stop breast feeding as babies do not usually bite the nipple, except occasionally in an attempt to relieve teething pains. The baby's tongue normally protrudes over the bottom teeth while sucking, thus protecting the nipple.

Teething gels that contain anesthetics can cause allergies and must be treated with caution; acetaminophen (paracetamol) may be used to relieve discomfort.

SEE ALSO *Infancy, Teeth*

TEMPERATURE

The temperature of the normal healthy human body is generally assumed to be 98.6°F (37°C), but may range from 97.2–100°F (36.2–37.8°C); temperatures ranging from 95.9–101.2°F (35.5–38.4°C) have also been recorded in healthy individuals. Temperature can only be taken accurately by using a thermometer (holding the hand to the forehead is not an accurate method of measurement). A person may sometimes appear to be hot when the core body temperature is actually normal.

The temperature can be taken in the mouth (orally) by placing a thermometer under the tongue; rectally, by inserting the thermometer a short distance into the rectum; or under the armpit (axilla). The rectal temperature is usually 1°F (0.5°C) higher than the oral temperature; the axillary temperature is usually 1°F (0.5°C) lower than the oral temperature. The temperature should always be taken by the same route for purposes of comparison in illness.

A child with a high fever, over 101°F (38.2°C), needs treatment to reduce their temperature in order to avoid the possibility of convulsions. This can be done by removing clothing, and bed clothes if necessary, and cooling the child with a tepid sponge. A tepid bath may also be used. Shivering is not the aim as this will raise the body's temperature. A fan may also help. Acetaminophen (paracetamol) or ibuprofen may be given to children to help reduce fever, but never aspirin, as it may cause Reye's syndrome. Aspirin is appropriate only for adults.

SEE ALSO *Convulsions, Fever, Reye's Syndrome, Temperature regulation*

TEMPERATURE REGULATION

Most organisms, humans included, are not able to maintain a body temperature that is significantly different from that of their environment for any length of time. Two categories of animals employ physiological mechanisms to maintain body temperature: warm-blooded creatures (endotherms), including mammals and birds, generate heat internally, while cold-blooded creatures (ectotherms), which include reptiles, use external heat to regulate body temperature.

Temperature regulation

The body has an in-built mechanism for maintaining a stable temperature. This mechanism is regulated by the hypothalamus in the brain. A change in external temperature is relayed to the hypothalamus by nerve endings in the surface of the skin. If the hypothalamus receives messages that the body is cold, it increases heat production in the body by increasing the metabolic rate. If the body is hot, the hypothalamus sends blood to the skin where heat can be lost through radiation, conduction, convection and evaporation.

Hypothalamus

Signals travelling via the nerves direct blood flow to organs or the skin, depending on the temperature of the body

Nerve receptors in the skin relay messages to the hypothalamus on body temperature

Skin and temperature

Both the dermal and epidermal layers of the skin are involved in regulating body temperature. When the body is hot, arteries dilate and blood flow to the skin increases, maximizing heat loss. The sweat glands are stimulated and release fluid, which evaporates and reduces the body's temperature. When the body is cold, the pores and arteries contract and the hairs of the skin stand up, providing an insulating layer which traps body heat close to the surface of the skin.

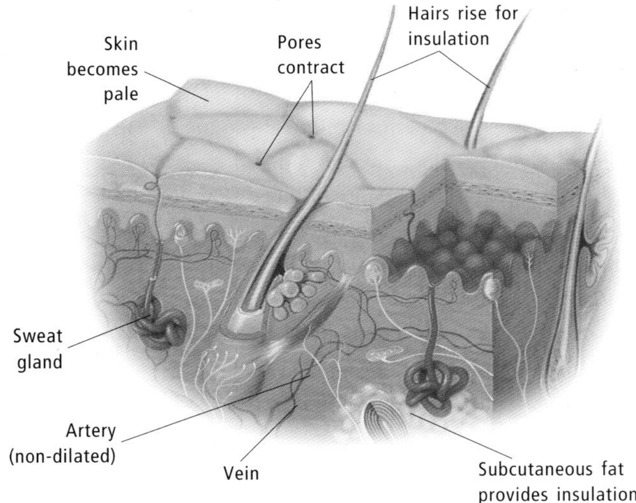
Skin reaction to cold
Skin becomes pale
Pores contract
Hairs rise for insulation
Sweat gland
Artery (non-dilated)
Vein
Subcutaneous fat provides insulation

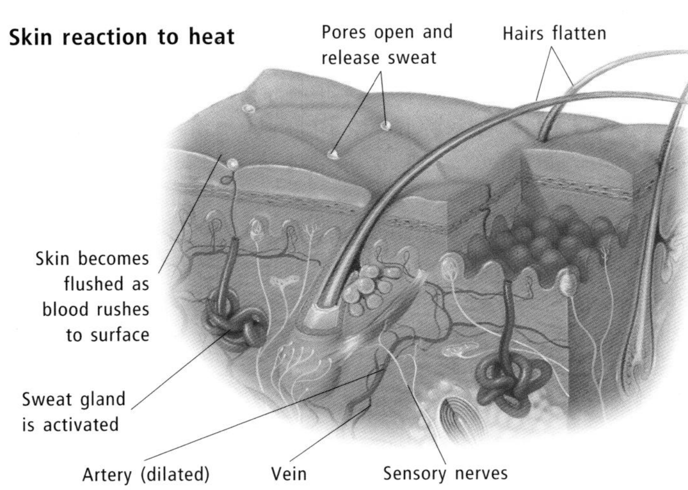
Skin reaction to heat
Pores open and release sweat
Hairs flatten
Skin becomes flushed as blood rushes to surface
Sweat gland is activated
Artery (dilated)
Vein
Sensory nerves

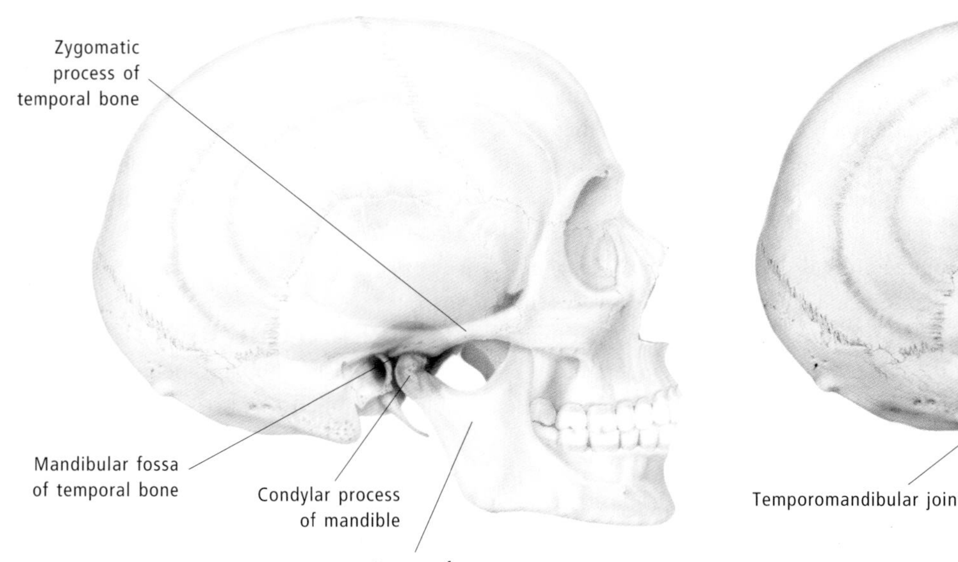

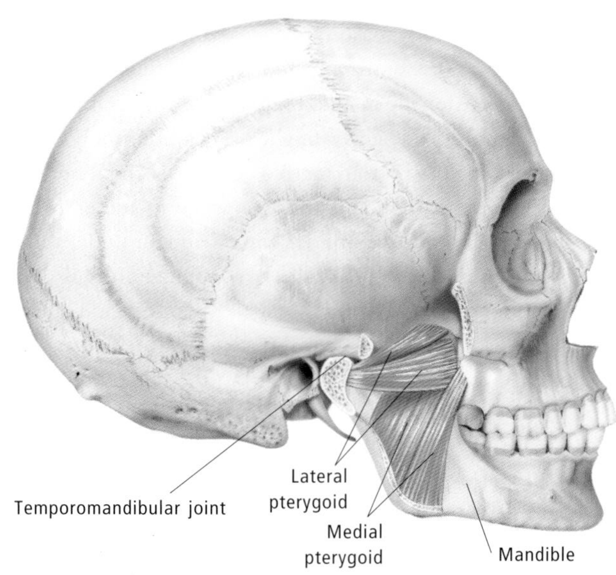

Temporomandibular joint syndrome

The temporomandibular joint has a complex action that allows movement up and down, side to side and backwards and forwards. Damage to cartilage in the joint or to the supporting muscles can result in temporomandibular joint syndrome. This may limit the action of the joint, cause clicking noises, or pain in the jaw muscles, neck or head.

The human body's usual core temperature ranges from 97.2–100°F (36.2–37.8°C). The core body temperature varies according to the time of day and is also affected by the environment, physical activity, food intake and emotions. Typically temperature is lowest early in the morning and highest in late afternoon, a normal part of the body's circadian rhythm.

Body temperature is the result of the balance between heat loss and heat production. Body heat is lost through radiation, which is affected by the rate of blood flow to the skin's surface; evaporation (the sweat glands can dissipate as many as 1,700 kilocalories (7,100 kilojoules) an hour; convection and conduction. The body's fat provides the insulation which helps to maintain the body temperature when exposed to hot or cold environments.

The part of the brain which regulates body temperature is the hypothalamus. When the body is heated, heat loss is initiated by messages sent to the hypothalamus; the blood vessels dilate and the body sweats. If the body temperature is too high (hyperthermia) the skin may become dry, deep, fast breathing will follow, and the patient may experience headaches, nausea and unconsciousness. When the body is exposed to cold stress, the first symptom of hypothermia is pain. This is followed by numbness, mental confusion, lethargy and irregular heartbeat.

A sharp rise in body temperature (hyperthermia) can trigger heat-related illnesses such as heat cramps, heat exhaustion and heatstroke. Hypothermia is a dangerous lowering of the body's temperature to below 95°F (35°C); there is a recorded case of survival after body temperature sunk to 57°F (13.9°C). Chilling is the first stage of cold injury; from this point body temperature can lower rapidly, leading to more serious cold injury. Frostnip is the next stage, when the skin blanches or loses its color. There may be numbness and as the area is rewarmed tingling may be felt. If the situation is not remedied frostbite may follow and crystals of ice may form in the tissues.

Babies and children are vulnerable to extremes of temperature, particularly cold, because they have a greater body surface compared to their weight than adults. However, babies and children do not need to be dressed differently than an adult in a similar environment. It is possible for babies to overheat when they are overdressed for the temperature. It is also possible for insufficient warm clothing to cause distress; this can happen where parents are overly concerned about sudden infant death syndrome and do not dress a baby warmly enough for sleep. The room temperature for a sleeping child should be kept around 68°F (20°C).

Fever occurs when the body's temperature is raised as a defense mechanism against infection or injury. As white blood cells are drawn toward the areas of the body where the infection is situated, chemicals are released into the bloodstream, causing the fever. Fever in itself is rarely harmful. As the temperature rises, fever and chills may be experienced together with mild dehydration. Very occasionally a child may suffer convulsions with a fever.

SEE ALSO *Convulsions, Fever, Heatstroke, Hyperthermia, Hypothermia, Skin, Sudden infant death syndrome, Sun exposure, Temperature*

TEMPORAL ARTERITIS

Temporal arteritis is a serious progressive disorder that involves inflammation of the arteries of the scalp, particularly those supplying blood to the temples and eyes. It is also known as giant cell arteritis and cranial arteritis. The swelling narrows the arteries and impedes blood flow, which can lead to severe headaches, sudden and permanent loss of sight in an eye, or a stroke. Temporal arteritis occurs almost exclusively in the over-50s, and most commonly in women aged 70-plus. The exact cause is unknown but, because it tends to afflict older people, it is thought likely that it is associated with the ageing process. Steroid medications and aspirin are commonly used in treatment.

SEE ALSO *Arteries*

TEMPOROMANDIBULAR JOINT SYNDROME

Temporomandibular joint (TMJ) syndrome is a term for a range of problems in the joint and surrounding muscles of the jaw that may produce pain, discomfort, clicking noises, aching or tender muscles, locking or restricted movement of the joint, neck pain, apparent toothache and headaches.

The action of the temporomandibular joints is complicated, allowing movements in three directions—hinging to open and close, sliding backward and forward, and moving from side to side. Between the jawbone (mandible) and the temporal bone of the skull is a cartilaginous disk which cushions the joint and can sometimes be displaced, as it is subject to great pressure during chewing.

Teeth-grinding (bruxism) during sleep can wear away biting surfaces, causing the teeth to meet unevenly ("bad bite"). This can cause jaw muscles (which must work together in a smooth and balanced way) to spasm, producing pain and headaches; the jaw may be displaced or lock in an abnormal position. Displaced disks rarely need surgery; teeth-grinding can be stopped by wearing a custom-made bite plate at night.

Osteoarthritis and rheumatoid arthritis can affect the joint and it is important to maintain mobility to avoid calcification of ligaments or fusion (ankylosis), which requires surgical correction.

In the absence of injury or other clear causes, muscular tension is often found to be the cause of TMJ syndrome. Rest and avoiding opening the jaw wide, even when yawning, may cure the problem, and reducing stress levels should also help.

SEE ALSO *Arthritis, Jaw, Joints, Teeth-grinding*

TENDINITIS

Tendinitis is inflammation of a tendon, the connective tissue which joins muscles to bones, commonly at the point of attachment. Tendons are liable to injury through repetitive action, as in manual occupations like typing; through hard use in vigorous sports; through trauma; or by degeneration. The tendons may suffer small tears or ruptures which accumulate gradually, over time becoming inflamed, painful and restricting movement.

A common cause of shoulder pain in middle age is painful arc syndrome, where pain is felt on raising the arm away from the body. It may begin after excessive use, after injury, or where there is calcification of the supraspinatus tendon in the joint. Dislocation of the shoulder will often tear the muscles or tendons of the rotator cuff. Biceps tendinitis can happen at any age, when repeated lifting of the arm damages tendons of the biceps muscle where they pass over the head of the humerus or upper arm bone. Pain is felt on raising the arm above shoulder level. Biceps tendinitis is a common cause of shoulder pain in throwing sports, when the tendon becomes irritated and inflamed; it may make a crackling sound (crepitus) on movement.

Elbow tendinitis or lateral epicondylitis ("tennis elbow") produces pain on opening a door or lifting a cup; it is caused by damage to the tendons joining the forearm extensor muscles to the elbow.

The Achilles tendon at the back of the heel can suffer tendinitis from running or jumping or repetitive movement. Swelling and tenderness may prevent walking. If the foot cannot be moved the tendon may have ruptured and will need surgical repair.

Regardless of where it occurs, the treatment of tendinitis is the same. The affected tendon must be rested—immobilized with a bandage, splint or temporary brace if necessary—to allow the inflammation and swelling to subside. Nonsteroidal anti-inflammatory medications taken by mouth, and heat or cold applied to the affected area will help reduce the pain and inflammation. Sometimes an injection of corticosteroid into the tendon may be needed. Occasionally surgery is indicated—if the condition does not improve or if the tendon has ruptured. The affected limb or extremity should not be used until completely pain free. Then physical therapy in the form of limb exercises can retain and improve the range of movement and help prevent freezing or stiffening of the joint. If the condition was caused by overuse, the contributing activity should be modified. Avoiding repetitive motion and overuse of that part of the body, and warming up by exercising at a relaxed pace before vigorous activity can help prevent the reoccurrence of tendinitis.

SEE ALSO *Achilles tendon, Ankle, Elbow, Rotator cuff muscle, Shoulder, Tendons, Tennis elbow, Tenosynovitis*

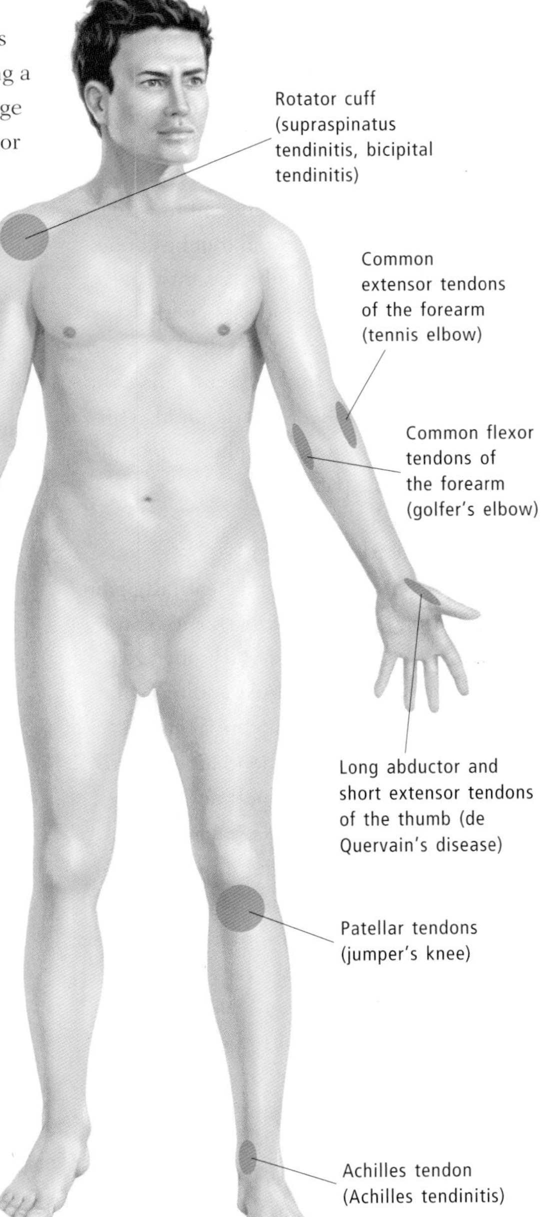

Tendinitis

Tendinitis is the inflammation of tendons and of tendon-muscle attachments due to excessive use. The illustration shows the tendons most commonly affected.

TENDONS

A tendon is a glistening white cord of connective tissue that attaches muscle to bone. It is similar in structure to a ligament, which connects bone to bone. Tendons play a critical role in the movement of the human body by transmitting the force created by muscles to move bones. In this way, they allow muscles to control movement from a distance. The fingers, for example, are moved by tendons with force supplied by the forearm muscles.

Like ropes, tendons are tough, fibrous and flexible. They are not, however, particularly elastic. If they were, much of the muscular force tendons are intended to carry would have dissipated before it had a chance to reach, let alone move, the bones.

Tendons are formed from the same components that make up other kinds of connective tissue, such as cartilage, ligament and bone. These components are collagen fibers, ground substance, and cells, which in the tendon are called fibrocytes. At the point where a tendon touches bone, the tendon fibers gradually pass into the substance of the bone and meld with it.

Some tendons run inside a fibrous sheath. Between the sheath and the tendon is a thin film of lubricant called synovial fluid. This arrangement helps tendons glide smoothly over surrounding parts.

Diseases and disorders

Inflammation of the tendon sheath is a painful condition known as tenosynovitis. Strain or trauma to a tendon sheath through repeated use, calcium deposits and high blood cholesterol levels are all potential causes. So too are diseases such as rheumatoid arthritis, gout or gonorrhea. Sometimes, during movement, a crackling noise occurs around the area of an inflamed tendon sheath.

Tenosynovitis is the underlying cause of two relatively common disorders responsible for pain in the hands and wrists—trigger finger and de Quervain's disease. In the case of trigger finger, the sheath through which the finger tendons run becomes swollen, restricting the movements of the tendons within and leading to a finger (or less commonly a thumb) becoming locked in a bent position. Trigger finger often affects people such as musicians, industrial workers and

Tendon microstructure

Tendons are constructed primarily of collagenic fibers arranged in a regular formation. This structure provides the strength needed to attach muscles to bones.

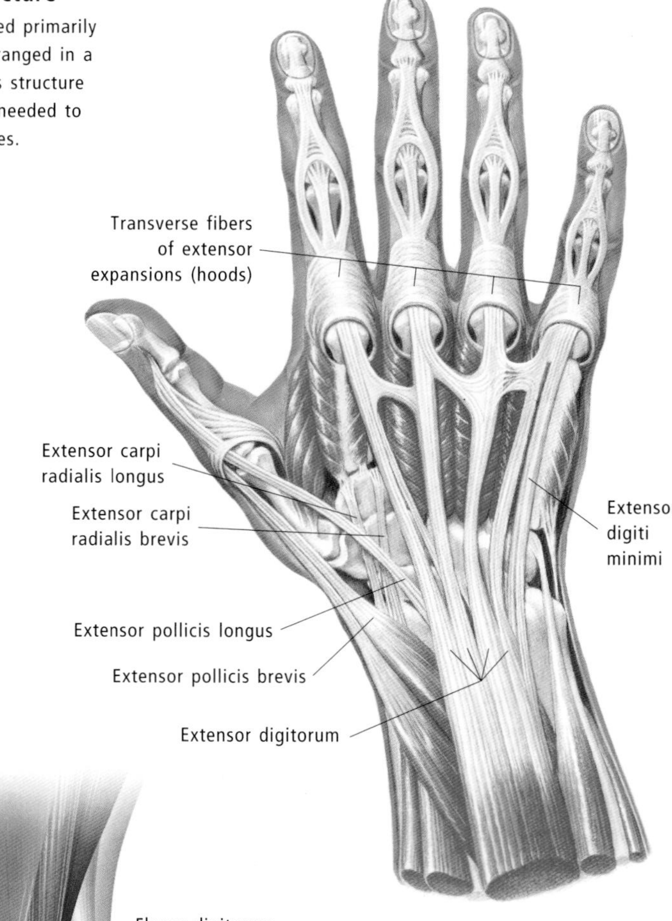

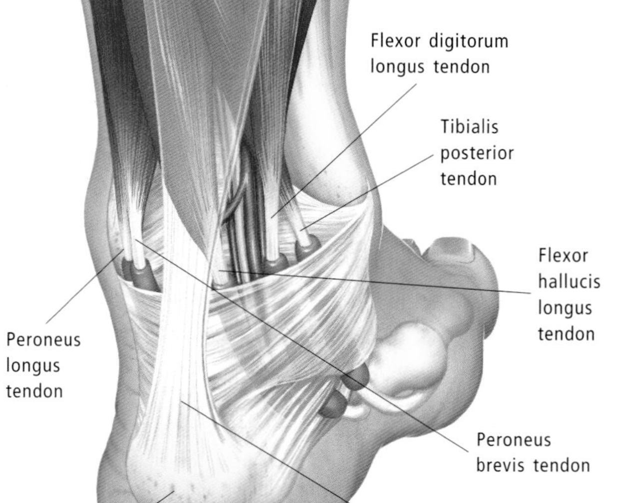

Tendon

Tendons are tough, fibrous tissues that join muscles to bones. In the hand, tendons link the fingers with the forearm muscles, allowing a full range of movement; while in the foot, the calf muscle is connected to the heel bone by the Achilles tendon.

T

farmers who use their fingers or thumbs in repetitive movements. The condition may also be caused by degenerative tissue changes associated with diseases such as rheumatoid arthritis and diabetes.

In de Quervain's disease, thickening of the sheath containing the specific tendons to the thumbs leads to pain in the wrists and along the back or base of the thumbs. A direct knock to the thumb or repetitive grasping with the thumb in situations such as gardening and racquet sports can provoke the condition. So too can the presence of inflammatory diseases such as rheumatoid arthritis.

Inflammation of a tendon itself leads to a condition known as tendinitis. It is most commonly caused by overuse or a sudden overstretching of a tendon. Both situations can lead to small tears or ruptures in a tendon. As tendons undergo a gradual process of degeneration with age, they weaken as people get older and become more prone to tendinitis. This may be why tendinitis in the rotator cuff tendons, in particular, is more common with age. These tendons help create the flexibility and huge range of movement normally permitted in the shoulders. Catching a heavy object with the arm extended or carrying out repetitive overhead activities with the arms can lead to rotator cuff tendinitis.

Tendinitis is often an underlying cause of repetitive strain injury (RSI), a painful disorder involving the hands, wrists or arms, produced by excessive or repetitive motion, such as typing on a keyboard.

The elbow is commonly afflicted by two types of tendinitis—"golfer's elbow" or medial epicondylitis, and "tennis elbow" or lateral epicondylitis.

Swinging a golf club, chopping wood with an axe, pitching a baseball and any other activity that requires repetitive gripping, grasping and turning of the hand and bending of the wrist can cause golfer's elbow. This condition is characterized by pain on the inside of the elbow.

With tennis elbow, the pain occurs in the upper forearm on the outer side of the elbow. It is caused by repetitive grasping and twisting actions such as those involved in swinging a tennis racquet, painting a house or using certain tools common in the carpentry trade. Over the last few years, tennis elbow has also started to appear in children who spend a lot of time playing hand-held computer games. Sufferers of tennis elbow not only experience pain, they can sometimes have difficulty actually straightening the forearm fully.

Another common form of tendinitis, known as "jumper's knee", affects the patellar tendon of the knee. As its name suggests, it often occurs in people playing jumping sports such as basketball and netball and is caused by the repeated impact of the force on the knee tendon that occurs when the foot hits the ground after jumping.

There are other sites in the legs where tendinitis can develop and about which sportspeople should be particularly careful. Achilles tendinitis—an inflammation of the large Achilles tendon that stretches from the calf muscles to the back of the heel—is common in runners, particularly sprinters. Long-distance runners tend to be more inclined to develop a form of tendinitis called iliotibial band syndrome, which produces pain along the outside of the knee. It is also a common affliction of dancers, cyclists and football players.

Treatment

Complete rupture of a tendon is rare and requires immediate medical attention and usually surgery. In the vast majority of cases, however, damage to tendons, or the sheaths surrounding them, responds well to ice treatments, elevation of the injury and rest, including immobilization of the affected area by strapping or even plaster, in severe cases. Non-steroidal anti-inflammatory drugs can help to reduce pain and swelling, and physical therapy will usually assist and accelerate the healing process. Steroid injections may sometimes be used in order to reduce severe pain and stiffness.

Occasionally, if tendinitis is failing to heal, surgery may be required. The extent of damage to soft tissues such as tendons can be assessed using the modern scanning technique known as magnetic resonance imaging (MRI).

SEE ALSO *Achilles tendon, Bones, Connective tissue, Elbow, Muscle, Tendinitis, Tenosynovitis, Tennis elbow, Trigger finger*

TENNIS ELBOW

"Tennis elbow" (lateral epicondylitis) refers to a strain of the muscles and tendons on the lateral side (outer or thumb side) of the forearm, near the elbow. These muscles are used for extending the wrist, as can occur in backhand strokes in tennis. Excess use can lead to tearing of the muscles or tendons and inflammation. Pain is felt at a point on the outer side of the elbow (near the lateral epicondyle) and may extend down the arm. It is aggravated by use. Although known as tennis elbow, this condition can also occur in people who never play sport.

Treatment includes resting the elbow and wrist, avoiding the movements which cause pain. Strapping the arm just below the elbow, ice packs and physiotherapy may help. Steroid injections can be used and surgery to the tendon may also be considered.

A similar condition, known as "golfer's elbow" (medial epicondylitis), can occur on the inner (medial) side of the elbow. It is due to strain in muscles used for flexing the wrist and hand, as can occur in playing golf. Like tennis elbow, the condition may occur in non-golfers. Treatment is similar to that outlined for tennis elbow.

SEE ALSO *Elbow, Muscle, Tendons*

TENOSYNOVITIS

Tenosynovitis is inflammation of a tendon and its tendon sheath, producing pain and restricting movement. Tendons, the strong connective tissues which attach muscles to bones, are often encased in fine protective sheaths through which they slide as joints are moved. The interior lining of the sheath produces a lubricating fluid to ease the tendon and allow free movement.

Inflammation reduces this lubrication and may also constrict the sheath around the tendon.

Overuse of joints and muscles, and repetitious practice of the same movement, as occurs in many sports, can cause irritation in tendon sheaths. Infections can produce inflammation and reduce the production of lubricating fluid. Certain occupations, such as keyboard operator, dentist and violinist, which involve repetitious movements of the hand, commonly produce tenosynovitis in the wrist.

When the wrist is affected, the condition may develop into carpal tunnel syndrome. Hands and shoulders are other areas that may be affected, although it can occur at any tendon site.

The symptoms of tenosynovitis are joint pain, stiffness and tenderness around the joint, pain on movement of a joint and difficulty straightening a joint. There may be swelling of the affected area.

The treatment is to rest or immobilize the tendon, as further use while the inflammation persists can lead to further damage, including a permanent thickening of the sheath and restricted motion of the affected muscle. The tendon can be immobilized by splinting the joint, or by means of a temporary brace. Nonsteroidal anti-inflammatory medications taken by mouth, and the application of heat or cold to the affected area will help reduce inflammation and pain. Sometimes corticosteroid drugs may be injected into the area to relieve inflammation. In severe cases, surgical release of the tendon may be needed.

Once the inflammation and pain has subsided, physical therapy in the form of limb exercises will strengthen muscles, prevent joint stiffness and help prevent recurrence. The condition is best prevented by making sure the tendon is not subjected to overuse, injury, strain, or excessive exercise.

SEE ALSO *Carpal tunnel syndrome, Ganglion, Joints, Tendinitis, Tendons*

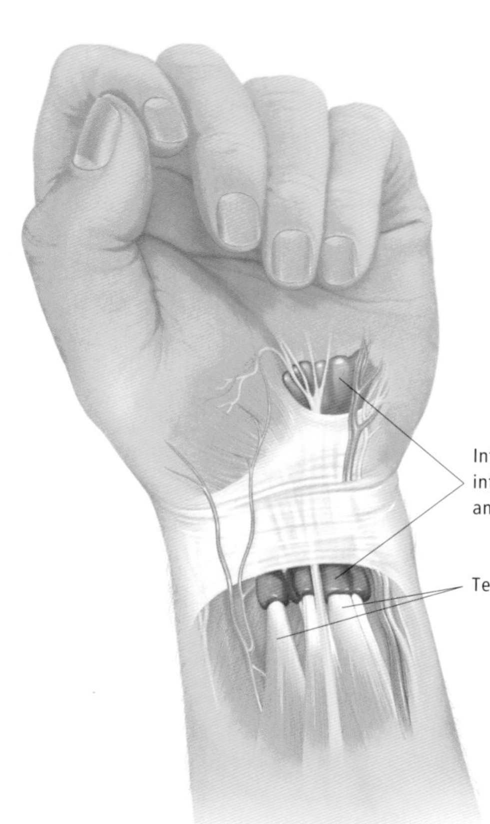

Tenosynovitis

Intense and continuous use of a tendon may result in tenosynovitis—the inflammation of a tendon and its sheath. This condition occurs mainly in the hands, wrists, feet and ankles.

TENSION HEADACHE

One of the most common type of headache, especially in adults and adolescents, tension headache is a result of the contraction of the neck and scalp muscles, which stretches the blood vessels, muscles and nerves in the skin and scalp, causing pain. Tension headaches often arise during an activity that causes the head to be held in one position for extended periods, such as when working at a computer keyboard or using industrial equipment over a long time. Sleeping with the neck in an abnormal position can also cause tension headache. People who suffer stress, depression, or anxiety are more susceptible to tension headaches than others.

The symptoms of tension headache are a dull ache, usually on both sides of the head, and worse in the scalp, temples, or back of the neck. Muscle stiffness also occurs in the neck or scalp. There are usually no other symptoms—a headache accompanied by visual disturbances, or an aura (an unusual sensation) is more likely to be a migraine.

General measures such as regular exercise and rest periods during work will help prevent tension headaches. Some people find meditation or relaxation exercises helpful. Mild analgesics such as acetaminophen or aspirin will help relieve pain, as will massage of the shoulders, neck, jaw and scalp. If a headache persists for longer than 24 hours a physician should be consulted.

SEE ALSO *Headaache, Migraine*

TERATOGEN

A condition, event or material substance that can cause physical defects in the developing fetus is called a teratogen. By altering the genetic makeup of cells during vital stages in the development of the embryo or fetus, teratogens produce congenital malformations, cancer, and other illnesses, depending upon the stage of pregnancy and the teratogen involved. There are over 2,000 known teratogenic agents. The more common ones include social drugs such as alcohol, cocaine and nicotine; medications, especially anticonvulsant drugs; environmental agents such as organic solvents, pesticides, lead and anesthetic gases; infectious diseases, especially rubella, cytomegalovirus, genital herpes, toxoplasmosis and chickenpox (varicella).

Avoiding exposure to teratogens is not always possible. For example, it has been estimated that there are more than 50,000 chemicals in common use in industrialized Western countries, and it has been estimated that as many as 20 percent of these may be teratogenic. However, there are some teratogens that can be avoided. Alcohol is a common cause of teratogenic disorders, affecting up to one in every 750 births. If consumed in excessive amounts, alcohol may cause growth retardation and low birth weight, slow development, learning disabilities and hyperactivity. Binge drinking may result in the baby having a small head circumference (microcephaly), intellectual disability and congenital heart disease, a syndrome known as fetal alcohol syndrome. Cigarette smoking during pregnancy also slows fetal growth and increases the risks of premature delivery and stillbirth.

All women should ensure they are protected against rubella (German measles) by vaccination if they have not already had the disease before becoming pregnant. Rubella is a viral infection which can lead to miscarriage if contracted in the first trimester, and to serious defects in the baby at any stage.

Because most drugs, alcohol and cigarettes are potential teratogens, complete abstinence during pregnancy is safest. Significantly elevated body temperature and radiation are also potential teratogens.

SEE ALSO *Fetal alcohol syndrome, Pregnancy, Rubella, Smoking*

T

TESTES

The testes, or testicles, are the major organs of reproduction in the male. They are two ovoid organs contained in the scrotum, a sac which lies directly behind the penis. In this location they are kept cooler by about 3.5°F (2°C) than within the body, functioning better at this lower temperature. The testes produce male sex hormones (primarily testosterone) and manufacture sperm, the microscopic cells which carry the man's genetic material to combine with that of the woman after fertilization of her ovum. The testes produce sperm continually from puberty to old age.

Testes develop from undifferentiated gonads in the fetus at about 6 weeks if a Y chromosome is present—the chromosome needed for the development of a male. When there is no Y chromosome, the gonads become ovaries. The testes at 8 weeks produce male hormones (androgens) which stimulate the growth of all the male sexual organs and inhibit the development of female organs. In rare cases organs of both sexes develop, resulting in a hermaphrodite.

In the fetus, the testes are located within the abdominal cavity close to the kidneys until the seventh or eighth month, when they descend through the inguinal canal (an opening in the abdominal wall) to the scrotum. Undescended testicles, a condition

Testes—posterior view

Contained in the scrotum, the testes are the main organs of reproduction in the male. They produce both sperm and the male sex hormones, including testosterone.

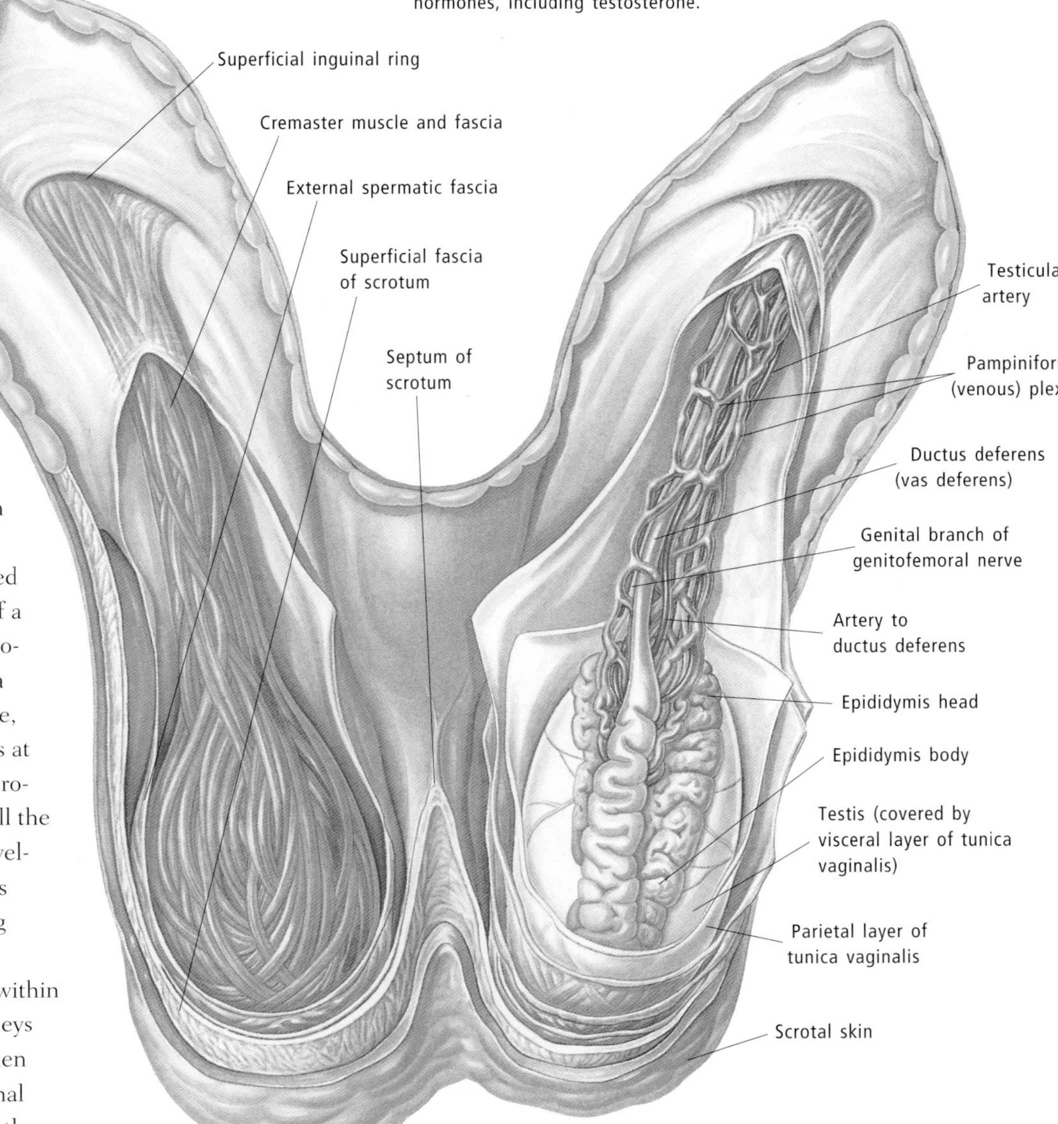

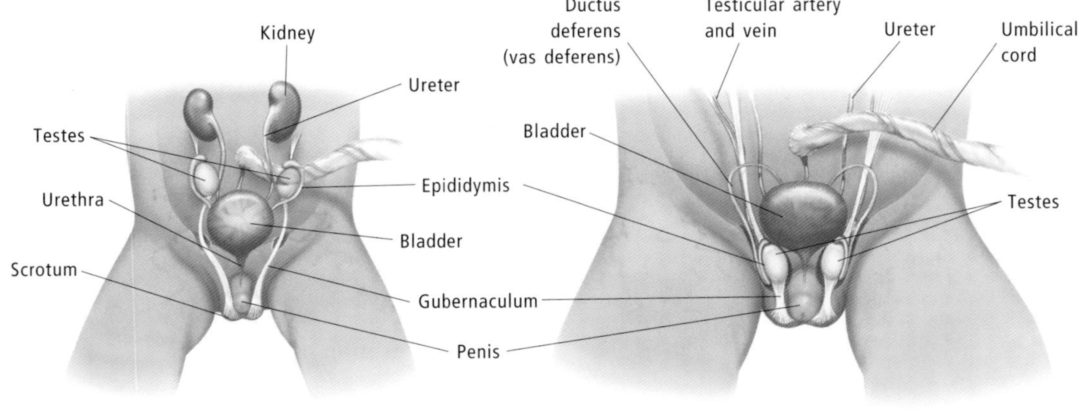

Development and descent of the testes

In the developing male fetus, the testes are located in the abdominal cavity near the kidneys until the seventh or eighth month. They then descend through the abdominal wall at the groin and enter the scrotum. They are accompanied by ducts, nerves, and blood vessels, all of which are contained in the spermatic cord.

T

known as cryptorchidism, can be corrected by surgery or by hormone injections. An inguinal hernia occurs when a loop of intestine passes through the inguinal canal with the testis.

At puberty the reproductive organs mature to become fully functional. This change is triggered by hormones released from the pituitary gland which enable the testes to start producing sperm and testosterone. The testes and penis grow larger at this time. Sperm are produced continually from puberty to old age at a rate of about 50,000 per minute, but taking about two and a half months to develop. Mature sperm leave the testicles through small ducts that lead into the epididymis. From here, they move into the seminal vesicles where they are stored until expulsion by ejaculation during orgasm. Sperm not expelled in ejaculations are reabsorbed by the body.

Diseases and disorders

A hydrocele is a usually painless, soft swelling due to fluid accumulation around a testicle which can be present at birth and if large may be corrected by surgery. A hematocele is a mass of blood that collects around a testicle, usually as a result of an injury; if large it may be removed surgically. Mumps, a viral disease that usually affects the salivary glands in the neck, can also cause pain and swelling in the testes (orchitis). If contracted after puberty it may permanently impair the ability to produce sperm. A varicocele is a mass of veins in the scrotum, like varicose veins, which can impair the production of healthy sperm by raising the temperature of the testes; the condition can be corrected by surgery. Testicular torsion, the twisting of one testicle and its spermatic cord, can be a congenital defect or result from injury or exertion; symptoms are pain and swelling, nausea and vomiting. Ultrasound may be used for diagnosis and the condition must be resolved within 24 hours as blood flow to the testicle is cut off, causing tissue death.

Testicular cancer is rare but is most often found in men between 15 and 35 years of age. It is not caused by injury but is often found on inspection after trauma. Generally painless, it often begins as a noticeable lump which can be detected by self-examination. Treatment is to remove the testicle (orchiectomy), which can be replaced by a cosmetic prosthesis if required; the other testicle will produce a normal amount of sperm and hormones. In prostate cancer, a complete orchiectomy may be performed to stop the production of testosterone, which some tumors need for growth.

Self-checking monthly by feeling each testicle between the thumb and forefinger can reveal early changes. Normal testicles are slightly soft but firm and smooth to the touch. Any hardness or lumpiness, or marked differences between testicles should be a signal for a medical check-up.

SEE ALSO *Hernia, Hormones, Hydrocele, Orchiectomy, Orchitis, Reproductive systems, Scrotum, Sperm, Testosterone*

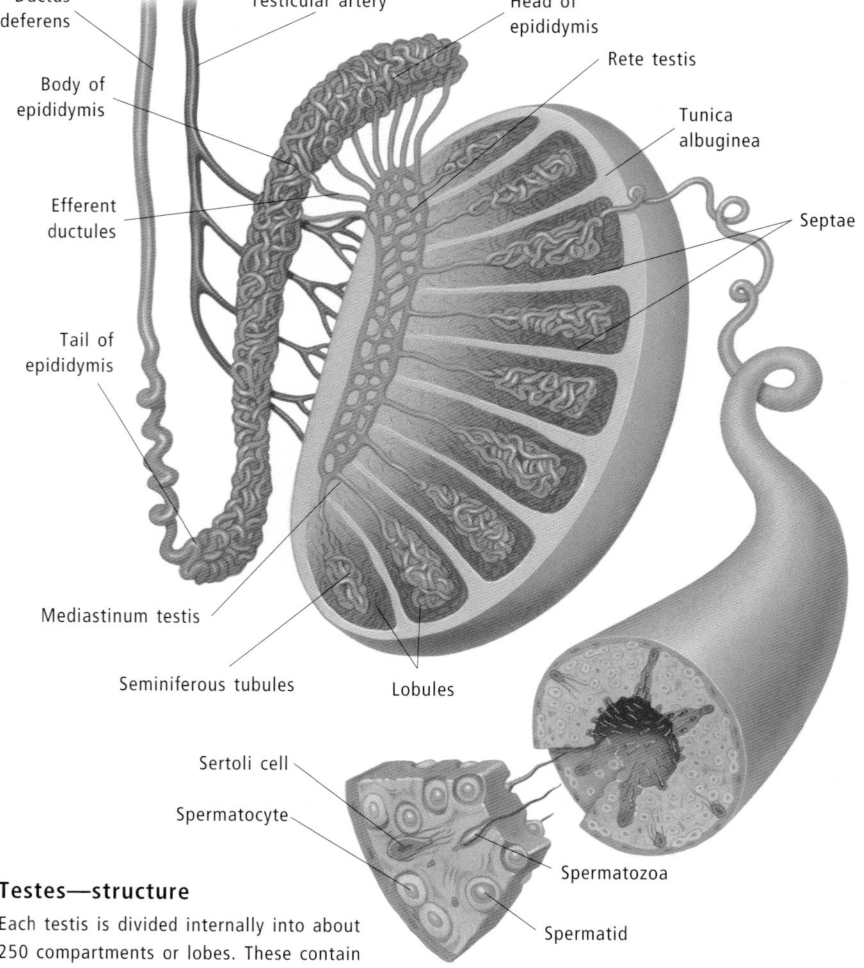

Testes—structure

Each testis is divided internally into about 250 compartments or lobes. These contain one to three very small convoluted tubules within which spermatozoa (sperm) are produced.

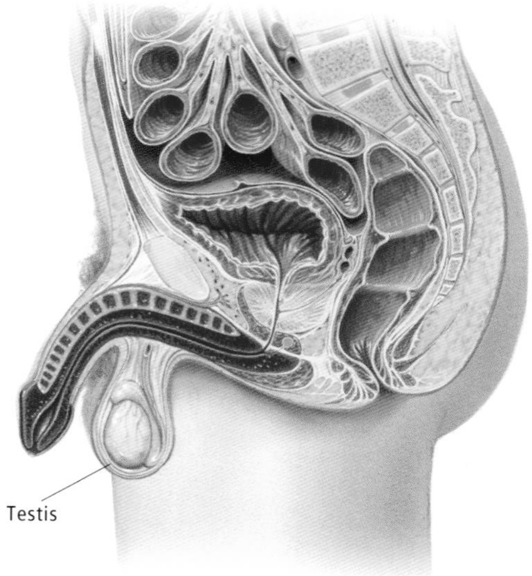

Location of the testes

Situated outside the body in the scrotum, the testes lie directly behind the penis.

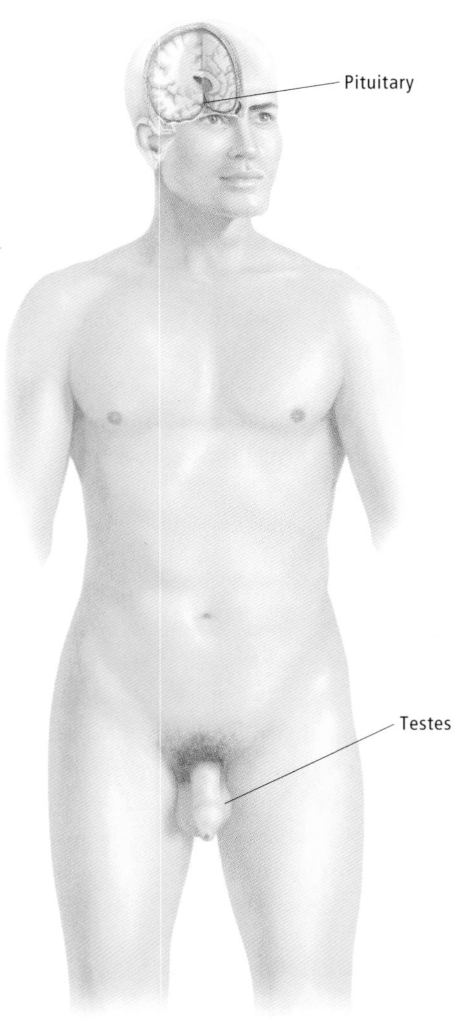

Testosterone

The hormone testosterone is produced by the testes under the control of the pituitary gland. Testosterone controls the development of male characteristics, such as facial hair and sperm production, and also plays a role in muscle growth and the body's metabolism.

TESTOSTERONE

Testosterone is the hormone responsible for the development of secondary sexual characteristics in the male. Secreted by the testes, it stimulates growth of facial and pubic hair, enlargement of the larynx and deepening of the voice, enlargement of the penis and testes, and an increase in muscle strength. Earlier in life, testosterone plays an important part in the development of external genitalia in the male fetus.

Testosterone production is controlled by the follicle stimulating hormone (FSH) and luteinizing hormone (LH). Both of these hormones are secreted by the front lobe of the pituitary gland. Small amounts of testosterone are also synthesized from cholesterol in the adrenal glands, ovaries and placenta.

Synthetic steroids similar to testosterone are used by athletes to promote muscle growth and improve performance, often with adverse side effects. Drugs based on synthetic testosterone have clinical uses such as the suppression of milk supply in lactating women and the treatment of female frigidity, breast cancer and testicular disorders.

SEE ALSO *Follicle stimulating hormone, Hormones, Pituitary gland*

TETANUS

Tetanus is an acute infectious disease, which occurs in both humans and animals, produced by the bacillus *Clostridium tetani* entering the body through a dirty wound, particularly a puncture wound. Symptoms include muscle stiffness and cramps, which appear first around the mouth and jaw (hence the disease's previous common name, lockjaw), a sore throat and difficulty breathing and swallowing, proceeding to severe muscle spasms and convulsions.

Tetanus can incubate for between 2 days and 2 weeks, but sometimes as long as 3 months; the longer the incubation period the milder the disease.

The severity of the symptoms is related to the amount of toxin produced by the bacterial infection and the resistance of the person to the disease. Of those who contract tetanus, 30–40 percent will die if they are not treated. In nearly half of tetanus cases no puncture wound is evident; any wound can serve as the entry point for tetanus germs, even a superficial abrasion. The spores of *Clostridium tetani* are most commonly found in topsoil and are spread by animal feces. They may also live on anything lying on the ground.

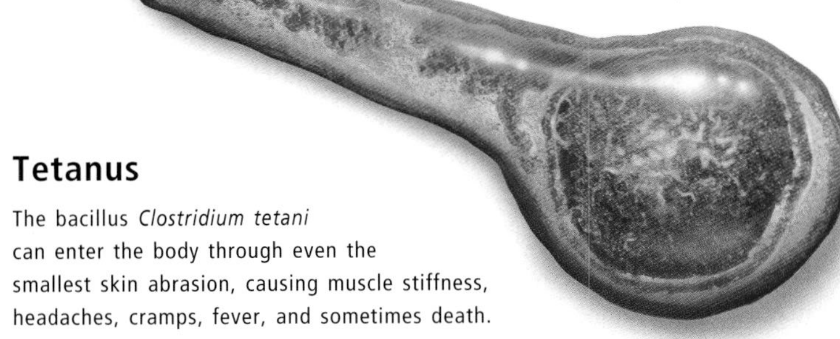

Tetanus

The bacillus *Clostridium tetani* can enter the body through even the smallest skin abrasion, causing muscle stiffness, headaches, cramps, fever, and sometimes death.

Tetanus is more prevalent in older people and agricultural workers who regularly come into contact with animal manure. Many incidences are caused by puncture wounds from rusty metal objects such as nails.

Wounds should be thoroughly cleaned and any dead tissue removed. Recovery from a tetanus attack does not guarantee immunity from the disease. Complications include hypertension, fractures of the spine or long bones, abnormal heartbeat, coma, general infection, blood clots in the lungs, pneumonia and death.

Immunization against tetanus is available as part of immunization programs in most industrialized countries, starting with babies from 6 weeks of age. It consists of a series of injections, the number depending on which type of tetanus toxoid is used; it is important that the immunization be repeated every 10 years. Redness and a hard lump are the most common side effects of the vaccine; if other side effects are noticed a medical check-up is a wise precaution. Accident victims are usually routinely administered with the vaccine. Treatment of tetanus includes antibiotics, sedatives and muscle relaxants.

SEE ALSO *Immunization, Infectious diseases*

TETANY

Tetany is a muscular spasm in the hands, feet and face, which is a symptom of a metabolic imbalance. This potentially life-threatening disease can be caused by abnormally low levels of calcium, potassium or magnesium in the blood or by an over-acid or over-alkaline condition of the body.

It is a painful condition in which the muscles of hands and feet cramp rhythmically and the larynx spasms, causing difficulty in

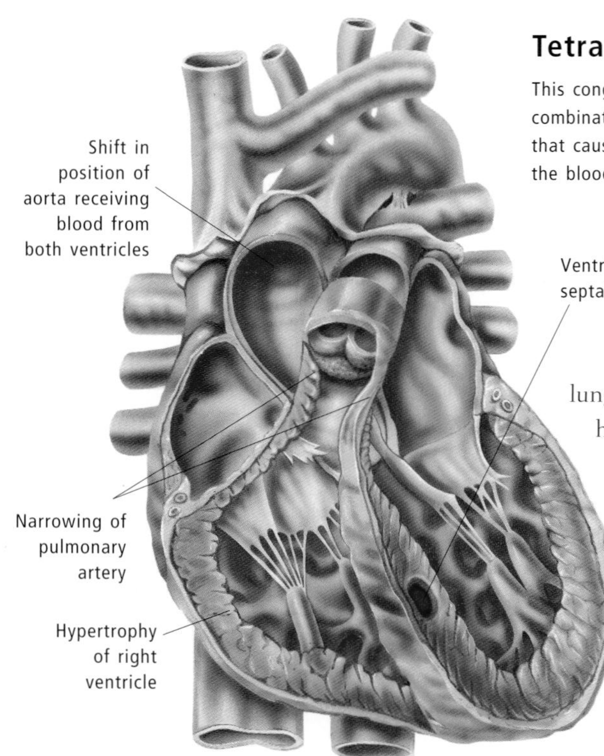

Tetralogy of Fallot

This congenital condition is a combination of four heart defects that cause low oxygen levels in the blood.

breathing, nausea, vomiting and convulsions. There may also be sensory abnormalities such as an odd feeling in the lips, tongue, fingers and feet, general muscle aches and spasms of the facial muscles.

The condition may accompany poorly controlled hypoparathyroidism, hypophosphatemia, osteomalacia, renal disorders or malabsorption syndromes. If caused by abnormal calcium levels, tetany may be associated with a vitamin D deficiency.

The aim of treatment is to restore metabolic balance, for example by intravenous administration of calcium in cases of calcium deficiency (hypocalcemia).

SEE ALSO *Acidosis, Alkalosis, Calcium, Potassium*

TETRALOGY OF FALLOT

Tetralogy of Fallot is a congenital disease of the heart; in other words, the basic disorder is present before the time of birth. The word tetralogy implies that there are four main abnormalities comprising the disease.

The two most important disorders are pulmonary stenosis and ventricular septal defect. Pulmonary stenosis is a severe narrowing of the pulmonary artery that leads from the right side of the heart to the lungs. Ventricular septal defect is a hole in the wall that separates the two ventricles, or main pumping chambers, of the heart.

In addition, there is a shift in the position of the aorta (the main artery passing from the heart to the rest of the body) so that it lies over the ventricular septal defect. The wall of the right ventricle thickens as a consequence of the narrowed pulmonary artery. The result of these disorders is that insufficiently oxygenated blood is pumped from the heart to the body. Blood flow to the lungs is decreased, which compounds the cyanotic effects. Children with this disease usually develop a blue tinge to the lips and mouth (cyanosis) within the first year of life. Breathlessness and fainting will become increasingly more severe and frequent. These episodes of fainting are referred to as "Tet spells".

It is estimated that about 50 in 100,000 infants develop tetralogy of Fallot, with a higher than normal incidence in children with Down syndrome. As with most congenital heart defects, the cause of this group of disorders is unknown, but prenatal occurrences thought to be associated with such conditions include viral illnesses, alcohol abuse, insufficient nutrition and diabetes. Treatment is by corrective surgery.

SEE ALSO *Congenital abnormalities, Cyanosis, Heart, Ventricular septal defect*

THALAMUS

The thalamus is an ovoid structure composed of a group of nerve cells lying deep within the brain. There are two thalami, lying on either side of the third ventricle, a fluid-filled space in the midline of the brain. A large bundle of nerve fibers, known as the internal capsule, lies to the side of each thalamus.

There are several parts of the thalamus, which serve as sensory relay centers between so-called "lower" parts of the central nervous system and the surface of the brain, the cerebral cortex. For example, sensory information from the retina in the eye is relayed through the thalamus to the visual cortex at the back of the brain. However, the thalamus is not a passive relay station—some of the information processing necessary for sensory perception must occur within the thalamus.

Other parts of the thalamus are motor, or muscle control, relay centers. The thalamus is involved in two "motor loops", circuits by which nerve impulses are transmitted from the motor parts of the cortex to nerve cells in the lower parts of the brain, back up to the thalamus and thence returned to the cortex. One of these loops involves the brain stem and cerebellum; the other involves the basal ganglia, which are large groups of nerve cells lying to the side and in front of each thalamus.

There are also parts of the thalamus that are said to be "non-specific" and have connections with the cortex, for which no clear functional significance is available at present.

SEE ALSO *Brain, Cerebral cortex, Nervous system*

THALASSEMIA

Also known as Cooley's anemia, Mediterranean anemia or hereditary leptocytosis, thalassemia is a group of hereditary diseases characterized by a deficiency of normal hemoglobin, the protein that transports oxygen to the tissues. The illness is caused by an imbalance in the alpha and beta protein globin chains which are needed for the production of hemoglobin.

Thalassemia major (homozygous thalassemia) may be diagnosed in the first year of life with symptoms of anemia and enlarged spleen and liver; by the age of 4, growth is stunted and bone deformities may be evident.

Thalassemia minor (heterozygous thalassemia) is characterized by mild anemia, often with no other symptoms.

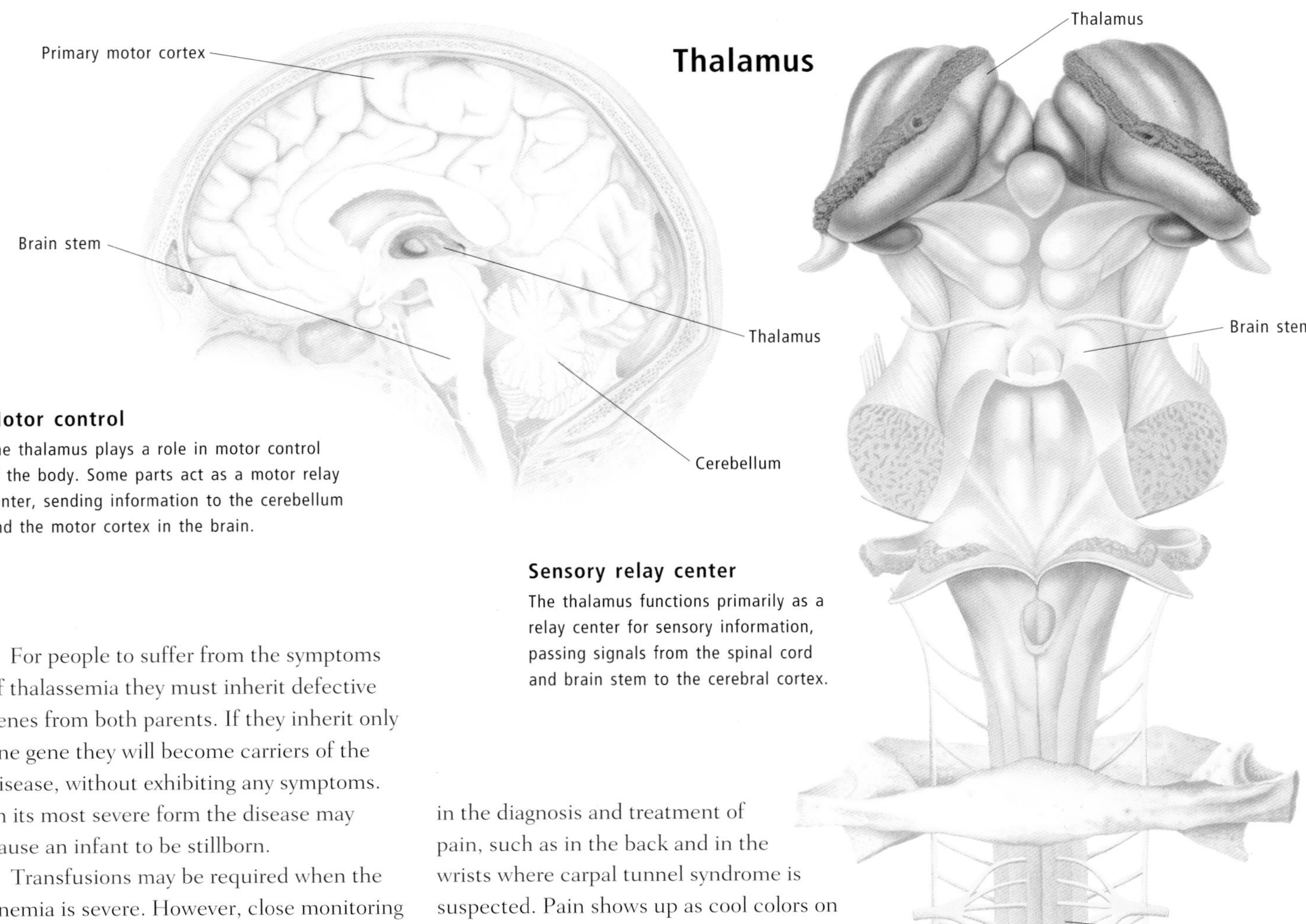

Motor control
The thalamus plays a role in motor control of the body. Some parts act as a motor relay center, sending information to the cerebellum and the motor cortex in the brain.

Sensory relay center
The thalamus functions primarily as a relay center for sensory information, passing signals from the spinal cord and brain stem to the cerebral cortex.

For people to suffer from the symptoms of thalassemia they must inherit defective genes from both parents. If they inherit only one gene they will become carriers of the disease, without exhibiting any symptoms. In its most severe form the disease may cause an infant to be stillborn.

Transfusions may be required when the anemia is severe. However, close monitoring is required as too much iron from the transfusions may cause damage to the liver, heart and endocrine systems. There is no cure for these diseases.

SEE ALSO *Anemia, Hemoglobin*

THERMOGRAPHY

Thermography is a technique involving measuring the temperature in different parts of the body by scanning with a heat-sensitive infrared camera. It is especially known for its use in the diagnosis of breast cancer by measuring skin temperature—a tumor is marginally hotter than surrounding tissue. Before the scan the skin is exposed to the air for 10 minutes to stabilize its temperature and increase the accuracy of the test.

The scanning procedure results in an infrared photo of the body's surface temperature, called a thermogram, which may show up such things as disease-causing plaque on the arteries of the heart, various cancers and infection. The procedure has also been used in the diagnosis and treatment of pain, such as in the back and in the wrists where carpal tunnel syndrome is suspected. Pain shows up as cool colors on the thermogram as it causes blood vessels in the skin to constrict, which reduces skin temperature. It is estimated that about a quarter of thermographic tests bring false positive responses, making the technique unreliable for the screening of serious disease such as cancer.

SEE ALSO *Atherosclerosis, Breast cancer*

THROAT

The throat is the front portion of the neck. Within it are the fauces, the opening that leads from the back of the mouth into the pharynx, and the pharynx itself, the cavity that connects the mouth, nose and larynx, which is situated behind the arch at the back of the mouth.

The nasal part of the pharynx, or nasopharynx, is the space just above the soft palate that joins with the back of the nose. It contains the adenoids and the openings of the eustachian tubes on each side (which lead to the middle ear). The oropharynx lies at the back of the mouth and contains the tonsils (one on each side) and the back of the tongue. The laryngeal pharynx connects the back of the throat to the voice box, or larynx, and the esophagus (gullet). At the top of the laryngeal pharynx is the epiglottis, a flap of tissue that lies just behind the base of the tongue. From the epiglottis the laryngeal pharynx leads downward to the esophagus. A separate passageway leads to the larynx.

During the action of swallowing, muscles in the walls of the throat lift the pharynx, pushing food down to the esophagus, and closing the epiglottis over the trachea so food and liquids do not pass into the trachea.

A sore throat is a symptom of many disorders, including colds, diphtheria, influenza, laryngitis, measles, infectious mononucleosis (glandular fever), pharyngitis and tonsillitis. Sore throats may be caused by bacteria such as *Streptococcus*, but most are caused

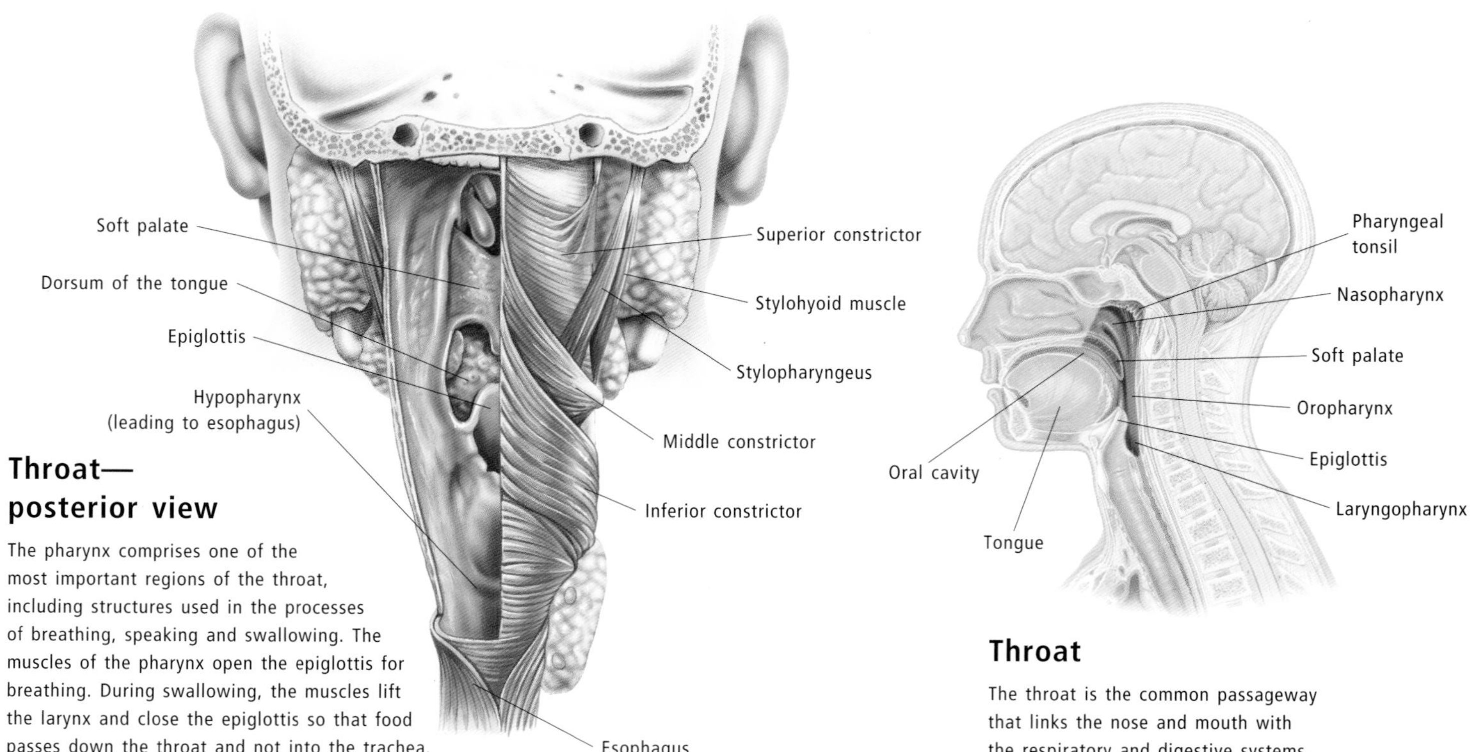

Throat—posterior view

The pharynx comprises one of the most important regions of the throat, including structures used in the processes of breathing, speaking and swallowing. The muscles of the pharynx open the epiglottis for breathing. During swallowing, the muscles lift the larynx and close the epiglottis so that food passes down the throat and not into the trachea.

Throat

The throat is the common passageway that links the nose and mouth with the respiratory and digestive systems.

by viruses; therefore, treating all sore throats with antibiotics (which do not cure viral infections) is inappropriate.

SEE ALSO *Adenoids, Digestive system, Epiglottis, Esophagus, Larynx, Pharynx, Trachea*

THROMBOANGIITIS OBLITERANS

In thromboangiitis obliterans, also known as Buerger's disease, clots and inflammation in the lining of blood vessels cause them to become constricted or blocked. The small and medium-sized arteries of the feet and legs are most commonly affected, although the hands may also be involved. Intermittent pain, blueness and eventual tissue damage and destruction result from reduced blood supply to affected areas. Painful ulcers, other infections and eventually gangrene requiring amputation can occur.

Pain in the hands and feet may be severe and accompanied by tenderness, tingling and burning sensations, which tend to be felt more during rest than when active. Foot pain is often felt in the arch. Other symptoms include skin changes or ulcers on the feet and hands. These extremities may feel cold or may be pale, red or a bluish color, with prominent cord-like veins. Symptoms of the disease may worsen if the sufferer is exposed to cold temperatures or experiences emotional stress.

The cause of thromboangiitis obliterans is unknown, but smoking is considered to be a trigger because the disease is most prevalent in cigarette-smoking men aged between 20 and 40 and rarely affects non-smokers. Stopping smoking also generally results in the partial healing of the affected area.

People with autoimmune diseases also have more risk of suffering from the disease. There is no cure and the goal of treatment is to control and reduce symptoms. As well as stopping smoking, it is helpful to avoid anything that restricts blood circulation, such as the cold. Staying warm and undertaking gentle exercise may help to increase circulation. In some cases, surgically cutting the nerves to the worst affected areas (sympathectomy) may offer pain control.

SEE ALSO *Arteries, Blood vessels, Smoking*

THROMBOCYTOPENIA

Thrombocytopenia is a reduction in the number of platelets circulating in the blood. Because platelets are essential for clotting, the main symptom of this disorder is abnormal bleeding, particularly into the skin where the blood forms bruises and small hemorrhages called petechiae, which appear as round purple-red spots. Mouth and nosebleeds are also common.

There is a range of possible causes of thrombocytopenia. One of the most frequent is an autoimmune disease called idiopathic thrombocytopenic purpura. This involves the production of antibodies against platelets by spleen and lymph tissue, resulting in the destruction of platelets in the spleen. As well as the characteristic bruising and skin hemorrhaging, this type of thrombocytopenia may also cause abnormal menstrual bleeding and sudden loss of blood in the intestinal tract. More children are affected than adults, mostly after viral infection, and often treatment is not necessary. In adults idiopathic thrombocytopenic purpura may develop into a chronic condition and does not usually follow viral infection.

Drug-induced non-immune thrombocytopenia is a reaction to certain drugs, some of which can damage bone marrow and slow the production of platelets. This is potentially fatal if it leads to bleeding in the brain or another vital organ. Other drugs may not affect the production of platelets but rather render them useless by ensuring that they cannot adhere to one another, a property

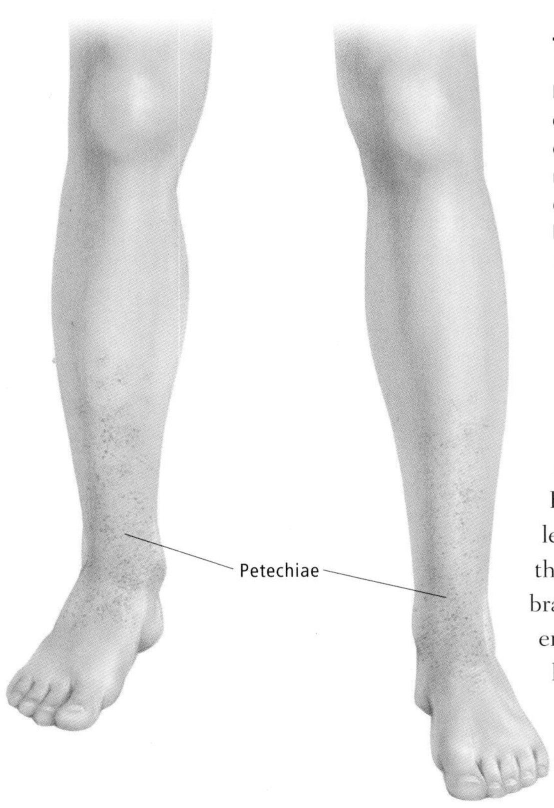

Thrombocytopenia

In this condition, reduced numbers of platelets in the blood inhibit clotting. This results in a distinctive rash of small red spots—usually on the legs—caused by abnormal bleeding into the skin. These spots are known as petechiae.

that is required for blood clotting. Drug-induced immune thrombocytopenia is the development of antibodies to blood platelets, either as a result of the direct use of certain drugs or, in the case of an affected fetus, due to drugs taken by the mother during pregnancy.

The condition may also occur with certain other diseases or infections, such as leukemia or AIDS, or as a reaction to particular drugs. Treatment depends on the cause.

Some forms of the illness will resolve themselves over time. Others may require treatments such as a transfusion of platelets. Complications can include bloody stools and vomiting blood.

SEE ALSO *AIDS, Autoimmune disease, Blood, Leukemia, Nosebleed, Platelets*

THROMBOEMBOLISM

Thromboembolism is the process of clot formation in a blood vessel (thrombosis) and its subsequent dislodgment and travel to another part of the circulation (embolism). When the thrombosis occurs in an artery, the dislodged fragment (embolus) travels to a more distant part of the arterial circulation until it obstructs a smaller branch. The blockage deprives the tissues in that area of their normal blood flow, cutting off their oxygen supply and causing death of the tissues in that organ or body part. Emboli from deep vein thrombosis in the legs or, occasionally, the arms travel to the right side of the heart and lodge in a branch of the pulmonary artery (pulmonary embolism). Alternatively an embolus may lodge in an artery in the extremities (especially in the legs and feet), the brain, the heart, or (less commonly) the bowel or kidney.

Thromboembolism is often associated with other conditions such as atherosclerosis (where a thrombus may form in the diseased area of an artery). It is more likely to affect people with blood diseases, those who are immobilized for long periods, and people with major illnesses such as cancer.

The symptoms of thromboembolism depend on where the embolus has lodged. In a limb or extremity it may cause pain and numbness; the limb will be cold and pale, lacking a pulse. Foot or leg ulcers and gangrene (death of tissue) may develop. In an internal organ the embolus usually causes pain and the loss of function of that organ—for example, stroke in the brain (causing paralysis); angina or myocardial infarction in the heart (which may cause heart failure or sudden death); and breathlessness and collapse in the lung.

Thromboembolism requires emergency treatment in hospital. Intravenous drugs are given—thrombolytic drugs such as streptokinase to break up the clot and anticoagulant medications such as heparin to prevent the development of new clots. Sometimes surgery is undertaken to remove the clot.

After recovery, oral anticoagulant drugs such as warfarin may need to be taken indefinitely.

SEE ALSO *Arteries, Blood vessels, Embolism, Pulmonary embolism, Thrombosis, Veins*

THROMBOLYTIC DRUGS

Thrombolytic therapy is treatment used to dissolve, or lyse, a clot. The drugs employed to dissolve clots act by enhancing the body's own anti-clotting mechanism, the fibrinolytic system. This is a series of proteins whose actions result in the breakdown of fibrin, the hard clot formed when the coagulation system is activated.

Thrombolytic therapy has been used mainly to treat coronary artery thrombosis which can cause heart attack. Studies have shown that thrombolytic therapy can significantly reduce the resulting damage to heart muscle and the risk of death from heart attack. However, the treatment must be given within hours of onset to be effective.

SEE ALSO *Coronary artery disease, Coronary thrombosis, Heart, Myocardial infarction, Thrombosis*

THROMBOSIS

Thrombosis is the formation of a clot, or thrombus, in a blood vessel. The blood is normally maintained in a liquid state within the circulation. However, a hemostatic system exists to allow the blood to clot in response to injury to a blood vessel. In disease states abnormal clotting may occur, leading to organ damage.

Disease may affect various aspects of the hemostatic system, which comprises the vessel wall and its lining endothelial cells, the platelet cells and the coagulation system. It may also affect the body's protective anti-clotting system, the fibrinolytic system.

Thrombosis may occur in arteries or veins, or in small vessels such as capillaries. The causes of these various forms of thrombosis vary.

Arterial thrombosis is generally caused by disease of the arterial wall, mostly due to atherosclerosis. This results in the irregular narrowing of blood vessels (plaque formation) and a later breakdown or ulceration of the smooth lining of the artery. Exposure of the raw surface of the artery causes platelet cells to adhere as a protective response. Eventually a clot will form and totally obstruct the vessel cavity (lumen). This deprives the organ supplied by the obstructed artery of oxygen and nutrients, and tissue death (infarction) occurs.

T

Thrombosis

Thrombosis is the formation of a blood clot (thrombus) inside an artery or vein which impedes blood flow. The total blockage of a blood vessel by thrombi can deprive organs of vital oxygen and nutrients and lead to the death of tissue (infarction).

Arterial thrombosis

The formation of thrombi in arteries is most commonly caused by atherosclerosis—a disease in which the blood vessels narrow and the lining of the vessel walls deteriorates.

THROMBUS

A thrombus is a blood clot inside a vein or artery. It can be dangerous if it severely impedes or stops the flow of blood, leading to a condition known as thrombosis. In cerebral thrombosis, a thrombus develops in an artery to the brain and can cause a stroke. A thrombus in an artery leading to cardiac muscle can lead to a heart attack. Certain factors predispose people to developing blood clots. These include slow blood circulation, the disease arteriosclerosis, prolonged use of the contraceptive pill,

The most common forms of serious infarction are myocardial infarction (heart attack), cerebral infarction (stroke) and peripheral arterial thrombosis leading to gangrene. Prevention of these forms of thrombosis includes treating the risk factors for atherosclerosis, such as hypertension and high cholesterol; anti-platelet drugs such as aspirin are often prescribed.

Venous thrombosis occurs most commonly in the deep veins of the legs, resulting in pain and swelling due to blockages in the blood leaving the legs. More serious consequences can occur if the clot detaches from the vein wall and travels to the lungs (pulmonary embolism). Venous thrombosis can occasionally occur in the brain or the intestines, with serious effects. Thrombosis in the veins may be related to disease of the vein wall, such as varicose veins. However, there are generally other contributory factors, such as sluggish circulation (stasis) or an alteration in the composition of the blood, making it clot more readily. This is generally due to an increase in proteins of the coagulation system and/or a decrease in the protective antifibrinolytic system.

Deep vein thrombosis is most likely to occur during periods of immobility, such as after an operation. Apart from the resulting venous stasis, there are changes in the blood during surgery which make a person less likely to bleed and more likely to clot. Similar changes occur during pregnancy, also increasing the risk of venous thrombosis.

It is increasingly recognized that some people inherit genes making them more susceptible to clotting. This tendency is known as thrombophilia and often explains why there is an increased incidence of clotting in some families, or why some pregnant women or some women taking the oral contraceptive develop thrombosis and others do not. The risk of venous thrombosis can be reduced by early mobilization after surgery and preventive treatment with anticoagulant drugs, such as heparin or warfarin.

SEE ALSO *Arteries, Atherosclerosis, Blood, Blood vessels, Capillaries, Cholesterol, Circulatory system, Gangrene, Hypertension, Myocardial infarction, Platelets, Pulmonary embolism, Stroke, Veins*

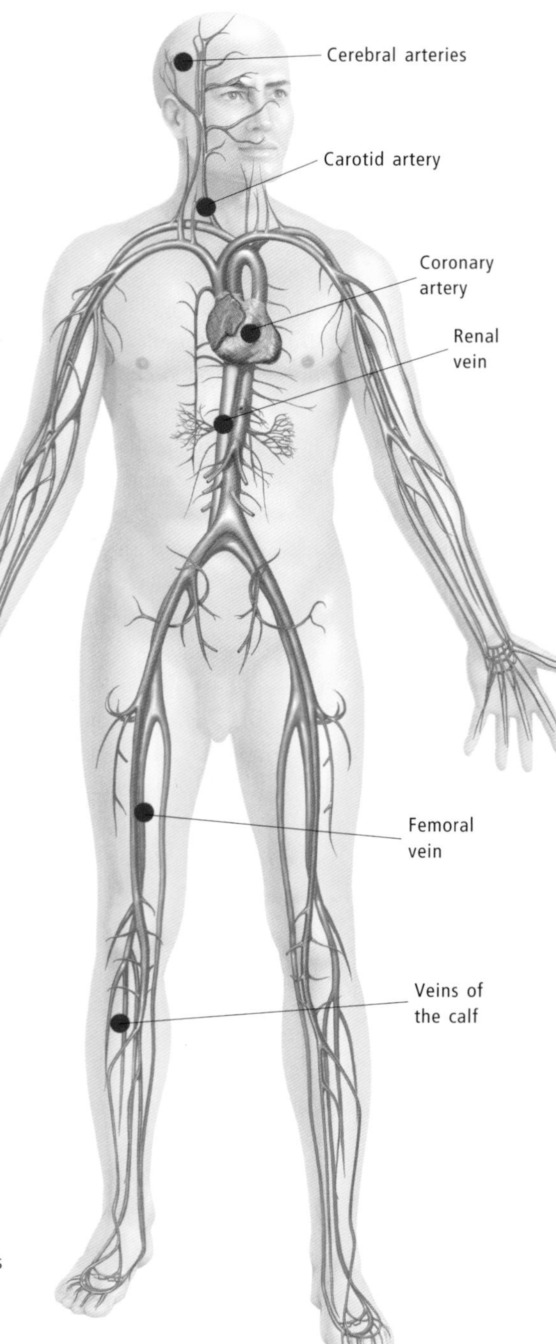

Thrombus sites

The most common sites of thrombus (blood clot) formation include the deep veins of the leg, the cerebral arteries (which may result in stroke), the renal veins and the arteries of the heart. In some cases the thrombus breaks free from its site of formation and becomes an embolus—a clot carried along in the bloodstream.

T

smoking and a serious injury. A thrombus that breaks away from the site where it formed is called an embolus.

SEE ALSO *Arteriosclerosis, Myocardial infarction, Stroke*

THUMBSUCKING

Many babies suck their thumbs while still in the uterus and can be born with blisters on the top lip, commonly referred to as sucking blisters. Although frowned upon in some societies, sucking the thumb (occasionally the fingers or some other part of the hand) is a comfort mechanism used by many babies and small children which is both emotionally comforting and physically harmless.

Children who continue to suck their thumbs into the school years, however, may be in need of emotional support or counseling, as such long-term sucking is often a replacement activity for some need. By this age the action of sucking may also damage the alignment of the teeth, a problem which can usually be rectified quite easily with orthodontic treatment if it does not right itself with time. The other result may be calluses on thumbs or fingers, but these too will disappear when the habit ceases. In most cases no treatment is needed.

SEE ALSO *Orthodontics, Teeth*

THYMUS GLAND

The thymus gland is found beneath the sternum, at about the level of the large vessels leaving the heart. It is much more obvious in children and adolescents, when it is active, than in adults, when it has shriveled to a fatty, fibrous remnant. At birth the thymus weighs about $^1/_2$ ounce (14 grams) and reaches about 1 ounce (28 grams) by puberty. In adults the gland reduces in weight again to only $^1/_2$ ounce (14 grams).

Although it is called a gland, the thymus is actually a lymph organ, producing T lymphocytes (a type of white blood cell) for distribution to the rest of the body. T lymphocytes are involved in the defense of the body against viruses and cancer cells, in delayed-type hypersensitivity reactions and in graft rejection.

If the thymus is removed from a newborn rat, other lymphoid organs in the body fail to develop and there is a decrease in the number of T lymphocytes in the blood. The animal is unable to make an adequate defense against viruses or to reject transplanted foreign tissue. Animals subsequently become weak, lose weight and die about 3–4 months after birth, due to widespread and overwhelming infections occurring throughout the body. Removal of the thymus in adults (sometimes advised for the treatment of the disease myasthenia gravis) does not have such serious effects because T lymphocytes have already been distributed throughout the body. In humans there are some diseases where T lymphocytes fail to develop. Children so affected will die soon after birth if untreated.

SEE ALSO *Lymphatic/Immune system, T cells*

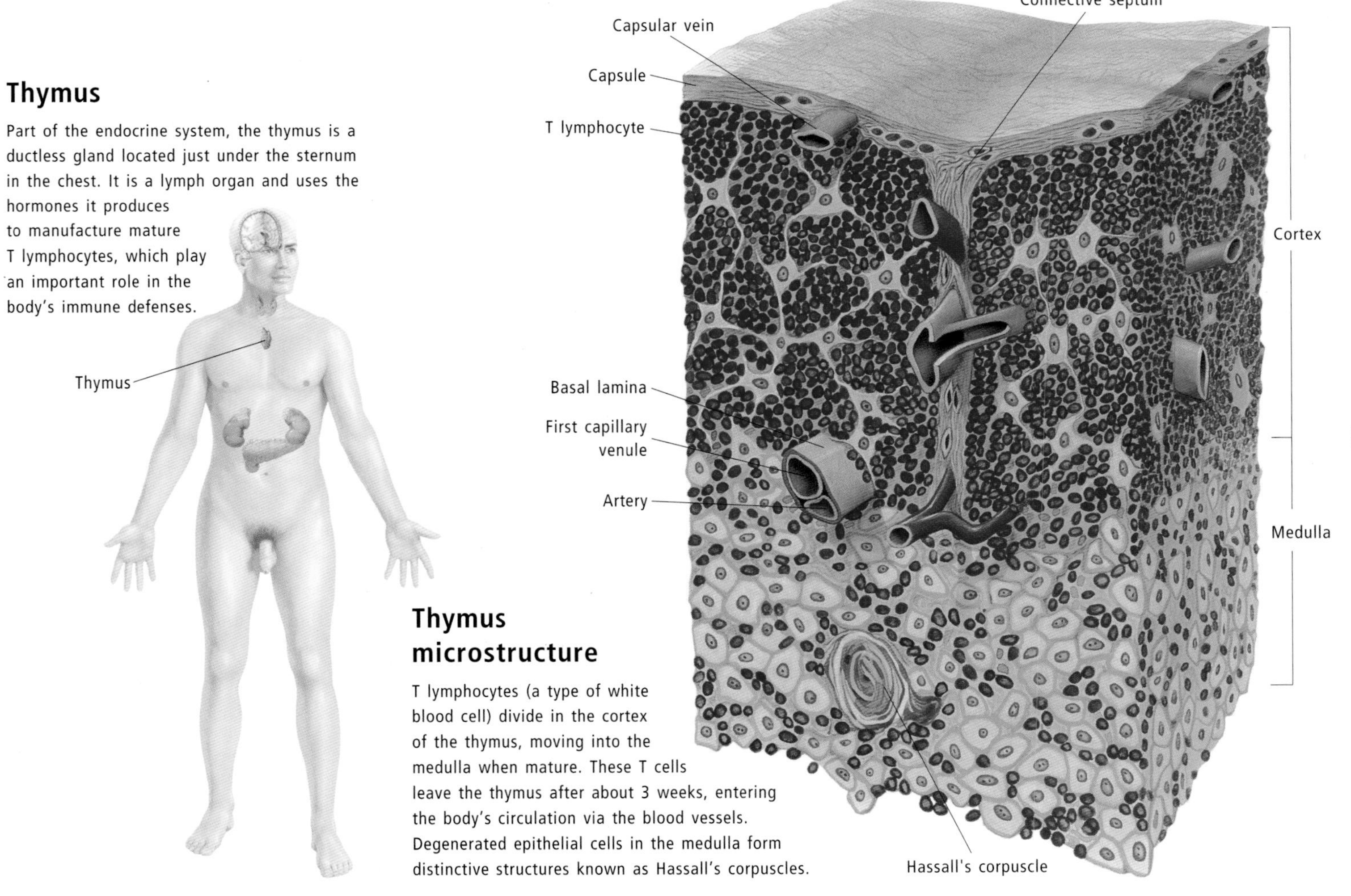

Thymus

Part of the endocrine system, the thymus is a ductless gland located just under the sternum in the chest. It is a lymph organ and uses the hormones it produces to manufacture mature T lymphocytes, which play an important role in the body's immune defenses.

Thymus microstructure

T lymphocytes (a type of white blood cell) divide in the cortex of the thymus, moving into the medulla when mature. These T cells leave the thymus after about 3 weeks, entering the body's circulation via the blood vessels. Degenerated epithelial cells in the medulla form distinctive structures known as Hassall's corpuscles.

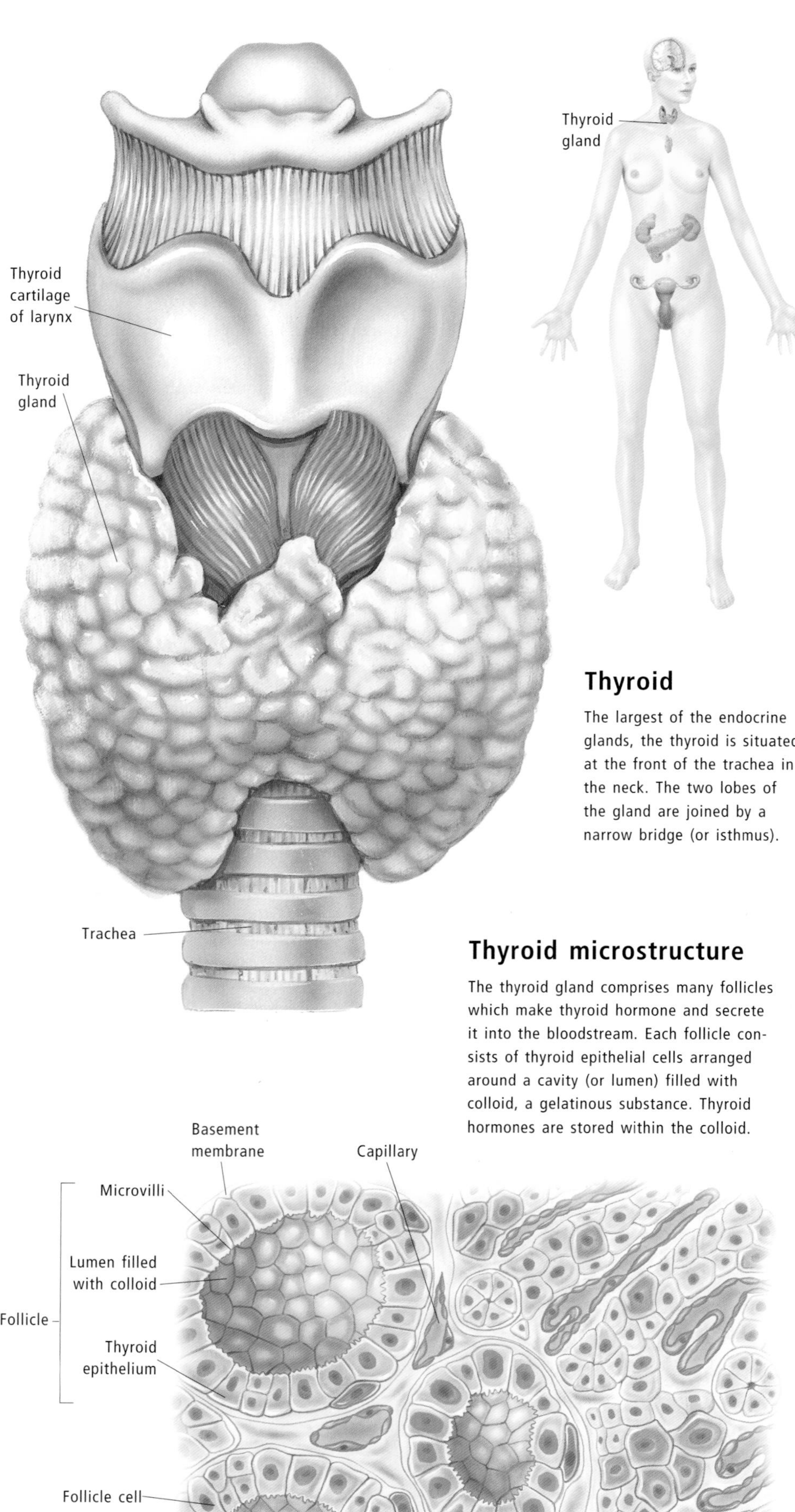

Thyroid

The largest of the endocrine glands, the thyroid is situated at the front of the trachea in the neck. The two lobes of the gland are joined by a narrow bridge (or isthmus).

Thyroid microstructure

The thyroid gland comprises many follicles which make thyroid hormone and secrete it into the bloodstream. Each follicle consists of thyroid epithelial cells arranged around a cavity (or lumen) filled with colloid, a gelatinous substance. Thyroid hormones are stored within the colloid.

THYROID GLAND

The thyroid gland is one of the endocrine glands, which secrete hormones directly into the bloodstream or body cavities. The thyroid gland consists of two lobes joined together in the midline by a narrow bridge or isthmus. It is located in the neck immediately below and in front of the voice box (larynx). The thyroid gland is very well supplied with blood by a series of arteries and lies in close proximity to several important nerves which supply the larynx. These nerves must be carefully identified and protected during surgery on the thyroid. Enlargement of the thyroid gland is known as a goiter. This may occur with either increased or decreased thyroid hormone production.

The thyroid gland is made up of many follicles, which are spherical or polygonal structures consisting of cells arranged around a cavity filled with a gelatinous substance called colloid.

The follicles of the thyroid gland make thyroid hormone and secrete it into the bloodstream. Thyroid hormone is composed of two different substances: thyroxine (also called T4, or tetraiodothyronine) and triiodothyronine (T3). Most thyroid hormone is made up of thyroxine. An essential component of both substances is iodine, found in the diet.

Thyroid hormone has several functions, the main one being to determine the metabolic rate of the body tissues, that is, how fast the tissues of the body will use up oxygen and produce waste materials. An excess of thyroid hormone will speed up metabolism and a deficiency will slow it down. Thyroid hormone is also necessary for the normal growth and development of children—too little thyroid hormone will produce short stature and mental retardation. The production of thyroid hormone is under the control of thyroid stimulating hormone (TSH), which is released from the pituitary gland. The presence of thyroid hormone in the bloodstream inhibits the production of TSH in a feedback loop control system. Between the thyroid follicles are parafollicular cells (C cells) which are responsible for the production and secretion of another hormone, calcitonin, which acts to reduce the concentration of calcium in the blood.

Diagnostic tests

Tests of the thyroid gland and its function include blood tests to determine the concentrations of thyroid hormone and thyroid-stimulating hormone in the blood, and isotope scans to determine the presence of "cold" or "hot" spots in the thyroid gland. Thyroid hormone concentration will be elevated in hyperthyroidism, while levels will be reduced in hypothyroidism or myxedema. Reduced levels of both TSH and thyroid hormone indicate a problem with the pituitary gland's production of TSH.

Diseases and disorders

Many diseases and disorders can affect the thyroid gland.

Hyperthyroidism

In hyperthyroidism (thyrotoxicosis), there is an increased level of thyroid hormone circulating in the blood. It may be due to a solitary hypersecretory thyroid nodule (Plummer's disease), a multinodular goiter with increased secretion, or excessive stimulation of the thyroid gland by factors circulating in the bloodstream, as seen in Graves' disease.

Patients experience symptoms reflecting the effects of excess circulating thyroid hormone, including nervousness, increased sweating, increased appetite, weight loss, muscular weakness, increased frequency of bowel movements, menstrual problems and intolerance to heat.

If blood levels of thyroid hormone reach dangerous heights during thyrotoxicosis, the patient may develop a condition known as thyroid storm. In this situation the patient will experience accentuated thyrotoxic symptoms, heart failure, grossly elevated fever and delirium.

Hyperthyroidism may be treated with the use of antithyroid drugs, radioactive iodine tablets, or surgery, depending on the patient's age, state of health and the size of the goiter.

Hypothyroidism

In hypothyroidism (also called myxedema) there is a reduced level of thyroid hormone in the blood. In this condition the patient will experience a puffy thickening of the skin below the eyes, and in the skin of the lips, fingers and legs. The patient will also complain of lethargy, the slowing of thought processes, weight gain and the loss of hair. Hypothyroidism in adults is most commonly seen in Hashimoto's disease and in endemic goiter, where iodine levels in the diet are low.

Graves' disease

Named after the Irish physician Robert James Graves, Graves' disease is the most common (though not the only) cause of hyperthyroidism (thyrotoxicosis). Also known as toxic diffuse goiter, it is an autoimmune disease, in which the body's own immune system attacks and inflames the thyroid gland. Antibodies to their own thyroid gland can be detected in the blood of people who have Graves' disease.

In this condition, the thyroid gland swells in size (develops into a goiter) and secretes excessive amounts of thyroid hormone into the bloodstream, causing thyrotoxicosis. The affected person experiences rapid heartbeat, tremor, increased sweating, weight loss (despite increased appetite), and weakness and fatigue.

A condition called exophthalmos often develops, in which the eyeballs protrude and the eyelids retract. This is caused by edema (fluid accumulation) in the tissues surrounding the eyeball in its socket. This eye protrusion usually responds to treatment of the excessive thyroid activity, but may cause loss of vision if not treated promptly.

Graves' disease is more common in women than in men and tends to run in families.

The condition is diagnosed by blood tests which show excess thyroid hormone in the blood, and a radioactive thyroid scan. There are several treatment options, including treatment with drugs such as propylthiouracil, and for severe cases the surgical removal of part of the thyroid gland, or oral administration of radioactive iodine.

Hashimoto's disease

Hashimoto's disease, also known as Hashimoto's thyroiditis or chronic lymphocytic thyroiditis, is a slowly developing persistent inflammation of the thyroid gland. Patients experience enlargement of the neck with pain and tenderness in the region of the thyroid. The enlargement of the thyroid gland may cause compression of the windpipe (trachea) and esophagus, resulting in difficulty in breathing and swallowing.

Like Graves' disease, it is an autoimmune disorder, affecting woman more often than men, and tends to run in families, but unlike Graves' disease, the inflammation may result in the undersecretion of thyroid hormone into the bloodstream, or hypothyroidism, the symptoms of which are intolerance to cold, weight gain, fatigue, constipation, joint stiffness and facial swelling.

Hashimoto's thyroiditis is often slow to develop, and is often associated with other autoimmune endocrine disorders such as diabetes mellitus or Addison's disease. High levels of thyroid autoantibodies are almost always present. Diagnosis can be made by a needle biopsy of the thyroid gland, with subsequent examination with a microscope.

Treatment may involve surgery to remove excess thyroid tissue which is compressing nearby structures. In mild cases, there may be no treatment required. Replacement therapy with thyroid hormone will be needed if there is hypothyroidism. In some patients, however, replacement therapy is associated with progression of the goiter.

Because Hashimoto's disease is slow to progress and often remains stable for many years, prospects for recovery are usually good.

Cretinism

Thyroid hormone is essential for brain development, and iodine is necessary for synthesis of thyroid hormone. In areas of the world where dietary iodine is inadequate, the fetus and neonate may not make sufficient thyroid hormone for normal brain maturation. In this condition, known as cretinism, the child will be intellectually disabled and have stunted growth. The face will be broad, emergence of the teeth will be delayed, and the tongue and mouth will be large. Parts of the world where this may occur are usually mountainous. Fortunately, supplementation of the diet with small amounts of iodine can completely prevent the problem.

Cretinism may also arise in children with congenital absence of the thyroid gland or in those who have a genetic defect in the enzymes that make thyroid hormone. In these children the condition may be remedied by thyroid hormone supplementation. Early diagnosis and treatment are essential.

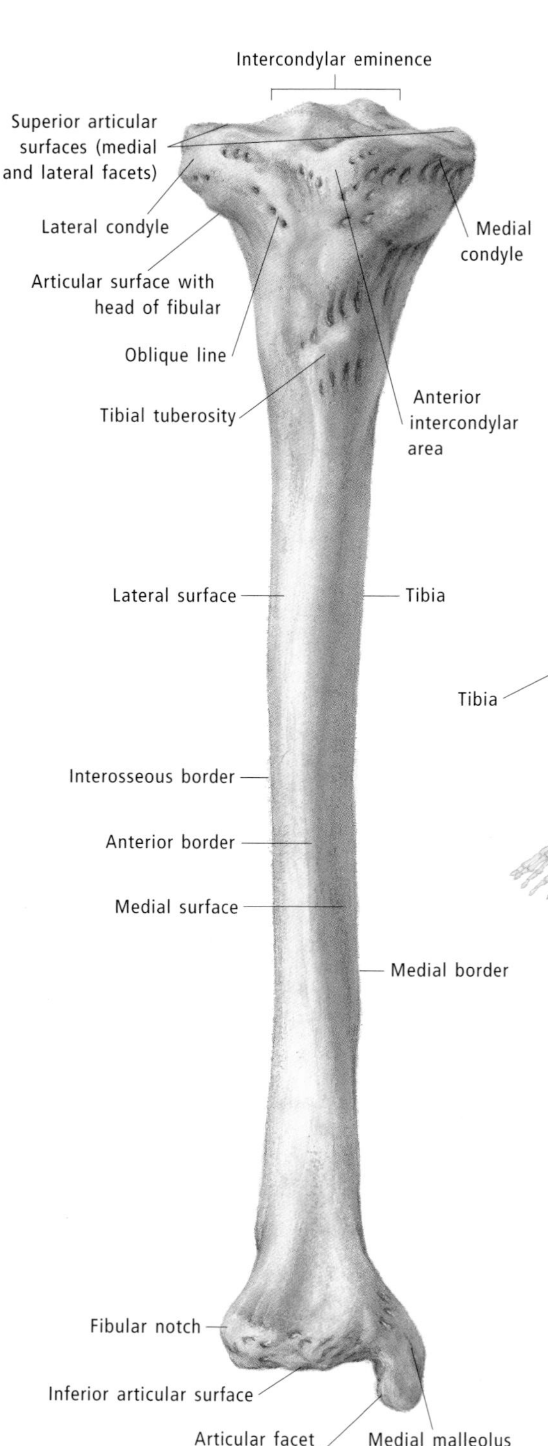

Tibia

The tibia or "shinbone" is the second-longest bone in the body. Joining with the femur, it helps form the knee joint, and combines with the fibula and the talus to form the ankle joint.

Tibia

Cancer

Cancers may arise from the thyroid gland, and are more common if there has been irradiation of the head and neck earlier in life. Thyroid cancers are of several different types. Those found in young patients (papillary adenocarcinoma) are usually slow-growing and spread outside the gland relatively late in the course of the disease. There are good survival rates for these tumors (over 80 percent after 10 years).

At the other extreme are the so-called undifferentiated thyroid cancers, which usually appear later in life and invade surrounding tissue in an aggressive manner. Survival rates with this kind of cancer are quite low (10–15 percent after 10 years). Patients with thyroid cancers complain of a painless lump in the neck, which gradually increases in size. They may also experience difficulty in swallowing and hoarseness of the voice, particularly if the nerves to the larynx have been damaged. Treatment is by surgery to remove the tumor and any involved lymph nodes, accompanied by radioactive iodine therapy. Aggressive tumors may need to be treated with chemotherapeutic agents. Tumors from the kidney, breast and lung sometimes spread to the thyroid gland, but they usually produce multiple lumps rather than one.

SEE ALSO *Cretinism, Endocrine glands, Glands, Goiter, Graves' disease, Hashimoto's disease, Hyperthyroidism, Hypothyroidism, Myxedema, Pituitary gland, Thyrotoxicosis*

THYROTOXICOSIS

Thyrotoxicosis or hyperthyroidism is caused by increased secretion of thyroid hormone into the bloodstream from the thyroid gland. The increased activity of the thyroid gland may be the result of an enlarged and hyperactive gland arising on its own, or to stimulation of the thyroid gland by antibodies in autoimmune disease (Graves' disease).

Patients complain of symptoms such as nervousness, weight loss with increased appetite, increased sweating, increased bowel movements, menstrual problems, rapid heart rate and a swelling in the neck (goiter).

In severe cases the condition may result in collapse and, if untreated, death—a condition sometimes called "thyroid storm".

Treatment is with drugs such as propylthiouracil, which block the production of thyroid hormone by the thyroid gland. Alternatives are the oral administration of radioactive iodine, which is taken up by the thyroid and destroys the gland's hormone-producing cells, or surgical removal of part of the gland.

SEE ALSO *Goiter, Graves' disease, Hyperthyroidism, Thyroid gland*

TIBIA

The tibia, or shin bone, is the inner and thicker of the two bones of the lower leg, the other being the fibula. It is also the second longest bone in the body, after the thighbone (femur). At its upper end, the tibia meets the femur to form the knee joint. At its lower end it meets with the fibula and a small bone called the talus to form the ankle joint. The small bump felt protruding on the inside of the ankle is part of the tibia that articulates with the talus. It is known as the medial malleolus. Pain along the tibia is often caused by shin splints (strain of the long flexor muscles of the toes).

A fracture of the tibia is a common injury, especially in childhood. It is usually caused by a direct blow to the child's leg, most often during a contact sport. In adults it may occur after weakening of the bone from repeated stress during jogging running or walking.

After the injury, there is severe pain in the leg at the fracture site, swelling of the tissue surrounding the fracture and, if the fracture is complete (that is, broken all the way through), the leg is deformed.

The fracture must be set under general anesthesia in hospital. X-rays of the tibia will confirm that the ends of the bone have been correctly aligned. The bone is held in place with a cast which extends above the knee and below the ankle. Healing usually takes 6–8 weeks. Then physical therapy is needed to restore muscle strength and eliminate stiffness in the ankle and knee.

SEE ALSO *Ankle, Femur, Fibula, Fractures, Knee, Leg, Shin splints*

T

TIC

A tic is the involuntary production of a movement or sound that occurs suddenly, rapidly, without conscious control, and may recur many times within a short period.

Movements are generally purposeless and may take the form of throat clearing, squinting, facial spasms, shrugs or jerks of the neck. More complex actions such as jumping or hopping are also tics. Vocal tics can involve repeated uttering of obscenities or generally unacceptable words, or of meaningless sounds.

Tics may be more frequent under stress or anxiety. They can be linked to emotional disturbance, obsessive behavior or developmental delays. Tics can range from mild to severe, and the affliction can be brief or long-lasting. Children, boys more than girls, often suffer transient tics which generally disappear without treatment. If the tics persist, the possibility of Tourette's syndrome must be considered.

Obsessive-compulsive disorder may produce behaviors similar to tics which are not classified as tics because they involve purposeful and conscious repetition; tics are purposeless and not the product of any identifiable abnormality.

SEE ALSO *Neuralgia, Obsessive-compulsive disorder, Tourette's syndrome*

TIC DOULOUREUX

Tic douloureux, or trigeminal neuralgia, is a disease of the trigeminal nerve, the principal sensory nerve in the face. The condition is marked by flashes of excruciating pain, which can be set off by touching a sensitive area of the face or by movements of the jaw. It can occur many times in a day and is usually felt in the cheek near the nose or above the temporomandibular joint.

This disorder is sometimes associated with compression of a nerve by an artery, and may be relieved by surgery, but generally the cause is unknown.

Normal pain relief does not work because of the spasmodic nature of the attacks, although antidepressant drugs may sometimes give temporary pain relief. Surgical destruction of the nerves is a possible treatment as a last resort.

SEE ALSO *Neuralgia*

TICKS

Ticks are small eight-legged arachnids related to mites and spiders. They feed by attaching themselves to the skin of humans and animals and sucking their blood. Although some people may experience a reaction to a tick, serious disease arises not so much from the tick itself but from diseases it transmits. Ticks can be the source of several diseases, including Lyme disease, Rocky Mountain spotted fever and Colorado tick fever.

Lyme disease is also known as Lyme arthritis. It is caused by the bacterium *Borrelia burgdorferi* and is transmitted by the bite of ticks carried on the bodies of animals, especially deer, field mice and other small rodents. It causes lethargy, muscle weakness, loss of coordination, and paralysis, which may affect the respiratory muscles. If diagnosed and treated early with antibiotics, the condition is usually curable.

Rocky Mountain spotted fever is caused by infection with microscopic parasites known as rickettsiae. Symptoms include a spotted rash, fever, muscle and joint pain, as well as nausea, vomiting and hallucinations. Treatment is with antibiotics. If left untreated, the disease can lead to heart failure, kidney failure, or death.

Colorado tick fever is a viral infection causing a flu-like illness, severe headache, sensitivity to light, and a rash. The symptoms last for about a week, and return after a few days of remission. Treatment is with rest, fluids and painkillers.

In tick-infested areas, it is best to wear protective clothing and use an insect repellent containing DEET (diethyltoluamide). To remove an attached tick, grasp it behind its head as close to the skin as possible, using fine-point tweezers or a tick remover. Gently pull the tick out sideways with a sharp twisting action. Hands should be washed with hot, soapy water, and the tweezers and bite disinfected. Do not attempt to kill the tick with alcohol, petroleum jelly, methylated spirits or any other substance as this causes the tick to inject more bacteria and toxins. Mass infestations of tiny (larval stage) ticks are best removed by soaking for 20 minutes in a deep, warm bath with one cup of bicarbonate of soda added.

SEE ALSO *Lyme disease, Rocky Mountain spotted fever*

TINEA

Tinea is a fungal infection caused by various species of either *Trichophyton* or *Microsporum*, which can grow on the skin, in the hair or the nails, creating visible signs such as dry, scaly, red or cracked skin, but no permanent damage. Ringworm, an infection of the skin causing reddish circular marks, is caused by a tinea fungus—despite the name, no worm is involved.

Tinea has become increasingly common in recent times because the spores can survive for long periods in flaked-off skin cells, which may be picked up on the bare feet from floor coverings. This is an easy method of transporting infection between users of hotel rooms and sports clubs, and between residents in private homes.

Tinea grows fast in warm moist areas of the body, particularly in skin folds. The skin rash is quite characteristic, appearing as a slightly raised patch with sharp borders, which, as it expands and spreads, leaves a dry or scaly clearing in the center. Between the toes it may cause painful itchy cracks in the skin and a characteristic unpleasant smell. Effects can vary from redness to blisters, which can become sites of secondary bacterial infection, particularly if blood circulation is poor.

Tinea infections are named after the part of the body where they are found and are as follows.

Tinea capitis affects the scalp, creating itchy red areas and hair loss.

Tinea corporis is tinea found on any part of the trunk, arms or legs, particularly in skin folds, where it will create red spots which spread as the fungus grows.

Tinea cruris, also called jock itch, is tinea in the groin. It affects men more than women and is often associated with wearing groin protectors.

Tinea pedis, or athlete's foot, is probably the most common form of this fungal infection, and usually presents as a patch of white scaly skin under the little toe; it may not be evident elsewhere.

Tinea unguium infects toenails and fingernails (onychomycosis), appearing as white or powdery patches, thickening the nail or causing it to fall off.

Tinea versicolor, an infection caused by the yeast *Pityrosporum orbiculare,* changes the color of skin and prevents tanning. People with dark skin may develop light patches, and those with light skin dark patches. There may be scaliness and irritation, but usually there is no pain or itching. Treatment is with antidandruff (selenium) shampoos, which may cause skin irritation. Pigmentation takes some time to return after clearing the infection, which may recur whenever conditions are favorable.

In most cases, tinea is easily recognizable by the physician. If there is doubt, a skin lesion biopsy (most commonly, scraping of the skin) can be performed followed by microscopic examination or culture, which shows the fungus responsible.

Most tinea infections are mild and can be treated with antifungal creams or powders, such as those that contain miconazole or clotrimazole. In some cases, topical corticosteroids may be added as well. In cases of severe or chronic infection, oral antifungal medications containing ketoconazole or sulconazole or another antifungal agent may be needed. Antibiotics may be needed to treat secondary bacterial infections. The condition may take up to 4–6 weeks to completely clear.

As the fungal spores are so hardy, it is important to eradicate them from shoes, socks and floor surfaces to avoid continual reinfection. Preventive measures are to ensure feet and toes are completely dry before dressing, to go without shoes and socks when indoors, to avoid skin contact with areas in common use at pools or gyms and to clean home floor coverings; it may also be wise to throw away shoes that have been worn for some time.

SEE ALSO *Antifungals, Ringworm*

Tinea sites

Tinea is a fungal infection of the skin, especially in warm moist areas of the body, such as between the toes and in the groin area.

Tinea

Ringworm

A popular name for tinea, ringworm is a fungal infection of the skin and is not caused by a worm.

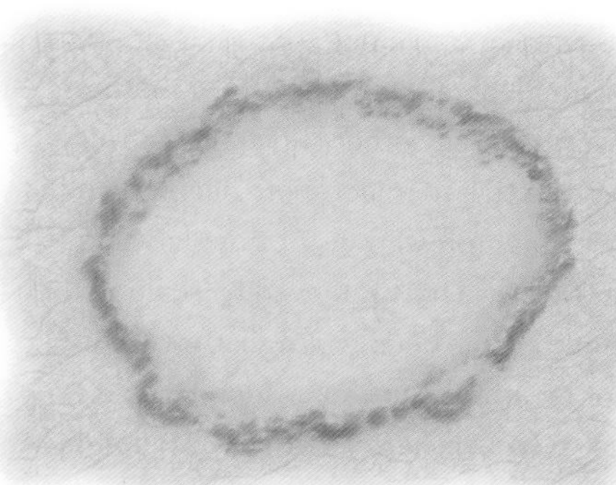

TINNITUS

Tinnitus is the sensation of hearing a sound in one or both ears when there is no external noise from the environment. The sound may be a buzzing or ringing, a high pitched hiss or whine, or more complex sounds, and may be continuous or intermittent.

Tinnitus is a symptom of a number of possible conditions. It is generally associated with ear damage from exposure to loud noise, or with age-related hearing loss, and can also follow a middle ear infection. A rushing noise may indicate vascular problems. Certain drugs, after long periods of use, can affect the inner ear.

Tinnitus can also be caused by tumors on, or injury to, the vestibulocochlear nerve; problems with the temporomandibular joint; otosclerosis, a stiffening of the bones (ossicles) of the middle ear; head and neck injury; and Menière's disease. Sometimes tinnitus may arise with no identifiable cause. It may be so severe as to interfere with concentration or sleep.

There is no cure, but to prevent the condition worsening, loud noise and drug use should be avoided. The noise can sometimes be masked by "filling silence" with more pleasant sounds such as a radio or softly ticking clock; users of hearing aids often report that this makes the tinnitus less intrusive. Some people find that the symptoms are worse when they are anxious or stessed.

There are a number of alternative therapies that may help to alleviate the symptoms of tinnitus. Herbalism practitioners prescribe ginkgo biloba, a stimulant for peripheral circulation, or black cohosh, an antispasmodic of the small blood vessels. Homeopathy suggests a number of specific remedies to treat various noises in the ear.

Hypnotherapists aim to either remove ringing in the ear or to lessen the patient's awareness of and reactions to the tinnitus if the sounds cannot be eliminated. Naturopathy suggests vitamin B complex, calcium, magnesium and potassium supplements. Traditional Chinese Medicine views an imbalance of the kidney energy as one possible cause of tinnitus. Acupuncture and Chinese herbs may bring relief in some cases.

SEE ALSO *Ear, Hearing, Menière's disease, Otosclerosis*

TISSUE

A tissue is a group or layer of cells of a similar kind, plus the material packaged between them, all of which function together for the same specialized purpose. There are four major types of tissue in the human body: epithelial, connective, muscular and nervous.

Epithelial tissue

Epithelial tissue, also known simply as epithelium, is made up of cells that are packaged so closely together there is virtually no room between them for any extra material. The cells are also arranged in continuous sheets in either single or multiple layers. Epithelial tissue has a wide range of roles including protection, excretion, absorption, sensory reception, secretion and reproduction. Compared to other tissue types, it is often exposed to a high degree of wear but has the capacity to renew itself relatively efficiently and quickly. Epithelium has a nerve supply but no direct blood supply. Vessels in neighboring tissue provide nutrients and carry out the removal of wastes.

Epithelial tissue is classified broadly into two main types. Glandular epithelium has a secretory function and forms both exocrine and endocrine glands. The second type, covering and lining epithelium, is more widespread. It forms the outermost layer of the skin and of some internal organs. It also lines the digestive, respiratory, reproductive and urinary systems as well as ducts, blood vessels and body cavities. Covering and lining epithelial tissue comes in either single or multiple layers and contains one of a number of different cell types, depending on the specific function of the tissue.

For example, simple squamous epithelium is a thin single-layered film that lines the air sacs of the lungs and allows for the diffusion of respiratory gases (oxygen and carbon dioxide) across its surface. In contrast, stratified squamous epithelium, which has a predominantly protective role, is a multi-layered variation which covers the tongue and forms tough moist surfaces such as the linings of the vagina, esophagus and mouth.

Connective tissue

Connective tissue is widespread in the body. The principal roles of connective tissue are to bind, support or strengthen organs or other tissues. It also functions inside the body to divide and compartmentalize other tissues and organ structures.

Structurally, connective tissue consists of cells linked together and supported by a matrix composed of protein fibers in a medium known as "ground substance". The ground substance can be in fluid, gel or solid form and is normally secreted by the cells of the connective tissue. The protein fibers come in three forms—collagen, elastin and reticular fibers—the proportions of which vary depending on the function of the tissue in which they are found. Each, however, provides support and strength along with flexibility. The molecules that form the protein fibers and ground substance are secreted by specialized connective tissue cells.

Other cells commonly found in connective tissue include disease-fighting macrophages, antibody-secreting plasma cells and mast cells, which produce histamine to stimulate the dilation of blood vessels at inflammation sites.

Humans have five main types of connective tissue: loose connective tissue, dense connective tissue, cartilage, bone and blood. Loose connective tissue includes adipose tissue, which is specialized for fat storage. One type of dense connective tissue, known as dense regular connective tissue, forms tendons and cartilage. Another, elastic connective tissue, is specialized for stretching and is found in the lungs, some artery walls and the vocal cords.

Cartilage comes in three forms: hyaline, fibrocartilage and elastic cartilage. Hyaline cartilage is the weakest and most abundant cartilage in the body. It covers the bones where they form synovial joints. Fibrocartilage forms a component of some other joints, which usually have a limited range of movement. Elastic cartilage is the hard material which can be felt in the external ear.

Muscle tissue

Muscle tissue accounts for up to 50 percent of total body weight in a healthy person, and comprises cells that are purpose-built for contraction. Muscle tissue equips the body for movement, helps transport substances around the body and produces as much as 85 percent of body heat. Through sustained contractions, muscle tissue also helps stabilize the body's posture and regulates the volume of internal organs such as the bladder.

There are three main forms of muscle tissue: skeletal, cardiac and smooth. The muscle fibers, or myofibers, of skeletal muscle are long, cylindrical, arranged parallel to each other and have a striped appearance under the microscope. This is the sort of muscle tissue that produces movements inside the limbs. It is usually attached to bones and is termed voluntary because one normally has conscious control over it.

Cardiac muscle cells are similar in that they too have a striped appearance. They are, however, branched and operate outside of conscious control. For this reason, cardiac muscle is known as involuntary. This is the muscle found in the heart; it cannot regenerate after being destroyed.

Smooth muscle tissue is also involuntary but it has no striations. This is the type of muscle found in the walls of blood vessels, in airways and inside the eye. Compared to the other muscle tissue types, it has reasonably good powers of regeneration.

Nervous tissue

Nervous tissue functions to sense changes both inside and outside the body, to analyze and interpret these sensory stimuli and to initiate a response. Nervous tissue forms the nervous system, which comprises the central nervous system (CNS) and the peripheral nervous system (PNS). The CNS includes the brain and spinal cord and is responsible for sorting and responding to stimuli, generating thoughts and emotions and forming and storing memories. All other nervous tissue in the body is included in the PNS, which collects sensory stimuli and transports it into the CNS, and then transports messages controlling the body's response out to the muscles, glands and sense organs.

Nervous tissue is composed of two main types of cells: neuroglia and neurons. Impulses travel around the body via the neurons. The glial cells, which are usually smaller and far more abundant, provide support and protection for the neurons. Types of neuroglia include astrocytes, oligodendrocytes, Schwann cells, microglia, ependymal cells and satellite cells. The glial cells function to maintain the proper biochemical environment required by neurons, fight invading microbes and produce material that physically supports and protects the neurons.

It is thought that, from about the age of 6 months, most human neurons lose the ability to reproduce themselves. As a result, when a neuron is destroyed completely it cannot be replaced. Some types of damage can, however, be repaired. Under certain conditions, nerve fibers in the PNS can regenerate after injury—but not in the case of the brain or the spinal cord. Damage to nervous tissue in these locations usually has some sort of permanent impact.

SEE ALSO *Cells, Collagen, Connective tissue, Muscle, Nervous system, Neurons*

Loose connective tissue

Lymphatic tissue

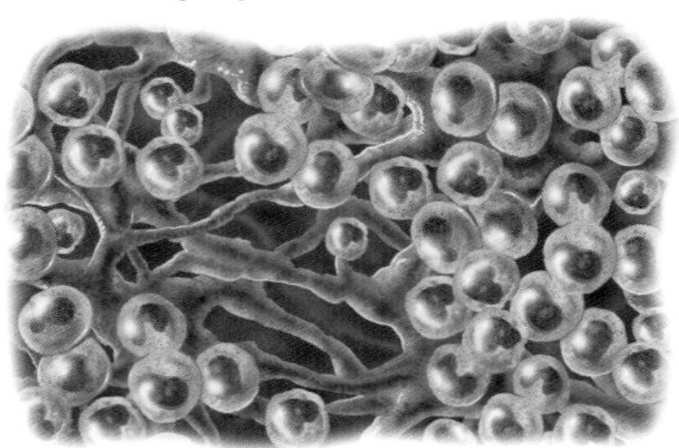

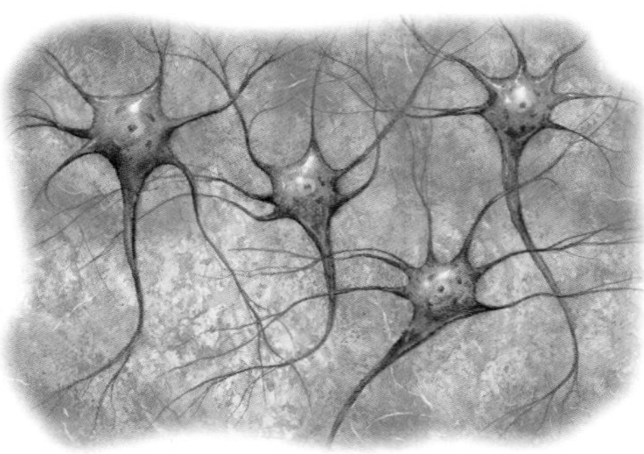

Neural tissue

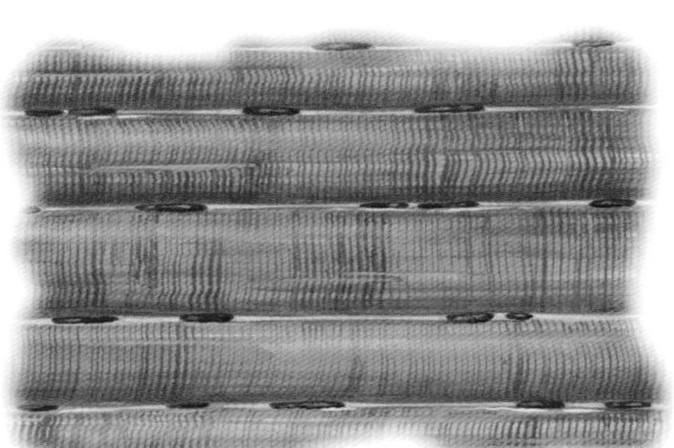

Skeletal muscle

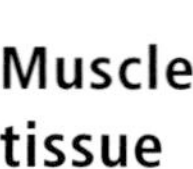

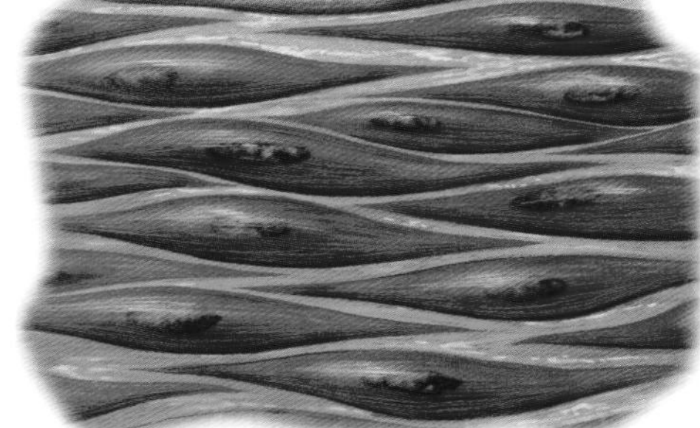

Smooth muscle

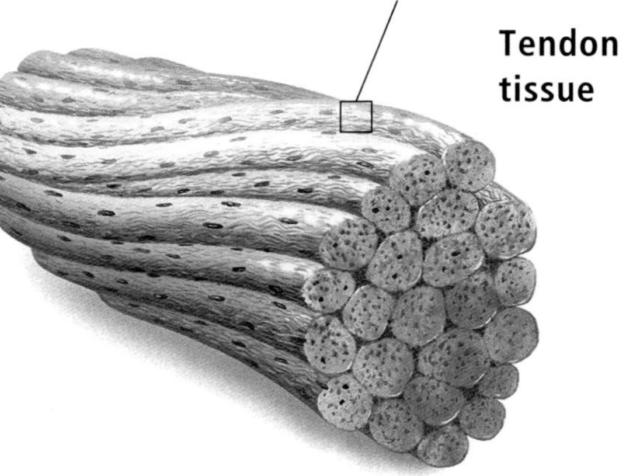

Tendon tissue

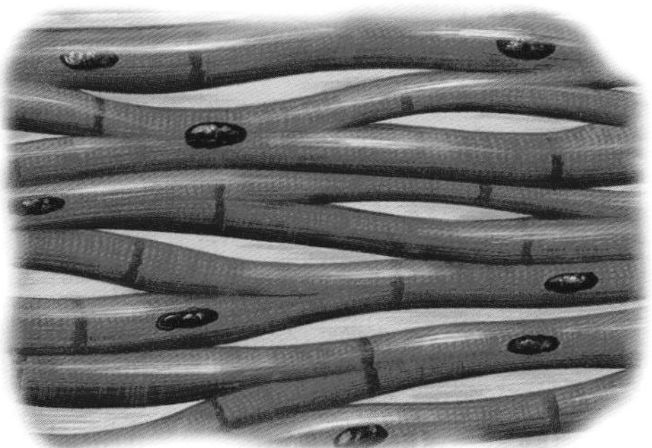

Cardiac muscle

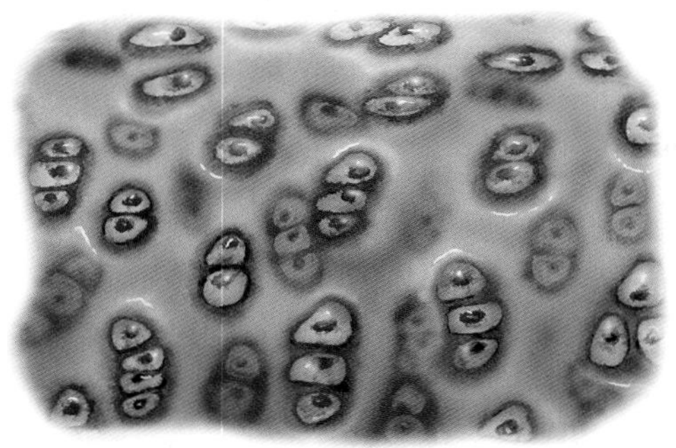

Hyaline cartilage

Fibrocartilage

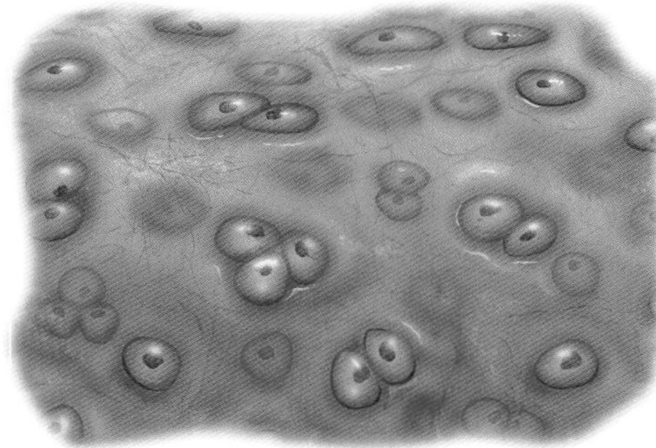

Elastic cartilage

Cartilage tissue

Tissue

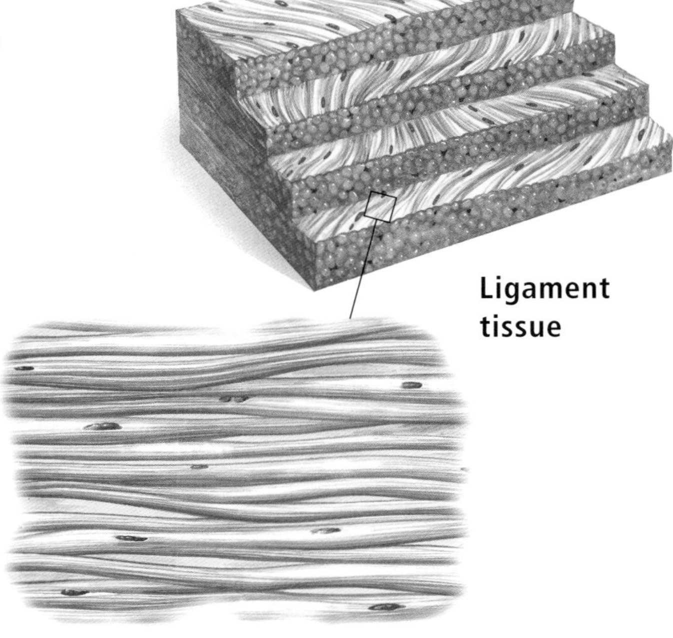

Ligament tissue

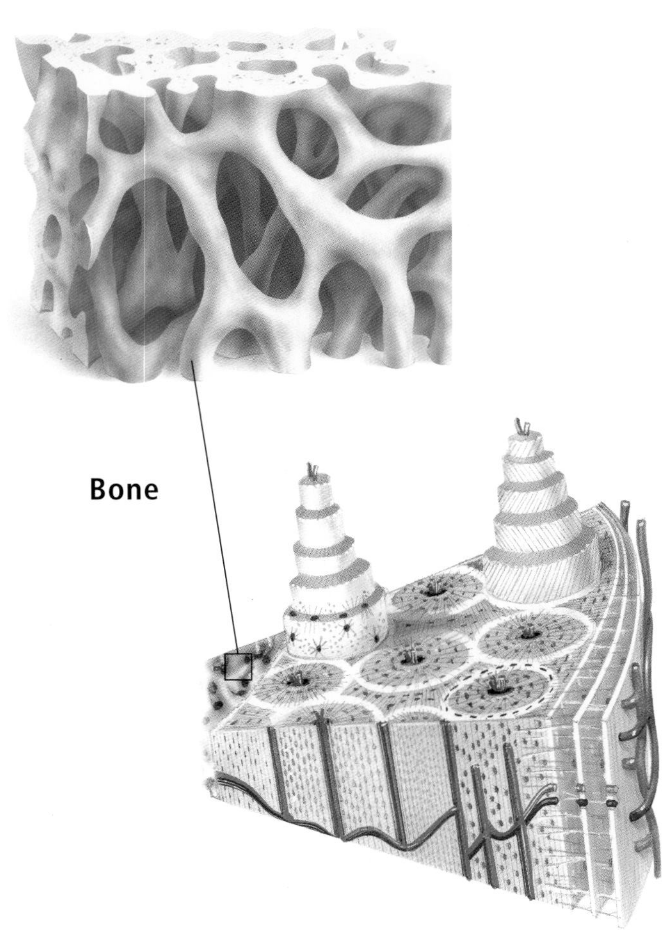

Bone

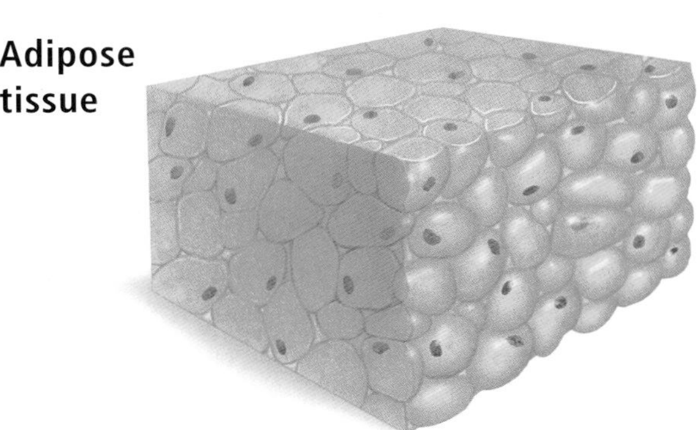

Adipose tissue

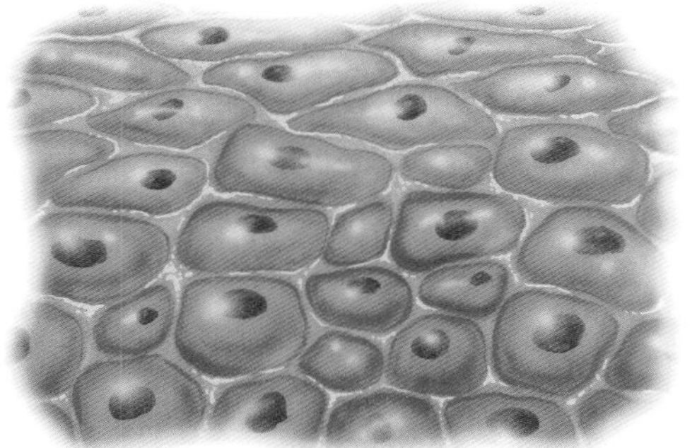

Epithelial tissue

TOILET TRAINING

There is no specific age when a child is ready to use a toilet. Up until the age of 15 months a child does not have the muscle control necessary to hold in the contents of the bladder or bowel until an appropriate moment. Emotional readiness is also an important element of toilet training; this sometimes does not develop until the end of the third year. Once children are aware of their bodily functions and of what society expects of them, by observing others, they will usually begin to use a toilet without much "training". Emotional stress or distress, anxiety over performance and fear of failure can all hinder the process.

It is advisable for parents to let children take their time in learning to use a toilet and to allow the child to proceed gradually at their own pace. In some societies a "potty" (chamberpot) is introduced before the toilet; children will usually progress naturally from this to a toilet before they reach school age. It is very important that children are also taught the importance of hygiene when they empty their bladder or bowels.

SEE ALSO *Bed-wetting*

TONGUE

The tongue is a muscular and sensory organ that is attached to the floor of the mouth. It has a dorsum or upper surface, a base attached to the floor of the mouth, a soft lower surface and a tip.

Structure and function

The tongue plays an important role in tasting, chewing and swallowing food, and in speech. Taste is sensed through the many taste receptors (taste buds) that are located on the dorsum of the tongue. The tongue's role during chewing is to move food around the mouth, pushing partially chewed food into position between the back teeth (molars). In swallowing, the tongue helps form a ball or bolus of food, which is gripped between the back of the tongue and the soft palate and squeezed backwards into the oropharynx.

During speech, the tongue makes contact with other structures in the mouth to help form consonants. Some consonants are formed by the tongue meeting the teeth (dental consonants like d, t), the soft palate (glottal consonants like g, k) or the hard palate (palatal consonants like n).

The dorsum of the tongue is studded with small projections called papillae, which come in three types. Filiform papillae are tiny cone-shaped elevations, which do not contain taste buds. Their role is to grip food and they are particularly well-developed in animals like cats which groom their fur with the tongue. Fungiform papillae are mushroom-shaped projections. They are less numerous than the filiform papillae, often contain taste buds and have a red appearance.

About two-thirds of the way back from the tongue's tip lies a V-shaped group of 7–12 vallate (also called circumvallae) papillae. These papillae have a central elevation, which is surrounded by a deep groove, much like a moat surrounding a castle. Taste buds located in the walls of the moat are continuously bathed in fluid, which clears food from the taste buds so that new taste stimuli can be tested. Other taste buds are located in nearby regions such as the palate, epiglottis and pharynx.

The pharyngeal part of the tongue behind the vallate papillae contains a lymphoid organ called the lingual tonsil. The lingual tonsil is involved in defending the body from microorganisms entering by the mouth.

The bulk of the tongue is made up of muscle, which can be divided into two main groups. The first group is called the intrinsic tongue muscles. They lie within the tongue itself and are responsible for changing its shape. Their fibers are arranged in three directions: vertical, longitudinal and horizontal. When vertical fibers contract they make the tongue thinner. When longitudinal fibers, which run the length of the tongue, contract, they make the tongue shorter. Horizontal fibers make the tongue narrower when they contract. Some people have a genetically determined ability to curl the tongue either upwards or downwards by controlling different groups of horizontal fibers separately.

Extrinsic tongue muscles, attached to the jaw, skull, palate and hyoid bones, are responsible for changing the position of the tongue. The hyoid bone is a small bone in the neck immediately below the jaw, which protects the airway from being crushed. The extrinsic muscles can move the tongue forward (genioglossus muscle), backward (styloglossus muscle), upward (palatoglossus muscle) and downward (hyoglossus muscle). Most of the tongue muscles are supplied by the hypoglossal nerve, which is one of the cranial nerves relaying messages to the brain.

The underside of the tongue is soft and kept very moist by salivary gland secretions. Beneath the tongue lie the openings of the ducts from the sublingual and submandibular salivary glands. The sublingual glands raise a ridge on the floor of the mouth on each side of the tongue's base. There is a midline ridge on the lower surface of the tongue called the frenulum. On each side of this ridge lie paired deep veins of the tongue, which are visible through the thin surface layer.

Diseases and disorders

Cancer of the tongue usually occurs in men aged between 40 and 80. It is often associated with heavy smoking, heavy drinking and poor oral hygiene. Most tongue cancers develop in the front two-thirds, particularly on the lateral border adjacent to the teeth. Tumors of the tongue often invade the floor of the mouth and may have spread to lymph nodes of the neck by the time diagnosis is made. The best form of treatment is surgical removal, including the removal of lymph nodes, and irradiation to kill cancer cells which may have spread to other neck structures. The chances of survival depend on the site of the cancer and whether spread to lymph nodes has occurred.

Those patients with cancers on the tip of the tongue have excellent rates of survival (greater than 80 percent after 5 years), while patients with cancers that have spread to the neck lymph nodes by the time of diagnosis have a very poor prognosis (less than 20 percent survive after 5 years).

Inflammation of the tongue (glossitis) may be due to many different causes. The tongue may be involved in oral yeast infections (oral thrush or candidiasis). In individuals who smoke and drink alcohol to excess, there may be degeneration of the tissues of the mouth, including the tongue, which may appear as flat white patches

Tongue—cross-section

The tongue is a muscular organ which is used in chewing, swallowing and speech. Taste buds are located in the papillae, which are projections on the upper surface of the tongue.

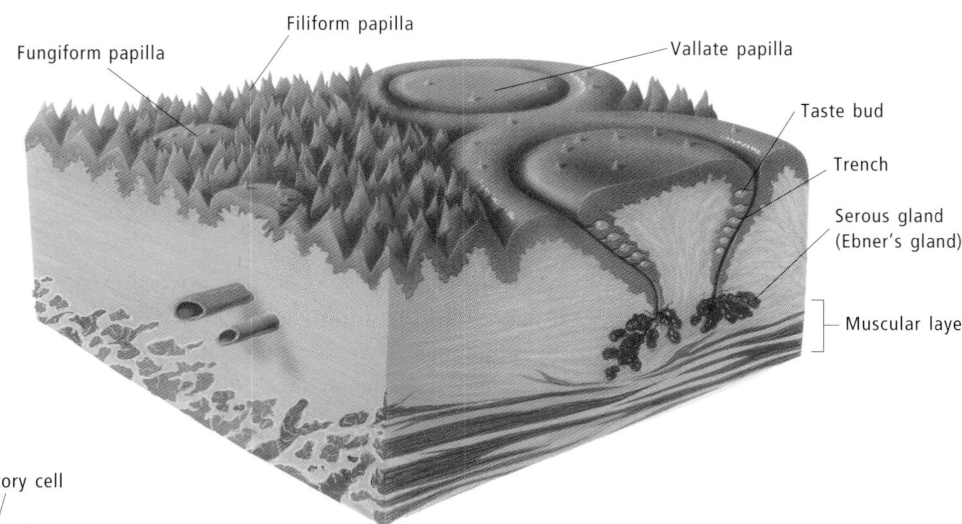

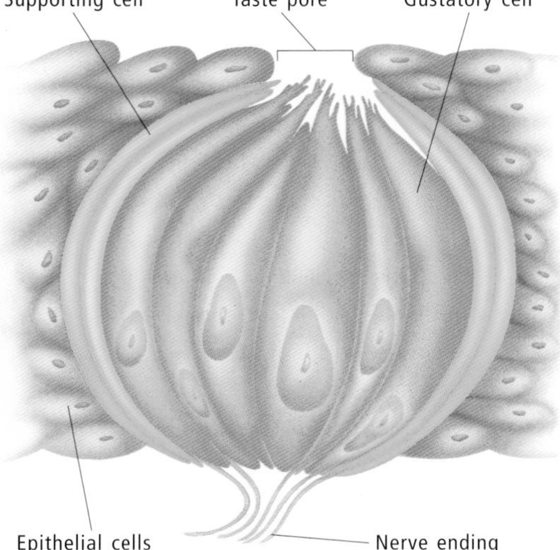

Tongue—taste

Taste buds are packed together in groups at various places on the tongue. These bundles of slender cells with hair-like branches are sensitive to sweet, salty, bitter and sour flavors.

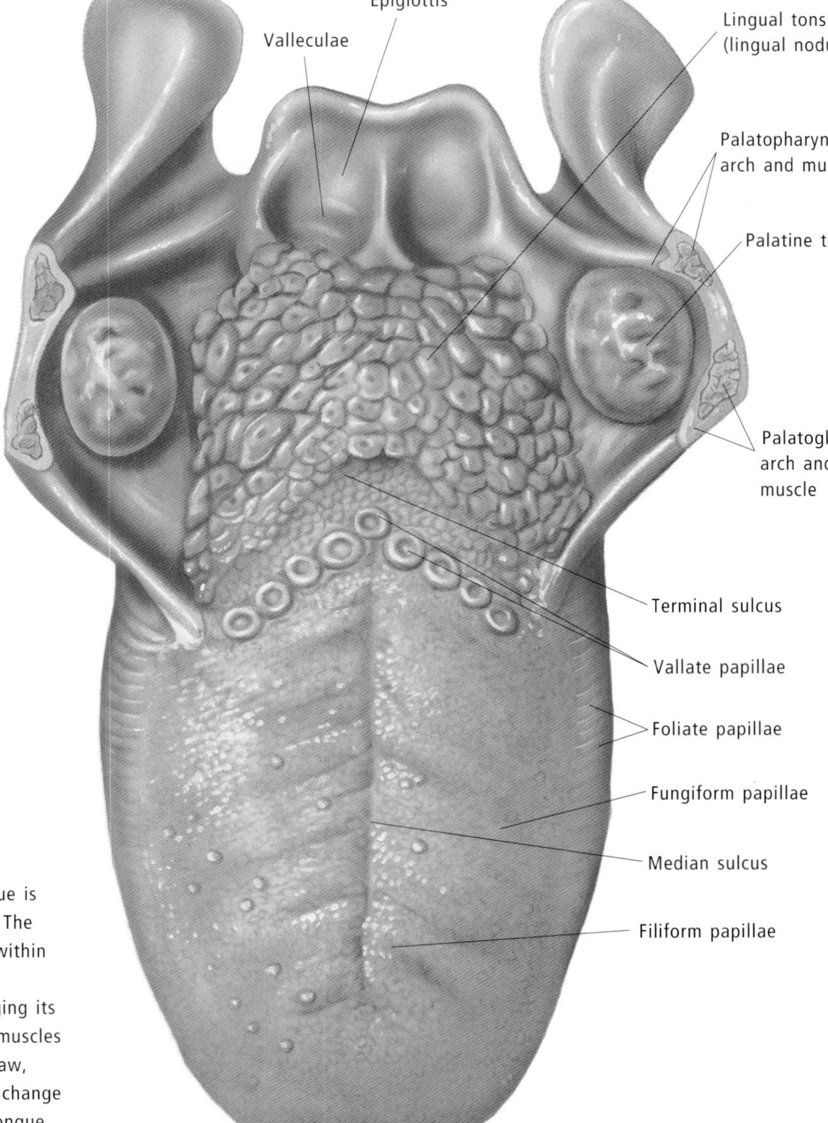

Tongue

The bulk of the tongue is made up of muscles. The intrinsic muscles lie within the tongue and are responsible for changing its shape. The extrinsic muscles are attached to the jaw, skull and palate and change the position of the tongue.

T

(leukoplakia) or as areas of redness (erythroplasia). The patient may experience a burning sensation in the affected areas, although many will have no symptoms at all. Patients with this type of degeneration should be advised to change their personal habits before cancer develops in the mouth tissues.

SEE ALSO *Glossitis, Mouth, Palate, Saliva, Speech, Taste*

TONOMETRY

Tonometry is the measurement of intraocular pressure (pressure within the eye), which is typically elevated in people with glaucoma. Various techniques are available, but applanation tonometry is considered to be the most accurate. This procedure involves bringing the measuring instrument into contact with the anesthetized cornea.

SEE ALSO *Cornea, Eye, Glaucoma*

TONSILS

The tonsils are lymphoid organs which lie under the surface lining of the mouth and throat. There are three sets of tonsils, named according to their position. The lingual tonsil lies on the back third of the tongue; the palatine tonsils lie on either side of the back of the tongue, between pillars of tissue which join the soft palate to the tongue; the pharyngeal or nasopharyngeal tonsils (adenoids) lie in the space behind the nose.

The tonsils are arranged around the entrance to the respiratory and digestive tracts to protect the body from bacteria and viruses which may enter from the mouth and nose. Tonsils produce lymphocytes, which cross into the mouth and throat.

Tonsillitis is inflammation of the tonsils, usually due to bacterial infection of the tonsillar tissue. The palatine tonsils have deep clefts, penetrating into their interior, which appear as pus-filled spots in tonsillitis. Patients with chronic tonsillitis will suffer from severe recurrent sore throats with fever. Frequent attacks of tonsillitis will require surgical removal of the tonsil, known as tonsillectomy. If the infection spreads from the palatine tonsil to the space around the soft palate, a pus-filled peritonsillar abscess will form. This disease is known as quinsy and requires high-dose intravenous antibiotics and surgical drainage.

SEE ALSO *Adenoids, Lymphocytes, Quinsy, Respiratory system, Throat*

TORTICOLLIS

Torticollis (or spasmodic torticollis) is a condition in which involuntary muscle spasms lead to prolonged contraction of the neck muscles. This causes the head to turn to one side, lean toward one shoulder or forward or backward, or to shake. Neck pain and headache may also occur. Symptoms increase gradually and usually plateau in 2–5 years. They may also spontaneously disappear in this time. Torticollis may be inherited or may result from neck trauma or nervous system damage.

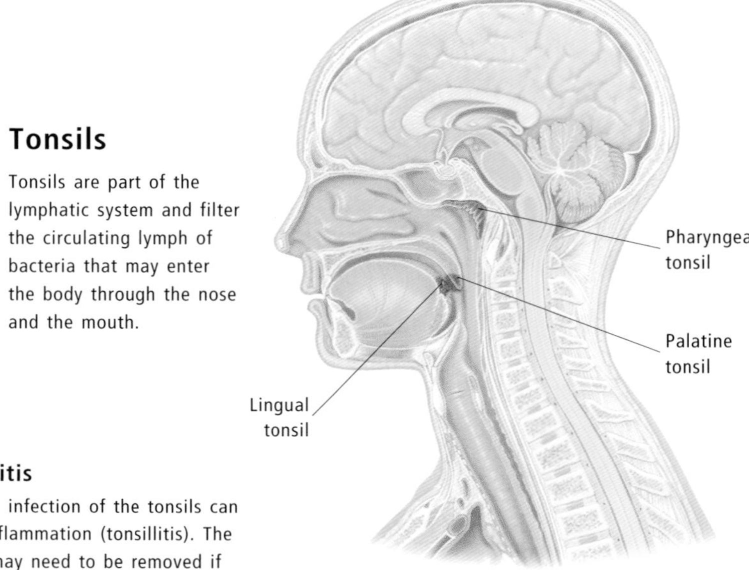

Tonsils

Tonsils are part of the lymphatic system and filter the circulating lymph of bacteria that may enter the body through the nose and the mouth.

Tonsillitis

Bacterial infection of the tonsils can cause inflammation (tonsillitis). The tonsils may need to be removed if infection recurs frequently.

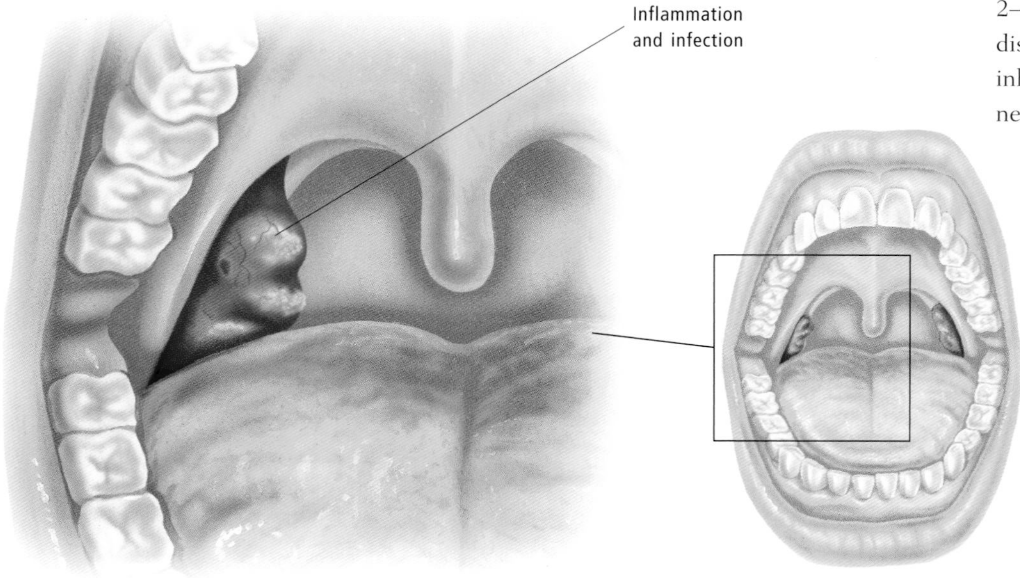

Palatine tonsils

The palatine tonsils are a pair of oval-shaped structures partially embedded in the mucous membrane on each side of the back of the throat.

Torticollis

Torticollis affects the muscles of the neck. Spasm of these muscles twists the neck so that the head is held in an abnormal position.

Sternocleidomastoid muscle

Babies may suffer from torticollis at birth due to the positioning of the head and neck in the uterus. Treatment involves stretching exercises, massage, traction or surgery, depending on the cause.

SEE ALSO *Neck*

TOUCH

The sense of touch, that is the perception of the skin coming in contact with an object, is also called the tactile sense. The surface of the skin has thousands of sensory nerve endings known as cutaneous receptors, which can detect different levels of pain, pressure and vibration, and temperatures ranging up to 113°F (45°C) and down to 50°F (10°C). The degreee of sensitivity to touch varies greatly over the body, as nerve endings are concentrated in particular parts of the body, such as the fingertips, lips and tongue. The fingertips can distinguish between objects which are barely 1/12 inch (2 millimeters) apart, whereas on the back of the hand, which has fewer receptors, the objects must be 2 inches (50 millimetres) apart before they can be defined as more than one object. Fingertips can also detect vibration of as little as one 10-millionth of a yard (meter). The whole body is usually receptive to touch. The area of skin served by one nerve fiber is called the receptive field of that fiber; receptive fields overlap. Body parts which are particularly sensitive to touch include the tongue, lips and fingertips. The tongue has roughly twice the concentration of pressure spots as a fingertip.

Touch is important to a newborn baby because it provides comfort and reassurance—the first skin to skin contact between a mother and her new baby is known to help in bonding their relationship. It is recognized that even babies in intensive care need to be touched in order to achieve optimal development. The sense of touch is also vital to the development and learning experiences of a baby. A baby uses touch to help learn about and understand the environment around it. The experience of different textures helps the baby to relate visual perceptions to touch. Touch continues to be an important part of communication, both good and bad, between humans throughout their lives.

A person touching a sharp spike or a hot surface will pull the hand away in a reflex action. There are other reflex actions which occur as a result of touch. In a newborn baby these include: the grasp reflex, which can also be found in the baby's foot; the Moro or startle reflex, which is used by doctors to test muscle tone; and the galant reflex, which is tested by gently stroking a finger along one side of a baby's back while supporting the baby under the abdomen. The baby's body will bend like a bow, pulling the pelvis towards the side stroked. This reflex indicates the state of development of the spinal nerves and will last until the baby is about 9 months old.

Certain medicines, injuries to the nervous system and illnesses can damage the peripheral nerves and impair the sense of touch. A lessening sense of pain, vibration, cold, heat, pressure and touch occurs with ageing.

Therapeutic touch is a school of alternative practice which believes that people who are ill have disturbed energy fields and that the hands of a trained person can move over the patient's body without touching to detect malalignments and re-pattern energy fields. There is no scientific evidence that this works, although it may have psychological benefits. Massage, however, the actual

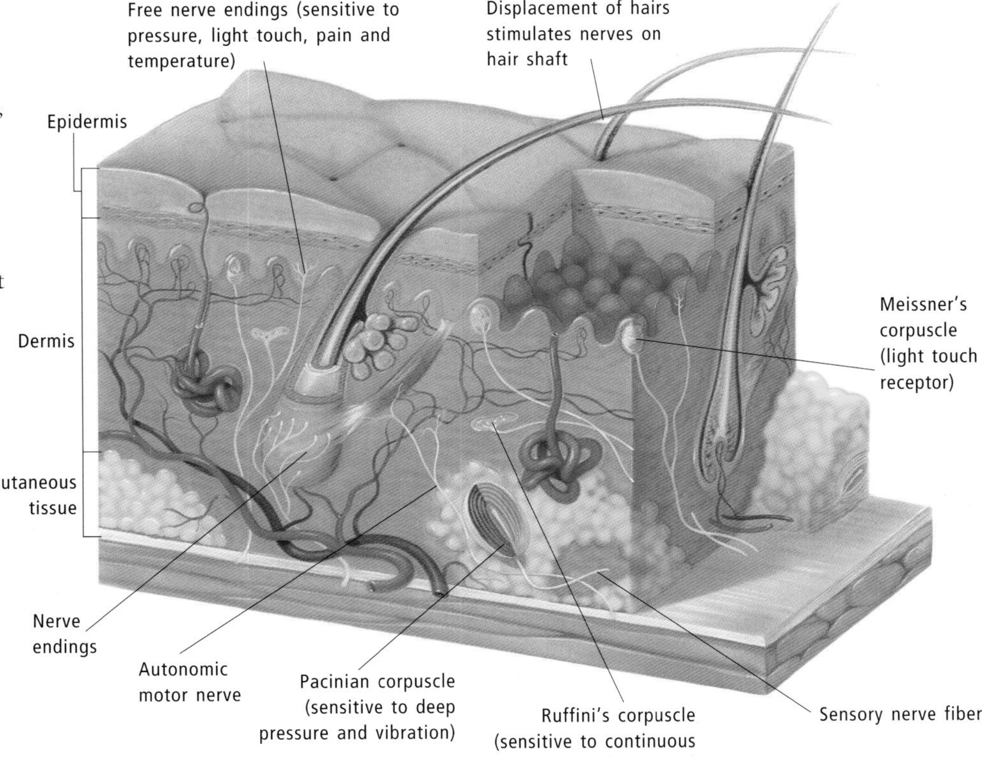

Touch receptors

The skin contains thousands of sensory nerve endings, known as cutaneous receptors, which are sensitive to temperature, pain, vibration and pressure. Each of the receptors is specially adapted to provide different types of sensory information.

touching of the body, is recognized as having a therapeutic effect on both the nervous and muscular systems and on the body's systemic circulation.

Massage is known to have been in use 3,000 years ago in China; it can relieve pain and reduce swelling, relax muscles and speed the healing process of sprain and strain injuries. Studies have found that massage improves the functioning of the nervous system and lowers stress hormone levels. It has also been found to be of benefit in a wide variety of maladies including asthma and migraine.

SEE ALSO *Hyperthermia, Hypothermia, Massage, Reflexes, Skin, Tongue*

Touch

Sensitivity

Sensitivity to touch varies greatly over the body depending on the number of nerve endings in different body parts. The fingertips, lips, and tongue are highly sensitive, containing many receptors. This allows them to send more information to the sensory cortex in the brain. Once this information has been processed, the motor part of the cortex coordinates an appropriate response, such as moving the hand away from a hot object.

Touch pathways

Touch receptors in the surface of the skin pass on their sensory information via the peripheral nervous system. Nerve impulses pass from the skin to peripheral nerves, then to the spinal nerve that innervates that region of the body. From here, the message is relayed up the spinal cord to processing centers in the brain stem and then to the cerebral cortex in the brain.

Spinal cord cross-section

Touch receptors relay information along the peripheral nerves to the spinal cord—part of the central nervous system. The dorsal gray matter of the cord contains groups of sensory cells that receive this information and pass the signals on to the brain.

TOURETTE'S SYNDROME

Tourette's syndrome, a disorder of the central nervous system, involves the involuntary production of sudden sounds and movements, the results of multiple motor and vocal tics. The movements are purposeless and generally recur many times in a day but they subside during sleep. Sometimes there is meaningless repetition of swearwords as part of this syndrome.

The symptoms may change frequently and vary in intensity, being worsened by stress and anxiety. In children the symptoms can even disappear just before a medical examination.

The condition generally starts in childhood or adolescence and affects three times as many males as females. It can sometimes be associated with learning difficulties or with hyperactivity.

Children can sometimes suffer transient tics, which last for a relatively short period and disappear spontaneously; diagnosis of Tourette's syndrome relies partly on the presence of tics for a period of time longer than one year.

SEE ALSO *Tics*

TOXEMIA

Toxemia is a type of blood poisoning caused by toxins, or poisons. Many bacterial infections, such as bacterial dysentery, diphtheria, food poisoning and tetanus, cause toxemia. It is possible to immunize against some diseases that cause toxemia, such as tetanus or diphtheria.

Toxemia of pregnancy (also known as eclampsia or preeclampsia) is a serious disturbance in blood pressure, kidney function and the central nervous system, which may occur in late pregnancy.

SEE ALSO ***Eclampsia, Preeclampsia, Septicemia***

TOXIC SHOCK SYNDROME

Toxic shock syndrome is a potentially fatal bacterial infection commonly associated with the use of highly absorbent tampons by menstruating women. A toxin produced by the *Staphylococcus aureus* bacterium causes fever, chills, headaches, rash and diarrhea about 5 days into a menstrual period.

This is accompanied by rapidly falling blood pressure and loss of body fluids, which induces shock. Other symptoms may include hallucinations, confusion, muscle pain, a sore throat and dry mouth, eyes and vagina. Women who have recently given birth, had surgery, used barrier type contraceptives or had a prior toxic shock infection have a greater risk of being infected.

It is not known exactly why the infection occurs. It is estimated that about 1 percent of menstruating women have the bacteria in their vaginas during a period. Changing tampons frequently or alternating them with sanitary pads is recommended as a means of reducing the risk of infection.

Hospitalization may be required, with the administration of antibiotics for the infection and intravenous fluids for the shock. Though rare, toxic shock syndrome also affects babies, young children and men, often as a result of *Staphylococcus aureus* bacterium entering the body via such things as skin wounds and boils.

SEE ALSO ***Shock, Staphylococcal infections***

TOXOCARIASIS

Toxocariasis is an infection by nematode worms of the genus *Toxocara*, parasites found in the gut of the dog and the cat. Infection by *T. canis* (found in dogs) is more common than infection by *T. cati* (found in cats). Eggs from the feces of dogs and cats, found in the soil, can be transferred directly to the mouth via the hands.

This infection may have no obvious symptoms, or quite mild symptoms, and can only be detected by a blood test to check the levels of eosinophils or a liver biopsy. The infection may disappear without treatment after 6–18 months.

If symptoms such as skin rash, enlarged spleen, recurring pneumonia or an eye lesion are present, treatment will be necessary, together with the worming of animals and the adoption of hygienic practices, such as washing hands more frequently.

SEE ALSO ***Infectious diseases, Worms***

TOXOPLASMOSIS

Toxoplasmosis is an infection caused by the parasite *Toxoplasma gondii*. It is usually acquired after eating raw or undercooked meat, raw eggs or unpasteurized milk containing infective cysts. The organism spreads from the intestines throughout the body, even crossing the placenta and infecting a fetus if a woman is pregnant.

Handling cat feces or soil contaminated with cat feces can also cause an infection. Most people have no symptoms, although sometimes there may be flu-like symptoms or a lymph gland may enlarge.

The main concern is infection during pregnancy, as the disease can seriously harm the developing fetus; people with weakened immune systems are also at greater risk of suffering serious illness. A month-long course of medication is the only effective cure for the condition.

SEE ALSO ***Food poisoning***

TRACHEA

The windpipe (trachea) is a $3\frac{1}{2}$–5 inch (9–12 centimeter) long and $\frac{3}{5}$ inch (1.5 centimeter) wide tube for the passage of air, beginning at the lower end of the voice box (larynx), and passing into the thoracic cavity where it terminates by dividing into the left and right main bronchi.

It is a fibro-elastic and muscular structure, reinforced by U-shaped cartilages. The cartilages prevent collapse of the airway, and the elastic fibers allow it to stretch and recoil with the movements of the larynx (which is used in swallowing and speech) and diaphragm (used in breathing). The back of the trachea is flat. Here, the ends of the cartilage are bridged by transversely oriented muscle (trachealis muscle), whose contractions reduce the diameter of the airway. The esophagus lies against this surface and expands into the gap in the cartilage when food is swallowed.

A tracheo-esophageal fistula is an abnormal opening between the esophagus and trachea. It can occur during development *in utero* or may be secondary to cancer, infection or trauma. It needs surgical correction.

The mucous membrane lining the trachea traps dust particles. Hair-like projections on the membrane (cilia), move the dust-laden mucus toward the throat where it may be swallowed or spat out. This clearing activity of the cilia is inhibited by smoking.

Since the larynx and trachea are the only air passage to the lungs, obstruction of the larynx (due to an allergic reaction, for example) may require surgical opening of the trachea (tracheostomy). The cavity, or lumen, of the trachea is very small in infants and inflammation of the trachea (tracheitis) can cause severe breathing difficulties.

SEE ALSO *Esophagus, Larynx, Pharynx, Tracheostomy*

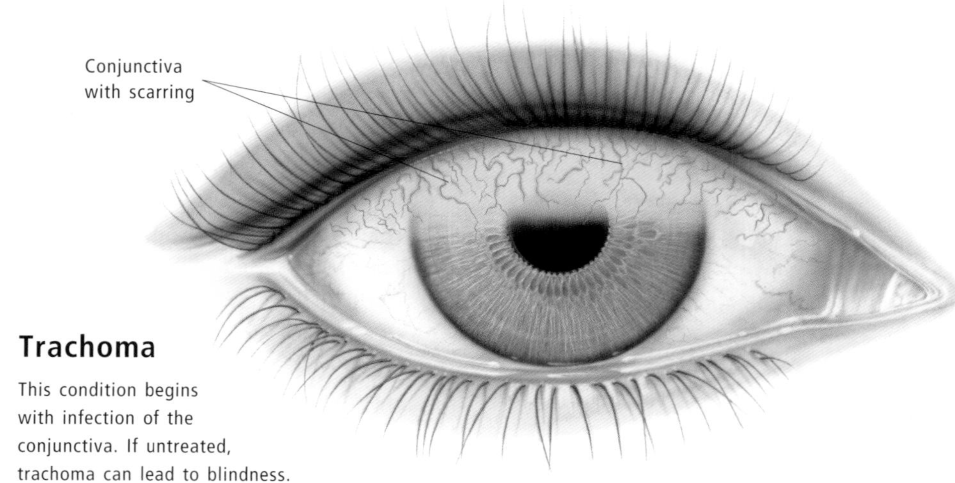

Trachoma

This condition begins with infection of the conjunctiva. If untreated, trachoma can lead to blindness.

TRACHEITIS

Tracheitis is inflammation of the trachea, or windpipe. It may be viral or bacterial, and is usually a mild condition in an adult. In young children, however, it can be a serious medical emergency. This is because in children the diameter of the trachea is much smaller than in adults, so the swelling of the lining of the trachea as a result of tracheitis may block the passage of air, causing severe difficulty in breathing, and ultimately even death.

The inflammation is usually caused by bacterium such as *Staphylococcus*, and usually follows a viral upper respiratory tract infection. The child has a high fever, looks very ill, and develops a high-pitched crowing sound when breathing in, called stridor.

A child with this condition must be taken to hospital immediately. An endotracheal tube (a breathing tube placed in the trachea) will need to be inserted to keep the airway open and allow oxygen to be administered. Intravenous antibiotics such as penicillins or cephalosporins are administered intravenously. If treatment is prompt, the child will recover fully.

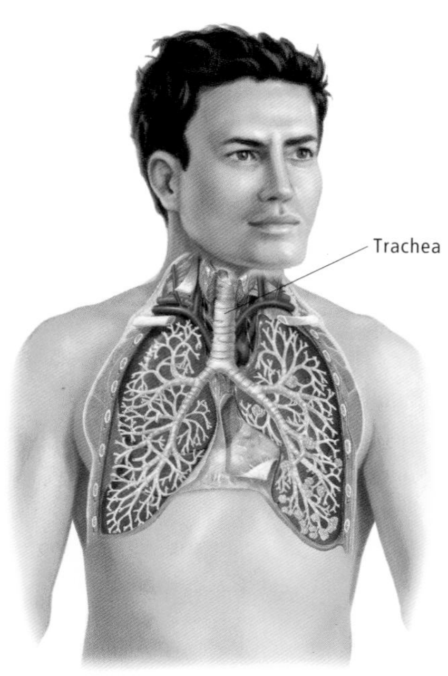

Trachea

The trachea is reinforced at the front and sides by a series of C-shaped rings of cartilage, which keep the passageway open. Gaps between the rings are occupied by muscle.

TRACHEOSTOMY

Tracheostomy is a surgical procedure in which an opening in the front of the windpipe (the trachea) is created to maintain a clear airway. A silicon tracheostomy tube is then placed in the opening. A tracheostomy is performed on someone who has had a mouth or chest injury or who has undergone a major operation, such as lung surgery. It is also performed on someone who needs to be on a mechanical ventilator for an extended period of time.

An emergency tracheostomy may need to be performed after an accident or injury if the normal airway is blocked by swelling or by blood.

SEE ALSO *Trachea*

Trachea

The trachea (windpipe) is the air passage that connects the larynx (voice box) and the two bronchi.

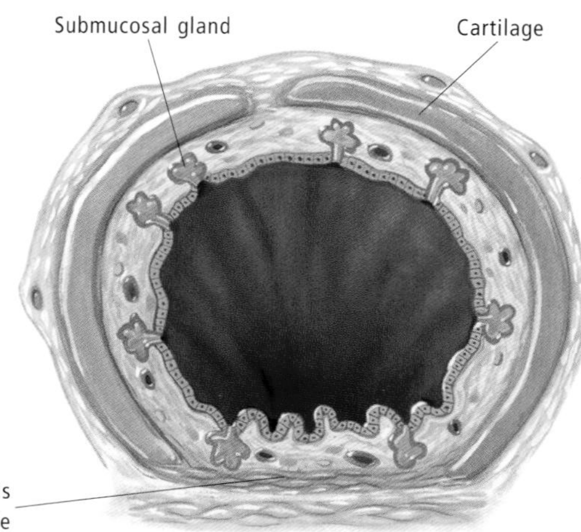

TRACHOMA

Also called granular conjunctivitis, trachoma is a disease of the eye caused by infection with the organism *Chlamydia trachomatis*. It is the world's most common cause of blindness, with as many as 500 million people affected around the world. The people affected are mainly in developing countries (as inadequate supply of running water often being a factor). The disease is spread by direct contact from person to person.

The condition begins slowly as a mild conjunctivitis which develops into a severe infection with copious amount of eye discharge. Erosions form in the cornea of the eye, which becomes infiltrated by blood vessels and scarred, causing blindness.

Trachoma is easily treated with antibiotics such as oral erythromycin. If treated early, the eye will recover completely. However, once scarring and blindness have occurred, vision usually cannot be restored. The condition is best prevented by improving sanitation and overcrowding in at-risk communities and educating them about the disease.

SEE ALSO *Blindness, Cornea, Eye, Eyelids*

TRACTION

Traction is the application of a pulling force to a part of the body, a technique used to align fractured bones to allow proper healing, and also used in physical therapy to overcome muscle tension, or to relieve pressure on bulging or herniated disks of the spine. Traction is generally applied by using weights to exert a sustained pull in one direction for a set period of time.

If applied to the spine (lumbar traction), the therapist may recline the patient and attach a fixed harness to restrain the upper body. A second harness is fitted around the hips or upper thighs and weights or a machine used to exert a carefully calculated degree of pull which is intended to straighten the spine and relieve pressure from the vertebrae on the disks.

In fractures of major bones such as the femur or pelvis, the patient may be similarly restrained in bed, with traction being applied by weights attached to the limb or a cast to ensure the bones knit in exact alignment. Traction may be applied for periods ranging from half an hour in physical therapy treatments to several months in the case of broken bones.

Some forms of exercise, notably yoga, use postures which place muscles under traction to properly align the spine and extend the range of available joint movement.

SEE ALSO *Physical therapy, Yoga*

TRANQUILIZERS

Tranquilizers, drugs which calm nervous activity, are of two types—antipsychotics and antianxiety drugs. The most commonly prescribed types of antianxiety drugs are the benzodiazepines, which are usually prescribed for anxiety states, panic or sleep problems, to control epileptic fits or the symptoms of alcohol withdrawal. Tranquilizers are absorbed into the bloodstream and affect the central nervous system, slowing down physical, mental and emotional responses. They can affect judgment, memory and the ability to concentrate, and cause drowsiness, dizziness, confusion and mood swings. In the long term they can be responsible for nausea, loss of libido, increased appetite and weight gain and lethargy. Taken at the same time as alcohol, painkillers or antihistamines (even cold remedies) they can cause unconsciousness and failure to breathe.

It is important to take tranquilizers only in the manner prescribed. Tranquilizers can easily become a drug of dependence when they are important to a person's daily life, even within 4–6 weeks of regular usage. Withdrawal creates its own set of symptoms—sleep problems, tension, muscle pain, panic attacks and depression—and must be undertaken carefully under medical supervision.

SEE ALSO *Antipsychotics, Drug dependence, Sedatives, Sleeping pills*

TRANSCUTANEOUS ELECTRICAL NERVE STIMULATION

Transcutaneous electrical nerve stimulation (TENS) is a pain-relieving treatment using a device that sends out electrical impulses to the nerves from electrodes attached to the surface of the skin. It works on the principle of counter-irritation—the electrical impulses suppress the original pain sensations by inhibiting the messages of the pain pathway to the brain.

The electrodes are usually placed on or near the site of the ache or pain, or on acupuncture points, in a technique known as electroacupuncture. TENS devices are used to relieve both acute and chronic pain, reducing the need for analgesic drugs.

SEE ALSO *Acupuncture, Pain*

TRANSIENT ISCHEMIC ATTACK

Transient ischemic attacks (commonly known as TIAs) are short episodes that result from the temporary obstruction of one of the small blood vessels carrying oxygen and other nutrients to the brain. The blockage is usually caused by a floating body (embolus) which gets lodged in one of these arteries, but frees itself after seconds or minutes. While the artery is blocked the brain tissue supplied by branches arising beyond the blockage is affected but, because it is only deprived of oxygen for a short time, function returns to normal once the floating body is freed and the blood supply to the tissue is restored.

The effects of a TIA usually last from a few seconds up to 10 minutes, but they can last as long as 24 hours. The effects will depend on which artery has been blocked, and may include temporary disturbances of vision or speech, dizziness, and numbness and/or weakness of one or more of the limbs or the face.

People who are suffering from heart disease, hardening of the arteries (atherosclerosis) or high blood pressure (hypertension) are the most at risk of having a TIA, which often precedes or accompanies the development of a stroke. Treatment usually involves the use of blood-thinning (anticoagulant) medications.

SEE ALSO *Arteries, Atherosclerosis, Blood vessels, Coronary artery disease, Hypertension, Stroke, Thrombus*

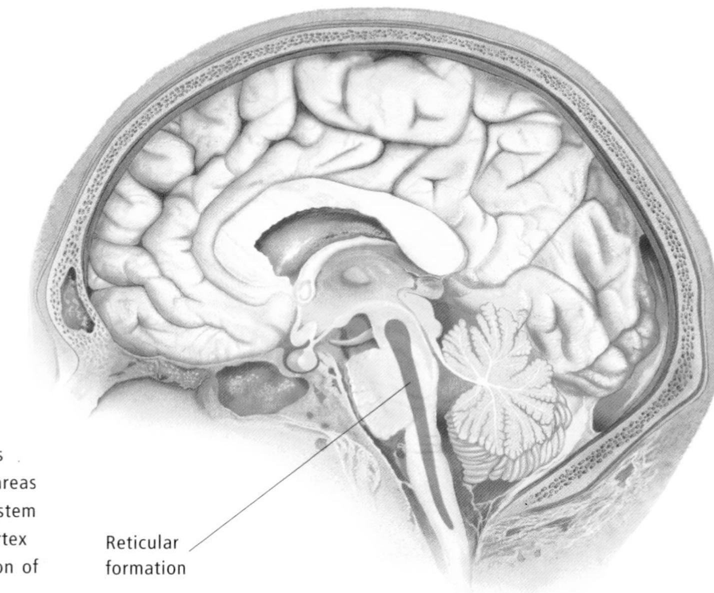

Tranquilizers

These drugs calm nervous activity and affect wide areas of the central nervous system including the cerebral cortex and the reticular formation of the brain.

TRANSPLANT SURGERY

Organ, tissue and limb transplant surgery, or grafts, means permanently transferring a tissue or organ from one part of the body to another, or from one person to another. The first records come from the sixth century BC, when Hindu doctors used skin flaps from the patient's own arm to repair damage to the nose. Kidneys were the first organs used in person-to-person transplants and are now the organ most commonly transplanted.

Current surgical techniques also make it possible to graft corneas, teeth, heart, lungs, liver, pancreas, cartilage, bone marrow, brain tissue, blood and skin to one person from another. More recently hip and knee joints have been transplanted, and even hands. Transplants of animal donor tissues to humans (xenotransplants) have also been made, and have included chimpanzee and baboon hearts, and heart valves and fetal brain cells from pigs. Some of these are highly experimental and are very contentious, largely due to the possibility of serious viral infections.

Autografts, where donor and host are the same person, pose no threat of tissue rejection, nor do grafts from one identical twin to another. A graft from any other source will stimulate rejection by the host because of the differences in histocompatibility antigens on the cell surfaces of donor and host tissues, which can quickly kill the implant. Immunosuppressive drugs are used to counter this reaction. Organ grafts are usually a long-term solution undertaken to sustain life in a chronically ill patient. Skin grafts may be short-term measures to prevent fluid loss and infection at burn sites while host tissue regenerates.

People who have decided that in the event of their death their organs can be used as transplants are referred to as organ donors. This information may be recorded on a card or driver's license. Organs are removed after death and transported to hosts, patients on a waiting list in priority of need. Transplant organs go to the patient on the waiting list who is nearest death, priority being given to those in whom earlier transplants have failed.

Transplant surgery is a very costly and uncertain procedure not funded by many private health insurers, and ethical questions stimulate much debate about the procedure. A black market in organs exists in some developing countries.

SEE ALSO *Bones, Eye, Grafting, Heart, Kidney*

TRANSSEXUALISM

Transsexualism is a condition in which a person sees himself or herself as a member of the opposite sex. Transsexualism occurs more frequently among men than in women. Transsexuals dislike their own sexual anatomy, feeling a strong need to act like and be treated like a member of the opposite sex. Some transsexuals undergo reassignment surgery to change their external anatomy to that of the opposite sex, in conjunction with hormone therapy to alter their sexual characteristics.

SEE ALSO *Sexual behavior, Sexuality*

Trapezius muscle

The trapezius muscle acts to steady the shoulder during arm movement. This muscle is flat and is situated at the back of the neck and upper chest.

TRAPEZIUS MUSCLE

The trapezius muscle is a flat, triangular muscle, lying under the skin of the back of the neck and upper part of the back of the chest. The triangular muscles on each side of the back meet in the midline, forming a trapezoidal (four-sided) shape.

The trapezius muscle arises, directly or through ligaments, from the spines of the vertebrae of the thorax and neck, and from the occipital bone of the cranium. The muscle fibers converge upon the shoulder, where they are attached to the collar bone (clavicle) and shoulder blade (scapula). The trapezius muscle acts mainly in steadying the shoulder during arm movements; it also assists in movements of the scapula.

SEE ALSO *Collar bone, Muscle, Scapula*

TRAUMA

Trauma is any injury, whether physical or psychological. A traumatic wound is an injury resulting from violence or external force. A broken bone, a burn, or a knocked-out tooth are all defined as trauma.

Trauma emergencies include dislocation and other serious bone and joint injuries. Extreme fear and apprehension, grief, witnessing or undergoing extremely disturbing experiences can cause psychological trauma, with long-lasting effects which may require counseling, medication and in some cases hospitalization.

SEE ALSO *Post-traumatic stress disorder*

TREMOR

A tremor is an involuntary shaking of the body or part of the body, caused by a neurological disease that interferes with the nerve supply of certain muscles. Tremors are seen in a range of neurological diseases, such as Parkinson's disease or alcoholic brain damage, or as a side effect of drugs such as antipsychotics. If there is no discernible cause, the condition is known as essential tremor.

A tremor may affect the whole body, or just certain areas such as the head, hands, arms or eyelids. A tremor may occur sporadically, or at regular intervals. Often a tremor worsens with voluntary movement or emotional stress and disappears during sleep. It may improve after consuming alcohol.

Treatment is directed at the underlying condition where possible. If the tremor prevents essential activities such as speaking or writing, drugs such as beta blockers, anticonvulsants or mild tranquilizers will help.

SEE ALSO *Parkinson's disease*

TRICHINOSIS

Trichinosis is a roundworm infection in which the parasite migrates through the body causing cystlike growths in the muscle fibers. The infection commonly occurs due to eating undercooked pork infected with larvae of the *Trichinella spiralis* roundworm. Pigs pick up the parasite by eating uncooked garbage. High temperatures kill the larvae; undercooking pork allows them to survive. The larvae mature and reproduce in the intestine, sending new larvae through the circulatory system to the muscles. In most cases there is little or no pain, but severe infection may result in muscular rheumatism. Treatment is by antiparasitic medication. Infection can be prevented by cooking meat thoroughly at 150°F (65°C) or more, or freezing it for 2 days at –16°F (–26°C).

SEE ALSO *Food poisoning, Worms*

TRICHURIASIS

Trichuriasis is an intestinal infection with the roundworm *Trichuris trichiura*, caused by eating the worm's eggs in contaminated food. The infection is common in tropical areas with poor sanitation, where soil is contaminated with feces. The larvae mature in the intestine and migrate to the colon where they multiply. It may produce no symptoms, but with heavy infestations can cause bloody diarrhea, weight loss, stomach pain and nausea. Extreme cases can result in dehydration and anemia. Treatment is by antiparasitic medication and prevention can be achieved by improving sanitary and waste disposal systems.

SEE ALSO *Roundworms, Worms*

TRICUSPID VALVE

The tricuspid valve is one of four valves that control the direction of blood flow through the heart. Comprising three triangular flaps of tissue, called cusps or leaflets, it is an opening between the right atrium and right ventricle of the heart. The closing of the tricuspid and other valves creates the heartbeat sound.

Blood flows from the veins into the right atrium and passes through the tricuspid valve into the right ventricle. The right ventricle then contracts and sends the blood through the pulmonary valve to the lungs. The tricuspid valve closes as the right ventricle contracts in order to prevent bloodflow back into the right atrium (regurgitation).

A disease-damaged tricuspid valve may cause regurgitation from ventricle to atrium to veins, reducing bloodflow to the lungs where fresh supplies of oxygen are gathered and transported back to the heart. The valve may be too narrow (stenotic), causing turbulence as blood passes through the constricted passage. This is heard as a rumbling murmur. The tricuspid valve may also be blocked or even absent due to congenital heart disease. Depending on the heart condition, an artificial valve may be surgically inserted to replace a damaged or abnormal one.

SEE ALSO *Circulatory system, Heart, Lungs, Ventricle*

TRIGEMINAL NERVE

The trigeminal nerve is the fifth cranial nerve that arises from the brain stem and passes to the face to supply skin on the face and scalp, the teeth, mucous membranes in the nose, mouth and eye, and the muscles responsible for chewing (muscles of mastication). It mainly contains sensory fibers which are involved in touch, pain and temperature. As its name implies, it has three components: ophthalmic, maxillary and mandibular.

The nerve divides not far from the brain stem, while still in the cranial cavity, and the three divisions pass out of the cranial cavity

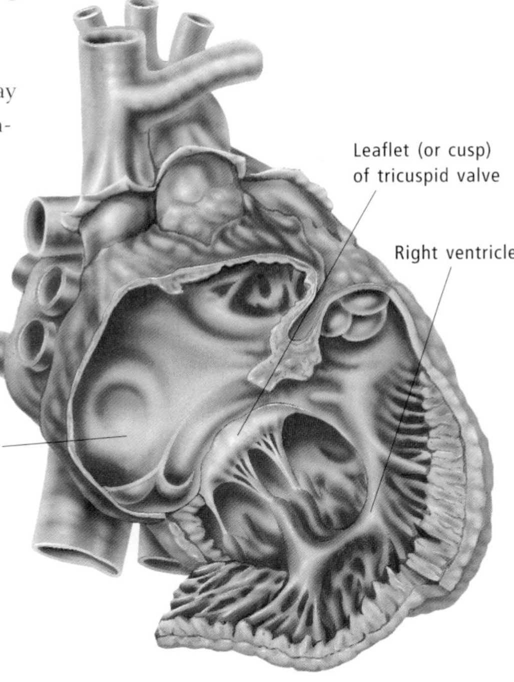

Tricuspid valve

This valve helps to control the direction of blood flow between the right atrium and right ventricle of the heart. Damage to the tricuspid valve may affect blood flow to the lungs.

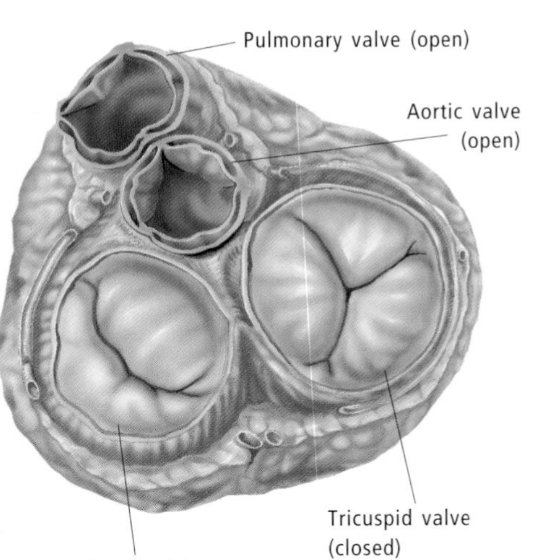

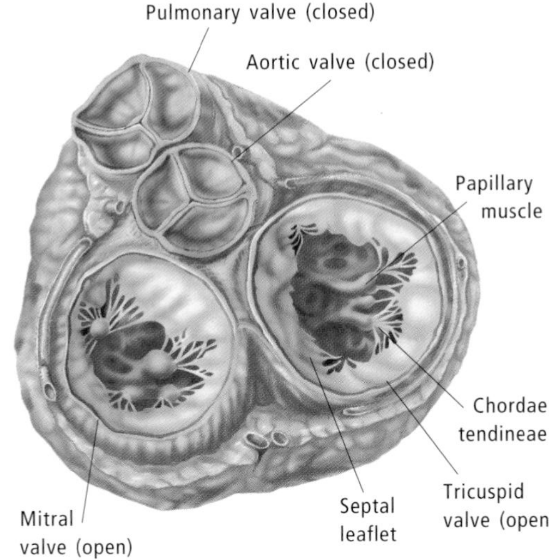

T

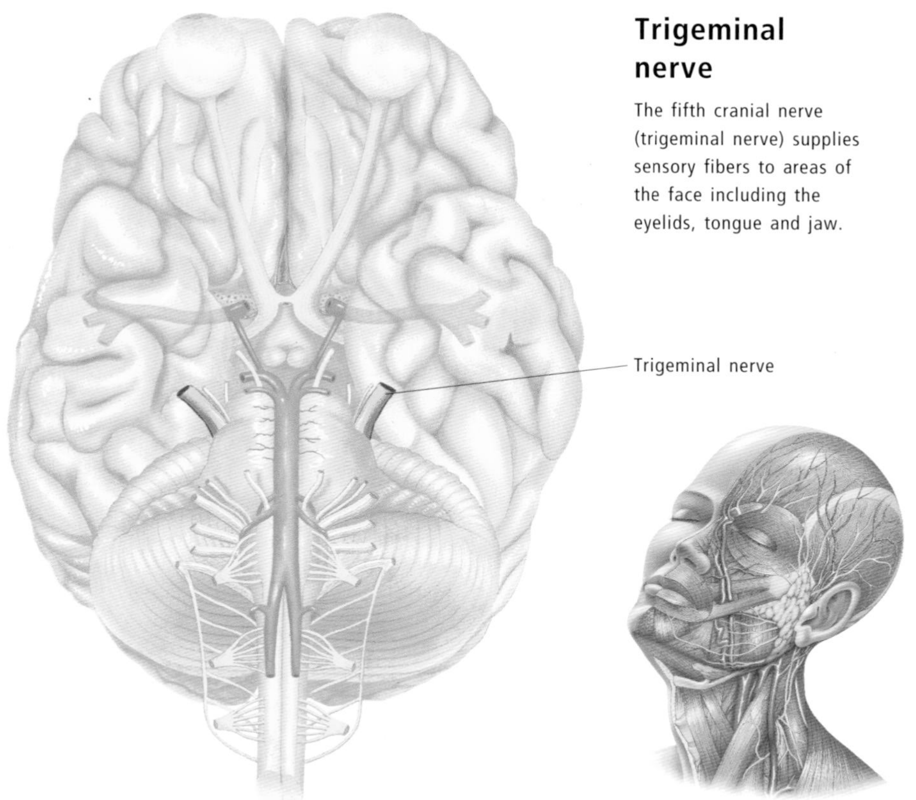

Trigeminal nerve

The fifth cranial nerve (trigeminal nerve) supplies sensory fibers to areas of the face including the eyelids, tongue and jaw.

through separate openings. The ophthalmic nerve supplies the skin of the upper eyelid, forehead and scalp as far back as the top of the head (vertex), part of the nose and the cornea. The maxillary nerve supplies skin on the temple and on the face from the lower eyelid to the upper lip. It also supplies the upper teeth, mucous membrane of the nose, hard and soft palate, and cheek. The largest branch, the mandibular nerve, supplies skin on the jaw, temple and ear, the lower teeth, mucous membrane of the floor of the mouth and the anterior two-thirds of the tongue. It is the only branch that supplies muscles, primarily the four muscles of mastication.

Trigeminal neuralgia (otherwise known as tic douloureux) is a disorder of the trigeminal nerve, the main sensory nerve in the face. It causes sudden, severe pain on one side of the face, in one of the areas supplied by the trigeminal nerve—usually along the second and third nerve divisions, which supply the lower face and jaw. The pain can be set off by touching a sensitive area of the face or by certain movements of the jaw whilst speaking, chewing or swallowing. The condition usually affects older women and over time the attacks may become more frequent. The cause is often unknown but it may be caused by a blood vessel or small tumor pressing on the nerve (which can be cured by surgery). In most cases however, there is no known cure for the disorder, so treatment is aimed at control of the pain. Unfortunatly this is not easy to achieve because of the spasmodic nature of the attacks. Mild over-the-counter analgesics such as aspirin or narcotic analgesics such as codeine may bring some relief. Anticonvulsants or antidepressants may also help. Surgical destruction of the nerve is a possible treatment as a last resort.

SEE ALSO *Nerves, Nervous system, Neuralgia, Tic douloureux*

TRIGGER FINGER

"Trigger finger" is a finger locked in the flexed or bent position, often a result of tenosynovitis, where the finger tendon is inflamed and swollen. As the finger is bent, the swollen tendon moves out of its sheath but does not slide back in to allow the finger to straighten. However, the finger can be straightened with additional effort or with pressure from the other hand, often with a snap (hence "trigger finger"). Treatment is usually rest or anti-inflammatory drugs.

SEE ALSO *Finger, Tendinitis, Tenosynovitis*

TUBAL STERILIZATION

Tubal sterilization, also called tubal ligation, is the surgical closing of the fallopian tubes to prevent future pregnancies. The fallopian (uterine) tubes allow passage of sperm cells to the ovum and movement of the fertilized ovum to the body of the uterus for implantation and development into a baby. Removal of a length of the tube, combined with clipping or tying of the cut ends, will prevent sperm reaching the ovum, thus sterilizing the woman. The procedure is performed in a hospital under general anesthesia by an gynecologist usually via a laparoscope (a telescopic tube). Recovery is quick, allowing the patient to return home the same day as the procedure. Strenuous exercise is best avoided for a few days, after which time work may be resumed. Normal sexual activity can be resumed when the woman feels ready, normally within a week. In a small number of cases—one out of 400 women—there is faulty closure of the tubes and the

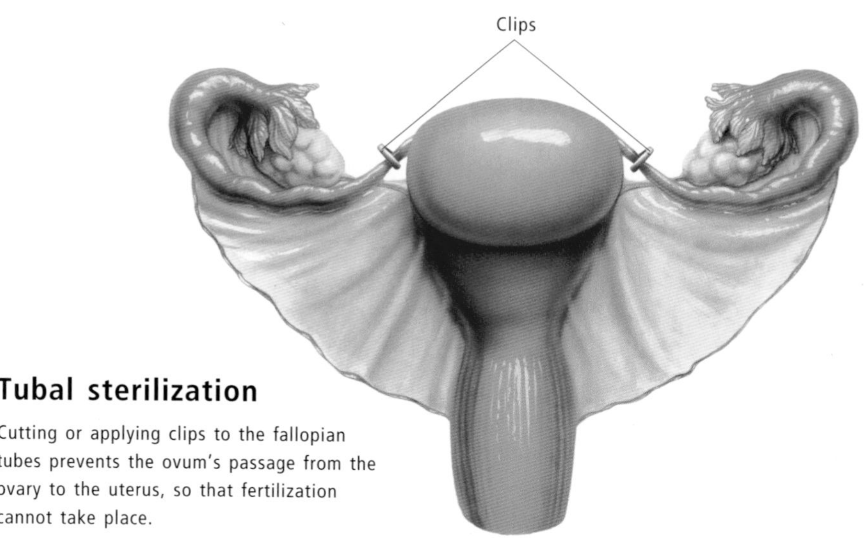

Tubal sterilization

Cutting or applying clips to the fallopian tubes prevents the ovum's passage from the ovary to the uterus, so that fertilization cannot take place.

chance of becoming pregnant again. This procedure may be reversed (with difficulty) by reparative microsurgery so it is suitable only for women who are certain that they wish to permanently prevent future pregnancies. It is not suitable as a temporary contraceptive measure.

SEE ALSO *Fallopian tubes, Sterilization*

TUBERCULOSIS

Tuberculosis is an infectious, inflammatory disease caused by bacteria belonging to the *Mycobacterium* group (usually *M. tuberculosis*). Infection of humans by *M. bovis* from cattle is now rare in industrialized nations, due to the eradication of this bacterium from cattle in these countries. Tuberculosis is primarily a disease of the lungs, but it may spread to other parts of the body, particularly in patients whose immune systems have been weakened and are in the last stages of the disease.

Tuberculosis was a common disease in Europe during the nineteenth century, but its prevalence began to decline when living conditions improved. At present in industrialized countries, tuberculosis is largely confined to people living in overcrowded and/or impoverished conditions, such as the very poor and homeless.

About 10–20 new cases per 100,000 population are diagnosed each year in industrialized nations, so it is still a very important public health problem. AIDS sufferers are at risk of contracting the disease, and it is becoming resistant to drug treatment. Another concern is that the disease may once again spread to the wider community if the quality of living conditions declines.

There are several predisposing factors to tuberculosis. Particular racial groups such as native North Americans and Inuits are more susceptible to the disease than people of European ancestry. Poor living conditions with overcrowding and malnutrition are major contributing factors, while smoking and other diseases such as alcoholism, diabetes mellitus and occupational lung diseases (silicosis) increase individual susceptibility to tuberculosis. A weakened immune system, due to AIDS or immunosuppressive drugs, may also increase the likelihood of the disease developing and advancing.

Initial infection with tuberculosis usually occurs in childhood. The bacteria are inhaled and cause a small patch of pneumonia in the middle or lower areas of the lung. The initial site develops a tubercle (hence the name of the disease), which is a clump of immune system and other cells surrounding a cavity filled with cheeselike material derived from dead lung tissue. The infection also spreads to lymph nodes in the center of the chest, but may not spread further at this stage. Children infected in this manner may have no symptoms at all, or complain only of a mild fever, cough and feeling unwell.

If the initial infection occurs in adults, the tubercle usually develops in the upper parts of the lung. In most cases this initial infection is halted and the bacteria are walled-off inside the tubercle. The bacillus can then lie dormant in the body for some years, with the possibility of it becoming active again at a later date. This secondary tuberculosis is common in people with a generally lowered resistance to disease.

The serious complications of tuberculosis arise when the bacteria escape from the initial site of infection and spread through the lung or the rest of the body. Widespread infection of the lung may cause the collapse of lung lobes and further infection of the pleural sacs around the lung. The bacteria may also spread via the bloodstream to the spleen, liver, kidneys, testes, fallopian tubes and brain membranes, with consequences ranging from sterility to death from overwhelming infection.

Treatment of tuberculosis is by the appropriate combination of antibiotics. The tuberculosis bacteria are likely to develop drug resistance if only a single drug

Tuberculosis

In this bacterial infection, inflammation of the passageways of the lungs results in the development of lesions and nodules or tubercles in the lungs. From here the infection may spread to the lymph nodes in the chest and to other organs in the body.

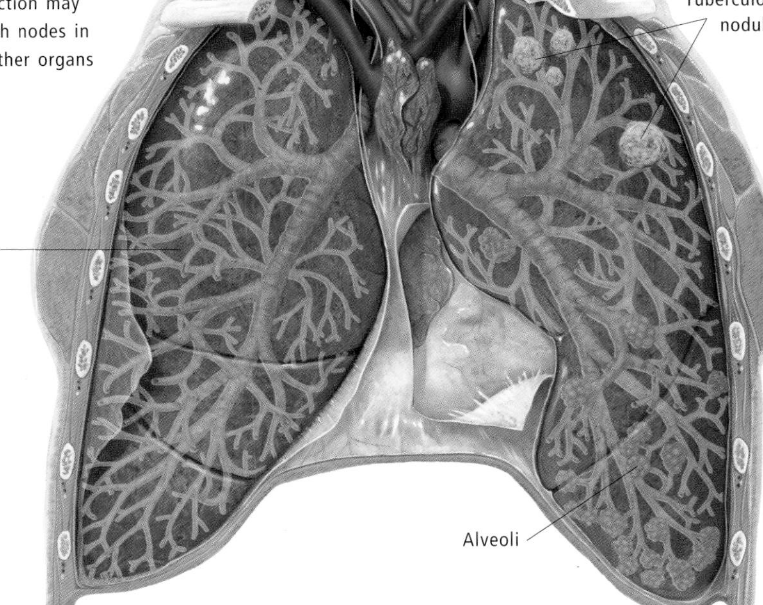

Tuberculosis bacteria

Tuberculosis is usually acquired by breathing in air which has tiny droplets of water containing the bacillus *Mycobacterium tuberculosis*.

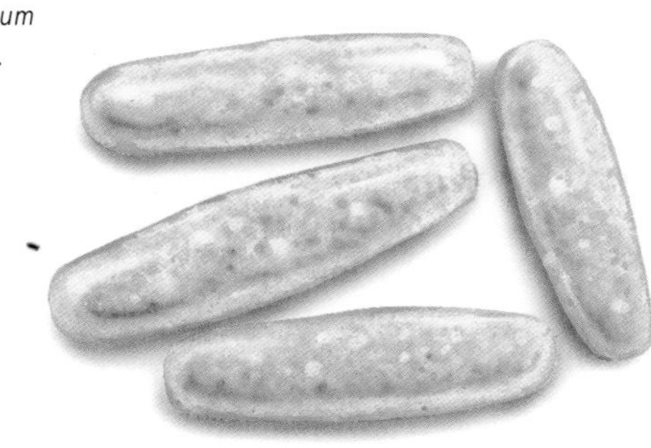

is used, so a combination of three drugs is usually given. Treatment must also continue for long periods to avoid recurrence. In those patients with extensive disease, up to 2 years of antibiotic treatment may be required.

SEE ALSO *Infectious diseases, Lungs*

TUMORS

A tumor (or neoplasm) is an abnormal growth or swelling of tissue. It may be cancerous (malignant) or noncancerous (benign). A malignant tumor is a neoplasm that grows and spreads throughout the body.

Malignant tumors can spread by extension into surrounding tissues, or beyond. They may spread to nearby lymph nodes via the lymphatic vessels, or to distant sites via blood vessels. This process is called metastasizing—an area of tumor that has derived from elsewhere in the body is called a metastasis, or a secondary (the original tumor is called a primary).

A benign tumor is a neoplasm that, if it grows, does so slowly, and does not spread or infiltrate other tissues of the body. The cells in benign tumors are similar under a microscope to the cells in the tissue they grow from. Cells in malignant tumors may look quite different. Not all cancers are tumors, however—cancers of the blood cells such as leukemia, for example, do not form growths.

Malignant tumors are more likely to be fatal (though in some circumstances benign tumors can cause death where their expansion destroys surrounding tissue, for example in the brain). On the other hand, some malignant tumors, such as some skin cancers, are treatable, especially if diagnosed early. Others grow so slowly that the affected person may die of some other condition—this is true of many men with prostate cancer. Much depends on the site of the tumor—cancer of the colon, for example, may be slow growing but is often fatal because it only causes symptoms at a late stage and is often not detected until it has grown and spread. Some benign tumors may eventually turn malignant and need to be treated.

The aim of treatment of a tumor is to destroy as much of it as possible without destroying normal tissue. This can be achieved by surgery, chemotherapy, radiation therapy or combinations of all of these.

SEE ALSO *Cancer*

TURNER'S SYNDROME

Turner's syndrome is a chromosome anomaly of females in which one of the two X chromosomes normally present in a female is absent. The disorder inhibits sexual development and causes infertility. A person with Turner's syndrome has short stature, a broad chest with widely spaced nipples, multiple birthmarks, coarctation (narrowing) of the aorta, and abnormalities of the eyes and bones. At puberty, the breasts fail to develop normally, and menstruation does not occur.

Although there is no cure for Turner's syndrome, after puberty, treatment with synthetic estrogen and progesterone can be given to replace the missing natural ovarian hormones. Normal secondary sexual characteristics should then develop and menstruation may occur. The affected person will remain infertile.

SEE ALSO *Chromosomal abnormalities, Chromosomes, Hormones*

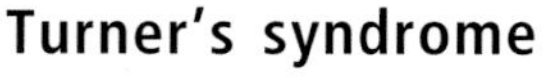

Turner's syndrome

The chromosomes carry the body's genetic information, with the X and Y chromosomes determining a person's sex. Normally a woman has two X chromosomes, but in Turner's syndrome there is only one X chromosome. Because some of the genetic information is missing, sexual development is impaired.

TWINS

The chance of a natural pregnancy being a multiple pregnancy varies according to heredity, age, race and the number of children a woman has already conceived.

Twins occur in approximately one out of every 86 natural pregnancies; the rate is higher in pregnancies resulting from infertility treatments. Seven out of ten pairs of twins are the result of two eggs being released by the woman's ovaries and fertilized at the same time, producing fraternal (dizygotic or non-identical) twins. Fraternal twins may be of different sex and develop with separate placentas (occasionally these may fuse into one). Identical (monozygotic) twins are produced after, rather than at the time of, conception, often after the fertilized egg has implanted itself into the uterine lining, when it splits into two. In this instance the twins will share a placenta and be of the same sex. Multiple births involving three or more babies, which are less common, occur through similar processes.

Twins, or a greater number of babies, fill the available space in the uterus more quickly than a singleton; the mother is at greater risk of hemorrhoids, heartburn, backache and premature (preterm) labor. The babies are also at greater risk of prematurity, poor fetal growth, perinatal death and, in the long term, cerebral palsy. Multiple pregnancies require additional support, though there is no medical evidence for the common belief that hospitalization for bed rest is beneficial.

SEE ALSO *Fertilization, Pregnancy*

TYPHOID

Also known as enteric fever, typhoid is a debilitating intestinal disease caused by infection with the bacterium *Salmonella typhi*. It is rare in the industralized countries. The disease incubates for between 1 and 2 weeks. Symptoms include headache, loss of appetite, fatigue and constipation, followed by abdominal pain and rosy spots on the abdomen and chest which last for 3–4 days, and diarrhea, which is the main problem; pneumonia may be a complication in severe cases. A blood test will determine if typhoid has been contracted. The disease can be treated with antibiotics.

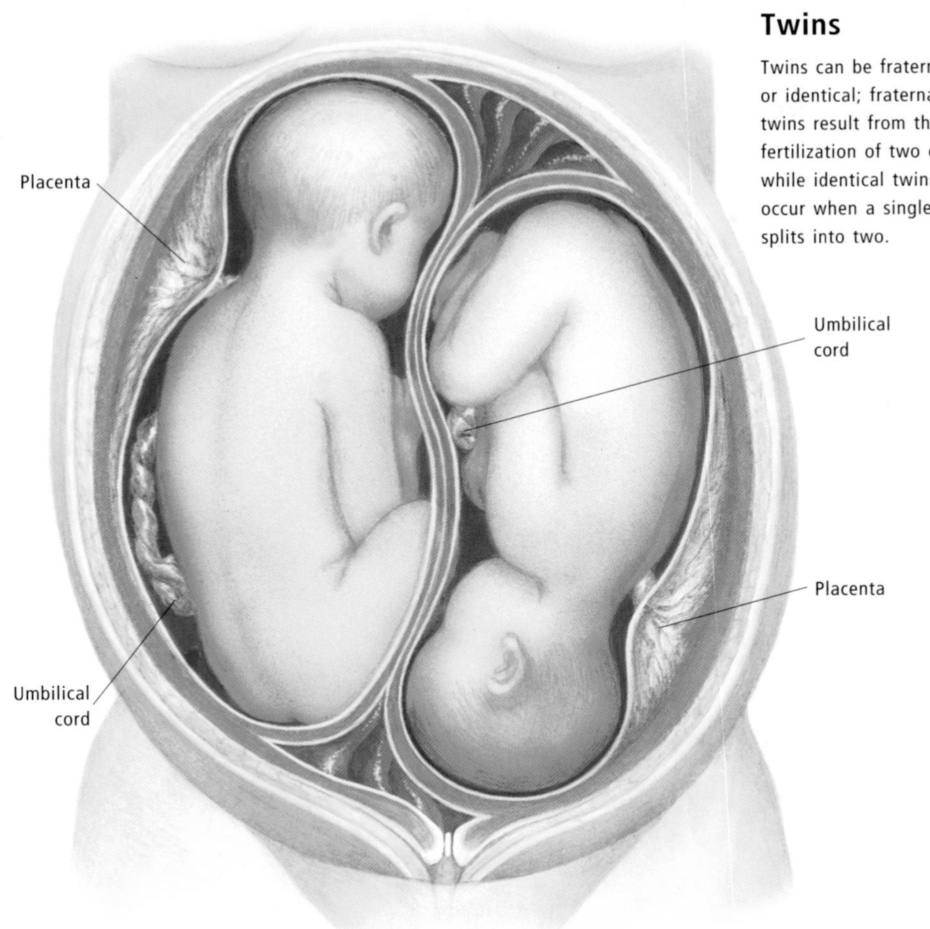

Twins

Twins can be fraternal or identical; fraternal twins result from the fertilization of two eggs, while identical twins occur when a single egg splits into two.

Typhoid vaccines give partial protection and the risk of the disease can be reduced by proper sanitation, good hygiene, by boiling or purifying all drinking water, pasteurizing milk and washing fruit and vegetables. People who have had typhoid may become carriers.

SEE ALSO *Gastroenteritis, Infectious diseases*

TYPHUS

Typhus is a general term for any of several related diseases caused by species of the microorganism *Rickettsia*, which are transmitted by a louse or a flea from infected rats or mice. They include epidemic typhus, endemic typhus and scrub typhus. Symptoms are fever, headache and the appearance of pink spots on all parts of the body except the face, hands and feet. Vomiting and delirium may occur. Antibiotics usually eradicate the infection.

Vaccines are available against epidemic and endemic typhus, but not scrub typhus. Insecticides, mite-repellent creams and clothing covering arms and legs are recommended in places where typhus is common.

SEE ALSO *Infectious diseases*

UVWXYZ

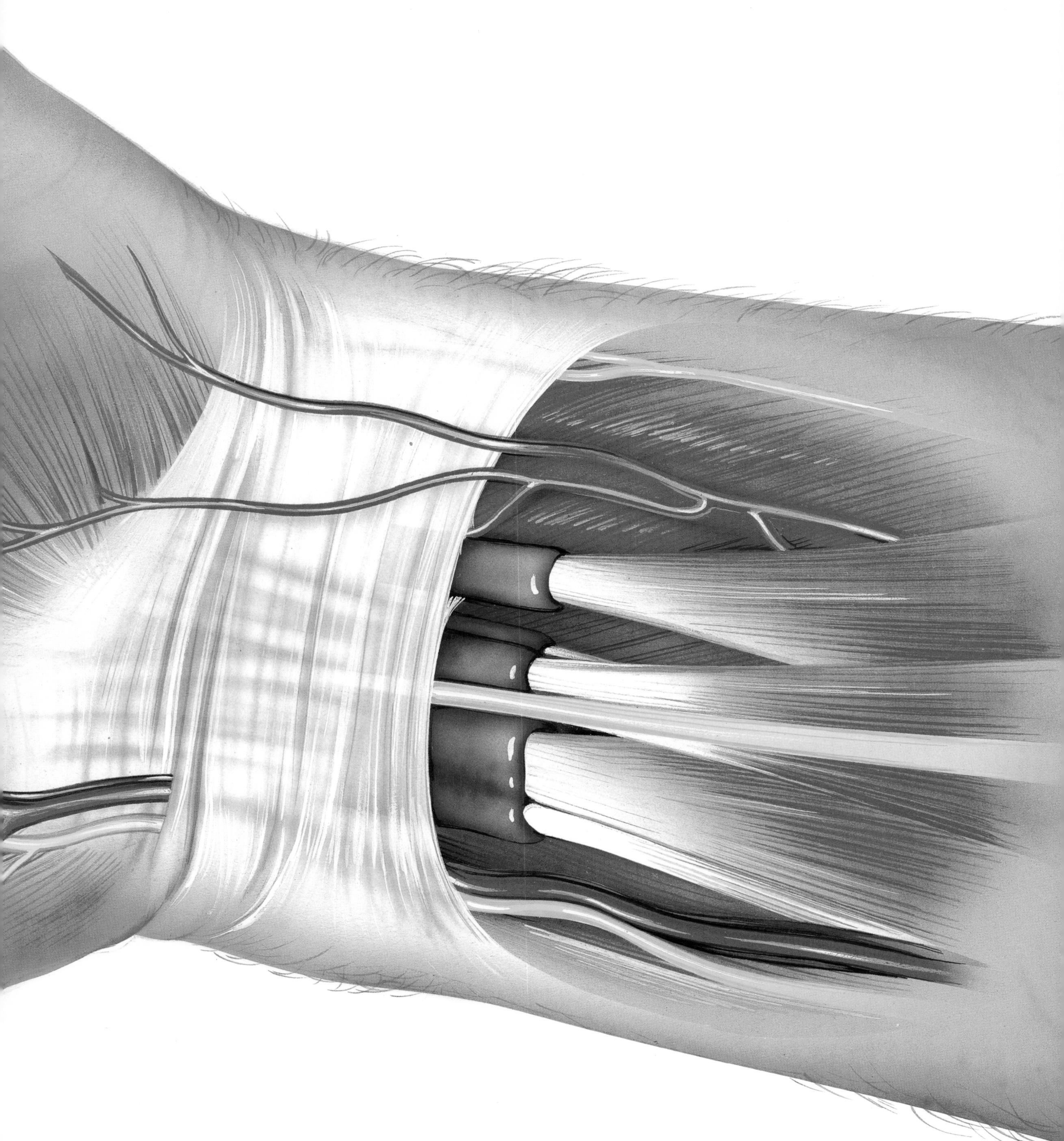

ULCER

An ulcer is a region where the surface layer of the skin, or the lining of an internal organ such as the gut or airway, has been lost. There is often loss of underlying tissue, so that the region has a punched-out appearance, as if a cookie-cutter has been used.

Ulcers may occur in many areas of the body. On the skin, decubitus ulcers (bedsores) can occur following prolonged and unrelieved pressure on the skin, sometimes associated with poor circulation. Some skin cancers may develop ulcers in their central regions, as seen with rodent ulcers (basal cell carcinomas). Varicose ulcers develop around the ankles, due to problems with drainage of venous blood from the skin of the leg. The cornea at the front of the eye may become ulcerated, with serious consequences for vision. Inside the mouth, aphthous ulcers may develop due to poor dentition, poor oral hygiene, excessive alcohol intake or cigarette smoking. Peptic ulcers develop in the upper gut, usually after the *Helicobacter pylori* bacterium has weakened and damaged the protective lining of the stomach or duodenum, allowing penetration by corrosive digestive juices. Multiple ulcers may occur in the colon and rectum in the condition known as ulcerative colitis.

SEE ALSO *Basal cell carcinoma, Cornea, Peptic ulcer, Ulcerative colitis*

ULCERATIVE COLITIS

Ulcerative colitis is predominantly a disease of the large bowel, although it may also involve the end of the small bowel. The disease usually arises between 15 and 20 years of age, although some patients develop the disease in their sixties. The disease involves loss of the surface lining of the bowel (ulceration) with bleeding. Patients complain of rectal bleeding and diarrhea, frequent discharges of watery stool mixed with blood, pus and mucus. Many patients have cramping abdominal pain, with fever, vomiting, weight loss and dehydration.

The complications of ulcerative colitis are very serious. About 30–40 percent of patients will develop cancer in the affected bowel within 20 years of onset. Other complications include a life-threatening dilation of the colon (toxic megacolon), which occurs in about 3 percent of patients; and perforation of the bowel in a further 3 percent.

Treatment may involve anti-inflammatory drugs, or surgery, particularly if chronic symptoms or cancer develop. Due to better treatment, the mortality rate is much lower now than 30 years ago.

SEE ALSO *Bowel cancer, Intestines, Rectum, Ulcer*

ULNA

The ulna and radius are the two bones of the forearm. The ulna lies on the medial (inner) side of the forearm, extending from the el-

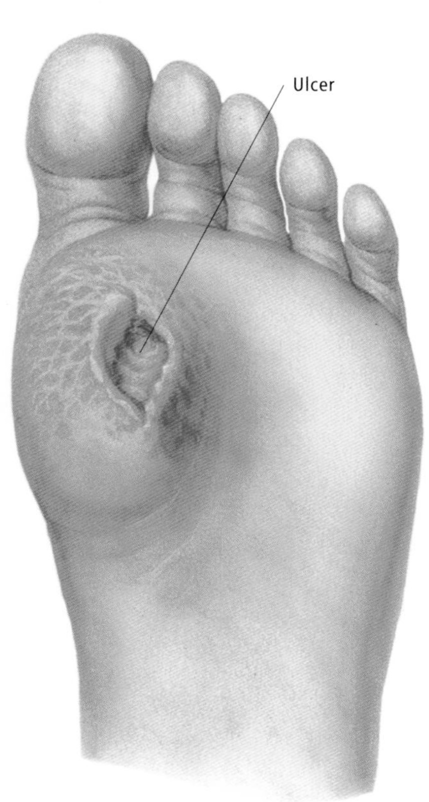

Foot ulcer

Diabetics often have poor circulation to the legs and feet and may develop ulcers in these areas. These ulcers often take a long time to heal.

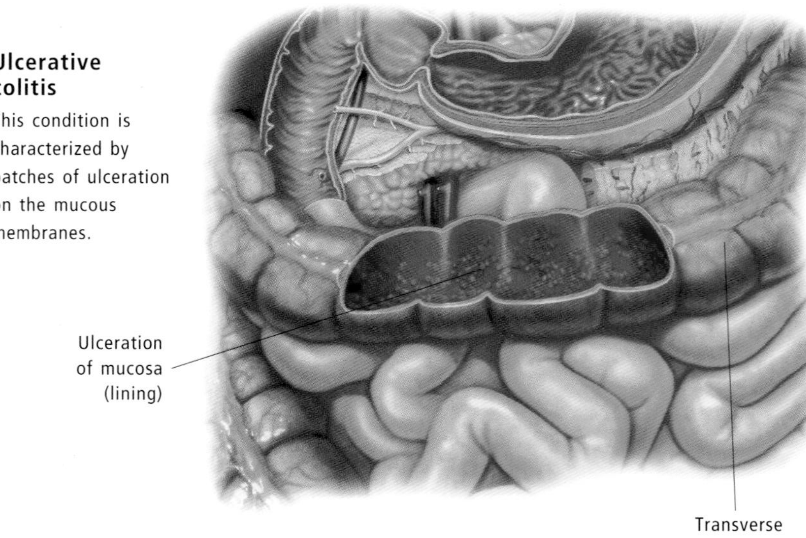

Ulcerative colitis

This condition is characterized by patches of ulceration on the mucous membranes.

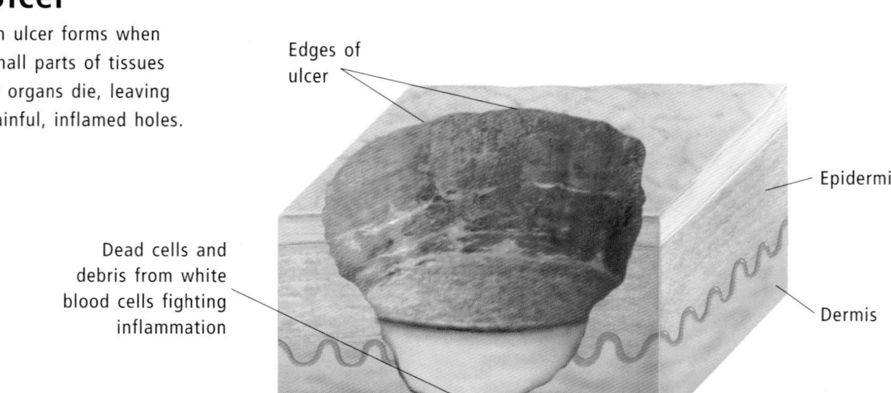

Ulcer

An ulcer forms when small parts of tissues or organs die, leaving painful, inflamed holes.

bow to the wrist. The ulna is a long bone of irregular cross-section, thickest at the elbow end and tapering towards the wrist. It projects above and behind the elbow. At the elbow, the ulna forms a hinge joint with the humerus. The radius articulates with the ulna at both ends, and is firmly bound to it along most of its length by a fibrous membrane which permits the radius to swing around the ulna, carrying the wrist with it. The ulna is not involved in the wrist joint. The ulna and radius are often fractured (resulting in a broken forearm).

SEE ALSO *Arm, Elbow, Humerus, Radius*

ULNAR NERVE

The ulnar nerve is one of the major nerves of the upper limb arising from the brachial plexus in the shoulder. It runs down the inner side of the upper arm, initially accompanying the brachial artery, winds around the inner side of the elbow joint to enter the forearm, and runs along the inner side of the forearm to enter the hand on the little-finger side. In the forearm, its position can be mapped by a line from the medial epicondyle of the humerus to the inner edge of the pisiform bone.

Branches of the ulnar nerve activate the flexor carpi ulnaris muscle and half of the flexor digitorum profundus muscle, and small muscles of the hand. The ulnar nerve provides sensation for the skin on the little-finger side of the hand. At the elbow, the ulnar nerve lies in a groove on the upper surface of the medial epicondyle, where it is liable to injury.

SEE ALSO *Arm, Elbow, Humerus, Ulna*

ULTRASOUND

Also known as ultrasonography or sonography, ultrasound is a diagnostic procedure that uses sound waves above 20,000 cycles per second to create an image. It produces excellent images of soft organs or organs filled with fluid; it is used to detect both cysts and solid tumors, to investigate the cause of abdominal pain and to guide the insertion of a needle during a needle biopsy or a test such as amniocentesis. During pregnancy ultrasound is used to confirm the age of the fetus, the position and/or health of the placenta, the number of babies and the physical development of the baby.

Ultrasound is usually performed as an outpatient procedure. A small amount of gel is applied to the skin over the area to be scanned, which improves the transmission of sound waves. The ultrasound transducer is moved backwards and forwards over the

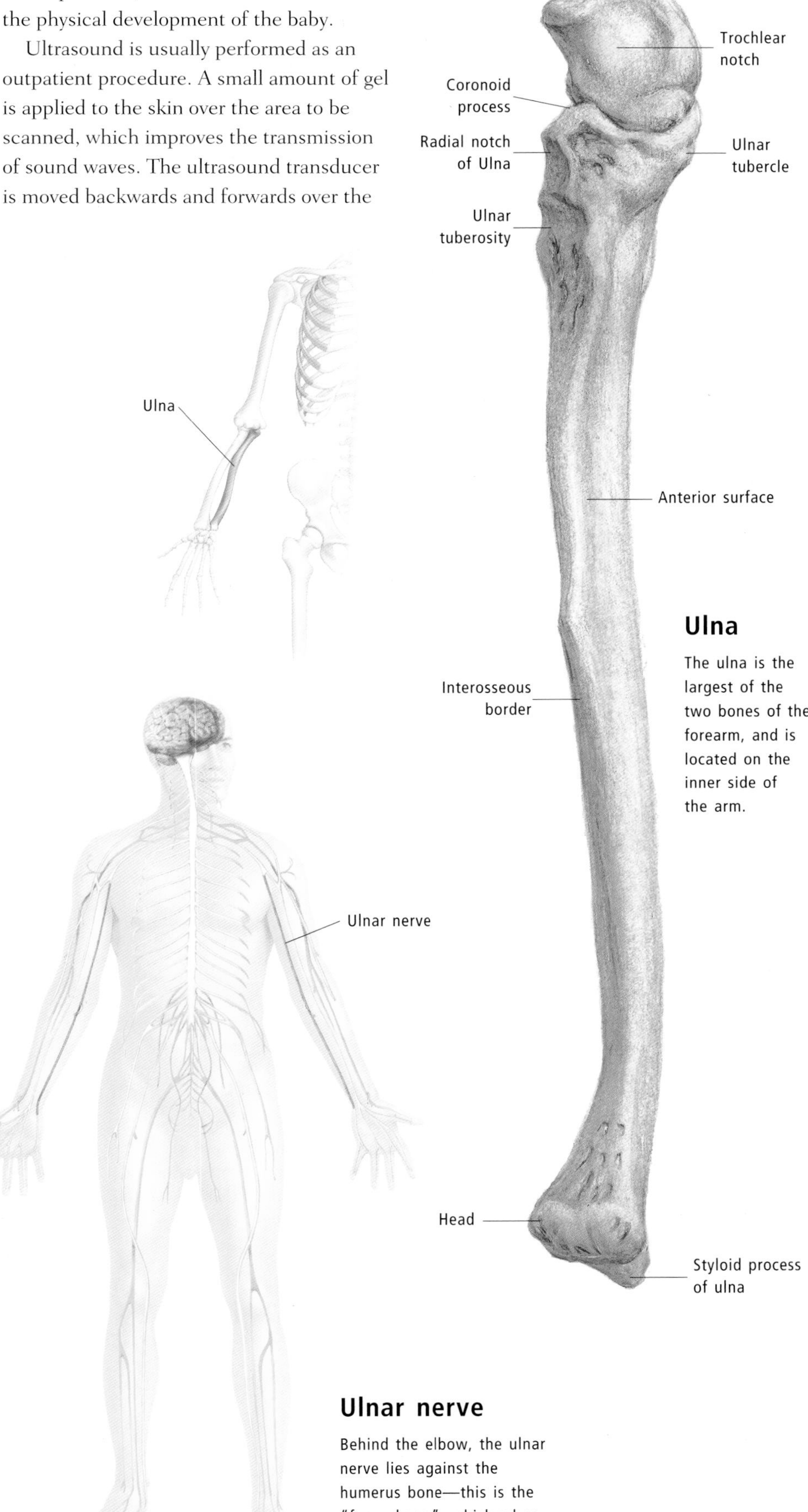

Ulna

The ulna is the largest of the two bones of the forearm, and is located on the inner side of the arm.

Ulnar nerve

Behind the elbow, the ulnar nerve lies against the humerus bone—this is the "funny bone", which when struck causes an odd sensation in the elbow area.

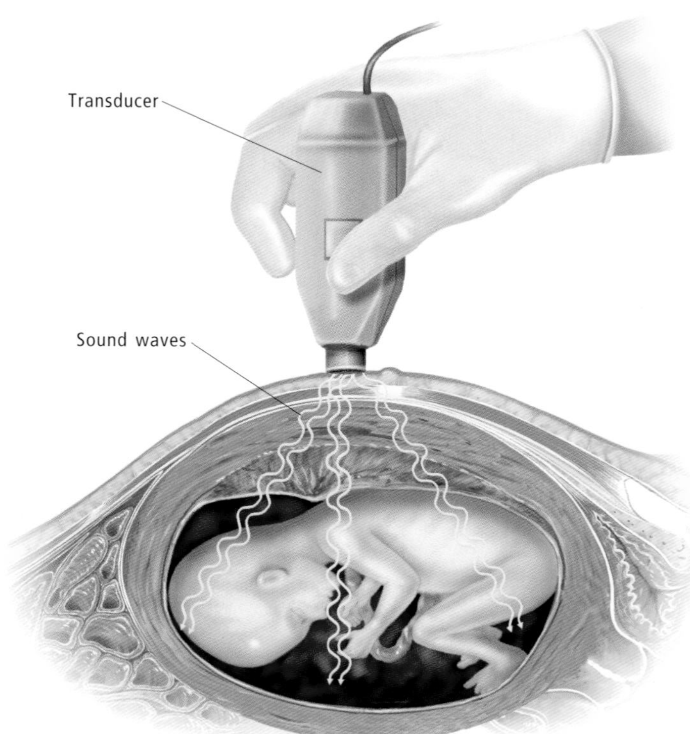

Ultrasound

This procedure uses sound waves to form a two-dimensional image of internal organs. It is commonly used in antenatal care to determine the health and development of the fetus. The transducer transmits reflections of the sound waves to a computer which converts them into an image on a screen.

area, transmitting the reflections of the sound waves to a computer, which converts them to an image on a screen.

Doppler ultrasonography is a specialized type of ultrasound used to investigate the flow of blood through blood vessels, and to look at the movement of parts of organs such as heart valves. Very high energy ultrasound produces a heating effect that is used in sports physical therapy to treat soft tissue injury. Ultrasound is also used in one form of lithotripsy, using the sound waves to shatter kidney stones.

In many industrialized societies ultrasound is treated as an expected part of antenatal care. It has many advantages over other methods of imaging, including the fact that the transmission of sound makes it safer than x-rays, which use ionizing radiation.

SEE ALSO *Amniocentesis, Biopsy, Doppler ultrasonography, Fetal development, Imaging techniques, Lithotripsy*

ULTRAVIOLET THERAPY

Ultraviolet (UV) therapy is a form of light therapy (or phototherapy) used to treat skin disorders. The patient stands undressed in a specially designed cabinet containing fluorescent light tubes. Ultraviolet light is administered as either longwave UV light energy (UVA) or shortwave UV light energy (UVB). One form of this treatment, known as PUVA, combines UVA light with psoralen medication, which renders the skin more responsive to the therapy. Ultraviolet therapy is principally used in the treatment of psoriasis, as well as for dermatitis, vitiligo and cutaneous T cell lymphoma.

SEE ALSO *Dermatitis, Psoriasis, Vitiligo*

UMBILICAL CORD

The umbilical cord serves to join the unborn baby (fetus) to the afterbirth (placenta), by which the fetus obtains nourishment from its mother. The fully developed cord is $\frac{1}{2}$–1 inch (1–2 centimeters) in diameter and about 20 inches (50 centimeters) long, but its length is very variable: 8–48 inches (20–120 centimeters). It contains two umbilical arteries and one umbilical vein, embedded in a mucoid connective tissue known as Wharton's jelly. It is covered by a thin layer of epithelium. Nourishment and oxygen pass from the placenta to the baby; waste products pass in the other direction.

Immediately after birth, blood from the placenta and umbilical cord passes into the baby. After delivery, the umbilical cord is tied in two places and cut between the ties (the ties prevent loss of blood). The remnants of the cord initially remain attached to the navel (umbilicus), then shrivel up and fall off after 3–4 days.

SEE ALSO *Childbirth, Placenta, Pregnancy*

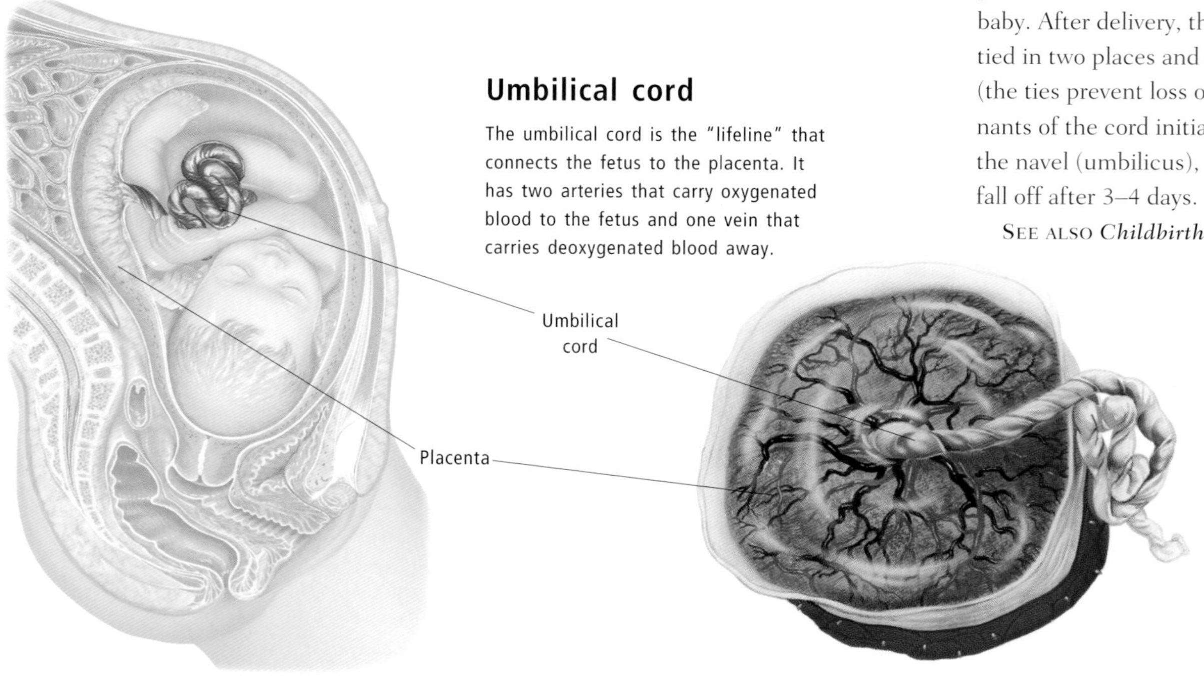

Umbilical cord

The umbilical cord is the "lifeline" that connects the fetus to the placenta. It has two arteries that carry oxygenated blood to the fetus and one vein that carries deoxygenated blood away.

UNCONSCIOUSNESS

An unconscious person is one who is hard to rouse or is unaware of their surroundings. Unconsciousness is caused by illness, injury or emotional shock. It may be temporary, as in fainting or blacking out, or it can be prolonged, as in coma. Depending on the cause, someone in a coma may never recover.

Unconsciousness has many causes; some of the more common include stroke, epilepsy, diabetic coma, drug overdose, concussion, low blood sugar (hypoglycemia) and heart attack. People who suffer from a medical condition that can cause unconsciousness should wear an identification bracelet or pendant, carry a card in a wallet, or have a special sticker on the back of their driver's license.

First aid is vital in the treatment of unconsciousness. Do not give an unconscious person food or drink. Do not leave an unconscious person alone. If the victim has stopped breathing, give artificial respiration and if the victim's heart has stopped, give external cardiac compression. Stop any bleeding with bandages and pressure, and call emergency medical services.

Anyone who has been unconscious for a period should see a physician even if they have apparently recovered, as it may signify an underlying illness or head injury.

SEE ALSO *Coma*

UREMIA

Uremia is the medical term for retention in the blood of urinary substances, normally caused by severe kidney failure. It occurs when the diseased kidney is no longer able to clear the blood of waste products such as creatinine, urea and ammonia. The term uremia has been used for over a century. It was originally used because it was presumed that the symptoms of renal failure were due to retention of abnormal amounts of urea in the blood. However, it is now clear that the symptoms of renal failure are attributable not so much to the accumulation of urea but to disturbances of water and electrolyte balance and the accumulation of many other endproducts of metabolism.

Uremia can cause a wide range of clinical symptoms. Symptoms vary from patient to patient, depending on the degree of reduction in renal function and the rapidity with which renal function is lost. At an early stage patients will often have no symptoms, but as renal function deteriorates, symptoms develop. Loss of appetite, nausea, hiccups and vomiting are the common initial symptoms of uremia. Stomach ulcers occur in one-quarter of uremic patients. The patient's skin often develops a sallow complexion (a yellow-brown appearance). This is due to the combined effect of impaired excretion of urinary pigments (urochromes) combined with anemia. High blood pressure (hypertension) is the most common complication of uremia. Fluid retention may result in congestive heart failure and/ or pulmonary edema (fluid in the lungs). Pericarditis (inflammation of the lining of the heart) may occur. The patient may experience disturbances of the nervous system that can include loss of concentration, memory loss and minor behavioral changes. A peripheral sensory neuropathy is common and results in loss of sensation, typically in the legs. Other symptoms include muscle cramps and muscle twitching. In terminal uremia patients become drowsy and finally sink into a coma.

Diabetes and high blood pressure are the commonest causes of uremia. Other causes include glomerulonephritis (inflammation of the kidney), analgesic nephropathy (due to long-term ingestion of large quantities of analgesics), systemic vascular disease (e.g. systemic lupus erythematosus), obstruction of the urinary tract (by congenital defect, kidney stones or tumors) and polycystic kidneys (a congenital abnormality).

The treatment is to correct the underlying kidney disease if possible. A diet low in protein, salts and water will help minimize the production of wastes by the body and alleviate symptoms. Eventually, kidney dialysis or a kidney transplant may be necessary.

SEE ALSO *Dialysis, Kidney, Transplant surgery*

Ureter

The muscular walls of the ureters propel urine from the kidneys to the bladder.

URETER

The ureters are two thin, muscular tubes that pass urine from the kidneys to the bladder. The walls of the ureters contain smooth muscles, which contract and propel urine in waves to the bladder.

The ureter may become blocked by a stone or a tumor. It may become inflamed, along with the rest of the urinary tract, in pyelonephritis.

Disorders of the ureter can be identified by a pyelogram, an x-ray taken after dye has been injected, showing the outline of the ureter and the other organs in the urinary tract.

SEE ALSO *Bladder, Kidney, Pyelonephritis, Urinary systems*

URETHRA

The urethra is the tube through which urine travels from the bladder to the outside of the body. In women, the urethra is short; it opens between the vagina and clitoris. The urethra is longer in men and also serves as the passage for semen. It passes through the prostate gland, where it is joined by the sperm ducts, and opens at the tip of the penis.

Various disorders may affect the urethra. It may become infected and inflamed (urethritis). Symptoms include pain on urinating (dysuria) and in men, a discharge from the

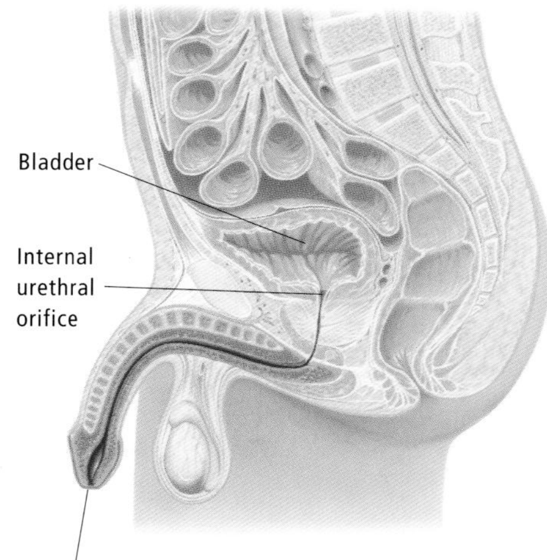

Male urethra

In men, the long urethral tube (usually 8 inches or 20 centimeters long) passes from the bladder through the prostate gland and penis. It transports urine and semen out of the body.

Female urethra

The female urethra is relatively short. As a result, invading bacteria can pass more easily into the body, leading to frequent bladder infections such as cystitis.

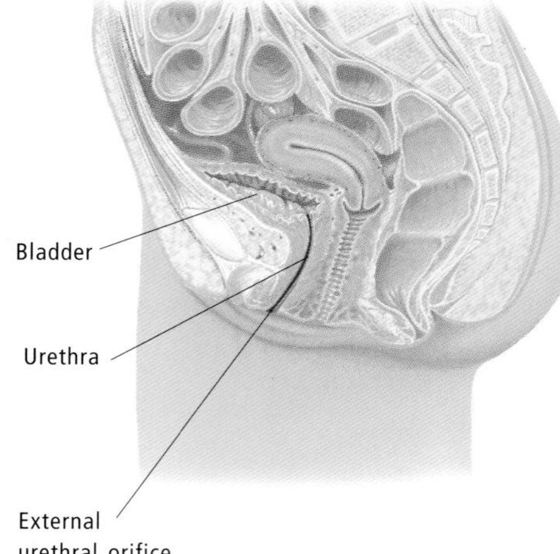

penis. Treatment is with an antibiotic appropriate for the particular microorganism causing the disease. Urethritis may result in scarring and narrowing of the urethra in men.

Epispadias is a congenital defect in which the urethra opens abnormally on the top of the penis, either in the head of, or along the entire length of, the penis. In hypospadias, the urethral opening appears on the underside of the penis. Both conditions cause urinary incontinence and sexual dysfunction in adulthood. Reconstructive surgery usually cures the defects.

SEE ALSO *Bladder, Epispadias, Hypospadias, Urethritis, Urinary incontinence*

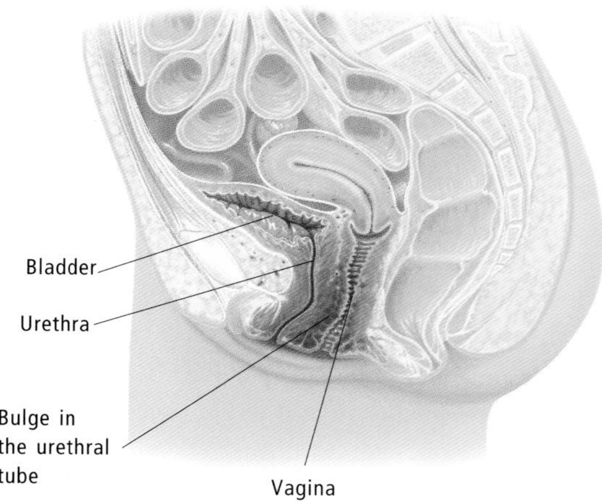

Urethrocele

A weakness in the vaginal wall can result in urethrocele, in which the urethral tube bulges against the vagina.

URETHRITIS

Urethritis is inflammation of the urethra—the tube through which urine travels from the bladder to the outside of the body. It often occurs with cystitis (inflammation of the bladder), prostatitis (inflammation of the prostate) or epididymitis (inflammation of the epididymis). Urethritis is often sexually transmitted, as in the case of gonorrhea and nonspecific or nongonococcal urethritis.

Symptoms are painful or burning urination, a frequent urge to urinate even when there is not much urine in the bladder, and a discharge that may be thick and yellow, or watery and white. A swab and culture of the discharge will identify the organism and help the physician to prescribe the correct antibiotic which usually cures the condition. Urethritis may result in scarring and narrowing of the urethra in men.

SEE ALSO *Bladder, Cystitis, Epididymitis, Gonorrhea, Prostatitis, Urethra*

URETHROCELE

A urethrocele is a bulge of the urethra (the tube that carries urine from the bladder to the outside of the body) along the front wall of the vagina. It is caused by a weakness in the vaginal wall, usually following childbirth. A minor urethrocele doesn't produce symptoms, but a larger one causes a lump inside the vaginal opening and may cause urinary incontinence. Surgery, performed through the vagina, will repair the weakness in the vaginal wall and the bulging urethra.

SEE ALSO *Bladder, Urethra, Urinary incontinence, Vagina*

URINALYSIS

Urinalysis is a test performed to analyze cells, proteins and other chemicals in the urine. It is used to detect disease, especially of the kidney and urinary tract. For example, the presence of blood in the urine (hematuria) may be due to a urinary tract infection, a stone, a polyp or cancer. Pus cells and bacteria may indicate urinary infection, while protein in the urine (proteinuria) may indicate nephritis or myeloma. Bilirubin in the urine may be a sign of jaundice, and glucose in the urine is usually caused by diabetes mellitus.

The sample of urine may be cultured for 24–48 hours. If bacterial colonies form in the culture it may be a sign of infection in the urinary tract. The culture will show the specific organism causing the infection and further tests can determine which antibiotics will kill it.

SEE ALSO *Cystitis, Kidney, Nephritis, Urinary systems, Urinary tract*

URINARY INCONTINENCE

The abnormal lack of voluntary control of the bladder in older children and adults is called incontinence. It may be caused by a neurological disorder or a disorder interfering with control of the sphincter muscle that normally closes the bladder—for example after pelvic surgery. In males, it may result from partial obstruction caused by enlargement of the prostate gland (prostatomegaly). Some women with prolapse (displacement) of the uterus develop stress incontinence as the uterus presses on the bladder and allows urine to escape when the woman coughs or laughs. It is important that the underlying cause of incontinence is treated. Leakage of urine can be managed by the use of waterproof undergarments with absorbent pads.

SEE ALSO *Bladder, Prolapse, Prostate gland*

URINARY TRACT

The urinary tract is a specialized filtering and recycling system that excretes certain fluid wastes produced by the body in the process of metabolism, such as urea, creatinine and ammonia. These wastes, along with excess water, are removed from the blood as urine by the two kidneys. Urine then passes through tubes called ureters into the bladder. From the bladder the urine passes out of the body through another tube called the urethra.

The urinary tract is subject to various disorders. Urinary tract infection is an infection of one or more parts of the urinary system, usually caused by bacteria. Urinary tract obstruction occurs when there is a blockage in the urethra, bladder or ureters. The condition may be congenital (existing from birth) or it may be caused by tumors or mineral deposits that form stones.

Diseases of the kidneys can lead to an accumulation of wastes in the blood, a condition called uremia. Cancers may form in the bladder or kidney. Diseases of the urinary tract are investigated by x-rays, pyelograms (x-rays taken after radiopaque dye has been injected, which show the outline of the urinary tract), cystoscopy (a tube inserted into the bladder through which the bladder can be viewed), CAT scans and ultrasound.

SEE ALSO *Bladder, Kidney, Urethra, Urinary systems*

URTICARIA

Urticaria (hives or nettle rash) is a skin rash in the form of wheals that are red, itchy and raised. It appears suddenly and may disappear just as quickly, leaving no trace or permanent damage. It can affect either sex and appear at any age. Urticaria of pregnancy may appear in the last two or three weeks and disappears after delivery. Urticaria can occur after illness, as a result of skin infection, or as the result of an allergic response when the chemical histamine is produced within the body. The rash may disappear as the allergic reaction subsides.

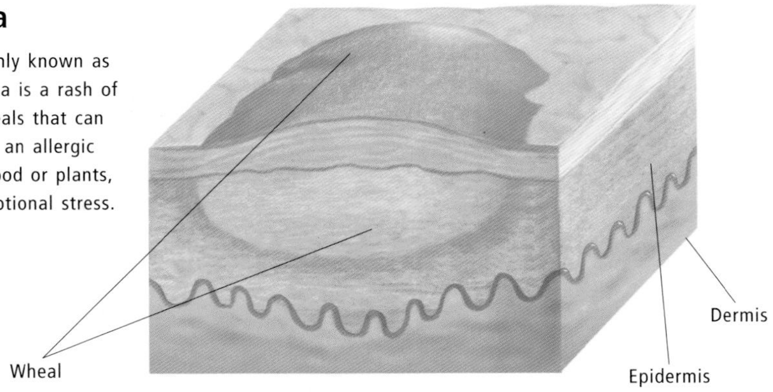

Occasionally urticaria may cause swellings in the throat and restrict breathing. If the rash appears to be below the skin surface and there is burning or pain rather than itching, a medical examination may be needed to establish whether it is urticaria or angioedema, a more serious condition.

Visible symptoms and the torment of itching can be relieved by taking a lukewarm bath with soothing additives, or by applying cool compresses to the rash. Medical advice should be sought in all cases where urticaria is persistent or is causing distress or discomfort. Drugs used in treatment include corticosteroid creams, antihistamines and, where there are breathing difficulties, epinephrine (adrenaline).

SEE ALSO *Allergies, Angioedema, Antihistamines*

Urticaria

More commonly known as hives, urticaria is a rash of itchy red wheals that can be caused by an allergic reaction to food or plants, illness or emotional stress.

UTERUS

The uterus (womb), the organ of gestation, is located in the pelvis, between the bladder and the rectum. It undergoes regular changes during the menstrual cycle. The non-pregnant uterus is pear shaped and flattened from front to back. It communicates with the vagina below. The two fallopian tubes open into its upper part, one on each side. In about 80 percent of women the uterus is anteverted (tilted forward); in the remaining 20 percent it is retroverted (tilted backwards). The uterus should be somewhat mobile and can be displaced vertically by a very distended bladder. This displacement is used to allow a clearer view of a non-pregnant uterus during ultrasound examination.

The uterus consists of the fundus (top), body and cervix. The wall of the body consists of an endometrium or inner lining adjacent to the central cavity; a thick muscular myometrium; and an outer layer of peritoneum or perimetrium. The endometrium contains large numbers of glands and blood vessels. It undergoes proliferation and secretion during much of the menstrual cycle, followed by sloughing of all but the deepest parts at menstruation. The remaining tissue forms the basis for regeneration of a new endometrium during the next cycle. The myometrium undergoes mild contractions during menstruation.

The uterus enlarges enormously in pregnancy and its hollow center is obliterated during the third month. It reaches the top of the pubic bone by about 12 weeks, the level of the umbilicus at about 20 weeks and the diaphragm at 36 weeks. The pregnant uterus also displaces or compresses adjacent abdominal organs.

The uterus is attached to the lateral walls of the pelvis by the broad ligament. Further support is provided by ligaments attached to the cervix, which cross the pelvic floor and attach to the walls of the pelvis. Pelvic floor muscles are also important in maintaining the uterus in its correct position. Damage or weakening of these supports can lead to a prolapsed uterus. In this condition the uterus and cervix become inverted and descend into the vagina or in extreme cases

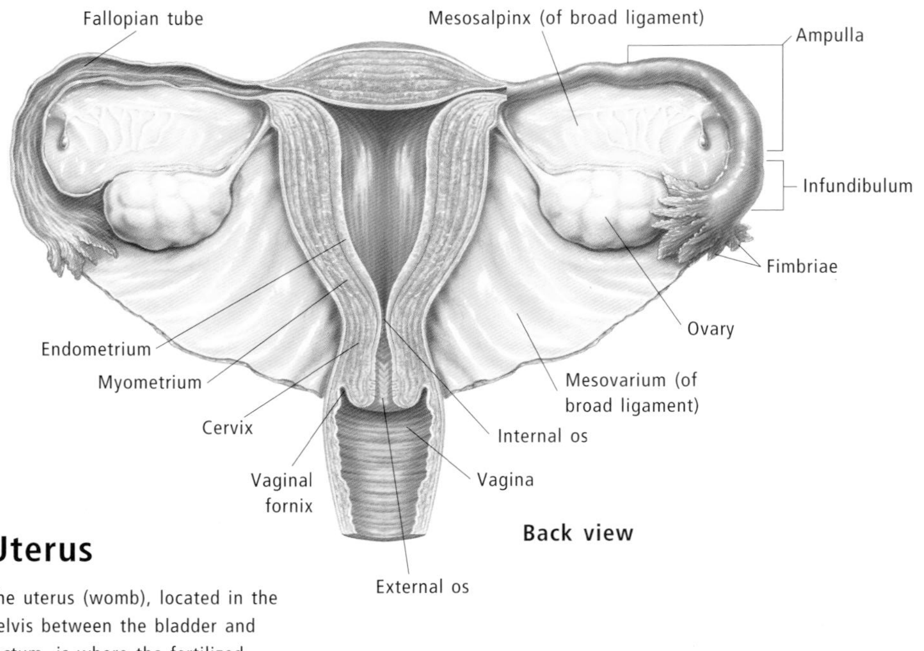

Uterus

The uterus (womb), located in the pelvis between the bladder and rectum, is where the fertilized ovum develops into an embryo and fetus.

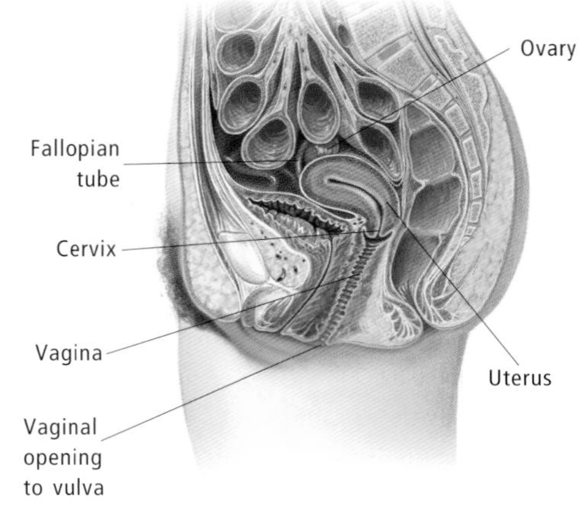

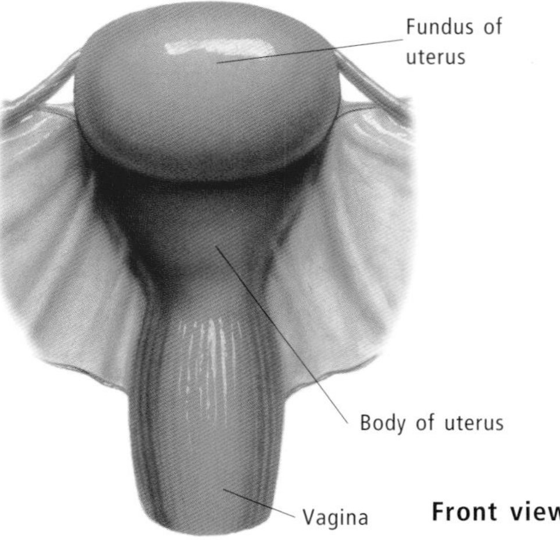

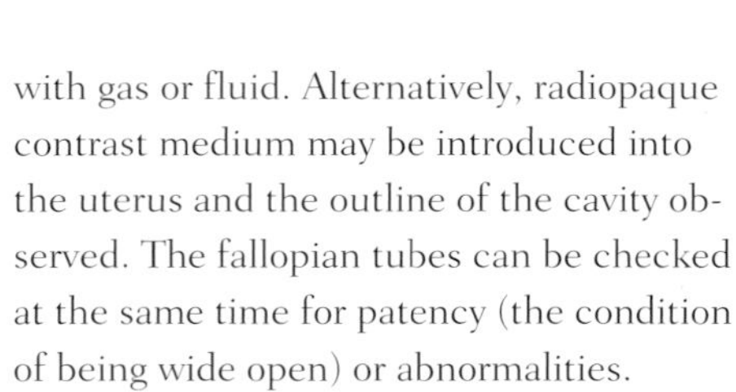

may protrude, along with the vagina, outside the body. The bladder and ureters (tubes connecting the kidneys to the bladder) may be inverted as well and this often causes acute urinary retention. The rectum and loops of intestine can also be involved.

The cervix has a thick muscular wall and a mucus-secreting lining which is not sloughed at menstruation. The mucus is usually thick and fills the cervical canal to form a protective plug and a barrier to sperm penetration. The mucus becomes thinner around the time of ovulation. Some of the mucus glands may become blocked and enlarged to form cysts. The layer of cells adjacent to the cervical canal, which connects the vagina to the uterus, is thin but becomes thicker just above the opening of the cervix with the vagina. This is where the majority of cervical carcinomas develop and, for this reason, pap smears are taken from this region. The cervical canal is comparatively narrow and has to be expanded under either local or general anesthetic in order to obtain a biopsy of the endometrium. A tissue sample is taken via curettage. Curettage can also be used as a treatment for abnormal uterine bleeding.

The internal structure of the uterus may be observed by passing a fiberoptic telescope through the cervix into the uterine cavity which has previously been inflated with gas or fluid. Alternatively, radiopaque contrast medium may be introduced into the uterus and the outline of the cavity observed. The fallopian tubes can be checked at the same time for patency (the condition of being wide open) or abnormalities.

Diseases and disorders

Cervical mucus resists the penetration of pathogens from the vagina. However, this protection is only partial, and the microbes responsible for pelvic inflammatory disease (PID) usually ascend from the vagina, although they may arise from an abdominal infection. Oral contraceptive users have a lower incidence of PID, apparently due to changes in the cervical mucus which render it more impervious to bacterial penetration.

The uterus is particularly vulnerable to infection after childbirth when there is an incomplete endometrial surface and possible damage to the cervix or when there are retained fragments of placenta. Infection may spread to adjacent organs or the bloodstream, leading to blood poisoning (septicemia) or puerperal fever. Permanent damage may follow, including chronic inflammation, adhesions and uterine displacement. Puerperal sepsis or fever is now uncommon due to improved obstetric care and antibiotics.

Fibroids (myomas or leiomyomas) commonly occur in the myometrium. These are benign tumors, consisting of spherical masses of muscle and fibrous tissue and ranging in size from minute to occasionally enormous. They are more frequent and likely to cause abnormal uterine bleeding in women over 35 years of age. Treatment involves the use of progestins, removal of the myoma, or hysterectomy.

The junction of the endometrium and myometrium is usually clearcut. In a sizeable minority of women, however, there is some growth of the endometrium into the myometrium, a condition known as adenomyosis. This is sometimes associated with endometriosis, fibroids or abnormal endometrial thickening. The tissue forming the adenomyosis may or may not respond to ovarian hormones. Adenomyosis may be symptomless or associated with menstrual discomfort or dysfunction. Treatment can be either surgical or hormonal. Adenomyosis may sometimes be associated with malignant changes.

Hysterectomy is surgical removal of the uterus. This is described as subtotal when

U

only the uterus is excised and total if both the uterus and cervix are removed. A radical hysterectomy involves removal of uterus, cervix, fallopian tubes, ovaries, the upper third of the vagina and at least some of the adjacent lymph nodes. Hysterectomy may be carried out via an abdominal incision or via an incision around the cervical opening (vaginal hysterectomy).

Complete absence of the uterus is rare but deformities resulting in either a bicornate (double) uterus or a single uterus divided by an internal septum can occur. These reflect the embryological origin of the uterus, which starts as two separate tubes which fuse during fetal life. A double or septate vagina may accompany bicornate uterus. The external genitalia, which have a separate embryological origin, are usually normal.

SEE ALSO *Cervix, Endometrium, Hysterectomy, Menstruation, Pap smear, Pelvic floor muscles, Pelvic inflammatory disease, Pregnancy, Reproductive systems, Retroversion of uterus*

VAGINA

The vagina is the passage connecting the uterus to the outside of the body. It is situated in the lower pelvis and pelvic floor and is located between the bladder and the rectum. The lower opening in virgin women is partly closed by a thin membrane called the hymen. The vaginal wall consists of a thick external muscle, an inner mucosa, and a cavity with the inner surfaces in direct contact. The cavity tilts slightly backwards and is at about 90° to the cervical canal, which connects the vagina with the cavity of the uterus. The vagina contains fluid consisting of cervical mucus and plasma from capillaries in the mucosa. The external opening of the cervix protrudes into the upper part of the vagina and is surrounded by a groove or fornix. The vagina is supported by the cervical ligaments and pelvic floor muscles.

The vagina and external cervix can be observed by expanding the vaginal cavity with the aid of a vaginal speculum.

The mucosa is lined with a thick layer of cells containing glycogen. The superficial cells are sloughed into the vaginal fluid and replaced by cell divisions deeper in the lining. The sloughed cells are broken down by bacteria (*Lactobacillus*), which are normal vaginal flora. The lactic acid thus produced discourages invasion by pathogens. If the *Lactobacilli* are destroyed, for example when antibiotics are administered, then yeast (candida) may proliferate and cause thrush. Symptoms are a white discharge (leukorrhea) and vulval itching.

There is little glycogen in the lining cells before puberty and vaginal infections are correspondingly more common. Glycogen also decreases after menopause and the vaginal mucosa becomes thin and prone to infection and irritation, leading to postmenopausal or atrophic vaginitis. Treatment is by topical or oral estrogens.

Diseases and disorders

Benign vaginal tumors can arise in the fibrous tissue of the vaginal wall or from remnants of embryonic tissue. These may be removed surgically if causing bleeding, discharge or local irritation. Vaginal malignancies are often the result of secondary spread from growths elsewhere. Primary vaginal carcinomas are more common in postmenopausal women. Treatment is either by irradiation, or by removal of the carcinoma or the entire vagina and possibly adjacent organs. Primary vaginal adenocarcinoma may occur in women under 25 who were exposed *in utero* to diethylstilboestrol (a non-steroidal synthetic estrogen) administered to their mothers early in pregnancy.

Vaginal prolapse can include a part of the bladder, which is pulled downwards through a weakness in the vaginal wall. This is termed a cystocele and can cause difficulties in urination. Surgical repair is usually the best treatment.

Fistulas are abnormal canals formed as a result of injury or occasionally as developmental abnormalities. Vaginal fistulas are the result of obstetric, surgical or accidental trauma or heavy irradiation. Fistulas connecting the vagina with the bladder cause continuous leakage of urine, causing physical damage and social embarrassment. Surgical closure is the most common treatment. Sometimes recent fistulas may close of their own accord if the bladder is drained continuously while the woman is maintained in a prone position. Fistulas can also connect the vagina to parts of the intestine, particularly the rectum (recto-vaginal fistula).

SEE ALSO *Candidiasis, Cystocele, Estrogens, Fistula, Prolapse, Reproductive systems, Vaginitis*

VAGINISMUS

Vaginismus is a condition in which spasm of the muscles at the entrance to the vagina precludes normal intercourse or renders it impossibly painful. It is usually psychological in origin and can arise from a fear of intercourse or of ensuing pregnancy. It can also follow traumas such as rape, painful childbirth, painful initial attempts at intercourse or intercourse too soon after gynecological surgery. It may occur even though sexual desire is quite strong. The woman may be sexually responsive to non-penetrative stimuli or capable of clitoral orgasm.

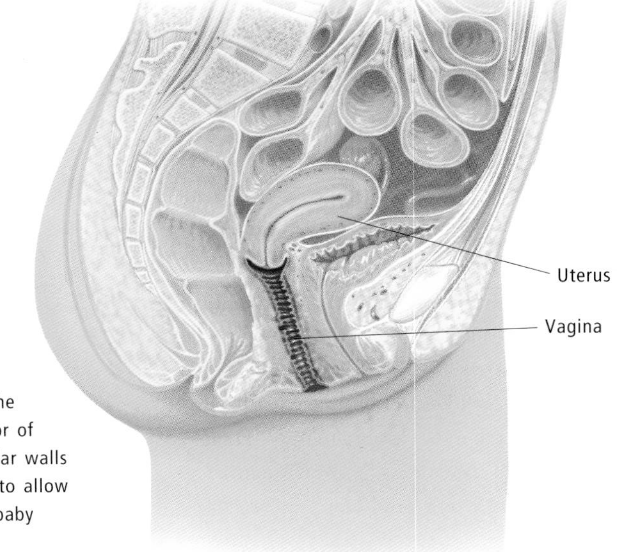

Vagina

The vagina is the passage that links the uterus to the exterior of the body. Its muscular walls are flexible enough to allow the passage of the baby during childbirth.

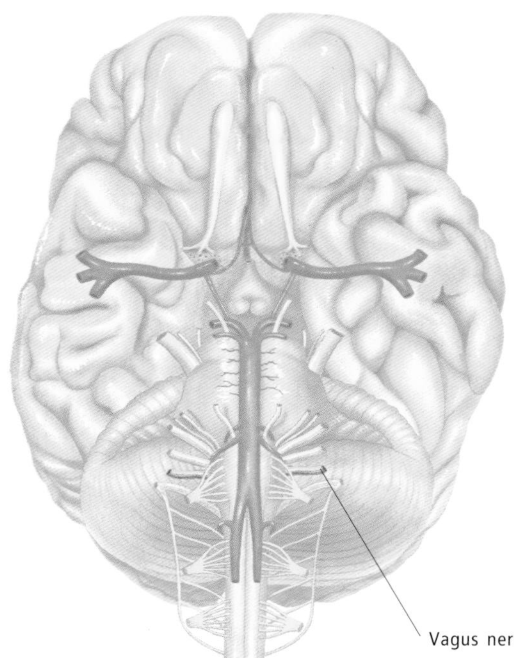

Vagus nerve

The tenth cranial nerve (vagus nerve) is involved in a variety of functions, such as sneezing, swallowing, coughing, speech, heartbeat, and the secretion of stomach acid.

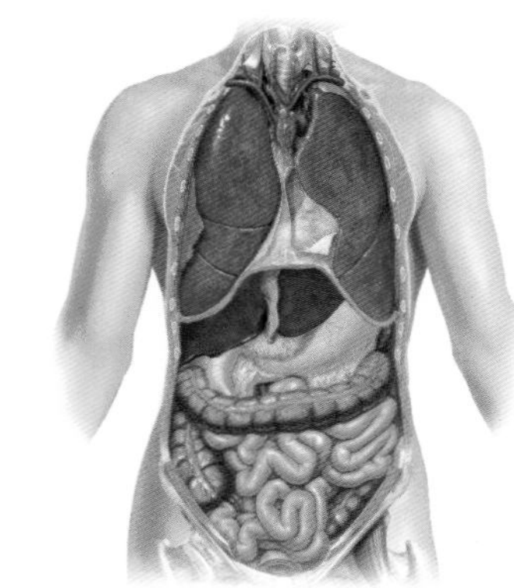

In the absence of organic problems, treatment for vaginismus is usually psychotherapy aimed at treating the fears underlying the condition. Gentle gradual dilation of the vaginal opening may also help.

SEE ALSO *Sexual intercourse, Vagina*

VAGINITIS

Vaginitis is a common gynecological complaint characterized by a discolored discharge and vaginal irritation and redness. Vaginitis is specific if it can be attributed to a particular irritative agent or bacterium. This is usually the case with vaginitis in women of reproductive age. Pre- and postmenopausal women have low levels of estrogen and the vaginal lining is very susceptible to a wide range of noxious agents. It is often impossible to pinpoint the cause of this type of vaginitis and it is described as non-specific.

One of the most common causes of vaginitis in young women is thrush resulting from infection with candida (yeast). Candida infections are not usually transmitted sexually and are due, in some cases, to loss of *Lactobacillus* as a result of antibiotic administration. Candida infections are especially prevalent in diabetes or pregnancy. Treatment is with fungicides. Vaginitis can also be the result of bacterial and protozoal infections, spread primarily by sexual contact.

The vaginal mucosa atrophies after menopause, with little glycogen produced to maintain an acid environment. This renders the vagina prone to infection or irritation leading to postmenopausal or atrophic vaginitis. This is characterized by tiny ulcers, often with a blood-stained discharge accompanied by itching or soreness. Ulceration may cause adhesions between the walls which partly obliterate the vaginal cavity. The condition is treated with estrogen pessaries or oral estrogens. These can cause uterine bleeding so are used only for a limited time.

SEE ALSO *Candidiasis, Estrogens, Menopause, Sexually transmitted diseases, Vagina*

VAGUS NERVE

The vagus or tenth cranial nerve is one of 12 cranial nerves which extend in pairs directly from the brain stem. The vagus nerve contains autonomic nerve fibers, which regulate functions in the body which operate without conscious control. It runs through the neck and thorax to the abdominal cavity and controls breathing, swallowing, speaking, heartbeat, the constriction of blood vessels and bronchial tubes, and digestion. It also conveys the sensation of taste to the brain from the throat.

The vagus nerve is only rarely damaged. One of its branches, the recurrent laryngeal nerve, may be damaged during surgery of the thyroid gland; this will paralyse muscles of the larynx, leading to hoarseness.

In vagotomy, the vagus nerve is cut adjacent to the esophagus to reduce secretion of hydrochloric acid as part of the treatment of stomach ulcer. While the vagus normally

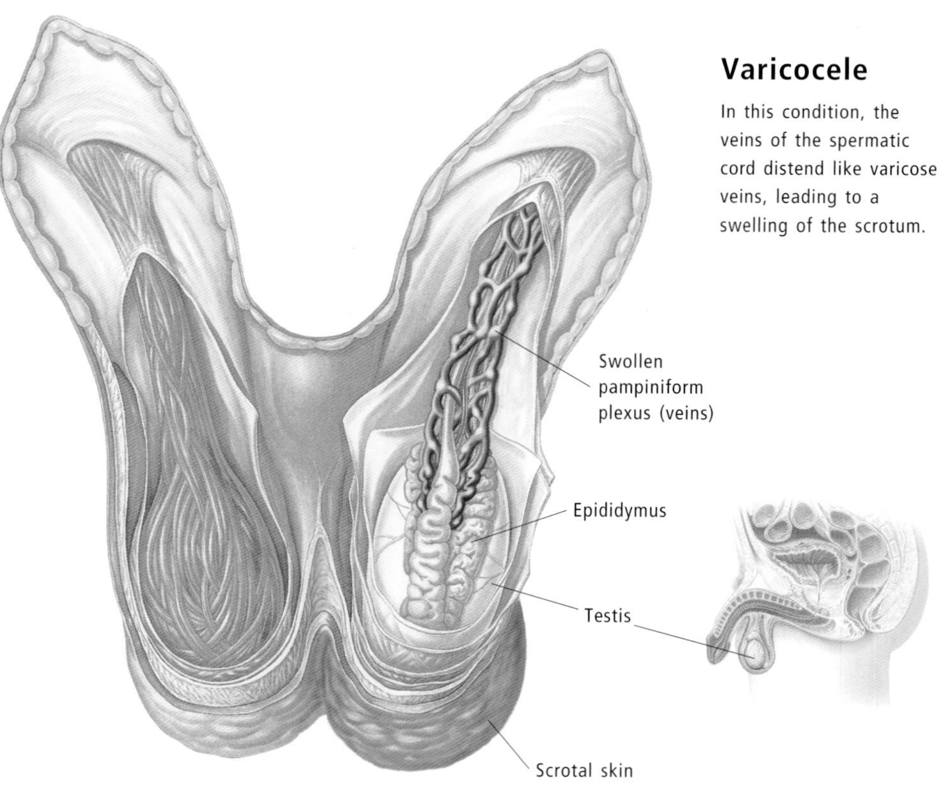

Varicocele

In this condition, the veins of the spermatic cord distend like varicose veins, leading to a swelling of the scrotum.

controls the stimulation of the stomach walls and lower sphincter, normal peristaltic action can continue without it. Vasovagal syncope is fainting caused by slowing of the heartbeat in response to signals from the vagus which arise during severe stomach cramps, through pain, fear or apprehension. The vagal response can, in cases of severe injury, completely inhibit normal movement of food through the bowels for several days. Heart arrhythmia, where the heart rate speeds up for no apparent reason, can sometimes be stopped by stimulation of the vagus nerve. In epilepsy, experiments using an implanted electronic device similar to a heart pacemaker are being used to stimulate the vagus nerve to stop or weaken seizures.

SEE ALSO *Arrythmia, Autonomic nervous system, Epilepsy, Nerves, Nervous system, Spinal cord*

VARICOCELE

A varicocele is a mass of enlarged and distended veins, similar to varicose veins, arising from the spermatic cord, which feels like a "mass of worms" on the testicle. The mass is more obvious when standing and often disappears on lying down, as blood pressure to it decreases. A varicocele more commonly develops on the left side and can result from defective valves in the testicular vein or by problems with the renal or kidney vein. A varicocele may produce an ache but is usually painless. If it prevents proper drainage of blood from the testes it may raise their temperature and reduce sperm production.

SEE ALSO *Fertility, Testes, Veins*

VARICOSE ULCER

Varicose ulcers, or venous stasis ulcers, occur on the leg just above the ankle. They are caused by problems with circulation in the leg. In the normal leg there is a set of valves which prevents backflow of venous blood from deep veins to surface veins when the calf muscles contract. If these valves become damaged or weakened, the surface veins are subjected to higher than normal internal pressure. This in turn interferes with the flow of blood through the small vessels supplying the skin around the ankle. The poor blood flow means that the skin becomes starved of nutrients and overloaded with waste products. Portions of the skin may die and ulcers result.

SEE ALSO *Circulatory system, Veins*

Varicose veins

Faults in the walls or valves of the veins, or the formation of blood clots, can disrupt blood flow in the veins of the legs causing swollen and knotted (varicose) veins. Faulty valves allow blood to pool, swelling and distending the veins.

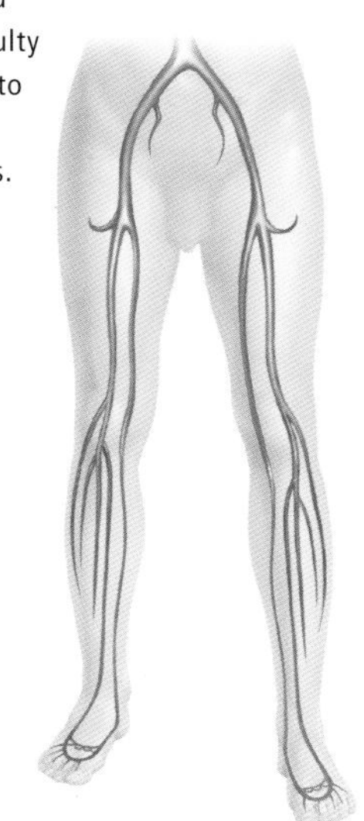

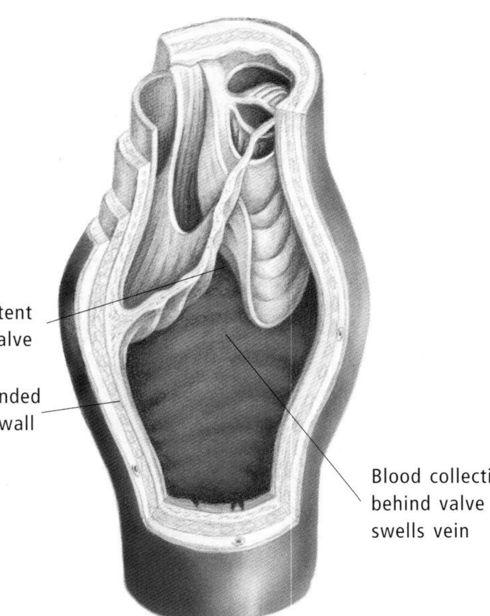

VARICOSE VEINS

Varicose veins are dilated, elongated, tortuous veins. They arise in the superficial veins of the leg—the great and small saphenous veins and their tributaries. Saphenous comes from the Greek word *saphenes*, meaning "obvious".

Varicose veins are defined as primary when they arise as a result of problems in the superficial veins themselves (many sufferers have a family history). Alternatively they may be secondary to the formation of clots (venous thrombosis) in the deep leg veins (deep vein thrombosis, DVT), or secondary to faulty valves in the veins that normally direct blood from the superficial veins into the deep leg veins. In the latter two cases, pressure in the superficial veins increases, either because blood cannot flow into the blocked deep veins, or because faulty valves in the communicating veins result in backflow into superficial veins when the leg muscles contract.

Valves in the veins may become incompetent when veins are overstretched by excessive pressure for long periods (weeks to months), for example when standing for prolonged periods or in pregnancy. The pressure causes the veins to become dilated but the valves do not increase in size, therefore affecting the efficiency of the valves. Elevating the legs and external compression with elastic support stockings can relieve varicose veins and relieve the swelling or edema in the lower leg that accompanies them.

Sluggish flow (stasis) of blood in varicose veins can affect the nourishment of the skin in the area, and even minor trauma can lead to the formation of a varicose ulcer. This is especially common over the subcutaneous surface of the tibia.

SEE ALSO *Circulatory system, Thrombosis, Varicose ulcer, Veins*

VASCULITIS

Vasculitis (angiitis) is a general term for a group of uncommon diseases causing inflammation of the blood vessels. Examples of vasculitis include Kawasaki disease, Behçet's disease, polyarteritis nodosa, Wegener's granulomatosis, Takayasu's arteritis, Churg-Strauss syndrome, giant cell arteritis (temporal arteritis) and Henoch Schönlein purpura. There is no known cure, but corticosteroids and immunosuppressants can help control the symptoms.

SEE ALSO *Autoimmune disease, Blood vessels*

VASECTOMY

Vasectomy is a surgical operation which involves cutting the two tubes (each called the ductus deferens or vas deferens) which run from the testes to the urethra. This prevents sperm reaching the seminal vesicles where they are held prior to ejaculation through the urethra during orgasm.

Vasectomy is a simple procedure that usually requires only a local anesthetic. There is some local bruising and discomfort but recovery takes only a few days. Sperm continue to be produced by the testes but they die and degenerate in the ductus deferens or in the epididymis. The other secretions which make up the seminal fluid are still produced and thus the man continues to ejaculate. After the operation it will take from 16–20 ejaculations to expel all the stored sperm and for the man to be declared infertile.

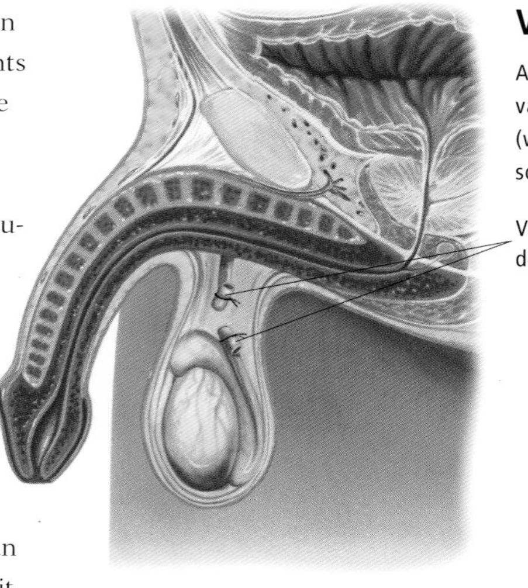

Vasectomy

A vasectomy involves severing the vas deferens tubes between the testes (where sperm is produced) and the urethra, so that sperm cannot leave the body.

Reversal of the operation is possible. It requires a general anesthetic and takes up to 2 hours, with recovery time related to the period spent anesthetized. About 60 percent of reversals succeed, enabling their subjects to father children. The best chances of success come with reversals performed less than 5 years after the original vasectomy and where the female partner is under 30 years of age and normally fertile.

Factors mitigating against success include the growth of fibrous tissue in the spermatic tubes and the production of antibodies to sperm after the vasectomy. Sperm may be frozen prior to vasectomy, for future use.

Vasectomy is the most effective form of contraception for men and may be done voluntarily for this purpose. It may also be done for prophylactic reasons where there is infection of the epididymis or testes.

SEE ALSO *Contraception, Reproductive systems, Sterilization, Testes*

VASODILATORS

Vasodilators are drugs that dilate small blood vessels, such as arterioles (small arteries) and venules (small veins). They increase blood flow to the tissues, lower the blood pressure of the circulation, and make the work load of the heart easier. Some, like nitroprusside and nitroglycerine, are used in ischemic heart disease and congestive heart failure, while others like hydralazine (a smooth muscle relaxant), diltiazem (a calcium channel blocker) and enalapril maleate (an ACE inhibitor) are used in the treatment of hypertension, often in combination with other hypertensive drugs such as diuretics and beta-blockers.

SEE ALSO *Arteries, Beta-blockers, Blood vessels, Calcium channel blockers, Hypertension*

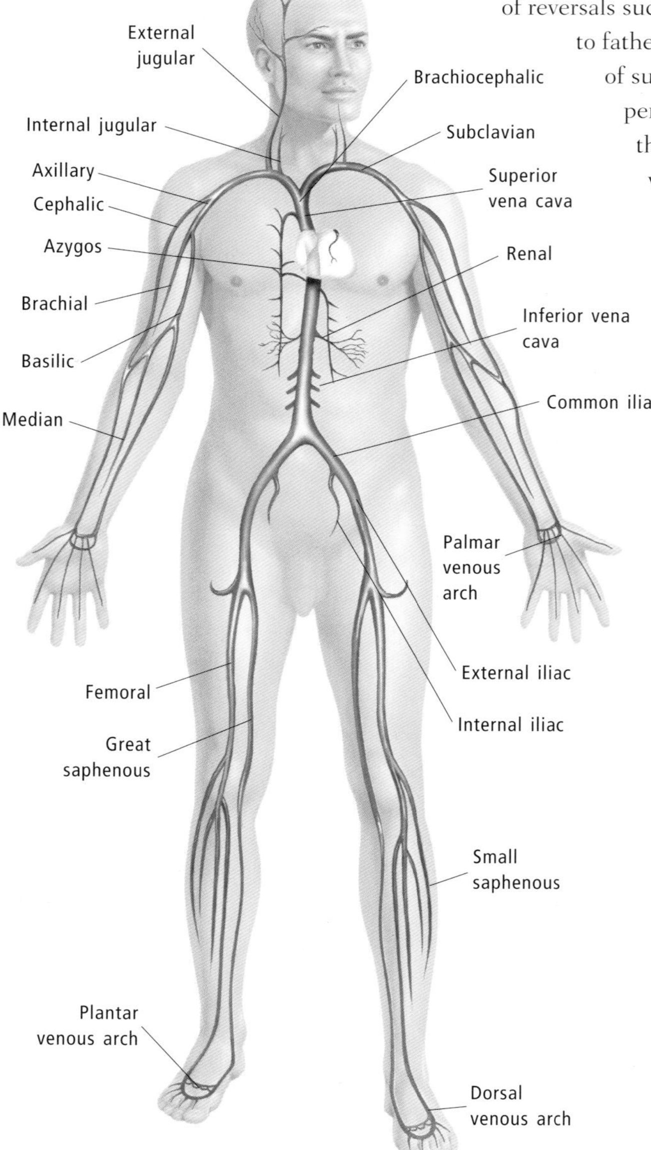

Veins

Deoxygenated blood travels back to the heart via a network of veins. Valves stop the blood from pooling in the veins, particularly where blood flow is fighting gravity (such as in the arms and legs).

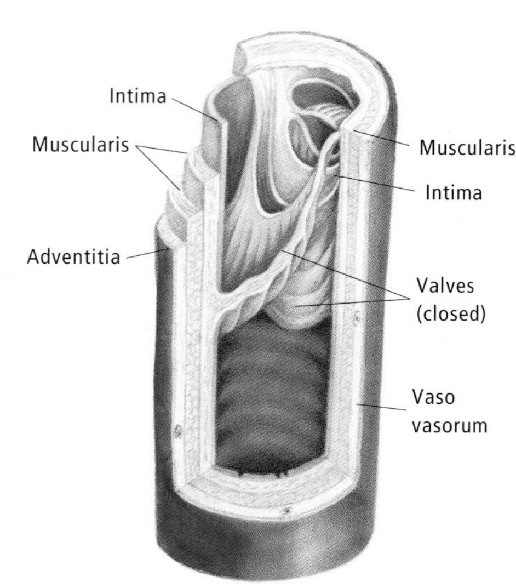

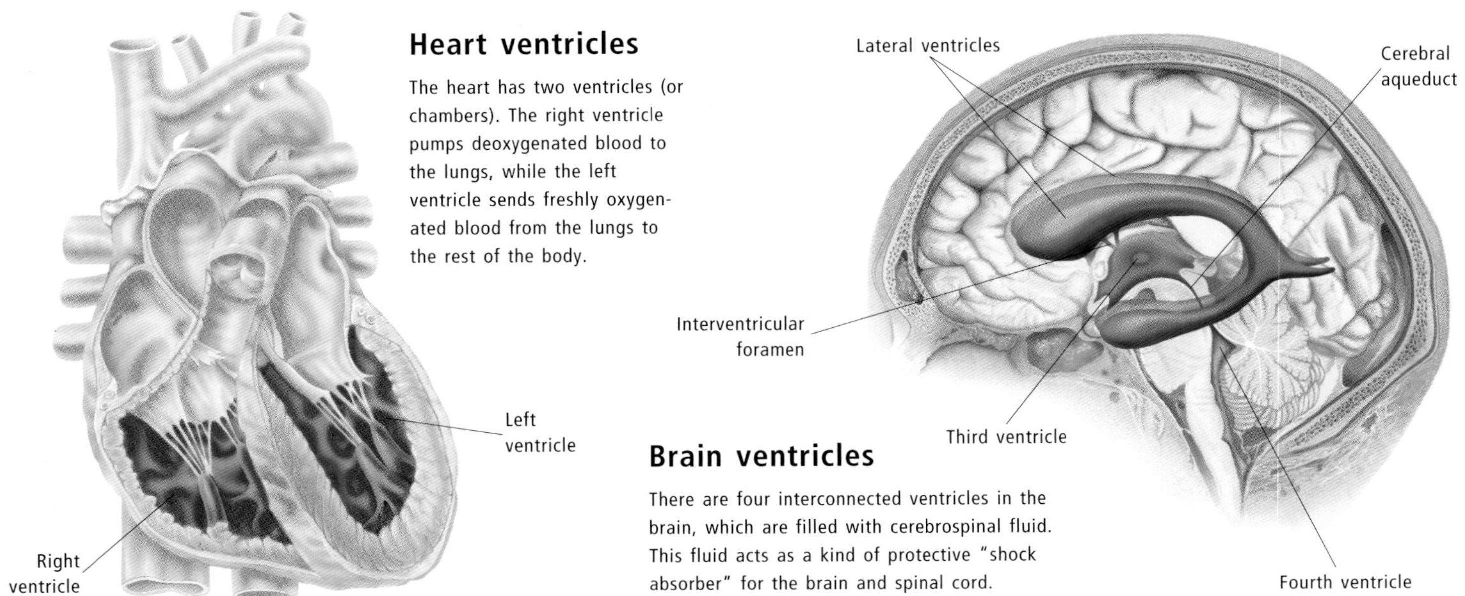

Heart ventricles

The heart has two ventricles (or chambers). The right ventricle pumps deoxygenated blood to the lungs, while the left ventricle sends freshly oxygenated blood from the lungs to the rest of the body.

Brain ventricles

There are four interconnected ventricles in the brain, which are filled with cerebrospinal fluid. This fluid acts as a kind of protective "shock absorber" for the brain and spinal cord.

VEINS

Veins are thin-walled, low-pressure blood vessels that return blood to the heart. The smallest veins are the venules, which commence at the venous end of capillaries. Veins receive tributaries from other veins and progressively increase in size as they approach the heart. Many, but not all, veins contain one-way valves.

The two largest veins in the body are the superior and inferior vena cavae, which drain into the heart from above and below respectively. The brachial, basilic and cephalic veins drain the upper limbs. They drain in turn into the axillary vein, which becomes the subclavian vein. The internal jugular vein, which drains the head and neck, joins the subclavian vein to form the brachiocephalic vein. The left and right brachiocephalic veins join to form the superior vena cava, which drains into the heart. The azygos vein, which drains the thoracic cavity, joins the superior vena cava just before it enters the heart.

The femoral vein drains the lower limb. It becomes the external iliac vein as it enters the trunk and is joined by the internal iliac vein from the pelvis to become the common iliac vein. The two common iliac veins join to form the inferior vena cava, which passes up the posterior abdominal wall. It is joined here by veins from the kidneys, gonads and back region, and just below the diaphragm by large veins from the liver. It passes through the diaphragm and almost immediately enters the heart.

Only a small number of veins in the trunk have valves; most are valveless. Blood in the trunk therefore flows according to pressure differences, making respiratory movements important in venous return. Inspiration creates a negative pressure within the thoracic cavity that not only draws air into the lungs but assists venous return to the heart.

Valves are common in veins within the limbs, where they assist the return of blood against the effect of gravity. They are particularly numerous in the lower limb. A large valve is also present in the lower end of the internal jugular vein, preventing the flow of blood back up toward the head and neck.

In the upper limb, most venous blood returns by the superficial veins which travel in the tissue just below the skin. In the lower limb, most venous blood returns by the deep veins which lie in compartments which contain muscles.

The contraction of nearby muscles compresses the veins and blood is forced by the valves in the direction of the heart. Blood then flows from superficial leg veins to the now empty deep veins, thus reducing pressure in the superficial veins.

Faulty valves in the veins communicating between the superficial and deep veins can lead to backflow of blood into the superficial veins when muscles contract. This results in the superficial veins becoming dilated and tortuous, otherwise known as varicose veins. Two of the superficial veins of the lower limb are named saphenous after the Greek word *saphenes*, meaning "obvious".

Stagnation of blood in veins can lead to the formation of blood clots (venous thrombosis). This most commonly occurs in the calves, and can be exacerbated by prolonged inactivity, such as bed rest or a long journey without exercise. Activation of the calf muscles can help to prevent pooling and stagnation of blood by assisting venous return from the area. The radiographic imaging of veins in the body is known as venography.

SEE ALSO *Circulatory system, Thrombosis, Varicose veins, Venography*

VENOGRAPHY

Venography is the x-ray examination of veins, usually to check for blood clots. Veins do not show up in an x-ray under normal conditions as the waves of electromagnetic radiation pass right through them. Instead, they need to be injected with a radiopaque dye that absorbs the x-rays, enabling the veins to be easily seen on the x-ray picture, or venogram. The injection is given under local anesthetic via a catheter that is inserted into a vein in the area of the body to be x-rayed.

SEE ALSO *Veins*

VENTRICLE

A ventricle is the term used for a small cavity or chamber in the brain and heart. The two lowest of the four chambers of the heart are called the right and left ventricles. The right ventricle pumps oxygen-depleted blood to the lungs via the pulmonary artery.

Vertebrae

The spine is made up of 33 vertebrae, which form a strong yet flexible housing for the spinal cord.

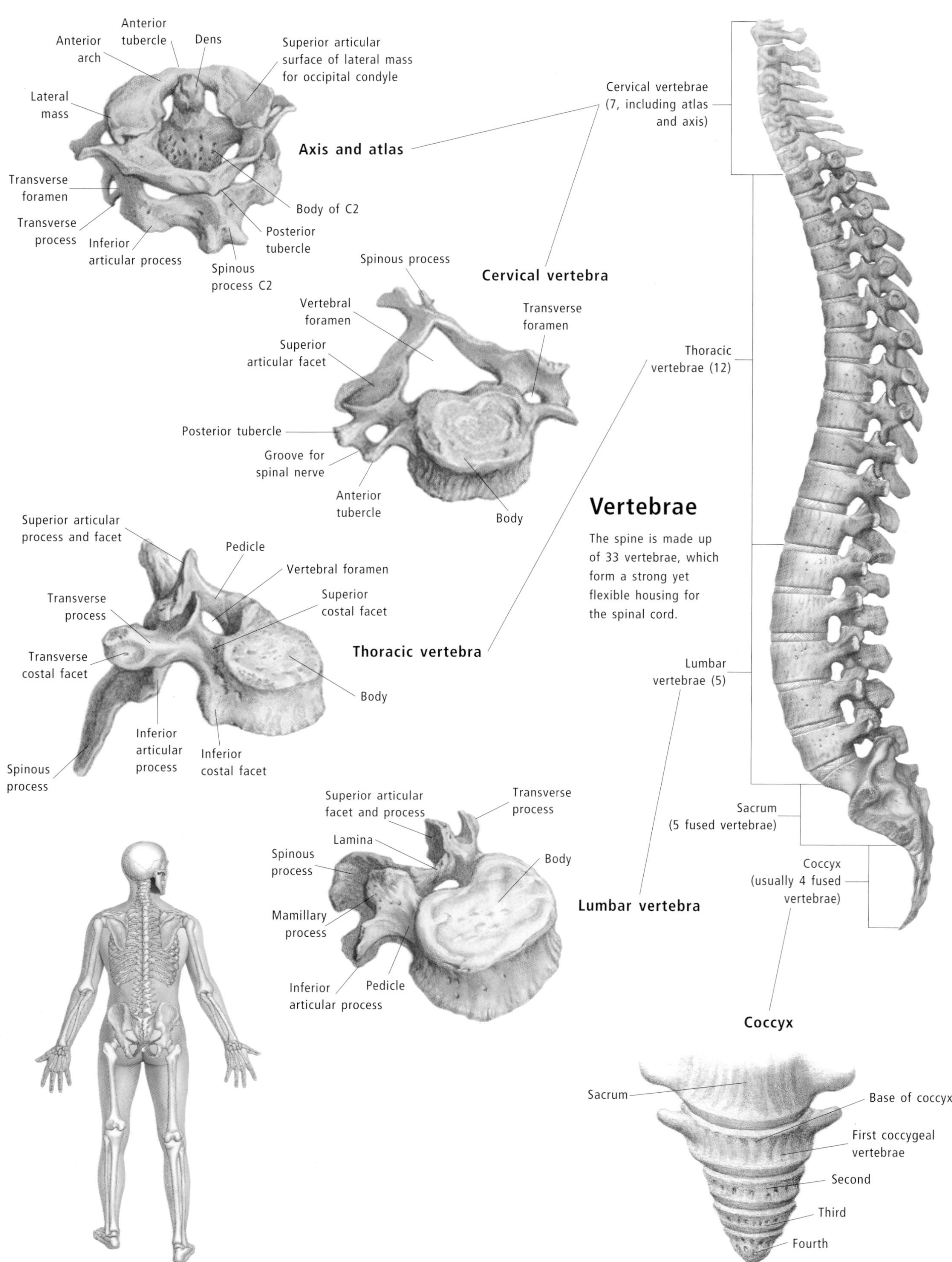

Axis and atlas
Anterior arch
Anterior tubercle
Dens
Superior articular surface of lateral mass for occipital condyle
Lateral mass
Transverse foramen
Transverse process
Inferior articular process
Spinous process C2
Posterior tubercle
Body of C2
Cervical vertebra
Spinous process
Vertebral foramen
Transverse foramen
Superior articular facet
Posterior tubercle
Groove for spinal nerve
Anterior tubercle
Body
Thoracic vertebra
Superior articular process and facet
Pedicle
Vertebral foramen
Superior costal facet
Transverse process
Transverse costal facet
Body
Inferior articular process
Inferior costal facet
Spinous process
Lumbar vertebra
Superior articular facet and process
Transverse process
Lamina
Body
Spinous process
Mamillary process
Inferior articular process
Pedicle
Cervical vertebrae (7, including atlas and axis)
Thoracic vertebrae (12)
Lumbar vertebrae (5)
Sacrum (5 fused vertebrae)
Coccyx (usually 4 fused vertebrae)
Coccyx
Sacrum
Base of coccyx
First coccygeal vertebrae
Second
Third
Fourth

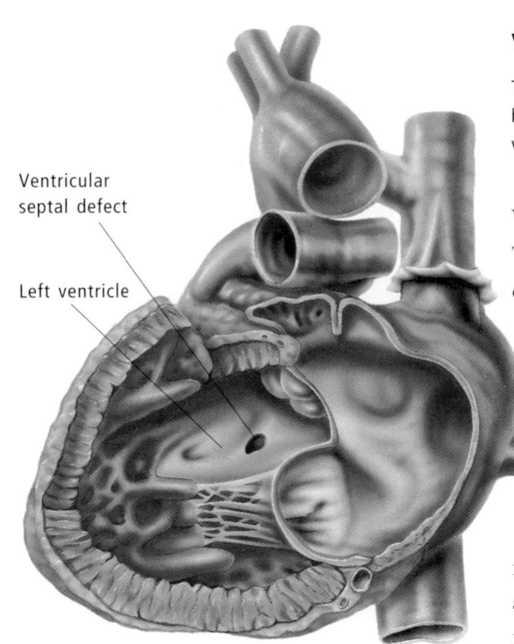

The more muscular left ventricle pumps oxygen-rich blood through the aorta to the rest of the body.

In the brain, there are four ventricles. These connect with each other, the central canal of the spinal cord, and the subarachnoid space surrounding the brain.

Specialized capillaries called choroid plexuses in the ventricles of the brain produce cerebrospinal fluid. This clear liquid fills the ventricles and the other cavities with which they are connected to create a protective cushion for the central nervous system.

SEE ALSO ***Brain, Heart, Spinal cord***

VENTRICULAR SEPTAL DEFECT

A ventricular septal defect (VSD) is a hole in the wall separating the two ventricles, or lower chambers, of the heart. Because of pressure differences between the two ventricles, blood passes through the hole from left to right. Blood in the left ventricle then leaks into the right ventricle with the result that more blood than normal is pumped to the lungs. This often produces chest infections and breathing difficulties. A large opening in a very small child can also cause symptoms of heart failure. Although small and medium-sized ventricular septal defects often close by themselves, surgery is usually needed to repair larger holes.

SEE ALSO ***Heart, Ventricle***

Ventricular septal defect

This congenital heart defect occurs when a hole forms in the membrane dividing the two ventricles of the heart.

VERTEBRAE

The vertebrae are the bony building blocks of the vertebral column (or spine). Individual vertebrae, separated by intervertebral disks, give the vertebral column both strength and flexibility. The vertebral column is comprised of seven cervical, twelve thoracic, five lumbar, five fused sacral and three to five fused coccygeal vertebrae.

The same basic elements are found in most vertebrae: a vertebral body; a vertebral arch comprising two pedicles and two laminae; and processes that project away from the arch. The bodies lie in front and are weight bearing. They increase in size as they progress down the spine. The body and vertebral arch form a bony housing for the vertebral canal, which protects the spinal cord and spinal nerve roots. The pedicles form the side walls of the foramen and the two laminae form the back walls. During fetal development the laminae fuse in the midline at the back; failure of fusion is known as spina bifida.

The backward-projecting spinous process and the two side-projecting transverse processes provide leverage for muscles that move the vertebral column. The articular processes project up and down from the left and right sides of the vertebral arch and form joints with the articular processes of adjacent vertebrae. The orientation of these joint surfaces affects the direction of movement between vertebrae.

Vertebrae may fracture as a result of trauma. Fracture or displacement may affect the spinal cord and associated nerves, and produce temporary or permanent loss of sensation and movement.

SEE ALSO ***Intervertebral disks, Skeletal system, Spine***

VERTIGO

Vertigo is a hallucination of movement, usually a feeling that the person or their surroundings is revolving. It may produce feelings of dizziness and confusion; intense vertigo may cause nausea and vomiting.

Vertigo may be caused by disorders of the inner ear, such as a blockage of the fluid in the semicircular canals, which regulate balance and detect movements of the head, or by disorders of the central nervous system. Vertigo is dangerous if experienced in high places and is an occupational hazard for divers and pilots, who are frequently in situations where there are no visual reference points. They may suffer spatial disorientation, becoming unable to properly judge their direction or speed of movement.

SEE ALSO ***Acrophobia, Dizziness, Semicircular canals***

VIRILIZATION

Normal virilization or masculinization is the appearance of male secondary sexual characteristics in the male. Virilization occurring in adult females or children usually indicates a serious underlying condition. It may be associated with hirsutism (abnormal male pattern hair growth) which is also a signal of an underlying disorder. In boys, the changes of puberty may appear early due to abnormal production of testosterone, the male sex hormone. This abnormal production of testosterone first accelerates bone growth and then stops it earlier than normal, resulting in lower final height. Treatment with synthetic hormones can achieve normal growth.

Virilization can occur in females (when it is also called virilism) when ovarian tumors produce the hormones testosterone and progesterone. If unchecked, the presence of these hormones will affect body shape, causing increasing muscularity and growth of facial and body hair. In addition, the breasts may atrophy or fail to develop, the voice deepens and the clitoris enlarges. Menstruation and ovulation both cease. Disorders of the adrenal gland in females, causing production of excessive quantities of androgens (male hormones), will create the same symptoms of virilization.

Girls who are deficient in adrenal hormones will appear normal at birth but may fail to undergo puberty or to menstruate. Urine tests can detect abnormal hormone levels and aid diagnosis of tumors or adrenal problems. Drug medication with dexamethasone can prevent adrenal production of androgens. Surgical removal of tumors or of the adrenal gland is sometimes necessary.

Viruses

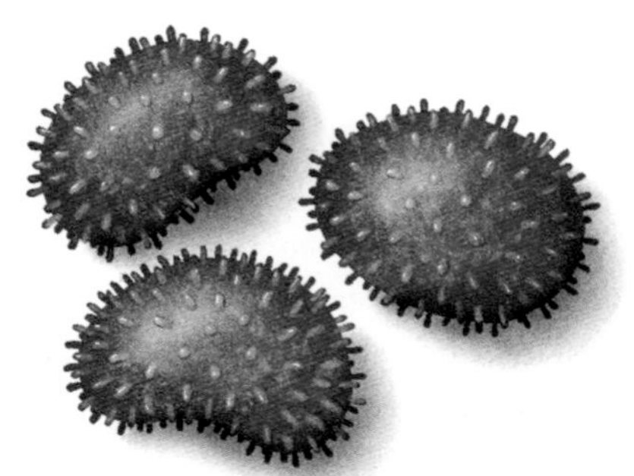
Influenza virus

Rotavirus

Cold virus

Polio virus

Herpes virus

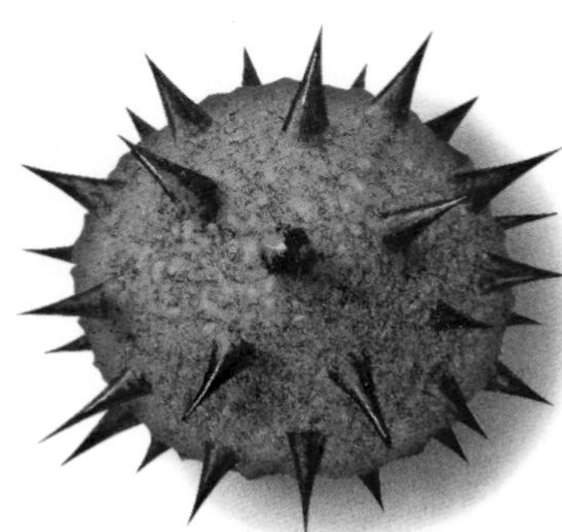
Wart virus

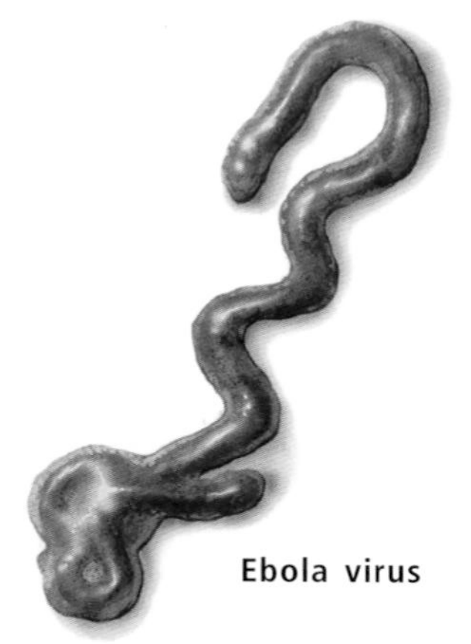
Ebola virus

The exposure of a female fetus to high levels of androgens (sex hormones) early in pregnancy, through drugs prescribed to prevent a miscarriage or the presence of a hormone-producing tumor in the mother, may result in genital abnormalities, with the external genitals developing a male appearance. This may include a greatly enlarged clitoris and absence of a vaginal opening, while the internal reproductive organs develop normally. This condition is known as female pseudohermaphroditism. Surgical reconstruction may be necessary to correct the genital abnormalities.

SEE ALSO *Adrenal glands, Hormones, Progesterone, Puberty, Testosterone*

Viruses

These tiny infectious organisms are much smaller than bacteria and vary considerably in shape and structure. In order to survive they must invade another cell, taking over their host's cellular machinery and using it to reproduce. Each virus has a preference for a different part of the body—the wart virus, for example, infects the skin; the polio virus attacks the nervous system.

VIRUSES

Viruses are a group of infectious organisms so small that they are only visible through electron microscopes. Just about all they contain is enough genetic material to duplicate themselves. They are much smaller than bacteria and cannot provide their own energy, nor can they replicate themselves outside living cells. They rely on invading another organism to survive, taking over its cellular machinery and using it to reproduce. Viruses infect all body tissues, but individual viruses show a preference for particular parts; for example, the poliomyelitis virus only infects part of the nervous system, the herpes virus infects the skin.

Some viruses cause acute disease lasting for only a short time and others cause recurring or chronic disease, while others do not cause any disease. The acute viral infections are of two types, local and systemic, as the result of the effect of the invading virus on the host.

Local infections occur at the site of the viral infection, such as the common cold, which infects the area around the nose, or enteritis, which causes bowel inflammation. Many viruses enter the body via the nose or mouth and begin their cycle of infection in the nose and throat. They then enter the bloodstream where they are spread to other parts of the body as in, for example, measles, mumps and chickenpox.

Other viral diseases are transmitted by the bites of insects, ticks and mites. These diseases begin in the skin or lymph nodes and spread rapidly into the bloodstream. Many viruses have an affinity for specific organs, for example, encephalitis and meningitis viruses affect the brain.

Some viruses remain in the tissues after the initial infection even though there are specific antibodies for them circulating in the blood and tissues. It is thought that these viruses reside inside cells where they are protected from antibodies, which are unable to penetrate the cell membrane. Measles and herpes viruses fit into this category.

Other viruses can remain in the body for a number of years before producing any symptoms.

Once a virus has entered the body it will find little resistance, apart from the presence of lymphocytes, a type of white blood cell that produces antibodies, and a small amount of interferon, which also helps to destroy viruses. After a few days the body begins to produce antibodies and greater amounts of interferon. Because viruses are so intimately involved in the vital processes of cells they are difficult to eradicate with medication without damaging the cells, although there are a few antiviral drugs. Antibiotics are ineffective against viruses because they work on elements found in bacteria which are not found in viruses.

Many viral diseases can be prevented by good hygiene. This means efficient sanitation and waste disposal combined with personal cleanliness and clean water. Immunization by vaccine can prevent epidemics caused by certain acutely infectious viruses and has been particularly effective against viruses such as smallpox and poliomyelitis. Some viruses are easier to immunize against than others. The common cold, which is caused by rhinoviruses, may prove impossible to immunize against because there are at least 100 antigenic types of the virus.

SEE ALSO *Antibodies, Bacteria, Chickenpox, Common cold, Encephalitis, Hepatitis, Herpes simplex, Infectious diseases, Measles, Meningitis, Multiple sclerosis, Mumps, Poliomyelitis, Ticks*

VISUALIZATION

Also known as creative visualization, this alternative therapy technique combines self-hypnosis, relaxation and the use of imagery to utilize the power of the mind to influence the body and emotions.

The use of visualization to support healing has become known through the work of American doctors Carl and Stephanie Simonton and Bernie Siegel. In their practices they encourage patients with cancer to visualize the tumor or cancer in their bodies and then to imagine it being eradicated or cured by specific images such as an attacking army of healthy blood cell soldiers or a healing waterfall.

Proponents of visualization believe it is effective for relaxation and pain relief. For example, patients might be asked to imagine themselves resting in a place of peace or being bathed in a succession of colors. In other cases patients might be encouraged to picture themselves full of energy or free from anxiety.

To practise visualization, patients sit or lie in a comfortable position, close their eyes, relax their muscles and slow their breathing before being guided into their visualization. Sometimes it is suggested they visualize a television screen which shows what they want to see.

Visualization may be used by holistic health practitioners, psychotherapists and hypnotherapists. It may also be practised alone with the aid of audiotapes.

SEE ALSO *Hypnotherapy, Meditation, Relaxation techniques*

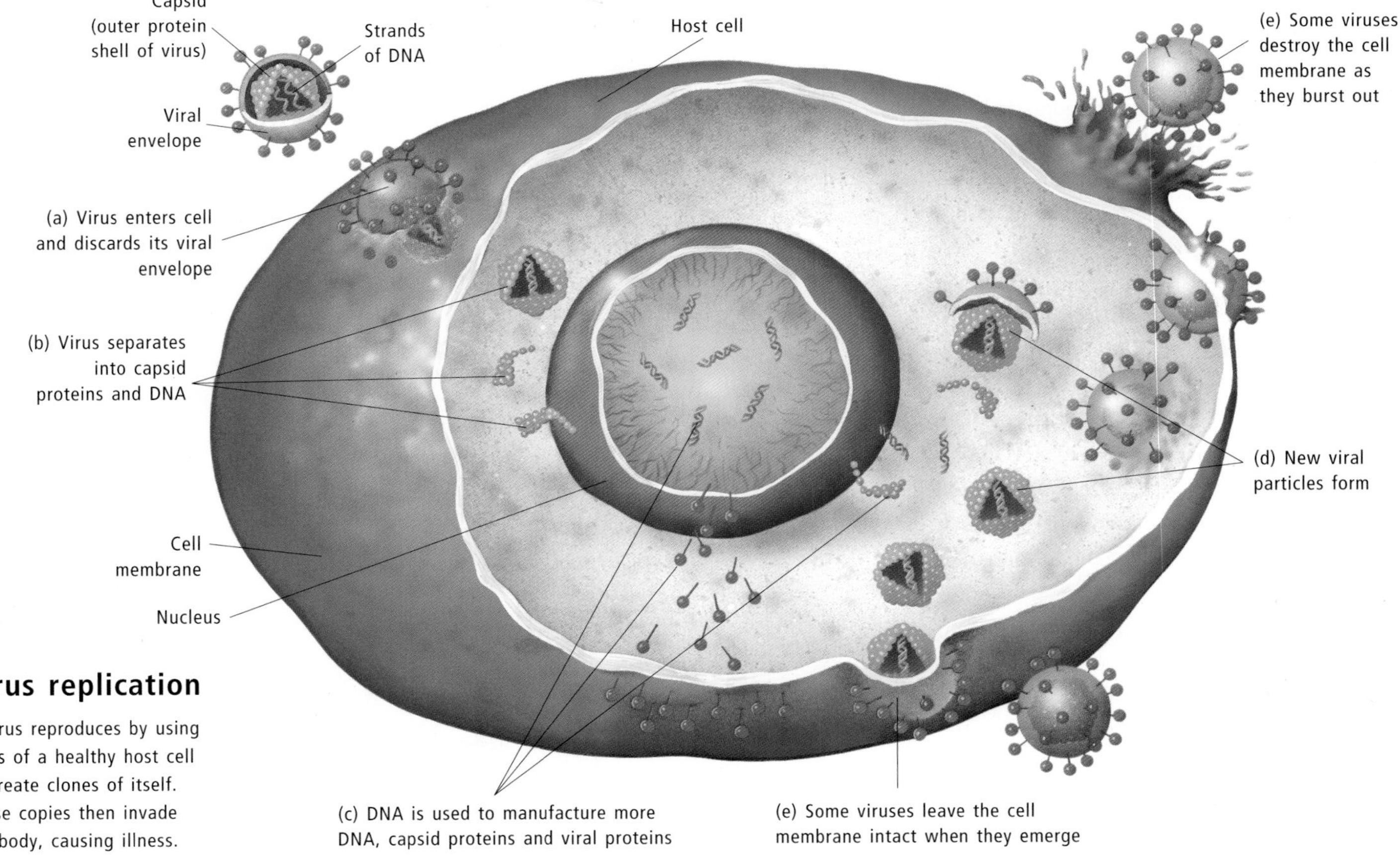
Capsid (outer protein shell of virus)
Strands of DNA
Viral envelope
Host cell
(e) Some viruses destroy the cell membrane as they burst out
(a) Virus enters cell and discards its viral envelope
(b) Virus separates into capsid proteins and DNA
(d) New viral particles form
Cell membrane
Nucleus
(c) DNA is used to manufacture more DNA, capsid proteins and viral proteins
(e) Some viruses leave the cell membrane intact when they emerge

Virus replication

A virus reproduces by using parts of a healthy host cell to create clones of itself. These copies then invade the body, causing illness.

V

VITAMINS

Vitamins are micronutrients, organic substances found in foods which are essential to the body but only in very small amounts, acting as catalysts in various chemical reactions. They may be either water-soluble or fat-soluble. Water-soluble vitamins are easily destroyed in cooking, not stored in the body for long periods, and any excess is usually excreted in the urine. They must be eaten regularly as deficiencies can develop relatively quickly. Vitamins of the B complex and vitamin C are water-soluble.

Fat-soluble vitamins are less easily destroyed in cooking and can be stored for long periods in body fat, making deficiencies slow to develop in adults. Deficiencies are still dangerous and may develop very quickly in babies and children. Vitamins A, D, E and K are fat-soluble.

Good nutrition, preferably involving breast feeding for at least the first year of life and eating a wide variety of foods from all food groups, should ensure adequate intake of all vitamins, in which case no benefits will be derived from vitamin or mineral supplements. A restricted diet with a very limited range or very small quantities of foods can result in a deficiency of one or several vitamins which may produce readily identifiable symptoms.

Self-dosing with vitamin supplements is unwise as some vitamins become toxic when taken in excess. The recommended daily allowances (RDAs) published by national health authorities are calculated as reference guides useful in planning the vitamin content of diets to avoid deficiencies. Excessive intakes usually arise from self-administration of supplements or from abnormally high consumption of highly concentrated food sources.

Vitamin A is obtained directly from food as retinol, retinal or retinoic acid, and indirectly as substances which are converted to vitamin A in the body (carotenoids and beta-carotene). It is important to the formation of visual purple in the eyes for normal vision and night vision, to growth and reproduction and nourishment of the epithelial cells, which line the mouth and airways, and for defence against infection.

Sources include liver, dairy products, and some fish oils. Beta-carotene is found in yellow and green vegetables such as pumpkin, carrots and spinach and fruits such as apricots, peaches and cantaloupe.

Deficiency comes only after several months when the body's stores are exhausted but is serious, causing susceptibility to infection and damage to the eyes with loss of night vision, dryness and ulceration of the whites and cornea (xerophthalmia), which can result in blindness. Excess vitamin A is toxic (early Arctic explorers died from excess vitamin A after eating polar bear liver), causing enlargement of the spleen and kidneys, headache, peeling skin, thickening bones and joint pain. Drinking excessive amounts of carrot juice may yellow the skin and the whites of the eyes.

Vitamin B_1 (thiamine) aids metabolization of carbohydrates and alcohol. Sources include wholegrain cereals, nuts, yeast and meats. The body stores only small quantities and a deficiency will appear in about a month where diet is inadequate.

Deficiency causes the tropical disease beriberi. Alcoholics are prone to thiamine deficiency and may develop Wernicke-Korsakoff syndrome. The symptoms are confusion, double vision, nystagmus (rapid uncontrolled eye movements) and lack of muscular coordination. Prompt treatment with direct injection of thiamine is indi-

Vitamin B1

The body can only store small quantities of this vitamin, which is needed to maintain nervous system function and for the metabolism of carbohydrates and alcohol.

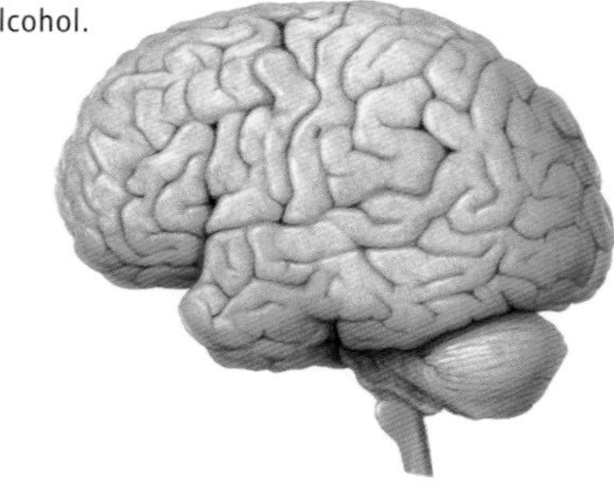

Vitamin B2

This vitamin helps to repair skin and body tissues; deficiency can cause dermatitis. It is also important for metabolic processes.

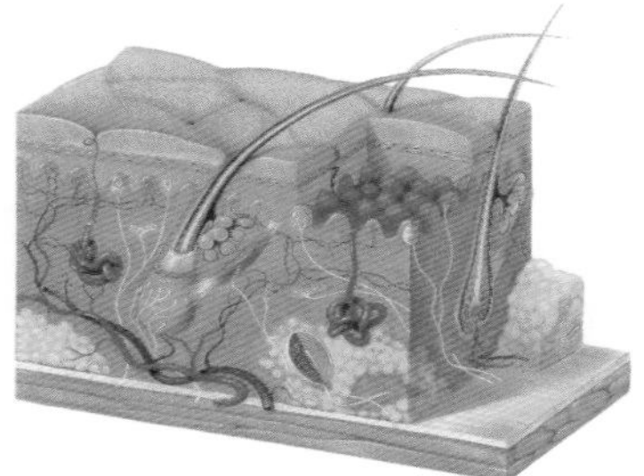

Vitamin B3

Absorbed from food or made in the body, vitamin B3 contributes to the health of the digestive organs, skin and nerves. It aids metabolism, helping the body break down food for energy.

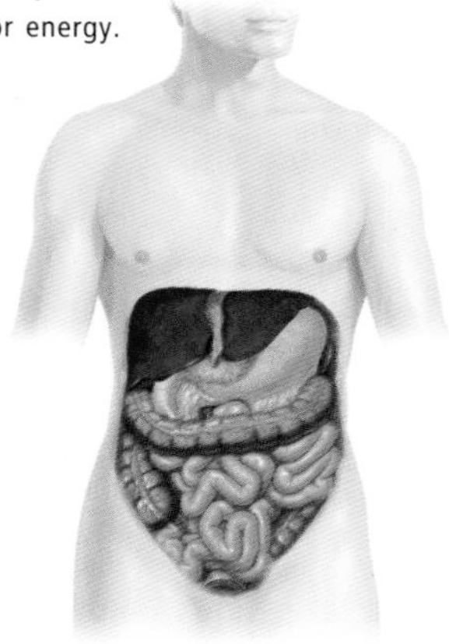

Vitamin B5

Vitamin B5 is essential for the formation of hemoglobin, fatty acids and cholesterol, and for the transmission of nerve impulses.

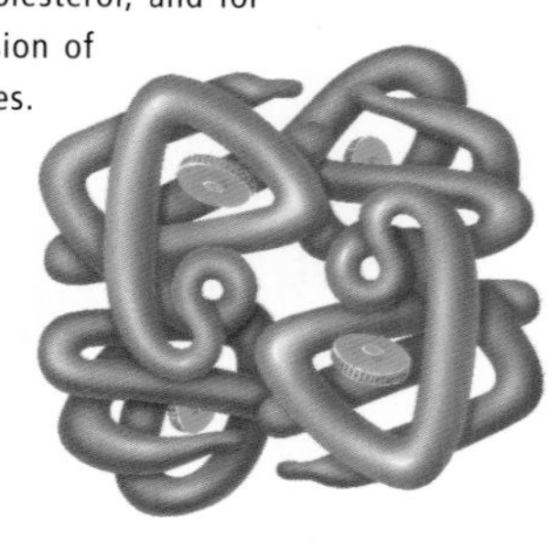

Vitamin A

Important for the formation of pigments needed for night and normal vision, this vitamin is also used for the growth and replication of epithelial cells and helps defend the body against infection.

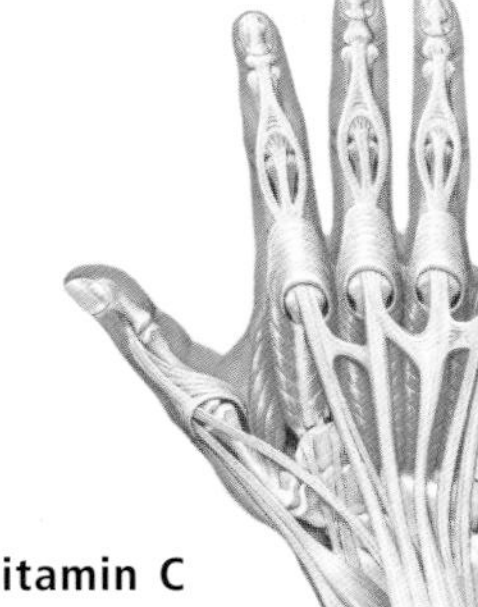

Vitamin C

An antioxidant, vitamin C helps to build collagen which is found in tendons and cartilage. Deficiencies in this vitamin cause the disease scurvy.

Vitamin D

Needed for the formation and growth of bones and teeth, vitamin D helps the body absorb calcium and phosphate. Deficiency causes skeletal problems, such as rickets in children and osteomalacia in adults.

Vitamin E

An important antioxidant, vitamin E prevents cell damage and extends the life of red blood cells.

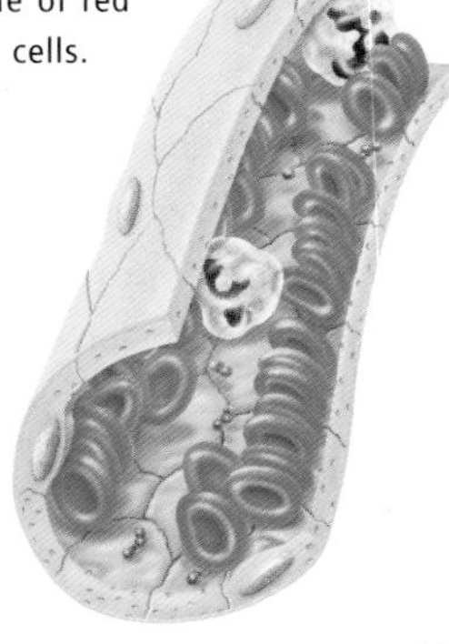

Vitamins

The body needs vitamins for the chemical reactions that make and repair cells, provide energy and maintain health. Vitamins are absorbed in the digestive tract. Fat-soluble vitamins (A, D, E and K) can be stored by the body, mainly in the liver. Water soluble vitamins (B, C, folacin and biotin) are absorbed quickly, but any excess is excreted in the urine. Poor diet can result in vitamin deficiencies, leading to diseases that affect the health of bones, muscles and other body tissues and organs.

Vitamin K

Vitamin K makes proteins needed for blood clotting, and for the bones and kidneys.

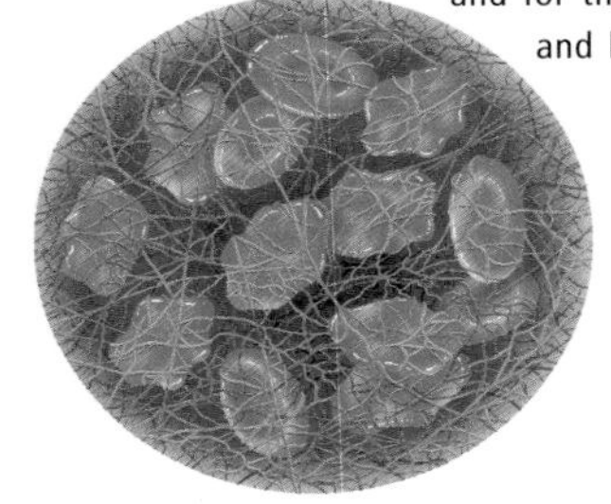

Vitamin B6

Vitamin B6 is important for the health of nerve cells and tissue and aids in the formation of red blood cells and proteins in the body.

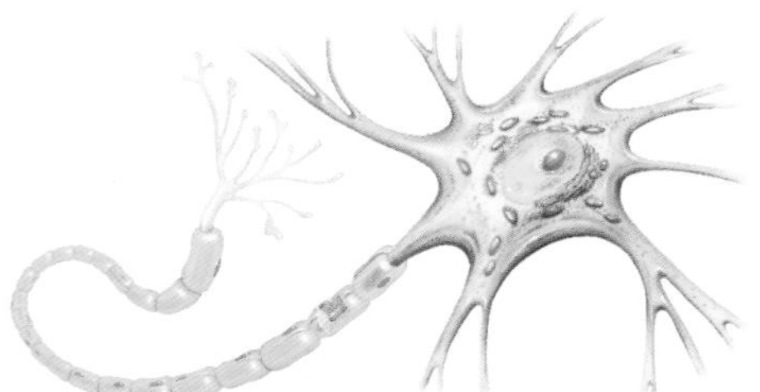

Vitamin B12

Deficiency in B12 causes anemia as this vitamin is essential for the production of red blood cells.

Folacin (folic acid)

Important for the formation of new body cells, folic acid is particularly important during the first 3 months of pregnancy as it helps prevent developmental defects in the fetus.

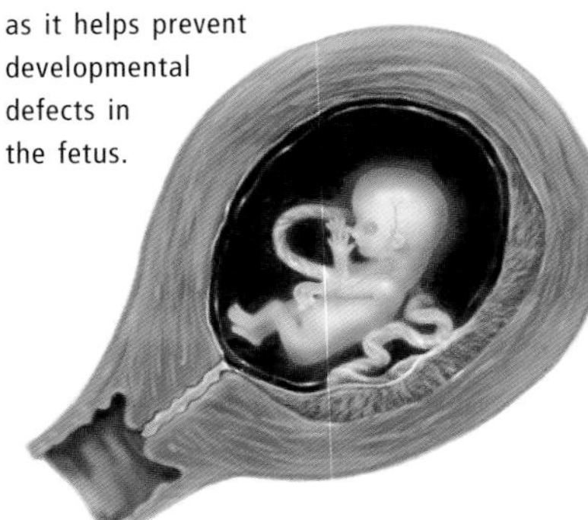

cated, although this may not prevent permanent brain damage.

Vitamin B_2 (riboflavin) is important for repairing skin and other body tissues. Sources include yeast, almonds, dairy foods, fish, meat and kidney. Riboflavin is easily destroyed by sunlight, which is why some countries have black milk bottles. Deficiency leads to cracked lips, dermatitis and susceptibility to infection. Excess is not toxic, as the excess is excreted in the urine.

Vitamin B_3 (niacin) can be made in the body from the aminoacid tryptophan or absorbed directly from food. It aids reactions within the body which break down foods to release energy. It is needed for the health of skin, digestive organs and nerves. Sources include cereals, flour, wholegrains, organ meats and poultry.

Deficiency causes pellagra, common in the southern USA early last century, where corn was the staple food. Symptoms are lack of appetite and muscular weakness, followed by diarrhea, dermatitis and dementia. These diseases have now been largely eradicated by changes in processing methods which retain essential nutrients and by widening the range of foods available. Excess intake, above 1,000 milligrams per day, causes unpleasant skin rashes and can lead to diabetes and gout.

Vitamin B_5 (pantothenic acid) is important to formation of hemoglobin, fatty acids and cholesterol, and transmission of nerve impulses. Sources include wholegrain foods, liver, kidney, beans, meat and poultry. Deficiency is rare but produces vomiting, pain, cramps, poor circulation and personality changes. Excess intake is also rare, but large doses can cause diarrhea.

Vitamin B_6 (pyridoxine, pyridoxamine, pyridoxal) helps digest protein and to build protein structures including antibodies, red blood cells and nerve tissue. Sources include some breakfast cereals, wheat germ, pork, fish, peanuts, potatoes, avocados, lentils and legumes. Deficiency brings mouth sores, fatigue, nausea, dizziness and muscle spasms. Excess intake, taking multiples of the RDA over a long period, can cause nerve damage.

Vitamin B_{12} (cyanocobalamin, cobalamin) is important in the manufacture of DNA and red blood cells, of tissue for nerve sheaths and in digestion of nutrients. Sources include animal foods, particularly liver, kidney and mushrooms. It also occurs in some fermented foods, where it occurs as a product of bacterial action (this is also thought to occur in the human intestine). Deficiency is very rare as body stores can last 5 years. Vegans, particularly babies and children, are most at risk of deficiency. An inability to absorb vitamin B_{12} causes pernicious anemia. Treatment is to give the vitamin by injection. Excess is not toxic even at high doses.

Folacin (folic acid) acts with vitamin B_{12} in many processes, including passing instructions from genes to cells to convey hereditary characteristics, making red blood cells and using fats in the body. Sources include chicken livers, yeast and yeast extracts, and leafy green vegetables.

As folacin is easily destroyed in cooking, deficiency is very common worldwide and can cause anemia, particularly in pregnancy, greatly increasing the risk of spina bifida and other neural tube defects in the fetus. This type of deficiency can be cured using yeast extract. Excess causes minimal toxic effects.

Biotin, originally known as vitamin H, is now recognized as a member of the B complex. Sources include liver, nuts and eggs, yeasts and bacteria in the intestine. Deficiency is rare since biotin is manufactured internally. Stores may be depleted by taking antibiotics. Symptoms are dermatitis, loss of appetite, nausea and high blood cholesterol. Excess causes no known toxic effects.

Vitamin C (ascorbic acid) helps to build collagen, the fibrous tissues of tendons and cartilage, maintains healthy bones and blood vessels, helps absorption of iron, prevents infection, is an antioxidant, may prevent development of cancer-causing substances, and helps the liver excrete waste products.

Sources include fresh vegetables and fruits. Vitamin C is stored for only 3 weeks in the body and should be replenished daily; in past times, sailors on long voyages were at risk of developing scurvy from lack of vitamin C. Babies get vitamin C from breast milk. Deficiency leads to scurvy, sometimes seen in alcoholics and drug-dependent people whose diets are grossly deficient, with weakness, bleeding gums, ulcers, joint pains and bruising. Excess intake is dangerous as it interferes with fertility, blood glucose levels and the effects of drugs, including aspirin, and can cause diarrhea, kidney stones and scurvy when excess intake ceases.

Vitamin D is vital for absorption of calcium and phosphate by bones. It can be made in the skin through exposure to sunlight and obtained in the diet from oily fish, dairy foods and as an ingredient of margarine.

Deficiency leads to rickets in children and osteomalacia in adults, with bone deformation and brittleness. Rare in the industrialized countries, vitamin D deficiency may occur in newborn babies in cultures where they are totally protected from exposure to sunlight for long periods. Excess intake is dangerous. Vitamin D is the most toxic vitamin in excess, causing stunted growth and weight loss, and depositing calcium in soft tissues such as heart, kidney and lungs. Sun exposure does not result in excess. Supplementing the diet is dangerous without medical supervision.

Vitamin E is an important antioxidant, preventing cell damage, ensuring normal life span of red blood cells and protecting against toxic chemicals. Despite claims it will prolong life and increase virility, there is no significant evidence for this. Sources include seeds, nuts and other plant foods, and seafood. Deficiency is rare but may cause anemia in newborn babies. Excess intake, at 20 times the RDA, causes nausea and indigestion.

Vitamin K (phylloquinone) makes proteins important for blood clotting and is used to make proteins in bones and kidneys. Sources include leafy green vegetables, cabbage, sprouts, liver, milk and eggs. Vitamin K is also made by bacteria in the human intestine.

Deficiency is rare, but occurs in adults because of inability to absorb it and in newborns whose intestines do not contain the bacteria that manufacture it. Deficiency in babies causes bleeding (hemorrhagic disease of the newborn), which is prevented by an injection given at birth. It is associated with diseases of the pancreas in alcoholics. Excess is not toxic, but very large doses may cause anemia.

SEE ALSO ***Anemia, Breast feeding, Diet, Minerals, Nutrition, Osteomalacia, Rickets, Scurvy, Sun exposure, Wernicke-Korsakoff syndrome***

V

VITILIGO

Up to 2 percent of the world's population, or some 50 million people, suffer from vitiligo. This disorder involves destruction of pigment-producing cells (melanocytes), which occur in the skin, linings of the mouth, nose, genital and rectal areas, and in the retinas. The result is white (pigment-free) patches on the skin. Hair growing at affected sites also turns white. The cause of vitiligo is unknown, although it is most prevalent in people with certain autoimmune disorders. One of the most beneficial treatments is psoralen photochemotherapy, which involves careful, controlled and long-term use of certain drugs combined with ultraviolet light exposure.

SEE ALSO *Autoimmune disease, Ultraviolet therapy*

Vitiligo

In this condition white patches develop on various parts of the body, such as the skin, as a result of damage to pigment-producing cells.

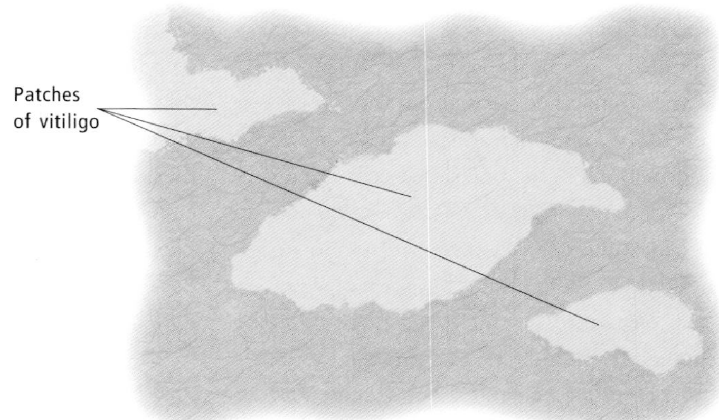

VOCAL CORDS

The vocal cords are a part of the voice box (larynx), situated in the neck, and are involved in breathing, speech and singing. The production of sound is generally due to vibration of the vocal cords. Each vocal cord consists of a ledge of elastic tissue extending across the cavity of the larynx. The term glottis is normally applied to the gap between the two vocal cords, or (sometimes) collectively to the gap, the vocal cords and the associated muscles.

The positions and tensions of the vocal cords are delicately controlled by laryngeal muscles. Air passes through the larynx and the glottis on its way to and from the lungs. During normal breathing, the vocal cords are separated by a moderate opening for unobstructed passage of air. During deep or forced breathing, the gap widens. For the production of shrill tones of speech or singing, the gap narrows and the cords are tensed. When air is forced through them, the cords vibrate, producing sound waves. The glottis can be fully closed to interrupt the passage of air.

Hoarseness is usually due to inflammation of, or damage to, the vocal cords. Another cause is accidental damage to the recurrent laryngeal nerve during thyroidectomy. Singers, who put the vocal cords under strain, are liable to develop nodules and cancer on the vocal cords.

SEE ALSO *Speech, Larynx*

VOLVULUS

A volvulus is a twisting of the intestine around itself, most commonly towards the lower end of the digestive tract—in the ileum, cecum or sigmoid colon of the bowel. It blocks the intestine and constricts the blood vessels serving the intestine. Abdominal pain and swelling, vomiting and constipation result. Surgery to untwist the volvulus is usually necessary. If gangrene has set in, the affected portion of the intestine must be removed. A volvulus in a very small child may relate to an intestinal malformation during fetal development. In older people, the twisting may be due to scar tissue caused by surgery or infection.

SEE ALSO *Digestive system, Intestines*

Vocal cords

The two pairs of mucous membranes that form the vocal cords sit in the larynx, on either side of the glottis.

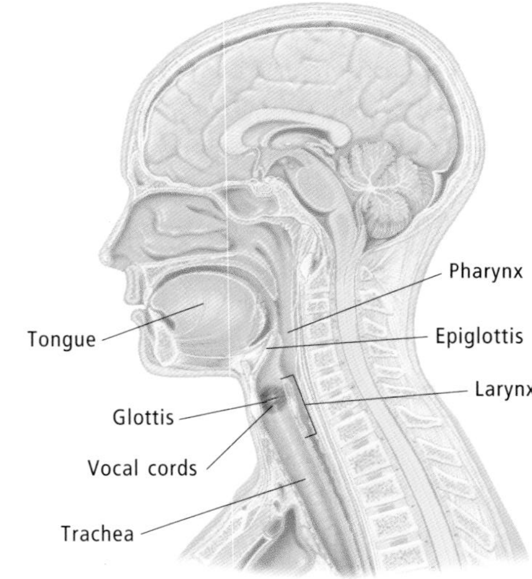

Root of tongue
Epiglottis
Glottis closed
Vocal folds
Vestibular fold
Vocal process of arytenoid cartilage

Vocal cords taut

When the gap between the vocal cords is almost closed, air passing through them makes them vibrate and creates sound waves.

Vocal cords relaxed

During breathing the vocal cords are separated. Air passes freely past them without making them vibrate, and so no sound is made.

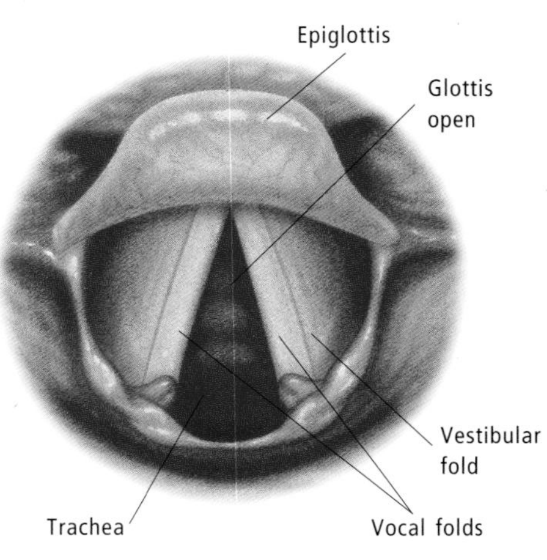

V

VOMITING

Vomiting, or emesis, is the forceful ejection of the stomach contents from the mouth by reversal of peristalsis, the normal muscular contractions of the digestive system. Nausea may or may not occur at the same time.

Vomiting may be caused by motion sickness, the use of certain drugs, an obstruction in the intestine, acute gastritis, injury to the head, appendicitis and pregnancy. The most common cause is the presence of a toxin, such as occurs in food poisoning, irritating the gut. Overindulgence in food and alcohol is another cause. Vomiting may be self-induced, particularly in people suffering from anorexia nervosa or bulimia.

Many babies posset (bring up a small amount after each feed), but this is not vomiting. True vomiting in a baby may be the symptom of a serious problem such as pyloric stenosis or a gastric illness, both of which require immediate medical help, or it may be the result of gastroesophageal reflux, which is common and not life-threatening. Because babies can dehydrate much more quickly than adults it is always important to seek medical reassurance.

Vomiting on an occasional basis during pregnancy is common; pregnancy nausea is even more common. Severe vomiting, or hyperemesis gravidarum, may require hospitalization; it disappears after the baby is born.

Vomiting blood (hematemesis) is very serious at any time and needs immediate evaluation by an expert. It can be caused by acute gastritis, a peptic ulcer, bleeding esophagal varices, or, more rarely, hemophilia, leukemia and other blood disorders.

An antiemetic is a drug that prevents vomiting. The three main types are phenothiazines, antihistamines and anticholinergics. Care should be taken if taking any of these medications as the side effects (especially drowsiness) can be quite severe.

SEE ALSO *Digestive system, Eating disorders, Food poisoning, Gastritis, Gastroesophageal reflux, Peristalsis, Pregnancy, Stomach*

VON WILLEBRAND'S DISEASE

Von Willebrand's disease is the most common inherited defect of the coagulation system. It results in a bleeding disorder similar to but generally milder than hemophilia. Unlike hemophilia, however, it affects males and females equally. It is due to a deficiency of von Willebrand factor, a protein involved in the interaction between platelet cells and a damaged blood vessel wall. Von Willebrand factor is present in the circulation complexed to Factor VIII, the clotting factor that is deficient in hemophilia. In severe von Willebrand's disease the Factor VIII level is low.

SEE ALSO *Blood vessels, Hemophilia, Platelets*

VULVA

The female external genitalia are collectively known as the vulva. They consist of paired folds, the labia majora, which are covered by skin and pubic hair and have a moist internal lining. The labia minora are fleshy folds within the labia majora which lie on either side of the vestibule containing the vaginal and urinary openings and mucus-secreting glands. The clitoris is erectile tissue like the penis and has erotic functions. The upper ends of the labia minora join around the clitoris. In some cultures, female genital mutilation is carried out. This usually involves dividing the clitoris and removing the labia.

Inflammation and irritation of the vulval skin can be the direct result of local irritants or be secondary to vaginal or urinary tract infection. Carcinoma of the vulva accounts for about 5 percent of all genital cancers and is usually treated with irradiation or surgery.

SEE ALSO *Clitoris, Penis, Vagina*

VULVITIS

The female external genitalia are collectively known as the vulva. Vulvitis describes any inflammation or irritation of this area with a variety of causes including local infections, allergic reactions or skin irritation resulting from vaginal discharges or urinary disorders. Vulvitis may also arise from changes in the skin of the vulva associated with a decline in circulating estrogens at menopause.

SEE ALSO *Menopause, Vagina, Vulva*

VULVOVAGINITIS

Vulvovaginitis is the result of a discharge from a vaginal inflammation or infection which produces a secondary irritation of the vulva (the external genitalia). In women of reproductive age, a common cause of vulvovaginitis is the vaginal discharge from thrush. Vulvovaginitis in childhood may be caused by infection or irritation from a foreign body in the vagina.

SEE ALSO *Vaginitis, Vulvitis*

Vulva

The vulva is the collective term for the external parts of a woman's genitals, including the labia majora, labia minora, mons pubis and clitoris.

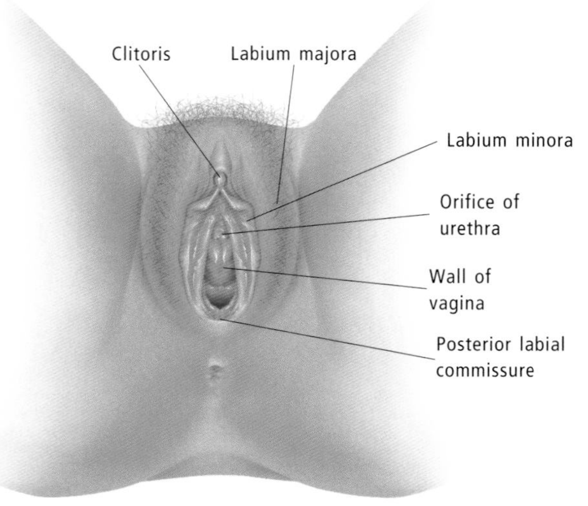

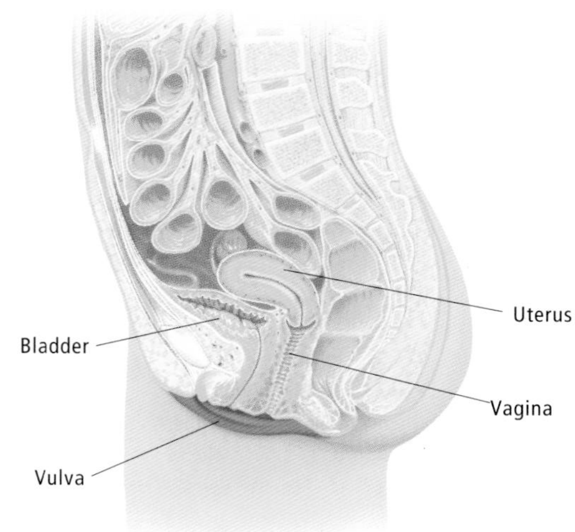

WARTS

Warts are benign tumors that occur in the outer layers of the skin. Typically, they appear as a raised, rough, round or oval lump that may be skin-colored, or lighter or darker than surrounding normal skin. Caused by the papillomavirus, they are mildly contagious and occur most often on the hands, feet, and face, though they may occur elsewhere.

Warts are often named for where they occur; plantar warts occur on the soles of the feet, genital warts in the skin on or around the genitalia. If they occur on the hands, arms or legs they are called common warts, or verrucae vulgaris. Multiple pinhead-sized warts occurring in children are called verrucae planae juveniles.

Warts usually cause no symptoms (though plantar warts may be painful) and disappear spontaneously within 2–3 years. If unsightly or painful they may be treated with an over-the-counter paint containing a mildly corrosive agent such as salicylic acid and/or lactic acid, which is applied daily for several weeks. They can be surgically removed with cryotherapy (freezing), electrocautery (burning), or laser treatment. Recurrence is common.

SEE ALSO *Genital warts, Skin, Viruses*

Warts

Caused by a virus, warts are small benign tumors that most commonly occur on the skin of the hands, feet and face.

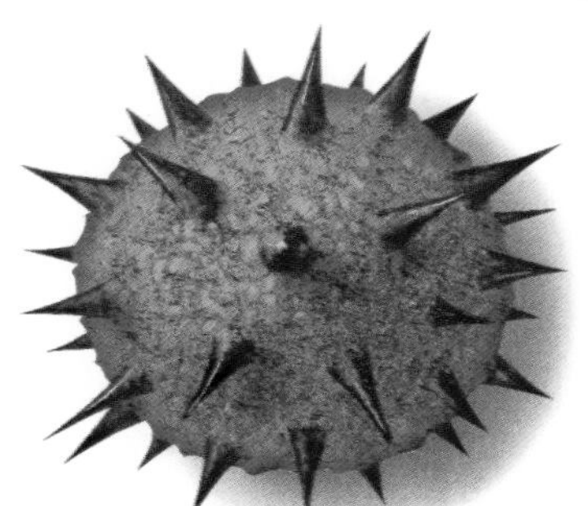

Wart virus

The papillomavirus is contagious and can be spread by scratching or rubbing infected skin.

WEIGHT

By definition, weight is the force with which a mass is attracted to the earth by gravity. When a person consumes more calories (or kilojoules) than is used through activity, body mass, and therefore weight, increases.

Pregnancy

During pregnancy the average weight gain in Western countries is around 26 pounds (12 kilograms); from 22–28½ pounds (10 to 13 kilograms) is thought to be ideal. One-third of this weight is made up of baby, placenta and amniotic fluid, one-third comprises an increase in breast tissue, other tissues and extra blood, and the remainder is body fat and retained water.

Babies and children

Growth and weight gain are important measures of healthy development in babies, and weight is among the first measurements taken of a newborn. When assessing a baby's weight it is important to take into account the baby's genetic inheritance and degree of prematurity, and the mother's health during pregnancy.

The growth charts used to assess a baby's growth are a valuable tool but need to be carefully interpreted, remembering that they show the range of weight of babies and children at various ages. The expected growth rate of children in industrialized countries is very different to that of children in less developed nations.

Weight charts need to be interpreted in conjunction with height charts to assess whether the baby or child is underweight or overweight. Not every child grows or gains weight at the same rate, so the overall pattern is necessary for a proper assessment. When a child is consistently overweight or underweight the cause needs to be investigated.

Failure to thrive means failure to gain weight, and in children up to the age of 2 is an indicator of serious illness or emotional or nutritional deprivation. Inadequate energy input, intestinal disease, heart and lung disease, metabolic conditions, congenital defects and emotional issues should all be investigated.

In many affluent countries childhood obesity is a growing problem. Obesity results in the creation of an abnormal number of fat cells, which may not disappear when weight is reduced, only losing some of their fat content. The cells retain a capacity for fat storage which gives the individual a tendency to become overweight in adolescence and adulthood. An overweight child can be disinclined to take part in physical activities. Obesity caused by poor eating habits can be worsened by the inactivity that results from sedentary leisure pursuits. The risk of becoming obese is greatest in children who have two obese parents; recent research indicates that genetic factors are important in determining obesity in adults.

Adults

Many women gain weight around the time of the menopause. In 90 percent of cases, this weight gain is the result of changes in lifestyle, not hormonal changes as is often thought. Women who remain physically active are less likely to increase their weight.

Weight-loss medicines, taken under medical supervision, and combined with a diet which reduces the daily calorie (kilojoule) intake, will help most obese people to lose weight. The best course is prevention; failing that, taking control of the amount of food consumed and exercise taken will help prevent health and lifestyle problems. Recent research suggests that metabolic and genetic disorders may cause obesity in some people.

SEE ALSO *Body Mass Index, Body shape, Diet, Nutrition, Obesity*

W

Wernicke-Korsakoff syndrome

Caused by a deficiency of thiamine, Wernicke-Korsakoff syndrome involves inflammation of the cerebellum, fourth ventricle and thalamus. This results in loss of motor skills, failing memory and general mental confusion.

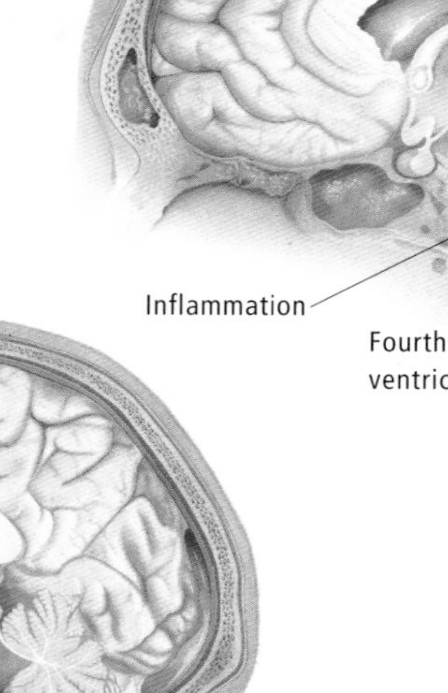

WERNICKE-KORSAKOFF SYNDROME

This syndrome is a combination of two disorders of the brain, Wernicke's encephalopathy and Korsakoff's amnesia, resulting from a deficiency in vitamin B_1 (thiamine). Long-term thiamine deficiency may become severe enough to affect the brain.

Wernicke's encephalopathy is an acute state involving confusion, memory loss and lack of muscular coordination, resulting when the supply of thiamine to the brain is depleted. This can happen after an alcoholic binge or after excessive vomiting in people who are generally undernourished. Thiamine deficiency is associated with alcoholism because alcoholics substitute alcohol for food and become generally malnourished.

The characteristics of Wernicke's encephalopathy are double vision, very rapid movements or paralysis of the eyes, mental confusion, drowsiness and uncoordinated walking. Emergency treatment is by direct injection of thiamine, but this may not prevent permanent brain damage.

People who recover from Wernicke's encephalopathy may suffer Korsakoff's amnesia or psychosis. Symptoms are mental confusion, loss of memory, apathy and delirium.

SEE ALSO *Alcoholism, Amnesia*

WHEEZING

Wheezing is a whistling sound heard in the chest when air passes through obstructed airways while breathing, especially when exhaling. It is one of the main symptoms of asthma. The sound is caused by the air passing through airways narrowed by muscle spasm, inflammation and the mucous secretion that occurs during asthma. Wheezing disappears when the asthma is treated. In severe asthma there may be no wheezing, as the bronchi may become so obstructed that no air can pass through.

SEE ALSO *Asthma, Breathing*

WHIPLASH

Whiplash is a term often applied to trauma to the cervical spine and tissues caused by rapid movement of the head and forceful flexion of the neck, causing pain, muscle spasm and limited motion. Treatment is usually protective support for the neck and back and sometimes the use of weights attached to head or legs to stretch the injured muscles and relieve pressure on the nerves.

SEE ALSO *Neck*

Whiplash

People involved in car accidents often suffer whiplash, as the sudden impact makes the head snap forward and then backwards, damaging the muscles and tissues of the neck and overstretching the cervical vertebrae.

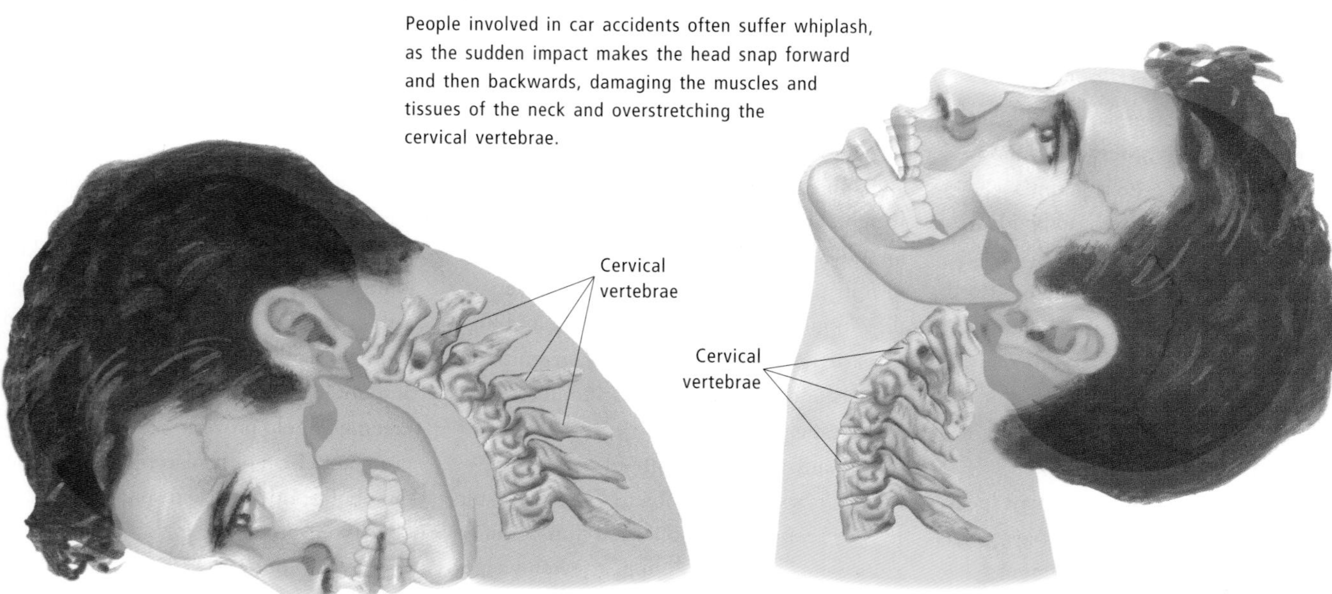

WHIPWORM

The whipworm (*Trichuris trichiura*) is a parasitic roundworm. Humans become the hosts for these worms when they eat uncooked food from crops grown in soil fertilized with sewage that has not been treated properly, or eat food prepared by infected handlers. The infection is known as trichuriasis and symptoms are abdominal pain and diarrhea; in small children complications such as intestinal blockage can result. Treatment with mebendazole is usually effective.

SEE ALSO *Trichuriasis, Worms*

WHITE BLOOD CELLS

Throughout life the body faces ongoing assault from thousands of different viruses, bacteria and other microbes, as well as a range of invertebrate parasites. The first lines of defense, the skin and mucous membranes, keep most of these potential invaders out. The comparative few that make it through to deeper tissues to cause disease face a barrage of attacks from the white blood cells (WBCs). Known also as leukocytes, WBCs are produced in red bone marrow and lymphatic tissue. There are five major types: neutrophils, eosinophils, basophils, monocytes and lymphocytes.

Most WBCs can "squeeze" through very small spaces to sites of infection in the body, a process referred to as emigration. These spaces include those between the cells of capillary walls. Neutrophils are the first to arrive at the site of an invasion. There they release bacteria-killing enzymes and ingest microorganisms and foreign particles by a process called phagocytosis. The monocytes arrive a little later but in much larger numbers, becoming macrophages once they migrate from the blood into tissues. They kill offending organisms and clean up debris associated with infection. Eosinophils also consume and engulf foreign material; in addition they release enzymes associated with allergic reactions which kill certain parasitic worms and protozoa. Basophils are also involved in inflammation and allergic reactions. Once they enter infected tissue they become mast cells, which release substances such as histamine that intensify the body's inflammatory response to foreign matter, producing hypersensitivity reactions.

White blood cells

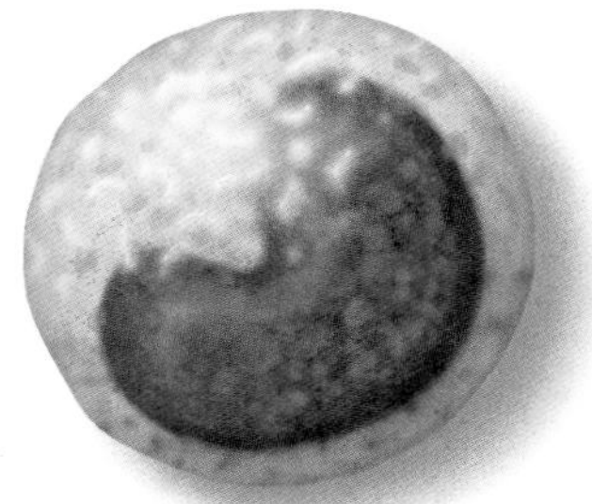

Monocyte
Monocytes circulate in the blood for 1–2 days before entering the body tissues to become macrophages.

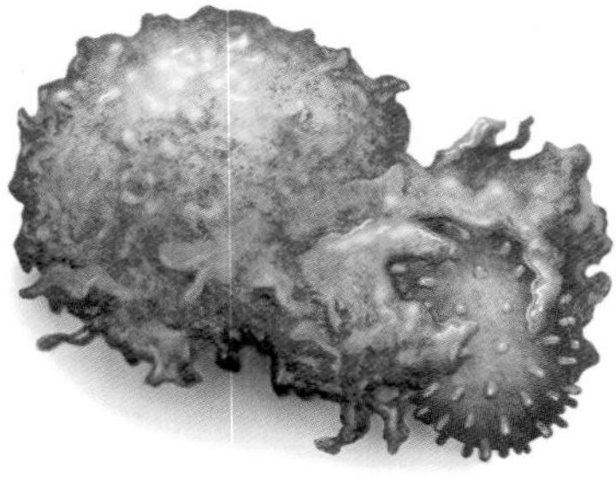

Macrophage
Macrophages fight infection by engulfing foreign organisms and debris.

Neutrophil
The front-line defense against bacterial invasions, neutrophils engulf and destroy microorganisms.

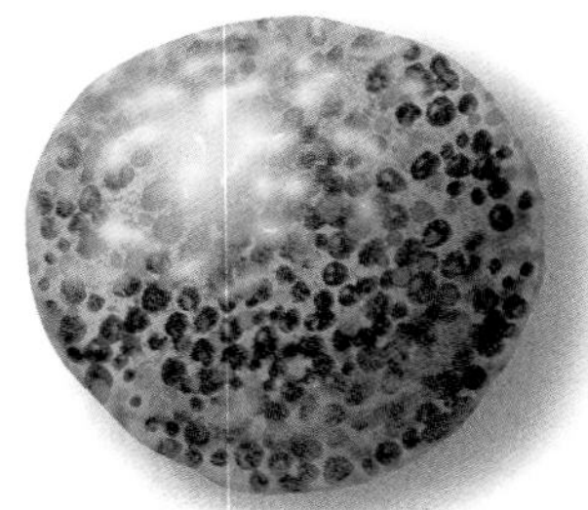

Basophil
These cells release substances that increase the body's response to invading allergens.

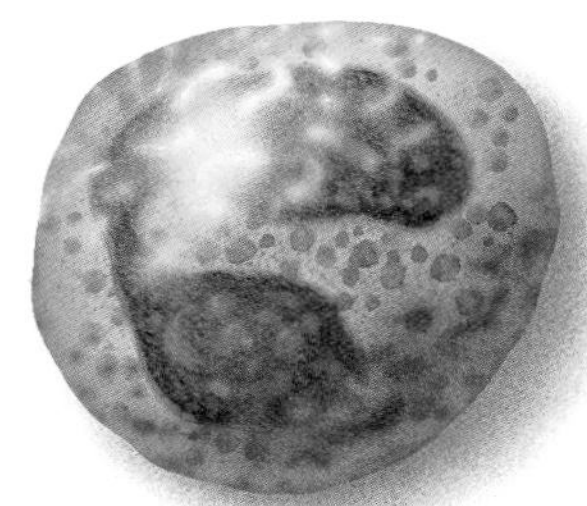

Eosinophil
Eosinophils release enzymes which cause allergic reactions and kill some parasites.

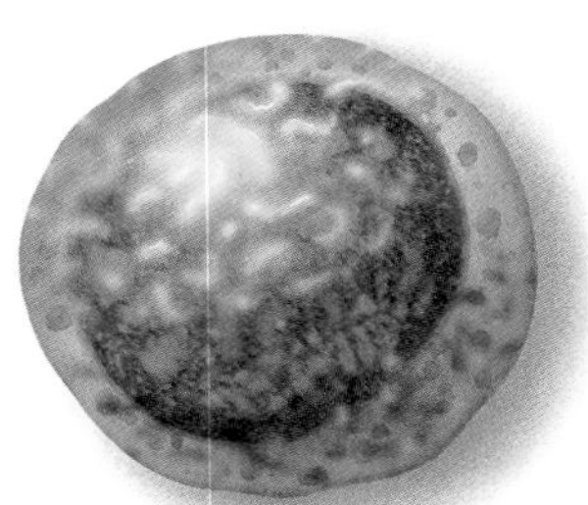

Lymphocyte
There are three types of lymphocyte. Natural killer cells and T cells attack foreign invaders directly; B cells make antibodies.

There are three types of lymphocytes: natural killer cells, T cells and B cells. Natural killer cells attack a wide variety of microorganisms and certain tumor cells. The T and B cells are directly involved in the body's immune responses. T cells combat viruses, fungi and cancer cells, and attack foreign tissue in organ transplants.

Before they can respond, T cells must become sensitized to a foreign invader. Different T cells learn to "recognize" different pathogens or harmful substances—there are literally millions of different T cells circulating in a healthy body. The situation is similar with B cells, which deal particularly well with bacteria and are highly effective at deactivating their toxins. Unlike T cells, B cells do not directly attack foreign material. Instead, they develop into plasma cells which secrete antibodies to do the work.

T and B cells can circulate in the body for years. The other WBCs are, like suicidal soldiers, eventually killed by their combat efforts—particularly by the toxic material they engulf. Their life spans are usually only a few days but during times of infection they may survive for only a matter of hours.

An increase in the number of WBCs in the blood usually indicates inflammation or infection. Because each WBC type plays a different role, the percentage of each type present in the blood helps diagnose disease. For example, a high eosinophil count suggests an allergic reaction or a parasitic worm infection. Normally, WBCs number between 5,000 and 10,000 per cubic milliliter of blood; over 10,000 suggests infection. An elevated WBC count is called leukocytosis and an abnormally low count is called leukopenia.

SEE ALSO *Blood, T cells*

WHITLOW

A pus-filled inflammation on the end of a finger or toe may be termed a whitlow. A herpetic whitlow is a swollen painful fingertip caused by the herpes simplex virus entering through a wound after exposure to infected oral or respiratory secretions; it may also occur as the result of nail-biting. Treatment may include the release of pus.

SEE ALSO *Herpes simplex*

WHOOPING COUGH

Whooping cough, also known as pertussis, is caused by the organism *Bordetella pertussis*. It is a serious, common and highly infectious illness in young children, particularly children under two years. It is spread by coughing, sneezing and close personal contact. Whooping cough incubates for between one and two weeks and can last for as long as three months. The affected person remains infectious for up to a month after the onset of the cough.

Beginning like a cold, whooping cough turns into exhausting coughing bouts with a characteristic whooping sound. Pneumonia is the most common complication and middle ear infections, nosebleeds, hemorrhages inside the eye, loss of appetite and dehydration are other possible complications.

Adults and older children who contract the disease are not likely to suffer as severely, but can still spread the disease. For those under two years, hospitalization is often necessary. Full immunization is the most sensible precaution.

SEE ALSO *Immunization, Infectious diseases*

Whitlow

Small fluid-filled blisters are a feature of herpetic whitlows, caused by the highly contagious herpes simplex virus.

WILSON'S DISEASE

A rare condition also known as hepatolenticular degeneration, Wilson's disease is a hereditary defect characterized by the accumulation of copper in organs such as the liver, brain, eyes, kidneys and bones, caused by a deficiency in the circulation of the copper-binding protein ceruloplasmin. This can lead to chronic hepatitis and cirrhosis. The eyes may develop a brown or green ring in the outer margin of the cornea, known as the Kayser-Fleischer ring. Wilson's disease usually appears in the second or third decade of life. Early diagnosis and treatment has the potential to reverse the effects of the disorder and prevent permanent damage.

Since Wilson's disease is an inherited disorder, relatives of a person diagnosed with the disease should be screened and treated early to prevent or minimize organ damage.

Wilson's disease

When the body cannot metabolize copper, dangerously high levels of the metal accumulate in the liver, brain, kidneys, bones and eyes. The appearance of brown or green rings in the eyes (Kayser-Fleischer rings) are the most obvious symptom of the disease.

WITHDRAWAL

Withdrawal is the reaction of the body and mind in a drug-dependent person when the effect of the substance of dependence wears off. It also refers to the period in which these effects are felt, typically when dependence is first being treated. Dependence on any substance involves craving; uncontrolled intake; physical or mental dependence; repeated use and increasing tolerance.

Repeated use causes the level of toxic substances in body tissues and bloodstream to rise. When use stops, these toxins are excreted and levels fall in the process of detoxification, which is the body's natural process of breakdown and excretion of waste. In the substance-dependent person, this fall in toxin levels triggers the craving and often results in harrowing physical and psychological withdrawal symptoms, including depression, suicidal impulses and life-threatening physical disorders, varying in degree with the particular substance (alcohol, street drugs, amphetamines or tranquilizers).

Withdrawal from alcohol and many drugs is characterized by trembling, restlessness, watery eyes and running nose, hallucinations, delusions, fever, dilated pupils, sweating, inability to sleep and excessively rapid heartbeat. Withdrawal from anti-anxiety drugs may cause panic attacks, deep depression, itching, muscle pain and sensitivity to light. Without medical attention, withdrawal symptoms may be serious enough to cause death.

Withdrawal because of failure of supply can provoke irrational or desperate behavior. Crime statistics in many industrialized nations show a high incidence of violations triggered by the need for money to obtain illegal drugs.

Withdrawal as a consequence of treatment for drug dependency is usually managed by physicians or counselors. They may use tranquilizers to relieve distress and replace illegal drugs with legal substances as a step toward breaking dependency.

Delirium tremens is a state of confusion and mental disorder induced by the withdrawal of alcohol. Alcohol withdrawal is sometimes treated with naltrexone to ease the cravings, or disulfiram, which causes nausea when alcohol is taken.

Heroin addiction is often treated with methadone, which is itself a potential substance of dependence. It can also be treated with naltrexone. Counseling often plays a vital part in managing the process of withdrawal.

SEE ALSO *Alcoholism, Delirium tremens, Detoxification, Drug dependence, Stimulants*

WORMS

A worm is an invertebrate animal with a soft slender body and no limbs. Four main groups cause parasitic infections in humans: flatworms (Platyhelminthes) such as the tapeworm, roundworms (Nematoda), ribbon worms (Nemertea) and segmented worms (Annelida). Infection is caused by ingestion of eggs or penetration of the skin by larvae.

The diseases caused by worms include the following.

Ankylostomiasis is an intestinal infection caused by the roundworms *Ancylostoma duodenale* and *Necator americanus*.

Ascariasis is an infection caused by *Ascaris lumbridoides*, an intestinal roundworm.

Elephantiasis is a chronic condition caused by the filiarial worms *Wuchereria bancrofti* or *Brugia malayi*, which enter the body through an infected mosquito.

Enterobiasis is a pinworm infection (threadworm, seatworm). It is caused by *Enterobius vermicularis* and spreads by transfer on the fingers after scratching the seat of infection, the anus. Eggs can also be inhaled as they drift in air.

Flukes of various kinds (Trematoda) can cause serious infections of the blood, liver, intestines and lungs. Intestinal flukes are transmitted from vegetation or freshwater fish; sheep liver flukes come from watercress containing cysts; clonorchiasis is caused by freshwater fish flukes; lung fluke infestations are transmitted from crabs and crayfish; schistosomiasis is caused by blood flukes entering the body from infested water.

Onchocerciasis is a serious infestation by the parasitic worm *Onchocerca volvulus*.

Strongyloidiasis is an intestinal infection by the threadworm *Strongyloides stercoralis*.

Tapeworm infections include intestinal infections by *Taenia saginata* (beef tapeworm) and *T. solium* (pork tapeworm). They may also include cysticercosis, infection by species of dwarf tapeworms, and, in sheepraising areas, echinococcosis, caused by the tapeworm *Echinococcus granulosus*, producing hydatid cysts.

Toxocariasis is an infection caused by *Toxocara canis* or *T. cati*, nematodes found in the dog and cat.

Trichinosis is an infection caused by the *Trichinella spiralis* worm, usually ingested from cysts in undercooked pork.

Trichuriasis is an infection caused by *Trichuris trichiura*, an intestinal roundworm also known as the whipworm.

SEE ALSO *Hookworm, Hydatid disease, Pinworms, Roundworm, Tapeworm, Trichinosis, Trichuriasis, Whipworm*

WRINKLES

Wrinkles are tiny ridges or furrows on the surface of the skin, associated with aging. They are caused by the gradual loss of elasticity in the skin that accompanies ageing. The elasticity of skin is due to the presence of fibers of the proteins elastin and collagen. In old age, there is a gradual reduction in the amount of elastin, and in the elastic properties of collagen, which lead to the appearance of wrinkles.

While the wrinkling of skin is a natural process which cannot be avoided, there are some environmental factors that will increase the rate at which they form, and these can be avoided. These include frequent exposure to sunshine and smoking. To minimize skin wrinkling, it is advisable to stop smoking, stay out of the sun as much as possible, wear protective clothing when outside, and use sunscreen. In some cases, the appearance of someone with early onset wrinkles can be improved with plastic surgery such as a facelift or browlift.

Wrinkle creams may be tried but their value is questionable and some, for example those containing female sex hormone (which stimulates regeneration of skin and improve its elastic properties), may have side effects if used frequently.

WRIST

The wrist (carpus) contains a group of eight bones, known as the carpal bones, which join the radius and ulna to the hand. This complex joint allows a wide range of movement, in which the hand can be bent forward (flexion) or backward (extension) or moved from side to side. Two of the carpal bones are particularly prone to injury. The scaphoid, which lies on the thumb side of the wrist and forms the floor of a region known as the "snuff box", can be fractured in a fall on an outstretched hand. The adjacent bone, the lunate, can dislocate fairly easily, and may cause a painful click during wrist movements.

The shape of the carpal bones forms a concavity or U-shape. The roof of this concavity is closed over by a dense band of connective tissue, forming the carpal tunnel. Long flexor tendons to the fingers and thumb pass through this tunnel, as well as the median nerve. Swelling within the tunnel can cause the median nerve to be compressed, and lead to carpal tunnel syndrome.

As well as the long flexor tendons that cross in front of the wrist through the carpal tunnel, long tendons associated with extension of the fingers and thumb pass across the back of the wrist. All these tendons are surrounded by synovial sheaths that lubricate them. These sheaths can get inflamed and painful, for example with overuse or in association with arthritis. Inflammation of two tendons to the thumb, a condition known as de Quervain's disease, causes pain which is exacerbated by gripping and twisting movements, as in wringing clothes. Resting the tendons by avoiding the painful movements usually helps, and anti-inflammatory medication may be recommended. The tendon sheaths can also form a small swelling or ganglion, usually on the back of the wrist. The ganglion may not be painful, but if necessary it can be removed surgically.

Three nerves cross the wrist to supply the skin and muscles of the hand—the median,

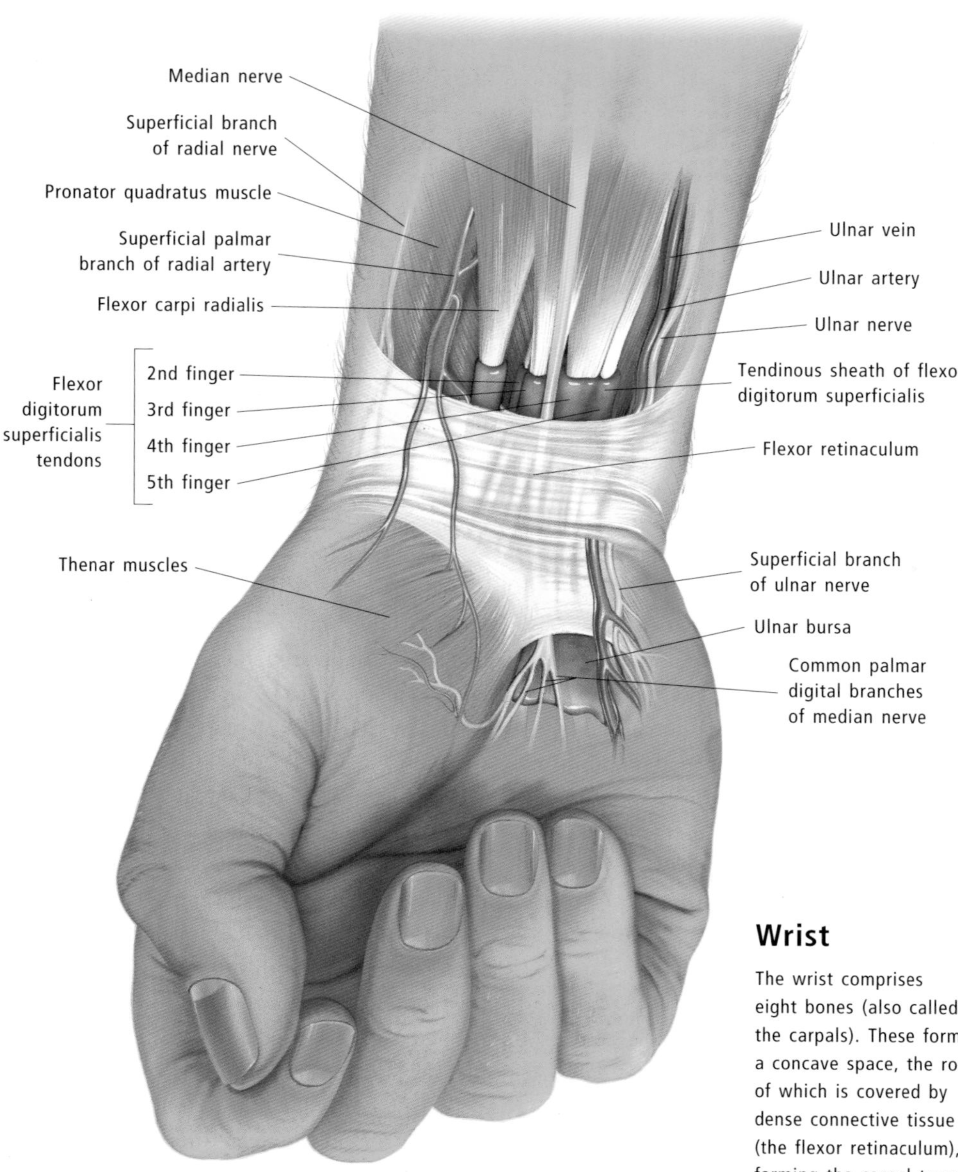

Wrist

The wrist comprises eight bones (also called the carpals). These form a concave space, the roof of which is covered by dense connective tissue (the flexor retinaculum), forming the carpal tunnel.

ulnar and radial nerves. Like the median nerve, the ulnar nerve can be compressed in a connective tissue tunnel (tunnel of Guyon) at the wrist. The ulnar nerve is particularly important for fine finger movements. The wrist is also crossed by two arteries, the ulnar and radial arteries. The pulse from the radial artery can be felt at the wrist, near the base of the thumb, while that for the ulnar artery is felt against the ulnar bone near the wrist.

The wrist is one of the joints commonly involved in rheumatoid arthritis. There is pain, joint stiffness and reduced movement, with joint deformity and swelling which may lead to carpal tunnel syndrome.

Osteoarthritis can occur in the wrist, especially if there has been a previous injury. Osteoarthritis is also common in the joint between the wrist and first metacarpal bone, which is involved in thumb movements (carpometacarpal joint). Arthritis in this joint can be the result of a common fracture of the metacarpal bone called Bennett's fracture. There is pain at the base of the thumb, aggravated by thumb movements. Treatment includes resting the joint, anti-inflammatory medication and steroid injections.

SEE ALSO *Carpal tunnel syndrome, Connective tissue, Ganglion, Hand, Joints, Osteoarthritis, Radial nerve, Radius, Rheumatoid arthritis, Tendons, Ulna, Ulnar nerve*

X CHROMOSOME

The cells of the human body each contain 23 pairs of chromosomes; one pair determines the sex of the individual, and consists of two X chromosomes (female) or one X and one Y chromosome (male). The sperm cell and the egg cell each have only 23 single chromosomes (one from each pair). When these cells unite the chromosomes pair up so the newly fertilized cell has 46 chromosomes (23 pairs).

At conception, there is one X chromosome present in the ovum, while the sperm may contain an X chromosome or a Y chromosome. If the united cell has two X chromosomes, the baby will be female, if there is an X and a Y chromosome the baby will be male.

SEE ALSO *Chromosomes, Fragile X syndrome, Y Chromosome*

X-RAY

X-rays are a form of electromagnetic radiation, similar to light but of a much shorter wavelength. They can penetrate soft tissue such as skin and muscle rather easily, but are absorbed by bones and other objects containing heavy atoms.

X-rays, or their penetration, are recorded or observed by use of photographic film or fluorescent screens, so they can therefore be used to study the internal structure of the body, particularly bones. Also observable are the presence and location of foreign objects, such as swallowed coins, and surgically-inserted needles and metal plates. Cavities, such as those of the gut, bladder, heart and blood vessels, can be studied by filling them with substances which are either radiopaque (for example, barium) or radiolucent (for example, carbon dioxide). The radiopaque substances offer resistance to x-rays, and appear as light areas on exposed film; the radiolucent substances permit their passage and appear as dark areas on exposed film.

Because x-rays are a form of ionizing radiation, they are potentially damaging to tissue. Excessive exposure to x-rays must be avoided. Exposure is normally minimized by employing a narrow beam of x-rays, covering sensitive parts of the body with lead-containing rubber shields, and using sensitive recording devices which require only low x-ray dosage. The damaging effects of x-rays can be of therapeutic value in the treatment of cancer and other tumors.

Cross-sectional pictures of body structures are obtained by computed axial tomography (CAT scanning), in which a series of x-ray images focused on different planes are analyzed by computer and presented as sections. CAT scans show soft tissue in more detail than plain x-rays.

SEE ALSO *Barium enema, Barium meal, CAT scan, Contrast x-rays, Imaging techniques*

XANTHELASMA

Xanthomas—flat, fatty, yellow deposits in the skin—are known as xanthelasmas when they affect the eyelids and surrounding area. In about half the number of people with this characteristic there is an association with high blood cholesterol and hyperlipidemia, and the appearance of xanthomas elsewhere on the body.

Seen most commonly in the elderly, xanthomas do not cause discomfort or disease. There is no treatment, though the spots may be removed for cosmetic reasons.

SEE ALSO *Cholesterol, Eyelids, Xanthoma*

XANTHOMA

A xanthoma is a small, firm, yellow to red-brown raised lesion that develops just beneath the skin and appears on the skin's surface as a nodule, papule, plaque or benign tumor. It is a painless deposit from the bloodstream of excess fats (lipids) such as cholesterol and triglycerides. Xanthomas can occur anywhere on the body but tend to be seen particularly on the elbows, knees, hands, feet, buttocks, joints and tendons.

Although they can be unsightly, xanthomas in themselves cause few problems. They may be indicators of a range of underlying metabolic disorders characterized by undesirable elevated blood lipid levels. For example, xanthomas can appear when the disease diabetes mellitus is poorly controlled.

Clustered around the joints in a condition known as xanthoma tuberosum, these nodules can suggest cirrhosis of the liver or certain thyroid disorders. In xanthoma tendinosum, xanthomas occur in clumps on the tendons and indicate a hereditary lipid storage disease. When they occur on the eyelids, xanthomas frequently indicate high cholesterol levels. The sudden appearance of large clusters on the legs, arms, buttocks or trunk indicate dangerously elevated triglyceride levels in the blood.

Most xanthomas disappear eventually, if the underlying cause is treated successfully.

SEE ALSO *Cholesterol, Fats, Xanthelasma*

Y CHROMOSOME

Chromosomes are the thread-like structures in cell nuclei that carry coded hereditary information. Normal humans have 46 chromosomes, arranged in 23 pairs, in each of their body cells. However, the sex cells (sperm and ova) each have only 23 single chromosomes. The sex chromosomes are labeled X and Y, the latter being responsible for the development of male characteristics. Sperm contain either an X or Y chromosome, but ova only ever contain the X chromosome. When a sperm fertilizes an ovum, the chromosomes combine to form the normal complement of 23 pairs. Only if the sperm carries a Y chromosome will the fertilized egg develop into a male.

The Y chromosome is roughly a third the length of the X chromosome, and apart from its role in determining maleness, is otherwise genetically inactive. This confers a biological advantage on the female, because if a male inherits a recessive gene on the X chromosome, for example the gene causing hemophilia, there is no second X chromosome with a dominant gene to counteract it. By contrast, a female who inherits the recessive disease-causing gene on the X chromosome from one parent, will probably inherit the normal, dominant gene from the other parent, and so probably will not develop the disease. The condition therefore is usually only seen in men (but is carried by women) and is termed sex-linked. Other examples of sex-linked conditions are red-green color blindness and night blindness.

SEE ALSO *Chromosomes, X chromosome*

YAWNING

In yawning, the mouth is opened very wide and a long deep breath is taken. Sometimes, the upper limbs are stretched, which may promote venous return. An involuntary act, a yawn is believed to be triggered by a need to get rid of accumulated carbon dioxide. Yawning typically occurs on waking from sleep, or when tired, but it may be of psychological origin.

SEE ALSO *Sleep*

YAWS

An infectious and debilitating disease of the skin and bones, yaws is also known as frambesia. Found in moist tropical regions of the world, it is most common in children aged 2–5 who wear few clothes, and live in areas where hygiene is poor. It is caused by the spirochete (spiral microorganism) *Treponema pertenue*, which enters the body through a break in the skin. Yaws is similar to syphilis but is not sexually transmitted.

Yaws has three stages, the first a single bump on the skin which gradually grows larger and is characterized by a wart-like thickening; this becomes fibrous and ulcerates, with a discharge. After about a month this will disappear and multiple eruptions of the same type develop. These lesions look similar to a raspberry. At this stage the disease may also affect the bones and joints. The third stage, which develops in 10 percent of sufferers, causes deformities which can resemble leprosy, and can also affect the spleen, brain and blood vessels.

Penicillin or another antibiotic may be used as a preventive measure as well as a treatment and is usually successful. Yaws is rarely fatal.

SEE ALSO *Infectious diseases*

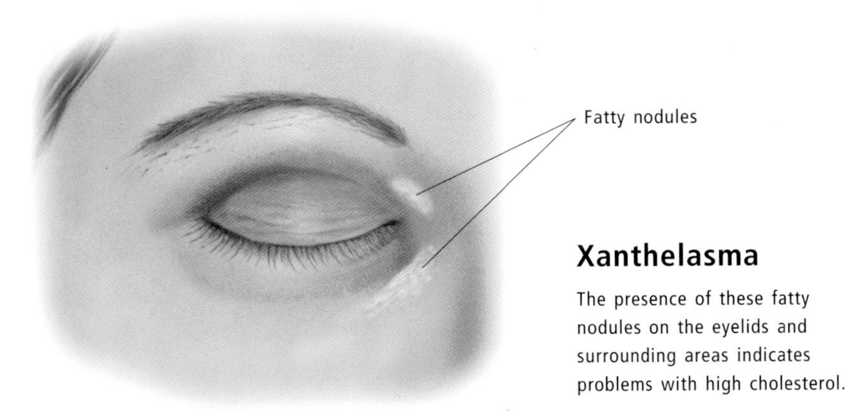

Xanthelasma

The presence of these fatty nodules on the eyelids and surrounding areas indicates problems with high cholesterol.

YELLOW FEVER

The bite of the mosquito *Aedes aegypti* can transmit the virus infection yellow fever to humans. Common in tropical climates, particularly Africa and South America, yellow fever is an acute infectious disease. There are two different patterns of transmission of the disease—either from person to person via the mosquito or from a mammalian host, often a monkey, to a forest mosquito and from there to a human.

Symptoms appear abruptly. Shivering, a high fever, severe headache, bone pains, dizziness, backache, nausea and vomiting strike suddenly, within three to six days of being infected. The virus destroys liver cells, and jaundice (yellowing of the skin) is common. While the majority of sufferers recover completely, others may become delirious and go into a coma, with death often the result. Those who recover have lifelong immunity. There is no cure and the only treatment is administration of intravenous fluids, anti-nausea medication, kidney dialysis and skilled medical care.

Immunization with an extremely mild yellow fever virus will give protection for 10 years. This vaccine cannot be given to children under the age of one.

SEE ALSO *Immunization, Viruses*

YOGA

The term yoga comes from the Sanskrit word *yuj*, which means "to bind together" or "union". In yoga this refers both to finding union between mind and body and to the experience of oneness that lies beyond the dualistic nature of the material world and the mind. Yoga was developed in India some four thousand years ago.

At first yoga was practised only by small numbers of spiritual disciples, who lived as recluses. They developed many of the postures of yoga from studying animals, which were seen to be healthier and more relaxed than humans.

The basic philosophies and practice of yoga were first written about in the second century BC by Patanjali in his yoga sutras, which summarize the eight limbs of yoga—*yamma*: moral codes of a universal nature; *niyama*: personal conduct; *asanas*: the practice of postures; *pranayama*: breath control; *pratyhara*: control of the senses; *dharana*: the power of concentration; *dhyana*: the stillness of meditation; and *samadhi*: contemplation and reflection.

The rise in popularity and spread of yoga throughout the world has taken place over the last 200 years. In the West, yoga is particularly popular for the physical effects of its postures, which promote flexibility and good health, and its relaxation and meditation practices, which help to reduce stress.

Yoga is particularly recommended for all stress-related illnesses, sciatica, back pain, emphysema, asthma, rheumatism, arthritis, digestive ailments and menstrual pain.

Techniques

Yoga utilizes an awareness of breath, body and mind. The major techniques, in the order they are practised in a typical hatha yoga class, are: physical postures (asanas), which are said to heal and maintain the physical body by increasing flexibility, strengthening the muscles and detoxifying and toning all the body systems; breathing exercises (pranayama), which are said to stimulate and increase the vital energy in the body and are also seen as helpful in calming the emotions and sharpening the mind; meditation (dhyana), which is believed to bring awareness of the inner reality, helping to transcend the illusions and stresses of external life; and total relaxation (yoga nidra), which achieves a deeply relaxed state by systematically guiding awareness through all the parts of the body.

Styles

There are a number of different yoga styles, some concentrating more on postures, others spending more time on relaxation and meditation. There is also a wide variation on the pace and degree of challenge involved in the practice of postures.

The three most common schools of yoga are Hatha yoga, Iyengar yoga and Oki yoga. In Hatha yoga, traditional postures are practised gently and slowly with breathing exercises, meditation and relaxation. They aim for a balance between energizing and relaxing practices to support overall well-being.

In Iyengar yoga, and its offshoot Astanga, the emphasis is on strengthening and maintaining the body through various postures, many of which are quite challenging.

Oki yoga is a Japanese version of yoga which focuses on the movement of *ch'i* (life energy) through the acupuncture meridians and which uses different postures in different seasons.

SEE ALSO *Exercise, Meditation, Relaxation techniques*

Yoga

The health benefits of yoga are achieved by exploiting the links between body and mind. Meditation and relaxation act on the hypothalamus and limbic system in the brain (which control autonomic functions such as breathing and heart rates, muscle tension and emotional state) to deliver physical benefits.

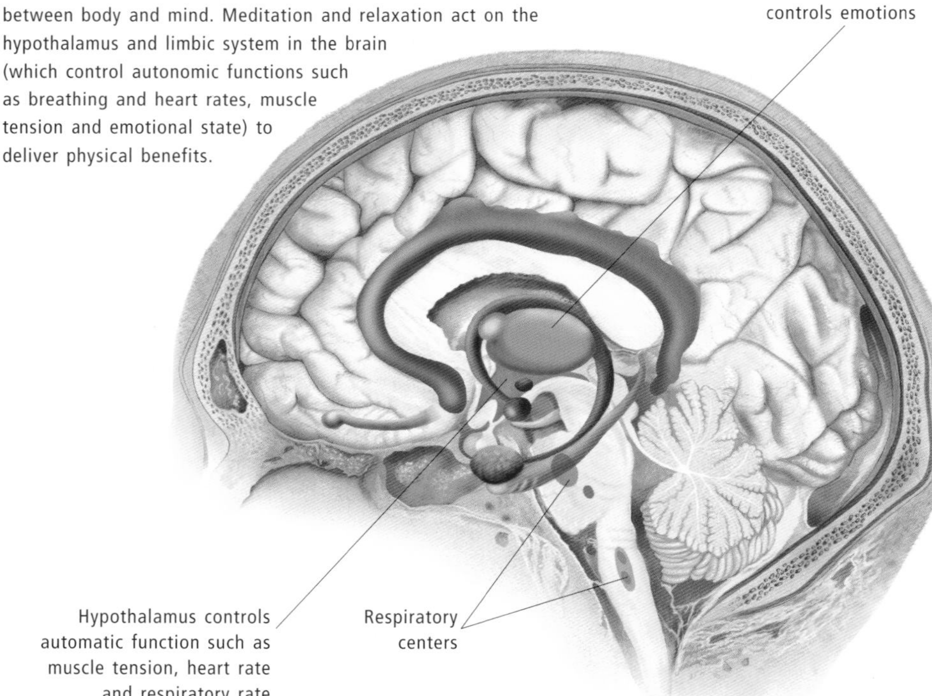
Limbic system controls emotions
Hypothalamus controls automatic function such as muscle tension, heart rate and respiratory rate
Respiratory centers

ZOLLINGER-ELLISON SYNDROME

This is an unusual disease caused by secretion of excess amounts of the hormone gastrin by tumors called gastrinomas. Gastrinomas most often arise from certain cells in the pancreas, although they may arise elsewhere in the duodenum or abdomen. The tumor may be small and very difficult to find. The gastrin produced by the tumor increases the secretion of acid by the stomach, causing stomach ulcers and problems with digestion. Patients may complain of upper abdominal pain and diarrhea.

Unlike other peptic ulcers, the pain is not easily relieved by antacids or milk. Treatment should ideally be to remove the gastrinoma if it can be found, or control the acid secretion with H_2 receptor blockers such as cimetidine.

SEE ALSO *Peptic ulcer, Stomach*

ZYGOTE

In a normal pregnancy, the ovum (egg) will be fertilized in the fallopian tube within 48 hours of intercourse.

This fertilized ovum, known as the zygote, begins to divide rapidly, first into two cells, then four, then eight, as it journeys down the fallopian tube, becoming a cluster of cells known as the blastocyst. About six days after fertilization the blastocyst implants itself into the uterine wall, where it will develop into the embryo.

SEE ALSO *Fertilization, Pregnancy, Reproductive systems*

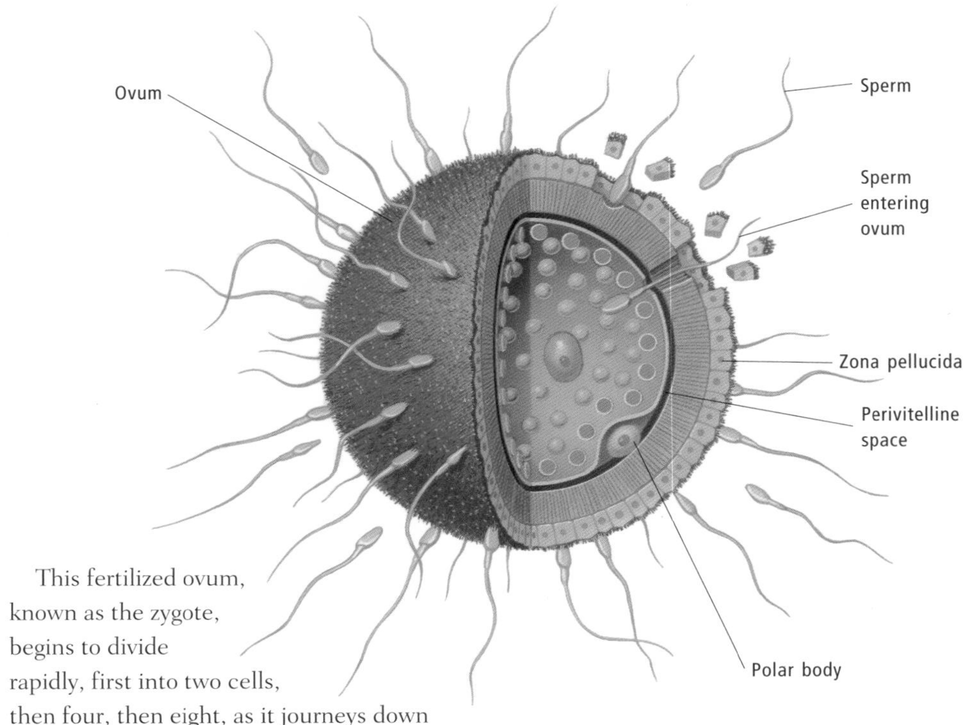

Zygote

A zygote is the cell created when a sperm enters and fertilizes an ovum, before it begins the process of division that will ultimately lead to the development of an embryo.

First Aid Emergency Guide

What is First Aid?

First aid is the initial care of the ill or injured. At any time, you may find yourself in a situation where someone has had an accident or is suffering from a sudden illness and needs help until a qualified health care professional, such as a doctor, registered nurse or ambulance officer, arrives.

The aims of first aid:

- promote a safe environment
- preserve life
- prevent injury or illness from becoming worse
- help promote recovery
- provide comfort to the ill or injured.

What a first aider should do:

- assess the situation quickly
- identify the nature of the injury or illness as far as possible
- manage the casualty promptly and appropriately
- arrange for Emergency Services to attend
- stay with the casualty until able to hand over to a health care professional
- give further help if necessary.

Other first aiders

The first aider who arrives first at the scene of an incident takes charge and stays in charge until handing over control. Any other first aider who arrives should offer to help the original first aider without trying to take over control. If you feel another first aider at the scene is more qualified to handle the situation, ask that person to take control. However, the most qualified person does not need to be in control, especially if another first aider already has matters well in hand.

Remember:

It must be stressed that reading this book, without attending a first aid course with its practical components, does not constitute a complete first aid education.

Emergency First Aid—The DRABC action plan

1 Check for DANGER—to you, to others and to the casualty.

2 Check for RESPONSE—shout and gently shake the shoulders. Is the casualty conscious or unconscious? If no response, go to 3. If responsive, go to 9.

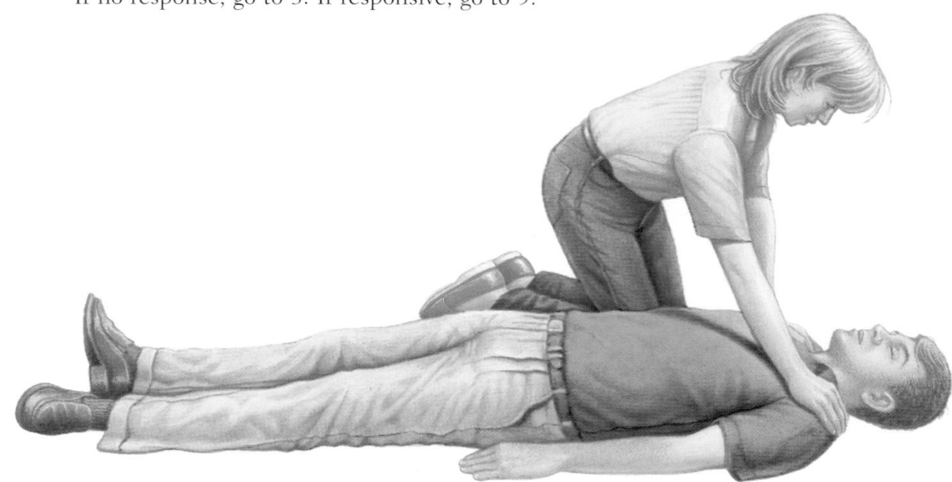

3 If no response, place the casualty in the recovery position.

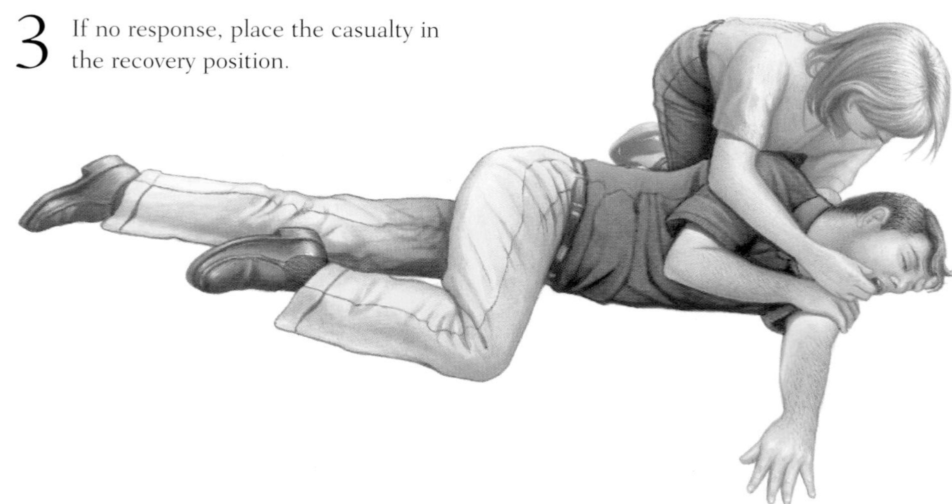

4 Check the AIRWAY—clear the mouth, tilt the head back to open the airway. Is the airway clear of objects? Is the airway open?

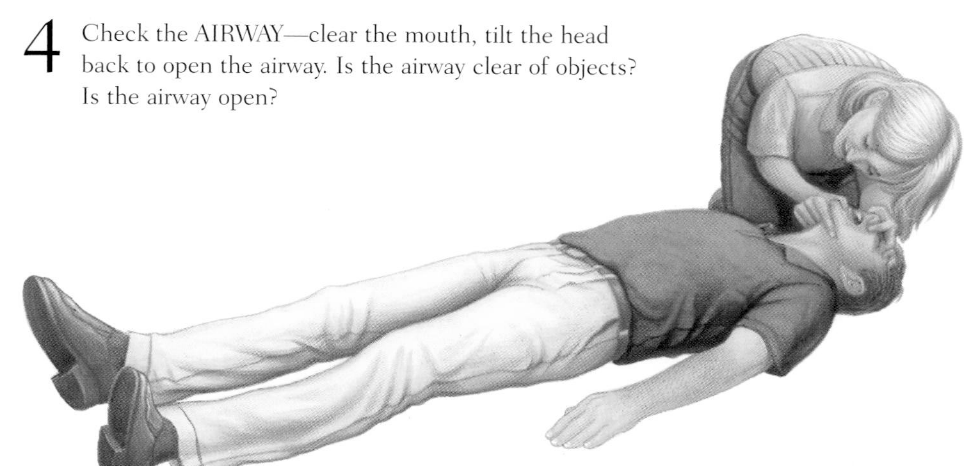

5 Check for BREATHING—look, listen and feel for breath. Is the chest rising and falling? Can you hear the casualty's breathing? Can you feel the breath on your cheek?
If the casualty is not breathing, go to 6.
If breathing, go to 10.

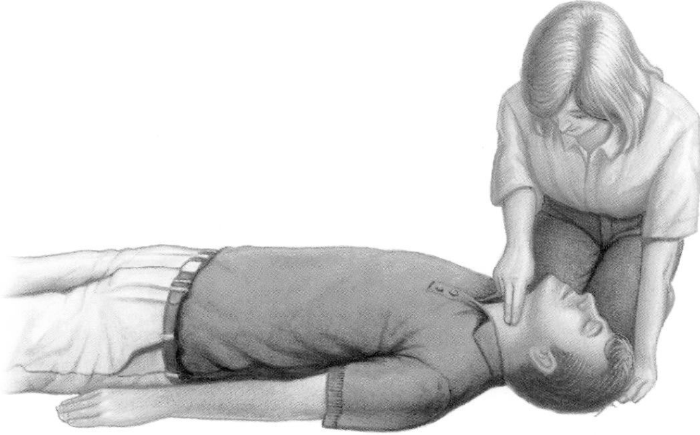

6 If not breathing—call the Emergency Services number for your area, then give two effective breaths.

7 Check for CIRCULATION—check the pulse at the neck. Can you feel a pulse? Can you see any obvious signs of life? If there is no pulse, go to 8. If the pulse is present, go to 11.

8 If there is no pulse, commence Cardiopulmonary Resuscitation (CPR):

- at a ratio of 15 compressions to 2 breaths in 15 seconds—4 cycles per minute for adults
- at a ratio of 5 compressions to 1 breath in 5 seconds—12 cycles per minute for children
- for both adults and children, check the pulse about every minute until medical aid arrives.

9 If responsive—manage any bleeding or injuries, monitor breathing and pulse, seek medical aid.

10 If breathing—leave casualty in the recovery position. Manage any bleeding or injuries, and seek medical aid. Check breathing and pulse regularly until medical aid arrives.

11 If the pulse is present but the casualty isn't breathing, continue Expired Air Resuscitation (EAR):

- at a ratio of 1 breath every 4 seconds for adults
- at a ratio of 1 breath every 3 seconds for children
- for both adults and children, check the pulse about every minute until medical aid arrives.

The Recovery Position

Adults and children (from age 1)

1 **Position casualty's legs:**

- kneel beside the casualty
- straighten the casualty's limbs
- lift the nearer leg at the knee so it is fully bent upwards.

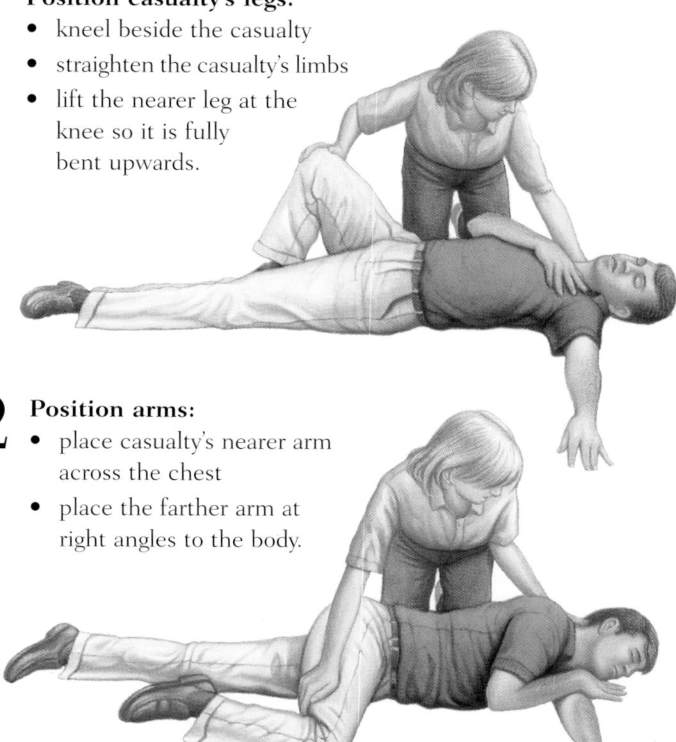

2 **Position arms:**

- place casualty's nearer arm across the chest
- place the farther arm at right angles to the body.

3 **Roll casualty into position:**

- roll casualty away from you onto their side
- keep the bent leg at right angles, with knee touching the ground to prevent casualty rolling onto their face.

4 **Make casualty steady:**

- make any adjustments necessary to ensure casualty does not roll.

5 **Ensure the airway is open.**

Infants (under 1 year)

- lay the infant face down on your forearm
- support the infant's head with your hand
- check the infant does not choke on their tongue or inhale vomit.

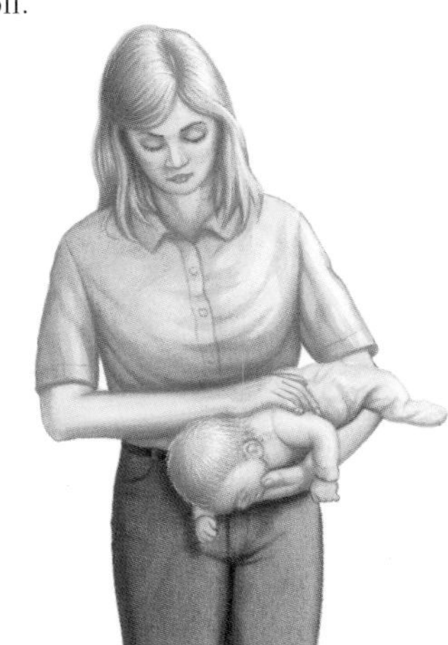

WARNING

If the casualty has head or neck injuries:

- ensure the head and neck are supported at all times
- do not allow rotation between the head and spine
- do not tilt the head back if neck injury is suspected.

FIRST AID

Expired Air Resuscitation (EAR) for adults

If breathing:

1 **Clear the airway:**
- place casualty in recovery position
- lift chin and open mouth
- use finger to remove any obvious obstruction
- tilt head back gently
- check breathing for up to 10 seconds.

If not breathing:

2 **Open airway:**
- turn casualty onto their back
- gently tilt the head back
- pinch the nose closed (use thumb and index finger)
- open mouth and maintain chin lift.

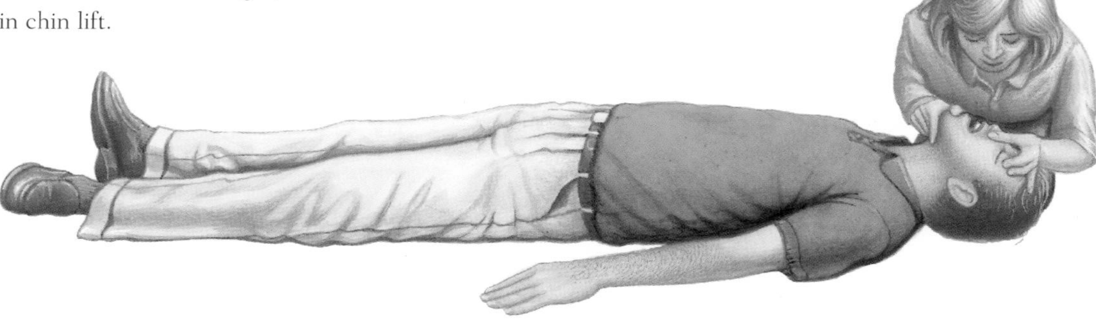

3 **Give EAR (mouth-to-mouth resuscitation):**
- take a full breath and place the lips on casualty's mouth (ensure a good seal)
- blow steadily into the mouth for 1–2 seconds
- watch for the chest to rise
- take mouth away and watch for the chest to fall
- take another breath and repeat the sequence, giving two effective breaths.

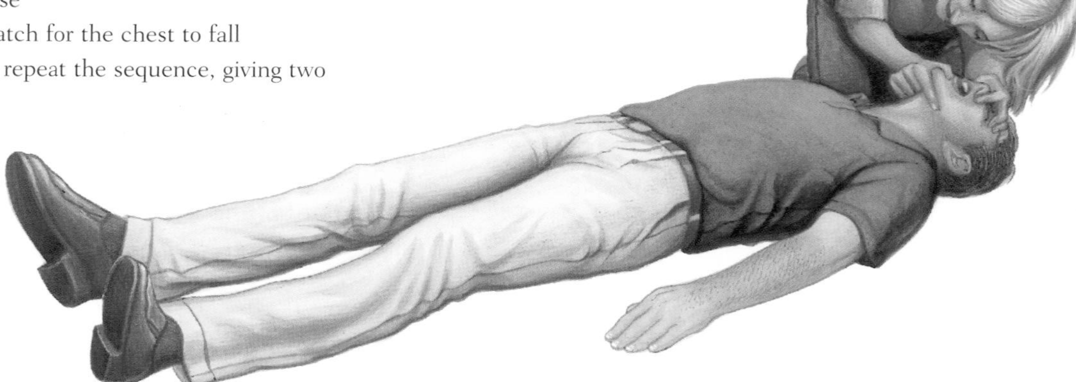

4 **Check for pulse:**
- check the pulse at the neck or wrist
- if pulse is absent, commence CPR
- if pulse is present, continue EAR at 15 breaths per minute
- recheck the pulse and look for other signs of recovery about every minute.

5 **Place in recovery position when breathing returns.**

Cardiopulmonary Resuscitation (CPR) for adults

1 **Position hands for CPR:**
- place casualty on their back
- find the groove at the neck between the collar bones
- find the lower end of the breast bone by running a finger along the last rib to the center of the body
- extend the thumb of each hand equal distances to meet in the middle of the breast bone

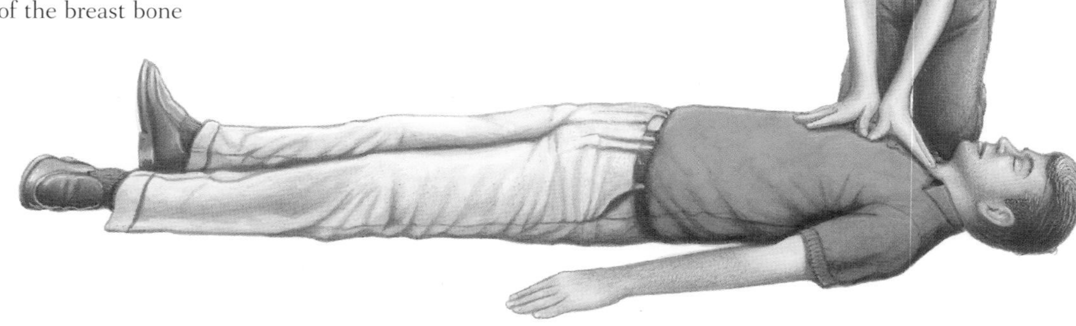

- keep the thumb of the left hand in position and place the heel of the right hand below it
- place the heel of the left hand on top of the right and interlock fingers of both hands.

2 **Commence chest compressions:**
- position yourself vertically above the casualty's chest
- with your arms straight, press down on the breast bone to depress it about 2 inches (4–5 centimeters)
- release the pressure.

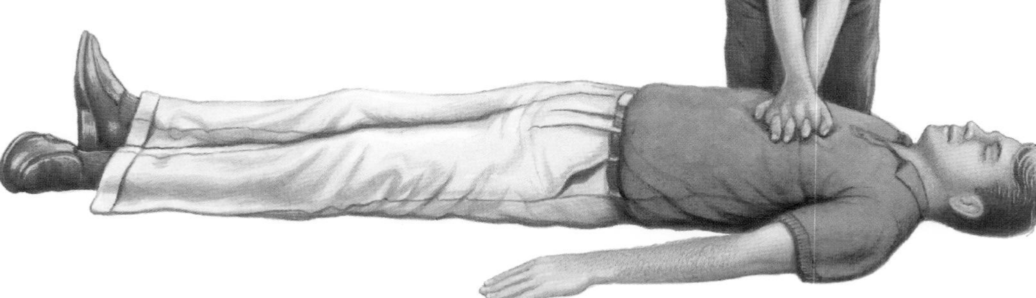

3 **Continue CPR:**
- complete 15 compressions
- give two effective breaths (EAR)
- continue compressions and breaths in a ratio of 15:2 at a rate of 4 cycles per minute
- check the pulse about every minute.

NOTE

CPR combines chest compressions with expired air resuscitation (EAR).

CPR is given when the casualty is not breathing and has no pulse.

Expired Air Resuscitation for children and infants

EAR for children (aged 1–8) and infants (under 1 year)

If breathing:

1 **Clear the airway:**
- place the infant/child in the recovery position
- tilt the head back very gently
- lift chin and open the mouth
- use a finger to remove any obvious obstruction
- check breathing for up to 10 seconds.

If not breathing:

2 **Open airway:**
- turn casualty onto back
- gently tilt head back slightly
- open mouth and lift chin.

3 **Give EAR (mouth-to-mouth resuscitation):**
- cover the mouth and nose with your mouth
- give two gentle breaths/puffs into the child or infant's mouth and nose
- check for the pulse—for an infant, on the inside upper arm; a child at the neck or wrist
- if pulse is absent, commence CPR
- if pulse is present, continue EAR at 20 breaths per minute
- recheck the pulse and look for other signs of recovery about every minute.

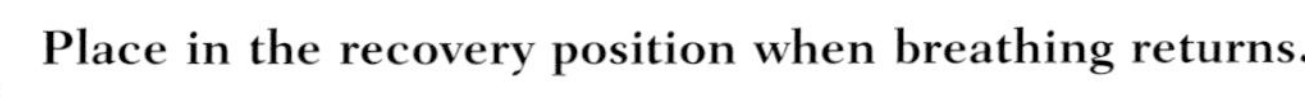

4 **Place in the recovery position when breathing returns.**

Cardiopulmonary Resuscitation for children and infants

CPR for children (aged 1–8)

- use the heel of one hand placed over the lower half of the breast bone to give chest compressions
- compress the chest approximately one-third the depth of the chest
- give 5 chest compressions in 3 seconds
- give one effective breath (EAR)
- continue compressions and breaths in a ratio of 5:1 at a rate of 12 cycles per minute
- check the pulse about every minute.

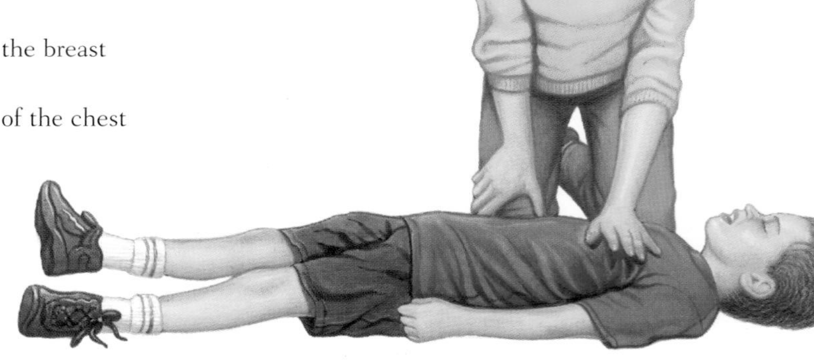

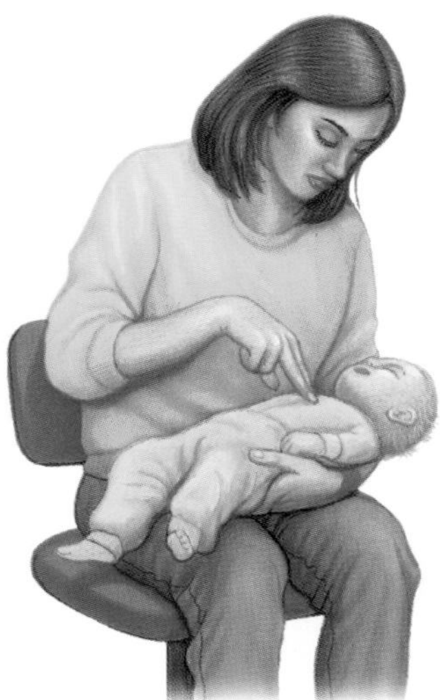

CPR for infants (under 1 year)

- place the tips of two fingers (index and middle) on the lower half of the breast bone
- compress the chest approximately one-third the depth of the chest
- give 5 chest compressions in 3 seconds
- give one effective breath (EAR)
- continue compressions and breaths in a ratio of 5:1 at a rate of 12 cycles per minute
- check the pulse about every minute.

NOTE

Adult EAR and CPR resuscitation techniques can be safely used on children over the age of 8 years.

For a newborn baby, chest compressions should not be attempted by anyone untrained in neonatal resuscitation.

Handling an emergency

Putting together a First Aid Kit:

A first aid kit should be kept in the home, car and workplace. It is important to ensure that you regularly check the contents of your first aid kit to make sure they are clean, packets are properly sealed, expiry dates have not been exceeded, and that you have replaced any previously used items.

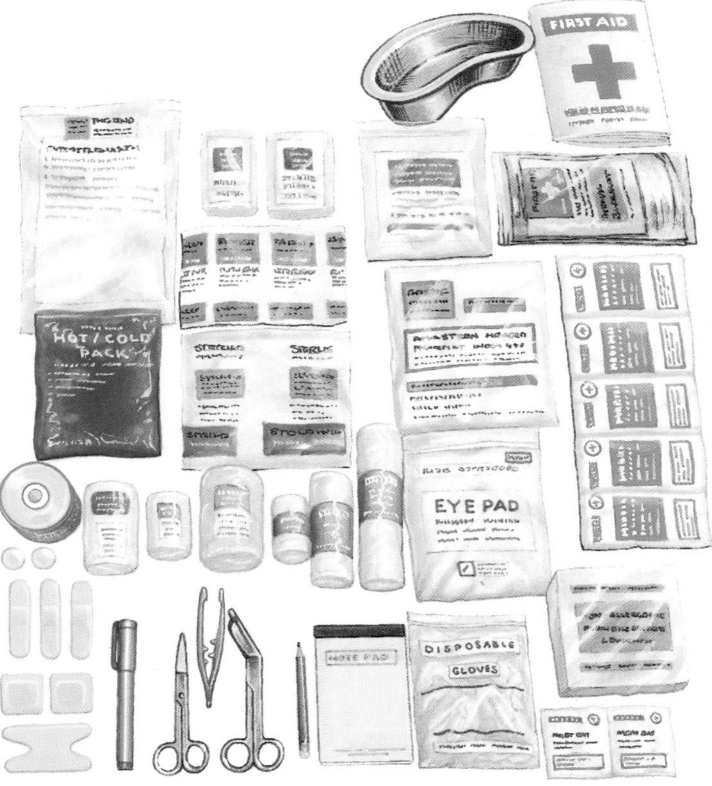

Although it is safer to use sterile bandages and dressings, there will be emergencies when you will not have a first aid kit immediately to hand. You will then have to use whatever materials you can find.

A basic first aid kit may contain:

Bandages

- two triangular bandages
- various crepe or conforming bandages of different sizes

Dressings

- non-adherent dressings
- various wound dressings
- adhesive shapes

Pads

- combine pads
- eye pads

Swabs

- gauze swabs
- alcohol swabs

Other

- adhesive tape
- disposable hand towels
- stainless steel scissors
- saline eyewash
- safety pins
- insect bite and sting lotion
- plastic bags
- stainless steel tweezers
- thermo blanket
- note pad and pencil
- disposable gloves.

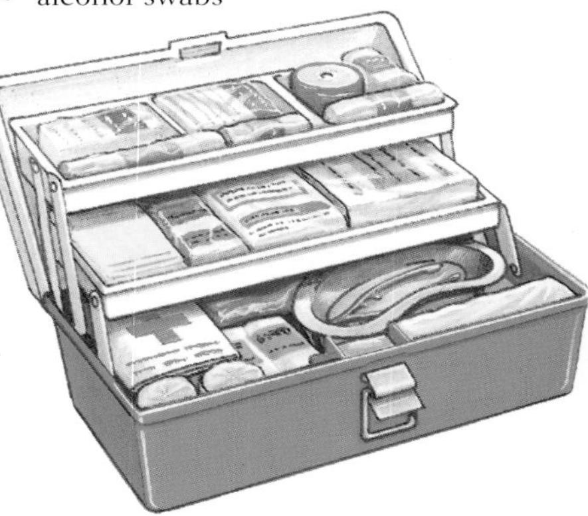

Lifting and moving casualties

Always try to give first aid where the casualty is found, as moving can result in further injury or make existing injuries worse. A casualty should only be moved if there is immediate danger—such as from a collapsing structure, traffic hazards, fire or poisonous fumes.

Moving a casualty

Use the quickest means available. Then make sure:

- there is no further danger
- the casualty has a clear airway and is able to breathe
- bleeding is controlled.

Before moving, consider:

- whether you can handle the size and weight of the person without injury to either of you
- what other help is available
- the type and seriousness of the injuries
- the terrain to be crossed
- the distance the casualty has to be moved
- whether a neck stabilizing collar should be applied before movement
- if travel or motion sickness may make the casualty worse.

WHEN LIFTING A CASUALTY, REMEMBER TO:

- bend at the knees
- keep your back straight and head up
- keep in a balance position
- keep your center of gravity low
- hold the weight close to your body for stability
- take small steps
- work as a team—someone must take the role of leader.

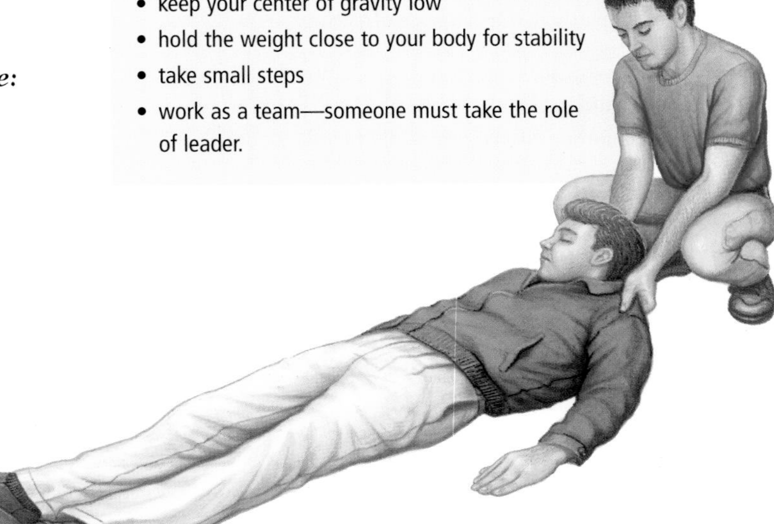

Asthma attack

If casualty is unconscious:

- follow DRABC
- seek medical aid urgently—call the Emergency Services number for your area.

If casualty is conscious:

1 **Make the casualty comfortable:**
- help the casualty into a comfortable position—usually sitting upright and leaning forward
- ensure adequate fresh air
- tell casualty to take slow, deep breaths.

2 **Help with administration of casualty's medication:**
- give 4 puffs of a reliever inhaler—casualty takes a breath with each puff
- if a spacer is available give 4 puffs, one at a time – casualty takes 4 breaths after each puff
- wait 4 minutes
- if no improvement, give another 4 puffs.

3 **If the attack continues:**
- call the Emergency Services number for your area
- in a severe attack, keep giving children 4 puffs every 4 minutes and adults 6–8 puffs every 5 minutes, until an ambulance arrives.

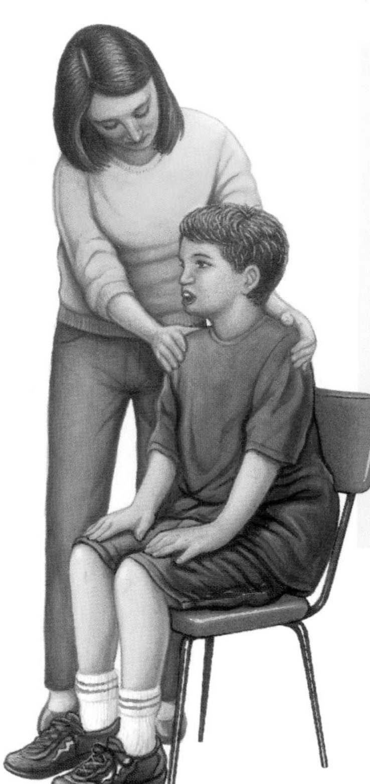

NOTE

If necessary, and where permitted under local legislation/regulations:

- use another person's reliever inhaler or use one from a first aid kit to assist a casualty with a severe asthma attack
- if someone is exhibiting difficulty breathing, but has not previously had an asthma attack, assist in giving 4 puffs of a reliever and continue with 4 puffs every 4 minutes if required, until an ambulance arrives.

Bleeding

Major wounds

1 **Apply pressure to the wound:**
- remove or cut the casualty's clothing to expose the wound
- apply direct pressure over wound
- cover wound with sterile dressing
- apply a pad.

2 **Raise and support injured part:**
- lie the casualty down
- raise the injured part above the level of the heart
- handle gently if you suspect a fracture.

3 **Bandage wound:**
- apply bandage firmly in place
- apply another dressing or pad if bleeding continues.

4 **Check circulation below the wound.**

5 **Seek medical aid if severe bleeding persists—call the Emergency Services number for your area.**

6 **Treat for shock.**

Minor wounds

- clean the wound thoroughly with gauze soaked in sterile or cooled boiled water, or under running tap water
- apply a non-stick dressing.

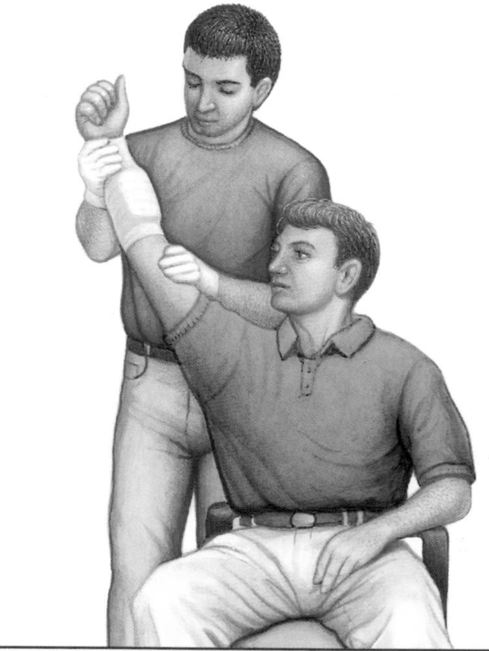

WARNING

Do not apply a tourniquet.

If bleeding from a limb does not stop, apply pressure with hand to pressure point.

If there is an embedded object in the wound, apply pressure either side of the wound and place pad around it before bandaging.

Wear gloves, if possible, to guard against infection.

If casualty becomes unconscious, follow DRABC action plan.

Dirty, penetrating or open wounds should be examined by a doctor, as tetanus or other serious infections may result.

Burns

1 **Remove casualty from danger:**
- follow DRABC
- if clothing is on fire STOP, DROP AND ROLL
- pull casualty to the ground
- wrap in blanket or similar
- roll casualty along ground until flames are extinguished.

2 **Cool the burnt area:**
- hold burnt area under cold running water for at least 10 minutes
- if a chemical burn, run cold water over burnt area for at least 20 minutes
- if a bitumen burn, run cold water over burnt area for 30 minutes
- if the burn is to the eye, flush the eye with water for 20 minutes.

3 **Remove any constrictions:**
- remove clothing and jewelry from burnt area (unless sticking to the burn).

4 **Cover the burn:**
- place sterile, non-stick dressing over the burn.

5 **Calm the casualty.**

6 **Seek medical aid urgently—call the Emergency Services number for your area.**

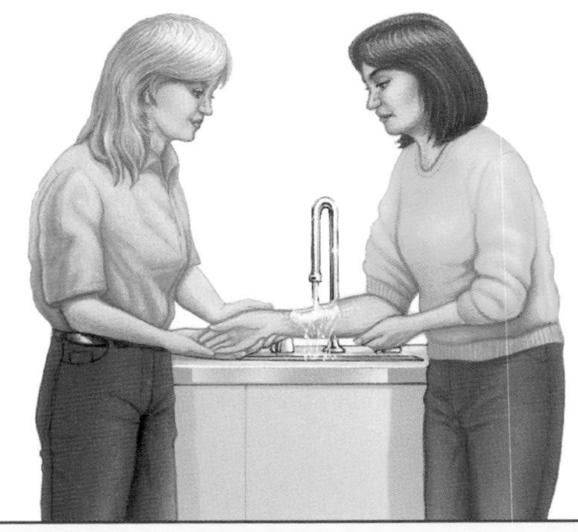

WARNING

Do not apply lotions, ointment or fat to burn.
Do not touch the injured areas or burst any blisters.
Do not remove anything sticking to the burn.
If the burn is large or deep, manage the casualty for shock.

Chest pain or discomfort

1 **Advise casualty to rest:**
- advise the casualty to stop any activity, and sit or lie down and rest.

2 **Casualty to take medication:**
- if casualty has medication for angina, get it and assist casualty in taking it.

3 **Seek urgent medical attention:**
- if unconscious, follow DRABC
- call the Emergency Services number for your area immediately
- do not drive the casualty to hospital, in case of cardiac arrest.

4 **Give aspirin:**
- give 300 milligrams (one tablet) of aspirin in water if ambulance help is delayed for more than 30 minutes
- no aspirin is given to those allergic to it, to asthmatics or to those on anti-coagulant medication (for example warfarin).

5 **Monitor vital signs:**
- monitor pulse, breathing, consciousness and skin color
- be prepared to give CPR.

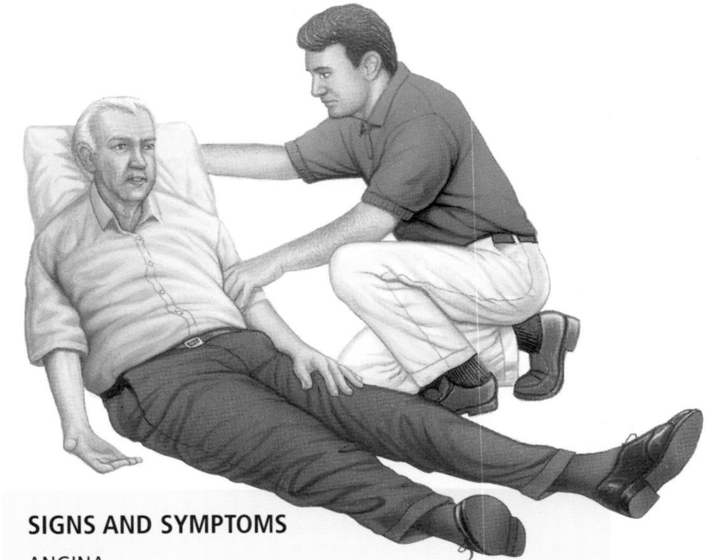

SIGNS AND SYMPTOMS

ANGINA
- pain or discomfort in the center of the chest
- pain radiating to neck and arms
- onset with exercise or emotional stress
- pain relieved by rest or medication.

HEART ATTACK

Signs and symptoms are similar to angina, and may include:
- severe, vise-like chest pain
- anxiety/confusion
- shortness of breath
- nausea/vomiting
- irregular pulse
- sometimes immediate collapse.

NOTE

Always treat chest pain or discomfort as a life-threatening situation

Choking

Adults and children (9 years and over)

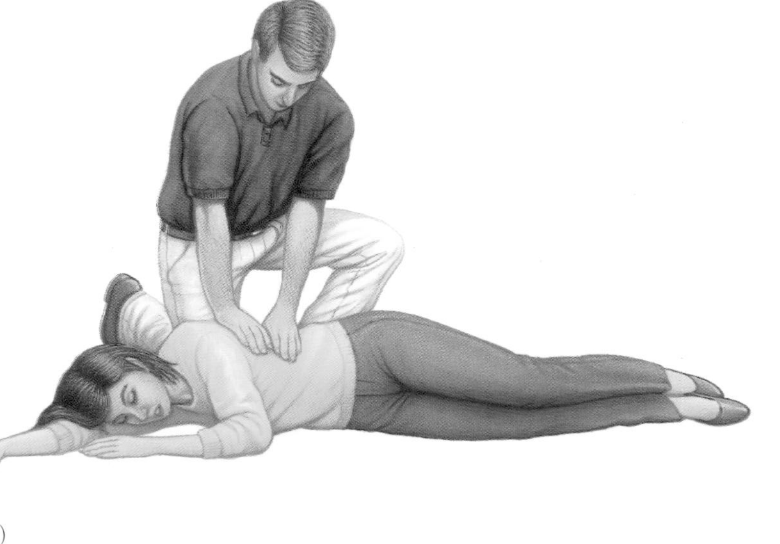

Partial blockage:

- encourage casualty to relax and breathe deeply
- ask casualty to cough
- if unsuccessful, bend casualty well forward and give 4 sharp blows between shoulder blades
- if unsuccessful, place the casualty on their side on the floor—call the Emergency Services number for your area.

Total blockage:

- lie casualty on their side on the floor
- give 4 sharp blows between the shoulder blades
- if unsuccessful, give 4 quick downward lateral chest thrusts (place your hands on the side of the chest, below the casualty's armpit)
- if unsuccessful—call the Emergency Services number for your area
- repeat steps until help arrives or blockage clears
- follow DRABC.

Child (1–8 years)

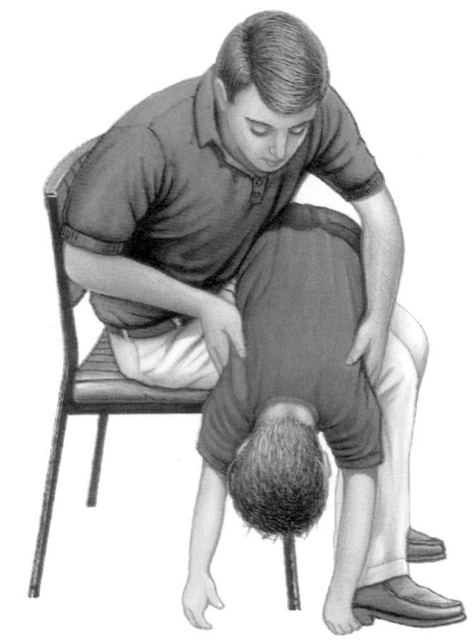

Partial blockage:

- ask the child to try to cough up the obstruction
- if unsuccessful, place child with head low and face down
- give 4 sharp blows between the shoulder blades.

Total blockage:

- place child face down on the floor or across your lap
- give 4 sharp blows between the shoulder blades
- if not breathing, give up to 4 quick, squeezing lateral chest thrusts on both sides simultaneously (place your hands below the child's armpits)
- if unsuccessful—call the Emergency Services number for your area
- repeat above steps until help arrives or blockage clears
- if not breathing, follow DRABC.

Infant (up to 1 year)

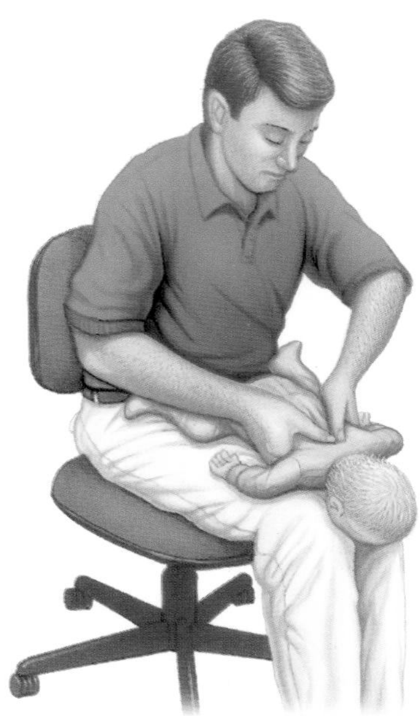

Partial blockage:

- lie infant face down on your forearm with their head low
- support the infant's head and shoulders on your hand
- give 4 sharp slaps between the shoulders
- check in the infant's mouth and remove any obstruction that has come loose
- if unsuccessful—call the Emergency Services number for your area.

Total blockage:

- place the infant face down on your lap
- give 4 sharp slaps between the shoulders and check for signs of breathing
- if not breathing, give 4 quick squeezing lateral chest thrusts on both sides simultaneously (place your hands below infant's armpits)
- check in infant's mouth and remove any obstruction that has come loose
- if unsuccessful—call the Emergency Services number for your area
- repeat above steps until help arrives or blockage clears
- follow DRABC.

Convulsions

Infantile convulsions

1 **During convulsions:**
- place the child on the floor for safety
- do not restrain the child.

2 **After convulsions:**
- follow DRABC
- turn the child onto their side
- remove excessive clothing or wrapping
- get medical aid urgently—call the Emergency Services number for your area.

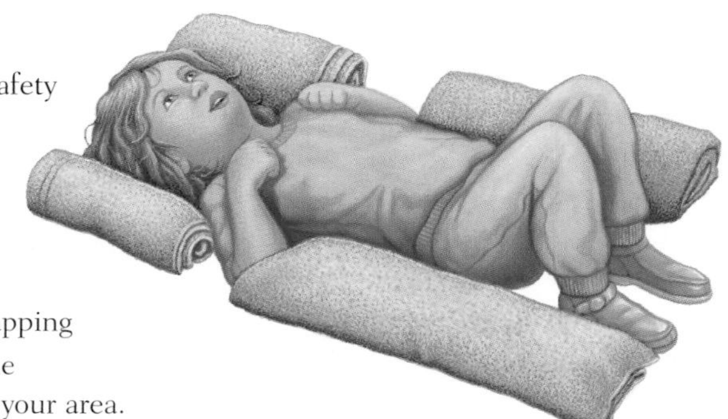

SIGNS AND SYMPTOMS
- fever
- twitching of face or limbs
- eyes rolling up
- congestion of face and neck
- blue face and lips
- stiffness of body with arched back
- unconsciousness.

WARNING
Do not cool the child by sponging or bathing.

Epileptic seizure

1 **Check breathing and pulse:**
- follow DRABC.

2 **Protect casualty:**
- protect from injury
- do not restrict movement
- do not place anything in the mouth.

3 **Manage injuries:**
- place on side as soon as possible
- manage injuries resulting from seizure
- do not disturb if casualty falls asleep
- continue to check airway, breathing and pulse.

4 **Seek medical aid if:**
- the seizure continues for more than 5 minutes
- another seizure quickly follows
- the person has been injured.

SIGNS AND SYMPTOMS
THE CASUALTY MAY:
- suddenly cry out
- fall to the ground
- have a congested and blue face and neck
- have jerky, spasmodic muscular movements
- froth at the mouth
- bite the tongue
- lose control of bladder and bowel.

Diabetic emergency

If casualty is unconscious:
- follow DRABC
- get medical aid urgently—call the Emergency Services number for your area.

If casualty is conscious, and signs suggest low blood sugar:
- give sweet food or drink (not diet, diabetic or sugar-free drinks) every 15 minutes until casualty recovers or medical aid arrives
- get medical aid urgently—call the Emergency Services number for your area.

If casualty is conscious, and signs suggest high blood sugar:
- allow casualty to self-administer insulin—do not administer but assist if required
- get medical aid urgently—call the Emergency Services number for your area
- give casualty sugar-free fluids to drink, if help is delayed.

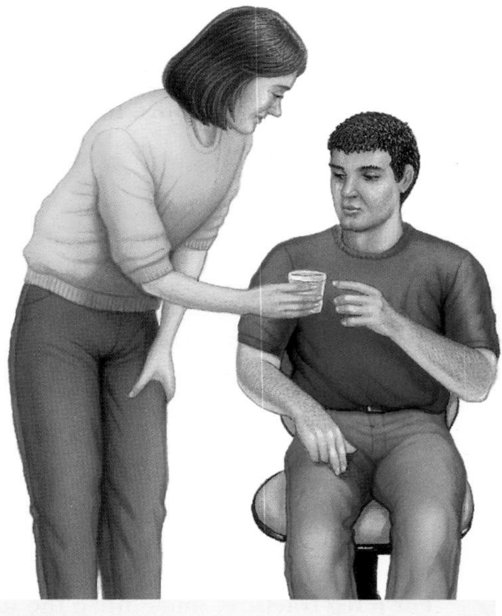

SIGNS AND SYMPTOMS

LOW BLOOD SUGAR
- pale
- hungry
- sweating
- weak
- confused
- aggressive

HIGH BLOOD SUGAR LEVELS
- thirsty
- needs to urinate
- hot dry skin
- smell of acetone on breath

NOTE
If you are not sure which form of diabetic emergency the casualty has, give a sweet drink. If the casualty has a high blood sugar emergency, then giving a sweet drink will not do undue harm.

Drug overdose

Persons who are under the influence of drugs or alcohol may be at risk of harming themselves or others through dangerous or violent behavior. In such a situation DO NOT put yourself at risk. If there is any risk to yourself call for assistance from Emergency Services. If the casualty collapses, check and maintain their airway. If the casualty becomes unconscious, perform EAR or CPR if required.

Fractures, dislocations, sprains and strains

Fractures and dislocations

1. **Follow DRABC.**
2. **Control any bleeding and cover any wounds.**
3. **Check for fractures:**
   - open, closed or complicated.
4. **Ask casualty not to move the injured part.**
5. **Immobilize the fracture:**
   - use broad bandages (where possible) to prevent movement at joints above and below the fracture
   - support the limb, carefully passing bandages under the natural hollows of the body
   - place a padded splint along the injured limb (under the leg for fractured kneecap)
   - place padding between the splint and the natural contours of the body and secure tightly
   - check that bandages are not too tight (or too loose) every 15 minutes.
6. **For a leg fracture, immobilize the foot and ankle:**
   - use figure of eight bandage.
7. **Watch for signs of loss of circulation to foot or hand.**
8. **Seek medical aid**—call the Emergency Services number for your area.

Electric shock

If a person has been electrocuted, check they are not still in contact with the electrical supply or you may also become a casualty.

1. **Switch off power if possible.**
2. **Remove casualty from the electrical supply without directly touching the casualty by using something that will not conduct electricity.**
3. **Follow DRABC.**
4. **Treat casualty as for a burn.**

NOTE

If the collar bone is fractured, support arm on injured side in a sling that goes under the elbow to support the arm against the chest with the fingers pointing up towards the opposite shoulder. If dislocation of a joint is suspected, rest, elevate and apply ice to the joint. It can be difficult for a first aider to tell whether the injury is a fracture, sprain or strain. If in doubt, always treat as a fracture.

SIGNS AND SYMPTOMS

Fracture and dislocation:
- pain at or near the site of the injury
- difficult or impossible normal movement
- loss of power
- deformity or abnormal mobility
- tenderness
- swelling
- discoloration and bruising.

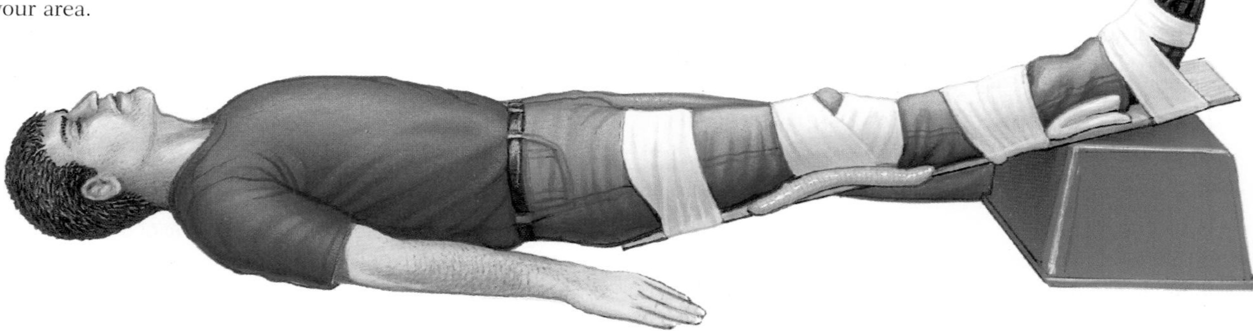

Sprains and strains

1 **Follow DRABC.**

2 **Follow RICE management plan:**
- R—rest casualty
- I—ice pack applied to injury for 15 minutes every 2 hours
- C—compression bandage over the injury
- E—elevate limb.

3 **Seek medical aid**—call the Emergency Services number for your area.

Head, eye and ear injuries

Head injuries

1 **Monitor breathing and pulse:**
- if casualty is unconscious, follow DRABC
- keep casualty's airway open with your fingers (if face badly injured).

2 **Support the head and neck:**
- support the casualty's head and neck during movement in case the spine is injured.

3 **Control bleeding:**
- place a sterile pad or dressing over the wound
- apply direct pressure to the wound unless you suspect a skull fracture
- if blood or fluid comes from ear, secure a sterile dressing lightly in place and allow to drain.

SIGNS AND SYMPTOMS
- altered or abnormal responses to commands and touch
- wounds to the scalp or face
- blood or clear fluid escaping from nose or ears
- pupils becoming unequal in size
- blurred vision
- loss of memory.

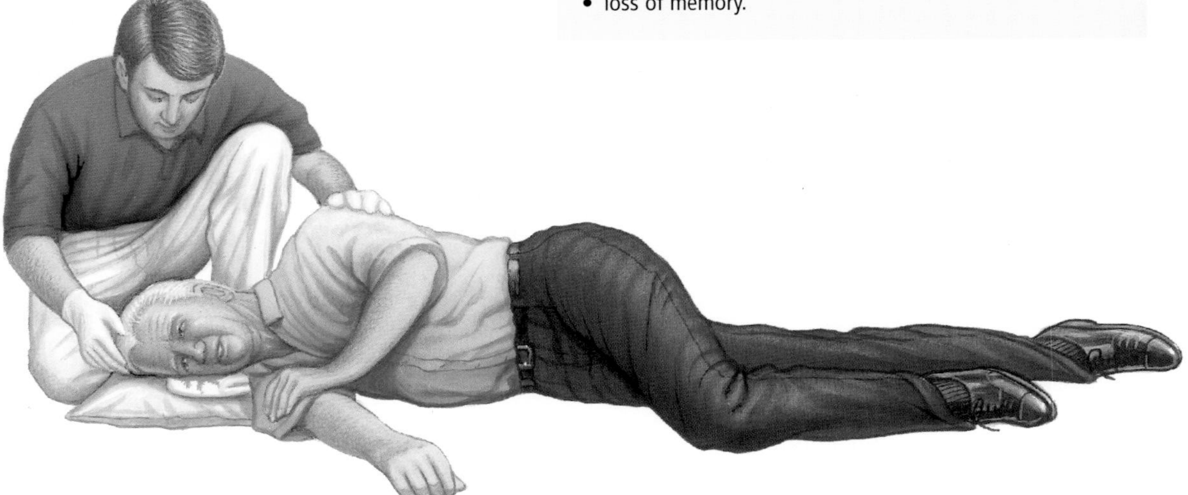

4 **Lie casualty down:**
- place casualty in a comfortable position with head and shoulders slightly raised
- be prepared to turn casualty onto their side if they vomit
- clear the airway quickly after vomiting.

5 **Seek medical aid urgently**—call the Emergency Services number for your area.

WARNING

Wear gloves, if possible, to protect against infection. If bleeding does not stop, reapply pressure to the wound and use another pad on top of the first.

Ear injuries

Ear injuries are common. Sport injuries and falls can damage the outer soft tissue. A direct blow to the head or pushing something into the ear may result in internal injury to the eardrum. Foreign objects—beads, stones, grass seeds—can become lodged in the canal. These can sometimes be removed by tilting the head to the side, pulling down on the earlobe and gently shaking the head.

Bleeding from within the ear:

- follow DRABC
- do not plug the ear canal
- do not administer drops of any kind
- allow fluid to drain freely
- place casualty on their side with the affected ear down
- place a sterile pad between the ear and the ground
- call the Emergency Services number in your area.

> **WARNING**
> Do not put anything in the ear to try and remove an object.

Eye injuries

1 **Support casualty's head:**
- support the casualty's head to keep it as still as possible
- ask casualty to try not to move their eyes.

2 **Flush eye with cool, flowing water:**
- if a chemical or heat burn, or there is smoke in the eyes, flush with water.

3 **Place dressing over eye:**
- place a sterile pad or dressing over the injured eye
- ask casualty to hold this in place
- bandage the dressing in place, covering the injured eye
- if there is an embedded object in the eye, lie casualty on their back, place pad around object and bandage in place.

4 **Seek urgent medical aid**—call the Emergency Services number for your area.

> **WARNING**
> Do not touch the eye or any contact lens.
> Do not allow casualty to rub the eye.
> Do not try to remove any object embedded in the eye.
> Do not apply pressure when bandaging the eye.

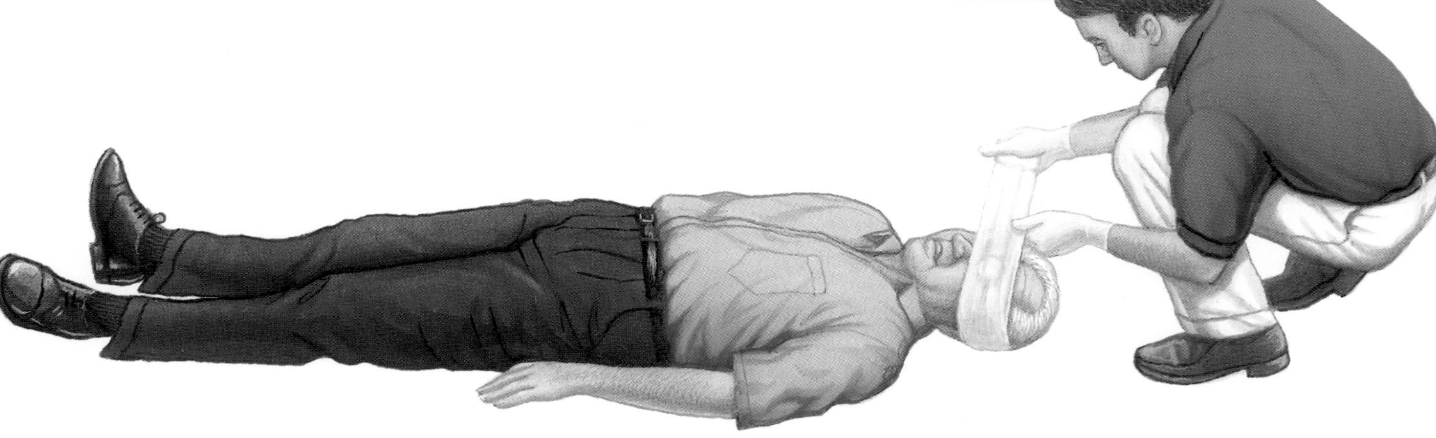

Gassing

Poisoning by inhalation occurs when a person breathes toxic fumes from a gas or substance. Such fumes usually cause breathing problems and can cause unconsciousness.

1 **Move casualty to fresh air being careful not to succumb to the gases or fumes yourself.**

2 **Loosen tight clothing.**

3 **If casualty is unconscious, perform EAR or CPR if required.**

Heat induced conditions

Heat exhaustion:

1 **Lie casualty down:**
- move casualty to lie down in a cool place with circulating air.

2 **Loosen tight clothing:**
- remove unnecessary garments.

3 **Sponge with cold water.**

4 **Give fluids to drink.**

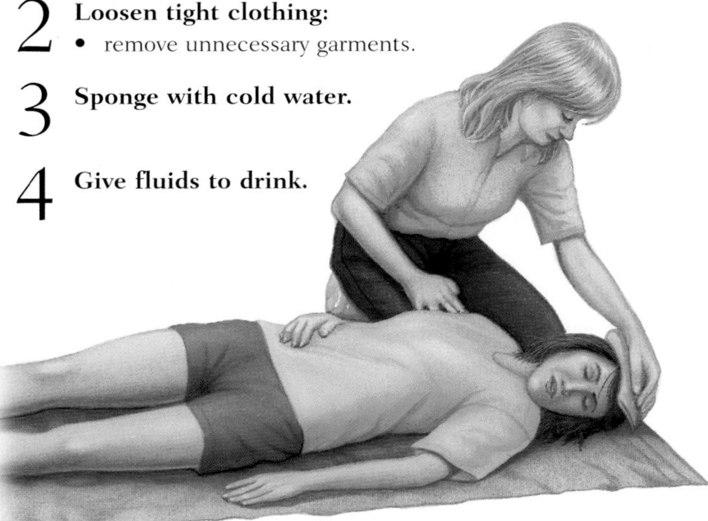

5 **Seek medical aid:**
- if casualty vomits
- if casualty does not recover promptly.

SIGNS AND SYMPTOMS
- feeling hot, exhausted and weak
- persistent headache
- thirst and nausea
- giddiness and faintness
- fatigue
- rapid breathing and shortness of breath
- pale, cool, clammy skin
- rapid, weak pulse.

Heatstroke

1 **Follow DRABC.**

2 **Apply cold packs or ice:**
- apply to neck, groin and armpits.

3 **Cover with a wet sheet.**

ADDITIONAL SYMPTOMS FOR HEATSTROKE:
- high body temperature
- flushed skin
- irritability and mental confusion may progress to seizure and unconsciousness.

Hypothermia

1 **Follow DRABC.**

2 **Remove the casualty to a warm, dry place.**

3 **Protect casualty:**
- protect the casualty and yourself from wind, rain, sleet, cold, as well as wet ground.

4 **Avoid excess activity or movement.**

5 **Maintain casualty in horizontal position.**

6 **Remove wet clothing.**

7 **Warm casualty:**
- place between blankets, in a sleeping bag, or wrap in a space blanket.

8 **Cover the head to maintain body heat.**

9 **Give warm drinks if conscious:**
- do not give alcohol.

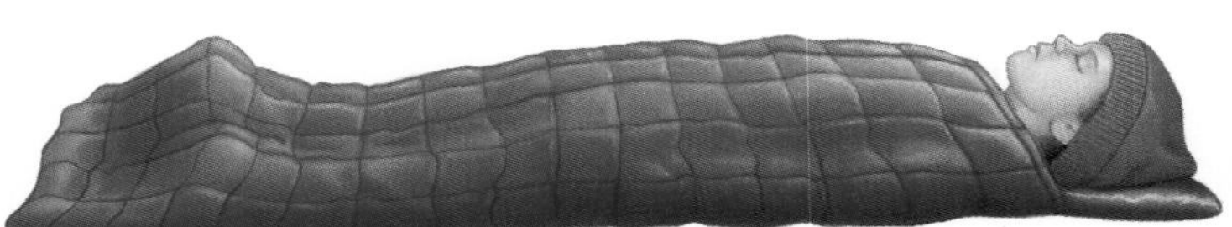

SIGNS AND SYMPTOMS

When body temperature falls, early warning signs may include:
- feeling cold
- shivering
- clumsiness and slurred speech
- apathy and irrational behavior
- heart rate may slow.

WARNING

Call the Emergency Services number for your area if the level of consciousness declines, shivering stops and the pulse is difficult to find. Use any other available forms of warming except direct radiant heat.

FIRST AID

Poisons, bites and stings

Poisoning

Poisons can be ingested, inhaled, absorbed or injected into the body. Most people are aware of potentially lethal venomous snakes or spiders in their area, and that poisonous fumes can be inhaled from a car exhaust or other toxic substance. However, many are not aware that some substances used in the home—cleaning products, pesticides, alcohol and medication—can also cause poisoning.

1 **Determine the type of poisoning:**
- if casualty is conscious, try to determine the type of poison taken.

2 **Seek medical advice urgently**—call the Emergency Services number for your area.

3 **Call the fire department if the area is contaminated with smoke, gases or fumes.**

4 **Monitor airway and breathing:**
- if casualty loses consciousness, follow DRABC.

SIGNS AND SYMPTOMS
- abdominal pain
- drowsiness
- nausea/vomiting
- burning pains from mouth to stomach
- difficulty in breathing
- tight chest
- blurred vision
- odors on breath
- change of skin color with blueness around lips
- sudden collapse.

WARNING

Do not attempt to induce vomiting unless advised to by the Emergency Services in your area.

Do not perform EAR on a casualty poisoned with cyanide.

Spider bites

For funnel-web spider, black widow and brown recluse spider bites follow the steps outlined for snakebites. For red-back spider bites apply an ice pack to the bitten area and seek medical aid.

SIGNS AND SYMPTOMS
- sharp pain
- profuse sweating
- nausea, vomiting, diarrhea.

ADDITIONAL SYMPTOMS FOR FUNNEL-WEB SPIDER BITE
- copious saliva
- confusion leading to coma
- muscular twitching
- breathing difficulty.

ADDITIONAL SYMPTOMS FOR RED-BACK SPIDER BITE
- intense pain, spreading
- small hairs stand on end.

Insect stings

While insect stings can be very painful, they are rarely fatal. They can, however, be dangerous for those who have an allergic reaction.

Management of insect stings:

1 **Follow DRABC.**

2 **If a severe allergic reaction, call the Emergency Services number in your area.**

3 **In cases of bee sting:**
- remove the sting by scraping sideways with your fingernail or the side of a sharp object, such as a knife.

4 **In cases of ticks:**
- if you can see an attached tick, grasp it behind its head as close to the skin as possible, using fine point tweezers or a tick remover
- gently pull the tick straight out with steady pressure
- wash your hands with hot, soapy water and disinfect the tweezers and the bite
- do not attempt to kill the tick with alcohol, petroleum jelly, methylated spirits or any other substance as this causes the tick to inject more bacteria and toxins
- mass infestations of tiny (larval stage) ticks are best removed by soaking for 20 minutes in a deep, warm bath with one cup of bicarbonate of soda added.

5 **Apply a cold compress to relieve pain if necessary.**

6 **Monitor airway, breathing and circulation, as in the DRABC action plan—give CPR if necessary.**

Snakebite

The following is based on the current guidelines on first aid for snakebite as agreed by the World Health Organisation Working Group on Natural Toxins:

1 **Check breathing and pulse:**
- if casualty is unconscious, follow DRABC.

2 **Calm casualty.**

3 **Apply pressure immobilization bandage:**
- apply a firm roller bandage starting just above the fingers or toes and moving up the limb as far as can be reached
- the bandage needs to be firm, as for a sprain, but not too tight.

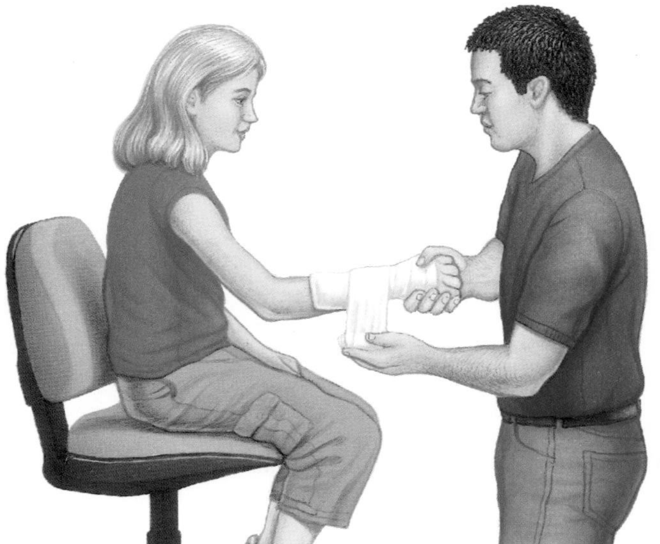

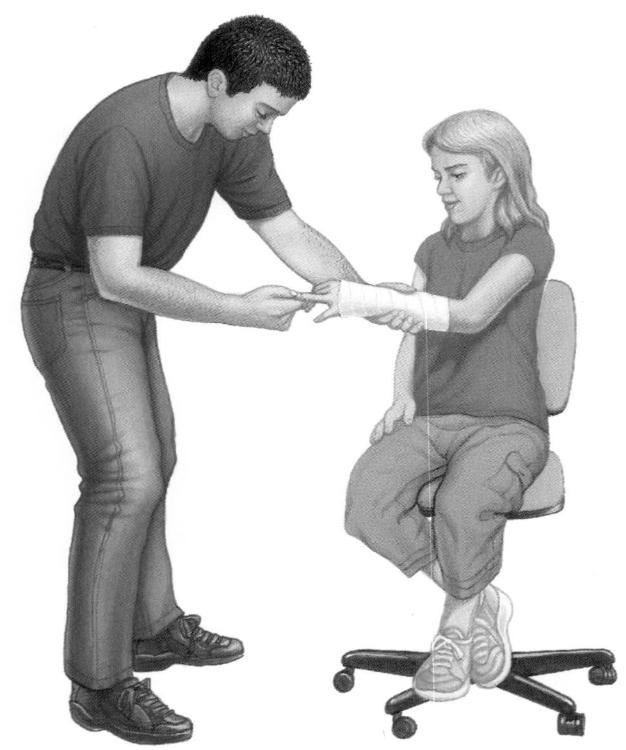

4 **Immobilize casualty:**
- apply a splint to immobilize the bitten limb
- check circulation in fingers or toes
- if possible, ensure the casualty does not move.

5 **Seek medical aid urgently—call the Emergency Services number for your area.**

NOTE

Applying a pressure immobilization bandage and splinting of the limb is recommended for managing snakebites which are not known to cause local tissue damage. These include all Australian snakes, and in other countries, the sea snakes, coral snakes, kraits, non-necrotic snakes, mambas and colubrids.

For bites by snakes that are known to cause local tissue damage, the pressure immobilization method is unlikely to do much harm with the exception of the viper and necrotic cobras. In these cases the management should only be to splint the limb.

NOTE

All snakebites must be treated as potentially lethal. The impact of the venom will be more rapid if one or more of the following cases exists:

- if the casualty is a child
- if the casualty has been physically active immediately following the bite
- if there have been multiple bites
- some species, such as the taipan and Russell's viper, are more likely than others to inject a lethal dose of venom.

SIGNS AND SYMPTOMS

- puncture marks
- nausea, vomiting, diarrhea
- headache
- double or blurred vision
- breathing difficulties
- drowsiness, giddiness
- pain or tightness in chest or abdomen
- respiratory weakness or arrest
- local tissue damage caused by snakes (e.g. some cobra venoms, many of the viper venoms and a few of the elapid venoms); Australian snakes do not cause tissue damage.

WARNING

Do not cut bitten area or try to suck venom out of wound.

Do not use a constrictive bandage (i.e. arterial tourniquet).

Do not try to catch the snake.

Do not wash venom off the skin as retained venom will assist identification (for Australian snakes venom only).

Shock

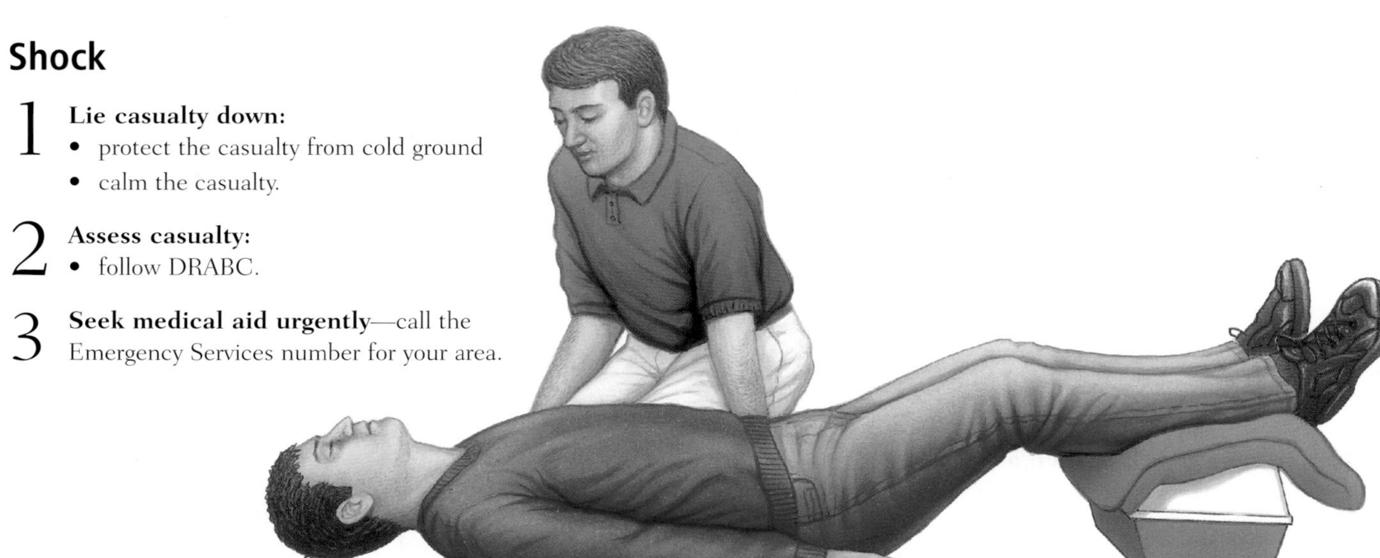

1 **Lie casualty down:**
- protect the casualty from cold ground
- calm the casualty.

2 **Assess casualty:**
- follow DRABC.

3 **Seek medical aid urgently**—call the Emergency Services number for your area.

4 **Manage any injuries:**
- control any bleeding
- raise the legs (unless fractured) above heart level
- dress any wounds or burns
- immobilize fractures.

5 **Ensure comfort:**
- loosen any tight clothing around neck, chest or waist
- maintain body warmth (do not heat)
- if thirsty, moisten lips (but give nothing to drink or eat).

6 **Monitor breathing and pulse:**
- maintain a clear and open airway.

7 **Place casualty in recovery position:**
- place in recovery position if casualty has difficulty breathing, is likely to vomit, or becomes unconscious.

SIGNS AND SYMPTOMS
- weak, rapid pulse
- cold, clammy skin
- rapid breathing
- faintness/dizziness
- nausea
- pale face, fingernails, lips.

Spinal injury

1 **Do not move casualty unless they are in danger.**

2 **Check breathing and pulse:**
- if casualty is unconscious, follow DRABC.

3 **Support the casualty's head and neck at all times:**
- place hands on the side of the head until other support is arranged
- apply a cervical or improvised collar to minimize neck movement.

4 **Give reassurance:**
- calm casualty.

5 **Seek medical aid urgently—call the Emergency Services number for your area.**

SIGNS AND SYMPTOMS
- pain at or below site of injury
- loss of sensation, or abnormal sensation, such as tingling, in hands or feet
- loss of movement or impaired movement below site of injury.

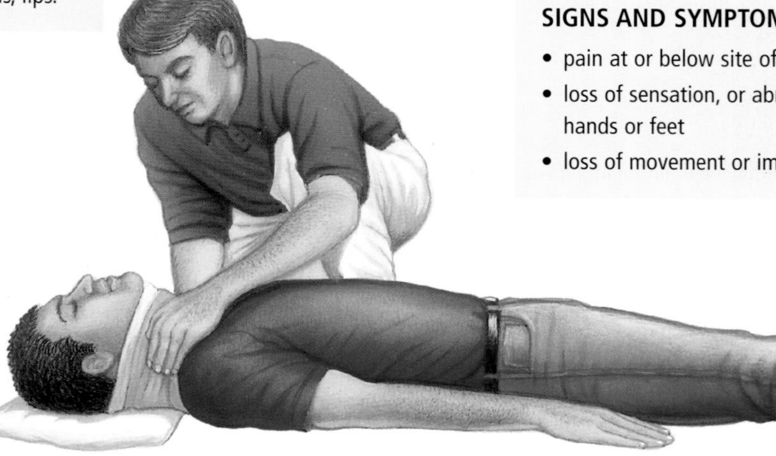

WARNING
If casualty is unconscious, place in recovery position.
If casualty is conscious, do not move, but support head.

Symptoms guide

This section provides information on common symptoms and associated diseases. You may find it useful to refer to this symptom guide if you would like to find out more information on a particular symptom, and what it may mean.

This symptoms guide **does not** replace your doctor, and should not be used as a guide to diagnosing medical conditions in yourself or a family member. Refer to your doctor or other appropriately qualified health professionals if you believe you or another person may have one of the diseases described.

LIST OF SYMPTOM ENTRIES

Abdominal distension
Abdominal pain
Arm and shoulder problems
Back deformity
Back pain
Bad breath (halitosis)
Blackouts, including fainting
Bones, fracture/brittleness
Bowel, bleeding from
Breast Lump
Breathing problems
Bruising
Chest pain
Constipation
Cough
Cramp
Diarrhea
Dizziness
Ear pain (earache)
Eye problems
Eyelid problems
Eyesight problems
Facial pain
Fatigue
Fever
Flatulence
Foot and ankle problems
Genital itching
Genital pain
"Glands", swollen
Gums, bleeding
Hair problems
Hallucinations
Hand and wrist problems
Headache
Hearing loss (deafness)
Heartburn
Hip problems
Hot flashes/flushes
Jaundice
Knee problems
Leg problems
Memory loss
Menstrual problems
Nail abnormalities
Nausea and vomiting
Neck problems
Nosebleed
Numbness and tingling
Palpitations
Seizures (known as "fits", including convulsions)
Sexual function problems
Skin problems
Sleep disturbances
Snoring
Speech problems
Swallowing problems
Throat problems
Tongue problems
Toothache
Tremor
Urination, difficult
Urination, frequent
Urination, painful
Vaginal problems
Voice problems
Weakness and paralysis
Weight gain
Weight loss
Wounds or sores, non-healing

How to use this guide

Symptoms are listed alphabetically, and usually contain the name of the affected body part. For example, if you would like information on pain in the eye, refer to *Eye problems* to find entries on pain and other problems relating to the eye.

Each entry includes a list of descriptions of various ways in which the symptom may be experienced. Look down the *Symptom characteristics* column until you find a description that best matches the symptom in which you are interested.

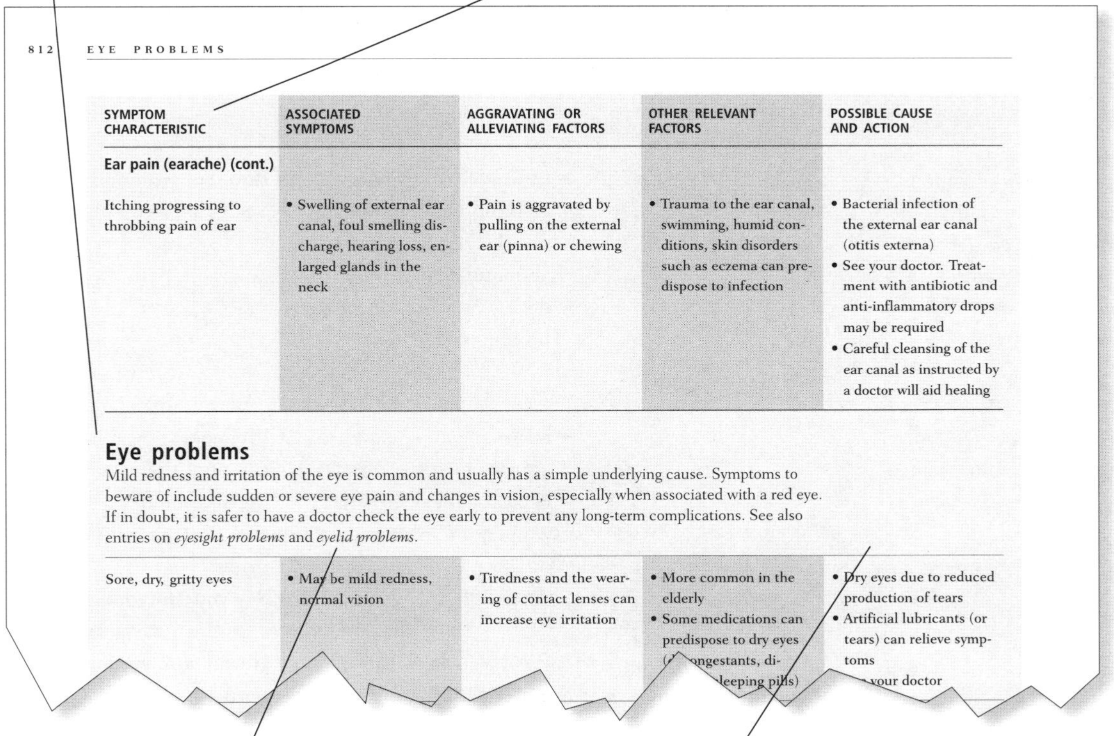

812 EYE PROBLEMS

SYMPTOM CHARACTERISTIC	ASSOCIATED SYMPTOMS	AGGRAVATING OR ALLEVIATING FACTORS	OTHER RELEVANT FACTORS	POSSIBLE CAUSE AND ACTION
Ear pain (earache) (cont.)				
Itching progressing to throbbing pain of ear	• Swelling of external ear canal, foul smelling discharge, hearing loss, enlarged glands in the neck	• Pain is aggravated by pulling on the external ear (pinna) or chewing	• Trauma to the ear canal, swimming, humid conditions, skin disorders such as eczema can predispose to infection	• Bacterial infection of the external ear canal (otitis externa) • See your doctor. Treatment with antibiotic and anti-inflammatory drops may be required • Careful cleansing of the ear canal as instructed by a doctor will aid healing

Eye problems
Mild redness and irritation of the eye is common and usually has a simple underlying cause. Symptoms to beware of include sudden or severe eye pain and changes in vision, especially when associated with a red eye. If in doubt, it is safer to have a doctor check the eye early to prevent any long-term complications. See also entries on *eyesight problems* and *eyelid problems*.

Sore, dry, gritty eyes	• May be mild redness, normal vision	• Tiredness and the wearing of contact lenses can increase eye irritation	• More common in the elderly • Some medications can predispose to dry eyes (…ongestants, di- … leeping pills)	• Dry eyes due to reduced production of tears • Artificial lubricants (or tears) can relieve symptoms • … your doctor

There is also a list of other symptoms that may be associated with the main symptom. Symptoms listed in the *Associated symptoms* column may not all occur at once, and not all of them must be present for the medical problem suggested under *possible cause* to be a likely explanation for the symptoms.

Diseases mentioned in the *possible cause* column suggest problems that may cause the symptoms described, but do not represent definitive diagnoses. Not all disease possibilities are listed, especially those that are less common.

You can read more about many of these symptoms, diseases and illnesses in the main A-Z section of this book.

The symptoms appear in alphabetical order and are listed above.

Abdominal distension

A wide variety of conditions may cause distension of the abdomen—causes range from pregnancy to conditions such as obstruction of the bowel that require urgent medical attention. More than one cause may be present at the same time. See also entries on *abdominal pain* and *flatulence*.

SYMPTOM CHARACTERISTIC	ASSOCIATED SYMPTOMS	AGGRAVATING OR ALLEVIATING FACTORS	OTHER RELEVANT FACTORS	POSSIBLE CAUSE AND ACTION
Mild distension, possibly with bloated sensation	• Flatulence, increased "rumbling" noises from the gut, abdominal discomfort	• Symptoms may be worsened by eating foods that ferment (e.g. the non-sugar sweetener sorbitol, milk, ice cream, fruit juices, onions, beans, celery, carrots, bananas, raisins, pretzels, bagels, wheat germ)	• Occasionally symptoms may occur in people with a history of malabsorption (inability to absorb foods properly in the gut) • A diet low in indigestible carbohydrates and lactose is less prone to fermentation and may alleviate the symptoms	• Increased gas in the stomach, small bowel or colon (flatulence) due to another disease or in a healthy person due to excessive fermentation of food by bacteria in the gut • See your doctor if you are worried or if symptoms persist
Generalized distension of the abdomen, with fullness in the flanks; may develop over days or weeks	• Shortness of breath and diminishing exercise tolerance (if heart disease is the cause) • Loss of appetite, nausea and tiredness (if liver disease is the cause) • Loss of appetite, weight loss and a general feeling of being unwell (if a tumor is the cause)		• Symptoms are more likely in a person with a history of heart problems, liver disease, heavy alcohol use, which can cause liver damage, or cancer	• Increased build up of fluid in the abdomen (ascites) • Causes include tumors, cirrhosis of the liver, heart failure • See your doctor at once
Rapidly developing generalized distension of the abdomen	• Rapid onset of abdominal pain that comes and goes in waves • Total constipation (inability to pass solids or gas) • Vomiting		• Bowel obstruction occurs more commonly in people who have had abdominal surgery, a hernia or other bowel problems	• Bowel obstruction • See your doctor at once
Distension in the lower area of the abdomen or pelvic area	• Difficulty passing urine, vague abdominal pain		• Ovarian cancer is more common with age and occasionally occurs in women under 35 years of age	• Pregnancy, ovarian cyst, tumor of the ovary or uterus, bladder distension due to retention of urine • See your doctor at once
Lump next to the umbilicus, near a surgical scar, or (in men) in the groin	• Painless	• Appears when straining or coughing or when you stand up (i.e. when pressure in the abdomen rises); lump then disappears spontaneously or can be pushed back	• Weakness in the abdominal wall may be caused by a congenital defect in the abdominal wall, a surgical incision, or muscle weakness due to obesity, pregnancy or wasting	• Hernia or inguinal hernia See your doctor

SYMPTOM CHARACTERISTIC	ASSOCIATED SYMPTOMS	AGGRAVATING OR ALLEVIATING FACTORS	OTHER RELEVANT FACTORS	POSSIBLE CAUSE AND ACTION
Lump that remains visible whether or not you are straining, coughing or standing	• Associated symptoms, if present, will depend on the cause			• Enlargement of an abdominal organ (e.g. liver or spleen), tumor, hernia that has become trapped • See your doctor at once

Abdominal pain

Abdominal pain may be related to any abdominal organ, and the type of pain will vary widely, depending on the cause. It is important to see your doctor or emergency room immediately if abdominal pain is severe or of sudden onset, since many common causes require immediate surgical intervention. See also entry on *abdominal distension*.

SYMPTOM CHARACTERISTIC	ASSOCIATED SYMPTOMS	AGGRAVATING OR ALLEVIATING FACTORS	OTHER RELEVANT FACTORS	POSSIBLE CAUSE AND ACTION
Episodes of pain in the upper abdomen, typically central and characterized as a burning sensation or heartburn	• Bitter fluid may return into the mouth from the stomach	• Symptoms may be aggravated by lying down • May be alleviated by antacids	• Symptoms may be brought on by stooping, straining or lying down	• Esophagitis caused by reflux • See your doctor
Episodes of pain in the upper abdomen, typically central but may also be on the right or left; may be characterized as a burning or gnawing sensation		• Pain is typically related to food, and may either occur before meals and be relieved by eating, antacids or vomiting, or may occur shortly after meals, sometimes making the person feel reluctant to eat	• The incidence of peptic ulcer is highest among people aged 30–50 years; may occur in teenagers and rarely in children • Ulcers are most frequently caused by a *Helicobacter pylori* infection or by the use of non-steroidal anti-inflammatory drugs	• Peptic ulcer • See your doctor
Episodes of colicky or constant pain in the upper abdomen, typically central or on the right side and of rapid onset; pain may radiate around the right side of the body into the shoulder and typically lasts for hours at a time	• Nausea • Sometimes vomiting • Sometimes yellowness of the skin may ensue (jaundice), possibly with darkened urine and pale stools	• This pain is not relieved by vomiting or antacids	• An episode may follow eating a fatty meal • Occurs in adults; women on oral contraceptives are at higher risk • May have a family history of gallstones	• Gallstones • See your doctor
Upper abdominal pain, gradually worsening and typically constant over hours or days before subsiding; pain may radiate directly through to the back	• Nausea, vomiting	• May be aggravated by food, drink or vomiting • Typically aggravated by lying down and alleviated by sitting up and leaning forward	• Symptoms may follow a bout of heavy drinking • May have background of alcohol use or gallstones	• Sudden-onset (acute) pancreatitis • See your doctor at once
Persistent upper abdominal pain, typically characterized as a constant background pain; pain may radiate directly through to the back	• May later develop weight loss or pale stools	• Pain may be aggravated by lying down and alleviated by sitting up and leaning forward	• May have background of alcohol use or gallstones	• Long-term (chronic) pancreatitis or pancreatic tumor • See your doctor

SYMPTOM CHARACTERISTIC	ASSOCIATED SYMPTOMS	AGGRAVATING OR ALLEVIATING FACTORS	OTHER RELEVANT FACTORS	POSSIBLE CAUSE AND ACTION
Abdominal pain (cont.)				
Constant discomfort on the right side of upper abdomen, typically felt as a dull ache	• Nausea, loss of appetite, tiredness, fever, eventually jaundice • Other symptoms depend on the cause • Shortness of breath, diminishing exercise tolerance and ankle swelling may occur with a heart problem • Loss of appetite, weight loss and a general feeling of being unwell may occur with a tumor		• Liver symptoms are more likely to occur in people with a history of heart disease, heavy alcohol users, cancer, recent intravenous drug use or blood transfusion, overseas travel, recent contact with a person with a similar illness	• Liver pain due to heart failure (causing swelling of the liver), viral hepatitis, hepatitis caused by heavy alcohol use, liver tumor • See your doctor
Rapid onset of diffuse cramping pains, typically centered around the central abdomen	• Diarrhea, nausea, vomiting, fever		• Symptoms may follow overseas travel or eating carelessly prepared food	• Gastroenteritis or food poisoning • Drink plenty of fluids • See your doctor if you are worried or if symptoms persist
Rapid onset of pain on the right side of the lower abdomen; the pain may either be constant or occur in waves; pain typically starts around the middle of the abdomen, then moves to the right lower abdomen	• Loss of appetite, nausea, vomiting, low fever		• Most common in children or young adults	• Appendicitis • This is a medical emergency • Go to the emergency room or call an ambulance immediately
Pains in the lower abdomen that may be cramping, occur in waves, or vague discomfort	• Change in bowel habit • May have blood or mucus in the stools	• Pain may be worse before defecation and alleviated by defecation or passing wind	• Cancer is a common cause in patients over 50, but can also occur in younger people • In older patients (> 70 years of age), bowel obstruction is one of the most common causes of abdominal pain requiring surgical intervention	• Inflammatory bowel disease or tumor of the colon • See your doctor • If severe pain, abdominal distension and total constipation (inability to pass solids or gas) occurs, this is a medical emergency • Go to the emergency room or call an ambulance immediately
Sudden severe pain on one flank, typically radiating from the loins around to the front of the abdomen and down to the groin	• May have a change in the color of your urine or blood in the urine • May be associated with nausea	• Passing a stone in the urine may cause severe pain	• May have a predisposing factor such as gout	• Kidney stone • This is a medical emergency • Go to the emergency room or call an ambulance immediately

SYMPTOM CHARACTERISTIC	ASSOCIATED SYMPTOMS	AGGRAVATING OR ALLEVIATING FACTORS	OTHER RELEVANT FACTORS	POSSIBLE CAUSE AND ACTION
Loin pain, typically a dull ache	• Fever • Passing urine more frequently • Painful urination		• May be a predisposing condition like an abnormality in the urinary tract or a disorder that impairs immune defenses • In women and infants, may occur without a predisposing factor	• Pyelonephritis (kidney infection) • See your doctor at once
Lower abdomen or pelvic pains in women	• Associated symptoms will depend on the underlying cause; there may be menstrual changes or difficulties or vaginal discharge		• Pain may be related to the menstrual cycle • Onset and severity will depend on underlying cause	• Problem of uterus or ovaries (e.g. endometriosis) • See your doctor
Severe, sharp, well localized abdominal pain; pain may be of abrupt onset, but sometimes is more gradual		• Pain aggravated by movement or coughing	• Predisposing conditions include peptic ulcer, abdominal aneurysm, hernia	• Peritonitis caused by appendicitis, perforation of a peptic ulcer, complication of abdominal aneurysm, strangulation or twisting of the bowel • This is a medical emergency. Go to the emergency room or call an ambulance immediately
Bouts of severe abdominal pain in an infant	• Screaming and drawing up the legs during the bouts of pain, vomiting, red stools		• Intussusception is most common during the first two years of life	• Intussusception • This is a medical emergency. Go to the emergency room or call an ambulance immediately

Arm and shoulder problems

Symptoms in the arm or shoulder often result from overuse, injury, and falls. Sporting activities and occupational tasks are common causes of problems in this area. Pain in the arm can also be a symptom of a heart attack, so see your doctor immediately if you experience unexplained pain. See also entry on *chest pain*.

SYMPTOM CHARACTERISTIC	ASSOCIATED SYMPTOMS	AGGRAVATING OR ALLEVIATING FACTORS	OTHER RELEVANT FACTORS	POSSIBLE CAUSE AND ACTION
Pain in the shoulder with movement, especially lifting the arm over the head; may occur following an injury or activity involving repetitive movements	• Tenderness and swelling in the area, weakness of the arm	• Symptoms are aggravated by further movement • Pushing and twisting movements (e.g. reaching behind the back, dressing) are often painful	• Lifting, twisting and sporting activities often cause these problems	• Tendinitis • Rest and apply ice • See your doctor if you are worried or if pain persists
Sharp pain in the arm or shoulder following vigorous activity	• Swelling, stiffness, tenderness	• Symptoms may be aggravated by movement of the arm	• Often occurs when sudden or unfamiliar stresses are placed on the arm (e.g. falls, lifting heavy objects, new exercise)	• Muscle strain or ligament sprain • Rest and apply ice • See your doctor if you are worried or if symptoms persist

SYMPTOM CHARACTERISTIC	ASSOCIATED SYMPTOMS	AGGRAVATING OR ALLEVIATING FACTORS	OTHER RELEVANT FACTORS	POSSIBLE CAUSE AND ACTION
Arm and shoulder problems (cont.)				
Sudden pain on the top of the shoulder; may be worse upon waking	• May be some redness and tenderness, limited movement	• Symptoms are usually aggravated by raising arm out to the side or twisting movement	• Can occur with overuse, infections, arthritis, injuries	• Bursitis • See your doctor for advice
Gradually worsening elbow pain that occurs with repeated movements	• Pain may spread down into the muscles in the forearm • May be tender to touch	• Symptoms are aggravated by further movement and alleviated by rest	• More likely to occur in those with weak wrist and arm muscles, and in tennis players using an incorrect backhand stroke	• Tennis elbow • Rest and apply ice • See your doctor if you are worried or if pain persists
Increasing shoulder pain and stiffness that has worsened over several weeks	• Limited movement in all directions	• Symptoms are aggravated by movement in most directions, especially away from the body	• Often occurs in older people, especially following an injury or shoulder/chest surgery	• Frozen shoulder • See your doctor
Intense arm pain following a fall or direct blow to the arm	• Arm or shoulder may be deformed	• Symptoms are aggravated by any attempt at movement		• Fracture or dislocation • See your doctor at once
Persistent, severe pain radiating from the chest down the left arm	• Shortness of breath, nausea, sweating • Feeling of chest being squeezed	• Pain does not change with arm movements	• Increased likelihood in a person who has previously had a heart attack or with a history of coronary heart disease	• Myocardial infarction (heart attack) • This is a medical emergency. Go to the emergency room or call an ambulance immediately

Back deformity

Abnormalities of the spine may occur due to an acquired disease, as a developmental problem in growing children, or as part of one of the syndromes of multiple anatomical abnormalities that are caused by genetic defects. Any unusual appearance of the spine should be checked by a doctor.

SYMPTOM CHARACTERISTIC	ASSOCIATED SYMPTOMS	AGGRAVATING OR ALLEVIATING FACTORS	OTHER RELEVANT FACTORS	POSSIBLE CAUSE AND ACTION
Sideways curvature of the spine (scoliosis) in an adolescent, visible while sitting erect and straight; spine is S-shaped or corkscrew shaped	• Postural problems, pain, fatigue of back muscles, visible disfigurement in severe cases		• The cause of idiopathic scoliosis unknown, but it is thought to be due to complex inherited causes • The condition is twice as common in females as males, and usually appears at around puberty	• Idiopathic scoliosis
Exaggeration of the normal outward curve of the spine at the level of the rib cage (kyphosis)	• Poor posture, fatigue or pain in back muscles		• Abnormal curvature may first appear in a young growing child	• Exaggerated kyphosis ("hunchback"), due to injury or a developmental abnormality • See your doctor
Exaggeration of the normal inward curve of the spine at the lower back (lordosis)	• Poor posture, fatigue or pain in back muscles		• Abnormal curvature may first appear in a young growing child	• Exaggerated lordosis ("swayback"), due to injury or a developmental abnormality • See your doctor

SYMPTOM CHARACTERISTIC	ASSOCIATED SYMPTOMS	AGGRAVATING OR ALLEVIATING FACTORS	OTHER RELEVANT FACTORS	POSSIBLE CAUSE AND ACTION
Sideways curvature of the spine (scoliosis) which worsens over time	• Difficulty running, jumping, hopping, muscle weakness, enlarged calf muscles, breathing problems • Children use their arms to pull themselves up from the ground after sitting or lying down • Spinal curvature may become painful over time		• Duchenne muscular dystrophy is a genetic disorder affecting only boys • The condition is present at birth, but signs only appear between 3–5 years of age	• Duchenne muscular dystrophy • See your doctor
Gradual development of a exaggerated outwards curvature (kyphosis) or sideways curvature of the spine (scoliosis) in an elderly person	• Multiple fractures of the vertebrae may result in "dowager's hump" • New vertebral fractures may be very painful, but pain usually subsides within weeks to months		• Osteoporosis is more common in women than men	• Osteoporosis • See your doctor
Exaggeration of the outward curve of the spine at the rib cage level (kyphosis), with flattening of the normal inward curve of the lower back in a young person with pain and stiffness	• Back stiffness and pain, chest pain arthritis and pain in other joints (e.g. knee, hip, heel), iritis, cardiovascular problems, bowel problems • Occasionally fatigue, fever, night sweats or loss of appetite may occur	• Stiffness may be worse in the morning	• Ankylosing spondylitis runs in families and is more common in men than women • The condition is relatively common in children in developing countries, but tends to occur in young adults in industrialized countries	• Ankylosing spondylitis • See your doctor

Back pain

The majority of cases of backache relate to the lower back. Low back pain is one of the most common symptoms that people experience. In adults, a majority of cases are based on a mechanical problem relating to posture, muscle strain, arthritis or disk problems. Sometimes, no physical cause is found.

In some circumstances, prompt and adequate early treatment of acute mechanical back pain may help to avoid progression to ongoing long-term pain, so do not hesitate to see your doctor. Back pain which is progressive, severe, persistent or associated with neurological symptoms such as weakness, numbness or tingling sensations always warrants a visit to a doctor. See also entry on *numbness and tingling*.

SYMPTOM CHARACTERISTIC	ASSOCIATED SYMPTOMS	AGGRAVATING OR ALLEVIATING FACTORS	OTHER RELEVANT FACTORS	POSSIBLE CAUSE AND ACTION
Vague back ache in an adult		• Tends to worsen as the day progresses	• More common with obesity, late pregnancy, or in people who are inactive or unfit	• Postural backache • If symptoms are mild, try gentle physical activity (e.g. swimming), maintain good posture when sitting and standing, avoid remaining in one position for long periods when sitting • See your doctor or a physical therapist if you are worried or if symptoms persist

SYMPTOM CHARACTERISTIC	ASSOCIATED SYMPTOMS	AGGRAVATING OR ALLEVIATING FACTORS	OTHER RELEVANT FACTORS	POSSIBLE CAUSE AND ACTION
Back pain (cont.)				
Steady ache not confined to a specific place, most often in the lower back; may begin suddenly during straining, twisting or unusual physical activity, or may start after such activities	• Stiffness	• Aggravated by movement but not by coughing or straining • May be relieved by lying still	• Adults or children • Commonly occurs as a sporting or occupational injury • Sometimes follows trauma, e.g. motor vehicle accident	• Acute muscle or ligament strain • Minor strains usually settle quickly and do not require medical attention • See your doctor or a physical therapist if you are worried or if symptoms persist
Sudden episodes of pain, usually in the lower back; often described as sharp and/or shooting in character; often radiates down into the buttock and leg	• Neurological symptoms may develop, such as tingling or some loss of sensation in the buttock or part of the leg	• Pain aggravated by bending (especially to the side), coughing/sneezing, laughing • May be alleviated by lying in the fetal position	• Pain may have been precipitated by trauma or an unusual movement • The pain may spontaneously go away for a time	• Intervertebral disk problem (e.g. herniated disk or disk protrusion) • See your doctor at once
Gradual onset of pain, usually in the lower back	• Similar symptoms in other joints, stiffness in the mornings	• Stiffness tends to gradually ease as the day progresses, pain tends to be worse with activity and eased by resting	• Not precipitated by physical activity or trauma • Osteoarthritis is more common with age; other forms of arthritis may occur in younger people	• Arthritis (e.g. osteoarthritis or rheumatoid arthritis) • See your doctor
Dull aching pain; may radiate to one side; most commonly in the middle or lower spine		• Worse with exertion, posture, movement, coughing	• May result from severe trauma, or minor or unnoticed trauma in a person with osteoporosis or a bone abnormality	• Vertebral fracture • See your doctor at once
Lower back ache, sometimes throbbing in nature	• May have stiffness, rash, other joints affected, or symptoms from the gastrointestinal, urinary or genital tract	• Characterized by being worse with rest, and alleviated by activity; this contrasts with mechanical causes of back pain	• Often in young adults or people with inflammatory disease of the bowel	• An inflammatory joint disorder • See your doctor
Unremitting continuous and possibly progressive pain, usually of gradual onset; may be deep, boring pain	• Weight loss, loss of appetite, malaise, fever, chills, nervous system problems	• Posture or motion typically have little effect on the pain	• Pathological lesions are rarely the cause of low back pain in adults; they are a more common underlying cause of pain higher up in the spine or low back pain in a child	• Cancer metastasis, cancer of the blood (e.g. leukemia), inflammation or infection • See your doctor at once

Bad breath (halitosis)

Most people have slightly bad breath when they first wake in the morning, because the normally physiological mechanisms that clean the mouth are inactive while sleeping. Transient bad breath may be of no particular significance or associated with an obvious short-term problem in the mouth or throat. Occasionally, persistent and genuinely bad breath results from serious underlying disorders of major bodily systems.

SYMPTOM CHARACTERISTIC	ASSOCIATED SYMPTOMS	AGGRAVATING OR ALLEVIATING FACTORS	OTHER RELEVANT FACTORS	POSSIBLE CAUSE AND ACTION
Transient, bad breath usually of easily recognizable attribution			• These causes are common and generally well recognized	• Lifestyle factors (e.g. smoking, drinking, eating certain foods such as garlic or onions) • See your doctor or dentist if you are worried or if symptoms persist
Persistent bad breath, may have a putrid odor			• These are the most common causes of halitosis	• Poor dental hygiene, rotten teeth, gingivitis, infections in the mouth or throat • See your doctor or dentist
Persistent bad breath; may have a putrid odor	• Cough, sputum, fever, headache (sinusitis)		• Sinusitis is the most common out of this group of conditions	• Respiratory infections resulting in build-up of stagnant secretions in the respiratory tract, sinusitis, lung diseases (e.g. lung abscess, lung cancer) • See your doctor at once
Characteristically, a sweet, fruity acetone smell on the breath	• Excessive thirst, increased urine volume, mental confusion, apathy, reduced awareness, which may progress to coma		• This type of diabetes typically begins before 40 years of age	• Uncontrolled Type I diabetes (insulin-dependent diabetes of juvenile-onset) • See your doctor at once • If drowsiness or coma is present, this is a medical emergency. Go to the emergency room or call an ambulance immediately
Persistent bad breath; characteristically, an ammonia or urinary smell on the breath	• Often associated with an unpleasant taste sensation • Many other symptoms may be associated including loss of appetite, weight loss, itchiness, headache, restlessness, hiccough, bruising, bleeding from the nose, drowsiness, nausea and vomiting, convulsions, muscle twitching		• Typically will have a known history of kidney disease and failure	• Chronic kidney failure • See your doctor • If drowsiness or coma is present, this is a medical emergency • Go to the emergency room or call an ambulance immediately

SYMPTOM CHARACTERISTIC	ASSOCIATED SYMPTOMS	AGGRAVATING OR ALLEVIATING FACTORS	OTHER RELEVANT FACTORS	POSSIBLE CAUSE AND ACTION
Bad breath (halitosis) (cont.)				
Persistent bad breath; variously described as a fishy, musty or mousy smell on the breath	• Fatigue, weight loss, fluid retention, general deterioration in health, yellowness of skin (jaundice) • There may be drowsiness, which may progress to coma		• May develop either as an rapidly progressive acute condition or due to liver problem	• Liver failure • See your doctor • If drowsiness or coma is present, this is a medical emergency. Go to the emergency room or call an ambulance at once

Blackouts, including fainting

Fainting results from a transient loss of consciousness. Lapses in awareness or falling to the ground suddenly without warning may also occur without loss of consciousness. Faints are more common in elderly people, who are also at greatest risk of injury from the resulting falls. In about 50 percent of cases, no cause is found.

SYMPTOM CHARACTERISTIC	ASSOCIATED SYMPTOMS	AGGRAVATING OR ALLEVIATING FACTORS	OTHER RELEVANT FACTORS	POSSIBLE CAUSE AND ACTION
Transient loss of consciousness with awareness that you are about to lose consciousness; occurs when upright, causing the person to fall to the ground	• Before losing consciousness, may have a feeling of weakness or lightheadedness, or dimness of vision • On waking, usually well oriented • May have milder episodes without loss of unconsciousness	• Episodes are transient because falling to the ground restores blood flow to the brain	• Fainting may be caused by pregnancy, standing in the sun for a long time, standing up while on medication for high blood pressure, sudden severe emotional stress, after a long bout of violent coughing, or as a response to pain, fear, injections, or the sight of blood	• Fainting • See your doctor if you are worried or if symptoms persist
Transient loss of consciousness often without warning; may occur when upright or when lying down	• Lightheadedness, palpitations, chest pain, or breathlessness preceding loss of consciousness • While unconscious, the person may be noticeably pale • On waking, the person is usually well oriented and quickly feels well again		• In some cases, fainting is precipitated by exercise • The risk is increased if the person is also dehydrated	• Heart disease • See your doctor at once
Transient lapse of consciousness—normal activity and awareness ceases briefly with or without falling or prior warning; may occur when upright or when lying down	• During the attack, may have fluttering of eyelids, rolling up of eyes, or there may be some jerking of the limbs or repeated simple muscle actions • May be confused for a period on waking		• Young person, or known history of epilepsy • Begins in childhood • May also experience other forms of epileptic seizure	• Epilepsy that does not involve convulsive movements • See your doctor
Falling to the ground suddenly without warning; may occur with or without loss of consciousness	• Sudden onset of persistent nervous system problems (e.g. blindness, weakness, pins and needles, numbness, difficulties with speech, lack of muscle coordination)		• More common with advancing age • Risk increased in people with hypertension, lipid abnormalities (e.g. high cholesterol), diabetes	• Stroke • This is a medical emergency • Go to the emergency room or call an ambulance at once

SYMPTOM CHARACTERISTIC	ASSOCIATED SYMPTOMS	AGGRAVATING OR ALLEVIATING FACTORS	OTHER RELEVANT FACTORS	POSSIBLE CAUSE AND ACTION
Sudden transient loss of consciousness, or falling to the ground, without warning	• There may be a sudden onset of transient neurological problems such as loss of vision, weakness, pins and needles, numbness, difficulties with speech, lack of muscle coordination, vertigo • These symptoms spontaneously resolve		• May have a history of cardiovascular disease or osteoarthritis of the neck • May have been precipitated by a particular movement of the head • More common with advancing age • Risk increased in people with hypertension, lipid abnormalities (e.g. high cholesterol), diabetes	• Transient ischemic attack • This is a medical emergency • Go to the emergency room or call an ambulance at once
Loss of consciousness, generally prolonged	• Before losing consciousness may experience confusion, sweating, possibly headache, faintness and weakness	• Loss of consciousness can usually be prevented by eating glucose candy or jelly beans and taking sugary drinks (e.g. fruit juice) as soon as the attack is recognized	• Person on medication to treat diabetes • May have missed a meal, exercised more than anticipated, or recently altered their diabetic medication	• Hypoglycemia (low blood sugar) • This is a medical emergency • Go to the emergency room or call an ambulance at once

Bones, fracture/brittleness

Suspected fractures always require immediate medical attention, especially when there is substantial blood loss, symptoms of nerve damage or any suggestion of damage to internal organs. If the injury may affect the spinal column—for example following a direct blow to the neck or back, falls from a height or high-speed accidents—great care must be taken to immobilize the spine until an ambulance arrives to transport the person to hospital.

SYMPTOM CHARACTERISTIC	ASSOCIATED SYMPTOMS	AGGRAVATING OR ALLEVIATING FACTORS	OTHER RELEVANT FACTORS	POSSIBLE CAUSE AND ACTION
Pain with loss of limb function and possibly also change in shape	• The skin overlying the fracture may be broken (open fracture) or intact (closed fracture) • There may be substantial blood loss, or damage to nerves or internal organs	• Pain is aggravated by any movement of the affected part	• Fractures may be caused by a heavy blow hitting or crushing a bone (direct force) or twisting, bending or compressing a bone (indirect force) • In adults, the break is usually through the full thickness of the bone • In children, the bones are more springy and incomplete fractures are common ("greenstick" fractures)	• Fracture • See your doctor at once • First aid involves controlling bleeding, covering any open wounds and supporting the limb in its most comfortable position
Broken bone following repeated activity that stresses a particular site (usually a limb)	• The most characteristic pattern of symptoms is pain that initially starts after the exercise or activity, then begins to occur during the activity and later is present at other times as well • There is no deformity and the limb functions normally		• Usually occurs in otherwise healthy active people	• Stress fracture • See your doctor at once

SYMPTOM CHARACTERISTIC	ASSOCIATED SYMPTOMS	AGGRAVATING OR ALLEVIATING FACTORS	OTHER RELEVANT FACTORS	POSSIBLE CAUSE AND ACTION
Bones, fracture/brittleness (cont.)				
Broken bone following slight trauma	• Pain with loss of limb function and possible deformity • Elderly women with long-term multiple fractures of the vertebrae may develop a hump at the top of the back	• Pain is aggravated by any movement of the affected part	• Pain or deformity of the bone before the fracture occurred suggests the cause may be a preexisting abnormality of the bone • There may have been previous episodes of fracture • Fractures of the hip, wrist and vertebrae are most commonly associated with osteoporosis • Osteoporosis is more common in women than men • Factors that increase risk of developing osteoporosis include inherited factors (family history, ethnicity), hormonal factors (menopause, ovarian problems, disease of thyroid gland), calcium deficiency, alcohol abuse, smoking, lack of exercise, or drug treatment	• Fracture due to an abnormality making the bone more fragile (pathological fracture) • Causes include osteoporosis, cancer with metastasis, blood cell abnormalities • See your doctor at once

Bowel, bleeding from

Bleeding from the bowel always warrants a visit to the doctor to determine the cause and, if blood loss has been substantial, to support the circulation. The most common cause is hemorrhoids, but more serious conditions such as bowel cancer are common and may be responsible for a bleed of any description. Serious pathologies need to be excluded by a doctor even if a minor ailment such as hemorrhoids is present. Some of the important causes in adults, such as hemorrhoids and rectal cancer, do not occur in children.

This table deals with bleeding through the rectum. Bleeding from the upper gastrointestinal tract (esophagus, stomach, duodenum) often causes vomiting of blood, which may either be fresh blood or darkened blood resembling coffee grounds.

SYMPTOM CHARACTERISTIC	ASSOCIATED SYMPTOMS	AGGRAVATING OR ALLEVIATING FACTORS	OTHER RELEVANT FACTORS	POSSIBLE CAUSE AND ACTION
Squirt or drip of fresh blood in toilet or on toilet paper after defecation	• Hemorrhoids are usually painless unless there are complications • A sensation of unsatisfied defecation or urgency signals a problem inside the rectum		• Straining to defecate predisposes to hemorrhoids	• Hemorrhoids, polyps, tumors • See your doctor
Small amount of fresh blood on toilet paper after defecation with sharp pain in the anus during or after defecating			• Straining to defecate may predispose to anal injuries	• Anal tear or break in tissue (fissure), tumor • See your doctor

SYMPTOM CHARACTERISTIC	ASSOCIATED SYMPTOMS	AGGRAVATING OR ALLEVIATING FACTORS	OTHER RELEVANT FACTORS	POSSIBLE CAUSE AND ACTION
Fresh blood mixed with stool or dark blood in stool, with or without blood clots	• No other symptoms or there may be diarrhea, constipation, abdominal pain, abdominal distension, weight loss, loss of appetite, general feeling of being unwell, symptoms of anemia (tiredness, lack of energy, breathlessness on exertion, pallor of skin or gums, fingernails) • Mucus may be passed with stools		• More likely in a person with personal or family history of polyps or bowel cancer • Conditions that predispose to bowel cancer include benign polyps, ulcerative colitis	• Bowel tumor, polyp, other problems of rectum or bowel • See your doctor
Episodes of bloody diarrhea	• Abdominal pain, aches, general feeling of being unwell, weight loss, fever, symptoms of anemia (tiredness, lack of energy, breathlessness on exertion, pallor of skin or gums, fingernails) • Mucus may be passed in stool		• Inflammatory bowel disease is most common in Jewish people (3–6 times higher than for non-Jewish racial or ethnic groups), and is higher among white racial groups than in black people or Asians • It commences most commonly at age 15–35 • The cause of inflammatory bowel disease is unknown	• An inflammatory bowel disease such as Crohn's disease or ulcerative colitis • See your doctor at once
Sudden onset of watery, bloody diarrhea or of smaller stools with blood, mucus and pus	• Abdominal pain, fever, aches, general feeling of being unwell • In children, high fever may develop so rapidly as to cause febrile seizures		• Dysentery is highly contagious, and is most common following travel or contact with others who have similar symptoms • Outbreaks are usually relatively mild in industrialized countries and most frequently occur in institutions such as schools • Outbreaks occurring in developing countries (or infections originating with a traveler to these countries) are more severe and sometimes fatal	• Dysentery, infection of the bowel • See your doctor at once • Dysentery is highly contagious, so contact the doctor's office or emergency department first to advise of symptoms
Bloody diarrhea of sudden onset	• Abdominal pain		• Most common in elderly people with a history of other cardiovascular disease, but no contact with dysentery	• Loss of blood supply to a portion of the bowel (ischemic colitis) • This is a medical emergency • Go to the emergency room or call an ambulance at once

SYMPTOM CHARACTERISTIC	ASSOCIATED SYMPTOMS	AGGRAVATING OR ALLEVIATING FACTORS	OTHER RELEVANT FACTORS	POSSIBLE CAUSE AND ACTION
Bowel, bleeding from (cont.)				
Heavy bleeding from the rectum	• Lightheadedness or fainting, confusion, severe thirst, feeling cold and clammy, pallor of skin, gums and nails		• Diverticulitis is more common in men than in women • Heavy bleeding is a rare complication of diverticulitis, which is usually associated with invisible or light bleeding	• Diverticulitis • This is a medical emergency • Go to the emergency room or call an ambulance at once
Melena (black tarry stools)	• May also vomit blood, either as fresh blood or darkened blood resembling coffee grounds		• Peptic ulcer can occur in any age group, but is relatively common in elderly people taking non-steroidal anti-inflammatory drugs for painful inflammatory conditions such as osteoarthritis or rheumatoid arthritis	• Bleeding from the esophagus, stomach, or duodenum, caused by a peptic ulcer, or gastritis, or dilated veins in the esophagus • This is a medical emergency • Go to the emergency room or call an ambulance at once
Blood in feces or red-colored stool in an infant	• Unwell with vomiting and bouts of abdominal pain and screaming		• Most common in children under 2 years	• Intussusception • This is a medical emergency • Go to the emergency room or call an ambulance at once

Breast lump

Most women will detect a lump in their breast at some time in their life. Most of these lumps are found to be benign on further assessment. Breast cancer has been found responsible for up to 25 percent of breast lumps and remains the most common cancer in women.

SYMPTOM CHARACTERISTIC	ASSOCIATED SYMPTOMS	AGGRAVATING OR ALLEVIATING FACTORS	OTHER RELEVANT FACTORS	POSSIBLE CAUSE AND ACTION
General breast lumpiness, tender breast lumps usually affecting both breasts, but occasionally a single lump only; lumps are soft, round and smooth; pain and tenderness may occur during menstrual cycles, usually of both breasts; lumps may come and go with menstrual cycles		• Pain and tenderness worse premenstrually • Sometimes symptoms may be alleviated by reducing intake of coffee, tea and chocolate	• Usually affects premenopausal women • Symptoms usually diminish or disappear after menopause	• Fibrocystic disease of the breast • See your doctor • If fibrocystic disease is diagnosed a well-fitted bra may help provide adequate support • Vitamin E supplementation may reduce symptoms
Firm, elastic breast lump that moves freely; usually a single smooth lump approximately 1½ inches (3–4 centimeters) in diameter	• Usually painless	• Lump may enlarge during adolescence or pregnancy	• Usually occurs in women 20–40 years of age	• Fibroadenoma • See your doctor

SYMPTOM CHARACTERISTIC	ASSOCIATED SYMPTOMS	AGGRAVATING OR ALLEVIATING FACTORS	OTHER RELEVANT FACTORS	POSSIBLE CAUSE AND ACTION
Hard or irregular breast lump which may be fixed in one position or attached to nearby tissues; usually only one breast is affected	• No other symptoms or pain (5 percent of patients), bloody or non-milky discharge from nipple, dimpling of the skin, tenderness or lumps under the armpit		• More common in women than in men • Most common after 40 years of age but may occur much earlier in women with a genetic predisposition	• Breast cancer • See your doctor at once
Firm single irregular lump, which may be attached to the skin	• Lump is painful and tender		• Gradual onset (over months) after breast trauma; the trauma involved may be subtle	• Abnormality in fat tissue • See your doctor
Single, tender breast lump that develops rapidly in a women who is breast feeding	• Pain and tenderness of lump, redness of the overlying skin, fever, chills		• Occurs during lactation	• Breast abscess • See your doctor

Breathing problems

Shortness of breath can be a gradually developing phenomenon or may be rapidly developing and life-threatening. Some of the more prominent causes of each are described in this section.

SYMPTOM CHARACTERISTIC	ASSOCIATED SYMPTOMS	AGGRAVATING OR ALLEVIATING FACTORS	OTHER RELEVANT FACTORS	POSSIBLE CAUSE AND ACTION
Long-term or repeated shortness of breath on exertion; onset gradual	• Shortness of breath on lying flat, waking up at night with shortness of breath which is relieved by sitting up, swelling of the legs, cough, wheeze may be present, gradual decline in exercise capacity, shortness of breath at rest	• Symptoms may be aggravated by lying down	• Chronic heart failure is most common in the middle-aged and elderly, and rarely occurs in younger people • Heart failure may follow rheumatic fever, heart attack/coronary artery disease, hypertension, arrhythmia, or heart valve abnormalities	• Chronic heart failure • See your doctor at once
Long-term or repeated shortness of breath on exertion; may progress gradually over many years	• Wheezing • Cough with sputum, often worse in the morning • Gradual decline in exercise capacity	• Sometimes alleviated by leaning forward or lying on stomach with head down	• Chronic obstructive lung disease is very much more common in smokers and in the elderly	• Chronic obstructive lung disease, bronchitis, emphysema • See your doctor
Long-term or repeated shortness of breath on exertion, occurring in episodes with no symptoms at other times	• Wheezing, persistent cough, usually without sputum	• Symptoms may be triggered by exposure to cigarette smoke or air pollution, exposure to pollens, cold air, exercise, respiratory infections	• History of hay fever or eczema; family history of asthma, eczema or allergies • Usually more frequent in winter, following a common cold or when pollen levels are high • May be exacerbated by exposure to pets or cigarette smoke	• Asthma • See your doctor • If breathing is difficult, or you suspect oxygen shortage, this is a medical emergency • Go to the emergency room or call an ambulance at once

SYMPTOM CHARACTERISTIC	ASSOCIATED SYMPTOMS	AGGRAVATING OR ALLEVIATING FACTORS	OTHER RELEVANT FACTORS	POSSIBLE CAUSE AND ACTION
Breathing problems (cont.)				
Long-term or repeated shortness of breath on exertion in a person working in a dusty environment; gradually progressive over a long period	• Cough		• Occupational exposure to coal, silica, asbestos	• Occupational lung disease • See your doctor
Acute shortness of breath at rest; onset may be sudden	• Chest pain if the episode is precipitated by a heart attack • May have a background history or recent worsening of shortness of breath on exertion and/or when lying flat, and/or waking up short of breath at night	• Breathlessness aggravated by lying down	• Pulmonary edema is more likely in a person with a history of this problem • May be caused by cardiac disease, lung infections, shock (e.g. cardiac surgery, serious infections, inhaled toxins)	• Pulmonary edema • This is a medical emergency • Go to the emergency room or call an ambulance at once
Sudden onset shortness of breath at rest	• Fever, chills, pain around the chest which is aggravated by breathing in		• Pneumonia is a relatively common condition in all age groups, but may be more likely with an inhaled foreign body, pre-existing lung diseases, immune suppression (e.g. other disease, medications)	• Pneumonia • See your doctor at once
Acute shortness of breath at rest; sudden onset	• Chest pain		• May occur spontaneously or as a result of chest trauma • Most often occurs in young healthy people without a prior lung problem • Predisposing factors include cystic fibrosis, chronic obstructive lung disease	• Pneumothorax • This is a medical emergency • Go to the emergency room or call an ambulance at once
Acute shortness of breath at rest	• Chest pain, dizziness, faintness, loss of consciousness, rapidly turning blue		• Predisposing factors to an embolus include the use of oral contraceptives in young women, recent surgery, recent childbirth, a long period of bed rest or immobility, history of a blood clot in the leg, abnormal heart rhythms	• Pulmonary embolism • This is a medical emergency • Go to the emergency room or call an ambulance at once

SYMPTOM CHARACTERISTIC	ASSOCIATED SYMPTOMS	AGGRAVATING OR ALLEVIATING FACTORS	OTHER RELEVANT FACTORS	POSSIBLE CAUSE AND ACTION
Very sudden shortness of breath at rest with choking; occurring while eating or where there is a high probability of a toddler inhaling a small object	• Severe distress with inability to take in air despite desperate efforts, collapse, blue skin and gums, loss of consciousness (in complete obstruction) • Rapid labored breathing with loud harsh noise while breathing in, gagging (in partial blockage of the airway)		• Inhalation is probable if onset while eating • In adults, this is more likely to occur if a person is intoxicated or has a reduced level of consciousness/awareness • Toddlers commonly inhale other objects	• Upper airway obstruction due to inhaled foreign body such as a piece of food • This is a medical emergency • Go to the emergency room or call an ambulance at once
Sudden shortness of breath at rest with choking; occurring when inhalation of food or a small object is unlikely	• Severe distress with inability to take in air despite desperate efforts, collapse, blue skin and gums, loss of consciousness (in complete obstruction) • Rapid labored breathing with loud harsh noise while breathing in, gagging (in partial blockage of the airway)		• Inflammation of the airways may be caused by an insect bite or sting, an allergic reaction to food or a new medication, inhalation of hot gases or other toxins • Eating peanuts is a relatively common cause of severe reaction, which may occur in a person without a known history of peanut allergy	• Upper airway obstruction due to swelling of structures in the throat • This is a medical emergency • Go to the emergency room or call an ambulance at once

Bruising

Bruising is a normal reaction to injury and is caused by blood leaking from damaged blood vessels under the skin. Bruises start off as a red mark, quickly turn blue then fade into a green or yellow color as they heal. Frequent or severe bruising after a minor injury could be a sign of an underlying disorder of the blood vessels or the ability of the blood to clot. Any unusual bruising should be checked by a doctor.

SYMPTOM CHARACTERISTIC	ASSOCIATED SYMPTOMS	AGGRAVATING OR ALLEVIATING FACTORS	OTHER RELEVANT FACTORS	POSSIBLE CAUSE AND ACTION
Bruise confined to a single area	• Pain, tenderness, may be a lump under the bruise if severe	• Cold compresses can reduce the bruising	• Bruising occurs in healthy people, usually after injury • Women tend to bruise more easily then men • Bruising is often more extensive in the elderly	• Bruise resulting from minor injury • Placing an ice pack over the injured site may reduce bruising • See your doctor if you are worried or if symptoms persist
Extensive dark purple bruises in an elderly person, often on arms or legs	• Pain, tenderness, may be a lump under the bruise if severe	• Cold compresses can reduce the bruising	• Usually a history of minor injury • Occurs in the elderly due to weakening of the blood vessels and skin	• Senile purpura (bruising due to old age) • Creams available from your pharmacist can speed healing of the bruise • See your doctor if you are worried or if symptoms persist

SYMPTOM CHARACTERISTIC	ASSOCIATED SYMPTOMS	AGGRAVATING OR ALLEVIATING FACTORS	OTHER RELEVANT FACTORS	POSSIBLE CAUSE AND ACTION
Bruising (cont.)				
Slow healing bruises	• Slow healing wounds, frequent infections, tingling and numbness in the hands or feet	• Improving blood sugar control can minimize complications of the disease	• May occur in people with a history of poorly controlled diabetes	• Diabetes • See your doctor
Bruising following minor injuries	• May be prolonged bleeding after cuts	• Cold compresses can reduce the bruising	• Medications that may be associated with increased bruising include aspirin, cortisone-type drugs (corticosteroids), non-steroidal anti-inflammatory drugs, blood thinning drugs (anticoagulants)	• Medication-related bruising • See your doctor
Development of bruising and tiny red dots on the skin	• Nosebleeds or bleeding from gums in severe cases • Heavy menstrual bleeding in young women	• Bruising settles as disorder resolves and clotting returns to normal	• Most common in children from 2– 4 years of age and young women • Illness may be prolonged in adults but is usually self-limiting in children without treatment	• Thrombocytopenia • See your doctor
Scattered bruises of varying ages, appearing over a period of weeks	• Severe fatigue, loss of appetite, pallor, episodes of fever, bone pain	• Treatment of underlying condition will improve the function of bone marrow and blood clotting	• May be a history of frequent infections	• Leukemia • See your doctor at once
Frequent, often severe bruising without significant injury; bruises may be firm and hard due to blood clotting under the skin	• Other signs of bleeding may be also present such as painful or swollen joints, excessive bleeding following cuts or dental extractions, blood in the urine • Symptoms of brain hemorrhage include irritability, drowsiness, headache, confusion, nausea, vomiting and double vision • Other internal bleeding may result in breathing problems, weakness, pallor or loss of consciousness	• Visible or internal bleeding may occur without any obvious trauma • Signs of bleeding (e.g. brain hemorrhage) may occur several days after an injury	• Hemophilia occurs only in males • The worldwide incidence is one in 10,000 males • Hemophilia is an inherited disorder, so there may be family history of a bleeding tendency	• Hemophilia or other bleeding disorder • See your doctor • If the person is bleeding or shows signs of internal bleeding, this is a medical emergency • Go to the emergency room or call an ambulance at once

Chest pain

Chest pain typically arises from the heart, lungs, chest wall or esophagus. Occasionally, chest pain is due to disease of upper abdominal structures such as the stomach or gallbladder. Any chest pain warrants full examination by a doctor.

SYMPTOM CHARACTERISTIC	ASSOCIATED SYMPTOMS	AGGRAVATING OR ALLEVIATING FACTORS	OTHER RELEVANT FACTORS	POSSIBLE CAUSE AND ACTION
Repeated episodes of central chest heaviness, pressure, tightness or discomfort occurring on exertion and relieved by rest; often the pain radiates into the neck and/or left arm, or the arm may feel numb or tingly; attacks usually last a few minutes, sometimes up to 15 minutes	• Shortness of breath or anxiety may be present	• Alleviated by rest or nitrate tablet taken under the tongue	• Angina pectoris occurs most frequently in the middle-aged or elderly • Rarely occurs in children with congenital heart problems	• Angina pectoris • See your doctor
Central burning pain radiating up the throat	• Bitter taste in the mouth or return of bitter fluids into the mouth from the stomach	• Relieved by antacids	• Heartburn occurs in adults and children and is a symptoms of gastroesophageal reflux • Attacks are often provoked by lying flat in bed at night, or bending over	• Heartburn • Avoid large meals, eating within a few hours of bedtime and any specific foods which provoke symptoms • See your doctor
Dull cramp-like central chest pain which occurs only after swallowing; the pain can be quite severe	• Difficulty swallowing		• Esophageal spasm may occur as a result of gastroesophageal reflux	• Esophageal spasm (a disturbance of the contractions of the esophagus which usually push food through to the stomach) • See your doctor
Severe central chest heaviness, pressure, tightness or discomfort which usually lasts more than 30 minutes; often the pain radiates into the neck and/or left arm; onset at rest or on exercise but without relief after resting	• Shortness of breath, sweating, cold, faintness, nausea or vomiting, palpitations • Symptoms may be relatively mild in a person with a past history of heart disease		• Myocardial infarction most commonly occurs in middle-aged or older people	• Myocardial infarction (heart attack) • This is a medical emergency • Go to the emergency room or call an ambulance at once
Sharp stabbing chest pain within a well-defined area, occurring on or worsened by breathing in	• Fever, cough with sputum that may contain pus, shortness of breath	• Pain is aggravated by taking a deep breath, or by coughing	• Pneumonia may result from a bacterial infection in previously healthy people, or due to lowering of resistance resulting from another illness (e.g. chronic obstructive pulmonary disease or cancer)	• Pneumonia • See your doctor at once

SYMPTOM CHARACTERISTIC	ASSOCIATED SYMPTOMS	AGGRAVATING OR ALLEVIATING FACTORS	OTHER RELEVANT FACTORS	POSSIBLE CAUSE AND ACTION
Chest pain (cont.)				
Sharp stabbing chest pain within a well-defined area, worse on breathing in; may affect one or both sides of the chest	• Shortness of breath • Coughing up blood	• Pain is aggravated by taking a deep breath, or by coughing	• Predisposing factors include a period of immobilization or bed rest, recent surgical procedure, recent childbirth, history of a blood clot in the leg, the use of oral contraceptives	• Loss of blood supply to an area of lung tissue (pulmonary infarct), usually due to blockage of blood vessels by a clot • See your doctor at once
Sudden onset of sharp localized pain on one side of the chest, worse on breathing in	• Shortness of breath	• Pain is aggravated by taking a deep breath, or by coughing	• Pneumothorax may occur in adults and children, either spontaneously or as a result of injury to the chest • Most often occurs in young healthy people without a prior lung problem • Predisposing factors include cystic fibrosis chronic obstructive lung disease	• Pneumothorax • See your doctor at once
Dull aching localized pain, usually on one side, and worse with movement (turning, twisting, bending), straining (e.g. lifting), possibly by coughing or deep breathing in	• Tenderness of the chest wall	• Aggravated by movement	• May follow trauma or unusual exertion	• Injury to the chest wall • See your doctor
Constant burning pain on one side of the chest followed by rash	• Painful blistering rash appears in the painful area a few days after the initial pain	• The pain is not affected by breathing, posture or exertion	• Shingles mainly occurs in adults over 60 years, and is due to reactivation of the same virus responsible for chickenpox • In children, chickenpox frequently causes a painful blistering rash on the chest	• Shingles • See your doctor at once
Sudden severe central chest pain	• Severe shortness of breath, fainting • Skin may be cold, clammy, pale		• Predisposing factors include a period of immobilization or bed rest, recent surgical procedure, recent childbirth, history of a blood clot in the leg, use of oral contraceptives	• Pulmonary embolism • This is a medical emergency • Go to the emergency room or call an ambulance at once

SYMPTOM CHARACTERISTIC	ASSOCIATED SYMPTOMS	AGGRAVATING OR ALLEVIATING FACTORS	OTHER RELEVANT FACTORS	POSSIBLE CAUSE AND ACTION
Sudden onset of severe tearing pain of the front or back of the chest which moves as time progresses; the pain often radiates through to the back or may be felt predominantly in the back of the chest; pain may also involve the arms, neck, trunk or legs	• Shortness of breath, fainting • Complications may cause symptoms in other bodily systems (e.g. paralysis of the legs, mental disturbances, bloody diarrhea)		• Most often occurs in middle-aged or elderly men with hypertension	• Tearing along the inside wall of the aorta (dissecting aneurysm) • This is a medical emergency • Go to the emergency room or call an ambulance at once
Central chest tightness or discomfort	• Shortness of breath, wheezing	• Symptoms may be triggered by exposure to cigarette smoke or air pollution, exposure to pollens, cold air, exercise, respiratory infections	• Asthma occurs more commonly in adults or children with a history of hay fever or eczema, or a family history of asthma, eczema or allergies • Usually more frequent in winter, following a common cold or when pollen levels are high • May be exacerbated by exposure to pets or cigarette smoke	• Asthma • See your doctor at once

Constipation

Constipation is the most common symptom relating to the gastrointestinal tract. Different people have different normal bowel habits—for a particular person it may be usual to pass anywhere between three stools per week and three per day. In most cases, constipation can be thought of in terms of a change away from an individual's usual pattern. Sometimes a person may by troubled by very hard stools or difficulty in expelling stools rather than a reduction in frequency.

Frequently the cause of constipation relates to lifestyle factors. Laxatives are not usually needed and can themselves cause constipation if used inappropriately, so it is preferable to seek medical advice before taking them. Occasionally serious underlying pathology is responsible, or constipation is a manifestation of disease in another bodily system. Prescription and over-the-counter medicines commonly cause or aggravate constipation.

SYMPTOM CHARACTERISTIC	ASSOCIATED SYMPTOMS	AGGRAVATING OR ALLEVIATING FACTORS	OTHER RELEVANT FACTORS	POSSIBLE CAUSE AND ACTION
Stools are dry and hard and may require straining to expel; the condition may be long-standing	• Vague discomfort in the abdomen • Children may also have a sense of bloating, irritability, soiling of underwear	• Can be alleviated by increasing your dietary fiber intake, which tends to increase the weight and water content of the stools and speed up their transit through the gut	• Most common in adults; may occur in children • Simple constipation is commonly due to a low-fiber diet, inadequate fluid intake, lack of exercise • May be triggered by any upset of eating or bowel routine (e.g. travel, recent bed rest or immobilization, recent dietary changes), ignoring the urge to have a bowel movement, recently toilet-trained children	• Simple constipation • Increase your dietary fiber intake from vegetables, fruits, and whole grains, avoid excessive intake of fatty or sugary foods, engage in some form of physical activity • See your doctor if you are worried or if symptoms persist, or if constipation occurs in a child

SYMPTOM CHARACTERISTIC	ASSOCIATED SYMPTOMS	AGGRAVATING OR ALLEVIATING FACTORS	OTHER RELEVANT FACTORS	POSSIBLE CAUSE AND ACTION
Constipation (cont.)				
Inconsistent frequency and/or character of stools; may be long-standing	• May have a sense of bloating or vague abdominal discomfort	• May be aggravated by stress	• Most commonly young adults, but may occur at any age	• Irritable bowel syndrome • See your doctor
Recent change from usual bowel habit or worsening of any pre-existing problem; may experience an early morning rush to go to the toilet	• Vague abdominal discomfort or crampy abdominal pains, blood or mucus in the stools, weight loss, loss of appetite, general feeling of being unwell • Laxative use less effective than previously		• More common with advancing age • Usually occurs after 40 years of age, but occasionally may occur at younger age • Predisposing conditions for bowel cancer include benign polyps, familial polyposis (an inherited condition in which many polyps form in the bowel at puberty), ulcerative colitis	• Bowel tumor • See your doctor
Passage of stools causes pain, so is consciously avoided by the person	• May be associated with urgent or painful desire to pass stools or fresh blood on the toilet paper		• May occur at any age • If an urgent or painful desire to pass stools is present, this points toward a potentially serious rectal lesion	• Anal tear/fissure, hemorrhoids, tumor of the anus or rectum • See your doctor
Stools are small, hard and are passed infrequently (e.g. once every few days); may be a recurrent problem	• Soiling of underwear		• Most likely in the elderly person • May be triggered by periods of bed rest or immobilization, poor fluid intake	• Feces wedged firmly in the rectum • See your doctor

Cough

Coughing is the body's way of clearing the airways of secretions or foreign material. A cough may be caused by any irritation or inflammation of the airways or lungs. Any persistent cough should be assessed by a doctor.

SYMPTOM CHARACTERISTIC	ASSOCIATED SYMPTOMS	AGGRAVATING OR ALLEVIATING FACTORS	OTHER RELEVANT FACTORS	POSSIBLE CAUSE AND ACTION
Rapid onset of cough that is dry or productive (produces phlegm)	• Runny nose, sore throat, fever, fatigue • If sputum is present it is usually clear or white	• Cough may be aggravated by cold air	• May follow recent contact with person with cough or cold • Often occurs in winter	• Infectious cough, often caused by a virus which causes irritation of the lining of the windpipe and the production of mucus • Usually self-limiting without treatment • See your doctor if you are worried or if symptoms persist

SYMPTOM CHARACTERISTIC	ASSOCIATED SYMPTOMS	AGGRAVATING OR ALLEVIATING FACTORS	OTHER RELEVANT FACTORS	POSSIBLE CAUSE AND ACTION
Acute onset of moist cough productive of phlegm	• Fever, shortness of breath, fatigue, sharp chest pain on breathing in due to inflammation of the pleura (pleurisy) • Sputum produced is yellow or green and may contain some blood	• Cough may be aggravated by cold air, smoky environment or exercise	• May follow recent cold or flu • More common in smokers	• Bronchitis or pneumonia caused by an infection • If the cause is bacterial, you may require treatment with antibiotics • See your doctor
Episodic dry cough with tight feeling in chest, often occurring at night or after exercise	• Wheeze, shortness of breath	• Usually more frequent in winter, following a common cold or when pollen levels are high • May be exacerbated by exposure to pets or cigarette smoke	• History of hay fever or eczema • Family history of asthma, eczema or allergies	• Asthma • Any episodic cough, especially if associated with wheeze should be assessed by a doctor • Management of acute episodes of asthma usually requires inhaled medications to open the airways (bronchodilator or "reliever" medication) • Continuous preventative medication may be required even when cough is not present • See your doctor if having difficulty breathing
Sudden onset of cough which persists, without other explanation (e.g. signs of a cold infection)	• Occasional wheeze		• History of choking • More common in children • Small objects such as peanuts or beads are commonly responsible	• Inhalation of a foreign body • See your doctor at once
Chronic cough, often productive of phlegm	• Shortness of breath on exertion, wheezing		• History of smoking or exposure to cigarette smoke	• Chronic bronchitis or chronic lung disease • See your doctor • Any change in the nature of a chronic "smoker's cough" should be checked by a doctor at once to rule out cancer of the airways (lung cancer)

Cramp

A cramp is a sudden, prolonged and painful contraction of one or a group of muscles. Although the term "cramp" is often used to describe abdominal pain (abdominal cramps) and period pain (menstrual cramps), this table will focus on cramps of voluntary muscles of the body. Muscular cramps occur very commonly and are usually benign. Occasionally they may indicate a serious underlying disease process so it is important to have any frequent or persistent cramps assessed by a doctor.

SYMPTOM CHARACTERISTIC	ASSOCIATED SYMPTOMS	AGGRAVATING OR ALLEVIATING FACTORS	OTHER RELEVANT FACTORS	POSSIBLE CAUSE AND ACTION
Sudden, prolonged and painful contraction of a small group of muscles	• If severe, tenderness and weakness may remain after the cramp has resolved	• Usually worse at night	• Most common in the elderly, often occurs in the calves	• Benign cramps • See your doctor

SYMPTOM CHARACTERISTIC	ASSOCIATED SYMPTOMS	AGGRAVATING OR ALLEVIATING FACTORS	OTHER RELEVANT FACTORS	POSSIBLE CAUSE AND ACTION
Cramp (cont.)				
Sudden, prolonged and painful contraction of muscles		• Occurs during or following strenuous exercise • Rest and gentle stretching of muscles can ease the spasm	• May occur after insufficient warm-up before strenuous exercise	• Benign cramps induced by exercise • Thorough warm-up and stretching before exercise can help prevent cramps • See your doctor if you are worried or if symptoms persist
Very prolonged painful contraction of muscles, usually in the extremities	• Occur during strenuous exercise involving excessive sweating	• Excessive sweating, heavy clothes, dehydration	• Sometimes known as "miner's cramps" or "stoker's cramps"	• Heat cramps • Replacement of depleted salts and water by consuming electrolyte enriched drinks may relieve symptoms • See your doctor if you are worried or if symptoms persist
Spasms of muscles in a particular position, usually the hands		• Aggravated by long periods of repetition of the same position or movements	• Common in writers using a pen, or musicians using repetitive fine hand movements	• Writers' cramp • Usually settles with rest • See a physical therapist or your doctor if cramps persist
Frequent generalized cramps in muscle groups anywhere in the body		• If electrolyte imbalance is present, correction of this (e.g. by hospital treatment) will alleviate cramps	• May be a sign of underlying neurological disease or electrolyte imbalance • Motor neuron disease is relatively rare, occurring in less than 0.01percent of people; more common in men than women, and occurs most often at around 60 years of age	• Motor neuron disease • See your doctor

Diarrhea

Diarrhea refers to the passing of frequent and abnormally loose or watery bowel actions. Diarrhea is often the result of gastrointestinal infection and lasts only a few days. Sometimes diarrhea can be caused by a more serious disease process. The consistency, color and frequency of the diarrhea will give valuable clues with regard to the underlying cause. Any prolonged or unusual diarrhea should be assessed by a doctor to rule out an underlying medical condition.

SYMPTOM CHARACTERISTIC	ASSOCIATED SYMPTOMS	AGGRAVATING OR ALLEVIATING FACTORS	OTHER RELEVANT FACTORS	POSSIBLE CAUSE AND ACTION
Abrupt onset of watery diarrhea; mucus often present but rarely blood; lasts 1–3 days	• Vomiting, mild abdominal pain, low-grade fever • May follow an upper respiratory tract infection	• Eating and drinking may aggravate diarrhea	• Very common in children, especially in winter • Highly contagious, spread by fecal–oral transmission	• Viral gastroenteritis • Oral rehydration is usually sufficient treatment • Medications to reduce nausea and vomiting, and acetaminophen (paracetamol) can be helpful • Contact your doctor for advice

SYMPTOM CHARACTERISTIC	ASSOCIATED SYMPTOMS	AGGRAVATING OR ALLEVIATING FACTORS	OTHER RELEVANT FACTORS	POSSIBLE CAUSE AND ACTION
Abrupt onset of watery diarrhea, moderate in quantity, lasting 1–3 days	• Generally painless, although mild abdominal cramps may be present • Low-grade fever or vomiting may be present	• Eating and drinking may aggravate diarrhea	• May be history of ingesting poorly prepared food or travel to South America, Africa or Asia	• A bacterial infection • See your doctor at once
Abrupt onset of watery diarrhea, copious in quantity, lasting 2–7 days	• Effortless vomiting usually follows the onset of diarrhea, nausea usually absent • Dehydration, muscle cramps • May cause serious, possibly fatal dehydration within hours		• Most common in developing countries including India, Bangladesh, African and Latin American countries • Often occurs in epidemics • Usually spread by drinking contaminated water • More common and serious in children	• Cholera • This is a medical emergency • Go to the emergency room or call an ambulance at once • Where medical help is unavailable, dehydration may be alleviated by maintaining fluid intake with solutions containing glucose and salt, or by breast feeding in babies
Abrupt onset of diarrhea containing blood or mucus, with an offensive odor	• High fever, aches and pains, nausea and vomiting, moderate to severe abdominal cramps, frequent urge to pass stool with little result	• Eating and drinking may aggravate diarrhea	• May be a history of travel to a developing country or simultaneous illness in people who have shared contaminated food	• Food poisoning • Antidiarrheal agents are not recommended for this type of diarrhea • See your doctor at once
Abrupt onset of watery diarrhea; symptoms may persist for weeks	• Mild abdominal pain, bloating, flatulence, malabsorption (passage of larger volume stools than normal due to inability to absorb food), low-grade fever	• Eating and drinking may aggravate diarrhea	• Often a history of travel • Common in children	• Infection with protozoal organism called giardia (giardiasis) • See your doctor
Abrupt onset of diarrhea while taking antibiotic medication	• Range from mild abdominal pain and bloating to severe abdominal cramps, fever and bloody diarrhea	• Cessation of antibiotics will generally relieve the symptoms	• May be simply a side effect caused by overgrowth of gastrointestinal flora or due to colitis caused by overgrowth of the bacteria *Clostridium difficile*	• Antibiotic-related diarrhea • See your doctor
Chronic intermittent diarrhea with mucus, sometimes alternating with constipation	• Abdominal pain, flatulence, bloating	• Emotional stress can aggravate symptoms • Increasing dietary fiber can improve symptoms	• Most common in young to middle-aged women	• Irritable bowel syndrome • See your doctor
Watery diarrhea; no mucus or blood	• Recent constipation, bloating and abdominal discomfort • No fever or other signs of infection • Fecal incontinence may occur	• Diet lacking in fiber can aggravate condition	• May be a history of chronic constipation • Watery stool leaks around the compacted feces	• Chronic constipation with overflow diarrhea • See your doctor

SYMPTOM CHARACTERISTIC	ASSOCIATED SYMPTOMS	AGGRAVATING OR ALLEVIATING FACTORS	OTHER RELEVANT FACTORS	POSSIBLE CAUSE AND ACTION
Diarrhea (cont.)				
Loose, bulky, offensively smelling stools	• Abdominal bloating and discomfort, flatulence, weight loss, signs of malnutrition or poor growth	• Worse with certain types of food such as dairy products or wheat products	• May be a history of gallbladder disease, disorders of the pancreas	• Poor absorption of food from the bowel due to lactose intolerance or celiac disease • Malabsorption • See your doctor
Gradual onset of frequent, loose stools containing blood and mucus	• Abdominal pain, weight loss, abdominal tenderness, bloating and passage of larger volume stools than normal due to inability to absorb food • May be associated arthritis or skin lesions	• Anti-inflammatory medication can relieve symptoms	• There may be a family history of inflammatory bowel disease	• Inflammatory bowel disease • Ulcerative colitis and Crohn's disease are the most common of these • See your doctor

Dizziness

Dizziness is a commonly reported symptom. The term "dizziness" is used to describe a variety of sensations such as lightheadedness, faintness, spinning or giddiness. Dizziness usually means either faintness (the feeling that precedes a faint) or vertigo (a false sense of movement). It is often a brief sensation, however persistent or frequent episodes of dizziness occasionally herald a serious medical condition so it is important to have these assessed by a doctor.

SYMPTOM CHARACTERISTIC	ASSOCIATED SYMPTOMS	AGGRAVATING OR ALLEVIATING FACTORS	OTHER RELEVANT FACTORS	POSSIBLE CAUSE AND ACTION
Faintness	• Lightheadedness, visual blurring, loss of vision, heaviness of limbs, loss of consciousness	• Raising legs may improve blood supply to the brain and alleviate the dizziness	• Usually a brief episode	• Faint caused by reduced blood supply to the brain • Causes include low blood pressure on standing, disturbance in heartbeat rhythm, dehydration • See your doctor at once
Sensation of movement or spinning	• Nausea	• Unfamiliar head movements or motion	• Commonly occurs while traveling in cars or on boats	• Motion sickness • Medication to relieve nausea and vomiting can relieve symptoms • See your doctor if you are worried or if symptoms persist
Sudden feeling of dizziness or spinning lasting a few seconds	• Nausea	• Occurs on changes to the position of the head such as rolling in bed	• Related to the blockage of fluid in the balance centers of the inner ear sometimes by tiny "stones"	• Benign paroxysmal positional vertigo • Your doctor can show you simple head movements to unblock the inner ear • Antiemetic medication can relieve symptoms • See your doctor

SYMPTOM CHARACTERISTIC	ASSOCIATED SYMPTOMS	AGGRAVATING OR ALLEVIATING FACTORS	OTHER RELEVANT FACTORS	POSSIBLE CAUSE AND ACTION
Severe episodes of dizziness with a sensation of spinning or linear movement	• Nausea, tendency to fall toward the side of the abnormality, rapid involuntary movements of the eyes	• Aggravated by movement of the head	• May occur only once or lead to recurrent episodes of vertigo	• Acute labyrinthitis caused by infection, poor blood supply to the inner ear or toxicity (drugs or alcohol) • See your doctor
Recurrent episodes of dizziness lasting 20 minutes to 2 hours	• Ringing in the ears (tinnitus), feeling of fullness of the ears, balance problems, nausea, hearing loss	• Reducing dietary salt, caffeine, alcohol may help control episodes	• May be caused by fluid in the canals of the inner ear	• Menière's disease • Full medical assessment is required • Investigations to rule out other causes of symptoms such as acoustic neuroma may be required • Diuretics can help prevent attacks, antiemetics can provide symptomatic relief • See your doctor

Ear pain (earache)

Ear pain is usually due to increased pressure in the middle ear or infection of the ear or surrounding structures. In addition to significant distress and discomfort, ear infections can lead to serious complications such as perforation of the eardrum or spread of an infection to the covering of the brain (meningitis). It is important to seek a doctor's advice, since antibiotic therapy may be needed.

SYMPTOM CHARACTERISTIC	ASSOCIATED SYMPTOMS	AGGRAVATING OR ALLEVIATING FACTORS	OTHER RELEVANT FACTORS	POSSIBLE CAUSE AND ACTION
Dull deep ear pain, feeling of fullness or pressure	• Nasal and sinus congestion, sore throat	• Swallowing can relieve the pressure in the middle ear	• Swelling and blockage of the tubes draining the middle ear results in increased pressure	• Fluid and pressure buildup in the middle ear • Treatment with decongestant medication may help improve the drainage from the middle ear • See your doctor if you are worried or if symptoms persist
Rapid onset of severe deep ear pain	• Fever, hearing loss, feeling of pressure in the ear, discharge if perforation of eardrum occurs, dizziness may occur if inner ear is involved	• Pulling on the external ear does not increase pain • Spontaneous perforation of the eardrum will relieve pain but prolong hearing loss	• Fever may be the only symptom in young children	• Infection of the middle ear (otitis media) caused by a virus or bacteria • See your doctor
Rapid onset of severe pain behind the ear	• Fever, swelling and tenderness over the mastoid (bony process behind the ear containing air cells that are linked to the middle ear)	• Pressure applied over the mastoid process increases the discomfort	• May be a history of otitis media as infection can spread from the middle ear to the mastoid • Meningitis is a complication of mastoid infection	• Bacterial infection of the mastoid air cells (mastoiditis) • See your doctor at once

SYMPTOM CHARACTERISTIC	ASSOCIATED SYMPTOMS	AGGRAVATING OR ALLEVIATING FACTORS	OTHER RELEVANT FACTORS	POSSIBLE CAUSE AND ACTION
Ear pain (earache) (cont.)				
Itching progressing to throbbing pain of ear	• Swelling of external ear canal, foul smelling discharge, hearing loss, enlarged glands in the neck	• Pain is aggravated by pulling on the external ear (pinna) or chewing	• Trauma to the ear canal, swimming, humid conditions, skin disorders such as eczema can predispose to infection	• Bacterial infection of the external ear canal (otitis externa) • See your doctor. Treatment with antibiotic and anti-inflammatory drops may be required • Careful cleansing of the ear canal as instructed by a doctor will aid healing

Eye problems

Mild redness and irritation of the eye is common and usually has a simple underlying cause. Symptoms to beware of include sudden or severe eye pain and changes in vision, especially when associated with a red eye. If in doubt, it is safer to have a doctor check the eye early to prevent any long-term complications. See also entries on *eyesight problems* and *eyelid problems*.

SYMPTOM CHARACTERISTIC	ASSOCIATED SYMPTOMS	AGGRAVATING OR ALLEVIATING FACTORS	OTHER RELEVANT FACTORS	POSSIBLE CAUSE AND ACTION
Sore, dry, gritty eyes	• May be mild redness, normal vision	• Tiredness and the wearing of contact lenses can increase eye irritation	• More common in the elderly • Some medications can predispose to dry eyes (decongestants, diuretics, sleeping pills)	• Dry eyes due to reduced production of tears • Artificial lubricants (or tears) can relieve symptoms • See your doctor
Sore, red eye, yellow sticky discharge, affecting one or both eyes	• Sensitivity to light, itching, burning, gritty feeling on moving the eyes, normal vision	• Rubbing eyes increases itching and discharge	• Highly contagious, often spreads from one eye to the other	• Conjunctivitis caused by a bacteria or virus • Gently cleanse eyes with cool water and avoid wearing contact lenses • See your doctor if you are worried or if symptoms persist
Rapid onset of red, painful eye	• Blurred vision, sensitivity to light, increased tear production, small pupil		• More common in people with joint diseases such as ankylosing spondylitis or Behçet's disease or other autoimmune diseases	• Iritis • See your doctor at once
Rapid onset of red, extremely painful eye on one side	• Nausea, vomiting and blurred vision, cornea may be hazy due to swelling, pupil becomes fixed and dilated in severe cases • Episode may be preceded by vision disturbances such as halos around lights	• Symptoms worsen at night when the pupil dilates • Some medications can make glaucoma worse such as some antidepressants or steroids	• May be a family history of glaucoma • More common in older people with diabetes or hypertension	• Glaucoma • See your doctor at once
Rapid onset of eye pain, oversensitivity to light and blurred vision on one side	• May be a visible white spot on the clear surface of the eye	• Movement of the eye aggravates pain	• May be a history of trauma to the eye such as a scratch	• Corneal ulceration due to infection, exposure or trauma • See your doctor at once

Eyelid problems

The eyelids protect the delicate surface of the eye, so any abnormality of the lid can affect the eye. Most problems of the eyelid are due to infection or structural weakening. See also entries on *eye problems* and *eyesight problems*.

SYMPTOM CHARACTERISTIC	ASSOCIATED SYMPTOMS	AGGRAVATING OR ALLEVIATING FACTORS	OTHER RELEVANT FACTORS	POSSIBLE CAUSE AND ACTION
In-turning of the eyelids	• Eyelashes rub the eye's surface causing irritation	• Worsens with age	• Lower lid affected more than the upper lid	• Entropion • See your doctor
Lower eyelid drooping outwards	• Watering of eye, irritation of eye, ulceration of the eye	• Cold wind and dust can cause irritation to eye due to exposure	• More common in the elderly and people with facial nerve damage	• Ectropion • See your doctor
Drooping of the upper eyelid	• Obstruction of visual field if pupil is obscured, brow ache, tired expression	• Worsens with age and when tired	• Can be a sign of nerve damage or muscular diseases such as muscular dystrophy or myasthenia gravis; occasionally present from birth (congenital ptosis)	• Ptosis • See your doctor
Firm, tender, red lump in or on the edge of the eyelid	• May point like a pimple, vision normal	• Rubbing the eye will aggravate the lump	• Inflammation or cysts in the glands within the eyelid margin (meibomian gland) may result in swelling that remains after healing	• Infection in a hair follicle or gland of the eyelid (stye) • Apply warm compresses and take mild analgesics • See your doctor if you are worried or if symptoms persist
Redness, soreness and scaling of the edge of the eyelid	• Itchiness of eyelid, vision normal • Eyelids may appear greasy, ulcerated or crusted	• Rubbing eyes can spread the infection	• Blepharitis most commonly occurs with acne rosacea or dandruff (seborrheic dermatitis)	• Inflammation of the eyelid (blepharitis) • Cleanse eyes gently with saline • Wash hands after touching eyes and use a clean tissue or cloth on each eye to avoid spreading infection from one eye to the other • See your doctor if you are worried or if symptoms persist
Redness, swelling and tenderness of the eyelid and surrounding face	• Fever, difficulty moving the eye or protrusion of the eyeball is a sign of severe infection	• Rubbing eyes will increase redness and swelling	• Common in children • Severe infection can lead to abscess of the eye-socket (orbit) or spread via the blood to the covering of the brain (meningitis)	• Inflammation within the tissue around the eye (periorbital cellulitis) • See your doctor at once

SYMPTOM CHARACTERISTIC	ASSOCIATED SYMPTOMS	AGGRAVATING OR ALLEVIATING FACTORS	OTHER RELEVANT FACTORS	POSSIBLE CAUSE AND ACTION

Eyesight problems

Disturbances of vision are very common. Whether vision is just blurred or there is complete or partial loss of eyesight, visual disturbance is a very distressing and disabling symptom. The eyes are extremely delicate organs and can be damaged by many diseases involving other parts of the body. This section will concentrate on conditions localized to the eye. See also entries on *eye problems* and *eyelid problems*.

SYMPTOM CHARACTERISTIC	ASSOCIATED SYMPTOMS	AGGRAVATING OR ALLEVIATING FACTORS	OTHER RELEVANT FACTORS	POSSIBLE CAUSE AND ACTION
Gradual onset of distorted vision, blurred vision especially when reading	• Central vision is affected but peripheral vision remains intact	• Tends to get worse with age	• Most common cause of loss of vision in the elderly	• Macular degeneration • Have your vision tested as you may need glasses • See your doctor if you are worried or if symptoms persist
Gradual onset of cloudy, foggy vision, distorted color, halos around lights	• Pupil of the eye may appear milky instead of black • Frequent changes in eyeglass prescription	• Vision is worse at night with glare from bright lights	• Cataracts are frequently a complication of diabetes	• Cataracts • See your doctor
Loss of parts of peripheral vision (visual field defects)	• Vision loss is the first symptom	• Early detection and treatment is the only way to prevent permanent vision loss • Those people at risk should be tested for glaucoma	• Risk factors include older age, black race, diabetes, hypertension, nearsightedness and a family history of glaucoma	• Glaucoma • See your doctor at once
Rapid development of hazy vision in one or both eyes lasting days to weeks	• Distortion of color, eye movements may be painful • Pupil is less reactive to light on the affected side	• Symptoms resolve without treatment	• Leads to an increased risk of developing multiple sclerosis	• Inflammation of the optic nerve (optic neuritis) • See your doctor at once
Rapid loss of vision in one eye	• Recent vision disturbances such as "floaters" (dark spots or shapes floating in the field of vision) due to previous small bleeds	• Symptoms depend of the size of the bleed into the vitreous humor (gel-like substance within the eye)	• Common in diabetics with disease of the blood vessels of the retina	• Hemorrhage into the fluid in the eye (vitreous hemorrhage) • See your doctor at once
Sudden loss of vision on one side	• Headache, tenderness of the temple area, pain in the jaw on chewing, fever • May be associated with muscle and joint pains and fatigue	• Anti-inflammatory drugs may relieve symptoms	• Rare disease occurring in the elderly • More common in women	• Temporal arteritis • See your doctor at once
Sudden, painless deterioration of vision in one eye	• Vision loss may be moderate to severe (unable to count fingers)	• Symptoms usually resolve over several months without treatment	• More common in people with glaucoma, atherosclerosis and high blood pressure	• Blockage of the central retinal vein • See your doctor at once

SYMPTOM CHARACTERISTIC	ASSOCIATED SYMPTOMS	AGGRAVATING OR ALLEVIATING FACTORS	OTHER RELEVANT FACTORS	POSSIBLE CAUSE AND ACTION
Sudden, complete, painless loss of vision in one eye	• Pupil does not react to light on one side	• Firm pressure on the eye may dislodge the obstruction	• More common in people with carotid artery atherosclerosis • Vision loss is often permanent	• Blockage of the central retinal artery • This is a medical emergency • Go to the emergency room or call an ambulance at once
Sudden painless loss of vision in one eye, like a curtain falling down	• Recent visual disturbances such as flashing lights or spots before the eyes	• Pressure on eye may aggravate vision loss	• May be a history of trauma, glaucoma, cataract surgery or nearsightedness	• Detached retina • This is a medical emergency • Go to the emergency room or call an ambulance at once

Facial pain

Facial pain can be a severe and distressing symptom. Facial neuralgia (recurrent stabbing, burning facial pain in a particular area of the face) may be severe, and do not respond well to simple painkillers. Any worrying facial pain should be assessed by a doctor.

SYMPTOM CHARACTERISTIC	ASSOCIATED SYMPTOMS	AGGRAVATING OR ALLEVIATING FACTORS	OTHER RELEVANT FACTORS	POSSIBLE CAUSE AND ACTION
Aching pain in the forehead, cheeks and upper jaw	• Feeling of pressure, nasal discharge, discharge from the back of the nose into throat, fever, tenderness of the forehead and facial bones	• Leaning forward can worsen pain	• May be a history of upper respiratory tract infection	• Sinus congestion or sinus infection (sinusitis) • Try decongestant medications from your pharmacist • See your doctor if you are worried or if symptoms persist
Episodes of sudden excruciating pain in the lips, gum, cheek or chin on one side of the face, lasting seconds to minutes	• Episodes occur regularly, day or night for several weeks	• Touching face, chewing, smiling, talking, blowing nose can trigger pain	• Usually occurs in the elderly • More common in women than men • There is usually no known cause	• Tic douloureux (trigeminal neuralgia) • See your doctor at once
Episodes of aching or burning pain on one side of the face	• Numbness, tingling in the same area	• Touching or moving the face can trigger an episode of pain	• May be a history of shingles	• Pain following shingles (post-zoster neuralgia) • See your doctor at once
Episodes of burning, stabbing pain, usually on one side of the face lasting up to an hour	• Numbness or tingling, may be followed by a headache	• Painkillers may relieve the pain	• May be a history of migraine • More common in women	• Migrainous neuralgia • See your doctor at once
Severe aching pain from the side of the face, in front of the ear on one side	• Tenderness over upper jaw joint (temporomandibular joint), malocclusion of teeth	• Chewing makes pain worse	• Usually occurs in elderly women • May be a history of rheumatoid arthritis	• Arthritis of the temporomandibular joint • See your doctor
Ache in the upper or lower jaw on one side	• Teeth sensitive to hot or cold, pain on chewing, feeling of pressure in jaw, may be fever	• Painkillers should relieve the pain	• May be a history of previous problems with teeth or fillings	• Tooth decay or abscess • Painkillers will ease the pain • See your dentist as soon as possible

Fatigue

Fatigue, or tiredness, is a common symptom that can occur after periods of exertion or following a poor night's sleep. However, in conjunction with other symptoms, it can also signal more serious medical problems.

SYMPTOM CHARACTERISTIC	ASSOCIATED SYMPTOMS	AGGRAVATING OR ALLEVIATING FACTORS	OTHER RELEVANT FACTORS	POSSIBLE CAUSE AND ACTION
Daytime fatigue and drowsiness	• Trouble falling asleep at night and/or difficulty sleeping through the night	• Stress and anxiety about inability to fall asleep or about personal problems	• Mild insomnia is common during pregnancy	• Insomnia • Try relaxation strategies before bed (e.g. taking a warm bath, reading for pleasure (not work-related reading), relaxation exercises) • Self-help information may be available at your pharmacy or hospital • See your doctor if you are worried or if symptoms persist
General leathargy that may limit daily activities	• Tendency to feel stressed or anxious		• Fatigue is common in those who try to do too much, or fit too much into their daily routine at the expense of rest and relaxation	• Lifestyle problems (e.g. overwork, lack of regular exercise, obesity, lack of sleep time) can contribute to fatigue • Try to change elements of lifestyle (e.g. exercise more, lose excess weight, cut down on excess workload where possible) • See your doctor if you are worried or if symptoms persist
Weakness and fatigue	• Dizziness, faintness, pale skin, loss of appetite, heart palpitations		• Commonly occurs with blood loss (e.g. after surgery or with repeated heavy periods) • Anemia may develop in pregnancy due to the increased demands placed on the mother's iron supplies	• Iron deficiency anemia • See your doctor
Debilitating fatigue that lasts for several months or longer, and becomes worse over time	• Persistent low-grade fever, aches and pains, weakness, swollen lymph nodes, joint pain, sore throat	• Fatigue is not from exertion and is not relieved by rest; however it can worsen following physical exertion	• This condition primarily affects young, urban professionals • The cause of this illness is not clear, but viruses, allergies, and hormonal imbalances may play some role • It may last for several months or years, but the majority or sufferers do recuperate	• Chronic fatigue syndrome • See your doctor

SYMPTOM CHARACTERISTIC	ASSOCIATED SYMPTOMS	AGGRAVATING OR ALLEVIATING FACTORS	OTHER RELEVANT FACTORS	POSSIBLE CAUSE AND ACTION
Fatigue that develops after starting new medication		• Not affected by physical activity or rest	• Medications that can cause fatigue include sleeping pills, cough and cold preparations, and blood pressure medication	• Medication side effect • See your doctor
Fatigue and lack of energy	• Persistent sadness and pessimism, change in appetite, difficulty sleeping or tendency to oversleep • May have thoughts of death or suicide	• May follow stressful life-changing events (e.g. death of a family member, loss of job, diagnosis of serious illness)	• Depression affects 25 percent of women, 10 percent of men, and 5 percent of adolescents at some time in their lives	• Depression • See your doctor at once
Extreme fatigue that develops quickly	• Sore throat, fever, chills headache, body aches, cough, nasal congestion		• Flu vaccination is recommended for those at risk or over 65 years of age	• Influenza • Rest as much as possible, drink plenty of fluids, take fever-reducing medication • See your doctor if you are worried or if symptoms persist
Fatigue, faintness, weakness	• Excessive thirst, frequent urination, increased appetite, weight loss, nausea, blurred vision • In women, frequent vaginal infections; in men, impotence • Recurring yeast infections in both sexes			• Diabetes • See your doctor at once
Fatigue that may progressively worsen	• Weight loss, cough (sometimes with bloody sputum), slight fever, night sweats, pain in the chest or back		• Lung cancer is most common among cigarette smokers • Tuberculosis occurs most frequently in Asia, Africa, the Middle East and Latin America	• Tuberculosis or lung cancer • See your doctor at once
Fatigue and weakness	• Shortness of breath, coughing, swelling of the abdomen or legs, rapid heartbeat	• Symptoms may worsen with exertion	• The risk of developing congestive heart failure is elevated in people with a history of cardiovascular disease, including hypertension or arrhythmia • Congestive heart failure may be triggered by infection, anemia, pregnancy or rheumatic fever	• Congestive heart failure • This is a medical emergency • Go to the emergency room or call an ambulance at once

Fever

Fever is defined as a body temperature higher than the normal 98.6°F (37°C) taken orally. Mild or short-term temperature rises are common with minor infections, but high or sustained fever can signal a potentially dangerous and serious infection. Fever is often accompanied by other symptoms, as outlined below, which may help identify the cause.

The first table that follows applies to fever in adults and children of all ages. The second table deals with some additional symptoms specific to infants and children.

Fever in adults and children of all ages

SYMPTOM CHARACTERISTIC	ASSOCIATED SYMPTOMS	AGGRAVATING OR ALLEVIATING FACTORS	OTHER RELEVANT FACTORS	POSSIBLE CAUSE AND ACTION
Fever—body temperature above 98.6°F (37°C)	• Flushed face, hot skin, sore throat, mild headache		• May follow exposure to people with similar symptoms	• Viral infection (e.g. cold or flu) • Take decongestant and fever-reducing medication • For any fever it is advisable to: – remove excess layers of clothing – drink plenty of fluids – take fever-reducing medication – have a lukewarm bath – check temperature every 4–6 hours • See your doctor if: – temperature remains at 102.2°F (39°C) or above in adults or 101.3°F (38.5°C) in children – fever lasts longer than 48 hours – the patient is pregnant – the patient is a child • In children, use a non-aspirin fever-reducing medication formulated for children • See your doctor if the fever does not respond quickly to medication or if the child has a sore throat or painful ear

SYMPTOM CHARACTERISTIC	ASSOCIATED SYMPTOMS	AGGRAVATING OR ALLEVIATING FACTORS	OTHER RELEVANT FACTORS	POSSIBLE CAUSE AND ACTION
Fever	• Aches, chills, nausea, vomiting, cramping, diarrhea		• Affects all age groups, but may cause life-threatening dehydration in the very young, the very ill and the elderly	• Gastroenteritis or other viral infection • Rest and follow standard advice for any fever: – remove excess layers of clothing – drink plenty of fluids – take a fever-reducing medication – have a lukewarm bath – check temperature every 4–6 hours • Use anti-diarrhea and anti-vomiting medications as advised by your pharmacist or doctor • See your doctor if vomiting lasts longer than 12 hours or if there is bloody diarrhea • See your doctor if you are worried or if symptoms persist
Fever	• Cough that is producing yellow or green mucus, rapid, light breathing, fatigue			• Respiratory infection (e.g. bronchitis or pneumonia) • See your doctor to assess the degree of lung congestion • Antibiotics may be required
Fever	• Severe headache, neck stiffness, drowsiness, vomiting, sensitivity to light		• May be confused and unable to respond well to questioning	• An infection in the area around the brain (meningitis) • This is a medical emergency • See your doctor or emergency department
Fevers that come and go over a period of weeks	• Sore throat, tiredness		• Infectious mononucleosis (glandular fever) with symptoms is most common in adolescents and adults • Although the infection is common in children, symptoms are generally milder and resemble a common cold, so the diagnosis is rarely made	• Prolonged viral illness such as infectious mononucleosis (glandular fever), other infection, or sign of another medical condition • See your doctor

SYMPTOM CHARACTERISTIC	ASSOCIATED SYMPTOMS	AGGRAVATING OR ALLEVIATING FACTORS	OTHER RELEVANT FACTORS	POSSIBLE CAUSE AND ACTION
Fever (cont.)				
Sudden onset of fever with simultaneous sore throat	• Headache		• Tends to occur during the colder months and can be precipitated by stress, overwork, exhaustion and when the body's immune system is fighting other infections	• Strep throat (streptococcal infection) • Rest and follow standard advice for any fever: – remove excess layers of clothing – drink plenty of fluids – take a fever-reducing medication – have a lukewarm bath – check temperature every 4–6 hours • See your doctor
High fever over 107.6°F (42°C)	• Flushed, dry, hot skin, rapid pulse, confusion, constricted pupils, seizures or fainting		• Follows exposure to hot weather or strenuous exercise in high temperatures, and dehydration	• Heatstroke, including sunstroke • Quickly move person to a cool place and cover body with cool, wet clothes • This is a medical emergency • Go to the emergency room or call an ambulance at once
Fever in a person taking medications for another medical condition			• May occur with anticancer chemotherapy (due to temporary immune system suppression), drugs used to treat invasive fungal infections, anticoagulants used in cardiovascular disease	• Fever can occur as a side effect of some medications • See your doctor—medication may be changed or dose altered
Fever	• Ear pain, hearing loss, feeling of fullness or fluid in the ear		• Fever may be the predominant sign in a child too young to indicate other symptoms	• Middle ear infection (otitis media) or outer ear infection (otitis externa) • Ear infections can lead to more serious problems if not treated, so see your doctor for assessment • Antibiotic treatment may be required • See your doctor
Fever	• Pain with urination or low back pain, tenderness on both sides of the lower back			• Kidney infection • You may require treatment with antibiotics • See your doctor at once

SYMPTOM CHARACTERISTIC	ASSOCIATED SYMPTOMS	AGGRAVATING OR ALLEVIATING FACTORS	OTHER RELEVANT FACTORS	POSSIBLE CAUSE AND ACTION
Fever	• Open sore or wound that is red • Red streaking on the arms or legs originating near the wound • Surrounding skin may be tender and hot; there may also be localized swelling			• Blood poisoning as a result of infection of the skin or lymphatic system • See your doctor at once

Fever in infants and children

SYMPTOM CHARACTERISTIC	ASSOCIATED SYMPTOMS	AGGRAVATING OR ALLEVIATING FACTORS	OTHER RELEVANT FACTORS	POSSIBLE CAUSE AND ACTION
Fever in a child aged under 3 months	• Lethargy, pale skin, irritability			• Fever in a baby should always be investigated to rule out serious infection • See your doctor at once
High fever over 101.3°F (38.5°C)	• Barking cough			• Croup • See a doctor as soon as possible • For any fever it is advisable to: – remove excess layers of clothing – drink plenty of fluids – take a fever-reducing medication – have a lukewarm bath – check temperature every 4–6 hours • See your doctor at once
Fever	• Blisters over face, back, neck and chest		• Occurs most commonly in children • May occur in adult not previously infected • Follows recent contact with person with chickenpox • Highly infectious, so common among childcare and hospital workers • Vaccination to prevent is now available in some countries	• Chickenpox • Chickenpox infection may be severe in adults, so ask medical advice at once • Take children with suspected chickenpox for assessment by a doctor, and keep child away from others who have not been infected • See your doctor • Chickenpox is highly contagious, so warn the doctor's office of the possibility of infection before attending

SYMPTOM CHARACTERISTIC	ASSOCIATED SYMPTOMS	AGGRAVATING OR ALLEVIATING FACTORS	OTHER RELEVANT FACTORS	POSSIBLE CAUSE AND ACTION
Fever (cont.)				
High fever, above 102°F (39°C)	• Seizure or convulsion may be triggered by high fever		• Three percent of children have at least one febrile convulsion • Cooling a feverish child in a lukewarm bath can help prevent a convulsion • A rapid rise in body temperature is more likely to cause seizures than a slow rise to the same temperature	• Febrile seizure • This requires immediate action • Ensure the airway is clear and turn child on to the side • Remove clothing and bathe or sponge with lukewarm water after the seizure has finished • See your doctor as soon as possible

Flatulence

Flatulence is the feeling or presence of gas in the stomach and intestines. A build-up of gas can cause a sensation of fullness or discomfort in the abdomen, which can lead to the passing of flatus (gas) through the anus or belching through the mouth. It is usually not harmful but can be a source of embarrassment for some people. See also entry on *abdominal distension*.

SYMPTOM CHARACTERISTIC	ASSOCIATED SYMPTOMS	AGGRAVATING OR ALLEVIATING FACTORS	OTHER RELEVANT FACTORS	POSSIBLE CAUSE AND ACTION
An uncomfortable, bloated feeling in the abdomen	• Bloating of abdomen, frequent passing of gas from the anus, abdominal pain	• Constipation may cause or worsen gas build-up in the bowel, by slowing the passage of food and increasing the chance of fermentation	• Flatulence may be caused by eating foods that ferment in the intestines and produce gas including beans, peas, wheat, oats, bran, cabbage, corn, brussels sprouts	• Dietary imbalance • Eat less of those foods likely to cause flatulence • This may require eliminating one food group at a time to see what leads to the flatulence • Anti-flatulent medications (e.g. charcoal tablets, simethicone) may also be useful • For constipation, eat foods rich in fiber and drink plenty of fluids • See your doctor if you are worried or if symptoms persist • See your doctor at once if abdominal pain is constant
Frequent passing of flatus, bloating of the abdomen following consumption of dairy foods	• Abdominal cramps, frothy diarrhea, vomiting	• Worsens after eating dairy products, disappears when these are eliminated from the diet	• More common in people from Asia, Africa and the subtropics, due to their low consumption of dairy products after infancy which leads to an underproduction of lactase, the enzyme that is necessary for digestion of lactose	• Lactose intolerance • See your doctor • Do not attempt to treat yourself or a child for lactose intolerance without medical advice • If lactose intolerance is confirmed, restrict consumption of dairy products, or take a lactase supplement to aid the digestion of lactose

SYMPTOM CHARACTERISTIC	ASSOCIATED SYMPTOMS	AGGRAVATING OR ALLEVIATING FACTORS	OTHER RELEVANT FACTORS	POSSIBLE CAUSE AND ACTION
Frequent belching (burping)		• Hurried eating or gulping, talking while eating, chewing gum, drinking carbonated (fizzy) drinks	• Dental problems and nose or mouth deformities may lead to belching due to an increase in swallowed air	• Too much air swallowed • Don't talk while eating, eat slowly and take small mouthfuls of food • Minimize chewing gum • Drink less carbonated drinks • See your doctor if you are worried or if symptoms persist
Increased passing of flatus, abdominal pain, bloating	• Constipation or diarrhea shortly after meals	• Abdominal pain usually relieved after passage of wind or bowel movement	• Overeating, bingeing or too much fat in the diet can bring on an episode	• Irritable bowel syndrome • Cause is unknown but may be related to stress, food sensitivities, eating irregularly • See your doctor

Foot and ankle problems

Most people experience occasional problems with the foot or ankle. Ankle sprains are one of the most common musculoskeletal injuries, while degenerative disorders such as gout and heel spurs may often affect people as they age.

SYMPTOM CHARACTERISTIC	ASSOCIATED SYMPTOMS	AGGRAVATING OR ALLEVIATING FACTORS	OTHER RELEVANT FACTORS	POSSIBLE CAUSE AND ACTION
Pain and swelling, usually on one side of the ankle, following twisting injury or fall	• Bruising, warmth	• May be aggravated by walking, but pain does not stop walking	• Most commonly affects the outer side of the ankle	• Injury to the ligaments in the ankle (ankle sprain) • Rest, apply ice, elevate the foot, use a compression bandage • See your doctor
Severe pain around the ankle following a fall, twisting injury, or direct blow to the ankle	• Swelling of the ankle and possibly foot and toes, throbbing, warmth, bruising, inability to walk	• Aggravated by walking or movement of the ankle		• Fracture or severe ligament sprain • Elevate the leg, apply ice • See your doctor at once
Pain under the heel and arch of the foot	• Maybe stiffness in the heel	• Prolonged walking or running	• Can lead to development of a heel spur (see directly below)	• Plantar fasciitis • See your doctor
Sharp pain under the heel	• May be some swelling	• Aggravated by walking, pressing on the heel	• May be more common in those with flat feet	• Excess growth of bone at the heel (spur) • See your doctor
Sudden onset of severe pain in the big toe, foot or ankle; pain often begins at night and may last for several days	• Swelling, skin over the affected area is usually red, hot, shiny and very tender to touch • May be fever and chills	• Aggravated by walking, anything pressing on the area (e.g. shoes, socks)	• Most commonly affects the big toe, but can affect many other joints in the body • Usually affects one or two joints at a time, and attacks recur	• Gout • See your doctor

SYMPTOM CHARACTERISTIC	ASSOCIATED SYMPTOMS	AGGRAVATING OR ALLEVIATING FACTORS	OTHER RELEVANT FACTORS	POSSIBLE CAUSE AND ACTION
Foot and ankle problems (cont.)				
Dull ache or pain at the back of the heel which travels up the back of the ankle and lower calf	• Mild swelling, tenderness, warmth at the back of the ankle	• Aggravated by running, jumping, walking, bicycling especially when first begin the activity	• More common in those with flat feet or tight muscles in the calf	• Inflammation of the Achilles tendon at the back of the ankle (tendinitis) • Avoid activities that cause pain • See your doctor for advice
Pain in the front part of the foot, usually during prolonged running or walking, or athletic activity	• May be some swelling, tenderness to touch	• Continuous, repeated activity especially running, walking	• More common in people whose feet have high arches	• Stress fracture • See your doctor

Genital itching

Genital itching is usually a symptom of infection or irritation of the genitals. It may occur in conjunction with genital pain (see following entry) and can be a symptom of some sexually transmitted diseases. See also entries on *genital pain* and *vaginal problems*.

SYMPTOM CHARACTERISTIC	ASSOCIATED SYMPTOMS	AGGRAVATING OR ALLEVIATING FACTORS	OTHER RELEVANT FACTORS	POSSIBLE CAUSE AND ACTION
Mildly itchy, raised growths on the vulva, penis or anus, which may develop a cauliflower-like appearance	• Mild pain, increased dampness or moisture in the area of the growths, increased discharge from the vagina or penis		• Although human papillomavirus infections are associated with some cancers (e.g. cervical cancer), most genital warts are caused by a different strain of human papillomavirus which does not cause cancer	• Genital warts • See your doctor
Itchy, painful rash around the vagina or on the penis	• In women, the vulva may be swollen and red, and there may be a thick, white discharge	• Sexual intercourse may increase discomfort	• Yeast infections can be a side effect of taking antibiotics, or may be triggered by stress, pregnancy, or use of the contraceptive pill • Candidiasis is most likely in women with diabetes or as a side effect of some antibiotics	• Candidiasis ("thrush") • or moniliasis infection • Wear cotton underwear and loose clothing • See your doctor
In females, itching, dryness and irritation of the vagina		• Sexual intercourse may be difficult and painful	• May occur in women following menopause, because a lack of estrogen causes dryness of the vagina	• Hormonal deficiency • Dryness can be relieved with vaginal lubricants • See your doctor if you are worried or if symptoms persist
Itching and burning of the genitals after sexual intercourse	• Redness or rash	• Symptoms may be aggravated by sexual intercourse	• Spermicides or other products used directly on the genitals may cause allergic reactions in susceptible people	• Allergic reaction • Discontinue use of spermicides • See your doctor

SYMPTOM CHARACTERISTIC	ASSOCIATED SYMPTOMS	AGGRAVATING OR ALLEVIATING FACTORS	OTHER RELEVANT FACTORS	POSSIBLE CAUSE AND ACTION
In females, irritation and itching inside and outside the vagina	• Inflammation or swelling, vaginal discharge, foul or fishy vaginal odor, dryness or discomfort during sexual intercourse, discomfort or burning with urination	• Symptoms may be aggravated by sexual intercourse		• Vaginitis • Vaginitis has a range of causes, including infections with bacteria, fungus, viruses • See your doctor

Genital pain

Pain in the genital area is usually the result of an infection, or may occur following injury. Sexually transmitted diseases are a common cause of infection, so it is important to practice safe sex to prevent further spread of these conditions, and consult your doctor for treatment. Any pain with sexual intercourse should be investigated by a doctor. See also entries on *genital itching* and *vaginal problems*.

SYMPTOM CHARACTERISTIC	ASSOCIATED SYMPTOMS	AGGRAVATING OR ALLEVIATING FACTORS	OTHER RELEVANT FACTORS	POSSIBLE CAUSE AND ACTION
Painful blisters on the genitals, which may break, weep and form sores; the first occurrence of blisters may last from 5 days to several weeks; further episodes are usually shorter and less severe, and usually occur less frequently	• Itchy, tingling sensation, swollen and tender lymph nodes in the groin, pain on urination, discharge from the urethra in men and vagina in women • Weakness or constipation may occur • Erectile dysfunction may occur in men	• Pain may be aggravated when urine comes into contact with the blisters	• Triggers for an episode may be stress, illness, sexual intercourse, menstruation • If a pregnant woman has an attack of genital herpes towards the end of her pregnancy, there is a risk of passing it on to the baby and causing serious problems such as brain damage; cesarean section may overcome this problem	• Genital herpes • Wear cotton underwear and loose clothing • See your doctor at once • Avoid sexual contact until medical advice is obtained
In women, tender swelling of the vaginal opening or swelling of one labia	• May be hot and painful to touch	• Sexual contact may aggravate pain		• Infection or abscess in a Bartholin's gland, or an infection of the labia • See your doctor at once
Burning sensation or pain with urination	• Frequent urge to urinate, even when bladder is empty • Urinating only small amounts • Burning sensation in lower abdomen, urine with a strong odor	• Lack of adequate fluid intake may prolong symptoms • Sexual contact may aggravate pain	• Cystitis is more common in women than in men • Infection may be triggered by sexual contact, use of diaphragm for birth control or use of urinary catheters	• Cystitis • Drink plenty of water • See your doctor
In men, tender and swollen tip of the penis		• Symptoms may be aggravated by sexual contact, pressure from tight clothing		• Infection of the head of the penis (balanitis) • See your doctor at once
In men, pain with ejaculation	• Blood in the semen, tenderness with bowel movements, or pain behind the penis or scrotum		• Sudden-onset prostatitis caused by a bacterial infection is most frequent in young men • Prostatitis may be triggered by the use of urinary catheters	• Prostatitis • See your doctor at once

SYMPTOM CHARACTERISTIC	ASSOCIATED SYMPTOMS	AGGRAVATING OR ALLEVIATING FACTORS	OTHER RELEVANT FACTORS	POSSIBLE CAUSE AND ACTION
Genital pain (cont.)				
In women, mild pain or discomfort while urinating	• Vaginal discharge, abdominal pain, rectal pain, sore throat		• Chlamydia is one of the most common sexually transmitted infections, and is most common in young, sexually active people • Most chlamydial infections do not cause any symptoms, so transmission is very common and easy	• Chlamydia • See your doctor at once • Avoid sexual contact until medical advice is obtained
In men, pain during urination	• Pus or mucus may be visible in urine		• Urethritis is the most common form of sexually transmitted disease • Occurs most frequently in sexually active young men	• Urethritis, caused by sexually transmitted infection • See your doctor at once
Painful urination in men or women	• Inflamed genitals after sexual intercourse • In males, discharge of pus from the penis • In females, vaginal discharge, urge to urinate frequently, abnormal menstrual bleeding • The infection may spread from the genitals to the urethra, rectum, conjunctiva, pharynx or cervix		• The incidence of gonorrhea is much higher in the USA than in other industrialized countries • Potential complications include inflammation of reproductive organs, peritonitis, inflammation around the liver, inflammation of the Bartholin's gland in women and epididymitis or abscess around the urethra in men, arthritis, dermatitis, endocarditis, meningitis, myocarditis or hepatitis	• Gonorrhea • See your doctor at once
Pain and tenderness in the genital area	• Bruising, possibly some discharge, urinary tract infection • Person may appear irritable or fearful	• Symptoms are aggravated by walking or sitting		• Sexual abuse or rape • See your doctor at once
Pain with sexual intercourse in women	• Bleeding after sexual intercourse, watery discharge from vagina, painful bowel movements, frequent urge to urinate		• Vaginal tumors are rare	• Tumor of the vagina • See your doctor at once

"Glands", swollen

The term "swollen glands" usually refers to swelling of the lymph nodes (also known as lymph glands) in the neck, armpit or groin. There are many causes of swollen lymph nodes, ranging from mild infections to serious disorders such as cancer. Swelling often goes down as the infection resolves, but if your glands stay swollen for more than two weeks consult your doctor.

SYMPTOM CHARACTERISTIC	ASSOCIATED SYMPTOMS	AGGRAVATING OR ALLEVIATING FACTORS	OTHER RELEVANT FACTORS	POSSIBLE CAUSE AND ACTION
Swollen, tender lymph nodes ("glands") in the neck, armpit or groin	• Skin over the nodes may be hot and red • There is usually an obvious site of infection nearby (e.g. an infected cut or sore, or a tooth, eye or ear infection) • Red lines may radiate from the site of infection towards the lymph nodes		• Inflammation of the lymph nodes (lymphadenitis) may occur with bacterial, viral or fungal infections	• Lymphadenitis • See your doctor
Swollen, lymph nodes in the neck	• Fever, fatigue, sore throat, headache		• Infectious mononucleosis occurs most commonly in young adults • The virus is contagious and is passed via kissing, coughing and sneezing; sometimes known as "the kissing disease"	• Infectious mononucleosis (glandular fever) • See your doctor
Swollen, tender lymph nodes in the neck	• Sore throat, headache, fever, bad breath, white spots on the tonsils	• Symptoms may be aggravated by moving the neck, swallowing or speaking		• Streptococcal infection ("strep throat") • See your doctor
Enlarged, non-tender lymph nodes throughout the body	• Fatigue, night sweats, weight loss, fever, severe itching all over the body • Lymph nodes enlarge slowly and are usually painless		• Non-Hodgkin's lymphoma is a relatively common cancer, and occurs most frequently in children and young adults • Hodgkin's disease occurs most commonly in young adults or in people over 50 years, and is more prevalent in men then women	• Cancer of the lymphatic system (lymphoma) (e.g. Hodgkin's lymphoma or non-Hodgkin's lymphoma) • See your doctor at once
Swollen lymph nodes in the neck, groin or armpit	• Weight loss, fatigue, tendency to bruise or bleed easily, loss of appetite • Anemia is common during the early stages of leukemia		• Leukemia may increase susceptibility to infections (e.g. tonsillitis, pneumonia) • Leukemia is most common in children and young adults	• Leukemia • See your doctor at once

SYMPTOM CHARACTERISTIC	ASSOCIATED SYMPTOMS	AGGRAVATING OR ALLEVIATING FACTORS	OTHER RELEVANT FACTORS	POSSIBLE CAUSE AND ACTION
"Glands", swollen (cont.)				
Swollen, inflamed lymph nodes just above the angle of the jaw, on one or both sides of the face	• Fever, fatigue, swelling of the lymph nodes under the tongue, testicular swelling in males, or abdominal pain	• Pain with chewing or swallowing	• Mumps is contagious, but less so than other infections such as measles or chickenpox • It is a preventable through immunization • In countries where mumps vaccination is widely practiced, mumps occurs most frequently in adults • Prior to routine vaccination it occurred most commonly in children • Mumps is spread by close contact	• Mumps • See your doctor

Gums, bleeding

Bleeding gums are usually a sign of gum disease, most often caused by poor oral hygiene. Smokers are more than twice as likely as non-smokers to develop gum disease, while other at-risk groups include people with diabetes, leukemia, and Crohn's disease.

SYMPTOM CHARACTERISTIC	ASSOCIATED SYMPTOMS	AGGRAVATING OR ALLEVIATING FACTORS	OTHER RELEVANT FACTORS	POSSIBLE CAUSE AND ACTION
Swollen, red gums that bleed easily, e.g. with brushing of the teeth or with eating	• Gums are tender when touched or when chewing food	• Eating can aggravate symptoms	• The hormonal changes of pregnancy can worsen the condition • Gingivitis is most commonly caused by poor oral hygiene, including inadequate brushing and flossing of the teeth	• Gingivitis • See your doctor or dentist
Bleeding, red gums	• Pus around the teeth, bad taste in the mouth, halitosis (bad breath) • Periodontitis may lead eventually to deepening of the pockets around the teeth, loose teeth, and loss of teeth	• Symptoms may be aggravated by eating	• Periodontitis occurs when gingivitis extends to the supporting structures of the teeth	• Periodontitis • See your dentist
Sudden onset of painful gums that bleed easily	• Fatigue, bad breath, excess saliva, appearance of gray-white mucus covering the gums	• Eating and swallowing may aggravate symptoms	• Poor oral hygiene predisposes to this condition, known as trench mouth; the term comes from World War I when many soldiers in the trenches developed the infection	• Bacterial infection of the mouth (Vincent's angina, Vincent's disease known as trench mouth) • See your dentist

SYMPTOM CHARACTERISTIC	ASSOCIATED SYMPTOMS	AGGRAVATING OR ALLEVIATING FACTORS	OTHER RELEVANT FACTORS	POSSIBLE CAUSE AND ACTION
Tendency to bleed easily from the gums and nose	• Swollen lymph nodes in the neck, groin or armpit, weight loss, fatigue, tendency to bruise easily, loss of appetite		• Increased susceptibility to infections (e.g. tonsillitis, pneumonia)	• Leukemia or serious infection (e.g. AIDS) • See your doctor at once
Extremely sore, swollen gums that bleed easily	• Earaches, symptoms similar to those of sinusitis, nosebleeds, fever, weight loss, cough, fatigue		• Wegener's granulomatosis is a rare disease occurring most commonly in white people • It occurs at any age, most common around 40 years	• Wegener's granulomatosis, a rare, serious disease • See your doctor at once

Hair problems

Hair loss or the growth of excessive hair can be a distressing symptom. While this may be a normal part of ageing, sometimes abnormal hair loss or growth can herald an underlying disorder. If your loss or gain of hair is worrying you, seek advice from your doctor. Many types of hair problems can be treated.

SYMPTOM CHARACTERISTIC	ASSOCIATED SYMPTOMS	AGGRAVATING OR ALLEVIATING FACTORS	OTHER RELEVANT FACTORS	POSSIBLE CAUSE AND ACTION
Gradual hair loss in the front or on the top of the head in men	• Affects middle-aged to elderly men		• May be a history of similar hair loss in male family members	• Male-pattern baldness • See your doctor
Gradual thinning or loss of hair all over the head, in a person taking medication	• Hair may fall out in clumps	• Hair loss will stop and new hair grow when medication ceased	• Person is taking a medication such as chemotherapy or steroids • Occasionally hair loss is a side effect of some anti-ulcer drugs, blood thinners or drugs to control blood pressure	• Medication-related hair loss • See your doctor
Gradual thinning or loss of hair all over the head in older adult women	• Hot flashes (flushes), mood swings, absentmindedness, irregular menstruation	• Gentle hair-care may prolong the life of ageing hair follicles	• Usually occurs in women over 50 years of age who may be undergoing menopause	• Hormonal changes related to ageing in women, or anemia (e.g. pernicious anemia or iron deficiency anemia) • See your doctor
Rapid thinning or loss of hair all over head	• Emotional or physical stress	• Rest and relaxation may reduce hair loss	• History of major surgery, childbirth or emotional stress	• Stress-related hair loss • Reduce stress • See your doctor if you are worried or symptoms persist
Small patches of hair falling out on the head	• Coin-shaped areas of baldness, healthy scalp and remaining hair is healthy	• No obvious cause or pattern to hair loss	• Usually resolves spontaneously • Occasionally can result in hair loss from the whole body	• Alopecia • See your doctor

SYMPTOM CHARACTERISTIC	ASSOCIATED SYMPTOMS	AGGRAVATING OR ALLEVIATING FACTORS	OTHER RELEVANT FACTORS	POSSIBLE CAUSE AND ACTION
Hair problems (cont.)				
Small patches of hair falling out on the head	• Oily, red or purple patches on scalp • May be similar lesion elsewhere on the body	• Scratching area can increase hair loss and increase inflammation	• Usually resolves over time but treatment may be necessary	• Dandruff (seborrheic dermatitis) or other skin diseases (e.g. fungal infection, lichen planus) • See your doctor at once
Excessive growth of dark coarse hair on face or body in a female	• May have deep voice or irregular periods	• Weight loss in the overweight can reduce the level of male hormone, reducing hair growth	• Person may be taking birth control pills, hormone supplements or anabolic steroids • Rarely, a tumor or the adrenal glands may produce excess male hormones	• Hirsutism due to excess male hormone (androgen) • See your doctor

Hallucinations

Hallucinations—hearing, seeing or feeling things that are not really there—are usually a symptom of mental illness, but may also occur in response to certain drugs, infections or as a result of alcohol withdrawal.

SYMPTOM CHARACTERISTIC	ASSOCIATED SYMPTOMS	AGGRAVATING OR ALLEVIATING FACTORS	OTHER RELEVANT FACTORS	POSSIBLE CAUSE AND ACTION
Hearing or seeing things that are not really there	• Excess physical activity and elation, irritability, hostility, easily distracted, impatient, false convictions of personal power, wealth and importance, paranoia, decreased need for sleep, increased sexual desire and risk-taking behavior (e.g. gambling) • Episodes usually emerge over a period of days to weeks, but may occur within a few hours (often morning)	• Symptoms may be aggravated by stress	• Symptoms usually develop rapidly, over a period of several days; while the collection of symptoms usually makes the diagnosis of mania straightforward, the person suffering from the disorder frequently denies there is anything wrong, so doctors usually have to obtain information from family members • Alcohol abuse or substance abuse often occur with bipolar disorder • Among patients with bipolar disorder, women are more prone to depressive episodes and men to manic episodes	• Mania • Mania most frequently occurs as a symptom of bipolar disorder ("manic-depression") • See your doctor

SYMPTOM CHARACTERISTIC	ASSOCIATED SYMPTOMS	AGGRAVATING OR ALLEVIATING FACTORS	OTHER RELEVANT FACTORS	POSSIBLE CAUSE AND ACTION
Hearing voices telling you what to do or saying things about you	• Visual hallucinations, delusions, disorganized speech, irrational behavior, stupor, rigidity or floppiness of limbs (catatonic behavior), lack of emotion, social withdrawal, lack of energy	• Symptoms may be aggravated by stress	• Schizophrenia is a relatively common psychotic disorder, affecting up to one in every 200 people at some time in their life • The likelihood of developing schizophrenia is greater if a family member has the disease • In males it most often develops in the teenage years to early 20s, and in females during their late 20s to mid-40s • Schizophrenia can be difficult to diagnose and usually requires assessment over several months	• Schizophrenia • This is a medical emergency • Go to the emergency room or call an ambulance at once
Seeing things that do not exist	• Sudden onset of symptoms such as confusion about the current time, date, location or identity, difficulty paying attention, loss of recent memory, inability to think logically, fever or other signs of infection, tremors, evidence of recent drug use		• If hallucinations occur with delirium they are usually visual • Delirium is not a mental disease, but can be caused by many disorders or conditions including dehydration, drug-intoxication, stroke or serious infections	• Delirium • See your doctor at once
Hearing things that are not really there, in a person with memory loss	• Gradual onset of symptoms such as forgetfulness of recent events, loss of memory, confusion, difficulty finding the right word to use, loss of ability to recognize people, places and objects, depression, fears, anxiety, wandering away		• If hallucinations occur with dementia, they are usually related to hearing voices or noises • Dementia can be an early sign of Alzheimer's disease, or occur in people with AIDS	• Dementia • See your doctor
Hearing voices that are accusing or threatening, causing fear and terror in a person with alcoholism; may last for several days	• Tremor, weakness, sweating, nausea • Symptoms of delirium tremens (high fever, confusion, sleeplessness, anxiousness, nightmares, profound depression, tremors, poor coordination)		• Symptoms usually begin 12–24 hours after a person with alcoholism stops drinking alcohol; if untreated, the person may develop delirium tremens (DTs) 2–10 days after cessation	• Hallucinations as a result of alcohol withdrawal in a person with alcoholism • See your doctor at once

SYMPTOM CHARACTERISTIC	ASSOCIATED SYMPTOMS	AGGRAVATING OR ALLEVIATING FACTORS	OTHER RELEVANT FACTORS	POSSIBLE CAUSE AND ACTION
Hallucinations (cont.)				
False hallucinations such as visual and auditory hallucinations that the sufferer understands are not real; sensations may be related (e.g. listening to music may cause colors to appear and move in time to the music)	• Impaired judgment, leading to dangerous decision making or accidents, panic, delusions, dilated pupils		• The ability to cope with the hallucinations depends on the user's experience and feelings of fear before taking the drug • An inexperienced user who is afraid is less able to cope and more likely to experience unpleasant hallucinations ("a bad trip") • Bad trips may cause temporary psychosis (a loss of contact with reality)	• Substance abuse involving hallucinogens such as LSD • See your doctor • Most users of hallucinogens do not seek medical treatment • A calm, dark room and quiet talk may help a user having a bad trip • If a user has prolonged psychosis, psychiatric treatment may be required

Hand and wrist problems

Problems in the wrist or hand can be caused by a variety of conditions, including overuse, injury and falls. The hands are also a common site for developing arthritis.

SYMPTOM CHARACTERISTIC	ASSOCIATED SYMPTOMS	AGGRAVATING OR ALLEVIATING FACTORS	OTHER RELEVANT FACTORS	POSSIBLE CAUSE AND ACTION
Pain in the wrist or hand following repeated movements	• May be some mild swelling, tingling	• Aggravated by continuing the repeated movements; alleviated by rest	• Inflammation of the tendons in the wrist or hand (tendinitis) may be caused by overuse • Healing is often delayed in people with arthritis, diabetes or gout	• Tendinitis • Try anti-inflammatory medication as advised by your pharmacist • See your doctor
Numbness, tingling, burning in the hand, wrist pain that shoots into the palm of the hand; may be worse at night	• Weakness, may be mild swelling	• Flexing the wrist, making a fist	• More common in women • Associated with occupations that involve repeated forceful movements of the wrist (e.g. using a screwdriver)	• Carpal tunnel syndrome • See your doctor
Pain and swelling following a fall or twisting injury	• Stiffness, bruising, limitation of movement	• May be aggravated by certain wrist movements		• Wrist sprain • See your doctor
Intense pain and swelling in the wrist following a fall, commonly onto an outstretched hand	• Hand may appear deformed (e.g. bent to the side)	• Aggravated by movement		• Fracture • See your doctor at once
Pain, swelling, stiffness in the wrist and/or finger joints, often worse after periods of inactivity	• Affected joints may feel hot, possible chills or fever • Can progress to cause deformities of the hand	• May be aggravated by movement	• Usually affects both hands/wrists at the same time • May have other joints that are affected • Affects more women than men	• Rheumatoid arthritis • See your doctor at once

SYMPTOM CHARACTERISTIC	ASSOCIATED SYMPTOMS	AGGRAVATING OR ALLEVIATING FACTORS	OTHER RELEVANT FACTORS	POSSIBLE CAUSE AND ACTION
Temporary patchy red and white discoloration of the fingers, usually following exposure to cold, may last for minutes or hours	• May be associated numbness, tingling, burning, feeling of pins and needles	• Alleviated by warming the hands	• Can also affect the feet • Most common in young women • More likely in smokers	• Raynaud's disease • See your doctor

Headache

Headache is the term used to describe any form of pain or discomfort in the head. It is an extremely common problem and one that most people have experienced. While most headaches are minor and easily treated with pain relievers, some warrant further medical investigation, and occasionally signal a more serious problem.

SYMPTOM CHARACTERISTIC	ASSOCIATED SYMPTOMS	AGGRAVATING OR ALLEVIATING FACTORS	OTHER RELEVANT FACTORS	POSSIBLE CAUSE AND ACTION
Dull, non-throbbing pain that feels like a vise around the head, squeezing both temples, extending into the neck	• Scalp or neck tenderness, tight or tender neck and shoulder muscles	• Symptoms may start after working in one position for several hours, or after driving; may be related to stress or anxiety		• Tension headache • Try relaxation techniques • Heat may help to relax neck and shoulder muscles, and analgesics may help the pain • See your doctor if you are worried or if symptoms persist
Mild-to-moderate headache generalized over the whole head, and may be throbbing	• Fever, aches, chills, nasal congestion, cough, nausea, vomiting or diarrhea		• Recent contact with infected person	• Viral infection such as a cold, flu or stomach virus • Ask your pharmacist for advice about medications to relieve symptoms • See your doctor if you are worried or if symptoms persist
Intense, throbbing, one-sided headache, may be centered around the eye; pain may last from a few hours to several days	• Vomiting and nausea may occur • In some people, the headache is preceded by a warning sign (aura), which may include visual disturbances such as flashing lights or spots • Oversensitivity to light, odors or sound may be experienced	• May be aggravated by bending forward, climbing stairs, or lying down (initially)	• Migraine may be triggered by certain foods (e.g. cheese, strawberries, chocolate) • In women, migraine may be associated with the menstrual cycle	• Migraine • Take analgesics such as acetaminophen (paracetamol) at once on onset of symptoms, and lie down • See your doctor if you are worried or if symptoms persist
Throbbing pain in the front of the head and around the eyes	• Feeling of pressure around the eyes and nose, thick nasal discharge	• May worsen with bending forward; may follow a recent cold or episode of hay fever	• Occurs with viral infections, allergies, deep sea diving or dental infections	• Sinusitis • Decongestants may be helpful to relieve symptoms • See your doctor if you are worried or if symptoms persist

SYMPTOM CHARACTERISTIC	ASSOCIATED SYMPTOMS	AGGRAVATING OR ALLEVIATING FACTORS	OTHER RELEVANT FACTORS	POSSIBLE CAUSE AND ACTION
Headache (cont.)				
Severe headache	• Stiff neck, vomiting, fever, drowsiness, delirium, unconscious, or have convulsions	• May be worsened by exposure to bright lights	• A child may be difficult to wake and have an unusual high-pitched moaning cry	• Meningitis • This is a medical emergency • Go to the emergency room or call an ambulance at once
Headache following recent injury to the head or after recently being knocked out	• Confusion, dizziness, memory loss • Worsening headaches, confusion, and increasing sleepiness over days or hours after injury		• History of trauma to the head	• Concussion or subdural hematoma • This is a medical emergency • Go to the emergency room or call an ambulance at once
Severe, piercing pain in and around one eye, lasting 30 minutes to several hours; headaches may occur one or more times a day for a period of weeks or months	• The affected eye may be bloodshot and watery • There may be associated nasal congestion and facial flushing	• Pain often occurs at night	• Occurs much more frequently in men than in women	• Cluster headache • See your doctor
Generalized headache in a person taking regular medication			• Occurs with regular or continuous use of medication	• Rebound headache • These headaches may occur with continuous use of certain medications such as nitrates (used to treat angina), or with overuse of analgesics or tranquilizers • See your doctor
Persistent, throbbing headache that begins first thing in the morning, and may lessen during the day	• Vomiting, nausea, fatigue, blurred vision, weakness • Headache may be unlike any other headache the person has had before	• May be worsened by changing positions (e.g. moving from lying down to standing)	• Hypertension causing these symptoms is relatively rare • Brain tumors are rare, and may be inherited or associated with exposure to ionizing radiation	• Severe hypertension or brain tumor • This is a medical emergency • Go to the emergency room or call an ambulance at once
Severe headache that begins suddenly	• Vomiting, limb weakness, double vision, slurred speech, difficulty swallowing, loss of consciousness			• Cerebral hemorrhage or aneurysm • This is a medical emergency • Go to the emergency room or call an ambulance at once

Hearing loss (deafness)

Significant loss of hearing is common, and can result from damage to the ear, disease of the ear or changes with age that damage the delicate structures enabling us to hear. Hearing loss is due to disturbances in the external or middle ear or abnormalities in the inner ear or neuronal (nerve) pathways. Any persistent loss of hearing should be assessed by a doctor to determine the type of hearing loss, possible causes and whether treatment is available which will restore hearing.

SYMPTOM CHARACTERISTIC	ASSOCIATED SYMPTOMS	AGGRAVATING OR ALLEVIATING FACTORS	OTHER RELEVANT FACTORS	POSSIBLE CAUSE AND ACTION
Intermittent hearing loss in one or both ears	• Usually no associated symptoms or pain	• Wax-softening drops may relieve hearing loss	• May have history of ear wax blockage	• Ear wax blockage (ceruminosis) • See your doctor • Do not try to remove the blockage yourself • You may damage the eardrum or small bones in the ear • Your doctor has special instruments to do this safely
Sudden-onset hearing loss in a child, without any history of ear infections	• Usually no other symptoms • May be itching or discomfort around the ear	• Pressure on the outside of the ear may increase discomfort	• Occurs most commonly in toddlers, who are likely to place small objects (e.g. buttons, beads, food) in their ear • Foreign bodies may be visible to the eye	• Foreign body in the ear canal • See your doctor • Do not try to remove the blockage yourself • You may damage the eardrum or small bones in the ear • Your doctor has special instruments to do this safely
Sudden hearing loss in one or both ears	• Fever, symptoms of a cold, discomfort ranging from a feeling of pressure in the ear to persistent, severe ache in one or both ears • Nausea and vomiting, dizziness or ringing in the ears	• Decongestants can aid drainage from the inner ear	• Most commonly occurs following a cold • Most common in children aged 3 months to 3 years, due to narrow eustachian tubes (tubes that allows pressure between the mouth or nose and ears to be equalized) • Eustachian tubes that are not fully developed may block easily with inflammation of the nose or throat, or with allergies	• Otitis media (viral or bacterial ear infection) commonly caused by a cold virus • Symptoms are caused by build-up of fluid • Perforation of the eardrum is a potential complication • This can lead to more prolonged but usually temporary hearing loss • See your doctor • See you doctor at once if the patient is a child
Gradual onset of hearing loss, usually in both ears	• High pitched sounds become hard to hear first followed by low pitched if deterioration continues	• Unprotected exposure to loud noise will cause further deterioration	• Commonly occurs in industrial workers exposed to loud noises, when correct ear-protection is not used • Can occur following just a few exposures to very loud sound	• Noise-induced hearing loss or occupational hearing loss • See your doctor

SYMPTOM CHARACTERISTIC	ASSOCIATED SYMPTOMS	AGGRAVATING OR ALLEVIATING FACTORS	OTHER RELEVANT FACTORS	POSSIBLE CAUSE AND ACTION
Hearing loss (deafness) (cont.)				
Gradual loss of hearing with age	• Initial reduction in ability to hear higher pitched noises, gradually affects whole hearing range		• Age-related hearing loss occurs in men more commonly than in women • Usually begins between ages 40–50 years	• Ageing-associated hearing loss (presbycusis) • See your doctor
Recurrent episodes of hearing loss, mainly low tone sounds, usually lasting 20 minutes to several hours	• Dizziness, ringing, rushing or buzzing sound in the ears (tinnitus), nausea, feeling of movement or dizziness (vertigo) • Occurs intermittently	• Reducing dietary salt, caffeine, alcohol may help control episodes	• Affects only one ear in the majority of people with the disease • May be caused by fluid in the canals of the inner ear	• Menière's disease • See your doctor • Antiemetics may provide symptomatic relief
Gradual onset of hearing loss on one side	• May have facial weakness on the same side		• Acoustic neuromas grow slowly and are more common in older people	• Acoustic neuroma (a benign tumor of nerve cells) • Tumors may grow large enough to put pressure on other structures (e.g. nerves in the face, jaw or mouth) • See your doctor
Gradual loss of hearing with age, usually in both ears	• May be associated with tinnitus and vertigo		• An inherited condition affecting approximately 1 percent of people	• Otosclerosis • See your doctor
Recent onset inability to hear high-pitched noise, in a person taking medication for another medical problem	• Ringing in the ears, dizziness		• Occurs mainly with antibiotics, particularly those used to treat serious infections in hospital	• Drug-induced ear damage • Check the consumer information on all the medications you take • See your doctor at once • Medications may be altered or stopped and blood tests may be required
Hearing loss in childhood	• Delayed language development		• Infection during pregnancy (e.g. rubella or cytomegalovirus) can cause congenital hearing loss in children • Repeated ear infections may cause deafness in children • Meningitis can lead to hearing loss in one or both ears • Any child with suspected hearing loss or delayed language development should have their hearing tested	• Congenital deafness, meningitis or otitis media • See your doctor

Heartburn

Heartburn does not involve the heart, but is a traditional name given to a symptom of a digestive problem that can often be relieved by indigestion medications. However, it is important to make sure the chest pain is not caused by angina or a heart attack.

SYMPTOM CHARACTERISTIC	ASSOCIATED SYMPTOMS	AGGRAVATING OR ALLEVIATING FACTORS	OTHER RELEVANT FACTORS	POSSIBLE CAUSE AND ACTION
Painful burning sensation in the chest, behind the breast bone, which may rise up to the throat	• Bitter taste in the mouth	• Large meals, fatty or spicy foods may cause symptoms • Lying down or bending may worsen symptoms • Smoking or alcohol may aggravate symptoms • Tight clothing or belts may make symptoms worse	• Typically occurs after food • Heartburn may occur during pregnancy but usually resolves after the baby is born	• Back-washing of food and stomach acid upwards into the esophagus (gastroesophageal reflux) • Take an antacid as advised by your pharmacist or doctor • Avoid foods that seem to cause the symptoms, and do not eat within 2 hours of going to bed • Quit smoking and reduce alcohol intake • Raise the head end of the bed 4 inches (10 centimeters) • Lose weight if you are overweight • See your doctor if you are worried or if symptoms persist
Intermittent pain behind the breast bone, which at first may not be easily distinguished from heartburn		• Worse with exercise, relieved by resting or rapidly acting nitrate drugs	• Most common in those with previous history of coronary heart disease	• Angina pectoris, a form of coronary heart disease • See your doctor at once • Failure to treat the cause of angina may result in a heart attack
Intense chest pain, which may at first be mistaken for severe heartburn	• Pain spreading to left arm or both arms; pain in jaw; feeling of chest being squeezed		• Increased likelihood in a person who has previously had a heart attack or with a history of coronary heart disease	• Heart attack (myocardial infarction) due to sudden loss of blood supply to a section of the heart muscle due to blockage of the coronary arteries supplying the heart muscle • This is a medical emergency • Go to the emergency room or call an ambulance at once

Hip problems

Hip problems often occur following a fall, especially in the elderly, or because of arthritis. Other causes of hip pain and stiffness include frequent running or problems with the cartilage in the hip joint.

SYMPTOM CHARACTERISTIC	ASSOCIATED SYMPTOMS	AGGRAVATING OR ALLEVIATING FACTORS	OTHER RELEVANT FACTORS	POSSIBLE CAUSE AND ACTION
Intense hip pain following a fall	• Leg may be held in an abnormal position, may develop swelling	• Standing, straightening the leg, lifting the leg	• More likely to occur in the elderly	• Hip fracture • See your doctor at once
Pain or clicking on the outside of the hip	• May be some tenderness or swelling	• Aggravated by activities involving repeated hip movement (e.g. running, bicycling, walking, climbing stairs)	• Often related to sporting activities	• Muscle strain, irritation of the sheath covering the muscles on the outer side of the thigh, or bursitis • Rest • See your doctor if you are worried or if symptoms persist
Stiffness and pain in one or both hips	• May have swelling and redness around the joints, stiffness and pain in other joints	• Stiffness often aggravated by long periods in one position • Pain aggravated by lots of walking or standing	• More likely in older people	• Arthritis • See your doctor for advice
In infants, clicking of the hip	• May be some pain when the hip is stretched, movement may be limited		• More common in girls than boys, also more common in babies born breech (buttocks first) or in those with a relative who has the same disorder	• Congenital dislocation of the hip • See your doctor
In teenagers, stiffness in the hip, pain and limping	• May also have pain in the knee or thigh • Affected leg may be twisted outward	• Aggravated by walking	• More common in overweight teens • Affects boys more than girls	• Dislocation of the top of the thigh bone (slipped capital femoral epiphysis) • See your doctor at once
In children, gradual onset of hip pain and stiffness; symptoms progress slowly	• Limping, wasting of thigh muscles, limited movements	• Aggravated by walking	• Most common in 5–10 year olds • Affects boys more than girls	• Degeneration of the top of the thigh bone (Perthes disease) • See your doctor
Shooting or burning pain in the back of one hip or buttock; pain may travel down the back of one leg	• May also have low back pain, numbness or tingling in the foot	• Aggravated by coughing, sneezing, bending, lifting	• More common in people with stiff backs or past back injury	• Sciatica • See your doctor

Hot flashes/flushes

Hot flashes/flushes is a classic symptom of menopause. Often symptoms are not severe enough to require treatment, but it is still worthwhile visiting your doctor to talk about the effects of menopause and possible strategies to prevent unnecessary discomfort. Certain conditions become much more common in women after menopause, especially heart disease and osteoporosis. See also entry on *skin problems* for other causes of flushing.

SYMPTOM CHARACTERISTIC	ASSOCIATED SYMPTOMS	AGGRAVATING OR ALLEVIATING FACTORS	OTHER RELEVANT FACTORS	POSSIBLE CAUSE AND ACTION
Episodes of sudden transient warmth and redness of the face, neck and upper chest in women	• Menstrual irregularities, nervousness, anxiety, irritability, fatigue, depression, urinary problems, vaginal dryness and irritation		• Frequency and severity varies greatly between individuals, usually begins in late 40s or early 50s	• Onset of menopause • See your doctor
Episodes of sudden transient warmth and redness of the face, neck and upper chest in a person taking hormonal medication		• Usually worst at commencement of course of medication and settles over time	• Hot flushes related to sex hormone changes may be associated with some medications (e.g. treatment for endometriosis or breast cancer in women, prostate cancer in men)	• Medication-related estrogen deficiency (women) or androgen deficiency (men) • See your doctor
Flushing of face and neck in a person taking medication			• Hot flushes may occur as a side effect of some medications (e.g. medications used in hypertension, Alzheimer's disease) or as an unusual reaction to a wide range of drugs	• Adverse effect of medication • See your doctor

Jaundice

Jaundice is a yellow discoloration of the skin and eyes due to excessive bile pigment (bilirubin) in the blood. Jaundice may be caused by abnormal breakdown of red blood cells releasing pigment into the blood (hemolytic anemia), inflammation or disease of the liver preventing excretion of bilirubin or obstruction of the flow of bile into the bowel. Jaundice always warrants a thorough medical assessment to determine the underlying cause.

SYMPTOM CHARACTERISTIC	ASSOCIATED SYMPTOMS	AGGRAVATING OR ALLEVIATING FACTORS	OTHER RELEVANT FACTORS	POSSIBLE CAUSE AND ACTION
Jaundice in a baby within the first 24 hours of life	• Sleepiness, poor feeding	• Dehydration may make the jaundice worse	• May be a history of jaundice in previous babies • Jaundice in the first 24 hours of life is always abnormal and is usually due to a mismatch of mother and baby's blood groups • High levels of jaundice can be dangerous to young babies	• Hemolytic anemia • See your doctor at once
Mild jaundice in a baby in the first few days of life	• Baby is otherwise well	• Dehydration may make the jaundice worse	• More common in breast fed babies and babies bruised during delivery	• Physiological jaundice • See your doctor

SYMPTOM CHARACTERISTIC	ASSOCIATED SYMPTOMS	AGGRAVATING OR ALLEVIATING FACTORS	OTHER RELEVANT FACTORS	POSSIBLE CAUSE AND ACTION
Jaundice (cont.)				
Gradual onset of jaundice or recurrent episodes of jaundice	• Color of urine and bowel movements are normal, spleen may be enlarged • Sickle cell disease can lead to sudden episodes of severe chest, abdominal or limb pain known as a sickle cell crisis	• Jaundice is more severe if underlying liver disease is present	• Pigment from red blood cells is released into the blood faster than the liver can excrete it; may be a history family history of abnormal red blood cells • Hemolytic anemia occurs in sickle cell disease, a genetic disorder of platelets which is more common among black racial groups	• Hemolytic anemia • See your doctor at once
Episode of jaundice lasting weeks to months	• Headache, fever, nausea, vomiting, abdominal pain, fatigue • Bowel movements may be pale, urine may be dark	• Jaundice fades as inflammation of the liver resolves	• Hepatitis A infection may result from eating contaminated food and is common with travel to a developing country • Intravenous drug use, unprotected sex and healthcare work involving the usage of needles increase a person's risk of contracting hepatitis B or C	• Viral hepatitis • See your doctor at once
Gradual onset of jaundice which is progressive	• Itchiness, loss of appetite, fatigue, weakness and muscle wasting, red palms, abdominal distension, vomiting blood or black sticky bowel movements, memory loss and confusion	• Excess alcohol or drugs that can damage the liver can increase the jaundice	• May be a history of hepatitis B or C infection, alcohol abuse or other liver disease	• Cirrhosis of the liver • See your doctor at once
Gradual onset of jaundice or recurrent episodes of jaundice	• Dark urine and pale bowel movements, itchiness, may be fever, abdominal pain or chills	• Jaundice fades once obstruction of the bile ducts is resolved	• Due to obstruction of the flow of bile from the liver to the bowel • May be a history of gallstones, liver disease or a family history of jaundice	• Obstructive jaundice • See your doctor at once
Gradual onset of jaundice in a person taking medications	• Itchiness	• Jaundice fades when medication is ceased	• Some antibiotics, anticonvulsant drugs, oral contraceptive pills and anesthetic agents can cause jaundice	• Medication-induced jaundice • See your doctor at once

Knee problems

Knee pain is a common symptom in all age groups. Problems range from mild pain under the kneecap to ligament tears requiring surgery. The knee is also a common site for developing arthritis.

SYMPTOM CHARACTERISTIC	ASSOCIATED SYMPTOMS	AGGRAVATING OR ALLEVIATING FACTORS	OTHER RELEVANT FACTORS	POSSIBLE CAUSE AND ACTION
Intermittent pain under the kneecap	• May be some tenderness when the kneecap is pushed down on the thigh bone (femur), may be some grating under the kneecap	• Aggravated by walking up and, particularly, down stairs or hills, aching when sitting for long periods of time, running, jumping	• Most common in people involved in sports or who have jobs requiring a lot of knee bending or walking up and down stairs	• Patellofemoral pain syndrome ("runner's knee") • Try to avoid activities that make the pain worse • See your doctor if you are worried or if symptoms persist
Intermittent pain inside the knee or along one side of the knee, often starts following a twisting injury	• Knee may lock, may feel blocked and unable to straighten it fully, may have clicking of the knee; some swelling may be present	• Aggravated by squatting or twisting	• More commonly occurs on the medial (inside) part of the knee	• Tearing of the cartilage in the knee (meniscus) • Apply ice and rest • See your doctor
Knee pain following a fall, twisting injury, hyperextension (knee forced straight) injury, or direct blow to the knee	• Popping sound at the time of injury, swelling that develops soon after the injury, giving way of the knee	• Giving way is aggravated by twisting movements or change of direction	• Common sporting injury and one of the most serious, often requiring surgery and extensive rehabilitation	• Tearing of one of the ligaments running through the knee joint from front to back (anterior cruciate ligament) • See your doctor
Long-term aching and stiffness in the knee which has become worse over a period of months	• Limited movement; the person may be unable to bend or straighten fully	• Pain is alleviated by rest, aggravated by a lot of activity • Stiffness is often worse in the morning	• More common in people over 50 years	• Osteoarthritis • See your doctor
Pain along the inner or outer knee, usually following a direct force to one side of the knee while the foot remains planted on the ground	• Tenderness on one side of the knee	• Twisting the leg while the foot stays on the ground	• Often occurs during sports such as soccer, football, skiing	• Damage to one or more of the ligaments on the inside or outside of the knee (collateral ligaments) • See your doctor
Pain, warmth and stiffness just below the kneecap	• Swelling and tenderness below the kneecap	• Bending, kneeling	• More common in people whose occupation requires frequent or prolonged kneeling	• Bursitis ("housemaid's knee") • See your doctor
Red, swollen knee	• Constant ache, swelling, fever, generally feeling unwell	• May be aggravated by movement	• Infection may spread through the blood, through a penetrating injury	• Osteomyelitis or joint infection (septic arthritis) • See your doctor at once

SYMPTOM CHARACTERISTIC	ASSOCIATED SYMPTOMS	AGGRAVATING OR ALLEVIATING FACTORS	OTHER RELEVANT FACTORS	POSSIBLE CAUSE AND ACTION

Leg problems

Leg problems can arise from a variety of conditions, from simple muscle strains to fractures and serious circulation disorders. See also entries on *knee problems, hip problems,* and *foot and ankle problems.*

SYMPTOM CHARACTERISTIC	ASSOCIATED SYMPTOMS	AGGRAVATING OR ALLEVIATING FACTORS	OTHER RELEVANT FACTORS	POSSIBLE CAUSE AND ACTION
Sudden pain in the leg associated with quick movement of the leg (e.g. kicking, sprinting, change of direction)	• Swelling, bruising	• Stretching or bending the leg but can still move it	• Common sporting injury, often affects hamstrings (muscles at back of thigh), quadriceps (muscles on the front of thigh) and calf muscles	• Muscle strain or tear • Rest and apply ice to the area • See your doctor
Severe, constant leg pain following an injury, fall or direct blow to the leg	• Swelling, may be some deformity of the leg	• Aggravated by attempts to walk or move the leg		• Fracture • This is a medical emergency • Go to the emergency room or call an ambulance at once
Intermittent pain over the front of the shin	• Maybe some pain when the shin is pressed	• Repetitive motion (e.g. running, bicycling, jumping, walking up and down hills)	• More common in those with flat feet, bow legs, knock knees	• Shin splints • See your doctor
Prominent veins in the legs	• Aching in the legs, foot swelling, itching	• Aggravated by standing for long periods of time • Alleviated by elevating the legs while lying down	• More common in women than men • Can worsen during pregnancy	• Varicose veins • Wear support stockings • See your doctor
Cramping pain in the calves, feet or hips while walking	• May develop numbness or tingling in the feet	• Aggravated by walking, especially quickly or up hills, usually alleviated by rest	• Risk is increased in people with abnormal cholesterol or triglyceride levels, diabetes, hypertension, men over 55 years old, women over 65 years old, those with a family history of cardiovascular disease, cigarette smokers, and those with obesity or little physical activity	• Peripheral vascular disease • See your doctor
Shooting or burning pain in the buttock and down the back of one leg	• May also have low back pain, numbness or tingling in the foot	• Aggravated by coughing, sneezing, bending, lifting	• More common in people with stiff backs or past back injury	• Sciatica • See your doctor
Pain and swelling in the back of the calf	• Warmth, pain when touched		• Most common following surgery or following long air flights or bus trips	• Deep venous thrombosis • This is a medical emergency • Go to the emergency room or call an ambulance at once

Memory loss

Among elderly people, memory loss is a common complaint. A family member may be the first to notice the problem. Dementia is a common cause of significant memory impairment in this age group, but correctable conditions or other causes may be discovered on medical assessment. Certain medications, such as sedatives, can precipitate sudden memory impairment.

SYMPTOM CHARACTERISTIC	ASSOCIATED SYMPTOMS	AGGRAVATING OR ALLEVIATING FACTORS	OTHER RELEVANT FACTORS	POSSIBLE CAUSE AND ACTION
Gradual onset of forgetfulness in everyday affairs, (e.g. misplacing things, difficulty remembering names, difficulty remembering things to be done)			• Typically occurs in an otherwise healthy person over 50 years	• Benign forgetfulness associated with age • Use memory aids such as lists and mnemonics • See your doctor if you are worried or if symptoms persist
Memory loss, usually developing gradually over months or years; memory progressively declines; ability to remember recent events is affected more than events that happened long ago	• Gradual relentless decline in thinking skills and overall mental function • Unusual behavior • Decline in standards of personal care		• Usually elderly people • Sometimes a correctable cause may be identified • Dementia may occur as a result of other diseases (e.g. AIDS)	• Dementia • See your doctor
Memory loss, usually of gradual onset over days or weeks	• Loss of concentration • Sadness • Lack of enjoyment in life • Difficulty sleeping • Low self-esteem		• May occur in any age group • Depression is a probable explanation if forgetfulness occurs in a young or middle-aged person • May have been precipitated by a personal loss	• Depression • See your doctor
Memory loss usually of rapid onset			• Any age group • A likely possibility if forgetfulness occurs in a young person or in middle age	• Alcohol (alcoholism) or drug abuse (drug dependence) • See your doctor
Sudden memory loss	• Headaches, vomiting, fever		• The risk of stroke is increased in people with a history of coronary heart disease, hypertension or other cardiovascular disease, abnormal cholesterol levels, and cigarette smokers • Professional fighters (e.g. boxers) are prone to trauma-related memory loss	• Brain tumor, infection (e.g. meningitis, encephalitis), stroke, severe or repeated trauma • See your doctor

Menstrual problems

Most menstrual problems warrant a full medical investigation, since they may indicate the presence of a disease that requires treatment. Although period pain or premenstrual syndrome may respond to simple self-treatment, it is important to ask your doctor's advice if symptoms persist or worsen.

SYMPTOM CHARACTERISTIC	ASSOCIATED SYMPTOMS	AGGRAVATING OR ALLEVIATING FACTORS	OTHER RELEVANT FACTORS	POSSIBLE CAUSE AND ACTION
Temporary emotional instability just prior to menstrual period	• Bloating or discomfort in lower abdomen, irritability, depression, tearfulness, inability to concentrate, sleep disturbances, fatigue, lethargy	• Symptoms usually disappear when menstruation begins • Caffeine may worsen irritability	• Approximately one-third of fertile women experience some premenstrual symptoms • The full premenstrual syndrome occurs in about 3–10 percent	• Premenstrual syndrome (PMS) • There is no standard treatment • Ask your pharmacist's advice on over-the-counter medication for bloating or pain • Vitamin B_6 supplements may help ease the symptoms • See your doctor if you are worried or if symptoms persist
Mild to moderate cramping pain during menstrual period		• Pain may be aggravated by flatulence or constipation • Pain may be alleviated by heat applied to the lower abdomen (e.g. a hot water bottle or bath)	• Period pain sufficiently severe to cause missed school or work days is common in teenagers and young women • Severe symptoms may suggest endometriosis	• Period pain (menstruation) • Try analgesic or non-steroidal anti-inflammatory drugs as recommended by your pharmacist • See your doctor if you are worried or if symptoms persist
Gradual onset of more pain than usual during and just before menstrual period	• Low back pain, period pain lasting more than 2–3 days and starting before the onset of bleeding • Spotting of small amounts of blood for 1–3 days prior to onset of period • Menstrual bleeding may be heavier than usual	• Pain in pelvic area may worsen during sexual contact • Pregnancy may temporarily resolve the problem, though symptoms may recur months or years later	• Endometriosis occurs in approximately 5–10 percent of women, and is more likely in women with a mother or sister with the disease, and in women who have never become pregnant • Endometriosis may result in infertility	• Endometriosis • See your doctor
More pain than usual during and just before menstrual period	• Fever, vaginal discharge with offensive odor, abnormal vaginal bleeding, abdominal pain, pain during urination • Onset of symptoms is usually gradual when caused by an intrauterine device (IUD)		• Pelvic inflammatory disease occurs almost exclusively in sexually active women • Pelvic inflammatory disease may result from infections (usually sexually transmitted infections), uterine surgery (e.g. dilation and curettage, insertion of IUD, cesarean section) or childbirth	• Pelvic inflammatory disease • See your doctor at once

SYMPTOM CHARACTERISTIC	ASSOCIATED SYMPTOMS	AGGRAVATING OR ALLEVIATING FACTORS	OTHER RELEVANT FACTORS	POSSIBLE CAUSE AND ACTION
Increased volume and length of menstrual bleeding in women with an intrauterine device (IUD)	• Spotting of blood between menstrual periods, increased pain during periods		• IUD may change the pattern of menstrual bleeding	IUD related adverse effect See your doctor
Excessive menstrual bleeding	• Pain during menstrual bleeding, longer than usual menstrual periods		• Fibroids are most common in women over 35 years old or who have had several pregnancies	• Uterine fibroids • See your doctor
Irregularity or cessation of menstrual periods in a woman who is not pregnant	• Fatigue or lethargy may occur with thyroid disease		• A menstrual period may occasional be missed in some women during the use of oral contraceptives • Excessive exercise or weight loss (e.g. during athletic training or anorexia nervosa) may cause cessation of menstrual periods	• Hormonal abnormality due to an ovarian problem, oral contraceptive use or a thyroid problem • See your doctor
Cessation of menstrual periods in sexually active women	• Breast tenderness, abdominal bloating or feeling of fullness, nausea		• All methods of contraception carry a slight chance of failure leading to pregnancy	• Pregnancy • Use pregnancy test kit—if positive, see your doctor • See your doctor if you are worried or if symptoms persist
Cessation of menstrual periods in women aged over 35 years	• Irritability, hot flushes (flashes)	• Estrogen supplements, plant estrogens or diets high in soy may relieve symptoms of menopause	• The onset of menopause most commonly occurs between the ages of 40–55 • Early menopause may occur from 35 years, or younger in rare cases	• Menopause • See your doctor
Recommencement of menstrual bleeding in a woman who has already gone through menopause	• Abdominal swelling or discomfort, vaginal discharge		• Some hormonal medications may cause uterine bleeding	• Uterine tumor or vaginal infection • See your doctor

SYMPTOM CHARACTERISTIC	ASSOCIATED SYMPTOMS	AGGRAVATING OR ALLEVIATING FACTORS	OTHER RELEVANT FACTORS	POSSIBLE CAUSE AND ACTION

Nail abnormalities

Injury and fungal infections are the most common causes of nail changes. Since some causes may indicate other conditions or permanently damage the nail bed, it is advisable to ask your doctor's advice on any nail abnormalities that does not heal quickly. If there is a build-up of skin crusts under the nail, do not attempt to remove debris from under the nail with manicure instruments until the condition has been checked by a doctor.

SYMPTOM CHARACTERISTIC	ASSOCIATED SYMPTOMS	AGGRAVATING OR ALLEVIATING FACTORS	OTHER RELEVANT FACTORS	POSSIBLE CAUSE AND ACTION
Crusty light-colored build-up under the nails	• Light-colored band at the end of the nail, vertical light-colored lines running from the nail tip towards the cuticle, lifting of nail, pain, crusty white skin between the fingers or toes	• Recent use of public showers or direct skin contact with a person with a fungal infection	• Toenails are more commonly affected than fingernails	• Fungal infection of the nail (onychomycosis) • These symptoms may also occur with psoriasis • See your doctor
Uneven ridges in the nail	• Bruising under the nail may have occurred some weeks before the nail begins to grow unevenly		• History of injury to the nail	• Nail bed injury • Nails may become misshapen due to trauma ranging from mild unnoticed stubbing of finger or toe, to an obvious cause like slamming the fingernail in a door • See your doctor if you are worried or if symptoms persist
Lifting of the hard part of the nail (the nail plate) from the soft tissue underneath (the nail bed)	• Pain, build-up of debris	• May be due to damage to the quick caused by scraping too deeply when cleaning under nails	• Fingernails are more commonly affected	• Psoriasis, fungal infections or nail injury • These symptoms may also occur for no known reason • Keep the nail area dry, keep the nail short, avoid scraping debris from under the nail and use only mild soap and shampoos • See your doctor if you are worried or if symptoms persist
Discoloration of nail plate (green)	• Moisture may be present under the nail	• Attempts to clean under the nail may cause spreading	• Commonly occurs with long fingernails	• Infection under the nail • See your doctor
Discoloration of the nail (red to black)	• Pain (feeling of uncomfortable pressure to severe throbbing pain)		• May follow known injury	• Bruise under the nail • Black discoloration may also follow the use of the antibiotic minocycline, or may indicate melanoma • See your doctor

SYMPTOM CHARACTERISTIC	ASSOCIATED SYMPTOMS	AGGRAVATING OR ALLEVIATING FACTORS	OTHER RELEVANT FACTORS	POSSIBLE CAUSE AND ACTION
Discoloration (blue, yellow, white)			• May be associated with medications or other medical conditions	• Nail discoloration may occur with the use of medications such as antimalarial drugs (blue) or antibiotics (white, black) • It also occurs with cirrhosis of the liver (white) or renal failure (red) • See your doctor
Thinning and roughening of all nails of toes and fingers	• Non-painful		• Occurs in pre-adolescent children	• "Twenty nail" dystrophy • Although it usually heals without treatment, it may indicate the onset of other skin diseases • See your doctor
Abnormal spoon-shaped concavity of nails (koilonychia)	• Fatigue, pallor (if anemia is cause) • Fatigue, joint pain (if hemochromatosis is the cause)		• This type of curvature may occur in children without any other condition • Hemochromatosis is an inherited condition that is most common in Caucasians	• Koilonychia may occur for no discernible reason, with iron deficiency anemia or with hemochromatosis • See your doctor
Exaggerated lengthwise curvature of nail (clubbing)	• Symptoms of underlying disease; caused by another medical condition • May also be boggy feeling around nail		• Parents or other relatives may have similar-shaped nails	• Clubbing may simply be hereditary, or can occur with liver, lung or heart diseases • See your doctor
Exaggerated curve of nails (over-curvature)	• There may be pain in the soft tissue at the sides of the nail		• Parents or other relatives may have similar-shaped nails	• May be due to ingrown toenail, or simply hereditary ("pincer" nail) • Avoid trimming outer edges of nail • See your doctor if you are worried or if symptoms persist
Swelling of the skin around the edges of the nail	• Pain	• Swelling may worsen following damage by rough manicure or injury to nail	• Manicure may cause damage to cuticle	• May follow injury or may occur with infections such as herpes, candidiasis ("thrush") • Keep the area clean and dry • See your doctor

SYMPTOM CHARACTERISTIC	ASSOCIATED SYMPTOMS	AGGRAVATING OR ALLEVIATING FACTORS	OTHER RELEVANT FACTORS	POSSIBLE CAUSE AND ACTION

Nausea and vomiting

Nausea and vomiting occur with many medical conditions, and the cause is not always obvious. Since some conditions that may cause these symptoms are potentially serious, it is advisable to consult a doctor if the problem does not resolve quickly. If symptoms recur, and/or are accompanied by any other unusual symptoms, you may need medical tests to find the problem. When a person vomits blood or has severe pain, the situation should be treated as an emergency and a doctor consulted at once.

SYMPTOM CHARACTERISTIC	ASSOCIATED SYMPTOMS	AGGRAVATING OR ALLEVIATING FACTORS	OTHER RELEVANT FACTORS	POSSIBLE CAUSE AND ACTION
Nausea and vomiting that does not occur within a short time of eating and seems unrelated to food eaten, in a person taking medication	• Unusual taste or general feeling of slight nausea between episodes	• There may be no distinct pattern	• Recent commencement of a new medication or combination	• Reaction to a medication • See your doctor if you are worried or if symptoms persist
Persistent nausea and vomiting over more than a week in women of child-bearing age	• Missed menstrual period	• Certain foods or smells may worsen symptoms • Symptoms may be consistently worse at certain times of day	• Non-predictable; a woman may experience morning sickness with one pregnancy but not a subsequent pregnancy	• "Morning sickness" of pregnancy • See your doctor • Avoid an empty stomach by eating frequent small meals • Nibbling dry crackers between meals and before getting out of bed may help
Nausea and vomiting after eating	• Diarrhea may follow	• Unable to tolerate food or liquids	• Symptoms occur after eating food that may have been kept too long or at incorrect temperature such as hot food kept warm several hours, or cold food that has been kept at room temperature or uncovered for several hours	• Bacterial contamination of food (food poisoning) • Take frequent small amounts of fluid, if tolerated • Typical cases of food poisoning will usually pass in under 12 hours • See your doctor if the person is severely ill and unable to drink fluids, if you are worried or if symptoms persist
Intermittent nausea and vomiting	• Burning pain high in the abdomen	• Worse after eating, especially spicy foods • Bland foods may relieve pain	• Use of anti-inflammatory medications for pain (prescription or non-prescription) may damage stomach lining • Ulcers are commonly caused by a bacterial infection and require antibiotics	• Gastritis, or ulcer of stomach or esophagus • If symptoms are mild and not persistent, use an antacid (your pharmacist may advise you on a suitable choice) • See your doctor

SYMPTOM CHARACTERISTIC	ASSOCIATED SYMPTOMS	AGGRAVATING OR ALLEVIATING FACTORS	OTHER RELEVANT FACTORS	POSSIBLE CAUSE AND ACTION
Recent onset nausea and vomiting	• Fever and cold or flu symptoms, diarrhea	• Inability to tolerate food or liquids		• Viral gastroenteritis • Rest and take frequent small amounts of fluids if tolerated (e.g. diluted soft drink or an electrolyte sachet from your pharmacist) • Your doctor or pharmacist may advise you further about treating specific symptoms • See your doctor if the person is unable to tolerate fluids, if you are worried or if symptoms persist
Nausea and vomiting with intermittent severe pain	• Pain in the upper right abdomen, fever	• Pain may worsen after eating greasy foods		• Gallbladder inflammation or gallstones • See your doctor if you are worried or if symptoms persist
Nausea and vomiting with steady worsening pain	• Recent onset abdominal pain in middle or lower right, fever		• Pain may begin as dull discomfort centrally and become more severe and localized to the right side	• Appendicitis or a bowel obstruction • This is a medical emergency • Go to the emergency room or call an ambulance at once
Nausea and vomiting in a person with diabetes			• High blood sugar on blood test using home monitoring kit and ketones on urine strip test	• Ketoacidosis, a complication of diabetes • This is a medical emergency • Go to the emergency room or call an ambulance at once
Vomiting in a baby or young child	• Crying, irritability or quietness, inability to become interested in toys		• Child under 2 vomiting for more than 6 hours, or child over 2 vomiting for more than 12 hours	• Viral infections are a common cause • Children may rapidly become dehydrated • See your doctor • If you suspect severe dehydration, go to the emergency room or call an ambulance at once
Vomiting in a baby or young child	• Uncontrollable crying, dark red diarrhea, unable to keep down any fluids		• Obstruction is relatively rare	• Intestinal obstruction • This is an emergency • Visit your doctor or the emergency room at once

SYMPTOM CHARACTERISTIC	ASSOCIATED SYMPTOMS	AGGRAVATING OR ALLEVIATING FACTORS	OTHER RELEVANT FACTORS	POSSIBLE CAUSE AND ACTION
Nausea and vomiting (cont.)				
Vomiting in a baby	• Forceful expulsion of stomach contents, persistent vomiting		• 20 percent of healthy babies vomit or regurgitate frequently enough to worry parents and cause them to seek medical advice • Approximately 7 percent of babies show more severe symptoms suggesting gastroesophageal reflux disease	• Stomach obstruction or reflux • Ask your doctor's advice to confirm the cause

Neck problems

Symptoms involving the neck may result from a wide variety of conditions. Infections in the body will often lead to swelling of the neck glands, while poor posture and arthritis can cause neck pain and stiffness.

SYMPTOM CHARACTERISTIC	ASSOCIATED SYMPTOMS	AGGRAVATING OR ALLEVIATING FACTORS	OTHER RELEVANT FACTORS	POSSIBLE CAUSE AND ACTION
Dull ache in the neck that comes on gradually, often when sitting or standing in one position for prolonged periods of time	• Tightness and ache across the shoulders and back of the head, headache	• May be aggravated by sitting in a slumped position, prolonged forward head posture (e.g. when typing or reading) • May also be aggravated by stress and anxiety • May be alleviated by moving the head and neck and changing positions frequently	• Common in those who have poor posture (e.g. rounded shoulders, slouched sitting, and in those whose work involves sitting at a desk or computer)	• Muscle fatigue or strain • Avoid prolonged neck positions and improve posture • See your doctor if you are worried or if symptoms persist
Neck stiffness that is present after sleep or periods of inactivity, gradually worsens over time	• Pain and limitation of movement, spine may be tender to touch	• Aggravated by periods of inactivity or following exercise • May be alleviated by moving the neck gently	• Most common in those aged over 40	• Osteoarthritis • See your doctor
Neck pain that develops after a jolt to the neck (e.g. a car stopping suddenly)	• Muscle spasm, stiffness, dizziness, headache • Severe injury can cause numbness and tingling in the arms and legs, weakness, difficulty walking	• May be aggravated by movements of the neck	• Most commonly develops after a car accident	• Whiplash injury • See your doctor at once • If there are severe symptoms (numbness, tingling, weakness, difficulty walking), this is a medical emergency • Go to the emergency room or call an ambulance at once
Swelling or a lump at the side or back of the neck	• Pain, fever, general feeling of illness	• Aggravated by touching the area, sometimes by neck movement	• There may be an infection near the area (e.g. strep (streptococcal) throat, scalp infection, ear infection)	• Enlarged lymph nodes caused by bacterial or viral infection • See your doctor

SYMPTOM CHARACTERISTIC	ASSOCIATED SYMPTOMS	AGGRAVATING OR ALLEVIATING FACTORS	OTHER RELEVANT FACTORS	POSSIBLE CAUSE AND ACTION
Intense neck pain that radiates into the shoulders and possibly down the arms	• Tingling or numbness in the hands, arm weakness	• Aggravated by neck movements, especially bending the head forward • May be aggravated by sneezing or coughing	• May follow an injury or begin after regular daily activities	• Vertebral disk injury causing pressure on a spinal nerve • See your doctor
Lumps in the neck that have been growing, or have been in the neck for more than 2 weeks	• Fatigue, fever, night sweats, weight loss		• Lumps are usually painless	• Tumor (e.g. lymphoma or leukemia) • See your doctor at once
Neck stiffness with a severe headache	• Vomiting, fever, drowsiness, may become delirious, unconscious or have convulsions	• Exposure to bright lights increases the pain	• A child may be difficult to wake or have a high-pitched cry	• Meningitis • This is a medical emergency • Go to the emergency room or call an ambulance at once

Nosebleed

Nosebleeds occur very commonly and are usually harmless. They usually happen infrequently and simple pressure to the nose is enough to control the bleeding. Sometimes bleeding can be severe and requires treatment by a doctor to prevent major blood loss. Any frequent or severe nosebleeds should be assessed by a doctor.

SYMPTOM CHARACTERISTIC	ASSOCIATED SYMPTOMS	AGGRAVATING OR ALLEVIATING FACTORS	OTHER RELEVANT FACTORS	POSSIBLE CAUSE AND ACTION
Spontaneous bleeding from the nose of mild to moderate severity	• Person is otherwise well	• Blowing the nose may increase bleeding	• No history of injury • Common in winter when cold dry air dries out the lining of the nose	• Nosebleed of unknown cause (idiopathic epistaxis) • Apply pressure by pinching the nose • See your doctor if you are worried or if symptoms persist
Mild to severe bleeding from the nose	• Nasal pain, swelling, nasal deformity	• Blowing the nose may increase bleeding	• History of injury	• Injury to the lining of the nose • Apply pressure by pinching the nose • See your doctor if you are worried or if symptoms persist
Recurrent episodes of mild to severe bleeding from the nose	• Red spidery spots on the skin and mucous membranes which become pale on pressure	• Irritation of the lining of the nose can increase bleeding	• May be a family history of blood vessel disorders	• Abnormality of the blood vessels of the nose (hereditary telangiectasia) • See your doctor
Recurrent episodes of mild to severe bleeding from the nose	• Headache, throbbing	• Stress or exertion may precipitate a bleed	• More common in the elderly • May be a history of hypertension	• Hypertension • Apply pressure by pinching the nose • See your doctor

SYMPTOM CHARACTERISTIC	ASSOCIATED SYMPTOMS	AGGRAVATING OR ALLEVIATING FACTORS	OTHER RELEVANT FACTORS	POSSIBLE CAUSE AND ACTION
Nosebleed (cont.)				
Sudden onset of moderate to severe bleeding from the nose	• No pain, easy bruising, prolonged bleeding after minor cuts	• Blowing the nose may increase bleeding	• May be a family history of bleeding problems such as hemophilia • Person may be taking blood thinners	• Bleeding disorder • Apply pressure by pinching the nose • See your doctor
Episodes of mild to severe bleeding from the nose	• Gradual onset of nasal obstruction, deafness (build up of fluid in the middle ear)	• Symptoms resolve when underlying condition is treated	• Vascular tumors of the nose usually occur in young men under the age of 25 years • Malignant tumors of the nose are common in Southeast Asia representing 20 percent of all malignant tumors	• Nasal tumor • See your doctor at once

Numbness and tingling

A feeling of numbness or tingling usually results from a malfunction in part of the body's nervous system. The symptoms may be caused by an isolated problem in one nerve, or may be part of a more serious degenerative disease. See also entry on *weakness and paralysis*.

SYMPTOM CHARACTERISTIC	ASSOCIATED SYMPTOMS	AGGRAVATING OR ALLEVIATING FACTORS	OTHER RELEVANT FACTORS	POSSIBLE CAUSE AND ACTION
Numbness or tingling in the hand, foot, arm or leg after being in one position	• May feel some mild stiffness when start to move	• Further aggravated by remaining in the same position • Alleviated by moving around		• Nerve compression • See your doctor if you are worried or if symptoms persist
Numbness or tingling in one arm or one leg	• Neck or back pain, weakness of the affected limb • In serious cases, may have difficulty urinating	• Aggravated by sitting, bending forward, sneezing, coughing	• The precise location of the symtoms defines which part of the back or neck is affected	• Pressure on a nerve caused by swelling of a ruptured or bulging vertebral disk in the spine • See your doctor at once
Numbness and tingling in the palm of the hand and wrist; may be worse at night	• Shooting pain into the hand, weakness, maybe mild swelling	• Flexing the wrist, making a fist	• More common in women • Also occurs in people who have to perform repeated forceful movements of the wrist (e.g. using a screwdriver)	• Carpal tunnel syndrome • See your doctor
Numbness or tingling in the hands and face, especially around the lips	• Palpitations, shaking, fear, anxiety	• Aggravated by stress, and fear of another attack	• Women are 2–3 times more likely to have an attack than men	• Panic attack • See your doctor if you are worried or if symptoms persist

SYMPTOM CHARACTERISTIC	ASSOCIATED SYMPTOMS	AGGRAVATING OR ALLEVIATING FACTORS	OTHER RELEVANT FACTORS	POSSIBLE CAUSE AND ACTION
Tingling or numbness in the arms, legs, trunk or face	• Loss of strength or dexterity, vision disturbances, dizziness, unusual tiredness, difficulty walking, trembling, loss of bladder control	• Aggravated by very warm weather, hot bath, fever	• More common among people who have lived in a temperate climate up to age 10 • Occurs much less commonly in those whose childhood was spent in a tropical climate, and extremely rare at the equator	• Multiple sclerosis • See your doctor at once
Numbness or tingling on one side of the body; symptoms usually start suddenly	• Weakness in hands or feet, confusion, dizziness, partial loss of vision or hearing, slurred speech, inability to recognize parts of the body, unusual movements, fainting		• More common with advancing age • Risk increased in people with cardiovascular disease (e.g. hypertension, coronary heart disease) lipid abnormalities (e.g. high cholesterol), diabetes	• Transient ischemic attack or stroke • This is a medical emergency • Go to the emergency room or call an ambulance at once

Palpitations

Palpitations is the term used to describe an uncomfortable awareness of your heartbeat. The palpitations may take the form of fluttering, throbbing, pounding or racing in the chest. The heart may feel as though it is beating irregularly. Palpitations may be harmless, but in certain cases they signal underlying heart disease.

SYMPTOM CHARACTERISTIC	ASSOCIATED SYMPTOMS	AGGRAVATING OR ALLEVIATING FACTORS	OTHER RELEVANT FACTORS	POSSIBLE CAUSE AND ACTION
Recurrent fluttering, racing, pounding, thumping in the chest; may have feeling of a strong pulse in the neck	• Chest discomfort, weakness, dizziness, shortness of breath		• There are many types of variation from normal heartbeat rhythm, some of which are serious • Arrhythmia is most commonly caused by heart disease, but may also occur with caffeine use, excessive alcohol, vigorous exercise	• Arrhythmia • See your doctor at once
Temporary racing, pounding, thumping in the chest; usually lasts for 10–20 minutes	• Trembling, dizziness, shortness of breath, feeling of choking, nausea, diarrhea, an out-of-body sensation, tingling in the hands, chills, fear of dying	• May be aggravated by stress, and the fear of further attacks	• Women are 2–3 times more likely than men to have these attacks	• Panic attack • See your doctor if you are worried or if symptoms persist
Racing heartbeat	• Shortness of breath on exertion, tiring easily, swelling in the legs and abdomen • May be sudden fever and flu-like symptoms	• May be aggravated by exertion	• Can occur as the result of infection, or in association with many diseases, or may have no identifiable cause	• Cardiomyopathy (disease of the heart muscle) • See your doctor at once

SYMPTOM CHARACTERISTIC	ASSOCIATED SYMPTOMS	AGGRAVATING OR ALLEVIATING FACTORS	OTHER RELEVANT FACTORS	POSSIBLE CAUSE AND ACTION
Palpitations (cont.)				
Awareness of forceful heartbeats, especially when lying on the left side	• Shortness of breath on exertion, swelling of the legs, chest pain, dizziness		• More common in those who have had rheumatic fever	• Heart valve disorder • See your doctor for advice
Sudden heavy pounding or thumping in the chest	• Pain in the middle of the chest that may spread down the left arm, sweating, shortness of breath, faintness, anxiousness, sense of impending doom	• Symptoms are not alleviated by rest	• Increased likelihood in a person who has previously had a heart attack or with a history of coronary heart disease	• Myocardial infarction (heart attack) • This is a medical emergency • Go to the emergency room or call an ambulance at once

Seizures (known as "fits", including convulsions)

Seizures result from an abrupt episode of abnormal electrical activity within the brain. There are many different types of seizures and many possible causes. Seizures may be generalized (generalized tonic-clonic convulsion also known as grand mal seizure) or localized to a particular part of the body (focal convulsion). Some seizures manifest as a brief aura followed by loss of awareness of surroundings. Any seizure warrants assessment by a doctor and often full medical investigation.

SYMPTOM CHARACTERISTIC	ASSOCIATED SYMPTOMS	AGGRAVATING OR ALLEVIATING FACTORS	OTHER RELEVANT FACTORS	POSSIBLE CAUSE AND ACTION
Repeated episodes of a generalized tonic-clonic seizure (grand mal seizure); begins with stiffness of limbs and jaw locking (tonic phase) followed by jerking of limbs (clonic phase) then a period of drowsiness and confusion (postictal phase)	• Urinary incontinence during fit	• Sleep deprivation, flickering lights, hyperventilation	• No fever or current illness	• Epilepsy • See your doctor at once
Repeated episodes of seizures that involve disturbances in the senses (sensory seizures)	• May have preceding aura involving visual and auditory hallucinations or distortions of taste and smell, followed by period of altered awareness sometimes associated with lipsmacking or repetitive movements (automatisms)	• May be brought on by sleep deprivation, flickering lights, hyperventilation		• Temporal lobe epilepsy • See your doctor at once
Brief generalized seizure in child under 5 years	• Fever • No signs of infection of the brain (encephalitis) or covering of the brain (meningitis), no history of epilepsy	• Rapid rise in temperature	• 3 percent of children have at least one febrile convulsion	• Simple febrile seizure of childhood • See your doctor at once

SYMPTOM CHARACTERISTIC	ASSOCIATED SYMPTOMS	AGGRAVATING OR ALLEVIATING FACTORS	OTHER RELEVANT FACTORS	POSSIBLE CAUSE AND ACTION
Repeated episodes of focal seizures (localized to a particular part of the body)	• Involuntary movements may occur in a single limb, one side of the body or involve eyes deviating to one side		• Indicates a localized lesion within the brain triggering the seizures	• Head injury is the most common cause in young adults, while cerebrovascular accidents (strokes) are the most common cause in the elderly • Congenital malformations of the brain, early meningitis or perinatal brain damage are common causes in children • This is a medical emergency • Go to the emergency room or call an ambulance at once
Generalized or focal convulsion	• Headache, drowsiness, neck stiffness, oversensitivity to light, fever	• May have preceding febrile illness	• May occur in previously healthy person	• Meningitis or encephalitis • This is a medical emergency • Go to the emergency room or call an ambulance at once
Isolated generalized or focal convulsion	• Headache, nervous system abnormalities, decreased consciousness, newly developed squint	• May follow head injury	• May indicate raised pressure within the confined space of the skull	• Brain tumor, abscess or cerebral hemorrhage • This is a medical emergency • Go to the emergency room or call an ambulance at once

Sexual function problems

Several problems limit sexual pleasure or the proper function of sex organs. See your doctor, since many problems affecting sexual function may be treated. Untreated sex problems can lead to relationship problems, depression and anxiety. See also entries on *genital pain* and *vaginal problems*.

SYMPTOM CHARACTERISTIC	ASSOCIATED SYMPTOMS	AGGRAVATING OR ALLEVIATING FACTORS	OTHER RELEVANT FACTORS	POSSIBLE CAUSE AND ACTION
In males, ejaculation before or immediately after intercourse begins	• Anxiety, frustration, depression	• May be aggravated by further worry about it happening	• More common in young men • Physical causes are rare, and most cases have a psychological cause	• Premature ejaculation • See your doctor if you are worried or if symptoms persist
In males, inability to have or keep an erection sufficient for sexual intercourse	• Anxiety, frustration, depression		• More likely as men get older • Physical disorders are the main cause, especially in men aged over 50	• Erectile dysfunction (impotence) • See your doctor
In males, pain during sexual contact	• May be redness or rash, or other symptoms of infection such as fever	• Symptoms are aggravated by continued sexual contact		• Infection (e.g. prostate, testes or urethra), allergic reaction to spermicide • See your doctor

SYMPTOM CHARACTERISTIC	ASSOCIATED SYMPTOMS	AGGRAVATING OR ALLEVIATING FACTORS	OTHER RELEVANT FACTORS	POSSIBLE CAUSE AND ACTION
Sexual function problems (cont.)				
Lack of sexual desire or inability to experience sexual pleasure	• Anxiety, frustration	• May be aggravated by stress, fatigue, anxiety, relationship problems	• More common in women than men • Physical and psychological causes can lead to this problem	• Arousal dysfunction • See your doctor
In females, pain during intercourse; pain may be in the vaginal area or deeper in the pelvis	• Vaginal discharge, itching, dryness	• May be aggravated by continued sexual contact	• Pelvic inflammatory disease and infections are most common among young, sexually active women • Endometriosis is most common among women with a family history of the disease, and in women who have never been pregnant • Hormonal imbalances causing vaginal dryness are more common following menopause	• Pelvic inflammatory disease, infections, hormonal imbalance, endometriosis • See your doctor
In females, inability to have intercourse due to contraction of the vaginal muscles	• Fear, anxiety, pain	• Fear of intercourse, pain, memories of unpleasant sexual experiences	• This is an involuntary response, outside the woman's control	• Vaginismus • See your doctor

SYMPTOM CHARACTERISTIC	ASSOCIATED SYMPTOMS	AGGRAVATING OR ALLEVIATING FACTORS	OTHER RELEVANT FACTORS	POSSIBLE CAUSE AND ACTION

Skin problems

The skin can show a very wide range of noticeable changes. It is important to check your skin regularly and report any changes to your doctor, since it is often difficult to tell the difference between significant changes (e.g. early skin cancers or eruptions due to other diseases) and unimportant ones, by appearance alone.

Changes in skin color

SYMPTOM CHARACTERISTIC	ASSOCIATED SYMPTOMS	AGGRAVATING OR ALLEVIATING FACTORS	OTHER RELEVANT FACTORS	POSSIBLE CAUSE AND ACTION
A longstanding spot that is brown (and a different color from the rest of the skin), unchanging in size or appearance; usually smooth and well defined; may be slightly raised or hairy	• None		• Moles commonly appear in childhood, during pregnancy or during treatment with medications containing estrogen • The pigment indicates that the lesion contains cells which produce melanin, a brown pigment present in the skin • Any change in a mole (e.g. itching, growing or spreading, becoming darker or lighter in color, changing shape, developing an irregular border, bleeding, becoming inflamed or ulcerated) may be a sign of cancer	• Mole • See your doctor • Although moles are harmless, any skin spot with this appearance should be examined by an expert to confirm that it is not a skin cancer
A new, growing or changing brown or blue-black pigmented lesion, usually irregular or asymmetric in shape and color; often over ¼ inch (0.5 centimeter) in diameter; may be bleeding or ulcerated	• Usually painless • May be itchy • Surrounding skin may be inflamed		• Melanoma occurs in all adult age groups but is rare in pre-pubescent children • Risk is increased in people with fair skin or hair, many freckles or moles, or moles of unusual appearance • Up to 50 percent of melanomas develop from moles • Sun exposure, especially before age 10, may predispose to melanoma	• Melanoma • See your doctor at once
Sharply defined white (depigmented) patches of skin			• Vitiligo may occur in people with a family history of the disease or in those with immune disorders	• Vitiligo • See your doctor

SYMPTOM CHARACTERISTIC	ASSOCIATED SYMPTOMS	AGGRAVATING OR ALLEVIATING FACTORS	OTHER RELEVANT FACTORS	POSSIBLE CAUSE AND ACTION
Changes in shape of skin surface				
Rash of pimples and pustules on face, chest and back	• Inflamed raised red spots, excessive oiliness, blocked pores (whiteheads, blackheads), scarring	• May be exacerbated by some foods or medications	• Acne is most common in teenagers but also occurs in 10–20 percent of adults	• Acne (acne vulgaris) • See your doctor
Unusual growth or ulcerated raised lump on the face	• May be itchy or painful		• Incidence increases with age • Skin cancers are most common on the face, but can develop on other sun-exposed areas of the body • Growth rate depends on the type of cancer; the growth may develop over a month or so, or slowly over many months	• Skin cancer • See your doctor
A well-defined, round swelling just under the skin of the scalp or back of the neck; typically the swelling feels smooth to firm and the surface is smooth and shiny; the swelling is attached to the skin and may have a central hole	• The swelling is painless and the overlying skin normal		• Cysts may occur at any age, but rarely before adolescence • Cysts grow slowly • There may be one or several cysts	• Sebaceous cyst • See your doctor
Small (pinpoint or pin head size) raised round pink or pearly shiny bumps with pits in the center			• Molluscum contagiosum is most common in children • Contacts (e.g. family members or friends) may also be affected • Commonly occurs on the face, eyelids or genital, but may develop on any area	• Molluscum contagiosum • See your doctor

SYMPTOM CHARACTERISTIC	ASSOCIATED SYMPTOMS	AGGRAVATING OR ALLEVIATING FACTORS	OTHER RELEVANT FACTORS	POSSIBLE CAUSE AND ACTION
Small red, warm, tender bump around a hair follicle, that develops suddenly	• Painful		• Boils may occur singly, or several may appear at the same time • Occasionally multiple boils in the same area result in inflammation of the whole area • Conditions that may predispose to boils include scratching of the skin, which allows bacteria to enter, illnesses which lower the body's resistance (e.g. diabetes)	• Boil • See your doctor
One or more small red bumps that appear suddenly and are randomly distributed, in a person exposed to insects	• Bumps are itchy	• Scratching may worsen inflammation and may cause open weeping sores	• May occur after spending time gardening or outdoors	• Insect bites • Calamine or other soothing lotions available from your pharmacist may relieve itching • See your doctor if you are worried or if symptoms persist
Red bumps or elevated red patches that appear suddenly, each of which lasts from a few hours to 2 days; may be white in the center	• Itching and tingling or a pricking sensation • Swelling around the mouth or throat, difficulty breathing	• Scratching may worsen inflammation and may cause open weeping sores	• Hives most often appear on the arms, legs or waist, but any part of the body may be affected • Common causes include food allergies, exposure to dusts, medicines, infections, heat or cold	• Hives (urticaria) • If needed, calamine or other soothing lotions as recommended by your pharmacist may relieve itching • See your doctor at once
Sudden appearance of bright red or dark red-blue tender deep-seated bumps or raised areas about 1–2 inches (2–5 centimeters) in diameter; usually on the front of both legs, occasionally on the outer forearms	• Lumps are painful • Fever, feeling of being generally unwell, joint pains, sore throat		• Most often affects 20–30 year olds, more commonly females • Erythema nodosum may occurs as a symptom of infection, drug reaction, or an underlying illness	• Skin eruption caused by inflammation within the skin (erythema nodosum) • See your doctor

Rashes

SYMPTOM CHARACTERISTIC	ASSOCIATED SYMPTOMS	AGGRAVATING OR ALLEVIATING FACTORS	OTHER RELEVANT FACTORS	POSSIBLE CAUSE AND ACTION
A tender, red, warm, swollen area of skin with an undefined border	• Fever		• May occur where skin is broken (e.g. a cut or scratch)	• Cellulitis • See your doctor

SYMPTOM CHARACTERISTIC	ASSOCIATED SYMPTOMS	AGGRAVATING OR ALLEVIATING FACTORS	OTHER RELEVANT FACTORS	POSSIBLE CAUSE AND ACTION
Skin problems–rashes (cont.)				
Small purplish-red bruise-like spots, may be flat or slightly raised	• Associated symptoms, if present, will depend on the underlying cause		• Purpura may be due to bruising, inflammation of capillaries, the use of cortisone-type medications (e.g. ointments or oral medications), diseases affecting the platelets, or serious infections	• Bleeding into the skin (purpura) due to medical condition affecting the blood or blood vessels • See your doctor at once
Red rash with tiny fluid-filled blisters; lesions tend to be dry and fragmented; may be swollen, scaly or develop painful cracks; the margins of the rash are often ill defined	• Severe itching • Skin may be dry in general • Other symptoms of allergies	• Itching is exacerbated by changes in temperature, mood and contact with irritating materials	• Symptoms may commence at any age, may occur intermittently or long-term, and may fluctuate in severity • Allergic dermatitis is most common in people with a family history of allergic diseases • May occur with other allergic conditions (e.g. asthma or hay fever)	• Eczema or dermatitis • See your doctor
Red rash with tiny fluid-filled blisters (vesicles) in an area exposed to an irritating substance; may be swollen or scaly	• May be itchy or sore	• Scratching may worsen inflammation and may cause open weeping sores	• Contact dermatitis)may occur following exposure to clothing, cosmetics, household detergents, occupational exposure to petroleum-based products, oils, solvents, paint, cement, rubber, resins, plants, or medicines which are applied directly to the skin • Contact dermatitis may occur on the shoulders, neck and scalp if the irritant is in the form of dust	• Contact dermatitis • Try to identify the cause by eliminating suspected substances • Avoid contact with the substance by wearing protective clothing • See your doctor if you are worried or if symptoms persist
Red rash or ring-like area; may be scaly	• Itchy • If the area affected is the scalp, hairs within the affected area tend to be broken		• May affect the nails, feet, hands, groin, trunk or scalp • Ringworm may follow contact with pets (e.g. dogs, cats or horses)	• Fungal infection (e.g. ringworm) • See your doctor
Reddish plaques covered with silvery scales; the margins are well defined	• Usually not itchy • Arthritis may occur	• Trauma, infections or emotional upsets may predispose to symptoms	• May affect any age group, but uncommon before 10 years of age and most common at 15–30 years of age • Usually develops gradually • Usually chronic	• Psoriasis • See your doctor

SYMPTOM CHARACTERISTIC	ASSOCIATED SYMPTOMS	AGGRAVATING OR ALLEVIATING FACTORS	OTHER RELEVANT FACTORS	POSSIBLE CAUSE AND ACTION
Rapid onset of well defined reddish, slightly scaly patches on the trunk; usually a single patch precedes the development of others by a week or so	• Patches may be slightly itchy • May also affect the arms and legs		• The cause of pityriasis rosea is unknown • Symptoms occur most commonly in spring and autumn • Any age group may be affected, most commonly young adults	• Pityriasis rosea • See your doctor
Sudden development of small round red target-like patches and bumps which are darker in the center than the outside of the lesion; may have blistering	• Feeling of being generally unwell, fever, sore throat, diarrhea		• Attacks may be triggered by medications, infections, cancer, pregnancy • Most commonly affects the back of the hands and forearms in a symmetrical fashion; may affect other areas	• Erythema multiforme, an inflammatory disease of the skin, which is usually a reaction to infection or medication • See your doctor
Flat blotchy red rashes, which begin 4 days after symptoms of a cold in a child; rashes may join up to form one larger red area	• Before the rash develops there may be a general feeling of being unwell, loss of appetite, fever, cough, runny nose, red watering eyes		• Measles is preventable by vaccination • Measles tends to be more severe in adults than in children	• Measles • Rest in bed and avoid contact with others, especially pregnant women • See your doctor • Measles is highly contagious, so warn the doctor's office of symptoms before you attend
Long-term redness of the cheeks, chin and central forehead, often with small round circumscribed bumps which may contain pus		• Before permanent redness develops, flushing may occur with heat, emotional reactions, alcohol, hot drinks or spicy foods	• Gradual onset • Begins after 30 years of age, typically in middle age • More common in women • More likely to develop in people who experience frequent pronounced flushing; flushing persists longer with repeated episodes until the condition becomes permanent	• Acne rosacea • See your doctor
Scaly rash across the nose and cheeks or forehead; spots are butterfly-shaped or round, with well defined margins	• Arthritis, joint pain, fever, hair loss, kidney problems		• Usually long-term • Onset is gradual • Women are twice as likely as males to develop lupus erythematosus • More common in African races (e.g. Afro-Americans) than white races	• Lupus erythematosus • See your doctor

SYMPTOM CHARACTERISTIC	ASSOCIATED SYMPTOMS	AGGRAVATING OR ALLEVIATING FACTORS	OTHER RELEVANT FACTORS	POSSIBLE CAUSE AND ACTION
Skin problems–rashes (cont.)				
Bright red rash on the cheeks ("slapped cheek"); after a day or two, rash typically also appears on the forearms and thighs	• Fever, general feeling of being unwell • Arthritis may occur in adults		• Most common in children aged 3–12 • Infection during pregnancy may cause fetal damage	• Fifth disease (erythema infectiosum), an infectious viral disease • Avoid contact with other people, especially pregnant women • See your doctor • Fifth disease is infectious, so warn the doctor's office of symptoms before you attend
Greasy, scaly round dirty-yellow or gray colored patches in hairy areas of the body such as the scalp; the patches may be pinhead to coin sized	• May be itchy or burning	• Scratching may cause open, inflamed or weeping sores	• Onset is gradual • Symptoms may occur in episodes or become long-term • Commonly affected areas include the scalp, eyelids, eyebrows, ears, chest, groin or between the buttocks • May occur in babies ("cradle cap")	• Dandruff (seborrheic dermatitis) • See your doctor
Blistering conditions				
Groups of bright red tiny fluid-filled blisters, which rupture and form crusts	• Rash is itchy • Fever (before blisters appear), feeling of being generally unwell • Adults may also experience aches and pains, headaches, serious nerve damage (rare)		• Rash mostly affects the trunk and face • Children are most often affected, especially between 2–8 years of age; condition is usually mild, but occasionally can be fatal • A person may be affected at any age if they have not previously had the condition • Severe illness occurs more often in adults	• Chickenpox • Rest, use calamine lotion or other medications recommended by your doctor or pharmacist to relieve itching, acetaminophen (paracetamol) for fever, daily bathing • Avoid scratching spots • See your doctor • Chickenpox is highly contagious, so warn the doctor's office of symptoms before you attend
Groups of tiny fluid-filled blisters in a band-like distribution on one side of the body; the vesicles usually rupture and crust over	• Severe pain in the area of the rash usually begins 1–2 days before the skin lesions		• Mostly occurs in adults • May recur	• Shingles • See your doctor at once

SYMPTOM CHARACTERISTIC	ASSOCIATED SYMPTOMS	AGGRAVATING OR ALLEVIATING FACTORS	OTHER RELEVANT FACTORS	POSSIBLE CAUSE AND ACTION
Small and larger blisters around the face and ears in a child	• Often itchy • Scratching can lead to further spread of the lesions		• May affect adults but more common in children	• Impetigo • Highly contagious • Other members of the household should avoid unnecessary contact with toweling or napkins that come into contact with the lesions • See your doctor
Multiple large blisters of the skin	• Not itchy, tender when the blister ruptures • After healing, area may remain darker than surrounding skin		• Pemphigus is a long-term disorder • Occurs mainly in the elderly; rarely occurs in people under 40 years of age	• Pemphigus/pemphigoid • See your doctor

Itching

SYMPTOM CHARACTERISTIC	ASSOCIATED SYMPTOMS	AGGRAVATING OR ALLEVIATING FACTORS	OTHER RELEVANT FACTORS	POSSIBLE CAUSE AND ACTION
Itching without other evidence of skin disease	• Associated symptoms will vary greatly depending on the specific cause			• No definable cause or liver disease, kidney disease, blood abnormalities, thyroid disease, human immunodeficiency virus (HIV) infection, tumors • See your doctor
Itchy, painful rash or raised red spots occurring during sea bathing	• Generalized inflamed rash or rash only in areas covered by clothing while swimming	• Thimble jellyfish reactions are exacerbated by clothing that traps the tiny creatures against the skin e.g. wearing T-shirts while swimming	• Causes vary with region e.g. thimble jellyfish reactions are common in Florida, USA and tend to occur in certain years, reactions to stinger tentacles are common in northeast Australia • Other creatures also known as "sea lice" cause tiny bites that may be painful rather than itchy	• Reaction to various marine irritants known as "sea lice" (e.g. thimble jellyfish, particles of broken stinging tentacles of marine stingers) • See your doctor
Intense itching that worsens at night; affects same areas on both sides of body in symmetrical pattern	• Dark wavy lines visible on skin of wrists, fingers, elbows, penis • Blisters, rash or pustules in skin folds (e.g. under breasts) • Face, scalp, neck or palms unaffected in adults but may be affected in infants	• Itching aggravated by hot showers • Scratching causes sores	• Scabies is contagious and is spread through personal contact • Outbreaks in developed countries tend to occur in institutions (e.g. nursing homes) • Symptoms begin 4–6 weeks after contact with an infected person	• Infestation by human itch mite (scabies) • See your doctor

SYMPTOM CHARACTERISTIC	ASSOCIATED SYMPTOMS	AGGRAVATING OR ALLEVIATING FACTORS	OTHER RELEVANT FACTORS	POSSIBLE CAUSE AND ACTION
Skin problems–itching (cont.)				
Extremely itchy areas ¾ inch (2 centimeters) diameter, followed by itching, burning for weeks; mostly on ankles or at areas where tight clothing is worn	• Blistering and bleeding		• Occurs in bushy, scrubby areas in tropics and sub-tropics, and occasionally temperate areas in warm weather • Other parasites (e.g. mites) may cause intense itching	• Infestation by harvest mite larvae (chiggers) • See your doctor
Itchy open weeping areas on head, neck, shoulders	• Oozing, crusting, matting of hair, infections, swollen painful “glands” (lymph nodes) • “Nits” (louse eggs) may be visible stuck to hairs		• Lice infestation is most common among pre-school and primary school-aged children	• Head lice infestation • See your doctor
Itching areas around neck or pubic area, armpits, eyelashes	• Thickened and darkened skin follows long-term infestations • “Nits” (louse eggs) may be visible stuck to hairs or clothing		• Body lice infestations occur mainly in the homeless and in people living in extreme poverty • Pubic lice are spread through direct contact or clothing	• Body lice or pubic lice • See your doctor

Sleep disturbances

Sleep problems are not uncommon in normal healthy people, but sleep disturbances can become extremely troubling and sometimes dangerous. Inappropriate use of sleeping pills can aggravate sleeping problems, so it is important to consult your doctor before using them.

SYMPTOM CHARACTERISTIC	ASSOCIATED SYMPTOMS	AGGRAVATING OR ALLEVIATING FACTORS	OTHER RELEVANT FACTORS	POSSIBLE CAUSE AND ACTION
Difficulty initiating or maintaining sleep	• Daytime fatigue • Depression may cause early morning waking • Drug and alcohol use may result in frequent waking during the night	• May be aggravated by irregular daytime naps or performing anxiety-producing tasks (e.g. work or non-relaxing chores) immediately before bedtime	• Insomnia may be caused by a change in the body clock, anxiety, depression, drug or alcohol use (e.g. inappropriate use of sedatives), psychiatric illness, physical discomfort due to medical disorders	• Insomnia • Undertake regular physical activity • Avoid heavy meals, alcohol or stimulants (e.g. coffee) at night • Avoid napping during the day • Go to bed and get up at the same time every day • Avoid lying in bed without sleeping for lengthy periods • If you haven’t fallen asleep within 30 minutes, get up, do something relaxing, and try again later • See your doctor if you are worried or if symptoms persist

SYMPTOM CHARACTERISTIC	ASSOCIATED SYMPTOMS	AGGRAVATING OR ALLEVIATING FACTORS	OTHER RELEVANT FACTORS	POSSIBLE CAUSE AND ACTION
Excessive daytime sleepiness; falling asleep when not stimulated	• Snoring	• Symptoms may be exacerbated by alcohol	• Sleepiness may occur in healthy people if they feel bored or tired or have slept poorly at night • Sleep apnea is most common among obese people, and in middle-aged and older adult men	• Sleep apnea • See your doctor
Brief irresistible attacks of sleep during the day in inappropriate situations or while active, e.g. while eating or talking; attacks are often frequent; usually the sleep attacks are refreshing and the person is easily woken from them	• Episodes of physical weakness set off by surprise or emotions, frightening hallucinations occurring during the transition to sleep or on waking, inability to move for a short period on waking		• Typically starts at 15–25 years of age	• Narcolepsy • See your doctor
Walking or talking during sleep; usually not recalled afterwards			• Sleepwalking commonly occurs in healthy children and occasionally in adults	• Sleepwalking • Ensure sleep is taken in a secure environment to reduce the risk of injuries/accidents while sleepwalking • Avoid drinking alcohol or coffee at night • See your doctor if you are worried or if symptoms persist
Waking from a frightening dream in a frightened or agitated state; usually able to remember the episode			• Nightmares commonly occur during the rapid eye movement phase of sleep in healthy adults and children • Some medications may cause nightmares	• Nightmares • See your doctor if you are worried or if symptoms persist
Waking suddenly in a very agitated and frightened state; the episodes are usually more severe and prolonged than with nightmares; usually unable to remember the episode	• Loud screaming on waking, rapid heartbeat and breathing, heavy sweating		• Most common in children around 5 or 6 years old; usually settles in adolescence • Sometimes, an epileptic disorder can cause sudden waking with agitation	• Night terrors • See your doctor
Hallucinations occurring during the transition to sleep or on waking			• Occurs in healthy people • More common in people with narcolepsy	• Hypnagogic hallucinations • See your doctor if you are worried or if symptoms persist

SYMPTOM CHARACTERISTIC	ASSOCIATED SYMPTOMS	AGGRAVATING OR ALLEVIATING FACTORS	OTHER RELEVANT FACTORS	POSSIBLE CAUSE AND ACTION
Sleep disturbances (cont.)				
Inability to move for a short period on waking			• Occurs in healthy people	• Sleep paralysis • See your doctor if you are worried or if symptoms persist

Snoring

Heavy snoring is a signal which may indicate an underlying problem, usually temporary obstruction of the windpipe (trachea) during sleep. Diagnosis and treatment are important for quality of life and long-term health, so consult your doctor for an assessment. See also entry on *sleep disturbances*.

SYMPTOM CHARACTERISTIC	ASSOCIATED SYMPTOMS	AGGRAVATING OR ALLEVIATING FACTORS	OTHER RELEVANT FACTORS	POSSIBLE CAUSE AND ACTION
Snoring during sleep, usually noticed by another person	• Daytime fatigue	• Aggravated when the person sleeps on the back • Alcohol and some medications may worsen snoring by relaxing the parts of the throat that cause snoring • Snoring may occur only during nasal congestion with hay fever or a cold	• Snoring is the sound of partially obstructed flow of air due the soft parts of the throat and mouth • 45 percent of adults snore at least occasionally, and 25 percent snore regularly • Heavy snoring is more common in overweight men and increases with age	• See your doctor if you are worried or if symptoms persist
Very loud snoring punctuated by long pauses in breathing, may be observed by sufferer's partner or room-mate	• Excessive daytime sleepiness due to poor quality of sleep • Tiredness, irritability, difficulty concentrating, loss of libido, morning headache, frequent waking during the night		• Most common in overweight middle-aged men • Predisposing factors include obesity, enlarged tonsils (especially in children), use of alcohol, sedatives/sleeping pills, neurological problems affecting the muscles around the windpipe	• Sleep apnea • Sleep on your side, lose weight if you are overweight, avoid drinking alcohol or using sedatives/sleeping pills • See your doctor

SYMPTOM CHARACTERISTIC	ASSOCIATED SYMPTOMS	AGGRAVATING OR ALLEVIATING FACTORS	OTHER RELEVANT FACTORS	POSSIBLE CAUSE AND ACTION

Speech problems

Speech or language problems are quite common in children. Have an audiologist check your child's hearing and if you are still concerned see a speech pathologist. The sudden onset of speech and/or language problems in adulthood are often indicative of an underlying medical problem. Therefore it is advisable to see your doctor and have the symptoms investigated.

SYMPTOM CHARACTERISTIC	ASSOCIATED SYMPTOMS	AGGRAVATING OR ALLEVIATING FACTORS	OTHER RELEVANT FACTORS	POSSIBLE CAUSE AND ACTION
The frequent repetition of sounds, usually at the beginning of words and sentences	• Eye blinking, head nodding or facial tension during speech	• Stressful situations or talking to unfamiliar people can make symptoms worse	• Often other members in the family have the same problem • More common in boys	• Stuttering • Children of any age who display signs of stuttering, particularly if it occurs with the associated symptoms, need to see a speech pathologist as soon as possible • Stuttering will not disappear if ignored • See your doctor if you are worried or if symptoms persist
A child with minimal speech	• Pointing or gesturing rather than talking	• Poor hearing	• Speech or language difficulties can run in families	• Language delay. If the child is not making babbling sounds by 12 months or producing some single words by 24 months see a speech pathologist • See your doctor if you are worried or if symptoms persist
Sudden onset of slurred speech	• Sudden difficulty thinking of words, getting words muddled up; knowing what you want to say but being unable to say it • Weakness on one side of the face or body • Difficulty understanding people		• More common with increasing age	• Transient ischemic attack or stroke • This is a medical emergency • Go to the emergency room or call an ambulance at once

Swallowing problems

Swallowing problems can occur in the mouth, throat or gullet (esophagus). The likelihood of swallowing difficulties increases with age. If symptoms occur see your doctor, as undetected swallowing problems can result in other health complications.

SYMPTOM CHARACTERISTIC	ASSOCIATED SYMPTOMS	AGGRAVATING OR ALLEVIATING FACTORS	OTHER RELEVANT FACTORS	POSSIBLE CAUSE AND ACTION
Food or drink keeps "going down the wrong way"; coughing or throat clearing during meals and/or when drinking	• Taking a longer time to eat and drink • Chest infections • Gradual loss of weight	• Fatigue usually makes swallowing more difficult • Some food or fluid may be more difficult to swallow than others	• Most likely in diseases of the nervous system	• Neurogenic dysphagia (nerve problem preventing normal use and coordination of swallowing muscles) • See your doctor

SYMPTOM CHARACTERISTIC	ASSOCIATED SYMPTOMS	AGGRAVATING OR ALLEVIATING FACTORS	OTHER RELEVANT FACTORS	POSSIBLE CAUSE AND ACTION
Swallowing problems (cont.)				
Food sticking in the throat		• Dry food tends to stick more often; drinking water often alleviates the problem	• May occur following damage caused by esophageal ulcers	• Narrowing of the esophagus • See your doctor
Indigestion/ heartburn	• Pain on swallowing • Coughing or choking on food after you have swallowed it • Coughing during the night • Husky voice	• Sleeping in a more upright position may help • Spicy foods can exacerbate the symptoms	• Typically occurs after food • Heartburn may occur during pregnancy but usually resolves after the baby is born	• Gastroesophageal reflux • See your doctor

Throat problems

Sore throats or discomfort when swallowing are common symptoms that often occur with viral infections and usually resolve without treatment. However, throat problems may sometimes indicate a more serious cause, so any persistent problem should always be checked by your doctor. See also the entry on *cough*.

SYMPTOM CHARACTERISTIC	ASSOCIATED SYMPTOMS	AGGRAVATING OR ALLEVIATING FACTORS	OTHER RELEVANT FACTORS	POSSIBLE CAUSE AND ACTION
Itchiness in the back of the mouth	• Dry or irritated feeling when swallowing • Urge to sneeze when attempt to rub area using the tongue • Watery discharge from nose or eyes	• Commonly occurs in spring or in dusty environment	• Common with other signs of allergy	• Allergic reaction (allergies) to airborne allergens (e.g. pollens) • Wait a few days to ensure the symptoms are not due to a respiratory viral infection like cold or flu • Ask your pharmacist or doctor for advice • Symptoms are usually readily relieved by medications such as oral anti-allergy tablets or nasal sprays • See your doctor if you are worried or if symptoms persist
Pain or discomfort on swallowing	• Sneeze, cough, headaches, swollen lymph nodes ("glands") under the jaw • Nasal discharge • Fever	• Worse on waking up		• Cold or flu (viral infection) • Rest, and see your pharmacist for advice on simple cough and cold remedies • See your doctor if you are worried or if symptoms persist

SYMPTOM CHARACTERISTIC	ASSOCIATED SYMPTOMS	AGGRAVATING OR ALLEVIATING FACTORS	OTHER RELEVANT FACTORS	POSSIBLE CAUSE AND ACTION
Pain or discomfort on swallowing	• Headache, swollen lymph nodes ("glands") under the jaw, fever, nausea, vomiting, diarrhea			• Viral gastroenteritis • Rest and drink plenty of fluids • Ask your doctor or pharmacist for advice on relieving symptoms • See your doctor if you are worried or if symptoms persist
Very sore throat, with white patches on the tonsils				• Bacterial streptococcal infection ("strep throat") or infectious mononucleosis (glandular fever) • See your doctor
Sore throat with cough	• Coughing mucus			• Bronchitis from cold or flu (viral infection) • See your doctor if you are worried or if symptoms persist
Sore throat with harsh barking cough in a child	• Fever			• Croup or epiglottitis • See your doctor at once
Sore throat	• Peeling skin within the mouth, inflammation and swelling of the tongue and gums		• Some medications may cause a strong inflammatory reaction in the mouth • Good oral hygiene, including brushing teeth and flossing gums may help prevent some oral infections	• Bacterial infection in the mouth (trench mouth) or reaction to prescription drugs • See your doctor or dentist

Tongue problems

Most problems affecting the tongue will resolve within a few days without treatment. However, it is important to have a medical assessment if symptoms recur or persist, since changes to the tongue may indicate other diseases.

SYMPTOM CHARACTERISTIC	ASSOCIATED SYMPTOMS	AGGRAVATING OR ALLEVIATING FACTORS	OTHER RELEVANT FACTORS	POSSIBLE CAUSE AND ACTION
Red, raw areas on tongue		• Discomfort may be increased by eating, drinking or use of mouthwashes	• Ulcers due to trauma; usually heal within a few days	• Ulcers due to trauma (e.g. false teeth or orthodontic braces) • See your doctor or dentist if you are worried or if symptoms persist

SYMPTOM CHARACTERISTIC	ASSOCIATED SYMPTOMS	AGGRAVATING OR ALLEVIATING FACTORS	OTHER RELEVANT FACTORS	POSSIBLE CAUSE AND ACTION
Tongue problems (cont.)				
Painful raw-looking white areas on or under tongue in an otherwise healthy person			• May occur with Crohn's disease or celiac disease	• Aphthous ulcers • Ulcers commonly occur in healthy people, and may be caused by herpes virus • See your doctor or dentist if you are worried or if symptoms persist
White spots surrounded by red area	• May be present on sides of mouth		• Most common in young children and babies, elderly people, or people with a suppressed immune system (e.g. diabetes, AIDS, taking cortisone-type drugs or chemotherapy for cancer)	• Oral candidiasis (thrush), a yeast infection • See your doctor
Enlarged tongue			• Occurs in developmental conditions such as Down syndrome	• Tumor or sign of another disease • See your doctor
Patchy pattern of raised light areas and flat red areas			• Patterns change over time	• "Geographic tongue" • A harmless inflammatory condition of the tongue • See your doctor
"Bald" or smooth appearance of tongue (loss of normal rough surface)	• May be painful			• Inflammation of tongue (glossitis), iron deficiency, vitamin deficiency or anemia • See your doctor
Inflammation and swelling of the tongue and gums	• Peeling skin within the mouth		• Some medications may cause a strong inflammatory reaction in the mouth • Good oral hygiene, including brushing teeth and flossing gums may help prevent some oral infections	• Bacterial infection in the mouth ("trench mouth") or reaction to prescription drugs • See your doctor or dentist
Bright or dark red tongue	• Fever		• Most common in young children	• Scarlet fever • See your doctor at once
Hairy appearance				• Overgrowth of normal projections on surface of tongue • See your doctor

SYMPTOM CHARACTERISTIC	ASSOCIATED SYMPTOMS	AGGRAVATING OR ALLEVIATING FACTORS	OTHER RELEVANT FACTORS	POSSIBLE CAUSE AND ACTION
Black or brown appearance			• Tobacco smoking or chewing may discolor the tongue	• Color changes due to antibiotics • See your doctor
Raised ulcer on edge of tongue with thickness or firmness of edges and surrounding areas			• Does not heal within a few days like common ulcers	• Cancer of the tongue • See your doctor at once

Toothache

Toothache warrants prompt attention, to maximize the chance of preserving the tooth. While problems involving pain in a tooth should generally be referred to a dentist, go immediately to the emergency room if a tooth is lost through injury outside your dentist's office hours.

SYMPTOM CHARACTERISTIC	ASSOCIATED SYMPTOMS	AGGRAVATING OR ALLEVIATING FACTORS	OTHER RELEVANT FACTORS	POSSIBLE CAUSE AND ACTION
Tooth knocked out by trauma to the mouth	• Pain in surrounding areas in the mouth		• In some circumstances, an otherwise healthy tooth that is accidentally knocked out may be saved	• This is a dental emergency • If a tooth has been completely knocked out, put it in a moist cool cloth or in your mouth to preserve it until you get to a dentist or emergency room • See your dentist or go to the emergency room at once
Pain in a specific tooth that is broken or chipped or a loose tooth				• If the chip has just occurred, keep chipped or broken off parts of tooth in a moist cool cloth • See your dentist at once
Pain in a specific tooth; initially pain occurs on exposure to hot and/or cold or when eating; may progress to continuous throbbing pain	• Pain may be continuous if there is inflammation or infection		• Poor dental hygiene increases the risk of tooth decay and cavities	• Tooth cavity or decay • See your dentist
Redness, swelling, tenderness and severe pain around a tooth and/or section of the gums	• May be swelling in the face		• May be preceded by other symptoms of tooth decay or periodontal disease, particularly if left untreated	• Dental abscess • See your dentist at once
Pain not necessarily related to a specific tooth	• Perhaps tenderness, gums may bleed easily on brushing or chewing, gums may be red and swollen, eventually loosening of the teeth may occur		• Usually starts with inflammation of the gums (gingivitis)	• Periodontal disease, most commonly inflammation of the supporting tissue around the teeth • See your dentist

Tremor

Tremor is a non-deliberate, rhythmic oscillation usually of the hands or head. It is relatively common in elderly people, or as a side effect of certain medications.

SYMPTOM CHARACTERISTIC	ASSOCIATED SYMPTOMS	AGGRAVATING OR ALLEVIATING FACTORS	OTHER RELEVANT FACTORS	POSSIBLE CAUSE AND ACTION
Coarse and rhythmical tremor of the hands at rest, sometimes the thumb moves over the fingers in a pill-rolling action	• Insidious onset of symptoms including slowness in initiating and performing movements, unusual shuffling or freezing up when walking and difficulties with balance and control of walking	• Tremor may disappear when actively using the hands and may be aggravated by emotion	• Most common among adults over 50 years of age	• Parkinson's disease • See your doctor
Fine trembling when using hands		• Aggravated when actively using the hands	• A normal tremor that is usually very subtle may be exaggerated by emotion, fatigue, cocaine, caffeine, advancing age, other medical conditions (e.g. thyroid disease), medications (e.g. drugs used in asthma), depression or other mood disturbances, epilepsy, psychiatric illness, withdrawal from alcohol dependency	• Physiological tremor—exaggeration of a slight tremor that is normally present in healthy people • See your doctor if you are worried or if symptoms persist
Trembling when using hands		• Alleviated by alcohol	• The tremor runs in the family	• Essential tremor • See your doctor
Coarse tremor when using hands		• Aggravated by actively using the hands in careful or precise movements	• Cerebellar disease may be due to biochemical, metabolic or toxic causes, problems of the immune system, tumors, abscess, loss of blood supply, hemorrhage, or bruising	• Cerebellar disease (disease or damage involving the part of the brain responsible for muscle tone, balance and coordination) • See your doctor
Coarse tremor of the head	• Difficulty maintaining balance, staggering when walking, jerkiness of movements, slurring of speech		• Genetically inherited tremors are relatively rare	• Age-related tremor, inherited condition, or a brain disease • See your doctor

SYMPTOM CHARACTERISTIC	ASSOCIATED SYMPTOMS	AGGRAVATING OR ALLEVIATING FACTORS	OTHER RELEVANT FACTORS	POSSIBLE CAUSE AND ACTION

Urination, difficult

The most common cause of difficulty on urinating is benign enlargement of the prostate, which frequently occurs in elderly men. However, any experience of difficulty urinating should be fully investigated by a doctor to ensure the cause is not serious and to determine whether your symptoms, or the condition responsible, may be treated. See also entries on *urination, painful* and *urination, frequent*.

SYMPTOM CHARACTERISTIC	ASSOCIATED SYMPTOMS	AGGRAVATING OR ALLEVIATING FACTORS	OTHER RELEVANT FACTORS	POSSIBLE CAUSE AND ACTION
In men, difficulty starting a urine stream	• Urine dribbling after urinating • Weak urine stream		• More common with ageing	• Prostate problems (e.g. enlargement, prostatitis or prostate cancer) • See your doctor at once
Feeling of incomplete emptying of bladder or difficulty in emptying	• Painful urination • Increase or decrease in urine volume		• History of urinary tract infections or other urinary problems • Genital injury (including childbirth)	• Urinary obstruction caused by a variety of conditions • See your doctor

Urination, frequent

Increase in the production or frequency of urination should be assessed by a doctor to ensure the cause is not potentially serious. Most common causes for these symptoms can be overcome or controlled, so there is no need to tolerate these symptoms without asking medical advice. See also entries on *urination, painful* and *urination, difficult*.

SYMPTOM CHARACTERISTIC	ASSOCIATED SYMPTOMS	AGGRAVATING OR ALLEVIATING FACTORS	OTHER RELEVANT FACTORS	POSSIBLE CAUSE AND ACTION
Frequent urge to urinate in a pregnant woman	• Less than usual volume in bladder	• Worse as pregnancy advances	• Common in pregnant women • Since other problems (e.g. diabetes) may be triggered by pregnancy, these symptoms should be assessed by a doctor	• The baby is pressing on the bladder • The problem should be resolved after birth • See your doctor
Involuntary leaking of urine		• Occurs with coughing, sneezing or exercise • May be worse during a bladder infection (cystitis), after drinking more fluids than usual or in cold weather	• Common in women after childbirth or with ageing	• Stress incontinence (weakness of bladder muscles causing leakage of urine) • See your doctor • Exercises may help strengthen the surrounding muscles • Severe cases may require surgery
Involuntary leaking of urine		• In elderly people with physical debility, difficulty moving about may exacerbate other causes of incontinence	• Some medications may cause bladder problems • Neurological disorders such as partial paralysis may result in incontinence	• Incontinence (other causes) • See your doctor
Producing more urine than usual			• Some medications cause increased urine production	• If you are taking medications, ask your pharmacist or doctor whether increased urine output is expected • See your doctor

SYMPTOM CHARACTERISTIC	ASSOCIATED SYMPTOMS	AGGRAVATING OR ALLEVIATING FACTORS	OTHER RELEVANT FACTORS	POSSIBLE CAUSE AND ACTION
Urination, frequent (cont.)				
Producing more urine than usual	• Discolored urine • Waking at night to urinate • Puffy swelling of extremities • Generally feeling unwell		• May occur with high blood pressure	• Kidney disease • See your doctor at once
Producing more urine than usual	• Excessive thirst, frequent urination, increased appetite, weight loss, nausea, blurred vision • In women, frequent vaginal infections; in men, impotence; recurring yeast infections in both sexes		• Diabetes is more common in people with obesity, hypertension, or a family history of diabetes	• Diabetes • See your doctor at once
In men, waking several times during the night to urinate	• Difficulty starting a urine stream • Urine dribbling after urinating		• More common with ageing	• Prostate problems (e.g. enlargement, prostatitis or prostate cancer) • See your doctor at once

Urination, painful

Any new occurrence of pain when urinating should be fully investigated by a doctor. For intermittent problems with which you are already familiar, like cystitis or genital herpes, your doctor or pharmacist can give advice on how to manage the problem when you recognize a new episode. See also entries on *urination, difficult* and *urination, frequent*.

SYMPTOM CHARACTERISTIC	ASSOCIATED SYMPTOMS	AGGRAVATING OR ALLEVIATING FACTORS	OTHER RELEVANT FACTORS	POSSIBLE CAUSE AND ACTION
Burning pain on urination	• Frequent urge to urinate, even when bladder is empty • Urinating only small amounts • Burning sensation in lower abdomen, urine with a strong odor	• Lack of adequate fluid intake may prolong symptoms • Sexual contact may aggravate pain	• Cystitis is more common in women than in men; infection may be triggered by sexual contact, use of diaphragm for birth control, or use of urinary catheters	• Cystitis • Drink plenty of water • See your doctor
Discomfort or burning pain on urination	• Cloudy urine, ache or stabbing pain in lower back, fever			• Kidney infection or kidney stones • See your doctor at once
Painful urination	• Pain under scrotum, difficulty urinating		• More common with ageing	• Prostate problems (e.g. prostatitis or prostate cancer) • See your doctor at once
Painful urination in sexually active men	• Discharge from tip of penis		• May follow recent sexual contact with a new partner	• Sexually transmitted infection of urinary tract (e.g. gonorrhea) • See your doctor at once • Avoid sexual contact until you obtain medical advice

SYMPTOM CHARACTERISTIC	ASSOCIATED SYMPTOMS	AGGRAVATING OR ALLEVIATING FACTORS	OTHER RELEVANT FACTORS	POSSIBLE CAUSE AND ACTION
Burning pain on urination	• Blisters or sores on external genital areas (may later become scabby) • Sore raw-feeling area inside vagina or on labia (women) • Vaginal discharge (women) • Discharge from infected sores • Burning pain in lower abdomen	• Urinating in a warm bath may alleviate scalding sensation • Outbreaks may be triggered by other viruses or stress	• New sores after others heal • Sores may become infected • First infection may cause flu-like symptoms	• Genital herpes • Wear cotton underwear and loose clothing • See your doctor at once • Avoid sexual contact until you obtain medical advice
In females, pain with sexual intercourse	• Bleeding after sexual intercourse, watery discharge from vagina, painful bowel movements, frequent urge to urinate		• Vaginal tumors are rare	• Tumor of the vagina • See your doctor at once

Vaginal problems

Some vaginal problems may be successfully treated with medications available from pharmacists. If you are unsure of the cause or if symptoms persist, see your doctor or sexual health clinic for a full sexual health check-up and to ensure possible infections do not result in fertility problems or other complications. See also entries on *genital pain* and *genital itching*.

SYMPTOM CHARACTERISTIC	ASSOCIATED SYMPTOMS	AGGRAVATING OR ALLEVIATING FACTORS	OTHER RELEVANT FACTORS	POSSIBLE CAUSE AND ACTION
Increased amount of discharge with normal light color, consistency and smell			• May be related to hormonal changes or new oral contraceptive	• Normal hormonal changes • See your doctor if the discharge changes or worries you
Thick white discharge forming clumps	• In women, the vulva may be swollen and red, and there may be a thick, white discharge	• Sexual intercourse may increase discomfort • Wearing tight clothing or synthetic underwear may worsen symptoms	• Yeast infections can be a side effect of taking antibiotics, or may be triggered by stress, pregnancy, or use of the contraceptive pill • Candidiasis is most likely in women with diabetes or as a side effect of some antibiotics	• Yeast infection (candidiasis) • Wear cotton underwear and loose clothing to allow air to the area • See your doctor
Greenish-yellow discharge with unpleasant smell			• Intense odor with only moderate amount of discharge	• Foreign object in vagina causing overgrowth of bacteria or yeasts that are naturally present • There may be an old tampon or contraceptive device in the vagina—check and remove • See your doctor if the discharge persists or if you cannot find a cause

SYMPTOM CHARACTERISTIC	ASSOCIATED SYMPTOMS	AGGRAVATING OR ALLEVIATING FACTORS	OTHER RELEVANT FACTORS	POSSIBLE CAUSE AND ACTION
Vaginal problems (cont.)				
Greenish-yellow discharge with unpleasant smell			• Recent sexual contact or new sexual partner in the last month	• Infection such as bacterial vaginosis or trichomoniasis (a parasitic infection) • See your doctor
Greenish-yellow discharge with unpleasant smell	• Pain in the lower abdomen, fever			• Pelvic inflammatory disease • See your doctor at once
Vaginal dryness	• Itching, irritation of vaginal lining		• No other symptoms	• Hormonal deficiency or undiagnosed infection • Lubricants to relieve itchiness or during sexual contact • See your doctor
Yellow discharge, may be thick like mucus	• Cervix bleeds when touched or scraped, abnormal menstrual bleeding, abdominal pain, fever, pain when urinating and pain and swelling of one or both labia		• May follow recent sexual contact with a new partner • The incidence of gonorrhea is much higher in the USA than in other industrialized countries • Potential complications include inflammation of reproductive organs, peritonitis, inflammation around the liver, inflammation of the Bartholin's gland in women and epididymitis or abscess around the urethra in men; arthritis, dermatitis, endocarditis, meningitis, myocarditis or hepatitis	• Gonorrhea • See your doctor or a sexual health clinic as soon as possible • Antibiotic treatment is important to prevent serious complications

Voice problems

Voice problems can occur for a number of different reasons. See your doctor if symptoms persist for more than two weeks. You may need to see an ear nose and throat doctor and speech pathologist who are the specialists in the diagnosis and management of voice disorders.

SYMPTOM CHARACTERISTIC	ASSOCIATED SYMPTOMS	AGGRAVATING OR ALLEVIATING FACTORS	OTHER RELEVANT FACTORS	POSSIBLE CAUSE AND ACTION
Husky voice, lasting longer than 2 weeks	• Throat pain • Upper respiratory tract infections (e.g. a cold) • Dry throat and the need to frequently throat clear	• Prolonged voice use, talking loudly and talking when tired exacerbates symptoms • Voice improves with voice rest, drinking water and avoiding smoking/ smoky environments	• People in occupations or lifestyles that involve constant voice use are predisposed to voice difficulties	• Functional voice loss • See your doctor

SYMPTOM CHARACTERISTIC	ASSOCIATED SYMPTOMS	AGGRAVATING OR ALLEVIATING FACTORS	OTHER RELEVANT FACTORS	POSSIBLE CAUSE AND ACTION
Sudden loss of voice	• May still be able to laugh and cough	• Stress		• Voice loss due to psychological causes (psychogenic voice loss) • See your doctor
Voice has a strangled, strained quality; voice breaks up during speech	• Can only speak with much effort	• Stressful situations can worsen voice quality but it can improve with laughing, singing and whispering		• Spasmodic dysphonia (spasm of vocal cords) • See your doctor

Weakness and paralysis

Weakness and paralysis are usually caused by disorders in the nervous system. Symptoms may involve the entire body, or be limited to one part such as an arm or leg. Paralysis (loss of muscle function) is a serious symptom and should be investigated by a doctor. See also entry on *numbness and tingling*.

SYMPTOM CHARACTERISTIC	ASSOCIATED SYMPTOMS	AGGRAVATING OR ALLEVIATING FACTORS	OTHER RELEVANT FACTORS	POSSIBLE CAUSE AND ACTION
Weakness or paralysis of the arms or legs	• Progressive numbness in the arms or legs, back or neck pain • Bladder, bowel and sexual functions may be affected	• May be aggravated by moving the neck or back	• Can occur following injury (e.g. broken neck or back), or due to a tumor, disease or infection	• Spinal cord damage • See your doctor at once
Weakness in one arm or one leg	• Neck or back pain, numbness and tingling of the affected limb	• Aggravated by bending, sitting, coughing, sneezing	• The precise location of the symptoms defines which part of the neck or back is affected	• Ruptured vertebral disk causing nerve compression • See your doctor at once
Weakness or paralysis on one side of the body, usually starts suddenly	• Tingling, confusion, dizziness, partial loss of hearing, slurred speech, inability to recognize parts of the body, unusual movements, fainting		• More common with advancing age • Risk increased in people with cardiovascular disease (e.g. hypertension, coronary heart disease) lipid abnormalities (e.g. high cholesterol), diabetes	• Transient ischemic attack or stroke • See your doctor at once
Weakness or paralysis in one part of the arm or leg, often after being in one position or following prolonged pressure to an area	• Numbness or tingling in the same area	• Aggravated by remaining in one position or continued pressure to an area • May be alleviated by moving around	• Can occur from prolonged postures such as sitting with legs crossed, sleeping on one arm • More likely in people who are unable to move around freely because of disability	• Single nerve injury • See your doctor
Profound weakness in both legs, then progresses upwards to both arms	• Tingling, numbness		• In the majority of cases, symptoms begin 3–21 days after a mild infection or surgery	• Guillain-Barré syndrome • This is a medical emergency • Go to the emergency room or call an ambulance at once

SYMPTOM CHARACTERISTIC	ASSOCIATED SYMPTOMS	AGGRAVATING OR ALLEVIATING FACTORS	OTHER RELEVANT FACTORS	POSSIBLE CAUSE AND ACTION
Weakness and paralysis (cont.)				
In males, progressive muscle weakness throughout the body, usually beginning in the muscles of the pelvis	• Muscles often enlarge • May also have trouble climbing stairs or getting out of a chair, frequent falls		• Usually first occurs in boys aged 3–7 years	• Muscular dystrophy • See your doctor at once
Weakness or paralysis on one side of the body	• Constant headache, poor balance and coordination, dizziness, double vision, loss of sensation, loss of hearing		• Most common in people with cancer in another part of the body	• Brain tumor • See your doctor at once

Weight gain

Weight gain usually relates to a mismatch between the intake and expenditure of calories. Sometimes, but infrequently, there is an underlying pathology of the brain and/or hormonal system. In children with obesity and short stature, congenital abnormalities must also be excluded. Weight gain due to fluid retention must be distinguished from that due to increased body fat so that appropriate treatment can be given.

SYMPTOM CHARACTERISTIC	ASSOCIATED SYMPTOMS	AGGRAVATING OR ALLEVIATING FACTORS	OTHER RELEVANT FACTORS	POSSIBLE CAUSE AND ACTION
Gradually progressive weight gain, usually generalized			• This is the most common cause of weight gain	• Overweight/obesity due to increased energy calorie intake or reduced physical activity • See your doctor
Recent weight gain in a woman of child-bearing age			• Commonly occurs in premenstrual phase and resolves after the period	• Normal weight fluctuation with menstrual cycle • See your doctor if you are worried or if symptoms persist
Weight gain after commencing a new medication	• May or may not have increased appetite		• The medication may either be increasing or restoring appetite, or causing retention of more fluid in the body • Drugs that may cause weight gain include corticosteroids, oral medications used in diabetes, the oral contraceptive pill, medications used in depression or schizophrenia	• Medication-induced weight gain • See your doctor if you are worried or if symptoms persist
Recent and rapid increase in weight over a day or two	• Deterioration in overall health, swollen legs, distended abdomen, swollen face, shortness of breath, waking up short of breath at night	• Symptoms may be aggravated or triggered by lying flat	• Diseases that may cause edema include heart failure, liver failure, kidney disease	• Edema • See your doctor

SYMPTOM CHARACTERISTIC	ASSOCIATED SYMPTOMS	AGGRAVATING OR ALLEVIATING FACTORS	OTHER RELEVANT FACTORS	POSSIBLE CAUSE AND ACTION
Weight gain that cannot be explained by excess calorie intake relative to physical activity	• An unusual distribution of the weight, unexplained increase in appetite, symptoms from other bodily systems, (e.g. headache, visual disturbances, excessive thirst, increased urine volume, inability to lose the weight using previously effective strategies, failure to gain height normally in a child)		• These causes are uncommon to rare	• Hormonal disorders, damage to the part of the brain which regulates appetite, congenital disorders • See your doctor

Weight loss

Unintentional weight loss is usually caused by serious underlying conditions. Cancer, gastrointestinal disease and depression are the most prominent causes. As with many other symptoms, a variety of medications can cause weight loss, so contact your doctor for advice if symptoms begin shortly after you start on a new medication. In about 25 percent of cases, no cause is identified.

SYMPTOM CHARACTERISTIC	ASSOCIATED SYMPTOMS	AGGRAVATING OR ALLEVIATING FACTORS	OTHER RELEVANT FACTORS	POSSIBLE CAUSE AND ACTION
Weight loss with reduced food intake; a substantial reduction in weight may occur rapidly	• Loss of weight and appetite may be the only early symptom, or there may be symptoms related to the specific bodily systems affected by the tumor		• Reduced food intake may be related to decreased appetite, a disturbed sense of taste, or nausea; energy requirements appear to increase	• Cancer • See your doctor at once
Weight loss with reduced food intake	• Other symptoms relate to the specific cause		• Reduction in eating may be due to pain, discomfort or nausea related to eating, or swallowing problems	• Inability to eat normally due to a peptic ulcer; disturbance of the contractions of the esophagus which usually push food through to the stomach; gallstones; problems with the mouth or teeth • See your doctor
Weight loss with reduced food intake	• Loss of concentration, sadness, lack of enjoyment in life, difficulty sleeping, low self-esteem, suicidal thoughts or feelings		• May affect any age group	• Depression • See your doctor
Weight loss with reduced food intake in teenage girls; extreme weight loss is typical	• Obsession with becoming thin through extremely strict dieting and exercise; exaggerated fear of becoming fat; distorted body image • Menstrual periods cease (or do not begin) because of starvation		• Girls and women are 10–20 times more likely to develop symptoms than boys or men	• Anorexia nervosa • See your doctor

SYMPTOM CHARACTERISTIC	ASSOCIATED SYMPTOMS	AGGRAVATING OR ALLEVIATING FACTORS	OTHER RELEVANT FACTORS	POSSIBLE CAUSE AND ACTION
Weight loss (cont.)				
Weight loss with reduced food intake	• Otherwise unwell • Other symptoms will depend on the particular cause			• Long-term or severe illnesses or infections • See your doctor
Weight loss despite normal appetite and adequate food intake	• Frequent stools, which may be pale and bulky, float in the toilet bowl and are difficult to flush, or have an unusually unpleasant smell		• Malabsorption may be due to liver disease, reduced stomach area after surgery to remove a tumor, or bowel surgery	• Malabsorption (inability to absorb digested nutrients through the bowel) • See your doctor
Weight loss despite normal appetite and adequate food intake	• Excessive thirst • Passing large amounts of urine		• This type of diabetes typically begins before 40 years of age	• Diabetes • See your doctor
Weight loss despite normal appetite and adequate food intake	• Intolerance of hot weather, increased anxiety, palpitations, excess sweating, itching		• May affect adults or children, females more often the males • The onset of symptoms is usually insidious over many months	• Thyrotoxicosis • See your doctor
Weight loss despite normal appetite and adequate food intake	• Fatigue, general feeling of being unwell, fever, diarrhea		• History of repeated infections • Risk of infection increased by unprotected sexual contact, sharing needles used for intravenous drug use, blood transfusion in a country without a system of routine screening for HIV	• Human immunodeficiency virus (HIV) infection • See your doctor

Wounds or sores, non-healing

Any wound that takes longer than normal to heal warrants investigation by your doctor, as slow-healing wounds may indicate an infection or significant problem affecting the whole body.

SYMPTOM CHARACTERISTIC	ASSOCIATED SYMPTOMS	AGGRAVATING OR ALLEVIATING FACTORS	OTHER RELEVANT FACTORS	POSSIBLE CAUSE AND ACTION
Area where normal skin surface has been lost and fails to heal (ulcer), especially if overgrown or sealed-looking at the edges	• May be itchy and/or painful		• Typically occurs in sun-exposed areas of the skin	• Skin cancer • See your doctor at once
Area where normal skin surface has been lost and fails to heal (ulcer) on the lower leg	• Long history of discomfort, swelling and skin changes of the lower leg		• History of disease of the leg veins (e.g. abnormal clotting or deep venous thrombosis) • Affects women more often than men	• Persistent ulcer that does not heal due to long-term abnormally high pressure in the leg veins (venous ulcer) • See your doctor at once

SYMPTOM CHARACTERISTIC	ASSOCIATED SYMPTOMS	AGGRAVATING OR ALLEVIATING FACTORS	OTHER RELEVANT FACTORS	POSSIBLE CAUSE AND ACTION
Area where normal skin surface has been lost and fails to heal (ulcer) on the tips of the toes or fingers or in areas subject to pressure	• Painful	• Discomfort is aggravated by pressure to the area	• History of disease in the arteries supplying blood to the affected area, or an injury affecting blood supply to the area	• Persistent ulcer that does not heal due to severe reduction of blood supply to the area (ischemic ulcer) • See your doctor at once
Area where normal skin surface has been lost and fails to heal (ulcer) in an area which suffers repeated trauma or pressure	• Painless • Numbness of the surrounding skin		• History of injury or disorder of the nerves supplying the affected area • The most common underlying cause is diabetes	• Persistent ulcer caused by repeated trauma to an area where the individual is unable to sense pain (neuropathic ulcer) • See your doctor at once
Area where normal skin surface has been lost and fails to heal (ulcer) in an area subjected to prolonged pressure while immobile in bed			• People who are elderly or physically incapacitated and unable to shift their weight are at risk • People with numbness who may not sense the need to shift their weight	• Bedsore • See your doctor at once
Persistent discharge from an unusual opening onto the skin	• Surrounding area may be painful or discolored		• May develop after a surgical procedure, after a traumatic injury which penetrates the skin, when a collection of pus (abscess) has drained through the skin, or when there is underlying tumor	• An infection or other problem below the surface of the skin • See your doctor at once
Failure in healing of a surgical wound	• Pain and discomfort of the operation site • Redness, tenderness, discharge from the wound		• The risk of wound infection is increased by contamination of a wound, damage to the surrounding skin or underlying tissues • More likely in people who are obese or poorly nourished, have reduced immune system function or chronic illness	• Wound infection • See your doctor at once
Area where normal skin surface has been lost and fails to heal (ulcer) on foot or lower leg in a person with diabetes			• Embedded foreign bodies of which the patient was unaware are commonly found in people with diabetic ulcers • Close control of blood sugar may help minimize the risk of foot ulcers	• Diabetic ulcer • See your doctor at once • Keep feet clean and dry at all times and wear properly fitted shoes • Inspect feet daily for callus, infection, abrasions or blisters

The Time of Your Life

DEVELOPMENTAL MILESTONES AND PREVENTIVE HEALTH ISSUES FOR WOMEN

WORLD HEALTH ORGANIZATION RECOMMENDED IMMUNIZATION SCHEDULE

This table shows a typical immunization schedule. While it highlights the main immunization recommendations for many regions, the schedule will vary from country to country, and dosing intervals and frequencies may be different. Furthermore, some high-risk areas will require additional vaccinations not listed here. Please consult your local health authority for the appropriate immunization schedule for your country. Certain immunizations are effective for a limited time and booster shots are required throughout life to maintain immunity.

DISEASE	Birth	2 months	4 months	6 months	12 months	12–18 months	4 years	10–13 years	15–19 years	50 years	65 + years
Hepatitis B	•	•	•	•				•*			
Diphtheria		•	•			•	•				
Tetanus		•	•			•	•		•	•	
Pertussis (whooping cough)		•	•			•	•				
Hemophilus influenzae B		•	•		•						
Polio		•	•	•			•		•		
Measles					•		•				
Mumps					•		•				
Rubella (German measles)					•		•				
Chickenpox (optional)						•**					
Pneumococcal infection											•***
Influenza											•****

* give 3 doses if not given as an infant. Second dose 1 month after first, third dose 5 months after second dose.

** can be given anytime after 12 months of age

*** give every 5 years from age 65

**** give every year from age 65

Birth–6 months

- At birth, babies have the ability to see about 8–12 inches (20–30 centimeters) in front of them and have fully developed hearing. The labia may be swollen.
- Within a few days of birth, babies develop a sense of taste and respond to their mother's voice and smell.
- First smile at 4–6 weeks.
- By 6 months, most babies can hold objects placed in their hand, focus in all directions, roll over and lift head and shoulders when lying on their stomach.

HEALTH CHECK

- Apgar score at 1 minute and 5 minutes after birth to assess color, heart rate, breathing, responsiveness, muscle tone. Length, weight and head circumference measured, plus thorough physical examination in first 12 hours after birth.
- Screening test at 4–5 days of age to detect presence of any rare metabolic diseases and some inherited diseases.
- Thorough physical examination at 6–8 weeks.
- Immunization at birth, 2 and 4 months. (See Schedule)

6–12 months

- First teeth usually appear by 6–8 months. Most babies can now sit with some support.
- By 9 months, babies are usually crawling, and may wave and clap hands. They may imitate sounds and will respond to own name.
- By 12 months of age, many babies will be walking by holding on to furniture, standing alone for a few seconds at a time and saying 1 or 2 single words.

HEALTH CHECK

- Immunization at 6 months and 12 months. (See Schedule)
- Physical and developmental examination may be done at 6–8 months.

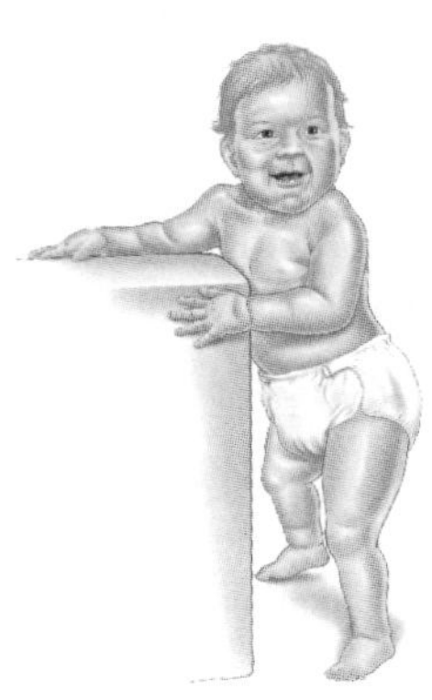

20–30 years

- Fertility peaks in the mid-20s, and this decade is the most likely time for childbearing to begin.
- Awareness of sexually transmitted diseases (STDs) and use of contraception is essential in all sexually active females.

HEALTH CHECK

- Physical examination every 2 years, including blood pressure, height and weight. From age 18, all women should have a Pap smear every 2 years.
- Breast self-examination should be done every month for life.
- Certain immunization boosters are necessary every 10 years. (See Schedule)

30–40 years

- Fertility declines, and risk of fetal abnormalities in the pregnant woman increases.
- Bone density starts to decline.

HEALTH CHECK

- Physical examination every 2 years, including blood pressure, height and weight. Pap smears continue every 2 years.
- Breast self-examination should be done every month.
- Cholesterol should be checked every 5 years.

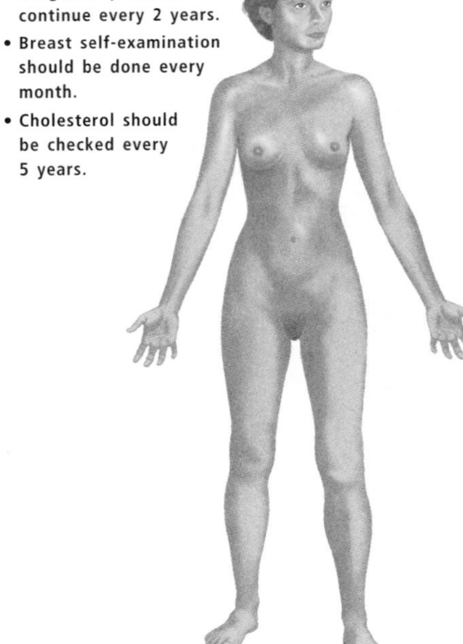

40–50 years

- Menopause usually commences, signifying the end of menstruation and fertility. Women may suffer hot flashes/flushes and other symptoms due to the decline in estrogen levels.
- Calcium and mineral content of bones decreases significantly.

HEALTH CHECK

- Physical examination every year, including blood pressure, height and weight, and clinical examination of breasts. Gynecological exam, including internal pelvic assessment every year. Pap smears, rectal examination and urine tests every year.
- Breast self-examination should be done every month.
- Mammograms may be done every 2 years.
- Eye test, including glaucoma screen, every 2 years.

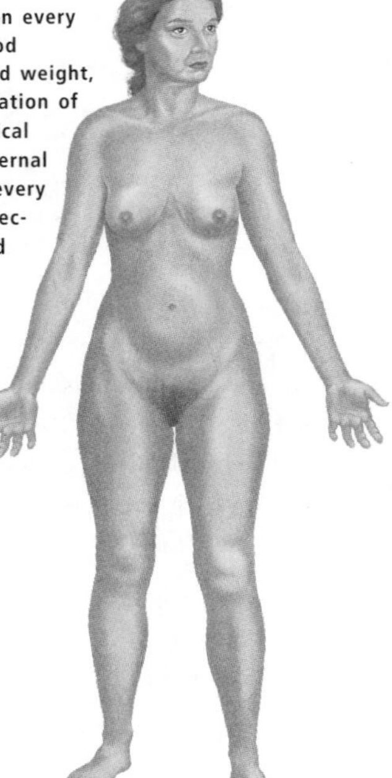

1–5 years

- The preschool years are a time of rapid development, and a time when a child's individuality becomes noticeable.
- At 18 months, she can walk well, stack blocks, throw a ball and push toys around the room.
- By her second birthday, she can run, walk up and down stairs and feed herself with a spoon. 2 year olds are easily frustrated and liable to throw temper tantrums. Vocabulary is expanding dramatically.
- 3–4 year olds learn to use simple sentences, and play involves more interaction with playmates. Girls are usually fully toilet-trained by this age.
- By age 4, girls have grown taller and appear slimmer, due to losing fat and gaining muscle. Most height increase involves the legs.

HEALTH CHECK

- Immunization at 12–18 months, and 4–5 years prior to school entry. (See Schedule)
- Development will be continually monitored at doctor's visits.

6–11 years

- These years are a time of rapid physical, intellectual and psychological growth.
- School begins at age 5–6, and girls start to develop close friendships, usually with other girls.
- Baby teeth begin to fall out around the sixth year.
- Reading and writing skills are developed and refined.
- For most girls, puberty begins after the age of 10. Signs of puberty include development of breasts and pubic hair, and a marked increase in physical size (growth spurt).
- Children of this age usually have the coordination and balance of an adult.

HEALTH CHECK

- Children who experience difficulties with schoolwork may be tested for attention deficit disorder (ADD) or learning problems such as dyslexia.
- Immunization boosters may be necessary. (See Schedule)

12–19 years

- Menstruation usually begins at 11–14 years of age, after which growth may slow down. Body fat increases around the hips and thighs, sweat glands develop further, and hormonal changes can start to cause skin problems.
- Eating disorders sometimes affect young women in this age group.

HEALTH CHECK

- Immunization at 10–13 years and 15–19 years. (See Schedule)
- Scoliosis screening is carried out at many schools. More girls than boys develop scoliosis—a sideways curvature of the spine.

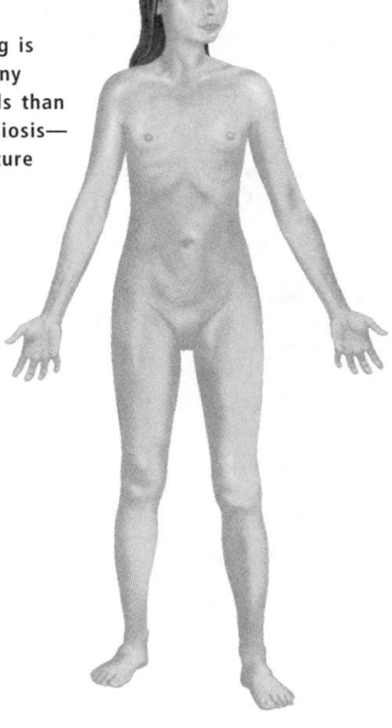

50–65 years

- Following menopause, bone density falls significantly. Lean body mass declines, and the metabolic rate decreases.

HEALTH CHECK

- Yearly screening continues, including blood pressure, height and weight, and clinical examination of breasts. Gynecological exam, including internal pelvic assessment and Pap smear every year. Rectal examination, urine tests and skin checks yearly. Eye test, including glaucoma screen, every 2 years.
- Additional annual screening following menopause is also necessary, including assessment of heart function, bone density and stools.
- Mammograms are recommended yearly.
- Sigmoidoscopy (visual examination of the rectum and lower colon) every 3–5 years is advised, and cholesterol screening every 5 years.

65–85 years

- By 65–70 years of age, a woman has half the bone density she had at age 30.
- There may be a decline in organ function, including the brain. Many older women will continue to be very active, but physical capabilities may become limited or more difficult.

HEALTH CHECK

- Yearly screening continues. Physical examination should include blood pressure, height and weight, and clinical examination of breasts. A gynecological examination, including internal pelvic exam and Pap smear, and rectal examination and urine tests are also advised. Yearly mammograms, as well as heart, bone, stool and cholesterol tests are recommended. Eye test, including glaucoma screen, every 2 years.
- Monthly breast self-examination should continue.
- Annual vaccination against influenza is advised.
- Pneumococcal immunization every 5 years.

85+ years

- Loss of bone density continues. About 30 percent of all women reaching 90 years of age will suffer a hip fracture due to weakened bones.
- The incidence of dementia continues to increase. Lapses of memory and difficulty learning new information are noticed in those affected.

HEALTH CHECK

- Yearly screening continues. Physical examination should include full gynecological examination, including Pap smear, rectal examination, blood pressure, height and weight, skin checks and clinical examination of breasts and urine tests.
- Blood tests for cholesterol and sugar.
- Yearly mammograms, as well as heart, bone density and stool tests are recommended.
- Pneumococcal and influenza immunizations continue.
- Eye test, including glaucoma screen, every 2 years.
- Monthly breast self-examination should continue.

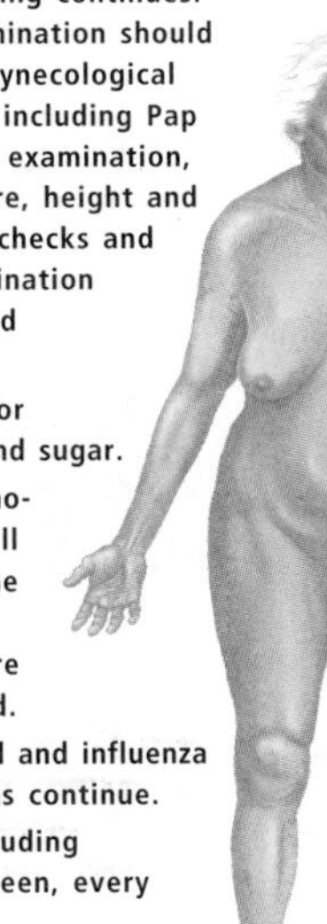

The Time of Your Life

DEVELOPMENTAL MILESTONES AND PREVENTIVE HEALTH ISSUES FOR MEN

WORLD HEALTH ORGANIZATION RECOMMENDED IMMUNIZATION SCHEDULE

This table shows a typical immunization schedule. While it highlights the main immunization recommendations for many regions, the schedule will vary from country to country, and dosing intervals and frequencies may be different. Furthermore, some high-risk areas will require additional vaccinations not listed here. Please consult your local health authority for the appropriate immunization schedule for your country. Certain immunizations are effective for a limited time and booster shots are required throughout life to maintain immunity.

DISEASE	Birth	2 months	4 months	6 months	12 months	12–18 months	4 years	10–13 years	15–19 years	50 years	65 + years
Hepatitis B	•	•	•	•				•*			
Diphtheria		•	•			•	•				
Tetanus		•	•			•	•		•	•	
Pertussis (whooping cough)		•	•			•	•				
Hemophilus influenzae B		•	•		•						
Polio		•	•	•			•		•		
Measles					•		•				
Mumps					•		•				
Rubella (German measles)					•		•				
Chickenpox (optional)						•**					
Pneumococcal infection											•***
Influenza											•****

* give 3 doses if not given as an infant. Second dose 1 month after first, third dose 5 months after second dose.

** can be given anytime after 12 months of age

*** give every 5 years from age 65

**** give every year from age 65

Birth–6 months

- At birth, babies have the ability to see about 8–12 inches (20–30 centimeters) in front of them and have fully developed hearing. Both testes should be present in the scrotum.
- Within a few days of birth, babies develop sense of taste and respond to their mother's voice and smell.
- First smile is usually at 4–6 weeks.
- By 6 months, most babies can hold objects placed in their hand, focus in all directions, roll over and lift head and shoulders when lying on their stomach.

HEALTH CHECK

- Apgar score at 1 minute and 5 minutes after birth to assess color, heart rate, breathing, responsiveness, muscle tone. Length, weight and head circumference measured, plus thorough physical examination in first 12 hours after birth.
- Screening test at 4–5 days of age to detect presence of any rare metabolic diseases and some inherited diseases.
- Thorough physical examination at 6–8 weeks.
- Immunization at birth, 2 and 4 months. (See Schedule)

6–12 months

- First teeth usually appear by 6–8 months. Most babies can now sit with some support.
- By 9 months, babies are usually crawling, and may wave and clap hands. They may imitate sounds and will respond to own name.
- By 12 months of age, most babies have tripled their birth weight. Many babies will be walking by holding on to furniture, standing alone for a few seconds at a time and saying 1 or 2 single words.

HEALTH CHECK

- Immunization at 6 months and 12 months. (See Schedule)
- Detailed physical and developmental examination may be done at 6–8 months.

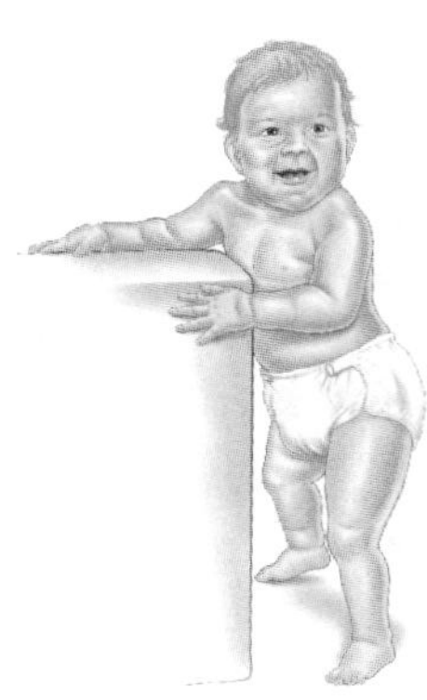

20–30 years

- Bones continue to broaden until the age of 20 in most males.
- Awareness of sexually transmitted diseases (STDs) and use of contraception is essential in all sexually active males.

HEALTH CHECK

- Regular physical examinations are recommended every 2 years, including height, weight, and blood pressure assessment.
- Testes should be clinically examined every 2 years, and self-examination is recommended every month.
- Certain immunization boosters are necessary every 10 years. (See Schedule)

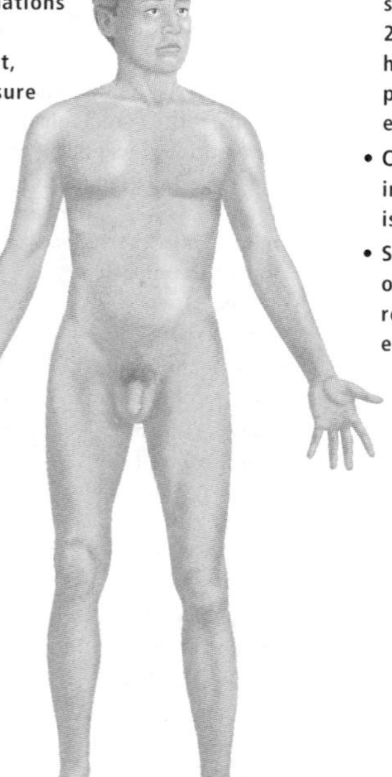

30–40 years

- Distribution of body fat may begin to change, becoming more prevalent around the abdomen.
- 30 percent of males in their 30s notice some hair loss.

HEALTH CHECK

- Regular physical exams should continue every 2 years, including height, weight, blood pressure, testicular examination.
- Cholesterol screening every 5 years is advised.
- Self-examination of testes is recommended every month.

40–50 years

- Metabolism may slow, causing a tendency to gain weight.
- Prostate enlargement usually begins around age 45.

HEALTH CHECK

- Physical examination every year, including height, weight, blood pressure, and clinical examination of testes. Rectal examination and urine tests yearly.
- Cholesterol screening should become more frequent, and may be tested every 1–2 years.
- Self-examination of testes is recommended every month.
- Eye exam, including glaucoma screening, is recommended every 2 years.

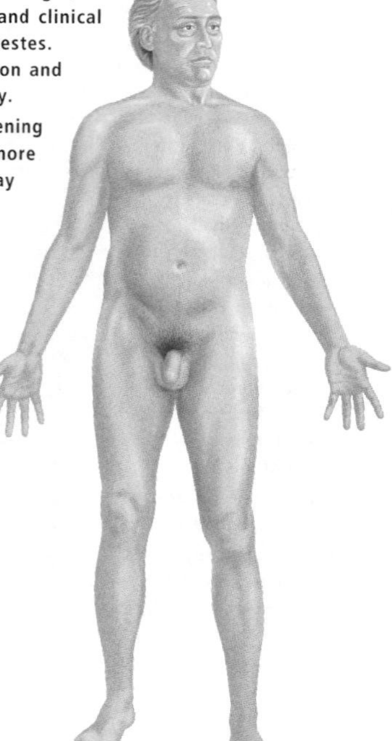

1–5 years

- The preschool years are a time of rapid development, and a time when a child's individuality becomes noticeable.
- At 18 months, he can walk well, stack blocks, throw a ball and push toys around the room.
- By his second birthday, he can run, walk up and down stairs, and feed himself with a spoon. 2 year olds are easily frustrated and liable to throw temper tantrums. Vocabulary is expanding dramatically.
- 3–4 year olds learn to use simple sentences, and play involves more interaction with playmates. Toilet-training in boys is usually complete by this time, although some boys may continue to have problems particularly at night.
- By age 4, boys have grown taller and appear slimmer, due to losing fat and gaining muscle. Most height increase involves the legs.

HEALTH CHECK

- Immunization at 18 months, and 4–5 years prior to school entry. (See Schedule)
- Development will be continually monitored at doctor's visits.

6–11 years

- These years are a time of rapid physical, intellectual and psychological growth.
- School begins at age 5–6, and boys start to develop close friendships, usually with other boys.
- Baby teeth begin to fall out around the sixth year.
- Reading and writing skills are developed and refined.
- Children of this age usually have the coordination and balance of an adult.

HEALTH CHECK

- Children who experience difficulties with schoolwork may be tested for attention deficit disorder (ADD) or learning problems such as dyslexia.
- Immunization boosters may be necessary. (See Schedule)

12–19 years

- Puberty in boys begins around 11–12 years. The testes and penis grow larger and the skin of the scrotum darkens. Pubic hair begins to appear.
- At the age of 12–13, boys have a growth spurt, growing rapidly in weight and height. The chest and shoulders become broader.
- At 13 or 14 the voice box begins to grow and the voice starts change. Many boys are able to ejaculate by this age.
- Underarm and facial hair, as well as sweat glands, typically begin to appear between 13 and 15 years of age.
- Height continues to increase until around 17–18 years of age.

HEALTH CHECK

- Immunization at 10–13 years and 15–19 years. (See Schedule)
- Screening for scoliosis (sideways curvature of the spine) is carried out at many schools.

50–65 years

- Prostate enlargement continues. Bone density falls.
- Hair loss is evident in 50 percent of men aged over 50.

HEALTH CHECK

- Yearly screening continues, including height, weight, blood pressure, clinical examination of testes, urine tests, skin checks and stool test. Self-examination of testes is recommended every month.
- Annual rectal examination and blood tests for prostate-specific antigen (a marker of prostate cancer).
- Sigmoidoscopy (visual study of the rectum and lower colon) every 3–5 years is advised.
- Eye exam, including glaucoma screening, is recommended every 2 years.
- Stress test and electrocardiogram (EKG) may be necessary, depending on overall health and family history of heart disease.

65–85 years

- Many older men will continue to be very active, but physical capabilities may become limited or more difficult. There may be a decline in organ function, including the brain.

HEALTH CHECK

- Yearly screening continues. Physical examination should include clinical examination of the testes and prostate, cholesterol measurements, height, weight, blood pressure, skin checks, heart tests and urine tests.
- Annual rectal examination, blood tests for prostate-specific antigen, and annual stool tests are necessary.
- Eye exam, including glaucoma screening, is recommended every 2 years.
- Yearly vaccination against influenza is advised.
- Pneumococcal immunization every 5 years.
- Self-examination of testes is recommended every month.

85+ years

- The incidence of dementia increases with age, affecting about 1 in 5 men over 85 years.
- Although age-related loss of bone density begins earlier and proceeds more rapidly in women, it is also a significant health problem in elderly men.
- Most elderly men remain independent.

HEALTH CHECK

- Yearly screening continues. Physical examination should include blood pressure check, rectal examination, height, weight, skin checks, heart tests and urine tests.
- Blood tests for cholesterol, sugar and prostate-specific antigen.
- Annual stool test for blood.
- Pneumococcal and influenza vaccinations continue.
- Tests for bone density are recommended.
- Self-examination of testes continues every month.

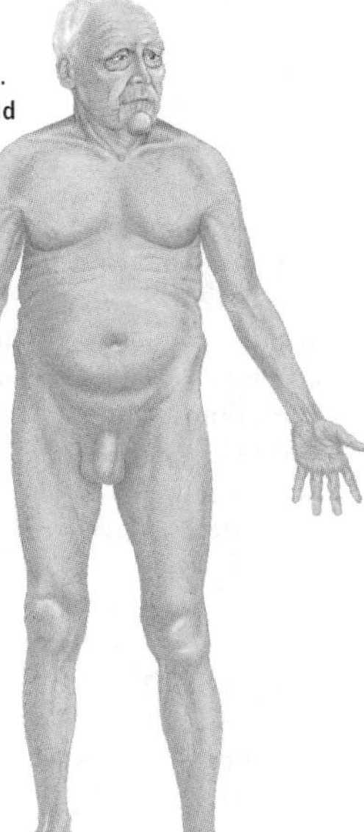

Index

Bold text denotes the main entry for a topic.

A

D

F

G

H

I

J

N

O

Q

S

T

U

V